Compact Disc World
Music At Your Fingertips!

DIAL 1·800·83·MUSIC (1·800·836·8742)
COMPACT DISC WORLD'S MAIL ORDER MUSIC HOTLINE

1·800·83·MUSIC
6 8 7 4 2

We are a mail order house carrying the largest selection of labels, artists & catagories. Our Director, Ira Hirsch, brings his 27 years of mail order experience to Compact Disc World's mail order operation.

- Classical
- Pop
- Jazz
- Shows
- Soundtracks
- Country
- R & B
- New Age
- Children's
- Languages
- Compact Discs
- Cassettes
- Videos
- Laser Discs
- Accessories

FOR INSTITUTIONS

We specialize in library and other institutional services.

All staff orders at same low discount prices

For library orders S&H free on order of 5 units or more

FOR INDIVIDUALS

We offer fantastic savings and prompt service.

Shipping and handling cost: $4.50 for order of any size

ALL MERCHANDISE GUARANTEED FACTORY FRESH.
All items in this catalog (including Spectrum) always available at great discount prices.
Rapid delivery: all shipments UPS (P.O. Box addresses shipped Parcel Post)

For courteous, knowledgeable and personal service call
1-800-836-8742 or fax 1-908-412-9050
or write:
Compact Disc World, P.O. Box 927, South Plainfield, NJ 07080

Compact Disc World

D1762123

SCHWANN *ARTIST* 1997

From the Editor

This 1997 edition of *Schwann Artist* is the essential companion to our quarterly publication, *Schwann Opus*. Whereas *Schwann Opus* lists recordings of works by composer, the *Artist* issue catalogs releases listed by performer—instrumentalist, vocalist, or ensemble.

This issue's cover story—Mark Swed's interview with the Los Angeles Philharmonic's Music Director, Esa-Pekka Salonen—describes a great success story. The LA Phil has succeeded in putting itself back on the map largely through the ideas, focus, and charisma of this conductor and composer.

Also in this issue, Mortimer Frank discusses what may prove to be Leonard Bernstein's greatest legacy—his potency as a music educator. I remember watching Bernstein's *Young Peoples Concerts* on television—who doesn't? Those too young to recall these nationally broadcast programs, which began in 1958 and continued for 15 years, can now see them on video. They're not just for kids.

This has been a year for debate on the issues faced by America's classical music industry. Amid the talk of diminishing audiences for symphonies and plummeting market shares in music sales I happened upon an item in the Sunday paper listing the five best-selling "classical music" recordings of all time. They were, in no particular order, The *Three Tenors*, *Chant*, *Three Tenors II*, and two CDs of various bits of well-worn repertoire performed by the London Symphony—these last two packaged by and sold in Victoria's Secret catalogues and stores alongside the bustiers and pantyhose. No wonder, then, that the classical guys at record companies, frantic for the next big thing, hire rock-and-roll radio promoters as marketing directors.

Perhaps the criticism should be leveled at the classical music industry itself, which apparently is suffering from an identity crisis. In *Who Killed Classical Music?* (Birch Lane Press, 1997), excerpted in this issue of *Schwann Artist*, UK music critic Norman Lebrecht chronicles his insights into the Machiavellian power plays and high drama behind the scenes in the classical business. As the official *bête noir* for the classical execs, Mr. Lebrecht's book should be required reading for the delegates of the American Symphony Orchestra League, who will be holding their annual conference this June in Washingtion, D.C.

Meanwhile, another pungent music critic, composer Virgil Thomson, waxed Delphic when he wrote in 1939 "…music still gets written, performed, and consumed, lots of it, in all categories. And neither the profession of writing it nor the trade of performing it is quite yet immobilized by friction with the businessmen who organize the dissemination of it… there is more good music around than ever gets through to the opera houses and to the trusts of concert management… There are musical activities of a popular nature and others of a recondite intellectual nature (far from popular) that enclose the nuclei of the next musical civilization… the official, the rich opera-and-concert world of today is the resplendent tail-end of a comet that has already gone around the corner."

—Kristina Melcher

The Beethoven Cycle Beethoven Would've Bought If Beethoven Had Bought CDs

"Unless you require period instruments, or you want a famous historical interpretation, this new series is ideal. [Conductor] Béla Drahos has trained his orchestra brilliantly, the performances are scrupulously faithful to the scores, and the tempi are flexible and up to date ... If you are starting a collection, this is the Beethoven cycle to have."
— **H.C. Robbins Landon, *BBC Music Magazine***

"These performances [of Symphonies 1 & 6] sparkle with life, suggesting the arrival (if he maintains this level) of a great conductor."
— **Leslie Gerber, *Classical Pulse!***

"This installment [Symphonies 3 & 8] offers edge-of-the-seat excitement, rich recorded sound and a bargain $5.99 price."
— **Jeff Bradley, *Denver Post***

"With this latest release [Symphonies 3 & 8] in the budget Beethoven cycle from Béla Drahos and the Nicolaus Esterházy Sinfonia, Naxos has done it again! This is the bargain *Eroica* of all time ... The Sinfonia plays faultlessly under Drahos ... in whose hands the ferocity of Beethoven's visionary epic resounds majestically ... Sonically, too, Naxos joins the big league with demonstration quality engineering ..."
— **Michael Jameson, *Classic CD***

BEETHOVEN
Symphonies No. 3 "Eroica" and No. 8
Nicolaus Esterházy Sinfonia
Béla Drahos

Beethoven The Symphonies
Béla Drahos
and the Nicolaus Esterházy Sinfonia.
Nos. 1 & 6 – 8.553474.
Nos. 3 & 8 – 8.553475.
Nos. 2 & 5 – 8.553476.
Nos. 4 & 7 – 8.553477.
No. 9 – 8.553478

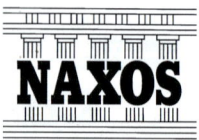

Call us at 800-75-NAXOS for a free catalog.

America's Guide to Classical Performers   19th Edition

SCHWANN
Artist 1997

SCHWANN PUBLICATIONS
1807 Second Street, Suite 101
Santa Fe, NM 87505
Tel: 505-988-2045
Fax: 505-992-4959
e-mail: schwann@vrd.com

Publisher Barney Cohen
Assistant Publisher Melanie Cullen

EDITORIAL
Features Editor Kristina Melcher
Managing Editor Ashley Benning
Copy Editors Jo Ann Baldinger, Richard Lehnert
Asst. to Features Editor Ralph Melcher
Contributing Editors Mortimer H. Frank, George Jellinek, Joan La Barbara, Fred Steiner, Mark Swed

LISTINGS
Listings Manager Becky Barnhart
Associate Editor Jennifer Alvarado
Editorial Assistants Bob Kasenchak, Jan Strance, Amy Williams, Jeffrey Clowdus, Susan Magee
Database Consultant Joe Patillo

ART & PRODUCTION
Art Director & Prod. Mgr. Benjamin Forde
Designer Hilary Wallace

BUSINESS OFFICE
PO Box 2057, Woodland, CA 95776
Tel: 916-661-6600   Fax: 916-661-7854

ADVERTISING & RETAIL SALES
Sales & Advertising Mgr. Michael J. Rohrig
Tel: 916-669-5161
Sales Analyst Ali Crawford
Tel: 916-661-7881

INDIVIDUAL SUBSCRIBERS
800-877-2693
or 518-436-9686 outside U.S.

SINGLE COPY SALES
800-888-8574
or 916-661-3395 outside U.S.
Fax: 800-999-1794

1997 Schwann Artist, 19th Edition, ISSN: 1080-6970

Schwann Artist is published annually for $19.95 plus S&H by Schwann Publications, 1280 Santa Anita Court, Woodland, CA 95776. Single copies of 1997 Schwann Artist may be obtained from Schwann Publications, P.O. Box 2057, Woodland, CA 95776.

© Schwann Publications. All rights reserved. No part of this publication may be reproduced or transmitted in any form or by any means, electronically, optically, or mechanically, including photocopy, recording, or any other information storage or retrieval system, without permission in writing from the publisher. The information contained in this publication is provided for reference uses only. No representations are made as to this publication's completeness or accuracy, although the publisher has made every effort to provide the most up-to-date and useful information possible. The publisher hereby expressly excludes all warranties.

member of

Give the gift of music.

Member of
NAIRD

ISBN: 1-57598-020-7
Printed in the USA

Features

6A   *L.A. Variations:*
An Interview with Esa-Pekka Salonen
Mark Swed

16A   *Learning with Lenny:*
The Ultimate Bernstein Legacy
Mortimer H. Frank

22A   *Orchestras That Matter:*
American Period-Instrument Orchestras
Bernard D. Sherman

26A   *The New World Symphony*
Larry Birnbaum

28A   *Book Excerpt:*
Going Off The Record
from Who Killed Classical Music?
Norman Lebrecht

Listings

1	Conductors
40	Orchestras & Ensembles
436	Instrumentalists
932	Choral Groups
1035	Vocalists
1490	Miscellaneous

Departments

4A	From the Editor
25A	Subscriber/Dealer Information
34A	How to Use Schwann Artist
35A	Symbols & Abbreviations
1494	Label Addresses

Cover Design Benjamin Forde
Cover Photo Gary Friedman/L.A. Times

Music Library Ref.
ML
156.2
.A75
1997

L.A. Variations
Mark Swed Interviews Esa-Pekka Salonen

The Vienna Philharmonic, an orchestra that guards its traditions more adamantly than any other, usually restricts its American visits to Carnegie Hall. But early in 1997 it returned to southern California for the first time in many years—and all hell broke loose. Women's groups, angered that throughout its long history the orchestra had refused to allow women full membership, threatened boycott and protest. The issue became page-one news in both the *Los Angeles Times* and the *New York Times*, and the orchestra was actually frightened into changing its policy.

This story exemplifies a classic clash of cultures, the values of the new world versus those of the old, and the power that the former now hold over the latter. The Vienna Philharmonic wandered just a little too close to the center of orchestral innovation, and now it has been forever altered. The West Coast can be like that.

Of course, the protest had quickly become bicoastal. Moreover, internal pressure to integrate had been mounting within the orchestra for some time. Nonetheless, this story reveals something of the spirit of a place where orchestral and musical culture are different from anywhere else. The attitudes found at the Los Angeles Philharmonic, now in its fourth season under music director Esa-Pekka Salonen, are beginning to attract international attention.

Los Angeles is perhaps the most unlikely place in the world to build an important orchestra. Much about the city is antithetical to everything an orchestra stands for. It is, for one thing, an extraordinarily pluralistic place, and—unlike many European cities that are suddenly being overwhelmed by cultural diversity—it has never had a single culture. Orchestras strive for uniformity, and the Vienna Philharmonic stands as the great model for achieving striking oneness of tone by restricting itself to players from a single musical tradition.

No one needs to be reminded that Los Angeles is also the entertainment capital of the world. Movies, television, and popular music not only form a significant part of the economy of Los Angeles, but also give the city its character. It is no coincidence that for the past three decades the Los Angeles Philharmonic has been led by glamorous music directors—Zubin Mehta, André Previn, and now Salonen. Carlo Maria Guilini, the Italian maestro who served as music director between Mehta and Previn, may seem uncharacteristic in this lineup, but he brought his own kind of European glamour.

Culture in Los Angeles does, however, have significant ties to European tradition, and nowhere more so than in classical music. With its opportunities in the movie industry and its weather, Los Angeles became a haven for émigré artists fleeing Hitler in the 1930s. They joined others who had come earlier from Europe and Russia, and suddenly southern California became the capital of music. Otto Klemperer was music director of the Los Angeles Philharmonic. Schoenberg, Stravinsky, Rachmaninoff, Heifetz, Piatigorsky, Rubinstein and Korngold all lived a few miles apart. Some of the émigrés adapted better than others, and there are wonderful photos depicting strange cultural collisions—such as the one of Schoenberg in summer whites, playing ping-pong in the back yard of his house across the street from the house that had been Shirley Temple's.

These émigrés set the tone for a new culture that could be built on the old. Los Angeles native John Cage, who idolized and studied with Schoenberg, felt empowered to make his own kind of radically new art. Michael Tilson Thomas, another native son, was shaped in part by the Russians with whom, early on, he came in contact—Heifetz, Piatigorsky, Stravinsky. And Korngold, along with other émigré composers, gave the movies their symphonic sound. Love it or hate it, Hollywood has been the greatest of all promulgators of symphonic music.

The Los Angeles Philharmonic itself is a case study in the weird combines of musical tradition and glitz. Under Otto Klemperer, music director from 1933 to 1939, it was a particularly imaginative ensemble. After Klemperer the orchestra went to the other extreme, taking the rare step of hiring an American conductor; but Alfred Wallenstein, who served from 1943 to 1956, was a competent traditionalist who brought the orchestra little innovation and only modest distinction.

The respected Dutch conductor Eduard van Beinum became music director in 1958 but suffered a heart attack the next year and died. Mehta became music director in 1962 and ushered the orchestra into an era of international renown. Young, dashing, and fearless, Mehta attempted the first real merger of old and new. His model for sound was pure Vienna, but his image was all show business. Mehta gave the orchestra the flair it sorely needed after Wallenstein, but he could never shake off the hint of superficiality that accompanied it.

With Guilini, who arrived in 1978, the pendulum moved again toward unfiltered European tradition, then swung right back with Previn in 1985. Previn, it was hoped, would be the perfect symbol for Los Angeles, a highly refined conductor with a Hollywood past as a film composer, a musician equally respected for his abilities to play jazz and Mozart. But Previn also demonstrated the danger of skirting musical schizophrenia. Not wanting to be reminded of his jazz career or his Hollywood youth (he told the press upon arrival that he didn't remember where he had put his Oscars), Previn proved to be an unbending traditionalist with only moderate popularity.

Esa-Pekka Salonen is the first conductor able to bridge Los Angeles's enormous cultural divides. This is doubly ironic because Salonen, who was born in Helsinki in 1958, comes from a country with very little ethnic diversity, and began his career as an intellectual modernist composer with little interest in the populist side of music making. Inadvertently, however, Salonen's conducting career—which originally was a sideline, a way of performing his and his colleagues' new music—is the one that turned out to be meteoric. He made his London debut in 1983, his American debut in 1984 with the Los Angeles Philharmonic, and in 1985, still in his early 20s, became principal conductor of the Swedish Radio Symphony (where he remained until 1994) and principal guest conductor of the L.A. Philharmonic.

It is probably safe to say that Salonen would not have had nearly the initial success he achieved in Los Angeles without his good looks. He is fair-haired and fit and favors jeans and T-shirts, just like a daytime soap star. Nor would he have become popular were he less dynamic on the podium. But he also would not have garnered the high respect that he merits without a phenomenal ear and an ability to clarify the thickest of textures and knottiest of rhythms.

Still, his four seasons in Los Angeles haven't been an easy adjustment for Salonen. He was promised certain things that have not come through, including a spectacular new concert hall designed by Frank O. Gehry. But the Disney Hall (named for Walt and Lillian Disney, thanks to a donation of $55 million by Lillian Disney) has yet to be built, and was almost abandoned when budget overruns drove the final cost to $250 million. Salonen arrived in Los Angeles just as it started to suffer financial recession along with devastation by earthquakes, riots, and floods. And his emphasis on the 20th-century repertoire and modernist music did not automatically win support from long-time subscribers. Salonen has had the further frustration of not being able to work in Los Angeles with the opera director Peter Sellars. Although they did collaborate on Debussy's *Pelléas et Mélisande* for the L.A. Opera, the projects that Salonen and Sellars have been involved in at Covent Garden (Hindemith's *Mathis der Maler*), the Theatre du Châtelet in Paris (Stravinsky's *The Rake's Progress*), and Salzburg (Ligeti's *Le Grand Macabre*) have not been optioned by the L.A. Opera.

Nor has it been easy for Salonen to assimilate. Centerless Los Angeles was a hard community to adapt to for someone who loved the life of high-powered conversations in European cafés. A dyed-in-the-wool Boulezian, Salonen also came to Los Angeles with a certain disdain for local culture. He ridiculed minimalism and called John Cage a charlatan. (Cage responded that he didn't know how that could be: "I was born in Los Angeles," he said.) Nor did he show any particular interest in West Coast traditions, in the music of Henry Cowell, Lou Harrison, or Harry Partch.

But Los Angeles has changed Salonen. He has lightened up musically. He admires the great success that Michael Tilson Thomas has had in San Francisco conducting West Coast music, realizing that it is one more example of how the West can provide new ideas for the future of the symphony. And he has developed a genuine regard for the work of John Adams, conducting his Chamber Symphony with tremendous verve. Salonen has lately taken a serious look at film music and recorded a disc of the music Bernard Herrmann wrote for Alfred Hitchcock and Martin Scorcese. This recording was an immediate smash hit.

Such projects seem to have changed Salonen as a composer as well. Although his success and responsibilities as a conductor, along with a family that includes two young daughters, leave little time to compose, he has completed a new orchestral work, *LA Variations*, that is a highly engaging showpiece for the Philharmonic. Its fanciful invention includes great motoric passages that owe something not just to Stravinsky but also to minimalism and movies. At the work's premiere early in 1997, Los Angeles Philharmonic subscribers responded with a sense of excitement that is rarely encountered in a symphony audience. A piece written for their orchestra, written in their time and place, written by their music director, is something exceedingly rare in orchestral life today.

Mark Swed: *One hears more and more that classical music is in trouble. Orchestras, we are told, are fighting to stay afloat and attract new audiences. All the indications are that*

The Los Angeles Philharmonic, itself, is a case study in the weird combines of musical tradition and glitz.

the classical-recording business can no longer sustain itself by constantly re-recording standard repertoire with new artists. Are you as pessimistic about the situation as so many in the business seem to be?

Esa-Pekka Salonen: No, not at all. I think we are very clearly at a turning point. Lots of the old structures have either fallen apart or are about to, not only in music, but politically and geographically. So as we enter a new era, certain phenomena get reevaluated, and no one can know exactly where this will lead.

But I don't see this turmoil necessarily as a negative thing. In fact, I think we need it. We need thorough analyses and we need new thinking. The problem at the moment is that we don't have a cultural philosophy that can cover all that is going on. We have, instead, either the German idea, which comes basically from Adorno and Dalhaus, where people get stuck in the idea of postmodern and never get out of it, or the more American way of thinking, which treats electronic media and mass media as the most important element in whatever the new culture will be. But very few people can actually handle both aspects of culture, can speak about Madonna and also speak about Ferneyhough.

Swed: *Does that mean you welcome the challenges that lie ahead?*

Salonen: I actually find them rather exciting, yes. We've got lots of practical problems—problems of funding, problems of marketing, problems of the mechanization of music by the electronic media. The Internet is completely wild. CD-ROM is very much coming but nobody knows quite how to handle that. Quite soon you will be able, with the speed of special ISDN lines, to actually have live picture and sound over the Internet, and this will completely change consumer consciousness.

Swed: *You say that we don't have a philosophy to deal with Ferneyhough and Madonna together. But hasn't it always been that way? The idea of sonata-allegro form was not identified by theorists until well into the 19th century, when it was already coming apart in the music. And some of today's young composers—say, Michael Torke, Aaron Kernis, David Lang, or the others in the Bang-on-a-Can movement—are equally at home with modernism and pop. Maybe the aesthetics necessarily have to come later.*

Salonen: Yes, absolutely. The philosophy that we have at the moment isn't actually connected to what's happening in reality. This is especially the case in Europe, where governments run the opera houses and symphony orchestras and put them in the hands of . . . well, I wouldn't say philosophers, but people who think about the arts on a theoretical level. But if their

thinking is not up-to-date we end up in a rather dangerous situation. I think the fact that the administration of the arts isn't able to keep up with what's really happening is the biggest threat at the moment. It's actually easier to keep up with what's happening in the U.S. because of the lack of government involvement.

Swed: *Does the audience have an effect on this equation as well?*

Salonen: If you ask audience members of our generation about their listening and consuming habits, you get a very eclectic picture. They might go to see this opera here or that symphony concert there, and then maybe they'll try some ethnic music or art rock. There used to be almost a sociological difference between classical and nonclassical music, but that has practically disappeared. If I think of my own habits, I realize that I'm also more eclectic than someone in my position would have been thirty years ago. So obviously we just have to react to this and find the right balance between presenting the various phenomena.

I don't think we are facing really monstrous obstacles. We need to be able to think in a more flexible way in order to overcome our problems. But I don't think the sole purpose of an arts organization is simply to exist. I don't think this will be the case, but if we were ever to end up in a situation where there was absolutely no function for us in the culture, I don't think there is any point in keeping up with the illusion that this is something valuable. I think we should just let go, because existence as such is not interesting enough. This is one of the problems in the strategic thinking in many cultural institutions. They plan for next week and the week after that and maybe the next year as well, but very few take the risk of thinking what will happen ten or fifteen years from now. Obviously if you do that you take a fiscal risk in the short run; but short-term thinking does not even guarantee survival, let alone development.

You mentioned the record companies, and surely they are experiencing failing sales and the difficulty of selling yet another Brahms cycle. But I think this is healthy. For me this is not the sign of a sick culture; for me this is common sense. If I go to a record store and want to buy a Brahms cycle, I must plow through the four hundred alternatives. The classics got a new lease on life from record buyers when the reformation movement started. So all of us started buying Norrington and Harnoncourt and Gardiner. I now wonder how long this can continue, but I'm not especially worried. I think that the companies should just record something else for a little while, and then come back to the classics in ten or fifteen years.

Swed: *The problem is the fear that the "something else" will be whatever crossover hit brings the quickest profit. It is not as though they are recording Ligeti cycles instead of Brahms cycles—except that in your case Sony Classical is doing just that, which is an amazing thing in the record industry these days.*

Salonen: It's a major commitment from the label, but there is also a private sponsor, Vincent Meyer, a Swiss banker who loves Ligeti's music. He's pumping an enormous amount of money into this, into the concert series, the opera, and the recorded cycle. Sometimes it takes an individual like that. If you look at the current big sellers, apart from the Three Tenors kind of stuff, almost all of it is less-recorded music, music that is interesting because of the repertoire value and not necessarily because of the conductor or the soloist. Which is also a healthy phenomenon.

Whatever you think of the Górecki piece (Symphony 3), at least people were listening to the music, and the fact that it was very well conducted by David Zinman and very well sung by Dawn Upshaw wasn't the point. The point was that it was this new piece that nobody had ever heard before. All of a sudden it became news. I think that is how it should be.

My role as a conductor is to try to find the balance, to try to present the great variety of everything there is for this particular kind of ensemble. And it's never static. If you have, say, Roger Norrington in town and he's conducting a Beethoven symphony and then the same piece is being conducted by Simon Rattle, you have two very interesting but different points of view, both modern and historically based at the same time. This phenomenon is so much a part of our life and our time that I don't even know what to call it. Obviously we have to see what's happening today and also we have to be interested in what's going to happen tomorrow, what is going to be written for symphony orchestra. I'm not worried at all about the future in this sense.

Swed: *What about the different pressures that get put on you? You have a board that employs you and has certain expectations; you have a marketing department that wants something else from you; you have more than one hundred players with their various and often conflicting personal and collective wants and needs; you have, as you've mentioned, varied audiences with their needs; and then you have yourself, your own needs as a musician and composer. Are there simply too many different pushes and pulls?*

I don't think the sole purpose of an arts organization is simply to exist... because existence as such is not interesting enough.

Swed: *A lot of the naysayers think that classical music is no longer vital because when they compare a modern performance of a Brahms symphony with, say, a Furtwängler recording, they find Furtwängler more interesting. What do you say to music lovers who want music to mean today exactly what it meant fifty or a hundred years earlier?*

Salonen: I am tempted to use a Spenglerian metaphor. I don't absolutely agree with [Oswald] Spengler in terms of his total vision about culture. But I do agree with him that whenever there is very clearly an end of a cycle in sight, people start saying that everything was better before, and that greatness—whatever that is, I don't quite know—was achieved earlier, that today nobody is able to achieve greatness. It's a normal phenomenon that happened toward the end of the Greek culture, then again at the end of the Roman Empire. At the end of the Medieval Era, when things started happening in Florence in the 1400s, lots of people were saying that the great days of mankind were over. Whenever we enter a new era there is this tremendous overdose of nostalgia. It's natural.

A symphony orchestra can easily fit into the modern culture if you think of it as a refurbished old building that has been fixed up with central heating and new windows. The basic shape remains from the past, but what's happening inside, the life, is of today. So I don't see a discrepancy there, because this happens in architecture every day. Old plays are being adapted every day. There is a big Shakespeare revival going on at the moment. Just look at *Romeo and Juliet*. All of a sudden everybody knows who Shakespeare is.

Salonen: To a certain extent, of course, there are. But I've tried to aim for variety and eclecticism in the total output of the Philharmonic rather than to have the Philharmonic accurately mirror my desires and tastes; that would be really too awesome a responsibility. So I try to make sure that the diet is varied and healthy. I think that is the only way. The greatest danger today is to concentrate on one narrow segment. Open-mindedness and variety are the key words.

Swed: *Still, the image of the orchestra is of you. Your picture has been all over town on billboards and banners for years now, and that does seem to leave the impression that the orchestra is you, and vice versa.*

Salonen: In the American system, the music director has a lot more to say and a lot more influence in the politics of an orchestra than in Europe, and American orchestras do mirror the music director's ideas more closely. But we just have to accept, however reluctantly, certain aspects of our culture, and one of those aspects is that ideas are rarely interesting and people are very interesting. So everything has to be filtered through somebody's face. A person represents this and that, and somehow it makes it easier for audiences to grasp and to understand and to follow. The same thing happens when you watch TV news. When a shooting drama occurs, it is delivered through the news anchor's mouth. Somebody has to tell the story. And in a sense I am the one who tells the great story of classical music to the community. I don't mean to sound pompous, but the symphony is one hundred and five people, a sea of faces, and therefore difficult to market in any other way. This is simply the way it works.

Somebody has to tell the story. And in a sense I am the one who tells the great story of classical music to the community.

I accept the responsibility for shaping the orchestra the way I think it should be shaped, for maintaining the principles of sound and articulation and intonation that should remain constant. But I try to keep other avenues open. The best orchestra is one without the sort of ego that says, "This is our sound." That is the European way. So I partly accept certain responsibilities and certain power and partly try to counteract them—and the balance is not always easy.

Swed: *How much does the environment, cultural and physical, affect this in Los Angeles?*

Salonen: Everything in Los Angeles is more challenging and more fascinating. The fact that everywhere orchestras, artists, and institutions are facing an uncertain future is very good, because it forces us to be avant-garde in the old sense of the word. When I speak of the avant-garde position for a symphony orchestra I'm not referring to the repertoire, but to playing a role in the forefront of society. In this part of the world, there is a very dense and important concentration of software makers. Much of the new media is concentrated in southern California, as well as a big part of the World Wide Web and other Internet resources. So at the moment this is the most exciting conducting position in the world, if you enjoy that sort of thing. And I do. It's constantly stimulating.

Swed: *Looking at the West Coast in general, there is all that new media in northern California; the San Francisco Symphony has a new lease on life; the Seattle Symphony is, for its size, one of the livelier in the country. This does seem to be where the new ideas are.*

Salonen: You could say this is part of the socioeconomic trend of the last two decades. The importance of the Atlantic is over; the Pacific is where it now happens. I'm not enough of an Adorno believer to say that music will necessarily reflect socioeconomic trends. But over the last couple of decades a lot of talent has moved to the West Coast. There are lots of very good brains on this side of America, and one of the characteristics of this side of the country is that people are willing to try new things. People here quite often started from nothing, and there is very little of the old European tradition, the families who have run things for hundreds of years, who go to the same schools and have always been supporters of the Philharmonic. It is not part of the life here.

But that not only makes it easier to try new things, it makes it almost a must. When you come here people expect you to do something that is challenging. Angelenos also expect to be entertained, which means that you can't keep repeating something, you have to always have new gags.

Swed: *There is also the other side of that equation. If the novelty level is not high enough, apathy sets in pretty quickly. That means that there is not a whole lot of depth to the musical community, and, indeed, it sometimes seems that there is not a real community at all for new music.*

Salonen: It's true that this is a difficult place for any kind of community feeling because of geography. Do you know the Ijsbreker Café in Amsterdam? It has been my dream for many years now to establish something of the kind here—a café that also has a concert hall, a hangout that serves both as a sort of community gathering spot and also a place where you can hear new music of all kinds. So if you can bear it, you listen to it, and if you can't you go to the bar and have a beer. If I have a free evening in Amsterdam, I always go to Ijsbreker.

Swed: *Do you see new ideas coming from other places besides Amsterdam?*

Salonen: In London orchestras are experts in survival. And although one can certainly learn more from their mistakes than their successes, what seems to work in terms of box office these days is thematic programming, mini-festivals, and mini-subscriptions. Within the season there might be two weekends of an in-depth experience of some composer or some period, or links between this art and that. I did three Ligeti concerts in London two weeks ago and sold out three times.

What I think also has to change, and is already changing, is the old-fashioned subscription idea that every Thursday you go to a concert. This doesn't seem to work any more. There is just too much going on, and people's tastes are too eclectic. They want more choices, and they don't want or need to buy somebody else's package, the package that is made for them by the wise guys at the Philharmonic.

Schwann Artist and Schwann Opus contributing editor Mark Swed is the chief music critic of the Los Angeles Times.

A Selected Discography of Esa-Pekka Salonen

BARTOK
Concerto for Orchestra;
Music for Strings, Percussion & Celesta
with Los Angeles Philharmonic
Sony Classical SK 62598

DALLIPICCOLA
Il Prigioniero; Canti di Prigionia
with Hynninen, Bryn-Julson, Haskin, Wedin, Alexandersson; Swedish Radio Symphony Orchestra & Radio Choir; Eric Ericson Chamber Choir
Sony Classical SK 68323

DEBUSSY
Images pour Orchestra; Prélude à l'après-midi d'un faune; La Mer
with Los Angeles Philharmonic
Sony Classical SK 62599

DEBUSSY
Nocturnes; La Damoiselle élue; Le Martyre de Saint Sébastien
with Dawn Upshaw, Paula Rasmussen, sopranos; Los Angeles Philharmonic
Sony Classical SK 58952

GRIEG
Peer Gynt (excerpts)
with Barbara Hendricks, soprano; Oslo Philharmonic
Sony Classical MK 44528

HAYDN
Symphonies 22, 78, 82
with Stockholm Chamber Orchestra
Sony Classical SK 45972

JOLIVET
Trumpet Concerto 2;
Concertino for Trumpet, Strings, & Piano;
TOMASI
Trumpet Concerto
with Wynton Marsalis, trumpet; C. Sheppard, piano; Philharmonia Orchestra
Sony Classical MK 42096

LUTOSLAWSKI
Piano Concerto; Symphony 2;
with Les Chantefleurs et Chantefables; Fanfare for the L.A. Philharmonic
with Paul Crossley, piano; Dawn Upshaw, soprano; Los Angeles Philharmonic
Sony Classical SK 67189

LUTOSLAWSKI
Symphonies 3 & 4;
Les Espaces du sommeil
with John Shirley-Quirk, baritone; Los Angeles Philharmonic
Sony Classical SK 66280

MESSIAEN
Des canyons aux étoiles; with Couleurs de la cité céleste; Oiseaux exotiques
with Paul Crossley, piano; London Sinfonietta
Sony Classical M2K 44762

MESSIAEN
Turangalîla Symphony;
LUTOSLAWSKI
Symphony 3; Les Espaces du sommeil
with Los Angeles Philharmonic; New Stockholm Chamber Orchestra
Sony Classical M2K 42271

Music for Films
HERRMANN
from Taxi Driver; Psycho; Fahrenheit 451; The Man Who Knew Too Much; Marnie; North by Northwest; Vertigo; Torn Curtain
with Los Angeles Philharmonic
Sony Classical SK 62700

NIELSEN
Flute Concerto;
Clarinet Concerto;
with Springtime on Funen; Lyric Humoresque; An Imaginary Trip to the Faeroe Islands; Prelude to Act II of Saul and David
with Swedish Radio Symphony Orchestra
Sony Classical SK 53276

NIELSEN
Symphony 1; Little Suite
with Swedish Radio Symphony Orchestra; New Stockholm CO
Sony Classical MK 42321

NIELSEN
Symphony 2;
with Aladdin (Incidental Music); Pan & Syrinx
Swedish Radio Symphony Orchestra & Radio Chorus
Sony Classical MK 44934

NIELSEN
Symphonies 3 & 6
with Swedish Radio Symphony Orchestra
Sony Classical SK 46500

NIELSEN
Symphony 4; *Helios*
with Swedish Radio Symphony Orchestra
Sony Classical MK 42093

NIELSEN
Symphony 5;
Maskarade (selections)
with Swedish Radio Symphony Orchestra
Sony Classical MK 44547

NIELSEN
Violin Concerto;
SIBELIUS
Violin Concerto
with Cho-Liang Lin, violin; Swedish Radio Symphony Orchestra
Sony Classical MK 44548

SAARIAHO
Du cristal; ... à la fumée
with Petri Alanko, alto flute; Anssi Karttunen, cello; Los Angeles Philharmonic
Ondine ODE 804

SALONEN
Mimo II; YTA I, II, III; Alto Saxophone Concerto; *Floof*
with Jorma Valjakka, oboe; Mikael Helasvuo, flute; Tuija Hakkila, piano; Anssi Karttunen, cello; Pekka Savijoki, saxophone; Anu Komsi, soprano; Finnish Radio Symphony Orchestra; Members of the Avanti! Chamber Orchestra
Finlandia 95607-2

SCHOENBERG
Piano Concerto;
LISZT
Piano Concertos 1 & 2
with Emmanuel Ax, piano; Los Angeles Philharmonic
Sony Classical SK 53289

SIBELIUS
Kullervo
with Los Angeles Philharmonic
Sony Classical SK 52563

SIBELIUS
Lemminkainen Suite; En Saga
with Los Angeles Philharmonic
Sony Classical SK 48067

SIBELIUS
Symphony 5;
Pohjola's Daughter
with Philharmonia Orchestra
Sony Classical MK 42366

STRAVINSKY
Apollon musagète; Concerto in D; Cantata
with Stockholm Chamber Orchestra; London Sinfonietta
Sony Classical SK 46667

STRAVINSKY
Concerto for Piano & Wind Instruments; Capriccio for Piano & Orchestra; Movements for Piano & Orchestra
with Paul Crossley, piano; London Sinfonietta
Sony Classical SK 45797

STRAVINSKY
Le Sacre du printemps; Symphony in 3 Movements
with Philharmonia Orchestra
Sony Classical SK 45796

STRAVINSKY
The Firebird; Jeu de cartes
with Philharmonia Orchestra
Sony Classical MK 44917

STRAVINSKY
Oedipus Rex
with Swedish Radio Orchestra
Sony Classical SK 48057

STRAVINSKY
Pétrouchka; Orpheus
with Philharmonia Orchestra
Sony Classical SK 53274

STRAVINSKY
Pulcinella; Renard the Fox; Ragtime; Octet
with London Sinfonietta
Sony Classical SK 45965

STRAVINSKY
Violin Concerto;
PROKOFIEV
Violin Concertos
with Cho-Liang Lin, violin; Los Angeles Philharmonic
Sony Classical SK 53969

TAKEMITSU
To the Edge of Dream; Vers, L'Arc-en-Ciel, Palma; Toward the Sea; Folios; 12 Songs for Guitar
with John Williams, guitar; London Sinfonietta
Sony Classical SK 46720

Valhalla Records — TO ORDER CALL (800) 222 6872

KENNETH LANE
WAGNERIAN ROMANTISCHER HELDENTENOR

•Reviews of 3rd CARNEGIE HALL (main hall) concert [solo "ALL-WAGNER"] 6/18/95:

¶"With impressive vocal skills and record-setting stamina heldentenor Kenneth Lane delivered the performance of a lifetime. For the first time ever a single-singer ALL-WAGNER program was sung in a major concert hall and virtuoso Kenneth Lane certainly gave the audience their money's worth. The athletic feat included all 9 heroic tenor roles . . . as well as all five *Wesendonck* songs [the first time ever sung in a major concert venue by a male voice] . . . effortlessly filled Carnegie Hall with tenor more dramatic & heroic than Wagner himself could have hoped for."
—**Stefan Jux,** Music Critic, *New Yorker Staats Zeitung*

¶"Kenneth Lane's All-Wagner solo concert marathon was <u>one of the extraordinary events of the century</u>. It's hard to imagine anyone daring to stand on the stage of the hallowed Carnegie Hall, and with no more than about a minute in between selections, peal forth in lustrous tones Wagnerian scenes from *RIENZI* to *PARSIFAL*, and then amazingly, add ALL of the *WESENDONCK LIEDER*. Each selection was treated as <u>an example of genuine introspection and committed vocal authority</u>. My own personal favorite was *TRISTAN* which captured the agony and ecstacy in the heartbroken hero, in <u>a voice that rode the crest of Wagnerian passion</u>."
—**Don Goldberg,** *Celebration Opera*, WRHU

¶"His voice easily filled the farthest reaches of Carnegie Hall . . . Mr. Lane's concert should be recorded in the *Guinness Book of Records* as a one-of-a-kind event."
—**Martin Kalmanoff,** Music Critic & Opera Composer [*Opera, Opera* (Saroyan), *The Harmfulness of Tobacco* (Eric Bentley) & *Just Say I Love Her*]

•Reviews of "WAGNER'S EPIC HEROES" CD:

¶"In this chronological survey of Wagner's output, Mr. Lane proved that dramatically and vocally he is that rare <u>real</u> heldentenor [heroic tenor]. The voice managed the upper regions with secure, ringing tones and a warm baritone color in the lower and middle registers. His prodigious talent for both vocal and histrionic expression literally and viscerally, demands viewing him in "live" opera performances, so strong is the impact that this recording conjures up visually in one's imagination!"
—**Laszlo Halasz,** Founder & First Artistic & Musical Director, New York City Opera

¶"Music to some enthusiasts is a quasi-religious experience. I am a moderately religious person, but the combination of Wagner and Kenneth Lane's voice makes conventional religion seem almost pedestrian !"
—**Brice M. Clagett,** Author/Critic/Attorney

¶"Kenneth Lane is certainly at home with the heroes! How many other tenors would (or could) attempt such an ambitious program? One would assume such a voice to come from a person of Valhallic proportions, as are most Wagnerian tenors. That he manages to maintain the support and heft for his heroic vocal undertakings and yet stay youthfully trim is certainly a tribute to his life-style and discipline. It must also come as a pleasant surprise to those who see him in operatic performances as well."
—Lawrence F. Holdridge, recordings' annotator, reviewer, radio commentator, and publisher of "The Record Auction" of Amityville, New York

¶"Hearing Kenneth Lane sing Wagner one is transported not only to the ideal aural realm of the Wagnerian heldentenor protagonist he is interpreting, but also convincingly to the entire Wagner canon, sensing the majesty, wide emotional outpourings and deeply-felt tenderness so palpably atmospheric of the Wagner we all imagined, but have not heard since the one and only Melchior."
—**Martin Kalmanoff,** Music Critic, opera composer
["The Bald Soprano" (Ionesco), "Insect Comedy" (Lewis Allan), *"Joy of Prayer,"* & "pop" standard "Just Say I Love Her"]

¶Lane's voice is indeed powerful and full of character. . . . He captures effectively the anguish of TRISTAN denouncing the cursed drink (and himself), the confusion of PARSIFAL confronting Kundry, the regret of the dying SIEGFRIED, the torture of OTELLO's jealousy. . . . It is also pleasant, these days when most would-be heldentenors are wimpy and characterless, to find a singer like Kenneth Lane, who has real dramatic power. . . . There is rich promise in his singing. . . . **WE NEED HIM!**
—**William Youngren,** Music Critic, FANFARE, March/April 1997

¶Kenneth Lane is a tenor with impressive credentials. . . . The evidence provided by [Lane's] "Amfortas! Die Wunde!" and "Nur eine Waffe taugt!" suggests that he'd be quite an imposing PARSIFAL. . . . [Lane's] three TRISTAN excerpts also tantalize with their power. . . . Noted: he does nail the two "B♭"s in "Dio! mi potevi scagliar! [Otello]"
—**James Miller,** Music Critic, *Fanfare*, March/April 1997

¶Lane's *Rienzi*——heartfelt, spiritual, even vibrato! Otello——great hi B♭ (!!) many, many very impressive points.
—**Eugene Kohn,** Metropolitan Opera Conductor

<<Continued next page>>

•Reviews of 2nd CARNEGIE HALL Concert & CD:
"CARNEGIE HALL TEN-LANGUAGES 'LIVE' SOLO DÉBUT" CD:

¶"Kenneth Lane's CDs are quite an achievement—displaying wide scope, fine musicianship and, above all, his stamina!"
——**George Jellinek,** host of the 2 nationally broadcast series,*The Vocal Scene & Vocal Gold;*
Author, *History Through the Opera Glass from the Rise of Caesar to the Fall of Napoleon*

¶"Not only does Lane have one of the most beautiful voices I have ever heard, but the style and feeling with which he sings qui te different pieces is unmatched in my experience. His renderings have an intensity, a warmth and an elegance that I have rarely encountered, a heroic quality—Melchior is the only comparison that comes to mind."
——**Brice M. Clagett,** Author/Critic/Attorney

¶"The size of Mr. Lane's voice is astounding, and he lives every word he sings. Lane's Florestan's aria (*Fidelio*) left me gasping! Only Roswaenge's had the same effect on me, but Lane's rendition contains a singularly up-tempo finale which is both a vocal and dramatic knock-out."
——**Joe Pearce,** Sec'y, Vocal Record Collectors' Society,
Contributor,*Opera Quarterly & The Record ollector*

¶"Huge, wide-ranging voice . . . heroic notes up to high B . . . a true dramatic tenor——a potential phenomenon——who can act with his voice as well as sing with it."
——**Bill Zakariasen,** *New York Concert Review*

¶"A true *Tenore di Forza!*"
——**Aida Favia-Artsay,** Author, Caruso on Records

•Reviews of 1st CARNEGIE HALL Concert [with dramatic soprano Norma Jean]:

¶*New York Times:* "stentorian tone"
¶*Musical Courier:* "voice of rare vocal beauty"
¶*New Yorker Staats-Zeitung:* "Kenneth Lane possesses unquestionable material, a well-developed technique which allows for his big tone production and the necessary endurance to go with it."
¶*Musical America:* "Kenneth Lane sang in no less than ten languages . . . Mr. Lane's . . . tenor voice was dark in quality and large enough to fill Carnegie Hall quite easily. The good-sized audience was quite enthusiastic."

•Reviews on tours:
Chicago American:: "an exciting voice" / *Houston Post*: : "a dramatic tenor of exceptional range & intensity" / *Montreal Gazette*: "a dramatic tenor with a bel canto quality" / *Vancouver Sun*: "a magnificent voice of pure quality & fine resonance" / *Toronto Telegram*: "a tenderness that belied the real strength of the voice"

On VALHALLA RECORDS CDs:
🍎 **(VAH-1595).** "Kenneth Lane, Wagnerian Heldentenor, WAGNER's EPIC HEROES"
🍎 **(VAH-1594).** "Kenneth Lane, Heldentenor, CARNEGIE HALL 'LIVE' SOLO DÉBUT in TEN LANGUAGES" [Italian, German, French, Spanish, Norwegian, Swedish, Latin, Hebrew, Yiddish, English]

SOON TO BE RELEASED:
🍎 **(VAH-1596).** "KENNETH LANE, WAGNERIAN ROMANTISCHER HELDENTENOR, WAGNER'S HEDONISTIC & PIOUS HEROES" including the Complete *Wesendonck Lieder,* with the Sofia (Bulgaria) State Opera Orchestra
🍎 **(VAH-1597).** "ALL-WAGNER CARNEGIE HALL 'LIVE' 6/18/95 CONCERT" [2-CD set, with *Wesendonck* Complete with Orchestra recorded in Europe]
🍎 **(VAH-1599).** "HEROES of the PEOPLE" CD with Orch. [Florestan, Samson, Rienzi, Otello, Arnold—8 high Cs, Rodrigue in Le Cid, Aeneas, Andrea Chénier, Sadko, Raoul, John of Leyden, Joseph in Egypt (Méhul), Rhadamès, Judas Maccabaeus, & Andrij's Prayer from Zaporozhets za Dunayem (Semyon Hulak-Artemovsky) & Andrij in Taras Bulba (Nicolai Lysenko) [both in Ukrainian].

CDs available (&, in 1998, Videocassettes) from H&B RECORDINGS DIRECT TEL: 1/800-222-6872 [USA, Canada, Puerto Rico] & Int'l Orders: USA Code + 210 545-0940; Int'l E-Mail: staff@hbdirect.com; Internet: http://www.hbdirect.com; FAX: 001 10 210-545-3968; Mailing Address: 12037 Starcrest Drive, San Antonio, Texas 78247, U.S.A.

AGENCY FOR OPERA PERFORMERS & VALHALLA RECORDS
(201) 335-0111/0112   FAX (201) 335-2882   E-Mail: ValhallRec@AOL.com

KENNETH LANE SINGS HIS FOURTH MAIN HALL CARNEGIE HALL CONCERT
Tuesday April 7, 1998, AT 8PM —ALL-WAGNER, WAGNER's EPIC HEROES—
including, all five monologues of Act Three of *TRISTAN*, scenes from ALL the *RING* music dramas, the usually-cut scenes of *RIENZI*, the Complete *Wesendonck Lieder* & CARNEGIE HALL PREMIÈRES of Songs by WAGNER .
Concert Season 1998-1999: Heroes of the People & Wagner's Hedonistic & Pious Heroes
Concert Season 1999-2000: "10 + 2"—A Concert of Vocal Masterpieces Sung in Twelve Languages, adding Russian & Ukrainian to the original TEN LANGUAGES Début Concert

Learning with Lenny:
The Ultimate Bernstein Legacy

Mortimer H. Frank

Almost smack in the middle of this tumultuous century a young, still somewhat unfocused musician who had displayed promising talent as a composer, conductor, and pianist burst upon the television scene with a stark cogency that changed forever the meaning of the term "music appreciation."

There he stood, italicized by intense lighting that cast shadows on a floor comprising a huge replica of the first page of the orchestral score of Beethoven's Fifth Symphony. He walked to the piano and played four notes: "Three Gs and an E-flat," he said, "nothing more. Baby-simple. Anyone might have thought of it, maybe. But out of them has grown the first movement of a great symphony, a movement so economical and consistent that almost every bar of it is a direct development of the opening notes." With these words, Leonard Bernstein emerged as an extraordinary educator.

To appreciate Bernstein's gift for explaining music, for making it comprehensible without violating its identity as music, one must first be aware of the varying degrees of futility that had stamped previous efforts at music education for the masses. Bernstein, to be sure, was not the first conductor to attempt what is called in literary circles *explication du texte*. With the advent of electrical technology in 1925, Leopold Stokowski recorded brief talks as part of his initial Victor sets of such warhorses as Beethoven's Seventh, Brahms's First, and Dvořák's "New World" symphonies. Stokowski noted that the Brahms was "like a song expressing the inner yearning of the soul." In counterpoint to this vague drivel was Stokowski's outlining of the work's themes, with illustrations provided on the piano—nothing very illuminating, but moderately informative if limited in scope by being confined to a four-minute, 78rpm side.

Far more insipid was the gibberish made up to fit the prominent themes from familiar masterpieces. To the "dawn" portion of Grieg's music for *Peer Gynt*, my fifth-grade class learned the words "morning is dawning and Peer Gynt is yawning and Grieg is too lazy to rise." And conductor Walter Damrosch offered these lyrics to the C-Major fanfares of the second movement of the Beethoven Fifth:

For the Hero has come,
Sound the trumpet and drum.
He has fought
The good fight
He has won.

Then there was the "tune detective," Sigmund Spaeth, who, among other things, showed how famous melodies from repertory staples were adapted in popular songs, a notable example being "I'm Always Chasing Rainbows" as an outgrowth of Chopin's Fantasie-Impromptu.

What all such feeble efforts on behalf of music education lacked was the kind of "appreciation" great art demands—discussion of that art in terms of the art itself. That such a discussion can have a broad-based clarity, cogency, and relevance without falling back on technical jargon was made patently obvious the day Leonard Bernstein stepped before the cameras on NBC's *Omnibus* program to discuss the Beethoven Fifth.

Fortunately, one does not have to rely on one's memory of that program. Sony has reissued the talk (delivered in four languages by Bernstein himself) on a single CD (SXK 47645) that also contains the conductor's New York Philharmonic recording of the entire Fifth Symphony. Although that performance is not always compelling, the commentary remains riveting.

Bernstein goes to the Beethoven Sketch Books and describes how the composer "rejected, rewrote, scratched out, tore up, and altered a passage as many as twenty times," leaving "a bloody record of a tremendous inner battle." But this inner battle is a far cry from Damrosch's ludicrous and meaningless "good fight." Bernstein orchestrates those rejected sketches and offers hypotheses about where they might have fit in the first movement's scheme.

What one learns from this extraordinary exercise has nothing to do with "fate knocking on the door" or any other

---

All photographs are from the *Young People's Concerts* which were broadcast on CBS from 1958 to 1973.

The miracle of so many of the *Young People's Concerts* is that they had relevance to audiences of every age.

extramusical idiocy. Rather, Bernstein's talk gives meaning to the notion that Classicism in music embodies a self-contained reductive style in which even the rests, the fermatas, and the simplest of triads become pregnant with drama and meaning. More than anything else, Bernstein reveals the way in which

Beethoven—to use the words F. Scott Fitzgerald applied to Tolstoy and all great artists—was "a taker outer." Unlike some of today's most offensive (and mindless) critics, Bernstein does not "deconstruct;" rather, he *reconstructs* the struggle that ultimately purged the first movement of anything extraneous and produced what is perhaps the tersest, most compact, and economical movement in the symphonic literature.

Bernstein's appearances on *Omnibus* proved that he was (in the best sense of the term) a television personality. Articulate, knowledgeable, and handsome, he spoke with a direct simplicity that was illuminating and comprehensible, a style ideally suited to what were then called "children's concerts." Under Bernstein they became *Young People's Concerts*, major events in what some people were beginning to call "the vast wasteland of television." The miracle of so many of them is that they had relevance to audiences of every age. Twenty-five of those concerts for "young people" have been re-issued on video cassettes. For this discussion I looked at six. Despite an occasional excess, they stand as models of taste and intelligence that continue to set standards for music education.

Consider, for example, the very first of the series, telecast on January 18, 1958. Its title—"What Does Music Mean?"—seems to raise a question unanswerable in the space of a one-hour format. Yet Bernstein goes at once to the heart of the issue. He enters, turns to the orchestra, and conducts the first half-minute of the finale of Rossini's Overture to *William Tell*. Then he stops, turns to his audience, and asks, "Okay, what do you think that music is all about?" After several shouted responses, he goes on, "That's just what I thought you'd say—cowboys, bandits, horses, the Lone Ranger." He then adds, "It's not about the Lone Ranger at all. It's about notes, E-flats and F-sharps. Music is never about anything. It's just about notes, sounds put together in such a way that we get pleasure out of listening to it."

This is the same attitude expressed by Toscanini when he said that the first movement of Beethoven's "Eroica" is not about Napoleon or any other hero; it is simply *Allegro con brio*. Bernstein's comment also echoes Stravinsky's notion that "music means nothing." As Bernstein goes on to say, "Music is never about something; it just is"—a welcome corrective to the extramusical nonsense tossed out by earlier "educators" in the name of "appreciation."

But having said that music is "never about anything," Bernstein proceeds to explain what the finale of the *William Tell* Overture *is* about: rhythm and "a good tune." He then shows how the opening of the finale is balanced by ascending and descending phrases that provide, as he puts it, a kind of "question and answer." In short, Bernstein is explaining music not with extramusical irrelevancies, but exclusively in terms of itself. This is, of course, the kind of analytical approach favored by Sir Donald Tovey, but with one key difference: technical terms are avoided and complex ideas emerge, as a result, with unfettered clarity. This is one of the most difficult of achievements, and surely the mark of the best criticism. And as I watched Bernstein engage his audience by having it sing part of the overture, I remembered that all *my* elementary-school music appreciation teacher could muster in presenting the finale of this overture was, "The first person to yell 'Hi-Yo Silver' will have to bring his mother to school."

Even when a work seems to invite extramusical associations, Bernstein cautions against them. In discussing the first movement of Beethoven's "Pastoral" Symphony, he notes that while the music has a subtitle ("Awakening of Joyful Feelings on Arrival in the Country"), it merely suggests joy, a joy that could be stimulated by anything, not necessarily the Austrian woods to which Beethoven often retreated. Similarly, in tackling "The Great Gate of Kiev" from Mussorgsky's *Pictures at an Exhibition*, Bernstein says that the music's grandeur suggests a magnificent gate only because the composer suggests it; it might just as well suggest the grandeur of the Mississippi River. Worth noting, too, is that this example, like all of those Bernstein chose for his "young" audience, is relatively short and thus not a strain on attention span.

On rare occasions Bernstein slips into the kind of excess that infected his interpretations during his earliest years with the New York Philharmonic. As an extension of his notion that music expresses feeling, he suggests that this feeling may be the one held by the composer when writing a particular piece. He amplifies this idea with a passage from Tchaikovsky's Fourth Symphony on which he imposed the words "I want it" to illustrate the ethos of "wanting." Here he is too subjective. Even if the music does suggest "wanting," itself an arguable notion, it doesn't follow that the composer himself felt wanting at the time he wrote it. Two of the most joyous works in the literature—Beethoven's Second Symphony and Stravinsky's Symphony in C—were written when their composers were deeply depressed: Beethoven over his growing deafness, and Stravinsky over the death of his daughter and his own confinement in a tuberculosis sanitarium. Like any artist, the composer affects a pose and assumes an artistic persona that may be quite different from the actual person.

Such lapses, however, are the exception, not the rule, and time and again one is reminded in watching these videos how clear and cogent Bernstein's explanations are. The telecast "What Is Sonata Form?" (November 6, 1964) clarifies the often misused term "form," which, as Bernstein notes, is used to define shape. Consequently to speak, as some writers do, of concerto form is to confuse the word with genre. More important, Bernstein clarifies not only the shape of sonata form but the harmonic underpinnings that give it dramatic tension. My only regret is that he does not state (as he once did on an *Omnibus* program) that sonata form, despite its recognizable shape, is not a prefabricated mold into which composers pour their music. But perhaps he felt this would be throwing too much at once to his young audience.

In the telecast of January 24, 1959, Bernstein tackles the question, "What Is Classical Music?" He distinguishes classical music from jazz, pop, and folk music by pointing out that it is meant to played by following notation as specifically as possible within the limitations and variations of human ability and taste. He goes on to define the Classical period, using Haydn as a prime exemplar. With the finale of that composer's Symphony 102, Bernstein does the seemingly impossible: he explains the jokes in the movement without killing their humor.

One may question, to be sure, Bernstein's distinction between Classicism and Romanticism, particularly his suggestion that Beethoven broke "Classical" rules to which Mozart and Haydn adhered. Surely it could be argued that, in their respective ways, Haydn and Mozart broke just as many rules, and that that was a source of their greatness.

In "What Makes Music Symphonic?," telecast on December 13, 1958, Bernstein speaks of how the sophisticated repetition that produces development lies at the heart of symphonic style, using examples from the standard repertory to make the point. Perhaps the highest compliment I can pay this talk is to say that it made me view works that I thought I knew all too well—the Beethoven "Eroica" and Tchaikovsky

Fourth Symphonies—from a new perspective. Again, there is no condescending here. Nor does Bernstein simply talk *at* his listeners; here he invites them to whistle the "Colonel Bogey March" as he uses it to illustrate a simple kind of development through repetition.

In "The Sound of an Orchestra," telecast on December 14, 1965, Bernstein says that a great orchestra should not have a sound of its own. Rather, it should be flexible so as to be able to produce a sonority most apt for the music at hand. He makes his point after performing the *Largo* from Haydn's Symphony 88 with a lushness and exaggeration that are all

wrong for Haydn, observing that such self-indulgent mannerisms exemplify "the sin of pride." Again he hits on the key issue of what lies at the core of the elusive quality we define as "good taste."

The last of the six *Young People's Concerts* to be considered here, "What Is a Melody?," televised on December 21, 1962, is devoted to what Bernstein terms "the meat and potatoes of music," its "main course." He builds distinctions among various types of melody; for example, the "theme-like" melodies of Beethoven on the one hand and, on the other, the more tuneful melodies exemplified by the famous second subject of the first movement of Tchaikovsky's "Pathétique" Symphony. Here Bernstein becomes a bit simplistic. The analogy he draws between that Tchaikovsky melody and the opening of the Beethoven Fifth is somewhat strained. But in this talk as in all the others, he makes you *think* about music, listen with the most attentive of ears, and contemplate music *qua* music intelligently and perceptively. And stimulating intelligent perception, after all, is what a great teacher does.

Though these three cassettes, each containing two telecasts, carry the Sony imprint, they are unnumbered and are available only from the Leonard Bernstein Society (800-382-6622). A brochure describing other available Bernstein videos can be obtained by writing to the Society at P.O. Box 3930, Milford, CT 06460.

More widely available are a number of videocassettes released by Kultur. Two of them, *Four Ways to Say Farewell* (Kultur 1445) and *The Little Drummer Boy* (Kultur 1444), are devoted to Mahler. The birth of widespread interest in Mahler was due not so much to his celebrated disciple, Bruno Walter, as to Bernstein. More than any other conductor, Bernstein brought Mahler to a broad public. He was the first to record all the composer's symphonies, and his identification with the music was so intense and complete that he once said, in a *High Fidelity* article, "I am Gustav Mahler."

This intense identification is apparent in the two videos. Indeed, in *Four Ways to Say Farewell*, some may find Bernstein's analysis of the Ninth Symphony too personal and subjective. The conductor who told young people that music is "only notes" speaks here of how this symphony's opening movement echoes Mahler's irregular heartbeat—biographically justifiable, perhaps, but ignoring the reality that, as great music, it must transcend such associations. Nonetheless, compelling insights are offered here, notably Bernstein's description of how the work marks the end of the Viennese symphonic tradition and the beginning of a new one. And let it not be forgotten that in the Vienna Philharmonic (with whom many snippets of the conductor's rehearsal of the work are shown) Bernstein was facing an orchestra that told him Mahler produced *"Scheissmusik."* Surely its mind change owes more than a little to Bernstein's efforts.

More compelling, however, is *The Little Drummer Boy*. Here Bernstein is brilliant in clarifying Mahler's Jewishness and illustrating it with musical examples of the Phrygian mode, cross-relation, and alternations of major and minor tonalities. And he goes on to show how Mahler overlaid the Viennese symphonic tradition with an ethos of diaspora. One

The *Young People's Concerts* became major events in what some people were beginning to call "the vast wasteland of television."

learns also how Mahler modified passages from *Des Knaben Wunderhorn* for use in the Symphony No. 2. Even those who find the work cluttered with excess should come away from Bernstein's analysis with an understanding that makes the music more meaningful and moving.

Utterly different but equally instructive is *"The Rite of Spring" in Rehearsal* (Kultur 1446), in which Bernstein rehearses the Schleswig-Holstein Music Festival Orchestra, a student ensemble, some of whose members were still in high school. The video is a model for conductors on how to deal with a remarkably skilled but inexperienced orchestra of less than world-class ability.

Bernstein begins their first meeting by asking for a two-octave C-Major scale starting on the lowest C of each instrument. They try it a few times, following his indications for dynamics, tempos, and attacks. Within five minutes he has a good idea of the group's responsiveness, intonation, and sonority. Interspersed in the rehearsal segments are comments from the young musicians; one of the most telling is, "Bernstein doesn't just beat time; he shows you."

He surely does, but he also knows not to push this student group too hard. At the end of the rehearsal he goes over a passage with the winds. After a few repetitions it is clear that they are incapable of producing what he wants, and he stops pursuing it. For anyone interested in how a gifted conductor rehearses, this should be required viewing.

No survey of Bernstein as educator would be complete without considering the six talks that comprised the 1973 Charles Eliot Norton lectures at Harvard. When the conductor (who graduated from Harvard in 1939) was invited to give these talks, many an eyebrow was raised. After all, some asked, did Broadway Lenny really deserve a place beside such a previous Norton luminary as Igor Stravinsky? But the result of those lectures—*The Unanswered Question* (Harvard University Press, 1976)—is every bit as rewarding as Stravinsky's *Poetics of Music*, the product of *his* Norton talks at Harvard.

In his introduction to *The Unanswered Question* Bernstein notes, "The pages that follow were written not to be read but listened to." On television the talks benefited from the charm of Bernstein's personality and from being able to hear him demonstrate his ideas on the piano. In book form that charm is partly lost, and the reader who cannot make sense of musical notation will not grasp in full the relevance of Bernstein's examples.

But enough can be gleaned, even by someone who cannot distinguish middle C from a B-flat, to reveal Bernstein not only as a profound musical thinker but as a commanding scholar as well. Inspired by Noam Chomsky's *Language and Mind*, he attempts to do with music what Chomsky did with language: to show, in effect, linguistic analogues in musical syntax, tackling such issues as phonology, semantics, and ambiguity as applied to music. Some of his analogies are strained, but there is no doubt that Bernstein's thinking fosters insights and appreciation in the richest sense of the terms. Space limitations prevent citing several examples, but one is worth looking at in some detail: a 30-page exegesis of the first movement of Beethoven's "Pastoral" Symphony.

This example is worth attention for two reasons. First, it develops the previously cited notion that Bernstein expresses about the "Pastoral" in one of his *Young People's Concerts*. Of greater importance, musical analysis simply does not get any better. In this case it is based upon exploding the ill-judged notion that the "Pastoral" (despite some suggestions to the contrary) should be heard in the context of a specific program. Instead it should be judged, in Bernstein's apt words, "not as a pastoral symphony but purely as Beethoven's Symphony 6 in F Major, Opus 68." He then proceeds to illustrate how the initial four measures of the work provide "the material out of which the whole first movement is going to grow."

To follow Bernstein's argument page by page is to discover how that movement is at once as grand and complex as the first movement of the "Eroica," yet as terse and economical as the opening movement of the Fifth Symphony. Indeed, what Bernstein provides here is criticism brought to an even higher level of sophistication, clarity, and aptness than he offered in his *Omnibus* excursion into the Fifth Symphony. And in the process he destroys the notion that Beethoven's even-numbered symphonies are less profound than the odd-numbered ones.

It is hard to imagine how Bernstein will be judged a half-century from now. Time plays strange tricks and can lead critics into peculiar byways, as some of the recent strictures leveled against Toscanini make clear. Certainly some of Bernstein's music is memorable, as are many of his finest recordings. But if I had to choose what I would want my grandchildren to take from him, the *Young People's Concerts* would have pride of place, with his writing to follow as they grew older. And that writing would also deserve consideration in any course I give in music criticism.

"I love to teach," Bernstein once said, "because I love to see people learn." In his pedagogical excursions, one becomes immersed not only in the conductor's love for music but in the music itself, taking from this immersion new awareness and appreciation of what great music is all about. It is a legacy to be proud of.

Mortimer H. Frank, contributing editor of Schwann Artist *and* Schwann Opus, *currently teaches at the Julliard School of Music. His forthcoming book,* Arturo Toscanini: The NBC Years, *will be published by Amadeus Press.*

ORCHESTRAS THAT MATTER

American Period-Instrument Orchestras

Bernard D. Sherman

If you wanted to start an early-music orchestra, you might find yourself wishing you lived on the other side of the Atlantic. In France or the Netherlands, your orchestra could benefit from the still-generous government arts funding; in England, you could draw upon the world's highest per-capita concentration of period-instrument virtuosos, who thrive due to an unequaled supply of studio gigs. And all three places offer large audiences of enthusiasts. Many American early-music experts have, in fact, found success after migrating overseas. Yet some who've stayed home have managed to create remarkable orchestras despite the more limited resources.

It's anyone's guess why New York has never quite taken to period orchestras, but it is obvious why San Francisco and Boston each support several: both areas are bursting with early-music devotees, and it was inevitable that some of them would start orchestras. Bostonians were the first to do so when, in 1973, Martin Pearlman founded what was then called Banchetto Musicale—one of those richly archaic names so beloved of early-music groups on both sides of the Atlantic. Under that name, the group gave the American period-instrument premieres of Rameau's *Zoroastre* and Mozart's *Don Giovanni* and *Magic Flute*. But when the group began to record for Telarc in 1992, it switched to a plain, unambiguously American title: **Boston Baroque**. European listeners told Telarc they preferred it, and, as Carole Friedman, the orchestra's executive director, says, "I always had to spell *and* explain the old name. With the new one, I only have to spell 'Baroque.'"

The group consists of a stable core of professional players and singers, augmented for certain works. Boston Baroque's *Messiah* won a Grammy nomination, and it brought Pearlman and group the distinction of being the first early-music players to perform on a Grammy Awards broadcast. The group's releases have all sold an average of 20,000 copies, which for classical music is quite respectable. Musically, too, its Brandenburg Concertos stand out in a crowded field, and its recording of the Robert Levin completion of the Mozart Requiem is a must-have for Mozartians.

Boston Baroque became well-known outside of Massachusetts only after Telarc began recording it. Something similar hap-

Left: Boston Baroque at Jordan Hall, New England Conservatory
Facing page: Tafelmusik

pened to the first American period-instrument band to gain international recognition, **Philharmonia Baroque Orchestra**; the recognition resulted from the group's CDs for Harmonia Mundi USA. Philharmonia started recording for the label after the British conductor Nicholas McGegan was appointed music director in 1985. The discs reflect McGegan's performing philosophy, in that they often preserve single long takes rather than patched-together studio concoctions on which—as McGegan puts it—"everything might be perfectly manicured but perfectly dead."

Philharmonia began almost informally in 1981 as a natural outgrowth of the San Francisco Bay Area's early-music scene, but has since developed into something that operates more or less like a standard orchestra. It now has a large base of subscribers—its concert series usually sell out—and a solid core of private and corporate donors. And instead of being the pick-up band so common in early music, it consists of a stable group of mostly local players (as does Boston Baroque). The years of working together have paid off: the musicians know each other's playing so well that they can respond to one another with the spontaneity of chamber players. You can hear this on the best of their recordings, such as their Harmonia Mundi disc of Rameau suites; one reviewer said this disc quickly persuades you that you're hearing "the most thrilling sounds of the late Baroque," and has an élan that Continental groups sometime miss in this composer. Other high points among their discs are the Corelli Concerti Grossi 1–6 Op. 6, and the Handel *Water Music*. (Philharmonia will, by the way, soon be recording for BMG Classics.)

Philharmonia's executive director, George Gelles, objects to the group's being pigeonholed as early-music "specialists." He points out that the Philharmonia's repertory covers as long a time span (1600 to 1850) as the repertory of, say, the San Francisco Symphony, which extends from 1750 to the present. Still, the opposite approach to repertory—that of specializing narrowly—can have its value. Among our period-instrument orchestras, the extreme example of specialization is probably the **Apollo Ensemble**—a group that plays only Haydn symphonies, and, to restrict things further, only those written before 1775. It was founded by John Hsu, a father figure among American viola da gamba players and an authority on Haydn, in order to complement his celebrated recordings of the composer's Baryton Trios. Hsu wanted to explore a more extrovert genre from the same period in Haydn's life—the symphony—by re-creating as closely as possible the constitution of Haydn's own orchestra.

Apollo consists of a select group of 14 early-music players who work with Hsu every summer, and the group does have some life outside the studio. Aside from concerts in New York, it will tour Europe this May, the culmination being a concert at the Esterházy palace, where most of Apollo's repertory was first played. Apollo's first CD features Symphonies 23, 35, and 42. The first-rate string playing is no surprise given the conductor's specialty, but I was also struck by the superb wind and horn playing. The CD and its follow-up (*The*

Hidden Haydn, Symphonies 12, 44, and 64) stand among the finest recordings of early and middle Haydn.

Toronto's **Tafelmusik** operates much more like Boston Baroque and Philharmonia Baroque, with a repertory stretching from Biber to Beethoven and a large audience of subscribers. Demand for tickets is so great, in fact, that Tafelmusik recently had to add an extra concert to its series. Violinist Jeanne Lamon has led the group's remarkably stable personnel since 1981; they also make recordings under the German conductor Bruno Weil. Like Philharmonia Baroque, Tafelmusik has won numerous record awards, and *Classic CD* went so far as to call the group "perhaps the world's finest period band." Good samples of its work with Lamon are the Handel *Water Music* (some regard this as the best recording of the piece) and Vivaldi *Four Seasons* (the *Penguin Guide's* Rosette winner). As for its recordings with Weil, some standouts are Haydn's "Paris" Symphonies and *Creation,* which, says *Gramophone,* conveys "the work's unique joy and exhilaration" better than other period-instrument recordings. *Classic CD* prefers it to all other recordings—including Karajan's, its previous benchmark in this work.

Tafelmusik has developed a following in Europe not only through its recordings but also through its international tours, which are far more frequent than those of other American period bands. The tours are funded partly by the government; being Canadian, Tafelmusik enjoys more government support than U.S. groups do, although its corporate support is significantly less than it would be in the States.

The only U.S. period-instrument orchestra with direct government ties is Kenneth Slowik's **Smithsonian Chamber Players,** which is sponsored by the Smithsonian Institution. Despite the museum connection, only a fraction of the group's funding comes from government sources, with the majority raised from the private sector (concert revenues go to the Smithsonian Institution). The funds are not sufficient to allow Slowik to try some things he would do very well, such as Wagner's *Siegfried Idyll* on period instruments; if he were in France or the Netherlands, government subsidies would make such things *faits accomplis*.

But Slowik has some remarkable accomplishments to his credit. The Cambridge University Press book *Choral Music on Record* called his Bach *St. John Passion*, on the Smithsonian house label, "unequivocally . . . the best of the period-instruments performances overall." Most interesting have been Slowik's two Deutsche Harmonia Mundi recordings of late-Romantic works for chamber orchestra. These break new ground for the early-music movement, both in the recent dates of the repertoire—they include some Schoenberg, Barber, and Richard Strauss—and in the approach to playing. In preparing the *Adagietto* from Mahler's Symphony 5, Slowik had his players listen to the first recording ever made of the piece, from 1926, led by Mahler's close friend Willem Mengelberg. The adoption of such practices as *portamento* and *rubato* makes Slowik's Mahler sound entirely unlike the clean-cut Wagner of Roger Norrington. Richard Taruskin, who has derided Norrington in the *New York Times* for trying to "de-Wagnerize Wagner," has praised Slowik for performances "far more shapely and eloquent, and more imbued with personal initiative, than our complacent cleaner-uppers have dreamt of in their note-bound philosophies." The Schoenberg *Verklärte Nacht* and Strauss *Metamorphosen* are equally moving and distinguished. Along with their other virtues, these recordings have the sense of discovery and commitment found in the best of pioneering early-music discs over the years.

Plenty of other early-music orchestras in the U.S. deserve the attention both of readers and of record companies, and some are managing to get on disc. Perhaps future articles will give them the coverage they warrant, but for the moment, the five listed above show how diverse American early-music orchestras can be, and how much they can accomplish in spite of the challenges they face.

Bernard D. Sherman is the author of Inside Early Music: Conversations with Performers *(Oxford University Press, 1997), and has written for* The Encyclopedia of Aesthetics *(OUP, 1998),* Early Music, Historical Performance, Fanfare, Piano and Keyboard, Strings, *and many other publications.*

Selected Discography of American Period-Instrument Orchestras

The Apollo Ensemble

HAYDN
Symphonies 35, 23, 42
Dorian DOR 90191

Hidden Haydn
HAYDN
Symphonies 12, 44, 64
Dorian DOR 90226

(Also recommended: John Hsu's recordings of the composer's intimate, affecting Baryton Trios, such as those on the disc Haydn Divertimenti, Dorian DOR 90233.)

Boston Baroque

BACH
Brandenburg Concertos
Telarc CD 80412 (2 CDs)

HANDEL
Messiah
Telarc CD 80322 (2 CDs)

MOZART
Requiem
(Robert Levin completion)
Telarc CD 80410

Philharmonia Baroque Orchestra

CORELLI
Concerti Grossi
Nos. 1-6, Op. 6
Harmonia Mundi USA
HMU 907014

HANDEL
Messiah
Harmonia Mundi USA
HMU 907050/52 (3 CDs)

HANDEL
Water Music
Harmonia Mundi USA
HMU 907010

RAMEAU
Orchestral Suites from *Naïs* and *Le Temple de la gloire*
Harmonia Mundi France
HMU 907121

The Smithsonian Chamber Players

BACH
St. John Passion
Smithsonian ND 0381 (2 CDs)

Metamorphosis
BARBER
Adagio for Strings;
ELGAR
Elegy and *Serenade;*
RICHARD STRAUSS
Metamorphosen
Deutsche Harmonia Mundi
05472-77343-2

Transfiguration
MAHLER
Adagietto
(from Symphony 5);
Quartet in F
(orchestrated from Beethoven String Quartet, Op. 95);
SCHOENBERG
Verklärte Nacht
Deutsche Harmonia Mundi
05472-77374-2

Tafelmusik
with Jeanne Lamon:

BACH
Brandenburg Concertos
Sony S2K 66289 (2 CDs)

(On the whole, I slightly prefer this version to Boston Baroque's, but in some concertos I would choose the opposite. Whatever your preference, both sets are superb.)

HANDEL
Water Music;
Suite from *Il pastor fido*
Sony SK 68257

VIVALDI
Four Seasons; with Sinfonia al Santo Sepolcro, RV. 169
Sony SK 48251

with Bruno Weil:

HAYDN
The Creation
Sony SX2K 57965 (2 CDs)

HAYDN
Symphonies 82, 83, 84
Sony SK 66295

HAYDN
Symphonies 85, 86, 87
Sony SK 66296

Opus Subscriptions

To order your subscription for *Schwann Opus* call or write:

Schwann Publications, Dept. 56A
49 Sheridan Avenue, Albany, NY 12210
Telephone: (800) 877-2693
Telephone: (518)-436-9686 outside U.S.

U.S. and Possessions	$39.95
Canada	$49.95
All Foreign	$79.00

Moving?
Send a copy of your current mailing label (address information) along with your new address. Indicate when the address change will take effect. Allow 8 weeks for address changes.

Single Copies

To order single copies of *Schwann Opus*, *Schwann Artist* and back issues (if available), call or write:

Sound Delivery
P.O. Box 2057, Woodland, CA 95776
Telephone: (800) 888-8574
Telephone: (916)-661-3395 outside U.S.
Fax: (800) 999-1794

	Opus	Artist
U. S. and Possessions	17.95	24.95
Canada	22.95	29.95
All Foreign	26.95	33.95

All prices include postage and handling. Please allow 6 to 8 weeks for delivery. Payment must accompany your order. All orders are payable in U.S. funds drawn on a U.S. bank.

Dealer/Newsstand Information

For new dealer/newsstand accounts, or changes in existing accounts, please call, fax, or write:

Schwann Publications
P.O. Box 2057, Woodland, CA 95776
Tel: (916) 669-5161, Fax: (916) 661-7854

Dealer/Newsstand Sales
If you're a record-store owner or newsstand dealer and would like to sell Schwann Publications - *Schwann Opus* or *Schwann Artist* - please write, fax, or call.

Changes in Existing Accounts
To make changes in your dealer/newsstand account, or for answers to any questions about your account, please write or call and have your customer account number handy. Allow 6 to 8 weeks for any changes you make in your account to be reflected in shipments and invoices.

Payment
All orders are payable in U.S. funds drawn on a U.S. bank.

Schwann Opus:
America's comprehensive guide to classical recordings. Published quarterly, Schwann Opus lists over 45,000 CD's, cassette tapes, laserdiscs and CD-Roms. Save by subscribing for a full year.

Schwann Artist:
The companion to Opus published annually. Schwann Artist includes more than 70,000 listings of CD's and cassette tapes, organized by artist name in these major sections: Orchestras & Ensembles, Conductors, Instrumental Soloists, Choral Groups and Vocalists.

ORCHESTRAS THAT MATTER

The New World Symphony

Larry Birnbaum

The New World Symphony is not an orchestra; it just sounds like one. In fact, the Miami Beach institution is a three-year fellowship program for conservatory graduates from around the country and the world—a sort of finishing school to prepare young musicians for permanent careers in major orchestras and other groups. But under the exuberant baton of artistic director Michael Tilson Thomas, this musical academy is also a first-rate working orchestra with an unusually broad and adventurous repertoire, whose concerts and recordings bear favorable comparison to those of more venerable and experienced professional ensembles.

"The New World Symphony appears from time to time as a performing unit, but its mission is educational," says Tilson Thomas, who established the program in 1987. "It performs as a symphony every two weeks or so, and between time it's functioning as a musical academy, with master classes, chamber-music coachings, private lessons, readings, career guidance, and all manner of other things. We try to give the players the opportunity to develop their creative and competitive edges to the fullest, because it's unknown to us and to them just where in the realm of music they're going to be going and which kinds of experiences will be the most valuable to them in the future."

The Symphony performs its share of Schubert, Brahms, and Mendelssohn, but it's known for its eclectic explorations of early, modern, American, Latin American, and other less familiar repertoire, from Pérotin to Piazzolla. Its albums include *Tangazo* (Argo), a collection of Latin American music; *Defining Dahl* (Argo), a tribute to the German émigré composer who was one of Tilson Thomas's teachers; and *Alma Brasileira* (RCA Red Seal), a sampling of Heitor Villa-Lobos's *Bachianas brasileiras* and his Chôros No. 10. Forthcoming releases include an album of Morton Feldman's works, and a set of jazz-flavored pieces by the likes of Stravinsky, Milhaud, and Gershwin, whose *Rhapsody in Blue* Tilson Thomas conducts from the keyboard.

"I don't like to repeat things that have already been done," says Tilson Thomas, "and where we've had the opportunity to do projects that give people an idea of the more unusual aspects of what we do, I thought it was important to do repertoire that was otherwise not available on recordings, and that stretched the listeners as well as the performers. I think there's a place for different repertoire and the cultivation of different audiences. And part of the strength of our educational program is that we give musicians not only the experience of playing Bach, Beethoven, and Mozart, but [also of] playing Steve Reich and Alban Berg and John Adams."

Left: Mark Niehaus, trumpet
Right: Brian Jones, percussion; John Burgardt, timpani; Tom Sherwood, percussion; Gabe Sobieski, percussion

Like his longtime friend and mentor Leonard Bernstein, Tilson Thomas is a world-class charmer who frequently uses the podium as a lectern—a skill he tries to teach his players. "The musicians work with coaches not only on their music but also on their ability to speak to an audience and give them an insight into what they're playing," he says. "It's tremendously gratifying for me when I hear some of them, who arrived rather scared and taciturn, learning to be comfortable in presenting their own personalities. I respect the view of traditionalists who have grown up with a particular view of the concert ritual, but we also need to make sure that new generations of music listeners come into the live-music experience and appreciate and understand it."

The New World Symphony came about through a confluence of dreams: Israeli-American cruise-line tycoon Ted Arison aspired to bring culture to his adopted home town, and Tilson Thomas sought to help music students pursue their careers. "For years I had been concerned about the transitional period in young musicians' lives," the conductor says, "because I was working with a lot of them in Tanglewood and other places and was always concerned to discover that many of them had no immediate plans upon graduation from school. Some mutual associates of ours knew that Ted wanted to make a project happen in Miami, so they brought the two of us together."

Arison converted the Lincoln Theatre, a movie house in the heart of the South Beach art-deco district, into a combination concert hall, office suite, and practice space, and refurbished two historic hotels to serve as dormitories. Recruiting fellows from such top schools as Juilliard, Peabody, Eastman, and the New England Conservatory, and from as far away as China, Syria, Latvia, and Brazil, the New World Symphony has become a Miami Beach fixture, and an anchor of the city's trend-setting revival. Since its first full season in 1988, the NWS has toured South and Central America, Europe, Israel, Japan, and throughout the United States, and has performed with such musical guests as Leonard Bernstein, Vladimir Feltsman, Anne-Sophie Mutter, Sarah Chang, and Midori.

The players, with an average age of 25, adapt readily to innovative repertoire, though not without cultivation. "It's interesting how many young musicians are actually rather conservative in their perspectives and need to be started in a more familiar place and gradually brought to a more daring one," Tilson Thomas says. "On the one hand, the musicians in the New World Symphony have very few preconceptions. Since they're learning everything for the first time, there's not much difference for them in learning a piece by Berio and learning one by Strauss. On the other hand, it's a challenge to try to bring them along very quickly through many years of experience that they don't necessarily have. It's always a stretch, for me as well as for them."

For all its conceptual breadth and youthful flair, however, the ensemble maintains a rigorous respect for tradition, reaching out to new audiences without pandering. "I don't know if crossover is the way I like to think about it," says Tilson Thomas. "I think we all accept now that there are many audiences for music, and we have to cultivate many audiences for there to be a healthy future for music. The issue is being able to play a diverse repertoire in a way that is idiomatic, a performance that feels right."

Larry Birnbaum writes about music for Down Beat, Pulse!, Newsday *and other publications.*

Selected Discography of The New World Symphony

Alma Brasiliera
VILLA-LOBOS
Bachianas brasileiras **4, 5, 7 & 9;**
Chôros **No. 10**
with Michael Tilson Thomas, conductor; Renée Fleming, soprano; BBC Singers
RCA Red Seal 09026-68538-2
(1997)

Defining Dahl
INGOLF DAHL
Concerto for Alto Saxophone; Hymn; Music for Brass Instruments; *The Tower of St. Barbara*
with Michael Tilson Thomas, conductor; John Harle, saxophone
Argo 444459-2

SCHOENFIELD
Concerto for Trumpet;
Four Parables; **Klezmer Rondos;**
Vaudeville
with John Nelson, conductor
Argo 440212-2

Tangazo:
Music of Latin America
CATURLA: *Tres danzas cubanas;*
CHÁVEZ: *Sinfonia india;*
COPLAND: *Danzón cubano;*
GINASTERA: Danzas del ballet *Estancia,* Op. 8a;
PIAZZOLLA: *Tangazo;*
ROLDÁN: Suite de
La rebambaramba; Rítmica V
REVUELTAS: *Sensemayá*
with Michael Tilson Thomas, conductor
Argo 436737-2

Going Off The Record from
Who Killed Classical Music?
Norman Lebrecht

What on earth is happening to classical music? Almost everywhere you care to look, audiences are waning, state and private subsidy is being cut, record sales are in freefall—and a handful of monopolistic agents and superstar soloists and conductors are becoming richer than ever before.

In Who Killed Classical Music? *I have tried to discover the hidden, previously untold history of the classical music business. It is a not unfamiliar tale of a cottage industry that became corporatized and lost sight of its purpose and its economic foundations in a rush for quick profit. When that happens to a razorblade factory, the firm goes bust and the world goes on. But when it befalls a core sector of our cultural heritage, the consequences can be devastating—not only for our time, but for all time to come.*

In the following excerpt, I take a look at where recorded music went out of the groove.

Norman Lebrecht, London, March 1997

The dawn before compact disc was unnervingly dark...

EMI, the British flagship, was sold off to the Thorn electronics concern. Decca, founded by Edward Lewis in 1929, was absorbed on his death in 1980 by the PolyGram group, a world-leading alliance of Philips and Deutsche Grammophon in which the Dutch manufacturer held 75% of the shares. The big music decisions were increasingly made by lightbulb and weapons manufacturers. It seemed only a matter of time before classical music was "rationalized," possibly to extinction.

Into this tenebrous prospect rose the compact disc, brightening record countenances with a laser beam. Gloom turned to boom as world retail sales of all recordings doubled in five years after 1985, from $12 billion to $24 billion. A tenth of this revenue was classical, as serious music reclaimed a double-figure market share for the first time in a generation. Ecstatic label chiefs ordered an increase in studio activity. They grew even more excited when the hidden benefits were revealed. By adding an unforeseen clarity to ancient recordings, compact disc made the great performances of yesteryear sound more glorious than ever before. Demand soared for Furtwängler and Toscanini, Heifetz and Kreisler, Caruso and Callas. To reissue them cost nothing more than a quick pressing and a royalty check. Classics were back in the black, and business quickly cottoned on to their reborn profitability.

Richard Branson, the airheads-to-airline entrepreneur, equipped his Virgin label with a classical wing. Steven Ross, head of Time-Warner, went on a classical rampage, buying Teldec in Germany, followed by Erato in France, Elektra Nonesuch in New York, Finlandia in Helsinki. Sony, the Japanese hardware company, took over Columbia Records. RCA Victor, the other apple-pie US label, was acquired for above its perceived market value by the German book conglomerate, Bertelsmann. When Branson got bored, EMI eagerly bought him out for just over $1 billion.

In the rock sector, the Japanese media group Matsushita bought out David Geffen, an independent producer, for half a billion dollars. Thorn spent $150 million on Chrysalis and $285 million for SBK. PolyGram, not to be outdone, paid over a billion dollars for A&M, Island and Motown. When the music finally stopped, four groups—Time-Warner, Sony-CBS, PolyGram, and Thorn-EMI—were heading the industry, with Matsushita-MCA and Bertelsmann-RCA some way behind. Together they commanded 85% of sales worth $26 billion a year. Of this total, classical turnover exceeded $2 billion, with the four majors holding three-quarters of the world market.

What triggered the takeover fever was not so much the teen appeal of Midori and Michael Jackson as the backlists of a century of recording which, on compact disc, were endlessly recyclable. After CD, there would be DAT, DCC, MiniDisc, and more besides. With better protection for copyrights and intellectual property, whoever owned the recorded past could control the multimedia future.

The classical controls at the reorganised majors were seized in the main by ex-Karajan aides. Günther Breest, his DG producer, became head of Sony Classical; Peter Andry, his EMI partner, became vice-president at Warner. Elsewhere, [Decca producer, John] Culshaw's trainees polished the Decca

---

From WHO KILLED CLASSICAL MUSIC? *Maestros, Managers and Corporate Politics* by Norman Lebrecht. Copyright © 1996 Norman Lebrecht. Published by arrangement with Carol Publishing Group. A Birch Lane Press Book.

> The major labels have become intoxicated by the taste of rock sales that they got from the Three Tenors—they have not only abandoned the classical business, they no longer understand it.

Sound and infiltrated Philips and DG. Across the classical labels there prevailed an air of collegiality that stopped just short of collusion. Producers might fight over a star, but they were of much the same mind when it came to consumer prices. Thus, by mysterious coincidence, new releases cost exactly the same, give or take a penny or two, on all good labels around the world. Odder still, reissues appeared at a uniform mid-price, while cut-outs and commercial failures were comparably priced at bargain level. There were accusations of price-rigging, especially when CD prices hit $28 in western Europe, but official inquiries regularly exonerated the industry. Its senior labels were simply behaving like elderly members of a Pall Mall club, following time-honored rules for which no one could remember the reason.

These cozy assumptions were, however, about to be exploded. In 1988, the year compact disc became a mass medium, a new line of digital classics appeared in British shops initially at a penny under £4. The packaging was crude and the artists unheard of, but the performances were acceptable and sometimes accomplished. The name on the spine was Naxos and the discs were made in Hong Kong. Over the next six years, Naxos breached the industry's price codes in all major territories and repertoire, trimming profits to a trickle.

The man who cracked the price cartel was a Frankfurt language teacher, Klaus Heymann, who had worked with the local US garrison in the Sixties and wound up in Hong Kong when his unit was posted to Vietnam. Wearying of the daily body count, he took to selling German cameras and hi-fis to GIs on furlough. When two of his suppliers, Bose and Revox, offered to stage concerts in support of their products, he booked the artists and imported records to sell in the foyer. By 1978, on his own reckoning, Heymann was the biggest record distributor in non-communist Asia. From there to making records was but a short step. Heymann's wife, Takao Nishizaki, a professional violinist, discovered a score by two Shanghai composers that detailed in glycerine sonorities the tragic fate of a maltreated working girl. The *Butterfly Lovers' Concerto* sold a quarter of a million copies in Hong Kong and was banned in Taiwan. "For the Chinese," said Heymann, "it's like the Mendelssohn and Beethoven and Tchaikovsky rolled into one." Mrs. Heymann soon filled football stadia with her soulful performances.

When compact disc arrived, Heymann was asked by a local businessman to provide a pack of the world's greatest classical music to be sold door-to-door in South Korea. Unable to organize sessions on short notice, he purchased 30 digital tapes, recorded in Bratislava, from a Slovak exile in Paris. Then his Korean partner went broke. "So there I was, stuck with 30 classical masters. I couldn't sell them at full price because these were unknown east European orchestras, although the performances were not too bad. I had to put them out on a budget label. That's how Naxos Records was born."

The discs went on sale in Hong Kong at six US dollars, "the cheapest CDs in the world." Woolworth's sold mountains of his discs in Britain, and Heymann booked more sessions in Bratislava and Ljubljana. "The orchestras were completely flexible," he relates. "If they had to cancel a concert to make a recording they would happily do so." If ten minutes were left at the end of a session, they would record an extra overture. He paid the players hard currency, 180 Deutschmarks ($105) each per record, or half as much again as their monthly salary. "For musicians in Bratislava it meant the difference between a life of hardship and a life of comfort," he maintained.

The conductors he used were often Westerners—an American, Stephen Gunzenhauser, whom he discovered in Lisbon, and Barry Wordsworth, conductor of London's Royal Ballet. While major labels fought over the winners of international piano competitions, Heymann picked up the players in fifth and sixth place. He paid conductors and soloists a flat fee of $1000 without further royalties. Underemployed radio producers and technicians provided studio supervision. Heymann himself claimed no specialist musical knowledge. A matter-of-fact businessman, his years in the East had barely touched a solid German mien, suspicious of flowery distractions. "Actually, I don't like to meet artists," he told the *Daily Telegraph*. "Many musicians have a certain charisma that lets them push you into doing things that don't make artistic or business sense. Also, you shouldn't like your artists, otherwise how can you be objective?"

He attacked the catalogue systematically, recording the complete symphonies of Beethoven, Brahms, Dvořák, Mozart, Tchaikovsky, Schubert, and Sibelius. Followed by the concertos, the chamber music, the string quartets, the solo sonatas. Integrality was no proof of artistic integrity, as ill-conceived Beethoven and Mahler interpretations would prove. The Dvořák cycle, on the other hand, was probably the best of its era, and the Beethoven piano sonatas, played by Stefan Vladar, got the pianist poached by Sony. Popular operas, all from eastern Europe, contained some superb singing.

Any music that was off the mainstream he released at full price on Marco Polo, his "label of discovery." Much of it was tedious note-spinning, but occasional revelations like Havergal Brian's monumental *Gothic* Symphony and the piano sonatas of Nikolai Myaskovsky won Heymann appreciable credibility among music buffs. Unwittingly, he was applying the Goddard Lieberson [of Columbia Records] law of making profitable releases pay for uneconomic esoterica.

As economic conditions worsened and major labels cut their output, Heymann attracted a superior class of ensemble. The BBC and Bournemouth orchestras recorded for Naxos for less than he paid in Bratislava. Pinchas Steinberg led Austrian Radio ensembles in Wagner operas. Naxos was becoming artistically competitive and commercially dangerous. Heymann was recording symphonies for one-fifth of major-label expenditure. He broke even at 2,500 sales, and often sold six times that figure in four years. In 1990, before penetrating America and Japan, he sold three million records. By the end of 1994 he was up to 10 million, with 50% annual growth. He employed a staff of seven, spent pennies on promotion, and cleared at least a dollar's profit on every disc sold. He was making 300 new records a year, and in Scandinavia was selling more than the rest of the classical record industry combined. In the United Kingdom he was third, just behind Decca and EMI but rising fast. One in every six classics bought around the world was a Naxos.

"The big companies stupidly created a star system, paying artists huge advances," he said. "Then they found they were having to delete good recordings to make room for releases by the people they had just signed up . . . Utterly stupid. I thought maybe we'd get to about 50 titles and then the majors would come at us with competition, and that would be the end," reflected Heymann. "But it didn't happen—though I think the majors wish they had taken notice in those days when we were so vulnerable."

Five years too late, the industry struck back with big-name reissues—Karajans and Kleibers for the price of an unknown Slovene. Heymann did not flinch. He had the distribution network, the repertoire, and the resources to meet the onslaught. "There's no question that he is causing us great pain," confided one label chief. "As long as he's around we shall have to keep discounting our product so heavily that we are making no money on it."

PolyGram's chief executive Alain Lévy admitted in his end-of-1993 accounts that budget competition was hurting his classical side. At the first glimmer of a rumor that Heymann was thinking of selling up, label bosses went flying to Hong Kong with sweetheart deals in their briefcases. Heymann was not interested—not even at $200 million, which seemed an inordinate price to offer for his pick'n'mix catalogue. Nevertheless, the industry clung to a belief that as Peking rule and his 60th birthday approached in 1997, Heymann would retire to Australia and they could close him down. "He'll record the whole repertoire and then sell out," said one label boss. They refused to believe that he was into classics for anything other than money. "The offers were very flattering." Heymann laughed. "But they still don't understand what I'm doing. My plans go beyond the year 2000, and I expect to offer a Naxos alternative to practically every classical work."

Heymann, having made his point, was now embarked on a crusade. "The major labels have become intoxicated by the taste of rock sales that they got from the Three Tenors," he said. "They have not only abandoned the classical business, they no longer understand it. You can make money in this business, but you've got to control your costs and have good repertoire ideas. I could live off my Johann Strauss edition—why didn't the major labels think of that first?"

"We are trying to get away from mass-merchandising," said Heymann, who now found himself in the front line, defending sound quality, refined artistry, and high production values, the tricolor of the traditional record industry. "People look at us in a completely different light from other bargain labels," he averred. "Critics are aware that we are also doing Marco Polo, that we are not just in business to make a quick buck. I invest every penny I make in new productions."

He hired a retiring producer from Decca to exert quality control over his output. Naxos would now carry only those recordings that bore a professional seal of approval (at worst, the rest could be shunted off on bottom-price catch-all labels).

A three-tier industry was taking shape—business class for star labels, cabin class for Naxos/Marco Polo, and both

CDs represented the shape of happiness to come—as the gleaming chalice of a sacrament that promised salvation through invention.

> "It's tragic: all we talk about nowadays is bottom line," said a major-label A&R chief. "We used to help artists plan careers... now we have to make projects pay, or drop the artist."

praying fervently that people would pay a little extra for quality rather than risk discomfort on the charter flights being scheduled by the undercutters. "There will always be new artists, and the public will always want to buy recordings by top artists who are performing today," declared BMG's chief confidently at an industry conference. There will also, he added in an undertone, be fewer new recordings made than ever before. By the end of 1995, a world leader like EMI was making just four classical recordings a month.

The elevator door has a serpentine design and a jugendstil blue-green coloring. The apartment is tall and airy, gracious as a ballroom and timeless as time past, a desired residence for dreamers and nostalgists. Bay windows bathe the rooms in winter sunlight, opening out onto an overhead U-bahn that every three or four minutes rattles commuters around Hamburg. Authentic to all appearances and elegant to a fault, this is the perfect home for a classical recording chief: reminiscent of bygone splendors, yet punctuated by forceful reminders of modern communications.

Roger Wright, artist and repertoire director of Deutsche Grammophon, the largest classical label, sits in front of a wall cabinet of compact discs and agonizes over production cuts. "These things won't wear out." He points despondently at the jewel-cased discs. "So how will we ever persuade people to buy another Beethoven cycle when the one they have got will last forever?"

His anguish, in a television interview, revealed a wormlike infestation that gnawed at the core of recording as it entered its second century. In 1983 Wright's company invested 100 million Deutschmarks in new technology. Switching from analogue to digital production, it urged music lovers to replace their fault-ridden vinyl recordings with immaculate compact discs. Impervious to cigarette ash and undamaged no matter how often you played them, CDs were the first records that did not have to be handled with surgical gloves and rock-steady hands.

Like a flight of swallows, compact discs took off across the wealthier hemisphere in a silvery cloud, a harbinger of the dawning information revolution. The uptake exceeded all expectations. In the fragile instant before the arrival of facsimile machines and home computers, before the implosion of global recession, compact disc represented the shape of happiness to come. It was the gleaming chalice of a sacrament that promised salvation through invention—*Vorsprung durch Technik,* in the jargon of German automakers—the defining gadget of an ephemeral yuppie generation. Along with AIDS, it would go down in history as the lasting emblem of the Eighties.

For classical recording, however, the rejuvenative elixir quickly wore off. In 1992 classical sales crashed by a quarter. By 1994 they were down to no more than 5% of the world market, which was still growing at a rate of 16% each year. Freak statistics made the classical figures look worse than they really were, but the underlying slump was undeniable. Not since the rise of radio in the late 1920s—when US record sales dropped from 104 million to six million in just five years—had the classical record industry felt so depressed. Then, as now, western economies were sluggish. But while previous recoveries were achieved by improving sound and extending choice, CD left little room for enhancement, and the range of music on sale had never been greater. Minor embellishments, such as Sony's 20-bit methodology and DG's four-dimensional 4D gimmick, might still be asseverated. But, for the vast majority of record buyers, compact disc was the *ultima vera.* Now, having bought a symphony, they need never buy it again.

"For the first time in history we now have perfect recorded sound," said the cellist Julian Lloyd Webber, "and, with this achievement, one of the prime historical reasons for re-recording a piece of music disappears." The commercial impetus, though, was unchanged—to keep musicians in work and the record business in profit. The situation had the poignancy of comic opera. Having boasted for a century of her purity and high fidelity, the heroine is rudely spurned when her immaculate status is validated.

These reflections dappled darkly around Roger Wright's living-room as he surveyed Deutsche Grammophon's tactical options. A pensive Englishman with the physique of a rugby fly-half and an impressive track record at the BBC and the Cleveland Orchestra, Wright was engaged to energize a company that lost its headlights when Herbert von Karajan and Leonard Bernstein died in 1989-90. DG, with its bright yellow shield and elegant packaging, was the classical leader, but its Hamburg head office was dumbstruck by the downturn. Wright himself was so worried that he sometimes walked into a record store and purchased new releases on rival labels—just to show the dealer that someone was still buying.

At DG, for the first time in memory, no one was taping a Beethoven cycle with a major orchestra. "There would have to be a compelling reason to record it again when we have digital Karajan, Bernstein, and Abbado," said Wright. Beethoven was a powerful brand name, and if Beethoven was unrecordable, the business was in trouble.

The economics were beginning to look absurd. It could cost $100,000 to record a Mahler symphony in Berlin, half a million to cast a Strauss opera in Vienna. Most records sold two or three thousand copies on first release. It would take a lifetime to earn back the outlay on a Berlin production.

Any rational analyst would have told the industry to quit recording and repackage the back catalogue. Wright's role was to find an excuse for continuing to make records, and his task was constrained by the dignity of his office. DG dared not stalk the catwalks of musical fashion without risking its hard-won authority. "The scrabbling around for pieces with quick-fix appeal is an embarrassment to us all," he sniffed, disdaining the half-million sales of Henryk Mikolai Górecki's meditative Third Symphony, which hit number six in the pop charts. "The trouble with chart hits is that no one will want to hear them next year," was the DG line. "We are concerned with building an enduring list of great music."

Yet the reality was that major labels had become overwhelmingly dependent on freak hits—Nigel Kennedy one year, Spanish monks the next—and on compilation discs designed to be played while driving a car, making love, or weeding the garden. These peripheral products accounted for the vast majority of classical sales. The traditional symphonic recording, like the traditional hardback novel, was being left on the shelf and was in danger of disappearing.

The star system that had sustained the classical record business since Caruso's day was now contributing to its demolition. Singers who used to be satisfied with a one-off check and a mess of post-session potage were demanding an unpayable ransom. The first Three Tenors concert in 1990 cost Decca half a million dollars in fees to Luciano Pavarotti, Plácido Domingo, and José Carreras, not bad for a warm evening's work. It sold millions of discs and videos, and left Domingo seething. "Decca obeyed the letter of the contract," he told journalists, "but as the concert sold so well they should have paid us more." Four years later, with the Los Angeles finals drawing near, the tenors changed the rules.

Acting through Pavarotti's outdoors-events impresario, Tibor Rudas, they staged a telephone auction for *Three Tenors II*. Six million pounds from EMI did not reach the reserve price, Sony dropped out at eight, and Decca's 10 million was vetoed by the grumpy Domingo. Warner stepped in with a winning offer of $16.5 million. The three tenors and their conductor would get a million each in advance and would earn four times as much by the end of the year in royalties and broadcast fees. "Thanks to the expansive international resources and expertise of the Warner Music Group, this remarkable reunion will reach a truly global audience," crowed Rudas. It would need to if anyone but the singers were to make any money on it.

"It is always better second time around," claimed Domingo—but better for whom? Certainly not for the record industry, which saw its stars pushed out of sight by a line of zeros, and least of all for opera houses that saw their prime attractions lured away by jamborees in open spaces.

Three Tenors II did roughly as well as could be expected, despite an appalling critical reception. Warners topped the charts and did not lose their corporate shirts, but the truly worrying statistic showed up in the industry's annual figures, where *Three Tenors II* outsold the next biggest "classical" record by a margin of nine discs to one. The new reality was that stars and their producers were no longer playing on the same side. The producers wanted to make the best operas and recitals achievable in modern times. The singers wanted to make the most money in history. The concept of a developing creative partnership was doomed, as stars flitted from one label to the next according to the sums they were offered.

Lifelong attachments like Sir Georg Solti's to Decca-London and Bob Dylan's to Sony-CBS were viewed as eccentric anachronisms. "Star artists are our major asset, and exclusivity is essential," protested Decca's outgoing president Roland Kommerell, but in the new climate both sides in future would be looking after number one.

The nightmare of Three Tenors millions was bound to prove calamitous for classical recording. In the past, when a label struck lucky with a freak hit, the profits were reinvested imaginatively. Decca plowed its Three Tenors pot into *Entartete Musik,* reviving valuable music that the Nazis had banned. EMI sank money from Nigel Kennedy's *Four Seasons* into young British artists. DG recycled Karajan cash into adventurous modernisms. Warner had spent its Górecki gold on a clutch of living composers.

These windfalls, though, were being ruled out by star greed. The record industry would no longer be able to take risks and extend the culture. Nor could it pay for the long-term development of new artists, an act of faith that could take years to redeem. EMI disclosed in 1994 that it had taken 15 years to break even on Simon Rattle. Without its commitment, an important conductor could have been mired in obscurity. "It's tragic: all we talk about nowadays is bottom line," said a major-label A&R chief. "We used to help artists plan careers, let them make mistakes and learn from them. Now we have to make projects pay, or drop the artist." Classical record companies needed one big hit a year to fund artist development. If limelight releases were rendered unprofitable by star demands, there would be no money to create stars of the future and the industry would fall back on its century-rich backlist, a museum of recorded music. The danger was known to industry chiefs and they were powerless to avert it. In these fretful circumstances, the bond between star and producer was frayed beyond repair. Stymied on the one side by an indestructible disc, and on the other by insatiable avarice, the classical record was reaching the end of its playline.

Norman Lebrecht is music columnist for London's Daily Telegraph. *His most recent books include* The Maestro Myth *(1991), and* The Companion to 20th Century Music *(1993).*

How to Use Schwann Artist

Schwann Artist contains currently available classical recordings listed by the name of the performing artist(s). It is divided into six sections:

CONDUCTORS: Each conductor's name is followed by the orchestras, ensembles and choral groups that he/she leads. Complete recording information can be found in the Orchestras & Ensembles and Choral Groups sections.

ORCHESTRAS & ENSEMBLES: Instrumental groups (including duos) and mixed vocal/instrumental groups. Ensemble member names, when available, are listed in brackets. Recordings are organized by conductor when available.

INSTRUMENTALISTS: Solo instrumentalists and members of ensembles.

CHORAL GROUPS: Vocal ensembles and choruses. For mixed vocal/instrumental ensembles, see Orchestras & Ensembles. Choral conductor names are listed when available.

VOCALISTS: Singers, speakers, and narrators.

MISCELLANEOUS: Performers of tape, electronic, and computer-generated music, and all others that don't fit into the above categories.

FINDING AN ARTIST
Performers are listed alphabetically by last name. Prefixes such as 'de' and 'van' are not usually included in an individual's last name.

We attempt to use one authoritative English-language name for each orchestra, ensemble, and choral group. Native-language names are kept when appropriate translations cannot be made. Most orchestras and opera houses and many ensembles are listed under their city name. For other groups, a city name may be included after the name for clarification.

WHAT'S IN A LISTING
The first line contains the performer's name. For individuals, instruments or vocal ranges are included.

The lines about recording information begin with composer and piece title or, in the case of compilations, with album title. Subsequent information may include: other artists on the piece, specific piece selections, recording location and date, and the language in which a piece is sung.

Label information follows, with label name, number of discs in the set (if more than one), and CD number. A SPARS Code—a three-letter code (each letter either A for analog or D for digital) explaining the recording, editing, and mastering processes used—will be given if available.

CONDUCTORS

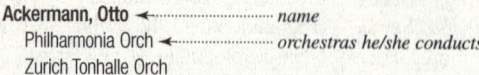

        Ackermann, Otto ← name
        Philharmonia Orch ← orchestras he/she conducts
        Zurich Tonhalle Orch

ORCHESTRAS & ENSEMBLES and CHORAL GROUPS

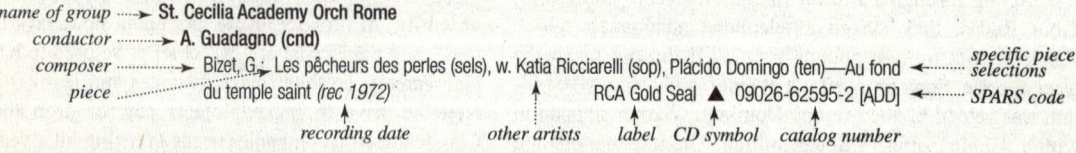

name of group → St. Cecilia Academy Orch Rome
conductor → A. Guadagno (cnd)
composer → Bizet, G.: Les pêcheurs des perles (sels), w. Katia Ricciarelli (sop), Plácido Domingo (ten)—Au fond ← *specific piece selections*
piece → du temple saint *(rec 1972)*   RCA Gold Seal ▲ 09026-62595-2 [ADD] ← SPARS code
       recording date   other artists   label   CD symbol   catalog number

---

INSTRUMENTALISTS and VOCALISTS

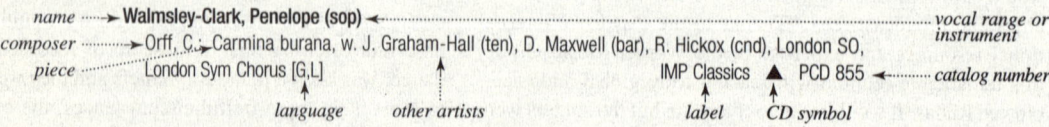

name → **Walmsley-Clark, Penelope (sop)** ← vocal range or instrument
composer → Orff, C.: Carmina burana, w. J. Graham-Hall (ten), D. Maxwell (bar), R. Hickox (cnd), London SO,
piece → London Sym Chorus [G,L]   IMP Classics ▲ PCD 855 ← catalog number
       language   other artists   label   CD symbol

The 1997 *Schwann Artist* listings are up-to-date as of the Spring 1997 *Schwann Opus*. Schwann listings are based on information supplied by manufacturers and distributors, and there is no charge to them for this service. Schwann Publications does not sell recordings. Our guides provide information you or your record dealer can use to order recordings directly from record labels and their authorized distributors.

We welcome your comments on this publication. Write to:
Letters to the Editor
Schwann Publications
1807 Second St., Suite 101, Santa Fe, NM 87505
or e-mail us at schwann@vrd.com

KEY TO SYMBOLS & ABBREVIATIONS USED IN SCHWANN ARTIST

Symbol	Meaning
▲	Compact Disc
△	MD (MiniDisc)
◆	Enhanced CD
■	Cassette Tape
□	DCC (Digital Compact Cassette)
acc	accordion
(D)	Digital recording
(m)	Mono recording
(m/s)	Contains both mono & stereo
alphn	alphorn
alt	alto
a sax	alto saxophone
archlt	archlute
arr.	arranged or arranged by
b cl	bass clarinet
b-bar	bass-baritone
band	bandoneon
bar	baritone
bar sax	baritone saxophone
bas hn	basset horn
bc	continuo
bgl	bugle
bgp	bagpipe
bn	bassoon
ca.	circa
cant	cantor
Cant(s)	Cantata(s)
car	carillons
cel	celeste/celesta
chit	chitorrone
chl	chalumeau
cl	clarinet
clvd	clavichord
cmpt	computer
cnd	conductor
cnt	cornet
CO	Chamber Orchestra
comp	complete
Con(s)	Concerto(s)
conc	concertina
ct	countertenor
cta	contralto
ctbn	contrabassoon
cym	cymbals
db	double bass
Divert(s)	Divertimento(s)
dlc	dulcimer
dr	drums
E hn	English horn
elec	electronics
eup	euphonium
Fant(s)	Fantasy(ies), Fantasia(s), Fantaisia(s), Fantasie(s)
fid	fiddle
fl	flute
flgl	flugelhorn
gam	gamelan
glock	glockenspiel
gtr	guitar
h-g	hurdy-gurdy
ham dlc	hammered dulcimer
harm	harmonium
hmc	harmonica
hn	horn
hp	harp
hpd	harpsichord
instrs	instruments
kbd	keyboard(s)
lib	libretto
lt	lute
mand	mandolin
mar	marimba
mez	mezzo-soprano
movt	movement
mt dlc	mountain dulcimer
nar	narrator
nat hn	natural horn
nat tpt	natural trumpet
ob	oboe
orchd	orchestrated or orchestrated by
Orch	Orchestra
org	organ
Ov(s)	Overture(s)
perc	percussion
Phil	Philharmonic
pic	piccolo
pnl	pianola
pno	piano
PO	Philharmonic Orchestra
psthn	posthorn
Qnt(s)	Quintet(s)
Qt(s)	Quartet(s)
rcr	recorder
Rhap(s)	Rhapsody(ies)
RPO	Radio Philharmonic Orchestra
RSO	Radio Symphony Orchestra
sels	selections
sgr	singer
shak	shakuhachi
sham	shamisen
shm	shawm
Sinf(s)	Sinfonia(s)
SO	Symphony Orchestra
Son(s)	Sonata(s)
sop	soprano
s sax	soprano saxophone
spt	septet
strs	strings
sxt	sextet
Sym(s)	Symphony(ies)
syn	synthesizer
ten	tenor
t sax	tenor saxophone
thb	theorbo
timp	timpani
tpt	trumpet
trans.	transcribed or transcribed by
trb	treble
trbn	trombone
trns fl	transverse flute
va	viola
Var(s)	Variation(s)
vc	cello
vc pic	violincello piccolo
vib	vibraphone
vih	vihuela
vir	virginal
vl	viol
vle	violone
vn	violin
voc	vocalist
w.	with
xyl	xylophone
zmz	zoomoozophone

ABBREVIATIONS used to indicate language of vocal recordings

A	Armenian
Cz	Czech
Da	Danish
D	Dutch
E	English
Fin	Finnish
F	French
G	German
He	Hebrew
Hun	Hungarian
I	Italian
J	Japanese
L	Latin
N	Norwegian
Pol	Polish
Port	Portuguese
R	Russian
Sla	Slavic
Sp	Spanish
Sw	Swedish
U	Ukranian
Yi	Yiddish

ABBREVIATIONS used for specialized indices

The works of some composers are usually identified not by the composer's own opus numbers, but by a particular Thematic index, compiled by a musicologist. Those in general use today are identified in our listings either by a single initial of the compiler or the title of the book, customarily known as a Werker-Verzeichnis, as follows:

BuxWV	[Karstadt] Buxtehude
BWV	[Schmieder] J.S. Bach
D.	[Deutsch] Schubert
H.	[Helm] C.P.E. Bach
H.	[Hoboken] Haydn
J.	[Jahns] Weber
K.	[Kirkpatrick] D. Scarlatti
K.	[Köchel] Mozart
L.	[Longo] D. Scarlatti
M.	[Marvin] Soler
RV.	[Ryom] Vivaldi
S.	[Searle] Liszt
SWV	[Bittinger] Schütz
Sz.	[Szöllösy] Bartók
W.	[Wotquenne] C.P.E. Bach
Z.	[Zimmermann] Purcell

Other Abbreviations appearing with composers' works:

WoO	Werk ohne Opuszahl [Work without an Opus number] Beethoven
K.Anh.	Köchel Anhang [Köchel appendix] Mozart

Notes

Opus Subscriptions

To order your subscription for *Schwann Opus* call or write:

Schwann Publications, Dept. 56A
49 Sheridan Avenue, Albany, NY 12210
Telephone: (800) 877-2693
Telephone: (518)-436-9686 outside U.S.

U.S. and Possessions	**$39.95**
Canada	**$49.95**
All Foreign	**$79.00**

Moving?
Send a copy of your current mailing label (address information) along with your new address. Indicate when the address change will take effect. Allow 8 weeks for address changes.

Single Copies

To order single copies of *Schwann Opus*, *Schwann Artist* and back issues (if available), call or write:

Sound Delivery
P.O. Box 2057, Woodland, CA 95776
Telephone: (800) 888-8574
Telephone: (916)-661-3395 outside U.S.
Fax: (800) 999-1794

	Opus	Artist
U. S. and Possessions	17.95	24.95
Canada	22.95	29.95
All Foreign	26.95	33.95

All prices include postage and handling. Please allow 6 to 8 weeks for delivery. Payment must accompany your order. All orders are payable in U.S. funds drawn on a U.S. bank.

Dealer/Newsstand Information

For new dealer/newsstand accounts, or changes in existing accounts, please call, fax, or write:

Schwann Publications
P.O. Box 2057, Woodland, CA 95776
Tel: (916) 669-5161, Fax: (916) 661-7854

Dealer/Newsstand Sales
If you're a record-store owner or newsstand dealer and would like to sell Schwann Publications - *Schwann Opus* or *Schwann Artist* - please write, fax, or call.

Changes in Existing Accounts
To make changes in your dealer/newsstand account, or for answers to any questions about your account, please write or call and have your customer account number handy. Allow 6 to 8 weeks for any changes you make in your account to be reflected in shipments and invoices.

Payment
All orders are payable in U.S. funds drawn on a U.S. bank.

Schwann Opus:
America's comprehensive guide to classical recordings. Published quarterly, Schwann Opus lists over 45,000 CD's, cassette tapes, laserdiscs and CD-Roms. Save by subscribing for a full year.

Schwann Artist:
The companion to Opus published annually. Schwann Artist includes more than 70,000 listings of CD's and cassette tapes, organized by artist name in these major sections: Orchestras & Ensembles, Conductors, Instrumental Soloists, Choral Groups and Vocalists.

Notes

CONDUCTORS

Aadland, Elvind
European Community CO
Aarburg, Alphons von
Capella Concertante
Zurich Boys' Choir
Abalyan, Boris
Lege Artis Chamber Choir
Abarius, Lionginal
Kaunas State Chorus
Lithuanian Radio–TV Chorus
Abbado, Claudio
Berlin PO
CO of Europe
Chicago SO
Dresden State Orch
Florence Maggio Musicale Orch
Florence Teatro Comunale Orch
London SO
Naples Alessandro Scarlatti RAI Orch
New Philharmonia Orch
Residentie Orch The Hague
Rome RAI SO
Royal Opera House Orch
La Scala Orch
Vienna PO
Vienna State Opera Orch
Abbado, Roberto
Bamberg SO
London SO
Munich RSO
Abbott, Graham
Australian Youth Orch
Abdullayev, Rauf
Moscow RSO
Ostankino Radio–TV Large SO
Abendroth, Hermann
Bayreuth Festival Orch
Berlin PO
Berlin Radio Orch
Berlin RSO
Leipzig Gewandhaus Orch
Leipzig RSO
Prague RSO
Abravanel, Maurice
Los Angeles PO
Brian Sullivan Orch
Utah SO
Abronovitch, Y.
Stockholm PO
Accardo, Salvatore
English CO
Italian Youth Orch
Philharmonia Orch
Prague CO
St. Cecilia Academy Orch Rome
Acciai, Giovanni
Collegium Vocale Nova Ars Cantandi
Schola Gregoriana
I Solisti del Madrigale
Acél, Ervin
Oradea PO
Szeged PO
Ackermann, Otto
Philharmonia Orch
Zurich Tonhalle Orch
Adam, F.
Strasbourg Opera Orch
Adams, Henrie
Artistica Buñol
Adams, John
London Sinfonietta
Orch of St. Luke's
Ader, B.
Tübingen Cantata Orch
Adigezalov, Yalchin
Moscow Radio–TV SO
Adler, Charles F.
Vienna Orch
Adler, Samuel
Berlin SO
Vienna State Opera Orch
Adolph, Henry
Camerata Slavonica
Slovak PO
Adriano
Czech–Slovak RSO Bratislava
Moscow SO
Slovak RSO Bratislava
Aerts, Karl
Concinite de Louvain Choir
Aeschbacher, Matthias
Lausanne CO
Agafonnikov, Igor
Alexandrov Red Army Choir
Ager, K.
Austrian Ensemble for New Music
Aghamir, Reza
Scapoli
Agostini, Federico
I Musici
Agrafiotis, Dimitri
Württemberg PO
Ahronovitch, Yuri
Bamberg SO

Ahronovitch, Yuri (cont.)
Budapest SO
London SO
Stockholm PO
Vienna SO
Akiyama, Kazuyoshi
American SO
Tokyo SO
Vancouver CO
Vancouver SO
Albert, Herbert
Naples Alessandro Scarlatti RAI Orch
Albert, Thomas
Fiori Musicali
Albert, Werner Andreas
Bamberg SO
Bavarian State Youth Orch
Cologne RSO
Frankfurt RSO
Hamburg State PO
Hanover North German Radio PO
Mediaeval Ensemble
Melbourne SO
Munich PO
NBC SO
North German RSO
Northwest German PO
Philharmonia Hungarica
Queensland SO
Rhenish PO
Rhineland–Palatinate State PO
Sydney SO
Winterthur Musicum Collegium
Alberth, Rudolf
Bavarian RSO
Albrecht, Gerd
Berlin RSO
Cologne RSO
Czech PO
Frankfurt RSO
Hamburg PO
Hamburg State Opera Orch
Hamburg State PO
Rome RAI SO
Aleksa, Jonas
Riga PO
Alessandrini, Rinaldo
Concerto Italiano
L'Europa Galante
Alexander, Gibson
Scottish CO
Alexander, John
Ancient Consort Singers
Pacific SO
Alexeiev, Nikolai
Musica Viva Ensemble
Alexeiev, V.
Collegium Musicum
Alfidi, J.
Philharmonia Bulgarica
Alfred, Donald E.
Westminster Concert Bell Choir
Aliberti, Armando
Festival Orch
Alin, Cecilia Rydinger
Kroumata Percussion Ensemble
Allain, Jean
Pasdeloup Concerts Association Orch
Alldis, John
Ensemble 1971
Allers, Franz
Graunke SO
Munich Bavarian State Opera Orch
Northwest German PO
Allwood, Ralph
Rodolfus Choir
Almeida, Antonio de
Bamberg SO
Barcelona Teatro Liceo Orch
Bournemouth SO
Camerata Provence Orch
Czech PO
Hong Kong PO
Irish National SO
London PO
Los Angeles CO
Monte Carlo Opera Orch
Moscow SO
Philharmonia Orch
Royal PO
Scottish CO
Almeida, Laurindo
Los Angeles CO
Alonso, Odón
Spanish National Radio–TV SO
Alonso, Victor
Concert de Les Arts
Alonso-Crespo, Eduardo
Cincinnati CO
Alsop, Marin
Colorado SO
Concordia Orch
String Fever
Altrichter, Petr
Czech PO

Altrichter, Petr (cont.)
Dvořák CO
Pardubice Chamber PO
Prague SO
Solist Band
Altschuler, V.
St. Petersburg Philharmony CO
Alwin, Karl
Vienna PO
Vienna State Opera Orch
Alwyn, Kenneth
BBC Concert Orch
Bournemouth Sinfonietta
Northern Sinfonietta of England
Philharmonia Orch
Prague PO
RTE Sinfonietta
Westminster PO
Alwyn, William
London PO
Ambache, Diana
Ambache CO
Amendola, Federico
Sicilian CO
Amfitheatrof, Daniel
EIAR Orch
MGM Studio SO
Pasdeloup Concerts Association Orch
Amos, David
Clarion Brass
City of London Sinfonia
Cracow PO
Crystal CO
Israel PO
Jerusalem SO
London SO
London SO Winds
New Russia Orch
Philharmonia Orch
Polish National RSO Katowice
Polish Radio–TV SO
Royal PO
Slovak State PO Košice
Ančerl, Karel
Berlin RSO
Czech PO
Dresden State Orch
Prague RSO
Prague SO
Toronto SO
Ancillotti, Mario
Symphonia Perusina
Anda, Géza
Salzburg Mozarteum Camerata Academica
Vienna SO
Andersen, Karsten
Bergen PO
Norwegian Wind Quintet
Norwegian Youth SO
Oslo PO
South Jutland SO
Andersson, Knud
New Orleans Opera Orch
Andersson, Per Ake
Norwegian National Opera Orch
André, Gunnar
Moscow RSO
Andreae, Marc
Bamberg SO
French National Orch
Swiss–Italian RSO
Swiss–Italian Radio–TV Orch
Andreassian, Nvart
Polychromie Ensemble
Andreescu, Horia
Bucharest George Enescu PO
Bucharest Virtuosi
Enescu State PO
Ploiesti PO
Romanian National RSO
Romanian Radio Orch
Romanian State Orch
Andreev, A.
Varna PO
Andretta, Giancarlo
Basel SO
Andrews, Paul
Slavyanka Men's Chorus San Francisco
Angelopoulos, Lycourgos
Greek Byzantine Choir
Angelov, Stoyan
Bulgarian RSO
Angerer, Hansjörg
Mozarteum Horn Players
Angerer, Paul
Concilium Musicum
English CO
Pforzheim CO
Southwest German CO Pforzheim
Vienna Concilium Musicum
Anguélov, Ivan
Monte Carlo PO
Angulo, José Luis
Santo Domingo de Silos Benedictine Monks' Choir

Angus, David
  Guildhall Chamber Ensemble
Anichanov, André
  St. Petersburg State SO
Anissimov, Alexander
  Irish National SO
  Moscow SO
Annovazzi, Napoleone
  Lucca Teatro Comunale del Giglio Orch
  Rome Opera Orch
Anosov, Nikolai
  Bolshoi Theater Orch
  Czech PO
  Moscow RSO
Ansermet, Ernest
  Decca String Orch
  Royal PO
  Walther Straram Orch
  Swiss Romande Orch
  Swiss Romande Orch members
Ansermet, Pierre
  Swiss Romande Orch
Antál, Mátyás
  Concentus Hungaricus
  Failoni CO
  Hungarian State Orch
Anthony, Pete
  Northwest Sinfonia
Antonellini, Vittorio
  I Solisti Aquilani
Antonini, Alfredo
  Bavarian RSO
  Oslo PO
  St. Cecilia Academy Orch Rome
Antonini, Giovanni
  Il Giardino Armonico Ensemble
Antonini, Pietro
  Cremona Musica Insieme Group
  Swiss-Italian Radio-TV Orch
Apelt, Arthur
  Berlin CO
  Berlin Staatskapelle
  Berlin State Orch
  Leipzig Gewandhaus Orch
Apolin, Alexander
  Pilsen RSO
Appia, E.
  Gabrieli Festival Orch
  RTF Orch
  Swiss Romande Orch
Appling, Elizabeth
  San Francisco Boys' Chorus
  San Francisco Chamber Singers
  San Francisco Girls' Chorus
Aprea, Bruno
  Graz SO
  Italian International Orch
Arabadjiev, Christo
  Philippopolis
Arámbarri, Jesús
  Madrid Concert Orch
  Spanish National Orch
Arbós, Enrique Fernández
  Madrid SO
Archer, Malcolm
  Bristol Cathedral Choir
  Bristol Cathedral Special Choirs
Archibald, Paul
  English Brass Ensemble
Ardal, Alf
  Canticum Novum CO
Arena, Maurizio
  Florence Maggio Musicale Orch
Argenta, Ataulfo
  London SO
  Paris Conservatory Societé des Concerts Orch
  Spanish National Orch
Argento, Pietro
  French National Orch
  Milan RAI SO
  Prague SO
  Swiss-Italian RSO
  Turin RAI SO
Argiris, Spiros
  RTBF SO
Arizcuren, Elias
  Conjunto Iberico Octet
Arman, Howard
  Innsbruck Woodwind Circle
  Salzburg Bach Choir
  Salzburg Baroque Ensemble
  Schütz Academy
Armand, Georges
  Toulouse CO
Armenian, Raffi
  Canadian Chamber Ensemble
  Kitchener-Waterloo SO
Armstrong, Donald
  New Zealand CO
Armstrong, Richard
  Welsh National Opera Orch
Arnell, Johann
  Berlin RSO
  Stockholm PO
Arnold, Malcolm
  Bournemoth SO
  City of Birmingham SO
  Grimethorpe Colliery Band

Arnold, Malcolm (cont.)
  London PO
  Philharmonia Orch
Arp, Klaus
  Kaiserslauten Radio Orch
  Southwest German RSO Baden-Baden
Arshavskaya, Ludmila
  Cantus Sacred Music Ensemble
Asahina, Takashi
  Osaka PO
Asbury, Stefan
  Asko Ensemble
  Oxford Camerata
Asensio, Enrique Garcia
  Madrid SO
Ash, Peter
  Downshire Players of London
Ashkenazy, Vladimir
  Berlin German SO
  Berlin RSO
  Boston SO
  Cleveland Orch
  (Royal) Concertgebouw Orch
  English CO
  Gothenburg SO
  Philharmonia Orch
  Royal PO
Asia, Daniel
  Musical Elements
Atherton, David
  BBC SO
  Eireann Radio-TV SO
  London PO
  London Sinfonietta
  London SO
  New Philharmonia Orch
Athinãos, Nikos
  Frankfurt State Orch
  Frankfurt on the Oder PO
  Frankfurt on the Oder State Orch
  Frankfurt on the Oder SO
Atlas, Dalia
  Camerata Atlas
  Israel Pro Musica Orch
  Philharmonia Hungarica
  Royal PO
Atterberg, Kurt
  Swedish RSO
Atzmon, Moshe
  BBC Welsh National SO
  Basel SO
  Malmö SO
  New Philharmonia Orch
  New PO
  North German RSO
  Royal PO
  World SO
Auberson, Jean-Marie
  Lausanne PO
  Romande Instrumental Group Rockband
  Vienna Opera Orch
Aubin, Tony
  French Radio Lyric Orch
Audoli, Jean-Walter
  Audoli Instrumental Ensemble
Auguin, Phillipe
  Helsingborg SO
Auriacombe, Louis
  Paris Conservatory Societé des Concerts Orch
  Toulouse CO
Austin, Christopher
  Brunel Ensemble
Austin, Richard
  Bournemouth Municipal Orch
Avalos, Francesco d'
  Hungarian State SO
  Philharmonia Orch
Avetisyan, Mikael
  Moscow Orch
Avshalomov, Jacob
  Portland Youth PO
  Portland Youth SO
Aykal, Gürer
  London SO
  North German RSO
  TRT String Orch
Ayo, Felix
  I Giovani Musici Italiani
  Pesaro Rossini Orch
  Symphonia Perusina
Azendrei, Janka
  Schola Hungarica
Azzolina, Mark
  Florida Symphonic Pops Orch
Babicky, František
  Brno State PO
Bach, Konrad
  Thüringian Saalfeld-Rudolstadt SO
  Thüringian SO
Baci, Ludovic
  Romanian National RSO
Baciu, Ion
  Cluj-Napoca PO
  Cluj-Napoca PO members
  Iasi Moldova PO
  Iasi Moldova PO Winds
Bäck, Sven-Erik
  Stockholm Chamber Choir
  Swedish Radio Choir

Backhouse, Jeremy
  Vasari Singers
Badea, Christian
  Columbus SO
  Royal PO
  Spoleto Festival Orch
Bader, Roland
  Berlin Cathedral Choir
  Berlin Domkapelle Instrumental Ensemble
  Berlin RSO
  Cologne RSO
  Cracow PO
  St. Hedwig's Cathedral Choir
  Stuttgart PO
Badura-Skoda, Paul
  Prague CO
Baekkelund, Kjell
  Gjovik Sinfonietta
Baer, P.
  Chevetogne Monks' Choir
Bagby, Benjamin
  Sequentia
Bailey, Mark
  Yale Russian Chorus
Baillie, A.
  London Sinfonietta
Bainbridge, Simon
  BBC SO
  Composers Ensemble
Bakala, Bretislav
  Brno RSO
  Brno State PO
Bakels, Kees
  Bournemouth SO
  Hilversum RSO
  Netherlands RSO
  Philharmonia Orch
Baker, Claude
  Indiana Univ New Music Ensemble
Balderi, Marco
  Swiss-Italian Orch
Baldner, Thomas
  Indiana Univ SO
Baldoon, John
  Federal Music Society members
  Federal Music Society Opera Company Orch
Balestracci, Sergio
  Santo Spirito Academy Orch
Baley, Virko
  Young Russia State SO Moscow
Balissat, Jean
  Swiss-Italian Radio-TV Orch
Ballista, Antonio
  Italian Virtuosi
Balogh, Attila
  Amati Ensemble
Balter, Alan
  Akron SO
Balzer, Wolfgang
  Rhenish PO
Bamert, Matthias
  BBC PO
  BBC SO
  Berlin RSO
  London Mozart Players
  London PO
  Philharmonia Orch
  Scottish CO
  Scottish National Orch
  Southwest German RSO Baden-Baden
Banchini, Chiara
  Ensemble 415
Bánfalvi, Béla
  Budapest Strings
  Kontra String Quartet
Bannwart, Roman
  Einsiedein & Lucerne Choralschola
Banzhaf, Helmut
  Pro Musica Sacra Orch
Banzo, Eduardo López
  Al Ayre Español
Barati, George
  Oslo PO
  Vienna State Opera Orch
Barballushi, Jetmir
  Albanian Radio-TV Orch
Barbirolli, John
  BBC SO
  Berlin PO
  Berlin State Opera Orch
  Czech PO
  English CO
  Hallé Orch
  Helsinki CO
  Helsinki SO
  London PO
  London String Orch
  London SO
  New Philharmonia Orch
  New York PO
  Philharmonia Orch
  Rome Opera Orch
  Rome Radio Orch
  Royal Opera House Orch Covent Garden
  Royal PO
  Stuttgart RSO
  Turin Radio Orch

Bardon, Claude
Caen Orch
Monte Carlo PO
Bardot, Francis
Altaïr SO
Paul Kuentz Orch
Barenboim, Daniel
Bayreuth Festival Orch
Berlin PO
Berlin State Opera Orch
Chicago SO
Cleveland Orch
English CO
London PO
London SO
New Philharmonia Orch
New York PO
Orch de Paris
Philharmonia Orch
Royal PO
Bareza, Nikša
Trieste Teatro Comunale Giuseppe Verdi Orch
Barlow, Alan
Royal PO
Barlow, Jeremy
Broadside Band
Barnea, Uri
Billings SO
Barnett, J.
National Orch Alumni Association members
Barney, Robert
Boston Gay Men's Chorus
Barra, Donald
Moscow PO
San Diego CO
Barrett, Michael
Brooklyn PO
Barrios, Eduardo Garcia
Baja California Orch
Barritt, Paul
London Divertimenti
Baršaï, Rudolf
Belgian Radio-TV French SO
CO of Europe
Cologne RSO
German Youth PO
Moscow CO
Moscow PO members
Moscow RSO
Bárta, Aleš
Prague CO
Bartholomée, Pierre
Brussels Radio-TV Instrumentalists
Liège PO
Philharmonic Concert Society
Bartle, Jean Ashworth
Toronto Children's Chorus
Bartoletti, Bruno
Bavarian RSO
Berlin State Opera Orch
Buenos Aires Teatro Colón Orch
Chicago Lyric Opera Orch
Florence Maggio Musicale Orch
Florence Teatro Comunale Orch
National PO
New Philharmonia Orch
Rome Opera Orch
St. Cecilia Academy Orch Rome
Venice Teatro La Fenice Orch
Bartos, Michael
Bronx Arts Ensemble
Polish National RSO Katowice
Barvinskij, O.
Ukrainian National SO
Barzin, Leon
Philharmonia Orch
Basarab, Mircea
Bucharest George Enescu PO
Bashford, Rodney
Grenadier Guards Band
Bashmet, Yuri
Moscow Soloists
Basile, Arturo
Italian Lyric Orch
Milan RAI SO
Naples Teatro San Carlo Orch
Rome Opera Orch
San Remo SO
Turin RAI Orch
Turin Radio-TV SO
Bass, Robert
Collegiate Orch
Batastini, Robert
Grace Lutheran Church Choir River Forest IL
St. Barbara Roman Catholic Church Choir Brookfield IL
Bateman, Paul
Prague PO
Royal Concert PO
Batík, Roland
Das Klein Orchester
London Little Orch
Bátiz, Enrique
London CO
London SO
Mexican State SO
Mexico City PO
Mexico Festival Orch

Bátiz, Enrique (cont.)
Mexico State SO
Philharmonia Orch
Royal Liverpool PO
Royal PO
Baude-Delhommais, Eric
Philidor Ensemble
Baudo, Serge
Bavarian RSO
Czech PO
London PO
London SO
Lyon National Chorus
Lyon National Orch
Orch de Paris
Paris Opera Orch
Prague SO
Royal College of Music Orch
Bauer, Peter
Joueurs de Flute
Bauert, Matthias
BBC PO
Bauer-Theussl, Franz
Slovak RSO Bratislava
Vienna Volksoper Orch
Baum, Hans-Dieter
Berlin RSO
Baumgartner, Andrew
Mount Angel Abbey Choir
Baumgartner, Rudolf
Lucerne Festival Strings
Bay, Peter
Nexus
Rochester PO
Bazhalkin, A. N.
Red Star Red Army Chorus
Beeser, Robert
Musical Elements
Beaudet, Jean-Marie
CBC Vancouver SO
Beck, John
Eastman Percussion Ensemble
Eastman Percussion Ensemble members
Bedford, Steuart
Aldeburgh Festival Ensemble
English CO
London SO
Scottish CO
Beecham, Thomas
BBC SO
Beecham Choral Society
Berlin PO
French National RSO
Helsinki PO
London PO
London SO
Metropolitan Opera Orch
New York PO
Philharmonia Orch
RCA Victor SO
Royal Opera House Orch
Royal PO
Swiss Romande Orch
Beegle, Raymond
New York Vocal Arts Ensemble
Gregg Smith Singers
Beek, Arie van
Auvergne CO
Rotterdam Conservatory Symphonic Band
Behr, Randall
Philharmonia Orch
Behrend, Siegfried
DZO CO
I Musici
Behrmann, Martin
Spandau Kantorei Berlin
Beier, Paul
Galilei Ensemble
Beinum, Eduard van
(Royal) Concertgebouw Orch
London PO
Beissel, Heribert
Hamburg SO
Slovak RSO Bratislava
Bélanger, M.
Montreal Metropolitan Orch
Belardi, Armando
São Paulo Teatro Municipale Orch
Bélis, Annie
Ensemble Kérylos
Bell, Robert Hunter
St. Mary Magdalene Church Choir Toronto
Bellemare, G.
Three Rivers SO
Bellezza, Vincenzo
Naples Teatro San Carlo Orch
Rome Opera Orch
Bellini, Gabriele
Eastern Netherlands Orch
Orkest van het Oosten
Sofia PO
Bellugi, Piero
Berlin RSO
Royal PO
La Scala Orch
Toscana Regional Orch
Turin RAI Orch
Turin Radio Orch

Belohlávek, Jiří
Brno State PO
Czech PO
New Czech CO
Prague RSO
Prague SO
Benda, Christian
Prague CO
Bender, Philippe
Cannes-Provence Alpes-Côte d'Azur Regional Orch
Bendix, Kurt
Stockholm Royal Opera House Orch
Ben-Dor, Gisèle
Israel CO
London SO
Sofia Soloists CO
Benedetti, Luigi
Gruppo di Canto Ambrosiano
Benedetti, Robert
Radio-Lyrique Orch
Benini, Maurizio
Irish National SO
Benjamin, Arthur
London SO
Benjamin, George
London Sinfonietta
Benjamin, Rick
Paragon Ragtime Orch
Bennett, Robert Russell
RCA Victor SO
Benoit, Philippe
Vivente Voce Choir
Ben-Yohanan, Dafna
Jerusalem Rubin Conservatory of Music & Dance Ankor Choir
Benzi, Roberto
Arnheim PO
Paris Opera Orch
Berezowsky, Nicolai
RCA Victor SO
Bergby, Ingar
Bit 20 Ensemble
Bergel, Erich
Budapest PO
Cape Town SO
Berger, Sven
Convivium Musicum
Berglund, Paavo
Bournemouth SO
Dresden Staatskapelle
Finnish RSO
Helsinki PO
New Philharmonia Orch
New Stockholm CO
Oslo PO
Royal Danish Orch
Stockholm PO
Beringer, Karl-Friedrich
Austro-Hungarian PO
Windsbach Boys' Choir
Berio, Luciano
Juilliard Ensemble
London Sinfonietta
Musique Vivante Ensemble
Philharmonia Orch
Berkeley, Lennox
London PO
Berkes, Kálmán
Budapest Wind Ensemble
Nicolaus Esterházy Sinfonia
Berki, László
Hungarian State Folk Ensemble Orch
Berkovsky, Daniel
Prague Festival Strings
Berlingen, Jean-Pierre
Normandy Orchestral Ensemble
Bernard, Anthony
Philharmonia Orch
Bernardi, Alfredo
CBC Vancouver SO
Bernardi, Mario
CBC Vancouver SO
Calgary PO
National Arts Center Canada Orch
Toronto SO
Bernart, Massimo de
Albanian Radio-TV Orch
Genoa Teatro Comunale Orch
Italian International Opera Orch
Italian PO
Lucca Teatro Comunale Giglio Orch
Montpellier PO
Piacenza SO
I Pomeriggi Musicali Orch
San Remo SO
Sicilian SO
Swiss-Italian Orch
Bernas, Richard
BBC Scottish SO
BBC SO
CSR Bratislava SO
Music Projects London
Bernasconi, Giorgio
Contrechamps Ensemble
Geneva Percussion Ensemble
Italian Accademia Strumentale
Bernatchez, Claude
Anonymus Ensemble

Bernbacher, K.
  Northwest German PO
Bernhardt, Robert
  Royal PO
Bernius, Frieder
  German Chamber PO
  German Wind Phil
  Musica Fiata
  Stuttgart Baroque Orch
  Stuttgart Chamber Choir
  Stuttgart CO
  Tafelmusik
  Württemberg CO
Bernstein, Elmer
  Royal PO
Bernstein, Leonard
  Bavarian RSO
  Berkshire Boys' Choirs
  Berlin PO
  Boston SO
  Chicago SO
  Columbia Jazz Combo
  Columbia SO
  (Royal) Concertgebouw Orch
  English Bach Festival Orch
  English CO
  French National Orch
  La Grande Ecurie et la Chambre du Roy
  Israel PO
  London SO
  Los Angeles PO
  Metropolitan Opera Orch
  National SO Washington D.C.
  New York City Ballet Orch
  New York City SO
  New York PO
  New York PO members
  Philadelphia Orch
  RCA Victor SO
  Royal Danish Orch
  St. Cecilia Academy Orch Rome
  St. Louis SO
  La Scala Orch
  Vienna PO
Berrettoni, Umberto
  La Scala Orch
Berrini, Marco
  Ars Cantica
Berry, Mary
  Cambridge Schola Gregoriana
  Schola Gregoriana
  Winchester Cathedral Choir
Berthelon, J.
  Maîtrise de la Loire
  Saratov Phil Choir
Bertini, Gary
  Dresden State Orch
  Stuttgart RSO
  Vienna SO
Bertola, Giulo
  Milan Angelicum CO
Bertolini, C.
  Rome Festival Orch
Bessler, Bernardo
  Brazilian CO
Best, Matthew
  City of London Sinfonia
  Corydon Orch
  Corydon Singers
  English CO
  Mediaeval Ensemble
  Westminster Cathedral Choristers
Betton, Joël
  Berlin Landeszupf Orch
Beuerle, Hans Michael
  Freiburg Bach Choir
  Anton Webern Choir Freiburg
Bezrukov, Georgy
  Bolshoi Theater SO Soloists
Bezzina, Gilbert
  Nice Baroque Ensemble
Bibl, Rudolf
  Vienna Volksoper Orch
Bidaud, Pierre-Alain
  Mélodia Brass Ensemble
Bielby, Jonathan
  Wakefield Cathedral Choir
Bigg, Julian
  Czech SO
Biggs, Hayes
  Musicians' Accord members
Bigot, Eugène
  Lamoureux Orch
  ORTF Lyric Orch
  Raugel Orch
Bihlmaier, Hans Norbert
  Copenhagen PO
Bilek, Zdenek
  Slovak PO
Binder, Erich
  Vienna Volksoper Orch
Bingelis, Petras
  Kaunas State Chorus
  Lithuanian Radio-TV Chorus
Binkley, Thomas
  Pro Arte Singers
  Studio of Early Music

Biondi, Fabio
  L'Europa Galante
Birney, Alan
  Pennsylvania Sinfonia Orch
  Pennsylvania Sinfonia Orch members
Birney-Smith, Richard
  Te Deum Singers
Bismuth, Patrick
  Concert Royal
Björlin, Ulf
  Cappella Coloniensis
  Royal PO
Blachly, Alexander
  Pomerium Musices
Black, Frank
  NBC SO
Black, Robert
  New York New Music Ensemble
  Prism CO
  Prism Orch
  Silesian PO
  Slovak RSO
  Speculum Musicae
  Warsaw National PO
  Warsaw PO
Black, Stanley
  London Festival Orch
  London SO
  Mantovani Orch
Blackley, John
  Schola Antiqua
Blagoeva, Adriana
  New CO
  Sofia Boys' Choir
Blake, Howard
  English CO
Blank, Emil
  Russian CO
Blankenburg, Elke Mascha
  Cologne Kurrende
  Cologne Youth Orch
  Leonarda Ensemble Cologne
  Clara Schumann Cologne Orch
Blarr, Oskar Gottlieb
  Ensemble 1971
Blazhkov, Igor
  Kiev SO
  Leningrad PO
Blech, Larry
  Berlin PO
  Berlin RSO
  Berlin State Opera Orch
  London SO
  Vienna State Opera Orch
Bleech, Harry
  Philharmonia Orch
Bliss, Arthur
  London CO
  London SO
  London SO Wind & Brass Ensemble
Blomstedt, Herbert
  Danish National RSO
  Dresden Staatskapelle
  Dresden State Orch
  Oslo PO
  San Francisco SO
  Stockholm PO
  Swedish RSO
Bloomfield, Theodore
  Rochester PO
Blum, D.
  Esterházy Orch
Bobescu, Jean
  Bucharest State Opera Orch
  Romanian Opera Orch
Boboc, Nicolae
  Arad PO
  Timisoara Banatul PO
Böck, Herbert
  Vienna Concentus Vocalis
  Vienna Youth Orch
Bodmer, Jacques
  Málaga City Orch
Boelzner, G.
  New York City Ballet Orch
Boesschoten, Gereon van
  Grimbergen Gregoriaans Abbey Monks' Choir
Boettcher, Wilfried
  Scottish CO
  Stuttgart PO
  Vienna Festival CO
Bogár, István
  Budapest Strauss Ensemble
  Budapest SO
Bogunia, Stanislav
  Solist Band
  Suk CO
Bohlin, Folke
  Lund Univ Male Voice Choir
Böhm, Karl
  Bavarian RSO
  Bayreuth Festival Orch
  Berlin German Opera Orch
  Berlin PO
  Dresden Staatskapelle
  Dresden State Opera Orch
  Dresden State Orch
  German Opera Orch

Böhm, Karl (cont.)
  Hamburg State Opera Orch
  Naples Teatro San Carlo Orch
  Philharmonia Orch
  Prague National Theater Orch
  San Francisco Opera Orch
  Saxon State Orch
  Vienna PO
  Vienna SO
  Vienna State Opera Orch
Bohn, Rüdiger
  Sinfonietta Tübingen
Bojesen, Michael
  Camerata
  Safri Duo
Bok, Joszef
  Warsaw PO
  Warsaw SO
Bolle, James
  Monadnock Music Festival Orch
  New Hampshire SO
Bolling, Claude
  Claude Bolling Big Band
Bollon, Fabrice
  Lisbon Gulbenkian Foundation CO
Bolton, Ivor
  Bournemouth Sinfonietta
  City of London Baroque Sinfonia
  English CO
  London PO
  Royal PO
  St. James' Baroque Players
Bonaventura, Mario di
  Hopkins Center Orch
Bonavera, Alfred
  English CO
Bonavolontà, Nino
  Rome SO
Boncompagni, Elio
  Hungarian RSO
  Turin RAI Orch
Bond, Victoria
  Shanghai SO
Bondarenko, Alexander
  Frescoes of Kiev
Bongartz, Heinz
  Berlin State Orch
  Dresden PO
  Dresden State Orch
  Leipzig Gewandhaus Orch
Bonnardot, Emmanuel
  Alla Francesca
Bonneau, Paul
  Luxembourg Radio-TV SO
Bonner, Gary
  Voices of the Azusa Pacific Univ
Bonynge, Richard
  Adelaide Opera Orch
  Bologna Teatro Comunale Orch
  Buenos Aires Teatro Colón Orch
  Catania Teatro Massimo Bellini Orch
  Chicago Lyric Opera Orch
  English CO
  Irish National SO
  London New SO
  London SO
  Monte Carlo Opera Orch
  National PO London
  Netherlands CO
  New Philharmonia Orch
  Polish National RSO Katowice
  Royal Opera House Orch
  San Francisco Opera Orch
  Scottish National Orch
  Swiss Romande Orch
  Welsh National Opera Orch
Borchgrevink, Hans M.
  Consortium Vocale
Bordignon, Mino
  Milan Chamber Music Choir
Borejko, Andrzej
  Poznan PO
Borin, Luciano
  Viotti CO
Borin, Per
  Dies Caniculares Festival Orch
Borries, Christian von
  Polish National RSO Katowice
Bosc, Rene
  Diagonales Brass & Percussion Ensemble
  Montpelier Brass Quintet
Boskovsky, Willi
  Boskovsky Ensemble
  Dresden State Opera Orch
  London PO
  Philharmonia Hungarica
  Johann Strauss Orch
  Vienna Mozart Ensemble
  Vienna PO
Bossard, Olivier
  Ligugé Abbey Monks' Choir
Bostock, Douglas
  Carlsbad SO
Botstein, Leon
  American SO
  Boston Pro Arte CO
  Chelsea Chamber Ensemble
  Hudson Valley Philharmonic String Quartet
  Hudson Valley Wind Quintet

▲ = CD ♦ = Enhanced CD △ = MD ■ = Cassette Tape □ = DCC

Botstein, Leon (cont.)
London PO
Botvay, Károly
Budapest Strings
New Bach Collegium Musicum
Bouchard, Denis
Canadian Forces Central Band
Boucher, Gilberte
Arpeggio CO
Boudreau, Walter
Montreal Metropolitan Orch
Boughton, William
English String Orch
English SO
London SO
Philharmonia Orch
Boulanger, Natalie
BBC SO
Boulez, Pierre
Bayreuth Festival Orch
BBC SO
Berlin PO
Chicago SO
Cleveland Orch
(Royal) Concertgebouw Orch
Domaine Musical Orch
Ensemble InterContemporain
French National Orch
The Hague PO
London SO
New Philharmonia Orch
New Philharmonia Strings
New York PO
Paris Conservatory Société des Concerts Orch
Paris Opera Orch
Philharmonia Orch
Royal Opera House Orch Covent Garden
Strasbourg Instrumental Percussion Group
Vienna PO
Boult, Adrian
BBC Scottish SO
BBC SO
Big SO
London New SO
London Orch Society
London PO
London SO
New Philharmonia Orch
Philharmonia Orch
Royal PO
Vienna State Opera Orch
Bouman, H.
Haydn-Héritage Ensemble
Bour, Ernest
Ensemble Modern
French National RSO
The Hague PO
Residentie Orch The Hague
Southwest RSO
Southwest German RSO Baden-Baden
Bourbon, Alix
Baroque Instrumental Ensemble
Bourbon, Maurice
Coeli et Terra Vocal Ensemble
Paris Métamorphoses Ensemble
Boutry, Roger
Republican Guard Orch of Harmony
Bouture, Didier
Harmonia Ensemble
Harmonia Nova Orch Ensemble
Boyd, John
Chicago Saxophone Quartet
Indiana State Univ Symphonic Wind Ensemble
Brabbins, Martyn
BBC Scottish SO
Philharmonia Orch
Bradshaw, Richard
Canadian Opera Company Orch
The Hague PO
Netherlands Ballet Orch
Bragg, George
Gregg Smith Singers
Braithwaite, Nicholas
London PO
New Zealand CO
Bräm, Thüring
Pardubice Philharmonic CO
Bramall, Anthony
Czech-Slovak RSO
Slovak PO
Brancusi, Cristian
Iasi Moldova Phil CO
Brand, Geoffrey
European Winds
London Winds
Brandl, Franz
Munich Madrigal Choir
Brebion, Jean
ORTF Lyric Orch
Brediceanu, Mihai
Bucharest George Enescu PO
Romanian Opera Orch
Brehm, Alvin
Group for Contemporary Music
Speculum Musicae members
Breiner, Paul
Camerata Cassovia
Capella Istropolitana
CSSR State PO

Breiner, Paul (cont.)
Czech State PO
Nicolaus Esterházy Sinfonia
Razumovsky Sinfonia
Breitner, T.
Budapest PO
Brembeck, Christian
Capella Istropolitana
Parthenia Baroque
Bremner, Tony
Australian PO
Philharmonia Orch
Bressan, Filippo Maria
Italian Virtuosi
Padua & Venice CO
Brett, Charles
Amaryllis Consort
Brett, Philip
Univ of California at Berkeley Chamber Chorus
Brezina, Alexander
Munich Wind Academy Soloists
Briccetti, Thomas
Bergamo Stabile Orch
Prague Virtuosi
Bride, Philip
French Instrumental Ensemble
Briggs, David
Truro Cathedral Choir
Briney, Bruce
Millar Brass Ensemble
Brion, Keith
Michigan State Univ Symphonic Band
New Sousa Band
Ohio State Univ Concert Band
Washington Winds
Britten, Benjamin
English CO
English Opera Group Orch
London SO
Boyd Neel String Orch
Royal Opera House Orch
Scottish CO
Britten, Tony
Royal PO
Brizio, Edoardo
Czech Radio-TV Orch
Prague PO
Prague SO
Brizzi, Aldo
Gruppo Musica Insieme
Nuovo Ensemble Italiano
Broedbent, Peter
Joyful Company of Singers
Brodsky, Vadim
Polish National RSO Katowice
Broeck, S. van den
New Flemish SO
Brook, Peter
Royal Shakespeare Company
Brooks, Tamara
Mendelssohn Club Chorus Philadelphia
New England Conservatory Jazz Big Band
New School of Music Orch
Brooks, William
Tuba Ensemble
Brookshire, Bradley
San Cassiano Musici
Brosse, D.
New Flemish SO
Brott, Boris
Hamilton PO
London SO
McGill CO
Nova Scotia Sym
Toronto Festival Pops Orch
Brough, Paul
Tewkesbury Abbey School Choir
Broughton, Bruce
London Sinfonietta
Sinfonia of London
Broussard, Maurice
Ottovoci Ensemble
La Primavera String Ensemble
Brouwer, Leo
Guitar Symphonietta
RCA Victor CO
Brown, Corrick
USSR Radio-TV Large Concert Orch
Brown, Earle
Avantgarde Ensemble
Brown, Iona
Academy of St. Martin in the Fields
Norwegian CO
Brown, Jonathan
Henry's Eight
Brown, Justin
Royal PO
Brown, Kyler
Virgin Consort
Brown, Mark
American SO
Collegium Aureum members
Gioia della Musica
Pro Cantione Antiqua
Brown, R.
Continuum Percussion Quartet
Brown, Timothy
Cambridge Univ Chamber Choir
Clare College Chapel Choir Cambridge

Brown, Timothy (cont.)
Clare College Choir Cambridge
Browne, Bruce
Choral Cross-Ties
Bruck, Charles
Netherlands Opera Orch
ORTF PO
Brüggen, Franz
Concerto Amsterdam
Orch of the 18th Century
Bruland, Sverre
Bergen PO
Brunelle, Philip
Minnesota Opera Orch
Minnesota Orch
Plymouth Festival Orch
Plymouth Music Series Ensemble Singers
Plymouth Music Series Orch
Plymouth Music Series Orch Soloists
Royal Swedish Opera Orch
Bruni, M.
Czech Phil Chorus
Prague CO
Brunner, Wolfgang
Salzburg Hofmusik
Buchler, Willy
Vienna Strauss Festival Orch
Buckley, Emerson
New York City Opera Orch
Buckley, Richard
BBC SO
Buder, Michael
Bamberg SO
Bugaj, Tomasz
Pamplona Pablo Sarasate Orch
Warsaw Sinfonia
Buketoff, Igor
Icelandic SO
New Philharmonia Orch
Oslo PO
Royal PO
Bullock, Ernest
Coronation Orch
Bultsevich, N.
Intercession Cathedral Church Choir
Bünte, Carl-August
Berlin SO
Buratto, Alan
Texas Boys' Choir
Burchard, Richard
Ars Femina Ensemble
Burfin, J.-M.
Württemberg PO
Burgin, Richard
Boston Brass Ensemble
Burgomeister, F.
Indianapolis Festival Orch
Burgon, Geoffrey
Endymion Ensemble
Burkh, Dennis
Janáček PO
Burkhard, Paul
Zurich Beromünster Orch
Burns, Stephen
American Concerto Orch
Burrichter, Ronald
Florida Musica Nova
Busca, Pietro
Ricercar Academy
Busch, Adolf
Adolf Busch Chamber Players
Busch, Fritz
Berlin State Opera Orch
Buenos Aires Teatro Colón Orch
Cologne RSO
Danish National RSO
Glyndebourne Festival Orch
New York PO
Stockholm PO
Winterthur SO
Büsser, Henri
Paris Opera Orch
Butt, Yondani
London SO
Philharmonia Orch
Royal PO
Bychkov, Semyon
Bavarian RSO
Berlin PO
Orch de Paris
Cable, Howard
Nova Scotia Sym
Cabré, Josep
Compañia Musical de las Americas
La Fidelissima Schola Gregoriense
Caetani, Oleg
Bamberg SO
Vienna SO
Caeyers, Jan
Beethoven Academy
Belgium New CO
Caiazza, Ivano
I Solisti Partenopei
Calabrese, Alfred
Britten Singers
Emory Univ Concert Choir
Caldwell, Sarah
Ekaterinburg PO
London SO

Callaway, Paul
  Washington National Cathedral Men & Boys' Choir
Calmel, Bernard
  Bernard Calmel Orch
Caltabiano, Ronald
  Society for New Music
Calvi, Gérard
  Théâtre Bouffes-Parisiens Orch & Ensemble
Cambreling, Sylvain
  Brussels Théâtre de la Monnaie Orch
  Monte Carlo PO
Cameron, Basil
  London PO
Camozzo, A.
  Bergamo Teatro Donizetti Orch
Campanella, Benno
  Bologna Teatro Comunale Orch
  Serenissima Pro Arte Orch
  Turin Teatro Regio Orch
  Venice Teatro La Fenice Orch
Campanino, Gigi
  Naples Teatro San Carlo Orch
Campbell, Jimmy
  Festival of the Sound Ensemble
Campori, Angelo
  Naples Teatro San Carlo Orch
Canin, Stuart
  New Century CO
Cantelli, Guido
  NBC SO
  New York PO
  New York Philharmonic SO
  Philharmonia Orch
  Rome RAI SO Soloists
  St. Cecilia Academy Orch Rome
  La Scala Orch
Cantryn, W.
  Amsterdam Baroque Orch
Cao, Pierre
  La Fenice Ensemble
  Luxembourg RSO
  Luxembourg Radio-TV SO
  Ricercar Consort
Capolongo, Paul
  Orch de Paris
Capp, Richard
  New York Philharmonia Virtuosi
Capuana, Franco
  Florence Maggio Musicale Orch
  Italian Lyric Orch
  Naples Teatro San Carlo Orch
  Rome Opera Orch
  St. Cecilia Academy Orch Rome
  La Scala Orch
  Trieste Teatro Comunale Giuseppe Verdi Orch
  Turin RAI SO
  Turin RSO
Carabetta, Samuel
  St. John's Episcopal Church Choir Lafayette Sq. Washington D.C.
Caracciolo, Franco
  Milan Italian Radio-TV Orch
  Naples Alessandro Scarlatti RAI Orch
  Naples RAI Orch
  Naples RAI SO
  Alessandro Scarlatti CO
Carchiolo, S.
  Catania Baroque Orch
Cardon, S.
  Grenoble Instrumental Ensemble
Carella, Giuliano
  Italian International Opera Orch
  Italian International Orch
  Loire PO
  Lucca Teatro Comunale Giglio Orch
Carewe, John
  Berlin RSO
  Bournemouth Sinfonietta
  Netherlands Ballet Orch
  Nice PO
Caridis, Miltiades
  Danish National RSO
  Oslo PO
  Vienna RSO
  Vienna State Opera Orch
Carignani, P.
  San Remo SO
Cariven, Marcel
  French Radio Lyric Orch
  ORTF Lyric Orch
Carlos, Wendy
  LSI PO
Carmichael, J. C.
  Furman Civic Wind Ensemble
  Mostly Modern Chamber Players
Carmichael, John
  National Festival Orch
Carmignola, Giuliano
  Sonatori de la Gioiosa Marca
Carney, Jonathan
  Royal PO
  Royal PO Chamber Ensemble
Caro, Roberto de
  Arpeggione Ensemble
Carpenter, Gary
  Slovak RSO Bratislava
Carraro, Massimiliano
  Graz SO
  Italian International Orch String Quartet

Carroll, Edward
  Washington Chamber Soloists
Cartigny, Gérard
  Liège SO
Carvalho, Eleazar de
  Paraiba SO
Carver, Lucinda
  Los Angeles Mozart Orch
Carwood, Andrew
  Cardinall's Musick
Casadei, Claudio
  Symphonia Perusina
Casadesus, Jean-Claude
  Cleveland Orch
  Lille National Orch
  Royal PO
Casals, Pablo
  Busch String Quartet
  Collegium Musicum
  Marlboro Festival Orch
  Perpignan Festival Orch
  Prades Festival Orch
Cassone, Gabriele
  Pian e Forte Ensemble
Cassuto, Alvaro
  Nova Filarmonia Portuguesa
Căstoiu, Iulian
  Romanian Patriarchate Choir
Catalucci, Gabriele
  In Canto CO
  In Canto di Terni Youth Orch
  Orch Giovanile In Canto
  Sassari SO
  Sassari SO Ensemble
Cavallaro, Angelo
  Marchigiana PO
Cave, Philip
  Magnificat Players
Cébron, Francis
  Paris Conservatory Societé des Concerts Orch
Ceccanti, Mauro
  Contempoensemble
Ceccato, Aldo
  Bergen PO
  London SO
  Naples Teatro San Carlo Orch
Celibidache, Sergiu
  Berlin PO
  Danish National RSO
  London SO
  Milan RAI SO
  Munich PO
  Naples Alessandro Scarlatti RAI Orch
  ORTF National Orch
  ORTF SO
  Rome Italian Radio-TV Orch
  Rome RAI Orch
  Rome RAI SO
  SDR SO
  South German RSO
  South German SO
  Southwest German RSO Baden-Baden
  Stuttgart RSO
  Swedish RSO
  Turin RAI Orch
  Turin RAI SO
  Turin Radio Orch
  Turin RSO
  Venice Teatro La Fenice Orch
  Vienna SO
Cellini, Renato
  Columbus Orch
  Mexican National Opera Orch
  New Orleans Opera Orch
  Palacio Bellas Artes Orch
  RCA Victor SO
Cera, Francesco
  Arte Musica Ensemble
Cerha, Friedrich
  Die Reihe Ensemble
Cesare, Fausto di
  Rara Ensemble
Chabanian, Levon
  St. Gayanée Chapel Armenian Liturgical Choir
Chailly, Riccardo
  Berlin RSO
  Bologna Teatro Comunale Orch
  Cleveland Orch
  (Royal) Concertgebouw Orch
  London Sinfonietta
  National PO
  National PO London
  La Scala Orch
Chakarov, E.
  Festival Sinfonietta
Chalabala, Zdenek
  Czech PO
  Prague National Theater Orch
Challender, Stuart
  Seymour Group
  Sydney SO
Chaloupka, Josef
  Prague National Theater Orch
Chancerelle, Xavier
  Paris Gregorian Choir
Chaney, Harold
  St. Ignatius of Antioch Choir New York

Charlet, Andre
  Brassus Chorale
  Romande Chamber Choir
  Swiss-Italian Radio Chorus
Charry, M.
  George Gershwin Festival Orch
Chaslin, Frederic
  Rouen SO
Chávez, Carlos
  New York Stadium SO
Chemin-Petit, Hans
  Berlin PO
Chen, Chiu-sen
  NHK SO
  Royal PO
  Yomiuri Nippon SO
Chen, David T. H.
  Taipei Municipal Chinese Classical Orch
Chen, Xieyang
  Shanghai SO
Chen, Zuohuang
  Czech RSO
  Slovak RSO Bratislava
Chenette, Stephen
  Hannaford Street Silver Band
Cherkasov, Gennadi
  Ostankino Radio-TV Large SO
Chernaik, David
  Apollo CO
Chernushenko, Vladislav
  Leningrad Glinka Choir
  St. Petersburg Cappella Orch
  St. Petersburg State Choir
Chiarappa, Carlo
  Accademia Bizantina
Childs, Barney
  Univ of Redlands Chamber Ensemble
Chivzhel, Eduard
  State SO
  Umeå Sinfonietta
  USSR RSO
Chmura, Gabriel
  Berlin RSO
  National Arts Center Canada Orch
  Stuttgart RSO
Christie, William
  Les Arts Florissants
  Cappella Coloniensis
  Corona
  Netherlands Chamber Choir
Christophers, Harry
  BBC PO
  (Royal) Concertgebouw CO
  The Sixteen
  The Sixteen Chorus
  The Sixteen Orch
Chung, Chai-Dong
  Seoul PO
Chung, Myung-Whun
  Bastille Opera Orch
  Bastille Orch
  (Royal) Concertgebouw Orch
  Gothenburg SO
  Northern Sinfonia of England
  Royal PO
  Saarbrück RSO
  Vienna PO
Ciacci, Diego Dini
  Le Cameriste
Cichewiecz, Dieter
  Hamburg das neue werk Ensemble
Cichirdan, Modest
  Craiova PO
Cichowicz, Vincent
  Millar Brass Ensemble
Ciepluch, G.
  Univ Circle Wind Ensemble
Cillario, Carlo Felice
  Angelicum CO
  Barcelona Teatro Liceo Orch
  London PO
  Milan Angelicum CO
  Milan RAI Orch
  Naples Teatro San Carlo Orch
  Royal Opera House Orch Covent Garden
  La Scala Orch
  Trieste Teatro Comunale Giuseppe Verdi Orch
Ciolkovitch, Vladimir
  Cossack Ensemble
Cipriani, Stelvio
  Bulgarian SO
Cirri, Riccardo
  Ars Cantus
Claire, Jean
  St. Peter's Abbey of Solesmes Monastic Choir
Claret, Gerard
  Andorra National CO
Clark, Keith
  Les Concerts du Monde
  Czech-Slovak RSO
  London PO
  Pacific SO
  Slovak PO
Clark, Richard Auldon
  KBS SO
  Manhattan CO
  New Zealand CO

Clark, Robert Haydon
  Consort of London
Clayton, Julian
  Chetham's CO
  Chetham's SO
Clemencic, René
  Alpe Adria Ensemble
  Guido d'Arezzo Orch
  Clemencic Consort
  Consort Fontegara
  Naples Scarlatti Vocal Ensemble
Clement, Andries
  Eindhovens Instrumental Ensemble
Clément, René
  Lyon Regional Conservatory Women's Voice Choir
Cleobury, Nicholas
  Aquarius
  Britten Sinfonia
  London Mozart Players
Cleobury, Stephen
  Brandenburg Consort
  Cambridge Chorus
  Cambridge Classical Players
  English CO
  King's College Choir Cambridge
  New London Orch members
  St. John's College Choir Cambridge
Cleva, Fausto
  American Opera Society Orch
  Monte Carlo Opera Orch
  RCA Italian Opera Orch
Cleve, G.
  Midsummer Mozart Festival Orch
Cloëz, Gustav
  Paris Opéra-Comique Orch
Cluytens, André
  Bayreuth Festival Orch
  French National Orch
  French National RSO
  Paris Conservatory Societé des Concerts Orch
  Paris Opera Orch
  Swiss-Italian RSO
  Turin RAI SO
  Vienna PO
Coates, Albert
  Barcelona Teatro Liceo Orch
  Berlin PO
  Cape Town SO
  London New SO
  London SO
Cochand, P.
  Classico CO Ensemble
Cock, Richard
  South African Broadcasting Corp National SO
Cohen, Elie
  Munich RSO
  Paris Opéra-Comique Orch
Cohen, Fred
  Musicians' Accord
Cohen, Joël
  Boston Camerata
  Camerata Mediterranea
  Ensemble de Tambours Provençaux
  Slovak RSO Bratislava
Coin, Christophe
  Baroque Instrumental Ensemble
  Limoges Baroque Ensemble
  Mosaïques Ensemble
Coker, Keller
  Medici Ensemble
Colacicchi, Luigi
  Milano Angelicum CO
Colino, Pablo
  St. Peter's Basilica Cappella Giulia Chorus Vatican City
Colleaux, Paul
  Stradivaria Ensemble
Colléeux, Paul
  Nantes Instrumental Ensemble
  Stradivaria Ensemble
Collingwood, Lawrence
  London SO
Collins, Anthony
  London New SO
  London New SO Strings
  London SO
Collins, Michael
  London Winds
Collura, Franco
  London PO
Colnot, Cliff
  Indiana Univ Harp Ensemble
  Univ of Chicago Contemporary Chamber Players
Colomer, Edmon
  English CO
  Orch de Cadaques
  Spanish National Youth Orch
Colonna, L.
  Naples Alessandro Scarlatti RAI Orch
Colson, Josep
  Belloc Abbey Monks' SO
Colusso, Flavio
  Seicentonovecento Ensemble
  Strumenti Antichi
Colwell, Dennis
  River City Brass Band
Comet, Catherine
  Grand Rapids SO

Comissiona, Sergiu
  Baltimore SO
  Helsinki PO
  Houston SO
  Jerusalem SO
  London Royal Promenade Orch
  London SO
  Stockholm PO
  Swedish RSO
  Utah SO
  Vancouver SO
Conca, Giuseppe
  Rome Opera Orch
Conde, S. Mas
  Limburg SO
Condie, Richard
  Royal PO
Conlon, James
  Cologne PO
  French National Orch
  Gürzenich Orch
  Orch de Paris
  Rotterdam PO
Conlon, Joan Catoni
  Pacific Northwest Chamber Chorus
  Univ of Washington Chorale
Connor, Bill
  Hallé Orch
Consoli, Achille
  EIAR Orch
Constant, Marius
  Ars Nova Ensemble
  Monte Carlo PO
Constantin, Marin
  Bucharest Madrigal Choir
  Madrigal Chamber Choir
Constantine, Andrew
  Irish National SO
Constantinides, Dinos
  Louisiana State Univ New Music Ensemble
Conta, Iosif
  Romanian National RSO
  Romanian Radio-TV Orch
Conte, Peter Richard
  St. Clement's Choir Philadelphia
Conway, William
  Goldberg Ensemble
Cooke, Richard
  English CO
Cooper, David
  Blackburn Cathedral Choir
Copland, Aaron
  Boston SO
  Columbia CO
  Columbia SO
  Czech PO
  London SO
  New Philharmonia Orch
  Symphony of the Air
Coppola, Piero
  London SO
  Pasdeloup Concerts Association Orch
  Pasdeloup Orch
Corazolla, Jan
  Rhenish CO
Corboz, Michel
  English Bach Baroque Orch
  Lausanne CO
  Lausanne Instrumental Ensemble
  Lausanne Vocal Ensemble
  Lisbon Gulbenkian Foundation CO
  Lisbon Gulbenkian Foundation Orch
Cordes, Manfred
  Weser-Renaissance Ensemble
Corp, Ronald
  New London Children's Choir
  New London Orch
Corporon, Eugene
  Cincinnati College Conservatory of Music Wind Sym
  Cincinnati Wind Sym
  North Texas College of Music Chamber Players
  North Texas College of Music Wind Sym
Cortes, Glen
  Icelandic SO
  Manhattan Chamber Sinfonia
  Manhattan School of Music Chamber Sinfonia
Cortot, Alfred
  Barcelona Pau Casals Orch
  Ecole Normale de Musique Orch
  Paris Ecole Normale CO
Cosmi, Gianfranco
  Lucca Teatro Comunale del Giglio Orch
Costa, D.
  Costa Orch
Costa, Othmar
  Vienna Kontrapunkte Ensemble
Couraud, Marcel
  Bamberg SO
  Stuttgart Pro Musica Orch
Couvert, Philippe
  St. Cecilia Academy Orch Rome
Cox, Ainslee
  Nuremberg SO
Craft, Robert
  Columbia Baroque Ensemble
  Columbia SO
  London SO
  Orch of St. Luke's

Crawford, Thomas
  Fairfield Orch
  New York Society Orch members
  Old Fairfield Academy Orch
Creed, Marcus
  Berlin Academy for Early Music
  Berlin RIAS Chamber Choir
  Berlin RSO
Crees, Eric
  London Sym Brass
Cremer, Curt
  Baden State Orch
  Stuttgart Pro Musica Orch
Crepin, Alain
  Belgian Air Force Symphonic Band
Crispini, Patrick
  European Concerts Orch
  Geneva Elans Orch Ensemble
Cristante, Lucio
  Collegium Vocale Nova Ars Cantandi
  Schola Gregoriana
Cristescu, Mircea
  Bucharest George Enescu PO
  Cluj-Napoca PO
Criswell, Patrick
  London SO
Croci, Cesare
  St. Petersburg State Academic Cappella SO
Crockett, Donald
  Los Angeles CO
Croft, J.
  Florida State Univ Band
Crossland, Anthony
  Wells Cathedral Choir
Crowther, Peter
  Sheffield Cathedral Choir
Crum, George
  London SO
Csaba, Péter
  Kuhmo Virtuosi
  New Stockholm CO
Cuendet, Olivier
  Lausanne CO
Cuiller, Daniel
  Stradivaria Ensemble
Culver, Andrew
  Long Beach Opera Orch
Cunningham, T.
  Brussels Choral Society
  Luc Capouillez Brass Ensemble
Currie, John
  Royal Scottish Orch
Curry, William Henry
  Episteme
  Orch of St. Luke's
Curtis, Alan
  Il Complesso Barocco
  I Fegi Armonici
  Sonatori de la Gioiosa Marca
  Tafelmusik
Cutt, Garry
  Grimethorpe Colliery Band
Czajkowski, Renard
  Poznan Philharmonic SO
Czarnecki, Vladislav
  Southwest German CO Pforzheim
Czepiel, Wojciech
  Łódz PO
Czigány, György
  Hungarian State Orch
Czyz, Henryk
  Cracow PO
  Łódzkiej Phil SO
Deetwyler, Jean
  Swiss-Italian Radio-TV Orch
Dahinden, Clemens
  Winterthur String Orch
Dahl, Mogens
  Jiyske Choir
Dähler, Jörg Ewald
  Bern CO
  Bernese Orch
Dailey, William
  Paul Whiteman Orch
Damgaard, Harry
  Norrköping SO
  Västerås SO
Damm, P.
  Bohdan Warchal Slovak CO
Danek, Petr
  Michael Consort
Daniel, Nicholas
  Divertimenti
  Haffner Wind Ensemble
Daniel, Paul
  BBC SO
  English Northern Philharmonia
  English Northern PO
  London SO
  Rotterdam PO
  Scottish CO
Danon, Oscar
  Belgrade National Opera Orch
  Brno State PO
  Metropolitan Orch
  RCA Victor SO
  Royal PO

Daragyozov, Dimiter
  Néophyte of Rila Choir
Darlington, Stephen
  Christ Church Cathedral Choir Oxford
  English String Orch
  Hanover Band
  Medici String Quartet
  St. Alban's Abbey Choir
Darlow, Denys
  London Handel Orch
Darman, Max Bragado
  Castilla y León SO
Daugherty, George
  RCA Victor SO
Dausgaard, Thomas
  Danish National RSO
  Royal PO
  Salomon Ensemble
David, A.
  BBC SO
  Toronto SO
David, Thomas Christian
  Tonkünstler Orch
Davidovac, I.
  Zagreb Youth Orch
Davidson, Arthur
  England Virtuosi
Davies, Dennis Russell
  American Composers Orch
  Bamberg SO
  Beethovenhalle Orch
  Brooklyn PO
  Cabrillo Festival Orch
  Jubilee Orch
  Orch of St. Luke's
  Paragon Ensemble
  Saarbrück RSO
  St. Luke's Chamber Ensemble
  St. Paul CO
  Stuttgart CO
  Stuttgart RSO
  Stuttgart State Opera Orch
Davies, Meredith
  BBC Northern SO
  London PO
  Royal PO
Maxwell Davies, Peter
  BBC PO
  Fires of London
  Royal PO
  Scottish CO
  Scottish National Orch
Davin, Patrick
  Rhineland–Palatinate State PO
Davis, Andrew
  BBC SO
  English CO
  London PO
  London SO
  New Philharmonia Orch
  Philharmonia Orch
  Toronto CO
  Toronto SO
Davis, Carl
  London PO
Davis, Colin
  Academy of St. Martin in the Fields
  Bavarian RSO
  Bavarian RSO Winds
  Bavarian SO
  BBC SO
  Boston SO
  City Lights Orch
  (Royal) Concertgebouw Orch
  Dresden Staatskapelle
  English CO
  London SO
  Netherlands Wind Ensemble
  Philharmonia Orch
  Royal Liverpool PO
  Royal Opera House Orch Covent Garden
  Royal PO
  Russian State SO
  Vienna PO
Davov, Y.
  Sofia PO
Dawson, James
  Oakland Univ Wind Sym
Deahl, Robert
  Texas Tech Univ Trombone Ensemble
Deáky, Z.
  Nuremberg SO
Dean, Timothy
  Pro Christe Orch
Debart, Dominique
  Basse Normandie Instrumental Ensemble
Dechant, Hermann
  Bamberg Youth Orch
  Collegium Aureum
  Musica Canterey Bamberg
Decker, Franz–Paul
  Montreal SO
  National Arts Center Canada Orch
  New Zealand SO
  Toronto SO
DeCormier, Robert
  Robert DeCormier Singers
  New York Choral Society

DeCormier, Robert (cont.)
  Vermont SO members
Decou, Emil
  Ensemble M
Defossez, René
  Belgian National Orch
  Liège SO
Deiss, Lucien
  Fathers of Saint–Esprit Chevilly
  Holy Spirit Fathers of Chevilly Choir
Dejmek, Zdenek
  Janáček CO
  Ostrava Janáček CO
Delacôte, Jacques
  Barcelona Teatro Liceo Orch
  Royal PO
Delage, Roger
  Nice PO
  Strasbourg Collegium Musicum Orch
Delcroix, Robert
  Basque Bayonne–Côte Orch
Delfs, Andreas
  German CO
  Swiss Youth SO
Delibozov, Tsanko
  Ruse PO
Deller, Alfred
  Baroque String Ensemble
  Consort of Viols
  Deller Consort
  King's Musick
  London Chamber Players
  Vienna Concentus Musicus
Deller, Mark
  Deller Consort
Delley, Claude
  Provence Camerata Genève
Delman, Vladimir
  Milan RAI SO
Delogu, Gaétano
  Czech PO
  Janáček CO
  Prague CO
  Prague SO
  Prague Virtuosi
Delvaux, Guy
  Artificii Musicali
DeMars, James
  Arizona State Univ Choirs
Demetriades, Dimitri
  Berlin RSO
Depoutot, René
  Nancy Concert Royal
DePreist, James
  Chicago SO
  Helsinki PO
  Juilliard Orch
  Los Angeles CO
  Malmö SO
  Monte Carlo PO
  Oregon SO
  Royal PO
  Royal Stockholm PO
Derde, John
  Kalken Gregorian Choir
Deruwe, Roger
  St. Salvator Cathedral Bruges Schola Gregoriana
  St. Saviour's Cathedral Choir
Dervaux, Pierre
  Orch de Paris
  Paris Opéra–Comique Orch
  Paris Opera Orch
Deryl, A.
  Budapest Orch
Desarzens, Victor
  Lausanne CO
  Lausanne SO
  Vienna Festival Orch
  Winterthur State Orch members
Deschamps, Anne–Marie
  Venance Fortunat
Descrieres, Georges
  Lower Normandy Instrumental Ensemble
Desderi, Claudio
  Camerata Musicale Orch
Desgraupes, Bernard
  Erwartung Ensemble
Desormiere, Roger
  French National RSO
  Oiseau–Lyre Orchestral Ensemble
Dessaints, Raymond
  Amati Ensemble
Dessau, Paul
  Berlin State Opera Orch
  Leipzig Gewandhaus Orch
Devos, Louis
  Musica Polyphonica
Devreese, Frédéric
  Brussels Belgian Radio–TV PO
Dexter, J.
  Mid–America Chorale
Diazmunoz, Eduardo
  Mexico State SO
Dickey, M.
  Michigan Chamber Players
Diemecke, Enrique
  Simón Bolívar SO
  Camerata de las Américas
  Mexican State SO

Dierksen, Uwe
  Pro Musica Nova
Diesenroth, M.
  Musikkorps des Wachtbataillons
Dimitrov, Dimiter
  Yoan Kukuzel–Angeloglasniyat Chamber Ensemble
Ding, Lucy
  Lira Chamber Chorus
Dirksen, Richard W.
  National Cathedral Choir
Dittrich, Michael
  Czech–Slovak RSO Bratislava
  Slovak RSO Bratislava
  Vienna Bella Musica Ensemble
Dixon, James
  Royal PO
  Univ of Iowa SO
Djurov, Plamen
  Sofia Soloists CO
Dmitriev, Alexander
  Leningrad PO
  St. Petersburg Philharmony Academic SO
  Stavanger SO
Dobra, János
  Hungarian Virtuosi CO, Budapest SO Winds
  Tomkins Vocal Ensemble
  Vienna–Szász CO
Dobrowen, Issay
  Vienna PO
Dobrzanski, J.
  Musica Antiquae Collegium Varsoviense
  Warsaw CO
Dobszay, László
  Schola Hungarica
Dods, Marcus
  London Concert Orch
Dohnányi, Christoph von
  Atlanta SO
  Cleveland Orch
  New Philharmonia Orch
  Vienna PO
Dohnányi, Ernst von
  Budapest PO
  London SO
Dohnányi, Oliver
  Capella Istropolitana
  CSSR State PO Košce
  Czech–Slovak RSO Bratislava
  Czech–Slovak Republic SO
  English CO
  Polish State PO
  Prague National Theater Orch
  Slovak PO
  Slovak RSO
  Slovak RSO Bratislava
Domarkas, Juozas
  Lithuanian National PO
  Slovak PO
Dombrecht, Paul
  Il Fondamento Ensemble
Domingo, Plácido
  London SO
  Munich RSO
  Philharmonia Orch
Donath, Klaus
  Suk CO
Dondeyne, Desire
  Musique des Gardiens de la Paix
Doneux, Edgar
  Belgian RSO
  RTBF New SO
Dopf, P. Hubert
  Vienna Hofburg Chapel Choir
Dorati, Antál
  Bamberg SO
  BBC SO
  Budapest Chamber Ensemble
  Budapest SO
  (Royal) Concertgebouw Orch
  Dallas SO
  Detroit SO
  European SO
  Handel Festival Orch
  Hungarian State Orch
  London SO
  Minneapolis SO
  National SO Washington D.C.
  Netherlands Radio PO
  New Philharmonia Orch
  Philharmonia Hungarica
  Residentie Orch The Hague
  Royal Opera House Orch Covent Garden
  Royal PO
  Royal Promenade CO
  Smithsonian Concerto Grosso
  Stockholm PO
  Univ of Minnesota Brass Band
Dorman, Zeev
  Israel PO members
Dorsey, T.
  Dorsey Orch
Douglass, David
  King's Noyse
Doussard, Jean
  ORTF Lyric Orch
Downes, Edward
  BBC PO
  London PO

Downes, Edward (cont.)
  New Philharmonia Orch
  Omroep Orch
  Royal Opera House Orch
  Sinfonia 21
Dragon, Carmen
  Hollywood Bowl Pops Orch
Drahos, Béla
  Nicolaus Esterházy Sinfonia
Dreier, Per
  London SO
  Norwegian Soloists
  Royal PO
Dressel, Heinz
  Folkwang CO
Drewanz, Hans
  Hamburg SO
Dreyfus, George
  Melbourne SO
  Queensland SO
Driesten, Roelof van
  Netherlands Ballet Orch
  Residentie Orch The Hague
  Rotterdam PO
Drinkell, David
  Belfast Cathedral Choir
Druckman, Jacob
  American Brass Quintet
Drummond, Dean
  Newband
Drury, Stephen
  New England Conservatory Avant-Garde Ensemble
Dshuraitis, A.
  Bolshoi Theater Orch
Duarte, Roberto
  Czech-Slovak RSO Bratislava
  Slovak RSO Bratislava
DuBois, Frans
  Chorale Caecilia
DuBois, Jean-Jacques
  French Concerts Orch
Duchable, François-René
  Strasbourg SO
Duczmal, Agnieszka
  Amadeus CO
  Polish Radio CO
  Poznan Polish Radio-TV CO
  Swiss CO
Dudarova, Veronika
  Moscow SO
  Russian SO
Dudea, G.
  Tîrgu Mures Philharmonic CO
Dufallo, Richard
  Amsterdam New Sinfonietta
  Festival CO
  Netherlands Wind Ensemble
  Rotterdam PO
Duftschmid, Lorenz
  Armonico Tributo Austria
Dumont, Cedric
  Basel RSO
Dun, Tan
  BBC Scottish SO
  Nine Songs Ensemble
Dunand, Robert
  Collegium Academicum Orch
  Geneva Collegium Academicum
Dunk, Roderick
  Travelling Opera Orch
Dunkel, Paul Lustig
  American Composers Orch
  Westchester PO
Dunn, Bruce Rodney
  Sinfonia of London
Dunn, Howard
  Chicago Chamber Brass
  Dallas Wind Sym
Dunn, Vivian
  City of Birmingham SO
  England SO
Dupaquier, Bernard
  Jura CO
Dutoit, Charles
  Beromünster Orch
  Boston SO
  (Royal) Concertgebouw Orch
  London PO
  London Sinfonietta
  Montreal PO
  Montreal Sinfonietta
  Montreal SO
  Philadelphia Orch
  Philharmonia Orch
  Royal PO
Duvier, E.
  Camerata Romana
Dvořák, J.
  Capella Istropolitana
Dyk, František
  Prague RSO
Earle, Hobart
  American Music Ensemble Vienna
  Odessa PO
Ebbinghouse, Bernard
  London PO
  London SO
Eben, David
  Schola Gregoriana Pragensis

Ebensberger, Gary
  Texas Schola Cantorum
Eberle, Christoph
  Capella Istropolitana
Eby, Anders
  Royal Stockholm PO
Eckertsen, Dean
  Milan Academy Orch
Edison, Noel
  Elora Festival Singers
Edlinger, Richard
  Capella Istropolitana
  CSSR State PO Košice
  Mozart Academy
  Mozart Festival Orch
  Romanian State PO
  Zagreb PO
Edwards, John Owen
  Munich SO
  National SO
Edwards, Sian
  English National Opera Orch
  London PO
  Royal Liverpool PO
Edwards, Terry
  London Sinfonietta
  London Sinfonietta Chorus
  London Voices
  St. Paul's Cathedral Choir
  St. Paul's Cathedral Choristers
Edwards, Warwick
  Scottish Early Music Consort
Effron, David
  Eastman Chamber Ensemble
  Eastman Philharmonia
  Rochester PO
Eggen, Christian
  Borealis Ensemble
  Cikada Ensemble
  Norwegian Broadcasting Orch
  Norwegian RSO
Ehmann, Wilhelm
  Gesamtleitung
  Westminster CO
  Westphalian Ensemble
  Westphalian Kantorei
Ehret, Ernst
  St. Michael Orch Munich
Ehrhardt, Werner
  Concerto Cologne
Ehrling, Sixten
  Danish National Orch
  Danish National RSO
  Gothenburg SO
  Juilliard Orch
  London SO
  Rilke Ensemble members
  Royal Stockholm PO
  Royal Swedish Opera Chorus
  Stockholm PO
  Stockholm Royal Opera House Orch
  Stockholm Symphonic Wind Orch
  Swedish CO
  Swedish RSO
Eichhorn, Kurt
  Berlin Baroque Trumpet Ensemble
  Bruckner Orch Linz
  La Dolcezza Ensemble
  Linz Brucknor Oroh
  Munich RSO
Eidelman, Cliff
  Seattle SO
Ek, Kerstin
  Orpheus Chamber Ensemble
  Täby Church Choir
Ekekian, Tigran
  Gostelradio Armenia Chamber Choir
Elder, Mark
  BBC SO
  City of Birmingham SO
  Orch of the Age of Enlightenment
  Rochester PO
  Royal Opera House Orch
Elgar, Edward
  London SO
  Royal Albert Hall Orch
Ellington, Duke
  Duke Ellington Orch
Ellis, Philip
  Royal PO
Ellis, Roger
  French Radio Lyric Orch
Elmendorff, Karl
  Bayreuth Festival Orch
  Saxon State Orch
Elmquist, M.
  Danish Radio Concert Orch
Elton-Brown, J.
  Mandolin Orch
Emilsson, Gudmondur
  Icelandic SO
Endo, Akira
  Crystal CO
  Los Angeles PO members
  Louisville Orch
Enescu, George
  Paris Conservatory Societé des Concerts Orch
  Paris SO

Enevold, Per
  Camerata Chamber Choir
  Danish National Radio Choir
Engstrom, Jan
  New Finnish SO
Enkoji, Masahiko
  Sendai PO
Entremont, Philippe
  Denver SO
  Vienna CO
Eötvös, Peter
  Asko Ensemble
  Ensemble Modern
Ephrikian, Angelo
  I Filarmonici
  Milan Complesso Barocco
  Milan Solisti
Epstein
  Royal PO
Epstein, David
  Boston Sym Chamber Players
  MIT SO
Epstein, Frank
  Collage New Music Ensemble
Equilbey, Laurence
  Accentus Chamber Choir
Erdei, Péter
  Budapest SO
Erdélyi, Miklos
  Budapest PO
Erede, Alberto
  Berlin PO
  Florence Maggio Musicale Orch
  Geneva Grand Théâtre Orch
  Japanese RSO
  Naples Teatro San Carlo Orch
  Parma Teatro Regio Orch
  Royal PO
  St. Cecilia Academy Orch Rome
Ericson, Eric
  Drottningholm Baroque Ensemble
  Stockholm Chamber Choir
  Stockholm Royal Conservatory Chamber Choir
  Swedish Radio Choir
Eriksson, C.
  Lyngby-Taarbaek SO
Erkens, Christoph
  Canticum
Ermakova, Lyudmila
  Russian State SO
Ermert, Herbert
  South Westphalian PO
Erminero, Bruno
  Turin RAI Orch
Ermler, Mark
  Bolshoi Theater Orch
  Moscow PO
  Royal Opera House Orch Covent Garden
  USSR RSO
Erne, B.
  Zurich Sprechchor
Erös, Peter
  Aalborg SO
  San Diego SO
  Stockholm PO
Erxleben, Michael
  New Berlin CO
  New Berlin SO
Eschenbach, Christoph
  Bamberg SO
  CO of Europe
  Hamburg PO
  Houston SO
  London PO
  Schleswig-Holstein Festival Orch
  South German RSO
Eschenburg, C.
  Capella Fidicinia Leipzig
Escher, Christof
  Linz Bruckner Orch
Eschwé, Alfred
  Austrian RSO
  CSR Bratislava SO
Esipov, Valery
  Russian CO
Esquieu, Yves
  Ensemble de Musique Ancienne Polyphonia Antiqua
Esser, Heribert
  Budapest SO
  Vienna SO
Estella, Enrique
  Concierto Montilla Orch
  Madrid CO
Estrada, Gregori
  Montserrat Escolania
  Montserrat Monastic Schola
Etcheverry, Jesus
  Paris Lyric Orch
Evans, Winsome
  Renaissance Players
Everett, S.
  Emory Wind Ensemble
Ewerhart, Rudolf
  Württemberg CO
Faberman, H.
  London SO
Fabien
  Timadéuc Abbey Monks' Choir

Fabre–Garrus, Bernard
　A Sei Voci
　Toulouse Saqueboutiers
Fabritiis, Oliviero de
　Arena di Verona Orch
　Bologna Teatro Comunale Orch
　Catania Teatro Massimo Bellini Orch
　Lisbon Teatro São Carlos Orch
　Milan RAI SO
　Naples Teatro San Carlo Orch
　National PO London
　NHK SO
　Palacio Bellas Artes Orch
　Rome Opera Orch
　Rome RAI Orch
　Rome Teatro Reale Opera Orch
　La Scala Orch
　Teatro La Gran Guardia Orch
　Trieste Teatro Comunale Giuseppe Verdi Orch
Facchin, Guido
　Tämmittam Percussion Ensemble
Fackler, Gerhard
　Arena di Verona Orch
Faerber, Jörg
　Berlin SO
　Württemberg CO
Fagan, Gerald
　Concert Players Orch
Fairfax, B.
　Polyphonia Orch
Faldner, Barry
　Chicago Sinfonia Orch
　Chicago Sinfonietta
　Chicago SO
Falk, Peter
　Berlin RSO
　Cologne RSO
　Vienna Opera Orch
　Vienna Volksoper Orch
Falletta, JoAnn
　Cabrillo Festival Orch
　English CO
　London SO
　New Zealand SO
　Women's PO
Fanal, D.
　Olsztyn State PO
Fang, Yuan
　Beijing RSO
Farberman, Harold
　All Star Percussion Ensemble
　Boston Chamber Ensemble
　Bournemouth Sinfonietta
　Bournemouth SO
　Helsingborg SO
　London PO
　London SO
　New PO members
　Prisma Chamber Players Copenhagen
　Stuttgart Philharmonia
Faris, Alexander
　London Promenade Orch
　Sadler's Wells Opera Orch
　Scottish CO
Farkač, Hynec
　Boemia CO
　Independent CO Boemia
Farncombe, Charles
　English Bach Festival Baroque Orch
　Philomusica Orch
Farnon, Robert
　Robert Farnon Orch
　London Festival Orch
　Munich RSO
　Royal PO
Farré-Fizio, Thérèse
　Gabriel Fauré Choir
Farrer, John
　Bournemouth SO
　English Sinfonia
　London PO
　Royal PO
Fasano, Renato
　Collegium Musicum Italicum Instrumental Ensemble
　Rome Virtuosi
Fedoseyev, Vladimir
　Fernseh SO
　Moscow Radio Grand SO
　Moscow RSO
　Moscow SO
　Ostankino Radio–TV Large SO
　Ostankino SO
　Philharmonia Orch
　USSR Radio–TV Large SO
　USSR RSO
　USSR SO
Fedotov, Viktor
　Kirov Orch
　London SO
　St. Petersburg Philharmony Academic SO
Feier, Jurij
　Bolshoi Theater Orch
Fei-yun, Liu Yuan
　Shanghai Conservatory
Fekete, Zoltán
　Prague SO
Felciano, R.
　Scripps Javanese Gamelan of Univ of California

Feldbrill, Victor
　National Arts Center Canada Orch
　Toronto SO
Felitsiant, V.
　Moscow Ancient Music Ensemble
Feltsman, Vladimir
　Orch of St. Luke's
Fenby, Eric
　Royal PO
Fennell, Frederick
　American SO
　Cleveland Sym Winds
　Dallas Wind Sym
　Eastman–Rochester Pops Orch
　Eastman Wind Ensemble
　Indiana Winds
　London Pops Orch
Fenton, Mark
　Ramsey Singers
Ferden, Bruce
　Cracow RSO
Ferenc, Tibor
　Hungarian National PO
Ferencsik, A.
　Budapest PO
　Budapest SO
　Hungarian State Opera Orch
　Hungarian State Orch
Ferencsik, János
　Brno State PO
　Budapest PO
　Budapest SO
　Czech PO
　Danish National RSO
　Hungarian PO
　Hungarian Radio–TV Chorus
　Hungarian RSO
　Hungarian State Opera Orch
　Hungarian State Orch
　London PO
Ferguson, Barry
　Rochester Choir
Ferrara, Franco
　Benedetto Marcello CO
Ferrari, Daniele
　Capriccio Italiano Ensemble
　I Giovani di Nuova Cameristica
　Milan Sinfonietta
Ferraris, Franco
　Brussels Théâtre de la Monnaie Orch
Ferré, Léo
　Liège SO
　Milan SO
Ferris, William
　William Ferris Chorale
Ferro, Gabriele
　Bologna Teatro Comunale Orch
　Capella Coloniensis
　Paris Lyon Opera Orch
　Rome Opera Orch
　La Scala Orch
　Sicilian SO
　Turin RAI Orch
　Welsh National Opera Orch
Fetler, D.
　Rochester CO
Fey, T.
　Schlierbach CO
Fiala, Petr
　Brno State PO
　Czech PO
Fidetzis, Byron
　Pasardjik SO
　Sophia PO
Fiedler, Arthur
　BBC Concert Orch
　Boston Pops Orch
　Boston SO
　Arthur Fiedler's Sinfonietta
　London SO
Fiedler, Max
　Berlin PO
Filaber, Andrzej
　Warsaw Cathedral Choir
Fillon, Jean-Luc
　Jazzogène Big Band
Fine, Irving
　Boston SO
Fiore, John
　Munich RSO
Fischer, Adám
　Austro-Hungarian Haydn Orch
　Budapest SO
　Hungarian National PO
　Hungarian State Orch
　Hungarian State SO
　Hungarian SO
　Royal PO
　Vienna CO
Fischer, Eduard
　Czech-Slovak RSO Prague
　Edwin Fischer CO
　Orch of St. Luke's
　Philharmonia Orch
　Royal Danish Orch
Fischer, György
　Cappella Coloniensis
　Vienna CO

Fischer, Iván
　Budapest Festival Orch
　Hungarian State Orch
　London SO
Fischer, Thierry
　Netherlands Wind Ensemble
　CO of Europe
Fischer-Dieskau, Dietrich
　Bavarian State Orch
　Czech PO
　London PO
　New PO
Fischer-Dieskau, Martin
　Czech-Slovak RSO Bratislava
　New Berlin CO
Fisher, Dennis W.
　North Texas College of Music Wind Sym
Fisher, John
　Venice Teatro La Fenice Orch
Fisk, Elliott
　Orch of St. Luke's
Fiskum, Bjarne
　Trondheim Soloists
Fistoulari, Anatole
　London SO
　New Philharmonia Orch
　Philharmonia Orch
　Royal PO
　Vienna State Opera Orch
Fjeldstad, Øivin
　Oslo PO
Flagello, Nicolas
　Rome CO
　Rome SO
Flämig, Martin
　Capella Fidicinia
　Dresden Kreuz Choir
　Dresden PO
Flath, Edwin
　California Bach Society CO
Fleisher, Leon
　Kennedy Center Theater Chamber Players
　New England Conservatory Orch
Flood, David
　Canterbury Cathedral Choir Lay Clerks
Flor, Claus Peter
　Bamberg SO
　Berlin SO
　(Royal) Concertgebouw Orch
　North German RSO
　Philharmonia Orch
　Royal PO
Florea, Christian
　Moldavian Radio–TV SO
Floreen, J. E.
　New Brunswick CO
Florêncio, José Maria
　Cracow Polish Radio–TV SO
　Polish Radio–TV SO
Florio, Antonio
　Capella della pietà de Turchini
Flugbeil, Hans
　Berlin Bach Orch
Flummerfeldt, Joseph
　New Jersey SO
　Westminster Choir
Flury, Urs Joseph
　Czech SO
　Prague Czech SO
Foley, Timothy
　Nonpareil Wind Band
Follert, U.-R.
　Breslau State PO
Folse, Bart
　Pro Arte Chorale
Fonville, John
　SONOR Ensemble of Univ of California San Diego members
Forbes Somerville, Murray
　Harvard Univ Choir
Forrai, Miklós
　Hungarian State Orch
Forrester, Thomas R.
　Philharmonia Orch
Förster, H.-R.
　Vogtland PO Greiz/Reichenbach
Forster, Karl
　Berlin SO
Fortner, Wolfgang
　Berlin RSO
Foss, Lukas
　Berlin SO
　Brooklyn PO
　Jerusalem SO
　Juilliard Orch
　Milwaukee SO
　Sheffield Ensemble
Foster, John
　Black Dyke Mills Band
Foster, Lawrence
　Barcelona SO
　Berlin RSO
　Birmingham SO
　City of Birmingham SO
　Hallé Orch
　Lausanne CO
　London SO
　Los Angeles PO
　Monte Carlo PO

Foster, Lawrence (cont.)
 Royal PO
Foster, Mark
 Asko Ensemble
 Itinéraire Ensemble
 Recherche Ensemble
Foster, Thomas
 Beverly Hills All Saints' Episcopal Church Choir
Fougstedt, Nils-Eric
 Finnish RSO
Fourestier, Louis
 ORTF Lyric Orch
Fournet, Jean
 Amsterdam Radio PO
 Czech PO
 Dutch RSO
 Groot Radio PO
 Lamoureux Orch
 Netherlands Radio PO
 ORTF Lyric Orch
 Rotterdam PO
 Swiss Festival Orch
 Tokyo Metropolitan SO
Fournillier, Patrick
 English CO
 Italian International Opera Orch
 Franz Liszt SO
 Picardie Orch
 Prague SO
 St.-Etienne Nouvel Orch
Fox, Frank
 FFB Orch
Françaix, Jean
 Saarbrück RSO
Francek, Josef
 Strauss Festival Orch
 Johann Strauss Orch
Franci, Carlo
 La Scala Orch
 Turin RAI SO
 Venice Teatro La Fenice Orch
Francis, Alun
 Basel RSO
 BBC Scottish SO
 Berlin RSO
 English CO
 Frankfurt RSO
 London SO
 New Philharmonia Orch
 Northwest CO Seattle
 Philharmonia Orch
 Saarbrück RSO
 Ulster Orch
Frandsen, John
 Copenhagen Opera Orch
 Danish National RSO
 South Jutland SO
Frank, Hans-Peter
 Helsingborg SO
Frankhauser, James
 Vancouver Cantata Singers
Franzetti, Carlos
 Buenos Aires Orch
 Modus Chamber Ensemble
 Orquesta Nova
Frascarelli, Angelo
 Capitol Chamber Artists
Fraser, Donald
 English CO
Freccia, Massimo
 New Philharmonia Orch
 RCA Victor SO
 Rome RAI SO
 Royal PO
Fredman, Myer
 London PO
 New Zealand SO
 Queensland SO
Freeman, James
 Orch 2001
 Orch 2001 members
Freeman, M.
 West End Orch
Freeman, Paul
 Berlin RSO
 Chicago Sinfonietta
 London PO
 London SO
 Mexican State SO
 Mexico City PO
 Moscow PO
 National Czech SO
 National Opera Orch
 Orch of the Americas
 Philharmonia Orch
 Royal PO
 Royal PO Soloists
 RTV SO
 Russian SO
 St. Petersburg PO
 Slovak National Orch
 Slovak PO
 Slovak RSO Bratislava
 Slovenian RSO
 Victoria SO
 Westphalian SO Recklinghausen
 Yugoslavia RSO
Freimuth, Heinz-Gurt
 Münster Wind Ensemble

Freisitzer, Roland
 Moscow Orch
Freitas Branco, Pedro de
 Madrid Concert Orch
Frémaux, Louis
 City of Birmingham SO
 London SO
 Paris Opera Orch Soloists
 Philharmonia Orch
French, John
 Philadelphia Concerto Soloists
Fricke, Heinz
 Bavarian RSO
 Berlin RSO
 Berlin State Opera Orch
 Munich RSO
Fricsay, Ferenc
 Bavarian RSO
 Bavarian State Orch
 Berlin RIAS Orch
 Berlin RIAS SO
 Berlin RSO
 Cologne RSO
 Vienna PO
 Vienna SO
Frieberger, Rupert Gottfried
 Collegium Musicum Pragense
 Heiligenberg Baroque Orch
Fried, Oskar
 Berlin PO
 Berlin State Opera Orch
Friedman, Lionel
 St. Andrew Camerata
 St. Cecilia CO
Friedmann, Samuel
 Rhenish PO
 Württemberg PO
Friend, Lionel
 BBC Scottish SO
 BBC SO
 Nash Ensemble
 Scottish CO members
Friesen, Heinz
 Amsterdam Wind Orch
 Concerto Rotterdam
Froelicher, Anatole
 Cracow SO
Fröhlich, Christian
 Berlin RSO
Froitzheim, Herbert
 Freiburg CO
Froment, Louis de
 Luxembourg RSO
 Luxembourg Radio-TV SO
Fromme, Wolfgang
 Collegium Vocale Cologne
Frontalini, Silvano
 Bacau PO
 Brussels Radio-TV SO
 Kaunas CO
 Lithuanian National SO
 Lituana di Vilnjus SO
 Minsk PO
 Moldavian National SO
 Moldavian Radio-TV SO
 Moldavian SO
 Warmia National Orch
 Warsaw Orch
Froschauer, Helmuth
 Cologne RSO
Frühbeck de Burgos, Rafael
 London SO
 Paris Opera Orch
Frykberg, Sten
 Helsingborg SO
 Norrköping SO
 Swedish RSO
Fuente, Eduardo de la
 Orch of the Americas
Fuente, Herrera de la
 Mexico City PO
 Mineria SO
 New Philharmonia Orch
 Orch of the Americas
 Xalapa SO
Fuente, Miguel de la
 La Follia Ensemble
Fujioka, Sachio
 BBC PO
Fuller, Albert
 Helicon
Funfgeld, Greg
 Bach Festival Orch
 Bethlehem Bach Choir
 Bethlehem Bach Festival Orch
Füri, Thomas
 Bern Camerata
Fürst, Janos
 Bamberg SO
 Helsinki PO
 New Irish CO
Furtwängler, Wilhelm
 Bayreuth Festival Orch
 Berlin PO
 Berlin State Opera Orch
 Berlin State Orch
 (Royal) Concertgebouw Orch
 Hamburg PO

Furtwängler, Wilhelm (cont.)
 London PO
 Lucerne Festival Orch
 NBC SO
 North German RSO
 Philharmonia Orch
 Rome RAI Orch
 Rome RAI SO
 Royal Opera House Orch Covent
 La Scala Orch
 Stockholm Concert Society Orch
 Stockholm PO
 Turin RAI Orch
 Turin RAI SO
 Vienna PO
 Vienna State Opera Orch
Fussell, Charles
 Collage New Music Ensemble
Gacazzeni, G.
 National PO London
Gafner, Hans
 Bern SO
Gagnepain, Bernard
 Academie Internationale de Sées
Gaigg, Michi
 L'Arpa Festante Baroque Orch
Gailis, Viesturs
 Thuringian SO
Gajard, Joseph
 Notre-Dame d'Argentan Abbey Monks' Choir
 St. Peter's Abbey of Solesmes Monastic Choir
Galante, Fabio
 L'Europa Galante
Gale, Simon
 Symphonic Rock Orch
Galliera, Alceo
 Monte Carlo Opera Orch
 Philharmonia Orch
 La Scala Orch
Gallois, Henri
 French Radio Lyric Orch
Galonski, S.
 Wroclaw Orch
Galway, James
 CO of Europe
 Danish National RSO
 Zagreb Solisti
Gamba, Piero
 London SO
Gamson, Arnold
 American Opera Society Orch
Gandolfi, Romano
 Prague Chamber Choir
 La Scala Chorus
Gantvarg, Mikhail
 St. Petersburg Soloists
Garaguly, Carl von
 Stockholm PO
Garant, Serge
 Quebec Society of Contemporary Music
Garbarino, Giuseppe
 Villa Marigola Festival Orch
Garben, Cord
 Berlin RSO
 North German Radio PO
Garcia, José-Luis
 English CO
Garcia-Bernalt, Bernardo
 Salamanca Univ Chamber Chorus
Garcia-Navarro, Luis A.
 English CO
 Philharmonia Orch
Gardelli, Lamberto
 Austrian RSO
 Bavarian RSO
 Berlin State Opera Orch
 Budapest PO
 Budapest SO
 Danish National RSO
 Drottningholm CO
 Hungarian State Opera Orch
 Hungarian State Orch
 Franz Liszt CO
 London String Orch
 Milan RAI SO
 Monte Carlo Opera Orch
 Munich RSO
 New Philharmonia Orch
 ORF SO
 Royal Opera House Orch Covent Garden
 Royal PO
 St. Cecilia Academy Orch Rome
 Vienna State Opera Orch
Gardiner, John Eliot
 CBC Vancouver SO
 English Baroque Soloists
 His Majesties Sagbutts & Cornetts
 Lyon Opera Orch
 Monte Carlo Opera Orch
 Monteverdi Choir London
 Monteverdi Orch
 North German RSO
 Orch Révolutionnaire et Romantique
 Paris Lyon Opera Orch
 Philharmonia Orch
 Vienna PO
Gardinon, Jean
 Paris Festival Orch

Gardner, Patrick
  Univ of Texas Concert Chorale
Garforth, David
  English CO
  Monte Carlo PO
  Royal Danish Orch
Garrido, Gabriel
  Luis Berger Ensemble
  Buenos Aires Affetti Ensemble
  Capella Cisplatina
  Elyma Ensemble
  Musica Antica Studio
Garvey, John
  Univ of Illinois New Music Ensemble
  Univ of Illinois New Music Ensemble members
Gatti, Daniele
  Bologna Teatro Comunale Orch
Gatto, Armando
  Bologna Teatro Comunale Orch
  Naples Teatro San Carlo Orch
  Nouvel PO
Gaubert, Philippe
  Concerts Straram Orch
  Paris Conservatory Société des Concerts Orch
  Paris SO
Gauk, Alexander
  All-Union RSO
  Moscow PO
  Moscow RSO
Gavazzeni, Gianandrea
  Catania Teatro Massimo Bellini Orch
  Emilia Romagna Arturo Toscanini SO
  Florence Maggio Musicale Orch
  Florence Teatro Comunale Orch
  Milan RAI SO
  National PO London
  Parma Teatro Regio Orch
  Rome Opera Orch
  Rome RAI SO
  Rome Radio-TV Orch
  Royal Opera House Orch Covent Garden
  La Scala Orch
  Trieste Teatro Comunale Giuseppe Verdi Orch
  Turin RAI Orch
  Turin RAI SO
  Venice Teatro La Fenice Orch
Gavazzeni, Giuseppe
  La Scala Orch
Geczy, Olga
  Lithuanian Opera Orch
Gee, Christopher-Lyndon
  Australian CO
  Sydney SO
Geese, Heinz
  Cologne RSO
Gelmetti, Gianluigi
  Bologna Teatro Comunale Orch
  Milan Italian Radio-TV Orch
  Rome Opera Orch
  Stuttgart RSO
  Turin RSO
  Tuscan Orch
  Venice Teatro La Fenice Orch
Gemignani, Paul
  Royal PO
Gendille, José-André
  Mans SO
Génetay, Claude
  National Museum CO
Georgescu, Remus
  Sofia PO
  Timisoara Banatul PO
  Timisoara PO
Georgia, Sister
  Pühtica Dormition Convent Choir
Georgiadis, John
  London Concert Orch
  London SO
  London Virtuosi
  Queensland PO
Gerecz, Arpad
  Lausanne CO
Gerelli, Ennio
  Milan RAI Orch
  Milan RAI SO
Gergiev, Valery
  Kirov Opera Orch
  Kirov Orch
  London SO
  Rotterdam PO
  San Francisco Opera Orch
  USSR RSO
  USSR Radio-TV Large SO
Gerhardt, A.
  London Royal Promenade Orch
  Utah SO
Gerhardt, Charles
  Grenadier Guards Band
  London National PO
  London SO
  Munich RSO
  National PO
  National PO London
  RCA Victor SO
  Royal PO
Geringas, David
  Czech Phil CO

Gervais, Michel-Marc
  Versailles National Masters
Gesseney, Christophe
  Euterpe
  Lausanne Euterpe Vocal Ensemble
Gester, Martin
  Parlement de Musique
Gharabekian, Aram
  Ukrainian Radio-TV SO
Ghent, Emmanuel
  Dithyrambos
Ghiaurov, Vladimir
  Plovdiv PO
  Sofia PO
Ghiglia, Erasmo
  Florence Teatro Comunale Orch
Ghione, Franco
  Don Milani Cultural Association Orch
  Lisbon Teatro São Carlos Orch
  La Scala Orch
  Turin RAI SO
Gibault, Claire
  Royal PO
Gibson, Alexander
  English CO
  London Festival Orch
  London New SO
  London PO
  London SO
  Philharmonia Orch
  Royal PO
  Royal Scottish National Orch
  Scottish CO
  Scottish Festival Brass Bands
  Scottish National Orch
Gibson, P.
  London SO
Gibson, Robert
  Univ of Maryland Flute Choir
Gieco, Enzo
  Agrupación Música
Gielen, Michael
  Berlin RSO
  Cincinnati SO
  Frankfurt Opera House & Museum Orch
  Hessian RSO
  London PO
  Naples Teatro San Carlo Orch
  Royal PO
  Saarland RSO
  Southwest German RSO Baden-Baden
  Stuttgart RSO
  Vienna Musikgesellschaft Orch
  Vienna Pro Musica Orch
Gier, Delta David
  Polish National RSO Katowice
Gilbert, David
  Manhattan School of Music Opera Orch
  Univ of Illinois Contemporary Chamber Players
Gilbert-Dyson, Peter
  Belmont Ensemble London
Gillesberger, Hans
  Chorus Viennensis
  Vienna Boys' Choir
  Vienna Orch
  Vienna State Opera Orch
  Vienna SO
Gilmour, Oliver
  St. John's Smith Square Orch
Gini, Roberto
  Camera Concerto
  Concerto Ensemble
Giorgi, Andrea
  Paris Opera Orch
Giovanetti, Reynald
  ORF SO
Gipson, Richard C.
  SoundStroke
Girard, André
  French Radio Lyric Orch
  ORTF Lyric Orch
Girault, Benoît
  National Police Orch of Harmony
Girod, Dirk
  Aargauer CO
Gispert, Enric
  Barcelona Ars Musica
Giulini, Carlo Maria
  Bavarian RSO
  Berlin PO
  Chicago SO
  (Royal) Concertgebouw Orch
  Florence Maggio Musicale Orch
  Hessian RSO
  London PO
  London SO
  Los Angeles PO
  Milan RAI Orch
  Milan RAI SO
  Naples Teatro San Carlo Orch
  New Philharmonia Orch
  Philharmonia Chorus
  Philharmonia Orch
  Residentie Orch The Hague
  Rome Opera Orch
  Rome RAI Orch
  Rome RAI SO
  Rome Radio Orch

Giulini, Carlo Maria (cont.)
  Royal Opera House Orch
  La Scala Orch
  Vienna PO
Giunta, Joseph
  Des Moines SO
Giuranna, Bruno
  Padua & Venice CO
Glaetzner, Burkhard
  New Bach Collegium Musicum
Gläser, Michael
  Bavarian RSO
  Munich RSO
Gleeson, Derek
  London PO
Glenton, Robert
  Orch of the Golden Age
Glière, Reinhold
  All-Union RSO
  Bolshoi Theater Orch
Glinka, Mihail
  Ljubljana SO
Globokar, Vinko
  Musique Vivante Ensemble
  Slovenian Radio Jazz Quintet
  Slovenian RSO
Glouzes, Jean
  Montpellier Vocal Ensemble
Glover, James
  London Mozart Players
  London PO
  Royal PO
Gloyd, Russell
  Cathedral Choral Society Orch
Glushchenko, Fedor
  BBC PO
  BBC Scottish SO
  Moscow PO
  Moscow State SO
  Philharmonia Orch
  Ukrainian CO
  Ukrainian State SO
Gmür, Hanspeter
  Budapest Camerata
  Camerata Budapest
  Failoni Orch
Gnedash, Vadim
  Ukrainian Radio-TV SO
  Ukrainian State SO
Goberman, Max
  New York Sinfonietta
Godfrey, Isidore
  D'Oyly Carte Opera Company Orch
  London New SO
  Royal Opera House Orch Covent Gardens
  Royal PO
Godwin, Anthony
  Palm Court Theater Orch
Goebel, Reinhard
  Cologne Musica Antiqua
Goehr, Walter
  Concerts de Paris SO
  London PO
  London SO
  Lucerne Festival Orch
  New Friends of Music Orch
  North German RSO
  Winterthur SO
Gohl, Matthias
  Black Elk Voices
Gold, Ernest
  Crystal CO
  Vienna Volksoper Orch
Goldberg, Szyman
  Netherlands CO
Golovanov, Nikolai
  All-Union RSO
  Bolshoi Theater Orch
  Leningrad PO
  Moscow Large RSO
  Moscow RSO
  Soviet State RSO
  USSR RSO
Golovshin, Igor
  Moscow State SO
  Moscow SO
  Russian State SO
  State SO
Golschmann, Vladimir
  American Festival Orch
  Columbia SO
  St. Louis SO
  Symphony of the Air
  Toronto SO
  Vienna State Opera CO
  Vienna State Opera Orch
Goltz, Gottfried von der
  Freiburg Baroque Orch
Golyshev, Alexander
  Bolshoi Theater Chamber Music Ensemble
Gonley, Stephanie
  English CO
Gönnenwein, Wolfgang
  Consortium Musicum
  German Bach Soloists
  Ludwigsburg Festival Orch
Goodall, Reginald
  Sadler's Wells Opera Orch
  Welsh National Opera Orch

Goodman, Al
  Music Project CO
Goodman, Peter Holman
  Parley of Instruments
Goodman, Roy
  Austro-Hungarian Haydn Orch
  Brandenburg Consort
  Brandenburg Orch
  European Community Baroque Orch
  Hanover Band
  London Vivaldi Orch
  Parley of Instruments
  Swedish RSO
Goodwin, Paul
  London Oboe Band
  Royal Welsh Fusiliers Regimental Band
Goossens, Eugene
  Cincinnati SO
  London SO
  Royal Albert Hall Orch
  Royal PO
  Vienna State Opera Orch
Gordon, D.
  New York Chamber SO
Gorenstein, Mark
  Russian SO
  Young Russia State SO Moscow
Goritzki, Johannes
  German Chamber Academy Orch
  New German Chamber Academy
Gorkovenko, Stanislav
  St. Petersburg New Philharmony Orch
  St. Petersburg Radio-TV SO
  St. Petersburg TV & Broadcast Company SO
Gorli, Sandro
  Divertimento Ensemble
Gorzynski, Zdzislaw
  Warsaw PO
  Warsaw State Opera House Orch
  Warsaw Teatr Wielki Orch
Gosman, Lazar
  Tchaikovsky CO
Gotti, T.
  Swiss-Italian RSO
Gottwald, Clytus
  Stuttgart Schola Cantorum
Gould, Morton
  Chicago SO
  Columbia Jazz Combo
  Morton Gould Orch
  Louisville Orch
Gouzes, André
  Dominican Friars of France
Govorov, Alexander
  St. Petersburg Soglasie Men's Choir
Goya, Dmitri
  Moldavian PO
Gracis, Ettore
  Bulgarian RSO
  Milan Pomeriggi Musicali Chamber SO
  La Scala Orch
  Turin RAI Orch
Graf, E.
  Salzburg Mozarteum Orch
  Vienna Opera Great SO
Graf, Hans
  Danish National RSO
  Salzburg Camerata Academica
  Salzburg Mozarteum Orch
Graf, Peter-Lukas
  English CO
  Lausanne CO
Graham, J.
  Speculum Musicae
Graham, Lowell
  American Promenade Orch
Graham-Jones, Ian
  Chichester Concert
Graunke, Kurt
  Graunke SO
Gräwe, Georg
  Grubenklang Orch
Gray, Bram
  Göteborg Brass Band
Grazioli, Giuseppe
  Harmonia Ensemble
Green, Gary
  Univ of Miami Wind Ensemble
Green, Phillip
  Garda Siochana Choir
  Philip Green Pops Concert Orch
Greenall, Matthew
  Elysian Singers London
  Endymion Ensemble
Greenberg, Noah
  New York Pro Musica
Gregor, Bohumil
  Czech PO
  Dvořák CO
  Prague CO
  Prague National Orch
  Prague National Theater Orch
Gregson, Edward
  Hallé Brass
  Northern Trombone Quartet
  RNCM Brass Ensemble
  Royal Northern College of Music Wind Orch

Greig, Don
  Orlando Consort
Gressier, Jules
  French National RSO
  French Radio Lyric Orch
  ORTF Lyric Orch
Grevillius, Nils
  Göteborg SO
  Stockholm PO
Grier, Francis
  Christ Church Cathedral Choir Oxford
Griffiths, Howard
  English CO
  Northern Sinfonia of England
  Royal PO
  Slovak RSO Bratislava
Grimbert, Jacques
  Paris Sorbonne Orch
Grin, Leonid
  Tampere PO
Grindenko, Anatoly
  Russian Patriarchate Choir
Gritton, Robin
  Datura Trombone Quartet
  Frankfurt RSO
Groh, Jack
  Univ of Arkansas Schola Cantorum
Gronostay, Uwe
  Berlin Radio Sinfonietta
  Berlin RIAS Chamber Choir
  Berlin RSO
  Danish National Radio Choir
  Netherlands Chamber Choir
Grossmann, Agnès
  Metropolitan Orch
Grossmann, Ferdinand
  Akademie Chamber Choir
  Pro Musica Orch
  Vienna Concert House Orch
  Vienna SO
Groves, Charles
  BBC SO
  BBC Scottish SO
  Bournemouth SO
  English CO
  English Sinfonia
  Liverpool PO
  London PO
  London SO
  Philharmonia Orch
  Pro Arte Orch
  Royal Liverpool PO
  Royal PO
Grube, Christian
  Berlin HDK Chamber Choir
  Berlin School of the Arts Chamber Choir
  Oriol Ensemble
Grüber, Arthur
  Berlin SO
  Berlin SO members
  Hamburg SO
  Philharmonia Hungarica
  Stuttgart Solisten
Gruber, Heinz Karl
  Ensemble Modern
  London Sinfonietta
Grundy, John
  Sydney Philharmonia Motet Choir
Grüner-Hegge, Odd
  Oslo PO
Grüss, Hans
  Capella Fidicinia
  Capella Fidicinia Dresden
  Capella Fidicinia Leipzig
Grylls, Karen
  Dorian Choir
Guadagno, Anton
  Academy of Music Orch
  American Opera Society Orch
  Arena di Verona Orch
  Cincinnati Summer Opera Association Orch
  Hartford Opera Orch
  London SO
  New Philharmonia Orch
  Philadelphia Lyric Opera Orch
  St. Cecilia Academy Orch Rome
  Santiago Teatro Municipale Orch
Gualda, Sylvio
  Radio France PO
Guanren, Gu
  Shanghai Chinese Folk Orch
Guarnieri, Antonio
  Rome RAI SO
  La Scala Orch
Gubert, Carlos
  Accademia Bach
  Padua Bach Academy CO
Gucht, Georges van
  Strasbourg Percussion Ensemble
Guest, Douglas
  Westminster Abbey Choir
Guest, George
  Academy of St. Martin in the Fields
  Argo CO
  City of London Sinfonia
  English CO
  King's College Choir Cambridge
  London Philomusica Antiqua

Guest, George (cont.)
  St. John's College Choir Cambridge
Guggenberger, P.
  Vienna Ensemble
Gui, Vittorio
  Berlin State Opera Orch
  EIAR Orch
  Florence Maggio Musicale Orch
  Glyndebourne Festival Orch
  London PO
  London SO
  Milan RAI SO
  Naples Teatro San Carlo Orch
  Palermo Teatro Massimo Orch
  Rome Opera Orch
  Rome Radio-TV SO
  Royal Opera Orch
  Royal PO
  Turin EIAR SO
  Venice Teatro La Fenice Orch
Guida, Guido Maria
  Berlin RSO
Guillard, Georges
  Ludwig String Quartet
Guingal, Alain
  French Lyric Orch
Guinjoan, Juan
  RTV SO
Gülke, Peter
  Berlin RSO
  Wuppertal SO
Güller, Bernhard
  South German Youth PO
  Stuttgart RSO
Gummersbach
  Rauber Quartet Society
Gundlach, Willi
  Dortmund Univ Chamber Choir
  Westphalia CO
Gunnarsson, Guomundur Oli
  Caput Ensemble
Gunzenhauser, Stephen
  BBC PO
  Capella Istropolitana
  Czech-Slovak RSO
  Czech-Slovak RSO Bratislava
  Czech-Slovak State PO
  Irish National SO
  Lisbon Gulbenkian Foundation Orch
  Polish National RSO Katowice
  Polish State PO
  Slovak PO
  Slovak RSO Bratislava
Gurlitt, Manfred
  Berlin PO
Guschlbauer, Theodore
  Bamberg SO
  Bournemouth SO
  Linz Bruckner Orch
  Lisbon Gulbenkian Foundation CO
  Strasbourg PO
  Vienna SO
Gusella, Mario
  Margherita Theater Orch
Gussev, Stanislav
  Moscow SO
  Yurlov Academic Choir
Guth, Peter
  Austrian RSO
  Capella Istropolitana
  Odense SO
  Strauss Festival Orch
Güttler, Ludwig
  Leipzig Bach Collegium
  Virtuosi Saxoniae
Gutwenger, Artur
  Lienz Chamber Choir
Guy, Hélène
  Provence Vocal Ensemble
Guyonnet, Jacques
  Geneva Collegium Academicum
Gyártó, Stefan
  Hamburg State Opera Orch
Hadari, Omri
  Cape Town SO
  South African National SO
Hadden, Nancy
  Circa 1500 Ensemble
Hadjidakis, Manos
  Athens Colours Orch
Haenchen, Hans
  Berlin CO
  Berlin RSO
  CPE Bach CO
  Netherlands PO
Haenisch, Konrad
  Essen Studio Choir
Haeren, Pascal van
  New England CO
Hage, Louis
  St. Esprit Univ Musicological Chorale
Hage, Paul Rouhana
  Lebanon Univ of the Holy Ghost Musical Institute Chorus
Hagen, Hans
  Vienna Unterhaltung Orch
Hager, Leopold
  Auvergne Orch
  English CO
  Luxembourg RSO

Hager, Leopold (cont.)
Luxembourg Radio–TV SO
Munich RSO
Netherlands CO
RTL SO
Salzburg Mozarteum Orch
Hahn, Klaus-Peter
Mannheim Kurpfälzisches CO
Haider, Friedrich
Munich RSO
Polish National RSO Cracow
Strasbourg PO
Swedish RSO
Tokyo PO
Hair, Graham
Australia Ensemble
Haitink, Bernard
Bavarian RSO
Bayer RSO
Berlin PO
Boston SO
(Royal) Concertgebouw Orch
Dresden Staatskapelle
London PO
London SO
Royal Opera House Orch
Vienna PO
Halaris, Christodoulos
Fine Instruments Orch
OP & PO Orch
Halasz, Michael
Bratislava RSO
Budapest Camerata
Budapest Failoni Orch
Czech RSO
Failoni Orch
Hagen PO
Irish National SO
Polish National RSO
Polish National RSO Katowice
Rhenish PO
Royal PO
Slovak PO
Zagreb Festival Orch
Halffter, Cristóbal
Madrid Instrumental Ensemble
Halffter, Ernesto
Champs Elysées Theater Orch
Séville Betica CO
Hall, William
William Hall Orch
Master Chorale of Orange County
Vienna Festival SO
Halsey, Louis
Allegri Singers
Elizabethan Singers
Halsey, Simon
City of Birmingham Sym Chorus
Halstead, Anthony
Hanover Band
Hamel, Marcel
ORTF Lyric Orch
Hamon, Pierre
Alla Francesca
Hancock, Gerre
St. Thomas Church Choir New York
St. Thomas Church Men & Boys' Choir New York
St. Thomas Men & Boys' Choir
Handford, Maurice
BBC Northern SO
Hallé Orch
Händler, Jack Martin
Dall'Arco CO
Handley, Vernon
BBC Northern SO
BBC PO
BBC SO
BBC Welsh National SO
Berlin RSO
Bournemouth SO
City of Birmingham SO
Hallé Orch
London PO
Malmö SO
Royal Liverpool Phil Choir
Royal Liverpool PO
Royal PO
Ulster Orch
Handt, Herbert
Lucchese CO
Toscana Accademia Strumentale
Hanke, Peter
Carmina Chamber Choir
Hannam, P.
Welsh Guards Band
Hannikainen, Tauno
Finnish RSO
London SO
Hansen, J.
St. Paul Youth Choir Aachen
Hansen, Richard
St. Cloud State Univ Wind Ensemble
Hanson, Gregg I.
Univ of Arizona Wind Orch
Hanson, Howard
Eastman–Rochester Orch
Mormon Youth SO
United States Air Force Band
World Youth SO Interlochen

Hantaï, Pierre
Le Concert Français
Hanuš, Tomáš
Prague Chamber PO
Harbison, John
Collage New Music Ensemble
Los Angeles Phil New Music Group
Hardin, L.
New York studio musicians
Harnoncourt, Nikolaus
CO of Europe
Concentus Musicus Soloists
(Royal) Concertgebouw Orch
Deller Consort
Dresden Staatskapelle
Leonhardt Consort
Residentie Orch The Hague
Vienna Concentus Musicus
Vienna Mozart Winds
Vienna PO
Vienna SO
Zurich Mozart Opera Orch
Zurich Opera Orch
Harrassowitz, Hermann
St. Lorenz Bach Choir Nuremberg
Harrell, Ray Evans
Magic Circle CO
Harrer, Uwe Christian
Vienna Boys' Choir
Harris, Roy
International String Congress Orch
Northwestern Univ Concert Choir
United States Air Force Academy Band members
Harrison, Guy Fraser
Oklahoma City SO
Hartemann, Jean-Claude
French Soloists
ORTF Lyric Orch
Harth-Bedoya, Miguel
Dianopolis Bulgarian CO
Harty, Hamilton
Hallé Orch
London PO
London SO
Harvey, Richard
Aquitaine Brass
London Brass
Hary, Béla
Transylvania PO Cluj
Haselböck, Martin
Vienna Academy
Hashimoto, Eiji
Ensemble for 18th Century Music
Hasler, Jean-Michel
Limoges Baroque Ensemble
Hauschild, Wolf-Dieter
Berlin RSO
Consortium Classicum
English CO
Leipzig RSO
Stuttgart PO
Hausegger, Siegmund von
Munich PO
Hautmann, J.
Lorraine PO
Havačak, L.
Prague CO
Hayman, Richard
Czech-Slovak RSO
Hayman SO
Slovak PO
Hayrabedian, Roland
Musicatreize
Strasbourg Percussion Ensemble
Hays, S. V.
Royal Artillery Band
Haza, Luis
London SO
Heath, Edward
English CO
Hetherington, Alan
Chicago String Ensemble
Hedwall, Lennart
Orebro CO
Heger, L.
English CO
Heger, Robert
Austrian RSO
Bavarian RSO
Berlin PO
Berlin Staatskapelle
Berlin State Opera Orch
Vienna PO
Vienna State Opera Orch
Hegyi, Ildikó
Albany SO
Concentus Hungaricus
Hegyi, Julius
Albany SO
Heider, Anne
His Majestie's Clerkes
Heider, Werner
Ars Nova
Nuremberg Ars Nova Ensemble
Heimans, Henri
Maastricht Municipal Orch
Heinrich, Siegfried
Polish National RSO Cracow

Heinrich, Siegfried (cont.)
Warsaw RSO
Heiss, John
New England Conservatory Jazz Big Band
Helasvuo, Pekka
Finlandia Sinfonietta
Finnish–Estonian Baroque Orch
Helbich, Wolfgang
Alsfeld Vocal Ensemble
Bremen Baroque Orch
Steintor Barock Bremen
Heldrich, Claire
New Music Consort
Heller, Alfred
Moscow RSO
Helles
Vienna SO
Hellmann, Diethard
Mainz Bach Choir
Mainz Bach Orch
Southwest German RSO Baden–Baden
Hellyer Jones, Jonathan
Cambridge Baroque Camerata
Helmrath, Michael
Munich Phil CO
Heltay, Laszlo
Argo CO
Brighton Festival Chorus
London PO
Hemberg, Eskil
Stockholm Univ Chorus
Heming, Capt. Peter
Her Majesty's Royal Marines Band Corps of Drums
Hempfling, Volker
Halle Handel Festival Orch
Henderson, Skitch
London SO
New York Pops Orch
RCA Victor SO
Hendl, Walter
Chicago SO
Dallas SO
RCA Victor SO
Hengelbrock, Thomas
Freiburg Baroque Orch
Henneberger, Jürg
Opera Nova Ensemble
Zurich New Music Ensemble
Hennig, Heinz
Hanover Boys' Choir
Hanover CO
London Baroque
Musica Fiata
North German Radio PO
Pro Cantione Antiqua
Henze, Hans Werner
Berlin PO
Ensemble Modern
Henzold, Olaf
AML Lucerne SO
Berlin RSO
Lucerne SO
Herbers, Werner
Ebony Band
Herbert, W.
New Orleans Opera Orch
Herbig, Günther
BBC PO
Berlin RSO
Berlin Soloists
Berlin State Orch
Berlin SO
Dresden PO
Royal PO
Southwest German RSO Baden–Baden
Toronto SO
Herbig, Lutz
Berlin SO
Herchet, Jörg
Hans Eisler New Music Group
Hercl, Josef
Prague Radio Chorus
Hermans, Eric
Studium Chorale
Herreweghe, Philippe
Les Arts Florissants
Champs Elysées Theater Orch
Chapelle Royale Choir
Chapelle Royale Orch
Chapelle Royale Vocal Enemble
Collegium Vocale
Collegium Vocale Orch
Européen Vocal Ensemble
Ghent Collegium Vocale
Ghent Collegium Vocale Orch
Musique Oblique Ensemble
Orch of the Age of Enlightenment
Organum Ensemble
Radio France PO
Royal Chapel European Vocal Ensemble
Toulouse Saqueboutiers
Herrmann, Bernard
Columbia SO
London Festival Players
London Festival Recording Ensemble
London PO
National PO
National PO London
New Philharmonia Orch

Herrmann, Bernard (cont.)
  Pro Arte Orch
Hess, Wolfgang
  Bonn Youth Ensemble
Heward, Leslie
  Hallé Orch
Heyerick, Florian
  Collegium Instrumentale Brugense
  Le Mercure Galant Baroque Orch
Hickox, Richard
  Academy of St. Martin in the Fields
  BBC PO
  BBC Welsh National Orch
  BBC Welsh National SO
  Bournemouth Sinfonietta
  Bournemouth SO
  Britten Singers
  City of London Baroque Sinfonia
  City of London School for Girls Orch
  City of London Sinfonia
  City of London Sinfonia members
  Collegium Musicum 90
  English Northern Philharmonia
  Haffner Wind Ensemble
  Richard Hickox Singers
  London SO
  Northern Sinfonia of England
  Royal Liverpool PO
  Royal PO
  Sinfonia 21
  Westminster Singers
Higginbottom, Edward
  Hanover Band
  King's Consort
  New College Choir Oxford
  Parley of Instruments
Hilbish, Thomas
  Univ of Michigan Chamber Choir
  Univ of Michigan SO members
Hill, David
  Academy of Ancient Music
  Bournemouth SO
  Brandenburg Consort
  Brandenburg Orch
  City of London Sinfonia
  London Baroque Brass
  Parley of Instruments
  Waynflete Singers
  Westminster Cathedral Choir
  Winchester Cathedral Choir
Hillier, Paul
  Hilliard Ensemble
  His Majesties Clerkes
  King's Noyse
  Theater of Voices
  Western Wind Chamber Chorus
Hills, Maj. Philip E.
  Grenadier Guards Band
Himpe, P.
  Londerzeel Youth SO
Hindemith, Paul
  Berlin PO
  French National Orch
  London SO
  Philharmonia Orch
  Vienna SO
Hinnells, Duncan
  European Chamber Opera Orch
Hinreiner, Ernst
  Salzburg Camerata Academica
  Salzburg Mozart Players
  Salzburg Mozarteum Camerata Academica
  Salzburg Mozarteum CO
  Salzburg Mozarteum Orch
  Salzburg RSO
Hirokami, Jun'ichi
  Bavarian RSO
  London SO
  Malmö SO
  Norrköping SO
  Royal PO
  Stockholm Symphonic Wind Orch
Hirsch, Hans Ludwig
  Accademia Instrumentalis Claudio Monteverdi
  Innsbruck CO
  Claudio Monteverdi Accademia Venice
  Musica Poetica Freiberg
Hirsch, Peter
  Young PO
Hladky, Vinzenz
  Vienna Pro Musica Orch
Hlasek, T.
  Hungarian Philharmonia
Hlaváček, Libor
  Ostrava Janáček CO
  Pardubice CO
  Pardubice State CO
  Prague CO
Hnyk, Jiri
  Czech Phil CO
Ho, Edith
  Church of the Advent Choir Boston
Hobson, Ian
  Sinfonia da Camera
Hochstrasser, Alois J.
  Lower Austria Tonkünst Orch
Hodkinson, Sydney
  Eastman Musica Nova Ensemble
  Rochester PO

Hoey, Choo
  Singapore SO
Hoffman, Joel
  Royal Festival Opera SO
Hofmann, Wolfgang
  Seiler CO
  Sinfonia Stuttgart
Hogwood, Christopher
  Academy of Ancient Music
  Amadeus Winds
  Handel & Haydn Society
  St. Paul CO
Hohstadt, Thomas
  Midland–Odessa SO
Holásek, L
  Capella Istropolitana
Holdridge, Lee
  London SO
  Los Angeles String Orch
  Royal PO
Holland, Florian
  Eastman Brass Quintet
Hollerung, Gábor
  Budapest Academic Choral Society
Holliger, Heinz
  Bern Camerata
  Bern Camerata String Ensemble
  CO of Europe
  Contrechamps Ensemble
  English CO
  Ensemble Modern
  German Youth PO
  Philharmonia Orch
  Saarbrück RSO
  Scharoun Ensemble
Hollingworth, Robert
  Fretwork
Hollreiser, Heinrich
  Austrian RSO
  Bamberg SO
  Dresden State Opera Orch
  German Opera Orch
  North German RSO
  Trieste PO
  Vienna Pro Musica Orch
  Vienna State Opera Orch
  Vienna SO
Holman, Peter
  Opera Restor'd
  Parley of Instruments
  Playford Consort
Holmquist, Ward
  Houston Grand Opera Orch
Holst, Gustav
  London SO
Holst, Imogen
  English CO
Holstein, Paul
  Southwest German Radio Children's Choir
Holten, Bo
  Ars Nova
  BBC Singers
Hötzel, Michael
  Philharmonia da Camera
Homolka, Miroslav
  Dvořák CO
Honeck, Manfred
  Bamberg SO
  Hungarian State Orch
  Munich RSO
Honegger, Arthur
  Paris Conservatory Societé des Concerts Orch
Honeyball, David
  London Brass Virtuosi
  Philharmonia Orch
Honeyman, Ian
  Il Seminario Musicale
Hoose, David
  Cantata Ensemble
  Cantata Singers
  Collage New Music Ensemble
  Dinosaur Annex Music Ensemble
Hopkins, John
  Melbourne SO
  New Zealand SO
  Queensland SO
  Slovak PO
  Sydney Conservatorium for Music Orch
  Victorian State Opera Orch
Horák, Vlastimil
  Bratislava Chamber Ensemble
Horenstein, Jascha
  American SO
  Bamberg SO
  BBC Northern SO
  BBC SO
  Berlin PO
  Colonne Concert Orch
  Hallé Orch
  London PO
  London SO
  Munich National Theatre Orch
  New Philharmonia Orch
  Paris Concerts Colonne Orch
  Pro Musica Orch
  Royal PO
  Southwest German RSO Baden-Baden
  Stockholm PO

Horenstein, Jascha (cont.)
  Vienna State Opera Orch
  Vienna SO
Horigome, Yozuko
  Tokyo Metropolitan SO
Horvat, Milan
  Copenhagen PO
  Slovenian PO
Hoskins
  HM Royal Marines Band
Houtmann, Jacques
  Lorraine PO
Hovhaness, Alan
  National PO London
  New Jersey Wind Sym
  Northwest Sinfonia
  Polyphonia Orch
  Royal PO
  Seattle SO
  Sevan PO
Howard, Michael
  Cantores in Ecclesia
Howarth, Elgar
  Bavarian RSO
  Gemini Ensemble
  Grimethorpe Colliery Band
  Jones Brass Ensemble
  London Sinfonietta
  Netherlands Radio PO
  Philharmonia Orch
  Residentie Orch The Hague
  Swedish RSO
Hrnčir, Josef
  Prague RSO
Hsu, John
  Apollo Ensemble
Hubad, Samo
  Zagreb Opera Orch
Huber-Contwig, E.
  Musica Nova Ensemble
Hug, Raimond
  Freiburg Baroque Soloists
Hug, Theo
  Bern Chamber Ensemble
  Bern Radio Chamber Ensemble
Huggett, Monica
  CBC Vancouver SO
  European Community Baroque Orch
  London Vivaldi Orch
  Orch of the Age of Enlightenment
  Sonnerie Ensemble
Hughes, Owain Arwel
  Aarhus SO
  BBC SO
  BBC Welsh National SO
  Danish National RSO
  Philharmonia Orch
  Royal PO
Hughes, Robert
  Metropolitan Opera Orch
  Oakland Youth Orch
Hugo, Robert
  Capella Regia Musicalis
Hulsmann, Kees
  Berkeley SO
Hultberg, Cortland
  Phoenix Chamber Choir
Humburg, Will
  Czech–Slovak RSO Bratislava
  Failoni CO
  Münster SO
Hunsberger, Donald
  Eastman–Dryden Orch
Hunt, Donald
  Donald Hunt Singers
  Worcester Cathedral Choir
Hünteler, Konrad
  Camerata of the 18th Century
Hurst, George
  BBC PO
  Bournemouth Sinfonietta
Husa, Karel
  Brno State PO
  Louisville Orch
  Orch de Paris Soloists
  Prague SO
  Stockholm RSO
Husmann, Mathias
  Magdeburg PO
Huss, Manfred
  Haydn Sinfonietta Vienna
Huybrechts, François
  Vienna PO
Hye–Knudsen, Johan
  Danish Radio Concert Orch
  Royal Danish Orch
Hyökki, Matti
  Helsinki Univ Chorus
Hzeil, S.
  Cleveland Orch
Iannitti, Francesco
  Giacomo Puccini Grosseto Chorale
Ickstadt, Alois
  Frankfurt Choir
  Hesse Radio Chorus
Iimori, Norichika
  Moscow RSO
Ilic, Vojislav
  Belgrade Radio–TV Chorus

Iliev, Constantin
  Philharmonia Bulgarica
  Sofia State PO
Imai, Nobuko
  London SO
Immerseel, Jos van
  Anima Eterna Orch
Inbal, Eliahu
  Arena di Verona Orch
  Berlin RSO
  (Royal) Concertgebouw Orch
  Fontenay Trio
  Frankfurt RSO
  French National Orch
  London PO
  London SO
  New Philharmonia Orch
  Philharmonia Orch
  Ramat Gan CO
  Swiss Romande Orch
  Venice Teatro La Fenice Orch
  Vienna SO
Indermühle, Thomas
  English CO
Ingebretsen, Kjell
  Kungliga Hovkapellet
  Royal PO
  Royal Stockholm Orch
  Swedish RSO
Inoue, Michiyoshi
  Netherlands CO
  New Japan PO
  Pro Musica Nipponia
  Royal PO
  South German RSO
  Tokyo Flute Ensemble
Ionescu-Galati, I.
  Brasov George Dima PO
Irving, Robert
  New York City Ballet Orch
  Royal PO
Isacson, Einar
  Lulea Chamber Choir
Iseler, Elmer
  CBC Vancouver SO
  Elmer Iseler Singers
  New York PO members
  Philadelphia Orch members
Ishii, Maki
  Tokyo Metropolitan SO
Ishimaru, Hiroshi
  Tokyo Metropolitan SO
Issakadze, Liana
  Georgian CO
Ivanoff, Vladimir
  Ensemble Saraband
  VOX
Ivanov, Konstantin
  Russian State SO
  USSR SO
Iwaki, Hiroyuki
  Melbourne SO
  New Japan PO
  Sydney SO
  Tokyo Metropolitan SO
Izquierdo, Juan Pablo
  Carnegie Mellon PO
  Latin American String Quartet
Izquierdo, Luis
  Carme Ensemble
  Czech PO
  Grand Canary PO
Jackson, Christopher
  Montreal Ancient Music Ensemble
  Montreal Studio de Musique Ancienne Orch
  Les Violons du Roy
Jackson, Don
  London SO
  Royal PO
Jackson, Douglas
  Hartt Contemporary Players
Jackson, Isaiah
  Berlin SO
  English CO
Jackson, Stephen
  BBC Sym Chorus
Jacob, W.
  Capella Sebaldina Nuremberg
Jacobs, René
  Berlin Academy for Early Music
  Concerto Cologne
  Concerto Vocale
  Ensemble 415
  Netherlands Chamber Choir
  Schola Cantorum Basiliensis Instrumental Ensemble
Jacquillat, Jean-Pierre
  Icelandic CO
  Lamoureux Concerts Orch
  Lamoureux Orch
Jaenike, M.
  Arte Antica
Jaffee, Michael
  Waverly Consort
Jagust, Mladen
  Belgrade Radio-TV Chorus
James, Robert
  James St. Bride's Church Choir

Jancsovics, Antal
  Budapest SO
Janigro, Antonio
  Milan RAI SO
  Vienna SO
  Zagreb RSO
  Zagreb Solisti
Janowski, Marek
  Dresden Staatskapelle
  French Radio PO
  German SO
  Leipzig Gewandhaus Orch
  Leipzig Opera Orch
  Munich RSO
  ORTF SO
  Philharmonia Orch
  Radio France PO
  Royal Liverpool PO
Jansons, Arvid
  Stockholm PO
Jansons, Mariss
  Berlin PO
  (Royal) Concertgebouw Orch
  Leningrad PO
  London PO
  Oslo PO
  Philadelphia Orch
  Philharmonia Orch
  St. Petersburg PO
Jaroff
  Don Cossack Choir
Jarre, Maurice
  London SO
  Royal PO
Järvi, Neeme
  Bamberg SO
  Bavarian RSO
  Bergen PO
  Chicago SO
  City of Birmingham SO
  Cologne RSO
  (Royal) Concertgebouw Orch
  Danish National RSO
  Detroit SO
  Estonian SO
  Estonian State SO
  Finnish RSO
  Gothenburg SO
  London PO
  London SO
  Lund's Student Choral Society
  Philharmonia Orch
  Royal Scottish National Orch
  Royal Stockholm PO
  Scottish National Orch
  Stockholm PO
  Stockholm Sinfonietta
  Swedish RSO
  Swiss Romande Orch
Järvi, Paavo
  Kroumata Percussion Ensemble
  Lyra Borealis Ensemble
  Malmö SO
  Royal Stockholm PO
  Scottish National Orch Wind Ensemble
  Tapiola Sinfonietta
Jarvinen, Arthur
  California EAR Unit
Jarvis, P.
  New Jersey Percussion Ensemble
Jean, Bernard
  Montreal Metropolitan Orch
Jean, Kenneth
  Czech-Slovak RSO Bratislava
  Hong Kong PO
  Slovak PO
Jean-Baptiste, Lucien
  l'Ile de la Cité Orch
Jeanes, Maj. E. W.
  Band of the Blues & Royals
Jeegers, Peit
  Piet Jeegers Clarinet Choir
Jeffers, Ron
  Oregon State Univ Choir
Jenkins, Glyn
  Bristol Bach Choir
Jenkins, Karl
  London PO
  Smith String Quartet
Jenkins, Newell
  Clarion Concerts Orch
  Clarion Music Society Orch
  New York Woodwind Soloists
Jennings, Joseph
  Chanticleer
Jensen, Jorgen Misser
  Danish Concert Band
Jensen, Thomas
  Danish National RSO
Jerome, Davis
  Mozart Festival Orch
Jia, Lu
  Trieste Teatro Comunale Giuseppe Verdi Orch
Jilek, Frantisek
  Brno Janáček Opera Orch
  Brno State PO
  Czech State PO
  Bohuslav Martinů CO

Jílek, Frantisek (cont.)
  Prague National Theater Orch
Jirous, Jiří
  Prague National Theater Orch
Jochum, Eugen
  Bamberg SO
  Bavarian Radio Chorus
  Bavarian RSO
  Bayreuth Festival Orch
  Berlin German Opera Orch
  Berlin PO
  (Royal) Concertgebouw Orch
  Dresden Staatskapelle
  German Opera Orch
  London PO
  London SO
  Swedish RSO
  Tölz SO
Joensen, Alice
  Fynske Chamber Choir
Joeres, Dirk
  Royal PO
  West German Sinfonia
Johanos, Donald
  Czech-Slovak RSO Bratislava
  Czech-Slovak RSO Prague
  Dallas SO
  Honolulu SO
Johansen, Svend Aaquist
  Danish Chamber Players
  South Jutland SO
Johansson, Bo
  Adolf Fredriks Girls' Choir
Johnson, A. Robert
  New York Philomusica
  New York Philomusica Winds
Johnson, Graham
  London Schubert Chorale
Johnson, Laurie
  Coldstream Guards Regimental Band
  Fanfare Trumpeters of the Scots Guards
  London Brass Chorale
  London Jazz Orch
  London PO
  London Studio SO
Johnson, Martha N.
  Sarum Consort
Johnson, Thor
  Peninsula Festival Orch
Jolivet, André
  Paris Opera Orch
Joly, Simon
  BBC Concert Orch
  BBC Singers
Jones, Barbara
  Stow Festival Orch
Jones, Brian
  Trinity Choir
Jones, Eric
  Eric Jones Orch
Jones, Geraint
  Geraint Jones Orch
Jones, Leslie
  London Little Orch
Jones, M.
  Zurich CO
Jones, Samuel
  Houston SO
Joó, Árpád
  Amsterdam PO
  Budapest SO
  London SO
  Philharmonia Orch
Joppich, Godehard
  Munich Benedictine Abbey Choral School
  Münsterschwarzach Abbey Monks' Choir
  Die Singphoniker
Jorda, Enrique
  London SO
  Pro Musica Orch
  San Francisco SO
Jordan, Armin
  Basel SO
  Lausanne CO
  Monte Carlo Opera Orch
  Monte Carlo PO
  Paris Chamber Ensemble
  Paris Orchestral Ensemble
  Swiss Romande Orch
  Swiss-Italian Orch
Jordania, Vakhtang
  KBS SO
Jørgensen, Jesper Grove
  Copenhagen Univ Choir
Josefowitz, D.
  Japan PO
Jouvet, Laurent
  Ganagobie Abbey Monks' Choir
Judd, James
  Argo SO
  CO of Europe
  English CO
  European Community Youth Orch
  Florida PO
  Hallé Orch
  London SO
  Royal PO
Junghänel, Konrad
  Cantus Cologne

Junghänel, Konrad (cont.)
Concerto Palatino
Concerto Palatino Choir
Gradus ad Parnassum
Vienna Hofburgkapelle Choir
Junkin, Jerry
Dallas Wind Sym
Jürgens, Jürgen
Camerata Accademica Hamburg
Concerto Amsterdam
Jurowski, Michail
Berlin German SO
Berlin RSO
Norrköping SO
Northwest German PO
Rhineland–Palatinate State PO
Kabasta, Oswald
Munich PO
Vienna SO
Kachanov, Nikolai
New York Russian Chamber Chorus
Kagel, Mauricio
Ars Acustica
Saarbrück RSO
South German RSO
Kahi, Vato
Georgian Festival Orch
Kajanus, Robert
Helsinki PO
London SO
Kajdasz, Edmund
Cantores Minores Wratislavienses
Polish Radio CO
Warsaw CO
Kajdasz, Wroclaw Edmund
Polish Radio Chorus
Wroclaw Orch
Kakhidze, Dzansug
Tbilisi SO
USSR Radio-TV Large SO
Kalinin, Nikolai
Ossipov Balalaika Orch
Kalinsky, B.
Prague SO
Kalitzke, Johannes
Musikfabrik NRW
North Rhine–Westphalia Musikfabrik
Kaljuste, Tõnu
Eric Ericson Chamber Choir
Estonian Phil Chamber Choir
Swedish Radio Choir
Tallinn CO
Kalmar, Carlos
Vienna SO
Kamen, Michael
Seattle SO
Kamirski, Wlodzimierz
Polish RSO
Polish Radio-TV SO
Warsaw Radio-TV Orch
Warsaw Theatr Wielk Orch
Kammler, Reinhard
Augsburg Cathedral Boys' Choir
Collegium Aureum
Munich Residenz CO
Kamp, Harry van der
Kapel Van de Lage Landen
Kamp, Salamon
Debrecen Kodaly Choir
Kämpf, Bernd
Neuwieder Chamber Chorus
Kamu, Okku
City of Birmingham SO
Copenhagen PO
English CO
Finlandia Sinfonietta
Finnish RSO
Gothenburg SO
Helsingborg SO
Helsinki PO
Helsinki RSO
London PO
Malmö SO
New Stockholm CO
Stockholm PO
Stockholm Sinfonietta
Swedish RSO
Kangas, Juha
Budapest SO
Marosensemble
Ostrobothnian CO
Prague Radio SO
Kantschieder, Paul
Masurian PO
Kaplan, Abraham
Camerata Singers
Camerata String Orch
Camerata SO
Kaplan, Gilbert
London SO
Kapp, Richard
Hamburg SO
Kiev Pro Musica
New York Philharmonia Virtuosi
Oberlin Baroque Ensemble
Philharmonia Hungarica
Philharmonia Virtuosi
Prague SO
Westphalia SO

Kapp, Richard (cont.)
Westphalia SO Recklinghausen
Karabtchevsky, Isaac
Brazil SO
Lower Austria Tonkünst Orch
Karajan, Herbert von
Bavarian RSO
Bayreuth Festival Orch
Berlin Opera Orch
Berlin PO
Berlin SO
Cologne RSO
(Royal) Concertgebouw Orch
Dresden Staatskapelle
Milan Italian Radio-TV Orch
Milan RAI SO
Orch de Paris
Paris SO
Philharmonia Orch
Prussian State Orch
RAI SO
RIAS SO
Rome Radio Orch
Rome RAI SO
La Scala Orch
Stockholm PO
Turin EIAR SO
Vienna PO
Vienna State Opera Orch
Vienna SO
Karas, Joza
Disman Radio Children's Choir
Disman Radio Children's Ensemble
Karolski, Thomas
Camerata Romana
Kashuro, Nikolai
Grajna Choir Minsk
Kaspszyk, Jacek
London SO
Philharmonia Orch
Polish National RSO Katowice
Karol Szymanowski State PO
Katajev, Vitaly
Northern Crown Soloists Ensemble
Katims, M.
Seattle SO
Katlewicz, Jerzy
Polish National RSO Katowice
Polish National SO
Warsaw PO
Katona, Anikó
Hungarian State Opera Orch
Katz, Arnold
Novosibirsk PO
USSR SO
Kaufman, Richard
Brandenburg PO
New Zealand SO
Nuremberg SO
Kawalla, Szymon
Koszalin State PO
Polish National RSO Cracow
Polish Radio-TV SO
Polish Radio-TV SO Cracow
Slovak RSO Bratislava
Kaye, Danny
Stockholm PO
Kazandjiev, Vassil
Bulgarian National RSO
Bulgarian PO
Bulgarian SO
Madrigal Chamber Ensemble
Sofia CO
Sofia Solisti CO
Zurich Baroque Strings
Keefe, Bernard
BBC SO
Keene, Christopher
Juilliard Orch
Syracuse SO
Keene, Dennis
Voices of Ascension
Voices of Ascension Orch
Kegel, Herbert
Dresden PO
Dresden State Orch
Leipzig RSO
Kegelmann, Gerald
Constitution Brass
Heidelberg Madrigal Choir
Heidelberg–Mannheim State Univ Chamber Choir
Kehr, Günter
Mainz CO
Keilberth, Joseph
Bavarian RSO
Bavarian State Opera Orch
Bavarian SO
Bayreuth Festival Orch
Cologne RSO
Stoccarda RSO
Stuttgart Reich RSO
Keitel, Wilhelm
Minsk Orch
Kektjiang, Lim
Gunma SO
Kelber, Wolfgang
Monteverdi Orch
Munich Monteverdi Orch
Heinrich Schütz Ensemble

Keller, Christoph
Zurich Chamber Ensemble
Kelly, Brett
Melbourne Academy
Kelly, Sherry Hill
Belmont Chorale
Kelterborn, Rudolf
Basel RSO
Basel RSO Winds
Swiss–Italian RSO
Kember, G.
Bavarian Radio Chorus
Kemmer, M.
RTL SO
Kempe, Rudolf
Bamberg SO
Bavarian RSO
Bavarian State Opera Orch
Berlin PO
Berlin Staatskapelle
Dresden Staatskapelle
Dresden State Chorus
Munich PO
Royal Opera House Orch
Royal PO
Saxon State Orch
Vienna PO
Kempen, Paul Van
Berlin PO
Berlin State Opera Orch
Berlin State Orch
German Opera Orch
Kendall, C.
20th Century Consort
Kendall, Christopher
Virtuoso Strings
Kennedy, Nigel
English CO
Kerstens, Huub
Netherlands Chamber Choir
Xenakis Ensemble
Kertész, István
Brighton Festival Chorus
French National RSO
Israel PO
London SO
Vienna PO
Vienna State Opera Orch
Kértesz, István
London SO
Keshishian, K.
St. Gayané Cathedral Choir
Kesling, Will
Utah State Univ Chamber Singers
Ketchum, Charles
Utah SO
Ketting, Otto
Netherlands Ballet Orch
Rotterdam Conservatory Ensemble
Rotterdam PO
Royal PO
Keulen, Geert van
Omroep Orch
Keuschnig, Peter
Berlin RSO
Khachaturian, Aram
Bolshoi Theater Orch
Moscow Radio Grand SO
Moscow RSO
Philharmonia Orch
Turin RAI SO
USSR Radio-TV Large SO
USSR Radio-TV Orch
USSR SO
Vienna PO
Khachaturian, Emin
Soviet Cinema Orch
USSR Cinema SO
USSR Ministry of Culture SO
Khaikin, Boris
Bolshoi Theater Orch
Kirov Opera Orch
Leningrad PO
Moscow RSO
USSR Radio-TV Large SO
Kharitonov, G.
Patriarchal Cathedral of the Epiphany Choir
Kibblewhite, Michael
East London Chorus
London PO
Kieft, Roland
Netherlands Jeugd SO
Kielland, Olar
Royal PO
Kim, Byung–Hwa
Korea State SO
Korean PO
Kim, Won–Mo
Prague CO
Royal Czech SO
King, Larry
Trinity Church Choir Wall Street
King, Robert
King's Consort
Musica da Camera
Kipnis, Igor
Connecticut Early Music Festival Ensemble

Kirchhoff, C.
  Ohio State Univ New Music Ensemble
Kirchner, Leon
  Boston Sym Chamber Players
Kirkman, Andrew
  Binchois Consort
Kitaienko, Dmitri
  Bergen PO
  Danish National RSO
  Danish Radio Concert Orch
  Moscow PO
  Moscow PO Strings
  USSR Radio-TV Large SO
Kiss, Eri
  Estonian National Male Choir
  Finnish National Opera Orch
  Malmö PO
  Royal Stockholm Orch
  Royal Swedish Orch
  Stockholm PO
Kletzow, Peter
  Claremont CO
Klava, Sigvard
  Riga Musicians
Klebel, B.
  Vienna Motet Choir
Klee, Bernhard
  Bavarian RSO
  Berlin RSO
  Berlin Staatskapelle
  Berlin State Chorus
  English CO
  Hanover Radio PO
Kleiber, Carlos
  Bavarian RSO
  Bavarian State Opera Orch
  Bavarian State Orch
  Bayreuth Festival Orch
  Chicago SO
  Cologne RSO
  Dresden State Opera Orch
  La Scala Orch
  SDR SO
  South German RSO
  Stuttgart RSO
  Stuttgart SO
  Vienna PO
  Vienna State Opera Orch
  Vienna SO
  West German RSO
Kleiber, Erich
  Bavarian State Opera Orch
  Berlin PO
  Berlin State Opera Orch
  Buenos Aires Teatro Colón Orch
  Cologne RSO
  (Royal) Concertgebouw Orch
  Florence Maggio Musicale Orch
  Florence Teatro Comunale Orch
  London PO
  Vienna PO
  Vienna SO
Klein, Kenneth
  London PO
  New York Virtuosi Chamber SO
Kleinert, Rolf
  Berlin RSO
Klemens, Mario
  Philharmonia Cassovia
  Prague Fisyo
  Prague Musici
Klement, Miloslav
  Symposium Musicum
Klemperer, Otto
  Bavarian RSO
  Berlin PO
  Berlin RSO
  Berlin State Opera Orch
  Cologne Gürzenich Orch
  Cologne RSO
  (Royal) Concertgebouw Orch
  French National RSO
  Lamoureux Concerts Orch
  Los Angeles PO
  New Philharmonia Orch
  Philadelphia Orch
  Philharmonia Orch
  Royal Opera House Orch
  Vienna PO
  Vienna SO
Kletzki, Paul
  Berlin PO
  Czech PO
  French National RSO
  Philharmonia Orch
  Swiss Romande Orch
  Vienna PO
Klikar, Pavel
  Prague Musica Antiqua
Klima, A.
  Prague RSO
  Prague SO
Klobucar, Berislav
  Vienna State Opera Orch
Klochkov, Vivian
  Orthodox Ensemble
  Orthodox Vocal Ensemble

Klöcker, Dieter
  Consortium Classicum
Klopfenstein, Hervé
  Lausanne Conservatory Ensemble
  Lausanne Conservatory Orch
  Youth Orch
Knall, Klaus
  Evangelische Singgemeinde Choirs
Knappertsbusch, Hans
  Bavarian State Opera Orch
  Bavarian State Orch
  Bayreuth Festival Orch
  Berlin German Opera Orch
  Berlin PO
  Berlin State Opera Orch
  London PO
  Munich PO
  North German RSO
  Swiss Romande Orch
  Vienna PO
  Vienna State Opera Orch
Knight, Erin
  New World SO
Knothe, Dietrich
  Berlin Radio Chorus
  Berlin RSO
  Berlin Soloists
  Capella Lipsiensis
  Dresden Capella Sagittariana
Knüsel, G.
  Essen CO
Knussen, Oliver
  BBC SO
  Da Capo Chamber Players
  Capricorn
  Cleveland Orch
  Danish National RSO
  Danish SO
  Lincoln Center Chamber Music Society
  London Sinfonietta
  Nash Ensemble
  Tanglewood Music Center Orch
Kobayashi, Ken-Ichiro
  Czech PO
Kober, Dietrich
  Chicago SO
Kobera, Walter
  Vienna Amadeus Ensemble
Koch, Helmut
  Berlin CO
  Berlin RSO
Koch, Olaf
  Leipzig SO
  Pomorska PO
  Thüringen PO
  USSR SO
Kocsár, Balázs
  Budapest SO
Kocsár, M.
  Franz Liszt CO
Kocsis, Zoltán
  Budapest Wind Ensemble
  Tomkins Vocal Ensemble
Koelble, Rainer
  Amati Ensemble
Koetsier, Jan
  Bavarian RSO
Kogan, Pavel
  Hanover North German Radio PO
  Moscow SO
  Russian State SO
Köhler, Axel
  Lautten Company
Köhler, Lutz
  HR Brass
Köhler, Siegfried
  Berlin SO
  Cologne RSO
  Düsseldorf CO
  Luxembourg RSO
  Philharmonia Hungarica
  Royal Stockholm Orch
  Stuttgart PO
  Swedish RSO
Kohlhaussen, W.
  Fonte di Musica CO
Koivula, Hannu
  Danish Radio Concert Orch
Koizumi, Kazuhiro
  Royal PO
  Winnipeg SO
Kojian, Varujan
  Hong Kong PO
  Monte Carlo PO
  Utah SO
Kojoukhar, V.
  USSR State SO
Kolb, B.
  Brooklyn College Percussion Ensemble
Kolchinsky, Camilla
  Polish National RSO Katowice
Kollár, Eva
  Concerto Armonico Budapest
  Monteverdi Chamber Choir
Kolman, B. H.
  Slovak State PO Košice
Kolobov, Evgeni
  New Opera Theater Orch

Komatsu, Kazuhiko
  Vent d'Orient Ensemble
Komives, Janos
  Ensemble Opus 95
Komor, V.
  Hungarian State Opera Orch
Kondrashin, Kiril
  Bavarian RSO
  (Royal) Concertgebouw Orch
  Czech PO
  Dresden State Orch
  London SO
  Moscow PO
  Moscow Philharmonic SO
  Moscow State SO
  Moscow Youth Orch
  RCA Victor SO
  Russian State SO
  Symphony of the Air
  USSR Radio-TV Large SO
  USSR State Orch
  USSR SO
  Vienna PO
Kongsted, Ole
  Capella Hafniensis
König, Gustav
  Berlin RIAS SO
König, Robert
  Bayreuth Festival Orch
  Bayreuth Festival Orch members
Kontarev, Vladimir
  Komi Republic Russian Chamber Choir
Konvalinka, Miloš
  Prague SO
Konwitschny, Franz
  Berlin RSO
  Berlin Staatskapelle
  Berlin State Opera Orch
  Dresden Staatskapelle
  Leipzig Gewandhaus Orch
  Leipzig Opera Orch
  Leipzig RSO
Koopman, Ton
  Amsterdam Baroque Orch
  Amsterdam Baroque Soloists
  Netherlands Chamber Choir
  Residentie Orch The Hague
  The Hague PO
Kopelman, Jozef
  Bratislava Chamber Soloists
  Capella Istropolitana
Kopilov, Aleksandr
  Bolshoi Theater Orch
Korchin, Leo
  Peterhoff Orch
  Renaissance CO
Kord, Kaziemierz
  Aventure Ensemble
  Polish National PO
  Southwest German RSO Baden-Baden
  Southwest German SO
  Warsaw National Philharmonic SO
  Warsaw PO
Korf, Anthony
  Parnassus Ensemble
Korkhin, Leo
  Collegium dell'Arte
  Orch del'Arte
  Peterhoff Orch
  Renaissance CO
Korn, Michael
  Concerto Soloists Instrumental Ensemble
  Philadelphia Singers
Korneiev, Alexander
  Moscow Chamber Ensemble
  Moscow Radio-TV SO
Körner, Ewald
  Slovak PO
Korngold, Erich Wolfgang
  Warner Brothers Orch
Korniev, Nikolai
  St. Petersburg Chamber Choir
Kórodi, Andras
  Budapest National Opera Orch
  Budapest PO
  Budapest SO
  Hungarian State Opera Orch
Koshouharov, I.
  Sofia Camerata Classica
Košler, Zdenek
  Czech PO
  Prague National Theater Orch
  Prague RSO
  Prague SO
  Prague SO members
  Slovak PO
  Slovak Radio Sym CO
  Talich String Quartet
Kostelanetz, André
  Columbia SO
  Kostelanetz Orch
  New York Philharmonic SO
  New York PO
  Philadelphia Orch
Kotik, Petr
  S.E.M. Ensemble Orch
Kotmel, Bohumil
  Czech PO

Koussevitzky, Serge
  Boston SO
Kout, Jiří
  Prague RSO
Koutnik, Tomáš
  Prague SO
  Slovak Radio Sym CO
Kovacevich, Stephen
  Australian CO
  Liverpool PO
  Royal Liverpool PO
Kovacic, Ernst
  Scottish CO
Kovács, János
  Budapest PO
  Hungarian State Opera Orch
  Hungarian State Orch
Kovalov, Alexey
  Moscow RSO
Kovatchev, Julian
  Sofia Festival Orch
  Trieste Teatro Comunale Giuseppe Verdi Orch
  Turin PO
Kozhouharov, I.
  Sofia Camerata Classica
  Sofia New Chamber Ensemble
Kozhukar, Vladimir
  USSR SO
  USSR SO String Group
Kraemer, Nikolas
  Capella Coloniensis
  London Sinfonietta
  Raglan Baroque Players
Kraft, William
  Los Angeles Percussion Ensemble
  Pittsburgh New Music Ensemble
  Voices of Change
Kralev, Stoyan
  Madrigal Chamber Ensemble
  Sofia Solisti CO
  Sofia Madrigal Ensemble
Kramer, G.
  Convivium Musicum Vindobonense
Kramer, Leo
  Belarus Minsk State PO
Kranjcevic, Vladimir
  Belgrade Radio–TV Chorus
Kraus, Herbert
  Vienna Mozart Ensemble
Kraus, Richard
  Bamberg SO
  Bayreuth Festival Orch
  Berlin PO
  Berlin RSO
  Cologne RSO
  West German Orch
Krauss, Clemens
  Bavarian State Opera Orch
  Bayreuth Festival Orch
  Berlin Reich RSO
  Stuttgart RSO
  Vienna PO
  Vienna State Opera Orch
  Vienna SO
Krautgartner, Karel
  Krautgartner Orch
Krček, Jaroslav
  Capella Istropolitana
  Musica Bohemica
Kročmor, Rudolf
  Bamberg SO
Kreder, Jean-Paul
  Nouvel PO
  ORTF Lyric Orch
Kreisler, Alexander von
  Cincinnati SO
Krenz, Jan
  Cracow Polish Radio-TV Orch
  Polish National RSO Katowice
  Polish National SO
  Sinfonia Varsovia String Ensemble
  Warsaw PO
Krimets, Konstantin
  Davydov SO
  Moscow SO
Krips, Josef
  London SO
  Prague CO
  RCA Victor SO
  Royal PO
  Symphony of the Air
  Vienna Festival Orch
  Vienna PO
  Vienna State Opera Orch
  Zurich Tonhalle Orch
Krivine, Emmanuel
  Bamberg SO
  Lyon National Chorus
  Lyon National Orch
  Netherlands CO
  Netherlands PO
  Philharmonia Orch
  Royal PO
  Sinfonia Varsovia
  Warsaw Sinfonia
Krombholc, Jaroslav
  Brno State PO
  Czech PO

Krombholc, Jaroslav (cont.)
  Munich RSO
  Prague National Theater Orch
  Prague RSO
Kröper, Andreas
  Prague Concertino Nutturno
Kubelik, Rafael
  Academy of St. Martin in the Fields
  Bavarian RSO
  Bavarian State Opera Orch
  Berlin PO
  Boston SO
  Chicago SO
  Czech PO
  Danish National RSO
  Philharmonia Orch
  Prague RSO
  Prague SO
  Royal Opera House Orch
  La Scala Orch
  Stockholm PO
  Turin RAI SO
  Vienna PO
Kuchar, Theodore
  Queensland SO
  Ukrainian National SO
  Ukrainian State SO
Kuentz, Paul
  Kuentz CO
  Paul Kuentz Orch
Kuhn, Bruson G.
  Dresden Staatskapelle
Kuhn, Gustav
  Bamberg SO
  Berlin RIAS Sinfonietta
  Berlin RSO
  Danish National RSO
  Marchigiana PO
  Munich RSO
  Salzburg Mozarteum Orch
Kühn, Pavel
  Czech PO
  Czech Radio Chorus
  Kühn Chamber Soloists
  Kühn Chorus
  Kühn Women's Chorus
  Prague CO
  Prague Radio Men's Chorus
  Prague Sinfonietta
  Prague SO
  Prague SO members
  Symposium Musicum
Kuijken, Barthold
  Octophorus
Kuijken, Sigiswald
  Orch of the Age of Enlightenment
  La Petite Bande
Kuijpers, Pierre
  Dutch Royal Military Band
Kujawsky, Eric
  Redwood Sym
Kulesha, Gary
  Composers Orch
Kuliberg, Erling
  Da Camera Choir
Kulinsky, Bohumil
  Bambini di Praga
  Prague Fisyo
  Prague PO
  Prague SO
Kulka, Janos
  Berlin PO
Kulling, Arthur
  Festspiel Orch members
Kuntzsch, Matthias
  Bochum SO
  Stuttgart PO
Kunzel, Erich
  Cincinnati Jazz Orch
  Cincinnati Pops Orch
  Cincinnati SO
  London SO
  Orch of St. Luke's
  Rochester Pops Orch
  Winnipeg SO
Kupferman, Meyer
  Bronx Arts Ensemble
  Music in the Mountains Festival Chamber Players
Kurczewski, Jerzy
  Ponzan Boys' Choir
Kurilo, Svetlana
  Kharkov Church of the Three Saints Choir
Kuroiwa, H.
  Hiroshima SO
Kurtz, Efram
  Philharmonia Chorus
  Philharmonia Orch
  Philharmonic SO
  Royal PO
Kurz, Dieter
  Stuttgart Ensemble
  Württemberg CO
Kussmaul, Jürgen
  Amsterdam Mozart Players
Kussmaul, Rainer
  Amsterdam Bach Soloists
Kuyiyama, Fumiaki
  Chorale OMP

Kvam, Terje
  Hanover Band
  Oslo Cathedral Choir
Kyhle, H.
  Stockholm Univ College of Music Orch
La Montaine, John
  Fredonia Singers
Labadie, Bernard
  Les Violons du Roy
  Walloon CO
Lacasse, M.
  Prefontaine Montreal Choeur Classique
Lajovic, Uros
  Berlin Radio Sinfonietta
  Berlin RSO
Lambert, Constant
  City of Birmingham SO
  Hallé Orch
  London PO
  Philharmonia Orch
  Royal Opera House Orch
  Sadler's Wells Opera Orch
Lambrecht, Heinz
  Vienna Volksoper Orch
Lamminmäki, Juhani
  Espoo CO
Lamneck, Esther
  New York Univ New Music Ensemble
Lamon, Jeanne
  Tafelmusik
Lamprecht, Franz
  Targu-Mures PO
Lampson, E.
  Hamburg Academy Orch
Lancelot, James
  Durham Cathedral Choir
Lanchbery, John
  Philharmonia Orch
  Royal Opera House Orch
Landau, Seigfried
  Westchester SO
  Westphalia SO
  Westphalia SO Recklinghausen
Landowski, Marcel
  Boulogne-Billancourt Orch Conservatory
  Colonne Association des Concerts Orch
  Harmonia Nova Orch Ensemble
  L'Itinéraire Ensemble
  Paris Conservatory Société des Concerts Orch
Lane, Louis
  Atlanta SO
  Cleveland Orch
  Cleveland Sinfonietta
Lanev, Emil
  Sofia SO
Lange, Mathieu
  Vienna Pro Musica Orch
Langstaff, John
  Revels Company
Länsiö, Tapani
  Polytech Choir
Lantos, Rezső
  Hungarian State Folk Ensemble Orch
Lanzillotta, Luigi
  Musica d'Oggi
Lara, Francisco
  Santo Domingo de Silos Benedictine Monks' Choir
Laredo, Jaime
  Scottish CO
Larsen, Ove Vedsten
  Aarhus CO
Larsson, C. Rune
  Stockholm PO
Lascae, Alexandru
  Arion Ensemble
  Moldavian PO
  Moldova Philharmonia
Lasserre, Françoise
  Champagne-Ardenne Akademia Regional Vocal Ensemble
  La Fenice Ensemble
Latham-König, Jan
  Cologne RSO
  Danish National RSO
  König Ensemble
  London PO
  Lucca Teatro Comunale del Giglio Orch
  Milan RAI SO
  Rome Opera Orch
  Venice Teatro La Fenice Orch
Latoszewski, Zygmunt
  Polish National RSO Katowice
  Warsaw Opera Orch
Laus, Michael
  Bournemouth SO
Lavigueur, Louis
  Louis Lavigueur Instrumental Ensemble
Law, Brian
  Thirteen Strings of Ottawa
Lawrence, Ashley
  BBC Concert Orch
  BBC Singers
Lawrence, Douglas
  Ormond College Choir Melbourne
Lawrence, Robert
  American Opera Society Orch
Lawrence-King, Andrew
  Harp Consort

Layer, Friedemann
  Montpellier Languedoc–Roussillon PO

Layfield, Malcolm
  Goldberg Ensemble
  London Bach Orch

Layton, Stephen
  Holst Singers
  London Choral Society
  London Schubert Chorale
  Polyphony

Lazar, Matthew
  Washington Music Ensemble
  Western Wind

Lazarev, Alexander
  BBC SO
  Bolshoi SO
  Bolshoi Theater Ensemble Soloists
  Bolshoi Theater Orch
  Bolshoi Theater SO Soloists
  Lausanne CO
  London PO
  Moscow PO
  USSR Radio–TV Large SO

Lazarof, Henri
  New Philharmonia Orch
  Utah SO

Leaper, Adrian
  Bratislava RSO
  Capella Istropolitana
  CSSR State PO Košice
  Czech State PO
  Czech–Slovak RSO Bratislava
  Gran Canaria PO
  Irish National SO
  London PO
  Polish National RSO Katowice
  Royal PO
  Slovak PO

LeBaron, Anne
  New Music Consort

Lecaudey, Jean-Pierre
  Orch de Chambre 13

Leck, Henry H.
  Indianapolis Children's Choir

Leconte, Jean–Michel
  French National RSO
  ORTF Lyric Orch

Ledger, Philip
  Academy of St. Martin in the Fields
  English CO
  King's College Choir Cambridge
  London Early Music Consort
  London Mozart Players
  London PO

Leeuw, Rienbert de
  Asko Ensemble
  The Hague Percussion Group
  Hilversum RSO
  Netherlands Chamber Choir
  Netherlands Radio CO
  Netherlands Wind Ensemble
  Schoenberg Ensemble
  Arnold Schoenberg Male Choir

Le Feuvre
  St. Anne de Kergonan Abbey Monks' Choir

Leger, Jean–Louis
  Hradec Kralove PO

Legrand, Michel
  Large SO
  Philharmonia Orch
  Prague PO

Lehár, Franz
  Vienna PO
  Vienna RSO
  Vienna SO
  Zurich RSO

Lehel, György
  Basel RSO
  Budapest RSO
  Budapest SO
  Czech PO
  Hungarian RSO
  Vienna SO

Lehmann, Wilfred
  Queensland SO

Leibowitz, René
  International SO
  London Festival Orch
  Paris Conservatory Société des Concerts Orch
  Paris Société des Concerts SO
  Pasdeloup Concerts Association Orch
  Royal PO
  Vienna State Opera Orch

Leiferkus, Sergei
  London Musici

Leifsson, Hákon
  Icelandic SO

Leighton Smith, Lawrence
  Debussy Trio
  London SO
  Louisville Orch
  Moscow PO

Leiner, Peter
  Contemporano Ensemble

Leinsdorf, Erich
  Boston SO
  Chicago SO
  Concert Arts SO

Leinsdorf, Erich (cont.)
  Czech PO
  London Phil SO
  London SO
  Los Angeles PO
  Metropolitan Opera Orch
  New Philharmonia Orch
  Philharmonia Orch
  Pittsburgh SO
  RCA Italian Opera Orch
  Rome Opera Orch
  Vienna PO

Leitner, Ferdinand
  Bâle SO
  Bavarian RSO
  Bavarian State Opera Orch
  Berlin PO
  Cappella Coloniensis
  Milan RAI SO
  Munich PO
  Residentie Orch The Hague
  Vienna SO

Leitner, Konrad
  Vienna Mozart Orch

Lenárd, Ondrej
  Bratislava RSO
  Czech RSO
  Czech SO
  Czech–Slovak RSO
  Czech–Slovak RSO Bratislava
  Czech–Slovak State Radio PO
  Polish State PO
  Slovak PO
  Slovak Radio Sym CO
  Slovak RSO Bratislava
  Vienna Strauss Festival Orch

Lencsés, Lajos
  South German Chamber Soloists

León, Tania
  Continuum Chamber Ensemble
  Musicians' Accord
  Musicians' Accord members
  Western Wind

Leonard, Peter
  Louisville Orch

Leonhard, Carl
  Stuttgart Radio Orch
  Stuttgart Reichssenders Orch

Leonhardt, Gustav
  Baroque Orch
  Leonhardt Consort
  Netherlands Bach Society Baroque Orch
  Orch of the Age of Enlightenment
  La Petite Bande

Lepak, Alexander
  Hartt Percussion Ensemble

Leppard, Raymond
  BBC Northern SO
  BBC SO
  Danske Strings members
  English CO
  Indianapolis SO
  Franz Liszt CO
  London PO
  National PO London
  New Philharmonia Orch
  Paris Lyon Opera Orch
  Prague CO
  Royal PO
  Santa Fe Opera Orch
  Scottish CO
  Turin RAI SO

Lerdahl, Fred
  Collage New Music Ensemble

LeRoux, J.-L.
  ORTF National Orch
  Performing Arts Orch
  San Francisco Contemporary Music Players

Leskovich, Bogo
  Rome RAI SO

Lesne, Brigitte
  Alla Francesca
  Discantus

Lesne, Gérard
  Il Seminario Musicale

Letonja, Marko
  Italian International Opera Orch

Letzbor, Gunar
  Ars Antiqua Austria

Levi, Yoel
  Atlanta SO
  Cleveland Orch
  London PO
  Philharmonia Orch

Levick, John
  Nebraska CO

Levine, David
  Cologne Classique Ensemble

Levine, Gilbert
  Berlin PO
  Berlin RSO
  Cracow PO
  English CO
  Royal PO

Levine, James
  Berlin PO
  Berlin SO
  Chicago SO
  Dresden Staatskapelle

Levine, James (cont.)
  English CO
  London SO
  Metropolitan Opera Orch
  Vienna PO

Levine, Joel
  Bayreuth Festival Orch
  Berlin PO
  Berlin SO
  Metropolitan Orch
  National PO London
  Philadelphia Orch
  Philharmonia Orch
  Ravinia Festival Ensemble
  Vienna PO
  Xalapa SO

Lewis, Anthony
  Academy of Ancient Music
  Brandenburg Consort
  St. Cecilia Academy Orch Rome

Lewis, Daniel
  Univ of Southern California SO

Lewis, Henry
  Milan RAI SO
  Rome RAI SO
  Royal PO
  Swiss Romande Orch
  Turin RSO

Lewis, J. Reilly
  Washington Bach Consort
  Washington National Cathedral Choral Society

Lewis, R. H.
  London PO
  London Sinfonietta
  London Sinfonietta Chorus
  Philharmonia Chamber Artists
  Philharmonia Orch
  Royal PO

Lewis, Vic
  Royal PO

Liang-Sheng, C.
  Geneva SO

Licata, Andrea
  Catania Teatro Massimo Bellini Orch
  Royal PO

Lief, Arthur
  New York CO

Lifchitz, Max
  Bronx Arts Ensemble
  North/South Consonance Ensemble

Ligeti, András
  Budapest PO
  Budapest SO
  Concentus Hungaricus
  Hungarian State Orch

Lilienthal, A.-H.
  Zurich Chamber Soloists

Lilje, Peeter
  Estonia Opera Company Orch
  Estonian SO

Liljefors, Mats
  Gävelborg SO
  St. Petersburg Hermitage Orch

Lindberg, Jacob
  Dowland Consort
  Drottningholm Baroque Ensemble

Linde, Hans–Martin
  Basel Schola Cantorum Instrumental Ensemble
  Cappella Coloniensis
  Chiaroscuro Ensemble
  Linde Consort

Ling, Jahja
  Royal PO
  Scottish CO

Lipkin, Arthur Bennett
  Oslo PO
  Royal PO

Litkov, Samuel
  Baltic CO
  St. Petersburg Festival Orch

Litschauer, Franz
  Vienna State Opera Men's Chorus

Litsova, L.
  Maîtrise de la Loire
  Saratov Phil Choir

Litton, Andrew
  Bournemouth SO
  Dallas SO
  English CO
  London PO
  Royal PO

Litton, James
  American Boychoir
  American SO
  Eighteenth Century Ensemble

Litvin, Carol
  Romanian RSO
  Romanian Radio–TV Orch

Lizzio, Alberto
  London Festival Orch
  Mozart Festival Orch
  Naples Solisti
  Philharmonia Slavonica
  San Marco Musici

Llewellyn, Grant
  BBC Welsh National SO
  Royal Flanders PO
  Royal Liverpool Orch

Llewellyn Jones, Brynmour
  Berlin Chamber Opera Orch
  Scharoun Ensemble
Lloyd, George
  Albany SO
  BBC Philharmonic Brass
  BBC PO
  Bournemouth SO
  City of London Sinfonia
  London SO
  Philharmonia Orch
  Welsh National Opera Orch
Lloyd-Jones, David
  English Northern Philharmonia
  French Radio Lyric Orch
  RTE Sinfonietta
Lloyd-Korsakov, David
  English Northern Philharmonia
Lockhart, James
  London PO
  Rhenish PO
  Rhine State PO
  Royal PO
Lockhart, Keith
  Boston Pops Orch
  Cincinnati CO
Loehrer, Edwin
  Lugano Chamber Society Chorus
  Lugano Chamber Society Instrumental Ensemble
  Lugano Chamber Society Orch
  Swiss-Italian Radio Chorus
  Swiss-Italian Radio-TV Orch
Logemann, Sally
  New York Renaissance Band
Loguin, Anders
  Falu Woodwind Quintet
  Kroumata Percussion Ensemble
  Omnibus Chamber Winds
Loibner, Wilhelm
  Vienna State Opera Orch
Lombard, Alain
  Bordeaux-Aquitaine National Orch
  Paris Opéra-Comique Orch
  Paris Opera Orch
  Residentie Orch The Hague
  Strasbourg PO
Lombardo, Fabio
  Gruppo Polifonico
  L'Homme Armé
Londeix, J.-M.
  International Saxophone Ensemble
London, Edwin
  Cleveland Chamber SO
  Ineluctable Modality
  Russian State SO
  Gregg Smith Singers
  Univ of Illinois Contemporary Chamber Players
Longhini, Marco
  Delitiæ Musicae Instrumental Ensemble
  Le Institutioni Harmoniche
  Verona Istitutioni Harmoniche
Loöcker, D.
  Consortium Classicum
Loomer, Diane
  Leoni Men's Chorus
Loosli, Théo
  Bern Chamber Ensemble
  Bern Radio Chamber Ensemble
  Bern Sinfonietta
  Bern SO
  Neuchâtelois SO
López-Cobos, Jesús
  Berlin RSO
  Cincinnati SO
  Lausanne CO
  New Philharmonia Orch
  Philharmonia Orch
  Royal PO
Lore, J.-P.
  French Oratorio Orch
  St. Yves Choral Association
  Guy Touvron Brass Ensemble
Loughran, James
  BBC SO
  Hallé Orch
  Philharmonia Orch
Löwlein, Hans
  Berlin State Opera Orch
Loy, M.
  Frankenland State SO
Lozano, Fernando
  Carlos Chávez SO
  Mexican State SO
  Mexico City PO
Lü, Shao-Chia
  New Russia Orch
Lubbock, John
  Orch of St. John
  St. John's Smith Square Orch
Lubin, Steven
  Mozartean Players
Lubman, Bradley
  June in Buffalo CO
  Tanglewood Music Center Fellows
Lucas, Andrew
  St. Paul's Cathedral Choir
Lucier, Alvin
  Brandeis Univ Chamber Chorus

Ludwig, Leopold
  Berlin RSO
  Dresden State Orch
  Hamburg State PO
  London SO
  North German RSO
  Vienna State Opera Orch
Ludwig, Thomas
  London SO
Luisi, Fabio
  Berlin German Opera Orch
  Emilia Romagna Arturo Toscanini SO
  Munich RSO
Lukács, Ervin
  Budapest SO
  Györ PO
  Hungarian State Opera Orch
  Hungarian State Orch
  Franz Liszt CO
Lukas, Viktor
  Lukas Consort
Lukáš, Z.
  Prague Chamber Soloists
Lukaszewski, Jan
  Schola Cantorum Gedanensis
Lumsden, Andrew
  Lichfield Cathedral Choir
Lumsden, David
  New College Choir Oxford
Lutoslawski, Witold
  BBC SO
  Polish National RSO Katowice
  Warsaw CO
  Warsaw PO
Lyndon-Gee, Christopher
  New Zealand SO
Lyng, Per
  Stockholm Symphonic Wind Orch
Lysy, Alberto
  Aquiles Delle-Vigne
  Camerata Lysy Gstaad
Maag, Peter
  Bamberg SO
  Bern SO
  Buenos Aires Teatro Colón Orch
  English CO
  London SO
  Naples Teatro San Carlo Orch
  New Philharmonia Orch
  Padua & Venice CO
  Philharmonia Hungarica
  La Scala Orch
  Turin RAI SO
  Venice PO
  Venice Teatro La Fenice Orch
  Vienna Volksoper Orch
Maazel, Lorin
  Bavarian RSO
  Berlin German Opera Orch
  Berlin PO
  Berlin RSO
  Cleveland Orch
  English CO
  French National Orch
  Lamoureux Orch
  London National PO
  London PO
  London SO
  Naples Alessandro Scarlatti RAI Orch
  New Philharmonia Orch
  Orch de Paris
  Orch National
  ORTF Orch
  Paris Opera Orch
  Philharmonia Orch
  Pittsburgh SO
  Rome RAI Orch
  Rome RAI SO
  St. Cecilia Academy Orch Rome
  La Scala Orch
  Vienna PO
  Vienna State Opera Orch
Macal, Zdenek
  London PO
  Milwaukee Sym Chorus
  Milwaukee SO
  New Jersey SO
  Philharmonia Orch
  Royal PO
McArthur, Edwin
  RCA Victor SO
  San Francisco Opera Orch
McCarthy, John
  London SO
  Royal PO
  Venice Solisti
McCreesh, Paul
  Gabrieli Consort
  Gabrieli Players
McCulloch, Derek
  Collegium Sagittarii
McCullogh, Donald
  McCullough Chorale
MacDonald, Ken
  Hawthorn Band–Australia's Champions
MacDonally, Capt.
  West Point Military Band

McFerrin, Bobby
  St. Paul CO
McGegan, Nicholas
  Arcadian Academy
  Capella Savaria
  English Bach Baroque Orch
  Freiburg Baroque Orch
  London SO
  Philharmonia Baroque Orch
  Romanesca
McGlaughlin, William
  Kansas City SO
McGlinn, John
  London Sinfonietta
  London Sinfonietta National PO
  New Princess Theater Orch
Machek, Miloš Alexander
  Bohuslav Martinů Philharmonic Brass
  Bonuslav Martinů PO
  Percussion Ensemble
McIntosh, Thomas
  London CO
Mackay, Andrew
  Sarum Consort
Mackerras, Charles
  Australian CO
  Basel SO
  BBC SO
  Brno State PO
  Czech PO
  Danish National RSO
  English CO
  London PO
  London SO
  New Philharmonia Orch
  Orch of St. Luke's
  Orch of St. Luke's members
  Orch of the Age of Enlightenment
  Paris Opera Orch
  Philharmonia Orch
  Prague CO
  Prague RSO
  Prague SO
  Royal Liverpool PO
  Royal PO
  San Francisco Opera Orch
  Scottish CO
  Vienna PO
  Vienna State Opera Orch
  Welsh National Opera Orch
Mackey, Steven
  San Francisco Contemporary Music Players
Mackintosh, Catherine
  Orch of the Age of Enlightenment
  Purcell Sinfony
McLeod, J.
  Polish Radio-TV SO
MacMillan, Ernest
  Toronto SO
MacMillan, James
  London CO
  Polyphony
  Royal Scottish National Orch
  Scottish CO
McMurrin, R.
  Coral Ridge Orch
McNeely, Joel
  Seattle SO
McPhee, Jonathan
  Boston Ballet Orch
  Griffin Music Ensemble
McRae, Paul Anthony
  Lake Forest SO
  London SO
Macura, Stanislav
  Czech PO
Maczewski, Winfried
  (Royal) Concertgebouw Orch
Maderna, Bruno
  Austrian RSO
  Bavarian RSO
  BBC SO
  Darmstadt International Chamber Ensemble
  Hilversum NOS Radio Orch
  Milan RAI SO
  North German RSO
  Rome RAI Orch
  Rome RAI SO
Maestri, Fabio
  In Canto CO
  Marchigiana PO String Group
  Musica d'Oggi
  Terni CO
Maga, Othmar
  Bamberg SO
  Bochum SO
  Philharmonia Hungarica
Maghini, Ruggero
  Milano Angelicum CO
Mägi, Paul
  Estonia Opera Company Orch
Magiera, Leone
  Modena Teatro Comunale Orch
Mahler, Fritz
  Hartford CO
  Hartford SO
Maier, Franzjosef
  Collegium Aureum

Maier, Franzjosef (cont.)
Montserrat Escolania
Maile, Hans
Berlin RSO
Maisky, Mischa
CO of Europe
Majone, R.
Turin RAI Orch
Maksymiuk, Jerzy
BBC Scottish SO
German Youth PO
Irish National SO
London PO
Polish CO
Polish National SO
Polish Radio-TV SO
Polish RSO
Malajoli, L.
La Scala Orch
Malát, Jiří
Pilsen RSO
Malcolm, George
English CO
Northern Sinfonia of England
Scottish CO
Malgoire, Jean-Claude
La Chambre du Roy
Compañia Musical de las Americas
English Bach Festival Orch
La Grande Ecurie et la Chambre du Roy
National CO
Venice Solisti
Malko, Nicolai
Philharmonia Orch
Malloch, William
Boston Early Music Soloists
Mallon, Kevin
Aradia Baroque Ensemble
Malov, Oleg
St. Petersburg Soloists
Maltsev, Anatoly
Red Army Chorus
USSR Ministry of Defense Orch
Maly, Milan
Prague National Theater Orch
Manahan, George
Richmond Sinfonia
Mancini, Henry
London SO
Mancini Pops Orch
Mandeal, Cristian
Cluj-Napoca PO
Mandrin, Emmanuel
Les Demoiselles de Saint-Cyr
Manduchi, Bonifacio
Fabio de Bologne Polyphonic Chorus
Mangiocavallo, Luigi
Academia Montis Regalis
Manley, Paul
Primavera CO
Mann, Tor
Stockholm PO
Swedish RSO
Manneke, Daan
Cappella Breda
Mannino, Franco
Milan RAI Orch
National Arts Center Canada Orch
Turin RAI Orch
Manolov, Dimiter
Philharmonia Bulgarica
Sofia National Opera Orch
Manos, George
National Gallery Vocal Arts Ensemble
Mansorov, Fuat
USSR Radio-TV Large SO
Mantle, Neil
Royal Scottish National Orch
Mantovani, Annunzio Paulo
Mantovani Orch
Manzano, Alvaro
Ecuador National SO
Manze, Andrew
Cologne La Stravaganza
Concerto Copenhagen
Mar, Norman del
BBC SO
Bournemouth Sinfonietta
City of Birmingham SO
London PO
New Philharmonia Orch
Philharmonia Orch
Royal PO
Marasch, Arkadi
Hallé Collegium Instrumentale
Marbà, Antoni Ros
Tenerife SO
Marchbank, Peter
South African Broadcasting Corp National SO
Marchi, Alessandro de
Armonico Theater Ensemble
Berlin Baroque Academy
Eufonia
Sigismondo D'India
Marchwicka, Ewa
Warsaw PO
Marco, Patrick
Budapest Orfeo Orch
Bernard Thomas CO

Mardirosian, Haig
St. Thomas Moore Cathedral Orch
Mardjani, Jahni
Georgian Festival Orch
Maresco, Carlo
Philadelphia Opera Orch
Margolis, Melvin
Fine Arts CO
Margraf, Horst-Tanu
Halle Handel Festival Orch
Mari, Jean-Baptiste
Paris Opera Orch
Marin, Ion
English CO
London SO
Philharmonia Orch
Venice Teatro La Fenice Orch
Vienna SO
Marinotti, B.
RTSI Orch
Marinov, Ivan
Bulgarian RSO
Sofia State PO
Sofia SO
Marinuzzi, Gino
EIAR Orch
Markevitch, Igor
Berlin PO
Japan PO
Lamoureux Concerts Orch
Lamoureux Orch
Lamoureux Orch members
Leipzig Gewandhaus Orch
London SO
Monte Carlo Opera Orch
Philharmonia Orch
Russian Radio Orch
Spanish National Radio-TV SO
Markiz, Lev
Amsterdam New Sinfonietta
Malmö SO
Malmö SO Chamber Ensemble
New Stockholm CO
Stockholm CO
Markowski, Andrzej
National PO London
Warsaw PO
Warsaw Philharmonic SO
Markson, Gerhard
Hagen PO
Irish National SO
Saarbrück RSO
Marlow, Richard
Fretwork
London Musici
Trinity College Choir Cambridge
Maros, Miklos
Strängnäs Sinfonietta Ensemble
Marosi, László
Budapest Symphonic Band
Marriner, Neville
Academy of St. Martin in the Fields
Academy of St. Martin in the Fields Chamber Ensemble
Cleveland Orch
German Bach Soloists
Holliger Wind Ensemble
Leipzig Gewandhaus Orch
London Festival Orch
London SO
London Strings
Los Angeles CO
Minnesota Orch
Netherlands Wind Ensemble
Northern Sinfonia of England
Philharmonia Orch
St. Mary's Chamber Players
Stuttgart Radio Orch
Stuttgart RSO
Marschik, Peter
Academy of London Orch
Marshall, Wayne
Aalborg SO
Marszalek
Cologne Radio Orch
Cologne RSO
Operetta Orch
Martignon, Claudio
Padua & Venice CO
Martin, Carolann
Arioso CO
Bournemouth Sinfonietta
Martin, Frank
Berlin PO
Lausanne CO
Luxembourg RSO
Swiss-Italian Orch
Martin, Karl
Musica d'Oggi
Martinez, Odaline de la
BBC PO
Lontano
Martini, Alberto
I Filarmonici
Accademia I Filarmonici
Martini, Jean
Buenos Aires Teatro Colón Orch
Frankfurt Baroque Orch

Martini, Louis
Jean-François Paillard CO
Martinon, Jean
French National Orch
French National RSO
Lamoureux Orch
ORTF National Orch
ORTF Orch
Orch de Paris
Paris Conservatory Societé des Concerts Orch
Martinotti, Bruno
Milan RAI SO
Martland, Steve
Steve Martland Band
Marturet, Eduardo
Berlin SO
Marty, Jean-Pierre
ORTF Lyric Orch
Martynov, Ravil
St. Petersburg State SO
Märzendorfer, Ernst
Austrian RSO
Berlin PO
Berlin RSO
Hungarian State Orch
Vienna CO
Vienna PO
Mascagni, Pietro
Berlin State Opera Orch
Holland Italian Opera Orch
La Scala Orch
Turin RSO
Masini, Gian-Franco
Barcelona SO
Grudgionz Festival Orch
Grudgionz Opera Theater Orch
Montpellier PO
ORTF Orch
Toscanini SO
Trieste Teatro Comunale Giuseppe Verdi Orch
Venezze di Rovigo Conservatory of Music Orch
Vienna SO
Mason, Capt. John R.
HM Royal Marines Band
Mason, David
Combattimento
London Sinfonietta
Massey, Roy
Hereford Cathedral Choir
Massini, Egizio
Romanian Opera Orch
Masson, Diego
Musique Vivante Ensemble
West Australian SO
Masur, Kurt
Atlanta SO
Czech PO
Dresden PO
Leipzig Gewandhaus Orch
Leipzig Opera Orch
London PO
New York PO
Mata, Eduardo
Simón Bolívar SO
La Camerata
Dallas SO
Frankfurt RSO
Latin American String Quartet
London SO
Mexican Soloists
New Philharmonia Orch
Philharmonia Orch
Swiss CO
Tambuco Camerata
Matačić, Lovro von
Lausanne CO
Philharmonia Orch
Vienna State Opera Orch
Matfei, Archmandrite
Trinity-St. Sergius Laura Monks' Choir
Troitse-Sergeyev Monastery Chorus
Matheson, John
BBC Concert Orch
Mathias, William
BBC Welsh National SO
Mathiesen, Askel
Denmark Concentus Musicus
Mathieson, Muir
London SO
London Sinfonia
Matl, Lubomir
Bordeaux-Aquitaine National Orch
Czech Phil Chorus
Czech PO
Dvořák CO
Irish National SO
Matsuo, Masataka
Hamilton College Orch
Matsuoka, Hakaru
Osaka PO
Mattes, Willy
Graunke SO
Mattran, Donald
Hartt Jazz Ensemble
Matukhov, Igor
Byelorussion Radio-TV SO
Matwej, Archmandrite
Moscow Religious Academy & Seminary

Matwej, Archmandrite (cont.)
 Zagorsk Monastery Monks' Choir
Matz, Peter
 New World SO
Mauceri, John
 Berlin German SO
 Berlin RIAS Chamber Ensemble
 Berlin RIAS Sinfonietta
 Berlin RSO
 Hollywood Bowl Orch
 Hollywood Bowl SO
 London SO
 New York City Opera Orch
 Scottish Opera Orch
Mauersberger, Rudolf
 Capella Fidicinia Dresden
 Dresden Church Choir
 Dresden Instrumental Ensemble
 Dresden Kreuz Choir
 Dresden PO Instrumental Group
 Dresden State Orch
 Leipzig Gewandhaus Orch
Maunas, Michel
 Pau Orch
Max, Hermann
 Das Kleine Konzert
Max, Robert
 Zemel Choir
Maxym, Robert
 Folkwang CO
Mayer, Uri
 Edmonton SO
 London Canada Orch
Mays, Walter
 Wichita State Univ Faculty Ensemble
Mazzucato, Giorgi
 Rovigo City Chorus
Measham, David
 London SO
 Melbourne SO
 National PO
 West Australian SO
Medina, Jesus
 Mexico International PO
Meditz, Gert
 New Vienna Soloists
Medlam, Charles
 London Baroque
 London Cornett & Sackbutt Ensemble
Medveczky, Adám
 Residentie Orch The Hague
Mefano, Paul
 Lyon Orch
 2E2M Ensemble
Megens, Wim
 De Ereprijs Orch
Mehl, Arnold
 Munich Bach Trumpet Ensemble
Mehrpohl, Udo
 Bavarian RSO
Mehta, M.
 American Youth SO
Mehta, Zubin
 Bavarian State Opera Orch
 Berlin PO
 Florence Maggio Musicale Orch
 Israel PO
 Israel PO members
 London PO
 Los Angeles PO
 New Philharmonia Orch
 New York PO
 New York PO Ensemble
 Rome Opera Orch
 Royal Opera House Orch Covent Garden
 Vienna PO
Meier, Jost
 Basel RSO
 Basel SO
 Biel Orchestral Society
 Da Camera Choir
 Prague Brixi CO
Meister, Christoph
 Prague Brixi CO
Meisters, Ine
 Trieste Teatro Comunale Giuseppe Verdi Orch
Melia, Roland
 St. Petersburg Chamber Ensemble
Melik-Pashayev, Alexander
 Bolshoi Opera Orch
 Bolshoi Theater Orch
Melkus, Eduard
 Vienna Capella Academica
Melles, Karl
 Vienna SO
Mellon, Agnès
 Il Seminario Musicale
Melville, Alan G.
 City of London Sinfonia
 English CO
Mende, Heinz
 Bavarian Radio Chorus
Mendoza, Alfredo
 Mexico City CO
Mendoze, Christian
 Musica Antiqua Ensemble
 Musica Antiqua Toulon
Mengelberg, Willem
 (Royal) Concertgebouw Orch

Mengelberg, Willem (cont.)
 New York PO
 New York Philharmonic SO
 Paris RSO
Menges, Herbert
 London SO
 Philharmonia Orch
Menier, Denis
 Wallonie Royal CO
Mentel, Jacek
 Polish National RSO Katowice
Menuhin, Yehudi
 Bach Festival Orch
 Bath Festival Orch
 Camerata Lysy
 Camerata Lysy Gstaad
 Czech State PO
 English CO
 English String Orch
 Menuhin Festival Orch
 Philharmonia Orch
 Royal PO
 Sinfonia Varsovia
Mercier, Jacques
 French Isles National Orch
 French National Orch
 Nouvel PO
 Turku PO
Mercurio, Steven
 Netherlands Radio PO
 Spoleto Festival Orch
Meredith, James
 Sonos Handbell Ensemble
Merithz, Claes
 Strängnäs Sinfonietta Ensemble
Mersson, Boris
 Montreux SO
 Rome Festival Orch
Merz, Florian
 Düsseldorf Classical PO
 South Westphalian PO
Merz, R.
 Zurich Sprechchor
Messner, Joseph
 Cathedral Choral Society Orch
 Cathedral Musician's Orch
 Salzburg Mozarteum Orch
Mester, Jorge
 London PO
 Louisville Orch
 Pasadena SO
 Symphony of the Air
Metzmacher, Ingo
 Ensemble Modern
 Hamburg State PO
Meylan, Jean
 Czech PO
 Prague RSO
Meyrowitz, Selmar
 Berlin State Opera Orch
Mezei, János
 Vienna-Szász PO
Miassojedov, Sergey
 Moscow Bach Center Orch
Michaels, Jost
 Bamberg SO
 Detmold Wind Ensemble
Michal, Luis
 Bavarian CO
Michalski, Carl
 Bavarian SO
 Graunke SO
 Vienna Volksoper Orch
Micheli, G.
 Emilia Romagna Arturo Toscanini SO
Michelucci, Roberto
 I Musici
Michielsen, Maarten
 Cappella Palestrina
 Koorproject Amersterdam
 Koorproject Rotterdam
Michniewski, Wojciech
 Gdansk SO
 Polish CO
 Polish National RSO Katowice
 Sinfonia Varsovia
Mihailovic, Duschan
 Russian CO
Mihály, András
 Budapest Chamber Ensemble
 Budapest CO
Mikael, J.
 Helsinki Festival Orch
Mikkelsen, Terje
 Lithuanian National SO
 Scapoli
Miladinovic, Dusan
 Belgrade National Opera Orch
Milhaud, Darius
 BBC SO
 Champs Élysées Theater Orch
 Concert Arts SO
 Czech PO
 French National RSO
 Paris Opera Orch
Milkov, Mikhail
 Bulgarian Radio-TV Chorus
 Bulgarian Radio-TV SO

Miller, David
 London Sinfonietta
Miller, David Alan
 Albany SO
 London SO
 Los Angeles PO
Miller, Gary
 New York City Gay Men's Chorus
Miller, Jonathan
 Chicago A Cappella
Millington, Andrew
 Guildford Cathedral Choir
Mills, Richard
 Tasmanian SO
Milnes, Eric
 Trinity Baroque Orch
Minin, Vladimir
 Moscow Chamber Choir
Minkowski, Marc
 Louvre Musicians
 Ricercar Academy
Minsky, Meir
 Orquestra Clássica do Porto
 Stuttgart RSO
Minter, Drew
 Ensemble 415
 Philharmonia Baroque Orch
Mintz, Shlomo
 Israel CO
Miskinis, Vytautas
 Azuoliukas Choir
Mitchell, Alasdair
 London PO
Mitchell, D.
 Partch Instrumentalists
Mitchell, George
 Trinity Chorale
Mitchell, H.
 National SO
Mitropoulos, Dimitri
 Cologne RSO
 Columbia SO
 (Royal) Concertgebouw Orch
 Florence Maggio Musicale Orch
 Florence Teatro Comunale Orch
 Metropolitan Opera Orch
 Minneapolis SO
 Minnesota Orch
 NBC SO
 New York PO
 Philharmonic SO
 Venice Teatro La Fenice Orch
 Vienna PO
 West German Radio Orch
Mitsumoto, Masatoshi
 Cracow RSO
Mnatsakanov, Walter
 Byelorussian Radio-TV SO
Moe, D.
 Oberlin Musical Union Orch
Moeckli, J.-P.
 Bern CO
Moglia, Alain
 Les Cuivres Francais
 Toulouse CO
 Toulouse National CO
Mogrelia, Andrew
 Czech State PO
 Czech-Slovak State PO
 Philharmonia Cassovia
 Prague Chamber Soloists
 Razumovsky Sinfonia
 Ukrainian CO
Molajoli, Lorenzo
 Milan SO
 La Scala Orch
Moles, Daniele
 Naples New Scarlatti Orch
Molinari-Pradelli, Francesco
 Dresden State Orch
 Florence Maggio Musicale Orch
 Milan RAI SO
 Naples Teatro San Carlo Orch
 Netherlands Opera Orch
 Reggio Emilia Teatro Municipale Orch
 Rome Opera Orch
 Rome Radio Orch
 Royal Opera House Orch
 St. Cecilia Academy Orch Rome
 Trieste Teatro Comunale Giuseppe Verdi Orch
 Turin RAI Orch
 Turin RAI SO
 Vienna State Opera Orch
Molino, Andrea
 Compania
 Gruppo Musica Insieme
 Turin Strings
Moll, Kevin
 Schola Discantus
Moltkau, Hans
 West Austrian SO
Monaco, Giulio
 Progetto Musica Instrumental Ensemble
Monteux, Pierre
 Boston Chamber Ensemble
 Boston SO
 Boston SO members
 Chicago SO

Monteux, Pierre (cont.)
(Royal) Concertgebouw Orch
Grande Orchestre Symphonique
London PO
London SO
Metropolitan Opera Orch
North German RSO
Paris Opéra-Comique Orch
Paris SO
San Francisco SO
Vienna PO

Montgomery, Kenneth
Bournemouth Sinfonietta
Hilversum RSO

Montgomery, Roger
Jane's Minstrels

Montorio, Daniel
Montilla Chorus

Mony, Walter
NSO RSO members
PACT Orch members

Moore, Ian
Cambridge Instrumental Ensemble
Cambridge Voices

Moore, Philip
Guildford Cathedral Choir

Moralt, Rudolf
Vienna State Opera Orch
Vienna SO

Morandi, Pier Giorgio
Budapest SO
Hungarian State Opera Orch

Morel, Christine
Claude Goudimel Ensemble

Morel, Jean-Paul
Columbia SO

Moren, Géo-Pierre
13 Etoiles Brass Band

Moretti, Riccardo
Bolshoi Theater SO
Bolshoi Theater SO Soloists

Moriarty, John
Central City Opera Orch
Copenhagen CO

Morricone, Ennio
Gruppo di Improvvisazione Nuova consonanza
London PO

Morris, Wyn
London PO
London Symphonica
New Philharmonia Orch

Mortensen, J. O.
Kalrup Girls' Choir

Mortimer, Harry
Massed Bands

Morton, Ralph
Quodlibet

Mosko, Stephen
Griffin Music Ensemble
Netherlands Wind Ensemble
San Francisco Contemporary Music Players

Moull, Geoffrey
Bielefeld PO

Mounk, Alicja
Tonhalle Orch

Moyse, Blanche Honegger
Orch of St. Luke's

Moyse, Louis
Marlboro Festival Ensemble

Mravinsky, Evgeny
Czech PO
Leningrad PO

Mtakiev, M.
Varna PO

Mucci, G.
Teatro La Gran Guardia Orch

Muck, Karl
Bayreuth Festival Orch
Berlin German Opera Orch
Berlin State Opera Orch
Berlin State SO

Mueller, Christoph
Cincinnati PO

Mueller, Otto-Werner
Juilliard Orch

Mugnai, Umberto
Palacio Bellas Artes Orch

Müller, Edoardo
Rome CO

Müller-Kray, Hans
Bern State Orch
South German RSO
Southwest German RSO
Stockholm RSO
Stuttgart RSO
Stuttgart South Radio Orch

Munch, Charles
Boston SO
Czech PO
French National RSO
National Orch
New Philharmonia Orch
ORTF National Orch
Paris Conservatory Société des Concerts Orch
Philadelphia Orch
Prague RSO
Rotterdam PO
Royal PO

Münch, Hans
Basel Orch
Basel SO

Münchinger, Karl
Ars Rediviva Orch Prague
Stuttgart CO
Stuttgart RSO

Munclinger, Milan
Ars Rediviva
Ars Rediviva Orch Prague
Prague CO

Mund, Uwe
Bamberg SO
Czech-Slovak RSO
Philharmonia Hungarica

Munih, Marko
Consortium Musicum Orch
Ljubljana RSO
Ljubljana SO

Munk, Ebbe
Copenhagen Boys' Choir
St. Annae Girls' Choir
Vox Danica Chamber Choir

Munrow, David
London Early Music Consort
St. Albans Abbey Boys' Choir

Müssauer, Manfred
Moravian PO

Mustonen, Andres
Hortus Musicus

Muti, Lorenzo
St. Stephen's CO

Muti, Riccardo
Berlin PO
Florence Maggio Musicale Orch
Florence Teatro Comunale Orch
Milan RAI Orch
New Philharmonia Orch
Philadelphia Orch
Philharmonia Orch
Rome Radio Orch
Rome RAI Orch
Rome RAI SO
Rome SO
Royal Opera House Orch
La Scala Orch
La Scala Orch Soloists
Venice Teatro La Fenice Orch
Vienna PO

Muus, Niels
Copenhagen Univ Choir

My, Dominique
Fa Ensemble
Paris String Quartet

Myrat, Alexander
Monte Carlo PO

Mysinski, Andrzej
Concerto Avenna
Warsaw Soloists

Nabarro, Malcolm
East of England Orch

Näf, C.
Amarillis Instrumental Ensemble

Näf, Fritz
Basel Madrigalists

Nagano, Kent
Berkeley SO
Hallé Orch
London PO
London Sinfonietta
London SO
Lyon Opera Orch
Paris Lyon Opera Orch
Philharmonia Orch

Nagy, Béla
Failoni CO

Nagy, Ferenc
Budapest MAV SO
Hungarian State Opera Orch

Nahon, Philippe
Ensemble Instrumental

Nanut, Anton
Ljubljana RSO
Ljubljana SO
Philharmonia Slavonica
Slovak SO
Slovenian Radio-TV Orch
Slovenian SO

Nanut, Marko Munih
Ljubljana SO

Naranjo, Wilfredo
Manzanillo Original Orch

Nash, Royston
D'Oyly Carte Opera Company Orch
Royal PO

Natanek, Adam
New Polish PO

Nazareth, Daniel
Slovak SO

Neal, Ronald
Dallas CO

Neale, Alasdair
New York CO Solisti
San Francisco SO

Neary, Martin
BBC SO
English CO
London Handel Orch

Neary, Martin (cont.)
New London Consort
Westminster Abbey Choir

Nebolsin, Vassily
Bolshoi Theater Orch

Nee, Thomas
La Jolla SO
SONOR Ensemble of Univ of California San Diego

Neel, Boyd
Boyd Neel String Orch

Negri, A. E.
Milan Euterpe Collegio Instrumental Ensemble

Negri, Vittorio
(Royal) Concertgebouw CO
English CO

Neidich, Charles
Mozzafiato

Nelson, John
Chicago Lyric Opera Chorus
Chicago Sym Chorus
Czech PO
Danish National RSO
English CO
Indianapolis SO
New World SO

Nelsson, Woldemar
Bayreuth Festival Orch

Németh, Gyula
Budapest PO
Budapest SO
Capella Savaria
Hungarian State Orch

Németh, Paul
Capella Savaria

Nerat, Harald
Salzburg CO

Neri, Fabio
Balzano Claudio Monteverdi Conservatory Youth Orch
Balzano Monteverdi Orch

Neschling, John
St. Gallen SO

Nestor, Leo
American Repertory Singers
National Shrine of the Immaculate Conception Choir Washington D.C.

Neuen, Donald
Eastman Musica Nova Ensemble

Neuhold, Günter
Flanders Royal PO
Rome RAI SO
Royal Flanders PO

Neumann, Horst
Leipzig Radio Chorus
Leipzig RSO
Leipzig RSO members

Neumann, Peter
Collegium Cartusianum
Cologne Chamber Choir
Cologne Instrumental Ensemble

Neumann, Václav
Brno State PO
Czech PO
Leipzig Gewandhaus Orch
Leipzig Opera Orch
Philharmonia Orch
Prague Chamber Soloists
Prague CO
Prague Percussion Ensemble
Prague Virtuosi
Southwest German RSO Baden-Baden
USSR Radio-TV SO

Neumeyr, Fritz
Collegium Terpsichore

Nevel, Erik van
Capella Sancti Michaelis
Concerto Palatino
Concerto Palatino Choir
Currende Instrumental Ensemble
Currende Vocal Ensemble
Ricercar Consort

Nevel, Paul van
Huelgas Ensemble

Newell, Robert
Canta-Sonare

Newman, A.
Madeira Festival Orch

Newman, Alfred
Hollywood Bowl SO

Newman, Anthony
Brandenburg Collegium
English CO
New Brandenburg Collegium
New York Arts Orch

Newman, David
London Metropolitan Orch

Newman, Mary Jane
Collegium Brass
New York Musica Antiqua

Newsome, Alec Evans
Besses o' th' Barn Band

Newsome, Edward Heath
Black Dyke Mills Band

Newsome, Roy
Besses o' th' Barn Band
Black Dyke Mills Band

Neyder
Vienna Boys' Choir

Nice, C.
Ljubljana SO

Nicholson, Paul
  Parley of Instruments
Nickoll, Harald
  Aachen Carmina Mundi
  Carmina Chamber Choir
Nicoara, Diodor
  Timisoara Banatul Phil Chorus
Nielson, K.
  Cantata Orch
Nikisch, Arthur
  Berlin PO
  London SO
Nikolayev, Leonid
  Moscow Conservatory Orch
  USSR Radio–TV Large SO
Nilson, Göran W.
  Gävelborg SO
  Norrköping SO
  Örebro SO
Nilsson, Torsten
  Oscar's Motet Choir
  Swedish Radio Chorus
Ninić, Tonko
  Zagreb Solisti
Niquet, Hervé
  Concert Spirituel Orch
  Concert Spirituel Vocal Ensemble
Niyazi
  Romanian Radio Orch
Noble, Anthony
  Farnborough Abbey Choir
Noble, Ray
  Fred Hartley Quintet
  New Mayfair Orch
Nobre, Marlos
  Musica Nova Philharmonia
Noda, Teruyuki
  NHK SO
Nolan, David
  London PO
Noll, William
  Atlanta Choral Guild
  Belgian French Community Youth Orch
  Ritz–Carlton Orch
Nopre, Gilles
  Rhenish PO
  Württemberg PO
Norjanen, Hannu
  Friends of Kuula
  Tapiola Chamber Choir
Norrington, Roger
  London Classical Players
  Orch of St. Luke's
  Schütz Choir London
Norris, Harry
  D'Oyly Carte Opera Company Orch
Noseda, Gianandrea
  Milan Giuseppe Verdi Large SO
Nosek, Václav
  Brno State PO members
Notev, Giorgio
  Pleven PO
Nott, Jonathan
  Moscow PO
Novik, Vladislav
  Ural Choir
Novotny, Břetislav
  Prague CO
Nowak, Grzegorz
  Bieler SO
  London SO
Nowakowski, Miczsław
  Sinfonia Varsovia
  Warsaw Chamber Opera Orch
Nozy, Norbert
  Belgian Guides Symphonic Band
Numajiri, Ryusuke
  Tokyo Metropolitan SO
Nussié, Olivier
  Goumoens-la-Ville
Nyman, Michael
  Michael Nyman Band
  Royal Liverpool Orch
Oberfrank, Géza
  Budapest MAV SO
  Budapest SO
  Failoni CO
  Hungarian State Opera Orch
  Hungarian State SO
Obsfeld, Frieder
  Westphalia PO
Ocejo, José Luis
  Laredo Instrumental Ensemble
Octors, Georges–Elie
  Wallonie Royal CO
  Walloon & French Community of Belgium CO
O'Donnell, James
  City of London Sinfonia
  His Majesties Sagbutts & Cornetts
  Pro Cantione Antiqua
  Westminster Cathedral Choir
Ogermann, Claus
  London SO
Öhrwall, Anders
  Drottningholm Baroque Ensemble
  Stockholm PO
Ohyama, Heiichiro
  Texas Festival Orch

Oistrakh, David
  Bergen PO
  Berlin PO
  Czech PO
  USSR SO
  Vienna PO
Oistrakh, Igor
  Prague Virtuosi
Olariu, Stelian
  Romanian Opera Orch
Oledzki, Bogdan
  Polish National RSO Katowice
Olefsky, P.
  Amatius Orch of New York
  English CO
Oliver, John
  John Oliver Chorale
Ollila, Tuomas
  Tampere PO
Olmi, Paolo
  Catania Teatro Massimo Bellini Orch
  Genoa Teatro Carlo Felice Orch
Olson, Robert
  Colorado MahlerFest Orch
Olszewska, M.
  Vienna PO
O'Neal, Michael
  Michael O'Neal Singers
O'Neal, Thomas
  Arizona State Univ Symphonic Band
Opdebeeck, Olivier
  Cori Spezzati Vocal Ensemble
Oramo, Sakari
  Finnish RSO
  Malmö SO
Orbelian, Constantine
  Moscow CO
O'Reilly, Graham
  William Byrd Ensemble
Oren, Daniel
  Bologna Teatro Comunale Orch
  Genoa Teatro Comunale Orch
  Rome Opera Orch
Orizio, Agostino
  Brescia & Bergamo Festival CO
  Gasparo da Salò Orch
Orlov, A.
  Moscow RSO
Ormandy, Eugene
  Brass Band
  Cleveland Orch
  Columbia SO
  Hollywood Bowl SO
  London SO
  Mendelssohn Club Chorus Philadelphia
  National SO Washington D.C.
  New York PO
  North German SO
  Philadelphia Orch
  Prades Festival Orch
  RCA Victor SO
  San Francisco Opera Orch
Ortmans, T.
  Studio Orch
Ortner, Erwin
  Austrian RSO
  CO of Europe
  Salzburg Baroque Ensemble
  Arnold Schoenberg Choir
Oskamp, Gérard
  Berlin SO
  Gothenburg SO
  Limburg SO
  Norske Bläsere
  Norwegian Winds
  Royal Flanders PO
Ossonce, Jean–Yves
  BBC Scottish SO
  New Zealand SO
Östman, Arnold
  Drottningholm Court Theater Orch
Ostrowsky, Avi
  Brussels Belgian Radio–TV PO
Otaka, Tadeaki
  BBC Welsh National Orch
  BBC Welsh National SO
  NHK SO
  Tokyo Metropolitan SO
  Tokyo PO
Otomo, Naoto
  New Japan PO
Otterloo, Willem van
  The Hague PO
  Vienna Festival Orch
Otto, Ralf
  Concerto Cologne
Ouderits, Leo
  BRTN PO Brussels
Oue, Eiji
  Minnesota Orch
Ovchinnikov, Vyacheslav
  USSR Radio–TV Large SO
Owen, C.
  Univ of Michigan Percussion Ensemble
Ozawa, Seiji
  Bavarian RSO
  Berlin PO
  Boston SO

Ozawa, Seiji (cont.)
  Chicago SO
  Dresden Staatskapelle
  English CO
  French National Orch
  London SO
  New Philharmonia Orch
  New York PO
  Orch de Paris
  Saito Kinen Orch
  San Francisco SO
  Toronto SO
  Vienna PO
Paray, P.
  Detroit SO
  London SO
  Monte Carlo Opera Orch
Pace, Marco
  Hungarian Radio–TV SO
Pacitti, Daniel
  Moldavian Radio–TV SO
Pacor, Giovanni
  Budapest CO
Pacquetceau, M. D.
  St. Marie de Maumont Nuns Choir
Page, Christopher
  Gothic Voices
Page, Robert
  Carnegie Mellon Concert Choir
  Carnegie Mellon PO
Paillard, Jean–François
  English CO
  Jean–François Paillard CO
Pál, Tamás
  Budapest CO
  Budapest SO
  Corelli CO
  Fricsay SO
  Hungarian State Orch
  Salieri CO
  Szeged SO
Palma, David
  Speculum Musicae
Palmer, Catherine
  Yorkminster Park Baptist Church Choir Toronto
Palmer, Michael
  American Sinfonia
  Rochester PO
Palmer, Rudolph
  Brewer Baroque CO
  Brewer CO
  Palmer CO
  Philomel Baroque CO
  St. Luke's Baroque Orch
Pálsson, P. P.
  Icelandic SO
Palumbo, Sante
  Sante Palumbo String Orch
Pancik, Josef
  Brno State PO
  Prague Chamber Choir
Paniagua, Eduardo
  Ancient Music Group
Paniagua, Gregorio
  Madrid Atrium Musicae
Panizza, Ettore
  Armed Forces Radio Orch
  Metropolitan Opera Orch
  New York Metropolitan Opera Orch
Panni, Marcello
  Munich RSO
  Naples Teatro San Carlo Orch
  Rome Opera CO
Pantillon, François
  Bern Vocal Ensemble
  Bieler SO
Panufnik, Andrzej
  BBC SO
  (Royal) Concertgebouw Orch
  New York Chamber SO
Panula, Jorma
  Aarhus SO
  Danish National RSO
  Gothenburg SO
  Helsinki PO
  Scandinavian Brass Ensemble
  Stockholm New CO
  Stockholm PO
Paoletti, Albert
  Rome Opera Orch
Papadopoulos, Marios
  City of Oxford Orch
  Royal PO
Papazian, Bedros
  Armenian Choir Sofia
  Sofia Orch Ensemble
Pappano, Antonio
  Philharmonia Orch
Parenti, M.
  Livorno Teatro La Gran Guardia Orch
Pařík, Ivan
  Prague CO
  Prague Sinfonietta
Parisi, Vittorio
  Mantova Orch
  Mantova Orch members
Parisot
  Yale Cellos

Parkes, Maj. Peter
  Black Dyke Mills Band
  Grimethorpe Colliery Band
  Williams Fairey Band

Parkman, Stefan
  Danish National Radio Chamber Choir
  Danish National Radio Choir
  Danish National Radio Choir Soloists
  Drottningholm Baroque Ensemble
  Stockholm Sinfonietta

Parmentier, Christian
  Hauts-de-Seine Plectrum Ensemble

Parmentier, Yves
  French Army Chorus
  Republican Guard Brass & Percussion

Parodi, Armando La Rosa
  Rome RAI Orch

Parodi, Rosa
  Naples Teatro San Carlo Orch

Parrott, Andrew
  Boston Early Music Festival Orch
  Taverner Consort
  Taverner Players

Parry, David
  English SO
  Philharmonia Orch
  Royal PO

Partch, Harry
  Gate 5 Ensemble

Pasquet, Nicolás
  Pécs SO
  Stuttgart PO

Pászti, Miklós
  Hungarian State Folk Ensemble Orch

Patanè, Franco
  Naples Teatro San Carlo Orch

Patanè, Giuseppe
  Bavarian State Opera Orch
  Bologna Teatro Comunale Orch
  Dresden State Orch
  Hungarian Radio-TV SO
  Hungarian State Opera Orch
  Hungarian State Orch
  Hungarian State SO
  Munich RSO
  National PO London
  Parma Teatro Regio Orch
  San Francisco War Memorial Opera House Orch
  La Scala Orch
  Vienna Volksoper Orch

Patenaude, G.
  Petits Chanteurs du Mont-Royal

Paternostro, Robert
  Berlin RSO
  Bulgarian RSO
  Cologne SO
  Hungarian State Opera Orch
  NHK Chamber Soloists
  Sofia SO
  Tokyo PO
  Tokyo SO
  Vienna SO

Patterson, Elizabeth C.
  Gloriae Dei Cantores

Patterson, Russell
  Kansas City Lyric Theater Orch
  Kansas City SO

Pauk, Alex
  Esprit Orch
  Nexus

Paulik, Anton
  Vienna State Opera Orch
  Vienna SO
  Vienna Volksoper Orch

Paulmüller, Alexander
  Stuttgart PO

Paumgartner, Bernhard
  Salzburg Mozarteum Orch

Pavlovich, Theodora
  Vassil Arnaudov Sofia Chamber Choir

Pay, Anthony
  Brodsky String Quartet
  English CO

Payn, William
  Rooke Chapel Choir

Paynter, John P.
  Northwestern Univ Sym Wind Ensemble

Peace, Paula
  Atlanta Chamber Players

Peacock, C.
  Heritage CO

Peerlman, Martin
  Banchetto Musicale
  Boston Baroque Orch

Pearson, Donald
  St. John's Episcopal Cathedral Choir Boy & Girls' Choir Denver
  St. John's Episcopal Cathedral Festival Orch

Peca, M.
  Rome Stradivari Ensemble

Peck, Benjamin
  New York Cornet & Sacbutt Ensemble

Pedersen, Ole
  Horsholm Percussion

Pederson, Ilonna
  Double Reed Ensemble
  New York Chamber Music

Pedrotti, Antonio
  Czech PO
  La Scala Orch

Peelman, Roland
  The Song Company

Peire, Patrick
  Capella Brugensis
  Collegium Instrumentale Brugense
  New Flemish SO

Peiretti, Rita
  Accademia dei Solinghi

Pelletier, Wilfrid
  Metropolitan Opera Orch

Peltz, Charles
  Buffalo Opera Sacra Orch

Pelucchi, Pierangelo
  Bergamo Collegium Musicum
  Collegium Musicum

Penderecki, Krzysztof
  Bamberg SO
  Karol Szymanowski State PO
  North German RSO
  Orch Giovanile Italiana
  Polish National RSO Katowice
  Royal Stockholm PO
  Sinfonia Varsovia

Peng, Cao
  Shanghai PO

Pennington, R.
  Royal Dragoon Guards Regimental Band

Penny, Andrew
  Irish National CO
  RTE Concert Orch
  RTE SO
  Royal Scottish National Orch
  Ukrainian National SO

Penrose, Timothy
  English Consort of Viols

Pepin, Jean-Paul
  Slovak PO

Perahia, Murray
  English CO

Pérès, Marcel
  Janequin Ensemble
  Organum Ensemble

Peress, Maurice
  New Palais Royale Orch
  Percussion Ensemble

Pérez, Victor Pablo
  Galicia SO
  Tenerife SO

Perick, Christof
  Berlin RSO
  Los Angeles CO

Perlea, Jonel
  Bamberg SO
  Florence Maggio Musicale Orch
  New York City Opera Orch
  Pro Musica Orch
  Rome Opera Orch
  Vienna SO

Perlman, Itzhak
  Israel PO

Perrenoud, Boris
  Vienna CO

Perret, P.
  Winston-Salem Piedmont Triad SO

Perriere, M.
  Festival SO

Perrin, Nigel
  Bath Camerata

Perry, William
  Capella Istropolitana
  Rome PO
  Slovak PO
  Vienna SO

Persichetti, Vincent
  New York String Orch

Pešek, Libor
  Bratislava Philharmonic CO
  Brno State PO
  Czech PO
  Dvořák CO
  Philharmonia Orch
  Prague Chamber Harmony
  Prague Chamber Soloists
  Prague CO
  Prague RSO
  Prague Wind Band
  Royal Liverpool Orch
  Royal Liverpool PO
  Royal PO
  Slovak PO

Peskó, Zoltan
  BBC SO
  Bologna Teatro Comunale Orch
  French National Orch
  Netherlands Radio PO
  Prague CO
  Southwest German RSO Baden-Baden

Peters, Reinhard
  Berlin PO

Petersen, Patricia
  Fortuna

Peterson, Edward
  Washington Winds

Petit, Jean-Claude
  French National Orch

Petit, Jean-Louis
  Avray Atelier Musique
  Avray CO
  Avray Ville Instrumental Ensemble
  Millière String Trio
  Jean-Louis Petit CO
  Transylvanian State PO Romania

Petitgirard, Laurent
  Classic Polonaise PO
  French SO
  Ljubljana RSO

Petkov, Dimiter
  Plovdiv PO

Petralia, Tito
  Milan RAI SO

Petrassi, Goffredo
  Milan Angelicum Instrumentalists
  Milan Italian Radio-TV Orch
  Turin RAI Radio-TV SO

Petró, János
  Pannon CO

Petronsky
  Slovak RSO Bratislava

Petrovici, Constantin
  Romanian Opera Orch

Peuvion, Jean-Pierre
  Liège New Music Ensemble

Pevzner, Boris
  Moscow Chamber Choral Theater

Pfaff, Luca
  Turin RAI Orch

Pfitzner, Hans
  Berlin New SO
  Berlin PO
  Berlin State Opera Orch

Phillips, M. H.
  SO of America

Phillips, Peter
  Eastern Connecticut SO
  Eastman Musica Nova
  Tallis Scholars

Phipps, Simon
  New Sadler's Wells Opera Orch

Piantini, Carlos
  Italian International Orch

Piazza, Enrico
  Milan RAI SO

Piccillo, Giuseppe
  Rome RAI SO

Picco, Guido
  Palacio Bellas Artes Orch

Pickett, Philip
  New London Collective
  New London Consort

Pidò, Evelino
  Palermo Teatro Massimo Orch

Pierlot, Philippe
  Ricercar Consort

Pierné, G.
  Colonne Orch

Pikler, Robert
  Sydney SO

Pilipchuk, Tamara
  Russian Chamber Choir

Pillement, Jérôme
  Bernard Thomas CO

Pillot, Laurent
  Berkeley SO

Pinchin, Harry
  Edmonton Wind Ensemble

Pini, Carl
  Academy of St. James
  Australian CO

Pinkas, Jiří
  Brno State PO
  Prague RSO

Pinner, Sue Ann
  Santa Barbara Regional Choir

Pinnock, Trevor
  English CO
  English Concert
  English Concert & Choir

Pio, Giusto
  London Astarte Orch

Pippin, Donald
  Stephen Hill Orch

Piquemal, Michel
  Jean-Walter Audoli Instrumental Ensemble
  Avignon-Provence Regional Lyric Orch
  Cannes Regional Chorus
  Cannes-Provence Alpes-Côte d'Azur Regional Orch
  Ensemble Vocal
  French Vittoria Regional Choir
  Harmonia Nova Orch Ensemble
  Nancy SO
  Orch de la Cité
  Michel Piquemal Vocal Ensemble
  Bernard Thomas CO

Pitamic, Alexander von
  Ljubljana SO
  South German PO

Pittman, Richard
  Boston Musica Viva

Pitz, Wilhelm
  Bayreuth Festival Orch

Planchart, Alejandro
  Capella Cordina

Plantes, Giles
  Claude-Gervaise Ensemble

Plasson, E.
  Toulouse National CO
Plasson, Michel
  Dresden PO
  Orféon Donostiarra
  Toulouse Capitole Orch
Platz, Robert
  Marstall Ensemble of the Bavarian State Opera
Pletnev, Mikhail
  German CO
  German Chamber PO
  Russian National Orch
Plotino, Antonio
  Genoa CO
  New Music Studium
Pohjola, Erkki
  Espoo CO
  Tapiola Children's Choir
  Tapiola Choir
Pohjola, Olli
  Avantil CO
Poiget, Christophe
  La Follia Ensemble
Pok, Frantisek
  Prague Rozmberk Consort
  Rozmberk Ensemble
Polgár, François
  Paris Opera Orch Soloists
Poliakin, Raoul
  New York Stadium SO
  Poliakin Orch
Polianski, Valéri
  Belarussian CO
  Russian PO
  Russian State SO
  Russian State Symphonic Cappella
  USSR Ministry of Culture Chamber Choir
Polivnick, Paul
  Alabama SO
  London SO
Polizzi, Antonino
  Budapest SO
  Prague SO
Pollack, Christian
  Slovak RSO Bratislava
  Slovak State PO Košice
Pollini, Maurizio
  CO of Europe
  English CO
  Vienna PO
Pomerantz, Stephen
  Budapest PO
Pommer, Max
  Berlin CO
  Helsinki PO
  Leipzig Gewandhaus Orch
  Leipzig New Bach Collegium Musicum
  Leipzig RSO
  New Bach Collegium Musicum
Pommier, Jean-Bernard
  Northern Sinfonia of England
  Philharmonia Orch
  Sinfonia Varsovia
Ponkin, Vladimir
  Moscow Contemporary Music Ensemble
  Moscow New PO
  St. Petersburg State Academic Cappella SO
Ponnelle, Pierre-Dominique
  Monte Carlo PO
  Munich Bach Soloists
  Nuremberg SO
Pons, Josep
  Barcelona Teatro Lliure CO
  Barcelona's Free Theater CO
Ponto, R.
  Oberlin Wind Ensemble
Poole, John
  BBC Singers
  Westminster Cathedral Choir
Popa, Aurelian Octav
  Quodlibet Musicum CO
Popa, Mircea
  Bucharest Opera & Ballet Theater Orch
Popescu, Paul
  Bucharest CO
  Bucharest Phil CO
  Romanian Radio-TV Orch
  Satu Mare PO
Popken, Ralf
  Freiburg Baroque Orch
Pople, Ross
  London Festival Orch
Popov, Kiril
  Sofia Choir of Priests
Popov, Victor
  Choral Arts Academy Men & Boys' Choir
  Moscow Choral Academy Men & Children's Choir
  Moscow Male Voice Choir
Popov, Viktor
  Moscow Academy Choir
  Moscow Contemporary Music Ensemble members
Popp, M.
  Estampie
Popsavov, Miroslav
  Rybin Choir Moscow
Porcelijn, David
  Asko Ensemble
  Netherlands Radio CO

Porcelijn, David (cont.)
  Netherlands Radio PO
  Netherlands Saxophone Quartet
  Stockholm Symphonic Wind Orch
  Sydney SO
Portal, M.
  Musique Vivante Ensemble
Posch, Michael
  Unicorn Ensemble
Posnak, P.
  Portland String Quartet
Pradella, Massimo
  Naples Alessandro Scarlatti RAI Orch
  Turin RAI SO
Pratt, Michael
  Group for Contemporary Music
Press, Maurice
  American String Quartet
Preston, Simon
  Academy of Ancient Music
  English CO
Prêtre, Georges
  Boston SO
  Chicago SO
  René DuClos Chorus
  French National Orch
  French National RSO
  London SO
  New Philharmonia Orch
  North German RSO
  Orch de Paris
  Paris Conservatory Societé des Concerts Orch
  Paris Opera Orch
  Philharmonia Orch
  Radio France PO
  RCA Italian Opera Orch
  Rome RAI SO
  Royal PO
  La Scala Orch
  Vienna SO
Previn, André
  Curtis Institute of Music SO
  London Collegium Musicum
  London SO
  Los Angeles PO
  New Albion Ensemble
  Orch of St. Luke's
  Pittsburgh SO
  Royal PO
  St. Louis SO
  Vienna PO
Previtali, Fernando
  Buenos Aires Teatro Colón Orch
  Milan RAI SO
  Naples Teatro San Carlo Orch
  Rome Opera Orch
  Rome RAI Orch
  Rome RAI SO
  St. Cecilia Academy Orch Rome
  Turin RAI Orch
  Turin Teatro Regio Orch
Price, Constance
  Vermont SO members
Price, Glenn
  Manhattan Percussion Ensemble
  Univ of Calgary Wind Ensemble
Priestman, Brian
  Belgian RSO
  Denver SO
  Leonhardt Consort
  London SO
  RTBF SO
Primavera, Joseph
  Philadelphia Youth Orch
Prin, Yves
  Radio France PO
Prinz, Johannes
  Vienna W. U. Choir
Pritchard, John
  BBC SO
  English CO
  Florence Maggio Musicale Orch
  Gürzenich Orch
  Glyndebourne Festival Orch
  London PO
  New Philharmonia Orch
  Philharmonia Orch
  Royal Liverpool PO
  Royal Opera House Orch
  St. Cecilia Academy Orch Rome
  Vienna PO
Prohaska, Felix
  Bach Guild Orch
  Vienna Festival Orch
  Vienna State Opera Orch
Proost, Walter
  San Remo SO
  Sinfonia D'Anvers
Prosser, Timothy
  Emmanuel College Chapel Choir Cambridge
Prossnitz, Walter
  English CO
Protheroe, Guy
  Spectrum
Proulx, Richard
  Cathedral Singers
Provatorov, Gaetane
  Moscow State SO
  USSR Radio-TV Large SO

Provatorov, Gaetane (cont.)
  USSR Radio-TV SO
Prüwer, Julius
  Berlin PO
Pryce-Jones, John
  Britannia Building Society Band
  Northern Ballet Theater Orch
Przybylski, Janusz
  Gdansk SO
  Warsaw SO
  Warschauer SO
Pugsley, Richard
  Gloriae Dei Ringers
Pulakka, T.
  Avantil CO
Pullan, Bruce
  Vancouver Bach Choir
Puppo, Michele di
  Banda Ruvomusica
Purvis, William
  Speculum Musicae
Pusztai, Tibor
  New River Chamber Players
  New World Chamber Ensemble
Quadri, Argeo
  Catania Teatro Massimo Bellini Orch
  Vincenzo Bellini Theater Orch
Quattrocchi, Fernand
  Lorraine PO
Queler, Eve
  Hungarian State Orch
  New York City Opera Orch
Questa, Angelo
  Milan RAI SO
  Naples Teatro San Carlo Orch
  Turin RAI Orch
  Turin RAI SO
  Turin RSO
Quinet, Fernand
  Belgian National Orch
Rachleff, L
  Oberlin Contemporary Music Ensemble
  Oberlin Wind Ensemble
Rachlevsky, Misha
  Kremlin CO
  Kremlin SO
Rachlin, E.
  Cambridge SO
Rachmaninoff, Sergei
  Philadelphia Orch
Rachmilovich, Jacques
  Santa Monica Orch
Rachon, Stefan
  Warsaw RSO
Rademann, Hans-Christoph
  Dresden Chamber Choir
  Munich Trombone Quartet
Radu, Valentin
  Ama Deus Ensemble
Radulescu, Horatiu
  French Flute Orch
Ragnarsson, Hjálmar
  Hljómeyki Chorus
Rahbari, Alexander
  Belgian Radio-TV Orch
  Belgian Radio-TV PO
  Brussels Belgian Radio-TV PO
  Brussels BRTN PO
  Brussels RTBF SO
  Czech PO
  Czech-Slovak RSO Bratislava
  London PO
  Slovak Radio New PO
Raichev, Rouslan
  Plovdiv PO
  Sofia PO
Raickovich, Miloš
  Moscow SO
Raine, Nic
  Prague PO
Raisin-Dadre, Denis
  Ensemble Doulce Mémoire
Raisky, Boris
  Belarussian State Radio-TV Orch
Rajski, Wojciech
  Musica Vitae
  Polish Chamber PO
Rajter, Ludovit
  Czech-Slovak RSO Bratislava
Ramin, Günther
  Leipzig Gewandhaus Orch
Rami, Franz
  Hassler Consort
Rampal, Jean-Pierre
  English CO
  French National Orch
  Hungarian Virtuosi CO
  Jerusalem Music Center CO
  Franz Liszt CO
  Salzburg Mozarteum Orch
Randa, Bernard
  SONOR Ensemble of Univ of California San Diego
Ranzani, Stefano
  La Scala Orch
Rapalo, Ugo
  Naples Alessandro Scarlatti RAI Orch
  Naples Teatro San Carlo Orch
Rapchak, Lawrence
  Chicago Chamber Opera

Rapè, Ernö
  Radio City Music Hall Orch
Rapf, Kurt
  Vienna Sinfonietta
Rapson, Penelope
  Fiori Musicali
Rasi, Alberto
  Italian Accademia Strumentale
Rasilainen, Ari
  Aalborg SO
  Jyvaskyla SO
  Tampere PO
Rasmussen, Frans
  Aalborg SO
  Aarhus SO
  Canzone Choir
  Collegium Musicum
  South Jutland SO
Rastvorova, Elena
  Moscow New Choir
Rathé, Filip
  Spectra Ensemble
Rathje, Per
  Pro Cantu
Ratiu, Miron
  Oradea PO
Rattle, Simon
  Berlin PO
  Birmingham Contemporary Music Group
  Bournemouth SO
  City of Birmingham SO
  Copenhagen Contemporary Players
  Great Britain National Youth Orch
  London PO
  London Sinfonietta
  London SO
  Nash Ensemble
  Northern Sinfonia of England
  Philharmonia Orch
  Royal Opera House Orch
Ratzinger, Georg
  Augsburg PO
  Munich Consortium Musicum
  Munich PO Soloists
  Munich Radio Orch
  Munich RSO
  Regensburg Cathedral Choir
Rauber, François
  St. Laurent Children's Choir
Ravel, Maurice
  Lamoureux Orch
  Mason–Murcie–Draper–Woodhouse–Dinsey–Tomlinson–James Septet
Ravens, Simon
  Musica Contexta
Ravier, Charles
  Polyphonique Ensemble
Read, J.
  Hürth Music School Orch
Redel, Kurt
  Camerata Labacensis
  English CO
  French Instrumental Ensemble
  Grenoble Instrumental Ensemble
  Luxembourg RSO
  Luxembourg Radio–TV SO
  Munich Pro Arte Orch
  Munich RSO
  New York City Opera Orch
  Philharmonia Hungarica
  Pro Arte Orch
  Rhine State PO
  Rhineland–Palatinate State PO
  Royal PO
  Slovak PO
  Talich CO
Reed, Alfred
  Senzoku Gakuen Symphonic Wind Orch
Reentovich, Y.
  Bolshoi Theater Violin Ensemble
Rees, Jonathan
  Scottish Ensemble
Rees, Owen
  A Capella Portugesa
  Cambridge Taverner Choir
Rees-Williams, Jonathan
  Lichfield Cathedral Choir
Reeves, Maj Colin
  HM Life Guards Concert Band
Reibold, Bruno
  Stuyvesant String Quartet
Reichel, Helmuth
  Zurich Bach Kantorei
Reichenberger, Hugo
  Vienna State Opera Orch
Reichert, Hubert
  Westphalia SO
Reichert, Manfred
  Ensemble 13
Reichwein, Leopold
  Vienna State Opera Orch
Reid, William
  Sadler's Wells Opera Orch
Reiner, Fritz
  Chicago SO
  Curtis Institute Student Orch
  London PO
  NBC SO

Reiner, Fritz (cont.)
  New York PO
  Pittsburgh SO
  RCA Victor SO
  Fritz Reiner SO
  Robin Hood Dell Orch Philadelphia
  Royal Opera House Orch
  Royal PO
  Vienna PO
Reinhardt, Rolf
  Luxembourg RSO
  Southwest German RSO Baden–Baden
Reiss, Scott
  Hesperus
Remenyi, János
  Hungarian Radio–TV Children's Chorus Girls' Voices
  Hungarian Radio–TV Male Chamber Choir
Remoortel, Edouard van
  London SO
  Monte Carlo Opera Orch
  Vienna Musikgesellschaft Orch
  Vienna SO
Rémy, Ludger
  Les Amis de Philippe
  Telemann CO
Rennert, Jonathan
  Parnassus String Ensemble
Renton, Frank
  Grimethorpe Colliery Band
Renz, Frederick
  New York Early Music Ensemble
Renz, Jany
  Early Music Ensemble
Renzetti, Donato
  London Sinfonietta Opera Orch
  Milan RAI SO
  Toscana Regional Orch
  Turin RAI Orch
  Tuscany Radio–TV Orch
Renzi, Armando
  Pro Civitate Christiana di Assisi Orch
Rescigno, Nicola
  American Opera Society Orch
  Dallas Civic Opera Orch
  Dallas SO
  London PO
  Mantova Teatro Sociale Orch
  Monte Carlo Opera Orch
  Monte Carlo PO
  National PO London
  Paris Conservatory Societé des Concerts Orch
  Paris Opera Orch
  Philharmonia Orch
  Rio de Janeiro Teatro Municipale Orch
  Royal Opera House Orch
  Stuttgart RSO
Reuber, Thomas
  Capella Piccola
  Capella Piccola Neuss
Reuter, Rolf
  Berlin Comic Opera Orch
  Berlin RSO
Revenaugh, Daniel
  Royal PO
Revzen, Joel
  St. Paul CO
Reyne, Hugo
  Marais SO
Reynish, Timothy
  Royal Northern College of Music Wind Orch
Reynolds, Alfred
  Hammersmith Lyric Theater Orch
  London Salon Ensemble
Reynolds, H. Robert
  Detroit Chamber Winds
Reynolds, Julian
  Concentus Bestiales
  European CO Per Musica
  Per Musica
Reynolds, R.
  Detroit Chamber Winds
Rezler, Arnold
  Polish National RSO Katowice
  Warsaw Opera Orch
Reznikoff, Iégor
  Vézelay Abbey Choir
Rezucha, Bystrik
  Massachusetts Wind Ensemble
  Slovak PO
  Slovak RSO Bratislava
  Slovak State PO Košce
Rice, JoAnn
  Florilegium Chamber Choir
Rich, Frederic C.
  Juilliard Orch members
Richard, André
  Rechérche Ensemble
Richman, James
  Concert Royal
Richman, Steven
  New York Harmonie Ensemble
Richter, Casper
  Brno State PO
Richter, Hans
  Southwest German CO Pforzheim
Richter, Karl
  Munich Bach Orch
Rickenbacher, Karl Anton
  Bamberg SO

Rickenbacher, Karl Anton (cont.)
  Bavarian RSO
  Berlin RSO
  Capella Cracoviensis
  London PO
Rickenbacker, Karl Anton
  Bamberg SO
Riddell, Wayne
  CBC Vancouver SO
Riedo, Paul
  St. Thomas Aquinas Church Choir
Rieger, Fritz
  Bavarian RSO
  Munich PO
Riesman, Michael
  Gavin Bryars Ensemble
  Philip Glass Ensemble
Rieu, André
  Amsterdam CO
Rifkin, Joshua
  Bach Ensemble
  Cappella Coloniensis
  (Royal) Concertgebouw CO
  London Brass Players
Rigacci, Bruno
  Bologna Teatro Comunale Orch
  Emilia Romagna Arturo Toscanini SO
  Florence Maggio Musicale Orch
Rignold, Hugo
  Philharmonia Orch
Riley, D.
  Toronto Ragtime Ensemble
Riley, Terry
  Buffalo New York State Univ Center of the Creative & Performing Arts members
  Shanghai Film Orch
Rilling, Helmuth
  Bach Collegium
  Bach Collegium Chorus
  Bach Ensemble
  Gächinger Kantorei
  Franz Liszt CO
  Oregon Bach Festival CO
  Oregon Bach Festival Orch
  Prague CO
  Stuttgart Bach Collegium
  Stuttgart Gächinger Kantorei
  Stuttgart Gedächtnis Figural Choir
  Stuttgart RSO
  Vienna Concentus Musicus
  Württemberg CO
Rimbu, Romeo
  Oradea PO
Rinkevičius, G.
  Lithuanian State SO
Rintoul, Richard
  Colburn CO
Riska, Astrid
  Jubilate Choir
Ristenpart, Karl
  Saar CO
Ritscher, Immaculata
  St. Hildegard Rüdesheim–Eibingen Benedictine Abbey Choir
Rivoli, Gianfranco
  Amsterdam PO
  Geneva RSO
  Madrid Radio–TV Orch
Rizzi, Carlo
  Bratislava RSO
  London PO
  London SO
  Piacenza SO
  Royal Opera House Orch
  San Remo SO
  Welsh National Opera Orch
Roa, Miguel
  Madrid SO
Robert, A.
  Montreal Chambristes
Robert, Guy
  Perceval Ensemble
Roberts, Gwyn
  Perihelion Ensemble members
Roberts, Timothy
  Invocation
Robertson, David
  Berlin SO
  Ensemble InterContemporain
  Monte Carlo PO
Robertson, Stewart
  Santa Fe SO
  Santa Fe SO Chamber Players
  Ukrainian National SO
  Ukrainian State SO
Robev, Georgi
  Bulgarian National Chorus
  Bulgarian Svetoslav Obretenov Choir
  Sofia PO
Robin, D.
  Vienna Mozart Orch
Robinson, Christopher
  St. George's Chapel Windsor Castle Choir
  St. John's College Choir Cambridge
  Worcester Cathedral Choir
Robinson, Paul
  Slovak State PO Košice
  Toronto CO
Robinson, Peter
  English National Opera Orch

Robinson, Stanford
  Philharmonia Orch
Rodan, Mendi
  Belgian National Orch
  Israel Sinfonietta
  Kol Israel SO
Rodgers Radcliffe, Stephen
  New York Chamber Ensemble
Rodzinski, Artur
  London Phil SO
  New York PO
  New York Philharmonic SO
  Rome RAI Orch
  Rome RAI Radio–TV SO
  Rome RAI SO
  Turin RAI SO
Rogers, Eric
  Royal PO
Rogers, Nigel
  Chiaroscuro Ensemble
  London Cornett & Sackbutt Ensemble
Rögner, Heinz
  Berlin CO
  Berlin Comic Opera Orch
  Berlin RSO
Rohan, Jiridřich
  Prague SO
Rojatti, Ezio
  Haydn Philharmonia
  Haydn Philharmonia Soloists
  Haydn PO Soloists
Rolek, Timm
  Chelsea Chamber Ensemble
Rolla, János
  Franz Liszt CO
  Zagreb Musici
Roller, A. C.
  Eastman Wind Ensemble
Rolston, Thomas
  Banff Festival Strings
Romagna, Emilia
  Toscanini SO
Ronald, Landon
  London New SO
  London PO
  London SO
Ronly–Riklis, S.
  Jerusalem SO
Rooley, Anthony
  Consort of Musicke
Rosado, L
  Orch dell'Angelicum
Rosbaud, Hans
  Amburgo RSO
  BBC SO
  Berlin PO
  Berlin RSO
  Berlin State Opera Orch
  Cologne RSO
  Netherlands Radio PO
  Paris Conservatory Societé des Concerts Orch
  Rome RAI Orch
  South German RSO
  Southwest German RSO Baden–Baden
Rose, Barry
  Guildford Cathedral Choir
  Guildford String Orch
  Pro Arte Orch
Rose, Gregory
  Circle & Singcircle
  Irish National SO
  London Jupiter SO
Rosekrans, Charles
  Hungarian State Orch
Rosen, Michael
  Oberlin Percussion Group
Rosenbaum, Harold
  New York Virtuoso Singers
Rosenberg, Manfred
  Brandenburg PO Potsdam
Rosenberg, R.
  Great Lakes CO
Rosenkrans, Charles
  Hungarian State Opera Orch
Rosensteiner, Florian
  CO Diagonal
Rosenstock, Milton
  National PO London
  New York Theater Ensemble
Rosenthal, Manuel
  French National Orch
  Paris Opera Orch
Rosenzweig, Morris
  Speculum Musicae
Ros–Marbá, Antonio
  Catalonia CO
  Madrid SO
  Netherlands CO
  Philharmonia Orch
  Seville Real SO
Ross, Robert A.M.
  Philadelphia Festival Choir members
  Voces Novae et Antiquae
Rossel, Roger
  Wallonie Opera Royal Orch
Rosser, John
  Viva Voce

Rossi, Mario
  BBC Concert Orch
  Cologne RSO
  Milan RAI Lyric Orch
  Naples RAI Orch
  Naples RAI SO
  Naples Teatro San Carlo Orch
  Rome Radio–TV SO
  Rome RAI Orch
  La Scala Orch
  Turin Radio Orch
  Turin RAI Orch
  Turin RAI SO
  Turin RSO
  Turin SO
  Vienna State Opera Orch
Rostropovich, Mstislav
  English CO
  London PO
  London SO
  National SO
  National SO Washington D.C.
  Orch de Paris
  Rotterdam PO
Rota, Marcello
  Swiss–Italian Orch
Rother, Artur
  Berlin City Opera Orch
  Berlin Large RSO
  Berlin PO
  Berlin Radio Orch
  Berlin RSO
  Berlin Staatskapelle
  Berlin State Opera Orch
Rothlisberger, Dana
  Towson State Univ Sym Band
Rothman, George
  Riverside SO
Rothstein, Jack
  Johann Strauss Orch
  Viennese Orch of London
Rotman, Hans
  Antwerp Kameropera Orch
  Warsaw PO
Rotter, Jorge
  Württemberg PO
Rotzsch, Hans–Joachim
  Leipzig Gewandhaus Orch
  Leipzig New Bach Collegium Musicum
  Leipzig St. Thomas Church Choir
  New Bach Collegium Musicum
Rouchon, Jean–Phillippe
  Maurice Ravel CO
  Philharmonia Orch
Roudenko, Andrei
  Russian Chamber Choir
  Voskreseniye Choir
Rouger, Denis
  Paris Sorbonne Orch
Rouits, Dominique
  Massy CO
Roussel, Jacques
  Antiqua Musica CO
Rousset, Christophe
  Talens Lyriques
Routley, Nicholas
  Sydney Chamber Choir
Rovatkey, Lajos
  Capella Agostino Steffani
  Cologne Chamber Choir
Rowell, Malcolm W.
  Univ of Massachusetts/Amherst Wind Ensemble
Rowicki, Witold
  Narodowej PO
  Polish National SO
  Royal PO
  Warsaw PO
  Warsaw Philharmonic SO
  Warsaw State Opera House Orch
Rozehnal, Jan
  Camerata Bratislava
  Czech–Slovak RSO Bratislava
  Slovak RSO Bratislava
Rozel, M. Lasserre de
  Cap–de–la–Madeleine Choir
  Petits Chanteurs de Trois–Rivières
  Petits Chanteurs du Mont–Royal
  Radio Canada Orch
Rozhdestvensky, Gennadi
  Azerbaijan SO
  BBC SO
  Bolshoi Theater Orch
  Czech PO
  Danish National RSO
  Leningrad PO
  London SO
  Moscow PO Soloists
  Moscow RSO
  Moscow State SO
  Philharmonia Orch
  Rotterdam PO
  Royal Stockholm PO
  Russian Ministry of Culture SO
  Russian State SO
  Russian State Symphonic Cappella
  Stockholm Concert Band
  Stockholm PO
  USSR Large SO

Rozhdestvensky, Gennadi (cont.)
  USSR Ministry of Culture SO
  USSR Radio–TV Large SO
  USSR Radio–TV SO
  USSR RSO
  USSR SO
  USSR State SO
  Vienna SO
Rózsa, Miklós
  MGM Studio Orch
  Royal PO
Rozsnyai, Zoltán
  Columbia Chamber SO
  Columbia SO
  Leipzig Gewandhaus Orch
  Philharmonia Hungarica
Rubányi, Vilmos
  Hungarian State Opera Orch
Rudel, Julius
  Amadeus Wind Ensemble
  Caramoor Festival Orch
  London SO
  New Philharmonia Orch
  New York City Opera Orch
  Orch of St. Luke's
  Paris Opera Orch
  Philadelphia Opera Orch
  Philharmonia Orch
  Prague Virtuosi
Rudin, Alexander
  Musica Viva CO
Rudner, Ola
  Malmö SO
Rudolf, Max
  Cincinnati SO
  Columbia SO
Ruhland, Konrad
  Munich Capella Antiqua
  Niederaltaich Scholars
Rulon, C. Bryan
  Musicians' Accord
Rundel, Peter
  Ensemble Modern
Rundell, C.
  Royal Northern College of Music Wind Orch
Runnells, Richard
  Melbourne Windpower
Runnicles, Donald
  Bavarian RSO
Rusmanis, Kriss
  Riga PO
Russell, Christopher
  Indiana Univ New Music Ensemble
Russell, Robert
  Choral Arts Society
Russell, Timothy
  Naples PO
  Pro Musica CO
  Pro Musica Chamber Players
Russo, J.
  National Festival Orch
Rutenberg, Peter
  Los Angeles Chamber Singers
Rutter, John
  Cambridge Singers
  City of London Sinfonia
  City of London Sinfonia members
  Clare College Orch
  Philip Jones Brass Ensemble
Ruud, Ole Kristian
  Bergen PO
  Trondheim SO
Ruzicka, Peter
  Berlin German SO
  Berlin RSO
  North German SO
Rybakova, Ariadna
  Moscow Patriarchal Choir
Rybin, Valery
  Valery Rybin Male Choir
Rybrant, S.
  Berlin PO
  Malmö SO
Rzaev, Nazim
  Bolshoi Theater Orch
Reich, Steve
  Brooklyn PO
Sabajno, Carlo
  Royal Opera House Orch Covent Garden
  La Scala Orch
Sabata, Victor de
  Berlin PO
  New York PO
  RAI Orch
  Rome CO
  La Scala Orch
  Turin RAI SO
Saccani, Rico
  Budapest PO
  Irish National SO
Sacchetti, Arturo
  Lugano Chamber Society Orch
Sacher, Paul
  Bâle SO
  Basel CO
  Basel RSO
  Philharmonia Orch
  Zurich Collegium Musicum

Sachs, Joel
  Continuum Chamber Ensemble
  New Juilliard Ensemble
Sackett, Andrew
  Tewkesbury Abbey School Choir
Sedin, Robert
  Lincoln Center Jazz Orch members
  Orch of St. Luke's members
  Princeton Composers Ensemble
Safir, Rachid
  Les Jeunes Solistes
Segrestano, Luigi
  Hymnus Orch
  Prague Musici
Seidenberg, Daniel
  Saidenberg Little Sym
St. Clair, Carl
  Pacific SO
  Toronto Sinfonietta
Saint-Cyr, André
  St. Benoît-du-Lac Abbey Monks' Choir
  St. Scholastica Priory Nuns' Choir Petersham MA
Sakari, Petri
  Icelandic SO
  Swedish CO
Sakssian, Haig
  Bell'Arte Orch
Salanne, Jean-Paul
  Domaine Musicale Orch
Salonen, Esa-Pekka
  Berlin PO
  Finnish RSO
  London Sinfonietta
  Los Angeles PO
  New Stockholm CO
  Oslo PO
  Philharmonia Orch
  Stockholm CO
  Stockholm Sinfonietta
  Swedish RSO
  Swedish RSO members
Salter, Hans
  Graunke SO
Salter, Robert
  Guildhall String Ensemble
Saltzman, Harry
  Sine Nomine Baroque Orch
  Sine Nomine Singers
Salwarowski, Jerzy
  Polish National RSO Katowice
Samale, Niccola
  Sinfonia Orch delle Marche
Samoilov, Yevgeni
  Moscow New Opera Orch
Samosud, Samuel
  All-Union RSO
  Bolshoi Theater Orch
  Moscow PO
Samuel, Gerhard
  CCM Contemporary Music Ensemble
  Cincinnati PO
  Oakland SO
  Oakland Youth Orch
  Royal PO
Sanchez, Emma
  Luis Berger Ensemble
  Capella Cisplatina
  Elyma Ensemble
Sand, Michael
  Arcangeli Baroque Strings
Sandberg, Herbert
  Royal Opera Orch
  Stockholm Royal Opera House Orch
Sander, Alexander
  Berlin RSO
Sanderling, Kurt
  BBC PO
  Berlin SO
  Cleveland Orch
  (Royal) Concertgebouw Orch
  Czech PO
  Danish National RSO
  Dresden Staatskapelle
  Leipzig Gewandhaus Orch
  Leningrad PO
  Philharmonia Orch
Sanderling, Stefan
  Irish National SO
  Royal PO
Sanderling, Thomas
  Berlin RSO
  London PO
  Turin PO
Sanders, John
  Gloucester Cathedral Choir
Sándor, Frigyes
  Franz Liszt CO
Sándor, János
  Budapest PO
  Győr PO
  Hungarian PO
  Hungarian State Opera Orch
  Hungarian State Orch
  London PO
  London SO
  Philharmonia Orch
Sanna, Sandro
  Berlin Radio Youth Orch

Sanna, Sandro (cont.)
  Montepulciano Arts Center Orch
Santi, Nello
  London SO
  Munich National Theater Orch
  ORTF Lyric Orch
  Royal PO
  Swiss–Italian Orch
  Turin Teatro Regio Orch
  Venice Teatro La Fenice Orch
Santi, P.
  Milan Virtuosi
Santini, Gabriele
  Naples Teatro San Carlo Orch
  Rome Opera Orch
  Rome RAI SO
  La Scala Orch
  Turin RAI Orch
  Turin RAI SO
Sanzogno, Nino
  Belgian Radio–TV Orch
  Chicago Lyric Opera Orch
  Florence Maggio Musicale Orch
  Milan RAI SO
  Naples Alessandro Scarlatti RAI Orch
  Palermo Teatro Massimo Orch
  Piacenza SO
  St. Cecilia Academy Orch Rome
  La Scala Orch
  Turin RAI SO
Sapszon, Ferenc
  Budapest MAV SO
  Budapest SO
  Hungarian State Opera Orch
Saraste, Jukka-Pekka
  Avantil CO
  Avanti Orch
  Bavarian RSO
  English CO
  Finnish RSO
  German Chamber PO
  Helsinki CO
  Scottish CO
  Umeå Sinfonietta
Serbu, Eugène
  European Master Orch
Sercos, Jean-Philippe
  Palais Royal Orch
Sardelli, Federico Maria
  Modo Antiquo
Sargent, Malcolm
  BBC SO
  D'Oyly Carte Opera Company Orch
  Leeds Philharmonic Society
  Liverpool PO
  London New SO
  London PO
  London SO
  Philharmonia Orch
  Pro Arte Orch
  Royal Choral Society
  Royal Liverpool PO
  Royal PO
  Vienna PO
Sassano, Salvatore
  Naples Teatro San Carlo Orch
Sassmannshaus, Kurt
  Starling CO
Satanowski, Robert
  Poznan Philharmonic SO
  Warsaw Opera Orch
  Warsaw Teatr Wielki Orch
Sato, Kotaro
  Tokyo Metropolitan SO
Satomaa, Tauno
  Candomino Choir
Sauvina, C.
  Frankenland State SO
Savage, Stephen
  Griffith Univ Ensemble
Savall, Jordi
  La Capella Reial de Catalunya
  Concert des Nations
  Hespèrion XX
Savina, Carlo
  Stockholm Royal Opera House Orch
Savini, Ino
  Barcelona Teatro Liceo Orch
Savino, Domenico
  Rome SO
Sawallisch, Wolfgang
  Bavarian RSO
  Bavarian State Opera Orch
  Bavarian State Orch
  Bayreuth Festival Orch
  Berlin RIAS SO
  Berlin RSO
  (Royal) Concertgebouw Orch
  Czech PO
  Leipzig Gewandhaus Orch
  London PO
  London SO
  Munich Winds
  NHK SO
  Philadelphia Orch
  Philharmonia Orch
  Rome RAI Orch
  La Scala Orch
  Swiss Romande Orch

Sawallisch, Wolfgang (cont.)
  Vienna SO
Sayer, Roger
  Rochester Cathedral Choir
Sbârcea, Petre
  Sibiu PO
Scaglia, Ferruccio
  Milan RAI SO
  Rome Italian Radio-TV Orch
Scapin, Massimo
  Laudis Cantores
Schaap, Jan
  Zaanstad Opera Orch
Schabasser, Josef
  Vienna Hofburg Chapel Choir
Schaenen, L.
  Chicago Lyric Opera Orch
Schäfer, Wolfgang
  Frankfurt Kantorei
  Freiburg Vocal Ensemble
Schaffner, Franz
  Lucerne City Wind Orch
Schalk, Franz
  Vienna PO
Scharoev, Anton
  Kiev National Phil CO
Schat, Peter
  Netherlands Wind Ensemble
Schebesta, Martin
  Academy of London Orch
Scheibe, Jo-Michael
  Univ of Miami Chorale
Schemahegumen, Dimitri
  Pochaev Lavra of the Dormiton Monks' Choir
Schenck, Andrew
  Atlantic Sinfonietta
  Chicago SO
  Ljubljana SO
  London SO
  New Zealand SO
Scherchen, Herman
  Cologne RSO
  Czech PO
  French National Orch
  French Radio-TV Orch
  Hessian RSO
  London Phil SO
  London SO
  Milan RAI SO
  North German RSO
  Northwest German PO
  Paris Opera Orch
  RTSI Orch
  Swiss-Italian RSO
  Swiss-Italian Radio-TV Orch
  Turin Radio Orch
  Vienna State Opera Orch
  Vienna State Opera Orch Soloists
  Vienna SO
Scherman, Thomas
  Little Orch Society
  Vienna State Opera Orch
Schermerhorn, Kenneth
  CSR Bratislava SO
  Czech-Slovak RSO
  Hong Kong PO
  Milwaukee SO
Schernus, Herbert
  Cologne German Radio Wind Quintet
  Cologne RSO
Scherzer, Ernst-Günther
  Vienna Operetta Orch
Scherzer, Manfred
  Dresden CO
Scheuber, K.
  Küsnacht Seminar Chamber Choir
  Zurich Ad Hoc Chorus
Schickele, Peter
  Turtle Mountain Naval Base Tactical Wind Ensemble
Schiff, Heinrich
  CO of Europe
  German Chamber PO
  Northern Sinfonia of England
  Philharmonia Orch
Schifrin, Lalo
  Hollywood CO
  London Studio SO
  Mexican State SO
Schillings, Max von
  Berlin State Opera Orch
  Berlin State Opera Orch members
  Berlin State Orch members
Scholl, Stefan
  Norwegian State Institute of Music Chamber Choir
Schippers, Thomas
  Cincinnati SO
  Columbia SO
  Florence Maggio Musicale Orch
  Juilliard Orch
  London SO
  New Philharmonia Orch
  New York Metropolitan Opera Orch
  New York PO
  RCA Italian Opera Orch
  Rome Opera Orch
  Rome RAI Orch
  Rome RAI SO
  St. Cecilia Academy Orch Rome
  La Scala Orch

Schippers, Thomas (cont.)
  Swiss Romande Orch
  Trieste PO
Schirmer, Ulf
  Vienna PO
Schlenck, John
  Vedantic Arts Ensemble
Schlingensiepen, Marc-Andreas
  Düsseldorf Choir
  Robert Schumann CO
Schmalstich, Clemens
  Berlin State Opera Orch
Schmeller, J.
  Ethel Smyth Ensemble
Schmelzer, Peter
  Prague Virtuosi
Schmid, Daniel
  Southern Bohemian Chamber PO Budweis
Schmid, Elmar
  Basel SO
Schmid, Erich
  Beromünster RSO
Schmidt, Hartmut
  Düsseldorf Choir
  Düsseldorf SO
  Niederrheinisch Community Choir
Schmidt, Ole
  Aarhus SO
  Danish National RSO
  Malmö SO
  Rhineland-Palatinate State PO
  Royal Northern College of Music CO
Schmidt-Boelcke, Werner
  Bavarian RSO
  FFB Orch
Schmidt-Gaden, Gerhard
  Collegium Aureum
  European Baroque Soloists
  Tölz Boys' Choir
Schmidt-Gertenbach, Volker
  Berlin SO
Schmidt-Isserstedt, Hans
  Berlin German Opera Orch
  Berlin PO
  Dresden Staatskapelle
  London SO
  North German RSO
  Stockholm PO
  Stockholm SO
Schmöhe, Georg
  Bamberg SO
  Berlin RSO
  Nuremberg SO
  Stuttgart PO
Schmolzi, Herbert
  Sarre CO
Schneebeli, Olivier
  Contrepoint Vocal Ensemble
  Marais SO
  Musica Aeterna
Schneider, Alexander
  CO of Europe
  Columbia SO
  English CO
  Marlboro Festival Orch
  Mostly Mozart Festival Orch
Schneider, Michael
  Bremen La Stagione
  Cologne Camerata
  La Stagione
Schneider, Peter
  Bayreuth Festival Orch
  Mannheim National Theater Orch
  Munich RSO
Schneider, Urs
  Bavarian RSO
  Capella Istropolitana
  Cologne RSO
  CSSR State PO Košice
  Czech-Slovak State PO
  Slovak PO
  Slovak State PO Košice
Schneiderhan, Wolfgang
  Berlin PO
Schneidt, Hanns-Martin
  Bamberg RSO
  Bavarian RSO
  Berlin RSO
  Munich Bach Orch
Schnitzler, Claude
  Bretagne Orch
  Brittany Orch
Scholes, Peter
  Aukland Philharmonia Orch
  New Zealand SO
Schöll, Klaus Rainer
  Mainz Wind Ensemble
Scholz, Alfred
  London Festival Orch
  London PO
  London SO
  New Philharmonia Orch
  Royal PO
  Vienna Volksoper Orch
Scholz, R.
  American CO
Schönherr, Max
  Austrian RSO

Schönwandt, Michael
  Berlin SO
  Collegium Musicum
  Copenhagen Collegium Musicum
  Danish National RSO
  Nice SO
  Royal Danish Orch
  South Jutland SO
  Tivoli SO
Schönwandt, Michael
  Danish SO
Schönzeler, Hans-Hubert
  Bournemouth Sinfonietta
  Melbourne SO
  West Australian SO
Schoonbroodt, Hubert
  Camerata Leodiensis
Schoorvaerts, P.
  Brussels Concert Band
Schreier, Manfred
  Stuttgart New Vocal Soloists
Schreier, Peter
  Austrian RSO
  Berlin CO
  Berlin Soloists
  CPE Bach CO
  Dresden Baroque Soloists
  Dresden Staatskapelle
  Scottish CO
Schröder, Jaap
  Concerto Amsterdam
  Drottningholm Baroque Ensemble
  Smithsonian CO
  Smithsonian Quartet
Schröder, Kurt
  Hessian RSO
Schuback, Thomas
  Drottningholm Baroque Ensemble
  Gothenburg CO
Schubert, Peter
  New Calliope Singers
Schubert, Wolfgang
  Graunke SO
Schüchter, Wilhelm
  Berlin Orch
  North German RSO
Schuler, David
  Church of St. Luke in the Fields Choir
Schüler, Johannes
  Berlin German Opera Orch
  Berlin State Opera Orch
Schuller, Gunther
  American Composers Orch
  Boston Pro Arte CO
  Collage New Music Ensemble
  Cologne RSO
  French Radio-TV PO
  Hanover North German Radio PO
  Houston Grand Opera Orch
  Lincoln Center Chamber Music Society
  Louisville Orch
  Melbourne SO
  Netherlands Radio PO
  New England Conservatory Ensemble
  New England Conservatory Ragtime Ensemble
  Saarbrück RSO
  St. Louis SO
Schultz, Stephen
  American Baroque
Schumacher, Richard
  Masterplayers
Schuman, William
  Adirondack CO
Schuricht, Carl
  Bavarian RSO
  Berlin PO
  Berlin Reich RSO
  Berlin State Orch
  (Royal) Concertgebouw Orch
  Frankfurt RSO
  French National Orch
  Hamburg SO
  Hessian RSO
  Monaco PO
  North German SO
  Paris National Orch
  Paris Opera Orch
  South German RSO
  South German SO
  Southwest German RSO Baden-Baden
  Stockholm RSO
  Stockholm SO
  Stuttgart RSO
  Swiss-Italian RSO
  Swiss Radio-TV Orch
  Swiss Romande Orch
  Vienna PO
Schurmann, Gerrard
  BBC SO
Schutze, Norbert
  Cologne RSO
  Händel Collegium
Schwartz, Magali
  Recherche Ensemble
Schwarz, Gerard
  American String Quartet
  English CO
  Hayashi Duo

Schwarz, Gerard (cont.)
  Juilliard Orch
  Juilliard String Quartet
  London SO
  Los Angeles CO
  Mostly Mozart Festival Orch
  Music Today Ensemble
  New York Chamber SO
  New York CO
  New York Trumpet Ensemble
  92nd St. Y Chamber SO
  92nd St. Y Chamber SO members
  Northwest Sinfonia
  Philadelphia Orch
  Scottish CO
  Seattle SO
  Carl Maria von Weber School for Music Soloists
Schwarz, Mario
  St. Gallen Collegium Musicum
Schwarz, Peter
  Berlin Ars Nova Ensemble
  Los Angeles CO
Schwarz, Rudolf
  London SO
Schweizer, Daniel
  Zurich SO
Scimone, Claudio
  Cappella Coloniensis
  Monte Carlo Opera Orch
  Philharmonia Orch
  Venice Solisti
Scott, John
  Royal PO
  Royal PO Pops
  St. Paul's Cathedral Choir
  St. Paul's Cathedral Special Choir
Scott, K. Lee
  Lee Scott Singers
Seal, Richard
  Salisbury Cathedral Choir
Seaman, Christopher
  Great Britain National Youth Orch
  Royal PO
Sebastian, Georges
  Berlin City Opera Orch
  Budapest RSO
  Czech PO
  Metropolitan Opera Orch
  Paris Opera Orch
Sebesta, Josef
  Prague Castle Brass Septet
Sebestyen, Ernö
  Bavarian RSO
  Berlin RIAS Sinfonietta
Sedares, James
  English CO
  London SO
  Louisville Orch
  New Zealand SO
  Phoenix SO
Sedazzari, Claudio Felice
  Schubert Camerata
Seebacher, Willi
  Leonhard Lechner Chamber Choir
Seeley, Gilbert
  Oregon Repertory Singers
Seelig, Timothy
  Dallas Wind Sym
  Dallas Women's Chorus
  Fort Worth CO
  Fort Worth Sym Brass
  Turtle Creek Chorale
Seeliger, Wolfgang
  Darmstadt CO
  Darmstadt Concert Choir
Seers, Jonathan
  Berlin RSO
Segal, Uri
  Lausanne CO
  Stuttgart RSO
Segarra, Ireneu
  Antics Escolans Orch
  Barcelona Ars Musicae Ensemble
  Montserrat Capella e Escolania
  Montserrat Escolania
Segerstam, Leif
  Austrian RSO
  Bamberg SO
  Danish National RSO
  Finnish RSO
  Helsinki CO
  Helsinki PO
  Kontra String Quartet
  Malmö SO
  Norrköping SO
  ORF SO
  Rhineland-Palatinate State PO
  Royal Stockholm PO
  Stockholm PO
  Swedish RSO
  Tampere PO
Seibel, Klauspeter
  German SO
  Kiel PO
Seifried, Reinhard
  Czech-Slovak State PO
  Irish National SO
Seipenbusch, Edgar
  Slovak PO

Šejna, Karel
Brno State PO
Czech PO
Semkow, Jerzy
Berlin PO
Cracow RSO
Polish National RSO Katowice
St. Louis SO
La Scala Orch
Warsaw PO
Sempé, Skip
Capriccio Stravagante
Senturia, M.
Univ of California SO
Serafin, Tullio
Florence Maggio Musicale Orch
Florence Teatro Comunale Orch
Milan RAI SO
Naples Teatro San Carlo Orch
Palermo Teatro Massimo Orch
Paris Opera Orch
Philharmonia Orch
Rome Opera Orch
Rome Radio-TV SO
Rome RAI SO
Royal Opera House Orch
St. Cecilia Academy Orch Rome
San Remo SO
La Scala Orch
Serebrier, José
Adelaide SO
Belgian RSO
Brno Czech State PO
Brno State PO
Czech State PO
English CO
London SO
Melbourne SO
Oslo PO
Philharmonia Orch
Rome RAI SO
Royal PO
Scottish CO
Scottish National Orch
Sicilian SO
Sydney SO
Sergeyev, Nikolai
Russian State Brass Orch
Serov, Eduard
Czech PO
Odense SO
Seurre, J.
Paris Harmonie Orch
Sewen, Marek
Cappella Arcis Varsoviensis
Warsaw CO
Warsaw Strings
Shallon, David
Bavarian RSO
Berlin RSO
Stuttgart RSO
Shambadal, Lior
Bamberg SO
Berlin Sinfonia
Shapey, Ralph
London Sinfonietta
Univ of Chicago Contemporary Chamber Players
Shaw, Robert
Academy of the Begynhof Amsterdam
Atlanta SO
Robert Shaw Chamber Singers
Robert Shaw Festival Singers
Robert Shaw Orch
Sheffer, Jonathan
Eos Ensemble
Shek, Henry
Gunma SO
Moscow SO
Shelley, Howard
City of London Sinfonia
London Mozart Players
Shepel, Oleg
Voronezh Chamber Choir
Shepherd, Adrian
Cantilena
Sheppard, P.
Parnassus Ensemble
Shereshevsky, Aaron
USSR State SO
Sherry, Fred
Speculum Musicae members
Shewan, Robert
Roberts Wesleyan College Chorale
Roberts Wesleyan College Wind Ensemble
Shewan, Stephen
Roberts Wesleyan College Brass Ensemble
Shilkret, Nathaniel
RCA Victor SO
Shipovalnikov, Aleksei
Slavyanka Men's Chorus
Shipway, Frank
Royal PO
Shostakovich, Maxim
Bavarian RSO
BBC SO
London PO
London SO
Montreal Musici

Shostakovich, Maxim (cont.)
Moscow RSO
New Philharmonia Orch
Prague SO
USSR Radio-TV Large SO
USSR Radio-TV SO
USSR SO
Shpiller, Ivan
Russian State SO
USSR Radio-TV Large SO
Shrock, Dennis
Canterbury Choral Society
Shulman, Daniel
Group for Contemporary Music
Light Fantastic Players
Speculum Musicae
Shumsky, E.
Pacific Rim Soloists
Sibert, Adolphe
Belgian Radio-TV Orch
ORTF Lyric Orch
Sie, Yip Wing
Hong Kong PO
Siede, Heiko
Telemann CO
Siegel, Laurenc
London PO
London SO
Philharmonia Orch
Royal PO
Sieghart, Martin
Bratislava RSO
Bruckner Orch Linz
Czech-Slovak RSO
Czech-Slovak State Radio PO
Linz Bruckner Orch
Mozart Academy
Polish State PO
Stuttgart CO
Vienna Concert Society
Vienna Concert Society Orch
Siegmann, Christian
Banda Classica
Siegwart, Peter
Luzern Opus Novum Ensemble
Zurich Collegium Musicum
Silantiev, Yury
All-Union Radio-TV Sym Variety Orch
Armenian Radio-TV Orch
Moscow RSO
Silipigni, Alfredo
Turin RAI SO
Sillito, Kenneth
Academy of St. Martin in the Fields
Silva, Luiz Alves da
Turicum Ensemble
Silva, Ruben
Moravian PO
Silver, Sheila
Musicians' Accord
Silverstein, Joseph
Bamberg SO
Utah SO
Silvestri, Constantin
Bournemouth SO
Philharmonia Orch
Romanian Radio-TV Orch
Simmons, Calvin
Los Angeles PO
Simms, James A.
Trinity Church Choir
Simon, Albert
Franz Liszt Academy Orch
Simon, Emil
Cluj-Napoca PO
Simon, Geoffrey
BBC SO
English CO
English CO Wind Ensemble
40 Cellos of the London PO
48 Violas of Academy of St. Martin in the Fields
Handel Festival Orch
London PO
London SO
Melbourne SO
Philadelphia Orch
Philharmonia Orch
Philharmonia Orch Off-stage Brass
Royal PO
Preston, Simon
(Royal) Concertgebouw CO
English CO
Westminster Abbey Choir
Westminster Abbey Orch
Simon, Stephen
London Philomusica Antiqua
New York Philomusica Antiqua
Simonetto, Alfredo
Milan Italian Radio-TV Orch
Milan RAI Lyric Orch
Milan RAI Orch
Milan RAI SO
Turin Radio-TV SO
Turin RAI Orch
Turin RAI SO
Simonov, Yuri
Bolshoi Theater Orch
London SO
Philharmonia Orch

Simonov, Yuri (cont.)
Royal PO
Sinaisky, Vasil
BBC PO
Moscow PO
Sinangil, Ali Dogan
Istanbul State Opera Orch
Istanbul State Opera Soloists
Sinclair, James
Orch New England
Singer, Kurt
Berlin State Opera Orch
Singher, Michael
Oberlin CO
Singleton, Kenneth
Denver Brass
Sinopoli, Giuseppe
Berlin German Opera Orch
Dresden Staatskapelle
German Opera Orch
New York PO
Philharmonia Orch
St. Cecilia Academy Orch Rome
Sitkovetsky, Dmitri
English CO
New European Strings
New European Strings CO
Prague Virtuosi
Sjökvist, Gustaf
Stockholm SO
Skidmore, Jeffrey
Baroque Orch
Ex Cathedra Baroque Orch
His Majesties Sagbutts & Cornetts
Skopal, Jiří
Boni Pueri Boys' Choir
Skripka, Sergei
Russian State Cinema Orch
Skrowaczewski, Stanislaw
Cologne RSO
French National Orch
Hallé Orch
London New SO
London SO
Minneapolis SO
Minnesota SO
Škvor, Petr
Dvořák CO
Pardubice CO
Philharmonic CO
Prague CO
Suk CO
Slatkin, Felix
Concert Arts Strings
Concert Arts Symphonic Band
Hollywood Bowl SO
St. Louis SO
Slatkin, Leonard
Bavarian RSO
Berlin RSO
Chicago SO
Juilliard Orch
London PO
London SO
Louisville Orch
Minnesota Orch
Munich RSO
National SO Washington D.C.
Philharmonia Orch
Royal PO
St. Louis SO
St. Louis SO members
Sleeper, Thomas
Univ of Miami SO
Sligter, Jurrien
Basho Ensemble
Slovák, Ladislav
Czech-Slovak RSO Bratislava
Leningrad Conservatory Academic SO
Melbourne SO
Prague SO
Slovak PO
Slowik, Kenneth
Smithsonian Chamber Players
Small, Howard Don
St. Mark's Cathedral Choir Minneapolis
Smetáček, Václav
Bologna SO
Czech PO
Prague CO
Prague RSO
Prague SO
Smith, Barry
St. Georges Singers
Smith, Craig
Emmanuel Music Chorus
Smith, Gregg
Adirondack CO
Dana Chorale
New York City Free-Lance Orch
Gregg Smith Singers
Smith, T.
Trinity Church Choir
Smola, Emmerich
Berlin RSO
BRTN PO
Southwest German RSO Baden-Baden
Snashall, John
English CO

Snell, Howard
  Brittania Building Society Band
  CWS Glasgow Band
  English CO
  London SO
  Royal PO
Sobol, Lawrence
  Orch de Paris Soloists
Sobotka, Wolfgang
  Capella Istropolitana
Söderblom, Ulf
  Finnish National Opera Orch
  Finnish RSO
  Helsinki PO
  Lahti SO
  Savonlinna Opera Festival Orch
Sollberger, Harvey
  Columbia Univ Group for Contemporary Music
  Group for Contemporary Music
  Indiana Univ New Music Ensemble
  Indiana Univ SO
  June in Buffalo CO
  San Diego SO Ensemble
  SONOR Ensemble of Univ of California San Diego members
  Speculum Musicae
Solomon, Izler
  Brandeis Festival Orch
  Columbus PO
  Indianapolis SO
  MGM Wind Orch
  RCA Victor SO
Solomon, Magen
  Redwood Sym
Solomons, Derek
  L'Estro Armonico
Soltesz, Stefan
  Munich RSO
  Vienna SO
Solti, Georg
  Bavarian RSO
  Bavarian State Opera Orch
  Bavarian SO
  Berlin PO
  CO of Europe
  Chicago Sym Chorus
  Chicago SO
  Cleveland Orch
  Cologne RSO
  (Royal) Concertgebouw Orch
  English CO
  Israel PO
  London PO
  London SO
  Naples Alessandro Scarlatti RAI Orch
  National PO London
  Orch de Paris
  Paris Opera Orch
  RCA Italian Opera Orch
  Rome Opera Orch
  Royal Opera House Orch Covent Garden
  St. Cecilia Academy Orch Rome
  La Scala Orch
  Vienna PO
  Vienna State Opera Chorus
  West German Radio Orch
  World Orch for Peace
Somary, Johannes
  Amor Artis Chamber Choir
  Amor Artis Orch
  Bronx Arts Ensemble
  English CO
  Polish National RSO Katowice
Sondeckis, Saulius
  Lithuanian CO
  St. Petersburg Camerata
Sothcott, John
  St. George's Canzona
Soudant, Herbert
  Sicilian SO
Sourisse, Jean
  Jean Sourisse Ensemble
  Vocal Audite Nova Ensemble
Sousa, John Philip
  Philadelphia Rapid Transit Company Band
  Sousa Band
Soustrot, Marc
  Loire PO
  Monte Carlo PO
Southgate, William
  New Zealand SO
Spada, Pietro
  Philharmonia Orch
  Philharmonia Orch Soloists
Spain, Anthony
  Northwest SO
Spalding, Richard
  Louisville Orch
Spanjaard, Ed
  Amsterdam New Sinfonietta
  Arditti String Quartet
  Caecilia Consort
  The Hague PO
  Netherlands Radio CO
  New Ensemble
Spano, Robert
  Bowling Green State Univ New Music Festival Ensemble
Sparf, Nils–Erik
  Drottningholm Baroque Ensemble

Spassky, Nicolas
  St. Nicolas Russian Orthodox Choir
Spassov, Boris
  Sofia National Opera Orch
Speach, Bernadette
  Bowery Ensemble
Speer, D.
  Contemporary Music Group
Sperber, S.
  Haifa SO
  Rinat & Israel Mandolin Ensemble
Spering, Christoph
  Das Neue Orch
Spicer, Paul
  Finzi Singers
  Finzi Wind Ensemble
Spiegelman, Joel
  Moscow PO
  Moscow RSO
Spieth, D.
  Lehigh Valley CO
Spivakov, Vladimir
  Moscow Virtuosi
Spohr, Dietburg
  Belcanto Ensemble Frankfurt
Sporken, Gerhard
  Liège New Music Ensemble
Springer, Alois
  Hamburg SO
  Luxembourg RSO
Springfels, Mary
  Newberry Consort
Spruit, Henk
  Netherlands Radio PO
Squires, S. E.
  Illinois CO
Stadlmair, Hans
  Bamberg SO
  Munich CO
Staicu, Paul
  Ciprian Porumbescu Conservatory Camerata CO
Stamic, P.
  International Festival Orch
Stamp, Jack
  Keystone Wind Ensemble
Stamp, Richard
  Academy of London Orch
  Toronto CO
Standage, Simon
  Academy of Ancient Music
  Collegium Musicum 90
Stanger, Russell
  Royal PO
Stanhope, David
  Seymour Group
  Tall Poppies Orch
Stanischeff, Christo
  ORF SO
Stankovsky, Robert
  Camerata Cassovia
  CSSR State PO Košice
  Czech PO
  Czech–Slovak RSO Bratislava
  Czech–Slovak RSO Prague
  Czech–Slovak State PO
  Philharmonia Cassovia
  Slovak RSO Bratislava
  Slovak State PO Košice
Stapleton, Robin
  Royal PO
Starek, Jiří
  Berlin RIAS Sinfonietta
  Berlin Radio Sinfonietta
  Stuttgart RSO
Starobin, David
  Speculum Musicae
Stassevitch, F.
  Budapest Chamber Ensemble
Steen, Jac van
  The Hague PO
  Netherlands Radio CO
Stefanov, Vassil
  Bulgarian RSO
  Philharmonia Bulgarica
  Sofia SO
Stefánsson, Jón
  Icelandic SO
  Langholtskirkju Choir
Stegmann, Bernd
  Berlin Vocal Ensemble
Steiger, Rand
  California EAR Unit
  California EAR Unit Yamaha Computer Assisted Music System
  SONOR Ensemble of Univ of California San Diego
Stein, Horst
  Bamberg SO
  Berlin State Opera Orch
  Swiss–Italian Orch
  Vienna PO
  Vienna State Opera Orch
  Vienna SO
Steinberg, Pinchas
  Austrian RSO
  Basel RSO
  Cologne RSO
  Czech–Slovak RSO Bratislava
  Munich RSO
  ORF SO

Stokowski, Leopold

Steinberg, Pinchas (cont.)
  RCA Victor SO
  Vienna ORF SO
Steinberg, William
  Berlin State Opera Orch
  Boston SO
  New York PO
  Philharmonia Orch
  Pittsburgh SO
  RCA Victor SO
Steiner, Fred
  National PO
Steiner, Heinrich
  Berlin RSO
Steinitz, Paul
  Collegium Sagittarii
Steinkopf, Hans
  Berlin RSO
Steinlucht, Arkady
  Mozarteum Orch
Steinsky, U.
  Scottish CO
Stenz, Markus
  Royal Scottish National Orch
Stephens, Harry
  The Sixteen Orch
Stephens, John
  American Camerata
  American Camerata for New Music
  Annapolis Brass Quintet
Stephenson, Allan
  South African National SO
Stephenson, Mark
  London Musici
Stern, Adam
  Basel Opera Mobile CO
  XTET
Stern, Gershon
  Israel SO
  Malmö SO
Stern, Isaac
  Columbia CO
  Columbia String Orch
  Jerusalem Music Center CO
  London SO
Stern, Michael
  Zurich Tonhalle Orch
Sternberg, Jonathan
  Zurich RSO
Sternefeld, Daniel
  Belgian National Orch
Stevens, Denis
  Accademia Monteverdiana Orch
Stevenson, C.
  Morhange Ensemble
Stewart, Warren
  Whole Noyse
Steyer, Arlette
  Maîtrise de Garçons de Colmar
Stiedry, Fritz
  Metropolitan Opera Orch
  New Friends of Music Orch
  Southern PO
Stiefel, Werner
  Bohuslav Martinů PO
Stier, Gothart
  Dresden Kreuz Choir
Stiglich, Irina
  Vassil Arnaudov Sofia Chamber Choir
Stobart, James
  Locke Brass Consort
Stock, David
  Pittsburgh New Music Ensemble
Stock, Frederick
  Chicago SO
Stokowski, Leopold
  All–American Youth SO
  American SO
  American SO Winds
  American Youth SO
  BBC SO
  Berlin PO
  Budapest RSO
  Chicago SO
  Czech PO
  Frankfurt RSO
  French National RSO
  Grenadier Guards Band
  Hilversum RSO
  Hollywood Bowl SO
  Houston SO
  Japan PO
  Leipzig Gewandhaus Orch
  Leopold Stokowski SO
  London PO
  London SO
  Los Angeles PO
  Metropolitan Opera Orch
  National PO
  National PO London
  NBC SO
  New Philharmonia Orch
  New Philharmonic Orch
  New York City SO
  New York Stadium SO
  Philadelphia Orch
  Philharmonic SO
  RCA Victor SO
  Residentie Orch The Hague

Stokowski, Leopold (cont.)
Royal PO
Southwest German RSO Baden-Baden
Stockholm PO
Stokowski SO
Swiss Romande Orch
Symphony of the Air
Stoll, Pierre
Paris SO
Stolz, Robert
Berlin German Opera Orch
Berlin SO
Vienna SO
Stone, Sayard
English CO
Storgårds, John
Wegelius CO
Zagros Ensemble
Storojev, M.
Montreal Musici
Storosum, Chaim
Collegium Musicum Judaicum Amsterdam
Stoutz, Edmond de
Zurich CO
Zurich Tonhalle Orch Winds
Stracke, Hans Richard
Philharmonia Hungarica
Stradelli, Victor de
London Festival Orch
London PO
London PO Festival Orch
Strange, Richard
Arizona State Univ Symphonic Band
Carnegie Mellon Concert Winds
Straram, Walther
Concerts Straram Orch
Walther Straram Orch
Straszynski, Andrzey
Polish National RSO Katowice
Stratta, Ettore
Baroque CO
Baroque Pops Orch
Festival Orch
Lille National Orch
Luxembourg RSO
Royal PO
Royal PO Strings
Stratton, Kerry
Hungarian State Orch
Moscow SO
Straube, Jörg
North German Figural Choir
Strauss, Eduard
Eduard Strauss Orch
Vienna Volksoper Orch
Strauss, Melvin
Longy Artists Ensemble
Strauss, Richard
Bavarian State Orch
Berlin PO
Berlin State Opera Orch
Tivoli SO
Vienna PO
Vienna State Opera Orch
Stravinsky, Igor
CBC Vancouver SO
Columbia Jazz Combo
Columbia SO
Grande Orchestre Symphonique
New York Philharmonic SO
North German RSO
Rome RAI SO
Royal PO
Swiss-Italian RSO
Walther Straram Orch
Streatfeild, Simon
Manitoba CO
Quebec SO
Strickland, William
Dumbarton Oaks Orch
Finnish RSO
Göteborg SO
Icelandic SO
Japan PSO
Oslo PO
Polish National RSO Katowice
Tokyo Imperial PO
Tokyo PO
Vienna SO
Stride, Fred
Fred Stride Orch
Stromberg, William T.
Moscow SO
Strugala, Tadeusz
Polish National RSO Katowice
Warsaw PO
Strydom, André
Cincinnati Contemporary Music Ensemble
Stryja, Karol
Polish National RSO Katowice
Polish State PO
Polish State PO Katowice
Silesian PO
Silesian Philharmonic SO
Slaska PO
Stryncl, Marek
Musica Florea
Stuart, Paul
Rochester Opera Theater Orch

Stubbs, Stephen
Tragicomedia
Studt, Richard
Bournemouth Sinfonietta
Stulen, Jan
Cologne RSO
Hilversum NOS Radio Orch
Hilversum RSO
Stultz, Marie
New England Merrimack College Treble Chorus
Treble Chorus of New England
Stupel, Ilya
Artur Rubinstein PO
Stupka, Frantisek
Czech PO
Prague RSO
Sturk, S.
Metropolitan Brass Ensemble
Stuurpp, Alda
Les Eléments
Stych, Jan
Brno State PO
Prague National Theater Orch
Suben, Joel Eric
Janáček PO
Polish National RSO Katowice
Slovak RSO Bratislava
Sudduth, James
Texas Tech Univ Symphonic Band
Suhubiette, Joel
Jacques Moderne Ensemble
Suitner, Otmar
Berlin Staatskapelle
Berlin State Opera Orch
Dresden Staatskapelle
Dresden State Opera Orch
Suk, Josef
Suk CO
Summerly, Jeremy
Oxford Camerata
Oxford Schola Cantorum
Sund, Robert
Orphei Drängar
Sung-jen, Hsu
Yomiuri Nippon SO
Surinach, Carlos
Athens SO
Paris RSO
Susskind, Walter
CBC Vancouver SO
Cincinnati SO
London SO
Philharmonia Orch
Philharmonic Orch
St. Louis SO
Sutej, Vjekoslav
Spalato National Theater Orch
Suzuki, Masaaki
Japan Bach Collegium
Svedlund, Thord
Camerata Romana
Gothenburg SO
Örebro CO
Umeå SO
Svejkovsky, Josef
Prague Trumpet Players Ensemble
Sveshnikov, Alexandr
USSR State Academic Choir
Svetlanov, Evgeni
Bolshoi Theater Orch
Bolshoi Theater SO Brass Section
London SO
Moscow RSO
Philharmonia Orch
Russia State SO
Russian Federation State SO
Russian State SO
Swedish RSO
USSR Radio-TV Large SO
USSR State Academy Orch
USSR State SO
USSR SO
Swann, Frederick
Crystal Cathedral Choir
Swarowsky, Hans
Bamberg PO
Bamberg SO
Czech PO
Prague National Theater Orch
Vienna Pro Musica Orch
Vienna State Opera Orch
Vienna SO
Swensen, Joseph
Tapiola Sinfonietta
Swierczewski, Michel
Lisbon Gulbenkian Foundation Orch
Swift, Daniel
CBC Vancouver SO
Swift, Maj Roger G.
Coldstream Guards Regimental Band
Swoboda, Henry
Vienna SO
Winterthur SO
Swoboda, Jerzy
Polish State PO
Silesian PO
Warsaw PO

Symeonides, A.
Bamberg SO
Symonette, Victor
Cologne RSO
Szabó, D.
Cantemus
Szabó, Miklós
Benjamin Britten Vocal Ensemble
Tátrai String Quartet
Szalinski, Antoni
Warsaw PO
Szegö, Péter
Anonymus Ensemble
Szekeres, Ferenc
Budapest Strings
Hungarian State Orch
Szell, George
Berlin PO
Berlin RSO
Cleveland Orch
Columbia SO
(Royal) Concertgebouw Orch
Czech PO
Dresden Staatskapelle
English CO
London PO
London SO
New York Metropolitan Opera Orch
New York Philharmonic SO
New York PO
RTF National Orch
Vienna PO
Szeryng, Henryk
English CO
Szöke, Tibor
Southwest German RSO Baden-Baden
Szostak, Zdzislav
Polish Radio-TV SO
Szüts, Péter
Concerto Armonico Budapest
Tabachnik, Michel
Basel RSO
Ensemble InterContemporain
Hanover North German Radio SO
Tabakov, Emil
Sofia PO
Sofia Solisti
Sofia Solisti CO
Tabbia, Dario
Ricercar Academy
Taglioni, Luigi
Camerata Nova Instrumental Ensemble
Talich, Václav
Czech PO
Czech PO Soloists
Stockholm PO
Talmi, Yoav
Golders Orch
Israel CO
Oslo PO
San Diego SO
Tamas
Hungarian Radio-TV SO
Tamas, J.
Aargauer SO
Tamayo, Arturo
Alternance Ensemble
Bavarian RSO
BBC SO
Berlin RSO
Consortium Classicum Soloists
Ensemble InterContemporain
Slovak RSO Bratislava
Tamura, Takuo
Pro Musica Nipponia
Tang, Jordan
Hong Kong PO
Tang, Mu Hai
Bavarian RSO
Royal Flemish PO
Sinfonia Varsovia
Tansini, Ugo
EIAR Orch
Tardue, Marc
Grenoble Instrumental Ensemble
Grenoble Instrumental String Ensemble
Tarr, Edward
HR Brass
Tate, Jeffrey
Bavarian RSO
Dresden Staatskapelle
English CO
English CO Wind Ensemble
French National Orch
Rotterdam PO
Royal Opera House Orch
Tatlow, Mark
Stockholm CO
Tátrai, Vilmos
Hungarian CO
Hungarian Wind Ensemble
London SO
Tavener, Alan
Cappella Nova
Taylor, Beverly
Project Ars Nova Ensemble
Taylor, Robert
Chorus Civitas CO

Tchakarov, Emil
 Sofia Festival Orch
 Sofia National Opera Orch
Tchernushenko, Alexander
 St. Petersburg State Academic Cappella SO
Tchernushenko, Vladislav
 Leningrad Glinka Academic Choir
 St. Petersburg Capella
 St. Petersburg Cappella Orch
 St. Petersburg State Academic Cappella SO
 Guy Touvron Brass Ensemble
Tchistiakov, Andreï
 Bolshoi Theater Orch
 Bolshoi Theater SO Soloists
 Moscow Choral Academy Choir
 Moscow Choral Academy Orch
 Moscow PO
 Russian State Choir
Tchivzhel, Edward
 Atlantic Sinfonietta
Temes, José Luis
 London PO
 Poznan
Temianka, Henri
 Temianka CO
Temirkanov, Yuri
 Berlin RSO
 Bolshoi Theater Orch
 Leningrad Bell Music Ensemble
 Leningrad Military Orch
 Leningrad PO
 Leningrad State Phil Academic SO
 Moscow PO
 New York PO
 Royal PO
 St. Petersburg PO
Temple, David
 London Phil Chamber Choir
Tenner, K.
 Vienna RSO
Tennstedt, Klaus
 Berlin PO
 Chicago SO
 London PO
 North German RSO
Terby, Fernand
 Brussels BRTN PO
Térey-Smith, Mary
 Capella Savaria
Terian, M.
 Moscow Conservatory Student Orch String Group
Terwilliger, E.
 Polish Chamber PO
Tetu, Bernard
 Lorraine PO
Tetzlaff, Christian
 German Chamber PO Winds
Teutsch, Karol
 Sinfonia Varsovia
 Warsaw CO
 Warsaw Philharmonic CO
Tevlin, Boris
 Moscow Tchaikovsky Conservatory Chamber Choir Women's Voices
Theis, Ernst
 Austrian Chamber Sym
Themel, Walter
 Udine CO
Theofanidis, Chris
 Barrow CO
Theuring, Günther
 Vienna Boys' Choir
Thielemann, Christian
 German Opera Orch
Thiemer, U.
 Vienna Opera Ball Orch
Thomas, Bernard
 London Pro Musica
 Bernard Thomas CO
Thomas, Jeffrey
 American Bach Soloists
Thomas, John Hugh
 BBC Welsh Chorus
Thomas, Kurt
 Leipzig Gewandhaus Orch
 Leipzig Opera Orch
Thomas, Patrick
 Bavarian RSO
 Melbourne SO
 Philharmonia Orch
 Sydney SO
Thomas, Ronald
 Australia Soloists
 Bournemouth Sinfonietta
Thome, Joel
 Orch of Our Time
Thompson, N.
 National Youth Ballet Orch
Thomson, B.
 English CO
 Hallé Orch
 London PO
 London SO
 Philharmonia Orch
 Royal Scottish National Orch
 Royal Scottish Orch
 Scottish National Orch
 Ulster Orch

Thomson, Bryden
 BBC Welsh National SO
Thomson, George
 Earplay
 Earplay members
Thomson, Virgil
 Philadelphia Orch
Thorby, Philip
 London Musica Antiqua
Thornton, Barbara
 Sequentia
Thunemann, Klaus
 I Musici
Thurlow, Alan
 Chichester Cathedral Choir
Tiboris, Peter
 Brno State PO
 Bohuslav Martinů PO
 Moscow Radio-TV SO
 Prague Virtuosi
 Sofia National Opera Orch
 Warsaw PO
Tichy, Jan Hus
 Prague National Theater Orch
Tieri, Emidio
 Florence Teatro Comunale Orch
Tietjen, Heinz
 Vienna State Opera Orch
Tigani, Roberto
 Sassari SO
Tihanyi, Laszlo
 Budapest SO
 Intermodulation Chamber Ensemble
Tikhonov, C.
 Moscow Helikon Theater Chamber Ensemble
Tilegant, Friedrich
 Southwest German CO Pforzheim
Tillai, Aurél
 Pécs Chamber Choir
Tilson Thomas, Michael
 Boston SO
 Buffalo PO
 Chicago SO
 Cleveland Orch
 Columbia Jazz Band
 (Royal) Concertgebouw Orch
 English CO
 Hungarian State Orch
 London Sinfonietta
 London SO
 Los Angeles PO
 New World Brass
 New World SO
 Orch of St. Luke's
 Philharmonia Orch
 San Francisco SO
 Utah SO
Tinsley, James
 Niagara Brass Ensemble
Tintner, Georg
 Nova Scotia Sym
Tippett, Michael
 Bath Festival Orch
 BBC PO
 English Northern Philharmonia
 Kalmar CO
Titner, G.
 Boston SO
 Canadian Brass
 New York PO members
Titov, Alexander
 New Philharmony Orch
 St. Petersburg Classical Music Studio Orch
 St. Petersburg Conservatory CO
 St. Petersburg New Classical Orch
 St. Petersburg New PO
 St. Petersburg New Philharmony Orch
Tjeknavorian, Loris
 Armenian PO
 London SO
 National PO London
 Royal Liverpool PO
Tobin, John
 English SO
Toffano, Giovanni
 Concentus Musicus Patavinus
 Venice Consort
Toffolo, L.
 Trieste Teatro Comunale Giuseppe Verdi Orch
Tomaro, Robert
 Silesian PO
Tomasi, Henri
 Paris SO
Tomita, Isao
 Plasma SO
Tomizawa, Yutaka
 Osaka PO
Tomlinson, Ernest
 Czech-Slovak RSO Bratislava
 Rossendale Male Voice Choir
 RTE Concert Orch
 Slovak RSO
 Slovak RSO Bratislava
Tomter, Lars Anders
 Norwegian CO
Tønnesen, Terje
 Norwegian CO

Topolski, Zlatko
 Vienna CO
 Vienna Tonkunstler Orch
Toporowski, Marek
 Concerto Polacco
Torke, Michael
 Philharmonia Orch
Tortelier, Yan Pascal
 BBC PO
 English CO
 Philharmonia Orch
 Scottish CO
 Ulster Orch
Törzs, Ivan
 Mecklenburg State Orch
Toscanini, Arturo
 BBC SO
 NBC SO
 New York Philharmonic SO
 New York PO
 Philadelphia Orch
 Philharmonia Orch
 La Scala Orch
 Stockholm PO
 Vienna PO
Toth, Gwendolyn
 ARTEK
Totsuka, N.
 Stockholm PO
Tovey, Bramwell
 Royal PO
 Winnipeg SO
Townhill, Dennis
 St. Mary's Episcopal Cathedral Choir Edinburgh
Toyama, Yuzo
 NHK SO
Toyoda, Koji
 Gunma SO
 Tchikashi Tanaka Ensemble
Trailescu, Cornel
 Romanian Opera Orch
Tranchant, Michel
 French Vocal Group
 Nouvel PO
Traphagen, Willis
 New York Harmonie Ensemble
Traunfellner, Claudius
 Vienna Co
 Vienna Chamber PO
Trautmann, Marc
 Pécs SO
Travis, Francis
 Basel RSO
 Zurich Tonhalle Orch
Tredici, David del
 Marlboro Festival Ensemble
 Marlboro Festival Players
Trench, Fiachra
 Irish National Film Orch
Trendell, David
 King's College Choir Cambridge
Trepte, Paul
 Ely Cathedral Choir
 Parley of Instruments
Trhlik, Otakar
 Ostrava Janáček PO
 Philharmonia Cassovia
 Prague RSO
 Prague SO
Trigos, Juan
 Sones Contemporaneos Ensemble
Trinca, F.
 Naples Accademic Musicale Solisti
Trojahn, Manfred
 German SO
Tschupp, Räto
 Aargauer SO
 Basel RSO
 Basel SO
 Frankfurt RSO
 Zurich Camerata
Ts'ong, Fou
 Polish CO
 Sinfonia Varsovia
Tuckwell, Barry
 English CO
 London SO
 Philharmonia Orch
Tuggle, J.
 Brandenburg PO
Tung, Ling
 Philharmonia Orch
Tuomela, T.
 Finnish National Opera Orch members
Turchak, S.
 Ukrainian State SO
Turco, Alberto
 In Dulci Jubilo
 Nova Schola Gregoriana
 Verona Cathedral Cappella Musicale
Turkovic, Milan
 Octagon Ensemble
 Vienna Radio Winds
Turner, Bruno
 Collegium Aureum
 Pro Cantione Antiqua
Turner, Gavin
 William Byrd Choir

Turnovsky, Martin
Prague SO
Stockholm Symphonic Wind Orch
Vienna Musikverein Orch

Turovsky, Yuli
Montreal Musici
Montreal SO members
Répercussion Ensemble

Tuttle, John
Exultate Chamber Singers

Tutu, Bernard
Toulouse Saqueboutiers

Tuxen, Erik
Danish National RSO

Tyler, James
London Early Music Group

Tzipine, Georges
French National RSO

Udaeta, Juan de
Granada City Orch

Ughi, Uto
St. Cecilia CO

Ugrin, Gábor
Hungarian State Chorus

Ukigaya, Takao
Hanover North German Radio PO
Hanover Radio PO
Philharmonia Pomorska
Pomeranian PO
Pomorska PO

Uljanov, Nicholas
Sofia PO

Unger, Heinz
CBC Vancouver SO

Unger, Wolfgang
Thüringian Academic Sing Circle

Urbanek, Pavel
Czech Brass Orch
Prague Festival Orch

Urbini, Pierluigi
Angelicum CO
Milan Angelicum Orch

Uridge, Michael
Musica Antiqua Ensemble

Urquhart, Peter
Capella Alamire

Ushakov, Igor
Valaam Singing Culture Institute Male Choir

Uy, Paul
Belgian Radio-TV French SO

Vachulka, L.
Prague Symposium Musicum

Vaglieri, Paolo
Milan CO

Vaillancourt, Lorranie
Les Evénements du Neuf
Nouvel Ensemble Moderne
Strasbourg Percussion Ensemble

Vajnar, František
Brno Janáček Opera Orch
Capella Istropolitana
Czech PO
Dvořák CO
Prague CO
Prague Collegium Musicum
Prague RSO
Suk CO

Valach, Jan
Philharmonia Hungarica

Valdes, Maximiano
Simón Bolívar SO
London SO
Nice PO

Válek, Roman
Baroque 1994 Ensemble

Válek, Vladimír
České Budejovice CO
Czech Phil CO
Czech PO
Czech RSO
Dvořák CO
Prague RSO
Prague SO

Valentin, Michael
Isaak Ensemble Heidelberg

Vanberg, Charles
Vanberg Viennese Soloists

Vandernoot, André
Belgian RSO
Philharmonia Orch

Van Dyke, G.
New Jersey Percussion Ensemble

Vann, Stanley
Peterborough Cathedral Choir

Vänskä, Osmo
Copenhagen PO
Icelandic SO
Lahti Chamber Ensemble
Lahti SO
Malmö SO
Stockholm PO
Tapiola Sinfonietta

Van Vactor, David
Hessian RSO

Vardi, Arie
Israel CO

Vardi, Emmanuel
Kapp Sinfonietta

Varga, Gilbert
BBC PO
Philharmonia Hungarica
Stuttgart RSO

Varineau, John
Royal Scottish National Orch

Vartolo, Sergio
Bologna San Petronio Cappella Musicale Orch
San Petronio Cappella Musicale
San Petronio Cappella Musicale Orch
San Petronio Cappella Musicale Soloists

Varviso, Silvio
Bayreuth Festival Orch
Rome Opera Orch
Vienna State Opera Orch

Vásáry, Tamás
Berlin PO
Bournemouth Sinfonietta
Northern Sinfonia of England
Philharmonia Orch

Vaselka, Josef
Czech Phil Chorus

Vashegyi, György
Budapest Orfeo Orch

Vass, George
Medici String Quartet
Oxford Camerata

Vassilov, S.
Bulgarian State PO

Vaszy, Viktor
Hungarian State Opera Orch

Vatŏs, T.
Danish National RSO

Vaughan Williams, Ralph
BBC SO

Vedernikov, Alexander
Moscow PO
Russian Philharmonia
Russian State SO

Végh, Sándor
Camerata Academica
International Musicians Seminar Soloists
Salzburg Camerata
Salzburg Camerata Academica
Salzburg Mozarteum Camerata Academica

Velardi, Esteban
Camerata Ligure
Josquino Salepico Chorus
Alessandro Stradella Consort

Velazco, Jorge
Berlin Radio Sinfonietta
Berlin SO

Veldhoven, J. van
Amsterdam Baroque Orch

Vella, Joseph
Sofia SO

Vellard, Dominique
Gilles Binchois Ensemble
Cantus Figuratus Ensemble
La Traditora

Velten, Hubert
CantArte Ensemble

Veltri, Michelangelo
Marseille Opera Orch
Scottish CO

Veneziani, Vittore
La Scala Orch

Venhoda, Miroslav
Chamber Ensemble of Early Instruments
Prague Madrigal Singers

Venzago, Mario
Basel RSO Soloists
Basel SO
German Chamber PO
Lucerne Festival Strings
Lucerne Singers
Swiss-Italian Radio-TV Orch
Swiss Phil Workshop

Verchi, Nino
Modena Teatro Comunale Orch

Verhoeff, Marcel
Bulgaria Male Voices
Russian Festival Ensemble

Vermeulen, Dirk
Flanders CO Sinfonia
Prima La Musica

Vernizzi, Fulvio
Groot Omroep Orch
Netherlands Radio Orch
Turin RAI Orch
Turin RSO

Verrot, Pascal
Bretagne Orch
Monte Carlo PO
Quebec SO
Texas Festival Orch

Veselka, Josef
Brno State PO
Czech Phil Chorus
Czech PO
Prague Phil Chorus

Vestri, A.
London Festival Orch

Vetere, I. Io
Giovanile Ambrosiano Ensemble

Vetö, Tamás
Aalborg SO
Copenhagen Univ Choir

Vetö, Tamás (cont.)
Danish National RSO
Odense SO
South Jutland SO
Swedish RSO

Vettori, Romano
Academy of Ancient Music Instumental Ensemble
Basso Generale

Vieru, Anatol
Romanian National RSO

Villa-Lobos, Heitor
French National Orch

Villiers, David de
Bielefeld PO
Cape Town SO

Vinogradov, Alexei
Moscow Contemporary Music Ensemble

Vinokourov, Arkadi
Kiev CO

Viotti, Marcello
Berlin German Opera Orch
English CO
Frankfurt RSO
Piacenza SO
Saarbrück RSO
Southwest German RSO Baden-Baden
Turin PO

Virumbrales, Luis Lozano
Alfonso X El Sabio Group

Vis, Lucas
Cologne RSO
(Royal) Concertgebouw Orch
Electronics Instrumental Ensemble
Frankfurt RSO
Mondriaan Quartet
Netherlands Ballet Orch
Netherlands PO
New Artis Orch
Residentie Orch The Hague

Visse, Dominique
Les Eléments Ensemble
Clément Janequin Ensemble

Vistisen, Flemming
Esbjerg Ensemble

Vizioli, Francesco
Italian International Orch

Vlach, Josef
Czech CO
Prague CO
Suk CO

Vlad, Alessio
St. Cecilia CO

Vlček, Oldřich
Prague CO
Prague Virtuosi

Vogel, Jaroslav
Brno State PO

Vogel, W.
Bucharest PO

Vogel, W. D.
Chopin PO

Vogt, Gerhard
Bavarian State Youth Plucked Instrument Orch

Volmer, Arvo
Estonian State SO

Vonk, Hans
Bavarian RSO
(Royal) Concertgebouw Orch
Dresden Staatskapelle
Dresden State SO
The Hague PO
Residentie Orch The Hague
Royal PO
Uttrecht SO

Vorhees, Donald
RCA Victor SO

Votto, Antonino
Florence Maggio Musicale Orch
Rio de Janeiro Teatro Municipale Orch
La Scala Orch
Trieste Teatro Comunale Giuseppe Verdi Orch
Turin RAI Orch
Turin RAI SO

Vriend, Jan Willem de
Combattimento Consort Amsterdam

Vronsky, Petr
Prague RSO
Slovak RSO Bratislava

Vuataz, R.
Swiss Romande RSO

Morris, W.
London PO
London Symphonica
London SO

Waart, Edo de
Dutch Radio PO
English CO
Minnesota Orch
Netherlands Radio PO
Netherlands Wind Ensemble
New Philharmonia Orch
New PO
Orch of St. Luke's
Philharmonia Orch
Rotterdam PO
Royal PO
San Francisco SO
Swiss Romande Orch

Wackenheim, Michel
  Strasbourg Cathedral Choir
Wadsworth, Derek
  Prague PO
Wagner, Roger
  Innsbruck SO
  Paris Conservatory Société des Concerts Orch
Wahl, B.
  Versailles CO
Wakasugi, Hiroshi
  Cologne RSO
  Leipzig Gewandhaus Orch
  Tokyo Metropolitan SO
  Tokyo PO
  Zurich Tonhalle Orch
Walden, Peter
  Raphaele Concert Orch
Waldhans, Jiří
  Brno State PO
Waldman, Frederic
  Musica Aeterna
Walker, John
  Riverside Choir New York
Wallace, John
  Wallace Collection
Wallberg, Heinz
  Bamberg SO
  Bavarian RSO
  Munich RSO
  Residentie Orch The Hague
  Swiss Romande Orch
Wallenstein, Alfred
  Berlin PO
  London New SO
  London SO
  Los Angeles PO
  Philadelphia Orch
  RCA Victor SO
  Standard SO
  Symphony of the Air
Wallez, Jean-Pierre
  French Instrumental Ensemble
  Harmonia Nova Orch
  Paris Orchestral Ensemble
  South Jutland SO
Wallfisch, Elizabeth
  Orch of the Age of Enlightenment
Walsh, Colin
  Lincoln Cathedral Choir
Walsh, Philip
  Wellington Cathedral Choir
Walter, Alfred
  BBC SO
  Brussels RTBF SO
  Budapest Strauss SO
  Budapest SO
  CSR SO Bratislava
  CSSR State PO Košice
  Czech–Slovak State PO
  Frankfurt on the Oder PO
  North German RSO
  Philharmonia Cassovia
  Rhenish PO
  Slovak State PO Košice
Walter, Bruno
  Bavarian State Opera Orch
  BBC SO
  Berlin PO
  Berlin State Opera Orch
  British SO
  Columbia SO
  (Royal) Concertgebouw Orch
  French National Orch
  London PO
  London SO
  Los Angeles PO
  Los Angeles Standard SO
  Mozart Festival Orch
  NBC SO
  New York Metropolitan Opera Orch
  New York Philharmonic SO
  New York PO
  New York SO
  Paris Conservatory Société des Concerts Orch
  Paris Mozart Festival Orch
  Philharmonic SO
  RCA Victor SO
  Rome Radio–TV SO
  Rome RAI SO
  Royal PO
  Salzburg Orch
  San Francisco Opera Orch
  Stockholm PO
  Symphony of the Air
  Vienna PO
  Vienna State Opera Orch
Walth, Gary
  Bismarck Mandan Civic Chorus
Walther, H.–J.
  Hamburg RSO
Walton, William
  London SO
  Philharmonia Orch
  Royal PO
Wand, Günter
  Berlin PO
  Chicago SO
  Cologne Gürzenich Orch

Wand, Günter (cont.)
  Cologne RSO
  North German RSO
Warchal, Bohdan
  Capella Istropolitana
  Slovak CO
Warchal, G.
  Slovak CO
Ward, Nicholas
  City of London Sinfonia
  Northern CO
Warland, Dale
  Macalester Concert Choir
  Dale Warland Singers
Warren, George Randolph
  Philharmonia Orch
Warren–Green, Christopher
  London CO
  Philharmonia Orch
  Philharmonia Orch members
  Wallace Collection
Washburn, Jon
  CBC Vancouver SO
  Purcell Quartet
  Vancouver Chamber Choir
Watanabe, Akeo
  Japan PO
Watkinson, Andrew
  City of London Sinfonia
Watson, Ian
  English CO
Watson, James
  Black Dyke Mills Band
  Desford Colliery Caterpillar Band
Watts, Maj S. A.
  Grenadier Guards Band
Watts, Thomas R.
  St. Amant Consort
Waybright, David
  Univ of Florida Wind Ensemble
Wayland, Newton
  Denver Sym Pops
  Greater Hoople Area Off–Season Philharmonic
  Rochester Pops Orch
Wealt, C.
  Toronto Chamber Winds
Webber
  Toronto Chamber Winds
Webber, Geoffrey
  Gonville & Caius College Choir Cambridge
Weber, Ekkehard
  La Gamba Freiburg
Weber, M.
  International Festival Orch
Wedd, Patrick
  Montreal Tudor Vocal Ensemble
Wedin, Jan–Olav
  Kalmar Läns CO
  Oskarshamn Ensemble
  Stockholm Chamber Ensemble
  Stockholm Sinfonietta
Wegrzyn
  Hanover Chamber Academy
Wehner, J.
  Philharmonia Cassovia
Wehnert, Wolfram
  Hesse Bach Collegium
  Marburg Bach Choir
Weigand, George
  Extempore String Ensemblo
Weigert, Hermann
  Bavarian RSO
Weigle, Jörg–Peter
  Dresden PO
  German Music School Orch
Weigle, Sebastian
  New Berlin CO
Weikert, Ralf
  Berlin German Opera Orch
  Venice Teatro La Fenice Orch
  Zurich Opera Orch
Weil, Bruno
  L'Archibudelli
  Classical Band
  Orch of the Age of Enlightenment
  Tafelmusik
  Tölz Boys' Choir
  Vienna SO
Weinberger, Gerhard
  German Bach Soloists
Weingartner, Felix von
  London PO
  London SO
  Paris Conservatory Société des Concerts Orch
  Royal PO
  Vienna PO
  Vienna State Opera Orch
Weisberg, Arthur
  Contemporary Chamber Ensemble
  Contemporary Chamber Players
  Ensemble 21
  New York PO
  Orch of the 20th Century
  Rutgers Univ Contemporary Chamber Ensemble
Weise, Klause
  Nice PO
Weiss, Donn
  UCLA Madrigal Singers

Weiss, Sidney
  Crystal CO
Weissmann, Frieder
  Berlin State Opera Orch
Welcher, D.
  Voices of Change
Weldon, George
  Liverpool PO
  Philharmonia Orch
Weller, Walter
  Basel SO
  City of Birmingham SO
  Philharmonia Orch
Wells, W.
  Carleton Orch members
Welser–Möst, Franz
  London PO
Welsh, John
  Fairfield Orch
Werner, Jean–Jacques
  Léon Barzin Orch
  Jeune PO
  Youth Orch
Wernick, Richard
  Univ of Pennsylvania Chamber Players
Werthen, Rudolf
  I Fiamminghi CO
West, Jeremy
  His Majesties Sagbutts & Cornetts
Westberg, Erik
  Erik Westberg Vocal Ensemble
Westbrook, James
  Univ of California Los Angeles Wind Ensemble
Westenburg, Richard
  Musica Sacra
  Musica Sacra Chorus
  St. John the Divine Cathedral Choir
Westerberg, Stig
  Drottningholm CO
  Helsingborg SO
  Kungl Hovkapellet
  Munich PO
  Musica Sveciae
  Royal Opera Orch
  Stockholm PO
  Swedish RSO
  Swedish RSO members
  Swedish SO
Westrip, Ian
  Philharmonia Orch
Wetton, Hilary Davan
  Holst Orch
  Milton Keynes City Orch
  Philharmonia Orch
  Royal PO
Wey, Fritz ter
  Aachen Boys' Choir
Weyand, Eckhard
  Stuttgart Hymnus Orch
Whigham, Jiggs
  HR Brass
White, Jack Noble
  Texas Boys' Choir
White, Robin
  Prague PO
Whiteman, Paul
  Paramount Studio Orch
  Sinatra Orch
  Paul Whiteman Orch
Whitfield, Peter
  Northern Light SO
Whitney, Robert
  Louisville Orch
Wich, Günther
  Philharmonia Hungarica
  South German CO
Wick, Denis
  London Wind Orch
Wickham, Edward
  Clerks' Group
Widekind, Flemming
  Athela Ensemble
Widmer, Ernst
  Collegium Academicum Soloists
Wiemann, M.
  Helmuth Stapff Group
Wiggelsworth, Mark
  BBC SO
  Premiere Ensemble
Wijnkoop, Alexander van
  Bern Camerata
Wiklund, Adolf
  Stockholm PO
Wikman, Thomas
  Music of the Baroque
Wilde, Barry
  London Serenata
Wildner, Johannes
  Camerata Cassovia
  Capella Istropolitana
  CSSR State PO Košice
  Czech–Slovak RSO
  Czech–Slovak RSO Bratislava
  Czech–Slovak State PO
  Philharmonia Cassovia
  Polish National RSO Katowice
  Polish State PO
  Slovak RSO Bratislava

Wildner, Johannes (cont.)
Slovak State PO Košice
Johann Strauss CO
Vienna Mozart Academy
Vienna SO Johann Strauss Ensemble

Wilkins, C.
Utah SO

Willcocks, David
Academy of St. Martin in the Fields
Bach Choir
English CO
King's College Choir Cambridge
London PO
London SO
New Philharmonia Orch
Philharmonia Orch
Royal College of Music Chamber Choir
Royal College of Music Orch
Royal PO
Thames CO
Wilbraham Brass Soloists

Willén, Niklas
Sundsvall CO

Williams, Howard
Bournemouth SO
Netherlands Ballet Orch
Pécs SO

Williams, Jan
Maelström Percussion Ensemble

Williams, John
Boston Pops Orch
London SO
St. Peter ad Vincula Choir within the Tower of London Chapel Royal

Williams, Julius P.
Bohuslav Martinů PO

Williams, Lyn
Queensland SO

Williams, Richard
London SO

Wills, Arthur
Ely Cathedral Choir

Wilson, R.
La Capella Ducale
Cologne Musica Fiata

Wilson, Ransom
Cologne Musica Fiata
Musica Fiata
New York Solisti

Wilson, Roland
Musica Fiata

Wimmer, Thomas
Accentus Ensemble

Winograd, Arthur
MGM Studio SO

Winschermann, Helmut
German Bach Soloists

Wise, Andrew
Eastern Netherlands Orch
Orkest van het Oosten

Wishart, Stevie
Sinfonye

Wislocki, Stanislaw
Polish National SO
Warsaw PO
Warsaw Philharmonic SO

Wissmer, Pierre
Luxembourg RSO
Swiss Romande Orch

Wit, Antoni
Cracow RSO
Gunma SO
Katowice Polish Radio-TV Orch
North German RSO
Polish National RSO Katowice

Witt, Fred
Mandolin Orch

Wodiczko, Bohdan
Polish National RSO Katowice

Woerkum, Martien van
Tilburgs Vocal Ensemble

Wohlert, Peter
Berlin CO
Berlin RSO
Berlin SO

Wojciechowski, Tadeusz
Polish National RSO Katowice

Wojnarowski, Henryk
Warsaw National Phil Chorus
Warsaw PO

Wöldike, Mogens
Vienna State Opera Orch

Wolf, Friedrich
St. Augustin Orch

Wolf, Robert
Leipzig RSO

Wolfe, Duain
Colorado Children's Chorale

Wolff, Albert
Lamoureux Orch
ORTF Lyric Orch
Paris Conservatory Societé des Concerts Orch
St. Paul CO

Wolff, Charles de
Amsterdam CO
(Royal) Concertgebouw Orch members

Wolff, Hugh
City of Birmingham SO
London SO

Wolff, Hugh (cont.)
New Jersey SO
Philharmonia Orch
St. Paul CO

Wolf-Ferrari, Manno
Florence Maggio Musicale Orch
Genoa Teatro Comunale Orch
Milan RAI Lyric Orch
Trieste Teatro Comunale Giuseppe Verdi Orch

Won, Kyung-Soo
Moscow PO

Wood, H. J.
BBC SO
Queen's Hall Orch

Wood, Henry
BBC SO
London PO
London SO
New Queen's Hall Orch
Queen's Hall Orch

Wood, James
Ensemble InterContemporain
New London Chamber Choir
New London Chamber Ensemble
Voronezh Chamber Choir

Woodcock, David
Oakham School Chapel Choir

Woods, Carlton
North Arkansas SO

Woodside, L.
Sinfonia Rubinstein

Woodward, Ralph B.
Salt Lake Children's Choir

Wooley, Robert
St. John's College Choir Cambridge

Woolfenden, Guy
Royal Northern College of Music Wind Orch

Wordsworth, Barry
BBC Concert Orch
BBC Welsh National SO
BBC Welsh SO
Capella Istropolitana
London PO
London SO
New Queen's Hall Orch
Royal Ballet Sinfonia
Royal Liverpool PO
Royal Opera House Orch
Royal PO
Slovak PO

Wright, Brian
London PO

Wright, Gordon
Philharmonia Hungarica

Wright, Jerome
Seattle Girls' Choir

Wright, Martin
(Royal) Concertgebouw Orch
Netherlands Radio PO

Wright, Rayburn
Eastman Jazz Ensemble

Wright, Simon
Philharmonia Orch
Philharmonia Orch members
Wallace Collection

Wulff, Bernhard
Aventure Ensemble

Wulstan, David
Clerkes of Oxenford

Wuorinen, Charles
American Composers Orch
Group for Contemporary Music
Group for Contemporary Music members
Lincoln Center Chamber Music Society
New Jersey Percussion Ensemble
Orch of St. Luke's
St. Luke's Chamber Ensemble

Wyner, Yehudi
Boston Chamber Players

Wyttenbach, Jürg
Bale SO
Cracow Polish Radio-TV SO
Cracow Radio-TV Polonaise Orch

Yablonski, Dimitri
Latvian National SO
Moscow SO

Yamada, Kazuo
Tokyo Metropolitan SO

Yampolsky, Viktor
Northwestern Univ SO
Sofia PO

Yannatos, James
Harvard-Radcliffe Orch

Yansons, A.
Leningrad PO

Yary, Antony
Pochaev Lavra of the Dormiton Monks' Choir

Yazaki, Hikotaro
Gunma SO

Yeh, John Bruce
DePaul Univ Wind Ensemble

Yestadt, James
Louisiana State Univ SO

Yinon, Israel
Bavarian Chamber PO
Brno State PO
Czech State PO
Kyndel String Quartet

Yip, Wing-Sie
Czech-Slovak State PO

Yoo, Scott
Metamorphosen CO

Young, Crawford
Ferrera Ensemble

Young, Kenneth
New Zealand SO

Ysaÿe, Eugène
Cincinnati SO

Yu, Dejong Victorin
Philharmonia Orch

Yuasa, Takuo
London PO

Yurlov, Alexander
Moscow PO

Yurovski, Mikhaïl
Moscow Forum Theater Orch

Zaboronok, Andrey
Bolshoi Theater Children's Choir

Zaffini, Clement
Provence Instrumental Ensemble

Zagrosek, Lothar
Austrian RSO
Bamberg SO
Berlin German SO
Berlin RSO
Cologne RSO
German SO
Leipzig Gewandhaus Orch
Leipzig Opera Orch
London Sinfonietta
Southwest German RSO Baden-Baden

Zajiček, Peter
Bratislava Musica Aeterna
Musica Aeterna

Zámbó, Istvan
Hungarian State Orch

Zander, Benjamin
Boston PO
New England Conservatory Youth PO

Zani, G.
Lucca Teatro Comunale Giglio Orch

Zanotelli, Hans
Berlin SO
Naples Solisti
Stuttgart Philharmonia Ensemble

Zapf, Gerd
Bavarian Brass Soloists of Munich

Zaun, Fritz
Berlin City Orch

Zdravkovich, Zoltan
Belgrade PO

Zecchi, Carlo
Czech PO

Zedda, Alberto
Collegium Instrumentale Brugense
Lausanne CO
Martina Franca Festival Orch
Milano Angelicum CO
Turin RAI SO
Turin RSO

Zehetmair, Thomas
German Chamber PO
Philharmonia Orch

Zender, Hans
Avantgarde Ensemble
Basel SO
Berlin RSO
Ensemble InterContemporain
Ensemble Modern
Munich Bavarian RSO
Saarbrück RSO

Zepnik, Karl
Landsberg Vocal Ensemble

Zhemchuzhin, Georgy
Dantchenko Moscow Stanislavsky Music Theater Orch

Zhuraitis, Algis
Bolshoi Theater Orch
Moscow PO
Russian Radio-TV SO
USSR Radio SO
USSR Radio-TV Orch

Zimerman, Krystian
Vienna PO

Zimmer, Hans E.
Berlin RSO
German SO

Zimmer, Richard
Philharmonia Cassovia

Zimmermann, Gerhardt
Louisville Orch
North Carolina SO

Zimmermann, H.
Academic SO
Berlin RSO

Zimmermann, Udo
Musica Viva Ensemble

Zinger, Pablo
Bronx Arts Ensemble

Zinman, David
Baltimore SO
Bavarian RSO
Berlin German SO
Berlin RSO
English CO
London Sinfonietta
London SO

▲ = CD ♦ = Enhanced CD △ = MD ■ = Cassette Tape ☐ = DCC

Zinman, David (cont.)
 Netherlands CO
 Orch of St. Luke's
 Philadelphia Orch
 Rochester PO
 Rotterdam PO
Zöbeley, Hans Rudolf
 Munich Motet Choir
 Munich Percussion Ensemble
 Munich Residenz Orch
 Munich SO
 Munich Trumpet Ensemble
Zöbeley, Martin
 Concerto di Viole
 Cornetti con Crema
 Group for Early Music
 Munich Early Music Group
Zollman, Ronald
 Basel SO
 Belgium Radio New SO Chamber Ensemble
 Northern Sinfonia of England
Zoltek, John
 Bohuslav Martinů PO
Zongjie, Han
 Chinese Central PO
Zukerman, Pinchas
 English CO
 English SO
 Los Angeles PO
 Los Angeles PO members
 Mostly Mozart Festival Orch
 National Arts Center Canada Orch
 St. Paul CO
Zukofsky, Paul
 BBC SO
 Icelandic SO
 Icelandic Youth Orch
 Juilliard Orch
 New York City Free-Lance Orch
 Prague SO
 Reykjavik CO
 Royal PO
 Sinfóluhljómsveit Aeskunnar
 Söngsveitin PO
Zuno, Ottavio
 Istanbul State SO
Zwilich, Ellen Taaffe
 New York PO Ensemble
Zyman, S.
 Chelsea Chamber Ensemble

ORCHESTRAS & ENSEMBLES

A Cumpagnia
Missa Coriscia in Monticellu, w. Nicole Casalonga (org/hpd) *(rec Mar. 18-23, 1994)* K617 ▲ 7043
Aalborg SO
P. Erös (cnd)
Nielsen, T.:Giardino magico Point ▲ PCD 5083 [ADD]
Norby, E.:Songs, w. Marianne Rorholm (sop)—Rilke Lieder Point ▲ PCD 5083 [ADD]
Pade, S.:Con Pno, w. Valeria Zanini (pno) Point ▲ PCD 5083 [ADD]
W. Marshall (cnd)
Gershwin, G.:An American in Paris Virgin Classics ▲ CDM 61247
Gershwin, G.:Cuban Ov Virgin Classics ▲ CDM 61247
Gershwin, G.:Girl Crazy (ov) Virgin Classics ▲ CDM 61247
Gershwin, G.:"I Got Rhythm" Vars, w. Wayne Marshall (pno) Virgin Classics ▲ CDM 61247
Gershwin, G.:Rhap in Blue, w. Wayne Marshall (pno) Virgin Classics ▲ CDM 61247
Gershwin, G.:Strike up the Band (ov) Virgin Classics ▲ CDM 61247 No24356 12472
A. Rasilainen (cnd)
Thommessen, O.A.:Woven in Stems, w. Marianne Hirsti (sop) Caprice ▲ CAP 21403
F. Rasmussen (cnd)
Gade, N.W.:Gefion, w. P. Høyer (bar) Kontrapunkt ▲ KPT 32149 [DDD]
Gade, N.W.:Die heilige Nacht Kontrapunkt ▲ KPT 32149 [DDD]
Gade, N.W.:Zion, w. P. Høyer (bar) Kontrapunkt ▲ KPT 32149 [DDD]
T. Vetö (cnd)
Nielsen, C.:Music of—sels from Hr. Oluf han rider; Tove; Amor og Digteren; Willemoes; Cosmus; En Aften paa Giske *(rec Aalborghallen, Aalborg, Denmark, Aug. 10-13, 1994)* BIS ▲ CD 641 [DDD]
Nørholm, I.:Con Vc, w. E. Bløndal Bengtsson (vc) Kontrapunkt ▲ 32099 [DDD]
Nørholm, I.:Con Vn, w. K. Suzumi (vn) Kontrapunkt ▲ 32099 [DDD]
Aargauer CO
K. Girod (cnd)
Wehrli, W.:Ein weltliches Requiem, w. R. Amsler (sop), D. Labusch (cta), B. Hunziker (ten), R. Strebel (bass), Aargauer Chamber Choir *(rec live Jan. 12, 1992)* Jecklin ▲ JS 276-2 [DDD]
Aargauer SO
J. Tamas (cnd)
Widmer, E.:Sinf in einem Satz *(rec Oct. 31, 1987)* Grammont ▲ CTSP 32-2 [ADD]
R. Tschupp (cnd)
Bertoni, F.:Orfeo ed Euridice, w. Jeannette Fischer (sop—Euridice), Julia Juon (mez—Orfeo), Steve Davislim (ten—Imeneo), Aarau New Canton School Choir *(rec Zurich Radio Studio, Oct 30-Nov 1, 1994)* Jecklin ▲ JEC 700
Aarhus Brass Quintet
Abrahamsen, H.:Round Paula ▲ PACD 82 [DAD]
Hartmann, J.P.E.:Org Music, w. Ulrik Spang-Hanssen (org)—Fant in a; Funeral March for Thorvaldsen; Fant in f, Op. 20; Funeral March for Oehlenschlaeger; Andante for Brass & Org; Son in g, Op. 58; Good Friday-Easter Morning, Op. 43; Funeral March for N.P. Nielsen; Festive tones [Opening Music for the University's Jubilee in 1879] *(rec Arhus Cathedral, Feb-May 1995)* Classico ▲ 127
Lorentzen, B.:Intrada Paula ▲ PACD 82 [DAD]
Nielsen, S.:Windscape Paula ▲ PACD 82 [DAD]
Nordentoft, A.:Studies Paula ▲ PACD 82 [DAD]
Nørgård, P.:Syn/Vision Paula ▲ PACD 82 [DAD]
Rasmussen, K.A.:Four, Five Paula ▲ PACD 82 [DAD]
Aarhus CO
O. V. Larsen (cnd)
Gade, N.W.:Novelletter, Op. 53 *(rec Ellevang Church, Aarhus, Denmark, 1981)* Paula ▲ PACD 12 [AAD]
Gade, N.W.:Novelletter, Op. 58 *(rec Ellevang Church, Aarhus, Denmark, 1981)* Paula ▲ PACD 12 [AAD]
Aarhus SO
O. A. Hughes (cnd)
Holmboe, V.:Sinf in memoriam *(rec Musikhuset Aarhus, Denmark, Jan 23 & 25, 1995)* BIS ▲ CD 695 [DDD]
Holmboe, V.:Sym 1 *(rec June 15, 1993)* BIS ▲ CD 605 [DDD]
Holmboe, V.:Sym 2 *(rec Musikhuset Aarhus, Denmark, Jan 23 & 25, 1995)* BIS ▲ CD 695 [DDD]
Holmboe, V.:Sym 3 *(rec Jan. 11-13, 1993)* BIS ▲ CD 605 [DDD]
Holmboe, V.:Sym 4, w. Jutland Opera Choir BIS ▲ CD 572 [DDD]
Holmboe, V.:Sym 5 BIS ▲ CD 572 [DDD]
Holmboe, V.:Sym 6 BIS ▲ CD 573 [DDD]
Holmboe, V.:Sym 7 BIS ▲ CD 573 [DDD]
Holmboe, V.:Sym 8 *(rec Musikhuset Aarhus, Denmark, June 7-8, 1993)* BIS ▲ CD 618 [DDD]
Holmboe, V.:Sym 9 *(rec Musikhuset Aarhus, Denmark, June 14-15, 1993)* BIS ▲ CD 618 [DDD]
Holmboe, V.:Sym 10 *(rec Jan. 11-13, 1993)* BIS ▲ CD 605 [DDD]
Holmboe, V.:Sym 11 *(rec Musikhuset Aarhus, Denmark, June 6-8, 1994)* BIS ▲ CD 728 [DDD]
Holmboe, V.:Sym 12 *(rec Musikhuset Aarhus, Denmark, June 6-8, 1994)* BIS ▲ CD 728 [DDD]
Holmboe, V.:Sym 13 *(rec Musikhuset Aarhus, Denmark, Jan 16, 1996)* BIS ▲ CD 728 [DDD]
J. Panula (cnd)
Nørgård, P.:Sym 2 Point ▲ PCD 5070
Nørgård, P.:Sym 4 Point ▲ PCD 5070
F. Rasmussen (cnd)
Gade, N.W.:Korsfarerne, w. Rorholm (mez), Westi (ten), Cold (bass), Aarhus Sym Chorus [Da] BIS ▲ CD 465 [DDD]
Lorentzen, B.:Con Ob, w. M. Hoffmann (ob) *(rec May 4-5 1992)* Marco Polo/Dacapo ▲ DCCD 9314 [DDD]
Lorentzen, B.:Regenbogen, w. M. Hoffmann (tpt) *(rec May 4-5 1992)* Marco Polo/Dacapo ▲ DCCD 9314 [DDD]
Poulenc, F.:Con for 2 Pnos, w. I. Thorson (pno), J. Thurber (pno) Olympia ▲ OLY 364 [DDD]
O. Schmidt (cnd)
Bentzon, N.V.:Sym 3 *(rec 1981)* Marco Polo/Dacapo ▲ DCCD 9102 [ADD]
Bentzon, N.V.:Sym 4 *(rec 1981)* Marco Polo/Dacapo ▲ DCCD 9102 [ADD]
Abbey Consort
Adeste Fideles! Christmas down the Ages, w. Emma Kirkby (sop), Abbey Ensemble, Westminster Abbey Choir [cnd:Martin Neary], English CO [cnd:Paul Willey] Sony Classical ▲ SK 62688 ■ ST 62688
Abbey Ensemble
Adeste Fideles! Christmas down the Ages, w. Emma Kirkby (sop), Abbey Consort, Westminster Abbey Choir [cnd:Martin Neary], English CO [cnd:Paul Willey] Sony Classical ▲ SK 62688 ■ ST 62688
Abbott O'Gorman Duo
Ravel, M.:Daphnis et Chloé (suite 2) [arr for Pno 4-Hands] Meridian ▲ MER 84300 [DDD]
Ravel, M.:Intro & Allegro [arr for Pno 4-Hands] Meridian ▲ MER 84300 [DDD]
Ravel, M.:Ma mère l'oye Meridian ▲ MER 84300 [DDD]
Ravel, M.:Rapsodie espagnole [arr for Pno 4-Hands] Meridian ▲ MER 84300 [DDD]
Ravel, M.:La Valse [arr for Pno 4-Hands] Meridian ▲ MER 84300 [DDD]
Abel-Steinberg-Winant Trio
Cowell, H.:Set of 5 New Albion ▲ NA 036 [DDD]
Harrison, L.:Varied Trio New Albion ▲ NA 015 [ADD]
Harrison, L.:Varied Trio New Albion ▲ NA 036 [DDD]
Satoh, S.:Toki No Mon New Albion ▲ NA 036 [DDD]

L'Academia d'Harmonia [Emilio Moreno (vn), Angel Sampedro (vn), Sergi Casademunt (vl), Albert Romani (hpd)]
Castro, F.J. de:Trattenimenti Armonici da Camera *(rec Barcelona, Feb 8-11, 1988)* RNE/Spanish National Radio ▲ AME 003 [DDD]
Academia Montis Regalis
L. Mangiocavallo (cnd)
Pugnani, G.:Ovs—Ovs from Sinfs 2 & 4-6 Opus 111 ▲ OPS 30151
Academia Wind Quintet
Danzi, F.:Qnts Ww, Op. 56—Nos. 1 & 2 Supraphon ▲ SUP 111264 [DDD]
Danzi, F.:Qnts Ww, Op. 68—Nos. 1 & 2 Supraphon ▲ SUP 111264 [DDD]
Academic Chamber Ensemble [Ventzislav Kindalov (fl), Dimiter Danchev (vn), Seta Baltayan (vc), Snezhana Barova (pno)]
Haydn, J.:Trio Vns & Continuo [1st vn arr V. Kindalov for fl] Gega ▲ GD 103 [DDD]
Yordanov, D.:Bonbonnière Fant [cavatina] Gega ▲ GD 103 [DDD]
Academic Chamber Ensemble [Ventzislav Kindalov (fl), Dimiter Danchev (vn), Snezhana Barova (pno)]
Martinů, B.:Madrigal Son Gega ▲ GD 103 [DDD]
Academic Chamber Ensemble [Ventzislav Kindalov (fl), Seta Baltayan (vc), Snezhana Barova (pno)]
Weber, C.M. von:Trio Fl Gega ▲ GD 103 [DDD]
Academic Chamber Ensemble [Ventzislav Kindalov (fl), Snezhana Barova (pno)]
Donizetti, G.:Son Fl & Pno Gega ▲ GD 103 [DDD]
Schnittke, A.:Suite in the Old Style [arr V. Kindalov for fl & pno] Gega ▲ GD 103 [DDD]
Academic SO
H. Zimmermann (cnd)
Paganini, N.:Con 6 Vn, w. R. Ricci (vn) One-Eleven ▲ URS 91080 [ADD]
Academica Quartet members
Franck, C.:Trios concertants, w. M. Sarbu (pno) Dynamic 2-▲ CD 21/1-2 [DDD]
Académie Internationale de Sées
B. Gagnepain (cnd)
Les Trois Maries:A Liturgical Play from the Middle Ages from Origny-Sainte-Benoîte, w. Paris Madrigal Choir Koch Schwann ▲ SCH 314252 [DDD]
Academy Chamber Ensemble
Mendelssohn, F.:Qnt 2 Strs Philips ▲ 420400-2 [ADD]
Academy for Old Music
Telemann, G.P.:Con Rcr & Fl, w. E. Hering (rcr), E.-B. Hilse (fl) LaserLight ▲ 15634 [DDD]
Academy of Ancient Music
C. Hogwood (cnd)
The Academy of Ancient Music B & W ▲ BW 001 [AAD/DDD]
Academy of Ancient Music L'Oiseau-Lyre ▲ 410553-2 OH ■ 410553-4
Bach, J.S.:Brandenburg Cons L'Oiseau-Lyre 2-▲ 414187-2 [DDD]
Bach, J.S.:Con 2 Hpd, w. Christophe Rousset (hpd) *(rec Henry Wood Hall, London, Aug 12-14, 1994)* L'Oiseau-Lyre ▲ 443326-2 [DDD]
Bach, J.S.:Con 4 Hpd, w. Christophe Rousset (hpd) *(rec EMI Studio No. 1, Abbey Road, London, Aug 5-8, 1993)* L'Oiseau-Lyre ▲ 443326-2 [DDD]
Bach, J.S.:Con 7 Hpd, w. Christophe Rousset (hpd) *(rec EMI Studio No. 1, Abbey Road, London, Aug 5-8, 1993)* L'Oiseau-Lyre ▲ 443326-2 [DDD]
Bach, J.S.:Con 3 for 2 Hpds L'Oiseau-Lyre ▲ 421500-2 [DDD]
Bach, J.S.:Cons for 3 Hpds (comp), w. C. Tilney (hpd), C. Rousset (hpd), D. Moroney (hpd) L'Oiseau-Lyre ▲ 433053-2 [DDD]
Bach, J.S.:Con for 4 Hpds, w. C. Tilney (hpd), C. Rousset (hpd), D. Moroney (hpd), C. Hogwood (hpd) L'Oiseau-Lyre ▲ 433053-2 [DDD]
Bach, J.S.:Cons Vn (comp), w. J. Schröder (vn) L'Oiseau-Lyre ▲ 400080-2 [DDD]
Bach, J.S.:Con 1 Vn, w. Jaap Schröder (vn) *(rec Kingsway Hall, London, Sept 14, 1981)* L'Oiseau-Lyre ▲ 443326-2 [DDD]
Bach, J.S.:Con Vn & Ob L'Oiseau-Lyre ▲ 421500-2 [DDD]
Bach, J.S.:Con for 2 Vns, w. J. Schröder (vn), C. Hirons (vn) L'Oiseau-Lyre ▲ 400080-2 [DDD]
Bach, J.S.:Con for 3 Vns L'Oiseau-Lyre ▲ 433053-2 [DDD]
Bach, J.S.:Suites Orch, BWV 1066-1069 L'Oiseau-Lyre 2-▲ 417834-2 [DDD]
The Baroque Experience L'Oiseau-Lyre 5-▲ 433523-2
Beethoven, L. van:Cons Pno (comp), w. S. Lubin (pno) L'Oiseau-Lyre 3-▲ 421408-2 [DDD]
Beethoven, L. van:Syms (comp), w. London Sym Chorus—[soloists in No. 9:Arleen Augér, Catherine Robbin, Anthony Rolfe Johnson, Gregory Reinhart] L'Oiseau-Lyre 6-▲ 425696-2 [DDD]
Beethoven, L. van:Sym 1 [period instrs] L'Oiseau-Lyre ▲ 414338-2 [DDD] ■ 414338-4
Beethoven, L. van:Sym 2 [period instrs] L'Oiseau-Lyre ▲ 414338-2 [DDD] ■ 414338-4
Beethoven, L. van:Sym 3, "Eroica" L'Oiseau-Lyre ▲ 417235-2 [DDD]
Beethoven, L. van:Sym 4 L'Oiseau-Lyre ▲ 417615-2 [DDD] □ 417615-5
Beethoven, L. van:Sym 5 L'Oiseau-Lyre ▲ 417615-2 [DDD]
Beethoven, L. van:Sym 6, "Pastorale" L'Oiseau-Lyre ▲ 421416-2 [DDD]
Beethoven, L. van:Sym 7 L'Oiseau-Lyre ▲ 425695-2 [DDD]
Beethoven, L. van:Sym 8 L'Oiseau-Lyre ▲ 425695-2 [DDD]
Beethoven, L. van:Sym 9, "Choral Sym" [G] L'Oiseau-Lyre ▲ 425517-2 [DDD]
Boyce, W.:Syms, Op. 2 L'Oiseau-Lyre ▲ 436761-2 [DDD]
Emma Kirkby Sings Mrs. Arne, w. Emma Kirkby L'Oiseau-Lyre ▲ 436132-2
Handel, G.F.:Messiah, w. Emma Kirkby (sop), Judith Nelson (mez), Carolyn Watkinson (cta), Paul Elliott (ten), David Thomas (bass) London 2-▲ 430488-2 [DDD]
Handel, G.F.:Orlando, w. Arleen Augér (sop), Emma Kirkby (sop), Catherine Robbin (mez), James Bowman (ct), David Thomas (bass) L'Oiseau-Lyre 3-▲ 430845-2 [DDD]
Handel, G.F.:Royal Fireworks Music L'Oiseau-Lyre ▲ 400059-2 [ADD]
Handel, G.F.:Solomon (arrival of the queen of Sheba) L'Oiseau-Lyre ▲ 410553-2 [ADD] ■ 410553-4
Handel, G.F.:Water Music (comp) L'Oiseau-Lyre ▲ 421476-2 [ADD]
Handel, G.F.:Water Music (suites) L'Oiseau-Lyre ▲ 400059-2 [ADD]
Haydn, J.:L'Anima del filosofo, or Orfeo ed Euridice, w. Cecilia Bartoli (mez), Uwe Heilmann (ten), Ildebrando d'Arcangelo (bass), Academy of Ancient Music Chorus L'oiseau Lyre ▲ 452 668-2
Haydn, J.:Con 1 Hn, w. Timothy Brown (hn) L'Oiseau-Lyre ▲ 417610-2 [DDD]
Haydn, J.:Con Org, Obs & Strs, H.XVIII/1, w. C. Hogwood (org) L'Oiseau-Lyre ▲ 417610-2 [DDD]
Haydn, J.:Con Tpt, w. Friedmann Immer (tpt) L'Oiseau-Lyre ▲ 417610-2 [DDD]
Haydn, J.:Die Schöpfung, w. Emma Kirkby (sop), Anthony Rolfe Johnson (ten), Michael George (bass), New College Choir Oxford [E] L'Oiseau-Lyre 2-▲ 430397-2 [DDD]
Haydn, J.:Syms (comp)—Nos. 6-9, 12, 13, 16, 40, 72 L'Oiseau-Lyre 3-▲ 433661-2 [DDD]
Haydn, J.:Syms (comp)—Nos. 1, 2, 4, 5, 10, 11, 18, 27, 32, 37 & 107 L'Oiseau-Lyre 3-▲ 436428-2 [DDD]
Haydn, J.:Syms (comp)—Nos 45-7, 51, 52, 64 L'Oiseau-Lyre 3-▲ 443777-2
Haydn, J.:Syms (comp)—Nos. 3, 14, 15, 17, 19, 20, 25, 33 & 36 L'Oiseau-Lyre 3-▲ 436592-2 [DDD]
Haydn, J.:Syms (comp)—Nos. 21-24, 28-31, 34 L'Oiseau-Lyre 3-▲ 430082-2 [DDD]
Haydn, J.:Syms (comp)—Nos. 35, 38, 39, 41, 58, 59, 65 L'Oiseau-Lyre 3-▲ 433012-2 [DDD]
Haydn, J.:Sym 26, "Lamentatione" L'Oiseau-Lyre 3-▲ 440222-2 [DDD]
Haydn, J.:Sym 42 L'Oiseau-Lyre 3-▲ 440222-2 [DDD]
Haydn, J.:Sym 43, "Mercury" L'Oiseau-Lyre 3-▲ 440222-2 [DDD]
Haydn, J.:Sym 44, "Trauer" L'Oiseau-Lyre 3-▲ 440222-2 [DDD]
Haydn, J.:Sym 48, "Maria Theresia" L'Oiseau-Lyre 3-▲ 440222-2 [DDD]
Haydn, J.:Sym 49, "La Passione" L'Oiseau-Lyre 3-▲ 440222-2 [DDD]

▲ = CD ♦ = Enhanced CD Δ = MD ■ = Cassette Tape □ = DCC

Academy of Ancient Music (cont.)
C. Hogwood (cnd) (cont.)
Haydn, J.:Sym 94, "Surprise Sym" [period instrs] L'Oiseau-Lyre ▲ 414330-2 [DDD]
Haydn, J.:Sym 108 L'Oiseau-Lyre 3-▲ 436592-2 [DDD]
Heinichen, J.D.:Con à 8, w. Amsterdam Loeki Stardust Quartet *(rec June 1992)* L'Oiseau-Lyre ▲ 436905-2 [DDD]
Marcello, B.:Con Rcrs, w. Amsterdam Loeki Stardust Quartet—in G *(rec June 1992)* L'Oiseau-Lyre ▲ 436905-2 [DDD]
Mozart, W.A.:Adagio Vn, K.261, w. S. Standage (vn) L'Oiseau-Lyre 2-▲ 433045-2 [DDD]
Mozart, W.A.:Arias, w. E. Kirkby (sop)—(opera arias) Il re pastore, K.208 *(Aer tranquillo e di sereni; L'amerò, sarò costante)*, Zaide, K.344 *(Ruhe sanft, mein holdes Leben; Trostlos schluchzet Philomele)*, (concert arias) Voi avete un cor fedele, K.217; Ah! lo previdi, K.272; Nehmt meinen Dank, ihr holden Gönner, K.383; Ch'io mi scordi di te, K.505 [G,I] L'Oiseau-Lyre ▲ 425835-2 [DDD]
Mozart, W.A.:Clemenza, w. Barbara Bonney (sop—Servilia), Cecilia Bartoli (mez—Sesto), Della Jones (mez—Vitellia), Diana Montague (mez—Annio), Uwe Heilman (ten—Tito), Giles Cachemaille (bar—Publio), Academy of Ancient Music Chorus London ("Editions de l'oiseau-lyre" series) 2-▲ 444131-2 [DDD]
Mozart, W.A.:Con Bn, w. D. Bond (bn) L'Oiseau-Lyre ▲ 417622-2 [DDD] □ 417622-5
Mozart, W.A.:Con Cl, w. Antony Pay (cl) L'Oiseau-Lyre ▲ 414339-2 [DDD]
Mozart, W.A.:Con Fl, K.313, w. L. Beznosiuk (fl) L'Oiseau-Lyre ▲ 417622-2 [DDD] □ 417622-5
Mozart, W.A.:Con Fl Hp, w. L. Beznosiuk (fl), F. Kelly (hp)—No. 1 L'Oiseau-Lyre ▲ 417622-2 [DDD] □ 417622-5
Mozart, W.A.:Cons Hn, w. Anthony Halstead (hn) L'Oiseau-Lyre ▲ 443216-2 [DDD]
Mozart, W.A.:Con Ob, K.314, w. Piquet (ob) L'Oiseau-Lyre ▲ 414339-2 [DDD]
Mozart, W.A.:Con 9 Pno, w. R. Levin (pno) *(rec Aug. 1993)* L'Oiseau-Lyre ▲ 443328-2 [DDD]
Mozart, W.A.:Con 11 Pno, w. Robert Levin (pno) L'oiseau-lyre ▲ 444571-2
Mozart, W.A.:Con 12 Pno, w. R. Levin (pno) *(rec Aug. 1993)* L'Oiseau-Lyre ▲ 443328-2 [DDD]
Mozart, W.A.:Con 13 Pno, w. Robert Levin (pno) L'oiseau-lyre ▲ 444571-2
Mozart, W.A.:Con 18 Pno, w. Robert Levin (pno) London ▲ 452051-2
Mozart, W.A.:Con 19 Pno, w. Robert Levin (pno) London ▲ 452051-2
Mozart, W.A.:Cons Vn, w. S. Standage (vn)—Nos. 1-5 L'Oiseau-Lyre 2-▲ 433045-2 [DDD]
Mozart, W.A.:Exsultate, w. Emma Kirkby (sop), Westminster Cathedral Boys' Choir [L] L'Oiseau-Lyre ▲ 411832-2 [DDD]
Mozart, W.A.:Kleine Nachtmusik L'Oiseau-Lyre ▲ 411720-2 [DDD]
Mozart, W.A.:Missa, K.317, w. E. Kirkby (sop), C. Robbin (mez), J.M. Ainsley (ten), M. George (bass), Winchester Cathedral Choir Argo ▲ 436585-2 [DDD]
Mozart, W.A.:Notturno Orchs, K.286 L'Oiseau-Lyre ▲ 411720-2 [DDD]
Mozart, W.A.:Rondo Hn, K.514, w. Anthony Halstead (hn) L'Oiseau-Lyre ▲ 443216-2 [DDD]
Mozart, W.A.:Rondo Pno Orch, K.386, w. Robert Levin (pno) London ▲ 444571-2
Mozart, W.A.:Rondo Vn, K.373, w. S. Standage (vn) L'Oiseau-Lyre 2-▲ 433045-2 [DDD]
Mozart, W.A.:Sacred Music, w. E. Kirkby (sop), Westminster Cathedral Boys' Choir—Regina coeli, K.108; Ergo interest, K.143; Regina coeli, K.127 [L] L'Oiseau-Lyre ▲ 411832-2 [DDD]
Mozart, W.A.:Serenata notturna L'Oiseau-Lyre ▲ 411720-2 [DDD]
Mozart, W.A.:Syms (comp) L'Oiseau-Lyre 2-▲ 417518-2 [ADD]
Mozart, W.A.:Syms (comp) L'Oiseau-Lyre 3-▲ 417841-2 [ADD]
Mozart, W.A.:Syms (comp) L'Oiseau-Lyre 3-▲ 417592-2 [ADD]
Mozart, W.A.:Syms (comp) L'Oiseau-Lyre 3-▲ 421104-2 [ADD]
Mozart, W.A.:Syms (comp) L'Oiseau-Lyre 3-▲ 421135-2 [ADD]
Music from the Time of Elizabeth I L'Oiseau-Lyre ▲ 433193-2 OH
The Original Sound, Vol. 2 L'Oiseau-Lyre 2-▲ 443267-2 [ADD/DDD]
Pachelbel, J.:Canon L'Oiseau-Lyre ▲ 410553-2 [ADD] ■ 410553-4
Pergolesi, G.B.:Salve regina in f, w. E. Kirkby (sop), J. Bowman (ct) L'Oiseau-Lyre ▲ 425692-2 [DDD]
Pergolesi, G.B.:Stabat mater, w. E. Kirkby (sop), J. Bowman (ct) L'Oiseau-Lyre ▲ 425692-2 [DDD]
Purcell, H.:Dido & Aeneas, w. Catherine Bott (sop—Dido), Emma Kirkby (sop—Belinda), Michael Chance (alt—Spirit), John Mark Ainsley (bar—Aeneas), David Thomas (bar—Sorceress) L'Oiseau-Lyre ▲ 436992-2 [DDD]
Purcell, H.:The Indian Queen, w. Catherine Bott (sop—Orazia/Married Woman), Emma Kirkby (sop—Indian Girl/Zempoalla/Cupid), John Mark Ainsley (ten—Indian Boy/Fame/Follower of Cupid/Aerial Spirits), Julian Podger (ten—Follower of Envy/Aerial Spirit), Gerald Finley (bar—Conjurer/Hymen/Follower of Cupid), Helen Parker (sgr—Aerial Spirits), David Thomas (bass—Envy/High Priest/Married Man/Follower of Cupid), Simon Berridge (sgr—Follower of Envy), Libby Crabtree (sgr—Follower of Hymen/Aerial Spirit), Tommy Williams (sgr—God of Dreams) *(rec Walthamstow Assembly Hall, London, July 1994)* L'Oiseau-Lyre ▲ 444339-2 [DDD]
Purcell, H.:Music for the Theater, w. E. Kirkby (sop), J. Nelson (sop), J. Bowman (ct), M. Hill (ten), R. Covey-Crump (ten), C. Keyte (bass), D. Thomas (bass) L'Oiseau-Lyre 6-▲ 425893-2 [ADD]
Purcell, H.:Music of, w. Catherine Bott (sop), Emma Kirkby (sop), James Bowman (alt), Anthony Rooley (lt), Monica Huggett (vn), Catherine Mackintosh (vn), Christophe Coin (vc), Paula Chateauneuf (gtr), Brandenburg Consort, Anthony Lewis (cnd), David Hill (cnd), St. Anthony Singers, Taverner Choir, Winchester Cathedral Choir—The Double Dealer; Come Ye Sons of Art; The Old Bachelor; Birthday Song for Queen Mary; Oedipus; King Arthur; Bonduca; The Fairy Queen; Son. No. 9 in F; Dido & Aeneas; Abdelazer; Bess of Bedlam; The Married Beau; Hear My Prayer, O Lord; Rejoice in the Lord Always L'Oiseau-Lyre ▲ 444620-2
Schickhardt, J.C.:Cons for 4 Rcrs, w. Amsterdam Loeki Stardust Quartet *(rec June 1992)* L'Oiseau-Lyre ▲ 436905-2 [DDD]
Telemann, G.P.:Cons (misc) L'Oiseau-Lyre ▲ 411949-2 [DDD]
Venice Preserv'd, w. Emma Kirkby (sop), Judith Nelson (mez), Nigel Rogers (ten) L'Oiseau-Lyre ▲ 425891-2 OH [ADD]
Vivaldi, A.:Cons Vc, w. C. Coin (vc)—5 concerti—RV. 401, 412, 413, 416, 418, 424 L'Oiseau-Lyre ▲ 421732-2 [DDD] □ 421732-5
Vivaldi, A.:Cons Vc, w. C. Coin (vc)—3 Concerti—RV.402, 406, 414 L'Oiseau-Lyre ▲ 433052-2 [DDD]
Vivaldi, A.:Cons Ob, w. F. de Bruine (ob)—in C, RV.447; in F, RV.457; in a RV.461; in a RV.463 London ▲ 433674-2
Vivaldi, A.:Cons Ob Vn, w. F. de Bruine (ob), S. Ritchie (vn)—in g, RV.460 L'Oiseau-Lyre ▲ 436172-2 [DDD]
Vivaldi, A.:Cons for 2 Obs, w. S. Hammer (ob), F. de Bruine (ob)—RV.535 London ▲ 433674-2
Vivaldi, A.:Cons Obs Cls, w. S. Hammer (ob), F. de Bruine (ob), E. Hoeprich (cl), A. Pay (cl)—RV.559 London ▲ 433674-2
Vivaldi, A.:Cons Orch—RV.394 L'Oiseau-Lyre ▲ 414329-2 [ADD]
Vivaldi, A.:Con for 2 Tpts L'Oiseau-Lyre ▲ 410553-2 [ADD] ■ 410553-4
Vivaldi, A.:Cons Rcr, w. Amsterdam Loeki Stardust Quartet—in A, RV.585, "in due cori" *(rec June 1992)* L'Oiseau-Lyre ▲ 436905-2 [DDD]
Vivaldi, A.:Cons Vn (misc), w. S. Ritchie (vn)—in D, RV.207; in e, RV.277; in A, RV.336; in G, RV.308; in c, RV.202 (Op. 11/1-5) L'Oiseau-Lyre ▲ 436172-2 [ADD]
Vivaldi, A.:Cons Vn, Op. 3/1-12, "L'estro armonico" L'Oiseau-Lyre 2-▲ 414554-2 [ADD]
Vivaldi, A.:Cons Vn, Op. 4, "La stravaganza", w. M. Huggett (vn) L'Oiseau-Lyre 2-▲ 417502-2 [DDD]
Vivaldi, A.:Cons Vn, Op. 8/1-12, "Il cimento dell'armonia e dell'inventione" L'Oiseau-Lyre 2-▲ 417515-2 [DDD]
Vivaldi, A.:Cons Vn, Op. 8/1-4, "The Four Seasons" L'Oiseau-Lyre ▲ 410126-2 [DDD]
Vivaldi, A.:Nisi Dominus, w. J. Bowman (ct) [L] L'Oiseau-Lyre ▲ 414329-2 [ADD]
Vivaldi, A.:Stabat Mater, w. J. Bowman (ct) L'Oiseau-Lyre ▲ 414329-2 [ADD]
S. Preston (cnd)
Bach, J.S.:Magnificat, BWV 243, w. E. Kirkby (sop), J. Nelson (sop), C. Watkinson (cta), P. Elliott (ten), D. Thomas (bass), Christ Church Cathedral Choir Oxford [E♭ version; L] L'Oiseau-Lyre ▲ 414678-2 [ADD]
Vivaldi, A.:Gloria, RV.589, w. J. Nelson (sop), E. Kirkby (sop), C. Watkinson (cta), P. Elliott (ten), D. Thomas (bass), Christ Church Cathedral Choir Oxford [L] L'Oiseau-Lyre ▲ 414678-2 [ADD]
S. Standage (cnd)
Bach, Joh. Christian:Adriano in Siria (ov) Chandos ("Chaconne" series) ▲ CHAN 0540 [DDD]
Bach, Joh. Christian:Sinf concertante Fl Chandos ("Chaconne" series) ▲ CHAN 0540 [DDD]

Academy of Ancient Music (cont.)
S. Standage (cnd) (cont.)
Bach, Joh. Christian:Sinfs, Op. 6—No. 6 Chandos ("Chaconne" series) ▲ CHAN 0540 [DDD]
Bach, Joh. Christian:Sinfs, Op. 18—Nos. 1 & 4 Chandos ("Chaconne" series) ▲ CHAN 0540 [DDD]
Academy of Ancient Music Chamber Ensemble
Kerle, J. de:Preces speciales pro salubri generalis Concili successu, w. Vox Hesperia *(rec Santa Maria Maggiore Church, Oct. 28-31, 1994)* Bongiovanni ▲ GB 5570 [DDD]
Schubert, Franz:Qnt Pno, D.667, w. S. Lubin (pno) L'Oiseau-Lyre ▲ 433848-2 [DDD]
Schubert, Franz:Songs (comp), w. J. M. Ainsley (ten)—Die Forelle, D.550; Am Strome, D.539; Auf dem See, D.543; Erlafsee, D.586; An eine Quelle, D.530; Der Jüngling am Bache, D.192; Der Schiffer, D.536 [G] L'Oiseau-Lyre ▲ 433848-2 [DDD]
Academy of Ancient Music Instumental Ensemble [Alberto Rossi (cnt), Giuliano Eccher (vl), Alberto guiliani (trbn), Ermes Giussani (trbn), Orietta Priore (trbn), Pietro Prosser (lt), Adriano Dallapè (org)]
R. Vettori (cnd)
Kerle, J. de:Preces speciales pro salubri generalis Concili successu, w. Vox Hesperia—Pro Concilio; Pro Populi Christiane unione; Contra Ecclesiae hostium furorem; contra eosdem hostes *(rec Church of S. Maria del Carmine, Rovereto)* Bongiovanni ▲ GB 5571 [DDD]
Academy of London Orch
P. Marschik (cnd)
Handel, G.F.:Messiah, w. Max Emanuel Cencic (sop), Charles Humphries (ct), Ivan Sharpe (ten), Robert Torday (b-bar), Martin Schebesta (cnd), Vienna Boys' Choir *(rec Symphony Hall, Birmingham & Barbican Center, London, Nov 17 & 19, 1994)* Capriccio 2-▲ 60068-2 [DDD]
R. Stamp (cnd)
Bach, J.S.:Con Ob d'amore, w. R. Still (ob d'amore) Virgin Classics ▲ CDZ 59686-2
Elgar, E.:Con Vc, w. M. Braunstein (va) Virgin Classics ▲ CDZ 59643
Marcello, A.:Con Ob & Strs, w. R. Still (ob) Virgin Classics ▲ CDZ 59686
Mozart, W.A.:Con 12 Pno, w. N. Rutman (pno) ASV Quicksilva ▲ CD QS 6022 [DDD]
Mozart, W.A.:Con 22 Pno, w. N. Rutman (pno) ASV Quicksilva ▲ CD QS 6022 [DDD]
Mozart, W.A.:Kleine Nachtmusik Virgin Classics ▲ 59533 [DDD]
Mozart, W.A.:Kleine Nachtmusik ASV Quicksilva ▲ ASQ 6184
Mozart, W.A.:Sym 33 ASV Quicksilva ▲ ASQ 6184
Mozart, W.A.:Sym 40 ASV Quicksilva ▲ ASQ 6184
Prokofiev, S.:Peter & the Wolf, w. J. Gielgud (nar) Virgin Classics ▲ 59533 [DDD]
Prokofiev, S.:Peter & the Wolf, w. John Gielgud (nar) Virgin Classics ("Ultraviolet" series) ▲ CUV 61137
Saint-Saëns, C.:Carnival of the Animals, w. J. Gielgud (nar) Virgin Classics ("Ultraviolet" series) ▲ CUV 61137
Saint-Saëns, C.:Carnival of the Animals, w. A. Nel (pno), K. Snell (pno) Virgin Classics ▲ 59533 [DDD]
Strauss, R.:Con Ob, w. R. Still (ob) Virgin Classics ▲ CDZ 59686
Strauss, R.:Metamorphosen Virgin Classics ▲ CDC 59538
Strauss, R.:Songs, w. G. Janowitz (sop) Virgin Classics ▲ CDC 59538
Academy of Music Orch
A. Guadagno (cnd)
Giordano, U.:Andrea Chénier, w. Montserrat Caballé (sop), Franco Corelli (ten), R. de Carlo (sgr), D. Dondi (sgr), G. Ellsworth (sgr), J. Fair (sgr), R. Falk (sgr), S. Felter (sgr), E. Green (sgr), H. Hicks (sgr), H. Krauss (sgr), L. Miller (sgr), N. Riggins (sgr), H. Salerno (sgr), Academy of Music Chorus Great Opera Performances 2-▲ GOP 766
Academy of St. James
C. Pini (cnd)
Bach, J.S.:Brandenburg Cons Omega 2-▲ OCD 1008/09 [DDD]
Academy of St. Martin in the Fields
Bach, J.S.:Cons Vn (comp), w. G. Kremer (vn) Philips ▲ 434730-2
Bach, J.S.:Con for 2 Vns, w. G. Kremer (vn) Philips ▲ 434730-2
Vivaldi, A.:Music of, w. Salvatore Accardo (vn), Frederico Agostini (vn), Heinz Holliger (ob), Ida Levin (vn), Aurele Nicolet (fl), Massimo Paris (va d'amore), Angel Romero (gtr), Celedonio Romero (gtr), Celine Romero (gtr), Henryk Szeryng (vn), Pinchas Zukerman (vn), English CO, I Musici, Naples Weekly International Soloists, St. Paul CO, Dresden Staatskapelle—The Four Seasons [Winter]; Con in D for Gtr [Largo]; Con in D for Fl, "Il gardellino" [Cantabile]; Con in C for Diverse Insts [Andante molto]; Con in g for Strs [Andante molto]; Con in D for 2 Vns & 2 Vcs [Largo]; Con in g for Ob, Vn, Ww & Strs [Larghetto]; Con in a for Gtr, "L'estro armonico" [Largo]; Con in F for 3 Vns [Andante]; Con in F for Fl [Largo]; Con in d for Va D'Amore [Largo]; Con in E for Vn & Strs, "Il riposo" [Allegro]; Con in G for Ob, Bn & Strs [Largo]; Con in B♭ for Vn & Strs [Largo]; Con in A for Gtr & Strs [Larghetto]; Con in E for Vn & Strs, "L'amoroso" [Allegro]; Con in G for Fl [Largo]; Con in A for Vn [Larghetto]; Con in c for Vn & Strs, "Il sospetto" [Andante]; Con in a for 2 Obs & Strs [Largo]; Con in g for Orch [Largo non molto]; Con in a for Vn [Largo]; Con in C for Ob [Adagio]; Con in g for Fl, "La notte" [Largo] Philips ▲ 454051-2 ■ 454 051-4
Walton, W.:Music of, w. London PO, Finzi Singers Chandos 23-▲ CHAN 9426 [DDD]
I. Brown (cnd)
Bach, J.S.:Con 8 Hpd, w. H. Holliger (ob) Philips ▲ 412851-2 [DDD]
Bach, J.S.:Con Ob, BWV 1053, w. H. Holliger (ob) Philips ▲ 412851-2 [DDD]
Bach, J.S.:Con in d Ob, w. H. Holliger (ob) Philips ▲ 412851-2 [DDD]
Bach, J.S.:Con Ob d'amore, w. H. Holliger (ob d'amore) Philips ▲ 412851-2 [DDD]
Barry Tuckwell, w. Barry Tuckwell (hn), English CO EMI Classics ("Doublefforte" series) 2-▲ CDFB 69395
Geminiani, F.:Con grossi, Op. 7 ASV ▲ ASV 724
Handel, G.F.:Cons Rcr, w. M. Petri (rcr)—1 con in F Philips ▲ 400075-2 [ADD]
Handel, G.F.:Hornpipe Philips ▲ 420397-2 [ADD]
Handel, G.F.:Son (Con) Obs Philips ▲ 420397-2 [ADD]
Haydn, J.:Con 1 Vc, w. Mstislav Rostropovich (vc) EMI Classics ▲ CDC 49305
Haydn, J.:Con 2 Vc, w. Mstislav Rostropovich (vc) EMI Classics ▲ CDC 49305
Marisa Robles, w. Marisa Robles (hp) London ("Serenata" series) ▲ 425723-2 [ADD]
Sammartini, G.:Cons Rcr, w. M. Petri (rcr)—in F Philips ▲ 400075-2 [ADD]
Stamitz, C.:Cons Cl, w. S. Meyer (cl)—No. 3 in B♭; No. 10 in B; No. 11 in E♭ EMI Classics ▲ CDC 54842 [DDD]
Stamitz, C.:Cons Cl, w. Sabine Meyer (cl) *(rec Concert Halls, Blackheath, Nov. 5-7, 1992)* EMI Classics ▲ CDC 55155 [DDD]
Stamitz, C.:Con Cl, w. S. Meyer (cl)—No. 3 in B♭; No. 10 in B; No. 11 in E♭ EMI Classics ▲ CDC 54842 [DDD]
Telemann, G.P.:Cons for 2 Hns, w. H. Baumann (hn), T. Brown (hn) Philips ▲ 412226-2 [DDD]
Telemann, G.P.:Cons Hns, w. H. Baumann (hn), T. Brown (hn), N. Hill (hn) Philips ▲ 412226-2 [DDD]
Telemann, G.P.:Cons Ob Orch, w. H. Holliger (ob)—Nos. 2-4, 6 & 8 Philips ("Digital Classics" series) ▲ 412879-2 [DDD]
Telemann, G.P.:Con in F Rcr Bn, w. M. Petri (rcr), K. Thunemann (bn) Philips ▲ 410041-2 [DDD]
Telemann, G.P.:Con Rcr, Fl, w. M. Petri (rcr), K. Bennett (fl) Philips ▲ 410041-2 [DDD]
Telemann, G.P.:Con in C Rcr, w. M. Petri (rcr) Philips ▲ 400075-2 [ADD]
Telemann, G.P.:Cons Tpt, w. H. Hardenberger (tpt), M. Laird (tpt), W. Houghton (tpt)—Concerto for 2 Trumpets & Strings; Concerto for Trumpet, 2 Oboes & Strings; Concerto for 3 Trumpets & Strings; Concerto for Trumpet & Strings Philips ("Digital Classics" series) ▲ 420954-2 [DDD]
Telemann, G.P.:Cons Vn—Nos. 3, 4, 8, 9, 11, in D, E, G, g, B♭ Philips ▲ 411125-2 [DDD]
Telemann, G.P.:Suite in a for Fl, w. M. Petri (rcr) Philips ▲ 410041-2 [DDD]
Vivaldi, A.:Cons Vc, w. H. Schiff (vc)—5 concerti—RV.401, 411-413, 418, 424 Philips ▲ 411126-2 [DDD]
Vivaldi, A.:Cons Mand, w. P. Romero (gtr)—3 concerti—RV.93, 425, 532 Philips ▲ 412624-2 [DDD]
Vivaldi, A.:Cons Rcr, w. M. Petri (rcr)—RV.443 Philips ▲ 400075-2
Vivaldi, A.:Cons Vn (misc), w. I. Brown (vn)—RV.356 Philips ▲ 412624-2 [DDD]
Vivaldi, A.:Cons Vn, Op. 8/1-4, "The Four Seasons", w. Iona Brown (vn) *(rec London, Sept 1995)* Hänssler Classic ▲ CD 98.017 [DDD]
Vivaldi, A.:Cons for 2 Vns, w. Iona Brown (vn), Johnathan Rees (vn), Briony Shaw (vn), Ralph de Souza (vn)—Nos. 3 & 10 *(rec London, Sept 1995)* Hänssler Classic ▲ CD 98.017 [DDD]

ORCH. & ENS.

Academy of St. Martin in the Fields (cont.)

C. Davis (cnd)

Mozart, W.A.:Complete Mozart Edition, w. C. Eda-Pierre (sop), N. Burrowes (sop), R. Tear (ten), S. Burrows (ten), John Alldis Choir Philips 2-▲ 422538-2 [ADD]

G. Guest (cnd)

Fauré, G.:Requiem, w. J. Bond (trb), B. Luxon (bar), St. John's College Choir Cambridge [L] London ("Jubilee" series) ▲ 430360-2 [ADD]

P. Ledger (cnd)

Bach, C.P.E.:Magnificat, w. F. Palmer (sop), H. Watts (cta), R. Tear (ten), S. Roberts (b-bar), King's College Choir Cambridge London ("Jubilee" series) ▲ 421148-2 [ADD]

Bach, J.S.:Christmas Oratorio, w. Elly Ameling (sop), Janet Baker (mez), Robert Tear (ten), Dietrich Fischer-Dieskau (bar), King's College Choir Cambridge *(rec 1976)* EMI Classics ("Doubleforte" series) 2-▲ CDFB 69503

Bach, J.S.:Magnificat, BWV 243, w. F. Palmer (sop), H. Watts (cta), R. Tear (ten), S. Roberts (b-bar), King's College Choir Cambridge London ("Jubilee" series) ▲ 421148-2 [ADD]

Charpentier, M.-A.:Te Deum in C, w. F. Lott (sop), I. Partridge (ten), S. Roberts (bar), P. Ledger (org), King's College Choir Cambridge EMI Classics ▲ CDM 63135

N. Marriner (cnd)

Academy of St. Martin in the Fields EMI Classics ▲ CDC 47391

Adam, A.:Giselle *(rec St. Jude's, London, Nov 21-23, 1994)* Capriccio ▲ 10568 [DDD]

Albinoni, T.:Adagio Org EMI Classics ▲ CDC 47391-2

Albinoni, T.:Cons à 5 Obs, Op. 9, w. Daniel Arrignon (ob)—No. 3 in F Classics for Pleasure ("Eminence" series) ▲ CFP 2235

Arie Amorose, w. Janet Baker (cta) Philips ("Collector" series) ▲ 434173-2 [ADD]

Avison, C.:Concerti grossi (12) Philips 2-▲ 438806-2

Bach, J.S.:The Art of the Fugue Philips ("Duo" series) 2-▲ 442556-2

Bach, J.S.:Brandenburg Cons—Nos. 4-6 Philips ▲ 400077-2 [ADD]

Bach, J.S.:Brandenburg Cons—Nos. 1, 2, 6 Philips ▲ 426088-2 [ADD]

Bach, J.S.:Brandenburg Cons—Nos. 1-3 Philips ▲ 400076-2 [ADD]

Bach, J.S.:Brandenburg Cons—Nos. 3, 4, 5 Philips ▲ 426089-2 [ADD]

Bach, J.S.:Cant 51, w. Helend Donath (sop) Classics for Pleasure ("Eminence" series) ▲ CFP 2235

Bach, J.S.:Cant 82, w. J. Baker (sop), R. Tear (ten), J. Shirley-Quirk (bar) London ("Jubilee" series) ▲ 430260-2 [ADD]

Bach, J.S.:Cant 159, w. J. Baker (sop), R. Tear (ten), J. Shirley-Quirk (bar) London ("Jubilee" series) ▲ 430260-2 [ADD]

Bach, J.S.:Cant 170, w. J. Baker (sop), R. Tear (ten), J. Shirley-Quirk (bar) London ("Jubilee" series) ▲ 430260-2 [ADD]

Bach, J.S.:Cons Hpd, BWV 1052-1058, w. A. Gavrilov (pno)—Nos. 1,6 & 7 EMI Classics ▲ CDD 64293-2 [DDD]

Bach, J.S.:Cons Hpd, BWV 1052-1058, w. A. Gavrilov (pno)—Nos. 1,2,4 & 5 EMI Classics ▲ CDD 64055-2 [DDD]

Bach, J.S.:Cons Hpd, BWV 1052-1058, w. A. Gavrilov (pno)—Nos. 1, 2, 4 & 5 EMI Classics ▲ CDM 65173

Bach, J.S.:Cons Hpd, BWV 1052-1058, w. A. Gavrilov (pno)—Nos. 3, 6 & 7 EMI Classics ▲ CDM 65174

Bach, J.S.:Con 2 Hpd, w. Neil Black (ob), Christopher Hogwood (bc), Nicholas Kraemer (bc) [trans for ob] *(rec St. John's, Smith Square, London, Aug 1974 & Feb 1975)* Boston Skyline ▲ BSD 127 [ADD]

Bach, J.S.:Con 4 Hpd, w. Neil Black (ob d'amore), Christopher Hogwood (bc), Nicholas Kraemer (bc) [trans for ob d'amore] *(rec St. John's, Smith Square, London, Aug 1974 & Feb 1975)* Boston Skyline ▲ BSD 127 [ADD]

Bach, J.S.:Con 1 for 2 Hpds, w. Carmel Kaine (vn), Tess Miller (ob), Christopher Hogwood (bc), Nicholas Kraemer (bc) [trans for vn & ob] *(rec St. John's, Smith Square, London, Aug 1974 & Feb 1975)* Boston Skyline ▲ BSD 127 [ADD]

Bach, J.S.:Con 2 for 3 Hpds, w. Carmel Kaine (vn), Ronald Thomas (vn), Richard Studt (vn), Christopher Hogwood (bc), Nicholas Kraemer (bc) [trans for 3 vn] *(rec St. John's, Smith Square, London, Aug 1974 & Feb 1975)* Boston Skyline ▲ BSD 127 [ADD]

Bach, J.S.:Cons Vn (comp), w. H. Szeryng (vn) Philips ▲ 422250-2 [ADD]

Bach, J.S.:Con Vn & Ob, w. G. Kremer (vn), Holliger (ob) Philips 2-▲ 426462-2 [ADD]

Bach, J.S.:Con Vn & Ob, w. G. Kremer (vn), Holliger (ob) Philips ▲ 434730-2

Bach, J.S.:Con for 2 Vns, w. H. Szeryng (vn), M. Hasson (vn) Philips 2-▲ 426462-2 [ADD]

Bach, J.S.:Con for 2 Vns, w. H. Szeryng (vn), M. Hasson (vn)—Air & Suite No. 3, BWV 1068 Philips ▲ 422250-2 [ADD]

Bach, J.S.:French Suites, w. A. Gavrilov (pno)—BWV 816 EMI Classics ▲ CDD 64293-2 [DDD]

Bach, J.S.:French Suites, w. A. Gavrilov (pno)—No. 5 EMI Classics ▲ CDM 65174

Bach, J.S.:Magnificat, BWV 243, w. B. Hendricks (sop), J. Rigby (sop), A. Murray (mez), U. Heilmann (ten), J. Hynninen (bar), *(chorus unknown)* EMI Classics ▲ CDC 54283-2

Bach, J.S.:Mass in b, BWV 232, w. M. Marshall (sop), J. Baker (mez), R. Tear (ten), S. Ramey (bass), *(chorus unknown)* [L] Philips 2-▲ 416415-2 [DDD]

Bach, J.S.:Mass in b, BWV 232, w. J. Kowalski (alt)—Qui sedes ad dextram patris; Agnus dei Capriccio ▲ 10 532 [DDD]

Bach, J.S.:St. Matthew Passion (sels), w. J. Kowalski (alt)—Du lieber Heiland du; Buss und Reu; Erbarme dich, erbarme dich, mein Gott; Erbarm' es Gott!; Können Tränen meiner Wangen Capriccio ▲ 10 532 [DDD]

Bach, J.S.:Suites Orch, BWV 1066-1069 Philips 2-▲ 426462-2 [ADD]

Bach, J.S.:Suites Orch, BWV 1066-1069 London ("Jubilee" series) ▲ 430378-2 [ADD]

Bach, J.S.:Suite 3 Orch London ▲ 452485-2 ■ 452 485-4

Barber, S.:Adagio Strs Argo ▲ 417818-2 [ADD]

Barry Tuckwell, w. Barry Tuckwell (hn), English CO EMI Classics ("Doubleforte" series) 2-▲ CDFB 69395

Beethoven, L. van:Romances Vn, w. J. Suk (vn) EMI Classics ▲ CDE 67765

Beethoven, L. van:Romances Vn, w. J. Suk (vn) Klavier ▲ KCD 11035 [DDD]

Beethoven, L. van:Romances Vn, w. D. Sitkovetsky (vn) Virgin Classics ▲ CDC 45001

Bellini, V.:Con in E♭ Ob, w. *(soloist unknown)* London ("Serenata" series) 2-▲ 430563-2 [ADD]

Bennett, Richard Rodney:Con A Sax, w. J. Harle (alt) EMI Classics ▲ CDC 54301

A Birthday Celebration Philips ▲ 442313-2

Boyce, W.:Syms, Op. 2 Capriccio ▲ CD 10421 [DDD]

Brahms, J.:Con Vn, w. Dmitry Sitkovetsky (vn) *(rec Henry Wood Hall, London, May 4-6, 1995)* Hänssler Classic ("Academy" series) ▲ CD 98.934 [DDD]

Bruch, M.:Con 1 Vn, w. J. Bell (vn) London ▲ 421145-2 [DDD] ■ 421145-4

Castelnuovo-Tedesco, M.:Con 1 Gtr, w. P. Romero (gtr) Philips ▲ 416357-2 [DDD]

Charpentier, M.-A.:Magnificat, w. D. Upshaw (sop), A. Murray (mez), E. Robinson (mez), J. Aler (ten), K. Moll (bass), Academy of St. Martin in the Fields Chorus EMI Classics ▲ CDC 54284

Charpentier, M.-A.:Te Deum in C, w. D. Upshaw (sop), A. Murray (mez), E. Robinson (mez), J. Aler (ten), K. Moll (bass), Academy of St. Martin in the Fields Chorus EMI Classics ▲ CDC 54284

Cherubini, L.:Ovs—ovs. to 7 operas, & 1 concert ov. EMI Classics ▲ CDC 54438

Cherubini, L.:Sons (2) Hn—No. 2 London ("Serenata" series) 2-▲ 430563-2 [ADD]

Copland, A.:Quiet City Argo ▲ 417818-2 [ADD]

Copland, A.:Quiet City *(rec St. John's, Smith Square, London, Oct 1975)* London 2-▲ 448261-2 [ADD]

Corelli, A.:Concerti grossi, Op. 6—complete London ("Serenata" series) 2-▲ 430560-2 [ADD]

Corelli, A.:Concerti grossi, Op. 6 London ("Double Decca" series) 2-▲ 443862-2

Cowell, H.:Hymn & Fuguing Tune 10, w. C. Nicklin (ob) Argo ▲ 417818-2 [ADD]

Debussy, C.:Rapsodie, w. J. Harle (sax) EMI Classics ▲ CDC 54301

Donizetti, G.:Qt in D Strs London ("Serenata" series) 2-▲ 430563-2

Dvořák, A.:Carnival Capriccio ▲ 10 386 [DDD]

Dvořák, A.:Othello Capriccio ▲ 10 386 [DDD]

Dvořák, A.:Serenade Strs Philips ▲ 400020-2 [DDD]

Dvořák, A.:Serenade Ww Philips ▲ 400020-2 [DDD]

Academy of St. Martin in the Fields (cont.)

N. Marriner (cnd) (cont.)

Dvořák, A.:Sym 9, "From the New World" Capriccio ▲ 10 386 [DDD]

Elgar, E.:In the South Collins Classics ▲ COL 1269 [DDD]

Elgar, E.:Serenade Strs ASV Quicksilva ▲ QS 6051 [ADD/DDD]

Elgar, E.:Serenade Strs ASV Quicksilva ▲ ASQ 6087 [ADD/DDD]

Elgar, E.:Sym 1 Collins Classics ▲ COL 1269 [DDD]

The English Connection ASV ▲ ASV 518 [DDD]

English Idyll, w.Julian Lloyd Webber (vc) Philips ▲ 442530-2

The French Connection ASV ▲ ASV 517 [DDD]

Giuliani, M.:Con 1 Gtr, w. P. Romero (gtr) Philips ▲ 420780-2 [ADD]

Giuliani, M.:Con 3 Gtr, w. P. Romero (gtr) Philips ▲ 420780-2 [ADD]

Giuliani, M.:Gtr Music, w. Pepe Romero (gtr)—includes Cons 1-3; Gran Son Eroica; Intro, Theme with Vars & Polonaise; Grande Overture; La Melanconia; Vars on a Theme by Handel; Variazioni Concertanti Philips ("Duo" series) 2-▲ 454 262-2

Glazunov, A.:Con Sax, w. J. Harle (sax) EMI Classics ▲ CDC 54301

Grieg, E.:Holberg Suite Philips ▲ 412727-2 [DDD]

Grieg, E.:Lyric Pieces—Op. 68/4 & 5 [arr Grieg for orch] Philips ▲ 412727-2 [DDD]

Grieg, E.:Peer Gynt, w. L. Popp (sop), Ambrosian Singers EMI Classics ▲ CDC 47003 [DDD]

Handel, G.F.:Arias, w. J. Kowalski (alt)—Behold a Virgin shall conceive; He was despised; O thou tellest good tidings to Zion [from *Messiah*]; Their land brought forth frogs [from *Israel in Egypt*]; Oh sacred oracles of truth [from *Belshazzar*]; May at last...[from *L'Allegro, il penseroso ed Il Moderato*] Capriccio ▲ 10 532 [DDD]

Handel, G.F.:Arias, w. K. Battle (sop)—Acis & Galatea—Oh, didst thou know...As when the dove; Giulio Cesare—E pur così in un giorno...Piangerò la sorte mia; Joshua—Oh! had I Jubal's lyre; L'Allegro, il Penseroso ed il Moderato—Sweet bird; Messiah—Rejoice greatly, o daughter of Zion; Solomon—Ev'ry sight these eyes behold; May peace in Salem...Will the sun forget to streak; Alcina—Ah! mio cor!; Tornami a vagheggiar [E,I] EMI Classics ▲ CDC 49179 [DDD]

Handel, G.F.:Concerti grossi, Op. 3 London ("Serenata" series) ▲ 430261-2 [ADD]

Handel, G.F.:Con grosso in C, "Alexanderfest" Philips ▲ 420397-2 [ADD]

Handel, G.F.:Con grosso in C, "Alexanderfest" Philips ▲ 434729-2

Handel, G.F.:Coronation Anthems (4) for George II, w. Academy Chorus [E] Philips ▲ 412733-2 [DDD]

Handel, G.F.:Messiah, w. Elly Ameling (sop), Anna Reynolds (alt), Philip Langridge (ten), Gwynne Howell (bass), Academy of St. Martin in the Fields Chorus *(rec St John's, Smith Square, London, Jan & July 1976)* London ("Double Decker" series) 2-▲ 444824-2 [ADD]

Handel, G.F.:Messiah, w. Sylvia McNair (sop), Anne Sofie von Otter (mez), Michael Chance (alt), Jerry Hadley (ten), Robert Lloyd (b-bar) [E] *(rec live, Dublin 4/13/92)* Philips 2-▲ 434695-2 [DDD]

Handel, G.F.:Messiah, w. Elly Ameling (sop), Anna Reynolds (mez), Philip Langridge (ten), Gwynne Howell (bass), Academy of St. Martin in the Fields Chorus [E] Argo ■ 421234-4

Handel, G.F.:Ovs—Alcina; Ariodante London ("Serenata" series) ▲ 430261-2 [ADD]

Handel, G.F.:Ovs, w. Ian Brown (pno)—Ov in D; Ov in B♭ Philips ▲ 420397-2 [ADD]

Handel, G.F.:Royal Fireworks Music Argo ▲ 414596-2 [ADD] ■ 414596-4

Handel, G.F.:Royal Fireworks Music Philips ▲ 420397-2 [ADD]

Handel, G.F.:Solomon (arrival of the queen of Sheba) Philips ▲ 420397-2 [ADD]

Handel, G.F.:Son à 5 for Vn & Obs Philips ▲ 420397-2 [ADD]

Handel, G.F.:Water Music (comp) Philips ▲ 434729-2

Handel, G.F.:Water Music (comp) Philips ▲ 416447-2 [ADD]

Handel, G.F.:Water Music (comp) Philips ■ 412924-4

Handel, G.F.:Water Music (comp) Argo ▲ 414596-2 [ADD]

Handel, G.F.:Water Music (comp) EMI Classics ▲ CDC 49810 [DDD]

Handel, G.F.:Water Music (suites) London ▲ 452485-2 ■ 452 485-4

Haydn, J.:Con 1 Vc, w. Heinrich Schiff (vc) Philips ▲ 420923-2 [DDD]

Haydn, J.:Con 1 Vc, w. Lynn Harrell (vc) EMI Classics ▲ CDM 64326

Haydn, J.:Con 2 Vc, w. Lynn Harrell (vc) EMI Classics ▲ CDM 64326

Haydn, J.:Con 2 Vc, w. András Schiff (vc) Philips ▲ 420923-2 [DDD]

Haydn, J.:Cons Hn, w. Barry Tuckwell (hn) London ("Serenata" series) ▲ 430633-2

Haydn, J.:Con Tpt, w. Alan Stringer (tpt) London ("Serenata" series) ▲ 430633-2

Haydn, J.:Con Tpt, w. Håkan Hardenberger (tpt) Philips ▲ 420203-2 [DDD] ■ 420203-4

Haydn, J.:Die Jahreszeiten, w. Edith Mathis (sop), Sigfried Jerusalem (ten), Dietrich Fischer-Dieskau (bar) Philips ("Duo" series) 2-▲ 438715-2

Haydn, J.:Mass 11, "Nelsonmesse", "Imperial Mass", "Coronation Mass", w. Elizabeth Vaughan (sop), Janet Baker (mez), King's College Choir Cambridge London ("Jubilee" series) ▲ 421146-2 [ADD]

Haydn, J.:Pno Music, w. Alfred Brendel (pno), Imogen Cooper (pno)—Andante w. Vars (H.XVII/6); Sons Nos. 49, 50 & 52 Philips 25-▲ 446920-2

Haydn, J.:Sym 59, "Fire" Philips ("Silver Line" series) ▲ 420866-2 [ADD]

Haydn, J.:Syms 82-87, "Paris Syms" Philips ("Duo" series) 2-▲ 438727-2

Haydn, J.:Sym 100, "Military" Philips ("Silver Line" series) ▲ 420866-2 [ADD]

Haydn, J.:Sym 101, "Clock" Philips ("Silver Line" series) ▲ 420866-2 [ADD]

Hertel, J.W.:Con Tpt, w. H. Hardenberger (tpt) Philips ▲ 420203-2 [DDD] ■ 420203-4

Honegger, A.:Con da camera, w. Aurèle Nicolet (fl), Heinz Holliger (E hn) *(rec St. John's, London, Oct. 8-11, 1991)* Philips ▲ 434105-2

Hummel, J.N.:Con Bn, w. K. Thunemann (bn) Philips ▲ 432081-2 [DDD]

Hummel, J.N.:Con in E♭ Tpt, S.49, w. H. Hardenberger (tpt) Philips ▲ 420203-2 [DDD] ■ 420203-4

Ives, C.:Sym 3 Argo ▲ 417818-2 [DDD] ■ 417818-4

Jacob, G.:Pieces Hmc, w. T. Reilly (hmc) Chandos ▲ CHAN 8617 [AAD]

Jeux d'Enfants, w. Christopher Hyde-Smith (fl/pic), Emma Johnson (cl), George MacDonald (cl), Gordon Back (pno), Mexico City PO, Mexico State SO, Royal PO [cnd:Enrique Bátiz], Northern Sinfonia of England ASV Quicksilva ▲ ASQ 6182

Lollipops Philips ("Solo" series) ▲ 442406-2

Mahler, G.:Songs from Rückert, w. Mitsuko Shirai (mez) Capriccio ▲ CD 10712 [DDD]

Martin, F.:Danses, w. Heinz Holliger (ob), Ursula Holliger (hp) *(rec St. John's, London, Oct. 8-11, 1991)* Philips ▲ 434105-2

Martinů, B.:Con Ob, w. Heinz Holliger (ob) *(rec St. John's, London, Oct. 8-11, 1991)* Philips ▲ 434105-2

Maw, N.:Life Studies I-VIII Continuum ▲ CCD 1030

Mendelssohn, F.:Con 1 Pno, w. Murray Perahia (pno) CBS ▲ MK 42401 [AAD]

Mendelssohn, F.:Con 2 Pno, w. M. Perahia (pno) CBS ▲ MK 42401 [AAD]

Mendelssohn, F.:Con in d Vn & Strs, w. V. Mullova (vn) Philips ▲ 432077-2 [DDD]

Mendelssohn, F.:Con in e Vn & Orch, Op. 64, w. J. Bell (vn) London ▲ 421145-2 [DDD] ■ 421145-4

Mendelssohn, F.:Con in e Vn & Orch, Op. 64, w. Dmitry Sitkovetsky (vn) *(rec Henry Wood Hall, London, May 4-6, 1995)* Hänssler Classic ("Academy" series) ▲ CD 98.934 [DDD]

Mendelssohn, F.:Con in e Vn & Orch, Op. 64, w. V. Mullova (vn) Philips ▲ 432077-2

Mendelssohn, F.:Elijah, w. Y. Kenny (sop), A.S. von Otter (mez), A. Rolfe Johnson (ten), T. Allen (bar) Philips 2-▲ 432984-2 [DDD]

Moody, J.:Little Suite, w. T. Reilly (hmc) Chandos ▲ CHAN 8617 [ADD]

Mozart, F.X.W.:Con Pno, Op. 14, w. Janet Colburn (pno) Audiofon ▲ CD 72038

Mozart, W.A.:Adagio & Fugue Strs Philips ▲ 416386-2 [DDD]

Mozart, W.A.:Adagio Vn, K.261, w. J. Suk (vn) Klavier ▲ KCD 11035 [DDD]

Mozart, W.A.:Andante Fl, K.315/285a, w. I. Grafenauer (fl) Philips ▲ 422339-2 [DDD]

Mozart, W.A.:Arias, w. C. Studer (sop)—arias from Die Zauberflöte, Le nozze di Figaro, Così fan tutte & Die Entführung aus dem Serail Philips ("Solo" series) ▲ 442410-2

Mozart, W.A.:Arias, w. B. Hendricks (sop), J. Sillman (org.), Academy Chorus EMI Classics ▲ CDC 49283

Mozart, W.A.:Ave verum corpus, w. K. Te Kanawa (sop), A. Sofie von Otter (mez), A. R. Johnson (ten), R. Lloyd (bass), Academy Chorus *(rec London, Mar. 10-12, 1993)* Philips ▲ 438999-2

Mozart, W.A.:Complete Mozart Edition Philips 6-▲ 422501-2 [ADD]

Mozart, W.A.:Complete Mozart Edition, w. A. M. Blasi (sop), S. McNair (sop), I. Vermillion (mez), J. Hadley (ten), C. H. Ahnsjö (ten) Philips 2-▲ 422535-2 [ADD]

▲ = CD ♦ = Enhanced CD Δ = MD ■ = Cassette Tape ▯ = DCC

Academy of St. Martin in the Fields (cont.)
N. Marriner (cnd) (cont.)

Mozart, W.A.:Complete Mozart Edition Philips 6-▲ 422502-2 [ADD]
Mozart, W.A.:Complete Mozart Edition Philips 5-▲ 422509-2 [ADD]
Mozart, W.A.:Con Bn, w. K. Thunemann (bn) Philips ▲ 422390-2 [DDD]
Mozart, W.A.:Con Cl, w. J. Brymer (cl) Philips ▲ 416483-2 [ADD]
Mozart, W.A.:Con Cl, w. K. Leister (cl) Philips ▲ 422390-2 [DDD]
Mozart, W.A.:Con Fl, K.313, w. I. Grafenauer (fl) Philips ▲ 422339-2 [DDD]
Mozart, W.A.:Con Fl Hp, w. I. Grafenauer (fl), M. Graf (hp) Philips ▲ 422339-2 [DDD]
Mozart, W.A.:Cons Hn, w. B. Tuckwell (hn) EMI Classics ▲ CDM 69569
Mozart, W.A.:Cons Hn, w. P. Damm (hn) Philips ▲ 422330-2 [DDD]
Mozart, W.A.:Con Ob, K.314, w. N. Black (ob) Philips ▲ 416483-2 [DDD]
Mozart, W.A.:Con Ob, K.314, w. H. Holliger (ob) Philips ▲ 411134-2 [DDD]
Mozart, W.A.:Con 5 Pno, w. Alfred Brendel (pno) Philips ▲ 416366-2 [DDD]
Mozart, W.A.:Con 6 Pno, w. Alfred Brendel (pno) Philips ▲ 416366-2 [DDD]
Mozart, W.A.:Con 8 Pno, w. Alfred Brendel (pno) Philips ▲ 411468-2 [DDD]
Mozart, W.A.:Con 9 Pno, w. A. Brendel (pno) Philips ("Duo" series) 2-▲ 442571-2
Mozart, W.A.:Con 15 Pno, w. A. Brendel (pno) Philips ▲ 400018-2 [DDD]
Mozart, W.A.:Con 15 Pno, w. A. Brendel (pno) Philips ("Duo" series) 2-▲ 442571-2
Mozart, W.A.:Con 19 Pno, w. *(pianist unknown)* Philips 2-▲ 442269-2
Mozart, W.A.:Con 20 Pno, w. Alfred Brendel (pno) Philips ♦ 0062635488
Mozart, W.A.:Con 20 Pno, w. A. Brendel (pno) Philips ("Concert Classics" series) ▲ 420867-2
Mozart, W.A.:Con 20 Pno, w. *(pianist unknown)* Philips 2-▲ 442269-2
Mozart, W.A.:Con 21 Pno Philips 2-▲ 442269-2
Mozart, W.A.:Con 21 Pno, w. Alfred Brendel (pno) Philips ♦ 0062635488
Mozart, W.A.:Con 21 Pno, w. Alfred Brendel (pno) Philips ▲ 400018-2 [DDD]
Mozart, W.A.:Con 22 Pno, w. A. Brendel (pno) Philips ("Duo" series) 2-▲ 442571-2
Mozart, W.A.:Con 23 Pno, w. Janet Colburn (pno) Audiofon ▲ CD 72038
Mozart, W.A.:Con 23 Pno, w. A. Brendel (pno) Philips ▲ 420487-2 [ADD]
Mozart, W.A.:Con 23 Pno Philips 2-▲ 442269-2
Mozart, W.A.:Con 24 Pno, w. A. Brendel (pno) Philips ("Concert Classics" series) ▲ 420867-2 [ADD]
Mozart, W.A.:Con 24 Pno Philips 2-▲ 442269-2
Mozart, W.A.:Con 25 Pno, w. A. Brendel (pno) Philips ("Duo" series) 2-▲ 442571-2
Mozart, W.A.:Con 26 Pno, w. A. Brendel (pno) Philips ▲ 411468-2 [DDD]
Mozart, W.A.:Con 27 Pno, w. A. Brendel (pno) Philips ("Duo" series) 2-▲ 442571-2
Mozart, W.A.:Con 27 Pno, w. A. Brendel (pno) Philips ▲ 420487-2 [ADD]
Mozart, W.A.:Con 1 Vn, w. A.-S. Mutter (vn) EMI Classics ▲ CDC 54302
Mozart, W.A.:Così fan tutte, w. K. Mattila (sop), E. Szmytka (sop), A. S. von Otter (mez), F. Araiza (ten), T. Allen (bar), J. van Dam (b-bar), Ambrosian Opera Chorus [I] Philips 3-▲ 422381-2 [DDD]
Mozart, W.A.:Dances & Marches Philips ▲ 416484-2 [DDD]
Mozart, W.A.:Don Giovanni, w. S. Sweet (sop), K. Mattila (sop), M. McLaughlin (sop), F. Araiza (ten), T. Allen (bar), S. Alaimo (b-bar), R. Lloyd (bass), Ambrosian Opera Chorus Philips 3-▲ 432129-2 [DDD]
Mozart, W.A.:Don Giovanni (sels), w. K. Mattila (sop), F. Araiza (ten), T. Allen (bar), R. Lloyd (bass) Philips ▲ 438494-2
Mozart, W.A.:Exsultate London ("Double Decker" series) 2-▲ 443009-2
Mozart, W.A.:Kleine Nachtmusik Philips ▲ 416386-2 [DDD]
Mozart, W.A.:March Hns, K.248 Klavier ▲ KCD 11035 [DDD]
Mozart, W.A.:Marches Orch, K.335 Philips ▲ 412725-2 [DDD]
Mozart, W.A.:Missa, K.317 London ("Double Decker" series) 2-▲ 443009-2
Mozart, W.A.:Missa, K.427, w. L. Marshall (sop), F. Palmer (sop), A. Rolfe Johnson (ten), G. Howell (bass), Academy Chorus [L] Philips ▲ 420891-2 [ADD]
Mozart, W.A.:Missa, K.427, w. K. Te Kanawa (sop), A. Sofie von Otter (mez), A. R. Johnson (ten), R. Lloyd (bass), Academy of St. Martin in the Fields Chorus *(rec London, Mar. 10-12, 1993)* Philips ▲ 438999-2
Mozart, W.A.:Music of Fantasy ▲ FCD 900 1791-2 ■ WAM 51791
Mozart, W.A.:Music of, w. Ferruccio Furlanetto (bass), Isaac Stern (vn), Canadian Brass—Eine kleine Nachtmusik; Syms 38 & 41; sels from Die Zauberflöte; plus others Sony Classical ("Greatest Hits" series) ▲ MLK 62682 ■ MLT 62682
Mozart, W.A.:Music of—includes Syms 40 & 41; Cons in d & C Pno; Con Fl Hp & Orch; Con in E♭ Hn; Con in A Cl; 3 German Dances; Divertimento in D; Eine Kleine Nachtmusik; Serenata notturna; A Musical Joke; Marriage of Figaro (sels) Philips 5-▲ 426 204-2
Mozart, W.A.:Music of Fantasy ▲ FCD 1205-2 ■ WAM 51205
Mozart, W.A.:Nozze di Figaro, w. L. Popp (sop), B. Hendricks (sop), A. Baltsa (mez), G. Raimondi (ten), J. Van Dam (bar), Ambrosian Opera Chorus [I] Philips 3-▲ 416370-2 [DDD]
Mozart, W.A.:Nozze di Figaro (sels), w. L. Popp (sop), B. Hendricks (sop), A. Baltsa (mez), G. Raimondi (ten), J. van Dam (b-bar), Ambrosian Opera Chorus [I] Philips ▲ 416870-2 [DDD]
Mozart, W.A.:Ovs—Le nozze di Figaro; Die Zauberflöte; Clemenza di Tito; Lucio Silla; Die Entführung aus dem Serail; Don Giovanni; Idomeneo, Così fan tutte; Impresario EMI Classics ▲ CDC 47014 [DDD] □ 0777-7-47014-5-7
Mozart, W.A.:Pno Music (misc), w. Alfred Brendel (pno), Imogen Cooper (pno)—Adagio K.540; Cons for Pno Nos. 10, 14, 15, 19, 21, 26, 27; Fant K.475; Rondo K.511; Sons Nos. 8, 11, 13, 14 Philips 25-▲ 446920-2
Mozart, W.A.:Requiem, w. I. Cotrubas (sop), H. Watts (cta), R. Tear (ten), J. Shirley-Quirk (bar), Academy of St. Martin in the Fields Chorus [L] London ▲ 417746-2 [ADD]
Mozart, W.A.:Requiem, w. S. McNair (sop), C. Watkinson (cta), F. Araiza (ten), R. Lloyd (b-bar), Academy Chorus [L] Philips ▲ 432087-2 [DDD]
Mozart, W.A.:Requiem London ("Double Decker" series) 2-▲ 443009-2
Mozart, W.A.:Rondo Hn, K.371, w. B. Tuckwell (hn) EMI Classics ▲ CDM 69569
Mozart, W.A.:Rondo Pno Orch, K.382, w. A. Brendel (pno) Philips ("Concert Classics" series) ▲ 420867-2 [ADD]
Mozart, W.A.:Rondo Vn, K.373, w. J. Suk (vn) Klavier ▲ KCD 11035 [DDD]
Mozart, W.A.:Serenade Ww, K.320 Philips ▲ 412725-2 [DDD]
Mozart, W.A.:Serenade Ww, K.361 Philips ▲ 412726-2 [DDD]
Mozart, W.A.:Sinf concertante Ob, K.Anh.9 [R.D. Levin's early 1980s revised edition] Philips ▲ 411134-2 [DDD]
Mozart, W.A.:Sinf concertante Vn, K.364, w. A.-S. Mutter (vn), B. Giuranna (va) EMI Classics ▲ CDC 54302
Mozart, W.A.:Syms (comp)—Nos. 1-20 Philips 6-▲ 422501-2 [ADD]
Mozart, W.A.:Syms (comp) EMI Classics ("Studio" series) 6-▲ CDMF 63856
Mozart, W.A.:Syms (comp)—Nos. 21-41 Philips 6-▲ 422502-2 [ADD]
Mozart, W.A.:Syms (comp)—Syms. 36, 38, 39, 40, 41 Philips 2-▲ 438332-2
Mozart, W.A.:Sym 24 EMI Classics ▲ CDC 49176 [DDD]
Mozart, W.A.:Sym 25 London ■ 411717-4
Mozart, W.A.:Sym 26 EMI Classics ▲ CDC 49176 [DDD]
Mozart, W.A.:Sym 27 EMI Classics ▲ CDC 49176 [DDD]
Mozart, W.A.:Sym 29 London ■ 411717-4
Mozart, W.A.:Sym 32 EMI Classics ▲ CDC 49176 [DDD]
Mozart, W.A.:Sym 40 EMI Classics ("Studio DDD" series) ▲ CDD 63897 [DDD]
Mozart, W.A.:Sym 41 EMI Classics ("Studio DDD" series) ▲ CDD 63897 [DDD]
Mozart, W.A.:Zauberflöte, w. K. Te Kanawa (sop), C. Studer (sop), E. Lind (sop), F. Araiza (ten), O. Bär (bar), S. Ramey (bass), Ambrosian Opera Chorus [G] Philips 2-▲ 426276-2 [DDD]
Mozart, W.A.:Zauberflöte (sels), w. K. Te Kanawa (sop), C. Studer (sop), E. Lind (sop), F. Araiza (ten), O. Bär (bar), S. Ramey (bass) Philips ▲ 438495-2
Musical Moments in the Garden, w. Bournemouth SO, English CO, Hollywood Bowl SO, Toulouse Orch, Philharmonia Orch, Toulouse CO, L. Auriacombe (cnd), T. Beecham (cnd), C. Davis (cnd), R. Hickox (cnd), M. Plasson (cnd), M. Sargent (cnd) Angel ▲ CDM 65203 ■ EG 65203
Pachelbel, J.:Canon Philips ▲ 416386-2 [DDD]
Paganini, N.:Con 1 Vn, w. V. Mullova (vn) Philips ▲ 422332-2 [DDD]
Respighi, O.:Ancient Airs & Dances—Set 3 Philips ▲ 420485-2 [DDD]

Academy of St. Martin in the Fields (cont.)
N. Marriner (cnd) (cont.)

Respighi, O.:La Boutique fantastique Philips ▲ 420485-2 [DDD]
Respighi, O.:The Fountains of Rome Philips ▲ 432133-2 [DDD] □ 432133-5
Respighi, O.:The Pines of Rome Philips ▲ 432133-2 [DDD] □ 432133-5
Respighi, O.:Trittico botticelliano EMI Classics 2-▲ CDFB 69358
Respighi, O.:Trittico botticelliano EMI Classics ▲ CDC 47844
Respighi, O.:Gli uccelli Philips ▲ 420485-2 [DDD]
Respighi, O.:Gli uccelli EMI Classics ▲ CDC 47844
Respighi, O.:Gli uccelli EMI Classics 2-▲ CDFB 69358
Rodrigo, J.:Concierto Andaluz, w. A. Romero (gtr), P. Romero (gtr) Philips ▲ 400024-2 [ADD]
Rodrigo, J.:Concierto de Aranjuez, w. P. Romero (gtr) Philips ▲ 438016-2
Rodrigo, J.:Concierto de Aranjuez, w. P. Romero (gtr) Philips ▲ 411440-2 [ADD]
Rodrigo, J.:Concierto de Aranjuez, w. P. Romero (gtr) Philips ("Spanish" series) ▲ 432828-2 [ADD]
Rodrigo, J.:Concierto madrigal, w. P. Romero (gtr), A. Romero (gtr) Philips ▲ 400024-2
Rodrigo, J.:Concierto madrigal, w. P. Romero (gtr), A. Romero (gtr) Philips ("Spanish" series) ▲ 432828-2 [ADD]
Rodrigo, J.:Concierto para una fiesta, w. P. Romero (gtr) Philips ▲ 411133-2 [DDD]
Rodrigo, J.:Fant para un gentilhombre, w. P. Romero (gtr) Philips ("Spanish" series) ▲ 432828-2 [ADD]
Rodrigo, J.:Fant para un gentilhombre, w. P. Romero (gtr) Philips ▲ 438016-2
Romero, C.:Concierto de Málaga, w. P. Romero (gtr) Philips ▲ 411133-2 [DDD]
Rossini, G.:Il barbiere di Siviglia (sels), w. A. Baltsa (mez), S. Burgess (mez), F. Araiza (ten), T. Allen (bar), D. Trimarchi (bar), R. Lloyd (bass) Philips ▲ 438498-2
Rossini, G.:La Cenerentola, w. C. Malone (sop), F. Palmer (sop), A. Baltsa (mez), F. Araiza (ten), S. Alaimo (bar), J. del Carlo (bass), R. Raimondi (bass), Ambrosian Chorus Philips ("Digital Classics" series) 3-▲ 420468-2 [DDD]
Rossini, G.:Ovs—William Tell; La Cenerentola; Semiramide; Barber of Seville; Italiana in Algeri; Otello; La gazza ladra; Scala di seta Philips ▲ 412893-2 [ADD]
Rossini, G.:Ovs—complete ovs. Philips 3-▲ 434016-2 [ADD]
Rossini, G.:Sons Str Qt London ("Serenata" series) 2-▲ 430563-2 [ADD]
Saint-Saëns, C.:Danse macabre Philips ▲ 420812-2 [DDD] ■ 420812-4
Scarlatti, A.:Cants, w. Helend Donath (sop)—Su le sponde del Tebro Classics for Pleasure ("Eminence" series) ▲ CFP 2235
Scarlatti, A.:Su le sponde del Tebro, w. Helen Donath (sop), Maurice André (tpt) EMI Classics ("Baroque" series) ▲ CDK 65735
Schubert, Franz:Rondo Vn, D.438, w. J. Suk (vn) Klavier ▲ KCD 11035 [DDD]
Sibelius, J.:Con Vn, w. Leila Josefowicz (vn) Philips ▲ 446131-2
Sibelius, J.:Karelia Suite Philips ▲ 412727-2 [DDD]
Sibelius, J.:The Swan of Tuonela Philips ▲ 412727-2 [DDD]
Stamitz, C.:Con Tpt, w. H. Hardenberger (tpt) Philips ▲ 420203-2 [DDD] ■ 420203-4
Stölzel, G.H.:Con Tpt, w. *(tpt unknown)* Classics for Pleasure ("Eminence" series) ▲ CFP 2235
Sullivan, A.:Music of—sels. from H.M.S. Pinafore, Yeoman of the Guard, Iolanthe, Di Ballo, Mikado, Pirates of Penzance, Macbeth, Gondoliers, Patience Philips ▲ 434916-2
Tausky, V.:Concertino Harm, w. T. Reilly (hmc) Chandos ▲ CHAN 8617 [ADD]
Tchaikovsky, P.:Con Vn, w. Leila Josefowicz (vn) Philips ▲ 446131-2
Tchaikovsky, P.:Manfred *(rec Nov. 19-21, 1992)* Capriccio ▲ 10 433 [DDD]
Tchaikovsky, P.:Marche slave *(rec Nov. 19-21, 1992)* Capriccio ▲ 10 433 [DDD]
Tchaikovsky, P.:Nutcracker Suite Philips ▲ 411471-2 [DDD]
Tchaikovsky, P.:Ov 1812 Capriccio ▲ CD 10 385 [DDD]
Tchaikovsky, P.:Romeo & Juliet Capriccio ▲ CD 10 401 [DDD]
Tchaikovsky, P.:Serenade Strs Philips ▲ 411471-2 [DDD]
Tchaikovsky, P.:Sym 4 Capriccio ▲ CD 10 401 [DDD]
Tchaikovsky, P.:Sym 6 Capriccio ▲ CD 10 385 [DDD]
Telemann, G.P.:Con Va London ("Jubilee" series) ▲ 430265-2 [ADD]
Telemann, G.P.:Don Quichotte (suite) London ("Jubilee" series) ▲ 430265-2 [ADD]
Telemann, G.P.:Ov Hamburger London ("Jubilee" series) ▲ 430265-2 [ADD]
Telemann, G.P.:Ov in D London ("Jubilee" series) ▲ 430265-2 [ADD]
Trumpet Concertos, w. Maurice André (tpt), Franz Liszt CO [cnd:Jesus Lopez-Cobos], Württemberg CO [cnd:Jörg Faerber], London PO [cnd:Jesus Lopez-Cobos], Philharmonia Orch [cnd:Riccardo Muti] EMI Classics 2-▲ CDZB 69152 [ADD]
Vaughan Williams, R.:Con Ob London ("British Collection" series) ▲ 421392-2 [ADD]
Vaughan Williams, R.:Con grosso London ("British Collection" series) ▲ 421392-2 [ADD]
Vaughan Williams, R.:Fant on Greensleeves Argo ▲ 414595-2 [ADD] ■ 421227-4
Vaughan Williams, R.:Fant on Greensleeves London ("British Collection" series) ▲ 421392-2 [ADD]
Vaughan Williams, R.:Fant on a Theme by Thomas Tallis Philips ▲ 442427-2
Vaughan Williams, R.:Fant on a Theme by Thomas Tallis Argo ▲ 414595-2 [ADD] ■ 421227-4
Vaughan Williams, R.:In the Fen Country Philips ▲ 442427-2
Vaughan Williams, R.:The Lark Ascending, w. I. Brown (vn) Argo ▲ 414595-2 [ADD] ■ 421227-4
Vaughan Williams, R.:Norfolk Rhap 1 Philips ▲ 442427-2
Vaughan Williams, R.:Romance Hmc, w. T. Reilly (hmc) Chandos ▲ CHAN 8617 [ADD]
Vaughan Williams, R.:Romance Hmc, w. T. Reilly (hmc) London ("British Collection" series) ▲ 421392-2 [ADD]
Vaughan Williams, R.:Variants of "Dives & Lazarus" Argo ▲ 414595-2 [ADD] ■ 421227-4
Vaughan Williams, R.:Variants of "Dives & Lazarus" Philips ▲ 442427-2
Vaughan Williams, R.:Vars Brass Band Philips ▲ 442427-2
Vaughan Williams, R.:The Wasps (ov) Philips ▲ 442427-2
Vieuxtemps, H.:Con 5 Vn, w. V. Mullova (vn) Philips ▲ 422332-2 [DDD]
Villa-Lobos, H.:Con Gtr, w. P. Romero (gtr) Philips ▲ 416357-2 [DDD]
Villa-Lobos, H.:Fant Sop Sax, w. J. Harle (sax) EMI Classics ▲ CDC 54301
Vivaldi, A.:Cons Vc, w. Kenneth Heath (vc)—in c London ■ 417100-4
Vivaldi, A.:Cons Diverse Instrs—RV.562a Philips ▲ 420482-2 [ADD]
Vivaldi, A.:Cons Diverse Instrs London ("Jubilee" series) ▲ 417777-2 [ADD]
Vivaldi, A.:Con for 2 Fls, w. W. Bennett (fl), F. Smith (fl) Philips ▲ 412892-2 [DDD]
Vivaldi, A.:Cons for 2 Hns, w. T. Brown (hn), D. Hill (hn)—RV.539 Philips ▲ 412892-2 [DDD]
Vivaldi, A.:Con for 2 Mands, w. J. Tyler (mand), Wootton (mand) Philips ▲ 412892-2 [DDD]
Vivaldi, A.:Con Ob Bn, w. C. Nicklin (ob), G. Sheen (bn) Philips ▲ 412892-2 [DDD]
Vivaldi, A.:Cons for 2 Obs, w. C. Nicklin (ob), B. Davis (ob)—RV.536 Philips ▲ 412892-2 [DDD]
Vivaldi, A.:Cons Tpt, w. Maurice André (tpt) or Bernard Soustrot (tpt), Iona Brown (vn)—in B♭ for Tpt & Vn Classics for Pleasure ("Eminence" series) ▲ CFP 2235
Vivaldi, A.:Con for 2 Tpts, w. Maurice André (tpt), Bernard Soustrot (tpt) Classics for Pleasure ("Eminence" series) ▲ CFP 2235
Vivaldi, A.:Con for 2 Tpts, w. Churchill (tpt), P. Jones (tpt) London ■ 417100-4
Vivaldi, A.:Cons Vn, Op. 3/1-12, "L'estro armonico" London ("Double Decker" series) 2-▲ 443476-2
Vivaldi, A.:Cons Vn, Op. 3/1-12, "L'estro armonico" London ("Serenata" series) 2-▲ 430557-2 [ADD]
Vivaldi, A.:Cons Vn, Op. 4, "La stravaganza" London ("Serenata" series) 2-▲ 430566-2 [ADD]
Vivaldi, A.:Cons Vn, Op. 4, "La stravaganza", w. Alan Loveday (vn)—RV.249 London ■ 417100-4
Vivaldi, A.:Cons Vn, Op. 8/1-4, "The Four Seasons", w. Alan Loveday (vn) Argo ▲ 414486-2 [ADD]
Vivaldi, A.:Cons Vn, Op. 8/1-4, "The Four Seasons", w. I. Brown (vn) Philips ▲ 420482-2 [ADD]
Vivaldi, A.:Cons Vn, Op. 9, "La Cetra"—No. 9 for 2 Violins London ■ 417100-4
Vivaldi, A.:Con Vn Obs, RV.563, w. I. Brown (vn), M. Laird (tpt), W. Houghton (tpt) Philips ▲ 412892-2 [DDD]
Vivaldi, A.:Cons for 4 Vns—RV.580 London ■ 417100-4
Vivaldi, A.:Gloria, RV.589, w. B. Hendricks (sop), A. Murray (mez), J. Rigby (mez), U. Heilmann (ten), J. Hynninen (bar), Academy Chorus EMI Classics ▲ CDC 54283
Vivaldi, A.:Gloria, RV.589, w. E. Vaughan (sop), J. Baker (mez), King's College Choir Cambridge London ("Jubilee" series) ▲ 421146-2 [ADD]
Walton, W.:As You Like It, w. C. Bott (sop) Chandos ▲ CHAN 8842 [DDD]
Walton, W.:As You Like It (sels), w. John Gielgud (nar)—Prelude; Moonlight Chandos ("7000" series) ▲ CHAN 7041

ORCH. & ENS.

Academy of St. Martin in the Fields (cont.)
N. Marriner (cnd) (cont.)
Walton, W.:Battle of Britain — Chandos ▲ CHAN 8870 [DDD]
Walton, W.:Escape Me Never (suite) — Chandos ▲ CHAN 8870 [DDD]
Walton, W.:Film Music, w. Westminster Choir — Chandos ▲ CHAN 8892 ■ CHAAB 1503
Walton, W.:Film Music — Chandos ▲ CHAN 8841 ■ CHAAB 1460
Walton, W.:Film Music — Chandos ▲ CHAN 8870 ■ CHAAB 1485
Walton, W.:Film Music — Chandos ▲ CHAN 8842 ■ CHAAB 1461
Walton, W.:Hamlet, w. J. Gielgud (nar) — Chandos ▲ CHAN 8842 [DDD]
Walton, W.:Hamlet (sels), w. John Gielgud (nar)—Fanfare; Soliloquy; The Ghost; The Question; To Be or Not to Be; Threnody; Finale — Chandos ("7000" series) ▲ CHAN 7041
Walton, W.:Henry V (shakespeare senario), w. Christopher Plummer (nar), Academy Chorus [E] — Chandos ▲ CHAN 8892 [DDD]
Walton, W.:Henry V (sels), w. Christopher Plummer (nar)—Prologue; Passacaglia on the Death of Falstaff; Touch Her Soft Lips & Part; St. Crispins Day; Againcourt — Chandos ("7000" series) ▲ CHAN 7041
Walton, W.:Macbeth (banquet & march) — Chandos ▲ CHAN 8841 [DDD]
Walton, W.:Major Barbara (shavian sequence) — Chandos ▲ CHAN 8841 [DDD]
Walton, W.:Richard III (shakespeare scenario), w. J. Gielgud (nar) — Chandos ▲ CHAN 8841 [DDD]
Walton, W.:Richard III (sels), w. John Gielgud (nar)—Prelude; Now Is the Winter of Our Discontent; The Princes in the Tower; Death of Richard & Finale — Chandos ("7000" series) ▲ CHAN 7041
Walton, W.:Spitfire Prelude & Fugue — Chandos ▲ CHAN 8870 [DDD]
Walton, W.:Three Sisters — Chandos ▲ CHAN 8870 [DDD]
Walton, W.:A Wartime Sketchbook — Chandos ▲ CHAN 8870 [DDD]
Weber, C.M. von:Andante & Rondo ungarese Bn, w. K. Thunemann (bn) — Philips ▲ 432081-2 [DDD]
Weber, C.M. von:Concertino Cl, w. A. Marriner (cl) — Philips ▲ 432146-2 [DDD]
Weber, C.M. von:Con Bn, w. K. Thunemann (bn) — Philips ▲ 432081-2 [DDD]
Weber, C.M. von:Con 1 Cl, w. A. Marriner (cl) — Philips ▲ 432146-2 [DDD]
Weber, C.M. von:Con 2 Cl, w. A. Marriner (cl) — Philips ▲ 432146-2 [DDD]
Weber, C.M. von:Sym 1 — ASV ▲ ASV 515 [DDD]
Weber, C.M. von:Sym 2 — ASV ▲ ASV 515 [DDD]
Wolf-Ferrari, E.:Ovs & Intermezzi—orchestral selections from I quattro rusteghi; Il campiello; Il segreto di Susanna; La dama boba; Il gioielli dell Madonna — EMI Classics ▲ CDC 54585
Marriner, Masur (cnd)
Beethoven, L. van:Contredanses, WoO 14, Leipzig Gewandhaus Orch — Philips 2-▲ 438706-2
Beethoven, L. van:German Dances, WoO 8, Leipzig Gewandhaus Orch — Philips 2-▲ 438706-2
Beethoven, L. van:Minuets Orch, WoO 7, Leipzig Gewandhaus Orch — Philips 2-▲ 438706-2
Beethoven, L. van:Ovs, Leipzig Gewandhaus Orch — Philips 2-▲ 438706-2
K. Sillito (cnd)
Bach, J.S.:Con 2 Vn, w. J. Williams (gtr)—& Andante from Sonata BWV 1003 [arr. Williams] — CBS ▲ MK 39560 [DDD]
Handel, G.F.:Ovs—Alcina; Ariodante; Rodrigo; Berenice; Solomon; Agrippina — Capriccio ▲ 10 420 [DDD]
D. Willcocks (cnd)
Bach, J.S.:Cant 147, w. King's College Choir Cambridge *(rec King's College Chapel, Cambridge, June, 1970)* — EMI Classics ▲ CDK 65334 [ADD]
Handel, G.F.:Chandos Anthems (11), w. April Cantelo (sop), Ian Partridge (ten), Andrew Davis (org), King's College Choir Cambridge—No. 10 only *(rec Chapel of King's College, Cambridge, 1967)* — London 2-▲ 443470-2 [ADD]
Pergolesi, G.B.:Magnificat in C, w. Elizabeth Vaughan (sop), Janet Baker (cta), Ian Partridge (ten), Christopher Keyte (bass), King's College Choir Cambridge *(rec 1966)* — London 2-▲ 443868-2 [ADD]

Academy of St. Martin in the Fields Chamber Ensemble
Academy Classics — Chandos ▲ CHAN 9216 [DDD]
All of the World's Most Beautiful Melodies!, w. McCann, Phillip (cnt), Gordon Langford (cnd), Roy Newsome (cnd), Peter Parkes (cnd), Black Dyke Mills Band, Sellers Engineering Band, Academy of St. Martin in the Fields Chamber Ensemble, Huddersfield Choral Society, Leeds Parish Church Boys Choir — Chandos ("Brass" series) 5-▲ CHN 4536(5)
Boccherini, L.:Qnts Gtr & Strs, w. P. Romero (gtr)—Op. 50/3 & 9 — Philips ▲ 426092-2 [ADD]
Boccherini, L.:Qnts Gtr & Strs, w. Pepe Romero (gtr)—includes La Ritirata de Madrid & Fandango — Philips 2-▲ 438769-2
Boccherini, L.:Qnts Gtr & Strs, w. P. Romero (gtr)—Op. 50/4, 5, 6 — Philips ▲ 420385-2 [ADD]
Brahms, J.:Sextet Strs, Op. 18 — Chandos ▲ CHAN 9151 [DDD]
Brahms, J.:Sextet Strs, Op. 36 — Chandos ▲ CHAN 9151 [DDD]
Debussy, C.:Danses sacrée et profane, w. S. Kanga (hp) — Chandos ▲ CHAN 8621 [DDD]
Dvořák, A.:Sextet — Chandos ▲ CHAN 8771 [DDD]
Enescu, G.:Oct Strs *(rec March 1992)* — Chandos ▲ CHAN 9131 [DDD]
Grainger, P.:Chamber Music—Molly on the Shore; Shallow Brown [w. Nicholas Spears (bar)]; Shepherds Hey!; Sussex Mummers' Carol; Handel in the Strand; Irish Tune from County Derry; The Immovable Do; My Robin Is to the Greenwood Gone; Mock Morris — Chandos ▲ CHAN 9346 [DDD]
Handel, G.F.:Sons Rcr, w. Michala Petri (rcr) — Philips ("Digital Classics" series) ▲ 412602-2 [DDD]
Leighton, K.:Fant-Octet — Chandos ▲ CHAN 9346 [DDD]
Martinů, B.:Serenade 2 — Chandos ▲ CHAN 8771 [DDD]
Martinů, B.:Sextet Strs — Chandos ▲ CHAN 8771 [DDD]
Mendelssohn, F.:Octet Strs — Philips ▲ 420400-2 [ADD]
Mendelssohn, F.:Octet Strs — Chandos ▲ CHAN 8790 [DDD]
Mozart, W.A.:Complete Mozart Edition, Grumiaux Trio — Philips 2-▲ 422513-2 [ADD]
Mozart, W.A.:Complete Mozart Edition — Philips 5-▲ 422504-2 [ADD]
Mozart, W.A.:Qt Ob, K.370 — Philips ▲ 422833-2 [ADD]
Mozart, W.A.:Qnt Cl, K.581 — Philips ▲ 422833-2 [ADD]
Mozart, W.A.:Qnt Hn, K.407 — Philips ▲ 422833-2 [ADD]
Nielsen, C.:Qnt Strs — Chandos ▲ CHAN 9258 [DDD]
Raff, J.:Octet Strs — Chandos ▲ CHAN 8790 [DDD]
Ravel, M.:Intro & Allegro, w. S. Kanga (hp), W. Bennett (fl), A. Marriner (cl) — Chandos ▲ CHAN 8621 [DDD]
Roussel, A.:Sérénade, w. S. Kanga (hp) — Chandos ▲ CHAN 8621 [DDD]
Saxophone Concertos, w. John Harle (sax) — EMI Classics ▲ CDC 54301
Schubert, Franz:Octet Ww, D.803 — Chandos ▲ CHAN 8585 [DDD]
Serenade, w. Reilly, Tommy (hmc) — Chandos ▲ CHAN 8486 [DDD]
Shostakovich, D.:Pieces Str Octet *(rec March 1992)* — Chandos ▲ CHAN 9131 [DDD]
Spohr, L.:Double Qt 3 — Hyperion ▲ CDA 66142 [DDD]
Spohr, L.:Double Qt 4 — Hyperion ▲ CDA 66142 [DDD]
Spohr, L.:Qnt Strs, Op. 91 — Chandos ▲ CHAN 9424
Spohr, L.:Sxt Strs — Chandos ▲ CHAN 9424
Strauss, R.:Capriccio (sels)—Sextet *(rec March 1992)* — Chandos ▲ CHAN 9131 [DDD]
Svendsen, J.:Octet Strs — Chandos ▲ CHAN 9258 [DDD]
Svendsen, J.:Romance Vn — Chandos ▲ CHAN 9258 [DDD]
Mozart, W.A.:Divert Str Qt, K.136 — Philips ▲ 412269-2 [DDD]
Mozart, W.A.:Kleine Nachtmusik — Philips ▲ 412269-2 [DDD]
Mozart, W.A.:Musikalischer Spass — Philips ▲ 412269-2 [DDD]

Academy of St. Martin in the Fields Chamber Ensemble [Malcolm Latchem (vn), Kenneth Sillito (vn), Robert Smissen (va), Stephen Tees (va), Stephen Orton (vc), Roger Smith (vc)]
Glazunov, A.:Qnt Strs — Chandos ▲ CHAN 9387 [DDD]
Tchaikovsky, P.:Souvenir de Florence — Chandos ▲ CHAN 9387 [DDD]

Accademia Bach
C. Gubert (cnd)
Fasch, J.F.:Cons (68) Var Instrs—in G for 2 Obs; in b for Ob & Fl; in a for Ob; in B♭ for 2 Obs *(rec Carceri d'Este Abbey, July 14-17, 1994)* — Dynamic ▲ CD 129 [DDD]
Fasch, J.F.:Ovs (96)—in G *(rec Carceri d'Este Abbey, July 14-17, 1994)* — Dynamic ▲ CD 129 [DDD]

Accademia Bizantina
Berio, L.:Duets for 2 Vns—Vol. 1, Nos. 1-34 — Denon/PCM Digital ▲ CO 75448
C. Chiarappa (cnd)
Bach, J.S.:Con Fl, Vn & Hpd, w. Carlo Chiarappa (vn) *(rec Il Liceo Musicale A. Masini di Forli, 1991)* — Denon 2-▲ CO 78970 [DDD]
Bach, J.S.:Con 1 Hpd, w. Carlo Chiarappa (vn) *(rec Il Liceo Musicale A. Masini di Forli, 1991)* — Denon 2-▲ CO 78970 [DDD]
Bach, J.S.:Con 5 Hpd, w. Carlo Chiarappa (vn) *(rec Il Liceo Musicale A. Masini di Forli, 1991)* — Denon 2-▲ CO 78970 [DDD]
Bach, J.S.:Con 1 for 2 Hpds, w. Carlo Chiarappa (vn) *(rec Il Liceo Musicale A. Masini di Forli, 1991)* — Denon 2-▲ CO 78970 [DDD]
Bach, J.S.:Con 2 for 3 Hpds, w. Carlo Chiarappa (vn) *(rec Il Liceo Musicale A. Masini di Forli, 1991)* — Denon 2-▲ CO 78970 [DDD]
Bach, J.S.:Cons Vn (comp), w. Carlo Chiarappa (vn) *(rec Il Liceo Musicale A. Masini di Forli, 1991)* — Denon 2-▲ CO 78970 [DDD]
Bach, J.S.:Con for 2 Vns, w. Carlo Chiarappa (vn) *(rec Il Liceo Musicale A. Masini di Forli, 1991)* — Denon 2-▲ CO 78970 [DDD]
Bach, J.S.:A Musical Offering, w. C. Chiarappa (vn) — Denon/PCM Digital ▲ DEN 75861 [DDD]
Berio, L.:Corale, "On Sequenza VIII" — Denon/PCM Digital ▲ CO 75448
Feo, F.:Salve regina, w. Lina Maria Akerlund (sop) — Denon ▲ CO 78904 [DDD]
Ghedini, G.F.:Con Vn, "Il Belprato", w. Carlo Chiarappa (vn) *(rec Rocca Sforzesca, Imola, Italy, July, 20-22, 1993)* — Denon ▲ CO 78916 [DDD]
Pergolesi, G.B.:Salve regina in a, w. Lina Maria Akerlund (sop) — Denon ▲ CO 78904 [DDD]
Pergolesi, G.B.:Stabat mater, w. Lina Maria Akerlund (sop), Giuseppe Zambon (ct) — Denon ▲ CO 78904 [DDD]
Respighi, O.:Ancient Airs & Dances, w. Carlo Chiarappa (vn)—Set No. 3 *(rec Rocca Sforzesca, Imola, Italy, July, 20-22, 1993)* — Denon ▲ CO 78916 [DDD]
Rota, N.:Con Strs *(rec Rocca Sforzesca, Imola, Italy, July, 20-22, 1993)* — Denon ▲ CO 78916 [DDD]
Schubert, Franz:Con Vn, w. Carlo Chiarappa (vn) *(rec Ravenna, Italy, Oct 27-29, 1987)* — Arts Music ▲ 447210-2 [DDD]
Schubert, Franz:German Dances Strs, D.90 *(rec Ravenna, Italy, Oct 27-29, 1987)* — Arts Music ▲ 447210-2 [DDD]
Schubert, Franz:Minuets & Trios, D.89 *(rec Ravenna, Italy, Oct 27-29, 1987)* — Arts Music ▲ 447210-2 [DDD]
Schubert, Franz:Polonaise Vn, w. Carlo Chiarappa (vn) *(rec Ravenna, Italy, Oct 27-29, 1987)* — Arts Music ▲ 447210-2 [DDD]
Schubert, Franz:Rondo Vn, D.438, w. Carlo Chiarappa (vn) *(rec Ravenna, Italy, Oct 27-29, 1987)* — Arts Music ▲ 447210-2 [DDD]
Tartini, G.:Cons Vn (misc), w. Carlo Chiarappa (vn)—in e, D.56; in G, D.78; in A, D.96; in b, D.125 *(rec Presso Museo S. Vitale, Revenna, Oct. 1-4, 1993)* — Denon ▲ DEN 78969 [DDD]
Vivaldi, A.:Cons Vn, Op. 8/1-12, "Il cimento dell'armonia e dell'inventione" — Denon ▲ CO 75352/75447 [DDD]

Accademia dei Solinghi
R. Peiretti (cnd)
Albinoni, T.:Fl Music, w. Enrico di Felice (German fl), Rita Peiretti (hpd)—Sons. in a, Nos. 3 in E, 5 in D & 6 in b; Cons. Nos. 1 in G & 2 in G — Stradivarius ▲ STV 33377 [DDD]

Accademia di Santa Cecilia Orch—see St. Cecilia Academy Orch Rome

Accademia I Filarmonici
A. Martini (cnd)
Mozart, W.A.:Adagio Fugue *(rec Sala Mozart, Palazzo Pizzini, Trento, Italy, Dec 1995)* — Arts ▲ 473592 [DDD]
Mozart, W.A.:Diverts Strs K.136-138 *(rec Sala Mozart, Palazzo Pizzini, Trento, Italy, Dec 1995)* — Arts ▲ 473592 [DDD]
Mozart, W.A.:Kleine Nachtmusik *(rec Sala Mozart, Palazzo Pizzini, Trento, Italy, Dec 1995)* — Arts ▲ 473592 [DDD]
Veracini, F.M.:Ovs—Nos. 1-6 *(rec Verona, Sala del Morone, Feb 18-20, 1995)* — Naxos ▲ 8.553412 [DDD]

Accademia Instrumentalis Claudio Monteverdi
H. L. Hirsch (cnd)
Albinoni, T.:Cons à 5 Obs, Op. 7, w. I. Gortizki (ob), J. Müller-Brincken (ob), J. E. Dähler (hpd)—Nos. 1,2 & 4 — Claves ■ C 601
Albinoni, T.:Cons à 5 Strs, Op. 10—No. 1 — Claves ■ C 601

Accademia Monteverdiana Orch
D. Stevens (cnd)
Gay, J.:The Beggar's Opera (sels), w. P. Clark (sop), A. Jenkins (sop), M. Cable (mez), E. Lane (mez), S. Minty (mez), E. Fleet (sgr), P. Hall (ten), V. Midgley (ten), N. Rogers (ten), J. Noble (bar), Accademia Monteverdiana Chorus—59 songs *(rec Aug. 1978)* — Koch Treasure ▲ 31621-2 [ADD]
Music in Honor of St. Thomas of Canterbury — Elektra/Nonesuch ■ 71292-4

Accademia Saxophone Quartet
Desenclos, A.:Quatuor — Nuova Era ▲ 7139 [DDD]
Françaix, J.:Petit Quatuor — Nuova Era ▲ 7139 [DDD]
French & American Music — Nuova Era ▲ NUO 7139 [DDD]
19th Century Music for Saxophones — Nuova Era ▲ NUO 7211 [DDD]

Accademia Strumentale Italiana
O Dolce Vita Mia, w. Invernizzi, Roberta (sop), Accademia Strumentale Italiana [cnd:Alberto Rasi] — Stradivarius ▲ STV 33396 [DDD]
G. Toffano (cnd)
Cantar Alla Pavana, w. Venice Consort *(rec Villa Beatrice, Monte Gemola, Baone, Padova, Oct 1995)* — Tactus ▲ TC 520002 [DDD]

Accentus Ensemble
Sephardic Romances:Music of the Spanish Jews from 1500 — Preiser ▲ PRE 90161 [DDD]
Spanish Popular & Court Music — Preiser ▲ PRE 90239 [AAD]
T. Wimmer (cnd)
Cancionero Musical de Palacio [Music of the Spanish Court] *(rec Lutheran Stadtpfarrkirche A. B., Vienna, May 9-12, 1995)* — Naxos ("Early Music" series) ▲ 8.553536 [DDD]
Sephardic Romances *(rec W.A.R. Studio, Vienna, Sept 1995)* — Naxos ▲ 8553617 [DDD]

Accordo Perfetto
Wilson, D.:Trio Vn — Redwood ▲ ESCD 45

Accroche Note Ensemble
Dillon, J.:Music of—Crossing Over; Ti-re-ti-ke-dha; Sgothan; Evening Rain; Come Live with Me; A Roaring Flame — Montaigne ▲ MO 782037

Acht Ensemble [Annette Fehrman (vn), Karin Schott (vn), Antonia Siegers (va), Ingo Zander (vc), Stefan Schäfer (db), Guido Schäfer (cl), Christoph Moinian (hn), Volker Tessmann (bn)]
Blanc, A.:Septet *(rec Kurhaus Hitzacker, Jan 1996)* — Thorofon ▲ CTH 2277 [DDD]
Thieriot, F.:Octet *(rec Kurhaus Hitzacker, Jan 1996)* — Thorofon ▲ CTH 2277 [DDD]

Act of Finding [Bruce Arnold (processed gtr), Thomas Buckner (sgr), Tom Hamilton (analog syn), Ratzo B. Harris (bass)]
Act Of Finding:Music of—To Dick Dickson; Another Family Resemblance; Quiet Is the Movt. of the Moon; Solos; Silent Travels; New Territory (Spring Collection); Fast Fast Fast Fast Fast Slow; Textural Threads; Can't See the Figure for the Ground; Destination A; Now & Then *(rec Systems Two, Brooklyn, NY)* — O.O. Discs ▲ OO 18

Ad Hoc String Quartet [Paul Vanderwerf (vn), David Belden (vn), Diedre Buckley (va), James Fellenbaum (vc)]
Rosner, A.:Qt 2 Strs — Albany ▲ TROY 210 [DDD]
Rosner, A.:Qt 3 Strs — Albany ▲ TROY 210 [DDD]
Rosner, A.:Qt 5 Strs — Albany ▲ TROY 210 [DDD]

▲ = CD ♦ = Enhanced CD Δ = MD ■ = Cassette Tape ▯ = DCC

Ad Hoc String Quartet [Paul Vanderwerf (vn), David Belden (vn), Diedre Buckley (va), Richard Yeo (vc)]
Shewan, S.:Qt 1 Strs — Albany ▲ TROY 149 [DDD]

Adelaide Opera Orch
R. Bonynge (cnd)
Donizetti, G.:L'elisir d'amore (sels), w. Luciano Pavarotti (ten)—Quanto è bella; Una furtiva lacrima *(rec 1965)* — Goldies ▲ GLD 63202 [ADD]

Adelaide SO
J. Serebrier (cnd)
Mennin, P.:Sym 9 — Finnadar ■ 90937-4
Poulenc, F.:La Voix humaine, w. C. Farley (sop) [F] — Chandos ▲ CHAN 8331 [DDD]

Adelaide Wind Quintet
Dreyfus, G.:Sextet, w. G. Winunguj (didjeridu) — Southern Cross ▲ SCCD 1024 [AAD]

Adelicia Ensemble
Weigl, V.:New England Suite — Gasparo ▲ GS 236

Les Adieux
Boccherini, L.:Qnt Pno, G.407-412—in E♭, G.410; in a, G.412 — Editio Classica ▲ 77053-2-RG [DDD]
Boccherini, L.:Qnt Pno, G.413-418—in e, G.415; in C, G.418 — Editio Classica ▲ 77053-2-RG [DDD]
Mozart, W.A.:Qnt Strs, K.174 — Deutsche Harmonia Mundi ▲ 77204-2 [DDD]
Mozart, W.A.:Qnt Strs, K.406 — Deutsche Harmonia Mundi ▲ 77204-2-RC [DDD]

Les Adieux Quartet
Music at the Time of Beaumarchais, w. Montserrat Figueras (sop), Lawrence Monteyro (sop), Raphel Oleg (vn), Miguel da Silva (va), Christophe Coin (vc), Marc Coppey (vc), José Miguel Moreno (gtr), Paul Badura-Skoda (pno), Philippe Cassard (pno), Eric Le Sage (pno), Bob Van Asperen (h — Valois ▲ V 4767

Adirondack CO
Barber, S.:A Hand of Bridge, w. C. Aks (sop), F. Kittelson (mez), W. Carney (ten), R. Muenz (bass), Gregg Smith Singers [E] — Premier ▲ PRCD 1009 [ADD]
Rorem, N.:Letters from Paris, w. Gregg Smith (cnd), Gregg Smith Singers — Vox Box ("The American Composers" series) 3-▲ CDX 3037

W. Schuman (cnd)
Schuman, W.:The Mighty Casey, w. R. Rees (sop), T. Bogdan (ten), R. Muenz (b-bar), Gregg Smith Singers, Long Island Choral Association [E] — Premier ▲ PRCD 1009 [ADD]

G. Smith (cnd)
Billings, W.:Anthems & Fuguing Tunes, w. Gregg Smith Singers—Chester; Be Glad Then America; Hopkinton; When Jesus Wept; The Lord Is Risen; A Virgin Unspotted; Boston; The Shepherd's Carol; I Am the Rose of Sharon; David's Lamentation; The Bird; Kittery; Cobham; Morpheus; Swift as an Indian Arrow Flies; Connection; Consonance; Jargon; Modern Music — Premier ▲ PRCD 1008 [ADD]
Blitzstein, M.:The Harpies, w. R. Rees (sop), T. Bogdan (ten), E. Najera (bar), et al., Gregg Smith Singers [E] — Premier ▲ PRCD 1009 [ADD]
Carter, E.:Songs, w. R. Rees (pno)—Warble for Lilac-Time; Voyage; 3 Poems of Robert Frost — CRI ▲ CD 648 [ADD]
Smith, Gregg:The Continental Harmonist Ballet, w. Gregg Smith Singers — Premier ▲ PRCD 1008 [ADD]
Smith, Gregg:Magnificat, w. R. Rees (sop), Gregg Smith Singers, Adirondack Festival Chorus — Premier ("Composer" series) ▲ PRCD 1020 [ADD/DDD]
Smith, Gregg:Prayer for Peace, w. Gregg Smith Singers, Adirondack Children's Choir, Adirondack Festival Chorus — Premier ("Composer" series) ▲ PRCD 1020 [ADD/DDD]
Smith, Gregg:Vars on a Bach Chorale, w. Gregg Smith Singers, Adirondack Festival Chorus — Premier ("Composer" series) ▲ PRCD 1020 [ADD/DDD]
Talma, L.:Voices of Peace, w. Rosalind Rees (sop), Scott Whittaker (ten), Charles Robert Stevens (bar), Gregg Smith Singers — Vox Box ("The American Composers" series) 3-▲ CDX 3037

Aeolian Chamber Players
Crumb, G.:Eleven Echoes of Autumn — CRI ■ ACS 6008
Rochberg, G.:Contra mortem et tempus — CRI ■ ACS 6013

Aeolian String Quartet [S. Humphreys (vn), R. Keenlyside (vn), M. Major (va), D. Simpson (vc)]
Mozart, W.A.:Divert Str Qt, K.136 — Saga Classics ▲ EC 3387
Mozart, W.A.:Qnt Cl, K.581, w. T. King (cl) — Saga Classics ▲ EC 3387
Schubert, Franz:Qnt Strs, D.956, w. B. Schrecker (vc) — Saga Classics ▲ 3368 [ADD]

Aequalis [F. Bronstein (pno), E. Mohr (vc), M. Parola (perc)]
Brody, M.:Commedia — New World ▲ 80412-2 [DDD]
Davidovsky, M.:Synchronism 6 — New World ▲ 80412-2 [DDD]
Gideon, M.:Son Vc & Pno — New World ▲ 80412-2 [DDD]
Steiger, R.:Trio In Memoriam — New World ▲ 80412-2 [DDD]
Ung, C.:Spiral — New World ▲ 80412-2 [DDD]

Affetti Musicali [Elisabeth Schwanda (rcr), Volker Mühlberg (vn), Bernward Lohr (hpd)]
Buonamente, G.B.:Il quarto libro de varie Sonate, Sinfonie, Gagliarde, Corrente e Brandi—Son ottava sopra La Romanesca *(rec Micahaelis-Kirche, Ronnenberg, Hannover, May 1995)* — Thorofon ▲ CTH 2279 [DDD]
Castello, D.:Sonate concertate in stil moderno—Terza son a 2 *(rec Micahaelis-Kirche, Ronnenberg, Hannover, May 1995)* — Thorofon ▲ CTH 2279 [DDD]
Fontana, G.B.:Sons—Son seconda *(rec Micahaelis-Kirche, Ronnenberg, Hannover, May 1995)* — Thorofon ▲ CTH 2279 [DDD]
Frescobaldi, G.:Il primo libro d'intavolatura di toccate di cembalo et organo—Toccata nona *(rec Micahaelis-Kirche, Ronnenberg, Hannover, May 1995)* — Thorofon ▲ CTH 2279 [DDD]
Marini, B.:Arfetti musicali—Cornera; Bocca; Zorzi; Martinenga; Albana; Candela *(rec Micahaelis-Kirche, Ronnenberg, Hannover, May 1995)* — Thorofon ▲ CTH 2279 [DDD]
Marini, B.:Sons, Syms & Retornelli—Sons prima, seconda & quarta; Son a 3 sopra La Monica *(rec Micahaelis-Kirche, Ronnenberg, Hannover, May 1995)* — Thorofon ▲ CTH 2279 [DDD]
Picchi, G.:Pieces Hpd—Ballo alla polacha; Todescha; Padoana ditta la ongara *(rec Micahaelis-Kirche, Ronnenberg, Hannover, May 1995)* — Thorofon ▲ CTH 2279 [DDD]
Rossi, S.:Il terzo libro de varie sonate, sinfonie, gagliarde, brandi e corrente—Son sopra porto celato il mio nobil pensiero *(rec Micahaelis-Kirche, Ronnenberg, Hannover, May 1995)* — Thorofon ▲ CTH 2279 [DDD]

Affetti Musicali [Éva Lax (mez), János Bal (rcr/fl), János Malina (rcr), László Borsódy (tpt), Erika Petőfi (vn), Csilla Vlyi (vc), Géza Klembala (org/hpd)]
Telemann, G.P.:Fortsetzung des Harmonischen Gottesdienstes—Der himmlischen Geister unzählbare Menge; Den Christen mischt Christus; Ach, reiner Geist!; Gott weiss!; Nach Finsternis und Todesschatten; Es fähret Jesus auf — Hungaroton ▲ HCD 31597 [DDD]

Affetti Musicali members [Alejandro Moguillansy (rcr), Carmen Leoni (hpd)]
Telemann, G.P.:Sons Rcr—in f *(rec The Netherlands, Jul 8-10, 1993)* — Emergo ▲ EC 3952 2 [DDD]

Affetti Musicali members [Alejandro Moguillansy (rcr), Makoto Akatsu (vn), Carmen Leoni (hpd)]
Telemann, G.P.:Trio Sons—in a, d & F for Rcr, Vn & Bc *(rec The Netherlands, Jul 8-10, 1993)* — Emergo ▲ EC 3952 2 [DDD]

Affetti Musicali members [Job ter Haar (vc), Carmen Leoni (hpd)]
Telemann, G.P.:Son in D Vc *(rec The Netherlands, Jul 8-10, 1993)* — Emergo ▲ EC 3952 2 [DDD]

Affetti Musicali members [Makoto Akatsu (vn), Carmen Leoni (hpd)]
Telemann, G.P.:Sons Vn—in A *(rec The Netherlands, Jul 8-10, 1993)* — Emergo ▲ EC 3952 2 [DDD]

Aglàia Ensemble
Bonporti, F.A.:Invenzioni (10) de camera — Stradivarius ▲ STR 33318 [DDD]

Aglàia Ensemble [Cinzia Barbagelata (vn), S. Gilardi (vn), M. Diatto (va), J. A. Guerrero (vc)]
Galuppi, B.:Concerti a quattro—Cons. in B♭, c, A, D, g, E♭ & G — Stradivarius ▲ STR 33316 [DDD]

Agrupación de Cámara Barcelona
The Early Recordings, 1942-1953, w. Victoria de los Angeles (sop), Gerald Moore (pno), Ivor Newton (pno), Ars Musicae Barcelona — Testament ▲ SBT 1087

Agrupación Música
E. Gieco (cnd)
L'espagne et le nouveau monde — Accord ▲ ACD 204362 [ADD]

Agrupación Música (cont.)
E. Gieco (cnd) (cont.)
Peru—Guatemala:Music of the Latin American Cathedrals, 16th through 18th Century Baroque Music from Unpublished Manuscripts — ARB ▲ 1425

Aguilar-Delgado Duo [David Aguilar, Imelda Delgado]
Doran, M.:Poem Fl — Protone ▲ NRPR 2201 [DDD]
Juon, P.:Son Fl — Protone ▲ NRPR 2201 [DDD]
Kuhlau, F.:Sons Fl, Op. 83—No. 3 in g only — Protone ▲ NRPR 2201 [DDD]
Molina, A.:Gigue — Protone ▲ NRPR 2201 [DDD]
Molina, A.:Sarabande — Protone ▲ NRPR 2201 [DDD]
Smith, Hale:Faces of Jazz—My Scarf is Yellow; The Broken Saxophone; Pooty's Blues; Day's End; Blooz; Following; Scrambled Eggs & Ernie; That's Mike; An Asphodel for Marcel; Goin' in a Hurry — Protone ▲ NRPR 2201 [DDD]

Aipponyi String Quartet
Haydn, J.:Qts Strs, Op. 33, "Russian Qts" — Ars Musici ▲ AM 1083-2 [DDD]

Aira String Quartet [Fabrizio Cipriani (vn), Marino Lagomarsino (vn), Ernest Braucher (va), Antonio Fantinuoli (vc)]
Viotti, G.B.:Qts Strs, G.112-114 *(rec Dynamic's Genoa, Apr 5-7, 1995)* — Dynamic ▲ CD 138 [DDD]

Akiko Tatsumi String Quartet [Akiko Tatsumi (vn), Kumie Taga (vn), Hiroshi Nakayama (va), Masaharu Kanda (vc)]
Yun, I.:Qnt Cl, w. Eduard Brunner (cl) *(rec Maebashi City Auditorium, Aug 31, 1984)* — Camerata ▲ 30CM 70 [AAD]
Yun, I.:Qnt Cl, w. Eduard Brunner (cl) *(rec Maebashi Shimin Bunka Kaikan, Aug 31-Sept 2, 1984)* — Camerata ▲ 25CM 356 [DDD]

Akron SO
A. Balter (cnd)
Baker, D.:Jazz Suite Cl, "3 Ethnic Dances", w. Alan Balter (cl) *(rec Masonic Auditorium, Cleveland, OH, Feb 22, 1993)* — Telarc ▲ CD 80409 [DDD]
Banfield, W.:Sym 6, "4 Songs for 5 American Voices", w. John English (tpt), Jack Schantz (tpt) *(rec Masonic Auditorium, Cleveland, OH, Feb 22, 1994)* — Telarc ▲ CD 80409 [DDD]

Al Ayre Español
E.L. Banzo (cnd)
Barroco Español, Vol. 1, w. Marta Almajano (sop) — Conifer Classics ▲ 75605-77325-2 [DDD]
Durón, S.:El Impossible mayor en amor le venze Amor *(rec Amsterdam, Sept 21-24, 1994)* — Deutsche Harmonia Mundi ▲ 05472-77336-2 [DDD]
Durón, S.:Veneo es de amor la embidia *(rec Amsterdam, Sept 21-24, 1994)* — Deutsche Harmonia Mundi ▲ 05472-77336-2 [DDD]
Literes, A.:Accis y Galatea *(rec Amsterdam, Sept 21-24, 1994)* — Deutsche Harmonia Mundi ▲ 05472-77336-2 [DDD]
Literes, A.:Los elementos *(rec Amsterdam, Sept 21-24, 1994)* — Deutsche Harmonia Mundi ▲ 05472-77336-2 [DDD]
Literes, A.:El estrago en la finesa *(rec Amsterdam, Sept 21-24, 1994)* — Deutsche Harmonia Mundi ▲ 05472-77336-2 [DDD]

Alabama Sacred Harp Convention
White Spirituals from the Sacred Harp — New World ▲ 80205-2 [AAD]

Alabama SO
P. Polivnick (cnd)
Kraft, William:Interplay, w. W. Samples, Jr. (vc) — Meet The Composer ▲ 79229-2 ■ 79229-4
Peck, R.:The Glory & the Grandeur — Albany ▲ TROY 040-2 [DDD]
Peck, R.:Signs of Life — Albany ▲ TROY 040-2 [DDD]

Alard String Quartet
Luening, O.:Legend, w. J. Ostryniec (ob), D. Rossi (va) — CRI ■ ACS 6011
Rainier, P.:Qt Strs — Leonarda ▲ LE 336
Swack, I.:Qt 3 Strs — Opus One ▲ 149

Alba Musica Kyo Ensemble
Landini & His Time:14th Century Italian Ars Nova — Channel Classics ▲ CCS 5793 [DDD]
Satoh, T.:Music of—A-I-i-c-e; Fuki no Kyoku; Hommage à Weiss; How Sweet is Mortal Sovrantyl; How Sweet Sour Music Is; Impromptu Elegiac Upon *Fuki no Kyoku*; Rockedy; Tawamure Uta — Channel Classics ▲ CCS 4692 [DDD]
Satoh, T.:Music of, w. C. Yamada (voc) [F, J]—Pèlerinage au Rollant (1981); Kobanashi (1985); Komori-uta (1982-91) — Channel Classics ▲ CCS 3291 [DDD]

Albanian Radio-TV Orch
J. Barballushi (cnd)
Calligaris, S.:Symphonic Dances—2nd Suite — Agora Musica ▲ AG 042.1 [DDD]
M. de Bernart (cnd)
Calligaris, S.:Con Pno, w. Sergio Calligaris (pno) — Agora Musica ▲ AG 042.1 [DDD]

Albany SO
Hadley, H.:Scherzo diabolique, w. I. Hegyi (vn) — New World ▲ NW 321-2 [DDD]
I. Hegyi (cnd)
Carpenter, J.A.:Sea Drift — New World ▲ NW 321-2 [DDD]
Chadwick, G.W.:Sym 2 — New World ▲ NW 339-2 [DDD]
Parker, H.:A Northern Ballad — New World ▲ NW 339-2 [DDD]
Porter, Q.:Dance in 3-Time — New World ▲ NW 321-2 [DDD]
J. Hegyi (cnd)
Laderman, E.:Pentimento — CRI ▲ CD 555 [DDD]
Mason, D.G.:Chanticleer — New World ▲ NW 321-2 [DDD]
Trimble, L.:Sym 3 — CRI ▲ CD 555 [DDD]
G. Lloyd (cnd)
Lloyd, G.:Music of, w. BBC PO, London SO—Sym No. 9 [finale]; Sym No. 5 [rondo]; Sym No. 6 [adagio]; Her Hair [from The Transformation of that Naked Ape]; Con No. 4 for Pno [1st movt]; Sym No. 11 [lento]; Sym No. 7 [vivo] — Albany ▲ TROY 075
Lloyd, G.:Sym 1 — Albany ▲ TROY 032-2 [DDD] ■ TROY 032-4 (D)
Lloyd, G.:Sym 4 — Albany ▲ AR 002-2 [DDD] ■ AR 002-4 (D)
Lloyd, G.:Sym 11 — Albany ▲ TROY 060-2 [DDD]
Lloyd, G.:Sym 12 — Albany ▲ TROY 032-2 [DDD] ■ TROY 032-4 (D)
D.A. Miller (cnd)
Torke, M.:Con Sax, w. John Harle (sax) *(rec Troy Savings Bank Music Hall, Troy, NY, Jan. 16, 1994)* — Argo ▲ 443529-2

Albemarle Ensemble
Persichetti, V.:King Lear — AmCam ▲ ACR 10305CD

Albéniz Guitar Duo [Thomas Kirchhoff (gtr), Burkhard Wolk (gtr)]
Albéniz Guitar Duo — FSM ("Fono" series) ▲ 97711 [DDD]
Albéniz Guitar Duo *(rec 1986)* — FSM ("Fono" series) ▲ 97706 [DDD]
Brouwer, L.:Per sonare a due — FSM ▲ FSM 97702 [DDD]
Carulli, F.:Serenades for 2 Gtrs, Op. 96/1-3 — FSM-Fono ▲ FCD 97707 [DDD]
Carulli, F.:Vars on 2 Russian Airs — FSM-Fono ▲ FCD 97707 [DDD]
Françaix, J.:Divert 2 Gtr — FSM ▲ FSM 97702 [DDD]
Jolivet, A.:Sérénade for 2 Gtrs — FSM ▲ FSM 97702 [DDD]
Piazzolla, A.:Tango Suite — FSM ▲ FSM 97702 [DDD]

Alberni String Quartet
Donizetti, G.:Qt 13 Strs — CRD ▲ 3366 [ADD]
Dvořák, A.:Waltzes Strs, B.105 *(rec 10-11/1988)* — CRD ▲ 3457 [DDD]
Mendelssohn, F.:Octet Strs, Medici String Quartet — Nimbus ▲ NI 5140 [DDD]
Mozart, W.A.:Qts Strs (misc)—Nos. 14-19, "The Haydn Quartets" — IMP Classics 3-▲ IMP BOXCD 19 [DDD]
Mozart, W.A.:Qt 14 Strs — IMP Classics ▲ PCD 958 [DDD]
Mozart, W.A.:Qt 15 Strs *(rec Jan. 1990)* — IMP Classics ▲ PCD 958 [DDD]
Mozart, W.A.:Qt 16 Strs — IMP Classics ▲ PCD 975 [DDD]
Mozart, W.A.:Qt 19 Strs — IMP Classics ▲ PCD 975 [DDD]
Puccini, G.:Crisantemi — CRD ▲ 3366 [ADD]

Alberni String Quartet (cont.)
Shostakovich, D.:Pieces Str Octet, Medici String Quartet — Nimbus ▲ NI 5140 [DDD]
Verdi, G.:Qt Strs — CRD ▲ CRD 3366
Wordsworth, W.:Qt 5 Strs — CRD ■ 4097
Wordsworth, W.:Qt 6 Strs — CRD ■ 4097

Alberni String Quartet members
Dvořák, A.:Bagatelles, Op. 47, w. V. Black (harm) *(rec 10–11/1988)* — CRD ▲ 3457 [DDD]
Dvořák, A.:Gavotte *(rec 10–11/1988)* — CRD ▲ 3457 [DDD]
Dvořák, A.:Miniatures, Op. 75a *(rec 10–11/1988)* — CRD ▲ 3457 [DDD]
Dvořák, A.:Terzetto *(rec 10–11/1988)* — CRD ▲ 3457 [DDD]

Albion Wind Ensemble
Beethoven, L. van:Qnt Pno, Ob, Cl, Hn & Bn, w. V. Perlemuter (pno) — Nimbus ▲ NI 5157 [DDD]
Mozart, W.A.:Qnt Pno, K.452, w. Vlado Perlemuter (pno) — Nimbus ▲ NI 5157 [DDD]

Albrecht String Quartet [Peter Biely (vn), Ivana Pristašová (vn), Peter Šesták (va), Jozef Lupták (vc)]
Godár, V.:Autumn Meditation *(rec Residence of Slovak Composers, Apr 1996)* — Slovart ▲ SR 0018-2-131 [DDD]
Godár, V.:Emmeleia *(rec Residence of Slovak Composers, Apr 1996)* — Slovart ▲ SR 0018-2-131 [DDD]
Godár, V.:Tenderness *(rec Residence of Slovak Composers, Apr 1996)* — Slovart ▲ SR 0018-2-131 [DDD]

Alcan String Quartet
Borodin, A.:Qt 2 Strs *(rec Oct. 1993)* — Analekta Fleur de Lys ▲ FL 2 3019
Brahms, J.:Qt 1 Strs *(rec 1/91)* — CBC ("Musica Viva" series) ▲ MVCD 1048 [DDD]
Debussy, C.:Qt Strs *(rec Oct. 1993)* — Analekta Fleur de Lys ▲ FL 2 3046
Enescu, G.:Oct Strs, w. Quebec String Quartet *(rec June 9–10, 1992)* — CBC ("Musica Viva" series) ▲ MVCD 1063 [DDD]
Haydn, J.:Qts Strs, Op. 76, "Erdődy Qts"—Op. 76/2 *(rec 1/91)* — CBC ("Musica Viva" series) ▲ MVCD 1048 [DDD]
Mendelssohn, F.:Octet Strs, w. Quebec String Quartet *(rec June 9–10, 1992)* — CBC ("Musica Viva" series) ▲ MVCD 1063 [DDD]
Mozart, W.A.:Qt 17 Strs — CBC ("Musica Viva" series) ▲ MVCD 1048 [DDD]
Wolf, H.:Italian Serenade *(rec Oct. 1993)* — Analekta Fleur de Lys ▲ FL 2 3019
Wolf, H.:Italian Serenade — Analekta ▲ An 29551

Alcatraz Ensemble
Danse Royale — Elektra/Nonesuch ▲ 79240-2 [DDD]
Visions & Miracles — Elektra/Nonesuch ▲ 79180-2 [DDD]

Aldeburgh Festival Ensemble
S. Bedford (cnd)
Britten, B.:The Turn of the Screw, w. F. Lott (sop), N. Secunde (sop), E. Hulse (sop), P. Cannan (mez), P. Langridge (ten), S. Pay (bar) — Collins Classics ▲ COL 7030 [DDD]

Alegria Ensemble
Carmina Burana XII — Pierre Verany ▲ 791092 [DDD]

Alexander & Daykin Piano Duo [Millette Alexander (pno), Frank Daykin (pno)]
Bach, J.S.:The Art of the Fugue [trans Erich Schwebsch] *(rec Music Hall, Tarrytown, NY, Mar 21–24, 1994)* — Connoisseur Society 2-▲ CD 4203

Alexander String Quartet [E. Pritchard (vn), F. Lifsitz (vn), P. Yarbrough (va), S. Wilson (vc)]
Bach, J.S.:Arias, w. Betsy Norden (sop), Bob Haley (tpt), Donald Foster (org)—(2) from Cantatas 21 & 36 [G] — Crystal ▲ CD 952 [DDD] ■ C 952
Bach, J.S.:Cant 51, w. Betsy Norden (sop), Bob Haley (tpt), Donald Foster (org) [G] — Crystal ▲ CD 952 [DDD] ■ C 952
Barber, S.:Dover Beach, w. N. Watson (bar) *(rec July 1992)* — Analekta ▲ CLCD 2009
Barber, S.:Serenade *(rec July 1992)* — Analekta ▲ CLCD 2009
Bresnick, M.:Qt 2 Strs, "Bucephalus" *(rec Sprague Hall, Yale Univ., July 25, 1985)* — CRI ▲ CD 682 [DDD]
Copland, A.:Movt Str Qt *(rec July 1992)* — Analekta ▲ CLCD 2009
Copland, A.:Pieces (2) Str Qt *(rec July 1992)* — Analekta ▲ CLCD 2009
Debussy, C.:Qt Strs — Gallo ▲ CD 512
Gershwin, G.:Lullaby, w. N. Watson (bar) *(rec July 1992)* — Analekta ▲ CLCD 2009
Greenberg, L.:Child's Play — Innova ▲ MN 111
Handel, G.F.:Arias, w. B. Norden (sop), B. Haley (tpt), D. Foster (hpd)—Destro dall' empia dite (from *Amadigi di Gaula*); Alle voci del bronzo guerriero (from Cantata No. 19, *O come chiare e belle*) [I] — Crystal ▲ CD 952 [DDD] ■ C 952
Hess, M.:About the Night — Innova ▲ MN 111
Lewis, P.S.:Beaming Contrasts, w. D. Tanenbaum (gtr) — New Albion ▲ NA 060 [DDD]
Lewis, P.S.:Journey to Still Water Pond, w. W. Winant (vib/mar) — New Albion ▲ NA 060 [DDD]
Lewis, P.S.:Night Lights — New Albion ▲ NA 060 [DDD]
Peterson, W.:Qt 2 Strs — Innova ▲ MN 111
Ravel, M.:Qt Strs — Gallo ▲ CD 512
Scarlatti, A.:Arias Sop, w. Betsy Norden (sop), Bob Haley (tpt), Donald Foster (hpd)—Con voce festiva; Mio tesoro [I] — Crystal ▲ CD 952 [DDD] ■ C 952
Dzubay, D.:Threnody after Josquin's *Mille regretz* — Innova ▲ MN 111

Alexander String Quartet members
Devienne, F.:Qts Bn, Op. 73, w. K. Walker (bn) — Gallo ▲ CD 472 [DDD]

Algae Trio [L. Van Marcke (hn), P. Koch (vn), D. Blumenthal (pno)]
Brahms, J.:Trio Hn *(rec Apr. 1993)* — Pavane ▲ ADW 7295 [DDD]
Cherubini, L.:Sons (2) Hn—No. 2 in F *(rec Apr. 1993)* — Pavane ▲ ADW 7295 [DDD]
Schumann, R.:Adagio & Allegro Hn *(rec Apr. 1993)* — Pavane ▲ ADW 7295 [DDD]

Alkan Trio [K. Lessing (vn), B. Schwarz (vc), R. Klaas (pno)]
Alkan, C.-V.:Chamber Music—Grand Duo concertant for Violin & Piano, Op. 21; Sonate de Concert for Cello & Piano, Op. 47; Trio for Piano, Violin & Cello, Op. 30 *(rec June 1991)* — Marco Polo ▲ 8.223383 [DDD]

Alkan Trio members
Bohnke, E.:Son Vc Pno — MD + G 2-▲ MDG 3250531 [DDD]
Bohnke, E.:Trio Pno — MD + G 2-▲ MDG 3250531 [DDD]

All Star Percussion Ensemble
H. Farberman (cnd)
All Star Percussion Ensemble II:Classics As Never Heard Before *(rec SUNY Performance Art Center, Aud C, Sept 14–15, 1994)* — Golden String ▲ GSCD 013A [DDD]
Beethoven, L. van:Sym 9, "Choral Sym"—Scherzo [arr Farberman] *(rec 1982)* — Allegretto ▲ ACD 8195
Beethoven, L. van:Sym 9, "Choral Sym"—Scherzo — MMG ▲ MCD 10007 [DDD]
Berlioz, H.:Sym fantastique—March — MMG ▲ MCD 10007 [DDD]
Berlioz, H.:Sym fantastique—March to the Scaffold [arr Farberman] *(rec 1982)* — Allegretto ▲ ACD 8195
Bizet, G.:Carmen (sels) — MMG ▲ MCD 10007 [DDD]
Bizet, G.:Carmen (suite 1) [arr Farberman] *(rec 1982)* — Allegretto ▲ ACD 8195
Pachelbel, J.:Canon [arr Farberman] *(rec 1982)* — Allegretto ▲ ACD 8195

All-American Youth SO
L. Stokowski (cnd)
Beethoven, L. van:Sym 5 *(rec 1940–41)* — Music & Arts ▲ CD 857 [ADD]
Brahms, J.:Sym 1 *(rec 1940–41)* — Music & Arts ▲ CD 857 [ADD]
Brahms, J.:Sym 4 *(rec 1940–41)* — Music & Arts ▲ CD 845 [ADD]
Dvořák, A.:Sym 9, "From the New World" *(rec 1940)* — Music & Arts ▲ CD 841 [AAD]
Mendelssohn, F.:A Midsummer Night's Dream (sels)—Scherzo *(rec 1940–41)* — Music & Arts ▲ CD 845 [ADD]
Ravel, M.:Boléro *(rec 1940)* — Music & Arts ▲ CD 841 [AAD]
Sibelius, J.:Sym 7 *(rec 1940)* — Music & Arts ▲ CD 841 [AAD]
Stokowski, L.:Transcriptions Orch—Andante sostenuto [Son. 2 Vn] *(rec 1940–41)* — Music & Arts ▲ CD 845 [ADD]

All-American Youth SO (cont.)
L. Stokowski (cnd) (cont.)
Strauss, R.:Tod und Verklärung *(rec 1940–41)* — Music & Arts ▲ CD 845 [ADD]

Allegri String Quartet
Stolen Gems, w. James Campbell (cl) *(rec 8/85)* — Marquis Classics ▲ ERAD 119 [DDD]

Allegri String Quartet [Peter Carter (vn), David Roth (vn), Roger Tapping (va), Bruno Schrecker (vc)]
Boccherini, L.:Qnts Fl, G.431–436, w. S. Francis (ob) — London ("Serenata" series) ▲ 433173-2 [ADD]
Ravel, M.:Intro & Allegro, w. V. McKeand (hp), C. Wincenc (fl), D. Campbell (cl) — Virgin Classics ▲ CDZ 59695
Ravel, M.:Intro & Allegro, w. Ieuan Jones (hp), William Bennett (fl), James Campbell (cl) *(rec All Saints' Church, East Finchley, London, Jan 12–20, 1994)* — Cala 2-▲ CACD 1018 [DDD]
Ravel, M.:Le Tombeau de Couperin, w. V. McKeand (hp), C. Wincenc (fl), D. Campbell (cl) — Virgin Classics ▲ CDZ 59695
Sirmen, M.L.:Qts Strs, Op. 3 *(rec All Saints Church, East Finchley, London, Jan 10–11, 1994)* — Cala ▲ CACD 1019 [DDD]

Allgäuer Horn Ensemble
Sacred Horn Music, w. U. Köbl (hn), M. Neukirchner (hn), C. Wulkopf (cta), J. Skudlik (org) — Ars Produktion ▲ FCD 368304

All-Union RSO
A. Gauk (cnd)
Chopin, F.:Con 1 Pno, w. H. Neuhaus (pno) — Russian Disc ▲ RUS 15007 [AAD]
Tchaikovsky, P.:Con Vn, w. D. Oistrakh (vn) *(rec 1939)* — Russian Disc ▲ RUS 15002 [AAD]
Tchaikovsky, P.:Vars on a Rococo Theme, w. S. Knushevitsky (vc) *(rec 1951)* — Russian Disc ▲ RUS 15002 [AAD]

R. Glière (cnd)
Glière, R.:Sheep's Spring (suite) *(rec 1947)* — Consonance ▲ 81-3000 [AAD]
Glière, R.:Sym 1 *(rec 1950)* — Consonance ▲ 81-3001 [AAD]
Glière, R.:Sym 2 *(rec 1949)* — Consonance ▲ 81 3002 [AAD]

N. Golovanov (cnd)
Scriabin, A.:Con Pno, w. H. Neuhaus (pno) — Russian Disc ▲ RUS 15 004 [AAD]

S. Samosud (cnd)
Puccini, G.:La Bohème (sels), w. Pavel Lisitsian (bar—Marseilles)—Duet of Roudolf & Marseilles [w. S. Lemeshev (ten—Roudolf)] *(rec 1954)* — Russian Compact Disc ("Talents of Russia" series) ▲ RCD 16025 [ADD]
Taneyev, S.:Duet for Romeo & Juliet, w. T. Lavrova (sop), S. Lemeshev (ten) *(rec 1954)* — Russian Disc ▲ RUS 15002 [AAD]

All-Union Radio-TV Sym Variety Orch
Silantiev, Mavisakhalyan (cnd)
Babadjanyan, A.:Music of, w. A. Arutiunyan (pno), Arno Babadjanyan (pno), B. Chekmenyov (gtr), A. Tarasov (gtr), A. Nikolayev (perc), Armenian Radio-TV Orch—Nocturne; Prelude & Vagarshapat Dance; Capriccio; Polyphonic Son; Exprompt; Armenian Rhap; Elegy in Commemoration of A. Khachaturyan; 6 Pictures; Melody & Humoresque; Fant on Give Me My Music Back; Fant on Dum spiro spero; Fant on Winer Love; Fant on Call Me; Piece for the Pno & Orch [Dreams] *(rec 1953–83)* — Russian Compact Disc ("Talents of Russia" series) ▲ RCD 16251 [ADD]

Alma Duo [Phyllis Kamrin (vn/va), Michael Goldberg (gtr)]
Albéniz, I.:Cantos de España—Cordoba [trans] *(rec St. Stephen's Church Belvedere CA, Feb 1991)* — Kameleon ▲ KA 9001 [DDD]
Ibert, J.:Histoires Pno—Dans la maison triste; La cage de crystal; La Meneuse de tortues d'or; Le cortege de Balkis [trans.] *(rec St. Stephen's Church, Belvedere, CA, Feb. 1991)* — Kameleon ▲ KA 9001 [DDD]
McGuire, E.:Fast Peace 3 *(rec St. Stephen's Church Belvedere CA, Feb. 1991)* — Kameleon ▲ KA 9001 [DDD]
Marais, M.:Suites VI & Hpd—No. 1 in d [trans.] *(rec St. Stephen's Church Belvedere CA, Feb. 1991)* — Kameleon ▲ KA 9001 [DDD]
Piazzolla, A.:Histoire du tango [trans.] *(rec St. Stephen's Church Belvedere CA, Feb. 1991)* — Kameleon ▲ KA 9001 [DDD]

Alma Music Amsterdam
Albinoni, T.:Cons Obs, w. H. de Vries (ob) — EMI Classics ▲ CDC 54664
Telemann, G.P.:Cons Ob Orch, w. H. de Vries (ob) — EMI Classics ▲ CDC 54664

Alma Musica Ensemble [Everard van Royen (fl), Haakon Stotijn (ob), Paul Godwin (vn), Johan van Helden (va), Carel van Leeuwen Boomkamp (vc), Gusta van Royen (hpd)]
Escher, R.:Le Tombeau de Ravel — Donemus ▲ CV 22

Almost Ensemble
Campo, F.:Qnt Vicento — Klavier ▲ KCD 11039 [DDD]
Flaherty, T.:Qnt, "Good Times" — Klavier ▲ KCD 11039 [DDD]
Heussenstamm, G.:Largo — Klavier ▲ KCD 11039 [DDD]
Kohn, K.:San Gabriel Set — Klavier ▲ KCD 11039 [DDD]

Alorian String Quartet [Alicia Huang (vn), Katherine McLin (vn), Amanda Grettie (va), Ellen Fuchs (vc)]
Rosner, A.:Qt 4 Strs — Opus One ▲ 150
Schubel, M.:Qt 3 Strs — Opus One ▲ CD 151

Alpe Adria Ensemble
R. Clemencic (cnd)
Mozart, W.A.:Bastien und Bastienne, w. Kirchner (sgr), Choy (sgr), Müller De Vries (sgr) [G] — Nuova Era 2-▲ 7106/07 [DDD]
Rousseau, J.-J.:Le Devin du village, w. Kirchner (sgr), Choy (sgr), Müller de Vries (sgr), Alpe Adria Chorus [F] — Nuova Era 2-▲ 7106/07 [DDD]

Alsace Polyphonique Ensemble
Chailly, J.:Choral Music, w. Strasbourg Univ Collegium Cantorum—Missa Solemnis; Salve Regina; Prière de Saint Françoise; Le cimetière marin — Skarbo ▲ SKR 3912 [DDD]

Altaïr SO
F. Bardot (cnd)
Mozart, W.A.:Missa, K.427, w. C. Pozderec (sop), M. C. LeBlanc (sop), F. Bardot (ten), L. Peintre (bar), Paris Opera Children's Choir [L] — Thésis ▲ THE11003

Altramar Medieval Music Ensemble [Angela Mariani (sgr), Allison Zelles (sgr), David Stattelman (sgr), Jann Cosart (vielle/rebec), Chris Smith (gittern/oud), Angela Mariani (hp), Allison Zelles (hp), David Stattleman (perc)]
St. Francis & the Minstrels of God *(rec St. Bridget's Catholic Church, Nolan Settlement, IA, Mar 1994)* — Dorian ▲ DOR 80143 [DDD]

Altramar Medieval Music Ensemble [Angela Mariani (sgr), David Stattleman (sgr), Jann Cosart (h-g/rebec), Angela Mariani (hp), Chris Smith (lt/gittern), David Stattleman (perc)]
Nova Stella:A Medieval Italian Christmas *(rec Church of the Immaculate Conception, Saint Mary-of-the-Woods, IN, Nov 1995 & Mar 1996)* — Dorian ▲ 80142 [DDD]

Ama Deus Ensemble
V. Radu (cnd)
Bach, J.S.:Magnificat, BWV 243, w. Julianne Baird (sop), Lorie Gratis (mez), David Price (ten), Kevin Deas (bass-bar), Bronwyn Fix-Keller (hpd) — Vox Classics ▲ VOX 7531
Bach, J.S.:Suite 3 Orch — Vox Classics ▲ VOX 7531
Handel, G.F.:Messiah, w. Julianne Baird (sop), Jennifer Lane (mez), David Price (ten), Kevin Deas (b-bar), Ama Deus Ensemble Chorus [period instruments; 1749 Covent Garden version] — Vox Classics 2-▲ VOX2 7502 [DDD]
Handel, G.F.:Messiah (sels), w. Julianne Baird (sop), Jennifer Lane (mez), David Price (ten), Kevin Deas (b-bar)—[Part 1] Sinf.; Comfort Ye My People; Every Valley Shall Be Exalted; And the Glory of the Lord; O Thou That Tellest Good Tidings to Zion; For Unto Us a Child is Born; Pifa; Rejoice Greatly o Daughter of Zion; He Shall Feed His Flock by Night; [Part 2] He was Despised and Rejected of Men; All We Like Sheep Have Gone Astray; Lift Up Your Heads, O Ye Gates; Why do the Nations So Furiously Rage Together; [Part 3] I Know That My Redeemer Liveth; Behold, I Tell You a Mystery; The Trumpet Shall Sound; Hallelujah — Vox Classics ▲ VOX 7508 [DDD]

46

▲ = CD ♦ = Enhanced CD Δ = MD ■ = Cassette Tape □ = DCC

Amadeus CO
A. Duczmal (cnd)
Bacewicz, G.:Con Strs *(rec Concert Hall of Adam Mickiewicz Univ, May–June 1992)* Conifer Classics ▲ CDCF 246 [DDD]
Bloch, E.:Concertino, w. M. M. Kofler (fl), H. Nicolai (va) *(rec 1990)* CPO ▲ CPO 999096–2 [DDD]
Bloch, E.:Con grosso 1 *(rec 1990)* CPO ▲ CPO 999096–2 [DDD]
Bloch, E.:Con grosso 2 *(rec 1990)* CPO ▲ CPO 999096–2 [DDD]
Bloch, E.:Episodes (4) *(rec 1990)* CPO ▲ CPO 999096–2 [DDD]
Dvořák, A.:Serenade Strs Arts ▲ 472872 [DDD]
Górecki, H.–M.:Con Pno, w. A. Górecka (pno) *(rec Concert Hall of Adam Mickiewicz Univ, May–June 1992)* Conifer Classics ▲ CDCF 246 [DDD]
Górecki, H.–M.:Pieces (3) in Old Style *(rec Concert Hall of Adam Mickiewicz Univ, May–June 1992)* Conifer Classics ▲ CDCF 246 [DDD]
Handel, G.F.:Serse, w. L. Atkinson (trb), D. Cole (sop), A. Terzian (mez), A. Andersson (ten), T. Allen (bar), Schumann–Halley (sgr), J. Teal (sgr) [I] *(rec live recording produced by "Studios Classique Berlin")* Koch Schwann 3–▲ CD SC 100 300 [DDD]
Haydn, J.:Con Hpd & Strs, H.XVIII/3, w. Elena Mouzalas (pno) Adda ▲ ADD 581228 [DDD]
Haydn, J.:Con Hpd & Strs, H.XVIII/4, w. Elena Mouzalas (pno) Adda ▲ ADD 581228 [DDD]
Haydn, J.:Con Hpd, Obs, Hns & Strs, H.XVIII/11, w. Elena Mouzalas (pno) Adda ▲ ADD 581228 [DDD]
Karlowicz, M.:Serenade Strs Polskie Nagrania ▲ PNCD 068 [DDD]
Kilar, W.:Orawa *(rec Concert Hall of Adam Mickiewicz Univ, May–June 1992)* Conifer Classics ▲ CDCF 246 [DDD]
Rooman, R.:Prelude, Aria & Sinf Vienna Modern Masters ▲ VMM 3014 [DDD]
Shostakovich, D.:Chamber Sym, Op. 110a *(rec Concert Hall of Adam Mickiewicz Univ, May–June 1992)* Conifer Classics ▲ CDCF 246 [DDD]
Suk, J.:Serenade Strs Polskie Nagrania ▲ PNCD 068 [DDD]
Szymanowski, K.:Étude Pno [arr A. Duczmal] *(rec Concert Hall of Adam Mickiewicz Univ, May–June 1992)* Conifer Classics ▲ CDCF 246 [DDD]
Tchaikovsky, P.:Serenade Strs Polskie Nagrania ▲ PNCD 068 [DDD]
Tchaikovsky, P.:Serenade Strs Arts ▲ 472872 [DDD]

Amadeus Ensemble
Brahms, J.:Sextet Strs, Op. 18, w. Alban Berg String Quartet members EMI Classics ▲ CDC 54216
Mozetich, M.:Dance, w. J. Petric (acc) CBC ("Musica Viva" series) ▲ MVCD 1038 [DDD]
Mozetich, M.:El Dorado, w. E. Goodman (hp) CBC ("Musica Viva" series) ▲ MVCD 1038 [DDD]
Mozetich, M.:Fant CBC ("Musica Viva" series) ▲ MVCD 1038 [DDD]
Mozetich, M.:Procession CBC ("Musica Viva" series) ▲ MVCD 1038 [DDD]

Amadeus Ensemble members
Barnes, M.:Divert Hp, w. E. Goodman (hp) CBC ("Musica Viva" series) ▲ MVCD 1054 [DDD]
Hoffmann, E.T.A.:Qnt Hp, w. Erica Goodman (hp) CBC ("Musica Viva" series) ▲ MVCD 1054 [DDD]
Ravel, M.:Intro & Allegro, w. E. Goodman (hp), S. Shulman (fl), S. McCartney (cl) CBC ("Musica Viva" series) ▲ MVCD 1054 [DDD]
Samuel–Rousseau, M.:Pastoral Vars on an Old Christmas Carol, w. E. Goodman (hp) CBC ("Musica Viva" series) ▲ MVCD 1054 [DDD]
Tournier, M.:Images, w. E. Goodman (hp) CBC ("Musica Viva" series) ▲ MVCD 1054 [DDD]

Amadeus String Quartet
Beethoven, L. van:Qts Strs (comp) Deutsche Grammophon 7–▲ 423473–2 [ADD]
Brahms, J.:Qt 1 Pno, w. Emil Gilels (pno) Deutsche Grammophon ("The Originals" series) ▲ 447407–2
Brahms, J.:Qnt Cl, w. K. Leister (cl) Deutsche Grammophon 3–▲ 419875–2 [ADD]
Brahms, J.:Qnt Pno, w. C. Eschenbach (pno) Deutsche Grammophon 3–▲ 419875–2 [ADD]
Brahms, J.:Qnt 1 Strs, w. Cecil Aronowitz (va) Deutsche Grammophon 3–▲ 419875–2 [ADD]
Brahms, J.:Qnt 2 Strs, w. Cecil Aronowitz (va) Deutsche Grammophon 3–▲ 419875–2 [ADD]
Brahms, J.:Sextet Strs, Op. 18, w. C. Aronowitz (va), A. Pleeth (vc) Deutsche Grammophon 3–▲ 419875–2 [ADD]
Brahms, J.:Sextet Strs, Op. 36, w. C. Aronowitz (va), A. Pleeth (vc) Deutsche Grammophon 3–▲ 419875–2 [ADD]
Haydn, J.:Qts Strs, Op. 54 Deutsche Grammophon 2–▲ 437134–2 [ADD]
Haydn, J.:Qts Strs, Op. 64, "Tost Qts" Deutsche Grammophon 3–▲ 431145–2 [ADD]
Haydn, J.:Qts Strs, Op. 71 Deutsche Grammophon 3–▲ 429189–2 [ADD]
Haydn, J.:Qts Strs, Op. 74 Deutsche Grammophon 3–▲ 429189–2 [ADD]
Haydn, J.:Qts Strs, Op. 76, "Erdödy Qts" Deutsche Grammophon 2–▲ 415867–2 [ADD]
Haydn, J.:Qts Strs, Op. 77, "Lobkowitz Qts" Deutsche Grammophon 3–▲ 429189–2 [ADD]
Haydn, J.:Qt Strs, Op. 103 Deutsche Grammophon 3–▲ 429189–2 [ADD]
Haydn, J.:The Seven Last Words of Christ on the Cross [string quartet version] Deutsche Grammophon 3–▲ 431145–2 [ADD]
Mozart, W.A.:Qts Fl, w. A. Blau (fl) Deutsche Grammophon 2–▲ 429819–2 [ADD]
Mozart, W.A.:Qts Strs (comp) Deutsche Grammophon 6–▲ 423300–2 [ADD]
Mozart, W.A.:Qnt Cl, K.581, w. G. De Peyer (cl) Deutsche Grammophon 2–▲ 429819–2 [ADD]
Mozart, W.A.:Qnt Cl, K.581, w. G. De Peyer (cl) Deutsche Grammophon 2–▲ 437137–2 [ADD]
Mozart, W.A.:Qnt Cl, K.581, w. Franz Klein (cl) Koch Schwann ▲ SCH 318092
Mozart, W.A.:Qnt Hn, K.407, w. G. Seifert (hn) Deutsche Grammophon 2–▲ 437137–2 [ADD]
Schubert, Franz:Qt 14 Strs Deutsche Grammophon ("Resonance" series) ▲ 427215–2 [ADD]
Schubert, Franz:Qnt Strs, D.956, w. Robert Cohen (vc)—Adagio *(rec Abbey Road Studios, London, Nov 10–11, 1994)* Argo ▲ 444873–2

Amadeus String Quartet members
Brahms, J.:Qt 1 Pno, w. M. Perahia (pno) CBS ▲ MK 42361 [DDD]
Mozart, W.A.:Qts Fl, w. A. Blau (fl) Deutsche Grammophon 2–▲ 437137–2 [ADD]
Mozart, W.A.:Qt Ob, K.370, w. L. Koch (ob) Deutsche Grammophon 2–▲ 437137–2 [ADD]

Amadeus Wind Ensemble
C. Hogwood (cnd)
Mozart, W.A.:Serenade Ww, K.361 L'Oiseau–Lyre ▲ 421437–2 [DDD]
J. Rudel (cnd)
Mozart, W.A.:Entführung (winds) MusicMasters ▲ 7001–2–C [DDD]
Mozart, W.A.:Zauberflöte (winds) MusicMasters ▲ 7001–2 C [DDD]

Amadinda Percussion Group
Cage, J.:Amores, w. Z. Kocsis (pno) Hungaroton ▲ HCD 12991 [DDD]
Cage, J.:4'33" Hungaroton ▲ HCD 12991 [DDD]
Cage, J.:Third Construction Hungaroton ▲ HCD 12991 [DDD]
Chávez, C.:Toccata for 6 Perc Hungaroton ▲ HCD 12991 [DDD]
Reich, S.:Music for Mallet Instruments, Voices & Electric Organ Hungaroton ▲ HCD 31358 [DDD]
Reich, S.:Music for Pieces of Wood Hungaroton ▲ HCD 31358 [DDD]
Reich, S.:Sextet Hungaroton ▲ HCD 31358 [DDD]
Varèse, E.:Ionisation Hungaroton ▲ HCD 12991 [DDD]

Amalia Ensemble
Clérambault, L.N.:Cants, w. I. Poulenard (sop), G. Ragon (ten)—Léandre et Héro (1713); Pirame et Tisbé (1713); L'Isle de Délos (1716); Apollon et Doris (1720) [F] *(rec 1/91)* Opus 111 ▲ OPS 39–9103 [DDD]

L'Amaltea Ensemble
Viadana, L. da:Vespri per l'Assunzione, w. S. Pozzer (sop), C. Calvino (alt), U. Müller Adam (ten), J. Clement (ten), S. Foresti (bass), Vox Hesperia, St. Marco Capella Musicale Fonè ▲ FON 92F 08 [DDD]

Amarillis Instrumental Ensemble
C. Näf (cnd)
Marx, K.:When Jesus Left His Mother, w. F. Staehelin (sgr), W. Pailer (bass), Feld Evangelistic Kantorei, Amarillis Vocal Ensemble [G] *(rec 6/89)* FSM ▲ FCD 97737 [DDD]

Amaryllis Consort
C. Brett (cnd)
English Madrigals, w. R. Aldwinckle (hpd) Allegro ▲ ALG PCD 873

Amaryllis Consort (cont.)
C. Brett (cnd) (cont.)
Italian Madrigals IMP Classics ("Masters" series) ▲ PCD 822 [DDD]

Amati Ensemble
Albinoni, T.:Adagio Org, w. J.–F. Gautier (org) *(rec Aug 1993)* Analekta ▲ AN 29504
Mozart, W.A.:Divert Hns Strs, K.334, w. Sharon String Quartet Arcobaleno ▲ AAOC 9389
Puccini, G.:Crisantemi *(rec Aug. 1993)* Analekta Fleur de Lys ▲ FL 2 3050
Spohr, L.:Nonet Strs, w. Sharon String Quartet Arcobaleno ▲ AAOC 9389
Verdi, G.:Qt Strs *(rec Aug. 1993)* Analekta Fleur de Lys ▲ FL 2 3050
A. Balogh (cnd)
Glazunov, A.:Elegy, Op. 105 *(rec Munich, Sept. 21–23, 1994)* Calig ▲ CAL 50940 [DDD]
Glazunov, A.:Suite Strs *(rec Munich, Sept. 21–23, 1994)* Calig ▲ CAL 50940 [DDD]
Glazunov, A.:Vars on a Russian Theme *(rec Munich, Sept. 21–23, 1994)* Calig ▲ CAL 50940 [DDD]
R. Dessaints (cnd)
Abril, A.G.:Music of, w. R. Boucher (gtr)—Concierto Mudéjar Analekta ▲ AN 29502
Brahms, J.:Hungarian Dances Orch *(rec Salle Pierre–Mercure, Montréal, Apr 1995)* Analekta Fleur de Lys ▲ FL 2 3010 [DDD]
Mendelssohn, F.:Sinfs Strs—Nos. 2 in D, 7 in d, 9 in c & 10 in b [Adagio–Allegro] Analekta ▲ AN 29503
La Ronde des Berceuses, w. Angèle Dubeau (vn) Analekta ▲ AN 28711 [DDD]
Rossini, G.:Sons Str Qt Analekta ▲ AN 29501
R. Koelble (cnd)
Baur, J.:Abbreviaturen *(rec July 7, 1973)* Koch Schwann ▲ SCH 311982 [ADD/DDD]

Amati Ensemble [Gil Sharon, Catalin Ilea, Idith Zvi, Gilah Yaron]
Schumann, C.:Romances Vn Arcobaleno ▲ AAOC 9361
Schumann, C.:Songs Arcobaleno ▲ AAOC 9361
Schumann, C.:Trio Pno Arcobaleno ▲ AAOC 9361

Amati String Quartet
Kelterborn, R.:Qt V Strs *(rec Oct. 20, 1989)* Grammont ▲ CTSP 35–2 [ADD]
Shostakovich, D.:Qt 3 Strs *(rec 1987)* Jecklin–Disco ▲ JD 620–2 [ADD]
Shostakovich, D.:Qt 7 Strs *(rec 1987)* Jecklin–Disco ▲ JD 620–2 [ADD]
Spohr, L.:Qt Strs, Op. 15/2—Op. 15/2 *(rec 1984)* Jecklin–Disco ▲ JD 593–2 [ADD]
Spohr, L.:Qt Strs, Op. 29/1—Op. 29/1 *(rec 1984)* Jecklin–Disco ▲ JD 593–2 [ADD]
Suter, R.:Qt 2 Strs Jecklin ▲ JD 690

Amatius Orch of New York
P. Olefsky (cnd)
Tchaikovsky, P.:Nocturne Vc, w. P. Olefsky (vc) Amatius Classics ▲ ACCD 1002 [DDD]
Tchaikovsky, P.:Pezzo capriccioso, w. P. Olefsky (vc) Amatius Classics ▲ ACCD 1002 [DDD]
Tcherepnin, A.:Mystère, w. H. Zheng (vc) Amatius Classics ▲ ACCD 1002 [DDD]

Ambache Chamber Ensemble [Adrian Levine (vn), Robert Smissen (va), Andrew Shulman (vc)]
Mozart, W.A.:Qts Pno, w. D. Ambache (pno)—K.493 Meridian ▲ CDE 84142
Mozart, W.A.:Qt Pno, K.493, w. Diana Ambache (pno) Meridian ▲ MER 84329 [AAD]
Mozart, W.A.:Sons Vn Pno (misc)—K.301 Meridian ▲ CDE 84142
Mozart, W.A.:Trio Pno, K.542, w. D. Ambache (pno) Meridian ▲ CDE 84142

Ambache Chamber Ensemble members [Adrian Levine (vn), Andrew Shulman (vc)]
Mozart, W.A.:Trio Pno, K.542, w. Diana Ambache (pno) Meridian ▲ MER 84329 [AAD]

Ambache CO
D. Ambache (cnd)
Mozart, W.A.:Con 8 Pno, w. D. Ambache (pno) IMP Classics ▲ PCD 931 [DDD]
Mozart, W.A.:Con 9 Pno, w. D. Ambache (pno) IMP Classics ▲ PCD 931 [DDD]
Mozart, W.A.:Con 21 Pno, w. D. Ambache (pno) Virgin Classics ▲ CDZ 59647
Mozart, W.A.:Con 25 Pno, w. D. Ambache (pno) Virgin Classics ▲ CDZ 59647
Mozart, W.A.:Rondo Pno Orch, K.386, w. D. Ambache (pno) IMP Classics ▲ PCD 931 [DDD]

Amburgo RSO
H. Rosbaud (cnd)
Schoenberg, A.:Moses und Aaron (sels), w. Amburgo Radio Chorus—Danza del Vitello d'Oro Stradivarius ▲ STV 10022 [ADD]

Amelite Consortium
Newman, Alfred:Robe, w. Viklarbo Chamber Ensemble Raptoria Caam ▲ RCD 1004
Newman, M.:Chamber Music, w. Viklarbo Chamber Ensemble—Solus for Violin & Cello; Ornitholites for Clairnet Qnt.; Dances for Deliverence for solo Violin Raptoria Caam ▲ RCD 1004

Amelite Consortium [M. Newman (vn), P. Kent (vn), V. Dimond (va), D. Smith (vc)]
Cox, R.:Music of, w. M. Walker (cl)—When April May *(rec April & May 1992)* Raptoria Caam ▲ RCD 1001
Fink, M.J.:Music of, w. M. Walker (cl)—Thread of Summer *(rec April & May 1992)* Raptoria Caam ▲ RCD 1001

Amelite Consortium [M. Newman (vn), P. Kent (vn), V. Dimond (va), G. Gottlieb (vc)]
Fox, J.:Music of, w. M. Walker (cl)—Between the Wheels *(rec April & May 1992)* Raptoria Caam ▲ RCD 1001
Newman, M.:Music of, w. M. Walker (cl)—Ornitholites *(rec April & May 1992)* Raptoria Caam ▲ RCD 1001
Walker, M.:Music of, w. M. Walker (cl)—Interlude I & II *(rec April & May 1992)* Raptoria Caam ▲ RCD 1001

American Bach Soloists
J. Thomas (cnd)
Bach, J.S.:Cant 8, w. J. Baird (sop), S. Rickards (alt), J. Thomas (ten), J. Weaver (bass) [G] Koch International Classics ▲ KIC 7163–2 [DDD]
Bach, J.S.:Cant 12 Koch International Classics ▲ KIC 7332 [DDD]
Bach, J.S.:Cant 18 Koch International Classics ▲ KIC 7332 [DDD]
Bach, J.S.:Cant 51, w. J. Baird (sop) [G] *(rec Apr & Oct 1990)* Koch International Classics ▲ KIC 7138–2 [DDD]
Bach, J.S.:Cant 54, w. D. Minter (ct) [G] *(rec Apr & Oct 1990)* Koch International Classics ▲ KIC 7138–2 [DDD]
Bach, J.S.:Cant 55, w. J. Thomas (ten) [G] *(rec Apr & Oct 1990)* Koch International Classics ▲ KIC 7138–2 [DDD]
Bach, J.S.:Cant 61 Koch International Classics ▲ KIC 7332 [DDD]
Bach, J.S.:Cant 78 Koch International Classics ▲ KIC 7234
Bach, J.S.:Cant 80 Koch International Classics ▲ KIC 7234
Bach, J.S.:Cant 82, w. W. Sharp (bar) [G] *(rec Apr & Oct 1990)* Koch International Classics ▲ KIC 7138–2 [DDD]
Bach, J.S.:Cant 106, "Actus tragicus", w. C. Brandes (sop), D. Minter (alt), W. Sharp (bar) Koch International Classics ▲ KIC 7164 [DDD]
Bach, J.S.:Cant 140 Koch International Classics ▲ KIC 7234
Bach, J.S.:Cant 140 Koch International Classics ▲ KIC 7610
Bach, J.S.:Cant 152 Koch International Classics ▲ KIC 7164 [DDD]
Bach, J.S.:Cant 156, w. S. Rickards (alt), J. Thomas (ten), J. Weaver (bass) [G] Koch International Classics ▲ KIC 7163–2 [DDD]
Bach, J.S.:Cant 161 Koch International Classics ▲ KIC 7164 [DDD]
Bach, J.S.:Cant 198, w. J. Nelson (sop), J. Malafronte (mez), J. Thomas (ten), W. Sharp (bar) [G] Koch International Classics ▲ KIC 7163–2 [DDD]
Bach, J.S.:Con for 4 Hpds, w. John Butt (hpd), Phebe Craig (hpd), Johathan Dimmock (hpd), Jeffrey Thomas (hpd) Koch International Classics ▲ KIC 7237 [DDD]
Bach, J.S.:Mass in b, BWV 232, w. William Sharp (bar) Koch International Classics ▲ KIC 7610
Bach, J.S.:Mass in b, BWV 232, w. J. Baird (sop), J. Nelson (sop), N. Zylstra, J. Lane, Z. Muñoz, S. Rickards, P. Romano, W. Sharp, J. Weaver (bass) Koch International Classics 2–▲ KIC 7194–2 [DDD]
Bach, J.S.:Psalms (4), w. Benita Valente (sop), Judith Malafronte (alt)—Psalm 51:Tilge, Höchter, meine Sünden Koch International Classics ▲ KIC 7237 [DDD]

American Baroque [Stephen Schultz (baroque fl), Elizabeth Blumenstock (baroque vn), Roy Wheldon (vl), Sarah Freiberg (baroque vc), Cheryl Ann Fulton (triple hp)]
S. Schultz (cnd)
Abel, C.F.:Qt Gtr, Fl, Vn & Vl—2nd movt. by R. Whelden New Albion ▲ NA 059
Telemann, G.P.:Qts, Book 4 Koch International Classics ▲ KIC 7031-2 [DDD] ■ 3-7031-4 (D)
Telemann, G.P.:Qts Vn—4 quartets—in A, D, G, g Amon Ra ▲ CD-SAR 39 [DDD]
Wheldon, R.:Music of, w. Karen Clark (alt)—I Was 16; Fugue State No. 1; I Was at a New Year's Eve Dance; Like a Passing River; The Graffiti on the Subway Cars; White Light Cant., New York 1980 [Sinf.; Right on 42nd Street; A Sudden Pang Seizes My Heart; On the Street It's Still Light; We're Out in the Boat]; Fugue State No. 2; Rucker Songs; So What's the Point; Adagio; What's the Point; Into the Light *(rec St. Stephen's Church, Belvedere, CA)* New Albion ▲ NA 072
American Brass Quintet
Felder, D.:Music of, w. Rachel Rudich (fl). June in Buffalo CO, Arditti String Quartet—Journal; Canzone XXXI; November Sky; 3rd Face; 3 Lines from 20 Poems Bridge ▲ BRI 9049 [DDD]
Roseman, R.:Double Qnt, w. New York Woodwind Quintet New World ▲ 80413-2 [DDD]
J. Barnett (cnd)
Riegger, W.:Movt Tpts, w. National Orch Alumni Association members CRI ▲ CD 572 [ADD]
Riegger, W.:Music for Brass, w. National Orch Alumni Association members CRI ▲ CD 572 [ADD]
Riegger, W.:Nonet, w. National Orch Alumni Association members CRI ▲ CD 572 [ADD]
Siegmeister, E.:Sextet Brass, w. G. Gottlieb (perc) Premier ("Composer" series) ▲ PRCD 1010 [ADD]
American Brass Quintet [Raymond Mase (tpt), Chris Gekker (tpt), David Wakefield (hn), Michael Powell (ten trbn), John D. Rojak (bass trbn)]
Adolphe, B.:Triskelion *(rec Mar 19–23, 1991)* Summit ▲ DCD 133 [DDD]
Bach, Jan:Triptych *(rec Music Division Recital Hall, SUNY College, Purchase, New York, Nov 2–8, 1993, Mar 14 & Apr 29, 1994)* Summit ▲ 187 [DDD]
Bland, E.:Qnt Brass Cambria ▲ CD 1026
Bolcom, W.:Qnt New World ▲ NW 377-2 [DDD]
Dennis, R.:Blackbird Vars *(rec Mar. 19–23, 1991)* Summit ▲ DCD 133 [DDD]
Druckman, J.:Other Voices New World ▲ NW 377-2 [DDD]
Ewazen, E.:Colchester Fant *(rec Mar. 19–23, 1991)* Summit ▲ DCD 133 [DDD]
Ewazen, E.:Frost Fire *(rec Recital Hall, SUNY Purchase, 1993)* Well-Tempered Productions ▲ WTP 5172 [DDD]
Felder, D.:Canzone XXXI *(rec Slee Hall, SUNY, Buffalo)* Bridge ▲ BCD 9049 [DDD]
Sampson, D.:Distant Voices *(rec Music Division Recital Hall, SUNY College, Purchase, New York, Nov 2–8, 1993, Mar 14 & Apr 29, 1994)* Summit ▲ 187 [DDD]
Sampson, D.:Morning Music *(rec Mar. 19–23, 1991)* Summit ▲ DCD 133 [DDD]
Schuller, G.:Qnt 2 Brass *(rec Music Division Recital Hall, SUNY College, Purchase, New York, Nov 2–8, 1993, Mar 14 & Apr 29, 1994)* Summit ▲ 187 [DDD]
Shapey, R.:Qnt Brass New World ▲ NW 377-2 [DDD]
Snow, D.:Dance Movts *(rec Mar. 19–23, 1991)* Summit ▲ DCD 133 [DDD]
Walker, G.:Music for Brass Albany ▲ TROY 154 [DDD]
Welcher, D.:Qnt Brass *(rec Music Division Recital Hall, SUNY College, Purchase, New York, Nov 2–8, 1993, Mar 14 & Apr 29, 1994)* Summit ▲ 187 [DDD]
Wright, M.:Qnt Brass New World ▲ NW 377-2 [DDD]
J. Druckman (cnd)
Druckman, J.:Dark Upon the Harp, w. J. DeGaetani (mez), J. Haas (perc), B. Herman (perc) [E] *(rec Aspen Music Festival 8/6/88)* Bridge ▲ BCD 9023 [ADD]
Balada, L.:Son Winds, w. J. Aley (tpt), D. Wakefield (hn), R. Borror (tenor trbn), R. Biddlecome (bass trbn) New World ▲ 80442-2
American Brass Quintet [Raymond Mase (tpts/flgl), Chris Gekker (tpts/flgl), David Wakefield (hn), Michael Powell (trbns), John D. Rojak (bass trbn)]
American Brass Quintet Delos ▲ DCD 3003 [DDD]
Fyre & Lightning:Consort Music of 1600 *(rec Joan & Irving Harris Concert Hall, Aspen Music Festival, Aspen, CO, Aug. 1994)* Summit ▲ DCD 181 [DDD]
The Yankee Brass Band New World ▲ 80312-2 [ADD]
American Camerata
J. Stephens (cnd)
American Camerata Performs AmCam ▲ ACR 10305
Krenek, E.:Capriccio Vc, w. E. Elsing (vc) AmCam ▲ ACR 10305CD
Moss, L.:Clouds AmCam ▲ ACR 10305CD
Moss, L.:Syms Brass, w. Annapolis Brass Quintet AmCam ▲ ACR 10305CD
Sapieyevski, J.:Mercury Con, w. A. Ghitalla (tpt) AmCam ▲ ACR 10305CD
Villa-Lobos, H.:Chôro 7 AmCam ▲ ACR 10305CD
American Camerata for New Music
Cyr, G.:Qt 2 Strs AmCam ▲ ACR 10303
J. Stephens (cnd)
Brandt, H.:Ghost Nets, w. L. Paer (db) AmCam ▲ ACR 10303
American Chamber Ensemble
Hindemith, P.:Qt Cl, Vn, Vc & Pno Leonarda ▲ LE 329
Weigl, V.:Songs of Remembrance [E] Leonarda ▲ LE 329
Zaimont, J.L.:From the Great Land [E] Leonarda ▲ LE 329
American CO
R. Scholz (cnd)
Mozart, W.A.:Con 12 Pno, w. M. Hess (pno) *(rec March 20, 1956)* Music & Arts 3-▲ CD 779 [AAD]
Mozart, W.A.:Con 27 Pno, w. M. Hess (pno) *(rec March 20, 1956)* Music & Arts 3-▲ CD 779 [AAD]
American Chamber Players
Bloch, E.:Qnt 1 Pno Koch International Classics ▲ KIC 7041-2 [DDD]
Bloch, E.:Qnt 2 Pno Koch International Classics ▲ KIC 7041-2 [DDD]
Harbison, J.:Twilight Music Koch International Classics ▲ KIC 7027-2 [DDD] ■ 3-7027-4 (D)
Harbison, J.:Vars Vn Koch International Classics ▲ KIC 7027-2 [DDD] ■ 3-7027-4 (D)
Mozart, W.A.:Trio Cl, K.498 Koch International Classics ▲ KIC 7029-2 [DDD] ■ 3-7029-4 (D)
Rochberg, G.:Qt Pno Koch International Classics ▲ KIC 7027-2 [DDD] ■ 3-7027-4 (D)
Stravinsky, I.:Duo Concertant Koch International Classics ▲ KIC 7078-2 [DDD]
Stravinsky, I.:Elégie Va Koch International Classics ▲ KIC 7078-2 [DDD]
Stravinsky, I.:L'Histoire du soldat Suite Vn Koch International Classics ▲ KIC 7078-2 [DDD]
Stravinsky, I.:Pieces Cl Koch International Classics ▲ KIC 7078-2 [DDD]
Stravinsky, I.:Vn Pno Arrangements—6 pieces from The Firebird, Le baiser de la fée & Mavra, arr Stravinsky for Violin & Piano, 1933–47 Koch International Classics ▲ KIC 7078-2 [DDD]
American Chamber Players [Loren Kitt (cl), Miles Hoffman (va), Lambert Orkis (pno)]
Bruch, M.:Trios Cl, Va & Pno, Op. 83 Koch International Classics ▲ KIC 7029-2 [DDD] ■ 3-7029-4 (D)
American Classics String Quartet
Gershwin, G.:Songs [newly arr. by John Stephens for string quartet]—By Strauss; The man I love; A foggy day; For you, for me, forever more; Nice work if you can get it AmCam ▲ ACR 10304 ■ ACR 10304
Kern, J.:Songs [seven songs arr. for string quartet, the first six by Charles Miller, the final one by John Stephens]—All the things you are; The way you look tonight; Smoke gets in your eyes; Once in a blue moon; The song is you; Bill AmCam ▲ ACR 10304 ■ ACR 10304
American Composers Orch
D. R. Davies (cnd)
Beaser, R.:Chorale Vars Argo ▲ 440337-2 [DDD]
Beaser, R.:Con Pno, w. P. Mia Paul (pno) Argo ▲ 440337-2 [DDD]
Beaser, R.:The 7 Deadly Sins, w. J. Opalach (b-bar) Argo ▲ 440337-2 [DDD]
Bolcom, W.:Con Vn, w. S. Luca (vn) Argo ▲ 433077-2 [DDD]
Bolcom, W.:Fant Concertante, w. J. Lyman Hill (va), E. Moye (vc) Argo ▲ 433077-2 [DDD]
Bolcom, W.:Sym 5 Argo ▲ 433077-2 [DDD]
Harrison, L.:Elegiac Sym MusicMasters ▲ 7021-2-C

American Composers Orch (cont.)
D. R. Davies (cnd) (cont.)
Harrison, L.:Suite Symphonic Strs *(rec Manhattan Center, New York, May 1994)* Argo ▲ 444560-2 [DDD]
Hovhaness, A.:Lousadzak, w. K. Jarrett (pno) MusicMasters ▲ 7021-2-C
Hovhaness, A.:Sym 2 MusicMasters ▲ 7021-2-C
McPhee, C.:Tabuh-Tabuhan, w. Peter Basquin (pno), Christopher Oldfather (pno) *(rec Manhattan Center, New York, May 1994)* Argo ▲ 444560-2 [DDD]
Sessions, R.:Sym 6 *(rec Manhattan Center, NY, May 1994)* Argo ▲ 444519-2 [DDD]
Sessions, R.:Sym 7 *(rec Manhattan Center, NY, May 1994)* Argo ▲ 444519-2 [DDD]
Sessions, R.:Sym 9 *(rec Manhattan Center, NY, May 1994)* Argo ▲ 444519-2 [DDD]
Thorne, F.:Sym 5 CRI ▲ CD 552 [DDD]
Ung, C.:Inner Voices *(rec Manhattan Center, New York, May 1994)* Argo ▲ 444560-2 [DDD]
P. Dunkel (cnd)
Biscardi, C.:At the Still Point, w. Jeanne Ingraham (vn), Susan Palma (fl), Gilbert Kalish (pno) *(rec Whitman Auditorium, Brooklyn College, NY, Feb. 1982)* CRI ▲ CD 686 [ADD]
Carter, E.:Holiday Ov *(rec 2/82)* CRI ▲ CD 610 [ADD]
Carter, E.:Holiday Ov CRI ■ ACS 6003
Carter, E.:Suite from Pocahontas *(rec 2/82)* CRI ▲ CD 610 [ADD]
Carter, E.:Sym 1 CRI ▲ CD 552 [DDD]
Carter, E.:Sym 1 CRI ■ ACS 6003
Picker, T.:Con Vn, w. R. Schulte (vn) *(rec 1982)* CRI ▲ CD 589 [ADD]
Roussakis, N.:Fire & Earth & Water & Air CRI ▲ CD 552 [DDD]
G. Schuller (cnd)
Helps, R.:Gossamer Noons, w. Bethany Beardslee (sop) *(rec Church of Holy Trinity, Mar 1978)* CRI ("American Masters" series) ▲ CD 717 [ADD]
C. Wuorinen (cnd)
Babbitt, M.:Con Pno, w. A. Feinberg (pno) New World ▲ 80346 [DDD]
American Concerto Orch
S. Burns (cnd)
Telemann, G.P.:Air de Trompette, w. Stephen Burns (tpt) *(rec Academy of Arts & Letters, New York City, Apr. 29–May 1, 1994)* Dorian Discovery ▲ DIS 80132 [DDD]
Telemann, G.P.:Cons Tpt, w. Stephen Burns (tpt)—in D for Tpt, Strs & Bc; in D for Tpt, 2 Obs, Bn & Hpd; in D for Tpt, Obs, Bn, Strs & Bc *(rec Academy of Arts & Letters, New York City, Apr. 29–May 1, 1994)* Dorian Discovery ▲ DIS 80132 [DDD]
Telemann, G.P.:Sons Tpt, w. Stephen Burns (tpt)—in D for Tpt, Strs & Bc *(rec Academy of Arts & Letters, New York City, Apr. 29–May 1, 1994)* Dorian Discovery ▲ DIS 80132 [DDD]
Telemann, G.P.:Suites Tpt, w. Stephen Burns (tpt)—in D for Tpt, Strs & Bc *(rec Academy of Arts & Letters, New York City, Apr. 29–May 1, 1994)* Dorian Discovery ▲ DIS 80132 [DDD]
American Festival Orch
V. Golschmann (cnd)
Harris, R.:Sym 4, "Folksong Sym", w. American Festival Chorus *(rec 1960; originally released)* Vanguard Classics ▲ OVC 4076 [ADD]
American Horn Quartet [D. Johnson (hn), C. Putnam (hn), K. Turner (hn), G. Winter (hn)]
Autumn ebs ▲ EBS 6046 [DDD]
Bernstein, L.:West Side Story (sels)—Suite [arr. Walter Perkins for 4 horns] ebs ▲ EBS 6038 [DDD]
Hindemith, P.:Son for 4 Hns ebs ▲ EBS 6038 [DDD]
Langley, J.W.:Qt for 4 Hns *(rec Dec. 1990)* ebs ▲ ebs 6008 [DDD]
Perkins, W.:Con for 4 Hns ebs ▲ EBS 6038 [DDD]
Shaw, L.E.:Fripperies *(rec Dec. 1990)* ebs ▲ ebs 6008 [DDD]
Turner, K.:Fanfare Barcs *(rec Dec. 1990)* ebs ▲ ebs 6008 [DDD]
Turner, K.:Qt 1 Hns *(rec Dec. 1990)* ebs ▲ ebs 6008 [DDD]
Turner, K.:Qt 2 Hns *(rec Dec. 1990)* ebs ▲ ebs 6008 [DDD]
Turner, K.:Qt 3 Hns ebs ▲ EBS 6038 [DDD]
American Music Ensemble Vienna
H. Earle (cnd)
Berger, T.:Con Manuale Albany ▲ TROY 066 [DDD]
Berger, T.:Malinconia und Rondo giocoso—Rondo Albany ▲ TROY 066
Chadwick, G.W.:Serenade *(rec live, 11/8/88)* Albany ▲ TROY 033-2 [ADD]
del Aguila, M.:Con Cl, w. W. Fuchs (cl) Albany ▲ TROY 066 [DDD]
del Aguila, M.:Herbsttag, w. M. Bayer St. Mary (fl), J. Farmer (bn), G. Mossyrsch (hp) Albany ▲ TROY 066 [DDD]
del Aguila, M.:Hexen, w. J. Farmer (bn) Albany ▲ TROY 066 [DDD]
Gilbert, H.F.:Suite CO *(rec live 11/8/88)* Albany ▲ TROY 033-2 [ADD]
American Opera Society Orch
F. Cleva (cnd)
Catalani, A.:La Wally, w. R. Tebaldi (sop), C. Bergonzi (ten), P. Glossop (bar), F. Corena (bass), American Opera Society Chorus *(rec Mar. 13, 1968)* Intaglio 2-▲ ING 764 [ADD]
A. Gamson (cnd)
Bellini, V.:I Capuleti e i Montecchi, w. L. Hurley (sop), G. Simionato (mez), R. Cassily (ten), E. Flagello (bass), American Opera Society Chorus [I] *(rec live, New York 10/14/58)* Melodram ("Connaisseur" series) 2-▲ CDM 27509 [ADD]
A. Guadagno (cnd)
Bellini, V.:La straniera, w. M. Caballé (sop), B. M. Casoni (cta), A. Zambon (ten), American Opera Society Chorus *(rec 1969)* Melodram 2-▲ MLO 270111 [DDD]
R. Lawrence (cnd)
Berlioz, H.:Les Troyens, w. R. Resnik (mez—Dido), E. Steber (sop—Cassandra), R. Cassily (ten—Aeneas), American Opera Society Chorus *(rec live, Carnegie Hall, 12/29/59 & 1/12/60)* VAI Audio 3-▲ VAIA 1006-3 [ADD]
N. Rescigno (cnd)
Bellini, V.:Il pirata, w. M. Callas (sop—Imogene), P. M. Ferraro (ten—Gualterio), Constantine Ego (bar—Ernesto), American Opera Society Chorus *(rec 1959)* EMI Classics ▲ CDMB 64938
Bellini, V.:Il pirata, w. M. Callas (sop), P. M. Ferraro (ten), C. Ego (bar), American Opera Society Chorus [I] *(rec live, New York 1/27/59)* Melodram 2-▲ MEL 26013
American Promenade Orch
L. Graham (cnd)
Busoni, F.:Lustspiel-Ov Klavier ▲ KCD 11053 [DDD]
Lalo, E.:Arlequin Klavier ▲ KCD 11053 [DDD]
Nicolai, O.:Lustigen Weiber von Windsor:Ov Klavier ▲ KCD 11053 [DDD]
Opening Night Klavier ▲ KCD 11049
Viotti, G.B.:Con 22 Vn, w. F. Sommer-Link (vn) Klavier ▲ KCD 11053 [DDD]
Weber, C.M. von:Die drei Pintos (sels)—Entre'acte [arr Mahler] Klavier ▲ KCD 11053 [DDD]
American Serenade Band
H.C. Smith (cnd)
The Golden Age of Brass:Virtuoso Solos, Vol. 1, w. David Hickman (cnt), Mark H. Lawrence (trbn) Summit ▲ DCD 114 [DDD]
The Golden Age of Brass, Vol. 3, w. M. Colburn (eup) Summit ▲ DCD 150 [DDD]
American String Quartet [Laurie Carney (vn), Peter Winograd (vn), Daniel Avshalomov (va), David Geber (vc)]
Brahms, J.:Qnt Pno, w. Lydia Artymiw (pno) *(rec Tuscon Winter Chamber Festival; Mar 10, 1995)* Arizona Friends of Chamber Music ▲ AFCD 19952
Dvořák, A.:Qt 9 Strs Elektra/Nonesuch ▲ 79126-2 [DDD]
Dvořák, A.:Qt 10 Strs Elektra/Nonesuch ▲ 79126-2 [DDD]
Mozart, W.A.:Qt 6 Strs [performed on matched set of Stradivarius instrs] *(rec SUNY, Purchase, NY, Feb 21–23, 1995)* MusicMasters ▲ 01612-67160-2
Mozart, W.A.:Qt 11 Strs MusicMasters ▲ 01612-67125-2
Mozart, W.A.:Qt 14 Strs MusicMasters ▲ 01612-67125-2
Mozart, W.A.:Qt 15 Strs MusicMasters ▲ 01612-67125-2
Mozart, W.A.:Qt 20 Strs [performed on matched set of Stradivarius instrs] *(rec SUNY, Purchase, NY, Feb 21–23, 1995)* MusicMasters ▲ 01612-67160-2

48 ▲ = CD ♦ = Enhanced CD Δ = MD ■ = Cassette Tape ◻ = DCC

American String Quartet (cont.)
Mozart, W.A.:Qt 21 Strs [performed on matched set of Stradivarius instrs] *(rec SUNY, Purchase, NY, Feb 21–23, 1995)* MusicMasters ▲ 01612-67160-2
Tsontakis, G.:Qts Strs New World ▲ 80414-2 [DDD]
M. Press (cnd)
Corigliano, J.:Poem in October, w. R. White (ten), T. Nyfenger (fl), B. Lucarelli (ob), J. Rabbai (cl), Maurice Press (hpd) RCA Gold Seal ▲ 60395-2-RG [ADD]
G. Schwarz (cnd)
Schoenberg, A.:Con Str Qt, w. New York CO Elektra/Nonesuch ▲ 79145-2 [DDD]
American SO
K. Akiyama (cnd)
Colgrass, M.:Concert Masters, w. Ronald Oakland (vn), Robert Rudie (vn), Masako Yanagita (vn) *(rec 1977)* Vox Box ("The American Composers" series) 2-▲ CDX 5158
Corigliano, J.:Con Ob, w. B. Lucarelli (ob) RCA Gold Seal ▲ 60395-2-RG [ADD]
Lees, B.:Con Vn, w. Ruggiero Ricci (vn) *(rec 1976)* Vox Box ("The American Composers" series) 2-▲ CDX 5158
L. Botstein (cnd)
Schubert, Franz:Fant Pno, D.940 [arr. Mottl for orch.] Koch International Classics ▲ KIC 7307 [DDD]
Schubert, Franz:German Dances Pno, D.820 Koch International Classics ▲ KIC 7307 [DDD]
Schubert, Franz:Son Pno 4-Hands, D.812 [arr. Joachim for orch.] Koch International Classics ▲ KIC 7307 [DDD]
M. Brown (cnd)
Gershwin, G.:An American in Paris Allegretto ▲ ACD 8034 [ADD] ■ ACS 8034
Gershwin, G.:Rhap in Blue, w. K. Perkins (pno) Allegretto ▲ ACD 8034 [ADD] ■ ACS 8034
F. Fennell (cnd)
Suesse, D.:Music of, w. Cy Coleman (pno), Dana Suesse (pno), Robert Barlow (hp), All City Concert Choir—Con Romantico for Pno & Orch; A Little Light Music; Young Man with Harp for Hp & Orch; The Blues [from Con in 3 Rhythms]; Coronach for Hp & Orch; Jazz Con for Combo & Orch; The Night Is Young & You're So Beautiful for Orch & Chorus *(rec Carnegie Hall, Dec 1974)* Premier ▲ PRCD 1055
J. Horenstein (cnd)
Mahler, G.:Sym 9 *(rec Nov. 10, 1969)* Music & Arts 4-▲ CD 785 [AAD]
J. Litton (cnd)
Bernstein, L.:Chichester Psalms, w. American Boychoir [He] MusicMasters ▲ 7049-2-C
Davidson, C.:I Never Saw Another Butterfly, w. American Boychoir—[E] MusicMasters ▲ 7049-2-C
L. Stokowski (cnd)
Bartók, B.:The Miraculous Mandarin (suite) *(rec Dec. 1969)* Intaglio ▲ ING 7421 [ADD]
Brahms, J.:Con 1 Pno, w. *(soloist unknown)* *(rec 1969)* Music & Arts ▲ CD 844 [AAD]
Canteloube, J.:Songs of Auvergne (sels), w. A. Moffo (sop)—7 songs RCA Gold Seal ▲ 7831-2-RG [ADD] ■ 7831-4-RG (CrO2)
Ives, C.:Robert Browning Ov *(rec 1966)* Sony Masterworks ("Portrait" series) ▲ MPK 46726 [ADD]
Ives, C.:Songs, w. Gregg Smith Singers, Ithaca College Concert Choir—Election (It Strikes Me That); Lincoln, the Great Commoner; Majority (or The Masses); They are there! (A War Song March) [E] *(rec 1967)* Sony Masterworks ("Portrait" series) ▲ MPK 46726 [ADD]
Ives, C.:Sym 4, w. New York Schola Cantorum *(rec 1965)* Sony Masterworks ("Portrait" series) ▲ MPK 46726 [ADD]
Josten, W.:Con sacro I–II, w. D. del Tredici (pno) CRI ▲ CD 597 [ADD]
Josten, W.:Jungle CRI ▲ CD 597 [ADD]
Rachmaninoff, S.:Vocalise, w. Anna Moffo (sop) RCA Gold Seal ▲ 7831-2-RG [ADD] ■ 7831-4-RG (CrO2)
Scriabin, A.:Etude Pno, Op. 2/1 [arr. for orchestra by Stokowski] *(rec 4/71)* Vanguard Classics ▲ OVC 8012 [ADD]
Tchaikovsky, P.:Sym 4 *(rec 4/71)* Vanguard Classics ▲ OVC 8012 [ADD]
Tchaikovsky, P.:Sym 5 Music & Arts 2-▲ MUA CD 944
Villa-Lobos, H.:Bachiana brasileira 5, w. A. Moffo (sop) RCA Victor ▲ 09026-61724-2 ■ 09026-61724-4 (CrO2)
Villa-Lobos, H.:Bachiana brasileira 5, w. Anna Moffo (sop) RCA Gold Seal ▲ 7831-2-RG [ADD] ■ 7831-4-RG (CrO2)
American SO members
Josten, W.:Canzona Seria CRI ▲ CD 597 [ADD]
American SO Winds
L. Stokowski (cnd)
Mozart, W.A.:Serenade Ww, K.361 Vanguard Classics ▲ OVC 8009 [ADD]
American Theater Orch
P. Gemignani (cnd)
Golden Days, w. Jerry Hadley (ten), Tony Randall (sgr), Mario Lanza (ten), Harvard Glee Club RCA Victor ▲ 09026-62681-2 ■ 09026-62681-2
In the Real World, w. Jerry Hadley (ten) RCA Victor ▲ 09026-61937-2
Standing Room Only:Broadway Favorites, w. Jerry Hadley (ten) RCA Victor ▲ 09026-61370-2 [ADD] ■ 09026-61370-4 (CrO2) □ 09026-61370-5
American Youth SO
M. Mehta (cnd)
Strauss, R.:Der Rosenkavalier (suite) Protone ▲ PRCD 1109 [ADD] ■ CSPR 159
Wagner, R.:Tristan und Isolde (sels) [arr. Stokowski] Protone ▲ PRCD 1109 [ADD] ■ CSPR 159
L. Stokowski (cnd)
Kodály, Z.:Te Deum, w. American Youth Chorus *(rec 1968)* Music & Arts ▲ CD 771 [AAD]
Americus Brass Band
Music of the Civil War Summit ▲ DCD 126 [DDD]
Amernet String Quartet
Premiere Chamber Works, w. Lambert Bloom, Sara (ob), various soloists Centaur ▲ CRC 2217 [DDD]
Sowerby, L.:Serenade Gasparo ▲ GSCD 315 [DDD]
Ames Piano Quartet [W. David (pno), M. Darlington (vn), L. Burkhalter (va), G. Work (vc)]
Brahms, J.:Qt 1 Pno *(rec Oct. 1993)* Dorian ▲ DOR 90194 [DDD]
Dvořák, A.:Qts Pno Strs, Opp. 23 & 87 Dorian ▲ DOR 90125 [DDD]
Fauré, G.:Qt 1 Pno Dorian ▲ DOR 90144 [DDD]
Fauré, G.:Qt 2 Pno Dorian ▲ DOR 90144 [DDD]
Schumann, R.:Qt Pno, Op. 47 *(rec Oct. 1993)* Dorian ▲ DOR 90194 [DDD]
Amherst Saxophone Quartet
Bach, J.S.:Music of—Solo Organ Concerto No. 1, BWV 592; Fantasia & Fugue in c, BWV 537; Fugue in G, BWV 577; Overture in g, BWV 1070; plus selections from Art of the Fugue, BWV 1080 (Nos. 1,3,5 & 9) & Orchestral Suites No. 1 in C, BWV 1066 (Nos. 2-7) & No. 2 in b, BWV 1067 (Badenerie) MCA Classics ▲ MCAD 6264 [DDD]
Foss, L.:Qt Saxes MCA Classics ▲ MCAD 10055
Mozart to Modern MCA Classics ▲ MCAD 10055 [DDD]
Amici Chamber Ensemble
Beethoven, L. van:Trio 7 Pno Summit ▲ SMT 151 [DDD]
Chan Ka Nin:Among Friends Summit ▲ SMT 151 [DDD]
Zemlinsky, A. von:Trio Cl Summit ▲ SMT 151 [DDD]
Amici Quartet [Joaquin Valdenpeñas (cl), Shmuel Ashkenasi (vn), David Hetherington (vc), Patricia Parr (pno)]
Chan Ka Nin:I Think That I Shall Never See... *(rec Humbercrest United Church, Toronto, Ontario)* Summit ▲ SMT 168 [DDD]
Messiaen, O.:Quatuor pour la fin du temps *(rec Humbercrest United Church, Toronto, Ontario)* Summit ▲ SMT 168 [DDD]
Amici String Quartet
Herrmann, B.:Qnt Cl, w. Robert Hill (cl) Unicorn-Kanchana ▲ UKCD 2069
Les Amis de Philippe
Bach, C.P.E.:Cons Hpd & Strs, w. Ludger Remy (hpd)—W.30, 37 & 38 CPO ▲ CPO 999350

Les Amis de Philippe (cont.)
L. Rémy (cnd)
Bach, C.P.E.:Sinfs Orch—H. 648, 649, 650, 653, 655 *(rec Nov 1995 & Jun 1996)* CPO ▲ 999418-2 [DDD]
AML Lucerne SO
O. Henzold (cnd)
Brun, F.:Sym 2 Gallo ▲ CD 838
Lauber, J.:Con Db, w. K. Thalmann (db) Gallo ▲ CD 838
Wagner, R.:Siegfried Idyll Gallo ▲ CD 838
Amor Artis Orch
J. Somary (cnd)
Bach, J.S.:Con Vn & Ob, w. Y. Waldman (vn), V. Brewer (ob) Omega ▲ OCD 1013 [DDD]
Corelli, A.:Con grosso, Op. 6/8, "Christmas Con" Omega ▲ OCD 1013 [DDD]
Handel, G.F.:Acis & Galatea, w. J. Baird (sop), L. Hirst (mez), S. Oosting (ten), J. Ostendorf (b-bar), Amor Artis Chorale [E] Newport Classic 2-▲ NC 60045 [DDD]
Mozart, W.A.:Requiem, w. Lorna Haywood (sop), D'Anna Fortunado (mez), Partick Romero (ten), John Cheek (bass), Amor Artis Chorale [period instrs] *(rec St. Jean Baptiste Church, New York City, Mar 1996)* Vox Classics ▲ VOX 7534 [DDD]
Saint-Saëns, C.:Requiem, w. Hewes (sgr), Weld (sgr), MacMaster (sgr), Watson (sgr), Amor Artis Chorale *(rec live)* Premier ▲ PRCD 1025 [DDD]
Vivaldi, A.:Cons Vn, Op. 8/1–4, "The Four Seasons", w. Y. Waldman (vn) Omega ▲ OCD 1013 [DDD]
D'Amore Duo [Vladimir Lande (ob), William Feasley (gtr)]
Cimarosa, D.:Con in C Ob Sonora ▲ SO 22573 [DDD]
Copper, L.:Le Montegnard Sonora ▲ SO 22573 [DDD]
Couperin, F.:Music of—Les Baricades Misterieuses; La Letiville; Les Tours de Passe-Passe; La Juliet Sonora ▲ SO 22573 [DDD]
Ibert, J.:Entracte Sonora ▲ SO 22573 [DDD]
Moriarty, M.:Simplicity Sonora ▲ SO 22573 [DDD]
Pilss, K.:Sonatine Ob Sonora ▲ SO 22573 [DDD]
David Amram Quartet
Rota, N.:Film Music Hannibal ▲ HNCD 9301
Amsterdam Bach Soloists
Bach, J.S.:Cons Vn (comp), w. Thomas Zehetmair (vn) Berlin Classics ▲ BER 1114 [DDD]
Bach, J.S.:Con Vn, BWV 1052, w. Thomas Zehetmair (vn) Berlin Classics ▲ BER 1114 [DDD]
Bach, J.S.:Con Vn, BWV 1058, w. Thomas Zehetmair (vn) Berlin Classics ▲ BER 1114 [DDD]
R. Kussmaul (cnd)
Haydn, J.:Con Org, Vn & Strs, H.XVIII/6, w. Robert Hill (hpd) Olympia ▲ OLY 428 [DDD]
Haydn, J.:Con 1 Vn, w. Ranier Kussmaul (vn) Olympia ▲ OLY 428 [DDD]
Haydn, J.:Con 3 Vn, w. Ranier Kussmaul (vn) Olympia ▲ OLY 428 [DDD]
Haydn, J.:Con 4 Vn, w. Ranier Kussmaul (vn) Olympia ▲ OLY 428 [DDD]
Amsterdam Baroque Orch
T. Koopman (cnd)
Bach, J.S.:St. John Passion, w. B. Schlick (sop), K. Wessel (alto), G. de Mey (ten), G. Turk (ten), K. Mertens (b-bar), P. Kooy (bass), Netherlands Bach Society Choir Erato 2-▲ 94675-2
Bach, J.S.:St. Matthew Passion, w. B. Schlick (sop), K. Wessel (alto), G. de Mey (ten), C. Pregardien (ten), P. Kooy (bass), W. Cantryn (cnd), J. van Veldhoven (cnd), Breda Sacred Choir, Netherlands Bach Society Boys' Choir Erato 2-▲ 2292-45814-2
Bach, J.S.:St. Matthew Passion, w. B. Schlick (sop), K. Wessel (alto), G. de Mey (ten), P. Kooy (bass) Erato 2-▲ 94676-2
Biber, H. von:Requiem à 15, w. E. Bongers (sop), A. Grimm (sop), K. Wessel (alt), P. de Groot (alt), M. Reyans (ten), S. Davies (ten), R. Steur (bass), K.-J. de Koning (bass), Amsterdam Baroque Choir Erato ▲ 91725
Biber, H. von:Vesperae longiores ac breviores una cum litaniis Laurentanis, w. E. Bongers (sop), A. Grimm (sop), K. Wessel (alt), P. de Groot (alt), M. Reyans (ten), S. Davies (ten), R. Steur (bass), K.-J. de Koning (bass), Amsterdam Baroque Choir Erato ▲ 91725
Charpentier, M.-A.:Motets for Double Choir, w. B. Schlick (sop), N. Zijlstra (sop), K. Wessel (alt), D. Visse (ct), H. van Berne (ten), C. Prégardien (ten), P. Kooy (bass), K. Martens (bass)—Canticum pro pace; Josué; Mors Saulis et Jonathae; Praelium Michaelis; Quam dilecta; 3 Leçons de Ténèbres Erato (Musifrance) ▲ 2292-45822-2 ZA
Handel, G.F.:Messiah, w. Marjanne Kweksilber (sop), James Bowman (ct), Paul Elliot (ten), G. Reinhart (bar), The Sixteen Erato 3-▲ 2292-45960-2
Handel, G.F.:La Rezurrezione, w. Nancy Argenta (sop), Barbara Schlick (sop), Guillemette Laurens (mez), Guy de Mey (ten), Klaus Mertens (bar) [I] Erato 2-▲ 2292-45617-2 [DDD]
Handel, G.F.:Water Music (comp) Erato ▲ 91716-2
Haydn, J.:Sym 83, "The Hen" Erato ▲ 2292-45807-2 ZK
Haydn, J.:Sym 84, "In Nomine Domini" Erato ▲ 2292-45807-2 ZK
Haydn, J.:Sym 85, "La Reine de France" Erato ▲ 2292-45807-2 ZK
Mozart, W.A.:Con Bn, w. *(soloist unknown)* Erato ▲ 91724-2
Mozart, W.A.:Con Fl Hp, w. *(soloists unknown)* Erato ▲ 91724-2
Mozart, W.A.:Con Ob, K.314, w. *(soloist unknown)* Erato ▲ 91724-2
Mozart, W.A.:Divert Hns Bn, K.205 Erato ▲ 2292-45713-2 [DDD]
Mozart, W.A.:Divert Ob, K.251 [period instrs] Erato ▲ 2292-45471-2 [DDD]
Mozart, W.A.:Diverts Str Qt, K.136–138 [period instrs] Erato ▲ 2292-45471-2 [DDD]
Mozart, W.A.:Kleine Nachtmusik Erato ▲ 2292-45713-2 [DDD]
Mozart, W.A.:March Hns, K.290 Erato ▲ 2292-45713-2 [DDD]
Mozart, W.A.:March Orch, K.249 Erato ▲ 45436-2
Mozart, W.A.:Requiem, w. B. Schlick (sop), C. Watkinson (cta), C. Prégardien (ten), H. van der Kamp (bass), Netherlands Bach Society Choir [L] Erato ▲ 2292-45472-2 [DDD] ■ 2292-45472-4
Mozart, W.A.:Serenade Vn, K.250 Erato ▲ 45436-2
Mozart, W.A.:Serenata notturna Erato ▲ 2292-45713-2 [DDD]
Mozart, W.A.:Sym 17 Erato ▲ 2292-45714-2
Mozart, W.A.:Sym 18 Erato ▲ 2292-45714-2
Mozart, W.A.:Sym 19 Erato ▲ 2292-45714-2
Mozart, W.A.:Sym 21 Erato ▲ 2292-45544-2 [DDD]
Mozart, W.A.:Sym 22 Erato ▲ 2292-45714-2
Mozart, W.A.:Sym 23 Erato ▲ 2292-45544-2 [DDD]
Mozart, W.A.:Sym 24 Erato ▲ 2292-45544-2 [DDD]
Mozart, W.A.:Sym 25 Erato ▲ 2292-45431-2
Mozart, W.A.:Sym 27 Erato ▲ 2292-45544-2 [DDD]
Mozart, W.A.:Sym 29 Erato ▲ 2292-45431-2
Mozart, W.A.:Sym 31 Erato 2-▲ 2292-45857-2
Mozart, W.A.:Sym 32 Erato ▲ 2292-45714-2
Mozart, W.A.:Sym 33 Erato ▲ 2292-45431-2
Mozart, W.A.:Sym 34 Erato 2-▲ 2292-45857-2
Mozart, W.A.:Sym 35 Erato 2-▲ 2292-45857-2
Mozart, W.A.:Sym 36 Erato 2-▲ 2292-45857-2
Mozart, W.A.:Sym 38 Erato 2-▲ 2292-45857-2
Mozart, W.A.:Sym 41 Erato 2-▲ 2292-45857-2
Mozart, W.A.:Sym (43), K.76 Erato ▲ 2292-45713-2
Purcell, H.:The Fairy Queen, w. C. Bott (sop), J. Thomas (ten), M. Schopper (bass), Amsterdam Baroque Choir Erato 2-▲ 98507-2
Amsterdam Baroque Soloists
Telemann, G.P.:Qt in G for Rcr, Ob, Vn & Cont Erato ▲ 94355-2
Telemann, G.P.:Sons Ob—Son. in C; Son. in f Erato ▲ 94355-2
Amsterdam CO
A. Rieu (cnd)
Handel, G.F.:Cons (16) Org, w. A. De Klerk (org)—No. 13 Sony Classical ("Essential Classics" series) ▲ SBK 47660; ■ SBT 47660

ORCH. & ENS.

Amsterdam CO (cont.)
A. Rieu (cnd) (cont.)
Haydn, J.:Con Org, Obs & Strs, H.XVIII/1, w. Albert De Klerk (org) Sony Classical ("Essential Classics" series) ▲ SBK 47660 ■ SBT 47660
Haydn, J.:Con Org, Vns & Bass Instrument, H.XVIII/5, w. Albert De Klerk (org) Sony Classical ("Essential Classics" series) ▲ SBK 47660 ■ SBT 47660
Haydn, J.:Con Org, Vns & Bass Instrument, H.XVIII/8, w. Albert De Klerk (org) Sony Classical ("Essential Classics" series) ▲ SBK 47660 ■ SBT 47660
Telemann, G.P.:Con Rcr, Fl, w. F. Brüggen (rcr), F. Vester (fl) Teldec ▲ 77620-2 [ADD]
Telemann, G.P.:Ouverture des Nations:anciens et mordernes Teldec ▲ 77620-2 [ADD]
C. de Wolff (cnd)
Bach, J.S.:St. John Passion, w. Holland Bach Choir—Eingangschor Vivace ▲ G 536
Handel, G.F.:Israel in Egypt, w. Holland Bach Choir—choruses Vivace ▲ G 536
Handel, G.F.:Judas Maccabaeus (sels), w. Holland Bach Choir—choruses Vivace G 536
Handel, G.F.:Messiah (sels), w. Holland Bach Choir—Choruses Vivace ▲ G 536
Amsterdam Guitar Trio
Bach, J.S.:Brandenburg Cons—Nos. 2,3,5 & 6, arranged for 3 guitars RCA Red Seal ▲ 6546-2-RC [DDD] ■ 6546-4-RC
Chopin, F.:Rondo for 2 Pnos [performers' transcription] RCA Red Seal ▲ 7800-2-RC [DDD]
Debussy, C.:Petite suite [performers' trans.] RCA Red Seal ▲ 7800-2-RC [DDD]
Debussy, C.:Suite bergamasque [performers' trans.] RCA Red Seal ▲ 7800-2-RC [DDD]
Scarlatti, D.:Sons Kbd—K.087, 098, 159, 206, 208, 299, 432, 443 [all arr. for 2 guitars]; K.030, 052, 096, 113, 135, 343, 417, 466 [all arr. for 3 guitars] *(rec Utrecht, June 6 & 7, 1993)* Emergo ▲ EC 3959 [DDD]
Vivaldi, A.:Cons Vn, Op. 8/1–4, "The Four Seasons" RCA Gold Seal ▲ 09026-61652-2
Amsterdam Loeki Stardust Quartet [Daniel Brüggen (rcr), Bertho Driever (rcr), Paul Leenhouts (rcr), Karel van Steenhoven (rcr)]
Boeke, K.:Lacrime, w. Kees Boecke (rcr) *(rec 1/91)* Channel Classics ▲ CCS 2891 [DDD]
Consort Songs, w. Connor Burrowes (trb), David Miller (lt/gtr) Channel Classics ▲ CCS 9196
Holborne, A.:Instrumental Consort Music, w. Kees Boecke (va da gamba)—Amoretta; Bona Speranza; Ecce quam bonum; The Funerals; Galliard; Image of Melancolly; Infernum; Muy Linda; Nec invideo; Paradizo; Pavana Ploravit; Sic semper soleo; The Sighes; Teares of the Muses *(rec 1/91)* Channel Classics ▲ CCS 2891 [DDD]
Italian Recorder Music L'Oiseau-Lyre ▲ 430246-2 OH [DDD]
Kemp, B.D.:Lieto Channel Classics ▲ CCS 8996
Keuris, T.:Passeggiate Channel Classics ▲ CCS 8996
Koomans, D.:The Jogger Channel Classics ▲ CCS 8996
Meijering, Chiel:Een Paard Met Vijf Poten Channel Classics ▲ CCS 8996
Meijering, Chiel:Sitting Ducks Channel Classics ▲ CCS 8996
Steenhoven, K. van:La chanteuse et le bois sauvage Channel Classics ▲ CCS 8996
Wagemans, P.J.:Kwartet Channel Classics ▲ CCS 8996
C. Hogwood (cnd)
Heinichen, J.D.:Con à 8, w. Academy of Ancient Music *(rec June 1992)* L'Oiseau-Lyre ▲ 436905-2 [DDD]
Marcello, B.:Con Rcrs, w. Academy of Ancient Music—in G *(rec June 1992)* L'Oiseau-Lyre ▲ 436905-2 [DDD]
Schickhardt, J.C.:Cons for 4 Rcrs, w. Academy of Ancient Music *(rec June 1992)* L'Oiseau-Lyre ▲ 436905-2 [DDD]
Telemann, G.P.:Con in a for 2 Rcrs *(rec June 1992)* L'Oiseau-Lyre ▲ 436905-2 [DDD]
Telemann, G.P.:Con in B♭ for 2 Rcrs *(rec June 1992)* L'Oiseau-Lyre ▲ 436905-2 [DDD]
Vivaldi, A.:Cons Rcr, w. Academy of Ancient Music—in A, RV.585, "in due cori" *(rec June 1992)* L'Oiseau-Lyre ▲ 436905-2 [DDD]
Amsterdam Mozart Players
Mozart, W.A.:Concertone Vns, w. V. Beths (vn), R. Kussmaul (vn) *(rec Mar. 1991)* Channel Classics ▲ CCS 3992 [DDD]
Mozart, W.A.:Sinf concertante Vn, K.364, w. R. Kussmaul (vn), J. Kussmaul (va) *(rec Mar. 1991)* Channel Classics ▲ CCS 3992 [DDD]
J. Kussmaul (cnd)
Mozart, W.A.:Cons Hn, w. J. Slagter (hn)—No. 1 [Allegro]; Nos. 2–4 Canal Grande ▲ CG 9211 [DDD]
Mozart, W.A.:Con 10 Pnos, w. M. Leonhard (pno), S. Grotenhuis (pno) *(rec Aug. 1990)* Channel Classics ▲ CCS 1190 [DDD]
Mozart, W.A.:Con Vn Pno, w. M. Leonhard (pno), R. Kussmaul (vn) *(rec Aug. 1990)* Channel Classics ▲ CCS 1190 [DDD]
Mozart, W.A.:Rondo Hn, K.514 (compl'd Süssmayer), w. J. Slagter (hn) Canal Grande ▲ CG 9211 [DDD]
Mozart, W.A.:Sym 29 *(rec Aug. 1990)* Channel Classics ▲ CCS 1190 [DDD]
Amsterdam New Sinfonietta
R. Dufallo (cnd)
Gershwin, G.:Porgy & Bess (sels)—Suite [arr anon for Str Orch & Jazz Sxt] Channel Crossings ▲ CCS 8395
L. Markiz (cnd)
Arensky, A.:Vars on a Theme of Tchaikovsky *(rec Oct & Dec 1990)* Globe ▲ GLO 6021 [DDD]
Beethoven, L. van:Qt 11 Strs, "Quartetto serioso" [orchd. Mahler] *(rec Waalse Kerk, Amsterdam, June 28–29, 1994)* BIS ▲ CD 674 [DDD]
Denisov, E.:Chamber Music Va, w. N. Imai (va), A. de Man (hpd) *(rec 6/91)* BIS ▲ CD 518 [DDD]
Denisov, E.:Con for 2 Vas, w. N. Imai (va), P. Vahle (va), A. de Man (hpd) *(rec 6/91)* BIS ▲ CD 518 [DDD]
Denisov, E.:Epitaph *(rec 6/91)* BIS ▲ CD 518 [DDD]
Denisov, E.:Vars on Bach's Chorale "Es ist genug" *(rec 6/91)* BIS ▲ CD 518 [DDD]
Hamburg, J.:Zey, w. Judith Mok (sop) NM Classics ▲ NM 92041
Janssen, G.:Zoek, w. Eleonore Pameijer (fl), Guuse Janssen (hpd) NM Classics ▲ NM 92041
Jeths, W.:Glenz, w. Peter Brunt (vn) NM Classics ▲ NM 92041
Mendelssohn, F.:Capriccio brillante, w. Ronald Brautigam (pno) *(rec Concertgebouw, Haarlem, Holland, May 18–20, 1995)* BIS ▲ CD 713 [DDD]
Mendelssohn, F.:Con in a Pno, Op. posth., w. Ronald Brautigam (pno) *(rec Concertgebouw, Haarlem, Holland, May 20–21, 1995)* BIS ▲ CD 718 [DDD]
Mendelssohn, F.:Con 1 Pno, w. Ronald Brautigam (pno) *(rec Concertgebouw, Haarlem, Holland, Aug 4, 1994)* BIS ▲ CD 718 [DDD]
Mendelssohn, F.:Con 2 Pno, w. Ronald Brautigam (pno) *(rec Concertgebouw, Haarlem, Holland, Aug 5, 1994)* BIS ▲ CD 718 [DDD]
Mendelssohn, F.:Cons (2) for 2 Pnos, w. Love Derwinger (pno), Roland Pöntinen (pno) *(rec Concertgebouw, Haarlem, Holland, Sept 20–22, 1994)* BIS ▲ CD 688 [DDD]
Mendelssohn, F.:Con in d Vn, Pno & Strs, w. Isabelle Van Keulen (vn), Ronald Brautigam (pno) *(rec Concertgebouw, Haarlem, Holland, July 4–5, 1995)* BIS ▲ CD 713 [DDD]
Mendelssohn, F.:Rondo brilliant, w. Ronald Brautigam (pno) *(rec Concertgebouw, Haarlem, Holland, May 18–20, 1995)* BIS ▲ CD 713 [DDD]
Mendelssohn, F.:Serenade & Allegro giocoso, w. Ronald Brautigam (pno) *(rec Concertgebouw, Haarlem, Holland, May 18–20, 1995)* BIS ▲ CD 713 [DDD]
Mendelssohn, F.:Sinfs Strs—Nos. 8 & 11 *(rec Concertgebouw, Haarlem, Holland, July 8–9 & Oct 4–5, 1995)* BIS ▲ CD 748 [DDD]
Mendelssohn, F.:Sinf 2 *(rec Aug. 13, 15 & 16, 1993)* BIS ▲ CD 643 [DDD]
Mendelssohn, F.:Sinf 3 *(rec Aug. 13, 15 & 16, 1993)* BIS ▲ CD 643 [DDD]
Mendelssohn, F.:Sinf 9 *(rec Aug. 13, 15 & 16, 1993)* BIS ▲ CD 643 [DDD]
Mendelssohn, F.:Sinf 10 *(rec Aug. 13, 15 & 16, 1993)* BIS ▲ CD 643 [DDD]
Schubert, Franz:Qt 14 Strs [orchd. Mahler] *(rec Waalse Kerk, Amsterdam, Apr. 19–20, 1994)* BIS ▲ CD 674 [DDD]
Shostakovich, D.:Chamber Sym, Op. 83a *(rec Oct & Dec. 1992)* Globe ▲ GLO 5093 [DDD]
Shostakovich, D.:Son Va, w. V. Mendelssohn (va) [arr. V. Mendelssohn for orch.] *(rec Oct & Dec. 1992)* Globe ▲ GLO 5093 [DDD]

Amsterdam New Sinfonietta (cont.)
L. Markiz (cnd) (cont.)
Tchaikovsky, P.:Andante cantabile, w. D. Ferschtman (vc) *(rec Oct. & Dec. 1990)* Globe ▲ GLO 6021 [DDD]
Tchaikovsky, P.:Elegy *(rec Oct. & Dec. 1990)* Globe ▲ GLO 6021 [DDD]
Tchaikovsky, P.:Nocturne Vc, w. P. Brunt (vn) *(rec Oct. & Dec. 1990)* Globe ▲ GLO 6021 [DDD]
Tchaikovsky, P.:Serenade Strs *(rec Oct./Dec. 1990)* Globe ▲ GLO 6021 [DDD]
E. Spanjaard (cnd)
Debussy, C.:Danses sacrée et profane, w. Ernestine Stoop (hp) *(rec Amsterdam & Utrecht)* Globe ▲ GLO 5144 [DDD]
Amsterdam Octet
Druschetzky, G.:Vars Wind Instrs Erasmus ▲ WVH 089
Hummel, J.N.:Parthia Erasmus ▲ WVH 089
Krommer, F.:Harmonie-Musik Erasmus ▲ WVH 089
Mysliveček, J.:Octets Ww—1 octet in E♭ Erasmus ▲ WVH 089
Amsterdam PO
A. Joó (cnd)
Brahms, J.:Con Vn & Vc, "Double Con", w. E. Verhey (vn), J. Starker (vc) Erasmus ▲ WVH 034 [DDD]
Brahms, J.:Tragic Ov Erasmus ▲ WVH 034 [DDD]
Dvořák, A.:Sym 9, "From the New World" *(rec Concertgebouw, Amsterdam, June 1985)* Arts ▲ 47242-2 [DDD]
Mahler, G.:Sym 1 *(rec Amsterdam, The Netherlands, July 1983)* Arts Music ▲ 47239-2 [DDD]
G. Rivoli (cnd)
Beethoven, L. van:Fant Pno, Op. 80, "Choral Fant", w. Lili Kraus (pno), Amsterdam Phil Chorus FNAC Music ("Via Classics" series) ▲ 642316
Amsterdam Piano Quartet
Debussy, C.:Jeux [transcribed for 4 Pianos by Maarten Bon] *(rec 1/92)* Channel Classics ▲ CCS 4992 [DDD]
Stravinsky, I.:Le Sacre du printemps Pno Channel Classics ▲ CCS 4992 [DDD]
Amsterdam Quartet [F. Brüggen (fl), J. Schröder (vn), A. Bylsma (vc), G. Leonhardt (hpd)]
Couperin, F.:Les Nations Teldec (Das alte Werke) 2-▲ 93689
Amsterdam Radio PO
J. Fournet (cnd)
Berlioz, H.:La Damnation de Faust, w. Régine Crespin (sop—Marguerite), Guy Fouché (ten—Faust), Michel Roux (bar—Méphistophélès), Peter van der Bilt (bass—Brander), Groot Omroepkoor *(rec Amsterdam, Mar 23, 1963)* Bella Voce 2-▲ BLV 107.202 [AAD]
Amsterdam Wind Orch
H. Friesen (cnd)
Bernstein, L.:Candide (sels)—Suite:The Best of All Possible Worlds; Westphalia Chorale and Battle Scene; Auto-da-fé; Glitter and Be Gay; Make Our Garden Grow *(rec Morgensterkerk, Wormerveer, the Netherlands, Feb 1994)* World Wind ▲ WWM 500.300
Bernstein, L.:On the Town—Lonely Town (Pas de deux) *(rec Morgensterkerk, Wormerveer, the Netherlands, Feb 1994)* World Wind ▲ WWM 500.300
Meij, J. de:Sym 2 *(rec Morgensterkerk, Wormerveer, the Netherlands, Feb 1994)* World Wind ▲ WWM 500.300
Anatolian String Quartet
Erkin, U.C.:Qt Strs Hungaroton ▲ HCD 31521 [ADD]
Saygun, A.A.:Qt 1 Strs Hungaroton ▲ HCD 31521 [ADD]
Ancient Instrument Ensemble Zurich
Renaissance Dances Odyssey ■ YT 60036
Ancient Instrumental Ensemble
Spanish Renaissance Music from the Old & New World, w. Ancient Consort Singers, Ancient Instrumental Ensemble *(rec 1980)* Entrée ▲ 0007-2 [ADD]
Ancient Music Group
E. Paniagua (cnd)
Alfonso El Sabio:Cantigas de Santa Maria, w. Valle de los Caídos Monastery School Children's Choir—Star of the Day; Prologue to the 5 Feasts; Dawn of All Dawns; Nativity of Holy Mary; Virginity; Trinity of Holy Mary; Mother of Jesus Christ; Mother of God; Old Woman & Child; Humanity of Holy Mary; Flower of All Flowers; Annunciation; Ave Maria; The Angels' Greeting; Purification-Candlemas; 7 Gifts; Nun & Gentleman; Assumption; Procession; Day of Judgment; Sybil-Judgement Sony Classical 2-▲ S2K 62284
Andorra National CO
G. Claret (cnd)
Casals, P.:Sant Martí del Canigo Nimbus ▲ NI 5482 [DDD]
Montsalvatge, X.:Concertino 1 + 13, w. Gerard Claret (vn) Nimbus ▲ NI 5482 [DDD]
Montsalvatge, X.:Postals illuminades Nimbus ▲ NI 5482 [DDD]
Toldrá, E.:Qt Strs [arr G. Claret for CO] Nimbus ▲ NI 5482 [DDD]
Toldrá, E.:Vistes al mar Nimbus ▲ NI 5482 [DDD]
Angeles String Quartet
The Cinema Classics Collection, Vol. 1, w. David Buechner (pno), London SO, New Zealand SO, Phoenix SO Koch International Classics ▲ KIC 7604
Korngold, E.W.:Qt 3 Strs Koch International Classics ▲ KIC 7325 [DDD]
Kreisler, F.:Qt Strs Koch International Classics ▲ KIC 7325 [DDD]
Angelicum CO
C. F. Cillario (cnd)
Leo, L.:La Morte di Abele, w. Emilia Cundari (sop—Angelo), Giuliana Matteini (sop—Abele), Adriana Lazzarini (mez—Eva), Ferrando Ferrari (ten—Caino), Paolo Montarsolo (bass—Adamo), Turin Polyphonic Chorus Dynamic 2-▲ CDL 144
P. Urbini (cnd)
Mendelssohn, F.:Con in d Vn, Pno & Strs, w. F. Gulli (vn), E. Cavallo (pno) Koch Treasure ▲ 31622-2 [ADD]
Armand Angster Clarinet System
Radulescu, H.:Inner Time II Montaigne ▲ MO 782030
Anima Eterna Orch
Mozart, W.A.:Cons Pno, w. J. van Immerseel (pno) Channel Classics 10-▲ CCS 0010 [DDD]
Mozart, W.A.:Cons Pno, w. J. van Immerseel (pno)—Nos. 22 & 23 *(rec Feb. 1991)* Channel Classics ▲ CCS 2491 [DDD]
Mozart, W.A.:Cons Pno, w. J. van Immerseel (pno)—Nos. 11, 13 & 14 *(rec July 1990)* Channel Classics ▲ CCS 0990 [DDD]
Mozart, W.A.:Cons Pno, w. J. van Immerseel (pno)—Nos. 18 & 19 *(rec Oct. 1990)* Channel Classics ▲ CCS 1991 [DDD]
Mozart, W.A.:Cons Pno, w. J. van Immerseel (pno)—Nos. 5 & 9 *(rec Mar. 1990)* Channel Classics ▲ CCS 0590 [DDD]
Mozart, W.A.:Cons Pno, w. J. van Immerseel (pno)—Nos. 15 & 16 *(rec Sept.–Oct. 1990)* Channel Classics ▲ CCS 1791 [DDD]
Mozart, W.A.:Cons Pno, w. J. van Immerseel (pno)—Nos. 8 & 12 *(rec Mar. 1990)* Channel Classics ▲ CCS 0690 [DDD]
Mozart, W.A.:Cons Pno, w. J. van Immerseel (pno)—Nos. 20 & 21 *(rec Oct. 1990 & Feb. 1991)* Channel Classics ▲ CCS 2391 [DDD]
Mozart, W.A.:Cons Pno, w. J. van Immerseel (pno)—Nos. 26 & 27 *(rec Mar. 1991)* Channel Classics ▲ CCS 2691 [DDD]
Mozart, W.A.:Cons Pno, w. J. van Immerseel (pno)—Nos. 24 & 25 *(rec Feb. 1991)* Channel Classics ▲ CCS 2591 [DDD]
Mozart, W.A.:Cons Pno, w. J. van Immerseel (pno)—Nos. 6 & 17 *(rec Sept.–Oct. 1990)* Channel Classics ▲ CCS 1891 [DDD]
Mozart, W.A.:Rondo Pno Orch, K.382, w. J. van Immerseel (pno) *(rec Mar. 1990)* Channel Classics ▲ CCS 0690 [DDD]

▲ = CD ♦ = Enhanced CD Δ = MD ■ = Cassette Tape □ = DCC

Anima Eterna Orch (cont.)
J. van Immerseel (cnd)
Mendelssohn, F.:Die Hochzeit des Camacho, w. R. Hofman (sop—Quiteria), A. Ulbrich (mez—Lucinda), S. Weir (ten—Basilio), H. Rhys-Evans (ten—Vivaldo), N. van der Meel (ten—Camacho), W. Wild (bar—Carrasco), U. Malmberg (bass—Sancho Panza), U. Cold (bass—Don Quixote), Aachen Boys Choir, Chor Modus Novus [G] *(rec Sept. 19–22, 1992)* Channel Classics 2-▲ CCS 5593 [DDD]
Mendelssohn, F.:Sym 4 Channel Classics ▲ CCS 6694 [DDD]
Mendelssohn, F.:Sym 5 Channel Classics ▲ CCS 6694 [DDD]
Schubert, Franz:Ovs—Die Zauberharfe Channel Classics ▲ CCS 4292 [DDD]
Schubert, Franz:Rosamunde (sels)—Ballet Music; Entr'acte Channel Classics ▲ CCS 4292 [DDD]
Annapolis Brass Quintet
Brass Bonanza, w. Berlin Brass Quintet, Dallas Brass Quintet, Metropolitan Brass Quintet, New York Brass Quintet, 1-5 Brass Quintet, St. Louis Brass Quintet Crystal ▲ CD 200 [ADD/DDD]
Christmas with Byrd & Brass, w. Charlie Byrd Trio Antigua ▲ DG 91-6
J. Stephens (cnd)
Moss, L.:Syms Brass, American Camerata AmCam ▲ ACR 10305CD
Anonymus Ensemble
Rue des jugleors:Instrumental & Vocal Music from the 12th to 14th Centuries *(rec Église Saint-Dominique, Quebec, Nov 1993)* Analekta ("Fleur de Lys" series) ▲ FL 2 3056 [DDD]
C. Bernatchez (cnd)
Llibre Vermell:La Route des pèlerins de Montserrat *(rec Nov. 1993)* Analekta ▲ AN 28001
P. Szegö (cnd)
Dubrovay, L.:Con for 11 Strs *(rec Academy of Music G. Dima in Cluj)* Hungaroton ("Classic" series) ▲ HCD 31572 [DDD]
Szegö, P.:Contrasts *(rec Academy of Music G. Dima in Cluj)* Hungaroton ("Classic" series) ▲ HCD 31572 [DDD]
Taranu, C.:Prolegomenes II *(rec Academy of Music G. Dima in Cluj)* Hungaroton ("Classic" series) ▲ HCD 31572 [DDD]
Antics Escolans Orch
I. Segarra (cnd)
Viola, A.:Choral Music, w. Montserrat Escolania—Missa "Alma Redemptoris Mater"; Beatus vir (Psalm 111); Laetatus sum (Psalm 121); Magnificat a 7 voces [L] Koch Schwann ▲ 3-1246-2 [DDD]
Antifonale Chamber Ensemble [Anders Hagberg (fl/ten sax), P. Dørge (gtr), I. Becker (syns/pno), K. Simonsen (b gtr), M. Carlsen (t sax), E. Hansen (gtr), K. Glak (pno), M. Mazur (dr)]
Blak, K.:Antifonale Tutl ▲ HJF 20
Antiqua Musica CO
J. Roussel (cnd)
Albinoni, T.:Cons à 5 Obs, Op. 7, w. Pierre Pierlot (ob)—No. 3 in B♭ *(rec Salle Wagram, Paris, Mar 1965)* EMI Classics ▲ CDK 65337 [ADD]
Couperin, F.:Les Nations (sels), w. Antoine Geoffroy-Dechaume (hpd) EMI Classics ▲ CDK 65732
Couperin, F.:La Pucelle, w. Antoine Geoffroy-Dechaume (hpd) EMI Classics ▲ CDK 65732
Anton String Quartet
Reger, M.:Qnt Cl, w. Steven Kanoff (cl) Accord ▲ ACD 204432 [DDD]
Antwerp Kameropera Orch
H. Rotman (cnd)
Mozart, W.A.:Arias—Dite almeno, K.479; Chi sa qual sia, K.582 CPO ▲ CPO 999104-2 [DDD]
Mozart, W.A.:Oca del Cairo CPO ▲ CPO 999104-2 [DDD]
Mozart, W.A.:Sposo deluso CPO ▲ CPO 999104-2 [DDD]
Anvance Ensemble
Wolpe, S.:Music of—Music for Any Instruments Col legno ▲ AU 31809
Anvers Sinfonia
W. Proost (cnd)
Mozart, W.A.:Arias, w. L. Hagen-William (b-bar)—10 opera arias from Betulia liberata, Così fan tutte, Don Giovanni, Finta semplice, Le nozze di Figaro, Zaide; 5 concert arias, K.513, 539, 549, 612, 621a Quantum ▲ QM 6896 [DDD] ■ QM 1991 (D)
Apollo CO
D. Chernaik (cnd)
Mendelssohn, F.:Sym 3 Meridian ▲ MER 84261 [DDD]
Mendelssohn, F.:Sym 4 Meridian ▲ MER 84261 [DDD]
Apollo Ensemble
J. Hsu (cnd)
Haydn, J.:Sym 12 *(rec Troy Savings Bank Music Hall, Troy, NY, June 1995)* Dorian ▲ DOR 90226 [DDD]
Haydn, J.:Sym 23 Dorian ▲ DOR 90191 [DDD]
Haydn, J.:Sym 35 Dorian ▲ DOR 90191 [DDD]
Haydn, J.:Sym 42 Dorian ▲ DOR 90191 [DDD]
Haydn, J.:Sym 44, "Trauer" *(rec Troy Savings Bank Music Hall, Troy, NY, June 1995)* Dorian ▲ DOR 90226 [DDD]
Haydn, J.:Sym 64, "Tempora mutantur" *(rec Troy Savings Bank Music Hall, Troy, NY, June 1995)* Dorian ▲ DOR 90226 [DDD]
Apollo String Quartet [Martin Válek (vn), Radek Krizanovsky (vn), Vladimír Kroupa (va), Pavel Verner (vc)]
Adams, J.L.:Dream in White on White *(rec May 1992)* New Albion ▲ NA 061
Dussek, J.L.:Qnt Pno, w. Hanus Barton (pno) Studio Matous ▲ MAT 20 [DDD]
Apollo String Quartet members
Dussek, J.L.:Qt Pno, w. Hanus Barton (pno) Studio Matous ▲ MAT 20 [DDD]
Apple Hill Chamber Players [M. Pearson (vn), B. Hauck (va), P. Cohen (vc), E. Stumacher (pno)]
Brahms, J.:Qt 3 Pno *(rec Apr. 22 & 23, 1991)* Centaur ▲ CRC 2158 [DDD]
Apple Hill Chamber Players [M. Pearson (vn), P. Cohen (vc), R. Merfeld (pno), E. Stumacher (pno)]
Dvorák, A.:Trio 1 Pno *(rec Apr. 25 & 26, 1991)* Centaur ▲ CRC 2158 [DDD]
Apple Hill Chamber Players [P. Levy (vn), R. Stout (vn), B. Hauck (va), P. Cohen (vc), R. Merfeld (pno)]
Harbison, J.:Qnt for 2 Vns Centaur ▲ CRC 2157 [DAD]
Shostakovich, D.:Qnt Pno Centaur ▲ CRC 2157 [DAD]
Apponyi String Quartet
Richter, F.X.:Sons (misc), w. Parlement de Musique—in B for Pno, Vn & Vc; in G for Fl & Db; in A for Hpd, Fl & Vc; in G for Pno, Vn & Vc Adda ▲ ADD 581226 [DDD]
Aquarius
N. Cleobury (cnd)
Davies, P.M.:The Boy Friend Collins Classics ▲ 10952 [DDD]
Davies, P.M.:The Devils Collins Classics ▲ 10952 [DDD]
Davies, P.M.:Seven In Nomine Collins Classics ▲ 10952 [DDD]
Falla, M. de:El amor brujo, w. Claire Powell (mez) Virgin Classics ("Ultraviolet" series) ▲ CUV 61138
Falla, M. de:El corregidor y la molinera, w. Jill Gomez (mez), Aquarius Virgin Classics ("Ultraviolet" series) ▲ CUV 61138
Aquilani Solisti
Vittorio Antonellini
Italian Mandolin Concertos, w. Ugo Orlandi (mand) Koch Schwann ▲ SCH 311171 [DDD]
Aquiles Delle-Vigne
A. Lysy (cnd)
Ravel, M.:Pavane pour une infante défunte Arcobaleno ▲ SBCD 6400 [DDD]
Aquitaine Brass
R. Harvey (cnd)
Fanfare for the Common Man, w. London Brass ASV ▲ ASV 870 [DDD]

Arad PO
N. Boboc (cnd)
Dittersdorf, K.D. von:Con Db, w. S. Thomasz (db) Olympia (Explorer) ▲ OCD 405 [AAD]
E. Rau (cnd)
Romanian Rhapsody, w. Romanian RSO, Cluj-Napoca PO [cnd:Emil Simon] Olympia ("Explorer" series) ▲ OCD 408 [AAD]
Aradia Baroque Ensemble
K. Mallon (cnd)
Caldara, A.:Sinfonie a 4 (12)—Nos. 5, "San Pietro in Cesarea" & 6, "St. Elena al Calvario" *(rec Toronto, Canada, Jan 1996)* Naxos ▲ 8.553772 [DDD]
Caldara, A.:Vaticini di pace, w. Mary Enid Hains (sop), Linda Dayiantis-Straub (sop), Jennifer Lane (mez), David Arnot (ten) *(rec Toronto, Canada, Jan 1996)* Naxos ▲ 8.553772 [DDD]
Arcadia
Veracini, F.M.:Sons [Sons. trans. for Fl]—not advised of selections Symphonia ▲ SYM 91S10 [DDD]
Arcadian Academy
N. McGegan (cnd)
Bach, J.S.:Cant 56, w. W. Parker (bass), Baroque Choral Guild [G] Harmonia Mundi USA ("Nightingale" series) ▲ HMN 907601
Bach, J.S.:Cant 82, w. W. Parker (bar), Baroque Choral Guild [G] Harmonia Mundi USA ("Nightingale" series) ▲ HMN 907601
Blow, J.:Songs, w. Christine Brandes (sop)—The Self Banished; It Grieves Me; Welcome, Welcome [prologue] *(rec Sept 18–21, 1994)* Harmonia Mundi France ▲ HMU 907167
Blow, J.:Songs, w. Christine Brandes (sop), Mary Springfels (va) Harmonia Mundi USA ▲ HMU 907167
Matteis, N.:Suites & Sonatas from *Ayres for the Violin*, w. N. McGegan (hpd)—Sonata in c (Book I, Nos. 46–49); Suite in g (Book II, Nos. 10–18); Suite in A (Book IV, Nos. 1–11); Sonata in C (Book IV, from Nos. 12–20); Suite in e (Book IV, from Nos. 21–29); Suite in d (Book IV, Nos. 33–36) Harmonia Mundi USA ▲ HMU 907067
Matteis, N.:Suites & Sonatas from *Ayres for the Violin* Harmonia Mundi USA ▲ HMU 907108
Purcell, H.:Music of, w. Christine Brandes (sop), Mary Springfels (va) Harmonia Mundi France ▲ HMU 907167
Purcell, H.:Pavan 3 for 2 Vns, w. Mary Springfels (vl) *(rec Sept 18–21, 1994)* Harmonia Mundi France ▲ HMU 907167
Purcell, H.:Sons for 2 Vns (misc), w. Mary Springfels (vl)—in B♭ & in F *(rec Sept 18–21, 1994)* Harmonia Mundi France ▲ HMU 907167
Purcell, H.:Songs, w. Christine Brandes (sop)—The Bashful Thames; So When the Glitt'ring Queen; Lord, What Is Man; Cupid, the Slyest Rogue Alive; Oh Lead Me to Some Peaceful Gloom; Dry Those Eyes; O Solitude; Amidst the Shades; When First Amintas; The Blessed Virgin's Expostulation; Fly Swift, Ye Hours; 'Twas within a Furlong *(rec Sept 18–21, 1994)* Harmonia Mundi France ▲ HMU 907167
Arcangeli Baroque Strings
M. Sand (cnd)
Vivaldi, A.:Cons Vn, Op. 3/1-12, "L'estro armonico", w. M. Sand (vn)—Nos. 1, 6–8, 10 & 11 Meridian ▲ MER 84225 [DDD]
Arcangelo Corelli Trio [A. Fackert (vn), P. Lamprecht (vl/vc), J. Vogelsänger (hpd/org)]
Castello, D.:Sons Vn—Nos. 5 & 8 *(rec Oct. 1992)* MD + G ▲ L 3476 [DDD]
Fontana, G.B.:Sons (18) Vns—Nos. 2 & 5 *(rec Oct. 1992)* MD + G ▲ L 3476 [DDD]
Uccellini, M.:Sons—Nos. 1 & 3 *(rec Oct. 1992)* MD + G ▲ L 3476 [DDD]
L'Archibudelli
Beethoven, L. van:Duet, WoO 32, "Mit 2 obligaten Augengläsern" Sony Classical ("Vivarte" series) ▲ SK 48076 [DDD]
Beethoven, L. van:Qnt for 2 Vns Sony Classical ("Vivarte" series) ▲ SK 48076 [DDD]
Beethoven, L. van:Sxt Hns, Op. 81b Sony Classical ("Vivarte" series) ▲ SK 48076 [DDD]
Beethoven, L. van:Trios Strs, Op. 9 Sony Classical ("Vivarte" series) ▲ SK 48190
Brahms, J.:Sextet Strs, Op. 18, w. Anner Bylsma (vc), Smithsonian Chamber Players Sony Classical ("Vivarte" series) ▲ SK 68252
Brahms, J.:Sextet Strs, Op. 36, w. Anner Bylsma (vc), Smithsonian Chamber Players Sony Classical ("Vivarte" series) ▲ SK 68252
Bruckner, A.:Intermezzo Str Qnt *(rec Amsterdam, May 3–6, 1994)* Sony Classical ▲ SK 66251 [DDD]
Bruckner, A.:Qt Strs *(rec Amsterdam, May 3–6, 1994)* Sony Classical ▲ SK 66251 [DDD]
Bruckner, A.:Qnt Strs *(rec Amsterdam, May 3–6, 1994)* Sony Classical ▲ SK 66251 [DDD]
Bruckner, A.:Rondo Str Qt *(rec Amsterdam, May 3–6, 1994)* Sony Classical ▲ SK 66251 [DDD]
Gade, N.W.:Octet, w. Smithsonian Chamber Players Sony Classical ("Vivarte" series) ▲ SK 48307
Haydn, M.:Qnts Strs—in B♭, C & G *(rec Austria, June 10–12, 1993)* Sony Classical ("Vivarte" series) ▲ SK 53987 [DDD]
Hummel, J.N.:Qt Cl, w. Charles Neidich (cl) *(rec Schloss Grafenegg, Reitschule, Austria, Sept. 19–22, 1993)* Sony Classical ▲ SK 57968 [DDD]
Mendelssohn, F.:Octet Strs, w. Smithsonian Chamber Players Sony Classical ("Vivarte" series) ▲ SK 48307
Mozart, W.A.:Divert Hns Strs, K.247 Sony Classical ("Vivarte" series) ▲ SK 46497
Mozart, W.A.:Divert Hns Strs, K.334 Sony Classical ("Vivarte" series) ▲ SK 46497
Mozart, W.A.:Divert Vn, K.246b Sony Classical ("Vivarte" series) ▲ SK 46702
Mozart, W.A.:Divert Vn, K.288 Sony Classical ("Vivarte" series) ▲ SK 46702
Mozart, W.A.:Duos Hns Sony Classical ("Vivarte" series) ▲ SK 46702
Mozart, W.A.:Duos Vn Sony Classical ("Vivarte" series) ▲ SK 46631
Mozart, W.A.:Grande Sestetto Concertante Sony Classical ("Vivarte" series) ▲ SK 46631
Mozart, W.A.:Marches Hns Sony Classical ("Vivarte" series) ▲ SK 46702
Mozart, W.A.:Musikalischer Spass Sony Classical ("Vivarte" series) ▲ SK 46702
Mozart, W.A.:Preludes & Fugues Str Trio—4 sels. Sony Classical ("Vivarte" series) ▲ SK 46497
Mozart, W.A.:Qnt Hn, K.407 Sony Classical ("Vivarte" series) ▲ SK 46702
Mozart, W.A.:Qnt Strs, K.515 *(rec Alte Reitschule, Schloss Grafenegg, Austria, June 28–July 1)* Sony Classical ▲ SK 66259 [DDD]
Mozart, W.A.:Qnt Strs, K.516 *(rec Alte Reitschule, Schloss Grafenegg, Austria, June 28–July 1)* Sony Classical ▲ SK 66259 [DDD]
Mozart, W.A.:Trio Vn, K.563 Sony Classical ("Vivarte" series) ▲ SK 46497
Onslow, G.:Qnts (34) Strs, w. Smithsonian Chamber Players—in c, Op. 38 [The Bullet]; in E, Op. 39; in b, Op. 40 Sony Classical ("Vivarte" series) ▲ SK 64308
Reicha, A.:Qnt Cl, Op. 89, w. Charles Neidich (cl) *(rec Schloss Grafenegg, Reitschule, Austria, Sept. 19–22, 1993)* Sony Classical ▲ SK 57968 [DDD]
Schubert, Franz:Octet Ww, D.803, w. Mozzafiato Sony Classical ("Vivarte" series) ▲ SK 66264
Schubert, Franz:Trio Strs, D.471 *(rec June 8–9, 1993)* Sony Classical ("Vivarte" series) ▲ SK 53982 [DDD]
Schubert, Franz:Trio Strs, D.581 *(rec June 8–9, 1993)* Sony Classical ("Vivarte" series) ▲ SK 53982 [DDD]
Spohr, L.:Double Qt 1, w. Smithsonian Chamber Players *(rec Jan. 21–24, 1993)* Sony Classical ▲ SK 53370 [DDD]
Spohr, L.:Qnts Strs, Op. 33, w. Smithsonian Chamber Players—in G *(rec Jan. 21–24, 1993)* Sony Classical ▲ SK 53370 [DDD]
Spohr, L.:Sxt Strs, w. Smithsonian Chamber Players *(rec Jan. 21–24, 1993)* Sony Classical ▲ SK 53370 [DDD]
Weber, C.M. von:Qnt Cl, w. Charles Neidich (cl) *(rec Schloss Grafenegg, Reitschule, Austria, Sept. 19–22, 1993)* Sony Classical ▲ SK 57968 [DDD]
B. Weil (cnd)
Haydn, J.:Ave regina, w. Marie-Claude Vallin (sop), Bob Van Asperen (org), Tölz Boys' Choir *(rec Bad Tolz, Germany, Jan. 2–4, 1993)* Sony Classical ("Vivarte" series) ▲ SK 53368 [DDD]
Haydn, J.:Lauda Sion, w. Ab Koster (nat hn), Knut Hasselmann (nat hn), Bob Van Asperen (org), Tölz Boys' Choir *(rec Bad Tolz, Germany, Jan. 2–4, 1993)* Sony Classical ("Vivarte" series) ▲ SK 53368 [DDD]

ORCH. & ENS.

L'Archibudelli (cont.)
B. Weil (cnd) (cont.)
Haydn, J.:Libera me, Domine, w. Bob Van Asperen (org), Tölz Boys' Choir *(rec Bad Tolz, Germany, Jan. 2–4, 1993)* Sony Classical ("Vivarte" series) ▲ SK 53368 [DDD]
L'Archibudelli [John Abberger (ob), Alayne Leslie (ob), Javier Bonet–Manrique (hn), Christoph Moinian (hn), Stefan Blonk (hn)]
Haydn, J.:Cassation Hns, w. Ab Koster (nat hn) Sony Classical ▲ SK 68253
Haydn, J.:Con 1 Hn, w. Ab Koster (nat hn) Sony Classical ▲ SK 68253
Haydn, J.:Divert Hn, Vn & Vc, H.IV/5, w. Ab Koster (nat hn) Sony Classical ▲ SK 68253
Haydn, J.:Divert for 2 Hns, Vns, Va & Db, H.II/21, w. Ab Koster (nat hn) Sony Classical ▲ SK 68253
Haydn, J.:Divert for 2 Hns, Vns, Va & Db, H.II/22, w. Ab Koster (nat hn) Sony Classical ▲ SK 68253
L'Archibudelli [V. Beths (vn), J. Kussmaul (va), A. Bylsma (vc)]
Beethoven, L. van:Serenade Strs, Op. 8 *(rec Nov. 22–25, 1992)* Sony Classical ▲ SK 53961 [DDD]
Beethoven, L. van:Trio Strs, Op. 3 *(rec Nov. 22–25, 1992)* Sony Classical ▲ SK 53961 [DDD]
L'Archibudelli [V. Beths (vn), L. van Dael (vn), J. Kussmaul (va), A. Bylsma (vc)]
Schubert, Franz:Qt 10 Strs *(rec June 8–9, 1993)* Sony Classical ("Vivarte" series) ▲ SK 53982 [DDD]
Arcis Wind Quintet
Barber, S.:Summer Music Ars Musici ▲ 5018
Berio, L.:Opus Number Zoo Ars Musici ▲ 5018
Danzi, F.:Qnts Ww, Op. 67—No. 2 Ars Musici ▲ 5018
Klughardt, A.:Qnt Winds Ars Musici ▲ 5018
Arctic Brass
Artic Brass Simax ▲ PSC 1074 [DDD]
Arden Trio
Ravel, M.:Trio Pno Delos ▲ DCD 3055
Saint-Saëns, C.:Trio 2 Pno Delos ▲ DCD 3055
Arditti String Quartet [Irvine Arditti (vn), Alexander Balanescu (vn), L. Andrade (va), Rohan de Saram (vc)]
Aperghis, G.:Triangle carré, w. Trio Le Cercle *(rec Apr 1990)* Montaigne ▲ MO 782002 [DDD]
Bartók, B.:Qt 4 Strs Gramavision ▲ 79439
Berg, A.:Lyric Suite Montaigne ▲ MO 789001
Berg, A.:Qt Strs Montaigne ▲ MO 789001
Bryars, G.:Epilogue ECM New Series ▲ 78118-21323-2
Bryars, G.:First Viennese Dance ECM New Series ▲ 78118-21323-2
Bryars, G.:Prologue ECM New Series ▲ 78118-21323-2
Bryars, G.:Qt 1 Strs, "Between the National & the Bristol" ECM New Series ▲ 78118-21323-2
Bryars, G.:Three Viennese Dances, w. Pascal Porgy (hn), Charles Fullbrook (perc) ECM New Series ▲ 78118-21323-2 [DDD]
Cage, J.:Four Mode ▲ mode 27
Cage, J.:Music for 4 for Str Qt *(rec live, Wesleyan University, 2/27/88)* Mode ▲ mode 17
Cage, J.:Pieces (30) Str Qt Mode ▲ mode 17
Cage, J.:Qt Strs Mode ▲ mode 27
Carter, E.:Elegy Va Etcetera ▲ KTC 1066
Carter, E.:Qt 1 Strs Etcetera ▲ KTC 1065
Carter, E.:Qt 2 Strs Etcetera ▲ KTC 1066
Carter, E.:Qt 3 Strs Etcetera ▲ KTC 1066
Carter, E.:Qt 4 Strs Etcetera ▲ KTC 1065
Cohn, S.:Eye of Chaos *(rec All Saints Church, Touting, England)* Albany ▲ TROY 159 [DDD]
Crawford, R.:Qt Strs Gramavision ▲ R21S 79440 ■ R41H 79440
Davis, D.:Bleeding Particles *(rec Warren Studios, UC San Diego)* Albany ▲ TROY 159 [DDD]
Dun, T.:Eight Colors *(rec Feb. 28, 1992)* CRI ▲ CD 655 [DDD]
Dusapin, P.:Qt Str Montaigne ▲ MO 782016
Dusapin, P.:Time Zones Montaigne ▲ MO 782016
Dutilleux, H.:Ainsi la nuit Montaigne ▲ MO 782016
Estrada, J.:Chamber Music, w. Stefano Scodanibbio (db) Montaigne ("Auvidis" series) ▲ MO 782056
Felder, D.:Music of, w. Rachel Rudich (fl), June in Buffalo CO, American Brass Quintet—Journal; Canzone XXXI; November Sky; 3rd Face; 3 Lines from 20 Poems Bridge ▲ BCD 9049 [DDD]
Felder, D.:Third Face *(rec Mastersound Astoria)* Bridge ▲ BCD 9049 [DDD]
Ferneyhough, B.:Adagissimo *(rec London, May 1989)* Montaigne ▲ MO 789002
Ferneyhough, B.:Qt 2 Strs *(rec London, May 1989)* Montaigne ▲ MO 789002
Ferneyhough, B.:Qt 3 Strs *(rec London, May 1989)* Montaigne ▲ MO 789002
Ferneyhough, B.:Qt 4 Strs, w. Brenda Mitchell (sop) Montaigne ▲ MO 782029
Ferneyhough, B.:Sons Str Qt *(rec London, May 1989)* Montaigne ▲ MO 789002
From Italy Montaigne ▲ MO 782042
From Vienna Montaigne ▲ MO 782027
Gaussin, A.:Chakra *(rec 4/90)* Montaigne ▲ MO 782002 [DDD]
Goldstein, B.:Aspen Qt *(rec Warren Studios, UC San Diego)* Albany ▲ TROY 159 [DDD]
Gubaidulina, S.:Qt 2 Strs Montaigne ▲ MO 789007
Gubaidulina, S.:Qt 3 Strs Gramavision ▲ 79439
Halffter, C.:Qt 3 Strs *(rec Madrid, Mar 1988)* Montaigne ▲ MO 789006
Harvey, J.:Qt 1 Strs Montaigne ▲ MO 782034
Harvey, J.:Qt 2 Strs Montaigne ▲ MO 782034
Henze, H.-W.:Qts 1–5 Strs Wergo 2-▲ WER 60114/15-50 [DDD]
Höller, Y.:Antiphon Montaigne ▲ MO 782036
Hosokawa, T.:Fragmente II, w. Pierre-Yves Artaud (fl) Montaigne ▲ MO 782078
Hosokawa, T.:Landscape I Montaigne ▲ MO 782078
Hosokawa, T.:Landscape II, w. Kaoru Nakayama (hp) Montaigne ▲ MO 782078
Hosokawa, T.:Landscape V, w. Mayumi Miyata (shō) Montaigne ▲ MO 782078
Kagel, M.:Pan, w. D. Wiesner (fl) *(rec 7/89)* Montaigne ▲ MO 789004 [DDD]
Kagel, M.:Qts Strs *(rec 7/89)* Montaigne ▲ MO 789004 [DDD]
Kurtág, G.:Hommage à Mihály András Montaigne ▲ MO 789007
Kurtág, G.:Officium breve in memoriam Andreae Szervánsky Montaigne ▲ MO 789007
Kurtág, G.:Qt Strs Montaigne ▲ MO 789007
Lachenmann, H.:Reigen seliger Geister Montaigne ▲ MO 782019
Ligeti, G.:The Ligeti Edition—String Quartets & Duets Sony Classical ▲ SK 62306
Ligeti, G.:Qt 1 Strs Wergo ▲ WER 60079-50
Ligeti, G.:Qt 2 Strs Wergo ▲ WER 60079-50
Lindberg, M.:Qnt Cl, w. Kari Kriikku (cl) Montaigne ▲ MO 782033
Lutoslawski, W.:Qt Strs Montaigne ▲ MO 789007
Mâche, F.-B:Eridan Montaigne ▲ MO 782002 [DDD]
Marco, Tomas:Espejo desierto *(rec Madrid, Mar 1988)* Montaigne ▲ MO 789006
Mason, B.:Qt Strs Bridge ▲ BCD 9045 [DDD]
Mira Fornés, R.:Caramelos para Zoe *(rec Madrid, Mar 1988)* Montaigne ▲ MO 789006
Nancarrow, C.:Qt 3 Strs Gramavision ▲ R21S 79440 ■ R41H 79440
1974—Arditti Quartet—1994 Montaigne ▲ MO 782070
Nono, L.:Fragmente-Stille Montaigne ▲ MO 789005
Pablo, L. de:Fragmento *(rec Madrid, Mar 1988)* Montaigne ▲ MO 789006
Platz, R.H.:Qt Strs Montaigne ▲ MO 782036
Ramos, R.:Pas encore *(rec Madrid, Mar 1988)* Montaigne ▲ MO 789006
Rasmussen, K.A.:Solos & Shadows *(rec Nov 1988)* Marco Polo/Dacapo 2-▲ DCCD 9003a/9003b [DDD]
Rasmussen, K.A.:Surrounded by Scales *(rec Nov. 1988)* Marco Polo/Dacapo 2-▲ DCCD 9003a/9003b [DDD]
Reynolds, R.:Coconino...a shattered landscape Gramavision ▲ R21S 79440 ■ R41H 79440
Rihm, W.:Qts Strs—No. 3 (1976); No. 5 (1981–83); No. 8 (1987–88) Montaigne ▲ MO 782001 [DDD]
Saariaho, K.:Nymphea Montaigne ▲ MO 782033
Scelsi, G.:Qt 5 Strs Salabert ▲ SCD 8904-5
Schnittke, A.:Qt 2 Strs Gramavision ▲ 79439
Schoenberg, A.:Qt in D Strs Montaigne 2-▲ MO 782025

Arditti String Quartet (cont.)
Schoenberg, A.:Qt 1 Strs Montaigne 2-▲ MO 782024
Schoenberg, A.:Qt 2 Strs, w. Dawn Upshaw (sop) Montaigne 2-▲ MO 782024
Schoenberg, A.:Qt 3 Strs Montaigne ▲ MO 782024
Schoenberg, A.:Qt 4 Strs Montaigne 2-▲ MO 782024
Schoenberg, A.:Trans Chamber Ensemble, w. Hakon Ausbö (harm), Michel Béroff (perc), Isabelle Berteletti (perc), Louise Bessette (pno), Marc Marder (db), Paul Meyer (cl), Michel Moraguès (fl)—Busoni:Berceuse élégiaque (1920); Mahler:Songs of a Wayfarer (1920) [w. Jean-Luc Chaignaud (baritone)]; Joh. Strauss:Kaiserwalzer (1925); Roses from the South (1921) Montaigne ▲ MO 789011 [DDD]
Schoenberg, A.:Verklärte Nacht, w. Thomas Kakusa (va), Valentin Erben (vc) Montaigne 2-▲ MO 782025
Sørensen, B.:Qts Strs—Alman (1983–84); Adieu (1986); Angels' Music (1987–88) *(rec Nov. 1988)* Marco Polo/Dacapo 2-▲ DCCD 9003a/9003b [DDD]
Sørensen, B.:Qts Strs Montaigne ▲ MO 782033
Spahlinger, M.:Apo Do Montaigne ▲ MO 782036
Stäbler, G.:Strike the ear... Koch Schwann ▲ SCH 311402 [DDD]
Stalvey, D.:Str Qt 1989 *(rec All Saints Church, Touting, England)* Albany ▲ TROY 159 [DDD]
Tiensuu, J.:Arsenic & Old Lace, w. Jukka Tiensuu (hpd) Montaigne ▲ MO 782033
U.S.A. Montaigne ▲ MO 782010 [DDD]
Webern, A.:Chamber Music—5 Movements; 6 Bagatelles; Qt. for Strs, Op. 28; Trio, Op. 20; Movt. for Str Trio; Qt for Strs, 1905; Slow Movt. for Str Qt. 1905; Rondo for Str Qt. (ca. 1906) Montaigne ▲ MO 789008
Webern, A.:Music of—Sätze, Op. 5; Bagatelles, Op. 9; Quartet, Op. 28; Quartet (1905); Trio, Op. 20; Satz (1925); Lansamer Satz (1905); Rondo (ca. 1906) Montaigne ▲ MO 789008 [DDD]
Xenakis, I.:Chamber Music, w. C. Helffer (pno)—Akea, Quintet for Piano & Strings (1986); À R. (Hommage to Ravel) for Piano (1987); Dikthas for Violin & Piano (1979); Embellie for Viola (1981); Evryali for Piano (1973); Herma for Piano (1960–61); Ikhoor for String Trio (1978); Kottos for Cello (1977); Mikka for Violin (1971); Mikka "S," for Violin (1976); Mists for Piano (1980); Nomos Alpha for Cello (1966); St/4 for String Quartet (1955–62); Tetora for String Quartet (1990); Tetras for String Quartet (1983) Montaigne 2-▲ MO 782005 [DDD]
Xenakis, I.:Tetras Gramavision ▲ R21S 79440 ■ R41H 79440
Zimmermann, W.:Festina lente Montaigne ▲ MO 782036
A. Brizzi (cnd)
Scelsi, G.:Khoom, w. Michiko Hirayama (sop), Frank Lloyd (hn), Maurizio Ben Omar (perc) Salabert ▲ SCD 8904-5
O. Henzold (cnd)
Lachenmann, H.:Tanzsuite mit Deutschlandlied, w. Berlin RSO Montaigne ▲ MO 782019
E. Spanjaard (cnd)
Harvey, J.:Scena, New Ensemble Montaigne ▲ MO 782034
Arditti String Quartet members
Harvey, J.:Lotuses, w. Felix Renggli (fl) Montaigne ▲ MO 782034
Scelsi, G.:Trio Strs Salabert ▲ SCD 8904-5
Schoenberg, A.:Weihnachtsmusik, w. Hakon Ausbö (harm), Louise Bessette (pno) Montaigne ▲ MO 789011 [DDD]
Arena di Verona Orch
O. de Fabritiis (cnd)
Verdi, G.:Ernani, w. I. Ligabue (sop), F. Corelli (ten), P. Cappuccilli (bar), R. Raimondi (bass), Arena di Verona Chorus *(rec live, Verona 7/15/72)* Golden Age of Opera 2-▲ GAO 131/32 [ADD]
G. Fackler (cnd)
Donizetti, G.:Requiem Mass, w. L. Pavarotti (ten), M. Cortez (ten), R. Bruson (bar), P. Washington (bass), Arena di Verona Chorus London ("Ovation" series) ▲ 425043-2 [ADD]
A. Guadagno (cnd)
Puccini, G.:La Bohème, w. Katia Ricciarelli (sop), Francisco Araiza (ten), Angelo Casertano (ten), Stefano Antonucci (bar), Claudio Giombi (bar), Paata Burchuladze (bass), Alfredo Mariotti (bass), Alberto Noli (bass), Andrea Piccinni (bass), Lauren Broglia (sgr), Limburg Cathedral Boys' Chorus Koch Schwann 2-▲ SCH 315922
Verdi, G.:Nabucco, w. Monica Pick-Hieronimi (sop), Anna Schiatti (sop), Mina Blum (sop), Angelo Casertano (ten), Gilberto Maffezzoni (ten), Paolo Gavanelli (bass), Paata Burchuladze (bass), Franco Federici (bass), Arena di Verona Chorus *(rec Berlin, Spring 1996)* Koch Schwann 2-▲ SCH CD 364272
E. Inbal (cnd)
Verdi, G.:Don Carlos, w. M. Caballé (sop), F. Cossotto (mez), P. Domingo (ten), P. Cappuccilli (bar), G. Petkov (bar), Arena di Verona Chorus [I] *(rec live 7/2/69)* Melodram 3-▲ MEL 37057 (m) [AAD]
Arensky Ensemble
Arensky, A.:Qt 2 Strs Meridian ▲ CDE 84211
Borodin, A.:Sextet Strs Meridian ▲ CDE 84211
Tchaikovsky, P.:Souvenir de Florence Meridian ▲ CDE 84211
Argo CO
G. Guest (cnd)
Pergolesi, G.B.:Stabat mater, w. Felicity Palmer (sop), Alfreda Hodgson (cta), David Hill (org), St. John's College Choir Cambridge *(rec 1978)* London 2-▲ 443868-2 [ADD]
L. Heltay (cnd)
Haydn, J.:Salve regina, H.XXIIIb/2, w. Arleen Auger (sop), Alfreda Hodgson (cta), Anthony Rolfe Johnson (ten), Gwynne Howell (bass), John Birch (db), London Chamber Choir *(rec St. Jude's, London, Feb 1979)* London 2-▲ 443027-2 [ADD]
Argo SO
J. Judd (cnd)
Myers, S.:Con Sop Sax, w. John Harle (sax) *(rec Studio 1, EMI, Abbey Road, London, July 21–22, 1993)* Argo ▲ 443529-2
Aria de Paris Flute Quintet
Flute Follies *(rec Sept. 1992)* Syrinx ▲ CSR 92103 [DDD]
Aria en Harmonie Quartet
Le Bal du kiosque à musique *(rec Dec. 1989)* Fonti Musicali ▲ FMD 183 [DDD]
Aria String Quartet [Thomas Füri (vn), Claudia Dora (vn), Christoph Schiller (va), Conradin Brotbek (vc)]
Schubert, Franz:Qt 8 Strs Novalis ▲ CD 150114 [DDD]
Schubert, Franz:Qt 13 Strs Novalis ▲ CD 150114 [DDD]
Ariadne String Quartet
Hays, S.:Tunings New World ▲ 805202 [DDD]
Ariel String Quartet
Herrmann, B.:Echoes Unicorn-Kanchana ▲ UKCD 2069
Ariel Wind Quintet
Child, P.:Qnt Winds CRI ▲ CD 605 [DDD]
Pinkham, D.:Advent Cant, w. C. Baum (hp), Boston Cecilia *(rec Dec. 1992)* Koch International Classics ▲ KIC 7180 [DDD]
Aries Brass Quintet
Aries Brass Quintet Centaur ▲ CRC 2083 [DDD]
Arion Ensemble
Baroque Chamber Music with Recorder, w. Verbruggen, Marion (rcr) Titanic ▲ Ti 177 [DDD]
Campra, A.:Cants françaises, w. Danièle Forget (sop)—Arion Analekta Fleur de Lys ▲ FL 2 3018
Clérambault, L.N.:Cants, w. Danièle Forget (sop)—Léandre et Héro; Orphée Analekta Fleur de Lys ▲ FL 2 3018
Un Concert en Nouvelle-France, w. Richard Duguay (ten) *(rec Église St-Paul-de-Joliette, Mar. 7–9, 1994)* CBC Records ("Musica Viva" series) ▲ MVCD 1081 [DDD]
Marais, M.:Music of—Suite in g for 2 Dessus & Bc Analekta ▲ ATM 29717
Mondonville, J.-J.C. de:Sons Hpd—No. 4 Analekta ▲ ATM 29717
Montéclair, M.P. de:Cants, w. Danièle Forget (sop)—Pan et Syrinx Analekta Fleur de Lys ▲ FL 2 3018
Quentin, J.-B.:Sons Fl, Vn & Vl—in a Analekta ▲ ATM 29717

52 ▲ = CD ♦ = Enhanced CD Δ = MD ■ = Cassette Tape ▯ = DCC

Arion Ensemble (cont.)
Telemann, G.P.:Cons (misc)—for Fl, Vn, Vl & Bc Analekta ▲ ATM 29717
Telemann, G.P.:Qts Vn—Quartet Nos. 4,5 & 6 CBC ("Musica Viva" series) ▲ MVCD 1040 [DDD]
Villeneuve, A. de:Music of—Premiere Suite in a for Fl & Vn Analekta ▲ ATM 29717

A. Lascae (cnd)
Bartók, B.:Divert Partridge ▲ 1126-2 [DDD]
Dvořák, A.:Waltzes Strs, B.105 Partridge ▲ 1118-2 [DDD]
Grieg, E.:Nordic Melodies, Op. 63 Partridge ▲ 1118-2 [DDD]
Prokofiev, S.:Visions fugitives [Rudolf Barshai's arr. for string orchestra] Partridge ▲ 1126-2 [DDD]
Purcell, H.:The Fairy Queen (orch suites) Partridge ▲ 1118-2 [DDD]
Rossini, G.:Sons Str Qt—Sonata No. 1 in G Partridge ▲ 1118-2 [DDD]
Tchaikovsky, P.:Souvenir d'un lieu cher, w. V. Beths (vn) [trans. for solo vn & strings A. Lascae] Partridge ▲ 1126-2 [DDD]

Arion Ensemble [C. Guimond (baroque fl), C. Rémillard (baroque vn), B. MacMillan (vl/baroque vc), H. Knox (hpd)]
Marais, M.:Pièces en trio *(rec July 1 & 2, 1993)* Analekta ▲ DD 71722
Quentin, J.-B.:Sons en trio Fls *(rec July 1 & 2, 1993)* Analekta ▲ DD 71722
Telemann, G.P.:Con in G Fl, Ob d'amore *(rec July 1 & 2, 1993)* Analekta ▲ DD 71722
Villeneuve, A. de:Conversations en manière de sonates *(rec July 1 & 2, 1993)* Analekta ▲ DD 71722

Arion Ensemble [H. Knox (hpd), C. Rémillard (vn)]
Mondonville, J.-J.C. de:Sons Hpd *(rec July 1 & 2, 1993)* Analekta ▲ DD 71722

Arion Quartet
Bach, J.S.:Trio Sons Org, BWV 525-530 *(rec Quebec, June 1996)* Analekta Fleur de Lys ▲ FL 23086 [DDD]

Arion Trio
Schubert, Franz:Adagio & Rondo concertante Vn, w. C. Veress (va) BIS 4-▲ CD 521/24 [DDD]
Schubert, Franz:Chamber Music Pno, w. C. Veress (va), A. Cincera (db) BIS 4-▲ CD 521/24 [DDD]
Schubert, Franz:Nocturne Pno BIS 4-▲ CD 521/24 [DDD]
Schubert, Franz:Qnt Pno, D.667, w. C. Veress (va), A. Cincera (db) BIS 4-▲ CD 521/24 [DDD]
Schubert, Franz:Trio Pno, D.28 BIS 4-▲ CD 521/24 [DDD]
Schubert, Franz:Trio 1 Pno BIS 4-▲ CD 521/24 [DDD]
Schubert, Franz:Trio 2 Pno BIS 4-▲ CD 521/24 [DDD]

Arion Trio [I. von Alpenheim (pno) I. Ozim (vn), W. Grimmer (vc)]
Mozart, W.A.:Divert Pno, K.254 BIS 2-▲ CD 513/14 [DDD]
Mozart, W.A.:Trios Pno (comp) BIS 2-▲ CD 513/14 [DDD]

Arion Trio [Pascal Devoyon (pno), Gérard Poulet (vn), Christoph Henkel (vc)]
Beethoven, L. van:Trio 1 Pno Arion ▲ ARN 68232 [DDD]
Beethoven, L. van:Trio 7 Pno Arion ▲ ARN 68232 [DDD]

Arioso CO
C. Martin (cnd)
Brockman, J.:Perihelion II Leonarda ▲ LE 327 [DDD]

Arioso String Quartet
Rosetti, F.A.:Qts Strs, Op. 6 CPO ▲ CPO 999338

Arioso Trio
Cory, E.:Designs *(rec 1981 & 1986)* CRI ▲ CD621 [ADD]

Arioso Wind Quintet
Barber, S.:Music of, w. Alexa Still (fl), Chicago SO, San Diego CO, Atlantic Sinfonietta, New Zealand SO, Capricorn, Repertory Singers—Capricorn Con; Canzone; Fadograph of a Yestern Scene; Cave of the Heart; Adagio for Strs; Souvenirs; Hermit Songs; To Be Sung on Water; The Lovers; Summer Music Koch International Classics ▲ KIC 7361
Harbison, J.:Qnt Winds Koch International Classics ▲ KIC 7262 [DDD]
Rochberg, G.:To the Dark Wood Koch International Classics ▲ KIC 7262 [DDD]
Rochberg, G.:Trio Cl Koch International Classics ▲ KIC 7262 [DDD]

D. Barra (cnd)
Barber, S.:Capricorn Con, San Diego CO Koch International Classics ▲ KIC 7206 [DDD]

Arizona State Univ Symphonic Band
T. O'Neal (cnd)
Stamp, J.:Be Thou My Vision *(rec Fisher Auditorium & Waller Hall, IUP Campus, May 1994, Jan & Feb 1995)* Citadel ▲ CTD 88111 [DDD]

R. Strange (cnd)
Ung, C.:Grand Spiral *(rec Gammage Auditorium, Tempe, AZ, 1990)* CRI ▲ CRI 710 [DDD/ADD]

Arlequin Trio [Salvador Espasa (fl), Pablo Riviere (va), Nicolás Daza (gtr)]
Maseda, E.P.:Miniatures RNE/Spanish National Radio ▲ 650003 [AAD]

Arman Ensemble [Deniz Arman Gelenbe (pno), Eric Pritchard (vn), Hsiao-mei Ku (vn), Jonathan Bagg (va), Fred Raimi (vc)]
Castelnuovo-Tedesco, M.:Qnt 1 Pno *(rec Forest Hills Baptist Church, Raleigh, NC, Aug & Nov 1995)* Albany ▲ TROY 191 [DDD]

Arman Ensemble [Deniz Arman Gelenbe (pno), Fritz Gearhart (vn), Brain Manker (vc)]
Castelnuovo-Tedesco, M.:Trio 1 Pno *(rec Forest Hills Baptist Church, Raleigh, NC, Aug & Nov 1995)* Albany ▲ TROY 191 [DDD]

Armed Forces Radio Orch
Mascagni, P.:Cavalleria rusticana (sels), w. Zinka Milanov (sop) *(rec 1938-1944)* Minerva ▲ MN A15 [ADD]
Mozart, W.A.:Don Giovanni (sels), w. Zinka Milanov (sop)—Don Ottavio, son morta...or sai che l'onore; Crudele...Non mi dir *(rec 1938-1944)* Minerva ▲ MN A15 [ADD]

E. Panizza (cnd)
Verdi, G.:Un ballo in maschera (sels), w. Zinka Milanov (sop)—Ecco l'orrido campo; Teco io sto; Morrò, ma prima in grazia *(rec 1938-1944)* Minerva ▲ MN A15 [ADD]

Armenian PO
L. Tjeknavorian (cnd)
Borodin, A.:In the Steppes of Central Asia ASV Quicksilva ▲ ASQ 6180
Borodin, A.:Prince Igor (Polovtsian dances) ASV Quicksilva ▲ ASQ 6180
Glinka, M.:Russlan & Ludmilla (ov) ASV Quicksilva ▲ ASQ 6180
Ippolitov-Ivanov, M.:Caucasian Sketches, Opp. 10 & 42—1 suite ASV ▲ ASV 773 [DDD]
Kabalevsky, D.:Colas Breugnon (suite) ASV ▲ ASV CD 967
Kabalevsky, D.:The Comedians ASV ▲ ASV CD 967
Kabalevsky, D.:Romeo & Juliet ASV ▲ ASV CD 967
Khachaturian, A.:The Battle of Stalingrad (suite) ASV ▲ ASV 859
Khachaturian, A.:Concert Waltz ASV ▲ ASV 964
Khachaturian, A.:Con Pno, w. Dora Serviarian-Kuhn (pno) ASV ▲ ASV 964
Khachaturian, A.:Dance Suite ASV ▲ ASV 964
Khachaturian, A.:Festive Poem ASV ▲ ASV 946 [DDD]
Khachaturian, A.:Funeral Ode in Memory of Lenin ASV ▲ ASV 946 [DDD]
Khachaturian, A.:Gayane (suites)—1 suite, "Sabre Dance" ASV ▲ ASV 773 [DDD]
Khachaturian, A.:Gayane (suites)—No. 2 ASV ▲ ASV 884 [DDD]
Khachaturian, A.:Greeting Ov ASV ▲ ASV 946 [DDD]
Khachaturian, A.:Lermontov Suite ASV ▲ ASV 946 [DDD]
Khachaturian, A.:Masquerade (ballet suite)—Waltz ASV ▲ ASV 773 [DDD]
Khachaturian, A.:Russian Fant ASV ▲ ASV 946 [DDD]
Khachaturian, A.:Spartacus (suites 1-3)—1 suite, "Onedin Line Theme" ASV ▲ ASV 773 [DDD]
Khachaturian, A.:Sym 1 ASV ▲ ASV 858
Khachaturian, A.:Sym 2 ASV ▲ ASV 859
Khachaturian, A.:Sym 3 ASV ▲ ASV 858
Khachaturian, A.:The Widow from Valencia ASV ▲ ASV 884 [DDD]
Mussorgsky, M.:Night ASV Quicksilva ▲ ASQ 6180
Prokofiev, S.:Cinderella (sels)—Suite No. 3 ASV ▲ ASV 886 [DDD]
Prokofiev, S.:Lt Kijé Suite ASV ▲ ASV 886 [DDD]
Prokofiev, S.:The Love for 3 Oranges (suite) ASV ▲ ASV 886 [DDD]

Armenian PO (cont.)
L. Tjeknavorian (cnd) (cont.)
Prokofiev, S.:Romeo & Juliet (suites) ASV ▲ ASV 885 [DDD]
Rimsky-Korsakov, N.:Christmas Eve (suite) ASV ▲ ASV 772
Rimsky-Korsakov, N.:Fairy Tale ASV ▲ ASV 771
Rimsky-Korsakov, N.:Golden Cockerel (suite) ASV ▲ ASV 772
Rimsky-Korsakov, N.:Sadko (song of india) ASV ▲ ASV 771
Rimsky-Korsakov, N.:Sadko Orch, Op. 5 ASV ▲ ASV 771
Rimsky-Korsakov, N.:Scheherazade ASV ▲ ASV 771
Rimsky-Korsakov, N.:The Tale of Tsar Saltan Orch, Op. 57 ASV ▲ ASV 772
Shostakovich, D.:Festive Ov ASV Quicksilva ▲ ASQ 6180
Tchaikovsky, P.:Eugene Onegin (sels)—Waltz & Polonaise ASV Quicksilva ▲ ASQ 6180
Tchaikovsky, P.:Romeo & Juliet ASV Quicksilva ▲ ASQ 6180
Tjeknavorian, L.:Danses fantastiques ASV ▲ ASV 884 [DDD]

Armenian Radio-TV Orch
Silantiev, Mavisakhalyan (cnd)
Babadjanyan, A.:Music of, w. A. Arutiunyan (pno), Arno Babadjanyan (pno), B. Chekmenyov (gtr), A. Tarasov (gtr), A. Nikolayev (perc), All-Union Radio-TV Sym Variety Orch—Nocturne; Prelude & Vagarshapat Dance; Capriccio; Polyphonic Son; Expromt; Armenian Rhap; Elegy in Commemoration of A. Khachaturyan; 6 Pictures; Melody & Humoresque; Fant on Give Me My Music Back; Fant on Dum spiro spero; Fant on Winer Love; Fant on Call Me; Piece for the Pno & Orch [Dreams] *(rec 1953-83)* Russian Compact Disc ("Talents of Russia" series) ▲ RCD 16251 [ADD]

Armenian-Canadian Chamber Ensemble
Wagner, R.:Siegfried Idyll CBC ("SM 5000" series) ▲ SMCD 5073 [DDD] ■ SMC 5073 (D)

Armin Rosin Trio
Blacher, B.:Divert Hänssler Classic ▲ 98.557 [DDD]
Damase, J.-M.:Trio Tpt Hänssler Classic ▲ 98.557 [DDD]
Koetsier, J.:Gran Trio Tpt, Trbn & Pno Hänssler Classic ▲ 98.557 [DDD]
Masterworks for Brass Hänssler Classic ▲ 98.557 [DDD]

Armin Strings
Duets:Ofra Harnoy & Friends, w. Harnoy, Ofra (vc), Michael Dussek (pno), Orford String Quartet, Maureen Forrester (cta), Andrew Davis (pno), Jeanne Baxtresser (fl), Catherine Wilson (pno), Paul Brodie (sax), Shauna Rolston (vc), Armin Strings, Canadian Piano Trio, Adele Armin (vn) Mastersound ▲ MST 30 [DDD]

Armonico Theater Ensemble
A. de Marchi (cnd)
Frescobaldi, G.:Missa sopra l'aria della monica, w. A. Cremonesi (org) Symphonia ▲ SYM 91S08 [DDD]
Handel, G.F.:Cants, w. Maria Cristina Kiehr (sop), Andreas Scholl (alt)—Il duello amoroso; Vendendo amor; La partenza; Nel dolce tempo; Sono liete, fortunate Accord ▲ ACD 204212 [DDD]

Armonico Tributo Austria
L. Duftschmid (cnd)
Schmelzer, J.H.:Ballet Suites, w. Lorenz Duftschmid (vl) Arcana ▲ ACA 33
Schmelzer, J.H.:Sons Instrs, w. Lorenz Duftschmid (vl) Arcana ▲ ACA 33

Armstrong Flute & Percussion Duo
Adams, J.L.:Songbirdsongs—Morningfieldsong; Apple Blossom Round; Meadowdance; Joyful Noise; Evensong *(rec Penn State Univ School of Music, University Park, May 1995)* Centaur ▲ CRC 2273 [DDD]
Dahl, I.:Duo concertante *(rec Penn State Univ School of Music, University Park, May 1995)* Centaur ▲ CRC 2273 [DDD]
Marttinen, T.:Alfa *(rec Penn State Univ School of Music, University Park, May 1995)* Centaur ▲ CRC 2273 [DDD]
Mols, R.:Interplay *(rec Penn State Univ School of Music, University Park, May 1995)* Centaur ▲ CRC 2273 [DDD]
Parker, P.:Beneath the Canopy—The Forest Beckons; Rivers Gently Flowing; Exotic Birds of Paradise; Twilight Calmness/Song of the Orchid; Python Dance *(rec Penn State Univ School of Music, University Park, May 1995)* Centaur ▲ CRC 2273 [DDD]
Vercoe, E.:Fantavia *(rec Penn State Univ School of Music, University Park, May 1995)* Centaur ▲ CRC 2273 [DDD]

Arnheim PO
R. Benzi (cnd)
Mahler, G.:Des Knaben Wunderhorn, w. J. Van Ness (cta), J. Bröcheler (bass) Ottavo ▲ OTT 79238 [DDD]

Arnold Quintet [Ettore Bongiovanni (hn), Leonardo Dosso (bn), Maurizio Longoni (cl), Francesco Pomarico (ob), Renato Rivolta (fl)]
Briccialdi, G.:Music of—Qnt in D, Op. 124; Qnts in B♭ series 10/2 & 3; Pot-pourri fantastique on themes from Il barbiere di Siviglia, series 10/4 Stradivarius ▲ STV 33331

Arnold Quintet [Renato Rivolta (fl), Francesco Pomarico (ob), Maurizio Longoni (cl), S. Paneblanco (hn), Leonardo Dosso (bn)]
Cambini, G.M.:Qnts (3) Ww Stradivarius ▲ STR 33310 [DDD]

L'Arpa Festante Baroque Orch
M. Gaigg (cnd)
Monn, G.M.:Syms—in G; in B♭; in E♭; in B♭ [a quattro]; in D; in A *(rec Neuss, Zeughaus, July 10-13, 1994)* CPO ▲ CPO 999273-2 [DDD]
Rameau, J.P.:Dardanus (sels)—Suite Amati ▲ CD 9206 [DDD]
Rameau, J.P.:Hippolyte et Aricie (orchestral suite) Amati ▲ CD 9206 [DDD]

Arpeggio CO
G. Boucher (cnd)
Vivaldi, A.:Cons Vc, w. Alexandre Debrus (vc)—RV.413 & 417 *(rec Studio Métamorphoses d'orphée)* Pavane ▲ ADW 7352 [DDD]
Vivaldi, A.:Con for 2 Vcs, w. Alexandre Debrus (vc) *(rec Studio Métamorphoses d'orphée)* Pavane ▲ ADW 7352 [DDD]
Vivaldi, A.:Cons Orch—in D & A *(rec Studio Métamorphoses d'orphée)* Pavane ▲ ADW 7352 [DDD]

Arpeggione Ensemble
Ibert, J.:Interludes Adda ▲ ADD 581060 [DDD]
Ibert, J.:Trio Vn, Vc & Hp Adda ▲ ADD 581060 [DDD]
Milhaud, D.:Scaramouche (transcriptions), *(instrumentation unknown)* Adda ▲ ADD 581060 [DDD]
Milhaud, D.:Suite Vn Adda ▲ ADD 581060 [DDD]
Roussel, A.:Sérénade Adda ▲ ADD 581060 [DDD]

R. de Caro (cnd)
Peri, J.:Euridice, w. Monica Benvenuti (sop—Ninfa I/Venere), Rossana Bertini (sop—Dafne/Ninfa II), Gloria Banditelli (cta—Euridice/Ninfa III/Tragedia/Proserpina), Mario Cecchetti (ten—Aminta/Radamanto), Paolo Da Col (ten—Tirsi), Gianpaolo Fagotto (ten—Orfeo), Giuseppe Zambon (ct—Arcetro), Sergio Foresti (bass—Caronte/Pastore), Furio Zanasi (bass—Plutone) *(rec Bologna, Italy, Nov 1992)* Arts Music 2-▲ 47276-2 [DDD]

Arraymusic Ensemble
Siddall, J.:Jakarta Sleep, w. D. Mott (sax) CBC ("Musica Viva" series) ▲ MVCD 1057 [DDD]

Arriaga String Quartet [Michaël Guttman (vn), Yvo Lintermans (vn), Ezequiel Larrea (va), Luc Tooten (vc)]
Amon, J.A.:Qt Hn, Op. 20/1, w. Luc Bergé (hn) Eufoda ▲ 1207 [DDD]
Devreese, G.:Qt Strs Phaedra ▲ 92 002 [DDD]
Hoffmeister, F.A.:Qnt Hn, w. Luc Bergé (hn) Eufoda ▲ 1207 [DDD]
Milhaud, D.:Qt 1 Strs *(rec Steurbaut Studios, Brussels, Nov. 1994)* Discover International ▲ DI 920290 [DDD]
Milhaud, D.:Qt 2 Strs *(rec Steurbaut Studios, Brussels, Nov. 1994)* Discover International ▲ DI 920290 [DDD]
Mozart, W.A.:Qnt Hn, K.407, w. Luc Bergé (hn) Eufoda ▲ 1207 [DDD]
Stich, J.V.:Qt Hn, w. Luc Bergé (hn) Eufoda ▲ 1207 [DDD]
Van Eechaute, P.:Qt 1 Strs Phaedra ▲ 92 002 [DDD]

ORCH. & ENS.

Ars Acustica
M. Kagel (cnd)
Kagel, M.:...Nach einer Lektüre von Orwell — Wergo ▲ WER 6305-2
Kagel, M.:Der Tribun — Wergo ▲ WER 6305-2
Ars Antiqua Austria
G. Letzbor (cnd)
Bach, J.S.:Brandenburg Con 4 — Symphonia ▲ SYM 94134
Bach, J.S.:Cons Vn (comp), w. Gunar Letzbor (vn) — Symphonia ▲ SYM 94134
Bach, J.S.:Con for 2 Vns, w. Gunar Letzbor (vn), Daniel Sepec (vn) — Symphonia ▲ SYM 94134
Weichlein, R.:Encaenia musices, w. Gunar Letzbor (vn), Daniel Sepec (vn), Herbert Lindsberger (va), Christoph Bitzinger (va), Michael Oman (vl), Gaetano Nasillo (vc), Roberto Sensi (vn), Andreas Lackner (nat tpt), Herbert Walser (nat tpt), Norbert Kirchner (hpd/org)—Sons. Nos. I in C, II in g, III in a, IV in E, V in C & VI in F — Symphonia ▲ SY 93S23
Ars Cantus
R. Cirri (cnd)
Cimarosa, D.:Con for 2 Fls, w. Marcello Gatti (fl), Federico Maria Sardelli (fl) *(rec Sept 7-10, 1995)* — Bongiovanni ▲ GB 2184 [DDD]
Cimarosa, D.:Con Hpd, w. Stefano Lorenzetti (hpd) *(rec Sept 7-10, 1995)* — Bongiovanni ▲ GB 2184 [DDD]
Cimarosa, D.:Il Maestro di cappella, w. Giorgio Gatti (bar) *(rec Sept 7-10, 1995)* — Bongiovanni ▲ GB 2184 [DDD]
Ars Femina Ensemble
R. Burchard (cnd)
Caccini, F.:La liberazione di Ruggiero dall'isola d'Alcina, w. Linda De Rungs (sop—Alcian/Vistola), Cecilia Amorocho (sgr—Melissa/Nunzia), Laura Lea Duckworth (sgr—Siren/Harpy), Eric Friedlander (sgr—Monster), L. Ernest Gross (sgr—Enchanted Cypress), Phoebe Jevtovic (sgr—Siren), James Rittenhouse (sgr—Ruggiero/Neptune), Sharon Sim (sgr—Siren), TimeChange *(rec Louisville, KY, 1993)* — Nannerl ▲ NR-ARS 003; ■ NR-ARS 003
Ars Instrumentalis Pragensis
Zelenka, J.D.:Sons Obs — Multisonic 2-▲ MUL 310217 [DDD]
Ars Nova
Schmidt, O.:The Öresund Sym, w. Kari Hamnøy (sop), Anders Lundh (ten), O. Schmidt (cnd), Malmö SO, Ars Nova *(rec Malmö Concert Hall, Sweden, Apr. 11-13, 1994)* — BIS ▲ CD 672 [DDD]
B. Holten (cnd)
Gombert, N.:Motets—Lugebat David Absalon; Musae Jovis [L] — Kontrapunkt ▲ 32008 [DDD]
Gombert, N.:Sacred Choral Music—Magnificat primi toni; Credo; Ave Maria; Si ignoras te; Ave salus mundi; Magnificat octavi toni — Kontrapunkt ▲ 32038 [DDD]
Holten, B.:Grundtvig Motets [Da] — Kontrapunkt ▲ 32016 [DDD]
Josquin Desprez:Chansons & Motets—Absalon, Fili Mi; Allegez Moy; Ave Maria; Carmen Gallicum Ludovici XI Regis Francorum; Je ne me puis tenis d'aimer; Nimphes des Bois; Pater Noster, Qui es in Caelis; Petite Camusette; Scaramella; Vive le Roy [F,L] *(rec 1992)* — Kontrapunkt ▲ 32110 [DDD]
Josquin Desprez:Missa de Beata Virgine [L] *(rec 1992)* — Kontrapunkt ▲ 32110 [DDD]
La Rue, P. de:Missa, "L'homme armé" [L] — Kontrapunkt ▲ 32008 [DDD]
La Rue, P. de:Missa pro defunctis [L] — Kontrapunkt ▲ 32001 [DDD]
New Music for Choir, w. Rilke Ensemble — Kontrapunkt ▲ 32016 [DDD]
Nørgård, P.:Wie ein Kind [G] — Kontrapunkt ▲ 32016 [DDD]
Ruders, P.:Motets—Preghiera Semplice (1981) & Psalm 86 (1985) [E,I] — Kontrapunkt ▲ 32016 [DDD]
Tallis, T.:Church Music, w. L.U. Mortensen (hpd)—Videte miraculum; Felix namque (I & II); Salvator mundi (I); O Nata lux [L] — Kontrapunkt ▲ 32003 [DDD]
Tallis, T.:The Lamentations of Jeremiah [L] — Kontrapunkt ▲ 32003 [DDD]
Wert, G. de:Sacred Music—Adesto dolori meo, O Deus; Ascendente Iesu un naviculam; Amwn, amen dico vobis; Egressus Iesus; Vox in Rama [L] — Kontrapunkt ▲ 32001 [DDD]
W. Heider (cnd)
Hölszky, A.:Requisiten — Koch Schwann ▲ 3-1062-2 [DDD]
Ars Rediviva
Benda, F.:Cons Hpd, w. J. Hála (hpd)—4 cons in G, D, g & C *(rec 1978)* — Supraphon ▲ 11 1001-2 [AAD]
M. Munclinger (cnd)
Bach, C.P.E.:Sinfs, H.663-666 — Vivace ▲ 589 [ADD]
Bach, J.S.:The Art of the Fugue *(rec 1979)* — Supraphon 2-▲ SUP 0087 [AAD]
Bach, J.S.:A Musical Offering — Supraphon 2-▲ SUP 0087 [AAD]
Benda, F.:Cons (3) Fl & Orch, w. A. Adorjan (fl) — Orfeo ▲ 151101 [DDD] ■ 151101 (D)
Handel, G.F.:Royal Fireworks Music — Supraphonet ▲ 11 1109-2 [AAD]
Handel, G.F.:Trio Sons—Trio Sonata in E, Op. 2/9 — Supraphonet ▲ 11 1109-2 [AAD]
Handel, G.F.:Water Music (suites)—Suite No. 1 in F *(rec 1973)* — Supraphonet ▲ 11 1109-2 [AAD]
Vivaldi, A.:Music of—Concerto in e for Bassoon & Strings; Concerti in D & g for Flute, Oboe, Violin, Bassoon & Continuo; Concerto in G for Oboe, Bassoon & Strings; Concerto in d for 2 Oboes & Strings; Concerto in a for Piccolo & Strings — Supraphon Collection ▲ 11 0608-2 [ADD]
Ars Rediviva Orch Prague
Bach, J.S.:Suites Orch, BWV 1066-1069 — Supraphon 3-▲ CD 111875 [DDD]
K. Münchinger (cnd)
Bach, J.S.:Brandenburg Cons — Supraphon 3-▲ CD 111875 [DDD]
Ars Subtilis Ytalica
Polyphonic Music of France & Italy, 1380-1410 — Arcana ▲ ACA 21 [DDD]
L'Art Pour L'Art Ensemble
Jahn, T.:Music of, w. N. Enna (sop)—selected vocal arrs. — Col Legno ▲ AU 31811
Yun, I.:Contrasts Vn — CPO ▲ CPO 999118 [DDD]
Yun, I.:Duo Vc — CPO ▲ CPO 999118 [DDD]
Yun, I.:Gagok — CPO ▲ CPO 999118 [DDD]
Yun, I.:Novelette Fl — CPO ▲ CPO 999118 [DDD]
Yun, I.:Sori — CPO ▲ CPO 999118 [DDD]
Artaria String Quartet
Boccherini, L.:Qnts Gtr & Strs, w. R. Savino (gtr)—Quintets I, II & III — Harmonia Mundi USA ▲ HUC 907039
Boccherini, L.:Qnts Gtr & Strs, w. R. Savino (gtr)—Quintets VII & VIII — Harmonia Mundi USA ▲ HMU 907069
Cleary, D.:Character Studies (5) *(rec Recital Hall, Viterbo College, La Crosse, Wisconsin, July 18-20, 1994)* — Centaur ▲ CRC 2251 [DDD]
Cleary, D.:Qt 1 Strs, "Inventing Situations" *(rec Recital Hall, Viterbo College, La Crosse, Wisconsin, July 18-20, 1994)* — Centaur ▲ CRC 2251 [DDD]
Cleary, D.:Qt 2 Strs, "Artaria" *(rec Recital Hall, Viterbo College, La Crosse, Wisconsin, July 18-20, 1994)* — Centaur ▲ CRC 2251 [DDD]
Giuliani, M.:Qnt Gtr, w. R. Savino (gtr) — Harmonia Mundi USA ▲ HMU 907069
Artaria Trio [R. Drinkall (pno), I. Gotkovsky (vn), N. Gotkovsky (vc)]
Beethoven, L. van:Trio 5 Pno *(rec Nov. 1990)* — Pyramid ▲ 13502 [DDD]
Schubert, Franz:Trio 1 Pno *(rec Nov. 1990)* — Pyramid ▲ 13502 [DDD]
Arte del Suono String Quartet [L. Bobesco (vn), S. Janssens (vn), J.-E. Homatas (va), J. Matthe (vc)]
Boccherini, L.:Qts Strs, G.242-247—No. 5 in D *(rec Jan. 1994)* — Pavane ▲ ADW 7309 [DDD]
Donizetti, G.:Qt 13 Strs *(rec Jan. 1994)* — Pavane ▲ ADW 7309 [DDD]
Puccini, G.:Crisantemi *(rec Jan. 1994)* — Pavane ▲ ADW 7309 [DDD]
Puccini, G.:Minuets Str Qt *(rec Jan. 1994)* — Pavane ▲ ADW 7309 [DDD]
Ysaÿe, E.:Vars on Paganini's Caprice No. 24 [arr. Jacques Ysaÿe for string quartet] *(rec Jan. 1994)* — Pavane ▲ ADW 7309 [DDD]

L'Arte dell'Arco
Boccherini, L.:Arias, w. Cristina Miatello (sop), Ensemble Barocco Padovano Sans Souci—Se non ti moro allato; Numi se giusti siete; Mi dona, mi rende quell'alma pietosa; Di giudice severo; Per quel paterno amplesso; Tornate sereni; Caro, son tua così; Deh respirar lasciatemi *(rec Armonia Ca' Bianca Hall, Apr 12-14, 1995)* — Dynamic ▲ CD 123 [DDD]
L'Arte dell'Arco [Giovanni Guglielmo (vn), Federico Guglielmo (vn), Carlo Lazari (vn), Mario Paladin (va), Pietro Bosna (vc), Franco Catalini (db), Federico Marincola (tiorba), Nicola Reniero (hpd)]
Vivaldi, A.:Cons Vn, Op. 9, "La Cetra" — Dynamic 2-▲ CDS 147/1-2 [DDD]
L'Arte dell'Arco [Giovanni Guglielmo (vn), Federico Guglielmo (vn), Pietro Bosna (vc), Andrea Coen (hpd)]
Locatelli, P.:Sons for 2 Vns, Op. 5 *(rec Rome, 1995)* — musicaimmagine ▲ MR 10036 [DDD]
L'Arte dell'Arco [Giovanni Guglielmo (vn), Federico Guglielmo (vn), Pietro Bosna (vc), Nicola Reniero (hpd)]
Vivaldi, A.:Trio Sons 2 Vns & Bc—R.60, 68, 70, 71, 74 & 77 *(rec Rome, 1992)* — musicaimmagine ▲ MR 10012 [DDD]
L'Arte dell'Arco [Giovanni Guglielmo (vn), Federico Guglielmo (vn), Pietro Bosna (vc)]
Viotti, G.B.:Music of—2 Trios for 2 Vns & Vc; 3 Serenades for 2 Vns *(rec Dynamic's, Genova, Italy, Dec 1-3, 1994)* — Dynamic ▲ CDS 101 [DDD]
Arte Musica Ensemble
Colonna, G.P.:Sacred Music—Nisi Dominus; Pulchra es; O caeli devota; Diffundite flores; Salve praetiosum; O lucidissima dies; Seconda lamentazione; Terza lamentazione *(rec Montepulciano, Siena, Italy, Nov 1995)* — Tactus ▲ TC 630301 [DDD]
F. Cera (cnd)
Gesualdo, D.C.:Madrigals—Book 4 (1596) — Tactus ▲ TC 560701 [DDD]
Artificii Musicali
Hasse, J.A.:Trio Sons, Op. 11 — Nuova Era ("Ancient Music" series) ▲ NUO 7176 [DDD]
G. Delvaux (cnd)
Handel, G.F.:Cants, w. Jean-Louis Bindi (bass)—Cuopre Talvolta il Cielo, H.98; Dalla Guerra Amorosa, H.102a; Spande Ancor a Mio Dispetto, H.165; Dal Fatale Momento, H.101b; Nell'Africane Selve, H.136a — Stradivarius ▲ STV 33425 [DDD]
Porpora, N.A.:Sinf da camera — Nuova Era ("Ancient Music" series) ▲ 7147 [DDD]
Artis String Quartet [Peter Schuhmayer (vn), Johannes Meissl (vn), Herbert Kefer (va), Othmar Müller (vc)]
Berg, A.:Lyric Suite — Orfeo ▲ 216901 [DDD]
Berg, A.:Qt Strs — Orfeo ▲ 216901 [DDD]
Brahms, J.:Qnt Pno, w. S. Vladar (pno) *(rec May 11-13, 1993)* — Sony Classical ▲ SK 58954 [DDD]
Dvořák, A.:Qt 14 Strs *(rec Sept. 27-29, 1992)* — Sony Classical ▲ SK 53288 [DDD]
Gielen, M.:Vars Str Qt — Sony Classical ▲ SK 48059
Mendelssohn, F.:Pieces Str Qt, Op. 81 — Accord 3-▲ ACD 201132 [DDD]
Mendelssohn, F.:Qt in E♭ Strs — Accord 3-▲ ACD 201132 [DDD]
Mendelssohn, F.:Qts (6) Strs, Opp. 12, 13 44/1-3 & 80 — Accord 3-▲ ACD 201132 [DDD]
Schoenberg, A.:Qt in D Strs — Orfeo ▲ 194901 [DDD] ■ MC 194901 (D)
Schubert, Franz:Qt Strs, D.3 — Sony Classical ▲ SK 52582
Schubert, Franz:Qt 14 Strs — Sony Classical ▲ SK 52582
Schumann, R.:Qnt Pno, w. S. Vladar (pno) *(rec May 11-13, 1993)* — Sony Classical ▲ SK 58954 [DDD]
Smetana, B.:Qt 1 Strs *(rec Sept. 27-29, 1992)* — Sony Classical ▲ SK 53288 [DDD]
Webern, A.:Bagatelles Str Qt — Sony Classical ▲ SK 48059
Webern, A.:Movts Str Qt — Sony Classical ▲ SK 48059
Webern, A.:Qt Strs, Op. 28 — Sony Classical ▲ SK 48059
Webern, A.:Rondo — Sony Classical ▲ SK 48059
Webern, A.:Slow Movt — Sony Classical ▲ SK 48059
Weigl, K.:Qt 3 Strs — Orfeo ▲ 216901 [DDD]
Wolf, H.:Intermezzo — Accord ▲ ACD 220802 [DDD]
Wolf, H.:Qt Strs — Accord ▲ ACD 220802 [DDD]
Wolf, H.:Serenade Str Qt — Accord ▲ ACD 220802 [DDD]
Zemlinsky, A. von:Qt 2 Strs — Orfeo ▲ 194901 [DDD] ■ MC 194901 (D)
Artistica Buñol
H. Adams (cnd)
Pasodobles — World Wind ▲ WWM 500.014
Reed, A.:Sym 2 *(rec Teatro Montecarlo, Buñol)* — World Wind ▲ WWM 500.008 [DDD]
Reed, A.:Sym 3 *(rec Teatro Montecarlo, Buñol)* — World Wind ▲ WWM 500.008 [DDD]
Reed, A.:Sym 4 *(rec Rodahal, Kerkrade, Jul 25, 1993)* — World Wind ▲ WWM 500.008 [DDD]
Artistrio
Villa-Lobos, H.:Trio 1 Pno — Masters of Art ▲ AAOC-9378
Villa-Lobos, H.:Trio 3 Pno — Masters of Art ▲ AAOC-9378
Les Arts Florissants
Monteverdi, C.:Combattimento — Harmonia Mundi France ▲ HMC 901426
W. Christie (cnd)
Campra, A.:Cants françaises—Arion, La Dispute de l'amour et de l'hymen, Les Femmes, Énée & Didon *(rec 1986)* — Musique d'Abord ▲ HMA 1901238
Charpentier, M.-A.:Actéon [F] — Musique d'Abord ▲ HMA 1901095
Charpentier, M.-A.:Les Arts florissants, w. C. Dussaut (sop), J. Feldman (sop), A. Mellon (sop), G. Laurens (mez), D. Visse (ct), P. Cantor (ten), G. Reinhart (bar) [F] — Musique d'Abord ▲ HMA 1901083
Charpentier, M.-A.:Assumpta est Maria — Harmonia Mundi France ▲ HMC 901298
Charpentier, M.-A.:In nativitatem Domini canticum [L] — Harmonia Mundi France ▲ HMC 905130
Charpentier, M.-A.:Litanies de la vierge — Harmonia Mundi France ▲ HMC 901298
Charpentier, M.-A.:Magnificat à 3 [F,L] — Harmonia Mundi France ▲ HMC 901082
Charpentier, M.-A.:Le Malade imaginaire, w. C. Brua (sop), N. Rime (sop), M. Zanetti (sop), D. Visse (ct), H. Crook (ten), J.-F. Gardeil (bar) [F] — Harmonia Mundi France ▲ HMC 901336
Charpentier, M.-A.:Médée, w. Isabelle Desrochers (sop—Cleone), Lorraine Hunt (sop—Medee), Noemi Rime (sop—Nerine), Monique Zanetti (sop—Creuse), Mark Padmore (ten—Jason), François Bazola (bar—Arcas), Jean-Marc Salzmann (bar—Oronte), Bernard Deletre (bass-Creon) — Erato 3-▲ 96558-2
Charpentier, M.-A.:Méditations (10) pour le Carême — Musique d'Abord ▲ HMA 1905151
Charpentier, M.-A.:Oratorios—Caecilia, Virgo et Martyr; Filius Prodigus; Magnificat [L] — Harmonia Mundi France ▲ HMC 90066
Charpentier, M.-A.:Pastorale sur la naissance de N.S. Jesu Christ [F,L] — Harmonia Mundi France ▲ HMC 901082
Charpentier, M.-A.:Le Reniement de Saint-Pierre — Musique d'Abord ▲ HMA 1905151
Charpentier, M.-A.:Te Deum, H. 146 — Harmonia Mundi France ▲ HMC 901298
Clérambault, L.N.:Cants, w. Noémi Rime (sop), Jean-Paul Fouchécourt (ten), Nicolas Rivenq (bass), Hiro Kurosaki (vn), Ryo Terakado (vn), Marc Hantaï (fl), Eric Bellocq (thb), Elisabeth Matiffa (b vl), Bruno Croscet (basse de vn)—Pyrame et Tisbé, La Muse de l'opéra ou les Caractères Lyriques, La Mort d'Hercule, Orphée — Musique d'Abord ▲ HMA 1901329
Couperin, F.:Music of, w. René Jacobs (alt), Gérard Lesne (alt), Kenneth Gilbert (hpd), Christophe Rousset (hpd), Phillippe Herreweghe (cnd), Chapelle Royale Choir—Hpd pieces; Tenebeae Lessons [sels] — Harmonia Mundi ("Great Baroque Composers" series) 3-▲ HMX 390870.72
Handel, G.F.:Concerti grossi, Op. 6—Nos. 1, 2, 6, 7 & 10 — Harmonia Mundi France ▲ HMC 901507
Handel, G.F.:Messiah, w. Sandrine Piau (sop), Barbara Schlick (sop), Andreas Scholl (alt), Mark Padmore (ten), Nathan Berg (bass) [1742 Dublin version] — Harmonia Mundi France 2-▲ HMC 901498/99
Lalande, M.-R. de:Motets, w. V. Gens (sop), S. Piau (sop), A. Steyer (sop), J.-P. Fouchécourt (ten), F. Piolino (ten), J. Corréas (bass) [L] — Harmonia Mundi France ▲ HMC 901351
Lalande, M.-R. de:Te Deum, w. V. Gens (sop), S. Piau (sop), A. Steyer (sop), J.-P. Fouchécourt (ten), F. Piolino (ten), J. Corréas (bass) [L] — Harmonia Mundi France ▲ HMC 901351
Lambert, M.:Airs de Cour [F] — Musique d'Abord ▲ HMA 1901123
Lully, J.-B.:Atys, w. Agnès Mellon (sop), Guillemette Laurens (mez), Guy de Mey (ten), Jean-François Gardeil (bar), Les Arts Florissants Chorus [F] — Harmonia Mundi France 3-▲ HMC 901257/59 [DDD];

▲ = CD ♦ = Enhanced CD Δ = MD ■ = Cassette Tape □ = DCC

Les Arts Florissants (cont.)
W. Christie (cnd) (cont.)
Lully, J.-B.:Music of, w. René Jacobs (alt), Gérard Lesne (alt), Kenneth Gilbert (hpd), Christophe Rousset (hpd), Phillippe Herreweghe (cnd), Chapelle Royale Choir—Hpd Pieces; 'Atys' excerpts; Dies Israe; Petits Motets Harmonia Mundi ("Great Baroque Composers" series) 3-▲ HMX 390870.72
Lully, J.-B.:Petits motets—the eleven motets from this group that have been authenticated as composed by Lully [L] Harmonia Mundi France ▲ HMC 901274 [DDD]
Monteverdi, C.:Madrigals—selections from Books 7 & 8 [I] Musique d'Abord ▲ HMA 1901068
Mozart, W.A.:Zauberflöte, w. Natalie Dessay (sop—Queen of the Night), Linda Kitchen (sop—Papagena), Rosa Mannion (sop—Pamina), Anna-Maria Panzarella (sop—First Lady), Doris Lamprecht (mez—Second Lady), Delphine Haidan (cta—Third Lady), Hans Peter Blochwitz (ten—Tamino), Steven Cole (ten—Monostatos), Chrisopher Josey (ten—First Priest/First Armed Man), Anton Scharinger (bar—Papageno), Reinhard Hagen (bass—Sarastro), Laurent Naouri (bass—Second Priest/Second Armed Man), Willard White (bass—Speaker) *(rec Paris Oct 2-9 1995)* Erato 2-▲ 12705-2 [DDD]
Purcell, H.:Dido & Aeneas, w. J. Feldman (sop), G. Laurens (mez), P. Cantor (ten) [E] Harmonia Mundi France ▲ HMC 905173
Purcell, H.:Dido & Aeneas, w. Véronique Gens (sop—Dido), Sophie Marin-Degor (sop—Belinda), Sophie Daneman (sop—2nd woman/1st witch), Gaëlle Mechaly (sop—2nd witch), Claire Brua (mez—Sorceress), Steve Dugardin (alt—Chorus), Jean-Paul Fouchécourt (ten—Spirit/Sailor), Nathan Berg (b-bar—Aeneas), Jonathan Arnold (bass—Chorus), William Christie (hpd) *(rec Massy Opera Theatre, Nov. 8-11, 1994)* Erato ▲ 98477-2 [DDD]
Rameau, J.P.:Anacreon Musique d'Abord ▲ HMA 1901090
Rameau, J.P.:Castor et Pollux, w. V. Gens (sop), A. Mellon (sop), H. Cook (ten), J. Corréas (bass) Harmonia Mundi France 3-▲ HMC 901435/37
Rameau, J.P.:Les Indes galantes, w. C. McFadden (sop), S. Piau (sop), I. Poulenard (sop), N. Rime (sop), M. Ruggeri (sop), H. Crook (ten), J.-P. Fouchecourt (ten), N. Rivenq (bar), J. Corréas (bass), B. Delétré (bass) [F] Harmonia Mundi France 3-▲ HMC 901367/69
Rameau, J.P.:Motets, w. S. Daneman (sop), N. Rime (sop), P. Agnew (ct), N. Rivenq (bar), N. Cavallier (bass)—In convertendo, Quam dilecta, Deus noster refugium *(rec June 8-12, 1994)* Erato ▲ 96967-2 [DDD]
Rameau, J.P.:Music of, w. René Jacobs (alt), Gérard Lesne (alt), Kenneth Gilbert (hpd), Christophe Rousset (hpd), Phillippe Herreweghe (cnd), Chapelle Royale Choir—Pieces; Les Indes Gallantes (sels) Harmonia Mundi ("Great Baroque Composers" series) 3-▲ HMX 390870.72
Rameau, J.P.:Music of, La Chapelle Royale, et al.—sels. from Anacréon; Harpsichord Suite in d; In Convertendo; Les Indes galantes *(rec 1981-83)* Harmonia Mundi Plus ▲ HMP 390808
Rameau, J.P.:Nélée et Myrthis, w. A. Mellon (sop—Myrthis), D. Michel-Dansac (sop—Maid), C. Pelon (sop—Maid), F. Semellaz (sop—Corinne), J. Corréas (bass—Nélée), Les Arts Florissants Chorus [F] *(rec 5/91)* Harmonia Mundi France ▲ HMC 901381
Rameau, J.P.:Pygmalion, w. A. Mellon (sop—Céphise), D. Michel-Dansac (sop—La Statue), S. Piau (sop—L'Amour), H. Crook (ten—Pygmalion), Les Arts Florissants Chorus [F] *(rec 5/91)* Harmonia Mundi France ▲ HMC 901381
Robbins, R.:Jefferson in Paris Angel ▲ CDQ 55311 ■ 4DQ 55311
Rossi, L.:Oratorio per la Settimana Santa Musique d'Abord ▲ HMA 1901297
Rossi, L.:Un peccator pentito Musique d'Abord ▲ HMA 1901297
Gesualdo, D.C.:Madrigali a cinque voci, Books I- VI (comp)—17 madrigals [I] Harmonia Mundi France ▲ HMC 901268 [DDD]

Alice Artzt Guitar Trio [Alice Artzt (gtr), Raymond Burley (gtr), Michel Rutscho (gtr)]
Bernstein, L.:West Side Story (sels)—Prologue/Something's Coming; Cha Cha; Tonight; Maria; I Feel Pretty; America; One Hand, One Heart; Gee, Officer Krupke; Somewhere; I Have a Love/Finale [all trans & arr R. Burley for 3 gtrs] Doremi ▲ 003 [DAD]
Chaplin, C.:Music of—Suite I:My Star/Wedding Theme [from A Countess from Hong Kong & The Circus]; The Deacon Presents/Opening Hymn, Jitters [from the Pilgrim]; A Dog's Life Theme/Mischief, Coffee & Cakes [from A Dog's Life]; With You, Dear, in Bombay; Suite II:Intro & Terry's Theme [from Limelight]; Love Interlude, Hurry Theme, Fanfare [from City Lights]; Smile [from Modern Times] [all trans & arr S. Abreu for 3 gtrs] Doremi ▲ 003 [DAD]
Gershwin, G.:Music of—Ballet from Primrose; Summertime; Prelude [all trans & arr R. Burley for 3 gtrs] Doremi ▲ 003 [DAD]

Graham Ashton Brass Ensemble
Family Carols, w. [cnd:David Willcocks], Bach Choir, Fanfare Trumpeters of the Royal Military School of Music, John Scott (org) Chandos ▲ CHAN 8973 [DDD]

Asko Ensemble
Ferneyhough, B.:Terrain, w. Irvine Arditti (vn) Montaigne ▲ MO 782029
Varèse, E.:Déserts Attacca ▲ Babel 9263-2 [DDD]
Varèse, E.:Intégrales Attacca ▲ Babel 9263-2 [DDD]
Varèse, E.:Ionisation Attacca ▲ Babel 9263-2 [DDD]
S. Asbury (cnd)
Torstensson, K.:Urban Songs, w. Charlotte Riedijk (sop) *(rec 1993 or 1994)* Donemus ▲ CV 32
Zuidam, R.:Freeze, w. Susan Narucki (sop—Patty Hearst), Gerrie de Vries (mez), Zeger Vandersteene (ten), Martin Hargrove (bass), Jaco Huijpen (bass) NM Classics 2-▲ NM 92047
P. Eötvös (cnd)
Machover, T.:Spectres Parisiens Bridge ▲ BCD 9002 ■ BC5-7002
Maderna, B.:Hyperion, w. P Walmsley-Clark (sop), B. Ganz (nar), J. Zoon (fl), Les Jeunes Solistes Vocal Ensemble Montaigne 2-▲ MO 782014 [DDD]
M. Foster (cnd)
Boogman, W.:La Disciplina Dei sentimenti, w. Charlotte Riedijk (nar), Jan Panis (sound projection), Hans Tutschku (sound projection), Asko Choir *(rec Muziekcentrum Vredenburg Utrecht, Netherlands, Dec 17, 1993)* Donemus ▲ CV 57 [DDD]
R. de Leeuw (cnd)
Andriessen, L.:Mausoleum, w. David Barick (bar), Charles van Tassel (bar), Schoenberg Ensemble Donemus ▲ CV 20
Messiaen, O.:Des Canyons aux étoiles, w. Schoenberg Ensemble, The Hague Percussion Ensemble Montaigne 2-▲ MO 782035
Torstensson, K.:The Last Diary, w. Palle Fuhr Jørgensen (nar), Schoenberg Ensemble *(rec The Hague, Netherlands, Mar 6 1995)* Donemus ▲ CV 57 [DDD]
D. Porcelijn (cnd)
Berio, L.:Tempi Concertati, w. L. Pameijer (fl), J. E. van Regteren Altena (vn) *(rec live, Amsterdam 3/6/90)* Attacca ▲ Babel 9057-4 [DDD]
Donatoni, F.:Cloches *(rec live, Groningen 3/8/90)* Attacca ▲ Babel 9057-4 [DDD]
Francesconi, L.:Plot in the Fiction, w. M. Schut (ob/E hn) *(rec live Groningen, 3/8/90)* Attacca ▲ Babel 9057-4 [DDD]
Loevendie, T.:Gassir, the Hero, w. Claron McFadden (sop—Partridge/Priestess), Timothy Wilson (alt—Shamsi), Christopher Gillett (ten—Safi), Robert Poulton (bar—Gassir), Lieuwe Visser (bass—Yemni), Roger Smeets (sgr—Rafi) *(rec live, Amsterdam Studios, June 14-15, 1993)* Donemus ▲ CV 35
Maderna, B.:Serenata 2 *(rec live 3/7/90)* Attacca ▲ Babel 9057-4 [DDD]
Torstensson, K.:Licks & Brains II, Netherlands Saxophone Quartet Donemus ▲ CV 13
Verbey, T.:Expulsie Donemus ▲ CV 31
Vriend, J.:Hallelujah II *(rec The Hague, Netherlands, Oct 13, 1988)* Donemus ▲ CV 57 [DDD]
Vries, K. de:Diafonia, w. R. Boelens (sop), G. de Vries (sop) Donemus ▲ CV 34

Aspen Music School Faculty members
Silverman, F.-E.:Passing Fancies New World ▲ NW 355-2 [DDD]
Silverman, F.-E.:Restless Winds New World ▲ NW 355-2 [DDD]

Aspen Wind Quintet members
Gannon, L.:Triad-O-Rama *(rec Sept. 1, 1993)* Catalyst ▲ 09026-61979-2 ■ 09026-61979-4

Aston Magna
Vivaldi, A.:Cons for 2 Vns—RV.511, 513 Elektra/Nonesuch ▲ 79056-2 [DDD] ■ 79056-4 (D)
Vivaldi, A.:Trio Sons 2 Vns & Bc—RV.63 & 75 Elektra/Nonesuch ▲ 79056-2 [DDD] ■ 79056-4 (D)

L'Astrée Ensemble [Ubaldo Rosso (trns fl), Massimo Gentili (trns fl), Pierluigi Fabretti (ob), Paolo Faldi (ob), Dileno Baldin (hn), Mary Knepper (hn), Sebastiano Cassará (vn), Luigi Mangiocavallo (vn), Stefano Veggetti (vc), Giancarlo Pavan (db), Giorgio Tabacco (hpd
Pugnani, G.:Ovs—No. 1 in D; No. 3 in B Symphonia ▲ SY 93S21

L'Astrée Ensemble members
Pugnani, G.:Qts Strs—No. 3 in A Symphonia ▲ SY 93S21
Pugnani, G.:Qnts Fl—No. 2 in F, Op. 1 Symphonia ▲ SY 93S21
Pugnani, G.:Qnts Fls Symphonia ▲ SY 93S21

L'Atelier String Trio [George Binkley (vn), Virginia Christensen (va), Roy Christensen (vc)]
Hindemith, P.:Trio 1 Gasparo ▲ 1009
Hindemith, P.:Trio 2 Gasparo ▲ 1009

Athela Ensemble
F. Widekind (cnd)
Gubaidulina, S.:Detto 2 Vc, w. H. Brendstrup (vc) Kontrapunkt ▲ KPT 32176 [DDD]

Athena Ensemble
Elgar, E.:Adagio cantabile & Andante con variazioni Chandos ("Collect" series) ▲ CHAN 6553 [ADD]
Elgar, E.:Dances (4) Chandos ("Collect" series) ▲ CHAN 6554 [ADD]
Elgar, E.:Harmony Music I-V—Nos. 1 & 5 Chandos ("Collect" series) ▲ CHAN 6553 [ADD]
Elgar, E.:Harmony Music I-V—Nos. 2-4 Chandos ("Collect" series) ▲ CHAN 6554 [ADD]
Elgar, E.:Intermezzos (5) Chandos ("Collect" series) ▲ CHAN 6553 [ADD]
Elgar, E.:Promenades (6) Chandos ("Collect" series) ▲ CHAN 6554 [ADD]
Gounod, C.:Petite Sym *(rec 1978)* Chandos ("Collect" series) ▲ CHAN 6543 [ADD]
Ibert, J.:Pièces brèves *(rec 1978)* Chandos ("Collect" series) ▲ CHAN 6543 [ADD]
Milhaud, D.:Le Cheminée du Roi René Chandos ("Collect" series) ▲ CHAN 6536 [ADD]
Milhaud, D.:Divert Ww Chandos ("Collect" series) ▲ CHAN 6536 [ADD]
Milhaud, D.:Pastorale Ob Chandos ("Collect" series) ▲ CHAN 6536 [ADD]
Milhaud, D.:Sketches Chandos ("Collect" series) ▲ CHAN 6536 [ADD]
Milhaud, D.:Suite d'après Corrette Chandos ("Collect" series) ▲ CHAN 6536 [ADD]
Nielsen, C.:Canto serioso Chandos ▲ CHAN 8680 [ADD]
Nielsen, C.:Fants Ob Chandos ▲ CHAN 8680 [ADD]
Nielsen, C.:Moderen—The fog is lifting; The children are playing; Faith and hope are playing Chandos ▲ CHAN 8680 [ADD]
Nielsen, C.:Qnt Ww Chandos ▲ CHAN 8680 [ADD]
Nielsen, C.:Serenata in vano Chandos ▲ CHAN 8680 [ADD]
Poulenc, F.:Sxt Pno *(rec 1978)* Chandos ("Collect" series) ▲ CHAN 6543 [ADD]
Triebensee, J.:Suite Chandos ("Collect" series) ▲ CHAN 6597 [ADD]

Athenaeum Enesco String Quartet
Boccherini, L.:Qnts Fl, G.419-424, w. A. Nicolet (fl)—Nos. 1, 5 & 6 Novalis ▲ 150082 [DDD]
Boccherini, L.:Qnts Fl, G.425-430, w. A. Nicolet (fl)—Nos. 2 & 4 Novalis ▲ 150082 [DDD]
Chausson, E.:Qt Strs Pierre Verany ▲ PV.792032 [DDD]
Enescu, G.:Qts Strs, Op. 22 CPO ▲ CPO 999068 [DDD]
Franck, C.:Qnt Pno, w. G. Tacchino (pno) Pierre Verany ▲ PV.792032 [DDD]
Kraus, J.M.:Qnt Fl, w. A. Nicolet (fl) Novalis ▲ 150082 [DDD]

Athens Byzantine Orch
Peloponnesius, P.:Music of—secular work in the 4th plagal mode FM ▲ FMR 705
Phokaeus, T.:Music of—Cherubic works in the 1st mode & 2nd plagel mode FM ▲ FMR 705

Athens Colours Orch
M. Hadjidakis (cnd)
Piazzolla, A.:Adiós Nonino, w. Astor Piazzolla (band) [arr for band, pno, hp & perc] *(rec Ancient Herod Odeon, Athens, Greece, July 3, 1990)* Milan ▲ 73138-35758-2
Piazzolla, A.:Con Band, w. Astor Piazzolla (band) *(rec Ancient Herod Odeon, Athens, Greece, July 3, 1990)* Milan ▲ 73138-35758-2
Piazzolla, A.:Tangos Band, w. Astor Piazzolla (band) *(rec Ancient Herod Odeon, Athens, Greece, July 3, 1990)* Milan ▲ 73138-35758-2

Athens SO
C. Surinach (cnd)
Glanville-Hicks, P.:Nausicaa, w. Teresa Stratas (sop—Nausicaa), Sophia Steffan (cta—Queen Arete), Michalis Heliotis (ten—Antinous/Priest), George Moutsios (ten—Eurymachus), Edward Ruhl (ten—Phemius), George Tsantikos (ten—Clytoneus), Vassilis Koundouris (bar—Messenger), John Modenos (bar—Aethon), Spiro Malas (bass—King Alcinous), Athens Sym Chorus *(rec Athens Festival, 1961)* CRI ▲ CD 695 [ADD]

Atlanta Chamber Players
H. Farberman (cnd)
Kramer, J.D.:Atlanta Licks, w. F. Weinstock (pno), L. Raley, P. Rehfeldt, London PO Leonarda ▲ LE 332
Kramer, J.D.:Music for Pno 3, w. F. Weinstock (pno), L. Raley, P. Rehfeldt, London PO Leonarda ▲ LE 332
Kramer, J.D.:Music for Pno 5, w. F. Weinstock (pno), L. Raley, P. Rehfeldt, London PO Leonarda ▲ LE 332
Kramer, J.D.:Musica Pro Musica, w. F. Weinstock (pno), L. Raley, P. Rehfeldt, London PO Leonarda ▲ LE 332
Kramer, J.D.:Renascence, w. F. Weinstock (pno), L. Raley, P. Rehfeldt, London PO Leonarda ▲ LE 332

Atlanta Chamber Players [Amy Porter (fl), David Hancock (vc), Paula Peace (pno)]
P. Peace (cnd)
Rorem, N.:Trio Fl *(rec Georgia State Univ Recital Hall, Atlanta, GA, Aug 5, 1995)* ACA Digital Recording ▲ CM 20038

Atlanta Chamber Players [Paula Peace (pno/cnd), Christopher Pulgram (vn), David Hancock (vc), Amy Porter (fl), Laura Ardan (cl), Paul Murphy (va), Carolyn Toll Hancock (vn)]
Amram, D.:Conversations *(rec Georgia State Univ Recital Hall, Atlanta, GA, July 29, 1995)* ACA Digital Recording ▲ CM 20038

Atlanta Chamber Players [Paula Peace (pno/cnd), Christopher Pulgram (vn), David Hancock (vc), Laura Ardan (cl), Paul Murphy (va), Carolyn Toll Hancock (vn)]
Copland, A.:Sextet Cl, Pno & Strs *(rec Georgia State Univ Recital Hall, Atlanta, GA, Aug 3, 1995)* ACA Digital Recording ▲ CM 20038

Atlanta Chamber Players [Paula Peace (pno/cnd), Christopher Pulgram (vn), Paul Murphy (va), David Hancock (vc)]
Harbison, J.:Trio Pno & Strs, "November 19, 1828" *(rec Georgia State Univ Recital Hall, Atlanta, GA, Oct 21, 1995)* ACA Digital Recording ▲ CM 20038

Atlanta SO
Duruflé, M.:Requiem, w. Blegen, Morris, Shaw, Atlanta Sym Chorus [L] Telarc ▲ CD 80135 [DDD]
L. Lane (cnd)
Copland, A.:Appalachian Spring (suite) Telarc ▲ CD-80078 [DDD]
Copland, A.:Fanfare for the Common Man Telarc ▲ CD-80078 [DDD]
Copland, A.:Rodeo Telarc ▲ CD-80078 [DDD]
Respighi, O.:The Fountains of Rome Telarc ▲ CD 80085 [DDD]
Respighi, O.:The Pines of Rome Telarc ▲ CD 80085 [DDD]
Respighi, O.:Gli uccelli Telarc ▲ CD 80085 [DDD]
Rorem, N.:Eagles New World ▲ NW 353-2 [DDD]
Rorem, N.:Sunday Morning New World ▲ NW 353-2 [DDD]
Singleton, A.:After Fallen Crumbs Meet The Composer ▲ 79231-2 ■ 79231-4
Singleton, A.:A Yellow Rose Petal Meet The Composer ▲ 79231-2 ■ 79231-4
Y. Levi (cnd)
The Artistry of Yoel Levi:The Telarc Collection, Vol. 8, w. Cleveland Orch
Barber, S.:Essay 1 Telarc ▲ CD 80250 [DDD]
Barber, S.:Essay 2 Telarc ▲ CD 80250 [DDD]
Barber, S.:Knoxville:Summer of 1915, w. S. McNair (sop) Telarc ▲ CD 80250 [DDD]
Barber, S.:Medea's Meditation & Dance of Vengeance Telarc ▲ CD 80250 [DDD]
Barber, S.:The School for Scandal Telarc ▲ CD 80250 [DDD]
Brahms, J.:Serenade 1 Orch *(rec 16-17, 1993)* Telarc ▲ CD 80349 [DDD]
Brahms, J.:Vars on a Theme by Haydn *(rec 16-17, 1993)* Telarc ▲ CD 80349 [DDD]
Copland, A.:Music for the Theatre Telarc ▲ CD-80201 [DDD]
Copland, A.:Sym 3 Telarc ▲ CD-80201 [DDD]
Hindemith, P.:Mathis der Maler (sym) Telarc ▲ CD 80195 [DDD]

Atlanta SO (cont.)

Y. Levi (cnd) (cont.)

Hindemith, P.:Nobilissima visione Telarc ▲ CD 80195 [DDD]
Hindemith, P.:Symphonic Metamorphosis on Themes of Carl Maria von Weber Telarc ▲ CD 80195 [DDD]
Kodály, Z.:Galanta Dances, w. Brice Andrus (hn), Laura Ardan (cl) *(rec Atlanta, 1995–96)* Telarc ▲ CD 80413 [DDD]
Kodály, Z.:Háry János (suite), w. James Barnes (cimbalom), Ted Gurch (sax), Reid Harris (va) *(rec Atlanta, 1995–96)* Telarc ▲ CD 80413 [DDD]
Kodály, Z.:Vars on a Hungarian Folk Song *(rec Atlanta, 1995–96)* Telarc ▲ CD 80413 [DDD]
Mahler, G.:Sym 5 *(rec Atlanta Symphony Hall, Woodruff Arts Center, Atlanta, GA, Feb 13–14, 1995)* Telarc ▲ CD 80394 [DDD]
Mendelssohn, F.:A Midsummer Night's Dream (sels)—Overture, Scherzo, Intermezzo, Nocturne, Wedding March Telarc ▲ CD 80318 [DDD]
Mendelssohn, F.:Sym 4 Telarc ▲ CD 80318 [DDD]
Mussorgsky, M.:Khovanshchina (prelude) Telarc ▲ CD 80296 [DDD]
Mussorgsky, M.:Night Telarc ▲ CD 80296 [DDD]
Mussorgsky, M.:Pictures at an Exhibition Telarc ▲ CD 80296 [DDD]
Paulus, S.:Concertante Orch New World ▲ NW 363–2 [DDD]
Paulus, S.:Sym Strs New World ▲ NW 363–2 [DDD]
Prokofiev, S.:Peter & the Wolf, w. P. Schickele (nar) [new text by Schickele] *(rec Mar. 20 & June 16, 1993)* Telarc ▲ CD 80350 [DDD] ■ CS 30350
Prokofiev, S.:Sym 1 Telarc ▲ CD 80289 [DDD]
Prokofiev, S.:Sym 5 Telarc ▲ CD 80289 [DDD]
Ravel, M.:Daphnis et Chloé, w. C. Smith (fl), Atlanta Sym Chorus *(rec May 24–25, 1993)* Telarc ▲ CD 80352 [DDD]
Ravel, M.:Pavane pour une infante défunte, w. Atlanta Sym Chorus *(rec May 24–25, 1993)* Telarc ▲ CD 80352 [DDD]
Rossini, G.:Ovs—Guillaume Tell; La Gazza ladra; L'Italiana in Algeri; Semiramide; La Scala di seta; Tancredi; Il barbieri di Siviglia *(rec Jan. 26, 1992 & May 26, 1)* Telarc ▲ CD 80334 [DDD]
Saint-Saëns, C.:Carnival of the Animals, w. P. Schickele (nar), R. Markham (pno), K. Broadway (pno) [poems by Schickele] *(rec Mar. 20 & June 16, 1993)* Telarc ▲ CD 80350 [DDD] ■ CS 30350
Saint-Saëns, C.:Con 2 Pno, w. A. Watts (pno) *(rec Symphony Hall, Woodruff Arts Center, Atlanta, GA, Nov. 21, 1994)* Telarc ▲ CD 80386 [DDD]
Schoenberg, A.:Pelleas und Melisande *(rec Atlanta, Mar. 5 & 7, 1994)* Telarc ▲ CD 80372
Schoenberg, A.:Verklärte Nacht *(rec Atlanta, Oct. 2, 1993)* Telarc ▲ CD 80372
Shostakovich, D.:Sym 5 Telarc ▲ CD 80215 [DDD]
Shostakovich, D.:Sym 8 *(rec Apr. 14, 1991)* Telarc ▲ CD 80291 [DDD]
Shostakovich, D.:Sym 9 Telarc ▲ CD 80215 [DDD]
Shostakovich, D.:Sym 10 Telarc ▲ CD 80241 [DDD]
Sibelius, J.:Karelia Suite Telarc ▲ CD 80320
Sibelius, J.:Pohjola's Daughter Telarc ▲ CD 80320
Sibelius, J.:En Saga Telarc ▲ CD 80320
Sibelius, J.:The Swan of Tuonela Telarc ▲ CD 80320
Sibelius, J.:Sym 1 Telarc ▲ CD 80246 [DDD]
Sibelius, J.:Sym 5 Telarc ▲ CD 80246 [DDD]
Stravinsky, I.:Pulcinella Suite [1949 revised version] Telarc ▲ CD 80266 [DDD]
Stravinsky, I.:Le Sacre du printemps Orch [1947 rev. ver.] Telarc ▲ CD 80266 [DDD]
Tchaikovsky, P.:Con 1 Pno, w. André Watts (pno) *(rec Symphony Hall, Woodruff Arts Center, Atlanta, GA, Aug. 1, 1994)* Telarc ▲ CD 80386 [DDD]
Torke, M.:Javelin *(rec Symphony Hall, Atlanta, GA, Nov 14, 1995)* Argo ▲ 452101–2 [DDD]
Torke, M.:Run *(rec Symphony Hall, Atlanta, GA, Nov 14, 1995)* Argo ▲ 452101–2 [DDD]

R. Shaw (cnd)

Adams, J.:Harmonium *(rec Atlanta, Nov 4–5, 1995)* Telarc ▲ CD 80365 [DDD]
Bach, J.S.:Magnificat, BWV 243, w. P. Jensen (sop), D. Upshaw (sop), M. Simpson (mez), D. Gordon (ten), W. Stone (bar), Atlanta Chamber Chorus Telarc ▲ CD 80194 [DDD]
Bach, J.S.:Mass in b, BWV 232, w. S. McNair (sop), G. Simpson (mez), D. Ziegler (mez), J. Aler (ten), W. Stone (bar), T. Paul (bass), Atlanta Chamber Chorus [L] Telarc 2–▲ CD 80233 [DDD]
Beethoven, L. van:Elegischer Gesang, "Sanft wie du lebtest", w. Atlanta Sym Chorus [chorus & string orch. performance] Telarc ▲ CD 80248 [DDD]
Beethoven, L. van:Mass, Op. 86, w. H. Schellenberg (mez), M. Simpson (mez), J. Humphrey (ten), M. Myers (ten), Atlanta Sym Chorus [L] Telarc ▲ CD 80248 [DDD]
Beethoven, L. van:Meeresstille und glückliche Fahrt, w. Atlanta Sym Chorus [G] Telarc ▲ CD 80248 [DDD]
Beethoven, L. van:Missa Solemnis, w. S. McNair (sop), Janice Taylor (mez), J. Aler (ten), T. Krause (bar), Atlanta Sym Chorus [L] Telarc 2–▲ CD 80150 [DDD]
Beethoven, L. van:Music of, w. K. Masur (cnd), Leipzig Gewandhaus Orch—sels. from Syms. 3,5,6,7 & 9, Pno Con. 5; Vn Con.; Egmont Ov.; Für Elise; Turkish March; Military Marches Nos. 1 & 2 Pro Arte ▲ CDM 820 ■ PCD 820
Beethoven, L. van:Music of, w. R. Serkin (pno), J. O'Conor (pno), Cleveland Orch—sels. from Syms. 5,6,7 & 9, Moonlight Son., Pno Con. 5, etc. Telarc ▲ CD 80240 [DDD] ■ CS 30240 (D)
Beethoven, L. van:Sym 9, "Choral Sym", w. B. Valente (sop), F. Kopleff (cta), J. Hadley (ten), J. Cheek (bass), Atlanta Sym Chorus Pro Arte ▲ CDD 245 [DDD]
Berlioz, H.:Les Nuits d'été, w. E. Ameling (sop) [F] Telarc ▲ CD 80084 [DDD]
Berlioz, H.:Requiem, "Grande Messe des Morts", w. J. Aler (ten), Atlanta Sym Chorus [L] Telarc 2–▲ CD 80109–2 [DDD]
Bernstein, L.:Chichester Psalms, w. Atlanta Sym Chorus [He] Telarc ▲ CD 80181 [DDD]
Bernstein, L.:Missa brevis, w. D. L. Ragin (ct), Atlanta Sym Chorus [L] Telarc ▲ CD 80181 [DDD]
Boito, A.:Mefistofele (sels), w. Cheek (sgr), Atlanta Sym Chorus—Prologue [I] Telarc 2–▲ CD 80109–2 [DDD]
Borodin, A.:Prince Igor (ov) Telarc ▲ CD 80039 [DDD]
Borodin, A.:Prince Igor (Polovtsian dances), w. Atlanta Sym Chorus [R] Telarc ▲ CD 80039 [DDD]
Brahms, J.:Alto Rhap, w. M. Horne (mez), Atlanta Sym Chorus [G] Telarc ▲ CD 80176 [DDD]
Brahms, J.:Con 1 Pno, w. P. Serkin (pno) Pro Arte ▲ CDD 266
Brahms, J.:Con 2 Pno, w. P. Serkin (pno) Pro Arte ▲ CDD 336 [DDD]
Brahms, J.:Ein Deutsches Requiem, w. A. Augér (sop), R. Stilwell (bar), Atlanta Sym Chorus [G] Telarc 2–▲ CD 80092 [DDD]
Brahms, J.:Gesang der Parzen, w. Atlanta Sym Chorus [G] Telarc ▲ CD 80176 [DDD]
Brahms, J.:Nänie, w. Atlanta Sym Chorus [G] Telarc ▲ CD 80176 [DDD]
Brahms, J.:Schicksalslied, w. Atlanta Sym Chorus [G] Telarc ▲ CD 80176 [DDD]
Britten, B.:War Requiem, w. L. Haywood (sop), A. Rolfe-Johnson (ten), B. Luxon (bar), Atlanta Sym Chorus [L] Telarc 2–▲ CD 80157 [DDD]
Choral Masterpieces, w. Atlanta Sym Chorus Telarc ▲ CD 80119 [DDD]
Christmas Favorites with Robert Shaw, w. Atlanta Sym Chorus Vox 90s ■ V9–9901
Christmas with Robert Shaw, w. Atlanta Sym Chorus Allegretto ▲ ACD 8409 [ADD]
Dvořák, A.:Te Deum, w. Atlanta Sym Chorus [L] Telarc ▲ CD 80287 [DDD]
Fauré, G.:Pelléas et Mélisande (suite) Telarc ▲ CD 80084 [DDD]
Fauré, G.:Requiem, w. J. Blegen (sop), J. Morris (bass), Atlanta Sym Chorus [L] Telarc ▲ CD 80135 [DDD]
Glass, Philip:The Canyon Sony Classical ▲ SK 46352 [DDD]
Glass, Philip:Itaipu, w. Atlanta Sym Chorus Sony Classical ▲ SK 46352 [DDD]
Grand & Glorious:Great Operatic Choruses, w. Atlanta Sym Chorus, A. Howard (asst choral cnd) Telarc ▲ CD 80333 [DDD]
Handel, G.F.:Messiah, w. Kaaren Erickson (sop), Sylvia McNair (sop), Alfreda Hodgson (cta), Jon Humphrey (ten), Richard Stilwell (bar), Atlanta Sym Chorus [E] Telarc 2–▲ CD 80093–2 [DDD]
Handel, G.F.:Messiah, w. Kaaren Erickson (sop), Sylvia McNair (sop), Alfreda Hodgson (cta), Jon Humphrey (ten), Richard Stilwell (bar), Atlanta Sym Chorus [E] Telarc ▲ CD 80103 [DDD]; ■ CS 30103 (D)
Haydn, J.:Die Schöpfung, w. Dawn Upshaw (sop), Jon Humphrey (ten), John Cheek (bass), Atlanta Chamber Chorus [E] Telarc 2–▲ CD 80298 [DDD]

Atlanta SO (cont.)

R. Shaw (cnd) (cont.)

Hindemith, P.:When Lilacs Last In The Dooryard Bloom'd, w. Jan DeGaetani (mez), William Stone (bar), Atlanta Sym Chorus [E] Telarc ▲ CD 80132 [DDD]
Janáček, L.:Slavonic Mass, w. C. Brewer (sop), M. Simpson (mez), K. Dent (ten), R. Roloff (bass), Atlanta Sym Chorus [Sla] Telarc ▲ CD 80287 [DDD]
Mahler, G.:Sym 8, w. Atlanta Sym Chorus [G] Telarc ▲ CD 80267 [DDD]
The Many Moods of Christmas, w. Atlanta Sym Chorus Telarc ▲ CD 80087 [DDD] ■ CS 30087 (D)
Mendelssohn, F.:Elijah, w. Barbara Bonney (sop), Henriette Schellenberg (sop), Florence Quivar (mez), Marietta Simpson (mez), Reid Bartelme (trb), Jerry Hadley (ten), Richard Clement (ten), Thomas Hampson (bar), Thomas Paul (bar), Atlanta Sym Chorus [E] *(rec Symphony Hall, Woodruff Arts Center, Atlanta, GA, Nov. 5–7, 1994)* Telarc 2–▲ CD 80389 [DDD]
Mozart, W.A.:Missa, K.427, w. Edith Wiens (sop), Delores Ziegler (mez), John Aler (ten), William Stone (bar), Atlanta Sym Chorus [L] Telarc 2–▲ CD 80150 [DDD]
Mozart, W.A.:Requiem, w. A. Augér (sop), D. Ziegler (mez), J. Hadley (ten), T. Krause (bar), Atlanta Sym Chorus [L] Telarc ▲ CD 80128 [DDD]
Orff, C.:Carmina burana, w. J. Blegen (sop), W. Brown (ten), H. Hagegård (bar), Atlanta Sym Chorus [G, L] Telarc ▲ CD 80056 [DDD]
Paulus, S.:Con Vn, w. W. Preucil (vn) New World ▲ NW 363–2 [DDD]
Poulenc, F.:Con Org, w. M. Murray (org) Telarc ▲ CD 80104 [DDD]
Poulenc, F.:Stabat mater, w. C. Goerke (sop), Atlanta Sym Chorus *(rec Atlanta, Nov. 7–8, 1993)* Telarc ▲ CD 80362 [DDD]
Rachmaninoff, S.:The Bells, w. Atlanta Sym Chorus *(rec Atlanta, Nov 4–5, 1995)* Telarc ▲ CD 80365 [DDD]
Rorem, N.:Str Sym New World ▲ NW 353–2 [DDD]
Schubert, Franz:Mass 2, w. D. Upshaw (sop), D. Gordon (ten), W. Stone (bass), Atlanta Sym Chorus [L] Telarc ▲ CD 80212 [DDD]
Schubert, Franz:Mass 6, w. B. Valente (sop), M. Simpson (mez), J. Humphrey (ten), G. Siebert (ten), M. Myers (ten), Atlanta Sym Chorus [L] Telarc ▲ CD 80212 [DDD]
Singleton, A.:Shadows Meet The Composer ▲ 79231–2 ■ 79231–4
Stravinsky, I.:The Firebird Suite Telarc ▲ CD 80039 [DDD]
Stravinsky, I.:Sym of Psalms, w. Atlanta Sym Chorus [L] Telarc ▲ CD 80254 [DDD]
Szymanowski, K.:Stabat Mater, w. C. Goerke (sop), M. Simpson (mez), V. Ledbetter (bar), Atlanta Sym Chorus *(rec Atlanta, Nov. 7–8, 1993)* Telarc ▲ CD 80362 [DDD]
Verdi, G.:Choruses, w. Atlanta Sym Chorus—from Aida, Don Carlos, Macbeth, Nabucco, Otello [I] Telarc 2–▲ CD 80152 [DDD] 2–■ CS 30152 (D)
Verdi, G.:Requiem Mass, w. V. Dunn (sop), D. Curry (cta), J. Hadley (ten), P. Plishka (bass), Atlanta Sym Chorus [L] Telarc 2–▲ CD 80152 [DDD] 2–■ CS 30152 (D)
Verdi, G.:Te Deum, w. Atlanta Sym Chorus [G] Telarc 2–▲ CD 80092 [DDD]
Verdi, G.:Te Deum, w. Atlanta Sym Chorus [L] Telarc 2–▲ CD 80109–2 [DDD]
Vivaldi, A.:Gloria, RV.589, w. D. Upshaw (sop), P. Jensen (sop), M. Simpson (mez), D. Gordon (ten), W. Stone (bar), Atlanta Chamber Chorus Telarc ▲ CD 80194 [DDD]
Walton, W.:Belshazzar's Feast, w. W. Stone (bar), Atlanta Sym Chorus [E] Telarc ▲ CD 80181 [DDD]

Atlantic Brass Quintet

All American Trombone, w. Ronald Barron (trbn), Fredrik Wanger (pno), Harvard Univ Wind Ensemble *(rec Sanders Theater, Harvard Univ; Symphony Hall, Boston; Morse Auditorium, Boston Univ, Nov 7, Dec 8–9, 1995)* Boston Brass ▲ BB 1003
A Joyous Christmas:Trumpets Sound, Voices Ring, w. American Boychoir MusicMasters ▲ 01612–67076–2 [DDD]

Atlantic Brass Quintet [J. Damian Foley (tpt), J. Luke (tpt), K. Owen (hn), J. Faieta (trbn), J. Manning (tuba)]

Bizet, G.:Carmen (suite 1) [trans. for brass quintet] *(rec Nov. 27–28, 1992)* MusicMasters ▲ 01612–67142–2 [DDD]
Liszt, F.:Hungarian Rhaps [trans. for brass quintet]— No. 2 *(rec Nov. 27–28, 1992)* MusicMasters ▲ 01612–67142–2 [DDD]
Mussorgsky, M.:Pictures at an Exhibition [trans. for brass quintet] *(rec Nov. 27–28, 1992)* MusicMasters ▲ 01612–67142–2 [DDD]

Atlantic Brass Quintet [Joseph Foley (tpt), Jeffrey Luke (tpt), R. Rasmussen (hn), John Faieta (trbn), John Manning (tuba)]

A Musical Voyage Summit ▲ DCD 119 [DDD] ■ DCD 119

Atlantic Sinfonietta

Barber, S.:Music of, w. Alexa Still (fl), Chicago SO, San Diego CO, New Zealand SO, Arioso Wind Quintet, Capricorn, Repertory Singers—Capricorn Con; Canzone; Fadograph of a Yestern Scene; Cave of the Heart; Adagio for Strs; Souvenirs; Hermit Songs; To Be Sung on Water; The Lovers; Summer Music Koch International Classics ▲ KIC 7361
Jolivet, A.:Chant de Linos [chamber version] Koch International Classics ▲ KIC 7016–2 [DDD] ■ 3–7016–4 (D)
Jongen, J.:Concert à cinq Koch International Classics ▲ KIC 7016–2 [DDD] ■ 3–7016–4 (D)

A. Schenck (cnd)

Barber, S.:Cave of the Heart Koch International Classics ▲ KIC 7019–2 [DDD] ■ 3–7019–4
Copland, A.:Appalachian Spring—original 13–instrument chamber version Koch International Classics ▲ KIC 7019–2 [DDD] ■ 3–7019–4
Hindemith, P.:Hérodiade Koch International Classics ▲ KIC 7051–2 [DDD]
Kurka, R.:The Good Soldier Schweik (suite) Koch International Classics ▲ KIC 7091–2 [DDD]
Menotti, G.C.:Errand into the Maze Koch International Classics ▲ KIC 7051–2 [DDD]
Milhaud, D.:La Création du monde Koch International Classics ▲ KIC 7091–2 [DDD]
More Music for Martha Graham Koch International Classics ▲ KIC 7051 [DDD]
Music for Martha Graham:The Original Versions Koch International Classics ▲ KIC 7019 [DDD]
Schuman, W.:Night Journey Koch International Classics ▲ KIC 7051–2 [DDD]
Weill, K.:Kleine Dreigroschenmusik Koch International Classics ▲ KIC 7091–2 [DDD]

E. Tchivzhel (cnd)

Dello Joio, N.:Diversion of Angels Koch International Classics ▲ KIC 7167–2 [DDD]
Dello Joio, N.:Exaltation of Larks Koch International Classics ▲ KIC 7167–2 [DDD]
Dello Joio, N.:Seraphic Dialogues Koch International Classics ▲ KIC 7167–2 [DDD]

Atlantic Sinfonietta members [B. Garner (instr), L. Martin (va), G. Benet (pno)]

Debussy, C.:Son Fl Koch International Classics ▲ KIC 7016–2 [DDD] ■ 3–7016–4 (D)

Atlantis Ensemble

Schubert, Franz:Octet Ww, D.803 Virgin Classics ▲ 59224 [DDD]

Atril5

Kupferman, M.:Flavors of the Stars Soundspells ▲ PAN 811308
Kupferman, M.:Ice Cream Con Soundspells ▲ SP 109

Audoli Instrumental Ensemble

J.-W. Audoli (cnd)

Britten, B.:Les Illuminations, w. C. Eda-Pierre (sop) [F] Arion ▲ ARN 68035 [DDD]
Britten, B.:Phaedra, w. C. Eda-Pierre (mez) [E] Arion ▲ ARN 68035 [DDD]
Britten, B.:Simple Sym [E] Arion ▲ ARN 68035 [DDD]
Pergolesi, G.B.:Concertino 2 Strs Arion ▲ ARN 68026 [DDD]
Pergolesi, G.B.:Con Vn, w. Y. Naganuma (vn) Arion ▲ ARN 68026 [DDD]
Pergolesi, G.B.:Salve regina in f, w. J. Bowman (ct) [L] Arion ▲ ARN 68026 [DDD]
Vivaldi, A.:Salve regina, RV.616, w. J. Bowman (ct) [L] Arion ▲ ARN 68026 [DDD]

M. Piquemal (cnd)

Ropartz, G.:Psalm 129, w. Vincent Le Texier (bar), French Vittoria Regional Choir Accord ▲ ACD 205132 [DDD]
Ropartz, G.:Requiem, w. Catherine Dubosc (sop), Jacqueline Mayeur (mez), Vincent Le Texier (bar), French Vittoria Regional Choir Accord ▲ ACD 205132 [DDD]

Audubon String Quartet

Bax, A.:Qnt Ob, w. P. Woods (ob) Telarc ▲ CD 80205 [DDD]
Bliss, A.:Qnt Cl, w. P. Woods (cl) Telarc ▲ CD 80205 [DDD]
Bliss, A.:Qnt Ob, w. Pamela Pecha (ob) IMP ("Classics" series) ▲ IMP 6701032
Britten, B.:Phantasy Qt, w. Pamela Pecha (ob) IMP ("Classics" series) ▲ IMP 6701032

56

▲ = CD ♦ = Enhanced CD Δ = MD ■ = Cassette Tape ▯ = DCC

Audubon String Quartet [D. Cleveland (vn), S. Smith (vn), D. Lederer (va), C. Shaw (vc)]
Fennelly, B.:Qt in 2 Movts *(rec 1980)* New World ▲ 80448-2
Audubon String Quartet [David Ehrlich (vn), David Salness (vn), Doris Lederer (va), Clyde Shaw (vc)]
Dohnányi, E. von:Qt 2 Strs *(rec LSU Recital Hall, Louisiana State Univ, Baton Rouge, July 23–25, 1995)* Centaur ▲ CRC 2309 [DDD]
Dohnányi, E. von:Qt 3 Strs *(rec LSU Recital Hall, Louisiana State Univ, Baton Rouge, July 23–25, 1995)* Centaur ▲ CRC 2309 [DDD]
Audubon String Quartet members
Britten, B.:Phantasy Qt, w. P. Woods (ob) Telarc ▲ CD 80205 [DDD]
Auer String Quartet
Weber, C.M. von:Intro, Theme & Vars Cl, w. Kálmán Berkes (cl) *(rec Scottish Church, Budapest, Aug. 23–27, 1994)* Naxos ▲ 8.553122 [DDD]
Weber, C.M. von:Qnt Cl, w. Kálmán Berkes (cl) *(rec Scottish Church, Budapest, Aug. 23–27, 1994)* Naxos ▲ 8.553122 [DDD]
Augsburg Early Music Ensemble
Et in terra pax:Sacred Music of the Middle Ages Christophorus ▲ 77139 [DDD]
Hildegard von Bingen & Her Time:Sacred Music of the 12th Century Christophorus ▲ CHR 74584 [DDD]
Hildegard Of Bingen:Sacred Songs Christophorus ▲ CHR 74584 [DDD]
Loves & Desires:Songs of the Trouvères *(rec Dec. 1991)* Christophorus ▲ CHR 77117 [DDD]
Monk Of Salzburg:Songs—57 secular songs Christophorus ▲ 77176
Planctus Mariae Christophorus ▲ 77147 [DDD]
Troubadours, Trouvères & Minnesingers Christophorus ▲ CD 74519
Augsburg PO
G. Ratzinger (cnd)
Schubert, Franz:Duetsche Messe, w. Munich RSO, Munich Radio Orch, Munich PO Soloists, Regensburg Cathedral Choir Ars Musici ▲ AM 0929 [DDD]
Aulos Ensemble [Anne Briggs (trns fl), Marc Schachman (baroque ob), Linda Quan (baroque vn), Myron Lutzke (baroque vc), Arthur Haas (hpd/org)]
A Baroque Christmas from the Metropolitan Museum of Art Concerts, w. Julianne Baird (sop) MusicMasters ▲ 01612-67119-2 ■ 01612-67119-4
Aulos Wind Quintet
Barber, S.:Summer Music *(rec 1989–90)* Koch Schwann ▲ 3-1153-2 [DDD]
Baur, J.:Quintetto pittoresco *(rec Jan. 31, 1989)* Koch Schwann ▲ SCH 311982 [ADD/DDD]
Briccialdi, G.:Qnt Ww, Op. 124 Koch Schwann ▲ CD 310 087 [DDD]
Cage, J.:Music for Ww *(rec 1989–90)* Koch Schwann ▲ 3-1153-2 [DDD]
Cambini, G.M.:Qnts (3) Ww—No. 3 Koch Schwann ▲ 310011 [DDD]
Carter, E.:Etudes (8) & a Fant *(rec 1989–90)* Koch Schwann ▲ 3-1153-2 [DDD]
Carter, E.:Qnt Ww *(rec 1989–90)* Koch Schwann ▲ 3-1153-2 [DDD]
Danzi, F.:Qnts Ww, Op. 67—No. 2 in e Koch Schwann ▲ 310011 [DDD]
Eisler, H.:Divert Wind Qnt Koch Schwann ▲ SCH 311632 [DDD]
Foerster, J.B.:Qnt Ww Koch Schwann ▲ CD 310 051 [DDD]
Haas, P.:Qnt Wind Koch Schwann ▲ CD 310 051 [DDD]
Hindemith, P.:Kleine Kammermusik Koch Schwann ▲ SCH 311632 [DDD]
Holst, G.:Qnt Winds Koch Schwann ▲ CD 310 100 [DDD]
Janácek, L.:Youth, w. K. Berger (b cl) Koch Schwann ▲ CD 310 051 [DDD]
Jolivet, A.:Sérénade Ob Koch Schwann ▲ CD 310 100 [DDD]
Lefebvre, C.:Suite Winds Koch Schwann ▲ CD 310 087 [DDD]
Nielsen, C.:Qnt Ww Koch Schwann ▲ CD 310 100 [DDD]
Pierne, P.:Suite pittoresque Koch Schwann ▲ CD 310 100 [DDD]
Reicha, A.:Qnt Ww, Op. 100/5 Koch Schwann ▲ 310011 [DDD]
Schoenberg, A.:Qnt Fl Koch Schwann ▲ SCH 311632 [DDD]
Schuller, G.:Suite Ww Ensemble *(rec 1989–90)* Koch Schwann ▲ 3-1153-2 [DDD]
Taffanel, P.:Qnt Ww Koch Schwann ▲ CD 310 087 [DDD]
Zemlinsky, A. von:Humoresque Koch Schwann ▲ CD 310 100 [DDD]
B. Güller (cnd)
Lindpaintner, P.J. von:Sinfs concertante, Stuttgart RSO *(rec 1984)* Koch Schwann ▲ CD 311 121 [ADD/DDD]
Aurelia Saxophone Quartet [Johan van der Linden (s sax), André Arends (a sax), Arno Bornkamp (t sax), Willem van Merwijk (bar sax)]
Piazzolla, A.:Music of, w. Gustavo Toker (band), Juan Pablo Dobal (pno)—Escualo; Adio Nonino; Caliente; Astor que Estas en Los Cielos; Contrabajeando; Cuatro Estaciones Porteñas; Vayamos al Diablo; Four, for Tango; Milonga del Angel; Contrabajissimo; Michelangelo 70; Fuga y Misterio; Variaciones de la Fuga *(rec live, De Rode Hoed, Amsterdam, June 26, 1994)* Etcetera ▲ KTC 1186
Auréole
Ibert, J.:Interludes [arr. for flute, viola & harp] Koch International Classics ▲ KIC 7102-2 [DDD]
Ravel, M.:Sonatine en Trio Koch International Classics ▲ KIC 7102-2 [DDD]
Auréole [L. Gilbert (fl), B. Allen (hp)]
Fauré, G.:Morceau de concours Fl & Hp Koch International Classics ▲ KIC 7102-2 [DDD]
Auréole [L. Gilbert (fl), M. Hammann (va), B. Allen (hp)]
Debussy, C.:Son Fl Koch International Classics ▲ KIC 7102-2 [DDD]
Genzmer, H.:Trio Fl, Va & Hp Koch International Classics ▲ KIC 7055-2 [DDD]
Gubaidulina, S.:The Garden of Joy & Sorrow Koch International Classics ▲ KIC 7055-2 [DDD]
Nielsen, C.:Moderen—The fog is lifting; The children are playing; Faith and Hope are playing Koch International Classics ▲ KIC 7055-2 [DDD]
Salzedo, C.:Sonatine en Trio Koch International Classics ▲ KIC 7102-2 [DDD]
Auréole [L. Gilbert (fl), M. Hammann (va)]
Devienne, F.:Duo Fl Koch International Classics ▲ KIC 7102-2 [DDD]
Aurora Ensemble
Corelli, A.:Trio Sons (misc)—Op. 1, Nos. 5,11 & 12; Op. 2, Nos. 7 & 10; Op. 3, No. 4; Op. 4, Nos. 1 & 4 [period instrs] Tactus ▲ TC 650302 [DDD]
Corelli, A.:Trio Sons (misc)—Op. 1, No. 9; Op. 2, Nos. 1 & 12; Op. 3, Nos. 9,11 & 12; Op. 4, Nos. 3 & 10 [period instrs] Tactus ▲ TC 650301 [DDD]
Scarlatti, A.:Lamentazioni par la Settimana Santa, w. C. Miatello (sop), G. P. Fagotto (ten) Symphonia ▲ SYM 92D17 [DDD]
Schmelzer, J.H.:Balletti, w. Labyrinto Ensemble di Viole—Nos. 3, 4, 5, 6, 8, 7 & 9 *(rec May 19–22, 1991)* Symphonia ▲ SY 91S07
Schmelzer, J.H.:Duodena selectarum sonatarum, w. Labyrinto Ensemble di Viole—Nos. 4, 6, 10, 11 & 12 *(rec May 19–22, 1991)* Symphonia ▲ SY 91S07
Schmelzer, J.H.:Die Fechtschule, w. Labyrinto Ensemble di Viole—Nos. 3, 4, 5, 6, 8, 7 & 9 *(rec May 19–22, 1991)* Symphonia ▲ SY 91S07
Schmelzer, J.H.:Sacro-profanus concentus musicus, w. Labyrinto Ensemble di Viole—Nos. 3, 4, 5, 6, 8, 7 & 9 *(rec May 19–22, 1991)* Symphonia ▲ SY 91S07
Schmelzer, J.H.:Serenata con altre arie; amento sopra la morte Ferdinandi III, w. Labyrinto Ensemble di Viole—Nos. 3, 4, 5, 6, 8, 7 & 9 *(rec May 19–22, 1991)* Symphonia ▲ SY 91S07
Aurora Ensemble [Enrico Gatti (vn), Odile Edouard (vn), Alain Gervreau (vc), Guido Morini (org/hpd)], Adriana Egivi (sgr), Sigrid Lee (sgr), Stefano Pilati (perc/sgr)]
The Art of the Violin in Italy During the 17th & 18th Centuries, Vol. 1 Symphonia ▲ SYM 90502 [DDD]
L'Arte del Violino Symphonia ▲ SY 91S11 [DDD]
Aurora String Quartet [Sharon Grebanier (vn), Mariko Smiley (vn), Basil Vendryes (va), Margaret Tait (vc)]
Macbride, D.:Dances Str Qt CRI ▲ CD 640 [DDD]
Mendelssohn, F.:Capriccio Str Qt *(rec May–Aug. 1993)* Naxos ▲ 8.550861 [DDD]
Mendelssohn, F.:Fugue Str Qt *(rec May–Aug. 1993)* Naxos ▲ 8.550861 [DDD]
Mendelssohn, F.:Qt 3 Strs *(rec May–Aug. 1993)* Naxos ▲ 8.550861 [DDD]

Aurora String Quartet (cont.)
Mendelssohn, F.:Qt 6 Strs *(rec May–Aug. 1993)* Naxos ▲ 8.550861 [DDD]
Aurora String Quartet [Sharon Grebanier (vn), Mariko Smiley (vn), Don Ehrlich (va), Mararet Tait (vc)]
Prokofiev, S.:Qt 1 Strs *(rec Fisher Hall, Santa Rosa, CA, Feb. 9–12, 1994)* Naxos ▲ 8.553136 [DDD]
Prokofiev, S.:Qt 2 Strs *(rec Fisher Hall, Santa Rosa, CA, Feb. 9–12, 1994)* Naxos ▲ 8.553136 [DDD]
Australia Ensemble
Berg, A.:Chamber Con Entr'acte ▲ ESCD 6507 [DDD]
Isaacs, M.:So It Does *(rec Sept. 27–Oct. 1, 1989)* Tall Poppies ▲ TP002 [DDD]
Mozart, W.A.:Qts Fl Tall Poppies ▲ TP 029
Mozart, W.A.:Qt Ob, K.370 Tall Poppies ▲ TP 029
Schoenberg, A.:Chamber Sym 1 Entr'acte ▲ ESCD 6507 [DDD]
Schoenberg, A.:Trio Strs Entr'acte ▲ ESCD 6507 [DDD]
Schubert, Franz:Der Hirt auf dem Felsen, w. J. Bates (sop), N. Westlake (cl), D. Bollard (pno) [G] *(rec July 1991)* Tall Poppies ▲ TP 011 [DDD]
Schubert, Franz:Qnt Strs, D.956, w. D. Pereira (vc) *(rec July 1991)* Tall Poppies ▲ TP 011 [DDD]
Vine, C.:Café Concertino *(rec Sept. 27–Oct. 1, 1989)* Tall Poppies ▲ TP002 [DDD]
Vine, C.:Café Concertino *(rec Sept. 1989)* Tall Poppies ▲ TP013 [DDD]
Wesley-Smith, M.:White Knight & Beaver *(rec Sept. 27–Oct. 1, 1989)* Tall Poppies ▲ TP002 [DDD]
Westlake, N.:Refractions at Summer Cloud Bay *(rec Sept. 27–Oct. 1, 1989)* Tall Poppies ▲ TP002 [DDD]
Whitehead, Gillian:Manutaki *(rec Sept. 27–Oct. 1, 1989)* Tall Poppies ▲ TP002 [DDD]
G. Hair (cnd)
Dallapiccola, L.:Divert in quattro esercizi, w. J. Manning (sop)—[I] Entr'acte ▲ ESCD 6504 [DDD]
Dallapiccola, L.:Liriche greche, w. J. Manning (sop)—[I] Entr'acte ▲ ESCD 6504 [DDD]
Dallapiccola, L.:Piccola musica notturna Entr'acte ▲ ESCD 6504 [DDD]
Australia Ensemble [Geoffrey Collins (fl), Alan Vivian (cl), David Bollard (pno)]
Sitsky, L.:Trio 6 Fl *(rec John Clancy Auditorium, Univ of New South Wales, 1993)* Vox Australis ▲ VAST 020-2 [DDD]
Australia Ensemble [Geoffrey Collins (fl), Alan Vivian (cl), Dene Olding (vn), Irina Morozova (va), Julian Smiles (vc), David Bollard (pno)]
Kerry, G.:Son da Camera *(rec John Clancy Auditorium, Univ of New South Wales, 1993)* Vox Australis ▲ VAST 020-2 [DDD]
Vine, C.:Miniature IV *(rec John Clancy Auditorium, Univ of New South Wales, 1993)* Vox Australis ▲ VAST 020-2 [DDD]
Australia Ensemble [Geoffrey Collins (fl), Alan Vivian (cl), Dimity Hall (vn), Irina Morozova (va), Julian Smiles (vc), David Bollard (pno)]
Kos, B.:Catena 2 *(rec John Clancy Auditorium, Univ of New South Wales, 1993)* Vox Australis ▲ VAST 020-2 [DDD]
Australia Ensemble [Geoffrey Collins (fl), Dimity Hall (vn), Irina Morozova (va), Julian Smiles (vc)]
Banks, D.:Divert Fl & Strs *(rec John Clancy Auditorium, Univ of New South Wales, 1993)* Vox Australis ▲ VAST 020-2 [DDD]
Australia Soloists
R. Thomas (cnd)
Tippett, M.:Little Music Chandos ("Collect" series) ▲ CHAN 6576 [ADD/DDD]
Australian CO
Sculthorpe, P.:Irkanda IV Southern Cross ▲ SCCD 1016 [ADD]
Sculthorpe, P.:Lament Strs Southern Cross ▲ SCCD 1016 [ADD]
Sculthorpe, P.:Port Essington Southern Cross ▲ SCCD 1016 [ADD]
Sculthorpe, P.:Son Strs Southern Cross ▲ SCCD 1016 [ADD]
C.L. Gee (cnd)
Respighi, O.:Ancient Airs & Dances Omega ▲ OCD 1007 [DDD]
Respighi, O.:Gli uccelli Omega ▲ OCD 1007 [DDD]
Strauss, R.:Der Bürger als Edelmann (suite) Omega ▲ OCD 1011 [DDD]
Stravinsky, I.:Pulcinella Omega ▲ OCD 1011 [DDD]
S. Kovacevich (cnd)
Beethoven, L. van:Con 5 Pno, "Emperor", w. Stephen Kovacevich (pno) Classics for Pleasure ("Eminence" series) ▲ CFP 2184 [DDD]
Beethoven, L. van:Grosse Fuge Str Qt Classics for Pleasure ("Eminence" series) ▲ CFP 2184 [DDD]
C. Mackerras (cnd)
Schubert, Franz:Sym 5 Omega ▲ OCD 1005 [DDD]
Schubert, Franz:Sym 6 Omega ▲ OCD 1005 [DDD]
C. Pini (cnd)
Tchaikovsky, P.:Serenade Strs Omega ▲ OCD 1010 [DDD]
Tchaikovsky, P.:Souvenir de Florence Omega ▲ OCD 1010 [DDD]
Australian PO
T. Bremner (cnd)
Herrmann, B.:Citizen Kane, w. R. Illing (sop) Preamble ▲ PRCD 1788 [DDD]
Herrmann, B.:The Magnificent Ambersons (film music) for Orchestra Preamble ▲ PRCD 1783 [DDD]
Australian Pops Orch
An Evening To Remember, w. Joan Sutherland (sop) DRG ▲ 13103
Australian Youth Orch
G. Abbott (cnd)
Christmas under Capricorn Tall Poppies ▲ TP 16
austraLYSIS members [Hazel Smith (nar), Roger Dean (sampler)]
Smith, Hazel:Simultaneity *(rec Sydney, 1993)* Tall Poppies ▲ TP 39 [DDD]
austraLYSIS members [Hazel Smith (vn), Roger Dean (pno), Harry Beckett (tpt), Ashley Brown (perc), Jim Fulkerson (trbn), Colin Lawson (cl), Marc Meggido (db), Geoff Warren (fl)]
Cresswell, L.:Organic Music *(rec London)* Tall Poppies ▲ TP 39 [DDD]
austraLYSIS members [Peter Jenkin (b cl), Roger Dean (sampler)]
Rue, R.:Nocturnal Windows *(rec Studio C, 2MBS-FM, 1993)* Tall Poppies ▲ TP 39 [DDD]
austraLYSIS members [Peter Jenkin (cl), Hazel Smith (vn), Roger Dean (db)]
Cresswell, L.:Soliloquy on a Lambent Tailpiece *(rec Studio C, 2MBS-FM, 1993)* Tall Poppies ▲ TP 39 [DDD]
austraLYSIS members [Peter Jenkin (cl), Roger Dean (pno)]
Dean, R.T.:TimeStrain *(rec Studio C, 2MBS-FM, 1993)* Tall Poppies ▲ TP 39 [DDD]
austraLYSIS members [Roger Dean (db), Stephanie McCallum (pno)]
Bright, C.:Night Db *(rec ABC, Sydney, 1990)* Tall Poppies ▲ TP 39 [DDD]
austraLYSIS members [Stephanie McCallum (pno), Hazel Smith (vn), Georg Pedersen (vc), Roger Dean (db), David Stanhope (cnd)]
Xenakis, I.:Morsima-Amorsima *(rec Studio C, 2MBS-FM, 1993)* Tall Poppies ▲ TP 39 [DDD]
Austria String Ensemble
Bruckner, A.:Qt Strs—Adagio movt Camerata ("After Hours Classics" series) ▲ 20 CM 423 [DDD]
Austrian Chamber Sym
E. Theis (cnd)
Milhaud, D.:Con Mar, w. Nebojša Jovan Zivkovic (mar/vib) *(rec Casino Zögernitz, Vienna, June 6–19, 1995)* Musicaphon ▲ M 56809 [DDD]
Milhaud, D.:Cortège funèbre *(rec Casino Zögernitz, Vienna, June 6–19, 1995)* Musicaphon ▲ M 56809 [DDD]
Radanovics, M.:Introversion *(rec Casino Zögernitz, Vienna, June 6–19, 1995)* Musicaphon ▲ M 56809 [DDD]
Austrian Ensemble for New Music
K. Ager (cnd)
Caprioli, A.:Serenata per Francesca, w. V. Fuchsberger (sgr), G. Schneider (vn), S. Winiarczyk (ob), A. Aigmüller (dr), R. Crow (instr), R. Huber (instr) *(rec 1987)* Pro Viva ▲ ISPV 148 CD [ADD]
Austrian Radio Orch
Operetta Recital, w. Bernd Weikl (bar), Austrian Radio Chorus [cnd:Kurt Eichorn] Orfeo ▲ 077831

ORCH. & ENS.

Austrian RSO
Korngold, E.W.:Music of — Cambria ▲ CD 1032
P. Angerer (cnd)
Christmas Songs, w. Carlo Bergonzi (ten), Vienna Children's Choir — Orfeo ▲ 030821
A. Eschwé (cnd)
Schmidt, F.:Concertante Variations on a Theme of Beethoven, w. D. Adam (pno) — Preiser ▲ 93395 [ADD]
Schmidt, F.:Vars on a Hussar's Song — Preiser ▲ 93395 [ADD]
L. Gardelli (cnd)
Verdi, G.:I due Foscari, w. K. Ricciarelli (sop), E. Connell (sop), J. Carreras (ten), V. Bello (ten), M. Antoniak (ten), P. Cappuccilli (bar), S. Ramey (bass), F. Handlos (bass), Austrian Radio Chorus — Philips 2-▲ 422426-2 [ADD]
P. Guth (cnd)
Strauss (II), Joh.:Orchestral Music—Elektrophor Polka, Op. 297; L'Enfantillage Polka, Op. 202; Es war so wunderschön March, Op. 467; Gut bürgerlich Polka, Op. 282; Industrie-Quadrille, Op. 35; Juristen-Ball-Tänze Waltz, Op. 177; Künstlerleben Waltz, Op. 316; Louischen Polka, Op. 339; Pasman Polka; Pasman Waltz; Sinngedichte Waltz, Op. 1; Sofien-Quadrille, Op. 75 *(rec May 1991)* — Marco Polo ▲ 8.223226 [DDD]
R. Heger (cnd)
Wagner, R.:Das Liebesverbot, w. H. Zadek (cta), L. Sorell (mez), A. Dermota (ten), K. Equiluz (ten), L. Welter (bar), Imdahl (sgr), Austrian Radio Chorus *(rec live, Vienna, 1962)* — Melodram 2-▲ MEL 27052 [AAD]
H. Hollreiser (cnd)
Cornelius, P.:Der Barbier von Bagdad, w. S. Jurinac (sop), H. Rössl-Majdan (mez), E. Majkut (ten), R. Schock (ten), A. Poell (bass-bar), G. Frick (bass), Austrian Radio Chorus [G] *(rec live Vienna, 1952)* — Verona 2-▲ 27050/51 (m) [AA
Cornelius, P.:Der Barbier von Bagdad, w. S. Jurinac (sop), H. Rössl-Majdan (mez), E. Majkut (ten), R. Schock (ten), A. Poell (bass-bar), G. Frick (bass), Austrian Radio Chorus *(rec live Vienna 1952)* — Melodram 2-▲ MEL 27050 (m) [AAD]
B. Maderna (cnd)
Alcalay, L.:Una strofa di Dante, w. Austrian Radio Chorus — Vienna Modern Masters ▲ VMM 3020 [AAD]
E. Märzendorfer (cnd)
Meyerbeer, G.:Les Huguenots, w. Jeanette Scovotti (sop—Urbain), Rita Shane (sop—Marguerite de Valois), Enriqueta Tarrès (sop—Valentine), Nicolai Gedda (ten—Raoul de Nangis), Justino Diaz (bass—Marcel), Dimiter Petkov (bass—Le Comte de Saint-Bris), Austrian Radio Chorus *(rec Vienna, Feb 17, 1971)* — Myto 2-▲ MCD 961141
E. Ortner (cnd)
Kaufmann, D.:Heiligenlegende, w. H. M. Kneihs (speaker), G. König (rcr), Austrian Radio Chorus — Vienna Modern Masters ▲ VMM 3020 [AAD]
M. Schönherr (cnd)
Korngold, E.W.:Orchestral Music—Much Ado About Nothing (5-part suite); Der Schneemann (Prelude & Serenade); Tomorrow (tone poem); Violanta (Prelude & Carnival) *(rec 1949 under the composer's supervision)*; Theme & Variations, Op. 42 *(rec 1955)* — Cambria ▲ CD 1066
P. Schreier (cnd)
Handel, G.F.:Acis & Galatea [arr Mozart], w. E. Mathis (sop), R. Gambill (ten), A R. Johnson (ten), R. Lloyd (b-bar), Austrian Radio Chorus [E] — Orfeo 2-▲ 133852 [DDD]
L. Segerstam (cnd)
Segerstam, L.:Con 1 Vn, w. H. Segerstam (vn) — BIS ▲ CD 84 [AAD]
Segerstam, L.:Patria — BIS ▲ CD 84 [AAD]
Segerstam, L.:Skizzen aus Pandora, w. H. Segerstam (vn) — BIS ▲ CD 84 [AAD]
Segerstam, L.:Songs of Experience, w. Taru Valjakka (sop) *(rec Grosses Konzerthaussaal, Vienna, Apr. 14, 1976)* — BIS ▲ CD 39 [AAD]
P. Steinberg (cnd)
Bellini, V.:Beatrice di Tenda, w. E. Gruberová (sop—Beatrice), V. Kasarova (mez—Agnese), D. Bernardini (ten—Orombello), B. Robinšak (ten—Anichino), I. Morosov (ten—Filippo Maria Visconti), D. Sumegi (bass—Rizzardo), Austrian Radio Chorus [I] *(rec live, Vienna Concert House 1/30 & 2/1/92)* — Nightingale Classics 2-▲ NC 070560-2 [DDD]
L. Zagrosek (cnd)
Einem, G. von:Dantons Tod, w. K. Laki (sop), I. Mayr (mez), H. Hiestermann (ten), W. Hollweg (ten), T. Adam (bass-bar), K. Rydl (bass), Austrian Radio Chorus [G] *(rec live, Salzburg, 8/13/83)* — Orfeo 2-▲ 102842 [ADD]
Gluck, C.W.:Paride ed Elena, w. I. Cotrubas (sop), S. Greenberg (sop), Fontana (sgr), F. Bonisolli (ten), Austrian Radio Chorus [I] *(rec 1983)* — Orfeo 2-▲ 118842 [DDD]
Martin, F.:Die Weise von Liebe und Tod des Cornets Christoph Rilke, w. M. Lipovšek (cta) [G] — Orfeo ▲ 164881 [DDD]
Schmidt, F.:Das Buch mit sieben Siegeln, w. Sylvia Greenberg (sop), Carolyn Watkinson (cta), Peter Schreier (ten), Thomas Moser (ten), Robert Holl (bass), Kurt Rydl (bass), Vienna State Opera Chorus [G] — Orfeo 2-▲ 143862 [DDD]
Smetana, B.:Triumph Sym — Marco Polo ▲ 8.223120 [ADD]
Austrian String Quartet
Pfitzner, H.:Qt 4 Strs — Vox Box 2-▲ CDX 5134 [ADD]
Austrian Tonkünstler Orch
H. Weigert (cnd)
Opera Arias, w. Astrid Varnay (sop) *(rec live, 6/19-20/51)* — Melodram ▲ CDM 16504 (m)
Austro-Hungarian Haydn Orch
A. Fischer (cnd)
Haydn, J.:Con 1 Vn, w. Rainer Küchl (vn) — Nimbus ▲ NI 5258 [DDD]
Haydn, J.:Con 4 Vn, w. Ranier Küchl (vn) — Nimbus ▲ NI 5258 [DDD]
Haydn, J.:March — Nimbus ▲ NI 5216 [DDD]
Haydn, J.:Ovs—La vera costanza — Nimbus ▲ NI 5341
Haydn, J.:Ovs—La fedeltà premiata — Nimbus ▲ NI 5135 [DDD]
Haydn, J.:Sinf concertante — Nimbus ▲ NI 5159 [DDD]
Haydn, J.:Syms (comp)—Nos. 1-20 *(rec Haydnsaal, Esterhzy Palace, Eisenstadt, Austria, 1989-91)* — Nimbus 5-▲ NI 5426/30 [DDD]
Haydn, J.:Sym 1 — Nimbus ▲ NI 5265 [DDD]
Haydn, J.:Sym 2 — Nimbus ▲ NI 5265 [DDD]
Haydn, J.:Sym 3 *(rec June 21-25, 1990)* — Nimbus ▲ NI 5407 [DDD]
Haydn, J.:Sym 4 — Nimbus ▲ NI 5265 [DDD]
Haydn, J.:Sym 5 — Nimbus ▲ NI 5265 [DDD]
Haydn, J.:Sym 6, "Le Matin" — Nimbus ▲ NI 5240-2 [DDD]
Haydn, J.:Sym 7, "Le Midi" — Nimbus ▲ NI 5240-2 [DDD]
Haydn, J.:Sym 8, "Le Soir" — Nimbus ▲ NI 5240-2 [DDD]
Haydn, J.:Sym 9 — Nimbus ▲ NI 5321 [DDD]
Haydn, J.:Sym 10 — Nimbus ▲ NI 5265 [DDD]
Haydn, J.:Sym 11 *(rec June 21-25, 1990)* — Nimbus ▲ NI 5407 [DDD]
Haydn, J.:Sym 12 — Nimbus ▲ NI 5321 [DDD]
Haydn, J.:Sym 13 — Nimbus ▲ NI 5321 [DDD]
Haydn, J.:Sym 18 *(rec Apr. 28 & May 2, 1991)* — Nimbus ▲ NI 5407 [DDD]
Haydn, J.:Sym 19 *(rec Apr. 28 & May 2, 1991)* — Nimbus ▲ NI 5407 [DDD]
Haydn, J.:Sym 20 *(rec Apr. 28 & May 2, 1991)* — Nimbus ▲ NI 5407 [DDD]
Haydn, J.:Sym 22, "Der Philosoph" — Nimbus ▲ NI 5392 [DDD]
Haydn, J.:Sym 22, "Der Philosoph" — Nimbus ▲ NI 5179 [DDD]
Haydn, J.:Sym 24 — Nimbus ▲ NI 5179 [DDD]
Haydn, J.:Sym 25 — Nimbus ▲ NI 5258 [DDD]
Haydn, J.:Sym 27 — Nimbus ▲ NI 5199 [DDD]
Haydn, J.:Sym 40 — Nimbus ▲ NI 5321 [DDD]
Haydn, J.:Sym 45, "Farewell" — Nimbus ▲ NI 5179 [DDD]
Haydn, J.:Sym 88 — Nimbus ▲ NI 5269 [DDD]

Austro-Hungarian Haydn Orch (cont.)
A. Fischer (cnd) (cont.)
Haydn, J.:Sym 88 — LaserLight ▲ 14 008 [DDD]
Haydn, J.:Sym 89 — Nimbus ▲ NI 5341
Haydn, J.:Sym 90 — Nimbus ▲ NI 5269 [DDD]
Haydn, J.:Sym 91 — Nimbus ▲ NI 5341
Haydn, J.:Sym 92, "Oxford" — Nimbus ▲ NI 5269 [DDD]
Haydn, J.:Syms 93-104, "The Salomon (or London) Syms" — Nimbus 5-▲ NI 5200/04 [DDD] ■ NC 5200/03
Haydn, J.:Sym 93 — Nimbus ▲ NI 5216 [DDD]
Haydn, J.:Sym 94, "Surprise Sym" — Nimbus ▲ NI 5159 [DDD]
Haydn, J.:Sym 95 — Nimbus ▲ NI 5216 [DDD]
Haydn, J.:Sym 96, "Miracle" — Nimbus ▲ NI 5135 [DDD]
Haydn, J.:Sym 97 — Nimbus ▲ NI 5199 [DDD]
Haydn, J.:Sym 98 — Nimbus ▲ NI 5199 [DDD]
Haydn, J.:Sym 99 — Nimbus ▲ NI 5230-2 [DDD]
Haydn, J.:Sym 100, "Military" — LaserLight ▲ 14 008 [DDD]
Haydn, J.:Sym 100, "Military" — Nimbus ▲ NI 5159 [DDD]
Haydn, J.:Sym 101, "Clock" — Nimbus ▲ NI 5105 [DDD]
Haydn, J.:Sym 102 — Nimbus ▲ NI 5135 [DDD]
Haydn, J.:Sym 104, "London" — Nimbus ▲ NI 5230-2 [DDD]
Haydn, M.:Con Fl, P.54 — Nimbus ▲ NI 5392 [DDD]
Haydn, M.:Con Fl, P.56 — Nimbus ▲ NI 5392 [DDD]
Haydn, M.:Syms — Nimbus ▲ NI 5392 [DDD]
R. Goodman (cnd)
Haydn, J.:Sym 103, "Drum Roll" — Nimbus ▲ NI 5105 [DDD]
Austro-Hungarian PO
K.-F. Beringer (cnd)
Brahms, J.:Alto Rhap, w. Lioba Braun (alt), Windsbach Boys' Choir *(rec Ansbach, July 1996)* — Hänssler Classic 2-▲ CD 98.134 [DDD]
Mendelssohn, F.:Sym 2, w. Pamela Coburn (sop), Lioba Braun (alt), Deon van der Walt (ten) *(rec Ansbach, July 1996)* — Hänssler Classic 2-▲ CD 98.134 [DDD]
Auvergne CO
A. van Beek (cnd)
de Fesch, W.:Music of, w. Gordan Nikolitch (vn)—Cons Grossi, Op. 2/6, Op. 3/3 & 4, Op. 5/2 & Op. 10/4 & 5; Cons for Vn, Op. 2/2 & 5, Op. 3/6 & Op. 5/5 — Olympia ▲ OLY 450 [DDD]
J.-J. Kantorow (cnd)
Canteloube, J.:Songs of Auvergne, w. M. Martin (sop) [trans. Jean-Guy Bailly for orch.] — Denon/PCM Digital ▲ DEN 75862 [DDD]
Leclair, J.-M.:Cons Vn, Op. 7, w. J.-J. Kantarow (vn)—No. 4 *(rec Basilique St. Julien de Brioude, Sept. 15-17, 1993)* — FNAC Music ▲ 592317 [DDD]
Locatelli, P.:L'arte del violino, w. J.-J. Kantarow (vn)—Harmonic Labrinth *(rec Basilique St. Julien de Brioude, Sept. 15-17, 1993)* — FNAC Music ▲ 592317 [DDD]
Mendelssohn, F.:Con in d Vn & Strs, w. J.-J. Kantarow (vn) *(rec Basilique St. Julien de Brioude, Sept. 15-17, 1993)* — FNAC Music ▲ 592317 [DDD]
Nocturne — Denon ▲ CO 75596 [DDD]
Tartini, G.:Son Vn "Devil's Trill", w. J.-J. Kantarow (vn) [trans M. O. Dupin for Violin & Orch.] *(rec Basilique St. Julien de Brioude, Sept. 15-17, 1993)* — FNAC Music ▲ 592317 [DDD]
Auvergne Orch
L. Hager (cnd)
Mozart, W.A.:Serenade Vn, K.250, w. Jean Jacques Kantorow (vn) — Denon ▲ CO 73870 [DDD]
Avalon Wind Quintet [Daniel Lampert (fl), Stefan Schilli (ob), Stefan Zimmer (cl), Christian Lampert (hn), Bernhard Straub (bn)]
Briccialdi, G.:Qnt Ww, Op. 124 *(rec Clara-Wieck-Auditorium, Sandhausen, Nov 28 - Dec 1, 1994)* — Naxos ▲ 8.553410 [DDD]
Cambini, G.M.:Qnts (3) Ww *(rec Clara-Wieck-Auditorium, Sandhausen, Nov 28 - Dec 1, 1994)* — Naxos ▲ 8.553410 [DDD]
Avantgarde Ensemble
Cage, J.:Music for 8 — MD + G ▲ MDG CD 6130701
Cage, J.:Music for 5—2 versions — MD + G ▲ MDG CD 6130701
Feldman, Morton:De Kooning — Wergo ▲ WER 62732
Feldman, Morton:For Frank O'Hara — Wergo ▲ WER 62732
Feldman, Morton:For Franz Kline — Wergo ▲ WER 62732
Feldman, Morton:Piece to Philip Guston — Wergo ▲ WER 62732
E. Brown (cnd)
Brown, E.:Event:Synergy II—2 versions *(rec Sender Freies Berlin, Jan 16-17, 1995)* — Hat Hut ("Now" series) ▲ CD 6177 [DDD]
H. Zender (cnd)
Schoenberg, A.:Kaiserwalzer — MD + G ▲ MDG 6130579 [DDD]
Schoenberg, A.:Little Pieces Pno — MD + G ▲ MDG 6130579 [DDD]
Schoenberg, A.:Phantasy Vn — MD + G ▲ MDG 6130579 [DDD]
Schoenberg, A.:Pierrot lunaire, w. Salome Kammer (nar) — MD + G ▲ MDG 6130579 [DDD]
Schoenberg, A.:Scherzo & Trio Str Qt — MD + G ▲ MDG 6130579 [DDD]
Avantgarde Ensemble [Salome Kammer (mez), Till Büning (vn), Ivo Bauer (va), Steffen Schleiermacher (pno)]
E. Brown (cnd)
Brown, E.:Windsor Jambs *(rec Sender Freies Berlin, Jan 16-17, 1995)* — Hat Hut ("Now" series) ▲ CD 6177 [DDD]
Avanti! CO
Lindberg, M.:Joy — Ondine ▲ ODE 784-2 [DDD]
Lindberg, M.:Marea — Ondine ▲ ODE 784-2 [DDD]
O. Pohjola (cnd)
Jokinen, E.:Con Acc, w. Matti Rantanen (acc) — Finlandia ▲ FIN 54404 [DDD]
Kortekangas, O.:Grand Hotel, w. E.-L. Saarinen (mez), S. Tiilikainen (bar), K. Laurikainen (nar), E.-O. Söderström (cnd), Finnish Chamber Chorus, Tapiola Chorus [Fin] — Ondine ▲ ODE 749-2 [ADD]
T. Pulakka (cnd)
Jolivet, A.:Con Fl, w. P. Alanko (fl) — Ondine ▲ ODE 802 [DDD]
J. Saraste (cnd)
Stravinsky, I.:Canzonetta — BIS ▲ CD 292 [DDD]
Stravinsky, I.:Pulcinella Suite — BIS ▲ CD 292 [DDD]
Avanti Orch
Stravinsky, I.:Danses concertantes — BIS ▲ CD 292
Stravinsky, I.:Pulcinella — BIS ▲ CD 292
Avanti! String Quartet
Hakola, K.:Qt Strs — Ondine ▲ ODE 739-2 [DDD]
Heininen, P.:Qt Strs — Ondine ▲ ODE 739-2 [DDD]
Heinió, M.:Qnt Pno, w. Jaana Karkkainen (pno) — Ondine ▲ ODE 865
Jokinen, E.:Qt 4 Strs — Ondine ▲ ODE 865
Kokkonen, J.:Qnt Pno, w. Jaana Karkkainen (pno) — Ondine ▲ ODE 865
Koskinen, J.:Qt Strs — Ondine ▲ ODE 739-2 [DDD]
Kurtág, G.:Hommage à Mihály András — Ondine ▲ ODE 739-2 [DDD]
Merilainen, U.:Qt 3 Strs — Ondine ▲ ODE 865
Avanti! String Quartet members
Crusell, B.H.:Qts (3) Cl, w. K. Kriikku (cl)—comp. — Ondine ▲ ODE 727-2 [DDD]
Avena Trio
Recital of French Music — Arcobaleno ▲ SBCD 2500 [DDD]
Aventure Ensemble
Aharonián, C.:Gente — Ars Musici ▲ AM 1147-2 [DDD]
Bruttger, T.:Monolith — Ars Musici ▲ AM 1147-2 [DDD]
Etkin, M.:Abgesang Mambo — Ars Musici ▲ AM 1147-2 [DDD]

▲ = CD ♦ = Enhanced CD Δ = MD ■ = Cassette Tape ◻ = DCC

Aventure Ensemble (cont.)
Luzuriaga, D.:Grave Bossa — Ars Musici ▲ AM 1147–2 [DDD]
Paraskevaïdis, G.:sendas — Ars Musici ▲ AM 1147–2 [DDD]
Riehm, R.:Sarca – il fiume Sarca — Ars Musici ▲ AM 1147–2 [DDD]
Rojko, U.:Atemaj — Ars Musici ▲ 1122
Rojko, U.:Glass Voices — Ars Musici ▲ 1122
Rojko, U.:Ottoki — Ars Musici ▲ 1122
Rojko, U.:Passing away — Ars Musici ▲ 1122
Rojko, U.:Tati — Ars Musici ▲ 1122
Rojko, U.:Whose Song — Ars Musici ▲ 1122
Schulhoff, E.:Bass Nightingale — Ars Musici ▲ 1071 [DDD]
Schulhoff, E.:Divertissement Ob — Ars Musici ▲ 1071 [DDD]
Schulhoff, E.:Wolkenpumpe — Ars Musici ▲ 1071 [DDD]
Varèse, E.:Octandre — Ars Musici ▲ AM 1147–2 [DDD]
Wolpe, S.:Anna Blume — Ars Musici ▲ 1071 [DDD]
Wolpe, S.:Son Ob — Ars Musici ▲ 1071 [DDD]

K. Kord (cnd)
Huber, N.A.:Air mit Sphinxes — Col Legno ▲ AU 31821
Huber, N.A.:Demijour — Col Legno ▲ AU 31821

B. Wulff (cnd)
Keller, M.:Zerblasen *(rec June 1994–Apr 1995)* — Jecklin ▲ JEC 310 [DDD]

Avignon–Provence Regional Lyric Orch
M. Piquemal (cnd)
Donizetti, G.:Messa di Gloria e Credo, w. Danielle Borst (sop), Hélène Jossoud (mez), Jean-Luc Viala (ten), Vincent Le Texier (bass-bar), Provence–Alpes–Côte d'Azur Regional Choir — Accord ▲ ACD 212142 [DDD]

Aviv String Quartet [H. Shaham (vn), J. McGross (vn), Y. Aloni (va), Z. Plesser (vc)]
Radzynski, J.:Music of, w. M. Beiser (vc), A Erez (pno), *(Qt. for Strings Y. Aloni (viola), A. Erez (Canto for Piano [rec 1991]),* M. Beiser, Z. Plesser *(5 Duets for 2 Cellos [rec 1992])* — CRI ▲ CD 649 [DDD]

Avray Atelier Musique
J.-L. Petit (cnd)
Arma, P.:Music of, w. Josette Morata (nar), Fabrice Moretti (sax), Régis Poulain (bn), Jean-Marie Cottet (pno), Alain Béghin (perc), Francis Petit (perc)—Phases contre phases for S Sax & Pno; Celui qui dort et dort for Nar, Bn, Xyl & Perc [after poems by Max Jacob]; 5 esquisses for Pno [from a Hungarian Theme]; Divertissement 1600 for Fls [w. Jean-Noël Catrice (fl), Béatrice Delpierre (fl), Pascale Haarscher (fl), Marie-Aude Menou (fl)]; 3 Regards for solo Ob [w. Jacques Vandeville (ob)]; Divert No. 6 for Cl & Pno [w. Dominique Vidal (cl)]; Parlando for solo Fl [w. Patrice Bocquillon (fl)] — REM ▲ REM 311266 [DDD]

Avray CO
Jolivet, A.:Rhapsodie à 7, w. J. Vandeville (ob), Millière String Trio — REM ▲ REM 311196 [DDD]

Avray Instrumental Ensemble
Chen, Q.:Yi, w. Jacques Di Donato (cl) — REM ▲ REM 311223 [DDD]
J.-L. Petit (cnd)
Chen, Q.:Feu d'Ombres, w. Fabrice Moretti (sax) — REM ▲ REM 311223 [DDD]
Chen, Q.:Poème Lyrique II, w. Ke-Long Shi (voice) — REM ▲ REM 311223 [DDD]

Azerbaijan SO
G. Rozhdestvensky (cnd)
Amirov, F.:Sym Strs — Olympia 2–▲ OLY 578 [ADD/DDD]

B & B Duo [Ron Borczon (gtr), Julie Burkert (fl)]
Hindemith, P.:Pieces (8) Fl & Pno [arr for Gtr & Fl] *(rec De La Ronde Hall, Baton Rouge, LA, 1993)* — Centaur ▲ CRC 2234 [DDD]
Kessner, D.:Circle Music II *(rec De La Ronde Hall, Baton Rouge, LA, 1993)* — Centaur ▲ CRC 2234 [DDD]
Kessner, D.:Intersonata *(rec De La Ronde Hall, Baton Rouge, LA, 1993)* — Centaur ▲ CRC 2234 [DDD]
Mozart, W.A.:Son 11 Pno [arr for Gtr & Fl] *(rec De La Ronde Hall, Baton Rouge, LA, 1993)* — Centaur ▲ CRC 2234 [DDD]

Babayaga String Quartet
Blue Rosin — Skylark ▲ SKY 9502

Bacau PO
S. Frontalini (cnd)
Mozart, W.A.:Arias, w. R. Panerai (bar)—Le nozze di Figaro:Non più andrai; Don Giovanni:Madamina, il catalogo è questo — Bongiovanni ▲ GB 2514 [DDD]
Verdi, G.:Arias, w. R. Panerai (bar)—Nabucco:Dioi di Giuda; Ernani:Gran Diol...O de' verd'anni miei; Rigoletto:Cortigiani, vil razza dannata; Il trovatore:Il balen del suo sorriso; La traviata:Di Provenza; Un ballo in maschera:Alla vita che t'arride; Eri tu che macchiavi quell'anima; Don Carlo:Per me giunto è il dì supremo; lo morrò, ma lieto in dor; Otello:Credo in un Dio crudel; Falstaff:L'onore — Bongiovanni ▲ GB 2514 [DDD]

Bach Collegium
H. Rilling (cnd)
Bach, Joh. Christian:Amadis des Gaules, w. Sonntag, Hobarth, Verebies, Wagner, Schöne, Gächinger Kantorei [G] — Hänssler Classic 2–▲ 98.963 [DDD]
Haydn, J.:Die Jahreszeiten, w. *(soloists unknown)*, Gächinger Kantorei — Hänssler Classic 2–▲ HAN 98982 [DDD]

Bach Ensemble
J. Rifkin (cnd)
Bach, J.S.:Cant 80 [G] — L'Oiseau-Lyre ▲ 417250–2 [DDD]
Bach, J.S.:Cant 80 — London ♦ 0062635471
Bach, J.S.:Cant 147 — London ♦ 0062635471
Bach, J.S.:Cant 147 [G] — L'Oiseau-Lyre ▲ 417250–2 [DDD]
Bach, J.S.:Magnificat, BWV 243, w. J. Bryden (sop), J. Baird (sop), J Gall (ct), F. Hoffmeister (ten), J. Opalach (bass) [L] — Pro Arte ▲ CDD 185 [DDD]
Bach, J.S.:Mass in b, BWV 232, w. J. Baird (sop), J. Nelson (sop), J. Dooley (ct), F. Hoffmeister (ten), J. Opalach (bass) [L] — Elektra/Nonesuch 2–▲ 79036–2 [DDD] 2–█ 79036–4 (D)
Hoffmann, M.:German Magnificat, w. J. Bryden (sop) [G] — Pro Arte ▲ CDD 185 [DDD]
H. Rilling (cnd)
Bach, J.S.:Cant 18, w. E. Csapò (sop), G. Schnaut (mez), A. Kraus (ten), W. Schöne (bass) [G] *(rec 1975)* — Hänssler Classic ▲ 98.877 [AAD]
Bach, J.S.:Cant 69, w. H. Donath (sop), J. Hamari (b-bar), A. Kraus (ten), W. Schöne (bass) *(rec Mar–Apr 1973)* — Hänssler Classic ▲ 98.829 [AAD]
Bach, J.S.:Cant 72, w. A. Augér (sop), H. Laurich (cta), W. Schöne (bass) [G] *(rec 1983)* — Hänssler Classic ▲ 98.875 [AAD]
Bach, J.S.:Cant 81, w. J. Hamari (mez), A. Kraus (ten), S. Nimsgern (b-bar) [G] *(rec 1984)* — Hänssler Classic ▲ 98.876 [AAD]
Bach, J.S.:Cant 83, w. H. Watts (cta), A. Kraus (ten), W. Heldwein (bass) [G] *(rec 1979)* — Hänssler Classic ▲ 98.875 [AAD]
Bach, J.S.:Cant 84, w. A. Augér (sop) [G] *(rec 1983)* — Hänssler Classic ▲ 98.877 [AAD]
Bach, J.S.:Cant 92, w. A. Augér (sop), G. Schreckenbach (cta), H. Watts (cta), A. Baldin (ten), P. Huttenlocher (bar) [G] *(rec 1980)* — Hänssler Classic ▲ 98.877 [AAD]
Bach, J.S.:Cant 97, w. H. Donath (sop), H. Gardow (sop), A. Kraus (ten), P. Huttenlocher (bar) *(rec Jan–Feb 1974)* — Hänssler Classic ▲ 98.835 [AAD]
Bach, J.S.:Cant 106, "Actus tragicus", w. E. Csapò (sop), H. Schwarz (cta), A. Kraus (ten), W. Schöne (bass) *(rec Jan 1975)* — Hänssler Classic ▲ 98.830 [AAD]
Bach, J.S.:Cant 119, w. A. Augér (sop), A. Murray (mez), A. Kraus (ten), W. Schöne (bass) *(rec Sept & Dec 1977 & Jan 197)* — Hänssler Classic ▲ 98.828 [AAD]
Bach, J.S.:Cant 120, w. H. Donath (sop), H. Laurich (cta), A. Kraus (ten), W. Schöne (bass) *(rec Mar–Apr 1973)* — Hänssler Classic ▲ 98.829 [AAD]
Bach, J.S.:Cant 125, w. M. Höffgen (mez), K. Equiluz (ten), W. Schöne (bass) [G] *(rec 1973)* — Hänssler Classic ▲ 98.876 [AAD]

Bach Ensemble (cont.)
H. Rilling (cnd) (cont.)
Bach, J.S.:Cant 144, w. A. Augér (sop), H. Watts (cta), A. Kraus (ten) [G] *(rec 1978)* — Hänssler Classic ▲ 98.876 [AAD]
Bach, J.S.:Cant 150, w. M. Schreiber (sop), M. Jetter (cta), P. Maus (ten), H.-F. Kunz (bass) *(rec June–July 1970)* — Hänssler Classic ▲ 98.835 [AAD]
Bach, J.S.:Cant 156, w. H. Laurich (cta), K. Equiluz (ten), W. Schöne (bass) [G] *(rec 1973)* — Hänssler Classic ▲ 98.875 [AAD]
Bach, J.S.:Cant 157, w. A. Kraus (ten), P. Huttenlocher (bar) *(rec Oct 1982, July 1983)* — Hänssler Classic ▲ 98.835 [AAD]
Bach, J.S.:Cant 193, w. A. Augér (sop), J. Hamari (cta) *(rec July 1983)* — Hänssler Classic ▲ 98.829 [AAD]
Bach, J.S.:Cant 196, w. D. Soffel (cta), A. Baldin (ten), N. Tüller (b-bar) *(rec Jan 1975)* — Hänssler Classic ▲ 98.828 [AAD]
Bach, J.S.:Cant 197, w. C. Cuccaro (sop), M. Georg (mez), P. Huttenlocher (bar) *(rec Feb 1984)* — Hänssler Classic ▲ 98.828 [AAD]
Bach, J.S.:Cant 198, w. A. Augér (sop), G. Schreckenbach (cta), A. Baldin (ten), P. Huttenlocher (bar) *(rec Sept 1983)* — Hänssler Classic ▲ 98.830 [AAD]
Bach, J.S.:Cant 200, w. M. Georg (cta) [G] *(rec 1984)* — Hänssler Classic 5–▲ 98.976

Bach Festival Orch
G. Funfgeld (cnd)
Bach, J.S.:Cant 56, w. D. Lichti (b-bar), Bethlehem Bach Choir [G] — Dorian ▲ DOR 90127 [DDD]
Bach, J.S.:Cant 63, w. S. McNair (sop), J. Taylor (mez), D. Gordon (ten), D. Lichti (b-bar), Bethlehem Bach Choir—plus Sanctus from Mass in b, BWV 232 [G] — Dorian ▲ DOR 90113 [DDD]
Bach, J.S.:Cant 65, w. D. Gordon (ten), D. Lichti (b-bar), Bethlehem Bach Choir [G] — Dorian ▲ DOR 90113 [DDD]
Bach, J.S.:Cant 140, w. H. Schellenberg (sop), D. Gordon (ten), D. Lichti (b-bar), Bethlehem Bach Choir [G] — Dorian ▲ DOR 90127 [DDD]
Y. Menuhin (cnd)
Bach, C.P.E.:Con Hpd & Strs, H.427, w. George Malcolm (hpd) — EMI Classics ("Baroque" series) ▲ CDK 65733

Bach Guild Orch
F. Prohaska (cnd)
Bach, J.S.:Cant 78, w. T. Stich-Randall (sop), D. Hermann (sop), A. Dermota (ten), H. Braun (bar), Bach Guild Chorus [G] *(rec May 1954)* — Vanguard Classics ("The Bach Guild" series) ▲ OVC 2009 [ADD]
Bach, J.S.:Cant 106, "Actus tragicus", w. T. Stich-Randall (sop), D. Hermann (sop), A. Dermota (ten), H. Braun (bar), Bach Guild Chorus [G] *(rec May 1954)* — Vanguard Classics ("The Bach Guild" series) ▲ OVC 2009 [ADD]

Bach–Mozart Ensemble Tokyo
Vivaldi, A.:Cons Bn, w. K. Dosaka (bn) *(rec June 22–26, 1992)* — Denon ▲ CO 75198 [DDD]
Vivaldi, A.:Cons Fl (misc), w. M. Arita (fl)—RV.438 & 440 *(rec June 22–26, 1992)* — Denon ▲ CO 75198 [DDD]; Denon ▲ CO 77288 [DDD]
Vivaldi, A.:Cons Fl, Op. 10, w. M. Arita (fl) — Denon ▲ CO 75198 [DDD]
Vivaldi, A.:Con Fl Ob, RV.107, w. M. Arita (fl), M. Homma (ob), N. Wakamatsu (vn), K. Dosaka (bn) *(rec June 22–26, 1992)* — Denon ▲ CO 75198 [DDD]
Vivaldi, A.:Cons Ob, w. M. Homma (ob)—RV.457 & 461 *(rec June 22–26, 1992)* — Denon ▲ CO 75198 [DDD]

Baden State Orch
C. Cremer (cnd)
Beethoven, L. van:Romances Vn, w. Susanne Lautenbacher (vn)—No. 1 — Special Music Co. ("Classics of the Heart" series) ▲ SCD 5196
Beethoven, L. van:Romances Vn, w. S. Lautenbacher (vn) — Allegretto ▲ ACD 8014 [ADD] █ ACS 8014

Badinage
Boismortier, J.B. de:Sons, Op. 26—No. 5 in g — Meridian ▲ MER 84335 [DDD]
Boismortier, J.B. de:Sons, Op. 50—No. 4 in d for Bn & Bc — Meridian ▲ MER 84335 [DDD]
Boismortier, J.B. de:Sons Fl, Op. 9—No. 4 in d — Meridian ▲ MER 84335 [DDD]
Boismortier, J.B. de:Sons Fl, Op. 91—Nos. 2 in g & 4 in d — Meridian ▲ MER 84335 [DDD]
Boismortier, J.B. de:Sons for 2 Vielles, Op. 27—No. 1 in C for Ob & Bc — Meridian ▲ MER 84335 [DDD]
Boismortier, J.B. de:Suites Hpd, Op. 59—No. 1 in c — Meridian ▲ MER 84335 [DDD]

Badinage [Paul Carroll (bn), Sally Civval (vc)]
Devienne, F.:Sons Bn, Op. 24—Nos. 3 in F & 5 in g — Meridian ▲ MER 84254 [DDD]

Badinage [Paul Carroll (fl), Sally Civval (vc), David Rowland (pno)]
Devienne, F.:Sons Fl—in C, Op. 13/2; in G, Op. 13/3; in D, Op. 68/1; in e, Op. 68/5 — Meridian ▲ MER 84254 [DDD]

Badinage [Paul Carroll (fl/rcr/bn/ob), Sally Civval (vc), David Rowland (hpd)]
Corrette, M.:Music of—Son in G for Bn & Bc, Op. 20/5; Son in e for Hpd & Fl, Op. 25/4; Suite in D for Hpd ; Son in e for Fl & Bc, Op. 13/2; Son in d for Ob & Bc [from L'ecole d'orphee]; Les Etoiles, rondeau for Hpd; Suite in C for Rcr & Bc [from Les Pieces]; La Furstemberg & Vars for Hpd [from Les Amusements du parnasse]; others — Meridian ▲ MER 84325 [DDD]

Judy Bailey Quintet
S. Challender (cnd)
Banks, D.:Music of, w. D. Burrows, Sydney SO—Nexus — Vox Australis ▲ VAST006–2 [DDD]

Baja California Orch
E. G. Barrios (cnd)
Kupferman, M.:Banners — Soundspells ▲ CD 113 [DDD]
Kupferman, M.:Con Gtr, w. Roberto Limón (gtr) — Soundspells ▲ CD 113 [DDD]
Kupferman, M.:Hexagon Skies, w. Roberto Limón (gtr) — Soundspells ▲ CD 114 [DDD]
Kupferman, M.:Hexagon Skies, w. Roberto Limón (gtr) — Soundspells ▲ CD 114 [DDD]
Kupferman, M.:Infinities Projections — Soundspells ▲ CD 114 [DDD]
Kupferman, M.:Infinities Projections — Soundspells ▲ CD 114 [DDD]

Balanescu String Quartet
Byrne, D.:High Life — Argo ▲ 436565–2 [DDD]
Lurie, J.:Stranger Than Paradise — Argo ▲ 436565–2 [DDD]
Moran, R.:Music from the Towers — Argo ▲ 436565–2 [DDD]
Nyman, M.:Qts Strs—Nos 1-3 — Argo ▲ 433093–2 [DDD]
Torke, M.:Chalk Str Qt — Argo ▲ 436565–2 [DDD]

Balanescu String Quartet [A. Balanescu (vn), C. Connors (vn), B. Hawkes (va), N. Cooper (vc)]
Abou-Khalil, R.:Arabian Waltz — Enja ▲ ENJ 9059
Volans, K.:Qt 2 Strs — Argo ▲ 440687–2 [DDD]
Volans, K.:Qt 3 Strs — Argo ▲ 440687–2 [DDD]

Balanescu String Quartet [Alexander Balanescu (vn), Clare Connors (vn), Andrew Parker (va), Sian Bell (vc)]
Bryars, G.:Qt 1 Strs, "Between the National & the Bristol" — Argo ▲ 448175–2 [DDD]
Bryars, G.:Qt 2 Strs — Argo ▲ 448175–2 [DDD]

Bâle SO
F. Leitner (cnd)
Bruckner, A.:Sym 6 *(rec 1992)* — Accord ▲ ACD 204372 [DDD]
P. Sacher (cnd)
Moret, N.:Hymnes, w. Heiner Kuehner (org) — Musiques Suisses ▲ CD 6103 [DDD]
J. Wyttenbach (cnd)
Huber, K.:Erinnere Dich an G. — Accord ▲ ACD 204532 [DDD]
Huber, K.:Ohne Grenze und Rand, w. Christoph Schiller (va) — Accord ▲ ACD 204532 [DDD]
Huber, K.:Protuberanzen—2 versions — Accord ▲ ACD 204532 [DDD]

Baltic CO
S. Litkov (cnd)
Haydn, J.:Sym 49, "La Passione" *(rec Vilnius Recording Studio, Vilnuis, Lithuania, Dec 1994)* — Infinity Digital ▲ QK 68429 [DDD]

Baltimore Consort
The Art of the Bawdy Song, w. The Merry Companions *(rec Oct. 1990)* — Dorian ▲ DOR 90155 [DDD]

Baltimore Consort (cont.)
Bright Day Star:Old Carols & Dance Tunes from the British Isles, Germany & Appalachia *(rec Jan. 1994)* Dorian ▲ DOR 90198 [DDD]
The Daemon Lover:Traditional Ballads & Songs of England, Scotland & America, w. Custer LaRue (sop) *(rec May 1992)* Dorian ▲ DOR 90174 [DDD]
On the Banks of Helicon:Early Music of Scotland Dorian ▲ DOR 90139 [DDD]
La Rocque 'n' Roll:Popular Music of Renaissance France Dorian ▲ DOR 90177 [DDD]
A Trip to Killburn:Playford Tunes & Their Ballads *(rec Troy Savings Bank Music Hall, Troy, NY, Jan 1996)* Dorian ▲ DOR 90238 [DDD]
Watkins Ale:Music of the English Renaissance Dorian ▲ DOR 90142 [DDD]

Baltimore Consort members [Mary Ann Ballard (vl), Mark Cudek (cittern/Renaissance gtr/baroque gtr/bass vl/lt/early wind instrs), Ronn McFarlane (lt)]
The True Lover's Farewell:Appalachian Folk Balads, w. Custer LaRue (sop) *(rec Troy Savings Bank Music Hall, Troy, NY, Sept. 1994)* Dorian ▲ DOR 90213 [DDD]

Baltimore SO
S. Comissiona (cnd)
Bassett, L.:Echoes from an Invisible World *(rec Baltimore, MD, Nov. 1979)* CRI ▲ CD 677 [ADD]
Brahms, J.:Qt 1 Pno [Schoenberg version] *(rec Elite Recordings, NYC, 1983)* Allegretto ▲ ACD 8196
Britten, B.:Diversions Pno, w. L. Fleisher (pno) Phoenix ▲ PHCD 122 [ADD]
Laderman, E.:Con Orch Phoenix ▲ PHCD 122 [ADD]
Lazarof, H.:Con Orch CRI ▲ CD 588 [ADD]
Ravel, M.:Alborada del gracioso Vanguard Classics ▲ OVC 4002 [ADD]
Ravel, M.:Boléro Vanguard Classics ▲ OVC 4002 [ADD]
Ravel, M.:Con Pno (left hand), w. L. Fleisher (pno) Vanguard Classics ▲ OVC 4002 [ADD]
Ravel, M.:Rapsodie espagnole Vanguard Classics ▲ OVC 4002 [ADD]

D. Zinman (cnd)
Albert, S.:Con Vc, w. Yo-Yo Ma (vc) *(rec Joseph Meyerhoff Hall, Baltimore, MD, Mar 6-7, 1993)* Sony Classical ▲ SK 57961 [DDD]; ■ ST 57961
Barber, S.:Adagio Strs Argo ▲ 436288-2 [DDD]
Barber, S.:Con Vc, w. Yo-Yo Ma CBS ▲ MK 44900 [DDD]
Barber, S.:Essay 1 Argo ▲ 436288-2 [DDD]
Barber, S.:Essay 2 Argo ▲ 436288-2 [DDD]
Barber, S.:Music for a Scene from Shelley Argo ▲ 436288-2 [DDD]
Barber, S.:The School for Scandal Argo ▲ 436288-2 [DDD]
Barber, S.:Sym 1 Argo ▲ 436288-2 [DDD]
Bartók, B.:Con Va, w. Yo-Yo Ma (alto vn) *(rec Joseph Meyerhoff Hall, Baltimore, MD, Mar. 6-7, 1993)* Sony Classical ▲ SK 57961 [DDD]; ■ ST 57961
Berlioz, H.:La Damnation de Faust (sels)—Minuet of the Will-o'-the-wisps; Dance of the sylphs; Rákóczy March Telarc ▲ CD 80164 [DDD]
Berlioz, H.:Hymne des Marseillais, w. S. McNair (sop), R. Leech (ten), Baltimore Sym Chorus Telarc ▲ CD 80164 [DDD]
Berlioz, H.:Ovs—Les francs-juges; Carnaval romain Telarc ▲ CD 80271 [DDD]
Berlioz, H.:Ovs—Benvenuto Cellini; Le Corsaire Telarc ▲ CD 80164 [DDD]
Berlioz, H.:Roméo et Juliette (sels)—Scène d'amour Telarc ▲ CD 80164 [DDD]
Berlioz, H.:Sym fantastique Telarc ▲ CD 80271 [DDD]
Berlioz, H.:Les Troyens (sels)—Trojan March; Royal Hunt & Storm Telarc ▲ CD 80164 [DDD]
Bloch, E.:Schelomo, w. Yo-Yo Ma (vc) *(rec Joseph Meyerhoff Hall, Baltimore, MD, Mar. 6-7, 1993)* Sony Classical ▲ SK 57961 [DDD]; ■ ST 57961
Britten, B.:Sym Vc, w. Yo-Yo Ma (vc) CBS ▲ MK 44900 [DDD]
Copland, A.:Billy the Kid (suite) Argo ▲ 440639-2 [DDD]
Copland, A.:Danzón Cubano Argo ▲ 440639-2 [DDD]
Copland, A.:El salón México Argo ▲ 440639-2 [DDD]
Dance Mix *(rec Joseph Meyerhoff Symphony Hall, Baltimore, Apr 9-10, 1994)* Argo ▲ 444454-2 [DDD]
Daugherty, M.:Bizarro Argo ▲ 452 103-2
Daugherty, M.:Metropolis Sym Argo ▲ 452 103-2
Elgar, E.:Cockaigne Telarc ▲ CD 80192 [DDD]
Elgar, E.:Enigma Vars Telarc ▲ CD 80192 [DDD]
Elgar, E.:Pomp & Circumstance Marches—Nos. 1 & 2 Telarc ▲ CD 80310 [DDD]
Elgar, E.:Salut d'amour Telarc ▲ CD 80192 [DDD]
Elgar, E.:Serenade Strs Telarc ▲ CD 80192 [DDD]
Elgar, E.:Sym 1 Telarc ▲ CD 80310 [DDD]
Glinka, M.:Russlan & Ludmilla (ov) *(rec Joseph Meyerhoff Symphony Hall, Baltimore, MD, Nov. 21, 1989)* Telarc ▲ CD 80378 [DDD]
Ippolitov-Ivanov, M.:Caucasian Sketches, Op. 10 *(rec Joseph Meyerhoff Symphony Hall, Baltimore, MD, May 28-29, 1994)* Telarc ▲ CD 80378 [DDD]
Ives, C.:Holidays, w. Baltimore Sym Chorus *(rec Joseph Meyerhoff Symphony Hall, Baltimore, MD, Sept 1994)* Argo ▲ 444860-2 [DDD]
Ives, C.:They Are There! *(rec Joseph Meyerhoff Symphony Hall, Baltimore, MD, Sept 1994)* Argo ▲ 444860-2 [DDD]
Ives, C.:Three Places in New England *(rec Joseph Meyerhoff Symphony Hall, Baltimore, MD, Sept 1994)* Argo ▲ 444860-2 [DDD]
Rachmaninoff, S.:Rhapsody on a Theme of Paganini, w. H. Gutiérrez (pno) Telarc ▲ CD 80193 [DDD]
Rachmaninoff, S.:Symphonic Dances *(rec Baltimore, May 28-29, 1994)* Telarc ▲ CD 80331 [DDD]
Rachmaninoff, S.:Sym 2 Telarc ▲ CD 80312 [DDD]
Rachmaninoff, S.:Sym 3 *(rec Baltimore, May 28-29, 1994)* Telarc ▲ CD 80331 [DDD]
Rachmaninoff, S.:Vocalise, w. S. McNair (sop) Telarc ▲ CD 80312 [DDD]
Rimsky-Korsakov, N.:Russian Easter Festival *(rec Joseph Meyerhoff Symphony Hall, Baltimore, MD, Nov. 26, 1991)* Telarc ▲ CD 80378 [DDD]
Rouse, C.:Phantasmata Meet The Composer ▲ 79230-2 ■ 79230-4
Rouse, C.:Sym 1 Meet The Composer ▲ 79230-2 ■ 79230-4
Schumann, R.:Sym 1 Telarc ▲ CD 80230 [DDD]
Schumann, R.:Sym 2 Telarc ▲ CD 80182 [DDD]
Schumann, R.:Sym 3 Telarc ▲ CD 80182 [DDD]
Schumann, R.:Sym 4 Telarc ▲ CD 80230 [DDD]
Stravinsky, I.:Fireworks Telarc ▲ CD 80270 [DDD]
Tchaikovsky, P.:Con 1 Pno, w. H. Gutiérrez (pno) Telarc ▲ CD 80193 [DDD]
Tchaikovsky, P.:Eugene Onegin (sels)—Polonaise *(rec Joseph Meyerhoff Symphony Hall, Baltimore, MD, Nov. 23, 1990)* Telarc ▲ CD 80378 [DDD]
Tchaikovsky, P.:Francesca da Rimini *(rec Joseph Meyerhoff Symphony Hall, Baltimore, MD, Jan. 23, 1990)* Telarc ▲ CD 80378 [DDD]
Tchaikovsky, P.:Romeo & Juliet Telarc ▲ CD 80228 [DDD]
Tchaikovsky, P.:Sym 4 Telarc ▲ CD 80228 [DDD]
Torke, M.:Bright Blue Music *(rec Joseph Meyerhoff Symphony Hall, Baltimore, MD, Sept 27-30, 1990)* Argo ▲ 452101-2 [DDD]
Torke, M.:Green *(rec Joseph Meyerhoff Symphony Hall, Baltimore, MD, Sept 27-30, 1990)* Argo ▲ 452101-2 [DDD]
Torke, M.:Music of—Ecstatic Orange; Green Music; Purple; Ash; Bright Blue Music Argo ▲ 433071-2 [DDD]

Balzano Claudio Monteverdi Conservatory Youth Orch
F. Neri (cnd)
Cimarosa, D.:Amor rende sagace, w. G. Bertagnolli (sop), D. Bruera (sop), C. Mantese (sop), M. Dalena (ten), E. Dara (bar), M. Nicolini (sgr) [I] *(rec live, Bolzano 7/25-27/91)* Bongiovanni 2-▲ GB 2126/27 [DDD]
Grétry, A.-E.-M.:Richard Coeur-de-lion, w. M. Pennichi (sop) Nuova Era 2-▲ NUO 7157 [DDD]

Balzano Monteverdi Orch
Paisiello, G.:Il mondo della luna, w. Gemma Bertagnolli (sop—Clarice), Enzo Dara (bar—Buonafede), Riccardo Ristori (bass—Cecco), Carla Di Censo (sgr—Flaminia), Daniele Gaspari (sgr—Ecclittico), Mattia Nicolini (sgr—Ernesto) *(rec Aug 4-6, 1993)* Bongiovanni 2-▲ GB 2173/74 [DDD]

Bamberg PO
H. Swarowsky (cnd)
Brahms, J.:Sym 2 Vivace ▲ 570 [ADD]
Brahms, J.:Sym 3 Vivace ▲ 570 [ADD]
Brahms, J.:Sym 4 Vivace 3-▲ E 321 [DDD]
Brahms, J.:Sym 4 Vivace ▲ 598 [ADD]
Brahms, J.:Tragic Ov Vivace 3-▲ E 321 [DDD]
Brahms, J.:Tragic Ov Vivace ▲ 598 [ADD]

Bamberg SO
Eybler, J.L.E. von:Con Cl, w. E. Brunner (cl) Tudor ▲ TUD 782 [DDD]
Gaspar Cassado Performs Cello Masterpieces, w. Gaspar Cassado (vc), Pro Musica Orch [cnd:Jonel Perlea] *(rec mid-late 1950s)* Vox Box 2-▲ CDX2 5502 [ADD]

R. Abbado (cnd)
Liszt, F.:Cons Pno, w. G. Oppitz (pno) RCA Red Seal ▲ 09026-60953-2
Liszt, F.:Fant on Hungarian Folk Tunes, w. G. Oppitz (pno) RCA Red Seal ▲ 09026-60953-2

Y. Ahronovitch (cnd)
Rubinstein, A.:Cons Vc, w. W. Thomas (vc) Koch Schwann ▲ CD 311 103 [DDD] ■ MC 211 103 (D)

W.A. Albert (cnd)
Pfitzner, H.:Con 1 Vc, w. D. Geringas (vc) CPO ▲ CPO 999135 [DDD]
Pfitzner, H.:Con 2 Vc, w. D. Geringas (vc) CPO ▲ CPO 999135 [DDD]
Pfitzner, H.:Con 3 Vc, w. D. Geringas (vc) CPO ▲ CPO 999135 [DDD]
Pfitzner, H.:Con Vn, w. S. Gawriloff (vn) CPO ▲ CPO 999079-2 [DDD]
Pfitzner, H.:Duo Vn, w. S. Gawriloff (vn), J. Berger (vc) CPO ▲ CPO 999079-2 [DDD]
Pfitzner, H.:Elegy & Round Dance CPO ▲ CPO 999136-2 [DDD]
Pfitzner, H.:Fant CPO ▲ CPO 999136-2 [DDD]
Pfitzner, H.:Das Fest auf Solhag CPO ▲ CPO 999080-2 [DDD]
Pfitzner, H.:Orch Music—includes Sym. in C#, Op. 36a; Elegy & Round Dance, Op. 45; Fantasy, Op. 56; Scherzo; Sym., Op. 46; Kleine Sym., Op. 44; Das Fest aus Solhaug (excerpts) CPO 5-▲ CPO 999249 [DDD]
Pfitzner, H.:Scherzo CPO ▲ CPO 999079-2 [DDD]
Pfitzner, H.:Sym in c# CPO ▲ CPO 999136-2 [DDD]
Pfitzner, H.:Sym in G CPO ▲ CPO 999080-2 [DDD]
Pfitzner, H.:Sym in C CPO ▲ CPO 999080-2 [DDD]

A. de Almeida (cnd)
Turina, J.:Danzas fantásticas RCA Red Seal ▲ 09026-60895-2
Turina, J.:La procesión del Rocio RCA Red Seal ▲ 09026-60895-2
Turina, J.:Ritmos RCA Red Seal ▲ 09026-60895-2
Turina, J.:Sinfonia sevillana RCA Red Seal ▲ 09026-60895-2

M. Andreae (cnd)
Haydn, J.:Con Tpt, w. Wolfgang Basch (tpt) Koch Schwann ▲ CD 311005 [DDD]
Mozart, L.:Con Tpt, w. W. Basch (tpt) Koch Schwann ▲ CD 311005 [DDD]
Reutter, J.G. von:Con 2 Tpt, w. W. Basch (tpt) Koch Schwann ▲ CD 311005 [DDD]
Telemann, G.P.:Con Tpt Strs in D, w. W. Basch (tpt) Koch Schwann ▲ CD 311005 [DDD]

M. Buder (cnd)
Genzmer, H.:Con for 4 Hns, w. Berlin PO Horns Koch Schwann ▲ 311 021 [DDD] ■ MC 110 021 (D)
Schumann, R.:Konzertstück Hns, w. Berlin PO Horns Koch Schwann ▲ 311 021 [DDD] ■ MC 110 021 (D)

O. Caetani (cnd)
Weber, C.M. von:Concertino Cl, w. E. Brunner (cl) Orfeo ▲ 067831 [DDD]
Weber, C.M. von:Con 1 Cl, w. E. Brunner (cl) Orfeo ▲ 067831 [DDD]
Weber, C.M. von:Con 2 Cl, w. E. Brunner (cl) Orfeo ▲ 067831 [DDD]

M. Couraud (cnd)
Bizet, G.:L'Arlésienne (suites) Allegretto ▲ ACD 8030 [ADD] ■ ACS 8030

D. R. Davies (cnd)
Hindemith, P.:Con Vc, w. János Starker (vc) *(rec Sinfonie an der Regnitz, Bamberg, July 19-21, 1994)* RCA Red Seal ▲ 09026-68027-2 [DDD]
Schumann, R.:Con Vc, w. Janos Starker (vc) *(rec Sinfonie an der Regnitz, Bamberg, July 19-21, 1994)* RCA Red Seal ▲ 09026-68027-2 [DDD]

A. Dorati (cnd)
Haydn, J.:Con Hpd & Strs, H.XVIII/3, w. Ilse von Alpenheim (pno) Vox Box 2-▲ CDX 5017 [ADD]
Haydn, J.:Con Hpd & Strs, H.XVIII/4, w. Ilse von Alpenheim (pno) Vox Box 2-▲ CDX 5017 [ADD]
Haydn, J.:Con Hpd, Vns & Bass Instrument, H.XVIII/9, w. Ilse von Alpenheim (pno) Vox Box 2-▲ CDX 5017 [ADD]
Haydn, J.:Con Hpd, Obs, Hns & Strs, H.XVIII/11, w. Ilse von Alpenheim (pno) Vox Box 2-▲ CDX 5017 [ADD]
Haydn, J.:Con Org & Strs, H.XVIII/2, w. Ilse von Alpenheim (hpd) Vox Box 2-▲ CDX 5017 [ADD]
Haydn, J.:Divert Hpd, Vns & Strs, H.XIV/4, w. Ilse von Alpenheim (pno) Vox Box 2-▲ CDX 5017 [ADD]
Haydn, J.:Life & Music of, w. Laszlo Varga (vc)—narration with selected excerpts from Syms. Nos. 11, 45, 82, 94, 96, 100, 101 & 104; Con. for Harpsichord; Mass No. 2, "Great Organ Mass"; Son. No. 48; Con. No. 1 for Violin; Qt. No. 76/3; Baryton Divert. 107; Musical Clock; Con. for Trumpet; Philemon and Baucis; Con. No. 2 for Horns; Mass in D♭; The Creation; Austrian National Anthem; plus the complete Con. No. 2 in D for Cello & Orch., H.VIIb/2 (Op.101) Vox Music Masters ("Music Masters" series) ▲ MMD 8508 [ADD] ■ MMC 8508

C. Eschenbach (cnd)
Schumann, R.:Sym 2 Virgin Classics ▲ CDC 59025
Schumann, R.:Sym 4 Virgin Classics ▲ CDC 59025

C. P. Flor (cnd)
Mendelssohn, F.:Capriccio brillante, w. Sergei Edelmann (pno) RCA Red Seal ▲ 7988-2-RC [DDD]
Mendelssohn, F.:Con 1 Pno, w. Sergei Edelmann (pno) RCA Red Seal ▲ 7988-2-RC [DDD]
Mendelssohn, F.:Con 2 Pno, w. S. Edelmann (pno) RCA Red Seal ▲ 7988-2-RC [DDD]
Mendelssohn, F.:Con in d Vn & Strs, w. K. Takezawa (vn) RCA Red Seal ▲ 09026-62512-2
Mendelssohn, F.:Con in e Vn & Orch, Op. 64, w. K. Takezawa (vn) RCA Red Seal ▲ 09026-62512-2
Mendelssohn, F.:A Midsummer Night's Dream (sels) RCA Red Seal ▲ 07863-57764-2
Mendelssohn, F.:Ovs—Athalie; Calm Sea & Prosperous Voyage; Hebrides; Hochzeit des Camacho; A Midsummer Night's Dream; Ruy Blas RCA Red Seal ▲ 07863-57905-2 [DDD]
Mendelssohn, F.:Sym 1 RCA Red Seal ▲ 09026-60391-2
Mendelssohn, F.:Sym 3 RCA Red Seal ▲ 09026-60893-2
Mendelssohn, F.:Sym 4 RCA Red Seal ▲ 09026-60893-2
Mendelssohn, F.:Sym 5 RCA Red Seal ▲ 09026-60391-2

J. Fürst (cnd)
Schumann, R.:Con Pno, w. P. Frankl (pno) Vox Box 2-▲ CDX 5027 [ADD]
Schumann, R.:Con Pno, w. P. Frankl (pno) Allegretto ▲ ACD 8166 [ADD] ■ ACS 8166
Schumann, R.:Intro & Allegro appassionato, Op. 92, w. P. Frankl (pno) Vox Box 2-▲ CDX 5027 [ADD]
Schumann, R.:Intro & Allegro appassionato, Op. 92, w. P. Frankl (pno) Allegretto ▲ ACD 8166 [ADD] ■ ACS 8166
Schumann, R.:Intro & Allegro, Op. 134, w. P. Frankl (pno) Vox Box 2-▲ CDX 5027 [ADD]
Schumann, R.:Intro & Allegro, Op. 134, w. P. Frankl (pno) Allegretto ▲ ACD 8166 [ADD] ■ ACS 8166
Tchaikovsky, P.:Oprichnik (sels)—Overture; Dance Vox Box 2-▲ CDX 5079 [ADD]
Tchaikovsky, P.:The Voyevoda (sels), Op. 3—Overture; Entr'acte & Dances of the Maids Vox Box 2-▲ CDX 5079 [ADD]

T. Guschlbauer (cnd)
Mozart, W.A.:Rondo Hn, K.371, w. Georges Barboteu (hn) Erato ▲ 94801-2
Mozart, W.A.:Sym 39 Erato ▲ 45939-2 [ADD] ■ 45939-4
Mozart, W.A.:Sym 40 Erato ▲ 45939-2 [ADD] ■ 45939-4
Mozart, W.A.:Sym 40—Allegro molto Erato ▲ 94682-2

▲ = CD ♦ = Enhanced CD Δ = MD ■ = Cassette Tape □ = DCC

Bamberg SO (cont.)

H. Hollreiser (cnd)

Bartók, B.:Cons Pno (comp), w. G. Sándor (pno), M. Gielen (cnd), Vienna SO *(rec 1958-59)* Vox Box ("Legends" series) 2-▲ CDX2 5506 [ADD]
Bruckner, A.:Sym 4, "Romantic" Allegretto ▲ ACD 8147 [ADD] ■ ACS 8147
Dvořák, A.:Sym 9, "From the New World" Allegretto ▲ ACD 8008 [ADD] ■ ACS 8008
Dvořák, A.:Sym 9, "From the New World"—Largo Special Music Co. ("Classics of the Heart" series) ▲ SCD 5196
Tchaikovsky, P.:Eugene Onegin (sels)—Polonaise; Waltz Vox Box 3-▲ CD3X 3026 [ADD]
Tchaikovsky, P.:Sym 5 Allegretto ▲ ACD 8004 [ADD] ■ ACS 8004
Wagner, R.:Ovs, Preludes & Orch Sels, w. H. Swarowsky (cnd)—Meistersinger; Lohengrin; Tannhäuser; Tristan & Isolde Allegretto ▲ ACD 8021 [ADD] ■ ACS 8021

M. Honeck (cnd)

Strauss, R.:Don Juan Berlin Classics ▲ BER 1137
Strauss, R.:Der Rosenkavalier (waltzes) Berlin Classics ▲ BER 1137
Strauss, R.:Symphonic Interludes Berlin Classics ▲ BER 1137

J. Horenstein (cnd)

Mahler, G.:Kindertotenlieder, w. N. Foster (bass) *(rec 1955)* Vox Box ("Legends" series) 2-▲ CDX2 5509 [ADD]
Mahler, G.:Lieder eines fahrenden Gesellen, w. Norman Foster (b-bar) *(rec Bamberg, 1954)* Vox Legends 2-▲ CDX2 5529
Strauss, R.:Don Juan *(rec Bamberg, 1954)* Vox Legends 2-▲ CDX2 5529
Strauss, R.:Till Eulenspiegels lustige Streiche *(rec Bamberg, 1954)* Vox Legends 2-▲ CDX2 5529
Strauss, R.:Tod und Verklärung *(rec Bamberg, 1954)* Vox Legends 2-▲ CDX2 5529
Wagner, R.:Lohengrin (preludes)—Act I *(rec Bamberg, 1954)* Vox Legends 2-▲ CDX2 5529
Wagner, R.:Tristan und Isolde (prelude & liebestod) *(rec Bamberg, 1954)* Vox Legends 2-▲ CDX2 5529

N. Järvi (cnd)

Dvořák, A.:Legends, Op. 59 BIS ▲ CD 436 [DDD]
Glazunov, A.:Concert Waltz 1 Orfeo ▲ 148101
Glazunov, A.:Concert Waltz 2 Orfeo ▲ 157101 [DDD]
Glazunov, A.:Lyric Poem Orfeo ▲ 157201 [DDD]
Glazunov, A.:Sym 2 Orfeo ▲ 148101
Glazunov, A.:Sym 3 Orfeo ▲ 157101 [DDD]
Glazunov, A.:Sym 4 Orfeo ▲ 148201
Glazunov, A.:Sym 6 Orfeo ▲ 157201 [DDD]
Glazunov, A.:Sym 7, "Pastoral" Orfeo ▲ 148201
Janácek, L.:Sinfonietta BIS ▲ CD 436 [DDD]
Martinů, B.:Sym 1 BIS ▲ CD 362
Martinů, B.:Sym 2 BIS ▲ CD 362
Martinů, B.:Sym 3 BIS ▲ CD 363
Martinů, B.:Sym 4 BIS ▲ CD 363
Martinů, B.:Sym 5 BIS ▲ CD 402
Martinů, B.:Sym 6 BIS ▲ CD 402
Pärt, A.:Perpetuum mobile BIS ▲ CD 434 [DDD]
Pärt, A.:Pro et contra, w. F. Helmerson (vc) BIS ▲ CD 434 [DDD]
Pärt, A.:Syms (comp) BIS ▲ CD 434 [DDD]
Tubin, E.:Kratt BIS ▲ CD 306 [DDD]
Tubin, E.:Sym 5 BIS ▲ CD 306 [DDD]

E. Jochum (cnd)

Beethoven, L. van:Ovs—Die Geschöpfe des Prometheus; Coriolan; Egmont; Fidelio; Leonore 1 & 3; Die Ruinen von Athen RCA Silver Seal ▲ 09026-61212-2 ■ 09026-61212-4
Mozart, W.A.:Maurerische Trauermusik Orfeo ▲ 045902
Mozart, W.A.:Sym 39 Orfeo ▲ 045901
Mozart, W.A.:Sym 40 Orfeo ▲ 045901
Mozart, W.A.:Sym 41 Orfeo ▲ 045902

R. Kempe (cnd)

Smetana, B.:The Bartered Bride, w. P. Lorengar (sop), F. Wunderlich (ten), G. Frick (bass), Bamberg RIAS Chorus [G] *(rec ca. 1963)* EMI Classics ("Studio" series) 2-▲ CDMB 64002

R. Kraus (cnd)

Grieg, E.:Peer Gynt Suites, Opp. 46 & 55 Deutsche Grammophon ("Resonance" series) ▲ 427204-2 [AAD]

R. Krečmer (cnd)

Dvořák, A.:Con Vc, w. W. Thomas-Mifune (vc) Koch Schwann ▲ SCH 311462 [DDD]
Dvořák, A.:Con Vc & Pno, w. W. Thomas-Mifune (vc) Koch Schwann ▲ SCH 311462 [DDD]

E. Krivine (cnd)

Brahms, J.:Academic Festival Ov Denon ▲ CO 78956
Brahms, J.:Syms (comp) *(rec Dominikanerbau, Bamberg, July 16-20 & Sept 30-Oct)* Denon 3-▲ CO 78956 [DDD]
Brahms, J.:Tragic Ov Denon 3-▲ CO 78956
Brahms, J.:Vars on a Theme by Haydn Denon ▲ CO 78956

P. Maag (cnd)

Salieri, A.:Con Fl, w. A. Nicolet (fl) Deutsche Grammophon ("Resonance" series) ▲ 427211-2 [ADD]

O. Maga (cnd)

Rimsky-Korsakov, N.:A May Night (ov) Vox Box 2-▲ CDX 5082 [ADD]
Rimsky-Korsakov, N.:Ov on Russian Themes Vox Box 2-▲ CDX 5082 [ADD]

M. A. G. Martinez (cnd)

Donizetti, G.:Requiem Mass, w. C. Studer (sop), H. Müller-Molinari (mez), A. Baldin (ten), J. P. Bogart (bass), J.-H. Rootering (bass), Bamberg Sym Chorus [L] Orfeo ▲ 172881 [DDD]

J. Michaels (cnd)

Berger, W.:Serenade Koch Schwann ▲ SCH 310722 [DDD]
Berger, W.:Vars & Fugue on an Original Theme Koch Schwann ▲ SCH 310722 [DDD]

U. Mund (cnd)

Suder, J.:Leider machen Leute, w. P. Coburn (sop), K. König (ten), M. Morgan (bar), W. Probst (bar), Bavarian Radio Chorus [G] Orfeo 2-▲ 124862 [DDD]

K. Penderecki (cnd)

Penderecki, K.:Con 2 Vc, w. B. Pergamenschikow (vc) Orfeo ▲ 285931 [DDD]
Penderecki, K.:Con Vn, w. C. Edinger (vn) Orfeo ▲ 285931 [DDD]

J. Perlea (cnd)

Beethoven, L. van:Con 5 Pno, "Emperor", w. G. Novaes (pno) Allegretto ▲ ACD 8026 [ADD] ■ ACS 8026
Beethoven, L. van:Con 5 Pno, "Emperor", w. G. Novaes (pno) *(rec 1950s)* Vox Box ("Legends" series) 2-▲ CDX2 5512 [ADD]
Beethoven, L. van:Life & Music of, w. G. Novaes (pno)—narration with selected excerpts from Syms. Nos. 3 & 5–9; Minuet, WoO 10/2; German Dances, WoO 8/1 & 2; Sonatina, Anh. 5/2; Sons. Nos. 14 & 23 for Piano, Opp. 27 & 57; Ovs., Opp. 43, 62 & 72; Con. for Violin, Op. 61; Con. No. 5 for Piano, Op. 73, plus a complete version of Con. No. 5 for Piano in E♭, Op. 73, "Emperor" Vox ("Music Masters" series) ▲ MMD 8507 [ADD] ■ MMC 8507
Berlioz, H.:Life & Music of—narration with selected excerpts from Benvenuto Cellini; Sym. fantastique, Op. 14; L'enfance du Christ, Op. 25; Harold in Italy, Op. 16; Trojan March; Rêverie et caprice, Op. 8; Lélio, Op. 14b; Le carnaval romain, Op. 9, La damnation de Faust, Op. 24 Vox ("Music Masters" series) ▲ MMD 8516 [ADD] ■ MMC 8516
Berlioz, H.:Sym fantastique Allegretto ▲ ACD 8012 [ADD] ■ ACS 8012
Brahms, J.:Hungarian Dances Orch—Nos. 1, 2, 5, 6, 7, 10, 17, 19, 21 Allegretto ▲ ACD 8018 [ADD] ■ ACS 8018

Bamberg SO (cont.)

J. Perlea (cnd) (cont.)

Brahms, J.:Life & Music of—narration with selected excerpts from Syms. Nos. 1–3; Cons. Nos. 1 & 2 for Piano, Opp. 15 & 83; Serenade, Op. 106/1; Con. for Violin, Op. 77; Capriccio, Op. 76/2; Hungarian Dances Nos. 1, 5 & 6; Lullaby, Op. 49/4; Vars., Opp. 35 & 56a; Rinaldo, Op. 50; Waltz, Op. 39/15; Love Song Waltzes, Op. 52/1; Academic Festival Ov., Op. 80; Qnt. for Clarinet, Op. 115; Tragic Ov., Op. 81 Vox ("Music Masters" series) ▲ MMD 8513 [ADD] ■ MMC 8513
Chopin, F.:Con 1 Pno, w. G. Novaes (pno) Allegretto ▲ ACD 8006 [ADD] ■ ACS 8006
Chopin, F.:Con 1 Pno, w. G. Novaes (pno) *(rec 1950s)* Vox Box ("Legends" series) 2-▲ CDX2 5513 [ADD]
Dvořák, A.:Life & Music of—narration with selected excerpts from Cypresses, B.152; Qt. in a, Op. 16; Syms. Nos. 8 & 9; Carnival Ov., Op. 92; Trio, Op. 90; Slavonic Dances, Opp. 46/1, 2, 6, 7 & 8 & 72/2 & 7; Qnt. for Strings, Op. 77; Stabat Mater, Op. 58; Qt., Op. 51; Scherzo capriccioso, Op. 66; Con. for Cello, Op. 104; Qt., Op. 96, "American"; Humoresque, Op. 108/7; Qnt. for Piano, Op. 81; Con. for Cello, Op. 104 Vox Music Masters (Music Masters) ▲ MMD 8511 [ADD] ■ MMC 8511
Dvořák, A.:Slavonic Dances (sels)—Op. 46/1,2,7,8 Allegretto ▲ ACD 8018 [ADD] ■ ACS 8018
Dvořák, A.:Slavonic Dances (sels)—No. 2 in e Special Music Co. ▲ SCD 5200
Fauré, G.:Elégie, w. G. Cassado (vc) Allegretto ▲ ACD 8143 [ADD] ■ ACS 8143
Grieg, E.:Life & Music of—narration with selected excerpts from Peer Gynt Suite, Op. 46/1 & 2; Lyric Suite, Op. 54/2 & 3; Elf Dance, Op. 12/4; Norwegian Dances, Op. 35/1 & 2; Elegiac Melodies, Op 34/2; Symphonic Dances, Op. 64/4; I Love Thee, Op. 5/3; Butterfly, Op. 43/1; Wedding Day at Troldhaugen, Op. 65/6; Con. Piano, Op. 16; Holberg Suite, Op. 40; Homage to Chopin; Sigurd Jorsalfar Suite, Op. 56/3 Vox Music Masters ("Music Masters" series) ▲ MMD 8505 [ADD] ■ MMC 8505
Grieg, E.:Peer Gynt Suites, Opp. 46 & 55—complete Op. 46; sels. from Op. 55 Allegretto ▲ ACD 8030 [ADD] ■ ACS 8030
Lalo, E.:Con Vc, w. G. Cassado (vc) Allegretto ▲ ACD 8143 [ADD] ■ ACS 8143
Rimsky-Korsakov, N.:Scheherazade Allegretto ▲ ACD 8003 [ADD] ■ ACS 8003
Rimsky-Korsakov, N.:Scheherazade—The Young Prince & Princess Special Music Co. ("Classics of the Heart" series) ▲ SCD 5196
Rossini, G.:La gazza ladra (ov) Special Music Co. ("Classics of the Heart" series) ▲ SCD 5196
Rossini, G.:Ovs—William Tell; Semiramide; Barber of Seville; Thieving Magpie; Cenerentola Allegretto ▲ ACD 8015 [ADD] ■ ACS 8015
Saint-Saëns, C.:Con 1 Vc, w. G. Cassado (vc) Allegretto ▲ ACD 8143 [ADD] ■ ACS 8143
Schubert, Franz:Con Vc, w. G. Cassado (vc) *(rec 1950s)* Vox Box ("Legends" series) 2-▲ CDX2 5502 [ADD]
Schumann, R.:Con Vc, w. G. Casado (vc) *(rec 1950s)* Vox Box ("Legends" series) 2-▲ CDX2 5502 [ADD]
Schumann, R.:Life & Music of—narration with selected excerpts from Syms. Nos. 3 & 4; Andante & Vars., Op.46; Symphonic Etudes, Op. 13; Toccata, Op. 7; Kreisleriana, Op. 16; Con. for Piano, Op. 54; Carnaval, Op. 9; Dedication, Op. 25/1; Papillons, Op. 2; "The Nut Tree", Op. 25/3; Qnt. for Piano, Op. 44; Album for the Young, Op. 68; Scenes from Childhood, Op. 15; Con. for Cello, Op. 129 Vox Music Masters ("Music Masters" series) ▲ MMD 8505 [ADD] ■ MMC 8505

K. A. Rickenbacher (cnd)

Bruckner, A.:Missa solemnis, w. C. Oelze (sop), C. Schubert (alt), J. Dümüller (ten), R. Hagen (bass), Bamberg Sym Chorus Virgin Classics ▲ CDC 59060
Bruckner, A.:Psalm 112, w. C. Oelze (sop), C. Schubert (alt), J. Dümüller (ten), R. Hagen (bass), Bamberg Sym Chorus Virgin Classics ▲ CDC 59060
Bruckner, A.:Psalm 114, w. C. Oelze (sop), C. Schubert (alt), J. Dümüller (ten), R. Hagen (bass), Bamberg Sym Chorus Virgin Classics ▲ CDC 59060
Bruckner, A.:Psalm 150, w. C. Oelze (sop), C. Schubert (alt), J. Dümüller (ten), R. Hagen (bass), Bamberg Sym Chorus Virgin Classics ▲ CDC 59060
Hartmann, K.A.:Gesangsszene, w. *(soloist unknown)* Koch Schwann ▲ SCH 312952 [DDD]
Hartmann, K.A.:Sinf tragica Koch Schwann ▲ SCH 312952 [DDD]
Hartmann, K.A.:Sym 2, "Adagio" Koch Schwann ▲ SCH 312952 [DDD]
Hindemith, P.:Mathis der Maler (sym) Virgin Classics ("Ultraviolet" series) ▲ CUV 61201
Hindemith, P.:Nobilissima visione Koch Schwann ▲ SCH 312992 [DDD]
Hindemith, P.:Neues vom Tage (concert ov) Virgin Classics ("Ultraviolet" series) ▲ CUV 61201
Hindemith, P.:Suite of French Dances Koch Schwann ▲ SCH 312992 [DDD]
Hindemith, P.:Symphonic Metamorphosis on Themes of Carl Maria von Weber Virgin Classics ("Ultraviolet" series) ▲ CUV 61201
Humperdinck, E.:Der Heirat wider Willen (ov) Koch Schwann ▲ SCH 311972 [DDD]
Humperdinck, E.:Humoreske Koch Schwann ▲ SCH 311972 [DDD]
Humperdinck, E.:Orchestral Suites—Hänsel und Gretel, Der blaue Vogel, Königskinder, Dornroschen Virgin Classics ▲ 59067 [DDD]
Humperdinck, E.:Shakespeare Suites 1 & 2 Koch Schwann ▲ SCH 311972 [DDD]

G. Schmöhe (cnd)

Ghedini, G.F.:Con for 2 Vcs, w. A. Meneses (vc), W. Thomas-Mifune (vc) *(rec 1/90)* Koch Schwann ▲ 311106 H1 [DDD]
Romberg, B.:Con Vcs, w. A. Meneses (vc), W. Thomas-Mifune (vc) Koch Schwann ▲ 311106 H1 [DDD]

H.-M. Schneidt (cnd)

Baur, J.:Con romano, w. Otto Winter (ob) Thorofon ▲ CTH 2270

L. Segerstam (cnd)

The Burlesque Trombone & Romantic Trombone Concertos, w. Christian Lindberg (trbn), Roland Pöntinen (pno) BIS ("BIS Twins" series) 2-▲ 318/378
David, Ferdinand:Concertino Trbn, w. C. Lindberg (trbn) BIS ▲ CD 378 [DDD]
Frumerie, G. de:Con Trbn, w. C. Lindberg (trbn) BIS ▲ CD 378 [DDD]
Grieg, E.:Con Pno, Op. 16, w. Roland Pöntinen (pno) BIS ("BIS Twins" series) 2-▲ CD 375/381
Grieg, E.:Con Pno, Op. 16, w. R. Pöntinen (pno) BIS ▲ CD 375
Grondahl, L.:Con Trbn, w. C. Lindberg (trbn) BIS ▲ CD 378 [DDD]
Guilmant, A.:Morceau symphonique, w. C. Lindberg (trbn) BIS ▲ CD 378 [DDD]
Tchaikovsky, P.:Con 1 Pno, w. R. Pöntinen (pno) BIS ▲ CD 375
Tchaikovsky, P.:Con 1 Pno, w. Roland Pöntinen (pno) BIS ("BIS Twins" series) 2-▲ CD 375/381

L. Shambadal (cnd)

Bruch, M.:Con 2 Vn, w. I. Turban (vn) *(rec Mar. 1992)* Claves ▲ CD 9318 [DDD]
Busoni, F.:Con Vn, w. I. Turban (vn) *(rec Mar. 1992)* Claves ▲ CD 9318 [DDD]
Strauss, R.:Con Vn, w. I. Turban (vn) *(rec Mar. 1992)* Claves ▲ CD 9318 [DDD]

J. Silverstein (cnd)

Schumann, C.:Con Pno, w. V. Jochum (pno) Tudor ▲ TUD 788 [DDD]

H. Stadlmair (cnd)

Droste-Hülshoff, A. von:Sinf concertante Koch Schwann ▲ SCH 311252 [DDD]
Druschetzky, G.:Sinf concertante Koch Schwann ▲ SCH 311252 [DDD]
Hummel, J.N.:Intro, Theme & Vars, w. *(soloist unknown)* Tudor ▲ TUD 782 [DDD]
Krommer, F.:Con Cl, w. E. Brunner (cl) Tudor ▲ TUD 782 [DDD]
Schacht, T. von:Cons Cl, w. D. Kloecker (cl), O. Link (cl), S. Wandel (cl)—in D & B for 1 Clarinet; in B for 2 Clarinets; in B for 3 Clarinets *(rec May 11-15, 1992)* Orfeo ▲ 290931 [DDD]
Schindelmeisser, L.:Sinf concertante Koch Schwann ▲ SCH 311252 [DDD]

H. Stein (cnd)

Reger, M.:Eine Ballettsuite Koch Schwann ▲ CD 311 150 [DDD]
Reger, M.:Con in Olden Style, w. H. Orlovsky (vn) Koch Schwann ▲ CD 313542 [DDD]
Reger, M.:Con Pno, w. G. Oppitz (pno) Koch Schwann ▲ CD 311058 [DDD]
Reger, M.:Con Vn, w. W. Forchert (vn) Koch Schwann ▲ CD 311 186 [DDD]
Reger, M.:Psalm 100, w. Bamberg Sym Chorus Koch Schwann ▲ SCH 312092 [DDD]
Reger, M.:Serenade Orch Koch Schwann ▲ SCH 315662
Reger, M.:Sinfonietta, w. H. Orlovsky (vn) Koch Schwann ▲ CD 313542 [DDD]
Reger, M.:Suite im alten Stil Koch Schwann ▲ SCH 315662
Reger, M.:Vars & Fugue on a Theme of Beethoven Koch Schwann ▲ 3-1141-2 [DDD]
Reger, M.:Vars & Fugue on a Theme of of J. A. Hiller Koch Schwann ▲ CD 311 150 [DDD]
Reger, M.:Vars & Fugue on a Theme by Mozart Koch Schwann ▲ 3-1141-2 [DDD]

ORCH. & ENS.

Bamberg SO (cont.)
H. Stein (cnd) (cont.)
Reger, M.:Die Weihe der Nacht, w. Bamberg Sym Chorus — Koch Schwann ▲ SCH 312092 [DDD]
H. Swarowsky (cnd)
Wagner, R.:Life & Music of—narration with selected excerpts from Die Meistersinger; Lohengrin; Faust; The Fairies; Siegfried; Rienzi; Der fliegende Holländer; Tannhäuser; Götterdämmerung; Tristan und Isolde; Die Walküre; Parsifal, plus H. Hollreiser, Bamberg SO performing Preludes to Act I & III, and Bridal Chorus from Lohengrin
Vox Music Masters ("Music Masters" series) ▲ MMD 8509 [ADD] ■ MMC 8509
A. Symeonides (cnd)
Gretchaninoff, A.:Suite Vc, w. W. Thomas (vc) — Koch Schwann ▲ 311008 [DDD]
Khachaturian, A.:Con Vc, w. W. Thomas (vc) — Koch Schwann ▲ 311008 [DDD]
H. Wallberg (cnd)
Feld, J.:Dramatic Fant, "The Days of August" *(rec 1985)* — Praga ▲ PR 255001
L. Zagrosek (cnd)
Bruch, M.:Con Cl & Va, w. E. Brunner (cl) — Koch Schwann ▲ CD 311065 [DDD]
Bruckner, A.:Qnt Strs [orchd. Hans Stadlmair] *(rec Bamberg, Nov. 2–4, 8 & 9, 1993)* — Orfeo ▲ 348951 [DDD]
Lutoslawski, W.:Con Ob, w. E. Brunner (ob), M. Graf (hp) — Koch Schwann ▲ CD 311065 [DDD]
Schoenberg, A.:Verklärte Nacht *(rec Bamberg, Feb. 7 & 8, 1994)* — Orfeo ▲ 348951 [DDD]
Strauss, R.:Duet-Concertino, w. E. Brunner (cl), M. Turkovič (bn), M. Graf (hp) — Koch Schwann ▲ CD 311065 [DDD]

Bamberg Sym String Quintet
Mendelssohn, F.:Qnts Strs, Opp. 18 & 87 — Concerto Bayreuth ▲ CBH 16011
Bamberg Youth Orch
H. Dechant (cnd)
Hoffmann, E.T.A.:Aurora, w. Thomas Rieger (trb), Maltraud Meier (mez), Siegfried Schulze (bass), Koch (sgr), Ohlmann (sgr), Bamberg Oratorio Chorus — Bayer 3–▲ 100276–78
Hoffmann, E.T.A.:Undine, w. Barbara Baier (sop—Berthalda), Heidrun Plesch (sop—Undine), Corinna Tippe (sop—Die Herzogin), Maria Hiefinger (mez—Fisherman's Wife), Achim Schamberger (ten—Der Herzog), Johannes Beck (bar—Ritter Huldbrand von Ringstetten), Michael Albert (bass—Fisherman), Ulrich Bosch (bass—Heilmann), Bernd Hofmann (bass—Kühleborn) — Bayer 3–▲ 100256/58 [DDD]
Banchetto Musicale
M. Pearlman (cnd)
Haydn, J.:Mass 11, "Nelsonmesse", "Imperial Mass", "Coronation Mass", w. Janet Baker (sop), Pamela Dellal (mez), Jeffery Thomas (ten), James Maddalena (bar) [L] — Arabesque ▲ Z 6560 [DDD]
Mozart, W.A.:Missa, K.317, w. S. Baker (sop), J. Malafronte (mez), F. Kelley (ten), J. Maddalena (bar) — Harmonia Mundi USA ▲ HMU 907021 ■
Mozart, W.A.:Vesperae solennes, w. S. Baker (sop), J. Malafronte (mez), F. Kelley (ten), J. Maddalena (bar) — Harmonia Mundi USA ▲ HMU 907021 ■
Band of the Blues & Royals
E. W. Jeanes (cnd)
Sousa, J.P.:Marches & Dances [most arrs. by Gordon Langford]—Washington Post; Hands across the sea; The Thunderer; High school cadets; El Capitan; The gladiator march; Manhattan Beach; Liberty Bell; Belle of Chicago; Semper Fidelis; Netional Fencibles; The Invincible eagle; King Cotton
Chandos ("Collect" series) ▲ CHAN 6517 [ADD]
Banda Classica
C. Siegmann (cnd)
Berger, W.:Serenade *(rec Radio Studio, Zurich, Feb. 23–25, 1994)* — Claves ▲ CD 9409 [DDD]
Hartmann, E.:Serenade *(rec Radio Studio, Zurich, Feb. 23–25, 1994)* — Claves ▲ CD 9409 [DDD]
Music for Wind Instruments — Koch Schwann ▲ SCH 310110 [DDD]
Strauss, R.:Suite Wws *(rec Radio Studio, Zurich, Feb. 23–25, 1994)* — Claves ▲ CD 9409 [DDD]
Banda Ruvomusica
M. di Puppo (cnd)
Amenduni, A.:Music of—Rassegnazione; Giorno di dolore; Vivo cordoglio; Triste ricordo *(rec Nov 20 & 21, 1993)* — Musicaimmagine ▲ 10035
Banff Camerata
Saint-Saëns, C.:Music of—Septet, Op. 65; Son. for Oboe & Piano, Op. 166; Wedding Cake, Op. 76; Fantaisie for Violin & Harp, Op. 124; Morceau de concert for Horn & Piano, Op. 94; Scherzo for Piano & Harmonium, Op. 8; Les cloches du soir, Op. 85 — Summit ▲ DCD 157 [DDD]
Banff Festival Strings
T. Rolston (cnd)
Bach, J.S.:Brandenburg Con 2, w. P. Bowman (ob), D. Hickman (tpt) *(rec Aug 6–8, 1990)* — Summit ▲ DCD 118 [DDD] ■ DCD 118
Hertel, J.W.:Con à 6, w. D. Hickman (tpt), P. Bowman (ob) *(rec Aug. 6–8, 1990)* — Summit ▲ DCD 118 [DDD] ■ DCD 118
Telemann, G.P.:Con Tpt Strs in D, w. D. Hickman (tpt) *(rec Aug. 6–8, 1990)* — Summit ▲ DCD 118 [DDD] ■ DCD 118
Vivaldi, A.:Con for 2 Tpts, w. D. Hickman (tpt), D. Carlsen (tpt) *(rec Aug. 6–8, 1990)* — Summit ▲ DCD 118 [DDD] ■ DCD 118
Bang on a Can [Maya Beiser (vc), Robert Black (db), Evan Ziporyn (cl), Mark Stewart (gtr), Lisa Moore (pno), Steven Schick (dr)]
Didkovsky, N.:Amalia's Secret *(rec The Hit Factory, New York, Oct 4–8, 1995)* — Sony Classical ▲ SK 62254 [DDD]
Gosfield, A.:The Manufacture of Tangles Ivory *(rec The Hit Factory, New York, Oct 4–8, 1995)* — Sony Classical ▲ SK 62254 [DDD]
Lang, D.:Cheating, Lying, Stealing *(rec The Hit Factory, New York, Oct 4–8, 1995)* — Sony Classical ▲ SK 62254 [DDD]
Pascoal, H.:Arapua *(rec The Hit Factory, New York, Oct 4–8, 1995)* — Sony Classical ▲ SK 62254 [DDD]
Bang on a Can members [Maya Beiser (vc), Lisa Moore (kbd), Mark Stewart (gtr), Steven Schick (perc)]
Vierk, L.V.:Red Shift *(rec The Hit Factory, New York, Oct 4–8, 1995)* — Sony Classical ▲ SK 62254 [DDD]
Bantam Orch [Guy Klucevsek (acc/melodica/pno), Sara Parkins (vn), Margaret Parkins (vc), Achim Tang (db)]
Klucevsek, G.:Music of—Rumbling; The Gunks; Urban Rite; Wave Hill; Tesknota; Stolen Memories; Donut Ask, Donut Tell; Regunkitation; Skating on Thin Air — Tzadik ▲ TZA CD 7018 [DDD]
Barbaroque Ensemble
Fučík, J.:Der alte Brummbär [arr for Bassoon, Clarinet, Cello, Double Bass & Barrel Organ] — Gallo ▲ CD 858 [DDD]
Handel, G.F.:Cons (16) Org—Op. 4/4 [arr for Barrel Org, Ob, Cl, Bn, Vc & Db] — Gallo ▲ CD 858 [DDD]
Lavergne, P.:Invariants — Gallo ▲ CD 858 [DDD]
Marcello, A.:Cons Ob—in d [arr for Ob, Bn, Vihuela, Db & Barrel Org] — Gallo ▲ CD 858 [DDD]
Weber, C.M. von:Concertino Ob [arr for Ob & Barrel Org] — Gallo ▲ CD 858 [DDD]
Charlie Barber & Band
Moran, R.:Cryptograms *(rec Chapel of Girard College, Philadelphia & Henry Wood Hall, London)* — Argo ▲ 444540–2 [DDD]
Barbican Trio
Lalo, E.:Trio 1 Pno — ASV ▲ ASV 899 [DDD]
Lalo, E.:Trio 2 Pno — ASV ▲ ASV 899 [DDD]
Lalo, E.:Trio 3 Pno — ASV ▲ ASV 899 [DDD]
Barcelona Ars Musicae
The Early Recordings, 1942–1953, w. Victoria de los Angeles (sop), Gerald Moore (pno), Ivor Newton (pno), Agrupación de Cámara Barcelona — Testament ▲ SBT 1087
E. Gispert (cnd)
Le Moyen Age Catalan — Harmonia Mundi ▲ HMA 190.051
I. Segarra (cnd)
Cererols, J.:Sacred Romances, w. Montserrat Capella e Escolania [period instrs] *(rec 1979?)* — Koch Treasure ▲ 31624–2 [ADD]

Barcelona Cello Ensemble
In Memoriam Pablo Casals, w. Lluís Claret (vc), Seon-Hee Myong (pno) — Valois ▲ V 4733
Barcelona Gran Teatro de Liceo Orch
Sings Catalan Songs, w. José Carreras (ten), Joan Casa — Sony Classical ▲ SK 47177
A. de Almeida (cnd)
Meyerbeer, G.:L'Africiane, w. Montserrat Caballe (sop—Selika), Christine Weidinger (sop—Inez), Miriam Ucelay (mez—Anna), Placido Domingo (ten—Vasco de Gama), Guillermo Sarabia (bar—Nelusko), Juan Thomas (b-bar—High Priest of Brahma), Dimiter Petkov (bass—Don Pedro), Juan Pons (bass—Don Diego), Eduardo Soto (bass—Grand Inquisitor), Barcelona Gran Teatro de Liceo Chorus *(rec Barcelona, Nov 27, 1977)* — Legato Classics 2–▲ LCD 208–2 [ADD]
C. F. Cillario (cnd)
Bellini, V.:Norma, w. Caballé (soprano—Norma), F. Cossotto (mez), B. Prevedi (ten), J. Carreras (ten), I. Vinco (bass), Barcelona Gran Teatro de Liceo Chorus [I] *(rec live, Barcelona 1/11/70)* — Melodram 2–▲ CDM 27089 [ADD]
Bizet, G.:Les Pêcheurs de perles, w. A. Maliponte (sop—Leila), A. Kraus (ten—Nadir), S. Bruscantini (bar—Zurga), Barcelona Gran Teatro de Liceo Chorus — Bongiovanni 2–▲ GB 516/17 [ADD]
A. Coates (cnd)
Rimsky-Korsakov, N.:The Legend of the Invisible City of Kitzeh (sels), w. Barcelona Gran Teatro de Liceo Chorus—Village Wedding Procession [Act 2]; The Battle of Kerzhenets [Act 3] *(rec Liceo Theater, Barcelona, 1928)* — Claremont ▲ GSE 785061
J. Delacôte (cnd)
Massenet, J.:Hérodiade, w. M. Caballé (sop—Salomé), D. Vejzovic (mez—Hérodiade), J. Carreras (ten—Jean), J. Pons (bar—Hérode), E. Serra (bar—Vitellius), V. Esteve (bar—High Priest), R. Kennedy (bass—Phanuel), Barcelona Gran Teatro de Liceo Chorus *(rec Jan. 6, 1984)* — Legato Classics 2–▲ LCD 182 [ADD]
I. Savini (cnd)
Verdi, G.:La forza del destino (sels), w. Raina Kabalvanska (sop), Carlo Bergonzi (ten), Barcelona Gran Teatro de Liceo Chorus *(rec live, Nov 13, 1972)* — Arkadia ▲ 499
Barcelona Pau Casals Orch
A. Cortot (cnd)
Brahms, J.:Con Vn & Vc, "Double Con", w. J. Thibaud (vn), P. Casals (vc) — Pearl 4–▲ PEAS 9935 (m) [AAD]
Brahms, J.:Con Vn & Vc, "Double Con", w. J. Thibaud (vn), P. Casals (vc) *(rec May 1929)* — EMI Classics 3–▲ 64057–2 (m) [ADD]
Brahms, J.:Con Vn & Vc, "Double Con", w. J. Thibaud (vn), P. Casals (vc) *(rec between May 11–12, 1929)* — Koch Historic 2–▲ 7705–2 [ADD]
Brahms, J.:Con Vn & Vc, "Double Con", w. Jacques Thibaud (vn), Pablo Casals (vc) — Dutton Laboratories ▲ DUT 5006 [ADD]
Brahms, J.:Con Vn & Vc, "Double Con", w. J. Thibaud (vn), P. Casals (vc) *(rec 1929 for HMV)* — Pearl ▲ PEA 9363 (m) [AAD]
Barcelona SO
L. Foster (cnd)
Bartók, B.:Con 2 Vn, w. Mark Kaplan (vn) [w. original coda] — Koch Schwann ▲ KIC CD 7387
Dohnányi, E. von:Con 2 Vn, w. Mark Kaplan (vn) — Koch Schwann ▲ KIC CD 7387
L. A. Garcia-Navarro (cnd)
Zarzuela Arias, w. Plácido Domingo (ten) — Acanta ▲ CD 49390
G.-F. Masini (cnd)
Verdi, G.:Arias, w. M. Caballé (sop)—7 arias & scenes from Ballo in maschera, Macbeth, Rigoletto, Trovatore, Vespri siciliani [I] — Acanta ▲ 49395
Barcelona Trio
Beethoven, L. van:Trio 1 Pno — Harmonia Mundi Plus ▲ HMP 3905205
Mendelssohn, F.:Trio 1 Pno — Harmonia Mundi France ▲ HMC 901335
Mendelssohn, F.:Trio 2 Pno — Harmonia Mundi France ▲ HMC 901335
Barcelona's Free Theater CO
J. Pons (cnd)
Albéniz, I.:Pepita Jimínez (suite), w. Susan Chilcott (sop), Francesc Garrigosa (ten), Barcelona Children's Choir — Harmonia Mundi France ▲ HMC 901537
Falla, M. de:El amor brujo, w. G. Ortega (mez) [Sp] — Harmonia Mundi France ▲ HMC 905213
Falla, M. de:Canciones populares españolas (7), w. V. de los Angeles (sop) — Harmonia Mundi France ▲ HMC 901432
Falla, M. de:Con Hpd, w. L. Vidal (hpd) — Harmonia Mundi France ▲ HMC 901432
Falla, M. de:El corregidor y la molinera, w. Gino Ortega (cantor) — Harmonia Mundi France ▲ HMC 901520
Falla, M. de:El gran teatro del mundo — Harmonia Mundi France ▲ HMC 901432
Falla, M. de:Psyché, w. V. de los Angeles (sop) — Harmonia Mundi France ▲ HMC 901432
Falla, M. de:El retablo de maese Pedro, w. G. Ortega (cantor) [Sp] — Harmonia Mundi France ▲ HMC 905213
Garcia Lorca, F.:Canciones, w. Gino Ortega (cant) — Harmonia Mundi France ▲ HMC 901520
Pablo, L. de:Tarde de Poetas, w. Luisa Castellani (sop), Jorge Chaminé (bar) — Harmonia Mundi France 2–▲ HMC 901568
Soler, J.:Chamber Con Pno, w. Lluís Vidal (pno) — Harmonia Mundi France ▲ HMC 905231
Soler, J.:Mahler Lieder, w. Virgínia Parramon (sop), Lluís Vidal (pno) — Harmonia Mundi France ▲ HMC 905231
Bargemusic [Ik-Hwan Bae (vn), Cynthia Phelps (va), Fred Sherry (vc), David Jolley (hn)]
Bach, J.S.:Brandenburg Cons — Koch International Classics 2–▲ KIC 7294
Bariano Trio [Noriko Fujii (sop), Barbara Peterson (fl), Janina Kuzma (hpd)]
London, E.:Sonnet Haiku *(rec Rockwell Studio, Cleveland, OH)* — New World ▲ 80477–2
Barkel String Quartet
The String Quartet in Sweden:A Cavalcade of Its History, w. Stockholm String Quartet, Garaguly String Quartet, Kyndel String Quartet, Ivan Ericson String Quartet, Grünfarb String Quartet, Skåne String Quartet, Hälsingborg String Quartet, Göteborg String Quartet, Galli Stri *(rec before 1951)* — Caprice 5–▲ CAP 21506 [AAD/ADD]
Barking Pumpkin Digital Gratification Consort
Zappa, F.:The Girl in the Magnesium Dress *(rec Utility Muffin Research Kitchen after 1984)* — Rykodisc ▲ RCD 10542
Zappa, F.:Jonestown *(rec Utility Muffin Research Kitchen after 1984)* — Rykodisc ▲ RCD 10542
Zappa, F.:Love Story *(rec Utility Muffin Research Kitchen after 1984)* — Rykodisc ▲ RCD 10542
Zappa, F.:Outside Now Again *(rec Utility Muffin Research Kitchen after 1984)* — Rykodisc ▲ RCD 10542
Barocco Padovano Sans Souci Ensemble
Albinoni, T.:Trattenimenti armonici per camera, w. Mario Folena (trns fl)—Nos. 1, 2 & 6–9 [trans anon in early 1700's] *(rec Chiesa della Natività della B.V. Maria ai Servi, Padova, Italy, Apr 24–25 & May 1, 1995)* — Dynamic ▲ CD 139 [DDD]
Barock Jazz Quintet
Marin, J.L.:Disco Gramofónico *(rec ZK Motorlet Prague Studio, Sept 4–6 & 14–15, 1986)* — Panton ▲ PAN 810884
Baroque Chamber Ensemble [Natalia Gerasimova (sgr), Igor Popkov (vn), Yuri Moukharlyamov (fl), Andrei Piskounov (ob), Sergey Moroz (vc), Victor Vasiliev (hpd)]
Bortnyansky, D.:Chamber Music—Alkid suite; Cant Ave Maria; Con Hpd; Quint Phabeus Suite; Son Hpd; Qnt in C — Russian Compact Disc ▲ RCD 10301 [DDD]
Bortnyansky, D.:Chamber Music—La Fête du signeur Sym & Aria; 8 Songs for Great Dutchess Yelizaveta Alekseyevna; Le Fils rival aria; Sinf Concertante in B — Russian Compact Disc ▲ RCD 10302 [DDD]
Baroque CO
The Best of Vivaldi, w. J.-F. Paillard (cnd), English CO, et al. — Victrola ("Victrola Best of" series) ▲ 60776–2–RV [ADD] ■ 60776–4–RV

Baroque CO (cont.)
  E. Stratta (cnd)
    Pachelbel's Canon, Albinoni's Adagio & Other Baroque Favorites
          Victrola ▲ 7821-2-RV [ADD] ■ 7821-4-RV
Baroque Chamber Players [James Pellerite (fl), Jerry Sirucek (ob), Murray Grodner (db), Wallace Hornibrook (hpd)]
  Barati, G.:Baroque Qt *(rec Indiana Univ, 1984)*   Centaur ▲ CRC 2286 [DDD]
Baroque de L'Ouest Ensemble
  Bernier, N.:Motets—Congratulamini   Ligia Digital ▲ 0202026
  Boismortier, J.B. de:Panis angelis   Ligia Digital ▲ 0202026
  Campra, A.:Motets—Cum invocarem   Ligia Digital ▲ 0202026
  Charpentier, M.-A.:Motets—Egredimini   Ligia Digital ▲ 0202026
  Daniélis, D.:Motets—Adoro te; Qui reminiscimi   Ligia Digital ▲ 0202026
  Mouret, J.-J.:Usquequo Domine   Ligia Digital ▲ 0202026
Baroque Instrumental Ensemble
  A. Bourbon (cnd)
    Dupuy, B.A.:Sacred Music, w. Isabelle Poulenard (sop), Jean-Louis Comorette (ct), Erik Gruchet (ten), Dominique Miraille (bar), Jean-Louis Bindi (bass), Toulouse Vocal Group—Noël; Motet; Magnificat
          Arion ▲ ARN 68330 [DDD]
  C. Coin (cnd)
    Boccherini, L.:Con Vc, G.476, w. C. Coin (vc)   Astrée ▲ E 8517 [DDD]
    Boccherini, L.:Con Vc, G.480, w. C. Coin (vc)   Astrée ▲ E 8517 [DDD]
    Boccherini, L.:Con Vc, G.482, w. C. Coin (vc)   Astrée ▲ E 8517 [DDD]
Baroque 1994 Ensemble
  R. Válek (cnd)
    Zelenka, J.D.:Miserere, ZWV 57, w. Czech Chamber Choir   Supraphon ▲ SUP 0052 [DDD]
    Zelenka, J.D.:Requiem, ZWV 48, w. Czech Chamber Choir   Supraphon ▲ SUP 0052 [DDD]
Baroque Orch
  Bach, J.S.:Cant 24, w. Residentie Chamber Choir The Hague   Erasmus ▲ WVH 152
  Bach, J.S.:Cant 182, w. Residentie Chamber Choir The Hague   Erasmus ▲ WVH 152
  R. Goodman (cnd)
    Odes on the Death of Henry Purcell, w. P. Holman (cnd), Parley of Instruments, Baroque Choir, R. Holton (sop), R. Covey-Crump (ten), C. Daniels (ten), S. Birchall (bass)
          Hyperion ▲ CDA 66578 [DDD]
    Purcell, H.:Music of, w. Parley of Instruments—sels from Dioclesian, King Arthur, The Fairy Queen, The Old Bachelor, Amphitryon, The Double Dealer, The Gordian Knot Untied, Abdelazer, Bonduca, others
          Hyperion 3-▲ CDA 67001/3
  G. Leonhardt (cnd)
    Bach, J.S.:Cant 27, w. Markus Schäfer (ten), Harry van der Kamp (bass), Tölz Boys' Choir
          Sony Classical ("Vivarte" series) ▲ SK 68265
    Bach, J.S.:Cant 34, w. Markus Schäfer (ten), Harry van der Kamp (bass), Tölz Boys' Choir
          Sony Classical ("Vivarte" series) ▲ SK 68265
    Bach, J.S.:Cant 41, w. Markus Schäfer (ten), Harry van der Kamp (bass), Tölz Boys' Choir
          Sony Classical ("Vivarte" series) ▲ SK 68265
  J. Skidmore (cnd)
    Vivaldi, A.:Sacred Choral Music, w. Ex Cathedra Choir—Versicle & Response, RV.593; Beatus Vir, RV.597; Hymn [from *Stabat Mater, RV 621*]; Canticle [from *Magnificat, RV.610*]
          ASV ("Gaudeamus" series) ▲ ASV 137 [DDD]
Baroque Pops Orch
  E. Stratta (cnd)
    Vivaldi, A.:Music of   RCA ■ ALK1-4980
Baroque String Ensemble
  A. Deller (cnd)
    Monteverdi, C.:Madrigals (book 8), w. Deller Consort
          Vanguard Classics ("The Bach Guild" series) ▲ OVC 2519 [ADD]
Baroque Strings
  Quantz, J.J.:Con in G Fl & Strs, w. A. Magnin (fl)   Gallo ▲ CD 372
  Vivaldi, A.:Cons Fl, Op. 10, w. A. Magnin (fl)—Nos. 2 & 3   Gallo ▲ CD 372
Barrow CO
  C. Theofanidis (cnd)
    Theofanidis, C.:Voices, w. Darla Barrow-Theofanidis (sop)   Albany ▲ TROY 158 [DDD]
Bartholdy Piano Quartet [Pier Narciso Masi (pno), Jörg-Wolfgang (vn), Matthias Buchholz (va), Franco Rossi (vc)]
  Franck, C.:Qt Strs   Entrée ▲ 0037
  Mendelssohn, F.:Qt 2 Pno *(rec Clara Wieck Auditorium, Heidelberg, Nov., 1991 & Dec. 1992)*
          Naxos ▲ 8.550967 [DDD]
  Mendelssohn, F.:Qt 3 Pno *(rec Clara Wieck Auditorium, Heidelberg, Nov., 1991 & Dec. 1992)*
          Naxos ▲ 8.550967 [DDD]
Bartók String Quartet [P. Komlós (vn), G. Hargitai (vn), G. Németh (va), L. Mező (vc)]
  Bartók, B.:Qt Strs (comp) *(rec June 5-10, 1991)*   Canyon 3-▲ EC 3698-2 [DDD]
  Beethoven, L. van:Qt 7 Strs   White Label ▲ HRC 153 [ADD]
  Beethoven, L. van:Qt 9 Strs   White Label ▲ HRC 153 [ADD]
  Brahms, J.:Qts Strs (comp) *(rec 1971-74)*   Hungaroton 3-▲ HCD 11591/93 [ADD]
  Brahms, J.:Qnt Cl, w. B. Kovács (cl)   Hungaroton ▲ HCD 11596
  Brahms, J.:Qnt Pno, w. D. Ránki (pno)   Hungaroton ▲ HCD 11596
  Brahms, J.:Qnt 1 Strs, w. G. Konrád (va) *(rec 1971-74)*   Hungaroton 3-▲ HCD 11591/93 [ADD]
  Brahms, J.:Qnt 2 Strs, w. G. Konrád (va) *(rec 1971-74)*   Hungaroton 3-▲ HCD 11591/93 [ADD]
  Brahms, J.:Sextet Strs, Op. 36, w. G. Konrád (va), E. Banda (vc) *(rec 1971-74)*
          Hungaroton 3-▲ HCD 11591/93 [ADD]
  Haydn, J.:Qts Strs, Op. 64, "Tost Qts"—No. 5 [The Lark]   Canyon Classics ▲ EC 3621
  Haydn, J.:Qts Strs, Op. 76, "Erdödy Qts"—Nos. 3 [Emperor] & 4 [Sunrise]   Canyon Classics ▲ EC 3621
  Mendelssohn, F.:Octet Strs, w. *(other artists unknown)*   Hungaroton ▲ HCD 31351
  Mendelssohn, F.:Qt 1 Strs   Hungaroton ▲ HCD 31107 [DDD]
  Mendelssohn, F.:Qt 3 Strs   Hungaroton ▲ HCD 31107 [DDD]
  Mozart, W.A.:Qts Strs (misc)—Nos. 14 & 15   White Label ▲ HRC 129 [ADD]
  Schoenberg, A.:Verklärte Nacht, w. *(other artists unknown)*   Hungaroton ▲ HCD 31351 [DDD]
Léon Barzin Orch
  J.-J. Werner (cnd)
    Hovhaness, A.:Music of, w. Annie Jodry (vn), Hasmig Surmélian (pno)—Lousadzak [Coming of Light] for Pno & Str Orch; Saris for Vn & Pno; Oror for Vn & Pno; Shatakh for Vn & Pno; Shatakh II; Khirgiz Suite for Vn & Pno; A Kirghiz Tala; Khirgiz III; Con No. 2 for Vn & Str Orch *(rec Paris, May 1995)*
          Media 7 ▲ MA 951001 [DDD]
Basel CO
  P. Sacher (cnd)
    Paul Sacher & New Music, w. Basel Percussion Ensemble, Zurich Collegium Musicum
          Ars Musici 3-▲ 1155
Basel Ensemble Galliarda
  F. Näf (cnd)
    Gesellige Zeit:German Lieder, Madrigals & Instrumental Music of the 16th & 17th Centuries, w. Basel Madrigalists   Musicaphon ▲ 506803
Basel Opera Mobile CO
  A. Stern (cnd)
    Grossmann, R.:Il President da Valdei, w. *(soloists unknown)* [Swiss Romanish language] *(rec 1989)*
          Jecklin-Disco ▲ JS 279-2 [ADD]
Basel Orch
  H. Münch (cnd)
    Brahms, J.:Con Vn, w. Adolf Busch (vn) *(rec Dec. 18, 1951)*   Music & Arts ▲ CD 861 [AAD]

Basel Percussion Ensemble
  P. Sacher (cnd)
    Paul Sacher & New Music, w. Basel CO, Zurich Collegium Musicum   Ars Musici 3-▲ 1155
Basel Percussion Trio [Gerhard Huber (perc), Siegfried Kutterer (perc), Thomas Waldner (perc)]
  Favre, P.:Sound Tales   Jecklin ▲ JS 304-2 [DDD]
  Zinsstag, G.:Diffractions   Jecklin ▲ JS 304-2 [DDD]
Basel RSO
  C. Dumont (cnd)
    Arnold, M.:Con Hmc, w. T. Reilly (hmc)   Chandos ▲ CHAN 9248 [DDD]
  A. Francis (cnd)
    Milhaud, D.:Sym 5   CPO ▲ CPO 999240 [DDD]
    Milhaud, D.:Sym 6   CPO ▲ CPO 999240 [DDD]
    Milhaud, D.:Sym 7   CPO ▲ CPO 999166 [DDD]
    Milhaud, D.:Sym 8   CPO ▲ CPO 999166 [DDD]
    Milhaud, D.:Sym 9   CPO ▲ CPO 999166 [DDD]
  R. Kelterborn (cnd)
    Kelterborn, R.:Relations, w. A. Burkhard *(rec Jan. 29, 1981)*   Grammont ▲ CTSP 35-2 [ADD]
  G. Lehel (cnd)
    Geiser, W.:Sym 2   Grammont ▲ CTSP 21-2 [ADD]
    Raff, J.:Sym 8   Tudor ▲ TUD 784 [ADD]
  J. Meier (cnd)
    Raff, J.:Ode au printemps, w. Peter Aronsky (pno)   Tudor ▲ TUD 784 [ADD]
  P. Sacher (cnd)
    Suter, R.:Son Orch *(rec 1974)*   Grammont ▲ CSTP 6-2 [AAD]
  P. Steinberg (cnd)
    Raff, J.:Konzert-Ov   Tudor ▲ TUD 786 [ADD]
  M. Tabachnik (cnd)
    Marti, H.:Mask   Grammont ▲ CTS P 22-2 [ADD]
  F. Travis (cnd)
    Raff, J.:Sym 10   Tudor ▲ TUD 786 [ADD]
  R. Tschupp (cnd)
    Moeschinger, A.:Con lyrique, w. I. Roth (sax)   Grammont ▲ CTSP 1-2 [ADD]
Basel RSO Soloists
  M. Venzago (cnd)
    Moser, R.:Wortabend, w. K. Graf (sop), N. Tüller (bass) [G]   Grammont ▲ CTSP 12-2 [ADD]
Basel RSO Winds
  R. Kelterborn (cnd)
    Kelterborn, R.:Sons Winds *(rec Sept. 1, 1987)*   Grammont ▲ CTSP 35-2 [ADD]
Basel Schola Cantorum Instrumental Ensemble
  H.-M. Linde (cnd)
    Schütz, H.:Danket dem Herren, denn er ist freundlich, w. Chiaroscuro Ensemble, Basel Boys' Choir
          EMI Classics ("Baroque" series) ▲ CDK 65736
Basel Serenata
  Pfiffner, E.:Cambiamenti concertanti, w. D. Doherty (ob), T. Waldner (dr) *(rec March 1992)*
          Pro Viva ▲ ISPV 170 [DDD]
Basel SO
  G. Andretta (cnd)
    Lalo, E.:Divert Orch   CPO ▲ CPO 999296 [DDD]
    Lalo, E.:Rapsodie norvégienne   CPO ▲ CPO 999296 [DDD]
    Lalo, E.:Scherzo   CPO ▲ CPO 999296 [DDD]
    Lalo, E.:Sym in g   CPO ▲ CPO 999296 [DDD]
  M. Atzmon (cnd)
    Pfiffner, E.:Componimento Org, w. M. Henking (org) *(rec Dec. 1980)*   Pro Viva ▲ ISPV 170 [ADD]
  A. Jordan (cnd)
    Debussy, C.:La Boîte à joujoux   Erato ▲ 2292-45819-2
    Dukas, P.:L'Apprenti sorcier   Erato ▲ 2292-45819-2
    Dukas, P.:Polyeucte   Erato ▲ 2292-45819-2
    Scriabin, A.:Con Pno, w. Karl-Andreas Kolly (pno)   Pan Classics ▲ 510079 [DDD]
  C. Mackerras (cnd)
    Hindemith, P.:Cupid & Psyche *(rec Stadtcasino Basel, Musiksaal & Ref. Kirche Arlesheim, Mar 1995)*
          Novalis ▲ 150118 [DDD]
    Hindemith, P.:The Four Temperaments, w. Bruno Canino (pno) *(rec Stadtcasino Basel, Musiksaal & Ref. Kirche Arlesheim, Mar 1995)*   Novalis ▲ 150118 [DDD]
    Hindemith, P.:Mathis der Maler (sym) *(rec Stadtcasino Basel, Musiksaal & Ref. Kirche Arlesheim, Mar 1995)*   Novalis ▲ 150118 [DDD]
  J. Meier (cnd)
    Suter, R.:Nocturnes Va, w. H. Fukai (va)   Jecklin ▲ JD 690
  H. Müller-Brühl (cnd)
    Beethoven, L. van:Die Geschöpfe des Prometheus *(rec 1970)*   Koch Schwann ▲ CD 316 070 [ADD]
  H. Münch (cnd)
    Beethoven, L. van:Romances Vn, w. Adolf Busch (vn) *(rec Dec. 18, 1951)*
          Music & Arts ▲ CD 861 [AAD]
  E. Schmid (cnd)
    Schmid, E.:Suite From Poetry by Rainer Maria Rilke, w. K. L. Okazaki (mez) [G] *(rec April 6, 1989)*
          Grammont ▲ CTSP 33-2 [ADD]
  R. Tschupp (cnd)
    Haller, H.:Ed è subito sera, w. P. Huttenlocher (bar) [I]   Grammont ▲ CTSP 10-2 [ADD]
  M. Venzago (cnd)
    Marescotti, A.-F.:Hymnes   Grammont ▲ CTSP 13-2
    Moser, R.:Wal, w. I. Roth (sax), B. Beaufreton (sax), M. Weiss (sax), J.-G. Koerper (sax), P. Egholm (sax)   Grammont ▲ CTSP 12-2 [ADD]
  W. Weller (cnd)
    Tchaikovsky, P.:Romeo & Juliet   Ars Musici ▲ AM 1140 [DDD]
    Tchaikovsky, P.:Sym 4   Ars Musici ▲ AM 1140 [DDD]
  H. Zender (cnd)
    Duggan, M.:Fragment & Caracol   Grammont ▲ CTSP 49-2
  R. Zollman (cnd)
    Popper, D.:Music of, w. Antonio Meneses (vc)—Con for Vc & Orch, Op. 24; Suite for Vc & Orch, Op. 50; Papillon, Op. 3/4; Tarantelle, Op. 33; Hungarian Rhap for Vc & Orch, Op. 86; Elfentanz, Op. 39
          Pan Classics ▲ 510075 [DDD]
    Saint-Saëns, C.:Ov de fête   Pan Classics ▲ 510078 [DDD]
    Saint-Saëns, C.:Phaéton   Pan Classics ▲ 510078 [DDD]
    Saint-Saëns, C.:Sym 2   Pan Classics ▲ 510078 [DDD]
    Saint-Saëns, C.:Tableaux symphoniques d'après la foi   Pan Classics ▲ 510078 [DDD]
Bash Ensemble [Richard Benjafield (perc), Chris Brannick (perc), Stephen Hiscock (perc), Andrew Martin (perc)]
  Launch   Sony Classical ▲ SK 69246
Basho Ensemble
  J. Sligter (cnd)
    Straesser, J.:Gedanken der Nacht, w. Ananda Goud (mez) *(rec live, Vredenburg, Utrecht, Jan. 17, 1993)*   Donemus ▲ CV 44
Basiliensis Trio [M. Mezger (rcr), Ekkehard Weber (vl), P. Simmonds (hpd)]
  Chamber Music for Recorder   Ars Musici ▲ 1105 [DDD]
Basque Bayonne-Côte Orch
  R. Delcroix (cnd)
    Chamouard, P.:Halabja   Skarbo ▲ SKR 3954
    Chamouard, P.:Sym 2   Skarbo ▲ SKR 3954

Basque Bayonne–Côte Orch (cont.)

R. Delcroix (cnd) (cont.)

Chamouard, P.:The Veils of Silence — Skarbo ▲ SKR 3954

Schubert, Franz:Mass 5, w. S. Chilcott (sop), R. Cyrille (alt), Vonk (ten), G. Schwarz (bass), Ametsa D'Irun Choir [L] — Forlane ▲ FOR 16649 [DDD]

Bassanova Duo

Mišek, A.:Son 1 Db *(rec July 1991)* — Partridge ▲ 1134–2 [DDD]

Mišek, A.:Son 2 Db *(rec 7/91)* — Partridge ▲ 1134–2 [DDD]

Skorzeny, F.:Sonatines Db *(rec 7/91)* — Partridge ▲ 1134–2 [DDD]

Basse Normandie Instrumental Ensemble

D. Debart (cnd)

Nyman, M.:Noises, w. Catherine Bott (sop), Hilary Summers (alt), Ian Bostridge (ten), Andrew Findon (sax), David Roach (sax) *(rec Caen, June 1991 & Abbey Road Studios, London, June 1993)* — Argo ▲ 440842–2 [DDD]

Stravinsky, I.:L'Histoire du soldat, w. Georges Descrieres (nar), Jean–Pierre Wallez (vn) — Forlane ▲ FRL 16580 [DDD]

Bastille Opera Orch

M.–W. Chung (cnd)

Berlioz, H.:Béatrice et Bénédict (sels), w. Kathleen Battle (sop), Bastille Opera Chorus—Je vais le voir *(rec Salle Gounod, Bastille Opera, Paris, Nov 1993 & June 1994)* — Deutsche Grammophon ▲ 447114–2 [DDD]

Charpentier, G.:Louise (sels), w. Kathleen Battle (sop)—Depuis le jour *(rec Salle Gounod, Bastille Opera, Paris, Nov 1993 & June 1994)* — Deutsche Grammophon ▲ 447114–2 [DDD]

Donizetti, G.:La fille du régiment (sels), w. Kathleen Battle (sop)—C'en est donc fait/Salut à la France! *(rec Salle Gounod, Bastille Opera, Paris, Nov 1993 & June 1994)* — Deutsche Grammophon ▲ 447114–2 [DDD]

Gounod, C.:Roméo et Juliette (sels), w. Kathleen Battle (sop)—Je veux vivre; Dieu! quel frisson/Amour, ranime mon courage *(rec Salle Gounod, Bastille Opera, Paris, Nov 1993 & June 1994)* — Deutsche Grammophon ▲ 447114–2 [DDD]

Mad About Love, w. Cheryl Studer (sop), Kiri Te Kanawa (sop), José Carreras (ten), Jerry Hadley (ten), Philharmonia Orch [cnd:Giuseppe Sinopoli], Boston SO [cnd:Seiji Ozawa], Vienna PO [cnd:John Eliot Gardiner, James Levine] — Deutsche Grammophon ▲ 449112–2 ■ 449112–4

Massenet, J.:Manon (sels), w. Kathleen Battle (sop)—Allons! il le faut!/Adieu, notre petite table; Suis–je gentille ainsi?/Obéissons, quand leur voix appelle *(rec Salle Gounod, Bastille Opera, Paris, Nov 1993 & June 1994)* — Deutsche Grammophon ▲ 447114–2 [DDD]

Messiaen, O.:Concert à Quatre, w. Catherine Cantin (fl), Heinz Holliger (ob), Yvonne Loriod (pno), Mstislav Rostropovich (vc) — Deutsche Grammophon ("4D Audio" series) ▲ 445947–2

Messiaen, O.:Eclair sur l'Au–Dela... — Deutsche Grammophon ▲ 439929–2

Messiaen, O.:Les Offrandes oubliées — Deutsche Grammophon ("4D Audio" series) ▲ 445947–2

Messiaen, O.:Un Sourire — Deutsche Grammophon ("4D Audio" series) ▲ 445947–2

Messiaen, O.:Le Tombeau resplendissant — Deutsche Grammophon ("4D Audio" series) ▲ 445947–2

Offenbach, J.:Belle Lurette (sels), w. Kathleen Battle (sop)—On s'amuse, on applaudit *(rec Salle Gounod, Bastille Opera, Paris, Nov 1993 & June 1994)* — Deutsche Grammophon ▲ 447114–2 [DDD]

Rimsky–Korsakov, N.:Scheherazade — Deutsche Grammophon ▲ 437818–2 [DDDD]

Saint–Saëns, C.:Samson et Dalila, w. W. Meier (mez), P. Domingo (ten), S. Ramey (bass), A. Fondary (bar), Bastille Opera Chorus — EMI Classics 2–▲ CDCB 54470

Saint–Saëns, C.:Sym 3, w. M. Matthes (org) — Deutsche Grammophon ▲ 435854–2

Shostakovich, D.:Lady Macbeth of Mtsensk, w. M. Ewing (sop), E. Zaremba (mez), P. Langridge (ten), H. Zednik (ten), A. Haugland (bass), A. Kotcherga (bass), K. Moll (bass), S. Larin (bass), Bastille Opera Chorus — Deutsche Grammophon 2–▲ 437511–2

Stravinsky, I.:The Firebird Suite — Deutsche Grammophon ▲ 437818–2 [DDD]

Thomas, A.:Hamlet (sels), w. Kathleen Battle (sop)—Mais quelle est cette belle/Pâle et blonde *(rec Salle Gounod, Bastille Opera, Paris, Nov 1993 & June 1994)* — Deutsche Grammophon ▲ 447114–2 [DDD]

Thomas, A.:Mignon (sels), w. Kathleen Battle (sop)—Oui, pour ce soir/Je suis Titania la blonde *(rec Salle Gounod, Bastille Opera, Paris, Nov 1993 & June 1994)* — Deutsche Grammophon ▲ 447114–2 [DDD]

Bastille Orch

Bizet, G.:L'Arlésienne (suites) — Deutsche Grammophon ▲ 431778–2 [DDD]

Bizet, G.:Carmen (suite 1) — Deutsche Grammophon ▲ 431778–2 [DDD]

Bizet, G.:Jeux d'enfants — Deutsche Grammophon ▲ 431778–2 [DDD]

Messiaen, O.:Turangalîla–sym, w. Y. Loriod (pno), J. Loriod (ondes Martenot) — Deutsche Grammophon ▲ 431781–2 [DDD]

Bath Festival Orch

Y. Menuhin (cnd)

Bach, J.S.:Brandenburg Cons—Nos. 4–6 — EMI Classics ▲ CDE 67761

Bach, J.S.:Brandenburg Cons—Nos. 1–3 — EMI Classics ▲ CDE 67760

Bach, J.S.:Brandenburg Con 2 — EMI Classics ("Baroque" series) ▲ CDK 65332

Beethoven, L. van:Fidelio, w. *(vocalists unknown)* — EMI Classics ▲ CDE 67762

Mozart, W.A.:Con 1 Vn, w. Y. Menuhin (vn) — EMI Classics ▲ CDE 67779

Mozart, W.A.:Con 3 Vn, w. Y. Menuhin (vn) — EMI Classics ▲ CDE 67779

Mozart, W.A.:Con 5 Vn, w. Y. Menuhin (vn) — EMI Classics ▲ CDE 67779

Purcell, H.:The Fairy Queen (sels), w. Joan Carlyle (sop), Yehudi Menuhin (vn)—Entry of Phoebus; Syms. [Acts 4 & 5]; Dance for the Haymakers; 1st Music; Dance for the Fairies; Prelude; 2nd Music; 1st Act Tune *(rec Abbey Road Studio 1, London, July 1965)* — EMI Classics ▲ CDK 65341 [ADD]

Purcell, H.:The Indian Queen (sels), w. Joan Carlyle (sop), Yehudi Menuhin (vn)—Tpt Tune; 4th Act Tune; I Attempt from Love's Sickness to Fly in Vain; Syms. [Acts 2 & 3]; 1st Music; Air *(rec Abbey Road Studio 1, London, July 1965)* — EMI Classics ▲ CDK 65341 [ADD]

Purcell, H.:King Arthur (sels), w. Joan Carlyle (sop), Yehudi Menuhin (vn)—Tpt Tune; 2nd Music; Sym.; Passacaglia; Aria of Venus; 2nd Act Tune *(rec Abbey Road Studio 1, London, July 1965)* — EMI Classics ▲ CDK 65341 [ADD]

Purcell, H.:Music for the Theater, w. Joan Carlyle (sop), Yehudi Menuhin (vn)—Bonduca [ov.]; The Old Bachelor [ov.]; Abdelazar [rondeau]; Bonduca [air]; Pausanias [air of Pandora:Sweeter than Roses or Cool Evening Breeze]; The Married Beau [jig]; Distressed Innocence [air]; Amphitryon [sarabande]; The Double Dealer [air] *(rec Abbey Road Studio 1, London, July 1965)* — EMI Classics ▲ CDK 65341 [ADD]

M. Tippett (cnd)

Tippett, M.:Fant Concertante on a Theme of Corelli — EMI Classics 2–▲ ZDMB 63522

Bath International Ensemble

Brahms, J.:Qnt Cl *(rec Univ of Cambridge, Dec 23–23 & 27–28, 1991)* — Cala ▲ CACD 1009 [DDD]

Brahms, J.:Qnt Pno *(rec Univ of Cambridge, Dec 23–23 & 27–28, 1991)* — Cala ▲ CACD 1009 [DDD]

Bavarian Brass Soloists Munich

G. Zapf (cnd)

Five Centuries of Music for Brass Ensemble — Calig ▲ CAL 50837 [DDD]

Bavarian CO

L. Michal (cnd)

Viotti, G.B.:Con 2 Vn, w. L. Michal (vn), M. Carfi (vn) — Calig ▲ CAL 50917 [DDD]

Viotti, G.B.:Sym Concertante 1, w. L. Michal (vn), M. Carfi (vn) — Calig ▲ CAL 50917 [DDD]

Viotti, G.B.:Sym Concertante 2, w. L. Michal (vn), M. Carfi (vn) — Calig ▲ CAL 50917 [DDD]

Bavarian Chamber PO

I. Yinon (cnd)

Haas, P.:Study — Koch Schwann ▲ SCH 313712 [DDD]

Karel, R.:Nonet — Koch Schwann ▲ SCH 313712 [DDD]

Klein, G.:Partita Strs — Koch Schwann ▲ SCH 313712 [DDD]

Schulhoff, E.:Double Con Fl, w. Jacque Zoon (fl), Monica Gutman (pno) — Koch Schwann ▲ SCH 313712 [DDD]

Bavarian RSO

Classics Go to the Movies Vol. 5, w. Hannes Käster (org), Salzburg Mozarteum Orch, Ludovic Spiess (ten), Virginia Zeani (sop), Rumanian Opera Orch, Rumanian Radio–TV Studio Orch, Sofia PO, Budapest SO, Philharmonia Orch — LaserLight ▲ 15 645

Bavarian RSO (cont.)

Wagner, R.:Ovs, Preludes & Orch Sels, w. Berlin PO, Bayreuth Festival Orch, Vienna PO, Berlin Opera Orch, H. von Karajan (cnd), R. Kubelik (cnd), K. Böhm (cnd), E. Jochum (cnd)—sels. from Rienzi, Die fliegende Holländer, Tannhäuser, Lohengrin, Parsifal, Die Meistersinger von Nürnberg, Die Walküre, Siegfried, Götterdämmerung *(rec 1958 & 1981)* — Deutsche Grammophon ("Double" series) 2–▲ 439687–2 [ADD]

R. Alberth (cnd)

Blacher, B.:Con 1 Pno, w. H. Göbel (pno) *(rec 1978)* — Thorofon ▲ CTH 2167 [ADD/DDD]

Orff, C.:Der Mond—Ein kleines Welttheater, w. Karl Erb (nar), Paul Kuen (ten—Lad 3), Josef Knapp (bar—Lad 2), Benno Kusche (bar—Lad 1), Georg Hann (bass—St. Peter), Georg Wieter (bass—Lad 4), Rudolf Wünzer (bass—The Farmer), Karl Hanft (sgr—Innkeeper), Willy Rösner (sgr—The Major), Bavarian Radio Chorus *(rec Studio 1, Bavarian Radio, Jan. 19–20, 1950)* — Calig ▲ CAL 50948 (m) [ADD]

A. Antonini (cnd)

Moszkowski, M.:Con Pno, w. D. Bar–Illan (pno)—& Etude in A♭, Op. 72/11 — InSync ■ C 4160

Moszkowski, M.:Con Pno, w. D. Bar–Illan (pno) — Audiofon ▲ CD 72006

Moszkowski, M.:Con Pno, w. David Bar–Illan (pno) — Audiofon ▲ CD 72065

B. Bartoletti (cnd)

Rossini, G.:Il barbiere di Siviglia (sels), w. G. d' Angelo (sop), G. Carturan (mez), N. Monti (ten), R. Capecchi (bar), G. Giorgetti (bar), C. Cava (bass), G. Tadeo (bass) — IMP Collectors Series ▲ IMPX 9022 [AAD]

S. Baudo (cnd)

Gluck, C.W.:Alceste, w. J. Norman (sop), N. Gedda (ten), B. Weikl (bar), T. Krause (bar), S. Nimsgern (b–bar), Bavarian Radio Chorus [French version] — Orfeo 3–▲ 027823 [DDD]

Gluck, C.W.:Alceste (sels), w. J. Norman (sop), N. Gedda (ten), B. Weikl (bar), T. Krause (bar), S. Nimsgern (b–bar), Bavarian Radio Chorus — Orfeo ▲ 027901 [DDD]

L. Bernstein (cnd)

Bartók, B.:Music for Strs, Perc & Cel *(rec live, 1983)* — Originals ▲ ORISH 814 [ADD]

Bartók, B.:Music for Strs, Perc & Cel — Hungaroton ▲ HCD 12631 [DDD]

Bernstein, L.:Divert — Hungaroton ▲ HCD 12631 [DDD]

Brahms, J.:Hungarian Dances Orch—No. 6 — Hungaroton ▲ HCD 12631 [DDD]

Haydn, J.:Mass 10, "Kriegsmesse", "Paukenmesse", w. Judith Blegen (sop), Brigette Fassbaender (mez), Claes Hakan Ahnsjö (ten), Hans Sotin (bass), Bavarian Radio Chorus [L] — Philips ▲ 412734–2 [DDD]

Mozart, W.A.:Ave verum corpus, w. Bavarian Radio Chorus *(rec live April 1990)* — Deutsche Grammophon ▲ 431791–2 [DDD] □ 431791–5

Mozart, W.A.:Exsultate, w. A. Augér (sop), Bavarian Radio Chorus *(rec live April 1990)* — Deutsche Grammophon ▲ 431791–2 [DDD] □ 431791–5

Mozart, W.A.:Missa, K.427, w. A. Augér (sop), F. von Stade (mez), F. Lopardo (ten), C. Hauptmann (bass), Bavarian Radio Chorus *(rec live April 1990)* — Deutsche Grammophon ▲ 431791–2 [DDD] □ 431791–5

Mozart, W.A.:Requiem, w. M. McLaughlin (sop), M. Ewing (sop), J. Hadley (ten), C. Hauptmann (bass), Bavarian Radio Chorus [L] — Deutsche Grammophon ▲ 427353–2 [DDD]

Schumann, R.:Sym 2 *(rec live, 1983)* — Originals ▲ ORISH 814 [ADD]

Wagner, R.:Tristan und Isolde (sels), w. H. Behrens (sop), Y. Minton (mez), P. Hofmann (ten), B. Weikl (bass), Bavarian Radio Chorus — Philips ▲ 438501–2

S. Bychkov (cnd)

Ruzicka, P.:The Blessed, the Damned *(rec Nov 1992)* — Thorofon ▲ CTH 2220

C. Davis (cnd)

Beethoven, L. van:Fidelio, w. Elizabeth Norberg–Schulz (sop—Marzelline), Deborah Voigt (sop—Lenore), Ben Heppner (ten—Florestan), Michael Schade (ten—Jaquino), Günter von Kanna‡en (b–bar—Don Pizarro), Matthias Hölle (bass—Rocco), Thomas Quasthoff (bass—Don Fernando), Bavarian Radio Chorus, Bavarian State Opera Men's Chorus *(rec Herkulessaal der Residenz, Munich, May 15–25, 1995)* — RCA Victor 2–▲ 09026–68344–2 [DDD]

Beethoven, L. van:Missa Solemnis, w. L. Orgonasova (sop), J. Rappé (ten), J.–H. Rootering (bass), Bavarian Radio Chorus — RCA Red Seal 2–▲ 09026–60967–2

Beethoven, L. van:Ovs—Coriolan, Die Geschöpfe des Prometheus, Leonore Nos. 1 & 3, Egmont, Fidelio, Die Ruinen von Athen — CBS ▲ MDK 44790 [DDD] ■ MDT 44790 (D)

Berg, A.:Con Vn, w. G. Kremer (vn) — Philips ▲ 412523–2 [DDD]

Berg, A.:Pieces Orch, Op. 6 — Philips ▲ 412523–2 [DDD]

Brahms, J.:Academic Festival Ov — RCA Red Seal ▲ 7980–2–RC [DDD]

Brahms, J.:Alto Rhap, w. N. Stutzmann (mez), Bavarian Radio Chorus — RCA Red Seal ▲ 09026–61201–2

Brahms, J.:Con 1 Pno, w. G. Oppitz (pno) — RCA Red Seal ▲ 09026–61618–2

Brahms, J.:Con 2 Pno, w. G. Oppitz (pno) — RCA Red Seal ▲ 09026–61619–2

Brahms, J.:Ein Deutsches Requiem, w. A. M. Blasi (sop), B. Terfel (b–bar), E. Schloter (org), Bavarian Radio Chorus [G] — RCA Red Seal ▲ 09026–60868–2

Brahms, J.:Gesang der Parzen, w. Bavarian Radio Chorus — RCA Red Seal ▲ 09026–61201–2

Brahms, J.:Marienlieder, w. Bavarian Radio Chorus — RCA Red Seal ▲ 09026–61201–2

Brahms, J.:Nänie, w. Bavarian Radio Chorus — RCA Red Seal ▲ 09026–61201–2

Brahms, J.:Schicksalslied, w. Bavarian Radio Chorus — RCA Red Seal ▲ 09026–61201–2

Brahms, J.:Sym 1 — RCA Red Seal ▲ 60382–2–RC [DDD] ■ 60382–4–RC (CrO2)

Brahms, J.:Sym 2 — RCA Red Seal ▲ 7980–2–RC [DDD]

Brahms, J.:Sym 3 — RCA Red Seal ▲ 60118–2–RC [DDD]

Brahms, J.:Sym 4 — RCA Red Seal ▲ 60383–2–RC [DDD]

Brahms, J.:Tragic Ov — RCA Red Seal ▲ 60118–2–RC [DDD]

Brahms, J.:Vars on a Theme by Haydn — RCA Red Seal ▲ 60382–2–RC [DDD] ■ 60382–4–RC (CrO2)

Bruckner, A.:Mass 3, w. K. Mattila (sop), M. Lipovšek (mez), T. Moser (ten), K. Moll (bass), Bavarian Radio Chorus [L] — Philips ▲ 422358–2 [DDD]

Dvořák, A.:Serenade Strs — Philips ("Solo" series) ▲ 442402–2

Elgar, E.:Con Vn, w. K. Takezawa (vn) — RCA Red Seal ▲ 09026–61612–2

Elgar, E.:Intro & Allegro, w. K. Takezawa (vn) — RCA Red Seal ▲ 09026–61612–2

Gounod, C.:Faust, w. K. Te Kanawa (sop), F. Araiza (ten), E. Nesterenko (bass), Bavarian Radio Chorus [F] — Philips 3–▲ 420164–2 [DDD]

Grieg, E.:Con Pno, Op. 16, w. M. Perahia (pno) — CBS ▲ MK 44899 [DDD]

Mahler, G.:Sym 4, w. Angela Maria Blasi (sop) *(rec Munich, Germany, Oct 13 & 14, 1993)* — RCA Red Seal ▲ 09026–62521–2 [DDD]

Mendelssohn, F.:A Midsummer Night's Dream (ov) — Orfeo ▲ 089841

Mendelssohn, F.:Sym 3 — Orfeo ▲ 089841

Mendelssohn, F.:Sym 4 — Orfeo ▲ 132851 [DDD]

Mendelssohn, F.:Sym 5 — Orfeo ▲ 132851 [DDD]

Mozart, W.A.:Complete Mozart Edition, w. B. Hendricks (sop), J. Varady (sop), S. Mentzer (mez), F. Araiza (ten), T. Allen (bar) — Philips 3–▲ 422537–2 [ADD]

Mozart, W.A.:Con Bn, w. *(soloist unknown)* — RCA Red Seal ▲ 09026–61927–2

Mozart, W.A.:Requiem, w. A. M. Blasi (sop), M. Lipovšek (mez), U. Heilmann (ten), J.–H. Rootering (bass), Bavarian Radio Chorus [L] — RCA Red Seal ▲ 09026–60599–2 [DDD] ■ 09026–60599–4 (CrO2) □ 09026–60599–5

Mozart, W.A.:Serenade Ww, K.320 — RCA Red Seal ▲ 09026–61927–2

Reger, M.:Eine Ballettsuite — Orfeo ▲ 090841 [DDD] ■ M 090841A (D)

Reger, M.:Vars & Fugue on a Theme of of J. A. Hiller — Orfeo ▲ 090841 [DDD] ■ M 090841A (D)

Saint–Saëns, C.:Samson et Dalila, w. J. Carreras (ten), A. Baltsa (mez), Summers (bar), Estes (bass), Burchuladze (bass), Bavarian Radio Chorus — Philips 2–▲ 426243–2 [DDD]

Saint–Saëns, C.:Samson et Dalila (sels), w. A. Baltsa (mez), J. Carreras (ten), D. George (ten), J. Summers (bar), S. Estes (bass), P. Burchuladze (bass) — Philips ▲ 438504–2

Schumann, R.:Con Vc, w. Yo Yo Ma (vc) — CBS 2–▲ M2K 44562 [ADD/DDD] 2–■ M2T 44562 (D)

Schumann, R.:Con Vc, w. Yo Yo Ma (vc) — CBS ▲ MK 42663 [DDD]

Schumann, R.:Con Pno, w. M. Perahia (pno) — CBS ▲ MK 44899 [DDD]

Stravinsky, I.:Oedipus Rex, w. J. Norman (sop), T. Moser (ten), S. Nimsgern (b–bar), R. Bracht (bass), Bavarian Radio Chorus [L] — Orfeo ▲ 071831 [DDD] ■ 071831 (D)

Tchaikovsky, P.:Serenade Strs — Philips ("Solo" series) ▲ 442402–2

Bavarian RSO (cont.)

C. Davis (cnd) (cont.)

Verdi, G.:Falstaff, w. S. Sweet (sop), M. Horne (mez), F. Lopardo (ten), R. Panerai (bar), A. Titus (bar), Bavarian Radio Chorus RCA Red Seal 2-▲ 09026-60705-2 [DDD]

Verdi, G.:Requiem Mass, w. C. Vaness (sop), F. Quivar (mez), D. O'Neill (ten), C. Colombara (bass), Bavarian Radio Chorus RCA Red Seal 2-▲ 09026-60902-2

Wagner, R.:Lohengrin (sels), w. Eva Marton (sop—Ortrud), Sharon Sweet (sop—Elsa von Brabant), Barbara Fleckenstein (sgr—Page), Marion Rambausek (sgr—Page), Atsuko Suzuki (sgr—Page), Gisela Ulmann (sgr—Page), Ben Heppner (ten—Lohengrin), Anton Rosner (ten—Nobleman), Heinrich Weber (ten—Nobleman), Sergei Leiferkus (bar—Friedrich von Telramund), Bryn Terfel (b-bar—King's Herald), Jan-Hendrik Rootering (bass—Henry the Fowler), Dankwart Siegele (sgr—Nobleman), Jürgen Weiss (sgr—Nobleman), Michael Gläser (cnd), Udo Mehrpohl (cnd), Bavarian Radio Chorus, Bavarian State Opera Chorus—Seht! Seht! [from Act 1, Scene 2]; Nun sei bedankt, mein lieber Schwan!; Wenn ich im Kampfe für dich siege; Welch holde Wunder muss ich sehen?; Nun höret mich und achtet wohl; Durch Gottes Sieg ist jetzt dein Leben mein [all from Act 1, Scene 3]; Treulich geführt ziehet dahin [from Act 3, Scene 1]; Wie hehr erkenn' ich unsrer Liebe Wesen!; Höchstes Vertrau'n hast du mir schon zu danken; Weh' nun ist all' unser Glück dahin! [all from Act 3, Scene 2]; In fernem Land, unnahbar euren Schritten [from Act 3, Scene 3] *(rec Munich, Mar 14–28, 1994)* RCA Red Seal ▲ 09026-68239-2 [DDD]

H. Fricke (cnd)

Hartmann, K.A.:Simplicius Simplicissimus, w. Helen Donath (sop) Wergo 2-▲ WER 6259-2

F. Fricsay (cnd)

Beethoven, L. van:Con 3 Pno, w. Annie Fischer (pno) *(rec 1957)* Enterprise ("Palladio" series) ▲ ENT PD 4213 (m)

Debussy, C.:Prélude à l'après-midi d'un faune *(rec 1953)* Enterprise ("Palladio" series) ▲ ENT PD 4213 (m)

Haydn, J.:Sym 98 *(rec 1954)* Enterprise ("Palladio" series) ▲ ENT PD 4213 (m)

Stravinsky, I.:Le Baiser de la fée *(rec live, 1956–61)* Enterprise (Document) ▲ ENT 954 [ADD]

Verdi, G.:Otello (sels) *(rec live 1956–61)* Enterprise (Document) ▲ ENT 954 [ADD]

L. Gardelli (cnd)

Gluck, C.W.:Iphigénie en Tauride, w. P. Lorengar (sop), F. Bonisolli (ten), D. Fischer-Dieskau (bar), W. Grönroos (bar), Bavarian Radio Chorus [F] Orfeo 2-▲ 052832 [DDD]

C.M. Giulini (cnd)

Schubert, Franz:Mass 6, w. Bavarian Radio Chorus *(rec live, Munich)* Sony Classical ▲ SK 69290

Schubert, Franz:Sym 4 *(rec Munich, Feb 27–28, 1993)* Sony Classical ▲ SK 66833 [DDD]

Schubert, Franz:Sym 8 *(rec Munich, Apr 24–28, 1995)* Sony Classical ▲ SK 66833 [DDD]

B. Haitink (cnd)

Brahms, J.:Alto Rhap, w. A. Hodgson (cta), Bavarian Radio Chorus [G] Orfeo ▲ 025821 [DDD]

Brahms, J.:Begräbnisgesang, w. Bavarian Radio Chorus [G] Orfeo ▲ 025821 [DDD]

Brahms, J.:Gesang der Parzen, w. Bavarian Radio Chorus [G] Orfeo ▲ 025821 [DDD]

Brahms, J.:Nänie, w. Bavarian Radio Chorus [G] Orfeo ▲ 025821 [DDD]

Mozart, W.A.:Zauberflöte, w. L. Popp (sop), E. Gruberova (sop), S. Jerusalem (ten), W. Brendel (bar), R. Bracht (bass), Bavarian Radio Chorus [G] EMI Classics 3-▲ CDCC 47951 [DDD]

Mozart, W.A.:Zauberflöte (sels), w. L. Popp (sop), E. Gruberova (sop), S. Jerusalem (ten), W. Brendel (bar), R. Bracht (bass), Bavarian Radio Chorus [G] EMI Classics ▲ CDC 47008 [DDD]

Wagner, R.:Götterdämmerung, w. E. Marton (sop), S. Jerusalem (ten), T. Hampson (bar), J. Tomlinson (bass) [G] EMI Classics 4-▲ CDCD 54485

Wagner, R.:Das Rheingold, w. M. Lipovšek (mez), J. Rappé (ten), H. Zednik (ten), P. Haage (ten), A. Schmidt (bar), T. Adam (b-bar), H. Tschammer (bass), K. Rydl (bass), J. Morris (bass) [G] EMI Classics 2-▲ CDCB 49853 [DDD]

Wagner, R.:Siegfried, w. K. Te Kanawa (sop), E. Marton (sop), S. Jerusalem (ten), P. Haage (ten), J. Morris (bass) [G] EMI Classics 4-▲ CDCD 54290

R. Heger (cnd)

Hindemith, P.:Concert Music Va & Large Chamber Orch, w. G. Schmid (va) Koch Schwann ▲ CD 310 045

Hindemith, P.:Kammermusik 5, w. G. Schmid (va) Koch Schwann ▲ SCH 313372 [ADD/DDD]

J. Hirokami (cnd)

Suder, J.:Con Pno, w. M. Höhenrieder (pno) Calig ▲ CAL 50888 [DDD]

E. Howarth (cnd)

Coates, G.:Sym 1, "Music on Open Strings" *(rec Munich, Nov 1980)* CPO ▲ CPO 999392-2 [DDD]

N. Järvi (cnd)

Glazunov, A.:Ov solennelle Orfeo ▲ 093201 [DDD] ■ M 093201

Glazunov, A.:Sym 1 Orfeo ▲ 093101 [DDD] ■ M 093101

Glazunov, A.:Sym 5 Orfeo ▲ 093101 [DDD] ■ M 093101

Glazunov, A.:Sym 8 Orfeo ▲ 093201 [DDD] ■ M 093201

Glazunov, A.:Wedding Procession Orfeo ▲ 093201 [DDD]

E. Jochum (cnd)

Bach, J.S.:Cant 51, w. Elisabeth Schwarzkopf (sop) *(rec Munich, 1951)* Bella Voce 2-▲ 107.201 [AAD]

Bach, J.S.:Mass in b, BWV 232, w. L. Marshall (sop), H. Töpper (mez), P. Pears (ten), K. Borg (bass), Bavarian Radio Chorus Philips 2-▲ 438739-2

Bach, J.S.:Mass in b, BWV 232, w. Helen Donath (sop), Brigitte Fassbaender (cta), Claes H. Ahnsjö (ten), Roland Hermann (bar), Robert Holl (bass), Bavarian Radio Chorus EMI Classics ("Doubleforte" series) 2-▲ CDFB 68640

Bach, J.S.:Mass in b, BWV 232, w. Bavarian Radio Chorus—Kyrie eleison *(rec Herkulessaal, Munich, Mar. & Apr. 1980)* EMI Classics ▲ CDK 65334 [ADD]

Beethoven, L. van:Die Ruinen von Athen (ov) Theorema ▲ TH 121217

Bruckner, A.:Mass 1, w. E. Mathis (sop), M. Schiml (mez), W. Ochman (ten), K. Ridderbusch (bass), Bavarian Radio Chorus Deutsche Grammophon ("The Originals" series) 2-▲ 447409-2

Bruckner, A.:Mass 1, w. E. Mathis (sop), M. Schiml (sop), W. Ochman (ten), K. Ridderbusch (bass), Bavarian Radio Chorus [L] Deutsche Grammophon 4-▲ 423127-2 [ADD]

Bruckner, A.:Mass 2, w. Bavarian Radio Chorus Deutsche Grammophon ("The Originals" series) 2-▲ 447409-2

Bruckner, A.:Mass 2, w. Bavarian Radio Chorus [L] Deutsche Grammophon 4-▲ 423127-2 [ADD]

Bruckner, A.:Mass 3, w. M. Stader (sop), C. Hellmann (mez), E. Haefliger (ten), K. Borg (bass), Bavarian Radio Chorus Deutsche Grammophon ("The Originals" series) 2-▲ 447409-2

Bruckner, A.:Mass 3, w. M. Stader (sop), A. Hellmann (alt), E. Haefliger (ten), K. Borg (bass), Bavarian Radio Chorus [L] Deutsche Grammophon 4-▲ 423127-2 [ADD]

Bruckner, A.:Syms (comp)—Berlin PO *(Nos. 1, 4, 7, 8 & 9)*, Bavarian RSO *(Nos. 2, 3, 5 & 6)* Deutsche Grammophon 9-▲ 429079-2 [ADD]

Haydn, J.:Mass 3, "Cäcilienmesse", w. Maria Stader (sop), Marga Höffgen (cta), Richard Holm (ten), Josef Greindl (bass), Bavarian Radio Chorus Deutsche Grammophon 2-▲ 437383-2 [ADD]

Haydn, J.:Mass 6, "Nikolai-messe", "6/4-Takt-Messe", w. Agnes Giebel (sop), Waldemar Kmentt (ten), Gottlob Frick (bass), Vienna Cathedral Choir, Vienna Boys' Choir Philips ("Two-Fers" series) 2-▲ 446175-2

Haydn, J.:Mass 7, "Kleine Orgelmesse", w. Agnes Giebel (sop), Waldemar Kmentt (ten), Gottlob Frick (bass), Vienna Cathedral Choir, Vienna Boys' Choir Philips ("Two-Fers" series) 2-▲ 446175-2

Haydn, J.:Die Schöpfung, w. Agnes Giebel (sop), Waldemar Kmentt (ten), Gottlob Frick (bass), Vienna Cathedral Choir, Vienna Boys' Choir Philips ("Two-Fers" series) 2-▲ 446175-2

Mussorgsky, M.:Boris Godunov, w. Martha Mödl (sop—Marina Mniszek), Lotte Schädle (sop—Xenia), Dorothea Siebert (mez—Fyodor), Hertha Töpper (mez—Xenia's wet-nurs), Karl Hermann Bennert (Boyer Khrushchyov), Lorenz Fehenberger (ten—Prince Shuysky), Hans Hopf (ten—Grigory), Karl Ostertag (ten—Missail), Hans Hotter (b-bar—Boris Godunov), Hermann Uhde (bar—Andrey Shchelkalov), Kurt Böhme (bass—Varlaam), Kim Borg (bass—Pimen), Kieth Engen (bass—Lewicki), Adolf Keil (bass—Nikitich), Benno Kusche (bar—Rangoni), Heinz Maria Linz (bass—Czernikowski), Bavarian Radio Chorus *(rec Munich, May 1957)* Myto 3-▲ MCD 953131

Wagner, R.:Der fliegende Holländer (ov) Theorema ▲ TH 121220

Wagner, R.:Lohengrin (preludes)—Act 1 Theorema ▲ TH 121220

Bavarian RSO (cont.)

E. Jochum (cnd) (cont.)

Weber, C.M. von:Der Freischütz, w. Irmgard Seefried (sop), Rita Streich (sop), Richard Holm (ten), Eberhard Wächter (bar), Kurt Böhme (b-bar), Bavarian Radio Chorus Deutsche Grammophon 2-▲ 439717-2 [ADD]

J. Keilberth (cnd)

Smetana, B.:The Bartered Bride, w. Dorothea Siebert (sop), Dagmar Hermann (mez), Maria von Ilosvay (mez), Hans Braun (bar), Kurt Böhme (bass), Bavarian Radio Chorus *(rec 1958)* Pantheon 2-▲ PHE 6652 (m)

R. Kempe (cnd)

Beethoven, L. van:Sym 8 *(rec 1975)* Originals ▲ ORISH 809 [ADD]

Tchaikovsky, P.:Sym 5 *(rec 1975)* Originals ▲ ORISH 809 [ADD]

B. Klee (cnd)

Mozart, W.A.:Con 21 Pno, w. Wilhelm Kempff (pno) Deutsche Grammophon ("Musikfest" series) ■ 415920-4

Mozart, W.A.:Con 22 Pno, w. W. Kempff (pno) Deutsche Grammophon ("Musikfest" series) ■ 415920-4

O. Klemperer (cnd)

Beethoven, L. van:Con 4 Pno, w. Leon Fleisher (pno), Berlin RSO, Cologne RSO Enterprise ("Palladio" series) ▲ ENT 4189 [ADD]

Beethoven, L. van:Sym 4, w. Berlin RSO, Cologne RSO Enterprise ("Palladio" series) ▲ ENT 4189 [ADD]

Beethoven, L. van:Sym 5, w. Berlin RSO, Cologne RSO Enterprise ("Palladio" series) ▲ ENT 4189 [ADD]

Brahms, J.:Sym 2, w. Berlin RSO, Cologne RSO Enterprise ("Palladio" series) ▲ ENT 4189 [ADD]

Mahler, G.:Sym 2, w. H. Harper (sop), J. Baker (mez) *(rec 1965)* Enterprise ("Document" series) ▲ ENT LV 937 [DDD]

Mendelssohn, F.:Die Hebriden *(rec live, May 23, 1969)* Originals ▲ ORI SH 917

Mendelssohn, F.:A Midsummer Night's Dream (comp), w. Edith Mathis (sop), Brigitte Fassbaender (mez), Bavarian Radio Chorus *(rec live, May 23, 1969)* Originals ▲ ORI SH 917

J. Koetsier (cnd)

Lortzing, A.:Die beiden Schützen, w. K. Nentwig (sop), P. Kuen (ten), B. Kusche (bar), K. Smitt-Walter (bar), M. Pröbstl (bass) *(rec 1950)* Memories 2-▲ MEM 4546 [ADD]

K. Kondrashin (cnd)

Tchaikovsky, P.:Con 1 Pno, w. Martha Argerich (pno) *(rec 1980)* Philips ▲ 446673-2

R. Kubelik (cnd)

Bach, J.S.:Con for 4 Hpds, w. Rudolf Kempe (pno), Fritz Rieger (pno), Wolfgang Sawallisch (pno), Rafael Kubelík (pno) *(rec 1972)* Arkadia ▲ 494

Beethoven, L. van:Con 1 Pno, w. R. Serkin (pno) *(rec live 1977)* Artists ▲ FED 67 [ADD]

Beethoven, L. van:Con 1 Pno, w. Rudolf Serkin (pno) *(rec live, 1968)* AS Disc ▲ ASD 2603

Beethoven, L. van:Con 2 Pno, w. R. Serkin (pno) *(rec live 1977)* Artists ▲ FED 67 [ADD]

Beethoven, L. van:Con 2 Pno, w. Rudolf Serkin (pno) *(rec live, 1968)* AS Disc ▲ ASD 2603

Beethoven, L. van:Con 4 Pno, w. A. Brendel (pno) Artists ▲ FED 47 [ADD]

Beethoven, L. van:Con 4 Pno, w. Alfred Brendel (pno) *(rec 1970)* Arkadia ▲ 494

Beethoven, L. van:Leonore 1 Artists ▲ FED 47 [ADD]

Berg, A.:Con Vn, w. H. Szeryng (vn) Deutsche Grammophon ("20th Century Classics" series) ▲ 431740-2 [ADD]

Berg, A.:Con Vn, w. H. Szeryng (vn) *(rec live 1975)* Artists ▲ FED 59 [ADD]

Berlioz, H.:Harold in Italy, w. *(soloist unknown)* Topazio ▲ TOP 260412

Brahms, J.:Syms (comp) Orfeo 3-▲ 070833 [DDD]

Bruckner, A.:Sym 6 *(rec live, 1971)* Originals ▲ ORI 861

Dvořák, A.:The Wild Dove Deutsche Grammophon 2-▲ 439663-2 [ADD]

Gluck, C.W.:Iphigénie en Tauride, w. S. Jurinac (sop), F. Wunderlich (ten), H. Prey (bar), K. Engen (bass), Bavarian Radio Chorus [1781 J.B. von Alxinger-Gluck German-language version] *(rec live, Munich 1965)* Myto 2-▲ 2 MCD 91544 [ADD]

Handel, G.F.:Judas Maccabaeus, w. Agnes Giebel (sop), Julianna Falk (cta), Fritz Wunderlich (ten), L. Welter (bar), Pöld (sgr), Bavarian Chorus [G] *(rec live 10/25/63)* Melodram 2-▲ MEL 28026 [AAD]

Handel, G.F.:Serse, w. Ingeborg Hallstein (sop), Fritz Wunderlich (ten), et al., Bavarian Radio Chorus [G] *(rec 10/22–28/62)* Verona 3-▲ 27032/34 (m) [AAD]

Haydn, J.:Mass 3, "Cäcilienmesse", w. Lucia Popp (sop), Doris Soffel (mez), Rudolf Laubenthal (ten), Kurt Moll (bass), Bavarian Radio Chorus [L] Orfeo 2-▲ 032822 [DDD]

Haydn, J.:Die Schöpfung, w. Margaret Marshall (sop), Lucia Popp (sop), Vinson Cole (ten), Bernd Weikl (bar), Gwynne Howell (bass), Bavarian Radio Chorus Orfeo 2-▲ 150852 [DDD] 2-■ 150852 (D)

Hindemith, P.:Kammermusik 5, w. G. Schmid (va) Koch Schwann ▲ CD 310 045

Hindemith, P.:Mathis der Maler (sym) *(rec 1977)* Originals ▲ ORISH 804 [ADD]

Hindemith, P.:Mathis der Maler, w. Urszula Koszut (sop), Trudeliese Schmidt (mez), Rose Wagemann (mez), William Cochran (ten), Donald Grobe (ten), James King (ten), Manfred Schmidt (ten), Dietrich Fischer-Dieskau (bar), Gerd Feldhoff (bass), Alexander Malta (bass), Peter Meven (bass), Karl Kreile (sgr), Bavarian Radio Chorus EMI Classics 2-▲ CDCC 55237

Hindemith, P.:Der Schwanendreher, w. G. Schmid (va) *(rec 1978)* Originals ▲ ORISH 804 [ADD]

Janácek, L.:Sinfonietta *(rec 1971)* Deutsche Grammophon ▲ 437254-2

Kubelík, R.:Cantate without Words *(rec 1981)* Panton ▲ PAN 811225

Kubelík, R.:Inventions & Interludes, w. Bavarian Radio Chorus *(rec Prague, 1993)* Panton ▲ PAN 811225

Kubelík, R.:Orphikon *(rec 1984)* Panton ▲ PAN 811225

Mahler, G.:Das Lied von der Erde, w. J. Baker (alt), W. Kmentt (ten) *(rec 1975)* Originals ▲ ORISH 806 [ADD]

Mahler, G.:Syms, w. Bavarian Radio Chorus Deutsche Grammophon 10-▲ 429042-2 [ADD]

Mahler, G.:Sym 9, w. J. Baker (alt), W. Kmentt (ten) *(rec 1975)* Originals ▲ ORISH 806 [ADD]

Mozart, W.A.:Con 21 Pno, w. Robert Casadesus (pno) *(rec 1971)* Arkadia ▲ 494

Mozart, W.A.:Con 21 Pno, w. C. Corzon (pno) *(rec 1975)* Artists ▲ FED 51 [ADD]

Mozart, W.A.:Con 23 Pno, w. C. Corzon (pno) *(rec 1975)* Artists ▲ FED 51 [ADD]

Mozart, W.A.:Con 5 Vn, w. H. Szeryng (vn) *(rec live 1975)* Artists ▲ FED 59 [ADD]

Mozart, W.A.:Don Giovanni, w. J. Varady (sop), A. Augér (sop), E. Mathis (sop), T. Moser (ten), A. Titus (bar), R. Panerai (bar), R. Scholze (bass), J.-H. Rootering (bass), Bavarian Radio Chorus [I] Eurodisc 3-▲ 7798-2 [DDD]

Mozart, W.A.:Exsultate, w. *(soloist unknown)* Deutsche Grammophon ▲ 429820-2 [ADD]

Mozart, W.A.:Sym 35 CBS ▲ MDK 44647 [ADD]

Mozart, W.A.:Sym 36 CBS ▲ MDK 44647 [ADD]

Mozart, W.A.:Sym 38 CBS ▲ MDK 44648 [ADD]

Mozart, W.A.:Sym 39 CBS ▲ MDK 44648 [ADD]

Mozart, W.A.:Sym 40 CBS ▲ MDK 44649 [ADD]

Mozart, W.A.:Sym 41 CBS ▲ MDK 44649 [ADD]

Schoenberg, A.:Con Pno, w. A. Brendel (pno) Deutsche Grammophon ("20th Century Classics" series) ▲ 431740-2 [ADD]

Schoenberg, A.:Con Vn, w. Z. Zeitlin (vn) Deutsche Grammophon ("20th Century Classics" series) ▲ 431740-2 [DDD]

Schoenberg, A.:Gurrelieder, w. I. Borkh (sop), H. Schachtschneider (ten), H. Töpper (mez), L. Fehenberger (ten), K. Engen (bass)—also includes songs by Berg, Schoenberg & Webern Deutsche Grammophon ("20th Century Classics" series) ▲ 431744-2 [ADD]

Schubert, Franz:Sym 9 *(rec live, 1978)* Artists ▲ FED 65 [ADD]

Schumann, R.:Manfred Ov *(rec 1978)* Sony Classical ("Essential Classics" series) ▲ SBK 48270 [ADD] ■ SBT 48270

Schumann, R.:Manfred Ov Odyssey 2-▲ MB2K 45680

Schumann, R.:Sym 1 Odyssey ▲ MBK 42603

Schumann, R.:Sym 1 Sony Classical ("Essential Classics" series) ▲ SBK 48269 [ADD] ■ SBT 48269

Schumann, R.:Sym 2 Sony Classical ("Essential Classics" series) ▲ SBK 48269 [ADD] ■ SBT 48269

Schumann, R.:Sym 3 *(rec 1979)* Sony Classical ("Essential Classics" series) ▲ SBK 48270 [ADD] ■ SBT 48270

Bavarian RSO (cont.)
R. Kubelik (cnd) (cont.)
Schumann, R.:Sym 3 — Odyssey ▲ MBK 42603
Schumann, R.:Sym 4 — Artists ▲ FED 47 [ADD]
Schumann, R.:Sym 4 *(rec 1978)* — Sony Classical ("Essential Classics" series) ▲ SBK 48270 [ADD] ■ SBT 48270
Smetana, B.:Dalibor, w. Sándor Kónya (ten), Franz Crass (bass), Gerd Nienstedt (bass), Bavarian Radio Chorus *(rec live, Munich, 1969)* — Serenissima 2–▲ SER 360169
Smetana, B.:Dalibor (sels), w. F. Weathers (sop), S. Konya (ten), G. Nienstedt (bass), Bavarian Radio Chorus—nine solo, duet & trio arias featuring tenor Sandor Konya as Dalibor, from Acts 1-3 *(rec live, Munich, 1968)* — Myto 2–▲ 2 MCD 92465 [ADD]
Smetana, B.:Hakon Jarl *(rec 1971)* — Deutsche Grammophon ▲ 437254–2
Smetana, B.:Má Vlast — Orfeo ▲ 115841 [DDD]
Smetana, B.:Prague Carnival *(rec 1971)* — Deutsche Grammophon ▲ 437254–2
Smetana, B.:Richard III *(rec 1971)* — Deutsche Grammophon ▲ 437254–2
Suk, J.:Asrael — Panton ▲ 81 1101–2
Tchaikovsky, P.:Romeo & Juliet *(rec live, 1972)* — Originals ▲ ORI 861
Wagner, R.:Die Meistersinger von Nürnberg, w. Gundula Janowitz (sop), Brigitte Fassbaender (mez), Sándor Kónya (ten), Gerhard Unger (ten), Thomas Helmsey (bar), Thomas Stewart (bar), Franz Crass (bass), Bavarian Radio Chorus *(rec 1967)* — Calig 4–▲ 5097174 [ADD]
Wagner, R.:Die Meistersinger von Nürnberg, w. G. Janowitz (sop), B. Fassbaender (mez), S. Kónya (ten), G. Unger (ten), T. Stewart (bar), F. Crass (bass), T. Hemsley (bass), Bavarian Radio Chorus [G] *(rec live, Munich, Oct. 1967)* — Myto 4–▲ 4 MCD 92569 [ADD]
Wagner, R.:Tannhäuser (ov) *(rec live, 1978)* — Artists ▲ FED 65 [ADD]
Weber, C.M. von:Oberon, w. B. Nilsson (sop), A. Augér (sop), J. Hamari (mez), P. Domingo (ten), H. Prey (bar) — Deutsche Grammophon ("Domingo Edition" series) ▲ 435406–2 [ADD]
Weber, C.M. von:Oberon, w. B. Nilsson (sop), A. Augér (sop), J. Hamari (mez), P. Domingo (ten), H. Prey (bar) — Deutsche Grammophon 2–▲ 419038–2 [ADD]
F. Leitner (cnd)
Busoni, F.:Doktor Faust, w. H. Hillebrecht (sop), W. Cochran (ten), D. Fischer-Dieskau (bar), K. C. Kohn (bass), Bavarian Radio Sym Chorus [G] — Deutsche Grammophon ("20th Century Classics" series) 3–▲ 427413–2 [ADD]
L. Maazel (cnd)
Schumann, R.:Con Vc, w. L. Harrell (vc) — Artists ▲ FED 54 [ADD]
Strauss, R.:Also sprach Zarathustra — RCA Red Seal ▲ 09026–68225–2
Strauss, R.:Don Juan — RCA Red Seal ▲ 09026–68225–2
Strauss, R.:Der Rosenkavalier (suite) — RCA Red Seal ▲ 09026–68225–2
Strauss, R.:Symphonia domestica *(rec Munich, Feb 6–7, 1995)* — RCA Red Seal ▲ 09026–68221–2 [DDD]
Strauss, R.:Tod und Verklärung *(rec Munich, Feb 6–7, 1995)* — RCA Red Seal ▲ 09026–68221–2 [DDD]
Tchaikovsky, P.:Sym 3 *(rec live 1991)* — Artists ▲ FED 54 [DDD]
B. Maderna (cnd)
Nono, L.:Per Bastiana *(rec live, Munich 11/20/70)* — Arkadia ▲ 027 [ADD]
S. Ozawa (cnd)
Beethoven, L. van:Con 1 Pno, w. M. Argerich (pno) *(rec live 1983)* — Artists ▲ FED 69 [ADD]
K. A. Rickenbacher (cnd)
Grieg, E.:Sym — Koch Schwann ▲ CD 311 118 [DDD]
Messiaen, O.:L'Ascension — Koch Schwann ▲ CD 311015 [DDD]
Messiaen, O.:Chronochromie — Koch Schwann ▲ CD 311015 [DDD]
Spohr, L.:Sym 9 — Orfeo ▲ 094841 [DDD]
Strauss, R.:Sym in d — Koch Schwann ▲ CD 311 118 [DDD]
F. Rieger (cnd)
Marschner, H.A.:Der Vampyr, w. Arleen Augér (sop), Donald Grobe (ten), Roland Hermann (bar), Nikolas Hillebrand (bass), Bavarian Radio Chorus *(rec live, Munich, 1974)* — Enterprise ("Documents" series) 2–▲ ENT 1009
Nicolai, O.:Lustigen Weiber, w. Erika Köth (sop), Hertha Töpper (mez), Maria Rogner (sgr), Hans Günter Nöcker (b–bar), Kim Borg (bass), Naan Pöld (sgr), Bavarian Chorus *(rec 1960's)* — Pantheon 2–▲ PHE 6660 (m)
D. Runnicles (cnd)
Humperdinck, E.:Hänsel und Gretel, w. H. Behrens (sop—Gertrud, the Stepmother), R. Ziesak (sop—Gretel), R. Joshua (sop—Sandman), C. Schäfer (sop—Dew Fairy), J. Larmore (mez—Hänsel), H. Schwarz (cta—Nibblewitch), B. Weikl (bar—Peter, the Father), Tölz Boys' Choir *(rec Munich, Feb. 1994)* — Teldec 2–▲ 94549–2 [DDD]
J.–P. Saraste (cnd)
Lindberg, M.:Kinetics — Ondine ▲ ODE 784–2 [DDD]
Rautavaara, E.:Con 2 Pno, w. R. Gothoni (pno) — Ondine ▲ ODE 757–2 [DDD]
W. Sawallisch (cnd)
Brahms, J.:Ein Deutsches Requiem, w. M. Price (sop), T. Allen (bar), Bavarian Radio Chorus [G] — Orfeo ▲ 039101
Pfitzner, H.:Das Käthchen von Heilbronn (ov) — Orfeo ▲ 168881 [DDD]
Pfitzner, H.:Palestrina (sels)—Preludes to Acts 1, 2 & 3 — Orfeo ▲ 168881 [DDD]
Pfitzner, H.:Die Rose vom Liebesgarten—Blütenwunder & Trauermarsch — Orfeo ▲ 168881 [DDD]
Schubert, Franz:Mass 4, w. H. Donath (sop), B. Fassbaender (mez), F. Araiza (ten), D. Fischer-Dieskau (bar), Bavarian Radio Chorus [L] — EMI Classics ("Studio" series) ▲ CDM 69222
Schubert, Franz:Mass 5, w. L. Popp (sop), B. Fassbaender (mez), A. Dallapozza (ten), D. Fischer-Dieskau (bar), Bavarian Radio Chorus [L] — EMI Classics ("Studio" series) ▲ CDM 69222
Schubert, Franz:Mass 6, w. H. Donath (sop), B. Fassbaender (mez), F. Araiza (ten), D. Fischer-Dieskau (bar), Bavarian Radio Chorus [L] — EMI Classics ("Studio" series) ▲ CDM 69223
Schubert, Franz:Offertorium, D.963, w. P. Schreier (ten), Bavarian Radio Chorus [L] — EMI Classics ("Studio" series) ▲ CDM 69223
Schubert, Franz:Tantum ergo, D.962, w. L. Popp (sop), B. Fassbaender (mez), A. Dallapozza (ten), D. Fischer-Dieskau (bar), Bavarian Radio Chorus [L] — EMI Classics ("Studio" series) ▲ CDM 69223
Strauss, R.:Elektra, w. C. Studer (sop), E. Marton (sop), M. Lipovsek (mez), H. Winkler (ten), B. Weikl (bar), Bavarian Radio Chorus — EMI Classics 2–▲ CDCB 54067
Strauss, R.:Die Frau ohne Schatten, w. C. Studer (sop), U. Vinzing (sop), H. Schwarz (mez), R. Kollo (ten), A. Muff (bass), Schmidt (sgr), Bavarian Radio Chorus [uncut version] [G] — EMI Classics 3–▲ CDCC 49074 [DDD]
Strauss, R.:Die Frau ohne Schatten, w. C. Studer (sop), U. Vinzing (sop), H. Schwarz (mez), R. Kollo (ten), A. Muff (bass), Schmidt (sgr), Bavarian Radio Chorus [G] — EMI Classics ▲ CDC 54494 [DDD]
Wagner, R.:Die Feen, w. L. E. Gray (sop), K. Lövaas (sop), K. Laki (sop), Anderson (sop), R. Alexander (sop), R. Hermann (bar), K. Moll (bass), Bavarian Radio Chorus [G] *(rec live, Munich Opera Fest. 1983)* — Orfeo 3–▲ 062833 [DDD]
Weber, C.M. von:Sym 1 — Orfeo ▲ 091841 [DDD]
Weber, C.M. von:Sym 2 — Orfeo ▲ 091841 [DDD]
W. Schmidt-Boelcke (cnd)
Lincke, P.:Frau Luna (sels), w. Ingeborg Hallstein (sop), Renata Tebaldi (sop), Willi Brokmeier (ten), Bavarian Radio Chorus [G] — Acanta ▲ CD 42484 [DDD]
U. Schneider (cnd)
Copland, A.:Con Cl, w. E. Brunner (cl) — Koch Schwann ▲ 3–1035–2 [DDD]
Hindemith, P.:Con Cl, w. E. Brunner (cl) — Koch Schwann ▲ 3–1035–2 [DDD]
Milhaud, D.:Con Cl, w. E. Brunner (cl) — Koch Schwann ▲ 3–1035–2 [DDD]
Milhaud, D.:Scaramouche Cl, w. E. Brunner (cl) — Koch Schwann ▲ 3–1035–2 [DDD]
H.–M. Schneidt (cnd)
Baur, J.:Musik mit R. Schumann — Thorofon ▲ CTH 2270
Bialas, G.:Aus der Matratzengruft, w. Bavarian Radio Chorus — CPO 2–▲ CPO 999204 [DDD]
C. Schuricht (cnd)
Brahms, J.:Tragic Ov — Theorema ▲ TH 121172
E. Sebestyen (cnd)
Stravinsky, I.:L'Histoire du soldat, w. P. Fricke (nar) *(rec Jan. 31, 1987)* — Calig ▲ CAL 50894 [DDD]

Bavarian RSO (cont.)
D. Shallon (cnd)
Glazunov, A.:Con ballata, w. B. Pergamenschikow (vc) — Koch Schwann ▲ CD 311 119 [DDD]
Glazunov, A.:Serenade espagnole, w. B. Pergamenschikow (vc) — Koch Schwann ▲ CD 311 119 [DDD]
Tishchenko, B.:Con Vc, w. B. Pergamenschikow (vc) — Koch Schwann ▲ CD 311 119 [DDD]
M. Shostakovich (cnd)
Shostakovich, D.:Con 1 Vc, w. H. Schiff (vc) — Philips ▲ 412526–2 [DDD]
Shostakovich, D.:Con 2 Vc, w. H. Schiff (vc) — Philips ▲ 412526–2 [DDD]
L. Slatkin (cnd)
Strauss, R.:Don Quixote, w. J. Starker (vc) — RCA Red Seal ▲ 09026–60561–2 [DDD]
Strauss, R.:Till Eulenspiegels lustige Streiche — RCA Red Seal ▲ 09026–60561–2 [DDD]
G. Solti (cnd)
Liszt, F.:Les Préludes — Originals ▲ ORISH 802 [ADD]
Tchaikovsky, P.:Sym 4 — Originals ▲ ORISH 802 [ADD]
A. Tamayo (cnd)
Kelemen, M.:Drammatico, w. Siegfried Palm (vc) *(rec Munich, Germany, Feb 22, 1991)* — BIS ▲ CD 742 [DDD]
M. Tang (cnd)
Taneyev, S.:Canzona Cl, w. W. Thomas–Mifune (vc) — Koch Schwann ▲ 3–1135–2 [DDD]
Taneyev, S.:Suite de Concert, w. W. Thomas–Mifune (vc) [arr vc & orch] — Koch Schwann ▲ 3–1135–2 [DDD]
J. Tate (cnd)
Humperdinck, E.:Hänsel und Gretel, w. B. Bonney (sop), E. Lind (sop), B. Hendricks (sop), A.S. von Otter (mez), H. Schwarz (mez), M. Lipovšek (mez), Andreas Schmidt (bar), Tölz Boys' Choir [G] — EMI Classics 2–▲ CDCB 54022 [DDD]
P. Thomas (cnd)
Yun, I.:Con Cl, w. E. Brunner (cl) — Camerata ▲ 30CM 46
Yun, I.:Piri Cl & Orch, w. E. Brunner (cl) — Camerata ▲ 30CM 46
H. Vonk (cnd)
Music of Tchaikovsky, w. Vienna SO [cnd:Yuri Ahronovitch], Budapest SO [cnd:András Ligeti] — Laserlight ♦ 90029 [CD–ROM; DDD]
Tchaikovsky, P.:Swan Lake (suite) — Capriccio ▲ 10 923 [DDD]
H. Wallberg (cnd)
Lortzing, A.:Zar und Zimmermann (sels), w. Lucia Popp (sop), Adalbert Kraus (ten), Hermann Prey (bar), Fritz Krenn (bass), Karl Ridderbusch (bass), Bavarian Radio Chorus [G] — Acanta 2–▲ CD 42424 [DDD]
H. Weigert (cnd)
Strauss, R.:Salome, w. Astrid Varnay (sop—Salome), Hertha Töpper (mez—Der Page der Herodias), Margarete Klose (cta—Herodias), Hans Hopf (ten—Narraboth), Karl Hoppe (ten—1st Nazarene), Karl Ostertag (ten—1st Jew), Julius Patzak (ten—Herodes), Hans Braun (bar—Jochanaan), Benno Kusche (bar—2nd Soldier), Adolf Keil (bass—1st Soldier), Hans Hermann Nissen (bass—Ein Kappadozier), Max Proebstl (bass—2nd Nazarene), Walter Carnotch (sgr—4th Jew), Emil Graf (sgr—3rd Jew), Paul Kaussen (sgr—2nd Jew), Hildegard Limmer (sgr—A slave), Georg Witter (sgr—5th Jew) *(rec June 21–25, 1953)* — Bella Voce 2–▲ BLV 7210 [AAD]
D. Zinman (cnd)
Mozart, W.A.:Con 20 Pno, w. C. Zacharias (pno) — EMI Classics ▲ CDC 49899
Mozart, W.A.:Con 21 Pno, w. C. Zacharias (pno) — EMI Classics ▲ CDC 49899
Bavarian RSO members
L. Bernstein (cnd)
Beethoven, L. van:Sym 9, "Choral Sym", w. Dresden State Orch members, Kirov Theatre Orch members, London SO members, New York PO members, Orch de Paris members, Bavarian Radio Chorus, Berlin Radio Chorus, Dresden Philharmonie Children's Chorus [G] *(rec live, Schauspielhaus, East Berlin, 12/25/89)* — Deutsche Grammophon ▲ 429861–2 [DDD] ■ 429861–4
Bavarian RSO Winds
C. Davis (cnd)
Mozart, W.A.:Serenade Ww, K.361 — RCA Red Seal ▲ 09026–60873–2
Mozart, W.A.:Serenade Ww, K.361 — RCA Gold Seal ▲ 09026–68113–2 [ADD]
Bavarian State Opera Marstall Ensemble
R. Platz (cnd)
Platz, R.H.:Dunkles Haus, w. Maria Husmann (sop—Woman), Michael Busch (bar—Man), Udo Zickwolf (nar—Child/Bird/Man), Carin Levine (a fl/b fl) *(rec 1991)* — Thorofon ▲ CTH 2170
Bavarian State Opera Orch
Wagner, R.:Tannhäuser (sels), w. Sylvia Sass (sop), Reiner Goldberg (ten), Hermann Prey (bar), Bavarian State Opera Chorus—Ov; Venusberg Bacchanal; Dich, teure halle, grüb' ich wieder; Freudig Begrüben wir die edle Halle; Intro; die Pilger sind's - Beglückt darf nun dich, o Heimat, ich schauen; plus others — Laserlight ▲ 14211 [DDD]
J. Keilberth (cnd)
Strauss, R.:Die ägyptische Helena, w. Annelies Kupper (sop—Aithra), Leonie Rysanek (sop—Helena), Ira Malaniuk (cta—Omniscient Seashell), Bernd Aldenhoff (ten—Menelas), Richard Holm (ten—Da-ud), Hermann Uhde (bar—Altair), Bavarian State Opera Chorus *(rec Munich Opera Festival, Prince Regent Theater, Aug 10, 1956)* — Orfeo d'or 2–▲ 424962
Strauss, R.:Die ägyptische Helena, w. L. Rysanek (sop), A. Kupper (sop), B. Aldenhoff (ten), H. Uhde (bar), Bavarian State Opera Chorus [G] *(rec live, Munich, 8/27/56)* — Melodram 2–▲ MEL 27066 (m) [AAD]
Strauss, R.:Der Rosenkavalier, w. Erika Köth (sop—Sophie), Annelie Waas (sop—Marianne), Claire Watson (sop—Marschallin), Hertha Töpper (mez—Octavian), Brigitte Fassbaender (cta—Annina), Gerhard Stolze (ten—Valzacchi), Fritz Wunderlich (ten—Singer), Otto Wiener (bar—Faninal), Kurt Böhme (bass—Baron), Bavarian State Opera Chorus *(rec Munich Opera Festival, National Theater, May 21, 1965)* — Orfeo d'or 3–▲ 425963
R. Kempe (cnd)
Strauss, R.:Feuersnot, w. Maud Cunitz (sop—Diemut), Antonia Fahberg (sop—Elsbeth), Irmgard Barth (mez—Wigelis), Liselotte Nölser (sgr—Margret), Karl Ostertag (ten—Schweiker), Marcel Cordes (bar—Kunrad), Kieth Engen (bass—Kofel), Karl Hoppe (bass—Hämerlein), Max Proebstl (bass—Ortolf), Georg Wieter (bass—Jörg), Bavarian State Opera Chorus *(rec Munich Opera Festival, Prince Regent Theater, Aug 14, 1958)* — Orfeo d'or 2–▲ 423962
Strauss, R.:Die Liebe der Danae (sels), w. L. Rysanek (sop), F. Frantz (b–bar)—eleven arias from Acts 1,2 & 3 [G] *(rec 1953)* — Melodram 3–▲ MEL 37061 (m) [AAD]
C. Kleiber (cnd)
Strauss, R.:Der Rosenkavalier, w. C. Watson (sop), B. Fassbaender (mez), K. Ridderbusch (bass) *(rec 1977)* — Exclusive 3–▲ EXL 49 [ADD]
E. Kleiber (cnd)
Strauss (II), Joh.:Die Fledermaus, w. J. Varady (sop), L. Popp (sop), A. Kollo (ten), H. Prey (bar), I. Rebroff (bass) [G] — Deutsche Grammophon 2–▲ 415646–2 [ADD]
H. Knappertsbusch (cnd)
Beethoven, L. van:Fidelio, w. S. Jurinac (sop), M. Stader (sop), H. Peerce (ten), Bavarian State Opera Chorus [G] *(rec ca. 1961)* — MCA Classics 2–▲ MCAD2–9809 [AAD]
Wagner, R.:Götterdämmerung, w. Birgit Nilsson (sop—Brünnhilde), Leonie Rysanek (sop—Gutrune), Gerda Sommerschuh (sop—Woglinde), Elisabeth Lindermeier (sop—Wellgunde), Ruth Michaelis (sop—Flohilde), Marianne Schech (sop—Dritte Norne), Ira Malaniuk (mez—Waltraute), Irmgarth Barth (mez—Erste Norne), Hertha Töpper (mez—Zweite Norne), Bernd Aldenhoff (ten—Siegfried), Hermann Uhde (bar—Gunther), Gottlob Frick (bass—Hagen), Bavarian State Opera Chorus *(rec live, Prinzregententheater, Sept. 1, 1955)* — Orfeo 4–▲ 356944 (m)
Wagner, R.:Götterdämmerung (sels), w. A. Varnay (sop), E. Grümmer (sop), B. Aldenhoff (ten), H. Uhde (bar), G. Frick (bass), J. Greindl (bass), Bayreuth Festival Orch, Bavarian State Opera Chorus, Bayreuth Festival Chorus [G] *(rec live 1955 & 1957)* — Melodram 4–▲ MEL 46106 (m) [AAD]
Wagner, R.:Tristan und Isolde, w. Helena Braun (sop—Isolde), Margarete Klose (mez—Brangäne), Günther Treptow (ten—Tristan), Paul Kuen (ten—Ein Hirte), Albrecht Peter (bar—Melot), Fritz Richard Bender (bar—Ein Steuermann), Ferdinand Frantz (b–bar—König Marke), Paul Schöffler (b–bar—Kurwenal), Bavarian State Opera Chorus *(rec live, Prinzregententheater, July 23, 1950)* — Orfeo 3–▲ 355

▲ = CD ♦ = Enhanced CD Δ = MD ■ = Cassette Tape □ = DCC

Bavarian State Opera Orch (cont.)

C. Krauss (cnd)

Puccini, G.:La Bohème, w. Trude Eipperle (sop), Hildegarde Ranczak (sop), Alfons Fügel (ten), Carl Kronenberg (bar), Georg Hann (bass), Georg Wieter (bass), Emil Graf (sgr), Otto Hillerbrandt (sgr), Karl Schmidt (sgr), Bavarian State Opera Chorus *(rec 1940)* Preiser 2-▲ PRE 90275

Strauss, R.:Capriccio (sels), w. V. Ursuleac (sop—Die Gräfin), F. Klarwein (ten—Flamand), H. Hotter (b-bar—Olivier), G. Hann (b-bar—La Roche), G. Wieter (bass—Der Haushofmeister) *(rec 1942)* Myto ▲ MCD 943104

Strauss, R.:Der Rosenkavalier, w. Adele Kern (sop), Viorica Ursuleac (sop), Georgine von Milinkovic (mez), Georg Hann (bass), Ludwig Weber (bass), Bavarian State Opera Chorus *(rec Munich, June 1942)* Preiser 3-▲ PRE 90218

Wagner, R.:Der fliegende Holländer, w. Viorica Ursuleac (sop), Luise Willer (mez), Karl Ostertag (ten), Hans Hotter (b-bar), Georg Hann (bass), Bavarian State Opera Chorus *(rec Mar 13–16, 1944)* Preiser 2-▲ PRE 90250 [ADD]

R. Kubelik (cnd)

Janácek, L.:Jenůfa, w. H. Hillebrecht (sop), A. Varnay (sop), W. Cochran (ten), Cox (sgr), Bavarian State Opera Chorus [G] *(rec live in Munich, Mar. 17, 1970)* Myto 2-▲ 2 MCD 90422 [ADD]

F. Leitner (cnd)

Strauss, R.:Salome, w. L. Rysanek (sop), A. Varnay (sop/mez), G. Stolze (ten), D. Fischer-Dieskau (bar) *(rec live, Monaco, 1971)* Melodram 2-▲ MEL 27098

Z. Mehta (cnd)

Wagner, R.:Tannhäuser, w. Nadine Secunde (sop), Waltraude Meier (mez), Rene Kollo (ten), Bernd Weikl (bar), Bavarian State Opera Chorus *(rec live, Munich, 1994)* Serenissima 3-▲ SER 360166

G. Patanè (cnd)

Verdi, G.:La traviata (sels), w. T. Stratas (sop), F. Wunderlich (ten), H. Prey (bar), Bavarian State Opera Chorus—substantial selections from Acts 1–3 *(rec live, Munich, 3/28/65)* Myto 2-▲ 2 MCD 91648 [ADD]

W. Sawallisch (cnd)

Wagner, R.:Die Meistersinger von Nürnberg, w. C. Studer (sop—Eva), B. Heppner (ten—Walther von Stolzing), B. Weikl (bar—Hans Sachs), S. Lorenz (b-bar—Sixtus Beckmesser), K. Moll (bass—Veit Pogner), Bavarian State Opera Chorus EMI Classics ▲ CDCD 55142

Wagner, R.:Ovs, Preludes & Orch Sels—Meistersinger Orfeo ▲ 161871 [DDD]

Wagner, R.:Rienzi, der Letzte der Tribunen, w. Cheryl Studer (sop—Irene), René Kollo (ten—Rienzi), Friedrich Lenz (ten—Gesandte), Norbert Orth (ten—Baroncelli), Bodo Brinkmann (bar—Paolo Orsini), Keith Engen (bass—Cecco del Vecchio), Raimund Grumbach (bass—Gesandte), Jan-Hendrik Rootering (bass—Steffano Colonna), Carmen Anhorn (sgr—Ein Friedensbote), Karl Helm (sgr—Kardinal Orvieto), John Janssen (sgr—Adriano), Alfred Kuhn (sgr—Gesandte), Hans Wilbrink (sgr—Gesandte), Bavarian State Opera Chorus *(rec live, July 6, 1983)* Orfeo d'or 3-▲ 346953

G. Solti (cnd)

Orff, C.:Antigonae, w. Christel Goltz (sop), Paul Kuen (ten), Karl Ostertag (ten), Benno Kusche (bar), Hermann Uhde (bar), N. Barth (bar), Bavarian State Opera Chorus *(rec Prinzregententheater, Jan. 12, 1951)* Orfeo d'or 2-▲ 407952

B. Walter (cnd)

Weber, C.M. von:Ovs *(rec 1954)* Legend ▲ LGD 114 [ADD]

Bavarian State Orch

D. Fischer-Dieskau (cnd)

Verdi, G.:Arias, w. Julia Varady (sop)—Ben io t'invenni [from Nabucco]; Tacea la notte; Timor di me [both from Il Trovatore]; È strano [w. Lothar Odinius (ten)]; Teneste la promessa-Attendo,attendo [both from La traviata]; Ecco l'orrido campo-Ma dall'arido stelo divulsa; Morrò, ma prima in grazia [both from Un ballo in maschera]; Pace, pace, mio dio [from La forza del destino] *(rec Studio 1, Bavarian Radio, Jan 23, 25, 26 & 28, 1995)* Orfeo ▲ 186951 [DDD]

Wagner, R.:Arias & Scenes, w. Julia Varady (sop), Peter Seiffert (ten), Bavarian State Chorus—Lohengrin:Ov; 'Wedding March & Chorus'; Tannhäuser:'Dich, teure Halle'; Ov Act 2; 'Gepriesen sei die Stunde; Walküre:'Ein Schwert verhiess mir der Vater' EMI Classics ▲ CDC 56138

F. Fricsay (cnd)

Beethoven, L. van:Fidelio (sels), w. L. Rysanek (sop), I. Seefried (sop), E. Haefliger (ten), F. Lenz (ten), D. Fischer-Dieskau (bar), K. Engen (bass), G. Frick (bass), Bavarian Opera Chorus—Overture, various arias & scenes, finale [G] IMP Collectors Series ▲ IMPX 9021 [AAD]

C. Kleiber (cnd)

Strauss, R.:Der Rosenkavalier, w. Claire Watson (sop—Feldmarschallin), Lucia Popp (sop—Sophie), Annelie Waas (sop—Marianne), Brigitte Fassbaender (mez—Octavian), Margaretthe Bence (ct—Annina), David Thaw (ten—Valzacchi), Karl Ridderbusch (bass—Baron Ochs), Benno Kusche (bass—Herr von Faninal), Albrecht Peter (bass—Police Inspector), Bavarian State Chorus *(rec live, Münchner Festspiele, July 20, 1974)* Arkadia 3-▲ 486 [ADD]

Verdi, G.:La traviata, w. I. Cotrubas (sop), G. Aragall (ten), R. Bruson (bar) [I] *(rec 1978)* Artists 2-▲ FED 45 [ADD]

H. Knappertsbusch (cnd)

Bruckner, A.:Sym 9 *(rec live, Monaco, 1958)* Arkadia ▲ 710 (m) [ADD]

Bruckner, A.:Sym 9 Music & Arts ▲ CD 896

W. Sawallisch (cnd)

Beethoven, L. van:Leonore 2 Orfeo ▲ 161871 [DDD]

Brahms, J.:Tragic Ov Orfeo ▲ 161871 [DDD]

Bruckner, A.:Sym 1 Orfeo ▲ 145851 [DDD]

Bruckner, A.:Sym 5 [original version], 1990/91) Orfeo ▲ 241911 [DDD]

Bruckner, A.:Sym 6 Orfeo ▲ 024821 [DDD]

Bruckner, A.:Sym 9 Orfeo ▲ 160851 ■ M 160851

Furtwängler, W.:Sym 3 *(rec live, Bavarian Radio National Theater, Munich, Jan 7, 1980)* Orfeo d'or ▲ CD 406961

Mozart, W.A.:Ovs—Die Zauberflöte Orfeo ▲ 161871 [DDD]

Strauss, R.:Arabella, w. H. Donath (sop), J. Varady (sop), D. Fischer-Dieskau (bar), A. Schmidt (bar), W. Berry (bass) Orfeo 2-▲ 169882 [DDD]

Verdi, G.:Ovs & Preludes—Forza del destino Orfeo ▲ 161871 [DDD]

Wagner, R.:Das Liebesverbot, w. Pamela Coburn (sop—Mariana), Friedrich Lenz (ten—Antonio), Hermann Prey (bar—Friedrich), Keith Engen (bass—Angelo), Raimund Grumbach (bass—Danieli/Wirt), Wolfgang Fassler (sgr—Luzio), Sabine Haas (sgr—Isabella/Claudios Schwester), Alfred Kuhn (sgr—Brighella/Chef der Sbirren), Hermann Sapell (sgr—Pontio Pilato), Robert Schunk (sgr—Claudio), Marianne Seibel (sgr—Dorella), Bavarian State Chorus *(rec July 9, 1983)* Orfeo d'or 3-▲ 345953

R. Strauss (cnd)

Strauss, R.:Eine Alpensinfonie *(rec 1941)* Koch Legacy ▲ 3-7132-2 H1

Strauss, R.:Eine Alpensinfonie *(rec 1940–41)* Preiser 2-▲ PRE 90205 [ADD]

Strauss, R.:Don Quixote, w. O. Uhl (vc) *(rec 1940–41)* Preiser 2-▲ PRE 90205 [ADD]

Strauss, R.:Festmusik zur Feier des 2600jährigen Bestehens des Kaiserreichs Japan *(rec 1940–41)* Preiser 2-▲ PRE 90205 [ADD]

Strauss, R.:Ein Heldenleben *(rec 1940–41)* Preiser 2-▲ PRE 90205 [ADD]

Bavarian State Youth Orch

W.A. Albert (cnd)

Suder, J.:Festival Mass, w. Natalia Kornewa (sop), Maria Neilau (alt), Vladimir Mostomoi (ten), Juri Dobrowolski (bass), Jessica Hartlieb (vn), Marlene Hinterberger (org), St. Petersburg Chamber Choir Calig ▲ CAL 50945 [DDD]

Bavarian State Youth Plucked Instrument Orch

G. Vogt (cnd)

Baumann, H.:Con Capriccioso, w. G. Tröster-Weyhofen (mand) Thorofon ▲ CTH 2146 [DDD]

Behrend, S.:Serenade Mand, w. G. Tröster-Weyhofen (mand) Thorofon ▲ CTH 2146 [DDD]

Starck, A.:Con Mand, w. G. Tröster-Weyhofen (mand) Thorofon ▲ CTH 2146 [DDD]

Tober-Vogt, E.:Carnival of Venice, w. G. Tröster-Weyhofen (mand) Thorofon ▲ CTH 2146 [DDD]

Vivaldi, A.:Con Mand, RV.425, w. G. Tröster-Weyhofen (mand) Thorofon ▲ CTH 2146 [DDD]

Bavarian SO

C. Davis (cnd)

Wagner, R.:Lohengrin, w. Sharon Sweet (sop—Elsa), Eva Marton (sop—Ortrud), Ben Heppner (ten—Lohengrin), Anton Rosner (ten—Nobleman), Heinrich Weber (ten—Nobleman), Jan-Hendrik Rootering (bar—Heinrich der Vögler), Sergei Leiferkus (bar—Friedrich von Telramund), Bryn Terfel (b-bar—King's Herald), Barbara Fleckenstein (sgr—Page), Atsuko Suzuki (sgr—Page), Gisela Ulmann (sgr—Page), Marion Rambausek (sgr—Page), Dankwart Siegele (sgr—Nobleman), Jürgen Weiss (sgr—Nobleman), Bavarian State Opera Chorus, Bavarian Radio Chorus *(rec Residenz Herkulesaal, Munich, May 14–28, 1994)* RCA Red Seal 3-▲ 09026-62646-2 [DDD]

J. Keilberth (cnd)

Janácek, L.:The Excursions of Mr. Brouček, w. Antonie Fahberg (sop—Piccolo), Wilma Lipp (sop—Málinka), Lilian Benningsen (cta—Fanny Nowak), Paul Kuen (ten—Trambahn-Kondukteur), Karl Ostertag (ten—Vorsitzender des Hausbesitzerverbandes), Fritz Wunderlich (ten—Mazal), Kurt Böhme (b-bar—Sakristan von St. Veit), Kieth Engen (bass—Würfl) *(rec live, Prinzregententheater, Nov. 19, 1959)* Orfeo 2-▲ 354942 (m)

C. Michalski (cnd)

Lehár, F.:Der Zarewitsch (sels), w. Christine Gorner (sop), Melita Muszely (sop), Fritz Wunderlich (ten), Willy Hagara (bar) Emperor Operetta ▲ KO 86341

G. Solti (cnd)

Strauss, R.:Eine Alpensinfonie *(rec 1986)* Originals ▲ ORISH 805 [DDD]

Bayer RSO

B. Haitink (cnd)

Wagner, R.:Der Ring des Nibelungen (sels), w. E. Marton (sop), C. Studer (sop), K. Te Kanawa (sop), M. Lipovšek (mez), S. Jerusalem (ten), R. Goldberg (ten), P. Haage (ten), J. Morris (bass) EMI Classics ▲ ZDC 54633

Baynov Piano Ensemble

Czerny, C.:Qt for 4 Pnos, Op. 816 Ars Produktion ▲ ARS 368331 [DDD]

Czerny, C.:Qt for 4 Pnos, Op. 230 Ars Produktion ▲ ARS 368331 [DDD]

Bayreuth Festival Horns

Es blies ein Jäger wohl in sein Horn Acanta ▲ 43469

Fantasies for 8 Horns Acanta ▲ 43800

Bayreuth Festival Orch

Wagner, R.:Die Meistersinger von Nürnberg, w. Maria Müller (sop), Max Lorenz (ten), Jaro Prohaska (bar), Josef Greindl (bass), Bayreuth Festival Chorus *(rec live, July–Aug 1943)* Grammofono 2000 4-▲ GRM 78602

Wagner, R.:Ovs, Preludes & Orch Sels, w. Berlin PO, Vienna PO, Bavarian RSO, Berlin Opera Orch, Karajan, Kubelik, Böhm, Jochum (cnds)—sels. from Rienzi, Die fliegende Holländer, Tannhäuser, Lohengrin, Parsifal, Die Meistersinger von Nürnberg, Die Walküre, Siegfried, Götterdämmerung *(rec 1958 & 1981)* Deutsche Grammophon ("Double" series) 2-▲ 439687-2 [ADD]

H. Abendroth (cnd)

Wagner, R.:Die Meistersinger von Nürnberg, w. H. Scheppan (sop), L. Suthaus (ten), E. Kunz (bar), P. Schöffler (b-bar), Bayreuth Festival Chorus *(rec 1943)* Preiser ▲ PRE 90174 [AAD]

D. Barenboim (cnd)

Wagner, R.:Das Rheingold, w. L. Finnie (mez—Fricka), G. Clark (ten—Loge), J. Tomlinson (bar—Wotan), B. Brinkmann (bar—Donner), Bayreuth Festival Chorus [G] Teldec 2-▲ 4509-91185-2

K. Böhm (cnd)

Beethoven, L. van:Sym 9, "Choral Sym", w. Bayreuth Festival Chorus Melodram ▲ CDM 18005

Wagner, R.:Der Ring des Nibelungen, w. B. Nilsson (sop), L. Rysanek (sop), K. Dvořaková (sop), M. Mödl (sop), A. Burmeister (mez), V. Soukupova (mez), E. Wohlfahrt (ten), W. Windgassen (ten), T. Stewart (bar), T. Adam (b-bar), G. Neidlinger (b-bar), K. Böhme (bass), G. Nienstedt (bass), Bayreuth Festival Chorus [G] *(rec live, 1966–67)* Philips 14-▲ 420325-2 [ADD]

Wagner, R.:Der Ring des Nibelungen (sels), w. Birgit Nilsson (sop—Brünnhilde), Leonie Rysanek (sop—Sieglinde), James King (ten—Siegmund), Wolfgang Windgassen (ten), Theo Adam (b-bar—Wotan), Gustav Neidlinger (b-bar), Josef Greindl (bass) *(rec Bayreuth, 1967)* Philips 2-▲ 454020-2

Wagner, R.:Siegfried, w. B. Nilsson (sop), W. Windgassen (ten), E. Wohlfahrt (ten), T. Adam (b-bar), G. Neidlinger (b-bar), Bayreuth Festival Chorus [G] Philips 4-▲ 412483-2 [ADD]

Wagner, R.:Tristan und Isolde, w. B. Nilsson (sop), C. Ludwig (mez), W. Windgassen (ten), E. Wächter (bar), M. Talvela (bass), Bayreuth Festival Chorus [G] *(rec Bayreuth Festival, 1966)* Deutsche Grammophon 3-▲ 419889-2 [ADD]

Wagner, R.:Tristan und Isolde, w. B. Nilsson (sop), C. Ludwig (mez), W. Windgassen (ten), E. Wächter (bar), M. Talvela (bass), Bayreuth Festival Chorus [G] Philips 3-▲ 434425-2 [ADD]

Wagner, R.:Die Walküre (act 1), w. Leonie Rysanek (sop), James King (ten), Gerd Nienstedt (bass) *(rec live, Bayreuth Festival)* Philips ("Solo" series) ▲ 442640-2

P. Boulez (cnd)

Wagner, R.:Götterdämmerung, w. G. Jones (sop), H. Jung (mez), F. Mazura (bar), H. Becht (bar), Bayreuth Festival Chorus [G] Philips 4-▲ 434424-2 [DDD]

Wagner, R.:Parcifal, w. G. Jones (sop), J. King (ten), T. Stewart (bar), D. McIntyre (b-bar), K. Ridderbusch (bass), F. Crass (bass), Bayreuth Festival Chorus [G] *(rec 1970)* Deutsche Grammophon 3-▲ 435718-2 [ADD]

Wagner, R.:Das Rheingold, w. H. Schwarz (mez), H. Zednik (ten), H. Becht (bar), D. McIntyre (b-bar), Bayreuth Festival Chorus [G] Philips 2-▲ 434421-2 [DDD]

Wagner, R.:Der Ring des Nibelungen, w. G. Jones (sop), H. Schwarz (mez), T. Altmeyer (ten), L. Hofmann (bass), D. McIntyre (b-bar), Bayreuth Festival Chorus Philips 32-▲ 434420-2 [ADD/DDD]

Wagner, R.:Siegfried, w. G. Jones (sop), H. Zednik (ten), H. Becht (bar), D. McIntyre (b-bar), Bayreuth Festival Chorus [G] Philips 3-▲ 434423-2 [DDD]

A. Cluytens (cnd)

Wagner, R.:Lohengrin, w. L. Rysanek (sop), A. Varnay (sop), S. Kónya (ten), E. Blanc (bar), Bayreuth Festival Chorus [G] *(rec live, 7/23/58)* Myto 3-▲ MCD 89002 (m) [ADD]

Wagner, R.:Die Meistersinger von Nürnberg (sels), w. W. Windgassen (ten), H. Hotter (b-bar), Bayreuth Festival Chorus—Monologue & Duet from Act 3 [G] *(rec live, 1957)* Arkadia 4-▲ 440 (m) [AAD]

K. Elmendorff (cnd)

Wagner, R.:Götterdämmerung, w. M. Fuchs (sop), H. Scheppan (sop), S. Svanholm (ten), R. Burg (bar), F. Dalberg (bass), Bayreuth Festival Chorus *(rec July 21, 1942)* Preiser 4-▲ PRE 90164 [AAD]

W. Furtwängler (cnd)

Beethoven, L. van:Syms (comp), w. E. Schwarzkopf (sop), E. Höngen (mez), H. Hopf (ten), O. Edelmann (bass), Vienna PO, Bayreuth Festival Chorus *(rec 1948–54)* EMI Classics 5-▲ CDHE 63606

Beethoven, L. van:Sym 9, "Choral Sym", w. Bayreuth Festival Chorus EMI Classics ▲ CDH 69801

Wagner, R.:Lohengrin (sels), w. Maria Müller (sop), Margarete Klose (mez), Franz Völker (ten), Joseph von Manowarda (bass), Bayreuth Festival Chorus—Prelude to Act III; Operatic sels. *(rec 1931)* Grammofono 2000 ▲ GRM 78515 [ADD]

E. Jochum (cnd)

Wagner, R.:Lohengrin, w. B. Nilsson (sop), A. Varnay (sop), W. Windgassen (ten), H. Uhde (bar), Bayreuth Festival Chorus *(rec live, Bayreuth 1954)* Melodram 3-▲ MEL 36104

H. von Karajan (cnd)

Wagner, R.:Die Meistersinger von Nürnberg, w. E. Schwarzkopf (sop), E. Kunz (ten), O. Edelmann (b-bar), Bayreuth Festival Chorus *(rec 1951)* Arkadia 4-▲ 224

Wagner, R.:Die Meistersinger von Nürnberg, w. E. Schwarzkopf (sop), I. Malaniuk (cta), H. Hopf (ten), G. Unger (ten), E. Kunz (bar), O. Edelmann (b-bar), F. Dalberg (bass), Bayreuth Festival Chorus [G] *(rec 1951)* EMI Classics ("Great Recordings of the Century" series) 4-▲ CDHD 63500 (m) [ADD]

Wagner, R.:Das Rheingold, w. P. Brivkalne (sop), I. Malaniuk (cta), R. Siewert (cta), Fritz (sgr), Pflanzl (ten), S. Björling (bar), W. Faulhaber (bass), L. Weber (bass), F. Dalberg (bass), Bayreuth Festival Chorus [G] *(rec live 8/1/51)* Melodram 2-▲ MEL 26107 (m) [AAD]

Wagner, R.:Das Rheingold, w. E. Schwarzkopf (sop), I. Malaniuk (cta), W. Windgassen (ten), S. Björling (bar), Pflanzl (sgr), Bayreuth Festival Chorus [G] *(rec live, 1951)* Arkadia 2-▲ 216 (m) [ADD]

Wagner, R.:Siegfried, w. A. Varnay (sop), R. Siewert (cta), B. Aldenhoff (ten), P. Kuen (ten), S. Björling (bar), H. Pflanzl (bass), F. Dalberg (bass), Bayreuth Festival Chorus [G] *(rec live 1951)* Melodram 4-▲ MEL 46106 (m) [AAD]

Bayreuth Festival Orch (cont.)
H. von Karajan (cnd) (cont.)
Wagner, R.:Tristan und Isolde, w. M. Mödl (sop), R. Vinay (ten), H. Hotter (b-bar), Bayreuth Festival Chorus *(rec 1955)* Arkadia 4-▲ 528 (m) [AAD]
Wagner, R.:Die Walküre (act 3), w. A. Varnay (sop—Brünnhilde), L. Rysanek (sop—Sieglinde), S. Björling (bar—Wotan) *(rec Aug. 12, 1951)* EMI Classics ▲ ZDH 64704
J. Keilberth (cnd)
Wagner, R.:Der fliegende Holländer, w. A. Varnay (sop), J. Traxel (ten), G. London (bar), A. van Mill (bass), Bayreuth Festival Chorus [G] *(rec live, Bayreuth, 7/25/56)* Myto 2-▲ 2 MCD 93175
Wagner, R.:Lohengrin, w. E. Steber (sop), A. Varnay (sop), W. Windgassen (ten), H. Uhde (bar), J. Greindl (bass), Bayreuth Festival Chorus *(rec live, Bayreuth Festival, 1953)* Teldec ("Historic" series) 4-▲ 93674
Wagner, R.:Tannhäuser, w. G. Brouwenstijn (sop), R. Vinay (ten), D. Fischer-Dieskau (bar), J. Greindl (bass), Bayreuth Festival Chorus *(rec live, Bayreuth, 1954)* Melodram 3-▲ MEL 36105
C. Kleiber (cnd)
Wagner, R.:Tristan und Isolde, w. C. Ligendza (sop—Isolde), Y. Minton (mez—Brangäne), H. Brilioth (ten—Tristan), K. Moll (bass—King Mark), Bayreuth Festival Chorus *(rec Bayreuth Festival, 1975)* Exclusive 3-▲ EXL 54 [ADD]
H. Knappertsbusch (cnd)
Wagner, R.:Der fliegende Holländer, w. A. Varnay (sop), W. Windgassen (ten), H. Uhde (bar), L. Weber (bass), Bayreuth Festival Chorus [G] *(rec live)* Arkadia 2-▲ 421 [ADD]
Wagner, R.:Götterdämmerung (sels), w. A. Varnay (sop), E. Grümmer (sop), B. Aldenhoff (ten), H. Uhde (bar), G. Frick (bass), J. Greindl (bass), Bavarian State Opera Orch, Bavarian State Opera Chorus, Bayreuth Festival Chorus [G] *(rec live 1955 & 1957)* Melodram 4-▲ MEL 46106 (m) [AAD]
Wagner, R.:Die Meistersinger von Nürnberg, w. L. Della Casa (sop), I. Malaniuk (cta), H. Hopf (ten), O. Edelmann (b-bar), K. Böhme (bass), Bayreuth Festival Chorus [G] *(rec live, 1952)* Arkadia 4-▲ 440 (m) [AAD]
Wagner, R.:Die Meistersinger von Nürnberg, w. E. Grümmer (sop), W. Windgassen (ten), T. Adam (b-bar), J. Greindl (bass), Bayreuth Festival Chorus [G] *(rec live, Bayreuth, 1960)* Melodram 4-▲ MEL 46103
Wagner, R.:Parsifal, w. I. Dalis (mez), J. Thomas (ten), G. London (bar), H. Hotter (b-bar), G. Neidlinger (b-bar), Bayreuth Festival Chorus [1962] [G] Philips 4-▲ 416390-2 [ADD]
Wagner, R.:Das Rheingold, w. E. Grümmer (sop), R. Gorr (mez), A. Andersson (ten), S. Konya (ten), T. Adam (b-bar), H. Hotter (b-bar), J. Greindl (bass), Bayreuth Festival Chorus [G] *(rec live 1958)* Arkadia 2-▲ 441 [AAD]
Wagner, R.:Der Ring des Nibelungen, w. Gré Brouwenstein (sop—Freia/Sieglinde), Ilse Hollweg (sop—Waldvogel), Gerda Lammers (sop—Ortlinde), Paula Lenchner (sop—Wellgunde/Gerhilde), Hilde Scheppan (sop—Helmwige), Astrid Varnay (sop—Brünnilde/3rd Norn), Lore Wissmann (sop—Woglinde), Maria von Ilosvay (mez—Flosshilde/Schwertleite/2nd Norn), Louise Charlotte Kamps (mez—Siegrune), Jean Madeira (mez—Erda/Rossweisse/1st Norn), Georgine van Milinkovic (mez—Fricka/Grimgerde), Elisabeth Schärtel (mez—Waltraute), Paul Kuën (ten—Mime), Ludwig Suthaus (ten—Loge), Josef Traxel (ten—Froh), Wolfgang Windgassen (ten—Siegmund/Siegfried), Alfons Herwig (bar—Donner), Hermann Uhde (bar—Gunther), Hans Hotter (b-bar—Wotan), Gustav Neidlinger (b-bar—Alberich), Josef Griendl (bass—Fasolt/Hunding/Hagen), Arnold van Mill (bass—Fafner), Bayreuth Festival Chorus *(rec live, Bayreuth, Aug 13-17, 1956)* Golden Melodram 14-▲ GM 1.001 [ADD]
Wagner, R.:Siegfried, w. A. Varnay (sop), W. Windgassen (ten), A. Andersson (ten), G. Stoltze (ten), H. Hotter (b-bar), J. Greindl (bass), Bayreuth Festival Chorus [G] *(rec live 1958)* Arkadia 4-▲ 443 [AAD]
Wagner, R.:Siegfried (sels), w. A. Varnay (sop), B. Aldenhoff (ten), Bayreuth Festival Chorus—Act 3 Scene 3 [G] *(rec live 1957)* Arkadia 4-▲ 443 [AAD]
R. König (cnd)
Wagner, R.:Siegfried Idyll Platz ▲ PLZ 629
R. Kraus (cnd)
Wagner, R.:Der fliegende Holländer, w. Maria Müller (sop), Joel Berglund (ten), Franz Völker (ten), Ludwig Hoffmann (bass), Bayreuth Festival Chorus *(rec live, Bayreuth, July 18, 1942)* Preiser 2-▲ PRE 90232 [ADD]
C. Krauss (cnd)
Wagner, R.:Parsifal (prelude) *(rec live, 1953)* Originals ▲ ORISH 825 [ADD]
J. Levine (cnd)
Wagner, R.:Parsifal, w. W. Meier (mez), P. Hofmann (ten), F. Mazura (bar), S. Estes (bass), H. Sotin (bass), M. Salminen (bass), Bayreuth Festival Chorus [1985] [G] Philips 4-▲ 434616-2 [DDD]
K. Muck (cnd)
Wagner, R.:Parsifal (sels), w. Bayreuth Festival Chorus—Festival of 1927, Act 1 & "Flower Maidens" scene from Act 2; Pistor, Brongeest, Hofmann, Berlin State Opera Orch. & Cho. (Act 3—1928) Opal ▲ CDS 9843 (m) [AAD]
Muck, Wagner (cnd)
Wagner, R.:Parsifal (sels), w. Fritz Wolff (ten), Alexander Kipnis (bass), Bayreuth Festival Chorus [1927]—Transformation Scene, Grail Scene, Flower Maidens Scene, Prelude to Act 3, Good Friday Music InSync ■ C 4137 (m)
W. Nelsson (cnd)
Wagner, R.:Der fliegende Holländer, w. L. Balsev (sop), R. Schunk (ten), S. Estes (bass), M. Salminen (bass), Bayreuth Festival Chorus [G] Philips 2-▲ 434599-2 [DDD]
Wagner, R.:Lohengrin, w. E. Connell (sop), N. Armstrong (sop), P. Hofmann (ten), L. Roar (bass), B. Weikl (bass), S. Vogel (bass), Bayreuth Festival Chorus CBS 3-▲ M3K 38594
W. Pitz (cnd)
Wagner, R.:Choruses, w. E. Schärtel (mez), J. Greindl (bass), Bayreuth Festival Chorus—choruses from Lohengrin, Götterdämmerung, Parsifal, Fliegende Holländer, Tannhäuser, Meistersinger Deutsche Grammophon ("Resonance" series) ▲ 429169-2 [ADD]
W. Sawallisch (cnd)
Wagner, R.:Der fliegende Holländer, w. L. Rysanek (sop), G. London (bar), J. Greindl (bass), Bayreuth Festival Chorus [G] *(rec live, Bayreuth 1959)* Melodram 2-▲ MEL 26101
Wagner, R.:Tannhäuser, w. A. Silja (sop), G. Bumbry (mez), W. Windgassen (ten), E. Wächter (bar), J. Greindl (bass), Bayreuth Festival Chorus [Dresden version with Paris Venusberg music] [G] Philips 3-▲ 434607-2 [ADD]
Wagner, R.:Tannhäuser, w. V. de Los Angeles (sop), G. Bumbry (mez), W. Windgassen (ten), G. Stolze (ten), D. Fischer-Dieskau (bar), T. Adam (b-bar), J. Greindl (bass), F. Crass (bass), Bayreuth Festival Chorus [G] *(rec 1961)* Myto 3-▲ MCD 93277
P. Schneider (cnd)
Wagner, R.:Lohengrin, w. C. Studer (sop), P. Frey (ten), M. Schenk (bass), Bayreuth Festival Chorus [G] Philips 4-▲ 434602-2 [DDD]
Wagner, R.:Lohengrin, w. C. Studer (sop), P. Frey (ten), M. Schenk (bass), Bayreuth Festival Chorus Philips 32-▲ 434420-2 [ADD/DDD]
Wagner, R.:Lohengrin (sels), w. C. Studer (sop), G. Schnaut (sop), P. Frey (ten), M. Schenk (bass), Bayreuth Festival Chorus Philips ▲ 438500-2
H. Tietjen, R. Strauss (cnd)
Max Lorenz:Recital, 1933-1957, w. Max Lorenz (ten), Maria Reining (sop), Berlin RSO [cnd:Artur Rother], German Large RSO [cnd:Rudolf Moralt, Max Schönherr, Anton Paulik], Hessen RSO [cnd:Kurt Schröder], Brenda Lewis (sop), Eberhard Wächter (ten), Wolfgang Zimmer (bar) *(rec 1933-57)* Myto ▲ MCD 934.88
S. Varviso (cnd)
Wagner, R.:Die Meistersinger von Nürnberg, w. Hannelore Bode (sop), Jean Cox (ten), Klaus Hirte (bar), Karl Ridderbusch (bass), Hans Sotin (bass), Bayreuth Festival Chorus [1974] Philips 32-▲ 434420-2 [ADD/DDD]
Wagner, R.:Die Meistersinger von Nürnberg, w. Hannelore Bode (sop), Jean Cox (ten), Klaus Hirte (bar), Karl Ridderbusch (bass), Hans Sotin (bass), Bayreuth Festival Chorus [1974] [G] Philips 4-▲ 434611-2 [ADD]
Bayreuth Festival Orch members
R. König (cnd)
Mozart, W.A.:Con 5 Vn, w. Elisabeth Glass (vn) Platz ▲ PLZ 629

Bayreuth Festival Orch members (cont.)
R. König (cnd) (cont.)
Schubert, Franz:Sym 5 Platz ▲ PLZ 629
BBC Concert Orch
K. Alwyn (cnd)
Addinsell, R.:Music of, w. Philip Martin (pno), Roderick Elms (pno)—Theme from Goodbye Mr. Chips; Invitation Waltz [from Ring Round the Moon]; The Smokey Mountains (con.); The Isle of Apples; The Prince & the Showgirl (sel.); Tom Brown's Schooldays [Ov.]; Festival; Journey to Romance; Fire Over England (suite); Theme from A Tale of Two Cities *(rec Golders Green Hippodrome, London, Apr. 20 & 21, 1994)* Marco Polo ("British Light Music" series) ▲ 8.223732 [DDD]
P. Bateman (cnd)
Soprano in Hollywood, w. Lesley Garrett (sop) Silva Classics ▲ SIL CD 6013
A. Fiedler (cnd)
Khachaturian, A.:Gayane (sels)—Dances IMP ("BBC Radio Classics" series) ▲ IMP 5691652
Liszt, F.:Con 1 Pno, w. Moura Lympany (pno) IMP ("BBC Radio Classics" series) ▲ IMP 5691652
Litolff, H.C.:Con Symphonique 4 (Scherzo)—Scherzo IMP ("BBC Radio Classics" series) ▲ IMP 5691652
Offenbach, J.:Gaîté Parisienne—3 Dances IMP ("BBC Radio Classics" series) ▲ IMP 5691652
Tchaikovsky, P.:Eugene Onegin (sels)—Polonaise IMP ("BBC Radio Classics" series) ▲ IMP 5691652
Tchaikovsky, P.:Marche slave IMP ("BBC Radio Classics" series) ▲ IMP 5691652
S. Joly (cnd)
Fauré, G.:Pavane Orch, w. BBC Singers IMP ("BBC Radio" series) ▲ IMP 5691482
A. Lawrence (cnd)
Bridge, F.:Summer IMP ("BBC Radio Classics" series) ▲ IMP 5691752
Delius, F.:Brigg Fair:An English Rhapsody IMP ("BBC Radio Classics" series) ▲ IMP 9128
Delius, F.:Dance Rhap 2 IMP ("BBC Radio Classics" series) ▲ IMP 9128
Delius, F.:In a Summer Garden IMP ("BBC Radio Classics" series) ▲ IMP 9128
Delius, F.:Irmelin (prelude) IMP ("BBC Radio Classics" series) ▲ IMP 9128
Delius, F.:Norwegian Suite IMP ("BBC Radio Classics" series) ▲ IMP 9128
J. Matheson (cnd)
Verdi, G.:La forza del destino, w. Martina Arroyo (sop—Donna Leonora), Janet Coster (mez—Preziosilla), Kenneth Bowen (ten—Trabuco), Kenneth Collins (ten—Don Alvaro), Peter Glossop (bar—Don Carlo), Roderick Kennedy (bass—Marquis), BBC Concert Chorus *(rec live, early 1980's)* Exclusive 2-▲ EXL 80 [ADD]
M. Rossi (cnd)
Verdi, G.:I vespri siciliani, w. J. Brumaire (sop), P. Bowden (mez), Bonhomme (sgr), Taylor (sgr), Baran (sgr), BBC Concert Chorus [original French version] *(rec live, London, 5/10/69)* Arkadia 3-▲ 456 [ADD]
B. Wordsworth (cnd)
Bennett, Richard Rodney:Con for Stan Getz, w. John Harle (sax) *(rec BBC Hippodrome, Golders Green, London, Mar. 11, 1993)* Argo ▲ 443529-2
Showcase:The Classics, w. Lucy Parham (pno) IMP ("Classics" series) ▲ IMP 6700662
Torch, S.:Music of—London Transport Suite [w. Mark Knowles (tuba)]; All Strings & Fancy Free [w. Martin Loveday (vn)]; Barbecue; Trapeze Waltz; Con Incognito [w. Philip Martin (pno)]; On a Spring Note; Bicycle Belles; Comic Cuts; Mexican Fiesta; Petite Valse [w. Roderick Elms (pno)]; Samba Sud; Shortcake Walk [w. Martin Loveday (vn)]; Slavonic Rhap [w. Philip Martin (pno), Clair Hiles (pno)]; Cresta run [w. Alasdair Malloy (xyl)]; Shooting Star; Going for a Ride; Duel for Drummers [w. Alasdair Malloy (perc), Stephen Webberly (perc)] *(rec Golden Green Hippodrome, London, 1992)* Marco Polo ▲ 8.223443 [DDD]
BBC Northern SO
M. Davies (cnd)
Mozart, W.A.:Missa, K.317, w. Janet Price (sop), Kevin Smith (ct), Anthony Rolfe-Johnson (ten), Graham Titus (bass), Leeds Phil Chorus IMP ("BBC Radio Classics" series) ▲ IMP 5691552
M. Handford (cnd)
Bantock, G.:Pagan Sym *(rec live, 1968)* Intaglio ▲ INCD 704-1 [ADD]
V. Handley (cnd)
Vaughan Williams, R.:Job IMP ("BBC Radio Classics" series) ▲ IMP 5691662
Vaughan Williams, R.:The Pilgrim's Progress, w. Delyth Jones (sop), Elsa Kendal (cta), Charles Groves (ten), Robin Leggate (ten), BBC Northern Singers IMP ("BBC Radio Classics" series) ▲ IMP 5691662
J. Horenstein (cnd)
Liszt, F.:A Faust Sym, w. J. Mitchinson (ten), BBC Northern Singers *(rec live Apr. 1972)* Music & Arts ▲ CD 744 [AAD]
Liszt, F.:A Faust Sym, w. J. Mitchinson (ten), BBC Northern Singers *(rec live)* Intaglio ▲ INCD 7141 [ADD]
Mahler, G.:Das Lied von der Erde, w. A. Hodgson (cta), J. Mitchinson (ten) *(rec live, Manchester, April 28, 1972)* Music & Arts ▲ CD 728-1 [AAD]
Nielsen, C.:Sym 3, w. A. Browning (sop), C. Wheatley (sgr) Intaglio ▲ ING 738 [ADD]
Schoenberg, A.:Chamber Sym 1 *(rec live, Sheffield 1970)* Intaglio ▲ INCD 7331 [ADD]
Sibelius, J.:Sym 5 *(rec live, Sheffield, 1970)* Intaglio ▲ INCD 7331 [ADD]
Wagner, R.:Eine Faust-Ov Intaglio ▲ INCD 7231 [ADD]
Wagner, R.:Eine Faust-Ov *(rec Apr. 1972)* Music & Arts ▲ CD 781 [ADD]
R. Leppard (cnd)
Debussy, C.:Images Orch IMP ("BBC Radio Classics" series) ▲ IMP 9136
Fauré, G.:Ballade Pno, w. Malcolm Binns (pno) IMP ("BBC Radio Classics" series) ▲ IMP 9136
Roussel, A.:Sym 3 IMP ("BBC Radio Classics" series) ▲ IMP 9136
BBC Phil Brass
G. Lloyd (cnd)
Lloyd, G.:Sym 10 Albany ▲ AR 015-2 [DDD] ■ AR 015-4 (D)
BBC PO
Davies, P.M.:Resurrection Collins Classics ▲ COL 7034 [DDD]
M. Bamert (cnd)
Dohnányi, E. von:Symphonic Minutes Chandos ▲ CHAN 9455
Dohnányi, E. von:Sym 2 Chandos ▲ CHAN 9455
Korngold, E.W.:Sinfonietta Chandos ▲ CHAN 9317 [DDD]
Korngold, E.W.:Sursum corda Chandos ▲ CHAN 9317 [DDD]
Mussorgsky, M.:Boris Godunov (sels)—Symphonic Synthesis [orchd Leopold Stokowski] *(rec New Broadcasting House, Manchester, England, June 28 & 29, 1995)* Chandos ▲ CHAN 9445
Mussorgsky, M.:Khovanshchina (orch sels)—Entr'acte to Act IV [orchd Leopold Stokowski] *(rec New Broadcasting House, Manchester, England, June 28 & 29, 1995)* Chandos ▲ CHAN 9445
Mussorgsky, M.:Night—Allegro [orchd Leopold Stokowski] *(rec New Broadcasting House, Manchester, England, June 28 & 29, 1995)* Chandos ▲ CHAN 9445
Mussorgsky, M.:Pictures at an Exhibition [orchd Leopold Stokowski] *(rec New Broadcasting House, Manchester, England, June 28 & 29, 1995)* Chandos ▲ CHAN 9445
Stokowski, L.:Transcriptions Orch—Bach—Toccata & Fugue in d; Air on the G String; Little Fugue in g; Sheep may safely graze; Prelude in b; Passacaglia & Fugue in c; Komm süsser Tod; Wir glauben all'an Einen Gott; Siciliano; Mein Jesu Chandos ▲ CHAN 9259 [DDD]
M. Bauert (cnd)
Stokowski Encores Chandos ▲ CHAN 9349 [DDD]
H. Christophers (cnd)
Ives, C.:The Unanswered Question Collins Classics ▲ COL 1446 [DDD]
Poulenc, F.:Répons des ténèbres, w. The Sixteen Collins Classics ▲ COL 1446 [DDD]
Stravinsky, I.:Sym of Psalms Collins Classics ▲ COL 1446 [DDD]
Tippett, M.:A Child Of Our Time, w. The Sixteen Collins Classics ▲ COL 1446 [DDD]
P. M. Davies (cnd)
Davies, P.M.:Caroline Mathilde (concert suite) *(rec 7/91)* Collins Classics ▲ 13082 [DDD]
Davies, P.M.:The Lighthouse, w. Neil Mackie (ten), Ian Comboy (bass), Christopher Keyte (bass) Collins Classics ▲ COL 1415 [DDD]
Davies, P.M.:Ojai Festival Ov *(rec 7/91)* Collins Classics ▲ 13082 [DDD]
Davies, P.M.:St. Thomas Wake *(rec 7/91)* Collins Classics ▲ 13082 [DDD]
Davies, P.M.:Sir Charles His Pavan Collins Classics ▲ 13902 [DDD]

BBC PO (cont.)
P. M. Davies (cnd) (cont.)
Davies, P.M.:Sym 1 Collins Classics ▲ COL 1435
Davies, P.M.:Sym 2 Collins Classics ▲ COL 1403 [DDD]
Davies, P.M.:Sym 3 Collins Classics ▲ COL 1416
Davies, P.M.:Threnody on a Plainsong for Michael Vyner *(rec 7/91)* Collins Classics ▲ 13082 [DDD]
Davies, P.M.:The Turn of the Tide, w. Manchester Cathedral Girl's Choir, Manchester Cathedral Boys' Choir, Manchester Cathedral Voluntary Boys' Choir, Manchester Grammar School Choir Collins Classics ▲ 13902 [DDD]
E. Downes (cnd)
Bantock, G.:Pagan Sym IMP ("BBC Radio Classics" series) ▲ IMP 5691592
Bax, A.:Northern Ballad 2 IMP ("BBC Radio Classics" series) ▲ IMP 5691592
Bax, A.:Northern Ballad 3, "Prelude to a Solemn Occasion" IMP ("BBC Radio Classics" series) ▲ IMP 5691592
Bax, A.:Tintagel IMP ("BBC Radio Classics" series) ▲ IMP 5691592
Berlioz, H.:Le Corsaire IMP ▲ IMP 2045
Borodin, A.:Prince Igor (ov) IMP ▲ IMP 2045
Brahms, J.:Academic Festival Ov IMP ▲ IMP 2045
Britten, B.:Our Hunting Fathers, w. Heather Harper (sop) IMP ("BBC Radio Classics" series) ▲ IMP 5691582
Elgar, E.:Sym 2 *(rec Mar. 1993)* Naxos ▲ 8.550635 [DDD]
Glière, R.:The Bronze Horseman Chandos ▲ CHAN 9379 [DDD]
Glière, R.:Con Hn, w. Richard Watkins (hn) Chandos ▲ CHAN 9379 [DDD]
Glière, R.:The Red Poppy Chandos ▲ CHAN 9160 [DDD]
Glière, R.:Sym 1 Chandos ▲ CHAN 9160 [DDD]
Glière, R.:Sym 2 Chandos ▲ CHAN 9071 [DDD]
Glière, R.:Sym 3, "Il'ya Muromets" Chandos ▲ CHAN 9041 [DDD]
Glière, R.:The Zaporozhy Cossacks Chandos ▲ CHAN 9071 [DDD]
Korngold, E.W.:Abschiedslieder, w. L. Finnie (cta) Chandos ▲ CHAN 9171 [DDD]
Korngold, E.W.:Sym in F# Chandos ▲ CHAN 9171 [DDD]
Mendelssohn, F.:Die schöne Melusina IMP ▲ IMP 2045
Miaskovsky, N.:Sym 5 *(rec Sept. 19, 1992)* Marco Polo ▲ 8.223499 [DDD]
Miaskovsky, N.:Sym 9 *(rec Dec. 1, 1992)* Marco Polo ▲ 8.223499 [DDD]
Respighi, O.:Ballad of the Gnomes, w. L. Mordkovich (vn) Chandos ▲ CHAN 9232 [DDD]
Respighi, O.:Belfagor Ov Chandos ▲ CHAN 9311 [DDD]
Respighi, O.:Con gregoriano, w. L. Mordkovich (vn) Chandos ▲ CHAN 9232 [DDD]
Respighi, O.:Con in modo misolidio, w. G. Tozer (pno) *(rec Jan. 7 & 8, 1994)* Chandos ▲ CHAN 9285 [DDD]
Respighi, O.:Con Pno, w. G. Tozer (pno) *(rec Jan. 7 & 8, 1994)* Chandos ▲ CHAN 9285 [DDD]
Respighi, O.:Corali Chandos ▲ CHAN 9311 [DDD]
Respighi, O.:Poema autunnale, w. L. Mordkovich (vn) Chandos ▲ CHAN 9232 [DDD]
Respighi, O.:Sinf drammatica Chandos ▲ CHAN 9213 [DDD]
Respighi, O.:Toccata Pno, w. G. Tozer (pno) Chandos ▲ CHAN 9311 [DDD]
Stevens, B.:Con Vc, w. A. Baillie (vc) Meridian ▲ CDE 84124
Stevens, B.:Con Vn, w. E. Kovacic (vn) Meridian ▲ CDE 84174
Stevens, B.:Sym 2 Meridian ▲ CDE 84174
Stevens, B.:Sym of Liberation Meridian ▲ CDE 84124
Suppé, F. von:Ovs—Light Cavalry IMP ("Concert Classics" series) ▲ IMP PCD 1101
Suppé, F. von:Ovs—Light Cavalry IMP ▲ IMP 2045
Wagner, R.:Die Meistersinger von Nürnberg (ov) IMP ▲ IMP 2045
S. Fujioka (cnd)
Yoshimatsu, T.:Con Gtr, "Pegasus Effect", w. Craig Ogden (gtr) Chandos ▲ CHAN 9438
Yoshimatsu, T.:Sym 2 Chandos ▲ CHAN 9438
Yoshimatsu, T.:Threnody to Toki Chandos ▲ CHAN 9438
F. Glushchenko (cnd)
Ippolitov-Ivanov, M.:Caucasian Sketches, Op. 10 Chandos ▲ CHAN 9321 [DDD]
Khachaturian, A.:Sym 3 Chandos ▲ CHAN 9321 [DDD]
Khachaturian, A.:Triumphal Poem Chandos ▲ CHAN 9321 [DDD]
S. Gunzenhauser (cnd)
Dvořák, A.:Carnival *(rec Mar. 23–24, 1992)* Naxos ▲ 8.550600 [DDD]
Dvořák, A.:In Nature's Realm *(rec Mar. 23–24, 1992)* Naxos ▲ 8.550600 [DDD]
Dvořák, A.:My Home *(rec Mar. 23–24, 1992)* Naxos ▲ 8.550600 [DDD]
Dvořák, A.:Othello *(rec Mar. 23–24, 1992)* Naxos ▲ 8.550600 [DDD]
Dvořák, A.:Vanda (ov) *(rec Mar. 23–24, 1992)* Naxos ▲ 8.550600 [DDD]
V. Handley (cnd)
Brian Kay's Sunday Morning:A Selection of Choral & Orchestral Favourites, w. Huddersfield Choral Society Chandos ("BBC Philharmonic" series) ▲ CHN 7025
G. Herbig (cnd)
Beethoven, L. van:Sym 4 IMP ("BBC Radio Classics" series) ▲ IMP 9123
Beethoven, L. van:Sym 5 IMP ("BBC Radio Classics" series) ▲ IMP 9123
Mahler, G.:Sym 5 IMP ("BBC Radio" series) ▲ IMP 5691432
Schubert, Franz:Sym 9 IMP ("BBC Radio" series) ▲ IMP 5691442
Strauss, R.:Tod und Verklärung IMP ("BBC Radio Classics" series) ▲ IMP 9122
Weber, C.M. von:Euryanthe (ov) IMP ("BBC Radio" series) ▲ IMP 5691442
R. Hickox (cnd)
Grainger, P.:Orchestral Music—In a Nutshell (suite); English Dance; Shepherd's Hey!; Blithe Bells; Green Bushes; Colonial Song; Harvest Hymn; Walking Tune; The Duke of Marlborough (fanfare); We Were Dreamers; Fisher's Boarding House; There Were 3 Friends Chandos ("The Grainger Edition" series) ▲ CHAN 9493
Respighi, O.:Aretusa, w. Linda Finnie (cta) Chandos ▲ CHAN 9453
Respighi, O.:Deità silvana, w. Ingrid Attrot (sop) [arr for voc & orch] Chandos ▲ CHAN 9453
Respighi, O.:Nebbie, w. Ingrid Attrot (sop) [arr for voc & orch] Chandos ▲ CHAN 9453
Respighi, O.:La Sensitiva, w. Linda Finnie (cta) Chandos ▲ CHAN 9453
G. Hurst (cnd)
Elgar, E.:Imperial March *(rec Apr. 1992)* Naxos ▲ 8.550634 [DDD]
Elgar, E.:Sym 1 *(rec Apr. 1992)* Naxos ▲ 8.550634 [DDD]
G. Lloyd (cnd)
Lloyd, G.:Charade Albany ▲ TROY 090 [DD]
Lloyd, G.:Con 1 Pno, w. M. Roscoe (pno) Albany ▲ TROY 037–2 [DDD] ■ TROY 037–4
Lloyd, G.:Con 2 Pno, w. M. Roscoe (pno) Albany ▲ TROY 037–2 [DDD] ■ TROY 037–4
Lloyd, G.:Con 3 Pno, w. K. Stott (pno) Albany ▲ TROY 019–2 [DDD] ■ TROY 019–4 (D)
Lloyd, G.:John Socman (ov) Albany ▲ AR 015–2 [DDD] ■ AR 015–4 (D)
Lloyd, G.:Music of, Albany SO, London SO—Sym No. 9 [finale]; Sym No. 6 [adagio]; Her Hair [from The Transformation of that Naked Ape]; Con No. 4 for Pno [1st movt]; Sym No. 11 [lento]; Sym No. 7 [vivo] Albany ▲ TROY 075
Lloyd, G.:Sym 2 Albany ▲ TROY 055–2 [DDD]
Lloyd, G.:Sym 3 Albany ▲ TROY 090 [DD]
Lloyd, G.:Sym 5 Albany ▲ TROY 022–2 [DDD] ■ TROY 022–4 (D)
Lloyd, G.:Sym 6 Albany ▲ AR 015–2 [DDD] ■ AR 015–C (D)
Lloyd, G.:Sym 7 Albany ▲ TROY 057–2 [DDD]
Lloyd, G.:Sym 9 Albany ▲ TROY 055–2 [DDD]
O. de la Martinez (cnd)
Smyth, E.:Con Vn Hn, w. Sophie Langdon (vn), Richard Watkins (hn) Chandos ▲ CHAN 9449
Smyth, E.:Serenade Chandos ▲ CHAN 9449
Smyth, E.:The Wreckers, w. Judith Howarth (sop), Anne-Marie Owens (mez), Annemarie Sand (mez), Justin Lavender (ten), Anthony Roden (ten), Peter Sidhom (bar), David Wilson-Johnson (bar), Brian Bannatyne-Scott (bass), Huddersfield Choral Society *(rec live, Royal Albert Hall, London, July 31, 1994)* Conifer Classics 2-▲ 75605–51250–2
K. Sanderling (cnd)
Mahler, G.:Sym 9 IMP ("BBC Radio Classics" series) ▲ IMP 5691562

BBC PO (cont.)
V. Sinaisky (cnd)
Szymanowski, K.:Sym 2 Chandos ▲ CHAN 9478
Szymanowski, K.:Sym 4, w. Howard Shelley (pno) Chandos ▲ CHAN 9478
M. Tippett (cnd)
Tippett, M.:Con Pno, w. M. Tirimo (pno) Nimbus ▲ NI 5301 [DDD]
Tippett, M.:Con Vn Va, w. E. Kovacic (vn), G. Caussé (va), A. Baillie (vc) Nimbus ▲ NI 5301 [DDD]
Y. P. Tortelier (cnd)
Dukas, P.:Polyeucte Chandos ▲ CHAN 9225 [DDD]
Dukas, P.:Sym in C Chandos ▲ CHAN 9225 [DDD]
Dutilleux, H.:L'Arbre de songes, w. Olivier Charlier (vn) Chandos ▲ CHAN 9504
Dutilleux, H.:Prière pour nous autres charnels, w. Martyn Hill (ten), Neal Davies (bar) Chandos ▲ CHAN 9504
Dutilleux, H.:Sonnets (2) de Jean Cassou, w. Neal Davies (bar) [arr bar & orch] Chandos ▲ CHAN 9504
Dutilleux, H.:Sym 1 Chandos ▲ CHAN 9194 [DDD]
Dutilleux, H.:Sym 2, "Le Double" Chandos ▲ CHAN 9194 [DDD]
Dutilleux, H.:Timbres, espace, mouvement avec interlude Chandos ▲ CHAN 9504
Fauré, G.:Ballade Pno, w. Kathryn Stott (pno) Chandos ▲ CHAN 9416 [DDD]
Fauré, G.:Dolly Chandos ▲ CHAN 9416 [DDD]
Fauré, G.:Elégie, w. Peter Dixon (vc) Chandos ▲ CHAN 9416 [DDD]
Fauré, G.:Fant Fl, w. Richard Davies (fl) Chandos ▲ CHAN 9416 [DDD]
Fauré, G.:Masques et bergamasques (suite) Chandos ▲ CHAN 9416 [DDD]
Fauré, G.:Pavane Chandos ▲ CHAN 9416 [DDD]
Fauré, G.:Pénélope (prelude) Chandos ▲ CHAN 9416 [DDD]
Gershwin, G.:An American in Paris Chandos ▲ CHAN 9325 [DDD]
Gershwin, G.:"I Got Rhythm" Vars, w. Howard Shelley (pno) Chandos ▲ CHAN 9325 [DDD]
Gershwin, G.:Ovs—Ovs. to Girl Crazy & Strike up the Band Chandos ▲ CHAN 9325 [DDD]
Gershwin, G.:Porgy & Bess (suite), "Catfish Row Suite", w. Howard Shelley (pno) Chandos ▲ CHAN 9325 [DDD]
Guilmant, A.:Sym 1, w. I. Tracey (org) Chandos ▲ CHAN 9271 [DDD]
Hindemith, P.:Con Vc, w. R. Wallfisch (vc) Chandos ▲ CHAN 9124 [DDD]
Hindemith, P.:The Four Temperaments, w. H. Shelley (pno) Chandos ▲ CHAN 9124 [DDD]
Hindemith, P.:Die Harmonie der Welt Chandos ▲ CHAN 9217 [DDD]
Hindemith, P.:Neues vom Tage (concert ov) Chandos ▲ CHAN 9060 [DDD]
Hindemith, P.:Nobilissima visione Chandos ▲ CHAN 9060 [DDD]
Hindemith, P.:Symphonia serena Chandos ▲ CHAN 9217 [DDD]
Hindemith, P.:Sym in E♭ for Concert Band Chandos ▲ CHAN 9060 [DDD]
Lutoslawski, W.:Con Orch Chandos ▲ CHAN 9421
Lutoslawski, W.:Mi-parti Chandos ▲ CHAN 9421
Lutoslawski, W.:Musique funèbre Chandos ▲ CHAN 9421
Poulenc, F.:Gloria Sop, w. Janice Watson (sop), BBC Singers Chandos ▲ CHAN 9341 [DDD]
Poulenc, F.:Stabat mater, w. Janice Watson (sop), BBC Singers Chandos ▲ CHAN 9341 [DDD]
Poulenc, F.:Con Org, w. I. Tracey (org) Chandos ▲ CHAN 9271 [DDD]
Roussel, A.:Bacchus et Ariane Chandos ▲ CHAN 9494
Roussel, A.:Le Festin de l'araignée Chandos ▲ CHAN 9494
G. Varga (cnd)
Lalo, E.:Con Vc, w. S. Rolland (vc) ASV ▲ ASV 867 [DDD]
Massenet, J.:Fant Vc, w. S. Rolland (vc) ASV ▲ ASV 867 [DDD]
Saint-Saëns, C.:Con 1 Vc, w. S. Rolland (vc) ASV ▲ ASV 867 [DDD]
BBC Scottish SO
British Music on Hyperion, w. Parley of Instruments, Roy Goodman (cnd), John Mark Ainsley (ten), Graham Johnson (pno), Salomon Quartet, Anthony Rolfe Johnson (ten), Royal PO, St. Paul's Cathedral Choir, Nash Ensemble, Martyn Hill (ten), Suasan Gritton (sop) Hyperion ▲ HYP 15
R. Bernas (cnd)
Goehr, A.:Sym in 1 Movt NMC ▲ NMC 23 [DDD]
A. Boult (cnd)
Bantock, G.:Hebridean Sym *(rec live, 1968)* Intaglio ▲ INCD 704–1 [ADD]
M. Brabbins (cnd)
Alkan, C.-V.:Cons (2) de camera, w. M.-A. Hamelin (pno) Hyperion ▲ CDA 66717
Glazunov, A.:Con 1 Pno, w. Stephen Coombs (pno) Hyperion ▲ CDA 66877
Glazunov, A.:Con 2 Pno, w. Stephen Coombs (pno) Hyperion ▲ CDA 66877
Goedicke, A.:Con Pno, w. Stephen Coombs (pno) Hyperion ▲ CDA 66877
Henselt, A. von:Con Pno, w. M.-A. Hamelin (pno) Hyperion ▲ CDA 66717
Henselt, A. von:Vars de concert, w. M.-A. Hamelin (pno) Hyperion ▲ CDA 66717
Maccunn, H.:The Dowie Dens o'Yarrow, w. Lisa Milne (sop), Janice Watson (sop), Jamie MacDougall (ten), Peter Sidhom (bar), Stephen Gadd (bass), Scottish Opera Chorus Hyperion ▲ CDA 66815
Maccunn, H.:Jeanie Deans (sels), w. Lisa Milne (sop), Janice Watson (sop), Jamie MacDougall (ten), Peter Sidhom (bar), Stephen Gadd (bass), Scottish Opera Chorus Hyperion ▲ CDA 66815
Maccunn, H.:Land of the Mountain & the Flood Hyperion ▲ CDA 66815
Maccunn, H.:Lay of Last Minstrel, w. Lisa Milne (sop), Janice Watson (sop), Jamie MacDougall (ten), Peter Sidhom (bar), Stephen Gadd (bass), Scottish Opera Chorus Hyperion ▲ CDA 66815
Maccunn, H.:Ship o' the Fiend, w. Lisa Milne (sop), Janice Watson (sop), Jamie MacDougall (ten), Peter Sidhom (bar), Stephen Gadd (bass), Scottish Opera Chorus Hyperion ▲ CDA 66815
Mackenzie, A.:Orchestral Music—Cricket on the Hearth Ov.; Twelfth Night Ov.; Benedictus; Scottish Rhap. No. 2; Coriolanus Incidental Music Hyperion ▲ CDA 66764
Wallace, W.:François Villon Hyperion ▲ CDA 66848
Wallace, W.:The Passing of Beatrice Hyperion ▲ CDA 66848
Wallace, W.:Sir William Wallace Hyperion ▲ CDA 66848
Wallace, W.:Sister Helen Hyperion ▲ CDA 66848
T. Dun (cnd)
Dun, T.:Music of—On Taoism; Orchestral Theatre I; Death & Fire Koch Schwann ▲ SCH 312982 [DDD]
A. Francis (cnd)
Albert, E. d':Con 1 Pno, w. Piers Lane (pno) Hyperion ▲ CDA 66747
Albert, E. d':Con 2 Pno, w. Piers Lane (pno) Hyperion ▲ CDA 66747
Pettersson, G.A.:Symphonic Movt CPO ▲ CPO 999281 [DDD]
Pettersson, G.A.:Sym 2 CPO ▲ CPO 999281 [DDD]
Pettersson, G.A.:Sym 13 CPO ▲ CPO 999224 [DDD]
Searle, H.:Sym 2 *(rec Studio 1, Glasgow, June 1995)* CPO ▲ CPO 999376–2 [DDD]
Searle, H.:Sym 3 *(rec Studio 1, Glasgow, June 1995)* CPO ▲ CPO 999376–2 [DDD]
Searle, H.:Sym 5 *(rec Studio 1, Glasgow, June 1995)* CPO ▲ CPO 999376–2 [DDD]
L. Friend (cnd)
Brian, H.:Con Vn, w. M. Bisengaliev (vn) *(rec Jan. 12–15, 1993)* Marco Polo ▲ 8.223479 [DDD]
Brian, H.:The Jolly Miller—Ov. *(rec Jan. 12–15, 1993)* Marco Polo ▲ 8.223479 [DDD]
Brian, H.:Sym 18 *(rec Jan. 12–15, 1993)* Marco Polo ▲ 8.223479 [DDD]
F. Glushchenko (cnd)
Dohnányi, E. von:Con 1 Pno, w. M. Roscoe (pno) Hyperion ▲ CDA 66684 [DDD]
C. Groves (cnd)
Elgar, E.:Caractacus, w. Scottish Phil Singers IMP ("BBC Radio Classics" series) ▲ IMP 5691802
Elgar, E.:Choral Songs (sels), w. Scottish Phil Singers—Give Unto the Lord IMP ("BBC Radio Classics" series) ▲ IMP 5691802
Elgar, E.:Froissart IMP ("BBC Radio Classics" series) ▲ IMP 5691802
Elgar, E.:Partsongs, Op. 26, w. Royal Scottish Academy of Music & Drama St. Cecilia Choir IMP ("BBC Radio Classics" series) ▲ IMP 5691802
Elgar, E.:Sospiri IMP ("BBC Radio Classics" series) ▲ IMP 5691802
Elgar, E.:Sursum corde IMP ("BBC Radio Classics" series) ▲ IMP 5691802
J. Maksymiuk (cnd)
Arensky, A.:Con Pno, w. S. Coombs (pno) Hyperion ▲ CDA 66624
Arensky, A.:Fant on Themes of Ryabinin, w. S. Coombs (pno) Hyperion ▲ CDA 66624

BBC Scottish SO (cont.)
J. Maksymiuk (cnd) (cont.)
Bortkiewicz, S.:Con 1 Pno, w. S. Coombs (pno) Hyperion ▲ CDA 66624
Grieg, E.:Lyric Pieces [arr. Grieg]—Evening in the Mountains, Op. 68/4; Cradle Song, Op. 68/5; Wedding Day at Troldhaugen, Op. 65/6 *(rec June 24–25, 1993)* Naxos ▲ 8.550864 [DDD]
Grieg, E.:Peer Gynt Suites, Opp. 46 & 55 *(rec June 24–25, 1993)* Naxos ▲ 8.550864 [DDD]
Grieg, E.:Sigurd Jorsalfar (suite) *(rec June 24–25, 1993)* Naxos ▲ 8.550864 [DDD]
Macmillan, J.:The Confession of Isobel Gowdie Koch Schwann ▲ 310502 [DDD]
Macmillan, J.:Tryst Koch Schwann ▲ 310502 [DDD]
Medtner, N.:Con 2 Pno, w. N. Demidenko (pno) Hyperion ▲ CDA 66580 [DDD]
Medtner, N.:Con 3 Pno, w. N. Demidenko (pno) Hyperion ▲ CDA 66580 [DDD]
Mendelssohn, F.:Cons (2) for 2 Pnos, w. S. Coombs (pno), I. Munro (pno) Hyperion ▲ CDA 66567 [DDD]
Moszkowski, M.:Con Pno, w. P. Lane (pno) Hyperion ▲ CDA 66452 [DDD]
Paderewski, I.J.:Con Pno, w. P. Lane (pno) Hyperion ▲ CDA 66452 [DDD]
The Romantic Piano Concerto, Vol. 1, w. P. Lane (pno) Hyperion ▲ CDA 66452 [DDD]
The Romantic Piano Concerto, Vol. 2, w. N. Demidenko (pno) Hyperion ▲ CDA 66580 [DDD]
J. Y. Ossonce (cnd)
Chabrier, E.:Briséïs, ou Les Amants de Corinthe, w. Kathryn Harries (sop), Simon Keenlyside (trb), Mark Padmore (ten), Michael George (bass), Joan Rodgers (sgr) Hyperion ▲ CDA 66803
BBC SO
D. Atherton (cnd)
Dickinson, P.:Con Org, w. J. Bate (org) EMI ▲ CDC7 47584 [DDD]
Dickinson, P.:Con Pno, w. H. Shelley (pno) EMI ▲ CDC7 47584 [DDD]
S. Bainbridge (cnd)
Bainbridge, S.:Fant Double Orch Continuum ▲ CCD 1020
M. Bamert (cnd)
Saxton, R.:Con Vn, w. T. Little (vn) Collins Classics ▲ 12832
Saxton, R.:I Will Awake the Dawn, w. BBC Sym Chorus Collins Classics ▲ 12832
Saxton, R.:In the Beginning Collins Classics ▲ 12832
J. Barbirolli (cnd)
Mahler, G.:Sym 4, w. H. Harper (sop) *(rec live, Prague, 1/16/67)* Intaglio ▲ INCD 7291 [ADD]
T. Beecham (cnd)
Gounod, C.:Faust, w. M. Licette (sop—Margarita), D. Vane (sop—Siebel), M. Brunskill (cta—Martha), H. Nash (ten—Faust), H. Williams (b-bar—Valentine), R. Easton (bass—Mephistopheles), R. Carr (bass—Wagner), BBC Sym Chorus Dutton Laboratories 2-▲ CDAX 2001 [ADD]
Handel, G.F.:Messiah, w. Dora Labbette (sop), Muriel Brunskill (cta), Hubert Eisdell (ten), Harold Williams (bar), BBC Choir *(rec 1927)* Pearl 2-▲ PEA 9456 [DDD]
R. Bernas (cnd)
Smalley, R.:Pulses NM Classics ▲ NMCD 017
N. Boulanger (cnd)
Boulanger, L.:Choral Music, w. J. Price (sop), BBC Sym Chorus—Psalm 24 (1916); Pie Jesu (1918) *(rec live Nov. 1968, London)* Intaglio ▲ INCD 703-1 [ADD]
Boulanger, L.:Du fond de l'abîme, w. B. Greevy (mez), I. Partridge (ten), BBC Sym Chorus *(rec live, London Nov. 1968)* Intaglio ▲ INCD 703-1 [ADD]
Fauré, G.:Requiem, w. J. Price (sop), J. Carol Case (bar), BBC Sym Chorus *(rec live, London Nov. 1968)* Intaglio ▲ INCD 703-1 [ADD]
P. Boulez (cnd)
Berg, A.:Pieces Orch, Op. 6 Enterprise ("Documents Live Recordings" Series) 2-▲ LV 915/916 (m) [ADD]
Berg, A.:Pieces Orch, Op. 6, Paris Conservatory Société des Concerts Orch Originals 2-▲ ORISH 855
Berg, A.:Pieces Orch, Op. 6 Sony Classical ("Pierre Boulez Edition" series) ▲ SMK 68331
Boulez, P.:Figures, Doubles, Prismes Erato ▲ 2292-45494-2 [DDD]
Boulez, P.:Pli selon pli, Portrait de Mallarmé, w. Halina Lukomska (sop) Sony Classical ("Pierre Boulez Edition" series) ▲ SMK 68335
Boulez, P.:Rituel Sony Classical ▲ SMK 45839 [DDD]
Boulez, P.:Le Soleil des eaux, w. P. Bryn-Julson (sop), BBC Singers [F] Erato ▲ 2292-45494-2 [DDD]
Boulez, P.:Le Visage Nuptial, w. P. Bryn-Julson (sop), E. Laurence (alt), BBC Singers [F] Erato ▲ 2292-45494-2 [DDD]
Brahms, J.:Gesang der Parzen, w. H. Harper (sop), H. Prey (bar), BBC Choral Society *(rec live July 20, 1973)* Memories 2-▲ HR 4493/94 [ADD]
Debussy, C.:Jeux Enterprise ("Documents Live Recordings" Series) 2-▲ LV 915/916 (m) [ADD]
Debussy, C.:Jeux, w. Paris Conservatory Société des Concerts Orch, BBC Sym Chorus Originals 2-▲ ORISH 855
Mahler, G.:Sym 2, w. F. Palmer (sop), T. Troyanos (alt), BBC Choral Society, London Phil Choir Enterprise 2-▲ LV 915/916
Mahler, G.:Sym 2, w. Felicity Palmer (sop/mez), Tatiana Troyanos (mez), Paris Conservatory Société des Concerts Orch, BBC Sym Chorus Originals 2-▲ ORISH 855
Mahler, G.:Sym 6 *(rec live, London, 1973)* Enterprise ("Documents" series) ▲ ENT LV 995
Mahler, G.:Sym 9 *(rec live, 1972)* AS Disc ▲ ASD 2509
Mahler, G.:Sym 9 *(rec live, Oct. 22, 1972)* Memories 2-▲ HR 4493/94 [ADD]
Ravel, M.:Poèmes de Mallarmé, w. J. Gomez (sop) [F] CBS ▲ MK 39023
Ravel, M.:Shéhérazade, w. H. Harper (sop) [F] CBS ▲ MK 39023
Schoenberg, A.:Begleitmusik zu einer Lichtspielszene Sony Classical ▲ SMK 48462 [ADD]
Schoenberg, A.:Chamber Sym 1 Sony Classical ▲ SMK 48462 [ADD]
Schoenberg, A.:Chamber Sym 2 Sony Classical 2-▲ SM2K 48456 [ADD]
Schoenberg, A.:Erwartung, w. J. Martin (sop) *(rec Apr. 14–15, 1977)* Sony Classical ▲ SMK 48466 [ADD]
Schoenberg, A.:Die glückliche Hand, w. S. Nimsgern (b-bar), BBC Singers *(rec Mar. 12, 1981)* Sony Classical ▲ SMK 48464 [ADD]
Schoenberg, A.:Gurrelieder, w. M. Napier (sop), Y. Minton (mez), J. Thomas (ten), K. Bowman (sgr), G. Reich (nar), S. Nimsgern (b-bar) *(rec Oct. 26–Dec. 06, 1974)* Sony Classical 2-▲ SM2K 48459 [ADD]
Schoenberg, A.:Die Jakobsleiter, w. Ensemble InterContemporain, BBC Singers Sony Classical ▲ SMK 48462 [ADD]
Schoenberg, A.:Moses und Aaron, w. R. Cassilly (ten), G. Reich (nar), Ensemble InterContemporain, BBC Singers *(rec Nov. 30–Dec. 06, 1974)* Sony Classical 2-▲ SM2K 48456 [ADD]
Schoenberg, A.:Ode to Napoleon, w. D. Wilson-Johnson (speaker), Ensemble InterContemporain *(rec Mar. 31, 1980)* Sony Classical ▲ SMK 48463 [ADD]
Schoenberg, A.:Orch Songs, Op. 22, w. Y. Minton (mez) *(rec Mar. 12, 1981)* Sony Classical 2-▲ SM2K 48459 [ADD]
Schoenberg, A.:Pieces Orch, Op. 16, w. Ensemble InterContemporain *(rec Sept. 23, 1976)* Sony Classical ▲ SMK 48463 [ADD]
Schoenberg, A.:Serenade Cl, w. J. Shirley-Quirk (bar), Ensemble InterContemporain *(rec Apr. 10, 1979)* Sony Classical ▲ SMK 48463 [ADD]
Schoenberg, A.:A Survivor from Warsaw, w. G. Reich (nar), BBC Sym Chorus *(rec 1976)* Sony Classical 2-▲ S2K 44571 [ADD/DDD]
Schoenberg, A.:Vars Orch, Op. 31 *(rec Sept. 23, 1976)* Sony Classical ▲ SMK 48464 [ADD]
Schumann, R.:Scenes from Goethe's "Faust", w. E. Mathis (sop), B. Rayner Cook (bar), D. Fischer-Dieskau (bar), G. Howell (bass), BBC Sym Chorus *(rec live, London, March 7, 1973)* Memories 2-▲ HR 4489/90 [ADD]
Stravinsky, I.:Pulcinella Suite Sony Classical (Pierre Boulez Edition) ▲ SK 45843
A. Boult (cnd)
Beethoven, L. van:Con 3 Pno, w. Solomon (pno) *(rec Bedford Grammar School, Aug 8, 9 & 12, 1944)* Dutton Laboratories ▲ DUT 7015 [ADD]
Beethoven, L. van:Con 4 Pno, w. M. Hess (pno) *(rec 1952)* Music & Arts 3-▲ CD 779 [AAD]
Brahms, J.:Con 2 Pno, w. A. Schnabel (pno) *(rec 1935 for EMI)* Pearl ▲ PEA 9399 (m) [AAD]
Elgar, E.:Con Vc, w. P. Casals (vc) *(rec 1945)* EMI Classics (Great Recordings of the Century) ▲ CDH 63498 (m) [ADD]
Mozart, W.A.:Con Hn, K.447, w. A. Brain (hn) EMI Classics ▲ CDM 64198

BBC SO (cont.)
A. Boult (cnd) (cont.)
Rawsthorne, A.:Con Strs IMP ("BBC Radio Classics" series) ▲ IMP 5691632
Tovey, D.F.:Con Vc, w. Pablo Casals (vc) *(rec live Nov. 17, 1937)* Symposium ▲ 1115
Vaughan Williams, R.:A Song of Thanksgiving, w. *(nar unknown)*, E. Suddaby (sop), BBC Children's Chorus Intaglio ▲ ING 757 [ADD]
Vaughan Williams, R.:Sym 3, w. Valerie Hill (sop) IMP ("BBC Radio Classics" series) ▲ IMP 5691642
Vaughan Williams, R.:Sym 6 IMP ("BBC Radio Classics" series) ▲ IMP 5691642
Vaughan Williams, R.:5 Tudor Portraits, w. P. Walker (sop), F. Harrison (alto), BBC Northern Singers Intaglio ▲ ING 757 [ADD]
Walton, W.:Sym 1 IMP ("BBC Radio Classics" series) ▲ IMP 5691782
R. Buckley (cnd)
Adams, J.:Shaker Loops IMP ("BBC Radio Classics" series) ▲ IMP 5691692
P. Daniel (cnd)
Birtwistle, H.:An Imaginary Landscape Collins Classics ▲ COL 1414
Birtwistle, H.:Nomos Collins Classics ▲ COL 1414
A. Davis (cnd)
Britten, B.:Peter Grimes (sea interludes & passacaglia), w. A. Davis Teldec ("British Line" series) ▲ 9031-73126-2 [DDD]
Britten, B.:Vars on a Theme of Frank Bridge Teldec ("British Line" series) ▲ 9031-73126-2 [DDD]
Britten, B.:The Young Person's Guide to the Orchestra Teldec ("British Line" series) ▲ 9031-73126-2 [DDD]
Delius, F.:Music of—Paris:The Song of a Great City; The Walk to Paradise Garden; In a Summer Garden; On Hearing the First Cuckoo in Spring; Summer Night on the River; Brigg Fair:An English Rhapsody Teldec ▲ 90845-2
Elgar, E.:Cockaigne Teldec ▲ 9031-73279-2 ZK
Elgar, E.:Enigma Vars Teldec ▲ 9031-73279-2 ZK
Elgar, E.:In the South Teldec ▲ 9031-74888-2 ZK
Elgar, E.:Intro & Allegro Teldec ▲ 9031-73279-2 ZK
Elgar, E.:The Music Makers, w. J. Rigby (mez), BBC Sym Chorus *(rec London, Aug. 1993)* Teldec ▲ 92374-2 [DDD]
Elgar, E.:Music of—Dream Children; Elegy; Sursum corda; Sospiri; Chanson de matin; Chanson de nuit; Salut d'amour *(rec London, Aug. 1993)* Teldec ▲ 92374-2 [DDD]
Elgar, E.:Pomp & Circumstance Marches—Nos. 1,3 & 4 Teldec ▲ 9031-73278-2 ■ 9031-73278-4
Elgar, E.:Serenade Strs Teldec ▲ 9031-73279-2 ZK
Elgar, E.:Sym 1 Teldec ▲ 9031-73278-2 ZK ■ 9031-73278-4
Elgar, E.:Sym 2 Teldec ▲ 9031-74888-2 ZK
Holst, G.:Egdon Heath, Homage to Hardy *(rec London, Dec. 1993)* Teldec ▲ 94541-2 [DDD]
Holst, G.:The Planets, w. A. Davis (org), BBC Sym Women's Chorus *(rec London, Dec. 1993)* Teldec ▲ 94541-2 [DDD]
Last Night of the Proms, w. Bryn Terfel (bar), Evelyn Glennie (mar), BBC Sym Chorus, BBC Singers *(rec Royal Albert Hall, Sep. 10, 1994)* Teldec ▲ 97868-2 [DDD]
Nielsen, C.:Maskarade—Overture Virgin Classics ▲ 59618 [DDD]
Nielsen, C.:Sym 4 Virgin Classics ▲ 59618 [DDD]
Nielsen, C.:Sym 5 Virgin Classics ▲ 59618 [DDD]
Sensual Classics II, w. A. Sultanov (pno), C. Katsaris (pno), Brodsky Quartet, London SO [cnd:M. Shostakovich], New York PO [cnd:Z. Mehta], Leipzig Gewandhaus Orch [cnd:K. Masur], 12 Cellos of the Berlin PO [cnd:A. Jordan, E. Inbal], et al. Teldec ▲ 92014-2 ■ 92014-4
Shostakovich, D.:Con 1 Vn, w. D. Sitkovetsky (vn) Virgin Classics ▲ CDC 59601
Shostakovich, D.:Con 2 Vn, w. D. Sitkovetsky (vn) Virgin Classics ▲ CDC 59601
Tippett, M.:The Mask of Time, w. F. Robinson (sop), S. Walker (mez), R. Tear (ten), J. Cheek (bass), BBC Sym Chorus EMI Classics ▲ ZDMB 64111
Vaughan Williams, R.:Fant on a Theme by Thomas Tallis Teldec (British Line) ▲ 9031-73127-2 [DDD] ■ 9031-73127-4
Vaughan Williams, R.:The Lark Ascending, w. T. Little (vn) Teldec (British Line) ▲ 9031-73127-2 [DDD] ■ 9031-73127-4
Vaughan Williams, R.:Sym 2 *(rec London, Mar. 1993)* Teldec ▲ 90858-2 [DDD]
Vaughan Williams, R.:Sym 4 Teldec ▲ 90844
Vaughan Williams, R.:Sym 5 Teldec ▲ 90844
Vaughan Williams, R.:Sym 6 Teldec (British Line) ▲ 9031-73127-2 [DDD] ■ 9031-73127-4
Vaughan Williams, R.:Sym 8 *(rec London, Mar. 1993)* Teldec ▲ 90858-2 [DDD]
C. Davis (cnd)
Bartók, B.:Cons Pno (comp), w. S. Kovacevich (pno), B. Haitink (cnd), Royal Concertgebouw Orch, London SO Philips 2-▲ 438812-2
Bartók, B.:Con 1 Pno, w. S. Bishop-Kovacevich (pno) Philips ("Silver Line" series) ▲ 426660-2 [ADD]
Bartók, B.:Con 2 Pno, w. S. Bishop-Kovacevich (pno) Philips ("Silver Line" series) ▲ 426660-2 [ADD]
Bartók, B.:Con 3 Pno, w. S. Bishop-Kovacevich (pno) Philips ("Silver Line" series) ▲ 426660-2 [ADD]
Beethoven, L. van:Cant on the Death of the Emperor Joseph II, w. K. Te Kanawa (sop), Y. Newman (mez), D. Barrett (bar), M. Langdon (bass), BBC Chorus, BBC Choral Society [G] *(rec live Oct. 7, 1970)* Intaglio ▲ INCD 7361 [ADD]
Beethoven, L. van:Con 1 Pno, w. S. Bishop-Kovacevich (pno) Philips ▲ 422968-2 [ADD]
Beethoven, L. van:Con 1 Pno, w. S. Bishop-Kovacevich (pno) Philips ("Duo" series) 2-▲ 442577-2
Beethoven, L. van:Con 2 Pno, w. S. Bishop Kovacevich (pno) Philips ("Duo" series) 2-▲ 442577-2
Beethoven, L. van:Con 2 Pno, w. S. Bishop Kovacevich (pno) Philips ▲ 422968-2 [ADD]
Beethoven, L. van:Con 3 Pno, w. S. Bishop Kovecevich (pno) Philips ("Duo" series) 2-▲ 442577-2
Beethoven, L. van:Con 4 Pno, w. S. Bishop Kovecevich (pno) Philips ("Duo" series) 2-▲ 442577-2
Grieg, E.:Con Pno, Op. 16, w. S. B. Kovacevich (pno) Philips ▲ 412923-2
Mozart, W.A.:Complete Mozart Edition, w. J. Norman (sop), M. Freni (sop), Y. Minton (mez), I. Wixell (bar), BBC Sym Chorus Philips 3-▲ 422540-2 [ADD]
Mozart, W.A.:Missa, K.317, w. BBC Sym Chorus Philips 2-▲ 438800-2
Mozart, W.A.:Missa, K.427, w. BBC Sym Chorus Philips 2-▲ 438800-2
Mozart, W.A.:Requiem, w. H. Donath (sop), Y. Minton (mez), A. Davies (ten), G Nienstedt (bass), John Alldis Choir [L] Philips ▲ 420353-2 [ADD]
Mozart, W.A.:Requiem, w. *(soloists unknown)*, BBC Sym Chorus Philips 2-▲ 438800-2
Schumann, R.:Con Pno, w. Bishop-Kovacevich (pno) Philips ▲ 412923-2 [ADD]
Walton, W.:Con Va, w. Peter Schidlof (va) IMP ("BBC Radio Classics" series) ▲ IMP 5691732
A. Dorati (cnd)
Berlioz, H.:Benvenuto Cellini, w. J. Carlyle (sop), J. Veasey (mez), K. Lewis (ten), Kentish, Cameron, Bushby, Garrard, Ward, BBC Sym Chorus [E] *(rec live, Royal Festival Hall, 1964)* Music & Arts 2-▲ CD 618 (m) [AAD]
M. Elder (cnd)
Benjamin, G.:Ringed by the Flat Horizon Nimbus ▲ NI 5075 [DDD]
Szymanowski, K.:Sym 4 IMP ("BBC Radio Classics" series) ▲ IMP 9124
P. Eötvös (cnd)
Reich, S.:The Desert Music, w. BBC Singers IMP ("BBC Radio Classics" series) ▲ IMP 5691692
L. Friend (cnd)
Brian, H.:Sym 3 Hyperion ▲ CDA 66334
C. Groves (cnd)
Bridge, F.:Enter Spring IMP ("BBC Radio Classics" series) ▲ IMP 5691752
Liszt, F.:Totentanz, w. M. Pollini (pno) *(rec live 1974 & 1979)* Artists ▲ FED 30 [ADD]
Schumann, R.:Gesänge der Frühe, w. M. Pollini (pno) *(rec live 1974 & 1979)* Artists ▲ FED 30 [ADD]
V. Handley (cnd)
Bliss, A.:Metamorphic Vars IMP ("BBC Radio Classics" series) ▲ IMP 5691682
J. Horenstein (cnd)
Bruckner, A.:Sym 5 *(rec Sept. 15, 1971)* Intaglio ▲ ING 754 [ADD]
Bruckner, A.:Sym 5 *(rec Royal Albert Hall, London, Oct 15, 1971)* Agorá Music ("Phoenix" series) ▲ PX 703.1 [ADD]
Bruckner, A.:Sym 9 [Alfred Orel edition] *(rec live, Royal Festival Hall, London 12/2/70)* Intaglio ▲ INCD 7091 [ADD]

70
▲ = CD ♦ = Enhanced CD Δ = MD ■ = Cassette Tape □ = DCC

BBC SO (cont.)
J. Horenstein (cnd) (cont.)
Bruckner, A.:Sym 9 *(rec Dec. 2, 1970)* Music & Arts ▲ CD 781 [AAD]
O. A. Hughes (cnd)
Sullivan, A.:Imperial March CPO ▲ CPO 999171 [DDD]
Sullivan, A.:In memoriam CPO ▲ CPO 999171 [DDD]
Sullivan, A.:Irish Sym CPO ▲ CPO 999171 [DDD]
Sullivan, A.:Victoria & Merry England (suites) CPO ▲ CPO 999171 [DDD]
B. Keefe (cnd)
Massenet, J.:Sapho, w. Jenny Hill (sop), Laura Sarti (mez), Bernard Dickerson (ten), Alexander Oliver (ten), Neilson Taylor (bar), George Macpherson (bass), Milla Andrew (sgr), BBC Sym Chorus *(rec live, 1973)* Memories 2–▲ MEM 4601 [AAD]
O. Knussen (cnd)
Holloway, R.:Con 2 Orch NM Classics ▲ NMCD 015
A. Lazarev (cnd)
Medtner, N.:Con 1 Pno, w. D. Alexeev (pno) Hyperion ▲ CDA 66744
Scriabin, A.:Con Pno, w. N. Demidenko (pno) Hyperion ▲ CDA 66680
Tchaikovsky, P.:Con 1 Pno, w. N. Demidenko (pno) Hyperion ▲ CDA 66680
R. Leppard (cnd)
Tippett, M.:Fant Concertante on a Theme of Corelli IMP ("BBC Radio Classics" series) ▲ IMP 9140
Tippett, M.:Sym 3, w. Josephine Barstow (sop) IMP ("BBC Radio Classics" series) ▲ IMP 9140
J. Loughran (cnd)
Elgar, E.:Sea Pictures, w. Janet Baker (mez) IMP ("BBC Radio Classics" series) ▲ IMP 5691672
W. Lutoslawski (cnd)
Lutoslawski, W.:Chain 2, w. Anne-Sophie Mutter (vn) Deutsche Grammophon ▲ 423696–2 [DDD]
Lutoslawski, W.:Chain 3 Deutsche Grammophon ▲ 431664–2 [DDD]
Lutoslawski, W.:Con Pno, w. K. Zimerman (pno) Deutsche Grammophon ▲ 431664–2 [DDD]
Lutoslawski, W.:Novelette Deutsche Grammophon ▲ 431664–2 [DDD]
Lutoslawski, W.:Partita Vn, Orch & Obbligato Pno, w. Anne-Sophie Mutter (vn), Phillip Moll (pno) Deutsche Grammophon ▲ 423696–2 [DDD]
C. Mackerras (cnd)
Martinů, B.:Double Con Pno, Tim, w. Harold Lester (pno) IMP ("BBC Radio Classics" series) ▲ IMP 9135
B. Maderna (cnd)
Mahler, G.:Sym 9 *(rec Mar. 31, 1971)* Arkadia ▲ 016 [ADD]
Ravel, M.:L'Heure espagnole, w. S. Danco (mez—Concepcion), J. Giraudeau (ten—Gonzalve), M. Hamel (ten—Torquemada), J. Cameron (bar—Ramiro), A. Vessières (bass—Gomez) *(rec Nov. 1960)* Stradivarius ▲ STR 10062 [ADD]
N. del Mar (cnd)
Delius, F.:A Mass of Life, w. K. Te Kanawa (sop), P. Bowden (mez), R. Dowd (ten), J. Shirley-Quirk (bar), BBC Sym Chorus *(rec live, London 5/3/71)* Intaglio 2–▲ INCD 702–2 [ADD]
Elgar, E.:The Music Makers, w. Sarah Walker (mez), BBC Singers, BBC Sym Chorus IMP ("BBC Radio Classics" series) ▲ IMP 5691672
Panufnik, A.:Sym 8 IMP ("BBC Radio Classics" series) ▲ IMP 9124
Rawsthorne, A.:Sym 3 *(rec 1968)* Lyrita ▲ SRCD 291
Strauss, R.:Eine Alpensinfonie IMP ("BBC Radio Classics" series) ▲ IMP 5691572
Strauss, R.:Con Ob, w. John Anderson (ob) IMP ("BBC Radio Classics" series) ▲ IMP 9138
D. Milhaud (cnd)
Milhaud, D.:L'Homme et son désir, w. Marion Davies (sop), Yvonne Newman (mez), David Barrett (ten), Anthony Holt (bass) IMP ("BBC Radio Classics" series) ▲ IMP 5691512
Milhaud, D.:Music for Indiana IMP ("BBC Radio Classics" series) ▲ IMP 5691512
Milhaud, D.:Sym 10 IMP ("BBC Radio Classics" series) ▲ IMP 5691512
Satie, E.:Jack in the Box IMP ("BBC Radio Classics" series) ▲ IMP 5691512
M. Neary (cnd)
Tavener, J.:Akathist of Thanksgiving, w. J. Bowman (ct), T. Wilson (ten), M. Baker (org), Westminster Abbey Choir, BBC Singers *(rec Jan. 21, 1994)* Sony Classical ▲ SK 64446 [DDD]
A. Panufnik (cnd)
Szymanowski, K.:Sym 3, w. Philip Langridge (ten), BBC Singers, BBC Sym Chorus IMP ("BBC Radio Classics" series) ▲ IMP 9124
Z. Peskó (cnd)
Dallapiccola, L.:Three Questions with 2 Answers Fonit Cetra ("Italia" series) ▲ FCT CDC 85
Maderna, B.:Aura Fonit Cetra ("Italia" series) ▲ FCT CDC 85
J. Pritchard (cnd)
Beethoven, L. van:Fant Pno, Op. 80, "Choral Fant", w. Edith Vogel (pno), BBC Sym Chorus, BBC Singers IMP ("BBC Radio Classics" series) ▲ IMP 9132
Beethoven, L. van:Leonore 1 IMP ("BBC Radio Classics" series) ▲ IMP 9132
Beethoven, L. van:Missa Solemnis, w. Ileana Cotrubas (sop), Kathleen Kuhlmann (mez), Robert Tear (ten), Gwynne Howell (bass), BBC Singers IMP ("BBC Radio Classics" series) ▲ IMP 5691552
Beethoven, L. van:Sym 7 IMP ("BBC Radio Classics" series) ▲ IMP 9132
Elgar, E.:In the South IMP ("BBC Radio Classics" series) ▲ IMP 9121
Elgar, E.:Sym 1 IMP ("BBC Radio Classics" series) ▲ IMP 9121
Rawsthorne, A.:Con 2 Pno, w. John Ogdon (pno) IMP ("BBC Radio Classics" series) ▲ IMP 5691762
Shostakovich, D.:Sym 11 IMP ("BBC Radio" series) ▲ IMP 5691422
Strauss, R.:Don Juan IMP ("BBC Radio Classics" series) ▲ IMP 5691572
Strauss, R.:Ein Heldenleben IMP ("BBC Radio Classics" series) ▲ IMP 9122
H. Rosbaud (cnd)
Togni, C.:Helian di Trakl, w. Dorothy Dorow (sop) Stradivarius ▲ STV DTM 90002 [ADD]
G. Rozhdestvensky (cnd)
Britten, B.:Spring Sym, w. Eiddwen Harrhy (sop), Linda Finnie (cta), Robert Tear (ten), BBC Sym Chorus, London Voices, Southend Boys' Choir IMP ("BBC Radio Classics" series) ▲ IMP 5691752
Delius, F.:A Song of the High Hills, w. BBC Sym Chorus, BBC Singers IMP ("BBC Radio Classics" series) ▲ IMP 9133
Janácek, L.:Ballad of Blanik IMP ("BBC Radio Classics" series) ▲ IMP 9135
Janácek, L.:Sinfonietta IMP ("BBC Radio Classics" series) ▲ IMP 9135
Janácek, L.:Taras Bulba IMP ("BBC Radio Classics" series) ▲ IMP 9135
Mahler, G.:Das Klagende Lied, w. Teresa Cahill (sop), Janet Baker (mez), Robert Tear (ten), Gwynne Howell (bass), BBC Sym Chorus IMP ("BBC Radio" series) ▲ IMP 5691412
Mussorgsky, M.:Sorochintsy Fair (sels), w. David Wilson Johnson (bar), BBC Sym Chorus, BBC Singers [E] IMP ("BBC Radio Classics" series) ▲ IMP 9139
Prokofiev, S.:Cons Vn (comp), w. I. Perlman (vn) EMI Classics ▲ CDC 47025 [DDD]
Prokofiev, S.:Poems, w. BBC Sym Chorus IMP ("BBC Radio" series) ▲ IMP 5691462
Tippett, M.:A Child Of Our Time, w. Jill Gomez (sop), Helen Watts (cta), Kenneth Wooliam (ten), John Shirley-Quirk (bar), BBC Sym Chorus IMP ("BBC Radio Classics" series) ▲ IMP 9130
Vaughan Williams, R.:Sancta civitas, w. Gareth Roberts (ten), Brian Rayner Cook (bar), BBC Singers, BBC Sym Chorus IMP ("BBC Radio Classics" series) ▲ IMP 9125
Vaughan Williams, R.:Sym 5 IMP ("BBC Radio Classics" series) ▲ IMP 9125
M. Sargent (cnd)
Beethoven, L. van:Con Vn, Op. 61, w. Josef Suk (vn) IMP ("BBC Radio Classics" series) ▲ IMP 5691612
Debussy, C.:La Mer IMP ("BBC Radio Classics" series) ▲ IMP 5691742
Dvořák, A.:Con Vn, w. Josef Suk (vn) IMP ("BBC Radio Classics" series) ▲ IMP 5691612
Elgar, E.:Con Vc, w. J. Du Pré (vc) *(rec live, Royal Albert Hall 1963)* Intaglio ▲ INCD 7351 [ADD]
Elgar, E.:Con Vc, w. P. Tortelier (vc) Testament ▲ TES SBT 2025 [ADD]
Grieg, E.:Songs, w. K. Flagstad (sop)—Spring, Op. 33/10; The Youth, Op. 33/9; On the way home, Op. 33/8; My goal, Op. 33/1; From Monte Pincio, Op. 39; The first meeting, Op. 21/1; Hope, Op. 26/1; A swan, Op. 25/2; Eros, Op. 70/1; I love thee, Op. 5/3 *(rec live, Royal Albert Hall , 9/7/57)* Arkadia 2–▲ 576 [ADD]
Holst, G.:Beni Mora EMI Classics ▲ CDC 49784
Holst, G.:Brook Green Suite EMI Classics ▲ CDC 49784
Holst, G.:Egdon Heath, Homage to Hardy EMI Classics ▲ CDC 49784

BBC SO (cont.)
M. Sargent (cnd) (cont.)
Holst, G.:First Choral Sym, w. H. Harper (sop), BBC Sym Chorus *(rec Jan. 3, 1964)* Intaglio ▲ ING 740 [ADD]
Holst, G.:The Perfect Fool EMI Classics ▲ CDC 49784
Ravel, M.:Shéhérazade Mez, w. Margaret Price (sop) IMP ("BBC Radio Classics" series) ▲ IMP 5691742
Sibelius, J.:Finlandia, Vienna PO EMI Classics ▲ CDE 67787
Sibelius, J.:En Saga, Vienna PO EMI Classics ▲ CDE 67787
Vaughan Williams, R.:Sym 1, w. Elaine Blighton (sop), John Cameron (bar), BBC Chorus, BBC Choral Society, Christchurch Harmonic Choir New Zealand *(rec 1965)* IMP ("BBC Radio" series) ▲ IMP 5691502
Vaughan Williams, R.:Sym 4 IMP ("BBC Radio Classics" series) ▲ IMP 9131
Wagner, R.:Wesendonck Songs, w. K. Flagstad (sop) *(rec 1953)* Memories 2–▲ HR 4456/57 [ADD]
G. Schurmann (cnd)
Schurmann, G.:Studies of Francis Bacon Chandos ▲ CHAN 9167 [ADD]
Schurmann, G.:Variants Chandos ▲ CHAN 9167 [ADD]
M. Shostakovich (cnd)
Berlioz, H.:Harold in Italy, w. Bruno Giuranna (va) IMP ("BBC Radio Classics" series) ▲ IMP 5691532
Shostakovich, D.:Con 2 Pno, w. Peter Donohoe (pno) IMP ("BBC Radio Classics" series) ▲ IMP 5691702
G. Simon (cnd)
Balcombe, R.:Greensleeves Suite, w. 40 Cellos of the London PO, Royal PO, Philharmonia Orch *(rec All Hallows Church, London, Jan 18 & Apr 2, 1993)* Cala ▲ CACD 104 [DDD]
Bernstein, L.:West Side Story (sels), w. 40 Cellos of the London PO, Royal PO, Philharmonia Orch—Tonight [arr. Balcombe] *(rec All Hallows Church, London, Jan 18 & Apr 2, 1993)* Cala ▲ CACD 104 [DDD]
Casals, P.:Sardana, w. 40 Cellos of the London PO, Royal PO, Philharmonia Orch *(rec All Hallows Church, London, Jan 18 & Apr 2, 1993)* Cala ▲ CACD 104 [DDD]
The London Viola Sound, w. 48 Violas of Academy of St. Martin in the Fields, English National Opera Orch, London PO *(rec Colosseum, Watford, UK, Jan 24, 1995)* Cala ▲ CACD 106 [DDD]
Rachmaninoff, S.:Vocalise, w. 40 Cellos of the London PO, Philharmonia Orch, Royal PO [arr. Balcombe] *(rec All Hallows Church, London, Jan 18 & Apr 2, 1993)* Cala ▲ CACD 104 [DDD]
Saint-Saëns, C.:Le Cygne, 40 Cellos of the London PO, Royal PO, Philharmonia Orch [arr. Balcombe] *(rec All Hallows Church, London, Jan 18 & Apr 2, 1993)* Cala ▲ CACD 104 [DDD]
L. Stokowski (cnd)
Falla, M. de:El amor brujo *(rec 1964)* Music & Arts ▲ CD 770 [AAD]
Mussorgsky, M.:Night *(rec 1963)* Music & Arts ▲ CD 765 [AAD]
Mussorgsky, M.:Pictures at an Exhibition *(rec 1963)* Music & Arts ▲ CD 765 [AAD]
Vaughan Williams, R.:Sym 8 IMP ("BBC Radio Classics" series) ▲ IMP 9131
Vaughan Williams, R.:Sym 8 *(rec 1964)* Music & Arts ▲ CD 770 [AAD]
A. Tamayo (cnd)
Dillon, J.:Music of—Ignis Noster; Helle Nacht Montaigne ▲ MO 782038
A. Toscanini (cnd)
Beethoven, L. van:Leonore (opera) *(rec between 1937 & 1939)* Enterprise ("Document" series) 2–▲ ENTLV 921 [ADD]
Beethoven, L. van:Leonore 1 Dutton Laboratories ▲ DUT 5004 [ADD]
Beethoven, L. van:Leonore 1 *(rec June 1, 1939)* Iron Needle ▲ IN 1310 [ADD]
Beethoven, L. van:Sym 1 *(rec Oct 25, 1937)* Iron Needle ▲ IN 1310 [ADD]
Beethoven, L. van:Sym 1 Dutton Laboratories ▲ DUT 5004 [ADD]
Beethoven, L. van:Sym 1 *(rec between 1937 & 1939)* Enterprise ("Document" series) 2–▲ ENTLV 921 [ADD]
Beethoven, L. van:Sym 4 Dutton Laboratories ▲ DUT 5004 [ADD]
Beethoven, L. van:Sym 4 *(rec between 1937 & 1939)* Enterprise ("Document" series) 2–▲ ENTLV 921 [ADD]
Beethoven, L. van:Sym 4 *(rec June 1, 1937)* Iron Needle ▲ IN 1310 [ADD]
Beethoven, L. van:Sym 6, "Pastorale" *(rec between 1937 & 1939)* Enterprise ("Document" series) 2–▲ ENTLV 921 [ADD]
Brahms, J.:Tragic Ov *(rec between 1937 & 1939)* Enterprise ("Document" series) 2–▲ ENTLV 921 [ADD]
Mozart, W.A.:Zauberflöte (sels)—Ov. *(rec between 1937 & 1939)* Enterprise ("Document" series) 2–▲ ENTLV 921 [ADD]
Verdi, G.:Requiem Mass, w. Zinka Milanov (sop), Libera me, Domine *(rec 1938–1944)* Minerva ▲ MN A15 [ADD]
R. Vaughan Williams (cnd)
Vaughan Williams, R.:Dona nobis pacem, w. R. Flynn (sop), R. Henderson (bar), BBC Sym Chorus [E,L] *(rec 11/36, broadcast transcr)* Pearl ▲ GEMMCD 9342 (m) [AAD]
Vaughan Williams, R.:Sym 4 *(rec 1937 for HMV)* Koch Legacy ▲ 3-7018-2 H1 (m)
Vaughan Williams, R.:Sym 4 Dutton Laboratories ▲ DUT CDAX 8011 [ADD]
A. Walter (cnd)
Furtwängler, W.:Sym 2 Marco Polo ▲ 8.223436
B. Walter (cnd)
Beethoven, L. van:Fidelio (ov) *(rec May 1934)* Grammofono 2000 ▲ GRM 78560
Beethoven, L. van:Fidelio (ov) *(rec 1934)* Iron Needle ▲ 1302 (m) [ADD]
Brahms, J.:Sym 4 *(rec 1934 for HMV)* Koch Legacy ▲ 3-7120-2 H1
Brahms, J.:Sym 4 *(rec May 1934)* Grammofono 2000 ▲ GRM 78560
Mozart, W.A.:Sym 39 *(rec May 1934)* Grammofono 2000 ▲ GRM 78560
Mozart, W.A.:Sym 39 EMI Classics ("Great Recordings of the Century" series) 3–▲ CDHC 63912
B. Walter, M. Sargent (cnd)
Wagner, R.:Arias & Scenes, w. K. Flagstad (sop), L. Melchior (ten), E. MacArthur (cnd) New York PO, RCA Victor SO, San Francisco Opera Orch—selections from Götterdämering; Tristan & Isolde; Lohengrin Memories 2–▲ HR 4456/57 [ADD]
M. Wiggelsworth (cnd)
Skempton, H.:Lento NMC ▲ NMC 5 [DDD]
H. Wood (cnd)
Bax, A.:Con Vc (1925), w. Beatrice Harrison (vc) Symposium ▲ SYM 1150
Bax, A.:Sym 3—1st movt [rehearsal excerpt] Symposium ▲ SYM 1150
Mozart, W.A.:Exsultate, w. Elizabeth Schumann (sop) Symposium ▲ SYM 1150
Mozart, W.A.:Rè pastore (sels) Symposium ▲ SYM 1150
Mozart, W.A.:Sinf concertante Vn, K.364 Symposium ▲ SYM 1150
Vaughan Williams, R.:Serenade to Music, w. Isobel Baillie (sop), Lilian Stiles-Allen (sop), Elsie Suddaby (sop), Eva Turner (sop), Margaret Balfour (cta), Muriel Brunskill (cta), Astra Desmond (cta), Mary Jarred (cta), Parry Jones (ten), Heddle Nash (ten), Frank Titterton (ten), Walter Widdop (ten), Roy Henderson (bar), Harold Williams (bar), Norman Allin (bass), Robert Easton (bass) *(rec Abbey Road, Oct 15, 1938)* Claremont ▲ CDGSE 785066
Vaughan Williams, R.:Serenade to Music, w. I. Baillie (sop), E. Suddaby (sop), S. Allen (sop), E. Turner (sop), M. Balfour (cta), A. Desmond (cta), M. Brunskill (cta), M. Jarred (cta), H. Nash (ten), W. Widdop (ten), P. Jones (ten), F. Titterton (ten), R. Henderson (bass), R. Easton (bass), H. Williams (bass), N. Allin (bass) [E] *(rec 10/15/38)* Pearl ▲ GEMMCD 9342 (m) [AAD]
H. J. Wood (cnd)
Vaughan Williams, R.:Serenade to Music, w. I. Baillie (sop), E. Suddaby (sop), S. Allen (sop), E. Turner (sop), M. Balfour (cta), A. Desmond (cta), M. Brunskill (cta), M. Jarred (cta), H. Nash (ten), W. Widdop (ten), P. Jones (ten), F. Titterton (ten), R. Henderson (bass), R. Easton (bass), H. Williams (bass), N. Allin (bass) Dutton Laboratories ▲ CDAX 8004 [ADD]
P. Zukovsky (cnd)
Schnabel, A.:Sym 1 *(rec Maida Vale, BBC Studios, London, Apr 26–28, 1994)* CP² ▲ CP² 109 [DDD]

BBC Welsh National Orch
R. Hickox (cnd)
Rubbra, E.:Sym 4 Chandos ▲ CHAN 9401 [DDD]
Rubbra, E.:Sym 10 Chandos ▲ CHAN 9401 [DDD]

BBC Welsh National Orch (cont.)
R. Hickox (cnd) (cont.)
Rubbra, E.:Sym 11 Chandos ▲ CHAN 9401 [DDD]
T. Otaka (cnd)
Firsova, E.:Cassandra—Andante *(rec Jan. 31, 1994)* BIS ▲ CD 668 [DDD]
Gubaidulina, S.:Pro et Contra *(rec Jan. 31, 1994)* BIS ▲ CD 668 [DDD]
Rachmaninoff, S.:Con 3 Pno, w. J. Lill (pno) Nimbus ▲ NI 5348 [DDD]
BBC Welsh National SO
M. Atzmon (cnd)
Mozart, W.A.:Ave verum, w. BBC Welsh Choral Society IMP ("BBC Radio" series) ▲ IMP 5691452
Mozart, W.A.:Maurerische Trauermusik, w. BBC Welsh Choral Society IMP ("BBC Radio" series) ▲ IMP 5691452
Mozart, W.A.:Requiem, w. Jennifer Smith (sop), Helen Watts (cta), Ian Partridge (ten), Stafford Dean (bass), BBC Choral Society IMP ("BBC Radio" series) ▲ IMP 5691452
V. Handley (cnd)
Williams, G.:Ballads Orch Lyrita ▲ SRCD 327
Williams, G.:Sym 2 Lyrita ▲ SRCD 327
R. Hickox (cnd)
Rubbra, E.:The Morning Watch, w. BBC Welsh National Chorus Chandos ▲ CHAN 9441
Rubbra, E.:Sym 2 Chandos ▲ CHAN 9481
Rubbra, E.:Sym 6 Chandos ▲ CHAN 9481
Rubbra, E.:Sym 9, w. Lynne Dawson (sop), Della Jones (alt), Stephen Roberts (bar), BBC Welsh National Chorus Chandos ▲ CHAN 9441
Tavener, J.:We Shall See Him As He Is, w. P. Rozario (sop), J. M. Ainsley (ten), A. Murgatroyd (ten), BBC Welsh National Chorus [E] Chandos ▲ CHAN 9128 [DDD]
O. A. Hughes (cnd)
Hughes, O.A.:Dewi Saint, w. Yvonne Kenny (sop), Martyn Hill (ten), David Wilson-Johnson (bar), BBC Welsh National Chorus [E] Chandos ▲ CHAN 8890 [DDD]
G. Llewellyn (cnd)
Chávez, C.:Con Trbn, w. Christian Lindberg (trbn) *(rec Brangwyn Hall, Swansea, Wales, Dec 14–15, 1995)* BIS ▲ CD 788 [DDD]
Mathias, W.:Con Ob, w. D. Cowley (ob) Nimbus ▲ NI 5343
Mathias, W.:Sym 3 Nimbus ▲ NI 5343
Rouse, C.:Con Trbn, w. Christian Lindberg (trbn) *(rec Brangwyn Hall, Swansea, Wales, Dec 14–15, 1995)* BIS ▲ CD 788 [DDD]
Thomas, A.R.:Meditation, w. Christian Lindberg (trbn) *(rec Brangwyn Hall, Swansea, Wales, Dec 14–15, 1995)* BIS ▲ CD 788 [DDD]
W. Mathias (cnd)
Mathias, W.:Sym 1 Nimbus ▲ NI 5260 [DDD]
Mathias, W.:Sym 2 Nimbus ▲ NI 5260 [DDD]
T. Otaka (cnd)
Denisov, E.:Con A Sax, w. Claude Delangle (sax) *(rec Brangwyn Hall, Swansea, Wales)* BIS ▲ CD 665 [DDD]
Denisov, E.:Peinture, w. David Buckland (ctbn) *(rec Brangwyn Hall, Swansea, Wales)* BIS ▲ CD 665 [DDD]
Elgar, E.:Intro & Allegro BIS ▲ CD 727
Elgar, E.:Sym 1 BIS ▲ CD 727
Franck, C.:Le Chasseur maudit Chandos ▲ CHAN 9342 [DDD]
Lutoslawski, W.:Chantefleurs et Chantefables, w. Valdine Anderson (sop) *(rec Brangwyn Hall, Swansea, Wales, July 27–28, 1995)* BIS ▲ CD 743 [DDD]
Lutoslawski, W.:Sym 3, w. Valdine Anderson (sop) *(rec Brangwyn Hall, Swansea, Wales, July 27–28, 1995)* BIS ▲ CD 743 [DDD]
Prokofiev, S.:Romeo & Juliet (suites)—sels. from all 3 suites Nimbus ▲ NI 5306 [DDD]
Rachmaninoff, S.:Con 3 Pno, w. *(pianist unknown)* [orch. Respighi] Nimbus ▲ NI 5311
Rachmaninoff, S.:The Isle of the Dead Nimbus ▲ NI 5344 [DDD]
Rachmaninoff, S.:Sym 1 Nimbus ▲ NI 5331
Rachmaninoff, S.:Sym 2 Nimbus ▲ NI 5322 [DDD]
Rachmaninoff, S.:Sym 3 Nimbus ▲ NI 5344 [DDD]
Rachmaninoff, S.:Vocalise Nimbus ▲ NI 5322 [DDD]
Schnittke, A.:Sym 6 *(rec Brangwyn Hall, Swansea, Wales, July 26–27, 1995)* BIS ▲ CD 747 [DDD]
Schnittke, A.:Sym 7, w. Nigel Seaman (tuba), David Buckland (ctbn), Michael Wright (db) *(rec Brangwyn Hall, Swansea, Wales, July 26–27, 1995)* BIS ▲ CD 747 [DDD]
Strauss, R.:Don Juan Nimbus ▲ NI 5235-2 [DDD]
Strauss, R.:Der Rosenkavalier (waltzes)—First waltz sequence Nimbus ▲ NI 5235-2 [DDD]
Strauss, R.:Till Eulenspiegels lustige Streiche Nimbus ▲ NI 5235-2 [DDD]
Strauss, R.:Tod und Verklärung Nimbus ▲ NI 5235-2 [DDD]
Takemitsu, T.:Dreamtime *(rec Brangwyn Hall, Swansea, Wales, Nov 7–8, 1995)* BIS ▲ CD 760 [DDD]
Takemitsu, T.:Fantasma Cantos, w. R. Stoltzman (cl) RCA Red Seal ▲ 09026-62537-2
Takemitsu, T.:A Flock Descends into the Pentagonal Garden *(rec Brangwyn Hall, Swansea, Wales, Nov 7–8, 1995)* BIS ▲ CD 760 [DDD]
Takemitsu, T.:Orion & Pleiades, w. Paul Watkins (vc) *(rec Brangwyn Hall, Swansea, Wales, Nov 7–8, 1995)* BIS ▲ CD 760 [DDD]
Takemitsu, T.:Quatrain II, w. R. Stoltzman (cl) RCA Red Seal ▲ 09026-62537-2
Takemitsu, T.:Star-Isle *(rec Brangwyn Hall, Swansea, Wales, Nov 7–8, 1995)* BIS ▲ CD 760 [DDD]
Takemitsu, T.:Waterways, w. R. Stoltzman (cl) RCA Red Seal ▲ 09026-62537-2
Takemitsu, T.:Waves, w. R. Stoltzman (cl) RCA Red Seal ▲ 09026-62537-2
Tchaikovsky, P.:Romeo & Juliet Nimbus ▲ NI 5306 [DDD]
B. Thomson (cnd)
Nielsen, C.:Sym 2 IMP ("BBC Radio" series) ▲ IMP 5691492
B. Wordsworth (cnd)
Bliss, A.:A Colour Sym Nimbus ▲ NI 5294 [DDD]
Bliss, A.:Metamorphic Vars Nimbus ▲ NI 5294 [DDD]
Beaux Arts Quartet
Cowell, H.:Qt 2 CRI ■ ACS 6005
Beaux Arts Trio
Beethoven, L. van:Trio 4 Pno, "Ghost" Philips ▲ 420716-2 [ADD]
Beethoven, L. van:Trio 4 Pno, "Ghost" Philips ▲ 412891-2 [ADD]
Beethoven, L. van:Trio 6 Pno, "Archduke" Philips ▲ 412891-2
Beethoven, L. van:Trio 9 Pno, "Kakadu" Philips ▲ 420231-2 [ADD]
Brahms, J.:Trios (comp) Philips 2-▲ 438365-2
Chausson, E.:Trio Vn Philips ▲ 411141-2 [DDD]
Fauré, G.:Qt 2 Pno Philips ▲ 434071-2 [DDD]
Haydn, J.:Trios Pno, Vn & Vc—H.XV/28-31 Philips ▲ 420790-2 [ADD]
Haydn, J.:Trios Pno, Vn & Vc—H.XV/24-27 Philips ▲ 422831-2 [ADD]
Korngold, E.W.:Trio Pno Philips ▲ 434072-2
Mendelssohn, F.:Trio 1 Pno Philips ▲ 416297-2 [DDD]
Mozart, W.A.:Complete Mozart Edition, w. Alfred Brendel (pno), Stephen Bishop Kovacevich (pno), Bruno Hoffmann (glass armonica) Philips 5-▲ 422514-2 [ADD]
Mozart, W.A.:Divert Pno, K.254 Philips ("Two-Fers" series) 2-▲ 446154-2
Mozart, W.A.:Qts Pno, w. Bruno Giuranna (va) Philips ▲ 410391-2 [DDD]
Mozart, W.A.:Trios Pno (comp) Philips ("Digital Classics" series) 3-▲ 422079-2
Rachmaninoff, S.:Trio élégiaque 1 Philips ▲ 420175-2 [DDD]
Rachmaninoff, S.:Trio élégiaque 2 Philips ▲ 420175-2 [DDD]
Saint-Saëns, C.:Trio 1 Pno Philips ▲ 434071-2 [DDD]
Schubert, Franz:Nocturne Pno Philips ▲ 422836-2 [ADD]
Schubert, Franz:Nocturne Pno Philips 2-▲ 438700-2
Schubert, Franz:Nocturne Pno Philips 2-▲ 412620-2 [DDD]
Schubert, Franz:Qnt Pno, D.667, w. S. Rhodes (va), Hörtnagel (db) Philips ▲ 420716-2 [ADD]
Schubert, Franz:Trio Pno, D.28 Philips 2-▲ 438700-2
Schubert, Franz:Trio Pno, D.28 Philips 2-▲ 412620-2 [DDD]

Beaux Arts Trio (cont.)
Schubert, Franz:Trio Pno, D.28 Philips ▲ 426096-2 [ADD]
Schubert, Franz:Trio 1 Pno Philips 2-▲ 438700-2
Schubert, Franz:Trio 1 Pno Philips ▲ 422836-2 [ADD]
Schubert, Franz:Trio 1 Pno Philips 2-▲ 412620-2 [DDD]
Schubert, Franz:Trio 2 Pno Philips 2-▲ 438700-2
Schubert, Franz:Trio 2 Pno Philips ▲ 426096-2 [ADD]
Schubert, Franz:Trio 2 Pno Philips 2-▲ 412620-2 [DDD]
Schumann, R.:Fantasiestücke Vn Philips ▲ 4321652
Schumann, R.:Qt Pno, Op. 47, w. S. Rhodes (va) Philips ▲ 420791-2 [ADD]
Schumann, R.:Qnt Pno, w. D. Bettelheim (vn), S. Rhodes (va) Philips ▲ 420791-2 [ADD]
Schumann, R.:Trios Pno (comp) Philips ▲ 432165-2
Shostakovich, D.:Qnt Pno Philips ▲ 432079-2 [DDD]
Shostakovich, D.:Trio 2 Pno Philips ▲ 432079-2 [DDD]
Tchaikovsky, P.:Trio Pno Philips ▲ 422400-2 [DDD]
Zemlinsky, A. von:Trio Cl Philips ▲ 434072-2
B. Haitink (cnd)
Beethoven, L. van:Con Vn, Vc & Pno, "Triple Con", w. London PO Philips ▲ 420231-2 [ADD]
Beaux Arts Trio [Jack Brymer (cl), Patrick Ireland (va), Stephen Kovacevich (pno)]
Mozart, W.A.:Trios Vn Vc Pno—K.254, 496, 502, 542, 548 & 564 Philips ("Two-Fers" series) 2-▲ 446154-2
Beaux Arts Trio [M. Pressler (pno), D. Guilet (vn), B. Greenhouse (vc)]
Beethoven, L. van:Trios Pno (comp) Philips 3-▲ 438948-2
Beaux Arts Trio [M. Pressler (pno), I. Cohen (vn), B. Greenhouse (vc)]
Brahms, J.:Qts Pno (comp), w. Walter Trampler (va) Philips ▲ 454017-2
Brahms, J.:Trio in A Pno (posth) Philips ▲ 454017-2
Rieti, V.:Trio Vn Premier ▲ PRCD 1033 [ADD]
Beaux Arts Trio [Menahem Pressler (pno), Ida Kavafian (vn), Peter Wiley (vc)]
Arensky, A.:Trio 1 Pno Philips ▲ 442781-2
Arensky, A.:Trio 2 Pno Philips ▲ 442781-2
Baker, D.:Roots II Philips ▲ 438866-2
Granados, E.:Trio Pno Philips ▲ 446 684-2
Rochberg, G.:Summer 1990 Philips ▲ 438866-2
Rorem, N.:Spring Music Philips ▲ 438866-2
Turina, J.:Círculo Philips ▲ 446 684-2
Turina, J.:Trio 1 Philips ▲ 446 684-2
Turina, J.:Trio 2 Pno Philips ▲ 446 684-2
K. Masur (cnd)
Beethoven, L. van:Con Vn, Vc & Pno, "Triple Con", w. Leipzig Gewandhaus Orch Philips ▲ 438005-2
Beaux Arts Trio [Stephen Kovacevich (pno), Jack Brymer (cl), Patrick Ireland (va)]
Mozart, W.A.:Trio Cl, K.498 Philips ("Two-Fers" series) 2-▲ 446154-2
Mozart, W.A.:Trios Pno (comp)—496, 502, 542, 548 & 564 Philips ("Two-Fers" series) 2-▲ 446154-2
Beecham SO
T. Beecham (cnd)
Sir Thomas Beecham, w. London PO *(rec 1910, 1912, 1916, 1918, 1)* Symposium 2-▲ SYM 1096/97
Beersheva Duo [S. Fuxon (pno), B. Berman (pno)]
Martin, F.:Etudes for 2 Pnos Gallo ▲ CD 633 [DDD]
Martin, F.:Ov & Foxtrot Gallo ▲ CD 633 [DDD]
Beethoven Academy
J. Caeyers (cnd)
Beethoven, L. van:Sym 1 *(rec 1995)* Musique D'Abord ▲ HMA 1901573
Beethoven, L. van:Sym 4 *(rec 1995)* Musique D'Abord ▲ HMA 1901573
Beethoven String Quartet
Shostakovich, D.:Qt 6 Strs *(rec 1977)* Praga ▲ PR 250077
Shostakovich, D.:Qt 9 Strs Consonance ▲ 81-3009 [AAD]
Shostakovich, D.:Qt 10 Strs Consonance ▲ 81-3009 [AAD]
Shostakovich, D.:Qt 11 Strs Consonance ▲ 81-3009 [AAD]
Shostakovich, D.:Qt 15 Strs Praga ▲ PR 254 043
Shostakovich, D.:Qnt Pno, w. D. Shostakovich (pno) *(rec 1940)* Multisonic ("Russian Treasures" series) ▲ 31 0179
Taneyev, S.:Qnt Pno Strs, w. Maria Yudina (pno) *(rec 1956–57)* Arlecchino ▲ ARLA 59
Beethoven String Quartet [Dmitri Tsiganov (vn), Nikolas Zabatnikov (vn), Fedor Druyinin (va), Sergei Shirinsky (vc)]
Shostakovich, D.:Qts Strs (comp)—Nos. 12, 13 & 14 *(rec 1968)* Consonance ▲ 81-3008 [AAD]
Beethoven String Quartet [Vasily Shirinsky (vn), Dmitri Tsiganov (vn), Vadim Borisovsky (va), Sergei Shirinsky (vc)]
Shostakovich, D.:Qts Strs (comp)—Nos. 7, 8 & 15 *(rec 1961)* Consonance ▲ 81-3006 [AAD]
Shostakovich, D.:Qts Strs (comp)—Nos. 1, 2 & 4 *(rec 1961)* Consonance ▲ 81-3005 [AAD]
Shostakovich, D.:Qts Strs (comp)—Nos. 3 & 6 *(rec 1960)* Consonance ▲ 81-3007 [AAD]
Shostakovich, D.:Qts Strs (comp)—Nos. 9, 10 & 11 *(rec 1965)* Consonance ▲ 81 3009 [AAD]
Shostakovich, D.:Qt 2 Strs Vanguard Classics ▲ OVC 8077 [ADD]
Shostakovich, D.:Qnt Pno, w. D. Shostakovich (pno) Vanguard Classics ▲ OVC 8077 [ADD]
Beethoven Trio Ravensberg
Rihm, W.:Fremde Szenen CPO ▲ CPO 999119 [DDD]
Spohr, L.:Trios Pno (comp) CPO 3-▲ CPO 999246 [DDD]
Volkmann, R.:Trio 1 Pno CPO ▲ CPO 999128 [DDD]
Volkmann, R.:Trio 2 Pno CPO ▲ CPO 999128 [DDD]
Beethoven Trio Vienna
Beethoven, L. van:Trio 4 Pno, "Ghost" Camerata ▲ 32CM-253
Beethoven, L. van:Trio 5 Pno Camerata ▲ 32CM-253
Mendelssohn, F.:Trio 1 Pno Camerata ▲ 32CM-141
Mozart, W.A.:Divert Pno Camerata 2-▲ 30CM-171-2
Mozart, W.A.:Trios Pno Vn (complete)—K.496, 502, 542, 548 & 564 Camerata 2-▲ 30CM-171-2
Schubert, Franz:Nocturne Pno *(rec Studio Baumgarten, Vienna, June 24, 1993)* Camerata 2-▲ 25CM-401-2 [DDD]
Schubert, Franz:Trio Pno, D.28 *(rec Studio Baumgarten, Vienna, June 17, 1995)* Camerata 2-▲ 25CM-401-2 [DDD]
Schubert, Franz:Trio 1 Pno *(rec Studio Baumgarten, Vienna, June 22–24, 1993)* Camerata 2-▲ 25CM 401 2 [DDD]
Schubert, Franz:Trio 2 Pno *(rec Studio Baumgarten, Vienna, Feb 14–17, 1995)* Camerata 2-▲ 25CM-401-2 [DDD]
Beethovenhalle Orch
D. R. Davies (cnd)
Beethoven, L. van:Coriolan Ov MusicMasters ▲ 1612-67121-2
Beethoven, L. van:Sym 3, "Eroica" MusicMasters ▲ 1612-67121-2
Kancheli, G.:Vom Winde beweint, w. K. Kashkashian (va) ECM New Series ▲ 78118-21471-2 [DDD]
Mendelssohn, F.:Die Hebriden MusicMasters 2-▲ 01612-67088-2
Mendelssohn, F.:Sym 1 MusicMasters 2-▲ 01612-67088-2
Mendelssohn, F.:Sym 2 MusicMasters 2-▲ 01612-67088-2
Mendelssohn, F.:Sym 3 MusicMasters 2-▲ 01612-67088-2
Pärt, A.:Festina lente ECM New Series ▲ 78118-21430-2 [DDD]; ■ 78118-21430-4
Begynhof Academy Amsterdam
Purcell, H.:Music of—Incassum Lesbia, Z.383 & O Dive custos, Z.504; High on a throne, Z.465; If music be the food of love, Z.379c; Dry those eyes (Ariel's Song from The Tempest), Z.631; Let Caesar & rania live, Z.335; Sonata No. 3 in d (from 12 Sonatas of Three Parts, 1683), Z.792; Sonata No. 6 in g (from 10 Sonatas of Four Parts, 1697), Z.807 Globe ▲ GLO 5029 [DDD]

▲ = CD ♦ = Enhanced CD Δ = MD ■ = Cassette Tape ▯ = DCC

Begynhof Academy Amsterdam (cont.)

R. Shaw (cnd)

Purcell, H.:Dido & Aeneas, w. C. Van Lunen (sop), R. A. Morgan (mez), D. Barick (bar) [E] Globe ▲ GLO 5020 [DDD]

Zelenka, J.D.:Lamentationes Jeremiae Prophetae, w. U. Groenewold (cta), H. Meens (ten), M. van Egmond (bass) [L] Globe ▲ GLO 5050 [DDD]

Beijing RSO

Y. Fang (cnd)

Yin, C.–Z.:Yellow River Con, w. R. Caramella (pno)—also includes Yunan Scenes Nuova Era ▲ 6722

Bekova Sisters [Eleonora Bekova (pno), Elvira Bekova (vn), Alfia Bekova (vc)]

Brahms, J.:Trio Cl Chandos ▲ CHAN 9400
Brahms, J.:Trio Hn Chandos ▲ CHAN 9400
Brahms, J.:Trio 1 Pno Chandos ("New Direction" series) ▲ CHAN 9340 [DDD]
Brahms, J.:Trio 2 Pno Chandos ("New Direction" series) ▲ CHAN 9340 [DDD]
Brahms, J.:Trio 3 Pno Chandos ▲ CHAN 9400
Elegy Chandos ▲ CHAN 9364 [DDD]
Martinů, B.:Trio 1 Pno Chandos ▲ CHAN 9452
Rachmaninoff, S.:Trio élégiaque 1 Chandos ("New Direction" series) ▲ CHAN 9329 [DDD]
Rachmaninoff, S.:Trio élégiaque 2 Chandos ("New Direction" series) ▲ CHAN 9329 [DDD]
Ravel, M.:Son Vn Vc Chandos ▲ CHAN 9452
Ravel, M.:Trio Pno Chandos ▲ CHAN 9452
Schubert, Franz:Nocturne Pno Chandos ▲ CHAN 9414 [DDD]
Schubert, Franz:Trio 2 Pno Chandos ▲ CHAN 9414 [DDD]
Tchaikovsky, P.:Songs, w. Sergej Larin (ten)—The Tender Stars Shone for Us, Op. 60/12; No, Only He Who's Known, Op. 6/6; Don Juan's Serenade, Op. 38/1; Amid the Noise of the Ball, Op. 38/3; Why Did I Dream of You, Op. 28/3; Mezza Notte; Night, Op. 60/9; Does the Day Reign?, Op. 47/6; To Forget So Soon; I Opened the Window, Op. 63/2; Rondel, Op. 65/6; This Moonlit Night, Op. 73/3; Disappointment, Op. 65/2; The Sun Has Set, Op. 73/4; I Shall Tell You Nothing, Op. 60/2; Amid Gloomy Days, Op. 73/5; Tell Me, of What in the Shade of the Branches, Op. 57/1; I Should Like a Single Word; Not a Word, O My Friend, Op. 6/2; It Was in Early Spring, Op. 38/2; A Tear Trembles, Op. 6/4; Why?, Op. 6/5; We Sat Together, Op. 73/1; O, If You Knew, Op. 60/3; Again I Am Alone, Op. 73/6 Chandos ▲ CHAN 9428 [DDD]

Belarus Minsk State PO

L. Kramer (cnd)

Benguerel, X.:Libre Vermell, w. Natalia Rudnjewa (mez), Belarus State Capella Chorus Minsk Koch Schwann 2–▲ SCH 314132

Belarussian CO

V. Polianski (cnd)

Arensky, A.:Vars on a Theme of Tchaikovsky Opus 111 ▲ OPS 57–9203 [DDD]
Tchaikovsky, P.:Serenade Strs Opus 111 ▲ OPS 57–9203 [DDD]

Belarussian State Radio–TV Orch

Smolsky, D.:Con. Vc, w. E. Ksaveriyev (vc) Olympia ▲ OCD 551 [AAD]
Smolsky, D.:Con 1 Dlc, w. E. Gladkov (dlc) Olympia ▲ OCD 551 [AAD]
Smolsky, D.:Con Vn, w. L. Gorelic (vn) Olympia ▲ OCD 551 [AAD]
Smolsky, D.:Ov Olympia ▲ OCD 551 [AAD]
Smolsky, D.:Sym 6 Olympia ▲ OCD 551 [AAD]

B. Raisky (cnd)

Glebov, E.:Fantastic Dances (5) Olympia ▲ OLY 552 [AAD]
Glebov, E.:The Little Prince Olympia ▲ OLY 552 [AAD]
Glebov, E.:Sym 5 Olympia ▲ OLY 552 [AAD]

Belcanto Ensemble Frankfurt

Eisler, H.:Woodbury–Liederbüchlein Koch Schwann ("Aulos" series) ▲ 314322 [DDD]
Schwehr, C.:Deutsche Tänze Koch Schwann ("Aulos" series) ▲ 314322 [DDD]
Van De Vate, N.:Cocaine Lil Koch Schwann ("Aulos" series) ▲ 314322 [DDD]

Belgian Air Force Symphonic Band

Kabalevsky, D.:The Comedians [arr. for band by Karel De Wolf] René Gailly ▲ CD 87036 [DDD]

A. Crepin (cnd)

The Comedians René Gailly ▲ CD 87036 [DDD]
Crepi, A.:Music of René Gailly ▲ CD 87074 [DDD]
Golden Jubilee of the Belgian Air Force *(rec Steurbaut Sound Recording Centre)* René Gailly ▲ CD 87124 [DDD]

Belgian Guides Symphonic Band

Belgian Guides Symphonic Band René Gailly ▲ CD 87056 [DDD]
Belgian Works for Symphonic Band, Vol. 1 René Gailly ▲ CD 87047 [DDD]
Belgian Works for Symphonic Band, Vol. 2 René Gailly ▲ CD 87057 [DDD]

N. Nozy (cnd)

Absil, J.:Roumaniana René Gailly ▲ CD 87047 [DDD]
Bach, J.S.:Air on the G String [orchd. W. Hautvast] René Gailly ▲ CD 87025 [DDD]
Bach, J.S.:Cons Org, BWV 592–597 [orchd. A. Prevost]—No. 3 in C, BWV 594 René Gailly ▲ CD 87025 [DDD]
Bach, J.S.:Fant & Fugue Org, BWV 537 [orchd. A. Prevost] René Gailly ▲ CD 87025 [DDD]
Bach, J.S.:Jesu bleibet meine Freude [orch. J. Moerenhout] René Gailly ▲ CD 87025 [DDD]
Bach, J.S.:Pastorale Org, BWV 590 [orchd. A. Prevost] René Gailly ▲ CD 87025 [DDD]
Bach, J.S.:Sheep May Safely Graze [orchd. A. Reed] René Gailly ▲ CD 87025 [DDD]
Bach, J.S.:Sinfs [orchd. W. Hautvast]—from Cantata "Ich lasse dich nicht, du segnest mich denn", BWV 157 René Gailly ▲ CD 87025 [DDD]
Bach, J.S.:Toccata & Fugue Org, BWV 565 [orchd. A. Prevost] René Gailly ▲ CD 87025 [DDD]
Belgian Military Marches, Vol. 1:Cavalry Marches René Gailly ▲ CD 87040 [DDD]
Belgian Military Marches, Vol. 2:Infantry Marches René Gailly ▲ CD 87055
Belgian Military Marches, Vol. 3:National Anthem René Gailly ▲ CD 87070 [DDD]
Berlioz, H.:Le Carnaval romain *(rec Steurbaut Sound Recording Ctr)* René Gailly ▲ CD87 105 [DDD]
Bernstein, L.:Candide (ov) René Gailly ▲ CD 87076 [DDD]
Bernstein, L.:On the Town—The Great Lover Displays Himself; Lonely Town; Times Square 1944 René Gailly ▲ CD 87076 [DDD]
Brotons, S.:Rebroll, w. Thomas Dieltjens (pno) René Gailly ▲ CD 87107 [DDD]
Falla, M. de:El sombrero de tres picos, w. Thomas Dieltjens (pno) René Gailly ▲ CD 87107 [DDD]
Gershwin, G.:Rhap in Blue, w. M. Mathijs (pno) René Gailly ▲ CD 87076 [DDD]
Gilson, P.:Richard III René Gailly ▲ CD 87047 [DDD]
Glorieux, F.:Movts Pno, w. R. Groslot (pno) René Gailly ▲ CD 87057 [DDD]
Gotkovsky, I.:Chant de la forêt, w. Vivente Voce Choir, Vocal Ensemble ex Tempore René Gailly ▲ CD 87058 [DDD]
Gotkovsky, I.:Con Sax, w. J. Leclercq (sax) René Gailly ▲ CD 87037 [DDD]
Gotkovsky, I.:Con Sym Band René Gailly ▲ CD 87037 [DDD]
Gotkovsky, I.:Fanfare René Gailly ▲ CD 87058 [DDD]
Gotkovsky, I.:Poème du feu René Gailly ▲ CD 87037 [DDD]
Gotkovsky, I.:Sym brillante René Gailly ▲ CD 87058 [DDD]
Gotkovsky, I.:Sym du printemps René Gailly ▲ CD 87058 [DDD]
Gould, M.:Jericho Rhap René Gailly ▲ CD 87076 [DDD]
Granados, E.:Danzas españolas (10), w. Thomas Dieltjens (pno) René Gailly ▲ CD 87107 [DDD]
Lalo, E.:Le Roi d'Ys (ov) *(rec Steurbaut Sound Recording Ctr)* René Gailly ▲ CD87 105 [DDD]
Legley, V.:Petite introduction pour une Fête Royale René Gailly ▲ CD 87057 [DDD]
Legley, V.:Sym 7 René Gailly ▲ CD 87047 [DDD]
Louel, J.:Sym 4 René Gailly ▲ CD 87057 [DDD]
Mendelssohn, F.:Ruy Blas (ov) *(rec Steurbaut Sound Recording Ctr)* René Gailly ▲ CD87 105 [DDD]
Rimsky–Korsakov, N.:Con Trbn, w. M. Becquet (trbn) René Gailly ▲ CD 87075 [DDD]
Rimsky–Korsakov, N.:Concertstück Cl, w. W. Boeykens (cl) René Gailly ▲ CD 87075 [DDD]
Rimsky–Korsakov, N.:Scheherazade René Gailly ▲ CD 87075 [DDD]
Rimsky–Korsakov, N.:Vars on a Theme of Glinka, w. J. van den Hauwe (ob) René Gailly ▲ CD 87075 [DDD]

Belgian Guides Symphonic Band (cont.)

N. Nozy (cnd) (cont.)

Rossini, G.:La gazza ladra (ov) *(rec Steurbaut Sound Recording Ctr)* René Gailly ▲ CD87 105 [DDD]
Shostakovich, D.:Festive Ov *(rec Steurbaut Sound Recording Ctr)* René Gailly ▲ CD87 105 [DDD]
Simonis, J.–M.:Eclosions (1991) René Gailly ▲ CD 87057 [DDD]
Smith, C.T.:Festival Vars René Gailly ▲ CD 87076 [DDD]
Strens, J.:Danse Funambulesque René Gailly ▲ CD 87047 [DDD]
Tchaikovsky, P.:Marche slave [trans. F. Rogister] René Gailly ▲ CD 87048 [DDD]
Tchaikovsky, P.:Ov 1812 [trans. H. Séha] René Gailly ▲ CD 87048 [DDD]
Tchaikovsky, P.:Romeo & Juliet [trans. M.H. Hindsley] René Gailly ▲ CD 87048 [DDD]
Verdi, G.:I vespri siciliani (ov) *(rec Steurbaut Sound Recording Ctr)* René Gailly ▲ CD87 105 [DDD]
Wagner, R.:Tannhäuser (ov) *(rec Steurbaut Sound Recording Ctr)* René Gailly ▲ CD87 105 [DDD]

Belgian National Orch

Ysaÿe, E.:Chant d'hiver, w. J. Rubenstein, M. Rodan Koch Schwann ▲ CD 311099 [DDD]
Ysaÿe, E.:Exil, w. J. Rubenstein, M. Rodan Koch Schwann ▲ CD 311099 [DDD]
Ysaÿe, E.:Extase, w. J. Rubenstein, M. Rodan Koch Schwann ▲ CD 311099 [DDD]
Ysaÿe, E.:Poème élégiaque Vn & Orch, w. J. Rubenstein, M. Rodan Koch Schwann ▲ CD 311099 [DDD]
Ysaÿe, E.:Scène au rouet, w. J. Rubenstein, M. Rodan Koch Schwann ▲ CD 311099 [DDD]

R. Defossez (cnd)

Absil, J.:Sym 2 *(rec Studio Fonior, Brussells, Sept 26, 1958)* Cypres ▲ CYP 3602

F. Quinet (cnd)

Absil, J.:Andante symphonique *(rec Brussells, Aug 20, 1952)* Cypres ▲ CYP 3602
Absil, J.:Con 1 Pno, w. André Dumortier (pno) *(rec Brussells, Aug 20, 1952)* Cypres ▲ CYP 3602

M. Rodan (cnd)

Ysaÿe, E.:Andante Vn, w. J. Rubenstein (vn) Koch Schwann ▲ CD 311099 [DDD]

D. Sternefeld (cnd)

Absil, J.:Serenade, Op. 44 *(rec Studio Fonior, Brussells, June 5, 1961)* Cypres ▲ CYP 3602

Belgian RSO

Marc Grauwels & Friends, w. Marc Grauwels (fl), Marie–Noelle de Callataÿ (sop), Hiroko Masaki (sop), Dennis James (glass hmc), Ingrid Procureur (hp), Yves Storms (gtr), Yvietta Matison (va), Mark Drobinsky (vc), Alain De Rijckere (bn), Daniel Blumenthal (pno), Frank Michiels (perc), Belgian RSO, et al. Syrinx 2–▲ 96101 [DDD]

E. Doneux (cnd)

Franck, C.:Grand Con 2 Pno, w. J.–C. Vanden Eynden (pno) Koch Schwann ▲ CD 311111 [DDD] ■ MC 211111 (D)
Franck, C.:Vars brillantes sur la ronde favorite de Gustave III, w. J.–C. Vanden Eynden (pno) Koch Schwann ▲ CD 311111 [DDD] ■ MC 211111 (D)

B. Priestman (cnd)

Fétis, F.J.:Fant symphonique, w. A. Froidebise (org) Koch Schwann ▲ CD 311097 [DDD]
Fétis, F.J.:Sym 1 Koch Schwann ▲ CD 311097 [DDD]

J. Serebrier (cnd)

Chausson, E.:Soir de fête Chandos ▲ CHAN 8369 [DDD]
Chausson, E.:Sym in B♭ Chandos ▲ CHAN 8369 [DDD]
Chausson, E.:The Tempest Chandos ▲ CHAN 8369 [DDD]
Serebrier, J.:Poema elegiaco Finnadar ■ 90937–4
Shostakovich, D.:5 Days–5 Nights (suite) RCA Red Seal ▲ 7763–2–RC [ADD]
Shostakovich, D.:The Gadfly (suite) RCA Red Seal ▲ 6603–2–RC [ADD] ■ 6603–4–RC
Shostakovich, D.:Hamlet (film music) RCA Red Seal ▲ 7763–2–RC [ADD]
Shostakovich, D.:King Lear (film music) RCA Red Seal ▲ 7763–2–RC [ADD]
Shostakovich, D.:Pirogov Suite RCA Red Seal ▲ 6603–2–RC [ADD] ■ 6603–4–RC

A. Vandernoot (cnd)

Franck, C.:Prélude, choral et fugue [orchd. Gabriel Pierné] Koch Schwann ▲ CD 311098 [DDD]

Belgian Radio–TV French SO

R. Barshaï (cnd)

Martinů, B.:Con 2 for 2 Vns, w. André Siwy (vn), Yaga Siwy (vn) *(rec 1989)* Discover International ▲ DI 920161 [DDD]
Prokofiev, S.:Son for 2 Vns, w. André Siwy (vn), Yaga Siwy (vn) *(rec 1989)* Discover International ▲ DI 920161 [DDD]
Szymanowski, K.:Con 2 Vn, w. André Siwy (vn) *(rec 1989)* Discover International ▲ DI 920161 [DDD]

P. Uy (cnd)

Carnet de bal Fonti Musicali ▲ FMD 187 [DDD]

Belgian Radio–TV Orch

A. Rahbari (cnd)

Bartók, B.:Con Orch *(rec 6/90)* Naxos ▲ 8.550261 [DDD]
Bartók, B.:Music for Strs, Perc & Cel *(rec 6/90)* Naxos ▲ 8.550261 [DDD]
Brahms, J.:Academic Festival Ov Naxos ▲ 8.550281 [DDD]
Brahms, J.:Serenade 1 Orch *(rec 6/90)* Naxos ▲ 8.550280 [DDD]
Brahms, J.:Serenade 2 Orch *(rec 3/90)* Naxos ▲ 8.550279 [DDD]
Brahms, J.:Sym 1 *(rec 6/90)* Naxos ▲ 8.550280 [DDD]
Brahms, J.:Sym 2 *(rec 3/90)* Naxos ▲ 8.550279 [DDD]
Brahms, J.:Sym 3 *(rec 1989)* Naxos ▲ 8.550278 [DDD]
Shostakovich, D.:Sym 5 Naxos ▲ 8.550427 [DDD]
Shostakovich, D.:Sym 9 Naxos ▲ 8.550427 [DDD]

N. Sanzogno (cnd)

Verdi, G.:Aida, w. Jessye Norman (sop), Yannula Pappas (mez), Walter Alberti (bar), Luigi Roni (b–bar), Belgian Radio–TV Chorus *(rec live, Paris, May 4, 1973)* Agorá ("Phoenix" series) 2–▲ 507

A. Sibert (cnd)

Lehár, F.:Der Graf von Luxemburg (sels), w. *(soloists unknown)*, Belgian Radio–TV Chorus Studio SM ▲ 2222
Lehár, F.:Das Land des Lächeins (sels), w. *(soloists unknown)*, Belgian Radio–TV Chorus Studio SM ▲ 2222
Lehár, F.:Die lustige Witwe, w. Teresa Stich–Randall (mez—Missia Palmieri), Monique Stiot (mez—Manon), Germaine Duclos (sgr—Praskovia), Linda Felder (sgr—Olga), Christiane Jacquin (sgr—Nadia), Jeannette Levasseur (sgr—Sylviane), Henri Legay (ten—Camille de Coutançon), Joseph Peyron (ten—Kromsky), Robert Destain (sgr—Baron Popoff), Michel Fauche (sgr—Pristich), Gérard Friedmann (sgr—Lerida), Jacques Gilet (sgr—Bogdanowitch), Jean Guy Henneveux (sgr—Prince Danilo), Serge Klin (sgr—Figg), Jacques Villa (sgr—D'Estillac), Belgian Radio–TV Chorus *(rec Grand Auditorium, Belgium, Apr 30, 1970)* Studio SM 2–▲ 2160 [AAD]
Strauss (II), Joh.:Eine Nacht in Venedig (sels), w. *(artists unknown)*, Belgian Radio–TV Chorus Studio SM ▲ 2222

Belgian Radio–TV PO

Classics Go to the Movies Vol. 2, w. Dresden PO, Budapest Festival Orch, Bulgarian TV–Radio SO, Bela Kovaks, Franz Liszt CO, Bruno Lazzaretti, Berlin RSO, Hungarian State Orch LaserLight ▲ 15 642

F. Devreese (cnd)

Devreese, G.:Tombelène, w. Brussels Belgian Radio–TV PO *(rec Brussels, 1993)* Marco Polo ▲ 8.223680 [DDD]

A. Rahbari (cnd)

Brahms, J.:Academic Festival Ov *(rec Belgian RTV Concert Hall, Brussels, Apr 27–May 5, 1989)* Naxos 4–▲ 8.504012 [DDD]
Brahms, J.:Con 2 Pno, w. J. Jandó (pno) *(rec June 3–4, 1992)* Naxos ▲ 8.550506 [DDD]
Brahms, J.:Sym 4 Naxos ▲ 8.550281 [DDD]
Brahms, J.:Sym 4 *(rec Belgian RTV Concert Hall, Brussels, Apr 27–May 5, 1989)* Naxos 4–▲ 8.504012 [DDD]
Brahms, J.:Tragic Ov *(rec Belgian RTV Concert Hall, Brussels, Apr 27–May 5, 1989)* Naxos 4–▲ 8.504012 [DDD]
Brahms, J.:Tragic Ov Naxos ▲ 8.550281 [DDD]
Brahms, J.:Vars on a Theme by Haydn *(rec 1989)* Naxos ▲ 8.550278 [DDD]
Shostakovich, D.:Sym 10 Naxos ▲ 8.550326 [DDD]

Belgian Radio–TV PO (cont.)
A. Rahbari (cnd) (cont.)
Stravinsky, I.:Jeu de cartes — Naxos ▲ 8.550472 [DDD]
Stravinsky, I.:Le Sacre du printemps Orch — Naxos ▲ 8.550472 [DDD]
Weber, C.M. von:Con 1 Pno, w. Dana Protopopescu (pno) *(rec Concert Hall of the Belgian Radio & Television, Brussels, May 16–18, 1994)* — Discover International ▲ DI 920222 [DDD]
Weber, C.M. von:Con 2 Pno, w. Dana Protopopescu (pno) *(rec Concert Hall of the Belgian Radio & Television, Brussels, May 16–18, 1994)* — Discover International ▲ DI 920222 [DDD]
Weber, C.M. von:Konzertstück Pno, w. Dana Protopopescu (pno) *(rec Concert Hall of the Belgian Radio & Television, Brussels, May 16–18, 1994)* — Discover International ▲ DI 920222 [DDD]

Belgian Wind Quintet [Jean Michel Tanguy (fl), Louis Op't Eynde (ob), Hedwig Swimberghe (cl), Herman Lemahieu (hn), Yves Bomont (bn)]
Arrieu, C.:Qnt Ww *(rec Concert Hall of the Belgian Radio & Television, Dec. 1988 & Jan. 1989)* — Discover International ▲ DI 920322 [DDD]
Barber, S.:Summer Music *(rec Concert Hall of the Belgian Radio & Television, Dec. 1988 & Jan. 1989)* — Discover International ▲ DI 920322 [DDD]
Beethoven, L. van:Qnt Pno, Ob, Cl, Hn & Bn *(rec Concert Hall of the Belgian Radio & Television, Dec. 1988 & Jan. 1989)* — Discover International ▲ DI 920322 [DDD]
Holst, G.:Qnt Winds *(rec Concert Hall of the Belgian Radio & Television, Dec. 1988 & Jan. 1989)* — Discover International ▲ DI 920322 [DDD]

Belgium New CO
J. Caeyers (cnd)
Hoffmeister, F.A.:Con for 2 Cls, w. Walter Boeykens (cl), Anne Boeykens (cl) — Musique d'abord ▲ HMA 1901433
Krommer, F.:Cons for 2 Cls, w. Anne Boeykens (cl), Walter Boeykens (cl) — Musique d'abord ▲ HMA 1901433

Belgium Radio New SO Chamber Ensemble
R. Zollman (cnd)
Grétry, A.-E.-M.:Le Jugement de Midas (sels), w. B. Degelin (sop), L. Devos (ten) — Koch Schwann ▲ SCH 310902 [ADD]

Belgrade National Opera Orch
O. Danon (cnd)
Tchaikovsky, P.:Mazeppa, w. Bakocevic (sgr), Cakarevic (sgr), Cangalovic (sgr), N. Mitic (bar), Belgrade National Opera Chorus [R] *(rec live, Berlin, 9/27/69)* — Myto 2-▲ 2 MCD 90527 [ADD]
D. Miladinovic (cnd)
Mussorgsky, M.:Boris Godunov, w. Cangalovic (sgr), Djokic (sgr), Milosevic (sgr), Petrovic (sgr), Belgrade National Opera Chorus *(rec live, La Fenice Theater, Venice, Jan. 3, 1967)* — Arkadia 3-▲ 492

Belgrade PO
Z. Zdravkovich (cnd)
Beethoven, L. van:Con 4 Pno, w. A. Benedetti Michelangeli (pno) — Exclusive ▲ EXL 17 [ADD]
Beethoven, L. van:Con 4 Pno, w. A. Benedetti Michelangeli (pno) — Legend ▲ LGD 100 [ADD]
Chopin, F.:Son Pno, Op. 35, w. A. Benedetti-Michelangeli (pno) — Legend ▲ LGD 100 [ADD]

Bell'Arte Ensemble
Mozart, W.A.:Preludes & Fugues Str Trio — Adagio ▲ ADG 91108 [ADD]
Mozart, W.A.:Trio Vn, K.563 — Adagio ▲ ADG 91108 [ADD]

Bell'Arte Orch
H. Sakssian (cnd)
Aprikian, G.:Naissance de David de Sassoun, w. Fabienne Chanoyan (sop—Angel), Anna Karakaya (mez—Queen Taline), Armand Arapian (bar—King Mehèr/Priest), Sipan-Komitas Choir Petit Chanteurs of Tebrotzassere School *(rec Ivry-sur-Seine, Jan 17–18, 1995)* — Studio SM ▲ D2514

Bell'Arte Trio [Elaine Comparone (hpd), Daniel Waitzman (fl), Marsha Heller (ob)]
Bach, J.C.F:Sons Hpd—in D — Premier ▲ PRCD 1051 [DDD]
Bach, J.C.F:Sons (14) Kbd & Fl— in C for Hpd & Fl; in d for Hpd & Ob — Premier ▲ PRCD 1051 [DDD]
Bach, J.C.F:Trios various Instrs, HW.VII/1–7—in C for Fl, Ob & Hpd; in e for Fl, Ob d'amore & Bc — Premier ▲ PRCD 1051 [DDD]
Joplin, S.:Music of—Elite Syncopations; Peacherine Rag; Augustan Club Waltz; Maple Leaf Rag; Rosebud March; Pleasant Moments; Gladiolus Rag; Eugenia; Bink's Waltz; Solace (mexican serenade); The Entertainer; The Easy Winners; Bethena (concert waltz); Magnetic Rag; Wall Street Rag; Euphonic Sounds *(rec Aug. 12–15, 1991 & Sept.)* — Premier ▲ PRCD 1043 [DDD]

Bellerive Trio
Milhaud, D.:Trio Vn — Koch Schwann ▲ 3-1310-2 [DDD]

Belloc Abbey Monks' SO
J. Colson (cnd)
Jour de Pâques/Jour de Joie, w. Belloc Abbey Monks' Choir — Studio SM ▲ 12 22 03 [ADD]

Belmont Ensemble London
P. Gilbert-Dyson (cnd)
Gorb, A.:Hymns Uproarious, w. B. Luxon (nar), S. Amit (nar) — Symposium ▲ SYM 1180
Walton, W.:Façade, w. B. Luxon (nar), S. Amit (nar) — Symposium ▲ SYM 1180
Watson, T.:Dick Whittington & His Cat, w. B. Luxon (nar), S. Amit (nar) — Symposium ▲ SYM 1180

Bennington Cello Quartet
Bacewicz, G.:Qt for 4 Vcs — Opus One ▲ 148
Davidson, T.:Dark Child Sings — Opus One ▲ 148
Hendrick, J.:Allegro — Opus One ▲ 148
Shawn, A.:Suite Vcs — Opus One ▲ 148
Tansman, A.:Mouvements — Opus One ▲ 148

Alban Berg String Quartet
Beethoven, L. van:Grosse Fuge Str Qt — EMI Classics 4-▲ CDC 47134 [DDD]
Beethoven, L. van:Qts Strs (comp)—Op. 59, 74, 95 — EMI Classics 3-▲ CDC 47130
Beethoven, L. van:Qts Strs (comp)—Op. 18, Nos. 2, 5 & 6; Op. 59, Nos. 2 & 3; Op. 95; Op. 132; Op. 133; Op. 135 *(rec live 1989)* — EMI Classics 4-▲ ZDCD 54592
Beethoven, L. van:Qts Strs (comp)—Op. 18, Nos. 1, 3 & 4; Op. 59, Nos. 1 & 3; Op. 74; Op. 127; Op. 130; Op. 131 *(rec live 1989)* — EMI Classics 4-▲ ZDCD 54587
Beethoven, L. van:Qts Strs (comp)—Op. 18 — EMI Classics 3-▲ CDC 47126
Beethoven, L. van:Qts Strs (comp)—Op. 127, 130, 131, 132, 135 — EMI Classics 4-▲ CDC 47134 [DDD]
Brahms, J.:Qts Strs (comp) — Teldec 2-▲ 95503-2
Brahms, J.:Qts Strs (comp) — EMI Classics ▲ ZDCB 54829
Debussy, C.:Qt Strs — EMI Classics ▲ CDC 47347 [DDD]
Dvořák, A.:Qt 12 Strs, "America" — EMI Classics ▲ CDC 54215
Dvořák, A.:Qt 13 Strs — Teldec 2-▲ 95503-2
Einem, G. von:Qt 1 Strs — EMI Classics ▲ CDC 54347
Haubenstock-Ramati, R.:Qt 2 Strs, "In memoriam Christl Zimmerli" — EMI Classics ▲ CDC 54347
Janácek, L.:Qt 1 Strs — EMI Classics ▲ CDC 55457
Janácek, L.:Qt 2 Strs — EMI Classics ▲ CDC 55457
Lanner, J.:Music of—Waltzes — EMI Classics ▲ CDC 54881
Mozart, W.A.:Music of, w. F. P. Zimmermann (vn), A. Dumay (vn), A. S. Mutter (vn), S. Meyer (cl), R. Vlatkovi (hn), C. Zacharias (pno), *(sels unknown)* — EMI Classics ▲ CDC 54165
Mozart, W.A.:Qts Strs (misc)—Nos. 14–23, K.387, 421, 428, 458, 464, 465, 499, 575, 589 & 590 "The Late Quartets" — Teldec 4-▲ 9031-72480-2 [ADD]
Mozart, W.A.:Qts Strs (misc)—Nos. 14–23, K.387, 421, 428, 458, 464, 465, 499, 575, 589 & 590 "The Late Quartets" — EMI Classics 5-▲ CDME 63858
Mozart, W.A.:Qt 17 Strs — Teldec ▲ 2292-43037-2
Mozart, W.A.:Qnt Strs, K.515, w. M. Wolf (va) — EMI Classics ▲ CDC 49085 [DDD]
Ravel, M.:Qt Strs — EMI Classics ▲ CDC 47347 [DDD]
Rihm, W.:Qt 4 Strs — EMI Classics ▲ CDC 54660
Schnittke, A.:Qt 4 Strs — EMI Classics ▲ CDC 54660
Schubert, Franz:Qt 13 Strs — EMI Classics ▲ CDC 47333 [DDD]
Schubert, Franz:Qt 14 Strs — EMI Classics ▲ CDC 47333 [DDD]
Schubert, Franz:Qnt Pno, D.667, w. E. Leonskaja (pno), G. Hörtnagel (db) — EMI Classics ▲ CDC 47448

Alban Berg String Quartet (cont.)
Schubert, Franz:Qnt Strs, D.956, w. A. Schiff (pno) — EMI Classics ▲ CDC 47018 ▯ 0777-7-47018-5-3
Schumann, R.:Qnt Pno, w. Philippe Entremont (pno) — EMI Classics ▲ CDC 55593
Smetana, B.:Qt 1 Strs — EMI Classics ▲ CDC 54215
Strauss (I), Joh.:Music of—Waltzes — EMI Classics ▲ CDC 54881
Strauss (II), Joh.:Waltzes — EMI Classics ▲ CDC 54881
Stravinsky, I.:Concertino Str Qt — EMI Classics ▲ CDC 54347
Stravinsky, I.:Double Canon — EMI Classics ▲ CDC 54347
Stravinsky, I.:Pieces Str Qt — EMI Classics ▲ CDC 54347

Alban Berg String Quartet members
Brahms, J.:Sextet Strs, Op. 18, w. Amadeus Ensemble — EMI Classics ▲ CDC 54216

Bergamo Collegium Musicum
P. Pelucchi (cnd)
Zingarelli, N.A.:La passione di Gesù Cristo, w. Ernesto Palacio (ten), Simone Alaimo (b-bar), Juan Diego Florez (sgr) *(rec S. Martino Church, Tirano, June 30, 1995)* — Agorá ▲ 018 [DDD]

Bergamo Stabile Orch
T. Briccetti (cnd)
Mayr, S.:La rosa bianca e la rosa rossa, w. Susanna Anselmi (sop), Anna Caterina Antonacci (sop), Silvia Mazzoni (mez), Luca Canonici (ten), Francesco Facini (bass), Danilo Serraiocco (bass) — Fonit Cetra ("Ricordi" series) 2-▲ FCT RFCD 2007

Bergamo Teatro la Donizetti Orch
A. Camozzo (cnd)
Donizetti, G.:Lucrezia Borgia (sels), w. L. Gencer (sop—Lucrezia), U. Grilli (ten—Gennaro)—sels. *(rec live, 10/4/71)* — Myto 2-▲ 2 MCD 92153 [ADD]

Bergen PO
K. Andersen (cnd)
Borgstrom, H.:Hamlet, w. E. Steen-Nøkleberg (pno) — NKF ▲ NKFCD 50026 [DDD]
Borgstrom, H.:The Thought — NKF ▲ NKFCD 50026 [DDD]
Braein, E.F.:Concertino, w. Ø. Gulbransen (fl) — Simax ▲ PSC 3117
Johansen, D.M.:Pan — Simax ▲ PSC 3119
Johansen, D.M.:Symphonic Vars — Simax ▲ PSC 3119
Saeverud, H.:Con Pno, w. J. H. Kayser (pno) — Norway Music ▲ ACD 4954
Saeverud, H.:Sinf dolorosa — Norway Music ▲ ACD 4953
Saeverud, H.:Sym 7 — Norway Music ▲ ACD 4953
S. Bruland (cnd)
Braein, E.F.:Capriccio, w. E. Knardahl (pno) — Simax ▲ PSC 3117
A. Ceccato (cnd)
Schumann, R.:Syms (comp) [all re-orchd. Mahler] — BIS ("BIS Twins" series) 2-▲ CD 361/394
Schumann, R.:Sym 1 [re-orchestrated version by Gustav Mahler] — BIS ▲ CD 361
Schumann, R.:Sym 2 [re-orchestrated version by Gustav Mahler] — BIS ▲ CD 361
Schumann, R.:Sym 3 [reorchestrated version by Gustav Mahler] — BIS ▲ CD 394 [DDD]
Valen, F.:Syms — Simax 2-▲ PSC 3101 [DDD]
N. Järvi (cnd)
Britten, B.:Peter Grimes (4 sea interludes) — BIS ▲ CD 420 [DDD]
Britten, B.:Sym Vc, w. T. Mørk (vc) — BIS ▲ CD 420 [DDD]
Britten, B.:The Young Person's Guide to the Orchestra — BIS ▲ CD 420 [DDD]
Pärt, A.:Cantus in Memory of Benjamin Britten — BIS ▲ CD 420 [DDD]
D. Kitayenko (cnd)
Concerto Sampler, w. Leif Ove Andsnes (pno), various artists — Virgin Classics 2-▲ CDC 59083
Debussy, C.:Prélude à l'après-midi d'un faune — Virgin Classics ▲ CDZ 59659
Dukas, P.:L'Apprenti sorcier — Virgin Classics ▲ CDZ 59659
Grieg, E.:Con Pno, Op. 16, w. L. O. Andsnes (pno) — Virgin Classics ▲ 59613 [DDD]
Liszt, F.:Con 2 Pno, w. L. O. Andsnes (pno) — Virgin Classics ▲ 59613 [DDD]
Mussorgsky, M.:Night — Virgin Classics ▲ CDZ 59659
Ravel, M.:Boléro — Virgin Classics ▲ CDZ 59659
Ravel, M.:Ma mère l'oye Orch — Virgin Classics ▲ CDZ 59659
Rimsky-Korsakov, N.:Antar — Chandos ▲ CHAN 9178 [DDD]
Rimsky-Korsakov, N.:Capriccio espagnol — Chandos ▲ CHAN 9178 [DDD]
Rimsky-Korsakov, N.:Capriccio espagnol — Chandos ("7000" series) 2-▲ CHAN 7029
Rimsky-Korsakov, N.:Con Pno, w. G. Tozer (pno) — Chandos ▲ CHAN 9229 [DDD]
Rimsky-Korsakov, N.:Russian Easter Festival, w. G. Tozer (pno) — Chandos ▲ CHAN 9229 [DDD]
Rimsky-Korsakov, N.:Russian Easter Festival — Chandos ("7000" series) 2-▲ CHAN 7029
Rimsky-Korsakov, N.:Sadko (sels) — Chandos ("7000" series) 2-▲ CHAN 7029
Rimsky-Korsakov, N.:Sadko Orch, Op. 5, w. G. Tozer (pno) — Chandos ▲ CHAN 9229 [DDD]
Rimsky-Korsakov, N.:Syms (comp) — Chandos ("7000" series) 2-▲ CHAN 7029
Rimsky-Korsakov, N.:Sym 3, w. G. Tozer (pno) — Chandos ▲ CHAN 9229 [DDD]
O.K. Ruud (cnd)
Prokofiev, S.:Con 3 Pno, w. L. O. Andsnes (pno) — Simax ▲ PSC 1060 [DDD]
Prokofiev, S.:Sym 7 — Simax ▲ PSC 1060 [DDD]

Bergen SO
D. Oistrakh (cnd)
Grieg, E.:Con Pno, Op. 16, w. S. Richter (pno) *(rec 1968)* — Intaglio ▲ ING 751 [ADD]

Bergen Wind Quintet
Barber, S.:Summer Music — BIS ▲ CD 291 [DDD]
Hall, P.:Four Tosserier, w. S. Kringlebotn (sop) [Nor] — Simax ("Norway in Music" series) ▲ PSC 3105 [DDD]
Hall, P.:Little Dance Suite [Nor] — Simax ("Norway in Music" series) ▲ PSC 3105 [DDD]
Hall, P.:Suite Wind Qnt [Nor] — Simax ("Norway in Music" series) ▲ PSC 3105 [DDD]
Hindemith, P.:Kleine Kammermusik — BIS ▲ CD 291 [DDD]
Jolivet, A.:Sérénade Ob — BIS ▲ CD 291 [DDD]
Nielsen, C.:Qnt Ww — BIS ▲ CD 428 [DDD]
Nielsen, C.:Wind Chamber Music—Allegretto for 2 Recorders (1931); Canto serioso for Horn & Piano (1913); Fantasy for Clarinet & Piano (*ca.* 1885); 2 Fantasy Pieces for Oboe & Piano, Op. 2 (1889); 3 Pieces from Die Moderen (incidental music), Op. 41 (1921); Quintet for Winds, Op. 43 (1922); Serenata in vano, Op. 68 (1914) — BIS ▲ CD 428 [DDD]
Saeverud, H.:Suite 1 Pno — BIS ▲ CD 291 [DDD]

Luis Berger Ensemble
G. Garrido (cnd)
Baroque Music at the Royal Audience of Charcas, w. Capella Cisplatina, Elyma Ensemble [cnd:Emma Sanchez], Cordoba Children's Choir *(rec Apr 19–24, 1996)* — K617 ▲ 7064 [DDD]

Bergerac Duo [Peter Ernst (gtr), Karin Scholz (gtr)]
Burkhart, F.:Toccata *(rec Dec 1994)* — Thorofon ▲ CTH 2274 [DDD]
Domeniconi, C.:Homenaje a Joaquin Rodrigo *(rec Dec 1994)* — Thorofon ▲ CTH 2274 [DDD]
Ginastera, A.:Dances (4)—Danza del trigo; Idilio crepuscular; Pequena danza *(rec Dec 1994)* — Thorofon ▲ CTH 2274 [DDD]
Kälberer, O.:Shiva *(rec Dec 1994)* — Thorofon ▲ CTH 2274 [DDD]
Petit, P.:Tarantelle Gtrs *(rec Dec 1994)* — Thorofon ▲ CTH 2274 [DDD]
Rodrigo, J.:Tonadilla *(rec Dec 1994)* — Thorofon ▲ CTH 2274 [DDD]
Veldhuis, J. ter:Diapason *(rec Dec 1994)* — Thorofon ▲ CTH 2274 [DDD]

Harald Bergersens Saxophone Quartet
Berg, O.:Qt Saxs *(rec 12/89 & 6/90)* — Victoria ▲ VCD 19059 [DDD]
Glazunov, A.:Qt Saxes *(rec 12/89 & 6/90)* — Victoria ▲ VCD 19059 [DDD]
Lacour, G.:Qt Saxes *(rec 12/89 & 6/90)* — Victoria ▲ VCD 19059 [DDD]

Berkeley SO
K. Hulsmann (cnd)
Lewis, P.S.:Con Vn, w. Kees Hulsmann (vn) *(rec Berkeley, CA, June 1995)* — New Albion ▲ NA 079

74 ▲ = CD ♦ = Enhanced CD Δ = MD ■ = Cassette Tape ▯ = DCC

Berkeley SO (cont.)
K. Nagano (cnd)
Martin, F.:Con Vn, w. Stuart Canin (vn) *(rec Los Medanos College, Pittsburgh, CA, Feb 25-26, 1995)* New Albion ▲ NA 086
Martin, F.:Maria-Triptychon, w. Sara Ganz (sop), Stuart Canin (vn) *(rec Los Medanos College, Pittsburgh, CA, Feb 25-26, 1995)* New Albion ▲ NA 086
L. Pillot (cnd)
Lewis, P.S.:Where the Heart Is Pure, w. Stephanie Friedman (mez) *(rec St. Stephen's Church, Belvedere, CA, Oct 1994 & June 1995)* New Albion ▲ NA 079
Berlin Academy for Early Music
Bach, J.S.:Suites Orch, BWV 1066-1069 Harmonia Mundi France 2-▲ HMC 901578.79
Homilius, G.A.:St. Matthew Passion, w. A. Monoyios (sop), U. Groenwald (cta), G. Türk, C. Prégardien (ten), K. Mertens (b-bar), H.-G. Wimmer (bass), Leverkusen Cappella Vocale Berlin Classics 2-▲ BER 1046 [DDD]
Music of the Berlin Court Berlin Classics ▲ BER 1025 [DDD]
Telemann, G.P.:Cants, w. R. Jacobs (ct)—Das Frauenzimmer verstimmt sich immer (aria); Vergiss dich selbst, mein schönster Engel (aria from the opera *Eginhard*); Meines bleibens ist nicht hier (cantata); Tirsis am Scheidewege (cantata); Nach Finsternis und Todesschatten (Cantata No. 27); An den Schlaf (The 5th Ode); Die Einsamkeit (for countertenor & harpsichord); Adagio in G (from Concerto grosso in e) Capriccio ▲ CD 10 338 [DDD]
M. Creed (cnd)
Handel, G.F.:Jephtha, w. Julia Gooding (sop), Christiane Oelze (sop), Catherine Denley (mez), Axel Köhler (ct), John Mark Ainsley (ten), Michael George (bass) *(rec June 1992)* Berlin Classics 2-▲ BER 1057-2 [DDD]
R. Jacobs (cnd)
Bach, J.S.:Cant 201, w. Maria Cristina Kiehr (sop), Andreas Scholl (ct), James Taylor (ten), Kurt Azeberger (ten), Roman Trekel (bar), Peter Lika (bass), Berlin Chamber Chorus Harmonia Mundi France 2-▲ HMC 901544.45
Bach, J.S.:Cant 205, w. Efrat Ben-Nunn (sop), Katharina Kammerloher (alt), Christoph Prégardien (ten), Klaus Häger (bass), Berlin Chamber Chorus Harmonia Mundi France 2-▲ HMC 901544.45
Bach, J.S.:Cant 213, w. Efrat Ben-Nun (sop), Andreas Scholl (ct), James Taylor (ten), Klaus Häger (bass), Berlin Chamber Chorus Harmonia Mundi France 2-▲ HMC 901544.45
Berlin Bach Orch
H. Flugbeil (cnd)
Buxtehude, D.:Cants, w. Greifswald Cathedral Choir—Wachet auf, ruft uns die Stimme, BuxWV 101; Jesu, meine Freude, BuxWV 60; Cantate Domino, BuxWV 12; Lauda Sion salvatorem, BuxWV68; Mit Fried und Freud ich fahr dahin, BuxWV 76; Befiehl dem Engel, dass er komm, BuxWV 10 *(rec Berlin, Wuppertal-Barmen, Herford, Apr. 1959, Jan. 1960 & Ju)* Cantate ▲ 57601
Berlin Baroque Academy
A. de Marchi (cnd)
Jommelli, N.:La Passione di Gesù Cristo, w. Debora Beronesi (sop), Anke Herrmann (sgr), Jeffrey Francis (ten), Maurizio Picconi (sgr), Eufonia, Sigismondo D'India *(rec Mar 31-Apr 4, 1996)* K617 2-▲ 7063 [DDD]
Berlin Baroque Company
Musik aus Sanssouci [Music from Sanssouci] Capriccio ▲ 10 477 [DDD]
Berlin Baroque Trumpet Ensemble
K. Eichhorn (cnd)
Erlebach, P.H.:Lobe, lobe den Herrn, w. La Dolcezza Ensemble, Capella Cantorum *(rec Berlin-Wilmersdorf, Aug 8-10, 1995)* Capriccio ▲ 10721 [DDD]
Krieger, J.P.:Gloria in excelsis deo, w. La Dolcezza Ensemble, Capella Cantorum *(rec Berlin-Wilmersdorf, Aug 8-10, 1995)* Capriccio ▲ 10721 [DDD]
Krieger, J.P.:Magnificat, w. La Dolcezza Ensemble, Capella Cantorum *(rec Berlin-Wilmersdorf, Aug 8-10, 1995)* Capriccio ▲ 10721 [DDD]
Zachow, F.W.:Von Himmel kam der Engel Schar, w. La Dolcezza Ensemble, Capella Cantorum *(rec Berlin-Wilmersdorf, Aug 8-10, 1995)* Capriccio ▲ 10721 [DDD]
Berlin Bassoon Quartet
Original Works for 3 Bassoons & Contrabassoon Classic Studio Berlin ▲ CS 12308 [DDD]
Berlin Brass Quintet
Brass Bonanza, w. Annapolis Brass Quintet, Dallas Brass Quintet, Metropolitan Brass Quintet, New York Brass Quintet, 1-5 Brass Quintet, St. Louis Brass Quintet Crystal ▲ CD 200 [ADD/DDD]
Berlin Chamber Ensemble
Françaix, J.:Heure du berger Pno MD + G ("Scene" series) ▲ MDG 6030557 [DDD]
Françaix, J.:Qnt Fl MD + G ("Scene" series) ▲ MDG 6030557 [DDD]
Françaix, J.:Qnt 2 Ww MD + G ("Scene" series) ▲ MDG 6030557 [DDD]
Berlin Chamber Opera Orch
B. Jones (cnd)
Henze, H.-W.:Elegy for Young Lovers, w. Regina Schudel (sop), Richard Lloyd Morgan (bass), Lawrence Richard (bass), Helmut Bernhofen (sgr), Bruno Fath (sgr), Aurelia Hajek (sgr), Silvia Weiss (sgr) *(rec Berlin)* Deutsche Schallplatten 2-▲ DS 1050
Järns, H.:Europa und der Stier Col Legno ▲ AU 31816
Berlin CO
H. Haenchen (cnd)
Telemann, G.P.:Cons Ob Orch, w. Burkhard Glaetzner (ob) *(rec 1978)* Berlin Classics ▲ BER 9210
Vivaldi, A.:Cons Ob, w. Burkhard Glaetzner (ob) *(rec 1978)* Berlin Classics ▲ BER 9210
H. Koch (cnd)
Mozart, W.A.:Arias, w. Peter Schreier (ten)—Per pietà, non ricerate, K.420; Misero! O sogno—Aura, che intorno, K.431 Berlin Classics ▲ BER 9129
Mozart, W.A.:Bastien und Bastienne, w. Adele Stolte (sop), Peter Schreier (ten), Theo Adam (bass) Berlin Classics ▲ BER 9129
Mozart, W.A.:Schauspieldirektor, w. Sylvia Geszty (sop), Peter Schreier (ten), Hermann Christian Polster (bass)—features complete dialog *(rec 1968)* Berlin Classics ▲ BER 9136 [DDD]
K. Masur (cnd)
Beethoven, L. van:Music of, w. Berlin State Orch, Leipzig Gewandhaus Orch, Suske Trio—Con for Piano in D, Op. 61; Son for Piano, Op. 14/1; Ländler; Minuets; Arias; plus others Berlin Classics 3-▲ BER 9131
M. Pommer (cnd)
Jochen Kowalski:Aria from Berlin's Operatic History, w. Jochen Kowalski (ct), C. Schornsheim (hpd), R. Alpermann (hpd), H. Friedrich (vc), Markus Stauch (db) Berlin Classics ▲ BER 1050 [DDD]
H. Rögner (cnd)
Wolf-Ferrari, E.:Serenade Strs Berlin Classics ▲ BER 9177
P. Schreier (cnd)
Bach, J.S.:Cants (misc), w. Edith Mathis (sop), Carolyn Watkinson (cta), Eberhard Büchner (ten), Peter Schreier (ten), Siegfried Lorenz (bar), Theo Adam (b-bar), Berlin Soloists Berlin Classics ▲ BER 9221
Bach, J.S.:Cant 36, w. Edith Mathis (sop), Peter Schreier (ten), Siegfried Lorenz (bar), Berlin Soloists Berlin Classics ▲ BER 9220
Bach, J.S.:Cant 202, "Wedding Cant", w. Edith Mathis (sop) Berlin Classics ▲ BER 9222
Bach, J.S.:Cant 203, w. Edith Mathis (sop), Peter Schreier (ten), Siegfried Lorenz (bar), Berlin Soloists Berlin Classics ▲ BER 9220
Bach, J.S.:Cant 205, w. Edith Mathis (sop), Carolyn Watkinson (alt), Julia Hamari (alt), Peter Schreier (ten), Siegfreid Lorenz (bass), Berlin Soloists Berlin Classics ▲ BER 9224
Bach, J.S.:Cant 206, w. Edith Mathis (sop), Carolyn Watkinson (alt), Peter Schreier (ten), Siegfried Lorenz (bass), Berlin Soloists Berlin Classics ▲ BER CD 9225
Bach, J.S.:Cant 207, w. Edith Mathis (sop), Carolyn Watkinson (alt), Julia Hamari (alt), Peter Schreier (ten), Siegfreid Lorenz (bass), Berlin Soloists Berlin Classics ▲ BER 9224
Bach, J.S.:Cant 209, w. Edith Mathis (sop), Peter Schreier (ten), Siegfried Lorenz (bar), Berlin Soloists Berlin Classics ▲ BER 9220
Bach, J.S.:Cant 210, w. Lucia Popp (sop) Berlin Classics ▲ BER 9222
Bach, J.S.:Cant 211, "Coffee Cant", w. Edith Mathis (sop), Peter Schreier (ten), Theo Adam (bass) Berlin Classics ▲ BER 9226

Berlin CO (cont.)
P. Schreier (cnd) (cont.)
Bach, J.S.:Cant 212, "Peasant Cant", w. Edith Mathis (sop), Peter Schreier (ten), Theo Adam (bass) Berlin Classics ▲ BER 9226
Bach, J.S.:Cant 215, w. Edith Mathis (sop), Carolyn Watkinson (alt), Peter Schreier (ten), Siegfried Lorenz (bass), Berlin Soloists Berlin Classics ▲ BER CD 9225
P. Wohlert (cnd)
Bach, J.S.:Brandenburg Cons—Nos. 1-3 LaserLight ▲ 15 508 [ADD]
Bach, J.S.:Brandenburg Cons—Nos. 4-6 LaserLight ▲ 15 509 [ADD]
Bach, J.S.:Brandenburg Con 1 Laserlight ▲ 15 508
Bach, J.S.:Brandenburg Con 2 Laserlight ▲ 15 508
Bach, J.S.:Brandenburg Con 3 Laserlight ▲ 15 508
Bach, J.S.:Con 3 Hpd Laserlight ▲ 15 508
Dvořák, A.:Serenade Strs LaserLight ▲ 15 605 [DDD]
Dvořák, A.:Slavonic Dances (comp)—Op. 72/1-8 Laserlight ▲ 15 605 [DDD]
Mozart, W.A.:Serenata notturna LaserLight ▲ 15 648 [DDD]
Mozart, W.A.:Serenata notturna LaserLight ▲ 15 862 [DDD]
Berlin Comic Opera Orch
R. Reuter (cnd)
Berlioz, H.:Lélio, "Le retourà la vie", w. M. Rabsilber (ten), B. Grabowski (bar), H.-P. Minetti (nar), Berlin Radio Chorus [F; narration G] Berlin Classics ▲ BER 2149 [DDD]
Handel, G.F.:L'Allegro, Il Penseroso ed il Moderato, w. V. Hruba-Freiberger (sop), D. Schellenberger-Ernst (sop), J. Kowalski (alt), F.Kapellmann (bass), Rabsilber (sgr), Berlin Radio Chorus Berlin Classics 2-▲ BER 1147 [DDD]
H. Rögner (cnd)
Theodorakis, M.:Sym 3, w. Els Bolkestein (sop), Berlin Radio Chorus Berlin Classics 2-▲ BER 1128 [ADD]
Berlin Domkapelle Instrumental Ensemble
R. Bader (cnd)
Mozart, L.:Missa solemnis, w. A. Augér (sop), G. Schreckenbach (mez), H. Laubenthal (ten), B. McDaniel (bar), St. Hedwig's Cathedral Choir [L] Koch Schwann ▲ CD 313028 [ADD]
Berlin German Opera House Orch
Opera Arias, w. Anders, Peter (ten) Teldec ▲ 95512-2 [ADD]
Berlin German Opera Orch
K. Böhm (cnd)
Mozart, W.A.:Nozze di Figaro (sels), w. G. Janowitz (sop), E. Mathis (sop), T. Troyanos (mez), D. Fischer-Dieskau (bar), H. Prey (bar)—Scenes & Arias Deutsche Grammophon ▲ 429822-2 [ADD]
E. Jochum (cnd)
Orff, C.:Carmina burana, w. Gundula Janowitz (sop), Gerhard Stolze (ten), Dietrich Fischer-Dieskau (bar), Berlin German Opera Chorus *(rec Ufa-Studio, Berlin, Oct 1967)* Deutsche Grammophon ▲ 447437-2 [ADD]
H. Knappertsbusch (cnd)
Wagner, R.:Parsifal (sels), w. E. Larcen (sop), H. Reimar (ten), C. Hartmann (bar), L. Weber (bass), Berlin German Opera Chorus—Act 3 *(rec 1943)* Enterprise ("Document" series) ▲ ENTLV 943 [ADD]
Wagner, R.:Parsifal (sels), w. Carl Hartmann (ten), Hans Reinmar (bar), Ludwig Weber (bass), Elsa Laren (sgr), Berlin German Opera Chorus—complete Act 3 *(rec Berlin, March 31, 1942)* Grammofono 2000 ▲ GRM 78555
F. Luisi (cnd)
Bellini, V.:Beatrice di Tenda, w. L. Aliberti (sop), C. Capasso (treble), M. Thompson (ten), P. Gavanelli (bass), Berlin German Opera Chorus Berlin Classics 2-▲ BER 1042 [DDD]
L. Maazel (cnd)
Dallapiccola, L.:Ulisse, w. C. Gayer (sop), E. Saedén (bar), V. von Halem (bass), A. Bernard (sgr), Berlin German Opera Chorus *(rec live, Berlin 9/28/68)* Stradivarius 2-▲ STR 10063 [ADD]
Verdi, G.:La traviata, w. P. Lorengar (sop), S. Malagu (mez), G. Aragall (ten), D. Fischer-Dieskau (bar), Berlin German Opera Chorus London ("Double Decker" series) 2-▲ 443000-2
K. Muck (cnd)
Wagner, R.:Parsifal, w. Gotthelf Pistor (ten), Cornelius Bronsgeest (bar), Ludwig Hofmann (bass), Berlin German Opera Chorus Preiser ▲ PRE 90270
H. Schmidt-Isserstedt (cnd)
Schumann, R.:Scenes from Goethe's "Faust", w. Lore Hoffman (sop), Walther Ludwig (ten), Karl Schmitt-Walter (bar), Berlin German Opera Chorus Enterprise ("The Radio Years" series) 2-▲ ENT RY 66
J. Schüler (cnd)
Flotow, F. von:Martha, w. Erna Berger (sop), Peter Anders (ten), Eugene Fuchs (bar), Josef Greindl (bass), Berlin German Opera Chorus Phonographe 2-▲ PHG 5050
G. Sinopoli (cnd)
Opera Choruses, w. Berlin German Opera Chorus Deutsche Grammophon [DDD] ◻ 415283-5
Strauss, R.:Salome, w. C. Studer (sop), L. Rysanek (sop), H. Hiestermann (ten), B. Terfel (b-bar) Deutsche Grammophon 2-▲ 431810-2 [DDD]
M. Viotti (cnd)
Bellini, V.:Il pirata, w. Lucia Aliberti (sop), Roberto Frontali (sgr), Stuart Neill (sgr), José Guadalupe Reyes (sgr), Berlin German Opera Chorus Berlin Classics 2-▲ BER 1115 [DDD]
R. Weikert (cnd)
Mozart, W.A.:Arias, w. D. Schellenberger (sop)—Alma grande e nobil core, K.578; Misera, dove son, K.369 EMI Classics ▲ CDC 55008
Mozart, W.A.:Clemenza (sels), w. D. Schellenberger (sop)—Non piu di fiori EMI Classics ▲ CDC 55008
Mozart, W.A.:Così fan tutte (sels), w. D. Schellenberger (sop)—Per pieta, Come scoglio EMI Classics ▲ CDC 55008
Mozart, W.A.:Don Giovanni (sels), w. D. Schellenberger (sop)—Mi tra di quel alma EMI Classics ▲ CDC 55008
Mozart, W.A.:Idomeneo (sels), w. D. Schellenberger (sop)—Zeffiretti EMI Classics ▲ CDC 55008
Mozart, W.A.:Nozze di Figaro (sels), w. D. Schellenberger (sop)—Porgi amor; Giunse alfin...Deh vieni non tardar EMI Classics ▲ CDC 55008
Mozart, W.A.:Zauberflöte (sels), w. D. Schellenberger (sop)—Ach ich fhl's EMI Classics ▲ CDC 55008
Peter Seiffert Sings Italian Arias, w. Peter Seiffert (ten) EMI Classics ▲ CDC 55010
Berlin German Opera Orch Soloists [A. Lange (tpt), P. Sharp (hn), W. Wiest (trbn)] (cnd)
Poulenc, F.:Son Tpt *(rec Sept. 8, 1991)* FSM-Adagio ▲ FCD 97 219
Berlin German Opera Orch Soloists [R. Schönemann, V. Knappe, A. Lange, T. Tomaszewski, G. Lösch]
Casella, A.:Serenata *(rec May 26 & June 1, 1992)* FSM-Adagio ▲ FCD 97 219
Berlin German SO
V. Ashkenazy (cnd)
Berg, A.:Early Songs, w. B. Balleys (mez) London ▲ 436567-2 [DDD]
Berg, A.:Lyric Suite—3 Pieces London ▲ 436567-2 [DDD]
Berg, A.:Orchesterlieder (5) nach Ansichtskartentexten von Peter Altenberg, w. B. Balleys (mez) London ▲ 436567-2 [DDD]
Berg, A.:Pieces Orch, Op. 6 London ▲ 436567-2 [DDD]
Stravinsky, I.:Capriccio, w. O. Mustonen (pno) *(rec Aug.-Sept. 1992)* London ▲ 440229-2 [DDD]
Stravinsky, I.:Con Pno Ww, w. O. Mustonen (pno) *(rec Aug.-Sept. 1992)* London ▲ 440229-2 [DDD]
Stravinsky, I.:Ebony Con, w. D. Askenazy (cl) *(rec Aug.-Sept. 1992)* London ▲ 440229-2 [DDD]
Stravinsky, I.:Movts Pno, w. O. Mustonen (pno) *(rec Aug.-Sept. 1992)* London ▲ 440229-2 [DDD]
M. Jurowski (cnd)
Shostakovich, D.:The Fall of Berlin (sels), w. Berlin RIAS Chamber Choir *(rec Church of Jesus Christ, Berlin-Dahlem, Germany, Mar 4-6, 1991)* Capriccio ▲ 10 405 [DDD]
Shostakovich, D.:Maxim Trilogy (sels), w. Berlin RIAS Chamber Choir—Youth of Maxim, Op. 41 (1934-5); Return of Maxim, Op. 45 (1936-7); Vyborg District, Op. 50 (1938) *(rec Room 1, German Radio Berlin, June 13-4, 1994)* Capriccio ▲ 10 561 [DDD]
Shostakovich, D.:Suite from Golden Mountains, w. Berlin RIAS Chamber Choir *(rec Room 1, German Radio Berlin, June 13-4, 1994)* Capriccio ▲ 10 561 [DDD]

Berlin German SO (cont.)
M. Jurowski (cnd) (cont.)
Shostakovich, D.:Zoya (sels), w. Berlin RIAS Chamber Choir *(rec Church of Jesus Christ, Berlin-Dahlem, Germany, Mar 4-6, 1991)* Capriccio ▲ 10 405 [DDD]
J. Mauceri (cnd)
Korngold, E.W.:Symphonic Serenade *(rec Church of Jesus Christ, Berlin, Apr. 1994)* London ("Entartete Musik" series) ▲ 444170-2 [DDD]
Korngold, E.W.:Theme & Vars for Orch *(rec Church of Jesus Christ, Berlin, Apr. 1994)* London ("Entartete Musik" series) ▲ 444170-2 [DDD]
Schulhoff, E.:The Flames, w. Jane Eaglen (sop—Donna Anna, Nun, Woman, Marguerite), Carola Höhn (sop—Shadow), Celina Lindsley (sop—Shadow), Regina Schudel (sop—Shadow), Iris Vermillion (mez—La Morte), Christiane Berggold (alt—Shadow), Kaja Borris (alt—Shadow), Elvira Dressen (alt—Shadow), Kurt Westi (ten—Don Juan), Johann-Werner Prein (bass—Commendatore), Gerd Wolf (bass—Harlequin), Berlin RIAS Chamber Choir *(rec Jesus-Christus Church, Berlin Dahlem, Oct 1993/Apr 1994)* London 2-▲ 444630-2 [DDD]
P. Ruzicka (cnd)
Pettersson, G.A.:Sym 15 CPO ▲ CPO 999223 [DDD]
Ruzicka, P.:Das Gesagnete CPO ▲ CPO 999223 [DDD]
L. Zagrosek (cnd)
Braunfels, W.:Die Vögel, w. Helen Kwon (sop—Nightingale), Wolfgang Holzmair (bar—Hoopoe), Matthias Gorne (b-bar—Prometheus), Michael Krause (sgr—Loyal Friend), Endrik Wottrich (sgr—Good Hope), Berlin Radio Chorus London ("Entartete Musik" series) ▲ 448 679-2
Schreker, F.:Die Gezeichneten, w. Elisabeth Connell (sop), Heinz Kruse (ten), Monte Pederson (bar), Alfred Muff (bass), László Polgar (bass) London 3-▲ 444442-2
D. Zinman (cnd)
Schumann, R.:Con Pno, w. Hélène Grimaud (pno) *(rec Paris 1995)* Erato ▲ 11727-2 [DDD]
Strauss, R.:Burleske, w. Hélène Grimaud (pno) *(rec Paris 1995)* Erato ▲ 11727-2 [DDD]
Berlin Guitar Ensemble
Berlin Guitar Ensemble *(rec Nov. 1992)* Thorofon ▲ CTH 2199 [DDD]
Berlin Instrumental Soloists
Haydn, J.:Cons for 2 Lire organizzata, w. W. von Karajan (org) Koch Schwann ▲ CD 311006 [ADD]
Berlin Landeszupf Orch
J. Betton (cnd)
Erdmann, D.:Music of—Divertissement für Zupforchester; Notturno for Recorder & Guitar Choir [w. M. Ripper (recorder)]; Serenata piccola Guitar Choir; Movimenti for Oboe, Zupforchester & Percussion [Birgit Schmieder (oboe), J. Kutay (percussion)]; Sonatine for Mandolin & Piano [w. E. Tonke & A. Suga]; Musik for Guitar Choir; Serenata für Zupforchester *(rec 1994)* Thorofon ▲ CTH 2213 [DDD]
Berlin Large RSO
A. Rother (cnd)
Beethoven, L. van:Con 5 Pno, "Emperor", w. Walter Gieseking (pno) Enterprise ("The Radio Years" series) 2-▲ ENT RY 66
Beethoven, L. van:Con 5 Pno, "Emperor", w. Walter Gieseking (pno) *(rec Sept 1944)* Enterprise ("The Piano Library" series) ▲ ENT 185
Brahms, J.:Sym 2, w. Walter Gieseking (pno) Enterprise ("The Radio Years" series) 2-▲ ENT RY 66
Berlin New SO
H. Pfitzner (cnd)
Schumann, R.:Sym 4 *(rec 1926)* Koch Legacy ▲ 3-7039-2
Berlin Octet
Beethoven, L. van:Septet Strs Berlin Classics ("Eterna" series) ▲ BER 2014 [DDD]
Berwald, F.:Septet Vn, "Grand Septet" Berlin Classics ▲ BER 9037 [ADD]
Kreutzer, C.:Grand Septet Berlin Classics ▲ BER 9037 [ADD]
Spohr, L.:Nonet Strs Berlin Classics ▲ BER 9012 [ADD]
Spohr, L.:Octet Strs Berlin Classics ▲ BER 9012 [ADD]
Witt, F.:Septet Cl Berlin Classics ("Eterna" series) ▲ BER 2014 [DDD]
Berlin Opera Orch
Wagner, R.:Ovs, Preludes & Orch Sels, w. Berlin PO, Bayreuth Festival Orch, Vienna PO, Bavarian RSO, H. von Karajan, R. Kubelik (cnd), K. Böhm (cnd), E. Jochum (cnd)—sels. from Rienzi, Die fliegende Holländer, Tannhäuser, Lohengrin, Parsifal, Die Meistersinger von Nürnberg, Die Walküre, Siegfried, Götterdämmerung *(rec 1958 & 1981)* Deutsche Grammophon ("Double" series) 2-▲ 439687-2 [ADD]
A. Rother (cnd)
Wagner, R.:Tristan und Isolde (sels), w. Martha Mödl (sop—Isolde), Johanna Blatter (mez—Brangäne), Wolfgang Windgassen (ten—Tristan)—Weh, ach wehel dies zu dulden [rec Nov 24., 1954]; Isoldel—Tristan! Geliebter! [rec Oct. 24, 1954]; Lausch', Geliebter!— Lass mich sterben! [rec Oct 24., 1954]; Mild und leise wie er lächelt [rec Oct 22., 1952] Teldec ("Historic" series) ▲ 95516-2 [ADD]
G. Sébastian (cnd)
Strauss, R.:Arias, w. K. Flagstad (sop)—from Elektra—Orest!...Orest! [from Recognition Scene] [G] *(rec live, 5/9/52)* Arkadia 2-▲ 576 (m) [ADD]
Strauss, R.:Arias, w. K. Flagstad (sop)—from Elektra—Orest!...Orest! [from Recognition Scene] [G] *(rec live, 5/9/52)* Melodram 2-▲ MEL 26514 (m) [AAD]
Strauss, R.:4 Last Songs, w. K. Flagstad (sop)—3 songs only, omitting Frühling *(rec live, 5/9 or 5/11/52)* Melodram 2-▲ MEL 26514 (m) [AAD]
Strauss, R.:4 Last Songs, w. K. Flagstad (sop)—3 songs only, omitting Frühling *(rec live, 5/9 or 5/11/52)* Arkadia 2-▲ 576 [ADD]
Wagner, R.:Arias & Scenes, w. Kirsten Flagstad (sop)—12 arias & scenes from Götterdämmerung, Parsifal, Tristan *(rec live 5/9 & 11/52)* Melodram 2-▲ MEL 26514 (m) [AAD]
Wagner, R.:Götterdämmerung (immolation scene), w. K. Flagstad (sop) [G] *(rec live, 5/9/52)* Arkadia 2-▲ 576 [ADD]
Wagner, R.:Tristan und Isolde (sels), w. K. Flagstad (sop)—Act 1 *(Wie lachend sie mir Lieder singen)*, Act 3 *(Tristan!...Ich bins, ich bins; Mild und leise [Liebestod])* [G] *(rec live May 9, 1952)* Arkadia 2-▲ 576 (m) [ADD]
Wagner, R.:Wesendonck Songs, w. K. Flagstad (sop) [G] *(rec live, 5/9 or 5/11/52)* Melodram 2-▲ MEL 26514 (m) [AAD]
Wagner, R.:Wesendonck Songs, w. K. Flagstad (sop) [G] *(rec live, 5/9 or 5/11/52)* Arkadia 2-▲ 576 [ADD]

Berlin Orch
W. Schüchter (cnd)
Straus, O.:Ein Walzertraum (sels), w. Melita Muszely (sop), Lisa Otto (sop), Rudolf Schock (ten), Bruno Fritz (bar), Berlin Chorus Emperor Operetta ▲ KO 86346
F. Zaun (cnd)
Paganini, N.:Con 1 Vn, w. G. Bustabo (vn)—1st movt., Allegro, w. cadenza by Wilhelmj *(rec 1940, orig. issued as Col)* Biddulph ▲ LAB 051 [ADD]
Berlin Philharmonia Ensemble
Schubert, Franz:Octet Ww, D.803 Denon/PCM Digital ▲ DEN 75671
Berlin Philharmonia String Quartet
Bärmann, H.J.:Qnt 3 Cl, w. D. Klöcker (cl) Orfeo ▲ 213901 [DDD]
Hindemith, P.:Qt 4 Strs *(rec Waldkirche Heiligensee, Berlin, Jan. 1995)* Thorofon ▲ CTH 2273 [DDD]
Küffner, J.:Intro, Theme & Vars, w. S. Meyer (cl) Denon/PCM Digital ▲ DEN 8098 [DDD]
Meyerbeer, G.:Qnt Cl, w. D. Klöcker (cl) Orfeo ▲ 213901 [DDD]
Mozart, W.A.:Kleine Nachtmusik, w. W. Güttler (db), M. Klier (hn) Denon/PCM Digital ▲ DEN 7229 [DDD]
Mozart, W.A.:Musikalischer Spass, w. N. Hauptmann (hn), M. Klier (hn) Denon/PCM Digital ▲ DEN 7229 [DDD]
Mozart, W.A.:Qnt Cl, K.581, w. S. Meyer (cl) Denon/PCM Digital ▲ DEN 8098 [DDD]
Mozart, W.A.:Qnt Cl, K.581, w. S. Meyer (cl) Denon ▲ CO 8003 [DDD]
Mozart, W.A.:Qnt Hn, K.407, w. Norbert Hauptmann (hn) Denon/Pcm Digital ▲ DEN 7229 [DDD]
Mozart, W.A.:Qnt Hn, K.407, w. Norbert Hauptmann (hn) Denon/PCM Digital ▲ DEN 8003 [DDD]
Schulhoff, E.:Qt 1 Strs *(rec Waldkirche Heiligensee, Berlin, Jan. 1995)* Thorofon ▲ CTH 2273 [DDD]

Berlin Philharmonia String Quartet (cont.)
Vivaldi, A.:Cons Pic, w. H. W. Dünshede (fl), W. Güttler (db), Motoi (hpd)—RV.441, 443, 444, 445 Denon ▲ 7076 [DDD]
Berlin Philharmonia String Quartet [D. Stabrawa (vn), C. Stadelmann (vn), N. Resa (va), J. Diesselhorst (vc)]
Beethoven, L. van:Qt 15 Strs *(rec 1992 & 1993)* Thorofon ▲ CTH 2182 [DDD]
Mendelssohn, F.:Pieces Str Qt, Op. 81 *(rec 1992 & 1993)* Thorofon ▲ CTH 2182 [DDD]
Berlin Philharmonia String Quartet members
Mozart, W.A.:Qt Ob, K.370, w. H. Schellenberger (ob) Denon/PCM Digital ▲ DC 8003 [DDD]
Berlin Philharmonic Academy Orch
Louis Ferdinand, Prince:Rondos, w. H. Göbel (pno) Thorofon ▲ CTH 2088 [DDD]
Berlin Philharmonic Academy Orch members
Copland, A.:Sextet Cl, Pno & Strs, w. H. Göbel (pno) Thorofon ▲ CTH 2012 [DDD]
Rheinberger, J.:Qt Pno, w. H. Göbel (pno) Thorofon ▲ CTH 2108 [DDD]
Rheinberger, J.:Sxt Fl, w. H. Göbel (pno) Thorofon ▲ CTH 2078 [ADD/DDD]
Rheinberger, J.:Sxt Fl *(rec 1989)* Thorofon 6-▲ BCTH 2161/6
Wolf-Ferrari, E.:Sinfonia da camera Thorofon ▲ CTH 2078 [ADD/DDD]
Berlin Philharmonic Brass Ensemble
H. von Karajan (cnd)
Christmas Adagio, w. Berlin PO Deutsche Grammophon ▲ 449924-2 ▮ 449924-4
Berlin Philharmonic Ensemble
Brahms, J.:Qt 1 Pno MD + G ▲ L 3464 [DDD]
Weber, C.M. von:Trio Fl MD + G ▲ L 3464 [DDD]
Berlin Philharmonic Horn Quartet
Live in Tokyo *(rec live, Tokyo, Jan 1992)* Seven Seas ▲ SVS 39
Berlin Philharmonic Octet
Beethoven, L. van:Septet Strs *(rec Teldec Studio, Berlin, Sept 10-13, 1995)* Nimbus ▲ NI 5461 [DDD]
Hindemith, P.:Octet Winds & Strs *(rec Teldec Studio, Berlin, Sept 10-13, 1995)* Nimbus ▲ NI 5461 [DDD]

Berlin Philharmonic Octet members
Brahms, J.:Qnt Cl Philips ("Duo" series) 2-▲ 446172-2
Brahms, J.:Qnt Pno, w. Werner Hass (pno) Philips ("Duo" series) 2-▲ 446172-2
Brahms, J.:Qnt 1 Strs Philips ("Duo" series) 2-▲ 446172-2
Brahms, J.:Qnt 2 Strs Philips ("Duo" series) 2-▲ 446172-2
Berlin PO
Beethoven, L. van:Con Vn, Vc & Pno, "Triple Con", w. Itzhak Perlman (vn), Yo-Yo Ma (vc), Daniel Barenboim (pno) EMI Classics ▲ CDC 55516
Beethoven, L. van:Fant Pno, Op. 80, "Choral Fant", w. Daniel Barenboim (pno) EMI Classics ▲ CDC 55516
Brahms, J.:Pno Music (misc), w. Alfred Brendel (pno), C. Abbado (cnd), H. Holliger (cnd), London SO—Ballades, Op. 10; Cons for Pno Nos. 1 & 2; Sxt-Vars Philips 25-▲ 446920-2
Grieg, E.:Con Pno, Op. 16, w. Walter Gieseking (pno) Music & Arts ▲ CD 925
Jurassic Classics, w. Kirov Orch, Vienna PO, London PO, Boston SO, V. Gergiev (cnd), A. Previn (cnd), C. Davis (cnd), N. Mariner (cnd) Philips ▲ 442599-2 ▮ 442599-4
Mad About Love, w. Cheryl Studer (sop), Kiri Te Kanawa (sop), José Carreras (ten), Jerry Hadley (ten), Philharmonia Orch [cnd:Giuseppe Sinopoli], Bastille Opera Orch [cnd:Myung-Whun Chung], Boston SO [cnd:Seiji Ozawa], Vienna PO [cnd:John Eliot Gardiner, James Levine] Deutsche Grammophon ▲ 449112-2 ▮ 449112-4
Wagner, R.:Ovs, Preludes & Orch Sels, w. Bayreuth Festival Orch, Vienna PO, Bavarian RSO, Berlin Opera Orch, H. von Karajan (cnd), R. Kubelik (cnd), K. Böhm (cnd), E. Jochum (cnd)—sels. from Rienzi, Die fliegende Holländer, Tannhäuser, Lohengrin, Parsifal, Die Meistersinger von Nürnberg, Die Walküre, Siegfried, Götterdämmerung *(rec 1958 & 1981)* Deutsche Grammophon ("Double" series) 2-▲ 439687-2 [ADD]
What a Wonderful Contrabass World!, w. New Colophonium Bass Quartet, Contrabass Quartet Camerata ▲ 32CM 60

C. Abbado (cnd)
Beethoven, L. van:Ah, perfido!, w. C. Studer (sop) Deutsche Grammophon ▲ 435617-2 [DDD]
Beethoven, L. van:Cons Pno (comp), w. Maurizio Pollini (pno) Deutsche Grammophon 3-▲ 439770-2 [DDD]
Beethoven, L. van:Egmont (ov) Deutsche Grammophon ▲ 435617-2 [DDD]
Beethoven, L. van:Fant Pno, Op. 80, "Choral Fant", w. E. Kissin (pno) Deutsche Grammophon ▲ 435617-2 [DDD]
Beethoven, L. van:Die Geschöpfe des Prometheus (sels), w. M. Argerich (pno), Berlin Singakademie *(rec May 23-25, 1993)* Sony Classical ▲ SK 53978 [DDD]
Beethoven, L. van:Leonore 2 Deutsche Grammophon ▲ 435617-2 [DDD]
Beethoven, L. van:Leonore Prohaska, w. Sylvia McNair (sop), Karoline Eichhorn (narr), Marie-Pierre Langlamet (hp), Sascha Reckert (glass hmc), Berlin Radio Chorus *(rec Great Hall, Philharmonie, Berlin)* Deutsche Grammophon ▲ 447748-2 [DDD]
Beethoven, L. van:Sym 9, "Choral Sym", w. Jane Eaglen (sop), Waltraud Meier (cta), Ben Heppner (ten), Bryn Terfel (bar), Swedish Radio Chorus, Eric Ericson Chamber Choir *(rec Salzburg Easter Festival, 1996)* Sony Classical ▲ SK 62634 ▲ SM 62634
Beethoven, L. van:Die Weihe des Hauses (incidental music), w. Sylvia McNari (sop), Byrn Terfel (bar), Bruno Ganz (narr), Berlin Radio Chorus *(rec Great Hall, Philharmonie, Berlin)* Deutsche Grammophon ▲ 447748-2 [DDD]
Brahms, J.:Alto Rhap, w. M. Lipovšek (mez), Ernst Senff Chorus [G] Deutsche Grammophon ▲ 427643-2 [DDD]
Brahms, J.:Con 1 Pno, w. A. Brendel (pno) Philips ▲ 420071-2 [DDD]
Brahms, J.:Con Vn, w. Viktoria Mullova (vn) Philips ▲ 438998-2
Brahms, J.:Gesang der Parzen, w. Berlin Radio Chorus Deutsche Grammophon ▲ 431790-2 [DDD] ▯ 431790-5
Brahms, J.:Nänie, w. Berlin Radio Chorus Deutsche Grammophon ▲ 435349-2 [DDD]
Brahms, J.:Schicksalslied, w. Ernst Senff Chorus [G] Deutsche Grammophon ▲ 429765-2 [DDD]
Brahms, J.:Schicksalslied, w. Leipzig Central German Radio Choir *(rec Philharmonie, Berlin, Feb. 26-28, 1993)* Sony Classical ▲ SK 53975 [DDD]
Brahms, J.:Sym 2 Deutsche Grammophon ▲ 427643-2 [DDD]
Brahms, J.:Sym 3 [G] Deutsche Grammophon ▲ 429765-2 [DDD]
Brahms, J.:Sym 4 Deutsche Grammophon ▲ 435349-2 [DDD]
Brahms, J.:Tragic Ov [G] Deutsche Grammophon ▲ 429765-2 [DDD]
Brahms, J.:Vars on a Theme by Haydn Deutsche Grammophon ▲ 435349-2 [DDD]
Dvořák, A.:The Noon Witch *(rec Philharmonie, Berlin, Nov. 16-19, 1993)* Sony Classical ▲ SK 64303 [DDD]
Dvořák, A.:Sym 8 *(rec Philharmonie, Berlin, Nov. 16-19, 1993)* Sony Classical ▲ SK 64303 [DDD]
Hindemith, P.:Kammermusik 1 EMI Classics ▲ CDC 56160
Hindemith, P.:Kammermusik 4, w. Kolja Blacher (vn) EMI Classics ▲ CDC 56160
Hindemith, P.:Kammermusik 5, w. Wolfram Christ (va) EMI Classics ▲ CDC 56160
Janácek, L.:Sinfonietta Deutsche Grammophon ("Masters" series) ▲ 445501-2 [DDD]
Liszt, F.:Prometheus, w. M. Argerich (pno), Berlin Singakademie *(rec May 23-25, 1993)* Sony Classical ▲ SK 53978 [DDD]
Mahler, G.:Kindertotenlieder, w. M. Lipvosek (mez) *(rec Sept. 3-4, 1992)* Sony Classical ▲ SK 53360 [DDD]
Mahler, G.:Songs from Rückert, w. M. Lipvosek (mez)—Ich bin der Welt abhanden gekommen *(rec Sept. 3-4, 1992)* Sony Classical ▲ SK 53360 [DDD]
Mahler, G.:Sym 1 Deutsche Grammophon ▲ 431769-2 [DDD] ▯ 431769-5
Mahler, G.:Sym 5 Deutsche Grammophon ▲ 437789-2
Mahler, G.:Sym 8, w. Sylvia McNair (sop), Andrea Rost (sop), Cheryl Studer (sop), Anne Sofie von Otter (mez), Rosemarie Lang (cta), Peter Seiffert (ten), Bryn Terfel (bar), Jan-Hendrik Rootering (bass), Berlin Radio Chorus, Prague Phil Chorus, Tölz Boys' Choir Deutsche Grammophon ("4D Audio" series) 2-▲ 445843-2

76 ▲ = CD ♦ = Enhanced CD Δ = MD ▮ = Cassette Tape ▯ = DCC

Berlin PO (cont.)

C. Abbado (cnd) (cont.)

Mendelssohn, F.:Midsummer Night's Dream (ov & incidental), w. Kenneth Branagh (nar), Sylvia McNair (sop), Angelika Kirchschlager (mez), Ernst Senff Chorus Women's Voices Sony Classical ▲ SK 62826
Mendelssohn, F.:Sym 4 Sony Classical ▲ SK 62826
Mozart, W.A.:Divert Ob, K.251 *(rec Nov. 28–29, 1992)* Sony Classical ▲ SK 53277 [DDD]
Mozart, W.A.:Marches Orch, K.335 *(rec Nov. 28–29, 1992)* Sony Classical ▲ SK 53277 [DDD]
Mozart, W.A.:Missa, K.427, w. A. Augér (sop), B. Bonney (sop), H.-P. Blochwitz (ten), Robert Holl (bass), Berlin Radio Chorus [L] Sony Classical ▲ SK 46671 [DDD]
Mozart, W.A.:Serenade Ww, K.320 *(rec Nov. 28–29, 1992)* Sony Classical ▲ SK 53277 [DDD]
Mozart, W.A.:Sinf Concertante, K.364, w. Rainer Kussmaul (vn), Wolfram Christ (va) Sony Classical ▲ SK 66859
Mozart, W.A.:Sym 23 Sony Classical ▲ SK 66859
Mozart, W.A.:Sym 28 Sony Classical ▲ SK 48063 [DDD]
Mozart, W.A.:Sym 29 Sony Classical ▲ SK 48063 [DDD]
Mozart, W.A.:Sym 35 Sony Classical ▲ SK 48063 [DDD]
Mozart, W.A.:Sym 36 Sony Classical ▲ SK 66859
Mussorgsky, M.:Boris Godunov, w. V. Valente (sop—Xenia), E. Gorochovskaya (mez—Nurse), L. Nichiteanu (mez—Fyodor), E. Zarmeba (mez—Hostess), M. Lipovšek (cta—Marina), P. Langridge (ten—Prince Shuisky), H. Wildhaber (ten—Misail), A. Fedin (ten—Simpleton), S. Leiferkus (bar—Rangoni), A. Kotcherga (bass—B. Godounov), A. Shagidullin (bass—Shchelkalov), S. Ramey (bass—Pimen), S. Larin (bass—Girgory), G. Nikolsky (bass—Varlaam), Tölz Boys' Choir, Berlin Radio Chorus, Slovak Phil Chorus *(rec Nov. 7–30, 1993)* Sony Classical 3-▲ S3K 58977 [DDD]
Mussorgsky, M.:Pictures at an Exhibition *(rec live, 1993)* Topazio ▲ TOP 26047
Mussorgsky, M.:Songs & Dances, w. Anatoly Kotcherga (bass)—Nos. 1–4 *(rec Philharmonie, Berlin, Feb. 18–20, 1994)* Sony Classical ▲ SK 66276 [DDD]
Mussorgsky, M.:Songs & Dances *(rec live, 1993)* Topazio ▲ TOP 26047
Nono, L.:Prometeo, w. I. Ade-Jesemann (sop), M. Bair-Ivenz (sop), S. Otto (alt), P. Hall (ten), U. Krumbiegel (nar), M. Schadock (nar), Freiburg Soloists Choir *(rec May 23–25, 1993)* Sony Classical ▲ SK 53978 [DDD]
Prokofiev, S.:Con 1 Pno, w. Yevgeny Kissin (pno) Deutsche Grammophon ▲ 439898-2
Prokofiev, S.:Con 3 Pno, w. Yevgeny Kissin (pno) Deutsche Grammophon ▲ 439898-2
Prokofiev, S.:Con 3 Pno, w. M. Argerich (pno) Deutsche Grammophon 3-▲ 435151-2 [ADD]
Prokofiev, S.:Con 3 Pno, w. Martha Argerich (pno) *(rec Jesus-Christus-Kirche, Berlin, May–June 1967)* Deutsche Grammophon ▲ 447438-2 [ADD]
Prokofiev, S.:Con 3 Pno, w. M. Argerich (pno) Deutsche Grammophon ▲ 415062-2 [AAD]
Ravel, M.:Con in G Pno, w. Martha Argerich (pno) *(rec Jesus-Christus-Kirche, Berlin, May–June 1967)* Deutsche Grammophon ▲ 447438-2 [ADD]
Reger, M.:An die Hoffnung, w. Karita Mattila (sop) *(rec Philharmonie, Berlin, Feb. 26–28, 1993)* Sony Classical ▲ SK 53975 [DDD]
Rihm, W.:Hölderlin-Fragmente, w. Johannes M. Kösters (bar) *(rec Philharmonie, Berlin, Feb. 26–28, 1993)* Sony Classical ▲ SK 53975 [DDD]
Schoenberg, A.:Con Pno, w. M. Pollini (pno) Deutsche Grammophon ▲ 427771-2 [DDD]
Schumann, R.:Con Pno, w. M. Pollini (pno) Deutsche Grammophon ▲ 427771-2 [DDD]
Schumann, R.:Con Pno, w. Maurizio Pollini (pno) Deutsche Grammophon ("Digital Midprice" series) ▲ 445522-2
Scriabin, A.:Sym 5, w. M. Argerich (pno), Berlin Singakademie *(rec May 23–25, 1993)* Sony Classical ▲ SK 53978 [DDD]
Strauss, R.:Burleske, w. M. Argerich (pno) *(rec Dec. 31, 1992)* Sony Classical ▲ SK 52565
Strauss, R.:Don Juan *(rec Dec. 31, 1992)* Sony Classical ▲ SK 52565
Strauss, R.:Hymnen von Friedrich Hölderlin, w. Karita Mattila (sop) *(rec Philharmonie, Berlin, Feb. 26–28, 1993)* Sony Classical ▲ SK 53975 [DDD]
Strauss, R.:Der Rosenkavalier (sels), w. K. Battle (sop), R. Fleming (sop), F. von Stade (mez), A. Schmidt (bar) *(rec Dec. 31, 1992)* Sony Classical ▲ SK 52565
Strauss, R.:Till Eulenspiegels lustige Streiche *(rec Dec. 31, 1992)* Sony Classical ▲ SK 52565
Tchaikovsky, P.:Con 1 Pno, w. Martha Argerich (pno) *(rec Berlin, Dec 1994)* Deutsche Grammophon ▲ 449816-2 [DDD]
Tchaikovsky, P.:Sym 5 *(rec Philharmonie, Berlin, Feb. 18–20, 1994)* Sony Classical ▲ SK 66276 [DDD]
Wagner, R.:Lohengrin (sels), w. C. Studer (sop), W. Meier (mez), S. Jerusalem (ten), B. Terfel (bar) Deutsche Grammophon ▲ 439768-2
Wagner, R.:Die Meistersinger von Nürnberg (sels), w. C. Studer (sop), W. Meier (mez), S. Jerusalem (ten), B. Terfel (bar) Deutsche Grammophon ▲ 439768-2
Wagner, R.:Tannhäuser (sels), w. C. Studer (sop), W. Meier (mez), S. Jerusalem (ten), B. Terfel (bar) Deutsche Grammophon ▲ 439768-2
Wagner, R.:Die Walküre (sels), w. C. Studer (sop), W. Meier (mez), S. Jerusalem (ten), B. Terfel (bar) Deutsche Grammophon ▲ 439768-2

H. Abendroth (cnd)

Wagner, R.:Eine Faust-Ov Enterprise ("The Radio Years" series) 2-▲ ENT RY 66

J. Barbirolli (cnd)

Mahler, G.:Sym 3, w. L. West (alt), St. Hedwig's Cathedral Choir [G] *(rec live, 3/8/69)* Arkadia 3-▲ 719 [ADD]
Mahler, G.:Sym 9 EMI Classics ("Studio" series) ▲ CDM 63115 [ADD]

D. Barenboim (cnd)

Beethoven, L. van:Con 1 Pno, w. D. Barenboim (pno) Sony Classical ▲ SK 45830 [DDD]
Beethoven, L. van:Con Vn, Op. 61, w. I. Perlman (vn) EMI Classics ▲ CDC 49567 [DDD]
Beethoven, L. van:Romances Vn, w. I. Perlman (vn) EMI Classics ▲ CDC 49567 [DDD]
Beethoven, L. van:Sym 7 *(rec West Berlin, 12 Nov. 1989)* Sony Classical ▲ SK 45830 [DDD]
Berlioz, H.:Sym fantastique CBS ▲ MK 39859 [DDD]
Brahms, J.:Con Vn, w. I. Perlman (vn) EMI Classics ▲ CDC 54580
Bruckner, A.:Sym 4, "Romantic" Teldec ▲ 73272-2
Bruckner, A.:Sym 7 Teldec ▲ 9031-77118-2
Bruckner, A.:Sym 9 *(rec live October 1990)* Teldec ▲ 9031-72140-2 [DDD]
Liszt, F.:Dante Sym, w. Berlin Radio Women's Chorus Teldec ▲ 77340
Mahler, G.:Des Knaben Wunderhorn, w. D. Fischer-Dieskau (bar) [G] Sony Classical ▲ SK 44935 [DDD]
Mahler, G.:Lieder eines fahrenden Gesellen, w. D. Fischer-Dieskau (bar) [G] Sony Classical ▲ SK 44935 [DDD]
Mozart, W.A.:Con 9 Pno, w. D. Barenboim (pno) Teldec ▲ 9031-73128-2 ZK [DDD]
Mozart, W.A.:Con 17 Pno, w. D. Barenboim (pno) Teldec ▲ 9031-73128-2 ZK [DDD]
Mozart, W.A.:Con 18 Pno, w. Daniel Barenboim (pno) *(rec live, Philharmonie Hall, Berlin, Apr. 1993)* Teldec ▲ 90674-2 [DDD]
Mozart, W.A.:Con 19 Pno, w. Daniel Barenboim (pno) *(rec live, Philharmonie Hall, Berlin, Apr. 1994)* Teldec ▲ 90674-2 [DDD]
Mozart, W.A.:Con 20 Pno, w. D. Barenboim (pno) Teldec 4-▲ 9031-72024-2 [DDD]
Mozart, W.A.:Con 20 Pno, w. D. Barenboim (pno) Teldec ▲ 9031-75710-2 [DDD]
Mozart, W.A.:Con 21 Pno, w. D. Barenboim (pno) Teldec 4-▲ 9031-72024-2 [DDD]
Mozart, W.A.:Con 21 Pno, w. D. Barenboim (pno) Teldec ▲ 9031-75710-2 [DDD]
Mozart, W.A.:Con 22 Pno, w. D. Barenboim (pno) Teldec ▲ 9031-75711-2 [DDD]
Mozart, W.A.:Con 22 Pno, w. D. Barenboim (pno) Teldec 4-▲ 9031-72024-2 [DDD]
Mozart, W.A.:Con 23 Pno, w. D. Barenboim (pno) Teldec 4-▲ 9031-72024-2 [DDD]
Mozart, W.A.:Con 23 Pno, w. D. Barenboim (pno) Teldec ▲ 9031-75711-2 [DDD]
Mozart, W.A.:Con 24 Pno, w. D. Barenboim (pno) Teldec ▲ 9031-75715-2 [DDD]
Mozart, W.A.:Con 24 Pno, w. D. Barenboim (pno) Teldec 4-▲ 9031-72024-2 [DDD]
Mozart, W.A.:Con 25 Pno, w. D. Barenboim (pno) Teldec ▲ 9031-75715-2 [DDD]
Mozart, W.A.:Con 25 Pno, w. D. Barenboim (pno) Teldec 4-▲ 9031-72024-2 [DDD]
Mozart, W.A.:Con 26 Pno, w. D. Barenboim (pno) Teldec ▲ 9031-75716-2 [DDD]
Mozart, W.A.:Con 26 Pno, w. D. Barenboim (pno) Teldec 4-▲ 9031-72024-2 [DDD]
Mozart, W.A.:Con 27 Pno, w. D. Barenboim (pno) Teldec 4-▲ 9031-72024-2 [DDD]
Mozart, W.A.:Con 27 Pno, w. D. Barenboim (pno) Teldec ▲ 9031-75716-2 [DDD]

Berlin PO (cont.)

D. Barenboim (cnd) (cont.)

Mozart, W.A.:Così fan tutte (sels), w. L. Cuberli (sop), J. Rodgers (sop), C. Bartoli (mez), J. Tomlinson (bass), Berlin RIAS Chamber Choir Erato ▲ 94821
Mozart, W.A.:Don Giovanni (sels), w. L. Cuberli (sop), J. Rodgers (sop), J. Tomlinson (bass), F. Furlanetto (bass), Berlin RIAS Chamber Choir Erato ▲ 94823
Mozart, W.A.:Nozze di Figaro (sels), w. L. Cuberli (sop), J. Rodgers (sop), C. Bartoli (mez), A. Schmidt (bar), Berlin RIAS Chamber Choir Erato ▲ 94822
Mozart, W.A.:Rondo Pno Orch, K.382, w. Daniel Barenboim (pno) *(rec live, Philharmonie Hall, Berlin, Apr. 1994)* Teldec ▲ 90674-2 [DDD]
Schubert, Franz:Rosamunde (sels) CBS 2-▲ M2K 42489 [DDD]
Schubert, Franz:Sym 1 CBS 2-▲ M2K 42489 [DDD]
Schubert, Franz:Sym 5 CBS ▲ MK 39671 [DDD]
Schubert, Franz:Sym 8 CBS ▲ MK 39676 [DDD] ■ IMT 39676 (D)

T. Beecham (cnd)

Mozart, W.A.:Zauberflöte, w. T. Lemnitz (sop), E. Berger (sop), I. Beilke (sop), H. Roswaenge (ten), H. Tessmer (ten), G. Hüsch (bar), W. Strienz (bass), Favre Chorus [without dialog; G] *(rec 1937–38 for HMV)* Pearl 2-▲ PEAS 9371 (m) [AAD]
Mozart, W.A.:Zauberflöte, w. T. Lemnitz (sop), E. Berger (sop), I. Beilke (sop), H. Roswaenge (ten), H. Tessmer (ten), G. Hüsch (bar), W. Strienz (bass), Favre Chorus [without dialog; G] *(rec 1937–38 for HMV)* EMI Classics ("Great Recordings of the Century" series) 2-▲ CDHB 61034 (m) [ADD]
Mozart, W.A.:Zauberflöte, w. T. Lemnitz (sop), E. Berger (sop), I. Beilke (sop), H. Roswaenge (ten), H. Tessmer (ten), G. Hüsch (bar), W. Strienz (bass), Favre Chorus [without dialog; G] *(rec 1937–38 for HMV)* Melodram 2-▲ MEL 27056 (m) [AAD]
Mozart, W.A.:Zauberflöte, w. E. Berger (sop), T. Lemnitz (sop), I. Beilke (sop), H. Roswaenge (ten), G. Hüsch (bar), W. Strienz (bass), Vereinigung Favres Soloists [G] *(rec Nov. 1937 & Feb.–Mar. 193)* Nimbus ("Prima Voce" series) 2-▲ NI 7827/8 (m) [ADD]

L. Bernstein (cnd)

Mahler, G.:Sym 9 *(rec live, 1979)* Deutsche Grammophon 2-▲ 435378-2 [DDD]

L. Blech (cnd)

Berlioz, H.:Le Carnaval romain *(rec 1927)* Koch Legacy ▲ 3-7072-2 H1

K. Böhm (cnd)

Mozart, W.A.:Con 21 Pno, w. S. Askenase (pno) Datum 2-▲ DAT 12305 [ADD]
Mozart, W.A.:Kleine Nachtmusik, w. T. Brandis (vn), G. Cappone (va) Deutsche Grammophon ("Resonance" series) ▲ 427208-2 [DDD]
Mozart, W.A.:Serenata notturna, w. T. Brandis (vn), G. Cappone (va) Deutsche Grammophon ("Resonance" series) ▲ 427208-2 [DDD]
Mozart, W.A.:Sinf concertante Vn, K.364, w. Thomas Brandis (vn), G. Cappone (va) Deutsche Grammophon ("Resonance" series) ▲ 427208-2 [DDD]
Mozart, W.A.:Sym 31 Deutsche Grammophon ("Resonance" series) ▲ 427210-2 [DDD]
Mozart, W.A.:Sym 35 Deutsche Grammophon ("Resonance" series) ▲ 429521-2 [ADD]
Mozart, W.A.:Sym 35 *(rec 1959, 1961 & 1966)* Deutsche Grammophon ("The Originals" series) 2-▲ 447416-2
Mozart, W.A.:Sym 36 *(rec 1959, 1961 & 1966)* Deutsche Grammophon ("The Originals" series) 2-▲ 447416-2
Mozart, W.A.:Sym 36 Deutsche Grammophon ("Resonance" series) ▲ 429521-2 [ADD]
Mozart, W.A.:Sym 38 *(rec 1959, 1961 & 1966)* Deutsche Grammophon ("The Originals" series) 2-▲ 447416-2
Mozart, W.A.:Sym 38 Deutsche Grammophon ("Resonance" series) ▲ 429521-2 [ADD]
Mozart, W.A.:Sym 39 *(rec 1959, 1961 & 1966)* Deutsche Grammophon ("The Originals" series) 2-▲ 447416-2
Mozart, W.A.:Sym 40 *(rec 1959, 1961 & 1966)* Deutsche Grammophon ("The Originals" series) 2-▲ 447416-2
Mozart, W.A.:Sym 40 Deutsche Grammophon ("Resonance" series) ▲ 427210-2 [ADD]
Mozart, W.A.:Sym 41 Deutsche Grammophon ("Resonance" series) ▲ 427210-2 [ADD]
Mozart, W.A.:Sym 41 *(rec 1959, 1961 & 1966)* Deutsche Grammophon ("The Originals" series) 2-▲ 447416-2
Mozart, W.A.:Zauberflöte (sels), w. E. Lear (sop), R. Peters (sop), L. Otto (sop), F. Wunderlich (ten), F. Lenz (ten), D. Fischer-Dieskau (bar), F. Crass (bass), Berlin RIAS Chamber Choir—Scenes & Arias Deutsche Grammophon ▲ 429825-2 [ADD] ■ 429825-4
Schubert, Franz:Syms (comp) Deutsche Grammophon 4-▲ 419318-2 [ADD]

P. Boulez (cnd)

Ravel, M.:Alborada del gracioso Deutsche Grammophon ▲ 439859-2
Ravel, M.:Une Barque sur l'océan Deutsche Grammophon ▲ 439859-2
Ravel, M.:Boléro Deutsche Grammophon ▲ 439859-2
Ravel, M.:Daphnis et Chloé Deutsche Grammophon ▲ 447057-2
Ravel, M.:Ma mère l'oye Orch Deutsche Grammophon ▲ 439859-2
Ravel, M.:Rapsodie espagnole Deutsche Grammophon ▲ 439859-2
Ravel, M.:La Valse Deutsche Grammophon ▲ 447057-2
Webern, A.:music of, w. Christiane Oelze (sop), Gerald Finley (bar), BBC Singers—Sym, Op. 21; Cants, Opp. 29 & 31; 3 Songs; Das Augenlicht; Vars, Op. 30; 5 Pieces Deutsche Grammophon ▲ 447 765-2

S. Bychkov (cnd)

Barber, S.:Adagio Strs Philips ▲ 434108-2
Elgar, E.:Intro & Allegro Philips ▲ 434108-2
Mozart, W.A.:Con 7 Pnos, w. K. Labèque (pno), M. Labèque (pno), S. Bychkov (pno) Philips ("Digital Classics" series) ▲ 426241-2
Mozart, W.A.:Con 10 Pnos, w. K. Labèque (pno), M. Labèque (pno) Philips ("Digital Classics" series) ▲ 426241-2 [DDD]
Shostakovich, D.:Sym 8 Philips ▲ 432090-2 [DDD]
Tchaikovsky, P.:Serenade Strs Philips ▲ 434108-2
Wolf, H.:Italian Serenade Philips ▲ 434108-2

S. Celibidache (cnd)

Bizet, G.:Sym 1 *(rec 1948–53)* Arlecchino ARL
Debussy, C.:Jeux *(rec 1948–53)* Arlecchino ARL
Debussy, C.:Petite suite *(rec 1948–53)* Arlecchino ARL
Roussel, A.:Little Suite *(rec 1948–53)* Arlecchino ARL
Shostakovich, D.:Sym 7 *(rec 1947)* Arlecchino ▲ ARL106
Shostakovich, D.:Sym 7 *(rec 1946)* Theorema ▲ TH 121122

H. Chemin-Petit (cnd)

Furtwängler, W.:Te Deum, w. E. Mathis (sop), J. Dooley (alt), S. Wagner (cta), G. Jelden (ten) *(rec live, 1967)* As Disc ▲ ASD 2506

A. Coates (cnd)

Tchaikovsky, P.:Sym 6 *(rec 1938)* GSE Claremont ▲ GSE 78 50 51

A. Erede (cnd)

Strauss, R.:Ariadne auf Naxos, w. Lisa Della Casa (sop—Ariadne), Lisa Otto (sop—Najade), Rudolf Schock (ten—Bacchus), Leonore Kirschstein (sgr—Echo), Nada Puttar (sgr—Dryade) Testament ▲ SBT 1036 [ADD]

M. Fiedler (cnd)

Brahms, J.:Con 2 Pno, w. Elly Ney (pno) *(rec 1937–41)* Pearl ▲ PEA 9170 [ADD]

O. Fried (cnd)

Liszt, F.:Mazeppa for Orch *(rec 1928)* In Sync ■ C 4128 (m)
Liszt, F.:Les Préludes *(rec 1928)* Koch Legacy ▲ 3-7146-2
Rimsky-Korsakov, N.:Scheherazade *(rec 1928)* Koch Legacy ▲ 3-7146-2
Stravinsky, I.:The Firebird Suite *(rec 1928)* Koch Legacy ▲ 3-7146-2
Wagner, R.:Eine Faust-Ov *(rec 1928)* In Sync ■ C 4128 (m)

Berlin PO (cont.)

W. Furtwängler (cnd)

Bach, J.S.:Air on the G String *(rec 1929–36)* Grammofono 2000 ▲ GRM 78574 (m)
Bach, J.S.:Brandenburg Con 3 *(rec 1930)* Symposium ▲ 1043 (m)
Bach, J.S.:Brandenburg Con 3 *(rec 1930)* Koch Legacy 2–▲ 370592
Bach, J.S.:Suite 3 Orch *(rec live Oct 24, 1948)* Music & Arts ▲ CD 708–1 [AAD]
Beethoven, L. van:Con 4 Pno, w. Conrad Hansen (pno) *(rec Oct.–Nov. 1943)* Music & Arts ▲ CD 839 [ADD]
Beethoven, L. van:Con 4 Pno, w. *(soloist unknown)* Arkadia 2–▲ 365
Beethoven, L. van:Con Vn, Op. 61, w. Erich Röhn (vn) *(rec Jan 9, 1944)* Iron Needle ▲ IN 1340 (m) [ADD]
Beethoven, L. van:Con Vn, Op. 61, w. Y. Menuhin (vn) *(rec live Sept 30, 1947)* Music & Arts ▲ CD 708–1 [AAD]
Beethoven, L. van:Coriolan Ov *(rec 1943)* Music & Arts ▲ CD 826 [AAD]
Beethoven, L. van:Coriolan Ov EMI Classics 2–▲ ZDHC 65513
Beethoven, L. van:Coriolan Ov *(rec June 27, 1943)* Iron Needle 3–▲ IN 1348/50 [ADD]
Beethoven, L. van:Coriolan Ov *(rec 1943)* Grammofono 2000 ▲ GRM 78502 [ADD]
Beethoven, L. van:Egmont (ov) *(rec 1933)* Iron Needle ▲ IN 1337 (m) [ADD]
Beethoven, L. van:Egmont (ov) *(rec 1929–36)* Grammofono 2000 ▲ GRM 78574 (m)
Beethoven, L. van:Leonore 2 EMI Classics 2–▲ ZDHC 65513
Beethoven, L. van:Ovs—Egmont *(rec ca. 1933)* Symposium ▲ 1043 (m)
Beethoven, L. van:Sym 3, "Eroica" *(rec live, Dec. 8, 1952)* AS Disc ▲ ASD 2900
Beethoven, L. van:Sym 3, "Eroica" *(rec Berlin, Dec. 8, 1952)* Music & Arts 2–▲ CD 869 [ADD]
Beethoven, L. van:Sym 3, "Eroica" *(rec 1930–1953)* Tahra 4–▲ FURT 1008/11
Beethoven, L. van:Sym 3, "Eroica" *(rec live 12/7/52)* Music & Arts ▲ CD 520 [AAD]
Beethoven, L. van:Sym 3, "Eroica" *(rec live, Berlin 12/52)* Arkadia ▲ 363 [ADD]
Beethoven, L. van:Sym 3, "Eroica" *(rec live 6/20/50)* Music & Arts ▲ CD 711–1 [AAD]
Beethoven, L. van:Sym 4 *(rec June 1943)* Music & Arts 2–▲ CD 824 [ADD]
Beethoven, L. van:Sym 4 *(rec June 30, 1943)* Iron Needle 3–▲ IN 1348/50 [ADD]
Beethoven, L. van:Sym 4 *(rec 1943)* Grammofono 2000 ▲ GRM 78502 [ADD]
Beethoven, L. van:Sym 5 *(rec May 25, 1947)* Music & Arts ▲ CD 789 [AAD]
Beethoven, L. van:Sym 5 *(rec June 1943)* Music & Arts 2–▲ CD 824 [ADD]
Beethoven, L. van:Sym 5 *(rec June 30, 1943)* Iron Needle 3–▲ IN 1348/50 [ADD]
Beethoven, L. van:Sym 5 *(rec 1943)* Grammofono 2000 ▲ GRM 78502 [ADD]
Beethoven, L. van:Sym 5 *(rec 1926 for Polydor)* Koch Legacy ▲ 370592
Beethoven, L. van:Sym 5 *(rec Berlin, May 23, 1954)* Music & Arts 2–▲ CD 869 [ADD]
Beethoven, L. van:Sym 5 *(rec 1930–1953)* Tahra 4–▲ FURT 1008/11
Beethoven, L. van:Sym 6, "Pastorale" *(rec May 25, 1947)* Music & Arts ▲ CD 789 [AAD]
Beethoven, L. van:Sym 6, "Pastorale" *(rec Mar. 1944)* Music & Arts 2–▲ CD 824 [ADD]
Beethoven, L. van:Sym 6, "Pastorale" Enterprise ("Sirio" series) ▲ ENT SO 530011
Beethoven, L. van:Sym 6, "Pastorale" *(rec Mar. 22 & 24, 1944)* Music & Arts ▲ CD 2001 [ADD]
Beethoven, L. van:Sym 6, "Pastorale" *(rec 1954)* Arkadia ▲ 504 (m) [AAD]
Beethoven, L. van:Sym 6, "Pastorale" Grammofono 2000 ▲ GRM 78551 (m)
Beethoven, L. van:Sym 6, "Pastorale" *(rec 1930–1953)* Tahra 4–▲ FURT 1008/11
Beethoven, L. van:Sym 7 *(rec Nov. 1943)* Music & Arts 2–▲ CD 824 [ADD]
Beethoven, L. van:Sym 9, "Choral Sym", w. Erna Berger (sop), Gertrude Pitzinger (cta), Walther Ludwig (ten), Rudolf Watzke (bass), Bruno Kittel Choir *(rec Queens Hall, London, May 1, 1937)* Music & Arts ▲ CD 818 [ADD]
Beethoven, L. van:Sym 9, "Choral Sym", w. Tilla Briem (sop), Elisabeth Höngen (cta), Peter Anders (ten), Rudolf Watzke (bass), Bruno Kittel Choir *(rec Mar 22, 1942)* Iron Needle 3–▲ IN 1348/50 [ADD]
Beethoven, L. van:Sym 9, "Choral Sym", w. Bruno Kittel Choir [G] *(rec live, Berlin 3/24/42)* Arkadia ▲ 357 (m) [ADD]
Beethoven, L. van:Sym 9, "Choral Sym", w. Tilla Briem (sop), Elisabeth Höngen (cta), Peter Anders (ten), Rudolf Watzke (bass), Bruno Kittel Choir *(rec 1942)* Grammofono 2000 ▲ GRM 78581
Berlin PO Symposium ▲ SYM 1043 (m)
Berlioz, H.:La Damnation de Faust (sels)—Marche hongroise *(rec 1930 for Polydor)* Koch Legacy 2–▲ 3–7073–2 K2
Brahms, J.:Con 2 Pno, w. E. Fischer (pno) Music & Arts 4–▲ CD 804 [ADD]
Brahms, J.:Con Vn, w. G. de Vito (vn) Music & Arts 4–▲ CD 804 [ADD]
Brahms, J.:Hungarian Dances Orch—Nos. 1 & 3 *(rec 1930 for Polydor)* Koch Legacy 2–▲ 3–7073–2 K2
Brahms, J.:Hungarian Dances Orch EMI Classics 2–▲ ZDHC 65513
Brahms, J.:Syms (comp) EMI Classics 2–▲ ZDHC 65513
Brahms, J.:Sym 1—Finale *(rec Jan. 23, 1945)* Music & Arts ▲ CD 805 [ADD]
Brahms, J.:Sym 4 Arkadia 2–▲ 365
Brahms, J.:Sym 4 *(rec live, 1942–43)* Grammofono 2000 ▲ GRM 78594 (m)
Brahms, J.:Vars on a Theme by Haydn *(rec Dec. 12–15, 1943)* Music & Arts ▲ CD 805 [ADD]
Brahms, J.:Vars on a Theme by Haydn *(rec live, 1942–43)* Grammofono 2000 ▲ GRM 78594 (m)
Bruckner, A.:Sym 5 *(rec Oct. 25–28, 1942)* Music & Arts ▲ CD 538 [AAD]
Bruckner, A.:Sym 6—Movts. 2, 3 & 4 *(rec Nov. 13–16, 1943)* Music & Arts ▲ CD 805 [ADD]
Bruckner, A.:Sym 7 *(rec live, Apr 23, 1951)* Theorema ▲ TH 121209
Bruckner, A.:Sym 7 [original version] *(rec Rome 5/1/51)* Music & Arts ▲ CD 698–1 (m) [AAD]
Bruckner, A.:Sym 7 *(rec live, Rome 5/1/51)* Arkadia ▲ 362 [ADD]
Bruckner, A.:Sym 7 *(rec live, Cairo, Egypt, Apr 23, 1951)* Music & Arts ▲ CD 894
Bruckner, A.:Sym 8 *(rec Berlin, Mar. 1949)* Originals ▲ ORISH 854 (m)
Bruckner, A.:Sym 8 [Haas edition] *(rec live, 3/15/49)* Music & Arts ▲ CD 624 (m) [AAD]
Bruckner, A.:Sym 9 [original version] *(rec Berlin, Oct 7, 1944)* Iron Needle ▲ IN 1333 [ADD]
Bruckner, A.:Sym 9 Enterprise ("Sirio" series) ▲ ENT SO 53004
Bruckner, A.:Sym 9 *(rec live Oct. 7, 1944, Berlin)* Music & Arts ▲ CD 730–1 [AAD]
The Early Recordings:1926–1937 Koch Legacy 2–▲ 3–7073–2 K2
Early Studio Recordings 1929–43, w. Vienna PO Music & Arts 4–▲ MUA CD 954
Grieg, E.:Con Pno, Op. 16, w. Walter Gieseking (pno) *(rec July 30, 1944)* Iron Needle 3–▲ IN 1348/50 [ADD]
Haydn, J.:Sym 88 *(rec Jesus–Christus Church, Berlin, Nov & Dec 1951)* Deutsche Grammophon ("The Originals" series) ▲ 447439–2 [ADD]
Hindemith, P.:Con Orch *(rec live, 6/12/50)* Music & Arts ▲ CD 713–1 [AAD]
Hindemith, P.:Die Harmonie der Welt *(rec live, 12/8/52)* Music & Arts ▲ CD 713–1 [AAD]
Mendelssohn, F.:Con in e Vn & Orch, Op. 64, w. Y. Menuhin (vn) EMI Classics ("Great Recordings of the Century" series) ▲ CDH 69799 (m) [ADD]
Mendelssohn, F.:Die Hebriden *(rec 1929–36)* Grammofono 2000 ▲ GRM 78574 (m)
Mendelssohn, F.:A Midsummer Night's Dream (ov) *(rec 1929)* Iron Needle ▲ IN 1337 (m) [ADD]
Mendelssohn, F.:Ovs—Overture to A Midsummer Night's Dream & The Hebrides Overture *(rec 1929 & 1930 for Polydor* Koch Legacy 2–▲ 3–7073–2 K2
Mozart, W.A.:Entführung (ov) *(rec 1929–36)* Grammofono 2000 ▲ GRM 78574 (m)
Mozart, W.A.:Kleine Nachtmusik *(rec ca. 1936/37 for Polydor)* Koch Legacy 2–▲ 370592
Mozart, W.A.:Kleine Nachtmusik *(rec 1929–36)* Grammofono 2000 ▲ GRM 78574 (m)
Mozart, W.A.:Nozze di Figaro (ov) *(rec 1933)* Iron Needle ▲ IN 1337 (m) [ADD]
Mozart, W.A.:Ovs—Die Entführung aus dem Serail & Le nozze di Figaro *(rec 1933 for Polydor)* Koch Legacy 2–▲ 3–7059–2
Mozart, W.A.:Sym 39 *(rec Feb 7, 1944)* Iron Needle ▲ IN 1340 (m) [ADD]
Pepping, E.:Sym 2 Arkadia 2–▲ 365
Pepping, E.:Sym 2 *(rec 1942–43)* Grammofono 2000 ▲ GRM 78510 [ADD]
Rossini, G.:La gazza ladra (sels)—Sinf *(rec 1930)* Iron Needle ▲ IN 1337 (m) [ADD]
Rossini, G.:La gazza ladra (ov) *(rec 1929–36)* Grammofono 2000 ▲ GRM 78574 (m)
Rossini, G.:Ovs—La gazza ladra & Barber of Seville *(rec 1930 & 1935 for Polydor)* Koch Legacy 2–▲ 370592
Schubert, Franz:Ovs—Rosamunde *(rec 1953)* Arkadia ▲ 525 (m) [AAD]
Schubert, Franz:Rosamunde (sels)—Overture, Ballet Music No. 2 & Entr'acte No. 3 *(rec 1929/30 for Polydor)* Koch Legacy 2–▲ 370592

Berlin PO (cont.)

W. Furtwängler (cnd) (cont.)

Schubert, Franz:Rosamunde (sels)—Overture, Ballet Mudic No. 2 & Entr'acte No. 3 *(rec ca. 1926–30)* Symposium ▲ 1043 (m)
Schubert, Franz:Rosamunde (sels)—Ov.; Ballet Music No. 2; Entr'Acte No. 3 *(rec 1930)* Enterprise ("Palladio" series) ▲ ENTPD 4176 [ADD]
Schubert, Franz:Sacred Music—Hymnisches Konzert *(rec 1942–43)* Grammofono 2000 ▲ GRM 78510 [ADD]
Schubert, Franz:Sym 9 *(rec 1942)* Music & Arts ▲ CD 826 [AAD]
Schubert, Franz:Sym 9 Theorema ▲ TH 121225
Schubert, Franz:Sym 9 *(rec 1942)* Enterprise ("Palladio" series) ▲ ENTPD 4176 [ADD]
Schubert, Franz:Sym 9 *(rec 1930–1953)* Tahra 4–▲ FURT 1008/11
Schubert, Franz:Sym 9 *(rec Jesus–Christus Church, Berlin, Nov & Dec 1951)* Deutsche Grammophon ("The Originals" series) ▲ 447439–2 [ADD]
Schubert, Franz:Sym 9 *(rec 1953)* Arkadia ▲ 525 (m) [AAD]
Schubert, Franz:Sym 9 *(rec Sept. 15, 1953)* Music & Arts ▲ CD 795 [AAD]
Schubert, H.:Hymnisches Konzert, w. Erna Berger (sop), Walther Ludwig (ten), *(organist unknown)* Arkadia 2–▲ 365
Schumann, R.:Con Pno, w. Walter Gieseking (pno) Enterprise ("The Piano Library" series) ▲ ENT PL 202
Schumann, R.:Con Pno, w. Walter Gieseking (pno) *(rec Berlin, Mar. 1–3, 1942)* Music & Arts ▲ CD 815 [AAD]
Sibelius, J.:Con Vn, w. G. Kulenkampff (vn) *(rec Feb. 7–8, 1943)* Music & Arts ▲ CD 799 [AAD]
Sibelius, J.:En Saga *(rec live, Berlin, Feb 2, 1943)* Grammofono 2000 ▲ GRM 78558
Sibelius, J.:En Saga, Vienna PO [2 versions] *(rec Feb. 7–8, 1943 & Sept. 25)* Music & Arts ▲ CD 799 [AAD]
Strauss (II), Joh.:Die Fledermaus (ov) *(rec 1937)* Iron Needle ▲ IN 1337 (m) [ADD]
Strauss (II), Joh.:Ovs—Die Fledermaus Overture *(rec 1937 for Polydor)* Koch Legacy 2–▲ 3–7073–2 K2
Strauss, R.:Don Juan Grammofono 2000 ▲ GRM 78551 (m)
Strauss, R.:Don Juan Enterprise ("Sirio" series) ▲ ENT SO 530011
Strauss, R.:Don Juan *(rec Feb. 15–17, 1942)* Music & Arts ▲ CD 829 [AAD]
Strauss, R.:Songs, w. P. Anders (ten)—4 Songs *(rec Feb. 15–17, 1942)* Music & Arts ▲ CD 829 [AAD]
Strauss, R.:Songs, w. P. Anders (ten) *(rec 2/42)* Arabesque ▲ Z 6082 (m)
Strauss, R.:Symphonia domestica *(rec 1/44)* Arabesque ▲ Z 6082 (m)
Strauss, R.:Till Eulenspiegels lustige Streiche *(rec 1930 for Polydor)* Koch Legacy 2–▲ 3–7073–2 K2
Strauss, R.:Till Eulenspiegels lustige Streiche *(rec Nov. 13–16, 1942)* Music & Arts ▲ CD 829 [AAD]
Stravinsky, I.:Le Baiser de la fée *(rec live, 5/18/53)* Music & Arts ▲ CD 713–1 [AAD]
Stravinsky, I.:Sym 1 Historical Performers ▲ HPS 8 [ADD]
Tchaikovsky, P.:Sym 6 *(rec Berlin, 1938)* Historical Performers ▲ HPS 14
Tchaikovsky, P.:Sym 6 *(rec Berlin, Oct–Nov 1938)* Grammofono 2000 ▲ GRM 78558
Wagner, R.:Götterdämmerung (siegfried's funeral) *(rec 1933 for Polydor)* Koch Legacy 2–▲ 3–7073–2 K2
Wagner, R.:Lohengrin (preludes)—prelude to Act I *(rec 1929–36)* Grammofono 2000 ▲ GRM 78574 (m)
Wagner, R.:Lohengrin (preludes), Act I Prelude *(rec 1930 for Polydor)* Koch Legacy 2–▲ 3–7073–2 K2
Wagner, R.:Ovs, Preludes & Orch Sels, Philharmonia Orch—Der fliegende Holländer; Tannhäuser; Lohengrin; Die Meistersinger von Nürnberg; Tristan und Isolde Historical Performers ▲ HPS 4 [ADD]
Wagner, R.:Ovs, Preludes & Orch Sels, Philharmonia Orch—orchestral excerpts from *Der fliegende Hollander; Gotterdämmerung; Lohengrin; Meistersinger von Nürnberg; Parsifal; Tannhaüser; Tristan und Isolde* & the Immolation Scene from *Götterdammerung* [w. Kirsten Flagstad (soprano)] *(rec 1938–1954)* EMI Classics ▲ CDHB 64935
Wagner, R.:Tristan und Isolde (prelude & liebestod) *(rec 1930)* Iron Needle ▲ IN 1337 (m) [ADD]
Wagner, R.:Tristan und Isolde (prelude & liebestod) *(rec 1930 for Polydor)* Koch Legacy 2–▲ 3–7073–2 K2
Weber, C.M. von:Der Freischütz (sels)—Ov. *(rec 1944)* Music & Arts ▲ CD 826 [AAD]
Weber, C.M. von:Der Freischütz (sels)—Overture & Prelude to Act 3 *(rec 1935 for Polydor)* Koch Legacy 2–▲ 3–7073–2 K2
Weber, C.M. von:Der Freischütz (sels)—Ov. *(rec Dec. 8, 1952)* Music & Arts ▲ CD 795 [AAD]
Weber, C.M. von:Der Freischütz (ov) *(rec 1935)* Iron Needle ▲ IN 1337 (m) [ADD]
Weber, C.M. von:Invitation to the Dance Orch *(rec 1932 for Polydor)* Koch Legacy 2–▲ 3–7073–2 K2
Weber, C.M. von:Invitation to the Dance Orch *(rec 1929–36)* Grammofono 2000 ▲ GRM 78574 (m)
Weber, C.M. von:Ovs—Oberon; Frieschutz; Eurianthe Historical Performers ▲ HPS 8 [ADD]
Weber, C.M. von:Ovs—Der Freischütz *(rec 1926 for Polydor)* Koch Legacy 2–▲ 370592

C. M. Giulini (cnd)

Beethoven, L. van:Sym 9, "Choral Sym", w. Ernst Senff Chorus [soloists J. Varady, J. van Nes, K. Lewis, S. Estes] Deutsche Grammophon ▲ 427655–2 [DDD]
Mahler, G.:Das Lied von der Erde, w. B. Fassbaender (mez), F. Araiza (ten) [G] Deutsche Grammophon ▲ 413459–2 [DDD]
Mozart, W.A.:Sinf concertante Ob, K.Anh.9 Sony Classical ▲ SK 48064 [DDD]
Mozart, W.A.:Sym 39 Sony Classical ▲ SK 48064 [DDD]
Mozart, W.A.:Sym 40 Sony Classical ▲ SK 47264
Mozart, W.A.:Sym 41 Sony Classical ▲ SK 47264
Verdi, G.:Pezzi sacri, w. S. Sweet (sop), Ernst Senff Chorus Sony Classical ▲ SK 46491
Vivaldi, A.:Credo, RV. 591, w. Ernst Senff Chorus Sony Classical ▲ SK 46491

M. Gurlitt (cnd)

Beethoven, L. van:Con Vn, Op. 61, w. J. Wolfsthal (vn) *(rec 1928 for Polydor)* Pearl ▲ PEA 9387 (m) [AAD]
Beethoven, L. van:Con Vn, Op. 61, w. Josef Wolfsthal (vn) [includes cadenzas by Joachim] Symposium ▲ SYM 1141

B. Haitink (cnd)

Bartók, B.:Bluebeard's Castle, w. Anne Sofie von Otter (mez—Judith), John Tomlinson (bass—Duke Bluebeard), Sandor Eles (nar) *(rec Berlin)* EMI Classics ▲ CDC 56162
Mahler, G.:Lieder eines fahrenden Gesellen, w. J. Norman (sop) Philips 2–▲ 426257–2 [DDD]
Mahler, G.:Sym 1 Philips ▲ 420936–2 [DDD]
Mahler, G.:Sym 2, w. S. McNair (sop), J. van Nes (cta), Ernst Senff Chorus Philips ▲ 438935–2
Mahler, G.:Sym 3, w. F. Quivar (cta), Ernst Senff Chorus Women's Voices, Tölz Boys' Choir Philips ▲ 432162–2
Mahler, G.:Sym 4, w. S. McNair (sop) Philips ▲ 434123–2
Mahler, G.:Sym 5 Philips ▲ 422355–2 [DDD]
Mahler, G.:Sym 6 Philips 2–▲ 426257–2 [DDD]
Mahler, G.:Sym 7 Philips 2–▲ 434997–2
Mahler, G.:Sym 10—Adagio Philips 2–▲ 434997–2
Schumann, R.:Adagio & Allegro Hn, w. H. Schiff (vc) [trans. for cello & orchestra] Philips ▲ 422414–2
Schumann, R.:Con Vc, w. H. Schiff (vc) Philips ▲ 422414–2
Schumann, R.:Fantasiestücke Cl, w. H. Schiff (vc) [cello & orch. trans.] Philips ▲ 422414–2
Schumann, R.:Stücke im Volkston, w. H. Schiff (vc) [cello & orch. trans.] Philips ▲ 422414–2

R. Heger (cnd)

Brahms, J.:Con 2 Pno, w. Walter Gieseking (pno)—movts 1 & 2 *(rec 1939–56)* Arbiter ▲ CD 103 [ADD]

H. W. Henze (cnd)

Henze, H.-W.:Syms (comp)—Nos. 1–5, London SO—No. 6 Deutsche Grammophon ("20th Century Classics" series) 2–▲ 429854–2 [ADD]

P. Hindemith (cnd)

Hindemith, P.:Mathis der Maler (sym) *(rec 1927–1934)* Koch Schwann ▲ CD 311342 [DDD]

J. Horenstein (cnd)

Bruckner, A.:Sym 7 *(rec ca. 1927/28 for Polydor)* Koch Legacy ▲ 3–7022–2 ■ 3–7022–4

78 ▲ = CD ♦ = Enhanced CD Δ = MD ■ = Cassette Tape □ = DCC

Berlin PO (cont.)
J. Horenstein (cnd) (cont.)
Haydn, J.:Sym 94, "Surprise Sym" *(rec 1929)* Koch Legacy ▲ 3-7054-2
Mozart, W.A.:Ovs—La Clemenza di Tito & Le nozze di Figaro *(rec 1929)* Koch Legacy ▲ 3-7054-2
Schoenberg, A.:Bach Trans *(rec 1929)* Koch Legacy ▲ 3-7054-2
Schubert, Franz:Sym 5 *(rec 1929)* Koch Legacy ▲ 3-7054-2
M. Jansons (cnd)
Shostakovich, D.:Con 1 Pno, w. Mikhail Rudy (pno), Ole Edvard Antonsen (tpt) EMI Classics ▲ CDC 55361
Shostakovich, D.:Sym 1 EMI Classics ▲ CDC 55361
E. Jochum (cnd)
Beethoven, L. van:Con Vn, Op. 61, w. Wolfgang Schneiderhan (vn) *(rec 1962 & 1967)* Deutsche Grammophon ("The Originals" series) ▲ 447403-2
Beethoven, L. van:Sym 6, "Pastorale" Theorema ▲ TH 121217
Brahms, J.:Con 1 Pno, w. E. Gilels (pno) Deutsche Grammophon 2-▲ 419158-2 [ADD]
Brahms, J.:Con 1 Pno, w. Emil Gilels (pno) *(rec Jesus-Christus Church, Berlin, June 1972)* Deutsche Grammophon ("The Originals" series) 2-▲ 447446-2 [ADD]
Brahms, J.:Con 1 Pno, w. E. Gilels (pno) Deutsche Grammophon ▲ 431595-2 [ADD]
Brahms, J.:Con 2 Pno, w. E. Gilels (pno) Deutsche Grammophon ("Galleria" series) ▲ 435588-2 [ADD]
Brahms, J.:Con 2 Pno, w. Emil Gilels (pno) *(rec Jesus-Christus Church, Berlin, June 1972)* Deutsche Grammophon ("The Originals" series) 2-▲ 447446-2 [ADD]
Brahms, J.:Con 2 Pno, w. E. Gilels (pno) Deutsche Grammophon 2-▲ 419158-2 [ADD]
Brahms, J.:Syms (comp) Deutsche Grammophon ("The Originals" series) ▲ 449 715-2
Brahms, J.:Sym 3 Theorema ▲ TH 121220
Bruckner, A.:Psalm 150, w. M. Stader (sop), Deutsche Opera Chorus [L] Deutsche Grammophon 4-▲ 423127-2 [ADD]
Bruckner, A.:Syms (comp), Bavarian RSO—Berlin PO *(Nos. 1, 4, 7, 8 & 9)*, Bavarian RSO *(Nos. 2, 3, 5 & 6)* Deutsche Grammophon 9-▲ 429079-2 [ADD]
Bruckner, A.:Te Deum, w. M. Stader (sop), S. Wagner (mez), E. Haefliger (ten), P. Lagger (bass), German Opera Chorus [L] Deutsche Grammophon 4-▲ 423127-2 [ADD]
H. von Karajan (cnd)
Albinoni, T.:Adagio Org Deutsche Grammophon ▲ 415301-2 [ADD]
Albinoni, T.:Adagio Org Deutsche Grammophon ▲ 413309-2 [DDD]
Albinoni, T.:Adagio Org Deutsche Grammophon ("Galleria" series) ▲ 419046-2 [ADD]
Art of Herbert von Karajan EMI Classics 4-▲ ZDMD 64563
Bach, J.S.:Brandenburg Cons Deutsche Grammophon 2-▲ 415374-2 [ADD]
Bach, J.S.:Brandenburg Cons Deutsche Grammophon ("Galleria" series) 2-▲ 431173-2 [ADD]
Bach, J.S.:Brandenburg Cons Deutsche Grammophon 2-▲ 437461-2 [ADD]
Bach, J.S.:Brandenburg Con 4 *(rec live, Berlin, 1970)* Foyer ▲ FOY 2038 [AAD]
Bach, J.S.:Mass in b, BWV 232, w. Gundula Janowitz (sop), Christa Ludwig (mez), Peter Schreier (ten), Karl Ridderbusch (bass), Vienna Choral Academy Deutsche Grammophon ("Double" series) 2-▲ 439696-2
Bach, J.S.:St. Matthew Passion, w. G. Janowitz (sop), C. Ludwig (mez), H. Laubenthal (ten), P. Schreier (ten), W. Berry (bar), D. Fischer-Dieskau (bar), Vienna Singverein, German Opera Chorus [G] Deutsche Grammophon 3-▲ 419789-2 [ADD]
Bach, J.S.:Suites Orch, BWV 1066-1069—BWV 1067 & 1068 only Deutsche Grammophon 2-▲ 437461-2 [ADD]
Bach, J.S.:Suite 2 Orch Deutsche Grammophon ("Galleria" series) 2-▲ 431173-2 [ADD]
Baroque Music Deutsche Grammophon ▲ 413309-2 GH [DDD]
Bartók, B.:Music for Strs, Perc & Cel EMI Classics ("Studio" series) ▲ CDM 69242 [ADD]
Beethoven, L. van:Con 3 Pno, w. M. Pollini (pno) *(rec Dec. 28, 1980)* Exclusive ▲ EXL 41 [AAD]
Beethoven, L. van:Con 3 Pno, w. G. Gould (pno) *(rec live, Berlin 1957)* Memories 2-▲ HR 4415/16 (m) [ADD]
Beethoven, L. van:Con Vn, Op. 61, w. A.-S. Mutter (vn) Deutsche Grammophon 4-▲ 415565-2 [ADD]
Beethoven, L. van:Con Vn, Op. 61, w. A.-S. Mutter (vn) Deutsche Grammophon ▲ 413818-2 [ADD]
Beethoven, L. van:Con Vn, Vc & Pno, "Triple Con", w. D. Oistrakh (vn), M. Rostropovich (vc), S. Richter (pno) EMI Classics ▲ CDM 64744
Beethoven, L. van:Con Vn, Vc & Pno, "Triple Con", w. A. S. Mutter (vn), Yo-Yo Ma (vc), M. Zeltser (pno) Deutsche Grammophon ▲ 415276-2 [ADD]
Beethoven, L. van:Coriolan Ov Deutsche Grammophon ▲ 415276-2 [ADD]
Beethoven, L. van:Coriolan Ov Deutsche Grammophon ("Galleria" series) ▲ 415833-2 [ADD]
Beethoven, L. van:Coriolan Ov Deutsche Grammophon ("The Originals" series) ▲ 447401-2
Beethoven, L. van:Coriolan Ov Deutsche Grammophon ▲ 439005-2 [DDD]
Beethoven, L. van:Egmont (ov) Deutsche Grammophon ▲ 415276-2 [ADD]
Beethoven, L. van:Fidelio (ov) Deutsche Grammophon ▲ 415276-2 [ADD]
Beethoven, L. van:Fidelio (ov) Deutsche Grammophon ▲ 439005-2 [DDD]
Beethoven, L. van:Fidelio (ov) Deutsche Grammophon ("Galleria" series) ■ 419051-4
Beethoven, L. van:Die Geschöpfe des Prometheus (ov) *(rec 1977)* Deutsche Grammophon ("Galleria" series) ▲ 415833-2 [ADD]
Beethoven, L. van:Leonore 3 Deutsche Grammophon ▲ 439005-2 [DDD]
Beethoven, L. van:Missa Solemnis, w. G. Janowitz (sop), C. Ludwig (mez), F. Wunderlich (ten), W. Berry (bass), Vienna Singverein [L] Deutsche Grammophon ("Galleria" series) 2-▲ 423913-2 [ADD]
Beethoven, L. van:Ovs—Die Geschöpfe desPrometheus; König Stephen; Die Ruinen von Athen; Egmont; Coriolan; Name-Day; Die Weihe des Hauses; Leonore 1, 2, 3; Fidelio Deutsche Grammophon ("Galleria" series) 2-▲ 427256-2 [ADD]
Beethoven, L. van:Ovs—Coriolan; Egmont; Fidelio; Leonore 3; Die Geschöpfe des Prometheus; Die Ruinen von Athen Deutsche Grammophon 6-▲ 429089-2 [ADD]
Beethoven, L. van:Die Ruinen von Athen (ov) *(rec 1977)* Deutsche Grammophon ("Galleria" series) ▲ 415833-2 [ADD]
Beethoven, L. van:Syms (comp)—[soloists in No. 9:Gundula Janowitz, Hilde Rössel-Majdan, Waldemar Kmentt, Walter Berry] *(rec 1963)* Deutsche Grammophon 5-▲ 429036-2 [ADD]
Beethoven, L. van:Syms (comp) [soloists in No. 9:Anna Tomowa-Sintow, Agnes Baltsa, Peter Schreier, José van Dam] *(rec 1975-76)* Deutsche Grammophon 6-▲ 429089-2 [ADD]
Beethoven, L. van:Sym 1 Deutsche Grammophon ▲ 439001-2 [DDD]
Beethoven, L. van:Sym 2 Deutsche Grammophon ▲ 439001-2 [DDD]
Beethoven, L. van:Sym 3, "Eroica" *(rec live, Vienna 1970)* Foyer ▲ FOY 2038 [AAD]
Beethoven, L. van:Sym 5 *(rec 1977)* Deutsche Grammophon ("Galleria" series) ■ 419051-4
Beethoven, L. van:Sym 6, "Pastorale" *(rec 1977)* Deutsche Grammophon ("Galleria" series) ▲ 415833-2 [ADD]
Beethoven, L. van:Sym 7 Grammofono 2000 ▲ GRM 78642
Beethoven, L. van:Sym 8 Deutsche Grammophon ▲ 439005-2 [DDD]
Beethoven, L. van:Sym 8 *(rec 1977)* Deutsche Grammophon ("Galleria" series) ■ 419051-4
Beethoven, L. van:Sym 9, "Choral Sym", w. G. Janowitz (sop), H. Rössel-Majdan (alt), W. Kmentt (ten), W. Berry (bass), Vienna Singverein Deutsche Grammophon ("The Originals" series) ▲ 447401-2
Beethoven, L. van:Sym 9, "Choral Sym", w. Vienna Singverein [G] *(rec 1976)* Deutsche Grammophon ("Galleria" series) ▲ 415832-2 [ADD] ■ 415832-4
Berg, A.:Lyric Suite—3 movts Deutsche Grammophon ("20th Century Classics" series) 3-▲ 427424-2 [ADD]
Berg, A.:Pieces Orch, Op. 6 Deutsche Grammophon 3-▲ 427424-2 [ADD]
Berlioz, H.:Sym fantastique Deutsche Grammophon ("Resonance" series) ▲ 429511-2 [ADD]
Bizet, G.:Carmen (sels), w. K. Ricciarelli (sop), A. Baltsa (mez), J. Carreras (ten), J. Van Dam (b-bar), Paris Opera Chorus [F] Deutsche Grammophon ▲ 413322-2 [DDD]
Borodin, A.:Prince Igor (Polovtsian dances) Deutsche Grammophon ("Galleria" series) ▲ 419063-2 [ADD]
Brahms, J.:Con 2 Pno, w. Hans Richter-Haaser (pno) Royal Classics ▲ ROY 6437
Brahms, J.:Con Vn, w. A.-S. Mutter (vn) Deutsche Grammophon 4-▲ 415565-2 [ADD/DDD]
Brahms, J.:Con Vn, w. Gidon Kremer (vn) EMI Classics 2-▲ CDFB 69334
Brahms, J.:Ein Deutsches Requiem, w. G. Janowitz (sop), E. Wächter (bar), Vienna Singverein [G] Deutsche Grammophon ("Galleria" series) ▲ 427252-2 [ADD]

Berlin PO (cont.)
H. von Karajan (cnd) (cont.)
Brahms, J.:Ein Deutsches Requiem, w. A. Tomowa-Sintow (sop), J. van Dam (b-bar), Vienna Singverein [G] *(rec 1976)* EMI Classics ▲ CDM 69229 [ADD]
Brahms, J.:Hungarian Dances Orch—Nos. 17-20 Deutsche Grammophon ("Resonance" series) ▲ 429156-2 [ADD]
Brahms, J.:Hungarian Dances Orch—Nos. 1, 3, 5, 6 & 17-20 *(rec Jesus-Christus-Kirche, Berlin, Sept 1959)* Deutsche Grammophon ▲ 447434-2 [ADD]
Brahms, J.:Syms (comp) Deutsche Grammophon 3-▲ 427602-2 [DDD]
Brahms, J.:Sym 1 *(rec 1963 & 1973)* Deutsche Grammophon ("The Originals" series) ▲ 447408-2
Brahms, J.:Sym 1 Deutsche Grammophon ▲ 423141-2 [DDD]
Brahms, J.:Sym 2 Deutsche Grammophon ▲ 429153-2 [ADD] ■ 429153-4
Brahms, J.:Sym 2 Deutsche Grammophon ▲ 423142-2 [DDD]
Brahms, J.:Sym 3 *(rec 1977)* Deutsche Grammophon ▲ 437645-2
Brahms, J.:Sym 3 Deutsche Grammophon ("Resonance" series) ▲ 429153-2 [ADD] ■ 429153-4
Brahms, J.:Sym 3 Deutsche Grammophon ▲ 431593-2 [ADD]
Brahms, J.:Sym 3 Deutsche Grammophon ▲ 427496-2 [DDD]
Brahms, J.:Sym 4 Deutsche Grammophon ▲ 431593-2 [ADD]
Brahms, J.:Sym 4 *(rec 1977)* Deutsche Grammophon ▲ 437645-2
Brahms, J.:Tragic Ov Deutsche Grammophon ▲ 427496-2 [DDD]
Brahms, J.:Tragic Ov Deutsche Grammophon 3-▲ 427602-2 [DDD]
Brahms, J.:Vars on a Theme by Haydn Deutsche Grammophon 3-▲ 427602-2 [DDD]
Brahms, J.:Vars on a Theme by Haydn Deutsche Grammophon ▲ 423142-2 [DDD]
Bruch, M.:Con 1 Vn, w. A.-S, Mutter (vn) Deutsche Grammophon 4-▲ 415565-2 [ADD/DDD]
Bruckner, A.:Syms (comp) Deutsche Grammophon 9-▲ 429648-2 [ADD/DDD]
Bruckner, A.:Sym 2 Deutsche Grammophon ▲ 415988-2 [DDD]
Les Chefs-d'Oeuvre du Violoncelle, w. Mstislav Rostropovich (vc), Israel PO [cnd:Leonard Bernstein] Deutsche Grammophon ("Double" series) 2-▲ 437952-2
Chopin, F.:Con 2 Pno, w. K. Zimmerman (pno) *(rec Sept. 1, 1980)* Exclusive ▲ EXL 41 [AAD]
Chopin, F.:Les Sylphides Deutsche Grammophon ("Galleria" series) ▲ 429163-2 [ADD]
Christmas Adagio, w. Berlin Philharmonic Brass Ensemble Deutsche Grammophon ▲ 449924-2 ■ 449924-4
Corelli, A.:Con grosso, Op. 6/8, "Christmas Con" Deutsche Grammophon ("Galleria" series) ▲ 419046-2 [ADD]
Debussy, C.:La Mer, Paris SO EMI Classics ▲ CDM 64357
Debussy, C.:La Mer Deutsche Grammophon ("Galleria" series) ▲ 427250-2 [ADD]
Debussy, C.:La Mer *(rec 1964 & 1965/66)* Deutsche Grammophon ("The Originals" series) ▲ 447426-2
Debussy, C.:Pelléas et Mélisande, w. N. Denize (mez), F. von Stade (mez), G. Raimondi (ten), R. Stilwell (bar), J. Van Dam (bass-bar), German Opera Chorus [F] EMI Classics 3-▲ CDCC 49350 [ADD]
Debussy, C.:Prélude à l'après-midi d'un faune Deutsche Grammophon ("Galleria" series) ▲ 427250-2 [ADD]
Delibes, L.:Coppélia (suite) Deutsche Grammophon ("Galleria" series) ▲ 429163-2 [ADD]
Dvořák, A.:Con Vc, w. Mstislav Rostropovich (vc) Deutsche Grammophon ("The Originals" series) ▲ 447413-2
Dvořák, A.:Con Vc, w. M. Rostropovich (vc) Deutsche Grammophon ▲ 413819-2 [ADD]
Dvořák, A.:Scherzo Capriccioso *(rec Jesus-Christus-Kirche, Berlin, Sept 1971)* Deutsche Grammophon ▲ 447434-2 [ADD]
Dvořák, A.:Serenade Strs Deutsche Grammophon ▲ 400038-2 [DDD]
Dvořák, A.:Slavonic Dances (sels)—Op.46/1, 3 & 7; Op. 72/ 2 & 8 *(rec Jesus-Christus-Kirche, Berlin, Sept 1959)* Deutsche Grammophon ▲ 447434-2 [ADD]
Dvořák, A.:Sym 8 *(rec 1979)* EMI Classics ▲ CDM 64325
Dvořák, A.:Sym 9, "From the New World" Grammofono 2000 ▲ GRM 78642
Dvořák, A.:Sym 9, "From the New World" *(rec 1959)* EMI Classics ▲ CDM 64325
Famous Ballets Deutsche Grammophon ("Double" series) 2-▲ 437404-2
Franck, C.:Symphonic Vars, w. A. Weissenberg (pno) EMI Classics ▲ CDM 64747
Grieg, E.:Holberg Suite Deutsche Grammophon ("Galleria" series) ▲ 419474-2 [ADD]
Grieg, E.:Peer Gynt Suites, Opp. 46 & 55 *(rec 1971)* Deutsche Grammophon ("Galleria" series) ▲ 419474-2 [ADD/DDD]
Grieg, E.:Sigurd Jorsalfar (suite) Deutsche Grammophon ("Galleria" series) ▲ 419474-2 [ADD/DDD]
Haydn, J.:Die Schöpfung, w. Gunalda Janowitz (sop), Fritz Wunderlich (ten), Dietrich Fischer-Dieskau (bass), Vienna Singverein *(rec 1966 & 1968)* Deutsche Grammophon ("Galleria" series) 2-▲ 435077-2 [ADD]
Haydn, J.:Sym 82, "The Bear" Deutsche Grammophon ("Digital Midprice" series) 2-▲ 445532-2 [DDD]
Haydn, J.:Sym 83, "The Hen" Deutsche Grammophon ("Digital Midprice" series) 2-▲ 445532-2 [DDD]
Haydn, J.:Sym 84, "In Nomine Domini" Deutsche Grammophon ("Digital Midprice" series) 2-▲ 445532-2 [DDD]
Haydn, J.:Sym 85, "La Reine de France" Deutsche Grammophon ("Digital Midprice" series) 2-▲ 445532-2 [DDD]
Haydn, J.:Sym 86 Deutsche Grammophon ("Digital Midprice" series) 2-▲ 445532-2 [DDD]
Haydn, J.:Sym 87 Deutsche Grammophon ("Digital Midprice" series) 2-▲ 445532-2 [DDD]
Haydn, J.:Syms 93-104, "The Salomon (or London) Syms" Deutsche Grammophon 5-▲ 429658-2 [DDD]
Haydn, J.:Sym 93 Deutsche Grammophon ("3D Classics" series) ▲ 427809-2 [DDD]
Haydn, J.:Sym 94, "Surprise Sym" Deutsche Grammophon ("3D Classics" series) ▲ 427809-2 [DDD]
Haydn, J.:Sym 100, "Military" Deutsche Grammophon ("3D Classics" series) ▲ 427809-2 [DDD]
Haydn, J.:Sym 103, "Drum Roll" Deutsche Grammophon ▲ 410517-2 [DDD]
Haydn, J.:Sym 104, "London" Deutsche Grammophon ▲ 410517-2 [DDD]
Herbert von Karajan EMI Classics ▲ CDM 64629
Hindemith, P.:Mathis der Maler (sym) EMI Classics ("Studio" series) ▲ CDM 69242 [ADD] ■ GNP 3 430 914
Honegger, A.:Sym 2, w. Fritz Wesenigk (tpt) *(rec French Church, St. Moritz, Aug 1969)* Deutsche Grammophon ("The Originals" series) ▲ 447435-2 [ADD]
Honegger, A.:Sym 3 *(rec Jesus-Christus Church, Berlin, Sept 1969)* Deutsche Grammophon ("The Originals" series) ▲ 447435-2 [ADD]
Karajan Adagio Deutsche Grammophon ▲ 445282-2
Karajan Adagio 2 *(rec Church of Jesus Christ, Berlin; Victoria Room, St. Moritz; French Church, St. Moritz; Philharmonie, Berlin; Mar 1964; Aug & Dec 1970;)* Deutsche Grammophon ▲ 449515-2 [ADD/DDD]
Karajan Festival Deutsche Grammophon 5-▲ 429436-2
Lehár, F.:Die lustige Witwe, w. E. Harwood (sop), T. Stratas (sop), W. Hollweg (ten), R. Kollo (ten), Z. Kelemen (bar), German Opera Chorus [G] *(rec 1972)* Deutsche Grammophon 2-▲ 435712-2 [ADD]
Liszt, F.:Fant on Hungarian Folk Tunes, w. Shura Cherkassky (pno) Deutsche Grammophon ("Galleria" series) ▲ 419862-2 [ADD]
Liszt, F.:Fant on Hungarian Folk Tunes, w. Shura Cherkassky (pno) Deutsche Grammophon 2-▲ 415967-2 [ADD]
Liszt, F.:Fant on Hungarian Folk Tunes, w. Shura Cherkassky (pno) Deutsche Grammophon ("Resonance" series) ▲ 429156-2 [ADD]
Liszt, F.:Hungarian Rhaps—Nos. 2, 5 & 12 Deutsche Grammophon 2-▲ 415967-2 [ADD]
Liszt, F.:Hungarian Rhaps—Nos. 5 & 12 Deutsche Grammophon ("Galleria" series) ▲ 419862-2 [ADD]
Liszt, F.:Hungarian Rhaps, w. S. Cherkassky (pno)—Nos. 2, 5, 6, 9, 12 & 14 Deutsche Grammophon ("Resonance" series) ▲ 429156-2 [ADD]
Liszt, F.:Hungarian Rhaps—No. 4 *(rec 1961 & 1967)* Deutsche Grammophon ("The Originals" series) ▲ 447415-2
Liszt, F.:Mazeppa Orch *(rec 1961 & 1967)* Deutsche Grammophon ("The Originals" series) ▲ 447415-2
Liszt, F.:Mephisto Waltz 1 Orch Deutsche Grammophon 2-▲ 415967-2 [ADD]

ORCH. & ENS.

Berlin PO (cont.)

H. von Karajan (cnd) (cont.)

Liszt, F.:Mephisto Waltz 1 Orch Deutsche Grammophon ("Galleria" series) ▲ 419862-2 [ADD]
Liszt, F.:Les Préludes Deutsche Grammophon 2-▲ 415967-2 [ADD]
Liszt, F.:Les Préludes *(rec 1961 & 1967)* Deutsche Grammophon ("The Originals" series) ▲ 447415-2
Mahler, G.:Kindertotenlieder, w. Christa Ludwig (mez) Deutsche Grammophon ("Double" series) 2-▲ 439678-2
Mahler, G.:Songs from Rückert, w. Christa Ludwig (mez) *(rec 1975–81)* Deutsche Grammophon ("Double" series) 2-▲ 439678-2
Mahler, G.:Sym 5 *(rec Jesus Christ Church, Berlin, Feb 1973)* Deutsche Grammophon ("The Originals" series) ▲ 447450-2 [ADD]
Mahler, G.:Sym 9 Deutsche Grammophon ("Double" series) 2-▲ 439678-2
Mahler, G.:Sym 9 Deutsche Grammophon ("Karajan Gold" series) 2-▲ 439024-2 [DDD]
Manfredini, F.:Con grosso, Op. 3/12 Deutsche Grammophon ▲ 419046-2 [ADD]
Marches Deutsche Grammophon 2-▲ 439690-2
Mendelssohn, F.:Con in e Vn & Orch, Op. 64, w. Anne-Sophie Mutter (vn) Deutsche Grammophon 4-▲ 415565-2 [ADD/DDD]
Mendelssohn, F.:Syms (comp) [Sym 2 w. Edith Mathis (sop), Liselotte Rebmann (sop), Werner Hollweg (ten), Deutsche Oper Chorus] *(rec 1971–2)* Deutsche Grammophon 3-▲ 429664-2 [ADD]
Mozart, W.A.:Con Bn, w. G. Piesk (bn) EMI Classics ▲ CDM 64355 [ADD]
Mozart, W.A.:Con Cl, w. K. Leister (cl) EMI Classics ▲ CDM 64355 [ADD]
Mozart, W.A.:Con Fl, K.313, w. A. Blau (fl), J. Galway (fl), F. Helmis (hp) EMI Classics ▲ CDM 69187
Mozart, W.A.:Con Fl Hp, w. A. Blau (fl), J. Galway (fl), F. Helmis (hp) EMI Classics ▲ CDM 69187
Mozart, W.A.:Con Ob, K.314, w. L. Koch (ob) EMI Classics ▲ CDM 64355 [ADD]
Mozart, W.A.:Con 3 Vn, w. A.S. Mutter (vn) Deutsche Grammophon ▲ 429814-2 [ADD]
Mozart, W.A.:Con 5 Vn, w. A.S. Mutter (vn) Deutsche Grammophon ▲ 429814-2 [ADD]
Mozart, W.A.:Divert Hns Strs, K.287 Deutsche Grammophon ("3D Classics" series) ▲ 431272-2 [DDD]
Mozart, W.A.:Diverts Str Qt, K.136–138 Deutsche Grammophon ▲ 429805-2 [ADD]
Mozart, W.A.:Don Giovanni, w. A. Tomowa-Sintow (sop), K. Battle (sop), A. Baltsa (mez), G. Winbergh (ten), S. Ramey (bass), F. Furlanetto (bass), P. Burchuladze (bass), German Opera Chorus [I] Deutsche Grammophon 3-▲ 419179-2 [DDD]
Mozart, W.A.:Don Giovanni (sels), w. A. Tomowa-Sintow (sop), K. Battle (sop), A. Baltsa (mez), G. Winbergh (ten), S. Ramey (bass), F. Furlanetto (bass), P. Burchuladze (bass), German Opera Chorus [I] Deutsche Grammophon ▲ 419635-2 [DDD]
Mozart, W.A.:Kleine Nachtmusik Deutsche Grammophon ▲ 429805-2 [ADD]
Mozart, W.A.:Kleine Nachtmusik Deutsche Grammophon ("3D Classics" series) ▲ 431272-2 [DDD]
Mozart, W.A.:Missa, K.317, w. A. Tomowa-Sintow (sop), A. Baltsa (mez), W. Krenn (ten), J. van Dam (b-bar), Vienna Singverein Deutsche Grammophon ▲ 429820-2 [ADD]
Mozart, W.A.:Missa, K.317, w. A. Tomowa-Sintow (sop), A. Baltsa (mez), W. Krenn (ten), J. van Dam (b-bar), Vienna Singverein [L] Deutsche Grammophon ("Galleria" series) 2-▲ 423913-2 [ADD]
Mozart, W.A.:Missa, K.427, w. B. Hendricks (sop), J. Perry (sop), P. Schreier (ten), B. Luxon (bar) Deutsche Grammophon ("Karajan Gold" series) ▲ 439012-2
Mozart, W.A.:Requiem, w. A. Tomowa-Sintow (sop), A. Baltsa (mez), W. Krenn (ten), J. van Dam (b-bar), Vienna Singverein [L] Deutsche Grammophon ("Galleria" series) ▲ 419867-2 [ADD] ■ 419867-4
Mozart, W.A.:Requiem, w. W. Lipp (sop), H. Rössl-Majdan (mez), A. Dermota (ten), W. Berry (bass), Vienna Singverein [L] *(rec 1961)* Deutsche Grammophon ("Resonance" series) ▲ 429160-2 [ADD] ■ 429160-4
Mozart, W.A.:Requiem, w. A. Tomowa-Sintow (sop), A. Baltsa (mez), W. Krenn (ten), J. van Dam (b-bar), Vienna Singverein Deutsche Grammophon ▲ 429821-2 [ADD] ■ 429821-4
Mozart, W.A.:Serenata notturna Deutsche Grammophon ▲ 429805-2 [ADD]
Mozart, W.A.:Serenata notturna Deutsche Grammophon ▲ 413309-2 [DDD]
Mozart, W.A.:Serenata notturna Deutsche Grammophon ("3D Classics" series) ▲ 431272-2 [DDD]
Mozart, W.A.:Sym 29 EMI Classics ▲ CDM 64327
Mozart, W.A.:Sym 29 Deutsche Grammophon 3-▲ 429668-2 [ADD]
Mozart, W.A.:Sym 29 EMI Classics ("Studio" series) 3-▲ CDMC 69882 [ADD]
Mozart, W.A.:Sym 32 Deutsche Grammophon 3-▲ 429668-2 [ADD]
Mozart, W.A.:Sym 33 Deutsche Grammophon 3-▲ 429668-2 [ADD]
Mozart, W.A.:Sym 35 Deutsche Grammophon 3-▲ 429668-2 [ADD]
Mozart, W.A.:Sym 35 EMI Classics ("Studio" series) 3-▲ CDMC 69882 [ADD]
Mozart, W.A.:Sym 36 EMI Classics ("Studio" series) 3-▲ CDMC 69882 [ADD]
Mozart, W.A.:Sym 36 Deutsche Grammophon 3-▲ 429668-2 [ADD]
Mozart, W.A.:Sym 38 EMI Classics ("Studio" series) 3-▲ CDMC 69882 [ADD]
Mozart, W.A.:Sym 38 Deutsche Grammophon 3-▲ 429668-2 [ADD]
Mozart, W.A.:Sym 39 Deutsche Grammophon 3-▲ 429668-2 [ADD]
Mozart, W.A.:Sym 39 EMI Classics ("Studio" series) 3-▲ CDMC 69882 [ADD]
Mozart, W.A.:Sym 40 Deutsche Grammophon 3-▲ 429668-2 [ADD]
Mozart, W.A.:Sym 40 EMI Classics ("Studio" series) 3-▲ CDMC 69882 [ADD]
Mozart, W.A.:Sym 40 EMI Classics ▲ CDM 64327
Mozart, W.A.:Sym 40 *(rec 1977)* Deutsche Grammophon ("Galleria" series) ▲ 435592-2 [ADD]
Mozart, W.A.:Sym 41 EMI Classics ("Studio" series) 3-▲ CDMC 69882 [ADD]
Mozart, W.A.:Sym 41 EMI Classics ▲ CDM 64327
Mozart, W.A.:Sym 41 *(rec 1977)* Deutsche Grammophon ("Galleria" series) ▲ 435592-2 [ADD]
Mozart, W.A.:Sym 41 Deutsche Grammophon 3-▲ 429668-2 [ADD]
Mozart, W.A.:Zauberflöte, w. Edith Mathis (sop), Karin Ott (sop), Janet Perry (sop), Anna Tomowa-Sintow (sop), Agnes Baltsa (mez), Hannah Schwarz (mez), Francisco Araiza (ten), Gottfried Hornik (bar), José Van Dam (b-bar), German Opera Chorus [G] Deutsche Grammophon 3-▲ 410967-2 [DDD]
Mozart, W.A.:Zauberflöte (sels), w. Edith Mathis (sop), Karin Ott (sop), Janet Perry (sop), Anna Tomowa-Sintow (sop), Agnes Baltsa (mez), Hannah Schwarz (mez), Francisco Araiza (ten), Gottfried Hornik (bar), José Van Dam (b-bar), German Opera Chorus [G] Deutsche Grammophon ▲ 415287-2 [DDD]
Mussorgsky, M.:Pictures at an Exhibition *(rec 1964 & 1965/66)* Deutsche Grammophon ("The Originals" series) ▲ 447426-2
Mussorgsky, M.:Pictures at an Exhibition Deutsche Grammophon ("Resonance" series) ▲ 429162-2 [ADD]
Nielsen, C.:Sym 4 Deutsche Grammophon ("Digital Midprice" series) ▲ 445518-2
Offenbach, J.:Gaîté Parisienne Deutsche Grammophon ("Galleria" series) ▲ 429163-2 [ADD]
Offenbach, J.:Ovs—Orphée aux enfers; Barbe-bleue; La Grande- Duchesse de Gérolstein; La belle Hélène; Vert-vert; Kakadu; Barcarolle, from Contes d'Hoffmann Deutsche Grammophon ▲ 400044-2 [DDD]
Pachelbel, J.:Canon Deutsche Grammophon ▲ 413309-2 [DDD]
Pachelbel, J.:Canon Deutsche Grammophon ("Galleria" series) ▲ 419046-2 [ADD]
Penderecki, K.:Polymorphia *(rec live, Berlin, 1968)* Foyer ▲ FOY 2038 [AAD]
Prokofiev, S.:Sym 1 Deutsche Grammophon ▲ 437253-2
Prokofiev, S.:Sym 5 *(rec 1969)* Deutsche Grammophon ▲ 437253-2
Puccini, G.:La Bohème, w. M. Freni (sop), E. Harwood (sop), L. Pavarotti (ten), R. Panerai (bar), German Opera Chorus [I] London 2-▲ 421049-2 [ADD] 2-■ 421049-4
Puccini, G.:La Bohème (sels), w. M. Freni (sop), E. Harwood (sop), L. Pavarotti (ten), R. Panerai (bar), German Opera Chorus London ▲ 421245-2 [DDD] ■ 421245-4
Puccini, G.:Tosca, w. K. Ricciarelli (sop), J. Carreras (ten), R. Raimondi (bass), German Opera Chorus [I] Deutsche Grammophon 2-▲ 413815-2 [ADD]
Ravel, M.:Alborada del gracioso EMI Classics ▲ CDM 64357
Ravel, M.:Boléro Deutsche Grammophon ("Galleria" series) ▲ 427250-2 [ADD]
Ravel, M.:Boléro *(rec 1964 & 1965/66)* Deutsche Grammophon ("The Originals" series) ▲ 447426-2
Ravel, M.:Daphnis et Chloé (suite 2) Deutsche Grammophon ("Galleria" series) ▲ 427250-2 [ADD]
Ravel, M.:La Valse EMI Classics ▲ CDM 64357

Berlin PO (cont.)

H. von Karajan (cnd) (cont.)

Respighi, O.:Ancient Airs & Dances—Set 3 Deutsche Grammophon ▲ 413822-2 [ADD]
Respighi, O.:The Fountains of Rome Deutsche Grammophon ▲ 413822-2 [ADD]
Respighi, O.:The Pines of Rome Deutsche Grammophon ▲ 413822-2 [ADD]
Rimsky-Korsakov, N.:Scheherazade Deutsche Grammophon ▲ 419063-2 [ADD]
Romantic Adagio Deutsche Grammophon ▲ 449900-2 ■ 449 900-4
Saint-Saëns, C.:Sym 3, w. P. Cochereau (org) Deutsche Grammophon ("Karajan Gold" series) ▲ 439014-2
Schoenberg, A.:Pelleas und Melisande Deutsche Grammophon ("20th Century Classics" series) 3-▲ 427424-2 [ADD]
Schoenberg, A.:Vars Orch, Op. 31 Deutsche Grammophon ("20th Century Classics" series) 3-▲ 427424-2 [ADD]
Schoenberg, A.:Vars Orch, Op. 31 Deutsche Grammophon ▲ 415326-2 [ADD]
Schoenberg, A.:Verklärte Nacht Deutsche Grammophon ▲ 415326-2 [ADD]
Schoenberg, A.:Verklärte Nacht Deutsche Grammophon ("20th Century Classics" series) 3-▲ 427424-2 [ADD]
Schubert, Franz:Syms (comp) EMI Classics ("Studio" series) 4-▲ CDMD 69884 [ADD]
Schubert, Franz:Sym 9 EMI Classics ▲ CDM 64628
Schumann, R.:Sym 1 *(rec 1963 & 1973)* Deutsche Grammophon ("The Originals" series) ▲ 447408-2
Shostakovich, D.:Sym 10 *(rec 1966)* Deutsche Grammophon ("Galleria" series) ▲ 429716-2 [ADD]
Shostakovich, D.:Sym 10 Deutsche Grammophon ▲ 413361-2 [DDD]
Shostakovich, D.:Sym 10 *(rec Berlin, Feb 1981)* Deutsche Grammophon ("Karajan Gold" series) ▲ 439036-2 [DDD]
Sibelius, J.:Con Vn, w. Gidon Kremer (vn) EMI Classics 2-▲ CDFB 69334
Sibelius, J.:Finlandia EMI Classics ▲ CDM 64331
Sibelius, J.:Karelia Suite EMI Classics ("Studio" series) ▲ CDM 69028 [DDD]
Sibelius, J.:Karelia Suite EMI Classics ▲ CDM 64331
Sibelius, J.:En Saga EMI Classics ▲ CDM 64331
Sibelius, J.:The Swan of Tuonela EMI Classics ▲ CDM 64331
Sibelius, J.:Sym 1 EMI Classics ("Studio" series) ▲ CDM 69028 [DDD]
Sibelius, J.:Sym 1 EMI Classics ("Studio DDD" series) ▲ CDD 63896 [DDD]
Sibelius, J.:Sym 2 EMI Classics ("Studio" series) ▲ CDM 69243 [DDD]
Sibelius, J.:Sym 6 EMI Classics ("Studio DDD" series) ▲ CDD 63896 [DDD]
Sibelius, J.:Tapiola Deutsche Grammophon ("Digital Midprice" series) ▲ 445518-2
Sibelius, J.:Tapiola EMI Classics ▲ CDM 64331
Smetana, B.:Má Vlast—Vysehrad & Moldau *(rec 1961 & 1967)* Deutsche Grammophon ("The Originals" series) ▲ 447415-2
Strauss (II), Joh.:Music of Deutsche Grammophon ▲ 410022-2 [DDD]
Strauss (II), Joh.:Waltzes—G'schichten aus dem Wienerwald; Auf der Jagd; Unter Donner und Blitz; Wiener Blut; An der schönen, blauen Donau; Kaiser Walzer; Annen Polka; Perpetuum mobile; Pizzicato Polka (written with Josef Strauss) Deutsche Grammophon ▲ 437255-2 [ADD]
Strauss (II), Joh.:Der Zigeunerbaron (ov) Grammofon 2000 ▲ GRM 78663
Strauss, Josef:Music of—Delirien; Pizzicato Polka (written with Johann Strauss, II) Deutsche Grammophon ▲ 437255-2 [ADD]
Strauss, R.:Eine Alpensinfonie Deutsche Grammophon ("Karajan Gold" series) ▲ 439017-2
Strauss, R.:Also sprach Zarathustra *(rec Jesus-Christus Church, Berlin, Jan & Mar 1973)* Deutsche Grammophon ("The Originals" series) ▲ 447441-2 [ADD]
Strauss, R.:Don Juan *(rec Jesus-Christus Church, Berlin, Dec 1972 & Jan 1973)* Deutsche Grammophon ("The Originals" series) ▲ 447441-2 [ADD]
Strauss, R.:Don Juan *(rec 1972)* Deutsche Grammophon ("Galleria" series) ▲ 429717-2 [ADD]
Strauss, R.:Don Quixote, w. A. Meneses (vc) Deutsche Grammophon ("Karajan Gold" series) (v▲ 439027-2 [DDD]
Strauss, R.:4 Last Songs, w. Gundula Janowitz (sop) Deutsche Grammophon ("The Originals" series) ▲ 447422-2
Strauss, R.:Ein Heldenleben *(rec Philharmonie, Berlin, Feb 1985)* Deutsche Grammophon ("Karajan Gold" series) ▲ 439039-2 [DDD]
Strauss, R.:Ein Heldenleben *(rec 1959)* Deutsche Grammophon ("Galleria" series) ▲ 429717-2 [ADD]
Strauss, R.:Metamorphosen Deutsche Grammophon ▲ 410892-2 [DDD]
Strauss, R.:Metamorphosen Deutsche Grammophon ("The Originals" series) ▲ 447422-2
Strauss, R.:Salome (dance) *(rec Jesus-Christus Church, Berlin, Dec 1972 & Jan 1973)* Deutsche Grammophon ("The Originals" series) ▲ 447441-2 [ADD]
Strauss, R.:Till Eulenspiegels lustige Streiche *(rec Jesus-Christus Church, Berlin, Dec 1972 & Jan 1973)* Deutsche Grammophon ("The Originals" series) ▲ 447441-2 [ADD]
Strauss, R.:Tod und Verklärung *(rec Philharmonie, Berlin, Jan 1982)* Deutsche Grammophon ("Karajan Gold" series) ▲ 439039-2 [DDD]
Strauss, R.:Tod und Verklärung Deutsche Grammophon ("The Originals" series) ▲ 447422-2
Strauss, R.:Tod und Verklärung Deutsche Grammophon ▲ 410892-2 [DDD]
Stravinsky, I.:Con Str *(rec French Church, St. Moritz, Aug 1969)* Deutsche Grammophon ("The Originals" series) ▲ 447435-2 [ADD]
Stravinsky, I.:Le Sacre du printemps Orch Deutsche Grammophon ("Resonance" series) ▲ 429162-2 [ADD]
Suppé, F. von:Ovs—Light Cavalry; Morning, Noon & Night in Vienna; Jolly Robbers; Beautiful Galatea; Poet & Peasant; Pique Dame Deutsche Grammophon 2-▲ 435712-2 [ADD]
Tchaikovsky, P.:Con 1 Pno, w. L. Berman (pno) Deutsche Grammophon ("Resonance" series) ▲ 429166-2 [ADD]
Tchaikovsky, P.:Con 1 Pno, w. E. Kissin (pno) Deutsche Grammophon ▲ 427485-2 [DDD] □ 427485-5
Tchaikovsky, P.:Con Vn, w. C. Ferras (vn) Deutsche Grammophon ("Resonance" series) ▲ 429166-2 [ADD]
Tchaikovsky, P.:Nutcracker Suite Deutsche Grammophon ▲ 419175-2 [ADD]
Tchaikovsky, P.:Nutcracker Suite Deutsche Grammophon ("Karajan Gold" series) ▲ 439021-2
Tchaikovsky, P.:Ov 1812 EMI Classics ▲ CDM 64871
Tchaikovsky, P.:Romeo & Juliet Deutsche Grammophon ("Karajan Gold" series) ▲ 439021-2
Tchaikovsky, P.:Serenade Strs Deutsche Grammophon ▲ 400038-2 [DDD]
Tchaikovsky, P.:Sleeping Beauty (sels) Deutsche Grammophon ▲ 419175-2 [ADD]
Tchaikovsky, P.:Swan Lake (sels) Deutsche Grammophon ▲ 419175-2 [ADD]
Tchaikovsky, P.:Sym 1 Deutsche Grammophon ▲ 431606-2 [ADD]
Tchaikovsky, P.:Sym 3 Deutsche Grammophon ▲ 431605-2 [ADD]
Tchaikovsky, P.:Sym 5 EMI Classics ▲ CDM 64871
Tchaikovsky, P.:Sym 5 Deutsche Grammophon ▲ 439019-2
Tchaikovsky, P.:Sym 6 Deutsche Grammophon ▲ 439020-2
Tchaikovsky, P.:Sym 6 Grammofono 2000 ▲ GRM 78653
Tchaikovsky, P.:Vars on a Rococo Theme, w. M. Rostropovich (vc) Deutsche Grammophon ▲ 413819-2 [ADD]
Tchaikovsky, P.:Vars on a Rococo Theme, w. Mstislav Rostropovich (vc) Deutsche Grammophon ("The Originals" series) ▲ 447413-2
Tchaikovsky, P.:Vars on a Rococo Theme, w. M. Rostropovich (vc) Deutsche Grammophon ▲ 431606-2 [ADD]
Vivaldi, A.:Cons Orch—RV. 151 Deutsche Grammophon ("Galleria" series) ▲ 419046-2 [ADD]
Vivaldi, A.:Cons Vn (misc), w. T. Brandis (vn)—RV.271 Deutsche Grammophon ("Galleria" series) ▲ 419046-2 [ADD]
Vivaldi, A.:Cons Vn, Op. 8/1-4, "The Four Seasons", w. M. Schwalbé (vn) Deutsche Grammophon ▲ 415301-2 [ADD]
Wagner, R.:Der fliegende Holländer, w. D. Vejzovic (sop), P. Hofmann (ten), J. Van Dam (b-bar), Kurt Moll (bass) [G] EMI Classics 2-▲ CDMB 64650
Wagner, R.:Lohengrin, w. A. Tomowa-Sintow (sop), D. Vejzovic (sop), A. Kollo (ten), S. Nimsgern (b-bar), K. Ridderbusch (bass), German Opera Chorus [G] EMI Classics ("Studio" series) 4-▲ CDMD 69314 [ADD]

▲ = CD ♦ = Enhanced CD Δ = MD ■ = Cassette Tape □ = DCC

Berlin PO (cont.)
H. von Karajan (cnd) (cont.)
Wagner, R.:Die Meistersinger von Nürnberg (sels)—Prelude to Act 3
Deutsche Grammophon ("Karajan Gold" series) ▲ 439022-2
Wagner, R.:Ovs, Preludes & Orch Sels—Meistersinger, Act 3
Deutsche Grammophon ▲ 413754-2 [DDD]
Wagner, R.:Ovs, Preludes & Orch Sels—Meistersinger, Ov.; Lohengrin, Perlude to Act 1; Tristan und Isolde, Perlude & Liebestod; Fliegende Holländer, Ov.; Tannhäuser, Ov. & Venusberg Music
EMI Classics ▲ CDM 64334
Wagner, R.:Ovs, Preludes & Orch Sels—Tannhäuser; Lohengrin; Der fliegende Holländer; Die Meistersinger von Nürnberg; Tristan und Isolde Enterprise ("Flowers") 2–▲ ENTBL 19 [ADD]
Wagner, R.:Parsifal, w. D. Vejzovic (sop), P. Hofmann (ten), J. Van Dam (b-bar), S. Nimsgern (b-bar), K. Moll (bass), German Opera Chorus [G] Deutsche Grammophon 4–▲ 413347-2 [DDD]
Wagner, R.:Der Ring des Nibelungen, w. R. Crespin (sop), G. Janowitz (sop), C. Ludwig (mez), H. Dernesch (mez), J. Vickers (ten), D. Fischer-Dieskau (bar), D. Thomas (bass) *(rec late 1960s)*
Deutsche Grammophon 15–▲ 435211-2 [ADD]
Wagner, R.:Der Ring des Nibelungen, w. R. Crespin (sop), G. Janowitz (sop), C. Ludwig (mez), H. Dernesch (mez), J. Vickers (ten), D. Fischer-Dieskau (bar), D. Thomas (bass) *(rec live at Salzburg Easter Festivals, 1967–1970)* Arkadia 12–▲ 223 (m) [ADD]
Wagner, R.:Der Ring des Nibelungen (orch sels)
Deutsche Grammophon ("Resonance" series) ▲ 429168-2 [ADD] ■ 429168-4
Wagner, R.:Tannhäuser (orch sels)—Ov.; Bacchanale
Deutsche Grammophon ("Karajan Gold" series) ▲ 439022-2
Wagner, R.:Tannhäuser (ov & venusberg) Deutsche Grammophon ▲ 413754-2 [DDD]
Wagner, R.:Tristan und Isolde, w. H. Dernesch (sop), C. Ludwig (mez), J. Vickers (ten), P. Schreier (ten), B. Weikl (bar), W. Berry (bass), K. Ridderbusch (bass), German Opera Chorus [G]
EMI Classics ("Studio" series) 4–▲ CDMD 69319 [ADD]
Wagner, R.:Tristan und Isolde (prelude & liebestod)
Deutsche Grammophon ("Karajan Gold" series) ▲ 439022-2
Webern, A.:Movts Str Qt
Deutsche Grammophon ("20th Century Classics" series) 3–▲ 427424-2 [ADD]
Webern, A.:Movts Str Qt Deutsche Grammophon ("20th Century Classics" series) ▲ 423254-2 [ADD]
Webern, A.:Passacaglia Deutsche Grammophon ▲ 423254-2 [ADD]
Webern, A.:Passacaglia Deutsche Grammophon 3–▲ 427424-2 [ADD]
Webern, A.:Pieces Orch, Op. 6 Deutsche Grammophon 3–▲ 427424-2 [ADD]
Webern, A.:Pieces Orch, Op. 6 Deutsche Grammophon ▲ 423254-2 [ADD]
Webern, A.:Sym, Op. 21 Deutsche Grammophon ▲ 423254-2 [ADD]
Webern, A.:Sym, Op. 21 Deutsche Grammophon 3–▲ 427424-2 [ADD]
R. Kempe (cnd)
Brahms, J.:Ein Deutsches Requiem, w. E. Grümmer (sop), D. Fischer-Dieskau (bar), St. Hedwig's Cathedral Choir [G] EMI Classics ▲ CDH 64705
Dvořák, A.:Sym 9, "From the New World" Royal Classics ▲ ROY 6440
Mahler, G.:Kindertotenlieder, w. D. Fischer-Dieskau (bar) [G] EMI Classics ▲ CDC 47657 (m) [ADD]
Wagner, R.:Die Meistersinger von Nürnberg, w. E. Grümmer (sop), M. Höffgen (cta), R. Schock (ten), G. Unger (ten), H. Prey (bar), B. Kusche (bar), F. Frantz (b-bar), G. Frick (bass) *(rec 1956)*
EMI Classics 4–▲ CDMD 64154
P. van Kempen (cnd)
Beethoven, L. van:Cons Pno (comp), w. W. Kempff (pno)
Deutsche Grammophon 3–▲ 435744-2 [ADD]
E. Kleiber (cnd)
Erich Kleiber Conducts Vol. 2, w. State Opera Orch *(rec 1928–36)* Preiser ▲ PRE CD 90287
Great Recordings, w. Czech PO, Berlin State Opera Orch, Mediaeval Ensemble
Preiser ▲ PRE 90229 [AAD]
Heuberger, R.:Der Opernball (ov) *(rec 1932, from Telefunken SK)* Biddulph ▲ WHL 002 [ADD]
Heuberger, R.:Der Opernball (ov) Teldec ("Historic" series) ▲ 95513-2 [ADD]
Heuberger, R.:Der Opernball (ov) Archipon ▲ ARC 102 (m) [ADD]
Lanner, J.:Music of—Die Schönbrunner, Op. 200 *(rec June 13, 1931)*
Teldec ("Historic" series) ▲ 95513-2 [ADD]
Reznicek, E.N. von:Donna Diana (ov) Archipon ▲ ARC 102 (m) [ADD]
Schubert, Franz:Sym 8 Theorema ▲ TH 121225
Strauss (II), Joh.:Music of—Kaiser-Walzer [rec Nov 10., 1931]; Accelerationen [rec June 25, 1932]; An der schönen blauen Donau [rec June 10, 1931]; Wein, Weib und Gesang [rec June 23, 1932]; Ov. from Die Fledermaus [rec June 19, 1933]; Ov. from Der Zigeunerbaron [rec June 19, 1933]
Teldec ("Historic" series) ▲ 95513-2 [ADD]
Strauss, Josef:Music of—Village Swallows Waltz *(rec 1933, from Telefunken E 1)*
Biddulph ▲ WHL 002 [ADD]
Strauss, R.:Der Rosenkavalier (waltzes) Grammofono 2000 ▲ GRM 78609 (m)
Strauss, R.:Der Rosenkavalier (waltzes) *(rec 1934 from Telefunken E 16)*
Biddulph ▲ WHL 002 [ADD]
Weber, C.M. von:Invitation to the Dance Orch Archipon ▲ ARC 102 (m) [ADD]
Weber, C.M. von:Invitation to the Dance Orch Grammofono 2000 ▲ GRM 78609 (m)
Weber, C.M. von:Invitation to the Dance Orch *(rec 1932)* Biddulph ▲ WHL 002 [ADD]
O. Klemperer (cnd)
Bruckner, A.:Sym 7 *(rec live Sept. 1958)* Music & Arts ▲ CD 751-1 (m) [AAD]
P. Kletzki (cnd)
Beethoven, L. van:Romances Vn, w. G. Kulenkampff (vn)—Op. 50 *(rec 1932 for Telefunken)*
Pearl ▲ PEA 9466 (m) [AAD]
Mozart, W.A.:Con 5 Vn, w. Szymon Goldberg (vn)—Adagio Symposium ▲ SYM 1141
H. Knappertsbusch (cnd)
Beethoven, L. van:Sym 3, "Eroica" *(rec Berlin, 1943)* Iron Needle ▲ 1322 [ADD]
Beethoven, L. van:Sym 3, "Eroica" *(rec 1942–43)* Preiser ▲ PRE 90976 [AAD]
Beethoven, L. van:Sym 5 *(rec live, 4/9/56)* Arkadia ▲ 723 [ADD]
Beethoven, L. van:Sym 8 *(rec live, 1/29/52)* Arkadia ▲ 723 [ADD]
Brahms, J.:Sym 3 *(rec 1942)* Preiser ▲ 90121 (m) [AAD]
Brahms, J.:Sym 3 Grammofono 2000 ▲ GRM 78522
Bruckner, A.:Sym 4, "Romantic" *(rec live, ca. 1942–44)* Music & Arts ▲ CD 249 (m) [AAD]
Bruckner, A.:Sym 4, "Romantic" *(rec Berlin, Mar 1944)* Grammofono 2000 ▲ GRM 78563 (m)
Bruckner, A.:Sym 4, "Romantic" *(rec Berlin, Sept 8, 1944)* Iron Needle ▲ IN 1344
Bruckner, A.:Sym 4, "Romantic" *(rec Sept. 8, 1944)* Preiser ▲ PRE 90226 [ADD]
Bruckner, A.:Sym 4, "Romantic" Enterprise ("Sirio" series) ▲ ENT SO 530013
Bruckner, A.:Sym 8 *(rec 1951)* Music & Arts ▲ CD 856 [AAD]
Bruckner, A.:Sym 9 *(rec 1950)* Music & Arts ▲ CD 219
Haydn, J.:Sym 94, "Surprise Sym" *(rec 1941)* Preiser ▲ 90121 (m) [AAD]
Liszt, F.:Les Préludes *(rec 1942–43)* Preiser ▲ PRE 90976 [AAD]
Mahler, G.:Kindertotenlieder, w. L. West (alt) [G] *(rec live, Berlin, 4/9/56)* Arkadia ▲ 710 (m) [ADD]
Nicolai, O.:Lustigen Weiber (ov) *(rec live 2/1/50)* Arkadia ▲ 723 [ADD]
Wagner, R.:Ovs, Preludes & Orch Sels—Ovs from Der Fliegende Holländer; Tannhäuser; Lohengrin; Die Walküre; Die Meistersinger; Parsifal *(rec 1928)* Preiser ▲ PRE 90286
R. Kraus (cnd)
Mahler, G.:Des Knaben Wunderhorn, w. E. Lear (sop), T. Stewart (bar) *(rec 1962 & 1983)*
VAI Audio ▲ VAIA 1061 (m) [ADD]
R. Kubelik (cnd)
Dvořák, A.:Syms (comp) Deutsche Grammophon 6–▲ 423120-2 [ADD]
Dvořák, A.:Sym 7 Deutsche Grammophon 2–▲ 439663-2 [ADD]
Dvořák, A.:Sym 8 Deutsche Grammophon 2–▲ 439663-2 [ADD]
Dvořák, A.:Sym 8 *(rec 1966 & 1972)* Deutsche Grammophon ("The Originals" series) ▲ 447412-2
Dvořák, A.:Sym 9, "From the New World"
Deutsche Grammophon ("Musikfest" series) ▲ 415915-2 [ADD]
Dvořák, A.:Sym 9, "From the New World" Deutsche Grammophon 2–▲ 439663-2 [ADD]

Berlin PO (cont.)
R. Kubelik (cnd) (cont.)
Dvořák, A.:Sym 9, "From the New World" *(rec 1966 & 1972)*
Deutsche Grammophon ("The Originals" series) ▲ 447412-2
Handel, G.F.:Royal Fireworks Music
Deutsche Grammophon ("Galleria" series) ▲ 419861-2 [ADD] ■ 419861-4
Handel, G.F.:Water Music (suites)
Deutsche Grammophon ("Galleria" series) ▲ 419861-2 [ADD] ■ 419861-4
Wagner, R.:Ovs, Preludes & Orch Sels—Siegfried Idyll; Lohengrin:Ov; Meistersinger:Ov; Tristan & Isolde:Prelude & Isolde's Death Theorema 3–▲ TH 121147/149
J. Kulka (cnd)
Chopin, F.:Con 2 Pno, w. T. Vásáry (pno)
Deutsche Grammophon ("Resonance" series) ▲ 429515-2 [ADD]
F. Leitner (cnd)
Beethoven, L. van:Con 4 Pno, w. Wilhelm Kempff (pno) *(rec 1961)*
Deutsche Grammophon ("The Originals" series) ▲ 447402-2
Beethoven, L. van:Con 5 Pno, "Emperor", w. Wilhelm Kempff (pno) *(rec 1961)*
Deutsche Grammophon ("The Originals" series) ▲ 447402-2
Mozart, W.A.:Con 8 Pno, w. Wilhelm Kempff (pno)
Deutsche Grammophon ("Double" series) 2–▲ 439699-2
Mozart, W.A.:Con 23 Pno, w. Wilhelm Kempff (pno)
Deutsche Grammophon ("Double" series) 2–▲ 439699-2
Mozart, W.A.:Con 24 Pno, w. Wilhelm Kempff (pno)
Deutsche Grammophon ("Double" series) 2–▲ 439699-2
Mozart, W.A.:Con 27 Pno, w. Wilhelm Kempff (pno)
Deutsche Grammophon ("Double" series) 2–▲ 439699-2
Tchaikovsky, P.:Nutcracker Suite
Deutsche Grammophon ("Resonance" series) ▲ 427219-2 [AAD] ■ 427219-4
G. Levine (cnd)
Schoenberg, A.:Pieces Orch, Op. 16 Deutsche Grammophon ▲ 419781-2 [DDD]
J. Levine (cnd)
Berg, A.:Pieces Orch, Op. 6 Deutsche Grammophon ▲ 419781-2 [DDD]
Berlioz, H.:Les Nuits d'été, w. A. S. von Otter (mez) [F] Deutsche Grammophon 2–▲ 427665-2 [DDD]
Berlioz, H.:Ovs—Benvenuto Cellini; Carnaval romain; Le Corsaire
Deutsche Grammophon 2–▲ 429724-2 [DDD]
Berlioz, H.:Requiem, "Grande Messe des Morts", w. L. Pavarotti (ten), Ernst Senff Chorus
Deutsche Grammophon 2–▲ 429724-2 [DDD]
Berlioz, H.:Roméo et Juliette, w. A. S. von Otter (sop), P. Langridge (ten), Morris (sgr), Ernst Senff Chorus [F] Deutsche Grammophon 2–▲ 427665-2 [DDD]
Berlioz, H.:Sym fantastique Deutsche Grammophon ▲ 431624-2 [DDD]
Debussy, C.:Images Orch Sony Classical ▲ SK 53284
Dukas, P.:L'Apprenti sorcier Deutsche Grammophon ▲ 419617-2 [DDD]
Dvořák, A.:Con Vn, w. S. Mintz (vn) Deutsche Grammophon ▲ 419618-2 [DDD]
Elgar, E.:Enigma Vars Sony Classical ▲ SK 53284
Haydn, J.:Die Schöpfung, w. Kathleen Battle (sop), Gösta Winbergh (ten), Kurt Moll (bass), Stockholm Radio Chorus, Stockholm Chamber Choir Deutsche Grammophon 2–▲ 427629-2 [DDD]
Mendelssohn, F.:Sym 3 Deutsche Grammophon ▲ 427670-2 [DDD]
Mendelssohn, F.:Sym 4 Deutsche Grammophon ▲ 427670-2 [DDD]
Saint-Saëns, C.:Sym 3, w. S. Preston (org) Deutsche Grammophon ▲ 419617-2 [DDD] □ 419617-5
Schoenberg, A.:Verklärte Nacht Deutsche Grammophon ▲ 435883-2
Schumann, R.:Sym 2 Deutsche Grammophon ▲ 423625-2 [DDD]
Schumann, R.:Sym 3 Deutsche Grammophon ▲ 423625-2 [DDD]
Sibelius, J.:Con Vn, w. S. Mintz (vn) Deutsche Grammophon ▲ 419618-2 [DDD]
Sibelius, J.:Finlandia Deutsche Grammophon ▲ 437828-2
Sibelius, J.:Sym 2 Deutsche Grammophon ▲ 437828-2
Sibelius, J.:Sym 4 Deutsche Grammophon ▲ 445865-2
Sibelius, J.:Sym 5 Deutsche Grammophon ▲ 445865-2
Sibelius, J.:Valse triste Deutsche Grammophon ▲ 437828-2
Smetana, B.:Má Vlast Deutsche Grammophon □ 431652-5
Strauss, R.:Metamorphosen Deutsche Grammophon ▲ 435883-2
Wagner, R.:Siegfried Idyll Deutsche Grammophon ▲ 435883-2
Webern, A.:Pieces Orch, Op. 6 Deutsche Grammophon ▲ 419781-2 [DDD]
L. Maazel (cnd)
Borodin, A.:In the Steppes of Central Asia Deutsche Grammophon ("Double" series) 2–▲ 437946-2
Dvořák, A.:Con Vc, w. Yo-Yo Ma (vc) CBS ▲ MK 42206 [DDD] ■ IMT 42206 (D) □ NM 42206
Dvořák, A.:Con Vc, w. Yo-Yo Ma (vc) CBS 2–▲ M2K 44562 [ADD/DDD] 2–■ M2T 44562 (D)
Dvořák, A.:Rondo, w. Yo Yo Ma (vc) CBS ▲ MK 42206 [DDD] ■ IMT 42206 (D) □ NM 42206
Dvořák, A.:Silent Woods, w. Yo Yo Ma (vc) CBS ▲ MK 42206 [DDD] ■ IMT 42206 (D) □ NM 42206
Mussorgsky, M.:Night Deutsche Grammophon ("Double" series) 2–▲ 437946-2
Mussorgsky, M.:Pictures at an Exhibition Deutsche Grammophon ("Double" series) 2–▲ 437946-2
Rachmaninoff, S.:Aleko (sels)—Intermezzo
Deutsche Grammophon ("Galleria" series) ▲ 435594-2 [DDD]
Rachmaninoff, S.:The Rock Deutsche Grammophon ("Galleria" series) ▲ 435594-2 [ADD]
Rachmaninoff, S.:Sym 1 *(rec 1983)* Deutsche Grammophon ("Galleria" series) ▲ 435594-2 [DDD]
Rachmaninoff, S.:Vocalise Deutsche Grammophon ("Galleria" series) ▲ 435594-2 [DDD]
Rimsky-Korsakov, N.:Capriccio espagnol, w. Lamoureux Orch
Deutsche Grammophon ("Double" series) 2–▲ 437946-2
Rimsky-Korsakov, N.:Golden Cockerel (suite), w. Lamoureux Orch
Deutsche Grammophon ("Double" series) 2–▲ 437946-2
Rimsky-Korsakov, N.:A May Night (ov), w. Lamoureux Orch
Deutsche Grammophon ("Double" series) 2–▲ 437946-2
Rimsky-Korsakov, N.:Russian Easter Festival, w. Lamoureux Orch
Deutsche Grammophon ("Double" series) 2–▲ 437946-2
Schumann, R.:Pno Music (misc), w. Alfred Brendel (pno), London SO—Abendleid; Adagio & Allegro; Con in a; Fant in C; Fantasiestücke; Kinderszenen; Kreisleriana; 3 Stücke in Volkston; 3 Romances; Symphonic Studies Philips 25–▲ 446920-2
Tchaikovsky, P.:Con Vn, w. G. Kremer (vn) Deutsche Grammophon ▲ 431609-2 [ADD]
Wagner, R.:Der Ring des Nibelungen (orch sels)—incl. Entry of the Gods into Valhalla, Ride of the Valkyries, Wotan's Farewell & Magic Fire Music, Forest Murmurs, Siegfried's Rhine Journey, Siegfried's Death & Funeral Music, Brünnhilde's Immolation & Final Scene
Telarc ▲ CD 80154 [DDD] ■ CS 30154 (D)
Yun, I.:Fanfare & Memorial *(rec live, Philharmonie Hall 12/11/88)* Arcadia ▲ ARC 1997-2 [DDD]
I. Markevitch (cnd)
Haydn, J.:Die Schöpfung, w. Irmgard Seefried (sop), Richard Holm (ten), Kim Borg (bass), St. Hedwig's Cathedral Choir Deutsche Grammophon ("Double" series) 2–▲ 437380-2
Mozart, W.A.:Missa, K.317, w. Maria Stader (sop), Sieglinde Wagner (mez), Helmut Krebs (ten), Josef Griendl (bass), St. Hedwig's Cathedral Choir Deutsche Grammophon 2–▲ 437383-2
F. Martin (cnd)
Martin, F.:Passacaglia Org [adapted for large orch. by Frank Martin] *(rec May 30, 1963)*
Jecklin-Disco ▲ JD 645-2 [ADD]
E. Märzendorfer (cnd)
La harpe du siècle:Hommage a Nicanor Zabaleta, w. Nicanor Zabaleta (hp), Berlin RSO, Paul Kuentz CO - [cnd:Paul Kuentz] Deutsche Grammophon ("Double" series) 2–▲ 439693-2
Mozart, W.A.:Con Fl Hp, w. Karlheinz Zoeller (fl), Nicanor Zabaleta (hp)
Deutsche Grammophon ▲ 427206-2 [AAD]
Z. Mehta (cnd)
Bartók, B.:Con 1 Vn, w. Midori (vn) Sony Classical ▲ SK 45941 [DDD]
Bartók, B.:Con 2 Vn, w. Midori (vn) Sony Classical ▲ SK 45941 [DDD]
Beethoven, L. van:Sym 5, w. Israel PO members *(rec live, Tel Aviv, 4/18/90)*
Sony Classical ▲ SK 45968

ORCH. & ENS.

Berlin PO (cont.)
Z. Mehta (cnd) (cont.)
Ben–Haim, P.:Sym 1, w. Israel PO members—Psalm movt *(rec live, Tel Aviv, 4/18/90)* Sony Classical ▲ SK 45968
Mozart, W.A.:Serenade Ww, K.361 *(rec Philharmonie, Berlin, Apr. 21–23, 1993)* Sony Classical ▲ SK 58950 [DDD]
Ravel, M.:La Valse, w. Israel PO members *(rec live in Tel Aviv, 4/18/90)* Sony Classical ▲ SK 45968
Strauss, R.:Eine Alpensinfonie Sony Classical ▲ SK 45800 [DDD]
Strauss, R.:Con 1 Hn, w. G. Seifert (hn) Sony Classical ▲ SK 45800 [DDD]
Strauss, R.:Con 2 Hn, w. Norbert Hauptmann (hn) Sony Classical ▲ SK 53267
Strauss, R.:Ein Heldenleben Sony Classical ▲ SK 53267
Strauss, R.:Salome, w. E. Martón (sop), B. Fassbaender (mez/sop), H. Zednik (ten), R. Lewis (ten), B. Weikl (bar) *(rec live)* Sony Classical 2–▲ S2K 46717
R. Muti (cnd)
Mozart, W.A.:Ave verum corpus, w. Stockholm Chamber Choir, Swedish Radio Chorus [L] EMI Classics ▲ CDC 49640
Mozart, W.A.:Requiem, w. P. Pace (sop), W. Meier (mez), F. Lopardo (ten), J. Morris (bass), Swedish Radio Chorus [L] EMI Classics ▲ CDC 49640 [DDD]
A. Nikisch (cnd)
Beethoven, L. van:Sym 5 Symposium ▲ 1087
Berlioz, H.:Le Carnaval romain Symposium ▲ 1087
Liszt, F.:Hungarian Rhaps—Nos. 2, 5, 6, 9, 12 & 14 Symposium ▲ 1087
D. Oistrakh (cnd)
Mozart, W.A.:Adagio Vn, K.261, w. D. Oistrakh (vn) EMI Classics ▲ CDM 64868
Mozart, W.A.:Con 4 Vn, w. D. Oistrakh (vn) EMI Classics ▲ CDM 64868
Mozart, W.A.:Con 4 Vn, w. D. Oistrakh (vn) EMI Classics ("Studio" series) ▲ CDM 69064
Mozart, W.A.:Con 5 Vn, w. D. Oistrakh (vn) EMI Classics ("Studio" series) ▲ CDM 69064
Mozart, W.A.:Con 5 Vn, w. D. Oistrakh (vn) EMI Classics ▲ CDM 64868
Mozart, W.A.:Rondo Vn, K.269, w. D. Oistrakh (vn) EMI Classics ▲ CDM 64868
Mozart, W.A.:Rondo Vn, K.373, w. D. Oistrakh (vn) EMI Classics ▲ CDM 64868
Mozart, W.A.:Sinf concertante Vn, K.364, w. I. Oistrakh (vn), D. Oistrakh (va) EMI Classics ▲ CDM 64632
S. Ozawa (cnd)
Bartók, B.:Con Va, w. W. Christ (va) Deutsche Grammophon ▲ 437993–2 [DDD]
Bartók, B.:Music for Strs, Perc & Cel Deutsche Grammophon ▲ 437993–2 [DDD]
Orff, C.:Carmina burana, w. E. Gruberova (sop), J. Aler (ten), T. Hampson (bar), Berlin Cathedral Boys' Choir, Shin–Yuh Kai Chorus [G, L] Philips ▲ 422363–2 [DDD] □ 422363–5
Prokofiev, S.:Lt Kijé Suite, w. Andreas Schmidt (bar) Deutsche Grammophon ▲ 435029–2 [DDD]
Prokofiev, S.:Sym 1 Deutsche Grammophon ▲ 435026–2 [DDD]
Prokofiev, S.:Sym 2 Deutsche Grammophon ▲ 435027–2 [DDD]
Prokofiev, S.:Sym 5 Deutsche Grammophon ▲ 435029–2 [DDD]
Prokofiev, S.:Sym 6 Deutsche Grammophon ▲ 435026–2 [DDD]
Prokofiev, S.:Sym 7 Deutsche Grammophon ▲ 435027–2 [DDD]
Wagner, R.:Ovs, Preludes & Orch Sels—Fliegende Höllander; Tannhaüser; Meistersinger; Tristan (Prelude & Liebestod) Philips ▲ 426271–2 [DDD] □ 426271–5
R. Peters (cnd)
Castelnuovo–Tedesco, M.:Con 1 Gtr, w. S. Behrend (gtr) Deutsche Grammophon ("Resonance" series) ▲ 427214–2 [AAD]
Rodrigo, J.:Concierto de Aranjuez, w. S. Behrend (gtr) Deutsche Grammophon ("Resonance" series) ▲ 427214–2 [AAD]
H. Pfitzner (cnd)
Beethoven, L. van:Sym 3, "Eroica" *(rec ca. 1930)* InSync ■ C 4146
Beethoven, L. van:Sym 3, "Eroica" *(rec 1929)* Preiser ▲ PRE 90201 [ADD]
Beethoven, L. van:Sym 8 *(rec 1929–33)* Preiser ▲ PRE 90221 [ADD]
Pfitzner, H.:Sym in C Preiser ▲ 90029 (m) [AAD]
J. Prüwer (cnd)
Chopin, F.:Con 1 Pno, w. A. Brailowsky (pno) *(rec 1928)* Danacord 2–▲ DACOCD 336/37 (m) [ADD]
Liszt, F.:Con 1 Pno, w. Alexander Brailowsky (pno) *(rec 1928)* Danacord 2–▲ DACOCD 338/339 (m) [ADD]
S. Rattle (cnd)
Liszt, F.:A Faust Sym, w. Peter Seiffert (ten), Prague Phil Chorus EMI Classics ▲ CDC 55220
H. Rosbaud (cnd)
Sibelius, J.:Finlandia *(rec Jesus Christ Church, Berlin, Nov 1954)* Deutsche Grammophon ("The Originals" series) ▲ 447453–2 [ADD]
Sibelius, J.:Karelia Suite *(rec Jesus Christ Church, Berlin, Mar 1957)* Deutsche Grammophon ("The Originals" series) ▲ 447453–2 [ADD]
Sibelius, J.:Scènes historiques—Festivo, Op. 25/3 *(rec Jesus Christ Church, Berlin, Nov 1954)* Deutsche Grammophon ("The Originals" series) ▲ 447453–2 [ADD]
Sibelius, J.:The Swan of Tuonela *(rec Jesus Christ Church, Berlin, Nov 1954)* Deutsche Grammophon ("The Originals" series) ▲ 447453–2 [ADD]
Sibelius, J.:Tapiola *(rec Jesus Christ Church, Berlin, Mar 1957)* Deutsche Grammophon ("The Originals" series) ▲ 447453–2 [ADD]
Sibelius, J.:Valse triste *(rec Jesus Christ Church, Berlin, Nov 1954)* Deutsche Grammophon ("The Originals" series) ▲ 447453–2 [ADD]
A. Rother (cnd)
Beethoven, L. van:Con 3 Pno, w. Eduard Erdmann (pno) *(rec 1920–33)* Enterprise ("Piano Library" series) ▲ ENT PL 215
S. Rybrant (cnd)
Alfvén, H.:A Boat with Flowers, w. E. Saeden (bar) Swedish Society ▲ SCD 1036
Alfvén, H.:Swedish Rhap 2, "Uppsala–rhapsodi" Swedish Society ▲ SCD 1036
V. de Sabata (cnd)
Kodály, Z.:Galanta Dances *(rec 1939)* Koch Legacy ▲ 3–7126–2 H1
Respighi, O.:Feste Romane *(rec 1939)* Koch Legacy ▲ 3–7126–2 H1
Rossini, G.:Guillaume Tell (ov) Theorema 2–▲ TH 121123/24
Verdi, G.:Ovs & Preludes—Aida—Prelude *(rec 1939)* Koch Legacy ▲ 3–7126–2 H1
E.–P. Salonen (cnd)
Prokofiev, S.:Romeo & Juliet (sels) CBS ▲ MK 42662 [DDD]
H. Schmidt–Isserstedt (cnd)
Brahms, J.:Con Vn, w. G. Kulenkampff (vn) *(rec 1936 for Telefunken)* Pearl ▲ PEA 9466 (m) [AAD]
Mendelssohn, F.:Con in e Vn & Orch, Op. 64, w. G. Kulenkampff (vn) *(rec 1935 for Telefunken)* Pearl ▲ PEA 9466 (m) [AAD]
Mendelssohn, F.:Con in e Vn & Orch, Op. 64, w. G. Kulenkampft (vn) *(rec Apr. 4, 1935)* Teldec ("Historic" series) ▲ 93672
Schumann, R.:Con Vn, w. G. Kulenkampft (vn) *(rec Dec. 20, 1937)* Teldec ("Historic" series) ▲ 93672
W. Schneiderhan (cnd)
Mozart, W.A.:Con 5 Vn, w. Wolfgang Schneiderhan (vn) *(rec 1962 & 1967)* Deutsche Grammophon ("The Originals" series) ▲ 447403–2
C. Schuricht (cnd)
Beethoven, L. van:Sym 3, "Eroica" *(rec 1964)* Originals 2–▲ ORISH 819 [ADD]
J. Semkow (cnd)
Chopin, F.:Con 1 Pno, w. T. Vásáry (pno) Deutsche Grammophon ("Resonance" series) ▲ 429515–2 [ADD]
G. Solti (cnd)
Beethoven, L. van:Missa Solemnis, w. Julia Varady (sop), Iris Vermillion (mez), Vinson Cole (ten), Rene Pape (bass), Kolja Blacher (vn), Berlin Radio Chorus London ▲ 444337–2 [DDD]
Strauss, R.:Also sprach Zarathustra London ▲ 452 603–2
Strauss, R.:Salome (dance) London ▲ 452 603–2
Strauss, R.:Till Eulenspiegels lustige Streiche London ▲ 452 603–2

Berlin PO (cont.)
G. Solti (cnd) (cont.)
Verdi, G.:Falstaff, w. E. Norberg–Schulz (sop—Nannetta), L. Serra (sop—Alice), S. Graham (mez—Meg Page), M. Lipovsek (cta—Miss Quickly), K. Begley (ten—Dr. Caius), P. Conti (ten—Ford), M. Luperi (ten—Pistol), J. Van Dam (b-bar—Falstaff), P. LeFebvre (bass—Bardolph), Berlin Radio Chorus London ▲ 440650–2 [DDD]
L. Stokowski (cnd)
Stravinsky, I.:Pétrouchka (suite) EMI Classics ("Full Dimensional Sound" series) ▲ CDM 65423
R. Strauss (cnd)
Cornelius, P.:Der Barbier von Bagdad (ov), Liszt–edited version of the Overture, rec 1928 for Polydor Koch Legacy ▲ 3–7119–2 H1
Gluck, C.W.:Iphigénie en Aulide (ov) [arr Richard Wagner] *(rec 1928 for Polydor)* Koch Legacy ▲ 3–7119–2 H1
Wagner, R.:Ovs, Preludes & Orch Sels—Der fliegende Holländer *(Overture)*, Tristan *(Act 1 Prelude) (rec 1928 for Polydor)* Koch Legacy ▲ 3–7119–2 H1
Weber, C.M. von:Ovs—Euryanthe *(rec 1928 for Polydor)* Koch Legacy ▲ 3–7119–2 H1
G. Szell (cnd)
Dvořák, A.:Con Vc, w. P. Fournier (vc) Deutsche Grammophon ("Resonance" series) ▲ 429155–2 [ADD]
K. Tennstedt (cnd)
Dvořák, A.:Sym 9, "From the New World" EMI Classics (Studio DDD) ▲ CDD 63900 [DDD]
Mendelssohn, F.:Sym 4 EMI Classics ("DDD Midline" series) ▲ CDD 64085 [DDD]
Schubert, Franz:Sym 9 EMI Classics ("DDD Midline" series) ▲ CDD 64085 [DDD]
Wagner, R.:Ovs, Preludes & Orch Sels—Dawn & Siegfried's Rhine Journey; Siegfried's Death & Funeral March [both from Götterdämmerung]; Preludes to Acts 1 & 2 [from Lohengrin]; Prelude to Act 1 [from Der Meistersinger von Nürnberg]; Entry of the Gods into Valhalla [from Das Rheingold]; Ov [from Rienzi]; Forest Murmers [from Siegfried]; Ov [from Tannhäuser]; Ride of the Valkyries; Wotan's Farewell; Magic Fire Music [all from Die Walküre] EMI Classics ("Doublefforte" series) 2–▲ CDFB 68616
T. Vásáry (cnd)
Mozart, W.A.:Con 26 Pno, w. T. Vasary (pno) Deutsche Grammophon ▲ 429810–2 [ADD]
A. Wallenstein (cnd)
Bloch, E.:Schelomo, w. P. Fournier (vc) Deutsche Grammophon ("Resonance" series) ▲ 429155–2 [ADD]
B. Walter (cnd)
Strauss, R.:Der Rosenkavalier (waltzes) *(rec 1930)* Iron Needle ▲ IN 1312 [ADD]
Strauss, R.:Salome (dance) *(rec 1930)* Iron Needle ▲ IN 1312 [ADD]
G. Wand (cnd)
Schubert, Franz:Sym 8 RCA Red Seal 2–▲ 09026–68314–2 [DDD]
Schubert, Franz:Sym 9 RCA Red Seal 2–▲ 09026–68314–2 [DDD]
Berlin PO Cellists
Pärt, A.:Fratres III ECM New Series ▲ 78118–21275–2 [DDD]; ■ 78118–21275–4
Berlin PO Horns [G. Seifert (hn), G. Köpp (hn), K. Wallendorf (hn), M. Klier (hn)]
Coenen, P.:Vars for 4 French Hns Koch Schwann ▲ 311 021 [DDD] ■ MC 110 021 (D)
Genzmer, H.:Con for 4 Hns, w. M. Buder (cnd), Bamberg SO Koch Schwann ▲ 311 021 [DDD] ■ MC 110 021 (D)
Schumann, R.:Konzertstück Hns, w. M. Buder (cnd), Bamberg SO Koch Schwann ▲ 311 021 [DDD] ■ MC 110 021 (D)
Berlin PO members
Strauss, R.:Qt Pno Koch Schwann ▲ SCH 311272 [DDD]
Suk, J.:Qt Pno Koch Schwann ▲ SCH 311272 [DDD]
Berlin PO Virtuosi
Handel, G.F.:Con Hp, w. Naoko Yoshino (hp)—Allegro moderato Sony Classical ▲ MLK 62369 [ADD/DDD]
Berlin PO Winds
Mozart, W.A.:Adagio Bas Hns, K.410/440d Orfeo ▲ 218911 [DDD]
Mozart, W.A.:Adagio Cl, K.Anh.94, in F Orfeo ▲ 188891 [DDD] ■ 188891 (D)
Mozart, W.A.:Adagio Cls, K.411 Orfeo ▲ 188891 [DDD] ■ 188891 (D)
Mozart, W.A.:Diverts—in E♭, K.166; in B♭, K.186; in E♭, K.Anh.226; in B♭, K.Anh.227 Orfeo ▲ 163881 [DDD] ■ 163881
Mozart, W.A.:Diverts—K.213, 240, 252, 253, 270 Orfeo ▲ 152861 [DDD]
Mozart, W.A.:Diverts Bas Hns, K.Anh.229—Nos. 1, 3 & 5 Orfeo ▲ 217901 [DDD]
Mozart, W.A.:Diverts Bas Hns, K.Anh.229—Nos. 2 & 4 Orfeo ▲ 218911 [DDD]
Mozart, W.A.:Duos Hns Orfeo ▲ 217901 [DDD]
Mozart, W.A.:Notturnos Sops, w. C. Schäfer (sop), G. Hintz (sop), D. Fischer–Dieskau (bar) Orfeo ▲ 218911 [DDD]
Mozart, W.A.:Nozze di Figaro (winds) Orfeo ▲ 218911 [DDD]
Mozart, W.A.:Più non si trovano, w. C. Schäfer (sop), G. Hintz (sop), D. Fischer–Dieskau (bar) Orfeo ▲ 218911 [DDD]
Mozart, W.A.:Serenade Ww, K.375 Orfeo ▲ 134851 ■ 134851
Mozart, W.A.:Serenade Ww, K.388 Orfeo ▲ 134851 ■ 134851
Triebensee, J.:Suite Orfeo ▲ 238911 [DDD]
Went, J.N.:Suite from *Le nozze di Figaro* for Ww Orfeo ▲ 238911 [DDD]
Berlin Philharmonic Wind Ensemble
Mozart, W.A.:Serenade Ww, K.361 Orfeo ▲ 188891 [DDD] ■ MC 188891 (D)
Berlin Philharmonic Wind Ensemble [Hansjörg Schellenberger (ob), Andreas Wittmann (ob), Karl Leister (cl), Peter Geisler (cl), Norbert Hauptmann (hn), Stefan Jezierski (hn), Daniele Damiano (bn), Henning Tog (bn)]
Went, J.N.:Suite from *Così fan tutte* for Ww Orfeo ▲ 260931 [DDD]
Went, J.N.:Suite from *Die Entführung* for Ww Orfeo ▲ 260931 [DDD]
Berlin Philharmonic Wind Quintet
Danzi, F.:Qnts Ww, Op. 56 BIS ▲ CD 552 [DDD]
Danzi, F.:Qnts Ww, Op. 67 BIS ▲ CD 532 [DDD]
Tomasi, H.:Printemps, w. M. Preis (sax) BIS ▲ CD 536 [DDD]
Berlin Philharmonic Wind Quintet [Michael Hasel (fl), Andreas Wittmann (ob), Walter Seyfarth (cl), Fergus McWilliam (hn), Henning Trog (bn)]
Bozza, E.:Scherzo BIS ▲ CD 536 [DDD]
Danzi, F.:Qnt Pno, Op. 54, w. Love Derwinger (pno) *(rec 1991 & 1992)* BIS ▲ CD 592 [DDD]
Danzi, F.:Qnts Ww, Op. 56, w. Love Derwinger (pno) *(rec 1991 & 1992)* BIS ▲ CD 592 [DDD]
Foerster, J.B.:Qnt Ww *(rec Nov. 17–22, 1992)* BIS ▲ CD 612 [DDD]
Françaix, J.:Qnt Fl BIS ▲ CD 536 [DDD]
Henze, H.–W.:L'autunno *(rec Berlin–Spandau, Sept 11–14, 1995)* BIS ▲ CD 752 [DDD]
Henze, H.–W.:Qnt Winds *(rec Berlin–Spandau, Sept 11–14, 1995)* BIS ▲ CD 752 [DDD]
Hindemith, P.:Kleine Kammermusik *(rec Berlin–Spandau, Sept 11–14, 1995)* BIS ▲ CD 752 [DDD]
Hindemith, P.:Septet Winds & Tpt, w. Thomas Clamor (tpt), Manfred Preis (b cl) *(rec Berlin–Spandau, Sept 11–14, 1995)* BIS ▲ CD 752 [DDD]
Kurtág, G.:Qnt Winds *(rec Jan. 19–22, 1994)* BIS ▲ CD 662 [DDD]
Ligeti, G.:Bagatelles *(rec Jan. 19–22, 1994)* BIS ▲ CD 662 [DDD]
Ligeti, G.:Pieces Wind Qnt *(rec Jan. 19–22, 1994)* BIS ▲ CD 662 [DDD]
Milhaud, D.:Le Cheminée du Roi René BIS ▲ CD 536 [DDD]
Orbán, G.:Qnt Ww *(rec Jan. 19–22, 1994)* BIS ▲ CD 662 [DDD]
Pilss, K.:Serenade Ww *(rec Nov. 17–22, 1992)* BIS ▲ CD 612 [DDD]
Reinecke, C.:Sextet Ww, w. M. Klier (hn) *(rec Nov. 17–22, 1992)* BIS ▲ CD 612 [DDD]
Szervánszky, E.:Qnt 1 Winds *(rec Jan. 19–22, 1994)* BIS ▲ CD 662 [DDD]
Zemlinsky, A. von:Humoresque *(rec Nov. 17–22, 1992)* BIS ▲ CD 612 [DDD]
Berlin Philharmonic Wind Quintet members
Danzi, F.:Qnt Ob, w. L. Derwinger (pno) BIS ▲ CD 552 [DDD]
Danzi, F.:Qnt Pno, Op. 53, w. L. Derwinger (pno) BIS ▲ CD 532 [DDD]

▲ = CD ♦ = Enhanced CD Δ = MD ■ = Cassette Tape □ = DCC

Berlin Radio Orch

H. Abendroth (cnd)

Schumann, R.:Con Pno, w. F. Wührer (pno) Berlin Classics ("Dokumente" series) ▲ BER 2052 [ADD]

A. Rother (cnd)

Strauss, R.:Feuersnot (sels), w. Maria Cebotari (sop), Paula Buchner (sop), Tiana Lemnitz (sop), Karl Schmitt-Walter (bar) *(rec 1943–44)* Preiser ▲ PRE 90222 [ADD]

Strauss, R.:Der Rosenkavalier (sels), w. Maria Cebotari (sop), Paula Buchner (sop), Tiana Lemnitz (sop), Karl Schmitt-Walter (bar) *(rec 1943–44)* Preiser ▲ PRE 90222 [ADD]

Strauss, R.:Salome (sels), w. Maria Cebotari (sop), Paula Buchner (sop), Tiana Lemnitz (sop), Karl Schmitt-Walter (bar)—Final Scene *(rec 1943–44)* Preiser ▲ PRE 90222 [ADD]

Verdi, G.:Aida (sels), w. Hilde Scheppan (sop), Margarete Klose (cta), Helge Roswaenge (ten), Hans Hotter (bar), Berlin State Opera Chorus [G] *(rec Nov. 21, 1942)* Preiser ▲ PRE 90219 [ADD]

Berlin Radio Sinfonietta

U. Gronostay (cnd)

Mozart, W.A.:Missa [longa], K.262, w. Regina Schudel (sop), Ulla Groenewold (cta), Peter Maus (ten), Berthold Possemeyer (bar), Berlin Radio Chamber Choir [L] Koch Schwann ▲ CD 313 021 [ADD/DDD]

Mozart, W.A.:Missa brevis, K.258, w. Regina Schudel (sop), Ulla Groenewold (cta), Peter Maus (ten), Berthold Possemeyer (bar), Berlin Chamber Chorus [L] Koch Schwann ▲ CD 313 021 [ADD/DDD]

U. Lajovic (cnd)

Mendelssohn, F.:Cons (2) for 2 Pnos, w. A. Paratore (pno), J. Paratore (pno) Koch Schwann ▲ CD 311 051 [ADD]

Mendelssohn, F.:Cons (2) for 2 Pnos, w. A. Paratore (pno), J. Paratore (pno) CBS ▲ MK 42523 [DDD]

R. Paternostro (cnd)

Arie Antiche, w. Renato Bruson (bar) Acanta ▲ 43310

J. Stárek (cnd)

Bruch, M.:Serenade Strs Koch Schwann ▲ CD 311067 [ADD]

Schubert, Franz:Ovs—Overture in c Koch Schwann ▲ CD 311067 [ADD]

Volkmann, R.:Serenade 3 Strs Koch Schwann ▲ CD 311067 [ADD]

Weber, C.M. von:Ecossaises Pno [arr Géza de Kresz for string orchestra] Koch Schwann ▲ CD 311067 [ADD]

J. Velazco (cnd)

Arriaga, J.C.:Sym in D Koch Schwann ▲ CD 311035 [DDD]

Sarrier, A.:Sinf in D Koch Schwann ▲ CD 311035 [DDD]

Soler, P.A.:Sons anciennes d'auters espagnols Koch Schwann ▲ CD 311035 [DDD]

Berlin RSO

Breezes from the Orient Vol. 1, w. Frankfurt RSO, various cnds Capriccio ▲ 10 379 [DDD]

Breezes from the Orient Vol. 2, w. Frankfurt RSO, various cnds Capriccio ▲ 10 380 [DDD]

Breezes from the Orient Vol. 3, w. Frankfurt RSO, various cnds Capriccio ▲ 10 381 [DDD]

Breezes from the Orient Vol. 4, w. Frankfurt RSO, various cnds Capriccio 2–▲ 10 403/04

Classics Go to the Movies Vol. 2, w. Dresden PO, Budapest Festival Orch, Bulgarian TV–Radio SO, Bela Kovaks, Franz Liszt CO, Bruno Lazzaretti, Hungarian State Orch LaserLight ▲ 15 642

Ernest Tomlinson, w. Frankfurt RSO, various cnds Marco Polo ("British Light Music" series) ▲ 8.223413 [DDD]

Gounod, C.:Faust (sels), w. Alexandrina Pendachanska (sop—Margarethe), Giuseppe Sabbatini (ten—Faust), György Melis (bar—Valentin), Nicolai Ghiaurov (bass—Méphistophélès), Nikola Ghiuselev (bass—Méphistophélès), Vienna SO, Hungarian State Opera Orch, Bulgarian RSO, Sofia SO, Bulgarian National Chorus, Bulgarian National Chorus Radio Choir—Intro; Vien ou bière; O sainte médaille...Avant de quitter ces lieux; Le veau d'or [all from Act 2]; Quel trouble inconnu me pénètre!...Salut! demeure chaste et pure; Je voudrais bien savoir...Il était un roi de Thule; Un bouquet!...O Dieu! que de bijoux [both from Act 3]; Gloire immortelle de nos aieux; Vous qui faites l'endormie [both from Act 4]; Intermezzo; Walpurgis Night [both from Act 5] Laserlight ▲ 14209 [DDD]

La harpe du siècle:Hommage a Nicanor Zabaleta, w. Nicanor Zabaleta (hp), Berlin PO [cnd:Ernst Märzendorfer], Paul Kuentz CO [cnd:Paul Kuentz] Deutsche Grammophon ("Double" series) 2–▲ 439693–2

Haydn Wood, w. Frankfurt RSO, various cnds Marco Polo ("British Light Music" series) ▲ 8.223402 [DDD]

Jochen Kowalski, w. Jochen Kowalski (ct) Capriccio ▲ 70416

Joseph Schmidt, w. Joseph Schmidt (ten), Rudolf Hindemith (cnd), Bruno Seidler-Winkler (cnd), Hermann Scherchen (cnd), Fritz Stiedry (cnd), Max von Schillings (cnd), unknown orchestra [cnd:Idris Lewis], General Motors SO, General Motors Sym Chorus [cnd:Erno Rapee, José Iturbi, Oscar Straus], et al. Koch Schwann ▲ SCH 312572 [ADD]

Korngold, E.W.:Sinfonietta Varèse Sarabande ▲ VSD 5311

Mysliveček, J.:Cons in C, D & F Vn, w. E. Sebestyen (vn) *(rec 1981)* Koch Treasure ▲ 31614–2 [ADD]

Robert Farnon, w. Frankfurt RSO, various cnds Marco Polo ("British Light Music" series) ▲ 8.223401 [DDD]

Schumann, R.:Carnaval Pno, w. P. Gülke Koch Schwann ▲ CD 311030 [DDD]

H. Abendroth (cnd)

Beethoven, L. van:Con Vn, Op. 61, w. D. Oistrakh (vn) *(rec live, Berlin 3/31/50)* Melodram ▲ MEL 18020 (m) [AAD]

Beethoven, L. van:Egmont (ov) *(rec live, Berlin 3/31/50)* Melodram ▲ MEL 18020 (m) [AAD]

Beethoven, L. van:Romances Vn, w. D. Oistrakh (vn)—Op. 40 *(rec live, Berlin 3/31/50)* Melodram ▲ MEL 18020 (m) [AAD]

Beethoven, L. van:Sym 3, "Eroica"—final movt. *(rec live, Berlin 3/31/50)* Melodram ▲ MEL 18020 (m) [AAD]

Mozart, W.A.:Notturno, K.286, w. Leipzig Gewandhaus Orch, Leipzig RSO Berlin Classics 2–▲ BER 9271

G. Albrecht (cnd)

Busoni, F.:Turandot, w. C. Lindsley (sop), J. Protschka (ten), R. Wörle (ten), R. Pape (bass), Berlin RIAS Chamber Choir Capriccio ▲ 60039 [DDD]

Casella, A.:Scarlattiana, w. Tanzini (pno) Koch Schwann ▲ CD 311054 [DDD]

Henze, H.-W.:Telemanniana Koch Schwann ▲ CD 311054 [DDD]

Hindemith, P.:Der Dämon Wergo ▲ WER 60132–50 [DDD]

Hindemith, P.:Mörder, Hoffnug der Frauen, w. Gabriele Schnaut (sop), Franz Grundheber (bar) Wergo ▲ WER 60132–50 [DDD]

Liszt, F.:Cantico del sol di Dan Francesco d'Assisi, w. Walton Grönroos (bar), Berlin RIAS Men's Chamber Choir Koch Schwann ▲ CD 311 055

Liszt, F.:Légendes [orch. versions] Koch Schwann ▲ CD 311 055

Meyerbeer, G.:Gli amori di Teolinda, w. Julia Varady (sop), J. Fadle (cl), Berlin RIAS Chamber Choir [I] Orfeo ▲ 054831 [DDD]

Reger, M.:Ein romantische Suite Koch Schwann ▲ CD 311011 [DDD]

Reger, M.:Tondichtungen nach Arnold Böcklin Koch Schwann ▲ CD 311011 [DDD]

Righini, V.:Te Deum, w. G. Resick (sop), M. Schiml (sop), R. Wohlers (ten), V. von Halem (bass), Berlin Radio Chorus [L] Koch Schwann ▲ CD 313052 [ADD]

Schumann, R.:Manfred, w. *(soloists unknown)*, Berlin RIAS Chamber Choir Koch Schwann ▲ SCH 310892 [DDD]

Spohr, L.:Con Str Qt, w. E. Sebestyen (vn), H. Ganz (vn), H. Beyerle (va), M. Ostertag (vc) Koch Schwann ▲ CD 311088 [DDD] ■ MC 211088 (D)

Spohr, L.:Jessonda (ov) Koch Schwann ▲ CD 311 069

Spohr, L.:Sym 3 Koch Schwann ▲ CD 311069

Spontini, G.:Olympia, w. J. Varady (sop), S. Toczyska (mez), F. Tagliavini (ten), D. Fischer-Dieskau (bar), G. Fortune (bass), J. Becker (bass), Berlin Radio Chorus [Paris version] Orfeo 2–▲ 137862 [DDD]

Villa-Lobos, H.:Bachiana brasileira 9 Koch Schwann ▲ CD 311054 [DDD]

Wolf, H.:Der Corregidor, w. H. Donath (sop), D. Soffel (mez), W. Hollweg (ten), P. Maus (ten), K. Moll (bass), D. Fischer-Dieskau (bar) [G] Koch Schwann 2–▲ CD 314 010

Zemlinsky, A. von:Eine florentinische Tragödie, w. D. Soffel (mez), K. Riegel (ten), G. Sarabia (bar) [G] Koch Schwann ▲ CD 314012 [DDD]

Berlin RSO (cont.)

G. Albrecht (cnd) (cont.)

Zemlinsky, A. von:Der Geburtstag der Infantin, w. B. Haldas (sop), I. Nielsen (sop), K. Riegel (ten), D. Weller (bass), Berlin RIAS Women's Chamber Choir [G] Koch Schwann ▲ CD 314 013 [DDD]

K. Ančerl (cnd)

Dvořák, A.:Requiem Mass, w. Elisabeth Rose (sop), Gertraud Prenzlow (cta), Peter Schreier (ten), Theo Adam (bass), Berlin Radio Chorus Forlane 2–▲ FRL 16636 [AAD]

J. Arnell (cnd)

Pettersson, G.A.:Sym 14 CPO ▲ CPO 999191 [ADD]

V. Ashkenazy (cnd)

Scriabin, A.:Rêverie London ▲ 430843–2 [DDD]

Scriabin, A.:Sym 3 London ▲ 430843–2 [DDD]

Scriabin, A.:Sym 4 London ▲ 430843–2 [DDD]

Strauss, R.:Con Ob, w. G. Hunt (ob) London ▲ 436415–2 [DDD]

Strauss, R.:Con Vn, w. B. Belkin (vn) London ▲ 436415–2 [DDD]

Strauss, R.:Duet-Concertino, w. D. Ashkenazy (cl), K. Walker (bn) London ▲ 436415–2 [DDD]

Stravinsky, I.:Sym in C *(rec June & Dec. 1991)* London ▲ 436416–2 [DDD]

Stravinsky, I.:Sym in 3 Movts *(rec June & Dec. 1991)* London ▲ 436416–2 [DDD]

Stravinsky, I.:Syms Ww *(rec June & Dec. 1991)* London ▲ 436416–2 [DDD]

R. Bader (cnd)

Donizetti, G.:Messa di Gloria e Credo, w. H. Mané (sop), G. Vighi (mez), P. Maus (ten), M. Machi (bass), St. Hedwig's Cathedral Choir [L] Koch Schwann ▲ CD 313031 [ADD]

Hoffmann, E.T.A.:Undine, w. Krisztina Láki (sop), R. Henry (sgr), Karl Ridderbusch (bass), St. Hedwig's Cathedral Choir *(rec Feb. 1982)* Koch Schwann 3–▲ SCH 310922 [DDD]

Kiel, F.:Der Stern von Bethlehem, w. M. Schiml (sop), H. Laubenthal (ten), St. Hedwig's Cathedral Choir [G] Koch Schwann ▲ CD 313032 [DDD]

Mozart, W.A.:Missa brevis, K.65, w. C. Malone (sop), G. Schreckenbach (mez), K. Markus (ten), W. Grönroos (bar), St. Hedwig's Cathedral Choir [L] Koch Schwann ▲ SCH 313021 [ADD/DDD]

Schubert, Franz:Stabat mater, w. G. Zeumer (sop), D. Ellenbeck (ten), E. G. Schramm (bass), Berlin Radio Chorus Koch Schwann ▲ CD 313 055 [ADD]

Wolf-Ferrari, E.:La vita nuova, w. Celina Lindsley (sop), George Fortune (bar), St. Hedwig's Cathedral Children's Choir Koch Schwann ▲ SCH 312672 [DDD]

M. Bamert (cnd)

Bottesini, G.:Duo Concertant on Themes from Bellini's *I Puritani*, w. M. Ostertag (vc), W. Güttler (db) Koch Schwann ▲ CD 311042 [DDD]

Bottesini, G.:Gran Duo Concertant, w. E. Sebestyen (vn), W. Güttler (db) Koch Schwann ▲ CD 311042 [DDD]

Bottesini, G.:Grande con for 2 Dbs, w. W. Güttler (db), K. Stoll (db) Koch Schwann ▲ CD 311042 [DDD]

Bottesini, G.:Grande con for 2 Dbs, w. W. Güttler (db) Koch Schwann ▲ SCH 313382 [ADD/DDD]

Raff, J.:Sym 5 Koch Schwann ▲ CD 311013 [ADD]

P. Bellugi (cnd)

Rossini, G.:La Cenerentola, w. B. Casoni (mez), U. Benelli (ten), S. Bruscantini (bar), A. Mariotti (bass), Berlin Radio Chorus [I] Acanta 2–▲ CD 43271 [DDD]

L. Blech (cnd)

Chopin, F.:Con 2 Pno, w. J. von Karolyi (pno) *(rec live, Berlin 6/4/50)* Melodram ▲ MEL 18025 (m/s) [AAD]

R. Chailly (cnd)

Grieg, E.:Con Pno, Op. 16, w. J. Bolet (pno) London ▲ 430719–2 [DDD]

Rachmaninoff, S.:Con 3 Pno, w. Martha Argerich (pno) *(rec live, Berlin)* Philips ▲ 446673–2

Schoenberg, A.:Gurrelieder, w. S. Dunn (sop), B. Fassbaender (mez), S. Jerusalem (ten), P. Haage (ten), H. Becht (bass), H. Hotter (nar), St. Hedwig's Cathedral Choir, Düsseldorf Municipal Choral Society [G] London 2–▲ 430321–2 [DDD]

Schumann, R.:Con Pno, w. J. Bolet (pno) London ▲ 430719–2 [DDD]

G. Chmura (cnd)

Schubert, Franz:Sym 7 Koch Schwann ▲ CD 311012 [ADD]

M. Creed (cnd)

Mozart, W.A.:Ave verum corpus, w. Berlin RIAS Chamber Choir [L] Capriccio ▲ 10169 [DDD]

Mozart, W.A.:Missa solemnis, K.139, w. M. Lindsay (sop), G. Schreckenbach (mez), W. Hollweg (ten), W. Grönroos (bar), Berlin RIAS Chamber Choir [L] Capriccio ▲ 10169 [DDD]

Mozart, W.A.:Missa solemnis, K.139, w. M. Lindsay (sop), G. Schreckenbach (mez), W. Hollweg (ten), W. Grönroos (bar), Berlin RIAS Chamber Choir [L] LaserLight ▲ 15 883 [DDD]

Mozart, W.A.:Sacred Music, w. Berlin RIAS Chamber Choir—Misericordias Domini, K.222; Inter natos mulierum, K.72; Sancta Maria, mater Dei, K.273; Venite populi, K.260 [L] LaserLight ▲ 15 883 [DDD]

Mozart, W.A.:Sacred Music, w. Berlin RIAS Chamber Choir—Misericordias Domini, K.222; Inter natos mulierum, K.72; Sancta Maria, mater Dei, K.273; Venite populi, K.260 [L] Capriccio ▲ 10169 [DDD]

Mozart, W.A.:Sacred Music, w. Berlin RIAS Chamber Choir—sels. from Ave verum corpus, K.618; Exsultate, jubilate, K.165; Misericordias Domini, K.222; Missa solemnis, K.139; Requiem; Venite populi, K.260; Vesperae de Domenica, K.321; Vesperae solennes de confessore, K.339 LaserLight ▲ 15 654 [DDD]

D. Demetriades (cnd)

Erdmann, D.:Con Mand, w. M. Kawaguchi (mand) MD + G ▲ L 3451 [DDD]

P. Falk (cnd)

Wusthoff, K.:Orchestral Music, w. Renate Erxleben (hp), Ernst-August Quelle (pno)—A Little Harp Serenade; Concertino for Piano & Orch; 3 Russian Fants for Piano & Orch Koch Schwann ▲ SCH 318062

Wusthoff, K.:Orchestral Music—All My Animals for Orch; Golf Games (concert waltz) for Orch; The Rain Fairy (ballet) for Orch; Slavonic Rhap for Orch Koch Schwann ▲ SCH 318072

W. Fortner (cnd)

Fortner, W.:Music of Berlin Classics ▲ BER 9209

L. Foster (cnd)

Waxman, F.:Ruth, w. George Shirley (nar) *(rec Berlin, Nov 25–26, 1993)* Capriccio ▲ 10711 [DDD]

Waxman, F.:The Spirit of St. Louis, w. George Shirley (nar) *(rec Berlin, Nov 25–26, 1993)* Capriccio ▲ 10711 [DDD]

A. Francis (cnd)

Pettersson, G.A.:Sym 9 CPO ▲ CPO 999231 [DDD]

P. Freeman (cnd)

Britten, B.:Scottish Ballad, w. J. Yarbrough (pno), R. Cowan (pno) Centaur ▲ CRC 2095 [DDD]

Khachaturian, A.:Con Pno, w. J. Pierce (pno) Phoenix ▲ PHCD 117 [DDD]

Vaughan Williams, R.:Con Pno, w. J. Yarbrough (pno), R. Cowan (pno) Centaur ▲ CRC 2095 [DDD]

H. Fricke (cnd)

Arias, w. Jochen Kowalski (ct) Capriccio ▲ CD 10 416 [DDD]

Chopin, F.:Les Sylphides Capriccio ▲ 10073 [DDD]

Delibes, L.:Coppélia (suite) Capriccio ▲ 10073 [DDD]

Delibes, L.:Coppélia (suite) LaserLight ▲ 15 616 [DDD]

F. Fricsay (cnd)

Bartók, B.:Con Orch Deutsche Grammophon ("The Originals" series) ▲ 447 443–2

Bartók, B.:Cons Pno (comp), w. Géza Anda (pno) Deutsche Grammophon ("The Originals" series) ▲ 447399–2

Mozart, W.A.:Con 20 Pno, w. C. Haskil (pno) *(rec Europa-Palast, Berlin, Jan. 10, 1954)* Myto 2–▲ 2 MCD 92361 [ADD]

Mozart, W.A.:Don Giovanni, w. I. Seefried (sop), S. Jurinac (sop), M. Stader (sop), E. Haefliger (ten), D. Fischer-Dieskau (bar), K. C. Kohn (bass) Deutsche Grammophon 3–▲ 437341–2

Mozart, W.A.:Entführung, w. S. Barabas (sop), R. Streich (sop), A. Dermota (ten), H. Krebs (ten), J. Greindl (bass), Berlin Radio Chorus [G] *(rec Jesus-Christuskirche, Berlin-Dahlem, Dec. 19–21, 1949)* Myto 2–▲ 2 MCD 92361 [ADD]

Mozart, W.A.:Nozze di Figaro, w. M. Stader (sop), I. Seefried (sop), H. Töpper (mez), D. Fischer-Dieskau (bar), R. Capecchi (bar), I. Sardi (bass) [G] *(rec 1960)* Deutsche Grammophon 3–▲ 437671–2

Berlin RSO (cont.)
F. Fricsay (cnd) (cont.)
Mozart, W.A.:Serenata notturna *(rec Titania-Palast, Berlin, Feb. 28, 1951)* Myto 2-▲ 2 MCD 92361 [ADD]
Schumann, R.:Con Pno, w. A. Cortot (pno) *(rec in concert, 1950s)* Melodram ▲ MEL 18018 (m)
Strauss (I), Joh.:Radetzky March Deutsche Grammophon ▲ 427217-2 [ADD]
Strauss (II), Joh.:Die Fledermaus, w. R. Streich (sop), A. Schlemm (mez), P. Anders (ten), H. Krebs (ten), Berlin Radio Chorus [G] *(rec live, Berlin, 11/8/49)* Melodram 2-▲ MEL 29001 (m) [AAD]
Strauss (II), Joh.:Music of—Fledermaus (overture); Annen-Polka; Kaiser-Walzer; Tritsch-Tratsch Polka; An der schönen, blauen Donau; Eljen a Magyar!; G'schichten aus dem Wienerwald Deutsche Grammophon ▲ 427217-2 [ADD]
Strauss (II), Joh.:Waltzes—Ouvertüre zu; Die Fledermaus; Annen-Polka; Kaiserwalzer; Tritsch-Tratsch-Polka; Radetzky-Marsch; An der schönen blauen Donau Eljen a Magyar; G'schichten aus dem Wiener Wald Deutsche Grammophon ("Resonance" series) ▲ 427217-2 [ADD]
C. Fröhlich (cnd)
Spohr, L.:Con 2 Vn, w. U. Hoelscher (vn) CPO ▲ CPO 999067 [DDD]
Spohr, L.:Con 3 Vn, w. U. Hoelscher (vn) CPO ▲ CPO 999145 [DDD]
Spohr, L.:Con 4 Vn, w. U. Hoelscher (vn) CPO ▲ CPO 999196 [DDD]
Spohr, L.:Con 5 Vn, w. U. Hoelscher (vn) CPO ▲ CPO 999067 [DDD]
Spohr, L.:Con 6 Vn, w. U. Hoelscher (vn) CPO ▲ CPO 999145 [DDD]
Spohr, L.:Con 7 Vn, w. Ulf Hoelscher (vn) CPO ▲ CPO 999232 [DDD]
Spohr, L.:Con 8 Vn, w. Ulf Hoelscher (vn) CPO ▲ CPO 999187 [DDD]
Spohr, L.:Con 9 Vn, w. Ulf Hoelscher (vn) CPO ▲ CPO 999232 [DDD]
Spohr, L.:Con 10 Vn, w. Ulf Hoelscher (vn) CPO ▲ CPO 999232 [DDD]
Spohr, L.:Con 11 Vn, w. U. Hoelscher (vn) CPO ▲ CPO 999196 [DDD]
Spohr, L.:Con 12 Vn, w. Ulf Hoelscher (vn) CPO ▲ CPO 999187 [DDD]
Spohr, L.:Con 12 Vn, w. U. Hoelscher (vn) CPO ▲ CPO 999145 [DDD]
Spohr, L.:Con 13 Vn, w. Ulf Hoelscher (vn) CPO ▲ CPO 999187 [DDD]
Spohr, L.:Ovs—Macbeth; Die Prüfung; Alruna; Die Eulenkönigin; Faust; Jessonda; Der Berggeist; Pietro von Abano; Der Alchymist CPO ▲ CPO 999093 [DDD]
C. Garben (cnd)
Mahler, G.:Songs, w. A. Schmidt (bar)—Ablösung im Sommer; Zu Strasburg auf der Schanz'; Nicht Wiedersehen; Um schlimme Kinder artig zu machen; Hans und Grete; Ich ging mit Lust durch einen grünen Wald; Frühlingsmorgen; Scheiden und Meiden; Erinnerung RCA Red Seal ▲ 09026-61184-2
Strauss, R.:Songs, w. A. Schmidt (bar)—Hymnus und Pilgers Morgenlied, Op. 33; Das Thal und das Einsame, Op. 51; Notturno, Op. 44 RCA Red Seal ▲ 09026-61184-2
B. Goldschmidt (cnd)
Testimonies of War:Kriegszeugnisse, 1914–45, w. London PO [cnd:N. Sheriff], Poznán PO [cnd:A. Borejko], BBC Sym Chorus Largo 2-▲ 5130 [DDD]
U. Gronostay (cnd)
Bruch, M.:Die Flucht der heiligen Familie, w. Berlin Radio Chorus [G] Koch Schwann ▲ CD 313013 [DDD]
Bruch, M.:Gruss an die heilige Nacht, w. G. Schreckenbach (mez), Berlin Radio Chorus [G] Koch Schwann ▲ CD 313013 [DDD]
Mozart, W.A.:Requiem, w. Edith Wiens (sop), Gabriele Schreckenbach (mez), Aldo Baldin (ten), Gerhard Faulstich (bar), Berlin RIAS Chamber Choir [L] LaserLight ▲ 15 882 [DDD]
Wolf, H.:Christnacht, w. Berlin Phil Chorus Koch Schwann ▲ SCH 313013 [DDD]
Wolf, H.:Christnacht, w. S. Inou-Heller (sop), M.-L. Wilke (mez), K. Thiem (bar), Berlin Radio Chorus [G] Koch Schwann ▲ CD 313013 [DDD]
G.M. Guida (cnd)
David, Felicien:Le Désert, w. O. Pascalin (nar), B. Lazzaretti (ten), St. Hedwig's Cathedral Choir Capriccio ▲ 10 379 [DDD]
Reyer, L.-E.-E.:Le Sélam, w. *(soloists unknown)*, St. Hedwig's Cathedral Choir Capriccio ▲ 10 380 [DDD]
Szymanowski, K.:Songs of the Infatuated Muezzin, w. G. Ottenthal (sop) Capriccio ▲ 10 379 [DDD]
P. Gülke (cnd)
Britten, B.:Canadian Carnival Koch Schwann ▲ 3-1034-2 [DDD]
Milhaud, D.:Le Carnaval d'Aix, w. K. Hellwig (pno) Koch Schwann ▲ 3-1034-2 [DDD]
Svendsen, J.:Norwegian Artists' Carnival Koch Schwann ▲ 3-1034-2 [DDD]
H. Haenchen (cnd)
Rheinberger, J.:Con 1 Org, w. A. Juffinger (org) Capriccio ▲ CD 10 336 [DDD]
Rheinberger, J.:Con 2 Org, w. A. Juffinger (org) Capriccio ▲ CD 10 336 [DDD]
Rheinberger, J.:Suite Org, w. A. Juffinger (org), E. Sebestyén (vn), M. Ostertag (vc) Capriccio ▲ CD 10 337 [DDD]
V. Handley (cnd)
Sibelius, J.:Music for Vn Orch, w. R. Holmes (vn)—Serenades in D & g, Op. 69, Nos. 1 & 2; Cantique & Devotion, Op. 77, Nos. 1 & 2; Six Humoresques, Op. 87/1 & 2 & Op. 89/1-4 Koch Schwann ▲ CD 311003 [ADD]
W.-D. Hauschild (cnd)
Auber, D.-F.:Fra Diavolo, w. H. Termer (sop), G. Neumann (ten), E. Büchner (bar) Berlin Classics ▲ BER 2140 [ADD]
Brahms, J.:Liebeslieder Waltzes SATB, w. Barbara Hoene (sop), Gisela Pohl (alt), Armin Ude (ten), Siegfried Lorenz (bar), Klaus Bässler (pno), Dieter Zechlin (pno) Berlin Classics ▲ BER 9269
Brahms, J.:Neue Liebeslieder Waltzes, w. Barbara Hoene (sop), Gisela Pohl (alt), Armin Ude (ten), Siegfried Lorenz (bar), Klaus Bässler (pno), Dieter Zechlin (pno) Berlin Classics ▲ BER 9269
Denisov, E.:Peinture, w. Günter Philipp (pno) Berlin Classics ▲ BER 9260
O. Henzold (cnd)
Lachenmann, H.:Tanzsuite mit Deutschlandlied, w. Arditti String Quartet Montaigne ▲ MO 782019
E. Inbal (cnd)
Liszt, F.:A Faust Sym, w. J. Zhang (ten), Berlin Radio Chorus Denon ▲ CO 75634 [DDD]
M. Jurowski (cnd)
Kancheli, G.:Sym 2 CPO ▲ CPO 999263 [DDD]
Kancheli, G.:Sym 7 CPO ▲ CPO 999263 [DDD]
Shostakovich, D.:Alone, w. Swetlana Katchur (sop), Wladimir Kazatchouk (ten), Berlin Radio Chorus *(rec Jesus Christ Church, Berlin-Dahlem, Sept 19-22, 1995)* Capriccio ▲ 10562 [DDD]
P. Keuschnig (cnd)
Sasse, K.-E.:Der Golem Capriccio ▲ CD 10467 [DDD]
B. Klee (cnd)
Mendelssohn, F.:Die Hochzeit des Camacho, w. R. Schudel (sop—Quiteria), C. Swanson (sop—Lucinda), C. Bieber (ten—Basilio), W. Mok (ten—Vivaldo), V. Horn (ten—Camacho), R. Lukas (bar—Carrasco), J. Becker (bass—Sancho Panza), W. Murray (bass—Don Quixote), Berlin Radio Chorus [G] Koch Schwann 2-▲ 314042 [DDD]
Zemlinsky, A. von:Lyric Sym, w. E. Söderström (sop), D. Duesing (bar) [G] Koch Schwann ▲ CD 311 053 [ADD]
Zemlinsky, A. von:Sinfonietta Koch Schwann ▲ CD 311 122 [ADD]
Zemlinsky, A. von:Songs to Poems by Maurice Maeterlinck, w. G. Linos (sop) [G] Koch Schwann ▲ CD 311 053 [ADD]
R. Kleinert (cnd)
Elgar, E.:Enigma Vars Berlin Classics ▲ BER 9270
Hindemith, P.:Philharmonisches Konzert Berlin Classics ▲ BER 9270
O. Klemperer (cnd)
Beethoven, L. van:Con 4 Pno, w. Leon Fleisher (pno), Bavarian RSO, Cologne RSO Enterprise ("Palladio" series) ▲ ENT 4189 [ADD]
Beethoven, L. van:Sym 4, w. Bavarian RSO, Cologne RSO Enterprise ("Palladio" series) ▲ ENT 4189 [ADD]
Beethoven, L. van:Sym 5, w. Bavarian RSO, Cologne RSO Enterprise ("Palladio" series) ▲ ENT 4189 [ADD]
Brahms, J.:Sym 2, w. Bavarian RSO, Cologne RSO Enterprise ("Palladio" series) ▲ ENT 4189 [ADD]
Mahler, G.:Sym 4, w. Elfriede Troetschel (sop) *(rec live, 1956)* Originals ▲ ORISH 823 [ADD]

Berlin RSO (cont.)
D. Knothe (cnd)
Schubert, Franz:Sacred Music, w. M. Hajossyova (sop), P. Schreier (ten), Berlin Radio Chorus—Offertorium, D.963; Offertorium, D.223; Tantum ergo, D.962; Psalm 23, D.706; An die Sonne, D.439; Offertorium, D.136; Salve Regina, D.106; Salve Regina, D.386; Psalm 92, D.953; Chor der Engel, D.440 [G,L] Capriccio ▲ 10096 [DDD]
H. Koch (cnd)
Beethoven, L. van:Music of, w. Sylvia Geszty (sop), Jozsef Reti (ten), Hermann Christian Polster (bass), Berlin State Orch, Berlin Soloists—Christ on the Mount of Olives (oratorio); Con in E♭ Pno; Irish Songs; Minuets; Canons; Epigrams; Joke Pieces; Incidental & Ballet Music Berlin Classics 3-▲ BER 9132
Handel, G.F.:Judas Maccabaeus, w. Gundula Janowitz (sop), Hertha Töpper (alt), Peter Schreier (ten), Ernest Haefliger (ten), Theo Adam (bass), Siegfried Vogel (bass), Berlin Radio Chorus Berlin Classics 2-▲ BER 9112
Haydn, J.:Die Schöpfung, w. Regina Werner (sop), Peter Schreier (ten), Theo Adam (bass), Berlin Radio Chorus Berlin Classics 2-▲ BER CD 9115
F. Konwitschny (cnd)
Bruckner, A.:Sym 2 [original version] *(rec 1951)* Berlin Classics ▲ BER 9173
R. Kraus (cnd)
Strauss, R.:4 Last Songs, w. E. Grümmer (sop) [G] *(rec 1970)* Melodram ▲ CDM 16523 [AAD]
G. Kuhn (cnd)
Cornelius, P.:Der Cid, w. Gertrud Ottenthal (sop), Ronnie Johansen (sgr), Robert Schunk (ten), Albert Dohmen (bar), Michael Schopper (bass), Endrik Wottrich (sgr), Berlin Radio Chorus Koch Schwann 2-▲ SCH 315222
U. Lajovic (cnd)
Bloch, E.:Sym Trbn, w. A. Rosin (trbn) Koch Schwann ▲ CD 311 086
Casella, A.:Sicilienne et burlesque Pno Trio, w. K.-B. Sebon (fl) [arr flute & orchestra] *(rec 1981)* Koch Treasure ▲ 316132 [ADD]
Chaminade, C.:Concertino Fl, w. K.-B. Sebon (fl) Koch Treasure ▲ 316132 [ADD]
Doppler, A.F.:Fant pastorale hongroise, w. K.-B. Sebon (fl) Koch Treasure ▲ 316132 [ADD]
Paganini, N.:Intro & Vars on "Dal tuo stellato soglio", w. G. Karr (db) [arr. Karr] Koch Schwann ▲ SCH 313382 [ADD/DDD]
Popp, W.:Fant brillante, w. K.-B. Sebon (fl) Koch Treasure ▲ 316132 [ADD]
Reger, M.:Romances Vn, w. H. Maile (vn) Koch Schwann ▲ CD 311 076 [ADD]
Reger, M.:Suite Vn Pno, w. H. Maile (vn) *(rec 1981)* Koch Schwann ▲ CD 311 122 [ADD]
Reger, M.:Symphonic Prologue for a Tragedy Koch Schwann ▲ CD 311 076 [ADD]
Saint-Saëns, C.:Tarantelle Fl, w. K.-B. Sebon (fl), J. Fadle (cl) [flute, clarinet & orchestra arr.] Koch Treasure ▲ 316132 [ADD]
Virtuoso Kettledrum Concertos, w. Werner Tharichen (timp) Koch Schwann ▲ SCH 311052
Works for Trombone & Orchestra, w. Armin Rosin (trbn) Koch Schwann ▲ SCH 311086
G. Levine (cnd)
Mussorgsky, M.:Pictures at an Exhibition LaserLight ▲ 14 012 [DDD]
J. López-Cobos (cnd)
Clarinet Concertos, w. Dieter Klöcker (cl) Koch Schwann ▲ SCH 311045
Dietrich, A.:Con Vn, w. H. Maile (vn) Koch Schwann ▲ CD 311070 [DDD]
Joachim, J.:Nocturne Vn, w. H. Maile (vn) Koch Schwann ▲ CD 311070 [DDD]
Mahler, G.:Totenfeier Koch Schwann ▲ 3-1204-2 [ADD]
L. Ludwig (cnd)
Hindemith, P.:Mathis der Maler, w. P. Lorengar (sop), D. Grobe (ten), D. Fischer-Dieskau (bar) [G]—sels Deutsche Grammophon ("20th Century Classics" series) 2-▲ 431741-2 [ADD]
Puccini, G.:Tosca, w. H. Ranczak (sop), H. Roswaenge (ten), G. Hann (bass) *(rec Oct. 1944)* Preiser 2-▲ PRE 90210 [ADD]
Weber, C.M. von:Abu Hassan, w. E. Schwarzkopf (sop), E. Witte (ten), M. Bohnen (bass), Berlin Radio Chorus [G] *(rec Germany 1941)* Forlane ▲ FOR 16572 (m) [AAD]
Weber, C.M. von:Abu Hassan, w. Elisabeth Schwarzkopf (sop), Erich Witte (ten), Michael Bohnen (bass), Berlin Radio Chorus Grammofono 2000 ▲ GRM 78650
L. Maazel (cnd)
Falla, M. de:El amor brujo, w. Grace Bumbry (mez) Deutsche Grammophon ("The Originals" series) ▲ 447414-2
Falla, M. de:El sombrero de tres picos (dances) Deutsche Grammophon ("The Originals" series) ▲ 447414-2
Mahler, G.:Sym 4, w. H. Harper (sop) *(rec 1969; remastered 1994)* FNAC Music ▲ 642314
Stravinsky, I.:The Firebird Suite Deutsche Grammophon ("The Originals" series) ▲ 447414-2
H. Maile (cnd)
Cirri, G.B.:Con Vc & Str, w. M. Nyikos (vc) Koch Schwann ▲ CD 311063 [DDD]
Vivaldi, A.:Cons Vc, w. M. Nyikos (vc)—2 concerti—RV.407, 410 Koch Schwann ▲ CD 311063 [DDD]
E. Märzendorfer (cnd)
Rodrigo, J.:Concert-Serenade, w. N. Zabaleta (hp) Deutsche Grammophon ("Resonance" series) ▲ 427214-2 [ADD]
J. Mauceri (cnd)
Korngold, E.W.:Between 2 Worlds, w. Alexander Frey (pno) *(rec Berlin, Apr. 1995)* London ("Entartete Musik" series) ▲ 444170-2 [DDD]
Korngold, E.W.:Das Wunder der Heliane, w. A. Tomowa-Sintow (sop), R. Runkel (cta), N. Gedda (ten), J. D. de Haan (ten), H. Welker (bar), R. Pape (bass) [G] London 3-▲ 436636-2 [DDD]
Weill, K.:Songs, w. U. Lemper (sop)—songs from Mahagonny, Three Penny Opera, Silverlake, One Touch of Venus, etc. London ▲ 425204-2 [DDD]
R. Paternostro (cnd)
Auber, D.-F.:Rondo Vc, w. M. Ostertag (vc) Koch Schwann ▲ 311039 [DDD] ■ 211039 (D)
Massenet, J.:Fant Vc, w. M. Ostertag (vc) Koch Schwann ▲ 311039 [DDD] ■ 211039 (D)
Popper, D.:Con Vc, Op. 24, w. M. Ostertag (vc) Koch Schwann ▲ 311039 [DDD] ■ 211039 (D)
C. Perick (cnd)
Schmidt, F.:Notre Dame, w. G. Jones (sop), J. King (ten), R. Laubenthal (ten), K. Moll (bass), St. Hedwig's Cathedral Choir, RIAS Chamber Chorus [G] Capriccio 2-▲ 10248/9 [DDD]
R. Reuter (cnd)
Pfitzner, H.:Der blumen Rache, w. Yvi Jänicke (cta), Yvonne Wiedstruck (sgr), Yaron Windmüller (voc), Berlin Radio Chorus CPO ▲ CPO 999158 [DDD]
Pfitzner, H.:Das dunkle Reich, w. Yvi Jänicke (cta), Yvonne Wiedstruck (voc), Yaron Windmüller (voc), Berlin Radio Chorus CPO ▲ CPO 999158 [DDD]
Pfitzner, H.:Fons salutifer, w. Yvi Jänicke (cta), Yvonne Wiedstruck (voc), Yaron Windmüller (voc), Berlin Radio Chorus CPO ▲ CPO 999158 [DDD]
K.A. Rickenbacher (cnd)
Beethoven, L. van:Cant on the Death of the Emperor Joseph II, w. Markus Schäfer (ten), Alan Titus (bar), Bodil Arnesen (sgr), Berlin Radio Chorus Koch Schwann ▲ SCH 314352 [DDD]
Beethoven, L. van:Di Flamme lodert, Op. 121, w. Bodil Arnesen (sop), Berlin Radio Chorus Koch Schwann ▲ SCH 314852
Beethoven, L. van:Di Flamme lodert, Op. 121b, w. Bodil Arnesen (sop), Berlin Radio Chorus Koch Schwann ▲ SCH 314852
Beethoven, L. van:In allen guten Stunden, w. Bodil Arnesen (sop), Berlin Radio Chorus Koch Schwann ▲ SCH 314852
Beethoven, L. van:Leonore Prohaska, w. Berlin Radio Chorus Koch Schwann ▲ SCH 314852
Beethoven, L. van:Marches (misc)—2 Marches for Military Music Koch Schwann ▲ SCH 314852
Beethoven, L. van:Meeresstille und glückliche Fahrt, w. Berlin Radio Chorus Koch Schwann ▲ SCH 314852
Beethoven, L. van:Music of, w. Berlin Radio Chorus—Wo sich die Pulse jugendlich jagen Koch Schwann ▲ SCH 314852
Beethoven, L. van:Triumphal March Koch Schwann ▲ SCH 314852
Françaix, J.:Preludes Koch Schwann ▲ CD 311060 [ADD]
Liszt, F.:Odes funèbres Koch Schwann ▲ SCH CD 317682
Liszt, F.:Tasso—Lamento e Trionfo Koch Schwann ▲ SCH CD 317682
Schreker, F.:Chamber Sym Koch Schwann ▲ CD 311 078

▲ = CD ♦ = Enhanced CD Δ = MD ■ = Cassette Tape □ = DCC

Berlin RSO (cont.)

K.A. Rickenbacher (cnd) (cont.)

Schreker, F.:Night Interlude — Koch Schwann ▲ CD 311 078
Schreker, F.:Prelude to a Drama — Koch Schwann ▲ CD 311 078
Schreker, F.:Valse lent — Koch Schwann ▲ CD 311 078

H. Rögner (cnd)

Mendelssohn, F.:Con in E for 2 Pnos, w. Vlastimil Lejsek (pno), Vera Lejskova (pno)—in E — Berlin Classics ▲ BER 9027 [ADD]
Wolf-Ferrari, E.:Ovs & Intermezzi — Berlin Classics ▲ BER 9177

H. Rosbaud (cnd)

Mahler, G.:Sym 7 *(rec 1952)* — Vox Box 2-▲ CDX2 5520

A. Rother (cnd)

Beethoven, L. van:Con 5 Pno, "Emperor", w. W. Gieseking (pno) *(rec 1944, Berlin)* — Melodram ▲ MEL 18023 (m) [AAD]
Beethoven, L. van:Con 5 Pno, "Emperor", w. Walter Gieseking (pno) *(rec Berlin, 1944)* — Music & Arts ▲ CD 815 [AAD]
Beethoven, L. van:Con 5 Pno, "Emperor", w. W. Gieseking (pno) *(rec 1944)* — Arkadia ▲ 588 [ADD]
Max Lorenz:Recital, 1933–1957, w. Max Lorenz (ten), Maria Reining (sop), Bayreuth Festival Orch [cnd:Heinz Tietjen, Richard Strauss], German Large RSO [cnd:Rudolf Moralt, Max Schönherr, Anton Paulik], Hessen RSO [cnd:Kurt Schröder], Brenda Lewis (sop), Eberhard Wächter (ten), Wolfgang Zimmer (bar) *(rec 1933–57)* — Myto ▲ MCD 934.88
Nicolai, O.:Lustigen Weiber, w. I. Bielke (sop), M. L. Schilp (mez), W. Ludwig (ten), G. Hann (bass), W. Streinz (bass), Berlin State Opera Chorus *(rec May 2, 1943)* — Preiser 2-▲ PRE 90208 [ADD]
Verdi, G.:La forza del destino (sels), w. H. Roswaenge (ten), H. Schlusnus (bar) *(rec 1942)* — Myto 2-▲ MCD 93279
Wagner, R.:Die Meistersinger von Nürnberg (sels), w. K. Wessel (alt), E. Kunz (bar), G. Hann (bass), Berlin Radio Chorus—Act 2 — Preiser ▲ PRE 90168 [AAD]

P. Ruzicka (cnd)

Mahler, G.:Bach Orchestral Works, w. M.–U. Senn (fl), P. Siegele (org), P. Schwarz (hpd) — Koch Schwann ▲ 3-1204-2 [ADD]
Ruzicka, P.:Etym, w. Philipp Moll (pno) *(rec Mar 1975)* — Thorofon ▲ CTH 2220

A. Sander (cnd)

Egk, W.:Geigenmusik, w. Hans Maile (vn) — Koch Schwann ▲ SCH 310752 [DDD]
Hartmann, K.A.:Con funèbre, w. Hans Maile (vn) — Koch Schwann ▲ SCH 310752 [DDD]
Zimmermann, B.A.:Con Vn, w. Hans Maile (vn) — Koch Schwann ▲ SCH 310752 [DDD]

T. Sanderling (cnd)

Pettersson, G.A.:Sym 8 — CPO ▲ CPO 999085 [ADD]
Shostakovich, D.:Michelangelo Suite Orch — Berlin Classics ▲ BERCD 9193

W. Sawallisch (cnd)

Beethoven, L. van:Sym 3, "Eroica" — Memories ▲ MEM 4545 [AAD]

G. Schmöhe (cnd)

Burgmüller, N.:Sym 2 — Koch Schwann ▲ CD 311010 [DDD]
Schumann, R.:Sym 4 [original version] — Koch Schwann ▲ CD 311010 [DDD]

H.–M. Schneidt (cnd)

Bizet, G.:Les Pêcheurs de perles (sels), w. B. Lazzaretti (ten), W. Glashof (bar)—Act 1 duet, "Au fond du temple saint" — Capriccio ▲ 10 380 [DDD]
Ravel, M.:Shéhérazade Mez, w. G. Pasino (mez) — LaserLight ▲ 14013 [DDD]
Ravel, M.:Shéhérazade Mez, w. G. Pasino (mez) — Capriccio ▲ 10 381 [DDD]
Rimsky-Korsakov, N.:Scheherazade — Capriccio ▲ 10 381 [DDD]
Strauss, R.:Salome (dance) — Capriccio ▲ 10 380 [DDD]

J. Seers (cnd)

Ravel, M.:La Valse — LaserLight ▲ 14013 [DDD]

D. Shallon (cnd)

Glazunov, A.:Con Sax, w. D. Bensmann (sax) — Koch Schwann ▲ SCH 313352 [DDD]
Wolf, H.:Songs (misc), w. M. Shirai (mez)—15 songs — Capriccio ▲ CD 10 335 [DDD]

L. Slatkin (cnd)

Gershwin, G.:Porgy & Bess (sels), w. R. Alexander (sop), S. Estes (bass), Berlin Radio Chorus [E] — Philips ▲ 412720-2 [DDD]

E. Smola (cnd)

Wusthoff, K.:Orchestral Music—The Schelde [suite]; Voyage to Greece; Old England Suite; Street Scenes — Koch Schwann ▲ SCH 318052 [DDD]

H. Steiner (cnd)

Gounod, C.:Faust, w. H. Singstreu (sop—Margarete), H. Rosvaenge (ten—Faust), M. Bohnen (bass—Mephistopheles), Berlin Radio Chorus *(rec 1938)* — Myto 2-▲ MCD 94196

H. Steinkopf (cnd)

Lortzing, A.:Wildschütz (sels), w. G. Hann (b-bar)—Fünftausend Taler *(rec 1943)* — Myto 2-▲ MCD 943103
Lortzing, A.:Zar und Zimmermann (sels), w. G. Hann (b-bar)—O cancta justitia!; Den hohen Herscher; Heil sei dem Tag *(rec 1943)* — Myto 2-▲ MCD 943103

G. Szell (cnd)

Strauss, R.:4 Last Songs, w. E. Schwarzkopf (sop) [G] — EMI Classics ▲ CDC 47276

A. Tamayo (cnd)

Busoni, F.:Berceuse élégiaque *(rec Aug. 17–20, 1992)* — Capriccio ▲ 10 480 [DDD]
Busoni, F.:Indianisches Tagebuch 2, "Gesang vom Reigen der Geister" *(rec Aug. 17–20, 1992)* — Capriccio ▲ 10 480 [DDD]
Busoni, F.:Lustspiel-Ov *(rec Aug. 17–20, 1992)* — Capriccio ▲ 10 480 [DDD]
Busoni, F.:Symphonic Suite *(rec Aug. 17–20, 1992)* — Capriccio ▲ 10 480 [DDD]

Y. Temirkanov (cnd)

Tchaikovsky, P.:Con 1 Pno, w. L. Berman (pno) [original version] — Koch Schwann ▲ CD 311 037 [DDD]

P. Wohlert (cnd)

Tchaikovsky, P.:Nutcracker (sels) — Laserlight ♦ 90023 [DDD]
Tchaikovsky, P.:Romeo & Juliet — LaserLight ▲ 15 633 [DDD]
Tchaikovsky, P.:Sleeping Beauty (suite) — LaserLight ▲ 15 633 [DDD]
Tchaikovsky, P.:Swan Lake (suite) — LaserLight ▲ 15 633 [DDD]

L. Zagrosek (cnd)

Hindemith, P.:Das Unaufhörliche, w. Ulrike Sonntag (sop), Robert Wörle (ten), Siegfried Lorenz (bar), Artur Korn (bass), Berlin Radio Chorus — Wergo 2-▲ WER 66032

H. Zender (cnd)

Bach, J.S.:The Art of the Fugue—orch. arr. Fritz Stiedry, 1941 — Koch Schwann ▲ CD 311032 [DDD]
Yun, I.:Con Vc, w. Siegfried Palm (vc) *(rec March 25, 1976)* — Camerata ▲ 30CM 22

H. E. Zimmer (cnd)

Indy, V. d':Fant sur des thèmes populaires français, w. Lajos Lences (ob) — Capriccio ▲ CD 10726 [DDD]
Rimsky-Korsakov, N.:Vars on a Theme of Glinka, w. Lajos Lences (ob) — Capriccio ▲ CD 10726 [DDD]
Schwencke, C.F.G.:Con Ob, w. Lajos Lences (ob) — Capriccio ▲ CD 10726 [DDD]
Weber, C.M. von:Concertino Ob, w. Lajos Lences (ob) — Capriccio ▲ CD 10726 [DDD]

H. Zimmermann (cnd)

Mozart, W.A.:Entführung (sels), w. W. Strienz (bass)—6 arias [G] — Melodram 2-▲ MEL 27056 (m) [AAD]

D. Zinman (cnd)

Koechlin, C.:Symphonic Poems based on Kipling's *The Jungle Book*—Seal Lullaby; Night-Song in the Jungle; Song of Kala Nag; Spring in the Forest; Mowgli; The Running; Night; The Law of the Jungle; The Meditation of Purun Bhagat; Les Bandar-log — RCA Red Seal 2-▲ 09026-61955-2

Berlin Radio Youth Orch

S. Sanna (cnd)

Bizet, G.:Don Procopio, w. Muscente (sgr), M. Gentile (sgr), Carmona (sgr), Barry (sgr), A. Antoniozzi (bar), Symbolon Ensemble Chorus [I] *(rec live 5/25/86)* — Bongiovanni 2-▲ GB 2043/44 [DDD]

Berlin Reich RSO

C. Krauss (cnd)

Strauss, R.:Ariadne auf Naxos, w. Erna Berger (sop), Viorica Ursuleac (sop), Helge Roswaenge (ten), Karl Hammes (bar) *(rec Berlin, 1935)* — Preiser ▲ PRE 90259

Berlin Reich RSO (cont.)

C. Schuricht (cnd)

Bruckner, A.:Sym 9 *(rec live Berlin, 1937)* — Archipon 2-▲ ARC 3.2/3 (m) [ADD]

Berlin RIAS Chamber Ensemble

J. Mauceri (cnd)

Weill, K.:Mahagonny, w. U. Lemper (sop), H. Jungwirth (sop), H. Wildhaber (ten), P. Haage (ten), T. Mohr (bar), S. Tremper (sgr), Jeffrey Cohen (pno) [G] — London ▲ 430168-2 [DDD]
Weill, K.:The Seven Deadly Sins, w. U. Lemper (sop), H. Jungwirth (sop), H. Wildhaber (ten), P. Haage (ten), T. Mohr (bar), S. Tremper (sgr) [G] — London ▲ 430168-2 [DDD]

Berlin RIAS Orch

F. Fricsay (cnd)

Bartók, B.:Music for Strs, Perc & Cel — Deutsche Grammophon ("The Originals" series) ▲ 447 443-2

Berlin RIAS Sinfonietta

J. Mauceri (cnd)

Weill, K.:Songs, w. U. Lemper (sop), London Voices—Bilbao Song; Surabaya Johnny; Was die Herren Matrosen sagen; Der Song von Mandelay; Das Lied vom Branntweinandler; Youkali; Les filles de Bordeaux; Le train du Ciel; Le grand Lustucru; Le roi d'Aquitaine; J'attends un navire; Tchaikovsky; One Life to Live; This Is New; A Song of Jenny; My Ship — London ▲ 436417-2 [DDD]
Weill, K.:The Threepenny Opera, w. U. Lemper (sop), Milva (sgr), S. Tremper (sgr), H. Dernesch (mez), R. Kollo (ten), M. Adorf (sgr), W. Reichmann (sgr), Berlin RIAS Chamber Choir [G] — London ▲ 430075-2 [DDD]

E. Sebestyen (cnd)

Reichardt, J.F.:Con Vn Orch *(rec 1980)* — Koch Treasure ▲ 31614-2 [ADD]
The Trombone, w. Armin Rosin (trbn), Michel Becquet (trbn), Berlin Trombone Quintet, Lorraine PO [cnd:Jacques Houtmann], Southwest German CO [cnd:Vladislav Czernedki] — Koch Schwann ▲ SCH 313342 [DDD]

J. Stárek (cnd)

Boccherini, L.:Syms, w. S. Prunnbauer (gtr), Jürgen Hollerbuhl (ob), B. Vestre (ob), Jörn Maatz (ob), H. Maile (vn), H. Ganz (vn), R. Forest (vc)—in C, G.495 (Op. 21/3) *(rec Dec. 1979)* — Koch Treasure ▲ 31612-2 [ADD]
Bossi, M.E.:Intermezzi Goldoniani *(rec 1979)* — Koch Treasure ▲ 31626-2 [ADD]
Donizetti, G.:Concertinos (4) solo Winds, w. J. Fadle (cl), K.–B. Sebon (fl), G. Passin (ob/ob d'amore) *(rec 1979)* — Koch Schwann ▲ CD 311 121 [ADD/DDD]
Reger, M.:Lyrisches Andante — Koch Schwann ▲ CD 311067 [ADD]
Reznicek, E.N. von:Serenade *(rec 1979)* — Koch Schwann ▲ CD 311 128 [ADD]
Tansman, A.:Musique de Cour, w. S. Prunnbauer (gtr) *(rec Dec. 1979)* — Koch Treasure ▲ 31612-2 [ADD]

J. Velazco (cnd)

Boccherini, L.:Con Vc, G.480, w. W. Boettcher (vc) — Koch Schwann ▲ CD 311101 [ADD]
Danzi, F.:Con Vc, w. W. Boettcher (vc) — Koch Schwann ▲ CD 311101 [ADD]

Berlin RIAS SO

F. Fricsay (cnd)

Mozart, W.A.:Exsultate, w. Maria Stader (sop) — Deutsche Grammophon 2-▲ 437383-2 [ADD]
Verdi, G.:Requiem Mass, w. Maria Stader (sop), Marjana Radev (mez), Helmut Krebs (ten), Kim Borg (bass), Berlin RIAS Chamber Choir, St. Hedwig Cathedral Choir *(rec Jesus–Christus Church, Berlin, Sept 1953)* — Deutsche Grammophon ("The Originals" series) ▲ 447442-2 [ADD]
Wagner, R.:Der fliegende Holländer, w. Annelies Kupper (sop—Senta), Sieglinde Wagner (mez—Mary), Ernst Haefliger (ten—Steersman), Wolfgang Windgassen (ten—Erik), Josef Metternich (ten—Dutchman), Josef Greindl (bass—Daland), Berlin RIAS Chamber Choir *(rec 1953)* — Deutsche Grammophon 2-▲ 439714-2 (m) [ADD]

G. König (cnd)

Mozart, W.A.:Litaniae Lauretanae, K.195, w. Maria Stader (sop), Berlin RIAS Chamber Choir — Deutsche Grammophon 2-▲ 437383-2
Mozart, W.A.:Missa, K.427, w. Maria Stader (sop), Berlin RIAS Chamber Choir — Deutsche Grammophon 2-▲ 437383-2
Mozart, W.A.:Vesperae de Dominica, w. Maria Stader (sop), Berlin RIAS Chamber Choir — Deutsche Grammophon 2-▲ 437383-2
Mozart, W.A.:Vesperae solennes, w. Maria Stader (sop), Berlin RIAS Chamber Choir — Deutsche Grammophon 2-▲ 437383-2

W. Sawallisch (cnd)

Beethoven, L. van:Leonore 3 — Memories ▲ MEM 4545 [AAD]

Berlin Saxophone Quartet [Detlef Bensmann (sax), Klaus Kreczmarsky (sax), Christof Griese (sax), Friedemann Graef (sax)]

Bach, J.S.:The Art of the Fugue — CPO 2-▲ CPO 999058-2 [DDD]
Berlin Saxophone Quartet — Koch Schwann ▲ SCH 313142 [DDD]
Bumcke, G.:Qts Saxs, Op. 23 — Koch Schwann ▲ CD 310055 [DDD]
Françaix, J.:Petit Quatuor — Koch Schwann ▲ CD 310055 [DDD]
Glazunov, A.:Qt Saxes — Koch Schwann ▲ CD 310055 [DDD]
Moulaert, R.:Andante, Fugue & Finale — Koch Schwann ▲ CD 310055 [DDD]
Moulaert, R.:Andante, Fugue & Finale — Koch Schwann ▲ SCH 313352 [DDD]
Schaeuble, H.:Duke Ellington Medley — Koch Schwann ▲ SCH 313352 [DDD]

Berlin Sinfonia

L. Shambadal (cnd)

Arutiunian, A.:Con Trbn, w. Branimir Slokar (trbn) *(rec Villa Siemens, Berlin, Feb 5–9, 1996)* — Claves ▲ CD 50-9606 [DDD]
Bloch, E.:Sym Trbn, w. Branimir Slokar (trbn) *(rec Villa Siemens, Berlin, Feb 5–9, 1996)* — Claves ▲ CD 50-9606 [DDD]
Grondahl, L.:Con Trbn, w. Branimir Slokar (trbn) *(rec Villa Siemens, Berlin, Feb 5–9, 1996)* — Claves ▲ CD 50-9606 [DDD]
Rota, N.:Con Trbn, w. Branimir Slokar (trbn) *(rec Villa Siemens, Berlin, Feb 5–9, 1996)* — Claves ▲ CD 50-9606 [DDD]

Berlin Soloists

Bach, J.S.:Cants (misc), w. Edith Mathis (sop), Carolyn Watkinson (cta), Eberhard Büchner (ten), Peter Schreier (ten), Siegfried Lorenz (bar), Theo Adam (b-bar), P. Schreier (cnd), Berlin CO — Berlin Classics ▲ BER 9221
Bach, J.S.:Cant 36, w. Edith Mathis (sop), Peter Schreier (ten), Siegfried Lorenz (bar), P. Schreier (cnd), Berlin CO — Berlin Classics ▲ BER 9220
Bach, J.S.:Cant 203, w. Edith Mathis (sop), Peter Schreier (ten), Siegfried Lorenz (bar), P. Schreier (cnd), Berlin CO — Berlin Classics ▲ BER 9220
Bach, J.S.:Cant 205, w. Edith Mathis (sop), Carolyn Watkinson (alt), Julia Hamari (alt), Peter Schreier (ten), Siegfreid Lorenz (bass), P. Schreier (cnd), Berlin CO — Berlin Classics ▲ BER 9224
Bach, J.S.:Cant 206, w. Edith Mathis (sop), Carolyn Watkinson (alt), Peter Schreier (ten), Siegfried Lorenz (bass), P. Schreier (cnd), Berlin CO — Berlin Classics ▲ BER CD 9225
Bach, J.S.:Cant 207, w. Edith Mathis (sop), Carolyn Watkinson (alt), Julia Hamari (alt), Peter Schreier (ten), Siegfreid Lorenz (bass), P. Schreier (cnd), Berlin CO — Berlin Classics ▲ BER 9224
Bach, J.S.:Cant 209, w. Edith Mathis (sop), Peter Schreier (ten), Siegfried Lorenz (bar), P. Schreier (cnd), Berlin CO — Berlin Classics ▲ BER 9220
Bach, J.S.:Cant 215, w. Edith Mathis (sop), Carolyn Watkinson (alt), Peter Schreier (ten), Siegfried Lorenz (bass), P. Schreier (cnd), Berlin CO — Berlin Classics ▲ BER CD 9225
Beethoven, L. van:Music of, w. Sylvia Geszty (sop), Jozsef Reti (ten), Hermann Christian Polster (bass), Koch (cnd), Berlin RSO, Berlin State Orch—Christ on the Mount of Olives (oratorio); Con in E♭ Pno; Irish Songs; Minuets; Canons; Epigrams; Joke Pieces; Incidental & Ballet Music — Berlin Classics 3-▲ BER 9132
Beethoven, L. van:Septet Strs — Teldec ("M Line" series) ▲ 97451-2
Brahms, J.:Qnt Cl, w. K. Leister (cl) — Teldec ▲ 2292-46429-2 [DDD]
Hindemith, P.:Octet Winds & Strs — Teldec ▲ 9031-73400-2
Mozart, W.A.:Qnt Cl, K.581, w. K. Leister (cl) — Teldec ▲ 2292-46429-2 [DDD]
Mozart, W.A.:Qnt Hn, K.407 — Teldec ("M Line" series) ▲ 97451-2
Prokofiev, S.:Ov on Hebrew Themes — Teldec ▲ 73400-2

ORCH. & ENS.

Berlin Soloists (cont.)
Prokofiev, S.:Qnt Ob Teldec ▲ 73400–2
Schütz, H.:Schwannengesang, w. J. Kowalski (alt), W. Marschall (ten), D. Knothe (cnd), Dreseden Capella Sagittariana, Berlin Radio Children's Choir Berlin Classics 2–▲ BER 1071 [DDD]

Berlin Spectrum Ensemble members [Mi-Kyung & P. Sporrong (violins), F. Dodge (cello)]
Helps, R.:Music of—Nocturne for String Quartet CRI ▲ CD 649 [DDD]

Berlin Spectrum Ensemble members [P. Sporrong (vn), B. Dean (va), F. Dodge (vc)]
del Tredici, D.:Trio Vn, Va & Vc *(rec 1987)* CRI ▲ CD 649 [DDD]
Street, T.:Trio Vn *(rec 1986)* CRI ▲ CD 649 [DDD]

Berlin Staatskapelle

A. Apelt (cnd)
Dvořák, A.:Rusalka (sels), w. A. Burmeister (mez), E. Mitzewa (mez), T. Adam (bass–bar) Berlin Classics ("Eterna" series) ▲ BER 2033 [ADD]

R. Heger (cnd)
Schillings, M. von:Glockenlieder, w. P. Anders (ten) [G] *(rec 5/20/43)* Acanta ▲ 43275 (m)
Wagner, R.:Wesendonck Songs, w. T. Lemnitz (sop) [G] *(rec 7/7/44)* Acanta ▲ 43275 (m)

R. Kempe (cnd)
Wagner, R.:Das Rheingold, w. L. Otto (sop), M. Muszely (sop), J. Blatter (mez), R. Stewart (mez), S. Wagner (mez), R. Schock (ten), H. Melchert (ten), F. Frantz (bass), B. Kusche (bass), J. Metternich (bass) *(rec Mar. 1959)* Berlin Classics ("Eterna" series) ▲ BER 2035 [ADD]

B. Klee (cnd)
Mozart, W.A.:Complete Mozart Edition, w. E. Mathis (sop), P. Schreier (ten), W. Hollweg (bar), I. Wixell (bar) Philips 2–▲ 422536–2 [ADD]
Nicolai, O.:Lustigen Weiber, w. H. Donath (sop), E. Mathis (sop), H. Schwarz (cta), P. Schreier (ten), K. Moll (bass), Berlin State Opera Chorus Berlin Classics 2–▲ BER 2115 [ADD]
Nicolai, O.:Lustigen Weiber, w. H. Donath (sop), E. Mathis (sop), H. Schwarz (mez), K. Ludwig (ten), K.–E. Mercker (ten), P. Schreier (ten), C. Dormoy (bar), B. Weikl (bar), K. Moll (bass), S. Vogel (bass), Berlin State Opera Chorus *(rec July 3, 1976)* Berlin Classics ("Eterna" series) ▲ BER 2046–2 [ADD]

F. Konwitschny (cnd)
Wagner, R.:Der fliegende Holländer, w. M. Schech (sop), S. Wagner (mez), G. Frick (ten), F. Wunderlich (ten), R. Schock (ten), D. Fischer–Dieskau (bar) Berlin Classics ("Eterna" series) 2–▲ BER 2097 [ADD]
Wagner, R.:Der fliegende Holländer (sels), w. Marianne Schech (sop), Fritz Wunderlich (ten), Dietrich Fischer–Dieskau (bar), Gottlob Frick (bass) Berlin Classics ▲ BER 9080 [ADD]

A. Rother (cnd)
Wagner, R.:Lohengrin, w. M. Müller (sop), F. Volker (ten), J. Prohaska (bar) [G] *(rec 1942)* Preiser 3–▲ 90043 (m) [AAD]

O. Suitner (cnd)
Brahms, J.:Hungarian Dances Orch Denon ▲ CO 74597 [DDD]
Bruckner, A.:Sym 1 Berlin Classics 2–▲ BER 1163
Bruckner, A.:Sym 4, "Romantic" Berlin Classics ▲ BER 1161
Bruckner, A.:Sym 5 Berlin Classics ▲ BER 1162
Bruckner, A.:Sym 8 Berlin Classics 2–▲ BER 1163
Dessau, P.:Einstein, w. Peter Schreier (ten), Theo Adam (bass), Reiner Suss (bass), Berlin State Opera Chorus Berlin Classics 2–▲ BER CD 9109
Dessau, P.:Leonce & Lena, w. C. Nossek (sop), E. Büchner (bar), R. Süss (bar) Berlin Classics ▲ BER 1074 [ADD]
Pfitzner, H.:Das Käthchen von Heilbronn (sels)—incidental music Berlin Classics ▲ BER 9026 [ADD]
Pfitzner, H.:Palestrina, w. C. Nossek (sop), R. Long (mez), P. Schreier (ten), S. Lorenz (bar), E. Wlaschiha (bass), Berlin State Opera Chorus Berlin Classics ▲ BER 1001
Reger, M.:Eine Ballettsuite Berlin Classics ▲ BER 9123
Reger, M.:Con in Olden Style, w. Heinz Schunk (vn), Karl Suske (vn) Berlin Classics ▲ BER 9123
Reger, M.:Vars & Fugue on a Theme of Beethoven Berlin Classics ▲ BER 9123
Schubert, Franz:Alfonso und Estrella, w. E. Mathis (sop), M. Falewicz (sop), P. Schreier (ten), H. Prey (bar), D. Fischer–Dieskau (bar), T. Adam (b–bar), Berlin Radio Chorus Berlin Classics 3–▲ BER 2156 [ADD]
Schubert, Franz:Sym 3 Denon/PCM Digital ▲ DEN 1253 [DDD]
Schubert, Franz:Sym 4 Denon/PCM Digital ▲ DEN 7759 [DDD]
Schubert, Franz:Sym 6 Denon/PCM Digital ▲ DEN 1253 [DDD]
Schubert, Franz:Sym 9 Denon/PCM Digital ▲ DEN 7371 [DDD]
Schumann, R.:Sym 1 Denon/PCM Digital ▲ DEN 1516 [DDD]
Schumann, R.:Sym 3 Denon/PCM Digital ▲ DEN 1516 [DDD]
Strauss, R.:Songs, w. Theo Adam (bass) Berlin Classics ▲ BER 9215
Strauss, R.:Symphonic Fant Berlin Classics ▲ BER 9026 [ADD]
Wagner, R.:Songs, w. Theo Adam (bass) Berlin Classics ▲ BER 9215
Wolf, H.:Penthesilea Berlin Classics ▲ BER 9026 [ADD]

Berlin State Opera Orch
Beethoven, L. van:Romances Vn, w. J. Wolfsthal (vn)—Op. 50 *(rec ca. 1925 for Polydor)* Pearl ▲ PEA 9387 (m) [AAD]
Opera Arias, w. Ivar Andrésen (bass) [var. cnds] *(rec 1927–29)* Preiser ("Lebendige Vergangenheit" series) ▲ PRE 89028 (m) [AAD]
Opera Arias, w. Franz Völker (ten) [var. cnds] Preiser ("Lebendige Vergangenheit" series) ▲ PRE 89005 (m) [AAD]
Tchaikovsky, P.:Con Vn, w. B. Huberman, W. Steinberg *(rec 1929 for Columbia Records)* The Classical Collector ▲ FDC 2003 (m) [AAD]
Vieuxtemps, H.:Con 4 Vn, w. Vâsa Příhoda (vn) Biddulph ▲ LAB 135
Wieniawski, H.:Con 2 Vn, w. Vâsa Příhoda (vn) Biddulph ▲ LAB 135

J. Barbirolli (cnd)
Wagner, R.:Tristan und Isolde (sels), w. F. Leider (sop), E. Marherr–Wagner (mez), L. Melchior (ten), L. Blech (cnd), A. Coates (cnd), London SO—Act 1 *(Doch nun von Tristan [Leider, Marherr–Wagner])*, Act 2 *(Isolde! Geliebter; O sink hernieder [Leider, Melchior])*, Act 3 *(Mild und leise [Leider]) [G] (rec late 1920s for HMV)* Legato Classics 2–▲ LCD 146–2 (m) [ADD]

D. Barenboim (cnd)
Beethoven, L. van:Sym 9, "Choral Sym", w. A. Marc (sop), I. Vermillion (mez), S. Jerusalem (ten), F. Struckmann (bar), Berlin State Opera Chorus Erato ▲ 94353–2

B. Bartoletti (cnd)
Verdi, G.:Il trovatore, w. R. Kabaivanska (sop), M. Cortez (ten), F. Bonisolli (ten), G. Zancanaro (bar), Berlin State Opera Chorus [I] Acanta 2–▲ CD 43301 [DDD]

L. Blech (cnd)
Beethoven, L. van:Con Vn, Op. 61, w. F. Kreisler (vn) *(rec 1926)* Pearl 2–▲ PEA 9996 [AAD]
Beethoven, L. van:Con Vn, Op. 61, w. F. Kreisler (vn) *(rec 1926)* Biddulph 2–▲ LAB 049 [ADD]
Beethoven, L. van:Con Vn, Op. 61, w. Fritz Kreisler (vn) Grammofono 2000 ▲ GRM 78575
Beethoven, L. van:Con Vn, Op. 61, w. F. Kreisler (vn) *(rec 1926 for HMV)* Music & Arts 2–▲ CD 290 (m) [AAD]
Brahms, J.:Con Vn, w. F. Kreisler (vn) *(rec 1927)* Biddulph 2–▲ LAB 049 [ADD]
Brahms, J.:Con Vn, w. F. Kreisler (vn) Music & Arts 2–▲ CD 290 (m) [AAD]
Brahms, J.:Con Vn, w. F. Kreisler (vn) *(rec 1926)* Pearl 2–▲ PEA 9996 [AAD]
Brahms, J.:Con Vn, w. Fritz Kreisler (vn) Grammofono 2000 ▲ GRM 78575
Liszt, F.:Hungarian Rhaps—No. 14 *(rec 1927–28)* Koch Legacy ▲ 3–7072–2 H1
Mendelssohn, F.:Con in e Vn & Orch, Op. 64, w. F. Kreisler (vn) *(rec 1926)* Pearl 2–▲ PEA 9996 [AAD]
Mendelssohn, F.:Con in e Vn & Orch, Op. 64, w. Fritz Kreisler (vn) Grammofono 2000 ▲ GRM 78575
Mendelssohn, F.:Con in e Vn & Orch, Op. 64, w. F. Kreisler (vn) *(rec 1926)* Music & Arts 2–▲ CD 290 (m) [AAD]
Mendelssohn, F.:Con in e Vn & Orch, Op. 64, w. F. Kreisler (vn) *(rec 1926)* Biddulph 2–▲ LAB 049 [ADD]
Mendelssohn, F.:Con in e Vn & Orch, Op. 64, w. Fritz Kreisler (vn) Enterprise ("Sirio" series) ▲ ENT SO 53009
Smetana, B.:The Moldau *(rec 1928)* Koch Legacy ▲ 3–7072–2 H1

Berlin State Opera Orch (cont.)

L. Blech (cnd) (cont.)
Wagner, R.:Der fliegende Holländer (sels), w. Friedrich Schorr (b–bar)—Die Frist ist um; Wie oft in Meeres *(rec 1929 HMV)* Pearl ▲ PEA 9944 (m) [AAD]
Wagner, R.:Die Meistersinger von Nürnberg (sels), w. E. Marherr–Wagner (mez), R. Hutt (ten), K. Jöken (bar), F. Schorr (b–bar), E. List (bass), L. Schützendorf (sgr), Berlin State Opera Chorus—Act 1:Hilf Gott! Will ich denn Schuster sein?; Das schöne Fest, Johannistag; Act 2:Johannistag! Johannistag!; Hab' ich heut' Singstund'?; Jerum! Jerum!; Act 3:Gleich, Meister! Hier!; Grüss' Gott, mein Evchen...Weilten die Stern' im lieblichen Tanz...O Sachs! Mein Freund!; Sankt Krispin, lobet ihn!; Silentium!...Wach' auf!; Verachtet mir die Meister nicht [G] *(rec Staatsoper unter den Linden, 5/22/28)* Pearl ▲ PEA 9340 (m) [AAD]

F. Busch (cnd)
Strauss, R.:Die ägyptische Helena (sels), w. R. Pauly–Dreesen (sop)—from Act 1 (Helen's awakening; Bei jener Nacht); from Act 2 (Funeral march; Zweite Brautnacht! Zaubernacht!) [G] *(rec 10/2/28 for Parlophone)* Pearl 2–▲ GEMMCDS 9365 (m) [AAD]

P. Dessau (cnd)
Dessau, P.:Puntila, w. Annelies Brumeister (mez—Lsins), Erich Witte (ten—Fredrick), Reiner Süss (bar—Johannes Puntila), Berlin State Chorus *(rec Berlin, May 1988)* Berlin Classics 2–▲ BER 2184 [ADD]

H. Fricke (cnd)
Lortzing, A.:Der Waffenschmied, w. E. Ebert (sop—Marie), G. Prenzlow (mez—Mariens), H. Neukirch (ten—Georg), G. Leib (bar—Ritter), H. Krämer (bass—Hans), Berlin State Opera Chorus Berlin Classics ("Eterna" series) ▲ BER 2036–2 [ADD]
Matthus, S.:Mirabeau, w. Carola Höhn (sop—Marie Antoinette), Carola Fischer (cta—Eveline Le Jay), Peter–Jürgend Schmidt (ten—Ludwig XVI), Jürgen Freier (bar—Honoré–Gabriel de Riqueti), Gerd Wolf (bass—Victor Riqueti), Berlin State Opera Chorus *(rec Berlin, 1989)* Berlin Classics 2–▲ BER 1075 [DDD]

O. Fried (cnd)
Beethoven, L. van:Sym 9, "Choral Sym", w. Bruno Kittel Choir [G] *(rec 1928 for Polydor)* Pearl ▲ PEA 9372 (m) [AAD]
Mahler, G.:Sym 2, w. G. Bindernagel (sop), E. Leisner (cta), Berlin Cathedral Choir *(rec 1923 for Polydor)* Pearl 2–▲ PEAS 9929 (m) [AAD]

W. Furtwängler (cnd)
Wagner, R.:Tannhäuser (ov) *(rec 1940)* Grammofono 2000 ▲ GRM 78515 [ADD]
Wagner, R.:Tristan und Isolde (acts 2 & 3), w. E. Schlüter (sop), M. Klose (cta), L. Suthaus (ten), J. Prohaska (ten), G. Frick (bass), Berlin State Opera Chorus [G] *(rec live, Berlin, 10/3/47)* Arkadia 2–▲ 358 [ADD]

L. Gardelli (cnd)
Verdi, G.:La traviata, w. M. Freni (sop), F. Bonisolli (ten), S. Bruscantini (bar), Berlin State Opera Chorus [I] Acanta 2–▲ CD 41644 [DDD]

V. Gui (cnd)
Cherubini, L.:Médée (sels), w. I. Borkh (sop—Medea), L. Suthaus (ten—Giasone), Berlin State Opera Chorus—3 soprano arias & 3 duets *(rec live, Berlin 1958)* Melodram 2–▲ CDM 27087 [ADD]

R. Heger (cnd)
Verdi, G.:Rigoletto, w. E. Berger (sop), R. Jacobs (alt), H. Roswaenge (ten), H. Schlusnus (bass), J. Greindl (bass), Berlin State Opera Chorus [G] *(rec 11/20–22/44)* Preiser 2–▲ 90036 (m) [AAD]

P.V. Kempen (cnd)
Dvořák, A.:Con Vn, w. Váša Příhoda (vn) *(rec live, Berlin, 1943)* Arkadia ▲ 623 [ADD]

E. Kleiber (cnd)
Erich Kleiber Conducts Vol. 2, w. Berlin PO *(rec 1928–36)* Preiser ▲ PRE CD 90287
Great Recordings, w. Berlin PO, Czech PO, Mediaeval Ensemble Preiser ▲ PRE 90229 [AAD]
Mozart, W.A.:Sym 39 *(rec 1927)* Koch Legacy ▲ 370112 (m) [DDD] ■ 370114 (m)

O. Klemperer (cnd)
Auber, D.–F.:Fra Diavolo (ov) *(rec 1926–31)* Symposium ▲ SYM 1042 (m)
Auber, D.–F.:Fra Diavolo (ov) *(rec 1929)* Iron Needle ▲ IN 1339 (m) [ADD]
Beethoven, L. van:Coriolan Ov *(rec 1926)* Iron Needle ▲ IN 1339 (m) [ADD]
Beethoven, L. van:Coriolan Ov *(rec 1926–31)* Symposium ▲ SYM 1042 (m)
Brahms, J.:Sym 1 *(rec Feb. 1928)* Koch Legacy ▲ 3–7053–2
Debussy, C.:Nocturnes, w. *(chorus unknown) (rec 1926–31)* Symposium ▲ SYM 1042 (m)
Debussy, C.:Nocturnes—Nuages & Fêtes *(rec 1926)* Iron Needle ▲ IN 1339 (m) [ADD]
Offenbach, J.:Le Belle Hélène (ov) *(rec 1929)* Iron Needle ▲ IN 1339 (m) [ADD]
Offenbach, J.:Le Belle Hélène (ov) *(rec 1926–31)* Symposium ▲ SYM 1042 (m)
Ravel, M.:Alborada del gracioso *(rec 1926)* Iron Needle ▲ IN 1339 (m) [ADD]
Ravel, M.:Alborada del gracioso *(rec 1926–31)* Symposium ▲ SYM 1042 (m)
Strauss, R.:Salome (dance) *(rec 5/25/28)* Koch Legacy ▲ 3–7053–2
Strauss, R.:Till Eulenspiegels lustige Streiche *(rec June 1929)* Koch Legacy ▲ 3–7053–2
Wagner, R.:Siegfried Idyll *(rec 1926–27)* Iron Needle ▲ IN 1339 (m) [ADD]
Wagner, R.:Siegfried Idyll *(rec 1926–31)* Symposium ▲ SYM 1042 (m)
Weill, K.:Kleine Dreigroschenmusik—Moritat von Mackie Messer; Ballade; Tango–Ballade; Kanonen–Song *(rec 1931)* Mastersound ▲ DFCD1–110 (m) [ADD]
Weill, K.:Kleine Dreigroschenmusik—Moritat von Mackie Messer; Ballade; Tango–Ballade; Kanonen–Lied *(rec 1931)* Koch Legacy ▲ 3–7053–2
Weill, K.:Kleine Dreigroschenmusik *(rec 1926–31)* Symposium ▲ SYM 1042 (m)

H. Knappertsbusch (cnd)
Mozart, W.A.:Sym 39 *(rec 1929)* Preiser ▲ PRE 90951 [ADD]

F. Konwitschny (cnd)
Wagner, R.:Tannhäuser, w. E. Grümmer (sop), M. Schech (sop), H. Hopf (ten), F. Wunderlich (ten), D. Fischer–Dieskau (bar), G. Frick (bass), Berlin State Opera Chorus [G] EMI Classics ("Studio" series) 3–▲ CDMC 63214 [ADD]

H. Löwlein (cnd)
Puccini, G.:Tosca (sels), w. G. Behms (sop—Tosca), *(other soloists unknown)*—6 arias [G] *(rec live, Berlin, 3/3/57)* Preiser ▲ 90103 (m) [ADD]

P. Mascagni (cnd)
Mascagni, P.:L'amico Fritz (sels)—Intermezzo *(rec 1927)* VAI Audio ▲ VAIA 1113 [ADD]
Mascagni, P.:Cavalleria rusticana (sels), w. José Riavez (ten)—Prelude; O Lola, bianca come fior... *(rec 1927)* VAI Audio ▲ VAIA 1113 [ADD]
Mascagni, P.:Guglielmo Ratcliff (sels)—Ratcliff's Dream, Act III *(rec 1927)* VAI Audio ▲ VAIA 1113 [ADD]
Mascagni, P.:Iris (sels)—Intro & Inno al sole [arr. for orch only]; Danza delle Guèchas *(rec 1927)* VAI Audio ▲ VAIA 1113 [ADD]
Mascagni, P.:I Rantzau (sels)—Prelude *(rec 1927)* VAI Audio ▲ VAIA 1113 [ADD]
Mascagni, P.:Visione lirica *(rec 1927)* VAI Audio ▲ VAIA 1113 [ADD]
Rossini, G.:Guillaume Tell (ov) *(rec 1927)* VAI Audio ▲ VAIA 1113 [ADD]

S. Meyrowitz (cnd)
Mahler, G.:Songs, w. S. Charles–Cahier (sgr)—Urlicht (from Knaben Wunderhorn) & Ich bin der Welt (from Rückert–Lieder) [G] *(rec 1930 for Ultraphon)* Pearl 2–▲ PEAS 9929 (m) [AAD]

K. Muck (cnd)
Wagner, R.:Ovs, Preludes & Orch Sels—Die Meistersinger [Prelude to Act 1]; Siegfried's Rheinfahrt; Trauermusik [both from Götterdämmerung]; Parsifal [Prelude to Act 1]; Tristan und Isolde [Prelude to Act 1]; Der Fliegende Holländer Ov; Tannhäuser Ov; Lohengrin [Prelude to Act 3] APR ▲ APR 5521 [ADD]
Wagner, R.:Ovs, Preludes & Orch Sels—Der fliegende Holländer:Ov.; Tristan und Isolde:Prelude Act 1; Götterdammerung:Rhine Journey & Funeral Music; Parsifal:Preludes to Acts 1 & 3; Die Meistersinger:Ov. Centaur ▲ CRC 2142 [ADD]

H. Pfitzner (cnd)
Beethoven, L. van:Sym 6, "Pastorale" *(rec ca.1929)* InSync ■ C 4146
Beethoven, L. van:Sym 6, "Pastorale" *(rec 1929–33)* Preiser ▲ PRE 90221 [ADD]
Pfitzner, H.:Duo Vn, w. M. Strub (vn), L. Hoelscher (vc) Preiser ▲ 90029 (m) [AAD]

▲ = CD ◆ = Enhanced CD Δ = MD ■ = Cassette Tape □ = DCC

Berlin State Opera Orch (cont.)

J. Prüwer (cnd)
Rosette Anday, w. Rosette Anday (cta), Vienna State Opera Orch [cnd:Carl Alwin], London SO [cnd:Robert Heger] Preiser ("Lebendige Vergangenheit" series) ▲ PRE 89046 (m) [AAD]

H. Rosbaud (cnd)
Beethoven, L. van:Con 1 Pno, w. Walter Gieseking (pno) *(rec 1930's)* APR ▲ APR 5511
Beethoven, L. van:Con 1 Pno, w. W. Gieseking (pno) *(rec Berlin 8/28/37)* The Classical Collector ▲ FDC 2008 [AAD]
Grieg, E.:Con Pno, Op. 16, w. Walter Gieseking (pno) *(rec Berlin, Apr 28–Oct 13, 1937)* APR ▲ APR 5513 [ADD]
Mozart, W.A.:Con 9 Pno, w. Walter Gieseking (pno) *(rec Berlin, Sept 29, 1936)* Iron Needle ▲ IN 1316 [ADD]
Mozart, W.A.:Con 9 Pno, w. W. Gieseking (pno) *(rec Berlin, Sept. 29, 1936)* APR ▲ APR 5511 [ADD]

A. Rother (cnd)
Wagner, R.:Rienzi, der Letzte der Tribunen (sels), w. Hilde Scheppan (sop), Margarete Klose (cta), Max Lorenz (ten), Jaro Prohaska (bar), Berlin State Opera Chorus *(rec 1941)* Preiser ▲ PRE 90223 [ADD]

Rother, Löwlein (cnd)
Martha Mödl Sings, w. Martha Mödl (sop) *(rec 1951–62)* Preiser ▲ PRE 90136 (m) [AAD]

M. von Schillings (cnd)
Wagner, R.:Götterdämmerung (rhine journey) *(rec 1927 for Polydor)* Preiser ▲ 90080 (m) [ADD]
Wagner, R.:Lohengrin (preludes)—Act 1 Prelude *(rec 1927 for Polydor)* Preiser ▲ 90080 (m) [ADD]
Wagner, R.:Parsifal (orch sels)—Act 1 Prelude, Flower Maidens Scene, Good Friday Music & Finale *(rec 1927 for Polydor)* Preiser ▲ 90080 (m) [ADD]
Wagner, R.:Siegfried (waldweben) *(rec 1927 for Polydor)* Preiser ▲ 90080 (m) [ADD]

C. Schmalstich (cnd)
Mozart, W.A.:Zauberflöte (sels), w. Marcel Wittrisch (ten), Alexander Kipnis (b), Maria Galvany (sop), Eide Norena (sop)—Dies Bildnis (Act 1); O Isis und Osiris; Der Hölle Rache; Ach, ich fühl's *(rec 1905–1944)* Minerva ▲ MN A14 [ADD]

J. Schüler (cnd)
Flotow, F. von:Martha, w. E. Berger (sop), P. Anders (ten), E. Fuchs (bar), J. Greindl (bass) *(rec 1944)* Berlin Classics 2–▲ BER 2163 [ADD]

B. Seidler-Winkler (cnd)
Opera Arias, w. Helge Roswaenge (ten) *rec 1936–1942 for HMV)* Preiser ("Lebendige Vergangenheit" series) ▲ PRE 89018 (m) [AAD]

K. Singer (cnd)
Brahms, J.:Alto Rhap, w. S. Onegin (mez), Berlin Doctors' Choir [G] *(rec 1929 from HMV 78 rpm discs)* Preiser ("Lebendige Vergangenheit" series) ▲ 89027 (m) [AAD]

H. Stein (cnd)
Leoncavallo, R.:Pagliacci, w. Melitta Muszely (sop), Rudolf Schock (ten), Josef Metternich (bar) *(rec 1959)* Berlin Classics ▲ BER 9102 [ADD]

W. Steinberg (cnd)
Tchaikovsky, P.:Con Vn, w. B. Huberman (vn) *(rec 8/16/29)* InSync ■ C 4166 (CrO2)
Tchaikovsky, P.:Con Vn, w. B. Huberman (vn) *(rec 1929)* Pearl ▲ GEMMCD 9332 (m) [AAD]

R. Strauss (cnd)
Beethoven, L. van:Sym 5 *(rec 1928)* Koch Legacy ▲ 3–7115–2 H1
Beethoven, L. van:Sym 5 *(rec 1928)* InSync ■ C 4128 (m)
Beethoven, L. van:Sym 7 *(rec 1926)* Koch Legacy ▲ 3–7115–2 H1
Mozart, W.A.:Ovs—Die Zauberflöte *(rec 1928 for Polydor)* Koch Legacy ▲ 371192
Mozart, W.A.:Sym 39 *(rec 1926)* Koch Legacy ▲ 370762
Mozart, W.A.:Sym 40 *(rec 1927)* Koch Legacy ▲ 370762
Mozart, W.A.:Sym 40 *(rec 1928 for Polydor)* Koch Legacy ▲ 371192
Mozart, W.A.:Sym 41 *(rec 1926)* Koch Legacy ▲ 370762
Strauss, R.:Der Bürger als Edelmann (suite) *(rec 1930 for Polydor)* Pearl ▲ PEA 9366 (m) [AAD]
Strauss, R.:Don Juan *(rec 1929 for Polydor)* Pearl ▲ PEA 9366 (m) [AAD]
Strauss, R.:Till Eulenspiegels lustige Streiche *(rec 1929 for Polydor)* Pearl ▲ PEA 9366 (m) [AAD]

O. Suitner (cnd)
Rossini, G.:Il barbiere di Siviglia, w. Ruth-Margaret Pütz (sop), Annelies Burmeister (mez), Peter Schreier (ten), Hermann Prey (bar), Franz Crass (bass), Fritz Ollendorff (bass) Berlin Classics 2–▲ BER 9021 [ADD]

B. Walter (cnd)
Mozart, W.A.:Sym 40 *(rec Jan 1929)* Iron Needle ▲ 1317 (m) [ADD]
Wagner, R.:Die Walküre (act 2), w. M. Fuchs (sop), E. Flesch (sop), L. Lehmann (sop), M. Klose (cta), L. Melchior (ten), H. Hotter (b-bar), A. Jerger (b-bar), E. List (bass) [G] *(rec 9/38 & 6/22/35)* EMI Classics ("References" series) ▲ CDH 64255
Wagner, R.:Die Walküre (act 2), w. M. Fuchs (sop), E. Flesch (sop), L. Lehmann (sop), M. Klose (cta), L. Melchior (ten), H. Hotter (b-bar), A. Jerger (b-bar), E. List (bass) [G] *(rec 9/38 & 6/22/35)* Danacord 2–▲ DACOCD 317/18 (m)

Weigert, Melichar (cnd)
Heinrich Sclusnus Liederalbum, w. Heinrich Schlusnus (bar), Franz Rupp (pno/org), *(rec between 1930–34)* Preiser 2–▲ PRE 89205 [ADD]

F. Weissmann (cnd)
Mozart, W.A.:Con 5 Vn, w. J. Wolfsthal (vn) *(rec 1928 for Parlophone)* Pearl ▲ PEA 9387 (m) [AAD]
Opera Arias & Duets, w. Meta Seinemeyer (sop) *(rec 1926–29 for Parlophon 7)* Preiser ("Lebendige Vergangenheit" series) ▲ PRE 89029 (m) [AAD]

Berlin State Opera Orch members

M. von Schillings (cnd)
Wagner, R.:Götterdämmerung (sels) *(rec Berlin, 1927–29)* Preiser ▲ PRE 90267

Berlin State Orch

S. Kurz (cnd)
Operatic Arias, w. Reiner Goldberg (ten) Capriccio ▲ 10056 [DDD]

H. Bongartz (cnd)
Beethoven, L. van:Egmont (incidental music), w. Elisabeth Breul (sop), Horst Schulze (spkr) Berlin Classics ▲ BER 9106
Beethoven, L. van:Egmont (ov) Berlin Classics ▲ BER 9106

W. Furtwängler (cnd)
Wagner, R.:Parsifal (prelude)—to Act I *(rec 1940)* Grammofono 2000 ▲ GRM 78515 [ADD]

G. Herbig (cnd)
Dessau, P.:Orchestermusik 4 Berlin Classics ▲ BER 2182 [ADD]

P. Van Kempen (cnd)
Brahms, J.:Con Vn, w. Gioconda de Vito (vn) A Classical Record ▲ ACR38–2
Dvořák, A.:Con Vn, w. Gioconda de Vito (vn) A Classical Record ▲ ACR38–2
Dvořák, A.:Con Vn, w. V. Prihoda (vn) *(rec live, Berlin 1937)* Melodram ▲ CDM 18037 [ADD]

H. Koch (cnd)
Beethoven, L. van:Music of, w. Sylvia Geszty (sop), Jozsef Reti (ten), Hermann Christian Polster (bass), Berlin RSO, Berlin Soloists—Christ on the Mount of Olives (oratorio); Con in E♭ Pno; Irish Songs; Minuets; Canons; Epigrams; Joke Pieces; Incidental & Ballet Music Berlin Classics 3–▲ BER 9132

K. Masur (cnd)
Beethoven, L. van:Music of, Berlin CO, Leipzig Gewandhaus Orch, Suske Trio—Con for Piano in D, Op. 61; Son for Piano, Op. 14/1; Ländler; Minuets; Arias; plus others Berlin Classics 3–▲ BER 9131

C. Schuricht (cnd)
Beethoven, L. van:Coriolan Ov *(rec 1937–41)* LYS ▲ LYS 130
Beethoven, L. van:Sym 3, "Eroica" *(rec 1937–41)* LYS ▲ LYS 130

Berlin State Orch members

M. von Schillings (cnd)
Wagner, R.:Die Meistersinger von Nürnberg (ov) *(rec Berlin, 1927–29)* Preiser ▲ PRE 90267
Wagner, R.:Tannhäuser (ov) *(rec Berlin, 1927–29)* Preiser ▲ PRE 90267
Wagner, R.:Tristan und Isolde (sels) *(rec Berlin, 1927–29)* Preiser ▲ PRE 90267

Berlin State SO

K. Muck (cnd)
Wagner, R.:Siegfried Idyll Opal ▲ CDS 9843 (m) [AAD]

Berlin String Quintet [D. Grevesmühl (vn), J. Pastor (vn), H. Sprenger (va), R. Kosubek (vc), M. Hussla (db)]
Mendelssohn, F.:Qnts Strs, Opp. 18 & 87 MD + G ▲ MDG 6030533
Mozart, W.A.:Qnt Strs, K.406 Regis Tro ▲ RTAC 004 [DDD]
Mozart, W.A.:Qnt Strs, K.516 Regis Tro ▲ RTAC 004 [DDD]

Berlin SO

S. Adler (cnd)
Gershwin, G.:Con Pno, w. E. List (pno) *(rec 1971)* Vox Box 2–▲ CDX 5069 [ADD]

S. Adler, I. Buketoff (cnd)
Gottschalk, L.M.:Music of, w. Trinidad Paniagua (sop), José Alberto Esteves (ten), Pablo Garcia (bar), Eugene List (pno), Cary Lewis (pno), Brady Millican (pno), Vienna State Opera Orch—Grande Tarantelle for Piano & Orchestra, Op. 67; Symphony No. 1, "La nuit des tropiques"; Symphony No. 2, "A Montevideo"; The Union (concert paraphrase on American national airs) for Piano & Orchestra, Op. 48; Variations on the Portuguese National Hymn for Piano & Orchestra, Op. 91; Grande fantaisie triomphale sur l'hymne national brésilien for Piano & Orchestra, Op. 69; Marche solennelle for Orchestra; Marcha triunfal y final de opera for Orchestra; Escenas campestres (opera in one act); Five Pieces for Piano Duet [Radieuse, Op. 72; Ses yeux, Op. 66; La Gallina, Op. 53; Ojos criollos, Op. 37; Pasquinade, Op. 59] Vox Box 2–▲ CDX 5009 [ADD]

C. A. Bunte (cnd)
Busoni, F.:Concertino Cl, w. Walter Triebskorn (cl) Vox Box 2–▲ CDX 5133
Busoni, F.:Divert Fl, w. Herman Klemeyer (fl) Vox Box 2–▲ CDX 5133
Busoni, F.:Konzertstück Pno, w. Frank Glazer (pno) Vox Box 2–▲ CDX 5133
Busoni, F.:Rondo arlecchinesco Vox Box 2–▲ CDX 5133
Verdi, G.:Aida (sels)—Prelude to Act I Intercord ▲ INT 892.923 [AAD]

J. Faerber (cnd)
Sinding, C.:Con Pno, w. R. Keller (pno) *(rec 1978)* Vox Box 2–▲ CDX 5068 [ADD]
Stavenhagen, B.:Con Pno, Op. 4, w. R. Keller (pno) *(rec 1978)* Vox Box 2–▲ CDX 5067 [ADD]

C. P. Flor (cnd)
Albert, E. d':Con Vc, w. Jürnjakob Timm (vc) Berlin Classics ▲ BER 9179
Beethoven, L. van:Cons Pno (comp), w. P. Rösel (pno) Berlin Classics 3–▲ BER 2136 [DDD]
Beethoven, L. van:Rondo Pno, WoO 6, w. P. Rösel (pno) Berlin Classics 3–▲ BER 2136 [DDD]
Cherubini, L.:Requiem Mass in c, w. Berlin Radio Chorus RCA Red Seal ▲ 60059–2–RC [DDD]
Glinka, M.:Russlan & Ludmilla (ov) RCA Red Seal ▲ 60119–2–RC [DDD]
Liszt, F.:Les Préludes RCA Red Seal ▲ 60119–2–RC [DDD]
Poulenc, F.:Con Org, w. J. Dalitz (org) Berlin Classics ▲ BER 2138 [DDD]
Saint-Saëns, C.:Sym 3, w. J. Dalitz (org) Berlin Classics ▲ BER 2138 [DDD]
Sibelius, J.:Finlandia RCA Red Seal ▲ 60119–2–RC [DDD]
Smetana, B.:The Moldau RCA Red Seal ▲ 60119–2–RC [DDD]
Tchaikovsky, P.:Ov 1812 RCA Red Seal ▲ 60119–2–RC [DDD]
Webern, A.:Songs, w. Roswitha Trexler (sop), Rolf-Dieter Arens (pno) Berlin Classics ▲ BER 9049 [DDD]

K. Forster (cnd)
Bach, J.S.:Cant 208, "Hunting Cant", w. Erika Köth (sop), Dietrich Fischer-Dieskau (bar), St. Hedwig's Cathedral Choir EMI Classics ("Baroque" series) ▲ CDK 65729

L. Foss (cnd)
Englund, S.E.:Con Cl, w. Richard Stoltzman (cl) *(rec Jesus-Christus-Kirche, Berlin, May 10–14, 1993)* RCA Red Seal ▲ 09026–61902–2 [DDD]
Foss, L.:Con Cl, w. Richard Stoltzman (cl) *(rec Jesus-Christus-Kirche, Berlin, May 10–14, 1993)* RCA Red Seal ▲ 09026–61902–2 [DDD]
McKinley, W.T.:Con 2 Cl, w. Richard Stoltzman (cl) *(rec Jesus-Christus-Kirche, Berlin, May 10–14, 1993)* RCA Red Seal ▲ 09026–61902–2 [DDD]

A. Grüber (cnd)
Hindemith, P.:Das Nusch-Nuschi—Dance Suite *(rec 1971)* Allegretto ▲ ACD 8191
Lutoslawski, W.:Dance Preludes Cl, Hp, Pno, Perc & Strs, w. Josef Masseli (cl) Vox Box 2–▲ CDX 5133
Lutoslawski, W.:Mala suita Vox Box 2–▲ CDX 5133
Lutoslawski, W.:Ov for Str Orch Vox Box 2–▲ CDX 5133

G. Herbig (cnd)
Albert, E. d':Con 2 Pno, w. Siegfried Stöckigt (pno) Berlin Classics ▲ BER 9179
Hartmann, K.A.:Sym 5, "Symphonie concertante" Berlin Classics ▲ BER 9048 [DDD]
Hartmann, K.A.:Sym 6 Berlin Classics ▲ BER 9048 [DDD]
Lutoslawski, W.:Funeral Music Berlin Classics ▲ BER CD 9166
Lutoslawski, W.:Livre Berlin Classics ▲ BER CD 9166
Schoenberg, A.:Pieces Orch, Op. 16 Berlin Classics ▲ BER CD 9166
Schoenberg, A.:Vars Orch, Op. 31 Berlin Classics ▲ BER CD 9166

L. Herbig (cnd)
Bruch, M.:Con for 2 Pnos, w. M. Borkofcky (pno), D. Hogan (pno) *(rec 1977)* Allegretto ▲ ACD 8169 [ADD] ■ ACS 8169

I. Jackson (cnd)
Herrmann, B.:Sinfonietta Str Orch Koch International Classics ▲ KIC 7152–2 [DDD]
Rózsa, M.:Andante Koch International Classics ▲ KIC 7152–2 [DDD]
Rózsa, M.:Con Str Orch Koch International Classics ▲ KIC 7152–2 [DDD]
Still, W.G.:Danzas de Panama Koch International Classics ▲ KIC 7154 [DDD]
Still, W.G.:La Guiablesse Koch International Classics ▲ KIC 7154 [DDD]
Waxman, F.:Sinfonietta Timp Koch International Classics ▲ KIC 7152–2 [DDD]

H. von Karajan (cnd)
Grieg, E.:Con Pno, Op. 16, w. K. Zimerman (pno) *(rec Sept. 1981)* Deutsche Grammophon ▲ 439015–2 [DDD]
Schumann, R.:Con Pno, w. K. Zimerman (pno) *(rec Sept. 1981)* Deutsche Grammophon ▲ 439015–2 [DDD]

S. Köhler (cnd)
Szymanowski, K.:Con 2 Vn, w. Fredell Lack (vn) Vox Box 2–▲ CDX 5133

J. Levine (cnd)
Haydn, J.:Mass 10, "Kriegsmesse", "Paukenmesse", w. Sylvia McNair (sop), Delores Ziegler (mez), Hans-Peter Blochwitz (ten), Andreas Schmidt (bar), Berlin RIAS Chamber Choir Deutsche Grammophon ▲ 435853–2
Mozart, W.A.:Missa, K.317, w. S. McNair (sop), D. Ziegler (mez), H.P. Blochwitz (ten), A. Schmidt (bar), Berlin RIAS Chamber Choir Deutsche Grammophon ▲ 435853–2
Schumann, R.:Manfred Ov Deutsche Grammophon ▲ 435856–2
Schumann, R.:Sym 1 Deutsche Grammophon ▲ 435856–2

E. Marturet (cnd)
Grieg, E.:Songs, w. Kari Lövaas (sop) Verdi Classics ▲ AU 32 116
Sibelius, J.:Songs, w. Kari Lövaas (sop) Verdi Classics ▲ AU 32 116
Strauss, R.:Songs, w. Kari Lövaas (sop) Verdi Classics ▲ AU 32 116

G. Oskamp (cnd)
Mozart, W.A.:Con 20 Pno, w. Roberte Mamou (pno) Verdi Classics ▲ AU 32 147
Mozart, W.A.:Con 24 Pno, w. Roberte Mamou (pno) Verdi Classics ▲ AU 32 147
Schumann, C.:Con Pno, w. Shoko Sugitani (pno) Verdi Classics ▲ AU 32 107
Schumann, R.:Con Pno, w. Shoko Sugitani (pno) Verdi Classics ▲ AU 32 107

D. Robertson (cnd)
Silvestrov, V.:Postludium, w. Alexei Lubimov (pno) *(rec Jesus-Christus-Kirche, Berlin, Jan 25–30, 1995)* Sony Classical ▲ SK 66825 [DDD]
Silvestrov, V.:Sym 5 *(rec Jesus-Christus-Kirche, Berlin, Jan 25–30, 1995)* Sony Classical ▲ SK 66825 [DDD]

K. Sanderling (cnd)
Beethoven, L. van:Sym 5 *(rec live 1984)* Capriccio ▲ 10018 [DDD]

Berlin SO (cont.)
K. Sanderling (cnd) (cont.)
Beethoven, L. van:Sym 5 — Laserlight ▲ 15 825 [DDD]
Shostakovich, D.:From Jewish Folk Poetry, w. Annelies Burmeister (mez), Maria Croonen (sgr), Peter Schreier (ten) — Berlin Classics ▲ BER 9016 [ADD]
Shostakovich, D.:Sym 1 — Berlin Classics ▲ BER 2181 [ADD]
Shostakovich, D.:Sym 5 — Berlin Classics ("Eterna" series) ▲ BER 2063 [ADD]
Shostakovich, D.:Sym 6 — Berlin Classics ▲ BER 2181 [ADD]
Shostakovich, D.:Sym 8 — Berlin Classics ("Eterna" series) ▲ BER 2064 [ADD]
Sibelius, J.:Finlandia — Berlin Classics ("Eterna" series) 4–▲ BER 2059 [ADD]
Sibelius, J.:Finlandia — Berlin Classics ▲ BER 9267
Sibelius, J.:Night Ride & Sunrise — Berlin Classics ("Eterna" series) 4–▲ BER 2059 [ADD]
Sibelius, J.:En Saga — Berlin Classics ("Eterna" series) 4–▲ BER 2059 [DDD]
Sibelius, J.:En Saga — Berlin Classics ▲ BER 9267
Sibelius, J.:Syms (comp) — Berlin Classics ("Eterna" series) 4–▲ BER 2059 [DDD]
Sibelius, J.:Sym 1 — Berlin Classics ▲ BER 9267
Sibelius, J.:Sym 2 — Berlin Classics ▲ BER 9273
Sibelius, J.:Sym 3 — Berlin Classics ▲ BER 9273
Sibelius, J.:Sym 4 — Berlin Classics ▲ BER CD 9274
Sibelius, J.:Sym 5 — Berlin Classics ▲ BER CD 9274
Sibelius, J.:Sym 6 — Berlin Classics ▲ BER 9281
Sibelius, J.:Sym 7 — Berlin Classics ▲ BER 9281
Tchaikovsky, P.:Sym 4 — Denon/PCM Digital ▲ DEN 8083 [DDD]
Tchaikovsky, P.:Sym 5 — Denon/PCM Digital ▲ DEN 8084 [DDD]
Tchaikovsky, P.:Sym 6 — Denon/PCM Digital ▲ DEN 8085 [DDD]
V. Schmidt-Gertenbach (cnd)
Chopin, F.:Allegro de concert, w. M. Ponti (pno) *(rec 1978)* — Vox Box 2–▲ CDX 5064 [ADD]
Litolff, H.C.:Con Symphonique 3, w. M. Ponti (pno) *(rec 1978)* — Vox Box 2–▲ CDX 5065 [ADD]
Mendelssohn, F.:Capriccio brillante, w. M. Ponti (pno) *(rec 1978)* — Vox Box 2–▲ CDX 5065 [ADD]
Rheinberger, J.:Con Pno, w. M. Ponti (pno) *(rec 1978)* — Vox Box 2–▲ CDX 5065 [ADD]
M. Schønwandt (cnd)
Berlioz, H.:Rêverie et caprice, w. J. Wagner (vn), Ernst Senff Chorus, Berlin Radio Choir — Kontrapunkt 2–▲ KPT 32143 [DDD]
Ravel, M.:Daphins et Chloé, w. Berlin Radio Chorus — Kontrapunkt ▲ KPT 32152 [DDD]
Schoenberg, A.:Con Vn, w. Michael Erxleben (vn) — Berlin Classics ▲ BER 1119 [DDD]
Stravinsky, I.:Con Vn, w. Michael Erxleben (vn) — Berlin Classics ▲ BER 1119 [DDD]
R. Stolz (cnd)
The Best of Johann Strauss, Jr., w. Vienna SO — Victrola ("Victrola Best of" series) ▲ 60774-2-RV [ADD] ■ 60774-4-RV
J. Velazco (cnd)
Gomezanda, A.:Danzas Mexicanas (6), w. Alan Marks (pno) — Koch Schwann ▲ SCH 310232
Gomezanda, A.:Fant Mexicana, w. Alan Marks (pno) — Koch Schwann ▲ SCH 310232
Gomezanda, A.:Logos, w. Wolfgang Boettcher (vc), Alan Marks (pno) — Koch Schwann ▲ SCH 310232
Gomezanda, A.:Xiuhtzitzquilo — Koch Schwann ▲ SCH 310232
P. Wohlert (cnd)
Tchaikovsky, P.:Ballet Suites — Laserlight ♦ 90022 [DDD]
Tchaikovsky, P.:The Nutcracker (sels) — LaserLight ▲ 15146
H. Zanotelli (cnd)
Albert, E. d':Tiefland, w. I. Strauss, Schock, Feldhoff, Sardi — Eurodisc 2–▲ 7797-2-RG [ADD]
Berlin SO members
A. Grüber (cnd)
Hindemith, P.:Hin und zurück, w. Barbara Miller (sop), Claus Bock (ten), Ulrich Schaible (bar), Helmut Kühnle (bass) *(rec 1971)* — Allegretto ▲ ACD 8191
Berlin Trombone Quintet
Berlin Trombone Quintet Vol 1 — Koch Schwann ▲ SCH 310089 [DDD]
Berlin Trombone Quintet Vol. 2:Music For Festive Occasions — Koch Schwann ▲ SCH 312062 [DDD]
The Trombone, w. Armin Rosin (trbn), Michel Becquet (trbn), Berlin RIAS Sinfonietta [cnd:Ernö Sebestyen], Lorraine PO [cnd:Jacques Houtmann], Southwest German CO [cnd:Vladislav Czernedki] — Koch Schwann ▲ SCH 313342 [DDD]
Die Berliner
Play Dance Music & Evergreens from the Salons der guten alten Zeit — Acanta ▲ 43802
Play Salon Music — Orfeo ▲ C 126901 A [DDD]
Berliner Conzert
Schenck, J.:L'Echo du Danube—Sonata Nos. 1,2,3 & 5 — MD + G ▲ L 3398 [DDD]
Bern Ad Hoc Ensemble
Moeschinger, A.:Cant, w. F. Lang (ten), N. Tüller (bass)—Prelude & Dialogue [F] — Grammont ▲ CTSP 1-2 [ADD]
Bern Camerata
Bach, C.P.E.:Sinfs, H.657–662, "Hamburg Syms" — Denon ▲ CO 73326 [DDD]
T. Füri (cnd)
Albinoni, T.:Adagio Org — Novalis ▲ 150004
Bach, J.S.:Brandenburg Con 3 — Novalis ▲ 150004
Baroque Festival — Novalis ▲ 150004-2 [DDD]
Geminiani, F.:Concerti grossi (misc)—Op. 3/1–6 — Novalis ▲ 150083 [DDD]
Manfredini, F.:Con grosso, Op. 3/12 — Novalis ▲ 150004
Pachelbel, J.:Canon — Novalis ▲ 150004
Purcell, H.:Pavane & Chaconne — Novalis ▲ 150004
Tartini, G.:Cons Vn (misc)— in d, D. 45; in e, D.56; in g, D.86 *(rec Dec. 1992)* — Novalis ▲ 150092 [DDD]
Veress, S.:Danze Transilvane — Grammont ▲ CTSP 16-2 [ADD]
Vivaldi, A.:Cons Orch—RV.109 — Novalis ▲ 150004
H. Holliger (cnd)
Veress, S.:Con Cl, w. T. Friedli (cl) — Grammont ▲ CTSP 16-2 [ADD]
Veress, S.:Musica concertante — ECM New Series ▲ 78118-21555-2 [DDD]
Veress, S.:Passacaglia concertante, w. Heinz Holliger (ob) — ECM New Series ▲ 78118-21555-2 [DDD]
A. van Wijnkoop (cnd)
Lehmann, H.U.:Dis-Cantus I, w. H. Holliger (ob) *(rec Nov. 1, 1972)* — Grammont ▲ CTS P 4-2
Bern Camerata String Ensemble
H. Holliger (cnd)
Yun, I.:Gong-Hu, w. Ursula Holliger (hp) *(rec Bremen Radio Studio, June 1985)* — Camerata ▲ 30CM 109 [AAD]
Bern Chamber Ensemble
Daetwyler, J.:Capriccio, Andante et Humoresque, w. H. Molnar (pic), J. Molnar (alphn), P. Falentin (tpt), A. Ramirez (perc) — Gallo ▲ CD 548 [AAD]
Daetwyler, J.:Con Tpt, w. P. Falentin (tpt), A. Ramirez (perc) — Gallo ▲ CD 548 [AAD]
Daetwyler, J.:Danses (3), w. A. Ramirez (perc) — Gallo ▲ CD 548 [AAD]
T. Hug (cnd)
Schoeck, O.:Elegie, w. A. Loosli (bass) *(rec 1967)* — Jecklin-Disco ▲ JD 510-2 [ADD]
T. Loosli (cnd)
Gerber, R.:Concertino Pno, w. M.-L. de Marval (pno) — Gallo ▲ CD 549 [AAD]
Gerber, R.:Danses espagnoles (3) — Gallo ▲ CD 549 [AAD]
Gerber, R.:Sym 2 — Gallo ▲ CD 549 [AAD]
Gerber, R.:Trois paysages de Breughel — Gallo ▲ CD 549 [AAD]
Bern CO
J. E. Dähler (cnd)
Zelenka, J.D.:Requiem in c, w. *(soloists unknown)*, Bern Chamber Choir [L] — Claves ▲ CD 8501 [DDD]
J.-P. Moeckli (cnd)
Schneider, U.P.:Orchesterbuch *(rec Sept. 14, 1982)* — Grammont ▲ CTSP 34-2 [ADD]
Bern Neue Horizonte Ensemble
Schneider, U.P.:Babel *(rec April 26, 1971)* — Grammont ▲ CTSP 34-2 [ADD]

Bern Radio Chamber Ensemble
T. Hug (cnd)
Flury, U.J.:Con Vn, w. U. J. Flury (vn) *(rec Phonag Tonstudio, March 4, 1977)* — Gallo ▲ CD 802 [ADD]
T. Loosli (cnd)
Schoeck, O.:Nachhall, w. A. Loosli (bass) *(rec 1973)* — Jecklin-Disco ▲ JD 535-2 [ADD]
Schoeck, O.:Songs (misc), w. A. Loosli (bass), K Grenacher (pno)—9 songs *(rec 1968)* — Jecklin-Disco ▲ JD 535-2 [ADD]
Bern Sinfonietta
Gerber, R.:Con E Hn, w. Peggy Wey-Ervin (E hn) — Gallo ▲ CD 862 [ADD]
Bern State Orch
H. Müller-Kray (cnd)
Schubert, Franz:Fierrabras, w. H. Plümacher (cta), F. Wunderlich (ten), R. Wolansky (bar), O. von Rohr (bass), Berlin RIAS Chamber Choir, South Swiss Radio Chorus—abridged performance *(rec 1959)* — Myto ▲ MCD 89001 [ADD]
Bern String Quartet
Moser, R.:Neigung *(rec Jan. 14, 1991)* — Jecklin ▲ JS 283-2 [ADD]
Reger, M.:Qts Strs, Op. 54 — CPO 3–▲ CPO 999069 [DDD]
Reger, M.:Qt Strs, Op. 74 — CPO 3–▲ CPO 999069 [DDD]
Reger, M.:Qt Strs, Op. 109 — CPO 3–▲ CPO 999069 [DDD]
Reger, M.:Qt Strs, Op. 121 — CPO 3–▲ CPO 999069 [DDD]
Schoeck, O.:Notturno, w. Niklaus Tüller (bar) — Accord ▲ ACD 220772 [AAD]
Bern String Quartet [Christine Ragaz (vn), Alexander van Wijnkoop (vn), Henrik Crafoord (va), Walter Grimmer (vc)]
Lachenmann, H.:Gran Torso — Col Legno ▲ AU 31804 [DDD]
Schmitt, F.:Qnt Pno, w. Werner Bartschi (pno) — Accord ▲ ACD 220982
Bern SO
Suter, H.:Le Laudi di San Francesco d'Assisi, w. A. Michael (sop), J. Winklet (alt), A. Baldin (ten), J. Will (bass), P. Laubschet (org), T. Loosli (cnd), Bern Bach Choir, Sekundar School Children's Choir — Ars Musici ▲ AM 1015-2 [DDD]
H. Gafner (cnd)
Burkhard, W.:Mass, Op. 85, w. K. Beidler (sop), M. Brodard (bass), Bern Gabrieli Chorus — Jecklin ▲ JD 687
P. Maag (cnd)
Mendelssohn, F.:Meeresstille — IMP Classics ▲ PCD 849 [DDD]
Mendelssohn, F.:Ovs—The Hebrides, Op. 26; Son & Stranger; The Fair Melusina, Op. 32 — IMP ▲ IMP 2003
Mendelssohn, F.:Sym 3 — IMP Classics ▲ PCD 849 [DDD]
Mendelssohn, F.:Sym 4 — IMP ("Concert Classics" series) ▲ IMP PCD 1097
Mendelssohn, F.:Sym 4 — IMP ▲ IMP 2003
Saint-Saëns, C.:Sym 3 — IMP Classics ▲ PCD 847 [DDD]
Saint-Saëns, C.:Sym 3, w. D. Chjorzempa (org) — IMP ▲ IMP 2010
Bernese Orch
J.E. Dähler (cnd)
Keiser, R.:Passions Oratorium, w. J. Bise (sop), M. Conrad (cta), G. Jelden (ten), U. Gilgen (bass), Bernese Chorus [G] *(rec Feb. 1971)* — Claves 2–▲ CD 9223/24 [ADD]
Beromünster Orch
C. Dutoit (cnd)
Perrin, J.:Con grosso, w. J. Perrin (pno) *(rec Radio Zürich, Mar 5, 1962)* — Grammont ▲ CTSP 45 [AAD]
Beromünster RSO
E. Schmid (cnd)
Mieg, P.:Mit Nacht, w. Ernst Haefliger (ten) *(rec 1966)* — Jecklin ▲ JS 314-2 [DDD]
Berwald String Quartet
Bäck, S.-E.:Qt 4 Strs — Caprice ▲ CAP 21490
Berwald, F.:Qnt Pno, w. S. Lindgren (pno) — Musica Sveciae ▲ MSCD 521 [DDD]
Rosenberg, H.:Qt 7 Strs — Caprice ▲ CAP 21353 [AAD/DDD]
Berwald String Quartet members
Bäck, S.-E.:Qnt Strs, "Exercitier" — Caprice ▲ CAP 21490
Besses o' th' Barn Band
R.N. Evans (cnd)
Around the World with the Besses — Chandos ("Collect" series) 2–▲ CHAN 6571/72 [ADD]
Hymns & Things — Chandos ▲ CHAN 4529 [DDD]
R. Newsome (cnd)
Bliss, A.:Belmont Vars — Chandos ("Brass" series) ▲ CHAN 4525 [DDD]
The British Bandsman Centenary Concert (1987), w. Massed Bands [cnd:Harry Mortimer], Black Dyke Mills Band [cnd:Maj. Peter Parkes], IMI Yorkshire Imperial Band [cnd:James Scott] — Chandos Brass ▲ CHAN 4513 [DDD]
Gregson, E.:Con Hn — Chandos ("Brass" series) ▲ CHAN 4526 [DDD]
Gregson, E.:Con Tuba — Chandos ("Brass" series) ▲ CHAN 4526 [DDD]
Howarth, E.:In Memoriam R.K. — Chandos ("Brass" series) ▲ CHAN 4525 [DDD]
Howells, H.:Triptych — Chandos ("Brass" series) ▲ CHAN 4525 [DDD]
Langford, G.:Rhaps Cnt — Chandos ("Brass" series) ▲ CHAN 4526 [DDD]
Langford, G.:Summer Scherzo — Chandos ("Brass" series) ▲ CHAN 4525 [DDD]
Newsome, R.:Northwest Passage — Chandos ("Brass" series) ▲ CHAN 4525 [DDD]
Martin Best Mediaeval Ensemble
Riquier, G.:Troubadour Songs — Nimbus ▲ NI 5261 [ADD]
Bethlehem Bach Festival Orch
G. Funfgeld (cnd)
Bach, J.S.:Arias, w. David Gordon (ten), Emily Newbold (fl), Loretta O'Sullivan (vc), Charlotte Mattax (hpd)—Ermunter dich [from Cant.180]; Der Ewigkeit [from Cant. 198]; Ach, schlage doch [from Cant. 95]; Benedictus [from Mass in b, BWV 232]; Woferne du [from Cant. 41]; O Seelenparadies [from Cant. 172]; Frohe Hirten [from Christmas Oratorio, BWV 248] *(rec St. Michael's Church, New York City, June 1994)* — Newport Classic ▲ NPD 85582 [DDD]
Biedermeier Ensemble
Musik des Biedermeier — Denon ▲ CO 72587 [DDD]
Walzer a la Paganini:Musik des Biedermeier III *(rec 1993)* — Denon ▲ CO 75779
Biedermeier Ensemble [Helmuth Puffler (vn), Bernhard Biberauer (vn), Edward Kudlak (va), Milan Sagat (db)]
Fahrbach (Jr.), P.:Dance Music—Jubel Csárdás, Op. 48; Brieftaube, Schnellpolka, Op. 19 *(rec Casino Zögernitz, Vienna, May 19–21, 1995)* — Denon ▲ CO 78823 [DDD]
Lanner, J.:Music of—Bruder halt! (galopp), Op. 16; Lenz-Blüthen (waltz), Op. 118; Leopoldstädter Ländler, Op. 35; Wiedner Kirchweih Ländler, Op. 13 *(rec Casino Zögernitz, Vienna, May 19–21, 1995)* — Denon ▲ CO 78823 [DDD]
Strauss (I), Joh.:Music of—Beliebte Annen Polka, Op. 137; Hof-Ball-Tänze Walzer, Op. 51; Sperl Galopp, Op. 42; Wiener Tivoli-Rutsh-Walzer, Op. 39 *(rec Casino Zögernitz, Vienna, May 19–21, 1995)* — Denon ▲ CO 78823 [DDD]
Strauss (II), Joh.:Waltzes—Demolirer Polka, Polka française, Op. 269; L'Enfantillage (Zäpperl Polka), Op. 202; Libeslieder-Walzer, Op. 114 *(rec Casino Zögernitz, Vienna, May 19–21, 1995)* — Denon ▲ CO 78823 [DDD]
Strauss, Josef:Music of—Aquarellen (waltz), Op. 258 *(rec Casino Zögernitz, Vienna, May 19–21, 1995)* — Denon ▲ CO 78823 [DDD]
Biedermeier Quintet [M. Root (fl), F. de Bruine (ob), E. Hoeprich (cl), C. Maury (hn), M. Vallon (bn)]
Danzi, F.:Qnts Ww, Op. 56—No. 1 *(rec Dec. 1993)* — Globe ▲ GLO 5114 [DDD]
Reicha, A.:Qnts Ww, Op. 88/2—No. 2 *(rec Dec. 1993)* — Globe ▲ GLO 5114 [DDD]
Biedermeier Quintet members [M. Root (fl), E. Hoeprich (cl), C. Maury (hn), M. Vallon (bn)]
Rossini, G.:Sons Str Qt [arr for fl, cl, hn & bn]—No. 4 in B♭ *(rec Dec. 1993)* — Globe ▲ GLO 5114 [DDD]

▲ = CD ♦ = Enhanced CD Δ = MD ■ = Cassette Tape □ = DCC

Biel Orchestral Society
J. Meier (cnd)
Meier, J.:Music of (Ascona; Music for Trbn & Orch [w. M. Bequet (trbn)]; Trio for Cello & Piano; Variations for solo Violin [w. H. Schneeberger (vn)] Grammont ▲ CTSP 42-2 [AAD]

Bielefeld PO
G. Moull (cnd)
Spohr, L.:Faust, w. C. Taha (sop), M. Vier (b-bar), E. von Jordis (bass), Bielefeld Opera Chorus [1852 version] *(rec live, June 1993)* CPO 2-▲ CPO 999247 [DDD]

D. de Villiers (cnd)
Krenek, E.:Der Sprūng über den Schatten, w. D. Amos (sop), L. Kemeny (sop), S. MacLean (mez), J. Dürmüller (ten), U. Neuweiler (ten), J. Pflieger (bar), T. Brüning (sgr), Bielefeld Phil Chorus [G] *(rec live, May 1989)* CPO 2-▲ CPO 999082-2 [DDD]

Bieler SO
G. Nowak (cnd)
Baer, W.:Con Vn, w. P. Milewsky (vn) Gallo ▲ CD 582 [DDD]
Martin, F.:Con Vn, w. P. Milewsky (vn) Gallo ▲ CD 582 [DDD]
Meier, J.:Trames I–IV, w. P. Milewsky (vn) Gallo ▲ CD 582 [DDD]

F. Pantillon (cnd)
Mozart, W.A.:Missa Solemnis, w. Christa Goetze (sop), Anna Schaffner (alt), Barnhard Gärtner (ten), Rudolf Rosen (bass), Philippe Laubscher (org), Pro Arte Chorale, Bern Vocal Ensemble
  Gallo ▲ CD 893 [DDD]
Pantillon, F.:Bethlehem, w. Christa Goetze (sop), Rudolf Rosen (nar), Philippe Laubscher (org), Pro Arte Chorale, Bern Vocal Ensemble Gallo ▲ CD 893 [DDD]

Big SO
A. Boult (cnd)
Elgar, E.:The Dream of Gerontius Beulah ▲ 3PD15 [ADD]
Elgar, E.:Sospiri Beulah ▲ 3PD15 [ADD]
Elgar, E.:Sym 2 Beulah ▲ 3PD15 [ADD]

Bilbao SO
J. López-Cobos (cnd)
Arriaga, J.C.:Agar, w. Angela Denning (sop) Discobi 2-▲ DIS 2002/1002
Arriaga, J.C.:Erminia, w. Angela Denning (sop) Discobi 2-▲ DIS 2002/1002
Arriaga, J.C.:Nada y mucho Discobi 2-▲ DIS 2002/1002
Arriaga, J.C.:O salutaris Discobi 2-▲ DIS 2002/1002

Bilitis Ensemble [Antonella De Angelis (fl), Amanda Patregnani (fl), Giusi Ciarla (hp), Annabella Palleri (hp), Annalisa Cialini (cel), Alessia Patregnani (voc)]
Bellafronte, R.:Danzarèa *(rec Chiese S. Maria Maggiore, Vasto, Jan 1995)*
  Bongiovanni ▲ GB 5049-2 [DDD]

Billings SO
U. Barnea (cnd)
Barnea, U.:Homage to Bach Innova ▲ MN 501
Hanson, H.:Pastorale Ob, w. Oscar Petty (ob) Innova ▲ MN 501
Haydn, J.:Con Ob, w. Oscar Petty (ob) Innova ▲ MN 501
Kay, U.:Brief Elegy, w. Oscar Petty (ob) Innova ▲ MN 501
Lombardo:Con Ob, w. Oscar Petty (ob) Innova ▲ MN 501
Martin, F.:Ballade Fl, w. S. Baron (fl) [orchestral version] CRS ▲ CD 8840
Piston, W.:Con Cl, w. J. Russo (cl) CRS ▲ CD 8840
Piston, W.:Con Fl, w. D. Baron (fl) CRS ▲ CD 8840
Rossini, J.:Con Vars Cl, w. C. Russo (cl) CRS ▲ CD 8840

Gilles Binchois Ensemble
Musica Humana, w. Françoise Atlan (mez), John Fleagle (ten/hp), Crawford Young (lt), Anonymous 4, Ensemble Discantus, Ensemble Organum, Gothic Voices, Greece Byzantine Choir, Hilliard Ensemble, Musica Nova, et al. L'Empreinte Digitale ▲ ED 13047
Le Puy Manuscript Virgin Classics ▲ CDC 59238

D. Vellard (cnd)
Banquet du Voeu 1454 [Feast of the Pheasant]:Music at the Court of Burgundy
  Virgin Classics ▲ CDC 59043
Dufay, G.:Missa, "Ecce ancilla Domini" Virgin Classics ▲ CDC 45050

Bingham String Quartet
Butler, M.:Songs & Dances from a Haunted Place *(rec July 11-12, 1991)*
  NM Classics ▲ NMCD 006 [DDD]
Cashian, P.:Qt 1 Strs *(rec July 11-12, 1991)* NM Classics ▲ NMCD 006 [DDD]
Ginastera, A.:Qnt Pno, w. A. Portugheis (pno) ASV ▲ ASV 902 [DDD]
Nicholls, D.:Qt Strs *(rec July 11-12, 1991)* NM Classics ▲ NMCD 006 [DDD]

Birmingham Contemporary Music Group
S. Rattle (cnd)
Schoenberg, A.:Erwartung, w. Phyllis Bryn-Julson (sop) EMI Classics ▲ CDC 55212

Birmingham SO
L. Foster (cnd)
Sauer, E. von:Con 1 Pno, w. Stephen Hough (pno) Hyperion ▲ CDA 66790
Scharwenka, X.:Con 4 Pno, w. Stephen Hough (pno) Hyperion ▲ CDA 66790

Bit 20 Ensemble
I. Bergby (cnd)
Nordheim, A.:Music of, w. Siri Torjesen (sop), Njål Sparbo (bar)—Magic Island; Tractatus; Part for 6 Basses; Aftonland [Evening Land]; 3 Voci; Part for Va, Hpd & Perc; Qt for Strs; Response for Org, Perc & Tape Norway Music 2-▲ CD 4990

Black Dyke Mills Band
All of the World's Most Beautiful Melodiesl, w. Phillip McCann (cnt), Gordon Langford (cnd), Roy Newsome (cnd), Peter Parkes (cnd), Sellers Engineering Band, Academy of St. Martin in the Fields Chamber Ensemble, Huddersfield Choral Society, Leeds Parish Church Boys Choir
  Chandos ("Brass" series) 5-▲ CHN 4536(5)
Bantock, G.:Prometheus Unbound Chandos Brass ▲ CHAN 4510 [DDD]
Bliss, A.:Kenilworth Chandos Brass ▲ CHAN 4506 [DDD]
Christmas Fantasy, w. Huddersfield Choral Society Chandos ▲ CHAN 8679 [AAD]
Fletcher, P.E.:Labour & Love Chandos Brass ▲ CHAN 4506 [DDD]
Hespe, G.W.:The Three Musketeers Chandos Brass ▲ CHAN 4506 [DDD]
Jenkins, C.:Life Divine Chandos Brass ▲ CHAN 4506 [DDD]
Live Brass, w. Massed Bands, James Shepherd Versatile Brass, Solna Brass, Brighouse & Rastrick Band, Don Lusher Trombone Ensemble *(rec live at the National Brass Band Festiva, Gala Concerts 1977, 1978, 1979)* Chandos Brass ▲ CHAN 6561 [ADD]
Lloyd, G.:Music of—Diversions on a Bass Theme; Evening Song; H.M.S. Trinidad; English Heritage
  Albany 2-▲ TROY 051-2 [DDD] ■ TROY 051-4
Lloyd, G.:Royal Parks Chandos Brass ▲ CHAN 4506 [DDD]
Mathias, W.:Vivat Regina Chandos Brass ▲ CHAN 4510 [DDD]
More of the World's Most Beautiful Melodies, w. Phillip McCann (cnt)
  Chandos Brass ▲ CHAN 4502 [DDD]
Rossini, G.:Music of [arr. for band]—4 Ovs. (Scala di seta, Cenerentola, Tancredi, William Tell), 2 Arias ("Una voce poco fa" & "Largo al factotum"), & La Danza
  Chandos ("Brass" series) ▲ CHAN 4505 [DDD]
Rubbra, E.:Vars on "The Shining River" Chandos Brass ▲ CHAN 4506 [DDD]
Vaughan Williams, R.:Vars Brass Band Chandos Brass ▲ CHAN 4510 [DDD]
Vinter, G.:James Cook-Circumnavigator Chandos ("Brass" series) ▲ CHAN 4508 [DDD]
The World's Most Beautiful Melodies, w. Phillip McCann (cnt) Chandos Brass ▲ CHAN 4501 [DDD]

J. Foster (cnd)
Lloyd, G.:Royal Parks Albany ▲ TROY 051-2 [DDD] ■ TROY 051-4

R.N. Heath (cnd)
Morning Cloud Chandos ▲ CHAN 4534 [ADD]

R. Newsome (cnd)
Ball, E.:Sinfonietta, "The Wayfarer" *(rec 1970s)* Chandos ("Brass" series) ▲ CHAN 4508 [ADD]

Newsome, Parkes (cnd)
Elgar, E.:Severn Suite Brass *(rec 1970s)* Chandos ("Brass" series) ▲ CHAN 4508 [ADD]
Fletcher, P.E.:An Epic Sym *(rec 1970s)* Chandos ("Brass" series) ▲ CHAN 4508 [ADD]

P. Parkes (cnd)
Black Dyke Plays Rossini Chandos Brass ▲ CHAN 4505 [DDD]
Blitz Chandos Brass ▲ CHAN 4504 [DDD]
The British Bandsman Centenary Concert (1987), w. Massed Bands [cnd:Harry Mortimer], Besses o' the Barn Band [cnd:Roy Newsome], IMI Yorkshire Imperial Band [cnd:James Scott]
  Chandos Brass ▲ CHAN 4513 [DDD]
Champions of Brass Chandos Brass ▲ CHAN 4510 [DDD]
Classic Brass Chandos ("Collect" series) ▲ CHAN 6539 [DDD]
The Complete Champions Chandos Brass ▲ CHAN 4509 [DDD]
The Concert Sound of the Black Dyke Mills Band Chandos Brass ▲ CHAN 4520 [DDD]
Famous Marches Chandos ("Collect" series) ▲ CHAN 6516 [DDD]
The John Foster Black Dyke Mills Band Celebrates 150 Years Chandos Brass ▲ CHAN 4516 [DDD]
Kings of Brass Chandos Brass ▲ CHAN 4517 [DDD]
Life Divine Chandos Brass ▲ CHAN 4506 [DDD]
The Lion & the Eagle Chandos ▲ CHAN 4528 [DDD]
Overtures Chandos Brass ▲ CHAN 4514 [DDD]
Russian Festival Chandos Brass ▲ CHAN 4519 [DDD]
Traditionally British Chandos ("Collect" series) ▲ CHAN 6515 [ADD]
A Tribute to Elgar, Delius & Holst Chandos Brass ▲ CHAN 4507 [DDD]
World Famous Marches Chandos ("Collect" series) ▲ CHAN 6565 [ADD]

J. Watson (cnd)
Great British Marches *(rec Manchester, 1994)* Doyen ▲ CD 039 [DDD]
Revelations *(rec Nov 1995)* Doyen ▲ CD 046 [DDD]
Walton, W.:Battle of Britain ASV ("White Line" series) ▲ ASV 2093 [DDD]
Walton, W.:Crown Imperial ASV ("White Line" series) ▲ ASV 2093 [DDD]
Walton, W.:The First Shout ASV ("White Line" series) ▲ ASV 2093 [DDD]
Walton, W.:Henry V (film suite) ASV ("White Line" series) ▲ ASV 2093 [DDD]
Walton, W.:Music for Children ASV ("White Line" series) ▲ ASV 2093 [DDD]
Walton, W.:A Wartime Sketchbook ASV ("White Line" series) ▲ ASV 2093 [DDD]

Blair String Quartet [Christian Teal (vn), Cornelia Heard (vn), John Kochanowski (va), Grace Mihi Bahng (vc)]
Kurek, M.:Qt 2 Strs *(rec Blair School of Music Recital Hall, 1995)* New World ▲ 80497-2

Blair Woodwind Quintet [Jane Kirchner (fl), Bobby Taylor (ob), Cassandra Lee (cl), Cynthia Estill (bn), Leslie Norton (hn)]
Kurek, M.:Matisse Impressions, w. James Helton (pno) *(rec Blair School of Music Recital Hall, 1995)*
  New World ▲ 80497-2

Boccherini String Quartet
Boccherini, L.:Qts Strs—in A, G.213 (Op. 39/8) Channel Classics ▲ CCS 3692 [DDD]
Boccherini, L.:Qnts Strs, w. Anner Bijlsma (vc)—Quintet in F, Op. 39/2 (G.338); Quintettino in E♭, Op. 27/4 (G.304) Channel Classics ▲ CCS 3692 [DDD]

Boccherini String Quartet members
Boccherini, L.:Trios Vn, G.95-100—in c, G.96 (Op. 14/2) Channel Classics ▲ CCS 3692 [DDD]

Bochum SO
M. Kuntzsch (cnd)
Bruch, M.:Con 1 Vn, w. R. Ricci (vn) Allegretto ▲ ACD 8169 [ADD] ■ ACS 8169

O. Mega (cnd)
Rimsky-Korsakov, N.:Christmas Eve (suite) Vox Box 2-▲ CDX 5082 [ADD]
Rimsky-Korsakov, N.:Fairy Tale Vox Box 2-▲ CDX 5082 [ADD]
Rimsky-Korsakov, N.:Fant on 2 Russian Themes, w. *(soloist unknown)* Vox Box 2-▲ CDX 5082 [ADD]
Rimsky-Korsakov, N.:Mlada (suite) Vox Box 2-▲ CDX 5082 [ADD]
Tchaikovsky, P.:Fatum Vox Box 2-▲ CDX 5079 [ADD]
Tchaikovsky, P.:The Storm Vox Box 2-▲ CDX 5079 [ADD]
Tchaikovsky, P.:The Tempest Vox Box 2-▲ CDX 5079 [ADD]

Boeckheler Piano Trio
Mendelssohn, F.:Trio 2 Pno Mastersound ▲ MST 28 [DDD]
Tchaikovsky, P.:Trio Pno Mastersound ▲ MST 28 [DDD]

Boehm Quintet
Carter, E.:Qnt Ww Premier ▲ PRCD 1006 [DDD]
Fine, I.:Partita Ww Premier ▲ PRCD 1006 [DDD]
Persichetti, V.:Pastoral Premier ▲ PRCD 1006 [DDD]
Piston, W.:Qnt Ww Premier ▲ PRCD 1006 [DDD]

Boehm Quintet [Sheryl Heinze (fl), P. Lanini (ob), S. Hartmann (cl), J. Anderer (hn), R. Wagner (bn)]
American Winds, Vol. 2:Jam Session Premier ▲ PRCD 1023 [DDD]

Boehm Quintet members
Piston, W.:Pieces Fl Premier ▲ PRCD 1006 [DDD]
Siegmeister, E.:10 Minutes Premier ▲ PRCD 1006 [DDD]

Boehm Quintet members [D. Starobin (gtr), J. Smirnoff (vn), G. Kalish (pno)]
Berger, A.:Qt Winds New World ▲ NW 360-2 [DDD]
Berger, A.:Trio New World ▲ NW 360-2 [DDD]

Boemia CO
H. Farkac (cnd)
Fasch, J.F.:Con Tpt & 2 Obs Rondo Grammofon ▲ RCD 8337
Haydn, J.:Con Tpt Rondo Grammofon ▲ RCD 8337
Horovitz, J.:Concertino Classico, w. Ole Andersen (tpt), Ketil Christensen (tpt)
  Rondo Grammofon ▲ RCD 8337
Hummel, J.N.:Con in E♭ Tpt, S.49 Rondo Grammofon ▲ RCD 8337
Tartini, G.:Con Tpt Rondo Grammofon ▲ RCD 8337
Trumpet Concertos, Vol. 2, w. Ketil Christensen (tpt), Ole Andersen (tpt), Lars Ole Schmidt (tpt)
  Rondo Grammofon ▲ RCD 8339
Vivaldi, A.:Con for 2 Tpts, w. Ole Andersen (tpt), Ketil Christensen (tpt)
  Rondo Grammofon ▲ RCD 8337

Walter Boeykens Ensemble
Beethoven, L. van:Septet Strs Harmonia Mundi France ▲ HMC 901518
Beethoven, L. van:Trio 7 Pno Harmonia Mundi France ▲ HMC 901518
Khachaturian, A.:Trio Cl Harmonia Mundi France ("Musique d'abord" series) ▲ HMA 1901419
Kókai, R.:Quartettino Harmonia Mundi France ("Musique d'abord" series) ▲ HMA 1901419
Messiaen, O.:Quatuor pour la fin du temps Harmonia Mundi France ▲ HMC 901348
Prokofiev, O.:Ov on Hebrew Themes
  Harmonia Mundi France ("Musique d'abord" series) ▲ HMA 1901419
Prokofiev, S.:Qnt Ob Harmonia Mundi France ▲ HMA 1901419
Weber, C.M. von:Grand duo concertant Cl, w. W. Boeykens (cl)
  Harmonia Mundi France ▲ HMC 901481
Weber, C.M. von:Qnt Cl, w. W. Boeykens (cl) Harmonia Mundi France ▲ HMC 901481
Weber, C.M. von:Vars on a Theme from *Silvana* Cl, w. W. Boeykens (cl)
  Harmonia Mundi France ▲ HMC 901481

Bohdan Warchal Slovak CO
P. Damm (cnd)
Britten, B.:Serenade, Op. 31, w. P. Schreier (ten) Campion ▲ 1313
Britten, B.:Simple Sym Campion ▲ 1313
Britten, B.:Vars on a Theme of Frank Bridge Campion ▲ 1313

Simón Bolívar SO
E. Diemecke (cnd)
Villa-Lobos, H.:Amazonas *(rec Aula Magna of the Universidad Central de Venezuela, Caracas, July & Aug 1995)* Dorian ▲ DOR 90228 [DDD]
Villa-Lobos, H.:Con 2 Vc, w. Andrés Díaz (vc) *(rec Aula Magna of the Universidad Central de Venezuela, Caracas, July & Aug 1995)* Dorian ▲ DOR 90228 [DDD]
Villa-Lobos, H.:Sym 4 *(rec Aula Magna of the Universidad Central de Venezuela, Caracas, July & Aug 1995)* Dorian ▲ DOR 90228 [DDD]
E. Mata (cnd)
Chávez, C.:Caballos de vapor (suite) Dorian 3-▲ DOR 98102 [DDD]
Chávez, C.:Caballos de vapor (suite) *(rec Central Univ. of Venezuela, Caracas, July 1994)* Dorian ▲ DOR 90211 [DDD]
Chávez, C.:Sym 2, "Sinf India" Dorian 3-▲ DOR 98102 [DDD]
Chávez, C.:Sym 2, "Sinf India" *(rec Nov. 1992 & July 1993)* Dorian ▲ DOR 90179 [DDD]
Estévez, A.:Florentino, el que cantó con el diablo, w. I. Alvarez (ten), W. Alvarado (bar), Simón Bolívar Orfeón Univ Schola Cantorum [L] *(rec 2 & 6/90)* Dorian Discovery ▲ DIS 80101 [DDD]
Estévez, A.:Mediodia en el Llano Dorian 3-▲ DOR 98102 [DDD]
Estévez, A.:Mediodia en el Llano *(rec Nov. 1992 & July 1993)* Dorian ▲ DOR 90179 [DDD]
Falla, M. de:El amor brujo, w. Marta Senn (mez) *(rec Aula Magna of Venezuela Central Univ., Caracas, July 1994)* Dorian ▲ DOR 90210 [DDD]
Falla, M. de:Canciones populares españolas (7), w. Marta Senn (mez) *(rec Aula Magna of Venezuela Central Univ., Caracas, July 1994)* Dorian ▲ DOR 90210 [DDD]
Falla, M. de:Homenajes (4) Orch *(rec Aula Magna of Venezuela Central Univ., Caracas, July 1994)* Dorian ▲ DOR 90210 [DDD]
Falla, M. de:El sombrero de tres picos (sels)—Suite 2 *(rec Aula Magna of Venezuela Central Univ., Caracas, July 1994)* Dorian ▲ DOR 90210 [DDD]
Falla, M. de:La vida breve, w. C. Angell (mez), M. Senn (mez), F. de la Mora (ten) [Sp] *(rec July 1993)* Dorian ▲ DOR 90192 [DDD]
Ginastera, A.:Estancia (sels)—Los trabajadores agricolas; Danza del trigo; Los peones de hacienda; Danza final "Malambo" *(rec Central Univ. of Venezuela, Caracas, July 1994)* Dorian ▲ DOR 90211 [DDD]
Ginastera, A.:Estancia (sels)—Los trabajadores agricolas; Danza del trigo; Los peones de hacienda; Danza final [Malambo] Dorian 3-▲ DOR 98102 [DDD]
Ginastera, A.:Pampeana 3 Dorian 3-▲ DOR 98102 [DDD]
Ginastera, A.:Pampeana 3 Dorian ▲ DOR 90178 [DDD]
Orbón, J.:Con grosso Dorian 3-▲ DOR 98102 [DDD]
Orbón, J.:Versiones sinfónicas *(rec Nov. 1992 & July 1993)* Dorian ▲ DOR 90179 [DDD]
Orbón, J.:Versiones sinfónicas Dorian 3-▲ DOR 98102 [DDD]
Revueltas, S.:Redes Dorian ▲ DOR 90178 [DDD]
Revueltas, S.:Redes Dorian 3-▲ DOR 98102 [DDD]
Revueltas, S.:Sensemayá Dorian 3-▲ DOR 98102 [DDD]
Revueltas, S.:Sensemayá Dorian ▲ DOR 90178 [DDD]
Villa-Lobos, H.:Bachiana brasileira 2 Dorian 3-▲ DOR 98102 [DDD]
Villa-Lobos, H.:Chôro 10 Dorian Discovery ▲ DIS 80101 [DDD]
Villa-Lobos, H.:Uirapuru Dorian 3-▲ DOR 98102 [DDD]
Villa-Lobos, H.:Uirapurú *(rec Central Univ. of Venezuela, Caracas, July 1994)* Dorian ▲ DOR 90211 [DDD]
M. Valdes (cnd)
Carreño, I.:Suite margariteña *(rec Aula Magna of the Universidad Central de Venezuela, Caracas, July 1995)* Dorian ▲ DOR 90227 [DDD]
Ginastera, A.:Ov to the Creole "Faust" *(rec Aula Magna of the Universidad Central de Venezuela, Caracas, July 1995)* Dorian ▲ DOR 90227 [DDD]
Guarnieri, C.M.:Dansa brasileira *(rec Aula Magna of the Universidad Central de Venezuela, Caracas, July 1995)* Dorian ▲ DOR 90227 [DDD]
Guarnieri, C.M.:Dansa negra *(rec Aula Magna of the Universidad Central de Venezuela, Caracas, July 1995)* Dorian ▲ DOR 90227 [DDD]
Guarnieri, C.M.:Dansa selvagem *(rec Aula Magna of the Universidad Central de Venezuela, Caracas, July 1995)* Dorian ▲ DOR 90227 [DDD]
Guarnieri, C.M.:Encantamento *(rec Aula Magna of the Universidad Central de Venezuela, Caracas, July 1995)* Dorian ▲ DOR 90227 [DDD]
Moncayo Garcia, J.P.:Huapango *(rec Aula Magna of the Universidad Central de Venezuela, Caracas, July 1995)* Dorian ▲ DOR 90227 [DDD]
Plaza, J.B.:Fuga romántica venezolana *(rec Aula Magna, Central Venezuela Univ, Caracas, July 1995)* Dorian ▲ DOR 90227 [DDD]
Revueltas, S.:El renacuajo Paseador *(rec Aula Magna of the Universidad Central de Venezuela, Caracas, July 1995)* Dorian ▲ DOR 90227 [DDD]
Simón Bolívar SO
E. Mata (cnd)
Orbón, J.:Con grosso, w. Latin American String Quartet Dorian ▲ DOR 90178 [DDD]
Claude Bolling Big Band
C. Bolling (cnd)
Cinemadreams Milan ▲ 73138-35751-2
Claude Bolling Trio
Bolling, C.:Con Gtr, w. A. LaGoya (gtr) Milan ▲ 73138-35646-2 ■ 73138-35646-4
Bolling, C.:Picnic Suite, w. J.-P. Rampal (fl), A. Lagoya (gtr) CBS ▲ MK 35864 ■ PMT 35864
Bolling, C.:Suite Vc, w. Yo-Yo Ma (vc) CBS ▲ MK 39059 ■ FMT 39059
Bolling, C.:Suite 1 Fl, w. J.-P. Rampal (fl) Milan ▲ 73138-35645-2 ■ 73138-35645-4
Bolling, C.:Suite Vn, w. P. Zukerman (vn) Milan ▲ 73138-35647-2 ■ 73138-35467-2
Bologna CO
L. Magiera (cnd)
Vincerò, w. Luciano Pavarotti (ten) *(rec Milan, May 27, 1990)* Replay ▲ 8005
Bologna I Filarmonici
Vivaldi, A.:Music of, w. Philharmonia Baroque Orch, Concerto Amsterdam, Boston Museum Trio, Clemencic Consort—sels. from Flute Concerto, RV.427 & 440; Four Seasons—Autumn; String Concerto, RV.129 & 152; Serenata a Tre, RV.690; Sonata, RV.2 *(rec 1970–86)* Harmonia Mundi Plus ▲ HMP 390810
Bologna SO
V. Smetáček (cnd)
Strauss, R.:4 Last Songs, w. M. Freni (sop) [G] *(rec live, 11/73)* Cantabile 2-▲ BIM 703-2
Bologna Teatro Comunale Orch
Kamen, Mageira (cnd)
Pavarotti & Friends 2, w. Luciano Pavarotti (ten), Nancy Gustafson (sop), Bryan Adams (sgr), Andreas Vollenweider (kbd) London ▲ 444460-2 ■ 444460-4
R. Bonynge (cnd)
Donizetti, G.:La favorita, w. F. Cossotto (mez), L. Pavarotti (ten), G. Bacquier (bar), N. Ghiaurov (bass), Bologna Teatro Comunale Chorus London 3-▲ 430038-2 [ADD]
Donizetti, G.:Maria Stuarda, w. J. Sutherland (sop), H. Tourangeau (mez), L. Pavarotti (ten), R. Soyer (bar), J. Morris (bass), Bologna Teatro Comunale Chorus [I] London 2-▲ 425410-2 [ADD]
B. Campanella (cnd)
Donizetti, G.:La fille du régiment, w. L. Serra (sop), M. Tagliasacchi (sop), W. Matteuzzi (ten), E. Dara (bar), Bologna Teatro Comunale Chorus [I] *(rec live, 2/16–26/89)* Nuova Era 2-▲ 6791/92 [DDD]
R. Chailly (cnd)
Puccini, G.:Manon Lescaut, w. K. Te Kanawa (sop), J. Carreras (ten), P. Coni (bar), I. Tajo (bass) [I] London 2-▲ 421426-2 [DDD]
Rossini, G.:La Cenerentola, w. C. Bartoli (mez—Cenerentola), F. Costa (mez—Clorinda), G. Banditelli (cta—Tisbe), W. Matteuzzi (ten—Don Ramiro), A. Corbelli (bar—Dandini), E. Dara (bar—Don Magnifico), M. Pertusi (bass—Alidoro), Bologna Teatro Comunale Chorus *(rec June 22–July 2, 1992)* London 2-▲ 436902-2 [DDD]

Bologna Teatro Comunale Orch (cont.)
R. Chailly (cnd) (cont.)
Rossini, G.:La Cenerentola (sels), w. Cecilia Bartoli (mez). Bologna Teatro Comunale Chorus—Nacqui all'affanno...Non più mesta *(rec 1992)* London ▲ 448300-2 [DDD]; ■ 448300-4
Verdi, G.:Rigoletto (sels), w. J. Anderson (sop), S. Verrett (mez), L. Pavarotti (ten), L. Nucci (bar), N. Ghiaurov (bass), Bologna Teatro Comunale Chorus London ▲ 436097-2 [DDD]
O. de Fabritiis (cnd)
Verdi, G.:Un ballo in maschera, w. Leyla Gencer (sop), Adriana Lazzarini (mez), Carlo Bergonzi (ten), Mario Zanasi (bar), Bologna Teatro Comunale Chorus *(rec live, Nov 28, 1961)* Arkadia 2-▲ 622
G. Ferro (cnd)
Rossini, G.:La scala di seta, w. Luciana Serra (sop), Oslavio di Credico (ten), William Matteuzzi (ten), Roberto Coviello (bar), Natale de Carolis (b-bar) Fonit Cetra ("Ricordi" series) 2-▲ FCT RFCD 2003
D. Gatti (cnd)
Rossini, G.:Arias, w. J. Anderson (sop), Bologna Teatro Comunale Chorus—arias from La Donna Del Lago, Semiramide, Otello, Guillaume Tell, Ermione, Il viaggio a Reims [I] London ▲ 436377-2 [DDD]
Rossini, G.:Armida, w. R. Fleming (sop), C. Bosi (ten), B. Fowler (ten), J. Francis (ten), D. Kaasch (ten), G. Kunde (ten), I. Zennaro (ten), I. D'Arcangelo (bass), S. Zadvorny (bass), Bologna Teatro Comunale Chorus *(rec Pesaro, Italy, Aug. 6–17, 1993)* Sony Classical 3-▲ S3K 58968 [DDD]
A. Gatto (cnd)
Verdi, G.:Macbeth, w. Grace Bumbry (mez—Lady Macbeth), Luciano Saldari (ten—Macduff), Paride Venturi (ten—Malcolm), Renato Bruson (bar—Macbeth), Agostino Ferrin (bass—Banquo), Bologna Teatro Comunale Chorus *(rec Bologna, Mar. 18, 1975)* Golden Age of Opera 2-▲ GAO 185/86 [ADD]
G. Patanè (cnd)
Rossini, G.:Il barbiere di Siviglia, w. C. Bartoli (mez), W. Matteuzzi (ten), L. Nucci (bar), P. Burchuladze (bass), Bologna Teatro Comunale Chorus [I] London 3-▲ 425520-2 [DDD]
Rossini, G.:Il barbiere di Siviglia (sels), w. C. Bartoli (mez), W. Matteuzzi (ten), L. Nucci (bar), P. Burchuladze (bass), Bologna Teatro Comunale Chorus London ▲ 440289-2 [DDD]
B. Rigacci (cnd)
Donizetti, G.:Pia de' Tolomei, w. Bologna Teatro Comunale Chorus Melodram 3-▲ CDM 37017
Bolshoi Theater Chamber Music Ensemble
A. Golyshev (cnd)
Stravinsky, I.:Songs, w. O. Romanko (sop), V. Samoilenki (pno)—The Cloud; 3 Songs; Cats' Lullabies; Lullaby; 2 Lyrics by K. Balmont; Pastorale; Pribautiki; 3 Stories for Children; 4 Russian Folk-Songs; Little Harmonic Ramuziana; In Memoriam Dylan T.; The Owl & the Pussy-cat; 3 Lyrics from Japanese Poetry; 3 Songs to Lyrics by Shakespeare; 2 Songs to Lyrics by S. Gorodestsky, Op. 6 MK ▲ MKA 417126 [DDD]
Bolshoi Theater Ensemble Soloists
A. Lazarev (cnd)
Stravinsky, I.:L'Histoire du soldat Suite Ensemble Allegretto ▲ ACD 8185 [ADD] ■ ACS 8185
Stravinsky, I.:Pribaoutki Allegretto ▲ ACD 8185 [ADD] ■ ACS 8185
Stravinsky, I.:Ragtime Allegretto ▲ ACD 8185 [ADD] ■ ACS 8185
Stravinsky, I.:Septet Cl Allegretto ▲ ACD 8185 [ADD] ■ ACS 8185
Bolshoi Theater Orch
N. Anosov (cnd)
Rimsky-Korsakov, N.:Capriccio espagnol, w. D. Oistrakh (vn), Moscow RSO *(rec 1960)* Multisonic ("Russian Treasures" series) ▲ 31 0186
Rimsky-Korsakov, N.:Scheherazade, Moscow RSO *(rec 1960)* Multisonic ("Russian Treasures" series) ▲ 31 0186
M. Ermler (cnd)
Borodin, A.:Prince Igor, w. Elana Obraztsova (mez—Konchakovna), Tatiana Tugarinova (mez—Yaroslavna), Vladimir Atlantov (ten—Vladimir Igoryevich), Artur Eisen (bass—Vladimir Galitsky), Ivan Petrov (bass—Igor Svyatoslavich), Alexander Vedernikov (bass—Konchak), Bolshoi Theater Chorus *(rec Moscow, 1969)* Melodiya ("The Russian Opera" series) 3-▲ 74321-29346-2 [ADD]
Glière, R.:Con Coloratura Sop, w. Evgenia Miroshnichenko (sop) *(rec 1974)* Consonance ▲ 81 3002 [AAD]
Tchaikovsky, P.:Queen of Spades, w. T. Milachkina (sop), V. Levko (mez), V. Atlantov (ten), Bolshoi Theater Chorus [R] Philips 3-▲ 420375-2 [ADD]
Ermler, Zhuraitis (cnd)
Rimsky-Korsakov, N.:The Maid of Pskov (sels), Moscow RSO—incidental music Multisonic ▲ MUL 310274
Rimsky-Korsakov, N.:Pan Voyevoda, Moscow RSO Multisonic ▲ MUL 310274
Rimsky-Korsakov, N.:Snow Maiden (suite), Moscow RSO Multisonic ▲ MUL 310274
J. Feier (cnd)
Delibes, L.:Coppélia (sels) Eurodisc ▲ 7935-2-RG [ADD]
R. Glière (cnd)
Glière, R.:Khrizis (suite) *(rec 1947)* Consonance ▲ 81-3000 [AAD]
N. Golovanov (cnd)
Mussorgsky, M.:Boris Godounov, w. Georgi Nelepp (ten), Maxim Mikhailov (bass), Mark Reizen (bass), *(other soloists unknown)*, Bolshoi Theater Chorus *(rec 1948)* Arlecchino 3-▲ ARL121/23
A. Khachaturian (cnd)
Khachaturian, A.:Funeral Ode in Memory of Lenin Russian Disc ▲ RUS 11063 [AAD]
B. Khaikin (cnd)
Tchaikovsky, P.:Eugene Onegin, w. G. Vishnevskaya (sop), L. Avdeyeva (mez), S. Lemeshev (ten), Belov (sgr), Petrov (sgr), Bolshoi Theater Chorus [R] *(rec ca. early '60s for Melodi)* Legato Classics 2-▲ LCD 163-2 (m) [ADD]
A. Kopilov (cnd)
Tchaikovsky, P.:The Nutcracker (sels) IMP Classics ▲ PCD 984 [DDD]
Tchaikovsky, P.:Sleeping Beauty (sels) IMP Classics ▲ PCD 982 [DDD]
A. Lazarev (cnd)
Gershwin, G.:Rhap in Blue, w. Timofei Dokschitzer (tpt) *(rec 1978)* RCA Gold Seal ▲ 74321-32045-2 [ADD]
Russian Opera Choruses, w. Bolshoi Theater Chorus Erato ▲ 91723-2 [DDD]
Shchedrin, R.:The Seagull Russian Disc ▲ RUS 10050 [AAD]
A. Melik-Pashayev (cnd)
Leoncavallo, R.:Pagliacci (sels), w. Pavel Lisitsian (bar—Silvio)—Prologue; Duet of Silvio & Nedda [w. N. Shpiller (sop—Nedda)] *(rec 1948)* Russian Compact Disc ("Talents of Russia" series) ▲ RCD 16025 [ADD]
Mussorgsky, M.:Boris Godunov, w. Irina Arkhipova (mez—Marina Mnishek), Evgenya Verbitskaya (mez—Nurse to Xenia), Valentina Klepatskaya (sgr—Fyodor), Tamara Sorokina (sgr—Xenia), Anton Grigoryev (ten—Simpleton), Vladimir Ivanovsky (ten—Grigory, the Pretender), Gyorgy Shulpin (bar—Prince Shuisky), Alexey Geleva (bass—Varlaam), Ivan Petrov (bass—Boris Godounov), Mark Reshetin (bass—Pimen), Alexi Ivanov (sgr—Andrei Shchelkalov), Evgeny Kibkalo (sgr—Rangoni), Bolshoi Theater Chorus *(rec Moscow, 1962)* Melodiya ("The Russian Opera" series) 3-▲ 74321-29349-2 [ADD]
Prokofiev, S.:War & Peace, w. Galina Vishnevskaya (sop—Natasha Rostovoa), Irina Arkhipova (mez—Hélène Bezukhova), Evgenya Verbitskaya (mez—Marya Akhrosimova), Alexi Maslennikov (ten—Anatole Kuragin), Vladimir Petrov (ten—Pierre Bezukhov), Pavel Lisitsian (bar—Napoleon), Alexi Krivchenya (bass—Field-Marshall Kutuzov), Evgeny Kibkalo (sgr—Prince Andrei Bolkonsky), Bolshoi Theater Chorus *(rec Moscow, 1961)* Melodiya ("The Russian Opera" series) 3-▲ 74321-29350-2 [ADD]
Tchaikovsky, P.:Queen of Spades, w. Elena Smolenskaya (sop), Evgenya Verbitskaya (mez), Georgi Nelepp (ten), Pavel Lisitsian (bar), Bolshoi Theater Chorus Arlecchino 3- ARL
V. Nebolsin (cnd)
Gounod, C.:Faust (sels), w. Pavel Lisitsian (bar—Valentin)—Valentin's Cavatina; Terzetto [w. A. Pirogov (bass—Mephisto), I. Kozlovsky (ten—Faust)]; Valentin's Death Scene *(rec 1954)* Russian Compact Disc ("Talents of Russia" series) ▲ RCD 16025 [ADD]

Bolshoi Theater Orch (cont.)
G. Rozhdestvensky (cnd)
Arutiunian, A.:Con Tpt, w. Timofei Dokschitzer (tpt) *(rec 1968)* RCA Gold Seal ▲ 74321-32045-2 [ADD]
Glazunov, A.:Album Leaf, w. Timofei Dokschitzer (tpt) *(rec 1968)* RCA Gold Seal ▲ 74321-32045-2 [ADD]
Prokofiev, S.:The Tale of the Stone Flower Russian Disc 2-▲ CD 11022 [AAD]
Shostakovich, D.:Sym 4 Russian Disc ▲ RUS 11190 [DDD]
Tchaikovsky, P.:The Nutcracker (sels) Monitor ■ 55014
Tchaikovsky, P.:Swan Lake (sels), w. Timofei Dokschitzer (tpt)—Neapolitan Dance *(rec 1968)* RCA Gold Seal ▲ 74321-32045-2 [ADD]
N. Rzaev (cnd)
Amirov, F.:The Arabian Nights Olympia 2-▲ OLY 578 [ADD/DDD]
S. Samosud (cnd)
Tchaikovsky, P.:Con Vn, w. David Ostrakh (vn) *(rec 1958–59)* Tuxedo ▲ TUXCD 1052
Y. Simonov (cnd)
Glinka, M.:Russlan & Ludmilla, w. Nina Fomina (sop—Gorislava), Bela Rudenko (sop—Ludmilla), Tamara Sinyavskaya (mez—Ratmir), Boris Morozov (bass—Farlaf), Evgeny Nesterenko (bass—Russlan), Valeri Yaroslavtsev (bass—Svetozar), Bolshoi Theater Chorus *(rec Moscow, 1978–1979)* Melodiya ("The Russian Opera" series) 3-▲ 74321-29348-2 [ADD]
Shchedrin, R.:Anna Karenina Russian Disc 2-▲ RUS 10030 [AAD]
Shostakovich, D.:The Golden Age *(rec 1982)* Russian Compact Disc 2-▲ RDCD 10009 [AAD]
E. Svetlanov (cnd)
Rachmaninoff, S.:Sym 2 Allegretto ▲ ACD 8183 [ADD] ■ ACS 8183
A. Tchistiakov (cnd)
Dargomyzhsky, A.:The Stone Guest Russian Season ▲ RUS 288113
Popular Scenes From Russian Operas, w. Bolshoi Theater Chorus, *(soloists unknown)* Russian Season ▲ LDC 288022 [DDD]
Rachmaninoff, S.:Aleko, w. Natalia Erassova (sop), Galina Borissova (cta), Vitaly Tarastchenko (ten), Vladimir Matorin (bass), Viatcheslav Potchapski (bass), Russian State Choir Russian Season 3-▲ CMX 388053
Rachmaninoff, S.:Francesca da Rimini, w. Maria Lapina (sop), Nilolaï Vassiliev (ten), Vitaly Tarastchenko (ten), Nikolaï Mechetniak (bar),Vladimir Matorin (bass), Russian State Choir Russian Season 3-▲ CMX 388053
Rachmaninoff, S.:The Miserly Knight, w. Mikhail Krutikov (sgr), Vladimir Kudriashov (sgr), Alexander Arkhipov (sgr), Vladislav Verestnikov (sgr), Piotr Gluboky (sgr), Russian State Choir Russian Season 3-▲ CMX 388053
Rimsky-Korsakov, N.:Kaschei the Immortal, w. I. Jourina (sop), N. Terentieva (mez), A. Arkhipov (ten), V. Verestnikov (bar), V. Matorin (bass), Yurloff Russian Choir [Russian] Russian Season ("Russian Season" series) ▲ LDC 288046 [DDD]
Rimsky-Korsakov, N.:A May Night, w. Maria Lapina (sop), Natalia Erassova (mez), Elena Okolycheva (cta), Alexander Arkhipov (ten), Vitaly Tarastchenko (ten), Piotr Glouboky (bass), Viatcheslav Potchapski (bass), Russian State Choir Russian Season 4-▲ CMX 388054
Shostakovich, D.:The Gamblers Russian Season ▲ RUS 288115
Y. Temirkanov (cnd)
Shchedrin, R.:Dead Souls, w. Larisa Avdeyeva (mez—Korobochka), Galina Borisova (mez—Plyushkin), Alexi Maslennikov (ten—Selifan), Vladislav Piavko (ten—Nozdryov), Vitali Vlasov (ten—Manilov), Boris Morozov (bass—Sobakevich), Alexander Voroshilo (sgr—Chichikov), Bolshoi Theater Chorus, Moscow Chamber Choir *(rec Moscow, 1982)* Melodiya ("The Russian Opera" series) 2-▲ 74321-29347-2 [ADD]
A. Zhuraitis (cnd)
Prokofiev, S.:Romeo & Juliet (sels)—highlights from the complete recording, Duet 34 IMP Classics ▲ PCD 983 [DDD]
Tchaikovsky, P.:Swan Lake (sels)—Valse [from Act 1]; Scene moderato; Scene allegro; Scene-allegro moderato; Assai quasi andante; Danse des cygnes [all from Act 2]; Danse hongroise; Danse russe; Danse espagnole; Danse napolitaine; Mazurka; Scène la sorties des ivites et la valse; Pas de deux; Scene-allegro [all from Act 3]; Scene-allegro; Scène finale [both from Act 4] IMP ("Classics" series) ▲ IMP 6700192
Tchaikovsky, P.:Swan Lake (sels) IMP Classics ▲ PCD 981 [DDD]
Bolshoi Theater String Quartet
Borodin, A.:Qt 1 Strs Multisonic ▲ MUL 310266
Bolshoi Theater SO
Baby Dance:A Toddler's Jump on the Classics, w. Bolshoi SO, Cleveland Orch, English Baroque Orch, Royal Concertgebouw Orch, A. Lazarev (cnd), J. E. Gardiner (cnd), T. Koopman (cnd), N. Harnoncourt (cnd), R. Leppard (cnd) Erato ▲ 96887-2 ■ 96887-4 ■ 97328-4 (blis
A. Lazarev (cnd)
Khachaturian, A.:Gayane (sels)—Sabre Dance Teldec ▲ 94677-2
Khachaturian, A.:Spartacus (sels)—Adagio for Spartacus and Phrygia Teldec ▲ 94677-2
Khachaturian, A.:Symphonic Suites Teldec ▲ 94677-2
Rachmaninoff, S.:Sym 2 *(rec Moscow, Jan. 25–28, 1994)* Erato ▲ 96360-2 [DDD]
Rachmaninoff, S.:Vocalise [arr. for orch.] *(rec Moscow, Jan. 25–28, 1994)* Erato ▲ 96360-2 [DDD]
Rimsky-Korsakov, N.:Capriccio espagnol Erato ▲ 94808
Rimsky-Korsakov, N.:Golden Cockerel (suite) Erato ▲ 94808
Rimsky-Korsakov, N.:A May Night (ov) Erato ▲ 94808
Rimsky-Korsakov, N.:Russian Easter Festival Erato ▲ 94808
Rimsky-Korsakov, N.:The Tsar's Bride Erato ▲ 94808
Tchaikovsky, P.:Eugene Onegin (sels)—Waltz & Polonaise Erato ▲ 2292-45964-2 ■ 2292-45964-4
Tchaikovsky, P.:Nutcracker Suite Erato ▲ 2292-45964-2 ■ 2292-45964-4
Tchaikovsky, P.:Sleeping Beauty (suite) Erato ▲ 2292-45963-2 ■ 2292-45963-4
Tchaikovsky, P.:Swan Lake (suite) Erato ▲ 2292-45963-2 ■ 2292-45963-4
The Ultimate Ballet Collection, w. Swiss Romande Orch [cnd:Armin Jordan] Erato ▲ 96969-2
Bolshoi Theater SO Brass Section
E. Svetlanov (cnd)
Shostakovich, D.:Festive Ov, w. Russian State SO *(rec Moscow, June 15–16, 1992)* Canyon Classics ▲ 3672 [DDD]
Bolshoi Theater SO Soloists
Glinka, M.:Chamber Music—Divert. on themes from Bellini's *La Sonnambula*; Vars. on a theme by Mozart for Harp; Nocturne in E♭ for Harp; Son. for Viola & Piano; Serenade on themes from Donizetti's *Anna Bolena* Russian Season ("Russian Season" series) ▲ LDC 288068
A. Lazarev (cnd)
Denisov, E.:Sun of the Incas, w. N. Lee (sop) Vox Box 2-▲ CDX 5121 [ADD]
Gubaidulina, S.:Concordanza Vox Box 2-▲ CDX 5121 [ADD]
Mansurian, T.:Rovem Vox Box 2-▲ CDX 5121 [ADD]
Schnittke, A.:Madrigals Sop, w. N. Lee (sop) Vox Box 2-▲ CDX 5121 [ADD]
A. Tchistiakov (cnd)
Rachmaninoff, S.:Aleko, w. Russian State Choir Russian Season ("Russian Season" series) ▲ LDC 288079
Rachmaninoff, S.:Francesca da Rimini, w. V. Taraschenko (ten), N. Vasiliev (bar), V. Matorin (bass) Russian Season ("Russian Season" series) ▲ LDC 288081
Rachmaninoff, S.:The Miserly Knight Russian Season ▲ LDC 288080
Bolshoi Theater Violin Ensemble
Y. Reentovich (cnd)
Debussy, C.:Clair de lune, w. Vera Dulova (hp) *(rec 1961)* Russian Compact Disc ("Talents of Russia" series) ▲ RCD 16204 [AAD]
Bonaventura Ensemble [Hermann Lechler (pno), Ulrich Wurlitzer (cl), Gerhard Zank (vc)]
Beethoven, L. van:Trio 7 Pno *(rec Studio 2, Bavarian Radio, Dec 14–15, 1995)* Calig ▲ CAL 50958 [DDD]
Brahms, J.:Trio Cl *(rec Studio 2, Bavarian Radio, Dec 18–19, 1995)* Calig ▲ CAL 50958 [DDD]
Bonn Telemann Ensemble [T. Habel-Thormé (rcr), N. Scheer, B. Wicke (org)]
Boismortier, J.B. de:Sons, Op. 34—No. 1 in g *(rec 1992)* FSM ▲ FCD 97759 [DDD]
Bonn Telemann Ensemble [T. Habel-Thormé (rcr), R. Jend (ob), N. Scheer (vn), M. Séché (bn), B. Wicke (org)]
Boismortier, J.B. de:Con Rec, Ob, Vn, Bn & Org *(rec 1992)* FSM ▲ FCD 97759 [DDD]
Naudot, J.-C.:Con Rcr—No. 1 in D *(rec 1992)* FSM ▲ FCD 97759 [DDD]
Bonn Youth Ensemble
W. Hess (cnd)
Alle Jahre wieder Bayer ▲ 100039
Bordeaux-Aquitaine National Orch
A. Lombard (cnd)
Berlioz, H.:Requiem, "Grande Messe des Morts", w. Jean-Luc Viala (ten), Lubomír Mátl (cnd), Prague Phil Chorus, Slovak Phil Choir Forlane ▲ FRL 16639 [DDD]
Bizet, G.:Carmen (sels), w. Léontina Vaduva (sop), Béatrice Uria-Monzon (mez), Christian Papis (ten), Vincent Le Texier (bar)—Toréador & other great arias Valois ▲ V 4769
Bloch, E.:Schelomo, w. Etienne Peclard (vc) Forlane ▲ FRL 16680 [DDD]
Chausson, E.:Poème Vn, w. Roland Daugareil (vn) Forlane ▲ FRL 16723 [DDD]
Lalo, E.:Sym espagnole, w. Roland Daugareil (vn) Forlane ▲ FRL 16723 [DDD]
Mozart, W.A.:Con 20 Pno, w. Emile Naoumoff (pno) Forlane ▲ FRL 16626 [DDD]
Mozart, W.A.:Con 24 Pno, w. Emile Naoumoff (pno) Forlane ▲ FRL 16626 [DDD]
Mussorgsky, M.:Boris Godunov (sels), w. P. Plishka (bass)—Coronation Scene, Monologue & Prayer & Death of Boris [R] Forlane ▲ FOR 16613 [DDD]
Prokofiev, S.:Sym-Con Vc, w. Etienne Peclard (vc) Forlane ▲ FRL 16680 [DDD]
Ravel, M.:L'Enfant et les sortilèges, w. M. Lagrange (sop), E. Vidal (sop), M. Damonte (mez), M. Mahé (mez), A. Chedel (cta), L. Pezzino (ten), M. Barrard (bar), V. le Texier (b-bar), Bordeaux Grand Théâtre Municipal Chorus [F] Valois ▲ V 4670
Verdi, G.:Arias, w. P. Plishka (bass)—five arias from Don Carlos, Macbeth, Nabucco, Vespri Siciliani [I] Forlane ▲ FOR 16613 [DDD]
Borealis Ensemble
C. Eggen (cnd)
Schoenberg, A.:Pierrot lunaire, w. A.-L. Berntsen (speaker) Victoria ▲ VCD 19088
Schoenberg, A.:Qt 2 Strs, w. A.-L. Berntsen (sop) Victoria ▲ VCD 19088
Boreas Wind Quintet [Joakim Dam Thomsen (ob), N. von Scholten (fl), A. E. Klett (cl), S. Haugland (bn), N. F. Jeppesen (hn)]
Blak, K.:Autumn with Frost Night Tutl ▲ FKT 6
Meitil, H.:Qnt 1 Ww Tutl ▲ FKT 6
Petersen, A.:Blåsarakvintett Tutl ▲ FKT 6
Bornus Consort
Pekiel, B.:Audite mortales Accord ▲ ACD 200692 [DDD]
Pekiel, B.:Missa brevis Accord ▲ ACD 200692 [DDD]
Pekiel, B.:Motets—3 sels Accord ▲ ACD 200692 [DDD]
M. Bornus-Szczycinski (cnd)
Zielenski, M.:Communiones totius anni, w. Kira Borescko (sop), Marcin Borus-Szczycinski (alt), Ryszard Minkiewicz (ten), Robert Hugo (org), Tallinn Linnamussikud Instrumental Ensemble, Tallin Linnamussikud Vocal Ensemble Urtext ▲ ACD 202662 [DDD]
Zielenski, M.:Offertoria totius anni, w. Kira Borescko (sop), Marcin Borus-Szczycinski (alt), Ryszard Minkiewicz (ten), Robert Hugo (org), Tallinn Linnamussikud Instrumental Ensemble, Tallin Linnamussikud Vocal Ensemble Urtext ▲ ACD 202662 [DDD]
Borodin String Quartet
The Lockenhaus Collection:Encore! Musical Jokes with Gidon Kremer and Friends, w. Martha Argerich (pno), et al. Philips ▲ 432252-2 PH [DDD]
Russian Miniatures Teldec ▲ 94572-2
Borodin String Quartet [M. Kopelman (vn), A. Abramenkov (vn), D. Shebalin (va), V. Berlinsky (vc)]
Beethoven, L. van:Grosse Fuge Str Qt *(rec live Dec. 12, 1991)* Russian Disc ▲ RD CD 11 087 [DDD]
Beethoven, L. van:Qt 11 Strs, "Quartetto serioso" MK ▲ MKA 418019 [AAD]
Borodin, A.:Qt 1 Strs EMI Classics ▲ CDC 47795 [DDD]
Borodin, A.:Qt 2 Strs EMI Classics ▲ CDC 47795 [DDD]
Brahms, J.:Qt 1 Strs *(rec Berlin, Jan. 1993)* Teldec ▲ 4509-90889-2 [DDD]
Brahms, J.:Qt 2 Strs Teldec ▲ 97461-2
Brahms, J.:Qt 3 Strs *(rec Berlin, Jan. 1993)* Teldec ▲ 4509-90889-2 [DDD]
Brahms, J.:Qnt Pno, w. Elizo Virzaladze (pno) Teldec ▲ 97461-2
Dvořák, A.:Qnt Pno, Op. 5, w. S. Richter (pno) Philips ▲ 412429-2 [ADD]
Dvořák, A.:Qnt Pno, Op. 81, w. S. Richter (pno) Philips ▲ 412429-2 [ADD]
Franck, C.:Qnt Pno, w. S. Richter (pno) Philips ▲ 432142-2 [DDD]
Haydn, J.:Qts Strs, Op. 64, "Tost Qts"—No. 5 MK ▲ MKA 418019 [AAD]
Haydn, J.:The Seven Last Words of Christ on the Cross *(rec Berlin, Oct. 1993)* Teldec ▲ 92373-2 [DDD]
Mahler, G.:Qt Pno [1 movt], w. L. Berlinsky (pno) Virgin Classics ▲ CDC 59040
Medtner, N.:Qnt Pno, w. E. Svetlanov (pno) Russian Disc ▲ RUS 11019 [DDD]
Schnittke, A.:Qt 3 Strs Virgin Classics ▲ CDC 59040
Schnittke, A.:Qnt Pno, w. L. Berlinsky (pno) Virgin Classics ▲ CDC 59040
Schoenberg, A.:Qt 2 Strs, w. L. Belobragina (sop) MK ▲ MKA 418019 [AAD]
Schubert, Franz:Qt 10 Strs Virgin Classics ▲ 59047 [DDD]
Schubert, Franz:Qt 12 Strs Virgin Classics ▲ 59047 [DDD]
Schubert, Franz:Qt 13 Strs Virgin Classics ▲ 59047 [DDD]
Schubert, Franz:Qnt Strs, D.956, w. Misha Milman (vc) *(rec Teldec Studio, Berlin, July 1994)* Teldec ▲ 94564-2 [DDD]
Shostakovich, D.:Elegy Str Qt *(rec live Dec. 12, 1991)* Russian Disc ▲ RD CD 11 087 [DDD]
Shostakovich, D.:Qt 2 Strs Virgin Classics ▲ CDC 59281
Shostakovich, D.:Qt 3 Strs Virgin Classics ▲ CDC 59041
Shostakovich, D.:Qt 7 Strs Virgin Classics ▲ CDC 59041
Shostakovich, D.:Qt 8 Strs Virgin Classics ▲ CDC 59041
Shostakovich, D.:Qt 8 Strs *(rec live Dec. 12, 1991)* Russian Disc ▲ RD CD 11 087 [DDD]
Shostakovich, D.:Qt 12 Strs *(rec July 13, 1970)* Intaglio ▲ ING 7561 [ADD]
Shostakovich, D.:Qt 12 Strs Virgin Classics ▲ CDC 59281
Shostakovich, D.:Qnt Pno, w. S. Richter (pno) *(rec July 17, 1966)* Intaglio ▲ ING 7561 [ADD]
Stenhammar, W.:Qt 3 Strs Swedish Society ▲ SCD 1032
Stenhammar, W.:Sentimental Romances, w. B. Lysell (vn) Swedish Society ▲ SCD 1032
Tchaikovsky, P.:Qt 1 Strs Teldec 2-▲ 90422-2
Tchaikovsky, P.:Qt 1 Strs EMI Classics 2-▲ ZDCB 49775
Tchaikovsky, P.:Qt 2 Strs EMI Classics 2-▲ ZDCB 49775
Tchaikovsky, P.:Qt 2 Strs Teldec 2-▲ 90422-2
Tchaikovsky, P.:Qt 3 Strs EMI Classics 2-▲ ZDCB 49775
Tchaikovsky, P.:Qt 3 Strs Teldec 2-▲ 90422-2
Tchaikovsky, P.:Souvenir de Florence Teldec 2-▲ 90422-2
Tchaikovsky, P.:Souvenir de Florence EMI Classics 2-▲ ZDCB 49775
Borodin Trio
Alyabiev, A.:Trio Pno Chandos ▲ CHAN 8975 [DDD]
Beethoven, L. van:Trios Pno (comp)—10 trios (excluding Op. 11) Chandos 4-▲ CHAN 8352 [DDD]
Brahms, J.:Trios (3) Pno Chandos 2-▲ CHAN 8334/35 [DDD]
Debussy, C.:Trio Pno Chandos ▲ CHAN 9016 [DDD]
Dvořák, A.:Trio 1 Pno Chandos ▲ CHAN 9172 [DDD]
Dvořák, A.:Trio 2 Pno Chandos ▲ CHAN 9172 [DDD]
Dvořák, A.:Trio 3 Pno Chandos ▲ CHAN 8320 [DDD]
Dvořák, A.:Trio 4 Pno, "Dumky" Chandos ▲ CHAN 8445 [DDD]
Haydn, J.:Trios Pno, Vn & Vc—H.XV/27 Chandos ▲ CHAN 8655 [DDD]
Martin, F.:Trio sur les mélodies populaires irlandaises Chandos ▲ CHAN 9016 [DDD]

ORCH. & ENS.

Borodin Trio (cont.)
Rachmaninoff, S.:Trio élégiaque 1 — Chandos ▲ CHAN 8341 [DDD]
Rachmaninoff, S.:Trio élégiaque 2 — Chandos ▲ CHAN 8341 [DDD]
Ravel, M.:Trio Pno — Chandos ▲ CHAN 8458
Schumann, R.:Fantasiestücke Vn — Chandos 2-▲ CHAN 8832/33 [DDD]
Shostakovich, D.:Qnt Pno, w. J. Horner (va), M. Zweig (vn) — Chandos ▲ CHAN 8342 [DDD]
Shostakovich, D.:Trio 2 Pno — Chandos ▲ CHAN 8342 [DDD]
Smetana, B.:Trio Pno — Chandos ▲ CHAN 8445 [DDD]
Taneyev, S.:Trio Pno — Chandos ▲ CHAN 8592 [DDD]
Tchaikovsky, P.:Album pour enfants — Chandos ▲ CHAN 8365 [DDD]
Tchaikovsky, P.:Trio Pno — Chandos ▲ CHAN 8975 [DDD]
Tchaikovsky, P.:Trio Pno — Chandos ▲ CHAN 8348 [DDD]
Turina, J.:Trio 1 Pno — Chandos ▲ CHAN 9016 [DDD]

Borodin Trio [Luba Edlina (pno), Rostislav Dubinsky (vn), Yuli Turovsky (vc)]
Arensky, A.:Trio 2 Pno — Chandos ▲ CHAN 8924 [DDD]
Beethoven, L. van:Trio 4 Pno, "Ghost" — Chandos ▲ CHAN 9296 [DDD]
Beethoven, L. van:Trio 6 Pno, "Archduke" — Chandos ▲ CHAN 9296 [DDD]
Brahms, J.:Qts Pno (comp), w. Rivka Golani (va) — Chandos 2-▲ CHAN 8809/10 [DDD]
Mozart, W.A.:Trios Pno (comp) — Chandos 2-▲ CHAN 8536/37 [DDD]
Prokofiev, S.:Ov on Hebrew Themes, w. E. Turovsky (vn), R. Golani (va), J. Campbell (cl) [orig. chamber version] — Chandos ▲ CHAN 8924 [DDD]
Shostakovich, D.:Songs Sop, Op. 127, w. N. Pelle (sop) — Chandos ▲ CHAN 8924 [DDD]

Borodin Trio [Luba Edlina (pno), Rostislav Dublinsky (vn), Laslzo Varga (vc)]
Spohr, L.:Trio 3 Pno — Chandos ▲ CHAN 9372 [DDD]
Spohr, L.:Trio 4 Pno — Chandos ▲ CHAN 9372 [DDD]

Boskovsky Ensemble
W. Boskovsky (cnd)
Bonbons Aus Wien:Rare Old Vienna Dances—The Willi Boskovsky Collection, Vol. 1 — Vanguard Classics ▲ OVC 8015 [ADD]
The Charm Of Old Vienna:Rare Old Vienna Dances, Vol. 2 — Vanguard Classics ▲ OVC 8016 [ADD]
Creampuffs From Vienna:Rare Old Vienna Dances, Vol. 3 *(rec 1962)* — Vanguard Classics ▲ OVC 8017 [ADD]

Boston Ballet Orch
J. McPhee (cnd)
Tchaikovsky, P.:The Nutcracker *(rec live)* — Boston Ballet Orchestra ▲ BBO103-32 [DDD]

Boston Baroque Orch
M. Pearlman (cnd)
Bach, J.S.:Brandenburg Cons [period instrs] — Telarc 2-▲ 2CD 80412 [DDD]
Bach, J.S.:Brandenburg Con 1 [period instrs] *(rec Jan 3–5, 1994)* — Telarc ▲ CD 80368 [DDD]
Bach, J.S.:Brandenburg Con 2 [period instrs] *(rec Jan 3–5, 1994)* — Telarc ▲ CD 80368 [DDD]
Bach, J.S.:Brandenburg Con 3 [period instrs] *(rec Jan 3–5, 1994)* — Telarc ▲ CD 80368 [DDD]
Bach, J.S.:Brandenburg Con 4 *(rec Jan 3–5, 1993)* — Telarc ▲ CD 80354 [DDD]
Bach, J.S.:Brandenburg Con 5 *(rec Jan 3–5, 1993)* — Telarc ▲ CD 80354 [DDD]
Bach, J.S.:Brandenburg Con 6 *(rec Jan 3–5, 1993)* — Telarc ▲ CD 80354 [DDD]
Handel, G.F.:Concerti grossi, Op. 6 [period instrs]—Nos. 1–6; — Telarc ▲ CD 80253 [DDD]
Handel, G.F.:Messiah, w. Karen Clift (sop), Catherine Robbin (mez), Bruce Fowler (ten), Victor Ledbetter (bar), Boston Baroque Chorus [E] — Telarc 2-▲ CD 80322 [DDD]
Handel, G.F.:Messiah (sels), w. Karen Clift (sop), Catherine Robbin (mez), Bruce Fowler (ten), Victor Ledbetter (bar), Boston Baroque Chorus—Sinfonia; Comfort ye, my people; Every valley shall be exalted; And the glory of the Lord; And He shall purify; Behold, a virgin shall conceive; O thou that tellest good tidings to Zion; For unto us a Child is born; Rejoice greatly, O daughter of Zion; His yoke is easy; All we like sheep; Lift up your heads; The Lord gave the word; Their sound is gone out; Why do the nations?; Let us break their bonds asunder; He that dwelleth in heaven; Thou shalt break them; Hallelujah; I know that my Redeemer liveth; Since by man came death; Behold, I tell you a mystery; The trumpet shall sound; Then shall be brought to pass; O death, where is thy sting?; But thanks be to God; Worthy is the Lamb...Amen *(rec May 18–22, 1992)* — Telarc ▲ CD 80348 [DDD]
Mozart, W.A.:Requiem, w. Ruth Ziesak (sop), Nancy Maultsby (mez), Richard Croft (ten), David Arnold (bar) [completion by Robert Levin; performed on period instruments] *(rec Campion Center, Weston, MA, Nov 2–3, 1994)* — Telarc ▲ CD 80410 [DDD]
Purcell, H.:Dido & Aeneas, w. Nancy Maultsby (sop—Dido), Susannah Waters (sop—Belinda), Margaret O'Keefe (sop—1st Witch), Sharon Baker (sop—2nd Woman), Laura Tucker (mez—Sorceress), Donna Ames (alt—Spirit), Richard Clement (ten—Sailor), Russell Braun (bar—Aeneas) — Telarc ▲ CD 80424 [DDD]
Purcell, H.:Music of—Ov; Rondeau; Air [all from Abdelazer]; Minuet & Air [from Gordian Knot Unty'd]; Curtain Tune on a Ground [from Timon of Athens]; Rondeau; Hornpipe; Ov; Dance for the Fairies; Chaconne [all from Fairy Queen]; Hornpipe on a Ground [from Married Beau] — Telarc ▲ CD 80424 [DDD]

Boston Brass Ensemble
Gabrieli, G.:Fant VI toni, w. E. Power Biggs (org) *(rec Harvard Univ, Cambridge, MA, 1959)* — Sony Classical ("Masterworks Heritage" series) ▲ MHK 62353 [ADD]
Gabrieli, G.:Intonationi d'organo, w. E. Power Biggs (org)—Del primo tono, secondo tono, terzo e quarto tono, ottavo tono, nono tono, dècimo tono, undicècimo tono & duodècimo tono *(rec Harvard Univ, Cambridge, MA, 1959)* — Sony Classical ("Masterworks Heritage" series) ▲ MHK 62353 [ADD]
R. Burgin (cnd)
Frescobaldi, G.:Music of, w. E. Power Biggs (org)—Toccatas in d & G; Canzoni Nos 1–5 in G, C, a, g & g *(rec Harvard Univ, Cambridge, MA, Mar 26, 27, 30 & 31, 1959)* — Sony Classical ("Masterworks Heritage" series) ▲ MHK 62353 [ADD]

Boston Chamber Ensemble
H. Farberman (cnd)
Molter, J.M.:Con 3 Tpt, w. Armando Ghitalla (tpt) *(rec Dec 1963 & Jan 1964)* — Crystal ▲ CD 760
P. Monteux (cnd)
Hummel, J.N.:Con in E Tpt, w. Armando Ghitalla (tpt) *(rec Dec 1963 & Jan 1964)* — Crystal ▲ CD 760

Boston Chamber Music Society
Brahms, J.:Qt 3 Pno — Northeastern ▲ NR 244-CD
Brahms, J.:Qnt Cl — Northeastern ▲ NR 243-CD
Brahms, J.:Trio Cl — Northeastern ▲ NR 243-CD
Brahms, J.:Trio 1 Pno — Northeastern ▲ NR 244-CD

Boston Chamber Players
Y. Wyner (cnd)
Wyner, Y.:Serenade Fl *(rec Jordan Hall, New England Conservatory of Music, Boston, Nov 6, 1977)* — CRI ("American Masters" series) ▲ CD 701 [ADD]

Boston Composers String Quartet
Pinkham, D.:Qt Strs *(rec Dec. 1992)* — Koch International Classics ▲ KIC 7180 [DDD]
Read, G.:Chamber Music, w. Janet Packer (vn), Gerald Berthiaume (cel), Leslie Stratton Norris (hp), Barbara Harbach (hpd), Joseph Holt (pno), Howard Karp (pno)—5 Aphorisms, Op. 150; Son. da Chiesa, Op. 61; Sonoric Fant. No. 1, Op. 102; Qt. 1 Strings, Op. 100 — Northeastern ▲ NOR 253 [DDD]
Read, G.:Qt 1 Strs *(rec Tsai Performance Center, Boston Univ., May, June & Nov. 1993)* — Northeastern ("Classical Arts, Contemporary" series) ▲ NR 253

Boston Early Music Festival Orch
A. Parrott (cnd)
Bach, J.S.:Con Fl, Vn & Hpd — EMI Classics 2-▲ ZDCB 54653-2
Bach, J.S.:Suites Orch, BWV 1066–1069 — EMI Classics 2-▲ ZDCB 54653-2
Mozart, W.A.:Church Sons—K.67 & 329 — Denon ▲ CO 79573 [DDD]
Mozart, W.A.:Laut verkünde unsre Freude, w. W. Hite (ten), W. Bastian (ten), W. Sharp (bar), Boston Early Music Festival Chorus [G] — Denon ▲ CO 77152 [DDD]
Mozart, W.A.:Missa, K.427, w. Nancy Armstrong (sop), Dominique Labelle (sop), Jeffery Thomas (ten), Richard Morrison (bass), Handel & Haydn Society Chorus [L] — Denon ▲ CO 79573 [DDD]
Mozart, W.A.:Requiem, w. J. Bryden (sop), M. Westbrook-Geha (mez), W. Hite (ten), S. Richardson (bar), Boston Early Music Festival Chorus [L] — Denon ▲ CO 77152 [DDD]

Boston Early Music Soloists
W. Malloch (cnd)
Bach, J.S.:Suites Orch, BWV 1066–1069—15-member ensemble performs the suites with one instrument to a part, on period instruments, & observing all repeats — Koch International Classics ▲ KIC 7037-2 [DDD]

Boston Museum Trio
Vivaldi, A.:Music of, w. Philharmonia Baroque Orch, Concerto Amsterdam, Clemencic Consort, Bologna I Filarmonici—sels. from Flute Concerto, RV.427 & 440; Four Seasons—Autumn; String Concerto, RV.129 & 152; Serenata a Tre, RV.690; Sonata, RV.2 *(rec 1970–86)* — Harmonia Mundi Plus ▲ HMP 390810

Boston Museum Trio [Daniel Stepner (vn), Laura Jeppesen (vl), John Gibbons (hpd)]
Bach, J.S.:Trio Sons (misc)—in G, BWV 1027; in D, BWV 1028; in g, BWV 1029 *(rec Waltham, MA, Oct 21 & 22, 1993)* — Centaur ▲ CRC 2198 [DDD]
Buxtehude, D.:Sons Vn, Vl & Continuo—4 sonatas—Op. 1/3, 4 & Op. 2/3, 6 — Musique d'Abord ▲ HMA 1901089
Marais, M.:La Gamme et autres morceaux de simphonie [period instrs] — Centaur ▲ CRC 2129
Marais, M.:Son à la Marésienne [period instrs] — Centaur ▲ CRC 2129
Marais, M.:Sonnerie [period instrs] — Centaur ▲ CRC 2129
Telemann, G.P.:Qts, Book 4, w. Christopher Krueger (fl) *(rec Slosberg Auditorium, Brandeis Univ, Waltham, MA, Aug 24–26, 1994)* — Centaur ▲ 2260 [DDD]
Vivaldi, A.:Sons Vn—RV.2,6,25 & 29, "Sonatas à Pisendel" — Musique d'Abord ▲ HMA 1901088 [ADD]

Boston Museum Trio members [Daniel Stepner (vn), John Gibbons (hpd)]
Bach, J.S.:Sons Vn—in G, BWV 1021; in e, BWV 1023 *(rec Waltham, MA, Oct 21 & 22, 1993)* — Centaur ▲ CRC 2198 [DDD]

Boston Musica Viva
Schwantner, J.:Consortium I, w. C. Pittman (fl) — Delos ▲ DCD 1011 [AAD]
Vercoe, E.:Herstory II [E] — Capstone ▲ CPS 8613
Wen-Chung, C.:Music of, New Music Consort, Speculum Musicae—Windswept Peaks; Suite for Hp & Ww Qnt; Echoes from the Gorge; Yü Ko — Albany ▲ TROY 155
R. Pittman (cnd)
Berio, L.:O King Orch — Delos ▲ DCD 1011 [AAD]
Child, P.:Ensemblance — Neuma ▲ 450-75 [DDD]
Crawford, R.:Movements (2) — Delos ▲ DCD 1012 [AAD]
Davidovsky, M.:Synchronism 3 — Delos ▲ DCD 1011 [AAD]
Harris, D.:Ludus II — Delos ▲ DCD 1011 [AAD]
Ives, C.:Largo — Delos ▲ DCD 1011 [AAD]
Lieberson, P.:Raising the Gaze — Neuma ▲ 450-79 [DDD]
Mekeel, J.:Corridors of Dream, w. *(soloist unknown)* — Delos ▲ DCD 1012 [AAD]
Musgrave, T.:Chamber Con 2 — Delos ▲ DCD 1012 [AAD]
Rands, B.:...in the receding mist CE — Neuma ▲ 450-79 [DDD]
Schwantner, J.:Consortium IV — Delos ▲ DCD 1011 [AAD]
Thow, J.:All Hallows — Neuma ▲ 450-79 [DDD]
Wilson, O.:A City Called Heaven — Neuma ▲ 450-79 [DDD]
Zwilich, E.T.:Chamber Sym *(rec July–Aug. 1980; originall)* — CRI ▲ CD 621 [ADD]

Boston Musica Viva [Nancy Cirillo (vn), Ronald Lowry (vc), William Wrzesion (cl), Hugh Hinton (pno)]
Chou Wen-Chung:Windswept Peaks — Albany ▲ TROY 155 [DDD]

Boston PO
B. Zander (cnd)
Mahler, G.:Sym 6 — IMP ("Masters" series) 2-▲ IMP DMCD 93
Stravinsky, I.:Le Sacre du printemps Orch — IMP Masters ▲ MCD 25 [DDD]

Boston Pops Orch
Strauss (II), Joh.:Waltzes — RCA ■ ALK1-4458
Strauss, Josef:Music of — RCA ■ ALK1-4458
A. Fiedler (cnd)
An American Salute — RCA Gold Seal ("Papillon Collection" series) ▲ 6806-2-RG [ADD] ■ 6806-4-RG
Anderson, L.:Music of *(rec Dec 1986)* — RCA Victrola ■ 5691-4 RV
Anderson, L.:Music of — RCA Victor ▲ 09026-61237-2 ■ 09026-61237-4 (CrO2)
A. Fiedler:The Collection — RCA Living Stereo 3-▲ 09026-68011-2
Basic 100 Vol. 30, w. Earl Wild (pno) — RCA Victor ▲ 09026-61727-2 ■ 09026-61727-4
Basic 100 Vol. 75 — RCA Victor ▲ 09026-68366-2 ■ 09026-68366-4
Bernstein, L.:Candide (ov) — RCA Victor ▲ 09026-68334-2 ■ 09026-68334-4
Bernstein, L.:Candide (ov) — RCA ■ RK 1033
Bernstein, L.:Fancy Free—sels. — RCA Gold Seal ▲ 6806-2-RG [ADD] ■ 6806-4-RG6
Bernstein, L.:Fancy Free (sels) *(rec 1958)* — RCA Living Stereo ▲ 09026-61501-2; ■ 09026-61505-4
Bernstein, L.:Fancy Free (sels)—Dances — RCA Victor ▲ 09026-68334-2 ■ 09026-68334-4
The Best of Handel, w. RCA Victor SO [cnd:Leopold Stokowski], et al. — Victrola ("Victrola Best of" series) ▲ 60771-2-RV [ADD] ■ 60771-4-RV
The Best of Mendelssohn, w. Philadelphia Orch [cnd:Eugene Ormandy], Leipzig Gewandhaus Orch [cnd:Kurt Masur], et al. — ("Victrola Best of" series)
Blockbusters from the Movies, w. Philadelphia Orch [cnd:Eugene Ormandy] — RCA Victor ▲ 09026-68080-2 ■ 09026-68080-4
Borodin, A.:In the Steppes of Central Asia — RCA Victrola ▲ 7813-2-RV [ADD] ■ 7813-4-RV
Borodin, A.:In the Steppes of Central Asia — RCA Living Stereo ▲ 09026-68132-2; ■ 09026-68132-4
Borodin, A.:Prince Igor (ov) — RCA Victrola ▲ 7813-2-RV [ADD] ■ 7813-4-RV
Borodin, A.:Prince Igor (ov) — RCA Living Stereo ▲ 09026-68132-2; ■ 09026-68132-4
Borodin, A.:Prince Igor (Polovtsian dances) — RCA Living Stereo ▲ 09026-68132-2 ■ 09026-68132-4
Borodin, A.:Prince Igor (Polovtsian dances) — RCA Victrola ▲ 7813-2-RV [ADD] ■ 7813-4-RV
Britten, B.:The Young Person's Guide to the Orchestra, w. Hugh Downs (nar) [commentary Eric Crozier; rec June 12, 1963] *(rec Symphony Hall, Boston, June 8, 1961)* — RCA Living Stereo ▲ 09026-68131-2 [ADD]; ■ 09026-68131-4
Chabrier, E.:España *(rec ca. 1956–60)* — RCA Gold Seal ▲ 09026-61497-2 ■ 09026-61497-4
Christmas at the Pops — RCA ▲ 09026-68266-2; ■ 09026-68266-4
A Christmas Festival with Arthur Fiedler & The Boston Pops — RCA Gold Seal ▲ 6428-2-RG [ADD] ■ 6428-4-RG
Christmas Sampler, w. Plácido Domingo (ten), James Galway (fl), Vienna Boys' Choir — RCA Victor ▲ 09026-61840-2 ■ 09026-61840-4
Cinema Classics 7:Classical Music Made Famous in Films — Naxos ▲ 8.551157 [DDD]
Cinema Classics 8:Classical Music Made Famous in Films — Naxos ▲ 8.551158 [DDD]
Cinema Classics 9:Classical Music Made Famous in Films — Naxos ▲ 8.551159 [DDD]
Classical Jukebox, w. Philadelphia Orch [cnd:Eugene Ormandy] — RCA Victor ▲ 09026-68121-2 ■ 09026-68121-4
Classical Music for Home Improvement, w. Philadelphia Orch [cnd:Ormandy] — RCA Victor ▲ 09026-61369-2 ■ 09026-61369-4 (CrO2)
Classics from the Crypt, w. Philadelphia Orch [cnd:Eugene Ormandy] — RCA Victor ▲ 09026-61238-2 ■ 09026-61238-4 (CrO2)
Copland, A.:El salón México — RCA Gold Seal ▲ 6806-2-RG [ADD] ■ 6806-4-RG6 (CrO2)
Enescu, G.:Romanian Rhap 1 — RCA Gold Seal ("Papillon Collection" series) ▲ 6530-2-RG [ADD] ■ 6530-4-RG
Everything You Wanted to Know about Classical Music, w. Philadelphia Orch [cnd:Eugene Ormandy] — RCA Victor ▲ 09026-61239-2 ■ 09026-61239-4 (CrO2)
Familiar Music for Family Fun — Victrola ■ ALK1-5383
Fiedler & Friends — RCA Gold Seal ▲ 09026-62578-2
Fiedler at the Ballet — RCA Gold Seal ▲ 09026-62577-2
Fiedler Encores — London ("Phase 4 Stereo" series) ▲ 448952-2

▲ = CD ♦ = Enhanced CD Δ = MD ■ = Cassette Tape □ = DCC

Boston Pops Orch (cont.)

A. Fiedler (cnd) (cont.)

Fiedler on the Roof RCA Victor ▲ 3201-2-RG [ADD] ■ 3201-4-RG
Fiedler's Favorite Marches RCA Victor ▲ 60700-2-RG [ADD] ■ 60700-4-RG
Fiedler's Greatest Hits RCA Victor ▲ 60835-2-RG ■ 60835-4-RG6
Gershwin IMP ("Collectors" series) ▲ IMPX 9013
Gershwin, G.:An American in Paris RCA Gold Seal ▲ 6519-2-RG [ADD] ■ 6519-4-RG (CrO2)
Gershwin, G.:An American in Paris RCA Victor ▲ 09026-61727-2; ■ 09026-61727-4 (CrO2)
Gershwin, G.:Con Pno, w. E. Wild (pno) RCA Victor ▲ 09026-61727-2; ■ 09026-61727-4 (CrO2)
Gershwin, G.:Con Pno, w. E. Wild (pno) RCA Gold Seal ▲ 6519-2-RG [ADD] ■ 6519-4-RG (CrO2)
Gershwin, G.:Cuban Ov RCA Gold Seal ▲ 6806-2-RG [ADD] ■ 6806-4-RG (CrO2)
Gershwin, G.:Cuban Ov RCA Victor ▲ 09026-68334-2 ■ 09026-68334-4
Gershwin, G.:Girl Crazy (suite) [orchd Leroy Anderson] *(rec Boston Sym Hall, June 1979)* London ("Phase 4 Stereo" series) ▲ 443900-2 [ADD]
Gershwin, G.:"I Got Rhythm" Vars, w. E. Wild (pno) RCA Gold Seal ▲ 6519-2-RG [ADD] ■ 6519-4-RG (CrO2)
Gershwin, G.:Of Thee I Sing (sels)—Ov; Wintergreen for President *(rec Boston Sym Hall, June 1979)* London ("Phase 4 Stereo" series) ▲ 443900-2 [ADD]
Gershwin, G.:Ovs—Oh, Kay!; Funny Face; Let 'em Eat Cake *(rec Boston Sym Hall, June 1979)* London ("Phase 4 Stereo" series) ▲ 443900-2 [ADD]
Gershwin, G.:Preludes (3) Pno [trans for orch Gregory Stone] *(rec Boston Sym Hall, June 1979)* London ("Phase 4 Stereo" series) ▲ 443900-2 [ADD]
Gershwin, G.:Rhap in Blue, w. E. Wild (pno) RCA Gold Seal ▲ 6519-2-RG [ADD] ■ 6519-4-RG (CrO2)
Gershwin, G.:Rhap in Blue, w. E. Wild (pno) RCA Victor ▲ 09026-61727-2; ■ 09026-61727-4 (CrO2)
Gershwin, G.:Second Rhap [arr Robert McBride] *(rec Boston Sym Hall, June 1979)* London ("Phase 4 Stereo" series) ▲ 443900-2 [ADD]
Gould, M.:American Salute RCA Gold Seal ▲ 6806-2-RG [ADD] ■ 6806-4-RG6 (CrO2)
Gould, M.:Interplay Pno—sels *(rec 1958)* RCA Living Stereo ▲ 09026-61501-2; ■ 09026-61501-4
Gounod, C.:Funeral March of a Marionette *(rec Symphony Hall, Boston, May 10, 1963)* RCA Living Stereo ▲ 09026-68131-2 [ADD] ■ 09026-68131-4
Great American Marches RCA Victor ■ AGK1-1334
Greatest Hits Polydor ■ 825088-4
Greatest Overtures, w. Chicago SO [cnd:Fritz Reiner] ▲ 60839-2-RG ■ 60839-4-RG
Grieg:Greatest Hits, w. Philadelphia Orch [cnd:Eugene Ormandy] RCA Victor ▲ 60832-2-RG ■ 60832-4-RG
Grieg, E.:Peer Gynt Suites, Opp. 46 & 55 *(rec Symphony Hall, Boston, May 20-21, 1957)* RCA Living Stereo ▲ 09026-68131-2 [ADD] ■ 09026-68131-4
Grofé, F.:Grand Canyon Suite RCA Gold Seal ▲ 6806-2-RG [ADD] ■ 6806-4-RG (CrO2)
Grofé, F.:Grand Canyon Suite RCA ■ RK 1033
Haydn, J.:Con Tpt, w. Al Hirt (tpt) RCA Victor ▲ 09026-61857-2; ■ 09026-61857-4
Hayman, R.:Kid Stuff—Children's Marching Song [Arnold]; March of the Siamese Children [Rodgers]; Mickey Mouse March [Dodd]; All around the Mulberry Bush; Mary Had a Little Lamb; London Bridge; Alouette *(rec Symphony Hall, Boston, Sept. 28, 1959)* RCA Living Stereo ▲ 09026-68131-2 [ADD]; ■ 09026-68131-4
Ibert, J.:Divert Orch *(rec 1956)* RCA Living Stereo ▲ 09026-61429-2 ■ 09026-61429-4
Irish Night at the Pops RCA Victor ▲ 60746-2-RG [ADD] ■ 60746-4-RG
Kay, H.:Cakewalk *(rec 1958)* RCA Living Stereo ▲ 09026-61501-2; ■ 09026-61501-4
Kay, H.:Stars & Stripes *(rec 1958)* RCA Living Stereo ▲ 09026-61501-2; ■ 09026-61501-4
Khachaturian, A.:Gayane (sels) RCA Victrola ▲ 7734-2-RV [DDD] ■ 7734-4-RV (CrO2)
Khachaturian, A.:Gayane (sels)—Lezghinka RCA Living Stereo ▲ 09026-68132-2 ■ 09026-68132-4
Khachaturian, A.:Masquerade (sels)—Galop RCA Living Stereo ▲ 09026-68132-2; ■ 09026-68132-4
Leroy Anderson's Greatest Hits RCA Victor ▲ 09026-61237-2 ■ 09026-61237-4 (CrO2)
Liszt, F.:Hungarian Rhaps RCA Victor ▲ 09026-62679-2 ■ 09026-62679-4
Liszt, F.:Hungarian Rhaps—No. 12 RCA ■ ALK1-4475
Liszt, F.:Mazeppa Orch RCA ■ ALK1-4475
Liszt, F.:Les Préludes RCA ■ ALK1-4475
Liszt, F.:Rakóczy March *(rec ca. 1956-60)* RCA Gold Seal ▲ 09026-61497-2 ■ 09026-61497-4
Liszt, F.:Rakóczy March RCA ■ ALK1-4475
The Little Drummer Boy:Christmas Favorites, w. Morton Gould (pno), New Philharmonia Orch, et al. RCA Victor ▲ 09026-61837-2 ■ 09026-61837-4
Loesser, F.:Hans Christian Andersen Medley—I'm Hans Christian Andersen; Thumbelina; Inch Worm; Anywhere I Wander; Wonderful Copenhagen *(rec Symphony Hall, Boston, June 27, 1960)* RCA Living Stereo ▲ 09026-68131-2 [ADD]; ■ 09026-68131-4
Lolly Pops Victrola ■ ALK1-4623
Lullaby RCA Victor ▲ 60876-2 [ADD] ■ 60876-4 (CrO2)
Neil Diamond Songbook Polydor ■ 6053
O Holy Night:Christmas Favorites, w. James Galway (fl), Richard Stoltzman (cl), Michala Petri (rcr), Emily Mitchell (hp), Canadian Brass RCA Victor ▲ 09026-61836-2 ■ 09026-61836-4
Offenbach, J.:Le Belle Hélène (ov) RCA ("Basic 100" series) ▲ 09026-68366-2 ■ 09026-68366-4
Offenbach, J.:Les Contes d'Hoffmann RCA ("Basic 100" series) ▲ 09026-68366-2 ■ 09026-68366-4
Offenbach, J.:Les Contes d'Hoffmann *(rec 1956)* RCA Living Stereo ▲ 09026-61429-2 ■ 09026-61429-4
Offenbach, J.:Gaîté Parisienne RCA Victrola ▲ 7734-2-RV [DDD] ■ 7734-4-RV (CrO2)
Offenbach, J.:Gaîté Parisienne RCA Living Stereo ▲ 09026-61847-2; ■ 09026-61847-4
Offenbach, J.:Gaîté Parisienne RCA ("Basic 100" series) ▲ 09026-68366-2 ■ 09026-68366-4
Offenbach, J.:Music of RCA ■ ALK1-4457
Offenbach, J.:Orphée aux enfers (sels)—Intermezzo RCA ("Basic 100" series) ▲ 09026-68366-2 ■ 09026-68366-4
100 Fiedler Favorites RCA Gold Seal 7-▲ 09026-62698-2
Opera without Singing Victrola ■ ALK1-5382 (m)
Orchestral Favorites London ("Weekend Classics" series) ▲ 430212-2 [AAD]
Overtures RCA Red Seal ▲ RCD1-5479
Pops around the World RCA Victor ▲ 09026-61544-2 ■ 09026-61544-4
Pops Christmas Party RCA Living Stereo ▲ 09026-61685-2 ■ 09026-61685-4
Pops Concert RCA Red Seal ▲ 6213-2-RC [ADD]
Pops Goes Christmas RCA Victor ■ RK 1304
Popular Favorites by Fiedler Pair ▲ PDC 2-1022 2-■ PDK 2-1022
Respighi, O.:La Boutique fantastique RCA Living Stereo ▲ 09026-61847-2; ■ 09026-61847-4
Rimsky-Korsakov, N.:Capriccio espagnol *(rec 1977)* LaserLight ▲ 15312 [DDD]
Rimsky-Korsakov, N.:Golden Cockerel (suite) *(rec ca. 1956-60)* RCA Gold Seal ▲ 09026-61497-2 ■ 09026-61497-4
Rimsky-Korsakov, N.:Golden Cockerel (suite) RCA ■ ALK1 4460
Rimsky-Korsakov, N.:Russian Easter Festival RCA Living Stereo ▲ 09026-68132-2 ■ 09026-68132-4
Rimsky-Korsakov, N.:Russian Easter Festival RCA Victrola ▲ 7813-2-RV [ADD] ■ 7813-4-RV
Rimsky-Korsakov, N.:Russian Easter Festival RCA Living Stereo ▲ 09026-68132-2; ■ 09026-68132-4
Rimsky-Korsakov, N.:The Tale of Tsar Saltan (orch sels)—Fight of the Bumblebee RCA Living Stereo ▲ 09026-68132-2 ■ 09026-68132-4
Rodgers, R.:Slaughter on 10th Avenue RCA Gold Seal ▲ 6806-2-RG [ADD] ■ 6806-4-RG (CrO2)
Rossini, G.:Ovs—William Tell RCA ■ ALK1 4460
Rossini, G.:Ovs—William Tell *(rec ca. 1956-60)* RCA Gold Seal ▲ 09026-61497-2 ■ 09026-61497-4

Boston Pops Orch (cont.)

A. Fiedler (cnd) (cont.)

Saint-Saëns, C.:Carnival of the Animals, w. Leo Litwin (pno), Samuel Lipman (pno), Martin Hoherman (vc), Hugh Downs (nar) [verses rec June 12, 1963] *(rec Symphony Hall, Boston, June 14, 1961)* RCA Living Stereo ▲ 09026-68131-2 [ADD]; ■ 09026-68131-4
Salute to Disney:Music from Disney Film Classics Deutsche Grammophon ▲ 447013-2 ■ 447013-4
Shchedrin, R.:Carmen RCA ■ 5689-4-RV
Stars & Stripes Forever:The Greatest Marches RCA Victor ▲ 60838-2-RG ■ 60838-4-RG6
Strauss Family Waltzes Victrola ■ ALK1-4458
Strauss, E.:Polkas & Waltzes—Bahn Frei; Doctrines RCA Living Stereo ▲ 09026-61688-2; ■ 09026-61688-4
Strauss (II), Joh.:Music of—Where the Citrons Bloom; Thunder & Lightening; 1001 Nights; Kriegsabenteur Schnell Polka; Fledermaus Polka; Roses from the South; Accelerations; Pizzicato Polka RCA Living Stereo ▲ 09026-61688-2; ■ 09026-61688-4
Strauss, Josef:Music of—Secret Attract/Dynamiden; Music of the Spheres; Pizzicato Polka RCA Living Stereo ▲ 09026-61688-2; ■ 09026-61688-4
Tchaikovsky, P.:Capriccio italien *(rec 1977)* LaserLight ▲ 15312 [DDD]
Tchaikovsky, P.:Eugene Onegin (sels) RCA Living Stereo ▲ 09026-68132-2 ■ 09026-68132-4
Tchaikovsky, P.:Eugene Onegin (sels) RCA Living Stereo ▲ 09026-68132-2; ■ 09026-68132-4
Tchaikovsky, P.:Marche slave RCA ■ ALK1 4460
Tchaikovsky, P.:Sleeping Beauty (sels) RCA Living Stereo ▲ 09026-68132-2 ■ 09026-68132-4
Tchaikovsky, P.:Swan Lake (sels) RCA Victrola ▲ 7879-2-RV [ADD] ■ 7879-4-RV
Tchaikovsky, P.:Swan Lake (suite) RCA Gold Seal ▲ 07863-55233-2 ■ 07863-55233-4
The Voices of Living Stereo, Vol. 2, w. Eileen Farrell (sop), Birgit Nilsson (sop), Roberta Peters (sop), Leontyne Price (sop), Galina Vishnevskaya (sop), Rosalind Elias (mez), Shirley Verrett (mez), Marian Anderson (cta), Maureen Forrester (cta), Sergio Franchi (ten), Mario Lanza (ten), Richard Lewis (ten), Jan Pee, Alexander Dedyukhin (pno), Franz Rupp (pno), Leo Taubman (pno), George Trovillo (pno), Charles Wadsworth (pno), Boston SO [cnd:Charles Munch], Chicago SO [cnd:Fritz Reiner], RCA Victor Orch, RCA Victor Chorus [cnd:Wa *(rec Boston & Chicago & New York & Rome, 1957-1964)* RCA Living Stereo ▲ 09026-68167-2 [ADD]
White Christmas Deutsche Grammophon ("Galleria" series) ▲ 419414-2 [ADD]
White Christmas Deutsche Grammophon ("Galleria" series) ▲ 419414-2 [ADD]
Wild Classics:A Celebration of Animals & Nature, w. James Galway (fl), Ofra Harnoy (vc), Martin Hoherman (vc), Emily Mitchell (hp), Michael Dussek (pno), Samuel Lipman (pno), Leo Litwin (pno), Gerhard Oppitz (pno), Isao Tomita (synths), Chicago SO [cnd:Fritz Reiner] RCA Red Seal ▲ 09026-68483-2 ■ 09026-68483-4

K. Lockhart (cnd)

Miller, G.:Music of, w. John Pizzarelli (gtr), King's Singers—Runnin' Wild; A String of Pearls; Moonlight Serenade; Chattanooga Choo-Choo; The Nearness of You; My Blue Heaven; Song of the Volga Boatmen; Sunrise Serenade; Kalamazoo; Serenade in Blue; The Anvil Chorus; St. Louis Blues March; A Nightingale Sang in Berkeley Square; American Patrol; Little Brown Jug; In the Mood *(rec Symphony Hall, Boston, May 30-June 1, 1996)* RCA Victor ▲ 09026-68598-2 [DDD] ■ 09026-68598-4

A. F. Williams (cnd)

Romance Classics Philips ▲ 456079-2

J. Williams (cnd)

Aisle Seat Philips ("Digital Classics" series) ▲ 411037-2
Albinoni, T.:Adagio Org Philips ▲ 416361-2 [DDD]
America, the Dream Goes on, w. James Ingram (sgr) Philips ▲ 412627-2 [DDD]
Bernstein, L.:Olympic Hymn, w. Tanglewood Festival Chorus *(rec Symphony Hall, Boston, MA, Jan 6, 10 & 13, 1996)* Sony Classical ▲ SK 62592 [DDD] ■ ST 62592
By Request:The Best of John Williams & The Boston Pops Philips ▲ 420178-2 [DDD] ■ 420178-4 (D)
Copland, A.:Fanfare for the Common Man Philips ▲ 412627-2 [DDD]
Fauré, G.:Pavane Orch Philips ▲ 416361-2 [DDD]
Gershwin, G.:An American in Paris Philips ("Digital Classics" series) ▲ 426404-2 [DDD]
Gershwin, G.:Porgy & Bess (symphonic picture) Philips ("Digital Classics" series) ▲ 426404-2 [DDD]
Gershwin, G.:Rhap in Blue, w. M. Dichter (pno) Philips ("Digital Classics" series) ▲ 426404-2 [DDD]
The Green Album Sony Classical ▲ SK 48224 ■ ST 48224
Holst, G.:The Planets, w. Tanglewood Festival Chorus Philips ▲ 420177-2 [DDD]
I Love a Parade Sony Classical ▲ SK 46747 [DDD] ■ ST 46747 (D)
Music of the Night:Pops on Broadway, 1990 Sony Classical ▲ SK 45567 [DDD] ■ ST 45567 (D)
On Stage Philips ▲ 412132-2 [DDD]
Out of This World Philips ▲ 411185-2 [DDD]
Pachelbel, J.:Canon Philips ▲ 416361-2 [DDD]
Pops in Love Philips ▲ 416361-2 [DDD]
Pops in Space Philips ("Digital Classics" series) ▲ 412884-2 [DDD]
Pops on Broadway Philips ▲ 416499-2 [DDD]
Pops on the March Philips ▲ 420804-2 [DDD]
Pops Stoppers:Greatest Hits of the Boston Pops Orchestra Philips ▲ 446520-2 ■ 446520-4
Ravel, M.:Pavane pour une infante défunte Philips ▲ 416361-2 [DDD]
Rózsa, M.:Ben-Hur (sels)—Parade of Charioteers *(rec Symphony Hall, Boston, MA, Jan 6, 10 & 13, 1996)* Sony Classical ▲ SK 62592 [DDD] ■ ST 62592
Salute Gene Kelly, Fred Astaire & Judy Garland Philips ▲ 454 727-2
Salute to Hollywood Philips ("Digital Classics" series) ▲ 422385-2 [DDD]
Satie, E.:Gymnopédies—Nos 1, 3 Philips ▲ 416361-2 [DDD]
Shostakovich, D.:Festive Ov *(rec Symphony Hall, Boston, MA, Jan 6, 10 & 13, 1996)* Sony Classical ▲ SK 62592 [DDD] ■ ST 62592
Space-taculars Philips ▲ 446728-2; ■ 446728-4
The Spielberg/Williams Collaboration Sony Classical ▲ SK 45997 △ SM 45997 ■ ST 45997
Suk, J.:Toward a New Life *(rec Symphony Hall, Boston, MA, Jan 6, 10 & 13, 1996)* Sony Classical ▲ SK 62592 [DDD] ■ ST 62592
Swing, Swing, Swing Philips ▲ 412626-2 [DDD] ■ 412626-4 (D)
Theodorakis, M.:Canto olympico, w. Tanglewood Festival Chorus *(rec Symphony Hall, Boston, MA, Jan 6, 10 & 13, 1996)* Sony Classical ▲ SK 62592 [DDD] ■ ST 62592
Williams on Williams:The Classic Spielberg Scores Sony Classical ▲ SK 68419 △ SM 68419 ■ ST 68419
Williams, John:The Olympic Spirit *(rec Symphony Hall, Boston, MA, Jan 6, 10 & 13, 1996)* Sony Classical ▲ SK 62592 [DDD] ■ ST 62592
Williams, John:Summon the Heroes *(rec Symphony Hall, Boston, MA, Jan 6, 10 & 13, 1996)* Sony Classical ▲ SK 62592 [DDD] ■ ST 62592
With a Song in My Heart, w. Jessye Norman (sop) Philips ▲ 412625-2 PH [DDD]

Boston Pro Arte CO

L. Botstein (cnd)

Kupferman, M.:Con Cl, w. P. Alexander (cl) CRI ▲ CD 575 [DDD]
Starer, R.:Con Vc, w. J. Starker (vc) *(rec Feb. 17, 1991)* CRI ▲ CD 618 [DDD]
Wernick, R.:Con Va, "Do Not Go Gentle...", w. W. Trampler (va) *(rec Oct. 7, 1989)* CRI ▲ CD 618 [DDD]
Wilson, R.:Con Bn, w. R. Wagner (bn) CRI ▲ CD 575 [DDD]
Wilson, R.:Con Pno, w. B. Uribe (pno) *(rec Feb. 16, 1992)* CRI ▲ CD 618 [DDD]
Wilson, R.:Suite Small Orch CRI ▲ CD 575 [DDD]

G. Schuller (cnd)

Paine, J.K.:St. Peter, w. J. Ommerlé (sop), A. Fortunato (mez), P. Kelly (ten), D. Evitts (bar), Back Bay Chorale [E] *(rec live in concert at Sanders Theater, Cambridge, Mass., 5/21/89)* GM 2-▲ 2027CD 2

Boston Shawn and Sackbut Ensemble

J. Cohen (cnd)

Nueva España:Close Encounters in the New World (1590-1690), w. Boston Camerata, Women's Choir of the Church Les Amis de la Sagesse, Schola Cantorum of Boston Erato ▲ 45977-2

Boston SO

Brahms, J.:Alto Rhap, w. Jard van Nes (cta), Tanglewood Festival Chorus Philips ▲ 442130-2

Boston SO (cont.)

Jurassic Classics, w. Berlin PO, Kirov Orch, Vienna PO, London PO, V. Gergiev (cnd), A. Previn (cnd), C. Davis (cnd), N. Mariner (cnd) Philips ▲ 442599-2 ■ 442599-4
Piano Greatest Hits, w. Artur Rubinstein (pno), Chicago SO, RCA Victor SO RCA Victor ▲ 09026-62662-2 ■ 09026-62662-4

V. Ashkenazy (cnd)

Sibelius, J.:Finlandia London ▲ 436566-2 [DDD]
Sibelius, J.:Romance Strs London ▲ 436566-2 [DDD]
Sibelius, J.:Sym 2 London ▲ 436566-2 [DDD]
Sibelius, J.:Valse triste London ▲ 436566-2 [DDD]

L. Bernstein (cnd)

Beethoven, L. van:Sym 7 *(rec live, Tanglewood Festival 8/19/90)* Deutsche Grammophon ▲ 431768-2 [DDD] ■ 431768-4
Britten, B.:Peter Grimes (4 sea interludes) *(rec live, Tanglewood Festival 8/19/90)* Deutsche Grammophon ▲ 431768-2 [DDD] ■ 431768-4
Liszt, F.:A Faust Sym, w. Kenneth Riegel (ten), Tanglewood Festival Chorus *(rec Symphony Hall, Boston, July 1976)* Deutsche Grammophon ("The Originals" series) ▲ 447449-2 [ADD]

A. Copland (cnd)

Copland, A.:Appalachian Spring *(rec 1959)* RCA Living Stereo ▲ 09026-61505-2; ■ 09026-61505-4
Copland, A.:Appalachian Spring (suite) *(rec 1959)* RCA Red Seal ▲ 09026-61505-2 ■ 09026-61505-4
Copland, A.:Appalachian Spring (suite) *(rec 1959)* RCA Gold Seal ▲ 6802-2-RG [ADD] ■ 6802-4-RG (CrO2)
Copland, A.:The Tender Land (suite) *(rec 1959)* RCA Living Stereo ▲ 09026-61505-2; ■ 09026-61505-4
Copland, A.:The Tender Land (suite) *(rec 1959)* RCA Gold Seal ▲ 6802-2-RG [ADD] ■ 6802-4-RG (CrO2)

C. Davis (cnd)

Sibelius, J.:Con Vn, w. Salvatore Accardo (vn) Philips ("Duo" series) 2-▲ 446160-2
Sibelius, J.:Finlandia Philips ("Duo" series) 2-▲ 446160-2
Sibelius, J.:The Swan of Tuonela Philips ("Duo" series) 2-▲ 446160-2
Sibelius, J.:The Swan of Tuonela Philips ("Solo" series) ▲ 442389-2
Sibelius, J.:Sym 1 Philips ("Duo" series) 2-▲ 446157-2
Sibelius, J.:Sym 2 Philips ("Solo" series) ▲ 442389-2
Sibelius, J.:Sym 2 Philips ("Duo" series) 2-▲ 446157-2
Sibelius, J.:Sym 3 Philips ("Duo" series) 2-▲ 446160-2
Sibelius, J.:Sym 4 Philips ("Duo" series) 2-▲ 446157-2
Sibelius, J.:Sym 5 Philips ("Duo" series) 2-▲ 446157-2
Sibelius, J.:Sym 6 Philips ("Duo" series) 2-▲ 446160-2
Sibelius, J.:Sym 7 Philips ("Duo" series) 2-▲ 446160-2
Sibelius, J.:Tapiola Philips ("Duo" series) 2-▲ 446160-2
Sibelius, J.:Valse triste Philips ("Solo" series) ▲ 442389-2

C. Dutoit (cnd)

Gubaidulina, S.:Offertorium, w. G. Kremer (vn) Deutsche Grammophon ▲ 427336-2 [DDD]

A. Fiedler (cnd)

Dvořák, A.:Carnival RCA Gold Seal ("Papillon Collection" series) ▲ 6530-2-RG [ADD] ■ 6530-4-RG
Dvořák, A.:Sym 9, "From the New World" RCA Gold Seal ("Papillon Collection" series) ▲ 6530-2-RG [ADD] ■ 6530-4-RG

I. Fine (cnd)

Fine, I.:Sym Phoenix ▲ PHCD 106 [AAD]

B. Haitink (cnd)

Brahms, J.:Nänie, w. Tanglewood Festival Chorus Philips ▲ 442 799-2
Brahms, J.:Sym 1 Philips ▲ 442 799-2
Brahms, J.:Sym 3 Philips ▲ 442130-2
Brahms, J.:Sym 4 Philips ▲ 434991-2

S. Koussevitzky (cnd)

The Art of Serge Koussevitzky *(rec 1936-44)* Pearl ▲ PEA 9179 [ADD]
Bartók, B.:Con Orch *(rec Dec 1, 1944)* Stradivarius ▲ STV 13614 [ADD]
Beethoven, L. van:Sym 2 *(rec 1929-39)* Pearl 2-▲ PEA 9185
Beethoven, L. van:Sym 8 *(rec 1929-39)* Pearl 2-▲ PEA 9185
Berlioz, H.:Le Carnaval romain BSO Classics ▲ BSO 441122
Brahms, J.:Con Vn, w. Jascha Heifetz (vn) *(rec 1935-41)* Pearl 2-▲ PEA 9167 [ADD]
Brahms, J.:Con Vn, w. Jascha Heifetz (vn) *(rec Symphony Hall, Boston, Apr 11, 1939)* RCA Gold Seal 2-▲ 09026-61735-2 [ADD]
Brahms, J.:Sym 1 Stradivarius ▲ STV 13614 [ADD]
Brahms, J.:Sym 3 *(rec 1938)* Pearl ▲ PEA 9237
Brahms, J.:Sym 4 *(rec 1945)* Pearl ▲ PEA 9237
Copland, A.:El salón México *(rec 1938 for Victor)* Pearl ▲ PEA 9492 (m) [AAD]
Corelli, A.:Music of—Suite for Str Orch [arr Pinelli] BSO Classics ▲ BSO 441122
Cowell, H.:Hymn & Fuguing Tune 2 *(rec 1944)* CRI ■ ACS 6005
Debussy, C.:Danse Pno, "Tarantelle styrienne" *(rec 1928-1938)* Pearl ▲ PEA 9090 [AAD]
Debussy, C.:La Mer *(rec 1928-1938)* Pearl ▲ PEA 9090 [AAD]
Debussy, C.:Prélude à l'après-midi d'un faune BSO Classics ▲ BSO 441122
Debussy, C.:Sarabande RCA Gold Seal ▲ 09026-61392-2
Fauré, G.:Elégie *(rec 1928-1938)* Pearl ▲ PEA 9090 [AAD]
Fauré, G.:Pelléas et Mélisande (suite) Biddulph ▲ WHL 044
Foote, A.:Suite Str Orch *(rec 1940 for Victor)* Pearl ▲ PEA 9492 (m) [AAD]
Grieg, E.:Elegaic Melodies, Op. 34—No. 2 Letzter Frühling [Last Spring] *(rec 1950)* RCA Red Seal ▲ 09026-61826-2
Hanson, H.:Sym 3 Biddulph ▲ WHL 044
Harris, R.:Sym 1 *(rec live, Carnegie Hall, New York 2/2/34 for Columbia Recor)* Pearl ▲ PEA 9492 (m) [AAD]
Harris, R.:Sym 3 *(rec 1939 for Victor)* Pearl ▲ PEA 9492 (m) [AAD]
Haydn, J.:Sym 94, "Surprise Sym" *(rec 1929-39)* Pearl 2-▲ PEA 9185
Haydn, J.:Sym 102 *(rec 1929-39)* Pearl 2-▲ PEA 9185
Koussevitsky, S.:Con Db—2nd movement Biddulph ▲ WHL 045
Liadov, A.:The Enchanted Lake Biddulph ▲ WHL 044
McDonald, H.:San Juan Capistrano *(rec 1939 for Victor)* Pearl ▲ PEA 9492 (m) [AAD]
Mendelssohn, F.:Sym 4 *(rec 1935-39)* Pearl ▲ PEA 9037 [ADD]
Mozart, W.A.:Sym 29 *(rec 1929-39)* Pearl 2-▲ PEA 9185
Mozart, W.A.:Sym 34 *(rec 1929-39)* Pearl 2-▲ PEA 9185
Mozart, W.A.:Sym 36 *(rec 1943-46)* LYS ▲ LYS 133
Mozart, W.A.:Sym 39 *(rec 1943-46)* LYS ▲ LYS 133
Mussorgsky, M.:Khovanshchina (prelude) Biddulph ▲ WHL 044
Mussorgsky, M.:Pictures at an Exhibition Pearl ▲ PEA 9020
Mussorgsky, M.:Pictures at an Exhibition RCA Gold Seal ▲ 09026-61392-2
Prokofiev, S.:Chout (suite)—finale RCA Gold Seal ▲ 09026-61657-2
Prokofiev, S.:Con 2 Vn, w. Jascha Heifetz (vn) *(rec Symphony Hall, Boston, Dec 20, 1937)* RCA Gold Seal 2-▲ 09026-61735-2 [ADD]
Prokofiev, S.:Con 2 Vn, w. J. Heifetz (vn) *(rec 12/20/37)* Biddulph ▲ LAB 018 [ADD]
Prokofiev, S.:Con 2 Vn, w. Jascha Heifetz (vn) *(rec 1935-41)* Pearl ▲ PEA 9167 [ADD]
Prokofiev, S.:Lt Kijé Suite *(rec 1939 for Victor/HMV)* Pearl ▲ PEA 9487 (m) [AAD]
Prokofiev, S.:The Love for 3 Oranges (scherzo & march)—includes both the 1929 & 1936 Victor/HMV recordings Pearl ▲ PEA 9487 (m) [AAD]
Prokofiev, S.:Peter & the Wolf, w. R. Hale (nar) *(rec 1939 for Victor/HMV)* Pearl ▲ PEA 9487 (m) [AAD]
Prokofiev, S.:Romeo & Juliet (suites)—Suite No. 2 RCA Gold Seal ▲ 09026-61657-2
Prokofiev, S.:Romeo & Juliet (suites)—No. 2 Biddulph ▲ WHL 045

Boston SO (cont.)

S. Koussevitzky (cnd) (cont.)

Prokofiev, S.:Sym 1 RCA Gold Seal ▲ 09026-61657-2
Prokofiev, S.:Sym 1 *(rec 1929 for Victor/HMV)* Pearl ▲ PEA 9487 (m) [AAD]
Prokofiev, S.:Sym 5 RCA Gold Seal ▲ 09026-61657-2
Rachmaninoff, S.:The Isle of the Dead Biddulph ▲ WHL 045
Rachmaninoff, S.:Vocalise [orchd by Rachmaninoff] Biddulph ▲ WHL 045
Ravel, M.:Boléro RCA Gold Seal ▲ 09026-61392-2
Ravel, M.:Daphnis et Chloé (suite 1) *(rec 1928-1938)* Pearl ▲ PEA 9090 [AAD]
Ravel, M.:Daphnis et Chloé (suite 2) RCA Gold Seal ▲ 09026-61392-2
Ravel, M.:La Valse RCA Gold Seal ▲ 09026-61392-2
Rimsky-Korsakov, N.:Dubinushka Biddulph ▲ WHL 044
Rimsky-Korsakov, N.:The Legend of the Invisible City of Kitzeh—Entr'acte Biddulph ▲ WHL 044
Satie, E.:Gymnopédies *(rec 1928-1938)* Pearl ▲ PEA 9090 [AAD]
Schubert, Franz:Sym 8 *(rec 1935-39)* Pearl ▲ PEA 9037 [ADD]
Schumann, R.:Sym 1 *(rec 1935-39)* Pearl ▲ PEA 9037 [ADD]
Shostakovich, D.:Sym 8—Adagio Biddulph ▲ WHL 045
Stravinsky, I.:Apollon musagète Pearl ▲ PEA 9020 [AAD]
Stravinsky, I.:Capriccio Pearl ▲ PEA 9020 [AAD]
Stravinsky, I.:Pétrouchka (suite) Pearl ▲ PEA 9020 [AAD]
Stravinsky, I.:Song of Volga Boatman (arr winds) Pearl ▲ PEA 9020
Tchaikovsky, P.:Chanson triste Biddulph ▲ WHL 045
Tchaikovsky, P.:Romeo & Juliet Biddulph 2-▲ WHL 034-35
Tchaikovsky, P.:Serenade Strs—Waltz only Biddulph 2-▲ WHL 034-35
Tchaikovsky, P.:Sym 4 Biddulph 2-▲ WHL 034-35
Tchaikovsky, P.:Sym 5 BSO Classics ▲ BSO 441122
Tchaikovsky, P.:Sym 5 Biddulph 2-▲ WHL 034-35
Tchaikovsky, P.:Sym 6 RCA Gold Seal ("Legendary Performers" series) ▲ 09026-60920-2
Tchaikovsky, P.:Sym 6 Biddulph 2-▲ WHL 034-35

R. Kubelik (cnd)

Smetana, B.:Má Vlast Deutsche Grammophon ("Galleria" series) ▲ 429183-2 [ADD]
Smetana, B.:The Moldau Deutsche Grammophon 2-▲ 439663-2 [ADD]

E. Leinsdorf (cnd)

Basic 100 Vol. 57 RCA Victor ▲ 09026-68082-2 ■ 09026-68082-4
Basic 100 Vol. 58, w. Artur Rubinstein (pno) RCA Victor ▲ 09026-68083-2 ■ 09026-68083-4
Basic 100 Vol. 74 RCA Victor ▲ 09026-68365-2 ■ 09026-68365-4
Basic 100 Vol. 77, w. Artur Rubinstein (pno) RCA Victor ▲ 09026-68454-2 ■ 09026-68454-4
Beethoven, L. van:Con 1 Pno, w. Artur Rubenstein (pno) RCA Victor ▲ 09026-68083-2; ■ 09026-68083-4
Beethoven, L. van:Con 1 Pno, w. A. Rubinstein (pno) RCA Red Seal ▲ 5674-2-RC [ADD]
Beethoven, L. van:Con 2 Pno, w. A. Rubinstein (pno) RCA Red Seal ▲ 5675-2-RC [ADD]
Beethoven, L. van:Con 3 Pno, w. A. Rubinstein (pno) RCA Red Seal ▲ 5675-2-RC [ADD]
Beethoven, L. van:Con 4 Pno, w. A. Rubinstein (pno) RCA Red Seal ▲ 5676-2-RC [ADD]
Beethoven, L. van:Con 4 Pno, w. Artur Rubenstein (pno) RCA Victor ▲ 09026-68083-2; ■ 09026-68083-4
Beethoven, L. van:Con 5 Pno, "Emperor", w. A. Rubinstein (pno) RCA Red Seal ▲ 5676-2-RC [ADD]
Beethoven, L. van:Die Geschöpfe des Prometheus (ov) RCA Victrola ▲ 60130-2-RV [ADD] ■ 60130-4-RV
Beethoven, L. van:Die Geschöpfe des Prometheus (ov) RCA Silver Seal ▲ 60786-2-RV [ADD] ■ 60786-4-RV
Beethoven, L. van:Sym 1 RCA Victrola ▲ 60128-2-RV [ADD] ■ 60128-4-RV
Beethoven, L. van:Sym 1 RCA Victor ▲ 09026-61720-2; ■ 09026-61720-4
Beethoven, L. van:Sym 2 RCA Victrola ▲ 60130-2-RV [ADD] ■ 60130-4-RV
Beethoven, L. van:Sym 3, "Eroica" RCA Victrola ▲ 7878-2-RV [ADD] ■ 7878-4-RV
Beethoven, L. van:Sym 3, "Eroica" RCA Silver Seal ▲ 60786-2-RV [ADD] ■ 60786-4-RV
Beethoven, L. van:Sym 3, "Eroica" RCA Victor ▲ 09026-61713-2; ■ 09026-61713-4
Beethoven, L. van:Sym 4 RCA Victrola ▲ 7745-2-RV [ADD] ■ 7745-4-RV
Beethoven, L. van:Sym 5 RCA Victrola ▲ 7745-2-RV [ADD] ■ 7745-4-RV
Beethoven, L. van:Sym 6, "Pastorale" RCA Victor ▲ 09026-61720-2; ■ 09026-61720-4
Beethoven, L. van:Sym 6, "Pastorale" RCA Victrola ▲ 7996-2-RV [ADD] ■ 7996-4-RV
Beethoven, L. van:Sym 7 RCA Victrola ▲ 7997-2-RV [ADD] ■ 7997-4-RV
Beethoven, L. van:Sym 8 RCA Victrola ▲ 60128-2-RV [ADD] ■ 60128-4-RV
Beethoven, L. van:Wellington's Victory, "Battle Sym"—The Battle ("Basic 100, Vol. 16") RCA Victor ▲ 09026-61713-2; ■ 09026-61713-4
The Best of Mozart, w. English CO [cnd:J.-F. Paillard], Chicago SO [cnd:F. Reiner], et al. Victrola ("Victrola Best of" series) ▲ 60773-2-RV [ADD] ■ 60773-4-RV
Brahms, J.:Academic Festival Ov RCA Victor ▲ 09026-68082-2; ■ 09026-68082-4
Brahms, J.:Con 1 Pno, w. V. Cliburn (pno) RCA Gold Seal ▲ 60357-2-RG [ADD] ■ 60357-4-RG (CrO2)
Brahms, J.:Hungarian Dances Orch—No. 5 RCA Victor ▲ 09026-68082-2; ■ 09026-68082-4
Brahms, J.:Sym 2 RCA Victor ▲ 09026-68082-2; ■ 09026-68082-4
Brahms, J.:Sym 2 RCA ■ 60129-4-RV
Fine, I.:Serious Song Phoenix ▲ PHCD 106 [AAD]
Lalo, E.:Sym espagnole, w. Ithzak Perlman (vn) RCA Victor ▲ 09026-68338-2 ■ 09026-68338-4
Mahler, G.:Sym 1 RCA ■ ALK1-4983
Mahler, G.:Sym 5 RCA Silver Seal ▲ 60482-2-RV [ADD] ■ 60482-4-RV (CrO2)
Mahler, G.:Sym 5 RCA ("Basic 100" series) ▲ 09026-68365-2 ■ 09026-68365-4
Mendelssohn, F.:A Midsummer Night's Dream (comp), w. Boston Sym Chorus RCA Victrola ▲ 7816-2-RV [ADD] ■ 7816-4-RV
Mendelssohn, F.:A Midsummer Night's Dream (sels), w. Boston Sym Chorus RCA Silver Seal ▲ 09026-60910-2 ■ 09026-60910-4
Mozart, W.A.:Kleine Nachtmusik RCA Gold Seal ▲ 09026-68113-2 [ADD]
Mozart, W.A.:Kleine Nachtmusik RCA Victrola ▲ 9305-2 [ADD] ■ 9305-4
Mozart, W.A.:Kleine Nachtmusik RCA Silver Seal ▲ 09026-60907-2 ■ 09026-60907-4
Mozart, W.A.:Sym 36 RCA Silver Seal ▲ 09026-60907-2 ■ 09026-60907-4
Mozart, W.A.:Sym 38 RCA ("Basic 100" series) ▲ 09026-68264-2 ■ 09026-68364-4
Mozart, W.A.:Sym 39 RCA Silver Seal ▲ 09026-60907-2 ■ 09026-60907-4
Mozart, W.A.:Sym 41 RCA Victrola ▲ 9305-2 [ADD] ■ 9305-4
Prokofiev, S.:Con 2 Vn, w. I. Perlman (vn) RCA Gold Seal ▲ 09026-61454-2
Scharwenka, X.:Con 1 Pno, w. Earl Wild (pno) *(rec Symphony Hall, Boston, MA, Jan 20, 1969)* Elan ▲ CD 2266 [ADD]
Schumann, R.:Con Pno, w. Artur Rubinstein (pno) RCA ("Basic 100" series) ▲ 09026-68454-2 ■ 09026-68454-4
Schumann, R.:Sym 4 RCA Victor ▲ 09026-61855-2; ■ 09026-61855-4
Schumann, R.:Sym 4 RCA Silver Seal ▲ 60488-2-RV [ADD] ■ 60488-4-RV (CrO2)
Sibelius, J.:Con Vn, w. I. Perlman (vn) *(rec ca. 1966/68)* RCA Gold Seal ▲ 07863-56520-2 [ADD] ■ 07863-56520-4
Strauss, R.:Arias, w. L. Price (sop), London SO, New Philharmonia Orch—selections from Ägyptische Helena *(Awakening Scene)*, Ariadne auf Naxos *(Es gibt ein Reich)*, Frau ohne Schatten *(Empress's Awakening Scene)*, Guntram *(Fass ich sie bang)*, Rosenkavalier *(Marschallin's Monologue)*, Salome *(Interlude & Final Scene)* [G] RCA Gold Seal ▲ 60398-2-RG [ADD] ■ 60398-4-RG (CrO2)
Stravinsky, I.:The Firebird Suite RCA Silver Seal ▲ 60541-2-RV [ADD] ■ 60541-4-RV
Tchaikovsky, P.:Con 1 Pno, w. Artur Rubinstein (pno) RCA ("Basic 100" series) ▲ 09026-68454-2 ■ 09026-68454-4
Tchaikovsky, P.:Con 1 Pno, w. A. Rubinstein (pno) RCA Gold Seal ▲ 09026-61262-2 ■ 09026-61262-4
Tchaikovsky, P.:Con 1 Pno, w. M. Dichter (pno) RCA Gold Seal ("Papillon Collection" series) ▲ 6526-2-RG [ADD] ■ 6526-4-RG
Tchaikovsky, P.:Con Vn, w. I. Perlman (vn) RCA Gold Seal ("Papillon Collection" series) ▲ 6526-2-RG [ADD] ■ 6526-4-RG

▲ = CD ♦ = Enhanced CD Δ = MD ■ = Cassette Tape □ = DCC

Boston SO (cont.)

E. Leinsdorf, C. Munch (cnd)

Basic 100 Vol. 37 RCA Victor ▲ 09026-61855-2 ■ 09026-61855-4
The Best of Beethoven, w. Jörg Demus (pno), et al. Victrola ("Victrola Best of" series) ▲ 60769-2-RV [ADD] ■ 60769-4-RV

P. Monteux (cnd)

Highlights from the Pierre Monteux Edition, w. San Francisco SO, Chicago SO RCA Gold Seal ▲ 09026-61978-2
The Pierre Monteux Edition, w. San Fransisco SO, RCA Victor Orch, Chicago SO RCA Gold Seal 15-▲ 09026-61893-2
Stravinsky, I.:Pétrouchka RCA Gold Seal ▲ 09026-61898-2
Stravinsky, I.:Pétrouchka RCA Gold Seal ("Papillon Collection" series) ▲ 6529-2-RG [ADD]
Stravinsky, I.:Le Sacre du printemps Orch RCA Gold Seal ("Papillon Collection" series) ▲ 6529-2-RG [ADD]
Stravinsky, I.:Le Sacre du printemps Orch RCA Gold Seal ▲ 09026-61898-2
Tchaikovsky, P.:Sym 4 RCA Gold Seal 2-▲ 09026-61901-2
Tchaikovsky, P.:Sym 5 RCA Gold Seal 2-▲ 09026-61901-2
Tchaikovsky, P.:Sym 6 RCA Gold Seal 2-▲ 09026-61901-2

P. Monteux, C. Munch (cnd)

The Age of Living Stereo:A Tribute to John Pfeiffer, w. Chicago SO [cnd:Fritz Reiner], NBC SO [cnd:Leopold Stokowski], RCA SO [cnd:Kiril Kondrashin] *(rec Boston & Chicago & New York, 1953-1961)* RCA Living Stereo 2-▲ 09026-68524-2 [ADD]

C. Munch (cnd)

Bach, J.S.:Brandenburg Cons—Nos. 1-3 RCA Victrola ■ ALK1-4488
Barber, S.:Adagio Strs RCA Gold Seal ▲ 09026-61424-2 ■ 09026-61424-4
Barber, S.:Medea's Meditation & Dance of Vengeance RCA Gold Seal ▲ 09026-61424-2 ■ 09026-61424-4
Basic 100 Vol. 7 RCA Victor ▲ 09026-61556-2 ■ 09026-61556-4
Basic 100 Vol. 24 RCA Victor ▲ 09026-61721-2 ■ 09026-61721-4
Basic 100 Vol. 56 RCA Victor ▲ 09026-68081-2 ■ 09026-68081-4
Basic 100 Vol. 65, w. Chicago SO [cnd:Fritz Reiner] RCA Victor ▲ 09026-68090-2 ■ 09026-68090-4
Beethoven, L. van:Con 1 Pno, w. S. Richter (pno) RCA Gold Seal ▲ 6804-2-RG [ADD]
Beethoven, L. van:Con Vn, Op. 61, w. J. Heifetz (vn) RCA Red Seal ▲ RCD1-5402
Beethoven, L. van:Con Vn, Op. 61, w. Jascha Heifetz (vn) *(rec Symphony Hall, Boston, Nov 27-28, 1955)* RCA Red Seal ▲ 09026-61742-2 [ADD]
Beethoven, L. van:Con Vn, Op. 61, w. J. Heifetz (vn) RCA ■ AGK1-5242
Beethoven, L. van:Leonore 3 RCA Gold Seal ▲ 6803-2-RG [ADD]
Beethoven, L. van:Sym 1 RCA Gold Seal ▲ 09026-61399-2 ■ 09026-61399-4
Beethoven, L. van:Sym 3, "Eroica" RCA Gold Seal ▲ 09026-61399-2 ■ 09026-61399-4
Beethoven, L. van:Sym 5 RCA Gold Seal ▲ 6803-2-RG [ADD]
Berlioz, H.:Béatrice et Bénédict (ov) *(rec Dec 1958)* RCA Victor Gold Seal 8-▲ 0902-668444-2 [ADD]
Berlioz, H.:Béatrice et Bénédict (ov) RCA Victor ▲ 09026-61721-2; ■ 09026-61721-4
Berlioz, H.:Benvenuto Cellini (ov) *(rec Apr 1959)* RCA Victor Gold Seal 8-▲ 0902-668444-2 [ADD]
Berlioz, H.:Le Carnaval romain *(rec Dec 1958)* RCA Victor Gold Seal 8-▲ 0902-668444-2 [ADD]
Berlioz, H.:Le Carnaval romain RCA Victor ▲ 09026-61721-2; ■ 09026-61721-4 (CrO2)
Berlioz, H.:Le Corsaire *(rec Dec 1958)* RCA Victor Gold Seal 8-▲ 0902-668444-2 [ADD]
Berlioz, H.:La Damnation de Faust, w. S. Danco (sop), D. Poleri (ten), M. Singher (bar), D. Gramm (bass), Harvard Glee Club [F] RCA Gold Seal 2-▲ 7940-2-RG [ADD]
Berlioz, H.:La Damnation de Faust, w. Suzanne Danco (sop), David Poleri (ten), Martial Singher (bar), Donald Gramm (bass), McHenry Boatwright (bass), Joseph de Pasquale (va), Louis Speyer (hn), Harvard Glee Club, Radcliffe Choral Society *(rec Feb 1954)* RCA Victor Gold Seal 8-▲ 0902-668444-2 [ADD]
Berlioz, H.:L'Enfance du Christ, w. Florence Kopleff (cta), Ceasare Valletti (ten), Gérard Souzay (bar), Lucien Oliver (bar), Giorgio Tozzi (bass), New England Conservatory Chorus *(rec Dec 1956)* RCA Victor Gold Seal 8-▲ 0902-668444-2 [ADD]
Berlioz, H.:L'Enfance du Christ, w. F. Kopleff (cta), C. Valletti (ten), G. Souzay (bar), G. Tozzi (bass), New England Conservatory Chorus RCA Gold Seal 2-▲ 09026-61234-2
Berlioz, H.:Harold in Italy, w. William Primrose (va) *(rec Nov 1954)* RCA Victor Gold Seal 8-▲ 0902-668444-2 [ADD]
Berlioz, H.:Harold in Italy, w. William Primrose (va) RCA Gold Seal ▲ 09026-62582-2
Berlioz, H.:Les Nuits d'été, w. Victoria de los Angeles (sop) *(rec Apr 1955)* RCA Victor Gold Seal 8-▲ 0902-668444-2 [ADD]
Berlioz, H.:Les Nuits d'été, w. V. de los Angeles (sop), M. Roggero (mez), L. Chabay (ten), Y. Sze (bass) RCA Gold Seal 2-▲ 09026-60681-2
Berlioz, H.:Ovs—Béatrice et Bénédict; Benvenuto Cellini; Le corsaire; Carnaval romain RCA Gold Seal ▲ 09026-61400-2 ■ 09026-61400-4
Berlioz, H.:Ovs—Béatrice et Bénédict RCA Gold Seal ▲ 6805-2-RG [ADD]
Berlioz, H.:Ovs—Carnaval romain; Le Corsaire RCA Silver Seal ▲ 60478-2-RV [ADD] ■ 60478-4-RV
Berlioz, H.:Requiem, "Grande Messe des Morts", w. Léopold Simoneau (ten), New England Conservatory Chorus *(rec Apr 1959)* RCA Victor Gold Seal 8-▲ 0902-668444-2 [ADD]
Berlioz, H.:Roméo et Juliette, w. M. Roggero (mez), L. Chabay (ten), Y. Sze (bass), Harvard Glee Club, Radcliffe Choral Society RCA Gold Seal 2-▲ 09026-60681-2
Berlioz, H.:Roméo et Juliette, w. Margaret Roggero (mez), Leslie Chabay (ten), Yi-Kwei Sze (bass), Harvard Glee Club, Radcliffe Choral Society *(rec Feb 1953)* RCA Victor Gold Seal 8-▲ 0902-668444-2 [ADD]
Berlioz, H.:Roméo et Juliette (sels) RCA Gold Seal ▲ 09026-61400-2 ■ 09026-61400-4
Berlioz, H.:Sym fantastique RCA Victrola ▲ 7735-2-RV [ADD] ■ 7735-4-RV
Berlioz, H.:Sym fantastique RCA Victor ▲ 09026-61721-2; ■ 09026-61721-4
Berlioz, H.:Sym fantastique *(rec Nov 1954)* RCA Victor Gold Seal 8-▲ 0902-668444-2 [ADD]
Berlioz, H.:Les Troyens (sels)—Royal Hunt & Storm *(rec Apr 1959)* RCA Victor Gold Seal 8-▲ 0902-668444-2 [ADD]
Berlioz, H.:Les Troyens (sels) RCA Gold Seal ▲ 09026-61400-2 ■ 09026-61400-4
Blackwood, E.:Sym 1 *(rec Nov. 1958)* Cedille ▲ CDR 90000 016 [ADD/DDD]
Brahms, J.:Sym 1 *(rec analog)* RCA Silver Seal ▲ 60788-2-RV [ADD/DDD] ■ 60788-4-RV
Brahms, J.:Sym 1 RCA Victrola ▲ 7812-2-RV [ADD] ■ 7812-4-RV
Brahms, J.:Sym 2 RCA Gold Seal ▲ 09026-60682-2
Brahms, J.:Sym 4 RCA Victor ▲ 09026-61855-2; ■ 09026-61855-4
Brahms, J.:Sym 4 RCA Silver Seal ▲ 09026-61206-2 ■ 09026-61206-4
Brahms, J.:Tragic Ov RCA Gold Seal ▲ 09026-60682-2
Chausson, E.:Sym in B♭ RCA Gold Seal ▲ 09026-60683-2
Chopin, F.:Con 2 Pno, w. A. Brailowsky (pno) RCA Gold Seal ▲ 09026-61656-2 [AAD]
Debussy, C.:La Damoiselle élue, w. V. de los Angeles (sop), C. Smith (mez), Radcliffe Choral Society [F] RCA Gold Seal 2-▲ 7940-2-RG [ADD]
Debussy, C.:Ibéria RCA Gold Seal ▲ 09026-60684-2
Debussy, C.:Images Orch RCA Living Stereo ▲ 09026-61956-2 [AAD]; ■ 09026-61956-4
Debussy, C.:Martyre de Saint Sébastian (fragments) RCA Gold Seal ▲ 09026-60684-2
Debussy, C.:La Mer RCA Gold Seal ▲ 6719-2-RG [ADD] ■ 6719-4-RG (CrO2)
Debussy, C.:La Mer *(rec 1956 & 1959)* RCA Living Stereo ▲ 09026-61500-2 ■ 09026-61500-4
Debussy, C.:Nocturnes—Nuages & Fêtes only RCA Gold Seal ▲ 6719-2-RG [ADD] ■ 6719-4-RG (CrO2)
Debussy, C.:Prélude à l'après-midi d'un faune RCA Gold Seal ▲ 6719-2-RG [ADD] ■ 6719-4-RG (CrO2)
Debussy, C.:Printemps (suite) RCA Gold Seal ▲ 6719-2-RG [ADD] ■ 6719-4-RG (CrO2)
Dvořák, A.:Con Vc, w. G. Piatigorsky (vc) *(rec 1957 & 1960)* RCA Gold Seal ▲ 09026-61498-2 ■ 09026-61498-4
Dvořák, A.:Sym 8 RCA Silver Seal ▲ 09026-61206-2 ■ 09026-61206-4
Elgar, E.:Intro & Allegro RCA Gold Seal ▲ 09026-61424-2 ■ 09026-61424-4

Boston SO (cont.)

C. Munch (cnd) (cont.)

Honegger, A.:Sym 2 RCA Gold Seal ▲ 09026-60685-2
Honegger, A.:Sym 5 RCA Gold Seal ▲ 09026-60685-2
Ibert, J.:Escales *(rec 1956 & 1959)* RCA Living Stereo ▲ 09026-61500-2
Indy, V. d':Sym on a French Mountain Air, w. Nicole Henriot-Schweitzer (pno) RCA Gold Seal ▲ 09026-62582-2
Mendelssohn, F.:Con in e Vn & Orch, Op. 64, w. Jascha Heifetz (vn) RCA Red Seal ▲ 5933-2-RC
Mendelssohn, F.:Con in e Vn & Orch, Op. 64, w. Jascha Heifetz (vn) *(rec Symphony Hall, Boston, Feb 23-25, 1959)* RCA Red Seal ▲ 09026-61743-2 [ADD]
Mendelssohn, F.:Sym 3 RCA Silver Seal ▲ 60483-2-RV [ADD] ■ 60483-4-RV (CrO2)
Mendelssohn, F.:Sym 4 RCA ▲ 09026-68090-2 ■ 09026-68090-4
Mendelssohn, F.:Sym 4 RCA Silver Seal ▲ 60483-2-RV [ADD] ■ 60483-4-RV (CrO2)
Milhaud, D.:La Création du monde RCA Gold Seal ▲ 09026-60685-2
Milhaud, D.:Suite provençale RCA Gold Seal ▲ 09026-60685-2
Poulenc, F.:Con Org, w. B. Zamkochian (org) RCA Gold Seal ▲ 60817-2-RG [ADD] ■ 60817-4-RG (CrO2)
Prokofiev, S.:Con 2 Vn, w. Jascha Heifetz (vn) *(rec Symphony Hall, Boston, Feb. 24, 1959)* RCA Red Seal ▲ 09026-61744-2 [ADD]
Prokofiev, S.:Con 2 Vn, w. J. Heifetz (vn) RCA Red Seal ▲ RCD1-7019
Rachmaninoff, S.:Con 3 Pno, w. B. Janis (pno) RCA Silver Seal ▲ 60540-2-RV [ADD] ■ 60540-4-RV
Ravel, M.:Boléro RCA Living Stereo ▲ 09026-61956-2 [AAD]; ■ 09026-61956-4 [DD
Ravel, M.:Boléro RCA Gold Seal ▲ 6522-2-RG [ADD] ■ 6522-4-RG (CrO2)
Ravel, M.:Daphins et Chloé, w. New England Conservatory Chorus *(rec 1955)* RCA Gold Seal ▲ 60469-2-RG [ADD]
Ravel, M.:Daphins et Chloé RCA Living Stereo ▲ 09026-61846-2
Ravel, M.:Daphins et Chloé, w. Alumi Chorus, New England Conservatory Chorus RCA Victor ▲ 09026-68081-2; ■ 09026-68081-4
Ravel, M.:Ma mère l'oye Orch RCA Gold Seal ▲ 6522-2-RG [ADD] ■ 6522-4-RG (CrO2)
Ravel, M.:Pavane pour une infante défunte RCA Gold Seal ▲ 6522-2-RG [ADD] ■ 6522-4-RG (CrO2)
Ravel, M.:Rapsodie espagnole RCA Living Stereo ▲ 09026-61956-2 [AAD]; ■ 09026-61956-4 [DD
Ravel, M.:Rapsodie espagnole RCA Gold Seal ▲ 6522-2-RG [ADD] ■ 6522-4-RG (CrO2)
Ravel, M.:La Valse RCA Living Stereo ▲ 09026-61956-2 [AAD]; ■ 09026-61956-4 [DD
Ravel, M.:La Valse RCA Gold Seal ▲ 6522-2-RG [ADD] ■ 6522-4-RG (CrO2)
Roussel, A.:Bacchus et Ariane (suite 2), w. New England Conservatory Chorus RCA Gold Seal ▲ 60469-2-RG [ADD]
Saint-Saëns, C.:Introduction & Rondo capriccioso, w. D. Oistrakh (vn) RCA Gold Seal ▲ 09026-60683-2
Saint-Saëns, C.:Le Rouet d'Omphale RCA Gold Seal ▲ 09026-61400-2 ■ 09026-61400-4
Saint-Saëns, C.:Sym 3, w. B. Zamkochian (org) *(rec 1956 & 1959)* RCA Living Stereo ▲ 09026-61500-2
Saint-Saëns, C.:Sym 3, w. B. Zamkochian (org) RCA Gold Seal ▲ 60817-2-RG [ADD] ■ 60817-4-RG (CrO2)
Schubert, Franz:Sym 8 RCA Silver Seal ▲ 60792-2-RV [ADD] ■ 60792-4-RV
Schubert, Franz:Sym 8 RCA Gold Seal ▲ 6803-2-RG [ADD]
Schubert, Franz:Sym 9 RCA Silver Seal ▲ 60792-2-RV [ADD] ■ 60792-4-RV
Schumann, R.:Genoveva (ov) RCA Gold Seal ▲ 09026-60682-2
Schumann, R.:Sym 1 RCA Silver Seal ▲ 60488-2-RV [ADD] ■ 60488-4-RV (CrO2)
Strauss, R.:Don Quixote, w. G. Piatigorsky (vc) RCA Gold Seal ▲ 09026-61485-2
Tchaikovsky, P.:Con Vn, w. I. Szeryng (vn) RCA ■ ALK1-4493
Tchaikovsky, P.:Romeo & Juliet RCA Gold Seal ▲ 09026-61563-2; ■ 09026-61563-4
Tchaikovsky, P.:Serenade Strs RCA Gold Seal ▲ 09026-61424-2 ■ 09026-61424-4
Tchaikovsky, P.:Sym 6 RCA Gold Seal ▲ 09026-61563-2; ■ 09026-61563-4
The Voices of Living Stereo, Vol. 2, w. Eileen Farrell (sop), Birgit Nilsson (sop), Roberta Peters (sop), Leontyne Price (sop), Galina Vishnevskaya (sop), Rosalind Elias (mez), Shirley Verrett (mez), Marian Anderson (cta), Maureen Forrester (cta), Sergio Franchi (ten), Mario Lanza (ten), Richard Lewis (ten), Jan Pee, Alexander Dedyukhin (pno), Franz Rupp (pno), Leo Taubman (pno), George Trovillo (pno), Charles Wadsworth (pno), Boston Pops Orch [cnd:Arthur Fiedler], Chicago SO [cnd:Fritz Reiner], RCA Victor Orch, et al. *(rec Boston & Chicago & New York & Rome, 1957-1964)* RCA Living Stereo ▲ 09026-68167-2 [ADD]
Wagner, R.:Götterdämmerung (immolation scene), w. E. Farrell (sop) RCA Gold Seal ▲ 09026-60686-2
Wagner, R.:Götterdämmerung (rhine journey) RCA ■ ALK1-4497
Wagner, R.:Tannhäuser (ov) RCA Gold Seal ▲ 09026-60686-2
Wagner, R.:Tannhäuser (ov & venusberg) RCA ■ ALK1-4497
Wagner, R.:Die Walküre (magic fire) RCA ■ ALK1-4497
Wagner, R.:Die Walküre (magic fire) RCA Gold Seal ▲ 09026-60686-2
Walton, W.:Con Vc, w. G. Piatigorsky (vc) *(rec 1957 & 1960)* RCA Gold Seal ▲ 09026-61498-2 ■ 09026-61498-4

S. Ozawa (cnd)

Bach, J.S.:Music of—orchestral transcriptions by Hideo Saito *(Partita in d)*, Schoenberg *(Prelude & Fugue in E♭)*, Stokowski *(Toccata in d)*, Stravinsky *(Choral Variations on "Vom Himmel hoch..")*, Webern *(Musical Offering)* Philips ▲ 432092-2 [DDD]
Barber, S.:Con Vn, w. Itzhak Perlman (vn) EMI Classics ▲ CDC 55360
Bartók, B.:Con Orch Philips ▲ 442783-2
Bartók, B.:Con 2 Vn, w. A.-S. Mutter (vn) Deutsche Grammophon ▲ 431626-2 [DDD] □ 431626-5
Bartók, B.:The Miraculous Mandarin, w. Tanglewood Festival Chorus Philips ▲ 442783-2
Beethoven, L. van:Cons Pno (comp), w. R. Serkin (pno) Telarc 3-▲ CD 80061 [DDD]
Beethoven, L. van:Con 2 Pno, w. R. Serkin (pno) Telarc ▲ CD 80064 [DDD]
Beethoven, L. van:Con 3 Pno, w. R. Serkin (pno) Telarc ▲ CD 80063 [DDD]
Beethoven, L. van:Con 4 Pno, w. R. Serkin (pno) Telarc ▲ CD 80064 [DDD]
Beethoven, L. van:Con 5 Pno, "Emperor", w. R. Serkin (pno) Telarc ▲ CD 80065 [DDD]
Beethoven, L. van:Egmont (ov) Telarc ▲ CD 80060 [DDD]
Beethoven, L. van:Fant Pno, Op. 80, "Choral Fant", w. R. Serkin (pno) Telarc ▲ CD 80063 [DDD]
Beethoven, L. van:Romances Vn, w. I. Stern (vn) CBS ▲ MK 37204 [DDD]
Beethoven, L. van:Sym 5 Telarc ▲ CD 80060 [DDD]
Berg, A.:Con Vn, w. Itzhak Perlman (vn) *(rec Symphony Hall, Boston, Feb & Nov 1978)* Deutsche Grammophon ("The Originals" series) ▲ 447445-2 [ADD]
Berlioz, H.:Requiem, "Grande Messe des Morts", w. Vincent Cole (ten), Tanglewood Festival Chorus RCA Red Seal ▲ 09026-62544-2
Bernstein, L.:Serenade, w. Itzhak Perlman (vn) EMI Classics ▲ CDC 55360
Britten, B.:Diversions Pno, w. L. Fleisher (pno) Sony Classical ▲ SK 47188 [DDD]
Dvořák, A.:Music of, w. Frederica von Stade (mez), Itzhak Perlman (vn), Yo-Yo Ma (vc), Rudolf Firkusny (pno), Czech Phil Chorus—Carnival Ov., Op. 92; Romance in f for Vn & Orch, Op. 11; Klid [Silent Woods] for Vc & Orch, Op. 68/5; Humoresque in G♭, Op. 101/1 & 7; Mesícku na nebi hlubokém [from Rusalka, Op. 114]; Psalm 149 for Chorus & Orch, Op. 79; Gypsy Songs for Voice & Piano, Op. 55/4 & 5; Allegro [from Trio for Vn, Vc & Pno, Op. 90]; Slavonic Dances, Op. 72/2 & 7 *(rec Smetana Hall, Prague, Dec. 16, 1993)* Sony Classical ("Front Line" series) ▲ SK 46687 [DDD]; ■ ST 46687
Fauré, G.:Dolly Deutsche Grammophon ▲ 423089-2 [DDD]
Fauré, G.:Elégie, w. J. Eskin (vc) Deutsche Grammophon ▲ 423089-2 [DDD]
Fauré, G.:Pelléas et Mélisande (suite), w. S. Hunt (sop) Deutsche Grammophon ▲ 423089-2 [DDD]
Foss, L.:American Pieces (3), w. Itzhak Perlman (vn) EMI Classics ▲ CDC 55360
Franck, C.:Sym in d Deutsche Grammophon ▲ 437827-2
Griffes, C.T.:The Pleasure Dome of Kubla Khan New World ▲ NW 273-2 [ADD]
Griffes, C.T.:Poems (3) of Fiona McLeod, w. P. Bryn-Julson (sop) [E] New World ▲ NW 273-2 [ADD]
Harbison, J.:Sym 1 *(rec 10/84)* New World ▲ 80331-2
Holst, G.:The Planets Philips ("Insignia" series) ▲ 434162-2 [DDD]
Ives, C.:Central Park in the Dark Deutsche Grammophon ("20th Century Classics" series) ▲ 423243-2 [ADD]

ORCH. & ENS.

Boston SO (cont.)
S. Ozawa (cnd) (cont.)
Ives, C.:Sym 4, w. Tanglewood Festival Chorus [E] Deutsche Grammophon ("20th Century Classics" series) ▲ 423243-2 [ADD]
Lieberson, P.:Con Pno, w. Peter Serkin (pno) New World ▲ NW 325-2 [DDD]
Liszt, F.:Cons Pno, w. K. Zimerman (pno) Deutsche Grammophon ▲ 423571-2 [DDD]
Liszt, F.:Totentanz, w. K. Zimerman (pno) Deutsche Grammophon ▲ 423571-2 [DDD]
Mad About Love, w. Cheryl Studer (sop), Kiri Te Kanawa (sop), José Carreras (ten), Jerry Hadley (ten), Philharmonia Orch [cnd:Giuseppe Sinopoli], Bastille Opera Orch [cnd:Myung-Whun Chung], Vienna PO [cnd:John Eliot Gardiner, James Levine] Deutsche Grammophon ▲ 449112-2 ■ 449112-4
Mahler, G.:Kindertotenlieder, w. J. Norman (sop) Philips 2-▲ 426249-2 [DDD]
Mahler, G.:Sym 1 Philips ▲ 422329-2 [DDD]
Mahler, G.:Sym 2, w. K. Te Kanawa (sop), M. Horne (mez), Tanglewood Festival Chorus [G] Philips 2-▲ 420824-2 [DDD]
Mahler, G.:Sym 3, w. Jessye Norman (sop), Tanglewood Festival Chorus, American Boychoir Philips ▲ 434909-2
Mahler, G.:Sym 6 Philips ▲ 434909-2
Mahler, G.:Sym 7 Philips 2-▲ 426249-2 [DDD]
Mahler, G.:Sym 8 [G L] Philips 2-▲ 410607-2 [DDD]
Mahler, G.:Sym 9 Philips 2-▲ 426302-2 [DDD]
Mahler, G.:Sym 10—Adagio only Philips 2-▲ 426302-2 [DDD]
Mendelssohn, F.:Con in e Vn & Orch, Op. 64, w. I. Stern (vn) CBS ▲ MK 37204 [DDD]
Mendelssohn, F.:A Midsummer Night's Dream (comp), w. Kathleen Battle (sop), Frederica von Stade (mez), Judi Dench (nar), Tanglewood Festival Chorus Deutsche Grammophon ▲ 439897-2
Moret, N.:En rêve, w. A.-S. Mutter (vn) Deutsche Grammophon ▲ 431626-2 [DDD] □ 431626-5
Orff, C.:Carmina burana, w. E. Mandac (sop), S. Kolk (ten), S. Milnes (bar), New England Conservatory Chorus [G, L] RCA Gold Seal ▲ 07863-56533-2 [ADD] ■ 07863-56533-4
Panufnik, A.:Sym 8 Hyperion ▲ CDA 66050 [DDD]
Poulenc, F.:Con Org, w. S. Preston (org) Deutsche Grammophon ▲ 437827-2
Poulenc, F.:Con for 2 Pnos, w. K. Labèque (pno), M. Labèque (pno) Philips ▲ 426284-2 [DDD]
Poulenc, F.:Gloria for Sop, w. K. Battle (sop), Tanglewood Festival Chorus [L] Deutsche Grammophon ▲ 427304-2 [DDD]
Poulenc, F.:Stabat mater, w. K. Battle (sop), Tanglewood Festival Chorus [L] Deutsche Grammophon ▲ 427304-2 [DDD]
Prokofiev, S.:Con 4 Pno, w. L. Fleisher (pno) Sony Classical ▲ SK 47188 [DDD]
Prokofiev, S.:Romeo & Juliet Deutsche Grammophon 2-▲ 423268-2 [DDD]
Ravel, M.:Alborada del gracioso Deutsche Grammophon ("Galleria" series) ▲ 415845-2 [ADD]
Ravel, M.:Une Barque sur l'océan Deutsche Grammophon ("Galleria" series) ▲ 415845-2 [ADD]
Ravel, M.:Boléro Deutsche Grammophon ("Galleria" series) ▲ 415845-2 [ADD]
Ravel, M.:Con Pno (left hand), w. L. Fleisher (pno) Sony Classical ▲ SK 47188 [DDD]
Ravel, M.:Menuet antique Deutsche Grammophon ("Galleria" series) ▲ 415845-2 [ADD]
Ravel, M.:Orchestral Music—Bolero; Menuet antique; La valse; Alborada del gracioso; Ma mère l'oye; Pavane pour une infante défunte; Le tombeau de Couperin; Rapsodie espagnole; Daphnis et Chloé; Une barque sur l'ocean; Valses nobles et sentimentales Deutsche Grammophon 3-▲ 439342-2
Ravel, M.:Orchestral Music—Boléro; La Valse; Rhap. espagnole; Mother Goose; Le Tombeau de Couperin; Valses Nobles & Sentimentales; Daphnis & Chloé Suite; Alborada del Gracioso; Menuet antique; Une Barque sur l'Océan *(rec 1974–75)* Deutsche Grammophon ("Double" series) 2-▲ 437392-2 [ADD]
Ravel, M.:Pavane pour une infante défunte Deutsche Grammophon ("Galleria" series) ▲ 415845-2 [ADD]
Ravel, M.:Shéhérazade Mez, w. F. von Stade (mez) [F] CBS ■ IMT 36665 (D)
Ravel, M.:La Valse Deutsche Grammophon ("Galleria" series) ▲ 415845-2 [ADD]
Schoenberg, A.:Con Vc, w. Yo-Yo Ma (vc) CBS ▲ MK 39863 [DDD]
Schoenberg, A.:Gurrelieder, w. J. Norman (sop), T. Troyanos (mez), J. McCracken (ten), D. Arnold (bar), Tanglewood Festival Chorus Philips 2-▲ 412511-2
Sessions, R.:Con Orch Hyperion ▲ CDA 66050 [DDD]
Sessions, R.:When Lilacs Last in the Dooryard Bloom'd, w. E. Hinds (sop), F. Quivar (mez), D. Cossa (bar), Tanglewood Festival Chorus [E] New World ▲ NW 296-2 [AAD]
Shostakovich, D.:Con Vn, Op. 125, w. G. Kremer (vn) Deutsche Grammophon ▲ 439890-2
Shostakovich, D.:Con 2 Vn, w. G. Kremer (vn) Deutsche Grammophon ▲ 439890-2
Sibelius, J.:Con Vn, w. V. Mullova (vn) Philips ▲ 416821-2 [DDD] □ 416821-5
Strauss, R.:Also sprach Zarathustra Philips ("Solo" series) ▲ 442645-2
Strauss, R.:Don Quixote, w. Yo Yo Ma (vc) CBS ▲ MK 39863 [DDD]
Strauss, R.:Ein Heldenleben Philips ("Solo" series) ▲ 442645-2
Stravinsky, I.:Con Vn, w. Itzhak Perlman (vn) *(rec Symphony Hall, Boston, Feb & Nov 1978)* Deutsche Grammophon ("The Originals" series) ▲ 447445-2 [ADD]
Tchaikovsky, P.:Con Vn, w. V. Mullova (vn) Philips ▲ 416821-2 [DDD] □ 416821-5
Tchaikovsky, P.:The Nutcracker Deutsche Grammophon 2-▲ 435619-2 [DDD]
Tchaikovsky, P.:Queen of Spades, w. M. Freni (sop), M. Forrester (cta), V. Atlantov (ten), D. Hvorostovsky (bar), Tanglewood Festival Chorus RCA Red Seal 3-▲ 09026-60992-2 [DDD]
Tchaikovsky, P.:Queen of Spades, w. M. Freni (sop), M. Forrester (cta), V. Atlantov (ten), D. Hvorostovsky (bar), Tanglewood Festival Chorus RCA Red Seal ▲ 09026-61227-2 [DDD] □ 09026-61227-5
Tchaikovsky, P.:Sleeping Beauty (suite) Deutsche Grammophon 2-▲ 435619-2 [DDD]
Tchaikovsky, P.:Swan Lake Deutsche Grammophon 2-▲ 415367-2 [ADD]
Vivaldi, A.:Cons Vn, Op. 8/1–4, "The Four Seasons", w. J. Silverstein (vn) Telarc ▲ CD 80070 [DDD] ■ CS 30070 (D)
Wilson, O.:Sinfonia *(rec 1984)* New World ▲ 80331-2

S. Ozawa, H. Wakasugi (cnd)
Takemitsu, T.:Music of, w. Tashi, Y. Nagano (mez), H. Ibe (gtr), M. Nagasako (hp), K. Abe (vib), Y. Takahashi (pno), R. Noguchi (fl), M. Hamada (lt), T. Koizumi (picc), S. Ueki (vn), Y. Hattori (vc), R. Stoltzman (cl), P. Serkin (pno)—Quatrain; Stanza I; Sacrifice; Ring; Valeria; A Flock Descends into the Pentagonal Garden Deutsche Grammophon ("20th Century Classics" series) ▲ 423253-2 [ADD]

G. Prêtre (cnd)
Berlioz, H.:Sym fantastique RCA Silver Seal ▲ 60478-2-RV [ADD] ■ 60478-4-RV

W. Steinberg (cnd)
Schubert, Franz:Sym 9 RCA Victrola ▲ 60127-2-RV [ADD] ■ 60127-4-RV

M. Tilson Thomas (cnd)
Ives, C.:Three Places in New England Deutsche Grammophon ("20th Century Classics" series) ▲ 423243-2 [ADD]
Ruggles, C.:Sun-treader Deutsche Grammophon ("20th Century Classics" series) ▲ 429860-2 [ADD]
Schuman, W.:Con Vn, w. P. Zukofsky (vn) Deutsche Grammophon ("20th Century Classics" series) ▲ 429860-2 [ADD]

G. Titner (cnd)
Beethoven, L. van:Egmont (ov), w. New York PO members, Canadian Brass Philips ("Digital Classics" series) ▲ 426487-2 [DDD]
Beethoven, L. van:Sym 5, w. New York PO members, Canadian Brass Philips ("Digital Classics" series) ▲ 426487-2 [DDD]
Beethoven, L. van:Wellington's Victory, "Battle Sym", w. New York PO members, Canadian Brass Philips ("Digital Classics" series) ▲ 426487-2 [DDD]

Boston SO Brass
Gabrieli, G.:Canzoni, w. Canadian Brass, New York PO Brass Players—13 canzoni CBS ▲ MK 44931 [DDD] ■ MT 44931 (D)

Boston SO Brass [Fred Mills (tpt), Ronald Romm (tpt), David Ohnanian (hn), Eugene Watts (trbn), Charles Daellenbach (tuba)]
Brass Busters, w. Canadian Brass, New York Phil Brass RCA Victor ▲ 09026-68076-2 ■ 09026-68076-4

Boston SO Chamber Players
Brahms, J.:Qnt Cl, w. Harold Wright (cl) Philips ▲ 442149-2
Brahms, J.:Qnt 1 Strs Elektra/Nonesuch ▲ 79068-2 [DDD]

Boston SO Chamber Players (cont.)
Brahms, J.:Qnt 2 Strs Elektra/Nonesuch ▲ 79068-2 [DDD]
Brahms, J.:Trio Cl Elektra/Nonesuch ■ 79076-4 (D)
Brahms, J.:Trio Hn Elektra/Nonesuch ■ 79076-4 (D)
Copland, A.:Qt Pno Elektra/Nonesuch ▲ 79168-2 [DDD] ■ 79168-4 (D)
Copland, A.:Sextet Cl, Pno & Strs Elektra/Nonesuch ▲ 79168-2 [DDD] ■ 79168-4 (D)
Dvořák, A.:Sextet Elektra/Nonesuch ▲ 79128-2
Harbison, J.:Qnt for 2 Vns, w. Gilbert Kalish (pno) Elektra/Nonesuch ▲ 79189-2 ■ 79189-4
Harbison, J.:Simple Daylight, w. Dawn Upshaw (sop) Elektra/Nonesuch ▲ 79189-2 ■ 79189-4
Harbison, J.:Words From Paterson, w. Sanford Sylvan (bar) Elektra/Nonesuch ▲ 79189-2 ■ 79189-4
Kirchner, L.:Trio Vn, w. L. Kirchner (pno) Elektra/Nonesuch ▲ 79188-2 [DDD]
Mozart, W.A.:Qnt Cl, K.581, w. Harold Wright (cl) Philips ▲ 442149-2
Schubert, Franz:Octet Ww, D.803 Elektra/Nonesuch ▲ 79046-2 [DDD]
Smetana, B.:Trio Pno Elektra/Nonesuch ▲ 79129-2
Stravinsky, I.:L'Histoire du soldat Suite Ensemble, Kocian String Quartet Praga ▲ PR 250057

D. Epstein (cnd)
Lerdahl, F.:Wake, w. B. Beardslee (sop) [E] CRI ▲ CD 580 [ADD/DDD]

L. Kirchner (cnd)
Kirchner, L.:Con Vn, Vc, Winds & Perc, w. L. Kirchner (pno) Elektra/Nonesuch ▲ 79188-2 [DDD]
Kirchner, L.:Music for Twelve Elektra/Nonesuch ▲ 79188-2 [DDD]

Boston SO members
P. Monteux (cnd)
Delibes, L.:Coppélia (suite) RCA Gold Seal ▲ 09026-61975-2
Delibes, L.:Sylvia (suite) RCA Gold Seal ▲ 09026-61975-2
Red, White & Brass, w. Canadian Brass, New York PO Philips ▲ 434276-2 PH [DDD] ■ 434276-4 PH

Boulogne-Billancourt Orch Conservatory
Landowski, Tzipine (cnd)
Landowski, M.:Music of, w. Nadine Sautereau (sop), Jean-Christophe Benoit (bar), Xavier Depraz (bass), Michel Bouquet (spkr), Gilbert Audin (bn), Evelyne Aïello, Didier Bouture, Ludovic Chevalier, Laurent Decker, Françoise Deslogères, Colonne Association des Concerts Orch, Paris Conservatory Société des Concerts Orch, L'Itinéraire Ensemble, Harmonia Nova Orch Ensemble—Con Bn; Con pour ondes Martenot; Femme sans passé; Hauts de Hurlevent; Horologe; Mouvement; Notes de Nuit; Souvenir d'un jardin d'enfance; Ventriloque Chamade 3-▲ 5639/40/41 [AAD/DDD]

Maurice Bourgue Wind Ensemble
Mozart, W.A.:Serenade Ww, K.361 Pierre Verany ▲ PVY 793031 [DDD]

Bournemouth Municipal Orch
R. Austin (cnd)
Delius, F.:Con Vn, w. M. Harrison (vn) *(rec live, 5/13/37)* Symposium ▲ 1075

Bournemouth SO
Jerusalem, w. Winchester Cathedral Choir [cnd:David Hill], Waynflete Singers Argo ▲ 430836-2 ZH [DDD]
Musical Moments in the Garden, w. Academy of St. Martin in the Fields, English CO, Hollywood Bowl SO, Toulouse Orch, Philharmonia Orch, Toulouse CO, L. Auriacombe (cnd), T. Beecham (cnd), C. Davis (cnd), R. Hickox (cnd), N. Marriner (cnd), M. Plasson (cnd), M. Sargent (cnd), et al. Angel ▲ CDM 65203 ■ EG 65203

Bournemouth Sinfonietta
Vivaldi, A.:Cons Vn, Op. 8/1–4, "The Four Seasons", w. R. Thomas (vn) Chandos ("Collect" series) ▲ CHAN 6510 [ADD]

K. Alwyn, R. Hickox (cnd)
Sullivan, A.:Music of, w. V. Masterson (sop), S. Armstrong (sop), R. Tear (ten), B. Luxon (bar), Northern Sinfonietta of England—sels. from all operettas of Gilbert & Sullivan EMI Classics ▲ CDM 64393

I. Bolton (cnd)
Bryars, G.:The Green Ray, w. J. Harle (sax) Argo ▲ 433847-2 [DDD]
Nyman, M.:Where the Bee Dances, w. J. Harle (sax) Argo ▲ 433847-2 [DDD]
Westbrook, M.:Bean Rows & Blues Shots, w. J. Harle (sax) Argo ▲ 433847-2 [DDD]

H. Farberman (cnd)
Druschetzky, G.:Con Ob & Timp, w. G. Hunt (oboe), J. Haas (timp) CRD ▲ 3449 [ADD]
Druschetzky, G.:Partita, w. J. Haas (timp) CRD ▲ 3449 [ADD]
Fischer, J.C. Christian:Sym for 8 Timp, w. J. Haas (timp) CRD ▲ 3449 [ADD]

R. Hickox (cnd)
Delius, F.:Brigg Fair:An English Rhapsody

G. Hurst (cnd)
Elgar, E.:Arthur (suite) Chandos ("Collect" series) ▲ CHAN 6582 [ADD]
Elgar, E.:Music of—Adieu; Burlesco from The Spanish Lady; Chanson de matin; Chanson de nuit; Dream Children; Gavotte (from Contrasts); Minuet from Beau Brummel; Salut d'amour; Sérénade lyrique; Soliloquy for Oboe & Orchestra; Sospiri; Sursum Corda; Three Bavarian Dances; Two Interludes from Falstaff; Waltz from Starlight Express; Woodland Interlude from Caractacus *(rec ca. 1975/76)* Chandos ("Collect" series) ▲ CHAN 6544 [ADD]
Elgar, E.:Music of—Sursum Corda, Op. 11; Sarabande (from *The Spanish Lady:Suite for Strings*); Minuet (from incidental music for *Beau Brummel*); Waltz (from *The Starlight Express*); Sospiri, Op. 70; Adieu (orchestral version) Chandos ▲ CHAN 8432 [ADD]
Elgar, E.:Serenade Strs Chandos ▲ CHAN 8375 [ADD]
Elgar, E.:The Starlight Express (suite), w. C. Glover (sop), J. Lawrenson (bar) Chandos ("Collect" series) ▲ CHAN 6582 [ADD]
Holst, G.:St. Paul's Suite Chandos ▲ CHAN 8375 [ADD]
Ireland, J.:Concertino pastorale Chandos ▲ CHAN 8375 [ADD]
Seascapes, w. Royal Scottish National Orch [cnd:A. Gibson], Ulster Orch [cnd:V. Handley], London PO [cnd:B. Thomson] Chandos ("Collect" series) ▲ CHAN 6538 [ADD/DDD]
Vaughan Williams, R.:Hymn-Tune Preludes Chandos ▲ CHAN 8432 [ADD]
Vaughan Williams, R.:Hymn-Tune Preludes Chandos ("Collect" series) ▲ CHAN 6545 [ADD]
Vaughan Williams, R.:The Poisoned Kiss (ov) Chandos ("Collect" series) ▲ CHAN 6545 [ADD]
Vaughan Williams, R.:The Poisoned Kiss (ov) Chandos ▲ CHAN 8432 [ADD]
Vaughan Williams, R.:The Running Set Chandos ▲ CHAN 8432 [ADD]
Vaughan Williams, R.:The Running Set Chandos ("Collect" series) ▲ CHAN 6545 [ADD]
Vaughan Williams, R.:Sea Songs Chandos ▲ CHAN 8432 [ADD]
Warlock, P.:Capriol Suite Chandos ▲ CHAN 8375 [ADD]

N. del Mar (cnd)
Bantock, G.:The Pierrot of the Minute Chandos ("Collect" series) ▲ CHAN 6566
Bridge, F.:Suite Str Orch Chandos ("Collect" series) ▲ CHAN 6566
Bridge, F.:Summer Chandos ("Collect" series) ▲ CHAN 6566
Bridge, F.:There Is a Willow Grows Aslant a Brook Chandos ("Collect" series) ▲ CHAN 6566
Butterworth, G.:Bredon Hill & Other Songs Chandos ("Collect" series) ▲ CHAN 6566
Delius, F.:Aquarelles (2) Chandos ("Collect" series) ▲ CHAN 6502 [ADD]
Delius, F.:Fennimore & Gerda (intermezzo) Chandos ("Collect" series) ▲ CHAN 6502 [ADD]
Delius, F.:Hassan [arr. Sir Thomas Beecham]—Intermezzo & Serenade Chandos ("Collect" series) ▲ CHAN 6502 [ADD]
Delius, F.:Irmelin (prelude) Chandos ("Collect" series) ▲ CHAN 6502 [ADD]
Delius, F.:Late Swallows Chandos ("Collect" series) ▲ CHAN 6502 [ADD]
Delius, F.:On Hearing the 1st Cuckoo Chandos ("Collect" series) ▲ CHAN 6502 [ADD]
Delius, F.:A Song Before Sunrise Chandos ("Collect" series) ▲ CHAN 6502 [ADD]
Delius, F.:Summer Night on the River Chandos ("Collect" series) ▲ CHAN 6502 [ADD]
Moeran, E.J.:Con Vc, w. Raphael Wallfisch (vc) Chandos ▲ CHAN 8456 [DDD]
Moeran, E.J.:Sinfonietta Chandos ▲ CHAN 8456 [DDD]
Vaughan Williams, R.:Flos Campi, w. F. Riddle (va), Bournemouth Chorus Chandos ("Collect" series) ▲ CHAN 6545 [ADD]
Vaughan Williams, R.:Suite Va, w. F. Riddle (va) Chandos ("Collect" series) ▲ CHAN 6545 [ADD]

C. Martin (cnd)
Gardner, K.:Rainforest Leonarda ▲ LE 327 [DDD]

96 ▲ = CD ♦ = Enhanced CD Δ = MD ■ = Cassette Tape □ = DCC

Bournemouth Sinfonietta (cont.)
C. Martin (cnd) (cont.)
Larsen, L.:Parachute Dancing Leonarda ▲ LE 327 [DDD]
Mamlok, U.:Elegy Leonarda ▲ LE 327 [DDD]
Richter, M.:Lament Leonarda ▲ LE 327 [DDD]
Van De Vate, N.:Journeys Leonarda ▲ LE 327 [DDD]
K. Montgomery (cnd)
Arne, T.:Syms (4)—Nos. 1, 2 & 4 EMI Classics ("Baroque" series) ▲ CDK 65730
Bach, Joh. Christian:Sinfs, Op. 9, w. Trevor Pinnock (hpd)—Sinf No. 2 in E♭ EMI Classics ("Baroque" series) ▲ CDK 65733
Bach, Joh. Christian:Sinfs, Op. 18, w. Trevor Pinnock (hpd)—Sinf No. 4 in D EMI Classics ("Baroque" series) ▲ CDK 65733
Grainger, P.:Folk Song Settings, w. M. Welsh (vc), Philip Martin (pno),—Blithe bells; Country gardens; Green bushes; Handel in the Strand; Mock morris; Molly on the shore; My Robin is to the greenwood gone; Shepherd's hey; Spoon River; Walking tune; Youthful rapture; Youthful Suite *(rec ca. 1979)* Chandos ("Collect" series) ▲ CHAN 6542 [ADD]
Grainger, P.:Music of—Youthful Suite; Blithe bells; Spoon River; My Robin is to the Greenwood gone; Green bushes; Country gardens; Mock morris; Youthful rapture; Shepherd's hey; Walking tune; Molly on the shore; Handel in the Strand Chandos ("Collect" series) ▲ CHAN 6542 [ADD]
Bournemouth Sinfonietta
H.-H. Schönzeler (cnd)
Rubbra, E.:Improvs on Virginal Pieces Chandos ("Collect" series) ▲ CHAN 6599 [ADD]
Rubbra, E.:Sym 10 Chandos ("Collect" series) ▲ CHAN 6599 [ADD]
Rubbra, E.:A Tribute Chandos ("Collect" series) ▲ CHAN 6599 [ADD]
R. Studt (cnd)
Bartók, B.:Divert *(rec Oct. 29–30, 1993)* Naxos ▲ 8.550979 [DDD]
Britten, B.:Simple Sym *(rec Oct. 29–30, 1993)* Naxos ▲ 8.550979 [DDD]
Britten, B.:Vars on a Theme of Frank Bridge *(rec Mar. 18–19, 1993)* Naxos ▲ 8.550823 [DDD]
Delius, F.:Aquarelles (2) *(rec Mar. 18–19, 1993)* Naxos ▲ 8.550823 [DDD]
Grieg, E.:Holberg Suite *(rec Winter Gardens, Bournemouth, UK, May 31–June 1, 1994)* Naxos ▲ 8.553106 [DDD]
Holst, G.:St. Paul's Suite *(rec Mar. 18–19, 1993)* Naxos ▲ 8.550823 [DDD]
Nielsen, C.:Little Suite *(rec Winter Gardens, Bournemouth, UK, May 31–June 1, 1994)* Naxos ▲ 8.553106 [DDD]
Stravinsky, I.:Con Str *(rec Oct. 29–30, 1993)* Naxos ▲ 8.550979 [DDD]
Svendsen, J.:Icelandic Melodies *(rec Winter Gardens, Bournemouth, UK, May 31–June 1, 1994)* Naxos ▲ 8.553106 [DDD]
Svendsen, J.:Norwegian Folk Melody *(rec Winter Gardens, Bournemouth, UK, May 31–June 1, 1994)* Naxos ▲ 8.553106 [DDD]
Svendsen, J.:Swedish Folk Melodies *(rec Winter Gardens, Bournemouth, UK, May 31–June 1, 1994)* Naxos ▲ 8.553106 [DDD]
Vaughan Williams, R.:Variants of "Dives & Lazarus" *(rec Mar. 18–19, 1993)* Naxos ▲ 8.550823 [DDD]
Walton, W.:Henry V (film suite) *(rec Oct. 29–30, 1993)* Naxos ▲ 8.550979 [DDD]
Warlock, P.:Capriol Suite *(rec Mar. 18–19, 1993)* Naxos ▲ 8.550823 [DDD]
Wirén, D.:Serenade Strs *(rec Winter Gardens, Bournemouth, UK, May 31–June 1, 1994)* Naxos ▲ 8.553106 [DDD]
R. Thomas (cnd)
Boyce, W.:Syms, Op. 2 CRD ▲ 3356
Britten, B.:Simple Sym Chandos ("Collect" series) ▲ CHAN 6592 [ADD]
Britten, B.:Vars on a Theme of Frank Bridge Chandos ("Collect" series) ▲ CHAN 6592 [ADD]
Vivaldi, A.:Cons Vn, Op. 8/1–12, "Il cimento dell'armonia e dell'inventione", w. R. Thomas (vn)—Nos. 7–12 Chandos ("Collect" series) ▲ CHAN 6578 [ADD]
T. Vásáry (cnd)
Honegger, A.:Concertino Pno & Orch, w. T. Vásáry (pno) Chandos ▲ CHAN 8993 [DDD]
Honegger, A.:Pastorale d'été Chandos ▲ CHAN 8993 [DDD]
Honegger, A.:Prélude, arioso et fughette sur le nom de BACH Chandos ▲ CHAN 8993 [DDD]
Honegger, A.:Sym 4 Chandos ▲ CHAN 8993 [DDD]
Martinů, B.:Sinfonietta giocosa Pno, w. J. Jacobson (pno) Chandos ▲ CHAN 8859 [DDD]
Martinů, B.:Sinfonietta Pno, w. J. Jacobson (pno) Chandos ▲ CHAN 8859 [DDD]
Martinů, B.:Toccata e due canzoni Chandos ▲ CHAN 8859 [DDD]
Respighi, O.:Adagio con variazioni Vc Orch, w. R. Wallfisch (vc) Chandos ▲ CHAN 8913 [DDD]
Respighi, O.:Il Tramonto, w. L. Finnie (mez) [!] Chandos ▲ CHAN 8913 [DDD]
Respighi, O.:Trittico botticelliano [!] Chandos ▲ CHAN 8913 [DDD]
Respighi, O.:Gli uccelli [!] Chandos ▲ CHAN 8913 [DDD]
Bournemouth SO
A. de Almeida (cnd)
Lalo, E.:Con Vc, w. Ofra Harnoy (vc) *(rec Wessex Hall, Dorset, England, May 11–12, 1995)* RCA Red Seal ▲ 09026–68420–2 [DDD]
Offenbach, J.:Andante Vc, w. Ofra Harnoy (vc) *(rec Wessex Hall, Dorset, England, May 11–12, 1995)* RCA Red Seal ▲ 09026–68420–2 [DDD]
Offenbach, J.:Con militaire, w. Ofra Harnoy (vc) *(rec Wessex Hall, Dorset, England, Jan 16–17, 1995)* RCA Red Seal ▲ 09026–68420–2 [DDD]
K. Bakels (cnd)
Vaughan Williams, R.:Sym 2 Naxos ▲ 8.550734 [DDD]
Vaughan Williams, R.:Sym 3, w. P. Rozario (sop) *(rec Nov. 12, 1992)* Naxos ▲ 8.550733 [DDD]
Vaughan Williams, R.:Sym 6 *(rec Nov. 12, 1993)* Naxos ▲ 8.550733 [DDD]
Vaughan Williams, R.:The Wasps (ov) *(rec Apr. 1993)* Naxos ▲ 8.550734 [DDD]
P. Berglund (cnd)
Britten, B.:Con Vn, w. I. Haendel (vn) EMI Classics ▲ CDM 64202
Grieg, E.:Symphonic Dances EMI Classics ("Doublefforte" series) 2–▲ CDFB 68649
Walton, W.:Con Vn, w. I. Haendel (vn) EMI Classics ▲ CDM 64202
H. Farberman (cnd)
Bazelon, I.:Entre Nous, w. Dorothy Lawson (vc) *(rec Poole Arts Centre, Poole, Dorset, England, June 6–7, 1995)* Albany ▲ TROY 174 [DDD]
Bazelon, I.:Sym 7, "Ballet for Orch" *(rec Poole Arts Centre, Poole, Dorset, England, June 6–7, 1995)* Albany ▲ TROY 174 [DDD]
Bazelon, I.:Sym 9, "Sunday Silence" *(rec Poole Arts Centre, Poole, Dorset, England, June 6–7, 1995)* Albany ▲ TROY 174 [DDD]
Farberman, H.:Con Jazz Drummer, w. L. Bellson (dr) BIS ("BIS Twins" series) 2–▲ CD 232/382 [DDD]
Farberman, H.:Con Jazz Drummer, w. L. Bellson (dr) BIS ▲ CD 382 [DDD]
Haydn, M.:Syms—in C, P.10; in C, P.12; in G, P.16; in C, P.19; in B♭, P.28; in F, P.30; in F, P.32; in D, P.43 Vox Box 2–▲ CDX 5020 [DDD]
J. Farrer (cnd)
Copland, A.:Billy the Kid (suite) IMP ("Classics" series) ▲ IMP 6700772
Copland, A.:Rodeo IMP ("Classics" series) ▲ IMP 6700772
Gershwin, G.:Porgy & Bess (symphonic picture) IMP ("Classics" series) ▲ IMP 6700772
C. Groves (cnd)
Delius, F.:On Hearing the 1st Cuckoo Saga Classics ▲ 3353 [ADD]
Elgar, E.:Intro & Allegro Saga Classics ▲ 3353 [ADD]
T. Guschlbauer (cnd)
Mozart, W.A.:Kleine Nachtmusik Erato ▲ 45939–2 [ADD] ■ 45939–4
V. Handley (cnd)
Simpson, R.:Sym 2 *(rec Dec. 1991 & July 1992)* Hyperion ▲ CDA 66505 [DDD]
Simpson, R.:Sym 4 *(rec Dec. 1991 & July 1992)* Hyperion ▲ CDA 66505 [DDD]
Simpson, R.:Sym 9 Hyperion ▲ CDA 66299 [DDD]
R. Hickox (cnd)
Britten, B.:Johnson over Jordan Chandos ▲ CHAN 9221 [DDD]
Britten, B.:Peter Grimes (4 sea interludes) Chandos ▲ CHAN 9221 [DDD]
Britten, B.:Suite on English Folk Tunes Chandos ▲ CHAN 9221 [DDD]

Bournemouth SO (cont.)
R. Hickox (cnd) (cont.)
Britten, B.:The Young Person's Guide to the Orchestra Chandos ▲ CHAN 9221 [DDD]
Delius, F.:Dance Rhap 1 Chandos ▲ CHAN 9355 [DDD]
Delius, F.:Dance Rhap 2 Chandos ▲ CHAN 9355 [DDD]
Delius, F.:Florida EMI Classics ▲ CDC 49932 [DDD]
Delius, F.:In a Summer Garden Chandos ▲ CHAN 9355 [DDD]
Delius, F.:North Country Sketches Chandos ▲ CHAN 9355 [DDD]
Delius, F.:Paris:The Song of a Great City EMI Classics ▲ CDC 49932 [DDD]
Delius, F.:Sea Drift, w. B. Terfel (bass–bar), Bournemouth Chorus Chandos ▲ CHAN 9214 [DDD]
Delius, F.:Songs of Farewell, w. B. Terfel (bass–bar), Bournemouth Chorus Chandos ▲ CHAN 9214 [DDD]
Delius, F.:Songs of Sunset, w. S. Burgess (mez), B. Terfel (bass–bar), Bournemouth Chorus Chandos ▲ CHAN 9214 [DDD]
Delius, F.:Walk to the Paradise Garden Chandos ▲ CHAN 9355 [DDD]
Mahler, G.:Das Klagende Lied, w. J. Rodgers (sop), L. Finnie (cta), H. P. Blochwitz (ten), Bath Festival Chorus, Waynflete Singers Chandos ▲ CHAN 9247 [DDD]
Tavener, J.:Theophany Chandos ▲ CHAN 9440
Tippett, M.:Con Orch, w. Timothy Walden (vc) Chandos ▲ CHAN 9384 [DDD]
Tippett, M.:Con Pno, w. Howard Shelley (pno) Chandos ▲ CHAN 9333 [DDD]
Tippett, M.:Fant Concertante on a Theme of Corelli Chandos ▲ CHAN 9233 [DDD]
Tippett, M.:Fant on a Theme from Handel Chandos ▲ CHAN 9233 [DDD]
Tippett, M.:New Year (suite) Chandos ▲ CHAN 9299 [DDD]
Tippett, M.:Praeludium Chandos ▲ CHAN 9276 [DDD]
Tippett, M.:Sym 1 Chandos ▲ CHAN 9333 [DDD]
Tippett, M.:Sym 2 Chandos ▲ CHAN 9299 [DDD]
Tippett, M.:Sym 3, w. F. Robinson (sop) Chandos ▲ CHAN 9276 [DDD]
Tippett, M.:Sym 4 Chandos ▲ CHAN 9233 [DDD]
Tippett, M.:Triple Con, w. Levon Chilingirian (vn), Simon Rowland–Jones (va), Philip de Groote (vc) Chandos ▲ CHAN 9384 [DDD]
Vaughan Williams, R.:Job EMI Classics ▲ CDC 54421
D. Hill (cnd)
Delius, F.:Winter Night *(rec Winchester Cathedral, Jan 10–13, 1994)* London ▲ 444130–2 [DDD]
Finzi, G.:In terra pax, w. Libby Crabtree (sop), Donald Sweeney (bass), Winchester Cathedral Choir, Waynflete Singers *(rec Winchester Cathedral, Jan 10–13, 1994)* London ▲ 444130–2 [DDD]
Ireland, J.:Songs, w. Nicholas Richardson (trb), Stephen Ryde–Weller (trb)—The Holy Boy *(rec Winchester Cathedral, Jan 10–13, 1994)* London ▲ 444130–2 [DDD]
Vaughan Williams, R.:Fant on Christmas Carols, w. Donald Sweeney (bass), David Dunnett (org), Winchester Cathedral Choir, Waynflete Singers *(rec Winchester Cathedral, Jan 10–13, 1994)* London ▲ 444130–2 [DDD]
Vaughan Williams, R.:Let Us Now Praise Famous Men, w. Winchester Cathedral Choir Argo ▲ 436120–2 [DDD]
Vaughan Williams, R.:O Clap Your Hands, w. Winchester Cathedral Choir Argo ▲ 436120–2 [DDD]
Vaughan Williams, R.:The Old 100th Psalm Tune, w. Winchester Cathedral Choir Argo ▲ 436120–2 [DDD]
Vaughan Williams, R.:Toward the Unknown, w. Winchester Cathedral Choir Argo ▲ 436120–2 [DDD]
Walton, W.:Coronation Te Deum, w. T. Byram–Wigfield (org), Winchester Cathedral Choir Argo ▲ 436120–2 [DDD]
Walton, W.:Orb & Sceptre Argo ▲ 436120–2 [DDD]
M. Laus (cnd)
Camilleri, C.:Con 1 Pno, w. A. de Groote (pno) Unicorn–Kanchana ▲ DKP CD 9150
Camilleri, C.:Con 2 Pno, w. A. de Groote (pno) Unicorn–Kanchana ▲ DKP CD 9150
Camilleri, C.:Con 3 Pno, w. A. de Groote (pno) Unicorn–Kanchana ▲ DKP CD 9150
A. Litton (cnd)
Bernstein, L.:Candide (ov) Virgin Classics ▲ CDC 59038
Bernstein, L.:Candide (ov) Virgin Classics ▲ CUV 61119
Bernstein, L.:Fancy Free Virgin Classics ▲ CDC 59038
Bernstein, L.:Fancy Free Virgin Classics ▲ CUV 61119
Bernstein, L.:Sym 2, "Age of Anxiety", w. J. Kahane (pno) Virgin Classics ▲ CUV 61119
Bernstein, L.:Sym 2, "Age of Anxiety", w. J. Kahane (pno) Virgin Classics ▲ CDC 59038
Gershwin, G.:Con Pno, w. A. Litton (pno) Virgin Classics ▲ CDZ 59693
Tchaikovsky, P.:Manfred Virgin Classics ▲ CDC 59230
Tchaikovsky, P.:Romeo & Juliet Virgin Classics ▲ CDC 59239 [DDD]
Tchaikovsky, P.:Romeo & Juliet Virgin Classics ("Ultraviolet" series) ▲ CUV 61267
Tchaikovsky, P.:Serenade Strs Virgin Classics ▲ CDC 59175
Tchaikovsky, P.:Sym 1 Virgin Classics ▲ ZDMC 59699
Tchaikovsky, P.:Sym 1 Virgin Classics ▲ 59588 [DDD]
Tchaikovsky, P.:Sym 2 Virgin Classics ▲ 59588 [DDD]
Tchaikovsky, P.:Sym 2 Virgin Classics ▲ ZDMC 59699
Tchaikovsky, P.:Sym 3 Virgin Classics ▲ ZDMC 59699
Tchaikovsky, P.:Sym 4 Virgin Classics ▲ ZDMC 59699
Tchaikovsky, P.:Sym 4 Virgin Classics ▲ CDC 59175
Tchaikovsky, P.:Sym 5 Virgin Classics ▲ ZDMC 59701
Tchaikovsky, P.:Sym 5 Virgin Classics ▲ 59598 [DDD]
Tchaikovsky, P.:Sym 6 Virgin Classics ▲ CDC 59239 [DDD]
Tchaikovsky, P.:Sym 6 Virgin Classics ("Ultraviolet" series) ▲ CUV 61267
Tchaikovsky, P.:Sym 6 Virgin Classics ▲ ZDMC 59701
Tchaikovsky, P.:The Tempest Virgin Classics ▲ 59598 [DDD]
Walton, W.:Belshazzar's Feast, w. Bryn Terfel (b–bar), Bournemouth Sym Chorus, L'Inviti, Waynflete Singers *(rec Winchester Cathedral, Feb 1995)* London ▲ 448134–2 [DDD]
Walton, W.:Con Vc, w. Robert Cohen (vc) London ▲ 443450–2
Walton, W.:Con Vn, w. Tasmin Little (vn) *(rec Guildhall, Southampton, Mar 1994)* London ▲ 444114–2 [DDD]
Walton, W.:Crown Imperial *(rec Winchester Cathedral, Feb 1995)* London ▲ 448134–2 [DDD]
Walton, W.:Henry V (film suite) *(rec Winchester Cathedral, Feb 1995)* London ▲ 448134–2 [DDD]
Walton, W.:Scapino *(rec Guildhall, Southampton, Mar 1994)* London ▲ 444114–2 [DDD]
Walton, W.:Sym 1 London ▲ 443450–2
Walton, W.:Sym 2 *(rec Guildhall, Southampton, Mar 1994)* London ▲ 444114–2 [DDD]
G. Lloyd (cnd)
Lloyd, G.:A Symphonic Mass, w. Brighton Festival Chorus Albany ▲ TROY 100 [DDD]
S. Rattle (cnd)
Mahler, G.:Sym 10 [version by Cooke, w. "slight adjustments" by Rattle] EMI Classics ▲ CDC 54406
C. Silvestri (cnd)
Simpson, R.:Con Pno, w. John Ogdon (pno) IMP ("BBC Radio Classics" series) ▲ IMP 5691762
H. Williams (cnd)
Donizetti, G.:Arias, w. Julstin Lavender (ten)—Un Ange, une Femme Inconnue; Je Ne Meritais Pas...Oijt Ta Voix M'Inspire; La Maitresse du Roi?...Ange St Pur [all from La Favorita]; Ingemisco [from Requiem]; Si Compia il Sacrificio...Io l'Amai [from Gabriella di Vergy] IMP ("Classics" series) ▲ IMP 6700102
Rossini, G.:Arias, w. Julstin Lavender (ten)—Ch Ascolto?...Ah Come Mai Non Senti Pieta [from Otello]; Ne M'Abandonne Point...Asile Hereditaire [from Guillaume Tell]; Cujus Animam Gementem [Stabat Mater]; Languir per una Bella & Oh Come il Cor di Giubilo [from L'Italiana in Algeri]; Avanons...Grand Dieu Faut...Il Qu'un Peuple [from Le siege de Corinthe] IMP ("Classics" series) ▲ IMP 6700102
M. Arnold (cnd)
Arnold, M.:Solitaire EMI Classics ▲ CDM 64044–2
Arnold, M.:Sym 1 EMI Classics ▲ CDM 64044
Bowed Piano Ensemble [Christopher Eisinger (pno), Amy Dounay (pno), Joshua Finch (pno), Talitha Jones (pno), Shawn Keener (pno), Lewis Keller (pno), Sally Rupert (pno), Stephen Scott (pno), Daniel Wiencek (pno), David Wilhelm (pno)]
Scott, S.:Vikings of the Sunrise:Fantasy on the Polynesian Star Path Navigators *(rec Packard Hall, Colorado College, Colorado Springs, Dec 9 & 10, 1995)* New Albion ▲ NA 084CD

Bowery Ensemble
B. Speach (cnd)
Speach, B.:Music of, w. J. Schanzer, L. Krech (trbn), J. Williams (gtr), A. de Mare (pno), Michael Pugliese (perc), T. Davis (speaker), et al.—Moto for Trombone, Percussion & Piano (1982); Pensées for Guitar (1983); Trajet for Trombone & Percussion (1983); Sonata for Piano (1986); Shattered Glass for Percussion (1987); Telepathy (Poetry/Music Suite) for Speaker, Contrabas Mode ▲ 16
Bowling Green State Univ New Music Festival Ensemble
R. Spano (cnd)
O'Brien, E.:Taking Measures, w. P. Makara (vn) Capstone ▲ CPS 8603
Bradshaw & Buono Piano Duo [David Bradshaw (pno), Cosmo Buono (pno)]
Bax, A.:The Poisoned Fountain Connoisseur Society ▲ CD 4171 [DDD]
Casella, A.:Pupazzetti Connoisseur Society ▲ CD 4171 [DDD]
Debussy, C.:Danses sacrée et profane [arr. Debussy] Connoisseur Society ▲ CD 4171 [DDD]
Debussy, C.:Petite suite Connoisseur Society ▲ CD 4171 [DDD]
Debussy, C.:Prélude à l'après-midi d'un faune [arr. Debussy, 1895] Connoisseur Society ▲ CD 4171 [DDD]
Ravel, M.:Frontispiece, w. Theodore Kelton (pno) Connoisseur Society ▲ CD 4171 [DDD]
Ravel, M.:Ma mère l'oye Pno Connoisseur Society ▲ CD 4171 [DDD]
Brahms Trio
Caprioli, A.:A la dolce Ombra *(rec 1987)* Pro Viva ▲ ISPV 148 CD [ADD]
Caprioli, A.:Trio Pno, Vn & Vc *(rec 1987)* Pro Viva ▲ ISPV 148 CD [ADD]
Brandeis Festival Orch
I. Solomon (cnd)
Berger, A.:Serenade Concertante CRI ▲ CD 622 (m) [ADD]
Brandeis-Bardin Ensemble
Zeisl, E.:Pno Trio Suite Harmonia Mundi USA ▲ HMU 907044
Zeisl, E.:Qt 2 Strs Harmonia Mundi USA ▲ HMU 907044
Brandenburg Collegium
A. Newman (cnd)
Mozart, W.A.:Kleine Nachtmusik—Romance Sony Classical ▲ MLK 62369 [ADD/DDD]
Brandenburg Consort
R. Goodman (cnd)
Avison, C.:Concerti grossi (12) Hyperion 2-▲ CDA 66891/92
Bach, J.S.:Brandenburg Cons Hyperion 2-▲ CDA 66711/12
Bach, J.S.:Brandenburg Cons Hyperion 2-▲ CDD 22001
Bach, J.S.:Suites Orch, BWV 1066–1069 Hyperion 2-▲ CDD 22002
Handel, G.F.:Almira (ov)—Ov No. 2 in g Hyperion ▲ CDA 66860
Handel, G.F.:Arias, w. Emma Kirkby (sop)—Vedrai s'a tuo dispetto [from Almira]; Perché viva il caro sposo [from Rodrigo]; Vo' far guerra [from Rinaldo]; Ah! spietato; Desterò dall' empia Dite [both from Amadigi di Gaula]; Ombre, piante [from Rodelinda]; Sinfonia; V' adoro, pupille [both from Giulio Cesare]; Cor di padre [from Tamerlano]; Scoglio d'immota fronte [from Scipione] Hyperion ▲ CDA 66860
Handel, G.F.:Messiah, w. Lynne Dawson (sop), Hilary Summers (cta), John Mark Ainsley (ten), Alastair Miles (bass), Stephen Cleobury (cnd), King's College Choir Cambridge [1752 version] Argo 2-▲ 440672-2 [DDD]
Handel, G.F.:Scipione (ov)—Ov; March Hyperion ▲ CDA 66860
Handel, G.F.:Silla (ov) Hyperion ▲ CDA 66860
Handel, G.F.:Tamerlano (ov) Hyperion ▲ CDA 66860
Rondeaux Royaux:Baroque Pops Hyperion ▲ CDA 66600
Vivaldi, A.:Arias, w. Emma Kirkby (sop)—Gelosia, tu gio rendi l'alma mia; Loombre, l'aure; Se mai senti spirati; Se in campo armato; Non mi lusinga vana speranza; Ferma Teodosiio; Ombre vane, Agitata da due venti; Non ti lusinghi, la credeltade Hyperion ▲ CDA 66745
Vivaldi, A.:Sinfs—Sinfs. from Tamerlano, Freiselda, Ottone in Villa Hyperion ▲ CDA 66745
Wassenaer, U.W. van:Concerti Armonici Hyperion ▲ CDA 66670
D. Hill (cnd)
Purcell, H.:Anthems, w. D. Dunnett (org), London Baroque Brass, Winchester Cathedral Choir—Funeral Sentences; Rejoice in the Lord Always; Jehova, Quam Multi Sunt Hostes; O God, Thou Art My God; Remember Not, Lord, Our Offences; Give Sentence with Me, O God; Hear My Prayer, O Lord; Voluntary in C; A Double Verse in G; O, I'm Sick of Life Argo ▲ 436833-2 [DDD]
Purcell, H.:Music for the Funeral of Queen Mary, w. D. Dunnett (org), London Baroque Brass, Winchester Cathedral Choir Argo ▲ 436833-2 [DDD]
Purcell, H.:Music of, w. Catherine Bott (sop), Emma Kirkby (sop), James Bowman (alt), Anthony Rooley (lt), Paula Chateauneuf (gtr), Monica Huggett (vn), Catherine Mackintosh (vn), Christophe Coin (vc), Academy of Ancient Music, David Hill (cnd), Anthony Lewis (cnd), St. Anthony Singers, Taverner Choir, Winchester Cathedral Choir—The Double Dealer; Come Ye Sons of Art; The Old Bachelor; Birthday Song for Queen Mary; Oedipus; King Arthur; Bonduca; The Fairy Queen; Son. No. 9 in F; Dido & Aeneas; Abdelazer; Bess of Bedlam; The Married Beau; Hear My Prayer, O Lord; Rejoice in the Lord Always London ("Editions de l'oiseau-lyre" series) ▲ 444620-2
Purcell, H.:My Beloved Spake, w. D. Dunnett (org), London Baroque Brass, Winchester Cathedral Choir Argo ▲ 436833-2 [DDD]
Brandenburg Orch
R. Goodman (cnd)
Mysliveček, J.:Cons Vn, w. Elizabeth Wallfisch (vn)—in B♭ Hyperion ▲ CDA 66840
Schubert, Franz:Rondo Vn, D.438, w. Elizabeth Wallfisch (vn) Hyperion ▲ CDA 66840
Spohr, L.:Con 8 Vn, w. Elizabeth Wallfisch (vn) Hyperion ▲ CDA 66840
Viotti, G.B.:Con 22 Vn, w. Elizabeth Wallfisch (vn) Hyperion ▲ CDA 66840
D. Hill (cnd)
Haydn, J.:Mass 7, "Kleine Orgelmesse", w. Linda Russell (alto), Catherine Wyn-Rogers (alt), William Kendall (ten), Michael George (bass), Winchester Cathedral Choir Hyperion ▲ CDA 66508 [DDD]
Haydn, J.:Mass 14, "Harmoniemesse", w. Linda Russell (alto), Catherine Wyn-Rogers (alt), William Kendall (ten), Michael George (bass), Winchester Cathedral Choir Hyperion ▲ CDA 66508 [DDD]
Brandenburg PO
R. Kaufman (cnd)
Korngold, E.W.:Captain Blood [reconstructed by John Morgan] *(rec Jesus Christ Church, Berlin)* Marco Polo ▲ 8.223607 [DDD]
Korngold, E.W.:Film Music—Charge of the Light Brigade; Juarez; Gunga Din; Devotion *(rec Jesus Christ Church, Berlin, Germany, Apr. 14–16, June 15–21, 1)* Marco Polo ▲ 8.223608 [DDD]
Rózsa, M.:The King's Thief [reconstructed by Christopher Palmer] *(rec Jesus Christ Church, Berlin)* Marco Polo ▲ 8.223607 [DDD]
Steiner, M.:The 3 Musketeers [arr. John Morgan] *(rec Jesus Christ Church, Berlin)* Marco Polo ▲ 8.223607 [DDD]
Young, V.:Scaramouche [reconstructed by William Stromberg] *(rec Jesus Christ Church, Berlin)* Marco Polo ▲ 8.223607 [DDD]
M. Rosenberg (cnd)
Original Motion Picture Scores Capriccio ▲ 10 469 [DDD]
J. Tuggle (cnd)
Khachaturian, A.:Spartacus, w. J. Schwab (vc), S. Grützmann (pno) *(rec Jan. 1993)* Divox ▲ CDX 39307 [DDD]
Brandis String Quartet [Thomas Brandis (vn), Peter Brem (vn), Wilfried Strehle (va), Wolfgang Boettcher (vc)]
Beethoven, L. van:Grosse Fuge Str Qt *(rec Concert Hall, Nimbus Foundation, Oct 27–29, 1994)* Nimbus ▲ NI 5465 [DDD]
Beethoven, L. van:Qt 4 Strs *(rec Oct. 14–17, 1992)* Nimbus ▲ NI 5353 [DDD]
Beethoven, L. van:Qt 5 Strs *(rec May 12, 1993)* Nimbus ▲ NI 5353 [DDD]
Beethoven, L. van:Qt 6 Strs *(rec Oct. 14–17, 1992)* Nimbus ▲ NI 5353 [DDD]
Beethoven, L. van:Qt 7 Strs Nimbus ▲ NI 5382 [DDD]
Beethoven, L. van:Qt 9 Strs Nimbus ▲ NI 5382 [DDD]
Brandis String Quartet (cont.)
Beethoven, L. van:Qt 13 Strs *(rec Concert Hall, Nimbus Foundation, Oct 27–29, 1994)* Nimbus ▲ NI 5465 [DDD]
Brahms, J.:Qnt 2 Strs, w. Brett Dean (va) *(rec Teldec-Studio, Berlin, Feb 23–26, 1996)* Nimbus ▲ NI 5488 [DDD]
Bruckner, A.:Qnt Strs, w. Brett Dean (va) *(rec Teldec-Studio, Berlin, Feb 23–26, 1996)* Nimbus ▲ NI 5488 [DDD]
Hindemith, P.:Qt 3 Strs *(rec Oct. 12–14, 1992)* Nimbus ▲ NI 5410 [DDD]
Mozart, W.A.:Qt 14 Strs Orfeo ▲ 041831 [DDD]
Mozart, W.A.:Qt 23 Strs Orfeo ▲ 041831 [DDD]
Schubert, Franz:Qt 4 Strs Nimbus ▲ NI 5313
Schubert, Franz:Qt 9 Strs Orfeo ▲ 113851 [DDD]
Schubert, Franz:Qt 10 Strs Orfeo ▲ 113851 [DDD]
Schubert, Franz:Qt 13 Strs *(rec Concert Hall of the Nimbus Foundation, Feb. 26, 1995)* Nimbus ▲ NI 5438 [DDD]
Schubert, Franz:Qt 14 Strs *(rec Concert Hall of the Nimbus Foundation, Feb. 26, 1995)* Nimbus ▲ NI 5438 [DDD]
Schubert, Franz:Qt 14 Strs Orfeo ▲ 017821 [DDD]
Schubert, Franz:Qt 15 Strs Orfeo ▲ 007821 [DDD]
Schulhoff, E.:Qt 1 Strs *(rec Oct. 12–14, 1992)* Nimbus ▲ NI 5410 [DDD]
Weill, K.:Qt Strs *(rec Oct. 12–14, 1992)* Nimbus ▲ NI 5410 [DDD]
J. Conlon (cnd)
Martinů, B.:Con Str Qt, w. French National Orch Erato ▲ 2292-45499-2 ZK
Martinů, B.:Ricercari, w. French National Orch Erato ▲ 2292-45499-2 ZK
Brasil Brass Quintet [Naílson Simões (tpt/flgl), Ayrton Benck (tpt/flgl), Cisneiro de Andrade (hn), Radegundis Feitosa (trbn/eup), Walmir Vieira (tuba)]
Manuel Do Espírito Santo, A.:Music of, w. Glauco Andreza (perc)—220 [arr. Adail Fernandes] *(rec Cultural Foundation Theatre, João Pessoa, Paraíba, Brazil, Mar 22–26, 1995)* Nimbus ▲ NI 5462 [DDD]
Segundo Sedícias, D.:Music of, w. Glauco Andreza (perc)—Trilogia matuta *(rec Cultural Foundation Theatre, João Pessoa, Paraíba, Brazil, Mar 22–26, 1995)* Nimbus ▲ NI 5462 [DDD]
Ursicino da Silva, J.:Music of, w. Glauco Andreza (perc)—Suite Recife; Gonzagueando; Concertino para Trompete; Brass Music No. 1; Marquinhos no frevo; Andrezza; Coletânea '93; Serenata no Capibaribe; Nairam; Tema para um trompetista *(rec Cultural Foundation Theatre, João Pessoa, Paraíba, Brazil, Mar 22–26, 1995)* Nimbus ▲ NI 5462 [DDD]
Villa-Lobos, H.:Cirandas Pno, w. Glauco Andreza (perc) [3 Cirandas arr. José Alberto Kaplan] *(rec Cultural Foundation Theatre, João Pessoa, Paraíba, Brazil, Mar 22–26, 1995)* Nimbus ▲ NI 5462 [DDD]
Brasov George Dima PO
I. Ionescu-Galati (cnd)
Constantinescu, P.:Con Str Orch *(rec 1981)* Olympia ▲ OCD 415 [AAD]
Brass Band
E. Ormandy (cnd)
Tchaikovsky, P.:Ov 1812, w. Philadelphia Orch, Mormon Tabernacle Choir CBS ■ MT 30447
Brass Ring
Brass Ring Crystal ▲ CD 561 ■ C 561
del Tredici, D.:Heavy Metal Alice Crystal ▲ CD 564
Druckman, J.:Dance with Shadows Crystal ▲ CD 564
Ewald, V.:Qnt 1 Brass Crystal ▲ CD 561 ■ C 561
Rorem, N.:Diversions Crystal ▲ CD 564
Brass Ring [Jay Lichtmann (tpt), Claire Newbold (tpt), Kirsten Bendixen (hn), David Kayser (trbn), Karl Kramer (tuba)]
Bach, J.S.:Clavier-Übung III—Wir Glauben all an einen Gott [arr for Brass Ensemble] Crystal ▲ CD 551
Gregson, E.:Qnt Brass Crystal ▲ CD 551
Henze, H.-W.:Fragmente aus einer Show Crystal ▲ CD 551
Hindemith, P.:Madrigals—4 sels [arr for Brass Ensemble] Crystal ▲ CD 551
Leclerc, F.:Par Monts et par vaux Crystal ▲ CD 551
Lutoslawski, W.:Mini Ov Crystal ▲ CD 551
Praetorius, M.:Terpsichore Crystal ▲ CD 551
Brassissimo Vienna [Freddy Staudigl (tpt/pic), Andreas Kretz (tpt), Marcus Schmidinger (hn), Johann Schodl (trbn), Martin Urban (tuba)]
Bach, J.S.:Music of, w. Martin Rieker (org)—Brandenburg Con No. 2, BWV 1047; Bourreé [from English Suite No. 2, BWV 807]; Wie sich ein Vater erbarmet; Lobet den Herrn [both from Psalm 150, BWV 225]; Rondeau; Badinerie [both from Suite No. 1 for Orch, BWV 1067]; Ertöt uns durch dein Güte, BWV 22; Nun danket alle Gott, BWV 79; Was Gott tut, das ist wohlgetan, BWV 75; Air [from Suite No. 3 for Orch, BWV 1068]; Wie will ich mich freuen, BWV 146; Wachet auf, ruft uns die Stimme, BWV 645; Halleluja [from Lobet den Herrn, alle Heiden, BWV 230]; Italian Con No. 1, BWV 971; Contrapunctus I & IX [from Art of the Fugue, BWV 1080]; Grosser Herr und starker König; Kommst du nun, Jesu, vom Himmel herunter, BWV 650; Jesu bleibet meine Freude, BWV 147; Ov [from Nun komm der Heiden Heiland, BWV 61]; Ach, mein herzliebstes Jesulein; Nun seid ihr wohl gerochen *(rec Halle, Germany, Sept 1–4, 1994)* Brassissimo ▲ BVR 2572775 [DDD]
Strauss (I), Joh.:Radetzky March, w. Ralf Kircher (perc), Rudolf Schmidinger (perc), Kevan Teherani (perc) *(rec Pfarrkirche Staatz, Nov 29–Dec 2, 1993)* Brassissimo ▲ BVR 2328517 [DDD]
Strauss (II), Joh.:Music of, w. Ralf Kircher (perc), Rudolf Schmidinger (perc), Kevan Teherani (perc)—Maskenball-Quadrille; Unter Donner und Blitz; Etwas Kleines; Kaiserwalzer; Annenpolka; Waldmeister-Ov; Leichtes Blut; Auf der Jagd; Pizzikato-Polka [composed w. Josef Strauss]; Elyen a Magyar; Perpetuum Mobile; Fledermaus-Ov *(rec Pfarrkirche Staatz, Nov 29–Dec 2, 1993)* Brassissimo ▲ BVR 2328517 [DDD]
Strauss, Josef:Music of, w. Ralf Kircher (perc), Rudolf Schmidinger (perc), Kevan Teherani (perc)—Ohne Sorgen; Moulinet-Polka; Pizzikato-Polka [composed w. Johann Strauss II]; Feuerfest *(rec Pfarrkirche Staatz, Nov 29–Dec 2, 1993)* Brassissimo ▲ BVR 2328517 [DDD]
Christmas with Brassissimo, w. Manfred Kaufmann (perc), Rudolf Schmidinger (perc) *(rec MG-SOUND Studios, Vienna)* Brassissimo ▲ BVR 5356400 [DDD]
Brass-zination
A Night at the Opera FSM ("Fono" series) ▲ 97701
Bratislava Camerata
J. Rozehnal (cnd)
Gallus, J.:Missa super "Sancta Maria" *(rec Church St. George of Svätý Jur, June & Aug 1995)* Slovart ▲ SR 0014-2-131 [DDD]
Harant, K.:Maria Kron *(rec Church St. George of Svätý Jur, June & Aug 1995)* Slovart ▲ SR 0014-2-131 [DDD]
Harant, K.:Missa quinis vocibus super Dolorosi martyr *(rec Church St. George of Svätý Jur, June & Aug 1995)* Slovart ▲ SR 0014-2-131 [DDD]
Harant, K.:Qui confidunt in Domino *(rec Church St. George of Svätý Jur, June & Aug 1995)* Slovart ▲ SR 0014-2-131 [DDD]
Zarewutius, Z.:Magnificats & Motets—Magnificats primi Toni & secondi Toni; Meine Seele erlebt den Herren; Ach, Christe Jesu Kindelein; Da Jesus geboren war; Das alte Jahr vergangen ist; Der Tag, der ist so freudenreich; O Jesu mi dulcissime; Wir loben all das Kindelein *(rec Bratislava, Oct. 1994)* Discover International ▲ DI 920252 [DDD]
Bratislava Chamber Ensemble
V. Horák (cnd)
Hummel, J.N.:Con Pno, Op. 34a, w. P. Kováč (pno) Koch Schwann ▲ CD 311120
Bratislava Chamber Soloists
J. Kopelman (cnd)
Elgar, E.:Serenade Strs *(rec Mirror Hall, Primacial Palace, Bratislava, Jan, Feb, & Oct, 1995)* Slovart ▲ SR 0012-2-131 [DDD]
Grieg, E.:Holberg Suite *(rec Mirror Hall, Primacial Palace, Bratislava, Jan, Feb, & Oct, 1995)* Slovart ▲ SR 0012-2-131 [DDD]
Tchaikovsky, P.:Serenade Strs *(rec Mirror Hall, Primacial Palace, Bratislava, Jan, Feb, & Oct, 1995)* Slovart ▲ SR 0012-2-131 [DDD]

Bratislava Musica Aeterna
P. Zajícek (cnd)
Zimmermann, A.:Con Bn — Trevak ▲ TRE 40010 [DDD]
Zimmermann, A.:Con Bns — Trevak ▲ TRE 40010 [DDD]
Zimmermann, A.:Con Db, w. R. Sasina (db) — Trevak ▲ TRE 40010 [DDD]
Zimmermann, A.:Con in D Db, w. R. Sasina (db) — Trevak ▲ TRE 40010 [DDD]
Zimmermann, A.:Con Hpd, w. M. Dobiášová (hpd) — Trevak ▲ TRE 40010 [DDD]
Zimmermann, A.:Grand Con Hpd, w. M. Dobiášová (hpd) — Trevak ▲ TRE 40010 [DDD]
Bratislava Philharmonic CO
L. Pešek (cnd)
Spohr, L.:Con 7 Vn, w. T. Nishizaki (vn) — Marco Polo ▲ 8.220406 [DDD]
Spohr, L.:Con 12 Vn, w. T. Nishizaki (vn) — Marco Polo ▲ 8.220406 [DDD]
Bratislava RSO
M. Halász (cnd)
Beethoven, L. van:Leonore 1 — Lydian ▲ LYD 18056
Beethoven, L. van:Leonore 2 — Lydian ▲ LYD 18057 [DDD]
Beethoven, L. van:Sym 3, "Eroica" — Lydian ▲ LYD 18056
Beethoven, L. van:Sym 6, "Pastorale" — Lydian ▲ LYD 18057 [DDD]
A. Leaper (cnd)
Yin, C.-Z.:Yellow River Con, w. Cheng-Zong Yin (pno) — Marco Polo ▲ 8.223412 [DDD]
Yin, C.-Z.:Yellow River Fant — Marco Polo ▲ 8.223408 [DDD]
O. Lenárd (cnd)
Italian & French Opera Arias, w. Peter Dvorský (ten) — Naxos ▲ 8.550343 [DDD]
Strauss (II), Joh.:Music of—Blue Danube (waltz), Op. 314; Roses from the South (waltz), Op. 388; Egyptian March, Op. 335; Emperor Waltz, Op. 437; Tritsch-Tratsch Polka, Op. 214; Viennese Blood (waltz), Op. 354; Persian March, Op. 289; 1001 Nights (waltz), Op. 346; Voices of Spring (waltz), Op. 410; Perpetuum mobile [Musical Joke], Op. 257; Pizzicato Polka [composed w. Josef Strauss] *(rec Concert Hall of Czecho-Slovak RSO, Bratislava, Jan. 11–21, 1988)* — Lydian ▲ 18060 [DDD]
Strauss, Josef:Music of—Village Swallows from Austria (waltz), Op. 164; Pizzicato Polka [composed w. Johann Strauss (II)] *(rec Concert Hall of Czecho-Slovak RSO, Bratislava, Jan. 11–21, 1988)* — Lydian ▲ 18060 [DDD]
Suchon, E.:The Whirlpool, w. G. Beňačková (sop), P. Dvorsky (ten), O. Malachovsky (bass) — Campion 2-▲ 1311/12 [DDD]
Tchaikovsky, P.:Fatum *(rec Bratislava, 1989)* — Lydian ▲ 18029 [DDD]
Tchaikovsky, P.:Sym 4 *(rec Bratislava, 1989)* — Lydian ▲ 18029 [DDD]
J. Pospíchal (cnd)
Wien, Wien, Schönes Wien, w. Marcela Cerno (sop), Miroslav Dvorsky (ten) — Supraphon ▲ SUP CD 3193
C. Rizzi (cnd)
Rossini, G.:Arias, w. E. Palacio (ten), Slovak Phil Chorus—8 Cantata Arias (1808–1824)—Pianto di Armonia sulla morte di Orfeo; Dolci aurette che spirate; La mia pace io già perdei; Se ostinata ancor non cedi; Giusto cielo i voti miei; Guidò Marte i nostri passi; Il pianto delle Muse in morte di Lord Byron [!] — Arkadia-Akademia ▲ 109 [DDD]
M. Sieghart (cnd)
Offenbach, J.:Ovs—Orpheus in the Underworld *(rec Concert Hall of the Czecho-Slovak Radio, Bratislava, Dec. 15–22, 1987)* — Lydian ▲ 18076 [DDD]
Strauss (II), Joh.:Ovs—Die Fledermaus; The Gypsy Baron *(rec Concert Hall of the Czecho-Slovak Radio, Bratislava, Dec. 15–22, 1987)* — Lydian ▲ 18076 [DDD]
Suppé, F. von:Ovs—Morning, Noon & Night in Vienna; The Beautiful Galatea; Light Cavalry; Poet & Peasant *(rec Concert Hall of the Czecho-Slovak Radio, Bratislava, Dec. 15–22, 1987)* — Lydian ▲ 18076 [DDD]
Bratislava String Trio [Pavel Bogacz (vn), Mikuláš Blaas (va), Peter Baran (vc)]
Hummel, J.N.:Qt Cl, w. Jozef Lupták (cl) *(rec Moyzes Hall of the Slovak Philharmonic, Bratislava, June 1995)* — Slovart ▲ SR 0011-2-131 [DDD]
Hummel, J.N.:Trio Strs (1801) *(rec Moyzes Hall of the Slovak Philharmonic, Bratislava, June 1995)* — Slovart ▲ SR 0011-2-131 [DDD]
Bratislava SO
V. Smetáček (cnd)
Sarti, G.:Russian Oratorio, w. Prague Phil Chorus — Studio SM ▲ 2456
Brazilian SO
I. Karabtchevsky (cnd)
Villa-Lobos, H.:Bachianas brasileiras (comp), w. Leila Guimaraes (sop), Nelson Freire (pno) *(rec June–Sept 1987)* — Iris 3-▲ 143/3 [ADD]
Julian Bream Consort
Fantasies, Ayres & Dances:Elizabethan & Jacobean Consort Music — RCA Red Seal ▲ 7801-2-RC [DDD]
Highlights from the Julian Bream Edition, w. Julian Bream (gtr), George Malcolm (hpd), John Eliot Gardiner (cnd), Monteverdi Orch — RCA Gold Seal ▲ 09026-61848-2
The Julian Bream Consort, Vol. 6 — RCA Gold Seal 2-▲ 09026-61589-2
Bremen Baroque Orch
W. Helbich (cnd)
Handel, G.F.:Te Deum, "Caroline", w. Mieke van der Sluis (sop), Graham Pushee (alt), Harry Van Berne (ten), Harry van der Kamp (bass), Alfelder Vocal Ensemble — CPO ▲ CPO 999244 [DDD]
Handel, G.F.:The Ways of Zion Do Mourn, w. Mieke van der Sluis (sop), Graham Pushee (alt), Harry van Berne (ten), Harry van der Kamp (bass), Alfelder Vocal Ensemble — CPO ▲ CPO 999244 [DDD]
Telemann, G.P.:Hamburger Admiralitätsmusik, w. Mieke van der Sluis (sop—Hammonia), Graham Pushee (ten—Themis), Rufus Müller (ten—Mercurius), Klaus Mertens (bass—Neptunius), David Thomas (bass—Mars), Michael Schopper (bass—Albis), Alsfeld Vocal Ensemble *(rec Nov 9, 1995)* — CPO 2-▲ CPO 999373-2 [DDD]
Telemann, G.P.:Kapitänmusik—1730 oratorio — CPO ▲ CPO 999109 [DDD]
Telemann, G.P.:Ov "Hamburger Ebb und Fluth" *(rec Nov 9, 1995)* — CPO 2-▲ CPO 999373-2 [DDD]
Bremen Chamber Phil Winds
Einem, G. von:Glück, Tod und Traum (sels) — Berlin Classics ▲ BER 1170
Tchaikovsky, P.:The Nutcracker (sels) — Berlin Classics ▲ BER 1170
Bremen La Stagione
M. Schneider (cnd)
Telemann, G.P.:Don Quichotte der Löwenritter, w. Academy of Ancient Music Vocal Ensemble — CPO ▲ CPO 999210
Brescia & Bergamo Festival CO
A. Orizio (cnd)
Boccherini, L.:Syms—G.506 in d — Fonè ▲ 86F 06-12 [ADD]
Haydn, J.:Con Org & Strs, H.XVIII/2, w. Nikita Magaloff (pno) — Fonè ▲ 86F 06-12 [ADD]
Locatelli, P.:Con Vn, w. M. Rizzi (vn) — Fonè ▲ 91F07 [DDD]
Locatelli, P.:Cons for 4 Vns—No. 6 — Fonè ▲ 87F 05-17 [DDD]
Locatelli, P.:Introduttioni teatrali & Concerti—No. 5 — Fonè ▲ 87F 05-17 [DDD]
Locatelli, P.:Introduttioni teatrali & Concerti — Fonè ▲ 91F07 [DDD]
Marcello, A.:Con Ob & Strs, w. M. Kühn (ob) — Fonè ▲ 87F 05-17 [DDD]
Vivaldi, A.:Cons Pic, w. Fabbriciani (pic)—in C — Fonè ▲ 87F 05-17 [DDD]
Vivaldi, A.:Cons Vn, Op. 3/1–12, "L'estro armonico"—No. 10 — Fonè ▲ 87F 05-17 [DDD]
Vivaldi, A.:Cons Vn, Op. 8/1–4, "The Four Seasons", w. G. Carmignola (vn) — Fonè ▲ 87 F04-16 [DDD]
Breslau State PO
U.-R. Follert (cnd)
Draeseke, F.:Mysterium:Christus, w. C. Bischoff (sop), A. Vogel (sop), E. Dersen (alt), K. Markus (ten), H.J. Ritzerfeld (ten), P. Langshaw (bar), B. Kämpff (bass), J. Sonnenschmidt (org), Evangelical Boys' Choir Palatine, Heilbronn Vocal Ensemble, Palatine Kurrende — Bayer 5-▲ 100175/79
Bretagne Orch
Copland, A.:Con Cl, w. Philippe Cuper (cl) — Accord ▲ ACD 243852 [DDD]
Françaix, J.:Con Cl, w. Philippe Cuper (cl) — Accord ▲ ACD 243852 [DDD]
Nielsen, C.:Con Cl, w. Philippe Cuper (cl) — Accord ▲ ACD 243852 [DDD]

Bretagne Orch (cont.)
C. Schnitzler (cnd)
Le Flem, P.:Fantaisie Pno, w. M.-C. Girod (pno) *(rec Oct. 22 & 25, 1993)* — Timpani ▲ 1C 1021 [DDD]
Le Flem, P.:La Magicienne de la Mer (sels)—2 Interludes *(rec Oct. 22 & 25, 1993)* — Timpani ▲ 1C 1021 [DDD]
Le Flem, P.:Sym 1 *(rec Oct. 22 & 25, 1993)* — Timpani ▲ 1C 1021 [DDD]
Martinů, B.:Con Ob, w. Thomas Indermühle (ob) — Camerata ▲ 30CM 346
Strauss, R.:Con Ob, w. Thomas Indermühle (ob) — Camerata ▲ 30CM 346
Vaughan Williams, R.:Con Ob, w. Thomas Indermühle (ob) — Camerata ▲ 30CM 346
Zimmermann, B.A.:Con Ob, w. Thomas Indermühle (ob) — Camerata ▲ 30CM 346
P. Verrot (cnd)
Ropartz, J.G.:Divertimento *(rec Quartz, Brest, Sept 11–12, 1995)* — Timpani ▲ 1034 [DDD]
Ropartz, J.G.:Pastorales *(rec Quartz, Brest, Sept 11–12, 1995)* — Timpani ▲ 1034 [DDD]
Ropartz, J.G.:Petite Sym *(rec Quartz, Brest, Sept 11–12, 1995)* — Timpani ▲ 1034 [DDD]
Ropartz, J.G.:Sérénade Champêtre *(rec Quartz, Brest, Sept 11–12, 1995)* — Timpani ▲ 1034 [DDD]
Ropartz, J.G.:Sons de Cloches *(rec Quartz, Brest, Sept 11–12, 1995)* — Timpani ▲ 1034 [DDD]
Brewer Baroque CO
R. Palmer (cnd)
Handel, G.F.:Muzio Scevola, w. Julianne Baird (sop—Clelia), Andrea Matthews (sop—Fidalma), Erie Mills (sop—Orazio), D'Anna Fortunato (mez—Muzio), Jennifer Lane (mez—Irene), Frederick Urrey (ten—Tarquino), John Ostendorf (b-bar—Porsenna) [period instrs] [!] *(rec 10/91)* — Newport Classic 2-▲ NPD 85540/2 [DDD]
Handel, G.F.:Siroe, Rè di Persia, w. Andrea Matthews (sop), Julianne Baird (mez), D'Anna Fortunato (mez), Steven Rickards (ct), Frederick Urrey (ten), John Ostendorf (b-bar) [period instrs] [!] — Newport Classic 3-▲ NCD 60125 [DDD]
Brewer CO
Battistin, J.B.:Héraclitie et Démocrite, w. D. Fortunato (mez), J. Ostendorf (b-bar), E. Brewer (hpd) [period instrs] *(rec 1985)* — Erasmus ▲ WVH 071 [DDD]
Clérambault, L.N.:Cants, w. D. Fortunato (mez), J. Ostendorf (bass-bar), E. Brewer (org)—Le Soleil vainqueur (1721); Léandre et Héro [from Livre II (1713)] *(rec 1985)* — Erasmus ▲ WVH 071 [DDD]
Handel, G.F.:Arias, w. Jan Opalach (bass) *(O Ruddier Than the Cherry [from Acis & Galatea]; Why Do the Nations [from Messiah]; Honor & Arms [from Samson])*, Jennifer Lane (mez) *(Ombra mai fu [from Serse]; Dopo notte [from Ariodante])*, Frederick Urrey (ten) *(Thou Shalt Break Them [from Messiah]; Where'er You Walk [from Semele])*, Julianne Baird (sop) *(Angels Ever Bright & Fair [from Theodora]; Deh, m'aiutate [from Imeneo])*, John Ostendorf (bar) *(Esser mia [from Imeneo]; Sorge nell'alma mia [from Imeneo])*, D'anna Fortunato (mez) *(Se potessero [from Imeneo])*, Madeline Tsingopoulos (mez) *(Lascia ch'io pianga [from Rinaldo])* [w. Edward Brewer (hpd)] *(rec Merklin Concert Hall, NYC & St. Jean Baptiste Church, NYC)* — Vox Classics ▲ VOX 7527
Handel, G.F.:Arias, w. J. Baird (sop)—Oh had I Jubal's Lyre [from *Joshua*]; *O Sleep why dost thou leave me* [from *Semele*]; Falsa immagine [from *Ottone*]; Lascia ch'io pianga [from *Rinaldo*]; Dopo notte [from *Ariodante*] — Newport Classic ▲ NPD 85568
Handel, G.F.:Berenice, w. Julianne Baird (sop—Berenice), Andrea Matthews (sop—Alessandro), D'Anna Fortunato (mez—Selene), Jennifer Lane (mez—Demetrio), Drew Minter (alt—Arsace), John McMaster (ten—Fabio), Jan Opalach (bass—Aristobolo) — Newport Classic 3-▲ NPD 85620/3 [DDD]
Handel, G.F.:Faramondo, w. Julianne Baird (sop—Clotilde), Mary Ellen Callahan (sop—Adolfo), D'Anna Fortunado (mez—Faramondo), Jennifer Lane (mez—Rosimonda), Drew Minter (alt—Gernando), Peter Castaldi (bar—Gustavo), Mark Singer (bar—Tebaldo), Edward Brewer (hpd) [period instrs] — Vox Classics 3-▲ VOX3 7536 [DDD]
Handel, G.F.:Imeneo, w. Julianne Baird (sop—Rosmene), Beverly Hoch (sop—Clomiri), D'Anna Fortunato (cta—Tirinto), Jan Opalach (bass—Argenio), John Ostendorf (bass—Imeneo), Edward Brewer (hpd) — Vox Box 2-▲ CDX 5135 [DDD]
Handel, G.F.:Joshua, w. Julianne Baird (sop), D'Anna Fortunato (mez), John Aler (ten), John Ostendorf (b-bar), Brewer Chorus [period instrs] — Newport Classic 2-▲ NPD 85515/1-2 [DDD]
Briccialdi Wind Quintet [Dante Milozzi (fl), Francesco di Rosa (ob), Stefano Ricci (cl), Patrick de Ritis (bn), David Kanarek (hn)]
Briccialdi, G.:Operatic Fants—Fant. on Rossini's Barbiere di Siviglia — Bongiovanni ▲ GB 5531 [DDD]
Briccialdi, G.:Qnts (3) Ww—Qnts (2) in B♭; Qnt in D, Op. 124 — Bongiovanni ▲ GB 5052-2 [DDD]
Cambini, G.M.:Qnts (3) Ww — Bongiovanni ▲ GB 5531 [DDD]
Danzi, F.:Qnts Ww, Op. 56—No. 1 — Bongiovanni ▲ GB 5052-2 [DDD]
Bridge Ensemble
Asia, D.:Ivory — Koch International Classics ▲ KIC 7313-2 [DDD]
Asia, D.:Qt Pno, w. Jonathan Shames (pno) — Koch International Classics ▲ KIC 7313-2 [DDD]
Asia, D.:Why(?) Jacob — Koch International Classics ▲ KIC 7313-2 [DDD]
Brighouse & Rastrick Band
Live Brass, w. Massed Bands, Black Dyke Mills Band, James Shepherd Versatile Brass, Solna Brass, Don Lusher Trombone Ensemble *(rec live at the National Brass Band Festiva, Gala Concerts 1977, 1978, 1979)* — Chandos ("Collect" series) ▲ CHAN 6561 [ADD]
Brindisi String Quartet
Britten, B.:Qt 2 Strs — Conifer Classics ▲ 74321-15006-2
Bridge, F.:Idylls (3) Str Qt — Conifer Classics ▲ 74321-15006-2
Bridge, F.:Qt 1 Strs — Continuum ▲ CON 1035 [DDD]
Bridge, F.:Qt 2 Strs — Continuum ▲ CON 1036 [DDD]
Bridge, F.:Qt 3 Strs — Continuum ▲ CON 1035 [DDD]
Bridge, F.:Qt 4 Strs — Continuum ▲ CON 1036 [DDD]
Holst, I.:Qt 1 Strs — Conifer Classics ▲ 74321-15006-2
Brio String Quartet
Haquinius, J.A.:Qt 1 Strs — Musica Sveciae ▲ MSCD 608
Britannia Building Society Band
J. Pryce-Jones (cnd)
The Best of Brass & Voices, w. Halifax Choral Society *(rec BBC Studio 7, 1995)* — Doyen ▲ CD 041 [DDD]
H. Snell (cnd)
Bowen, B.:Eup Music, w. Robert Childs (eup) — Doyen ▲ CD 002 [DDD]
Byrd, W.:The Earl of Oxford's March [arr E. Howarth] *(rec BBC Studio 7, Manchester)* — Doyen ▲ CD 011 [DDD]
Curnow, J.:Rhap Eup, w. Nicholas Childs (eup) — Doyen ▲ CD 002 [DDD]
Fascinating Rhythm, w. Simone Rebello (perc), Edwards Jazz Quartet, Stewart Death (pno) — Doyen ▲ CD 024 [DDD]
Gershwin, G.:Girl Crazy (sels)—Embracable You [arr E. Howarth] *(rec BBC Studio 7, Manchester)* — Doyen ▲ CD 011 [DDD]
Golland, J.:Con 1 Eup, w. Robert Childs (eup) — Doyen ▲ CD 002 [DDD]
Howarth, E.:American Dream *(rec BBC Studio 7, Manchester)* — Doyen ▲ CD 011 [DDD]
Howarth, E.:The Bandsman's Tale, w. Julian Kelly (elec pno) *(rec BBC Studio 7, Manchester)* — Doyen ▲ CD 011 [DDD]
Howarth, E.:In Memoriam R.K. *(rec BBC Studio 7, Manchester)* — Doyen ▲ CD 011 [DDD]
Mussorgsky, M.:Pictures [arr E. Howarth] *(rec BBC Studio 7, Manchester)* — Doyen ▲ CD 011 [DDD]
Phillips, John:Romance, w. Robert Childs (eup), Nicholas Childs (eup) — Doyen ▲ CD 002 [DDD]
Sparke, P.:Fant Eup, w. Nicholas Childs (eup) — Doyen ▲ CD 002 [DDD]
Stephens, D.:Rhap Eup, w. Nicholas Childs (eup) — Doyen ▲ CD 002 [DDD]
British SO
B. Walter (cnd)
Beethoven, L. van:Con Vn, Op. 61, w. Joseph Szigeti (vn) *(rec 1932)* — Iron Needle ▲ 1302 (m) [ADD]
Beethoven, L. van:Con Vn, Op. 61, w. J. Szigeti (vn) *(rec 1932)* — Pearl ▲ PEA 9345 (m) [AAD]
Mozart, W.A.:Nozze di Figaro (ov) *(rec Apr 15, 1932)* — Iron Needle ▲ 1317 (m) [ADD]
Wagner, R.:Arias & Scenes, w. Royal PO—Prelude to Act I [2 versions]; Transformation Scene [both fromParsifal]; Venusberg Music [from Tannhäuser]; Rienzi Ov; Liebestod [from Tristan & Isolde]; Preludes to Acts I & III; Dance of the Apprentices & Entrance of the Masters [all from Die Meistersinger von Nürnberg] — VAI Audio ▲ VAIA 1114 [ADD]

British SO (cont.)
B. Walter (cnd) (cont.)
Wagner, R.:Ovs, Preludes & Orch Sels, w. Royal PO—Prelude to Act 3 [from Lohengrin]; Parsifal; Ov. [from Der fliegende Holländer]; Siegfried's Journey to the Rhine & Funeral March [from Götterdämmerung] *(rec 1925–27 & 1931)* VAI Audio ▲ VAIA 1059
H. Wood (cnd)
Sir H. J. Wood Conducts Proms Favourites, w. Queen's Hall Orch, London PO, London SO *(rec between Nov. 1929 & March)* Dutton Laboratories ▲ DUT 8008 [ADD]
Brittany Orch
C. Schnitzler (cnd)
Martinů, B.:Con Ob, w. T. Indermühle (ob) *(rec Rennes Opéra, France)* Camerata ▲ ACC 120 [DDD]
Strauss, R.:Con Ob, w. T. Indermühle (ob) *(rec Rennes Opéra, France)* Camerata ▲ ACC 120 [DDD]
Vaughan Williams, R.:Con Ob, w. T. Indermühle (ob) *(rec Rennes Opéra, France)* Camerata ▲ ACC 120 [DDD]
Zimmermann, B.A.:Con Ob, w. T. Indermühle (ob) *(rec Rennes Opéra, France)* Camerata ▲ ACC 120 [DDD]
Britten Sinfonia
N. Cleobury (cnd)
Britten, B.:Les Illuminations, w. John Mark Ainsley (ten) EMI Classics ▲ CDM 65899
Britten, B.:Nocturne, w. John Mark Ainsley (ten) EMI Classics ▲ CDM 65899
Britten, B.:Serenade, Op. 31, w. John Mark Ainsley (ten) EMI Classics ▲ CDM 65899
Strauss, R.:Con 1 Hn, w. David Pyatt (hn) Classics for Pleasure ("Eminence" series) ▲ CFP 2238
Strauss, R.:Con 2 Hn, w. David Pyatt (hn) Classics for Pleasure ("Eminence" series) ▲ CFP 2238
Strauss, R.:Duet-Concertino, w. Joy Farrall (cl), Julie Andrews (bn) Classics for Pleasure ("Eminence" series) ▲ CFP 2238
Strauss, R.:Serenade Ww Classics for Pleasure ("Eminence" series) ▲ CFP 2238
Britten String Quartet [P. Manning (vn), K. Pascoe (vn), P. Lale (va), A. Shulman (vc)]
Beethoven, L. van:Qt 13 Strs *(rec 3/89)* Collins Classics ▲ 12982 [DDD]
Britten, B.:Qt Strs (comp) Collins Classics 5-▲ 70222 [DDD]
Britten, B.:Qt 1 Strs *(rec 5/90)* Collins Classics ▲ 11152 [DDD]
Britten, B.:Qt 2 Strs Collins Classics ▲ 10252 [DDD]
Britten, B.:Qt 3 Strs Collins Classics ▲ 10252 [DDD]
Britten, B.:Simple Sym [arr. string quartet] *(rec 8/89)* Collins Classics ▲ 11152 [DDD]
Britten, B.:Simple Sym Collins Classics 5-▲ 70222 [DDD]
Cooke, A.:Qnt Cl, w. T. King (cl) Hyperion ▲ CDA 66428 [DDD]
Dvořák, A.:Qt 9 Strs EMI Classics ▲ CDC 54413
Dvořák, A.:Qt 12 Strs, "America" EMI Classics ▲ CDC 54413
Elgar, E.:Qt Strs Collins Classics 5-▲ 70222 [DDD]
Elgar, E.:Qt Strs Collins Classics ▲ COL 1280 [DDD]
Frankel, B.:Qnt Cl, w. T. King (cl) Hyperion ▲ CDA 66428 [DDD]
Fuchs, R.:Qnt Cl, w. T. King (cl) Hyperion ▲ CDA 66479 [DDD]
Holbrooke, J.:Eilan Shona, w. T. King (cl) Hyperion ▲ CDA 66428 [DDD]
Howells, H.:Rhapsodic Qnt, w. T. King (cl) Hyperion ▲ CDA 66428 [DDD]
Maconchy, E.:Qnt Cl, w. T. King (cl) Hyperion ▲ CDA 66428 [DDD]
Ravel, M.:Qt Strs EMI Classics ▲ CDC 54346
Romberg, A.:Qnt Cl, w. T. King (cl) Hyperion ▲ CDA 66479 [DDD]
Schnittke, A.:Qt 3 Strs *(rec 3/89)* Collins Classics ▲ 12982 [DDD]
Stanford, C.V.:Fants Cl, w. T. King (cl) Hyperion ▲ CDA 66479 [DDD]
Tippett, M.:Qts Strs Collins Classics 2-▲ 70062 [DDD]
Tippett, M.:Qts Strs Collins Classics 5-▲ 70222 [DDD]
Vaughan Williams, R.:On Wenlock Edge EMI Classics ▲ CDC 54346
Vaughan Williams, R.:Qt 1 Strs EMI Classics ▲ CDC 54346
Walton, W.:Qt Strs Collins Classics ▲ COL 1280 [DDD]
Walton, W.:Qt Strs Collins Classics 5-▲ 70222 [DDD]
Brixi CO Prague
C. Meister (cnd)
Bach, J.S.:Cons Vn (comp), w. Gilles Colliard (vn) *(rec Studio Martinek, Prague, Sept 5–8, 1994)* Doron ▲ DRC 5005 [DDD]
Bach, J.S.:Con Vn & Ob, w. Gilles Colliard (vn), Isaac Duarte (ob) *(rec Studio Martinek, Prague, Sept 5–8, 1994)* Doron ▲ DRC 5005 [DDD]
Bach, J.S.:Con for 2 Vns, w. Gilles Colliard (vn), Saskia Lethiec (vn) *(rec Studio Martinek, Prague, Sept 5–8, 1994)* Doron ▲ DRC 5005 [DDD]
Brno Czech State PO
J. Serebrier (cnd)
Smetana, B.:The Bartered Bride (ov) Conifer Classics ▲ 75605-51522-2
Smetana, B.:The Moldau Conifer Classics ▲ 75605-51522-2
Brno Janáček Opera Orch
F. Jílek (cnd)
Janácek, L.:The Beginning of a Romance, w. Brno Janáček Opera Chorus Multisonic ▲ MUL 310245
Janácek, L.:Fate, w. Magdaléna Hajóssyová (sop), Vladimír Krejčík (ten), Vilém Přibyl (ten), Brno Janáček Opera Chorus Supraphon ▲ SUP 0045 [AAD]
Janácek, L.:Jenůfa, w. G. Beňačková (sop—Jenufa), N. Kniplová (mez—Kostelnička Buryja), V. Krejčík (ten—Steva Buryja), V. Přibyl (ten—Laca Klemen), Brno Janáček Opera Chorus [Cz] *(rec 1977–8)* Supraphon 2-▲ 10 2751-2 [AAD]
Martinů, B.:Alexandre bis, w. J. Krátká (sop), A. Barová (mez), R. Novák (ten), R. Tuček (bar) Supraphon ▲ SUP 11 2140 [AAD]
Martinů, B.:Comedy on the Bridge, w. J. Krátká (sop), A. Barová (mez), R. Novák (ten), R. Tuček (bar) Supraphon ▲ SUP 11 2140 [AAD]
F. Vajnar (cnd)
Smetana, B.:The Kiss, w. Eva Deplotová (sop), Libuše Márová (mez), Leo Marian Vodička (ten), Brno Janáček Opera Chorus Supraphon 2-▲ SUP 112180 [AAD]
Brno RSO
B. Bakala (cnd)
Janácek, L.:Amarus, w. *(soloists unknown),* Moravian-Academic Choral Society, 1954) Panton ▲ PAN 811242
Janácek, L.:The Danube Orch *(rec live, 1952)* Multisonic ("Prague Spring Collection" series) ▲ 31 0184 [ADD]
Janácek, L.:Šárka, w. A. Nováková (sop), A. Jurecka (ten), J. Válka (ten), K. Kunc (bass), Brno Radio Chorus *(rec live, 1953)* Multisonic ("Prague Spring Collection" series) ▲ 31 0154 [ADD]
Janácek, L.:Sinfonietta, w. Moravian-Academic Choral Society *(rec 1955)* Panton ▲ PAN 811264
Janácek, L.:Sinfonietta *(rec live, 1952)* Multisonic ("Prague Spring Collection" series) ▲ 31 0184 [ADD]
Janácek, L.:Taras Bulba *(rec live, 1952)* Multisonic ("Prague Spring Collection" series) ▲ 31 0184 [ADD]
Janácek, L.:Taras Bulba, w. Moravian-Academic Choral Society *(rec 1952)* Panton ▲ PAN 811264
Brno State PO
F. Babicky (cnd)
Saudek, V.:Con Pno, w. Tomás Visek (pno) Panton ▲ PAN 811012
Simon, L.:Con Pno, w. Tomás Visek (pno) Panton ▲ PAN 811012
B. Bakala (cnd)
Beethoven, L. van:Con 1 Pno, w. S. Richter (pno) *(rec 1956)* Praga ▲ PR 254024
Beethoven, L. van:Con 3 Pno, w. S. Richter (pno) *(rec 1956)* Praga ▲ PR 254024
J. Bělohlávek (cnd)
Fibich, Z.:Sym 3 *(rec 8/81)* Supraphon ("Collection" series) ▲ 110657-2 [ADD]
Khachaturian, A.:Gayane (sels)—Dance of the Rose Maidens, Lezghinka & Sabre Dance Supraphon Collection ▲ 11 0643-2 [ADD]
Khachaturian, A.:Masquerade (sels)—Valse Supraphon Collection ▲ 11 0643-2 [ADD]
O. Danon (cnd)
Balakirev, M.:Ov on Czech Themes Supraphon Collection ▲ 11 0622-2 [ADD]
Glinka, M.:Kamarinskaya Supraphon ("Collection" series) ▲ 11 0622-2 [ADD]

Brno State PO (cont.)
O. Danon (cnd) (cont.)
Rimsky-Korsakov, N.:Russian Easter Festival Supraphon Collection ▲ 11 0622-2 [ADD]
Tchaikovsky, P.:Marche slave Supraphon Collection ▲ 11 0622-2 [ADD]
J. Ferencsik (cnd)
Bartók, B.:Con 1 Vn, w. A. Gertler (vn) Supraphon Collection ▲ 11 0632-2 [ADD]
K. Husa (cnd)
Husa, K.:The Trojan Women (sels)—Prologue [Smoldering Troy]; Cassandra; Lullaby; Death of Astyanax; Hecuba's Lament, Fanfare & Epilogue Phoenix ▲ PHCD 128
F. Jílek (cnd)
Dvořák, A.:Con Pno, w. Radoslav Kvapil (pno) Supraphon ▲ SUP 3067
Fibich, Z.:The Atonement of Tantalus, w. Kühn Chorus Supraphon 6-▲ SUP CD 3037
Fibich, Z.:Hippodamia's Death, w. Kühn Chorus Supraphon 6-▲ SUP CD 3037
Janácek, L.:Adagio Supraphon ▲ SUP 111521 [DDD]
Janácek, L.:Ballad of Blanik Supraphon ▲ SUP 111521 [DDD]
Janácek, L.:Con Vn, w. I. Zenatý (vn) *(rec Jan. 22–25, 1992)* Supraphon ▲ 111522-2 [DDD]
Janácek, L.:The Cossak Dance Supraphon ▲ SUP 111521 [DDD]
Janácek, L.:The Danube Sop & Orch, w. K. Dvořákové (sop), J. Beneš *(rec Jan. 22–25, 1992)* Supraphon ▲ 111522-2 [DDD]
Janácek, L.:The Fiddler's Child Supraphon ▲ SUP 111521 [DDD]
Janácek, L.:Idyll Supraphon ▲ SUP 111520 [DDD]
Janácek, L.:Jealousy Supraphon ▲ SUP 111521 [DDD]
Janácek, L.:Lachian Dances Supraphon ▲ SUP 111520 [DDD]
Janácek, L.:Schluck und Jau, w. M. Gajdošová (vn), J. Beneš *(rec Jan. 22–25, 1992)* Supraphon ▲ 111522-2 [DDD]
Janácek, L.:Serbian Reel Supraphon ▲ SUP 111521 [DDD]
Janácek, L.:Sinfonietta *(rec Apr. 14–16, 1986)* Supraphon ▲ 111522-2 [DDD]
Janácek, L.:Slavonic Mass, w. Gabriela Benackova (sop), Eva Randova (cta), Vilem Pribyl (ten), Sergej Kopack (bass), Josef Veselka (cnd), Czech Phil Chorus *(rec 1979)* Supraphon ▲ SUP CD 3045
Janácek, L.:Suite Orch, Op. 3 Supraphon ▲ SUP 111521 [DDD]
Janácek, L.:Suite Str Orch Supraphon ▲ SUP 111520 [DDD]
Janácek, L.:Taras Bulba Supraphon ▲ SUP 111521 [DDD]
Martinů, B.:Špalíček, w. A. Kratochvilová (sop), M. Kopp (ten), R. Novák (bass), Kantiléna Children's Chorus [Cz] Supraphon 2-▲ 11 0752-2 [DDD]
Novák, V.:Eternal Longing Supraphon ▲ SUP 3049
Novák, V.:Nikotina Supraphon ▲ SUP 3050
Novák, V.:Signorina Gioventu Supraphon ▲ SUP 3049
Novák, V.:Toman Supraphon ▲ SUP 3050
J. Krombholc (cnd)
Fibich, Z.:The Courtship of Pelops, w. Kühn Chorus Supraphon 6-▲ SUP CD 3037
O. Lenárd (cnd)
Famous Opera Arias, w. Eva Randová (mez) *(rec live 1992)* Supraphon ▲ SUP 1118546
C. Mackerras (cnd)
Martinů, B.:The Greek Passion, w. Helen Field (sop), John Mitchinson (ten), Phillip Joll (b-bar), John Tomlinson (bass), Czech Phil Chorus [E] *(rec 1981)* Supraphon 2-▲ 10 3611-2 [DDD]
V. Neumann (cnd)
Roussel, A.:Sym 3 *(rec Nov. 4–6, 1963)* Supraphon ("Collection" series) ▲ 11 0681-2 [ADD]
L. Pešek (cnd)
Elgar, E.:Con Vc, w. M. Fukačová (vc) *(rec 6/89)* Supraphon ▲ 110390-2 [DDD]
Tchaikovsky, P.:Pezzo capriccioso, w. M. Fukačová (vc) Supraphon ▲ 110390-2 [DDD]
Tchaikovsky, P.:Vars on a Rococo Theme, w. M. Fukačová (vc) Supraphon ▲ 110390-2 [DDD]
J. Pinkas (cnd)
Dvořák, A.:The Jacobin, w. D. Šounová-Broukov (sop), V. Přibyl (ten), K. Berman (bass), Kühn Chorus Supraphon 2-▲ SUP 11 2190 [AAD]
Dvořák, A.:The Jacobin (sels), w. Marcela Machotková (sop), Beno Blachut (ten), Vilém Přibyl (ten) Supraphon ▲ SUP 112250 [AAD]
C. Richter (cnd)
Zawinul, J.:Stories of the Danube, w. Bruhan Ocal (voc/perc), Joe Zawinul (kbd), Walter Grassman (dr) Philips ▲ 454143-2
K. Šejna (cnd)
Novák, V.:Slovak Suite *(rec July 1968)* Supraphon ("Collection" series) ▲ 11 0682-2 [ADD]
J. Serebrier (cnd)
Dvořák, A.:Sym 9, "From the New World" *(rec Brno, Czech Republic, Feb 1995)* Conifer Classics ▲ 75605-51522-2 [DDD]
Smetana, B.:Má Vlast—Vltava *(rec Brno, Czech Republic, Feb 1995)* Conifer Classics ▲ 75605-51522-2 [DDD]
J. Štych (cnd)
Fibich, Z.:Šárka, w. Eva Deplotová (sop), Eva Randová (mez), Vilém Přibyl (ten), Vaclav Zítek (bar), J. Pancik (cnd), Janáček Opera Chorus *(rec 1978)* Supraphon 2-▲ SUP 0036
L. Svárovský (cnd)
Albinoni, T.:Cons Tpt, w. Jaroslav Halír (tpt)—in B♭ Panton ▲ PAN 811368
Hummel, J.N.:Con in E♭ Tpt, S.49, w. Jaroslav Halír (tpt) Panton ▲ PAN 811368
Janácek, L.:Music of, w. Zuzana Lapciková (sop), Pavla Dittmannová (cta), Petr Julícek (ten), Petr Fiala (cnd), Brno Czech Phil Chorus—Rákos Rákoczy (ballet); folk songs, choruses & dances Supraphon ▲ SUP CD 3129
Wayne, H.:Sym 4 New Millennium ▲ 61596
Wayne, H.:Sym 5 *(rec Czech Radio, Brno, Czech Republic, Apr 15–17, 1993)* New Millenium ▲ 61595
P. Tiboris (cnd)
Beethoven, L. van:Sym 9, "Choral Sym", w. Janáček Opera Chorus [soloists:L. A. Myers, I. Sameth, J. Clark, R. Conant]; [Mahler's re-orchestration] *(rec 12/91)* Bridge ▲ BCD 9033
Mahler, G.:Beethoven's Sym 9, w. Leah Anne Myers (sop), Ilene Sameth (mez), James Clark (ten), Richard Conant (bass), Janáček Opera Chorus Bridge ▲ BCD 9033 [DDD]
J. Waldhans (cnd)
Fibich, Z.:Sym 2 *(rec 3/76)* Supraphon ("Collection" series) ▲ 110657-2 [ADD]
I. Yinon (cnd)
Ullmann, V.:Con Pno, w. K. Richter (pno) Bayer ▲ 100228 [DDD]
Ullmann, V.:Sym 2 Bayer ▲ 100228 [DDD]
Ullmann, V.:Vars, Fant & Double Fugue Bayer ▲ 100228 [DDD]
Brno State PO members
V. Nosek (cnd)
Martinů, B.:The Amazing Flight *(rec Studio Dukla Brno, Feb 2, 1995)* Panton ("Protokol XX" series) ▲ PAN 811417 [DDD]
Martinů, B.:The Butterfly That Stamped *(rec Studio Dukla Brno, Aug 27, 1976)* Panton ("Protokol XX" series) ▲ PAN 811417 [ADD]
Martinů, B.:Echec au roi, w. Anna Barová (alt) *(rec Studio Dukla Brno, Aug 27, 1976)* Panton ("Protokol XX" series) ▲ PAN 811417 [ADD]
Broadside Band [Jeremy Barlow (rcrs/perc), Sharon Lindo (vns/rcr), George Weigand (lt/mandore/cittern/gtr), Rosemary Thorndycraft (b vl/h-g), Ben Sansom (vn), Marilyn Sansom (vc)]
J. Barlow (cnd)
Arbeau, T.:Orchésographie Harmonia Mundi France ▲ HMC 901152
Il Ballarino Hyperion ▲ CDA 66244 [DDD]
Danses populaires françaises Harmonia Mundi ▲ HMC 90.1152
English Country Dances Saydisc ▲ CDSDL 393 [DDD]
Gay, J.:The Beggar's Opera, w. S. Walker (mez), B. Hoskins (sgr), A. Thompson (ten), C. Daniels (ten), I. Caddy (b-bar) [E] Hyperion 2-▲ CDA 66591/92
Gay, J.:The Beggar's Opera (sels), w. P. Kwella (sop), P. Elliott (ten)—9 songs in 30 versions [E] Harmonia Mundi France ▲ HMC 901071
John Playford's Popular Tunes Amon Ra ▲ CDSAR 28

Broadside Band
(lt/mandore/cittern/gtr), Rosemary Thorndycraft (b vl/h-g), Ben Sansom (vn), Marilyn (cont.)
J. Barlow (cnd) (cont.)
Old English Nursery Rhymes, w. Vivien Ellis (sop), Tim Laycock (sgr) *(rec Valley Recordings, Littleton-on-Severn, Feb 1996)* Saydisc ▲ CDSDL 419
Popular Tunes in 17th Century England Harmonia Mundi ("Musique d'Abord" series) ▲ HMA 1901039 ■

Brodsky String Quartet
Brodsky Unlimited Teldec ▲ 2292-46015-2
Sensual Classics II, w. A. Sultanov (pno), C. Katsaris (pno), London SO [cnd:M. Shostakovich], New York PO [cnd:Z. Mehta], BBC SO [cnd:A. Davis], Leipzig Gewandhaus Orch [cnd:K. Masur], 12 Cellos of the Berlin PO [cnd:A. Jordan, E. Inbal], et al. Teldec ▲ 92014-2 ■ 92014-4

Brodsky String Quartet [Michael Thomas (vn), Ian Belton (vn), Paul Cassidy (va), Jacquelin Thomas (vc)]
Borodin, A.:Qt 2 Strs Teldec ▲ 2292-46319-2 [DDD]
Costello, E.:The Juliet Letters, w. Elvis Costello (sgr) Warner Bros. ▲ 9 45180-2
Delius, F.:Qt Strs ASV ▲ ASV 526 [DDD]
Elgar, E.:Qt Strs ASV ▲ ASV 526 [DDD]
Haydn, J.:Qts Strs, Op. 54—No. 2 in C Silva Classics ▲ SIL 6012
Haydn, J.:Qts Strs, Op. 54—No. 2 *(rec Feb 1996)* Silva Screen ▲ SILKD 6012 [DDD]
Mozart, W.A.:Adagio & Fugue Silva Classics ▲ SIL 6012
Mozart, W.A.:Adagio & Fugue *(rec Feb 1996)* Silva Screen ▲ SILKD 6012 [DDD]
Mozart, W.A.:Qt 17 Strs *(rec Feb 1996)* Silva Screen ▲ SILKD 6012 [DDD]
Mozart, W.A.:Qt 17 Strs Silva Classics ▲ SIL 6012
Shostakovich, D.:Qts Strs (comp) Teldec 6-▲ 9031-71702-2 [DDD]
Shostakovich, D.:Qt 1 Strs Teldec ▲ 2292-46009-2-ZK [DDD]
Shostakovich, D.:Qt 3 Strs Teldec ▲ 2292-46009-2-ZK [DDD]
Shostakovich, D.:Qt 4 Strs Teldec ▲ 2292-46009-2-ZK [DDD]
Shostakovich, D.:Qt 6 Strs Teldec ▲ 9031-73108-2 ZK
Shostakovich, D.:Qt 7 Strs Teldec ▲ 2292-44919-2-ZK
Shostakovich, D.:Qt 8 Strs Teldec ▲ 2292-44919-2-ZK
Shostakovich, D.:Qt 9 Strs Teldec ▲ 2292-44919-2-ZK
Shostakovich, D.:Qt 10 Strs Teldec ▲ 9031-73108-2 ZK
Shostakovich, D.:Qt 11 Strs Teldec ▲ 9031-73109-2 ZK
Shostakovich, D.:Qt 12 Strs Teldec ▲ 9031-73109-2 ZK
Shostakovich, D.:Qt 13 Strs Teldec ▲ 9031-73109-2 ZK
Shostakovich, D.:Qt 14 Strs Teldec ▲ 9031-73108-2 ZK
Tchaikovsky, P.:Qt 3 Strs Teldec ▲ 2292-46319-2 [DDD]
A. Pay (cnd)
Mozart, W.A.:Qnt Cl, K.581, w. Joan Enric Lluna (bas hn) Cala ▲ CAL 88010 [DDD]

Bronx Arts Ensemble
Kupferman, M.:Qnt Bn, w. W. Scribner (bn) Soundspells ▲ CD 108 [DDD]
Kupferman, M.:Qnt Cl, w. P. Alexander (cl) Soundspells ▲ CD 108 [DDD]
Rheinberger, J.:Nonet Fl Thorofon ▲ CTH 2061 [DDD]
Rheinberger, J.:Nonet Fl *(rec 1981)* Thorofon 6-▲ BCTH 2161/6
Surinach, C.:Qt Pno, w. I. Chorberg (vn), P. Zinger (pno) *(rec 1992)* New World ▲ 80428-2
M. Kupferman (cnd)
Kupferman, M.:Images of Chagall Soundspells ▲ SP 103
M. Lifchitz (cnd)
Campos-Parsi, H.:Sonetos Sagrados [Sp] New World ▲ NW 379-2 [DDD]
Lifchitz, M.:Yellow Ribbons—Nos. 11,12 & 15 New World ▲ NW 379-2 [DDD]
Sierra, R.:Doña Rosita la Soltera [Sp] New World ▲ NW 379-2 [DDD]
Sierra, R.:Salsa para Vientos [Sp] New World ▲ NW 379-2 [DDD]
J. Somary (cnd)
Freeman, J.:Suite Org, w. Alberto Bird (org) Premier ▲ PRCD 1042 [DDD]
Somary, J.:Songs of Innocence, w. Andrea Matthews (sop), Zheng Zhou (bar) Premier ▲ PRCD 1042 [DDD]
Somary, J.:3 Is Company Premier ▲ PRCD 1042 [DDD]
P. Zinger (cnd)
Surinach, C.:Cantares, w. Rachel Rosales (sop) [E] New World ▲ 80505-2
Surinach, C.:Cantos Bereberes New World ▲ 80505-2
Surinach, C.:Chansons et Danses Espagnoles New World ▲ 80505-2
Surinach, C.:Con Str Orch, w. I. Chorberg (vn) *(rec 1992)* New World ▲ 80428-2
Surinach, C.:Doppio Concertino, w. P. Zinger (pno) *(rec 1992)* New World ▲ 80428-2
Surinach, C.:Hollywood Carnival—Opening; Charlie Chaplin; Parade of Beauties; Epitaph to the Silent Movies; Stereophonism; Pasodoble in Technicolor New World ▲ 80505-2
Surinach, C.:Songs of Spain, w. Rachel Rosales (sop) New World ▲ 80505-2
Surinach, C.:Tientos—Plaintive; Sorrowful; Joyful New World ▲ 80505-2

Bronx Arts Ensemble [Gerald Tarack (vn), Browning Cramer (vn), Sandra Robbins (va), Jill Jaffe (va), Lutz Rath (vc)]
Bruch, M.:Qnt Strs *(rec Holy Trinity Church, New York City, 1991-94)* Premier ▲ PRCD 1048 [DDD]

Bronx Arts Ensemble [Gerald Tarack (vn), Browning Cramer (vn), Victoria Stewart (vn), Martha Mott (vn), Susan Follari (va), Carl Johansen (va), Lutz Rath (vc), Dean Crandall (db)]
Bruch, M.:Octet Strs *(rec Holy Trinity Church, New York City, 1991-94)* Premier ▲ PRCD 1048 [DDD]

Bronx Arts Ensemble [Paul Gallo (cl), William Scribner (bn), Sharon Moe (hn), Gerald Tarack (vn), Browning Cramer (vn), Lutz Rath (vc), Dean Crandall (db)]
Bruch, M.:Septet Cl *(rec Holy Trinity Church, New York City, 1991-94)* Premier ▲ PRCD 1048 [DDD]

Brooklyn College Center for Computer Music
Halac, J.:Computer Music—India vieja, sincretismo #1; Ball, sincretismo #4; Illegal Edge; Uitotos, sincretismo #2; Cueca; Maturity, sincretismo #3 Centaur ▲ CRC 2189 [DDD]

Brooklyn College Percussion Ensemble
B. Kolb (cnd)
Kolb, B.:Spring River Flowers Moon Night, w. D. Sarobin (gtr/mand) CRI ■ C 361
Kolb, B.:Spring River Flowers Moon Night, w. D. Sarobin (gtr/mand) CRI ▲ CD 576 [ADD]

Brooklyn PO
M. Barrett (cnd)
Barlow, W.:The Winter's Past, w. H. Lucarelli (ob) Koch International Classics ▲ KIC 7187 [DDD]
Bloom, Robert:Narrative, w. H. Lucarelli (ob) Koch International Classics ▲ KIC 7187 [DDD]
Bloom, Robert:Requiem, w. H. Lucarelli (ob) Koch International Classics ▲ KIC 7187 [DDD]
Corigliano, J.:Aria Ob & Str, w. H. Lucarelli (ob) Koch International Classics ▲ KIC 7187 [DDD]
Wilder, A.:Con Ob, w. H. Lucarelli (ob) Koch International Classics ▲ KIC 7187 [DDD]
Wilder, A.:Piece Ob, w. H. Lucarelli (ob) Koch International Classics ▲ KIC 7187 [DDD]
D. R. Davies (cnd)
Glanville-Hicks, P.:Etruscan Con, w. K. Jarrett (pno) MusicMasters ▲ 01612-67089-2
Glass, Philip:Low Sym Philips ▲ 438150-2 [DDD] ■ 438150-4
Harrison, L.:Pastorales (7) MusicMasters ▲ 01612-67089-2
McPhee, C.:Balinese Ceremonial Music, w. Stephen Drury (pno), Yukiko Takagi (pno) MusicMasters ("Classics" series) ▲ 01612-67159-2
McPhee, C.:Con Pno, w. Stephen Drury (pno) MusicMasters ("Classics" series) ▲ 01612-67159-2
McPhee, C.:Nocturne MusicMasters ("Classics" series) ▲ 01612-67159-2
McPhee, C.:Sym 2, "Pastorale" MusicMasters ("Classics" series) ▲ 01612-67159-2
Riley, T.:June Buddhas MusicMasters ▲ 01612-67089-2
L. Foss (cnd)
Blitzstein, M.:Con Pno, w. M. Barrett (pno) CRI ▲ CD 554 [DDD]
Fine, I.:Notturno, w. J. Lyman Hill (va), A. Hess (hp) CRI ▲ CD 574 [ADD]
Foss, L.:Orpheus & Euridice, w. Y. Menuhin (vn), E. Michell (vn) New World ▲ NW 375-2 [DDD]
Foss, L.:Renaissance Con, w. C. Wincenc (fl) New World ▲ NW 375-2 [DDD]
Foss, L.:Salomon Rossi Suite New World ▲ NW 375-2 [DDD]
Picker, T.:Keys to the City, w. T. Picker (pno) CRI ▲ CD 554 [DDD]

Brooklyn PO (cont.)
L. Foss (cnd) (cont.)
Weber, C.M. von:Andante & Rondo ungarese Bn, w. J. Manasse (cl) [newly arranged by James Cohn for clarinet & orchestra] XLNT ▲ CD 18005 [DDD]
Weber, C.M. von:Concertino Cl, w. J. Manasse (cl) XLNT ▲ CD 18005 [DDD]
Weber, C.M. von:Con 1 Cl, w. J. Manasse (cl) XLNT ▲ CD 18005 [DDD]
Weber, C.M. von:Con 2 Cl, w. J. Manasse (cl) XLNT ▲ CD 18005 [DDD]
S. Reich, M. Tilson Thomas (cnd)
Reich, S.:The Desert Music, w. Ensemble, Brooklyn Phil Chorus Elektra/Nonesuch ▲ 79101-2 [DDD] ■ 79101-4 (D)

Broyhill Chamber Ensemble [Gil Morgenstern (vn), Nardo Poy (va), Käthe Jarka (vc)]
Chumbley, R.:Self Studies (3), w. Shirley Irek (pno) *(rec Appalachian State Univ, July 1995)* MMC ▲ MMC 2041 [DDD]
Copland, A.:Qt Pno, w. Robert Chumbley (pno) *(rec Appalachian State Univ, July 1995)* MMC ▲ MMC 2041 [DDD]
McKinley, W.T.:Qt 1 Pno, w. Brian Zeger (pno) *(rec Appalachian State Univ, July 1995)* MMC ▲ MMC 2041 [DDD]

Dave Brubeck Quartet [Dave Brubeck (pno), Bobby Militello (sax), Jack Six (db), Randy Jones (dr)]
R. Gloyd (cnd)
Brubeck, D.:To Hope!:A Celebration, w. Shelley Waite (sop), Mark Bleeke (ten), Kevin Deas (b-bar), Cathedral Choral Society Orch, Cathedral Choral Society Chorus *(rec Washington National Cathedral, Washington, D.C., June 12, 1995)* Telarc ▲ CD 80430 [DDD]

Bruckner Orch Linz
K. Eichhorn (cnd)
Bruckner, A.:Sym 2 [edited W. Carragan] Camerata 2-▲ 30CM 195/96
Bruckner, A.:Sym 2 *(rec Brucknerhaus, Linz, Mar. 25-28, 1991)* Camerata 2-▲ 15CM 379/80 [DDD]
Bruckner, A.:Sym 5 [Nowak edition] Camerata 2-▲ 25CM 335/36
Bruckner, A.:Sym 6 Camerata ▲ 30CM 345
Bruckner, A.:Sym 8 [1890 Nowak edition] Camerata ▲ 32CM 225
Bruckner, A.:Sym 9 [W. Carragan's 1983 completed version] Camerata 2-▲ 30CM 275/76 [DDD]
M. Sieghart (cnd)
Bruckner, A.:Sym 1 [Linz version] *(rec Brucknerhaus, Linz, Apr 10-11, 1995)* Camerata ▲ 30CM 367 [DDD]

Bruges Belfry Bells
Four Centuries of Chimes Music René Gailly ▲ CD 88904 [DDD]

Brunel Ensemble
C. Austin (cnd)
Lutyens, E.:Music of, w. Teresa Cahill (sop)—Bagatelles; O saisons, o chateaux Cala ▲ CAL CACD 77005
McCabe, J.:Red Leaves, w. Teresa Cahill (sop) Cala ▲ CAL CACD 77005
Saxton, R.:Music of—Birthday Piece for Richard Rodney Bennett [w. Teresa Cahill (sop)]; Elijah's Vn Cala ▲ CAL CACD 77005
Williamson, M.:Sym 7, w. Teresa Cahill (sop) Cala ▲ CAL CACD 77005

Brussels Belgian Radio-TV PO
F. Devreese (cnd)
Devreese, F.:Con 2 Pno, w. D. Blumenthal (pno) *(rec Jan. 26, 1991)* Marco Polo ▲ 8.223505 [DDD]
Devreese, F.:Con 3 Pno, w. D. Blumenthal (pno) *(rec Nov. 19-22, 1991)* Marco Polo ▲ 8.223505 [DDD]
Devreese, F.:Con 4 Pno, w. D. Blumenthal (pno) *(rec Nov. 19-22, 1991)* Marco Polo ▲ 8.223505 [DDD]
Devreese, F.:Film Music—Benvenuta; Un Soir, un Train; L'Oeuvre au noir; Belle Marco Polo ▲ 8.223681 [DDD]
Devreese, G.:Concertino Vc, w. V. Spanoghe (vc) [1992 version] *(rec Brussels, 1993)* Marco Polo ▲ 8.223680 [DDD]
Devreese, G.:Con 1 Vn, w. G. De Neve (vn) *(rec Brussels, 1993)* Marco Polo ▲ 8.223680 [DDD]
Devreese, G.:Tombelène, w. F. Devreese *(rec Brussels, 1993)* Marco Polo ▲ 8.223680 [DDD]
A. Ostrowsky (cnd)
Mahler, G.:Sym 5 *(rec Concert Hall of the Belgian Radio & Television, 1994)* Discover International ▲ DI 920220 [DDD]
A. Rahbari (cnd)
Beethoven, L. van:Egmont (ov), w. M. Gauci (sop) Discover International ▲ DICD 920114 [DDD]
Beethoven, L. van:Sym 3, "Eroica" *(rec Feb. 1990)* Naxos ▲ 8.550407 [DDD]
Beethoven, L. van:Sym 8 *(rec Feb. 1990)* Naxos ▲ 8.550407 [DDD]
Beethoven, L. van:Sym 9, "Choral Sym", w. M. Gauci (sop), Bruges Cantores Oratorio Choir Discover International ▲ DICD 920151 [DDD]
Blockx, J.:Flemish Dances *(rec Brussels, 2/91)* Marco Polo ▲ 8.223418 [DDD]
Boeck, A. de:Fant on 2 Flemish Folksongs *(rec Brussels, 2/91)* Marco Polo ▲ 8.223418 [DDD]
Brahms, J.:Serenade 1 Orch *(rec Brussels, June 1990)* Naxos ▲ 8.553227 [DDD]
Debussy, C.:Berceuse héroïque *(rec May 19-22, 1992)* Naxos ▲ 8.550505 [DDD]
Debussy, C.:Images Orch *(rec May 19-22, 1992)* Naxos ▲ 8.550505 [DDD]
Debussy, C.:Marche écossaise sur un thème populaire *(rec May 19-22, 1992)* Naxos ▲ 8.550505 [DDD]
Debussy, C.:Martyre de Saint Sébastien (complete) *(rec May 19-22, 1992)* Naxos ▲ 8.550505 [DDD]
Debussy, C.:La Mer *(rec 11/89)* Naxos ▲ 8.550262 [DDD]
Debussy, C.:Nocturnes *(rec 11/89)* Naxos ▲ 8.550262 [DDD]
Debussy, C.:Prélude à l'après-midi d'un faune *(rec 11/89)* Naxos ▲ 8.550262 [DDD]
Debussy, C.:Rapsodie, w. S. Rahbari (sax) Marco Polo ▲ 8.223374
Gilson, P.:La Mer *(rec Brussels 2/91)* Marco Polo ▲ 8.223418 [DDD]
Glazunov, A.:Con Sax, w. S. Rahbari (sax) Marco Polo ▲ 8.223374
Ibert, J.:Concertino da camera, w. S. Rahbari (sax) Marco Polo ▲ 8.223374
Meulemans, A.:Sym 3 Marco Polo ▲ 8.223418 [DDD]
Milhaud, D.:Scaramouche Sax, w. S. Neidenbach-Rahbari (sax) Marco Polo ▲ 8.223374
Mortelmans, L.:Morning Mood Marco Polo ▲ 8.223418 [DDD]
Poot, M.:Cheerful Ov Marco Polo ▲ 8.223418 [DDD]
Rachmaninoff, S.:Con 2 Pno, w. David Lively (pno) *(rec Concert Hall of the Belgian Radio & Television, Brussels, May 19-21, 1994)* Discover International ▲ DI 920221 [DDD]
Rachmaninoff, S.:Con 3 Pno, w. David Lively (pno) *(rec Concert Hall of the Belgian Radio & Television, Brussels, May 19-21, 1994)* Discover International ▲ DI 920221 [DDD]
Saxophone & Orchestra, w. Sohre Rahbari (a sax) Marco Polo ▲ 8.223374
Schubert, Franz:Sym 9 *(rec June 12-15, 1991)* Naxos ▲ 8.550502 [DDD]
Schumann, R.:Intro & Allegro appassionato, Op. 92, w. J. Jandó (pno) *(rec June 3-4, 1992)* Naxos ▲ 8.550506 [DDD]
Soprano Arias from Italian Operas, w. Miriam Gauci (sop) *(rec Jan. 14-17, 1992)* Naxos ▲ 8.550606 [DDD] ▲ 7.550606 [DDD]

Brussels BRTN PO
L. Ouderits (cnd)
Celis, F.:Musica per undeci *(rec BRTN-Concerthall, Apr 25, 1987)* Phaedra ▲ 92 003 [DDD]
A. Rahbari (cnd)
Beethoven, L. van:Con 5 Pno, "Emperor", w. J. Stancul (pno) Discover International ▲ DICD 920160 [DDD]
Debussy, C.:Marche écossaise sur un thème populaire, w. A. Rahbari (cnd), Brussels BRT PO, Brussels Belgian Radio-TV PO *(rec May 19-22, 1992)* Naxos ▲ 8.550505 [DDD]

ORCH. & ENS.

Brussels BRTN PO (cont.)
E. Smola (cnd)
Lehár, F.:Music of, w. H. Martinpelto (sop), Z. Terzakis (ten)—Die lustige Witwe *(Ov.)*, Paganini *(Gern hab' ich die Frau'n geküsst; Niemand liebt dich so wie ich)*, Der Graf von Luxemburg *(Es duftet nach Trèfle incarnat; Faschungsmarsch)*, Friederike *(O Mädchen, mein Mädchen)*, Zigeunerliebe *(Hör' ich Cymbalklänge; Zorika, Zorika)*, Schön ist die Welt *(Schön ist die Welt)*, Das Land des Lächelns *(Chinesischer Tanz; Dein ist mein ganzes Herz)*, Eva *(Fräulein Frau das klingt doch nicht gewöhnlich; Nur das eine Wort sprich es aus)*, Giuditta *(Intermezzo; Du bist meine Sonne; Herr Käpitan, der Weg ist weit; Schönste der Frau'n; Freunde, das Leben ist lebenswert)* Eufoda ▲ EUF 1188 [DDD]
F. Terby (cnd)
Celis, F.:Cantilena *(rec BRTN–Concerthall, Mar 20, 1981)* Phaedra ▲ 92 003 [DDD]
Celis, F.:Preludio e Narrazione, w. Jacqueline van Quaille (sop) *(rec BRTN–Concerthall, Dec 14, 1985)* Phaedra ▲ 92 003 [DDD]
Celis, F.:Sinf III *(rec BRTN–Concerthall, Dec 15, 1989)* Phaedra ▲ 92 003 [DDD]
Dvořák, A.:Con Vc, w. Edmond Baeyens (vc) *(rec Belgian Radio-TV Concerthall, Jan 1978)* Phaedra ▲ 492 002 [ADD]
Schumann, R.:Con Vc, w. Edmond Baeyens (vc) *(rec Belgian Radio–TV Concerthall, May 1978)* Phaedra ▲ 492 002 [ADD]

Brussels Concert Band
P. Schoorvaerts (cnd)
Just between Friends René Gailly ▲ CD 69002 [DDD]

Brussels Double Bass Quartet
Brussels Double Bass Quartet Pavane ▲ ADW 7254

Brussels Radio-TV Instrumentalists
P. Bartholomée (cnd)
Franck, C.:Messe solennelle, w. L. Devos (ten), Brussels Radio-TV Chorus [L] *(rec 1976)* Koch Schwann ▲ 3-1044-2 [ADD]

Brussels Radio-TV SO
S. Frontalini (cnd)
Donizetti, G.:Ovs—Roberto Devereux; Il diluvio universale; Betly; Zoraida di Granata; Gabriella di Vergy; Alina, regina di Golconda; Una follia; Il falegname di Livonia Bongiovanni ▲ GB 2049 [DDD]

Brussels RTBF SO
A. Rahbari (cnd)
Stravinsky, I.:The Firebird Suite [1919 version] *(rec 1/90)* Naxos ▲ 8.550263 [DDD]
Stravinsky, I.:Pétrouchka [1947 version] *(rec 1/90)* Naxos ▲ 8.550263 [DDD]
A. Walter (cnd)
Bériot, C.-A. de:Con 1 Vn, "Military", w. T. Nishizaki (vn) Marco Polo ▲ 8.220440 [DAD]
Bériot, C.-A. de:Con 8 Vn, w. T. Nishizaki (vn) Marco Polo ▲ 8.220440 [DAD]
Bériot, C.-A. de:Con 9 Vn, w. T. Nishizaki (vn) Marco Polo ▲ 8.220440 [DAD]
Furtwängler, W.:Sym 3 Marco Polo ▲ 8.223105

Brussels String Quartet [Zygmunt Marek Kowalski (vn), Tomiko Shida (vn), Yves Cortvrint (va), Luc Dewez (vc)]
Borodin, A.:Qt 1 Strs Ricercar ▲ 161146
Borodin, A.:Qt 2 Strs Ricercar ▲ 161146

Brussels Théâtre de la Monnaie Orch
S. Cambreling (cnd)
Offenbach, J.:Les Contes d'Hoffmann, w. L. Serra (sop), R. Plowright (sop), J. Norman (sop), A. Murray (mez), J. Taillon (mez), N. Shicoff (ten), A. Oliver (ten), R. Tear (ten), J. Van Dam (b-bar), D. Duesing (bar), K. Rydl (bass) [F] EMI Classics 3-▲ CDCC 49641 [DDD]
F. Ferraris (cnd)
Verdi, G.:Otello (sels), w. K. Ricciarelli (sop), M. del Monaco (ten), A. Protti (bar) *(rec Nov. 9, 1972)* Standing Room Only 2-▲ SRO 169-2

Gavin Bryars Ensemble [J. McCarthy (rcr), R. Heaton (cl), A. Balanescu (vn), M. Allen (vib), J. White (pno), G. Bryars (db)]
Bryars, G.:Sub Rosa ECM New Series ▲ 78118-21533-2 [DDD]
M. Riesman (cnd)
Bryars, G.:Jesus' Blood Never Failed Me Yet, w. T. Waits (sgr) Philips ▲ 438823-2

Buccina Ensemble
Bares, P.:Mass for 4 Brass Instrs Pro Viva ▲ ISPV 166
Bares, P.:Mass for 3 Voices Pro Viva ▲ ISPV 166

Bucharest CO
P. Popescu (cnd)
Popovici, D.:Codex Canon *(rec 1972)* Electrecord ▲ ELCD 102 [AAD]

Bucharest George Enescu PO
H. Andreescu (cnd)
Enescu, G.:Sym 2 Marco Polo ▲ 8.223142
M. Basarab (cnd)
Constantinescu, P.:The Nativity, w. E. Petrescu (sop), M. Kessler (mez), V. Teodorian (ten), H. Bömches (bass), Bucharest George Enescu Phil Chorus *(rec 1977)* Olympia ▲ OCD 402 [AAD]
M. Brediceanu (cnd)
Enescu, G.:Sym 1 Marco Polo ▲ 8.223141
M. Cristescu (cnd)
Mozart, W.A.:Con Cl, w. A. O. Popa (cl) *(rec 1971)* Electrecord ▲ ELCD 108 [AAD]
Weber, C.M. von:Con 1 Cl, w. A. O. Popa (cl) *(rec 1971)* Electrecord ▲ ELCD 108 [AAD]
Weber, C.M. von:Con 2 Cl, w. A. O. Popa (cl) *(rec 1971)* Electrecord ▲ ELCD 108 [AAD]

Bucharest Opera & Ballet Theater Orch
M. Popa (cnd)
Leoncavallo, R.:Pagliacci, w. Arta Florescu (sop—Nedda), Cornel Stavru (ten—Canio), Valentin Teodorian (ten—Beppe), Nicolae Herlea (bar—Tonio), Ladislau Konya (bar—Silvio), Bucharest Opera & Ballet Theater Chorus *(rec 1966)* Vox Box 2-▲ CDX 5161
Mascagni, P.:Cavalleria rusticana, w. Marina Krilovici (sop—Santuzza), Viorica Cortez (mez—Lola), Milka Nistor (mez—Lucia), Cornel Stavru (ten—Turiddu), David Ohanesian (bar—Alfio), Bucharest Opera & Ballet Theater Chorus *(rec 1966)* Vox Box 2-▲ CDX 5161

Bucharest PO
W. Vogel (cnd)
Barber, S.:Adagio Strs Gallo ▲ CD 742
Gerber, R.:The Old Farmer's Almanac Gallo ▲ CD 742

Bucharest State Opera Orch
J. Bobescu (cnd)
Verdi, G.:La traviata (sels), w. V. Zeani (sop), Buzea (sgr), Herlea (sgr) [I] Allegretto ▲ ACD 8084 [ADD] ▮ ACS 8084

Bucharest Virtuosi
H. Andreescu (cnd)
5 Centuries of German Music in Transylvania, w. Georgeta Stoleriu (sop), Adrian Petrescu (ob), René Cristian Popescu (vn), Gabriel Bala (va), Stefan Thomasz (db), Nicolae Licaret (hpd) Electrecord ▲ ELC EDC 168 [DDD]

Buchberger Quartet
Hindemith, P.:Ov to the "Flying Dutchman" *(rec 1989-90)* Wergo ▲ WER 6197-2 [DDD]
Hindemith, P.:Qnt Cl *(rec 1989-90)* Wergo ▲ WER 6197-2 [DDD]
Hindemith, P.:Repertoire for Military Orchestra "Minimax" *(rec 1989-90)* Wergo ▲ WER 6197-2 [DDD]

Budapest Brass Quintet
Brown, R.:Concertino, w. Alice Giles (hp) Koch Schwann ▲ SCH 311732
Schmidt, W.:Music for Scrimshaws, w. Alice Giles (hp) Koch Schwann ▲ SCH 311732

Budapest Camerata
H. Gmür (cnd)
Bach, Joh. Christian:Sinf concertante, T.284/4 *(rec Festetich Castle, Budapest, Mar 1994)* Naxos ▲ 8.553085 [DDD]

Budapest Camerata (cont.)
H. Gmür (cnd) (cont.)
Bach, Joh. Christian:Sinf concertante, T.284/6, w. Ildiko Line (vn), Violetta Eckhardt (vn), Marianna Kruzse (ob) *(rec Festetich Castle, Budapest, Mar 1994)* Naxos ▲ 8.553085 [DDD]
Bach, Joh. Christian:Sinfs Obs, Op. 3 *(rec Festetich Castle, Budapest, Mar 1994)* Naxos ▲ 8.553083 [DDD]
Bach, Joh. Christian:Sinfs, Op. 6 *(rec Festetich Castle, Budapest, Mar 1994)* Naxos ▲ 8.553084 [DDD]
Bach, Joh. Christian:Sinfs, Op. 9—No. 1 in B♭; No. 2 in E♭; No. 3 in B♭ *(rec Festetich Castle, Budapest, Mar 1994)* Naxos ▲ 8.553085 [DDD]
M. Halász (cnd)
Pergolesi, G.B.:Orfeo, w. Julia Faulkner (sop) *(rec Festetich Castle, Budapest, Sept. 1994)* Naxos ▲ 8.550766 [DDD]
Pergolesi, G.B.:Stabat mater, w. Julia Faulkner (sop), Anna Gonda (alt) *(rec Festetich Castle, Budapest, Sept. 1994)* Naxos ▲ 8.550766 [DDD]
L. Kovács (cnd)
Donizetti, G.:Concertinos (misc)—in c for Fl & CO; in F for Ob & CO; in d for Vn, Vc & Orch.; in G for E Hn & Orch.; in B♭ for Cl & Orch. *(rec Festetich Castle, Budapest, June 5–11, 1994)* Marco Polo ▲ 8.223701 [DDD]
Donizetti, G.:Sinfs (misc)—in g for Ww; in d on the Death of A. Capuzzi *(rec Festetich Castle, Budapest, June 5–11, 1994)* Marco Polo ▲ 8.223701 [DDD]

Budapest Chamber Ensemble
A. Dorati (cnd)
Bartók, B.:Village Scenes, w. Faragó (sop), Adám (sop), Győr Girls' Choir [Slovak] Hungaroton ▲ HCD 31047 [ADD]
A. Mihály (cnd)
Durkó, Z.:Iconography 2, w. Ferenc Tarjáni (hn) *(rec 1972)* Hungaroton ▲ HCD 31654 [AAD]
F. Stassevitch (cnd)
Mozart, W.A.:Con 3 Vn, w. R. Ricci (vn) One-Eleven ▲ URS 91040 [ADD]
Mozart, W.A.:Con 3 Vn, w. R. Ricci (vn) One-Eleven ▲ URS 93010 [ADD]
Prokofiev, S.:Con 2 Vn, w. R. Ricci (vn) One-Eleven ▲ URS 93010 [ADD]
Respighi, O.:Con gregoriano, w. R. Ricci (vn) One-Eleven ▲ URS 93010 [ADD]

Budapest CO
A. Mihály (cnd)
Boulez, P.:Improvisations sur Mallarmé I & II, w. E. Sziklay (sop) [F] Hungaroton ▲ HCD 11385 [ADD]
Schoenberg, A.:Pierrot lunaire, w. E. Sziklay (speaker) [G] Hungaroton ▲ HCD 11385 [ADD]
Webern, A.:Canons on Latin Texts, w. Erika Sziklay (sop) [L] Hungaroton ▲ HCD 11385 [ADD]
Webern, A.:Songs, Op. 8, w. E. Sziklay (sop) [G] Hungaroton ▲ HCD 11385 [ADD]
G. Pacor (cnd)
Schubert, Franz:Qt 14 Strs [orchd. Mahler] RS Applausi ▲ 6367-08
T. Pál (cnd)
Hummel, J.N.:Con Pno, Op. 85, w. Hae-won Chang (pno) *(rec Budapest, May 28–30, 1987)* Naxos ▲ 8.550837 [DDD]
Hummel, J.N.:Con Pno, Op. 89, w. Hae-won Chang (pno) *(rec Budapest, May 28–30, 1987)* Naxos ▲ 8.550837 [DDD]

Budapest Collegium Musicum
Hungarian Baroque Songs & Dances, w. Drew Minter (ct) White Label ▲ HRC 183 [ADD]

Budapest Concert Orch
J. Acs (cnd)
Live from Budapest, w. Berle Sanford Rosenberg (ten) *(rec live in concert, 8/24/90)* Olympia ▲ OLY 370 [DDD]

Budapest Failoni Orch
M. Halász (cnd)
Schubert, Franz:Sym 1 *(rec Italian Institute, Budapest, Mar. 1994)* Naxos ▲ 8.553093 [DDD]
Schubert, Franz:Sym 2 *(rec Italian Institute, Budapest, Mar. 1994)* Naxos ▲ 8.553093 [DDD]
Schubert, Franz:Sym 6 *(rec Italian Institute, Budapest, Mar. 1994)* Naxos ▲ 8.553094 [DDD]

Budapest Festival Horn Quartet [Miklós Nagy (hn), László Rákos (hn), László Gál (hn), Tibor Maruzsa (hn)]
Cornologia, w. Zoltán Varga (timp/perc), Dimitris Politis (gtr), Ferenc Gayer (db/bass gtr), János Weszely (dr), Sándor Balogh (pno) *(rec Hungaroton Classic Studio, Feb 15-16, 1996)* Hungaroton ▲ HCD 31652 [ADD/DDD]

Budapest Festival Orch
Classics Go to the Movies Vol. 2, w. Dresden PO, Bulgarian TV-Radio SO, Bela Kovaks, Franz Liszt CO, Bruno Lazzaretti, Berlin RSO, Hungarian State Orch LaserLight ▲ 15 642
I. Fischer (cnd)
Bartók, B.:Con Orch Hungaroton ▲ HCD 31167 [DDD]
Bartók, B.:Cons Pno (comp), w. Zoltán Kocsis (pno) Philips ▲ 446368-2
Bartók, B.:Con 1 Vn, w. Thomas Zehetmair (vn) Berlin Classics ▲ BER 1134 [DDD]
Bartók, B.:Con 2 Vn, w. Thomas Zehetmair (vn) Berlin Classics ▲ BER 1134 [DDD]
Bartók, B.:Dance Suite Hungaroton ▲ HCD 31167 [DDD]
Brahms, J.:Hungarian Dances Orch Hungaroton ▲ HCD 12571 [DDD]
Liszt, F.:Mazeppa Orch Harmonia Mundi Plus ("Plus" series) ▲ HMP 3903049
Liszt, F.:Mephisto Waltz 1 Orch Harmonia Mundi Plus ("Plus" series) ▲ HMP 3903049
Liszt, F.:Les Préludes Harmonia Mundi Plus ("Plus" series) ▲ HMP 3903049
Liszt, F.:Tasso—Lamento e Trionfo Harmonia Mundi Plus ("Plus" series) ▲ HMP 3903049
Strauss (II), Joh.:Music of—Éljen a Magyar; Tritsch-Tratsch Polka; Die Libelle; Auf der Jagd; Neue Pizzicato Polka; Perpetuum mobile; Pizzicato Polka [written w. Josef Strauss] Harmonia Mundi Plus ▲ HMP 3903016
Strauss, Josef:Music of—Die Emanzipierte; Pizzicato Polka [written w. Johann Strauss II] Harmonia Mundi Plus ▲ HMP 3903016

Budapest MÁV SO
Oberfrank, Gardelli (cnd)
Verdi, G.:Arias, w. Sylvia Sass (sop), Giorgio Lamberti (ten), Kolos Kováts (bass), Hungarian State Opera Orch, Béla Pödör (cnd), Ferenc Sapszon (cnd), Ferenc Nagy (cnd), Hungarian People's Army Male Chorus, Hungarian Radio-TV Chorus, Hungarian State Opera Chorus—Vieni, o Levita!...Tu sul labbro [from Nabucco]; Verginil...Il ciel per ora...Sciagurata! Hai tu creduto; Qui posa il fianco [both from I Lombardi]; Che mai vegg'io...Infelice! E tu credevi...; Vigili pure il ciel...Iddio n'ascolti [both from Ernani]; Mentre gonfiarsi l'anima [from Attila]; Studia il passo...Come dal ciel precipita! [from Macbeth]; O patria, o cara patria...O tu, Palermo [from I vespri Siciliani]; A te l'estremo addio... [from Simon Boccanegra]; Ella giammai m'amò [from Don Carlo] Hungaroton ("Great Hungarian Voices" series) ▲ HCD 31650 [ADD/DDD]

Budapest National Opera Orch
A. Kórodi (cnd)
Waydicth, G. von:The Caliph's Magician, w. Júlia Pászthi (sop—Eunuch), Sándor Palcso (ten—The Emir), István Rozsos (ten—Nawab), Zsolt Bende (bar—The Magician), Arpád Kishegyi (sgr—Djinn), András Nagy-Soljom (sgr—The Caliph), Csaba Ötvös (sgr—Djinn), Csilla Ötvös (sgr—Odalisk), Budapest National Opera Chorus *(rec 1975)* VAI Audio 2-▲ VAIA 1095-2 [ADD]

Budapest Orch
A. Deryl (cnd)
Massenet, J.:Music of Auvidis Travelling ▲ K 1008 ▮
Schubert, Franz:Music of Auvidis Travelling ▲ K 1008 ▮
Schumann, R.:Music of Auvidis Travelling ▲ K 1008 ▮

Budapest Orfeo Orch
G. Vashegyi (cnd)
Mozart, W.A.:Ave verum corpus, w. Noemi Rime (sop), Christine Batty (mez), Stuart Patterson (ten), Bernard Deletre (bass), Patrick Marco (cnd), Maitrise de Paris Pierre Verany ▲ PVY 730058 [DDD]
Mozart, W.A.:Missa, K.317, w. Noemi Rime (sop), Christine Batty (mez), Stuart Patterson (ten), Bernard Deletre (bass), Patrick Marco (cnd), Maitrise de Paris Pierre Verany ▲ PVY 730058 [DDD]
Mozart, W.A.:Vesperae solennes, w. Noemi Rime (sop), Christine Batty (mez), Stuart Patterson (ten), Bernard Deletre (bass), Patrick Marco (cnd), Maitrise de Paris Pierre Verany ▲ PVY 730058 [DDD]

▲ = CD ♦ = Enhanced CD Δ = MD ▮ = Cassette Tape ▯ = DCC

Budapest PO
Classics Go to the Movies Vol. 4, w. Budapest SO, Salzburg Mozarteum Orch, Christian Altenburger, Ernst Mayer-Schieming, German Bach Soloists, Sofia National Opera Orch LaserLight ▲ 15 644
E. Bergel (cnd)
Chopin, F.:Con 1 Pno, w. B. Rigutto (pno) Denon ▲ CO 75637 [DDD]
Chopin, F.:Con 2 Pno, w. B. Rigutto (pno) Denon ▲ CO 75637 [DDD]
T. Breitner (cnd)
Schumann, R.:Sym 1 Laserlight ▲ 15 827 [DDD]
Schumann, R.:Sym 2 Laserlight ▲ 15 827
E. Dohnányi (cnd)
Mozart, W.A.:Con 17 Pno, w. E. von Dohnányi (pno) *(rec 1928 for Columbia Records)* Koch Schwann ▲ CD 311136 (m) [ADD]
M. Erdélyi (cnd)
Bartók, B.:Pieces Orch, Sz.51 Hungaroton ▲ HCD 31050
A. Ferencsik (cnd)
Kodály, Z.:Con Orch Hungaroton ▲ HCD 12190
Rimsky-Korsakov, N.:Scheherazade Vivace 2-▲ G 212 [DDD/ADD]
Weber, C.M. von:Ovs—Oberon Overture Vivace 2-▲ G 212 [DDD/ADD]
J. Ferencsik (cnd)
Bartók, B.:Bluebeard's Castle, w. K. Palánkay (sop), M. Székely (bass) [Hun] *(rec 1956)* Hungaroton ▲ HCD 11001 (m) [ADD]
Erkel, F.:Bánk Bán, w. K. Agay (sop), E. Komlóssy (cta), J. Réti (ten), J. Simándy (ten), S. Sólyom-Nagy (bar), Hungarian State Opera Chorus [Hun] *(rec 1969)* Hungaroton 2-▲ HCD 11376/77 [ADD]
Kodály, Z.:Háry János (suite) Hungaroton ▲ HCD 12190
L. Gardelli (cnd)
Mendelssohn, F.:Die Hebriden White Label ▲ HRC 168 [ADD]
Mussorgsky, M.:Night White Label ▲ HRC 168 [ADD]
Respighi, O.:The Pines of Rome White Label ▲ HRC 168 [ADD]
Tchaikovsky, P.:Romeo & Juliet White Label ▲ HRC 168 [ADD]
A. Kórodi (cnd)
Bartók, B.:Con Va, w. G. Németh (va) Hungaroton ▲ HCD 31050
Chopin, F.:Concerto No. 1 in e for Piano & Orchestra, Op. 11 (1830), w. Sandor Falvai (pno) Laserlight ♦ 90016 [DDD]
Chopin, F.:Con 1 Pno, w. S. Falvai (pno) LaserLight ▲ 14 003 [DDD]
Famous Marches & Dances Laserlight ▲ 15 621
Goldmark, K.:Ovs—Sakuntala, Op. 13; Im Frühling, Op. 36; Der gefesselte Prometheus, Op. 38; In Italien, Op. 49 Hungaroton ▲ HCD 12552 [DDD]
Opera Intermezzi Capriccio ▲ CDC 10080
J. Kovács (cnd)
Mendelssohn, F.:A Midsummer Night's Dream (sels) Laserlight ▲ 15 623
Mendelssohn, F.:A Midsummer Night's Dream (sels) LaserLight ▲ 15526 [DDD]
Schubert, F.:Music of Schubert, w. Jenö Jandó (pno), Colorado String Quartet Laserlight ♦ 90032 [DDD]
Mendelssohn, F.:Ovs Laserlight ▲ 15 526 [DDD]
Mendelssohn, F.:Sym 4 Laserlight ▲ 15 526 [DDD]
Schubert, Franz:Ovs—Rosamunde Laserlight ▲ 15 823
Schubert, Franz:Rosamunde Laserlight ▲ 15 527 [DDD]
Schubert, Franz:Rosamunde (sels)—Overture LaserLight ▲ 15 823 [DDD]
Schubert, Franz:Sym 3 Laserlight ▲ 15 823
Schubert, Franz:Sym 8 Laserlight ▲ 15 823 [DDD]
Schubert, Franz:Sym 8 Laserlight ▲ 15 527 [DDD]
A. Ligeti (cnd)
Tchaikovsky, P.:Con 1 Pno, w. Jenö Jando (pno)—Andante semplice LaserLight ▲ 14 224
Tchaikovsky, P.:Con 1 Pno, w. J. Jando (pno) Laserlight ▲ 15 516 [DDD]
Tchaikovsky, P.:Con 1 Pno, w. J. Jando (pno) Capriccio ▲ 10 921 [DDD]
G. Németh (cnd)
Mozart, W.A.:Con 3 Vn, w. D. Kovács (vn) White Label ▲ HRC 154 [ADD]
Mozart, W.A.:Con 5 Vn, w. D. Kovács (vn) White Label ▲ HRC 154 [ADD]
S. Pomerantz (cnd)
Beethoven, L. van:Sym 6, "Pastorale" *(rec Italian Institute, Budapest, Aug 9–11, 1994)* Doremi ▲ 71116 [DDD]
Beethoven, L. van:Sym 7 *(rec Italian Institute, Budapest, Aug 9–11, 1994)* Doremi ▲ 71116 [DDD]
R. Saccani (cnd)
Liszt, F.:Con 1 Pno, w. J. Rose (pno) Vox Box 2-▲ CDX 5106 [DDD]
Liszt, F.:Con 2 Pno, w. J. Rose (pno) Vox Box 2-▲ CDX 5106 [DDD]
Liszt, F.:Totentanz, w. J. Rose (pno) Vox Box 2-▲ CDX 5106 [DDD]
J. Sándor (cnd)
Bizet, G.:L'Arlésienne (suites) LaserLight ▲ 15 614 [DDD]
Bizet, G.:Carmen (suites) LaserLight ▲ 15 614 [DDD]
Bruch, M.:Con 1 Vn, w. M. Szenthelyi (vn) Laserlight ▲ 15 615
Delibes, L.:Sylvia LaserLight ▲ 15 616 [DDD]
Devienne, F.:Con Fl, w. J. Szebenyi (fl) Vivace ▲ E 562 [ADD]
Gershwin, G.:An American in Paris LaserLight ▲ 15 606 [DDD]
Gershwin, G.:Rhap in Blue, w. J. Jandó (pno) LaserLight ▲ 15 606 [DDD]
Gold & Silver, w. Hungarian State Orch White Label ▲ HRC 065
Gounod, C.:Faust (ballet music) LaserLight ▲ 15 616 [DDD]
Grieg, E.:Con Pno, Op. 16, w. J. Jandó (pno) LaserLight ▲ 15 617 [DDD]
Grieg, E.:Peer Gynt Suite 1 LaserLight ▲ 15 617 [DDD]
Haydn, M.:Con Fl, P.54, w. János Szebenyi (fl) Vivace ▲ E 562 [ADD]
Haydn, M.:Serenade White Label ▲ HRC 100 [ADD]
Haydn, M.:Sym in D White Label ▲ HRC 100 [ADD]
Mussorgsky, M.:Night LaserLight ▲ 14 012 [DDD]
Rosetti, F.A.:Con Fl, w. J. Szebenyi (fl) Vivace ▲ E 562 [ADD]
Budapest Piano Duet [Tamás Kereskedö (pno), Zoltán Pozsgai (pno)]
Liszt, F.:Symphonic Poems—Les préludes; Hungaria; Hunnenschlacht [all trans Liszt] *(rec Hungaroton Classic LTD Studios, 1995)* Hungaroton ▲ HCD 31620 [DDD]
Budapest Quartet
Brahms, J.:Qts Strs (comp)—Op. 51, No. 2 Biddulph 2-▲ LAB 120–21
Brahms, J.:Qnt 1 Strs, w. Alfred Hobday (va) Biddulph 2-▲ LAB 120–21
Brahms, J.:Qnt 2 Strs, w. Alfred Hobday (va) Biddulph 2-▲ LAB 120–21
Brahms, J.:Sextet Strs, Op. 36, w. Alfred Hobday (va), Anthony Pini (vc) Biddulph 2-▲ LAB 120–21
Budapest RSO
G. Lehel (cnd)
Ravel, M.:Daphnis et Chloé (suite 1) LaserLight ▲ 14013 [DDD]
G. Sébastian (cnd)
Bartók, B.:Bluebeard's Castle, w. Mihály Székely (bass), *(other soloists unknown)* *(rec 1951)* Arlecchino ▲ ARL109
L. Stokowski (cnd)
Kodály, Z.:Háry János (suite) *(rec 1967)* Music & Arts ▲ CD 771 [AAD]
Budapest Strauss Ensemble
I. Bogár (cnd)
Wedding Celebrations *(rec Apr. 5–7, 1993)* Naxos ▲ 8.550900 [DDD]
Wedding Music, w. B. Hoch (org) *(rec 1992)* Naxos ▲ 8.550790 [DDD]

Budapest Strauss SO
A. Walter (cnd)
Straus, O.:Music of—Rund um die Liebe:Ov.; Einzugs March; Walzerträume Waltz; G'stellte Mädl'n Polka; Alt-Weiner Reigen, Op. 45; Komm, komm, Held meiner Träme Waltz & L'amour m'emporte Waltz [w. V. Kincses (soprano)]; Bulgaren Marsch; Didi Marsch; Die Schlossparade Marsch; Valse lente; Menuett à la cour; Tragant Waltz; Eine Ballnacht Waltz; Der Reigen Concert Waltz *(rec Apr. 1–4, 1993)* Marco Polo ▲ 8.223596 [DDD]
Strauss, Josef:Music of—Kakadu-Quadrille, Op. 276; Marien-Klänge, Walzer, Op. 214; Etiquette, Polka française, Op. 208; Thalia, Polka Mazur, Op. 195; Gablenz-Marsch, Op. 159; Angelica-Polka française, Op. 123; Fantasiebilder, Walzer, Op. 151; Moulinet-Polka française, Op. 57; Bauern-Polka Mazur, Op. 10; Wiegenlieder, Walzer, Op. 18; Eislauf, Polka schnell, Op. 261 *(rec Italian Institute, Budapest, Mar. 29–31, 1993)* Marco Polo ▲ 8.223561 [DDD]
Budapest String Quartet
Beethoven, L. van:Grosse Fuge Str Qt Sony Classical ("Essential Classics" series) ▲ SBK 47665 ■ SBT 47665
Beethoven, L. van:Qts Strs (comp)—Quartet Nos. 1–6, Op. 18 *(rec 1951–2)* Sony Masterworks ("Portrait" series) 2-▲ MP2K 52531 (m) [ADD]
Beethoven, L. van:Qt 7 Strs Sony Classical ("Essential Classics" series) ▲ SBK 46545 [ADD] ■ SBT 46545
Beethoven, L. van:Qt 8 Strs Sony Classical ("Essential Classics" series) ▲ SBK 46545 [ADD] ■ SBT 46545
Beethoven, L. van:Qt 9 Strs Sony Classical ("Essential Classics" series) ▲ SBK 47665 ■ SBT 47665
Beethoven, L. van:Qt 10 Strs, "Harp" Sony Classical ("Essential Classics" series) ▲ SBK 47665 ■ SBT 47665
Brahms, J.:Qt 1 Strs *(rec 1963)* Sony Masterworks ("Portrait" series) ▲ MPK 45686 [ADD]
Brahms, J.:Qt 3 Strs *(rec 1963)* Sony Masterworks ("Portrait" series) ▲ MPK 45553 [ADD]
Brahms, J.:Qt 3 Strs Biddulph 2-▲ LAB 120–21
Brahms, J.:Qnt Cl, w. D. Oppenheim (cl) *(rec 1959)* Sony Masterworks ("Portrait" series) ▲ MPK 45553 [ADD]
Brahms, J.:Qnt Pno, w. R. Serkin (pno) *(rec 1963)* Sony Masterworks ("Portrait" series) ▲ MPK 45686 [ADD]
Dvořák, A.:Qt 12 Strs, "America" Biddulph ▲ LAB 140
Grieg, E.:Qt Strs, Op. 27 *(rec 1938)* RCA Red Seal ▲ 09026-61826-2
Mozart, W.A.:Kleine Nachtmusik, w. J. Levine (db) Sony Classical 3-▲ SM3K 46527
Mozart, W.A.:Qts Strs (misc)—Nos. 14–19, "The Haydn Quartets" Sony Classical 2-▲ SM2K 47219
Mozart, W.A.:Qt 17 Strs Biddulph ▲ LAB 140
Mozart, W.A.:Qt 19 Strs *(rec 1932)* EMI Classics ("Great Recordings of the Century" series) ▲ CDH 63697 (m) [ADD]
Mozart, W.A.:Qt 20 Strs *(rec 1934)* EMI Classics ("Great Recordings of the Century" series) ▲ CDH 63697 (m) [ADD]
Mozart, W.A.:Qnt Cl, K.581, w. B. Goodman (cl) *(rec 1938)* EMI Classics ("Great Recordings of the Century" series) ▲ CDH 63697 (m) [ADD]
Mozart, W.A.:Qnt Cl, K.581, w. D. Oppenheim (cl) Sony Classical 3-▲ SM3K 46527
Mozart, W.A.:Qnt Cl, K.581, w. Benny Goodman (cl) Iron Needle ▲ 1306
Mozart, W.A.:Qnt Cl & Strs, w. Benny Goodman (cl) Enterprise ("The Radio Years" series) ▲ ENT RY 60
Mozart, W.A.:Qnt Cl, K.581, w. Benny Goodman (cl) Biddulph ▲ LAB 140
Mozart, W.A.:Qnts Strs, w. W. Trampler (va) Sony Classical 3-▲ SM3K 46527
Nanes, R.:Qts Strs—Nos. 1–5 (1978–88) Delfon 2-▲ CD 7080 [DDD]
Schubert, Franz:Qt 13 Strs *(rec 1953)* Sony Masterworks ("Portrait" series) ▲ MPK 45696 [ADD]
Schubert, Franz:Qt 14 Strs *(rec 1953)* Sony Masterworks ("Portrait" series) ▲ MPK 45696 [ADD]
Schumann, R.:Qnt Pno, w. P. Serkin (pno) CBS ▲ MYK 37256 [ADD] ■ MYT 37256
Budapest String Quartet [Josef Roisman (vn), Alexander Schneider (vn), Boris Kroyt (va), Mischa Schneider (vc)]
Haydn, J.:Qts Strs, Op. 64, "Tost Qts"—No. 5 *(rec Aug 3, 1940)* Bridge ("Great Performances from the Library of Congress" series) ▲ BRI 9067
Haydn, J.:Qts Strs, Op. 76, "Erdődy Qts"—No. 5 in D *(rec Mar 29, 1941)* Bridge ("Great Performances from the Library of Congress" series) ▲ BRI 9067
Mozart, W.A.:Qt 17 Strs *(rec 1934–40)* Enterprise ("Strings" series) ▲ ENT QT 99300
Budapest String Quartet [Josef Roisman (vn), Alexander Schneider (vn), Istvan Ipolyi (va), Mischa Schneider (vc)]
Mozart, W.A.:Qt 20 Strs *(rec 1934–40)* Enterprise ("Strings" series) ▲ ENT QT 99300
Budapest String Quartet [Josef Roisman (vn), Jac Gorodetzky (vn), Boris Kroyt (va), Mischa Schneider (vc)]
Rachmaninoff, S.:Qt Strs (1889) *(rec Coolidge Auditorium, Library of Congress, Apr 4, 1952)* Bridge ▲ BRIDGE 9063
Rachmaninoff, S.:Qt Strs (?1896) *(rec Coolidge Auditorium, Library of Congress, Apr 4, 1952)* Bridge ▲ BRIDGE 9063
Budapest String Quartet [Josef Roismann (vn), Edgar Ortenberg (vn), Boris Kroyt (va), Mischa Schneider (vc)]
Brahms, J.:Qnt Pno, w. George Szell (pno) *(rec Coolidge Auditorium, Library of Congress, Oct 11, 1945)* Bridge ▲ BCD 9062
Budapest String Quartet members
Mozart, W.A.:Qts Pno, w. G. Szell (pno) *(rec 1946)* Sony Masterworks ("Portrait" series) ▲ MPK 47685 [ADD]
Mozart, W.A.:Qts Pno, w. M. Horszowski (pno)—K.478 Sony Classical 3-▲ SM3K 46527
Schubert, Franz:Qnt Pno, D.667, w. M. Horszowski (pno), J. Levine (db) Sony Classical ("Essential Classics" series) ▲ SBK 46343 [ADD] ■ SBT 46343
Budapest String Quartet members [Josef Roisman (vn), Boris Kroyt (va), Mischa Schneider (vc)]
Beethoven, L. van:Qt Pno, Op. 16, w. Mieczyslaw Horszowski (pno) *(rec Apr 7, 1955)* Bridge ("Great Performances from the Library of Congress" series) ▲ BRI 9067
Budapest String Quartet members [Josef Roisman (vn), Mischa Schneider (vc)]
Haydn, J.:Trios Pno, Vn & Vc, w. Mieczyslaw Horszowski (pno)—Rondo all'Ongarese [from Trio in G] *(rec Apr 7, 1955)* Bridge ("Great Performances from the Library of Congress" series) ▲ BRI 9067
Budapest String Quartet members [Josef Roismann (vn), Boris Kroyt (va), Mischa Schneider (vc)]
Schubert, Franz:Qnt Pno, D.667, w. Georges Moleux (db), George Szell (pno) *(rec Coolidge Auditorium, Library of Congress, May 16, 1946)* Bridge ▲ BCD 9062
Budapest Strings
Bach, Joh. Christian:Sinf concertante, T.289/4, w. János Bálint (fl), Lajos Lencsés (ob), Béla Bánfalvi (vn), Károly Botvay (vc) *(rec Budapest)* Capriccio ▲ 10509 [DDD]
Bach, Joh. Christian:Sinf concertante, T.284/6, w. Béla Bánfalvi (vn), Zsuzsanna Németh (vn), Lajos Lencsés (ob) *(rec Budapest)* Capriccio ▲ 10509 [DDD]
Bach, Joh. Christian:Sinf concertante, T.284/4, w. Béla Bánfalvi (vn), Károly Botvay (vc) *(rec Budapest)* Capriccio ▲ 10509 [DDD]
Bach, J.S.:Con Vn & Ob, w. Béla Bánfalvi (vn), Emilia Csánky (ob) *(rec Unitarian Church, Budapest, Nov 1991)* Naxos ▲ 8.553028 [DDD]
Bach, J.S.:Easter Oratorio, w. Béla Bánfalvi (vn), Emilia Csánky (ob)—Adagio *(rec Unitarian Church, Budapest, Nov 1991)* Naxos ▲ 8.553028 [DDD]
Chausson, E.:Poème Vn Capriccio ▲ 10 527 [DDD]
Classics Go to the Movies Vol. 3, w. Hungarian State Orch, Lajos Meyer, Leonhard Hokanson (pno), Carmerata Labacensis, Budapest SO, Prague Festival Orch LaserLight ▲ 15 643
Elgar, E.:Serenade Strs Capriccio ▲ 10 527 [DDD]
Endler, J.S.:Sinf, w. Reinhold Friedrich (tpt) Capriccio ▲ 10 529 [DDD]
Famous Baroque Concerti *(rec Unitarian Church, Budapest, Nov. 1991)* Naxos ▲ 8.553028 [DDD]
Fasch, J.F.:Cons (68) Var Instrs, w. Reinhold Friedrich (tpt)—Concerto in D; Concerto à 8 in D Capriccio ▲ 10 529 [DDD]

ORCH. & ENS.

Budapest Strings (cont.)
Gershwin, G.:Porgy & Bess (sels)—I got Plenty o'Nuttin; Summertime; I love you Porgy; It Ain't Necesarily So; Bess, You Is My Woman Now — Laserlight ▲ 15 606
Gershwin, G.:Porgy & Bess (suite), "Catfish Row Suite"—I got plenty of nuttin'; Summertime; I loves you Porgy; It ain't necessarily so; Bess you is my woman now — LaserLight ▲ 15 606 [DDD]
Handel, G.F.:Concerti grossi, Op. 6—No. 1 *(rec Unitarian Church, Budapest, Nov. 1991)* — Naxos ▲ 8.553028 [DDD]
Handel, G.F.:Cons (16) Org, w. E. Achim (org) [organ of the Franciscan church at Vác, Hungary]—Op. 4 — Capriccio ▲ 10 533 [DDD]
Handel, G.F.:Solomon (arrival of the queen of Sheba) *(rec Unitarian Church, Budapest, Nov. 1991)* — Naxos ▲ 8.553028 [DDD]
Rózsavölgyi, M.:Csárdás, w. B. Bánfalvi (vn) — Capriccio ▲ 10 528 [DDD]
Serenade — Laserlight ▲ 15 505
Suk, J.:Serenade Strs — Capriccio ▲ 10 527 [DDD]
Telemann, G.P.:Con Tpt Strs in D, w. Reinhold Friedrich (tpt) — Capriccio ▲ 10 529 [DDD]
Telemann, G.P.:Ovs—in D — Capriccio ▲ 10 529 [DDD]
Vivaldi, A.:Cons & Sinfs—Concerti, RV.110, 118, 123, 127, 136, 142, 145, 156, 159, 161 *(rec 6/91)* — Nuova Era ▲ 7047 [DDD]
Vivaldi, A.:Cons & Sinfs—Symphony, RV.131; 8 Concerti—RV.109, 120, 126, 129 ("Madrigalesco"), 134, 143, 151 ("alla rustica") & 155 — Nuova Era ▲ 6937 [DDD]
Vivaldi, A.:Cons & Sinfs—6 Concerti—RV.113, 121, 128, 133, 152, 164; 3 Sinfonias—RV.112, 132, 149; Sonata à 4, "Al Santo Sepolcro" — Nuova Era ▲ 7113 [DDD]
Vivaldi, A.:Cons for 2 Gtrs, w. Béla Sztankovits (gtr), Zoltán Tokos (gtr) *(rec Unitarian Church, Budapest, Nov. 1991)* — Naxos ▲ 8.553028 [DDD]
Vivaldi, A.:Con for 2 Mands, w. Béla Sztankovits (gtr), Zoltán Tokos (gtr) *(rec Unitarian Church, Budapest, Nov 1991)* — Naxos ▲ 8.553028 [DDD]
Vivaldi, A.:Cons Ob, w. Emilia Csánky (ob)—in a, RV.461 *(rec Unitarian Church, Budapest, Nov. 1991)* — Naxos ▲ 8.553028 [DDD]
Vivaldi, A.:Cons for 2 Vns, w. Béla Bánfalvi (vn), Zsuzsa Németh (vn)—in G, RV.516 *(rec Unitarian Church, Budapest, Nov. 1991)* — Naxos ▲ 8.553028 [DDD]
Vivaldi, A.:Con for 2 Vns, RV.523, w. Béla Sztankovits (gtr), Zoltán Tokos (gtr) [arr 2 gtrs] *(rec Unitarian Church, Budapest, Nov. 1991)* — Naxos ▲ 8.553028 [DDD]
Vivaldi, A.:Music of, w. Capella Istropolitana, Concentus Hungaricus, Dall'Arco CO—selections from The Four Seasons; Flautino Con. in C; Flute Con. in F; Flute Con. in a, RV.108; Con. in B♭ for 2 Trumpets; Concerti, Op. 3/4, 8, 10 & 11; Oboe Con., Op. 8/9; Violin Con., Op. 8/5 & 12; Lute Con. in D; Il Gardellino — Naxos ▲ 8.551105 [DDD]
Wolf, H.:Italian Serenade — Capriccio ▲ 10 527 [DDD]

B. Bánfalvi (cnd)
Bach, Joh. Christian:Sinf concertante, T.287/2, w. Lajos Lencsés (ob), Emilia Csánky (ob), Károly Botvay (vc) *(rec Budapest, Feb 10–13, Apr 28–May 1)* — Capriccio ▲ 10509 [DDD]
Concierto de Aranjuez, w. Zoltan Tokos, Monika (gtr), Jürgen Rost (gtr) — LaserLight ▲ 15602 [DDD]
Csermák, A.G.:Hungarian Dances (6) — Capriccio ▲ 10 528 [DDD]
Csermák, A.G.:Vaterlandsliebe — Capriccio ▲ 10 528 [DDD]
Handel, G.F.:Ode for St. Cecilia's Day — Laserlight ▲ 15 607
Handel, G.F.:Solomon (sels) — Laserlight ▲ 15 607
Handel, G.F.:Water Music (comp) — Laserlight ▲ 15 607
Handel, G.F.:Water Music (suites)—Suites 1–3; also, Ode for St. Cecilia's Day—minuet; Solomon—Sinfonia from Act 3 — LaserLight ▲ 15607 [DDD]
Kauer, F.:New Hungarian Dances — Capriccio ▲ 10 528 [DDD]
Rodrigo, J.:Concierto de Aranjuez, w. Z. Tokos (gtr) — Laserlight ▲ 15 602 [DDD]
Weiner, L.:Divert 1 Str Orch — Capriccio ▲ 10 528 [DDD]

K. Botvay (cnd)
Classical Favorites for Strings:Nocturnes, Songs, Arias & Etudes — LaserLight ▲ 14039 [DDD]
Classical Favorites for Strings:Songs, Romances & Dances — LaserLight ▲ 14040 [DDD]
Handel, G.F.:Cons (16) Org, w. G. Lehotka (org)—Op. 4/2, 4 & 5 & Op. 7/4 — LaserLight ▲ 15 629 [DDD]
Mercadante, S.:Cons (6) Fl (1819), w. M. Hegedűs (fl)—in e — LaserLight ▲ 15634 [DDD]
Mercadante, S.:Con in e Fl, Op. 57, w. M. Hegedűs (fl) — LaserLight ▲ 14037 [DDD]
Vivaldi, A.:Cons Diverse Instrs, w. L. Mayer (mand), B. Glaetzner (ob), Güttler (tpt), Sandau (tpt), M. Pommer (cnd), New Bach Collegium Musicum — LaserLight ▲ 15518 [DDD]
Vivaldi, A.:Cons Ob, w. B. Glaetzner (ob)—RV.454 — Laserlight ▲ 15 518
Vivaldi, Antonio:Concertos (4) for Violin, Strings & Continuo, Op. 8/1–4 (RV.269, 293, 297, 315), "The Four Seasons" — Laserlight ♦ 90012 [DDD]
Vivaldi, A.:Cons Vn, Op. 8/1–4, "The Four Seasons", w. B. Banfalvi (vn) — Laserlight ▲ 15 518 [DDD]

F. Szekeres (cnd)
Albinoni, T.:Magnificat [L] — Hungaroton ▲ HCD 31259 [DDD]
Caldara, A.:Magnificat, w. M. Szűcs (sop), K. Takács (cta), D. Gulyás (ten), T. Bátor (bass), Budapest Madrigal Choir [L] — Hungaroton ▲ HCD 31259 [DDD]
Sammartini, G.B.:Magnificat in B♭, w. Szűcs (sop), Takács (alt), Gulyás (ten), Bátor (bass), Budapest Madrigal Choir [L] — Hungaroton ▲ HCD 31259 [DDD]
Vivaldi, A.:Magnificat, RV.610, w. T. Takács (mez), D. Gulyás (ten), T. Bátor (bass), R. Szűcs (bass), Budapest Madrigal Choir [L] — Hungaroton ▲ HCD 31259 [DDD]
Vivaldi, A.:Magnificat, RV.611, w. T. Takács (mez), J. Németh (mez), Bátori (sgr), Kovács (sgr), Szőkefalvi-Nagy (sgr), Budapest Madrigal Choir [L] — Hungaroton ▲ HCD 31259 [DDD]

Budapest Symphonic Band

L. Marosi (cnd)
Bogár, I.:Con Tuba, w. József Bazsinka (tuba), Gusztáv H *(rec Jul 3–7, 1995)* — Hungaroton ▲ HCD 31612 [DDD]
Dubrovay, L.:Buzzing - Polka, w. József Bazsinka (tuba), Gusztáv H *(rec Jul 3–7, 1995)* — Hungaroton ▲ HCD 31612 [DDD]
Hidas, F.:Folksongs of Békés County, w. József Bazsinka (tuba), Gusztáv H *(rec Jul 3–7, 1995)* — Hungaroton ▲ HCD 31612 [DDD]
Hidas, F.:Folksongs of the Balaton, w. József Bazsinka (tuba), Gusztáv H *(rec Jul 3–7, 1995)* — Hungaroton ▲ HCD 31612 [DDD]
Lendvay, K.:The Last Message from Maestro Tchaikovsky, w. József Bazsinka (tuba), Gusztáv H *(rec Jul 3–7, 1995)* — Hungaroton ▲ HCD 31612 [DDD]
Ránki, G.:The Magic Potion, w. József Bazsinka (tuba), Gusztáv Hóna (harsona/bn) *(rec Jul 3–7, 1995)* — Hungaroton ▲ HCD 31612 [DDD]
Ránki, G.:The Tales of Father Goose, w. József Bazsinka (tuba), Gusztáv Hóna (harsona/bn) *(rec Jul 3–7, 1995)* — Hungaroton ▲ HCD 31612 [DDD]

Budapest SO
Classics Go to the Movies Vol. 1, w. Hungarian State Opera Orch, Vienna Strauss Orch, Jenő Jandó (pno), Plovdiv PO, Dresden PO, New Leipzig Bach Collegium Musicum — LaserLight ▲ 15 641
Classics Go to the Movies Vol. 3, w. Hungarian State Orch, Lajos Meyer, Budapest Strings, Leonhard Hokanson (pno), Carmerata Labacensis, Prague Festival Orch — LaserLight ▲ 15 643
Classics Go to the Movies Vol. 4, w. Budapest PO, Salzburg Mozarteum Orch, Christian Altenburger, Ernst Mayer-Schieming, German Bach Soloists, Sofia National Opera Orch — LaserLight ▲ 15 644
Classics Go to the Movies Vol. 5, w. Hannes Käster (org), Salzburg Mozarteum Orch, Bavarian RSO, Ludovic Spiess (ten), Virginia Zeani (sop), Rumanian Opera Orch, Rumanian Radio–TV Studio Orch, Sofia PO, Philharmonia Orch — LaserLight ▲ 15 645
Music at the Time of Beaumarchais, w. Montserrat Figueras (sop), Lawrence Monteyro (sop), Raphel Oleg (vn), Miguel da Silva (va), Christophe Coin (vc), Marc Coppey (vc), José Miguel Moreno (gtr), Paul Badura-Skoda (pno), Philippe Cassard (pno), Eric Le Sage (pno), et al. — Valois ▲ V 4767

I. Bogár (cnd)
Brahms, J.:Hungarian Dances Orch — Naxos ▲ 8.550110 [DDD] Δ 7.550110 [DDD]

T. Bródy (cnd)
Make Wonder:Songs from Operettas, w. Magda Kalmár (sop), Éva Kőteles (sgr), Judit Takács (sgr), Bori Szita (sgr), Hungarian State Orch [cnd:András Sebestyén] — Hungaroton ▲ HCD 16613 [AAD]

Budapest SO (cont.)

A. Dorati (cnd)
Bartók, B.:Cant Profana, "The Giant Stags", w. József Réti (ten), József Gregor (bass), Hungarian Radio–TV Chorus — Hungaroton ▲ HCD 31503 [ADD]
Bartók, B.:Choruses (7), w. Liszt Academy Chamber Chorus — Hungaroton ▲ HCD 31047 [ADD]

H. Esser (cnd)
Beethoven, L. van:Con 3 Pno, w. A. Fischer (pno) *(rec 1966)* — Hungaroton ▲ HCD 31493 [ADD]

A. Ferencsik (cnd)
Liszt, F.:Missa solemnis, w. V. Kincses (mez), T. Takács (mez), G. Korondy (ten), J. Gregor (bass), Budapest Sym Chorus [L] — Hungaroton ▲ HCD 11861

J. Ferencsik (cnd)
Bartók, B.:Rhaps (2) Vn & Orch, w. D. Kovács (vn) — Hungaroton ▲ HCD 31050

A. Fischer (cnd)
Rossini, G.:Ovs—Italiana in Algeri, Barber of Seville, William Tell, Semiramide, Signor Bruschino, La gazza ladra — White Label ▲ HRC 052

L. Gardelli (cnd)
Cherubini, L.:Médée, w. M. Kalmar (sop), S. Sass (sop), T. Takacs (mez), V. Luchetti (ten), K. Kovats (bass), Hungarian Radio Chorus [I] — Hungaroton 2–▲ HCD 11904/05
Vivaldi, A.:Cons Vn, Op. 8/1–4, "The Four Seasons", w. Dénes Kovács (vn) — Classical Diamonds ▲ CLD 4009 [ADD]

G. Györványi-Ráth (cnd)
Dohnányi, E. von:Con 1 Pno, w. L. Baranyay (bn) — Hungaroton ▲ HCD 31555 [DDD]
Dohnányi, E. von:Con 2 Pno, w. L. Baranyay (bn) — Hungaroton ▲ HCD 31555 [DDD]

A. Jancsovics (cnd)
Kallinikov, V.:The Cedar & the Palm — Marco Polo ▲ 8.223135 [DDD]
Kallinikov, V.:Epic Poem — Marco Polo ▲ 8.223135 [DDD]
Kallinikov, V.:The Nymphs — Marco Polo ▲ 8.223135 [DDD]
Kallinikov, V.:Tsar Boris — Marco Polo ▲ 8.223135 [DDD]

A. Joó (cnd)
Liszt, F.:Symphonic Poems — Hungaroton 5–▲ HCD 12677/81
Mendelssohn, F.:Con in e Vn & Orch, Op. 64, w. E. Verhey (vn) — Vivace ▲ E 555 [DDD]
Mendelssohn, F.:Con in e Vn & Orch, Op. 64, w. E. Verhey (vn)—Das Konzert, Vol. 1 — Vivace 2–▲ G 107/108 [DDD/ADD]
Mendelssohn, F.:Con in e Vn & Orch, Op. 64, w. E. Verhey (vn) — Vivace 3–▲ E 324 [ADD/DDD]
Mendelssohn, F.:Con in e Vn & Orch, Op. 64, w. E. Verhey (vn) — Laserlight ▲ 15 615 [DDD]
Mendelssohn, F.:Con in e Vn & Orch, Op. 64, w. E. Verhey (vn) — Sound 2–▲ E 220 [DDD]
Tchaikovsky, P.:Con Vn, w. E. Verhey (vn)—Das Konzert, Vol. 2 — Vivace 2–▲ G 117/118 [DDD]
Tchaikovsky, P.:Con Vn, w. E. Verhey (vn) — Vivace ▲ E 555 [DDD]
Tchaikovsky, P.:Con Vn, w. E. Verhey (vn) — Sound 2–▲ E 220 [DDD]
Tchaikovsky, P.:Con Vn, w. E. Verhey (vn) — Laserlight ▲ 15 516
Tchaikovsky, P.:Con Vn, w. E. Verhey (vn) — Capriccio ▲ 10 921 [DDD]
Tchaikovsky, P.:Con Vn, w. E. Verhey (vn) — Vivace 3–▲ E 324 [ADD/DDD]

B. Kocsár (cnd)
Liszt, F.:Fant on Hungarian Folk Tunes, w. György Oracecz (pno) *(rec Italian Cultural Institute, Budapest, June 26–27, 1992)* — Hungaroton ▲ HCD 31461 [DDD]
Liszt, F.:Hungarian Rhaps—No. 14 *(rec Italian Cultural Institute, Budapest, Aug. 14, 1992)* — Hungaroton ▲ HCD 31461 [DDD]
Liszt, F.:Totentanz, w. György Oracecz (pno)—also solo pno version *(rec Italian Cultural Institute, Budapest, Apr. 21–22, 1992)* — Hungaroton ▲ HCD 31461 [DDD]

A. Kórodi (cnd)
Liszt, F.:Hungarian Rhaps—Nos. 2, 5, 6, 9, 12 & 14 — Capriccio ▲ CDC 10077 [DDD]

G. Lehel (cnd)
Bach, J.S.:Con 1 Vn, w. Andre Gertler (vn) — Hungaroton ▲ HCD 31635
Beethoven, L. van:Romances Vn, w. D. Kovács (vn) — White Label ▲ HRC 147 [ADD]
Debussy, C.:Prélude à l'après-midi d'un faune — LaserLight ▲ 15528 [DDD]
Dukas, P.:L'Apprenti sorcier — LaserLight ▲ 15528 [DDD]
Durkó, Z.:Altamira, w. Hungarian Radio–TV Chamber Chorus *(rec 1972)* — Hungaroton ▲ HCD 31654 [AAD]
Durkó, Z.:Burial Prayer, w. Attila Fülöp (ten), Endre Ütő (bass), Ferenc Sapszon (cnd), Hungarian Radio–TV Chorus *(rec 1975)* — Hungaroton ▲ HCD 31654 [AAD]
Liszt, F.:Dante Sym, w. Budapest Sym Chorus — Hungaroton ▲ HCD 11918
Liszt, F.:Hungarian Coronation Mass, w. V. Kincses (sop), T. Tákacs (mez), D. Gulyas (ten), L. Polgar (bass), Hungarian Radio Chorus [L] — Hungaroton ▲ HCD 12148
Mozart, W.A.:Con 4 Vn, w. D. Kovács (vn) — White Label ▲ HRC 154 [ADD]
Rachmaninoff, S.:Con 2 Pno, w. Jenő Jandó (pno) *(rec Italian Institute, Budapest, Feb 9–10 & Apr 5–7, 1988)* — Naxos 4–▲ 8.504011 [DDD]
Rachmaninoff, S.:Con 2 Pno, w. J. Jandó (pno) — Naxos ▲ 8.550117 [DDD]
Rachmaninoff, S.:Rhapsody on a Theme of Paganini, w. J. Jandó (pno) — Naxos ▲ 8.550117 [DDD]
Rachmaninoff, S.:Rhapsody on a Theme of Paganini, w. Jenő Jandó (pno) *(rec Italian Institute, Budapest, Feb 9–10 & Apr 5–7, 1988)* — Naxos 4–▲ 8.504011 [DDD]
Ravel, M.:Rapsodie espagnole — LaserLight ▲ 15528 [DDD]
Rimsky-Korsakov, N.:Capriccio espagnol — LaserLight ▲ 15528 [DDD]
Wagner, R.:Music of, w. Sofia RSO [cnd:Vassil Kazandjiew] — Laserlight ♦ 90028 [DDD]
Wagner, R.:Ovs, Preludes & Orch Sels, w. Y. Ahronovitch (cnd), Vienna SO—Fliegende Holländer, Lohengrin, Meistersinger, Parsifal, Tannhäuser, Tristan und Isolde — LaserLight ▲ 15 521 [DDD]

A. Ligeti (cnd)
Bartók, B.:Con 1 Pno, w. Jenő Jandó (pno) *(rec Italian Institute, Budapest, Feb. 14–18, 1994)* — Naxos ▲ 8.550771 [DDD]
Bartók, B.:Con 2 Pno, w. Jenő Jandó (pno) *(rec Italian Institute, Budapest, Feb. 14–18, 1994)* — Naxos ▲ 8.550771 [DDD]
Bartók, B.:Con 3 Pno, w. Jenő Jandó (pno) *(rec Italian Institute, Budapest, Feb. 14–18, 1994)* — Naxos ▲ 8.550771 [DDD]
Grieg, E.:Con Pno, Op. 16, w. J. Jandó (pno) — Naxos ▲ 8.550118 [DDD]
Grieg, E.:Con Pno, Op. 16, w. Jenő Jandó (pno) *(rec Italian Institute, Budapest, Mar 1–6, 1988)* — Naxos ▲ 8.553267 [DDD]
Liszt, F.:Con 2 in A for Pno, Orch, S.125 (1839; rev 1849–61), w. Jenő Jando (pno) — Laserlight ♦ 90021 [DDD]
Liszt, F.:Fant on Hungarian Folk Tunes, w. J. Jandó (pno) — LaserLight ▲ 15631 [DDD]
Liszt, F.:Fant on Themes from Beethoven's *Ruins of Athens*, w. J. Jandó (pno) — LaserLight ▲ 14011 [DDD]
Liszt, F.:Grand fantaisie symphonique on Berlioz's *Lélio*, w. J. Jandó (pno) — LaserLight ▲ 14011 [DDD]
Liszt, F.:Malédiction, w. J. Jandó (pno) — LaserLight ▲ 14011 [DDD]
Liszt, F.:Polonaise brillante, w. J. Jandó (pno) — LaserLight ▲ 15631 [DDD]
Liszt, F.:Totentanz, w. J. Jando (pno) — LaserLight ▲ 15630 [DDD]
Liszt, F.:Wandererfantasie, w. J. Jando (pno) — LaserLight ▲ 15630 [DDD]
Mahler, G.:Das Klagende Lied, w. Katalin Szendrényi (sop), Klára Takács (cta), Dénes Gulyás (ten), Péter Erdei (cnd), Hungarian Radio–TV Chorus — Classical Diamonds ▲ CLD 4010 [DDD]
Mahler, G.:Sym 10—Adagio — Classical Diamonds ▲ CLD 4010 [DDD]
Schumann, R.:Con Pno, w. J. Jandó (pno) — Naxos ▲ 8.550118 [DDD]
Sugár, R.:Con in Memoriam *(rec Italian Cultural Institute, Budapest, Mar 19–23, 1991)* — Hungaroton ▲ HCD 31189 [DDD]
Sugár, R.:Epilógus *(rec Italian Cultural Institute, Budapest, Mar 19–23, 1991)* — Hungaroton ▲ HCD 31189 [DDD]
Sugár, R.:Sinf a variazione *(rec Italian Cultural Institute, Budapest, Mar 19–23, 1991)* — Hungaroton ▲ HCD 31189 [DDD]
Tchaikovsky , P.:Music of, w. Bavarian RSO [cnd:Hnas Vonk], Vienna SO [cnd:Yuri Ahronovitch] — Laserlight ♦ 90029 [DDD]

E. Lukács (cnd)
Mozart, W.A.:Con 20 Pno, w. Annie Fischer (pno) *(rec 1965)* — Hungaroton ▲ HCD 31492

▲ = CD ♦ = Enhanced CD Δ = MD ■ = Cassette Tape □ = DCC

Budapest SO (cont.)
E. Lukács (cnd) (cont.)
Mozart, W.A.:Con 21 Pno, w. Annie Fischer (pno) *(rec 1965)* Hungaroton ▲ HCD 31492
Mozart, W.A.:Rondo Pno, K.382, w. Annie Fischer (pno) *(rec 1965)* Hungaroton ▲ HCD 31492
M. Maros (cnd)
Maros, M.:Music of, w. Ilona Maros (sop), John-Edward Kelly (sax), J. Kangas (cnd), Ostrobothnian CO, Prague Radio SO, Marosensemble—Sym No. 1; 4 Songs [from Gitanjali]; Sinf concertante [Sym No. 3]; Con for A Sax & Orch Phono Suecia ▲ PHN 23 [DDD]
P. G. Morandi (cnd)
Mendelssohn, F.:Con in d Vn & Strs, w. J. Bálint (fl) Hungaroton ▲ HCD 31481 [DDD]
Mendelssohn, F.:Con in e Vn & Orch, Op. 64, w. J. Bálint (fl) Hungaroton ▲ HCD 31481 [DDD]
Paganini, N.:Con 2 Vn, w. J. Bálint (fl)—3rd movt. Hungaroton ▲ HCD 31481 [DDD]
G. Németh (cnd)
Chopin, F.:Con 1 Pno, w. István Székely (pno) *(rec Italian Institute, Budapest, Mar 29–Apr 1, 1988)* Naxos 4–▲ 8.504011 [DDD]
Chopin, F.:Con 1 Pno, w. I. Székely (pno) Naxos ▲ 8.550123 [DDD] ∆ 7.550123 [DDD]
Chopin, F.:Con 2 Pno, w. István Székely (pno) *(rec Italian Institute, Budapest, Mar 29–Apr 1, 1988)* Naxos 4–▲ 8.504011 [DDD]
Chopin, F.:Con 2 Pno, w. I. Székely (pno) Naxos ▲ 8.550123 [DDD] ∆ 7.550123 [DDD]
G. Oberfrank (cnd)
Lehár, F.:Giuditta (sels), w. Katalin Pitti (sop), Győző Leblanc (sgr), Hungarian Radio-TV Chorus [Hun] Hungaroton ▲ HCD 16809 [ADD]
Lehár, F.:Das Land des Lächelns (sels), w. Házy (sop), Magda Kalmár (sop), Szimándy (sgr), Bende (sgr), Hungarian Radio-TV Chorus [Hun] Hungaroton ▲ HCD 16809 [ADD]
Lehár, F.:Waltzes—"Gold and Silver" Waltz, Op. 79 Hungaroton ▲ HCD 16809 [ADD]
A. Polizzi (cnd)
Beethoven, L. van:Syms (comp), Prague SO *(rec 1986 & 1990–94)* Harmonia Mundi France 6–▲ HMX 2905225.30
Wagner, R.:Götterdämmerung (siegfried's funeral), Prague SO *(rec 1986 & 1990–94)* Harmonia Mundi France 6–▲ HMX 2905225.30
T. Pál (cnd)
Beethoven, L. van:Fidelio (ov) Capriccio ▲ 10 914 [DDD]
Beethoven, L. van:Leonore 2 Capriccio ▲ 10 914 [DDD]
Mozart, W.A.:Sym 35 *(rec Italian Institute, Budapest, Feb. 16–22, 1987)* Lydian ▲ 18059 [DDD]
Mozart, W.A.:Sym 36 *(rec Italian Institute, Budapest, Feb. 16–22, 1987)* Lydian ▲ 18059 [DDD]
L. Tihanyi (cnd)
Tihanyi, L.:Enodios Hungaroton ▲ HCD 31352
Tihanyi, L.:Krios Hungaroton ▲ HCD 31352
A. Walter (cnd)
Spohr, L.:Faust (ov) Marco Polo ▲ 8.223122 [DDD]
Spohr, L.:Jessonda (ov) Marco Polo ▲ 8.223122 [DDD]
Spohr, L.:Sym 4 Marco Polo ▲ 8.223122 [DDD]
Budapest SO Winds
J. Dobra (cnd)
Fauré, G.:Requiem, w. D. Karasszon (org), E. Maros (hp), Hungarian Virtuosi CO, Tomkins Vocal Ensemble Hungaroton ▲ HCD 31424 [DDD]
Budapest Wind Ensemble
Beethoven, L. van:Qnt Pno, Ob, Cl, Hn & Bn, w. Z. Kocsis (pno) Musique d'Abord ∆ HMA 1903020
Mozart, W.A.:Qnt Pno, K.452, w. Z. Kocsis (pno) Musique d'Abord ∆ HMA 1903020
Mozart, W.A.:Serenade Ww, K.375—sels. LaserLight ▲ 15 648 [DDD]
Mozart, W.A.:Serenade Ww, K.388—sels. LaserLight ▲ 15 648 [DDD]
K. Berkes (cnd)
Druschetzky, G.:Music of—Music for Wind Instrs; Partitas in B♭, E & C; Vars, Rondos & Marches Hungaroton ▲ HCD 31618
Z. Kocsis (cnd)
Mozart, W.A.:Serenade Ww, K.361 Musique d'Abord ▲ HMA 1903051
Mozart, W.A.:Serenade Ww, K.388 Musique d'Abord ▲ HMA 1903051
Buenos Aires Affetti Ensemble
G. Garrido (cnd)
Les Chemins du Baroque (The Paths of the Baroque), w. Elyma Vocal Ensemble, Elyma Instrumental Ensemble, Cordoba Children's Choir Garrado, Compañia Musical de las Americas, Maîtrise National de Versailles, La Grande Ecurie et la Chambre du Roy [cnd:Jean-Claude Malgoire], Compañia Musical de las Americas, La Fenice [cnd:Josep Cabré], et al. K617 ("First 4 volumes of K617" series) ▲ 7042
Les Chemins du Baroque [The Paths of the Baroque], Vol. 4:Domenico Zipoli's Vepres de San Ignaci, w. Cantores de Cordoba Children's Chorus K617 ▲ 7027 [DDD]
Zipoli, D.:Choral Music, w. Cristina Garcia Banegas (org), Ensemble Elyma, Cordoba Children's Chorus—Misa brevis; O gloriosa virgunum; Sacris solemnis; Tantum ergo; Letania I in c; Letania II in f; Ave maris stella; Zoipaqui; Deus in adjutorium; Dixit Dominus K617 ▲ 7036
Zipoli, D.:Vepres de San Ignacio, w. Cordoba Children's Chorus K617 ▲ 7027 [DDD]
Buenos Aires Orch
C. Franzetti (cnd)
Franzetti, C.:Aubade, w. Buenos Aires Teatro Colón Chorus *(rec Ion Studios, Buenos Aires, Argentina, 1985)* Premier ▲ PRCD 1044 [DDD]
Buenos Aires Quintet
E. Stratta (cnd)
The Symphonic Tango, w. Royal PO Strings Teldec ▲ 9031-76997-2 ■ 9031-76997-4
Buenos Aires Teatro Colón Orch
B. Bartoletti (cnd)
Rossini, G.:Il barbiere di Siviglia, w. T. Berganza (mez), R. Casellato (ten), S. Bruscantini (bar), G. Tozzi (bass), Buenos Aires Teatro Colón Chorus [I] *(rec 1969)* Golden Age of Opera 2–▲ GAO 149/50
R. Bonynge (cnd)
Bellini, V.:Norma, w. J. Sutherland (sop), F. Cossotto (mez), C. Craig (ten), I. Vinco (bass), Buenos Aires Teatro Colón Chorus *(rec live 7/2/69)* Ediciones Teatro Colon 3–▲ ETC 101 [AAD]
F. Busch (cnd)
Wagner, R.:Der fliegende Holländer, w. M. Lawrence (sop), F. Destal (bar), A. Kipnis (bass), Buenos Aires Teatro Colón Chorus [G] *(rec live broadcast 9/19/36)* Pearl 2–▲ PEAS 9910 (m) [ADD]
E. Kleiber (cnd)
Wagner, R.:Götterdämmerung (immolation scene), w. K. Flagstad (sop) [G] *(rec live broadcast, Sept. 1948)* Pearl 2–▲ PEAS 9910 (m) [ADD]
Wagner, R.:Tristan und Isolde (sels), w. K. Flagstad (sop), V. Ursuleac (sop), S. Svanholm (ten), H. Hotter (b-bar), Buenos Aires Teatro Colón Chorus—highlights from Acts 1–3 [G] *(rec live, 1948)* Melodram 2–▲ MEL 25007 (m) [AAD]
P. Maag (cnd)
Offenbach, J.:Les Contes d'Hoffmann, w. H. Harper (sop), Bakocevic (sgr), M. Mesplé (sop), S. Kónya (ten), G. Bacquier (bar), Buenos Aires Teatro Colón Chorus [F] *(rec live, Buenos Aires 8/3/70)* Melodram 2–▲ MEL 27090 [ADD]
J.E. Martini (cnd)
Donizetti, G.:Lucia di Lammermoor, w. B. Sills (sop), A. Kraus (ten), G. Mastromei (bar), V. de Narke (bass), Buenos Aires Teatro Colón Chorus *(rec 1968)* Arkadia 2–▲ 474
F. Previtali (cnd)
Verdi, G.:Rigoletto, w. Renata Scotto (sop—Gilda), Stella Maris Silva (sop—Giovanna), Martha Carrizo (mez—Page), Carmen de la Mata (mez—Countess Ceprano), Noemi Souza (cta—Maddalena), Horacio Mastrango (ten—Borso), Richard Tucker (ten—Duke of Mantua), Cornell MacNeil (bar—Rigoletto), Riccardo Yost (bar—Marullo), Guerrino Boschetti (bass—Usher), Tulio Gagliardo (bass—Count Ceprano), Victor de Narké (bass—Monterone), William Wilderman (bass—Sparafucile), Buenos Aires Teatro Colón Chorus *(rec Colon Theater, Buenos Aires, Aug. 22, 1967)* Legato Classics 2–▲ LCD 198–2
Buffalo Guitar Quartet
Chobanian, L.:Sonics New World ▲ NW 384–2 [DDD]
Hartley, W.S.:Qt Gtrs New World ▲ NW 384–2 [DDD]
Ortiz-Alvarado, W.:Abrazo New World ▲ NW 384–2 [DDD]

Buffalo Guitar Quartet (cont.)
Pearson, S.F.:Mummychogs New World ▲ NW 384–2 [DDD]
Piorkowski, J.:The Struggle of Jacob New World ▲ NW 384–2 [DDD]
Buffalo New York State Univ Center of the Creative & Performing Arts members
T. Riley (cnd)
Riley, T.:In C CBS ▲ MK 07178 [ADD]
Buffalo Opera Sacra Orch
C. Peltz (cnd)
Honegger, A.:Christophe Colomb, w. E. Knecht (speaker—Queen Isabella), S. Rawson (speaker—The Magician), N. Garvey (speaker—Christopher Columbus), A. Furnival (speaker—King Ferdinand), D. McCabe (bar), Buffalo Opera Sacra Chorus [E] *(rec Buffalo, New York, Oct. 30–31, 1992)* Mode ▲ MOD 35 [DDD]
Buffalo PO
M. Tilson Thomas (cnd)
Gershwin, G.:Ovs [arr. Don Rose]—Oh, Kay!; Funny Face; Girl Crazy; Strike Up The Band; Of Thee I Sing; Let 'Em Eat Cake CBS ▲ MK 42240 [ADD]
Bugaku Percussion Ensemble [Haruo Suzuki (perc), Yasuo Yamamura (perc), Norifumi Shimazu (perc), Aya Motohashi (perc)]
Peebles, S.:Phoenix Calling, w. Ikuo Kakehashi (shô), Sarah Peebles (shô), Andy Morris (perc) *(rec live, Shukōji Temple, Kawasaki)* Innova ▲ 506
Bulgarian National PO
V. Kazandjiev (cnd)
Pergolesi, G.B.:Stabat mater, w. T. Genova (sop), Bozhkova (sgr), Bulgarian Phil Chorus [L] Vivace 2–▲ 140141 [ADD/DDD]
Bulgarian National RSO
Shostakovich, D.:Con 1 Vn, w. N. Gotkovsky (vn) Pyramid ▲ PYR 13493
Shostakovich, D.:Con 2 Vn, w. N. Gotkovsky (vn) Pyramid ▲ PYR 13493
Bulgarian National SO
L. Denev (cnd)
The Other Portrait, w. Ken Peplowski (cl), Ken Peplowski (t sax), Ken Peplowski Jazz Quartet [Ken Peplowski (cl), Ben Aronov (pno), Greg Cohen (db), Chuck Redd (dr)] Concord Concerto ▲ CCD 42043 [DDD]
Bulgarian RSO
Gounod, C.:Faust (sels), w. Alexandrina Pendachanska (sop—Margarethe), Giuseppe Sabbatini (ten—Faust), György Melis (bar—Valentin), Nicolai Ghiaurov (bass—Méphistophélès), Nikola Ghiuselev (bass—Méphistophélès), Berlin RSO, Vienna SO, Hungarian State Opera Orch, Sofia SO, Bulgarian National Chorus, Bulgarian National Chorus Radio Choir—Intro; Vien ou bière; O sainte médaille...Avant de quitter ces lieux; Le veau d'or [all from Act 2]; Quel trouble inconnu me pénètre!...Salut! demeure chaste et pure; Je voudrais bien savoir...Il était un roi de Thule; Un bouquet!...O Dieu! que de bijoux [both from Act 3]; Gloire immortelle de nos aieux; Vous qui faites l'endormie [both from Act 4]; Intermezzo; Walpurgis Night [both from Act 5] Laserlight ▲ 14209 [DDD]
S. Angelov (cnd)
Rimsky-Korsakov, N.:Snow Maiden, w. Stefka Evstatieva (sop—Kupava), Elena Zemenkova (sop—Snow Maiden), Alexandrina Milcheva (mez—Spring Fairy), Vessela Zorova (mez—wife), Stefka Mineva (alt—Lehl), Avram Andreev (ten—Tsar), Lyubomir Dyakovski (ten—Cottager, Sprite), Lyubomir Videnov (bar—Misgir), Nicola Ghiuselev (bass—King), Bulgarian National Chorus *(rec Sofia, 1985)* Capriccio 3–▲ 10749–51 [DDD]
E. Gracis (cnd)
Beethoven, L. van:Fidelio (sels), w. Boris Christoff (bass), Bulgarian National Chorus—Aria of Piazarro Forlane ▲ FRL 16651 [AAD]
Gluck, C.W.:Iphigénie en Aulide (sels), w. Boris Christoff (bass), Bulgarian National Chorus—Récitatif & Aria of Agamemnon Forlane ▲ FRL 16651 [AAD]
Monteverdi, C.:Arias & Duets, w. Boris Christoff (bass), Bulgarian National Chorus—Aria of Seneca [from The Coronation of Poppee] Forlane ▲ FRL 16651 [AAD]
Mozart, W.A.:Arias, w. Boris Christoff (bass), Bulgarian National Chorus—Cosi dunque tradisci Forlane ▲ FRL 16651 [AAD]
Rameau, J.P.:Dardanus (sels), w. Boris Christoff (bass), Bulgarian National Chorus—Aria of Antenor Forlane ▲ FRL 16651 [AAD]
Recital, w. Boris Christoff (bass), Bulgarian Radio Sym Chorus Forlane ▲ FOR 16651 [AAD]
Verdi, G.:Macbeth (sels), w. Boris Christoff (bass), Bulgarian National Chorus—Récitative & Aria of Banco Forlane ▲ FRL 16651 [AAD]
V. Kazandjiev (cnd)
Brahms, J.:Con 1 Pno, w. I. Drenikov (pno) Pierre Verany ▲ PV.791012 [DDD]
Macdowell, E.:Con 1 Pno, w. T. Tirino (pno) Centaur ▲ CRC 2149 [DDD]
Macdowell, E.:Con 2 Pno, w. T. Tirino (pno) Centaur ▲ CRC 2149 [DDD]
I. Marinov (cnd)
Glazunov, A.:Con Vn, w. Angèle Dubeau (vn) Analekta ▲ AN 28707
Glazunov, A.:The Seasons Analekta ▲ AN 28707
Glazunov, A.:The Seasons, w. A. Dubeau (vn) Analekta Fleur de Lys ▲ FL 2 3045
Sibelius, J.:Con Vn, w. Angèle Dubeau (vn) Analekta ▲ AN 28705 [DDD]
Sibelius, J.:Con Vn, w. Angèle Dubeau (vn) Analekta ("Fleur de Lys" series) ▲ FL 23045
Sibelius, J.:Finlandia Analekta ▲ AN 28705 [DDD]
Sibelius, J.:The Swan of Tuonela Analekta ▲ AN 28705 [DDD]
Sibelius, J.:Valse triste Analekta ▲ AN 28705 [DDD]
I. Stefanov (cnd)
Mozart, W.A.:Cosi fan tutte (sels), w. Anna Tomowa-Sintow (sop)—Come scoglio; Un'aura amorosa LaserLight ▲ 15 890 [DDD]
Bulgarian Radio-TV SO
M. Milkov (cnd)
Orff, C.:Catulli Carmina, w. E. Stoyanova (sop), K. Kaludov (ten), Bulgarian Radio-TV Chorus [L] *(rec live in Sofia, 1988)* Forlane ▲ FOR 16610 [DDD]
Bulgarian State PO
S. Vassilov (cnd)
Beethoven, L. van:Con Vn, Op. 61, w. R. Ricci (vn) One-Eleven ▲ URS 91050 [ADD]
Bulgarian String Quartet
Schubert, Franz:Qnt Strs, D.956, w. R. Pidoux (vc) Musique d'Abord ▲ HMA 190980
Bulgarian SO
S. Cipriani (cnd)
Cinema & Musica:L'Immagine Italia CAM ▲ CVS 019
V. Kazandjiev (cnd)
Stoyanov, V.:Con 1 Pno, w. B. Nedeltchev (pno) Gega ▲ GD 107 [DDD]
Vladigerov, P.:Con 3 Pno, w. B. Nedeltchev (pno) Gega ▲ GD 107 [DDD]
Adolf Busch Chamber Players [E. Rothwell (ob), A. Brain (hn), M. Moyse (fl), R. Serkin (pno)]
A. Busch (cnd)
Bach, J.S.:Brandenburg Cons, w. A. Busch (vn) *(rec mid 1930s)* EMI Classics (Great Recordings of the Century) 3–▲ ZDHC 64047–2
Bach, J.S.:Suites Orch, BWV 1066–1069, w. A. Busch (vn) *(rec mid 1930s)* EMI Classics ("Great Recordings of the Century" series) 3–▲ CDHC 64047–2
Busch String Quartet
Great Violinists, Vol. 5 Symposium ▲ SYM 1109
Busch String Quartet [A. Busch (vn), G. Andreasson (vn), K. Doktor (va), H. Busch (vc)]
Beethoven, L. van:Qt 7 Strs *(rec 1942)* Sony Masterworks ("Portrait" series) ▲ MPK 47687 [ADD]
Beethoven, L. van:Qt 9 Strs *(rec between 1932–37)* Preiser 6–▲ PRE 90172 [AAD]
Beethoven, L. van:Qt 11 Strs, "Quartetto serioso" *(rec between 1932–37)* Preiser 6–▲ PRE 90172 [AAD]
Beethoven, L. van:Qt 13 Strs *(rec 1941)* Sony Masterworks ("Portrait" series) ▲ MPK 47687 [ADD]
Beethoven, L. van:Qt 14 Strs *(rec between 1932–37)* Preiser 6–▲ PRE 90172 [AAD]
Beethoven, L. van:Qt 15 Strs *(rec between 1932–37)* Preiser 6–▲ PRE 90172 [AAD]
Brahms, J.:Qt 2 Pno, w. R. Serkin (pno), A. Busch (vn) *(rec 1938)* EMI Classics ▲ CDH 64702

Busch String Quartet (cont.)
Brahms, J.:Qt 1 Strs, w. R. Kell (cl) EMI Classics ▲ CDH 64932
Brahms, J.:Qnt Cl, w. R. Kell (cl) EMI Classics ▲ CDH 64932
Brahms, J.:Qnt Pno, w. R. Serkin (pno), A. Busch (vn) *(rec 1938)* EMI Classics ▲ CDH 64702
Schubert, Franz:Qt 8 Strs *(rec 1931–38)* Pearl 2–▲ PEA 9141 [ADD]
Schubert, Franz:Qt 14 Strs *(rec mid-1930s)* EMI Classics ("Great Recordings of the Century" series) ▲ CDH 69795 (m) [ADD]
Schubert, Franz:Qt 14 Strs *(rec 1931–38)* Pearl 2–▲ PEA 9141 [ADD]
Schubert, Franz:Qt 15 Strs *(rec late 1930s)* EMI Classics ("Great Recordings of the Century" series) ▲ CDH 69795 (m) [ADD]
Schubert, Franz:Qt 15 Strs *(rec 1931–38)* Pearl 2–▲ PEA 9141 [ADD]

Busch String Quartet members
Brahms, J.:Qt 2 Pno, w. A. Rubinstein (pno) *(rec 1932)* Biddulph ▲ LAB 027 [ADD]
Schubert, Franz:Trio 2 Pno, w. Rudolf Serkin (pno) *(rec 1931–38)* Pearl 2–▲ PEA 9141 [ADD]

Busoni String Quartet [Kolbjørn Holthe (vn), Eilev Skinnarmo (vn), Jennifer Harris Cassin (va), Dan Cassin (vc)]
Busoni, F.:Qt 1 Strs *(rec LSU Recital Hall, Louisiana State University, Baton Rouge, LA, Apr 15–16, 1995)* Centaur ▲ 2268 [DDD]
Busoni, F.:Qt 2 Strs *(rec LSU Recital Hall, Louisiana State University, Baton Rouge, LA, Apr 15–16, 1995)* Centaur ▲ 2268 [DDD]

Byelorussian Radio-TV SO
W. Mnatsakanov (cnd)
Shostakovich, D.:Alone, w. Igor Matukhov (cnd), Minsk Chamber Choir—sels *(rec Byelorussian Radio Committe Studio, Minsk, Nov 1995)* Russian Disc ▲ RDCD 10007 [DDD]
Shostakovich, D.:The Young Guard [arr Levon Avtomyan, 1954] *(rec Byelorussian Radio Committe Studio, Minsk, Feb 1995)* Russian Compact Disc ▲ RDCD 10002 [DDD]
Shostakovich, D.:Zoya, w. Minsk Chamber Choir *(rec Byelorussian Radio Committe Studio, Minsk, Feb 1995)* Russian Compact Disc ▲ RDCD 10002 [DDD]

William Byrd Ensemble
Gibbons, O.:Instrumental & Vocal Music, w. Andrew Lawrence King (org/hp), Graham O'Reilly (cnd), The Occasional Byrd—The Eyes of All Wait upon Three; Do Not Repine, Fair Sun; Trust Not Too Much, Fair Youth; Blessed Are All They That Fear the Lord; O God, the King of Glory; In Nomine; The Cries of London; The Lord of Salisbury His Pavin; Sing unto the Lor, O Ye Saints of His; If Ye Be Risen Again with Christ; See, See, the Word is Incarnate; What is Our Life? Adda ▲ ADD 581169 [DDD]
Palestrina, G.:The Song of Songs Jade ▲ 28337-2

Charlie Byrd Trio
Christmas with Byrd & Brass, w. Annapolis Brass Quintet Antigua ▲ DG 91-6

Cabaza Percussion Quartet
Brodmann, H.-G.:Greetings to Hermann CPO ▲ CPO 999088-2 [AAD]
Cage, J.:Second Construction CPO ▲ CPO 999344
Heider, W.:Gallery CPO ▲ CPO 999088-2 [AAD]
Heider, W.:Gong Game CPO ▲ CPO 999344
Hummel, B.:Frescoes '70 CPO ▲ CPO 999088-2 [AAD]
Ohana, M.:Etudes Chorégraphiques CPO ▲ CPO 999088-2 [AAD]
Reich, S.:Music for Pieces of Wood CPO ▲ CPO 999088-2 [AAD]
Schmidt, R.:B-A-C-H Perc Qt CPO ▲ CPO 999344

Cabrillo Festival Orch
D.R. Davies (cnd)
Harrison, L.:Sym 3 *(rec Cabrillo Music Festival, Santa Cruz, CA, 1982)* MusicMasters ▲ 7073-2-C [DDD]
J. Falletta (cnd)
Adams, J.L.:The Far Country of Sleep *(rec July 1991)* New Albion ▲ NA 061

Caecilia Consort
E. Spanjaard (cnd)
Andriessen, L.:Sym Open Strs Attacca ▲ Babel 9267-6 [DDD]

Caen Orch
Rameau, J.P.:Concerts transcrits en sextuor, w. Mireille Lagace (hpd) Approche ▲ 6838
C. Bardon (cnd)
Constant, M.:Cent-trois regards dans l'eau, w. R. Milosi (vn) *(rec Feb. 25–27, 1994)* Chamade ▲ 5606 [DDD]
Tanguy, É.:Con Fl, w. P.-Y. Artaud (fl) *(rec Feb. 25–27, 1994)* Chamade ▲ 5606 [DDD]
Tanguy, É.:Con Vn, w. R. Milosi (vn) *(rec Feb. 25–27, 1994)* Chamade ▲ 5606 [DDD]

Calefax Reed Ensemble
Brumel, A.:Motets—Languiente miseris; Nato canunt omnia [arr. R. Hekkema] *(rec June 16–19, 1992)* Canal Grande ▲ CG 9321 [DDD]
Debussy, C.:Children's Corner MD + G ▲ MDG 6190658
Debussy, C.:Épigraphes antiques [arr chamber ensemble] MD + G ▲ MDG 6190658
Doest, T. ter:Circusmuziek *(rec June 16–19, 1992)* Canal Grande ▲ CG 9321 [DDD]
Ockeghem, J.:Missa "Fors seulement" [arr. Lucas van Helsdingen]—Kyrie; Gloria; Credo *(rec June 16–19, 1992)* Canal Grande ▲ CG 9321 [DDD]
Ravel, M.:Le Tombeau de Couperin MD + G ▲ MDG 6190658
Shostakovich, D.:Preludes & Fugues Pno [arr. Eduard Wesly]—Nos. 1, 4, 7 & 8 *(rec June 16–19, 1992)* Canal Grande ▲ CG 9321 [DDD]

Calgary PO
M. Bernardi (cnd)
Bartók, B.:Con 3 Pno, w. J. Coop (pno) CBC ("SM 5000" series) ▲ SMCD 5124 [DDD]
Coulthard, J.:Music to St. Cecilia, w. P. Wedd (org) CBC ("SM 5000" series) ▲ SMCD 5113 [DDD]
Elgar, E.:Con Vc, w. Shauna Rolston (vc) *(rec Calgary Centre for the Performing Arts, Mar 15–16, 1994)* CBC ("SM 5000" series) ▲ SM5 5153 [DDD]
Forsyth, M.:Con Pno, w. J. Coop (pno) CBC ("SM 5000" series) ▲ SMCD 5124 [DDD]
Glazunov, A.:Chant du ménéstrel, w. Shauna Rolston (vc) *(rec Calgary Centre for the Performing Arts, Mar 15–16, 1994)* CBC ("SM 5000" series) ▲ SM5 5153 [DDD]
Glitter & Be Gay, w. Tracy Dahl (coloratura sop) *(rec May 14–16, 1992)* CBC Records ("SM 5000" series) ▲ SMCD 5125 [DDD]
Jongen, J.:Symphonie Concertante, w. P. Wedd (org) CBC ("SM 5000" series) ▲ SMCD 5113 [DDD]
Mendelssohn, F.:Die Hebriden *(rec Calgary Centre for the Performing Arts, Calgary, Feb. 17–18, 1992)* CBC ("SM 5000" series) ▲ SM5 5144 [DDD]
Mendelssohn, F.:Sym 1 *(rec Calgary Centre for the Performing Arts, Calgary, Feb. 17–18, 1992)* CBC ("SM 5000" series) ▲ SM5 5144 [DDD]
Mendelssohn, F.:Sym 5 *(rec Calgary Centre for the Performing Arts, Calgary, Feb. 17–18, 1992)* CBC ("SM 5000" series) ▲ SM5 5144 [DDD]
Mozart, W.A.:Ovs—Le nozze di Figaro, K.492; Così fan tutte, K.588; Don Giovanni, K.527; Die Entführung aus dem Serail, K.384; Mitridate, rè di Ponto, K.74; La clemenza di Tito, K.621; Idomeneo, rè di Creta, K.366; Der Schauspieldirektor, K.486; Die Zauberflöte, K.620; La finta semplice, K.46a; Bastien und Bastienne, K.46b; Lucio Silla, K.135 *(rec Jack Singer Hall, Calgary Centre for the Performing Arts)* CBC ("SM 5000" series) ▲ SM5 5149 [DDD]
Opera Arias, w. Allan Monk (bar) CBC Records ("SM 5000" series) ▲ SMCD 5102 [DDD] ■ SMC 5102 (D)
Popper, D.:Hungarian Rhap, w. Shauna Rolston (vc) *(rec Calgary Centre for the Performing Arts, Mar 15–16, 1994)* CBC ("SM 5000" series) ▲ SM5 5153 [DDD]
Poulenc, F.:Con Org, w. P. Wedd (org) CBC ("SM 5000" series) ▲ SMCD 5113 [DDD]
Prokofiev, S.:Con 1 Pno, w. J. Coop (pno) CBC ("SM 5000" series) ▲ SMCD 5124 [DDD]
Saint-Saëns, C.:Con 1 Vc, w. Shauna Rolston (vc) *(rec Calgary Centre for the Performing Arts, Mar 15–16, 1994)* CBC ("SM 5000" series) ▲ SM5 5153 [DDD]
Schuller, G.:Con Org, w. James Diaz (org) *(rec live, Jack Singer Concert Hall, Calgary, Alberta, Oct. 14, 1994)* New World ▲ 80492-2
Schumann, R.:Konzertstück Hns CBC ("SM 5000" series) ▲ SMCD 5092 [DDD] ■ SMC 5092 (D)
Schumann, R.:Ov, Scherzo & Finale CBC ("SM 5000" series) ▲ SMCD 5067 [DDD]
Schumann, R.:Sym 1 CBC ("SM 5000" series) ▲ SMCD 5082 [DDD] ■ SMC 5082 (D)

Calgary PO (cont.)
M. Bernardi (cnd) (cont.)
Schumann, R.:Sym 2 CBC ("SM 5000" series) ▲ SMCD 5067 [DDD]
Schumann, R.:Sym 4 CBC ("SM 5000" series) ▲ SMCD 5082 [DDD] ■ SMC 5082 (D)
Song to the Moon, w. Joanne Kolomyjec (sop) *(rec Centre for Performing Arts, Calgary, AB, May 2–4, 1993)* CBC Records ("SM 5000" series) ▲ SMCD 5138 [DDD]
Tchaikovsky, P.:Andante cantabile, w. Shauna Rolston (vc) *(rec Calgary Centre for the Performing Arts, Mar 15–16, 1994)* CBC ("SM 5000" series) ▲ SM5 5153 [DDD]

California Bach Society CO
E. Flath (cnd)
Bach, J.S.:Cant 118, w. E. Flath (org), California Bach Society Chorus, Valley Choral Society [G] Bainbridge ▲ BCD 2502 [DDD]
Kobialka, D.:Antiphony Across..., w. E. Flath (org), California Bach Society Chorus, Valley Choral Society Bainbridge ▲ BCD 2502 [DDD]

California EAR Unit
A. Jarvinen (cnd)
Jarvinen, A.:Music of—Vulture's Garden; Edible Black Ink; Murphy-Nights; Count Your Change; Clean Your Gun; Paces of Yu; Eye in the Wall of Meat; Queen of Spain *(rec 1990–96)* O.O. Discs ▲ OO 28 [DDD]
R. Steiger (cnd)
Subotnick, M.:The Key to Songs, w. Rand Steiger (cmpt) New Albion ▲ NA 012
Subotnick, M.:Return, w. Rand Steiger (cmpt) New Albion ▲ NA 012

California EAR Unit [Dorothy Stone (fl), Erika Duke-Kirkpatrick (vc), Amy Knoles (perc)]
Kim, B.-K.:Epitaph Cambria ▲ CD 1046

California EAR Unit [Dorothy Stone (fl), James Rohrig (cl), Amy Knoles (perc), Arthur Jarvinen (perc), Lorna Eder (pno), Robin Lorentz (vn), Erika Duke-Kirkpatrick (vc)]
R. Steiger (cnd)
Baley, V.:Dreamtime *(rec Trompe l'oreille, Fullerton, CA, Sept 18–19 & Oct 14–15, 1)* Cambria ▲ CD 1090

Calliope
Schickele, P.:Bestiary:A Music Theater Piece, w. P. Schickele (nar) Vanguard Classics ▲ OVC 4066

Calliope [Lucy Bardo, Lawrence Benz, Allan Dean, Ben Harms, Frederic Hand]
Calliope Dances:A Renaissance Revel Elektra/Nonesuch ▲ 79039-2 [DDD] ■ 79039-4 (D)
Calliope:Diversions Summit ▲ DCD 112 [DDD]
Calliope Festival:An Italian Renaissance Revel Elektra/Nonesuch ■ 79069-4 (D)

Bernard Calmel Orch
Daniel-Lesur, D.J.Y.:Orchestral Music—Symphonie de danses; Nocturne; Vars. for Piano & Strings; Stele a la memoir d'un jeune fille; Serenade Pavane ▲ ADW 7302
B. Calmel (cnd)
Kaufmann, S.:Cantabile, w. Philippe Pennanguer (vc) *(rec Feb 1996)* Pavane ▲ ADW 7362 [DDD]
Kaufmann, S.:Elégie *(rec Feb 1996)* Pavane ▲ ADW 7362 [DDD]
Kaufmann, S.:Et si un jour, w. Béatrice Barbary (sop), Marielle Rousseau Vocal Ensemble *(rec Feb 1996)* Pavane ▲ ADW 7362 [DDD]
Kaufmann, S.:Un Matin à varsovie, w. Béatrice Barbary (sop), Philippe Pennanguer (vc), Serge Kaufmann (nar) *(rec Feb 1996)* Pavane ▲ ADW 7362 [DDD]
Kaufmann, S.:Le Temps déchiré, w. Anna Holroyd (mez) *(rec Feb 1996)* Pavane ▲ ADW 7362 [DDD]

Cambridge Baroque Camerata
J.H. Jones (cnd)
Benda, F.:Con in G Fl & Strs, w. N. McLaren (fl) [period instrs] Amon Ra ▲ CD-SAR 52 [DDD]
Naudot, J.-C.:Cons Fl, w. N. McLaren (fl)—No. 1 [period instrs] Amon Ra ▲ CD-SAR 52 [DDD]
Quantz, J.J.:Con in e Fl & Strs, w. N. McLaren (fl) [period instrs] Amon Ra ▲ CD-SAR 52 [DDD]
Tartini, G.:Con in G Fl, w. N. McLaren (fl) [period instrs] Amon Ra ▲ CD-SAR 52 [DDD]

Cambridge Classical Players
S. Cleobury (cnd)
Mozart, W.A.:Ave verum corpus, w. King's College Choir, Hilliard Ensemble [L] EMI Classics ▲ CDC 49672 [DDD]
Mozart, W.A.:Vesperae de Dominica, w. L. Dawson (sop), E. James (mez), R. Covey-Crump (ten), P. Hillier (bass), Hilliard Ensemble, King's College Choir [L] EMI Classics ▲ CDC 49672 [DDD]
Mozart, W.A.:Vesperae solennes, w. L. Dawson (sop), E. James (mez), R. Covey-Crump (ten), P. Hillier (bass), Hilliard Ensemble, King's College Choir [L] EMI Classics ▲ CDC 49672 [DDD]

Cambridge Instrumental Ensemble
I. Moore (cnd)
Rütti, C.:Verena, die Quelle, w. Silja Walter (nar), Cambridge Voices Herald 2–▲ HAVPCD 186 [DDD]

Cambridge Musick [Robert Ehrlich (rcr), Andrew Manze (vn), Mark Levy (vl), Richard Egarr (hpd)]
Handel, G.F.:Sons Rcr—HWV 360, 362, 365, 367, 369, 377 *(rec Utrecht, Aug 1995)* Globe 2–▲ GLO 6032 [DDD]
Handel, G.F.:Son Va *(rec Utrecht, Aug 1995)* Globe 2–▲ GLO 6032 [DDD]
Handel, G.F.:Sons Vn—in d, HWV 359a; in A, HWV 361; in D, HWV 371; Violin movement in a, HWV 408; Violin movement (Allegro) in c, HWV 412 *(rec Utrecht, Aug 1995)* Globe 2–▲ GLO 6032 [DDD]
Handel, G.F.:Trio Sons—Op 2/1&4 *(rec Utrecht, Aug 1995)* Globe 2–▲ GLO 6032 [DDD]

Cambridge SO
E. Rachlin (cnd)
Tchaikovsky, P.:Sérénade mélancolique, w. C. Glenn (vn) Vox Box 3–▲ CD3X 3026 [ADD]
Tchaikovsky, P.:Souvenir d'un lieu cher, w. C. Glenn (vn) [orch. Glazunov] Vox Box 3–▲ CD3X 3026 [ADD]
Tchaikovsky, P.:Valse-Scherzo Vn, w. C. Glenn (vn) Vox Box 3–▲ CD3X 3026 [ADD]

Camera Concerto
R. Gini (cnd)
Vivaldi, A.:Cants, w. C. Calvi (cta)—2 Cantatas—"Amor hai vinto," R.683; "Cessate, omai cessate," RV.684 [I] Nuova Era ("Ancient Music" series) ▲ 6877 [DDD]
Vivaldi, A.:Stabat Mater Cta, w. C. Calvi (cta) [L] Nuova Era ("Ancient Music" series) ▲ 6877 [DDD]

La Camerata
E. Mata (cnd)
Chávez, C.:Energia *(rec Sala Nezahualcóyotl, Mexican National Independent Univ., Oct. 1994)* Dorian ▲ DOR 90215 [DDD]
Chávez, C.:La hija de Cólquide Ww *(rec Sala Nezahualcóyotl, Mexican National Independent Univ., Oct. 1994)* Dorian ▲ DOR 90215 [DDD]

La Camerata
Barber, S.:Prayers of Kierkegaard, w. S. Skov (pno), J. Koch (pno), C. Bjørkøe (pno), Safri Duo Danica ▲ DCD 8154
Britten, B.:Flower Songs, w. S. Skov (sop), J. Koch (pno), C. Bjørkøe (pno), Safri Duo Danica ▲ DCD 8154
Nørholm, I.:Songs, w. S. Skov (sop), J. Koch (pno), C. Bjørkøe (pno), Safri Duo—Song at Sunset Danica ▲ DCD 8154
M. Bojesen (cnd)
Grainger, P.:Songs, w. S. Skov (sop), J. Koch (pno), C. Bjørkøe (pno), Safri Duo—No Nighean Dhu; O Mistress Mine; 6 Dukes Went a-Fishing; Mary Thompson; Old Irish Tune Danica ▲ DCD 8154

Camerata Academica
S. Végh (cnd)
Mozart, W.A.:Con 24 Pno, w. A. Schiff (pno) London ▲ 425791-2 [DDD]
Mozart, W.A.:Con 25 Pno, w. A. Schiff (pno) London ▲ 425791-2 [DDD]

Camerata Academica Novi Sad
Despic, D.:Meditations (3), w. Ksenija Jankovic (vc) Emergo ▲ EC 3950 [DDD]
Detoni, D.:Forgotten Music Emergo ▲ EC 3950 [DDD]
Maric, L.:Ostinato super thema octoicha, w. Gordana Marjanovic (pno), Inge Frimout-hei (hp) Emergo ▲ EC 3951 [DDD]
Slavenski, J.:Slavenska son, w. Maja Jokanovic (vn), Gordana Marjanovic (pno) Emergo ▲ EC 3950 [DDD]

Camerata Academica Novi Sad (cont.)
Tickmayer, S.K.:Music of Forgotten Times, w. Borislav Čičvački (ob) Emergo ▲ EC 3950 [DDD]

Camerata Atlas
D. Atlas (cnd)
Arensky, A.:Vars on a Theme of Tchaikovsky IMP Classics ▲ IMP PCD 1083 [DDD]
Suk, J.:Serenade Strs IMP Classics ▲ IMP PCD 1083 [DDD]
Tchaikovsky, P.:Serenade Strs IMP Classics ▲ IMP PCD 1083 [DDD]

Camerata Bariloche
Sammartini, G.:Giuseppe St. Martini's Cons Hpd, w. M. Cosachov (hpd), No. 1 in A FSM–Adagio ▲ FCD 91118 [DDD]
Zorzi, J.C.:Adagio elegíaco *(rec Troy Savings Bank Music Hall, Troy, NY, Feb. 1994)* Dorian ▲ DOR 90202 [DDD]

Camerata Bariloche CO
Arizaga, R.:Passacaglia *(rec Troy, NY, Jan 1994)* Dorian ▲ DOR 90201
Bragato, J.:Graciala y Buenos Aires, w. *(soloist unknown) (rec Troy, NY, Jan. 1994)* Dorian ▲ DOR 90201
Gianneo, L.:Piezas criollas (3)—No. 1 [Lamento quichua] *(rec Troy Savings Bank Music Hall, Troy, NY, Feb. 1994)* Dorian ▲ DOR 90202 [DDD]
Ginastera, A.:Impresiones de la Puna, w. Claudio Barile (fl) *(rec Troy Savings Bank Music Hall, Troy, NY, Feb. 1994)* Dorian ▲ DOR 90202 [DDD]
Guastavino, C.:Cantilenas Argentinas (3) y Final *(rec Troy Savings Bank Music Hall, Troy, NY, Feb. 1994)* Dorian ▲ DOR 90202 [DDD]
Guastavino, C.:Jeromita Linares, w. Pablo Cohen (gtr) *(rec Troy Savings Bank Music Hall, Troy, NY, Feb. 1994)* Dorian ▲ DOR 90202 [DDD]
Piazzolla, A.:Suite Ob *(rec Troy, NY, Jan. 1994)* Dorian ▲ DOR 90201
Piazzolla, A.:Suite punta del este *(rec Troy, NY, Jan. 1994)* Dorian ▲ DOR 90201
Piazzolla, A.:Tangos Str Orch *(rec Troy, NY, Jan. 1994)* Dorian ▲ DOR 90201
Sammartini, G.B.:Con Hpd, w. M. Cosachov (hpd) FSM–Adagio ▲ FCD 91118 [DDD]

Camerata Cassovia
P. Breiner (cnd)
Bach, J.S.:Con 1 Hpd, w. G. Garcia (gtr) [arr. Garcia from Con. 1 for Harpsichord, BWV 1052], June 6–8, 1990) Naxos ▲ 8.550274 [DDD]
Vivaldi, A.:Cons Gtr, w. G. Garcia (gtr) [all arr. Garcia]—in D, RV.93; in e, RV.277; in C, RV.425; in d, RV.540 (w. Karol Petroczi [viol]) Naxos ▲ 8.550274 [DDD]
R. Stankovsky (cnd)
Haydn, J.:Con Hpd & Strs, H.XVIII/4, w. Hae.–won Chang (pno) *(rec Sept. 7–12, 1992)* Naxos ▲ 8.550713 [DDD]
Haydn, J.:Con Hpd, Vns & Bass Instrument, H.XVIII/9, w. Hae–won Chang (pno) *(rec Sept. 7–12, 1992)* Naxos ▲ 8.550713 [DDD]
Haydn, J.:Con Hpd, Obs, Hns & Strs, H.XVIII/11, w. Hae–won Chang (pno) *(rec Sept. 7–12, 1992)* Naxos ▲ 8.550713 [DDD]
Haydn, J.:Con Org, Vns & Bass Instrument, H.XVIII/7, w. Hae–won Chang (pno) *(rec Sept. 7–12, 1992)* Naxos ▲ 8.550713 [DDD]
J. Wildner (cnd)
Giuliani, M.:Con 1 Gtr, w. D. Linhares (gtr) Naxos ▲ 8.550483 [DDD]
Haydn, J.:Sym 94, "Surprise Sym" Lydian ▲ LYD 18081 [DDD]
Haydn, J.:Sym 100, "Military" Lydian ▲ LYD 18081 [DDD]
Haydn, J.:Sym 101, "Clock" Lydian ▲ LYD 18081 [DDD]
Moreno Torroba, F.:Sonatina Gtr Orch, w. D. Linhares (gtr) Naxos ▲ 8.550483 [DDD]
Vivaldi, A.:Cons Gtr, w. D. Linhares (gtr)—Concerti RV.82, 93 & 540 transcribed for guitar & orchestra Naxos ▲ 8.550483 [DDD]

Camerata de las Américas
E. Diemecke (cnd)
Revueltas, S.:Music of, w. Lourdes Ambriz (sop), Jesús Suaste (bar), Latin American String Quartet, Juan D. Tercero Vocal Octet—Troka; Cuauhnáhuac; The Owl; Frogs; Duet for Duck & Canary; Why Do You Believe?; Walking; Scenes from Childhood; 4 Little Pieces; The Knifesharpener; Market; Sensemayá *(rec Mexico City, Sept 1996)* Dorian ▲ 90244 [DDD]

Camerata Labacensis
Classics Go to the Movies Vol. 3, w. Hungarian State Orch, Lajos Meyer, Budapest Strings, Leonhard Hokanson (pno), Budapest SO, Prague Festival Orch LaserLight ▲ 15 643
K. Redel (cnd)
Mozart, W.A.:Con Hn, K.412, w. J. Falout (hn) PMG ("Vienna Master" series) ▲ CD 160224 [DDD]
Mozart, W.A.:Con Hn, K.447, w. J. Falout (hn) Sound 2–▲ CDN 115/116 [DDD]
Mozart, W.A.:Con Hn, K.447, w. J. Falout (hn) PMG ("Vienna Master" series) ▲ CD 160224 [DDD]
Mozart, W.A.:Con Hn, K.447, w. J. Falout (hn) Vivace ▲ 549 [DDD]
Mozart, W.A.:Con Ob, K.314, w. B. Rogelja (ob) PMG ("Vienna Master" series) ▲ CD 160224 [DDD]
Mozart, W.A.:Con Ob, K.314, w. B. Rogelja (ob) Sound 2–▲ CDN 115/116 [DDD]
Mozart, W.A.:Con Ob, K.314, w. B. Rogelja (ob) Vivace ▲ 549 [DDD]
Mozart, W.A.:Con 9 Pno, w. L. Hokanson (pno) PMG ("Vienna Master" series) ▲ CD 160212 [DDD]
Mozart, W.A.:Con 9 Pno, w. L. Hokanson (pno) Vivace 3–▲ E 313 [DDD]
Mozart, W.A.:Con 17 Pno, w. L. Hokanson (pno) Vivace 3–▲ E 313 [DDD]
Mozart, W.A.:Con 17 Pno, w. L. Hokanson (pno) PMG ("Vienna Master" series) ▲ CD 160212 [DDD]

Camerata Leodiensis
H. Schoonbroot (cnd)
Mahaut, A.:Cons Fl, w. B. Giaux (fl)—(2) in d & e Koch Schwann ▲ CD 311100 [DDD]
Mahaut, A.:Sinfs Strs, w. D. Huybrechts (va)—No. 1 in F, No. 2 in D & Op. 2, No. 4 in c; Sinfonia in A for Viola, Strings & Continuo, Op. 2, No. 6 Koch Schwann ▲ CD 311100 [DDD]

Camerata Ligure
E. Velardi (cnd)
Stradella, A.:Susanna, w. S. Piccollo (sop), L. Bertotti (sop), M. Lazzara (cta), M. Nuvoli (ten), M. Perrella (bass) [period instrs] [I] Bongiovanni 2–▲ GB 2121/22 [DDD]

Camerata Lysy Gstaad
A. Lysy (cnd)
Haydn, J.:Con 1 Vn, w. Alberto Lysy (vn) *(rec Kirche Saanen–Gstaad, Nov 1979 & Feb 1983)* Claves ▲ CD 508303 [DDD]
Haydn, J.:Con 3 Vn, w. Alberto Lysy (vn) *(rec Kirche Saanen–Gstaad, Nov 1979 & Feb 1983)* Claves ▲ CD 508303 [DDD]
Haydn, J.:Con 4 Vn, w. Alberto Lysy (vn) *(rec Kirche Saanen–Gstaad, Nov 1979 & Feb 1983)* Claves ▲ CD 508303 [DDD]
Y. Menuhin (cnd)
Bach, J.S.:Cons Vn (comp), w. A. Lysy (vn) Discover International ▲ DICD 920138 [DDD]
Bach, J.S.:Con 2 Vn, w. A. Lysy (vn) Discover International ▲ DICD 92140 [DDD]
Bach, J.S.:Con Vn, BWV 1058, w. A. Lysy (vn) Discover International ▲ DICD 920138 [DDD]
Telemann, G.P.:Cons Vn, w. A. Lysy (vn) Discover International ▲ DICD 92140 [DDD]

Camerata Mediterranea
J. Cohen (cnd)
Lo Gai Saber:Troubadours and Minstrels, 1100–1300, w. Anne Azema (voc), François Harismendy (voc), Jean–Luc Madier (voc), Cheryl Ann Fulton (hp), Joel Cohen (instr), Shira Kammen (instr) Erato ▲ 2292–45647–2 [DDD]

Camerata Mediterranea [A. Azema (voc), J.–L. Madier (voc), F. Harismendy (voc), M. Tindemans (fid), C. A. Fulton (hp), J. Cohen (cnd/voc/oriental lt)]
de Ventadorn, B.:Le Fou sur le pont *(rec Abbey of Nouaillé–Maupertuis, France, Sept. 8–15, 1993)* Erato ▲ 4509–94825–2 [DDD]

Camerata Musicale Orch
C. Desderi (cnd)
Rossini, G.:La pietra del paragone, w. M. C. Nocentini (sop), A. Trovarelli (mez), H. M. Molinari (cta), P. Barbacini (ten), V. Di Matteo (bar), R. Scaltriti (bar), A. Svab (bar), P. Rumetz (bass), Modeno Teatro Comunale Chorus [I] *(rec 1992)* Nuova Era 2–▲ 7132/33 [DDD]

Camerata Nova Instrumental Ensemble
L. Taglioni (cnd)
Lassus, O. de:Choral Music, w. Camerata Nova—Villanelle alla Napoletana Stradivarius ▲ STV 33374

Camerata of the 18th Century
Telemann, G.P.:Musique de Table—Concerto in A for Flute, Violin, Cello, Strings & Basso Continuo; Suite in e for 2 Flutes, Strings & Basso Continuo; Quartet in G for Flute, Oboe, Violin & Basso Continuo *(rec Aug. 31–Sept. 5, 1992)* MD + G ▲ L 3472 [DDD]
K. Hünteler (cnd)
Bach, Joh. Christian:Qnts Fl, Op. 11 MD + G ▲ MDG 3110613
Haydn, J.:Sym 93 [arr J. P. Solomon for fl, strs & bc] MD + G ▲ MDG CD 3110716
Haydn, J.:Sym 94, "Surprise Sym" [arr J. P. Solomon for fl, strs & bc] MD + G ▲ MDG CD 3110716
Haydn, J.:Sym 97 [arr J. P. Solomon for fl, strs & bc] MD + G ▲ MDG CD 3110716
Telemann, G.P.:Musique de Table—Set 2 MD + G ▲ MDG 3110473
Telemann, G.P.:Musique de Table—Set 3 MD + G ▲ MDG 3110474
Telemann, G.P.:Musique de Table MD + G 4–▲ MDG 3110580
Telemann, G.P.:Musique de Table—Set 1 [period instrs] MD + G ▲ MDG 3110472
Vivaldi, A.:Cons Fl, Op. 10, w. Konrad Hünteler (fl) [Denner fl] MD + G ▲ MDG 3110640

Camerata Provence Orch
A. de Almeida (cnd)
Boieldieu, F.–A.:Le Calife de Bagdad, w. L. Mayo (sop), J. Michelini (sop), C. Cheriez (mez), L. Dale (ten), H. Rhys–Evans (ten), Provence Camerata Chorus [F] Sonpact ▲ SPT 93007 [DDD]

Camerata Romana
Grieg, E.:Music of, w. Göran Marcusson (fl)—Bröllopsdag på Troldhaugen; Våren; Jeg elsker Dig Intim Musik ▲ INT 23 [DDD]
Koch, E. von:Con Ob, w. Mårtin Larsson (ob) Intim Musik ▲ INT 33
Larsson, L.–E.:Concertinos, w. Mårtin Larsson (ob)— for oboe [No. 2] Intim Musik ▲ INT 33
Larsson, L.–E.:Concertinos—Nos. 1 for Fl; 2 for Ob; 3 for Cl; 4 for Bn; 5 for Hn; 6 for Tpt; 7 for Trbn Intim Musik ▲ INT 30
Larsson, L.–E.:Concertinos, w. Jan Stigmer (vn), Per–Ola Lindberg (va), Bjøorg Vaernes (vc), Ingalill Hillerud (db), Joakim Kallhed (pno)—Nos. 8–12 Intim Musik ▲ INT 31
Larsson, L.–E.:Concertinos, w. Göran Marcusson (fl)—for Fl Intim Musik ▲ INT 23 [DDD]
Lindberg, O.:Music of, w. Göran Marcusson (fl)—Gammal fäbodpsalm Intim Musik ▲ INT 23 [DDD]
Linde, B.:Miniature Suite, w. Mårtin Larsson (ob) Intim Musik ▲ INT 33
Roman, J.H.:Con Fl, w. Göran Marcusson (fl) Intim Musik ▲ INT 23 [DDD]
Roman, J.H.:Con Ob d'Amore, w. Mûrtin Larsson (ob) Intim Musik ▲ INT 33
E. Duvier (cnd)
Bach, J.S.:Cons Vn (comp), w. J. Brezina (vn) PMG ("Vienna Master" series) ▲ CD 160101 [DDD]
Bach, J.S.:Con for 2 Vns, w. J. Brezina (vn), F. Elias (vn) PMG ("Vienna Master" series) ▲ CD 160101 [DDD]
T. Karolski (cnd)
Bach, J.S.:Cons Vn (comp), w. A. Stadlmayer (vn) Vivace ▲ E 506
Bach, J.S.:Con for 2 Vns, w. A. Stadlmayer (vn), T. Brodzky (vn) Vivace ▲ E 506
T. Svedlund (cnd)
Roman, J.H.:Con Fl, w. Göran Marcusson (fl) Intim Musik ▲ INT 32
Roman, J.H.:Con Ob, w. Mårten Larsson (ob) Intim Musik ▲ INT 32
Roman, J.H.:Cons (4) Vn, w. Jan Stigmer (vn)—in d & f Intim Musik ▲ INT 32

Camerata Schubert
C.F. Sedazzari (cnd)
Mercadante, S.:Fant concertante on Themes from Orazi e Curiazi, w. Luca Truffelli (fl), Gian–Luca Petrucci (fl d'amore) Bongiovanni ▲ GB 2199 [DDD]
Mercadante, S.:Sinf concertante 1, w. Luca Truffelli (fl), Roberto Saltini (cl), Giovanni Sora (cl), Andrea Mastini (cnt) Bongiovanni ▲ GB 2199 [DDD]
Mercadante, S.:Sinf concertante 2, w. Luca Truffelli (fl), Roberto Saltini (cl), Andrea Mastini (cnt) Bongiovanni ▲ GB 2199 [DDD]
Mercadante, S.:Sinf concertante 3, w. Luca Truffelli (fl), Roberto Saltini (cl), Giovanni Sora (cl), Andrea Mastini (cnt) Bongiovanni ▲ GB 2199 [DDD]

Camerata Slavonica
H. Adolph (cnd)
Mozart, W.A.:Kleine Nachtmusik Special Music Co. ▲ SCD 5200

Camerata String Orch
A. Kaplan (cnd)
Starer, R.:Con a 3, w. J. Rabbai (cl), G. Schwarz (tpt), P. Brevig (trbn) *(rec 1972)* CRI ▲ CD 612 [ADD]

Camerata String Quartet
Lekeu, G.:Méditation Ricercar ▲ RIS 107099 [DDD]
Lekeu, G.:Molto Adagio, sempre cantate doloroso Ricercar ▲ RIS 107099 [DDD]
Rheinberger, J.:Qt 1 Strs Thorofon ▲ CTH 2102 [DDD]
Rheinberger, J.:Qt 1 Strs *(rec 1991)* Thorofon 6–▲ BCTH 2161/6
Rheinberger, J.:Qt 3 Strs *(rec 1991)* Thorofon 6–▲ BCTH 2161/6
Rheinberger, J.:Qt 3 Strs Thorofon ▲ CTH 2102 [DDD]

Camerata SO
A. Kaplan (cnd)
Mennin, P.:Sym 4, w. Camerata Singers Phoenix ▲ PHCD 107 [AAD]

Camerata Tallinn [Jaan Oun (dir/fl), Ulrika Kristian (vn), Heiki Mätlik (gtr)]
Eespere, R.:Trivium *(rec Merchant Guild, Tallinn/Estonia, 1994)* Catalyst ▲ 09026–68331–2 [DDD/ADD]

Camerata Trajectina [S. van Grootel (sop), S. Buwalda (cta), M. van Altena (ten), J. Boswinkel (bass), S. Coolen (rcr/vl), L.P. Grijp (lt/cither), E. Beijer (vn/vl)]
Clemens Non Papa, J.:Souterliedekens—Psalm 35; Hymn of Mary; Het daghet inden oosten; Vier Dansliedekens; Die Nachtegael die sanck een Liedt; Een liedt eerbaer van de lidfste claer; Ick quam tot eenen dansse; Tyrranich werk spoortmen nu alle weghen; Doen Hanseleijn over de heyde reed; Het reghende seer ende ick worde nat; Alder hande Danserye; Een oude man sprak een meysken an *(rec Oct. 1993)* Globe ▲ GLO 6020 [DDD]
Mes, G.:Music of—Psalms 3, 4, 31, 35 & 39; Lofzang van Zacharias; Ick seg adieu [arr.] *(rec Oct. 1993)* Globe ▲ GLO 6020 [DDD]

Camerata Trajectina [Suze van Grootel (sop), Nico van der Meel (ten), Tom Sol (bar), Saskia Coolen (fl/rcr/va da gamba), Erik Beijer (fid/va da gamba), Louis Peter Gripp (lt/thb/cittern), Johannes Leertouwer (vn), Wanda Visser (vn), Ursula Dütchler (hpd/org)]
Grace & Peace:16th & 17th Century Mennonite Music from the Netherlands *(rec Utrecht, Sept 1995)* Globe ▲ GLO 6038 [DDD]
The Musical World of Jan Steen, Painter & Story Teller Globe ▲ GLO 6040

Camerata Vistula
Górecki, H.–M.:Lerchenmusik Olympia ▲ OCD 343 [DDD]
Lutosławski, W.:Dance Preludes Cl, Hp, Pno, Perc & Strs Olympia ▲ OCD 343 [DDD]
Prokofiev, S.:Ov on Hebrew Themes Olympia ▲ OCD 343 [DDD]

Camerata Woodwind Quintet
Karlins, M.W.:Qnt 1 Winds Opus One ▲ CD 154
Karlins, M.W.:Qnt 2 Winds Opus One ▲ CD 154

Le Cameriste
D.D. Ciacci (cnd)
Gymnopédies *(rec Trento, Italy, May 1994)* Arts ▲ 447271–2 [DDD]
A. Trentin (cnd)
Albinoni, T.:Cons à 5 Strs, Op. 5, w. Le Cameriste—Nos. 7–12 *(rec Studiosintesi, Montepulciano, Italy)* Tactus ▲ TC 670102 [DDD]
Albinoni, T.:Cons à 5 Strs, Op. 5, w. Le Cameriste—Nos. 1–6 *(rec Studiosintesi, Montepulciano, Italy)* Tactus ▲ TC 670101 [DDD]

Cameron Highlanders Pipes & Drums
Advance Bandleader ▲ BND 5108 [DDD]

Campion–Vachon Duo [Guy Campion (pno), Mario Vachon (pno)]
Gershwin, G.:The George Gershwin Songbook [arr for 2 pnos] *(rec St Augustin de Mirabel School, Québec, July 1995)* Analekta ▲ AN 29255 [DDD]
Satie, E.:Aperçus désagréables *(rec Salle Henri-Gagnon, Quebec)* Analekta Fleur de Lys ▲ FL 2 3040
Satie, E.:La belle excentrique *(rec Salle Henri-Gagnon, Quebec)* Analekta Fleur de Lys ▲ FL 2 3040
Satie, E.:En habit de cheval *(rec Salle Henri-Gagnon, Quebec)* Analekta Fleur de Lys ▲ FL 2 3040
Satie, E.:Morceaux en forme de poire *(rec Salle Henri-Gagnon, Quebec)* Analekta Fleur de Lys ▲ FL 2 3040
Satie, E.:Parade [concert reduction for Pno 4-Hands, Siren, Lottery Wheel, Water Puddles, Typewriter & Revolver] *(rec Salle Henri-Gagnon, Quebec)* Analekta Fleur de Lys ▲ FL 2 3040
Satie, E.:Petites pièces montées *(rec Salle Henri-Gagnon, Quebec)* Analekta Fleur de Lys ▲ FL 2 3040

Canadian Brass
Basic 100 Vol. 34, w. English CO Brass RCA Victor ▲ 09026-61852-2 ■ 09026-61852-4
Gabrieli, G.:Canzoni, w. Boston SO Brass Players, New York PO Brass Players—13 canzoni CBS ▲ MK 44931 [DDD] ■ MT 44931 (D)
Handel, G.F.:Water Music (suites) RCA Gold Seal ▲ RCD1-3554; ■ ARK1-3554
It's Good to Be the King:Musical Delights for Kings, Queens, Princes & Royalty, w. Claudio Abbado (cnd), Eugene Ormandy (cnd), Esa-Pekka Salonen (cnd), Michael Tilson Thomas (cnd), Chicago SO, Philadelphia Orch, Royal PO, Tafelmusik Sony Classical ▲ SFK 57483 ■ SFT 57483
Monteverdi, C.:Music of—sels from Christmas Vespers & Vespro della Beata Vergine [arr for brass; w. principal brass players of the Boston SO & New York PO] CBS ▲ MK 44931 [DDD] ■ MT 44931 (D)
Mozart, W.A.:Music of, *(sels unknown)* CBS ▲ MK 44545 [DDD] ■ MT 44545 (D)
O Holy Night:Christmas Favorites, w. James Galway (fl), Richard Stoltzman (cl), Michala Petri (rcr), Emily Mitchell (hp), Boston Pops Orch [cnd:Arthur Fiedler] RCA Victor ▲ 09026-61836-2 ■ 09026-61836-4
Pachelbel, w. Jean-Pierre Rampal (fl), Igor Kipnis (hpd), Raymond Leppard (cnd), John Williams (gtr), E. Power Biggs (org), et al. Sony Classical ("Greatest Hits" series) ▲ MLK 62680 ■ MLT 62680
Pachelbel, J.:Canon CBS ▲ MK 39515 ■ MT 39515
Pachelbel, J.:Canon RCA Red Seal ▲ RCD1-4733 ■ ARK1-4733
Pachelbel, J.:Canon RCA Gold Seal ▲ RCD1-3554 ■ ARK1-3554
Pachelbel, J.:Canon CBS ▲ MK 39035 [DDD]
Vivaldi, A.:Cons Vn, Op. 8/1-4, "The Four Seasons" [trans. Frackenpohl] CBS ▲ MK 42095 ■ MT 42095

E. Iseler (cnd)
Gabrieli, G.:Music of, w. New York PO members, Philadelphia Orch members Philips ▲ 438392-2

J. Levine (cnd)
The Bells of St. Genevieve & Other Baroque Favorites, w. English CO, James Galway (fl), Vladimir Spivakov (vn), Pinchas Zukerman (vn), et al. RCA Victor ▲ 09026-61002-2 [DDD] ■ 09026-61002-4 (CrO2) □ 09026-61002-5

N. Marriner (cnd)
Mozart, W.A.:Music of, w. Ferruccio Furlanetto (bass), Isaac Stern (vn), Academy of St. Martin in the Fields—Eine kleine Nachtmusik; Syms 38 & 41; sels from Die Zauberflöte; plus others Sony Classical ("Greatest Hits" series) ▲ MLK 62682 ■ MLT 62682

G. Titner (cnd)
Beethoven, L. van:Egmont (ov), w. Boston SO, New York PO members Philips ("Digital Classics" series) ▲ 426487-2 [DDD]
Beethoven, L. van:Sym 5, w. Boston SO, New York PO members Philips ("Digital Classics" series) ▲ 426487-2 [DDD]
Beethoven, L. van:Wellington's Victory, "Battle Sym", w. Boston SO, New York PO members Philips ("Digital Classics" series) ▲ 426487-2 [DDD]

Canadian Brass [Frederic Mills (tpt), Ronald Romm (tpt), David Ohnanian (hn), Eugene Watts (trbn), Charles Daellenbach (tuba)]
Albinoni, T.:Adagio Org CBS ▲ MK 39035 [DDD]
Bach, J.S.:The Art of the Fugue CBS ▲ MK 44501 [DDD] ■ MT 44501 (D)
Bach, J.S.:Passacaglia & Fugue Org RCA Gold Seal ▲ RCD1-3554 ■ ARK1-3554
Bach, J.S.:Sheep May Safely Graze RCA Gold Seal ▲ RCD1-3554 ■ ARK1-3554
Bach, J.S.:Toccata & Fugue Org, BWV 565 RCA Gold Seal ▲ RCD1-3554 ■ ARK1-3554
Bach, J.S.:Toccata & Fugue Org, BWV 565 RCA Red Seal ▲ RCD1-4733 ■ ARK1-4733
Baroque Brass:Basic 100, Vol. 34, w. English CO Brass RCA Victor ▲ 09026-61854-2 ■ 09026-61854-4 (CrO2)
Basin Street CBS ▲ MK 42367 [DDD] ■ FMT 42367 (D)
Best of the Canadian Brass CBS ▲ MK 45744 [DDD] ■ FMT 45744 (D)
Bolero & Other Blockbusters RCA Victor ▲ 09026-68109-2 ■ 09026-68109-4
Brass Busters, w. New York Phil Brass, Boston Sym Brass RCA Victor ▲ 09026-68076-2 ■ 09026-68076-4
Brass on Broadway, w. Luther Henderson (kbd), Edward Metz (perc), Star of Indiana Drummers Philips ▲ 442133-2
The Canadian Brass Go for Baroque! RCA ▲ 09026-68107-2; ■ 09026-68107-4
Canadian Brass Live! CBS ▲ MK 39515 ■ MT 39515
Champions ▲ MK 37797 ■ PMT 37797
Christmas with the Canadian Brass, w. John Grady RCA Gold Seal ▲ RCD1-4132 ■ ARK1-4132
Clarke, J.:Tpt Voluntary *(rec Glenn Gould Studio, Toronto, OT, Jan. 30- Feb. 3, 1995)* RCA Red Seal ▲ 09026-68257-2 [DDD]; ■ 09026-68257-4
Encore Musica Viva ▲ MVCD 1011 [ADD]
English Renaissance Music CBS ▲ MK 45792 [DDD] ■ MT 45792 (D)
The Essential Canadian Brass Philips ▲ 432571-2 PH [DDD] ■ 432571-4 PH (D) □ 432571-5
Gabrieli, G.:Son pian' e forte CBS ▲ MK 39035 [DDD]
Gershwin, G.:Music of—Strike up the band!; Someone to watch over me; Medley, "The Rhythm Series" (Clap yo' hands/Fidgety feet/Fascinating rhythm/I got rhythm); A foggy day; Nice work if you can get it; The man I love; Rialto ripples; Piano Preludes Nos. 1-3 RCA Red Seal ▲ 6490-2-RC [DDD] ■ 6490-4-RC (D)
Gershwin, G.:Porgy & Bess (sels) RCA Red Seal ▲ 6490-2-RC [DDD] ■ 6490-4-RC (D)
Greatest Hits RCA Red Seal ▲ RCD1-4733 ■ ARK1-4733
Handel, G.F.:Concerti grossi, Op. 3—Andante & Allegro [from No. 4] *(rec Glenn Gould Studio, Toronto, OT, Jan. 30- Feb. 3, 1995)* RCA Red Seal ▲ 09026-68257-2 [DDD]; ■ 09026-68257-4
Handel, G.F.:Samson (sels)—Let the Bright Seraphim *(rec Glenn Gould Studio, Toronto, OT, Jan. 30- Feb. 3, 1995)* RCA Red Seal ▲ 09026-68257-2 [DDD]; ■ 09026-68257-4
Handel, G.F.:Serse (sels)—Largo; Allegro; Bourree *(rec Glenn Gould Studio, Toronto, OT, Jan. 30- Feb. 3, 1995)* RCA Red Seal ▲ 09026-68257-2 [DDD]; ■ 09026-68257-4
Handel, G.F.:Solomon (arrival of the queen of Sheba) *(rec Glenn Gould Studio, Toronto, OT, Jan. 30- Feb. 3, 1995)* RCA Red Seal ▲ 09026-68257-2 [DDD]; ■ 09026-68257-4
Handel, G.F.:Water Music (suites) *(rec Glenn Gould Studio, Toronto, OT, Jan. 30- Feb. 3, 1995)* RCA Red Seal ▲ 09026-68257-2 [DDD]; ■ 09026-68257-4
High, Bright, Light & Clear:The Glory of Baroque Brass RCA Red Seal ▲ RCD1-4574 [DDD] ■ ARE1-4574 (D)
In Berlin CBS ▲ MK 39035 [DDD]
More Greatest Hits RCA Red Seal ▲ 5628-2-RC [DDD] ■ 5628-4-RC (CrO2)
Noël, w. Canadian Brass Jazz All-Stars, Angel Romero (gtr), *(children's choir unknown)*, Richard Stoltzman (cl), Harolyn Blackwell (sop), Jerry Hadley (ten), King's Singers, James Galway (fl) *(rec Apr. 17-20, 1994)* RCA Victor ▲ 09026-62683-2 ■ 09026-62683-4
Plays Great Baroque Music RCA Gold Seal ▲ RCD1-3554 ■ ARK1-3554
Purcell, H.:Abdelazer, or The Moor's Revenge—Suite *(rec Glenn Gould Studio, Toronto, OT, Jan. 30- Feb. 3, 1995)* RCA Red Seal ▲ 09026-68257-2 [DDD]; ■ 09026-68257-4
Purcell, H.:The Fairy Queen (sels)—Suite *(rec Glenn Gould Studio, Toronto, OT, Jan. 30- Feb. 3, 1995)* RCA Red Seal ▲ 09026-68257-2 [DDD]; ■ 09026-68257-4

Canadian Brass (cont.)
Purcell, H.:Fant Vls, Z.745 *(rec Glenn Gould Studio, Toronto, OT, Jan. 30- Feb. 3, 1995)* RCA Red Seal ▲ 09026-68257-2 [DDD]; ■ 09026-68257-4
Purcell, H.:Tpt Tune, Z.t678 *(rec Glenn Gould Studio, Toronto, OT, Jan. 30- Feb. 3, 1995)* RCA Red Seal ▲ 09026-68257-2 [DDD]; ■ 09026-68257-4
Red, White & Brass, w. Boston SO members, New York PO Philips ▲ 434276-2 PH [DDD] ■ 434276-4 PH
Renaissance Men RCA ▲ 09026-68108-2; ■ 09026-68108-4
Tallis, T.:Church Music—In nomine II *(rec Glenn Gould Studio, Toronto, OT, Jan. 30- Feb. 3, 1995)* RCA Red Seal ▲ 09026-68257-2 [DDD]; ■ 09026-68257-4
Tallis, T.:Songs—Solfaing Song *(rec Glenn Gould Studio, Toronto, OT, Jan. 30- Feb. 3, 1995)* RCA Red Seal ▲ 09026-68257-2 [DDD]; ■ 09026-68257-4
Toccata, Fugues & Other Diversions Omega Classics ▲ OCD 3014 [ADD]
The Village Band RCA Red Seal ▲ RCD1-4436 ■ ARE1-4436

Canadian Brass [Ronald Romm (tpt), Jens Lindemann (tpt/flgl), David Ohanian (hn), Eugene Watts (trbn), Charles Daellenbach (tuba)]
Bernstein, L.:Music of—America [w. Larry Weeks (tpt), Harcus Hennigar (hn), Gordon Sweeney (trbn), Brian Leonard (perc), Dick Smith (perc), Tom Szczesniak (kbd)]; Make Our Garden Grow; Jet Song [w. Brian Leonard (perc), Dick Smith (perc)]; Maria [w. Larry Weeks (tpt), James Spragg (tpt), Harcus Hennigar (hn), Gordon Sweeney (trbn), Jeff Hall (b trbn), David Young (bass), Tom Szczsniak (kbd), Ted Warren (dr), Christopher Derrick (voc)]; Something's Coming [w. Brian Leonard (perc) Dick Smith (perc)]; A Simple Song [w. Brian Leonard (perc), Dick Smith (perc), Tom Szczsniak (kbd)]; Alleluia [w. Tom Szczsniak (kbd), David Young (bass), Ted Warren (dr)]; A Boy Like That/I Have A Love; Best of All Possible Worlds [w. Larry Weeks (tpt), James Spragg (tpt), Harcus Hennigar (hn), Gordon Sweeney (trbn), Jeff Hall (b trbn), David Young (bass), Ted Warren (dr) Tom Szczsniak (kbd)]; One Hand, One Heart; Tonight [w. Brian Leonard (perc), Dick Smith (perc)]; I Feel Pretty [w. Brian Leonard (perc)]; Somewhere [w. Harcus Hennigar (hn), Gordon Sweeney (trbn), Tom Szczsniak (kbd), Brian Leonard (perc)]; Gee, Officer Krupke [all arr C. Dedrick] BMG ▲ 09026-68633-2 [DDD]

Canadian Brass Jazz All-Stars
Noël, w. Canadian Brass, Angel Romero (gtr), *(children's choir unknown)*, Richard Stoltzman (cl), Harolyn Blackwell (sop), Jerry Hadley (ten), King's Singers, James Galway (fl) *(rec Apr. 17-20, 1994)* RCA Victor ▲ 09026-62683-2 ■ 09026-62683-4

Canadian Chamber Ensemble
R. Armenian (cnd)
Dvořák, A.:Serenade Ww CBC ("SM 5000" series) ▲ SMCD 5073 [DDD] ■ SMC 5073 (D)
Forsyth, M.:Fanfare & (3) Masquerades Centrediscs ▲ CMC CD 3488
Françaix, J.:Sérénade CBC ("SM 5000" series) ▲ SMCD 5073 [DDD]; ■ SMC 5073 (D)
Kulesha, G.:Chamber Con 3 Centrediscs ▲ CMCCD 3488
McCauley, W.:Miniatures 10 Winds *(rec Centre in the Square, Kitchener, May 23 & Oct 2, 1991)* CBC ▲ 5159 [DDD]
Milhaud, D.:Création du monde *(rec Centre in the Square, Kitchener, May 23 & Oct 2, 1991)* CBC ▲ 5159 [DDD]
Schafer, R.M.:Con Hpd Centrediscs ▲ CMCCD 3488
Stravinsky, I.:Instr Miniatures *(rec Centre in the Square, Kitchener, May 23 & Oct 2, 1991)* CBC ▲ 5159 [DDD]
Stravinsky, I.:Octet *(rec Centre in the Square, Kitchener, May 23 & Oct 2, 1991)* CBC ▲ 5159 [DDD]
Stravinsky, I.:Ragtime *(rec Centre in the Square, Kitchener, May 23 & Oct 2, 1991)* CBC ▲ 5159 [DDD]

Canadian Forces Central Band
D. Bouchard (cnd)
Canada Remembers Bandleader ▲ BND 5105 [DDD]

Canadian Opera Company Orch
R. Bradshaw (cnd)
Rossini, G.:Ermione (sels), w. Canadian Opera Company Chorus—Sinf *(rec George Weston Recital Hall, Ford Centre for the Performing Arts, North York, Ontario, Dec 20-23, 1994)* CBC ("SM 5000" series) ▲ SM5 5148 [DDD]
Rossini, G.:Giunone, w. Wendy Nielsen (sop—Giunone), Canadian Opera Company Chorus *(rec George Weston Recital Hall, Ford Centre for the Performing Arts, North York, Ontario, Dec 20-23, 1994)* CBC ("SM 5000" series) ▲ SM5 5148 [DDD]
Rossini, G.:Mosè in Egitto (sels), w. Wendy Nielsen (sop—Elcia), Anita Krause (mez—Amenosi), Richard Margison (ten—Aronne), Gary Relyea (b-bar—Mosè), Canadian Opera Company Chorus—Scena, Coro & Preghiera [Dal tuo stellato soglio] *(rec George Weston Recital Hall, Ford Centre for the Performing Arts, North York, Ontario, Dec 20-23, 1994)* CBC ("SM 5000" series) ▲ SM5 5148 [DDD]
Verdi, G.:Alzira (sels), w. Stephen McClare (ten—Otumbo), Richard Margison (ten—Zamoro), Gary Relyea (b-bar—Alvaro), Canadian Opera Company Chorus—Il prigioniero [prologue] *(rec George Weston Recital Hall, Ford Centre for the Performing Arts, North York, Ontario, Dec 20-23, 1994)* CBC ("SM 5000" series) ▲ SM5 5148 [DDD]
Verdi, G.:Ernani (sels), w. Richard Margison (ten—Ernani), Gary Relyea (b-bar—Don Silva), Canadian Opera Company Chorus—Conspiracy [An alliance; Let the Lion of Castile Rise Again] *(rec George Weston Recital Hall, Ford Centre for the Performing Arts, North York, Ontario, Dec 20-23, 1994)* CBC ("SM 5000" series) ▲ SM5 5148 [DDD]
Verdi, G.:Giovanna d'Arco (sels)—Sinf *(rec George Weston Recital Hall, Ford Centre for the Performing Arts, North York, Ontario, Dec 20-23, 1994)* CBC ("SM 5000" series) ▲ SM5 5148 [DDD]
Verdi, G.:Inno delle nazioni, w. Richard Margison (ten—Bardo), Canadian Opera Company Chorus *(rec George Weston Recital Hall, Ford Centre for the Performing Arts, North York, Ontario, Dec 20-23, 1994)* CBC ("SM 5000" series) ▲ SM5 5148 [DDD]
Verdi, G.:Macbeth (sels), w. Canadian Opera Company Chorus—Scottish Exiles' Chorus [Patria oppressa!] *(rec George Weston Recital Hall, Ford Centre for the Performing Arts, North York, Ontario, Dec 20-23, 1994)* CBC ("SM 5000" series) ▲ SM5 5148 [DDD]
Verdi, G.:Nabucco (sels), w. Canadian Opera Company Chorus—Chorus of the Hebrew Slaves [Va, pensiero, sull'ali dorate] *(rec George Weston Recital Hall, Ford Centre for the Performing Arts, North York, Ontario, Dec 20-23, 1994)* CBC ("SM 5000" series) ▲ SM5 5148 [DDD]

Canadian Piano Trio
Duets:Ofra Harnoy & Friends, w. Ofra Harnoy (vc), Michael Dussek (pno), Orford String Quartet, Maureen Forrester (cta), Andrew Davis (pno), Jeanne Baxtresser (fl), Catherine Wilson (pno), Paul Brodie (sax), Shauna Rolston (vc), Armin Strings, Adele Armin (vn) Mastersound ▲ MST 30 [DDD]

Canaria Grand PO
G. P. Sanzogno (cnd)
The Art of Alfredo Kraus, w. Alfredo Kraus (ten), Edemiro Arnaltes (pno) RNE/Spanish Radio 3-▲ 65015/16/17.

Cannes-Provence Alpes-Côte d'Azur Regional Orch
P. Bender (cnd)
Caplet, A.:Le miroir de Jésus, w. R. Allouche (mez), Maîtrise Gabriel Fauré Sonpact ▲ SPT 94010 [DDD]
Milhaud, D.:Le Carnaval d'Aix, w. R. Caramella (pno) Nuova Era ▲ 7130 [DDD]
Milhaud, D.:Concertino d'hiver, w. J. Douay (trbn) Nuova Era ▲ 7130 [DDD]
Milhaud, D.:Fant pastorale, w. R. Caramella (pno) Nuova Era ▲ 7130 [DDD]
Milhaud, D.:Suite provençale Nuova Era ▲ 7130 [DDD]
M. Piquemal (cnd)
Cornelius, P.:Stabat Mater, w. D. Borst (sop), J. Mayeur (cta), J.-L. Viala (ten), F. Vassar (bass-bar), Cannes Regional Chorus Musique d'Abord ▲ HMA 1905206

Cantabile Trio [H.-J. Wegner (fl), G. Larisch (vc), C. Kroeker (pno)]
Damase, J.-M.:Sonate en concert Thorofon ▲ CTH 2135 [DDD]
Dussek, J.L.:Trio Son Pno, Op. 65 *(rec 1993)* Thorofon ▲ CTH 2151 [DDD]
Goossens, E.:Impressions (5) of a Holiday Thorofon ▲ CTH 2135 [DDD]
Gyrowetz, A.:Divertissement Pno *(rec 1993)* Thorofon ▲ CTH 2151 [DDD]
Kozeluch, L.:Son 2 Fl *(rec 1993)* Thorofon ▲ CTH 2151 [DDD]
Manziarly, M. de:Trio Fl, Vc & Pno Thorofon ▲ CTH 2135 [DDD]
Pierné, G.:Son da camera Fl Thorofon ▲ CTH 2135 [DDD]

▲ = CD ♦ = Enhanced CD Δ = MD ■ = Cassette Tape □ = DCC

CantArte Ensemble
H. Velten (cnd)
Gregorian Chants:Advent *(rec Dominikanerkirche Adlersberg, Sept 23–25, 1994)* Capriccio ▲ 10593 [DDD]
Gregorian Chants:Christmas *(rec Klosterkirche Pielenhofen, Feb 24–26, 1995)* Capriccio ▲ 10701 [DDD]
Canta-Sonare
R. Newell (cnd)
Newell, R.:New London Capstone ▲ CPS 8618
Cantata Ensemble
D. Hoose (cnd)
Harbison, J.:The Flight into Egypt, w. Roberta Anderson (sop), Sanford Sylvan (bar), Cantata Singers [E] New World ▲ 80395-2 [DDD]
Canterbury Cellists [Elizabeth Bone (vc), Ashley Brown (vc), Alexander Ivashkin (vc), Natalia Pavlutskaya (vc), Julie Platt (vc)]
Prokofiev, S.:Concertino [arr M. Rostropovich for vc ensemble] *(rec School of Music, Auckland Univ & St. Barnabas Church, Christchurch)* Manu ▲ 1517
Canticum Novum CO
A. Ardal (cnd)
Bach, J.S.:Cant 82, w. Knut Skram (bass), Brynjar Hoff (ob) *(rec Greverud Church, Oslo, Norway, June 8 & 9 & Sept 23, 197)* BIS ▲ CD 101 [AAD]
Cantilena
A. Shepherd (cnd)
Abel, C.F.:Syms, Op. 7 Chandos ▲ CHAN 8648 [DDD]
Arne, T.:Favourite Cons (6), w. R. Bevan Williams (org) Chandos 2-▲ CHAN 8604/05 [DDD]
Arne, T.:Syms (4) Chandos ▲ CHAN 8403 [DDD]
Boccherini, L.:Syms—in D, G.490; in C, G.505; in d, G.506; in A G.511; in B♭ G.514; in d, G.517; in A G.518 Chandos 2-▲ CHAN 8414/15 [DDD]
Boyce, W.:Con grossi (3) Chandos ("Collect" series) ▲ CHAN 6541 [ADD]
Boyce, W.:Ovs (12)—Nos. 11 & 12 Chandos ("Collect" series) ▲ CHAN 6541 [ADD]
Corelli, A.:Concerti grossi, Op. 6—comp. Chandos 3-▲ CHAN 8336/38 [DDD]
Dittersdorf, K.D. von:Syms (Metamorphoses) Chandos 2-▲ CHAN 8564/65 [DDD]
Haydn, J.:Sym 22, "Der Philosoph" Chandos ("Collect" series) ▲ CHAN 6579 [DDD]
Haydn, J.:Sym 24 Chandos ("Collect" series) ▲ CHAN 6579 [DDD]
Haydn, J.:Sym 30, "Alleluja" Chandos ("Collect" series) ▲ CHAN 6579 [DDD]
Haydn, J.:Sym 43, "Mercury" Chandos ("Collect" series) ▲ CHAN 6590 [DDD]
Haydn, J.:Sym 44, "Trauer" Chandos ("Collect" series) ▲ CHAN 6590 [DDD]
Haydn, J.:Sym 49, "La Passione" Chandos ("Collect" series) ▲ CHAN 6590 [DDD]
Hebden, J.:Cons Strs Chandos ▲ CHAN 8339
Cantus Cologne
Schein, J.H.:Israels Brünnlein—Unser Leben währet siebzig Jahr; Ach Herr, ach meiner schone; Da Jakob vollendet hatte; Ich lasse dich nicht; Die mit Tränen sähen; Oh Herr, ich bin dein Knecht; Herr, lass meine Klage; Ist nicht Ephraim mein teurer Sohn; Ich bin die Wurzel des Geschlechtes David; Ich freue mich im Herren; Was betrübst du dich, meine Seele; Nu danket alle Gott *(rec St. Osdag Church, Mandelsloh, Feb 13–16, 1995)* Deutsche Harmonia Mundi ▲ 05472-77359-2 [DDD]
Schein, J.H.:Vom Himmel hoch da komm ich her *(rec St. Osdag Church, Mandelsloh, Feb 13–16, 1995)* Deutsche Harmonia Mundi ▲ 05472-77359-2 [DDD]
K. Junghänel (cnd)
Bach, Joh. Christoph:Motets & Cants—Fürchte dich nicht; Der Gerechte, ob er gleich zu zeitlich stirbt Deutsche Harmonia Mundi ▲ 05472-77305-2
Bach, J.M.:Motets—Halt, was du hast; Fürchtet euch nicht Deutsche Harmonia Mundi ▲ 05472-77305-2
Carissimi, G.:Jephte Deutsche Harmonia Mundi ▲ 05472-77322-2 [DDD]
Marazzoli, M.:Per il giorno della resurrezione Deutsche Harmonia Mundi ▲ 05472-77322-2 [DDD]
Marazzoli, M.:San Tommaso Deutsche Harmonia Mundi ▲ 05472-77322-2 [DDD]
Monteverdi, C.:Vespro della Beata Vergine, w. Konrad Junghänel (lt), Concerto Palatino *(rec Sept 8–12, 1994)* Deutsche Harmonia Mundi 2-▲ 05472-77332-2 [DDD]
Pachelbel, J.:Motets—Jauchzet dem Herrn; Nun Danket alle Gott; Exsurgat Deus; Troste uns Gott; Der Herr ist König und herrlich geschmuckt; Gott ist unser Zuversicht; Paratum cor meum Deus; Der Herr ist König; Singet dem Herrn; Jauchzet Gott, alle Lande Deutsche Harmonia Mundi ▲ 05472-77305-2
Pachelbel, J.:Music for Vespers—Magnificat Deutsche Harmonia Mundi ▲ 05472-77305-2
Il Pastor Fido Deutsche Harmonia Mundi ▲ 05472-77240-2
Rosenmüller, J.:Vespro della Beata Vergine, w. Concerto Palatino Harmonia Mundi 2-▲ HMC 901611.12
Cantus Cologne [Jean Tubery (cnt/muet/rcr), Christina Pluhar (triple hp), Matthias Spaeter (archlt), Jean-Marc Aymes (org/hpd)]
Schein, J.H.:Opella Nova II, w. La Fenice Ensemble—Mach dich auf, werde Licht, Zion; Magnificat; Warum betrübst du dich, mein Herz, Vater unser, der du bist im Himmel *(rec St. Osdag Church, Mandelsloh, Feb 13–16, 1995)* Deutsche Harmonia Mundi ▲ 05472-77359-2 [DDD]
Cantus Cologne [Johanna Koslowsky (sop), David Cordier (alt), Wilfried Jochens (ten), Gerd Türk (ten), Franz-Josef Selig (bass), Konrad Junghänel (lt), Carsten Lohff (hpd/org)]
Albert, H.:Musicalische—17 sels Ars Musici ▲ 3026 [DDD]
Cantus Figuratus Ensemble
D. Vellard (cnd)
Agricola, A.:Motets, w. La Traditora—Da pacem Domine; O quam glorifica K617 ▲ 7056
Compère, L.:Motet-Chansons, La Traditora—O vos Omnes K617 ▲ 7056
Compère, L.:Motets, La Traditora—Crux triumphans K617 ▲ 7056
Josquin Desprez:Motets, La Traditora—In pace in idipsum K617 ▲ 7056
Lasson, M.:Motets, La Traditora—Congratulamini mihi; Virtute magna; Anthoni pater inclyte K617 ▲ 7056
Obrecht, J.:Motets, La Traditora—Si sumpsero K617 ▲ 7056
Therache, P. de:Missa 'O vos omnes', La Traditora K617 ▲ 7056
Therache, P. de:Motets, La Traditora—Verbum bonum et suave K617 ▲ 7056
Cape Town SO
E. Bergel (cnd)
Chopin, F.:Con 1 Pno, w. Steven de Groote (pno) *(rec City Hall, Cape Town, Aug. 7, 1986)* Claremont ▲ GSE 1536 [ADD]
A. Coates (cnd)
Mendelssohn, F.:Elijah, w. Johanna Uys Melodic Choir *(rec live, 1952)* GSE Claremont ▲ GSE 78 50 54
Mendelssohn, F.:Elijah (sels), w. Melodic Choir—Hear Ye Israel, Be Not Afraid Claremont ▲ GSE 78 50 54
O. Hadari (cnd)
Beethoven, L. van:Con 2 Pno, w. Steven de Groote (pno) *(rec City Hall, Cape Town, Aug. 21, 1988)* Claremont ▲ GSE 1536 [ADD]
D. de Villiers (cnd)
Beethoven, L. van:Con 4 Pno, w. S. de Groote (pno) Vivace 3-▲ E 322 [DDD]
Brahms, J.:Con 2 Pno, w. S. de Groote (pno) Vivace 3-▲ E 323 [DDD]
Brahms, J.:Con 2 Pno, w. S. de Groote (pno) Vivace ▲ 592 [DDD]
Rachmaninoff, S.:Con 2 Pno, w. S. de Groote (pno) Vivace 3-▲ E 322 [DDD]
Capella Academica Vienna
Bach, Joh. Christian:Qnt Fl, Op. 22/1 Capriccio ▲ 10166 [DDD]
E. Melkus (cnd)
Bach, Joh. Christian:Cons Hpd, T.292/1, w. I. Haebler (pno) Philips 2-▲ 438712-2
Bach, Joh. Christian:Semi Cons Hpd, w. I. Haebler (pno) Philips 2-▲ 438712-2
Organ Concertos of the Classical Era, w. Franz Haselböck (org) Hänssler Classic ▲ 98.575 [DDD]

Capella Agostino Steffani
L. Rovatkay (cnd)
Caldara, A.:Stabat Mater, w. Monika Frimmer (sop), Gloria Banditelli (mez), Gerd Türk (ten), Peter Frank (bass), Westphalia Kantorei EMI Classics ▲ CDC 54845
Pergolesi, G.B.:Stabat mater, w. Monika Frimmer (sop), Gloria Banditelli (mez), Gerd Türk (ten), Peter Frank (bass), Westphalia Kantorei EMI Classics ▲ CDC 54845
Steffani, A.:Enrico Leone, w. R. Popken (alt), M. Frimmer (sop), S. Szameit (sop), N. Yoko (cta), C. Guber (cta), D. Diwiak (ten), G. Faulstich (bar) [period instrs] [I] Calig ▲ CAL 50855 [DDD]
Vivaldi, A.:Son al St. Sepolcro, w. Monika Frimmer (sop), Gloria Banditelli (mez), Gerd Türk (ten), Peter Frank (bass), Westphalia Kantorei EMI Classics ▲ CDC 54845
Capella Antiqua
K. Ruhland (cnd)
Medieval Christmas Music, w. Niederaltaich Scholars Sony Classical ("Vivarte" series) ▲ SK 45946
Capella Antiqua Bambergensis
E Dame Jolie:Music of Princes, Knights & Thieves Koch Schwann ▲ SCH 310372 [DDD]
Musikalisches Tafelkonfekt Koch Schwann ▲ SCH 310382 [DDD]
Capella Brugensis
P. Peire (cnd)
de Fesch, W.:Missa pascalis, Collegium Instrumentale Brugense Eufoda ▲ 1173 [DDD]
Fiocco, J.-H.:Music of, w. Collegium Instrumentale Brugense—Missa Sanctae Caeciliae Eufoda ▲ 1173 [DDD]
Gluck, C.W.:Orfeo ed Euridice, w. M.-N. de Callatay (sop), E. Podles (mez), Collegium Instrumentale Brugense[original instruments] Forlane 2-▲ FOR 16720 [DDD]
Kennis, W.J.:Arrangements of W. A. Mozart's Sacred Music, w. Collegium Instrumentale Brugense—Ave verum; Confitebor in D; Laudate pueri; Pange lingua; Quis te comprehendat [L] Eufoda ▲ 1152 [DDD]
Mozart, W.A.:Music of, w. Philip Defrancq (ten), Reginaldo Pinheiro (ten), Jan Van Der Crabben (bar), Jan Vermeulen (pno), Guy Penson (org), Collegium Instrumentale Brugense—Zerfliesset heut', geliebte Brüder [song]; Dir Seele des Weltalls [cant]; O heiliges Band der Freundschaft [song]; Die ihr einem Neuen Grade [Maurer-Geselienlied]; Die Maurerfreude [cant]; Maurerische Trauermusik; Die ihr der unermesslichen Weltalls Schöpfer ehrt [Kleine deutsche Kantate]; Laut verkünde unsre Freude [Eine kleine Freimaurerkantate]; Lasst uns mit geschlugnen Händen [hymn]; Ihr unsre neuen Leiter [song] *(rec Studio Steurbaut, Gent, Dec 1992)* René Gailly ▲ 92013 [DDD]
Mozart, W.A.:Sacred Music, w. Collegium Instrumentale Brugense—Veni Sancte Spritus, K.47; Regina coeli, K.127; Exsultate, jubilate, K.165; Sub tuum praeisium, K.198; Misericordias Domini, K.222; Sancta Maria, mater Dei, K.273; Regina coeli, K.276; Alma Dei creatoris, K.277; Ave verum corpus, K.618 Forlane ▲ FOR 16714 [DDD]
A. Zedda (cnd)
Rossini, G.:Tancredi, w. Sumi Jo (sop—Amenaide), Lucretia Lendi (mez—Roggiero), Anna Maria di Micco (mez—Isaura), Ewa Podles (cta—Tancredi), Stanford Olsen (ten—Argirio), Pietro Spagnoli (bar—Orbazzano), Ewald Demeyere (hpd), Lieven Baert (vc), Franck Coryn (db), Collegium Instrumentale Brugense *(rec Poissy Theatre & Centre Musical-Lyrique-Phonographique, Ile de France, Jan. 26–31, 1994)* Naxos ("Opera Classics" series) 2-▲ 8.660037/38 [DDD]
Capella Cisplatina
G. Garrido (cnd)
Baroque Music at the Royal Audience of Charcas, w. Elyma Ensemble, Luis Berger Ensemble [cnd:Emma Sanchez], Cordoba Children's Choir *(rec Apr 19–24, 1996)* K617 ▲ 7064 [DDD]
Capella Clementina
H. Müller-Brühl (cnd)
Baroque Concertos, w. Cologne CO *(rec 1971 and 1978)* Koch Treasure ▲ SCH 316152 [ADD]
Capella Clementina [Josef Niessen (vn), Hajo Bäss (vn), Wilfried Engel (va), Philipp Bosbach (vc), Claus Körfer (db), Roswitha Trimborn (cem), Helmut Müller- Brühl (cnd)]
Hasse, J.A.:Piramo e Tisbe, w. Barbara Schlick (sop), Suzanne Gari (sop), Michel LeCocq (ten) Koch Schwann 2-▲ SCH 310882 [DDD]
Vivaldi, A.:Cons Flautino, w. Conrad Steinmann (rcr) [period instrs]—RV.444 & 445 *(rec Schloss Hohenems, Austria)* Claves ("Favor Collection" series) ▲ CLF 0804-9 [ADD]
Vivaldi, A.:Cons Fl, Op. 10, w. Conrad Steinmann (rcr) [period instrs]—No. 2 in g [La notte] *(rec Schloss Hohenems, Austria)* Claves ("Favor Collection" series) ▲ CLF 0804-9 [ADD]
Vivaldi, A.:Cons Rcr, w. Conrad Steinmann (rcr) [period instrs]—in c, RV.441 *(rec Schloss Hohenems, Austria)* Claves ("Favor Collection" series) ▲ CLF 0804-9 [ADD]
Capella Coloniensis
Roman, J.H.:Con grosso, w. U. Björlin (ob) Capriccio ▲ 10 624 [DDD]
U. Björlin (cnd)
Frederick II:Con Fl, w. K. Hünteler (fl) LaserLight ▲ 14036 [DDD]
Haydn, J.:Sym 50 LaserLight ▲ 15 830 [DDD]
Haydn, J.:Sym 87 LaserLight ▲ 15 830 [DDD]
Haydn, J.:Sym 89 LaserLight ▲ 15 830 [DDD]
Mozart, W.A.:Con 12 Pno, w. M. Migdal (pno) LaserLight ▲ 15 870 [DDD]
Mozart, W.A.:Con 25 Pno, w. M. Migdal (pno) LaserLight ▲ 15 870 [DDD]
Mozart, W.A.:Con 7 Vn, w. H. Kurosaki (vn) Capriccio ▲ 10 620 [DDD]
Roman, J.H.:Drottningholmsmusiquen Capriccio ▲ 10 624 [DDD]
W. Christie (cnd)
Bach, C.P.E.:Die Israeliten in der Wüste, w. L. Lootens (sop), B. Schlick (sop), H. Meens (ten), S. Barcoe (sgr), Corona Musique d'Abord ▲ HMA 1901321
Hasse, J.A.:Cleofide, w. Emma Kirkby (sop), Agnès Mellon (sop), Randall Wong (ct), Dominique Visse (ct), Derek Lee Ragin (ct), David Cordier (alt) [I] Capriccio 4-▲ 10193/96 [DDD]
G. Ferro (cnd)
Rossini, G.:La Cenerentola, w. E. Ravaglia (sop), L. V. Terrani (mez), F. Araiza (ten), E. Dara (bar), Cologne Radio Chorus [I] Sony Classical 2-▲ S2K 46433 [ADD]
Rossini, G.:L'italiana in Algeri, w. L. V. Terrani (mez), L. Rizzi (cta), W. Ganzarolli (bar), E. Dara (bar), Cologne Radio Chorus [period instrs] [I] CBS 2-▲ M2K 39048 [ADD]
G. Fischer (cnd)
Telemann, G.P.:Con Rcr, w. G. Höller (rcr), K. Hünteler (trns fl) LaserLight ▲ 14036 [DDD]
N. Kraemer (cnd)
Mozart, W.A.:Con 9 Pno, w. L. Nicholson (pno) Capriccio ▲ 10 621 [DDD]
Mozart, W.A.:Con 12 Pno, w. L. Nicholson (pno) Capriccio ▲ 10 622 [DDD]
Mozart, W.A.:Con 13 Pno, w. L. Nicholson (pno) LaserLight ▲ 15 871 [DDD]
Mozart, W.A.:Con 13 Pno, w. L. Nicholson (pno) Capriccio ▲ 10 623 [DDD]
Mozart, W.A.:Con 18 Pno, w. L. Nicholson (pno) Capriccio ▲ 10 622 [DDD]
Mozart, W.A.:Con 21 Pno, w. L. Nicholson (pno) Capriccio ▲ 10 621 [DDD]
Mozart, W.A.:Con 23 Pno, w. L. Nicholson (pno) LaserLight ▲ 15 871 [DDD]
Mozart, W.A.:Con 23 Pno, w. L. Nicholson (pno) Capriccio ▲ 10 623 [DDD]
F. Leitner (cnd)
Gluck, C.W.:Orfeo ed Euridice, w. Ruth-Margret Pütz (sop), Elisabeth Söderström (sop), Dietrich Fischer-Dieskau (bar), Cologne Radio Chorus *(rec live, Cologne, Nov. 8, 1964)* Orfeo d'or 2-▲ 391952
Handel, G.F.:Alcina, w. J. Sutherland (sop), N. Proctor (cta), van Dick (sgr), Cologne Radio Chorus [I] *(rec live, 1959)* Verona 3-▲ 27011/13 (m) [AAD]
Handel, G.F.:Alcina, w. J. Sutherland (sop), N. Procter (cta), N. Monti (ten), F. Wunderlich (ten), T. Hemsley (bar), Cologne Radio Chorus Melodram 3-▲ CDM 37002
Handel, G.F.:Alcina (sels), w. J. Sutherland (sop)—(2 arias) Di, cor mio, quanto t'amai; Ah! mio cor! scherrito sei [I] *(rec live May 15, 1959)* Myto 2-▲ 2 MCD 90529 [ADD]
H.-M. Linde (cnd)
Mozart, W.A.:Sym 25 Capriccio ▲ 10 620 [DDD]
Mozart, W.A.:Sym 31 Capriccio ▲ 10 620 [DDD]
J. Rifkin (cnd)
Mozart, W.A.:Sym 32 [period instrs] Capriccio ▲ CD 10728 [DDD]

ORCH. & ENS.

Capella Coloniensis (cont.)
C. Scimone (cnd)
Vivaldi, A.:La Sena festeggiante, w. L Cuberli (sop), H. Müller-Molinari (mez), S. Nimsgern (b-bar) Cetra Classic ▲ CDC 25 [AAD]
Capella Compostelana
Vaquedano, J. de:Villancicos—Pan por pan; Peregrino espera; Que gira, que buela; O Crux, Ave; Quien de las flores; que le diré a esta bella zagala; Interveniat pro Nobis; Al ver un infante; Contra los villancicos de noche Buena; Diga la admiración; Ha de la tumba sacra [Sp & L] Fonti Musicali ▲ FMD 200 [DDD]
Capella Concertante
A. von Aarburg (cnd)
Haydn, M.:Missa Sancti Leopoldi in festo Innocentium, w. R. Zela, A. Schram (sop), O. Messerli (alto), Zurich Boys' Choir [L] *(rec 12/89)* Tudor ▲ 754 [DDD]
Haydn, M.:Vesperae pro festo Sanctorum Innocentium, w. L. Tsimitselis (sop), A. Schram (sop), O. Messerli (alt), Zurich Boys' Choir [L] *(rec 12/89)* Tudor ▲ 754 [DDD]
Capella della pietà de Turchini
A Neapolitan Vespers of the Blessed Virgin Mary, 1632 Symphonia ▲ SYM 91S04 [DDD]
Oh Cielo, Oh Ammore:Baroque Neopolitan Cantatas, Vol. 1, w. Pino de Vittorio Symphonia ▲ SYM 91S07 [DDD]
A. Florio (cnd)
Caresana, C.:Per la Nascita del Verbo Opus 111 ▲ OPS 30-152
Sui Palchi Delle Stelle:Sacred Music in the Neapolitan Conservatories at the Time of Francesco Provenzale, w. Antonella Ippolito (sop), Jane Haughton (sop), Daniela del Monaco (alt), Sebastiano Cassarà (vn), Rosario Di Meglio (vn), Antonella Bologna (va), Paolo Dionisio (vl), Antonio Florio (vc), Pierluigi Ciappareli (thb), Enrico Baiano (org/hpd) Symphonia ▲ SY 93S20 [DDD]
Capella Ensemble
Music of the Napolenic Era Inside Sounds ▲ ISC 111 [DDD]
Capella Istropolitana
Bach, J.S.:Music of—Ave Maria; In Dulci Jubilo; Mein Jesu; Nun komm, der Heiden; Sheep May Safely Graze; Wachet auf; also, selections from Brandenburg Con. 1-3; Double Con.; Suites 2-4; Violin Con. in a & in E Naxos ▲ 8.551106 [DDD]
Beethoven, L. van:Music of, w. J. Jandó (pno), et al., CSR SO Bratislava, Slovak PO—Egmont & Fidelio Ovs.; Für Elise; sels. from Pno Son. 8 & 14; Sym. 3, 5 & 6; Pno Con. 4 & 5; Vn Con. Naxos ▲ 8.551101 [DDD] Δ 7.551101 [DDD]
Mozart, W.A.:Arias, w. A. Martin (bar), D. Robin (cnd), Vienna Mozart Orch—arias & duets from Entführung aus dem Serail, Così fan tutte, Don Giovanni, Die Zauberflöte, Le nozze di Figaro [G,I] Naxos ▲ 8.550435 [DDD]
Mozart, W.A.:Music of—sels. from Eine kleine; Son., K.310 Pno; Qt Strs, K.458; Syms 25, 40 & 41; Con Cl; Divert K.136; Con 1 Fl; Serenata Notturna; Con 3 Vn; Con 21 Pno Naxos ▲ 8.551103 [DDD] Δ 7.551103 [DDD]
Vivaldi, A.:Music of, w. Concentus Hungaricus, Dall'Arco CO, Budapest Strings—selections from The Four Seasons; Flautino Con. in C; Flute Con. in F; Flute Con. in a, RV.108; Con. in B♭ for 2 Trumpets; Concerti, Op. 3/4, 8, 10 & 11; Oboe Con., Op. 8/9; Violin Con., Op. 8/5 & 12; Lute Con. in D; Il Gardellino Naxos ▲ 8.551105 [DDD]
P. Breiner (cnd)
Boccherini, L.:Con Vc, G.482, w. L. Kanta (vc) *(rec 9/87)* Naxos ▲ 8.550059 [DDD]
Haydn, J.:Con 1 Vc, w. L. Kanta (vc) *(rec 9/87)* Naxos ▲ 8.550059 [DDD]
Haydn, J.:Con 2 Vc, w. L. Kanta (vc) *(rec 11/88)* Naxos ▲ 8.550059 [DDD]
C. Brembeck (cnd)
Bach, J.S.:Cant 199, w. F. Wagner (sop) [G] *(rec May 1991)* Naxos ▲ 8.550431 [DDD]
Bach, J.S.:Cant 202, "Wedding Cant", w. F. Wagner (sop) [G] *(rec May 1991)* Naxos ▲ 8.550431 [DDD]
Bach, J.S.:Cant 209, w. F. Wagner (sop) [G] *(rec May 1991)* Naxos ▲ 8.550431 [DDD]
O. Dohnányi (cnd)
Bach, J.S.:Cons Vn (comp), w. T. Nishizaki (vn) *(rec 1989)* Naxos ▲ 8.550194 [DDD]
Bach, J.S.:Con for 2 Vns, w. T. Nishizaki (vn), A. Jablokov (vn) *(rec 1989)* Naxos ▲ 8.550194 [DDD]
Beethoven, L. van:Contredanses, WoO 14 *(rec June 1989)* Naxos ▲ 8.550433 [DDD]
Beethoven, L. van:Dances, WoO 17 *(rec June 1989)* Naxos ▲ 8.550433 [DDD]
Beethoven, L. van:German Dances, WoO 42 *(rec June 1989)* Naxos ▲ 8.550433 [DDD]
Beethoven, L. van:Minuets Orch, WoO 7 *(rec June 1989)* Naxos ▲ 8.550433 [DDD]
Respighi, O.:Bach Transcriptions, w. T. Nishizaki (vn)—Son. for Violin & Basso Continuo, BWV.1023 trans. for violin & strings *(rec 1989)* Naxos ▲ 8.550194 [DDD]
J. Dvořák (cnd)
Bach, J.S.:Orchestral Trans—Prelude in b (Stokowski); Siciliano (J. Dvorák); Wachet auf, ruft uns die Stimme (G. Bantock) *(rec Jan-Mar 1989)* Naxos ▲ 8.550244 [DDD]
Bach, J.S.:Ov, BWV 1070 *(rec Jan-Mar 1989)* Naxos ▲ 8.550245 [DDD]
Bach, J.S.:Suites Orch, BWV 1066-1069—Nos. 1-3 [No. 3 arr Joachim Raff] *(rec Jan-Mar 1989)* Naxos ▲ 8.550244 [DDD]
Bach, J.S.:Suite 3 Orch *(rec Jan-Mar 1989)* Naxos ▲ 8.550245 [DDD]
C. Eberle (cnd)
Mozart, W.A.:Con 20 Pno, w. Peter Lang (pno) *(rec Concert Hall of Czecho-Slovak Radio, Bratislava, May 3-8, 1988)* Lydian ▲ 18028 [DDD]
Mozart, W.A.:Con 21 Pno, w. Peter Lang (pno) *(rec Concert Hall of Czecho-Slovak Radio, Bratislava, May 3-8, 1988)* Lydian ▲ 18028 [DDD]
R. Edlinger (cnd)
Baroque Favorites Naxos ▲ 8.550102 [DDD]
Best Of Baroque Music Naxos ▲ 8.550014 [DDD]
Mozart, W.A.:Con Fl Hp, w. J. Válek (fl), H. Müllerová (hp) *(rec 1988)* Naxos ▲ 8.550159 [DDD]
Mozart, W.A.:Divert Hns Bn, K.205 *(rec March 1988)* Naxos ▲ 8.550108 [DDD]
Mozart, W.A.:Diverts Str Qt, K.136-138 *(rec March 1988)* Naxos ▲ 8.550108 [DDD]
Mozart, W.A.:Sinf concertante Ob, K.Anh.9 *(rec 1988)* Naxos ▲ 8.550159 [DDD]
Telemann, G.P.:Cons (misc), w. L. Kyselak (va), Z. Tylšar (hn), B. Tylšar (hn), A. Hoelbling (vn) Q. Hoelbling (vn), A. Jablokov (vn)—Viola Con. in G; Concerto in F for 3 Violins; Concerto for 2 Horns Naxos ▲ 8.550156 [DDD] Δ 7.550156 [DDD]
Telemann, G.P.:Suite Rcr, w. J. Stivín (rcr) Naxos ▲ 8.550156 [DDD] Δ 7.550156 [DDD]
S. Gunzenhauser (cnd)
Chen, G.:Songs, w. Takako Nishizaki (vn) [arr. for solo violin & orchestra]—Bells from the Temple; Flowing Water and Floating Clouds; The Hungry Horse Rattles His Bridle *(rec Shatin Town Hall, Hong Kong, June 23, 1987)* Marco Polo ("Chinese Composers" series) ▲ 8.223908 [DDD]
Mozart, W.A.:Adagio Vn, K.261, w. T. Nishizaki (vn) Naxos ▲ 8.550418 [DDD]
Mozart, W.A.:Con 3 Vn, w. T. Nishizaki (vn) Naxos ▲ 8.550418 [DDD]
Mozart, W.A.:Con 4 Vn, w. T. Nishizaki (vn) *(rec Nov. 1989)* Naxos ▲ 8.550332 [DDD]
Mozart, W.A.:Con 5 Vn, w. T. Nishizaki (vn) Naxos ▲ 8.550418 [DDD]
Mozart, W.A.:Rondo Vn, K.373, w. T. Nishizaki (vn) Naxos ▲ 8.550418 [DDD]
Mozart, W.A.:Sinf concertante Vn, K.364, w. T. Nishizaki (vn), L. Kyselak (va) *(rec Nov. 1989)* Naxos ▲ 8.550332 [DDD]
Vivaldi, A.:Cons Orch—RV.151, "Concerto alla Rustica" Naxos ▲ 8.550056 [DDD] Δ 7.550056 [DDD]
Vivaldi, A.:Cons Vn, Op. 8/1-4, "The Four Seasons", w. T. Nishizaki (vn) Naxos ▲ 8.550056 [DDD] Δ 7.550056 [DDD]
P. Guth (cnd)
Haydn, J.:Minuetti, H.IX/16 CPO ▲ CPO 999108 [DDD]
J. Kopelman (cnd)
Handel, G.F.:Concerti grossi, Op. 3—No. 3 Naxos ▲ 8.550157 [DDD]
Handel, G.F.:Concerti grossi, Op. 6—Nos. 4-6 *(rec 5/88)* Naxos ▲ 8.550157 [DDD]
J. Kopelman (cnd)
Mozart, W.A.:Cons Hn, w. M. Stevove (hn) *(rec Nov. 1988)* Naxos ▲ 8.550148 [DDD]
Vivaldi, A.:Cons Vn, Op. 3/1-12, "L'estro armonico", w. J. Kopelman (vn)—Nos. 1, 2, 4, 7, 8, 10 & 11 Naxos ▲ 8.550160 [DDD]

Capella Istropolitana (cont.)
J. Krček (cnd)
Christmas Concerti *(rec Jan. & Mar. 1989 & June &)* Naxos ▲ 8.550567 [DDD]
Corelli, A.:Concerti grossi, Op. 6—Nos. 1-6 *(rec 1990)* Naxos ▲ 8.550402 [DDD]
Corelli, A.:Concerti grossi, Op. 6—Nos. 7-12 *(rec 1990)* Naxos ▲ 8.550403 [DDD]
Dvořák, A.:Serenade Strs *(rec 5/90)* Naxos ▲ 8.550419 [DDD]
Handel, G.F.:Messiah (sels), w. L. Holásek (cnd), Bratislava City Chorus—choruses *(rec 9/89)* Naxos ▲ 8.550317 [DDD]; Δ 7.550317 [DDD]
Italian Concerti Grossi *(rec Mar. 1993)* Naxos ▲ 8.550877 [DDD]
Locatelli, P.:Concerti grossi—Nos. 1-6 *(rec Moyzes Hall, Sept 1994 & Feb 1995)* Naxos ▲ 8.553445 [DDD]
Suk, J.:Serenade Strs *(rec 5/90)* Naxos ▲ 8.550419 [DDD]
A. Leaper (cnd)
Bridge, F.:Lament Strs Naxos ▲ 8.550331 [DDD]
Dowland, J.:Galliards—Galliard a 5 Naxos ▲ 8.550331 [DDD]
Elgar, E.:Elegy Strs Naxos ▲ 8.550331 [DDD]
Elgar, E.:Intro & Allegro Naxos ▲ 8.550331 [DDD]
Elgar, E.:Serenade Strs Naxos ▲ 8.550331 [DDD]
Grieg, E.:Elegaic Melodies, Op. 34 *(rec 4/89)* Naxos ▲ 8.550330 [DDD]
Grieg, E.:Melodies, Op. 53 *(rec 4/89)* Naxos ▲ 8.550330 [DDD]
Parry, H.:An English Suite Naxos ▲ 8.550331 [DDD]
Parry, H.:Lady Radnor's Suite Naxos ▲ 8.550331 [DDD]
Sibelius, J.:Andante festivo *(rec 4/89)* Naxos ▲ 8.550330 [DDD]
Sibelius, J.:Canzonetta *(rec 4/89)* Naxos ▲ 8.550330 [DDD]
Sibelius, J.:Rakastava Strs *(rec 4/89)* Naxos ▲ 8.550330 [DDD]
Sibelius, J.:Romance Strs *(rec 4/89)* Naxos ▲ 8.550330 [DDD]
W. Perry (cnd)
Molter, J.M.:Con in D Tpt, w. A. Ghitalla (tpt) Premier ▲ PRCD 1027 [DDD]
U. Schneider (cnd)
Daetwyler, J.:Dialog mit der Natur, w. J. Molnár (alphn) Marco Polo ▲ 8.223101 [DDD]
Farkas, F.:Concertino rustico, w. J. Molnár (alphn) Marco Polo ▲ 8.223101 [DDD]
Mozart, L.:Sym in G, "Sinf pastorella", w. J. Molnár (alphn) Marco Polo ▲ 8.223101 [DDD]
P. Škvor (cnd)
Famous Trumpet Concerti, w. Miroslav Kejmar (tpt) *(rec 1/89)* Naxos ▲ 8.550243 [DDD]
W. Sobotka (cnd)
Mozart, W.A.:Divert Hns Strs, K.247 Naxos ▲ 8.550026 [DDD] Δ 7.550026 [DDD]
Mozart, W.A.:Kleine Nachtmusik Naxos ▲ 8.550026 [DDD] Δ 7.550026 [DDD]
Mozart, W.A.:Serenata notturna Naxos ▲ 8.550026 [DDD] Δ 7.550026 [DDD]
F. Vajnar (cnd)
Fiala, J.:Con for 2 Hns, w. Z. Tylšar (hn), B. Tylšar (hn) Naxos ▲ 8.550459 [DDD]
Pokorny, F.X.:Con Hns, w. Z. Tylšar (hn), B. Tylšar (hn) Naxos ▲ 8.550459 [DDD]
Rosetti, F.A.:Con for 2 Hns, w. Z. Tylšar (hn), B. Tylšar (hn)—Concerti in A♭ & E♭ Naxos ▲ 8.550459 [DDD]
B. Warchal (cnd)
Bach, J.S.:Brandenburg Cons—Nos. 1-3 Naxos ▲ 8.550047 [DDD]
Bach, J.S.:Brandenburg Cons—Nos. 4-6 Naxos ▲ 8.550048 [DDD] Δ 7.550048 [DDD]
Handel, G.F.:Royal Fireworks Music Naxos ▲ 8.550109 [DDD]; Δ 7.550109 [DDD]
Handel, G.F.:Water Music (comp) Naxos ▲ 8.550109 [DDD]; Δ 7.550109 [DDD]
J. Wildner (cnd)
Mozart, W.A.:Arias, w. J. Dickie (ten)—arias from Clemenza di Tito, Così fan tutte, Don Giovanni, Entführung aus dem Serail, Die Zauberflöte *(rec Dec. 1989)* Naxos ▲ 8.550383 [DDD]
Mozart, W.A.:Con 1 Vn, w. T. Nishizaki (vn) Naxos ▲ 8.550414 [DDD]
Mozart, W.A.:Con 2 Vn, w. T. Nishizaki (vn) *(rec April 3-9, 1990)* Naxos ▲ 8.550414 [DDD]
Mozart, W.A.:Così fan tutte, w. J. Borowska (sop—Fiordiligi), P. Coles (sop—Despina), R. Yachmi (mez—Dorabella), J. Dickie (ten—Ferrando), A. Martin (bar—Guglielmo), P. Mikulaš (b-bar—Don Alfonso), Slovak Phil Chorus [I] *(rec Feb.-Mar. 1990)* Naxos 3-▲ 8.660008/10 [DDD]
Mozart, W.A.:Così fan tutte (sels), w. Joanna Borowska (sop—Fiordiligi), Priti Coles (sop—Despina), Rohangiz Yachmi (mez—Dorabella), John Dickie (ten—Ferrando), Andrea Martin (bar—Guglielmo), Peter Mikulaš (bass—Don Alfonso), Milada Synkova (hpd), Slovak Phil Chorus—Ov.; [Act I] La mia Dorabella capace non è; È la fede della femmine; Una bella serenata; Ah guarda, sorella; Vorrei dir, e cor non ho; Sento, o Dio; Bella vita militar!; Soave sia il vento; Smanie implacabili; In uomini, in soldati; Alla bella Despinetta; Come Scoglio; Non siate ritrosi; Un'aura amorosa; [Act II] Una donna a quindici anni; Prenderò quel brunettino; La mano a me date; Ei parte...senti...ah no!; Donne mie la fate a tanti a tanti; Fra gle amplessi; Fortunato l'uom che prende *(rec Slovak Philharmonic Moyzes Hall, Bratislava, Feb.-Apr. 1990)* Naxos ▲ 8.553172 [DDD]
Mozart, W.A.:Dances & Marches—German Dances, K.586, 600, 602 & 605 Naxos ▲ 8.550412 [DDD]
Mozart, W.A.:March Orch, K.249 *(rec Apr. 1990)* Naxos ▲ 8.550333 [DDD]
Mozart, W.A.:Rondo Vn, K.269, w. T. Nishizaki (vn) Naxos ▲ 8.550414 [DDD]
Mozart, W.A.:Serenade Vn, K.250, w. T. Nishizaki (vn) *(rec Apr. 1990)* Naxos ▲ 8.550333 [DDD]
Saint-Saëns, C.:Andante Vn, w. T. Nishizaki (vn) Naxos ▲ 8.550414 [DDD]
B. Wordsworth (cnd)
Beethoven, L. van:Con 1 Pno, w. S. Vladar (pno) *(rec 10/88)* Naxos ▲ 8.550190 [DDD]
Beethoven, L. van:Con 2 Pno, w. S. Vladar (pno) Naxos ▲ 8.550121 [DDD]
Beethoven, L. van:Con 2 Pno, w. Stefan Vladar (pno) *(rec Slovak Philharmonic Concert Hall, Bratislava, Mar 1988)* Naxos 4-▲ 8.504011 [DDD]
Beethoven, L. van:Con 3 Pno, w. S. Vladar (pno) Naxos ▲ 8.550122 [DDD]
Beethoven, L. van:Con 4 Pno, w. Stefan Vladar (pno) *(rec Concert Hall, Bratislava, Mar 1988)* Naxos ▲ 8.553266 [DDD]
Beethoven, L. van:Con 4 Pno, w. S. Vladar (pno) Naxos ▲ 8.550122 [DDD]
Beethoven, L. van:Con 5 Pno, "Emperor", w. Stefan Vladar (pno) *(rec Slovak Philharmonic Concert Hall, Bratislava, Mar 1988)* Naxos 4-▲ 8.504011 [DDD]
Beethoven, L. van:Con 5 Pno, "Emperor", w. S. Vladar (pno) Naxos ▲ 8.550121 [DDD]
Beethoven, L. van:Con 5 Pno, "Emperor", w. Stefan Vladar (pno) *(rec Concert Hall, Bratislava, Mar 1988)* Naxos ▲ 8.553266 [DDD]
Haydn, J.:Sym 44, "Trauer" *(rec 6/89)* Naxos ▲ 8.550287 [DDD]
Haydn, J.:Sym 45, "Farewell" *(rec 12/89)* Naxos ▲ 8.550382 [DDD]
Haydn, J.:Sym 48, "Maria Theresia" *(rec 12/89)* Naxos ▲ 8.550382 [DDD]
Haydn, J.:Sym 82, "The Bear" Naxos ▲ 8.550139 [DDD]
Haydn, J.:Sym 83, "The Hen" Naxos ▲ 8.550114 [DDD] Δ 7.550114 [DDD]
Haydn, J.:Sym 85, "La Reine de France" *(rec 3/90)* Naxos ▲ 8.550387 [DDD]
Haydn, J.:Sym 88 *(rec 6/89)* Naxos ▲ 8.550287 [DDD]
Haydn, J.:Sym 92, "Oxford" *(rec 3/90)* Naxos ▲ 8.550387 [DDD]
Haydn, J.:Sym 94, "Surprise Sym" Naxos ▲ 8.550114 [DDD] Δ 7.550114 [DDD]
Haydn, J.:Sym 96, "Miracle" Naxos ▲ 8.550139 [DDD]
Haydn, J.:Sym 100, "Military" Naxos ▲ 8.550139 [DDD]
Haydn, J.:Sym 101, "Clock" Naxos ▲ 8.550114 [DDD] Δ 7.550114 [DDD]
Haydn, J.:Sym 102 *(rec 12/89)* Naxos ▲ 8.550382 [DDD]
Haydn, J.:Sym 103, "Drum Roll" *(rec 3/90)* Naxos ▲ 8.550387 [DDD]
Haydn, J.:Sym 104, "London" *(rec 6/89)* Naxos ▲ 8.550287 [DDD]
Mozart, W.A.:Ovs—(18) Apollo et Hyacinthus; Bastien; Lucio Silla; La finta giardiniera; Il rè pastore; Idomeneo; Die Entführung aus dem Serail; Der Schauspieldirektor; Don Giovanni; Le nozze di Figaro; Così fan tutte; Die Zauberflöte; Mitridate, rè di Ponto; La clemenza di Tito *(rec Sept. 6-9 1988)* Naxos ▲ 8.550185 [DDD]
Mozart, W.A.:Ovs—Apollo et Hyacinthus, K.38; Bastien und Bastienne, K.50; Mitridate, rè di Ponto, K.87; Lucio Silla, K.135; La finta giardiniera, K.196; Il rè pastore, K.208; Idomeneo, K.366; Die Entführung aus dem Serail, K.384; Der Schauspieldirektor, K.486; Marriage of Figaro, K.492; Don Giovanni, K.527; Così fan tutte, K.588; Magic Flute, K.620; La clemenza di Tito, K.621 *(rec Czechoslovak Radio Concert Hall, Bratislava, Sept 6-9, 1988)* Naxos 4-▲ 8.504013 [DDD]

110 ▲ = CD ♦ = Enhanced CD Δ = MD ■ = Cassette Tape □ = DCC

Capella Istropolitana (cont.)
B. Wordsworth (cnd) (cont.)
Mozart, W.A.:Sym 25 — Naxos ▲ 8.550113 [DDD]
Mozart, W.A.:Sym 27 — Naxos ▲ 8.550264 [DDD]
Mozart, W.A.:Sym 28 — Naxos ▲ 8.550164 [DDD]
Mozart, W.A.:Sym 29 — Naxos ▲ 8.550119 [DDD]
Mozart, W.A.:Sym 30 — Naxos ▲ 8.550119 [DDD]
Mozart, W.A.:Sym 31 — Naxos ▲ 8.550164 [DDD]
Mozart, W.A.:Sym 32 — Naxos ▲ 8.550113 [DDD]
Mozart, W.A.:Sym 33 — Naxos ▲ 8.550264 [DDD]
Mozart, W.A.:Sym 34 — Naxos ▲ 8.550186 [DDD]
Mozart, W.A.:Sym 35 — Naxos ▲ 8.550186 [DDD]
Mozart, W.A.:Sym 36 — Naxos ▲ 8.550264 [DDD]
Mozart, W.A.:Sym 38 — Naxos ▲ 8.550119 [DDD]
Mozart, W.A.:Sym 39 — Naxos ▲ 8.550186 [DDD]
Mozart, W.A.:Sym 40 *(rec June 1988)* — Naxos ▲ 8.550299 [DDD]
Mozart, W.A.:Sym 40 — Naxos ▲ 8.550164 [DDD]
Mozart, W.A.:Sym 41 *(rec Mar. 1988)* — Naxos ▲ 8.550299 [DDD]
Mozart, W.A.:Sym 41 — Naxos ▲ 8.550113 [DDD]

Capella Nova
A. Tavener (cnd)
Black, J.:Sacred Music—Ane Lesson upone the Feftie Psalme — ASV ("Gaudeamus" series) ▲ ASV 136 [DDD]
Carver, R.:Cantate Domino — ASV ("Gaudeamus" series) ▲ ASV 136 [DDD]
Carver, R.:Sacred Choral Music (comp)—Dum sacrum mysterium; Two Motets [L] — ASV ("Gaudeamus" series) ▲ CD GAU 124 [DDD]
Carver, R.:Sacred Choral Music (comp)—Mass for Six Voices; Mass "L'homme armé" for Four Voices [L] — ASV ("Gaudeamus" series) ▲ CD GAU 126 [DDD]
Carver, R.:Sacred Choral Music (comp)—Mass "Fera Pessima" for Five Voices; Mass "Pater Creator Omnium" for Four Voices [L] — ASV ("Gaudeamus" series) ▲ CD GAU 127 [DDD]

Capella Piccola Neuss
T. Reuber (cnd)
Fux, J.J.:La Fede sacrilega nella morte del Precursor San Giovanni Battista, "Johannes der Täufer", w. J. Koslowsky (sop), M. Lins (sop), H. Helling (cta), J. Calaminus (ten), G. Schwarz (bass) [period instrs] [I] — Thorofon 2-▲ CTH 2071/72 [DDD]

Capella Regis Musicalis
R. Hugo (cnd)
Michna, A.V.:Sacred Music, w. M. Bornus-Szczycinski (sgr), M. Cechalová (sgr), J. Lewitová (sgr), M. Pospí il (sgr), M. Predota (sgr)—Missa V à 5 et à 7 si placet; Cantiones pro Defunctis; Missa VI pro Defunctis à 6 et à 10; Requiem — Studio Matou ▲ MAT 1 [DDD]
Zelenka, J.D.:Il penitenti al sepolchro del Redentore, w. Magdaléna Kozená (alt—Maddalena), Martin Prokeš (ten—Davidde), Michael Pospíšil (bass) *(rec St Franciscus Church of the Convent of St Agnes of Bohemia, Prague, Nov 1994)* — Panton ▲ 811389-2 [DDD]

Capella Reial de Catalunya
J. Savall (cnd)
El Cant de la Sibil-la, Vol. 1, w. Montserrat Figueras (sop) — Fontalis ▲ ES 8705

Capella Rudolphina
Mirabile Mysterium, w. Duodena Cantitans — Supraphon ▲ SUP 0192
P. Danek (cnd)
Music From the Time of Prince Rudolf II, w. Michael Consort, Duodena Cantitans — Supraphon ▲ SUP 112176 [DDD]

Capella Sancti Michaelis
E. van Nevel (cnd)
Biber, H. von:Requiem à 15, w. G. de Reyghere (sop), J. Feldman (sop), J. Bowman (ct), I. Honeyman (ten), M. van Egmond (bass), Ricercar Consort [L] *(rec 5/90)* — Ricercar ▲ RIC 81063 [DDD]
Kerll, J.C.:Missa pro defunctis, w. G. de Reyghere (sop), J. Bowman (alt), I. Honeyman (ten), G. de Mey (ten), M. van Egmond (bass), Ricercar Consort [L] *(rec 5/90)* — Ricercar ▲ RIC 81063 [DDD]

Capella Savaria
Naudot, J.-C.:Cons Fl, w. Pál Németh (fl) — Hungaroton ▲ HCD 31600 [DDD]
N. McGegan (cnd)
Handel, G.F.:Agrippina, w. S. Bradshaw (sop), W. Hill (sop), L. Saffer (sop), G. Banditelli (cta), D. Minter (alt), R. Popken (alt), B. Szilágyi (bar), M. Dean (b-bar), N. Isherwood (bass) [period instrs] [I] — Harmonia Mundi USA 3-▲ HMU 907063/65 ■ HMU 407063/65
Handel, G.F.:Brockes-Passion, w. K. Farkas (sop), M. Zádori (sop), D. Minter (alt), J. Bándi (ten), M. Klietmann (ten), G. de Mey (ten), I. Gáti (bar), Hallé State Chorus [period instrs] [G] — Hungaroton 3-▲ HCD 12734/36 [DDD]
Telemann, G.P.:Brockes Passion, w. M. Zádori (sop), A. Markert (cta), M. Klietmann (ten), G. De Mey (ten), I. Gáti (bar), Hallé State Chorus [period instrs] — Hungaroton 3-▲ HCD 31130/32 [DDD]
Vivaldi, A.:Juditha triumphans devicta Holofernes barbarie, w. M. Zádori (sop), J. Németh (mez), K. Gémes (mez), G. Banditelli (cta), A. Markert (cta), Savaria Vocal Ensemble [L] — Hungaroton 2-▲ HCD 31063/64 [DDD]
G. Németh (cnd)
Handel, G.F.:St. John Passion, w. Mária Z(ádori (sop), Judit Németh (mez), Charles Brett (ct), Martin Klietmann (ten), Jósef Moldvay (bass) — Hungaroton ▲ HCD 12908 [DDD]
P. Németh (cnd)
Bruhns, N.:Jauchzet dem Herren alle Welt, "Psalm 100", w. M. Klietmann (ten) [period instrs]; [G] — Hungaroton ▲ HCD 31134 [DDD]
Esterházy, P.:Harmonia caelestis, w. M. Fers (sop), M. Zádori (sop), K. Gémes (mez), K. Károlyi (cta), G. Kállay (ten), J. Moldvay (bass), Savaria Vocal Ensemble [period instrs] [L] — Hungaroton 2-▲ HCD 31148/49 [DDD]
Fux, J.J.:Plaudite, sonat tuba, w. M. Klietmann (ten), E. H. Tarr (tpt) [period instrs] [L] — Hungaroton ▲ HCD 31134 [DDD]
Graun, K.H.:Der Tod Jesu, w. M. Zádori (sop), M. Fers (sop), M. Klietmann (ten), K. Mertens (b-bar) — Musique d'Abord ▲ HMA 1903061
Handel, G.F.:Cons (16) Org, w. F. Haseböck (org)—5 sels. — Hänssler Classic ▲ 98940 [DDD]
Monteverdi, C.:Salve, o Regina, w. M. Klietmann (ten) [period instrs] [L] — Hungaroton ▲ HCD 31134 [DDD]
A Musical Grand Tour, w. Concerto Amsterdam [cnd:Jaap Schröder], Ensemble 415 [cnd:Chiara Banchini], Philharmonia Baroque [cnd:Nicholas McGegan], et al. — Harmonia Mundi ▲ HMUK 986001
Pergolesi, G.B.:La serva padrona, w. K. Farkas (sop), J. Gregor (bass) [period instrs] [F,I] — Hungaroton ▲ HCD 12846 [DDD]
Schütz, H.:Kleine geistliche Konzerte (sels), w. M. Klietmann (ten) [period instrs]—5 selections—SWV.282, 285, 306, 308, 309 [G] — Hungaroton ▲ HCD 31134 [DDD]
Schütz, H.:Symphoniae sacrae (sels), w. M. Klietmann (ten) [period instrs]—2 selections—Paratum cor meum, SWV.257; Singet dem Herren ein neues Lied, SWV.342 [G,L] — Hungaroton ▲ HCD 31134 [DDD]
Vivaldi, A.:Cons Ob, w. M. Wolf (ob/rcr)—RV.450, 454, 457, 442, 535, 545 & 557 *(rec 1991)* — Musique d'Abord ▲ HMA 1903018
Vivaldi, A.:Motets, w. M. Zádori (sop)—Canta in prato, ride in monte, RV.623; O qui coeli terraeque serenitas, RV.631; Nulla in mundo pax sincera, RV.630; In furore iustissimae irae, RV.626; Carae rosae respirate, RV.624; Vos aurae per montes, RV.634 *(rec 1992)* — Musique d'Abord ▲ HMA 1903063
Werner, G.J.:Debora, w. W. Hill (sop), G. Banditelli (mez), M. Klietmann (ten), K. Mertens (b-bar) — Quintana ▲ QUI 903062
M. Térey-Smith (cnd)
Rameau, J.P.:Abaris Suite [period instrs] *(rec Köszeg Castle, Mar 1995)* — Naxos ▲ 8.553388 [DDD]
Rameau, J.P.:La Naissance d'Osiris [period instrs] *(rec Köszeg Castle, Mar 1995)* — Naxos ▲ 8.553388 [DDD]

Capella Sebaldina Nuremberg
W. Jacob (cnd)
Pachelbel, J.:Magnificat, w. A. Jacob (org) — Entrée ▲ 0050 [ADD]
Pachelbel, J.:Missa brevis, w. A. Jacob (org) — Entrée ▲ 0050 [ADD]
Pachelbel, J.:Motets, w. A. Jacob (org)—Singet dem Herrn ein neues Lied; Der Herr ist König; Nun danket alle Gott; Jauchzet dem Herrn; Exsurgat Deus; Tröste uns Gott; Gott ist unsre Zuversicht — Entrée ▲ 0050 [ADD]

Capilla Flamenca
Renaissance-polyfonie in Brugge:The Songbook of Zeghere van Male — Eufoda ▲ EUF 1155 [DDD]

Capitol Chamber Artists
Chadabe, J.:Rhythms VI — Centaur ▲ CRC 2071 [DDD]
Eastham, C.:Duo Fl — Centaur ▲ CRC 2071 [DDD]
Walker, G.:Poem — Centaur ▲ CRC 2071 [DDD]
Willey, J.:A Little Quartet — Centaur ▲ CRC 2071 [DDD]
A. Frascarelli (cnd)
Walker, G.:Poem, w. Ian Walker (nar) — Albany ▲ TROY 154 [DDD]

Capitol SO
C.D. Newman (cnd)
The Orchestra Sings:Great Operatic Themes for Orchestra, w. Hollywood Bowl SO — Angel ▲ CDM 65430 ■ EG 65430

Cappella Arcis Varsoviensis
M. Sewen (cnd)
Jarzebski, A.:Music of—complete works — Olympia ▲ OLY 393 [ADD]

Cappella Concinite
Brahms, J.:Songs—Die Entführung; Minnelied; Erlaube mir, feins Mädchen; Ständchen-Verstohlen geht der Mond auf; Altes Minnelied; Da unten im Tale; Wiegenlied *(rec Nov. 8, 22 & 29, 1986)* — Eufoda ▲ 1112
Mendelssohn, F.:Songs—(6) Duets, Op. 63; (3) Duets, Op. 77/1; (3) Folksongs Nos. 1 & 2 *(rec Nov. 8, 22 & 29, 1986)* — Eufoda ▲ 1112
Schumann, R.:Songs—OP. 69/1, 3 & 6; Op. 91/4 *(rec Nov. 8, 22 & 29, 1986)* — Eufoda ▲ 1112

Capriccio Ensemble
Krommer, F.:Sinf Concertante, w. P.-L. Graf (fl), H. R. Stalder (cl), T. Wicky (vn) — Tudor ▲ 757 [DDD]
Schnyder von Wartensee, X.:Con for 2 Cls, w. H. R. Stalder (cl), T. Friedli (cl) — Tudor ▲ 757 [DDD]

Capriccio Italiano Ensemble
D. Ferrari (cnd)
Ricci, F.P.:Dies irae, w. Concentus Musicae Antiqua — Nuova Era ▲ NUO 7244
Ricci, F.P.:Miserere, w. Concentus Musicae Antiqua — Nuova Era ▲ NUO 7243
Ricci, F.P.:Stabat Mater, w. Concentus Musicae Antiqua — Nuova Era ▲ NUO 7243
Sammartini, G.B.:Cants for the Fridays in Lent, w. Silvia Mapelli (sop), Caterina Calvi (cta), Vito Martino (ten)—Il pianto delle pie Donne; Pianto di Maddalena al Sepolcro — Nuova Era ▲ NUO CD 7269
Sammartini, G.B.:Cants for the Fridays in Lent, w. Silvia Mapelli (sop), Caterina Calvi (alt), Vito Martino (ten)—Il Pianto Delle Pie Donne, J.118; Pianto di Maddalena al Sepolcro, J.120 — Enterprise ("Tiziano" series) ▲ ENT TZ 96007 [DDD]

Capriccio Salon Ensemble
Portrait — Canal Grande ▲ CG 9212 [DDD]

Capriccio Stravagante
Monteverdi, C.:Combattimento — Deutsche Harmonia Mundi ▲ 05472-77190-2
Monteverdi, C.:Lamento d'Arianna — Deutsche Harmonia Mundi ▲ 05472-77190-2
S. Sempé (cnd)
Canto Mediterraneo, w. Laurens, Guillemette (sop) — Astrée ▲ 8548
Capriccio Stravagante — Deutsche Harmonia Mundi ▲ 05472-77190-2
Couperin, F.:Pièces de violes avec la bass chifrée, w. Jay Bernfeld (vl) *(rec New York, 1993)* — Deutsche Harmonia Mundi ▲ 05472-77315-2 [DDD]
Couperin, F.:La Sultane, w. Jay Bernfeld (vl) *(rec New York, 1993)* — Deutsche Harmonia Mundi ▲ 05472-77315-2 [DDD]
Couperin, F.:La Superbe, w. Jay Bernfeld (vl) *(rec New York, 1993)* — Deutsche Harmonia Mundi ▲ 05472-77315-2 [DDD]
Couperin, F.:Vl Music, w. Jay Bernfeld (vl)—Le Dodo ou l'amour au berceau *(rec New York, 1993)* — Deutsche Harmonia Mundi ▲ 05472-77315-2 [DDD]
Lully, J.-B.:Divertissements, w. G. Laurens (mez) — Deutsche Harmonia Mundi ▲ 77218-2-RC [DDD]
Monteverdi & His Time, w. Guillemette Laurens (mez) — Deutsche Harmonia Mundi ▲ 05472-77200-2 [DDD]
Purcell, H.:Music of, w. S. Sempé (hpd) — Deutsche Harmonia Mundi ▲ 05472-77252-2

Capriccio Stravagante [Manfredo Kraemer (vn), Michel Murgier (vc), Skip Sempé (hpd/cem)]
Veracini, F.M.:Sonate accademiche *(rec Grace Rainey Rogers Auditorium, Metropolitan Museum of Art, New York City, Aug 1993)* — Deutsche Harmonia Mundi ▲ 05472-77314-2 [DDD]

Capriccioso Duo [Gertrud Weyhofen (mand), Michael Tröster (gtr)]
Duo Capriccioso — Thorofon ▲ CTH 2092 [DDD]
The Sounding Joy:Music for the Winter Holidays

Capricorn
Barber, S.:Music of, w. Alexa Still (fl), Chicago SO, San Diego CO, Atlantic Sinfonietta, New Zealand SO, Arioso Wind Quintet, Repertory Singers—Capricorn Con; Canzone; Fadograph of a Yestern Scene; Cave of the Heart; Adagio for Strs; Souvenirs; Hermit Songs; To Be Sung on Water; The Lovers; Summer Music — Koch International Classics ▲ KIC 7361
Glinka, M.:Grand Sextet — Hyperion ▲ CDA 66163 [AAD]
Højsgaard, E.:Pale Landscape *(rec London, Jan. 17-18, 1993)* — Marco Polo/Dacapo ▲ 8.224008 [DDD]
Rasmussen, K.A.:Italian Con *(rec London, Jan. 17-18, 1993)* — Marco Polo/Dacapo ▲ 8.224008 [DDD]
Rimsky-Korsakov, N.:Qnt Fl — Hyperion ▲ CDA 66163
Schnittke, A.:Madrigals, w. Sarah Leonard (sop) — Hyperion ▲ CDA 66885
Schnittke, A.:Qnt Pno — Hyperion ▲ CDA 66885
Schnittke, A.:Serenade — Hyperion ▲ CDA 66885
Schnittke, A.:Trio Strs — Hyperion ▲ CDA 66885
O. Knussen (cnd)
Ruders, P.:Nightshade — Bridge ▲ BCD 9037 [DDD]

Capricorn [A. Lamb (cl), T. Mason (vc), C. Edwards (pno)]
Nordentoft, A.:Nervous Saurian *(rec London, Jan. 17-18, 1993)* — Marco Polo/Dacapo ▲ 8.224008 [DDD]

Capricorn members [A. Lamb (cl), L. Hatfield (instr), T. Mason (vc), C. Edwards (pno)]
Rosing-Schow, N.:Inner Voices *(rec London, Jan. 17-18, 1993)* — Marco Polo/Dacapo ▲ 8.224008 [DDD]

Capricorn members [E. Layton (vn), A. Lamb (cl), C. Edwards (pno)]
Ruders, P.:Vox in Rama — Bridge ▲ BCD 9037 [DDD]

CAPUT Ensemble
Clementi, A.:Music of—Adagio; Impromptu; Berceuse; Scherzo; Triplum — Stradivarius ▲ STR 33336 [DDD]
Nova, R.:Music of—Sex Nova Organa; Sequentia; Carved Out; Sequentia Super Sex Nova Organa — Stradivarius ▲ STR 33336 [DDD]
Tómasson, H.:Kvartett II — Music from Iceland ▲ ITM 707
Tómasson, H.:Octette — Music from Iceland ▲ ITM 707
Tómasson, H.:Spírall — Music from Iceland ▲ ITM 707
G. O. Gunnarsson (cnd)
Birgisson, S.S.:Qt Strs *(rec Feb-July 1995)* — Music From Iceland ▲ ITM 808 [DDD]
Grímsson, L.H.:Tales from a Forlorn Fortress *(rec Feb 1994)* — Music From Iceland ▲ ITM 808 [DDD]
Ingólfsson, A.:Vink II *(rec Feb-July 1995)* — Music From Iceland ▲ ITM 808 [DDD]
Leifs, J.:Icelandic Dances [arr Atli Heimir Sveinsson for Fl, Cl, Vn, Vc & Pno] *(rec Feb-July 1995)* — Music From Iceland ▲ ITM 808 [DDD]

ORCH. & ENS.

CAPUT Ensemble (cont.)
G. O. Gunnarsson (cnd) (cont.)
Másson, A.:Elja *(rec Feb–July 1995)* Music From Iceland ▲ ITM 808 [DDD]
Ragnarsson, H.:Romanza *(rec Feb–July 1995)* Music From Iceland ▲ ITM 808 [DDD]
Tómasson, H.:Trio Animato *(rec Feb–July 1995)* Music From Iceland ▲ ITM 808 [DDD]
Caramoor Festival Orch
Janácek, L.:Nursery Rhymes, w. J. Rudel Phoenix ▲ PHCD 109 [AAD]
J. Rudel (cnd)
Janácek, L.:Capriccio, w. H. Somer (pno) Phoenix ▲ PHCD 109 [AAD]
Janácek, L.:Concertino Pno, w. H. Somer (pno) Phoenix ▲ PHCD 109 [AAD]
Janácek, L.:Youth Phoenix ▲ PHCD 109 [AAD]
Caravaggio Ensemble
Bravo Bassoon, w. Daniel Smith (bn), Jonathan Still (pno) ASV ▲ ASV 2078 [DDD]
Carillon Brass
Carillon Christmas *(rec Kettering 7th Day Adventist Church, Dayton, OH, Apr. 5–7, 1992)* Integra Classic ▲ IMCD 920 [DDD]
Carlsbad SO
D. Bostock (cnd)
Dvořák, A.:Romance Vn, w. Vladislav Linetzky (vn) *(rec Lazne III, Karlovy Vary, Czech Republic, Jan 13–15, 1996)* Classico ▲ CLASSCD 150
Fibich, Z.:Idyll, w. Jaroslav Kubricht (cl) *(rec Lazne III, Karlovy Vary, Czech Republic, Jan 13–15, 1996)* Classico ▲ CLASSCD 150
Fučík, J.:Der alte Brummbär, w. Marek Rothbauer (bn) *(rec Lazne III, Karlovy Vary, Czech Republic, Jan 13–15, 1996)* Classico ▲ CLASSCD 150
Fučík, J.:Marinarella *(rec Lazne III, Karlovy Vary, Czech Republic, Jan 13–15, 1996)* Classico ▲ CLASSCD 150
Labitzky, A.:Ouverture characteristique *(rec Lazne III, Karlovy Vary, Czech Republic, Jan 13–15, 1996)* Classico ▲ CLASSCD 150
Labitzky, J.:Carlsbad Waltz *(rec Lazne III, Karlovy Vary, Czech Republic, Jan 13–15, 1996)* Classico ▲ CLASSCD 150
Nedbal, O.:Valse triste *(rec Lazne III, Karlovy Vary, Czech Republic, Jan 13–15, 1996)* Classico ▲ CLASSCD 150
Smetana, B.:Orchestral Music—Jump-Dance of the Clowns *(rec Lazne III, Karlovy Vary, Czech Republic, Jan 13–15, 1996)* Classico ▲ CLASSCD 150
Carme Ensemble
Mozart, W.A.:Serenade Ww, K.361 Nuova Era ▲ 6968 [DDD]
L. Izquierdo (cnd)
Falla, M. de:El amor brujo, w. M. Senn (mez) [original ver.] [Sp] Nuova Era ▲ 6809 [DDD]
Falla, M. de:Canciones populares españolas (7), w. M. Senn (mez) [Sp] Nuova Era ▲ 6809 [DDD]
Carmina String Quartet [Matthais Enderle (vn), Susanne Frank (vn), Wendy Champney (va), Stephan Goerner (vc)]
Brahms, J.:Qt 1 Strs *(rec Apr. 16–21, 1993)* Denon/PCM Digital ▲ DEN 75756 [DDD]
Brahms, J.:Qt 2 Strs *(rec Apr. 16–21, 1993)* Denon/PCM Digital ▲ DEN 75756 [DDD]
Debussy, C.:Qt Strs *(rec Feb. 1992)* Denon ▲ CO 75164 [DDD]
Fuchs, R.:Qnt Cl, w. Paul Meyer (cl) *(rec Landgasthof Riehen, Switzerland, Apr 2, 3 18 & 19, 1995)* Denon ▲ CO 78801 [DDD]
Haydn, J.:Qts Strs, Op. 76, "Erdődy Qts"—Nos. 1–3 *(rec La Chaux-de-Fonds, Switzerland, Dec. 1993)* Denon ▲ CO 75970 [DDD]
Haydn, J.:Qts Strs, Op. 76, "Erdődy Qts"—Nos. 4–6 *(rec Musica Théâtre, La Chaux-de-Fonds, Switzerland, Jan. 1995)* Denon ▲ CO 78963 [DDD]
Mendelssohn, F.:Qt 2 Strs Denon ▲ CO 79527 [DDD]
Mendelssohn, F.:Qt 6 Strs Denon ▲ CO 79527 [DDD]
Ravel, M.:Qt Strs *(rec Feb. 1992)* Denon ▲ CO 75164 [DDD]
Szymanowski, K.:Qt 1 Strs Denon ▲ CO 79462 [DDD]
Szymanowski, K.:Qt 2 Strs Denon ▲ CO 79462 [DDD]
Weber, C.M. von:Qnt Cl, w. Paul Meyer (cl) *(rec Landgasthof Riehen, Switzerland, Apr 2, 3 18 & 19, 1995)* Denon ▲ CO 78801 [DDD]
Webern, A.:Slow Movt Denon ▲ CO 79462 [DDD]
Wettstein, P.:Janus *(rec May 6, 1991)* Jecklin ▲ JS 283-2 [ADD]
Carnegie Chamber Players
Moravec, P.:Circular Dreams CRI ▲ CD 641 [DDD]
Carnegie Mellon Concert Winds
R. Strange (cnd)
Balada, L.:Con Pno, w. H. Franklin (pno) New World ▲ 80442-2
Carnegie Mellon PO
J.P. Izquierdo (cnd)
Balada, L.:Escenas borrascosas, w. Kay Shackleton-Williams (sop—Isabel), Nancy Maria Balach (mez—Beatriz), Matthew Walley (ten—Colón), Robert Page (cnd), Carnegie Mellon Concert Choir, Carnegie Mellon Repertory Chorus *(rec Carnegie Music Hall, Pittsburgh, PA, Apr 7–8, 1994)* New World ▲ 80498-2
Vali, R.:Movts Str Qt, w. Latin American String Quartet *(rec Carnegie Music Hall, Carnegie, PA, Mar. 11 & 14, 1993)* New Albion ▲ NAO 77
Carnival Band
Sing Lustily & with Good Courage:Gallery Hymns of the 18th & Early 19th Centuries, w. Maddy Prior (voc) Saydisc ▲ CDSDL 383 [DDD]
A Tapestry of Carols, w. Maddy Prior (voc) Saydisc ▲ CDSDL 366 [DDD] ■ CSDL 366 (D)
Caspar da Salo Quartet
Haydn, J.:Qts Strs, Op. 1—No. 1 only PMG ("Vienna Master" series) ▲ CD 160209 [DDD]
Haydn, J.:Qts Strs, Op. 64, "Tost Qts"—Nos. 4–6 PMG ("Vienna Master" series) ▲ CD 160117 [DDD]
Haydn, J.:Qts Strs, Op. 64, "Tost Qts"—No. 5 PMG ("Vienna Master" series) ▲ CD 160209 [DDD]
Haydn, J.:Qts Strs, Op. 76, "Erdődy Qts"—No. 3 PMG ("Vienna Master" series) ▲ CD 160209 [DDD]
Caspar da Salo Quintet
Schubert, Franz:Qnt Pno, D.667 PMG ("Vienna Master" series) ▲ CD 160111 [DDD]
Cassatt String Quartet [M. Otani (vn), S. A. Lim (vn), M. Oshima (va), A. Cholakian (vc)]
Davidson, T.:Cassandra Sings *(rec Jan. 18–21, 1993)* CRI ▲ CD 671 [DDD]
Godfrey, D.:Intermedio *(rec Jan. 18–21, 1993)* CRI ▲ CD 671 [DDD]
Hovda, E.:Lemniscates *(rec Jan. 18–21, 1993)* CRI ▲ CD 671 [DDD]
Waggoner, A.:A Song:Strophic Vars *(rec Jan. 18–21, 1993)* CRI ▲ CD 671 [DDD]
Wolfe, J.:Four Marys Point Music ▲ 454054-2
Wolfe, J.:Four Marys *(rec Jan. 18–21, 1993)* CRI ▲ CD 671 [DDD]
Castalian Band
Haydn, J.:Sons Pno—No. 39 for Pno & Vn *(rec East Woodhay Church, Newbury, Dec 1990)* Musicaphon ▲ M 56817 [DDD]
Haydn, J.:Songs—The Minstrel; The Blythsome Bridal; The Border Widow's Lament; Mary's Dream; The Braes of Ballochmyle; Rattling Roaring Willy; Deil Tak the War; Up in the Morning Early; The Tears of Caledonia; Happy Dick Dawson; MacGregor of Ruara's Lament; Jenny's Bawbee *(rec East Woodhay Church, Newbury, Dec 1990)* Musicaphon ▲ M 56817 [DDD]
Haydn, J.:Trios Pno, Vn & Vc—in d/D *(rec East Woodhay Church, Newbury, Dec 1990)* Musicaphon ▲ M 56817 [DDD]
Castellani-Andriaccio Duo [Joanne Castellani (gtr), Michael Andriaccio (gtr)]
Danzas & More Fleur de Son ▲ FDS 57916-2 [ADD]
1685:A Glorious Triology Fleur de Son ▲ FDS 57917-2 [DDD]
Under the Palms Fleur de Son ▲ FDS 57918 [DDD]
Castilla y León SO
M.B. Darman (cnd)
Mendelssohn, F.:Con in d Vn & Strs, w. Felix Ayo (vn) *(rec Estudios Cinearte, Madrid, July 14, 1992)* Dynamic ▲ CD 153 [DDD]
Mendelssohn, F.:Con in d Vn, Pno & Strs, w. Felix Ayo (vn), Emma Jimenez (pno) *(rec Estudios Cinearte, Madrid, Apr 12, 1992)* Dynamic ▲ CD 153 [DDD]

Castle Trio
Beethoven, L. van:Trio 2 Pno Virgin Classics ▲ CDC 59220
Beethoven, L. van:Trio 4 Pno, "Ghost" [period instrs] Smithsonian Collection ▲ ND 036 [DDD]
Beethoven, L. van:Trio 5 Pno [period instrs] Smithsonian Collection ▲ ND 036 [DDD]
Beethoven, L. van:Trio 6 Pno, "Archduke" Virgin Classics ▲ 59044 [DDD]
Beethoven, L. van:Trio 7 Pno [violin version] Virgin Classics ▲ CDC 59220
Beethoven, L. van:Trio 8 Pno Virgin Classics ▲ CDC 59220
Beethoven, L. van:Trio 9 Pno, "Kakadu" Virgin Classics ▲ 59044 [DDD]
Beethoven, L. van:Trio 10 Pno Virgin Classics ▲ 59044 [DDD]
Dvořák, A.:Trio 4 Pno, "Dumky" Smithsonian Collection ▲ ND 034 [DDD]
Schubert, Franz:Trio Pno, D.28 Virgin Classics ▲ CDC 59303
Schubert, Franz:Trio 2 Pno Virgin Classics ▲ CDC 59303
Smetana, B.:Trio Pno Smithsonian Collection ▲ ND 034 [DDD]
Castleman/Hodgkinson Violin-Piano Duo [Charles Castleman (vn), Randall Hodgkinson (pno)]
Antheil, G.:Son 2 Vn—re-creation of Antheil's 1927 Carnegie Hall concert MusicMasters ▲ 01612-67094-2 [DDD]
Catalonia CO
A. Ros-Marbá (cnd)
Haydn, J.:The Seven Last Words of Christ on the Cross Studio SM 2-▲ 2441
Catania Baroque Orch
S. Carchiolo (cnd)
Hasse, J.A.:Larinda e Vanesio, w. Silvia Piccollo (sop—Larinda), Giorgio Gatti (bar—Vanesio) *(rec Sept. 29, 1992)* Bongiovanni ▲ GB 2137
Catania Teatro Massimo Bellini Orch
R. Bonynge (cnd)
Paisiello, G.:Nina, o sia La pazza per amore, w. M. Bolgan (sop), F. Pediconi (sop), D. Bernardini (ten), F. Musinu (bass), G. Surian (bass), Catania Teatro Massimo Bellini Chorus [I] *(rec live 1989)* Nuova Era 2-▲ 6872/73 [DDD]
O. de Fabritiis (cnd)
Massenet, J.:Thaïs, w. R. Kabaivanska (sop), S. Bruscantini (bar), Catania Teatro Massimo Bellini Chorus [I] *(rec live, 4/3/69)* Golden Age of Opera 2-▲ GAO 121/122 [ADD]
G. Gavazzeni (cnd)
Bellini, V.:I Puritani, w. A. Maliponte (sop—Elvira), A. di Stasio (sop—Enrichetta di Francia), A. Kraus (ten—Lord Arturo Talbo), A. Pedroni (ten—Bruno Roberton), P. Cappuccilli (bar—Sir Riccardo Forth), R. Raimondi (bass—Sir Giorgio), Catania Teatro Massimo Bellini Chorus *(rec Feb. 6, 1972)* Ornamenti 2-▲ FE 107 [ADD]
Verdi, G.:Ernani, w. Licia Galvano (sop—Giovanna), Leyla Gencer (sop—Elvira), Carlo Bergonzi (ten—Ernani), Nino Valori (ten—Don Riccardo), Piero Cappuccilli (bar—Don Carlo), Alessandro Cassis (bar—Jago), Ruggero Raimondi (bass—Don Ruy Gomez de Silva), Catania Teatro Massimo Bellini Chorus *(rec live, Catania, Jan 15, 1972)* Arkadia 2-▲ 621 [ADD]
A. Licata (cnd)
Bellini, V.:Adelson e Salvini, w. A. Nafé (mez), F. Previati (bar), Catania Teatro Massimo Bellini Chorus Nuova Era 2-▲ NUO 7154 [DDD]
Bellini, V.:Bianca e Fernando, w. Y. O. Shin (sop), G. Kunde (ten), W. Coppola (ten), A. Tomicich (bass), Catania Teatro Massimo Bellini Chorus Nuova Era 2-▲ NUO 7076 [DDD]
Marinuzzi, G.:Jacquerie, w. Ilaria Galgani (sop), Antonio Salvadori (bar), Miro Solman (sgr), Martine Surais (sgr), Catania Teatro Massimo Bellini Chorus *(rec Catania, 1994)* Nuova Era 2-▲ NUO 7200 [DDD]
P. Olmi (cnd)
Bellini, V.:Zaira, w. K. Ricciarelli (sop), A. Papadjakou (cta), R. Vargas (ten), S. Alaimo (ten), Catania Teatro Massimo Bellini Chorus [I] *(rec live 1990)* Nuova Era 2-▲ 6982/83 [DDD]
Bellini, V.:Zaira (sels), w. K. Ricciarelli (sop), R. Vargas (ten), Catania Teatro Massimo Bellini Chorus Nuova Era ▲ NUO 7187 [DDD]
A. Quadri (cnd)
Bellini, V.:I Puritani (sels), w. G. Tucci (sop), L. Pavarotti (ten), A. Protti (bar), R. Raimondi (bass), Catania Teatro Massimo Bellini Chorus [I] *(rec live, Catania 3/22/68)* Verona 3-▲ 27029/31
Bellini, V.:I Puritani (sels), w. G. Tucci (sop), L. Pavarotti (ten), A. Protti (bar), R. Raimondi (bass), Catania Teatro Massimo Bellini Chorus [I] *(rec live, Catania 3/22/68)* Melodram ▲ MEL 15001
Cathedral Choral Society Orch
R. Gloyd (cnd)
Brubeck, D.:To Hope!:A Celebration, w. Shelley Waite (sop), Mark Bleeke (ten), Kevin Deas (b-bar), Dave Brubeck Quartet [Dave Brubeck (pno), Bobby Militello (sax), Jack Six (db), Randy Jones (dr)], Cathedral Choral Society Chorus *(rec Washington National Cathedral, Washington, D.C., June 12, 1995)* Telarc ▲ CD 80430 [DDD]
J. Messner (cnd)
Mozart, W.A.:Requiem, w. Hanna Seebach-Ziegler (sop), Jella von Braun (alt), Hermann Gallos (ten), Richard Mayr (bass), Salzburg Cathedral Choir *(rec Aug 9, 1931)* Orfeo d'or ("Festspiel Dokumente" series) ▲ 396951
Cathedral Musician's Orch
J. Messner (cnd)
Mozart, W.A.:Requiem, w. Salzburg Cathedral Choir Orfeo d'or ▲ 409951
Catherine Wilson Trio [Catherine Wilson (pno), Adele Armin (vn), Jack Mendelsohn (vc)]
Bloch, E.:Nocturnes (3) Doremi ▲ DHR 71112 [DDD]
Fauré, G.:Trio Doremi ▲ DHR 71112 [DDD]
Schubert, Franz:Nocturne Pno Doremi ▲ DHR 71112 [DDD]
Widor, C.M.:Pièces Pno Doremi ▲ DHR 71112 [DDD]
CBC Vancouver Orch
M. Bernardi (cnd)
Coulthard, J.:The Bird of Dawning Singeth All Night Long, w. CBC Vancouver SO CBC ("SM 5000" series) 2-▲ SMCD 5050-2 [DDD]
CBC Vancouver SO
J.-M. Beaudet (cnd)
Schoenberg, A.:Con Pno, w. Glenn Gould (pno) *(rec Dec. 21, 1953)* CBC ("Perspective" series) ▲ PSCD 2008 (m) [ADD]
A. Bernardi (cnd)
Herbert, V.:Sunset CBC ("SM 5000" series) 2-▲ SMCD 5050-2 [DDD]
M. Bernardi (cnd)
Bach, J.S.:Brandenburg Cons—Nos. 1–6 CBC ("SM 5000" series) 2-▲ SMCD 5028-2 [DDD] 2-■ SMC 5028-2 (D)
Bach, J.S.:Con 1 Hpd, w. A. Hewitt (pno) CBC ("SM 5000" series) ▲ SMCD 5065 [DDD] ■ SMC 5065 (D)
Bach, J.S.:Con 2 Hpd, w. A. Hewitt (pno) CBC ("SM 5000" series) ▲ SMCD 5065 [DDD] ■ SMC 5065 (D)
Bach, J.S.:Con 5 Hpd, w. A. Hewitt (pno) CBC ("SM 5000" series) ▲ SMCD 5065 [DDD] ■ SMC 5065 (D)
Barber, S.:Adagio Strs CBC ("SM 5000" series) 2-▲ SMCD 5050-2 [DDD]
Berlioz, H.:Les Nuits d'été, w. Linda Maguire (mez) *(rec The Orpheum, Vancouver, B.C., Apr. 2, 5 & 6, 1993)* CBC ("SM 5000" series) ▲ SMCD 5137 [DDD]
Canadian & American Music for Chamber Orchestra CBC Records ("SM 5000" series) 2-▲ SMCD 5050-2 [DDD]
Cardy, P.:Virelai, w. J. Rapson (cl) CBC ("SM 5000" series) ▲ SMCD 5094 [DDD]
Copland, A.:Quiet City CBC ("SM 5000" series) 2-▲ SMCD 5050-2 [DDD]
Corigliano, J.:Elegy CBC ("SM 5000" series) 2-▲ SMCD 5050-2 [DDD]
Coulthard, J.:The Bird of Dawning Singeth All Night Long, w. CBC Vancouver Orch. CBC ("SM 5000" series) 2-▲ SMCD 5050-2 [DDD]
Coulthard, J.:Songs, w. Linda Maguire (mez)—The White Rose; Innocence; Cradle Song; Frolic *(rec The Orpheum, Vancouver, B.C., Apr. 2, 5 & 6, 1993)* CBC ("SM 5000" series) ▲ SMCD 5137 [DDD]
Debussy, C.:Petite suite CBC ("SM 5000" series) ▲ SMCD 5122 [DDD]

▲ = CD ♦ = Enhanced CD Δ = MD ■ = Cassette Tape □ = DCC

CBC Vancouver SO (cont.)
M. Bernardi (cnd) (cont.)
Diamond, D.:Rounds CBC ("SM 5000" series) 2-▲ SMCD 5050-2 [DDD]
Fauré, G.:Pelléas et Mélisande (suite) CBC ("SM 5000" series) ▲ SMCD 5122 [DDD]
Forsyth, M.:Sketches from Natal CBC ("SM 5000" series) ▲ SMCD 5135 [DDD]
Frumerie, G. de:Pastoral Suite, w. Kathleen Rudolph (fl), *(harpist unknown) (rec Orpheum, Vancouver, British Columbia, Mar 1-2, 1992)* CBC ▲ SMCD 5157 [DDD]
Grieg, E.:Elegaic Melodies, Op. 34 CBC ("SM 5000" series) ▲ SMCD 5064 [DDD] ■ SMC 5064 (D)
Grieg, E.:Holberg Suite CBC ("SM 5000" series) ▲ SMCD 5064 [DDD] ■ SMC 5064 (D)
Grieg, E.:Lyric Pieces—Op. 68/4-5 *(rec Orpheum, Vancouver, British Columbia, Mar 1-2, 1992)* CBC ▲ SMCD 5157 [DDD]
Griffes, C.T.:Poem Fl CBC ("SM 5000" series) 2-▲ SMCD 5050-2 [DDD]
Handel, G.F.:Con Hp, w. Hugh McLean (org) [arr org & orch] CBC ▲ 5163 [DDD]
Handel, G.F.:Water Music (comp) CBC ("SM 5000" series) ▲ SMCD 5032 [DDD]; ■ SMC 5032 (D)
Ives, C.:The Unanswered Question CBC ("SM 5000" series) 2-▲ SMCD 5050-2 [DDD]
Komorous, R.:Serenade Strs CBC ("SM 5000" series) 2-▲ SMCD 5050-2 [DDD]
Larsson, L.-E.:Pastoralsvit *(rec Orpheum, Vancouver, British Columbia, Mar 1-2, 1992)* CBC ▲ SMCD 5157 [DDD]
Larsson, L.-E.:En Vintersaga, w. *(soloist unknown) (rec Orpheum, Vancouver, British Columbia, Mar 1-2, 1992)* CBC ▲ SMCD 5157 [DDD]
McDougall, I.:Andante CBC ("SM 5000" series) 2-▲ SMCD 5050-2 [DDD]
McDougall, I.:Con Cl, w. S. McCartney (cl) CBC ("SM 5000" series) ▲ SMCD 5094 [DDD]
Maurice, P.:Tableaux de Provence, w. J. Nolan (sax) CBC ("SM 5000" series) ▲ SMCD 5135 [DDD]
Milhaud, D.:Le Globe-trotter CBC ("SM 5000" series) ▲ SMCD 5135 [DDD]
Mozart, W.A.:Con Fl Hp, w. N. Shulman (fl), J. Loman (hp) CBC ("SM 5000" series) ▲ SMCD 5133 [DDD]
Mozart, W.A.:Con 9 Pno, w. A. Cheng (pno) CBC ("SM 5000" series) ▲ SMCD 5104 [DDD] ■ SMC 5104 (D)
Mozart, W.A.:Con 17 Pno, w. A. Cheng (pno) CBC ("SM 5000" series) ▲ SMCD 5104 [DDD] ■ SMC 5104 (D)
Mozart, W.A.:Sinf concertante Vn, K.364, w. J. Israelievitch (vn), S. Dann (va) CBC ("SM 5000" series) ▲ SMCD 5133 [DDD]
Mozart, W.A.:Sym 16 CBC ("SM 5000" series) ▲ SMCD 5133 [DDD]
Mozart, W.A.:Sym 25 CBC ("SM 5000" series) ▲ SM5 5150 [DDD]
Mozart, W.A.:Sym 41 CBC ("SM 5000" series) ▲ SM5 5150 [DDD]
Nielsen, C.:Little Suite CBC ("SM 5000" series) ▲ SMCD 5064 [DDD] ■ SMC 5064 (D)
Poulenc, F.:Sinfonietta CBC ("SM 5000" series) ▲ SMCD 5122 [DDD]
Respighi, O.:Il Tramonto, w. Linda Maguire (mez) *(rec The Orpheum, Vancouver, B.C., Apr. 2, 5 & 6, 1993)* CBC ("SM 5000" series) ▲ SMCD 5137 [DDD]
Ridout, G.:George III his Lament CBC ("SM 5000" series) 2-▲ SMCD 5050-2 [DDD]
Riisager, K.:Little Ov *(rec Orpheum, Vancouver, British Columbia, Mar 1-2, 1992)* CBC ▲ SMCD 5157 [DDD]
Satie, E.:Jack in the Box CBC ("SM 5000" series) ▲ SMCD 5122 [DDD]
Schubert, Franz:Sym 6 CBC ("SM 5000" series) ▲ SMCD 5070 [DDD] ■ SMC 5070 (D)
Sibelius, J.:Valse triste CBC ("SM 5000" series) ▲ SMCD 5064 [DDD] ■ SMC 5064 (D)
Somers, H.:Picasso Suite:Light Music *(rec The Orpheum, Vancouver, B.C., Mar 6-7, 1992)* CBC ▲ 5161 [DDD]
Sowande, F.:African Suite CBC ("SM 5000" series) ▲ SMCD 5135 [DDD]
Stravinsky, I.:Apollon Musagète *(rec The Orpheum, Vancouver, B.C., Mar 6-7, 1992)* CBC ▲ 5161 [DDD]
Stravinsky, I.:Pulcinella Suite *(rec The Orpheum, Vancouver, B.C., Mar 6-7, 1992)* CBC ▲ 5161 [DDD]
Thrower, J.:Improv on a Blue Theme, w. J. Valdepeñas (cl) CBC ("SM 5000" series) ▲ SMCD 5094 [DDD]
Wagner, R.:Wesendonck Songs, w. Linda Maguire (mez) *(rec The Orpheum, Vancouver, B.C., Apr. 2, 5 & 6, 1993)* CBC ("SM 5000" series) ▲ SMCD 5137 [DDD]
Willan, H.:Overture to an Unwritten Comedy CBC ("SM 5000" series) 2-▲ SMCD 5050-2 [DDD]
Willan, H.:Poem CBC ("SM 5000" series) 2-▲ SMCD 5050-2 [DDD]
Wirén, D.:Serenade Strs—Marcia *(rec Orpheum, Vancouver, British Columbia, Mar 1-2, 1992)* CBC ▲ SMCD 5157 [DDD]

J.E. Gardiner (cnd)
Geminiani, F.:The Enchanted Forest, w. Elizabeth Wilcock (vn), Stanley Ritchie (vn), Susie Napper (vc), Janet See (fl), Barbara Kallaur (fl), Patrick Wedd (hpd) CBC ▲ 5163 [DDD]

M. Huggett (cnd)
Handel, G.F.:The Alchymist, w. Nancy Argenta (sop) [I] CBC ("SM 5000" series) ▲ SMCD 5091 [DDD]; ■ SMC 5091 (D)
Handel, G.F.:Alcina (sels), w. N. Argenta (sop)—2 arias & several orchestral sels. [I] CBC ("SM 5000" series) ▲ SMCD 5091 [DDD]; ■ SMC 5091 (D)
Purcell, H.:Music for the Theater, w. N. Argenta (sop)—sels. from *The Fairy Queen* (2 arias), *King Arthur* (overture & 5 sels.), & *The Married Beau* (overture & 9 sels.) [E] CBC ("SM 5000" series) ▲ SMCD 5091 [DDD] ■ SMC 5091 (D)

E. Iseler (cnd)
Coulthard, J.:Quebec May, w. Elmer Iseler Singers—[E,F] CBC ("SM 5000" series) ▲ SMCD 5115 [DDD]
Glick, S.I.:Sing Unto the Lord a New Song, w. Elmer Iseler Singers [E,Heb] CBC ("SM 5000" series) ▲ SMCD 5115 [DDD]
Holman, D.:Night Music, w. Elmer Iseler Singers [E] CBC ("SM 5000" series) ▲ SMCD 5115 [DDD]
Somers, H.:Chansons de la Nouvelle-France, w. Elmer Iseler Singers [F] CBC ("SM 5000" series) ▲ SMCD 5115 [DDD]

W. Riddell (cnd)
Bach, J.S.:Cant 140, w. Rosemarie Landry (sop), Ben Heppner (ten), Mark Pedrotti (bass), Tudor Singers of Montreal CBC ▲ 5163 [DDD]

I. Stravinsky (cnd)
Stravinsky, I.:Sym in C *(rec 1962)* CBS ▲ MK 42434 [ADD]
Stravinsky, I.:Sym of Psalms, w. Toronto Festival Singers [rev. ver.] [L] *(rec 1963)* CBS ▲ MK 42434 [ADD]

W. Susskind (cnd)
Mozart, W.A.:Con 24 Pno, w. Glenn Gould (pno) *(rec 1961)* Sony Classical ("Glenn Gould Edition" series) ▲ SMK 52626 [ADD]

D. Swift (cnd)
Lalo, E.:Aubades CBC ▲ SMCD 5152 [DDD]
Milhaud, D.:Rag-Caprices CBC ▲ SMCD 5152 [DDD]
Ropartz, G.:Serenade Strs CBC ▲ SMCD 5152 [DDD]
Sauguet, H.:Le cigale et la fourmi CBC ▲ SMCD 5152 [DDD]
Sauguet, H.:Les Forains CBC ▲ SMCD 5152 [DDD]
Sauguet, H.:La Nuit CBC ▲ SMCD 5152 [DDD]

H. Unger (cnd)
Beethoven, L. van:Con 3 Pno, w. G. Gould (pno) CBC ("Perspective" series) ▲ PSCD 2004 (m) [ADD]

J. Washburn (cnd)
Bernhard, C.:Missa "Durch Adams Fall", w. Henriette Schellenberg (sop), Laverne G' Froerer (mez), Keith Boldt (ten), George Roberts (bar), Vancouver Chamber Choir *(rec Ryerson United Church & The Orpheum, Vancouver, May 4-7, 1992)* CBC ▲ 5160 [DDD]
Fauré, G.:Messe basse, w. Henriette Schellenberg (sop), Laverne G' Froerer (mez), Keith Boldt (ten), George Roberts (bar), Vancouver Chamber Choir [orchd J. Washburn] *(rec Ryerson United Church & The Orpheum, Vancouver, May 4-7, 1992)* CBC ▲ 5160 [DDD]
Haydn, J.:Mass 7, "Kleine Orgelmesse", w. Henriette Schellenberg (sop), Laverne G' Froerer (mez), Keith Boldt (ten), George Roberts (bar), Vancouver Chamber Choir *(rec Ryerson United Church & The Orpheum, Vancouver, May 4-7, 1992)* CBC ▲ 5160 [DDD]

CBC Vancouver SO (cont.)
J. Washburn (cnd) (cont.)
Raminsh, I.:Choral Music, w. Vancouver Chamber Choir—And I think over again; Ave Maria; Ave, verum corpus; Come, My Light; The Great Sea; Magnificat; Songs of the Lights [E,L] CBC ("SM 5000" series) ▲ SMCD 5116 [DDD]
Weber, C.M. von:Missa sancta 2, w. Henriette Schellenberg (sop), Laverne G' Froerer (mez), Keith Boldt (ten), George Roberts (bar), Vancouver Chamber Choir *(rec Ryerson United Church & The Orpheum, Vancouver, May 4-7, 1992)* CBC ▲ 5160 [DDD]

CCM Contemporary Music Ensemble
G. Samuel (cnd)
Samuel, G.:Nocturne on an Impossible Dream, w. Yehonatan Berick (vn), Helen Russell (cl), Alonzo Alexander (pno) *(rec Corbett Auditorium, Cincinnati Conservatory, OH)* Acoma ▲ GXD 5733 [DDD]
Smoot, R.J.:Con Gtr, w. Lynn Harting-Ware (gtr) *(rec Corbett Auditorium, Cincinnati Conservatory, OH)* Acoma ▲ GXD 5733 [DDD]
Ware, P.:Kabah *(rec Corbett Auditorium, Cincinnati Conservatory, OH)* Acoma ▲ GXD 5733 [DDD]

CELLO [Laura Bontrager (vc), Maria Kitsopoulos (vc), Maureen McDermott (vc), Caryl Paisner (vc)]
Subliminal Blues & Greens *(rec Troy Savings Bank Music Hall, Troy, NY)* d'Note Classics ▲ DND 1011 [DDD]

Cello Octet Conjunto Ibérico
E. Arizcuren (cnd)
Cello Octet Conjunto Ibérico, w. Claron McFadden (sop) *(rec 1992)* Canal Grande ▲ CG 9323 [DDD]

Center City Brass Quintet
Arnold, M.:Qnt Brass Collins ▲ COL 1489
Bozza, E.:Sonatine Collins ▲ COL 1489
Calvert, M.:Suite from the Monteregian Hills Collins ▲ COL 1489
Dahl, I.:Music for Brass Collins ▲ COL 1489
Ewald, V.:Qnt 1 Brass Collins ▲ COL 1489
Maurer, L.:Pieces Brass Qnt Collins ▲ COL 1489

Center for New Music Ensemble
Lewis, P.T.:Music of, w. J. Ferrell (vn), J. Avery (pno), S. Schick (perc), Peter Tod Lewis (elec), Columbia String Quartet—Bricolage (1979); Gestes (1973); Manestar (1970); ...of bells...and time (1967); Signs & Circuits—String Quartet No. 2 (1969) *(rec 1978-82)* CRI ▲ CD 619 [ADD]

Central City Opera Orch
J. Moriarty (cnd)
Moore, D.:Ballad of Baby Doe, w. Jan Grissom (sop—Baby Doe), Dana Kreuger (mez—Augusta), Myrna Paris (cta—Mama), Brian Steele (bar—Horace), Mark Freiman (b-bar—W. J. Bryan), Central City Opera Chorus *(rec Central City, CO)* Newport Classic 2-▲ NPD 85593/2 [DDD]

Le Cercle Trio [Willy Coquillat (perc), Jean-Pierre Drouet (perc), Gaston Sylvestre (perc)]
Aperghis, G.:Triangle carré, w. Arditti String Quartet *(rec Apr 1990)* Montaigne ▲ MO 782002 [DDD]
Reibel, G.:Rabelais ou la Naissance du Verbe Musique Francaise d'Aujourd'hui ("Collection MFA-Radio France" series) ▲ MFA 216002
Xenakis, I.:Okho *(rec 4/90)* Montaigne ▲ MO 782002 [DDD]

Ceské Budejovice CO
V. Válek (cnd)
Gerber, R.:Suites françaises (3)—No. 3 Gallo ▲ CD 861 [ADD]

Chagall Trio [Nicoline Kraamwinkel (vn), Tim Gill (vc), Julian Rolton (pno)]
Smyth, E.:Trios Vn—in d Meridian ▲ MER 84286 [DDD]

Chagall Trio members [Nicoline Kraamwinkel (vn), Julian Rolton (pno)]
Smyth, E.:Son Vn Meridian ▲ MER 84286 [DDD]

Chagall Trio members [Tim Gill (vc), Julian Rolton (pno)]
Smyth, E.:Son Vc Meridian ▲ MER 84286 [DDD]

Chalumeau Quintet
Lachner, F.P.:Octet, w. S. Meyer (cl), N. Frisch (hn), J. Steinbrecher (bn) Ambitus ▲ 97825 [DDD]
Lachner, F.P.:Qnt Winds Ambitus ▲ 97825 [DDD]

Chalumeau Trio [Bernhard Veil (cl), Dorothea Borth (vc), Bettina Heinz (pno)]
Brahms, J.:Trio Cl Bayer ▲ 800877
Glinka, M.:Trio pathétique [trans for cl, vc & pno] Bayer ▲ 800877
Komma, K.M.:Trio Cl Bayer ▲ 800877

Chamäleon Kammermusik Ensemble [Jonathan Allen (vn), Bernd Haag (va), Luzius Gartmann (vc), Madeline Nussbaumer (pno)]
Juon, P.:March Vc & Pno Gallo ▲ CD 876 [ADD]
Juon, P.:Rhap Pno Gallo ▲ CD 876 [ADD]

Chamäleon Kammermusik Ensemble [Jonathan Allen (vn), Luzius Gartmann (vc), Madeline Nussbaumer (pno)]
Juon, P.:Trio-Miniaturen Gallo ▲ CD 876 [ADD]

Chamäleon Kammermusik Ensemble [Jonathan Allen (vn), Madeline Nussbaumer (pno)]
Juon, P.:Son Vn Gallo ▲ CD 876 [ADD]
Juon, P.:Stücke (4) Vn & Pno Gallo ▲ CD 876 [ADD]

Chamber Ensemble of Early Instruments
M. Venhoda (cnd)
Blow, J.:Songs, w. T. Penrose (ct), J. Griffett (ten)—Welcome Ev'ry Guest; Ah, Heav'n! What Is't I Hear; Loving Above Himself; If I My Celia Could Persuade; The Fair Lover And His Black Mistress; Why Weeps Asteria?; The Spheres, Those Instruments Divine; Hark! How the Wakened Strings Resound Campion ▲ 1323 [DDD]

Chamber Music Northwest
Brahms, J.:Qnt Cl, w. D. Shifrin (cl) Delos ▲ DE 3066 [DDD]
Brahms, J.:Qnt 2 Strs, w. Walter Trampler (va) Delos ▲ DE 3066 [DDD]
Mozart, W.A.:Qnt Cl, K.581, w. David Shifrin (cl) Delos ▲ DCD 3020 [DDD]
Schiff, D.:Divertimento from "Gimpel the Fool" [He] Delos ▲ DE 3058 [DDD]
Schiff, D.:Scenes from Adolescence [He] Delos ▲ DE 3058 [DDD]
Schiff, D.:Suite from Sacred Service [He] Delos ▲ DE 3058 [DDD]

Chamber Music Northwest members [Eriko Sato (vn), David Shifrin (cl), Fred Sherry (vc), David Oei (pno)]
Schickele, P.:Qt Cl Vanguard Classics ▲ OVC 4066

Chamber Opera Quintet [Theo Mertens, François van Kerckhoven, Alex van Aeken, José Schyns, Gerard Peeters]
Virtuoze Miniaturen *(rec Oct.-Dec. 1987)* Eufoda ▲ EUF 1122 [DDD]

CO Diagonal
F. Rosensteiner (cnd)
Gubaidulina, S.:The Seven Last Words, w. Julius Berger (vc), Stefan Hussong (acc) Wergo ▲ WER 6263-2

CO of Europe
Bach, J.S.:Brandenburg Cons—Nos. 1-6 Deutsche Grammophon 2-▲ 431660-2 [DDD]
Bach, J.S.:Cons Hpd, BWV 1052-1058, w. A. Schiff (hpd) London 2-▲ 425676-2 [DDD]
C. Abbado (cnd)
Mozart, W.A.:Con 17 Pno, w. Maria João Pires (pno) *(rec Teatro Comunale, Ferrara, June 1993)* Deutsche Grammophon ▲ 439941-2 [DDD]
Mozart, W.A.:Con 21 Pno, w. Maria João Pires (pno) *(rec Teatro Comunale, Ferrara, June 1993)* Deutsche Grammophon ▲ 439941-2 [DDD]
Prokofiev, S.:March, Op. 99 Deutsche Grammophon 3-▲ 435151-2
Prokofiev, S.:Ov on Hebrew Themes Deutsche Grammophon ▲ 429396-2 [DDD] ▢ 429396-5
Prokofiev, S.:Ov on Hebrew Themes Deutsche Grammophon 3-▲ 435151-2 [ADD]
Prokofiev, S.:Peter & the Wolf, w. Sting (nar) Deutsche Grammophon ▲ 429396-2 [DDD] ▢ 429396-5
Prokofiev, S.:Sym 1 Deutsche Grammophon 3-▲ 435151-2 [ADD]
Rossini, G.:Il barbiere di Siviglia, w. K. Battle (sop), P. Domingo (ten), F. Lopardo (ten), L. Gallo (bar), R. Raimondi (bass) [I] Deutsche Grammophon 2-▲ 435763-2

ORCH. & ENS.

CO of Europe (cont.)

C. Abbado (cnd) (cont.)

Rossini, G.:Ovs—Barber of Seville, William Tell, Cenerentola, Italiana in Algeri, La gazza ladra, Scala di seta, Semiramide — Deutsche Grammophon ▲ 431653-2 [DDD]
Schubert, Franz:Fierrabras, w. K. Mattila (sop), C. Studer (sop), R. Gambill (ten), T. Hampson (bar), R. Holl (bass), L. Polgar (bass), Arnold Schoenberg Choir [G] *(rec live)* — Deutsche Grammophon 2-▲ 427341-2 [DDD]
Schubert, Franz:Mass 2, w. B. Bonney (sop), B. Poschner (ten), M. Hintermeier (cta), J. A. Pita (ten), A. Schmidt (bar) — Deutsche Grammophon ▲ 435486-2
Schubert, Franz:Rosamunde, w. A.-S. von Otter (mez), Ernst Senff Chorus — Deutsche Grammophon ▲ 431655-2 [DDD]
Schubert, Franz:Rosamunde (sels)—Overture only — Deutsche Grammophon ▲ 423656-2 [DDD]
Schubert, Franz:Rosamunde (sels)—Ov. — Deutsche Grammophon 5-▲ 423651-2 [DDD]
Schubert, Franz:Son Pno 4-Hands, D.812 — Deutsche Grammophon 5-▲ 423651-2 [DDD]
Schubert, Franz:Son Pno 4-Hands, D.812 — Deutsche Grammophon ▲ 423655-2 [DDD]
Schubert, Franz:Syms (comp) — Deutsche Grammophon 5-▲ 423651-2 [DDD]
Schubert, Franz:Sym 1 — Deutsche Grammophon ▲ 423652-2 [DDD]
Schubert, Franz:Sym 2 — Deutsche Grammophon ▲ 423652-2 [DDD]
Schubert, Franz:Sym 3 — Deutsche Grammophon ▲ 423653-2 [DDD]
Schubert, Franz:Sym 4 — Deutsche Grammophon ▲ 423653-2 [DDD]
Schubert, Franz:Sym 5 — Deutsche Grammophon ▲ 423654-2 [DDD]
Schubert, Franz:Sym 8 — Deutsche Grammophon ▲ 423655-2 [DDD]
Schubert, Franz:Sym 9 — Deutsche Grammophon ▲ 423656-2 [DDD]
Schumann, R.:Requiem Mignon, w. B. Bonney (sop), B. Poschner (ten), M. Hintermeier (cta), J. A. Pita (ten), A. Schmidt (bar) — Deutsche Grammophon ▲ 435486-2
Vivaldi, A.:Cons Diverse Instrs, w. V. Mullova (vn) — Philips ▲ 420216-2 [DDD]
Vivaldi, A.:Cons Vn, Op. 8/1-4, "The Four Seasons", w. V. Mullova (vn) — Philips ▲ 420216-2 [DDD]

R. Barshaï (cnd)

Shostakovich, D.:Chamber Sym, Op. 73a [trans Barshai] — Deutsche Grammophon ▲ 435386-2
Shostakovich, D.:Chamber Sym, Op. 83a — Deutsche Grammophon ▲ 435386-2
Shostakovich, D.:Chamber Sym, Op. 110a — Deutsche Grammophon ▲ 429229-2 [DDD]
Shostakovich, D.:Chamber Sym, Op. 118a — Deutsche Grammophon ▲ 429229-2 [DDD]

C. Eschenbach (cnd)

Schnittke, A.:Con 2 Vn, w. G. Kremer (vn) — Teldec ▲ 94540-2

T. Fischer (cnd)

Martin, F.:Con for 7 Winds — Deutsche Grammophon ▲ 435383-2 [DDD]
Martin, F.:Etudes Str Orch — Deutsche Grammophon ▲ 435383-2 [DDD]
Martin, F.:Polyptyque (6 images de la Passion du Christ) — Deutsche Grammophon ▲ 435383-2 [DDD]

J. Galway (cnd)

Mozart, W.A.:Andante Fl, K.315/285a, w. J. Galway (fl) — RCA Red Seal 2-▲ 7861-2-RC [DDD]
Mozart, W.A.:Cons Fl, w. James Galway (fl) — RCA Red Seal 2-▲ 7861-2-RC [DDD]
Mozart, W.A.:Con Fl Hp, w. James Galway (fl), M. Robles (hp) — RCA Red Seal 2-▲ 7861-2-RC [DDD]
Mozart, W.A.:Divert Hns Strs, K.334, w. James Galway (fl)—Menuetto — RCA Red Seal 2-▲ 7861-2 [DDD]
Mozart, W.A.:Kleine Nachtmusik — RCA Red Seal 2-▲ 7861-2 [DDD]
Mozart, W.A.:Son 11 Pno, w. J. Galway (fl)—Rondo — RCA Red Seal 2-▲ 7861-2-RC [DDD]

J. E. Gardiner (cnd)

Music for Cello & Orchestra, w. Steven Isserlis (vc) — Virgin Classics ▲ CDC 59595 [DDD]

N. Harnoncourt (cnd)

Beethoven, L. van:Die Geschöpfe des Prometheus *(rec Musikverein, Vienna, Nov., 1993)* — Teldec ▲ 90876-2 [DDD]
Beethoven, L. van:Missa Solemnis, w. M. Lipovsek (mez), R. Holl (bass), E. Ortner (cnd), Arnold Schoenberg Choir — Teldec 2-▲ 9031-74884-2
Beethoven, L. van:Syms (comp)—[soloists in No. 9:C. Margiono, B. Remmert, R. Schasching, R. Hall, Arnold Schoenberg Chorus] — Teldec 5-▲ 2292-46452-2-ZC
Beethoven, L. van:Sym 1 — Teldec ▲ 9031-75708-2-ZK
Beethoven, L. van:Sym 2 — Teldec ▲ 9031-75712-2-ZK
Beethoven, L. van:Sym 3, "Eroica" — Teldec ▲ 9031-75708-2-ZK
Beethoven, L. van:Sym 4 — Teldec ▲ 9031-75714-2-ZK
Beethoven, L. van:Sym 5 — Teldec ▲ 9031-75712-2-ZK
Beethoven, L. van:Sym 6, "Pastorale" — Teldec ▲ 9031-75709-2-ZK
Beethoven, L. van:Sym 7 — Teldec ▲ 9031-75714-2-ZK
Beethoven, L. van:Sym 8 — Teldec ▲ 9031-75709-2-ZK
Beethoven, L. van:Sym 9, "Choral Sym", w. Arnold Schoenberg Choir — Teldec ▲ 9031-75713-2-ZK
Mendelssohn, F.:Die erste Walpurgisnacht, w. B. Remmert (alt), U. Heilman (ten), T. Hampson (bar), R. Pape (bass) — Teldec ▲ 74882-2
Mendelssohn, F.:A Midsummer Night's Dream (comp), w. P. Coburn (sop), E. von Magnus (alt/nar), C. Bantzer (nar) — Teldec ▲ 74882-2
Mendelssohn, F.:Sym 3 — Teldec ▲ 9031-72308-2 ZK
Mendelssohn, F.:Sym 4 — Teldec ▲ 9031-72308-2 ZK
Mozart, W.A.:Arias, w. E. Gruberova (sop)—concert arias K.217, 368, 369, 374, 416, 418, 419, 538 — Teldec ▲ 9031-72302-2 ZK
Mozart, W.A.:Sym 38 — Teldec ▲ 90866-2
Mozart, W.A.:Sym 39 — Teldec ▲ 90866-2
Mozart, W.A.:Sym 40 — Teldec ▲ 93667-2
Mozart, W.A.:Sym 41 — Teldec ▲ 93667-2
Schumann, R.:Con Pno, w. M. Argerich (pno) *(rec Graz, Germany, July 1992)* — Teldec ▲ 90696-2 [DDD]
Schumann, R.:Con Vn, w. G. Kremer (vn) *(rec Graz, Germany, July 1994)* — Teldec ▲ 90696-2 [DDD]
Schumann, R.:Sym 3 *(rec Graz, Germany, June 1993)* — Teldec ▲ 90867-2 [DDD]
Schumann, R.:Sym 4 *(rec Graz, Germany, July 1994)* — Teldec ▲ 90867-2 [DDD]

H. Holliger (cnd)

Berg, A.:Chamber Con, w. O. Maisenberg (pno), T. Zehetmair (vn) — Teldec ▲ 2292-46019-2 [DDD]
Schoenberg, A.:Begleitmusik zu einer Lichtspielszene *(rec Berlin, Sept. 1992)* — Teldec ▲ 9031-77314-2 [DDD]
Schoenberg, A.:Chamber Sym 1 — Teldec ▲ 2292-46019-2 [DDD]
Schoenberg, A.:Chamber Sym 2 *(rec Berlin, Sept. 1992)* — Teldec ▲ 9031-77314-2 [DDD]
Schoenberg, A.:Verklärte Nacht *(rec Berlin, Sept. 1992)* — Teldec ▲ 9031-77314-2 [DDD]

J. Judd (cnd)

Beethoven, L. van:Die Geschöpfe des Prometheus (ov) — IMP Masters ▲ PCD 805 [DDD]
Fauré, G.:Pavane Orch — IMP Masters ▲ PCD 805 [DDD]
Mozart, W.A.:Divert Str Qt, K.136 — IMP Masters ▲ PCD 805 [DDD]
Rossini, G.:Ovs—Barber of Seville — IMP Masters ▲ PCD 805 [DDD]
Wagner, R.:Siegfried Idyll — IMP Masters ▲ PCD 805 [DDD]

M. Maisky (cnd)

Haydn, J.:Con 1 Vc, w. Mischa Maisky (vc) — Deutsche Grammophon ▲ 419786-2 [DDD]
Haydn, J.:Con 2 Vc, w. Mischa Maisky (vc) — Deutsche Grammophon ▲ 419786-2 [DDD]
Haydn, J.:Con 4 Vn, w. Mischa Maisky (vc) [arr. for cello & orch.] — Deutsche Grammophon ▲ 419786-2 [DDD]

M. Pollini (cnd)

Rossini, G.:La donna del lago, w. K. Ricciarelli (sop), L. V. Terrani (mez), D. Raffanti (ten), S. Ramey (bass), Prague Phil Chorus [I] — CBS 2-▲ M2K 39311 [DDD]

H. Schiff (cnd)

Schnittke, A.:Con grosso 1, w. Gidon Kremer (vn), Tatiana Grindenko (vn), Yuri Smirnov (hpd/pno) — Deutsche Grammophon ("Digital Midprice" series) ▲ 445520-2
Schnittke, A.:Moz-Art à la Haydn, w. G. Kremer (vn) — Deutsche Grammophon ▲ 429413-2 [DDD]
Schnittke, A.:Moz-Art à la Haydn, w. Gidon Kremer (vn), Tatiana Grindenko (vn) — Deutsche Grammophon ("Digital Midprice" series) ▲ 445520-2
Schnittke, A.:Quasi una son, w. Gidon Kremer (vn) — Deutsche Grammophon ("Digital Midprice" series) ▲ 445520-2

CO of Europe (cont.)

H. Schiff (cnd) (cont.)

Schnittke, A.:Quasi una son, w. G. Kremer (violin) — Deutsche Grammophon ▲ 429413-2 [DDD]

A. Schneider (cnd)

Bach, J.S.:Con Vn & Ob, w. M. Blankestijn (vn), D. Boyd (ob) — ASV ("CO of Europe" series) ▲ CDCOE 803 [DDD]
Mozart, W.A.:Cons Hn, w. Gail Williams (hn) — ASV ("CO of Europe" series) ▲ CDCOE 805 [DDD]
Mozart, W.A.:Serenade Ww, K.361 — ASV ("CO of Europe" series) ▲ CDCOE 804 [DDD]
Mozart, W.A.:Serenade Ww, K.375 — ASV ("CO of Europe" series) ▲ CDCOE 802 [DDD]
Mozart, W.A.:Serenade Ww, K.388 — ASV ("CO of Europe" series) ▲ CDCOE 802 [DDD]
Mozart, W.A.:Sinf concertante Ob, K.Anh.9 — ASV ("CO of Europe" series) ▲ CDCOE 803 [DDD]
Vivaldi, A.:Cons Orch—RV.556 — ASV ("CO of Europe" series) ▲ CDCOE 803 [DDD]

G. Solti (cnd)

Mozart, W.A.:Così fan tutte, w. Renée Fleming (sop—Fiordiligi), Adelina Scarabelli (sop—Despina), Anne Sofie Von Otter (mez—Dorabella), Frank Lopardo (ten—Ferrando), Olaf Bar (bar—Guglielmo), Michele Pertusi (bass—Don Alfonso) — London 3-▲ 444174-2
Mozart, W.A.:Sym 40 — London ▲ 414334-2 [DDD]
Mozart, W.A.:Sym 40 — London ("Jubilee" series) ▲ 430437-2 [ADD]
Mozart, W.A.:Sym 41 — London ("Jubilee" series) ▲ 430437-2 [ADD]
Mozart, W.A.:Sym 41 — London ▲ 414334-2 [DDD]
The Solti Edition, w. Chicago SO, London PO, London SO, Vienna PO, New Philharmonia Orch, Royal Opera House Orch — London 25-▲ 436600-2

CO of Europe Soloists

Mozart, W.A.:Serenade Ww, K.361 — Teldec ▲ 2292-46471-2 [DDD]

CO of Europe Soloists [Douglas Boyd (ob), Rachel Frost (ob), Matthew Wilkie (bn), Enno Senft (db), Ursula Duetschler (hpd)]

Zelenka, J.D.:Sons Obs *(rec The Warehouse, London, Apr 7-13, 1995)* — Claves 2-▲ CD 9511/12 [DDD]

CO of Europe Wind Soloists

Mozart, W.A.:Diverts—complete for winds — Teldec 5-▲ 2292-46472-2

Champ d'Action

Brewaeys, L.:Trajet, w. Johan Bossers (pno) *(rec Blauwe Zaal, deSingel, Oct. 1994)* — Megadisc ▲ 7869
de Visscher, E.:Stille und Lärm *(rec Blauwe Zaal, deSingel, Oct. 1994)* — Megadisc ▲ 7869
Haene, F. d':Inert Reacting Substance of ( ) *(rec Blauwe Zaal, deSingel, Oct. 1994)* — Megadisc ▲ 7869
Logghe, G.:Time before & time after *(rec Blauwe Zaal, deSingel, Oct. 1994)* — Megadisc ▲ 7869
Verstockt, S.:Apeiron *(rec Blauwe Zaal, deSingel, Oct. 1994)* — Megadisc ▲ 7869

Champs Elysées Theater Orch

E. Halffter (cnd)

Falla, M. de:El retablo de maese Pedro, w. Seoane (sop), Gonzalo (sgr), Navarro (sgr) *(rec ca. 1959)* — MCA Classics ▲ MCAD 10481 (m/s) [ADD]

P. Herreweghe (cnd)

Beethoven, L. van:Missa Solemnis, w. Rosa Mannion (sop), Birgit Remmert (alt), James Taylor (ten), Cornelius Hauptmann (bass), Chapelle Royale Choir, Collegium Vocale *(rec Auditorium Stravinski de Montreux, Feb. 20-21, 1995)* — Harmonia Mundi France ▲ HMC 901557
Berlioz, H.:Herminie, w. Mireille Delunsch (sop) — Harmonia Mundi France ▲ HMC 90152
Berlioz, H.:Les Nuits d'été, w. Brigitte Balleys (mez) — Harmonia Mundi France ▲ HMC 90152
Brahms, J.:Ein Deutsches Requiem, w. Christiane Oelze (sop), Gerald Finley (bar), Chapelle Royale Choir, Collegium Vocale — Harmonia Mundi ▲ HMC 901608 ■ HMC 401608
Mendelssohn, F.:Elijah, w. La Chapelle Royale Orch, Collegium Vocale — Harmonia Mundi France 2-▲ HMC 901463/64
Mendelssohn, F.:Die Hebriden — Harmonia Mundi France ▲ HMC 901502
Mendelssohn, F.:A Midsummer Night's Dream (comp), w. Sandrine Piau (sop), Delphine Collot (sop) — Harmonia Mundi France ▲ HMC 901502
Mendelssohn, F.:St. Paul, w. Melanie Diener (sop), Annette Markert (mez), James Taylor (ten), Matthias Görne (bass), Chapelle Royale Choir, Collegium Vocale *(rec Stravinsky Auditorium, Montreaux)* — Harmonia Mundi France 2-▲ HMC 901584.85
Mozart, W.A.:Maurerische Trauermusik — Harmonia Mundi France ▲ HMX 29001393
Mozart, W.A.:Missa, K.427, w. C. Oelze (sop), J. Larmore (mez), S. Weir (ten), P. Kooy (bass), Chapelle Royale Choir, Collegium Vocale — Harmonia Mundi France ▲ HMC 901393
Mozart, W.A.:Missa, K.427, w. Jennifer Larmore (sop), Christiane Oelze (sop), Scot Weir (ten), Peter Kooy (bass), Chapelle Royale Choir, Collegium Vocale — Harmonia Mundi France ▲ HMX 29001393
Schumann, R.:Con Pno, w. Andreas Staier (pno) [J. B. Streicher fortepno, ca. 1850] — Harmonia Mundi ▲ HMC 901555
Schumann, R.:Sym 2 — Harmonia Mundi ▲ HMC 901555

D. Milhaud (cnd)

Milhaud, D.:Le Boeuf sur le toit — EMI Classics ▲ CDC 54604
Milhaud, D.:Le Boeuf sur le toit — Studio SM ▲ 2516
Milhaud, D.:La Création du monde — EMI Classics ▲ CDC 54604
Milhaud, D.:La Création du monde — Studio SM ▲ 2516

Chandos Concert Orch

S. Barry (cnd)

Treasures of Operetta I, w. Marilyn Hill Smith (sop), Peter Morrison (bar) — Chandos ▲ CHAN 8362 [DDD]
Treasures of Operetta II, w. Marilyn Hill Smith (sop), Peter Morrison (bar), Ambrosian Singers — Chandos ▲ CHAN 8561 [DDD]
Treasures of Operetta III, w. Marilyn Hill Smith (sop), Peter Morrison (bar), Chandos Singers — Chandos ▲ CHAN 8759 [DDD]

Change Ringing Handbell Group

Ringing Clear:The Art of Handbell Ringing, w. Sound in Brass Handbells, Launton Handbell Ringers, Four in Hand Grosmont Handbell Ringers — Saydisc ▲ CDSDL 333 [AAD]

Chanticleer Sinfonia

Mexican Baroque, w. [cnd:Joseph Jennings], Chanticleer — Teldec ▲ 96353

Chapelle du Québec Ensemble

Fauré, G.:Music of—Tantum Ergo, Op. 55; Ecce Fidelis Servus, Op. 54; O Calutaris, Op. 47/1; maria Mater Gratiae, Op. 47/2; Ave Maria, Op. 93; Salve Regina, Op. 67/1; Tantum Ergo, sans Op.; Ave Maria, Op. posth.; Ave Verum, Op. 65/1; Tantum Ergo, Op. 65/2; Sancta Mater, sans Op.; Ave Maria, Op. 67/2; Tu es Petrus, sans Op.; Cantique de Jean Racine, Op. 11; Il est Né Le Divin Enfant; Noël d'enfants; Les anges dans nos campagnes; Noël, Op. 43/1; En prière, sans Op. — Adès ▲ ADE 202132 [DDD]

La Chapelle Royale

Bach, J.S.:Music of, w. R. Jacobs (ct), G. Murray (org), Ensemble 415, Collegium Vocale—selections from Cantatas 35, 78 & 82, St. John Passion, St. Matthew Passion, & the Well-tempered Clavier; Chorale Prelude, BWV 622; Flute Sonata, BWV 1034; Toccata & Fugue in d *(rec 1969-88)* — Harmonia Mundi Plus ▲ HMP 390801

W. Christie (cnd)

Rameau, J.P.:Music of, Les Arts Florissants, et al.—sels. from Anacréon; Harpsichord Suite in d; In Convertendo; Les Indes galantes *(rec 1981-83)* — Harmonia Mundi Plus ▲ HMP 390808

P. Herreweghe (cnd)

Bach, J.S.:Cant 56, w. P. Kooy (bass) — Harmonia Mundi France ▲ HMC 901365
Bach, J.S.:Cant 78 [G] — Harmonia Mundi France ▲ HMC 901270
Bach, J.S.:Cant 80, w. Barbara Schlick (sop), Agnès Mellon (sop), Gérard Lesne (ct), Howard Crook (ten), Peter Kooy (bass), Collegium Vocale — Harmonia Mundi France Δ HMC 6901326
Bach, J.S.:Cant 82, w. P. Kooy (bass) — Harmonia Mundi France ▲ HMC 901365
Bach, J.S.:Cant 158, w. P. Kooy (bass) — Harmonia Mundi France ▲ HMC 901365
Bach, J.S.:Cant 198 [G] — Harmonia Mundi France ▲ HMC 901270
Bach, J.S.:Magnificat, BWV 243, w. A. Mellon (sop), B. Schlick (sop), G. Lesne (ct), H. Crook (ten), P. Kooy (bass), Collegium Vocale [L] — Harmonia Mundi France ▲ HMC 901326
Bach, J.S.:Motets, BWV 225-30, w. Ghent Collegium Vocale — Harmonia Mundi France ▲ HMC 901231

La Chapelle Royale (cont.)
P. Herreweghe (cnd) (cont.)
Bach, J.S.:St. John Passion, w. B. Schlick (sop), C. Patriasz (cta), H. Crook (ten), W. Kendall (ten), P. Kooy (bass), P. Lika (bass), Ghent Collegium Vocale [G] — Harmonia Mundi France 2-▲ HMC 901264/65 [DDD]
Bach, J.S.:St. Matthew Passion, w. B. Schlick (sop), R. Jacobs (ct), H. P. Blochwitz (ten), H. Crook (ten), U. Cold (bass), P. Kooy (bass), Ghent Collegium Vocale [G] — Harmonia Mundi France 3-▲ HMC 901155/57
Brahms, J.:Motets (misc), w. Ghent Collegium Vocale—Opp. 29, 74 & 110 [G] — Harmonia Mundi France ▲ HMC 901122
Campra, A.:Messe de Requiem, w. E. Baudry (sop), M. Zanetti (sop), J. Benet (ten), J. Elwes (ten), S. Varcoe (bar) [L] — Harmonia Mundi France ▲ HMC 901251
du Mont, H.:Motets pour la chapelle du roy, w. Chapelle Royale Choir—Memorare, Dialogus de anima, Magnificat, Super Flumina Babylonis [L] *(rec July 1981)* — Musique d'Abord ▲ HMA 1901077
Hassler, H.L.:Vater unser im Himmelreich — Harmonia Mundi France ▲ HMC 901401
Lalande, M.–R. de:Dies Irae, w. P. Kwella (sop), L. Perillo (sop), H. Crook (ten), H. Lamy (ten), P. Harvey (bar), Chapelle Royale Choir [L] — Harmonia Mundi France ▲ HMC 901352
Lalande, M.–R. de:Miserere mei, Deus, w. P. Kwella (sop), L. Perillo (sop), H. Crook (ten), H. Lamy (ten), P. Harvey (bar), Chapelle Royale Choir [L] — Harmonia Mundi France ▲ HMC 901352
Lechner, L.:Choral Music—Motet—Si bona suscepimus — Harmonia Mundi France ▲ HMC 901401
Lully, J.–B.:Armide, w. V. Gens (sop), N. Rime (sop), G. Laurens (mez), H. Crook (ten), G. Ragon (ten), Collegium Vocale [F] — Harmonia Mundi France 2-▲ HMC 901456/57
Mendelssohn, F.:Elijah, w. Champs Élysées Theater Orch, Collegium Vocale — Harmonia Mundi France 2-▲ HMC 901463/64
Mendelssohn, F.:Psalm 42, w. E. Harrhy (sop), H. Lamy (ten), P. Kooy (bass), Ghent Collegium Vocale [G] — Harmonia Mundi France ▲ HMC 901272 [DDD]
Mendelssohn, F.:Psalm 115, w. E. Harrhy (sop), Ghent Collegium Vocale [G] — Harmonia Mundi France ▲ HMC 901272 [DDD]
Mendelssohn, F.:Verleih uns Frieden, w. Ghent Collegium Vocale [G] — Harmonia Mundi France ▲ HMC 901272 [DDD]
Rameau, J.P.:Les Indes Galantes (syms) *(rec June 1983)* — Musique d'Abord ▲ HMA 1901130 [ADD]

La Chapelle Royale Orch Soloists
Charpentier, M.–A.:Miserere:Psalmus 50 — Harmonia Mundi France ▲ HMC 901185 [ADD]
Charpentier, M.–A.:Motet pour une longue offrande — Harmonia Mundi France ▲ HMC 901185 [ADD]
Charpentier, M.–A.:Pour la seconde fois que le saint sacrement vient au même reposoir — Harmonia Mundi France ▲ HMC 901185 [ADD]
Charpentier, M.–A.:Pour le saint sacrement au reposoir — Harmonia Mundi France ▲ HMC 901185 [ADD]

Charis Ensemble
Kreutzer, C.:Grand Septet — MD + G ▲ L 3232 [DDD]
Witt, F.:Septet Cl — MD + G ▲ L 3232 [DDD]

Charivari Agréable
Marais, M.:Pièces de viole (misc)—Suite in F/f; Suite in e/G; Caprice ou Sonate; Suite in D/d — ASV/Gaudeamus ▲ ASV 152

Carlos Chávez SO
F. Lozano (cnd)
Jiménez, M.B.:Angelus — Forlane 2-▲ FOR 16712 [DDD]
Jiménez, M.B.:El Chueco — Forlane 2-▲ FOR 16712 [DDD]
Jiménez, M.B.:Noche en Morelia — Forlane 2-▲ FOR 16712 [DDD]
Jiménez, M.B.:Three Cards of Mexico — Forlane 2-▲ FOR 16712 [DDD]
Jiménez-Mabarak, C.:Ballad of the Tabasco River — Forlane 2-▲ FOR 16712 [DDD]
Jiménez-Mabarak, C.:Portrait Gallery — Forlane 2-▲ FOR 16712 [DDD]
Jiménez-Mabarak, C.:Sym in 1 Movement — Forlane 2-▲ FOR 16712 [DDD]
Latin American Music — Forlane ▲ FOR 16736 [DDD]
Morales, M.:Ildegonda, w. Violeta Dávalos (sgr—Ildegonda), Grace Echauri (sgr—Idelbene), Raúl Hernández (sgr—Rizzardo), Ricardo Santin (sgr—Rolando), Escuola Nacional de Música Chorus — Forlane 2-▲ FRL 16739 [DDD]
Musica Latinoamericana de Concierto — Spartacus ▲ 21033
Ponce, M.:Concierto del sur, w. Alfonso Moreno (gtr) — Forlane ▲ FRL 16733 [DDD]
Ponce, M.:Concierto del sur, w. Alfonso Moreno (gtr) — Forlane ▲ FRL 16757
Ponce, M.:Concierto del sur, w. Juan Carlos Laguna (gtr) — Forlane ▲ FOR 16736 [DDD]
Rodrigo, J.:Concierto de Aranjuez, w. Juan Carlos Laguna (gtr) — Forlane ▲ FRL 16757
Rodrigo, J.:Concierto de Aranjuez, w. Juan Carlos Laguna (gtr) — Forlane ▲ FRL 16733 [DDD]
Rodrigo, J.:Concierto de Aranjuez, w. Alfonso Moreno (gtr) — Forlane ▲ FOR 16736 [DDD]
Villa-Lobos, H.:Con Gtr, w. Rafael Jimenez (gtr) — Forlane ▲ FRL 16733 [DDD]
Villa-Lobos, H.:Con Gtr, w. Rafael Jimenez (gtr) — Forlane ▲ FRL 16757
Villa-Lobos, H.:Con Gtr, w. Rafael Jimenez (gtr) — Forlane ▲ FOR 16736 [DDD]

Chelsea Chamber Ensemble
L. Botstein (cnd)
Brahms, J.:Serenade 1 Orch [1st version for nonet; reconstrd. Alan Boustead] *(rec Feb. 24, 1993)* — Vanguard Classics ▲ OVC 8049 [DDD]
T. Rolek (cnd)
Fennimore, J.:Eventide, w. K. Williams (sop), H. Johnsson (mez), P. Creech (ten) [E] — Albany ▲ TROY 023-2 [ADD]
S. Zyman (cnd)
Zyman, S.:Con Pno, w. M. Conti (pno) — Antilles/New Directions ▲ 91055-2 ■ 91055-4
Zyman, S.:Qnt Pno, w. M. Conti (pno) — Antilles/New Directions ▲ 91055-2 ■ 91055-4

Cherubini String Quartet
Plaisir d'Amour - Mélodies Françaises, w. Barbara Hendricks (sop), Michel Dalberto (pno) — EMI Classics ▲ CDC 55388
Reimann, A.:Unrevealed, w. D. Fischer-Dieskau (bar) — Orfeo ▲ 212901

Chester String Quartet [Aaron Berofsky (vn), Kathryn Botapek (vn), David Harding (va), Tom Rosenberg (vc)]
Barber, S.:Qt Strs — Koch International Classics ▲ KIC 7069-2
Kernis, A.J.:100 Greatest Dance Hits, w. David Tanenbaum (gtr) *(rec Manhattan Center Studios, New York, May 31–June 3, 1995)* — New Albion ♦ NA 083CD
Piston, W.:Qt 1 Strs — Koch International Classics ▲ KIC 7069-2
Porter, Q.:Qt 3 Strs — Koch International Classics ▲ KIC 7069-2

Chestnut Brass Company
Davison, J.:Qnt 1 Brass — Crystal ▲ CD 562
Johnson, F.:Concert Band Marches & Dance Music, w. Friends—Music of Francis Johnson & his Contemporaries:Early 19th-Century Black Composers — MusicMasters ▲ 7029-2-C [DDD]
Pastime with Good Company — Crystal ▲ CD 562 ■ C 562
Roger, D.:Sepplique et Polychromie — Crystal ▲ CD 562 ■ C 562
W. Noll (cnd)
The Joy of Christmas, w. Anthony Newman (org), Choral Guild of Atlanta, Choral Guild of Atlanta Brass & Percussion, Benjamin Harms (timp), Walter Huff (org) — Sony Classical ▲ SFK 62698 ■ SFT 62698

Chetham's CO
J. Clayton (cnd)
Mozart, W.A.:Con Cl, w. Mark van de Wiel (b cl) — Olympia ▲ OLY 484 [DDD]
Sssmayr, F.X.:Con Movt Bas Cl, w. Mark van de Wiel (b cl) — Olympia ▲ OLY 484 [DDD]
Woolrich, J.:Si va Facendo Notte, w. Mark van de Wiel (b cl) — Olympia ▲ OLY 484 [DDD]

Chetham's SO
Stevenson, R.:Con 1 Pno, w. M. McLachlan (pno) — Olympia ▲ OLY 429 [DDD]
Stevenson, R.:Con 2 Pno, w. M. McLachlan (pno) — Olympia ▲ OLY 429 [DDD]
Tcherepnin, A.:Con 1 Pno, w. Murray McLachlan (pno) — Olympia ▲ OLY 440 [DDD]
Tcherepnin, A.:Con 2 Pno, w. M. McLachlan (pno) — Olympia ▲ OLY 439 [DDD]
Tcherepnin, A.:Con 3 Pno, w. M. McLachlan (pno) — Olympia ▲ OLY 439 [DDD]
Tcherepnin, A.:Con 4 Pno, w. Murray McLachlan (pno) — Olympia ▲ OLY 440 [DDD]
Tcherepnin, A.:Con 5 Pno, w. Murray McLachlan (pno) — Olympia ▲ OLY 440 [DDD]

Chetham's SO (cont.)
Tcherepnin, A.:Con 6 Pno, w. M. McLachlan (pno) — Olympia ▲ OLY 439 [DDD]

Chiaroscuro Ensemble
Dufay, G.:Chansons—"Resvelons nous" and "Bon jour, bon mois" — Nuova Era ("Ancient Music" series) ▲ 6741 [DDD]
Dufay, G.:Missa, "Se la face ay pale" — Nuova Era ("Ancient Music" series) ▲ 6741 [DDD]
H.–M. Linde (cnd)
Schütz, H.:Danket dem Herren, denn er ist freundlich, w. Basel Schola Cantorum Instrumental Ensemble, Basel Boys' Choir — EMI Classics ("Baroque" series) ▲ CDK 65736

Chicago Baroque Ensemble
Vivaldi, A.:Cants, w. Patrice Michaels Bedi (sop)—All'ombra di sospetto, R.178; Lungi dal vago volto, R.680 *(rec St. Luke's Church, Evanston, IL, May–Aug 1995)* — Cedille ▲ CDR 90000 025 [DDD]
Vivaldi, A.:Cons Fl (misc)—in G, R.436 *(rec St. Luke's Church, Evanston, IL, May–Aug 1995)* — Cedille ▲ CDR 90000 025 [DDD]
Vivaldi, A.:Cons Orch—in d for Strs, R.128 *(rec St. Luke's Church, Evanston, IL, May–Aug 1995)* — Cedille ▲ CDR 90000 025 [DDD]
Vivaldi, A.:Motets, w. Patrice Michaels Bedi (sop)—Nulla in mundo pax sincera, R.630; Londe mala, umbrae, terrores, R.629 *(rec St. Luke's Church, Evanston, IL, May–Aug 1995)* — Cedille ▲ CDR 90000 025 [DDD]
Vivaldi, A.:Sons Vc—in B♭, Op. 14/4 [R.45] *(rec St. Luke's Church, Evanston, IL, May–Aug 1995)* — Cedille ▲ CDR 90000 025 [DDD]

Chicago Brass Ensemble
Gabrieli, G.:Sacrae symphoniae, w. Philadelphia Brass Ensemble, Cleveland Brass Ensemble—Canzon Septimi Toni Nos 1 & 2; Canzon Duodecimi Toni; Canzon a 12 in Echo; Canzon Quarti Toni; Canzon Primi Toni; Canzon Noni Toni; Son Octavi Toni; Son pian' e forte *(rec Philadelphia, 1968)* — Sony Classical ("Masterworks Heritage" series) ▲ MHK 62353 [ADD]

Chicago Brass Quintet
Chicago Brass Quintet — Crystal ■ C211
Hopkins, J.:Qnt 1 Brass — Crystal ■ C211
Mattern, J.:Son Breve — Crystal ■ C211
Merry Christmas — Centaur ▲ CRC 2037

Chicago Chamber Brass
Christmas with, w. Glen Ellyn Children's Chorus — Crystal ▲ CD 430
Fireworks for Brass — Pro Arte ▲ CDM 805 ■ PCD 805
H. Dunn (cnd)
The Brass & the Band, w. Dallas Wind Sym — Crystal ▲ CD 431 [DDD] ■ C 431 (D)

Chicago Chamber Musicians
Diamond, D.:Chaconne *(rec Bennet Hall, Ravinia, Highland Park, IL)* — Cedille ▲ CDR 90000 023 [DDD]
Diamond, D.:Concert Piece Hn *(rec Bennet Hall, Ravinia, Highland Park, IL)* — Cedille ▲ CDR 90000 023 [DDD]
Diamond, D.:Partita Ob, Bn & Pno *(rec Bennet Hall, Ravinia, Highland Park, IL)* — Cedille ▲ CDR 90000 023 [DDD]
Diamond, D.:Qnt Fl *(rec Bennet Hall, Ravinia, Highland Park, IL)* — Cedille ▲ CDR 90000 023 [DDD]
Diamond, D.:Qnt Winds *(rec Bennet Hall, Ravinia, Highland Park, IL)* — Cedille ▲ CDR 90000 023 [DDD]

Chicago Chamber Opera
L. Rapchak (cnd)
Rapchak, L.:The Lifework of Juan Diaz, w. C. Loverde (sop), R. Hovencamp (sgr), R. Alderson (sgr), D. Rowader (sgr) — Albany ▲ TROY 091 [DDD]

Chicago CO
D. Kober (cnd)
Handel, G.F.:Life & Music of—narration & selected excerpts from Water Music; Israel in Egypt; Con. Nos. 5, 13 & 16 for Organ; Messiah; Ovs. [from *Faithful Shepherd; Terpsichore; Rodelinda; Ezio; Alexander's Feast*]; Julius Caesar:Aria of Ptolemy & Finale; Son. No. 1 in B♭; Con. Grosso, Op. 6/5 & 6; Messiah:"Every Valley Shall Be Exalted"; Fant. in C; Harmonious Blacksmith; Largo [from *Serse*]; Hallelujah Amen [from *Judas Maccabeus*] — Vox Music Masters ("Music Masters" series) ▲ MMD 8506 [ADD] ■ MMC 8506
Handel, G.F.:Water Music (comp) — Allegretto ▲ ACD 8042 [ADD] ■ ACS 8042
Nielsen, C.:Con Cl, w. J. B. Yeh (cl) — Centaur ▲ CRC 2024 [DDD]
Nielsen, C.:Con Fl, w. M. Stolper (fl) — Centaur ▲ CRC 2024 [DDD]
Prokofiev, S.:Sinfonietta, Op. 5 — Centaur ▲ CRC 2154
Prokofiev, S.:Son Fl, w. J. B. Yeh (cl) [arr. Kennan as Con. for Clarinet & Orch.] — Centaur ▲ CRC 2154
Prokofiev, S.:Summer Day — Centaur ▲ CRC 2154

Chicago Ensemble
La Flûte Lumineuse, w. Susan Levitin (fl), Gerald Rizzer (pno) *(rec WFMT Studios, Chicago)* — Mark ▲ MCD 1939

Chicago Lyric Opera Orch
B. Bartoletti (cnd)
Donizetti, G.:Don Pasquale, w. Ileana Cotrubas (sop), Alfredo Kraus (ten), Wladimiro Ganzarolli (bar), Vincente Sardinero (bar), Sutliff (sgr), Chicago Lyric Opera Chorus *(rec live, Chicago, Nov. 2, 1974)* — Arkadia 2-▲ 490
R. Bonynge (cnd)
Donizetti, G.:La fille du régiment, w. J. Sutherland (sop), R. Resnik (mez), A. Kraus (ten), S. Maias (bass), Chicago Lyric Opera Chorus [F] *(rec Nov. 20, 1973)* — Myto 2-▲ MCD 93276
L. Schaenen (cnd)
Weisgall, H.:Six Characters in Search of an Author, w. E. Byrne (sop—Stepdaughter), S. Foster (sop—Prompter), E. Furtal (sop—Coloratura), J. King (mez—Mezzo), N. Maultsby (mez—Mother), P. LoVerne (cta—Madame Pace), D. Pritchett (alt—Wardrobe Mistress), B. Fowler (ten—Tenore Boffo), K. Anderson (ten—Director), A. Schroeder (bar—Accompanist), P. Zawisza (bar—Stage Manager), R. Orth (bar—Father), G. Lehman (bar—Son), M. Wadsworth (b-bar—Basso Cantante), Lyric Opera Center Chorus *(rec Chicago, June 14 & 16, 1990)* — New World 2-▲ 80454-2

Chicago Pro Musica
Bowles, P.:Music for a Farce — Reference ▲ RR 29CD [DDD]
Martinů, B.:La Revue de Cuisine — Reference ▲ RR 29CD
Nielsen, C.:Serenata in vano — Reference ▲ RR 16CD [DDD]
Rimsky-Korsakov, N.:Capriccio espagnol — Reference ▲ RR 17CD [DDD]
Scriabin, A.:Waltz Pno — Reference ▲ RR 16CD [DDD]
Strauss, R.:Till Eulenspiegels lustige Streiche [arr. by F. Hasenöhrl for violin, winds & bass] — Reference ▲ RR 16CD [DDD]
Stravinsky, I.:L'Histoire du soldat Suite Ensemble — Reference ▲ RR 17CD [DDD]
Varèse, E.:Octandre — Reference ▲ RR 29CD [DDD]
Walton, W.:Façade [orig. chamber ensemble version, but without recitation] — Reference ▲ RR 16CD [DDD]
Weill, K.:Kleine Dreigroschenmusik — Reference ▲ RR 29CD [DDD]

Chicago Radio Orch
G. Merola (cnd)
Chicago 1950, w. Giuseppe Di Stefano (ten), Bidu Sayao (sop), Renata Tebaldi (sop) — Myto ▲ MCD 924.67 [ADD]

Chicago Saxophone Quartet
J. Boyd (cnd)
Andriessen, J.:Con grosso Sax Qt, w. Indiana State Univ Symphonic Wind Ensemble *(rec 1994)* — Truemedia ▲ D 94127
Barker, W.:Capriccio Sax Qt, Indiana State Univ Symphonic Wind Ensemble *(rec 1994)* — Truemedia ▲ D 94127

Chicago Saxophone Quartet [Wayne Richard, Paul Bro, Roger Birkeland, James Kasprzyk]
Chicago Saxophone Quartet *(rec Apr. & May 1989)* — Centaur ▲ CRC 2086 [DDD]

Chicago Sinfonia Orch

B. Faldner (cnd)

- Debussy, C.:Sym in b — Koch International Classics ▲ KIC 7067-2 [DDD]
- Milhaud, D.:Chamber Sym 5 — Koch International Classics ▲ KIC 7067-2 [DDD]

Chicago Sinfonietta

- Gounod, C.:Petite Sym — Koch International Classics ▲ KIC 7067-2 [DDD]

P. Freeman (cnd)

- Cordero, R.:Miniatures (8) *(rec Lund Auditorium, Rosary College, River Forest, IL, May 10, 1995)* — Intersound ▲ 3534
- Ganz, R.:Con Pno, w. Ramon Salvatore (pno) *(rec Lund Auditorium, River Forest, IL, Feb 27, 1996)* — Cedille ▲ CDR 90000 028 [DDD]
- Hailstork, A.:An American Port of Call *(rec Lund Auditorium, Rosary College, River Forest, IL, May 10, 1995)* — Intersound ▲ 3534
- Hailstork, A.:Epitaph:In Memoriam, Martin Luther King, Jr. *(rec Lund Auditorium, Rosary College, River Forest, IL, May 10, 1995)* — Intersound ▲ 3534
- Macdowell, E.:Con 1 Pno, w. D. Han (pno) — Pro Arte/Fanfare ▲ CDS 3412 [DDD]
- Macdowell, E.:Con 2 Pno, w. D. Han (pno) — Pro Arte/Fanfare ▲ CDS 3412 [DDD]
- Macdowell, E.:Poème erotique — Pro Arte/Fanfare ▲ CDS 3412 [DDD]
- Mozart, F.X.W.:Con Pno, Op. 25, w. G. Johannesen (pno) — Centaur ▲ CRC 2062 [DDD]
- Mozart, L.:Bauernhochzeit, w. J. Bettridge (bgp) — Centaur ▲ CRC 2062 [DDD]
- Mozart, W.A.:Petits riens (sels) — Centaur ▲ CRC 2062 [DDD]
- Shostakovich, D.:Con 1 Pno, w. D. Han (pno), J. Henes (tpt) — Pro Arte ▲ CDD 551 [DDD]
- Shostakovich, D.:5 Days–5 Nights (sels)—"Liberated Dresden" section — Pro Arte ▲ CDD 551 [DDD]
- Shostakovich, D.:The Gadfly (suite)—Overture, Romance & Galop — Pro Arte ▲ CDD 551 [DDD]
- Shostakovich, D.:Hamlet (incidental)—Introduction, Ball at the Palace, In the Garden, Scene of the Posining, Duel and Death of Hamlet — Pro Arte ▲ CDD 551 [DDD]
- Shostakovich, D.:Tahiti Trot — Pro Arte ▲ CDD 551 [DDD]
- Williams, James:Sym for the Sons of Nam *(rec Lund Auditorium, Rosary College, River Forest, IL, May 10, 1995)* — Intersound ▲ 3534

Chicago String Ensemble

A. Heatherington (cnd)

- Bloch, E.:Con grosso 1, w. D. Schrader (pno) *(rec June 2 & 3, 1992)* — Centaur ▲ CRC 2140 [DDD]
- Chajes, J.:Israeli Melodies (6) *(rec June 2 & 3, 1992)* — Centaur ▲ CRC 2140 [DDD]
- Gould, M.:Holocaust Suite *(rec June 2 & 3, 1992)* — Centaur ▲ CRC 2140 [DDD]
- Pasatieri, T.:Yizkor *(rec June 2 & 3, 1992)* — Centaur ▲ CRC 2140 [DDD]

Chicago SO

- Barber, S.:Music of, w. Alexa Still (fl), San Diego CO, Atlantic Sinfonietta, New Zealand SO, Arioso Wind Quintet, Capricorn, Repertory Singers—Capricorn Con; Canzone; Fadograph of a Yestern Scene; Cave of the Heart; Adagio for Strs; Souvenirs; Hermit Songs; To Be Sung on Water; The Lovers; Summer Music — Koch International Classics ▲ KIC 7361
- It's Good to Be the King:Musical Delights for Kings, Queens, Princes & Royalty, w. Claudio Abbado (cnd), Eugene Ormandy (cnd), Esa-Pekka Salonen (cnd), Michael Tilson Thomas (cnd), Canadian Brass, Philadelphia Orch, Royal PO, Tafelmusik — Sony Classical ▲ SFK 57483 ■ SFT 57483
- Piano Greatest Hits, w. Artur Rubinstein (pno), Boston SO, RCA Victor SO — RCA Victor ▲ 09026-62662-2 ■ 09026-62662-4
- The Tsar, w. Philadelphia Orch [cnd:Eugene Ormandy], André Kostelanetz (cnd), Jennie Tourel (mez), Claudio Abbado (cnd), et al. — Sony Classical ("Greatest Hits" series) ▲ MLK 62683 ■ MLT 62683

C. Abbado (cnd)

- Bartók, B.:Con 1 Pno, w. M. Pollini (pno) — Deutsche Grammophon ▲ 415371-2 [ADD]
- Bartók, B.:Con 2 Pno, w. M. Pollini (pno) — Deutsche Grammophon ▲ 415371-2 [ADD]
- Brahms, J.:Con Vn & Vc, "Double Con", w. I. Stern (vn), Yo-Yo Ma (vc) — CBS ▲ MK 42387 [DDD]
- Mahler, G.:Songs from Rückert, w. H. Schwarz (mez) [G] — Deutsche Grammophon ("Galleria" series) 2-▲ 423928-2 [ADD/DDD]
- Mahler, G.:Sym 2, w. C .Neblett (sop), M. Horne (mez), Chicago Sym Chorus [G] — Deutsche Grammophon ("Galleria" series) 2-▲ 427262-2 [ADD]
- Mahler, G.:Sym 5 — Deutsche Grammophon ("Galleria" series) ▲ 427254-2 [ADD]
- Mahler, G.:Sym 6 — Deutsche Grammophon ("Galleria" series) ▲ 423928-2 [ADD/DDD]
- Mahler, G.:Sym 7 — Deutsche Grammophon ("Masters" series) ▲ 445513-2 [DDD]
- Prokofiev, S.:Cons Vn (comp), w. S. Mintz (vn) — Deutsche Grammophon 3-▲ 435151-2 [ADD]
- Prokofiev, S.:Cons Vn (comp), w. S. Mintz (vn) — Deutsche Grammophon ▲ 410524-2 [DDD]
- Prokofiev, S.:Lt Kijé Suite — Deutsche Grammophon ("The Originals" series) ▲ 447419-2
- Prokofiev, S.:Lt Kijé Suite — Deutsche Grammophon 3-▲ 435151-2 [ADD]
- Prokofiev, S.:Lt Kijé Suite — Deutsche Grammophon ▲ 419603-2 [DDD]
- Prokofiev, S.:Scythian Suite — Deutsche Grammophon ("The Originals" series) ▲ 447419-2
- Prokofiev, S.:Scythian Suite — Deutsche Grammophon 3-▲ 435151-2 [ADD]
- Tchaikovsky, P.:Marche slave — Sony Classical ▲ SK 47179
- Tchaikovsky, P.:Marche slave — CBS ▲ MK 42368 [DDD]
- Tchaikovsky, P.:Ov 1812 — Sony Classical ▲ SK 45939
- Tchaikovsky, P.:Ov 1812 — Sony Classical ▲ SK 47179
- Tchaikovsky, P.:Romeo & Juliet — Sony Classical ▲ SK 47179
- Tchaikovsky, P.:Romeo & Juliet — CBS ▲ MK 44911 [DDD]
- Tchaikovsky, P.:Sym 1 — Sony Classical ▲ SK 48056
- Tchaikovsky, P.:Sym 2 — CBS ▲ MK 39359 [DDD]
- Tchaikovsky, P.:Sym 3 — Sony Classical ▲ SK 45939
- Tchaikovsky, P.:Sym 4 — CBS ▲ MK 44911 [DDD]
- Tchaikovsky, P.:Sym 5 — CBS ▲ MK 42094 [DDD]
- Tchaikovsky, P.:The Tempest — CBS ▲ MK 39359 [DDD]
- Tchaikovsky, P.:The Tempest — Sony Classical ▲ SK 47179
- Tchaikovsky, P.:The Voyevoda, Op. 78 — CBS ▲ MK 42094 [DDD]

D. Barenboim (cnd)

- Beethoven, L. van:Con Vn, Op. 61, w. P. Zukerman (vn) — Deutsche Grammophon ▲ 435099-2 [ADD]
- Berio, L.:Contiuo Orch — Teldec ▲ 4509-66596-2 [DDD]
- Brahms, J.:Ein Deutsches Requiem, w. J. Williams (sop), T. Hampson (bass), Chicago Sym Chorus [G] — Erato ▲ 92856-2
- Brahms, J.:Syms (comp) — Erato 4-▲ 94817
- Carter, E.:Partita Orch — Teldec ▲ 4509-66596-2 [DDD]
- Corigliano, J.:Sym 1, Corigliano's First Symphony is a work, in the composer's words, "generated by feelings of loss, anger & frustration" stemming from the loss of many friends & colleagues to the AIDS epidemic over the past decade.) — Erato ▲ 2292-45601-2 [DDD]
- Dvořák, A.:Con Vc, w. J. Du Pré (vc) — EMI Classics ▲ CDC 47614
- Elgar, E.:Con Vn, w. Itzhak Perlman (vn) — Deutsche Grammophon ("Masters" series) ▲ 445564-2
- Mendelssohn, F.:Con in e Vn & Orch, Op. 64, w. I. Perlman (vn) — Erato ▲ 91732-2
- Ravel, M.:Alborada del gracioso — Erato ▲ 2292-45766-2 ZK
- Ravel, M.:Boléro — Erato ▲ 2292-45766-2 ZK
- Ravel, M.:Daphnis et Chloé (suite 2) — Erato ▲ 2292-45766-2 ZK
- Ravel, M.:Pavane pour une infante défunte — Erato ▲ 2292-45766-2 ZK
- Ravel, M.:Rapsodie espagnole — Erato ▲ 2292-45766-2 ZK
- Rimsky-Korsakov, N.:Scheherazade, w. S. Magad (vn) — Erato ▲ 91717-2 [DDD]
- Rimsky-Korsakov, N.:The Tale of Tsar Saltan Orch, Op. 57, w. S. Magad (vn) — Erato ▲ 91717-2
- Strauss, R.:Eine Alpensinfonie — Erato ▲ 45997-2
- Strauss, R.:Don Juan *(rec in Orchestra Hall, Chicago, 5/28/91)* — Erato ▲ 2292-45625-2 [DDD]
- Strauss, R.:Don Quixote, w. J. Sharp (vc) *(rec in Orchestra Hall, Chicago, 5/28/91)* — Erato ▲ 2292-45625-2 [DDD]
- Strauss, R.:Ein Heldenleben — Erato ▲ 2292-45621-2 [DDD]
- Strauss, R.:Symphonic Fant — Erato ▲ 45997-2
- Strauss, R.:Till Eulenspiegels lustige Streiche — Erato ▲ 2292-45621-2 [DDD]
- Takemitsu, T.:Visions — Teldec ▲ 4509-66596-2 [DDD]
- Tchaikovsky, P.:Capriccio italien — Deutsche Grammophon ("Digital Midprice" series) ▲ 445523-2

Chicago SO (cont.)

D. Barenboim (cnd) (cont.)

- Tchaikovsky, P.:Francesca da Rimini — Deutsche Grammophon ("Digital Midprice" series) ▲ 445523-2
- Tchaikovsky, P.:Ov 1812 — Deutsche Grammophon ("Digital Midprice" series) ▲ 445523-2
- Tchaikovsky, P.:Romeo & Juliet — Deutsche Grammophon ("Digital Midprice" series) ▲ 445523-2
- Verdi, G.:Requiem Mass, w. A. Marc (sop), W. Meier (mez), P. Domingo (ten), F. Furlanetto (bass), Chicago Sym Chorus — Erato 2-▲ 96357-2
- Waltzes & Polkas — Erato ▲ 45998-2

L. Bernstein (cnd)

- Shostakovich, D.:Sym 1 — Deutsche Grammophon 2-▲ 427632-2 [DDD]
- Shostakovich, D.:Sym 7 — Deutsche Grammophon 2-▲ 427632-2 [DDD]

P. Boulez (cnd)

- Bartók, B.:Cant Profana, "The Giant Stags", w. J. Aler (ten), J. Tomlinson (bass), Chicago Sym Chorus — Deutsche Grammophon ▲ 435863-2 [DDD]
- Bartók, B.:Con Orch — Deutsche Grammophon ▲ 437826-2 [DDD]
- Bartók, B.:Dance Suite — Deutsche Grammophon ("4D Audio" series) ▲ 445825-2
- Bartók, B.:Divert — Deutsche Grammophon ("4D Audio" series) ▲ 445825-2
- Bartók, B.:Hungarian Sketches — Deutsche Grammophon ("4D Audio" series) ▲ 445825-2
- Bartók, B.:The Miraculous Mandarin, w. Chicago Sym Chorus *(rec Orchestra Hall, Chicago, Dec 1994)* — Deutsche Grammophon ▲ 447747-2 [DDD]
- Bartók, B.:Music for Strs, Perc & Cel, w. Chicago Sym Chorus *(rec Orchestra Hall, Chicago, Dec 1994)* — Deutsche Grammophon ▲ 447747-2 [DDD]
- Bartók, B.:Pictures Orch — Deutsche Grammophon ("4D Audio" series) ▲ 445825-2
- Bartók, B.:Pieces Orch, Sz.51 — Deutsche Grammophon ▲ 437826-2 [DDD]
- Bartók, B.:The Wooden Prince — Deutsche Grammophon ▲ 435863-2 [DDD]
- Schoenberg, A.:Pelleas und Melisande — Erato ▲ 2292-45827-2-ZK
- Schoenberg, A.:Vars Orch, Op. 31 — Erato ▲ 2292-45827-2-ZK

J. DePreist (cnd)

- Blackwood, E.:Sym 5 *(rec live May & June 1992)* — Cedille ▲ CDR 90000 016 [ADD/DDD]

B. Faldner (cnd)

- Milhaud, D.:Chamber Sym 1 — Koch International Classics ▲ KIC 7067-2 [DDD]
- Milhaud, D.:Chamber Sym 2 — Koch International Classics ▲ KIC 7067-2 [DDD]
- Milhaud, D.:Chamber Sym 3 — Koch International Classics ▲ KIC 7067-2 [DDD]

C.M. Giulini (cnd)

- Berlioz, H.:Roméo et Juliette (sels) — EMI Classics ("Doubleforte" series) 2-▲ CDFB 68586
- Brahms, J.:Con Vn, w. I. Perlman (vn) — EMI Classics ▲ CDC 47166
- Bruckner, A.:Sym 9 — EMI Classics ▲ CDM 65177
- Dvořák, A.:Sym 9, "From the New World" — Deutsche Grammophon ("Galleria" series) ▲ 423882-2 [ADD]
- Mahler, G.:Sym 9 — Deutsche Grammophon ("Double" series) 2-▲ 437467-2
- Schubert, Franz:Sym 8 — Deutsche Grammophon ▲ 423882-2 [ADD]
- Schumann, R.:Con Pno, w. A. Rubinstein (pno) — RCA Red Seal ▲ 6255-2-RC [ADD]
- Schumann, R.:Con Pno, w. *(pno unknown)* — RCA Victor ▲ 09026-62677-2 ■ 09026-62677-4
- Tchaikovsky, P.:Romeo & Juliet — EMI Classics ▲ CDE 67789
- Tchaikovsky, P.:Sym 6 — EMI Classics ▲ CDE 67789

M. Gould (cnd)

- Tchaikovsky, P.:Waltzes—from Eugene Onegin, Nutcracker, Sleeping Beauty, Swan Lake, etc. — RCA Victrola ▲ 60134-2-RV [ADD] ■ 60134-4-RV

W. Hendl (cnd)

- Macdowell, E.:Con 2 Pno, w. Van Cliburn (pno) — RCA Living Stereo ▲ 09026-68480-2 ■ 09026-68480-4
- Macdowell, E.:Con 2 Pno, w. V. Cliburn (pno) — RCA Gold Seal ▲ 60420-2-RG [ADD] ■ 60420-4-RG (CrO2)
- Prokofiev, S.:Con 3 Pno, w. V. Cliburn (pno) — RCA Red Seal ▲ 6209-2-RC [ADD]
- Prokofiev, S.:Con 3 Pno, w. Van Cliburn (pno) *(rec 1960)* — RCA Living Stereo ▲ 09026-62691-2 [ADD]; ■ 09026-62691-4
- Saint-Saëns, C.:Introduction & Rondo capriccioso, w. Friedman (vn) — RCA Silver Seal ▲ 09026-61210-2 ■ 09026-61210-4
- Sibelius, J.:Con Vn, w. Jascha Heifetz (vn) *(rec Orchestra Hall, Chicago, Jan. 10 & 12, 1959)* — RCA Red Seal ▲ 09026-61744-2 [ADD]
- Sibelius, J.:Con Vn, w. J. Heifetz (vn) — RCA Red Seal ▲ RCD1-7019

N. Järvi (cnd)

- Hindemith, P.:Con Orch — Chandos ▲ CHAN 9000 [DDD]
- Kodály, Z.:Galanta Dances — Chandos ▲ CHAN 8877 [DDD]
- Kodály, Z.:Háry János (suite) — Chandos ▲ CHAN 8877 [DDD]
- Kodály, Z.:Vars on a Hungarian Folk Song — Chandos ▲ CHAN 8877 [DDD]
- Mussorgsky, M.:Pictures at an Exhibition — Chandos ▲ CHAN 8849 [DDD]
- Schmidt, F.:Sym 3 — Chandos ▲ CHAN 9000 [DDD]
- Scriabin, A.:Sym 4 — Chandos ▲ CHAN 8849 [DDD]

C. Kleiber (cnd)

- Butterworth, G.:English Idylls—No. 1 *(rec 1978)* — Artists 2-▲ FED 45 [ADD]

R. Kubelik (cnd)

- Bartók, B.:Music for Strs, Perc & Cel — Mercury Living Presence ▲ 434378-2 (m)
- Mussorgsky, M.:Pictures — Mercury Living Presence ▲ 434378-2 (m)
- Smetana, B.:Má Vlast — Mercury Living Presence ▲ 434379-2 (m)

E. Leinsdorf (cnd)

- Brahms, J.:Con 2 Pno, w. S. Richter (pno) *(rec 1960)* — RCA Gold Seal ▲ 07863-56518-2 [ADD] ■ 07863-56518-4

J. Levine (cnd)

- Anne-Sophie Mutter, w. Anne-Sophie Mutter (vn) — Deutsche Grammophon ▲ 437093-2 GH
- Babbitt, M.:Correspondences — Deutsche Grammophon ▲ 431698-2 [DDD]
- Bartók, B.:Con Orch — Deutsche Grammophon ▲ 429747-2 [DDD]
- Bartók, B.:Music for Strs, Perc & Cel — Deutsche Grammophon ▲ 429747-2 [DDD]
- Beethoven, L. van:Cons Pno (comp), w. A. Brendel (pno) *(rec live)* — Philips 3-▲ 411189-2 [DDD]
- Beethoven, L. van:Con 1 Pno, w. A. Brendel (pno) — Philips ▲ 412787-2 [DDD]
- Beethoven, L. van:Con 2 Pno, w. A. Brendel (pno) — Philips ▲ 412787-2 [DDD]
- Beethoven, L. van:Con 3 Pno, w. A. Brendel (pno) — Philips ▲ 412788-2 [DDD]
- Beethoven, L. van:Con 4 Pno, w. A. Brendel (pno) — Philips ▲ 412788-2 [DDD]
- Beethoven, L. van:Con 5 Pno, "Emperor", w. A. Brendel (pno) — Philips ▲ 412789-2 [DDD]
- Beethoven, L. van:Pno Music (misc), w. Alfred Brendel (pno)—Andante for Pno, WoO 57; Bagatelles for Pno, Op. 126 & WoO 59; Cons for Pno Nos. 4 & 5; Ecossaises; Sons Op. 2/3, 22, 31/3, 57, 78, 106, 109; Vars for Pno:Op. 34, 35, 120 & WoO 70 & 79 — Philips 25-▲ 446920-2
- Berg, A.:Con Vn, w. A.-S. Mutter (vn) — Deutsche Grammophon ▲ 437093-2
- Brahms, J.:Ein Deutsches Requiem, w. K. Battle (sop), H. Hagegard (bar), Chicago Sym Chorus [G] *(rec ca. 1984)* — RCA Gold Seal ▲ 09026-61349-2 ■ 09026-61349-4
- Brahms, J.:Sym 3 — RCA Victor ▲ 09026-61849-2; ■ 09026-61849-4 (CrO2)
- Bruch, M.:Kol Nidrei, w. M. Heimovitz (vc) — Deutsche Grammophon ▲ 427323-2 [DDD]
- Cage, J.:Atlas Eclipticalis — Deutsche Grammophon ▲ 431698-2
- Carter, E.:Vars Orch — Deutsche Grammophon ▲ 431698-2
- Gershwin, G.:An American in Paris — Deutsche Grammophon ▲ 431625-2
- Gershwin, G.:Cuban Ov — Deutsche Grammophon ▲ 431625-2
- Gershwin, G.:Porgy & Bess (suite), "Catfish Row Suite" — Deutsche Grammophon ▲ 431625-2
- Gershwin, G.:Rhap in Blue — Deutsche Grammophon ▲ 431625-2
- Holst, G.:The Planets, w. Chicago Sym Chorus — Deutsche Grammophon ▲ 429730-2 [DDD] □ 429730-5
- Lalo, E.:Con Vc, w. M. Heimovitz (vc) — Deutsche Grammophon ▲ 427323-2 [DDD]
- Mahler, G.:Sym 3, w. M. Horne (mez) [G] — RCA Red Seal 2-▲ RCD2-1757
- Mozart, W.A.:Con 21 Pno, w. A. Rubinstein (pno) — RCA Victor ▲ 09026-61708-2; ■ 09026-61708-4
- Mozart, W.A.:Sym 40 — RCA Victor ▲ 09026-61708-2; ■ 09026-61708-4

116

▲ = CD ♦ = Enhanced CD Δ = MD ■ = Cassette Tape □ = DCC

Chicago SO (cont.)

J. Levine (cnd) (cont.)

Mozart, W.A.:Sym 40 *(rec 1981)* RCA Gold Seal ▲ 09026-61397-2 ■ 09026-61397-4
Mozart, W.A.:Sym 41 RCA Victor ▲ 09026-61708-2; ■ 09026-61708-4
Mozart, W.A.:Sym 41 *(rec 1981)* RCA Gold Seal ▲ 09026-61397-2 ■ 09026-61397-4
Orff, C.:Carmina burana, w. J. Anderson (sop), P. Creech (ten), B. Weikl (bar), Chicago Sym Chorus [G,L] Deutsche Grammophon ▲ 415136-2 [DDD] ■ 415136-4
Prokofiev, S.:Sym 1 Deutsche Grammophon ▲ 439912-2
Prokofiev, S.:Sym 5 Deutsche Grammophon ▲ 439912-2
Rihm, W.:Gesungene Zeit, w. A.-S. Mutter (vn) Deutsche Grammophon ▲ 437093-2
Saint-Saëns, C.:Con 1 Vc, w. M. Heimovitz (vc) Deutsche Grammophon ▲ 427323-2 [DDD]
Schuller, G.:Spectra Deutsche Grammophon ▲ 431698-2
Stravinsky, I.:Oedipus Rex, w. F. Quivar (mez), P. Langridge (ten), D. Kaasch (ten), J. Morris, J.-H. Rootering (bass), J. Bastin (bass), Chicago Sym Chorus Deutsche Grammophon ▲ 435872-2

P. Monteux (cnd)

Franck, C.:Pièce héroïque [orchd.] RCA Gold Seal ▲ 09026-61900-2
Franck, C.:Sym in d RCA Gold Seal ▲ 09026-61900-2
Franck, C.:Sym in d RCA Gold Seal ▲ 6805-2-RG [ADD]
Highlights from the Pierre Monteux Edition, w. San Francisco SO, Boston SO RCA Gold Seal ▲ 09026-61978-2
The Pierre Monteux Edition, w. San Fransisco SO, RCA Victor Orch, Boston SO RCA Gold Seal 15-▲ 09026-61893-2

S. Ozawa (cnd)

Rimsky-Korsakov, N.:Scheherazade EMI Classics ▲ CDE 67784
Stravinsky, I.:Le Sacre du printemps Orch RCA Silver Seal ▲ 60541-2-RV [ADD] ■ 60541-4-RV

G. Prêtre (cnd)

Rachmaninoff, S.:Con 3 Pno, w. A. Weissenberg (pno) RCA Gold Seal ▲ 09026-61396-2

F. Reiner (cnd)

The Age of Living Stereo:A Tribute to John Pfeiffer, w. Boston SO [cnd:Pierre Monteux, Charles Munch], NBC SO [cnd:Leopold Stokowski], RCA SO [cnd:Kiril Kondrashin] *(rec Boston & Chicago & New York, 1953-1961)* RCA Living Stereo 2-▲ 09026-68524-2 [ADD]
Albéniz, I.:Iberia Suite *(rec Orchestral Hall, Chicago, Apr. 26, 1958)* RCA Living Stereo ▲ 09026-62586-2 [ADD]; ■ 09026-62586-4
Albéniz, I.:Navarra [trans. Enrique Arbós] *(rec Orchestral Hall, Chicago, Apr. 26, 1958)* RCA Living Stereo ▲ 09026-62586-2 [ADD]; ■ 09026-62586-4
Bartók, B.:Con Orch RCA Living Stereo ▲ 09026-61504-2; ■ 09026-61504-4
Bartók, B.:Con Orch RCA Gold Seal ▲ 60175-2 RG [ADD] ■ 60175-4 RG (CrO2)
Bartók, B.:Hungarian Sketches RCA Living Stereo ▲ 09026-61504-2; ■ 09026-61504-4
Bartók, B.:Music for Strs, Perc & Cel RCA Gold Seal ▲ 60175-2-RG [ADD] ■ 60175-4-RG (CrO2)
Bartók, B.:Music for Strs, Perc & Cel RCA Living Stereo ▲ 09026-61504-2 ■ 09026-61504-4
Basic 100 Vol. 65, w. Boston SO [cnd:Charles Munch] RCA Victor ▲ 09026-68090-2 ■ 09026-68090-4
Basic 100 Vol. 72 RCA Victor ▲ 09026-68363-2 ■ 09026-68363-4
Beethoven, L. van:Con 4 Pno, w. V. Cliburn (pno) RCA Gold Seal ▲ 7943-2-RG [ADD] ■ 7943-4-RG
Beethoven, L. van:Con 5 Pno, "Emperor", w. V. Cliburn (pno) RCA Gold Seal ▲ 7943-2-RG [ADD] ■ 7943-4-RG
Beethoven, L. van:Con 5 Pno, "Emperor", w. V. Cliburn (pno) RCA Living Stereo ▲ 09026-61961-2 [AAD]; ■ 09026-61961-4
Beethoven, L. van:Coriolan Ov RCA Silver Seal ▲ 60534-2-RV [ADD] ■ 60534-4-RV
Beethoven, L. van:Coriolan Ov RCA Gold Seal ▲ 09026-60962-2
Beethoven, L. van:Coriolan Ov RCA Red Seal ▲ RCD1-5403
Beethoven, L. van:Fidelio (ov) RCA Red Seal ▲ RCD1-5403
Beethoven, L. van:Fidelio (ov) RCA Gold Seal ▲ 09026-60962-2
Beethoven, L. van:Sym 1 RCA Gold Seal ▲ 60002-2-RG [ADD] ■ 60002-4-RG
Beethoven, L. van:Sym 3, "Eroica" RCA Gold Seal ▲ 09026-60962-2
Beethoven, L. van:Sym 5 RCA Red Seal ▲ RCD1-5403
Beethoven, L. van:Sym 6, "Pastorale" RCA Gold Seal ▲ 60002-2-RG [ADD] ■ 60002-4-RG
Beethoven, L. van:Sym 9, "Choral Sym" [G] RCA Gold Seal ("Papillon Collection" series) ▲ 6532-2-RG [ADD] ■ 6532-4-RG
Beethoven, L. van:Sym 9, "Choral Sym", w. P. Curtin (sop), F. Kopleff (cta), J. McCollum (ten), D. Gramm (bass) RCA Gold Seal ▲ 09026-61795-2
Berlioz, H.:Les Nuits d'été, w. L. Price (sop) RCA Gold Seal 2-▲ 09026-61234-2
The Best of Mozart, w. Boston SO [cnd:E. Leinsdorf], English CO [cnd:J.-F. Paillard], et al. Victrola ("Victrola Best of" series) ▲ 60773-2-RV [ADD] ■ 60773-4-RV
The Best of Tchaikovsky, w. Philadelphia Orch [cnd:E. Ormandy], J. Browning (pno), London SO [cnd:S. Ozawa], et al. Victrola ("Victrola Best of" series) ▲ 60775-2-RV [ADD] ■ 60775-4-RV
Borodin, A.:Prince Igor (prelude, act 3) RCA Red Seal ▲ 5602-2-RC [ADD]
Brahms, J.:Con 1 Pno, w. A. Rubinstein (pno) RCA Gold Seal ▲ 09026-61263-2 ■ 09026-61263-4
Brahms, J.:Con 2 Pno, w. Van Cliburn (pno) RCA Living Stereo ▲ 09026-68480-2 ■ 09026-68480-4
Brahms, J.:Con 2 Pno, w. V. Cliburn (pno) RCA Gold Seal ▲ 7942-2-RG [ADD] ■ 7942-4-RG (CrO2)
Brahms, J.:Con 2 Pno, w. E. Gilels (pno) RCA Silver Seal ▲ 60536-2-RV [ADD] ■ 60536-4-RV
Brahms, J.:Con Vn, w. J. Heifetz (vn) *(rec 1955 & 1957)* RCA Gold Seal ▲ 09026-61495-2 ■ 09026-61495-4
Brahms, J.:Con Vn, w. J. Heifetz (vn) RCA Red Seal ▲ RCD1-5402
Brahms, J.:Con Vn, w. Jascha Heifetz (vn) *(rec Orchestra Hall, Chicago, Feb 21-22, 1955)* RCA Red Seal ▲ 09026-61742-2 [ADD]
Brahms, J.:Sym 3 RCA Gold Seal ▲ 09026-61793-2
Debussy, C.:Ibéria RCA Gold Seal ▲ 60179-2-RG [ADD]
Debussy, C.:La Mer RCA Living Stereo ▲ 09026-68079-2
Debussy, C.:La Mer RCA Gold Seal ▲ 09026-60875-2 [ADD] ■ 09026-60875-4
Dvořák, A.:Carnival RCA Living Stereo ▲ 09026-62587-2; ■ 09026-62587-4
Dvořák, A.:Carnival RCA Silver Seal ▲ 60537-2-RV [ADD] ■ 60537-4-RV
Dvořák, A.:Sym 9, "From the New World" RCA ■ ALK1-4463
Dvořák, A.:Sym 9, "From the New World" RCA Living Stereo ▲ 09026-62587-2; ■ 09026-62587-4
Falla, M. de:El amor brujo, w. Leontyne Price (sop) *(rec Orchestral Hall, Chicago, Mar. 4, 1963)* RCA Living Stereo ▲ 09026-62586-2 [ADD]; ■ 09026-62586-4
Falla, M. de:El sombrero de tres picos (sels)—The Neighbor's dance; The Miller's Dance; Final Dance *(rec Orchestral Hall, Chicago, Apr. 26, 1958)* RCA Living Stereo ▲ 09026-62586-2 [ADD]; ■ 09026-62586-4
Falla, M. de:La vida breve (interlude & dance 1), w. Leontyne Price (sop) *(rec Orchestral Hall, Chicago, Apr. 26, 1958)* RCA Living Stereo ▲ 09026-62586-2 [ADD]; ■ 09026-62586-4
Glinka, M.:Russlan & Ludmilla (ov) RCA ■ ALK1-4973
Glinka, M.:Russlan & Ludmilla (ov) RCA ("Basic 100" series) ▲ 09026-68363-2 ■ 09026-68363-4
Glinka, M.:Russlan & Ludmilla (ov) RCA Gold Seal ▲ 60176-2-RG [ADD] ■ 60176-4-RG (CrO2)
Granados, E.:Goyescas (intermezzo) *(rec Orchestral Hall, Chicago, Apr. 26, 1958)* RCA Living Stereo ▲ 09026-62586-2 [ADD] ■ 09026-62586-4
Greatest Overtures, w. A. Fiedler (cnd), Boston Pops Orch ▲ 60839-2-RG ■ 60839-4-RG
Haydn, J.:Sym 88 *(rec 1960)* RCA Gold Seal ▲ 09026-60729-2 ■ 09026-60729-4
Hovhaness, A.:Sym 2 RCA Red Seal ▲ 5733-2-RC
Hovhaness, A.:Sym 2 RCA Living Stereo ▲ 09026-61957-2
Humperdinck, E.:Hänsel und Gretel (sels) RCA Gold Seal ▲ 09026-61792-2
Johann Strauss:Greatest Hits RCA Victor ▲ 60844-2-RG ■ 60844-4-RG
Kabalevsky, D.:Colas Breugnon (ov) RCA Red Seal ▲ 5602-2-RC [ADD]
Liszt, F.:Mephisto Waltz 1 Orch *(rec Orchestra Hall, Chicago, Dec 10, 1955)* RCA Living Stereo ▲ 09026-61246-2 [ADD]
Liszt, F.:Totentanz, w. B. Janis (pno) *(rec 1959)* RCA Gold Seal ▲ 09026-61250-2 ■ 09026-61250-4

Chicago SO (cont.)

F. Reiner (cnd) (cont.)

Mahler, G.:Das Lied von der Erde, w. M. Forrester (cta), R. Lewis (ten) [G] RCA Gold Seal ▲ 60178-2-RG [ADD]
Mendelssohn, F.:Die Hebriden RCA Victor ▲ 09026-68090-2; ■ 09026-68090-4
Mendelssohn, F.:Sym 5 RCA ▲ 09026-68090-2 ■ 09026-68090-4
Mendelssohn, F.:Sym 5 RCA Victor ▲ 09026-68090-2; ■ 09026-68090-4
Mozart, W.A.:Kleine Nachtmusik RCA Gold Seal ▲ 09026-62585-2
Mozart, W.A.:Ovs—Don Giovanni RCA Silver Seal ▲ 60484-2 [ADD] ■ 60484-4 (CrO2)
Mozart, W.A.:Sym 39 RCA Gold Seal ▲ 09026-62585-2
Mozart, W.A.:Sym 40 RCA Gold Seal ▲ 09026-62585-2
Mussorgsky, M.:Night RCA Red Seal ▲ 5602-2-RC [ADD]
Mussorgsky, M.:Night RCA Living Stereo ▲ 09026-61958-2 [AAD]; ■ 09026-61958-4 [DD
Mussorgsky, M.:Pictures at an Exhibition RCA Living Stereo ▲ 09026-61958-2 [AAD]; ■ 09026-61958-4
Mussorgsky, M.:Pictures at an Exhibition *(rec 1957)* RCA Gold Seal ▲ 09026-61401-2 ■ 09026-61401-4
Prokofiev, S.:Alexander Nevsky, w. R. Elias (mez), Chicago Sym Chorus [E] RCA Gold Seal ▲ 60176-2-RG [ADD] ■ 60176-4-RG (CrO2)
Prokofiev, S.:Alexander Nevsky RCA ("Basic 100" series) ▲ 09026-68363-2 ■ 09026-68363-4
Prokofiev, S.:Lt Kijé Suite RCA ("Basic 100" series) ▲ 09026-68363-2 ■ 09026-68363-4
Prokofiev, S.:Lt Kijé Suite RCA Gold Seal ▲ 60176-2 RG [ADD] ■ 60176-4 RG (CrO2)
Prokofiev, S.:Lt Kijé Suite RCA Living Stereo ▲ 09026-61957-2
Rachmaninoff, S.:Con 2 Pno, w. V. Cliburn (pno) RCA Living Stereo ▲ 09026-61961-2 [AAD]; ■ 09026-61961-4 [DD
Rachmaninoff, S.:Con 2 Pno, w. Artur Rubinstein (pno) RCA Red Seal ▲ RCD1-4934 ■ ARE1-4934
Rachmaninoff, S.:Con 2 Pno, w. Van Cliburn (pno) RCA Red Seal ▲ 07863-55912-2 [ADD] ■ 07863-55912-4
Rachmaninoff, S.:The Isle of the Dead RCA Victor ▲ 09026-68022-2; ■ 09026-68022-4
Rachmaninoff, S.:The Isle of the Dead *(rec 1957)* RCA Gold Seal ▲ 09026-61250-2 ■ 09026-61250-4
Rachmaninoff, S.:Rhapsody on a Theme of Paganini, w. Artur Rubinstein (pno) RCA Red Seal ▲ RCD1-4934 ■ ARE1-4934
Ravel, M.:Alborada del gracioso RCA Gold Seal ▲ 60179-2-RG [ADD]
Ravel, M.:Pavane pour une infante défunte *(rec 1957)* RCA Gold Seal ▲ 09026-61250-2 ■ 09026-61250-4
Ravel, M.:Pavane pour une infante défunte RCA Gold Seal ▲ 60179-2-RG [ADD]
Ravel, M.:Rapsodie espagnole RCA Gold Seal ▲ 60179-2-RG [ADD]
Ravel, M.:Rapsodie espagnole *(rec 1956)* RCA Gold Seal ▲ 09026-61250-2 ■ 09026-61250-4
Ravel, M.:Valses nobles et sentimentales RCA Gold Seal ▲ 60179-2-RG [ADD]
Respighi, O.:The Fountains of Rome *(rec 1959)* RCA Gold Seal ▲ 09026-61401-2 ■ 09026-61401-4
Respighi, O.:The Fountains of Rome RCA Living Stereo ▲ 09026-68079-2
Respighi, O.:The Pines of Rome *(rec 1959)* RCA Gold Seal ▲ 09026-61401-2 ■ 09026-61401-4
Respighi, O.:The Pines of Rome RCA Living Stereo ▲ 09026-68079-2
Rimsky-Korsakov, N.:Scheherazade RCA Gold Seal ▲ 09026-60875-2 [ADD] ■ 09026-60875-4
Rimsky-Korsakov, N.:Scheherazade, w. Sidney Harth (vn) *(rec Orchestra Hall, Chicago, Feb 8, 1960)* RCA Living Stereo ▲ 09026-68168-2 [ADD]
Rossini, G.:Ovs—Barber of Seville, Cenerentola, Gazza ladra, Scala di seta, Signor Bruschino, William Tell RCA Gold Seal ▲ 60387-2-RG [ADD] ■ 60387-4-RG (CrO2)
Schubert, Franz:Sym 5 RCA Gold Seal ▲ 09026-61793-2
Schubert, Franz:Sym 8 RCA Red Seal ▲ RCD1-5403
Schumann, R.:Con Pno, w. Van Cliburn (pno) *(rec 1960)* RCA Living Stereo ▲ 09026-62691-2 [ADD]; ■ 09026-62691-4
Schumann, R.:Con Pno, w. V. Cliburn (pno) RCA Gold Seal ▲ 60420-2-RG [ADD] ■ 60420-4-RG (CrO2)
Smetana, B.:The Bartered Bride (ov) RCA Living Stereo ▲ 09026-62587-2; ■ 09026-62587-4
Strauss (II), Joh.:Music of—Artist's life; Vienna blood waltz; Treasure waltz; Roses from the south; Blue Danube; Emperor waltz; Morning papers; Thunder and lightning polka RCA Gold Seal ▲ 60177-2-RG [ADD]
Strauss (II), Joh.:Waltzes—Morning Papers; Emperor Waltz; On the Beautiful Blue Danube; Vienna Blood; Roses from the South; Treasure Waltz; Thunder & Lightning *(rec 1957 & 1960)* RCA Living Stereo ▲ 09026-68160-2 [ADD]; ■ 09026-68160-4
Strauss, Josef:Music of—Village Swallows *(rec 1957 & 1960)* RCA Living Stereo ▲ 09026-68160-2 [ADD]; ■ 09026-68160-4
Strauss, Josef:Music of—2 waltzes:My life is love and laughter; Village swallows RCA Gold Seal ▲ 60177-2-RG [ADD]
Strauss, R.:Also sprach Zarathustra RCA Victor ▲ 09026-61709-2; ■ 09026-61709-4
Strauss, R.:Also sprach Zarathustra *(rec 1962)* RCA Gold Seal ("Papillon Collection" series) ▲ 6722-2-RG [ADD]
Strauss, R.:Also sprach Zarathustra *(rec 1954)* RCA Gold Seal ▲ 09026-61494-2 ■ 09026-61494-4
Strauss, R.:Also sprach Zarathustra RCA Gold Seal ▲ 09026-60930-2
Strauss, R.:Der Bürger als Edelmann (suite) RCA Gold Seal ▲ 09026-60930-2
Strauss, R.:Burleske, w. B. Janis (pno) RCA Gold Seal ▲ 09026-61796-2
Strauss, R.:Don Juan RCA Living Stereo ▲ 09026-68170-2 ■ 09026-68170-4
Strauss, R.:Don Juan RCA Red Seal ▲ RCD1-5408
Strauss, R.:Don Quixote, w. A. Janigro (vc) RCA Gold Seal ▲ 09026-61796-2
Strauss, R.:Don Quixote RCA Living Stereo ▲ 09026-68170-2 ■ 09026-68170-4
Strauss, R.:Elektra (sels), w. I. Borkh (sop)—Elektra's Soliloquy, Recognition Scene, & Finale RCA Gold Seal ▲ 09026-60874-2 [ADD] ■ 09026-60874-4
Strauss, R.:Ein Heldenleben *(rec 1954)* RCA Gold Seal ▲ 09026-61494-2 ■ 09026-61494-4
Strauss, R.:Ein Heldenleben RCA Red Seal ▲ RCD1-5408
Strauss, R.:Ein Heldenleben RCA Victor ▲ 09026-61709-2; ■ 09026-61709-4
Strauss, R.:Der Rosenkavalier (waltzes) *(rec 1957 & 1960)* RCA Living Stereo ▲ 09026-68160-2 [ADD]; ■ 09026-68160-4
Strauss, R.:Der Rosenkavalier (waltzes) RCA Gold Seal ▲ 09026-60930-2
Strauss, R.:Salome (sels), w. I. Borkh (sop)—Dance of the Seven Veils & Final Scene RCA Gold Seal ▲ 09026-60874-2 [ADD] ■ 09026-60874-4
Strauss, R.:Symphonia domestica RCA Gold Seal ▲ 60388-2-RG [ADD]
Stravinsky, I.:Le Chant du rossignol RCA Red Seal ▲ 5733-2-RC [ADD]
Stravinsky, I.:Le Chant du rossignol *(rec Orchestra Hall, Chicago, Nov 3, 1956)* RCA Living Stereo ▲ 09026-68168-2 [ADD]
Stravinsky, I.:Divert Orch RCA Red Seal ▲ 5733-2-RC [ADD]
Stravinsky, I.:Divert Orch RCA Living Stereo ▲ 09026-61957-2
Tchaikovsky, P.:Con Vn, w. J. Heifetz (vn) *(rec 1955 & 1957)* RCA Gold Seal ▲ 09026-61495-2 ■ 09026-61495-4
Tchaikovsky, P.:Con Vn, w. Jascha Heifetz (vn) *(rec Orch Hall, Chicago, Apr 19, 1957)* RCA Red Seal ▲ 09026-61743-2 [ADD]
Tchaikovsky, P.:Con Vn, w. J. Heifetz (vn) RCA Red Seal ▲ 5933-2-RC
Tchaikovsky, P.:Ov 1812 *(rec Orchestra Hall, Chicago, Jan 7, 1956)* RCA Living Stereo ▲ 09026-61246-2 [ADD]
Tchaikovsky, P.:Suite 1—5th movt., March RCA Red Seal ▲ 5602-2-RC [ADD]
Tchaikovsky, P.:Sym 6 RCA ■ ALK1-4464
Tchaikovsky, P.:Sym 6 *(rec Orchestra Hall, Chicago, Apr 16 & 17, 1957)* RCA Living Stereo ▲ 09026-61246-2 [ADD]
Tchaikovsky, P.:Sym 6—5th movt., March RCA Red Seal ▲ 5602-2-RC [ADD]

Chicago SO (cont.)

F. Reiner (cnd) (cont.)

The Voices of Living Stereo, Vol. 2, w. Eileen Farrell (sop), Birgit Nilsson (sop), Roberta Peters (sop), Leontyne Price (sop), Galina Vishnevskaya (sop), Rosalind Elias (mez), Shirley Verrett (mez), Marian Anderson (cta), Maureen Forrester (cta), Sergio Franchi (ten), Mario Lanza (ten), Richard Lewis (ten), Jan Pee, Alexander Dedyukhin (pno), Franz Rupp (pno), Leo Taubman (pno), George Trovillo (pno), Charles Wadsworth (pno), Boston Pops Orch [cnd:Arthur Fiedler], Boston SO [cnd:Charles Munch], RCA Victor Orch, RCA Victor Chorus [cnd:Wa *(rec Boston & Chicago & New York & Rome, 1957–1964)* RCA Living Stereo ▲ 09026-68167-2 [ADD]
Weber, C.M. von:Invitation to the Dance Orch *(rec 1957)* RCA Gold Seal ▲ 09026-61250-2 ■ 09026-61250-4
Weber, C.M. von:Invitation to the Dance Orch *(rec 1957 & 1960)* RCA Living Stereo ▲ 09026-68160-2 [ADD]; ■ 09026-68160-4
Weinberger, J.:Schwanda der Dudelsackpfeifer (polka & fugue) RCA Living Stereo ▲ 09026-62587-2; ■ 09026-62587-4
Wild Classics:A Celebration of Animals & Nature, w. James Galway (fl), Ofra Harnoy (vc), Martin Hoherman (vc), Emily Mitchell (hp), Michael Dussek (pno), Samuel Lipman (pno), Leo Litwin (pno), Gerhard Oppitz (pno), Isao Tomita (synths), Boston Pops Orch [cnd:Arthur Fiedler] RCA Red Seal ▲ 09026-68483-2 ■ 09026-68483-4

G. Reiner (cnd)

Wagner, R.:Ovs, Preludes & Orch Sels—sels. from Die Meistersinger von Nürnberg; Götterdämmerung, Lohengrin & Tannhäuser RCA Gold Seal ▲ 09026-61792-2

A. Schenck (cnd)

American Portraits, w. London SO [cnd:J. Sedares], New York Festival of Song [cnd:Jo Ann Faletta, et al.] Koch International Classics ▲ KIC 7233 [DDD]
Barber, S.:The Lovers, w. D. Duesing (bar), Chicago Sym Chorus [E], 10/91) Koch International Classics ▲ KIC 7125-2 [DDD]
Barber, S.:Prayers of Kierkegaard, w. S. Reese (sop), Chicago Sym Chorus [E], 10/91) Koch International Classics ▲ KIC 7125-2 [DDD]

L. Slatkin (cnd)

Bruch, M.:Con 1 Vn, w. C.-L. Lin (vn) CBS ▲ MK 42315 [DDD]
Bruch, M.:Con 1 Vn, w. C.-L. Lin (vn) CBS ▲ MDK 44902 [DDD] ■ MDT 44902 (D)
Bruch, M.:Scottish Fant Vn, w. Cho-Liang Lin (vn) CBS ▲ MK 42315 [DDD]

G. Solti (cnd)

Bach, J.S.:Mass in b, BWV 232, w. F. Lott (sop), A. S. von Otter (mez), H. P. Blochwitz (ten), W. Shimell (bar), G. Howell (b-bar), Chicago Sym Chorus London 2-▲ 430353-2 [DDD]
Bach, J.S.:St. Matthew Passion, w. K. Te Kanawa (sop), A. S. von Otter (mez), H. P. Blochwitz (ten), A. Rolfe Johnson (ten), O. Bär (bar), T. Krause (bass), Chicago Sym Chorus, Glen Ellyn Children's Chorus [G] London 3-▲ 421177-2 [DDD]
Bach, J.S.:St. Matthew Passion (sels), w. K. Te Kanawa (sop), A. S. von Otter (mez), H. P. Blochwitz (ten), A. Rolfe Johnson (ten), O. Bär (bar), T. Krause (bass), Chicago Sym Chorus, Glen Ellyn Children's Chorus [G] London ▲ 425691-2 [DDD]
Bartók, B.:Con Orch London ▲ 417754-2 [DDD]
Bartók, B.:Con 1 Vn, w. K.-W. Chung (vn) London ▲ 425015-2 [DDD/ADD]
Bartók, B.:Divert London ▲ 430352-2 [DDD] □ 430352-5
Bartók, B.:Hungarian Sketches London ▲ 443444-2
Bartók, B.:The Miraculous Mandarin (suite) London ▲ 430352-2 [DDD] □ 430352-5
Bartók, B.:Music for Strs, Perc & Cel London ▲ 430352-2 [DDD] □ 430352-5
Bartók, B.:Romanian Dances London ▲ 443444-2
Beethoven, L. van:Con 2 Pno, w. V. Ashkenazy (pno) London ▲ 417703-2 [ADD]
Beethoven, L. van:Con 3 Pno, w. V. Ashkenazy (pno) London ▲ 417740-2 [ADD]
Beethoven, L. van:Con 4 Pno, w. V. Ashkenazy (pno) London 2-▲ 436380-2 [ADD]
Beethoven, L. van:Con 4 Pno, w. V. Ashkenazy (pno) London ▲ 417740-2 [ADD]
Beethoven, L. van:Con 5 Pno, "Emperor", w. V. Ashkenazy (pno) London ▲ 417703-2 [ADD]
Beethoven, L. van:Con 5 Pno, "Emperor", w. V. Ashkenazy (pno) London 2-▲ 436380-2 [ADD]
Beethoven, L. van:Egmont (ov) London ♦ 0062635457
Beethoven, L. van:Egmont (ov) London ▲ 430087-2 [DDD]
Beethoven, L. van:Fidelio, w. H. Behrens (sop), S. Ghazarian (sop), P. Hofmann (ten), T. Adam (b-bar), H. Sotin (bass), Chicago Sym Chorus [G] London 2-▲ 410227-2 [DDD]
Beethoven, L. van:Leonore 3 London ▲ 421773-2 [DDD]
Beethoven, L. van:Syms (comp), w. Chicago Sym Chorus [soloists in No. 9:Jessye Norman, Reinhild Runkel, Robert Schunk, Hans Sotin] [G] London 6-▲ 430400-2 [DDD]
Beethoven, L. van:Sym 1 London ▲ 430320-2 [DDD]
Beethoven, L. van:Sym 2 London ▲ 430320-2 [DDD]
Beethoven, L. van:Sym 3, "Eroica" London ▲ 430087-2 [DDD]
Beethoven, L. van:Sym 3, "Eroica" London ♦ 0062635457
Beethoven, L. van:Sym 4 London ▲ 421580-2 [DDD]
Beethoven, L. van:Sym 5 London ▲ 421580-2 [DDD]
Beethoven, L. van:Sym 6, "Pastorale" London ▲ 417765-2 [ADD]
Beethoven, L. van:Sym 6, "Pastorale" London ▲ 421773-2 [DDD]
Beethoven, L. van:Sym 7 London ▲ 425525-2 [DDD] ■ 425525-4
Beethoven, L. van:Sym 8 London ▲ 425525-2 [DDD] ■ 425525-4
Beethoven, L. van:Sym 8 London ▲ 417765-2 [ADD]
Beethoven, L. van:Sym 9, "Choral Sym", w. Chicago Sym Chorus [soloists P. Lorengar, Y. Minton, S. Burrows, M. Talvela] London ("Jubilee" series) ▲ 430438-2 [ADD]
Beethoven, L. van:Sym 9, "Choral Sym", w. Chicago Sym Chorus [G] London ▲ 417800-2 [DDD] ■ 417800-4
Berlioz, H.:La Damnation de Faust, w. F. von Stade (mez), K. Riegel (ten), J. Van Dam (b-bar), Chicago Sym Chorus London 2-▲ 414680-2 [DDD]
Berlioz, H.:Ovs—Les francs-juges London ("Jubilee" series) ▲ 430441-2 [ADD]
Berlioz, H.:Sym fantastique London ("Jubilee" series) ▲ 430441-2 [ADD]
Brahms, J.:Ein Deutsches Requiem, w. K. Te Kanawa (sop), B. Weikl (bar), Chicago Sym Chorus [G] London 2-▲ 414627-2 [ADD]
Brahms, J.:Sym 4 London ("Jubilee" series) ▲ 430440-2 [ADD]
Brahms, J.:Vars on a Theme by Haydn London ("Jubilee" series) ▲ 430440-2 [ADD]
Brahms, J.:Vars on a Theme by Haydn London 2-▲ 414627-2 [ADD]
Bruckner, A.:Sym 1 [Linz version, 1865–66] *(rec Orchestra Hall, Chicago, IL, Feb 1995)* London ▲ 448898-2 [DDD]
Bruckner, A.:Sym 2 *(rec Oct. 12 & 14, 1991)* London ▲ 436844-2 [DDD]
Bruckner, A.:Sym 3, "Wagner" London ▲ 440316-2
Bruckner, A.:Sym 8 [1890 Nowak edition] London ▲ 430228-2 [DDD]
Classical Ecstasy—Classics for a New Age, w. English CO [cnd:Alexander Schneider], London PO [cnd:Leonard Slatkin], Philadelphia Orch [cnd:James Levine], Philharmonia Orch [cnds:Andrew Litton, Henry Lewis], RCA Italiana Opera Orch [cnd:Francesco Molinari-Pradelli], RCA RCA Gold Seal ▲ 74321-23041-2 [ADD/DDD]
Debussy, C.:La Mer London ▲ 436468-2 [DDD]
Debussy, C.:Nocturnes, w. Chicago Sym Chorus London ▲ 436468-2 [DDD]
Debussy, C.:Prélude à l'après-midi d'un faune London ▲ 417704-2 [ADD]
Debussy, C.:Prélude à l'après-midi d'un faune London ("Jubilee" series) ▲ 430444-2 [ADD]
Debussy, C.:Prélude à l'après-midi d'un faune, w. Chicago Sym Chorus London ▲ 436468-2 [DDD]
Handel, G.F.:Messiah, w. Kiri Te Kanawa (sop), Anne Gjevang (mez), Richard Lewis (ten), Gwynne Howell (bass), Chicago Sym Chorus [E] London 2-▲ 414396-2 [DDD]
Handel, G.F.:Messiah (sels), w. Chicago Sym Chorus—choruses [E] London ("Jubilee" series) ▲ 430734-2 [DDD]
Handel, G.F.:Messiah (sels), w. Kiri Te Kanawa (sop), Anne Gjevang (mez), Richard Lewis (ten), Gwynne Howell (bass), Chicago Sym Chorus—arias & choruses London ▲ 430098-2 [DDD] ■ 430098-4
Haydn, J.:Die Schöpfung (sels), w. Norma Burrowes (sop), Rüdger Wohlers (ten), James Morris (bass), Chicago Sym Chorus London ("Jubilee" series) ▲ 430739-2 [DDD]

Chicago SO (cont.)

G. Solti (cnd) (cont.)

Haydn, J.:Die Schöpfung, w. Ruth Ziesak (sop—Eve & Gabriel), Herbert Lippert (ten—Uriel), Rene Papé (bass—Raphael), Anton Scharinger (bass—Adam), Chicago Sym Chorus London 2-▲ 443445-2 [DDD]
Kodály, Z.:Háry János (suite) London ▲ 443444-2
Liszt, F.:A Faust Sym, w. S. Jerusalem (ten), Chicago Sym Chorus [G] London ▲ 417399-2 [DDD]
Liszt, F.:Hungarian Rhaps London ▲ 443444-2
Liszt, F.:Mephisto Waltz 1 Orch London ▲ 443444-2
Mahler, G.:Sym 1 London ▲ 411731-2 [DDD]
Mahler, G.:Sym 2, w. I. Buchanan (sop), M. Zakai (cta), Chicago Sym Chorus [G] London 2-▲ 410202-2 [DDD]
Mahler, G.:Sym 4, w. K. Te Kanawa (sop) [G] London ▲ 410188-2 [DDD]
Mahler, G.:Sym 5 London ("Jubilee" series) ▲ 430443-2 [ADD]
Mahler, G.:Sym 5 London ▲ 414321-2 [DDD]
Mahler, G.:Sym 5 *(rec 1991)* London ▲ 433329-2 [DDD] ■ 433329-4
Mahler, G.:Sym 7 London 2-▲ 414675-2 [ADD]
Mahler, G.:Sym 8, w. A. Augér (sop), H. Harper (sop), L. Popp (sop), Y. Minton (mez), H. Watts (cta), A. Kollo (ten), J. Shirley-Quirk (bar), M. Talvela (bass), Vienna State Opera Chorus, Vienna Boys' Choir, Vienna Singverein [G,L] London 2-▲ 414493-2 [ADD]
Mendelssohn, F.:Sym 3 London ▲ 414665-2 [DDD]
Mendelssohn, F.:Sym 4 London ▲ 414665-2 [DDD]
Mussorgsky, M.:Pictures at an Exhibition London ("Jubilee" series) ▲ 430446-2 [DDD]
Mussorgsky, M.:Pictures at an Exhibition London ▲ 417754-2 [DDD]
Prokofiev, S.:Romeo & Juliet (sels) London ▲ 430731-2 [DDD]
Prokofiev, S.:Sym 1 London ▲ 430731-2 [DDD]
Prokofiev, S.:Sym 1 London ("Jubilee" series) ▲ 430446-2
Ravel, M.:Boléro London ▲ 417704-2 [ADD]
Ravel, M.:Boléro London ("Jubilee" series) ▲ 430444-2 [ADD]
Ravel, M.:Le Tombeau de Couperin London ("Jubilee" series) ▲ 430444-2 [ADD]
Schoenberg, A.:Moses und Aaron, w. B. Bonney (sop), M. Zakai (cta), P. Langridge (ten), F. Mazura (bar), A. Haugland (bass), Chicago Sym Chorus, Glen Ellyn Children's Chorus [G] London 2-▲ 414264-2 [DDD]
Shostakovich, D.:Sym 8 London ▲ 425675-2 [DDD]
The Solti Edition, w. London PO, London SO, Vienna PO, New Philharmonia Orch, Royal Opera House Orch, CO of Europe London 25-▲ 436600-2
Strauss, R.:Also sprach Zarathustra London ("Jubilee" series) ▲ 430445-2
Strauss, R.:Don Juan London ("Jubilee" series) ▲ 430445-2
Strauss, R.:Till Eulenspiegels lustige Streiche London ("Jubilee" series) ▲ 430445-2 [ADD]
Stravinsky, I.:Jeu de cartes London ▲ 443775-2
Stravinsky, I.:Pétrouchka [orig. 1911 version] London ▲ 443775-2
Stravinsky, I.:Le Sacre du printemps Orch London ▲ 417704-2 [ADD]
Tchaikovsky, P.:Nutcracker Suite London ("Jubilee" series) ▲ 430707-2 [DDD]
Tchaikovsky, P.:Ov 1812 London ("Jubilee" series) ▲ 430446-2 [DDD]
Tchaikovsky, P.:Romeo & Juliet London ("Jubilee" series) ▲ 430442-2 [ADD]
Tchaikovsky, P.:Romeo & Juliet London ("Jubilee" series) ▲ 430707-2 [DDD]
Tchaikovsky, P.:Romeo & Juliet London ("Jubilee" series) ▲ 430745-2 [DDD]
Tchaikovsky, P.:Swan Lake (sels) London ▲ 425516-2 [DDD]
Tchaikovsky, P.:Swan Lake (suite) London ("Jubilee" series) ▲ 430707-2 [DDD]
Tchaikovsky, P.:Sym 4 London ("Jubilee" series) ▲ 430745-2 [DDD]
Tchaikovsky, P.:Sym 5 London ▲ 425516-2 [DDD]
Tchaikovsky, P.:Sym 6 London ("Jubilee" series) ▲ 430442-2 [ADD]
Tippett, M.:Byzantium, w. F. Robinson (sop) London ▲ 433668-2 [DDD]
Tippett, M.:Suite in D London 3-▲ 425646-2 [ADD/DDD]
Tippett, M.:Sym 4 London ▲ 433668-2 [DDD]
Verdi, G.:Choruses, w. Chicago Sym Chorus—from Aida, Ballo in maschera, Macbeth, Nabucco, Otello, Requiem, Trovatore [I] London ▲ 430226-2 [DDD] □ 430226-5
Verdi, G.:Otello, w. K. Te Kanawa (sop), L. Pavarotti (ten), L. Nucci (bar), Chicago Sym Chorus [I] London 2-▲ 433669-2 [DDD]
Wagner, R.:Der fliegende Holländer, w. Martin (sop), A. Kollo (ten), N. Bailey (bar), M. Talvela (bass), Chicago Sym Chorus [G] London 2-▲ 414551-2 [ADD]
Wagner, R.:Die Meistersinger von Nürnberg, w. *(soloists unknown)* London ▲ 452 606-2
Wagner, R.:Ovs, Preludes & Orch Sels—Fliegende Holländer & Tannhäuser Ovs.; Die Meistersinger, Act 1 Prelude; Prelude & Liebestod from Tristan London ("Jubilee" series) ▲ 430448-2 [ADD]
Weiner, L.:Prinz Csongor und die Kobolde London ▲ 443444-2

F. Stock (cnd)

Beethoven, L. van:Con 4 Pno, w. A. Schnabel (pno) RCA Gold Seal ▲ 09026-61393-2
Beethoven, L. van:Con 5 Pno, "Emperor", w. A. Schnabel (pno) RCA Gold Seal ▲ 09026-61393-2
Tchaikovsky, P.:Con Vn, w. N. Milstein (vn) *(rec 1940)* Biddulph ▲ LAB 063 [ADD]

L. Stokowski (cnd)

Rimsky-Korsakov, N.:Russian Easter Festival RCA Silver Seal ▲ 60487-2-RV [DDD] ■ 60487-4-RV (CrO2)

K. Tennstedt (cnd)

Mahler, G.:Sym 1 *(rec live)* EMI Classics ▲ CDC 54217

M. Tilson Thomas (cnd)

Ives, C.:Central Park in the Dark CBS ▲ MK 42381 [DDD]
Ives, C.:Holidays, w. Chicago Sym Chorus CBS ▲ MK 42381 [DDD]
Ives, C.:Sym 1 Sony Classical ▲ SK 44939 [DDD]
Ives, C.:Sym 4, w. Chicago Sym Chorus—also including choral performances of five American hymns which are quoted by Ives in his Fourth Symphony Sony Classical ▲ SK 44939 [DDD]
Ives, C.:The Unanswered Question [both the original & the revised version] CBS ▲ MK 42381 [DDD]

G. Wand (cnd)

Brahms, J.:Sym 1 RCA Red Seal ▲ 60428-2-RC [DDD]

Chicago Sym Winds

Grieg, E.:Lyric Pieces—4 sels. Sheffield Lab ("Salon" series) ▲ SLS 506
Mozart, W.A.:Serenade Ww, K.375 Sheffield Lab ("Salon" series) ▲ SLS 506

Chichester Concert

I. Graham-Jones (cnd)

Marsh, J.:A Conversation Sym [period instrs] Olympia ("Explorer" series) ▲ OCD 400 [DDD]
Marsh, J.:Sym 1 [period instrs] Olympia ("Explorer" series) ▲ OCD 400 [DDD]
Marsh, J.:Sym 3 [period instrs] Olympia ("Explorer" series) ▲ OCD 400 [DDD]
Marsh, J.:Sym 4 [period instrs] Olympia ("Explorer" series) ▲ OCD 400 [DDD]
Marsh, J.:Sym 6 [period instrs] Olympia ("Explorer" series) ▲ OCD 400 [DDD]

Chieftains

Carol of the Drum, w. Emily Mitchell (hp), Richard Stoltzman (cl), Michala Petri (rcr), James Galway (fl), Hampton String Quartet, Royal PO, Boys' Choir of Harlem RCA Victor ▲ 09026-61839-2 ■ 09026-61839-4

Chilingirian String Quartet

Arriaga, J.C.:Qts (3) Strs CRD 2-▲ CRD 33123 [ADD]
Aslamazyan, S.:Armenian Suite Positively Armenian ■ PA 107C
Bartók, B.:Qt Strs (comp)—Nos. 3,4 & 5 Chandos ▲ CHAN 8634 [DDD]
Bartók, B.:Qt Strs (comp)—Nos. 1 & 2 Chandos ▲ CHAN 8588 [DDD]
Bartók, B.:Qt Strs (comp)—No. 6 Chandos ▲ CHAN 8660 [DDD]
Bartók, B.:Qnt Pno & Strs, w. S. Deroote (pno) Chandos ▲ CHAN 8660 [DDD]
Bazil, L.:The Abandoned Churches of Ani Positively Armenian ■ PA 107C
Dvořák, A.:Cypresses Chandos ▲ CHAN 8826 [DDD]
Dvořák, A.:Gavotte Chandos ▲ CHAN 9173 [DDD]
Dvořák, A.:Miniatures, Op. 75a Chandos ▲ CHAN 9173 [DDD]
Dvořák, A.:Notturno, w. D. McTier (db) Chandos ▲ CHAN 9046 [DDD]
Dvořák, A.:Qt Movt Chandos ▲ CHAN 8874 [DDD]

▲ = CD ♦ = Enhanced CD Δ = MD ■ = Cassette Tape □ = DCC

Chilingirian String Quartet (cont.)
Dvořák, A.:Qts Strs (comp)—Nos. 8 & 9 — Chandos ▲ CHAN 8755 [DDD]
Dvořák, A.:Qts Strs (comp)—Nos. 12 & 14 — Chandos ▲ CHAN 8919 [DDD]
Dvořák, A.:Qts Strs (comp)—No. 13 — Chandos ▲ CHAN 8874 [DDD]
Dvořák, A.:Qts Strs (comp)—Nos. 10 & 11 — Chandos ▲ CHAN 8837 [DDD]
Dvořák, A.:Qts Strs (comp)—No. 7 in a, Op. 16 — Chandos ▲ CHAN 8826 [DDD]
Dvořák, A.:Qnt Pno, Op. 81, w. J. Menuhin (pno) — Chandos ▲ CHAN 9173 [DDD]
Dvořák, A.:Qnt Strs, Op. 77, w. D. McTier (db) — Chandos ▲ CHAN 9046 [DDD]
Dvořák, A.:Qnt Strs, Op. 97, w. S. Rowland-Jones (va) — Chandos ▲ CHAN 9046 [DDD]
Dvořák, A.:Terzetto — Chandos ▲ CHAN 9173 [DDD]
Dvořák, A.:Waltzes Strs, B.105 — Chandos ▲ CHAN 8874 [DDD]
Elgar, E.:Qt Strs — EMI Classics ▲ CDM 65099
Elgar, E.:Qnt Pno Strs — EMI Classics ▲ CDM 65099
Haydn, J.:Qts Strs, Op. 71 — Chandos ▲ CHAN 9146 [DDD]
Khachaturian, A.:Double Fugue — Positively Armenian ■ PA 107C
Korngold, E.W.:Qt 1 Strs — RCA Gold Seal ▲ 7889-2-RG [ADD]
Korngold, E.W.:Qt 3 Strs — RCA Gold Seal ▲ 7889-2-RG [ADD]
Mirzoyan, E.:Qt Strs — Positively Armenian ■ PA 107C
Mozart, W.A.:Qt Ob, K.370, w. G. Hunt (ob) — Classics for Pleasure ▲ CDCFP 4377 [ADD]
Mozart, W.A.:Qts Strs (misc)—Nos. 16 & 17 — CRD ▲ 3363 [ADD]
Mozart, W.A.:Qts Strs (misc)—Nos. 14 & 15 — CRD ▲ 3362 [ADD]
Mozart, W.A.:Qts Strs (misc)—Nos. 18 & 19 — CRD ▲ 3364 [ADD]
Mozart, W.A.:Qt 20 Strs — CRD ▲ 3427
Mozart, W.A.:Qt 21 Strs — CRD ▲ 3427
Mozart, W.A.:Qt 22 Strs — CRD ▲ 3428
Mozart, W.A.:Qt 23 Strs — CRD ▲ 3428
Mozart, W.A.:Qnt Cl, K.581, w. A. Marriner (cl) — Classics for Pleasure ▲ CDCFP 4377 [ADD]
Panufnik, A.:Qt 1 Strs — Conifer Classics ▲ 74321-16190-2
Panufnik, A.:Qt 2 Strs — Conifer Classics ▲ 74321-16190-2
Panufnik, A.:Qt 3 Strs — Conifer Classics ▲ 74321-16190-2
Panufnik, A.:Sxt Strs, w. Roger Chase (va), Stephen Orion (vc) — Conifer Classics ▲ 74321-16190-2
Panufnik, A.:Song to the Virgin — Conifer Classics ▲ 74321-16190-2
Pärt, A.:Fratres I [quartet version] — Virgin Classics ▲ CDC 45023
Pärt, A.:Summa [quartet version] — Virgin Classics ▲ CDC 45023
Prokofiev, S.:Qt 1 Strs — Chandos ▲ CHAN 8929 [DDD]
Prokofiev, S.:Qt 2 Strs — Chandos ▲ CHAN 8929 [DDD]
Schubert, Franz:Qt 13 Strs — Nimbus 2-▲ NI 5048/49
Schubert, Franz:Qt 14 Strs — Nimbus 2-▲ NI 5048/49
Schubert, Franz:Qt 15 Strs — Nimbus 2-▲ NI 5048/49
Stravinsky, I.:Pieces Str Qt — Chandos ("Collect" series) ▲ CHAN 6535 [ADD]
Tavener, J.:Qt 1 Strs — Virgin Classics ▲ CDC 45023
Tavener, J.:Qt 2 Strs — Virgin Classics ▲ CDC 45023
Wood, Hugh:Qts Strs — Conifer Classics ▲ 75605-51239-2 [DDD]

Chilingirian String Quartet [L. Chilingirian (vn), M. Butler (vn), S. Rowland-Jones (va), P. de Groote (vc)]
Berwald, F.:Qt 1 Strs — CRD ▲ CRD 3361 [ADD]
Wikmanson, J.:Qt 2 Strs — CRD ▲ CRD 3361 [ADD]

Chilingirian String Quartet [Levon Chilingirian (vn), Charles Stewart (vn), Simon Rowland-Jones (va), Philip De Groote (vc)]
Arriaga, J.C.:Qts (3) Strs — CRD 2-▲ CRD 3312/13
Firsova, E.:Qt 4 Strs, "Amoroso" *(rec All Saints' Church, Petersham, Surrey, England)* — Conifer Classics ▲ 75605-51252-2 [DDD]
Mozart, W.A.:Qt 14 Strs — CRD ▲ CRD 3362
Mozart, W.A.:Qt 15 Strs — CRD ▲ CRD 3362
Roslavets, N.:Qt 3 Strs *(rec All Saints' Church, Petersham, Surrey, England)* — Conifer Classics ▲ 75605-51252-2 [DDD]
Schnittke, A.:Canon in memoriam Igor Stravinsky *(rec All Saints' Church, Petersham, Surrey, England)* — Conifer Classics ▲ 75605-51252-2 [DDD]
Smirnov, D.:Qt 2 Strs *(rec All Saints' Church, Petersham, Surrey, England)* — Conifer Classics ▲ 75605-51252-2 [DDD]
Stravinsky, I.:Pieces Str Qt *(rec All Saints' Church, Petersham, Surrey, England)* — Conifer Classics ▲ 75605-51252-2 [DDD]
Wikmanson, J.:Qt 2 Strs — CRD 2-▲ CRD 3312/13

Chilingirian String Quartet members
Mozart, W.A.:Qts Fl, w. S. Milan (fl) — Chandos ▲ CHAN 8872 [DDD]

Chinese Central PO
H. Zongjie (cnd)
Beethoven, L. van:Con Vn, Vc & Pno, "Triple Con", w. P. León (vn), P. Corostola (vc), L. Milà (pno) — Regis Tro ▲ RTAC 003 [DDD]

Chinook Trio [S. Hoeppner (fl), A. Forsyth (vc), G. Saarinen (pno)]
Beethoven, L. van:Trio Fl, WoO 37 — Marquis ▲ MAR 141
Czerny, C.:Fant concertante — Marquis ▲ MAR 141
Hummel, J.N.:Adagio, Vars & Rondo on "Schöne Minka" — Marquis ▲ MAR 141
Kuhlau, F.:Grand Trio [arr fl, vc & pno] — Marquis ▲ MAR 141

Chitarristico Trio [Fabio Renato d'Ettorre (gtr), Arturo Tallini (gtr), Fernando Lepri (gtr)]
Amoroso, A.:Trio Gtrs — Musik Strasse ▲ MC 2103
Ettorre, F.R. d':Suite Gallega — Musik Strasse ▲ MC 2103
Ferranti, M.Z. de:Polonaise concertante [ed. Chanterelle] — Musik Strasse ▲ MC 2103
Mozart, W.A.:Fant Pno, K.475 [trans Luciano Chailly for 3 gtrs] — Musik Strasse ▲ MC 2103
Vivaldi, A.:Con for 2 Mands [trans. d'Ettore, Tallini & Lepri for 3 gtrs] — Musik Strasse ▲ MC 2103

Chopin CO
W.D. Vogel (cnd)
Bellini, V.:Sinf breve in D — Dynamic ▲ CD 79 [DDD]
Cimarosa, D.:Sinf in D — Dynamic ▲ CD 79 [DDD]
Clementi, M.:Sinf in D — Dynamic ▲ CD 79 [DDD]
Paisiello, G.:Sinf in D — Dynamic ▲ CD 79 [DDD]
Rossini, G.:Sinf "di Bologna" — Dynamic ▲ CD 79 [DDD]
Salieri, A.:Sinf, "Veneziana" — Dynamic ▲ CD 79 [DDD]

Chopin Trio [Bogumil Nowicki (pno), Bartosz Bryla (vn), Pawel Frejdlich (vc)]
Chopin, F.:Trio Pno *(rec Warsaw Philharmony Hall, Nov 11, 1992)* — Canyon Classics ▲ 238
Mozart, W.A.:Divert Pno, K.254 *(rec National Philharmonic Concert Hall, Warsaw, Aug–Oct 1990)* — Polskie Nagrania 2-▲ PNCD 127/1-2 [DDD]
Mozart, W.A.:Trios Pno (comp) *(rec National Philharmonic Concert Hall, Warsaw, Aug–Oct 1990)* — Polskie Nagrania 2-▲ PNCD 127/1-2 [DDD]

Choral Guild of Atlanta Brass & Percussion
The Joy of Christmas, w. Anthony Newman (org), Chestnut Brass Company [cnd:William Noll], Choral Guild of Atlanta, Benjamin Harms (timp), Walter Huff (org) — Sony Classical ▲ SFK 62698 ■ SFT 62698

Chorus Civitas CO
R. Taylor (cnd)
Vaughan Williams, R.:Epithalamion, w. Edward Scott Hendricks (bar), Chorus Civitas *(rec The Stockade, Baton Rouge, Apr 24 & 27, 1995)* — Centaur ▲ CRC 2299 [DDD]
Vaughan Williams, R.:An Oxford Elegy, w. Gerard Killebrew (nar), Chorus Civitas *(rec The Stockade, Baton Rouge, Apr 24 & 27, 1995)* — Centaur ▲ CRC 2299 [DDD]

Christopher String Quartet
Malipiero, G.-F.:Qt 1 Strs — Indiana Univ School of Music ▲ IUSM 01 [DDD]
Turina, J.:La oracion del torero [arr Str Qt] — Indiana Univ School of Music ▲ IUSM 01 [DDD]
Weigl, K.:Qt 1 Strs — Indiana Univ School of Music ▲ IUSM 01 [DDD]

Chung Trio [M.-W. Chung (pno), K.-W. Chung (vn), M.-W. Chung (vc)]
Beethoven, L. van:Trio 1 Pno — EMI Classics ▲ CDC 54579
Beethoven, L. van:Trio 4 Pno, "Ghost" — EMI Classics ▲ 54579

I Ciarlatani
Codex Manesse:The Great Heidelberg Song Manuscript — Christophorus ▲ CHR 77192 [DDD]
Renaissance Music at the Court in Heidelberg — Christophorus ▲ CHR 77184 [DDD]

Cicashi Tanaka Ensemble
Tchaikovsky, P.:Serenade Strs—Larghetto elegiaco movt — Camerata ("After Hours Classics" series) ▲ 20 CM 423 [DDD]

Cikada Ensemble
C. Eggen (cnd)
Thoresen, L.:AbUno — Norway Music ▲ ACD 4968
Thoresen, L.:Qudrat — Norway Music ▲ ACD 4968

Cikada String Quartet
Crumb, G.:Black Angels (Images I) — Cala ▲ CAL 77001
Lutoslawski, W.:Qt Strs — Cala ▲ CAL 77001
Webern, A.:Qt Strs, Op. 28 — Cala ▲ CAL 77001

Cincinnati CO
E. Alonso-Crespo (cnd)
Alonso-Crespo, E.:Juana, la loca (sels)—Ov; Ballet Music *(rec Emory Theater, Cincinnati, OH, Jan 24, 1994)* — Ocean ▲ OR 101 [DDD]
Alonso-Crespo, E.:Ovs & Dances — Ocean ▲ ORC 101
Alonso-Crespo, E.:Putzi (sels)—Mephisto (waltz) *(rec Emory Theater, Cincinnati, OH, Jan 24, 1994)* — Ocean ▲ OR 101 [DDD]
Alonso-Crespo, E.:Yubarta (ov) *(rec Emory Theater, Cincinnati, OH, Jan 24, 1994)* — Ocean ▲ OR 101 [DDD]
K. Lockhart (cnd)
Galbraith, N.:Con 1 Pno, w. Ralph Zitterbart (pno) *(rec Emory Theater, Cincinnati, OH, Jan 24, 1994)* — Ocean ▲ OR 101 [DDD]

Cincinnati College Conservatory of Music Wind Sym
E. Corporon (cnd)
American Variations *(rec Corbett Auditorium, July 25–28, 1994)* — Klavier ▲ KCD 11060 [DDD]
Bernstein, L.:Candide (ov) — Klavier ▲ KCD 11048 [DDD]
Bernstein, L.:Music of—Slava — Klavier ▲ KCD 11030 [DDD]
Cincinnati College-Conservatory of Music Wind Symphony — Klavier ▲ KCD 11042 [DDD]
Colgrass, M.:Winds of Nagual *(rec Corbett Auditorium, May 26–27, 1990)* — Klavier ▲ KCD 11064 [DDD]
Copland, A.:Emblems — Klavier ▲ KCD 11030 [DDD]
Copland, A.:An Outdoor Ov — Klavier ▲ KCD 11048 [DDD]
Copland, A.:El salón México — Klavier ▲ KCD 11048 [DDD]
Dahl, I.:Sinfonietta — Klavier ▲ KCD 11030 [DDD]
Diamond, D.:Hearts Music *(rec Corbett Auditorium, May 26–27, 1990)* — Klavier ▲ KCD 11064 [DDD]
Diamond, D.:Tantivy — Klavier ▲ KCD 11051
Druckman, J.:In Memoriam Vincent Persichetti — Klavier ▲ KCD 11051
Druckman, J.:Paean — Klavier ▲ KCD 11051
Gershwin, G.:Rhap in Blue, w. W. Black (pno) [scored Grofé] — Klavier ▲ KCD 11047 [DDD]
Gillingham, D.:Songs of the Night *(rec Corbett Auditorium, May 30 & 31, 1992)* — Klavier ▲ KCD 11066 [DDD]
Gilmore, B.:Folksongs (5), w. Barbara Paré (sop) *(rec Corbett Auditorium, May 30 & 31, 1992)* — Klavier ▲ KCD 11066 [DDD]
Grainger, P.:Folk Song Settings—Irish Tune from County Derry; The Gum-Suckers March *(rec White Recital Hall, Univ of Missouri, Kansas City, Feb 23, 1991)* — Klavier ▲ KCD 11067 [DDD]
Gregson, E.:Celebration, w. M. Kane (tpt), J. Burgess (tpt), D. Papp (tpt) — Klavier ▲ KCD 11047 [DDD]
Hartley, W.S.:Con Winds *(rec Corbett Auditorium, May 26–27, 1990)* — Klavier ▲ KCD 11064 [DDD]
Kurka, R.:The Good Soldier Schweik (suite) — Klavier ▲ KCD 11051
Maslanka, D.:A Child's Garden — Klavier ▲ KCD 11030 [DDD]
Maw, N.:American Games — Klavier ▲ KCD 11047 [DDD]
Murray, L.:Ronald Searle Suite *(rec Corbett Auditorium, May 26–27, 1990)* — Klavier ▲ KCD 11064 [DDD]
Nelson, R.:Aspen Jubilee *(rec Corbett Auditorium, May 26–27, 1990)* — Klavier ▲ KCD 11064 [DDD]
Persichetti, V.:Mascarade *(rec Corbett Auditorium, May 30 & 31, 1992)* — Klavier ▲ KCD 11066 [DDD]
Persichetti, V.:Sym 6 — Klavier ▲ KCD 11047 [DDD]
Piston, W.:Turnbridge Fair — Klavier ▲ KCD 11030 [DDD]
Reed, H.O.:La Fiesta Mexicana — Klavier ▲ KCD 11048 [DDD]
Schmitt, F.:Dionysiaques *(rec Corbett Auditorium, May 30 & 31, 1992)* — Klavier ▲ KCD 11066 [DDD]
Schoenberg, A.:Theme & Vars Band — Klavier ▲ KCD 11047 [DDD]
Schuman, W.:Chester Ov — Klavier ▲ KCD 11048 [DDD]
Schuman, W.:George Washington Bridge — Klavier ▲ KCD 11048 [DDD]
Skalkottas, N.:Greek Dances—Epirotikos; Kalamatianos; Sifneikos; Kritikos *(rec White Recital Hall, Univ of Missouri, Kansas City, Feb 23, 1991)* — Klavier ▲ KCD 11067 [DDD]
Stamp, J.:Gavorkna Fanfare *(rec White Recital Hall, Univ of Missouri, Kansas City, Feb 23, 1991)* — Klavier ▲ KCD 11067 [DDD]
Tcherepnin, I.:Statue *(rec White Recital Hall, Univ of Missouri, Kansas City, Feb 23, 1991)* — Klavier ▲ KCD 11067 [DDD]
Tippett, M.:Mosaic *(rec White Recital Hall, Univ of Missouri, Kansas City, Feb 23, 1991)* — Klavier ▲ KCD 11067 [DDD]
Weinstein, M.:Con Ww *(rec White Recital Hall, Univ of Missouri, Kansas City, Feb 23, 1991)* — Klavier ▲ KCD 11067 [DDD]
Wilson, D.:Piece of Mind — Klavier ▲ KCD 11051
Zappa, F.:Dog-Breath Vars *(rec Corbett Auditorium, May 30 & 31, 1992)* — Klavier ▲ KCD 11066 [DDD]
Zappa, F.:Envelopes *(rec Corbett Auditorium, May 30 & 31, 1992)* — Klavier ▲ KCD 11066 [DDD]

Cincinnati Contemporary Music Ensemble [Kelly Spicer (bn), Elizabeth Rankin (vn), Michael Wheatly (vn), Elizabeth Council (va), Whitney Griggs (vc)]
A. Strydom (cnd)
Zaidel-Rudolph, J.:Masada — Claremont ▲ GSE 1532

Cincinnati Jazz Orch
E. Kunzel (cnd)
Gershwin, G.:Rhap in Blue, w. W. Tritt (pno) [original jazz band orchestration of 1924, including 48 bars, mostly solo piano, cut prior to the premiere] — Telarc ▲ CD 80166 [DDD] ■ CS 30166 (D)

Cincinnati PO
C. Mueller (cnd)
Françaix, J.:Con Cl, w. Dimitri Ashkenazy (cl) — Pan Classics ▲ 510082 [DDD]
Moser, R.:Con Cl, w. Dimitri Ashkenazy (cl) — Pan Classics ▲ 510082 [DDD]
Rimsky-Korsakov, N.:Concertstück Cl, w. Dimitri Ashkenazy (cl) — Pan Classics ▲ 510082 [DDD]
Taneyev, S.:Canzona Cl, w. Dimitri Ashkenazy (cl) — Pan Classics ▲ 510082 [DDD]
G. Samuel (cnd)
Beethoven, L. van:Sym 9, "Choral Sym", w. CCM Chorus — Centaur ▲ CRC 2107
Blumenfeld, H.:Ange de flamme et de glaçe, w. Christine Schadeberg (sop), Randall Gremillion (bass) — Centaur ▲ CRC 2277
Blumenfeld, H.:La Face cendrée, w. Christine Schadeberg (sop), Randall Gremillion (bass) — Centaur ▲ CRC 2277
Blumenfeld, H.:Illuminations, w. Christine Schadeberg (sop), Randall Gremillion (bass) — Centaur ▲ CRC 2277
Handel, D.:Acquainted with the Night — Vienna Modern Masters ▲ VMM 3011 [DDD]
Handel, D.:Kyushu — Vienna Modern Masters ▲ VMM 3006 [DDD]
Ives, C.:Orchestral Set 2 *(rec Oct. 30 & 31, 1993)* — Centaur ▲ CRC 2205 [DDD]

Cincinnati PO (cont.)
G. Samuel (cnd) (cont.)
Ives, C.:The Unanswered Question *(rec Oct. 30 & 31, 1993)* Centaur ▲ CRC 2205 [DDD]
Ives, C.:Universe Sym *(rec Jan. 29, 1994)* Centaur ▲ CRC 2205 [DDD]
Schubert, Franz:Der Graf von Gleichen, w. Gwendolyn Coleman (sop), Karen Driscoll (sop), Tracy Thomas (sop), Brad Diamond (ten), John M. Koch (bar), CCM Chamber Choir *(rec Corbett Auditorium, Univ of Cincinnati, Mar 12–13, 1994)* Centaur 2-▲ 2281/2282 [DDD]
Schubert, Franz:Sym in E *(rec April 1992)* Centaur ▲ CRC 2139 [DDD]
Thome, D.:The Ruins of the Heart, w. M. Henderson (sop) Centaur ▲ CRC 2144 [DDD]
Cincinnati Pops Orch
E. Kunzel (cnd)
Amen:A Gospel Celebration, w. Azusa Pacific Univ Choir, Central State Univ Chorus, Cincinnati Pops Chorale, Jennifer Holliday (sgr), Maureen McGovern (sgr), Lou Rawls (sgr) *(rec Feb. 28–Mar. 1, 1993)* Telarc ▲ CD 80315 [DDD] ■ CD 80315
American As Apple Pie Vox Box 3-▲ CD3X 3035 [ADD]
American Jubilee Telarc ▲ CD 80144 [DDD] ■ CS 30144 (D)
American Piano Classics Telarc ▲ CD 80112 [DDD]
Anderson, L.:Con Pno, w. S. Goodyear (pno) Telarc ▲ CD 80112 [DDD]
Big Band Hit Parade Telarc ▲ CD 80177 [DDD] ■ CS 30177 (D)
Bond & Beyond Telarc ▲ CD 80251 [DDD] ■ CS 30251 (D)
Chiller Telarc ▲ CD 80189 [DDD] ■ CS 30189 (D)
Christmas with the Pops Telarc ▲ CD 80226 [DDD] ■ CS 30226 (D)
Classics of the Silver Screen Telarc ▲ CD 80221 [DDD] ■ CS 30221 (D)
Copland, A.:Appalachian Spring (suite) *(rec Cincinnati Music Hall, 1989–95)* Telarc ▲ CD 80339 [DDD]
Copland, A.:Billy the Kid (suite) *(rec Cincinatti Music Hall, 1989–95)* Telarc ▲ CD 80339 [DDD]
Copland, A.:Fanfare for the Common Man *(rec Cincinatti Music Hall, 1989–95)* Telarc ▲ CD 80339 [DDD]
Copland, A.:Inaugural Fanfare Telarc ▲ CD–80117 [DDD]
Copland, A.:John Henry Telarc ▲ CD–80117 [DDD]
Copland, A.:Jubilee Var on a Theme by Goossens Telarc ▲ CD–80117 [DDD]
Copland, A.:Lincoln Portrait, w. K. Hepburn (nar) [E] Telarc ▲ CD–80117 [DDD]
Copland, A.:Old American Songs (set 1), w. S. Milnes (bar) [E] Telarc ▲ CD–80117 [DDD]
Copland, A.:An Outdoor Ov Telarc ▲ CD–80117 [DDD]
Copland, A.:Quiet City, w. Phillip Collins (tpt), William Harrod (E hn) *(rec Cincinatti Music Hall, 1989–95)* Telarc ▲ CD 80339 [DDD]
Copland, A.:Rodeo *(rec Cincinatti Music Hall, 1989–95)* Telarc ▲ CD 80339 [DDD]
Copland, A.:The Tender Land (sels), w. S. Milnes (bar)—The Promise of Living [E] Telarc ▲ CD–80117 [DDD]
The Dance Vox Box 2-▲ CDX 5130 [DDD]
A Disney Spectacular Telarc ▲ CD 80196 [DDD] ■ CS 30196 (D)
Down on the Farm Telarc ▲ CD 80263 [DDD] ■ CS 30263 (D)
Dukas, P.:L'Apprenti sorcier Telarc ▲ CD 80115 [DDD] ■ CS 30115 (D)
Fantastic Journey Telarc ▲ CD 80231 [DDD] ■ CS 30231 (D)
The Fantastic Leopold Stokowski:Transcriptions for Orchestra *(rec Sept. 17, 1985, May 11, 1)* Telarc ▲ CD 80338 [DDD]
Fiesta! Telarc ▲ CD 80235 [DDD] ■ CS 30235 (D)
Gershwin, G.:Con Pno, w. W. Tritt (pno) Telarc ▲ CD 80166 [DDD] ■ CS 30166 (D)
Gershwin, G.:"I Got Rhythm" Vars, w. W. Tritt (pno) Telarc ▲ CD 80166 [DDD] ■ CS 30166 (D)
Gershwin, G.:Porgy & Bess (suite), "Catfish Row Suite" Telarc ▲ CD 80086 [DDD] ■ CS 30086 (D)
Gershwin, G.:Rialto Ripples Rag, w. W. Tritt (pno) Telarc ▲ CD 80166 [DDD] ■ CS 30166 (D)
Gershwin, G.:Second Rhap, w. S. Goodyear (pno) Telarc ▲ CD 80112 [DDD]
Gottschalk, L.M.:Grande Tarantelle, w. W. Tritt (pno) Telarc ▲ CD 80112 [DDD]
Gould, M.:Interplay Pno, w. W. Tritt (pno) Telarc ▲ CD 80112 [DDD]
Grofé, F.:Grand Canyon Suite Telarc ▲ CD 80086 [DDD] ■ CS 30086 (D)
Happy Trails:Round-Up 2 Telarc ▲ CD 80191 [DDD] ■ CS 30191 (D)
Hollywood's Greatest Hits, Vol. 1:17 Telarc ▲ CD 80168 [DDD] ■ CS 30168 (D)
Hollywood's Greatest Hits, Vol. 2 Telarc ▲ CD 80319 ■ CS 80319
Ibert, J.:Divert Orch Telarc ▲ CD 80294 [DDD] ■ CS 30294 (D)
International Salute Vox Box 2-▲ CDX 5132 [ADD/DDD]
Kreisler, F.:Vn Pieces, w. Robert McDuffie (vn)—Midnight Bells; Poupée Valsante; Tambourin Chinois; Liebesleid; Caprice Viennois; Schön Rosmarin; La Chasse; Liebesfreud; Serenade from 'Frasquita', Viennese Melody; Rondino *(rec Music Hall, Cincinatti, OH, Nov 11 & 13, 1995)* Telarc ▲ CD 80402 [DDD]
Lehár, F.:Music of, w. Robert McDuffie (vn)—Con Vn; Magyar Ábránd; Vergissmennicht *(rec Music Hall, Cincinatti, OH, Nov 11 & 13, 1995)* Telarc ▲ CD 80402 [DDD]
Liszt, F.:Les Préludes Telarc ▲ CD 80115 [DDD] ■ CS 30115 (D)
Mancini's Greatest Hits Telarc ▲ CD 80183 [DDD] ■ CS 30183 (D)
Movie Love Themes, w. William Tritt (pno) Telarc ▲ CD 80243 [DDD] ■ CS 30243 (D)
Offenbach, J.:Con militaire, w. O. Harnoy (vc) Vox Box 2-▲ CDX 5131
Offenbach, J.:Dance Music—Les belles américaines; Galop from Geneviève de Brabant Telarc ▲ CD 80294 [DDD] ■ CS 30294 (D)
Offenbach, J.:Gaîté Parisienne Vox Box 2-▲ CDX 5131
Offenbach, J.:Gaîté Parisienne Telarc ▲ CD 80294 [DDD] ■ CS 30294 (D)
Offenbach, J.:Music of—Grand Orch. [Ov.]; Souvenir d'Aix-les-Bains Valse; Schüler Polka; American Eagle Waltz [w. P. Collins (trumpet)]; La Bell Hélène; l'Ile de Tulipatan Vox Box 2-▲ CDX 5131
Overtures Telarc ▲ CD 80116 [DDD] ■ CS 30116 (D)
Pomp & Pizazz Telarc ▲ CD 80122 [DDD] ■ CS 30122 (D)
Pops Play Puccini:Puccini without Words Telarc ▲ CD 80260 [DDD] ■ CS 30260 (D)
Rimsky-Korsakov, N.:Mlada (procession) Telarc ▲ CD 80115 [DDD] ■ CS 30115 (D)
Rimsky-Korsakov, N.:Snow Maiden (dance) Telarc ▲ CD 80115 [DDD] ■ CS 30115 (D)
Rodgers & Hammerstein:Songbook for Orchestra Telarc ▲ CD 80278 [DDD] ■ CS 30278 (D)
Rodgers, R.:The Sound of Music, w. E. Farrell (sop), F. von Stade (mez), Håkan Hagegård (ten), B. Daniels (sgr), L. D. von Schlanbusch (sgr), et al., May Festival Chorus [1987 studio cast] Telarc ▲ CD 80162 [DDD] ■ CS 30162
Round-Up Telarc ▲ CD 80141 [DDD] ■ CS 30141 (D)
Sailing Telarc ▲ CD 80292 [DDD] ■ CS 30292 (D)
Saint-Saëns, C.:Samson et Dalila (Bacchanale) Telarc ▲ CD 80115 [DDD] ■ CS 30115 (D)
Sieczynski, R.:Wien Wien nur du Allein, w. Robert McDuffie (vn) *(rec Music Hall, Cincinatti, OH, Nov 11 & 13, 1995)* Telarc ▲ CD 80402 [DDD]
Star Tracks Telarc ▲ CD 80094 [DDD] ■ CS 30094 (D)
Star Tracks II Telarc ▲ CD 80146 [DDD] ■ CS 30146 (D)
The Stokowski Sound:Transcriptions for Orchestra by Leopold Stokowski Telarc ▲ CD 80129 [DDD]
Strauss, E.:Polkas & Waltzes—Bahn frei polka, Op. 45 Telarc ▲ CD 80098 [DDD] ■ CS 30098 (D)
Strauss (I), Joh.:Radetzky March Telarc ▲ CD 80098 [DDD] ■ CS 30098 (D)
Strauss (II), Joh.:Hochzeitspräludium, w. Robert McDuffie (vn) [arr Erich Kunzel for Orch] *(rec Music Hall, Cincinatti, Ohio, Nov 11 & 13, 1995)* Telarc ▲ CD 80402 [DDD]
Strauss (II), Joh.:Music of—9 waltzes & polkas Telarc ▲ CD 80098 [DDD] ■ CS 30098 (D)
Strauss, Josef:Music of—Feuerfest & Pizzicato polkas Telarc ▲ CD 80098 [DDD] ■ CS 30098 (D)
Ein Straussfest II Telarc ▲ CD 80314 [DDD] ■ CS 30314
Symphonic Spectacular Telarc ▲ CD 80170 [DDD] ■ CS 30170 (D)
Symphonic Star Trek *(rec Music Hall, Cincinnati, OH, 1983-1995)* Telarc ▲ CD 80383
Time Warp Telarc ▲ CD 80106 [DDD] ■ CS 30106 (D)
Trumpet Spectacular, w. Doc Severinsen (flgl) Telarc ▲ CD 80223 [DDD] ■ CS 30223 (D)

Cincinnati Pops Orch (cont.)
E. Kunzel (cnd) (cont.)
Verdi, G.:Orchestral Sels—Grand Entrance:"Su! del Nilo al sacro lido"; Ritorna vincitor!"; "L'insana parola"; Act I:"Celeste Aida"; Act II:"Gloria all'Egitto"; Egyptian March;"Vieni, o guerriero vindice" [all selections from Aida]; "Ave Maria" [from Otello]; Act II:"Vedil le fosche notturne spoglie"; Act III:"Di quella pira" [both from Il Trovatore]; Prelude; Act I:Introduction; "Brindisi"; Waltz; "Un dì felice"; "Sempre libera degg'io"; Act II:"Di Provenza il mar, il suol" [all selctions from La Traviata]; Act I:"Questa o quella"; Act II:"Caro nome"; Act IV:"La donna è mobile"; "Un di, se ben rammentomi" [all selctions from Rigoletto]; Act III:Finale "Tutto nel mondo è burla" [from Falstaff]; Act III:"Va, pensiero" [from Nabucco] *(rec Music Hall, Cincinnati, Ohio, Jan. 17–18, 1994)* Telarc ▲ CD 80364 [DDD]
The Very Best of Erich Kunzel & the Cincinnati Pops Telarc ▲ CD 80401 [DDD]
Victory At Sea Telarc ▲ CD 80175 [DDD] ■ CS 30175 (D)
Weinberger, J.:Schwanda der Dudelsackpfeifer (polka & fugue) Telarc ▲ CD 80115 [DDD] ■ CS 30115 (D)
Williams, John:Film Music—Stars Wars Trilogy; Superman; Close Encounters; E.T.; Raiders of the Lost Ark Telarc ▲ CD 80094 ■ CS 30094
Young at Heart Telarc ▲ CD 80245 [DDD] ■ CS 30245 (D)
Cincinnati Summer Opera Association Orch
A. Guadagno (cnd)
Bizet, G.:Carmen, w. Cooper (sgr), Dunn (sgr), P. Domingo (ten), F. Guarrera (bar), Cincinnati Summer Opera Association Chorus [F] *(rec live 7/19/68)* Melodram 2-▲ MEL 27034 (m) [AAD]
Cincinnati SO
M. Gielen (cnd)
Beethoven, L. van:Sym 3, "Eroica" *(rec 1980)* Vox Box 2-▲ CDX 5137 [DDD]
Berg, A.:Lulu (suite), w. Kathleen Battle (sop) *(rec 1981)* Vox Box 2-▲ CDX 5136 [DDD]
Berg, A.:Lyric Suite *(rec 1981)* Vox Box 2-▲ CDX 5136 [DDD]
Busoni, F.:Studies for Doktor Faust *(rec 1983)* Vox Box 2-▲ CDX 5137 [DDD]
Busoni, F.:Turandot (suite), w. May Festival Chorus Women's Voices *(rec 1983)* Vox Box 2-▲ CDX 5137 [DDD]
Carter, E.:Con Pno, w. U. Oppens (pno) *(rec live, 10/5–6/84)* New World ▲ NW 347-2 [DDD/ADD] ■ NW 347-4
Carter, E.:Vars Orch *(rec live, 10/22/85)* New World ▲ NW 347-2 [ADD/DDD] ■ NW 347-4
Lutoslawski, W.:Con Ob, w. Heinz Holliger (ob), Ursula Holliger (hp) *(rec 1983)* Vox Box 2-▲ CDX 5136 [DDD]
Strauss, R.:Con Ob *(rec 1983)* Vox Box 2-▲ CDX 5136 [DDD]
Strauss, R.:Metamorphosen *(rec 1983)* Vox Box 2-▲ CDX 5136 [DDD]
Strauss, R.:Tod und Verklärung *(rec 1984)* Vox Box 2-▲ CDX 5136 [DDD]
E. Goossens (cnd)
Walton, W.:Con Vn, w. Jascha Heifetz (vn) *(rec 1935–41)* Pearl ▲ PEA 9167 [ADD]
A. von Kreisler (cnd)
Grieg, E.:Con Pno, Op. 16, w. S. Eisenberger (pno) [previously unpublished] *(rec live 4/4/38)* Pearl ▲ PEA 9933 (m) [AAD]
E. Kunzel (cnd)
Beethoven, L. van:Wellington's Victory, "Battle Sym" Telarc ▲ CD 80079 [DDD]
Gershwin, G.:An American in Paris Telarc ▲ CD 80058 [DDD]
Gershwin, G.:Rhap in Blue, w. E. List (pno) Telarc ▲ CD 80058 [DDD]
Liszt, F.:Battle of the Huns Telarc ▲ CD 80079 [DDD]
Liszt, F.:Hungarian Battle March Telarc ▲ CD 80079 [DDD]
Tchaikovsky, P.:Ov 1812 Telarc ▲ CD 80041 [DDD] ■ CS 30041 (D)
J. López-Cobos (cnd)
Bizet, G.:L'Arlésienne (suites)—Suite No. 1 Telarc ▲ CD 80224 [DDD]
Bizet, G.:Carmen (suite 1) Telarc ▲ CD 80224 [DDD]
Bizet, G.:Sym 1 Telarc ▲ CD 80224 [DDD]
Bruckner, A.:Sym 4, "Romantic" [original 1874 version] Telarc ▲ CD 80244 [DDD]
Bruckner, A.:Sym 6 Telarc ▲ CD 80264 [DDD]
Bruckner, A.:Sym 7 Telarc ▲ CD 80188 [DDD]
Bruckner, A.:Sym 8 *(rec Mar. 14–15, 1993)* Telarc ▲ CD 80343 [DDD]
Bruckner, A.:Sym 9 Telarc ▲ CD 80299 [DDD]
Falla, M. de:Homenajes (4) Orch Telarc ▲ CD 80149 [DDD]
Falla, M. de:El sombrero de tres picos, w. Quivar (mez) [Sp] Telarc ▲ CD 80149 [DDD]
Falla, M. de:La vida breve, w. A. Nafé (mez), A. Ordóñez (ten), May Festival Chorus [Sp] Telarc ▲ CD 80317 [DDD]
Falla, M. de:La vida breve (interlude & dance 1) Telarc ▲ CD 80149 [DDD]
Franck, C.:Le Chasseur maudit Telarc ▲ CD 80247 [DDD]
Franck, C.:Sym in d Telarc ▲ CD 80247 [DDD]
Mahler, G.:Kindertotenlieder, w. A. Schmidt (bar) [G] Telarc ▲ CD 80269 [DDD]
Mahler, G.:Lieder eines fahrenden Gesellen, w. A. Schmidt (bar) [G] Telarc ▲ CD 80269 [DDD]
Mahler, G.:Songs from Rückert, w. A. Schmidt (bar) [G] Telarc ▲ CD 80269 [DDD]
Mahler, G.:Sym 9 *(rec Cincinnati Music Hall, May 1996)* Telarc 2-▲ CD 80426 [DDD]
Rachmaninoff, S.:Études-tableaux, Opp. 33 & 39—Opp. 33/7, 39/2, 6, 7 & 9 [arr O. Respighi for orch] *(rec Cincinnati, 1995)* Telarc ▲ CD 80396 [DDD]
Ravel, M.:Alborada del gracioso Telarc ▲ CD 80171 [DDD] ■ CS 30171 (D)
Ravel, M.:Boléro Telarc ▲ CD 80171 [DDD] ■ CS 30171 (D)
Ravel, M.:Rapsodie espagnole Telarc ▲ CD 80171 [DDD] ■ CS 30171 (D)
Ravel, M.:La Valse Telarc ▲ CD 80171 [DDD] ■ CS 30171 (D)
Ravel, M.:Valses nobles et sentimentales Telarc ▲ CD 80171 [DDD] ■ CS 30171 (D)
Respighi, O.:La Boutique fantastique *(rec Cincinatti, 1995)* Telarc ▲ CD 80396 [DDD]
Respighi, O.:Brazilian Impressions *(rec May 2–3, 1993)* Telarc ▲ CD 80356 [DDD]
Respighi, O.:Vetrate di chiesa *(rec May 2–3, 1993)* Telarc ▲ CD 80356 [DDD]
Strauss, R.:Burleske, w. Jeffrey Kahane (pno), Eugene Espino (timp) *(rec Music Hall, Cincinnati, OH, Oct. 2–3, 1994)* Telarc ▲ CD 80371 [DDD]
Strauss, R.:Festliches Präludium, w. Michael Chertok (org) *(rec Music Hall, Cincinnati, OH, Oct. 2–3, 1994)* Telarc ▲ CD 80371 [DDD]
Strauss, R.:Der Rosenkavalier (suite) *(rec Music Hall, Cincinnati, OH, Oct. 2–3, 1994)* Telarc ▲ CD 80371 [DDD]
Strauss, R.:Salome (dance) *(rec Music Hall, Cincinnati, OH, Oct. 2–3, 1994)* Telarc ▲ CD 80371 [DDD]
Villa-Lobos, H.:Bachiana brasileira 2 *(rec Music Hall, Cincinnati, Ohio, Apr 23–24, 1995)* Telarc ▲ CD 80393 [DDD]
Villa-Lobos, H.:Bachiana brasileira 4 *(rec Music Hall, Cincinnati, Ohio, Apr 23–24, 1995)* Telarc ▲ CD 80393 [DDD]
Villa-Lobos, H.:Bachiana brasileira 8 *(rec Music Hall, Cincinnati, Ohio, Apr 23–24, 1995)* Telarc ▲ CD 80393 [DDD]
Wagner, R.:Ovs, Preludes & Orch Sels—Die Meistersinger von Nürnberg:Prelude Act I; Rienzi:Ov.; Faust Ov.; Die fliegene Holländer:Ov.; Tristan und Isolde:Prelude; Liebestod; Tannäuser:Ov. *(rec Mar. 21–22, 1994)* Telarc ▲ CD 80379 [DDD]
M. Rudolf (cnd)
Gutche, G.:Sym 5 CRI ■ C 189
Schuller, G.:Con Pno, w. J. Rosenblum Kirstein (pno) GM ▲ GM 2044
T. Schippers (cnd)
Rossini, G.:Ovs—La Gazza Ladra; Semiramide; Guilaume Tell; Tancredi; La Cenerentola *(rec 1976)* Vox Box 2-▲ CDX 5141 [ADD]
Rossini, G.:Stabat Mater, w. Sung-Sook Lee (sop), Florence Quivar (mez), Kenneth Riegel (ten), Paul Plishka (bass), May Festival Chorus *(rec 1975)* Vox Box 2-▲ CDX 5141 [ADD]
Schubert, Franz:Sym 8 *(rec 1976)* Vox Box 2-▲ CDX 5138 [ADD]
Schubert, Franz:Sym 9 *(rec 1976)* Vox Box 2-▲ CDX 5140 [ADD]
Strauss, R.:Don Juan *(rec 1976)* Vox Box 2-▲ CDX 5140 [ADD]
Strauss, R.:Der Rosenkavalier (waltzes) *(rec 1976)* Vox Box 2-▲ CDX 5140 [ADD]
Strauss, R.:Salome (dance) *(rec 1976)* Vox Box 2-▲ CDX 5140 [ADD]
Strauss, R.:Till Eulenspiegels lustige Streiche *(rec 1976)* Vox Box 2-▲ CDX 5140 [ADD]

120 ▲ = CD ♦ = Enhanced CD Δ = MD ■ = Cassette Tape □ = DCC

Cincinnati SO (cont.)
W. Susskind (cnd)
Mahler, G.:Das Lied von der Erde, w. Lili Chookasian (cta), Richard Cassilly (ten) *(rec 1978)* Vox Box 2-▲ CDX 5138 [ADD]
Mendelssohn, F.:A Midsummer Night's Dream (sels)—Ov.; Scherzo; Nocturne; Wedding March *(rec 1978)* Vox Box 2-▲ CDX 5138 [ADD]
Shostakovich, D.:Sym 1 *(rec 1979)* Vox Box 2-▲ CDX 5139 [ADD]
Shostakovich, D.:Sym 2 *(rec 1979)* Vox Box 2-▲ CDX 5139 [ADD]
Tchaikovsky, P.:Con 2 Pno, w. Shura Cherkassky (pno) *(rec 1981)* Vox Box 2-▲ CDX 5139 [ADD]
E. Ysaÿe (cnd)
Rimsky-Korsakov, N.:Scheherazade—1st & 3rd movts. Symposium ▲ 1045
Cincinnati Wind Sym
E. Corporon (cnd)
Adams, J.:Short Ride in a Fast Machine Klavier ▲ KCD 11058
Freund, D.W.:Jug Blues & Fat Pickin' Klavier ▲ KCD 11059
Gregson, E.:The Sword & the Crown Klavier ▲ KCD 11059
Harbison, J.:Three City Blocks Klavier ▲ KCD 11059
Hindemith, P.:Sym in B♭ for Concert Band Klavier ▲ KCD 11059
Margolis, J.:Terpsichore Klavier ▲ KCD 11058
Milhaud, D.:Suite Française Klavier ▲ KCD 11058
Nelson, R.:Passacaglia Orch Klavier ▲ KCD 11058
Rands, B.:Ceremonial Klavier ▲ KCD 11059
Stravinsky, I.:Circus Polka Klavier ▲ KCD 11059
Ticheli, F.:Postcard Klavier ▲ KCD 11058
Il Cinquecento
Come away, Sweet Love Christophorus ▲ CHR 77126 [DDD]
Ciompi String Quartet [Bruce Berg (vn), Claudia Bloom (vn), Jonathan Bagg (va), Frederic Raimi (vc)]
Beethoven, L. van:Qt 10 Strs, "Harp" *(rec live to two-track)* Sheffield Lab ("Salon" series) ▲ SLS 503 [A–D]
Bolle, J.:Qt Strs Gasparo ▲ GSCD 317 [DDD]
Bridge, F.:Qt 4 Strs *(rec live to two-track)* Sheffield Lab ("Salon" series) ▲ SLS 503 [ADD]
Copland, A.:Movt Str Qt Albany ▲ TROY 073 [DDD]
Jaffe, S.:Qt 1 Strs Albany ▲ TROY 073 [DDD]
Suderburg, R.:Chamber Music V, w. E. Suderburg—Tape [mixed from voices of Stevenson, Eisenhower & crowd applause] Delfon ▲ DRS 2127 [DDD]
Ward, R.:Qt 1 Strs Albany ▲ TROY 073 [DDD]
Wheelock, D.:Qt 3 Strs Albany ▲ TROY 139 [DDD]
Wheelock, D.:Qt 4 Strs Albany ▲ TROY 139 [DDD]
Ciosoni Trio [T. Lane (fl), E. Mandat (cl), M. Cameron (db)]
Martirano, S.:UIUS & Just fa' Laffs *(rec Dec. 1992)* Centaur ▲ CRC 2170 [DDD]
Ciprian Porumbescu Conservatory Camerata CO
P. Staicu (cnd)
Mozart, W.A.:Cons Hn, w. P. Staicu (hn) Electrecord ▲ ELCD 107 [AAD]
Circa 1500 Ensemble
The Flower of All Ships:Tudor Court Music from the Time of the Mary Rose CRD ▲ CD 3448 [DDD]
Music from the Spanish Kingdoms CRD ▲ 3447 [DDD]
O Lusitano:Portuguese Vilancetes, Cantigas & Romances, w. Gérard Lesne (ct) Virgin Classics ▲ 59071 [DDD]
Renaissance Music from the Courts of Mantua & Ferrara Chandos ("Chaconne" series) ▲ CHAN 0524 [DDD]
N. Hadden (cnd)
New Fashions:Cries & Ballads of London, w. Redbyrd CRD ▲ CD 3487 [DDD]
Circe Wind Quintet
Damaré, E.:Music of, w. Jean-Louis Beaumadier (petite fl), Christophe Poiget (vn), Marc Giradot (ophicleide/tuba), La Follia Instrumental Ensemble—La Capricieuse, Op. 270; Feux follets, Op. 378; Les Échos des bois, Op. 220; Le Merle blanc, Op. 161; Tarentelle, Op. 391; L'Oiseau et les roses, Op. 153; Le Tourbillon, Op. 212; L'Alouette, Op. 172; Pizzicato, Op. 426; La Danse des grillons, Op. 380 *(rec 1996)* Calliope ▲ CAL 9869 [DDD]
City Lights Orch
C. Davis (cnd)
Chaplin, C.:City Lights Silva America ▲ SSD 1054
City of Birmingham SO
M. Arnold (cnd)
Arnold, M.:Con for 2 Pnos, w. P. Sellick (pno), C. Smith (pno) EMI Classics ▲ CDM 64044-2
V. Dunn (cnd)
Sullivan, A.:The Merchant of Venice Klavier ■ KC 521
Sullivan, A.:Ovs—In Memoriam Klavier ■ KC 521
Sullivan, A.:The Tempest, England SO Klavier ▲ KCD 11033
Sullivan, A.:The Tempest Klavier ■ KC 521
M. Elder (cnd)
Shostakovich, D.:Allegedly Murdered—Orchestral Suite [completed by McBurney] *(rec Symphony Hall, Birmingham, England, Dec 16-18, 1992)* United ▲ CAL 88001 [DDD]
Shostakovich, D.:Fragments *(rec Symphony Hall, Birmingham, England, Dec 16–18, 1992)* United ▲ CAL 88001 [DDD]
Shostakovich, D.:Hamlet (incidental) *(rec Birmingham Town Hall, June 13–15, 1994)* Cala ▲ CACD 1021 [DDD]
Shostakovich, D.:Hamlet (incidental), w. David Wilson-Johnson (bar) United ▲ UNI 88050
Shostakovich, D.:King Lear (incidental), w. David Wilson-Johnson (bar) United ▲ UNI 88050
Shostakovich, D.:King Lear (incidental) *(rec Birmingham Town Hall, June 13–15, 1994)* Cala ▲ CACD 1021 [DDD]
Shostakovich, D.:Songs, Op. 46, w. Dimitri Kharitonov (bass) [orchd Shostakovich, completed McBurney] *(rec Symphony Hall, Birmingham, England, Dec 16–18, 1992)* United ▲ CAL 88001 [DDD]
Shostakovich, D.:Suite 1 Jazz Orch *(rec Symphony Hall, Birmingham, England, Dec 16–18, 1992)* United ▲ CAL 88001 [DDD]
L. Foster (cnd)
Cherubini, L.:Ovs—Ali Baba; Anacréon; Faniska; 2 Journées; Abencérages; Hôtellerie Portugaise; Lodoiska; Médée Claves ▲ 9513
L. Frémaux (cnd)
Berlioz, H.:Benvenuto Cellini (sels) Klavier ▲ KCD 11010 [ADD]
Berlioz, H.:Le Carnaval romain Klavier ▲ KCD 11012 [ADD]
Berlioz, H.:La Damnation de Faust (sels)—Danse of the Sylphs; Minuet of the Will-O'The-Wisps Klavier ▲ KCD 11007 [ADD]
Berlioz, H.:La Damnation de Faust (sels)—March hongroise Klavier ▲ KCD 11029 [ADD]
Berlioz, H.:Marche funèbre—orch only Klavier ▲ KCD 11010 [ADD]
Berlioz, H.:Marche funèbre Klavier ▲ KCD 11012 [ADD]
Berlioz, H.:Music of, w. City of Birmingham Sym Chorus—Ovt., Le carnaval romain, Op. 9; Funeral March for Hamlet, Op. 18/3; Hungarian March; Dance of Sylphs; Minuet of the Will-o'-wisps; Ovt., Benvenuto Cellini, Op. 23; The Trojans (selections) Klavier ■ KC 553
Berlioz, H.:Music of—Dance of the Sylphs; Minuet of the Will-O'The-Wisps Klavier ▲ KCD 11007 [ADD]
Berlioz, H.:Ovs—Roman Carnival; Benvenuto Cellini Klavier ▲ KCD 11040
Berlioz, H.:Les Troyens (sels) Klavier ▲ KCD 11010 [ADD]
Berlioz, H.:Les Troyens (sels)—The Royal Hunt and Storm Klavier ▲ KCD 11029 [ADD]
Bizet, G.:Roma Klavier ▲ KCD 11012 [ADD]
Bizet, G.:Sym 1 Klavier ▲ KCD 11012 [ADD]
Fauré, G.:Ballade Pno, w. J. Ogdon (pno) Klavier ▲ KCD 11011 [ADD]
Litolff, H.C.:Con Symphonique 4, w. J. Ogdon (pno)—Scherzo Klavier ▲ KCD 11011 [ADD]

City of Birmingham SO (cont.)
L. Frémaux (cnd) (cont.)
Litolff, H.C.:Con Symphonique 4, w. J. Ogdon (pno) Klavier ■ KC 527
Massenet, J.:Le Cid (ballet suite) Klavier ▲ KCD 11007 [ADD] ■ KC 522
Massenet, J.:Suite 4 Klavier ▲ KCD 11007 [ADD]
Massenet, J.:La Vierge—Last Sleep of the Virgin Klavier ▲ KCD 11007 [ADD]
Offenbach, J.:Le Belle Hélène Klavier ▲ KCD 11007 [ADD]
Offenbach, J.:Dance Music—La Belle Helene Klavier ▲ KCD 11007 [ADD]
Offenbach, J.:Ovs—Orpheus in the Underworld; The Grand Duchess of Gerolstein; La Belle Helene; Barbe-bleu; La Vie Parisienne Klavier ■ KC 11040 [ADD]
Saint-Saëns, C.:Carnival of the Animals, w. J. Ogdon (pno), B. Lucas (pno) Klavier ■ KC 527
Saint-Saëns, C.:Carnival of the Animals, w. J. Ogdon (pno), B. Lucas (pno) Klavier ▲ KCD 11011 [ADD]
Saint-Saëns, C.:Sym 3, w. C. Robinson (org) Klavier ▲ KCD 11010 [ADD]
Saint-Saëns, C.:Sym 3, w. Christopher Robinson (org) Royal Classics ▲ ROY 6440
Saint-Saëns, C.:Sym 3, w. C. Robinson (organ)—Mvts. 1 & 2 Klavier ■ KC 526
Saint-Saëns, C.:Wedding Cake, w. M. de la Pau (pno) Klavier ▲ KCD 11011 [ADD]
Walton, W.:Coronation Te Deum, w. City of Birmingham Sym Chorus EMI Classics ▲ CDM 64201
Walton, W.:Crown Imperial EMI Classics ▲ CDM 64201
Walton, W.:Façade (suites) EMI Classics ▲ CDM 64201
Walton, W.:Gloria, w. B. Robotham (sop), A. Rolfe Johnson (ten), B. Rayner Cook, Worcester Cathedral Choristers EMI Classics ▲ CDM 64201
Walton, W.:Orb & Sceptre EMI Classics ▲ CDM 64201
V. Handley (cnd)
Vaughan Williams, R.:On Wenlock Edge, w. R. Tear (ten) [orch. version] EMI Classics ▲ CDM 64731
N. Järvi (cnd)
Weber, C.M. von:Concertino Cl, w. J. Hilton (cl) Chandos ▲ CHAN 8305 [DDD]
Weber, C.M. von:Con 1 Cl, w. J. Hilton (cl) Chandos ▲ CHAN 8305 [DDD]
Weber, C.M. von:Con 2 Cl, w. J. Hilton (cl) Chandos ▲ CHAN 8305 [DDD]
O. Kamu (cnd)
Shostakovich, D.:Sym 13, w. N. Storojev (bass), City of Birmingham Sym Chorus [R] Chandos ▲ CHAN 8540 [DDD]
C. Lambert (cnd)
Tchaikovsky, P.:Romeo & Juliet *(rec Feb. 24, 1941)* Dutton Laboratories ▲ CDLX 7006 [ADD]
N. del Mar (cnd)
Vaughan Williams, R.:Fant on a Theme by Thomas Tallis, w. City of Birmingham Sym Chorus Klavier ▲ KCD 11034 [DDD]
Vaughan Williams, R.:Norfolk Rhap 1, w. City of Birmingham Sym Chorus Klavier ▲ KCD 11034 [DDD]
Vaughan Williams, R.:Toward the Unknown, w. City of Birmingham Sym Chorus Klavier ▲ KCD 11034 [DDD]
Vaughan Williams, R.:Variants of "Dives & Lazarus", w. City of Birmingham Sym Chorus Klavier ▲ KCD 11034 [DDD]
S. Rattle (cnd)
Adams, J.:The Chairman Dances EMI Classics ▲ CDC 55051
Adams, J.:Harmonielehre EMI Classics ▲ CDC 55051
Adams, J.:Short Ride in a Fast Machine EMI Classics ▲ CDC 55051
Adams, J.:Tromba lontana EMI Classics ▲ CDC 55051
Arnold, M.:Con Gtr, w. J. Bream (gtr) EMI Classics ▲ CDC 54661-2
Bartók, B.:Con Orch EMI Classics ▲ CDC 55094
Bartók, B.:Con 1 Pno, w. P. Donohoe (pno) EMI Classics ▲ CDC 54871
Bartók, B.:Con 3 Pno, w. P. Donohoe (pno) EMI Classics ▲ CDC 54871
Bartók, B.:Con for 2 Pnos, w. K. Labeque (pno), M. Labeque (pno), S. Gualda (perc), J.-P. Drouet (perc) EMI ▲ CDC 47446
Bartók, B.:Con 2 Vn, w. K.-W. Chung (vn) EMI Classics ▲ CDC 54211
Bartók, B.:The Miraculous Mandarin, w. City of Birmingham Sym Chorus EMI Classics ▲ CDC 55094
Bartók, B.:Rhaps (2) Vn & Orch, w. K.-W. Chung (vn) EMI Classics ▲ CDC 54211
Berg, A.:Lulu (suite), w. A. Auger (sop) EMI ▲ CDC 49857
Brahms, J.:Qt 1 Pno, w. A. Schoenberg (pno) EMI Classics 2-▲ CDCB 47300
Britten, B.:An American Ov *(rec 5/84)* EMI Classics 2-▲ CDCB 54270 [DDD]
Britten, B.:Ballad of Heroes, w. R. Tear (ten), City of Birmingham Sym Chorus [E] *(rec 7/90)* EMI Classics 2-▲ CDCB 54270 [DDD]
Britten, B.:The Building of the House, w. City of Birmingham Sym Chorus [E] *(rec 7/90)* EMI Classics 2-▲ CDCB 54270 [DDD]
Britten, B.:Canadian Carnival, w. City of Birmingham Sym Chorus *(rec 4/82)* EMI Classics 2-▲ CDCB 54270 [DDD]
Britten, B.:Chanson françaises (4), w. J. Gomez (sop) [F] *(rec 4/82)* EMI Classics 2-▲ ZDCB 54270 [DDD]
Britten, B.:Diversions Pno, w. P. Donohoe (pno) *(rec 7/90)* EMI Classics 2-▲ CDCB 54270 [DDD]
Britten, B.:Praise We Great Men, w. A. Hargan (sop), M. King (alt), R. Tear (ten), W. White (bass), City of Birmingham Sym Chorus [E] *(rec July, 1990)* EMI Classics 2-▲ CDCB 54270 [DDD]
Britten, B.:Russian Funeral Music EMI Classics ▲ CDC 55473
Britten, B.:Scottish Ballad, w. P. Donohoe (pno), P. Fowke (pno) *(rec 4/82)* EMI Classics 2-▲ CDCB 54270 [DDD]
Britten, B.:Sinf da requiem *(rec 5/84)* EMI Classics 2-▲ CDCB 54270 [DDD]
Britten, B.:Sinf da requiem EMI Classics ▲ CDM 64870
Britten, B.:Suite on English Folk Tunes *(rec 5/84)* EMI Classics 2-▲ CDCB 54270 [DDD]
Britten, B.:War Requiem, w. E. Söderström (sop), R. Tear (ten), T. Allen (bar), City of Birmingham Sym Chorus, Christ Church Boys' Chorus [E,L] EMI Classics 2-▲ CDCB 47033
Britten, B.:Young Apollo, w. P. Donohoe (pno), F. Kok (vn), J. Ballard (vn), P. Cole (va), M. Kaznowski (vc) *(rec 4/82)* EMI Classics 2-▲ CDCB 54270 [DDD]
Debussy, C.:Images Orch EMI ▲ CDC 49947
Debussy, C.:Jeux EMI ▲ CDC 49947
Debussy, C.:Le Roi Lear (sels) EMI ▲ CDC 49947
Doyle, P.:Henry V, w. P. Doyle (bar), Stephen Hill Singers Angel ▲ CDC 49919 ■ 4DS 49919
Elgar, E.:Enigma Vars EMI Classics ▲ CDC 55001
Elgar, E.:Falstaff EMI Classics ▲ CDC 55001
Elgar, E.:Grania & Diarmid (sels)—Incidental Music; Funeral March EMI Classics ▲ CDC 55001
Gershwin, G.:Con Pno, w. P. Donohoe (pno) EMI Classics ▲ CDC 54280
Gershwin, G.:Con Pno, w. P. Donohoe (pno) EMI Classics ("American Composer" series) ▲ CDM 64305
Grieg, E.:Con Pno, Op. 16, w. L. Vogt (pno) EMI Classics ▲ CDC 54746
Guide to the Orchestra Cambrix Publishing ♦ CPO 70
Haydn, J.:Die Schöpfung, w. Arleen Augér (sop), Philip Langridge (ten), David Thomas (bass), City of Birmingham Sym Chorus [E] EMI Classics 2-▲ CDCB 54159 [DDD]
Haydn, J.:Sym 60, "Il Distratto" EMI Classics ▲ CDC 54297 ◻ 0777-7-54297-5-6
Haydn, J.:Sym 70 EMI Classics ▲ CDC 54297 ◻ 0777-7-54297-5-6
Haydn, J.:Sym 90 EMI Classics ▲ CDC 54297 ◻ 0777-7-54297-5-6
Henze, H.-W.:Barcarola EMI Classics ▲ CDC 54762
Henze, H.-W.:Sym 7 EMI Classics ▲ CDC 54762
Janácek, L.:Sinfonietta, w. City of Birmingham Sym Chorus EMI ▲ CDC 47504
Janácek, L.:Slavonic Mass, w. F. Palmer (sop), A. Gunson (mez), M. King (mez), J. Mitchinson (ten), J. Parker-Smith (org), City of Birmingham Sym Chorus EMI ▲ CDC 47504
Mahler, G.:Das Klagende Lied, w. H. Döse (sop), A. Hodgson (cta), R. Tear (ten), S. Rae, City of Birmingham Sym Chorus EMI ▲ CDC 47089
Mahler, G.:Sym 1 EMI Classics ▲ CDC 54647
Mahler, G.:Sym 2, w. A. Augér (mez), J. Baker (mez), City of Birmingham Sym Chorus [G] EMI Classics 2-▲ CDCB 47962 [DDD]
Mahler, G.:Sym 6 EMI Classics 2-▲ CDCB 54047 [DDD]
Mahler, G.:Sym 7 *(rec live)* EMI Classics ▲ CDC 54344
Mahler, G.:Sym 10 EMI Classics 2-▲ CDCB 47300
Maw, N.:Odyssey EMI Classics 2-▲ CDCB 54277
Messiaen, O.:Turangalîla-sym EMI Classics 2-▲ CDCB 47463 [DDD]

ORCH. & ENS.

City of Birmingham SO (cont.)
S. Rattle (cnd) (cont.)
Prokofiev, S.:Scythian Suite EMI Classics ▲ CDC 54577
Prokofiev, S.:Sym 5 EMI Classics ▲ CDC 54577
Rachmaninoff, S.:Con 2 Pno, w. Cécile Ousset (pno) EMI ▲ CDC 47223
Rachmaninoff, S.:Rhapsody on a Theme of Paganini, w. C. Ousset (pno) EMI ▲ CDC 47223
Ravel, M.:Alborada del gracioso EMI Classics ▲ CDC 54204
Ravel, M.:Boléro EMI Classics ▲ CDC 54303 □ 0777-7-54303-5-6
Ravel, M.:Con Pno (left hand), w. C. Ousset (pno) EMI Classics ▲ CDC 54158
Ravel, M.:Con in G Pno, w. C. Ousset (pno) EMI Classics ▲ CDC 54158
Ravel, M.:Daphnis et Chloé EMI Classics ▲ CDC 54303 □ 0777-7-54303-5-6
Ravel, M.:Fanfare EMI Classics ▲ CDC 54204
Ravel, M.:Ma mère l'oye Orch EMI Classics ▲ CDC 54204
Ravel, M.:Shéhérazade Mez, w. M. Ewing (sop) EMI Classics ▲ CDC 54204
Ravel, M.:Le Tombeau de Couperin EMI Classics ▲ CDC 54158
Ravel, M.:La Valse EMI Classics ▲ CDC 54204
Rodrigo, J.:Concierto de Aranjuez, w. J. Bream (gtr) EMI Classics ▲ CDC 54661
Schoenberg, A.:Chamber Sym 1 EMI Classics ▲ CDC 55212
Schoenberg, A.:Pieces Orch, Op. 16 EMI ▲ CDC 49857
Schoenberg, A.:Vars Orch, Op. 31 EMI Classics ▲ CDC 55212
Schumann, R.:Con Pno, w. L. Vogt (pno) EMI Classics ▲ CDC 54746
Shostakovich, D.:Sym 4 EMI Classics ▲ CDC 55473
Shostakovich, D.:Sym 10, Philharmonia Orch EMI Classics ▲ CDM 64870
Sibelius, J.:Con Vn, w. N. Kennedy (vn) EMI Classics ▲ CDC 54559 [DDD] ■ 4DS 54559
Sibelius, J.:Syms (comp) EMI Classics 4–▲ CDMD 64118
Stravinsky, I.:Apollon musagète EMI Classics ▲ CDC 49636 [DDD]
Stravinsky, I.:Le Sacre du printemps Orch EMI Classics ▲ CDC 49636 [DDD]
Stravinsky, I.:Scherzo à la russe EMI Classics ▲ CDC 49178 [DDD]
Stravinsky, I.:Studies Orch [1952 vers.] EMI Classics ▲ CDC 49178 [DDD]
Stravinsky, I.:Sym in 3 Movts EMI ▲ CDC 49053
Szymanowski, K.:Con 1 Vn, w. Thomas Zehetmair (vn) EMI Classics ▲ CDC 55607
Szymanowski, K.:Con 2 Vn, w. Thomas Zehetmair (vn) EMI Classics ▲ CDC 55607
Szymanowski, K.:Litany to the Virgin Mary, w. E. Szmytka (sop), F. Quivar (cta), J. Garrison (ten), J. Connell (bass), City of Birmingham Sym Chorus EMI Classics ▲ CDC 55121
Szymanowski, K.:Stabat Mater, w. E. Szmytka (sop), F. Quivar (mez), J. Connell (bass), City of Birmingham Sym Chorus EMI Classics ▲ CDC 55121
Szymanowski, K.:Sym 3, w. J. Garrison (ten), City of Birmingham Sym Chorus EMI Classics ▲ CDC 55121
Takemitsu, T.:To the Edge of Dream, w. J. Bream (gtr) EMI Classics ▲ CDC 54661
Turnage, M.-A.:Drowned Out EMI Classics ▲ CDC 55091
Turnage, M.-A.:Kai EMI Classics ▲ CDC 55091
Turnage, M.-A.:Momentum EMI Classics ▲ CDC 55091
Turnage, M.-A.:3 Screaming Popes EMI Classics ▲ CDC 55091
Turnage, M.-A.:3 Screaming Popes EMI ▲ C25G 15897
Walton, W.:Con Vc, w. L. Harrell (vc) EMI Classics ▲ CDC 54572
Walton, W.:Sym 1 EMI Classics ▲ CDC 54572
Webern, A.:Pieces Orch, Op. 6 EMI ▲ CDC 49857
Weill, K.:The Seven Deadly Sins, w. E. Ross (sop), A. R. Johnson (ten), I. Caley (ten), M. Rippon (bass), J. Tomlinson (bass) EMI Classics ▲ CDM 64739
S. Rattle, V. Handley (cnd)
Butterworth, G.:Songs (3) Voc & Strs, w. R. Tear (ten), T. Allen (bar) EMI Classics ▲ CDM 64731
Elgar, E.:Songs, w. R. Tear (ten), T. Allen (bar) EMI Classics ▲ CDM 64731
Vaughan Williams, R.:Songs of Travel, w. T. Allen (bar) [orch. version] EMI Classics ▲ CDM 64731
W. Weller (cnd)
Beethoven, L. van:Cons Pno (comp), w. J. Lill (pno) Chandos 3–▲ CHAN 9084/86 [DDD]
Beethoven, L. van:Con 5 Pno, "Emperor", w. John Lill (pno) Chandos ▲ CHAN 7028
Beethoven, L. van:Coriolan Ov Chandos ▲ CHAN 7028
Beethoven, L. van:Die Geschöpfe des Prometheus (ov) Chandos ▲ CHAN 7028
Beethoven, L. van:Leonore 3 Chandos ▲ CHAN 7028
Beethoven, L. van:Syms (comp), w. City of Birmingham Sym Chorus Chandos 5–▲ CHAN 7042
Beethoven, L. van:Sym 1 Chandos ▲ CHAN 8751 [DDD]
Beethoven, L. van:Sym 2 Chandos ▲ CHAN 8752 [DDD]
Beethoven, L. van:Sym 3, "Eroica" Chandos ▲ CHAN 8751 [DDD]
Beethoven, L. van:Sym 4 Chandos ▲ CHAN 8753 [DDD]
Beethoven, L. van:Sym 5 Chandos ▲ CHAN 8752 [DDD]
Beethoven, L. van:Sym 7 Chandos ▲ CHAN 8753 [DDD]
Beethoven, L. van:Sym 8 Chandos ▲ CHAN 8754 [DDD]
Beethoven, L. van:Sym 10 Chandos ("Collect" series) ▲ CHAN 6501 [DDD]
Beethoven, L. van:Sym 10 Chandos 5–▲ CHAN 7042
H. Wolff (cnd)
Kernis, A.J.:Invisible Mosaic III Argo ▲ 448 900-2
Kernis, A.J.:Sym 2 Argo ▲ 448 900-2
City of Birmingham SO members
Kernis, A.J.:Qt Strs Argo ▲ 448 900-2
City of London Baroque Sinfonia
I. Bolton (cnd)
Handel, G.F.:Arias, w. R. White (ten) Virgin Classics ▲ CDZ 59644
R. Hickox (cnd)
Monteverdi, C.:Incoronazione, w. A. Augér (soprano—Poppea), D. Jones (mez—Nerone), L. Hirst (mez—Ottavia), J. Bowman (ct—Ottone) Virgin Classics ▲ CDCC 45082
Monteverdi, C.:Incoronazione, w. A. Augér (sop), S. Leonard (sop), D. Jones (mez), L. Hirst (mez), J. Bowman (ct), G. Reinhart (bass). Virgin Classics 3–▲ CDCC 59524
City of London Brass Quintet
A Little Christmas Music, w. King's Singers, Kiri Te Kanawa (sop), City of London Sinfonia [cnd:R. Hickox] EMI Classics ▲ CDC 49909
City of London School for Girls Orch
R. Hickox (cnd)
Britten, B.:Psalm 150, w. City of London School for Girls Chorus, City of London School for Boys Chorus [E] Chandos ▲ CHAN 8855 [DDD]
Britten, B.:Welcome Ode, w. City of London School for Girls Chorus, City of London School for Boys Chorus [E] Chandos ▲ CHAN 8855 [DDD]
City of London Sinfonia
American Music Sampler, w. Gomez, Jill (sop), Crispian Steele (tpt), Helen McQueen (E hn), Wayne Marshall (pno), City of London Sinfonia [cnd:R. Hickox] Virgin Classics 2–▲ CDC 59089
Christmas Day in the Morning, w. Cambridge Singers, Stephen Varcoe (bar), City of London Sinfonia [cnd:John Rutter] Collegium ▲ COLCD 121 ■ COLCS 121
Christmas Night:Carols of the Nativity, w. [cnd:John Rutter], Cambridge Singers Collegium ▲ COLCD 106 [DDD] ■ COLC 106 (D)
La Flûte enchantée, w. Milan, Susan (fl), City of London Sinfonia [cnd:Richard Hickox] Chandos ▲ CHAN 8840 [DDD]
If There Were Dreams to Sell:English Orchestral Songs, w. Varcoe, Stephen (bar), City of London Sinfonia [cnd:Richard Hickox] Chandos ▲ CHAN 8743 [DDD]
A Little Christmas Music, w. King's Singers, Kiri Te Kanawa (sop), City of London Brass Quintet, City of London Sinfonia [cnd:R. Hickox] EMI Classics ▲ CDC 49909
M. Best (cnd)
Vaughan Williams, R.:Choral Hymns, w. J. Bowen (ten), Corydon Singers [E] Hyperion ▲ CDA 66569 [DDD]
Vaughan Williams, R.:Magnificat, w. C. Wyn-Rogers (alt), Corydon Singers [E] Hyperion ▲ CDA 66569 [DDD]

City of London Sinfonia (cont.)
M. Best (cnd) (cont.)
Vaughan Williams, R.:The Old 100th Psalm Tune, w. Corydon Singers [E] Hyperion ▲ CDA 66569 [DDD]
Vaughan Williams, R.:The Shepherds of the Delectable Mountains, w. L. Kitchen (sop), J.-M. Ainsley (ten), A. Thompson (ten), A. Opie (bar), B. Terfel (b-bar), J. Best (bass) [E] Hyperion ▲ CDA 66569 [DDD]
Vaughan Williams, R.:A Song of Thanksgiving, w. John Gielgud (nar), L. Dawson (sop), London Oratory Junior Choir [E] Hyperion ▲ CDA 66569 [DDD]
B. Broughton (cnd)
Rózsa, M.:Ivanhoe Intrada ▲ ITDCD 7055 [DDD]
Rózsa, M.:Julius Caesar, w. Sinfonia Chorus Intrada ▲ ITDCD 7056
B. R. Dunn (cnd)
Baker, M.C.:Through the Lions' Gate *(rec Abbey Road Studios, London, 1993)* Summit ▲ SMT 182 [DDD]
G. Guest (cnd)
Charpentier, M.-A.:Messe de minuit pour Noël, w. St. John's College Choir Cambridge [L] Chandos ▲ CHAN 8658 [DDD]
Poulenc, F.:Motets (4) pour le temps de Noël, w. St. John's College Choir Cambridge [L] Chandos ▲ CHAN 8658 [DDD]
Poulenc, F.:Motets (4) pour un temps de pénitence, w. St. John's College Choir Cambridge [L] Chandos ▲ CHAN 8658 [DDD]
Poulenc, F.:Salve regina, w. St. John's College Choir Cambridge [L] Chandos ▲ CHAN 8658 [DDD]
R. Hickox (cnd)
Alwyn, W.:Autumn Legend, w. N. Daniel (E hn) Chandos ▲ CHAN 9065 [DDD]
Alwyn, W.:Con grosso 1 Chandos ▲ CHAN 8866 [DDD]
Alwyn, W.:Con grosso 2 Chandos ▲ CHAN 8866 [DDD]
Alwyn, W.:Con grosso 3 Chandos ▲ CHAN 8866 [DDD]
Alwyn, W.:Con Ob, w. N. Daniel (E hn) Chandos ▲ CHAN 8866 [DDD]
Alwyn, W.:Lyra Angelica, w. R. Masters (hp) Chandos ▲ CHAN 9065 [DDD]
Alwyn, W.:Pastoral Fant, w. S. Tees (va) Chandos ▲ CHAN 9065 [DDD]
Alwyn, W.:Tragic Interlude Chandos ▲ CHAN 9065 [DDD]
Barber, S.:Adagio Strs Virgin Classics ▲ CDC 59520-2 [DDD]
Barber, S.:Knoxville:Summer of 1915, w. J. Gomez (sop) [E] Virgin Classics ▲ 59520 [DDD]
Beethoven, L. van:Con 1 Pno, w. C. Ortiz (pno) IMP Masters ▲ PCD 854 [DDD]
Beethoven, L. van:Con 2 Pno, w. C. Ortiz (pno) IMP Masters ▲ PCD 854 [DDD]
Beethoven, L. van:Con 3 Pno, w. C. Ortiz (pno) IMP Classics ▲ PCD 879 [DDD]
Beethoven, L. van:Con 4 Pno, w. C. Ortiz (pno) IMP Classics ▲ PCD 879 [DDD]
Beethoven, L. van:Con 5 Pno, "Emperor", w. Cristina Ortiz (pno) IMP ("Classic" series) ▲ IMP 2038
Beethoven, L. van:Con Vn, Op. 61, w. Mayumi Seiler (vn) Virgin Classics ("Ultraviolet" series) ▲ CUV 61117
Beethoven, L. van:Coriolan Ov Virgin Classics ("Ultraviolet" series) ▲ CUV 61117
Berlioz, H.:Les Nuits d'été, w. J. Baker (mez) Virgin Classics ("Ultraviolet" series) ▲ CUV 61118
Berlioz, H.:Songs, w. J. Baker (mez)—Zaïde, Op. 19/1; La belle voyageuse, Op. 2/4; La captive, Op. 12; Les nuits d'été, Op. 7 Virgin Classics ▲ CDC 59622
Brahms, J.:Alto Rhap, w. J. Baker (mez), London Sym Chorus Virgin Classics ▲ CDC 59589
Britten, B.:Cant misericordium, w. J. M. Ainsley (ten), S. Varcoe (bar), Britten Singers [L] Chandos ▲ CHAN 8997 [DDD]
Britten, B.:A Midsummer Night's Dream, w. J. Gomez (sop), D. Jones (sop), J. Bowman (ct), N. Bailey (bar), H. Herford (bar) Virgin Classics ▲ CDCB 59305
Britten, B.:A Midsummer Night's Dream Virgin Classics ▲ CDC 59305
Britten, B.:Noye's Fludde Virgin Classics ("Ultraviolet" series) ▲ CUV 61122
Britten, B.:Peter Grimes, w. London Sym Chorus Chandos 2–▲ CHAN 9447/8
Britten, B.:The Rape of Lucretia (sels), w. C. Pierard (sop), P. Rozario (sop), A. Gunson (mez), J. Rigby (cta), N. Robson (ten), D. Maxwell (bar), A. Opie (bar), A. Miles (bass) Chandos 2–▲ CHAN 9254/55 [DDD]
Britten, B.:Serenade, Op. 31 Virgin Classics ("Ultraviolet" series) ▲ CUV 61122
Bush, G.:Farewell, Earth's Bliss, w. S. Varcoe (bar) [E] Chandos ▲ CHAN 8864 [DDD]
Bush, G.:Songs (4) from The Hesperides, w. S. Varcoe (bar) [E] Chandos ▲ CHAN 8864 [DDD]
Bush, G.:A Summer Serenade, w. A. Thompson (ten), Westminster Singers [E] Chandos ▲ CHAN 8864 [DDD]
Butterworth, G.:Songs (3) Voc & Strs, w. S. Varcoe (b-bar) [E] Chandos ▲ CHAN 8743 [DDD]
Butterworth, G.:Songs (6) from *A Shropshire Lad*, w. S. Varcoe (b-bar) [E] Chandos ▲ CHAN 8743 [DDD]
Chaminade, C.:Concertino Fl, w. S. Milan (fl) Chandos ▲ CHAN 8840 [DDD]
Copland, A.:Appalachian Spring (suite) Virgin Classics ▲ 59520 [DDD]
Copland, A.:Quiet City, w. C. Steele-Perkins (tpt), H. McQueen (E hn) Virgin Classics ▲ 59520 [DDD]
Dyson, G.:Children's Suite Chandos ▲ CHAN 9369 [DDD]
Dyson, G.:Con da Camera Chandos ▲ CHAN 9076 [DDD]
Dyson, G.:Con da Chiesa Chandos ▲ CHAN 9076 [DDD]
Dyson, G.:Con Leggiero, w. Eric Parkin (pno) Chandos ▲ CHAN 9076 [DDD]
Dyson, G.:Con Vn, w. Lydia Mordkovitch (vn) Chandos ▲ CHAN 9369 [DDD]
Dyson, G.:Sym in G Chandos ▲ CHAN 9200 [DDD]
Elgar, E.:Intro & Allegro EMI Classics ▲ CDC 54407
Elgar, E.:Songs, w. S. Varcoe (bass-bar)—Pleading, Op. 48/1; Twilight, Op. 59/6 [E] Chandos ▲ CHAN 8743 [DDD]
Finzi, G.:Let us garlands bring, w. S. Varcoe (bar) [E] Chandos ▲ CHAN 8743 [DDD]
Finzi, G.:Requiem da Camera, w. S. Varcoe (bar), Britten Singers [E] Chandos ▲ CHAN 8997 [DDD]
Gershwin, G.:Rhap in Blue, w. W. Marshall (pno) Virgin Classics ▲ CDZ 59693
Gershwin, G.:Rhap in Blue, w. W. Marshall (pno) [original Paul Whiteman Orchestra arr.] Virgin Classics ▲ 59520 [DDD]
Ginastera, A.:Con Hp, w. R. Masters (hp) Chandos ▲ CHAN 9094 [DDD]
Glière, R.:Con Coloratura Sop, w. E. Hulse (sop) Chandos ▲ CHAN 9094 [DDD]
Glière, R.:Con Hp, w. R. Masters (hp) Chandos ▲ CHAN 9094 [DDD]
Godard, B.:Suite de trois morceaux, w. S. Milan (fl) Chandos ▲ CHAN 8840 [DDD]
Handel, G.F.:Water Music (suites)—in F, D & G IMP ▲ IMP 2004
Holloway, R.:Romanza, w. E. Gruenberg (vn) Chandos ▲ CHAN 9228 [DDD]
Holloway, R.:Sea Surface Full of Clouds, w. P. Walmsley-Clark (sop), M. Cable (mez), C. Brett (alt), M. Hill (ten) Chandos ▲ CHAN 9228 [DDD]
Holst, G.:A Choral Fant, w. London Sym Chorus, Joyful Company of Singers Chandos ▲ CHAN 9437
Holst, G.:A Dirge for 2 Veterans, w. London Sym Chorus Chandos ▲ CHAN 9437
Holst, G.:The Dream-City, w. P. Kwella (sop) [E] Hyperion ▲ CDA 66099 [DDD]
Holst, G.:Music of—Double Con., Op. 49; Fugal Con., Op. 40/2; Lyric Movement; Brook Green Suite; St. Paul's Suite; Songs without Words, Op. 22 Chandos ▲ CHAN 9270 [DDD]
Holst, G.:Ode to Death, w. London Sym Chorus, Joyful Company of Singers Chandos ▲ CHAN 9437
Holst, G.:Partsongs (7), Op. 44, w. London Sym Chorus, Joyful Company of Singers Chandos ▲ CHAN 9437
Holst, G.:Psalms 86 & 148, w. J. Alley (org), Britten Singers [E] Chandos ▲ CHAN 8997 [DDD]
Holst, G.:Savitri, w. F. Palmer (sop), P. Langridge (ten), S. Varcoe (bar), Hickox Singers Hyperion ▲ CDA 66099 [DDD]
Howells, H.:Con Strs Chandos ▲ CHAN 9161 [DDD]
Howells, H.:Elegy Va & Str Qt Chandos ▲ CHAN 9161 [DDD]
Howells, H.:Serenade Strs Chandos ▲ CHAN 9161 [DDD]
Howells, H.:Suite Strs Chandos ▲ CHAN 9161 [DDD]
Ibert, J.:Divert Orch Virgin Classics ▲ CDZ 59695
Ireland, J.:Concertino pastorale Chandos ▲ CHAN 9376 [DDD]
Ireland, J.:A Downland Suite Chandos ▲ CHAN 9376 [DDD]
Ireland, J.:Poem Chandos ▲ CHAN 9376 [DDD]
Ireland, J.:Symphonic Studies Chandos ▲ CHAN 9376 [DDD]
Martin, F.:Ballade Fl, w. S. Milan (fl), M. Dussek (pno) Chandos ▲ CHAN 8840 [DDD]

▲ = CD ♦ = Enhanced CD Δ = MD ■ = Cassette Tape □ = DCC

City of London Sinfonia (cont.)
R. Hickox (cnd) (cont.)
Martinů, B.:Con Str Qt, Endellion String Quartet — Virgin Classics ▲ 59575 [DDD]
Martinů, B.:Double Con Pno, Tim — Virgin Classics ▲ 59575 [DDD]
Martinů, B.:Sinfonia concertante Ob — Virgin Classics ▲ 59575 [DDD]
Mendelssohn, F.:Hear my prayer, w. J. Baker (mez) — Virgin Classics ▲ CDC 59589
Mendelssohn, F.:Psalm 42, w. J. Baker (mez), London Sym Chorus — Virgin Classics ▲ CDC 59589
Mendelssohn, F.:Songs (4) (1830), w. J. Baker (mez), F. Lloyd (hn), R. Masters (hp), London Sym Chorus — Virgin Classics ▲ CDC 59589
Mozart, W.A.:Con Cl, w. David Campbell (cl) — IMP ▲ IMP 2011
Mozart, W.A.:Con Fl Hp, w. Philippa Davies (fl), Rachel Masters (hp) — IMP ▲ IMP 2011
Mozart, W.A.:Con Fl Hp, w. S. Milan (fl), S. Kanga (hp) — Chandos ▲ CHAN 9051 [DDD]
Mozart, W.A.:Cons Hn, w. Richard Watkins (hn) — IMP Classics ▲ PCD 865 [DDD]
Mozart, W.A.:Con Hn, K.412, w. Richard Watkins (hn) — IMP ▲ PCD 2013
Mozart, W.A.:Con Hn, K.417, w. Richard Watkins (hn) — IMP ▲ PCD 2013
Mozart, W.A.:Con Hn, K.447, w. Richard Watkins (hn) — IMP ▲ PCD 2013
Mozart, W.A.:Con Hn, K.495, w. Richard Watkins (hn) — IMP ▲ PCD 2013
Mozart, W.A.:Con Ob, K.314, w. D. Theodore (ob) — Chandos ▲ CHAN 9051 [DDD]
Mozart, W.A.:Rondo Hn, K.371, w. R. Watkins (hn) — IMP Classics ▲ PCD 865 [DDD]
Mozart, W.A.:Rondo Hn, K.371, w. Richard Watkins (hn) — IMP ▲ PCD 2013
Quilter, R.:Shakespeare Songs, Op. 6, w. S. Varcoe (b–bar) [E] — Chandos ▲ CHAN 8743 [DDD]
Respighi, O.:La Sensitiva, w. J. Baker (mez) — Virgin Classics ("Ultraviolet" series) ▲ CUV 61118
Rossini, G.:Arias, w. D. Jones (mez), Richard Hickox Singers—nine arias, from Adelaide di Borgogna, Barbiere di Siviglia, Bianca e Falliero, Cenerentola, Donna del Lago, Italiana in Algeri, Otello, Signor Bruschino [I] — Chandos ▲ CHAN 8865 [DDD]
Rossini, G.:Stabat Mater, w. H. Field (sop), D. Jones (mez), A. Davies (ten), R. Earle (bass), London Sym Chorus [L] — Chandos ▲ CHAN 8780 [DDD]
Saint-Saëns, C.:Airs de ballet d' *Ascanio*, w. S. Milan (fl) — Chandos ▲ CHAN 8840 [DDD]
Salieri, A.:Con Fl, w. S. Milan (fl), D. Theodore (ob) — Chandos ▲ CHAN 9051 [DDD]
Schubert, Franz:Sym 3 — IMP Classics ▲ PCD 848 [DDD]
Schubert, Franz:Sym 8 — IMP Classics ▲ PCD 848 [DDD]
Strauss, R.:Con Ob, w. N. Daniel (ob) — Chandos ▲ CHAN 9286 [DDD]
Stravinsky, I.:Danses concertantes — Virgo ▲ CDZ 61107
Stravinsky, I.:Pulcinella, w. A. Murray (mez), M. Hill (ten), D. Thomas (bass) — Virgo ▲ CDZ 61107
Tavener, J.:Elis Thanaton, w. Patricia Rozario (sop), Stephen Richards (bass) — Chandos ▲ CHAN 9440
Tippett, M.:Divert on Sellinger's Round — Chandos ▲ CHAN 9409 [DDD]
Tippett, M.:The Heart's Assurance, w. John Mark Ainsley (ten) — Chandos ▲ CHAN 9409 [DDD]
Tippett, M.:Little Music — Chandos ▲ CHAN 9409 [DDD]
Vaughan Williams, R.:Fant on a Theme by Thomas Tallis — EMI Classics ▲ CDC 54407
Vaughan Williams, R.:Songs, w. S. Varcoe (b–bar)—3 songs from *The House of Life*—Love-Sight; Silent Noon; Heart's Haven [E] — Chandos ▲ CHAN 8743 [DDD]
Walton, W.:Anon in Love, w. M. Hill (ten) [E] — Chandos ▲ CHAN 8824 [DDD]
Walton, W.:Christopher Columbus (suite), w. L. Finnie (mez), A. Davies (ten), Westminster Singers [E] — Chandos ▲ CHAN 8824 [DDD]
Walton, W.:Son Str Orch — EMI Classics ▲ CDC 54407
Walton, W.:A Song for the Lord Mayor's Table, w. J. Gomez (sop) [E] — Chandos ▲ CHAN 8824 [DDD]
Walton, W.:Songs after Edith Sitwell, w. J. Gomez (sop) [E] — Chandos ▲ CHAN 8824 [DDD]
Walton, W.:The Twelve, w. P. Forbes (sop), R. Gleave (mez), S. Gay (alt), J. Oxley (ten), P. Harvey (bar) [E] — Chandos ▲ CHAN 8824 [DDD]

D. Hill (cnd)
Fauré, G.:Requiem, w. Harry Escott (trb), David Wilson-Johnson (bar), Westminster Cathedral Choir — IMP ▲ PCD 2015

G. LLoyd (cnd)
Handel, G.F.:Con Eup, w. J.–P. Chevailler (eup) — Albany ▲ TROY 201-2 [DDD]; ■ TROY 201-4 (D)

J. Laredo (cnd)
Baroque Beauties, w. Scottish CO, City of London Sinfonia [cnd:R. Hickox], E. Ritchie (sop), Bowman (ct), J. Purvis (pno) — Pickwick ("The Orchid" series) ▲ PICORCD 11010

G. Lloyd (cnd)
Danzi, F.:Con Bn, w. J.–P. Chevailler (eup) — Albany ▲ TROY 201-2 [DDD] ■ TROY 201-4 (D)
Mozart, W.A.:Con Bn, w. J.–P. Chevailler (eup) — Albany ▲ TROY 201-2 [DDD] ■ TROY 201-4 (D)

A.G. Melville (cnd)
Boughton, R.:Bethlehem, w. Holst Singers, New London Children's Choir [adapted] — Hyperion ▲ CDA 66690

J. O'Donnell (cnd)
Stravinsky, I.:Canticum sacrum, w. J. M. Ainsley (ten), S. Roberts (bar), Westminster Cathedral Choir — Hyperion ▲ CDA 66437
Stravinsky, I.:Mass, w. Westminster Cathedral Choir — Hyperion ▲ CDA 66437
Stravinsky, I.:Sym of Psalms, w. Westminster Cathedral Choir — Hyperion ▲ CDA 66437

J. Rutter (cnd)
Bach, J.S.:Music of [trans. for orch.]—Sinfs. from Cants. 29 & 156; Sonatina from Cant. 106; Wir eilen mit schwachen, doch emsigen Schritten (duet from Cant. 78); Sheep may safely graze (from Cant. 208); Zion hört die Wächter singen (from Cant. 140); Vergnügte Ruh (aria from Cant. 170); Sinfonia (Pastoral Sym.) from the Christmas Oratorio; Bourée & Badinerie from Orchestral Suite No. 2 in b; Air & Gavotte from Orchestral Suite No. 3 in D; Bist du bei mir; Harpsichord Con. in E (1st movt.); Oboe & Violin Con. in d (2nd movt.) — American Gramaphone ▲ AGCD 592 ■ AGC 592
The Handel Collection — American Gramaphone ▲ AGCD 590 [DDD] ■ AGC 590 (D)
Handel, G.F.:Music of—Con Hrp B♭, Op. 4/6 [w Harry Bicket (hpd), Rachel Masters, (hrp)]; Con Ob 1 B♭ [(Nicholas Daniel, ob)]; Con Org F, Op. 4/5 [John Scott (org)]; 3 selections from solo Hpd Suites (Harmonious Blacksmith; Sarabande; Gigue) [Harry Bicket (hpd)] — American Gramaphone ▲ AGCD 590 [DDD]; ■ AGC 590 (D)
The Mozart Collection — American Gramaphone ▲ AGCD 586 ■ AGC 586
Mozart, W.A.:Music of—Ovs. to Le nozze di Figaro & Die Zauberflöte; plus various sym. & con. movts. — American Gramaphone ▲ AGCD 586 ■ AGC 586
Poulenc, F.:Gloria Sop, w. D. Deam (sop), Cambridge Singers [L] — Collegium ▲ COLCD 108 [DDD] ■ COLC 108 (D)
Poulenc, F.:Litanies à la vierge noire, w. Cambridge Singers [L] — Collegium ▲ COLCD 108 [DDD] ■ COLC 108 (D)
Rutter, J.:Anthems, w. Cambridge Singers—I Will Lift Up Mine Eyes" [E] — Collegium ▲ COLCD 103 [DDD] ■ COLC 103 (D)
Rutter, J.:Anthems, w. Cambridge Singers—10 anthems [E] — Collegium ▲ COLCD 100 [DDD] ■ COLC 100 (D)
Rutter, J.:Church Music, w. Cambridge Singers—Te Deum; Be thou my vision; I believe in springtime; Lord, make me an instrument of thy peace; O be joyful in the Lord; All creatures of our God and King; A choral fanfare; As the bridegroom to his chosen; Christ the Lord is risen again; Thy perfect love; The Lord is my light and my salvation; Go forth into the world in peace; Now thank we all our God — Collegium ▲ COLCD 112 [DDD] ■ COLC 112 (D)
Rutter, J.:Requiem, w. C. Ashton (sop), D. Deam (sop). Cambridge Singers [E,L] — Collegium ▲ COLCD 103 [DDD] ■ COLC 103 (D)

H. Shelley (cnd)
Mozart, W.A.:Con 21 Pno, w. Howard Shelley (pno) — IMP ▲ IMP 2007
Mozart, W.A.:Con 24 Pno, w. Howard Shelley (pno) — IMP ▲ IMP 2007

N. Ward (cnd)
Barbirolli, J.:Con on Themes of Peroglisi, w. Anthony Camden (ob) *(rec East Finchley, England, Apr 1995)* — Naxos ▲ 8.553433 [DDD]
Bellini, V.:Con in E♭ Ob, w. Anthony Camden (ob) *(rec East Finchley, England, Apr 1995)* — Naxos ▲ 8.553433 [DDD]
Cimarosa, D.:Con in C Ob, w. Anthony Camden (ob) *(rec East Finchley, England, Apr 1995)* — Naxos ▲ 8.553433 [DDD]
Corelli, A.:Con Ob, w. Anthony Camden (ob) *(rec East Finchley, England, Apr 1995)* — Naxos ▲ 8.553433 [DDD]

City of London Sinfonia (cont.)
N. Ward (cnd) (cont.)
Fiorillo, F.:Sinf concertante, w. Anthony Camden (ob), Julia Girdwood (ob)—in F *(rec East Finchley, England, Apr 1995)* — Naxos ▲ 8.553433 [DDD]
Handel, G.F.:Cons (3) Ob, w. Anthony Camden (ob) *(rec All Saints Church, East Finchley, Apr 24 & 27, 1995)* — Naxos ▲ 8.553430 [DDD]
Handel, G.F.:Hpd Music, w. Anthony Camden (ob)—Air in g & Rondo in G [orchd A. Camden] *(rec All Saints Church, East Finchley, Apr 24 & 27, 1995)* — Naxos ▲ 8.553430 [DDD]
Handel, G.F.:Ottone, Rè di Germania (ov), w. Anthony Camden (ob), Julia Girdwood (ob) *(rec All Saints Church, East Finchley, Apr 24 & 27, 1995)* — Naxos ▲ 8.553430 [DDD]
Handel, G.F.:Suites Hpd, w. Anthony Camden (ob), Julia Girdwood (ob)—in g [trans by A. Camden] *(rec All Saints Church, East Finchley, Apr 24 & 27, 1995)* — Naxos ▲ 8.553430 [DDD]
Righini, V.:Con Ob, w. Anthony Camden (ob) *(rec East Finchley, England, Apr 1995)* — Naxos ▲ 8.553433 [DDD]

A. Watkinson (cnd)
Vivaldi, A.:Con for 2 Tpts, w. C. Steele-Perkins (tpt), M. Meeks (tpt), N. Ward (vn), A. Watkinson (vn) — Virgin Classics ▲ CDZ 59651
Vivaldi, A.:Cons Vn, Op. 8/1–4, "The Four Seasons", w. A. Watkinson (vn) — Virgin Classics ▲ CDZ 59651

City of London Sinfonia members
R. Hickox (cnd)
Walton, W.:Façade, w. S. Walton (nar), Richard Baker (nar) [E] — Chandos ▲ CHAN 8869 [DDD]
J. Rutter (cnd)
Fauré, G.:Requiem, w. C. Ashton (sop), S. Varcoe (bar), Cambridge Singers [1893 ver.] [L] — Collegium ▲ COLCD 109 [DDD] ■ COLC 109 (D)

City of Oxford Orch
M. Papadopoulos (cnd)
Albinoni, T.:Adagio Org *(rec St. Barnabas Church, Oxford, May 23–24, 1994)* — IMP ("Classics" series) ▲ IMP PCD 1104
Corelli, A.:Con grosso, Op. 6/8, "Christmas Con" *(rec St. Barnabas Church, Oxford, May 23–24, 1994)* — IMP ("Classics" series) ▲ IMP PCD 1104
Handel, G.F.:Solomon (arrival of the queen of Sheba) *(rec St. Barnabas Church, Oxford, May 23–24, 1994)* — IMP ("Classics" series) ▲ IMP PCD 1104
Handel, G.F.:Water Music (suites)—No. 3 in G *(rec St. Barnabas Church, Oxford, May 23–24, 1994)* — IMP ("Classics" series) ▲ IMP PCD 1104
Purcell, H.:The Fairy Queen (sels)—Suite *(rec St. Barnabas Church, Oxford, May 23–24, 1994)* — IMP ("Classics" series) ▲ IMP PCD 1104
Torelli, G.:Con for 2 Tpts *(rec St. Barnabas Church, Oxford, May 23–24, 1994)* — IMP ("Classics" series) ▲ IMP PCD 1104
Vivaldi, A.:Cons Vn, Op. 8/1–4, "The Four Seasons"—No. 4 in f *(rec St. Barnabas Church, Oxford, May 23–24, 1994)* — IMP ("Classics" series) ▲ IMP PCD 1104

Clare College Orch
J. Rutter (cnd)
Carols from Clare College Cambridge, w. Clare College Chapel Choir Cambridge — EMI Classics ▲ CDM 69950

Claremont CO
P. Klatzow (cnd)
Klatzow, P.:Con Cl, w. Mathew Reid (cl) — Claremont ▲ GSE 1524

Claremont String Quartet [Marc Gottlieb (vn), Vladimir Weisman (vn), Scott Nickrenz (va), Irving Klein (vc)]
Jacobi, F.:Hagiographia — CRI ("American Masters" series) ▲ CD 703 [ADD]

Clarinesque Ensemble
Somebody Loves Me:Music for 4 Clarinets — Signum ▲ 63-00

Clarion Brass
D. Amos (cnd)
Rosner, A.:Magnificat, w. St. Paul's Cathedral Choir [L] — Laurel ▲ LR 849CD [ADD/DDD]

Clarion Concerts Orch
N. Jenkins (cnd)
Cherubini, L.:Mass in d, w. Patricia Wells (sop), Maureen Forrester (cta), George Shirley (ten), Justino Diaz (bass), Clarion Concerts Chorus *(rec Vanguard's 23rd Street Recording Studio)* — Vanguard Classics ▲ SVC-44 [AAD]
Rossini, G.:La pietra del paragone, w. A. Elgar (sop), B. Wolff (mez), E. Bonazzi (mez), J. Carreras (ten), J. Reardon (bar), R. Murcell (bar), A. Foldi (b–bar), J. Diaz (bass), Clarion Concerts Chorus [I] *(rec ca. 1972)* — Vanguard Classics 3–▲ OVC 8043/45 [ADD]

Clarion Ensemble
Clarion Ensemble — Amon Ra ▲ CDSAR 30 [DDD]

Clarion Music Society Orch
N. Jenkins (cnd)
Dittersdorf, K.D. von:Arcifanfano, King of Fools, or It's Always Too Late to Learn, w. P. Brooks (sop), A. Russell (sop), E. Steber (sop), J. McCollum (ten), J. Sopher (ten), H. Rehfuss (bar), D. Smith (bar), Clarion Music Society Chorus [E] *(rec live, New York 1965)* — VAI Audio 2–▲ VAIA 1010–2 (m) [ADD]

Classic Polonaise PO
L. Petitgirard (cnd)
Petitgirard, L.:Le Légendaire, w. A. Dumay (vn), Cracow Polish Radio–TV Chorus — Orchestre Symphonique France ▲ OSF 49013 [DDD]

Classic Trio [Geoffery Haydock (cl), Alexander Volpov (vc), Penelope Smith (pno)]
Beethoven, L. van:Trio 7 Pno — ASV/Quicksilva ▲ ASQ CD 6187
Brahms, J.:Trio Cl — ASV/Quicksilva ▲ ASQ CD 6187
Glinka, M.:Trio pathétique [arr for cl, vc & pno] — ASV/Quicksilva ▲ ASQ CD 6187

Classical Band
B. Weil (cnd)
Schubert, Franz:Sym 8 — Sony Classical ("Vivarte" series) ▲ SK 48132
Schubert, Franz:Sym 9 — Sony Classical ("Vivarte" series) ▲ SK 48132

Classical Brass
The Joy of Christmas, w. National Cathedral Choral Society — Centaur ▲ CRC 2132

Classical Guitar Duo [Julian Gray (gtr), Ronald Pearl (gtr)]
Handel, G.F.:Chaconne Hpd [arr. for gtrs] *(rec Troy Savings Bank Music Hall, Troy, NY, May & June 1994)* — Dorian ▲ DOR 90209 [DDD]
Handel, G.F.:Rodelinda, Regina de' Longobardi (sels)—Ov. [arr. for gtrs] *(rec Troy Savings Bank Music Hall, Troy, NY, May & June 1994)* — Dorian ▲ DOR 90209 [DDD]
Scarlatti, D.:Sons Kbd—K.33, 137, 213, 215, 227 & 491 [arr. for gtrs] *(rec Troy Savings Bank Music Hall, Troy, NY, May & June 1994)* — Dorian ▲ DOR 90209 [DDD]

Classical String Quartet
Mozart, W.A.:Qt 14 Strs [period instrs] — Titanic ▲ Ti 154 [DDD]
Mozart, W.A.:Qt 17 Strs [period instrs] — Titanic ▲ Ti 154 [DDD]

Classical Winds
Beethoven, L. van:Octet, Op. 103 [period instrs] — Amon Ra ▲ CD-SAR 26 [DDD]
Beethoven, L. van:Sxt Winds, Op. 71 [period instrs] — Amon Ra ▲ CD-SAR 26 [DDD]
Mozart, W.A.:Diverts Bas Hns, K.Anh.229 [period instrs]—Nos. 1–4 — Amon Ra ▲ CD-SAR 25 [DDD]

Classico CO Ensemble
P. Cochand (cnd)
Pachelbel, J.:Canon, w. L. Chan (vn), P. Cochand (vn) *(rec Oct. 19–21, 1992)* — Gallo ▲ CD 723 DAD
Richter, F.X.:Grandes simphonies, w. L. Chan (vn), P. Cochand (vn)—in G *(rec Oct. 19–21, 1992)* — Gallo ▲ CD 723 DAD
Telemann, G.P.:Don Quichotte (suite), w. L. Chan (vn), P. Cochand (vn) *(rec Oct. 19–21, 1992)* — Gallo ▲ CD 723 DAD
Vivaldi, A.:Cons Vn, Op. 3/1–12, "L'estro armonico", w. L. Chan (vn), P. Cochand (vn) *(rec Oct. 19–21, 1992)* — Gallo ▲ CD 723 DAD

Classico Italiano Octet
Beethoven, L. van:Fidelio (sels)—Harmoniemusik von Wenzel Sedlak Stradivarius ▲ STV 33370 [DDD]
Donizetti, G.:Sinfs (misc)—in g Stradivarius ▲ STV 33370 [DDD]
Schubert, Franz:Minuet & Finale Stradivarius ▲ STV 33370 [DDD]
Claude-Gervaise Ensemble
G. Plantes (cnd)
Music in the Age of Leonardo Da Vinci Musica Viva ▲ MVCD 1022 [DDD]
Claudel String Quartet
Dvořák, A.:Qt 10 Strs ISBA ▲ ISB 5015
Dvořák, A.:Qnt Pno, Op. 81, w. Marie Fabi (pno) ISBA ▲ ISB 5015
Clemencic Consort
Carmina Burana Harmonia Mundi ▲ HMC 90335 ■
Danses anciennes de Hongrie et de Transylvanie Harmonia Mundi ▲ HMA 190.1003
La Fête de l'Ane Harmonia Mundi ▲ HMC 901036
Le Roman de fauvel Harmonia Mundi ("Musique d'Abord" series) ▲ HMA 190994 ■
Schmelzer, J.H.:Balletti Preiser ▲ 93389 [DDD]
Schmelzer, J.H.:Die Fechtschule Preiser ▲ 93389 [DDD]
Schmelzer, J.H.:Sacro-profanus concentus musicus Preiser ▲ 93389 [DDD]
Schmelzer, J.H.:Serenata con altre arie; amento sopra la morte Ferdinandi III Preiser ▲ 93389 [DDD]
Troubadours Harmonia Mundi ▲ HMC 90396
Vivaldi, A.:Music of, Philharmonia Baroque Orch, Concerto Amsterdam, Boston Museum Trio, Bologna I Filarmonici—sels. from Flute Concerto, RV.427 & 440; Four Seasons—Autumn; String Concerto, RV.129 & 152; Serenata a Tre, RV.690; Sonata, RV.2 *(rec 1970–86)* Harmonia Mundi Plus ▲ HMP 390810
R. Clemencic (cnd)
Carmina Burana *(rec mid-1970s)* Harmonia Mundi 3-▲ HMA 190336.38
Clemencic, R.:Molière Musique D'Abord ▲ HMA 1901020
Dufay, G.:Missa, "Ecce ancilla Domini" Musique d'Abord ▲ HMA 190939
Dufay, G.:Missa, "Sine nomine" Musique d'Abord ▲ HMA 190939
Fux, J.J.:Dafne in Lauro, w. L. Akerlund (sop), S. Piccollo (sop), M. van der Sluis (sop), G. Lesne (alt), M. Klietmann (ten), La Cappella Vocal Ensemble [I] Nuova Era ("Ancient Music" series) 2-▲ 6930/31 [DDD]
Keiser, R.:Croesus, w. P. Grigorova (sop), M. Klietmann (ten), S. Mizugushi (bass), La Cappella Vocal Ensemble [G] Nuova Era ("Ancient Music" series) 2-▲ 6934/35 [DDD]
Monteverdi, C.:Combattimento [I] Musique d'Abord ▲ HMA 190986
Pergolesi, G.B.:Stabat mater Accord ▲ ACD 200062 [DDD]
Pergolesi, G.B.:Salve regina in F Accord ▲ ACD 200062 [DDD]
Rue, P. de la:Missa pro defunctis Accord ▲ ACD 201212 [DDD]
Scarlatti, A.:Venere e Adone:Il Giardino d'amore Accord ▲ ACD 200082 [DDD]
Senfl, L.:Vocal Music—Motet pour St. Paul; Lied Autobiographique; Chants d'amour, chants à boire & à danser; Ode d'Horace; Ode funèbre pour l'Empereur Maximilien Accord ▲ ACD 220632 [DDD]
Torrejón Y Velasco, T. de:La purpura de la rosa, w. M. van der Sluis (sop), P. Mildenhall (sop), J. Benet (ten), A. Martin (bar), La Cappella Vocal Ensemble [Sp] Nuova Era ("Ancient Music" series) ▲ 6936 [DDD]
Vivaldi, A.:L'Olimpiade, w. L. Meeuwsen (sop), M. van der Sluis (sop), E. von Magnus (alt), G. Lesne (alt), A. Christofelis (alt), W. Oberholtzer (bar), A. Walker Schultze (bass), La Cappella Vocal Ensemble [I] *(rec live, Paris, 2/8–10/90)* Nuova Era ("Ancient Music" series) 2-▲ 6932/33 [DDD]
Clemencic Consort [René Clemencic (fl), Luigi Mangiocavallo (vn), Edward Smith (hpd), Luciano Contini (lt), Claudio Ronco (vc)]
Veracini, F.M.:Sons Vn (1716) Accord ▲ ACD 202112 [DDD]
Clementi Quartet
Mozart, W.A.:Sym 35 [arr Clementi for Pno, Fl, Vn & Vc] Agorá ▲ 004
Mozart, W.A.:Sym 36 [arr Clementi for Pno, Fl, Vn & Vc] Agorá ▲ 003
Mozart, W.A.:Sym 38 [arr Clementi for Pno, Fl, Vn & Vc] Agorá ▲ 003
Mozart, W.A.:Sym 39 [arr Clementi for Pno, Fl, Vn & Vc] Agorá ▲ 004
Mozart, W.A.:Sym 40 [arr Clementi for Pno, Fl, Vn & Vc] Agorá ▲ 003
Mozart, W.A.:Sym 41 [arr Clementi for Pno, Fl, Vn & Vc] Agorá ▲ 004
Clementi Quartet [Fabio Bidini (pno), Tamás Kocsis (vn), Laura Bruton (va), Alexis Pia Gerlach (vc)]
Brahms, J.:Qts Pno (comp) *(rec Mesquite Performing Arts Center, Texas, Apr 1996)* EPR 2-▲ EPR 9611/2 [DDD]
Clementi Trio Cologne
Schoenberg, A.:Verklärte Nacht [violin-cello-piano arr. by Edward Steuermann] Largo ▲ 5111 [DDD]
Cleveland Brass Ensemble
Gabrieli, G.:Sacrae symphoniae, w. Philadelphia Brass Ensemble, Chicago Brass Ensemble—Canzon Septimi Toni Nos 1 & 2; Canzon Duodecimi Toni; Canzon a 12 in Echo; Canzon Quarti Toni; Canzon Primi Toni; Canzon Noni Toni; Son Octavi Toni; Son pian' e forte *(rec Philadelphia, 1968)* Sony Classical ("Masterworks Heritage" series) ▲ MHK 62353 [ADD]
Cleveland Chamber SO
E. London (cnd)
Burt, G.:Exit Music III GM ▲ GM 2045
Finney, R.L.:Narrative Vc, w. Norman Fischer (vc) Albany ▲ TROY 208 [DDD]
Harris, D.:Music of— *(Mermaid Vars.)*, Janice Meyerson (mez), Richard Pittman (cnd), Boston Musica Viva *(For the Night to Wear)*, Veronica Jochum (pno) *(Balladen)*, Susan Davenny Wyner (sop), Yehudi Wyner (pno) *(Of Harford in a Purple Light)*, Janice Meyerson (mez), Hugh Hinton (pno) *(Les Mains)*, Lucy Shelton (sop), Craig Kirchhoff (cnd), Ohio State Univ. Faculty Ensemble *(Pierrot Lieder)*, Composers String Quartet *(Qt. for Strs)*, Paul Zukofsky (vn), Gilbert Kalish (pno) *(Fant. for Vn & Pno)*, Sydney Hodkinson (cnd), St. Paul CO *(Ludus)* CRI ▲ CD 666 [ADD]
London, E.:Before the World Was Made, w. Christine Schadeberg (sop) Albany ▲ TROY 208 [DDD]
London, E.:In Heinrich's Shoes *(rec Waetjen Hall, Cleveland, OH)* New World ▲ 80477-2
London, E.:Two A'Marvell's FOR WORDS, w. Philip Larson (b-bar) GM ▲ GM 2045
Martirano, S.:LON/dons GM ▲ GM 2039
Miller, E.J.:Beyond the Wheel, w. Kay Stern (vn) GM ▲ GM 2045
Powell, Morgan:Red White & Black Blues *(rec Cleveland, OH, Sept 24, 1992.* New World ▲ 80499-2
Rands, B.:London Serenade GM ▲ GM 2039
Read Thomas, A.:Vigil, w. Norman Fischer (vc) GM ▲ GM 2045
Reynolds, R.:The Dream of the Infinite Rooms GM ▲ GM 2039
Thorne, F.:Sym 6 Albany ▲ TROY 208 [DDD]
Cleveland Duo [S. Warner (vn), C. G. Warner (pno)]
Bartók, B.:Duos (44)—Nos. 11,23,28,30,32,35,36,38,39,41,42 & 44 Cappella ▲ [no stock number] [DDD]
Brahms, J.:Scherzo Vn Cappella ▲ [no stock number] [DDD]
Debussy, C.:Son Vn Cappella ▲ [no stock number] [DDD]
Eychenne, M.:Cantilène et Danse, w. J. Umble (sax) Dana Recording Project ▲ DRP 5 [DDD]
Milhaud, D.:Son 2 Vn Cappella ▲ [no stock number] [DDD]
Morawetz, O.:Duo Vn Cappella ▲ [no stock number] [DDD]
Cleveland Orch
Baby Dance:A Toddler's Jump on the Classics, w. Bolshoi SO, English Baroque Orch, Royal Concertgebouw Orch, A. Lazarev (cnd), J. E. Gardiner (cnd), T. Koopman (cnd), N. Harnoncourt (cnd), R. Leppard (cnd) Erato ▲ 96887-2 ■ 96887-4 ■ 97328-4 (blis
Dvořák, A.:Sym 9, "From the New World", w. G. Szell (cn) CBS ▲ MYK 37763 [ADD] ■ MYT 37763
V. Ashkenazy (cnd)
Beethoven, L. van:Cons Pno (comp), w. V. Ashkenazy (pno) London 3-▲ 421718-2 [DDD]
Beethoven, L. van:Con 3 Pno, w. V. Ashkenazy (pno) London ☐ 433321-5
Beethoven, L. van:Con 4 Pno, w. V. Ashkenazy (pno) London ☐ 433321-5
Beethoven, L. van:Fant Pno, Op. 80, "Choral Fant", w. V. Ashkenazy (pno) London 3-▲ 421718-2 [DDD]
Brahms, J.:Sym 1 London ▲ 436289-2

Cleveland Orch (cont.)
V. Ashkenazy (cnd) (cont.)
Brahms, J.:Sym 2 London ▲ 433549-2
Brahms, J.:Sym 3 London ▲ 433548-2 [DDD]
Brahms, J.:Sym 4 London ▲ 436853-2 [DDD]
Brahms, J.:Vars on a Theme by Haydn London ▲ 433548-2 [DDD]
Dvořák, A.:Carnival London ▲ 433548-2 [DDD]
Dvořák, A.:Othello London ▲ 436289-2
Dvořák, A.:Serenade Strs London ▲ 433549-2
Prokofiev, S.:Cinderella London 2-▲ 410162-2 [DDD]
Rachmaninoff, S.:Con 1 Pno, w. Jean-Yves Thibaudet (pno) *(rec Severance Hall, Cleveland, Ohio, Apr 25, 1994)* London ▲ 448219-2
Rachmaninoff, S.:Con 2 Pno, w. Jean-Yves Thibaudet (pno) *(rec Severance Hall, Cleveland, Ohio, Apr 25, 1994)* London ▲ 448219-2
Rachmaninoff, S.:Con 2 Pno, w. J.-Y. Thibaudet (pno) London ▲ 440653-2 [DDD]
Rachmaninoff, S.:Con 3 Pno, w. Jean-Yves Thibaudet (pno) *(rec Severance Hall, Cleveland, Ohio, Apr 25, 1994)* London ▲ 448219-2 [DDD]
Rachmaninoff, S.:Rhapsody on a Theme of Paganini, w. J.-Y. Thibaudet (pno) London ▲ 440653-2 [DDD]
Ravel, M.:Ma mère l'oye Orch London ▲ 430413-2 [DDD]
Ravel, M.:Rapsodie espagnole London ▲ 430413-2 [DDD]
Ravel, M.:La Valse London ▲ 430413-2 [DDD]
Ravel, M.:Valses nobles et sentimentales London ▲ 430413-2 [DDD]
Tchaikovsky, P.:Con Vn, w. J. Bell (vn) London ▲ 421716-2 [DDD]
Wieniawski, H.:Con 2 Vn, w. J. Bell (vn) London ▲ 421716-2 [DDD]
D. Barenboim (cnd)
Lalo, E.:Con Vc, w. Jacqueline Du Pré (vc) *(rec live, Severance Hall, Boston, 1973)* EMI Classics ▲ CDC 55528
P. Boulez (cnd)
Debussy, C.:Images Orch Deutsche Grammophon ▲ 435766-2 [DDD]
Debussy, C.:Jeux Deutsche Grammophon ("4D Audio" series) ▲ 439896-2
Debussy, C.:La Mer Deutsche Grammophon ("4D Audio" series) ▲ 439896-2
Debussy, C.:Nocturnes Deutsche Grammophon ("4D Audio" series) ▲ 439896-2
Debussy, C.:Orchestral Music, w. Philharmonia Orch—Images pour orchestre; Jeux; La Mer; Nocturnes; Prélude à l'après-midi d'un faune; Printemps Odyssey 2-▲ MB2K 45620
Debussy, C.:Orchestral Music, w. New Philharmonia Orch—La mer; Nocturnes; Printemps; Rapsodie; Prélude à l'après-midi d'un faune; Jeux; Images; Danses sacrée et profane Sony Classical ("Pierre Boulez Edition" series) 2-▲ SM2K 68327
Debussy, C.:Prélude à l'après-midi d'un faune Deutsche Grammophon ▲ 435766-2 [DDD]
Debussy, C.:Première rapsodie Deutsche Grammophon ("4D Audio" series) ▲ 439896-2
Debussy, C.:Printemps (suite) Deutsche Grammophon ▲ 435766-2 [DDD]
Mahler, G.:Sym 7 *(rec Masonic Auditorium, Cleveland, Nov 1994)* Deutsche Grammophon ▲ 447756-2 [DDD]
Ravel, M.:Con Pno (left hand), w. P. Entremont (pno) Sony Classical ("Essential Classics" series) ▲ SBK 46338 [ADD] ■ SBT 46338
Ravel, M.:Con in G Pno, w. P. Entremont (pno) Sony Classical ("Essential Classics" series) ▲ SBK 46338 [ADD] ■ SBT 46338
Ravel, M.:Orchestral Music, w. New York PO—including Alborada del gracioso, Boléro, Daphnis et Chloé (complete), Ma Mère l'Oye, Rapsodie espagnole, La Valses, Valses nobles et sentimentales Sony Classical 3-▲ SM3K 45842 [DDD]
Stravinsky, I.:Le Sacre du printemps for Orch CBS ▲ MK 42395 [AAD]
Stravinsky, I.:Le Sacre du printemps for Orch CBS ▲ MYK 37764 [ADD] ■ MYT 37764
Stravinsky, I.:Le Sacre du printemps for Orch Deutsche Grammophon ▲ 435769-2 [DDD]
R. Chailly (cnd)
Gershwin, G.:An American in Paris London ▲ 417326-2 [DDD]
Gershwin, G.:Cuban Ov London ▲ 417326-2 [DDD]
Gershwin, G.:Lullaby London ▲ 417326-2 [DDD]
Gershwin, G.:Rhap in Blue, w. K. Labèque (pno), M. Labèque (pno) London ▲ 417326-2 [DDD]
C. von Dohnányi (cnd)
Bartók, B.:Con Orch London ▲ 425694-2 [DDD]
Bartók, B.:Music for Strs, Perc & Cel London ▲ 443173-2 [DDD]
Beethoven, L. van:Leonore 3 Telarc 5-▲ CD 80200 [DDD]
Beethoven, L. van:Leonore 3 Telarc ▲ CD 80145 [DDD]
Beethoven, L. van:Music of, w. R. Serkin (pno), J. O'Conor (pno), R. Shaw (cnd), Atlanta SO—sels. from Syms. 5,6,7 & 9, Moonlight Son., Pno Con. 5, etc. Telarc ▲ CD 80240 [DDD] ■ CS 30240 (D)
Beethoven, L. van:Syms (comp)—[SATB soloists in No. 9 are Carol Vaness, Janice Taylor, Siegfried Jerusalem & Robert Lloyd] Telarc 5-▲ CD 80200 [DDD]
Beethoven, L. van:Sym 1 Telarc ▲ CD 80187 [DDD]
Beethoven, L. van:Sym 2 Telarc ▲ CD 80187 [DDD]
Beethoven, L. van:Sym 3, "Eroica" Telarc ▲ CD 80090 [DDD]
Beethoven, L. van:Sym 4 Telarc ▲ CD 80198 [DDD]
Beethoven, L. van:Sym 5 Telarc ▲ CD 80163 [DDD] ■ CS 30163 (D)
Beethoven, L. van:Sym 6, "Pastorale" Telarc ▲ CD 80145 [DDD]
Beethoven, L. van:Sym 7 Telarc ▲ CD 80163 [DDD] ■ CS 30163 (D)
Beethoven, L. van:Sym 8 Telarc ▲ CD 80198 [DDD]
Beethoven, L. van:Sym 9, "Choral Sym", w. Cleveland Orch Chorus [G] Telarc ▲ CD 80120 [DDD] ■ CS 30120 (D)
Berlioz, H.:Sym fantastique London ▲ 430201-2 [DDD]
Brahms, J.:Con Vn, w. Joshua Bell (vn) London ▲ 444811-2
Brahms, J.:Syms (comp) Teldec 4-▲ 2292-44972-2 [DDD]
Brahms, J.:Sym 2 Teldec ▲ 2292-42429-2
Brahms, J.:Sym 3 Teldec ▲ 92144
Brahms, J.:Sym 3 Teldec ▲ 2292-43711-2
Brahms, J.:Sym 4 Teldec ▲ 92144
Brahms, J.:Sym 4 Teldec ▲ 2292-43465-2
Brahms, J.:Tragic Ov Teldec 4-▲ 2292-44972-2 [DDD]
Brahms, J.:Tragic Ov Teldec ▲ 2292-43711-2
Brahms, J.:Vars on a Theme by Haydn Teldec ▲ 2292-42429-2 ■ 2292-42429-4
Brahms, J.:Vars on a Theme by Haydn Teldec 4-▲ 2292-44972-2 [DDD]
Bruckner, A.:Sym 4, "Romantic" London ▲ 430099-2 [DDD] ☐ 430099-5
Bruckner, A.:Sym 5 London ▲ 433318-2
Bruckner, A.:Sym 6 *(rec Oct. 7, 1991)* London ▲ 436153-2 [DDD]
Bruckner, A.:Sym 7 London ▲ 430841-2 [DDD]
Busoni, F.:Con Pno, Op. 39, w. G. Ohlsson (pno), Cleveland Chorus [G] Telarc ▲ CD 80207 [DDD]
Dvořák, A.:Slavonic Dances (comp) London ▲ 430171-2 ☐ 430171-5
Dvořák, A.:Sym 6 London ▲ 430204-2 [DDD]
Dvořák, A.:Sym 7 London 2-▲ 421082-2 [DDD]
Dvořák, A.:Sym 7 London ▲ 430728-2 [DDD]
Dvořák, A.:Sym 8 London 2-▲ 421082-2 [DDD]
Dvořák, A.:Sym 8 London ▲ 430728-2 [DDD]
Dvořák, A.:Sym 9, "From the New World" London ▲ 414421-2 [DDD]
Ives, C.:Sym 4 London ▲ 443172-2
Ives, C.:The Unanswered Question London ▲ 443172-2
Janácek, L.:Capriccio London ▲ 443173-2
Janácek, L.:Taras Bulba London ▲ 430204-2 [DDD]
Lutoslawski, W.:Con Orch London ▲ 425694-2 [DDD]
Lutoslawski, W.:Musique funèbre London ▲ 430844-2 [DDD]
Mahler, G.:Sym 1 London ☐ 425718-5
Mahler, G.:Sym 4, w. D. Upshaw (sop) *(rec May 1992)* London ▲ 440315-2 [DDD]
Mahler, G.:Sym 6 London 2-▲ 436240-2 [DDD]

Cleveland Orch (cont.)
C. von Dohnányi (cnd) (cont.)
Martinů, B.:Con Str Qt London ▲ 443173-2 [DDD]
Mendelssohn, F.:Die erste Walpurgisnacht, w. Cleveland Orch Chorus [G] Telarc ▲ CD 80184 [DDD]
Mendelssohn, F.:Sym 3 Telarc ▲ CD 80184 [DDD]
Mozart, W.A.:Con Fl Hp, w. *(soloists unknown)* London ▲ 443175-2 [DDD]
Mozart, W.A.:Kleine Nachtmusik London ▲ 443175-2 [DDD]
Mozart, W.A.:Sinf concertante Vn, K.364 London ▲ 443175-2 [DDD]
Mozart, W.A.:Sym 35 London 3-▲ 436421-2 [DDD]
Mozart, W.A.:Sym 36 London 3-▲ 436421-2 [DDD]
Mozart, W.A.:Sym 38 London 3-▲ 436421-2 [DDD]
Mozart, W.A.:Sym 39 London 3-▲ 436421-2 [DDD]
Mozart, W.A.:Sym 40 London 3-▲ 436421-2 [DDD]
Mozart, W.A.:Sym 41 London 3-▲ 436421-2 [DDD]
Mussorgsky, M.:Night [composer's original version]
Teldec ("Digital Experience" series) ▲ 9031-77600-2 AW [DDD] ■ 9031-77600-4
Mussorgsky, M.:Pictures at an Exhibition
Teldec ("Digital Experience" series) ▲ 9031-77600-2 AW [DDD] ■ 9031-77600-4
Ravel, M.:Alborada del gracioso Teldec ("M Line" series) ▲ 97439-2
Ravel, M.:Boléro Teldec ("M Line" series) ▲ 97439-2
Ravel, M.:Daphnis et Chloé (suite 2) Teldec ("M Line" series) ▲ 97439-2
Ravel, M.:La Valse Teldec ("M Line" series) ▲ 97439-2
Schoenberg, A.:Pieces Orch, Op. 16 London 2-▲ 436240-2 [DDD]
Schubert, Franz:Sym 9 Telarc ▲ CD 80110 [DDD]
Schumann, R.:Con Vn, w. Joshua Bell (vn) London ▲ 444811-2
Schumann, R.:Sym 1 London ▲ 421439-2 [DDD]
Schumann, R.:Sym 2 London ▲ 421439-2 [DDD]
Schumann, R.:Sym 3 London ▲ 421643-2 [DDD]
Schumann, R.:Sym 4 London ▲ 421643-2 [DDD]
Shostakovich, D.:Sym 10 London ▲ 430844-2 [DDD]
Strauss, R.:Ein Heldenleben London ▲ 436444-2 [DDD]
Strauss, R.:Till Eulenspiegels lustige Streiche London ▲ 436444-2 [DDD]
Tchaikovsky, P.:Eugene Onegin (sels)—Polonaise Telarc ▲ CD 80130 [DDD]
Tchaikovsky, P.:Sym 6 Telarc ▲ CD 80130 [DDD]
Varèse, E.:Amériques London ▲ 443172-2
Wagner, R.:Das Rheingold, w. Gabriele Fontana (sop—Woglinde), Nancy Gustafson (sop—Freia), Ildiko Komlosi (mez—Wellgunde), Hanna Schwarz (mez—Fricka), Elena Zaremba (mez—Erda), Margareta Hintermeier (cta—Flosshilde), Kim Begley (ten—Loge), Peter Schreier (ten—Mime), Thomas Sunnegardh (ten—Froh), Robert Hale (bass-bar—Wotan), Walter Fink (bass—Fafner), Franz-Josef Kapellmann (bass—Alberich), Jan-Hendrik Rootering (bass—Fasolt), Eike Wilm Schulte (bass—Donner) *(rec Severance Hall, Cleveland, Ohio, Dec 1993)* London 2-▲ 443690-2
Weber, C.M. von:Invitation to the Dance for Orch London ▲ 430201-2 [DDD]
Webern, A.:Bach Transcription *(rec Oct. 7, 1991)* London ▲ 436153-2 [DDD]
Webern, A.:Im Sommerwind London 2-▲ 436240-2 [DDD]
Webern, A.:Pieces Orch, Op. 6 London 3-▲ 436421-2 [DDD]
Webern, A.:Pieces Orch, Op. 10 London 3-▲ 436421-2 [DDD]
Webern, A.:Sym, Op. 21 London 3-▲ 436421-2 [DDD]
Webern, A.:Vars Orch London 3-▲ 436421-2 [DDD]
O. Knussen (cnd)
Copland, A.:Grohg London ▲ 443203-2 [DDD]
Copland, A.:Hear ye! Hear ye! London ▲ 443203-2 [DDD]
Copland, A.:Prelude London ▲ 443203-2 [DDD]
L. Lane (cnd)
Copland, A.:An Outdoor Ov Sony Classical ("Essential Classics" series) ▲ SBK 62401 ■ SBT 62401
Copland, A.:Rodeo (sels)—3 Dance Episodes
Sony Classical ("Essential Classics" series) ▲ SBK 62401 ■ SBT 62401
Y. Levi (cnd)
The Artistry of Yoel Levi:The Telarc Collection, Vol. 8, w. Atlanta SO
Prokofiev, S.:Romeo & Juliet (sels) Telarc ▲ CD 80089 [DDD]
Sibelius, J.:Finlandia Telarc ▲ CD 80095 [DDD]
Sibelius, J.:Sym 2 Telarc ▲ CD 80095 [DDD]
L. Maazel (cnd)
Beethoven, L. van:Fidelio (ov) Odyssey ■ YT 42484
Beethoven, L. van:Leonore 3 Odyssey ■ YT 42484
Beethoven, L. van:Syms (comp) *(rec 1970s)* CBS 5-▲ M5K 45532
Beethoven, L. van:Sym 1 Odyssey ■ YT 42479
Beethoven, L. van:Sym 6, "Pastorale" Odyssey ■ YT 42483
Beethoven, L. van:Sym 7 Odyssey ■ YT 42484
Beethoven, L. van:Sym 8 Odyssey ■ YT 42479
Beethoven, L. van:Sym 9, "Choral Sym" [G] CBS ▲ MK 38868
Beethoven, L. van:Sym 9, "Choral Sym"—final movt. Odyssey ■ YT 42485
Beethoven, L. van:Wellington's Victory, "Battle Sym" Odyssey ■ YT 42482
Berlioz, H.:Sym fantastique Telarc ▲ CD 80076 [DDD]
Gershwin, G.:An American in Paris London ▲ 417716-2 [ADD]
Gershwin, G.:Cuban Ov London ▲ 417716-2 [ADD]
Gershwin, G.:Cuban Ov London ▲ 436570-2 (m) [ADD]
Gershwin, G.:Rhap in Blue, w. I. Davis (pno) London ▲ 417716-2 [ADD]
Mussorgsky, M.:Night Telarc ▲ CD 80042 [DDD]
Mussorgsky, M.:Pictures at an Exhibition Telarc ▲ CD 80042 [DDD]
Scriabin, A.:Sym 4 London ▲ 417252-2 [ADD]
Shostakovich, D.:Sym 5 *(rec Apr. 5, 1981)* Telarc ▲ CD 82001 [DDD]
Strauss, R.:Don Juan CBS ▲ MDK 44909 [DDD]
Strauss, R.:Till Eulenspiegels lustige Streiche CBS ▲ MDK 44909 [DDD]
Strauss, R.:Tod und Verklärung CBS ▲ MDK 44909 [DDD]
Stravinsky, I.:Le Sacre du printemps for Orch *(rec May 14, 1980)* Telarc ▲ CD 82001 [DDD]
Stravinsky, I.:Le Sacre du printemps for Orch Telarc ▲ CD 80054 [DDD]
Tchaikovsky, P.:Nutcracker Suite Telarc ▲ CD 80068 [DDD]
Tchaikovsky, P.:Romeo & Juliet Telarc ▲ CD 80068 [DDD]
Tchaikovsky, P.:Romeo & Juliet Telarc ▲ CD 82002
Tchaikovsky, P.:Sym 4 CBS ▲ MDK 44784 [DDD]
Tchaikovsky, P.:Sym 4 Telarc ▲ CD 82002
Tchaikovsky, P.:Sym 5 CBS ▲ MDK 44785 [DDD]
Tchaikovsky, P.:Sym 6 CBS ▲ MDK 44786 [DDD]
N. Marriner (cnd)
Schumann, R.:Con Vc, w. L. Harrell (vc) London ("Jubilee" series) ▲ 430743-2 [DDD]
K. Sanderling (cnd)
Shostakovich, D.:Sym 15 Erato ▲ 2292-45815-2 ZK
G. Solti (cnd)
Beethoven, L. van:Cons Pno (comp), w. V. Ashkenazy (pno) London 3-▲ 425582-2 [ADD]
G. Szell (cnd)
Beethoven, L. van:Cons Pno (comp), w. L. Fleisher (pno)
Sony Classical ("Essential Classics" series) 3-▲ SB3K 48397
Beethoven, L. van:Cons Pno (comp), w. L. Fleisher (pno) CBS 3-▲ M3K 42445
Beethoven, L. van:Con 1 Pno, w. L. Fleisher (pno) Odyssey ■ YT 35928
Beethoven, L. van:Con 1 Pno, w. L. Fleisher (pno)
Sony Classical ("Essential Classics" series) ▲ SBK 47658 ■ SBT 47658
Beethoven, L. van:Con 1 Pno, w. Emil Gilels (pno)
EMI Classics ("Doublefforte" series) 2-▲ CDFB 69506
Beethoven, L. van:Con 2 Pno, w. L. Fleisher (pno)
Sony Classical ("Essential Classics" series) ▲ SBK 48165 ■ SBT 48165

Cleveland Orch (cont.)
G. Szell (cnd) (cont.)
Beethoven, L. van:Con 2 Pno, w. L. Fleisher (pno) Odyssey ■ YT 35928
Beethoven, L. van:Con 2 Pno, w. Emil Gilels (pno)
EMI Classics ("Doublefforte" series) 2-▲ CDFB 69506
Beethoven, L. van:Con 3 Pno, w. L. Fleisher (pno)
Sony Classical ("Essential Classics" series) ▲ SBK 47658 ■ SBT 47658
Beethoven, L. van:Con 3 Pno, w. Emil Gilels (pno)
EMI Classics ("Doublefforte" series) 2-▲ CDFB 69506
Beethoven, L. van:Con 4 Pno, w. L. Fleisher (pno) CBS ▲ MYK 37762 [ADD] ■ MYT 37762
Beethoven, L. van:Con 4 Pno, w. L. Fleisher (pno) Odyssey ■ YT 35490
Beethoven, L. van:Con 4 Pno, w. Emil Gilels (pno)
EMI Classics ("Doublefforte" series) 2-▲ CDFB 69506
Beethoven, L. van:Con 4 Pno, w. L. Fleisher (pno)
Sony Classical ("Essential Classics" series) ▲ SBK 48165 ■ SBT 48165
Beethoven, L. van:Con 5 Pno, "Emperor", w. L. Fleisher (pno) Odyssey ■ YT 35491
Beethoven, L. van:Con 5 Pno, "Emperor", w. Emil Gilels (pno)
EMI Classics ("Doublefforte" series) 2-▲ CDFB 69509
Beethoven, L. van:Egmont (ov)
Sony Classical ("Essential Classics" series) ▲ SBK 46532 [ADD] ■ SBT 46532
Beethoven, L. van:Egmont (ov) Sony Classical ("Essential Classics" series) 5-▲ SB5K 48396
Beethoven, L. van:Fidelio (ov) Sony Classical ("Essential Classics" series) 5-▲ SB5K 48396
Beethoven, L. van:Fidelio (ov)
Sony Classical ("Essential Classics" series) ▲ SBK 46533 [ADD] ■ SBT 46533
Beethoven, L. van:König Stephen (ov)
Sony Classical ("Essential Classics" series) ▲ SBK 48158 ■ SBT 48158
Beethoven, L. van:König Stephen (ov) Sony Classical ("Essential Classics" series) 5-▲ SB5K 48396
Beethoven, L. van:Leonore 1 Odyssey ■ YT 42485
Beethoven, L. van:Syms (comp) Sony Classical ("Essential Classics" series) 5-▲ SB5K 48396
Beethoven, L. van:Sym 1
Sony Classical ("Essential Classics" series) ▲ SBK 46532 [ADD] ■ SBT 46532
Beethoven, L. van:Sym 2 CBS ▲ MYK 38469 [ADD] ■ MYT 38469
Beethoven, L. van:Sym 2 Sony Classical ("Essential Classics" series) ▲ SBK 47651 ■ SBT 47651
Beethoven, L. van:Sym 3, "Eroica"
Sony Classical ("Essential Classics" series) ▲ SBK 46328 [ADD] ■ SBT 46328
Beethoven, L. van:Sym 3, "Eroica" CBS ▲ MYK 37222 [ADD] ■ MYT 37222
Beethoven, L. van:Sym 4 Odyssey ■ YT 34600
Beethoven, L. van:Sym 4 Sony Classical ("Essential Classics" series) ▲ SBK 48158 ■ SBT 48158
Beethoven, L. van:Sym 5 Sony Classical ("Essential Classics" series) ▲ SBK 47651 ■ SBT 47651
Beethoven, L. van:Sym 6, "Pastorale"
Sony Classical ("Essential Classics" series) ▲ SBK 46532 [ADD] ■ SBT 46532
Beethoven, L. van:Sym 7 Sony Classical ("Essential Classics" series) ▲ SBK 48158 ■ SBT 48158
Beethoven, L. van:Sym 8 *(rec 1961)* CBS ▲ MYK 37773 [ADD] ■ MYT 37773
Beethoven, L. van:Sym 8
Sony Classical ("Essential Classics" series) ▲ SBK 46328 [ADD] ■ SBT 46328
Beethoven, L. van:Sym 9, "Choral Sym"
Sony Classical ("Essential Classics" series) ▲ SBK 46533 [ADD] ■ SBT 46533
Beethoven, L. van:Sym 9, "Choral Sym" Odyssey ▲ MBK 42532 [ADD] ■ YT 34625
Brahms, J.:Academic Festival Ov
Sony Classical ("Essential Classics" series) ▲ SBK 46330 [ADD] ■ SBT 46330
Brahms, J.:Academic Festival Ov Sony Classical ("Essential Classics" series) 3-▲ SB3K 48398
Brahms, J.:Academic Festival Ov CBS ▲ MYK 37778 [ADD] ■ MYT 37778
Brahms, J.:Academic Festival Ov Odyssey 3-▲ MB3K 45823
Brahms, J.:Con 1 Pno, w. R. Serkin (pno)
Sony Classical ("Essential Classics" series) ▲ SBK 48166 ■ SBT 48166
Brahms, J.:Con 1 Pno, w. R. Serkin (pno) CBS ▲ MYK 37803 [ADD] ■ MYT 37803
Brahms, J.:Con 1 Pno, w. L. Fleisher (pno) Odyssey ■ YT 31273
Brahms, J.:Con 1 Pno, w. R. Serkin (pno) CBS ▲ MK 42261 [ADD]
Brahms, J.:Con 2 Pno, w. R. Serkin (pno) CBS ▲ MYK 37258 [ADD] ■ MYT 37258
Brahms, J.:Con 2 Pno, w. L. Fleisher (pno) Odyssey ■ YT 32222
Brahms, J.:Con 2 Pno, w. R. Serkin (pno) *(rec Jan. 21-22, 1966)*
Sony Classical ▲ SBK 53262 ■ SBT 53262
Brahms, J.:Con 2 Pno, w. R. Serkin (pno) CBS ▲ MK 42262 [ADD]
Brahms, J.:Con Vn & Vc, "Double Con", w. D. Oistrakh (vn), M. Rostropovich (vc)
EMI Classics ▲ CDM 64744
Brahms, J.:Ein Deutsches Requiem, w. *(chorus unknown)* Melodram ▲ CDM 17503
Brahms, J.:Hungarian Dances Orch—Nos. 17-21
Sony Classical ("Essential Classics" series) 3-▲ SB3K 48398
Brahms, J.:Syms (comp) Odyssey 3-▲ MB3K 45823
Brahms, J.:Syms (comp) Sony Classical ("Essential Classics" series) 3-▲ SB3K 48398
Brahms, J.:Sym 1 Sony Classical ("Essential Classics" series) ▲ SBK 46534 [ADD] ■ SBT 46534
Brahms, J.:Sym 1 CBS ▲ MYK 37775 [ADD] ■ MYT 37775
Brahms, J.:Sym 2 Sony Classical ("Essential Classics" series) ▲ SBK 47652 ■ SBT 47652
Brahms, J.:Sym 2 CBS ▲ MYK 37776 [ADD] ■ MYT 37776
Brahms, J.:Sym 3 Sony Classical ("Essential Classics" series) ▲ SBK 47652 ■ SBT 47652
Brahms, J.:Sym 3 CBS ▲ MYK 37777 [ADD] ■ MYT 37777
Brahms, J.:Sym 4 Sony Classical ("Essential Classics" series) ▲ SBK 46330 [ADD] ■ SBT 46330
Brahms, J.:Sym 4 CBS ▲ MYK 37778 [ADD] ■ MYT 37778
Brahms, J.:Tragic Ov Odyssey 3-▲ MB3K 45823
Brahms, J.:Tragic Ov Sony Classical ("Essential Classics" series) ▲ SBK 46330 [ADD] ■ SBT 46330
Brahms, J.:Tragic Ov CBS ▲ MYK 37776 [ADD] ■ MYT 37776
Brahms, J.:Tragic Ov Sony Classical ("Essential Classics" series) 3-▲ SB3K 48398
Brahms, J.:Vars on a Theme by Haydn CBS ▲ MYK 37777 [ADD] ■ MYT 37777
Brahms, J.:Vars on a Theme by Haydn Sony Classical ("Essential Classics" series) 3-▲ SB3K 48398
Brahms, J.:Vars on a Theme by Haydn Odyssey 3-▲ MB3K 45823
Bruckner, A.:Sym 3, "Wagner" *(rec Jan. 28-29, 1966)*
Sony Classical ("Essential Classics") 2-▲ SB2K 53519 [ADD]
Bruckner, A.:Sym 8 *(rec Jan. 28-29, 1966)*
Sony Classical ("Essential Classics") 2-▲ SB2K 53519 [ADD]
The Cleveland Orchestra CBS Masterworks ▲ MDK 46286 [AAD] ■ MGT 46286
Dvořák, A.:Carnival CBS ▲ MYK 36716 ■ MYT 36716
Dvořák, A.:Carnival CBS ▲ MK 42417 [ADD]
Dvořák, A.:Slavonic Dances (comp) Sony Classical (Essential Classics) ▲ SBK 48161 ■ SBT 48161
Dvořák, A.:Slavonic Dances (comp)—Op. 46 Odyssey ■ YT 34626
Dvořák, A.:Slavonic Dances (sels)—Op. 46, Nos. 1 & 3; Op. 72, Nos. 2 & 7
CBS ▲ MYK 36716 ■ MYT 36716
Dvořák, A.:Slavonic Dances (sels)—Nos. 1 & 8 *(rec 1962 & 1964)* CBS ▲ MK 42417 [ADD]
Dvořák, A.:Slavonic Dances (sels)—Opp. 46/3 & 72/2
EMI Classics ("Doublefforte" series) 2-▲ CDFB 69509
Dvořák, A.:Sym 8 CBS ▲ MYK 38470 [ADD] ■ MYT 38470
Dvořák, A.:Sym 8 EMI Classics ("Doublefforte" series) 2-▲ CDFB 69509
Dvořák, A.:Sym 9, "From the New World" *(rec 1959)* CBS ▲ MK 42417 [ADD]
Franck, C.:Symphonic Vars, w. L. Fleisher (pno) *(rec 1956)*
CBS ▲ MYK 37812 (m) [ADD] ■ MYT 37812 (m)
Grieg, E.:Peer Gynt Suite 1 CBS ▲ MLK 39435 [ADD] ■ MT 39435
Haydn, J.:Sym 92, "Oxford"
Sony Classical ("Essential Classics" series) ▲ SBK 46332 [ADD] ■ SBT 46332
Haydn, J.:Syms 93-98 Odyssey 2-▲ MB2K 45673
Haydn, J.:Sym 93 CBS ▲ MYK 37761 [ADD] ■ MYT 37761
Haydn, J.:Sym 94, "Surprise Sym" CBS ▲ MYK 37761 [ADD] ■ MYT 37761

ORCH. & ENS.

Cleveland Orch (cont.)
G. Szell (cnd) (cont.)
Haydn, J.:Sym 94, "Surprise Sym" Sony Classical ("Essential Classics" series) ▲ SBK 46332 [ADD] ■ SBT 46332
Haydn, J.:Sym 96, "Miracle" Sony Classical ("Essential Classics" series) ▲ SBK 46332 [ADD] ■ SBT 46332
Hindemith, P.:Symphonic Metamorphosis on Themes of Carl Maria von Weber *(rec Oct. 10, 1964)* Sony Classical ▲ SBK 53258 ■ SBT 53258
Janácek, L.:Sinfonietta *(rec Cleveland, OH, Oct 15, 1965)* Sony Classical ("Essential Classics" series) ▲ SBK 62404 ■ SBT 62404
Kodály, Z.:Háry János (suite) Sony Classical ("Essential Classics" series) ▲ SBK 48162 ■ SBT 48162
Kodály, Z.:Háry János (suite) *(rec 1969)* CBS ▲ MYK 38527 [AAD] ■ MYT 38527
Mahler, G.:Sym 4, w. J. Raskin (sop) [G] CBS ▲ MYK 37225 [ADD] ■ MYT 37225
Mahler, G.:Sym 4, w. J. Raskin (sop) [G] CBS ▲ MK 42416 [ADD]
Mahler, G.:Sym 4, w. J. Raskin (sop) Sony Classical ("Essential Classics" series) ▲ SBK 46535 [ADD] ■ SBT 46535
Mahler, G.:Sym 6 Sony Classical ("Essential Classics" series) ▲ SBK 47654 ■ SBT 47654
Mahler, G.:Sym 10 *(rec Nov. 1, 1958)* Sony Classical ▲ SBK 53259 ■ SBT 53259
Mendelssohn, F.:Die Hebriden Sony Classical ("Essential Classics" series) ▲ SBK 46536 [ADD] ■ SBT 46536
Mendelssohn, F.:A Midsummer Night's Dream (sels) CBS ▲ MYK 37760 ■ MYT 37760
Mendelssohn, F.:A Midsummer Night's Dream (sels)—Overture, Scherzo, Nocturne, Intermezzo, Wedding March *(rec 1967)* Sony Classical ("Essential Classics" series) ▲ SBK 48264 [ADD] ■ SBT 48264
Mendelssohn, F.:Sym 3 Sony Classical ("Essential Classics" series) ▲ SBK 46536 [ADD] ■ SBT 46536
Mendelssohn, F.:Sym 4 CBS ▲ MYK 37760 ■ MYT 37760
Mendelssohn, F.:Sym 4 Sony Classical ("Essential Classics" series) ▲ SBK 46536 [ADD] ■ SBT 46536
Mozart, W.A.:Adagio Vn, K.261, w. Isaac Stern (vn) Sony Classical 3–▲ SM3K 66475
Mozart, W.A.:Con Cl, w. Robert Marcellus (cl) *(rec Cleveland, OH, Oct 21, 1961)* Sony Classical ("Essential Classics" series) ▲ SBK 62424 [ADD] ■ SBT 62424
Mozart, W.A.:Con Cl, w. Robert Marcellus (cl) *(rec 1961)* CBS ▲ MYK 37810 [AAD] ■ MYT 37810
Mozart, W.A.:Con 21 Pno, w. R. Casadesus (pno) CBS ▲ MYK 38523 [AAD] ■ MYT 38523
Mozart, W.A.:Con 21 Pno, w. R. Casadesus (pno) Sony Classical 3–▲ SM3K 46519
Mozart, W.A.:Con 24 Pno, w. R. Casadesus (pno) CBS ▲ MYK 38523 [AAD] ■ MYT 38523
Mozart, W.A.:Con 24 Pno, w. R. Casadesus (pno) Sony Classical 3–▲ SM3K 46519
Mozart, W.A.:Con 25 Pno, w. Leon Fleisher (pno) CBS 3–▲ M3K 42445
Mozart, W.A.:Con 25 Pno, w. Leon Fleisher (pno) CBS ▲ MYK 37762 [ADD] ■ MYT 37762
Mozart, W.A.:Cons Vn, w. Isaac Stern (vn)—Nos. 1-5 Sony Classical 3–▲ SM3K 66475
Mozart, W.A.:Exsultate, w. Judith Raskin (sop) [L] *(rec 1964)* CBS ▲ MK 42416 [ADD]
Mozart, W.A.:Kleine Nachtmusik CBS ▲ MK 42418 [ADD]
Mozart, W.A.:Kleine Nachtmusik *(rec 1968)* Sony Classical ("Essential Classics" series) ▲ SBK 48266 [ADD] ■ SBT 48266
Mozart, W.A.:Music of, w. P. Entremont (pno), *(sels unknown)* CBS ▲ MLK 39436 ■ MT 39436
Mozart, W.A.:Rondo Vn, K.373, w. Isaac Stern (vn) Sony Classical 3–▲ SM3K 66475
Mozart, W.A.:Serenade Ww, K.320 *(rec 1969)* Sony Classical ("Essential Classics" series) ▲ SBK 48266 [ADD] ■ SBT 48266
Mozart, W.A.:Sinf concertante Vn, K.364, w. Isaac Stern (vn) Sony Classical 3–▲ SM3K 66475
Mozart, W.A.:Sinf concertante Vn, K.364, w. R. Druian (vn), A. Skernick (va) *(rec 1963)* CBS ▲ MYK 37810 [AAD] ■ MYT 37810
Mozart, W.A.:Sym 35 Sony Classical ("Essential Classics" series) ▲ SBK 46333 [ADD] ■ SBT 46333
Mozart, W.A.:Sym 35 CBS ▲ MYK 38472 [ADD] ■ MYT 38472
Mozart, W.A.:Sym 39 CBS ▲ MYK 38472 [ADD] ■ MYT 38472
Mozart, W.A.:Sym 40 CBS ▲ MK 42418 [ADD]
Mozart, W.A.:Sym 40 Sony Classical ("Essential Classics" series) ▲ SBK 46333 [ADD] ■ SBT 46333
Mozart, W.A.:Sym 40 CBS ▲ MYK 37220 ■ MYT 37220
Mozart, W.A.:Sym 41 CBS ▲ MYK 37220 ■ MYT 37220
Mozart, W.A.:Sym 41 CBS ▲ MK 42418 [ADD]
Mozart, W.A.:Sym 41 Sony Classical ("Essential Classics" series) ▲ SBK 46333 [ADD] ■ SBT 46333
Mussorgsky, M.:Pictures at an Exhibition Sony Classical ("Essential Classics" series) ▲ SBK 48162 ■ SBT 48162
Prokofiev, S.:Con 1 Pno, w. G. Graffman (pno) CBS ▲ MYK 37806 [ADD] ■ MYT 37806
Prokofiev, S.:Con 3 Pno, w. G. Graffman (pno) CBS ▲ MYK 37806 [ADD] ■ MYT 37806
Prokofiev, S.:Lt Kijé Suite CBS ▲ MYK 38527 [AAD] ■ MYT 38527
Prokofiev, S.:Lt Kijé Suite Sony Classical ("Essential Classics" series) ▲ SBK 48162 ■ SBT 48162
Rachmaninoff, S.:Rhapsody on a Theme of Paganini, w. Leon Fleisher (pno) *(rec 1956)* CBS ▲ MYK 37812 (m) [ADD]
Schubert, Franz:Sym 8 *(rec 1960)* Sony Classical ("Essential Classics" series) ▲ SBK 48268 [ADD] ■ SBT 48268
Schubert, Franz:Sym 9 Odyssey ▲ YT 30669
Schubert, Franz:Sym 9 *(rec 1957)* Sony Classical ("Essential Classics" series) ▲ SBK 48268 [ADD] ■ SBT 48268
Schumann, R.:Con Pno, w. L. Fleisher (pno) Odyssey ▲ YT 30668
Schumann, R.:Manfred Ov *(rec Jan 21, 1959)* Sony Classical ("Masterworks Heritage" series) 2–▲ MH2K 62349 [ADD]
Schumann, R.:Syms (comp) *(rec 1958–1960)* Sony Classical ("Masterworks Heritage" series) 2–▲ MH2K 62349 [ADD]
Schumann, R.:Sym 1 CBS ▲ MYK 38468 [AAD] ■ MYT 38468
Schumann, R.:Sym 4 CBS ▲ MYK 38468 [AAD] ■ MYT 38468
Smetana, B.:The Bartered Bride (dances)—3 Dances—Polka, Furiant & Dance of the Comedians *(rec 1963)* Sony Classical ("Essential Classics" series) ▲ SBK 48279 [ADD] ■ SBT 48279
Smetana, B.:The Bartered Bride (dances) CBS ▲ MYK 36716 ■ MYT 36716
Smetana, B.:The Moldau *(rec 1963)* Sony Classical ("Essential Classics" series) ▲ SBK 48264 [ADD] ■ SBT 48264
Smetana, B.:The Moldau CBS ▲ MYK 36716 ■ MYT 36716
Smetana, B.:The Moldau *(rec 1963)* CBS ▲ MK 42417 [ADD]
Strauss (II), Joh.:Music of Odyssey ▲ YT 30053
Strauss, Josef:Music of—waltzes CBS 2–■ MGT 35918
Strauss, R.:Don Juan *(rec 1957)* Sony Classical ("Essential Classics" series) ▲ SBK 48272 [ADD] ■ SBT 48272
Strauss, R.:Don Juan CBS ▲ MYK 36721 ■ MYT 36721
Strauss, R.:Symphonia domestica *(rec Jan. 10, 1964)* Sony Classical ("Essential Classics" series) ▲ SBK 53511 [ADD] ■ SBT 53511
Strauss, R.:Till Eulenspiegels lustige Streiche CBS ▲ MYK 36721 ■ MYT 36721
Strauss, R.:Till Eulenspiegels lustige Streiche *(rec 1957)* Sony Classical ("Essential Classics" series) ▲ SBK 48272 [ADD] ■ SBT 48272
Strauss, R.:Tod und Verklärung *(rec Mar. 29–30, 1957)* Sony Classical ("Essential Classics" series) ▲ SBK 53511 [ADD] ■ SBT 53511
Stravinsky, I.:The Firebird Suite Sony Classical (Essential Classics) ▲ SBK 47664 ■ SBT 47664
Stravinsky, I.:Pétrouchka (suite) Sony Classical (Essential Classics) ▲ SBK 47664 ■ SBT 47664
Tchaikovsky, P.:Con 1 Pno, w. G. Graffman (pno) CBS ▲ MYK 37263 [ADD] ■ MYT 37263
Wagner, R.:Eine Faust-Ov Sony Classical ("Essential Classics" series) ▲ SBK 62403 ■ SBT 62403
Wagner, R.:Der fliegende Holländer (ov) Sony Classical ("Essential Classics" series) ▲ SBK 62403 ■ SBT 62403
Wagner, R.:Götterdämmerung (rhine journey & funeral) CBS ▲ MYK 36715 ■ MYT 36715
Wagner, R.:Lohengrin (preludes), w. E. Ormandy (cnd), Philadelphia Orch—Acts 1 & 3 Sony Classical ("Essential Classics" series) ▲ SBK 62403 ■ SBT 62403
Wagner, R.:Die Meistersinger von Nürnberg (prelude/act 1) CBS ▲ MLK 39438 ■ MT 39438
Wagner, R.:Ovs, Preludes & Orch Sels—Fliegende Holländer, Meistersinger, Tannhäuser CBS ▲ MYK 38486 [ADD] ■ MYT 38486

Cleveland Orch (cont.)
G. Szell (cnd) (cont.)
Wagner, R.:Rienzi, der Letzte der Tribunen (ov) Sony Classical ("Essential Classics" series) ▲ SBK 62403 ■ SBT 62403
Wagner, R.:Der Ring des Nibelungen (orch sels) CBS ▲ MYK 36715 ■ MYT 36715
Wagner, R.:Tannhäuser (ov) CBS ▲ MYK 38486 ■ MYT 38486
Wagner, R.:Tristan und Isolde (prelude & liebestod) CBS ▲ MYK 38486 [ADD] ■ MYT 38486
Wagner, R.:Die Walküre (magic fire) CBS ▲ MYK 36715 ■ MYT 36715
Wagner, R.:Die Walküre (ride of the valkyries) CBS ▲ MYK 36715 ■ MYT 36715
M. Tilson Thomas (cnd)
Orff, C.:Carmina burana, w. J. Blegen (sop), K. Riegel (ten), P. Binder (bar), Cleveland Orch Chorus [G, L] CBS ▲ MK 33172 [ADD]
Cleveland Orch String Quartet [D. Majeske (vn), B. Goldschmidt (vn), R. Vernon (va), S. Geber (vc)]
Brahms, J.:Qnt Pno, w. V. Ashkenazy (pno) London ▲ 425839–2 [DDD]
Chausson, E.:Con Vn, Pno & Str Qt, w. L. Maazel (vn), I. Margalit (pno) *(rec 1979)* Telarc ▲ CD 80046 [DDD]

Cleveland Sinfonietta
L. Lane (cnd)
Vaughan Williams, R.:The Lark Ascending, w. Rafael Druian (vn) Sony Classical ("Essential Classics" series) ▲ SBK 62645 ■ SBT 62645
Cleveland String Quartet [William Preucil (vn), Peter Salaff (vn), James Dunham (va), Paul Katz (vc)]
Adler, S.:Qt 7 Strs CRI ▲ CD 608 [DDD]
Beethoven, L. van:Grosse Fuge Str Qt *(rec Worcester, MA, 1995)* Telarc ▲ CD 80422 [DDD]
Beethoven, L. van:Qt 1 Strs *(rec Mechanics Hall, Worcester, MA, Sept. 23–24, 1993)* Telarc ▲ CD 80382 [DDD]
Beethoven, L. van:Qt 2 Strs *(rec Mechanics Hall, Worcester, MA, Sept. 23–24, 1993)* Telarc ▲ CD 80382 [DDD]
Beethoven, L. van:Qt 3 Strs *(rec Mechanics Hall, Worcester, MA, Sept. 23–24, 1993)* Telarc ▲ CD 80382 [DDD]
Beethoven, L. van:Qt 4 Strs *(rec Mechanics Hall, Worcester, MA, May 17–20, 1993)* Telarc ▲ CD 80414 [DDD]
Beethoven, L. van:Qt 5 Strs *(rec Mechanics Hall, Worcester, MA, May 5 & 8, 1994)* Telarc ▲ CD 80414 [DDD]
Beethoven, L. van:Qt 6 Strs *(rec July 25–30, 1991)* Telarc ▲ CD 80229 [DDD]
Beethoven, L. van:Qt 7 Strs *(rec May 12–16, 1992)* Telarc ▲ CD 80229 [DDD]
Beethoven, L. van:Qt 8 Strs *(rec July 25–30, 1991 & May 12)* Telarc ▲ CD 80268 [DDD]
Beethoven, L. van:Qt 9 Strs *(rec July 25–30, 1991 & May 12)* Telarc ▲ CD 80268 [DDD]
Beethoven, L. van:Qt 10 Strs, "Harp" *(rec Sept. 28– Oct. 3, 1992)* Telarc ▲ CD 80351 [DDD]
Beethoven, L. van:Qt 11 Strs, "Quartetto serioso" *(rec July 25–30, 1991)* Telarc ▲ CD 80351 [DDD]
Beethoven, L. van:Qt 13 Strs *(rec Worcester, MA, 1995)* Telarc ▲ CD 80422 [DDD]
Borodin, A.:Qt 2 Strs Telarc ▲ CD 80178 [DDD]
Brahms, J.:Qt 1 Strs *(rec Sept. 20–24, 1993)* Telarc ▲ CD 80346 [DDD]
Brahms, J.:Qt 2 Strs *(rec Sept. 20–24, 1993)* Telarc ▲ CD 80346 [DDD]
Corigliano, J.:Qt Strs *(rec Mechanics Hall, Worcester, MA; Dec 11–15, 1995)* Telarc ▲ CD–80415 [DDD]
Debussy, C.:Qt Strs Telarc ▲ CD 80111 [DDD]
Dvořák, A.:Qt 12 Strs, "America" Telarc ▲ CD 80283 [DDD]
Dvořák, A.:Qt 14 Strs Telarc ▲ CD 80283 [DDD]
Haydn, J.:Qts Strs, Op. 76, "Erdődy Qts"—No. 5 only *(rec Mechanics Hall, Worcester, MA; Dec 11–15, 1995)* Telarc ▲ CD–80415 [DDD]
Mendelssohn, F.:Octet Strs, Meliora String Quartet Telarc ▲ CD 80142 [DDD]
Mendelssohn, F.:Qt 2 Strs Telarc ▲ CD 80142 [DDD]
Mozart, W.A.:Qt 14 Strs Telarc ▲ CD 80297 [DDD]
Mozart, W.A.:Qt 15 Strs Telarc ▲ CD 80297 [DDD]
Ravel, M.:Qt Strs Telarc ▲ CD 80111 [DDD]
Schubert, Franz:Qt 13 Strs Telarc ▲ CD 80225 [DDD]
Schubert, Franz:Qnt Pno, D.667, w. A. Brendel (pno) Philips ▲ 400078–2 [ADD]
Schubert, Franz:Qnt Strs, D.956, w. Yo Yo Ma (vc) CBS ▲ MK 39134 [DDD] ■ IMT 39134
Schumann, R.:Qt Pno, Op. 47, w. E. Ax (pno) RCA Red Seal ▲ 6498–2–RC [DDD]
Schumann, R.:Qnt Pno, w. E. Ax (pno) RCA Red Seal ▲ 6498–2–RC [DDD]
Smetana, B.:Qt 1 Strs Telarc ▲ CD 80178 [DDD]
Cleveland String Quartet members
Schubert, Franz:Qnt Pno, D.667, w. J. O'Conor (pno), J. VanDemark (db) Telarc ▲ CD 80225 [DDD]
Cleveland Sym Winds
F. Fennell (cnd)
Arnaud, L.:Fanfares (3) Telarc ▲ CD 80099 [DDD]
Bach, J.S.:Fant Org, BWV 572—Gravement section Telarc ▲ CD 80038 [DDD]
Grainger, P.:Lincolnshire Posy Telarc ▲ CD 80099 [DDD]
Handel, G.F.:Royal Fireworks Music Telarc ▲ CD 80038 [DDD]
Holst, G.:Suites for Band Telarc ▲ CD 80038 [DDD]
Stars & Stripes Telarc ▲ CD 80099 [DDD]
Vaughan Williams, R.:English Folk Song Suite Telarc ▲ CD 80099 [DDD]
Closane Trio
Lund, E.:Concensus Fences *(rec live 1992)* Opus One ▲ CD 164
Cluj–Napoca Collegium Musicum Academicum Ensemble
Boismortier, J.B. de:Sons, Op. 34—No. 1 *(rec 6/81)* Electrecord ▲ ELCD 127 [AAD]
Couperin, F.:Concerts royaux (4) *(rec 6/81)* Electrecord ▲ ELCD 127 [AAD]
Quentin, J.–B.:Son Fl, Vn & Vl in e *(rec 1981)* Electrecord ▲ ELCD 127 [AAD]
Cluj–Napoca G. Dima Conservatory Percussion Ensemble
Terényi, E.:Swing Suite Electrecord ▲ ELCD 124 [AAD]
Terényi, E.:Vivaldiana, w. G. Costea, E. Botár, C. Mandeal, Cluj–Napoca CO *(Vivaldiana)*, Costea, et al. *(Gallant Dances)*, P. Szeles, G. Dudea, Tîrgu Mures Phil. CO *(Baroque Rhap.)*, "G. Dima" Conservatory Percussion Ensemble of Cluj–Napoca *(Swing Suite)* Electrecord ▲ ELCD 124 [AAD]
Cluj–Napoca PO
I. Baciu (cnd)
Enescu, G.:Sym 3, w. Cluj–Napoca Phil Chorus Marco Polo ▲ 8.223143
M. Cristescu (cnd)
Dittersdorf, K.D. von:Con Fl, w. G. Costea (fl) Olympia (Explorer) ▲ OCD 405 [AAD]
C. Mandeal (cnd)
Haydn, J.:Con for 2 Hns, w. Vasile Oprea (hn), Daian Lung (hn) Electrecord ▲ ELCD 107 [AAD]
Schumann, R.:Konzertstück Hns, w. V. Oprea (hn), D. Lung (hn), A. Marc (hn), T. Tulbure (hn) Electrecord ▲ ELCD 107 [AAD]
E. Simon (cnd)
Romanian Rhapsody, w. C. Litvin (cnd), Romanian RSO, Eliodor Rau (cnd), Arad PO Olympia ("Explorer" series) ▲ OCD 408 [AAD]
Taranu, C.:Sym 2 Olympia ▲ OCD 416 [AAD]
Cluj–Napoca PO members
I. Baciu (cnd)
Enescu, G.:Chamber Sym Marco Polo ▲ 8.223143
Cluster Ensemble
Cluster Ensemble Ondine ▲ ODE 808 [DDD]
Coffee Club Orch
Shakin' the Blues away Angel ▲ CDQ 54390
Cohen Piano Trio [Anthya Rael (pno), Raymond Cohen (vn), Robert Cohen (vc)]
Dvořák, A.:Trios Pno, Opp. 21, 26, 65, 90 *(rec Rosslyn Hill Chapel, London, Apr 15, 17, 27 & 29, 1980)* CRD 2–▲ CRD 3386/87 [ADD]

126 ▲ = CD ♦ = Enhanced CD Δ = MD ■ = Cassette Tape ▯ = DCC

Cohen Piano Trio members [Raymond Cohen (vn), Anthya Rael (pno)]
Dvořák, A.:Romantic Pieces, Op. 75 *(rec Rosslyn Hill Chapel, London, Apr 15, 17, 27 & 29, 1980)* CRD 2-▲ CRD 3386/87 [ADD]

Colburn CO
R. Rintoul (cnd)
Elgar, E.:Intro & Allegro Ambassador ▲ ARC 1009 [DDD]
Sibelius, J.:Rakastava Strs Ambassador ▲ ARC 1009 [DDD]
Strauss, R.:Metamorphosen Ambassador ▲ ARC 1009 [DDD]

Coldstream Guards Regimental Band
Holst, G.:Suites for Band Bandleader ▲ BNA 5002 [DDD]
Music from the 1994 Royal Tournament, w. Grenadier Guards Band, Irish Guards Band, Life Guards Band, Welsh Guards Band, et al. Bandleader ▲ BND 5094 [DDD]
Vaughan Williams, R.:English Folk Song Suite Bandleader ▲ BNA 5002 [DDD]
Vaughan Williams, R.:Toccata marziale Bandleader ▲ BNA 5002 [DDD]
L. Johnson (cnd)
Johnson, Laurie:Music of, w. W. Davies (org), London PO, London Jazz Orch, London Studio SO, Fanfare Trumpeters of the Scots Guards, London Brass Chorale—Royal Tour (suite); Symphony (Synthesis) for Combined Jazz & Symphony Orchestras (1969); Three Paintings by Lautrec; The Wind in the Willows (1985) *(rec 1969–82)* Unicorn-Kanchana ▲ UKCD 2057 [DDD/ADD]
R.G. Swift (cnd)
Marches, Vol. 1 Denon ▲ CO 73806 [DDD]
Marches, Vol. 2:Music of America & Continental Europe Denon ▲ CO 73807 [DDD]
National Anthems, Vol. 1 Denon ▲ CO 74500 [DDD]
National Anthems, Vol. 2 Denon ▲ CO 74501 [DDD]

Collage New Music Ensemble
Gruenberg, L.:Diversions, Op. 32 GM ▲ GM 2015CD
Lazarof, H.:Divert Cl, w. F. Epstein (perc) Delos ▲ DE 3124 [DDD]
McLennan, J.S.:Essay GM ▲ GM 2019 CD
F. Epstein (cnd)
Lazarof, H.:Necompe *(rec Seiji Ozawa Hall, Tanglewood, Lenox, MA, July 10, 1994)* Laurel ▲ LR 856 [DDD]
C. Fussell (cnd)
Bazelon, I.:Legends & Love Letters, w. J. Heller (sop), F. Epstein (perc), C. Oldfather (pno), R. Annis (cl), J. Scolnik (fl), J. Moerchel (vc) Albany ▲ TROY 054 [DDD]
J. Harbison (cnd)
Harbison, J.:Samuel Chapter, w. Larson (sop) [E] Elektra/Nonesuch ▲ 79129-2 [DDD]
D. Hoose (cnd)
Child, P.:Clare Cycle, w. J. Heller (sop) [E] CRI ▲ CD 605 [DDD]
F. Lerdahl (cnd)
Lerdahl, F.:Eros, w. B. Morgan (mez) [E] CRI ▲ CD 580 [ADD/DDD]
G. Schuller (cnd)
Geller, T.:Where Silence Reigns, w. S. Sylvan (bar) GM ▲ GM2032CD
Gruenberg, L.:The Creation, w. W. Brown (ten) [E] GM ▲ GM 2015CD

Collage New Music Ensemble [J. Smirnoff (vn/va), J. Moerschel (vc), S. Drury (pno)]
Grainger, P.:Chamber Music—Handel in the Strand (1912); Harvest Hymn (1932); Lord Peter's Stable-Boy (1927); My Robin is to the Greenwood Gone; Colonial Song (1911) *(all for trio)*; Scandinavian Suite (1902); The Maiden & the Frog (1925); Youthful Rapture (1901) *(all for cello & piano)*; Mock Morris (1914); The Sussex Mummers' Christmas Carol (1911); Molly on the Shore (1907) *(all for violin & piano)*; Arrival Platform Humlet (1912) *(for viola)* Northeastern ("Classical Arts" series) ▲ NR 228-CD

Collage New Music Ensemble [Randolph Bowman (fl), Robert Annis (cl), Ronan Lefkowitz (vn), Joel Moerschel (vc), Christopher Oldfather (pno), Frank Epstein (perc)]
G. Schuller (cnd)
Imbrie, A.W.:Pilgrimage GM ▲ GM 2019 CD

Collegiate Orch
R. Bass (cnd)
Strauss, R.:Friedenstag, w. A. Marc (sop), R. Roloff (bass), Collegiate Chorale [G] *(rec in concert at Carnegie Hall, 11/19/89)* Koch International Classics ▲ KIC 7111-2 [DDD]

Collegio Vocale e Strumentale Euterpe
Willaert, A.:Madrigals—Le vecchie per invidie sono pazze; Madonn'io non lo so; Un giorno mi prego, una vedovella; O bene mio; Cingari simo; Se pur ti guardo; Occhio non fu giamai; Zola zentil; Sempre mi ride sta donna; Quando di rosed'oro; A quando quand'havea; O dolce vita mia; Madonna mia famme bon'offerta; Sospiri miei; E se per gelosia; Vecchie letrose Stradivarius ▲ STR 33311 [DDD]
Willaert, A.:Ricercars—Ricercare I; Ricecare X; Ricecare a tre voci Stradivarius ▲ STR 33311 [DDD]

Collegium Academicum Orch
R. Dunand (cnd)
Mozart, W.A.:Arias, w. Gabriel Bacquier (b-bar)—Der Schausspieldirektor; Airs de concert italiens pour basse; Grand airs d'opéras Gallo ▲ CD 816

Collegium Academicum Soloists
E. Widmer (cnd)
Widmer, E.:Caititi-Lua Nova, w. S. Stenhammar (sop) *(rec May 23, 1980)* Grammont ▲ CTSP 32-2 [ADD]

Collegium Aureum
Bach, C.P.E.:Con doppio, w. G. Leonhardt (hpd), A. Curtis (hpd) Editio Classica ▲ 77061-2 [ADD]
Bach, C.P.E.:Con Hpd & Strs, H.427, w. G. Leonhardt (hpd) Editio Classica ▲ 77061-2 [ADD]
Bach, C.P.E.:Con Ob, H.468, w. H. Hücke (ob) Editio Classica ▲ 77061-2-RG [ADD]
Bach, C.P.E.:Magnificat, w. Elly Ameling (sop)—Quia Respexit Deutsche Harmonia Mundi ▲ 74321-26613-2
Bach, J.S.:Cant 202, "Wedding Cant", w. E. Ameling (sop) Editio Classica 2-▲ 77151-2-RG [ADD]
Bach, J.S.:Cant 209, w. E. Ameling (sop) Editio Classica 2-▲ 77151-2-RG [ADD]
Bach, J.S.:Cant 211, "Coffee Cant", w. E. Ameling (sop), G. English (ten), S. Nimsgern (b-bar) Editio Classica 2-▲ 77151-2-RG [ADD]
Bach, J.S.:Cant 212, "Peasant Cant", w. E. Ameling (sop), G. English (ten), S. Nimsgern (b-bar) Editio Classica 2-▲ 77151-2-RG [ADD]
A Baroque Christmas RCA Gold Seal ▲ 09026-61882-2
Beethoven, L. van:Con 4 Pno, w. P. Badura-Skoda (pno) Editio Classica ▲ 77063-2-RG [ADD]
Beethoven, L. van:Con Vn, Vc & Pno, "Triple Con", w. F. Maier (vn), A. Bylsma (vc), P. Badura-Skoda (pno) Editio Classica ▲ 77063-2-RG [ADD]
Greatest Hits of 1750, w. Leonhardt Ensemble, La Petite Bande, et al. Pro Arte ▲ CDM 817
Mozart, W.A.:Con Cl, w. *(soloist unknown)* [period instrs] RCA Victrola ▲ 77509-2-RV [ADD] ■ 77509-4-RV
Mozart, W.A.:Con Ob, K.314, w. *(soloist unknown)* [period instrs] RCA Victrola ▲ 77509-2-RV [ADD] ■ 77509-4-RV
Mozart, W.A.:Qts Fl [period instrs] RCA Victrola ▲ 77517-2 [ADD] ■ 77517-4
Mozart, W.A.:Qt Ob, K.370 [period instrs] RCA Victrola ▲ 77513-2 [ADD] ■ 77513-4
Mozart, W.A.:Qnt Cl, K.581 [period instrs] RCA Victrola ▲ 77513-2 [ADD] ■ 77513-4
Mozart, W.A.:Qnt Hn, K.407 [period instrs] RCA Victrola ▲ 77513-2 [ADD] ■ 77513-4
Mozart, W.A.:Sym 40 [period instrs] RCA Victrola ▲ 77533-2 [ADD] ■ 77533-4
Mozart, W.A.:Sym 41 [period instrs] RCA Victrola ▲ 77533-2 [ADD] ■ 77533-4
Pachelbel, J.:Canon Pro Arte ▲ CDD 215
Pergolesi, G.B.:La serva padrona, w. M. Bonifaccio (sop), S. Nimsgern (b-bar) [I] Deutsche Harmonia Mundi ▲ 77184-2-RC [DDD]
Telemann, G.P.:Con Tpt Strs in D Pro Arte ▲ CDD 215
H. Dechant (cnd)
Gassmann, F.L.:La Contessina, w. Susanne Ganglberger (sop—Vespina), Elisabeth Mayer (sop—Contessina), Barbara Eisschiel (mez—Lindoro), Hermann Diller (ten—Gazzetta), Kurt Köller (bar—Pancrazio), Joseph Pichler (Graf Baccellone) Bayer 2-▲ BR 100 252/3 [DDD]

Collegium Aureum (cont.)
H. Hennig (cnd)
Monteverdi, C.:Vespro della Beata Vergine, w. Pro Cantione Antiqua, Musica Fiata, Hanover Boys' Choir Ars Musici 2-▲ 1000 [AAD]
R. Kammler (cnd)
Mozart, W.A.:Missae Breves, w. Augsburg Cathedral Boys' Choir—in G, K.49; in d, K.65; in F, K.192; in D, K.194; in C, K.220; in B♭, K.275; in C, K.258; in C, K.259 [L] Deutsche Harmonia Mundi 2-▲ 77090-2-RC [DDD]
F. Maier (cnd)
Authentic Baroque ("Pachelbel Kanon & Other Baroque Hits") Pro Arte ▲ CDD 215
Bach, J.S.:Cant 202, "Wedding Cant", w. Elly Ameling (sop) Deutsche Harmonia Mundi ▲ 74321-26614-2
Bach, J.S.:Cant 211, "Coffee Cant", w. Elly Ameling (sop)—Ei, wie schmeckt der Coffee susse Heute noch, heute noch Deutsche Harmonia Mundi ▲ 74321-26614-2
Bach, J.S.:Cant 212, "Peasant Cant", w. Elly Ameling (sop)—Klein Zschocher Deutsche Harmonia Mundi ▲ 74321-26614-2
Christmas Concerti Editio Classica ▲ 77048-2-RG [ADD] ■ 77048-4-RG (CrO2)
Missa Salisburgensis, w. Montserrat Escolania, Tolz Boys' Choir Deutsche Harmonia Mundi ▲ 77050-2-RC [DDD]
B. Turner (cnd)
Lassus, O. de:Magnificat, w. Pro Cantione Antiqua Editio Classica ▲ 77066-2-RG [ADD]
Lassus, O. de:Motets, w. Pro Cantione Antiqua Editio Classica ▲ 77066-2-RG [ADD]
Lassus, O. de:Requiem, w. Pro Cantione Antiqua Editio Classica ▲ 77066-2-RG [ADD]

Collegium Aureum members
M. Brown (cnd)
Purcell, H.:Music of, w. Pro Cantione Antiqua—Incidental Music from Oedipus; Rounds & Catches [Christchurch Bells; I Gave Her Cakes & Ale; He That Drinks Is Immortal; Tom the Taylor; Sir Walter; My Lady's Coachman John; As Roger Last Night]; 'Tis Wine Was Made to Rule the Day; Arise Ye Subterranean Winds; Lost Is My Quiet Forever; When the Cock Begins to Crow; Hark, How the Wild Musicians; Not All My Torments; Laudate Ceciliam Ars Musici ▲ 1141 [ADD]

Collegium Brass
Bach, J.S.:Chorale Preludes Org, w. Mary Jane Newman (org)—BWV 79, Now Thank We All Our God *(rec Presbyterian Church, Mt. Kisco, NY, Aug 26–27, 1995)* Helicon ▲ HE 1006 [DDD]
Handel, G.F.:Royal Fireworks Music, w. Mary Jane Newman (org), Jeffery Milarsky (timp) [arr Newman for org, 3 tpt & timp] *(rec Presbyterian Church, Mt. Kisco, NY, Aug 26–27, 1995)* Helicon ▲ HE 1006 [DDD]
Telemann, G.P.:Con Tpt Strs in D, w. Rich Kelley (tpt)—Adagio *(rec Presbyterian Church, Mt. Kisco, NY, Aug 26–27, 1995)* Helicon ▲ HE 1006 [DDD]
M. J. Newman (cnd)
Handel, G.F.:Semele, w. Kirstan Norderval (sop)—Where're You Walk *(rec Presbyterian Church, Mt. Kisco, NY, Aug 26–27, 1995)* Helicon ▲ HE 1006 [DDD]

Collegium Cartusianum
P. Neumann (cnd)
Durante, F.:Lamentationes Jeremiae Prophetae, w. Mechthild Bach (sop), Monika Frimmer (sop), Margarete Joswig (sgr), Cologne Chamber Choir CPO ▲ CPO 999325
Mozart, W.A.:Missa, K.427, w. Monika Frimmer (sop), Barbara Schlick (sop), Christoph Prégardien (ten), Klaus Mertens (bass), Cologne Chamber Choir Virgin Classics ▲ CDM 61167

Collegium dell'Arte
L. Korkhin (cnd)
Vivaldi, A.:Con Ob Bn, w. Sergei Bliznetzov (ob), Sergei Blashenov (bn) Infinity Digital ▲ QK 66724 [DDD]
Vivaldi, A.:Cons Obs Cls Infinity Digital ▲ QK 66724 [DDD]

Collegium dell'Arte [A. Zes (ob), S. Shedrin (ob), D. Krasnik (bn), A. Degtjarenko (bn), V. Tatanusitch (hn), Y. Moshevelov (hn)]
Mozart, W.A.:Divert Obs, K.253 Infinity Digital ▲ QK 57230
Mozart, W.A.:Divert Obs, K.270 Infinity Digital ▲ QK 57230

Collegium Instrumentale Brugense
Mystery Circles, w. Noordlimburgs Men's Chorus Eufoda ▲ EUF 1144 [DDD]
F. Heyerick (cnd)
Bréval, J.B.:Sym concertante, w. Berten D'Hollander (fl), Luc Loubry (bn) Arcobaleno ▲ AAOC 9324
Mozart, W.A.:Con Bn, w. Luc Loubry (bn) Arcobaleno ▲ AAOC 9324
Vivaldi, A.:Con Fl Bn, w. Berten D'Hollander (fl), Luc Loubry (bn) Arcobaleno ▲ AAOC 9324
P. Peire (cnd)
Bach, J.S.:Cons for 3 Hpds (comp), w. F. Braley (pno), S. Prutsman (pno), B. Ganz (pno) René Gailly ▲ CD 87065 [DDD]
Benda, F.:Con in e Fl & Orch, w. E. Dequeker (fl) Eufoda ▲ 1172 [DDD]
Brehy, H.-P.:Usquequo Domine Eufoda ▲ 1133 [DDD]
Danzi, F.:Cons (4) Fl, w. E. Dequeker (rcr)—Op. 31 Eufoda ▲ 1172 [DDD]
de Fesch, W.:Missa pascalis, Capella Brugensis Eufoda ▲ 1173 [DDD]
Devienne, F.:Con 4 Fl, w. E. Dequeker (rcr) Eufoda ▲ 1172 [DDD]
Famous Arias, w. Ewa Podles (sop) Forlane ▲ FOR 16620 [DDD]
Fiocco, J.-H.:Libera me Domine, w. Westvlaams Vocal Ensemble Eufoda ▲ 1133 [DDD]
Fiocco, J.-H.:Music of, w. Capella Brugensis—Missa Sanctae Caeciliae Eufoda ▲ 1173 [DDD]
Fiocco, J.-H.:Tandem fulget, w. Westvlaams Vocal Ensemble Eufoda ▲ 1133 [DDD]
Gluck, C.W.:Arias, w. Ewa Podles (mez)—sels from Orfeo ed Euridice & Iphegénie en Aulide Forlane ▲ FRL 16620 [DDD]
Gluck, C.W.:Orfeo ed Euridice, w. M.-N. de Callatay (sop), E. Podles (mez), Capella Brugensis [original instruments] Forlane 2-▲ FOR 16720 [DDD]
Handel, G.F.:Arias, w. E. Podles (mez)—sels from Rinaldo Forlane ▲ FRL 16620 [DDD]
Helmont, C.J. van:Cantate Domino canticum novum Eufoda ▲ 1133 [DDD]
Helmont, C.J. van:Magnificat anima mea Dominum Eufoda ▲ 1133 [DDD]
Helmont, C.J. van:Victimae Paschali laudes Eufoda ▲ 1133 [DDD]
Kennis, W.J.:Arrangements of W. A. Mozart's Sacred Music, w. Capella Brugensis—Ave verum; Confitebor in D; Laudate pueri; Pange lingua; Quis te comprehendat [L] Eufoda ▲ 1152 [DDD]
Maldere, P. van:Sinfs (misc)—Sinf No. 23 in E♯, Op. 4; Sinf No. 18 in A; Sinf No. 38 in D; Sinf No. 43 in D Eufoda ▲ 1206 [DDD]
Marcello, B.:Arias, w. Ewa Podles (mez)—sels from Quella Fiamma Che M'Accende Forlane ▲ FRL 16620 [DDD]
Mozart, W.A.:Con 7 Pnos, w. F. Braley (pno), S. Prutsman (pno), B. Ganz (pno) René Gailly ▲ CD 87065 [DDD]
Mozart, W.A.:Music of, w. Philip Defrancq (ten), Reginaldo Pinheiro (ten), Jan Van Der Crabben (bar), Jan Vermeulen (pno), Guy Penson (org), Capella Brugensis—Zerfliesset heut', geliebte Brüder [song]; Dir Seele des Weltalls [cant]; O heiliges Band der Freundschaft [song]; Die ihr einem Neuen Grade [Maurer-Geselienlied]; Die Maurerfreude [cant]; Maurerische Trauermusik; Die ihr der unermesslichen Weltalls Schöpfer ehrt [Kleine deutsche Kantate]; Laut verkünde unsre Freude [Eine kleine Freimaurerkantate]; Lasst uns mit geschlungen Händen [hymn]; Ihr unsre neuen Leiter [song] *(rec Studio Steurbaut, Gent, Dec 1992)* René Gailly ▲ 92013 [DDD]
Mozart, W.A.:Sacred Music, w. Capella Brugensis—Veni Sancte Spritus, K.47; Regina coeli, K.127; Exsultate, jubilate, K.165; Sub tuum praeisium, K.198; Misericordias Domini, K.222; Sancta Maria, mater Dei, K.273; Regina coeli, K.276; Alma Dei creatoris, K.277; Ave verum corpus, K.618 Forlane ▲ FOR 16714 [DDD]
Purcell, H.:Arias, w. Ewa Podles (mez)—sels from Dido & Aeneas Forlane ▲ FRL 16620 [DDD]
Vivaldi, A.:Arias, w. Ewa Podles (mez)—sels from Orlando Furioso & Bajazet Forlane ▲ FRL 16620 [DDD]

ORCH. & ENS.

Collegium Instrumentale Brugense (cont.)
A. Zedda (cnd)
Rossini, G.:Tancredi, w. Sumi Jo (sop—Amenaide), Lucretia Lendi (mez—Roggiero), Anna Maria di Micco (mez—Isaura), Ewa Podles (cta—Tancredi), Stanford Olsen (ten—Argirio), Pietro Spagnoli (bar—Orbazzano), Ewald Demeyere (hpd), Lieven Baert (vc), Franck Coryn (db), Capella Brugensis *(rec Poissy Theatre & Centre Musical-Lyrique-Phonographique, Ile-de France, Jan. 26–31, 1994)* Naxos ("Opera Classics" series) 2-▲ 8.660037/38 [DDD]

Collegium Musicum
Handel, G.F.:Cons (16) Org, w. H. Gehann (org) LaserLight ▲ 15502 [ADD]
V. Alexeiev (cnd)
Handel, G.F.:Concerti grossi, Op. 3—Nos. 2, 3 & 5 Infinity Digital ▲ QK 64293 [DDD]
Handel, G.F.:Cons (3) Ob, w. V. Hussu (ob) Infinity Digital ▲ QK 64293 [DDD]
Handel, G.F.:Solomon (sels)—Ov.; Arrival of the Queen of Sheba Infinity Digital ▲ QK 64293 [DDD]
P. Casals (cnd)
Mozart, W.A.:Arias, w. V. de los Angeles (sop)—aria from Idomeneo *(rec live July 9, 1959)* Music & Arts 4-▲ CD 689 (m) [AAD]
P. Pelucchi (cnd)
Mayr, S.:La Passione, w. Ernesto Palacio (ten), Riccardo Ristori (bass) Agorá 2-▲ 005
F. Rasmussen (cnd)
Gade, N.W.:Elverskud, w. L. Balslev (sop), E. Guillaume (mez), M. Melbye (bar), Canzone Choir [Da] Kontrapunkt ▲ 32070 [DDD]
Gade, N.W.:Kalanus, w. M. Rørholm (mez), N. Gedda (ten), L. Mróz (bar), Canzone Choir Kontrapunkt ▲ 32072 [DDD]
M. Schønwandt (cnd)
Gade, N.W.:Sym 3 *(rec March 18–20, 1988)* Marco Polo ▲ DCCD 9004
Gade, N.W.:Sym 5, w. Amalie Malling (pno) *(rec March 18–20, 1988)* Marco Polo ▲ DCCD 9004
Strauss, R.:Con Ob, w. B.C. Nielsen (ob) Kontrapunkt ▲ 32039 [DDD]

Collegium Musicum Italicum Instrumental Ensemble
R. Fasano (cnd)
Gluck, C.W.:Orfeo ed Euridice, w. A. Moffo (sop), J. Raskin (sop), S. Verrett (mez), Rome Virtuosi RCA Gold Seal 2-▲ 7896-2-RG [ADD]

Collegium Musicum 90
Telemann, G.P.:Duos, w. S. Standage (vn)—Canonic Duos Chandos ("Chaconne" series) ▲ CHAN 0549 [DDD]
R. Hickox (cnd)
Bach, J.S.:Magnificat, BWV 243, w. T. Bonner (sop), E. Kirkby (sop), M. Chance (ct), J. M. Ainsley (ten), S. Varcoe (b-bar) Chandos ("Chaconne" series) ▲ CHAN 0518 [DDD]
Bach, J.S.:Mass in b, BWV 232, w. N. Argenta (sop), C. Denley (mez), M. Tucker (ten), S. Varcoe (b-bar) Chandos ("Chaconne" series) 2-▲ CHAN 0533/34 [DDD]
Handel, G.F.:Messiah, w. Joan Rodgers (sop), Della Jones (mez), Christopher Robson (ct), Philip Langridge (ten), Bryn Terfel (b-bar) [period instrs] [E] Chandos ("Chaconne" series) 2-▲ CHAN 0522/23 [DDD]
Haydn, J.:Mass 7, "Kleine Orgelmesse" Chandos ▲ CHAN 0592
Haydn, J.:Mass 12, "Theresienmesse", w. Janine Watson (sop), Pamela Helen Stephen (mez), Mark Padmore (ten), Stephen Varcoe (bass) Chandos ▲ CHAN 0592
Purcell, H.:Dido & Aeneas, w. Rebecca Evans (sop—Belinda), Maria Ewing (sop—Dido), Mary Plazas (sop—1st witch), Patricia Rozario (sop—2nd woman), Sally Burgess (mez—Sorceress), Pamela Helen Stephens (mez—2nd witch), James Bowman (ct—Spirit), Jamie MacDougal (ten—Sailor), Karl Daymond (bar—Aeneas) Chandos ("Early Music" series) ▲ CHAN 0586 [DDD]
Purcell, H.:The Prophetess, or The History of Dioclesian, w. C. Pierard (sop), J. Bowman (alt), J. M. Ainsley (ten), I. Bostridge (ten), M. George (bass)—Masque Chandos ("Chaconne" series) ▲ CHAN 0558 [DDD]
Purcell, H.:The Prophetess, or The History of Dioclesian, w. Catherine Pierard (sop), James Bowman (alt), John Mark Ainsley (ten), Michael George (bass) Chandos ▲ CHAN 0569/70 [DDD]
Purcell, H.:Timon of Athens, w. I. Davies (trb), C. de la Hoyde (trb), J. Bowman (alt), J. M. Ainsley (ten), M. George (bass)—Masque Chandos ("Chaconne" series) ▲ CHAN 0558 [DDD]
Telemann, G.P.:Cants, w. P. Kwella (sop), C. Denley (mez), S. Roberts (b-bar), M. George (bass)—Die Donner Ode Chandos ("Chaconne" series) ▲ CHAN 0548 [DDD]
Telemann, G.P.:Motets, w. P. Kwella (sop), C. Denley (mez), S. Roberts (b-bar), M. George (bass)—Deus judicium tuum Chandos ("Chaconne" series) ▲ CHAN 0548 [DDD]
Vivaldi, A.:Gloria, RV.589, w. E. Kirkby (sop), T. Bonner (sop), M. Chance (ct) Chandos ("Chaconne" series) ▲ CHAN 0518 [DDD]
S. Standage (cnd)
Albinoni, T.:Cons à 5 Obs, Op. 7, w. Anthony Robson (ob)—Nos. 3 in B♭, 6 in D, 9 in F & 12 in C Chandos ("Chaconne" series) ▲ CHAN 0579 [DDD]
Albinoni, T.:Cons à 5 Obs, Op. 9, w. Anthony Robson (ob)—Nos. 2 in d, 5 in C, 8 in g & 11 in B♭ Chandos ("Chaconne" series) ▲ CHAN 0579 [DDD]
Aubert, J.:Cons, Op. 17—Nos. 1 & 6 Chandos ("Early Music" series) ▲ CHAN 0577 [DDD]
Aubert, J.:Cons, Op. 26—No. 4 Chandos ("Early Music" series) ▲ CHAN 0577 [DDD]
Aubert, J.:Concerts de simphonies—Suites Nos. 2 in D & 5 in F Chandos ("Early Music" series) ▲ CHAN 0577 [DDD]
Bach, J.S.:Cons Vn (comp), w. Simon Standage (vn) Chandos ("Chaconne" series) ▲ CHAN 0594
Bach, J.S.:Con Vn, BWV 1052 *(rec April 1992)* Chandos ("Chaconne" series) ▲ CHAN 0530 [DDD]
Bach, J.S.:Con Vn, BWV 1058 *(rec Apr 1992)* Chandos ("Chaconne" series) ▲ CHAN 0530 [DDD]
Bach, J.S.:Con for 2 Vns, w. Micaela Comberti (vn), Simon Standage (vn) Chandos ("Chaconne" series) ▲ CHAN 0594
Bach, J.S.:Con for 3 Vns, w. Micaela Comberti (vn), Miles Golding (vn), Simon Standage (vn) Chandos ("Chaconne" series) ▲ CHAN 0594
Bonporti, F.A.:Concerti (10) à Quattro, Op. 11 *(rec Apr. 1992)* Chandos ("Chaconne" series) ▲ CHAN 0530 [DDD]
Handel, G.F.:Apollo e Dafne, w. N. Argenta (sop), M. George (bass) Chandos ("Early Music" series) ▲ CHAN 0583 [DDD]
Handel, G.F.:Crudel tiranno amor, w. Nancy Argenta (sop) Chandos ("Early Music" series) ▲ CHAN 0583 [DDD]
Leclair, J.-M.:Cons Vn, Op. 7, w. Simon Standage (vn)—No. 1 Chandos ("Early Music" series) ▲ CHAN 0589 [DDD]
Leclair, J.-M.:Cons Vn, Op. 7, w. S. Standage (vn)—Nos. 2 in D & 5 in a Chandos ("Chaconne" series) ▲ CHAN 0551 [DDD]
Leclair, J.-M.:Cons Vn, Op. 10, w. S. Standage (vn)—Nos. 1 in B♭ & 5 in e Chandos ("Chaconne" series) ▲ CHAN 0551 [DDD]
Leclair, J.-M.:Cons Vn, Op. 10, w. Simon Standage (vn)—Nos. 3, 4 & 6 Chandos ("Early Music" series) ▲ CHAN 0589 [DDD]
Marcello, A.:Cons Vn, w. Simon Standage (vn) Chandos ("Chaconne" series) ▲ CHAN 0563 [DDD]
Marcello, A.:Con Vn, w. Simon Standage (vn) Chandos ("Chaconne" series) ▲ CHAN 0563 [DDD]
Telemann, G.P.:Le Changeante Chandos ("Chaconne" series) ▲ CHAN 0519 [DDD]
Telemann, G.P.:Con for 2 Chls, w. Michael Harris (chl), Colin Lawson (chl) *(rec Goldsmiths' College, Apr 24–26, 1995)* Chandos ("Chaconne" series) ▲ CHAN 0593
Telemann, G.P.:Con Fl Vn in e, w. R. Brown (fl), S. Standage (vn) Chandos ("Chaconne" series) ▲ CHAN 0519 [DDD]
Telemann, G.P.:Cons for 2 Fls, w. R. Brown (fl), S. Peasgood (fl), S. Standage (vn), J. Coe (vc)—(1) in D Chandos ("Chaconne" series) ▲ CHAN 0512 [DDD]
Telemann, G.P.:Con Va, w. Simon Standage (va) *(rec Goldsmiths' College, Apr 24–26, 1995)* Chandos ("Chaconne" series) ▲ CHAN 0593
Telemann, G.P.:Cons in a & E Vn, w. S. Standage (vn) Chandos ("Chaconne" series) ▲ CHAN 0519 [DDD]
Telemann, G.P.:Cons in f# & G Vn, w. S. Standage (vn) Chandos ("Chaconne" series) ▲ CHAN 0512 [DDD]
Telemann, G.P.:Con in G for 2 Vns, w. S. Standage (vn), M. Comberti (vn) Chandos ("Chaconne" series) ▲ CHAN 0512 [DDD]

Collegium Musicum 90 (cont.)
S. Standage (cnd) (cont.)
Telemann, G.P.:Music of—Trio Sonata in E♭ for 2 Violins & Continuo; Singe-, Spiel- und Generalbass-Übungen (songs); Flute Suite No. 5; Moral Cantata—Happiness; Sonata in e for 2 Violins; 24 Serious & Lighthearted Odes (selections); Flute Quartet in G Chandos ("Chaconne" series) ▲ CHAN 0525 [DDD]
Telemann, G.P.:Ov Alster Chandos ("Chaconne" series) ▲ CHAN 0547 [DDD]
Telemann, G.P.:Ov burlesque Chandos ("Chaconne" series) ▲ CHAN 0512 [DDD]
Telemann, G.P.:Son 2 Chls, w. Michael Harris (chl), Colin Lawson (chl) *(rec Goldsmiths' College, Apr 24–26, 1995)* Chandos ("Chaconne" series) ▲ CHAN 0593
Telemann, G.P.:Sonates Corellisantes Chandos ("Chaconne" series) ▲ CHAN 0549 [DDD]
Telemann, G.P.:Suites Orch—in B♭, "Völker Ov"; in G, "Nations anciens et modernes" *(rec Goldsmiths' College, Apr 24–26, 1995)* Chandos ("Chaconne" series) ▲ CHAN 0593
Telemann, G.P.:Suite Orch Chandos ("Chaconne" series) ▲ CHAN 0547 [DDD]
Telemann, G.P.:Syms—Grillen Symphonie Chandos ("Chaconne" series) ▲ CHAN 0547 [DDD]
Vivaldi, A.:Con for 2 Vcs, w. J. Coe (vc), D. Watkin (vc) Chandos ("Chaconne" series) ▲ CHAN 0528 [DDD]
Vivaldi, A.:Con Ob Vns, w. A. Robson (ob), S. Standage (vn), M. Comberti (vn) Chandos ("Chaconne" series) ▲ CHAN 0528 [DDD]
Vivaldi, A.:Cons for 2 Obs, w. A. Robson (ob), C. Latham (ob)—RV.535 in d Chandos ("Chaconne" series) ▲ CHAN 0528 [DDD]
Vivaldi, A.:Cons Vn (misc), w. S. Standage (vn) *(rec April 1992)* Chandos ("Chaconne" series) ▲ CHAN 0530 [DDD]

Collegium Musicum Pragense
Druschetzky, G.:Music of Supraphon ▲ SUP 11 0097 [DDD]
Haydn, J.:Mass 1a, Missa 'Rorate coeli desuper', w. G. Öhlinger (sop), M. Bayer (alt), M. Klietmann (ten), A. Lebeda (bass), D. de Rooij an der Reil (org) Christophorus ▲ CD 74541 [DDD]
Haydn, J.:Mass 7, "Kleine Orgelmesse", w. G. Öhlinger (sop), M. Bayer (alt), M. Klietmann (ten), A. Lebeda (bass) Christophorus ▲ CD 74541 [DDD]
Hummel, J.N.:Parthia *(rec 1973)* Tuxedo ▲ TUXCD 1026
Krommer, F.:Music of—Partita for 2 Oboes, 2 Clarinets, 2 Horns, 2 Bassoons & Double Bassoon Supraphon ▲ SUP 11 0097 [DDD]
Masek, V.:Music of—Serenata in D a due chori Supraphon ▲ SUP 11 0097 [DDD]
Mysliveček, J.:Octet 2 Ww Supraphon ▲ SUP 11 0097 [DDD]
R. G. Frieberger (cnd)
Buxtehude, D.:Cants, w. Heiligenberg Baroque Orch—Alles, was ihr tut; Befiehl dem Engel, dass er komm; Ich habe List abzuscheiden; Jesu, meine Freud Christophorus ▲ CD 74588
Schein, J.H.:Cants, w. Heiligenberg Baroque Orch—An Wasserflüssen Babylon Christophorus ▲ CD 74588
Schütz, H.:Motets, SWV 53–60 [L] Christophorus ▲ CD 74587 [DDD]
Schütz, H.:St. John Passion [G] Christophorus ▲ CD 74587 [DDD]

Collegium Musicum Pragense [G. Öhlinger (sop), M. Bayer (alt), M. Klietmann (ten), A. Lebeda (bass)]
Haydn, J.:Salve regina, H.XXIIIb/2, w. D. de Rooij an der Reil (org) Christophorus ▲ CD 74541 [DDD]

Collegium Musicum Soloists
Ibert, J.:Aria Cl & Pno Kontrapunkt ▲ KPT 32202
Ibert, J.:Entracte Kontrapunkt ▲ KPT 32202
Ibert, J.:Interludes Kontrapunkt ▲ KPT 32202
Ibert, J.:Le Jardinier de Samos (suite) Kontrapunkt ▲ KPT 32202
Ibert, J.:Jeux Kontrapunkt ▲ KPT 32202
Ibert, J.:Pièces brèves Kontrapunkt ▲ KPT 32202
Saint-Saëns, C.:Airs de ballet d'Ascanio Kontrapunkt 2-▲ 32062/63 [DDD]
Saint-Saëns, C.:Caprice sur des airs danoises et russes Kontrapunkt 2-▲ 32062/63 [DDD]
Saint-Saëns, C.:Cavatina Trbn Kontrapunkt 2-▲ 32062/63 [DDD]
Saint-Saëns, C.:Odelette Fl Kontrapunkt 2-▲ 32062/63 [DDD]
Saint-Saëns, C.:Rêverie du soir [arr for ob, fl & pno] Kontrapunkt 2-▲ 32062/63 [DDD]
Saint-Saëns, C.:Romance Fl Kontrapunkt 2-▲ 32062/63 [DDD]
Saint-Saëns, C.:Romance Hn, Op. 36 Kontrapunkt 2-▲ 32062/63 [DDD]
Saint-Saëns, C.:Romance Hn, Op. 67 Kontrapunkt 2-▲ 32062/63 [DDD]
Saint-Saëns, C.:Spt Tpt Kontrapunkt 2-▲ 32062/63 [DDD]
Saint-Saëns, C.:Son Bn Kontrapunkt 2-▲ 32062/63 [DDD]
Saint-Saëns, C.:Son Cl Kontrapunkt 2-▲ 32062/63 [DDD]
Saint-Saëns, C.:Son Ob Kontrapunkt 2-▲ 32062/63 [DDD]
Saint-Saëns, C.:Tarantelle Fl Kontrapunkt 2-▲ 32062/63 [DDD]

Collegium Musicum Soloists [Michael Beier (fl), Toke Lund Christiansen (fl), Niels Thomsen (cl), Asger Svendsen (bn)]
Ibert, J.:Movements for 2 Fls Kontrapunkt ▲ KPT 32202

Collegium Pro Musica
Instrumental Music in Genoa in the 17th Century Dynamic ▲ CD 75 [DDD]
Scarlatti, A.:Cants, w. S. Picollo (sop), R. Balconi (ten), S. Bagliano (rcr)—includes Clori mia, Clori bella; Filli che esprime la sua fede a Fileno; Ardo e ver per te d'amore; Tu sei quella che al nime sembri giusta, plus others Nuova Era ("Ancient Music" series) ▲ NUO 7162 [DDD]

Collegium Pro Musica [Stefano Bagliano (rcr), Enrico Bronzi (vc), Antonio Fantinuoli (vc), Claudio Tumeo (tt), Piero Barbareschi (hpd)]
Marcello, B.:Sons Rcr *(rec Genoa, Italy, Oct 9–11, 1995)* Dynamic ▲ CD 155 [DDD]

Collegium Pro Musica [Stefano Bagliano (rcr), Fabrizio Cipriani (vn), Enrico Bronzi (vc), Sirio Restani (hpd)]
Vivaldi, A.:Cons Diverse Instrs—in F, R.100; in D, R.92; in g, R.106; in D, R.84; in D, R.91; in g, R.103 *(rec Montevarchi, Italy, May 15–17, 1995)* Dynamic ▲ CD 156 [DDD]

Collegium Sagittarii
D. McCulloch (cnd)
Schütz, H.:The 7 Words of Jesus Christ on the Cross, w. Paul Steinitz (cnd), London Bach Society Choir Cantate ▲ 57615 [AAD]

Collegium 1704
Zelenka, J.D.:Con à 8 Supraphon ▲ SUP 0009
Zelenka, J.D.:Hipocondrie à 7 Supraphon ▲ SUP 0009
Zelenka, J.D.:Ov & Concertanti Supraphon ▲ SUP 0009
Zelenka, J.D.:Sinfonia & Concertanti Supraphon ▲ SUP 0009
Zelenka, J.D.:Son 3 CO Supraphon ▲ SUP 0009

Collegium Terpsichore
Praetorius, M.:Terpsichore, w. S. Behrend (gtr), S. Fink (perc), Ulsamer Collegium—36 sels IMP Collectors Series ▲ IMPX 9026 [AAD]
F. Neumeyr (cnd)
Dance Music of the High Renaissance *(rec 1971 & 1973)* Boston Skyline ▲ BSD 118 [ADD]

Collegium Tubicense Ulm
Christmas Concert, w. Dach, Simon, Ulmer Brass Ensemble, Holzbläser Ensemble, Holzbläser CO Christophorus ▲ CD 74585

Collegium Vocale Orch
P. Herreweghe (cnd)
Bach, J.S.:Cant 11, "Ascension Oratorio", w. B. Schlick (sop), C. Patriasz (cta), C. Prégardien (ten), P. Kooy (bass) Harmonia Mundi France ▲ HMC 901479
Bach, J.S.:Cant 73, w. B. Schlick (sop), H. Crook (ten), P. Kooy (bass), Collegium Vocale Virgin Classics ▲ CDC 59237-2
Bach, J.S.:Cant 105, w. B. Schlick (sop), G. Lesne (mez), H. Crook (ten), P. Kooy (bass), Collegium Vocale Virgin Classics ▲ CDC 59237-2
Bach, J.S.:Cant 131, w. B. Schlick (sop), G. Lesne (mez), H. Crook (ten), P. Kooy (bass), Collegium Vocale Virgin Classics ▲ CDC 59237-2
Bach, J.S.:Mass in b, BWV 232, w. B. Schlick (sop), C. Patriasz (cta), C. Brett (ct), H. Crook (ten), P. Kooy (bass), Collegium Vocale [L] Virgin Classics ("Veritas" series) 2-▲ CDCB 59517-2 [DDD]

▲ = CD ♦ = Enhanced CD Δ = MD ■ = Cassette Tape □ = DCC

Cologne Camerata
Florilegium Musicale — Deutsche Harmonia Mundi ▲ 77172-2-RC [DDD]
Handel, G.F.:Sons Rcr, w. Sabine Bauer (rcr), Michael Schneider (rcr)—8 Sonatas—Op. 1, Nos. 2, 4, 7 & 11; Sonatas in B♭, d & G; Sonata in F for 2 Recorders — Editio Classica ▲ 77104-2-RG [DDD]
Telemann, G.P.:Cons (misc)—Con Rcr Fl Strs in e; Con Ob Vn Strs in c; Con 2 Fls Strs in a; Con Fl Strs in b; Con 2 Obs Vc Strs in D; Con Ob Vn 2 Fls in B♭, *(Feb 1996)* — Deutsche Harmonia Mundi ▲ 05472-77367-2 [DDD]
Telemann, G.P.:Con Bn — Deutsche Harmonia Mundi ▲ 77201-2-RC [DDD]
Telemann, G.P.:Con Fl Strs in D — Deutsche Harmonia Mundi ▲ 77201-2-RC [DDD]
Telemann, G.P.:Con Ob Strs — Deutsche Harmonia Mundi ▲ 77201-2-RC [DDD]
Vivaldi, A.:Cons Rcr—RV.441-445 — Editio Classica ▲ 77016-2-RG [DDD]
M. Schneider (cnd)
Sammartini, G.B.:Son Orch — Deutsche Harmonia Mundi ▲ 05472-77323-2 [DDD]
Sammartini, G.B.:Trio Strs — Deutsche Harmonia Mundi ▲ 05472-77323-2 [DDD]
Sammartini, G.:Con Vc — Deutsche Harmonia Mundi ▲ 05472-77323-2 [DDD]
Sammartini, G.:Con in E♭ Ob — Deutsche Harmonia Mundi ▲ 05472-77323-2 [DDD]
Sammartini, G.:Cons Rcr—in F — Deutsche Harmonia Mundi ▲ 05472-77323-2 [DDD]
Sammartini, G.:Trio Strs — Deutsche Harmonia Mundi ▲ 05472-77323-2 [DDD]
Telemann, G.P.:Ovs—Suites in D & in A — Deutsche Harmonia Mundi ▲ 05472-77324-2 [DDD]

Cologne Camerata [Karl Kaiser (fl), Rainer Zipperling (vc), Sabine Bauer (hpd/pno)]
Richter, F.X.:Sons Vn—3 sons — CPO ▲ 999440-2 [DDD]

Cologne Camerata [Karl Kaiser (trns fl), Michael Schneider (rcr), Hans-Peter Westermann (ob), Mary Utiger (vn), Rainer Zipperling (vl/vc), Ghislaine Wauters (vl), Yasunori Imamura (thb), Sabine Bauer (hpd/org), Harald Hoeren (hpd/org)]
Telemann, G.P.:Trio Sons—Trio in c for Rcr, Ob & Cont; Trio in G for Vl, Hpd obl & Cont; Trio in g for Vn, Ob & Cont; Trio in A for Fl, Hpd obl & Cont; Trio in a for Rcr, Vn & Cont; Trio for Fl, Vl & Cont; Trio in F for Rcr, Vl & Cont; Trio in B♭ for Rcr, Hpd obl & Cont; Trio in E for Fl, Vn & Cont; Trio in D for Vn, Vl & Cont; Trio in d for Fl, Ob & Cont; Trio in E♭ for Ob, Hpd obl & Cont *(rec DeutschlandRadio Cologne, Oct 13-18, 1994 & Mar 21-)* — Deutsche Harmonia Mundi 4-▲ 05472-77361-2 [DDD]

Cologne Camerata members
Telemann, G.P.:Sons Fl & Hpd—in D & G *(rec DeutschlandRadio Cologne, Oct 13-18, 1994 & Mar 21-)* — Deutsche Harmonia Mundi 4-▲ 05472-77361-2 [DDD]
Telemann, G.P.:Sons Ob—in B♭ & e *(rec DeutschlandRadio Cologne, Oct 13-18, 1994 & Mar 21-)* — Deutsche Harmonia Mundi 4-▲ 05472-77361-2 [DDD]
Telemann, G.P.:Sons Rcr—in d & C *(rec DeutschlandRadio Cologne, Oct 13-18, 1994 & Mar 21-)* — Deutsche Harmonia Mundi 4-▲ 05472-77361-2 [DDD]
Telemann, G.P.:Sons Vl Continuo—in a & e *(rec DeutschlandRadio Cologne, Oct 13-18, 1994 & Mar 21-)* — Deutsche Harmonia Mundi 4-▲ 05472-77361-2 [DDD]
Telemann, G.P.:Sons Vn—in F & A *(rec DeutschlandRadio Cologne, Oct 13-18, 1994 & Mar 21-)* — Deutsche Harmonia Mundi 4-▲ 05472-77361-2 [DDD]
Telemann, G.P.:Suites Hpd—in C & F *(rec DeutschlandRadio Cologne, Oct 13-18, 1994 & Mar 21-)* — Deutsche Harmonia Mundi 4-▲ 05472-77361-2 [DDD]

Cologne CO
Six Venetian Concerti, w. Christian Mendoze (rcr) — Pierre Verany ▲ 787093 [DDD]
H. Müller-Brühl (cnd)
Bach, Joh. Christian:Con Fl, w. K. B. Sebon (fl) — Koch Schwann ▲ CD 311081 [ADD]
Bach, J.C.F:Sinfs, HW.I/1-4 — Koch Schwann 2-▲ SCH 310482 [ADD]
Bach, J.C.F:Sinf, HW.I/3 — Koch Schwann ▲ CD 311081 [ADD]
Bach, J.C.F:Sinf, HW.I/6 — Koch Schwann 2-▲ SCH 310482 [ADD]
Bach, J.C.F:Sinf, HW.I/10 — Koch Schwann 2-▲ SCH 310482 [ADD]
Bach, J.C.F:Sinf, HW.I/20 — Koch Schwann 2-▲ SCH 310482 [ADD]
Bach, W.F.:Sym, F.67 — Koch Schwann ▲ CD 311081 [ADD]
Baroque Concertos, w. Capella Clementina *(rec 1971 and 1978)* — Koch Treasure ▲ SCH 316152 [ADD]
Haydn, J.:Cassation Hns — Koch Schwann ▲ CD 316 026 [ADD]
Haydn, J.:Con for 2 Hns, w. Erich Penzel (hn), Walter Lexutt (hn) — Koch Schwann ▲ CD 316 026 [ADD]
Haydn, J.:Sym 55, "Der Schulmeister" — Koch Schwann ▲ CD 316051 [ADD]
Mozart, W.A.:Missa, K.427, w. S. Meinardus (sop), H.-J. Möhring (fl), G. Passin (ob), F. Essmann (bn)—Et incarnatus est [L] *(rec May 1968)* — Koch Treasure ▲ 316182 [ADD]

Cologne Classique Ensemble
Glinka, M.:Grand Sextet — Koch Schwann ▲ CD 310034 [ADD]
Rimsky-Korsakov, N.:Sextet Vns — Koch Schwann ▲ CD 310034 [ADD]
D. Levine (cnd)
Schumann, R.:Qt Pno in c — Koch Treasure ▲ 31627-2 [ADD]

Cologne Clementi Trio
Zemlinsky, A. von:Trio Cl [violin-cello-piano arr. by Edward Steuermann] — Largo ▲ 5111 [DDD]

Cologne Divitia Ensemble
Handel, G.F.:Cants, w. D .L. Ragin (ct)—4 cantatas—"Careo sempre di gloria"; "Lungi da me pensier tiranno"; Siete rose ruggiadose"; "Udite il mio consiglio" [I] — Channel Classics ▲ CCS 0890 [DDD]

Cologne Divitia Ensemble [A Gangler (ob), Hartig (vc), Samuels (hpd)]
Handel, G.F.:Sons Ob—Op. 1/8 in c & Op. 1/5 F [period instrs] — Channel Classics ▲ CCS 0890 [DDD]

Cologne Flautando [Katharina Hess (fl), Susanne Hochscheid (fl), Lucia Mense (fl), Ursula Thelen (fl)]
La Spiritata *(rec Honrath Church, Cologne, May 3-5, 1996)* — Ars Musici ▲ AME 3027-2 [DDD]

Cologne Gürzenich Orch
O. Klemperer (cnd)
Mozart, W.A.:Con 20 Pno, w. C. Haskil (pno) — Legend ▲ LGD 113 [ADD]
Mozart, W.A.:Con 27 Pno, w. C. Haskil (pno) — Legend ▲ LGD 113 [ADD]
G. Wand (cnd)
Haydn, J.:Die Schöpfung, w. Jeannette van Dijck (sop), Peter Schreier (ten), Theo Adam (bass), Hans Plumacher (vc), Heinz Detering (db), Fritz Lehan (hpd), Cologne Gürzenich Chorus — Accord 2-▲ ACD 200422 [AAD]

Cologne Instrumental Ensemble
P. Neumann (cnd)
Monteverdi, C.:Madrigals, w. Cologne Chamber Choir—8 selections from Books 2,5,6 & 8 [I] — MD + G ▲ L 3081 [DDD]

Cologne Kurrende
E.M. Blankenburg (cnd)
Martinez, M.:Music of, w. Clara Schumann Cologne Orch—Psalm Cants; In Exitu Israel; Dixit Dominus — Koch Schwann ▲ SCH 317382

Cologne La Stravaganza
A. Manze (cnd)
Handel, G.F.:Con grosso in C, "Alexanderfest" *(rec Feb. 6-9, 1992)* — Denon ▲ CO 79943 [DDD]
Handel, G.F.:Cons (16) Org, w. C. Lehman (org) *(rec Feb. 6-9, 1992)* — Denon ▲ CO 79943 [DDD]
Handel, G.F.:Royal Fireworks Music *(rec Feb. 6-9, 1992)* — Denon ▲ CO 79943 [DDD]
Handel, G.F.:Solomon (arrival of the queen of Sheba) *(rec Feb. 6-9, 1992)* — Denon ▲ CO 79943 [DDD]
Handel, G.F.:Water Music (suites) *(rec Feb. 6-9, 1992)* — Denon ▲ CO 79943 [DDD]

Cologne Musica Antiqua
Couperin, F.:Les Nations — Archiv ("Galleria" series) 2-▲ 427164-2 [DDD]
Sonatas & Motets of the Italian Baroque, w. Cologne Vocal Consort — Koch Schwann ▲ SCH 310602 [ADD]
Telemann, G.P.:Con for 2 Rcrs, Bn — Archiv ▲ 413788-2 [DDD]
R. Goebel (cnd)
Bach, J.S.:The Art of the Fugue — Archiv ("3D Baroque" series) ▲ 431704-2 [DDD]
Bach, J.S.:Brandenburg Cons — Archiv 2-▲ 423116-2 [DDD]

Cologne Musica Antiqua (cont.)
R. Goebel (cnd) (cont.)
Bach, J.S.:Brandenburg Cons—Nos. 1-3 [period instrs] *(rec Cologne, June 1986)* — Archiv ▲ 447287-2 [DDD]
Bach, J.S.:Brandenburg Cons—Nos. 4-6 — Archiv ("3D Baroque" series) ▲ 431702-2 [DDD]
Bach, J.S.:Brandenburg Cons—Nos. 1-3 — Archiv ("3D Baroque" series) ▲ 431701-2 [DDD]
Bach, J.S.:Brandenburg Cons—Nos. 4-6 [period instrs] *(rec Cologne, Feb 1987)* — Archiv ▲ 447288-2 [DDD]
Bach, J.S.:Con Fl, Vn & Hpd — Archiv 2-▲ 423116-2 [DDD]
Bach, J.S.:Suites Orch, BWV 1066-1069 — Archiv 2-▲ 415671-2 [DDD]
Bach, J.S.:Suite 1 Orch [period instrs] *(rec Cologne, May 1986)* — Archiv ▲ 447287-2 [DDD]
Bach, J.S.:Suite 4 Orch [period instrs] *(rec Cologne, May 1985)* — Archiv ▲ 447288-2 [DDD]
Baroque Chamber Music *(rec 1974-75)* — Koch Schwann ▲ SCH 310612 [ADD]
Biber, H. von:Son jucunda — Archiv ▲ 429230-2 [DDD]
Biber, H. von:Son Strs, "Die Bauernkirchfahrt" — Archiv ▲ 429230-2 [DDD]
Biber, H. von:Son Strs, "Campanarum" — Archiv ▲ 429230-2 [DDD]
Cologne Musica Antiqua — Archiv ▲ 415296-2 AH [ADD]
Gluck, C.W.:Alessandro — Archiv ▲ 445824-2
Handel, G.F.:Cants, w. A. von Otter (mez)—Haec est Regina virginum, HWV 235; Ah! che troppo ineguali, HWV 230; Donna, che in ciel di tanta luce splendi, HWV 233; Il pianto di Maria [Giunta l'ora fatal], HWV 234 *(rec Cologne, Mar & Aug 1993)* — Archiv Produktion ▲ 439866-2 [DDD]
Handel, G.F.:Trio Sons—No. 10 in G for 2 Vn & Bc, Op. 5/4 — Deutsche Grammophon ▲ 447285-2
Heinichen, J.D.:Dresden Cons — Archiv ▲ 437849-2 [DDD]
Heinichen, J.D.:Dresden Cons — Archiv ▲ 437549-2
Heinichen, J.D.:Sacred Music—Lamentationes Jeremiae prophetae; Beatus vir; Alma mater redemptoris; Nisi Dominus aedificaverit; De profundis; Nicht das Band, das dich bestricket; Warum toben die Heiden; Pastorale in A *(rec Melanchthon Church, Cologne, Oct 1994 & Jan 1995)* — Archiv 2-▲ 447092-2 [DDD]
Italian Baroque Concerti — Archiv ▲ 435393-2 AH [DDD]
Pachelbel, J.:Canon — Deutsche Grammophon ▲ 447285-2
Rebel, J.-F.:Les Élémens — Archiv ▲ 445824-2
Telemann, G.P.:Con for 2 Chls — Archiv ▲ 419633-2 [DDD]
Telemann, G.P.:Cons Fl (misc) — Archiv ▲ 419633-2 [DDD]
Telemann, G.P.:Con for 3 Obs — Archiv ▲ 419633-2 [DDD]
Telemann, G.P.:Con Rcr, Fl — Archiv ▲ 419633-2 [DDD]
Telemann, G.P.:Con Tpt Strs in D — Archiv ▲ 419633-2 [DDD]
Telemann, G.P.:Con Tpt Vn — Archiv ▲ 419633-2 [DDD]
Telemann, G.P.:Music of—Son in e for 7 inst — Archiv ▲ 445824-2
Telemann, G.P.:Musique de Table — Archiv 4-▲ 427619-2 [DDD]
Telemann, G.P.:Musique de Table (sels)—sels. — Archiv ▲ 429774-2 [DDD]
Vivaldi, A.:Trio Sons 2 Vns & Bc—in d, R.63 (Op. 1/12) — Deutsche Grammophon ▲ 447285-2

Cologne Musica Fiata
R. Wilson (cnd)
Monteverdi, C.:Selva morale e spirituale (sels), w. La Capella Ducale *(rec Nov. 11-13, 1992)* — Sony Classical ▲ SK 53363 [DDD]
Picchi, G.:Canzoni da sonar, w. La Capella Ducale *(rec Nov. 11-13, 1992)* — Sony Classical ▲ SK 53363 [DDD]

Cologne Philharmonic Cellists
Cellicatissimo:Light Tunes For Serious Cellists — Koch Schwann ▲ SCH 311522 [DDD]

Cologne PO
J. Conlon (cnd)
Weber, C.M. von:Oberon, w. D. Voigt (sop), D. Ziegler (mez), G. Lakes (ten), B. Heppner (ten), Cologne Opera Chorus — EMI Classics 2-▲ CDCB 54739
Zemlinsky, A. von:Der Geburtstag der Infantin, w. Soile Isokoski (sop), Iride Martinez (sgr), Andrew Collis (sgr), David Kuebler (ten), Juanita Lascarro (sgr), Machiko Obata (sgr), Anne Schwanewilms (sgr), Natalie Karl (sgr), Martina Rüping (sgr), Franfurter Kantorei (sgr), Gürzenich Orch *(rec Cologne, Feb 1996)* — EMI Classics 2-▲ CDCB 56208
Zemlinsky, A. von:Die Seejungfrau, w. Gürzenich Orch — EMI Classics ▲ CDC 55515
Zemlinsky, A. von:Sinfonietta, w. Gürzenich Orch — EMI Classics ▲ CDC 55515

Cologne Piano Duo [Elzbieta Kalvelage (pno), Michael Krücker (pno)]
Mendelssohn, F.:Allegro brillant — Koch Schwann ▲ SCH 315802 [DDD]
Moscheles, I.:Grande Son Pno 4-Hands — Koch Schwann ▲ SCH 315802 [DDD]
Moszkowski, M.:Pno 4-Hands Music—Album espagnol, Op. 21; Polish Folk Dances, Op. 55; Aus aller Herren Länder, Op. 23; German Round Dances, Op. 25; Spanish Dances, Op. 12 — Koch Schwann ▲ SCH 312392
Moszkowski, M.:Pno 4-Hands Music—New Spanish Dances; 5 Waltzes — Koch Schwann ▲ SCH 315802 [DDD]

Cologne Radio Orch
Marszalek (cnd)
Kálmán, I.:Die Csárdásfürstin (sels), w. E. Köth (sop), F. Fehringer (ten), B. Kusche (bar), Heusser (sgr), Hofmann (sgr), Cologne Radio Chorus [G] — Acanta ▲ CD 42435 [DDD]
Kálmán, I.:Gräfin Mariza, w. A. Görner (sop), F. Wunderlich (ten), B. Kusche (bar), Hartung (sgr), Hofmann (sgr), Cologne Radio Chorus [G] — Acanta ▲ CD 42479 [DDD]

Cologne RSO
W.A. Albert (cnd)
Françaix, J.:Divert Bn, w. Dag Jensen (bn) — Capriccio ▲ CD 10579 [DDD]
Hummel, J.N.:Con Bn, w. Dag Jensen (bn) — Capriccio ▲ CD 10579 [DDD]
Jolivet, A.:Con Bn, w. Dag Jensen (bn) — Capriccio ▲ CD 10579 [DDD]
Mozart, W.A.:Con Bn, w. Dag Jensen (bn) — Capriccio ▲ CD 10579 [DDD]
G. Albrecht (cnd)
Hindemith, P.:Mathis der Maler, w. Josef Protschka (ten), Hermann Winkler (ten), Roland Hermann (bar), Victor von Halem (bass), Harold Stamm (bass) — Wergo 3-▲ WER 6255-2
Ruzicka, P.:Metamorphoses on a Sound Plane by Joseph Haydn — CPO ▲ CPO 999053 [DDD]
Schoeck, O.:Massimilla Doni, w. E. Mathis (sop), A. Küttenbaum (mez), H. Winkler (ten), H. Stamm (bass), Cologne Radio Chorus [G] — Koch Schwann 2-▲ CD 314025 [DDD]
R. Bader (cnd)
Mozart, F.X.W.:Cons Pno, w. K. Hellwig (pno) — Koch Schwann ▲ CD 311004 [ADD]
R. Barshaï (cnd)
Baur, J.:Sinfonische Metamorphosen — Thorofon ▲ CTH 2270
F. Busch (cnd)
Verdi, G.:Un ballo in maschera, w. Martha Mödl (sop—Ulrica), Walburga Wegner (sop—Amelia), Anny Schlemm (mez—Oscar), Lorenz Fehenberger (ten—Ricardo), Dietrich Fischer-Dieskau (bar—Renato), Wilhelm Schirp (bass—Samuel), Willy Schoneweib (bass—Tom), Gunther Wilhelms (bass—Silvan), Fritz Augustin (sgr—Ein Richter), Friedrich Himmelmann (sgr—Ein Diener Amelia), Bernhard Alois Zimmermann (cnd), Cologne Radio Chorus — Calig 2-▲ 50946/47 (m) [ADD]
P. Falk (cnd)
Künneke, E.:The Alluring Flame, w. Birgit Fandrey (sgr—Dolores), Christianne Hossfeld (sgr—Lisbeth), Maria Mallé (sgr), Jürgen Sacher (ten—Master), Ralf Lukas (bar—Hoffman), Gerd Grochowski (sgr—1st Neighbor), Gerhard Peters (sgr—Friedrich), Zoran Todorovic (sgr—Jacinto), Theodor Weimer (sgr—2nd Neighbor), Cologne Radio Chorus *(rec Cologne, Nov 7-26, 1994)* — Capriccio ▲ 10753 [DDD]
F. Fricsay (cnd)
Rossini, G.:Stabat Mater, w. E. Grümmer (sop), M. von Ilosvay (mez), C. Ludwig (mez), H. Fehn (bass), Cologne Radio Chorus [L] *(rec 1953)* — Melodram ▲ CDM 16523 [AAD]
Stravinsky, I.:Con Vn, w. A. Grumiaux (vn) — Originals ▲ ORISH 818 [ADD]
H. Froschauer (cnd)
Kreutzer, C.:Das Nachtlager in Granada, w. R. Klepper (sop), M. Pabst (ten), H. Prey (bar), Cologne Radio Chorus — Capriccio ▲ 60029 [DDD]
H. Geese, E. Künneke (cnd)
Künneke, E.:Der Vetter aus Dingsda (sels), w. G. Van Jüten (sop), Kollo (ten), B. Kusche (bar), Wolff (sgr), Breck (sgr), Cologne Radio Chorus [G] — Acanta ▲ CD 43460 [DDD]

ORCH. & ENS.

Cologne RSO (cont.)
H. Geese, E. Smola (cnd)
Mackeben, T.:Music of—Paris, du bist die schönste Stadt der Welt [from "Patrioten", 1937]; Bei dir war es immer so schön; Amorcito mio; Mein kleiner Teddybär [from "Anita & der Teufel", 1940]; Nur nicht aus Liebe weinen [from "Es war eine rauschende Ballnacht", 1939]; Münch'ner G'schichten [from "Bal paré", 1940]; Ich bin auf der Welt um glücklich zu sein [from "Mädchen in Weiss", 1936]; Drei Sterne sah ich scheinen; Eine Frau wird erst schön durch die Liebe [from "Heimat", 1938]; Fantasie über drei Lieder [from "Das Herz der Königen]; Walzer der Freude [from "Der goldene Käfig", 1943]; Frauen sind keine Engel; Tanz auf dem Vulkan; Bel Ami *(rec West German Radio, Cologne, Jan 11–14 & 30, 1994)* Capriccio ▲ 10 705 [DDD]
N. Järvi (cnd)
Mozart, W.A.:Don Giovanni, w. S. Ghazarian (sop), G. Ottenthal (sop), P. Pace (sop), G. Sabbatini (ten), R. Bruson (bar), A> Rinaldi-Miliani (bar), F. De Grandis (bass), N. Ghiuselev (bass), Cologne Radio Chorus [I] Chandos 3-▲ CHAN 8920/22 [DDD]
H. von Karajan (cnd)
Orff, C.:De temporum fine comoedia, w. C. Ludwig (mez), P. Schreier (ten), J. Greindl (bass), Cologne Radio Chorus [L] Deutsche Grammophon ("20th Century Classics" series) ▲ 429859-2 [ADD]
J. Keilberth (cnd)
Hindemith, P.:Cardillac, w. Leonore Kirschstein (sop), Donald Grobe (ten), Dietrich Fischer-Dieskau (bar) [G] Deutsche Grammophon ("20th Century Classics" series) 2-▲ 431741-2 [ADD]
C. Kleiber (cnd)
Beethoven, L. van:Sym 7 *(rec live, 1972)* Originals ▲ ORISH 813 [ADD]
Haydn, J.:Sym 94, "Surprise Sym" *(rec live, 1972)* Originals ▲ ORISH 813 [ADD]
E. Kleiber (cnd)
Schubert, Franz:Sym 9 *(rec 1953)* Memories ▲ MEM 4569 [ADD]
O. Klemperer (cnd)
Beethoven, L. van:Con 4 Pno, w. Leon Fleisher (pno), Bavarian RSO, Berlin RSO Enterprise ("Palladio" series) ▲ ENT 4189 [ADD]
Beethoven, L. van:Sym 4, w. Bavarian RSO, Berlin RSO Enterprise ("Palladio" series) ▲ ENT 4189 [ADD]
Beethoven, L. van:Sym 5, w. Bavarian RSO, Berlin RSO Enterprise ("Palladio" series) ▲ ENT 4189 [ADD]
Brahms, J.:Sym 2, w. Bavarian RSO, Berlin RSO Enterprise ("Palladio" series) ▲ ENT 4189 [ADD]
Bruckner, A.:Sym 8 *(rec live, 6/7/57)* Arkadia ▲ 704 (m) [ADD]
Mahler, G.:Kindertotenlieder, w. G. London (bar) [G] *(rec live, Cologne, 10/17/55)* Arkadia 2-▲ 578 (m) [ADD]
R. Kraus (cnd)
Wagner, R.:Lohengrin, w. H. Braun (sop—Ortrud), T. Epperle (sop—Elsa von Brabant), P. Anders (ten—Lohengrin), C. Kronenberg (bar—Frederich von Telramund), J. Greindl (bass—Heinrich der Vogler), Cologne Radio Chorus *(rec Nov. 1951)* Myto 3-▲ MCD 93485
S. Köhler (cnd)
Straus, O.:The Merry Nibelungs, w. Lisa Griffith (sop—Kriemhild), Gudrun Volkert (sop—Brunhilde), Daphne Evangelatos (cta—Ute), Gabriele Henkel (sgr—Giselher), Christine Mann (sgr—Vogel), Hein Heidbüchel (ten—Volker), Martin Gantner (sgr—Gunther), Gerd Grochowski (sgr—Dankwart), Michael Nowak (sgr—Siegfried), Josef Otten (sgr—Hagen), Cologne Radio Chorus *(rec Cologne, Jan 31–Feb 17, 1995)* Capriccio ▲ 10752 [DDD]
J. Latham-König (cnd)
Hindemith, P.:Neues vom Tage, w. Elisabeth Werres (sop), R. Ries (sgr), Claudio Nicolai (bar) [G] Wergo 2-▲ WER 6192/93-2
Weill, K.:Aufstieg und Fall der Stadt Mahagonny, w. A. Silja (sop), A. Schlemm (mez), W. Neumann (ten), T. Lehrberger (ten), K. Hirte (bar), Cologne Radio Chorus [G] Capriccio 2-▲ CD 10160/1 [DDD]
Marszalek (cnd)
Jessel, L.:Schwarzwaldmädel (sels), w. E. Lind (sop), F. Fehringer (ten), B. Kusche (bar), Hofmann (sgr), Schörg (sgr), Schubart (sgr), Cologne Radio Chorus [G] Acanta ▲ CD 42552 [DDD]
Künneke, E.:Die grosse Sünderin (sels), w. M. Cunitz (sop), R. Schock (ten), Bajew (sgr), Gehly (sgr), Rau (sgr), Schröder (sgr), Weigelt (sgr), Cologne Radio Chorus [G] Acanta ▲ CD 42483 [DDD]
Lehár, F.:Paganini (sels), w. A. Schlemm (mez), Lisolette Losch (sop), P. Anders (ten), Gehly (sgr), Hofmann (sgr), Schneider (sgr), Cologne Radio Chorus [G] Acanta ▲ CD 43810 [DDD]
Strauss (II), Joh.:Der Zigeunerbaron (sels), w. S. Jurinac (sop), W. Hollweg (ten), P. Anders (ten), K. Schmitt-Walter (bar), Schneider (sgr), G. Hann (bass), Cologne Radio Chorus [G] Acanta ▲ CD 43807 [DDD]
D. Mitropoulos (cnd)
Mahler, G.:Sym 6 *(rec 1959)* Arkadia ▲ 522 (m) [AAD]
H. Rosbaud (cnd)
Mahler, G.:Das Lied von der Erde, w. Grace Hoffman (mez), Ernst Haefliger (ten) *(rec live, Cologne, Germany, Apr 18, 1955)* Agorá Music ("Phoenix" series) ▲ 701 [ADD]
M. Rossi (cnd)
Mozart, W.A.:Thamos, w. T. Stich-Randall (mez), A. Deloire (mez), J. Traxel (ten), T. Adam (b-bar), Cologne Radio Chorus [G] *(rec live, Cologne May 20, 1956)* Melodram 3-▲ CDM 37084 [AAD]
H. Scherchen (cnd)
Reger, M.:Serenade Orch *(rec Cologne, 1958)* Originals ▲ ORISH 827 [ADD]
Schoenberg, A.:Pelleas und Melisande *(rec Cologne, 1958)* Originals ▲ ORISH 827 [ADD]
Schoenberg, A.:Pelleas und Melisande *(rec July 10, 1958)* Arkadia ▲ 769 [ADD]
H. Schernus (cnd)
Cornelius, P.:Stabat Mater, w. B. Scherler (mez), M. Schmidt (ten), S. Nimsgern (bass-bar), R. Didusch (sgr), Cologne Radio Chorus [L] *(rec 1978)* Koch Schwann ▲ 3-1086-2 [ADD]
U. Schneider (cnd)
Backofen, J.G.:Con for 2 Cls, w. F. Klein (cl), E. Klein (cl) Koch Schwann ▲ CD 311001 [DDD]
Stamitz, C.:Con for 2 Cls, w. F. Klein (cl), E. Klein (cl) Koch Schwann ▲ CD 311001 [DDD]
G. Schuller (cnd)
Schulhoff, E.:Con Pno, w. Michael Rische (pno) Koch Schwann ▲ SCH 315972 [DDD]
Schulhoff, E.:Sym 5 Koch Schwann ▲ SCH 315972 [DDD]
N. Schutze (cnd)
Schultze, N.:Das kalte Herz, w. Grit van Jüten (sop), Elisabeth Steiner (mez), Heinz Kruse (ten), Detelf Zywietz (sgr), Händel Collegium Koch Schwann 2-▲ SCH 318002 [DDD]
S. Skrowaczewski (cnd)
Prokofiev, S.:Romeo & Juliet (suites) Denon ▲ DEN 78840
G. Solti (cnd)
Verdi, G.:Requiem Mass, w. Gré Brouwenstijn (sop), Oralia Dominguez (mez), Giuseppe Zampieri (ten), Nicola Zaccaria (bass), Cologne Radio Chorus *(rec Nov 17, 1958)* Bella Voce 2-▲ 107.201 [AAD]
P. Steinberg (cnd)
Anderson, L.:Music of—19 compositions LaserLight ▲ 15 248
J. Stulen (cnd)
Schillings, M. von:Hexenlied, w. M. Möll (nar) CPO ▲ CPO 999233 [DDD]
Schillings, M. von:Symphonic Prologue to King Oedipus by Sophocles CPO ▲ CPO 999233 [DDD]
Schillings, M. von:Tanz der Blumen CPO ▲ CPO 999233 [DDD]
Schillings, M. von:Ein Zwiegespräch CPO ▲ CPO 999233 [DDD]
V. Symonette (cnd)
Weill, K.:Songs, w. Steven Kimbrough (bar)—Songs from Firebrand of Florence; Love Life; One Touch of Venus; Knickerbocker Holiday; Johnny Johnson Koch Schwann ▲ SCH CD 314162
L. Vis (cnd)
Ruzicka, P.:Torso *(rec Dec 1973)* Thorofon ▲ CTH 2220
H. Wakasugi (cnd)
Brahms, J.:Qt 1 Pno [Arnold Schoenberg's 1937 orch.] Koch Schwann ▲ CD 311 034 [ADD]
G. Wand (cnd)
Bruckner, A.:Syms (comp)—Nos. 1-9 RCA Gold Seal 10-▲ 60075-2-RG [ADD]
Schumann, R.:Con Pno, w. W. Gieseking (pno) *(rec live, Essen 1/8/51)* Arkadia ▲ 588 [ADD]

Cologne RSO (cont.)
L. Zagrosek (cnd)
Weill, K.:The Seven Deadly Sins, w. D. Bierett (sop), D. Ellenbeck (ten) Capriccio ▲ 60028 [DDD]
Cologne Salon Orch
Music at the Coffee Houses of Cologne Ars Musici ▲ 8000
Salon Music, Vol. 1 RCA Victor ▲ 09478-69295-2 [ADD]
Salon Music, Vol. 2 RCA Victor ▲ 09478-69296-2 [ADD]
Salon Music, Vol. 3 RCA Victor ▲ 09478-69297-2 [ADD]
Stolz, R.:Music of, w. Le Nouveau Salon—Ein Abend mit Robert Stolz; A klane Drahrerei; Hysterie; Türkischer Marsch; Träume an der Donau; Tief berauscht mich dein Haar; Spiel auf deiner Geige; Fünf-Uhr-Tee bei Robert Stoltz; Ungeküsst sollst du nicht schlafen geh'n; Oft genügt ein Gläschen Sekt; O süsse Señorita, sag' nicht nein Ars Musici ▲ AMS 8006-2 [DDD]
Cologne SO
R. Paternostro (cnd)
Wagner, R.:Arias & Scenes, w. G. Jones (sop)—Götterdämmerung:Immolation Scene (Act 3); Lohengrin:Elsas Traumerzählung (Act 1); Tannhäuser:Hallenarie (Act 2); Gebet der Elisabeth (Act 3); Tristan und Isolde:Prelude & Liebestod [G] Chandos ▲ CHAN 8930 [DDD]
Wagner, R.:Götterdämmerung (immolation scene), w. G. Jones (sop) [G] Chandos ▲ CHAN 8930 [DDD]
Cologne Youth Orch
Peeters, F.:Con Org Orch, w. P. Wisskirchen (org) Motette ▲ MOT CD 40161 [DDD]
E.M. Blankenburg (cnd)
Mendelssohn, Fanny:Oratorio, w. I. Lippitz (sop), Annemarie Fischer-Kunz (cta), H. Hatano (ten), T. Thomaschke (bass), Cologne Youth Chorus CPO ▲ CPO 999009-2 [DDD]
Colonne Association des Concerts Orch
M. Landowski, G. Tzipine (cnd)
Landowski, M.:Music of, w. Nadine Sautereau (sop), Jean-Christophe Benoit (bar), Xavier Depraz (bass), Michel Bouquet (spkr), Gilbert Audin (bn), Evelyne Aïello, Didier Bouture, Ludovic Chevalier, Laurent Decker, Françoise Deslogères, Boulogne-Billancourt Orch Conservatory, Paris Conservatory Société des Concerts Orch, L'Itinéraire Ensemble, Harmonia Nova Orch Ensemble—Con Bn; Con pour ondes Martenot; Femme sans passé; Hauts de Hurlevent; Horologe; Mouvement; Notes de Nuit; Souvenir d'un jardin d'enfance; Ventriloque Chamade 3-▲ 5639/40/41 [AAD/DDD]
Colonne Concerts Orch
J. Horenstein (cnd)
Ravel, M.:Con Pno (left hand), w. Vlado Perlemuter (pno) Accord ▲ ACD 201052 [AAD]
Ravel, M.:Con in G Pno, w. Vlado Perlemuter (pno) Accord ▲ ACD 201052 [AAD]
P. Paray (cnd)
The Early Recordings, w. Jeanne-Marie Darré (pno), Paris Conservatory Orch [cnd:A. Cluytens] *(rec between 1922 & 1947)* VAI Audio 2-▲ VAIA/IPA 1065 (m) [ADD]
Colonne Orch
G. Pierné (cnd)
Ravel, M.:Pavane pour une infante défunte *(rec Paris, 1929 from American Decca)* Music & Arts ▲ CD 703-1 [AAD]
Colorado College New Music Ensemble
Scott, S.:Minerva's Web New Albion ▲ NA 026 [DDD]
Scott, S.:The Tears of Niobe New Albion ▲ NA 026 [DDD]
Colorado MahlerFest Orch
R. Olson (cnd)
Mahler, G.:Sym 8, w. Oksana Krovytska (sop—Magna Peccatrix), Sheila Smith (sop—Una poenitentium), Shauna Southwick (sop—Mater gloriosa), Kristine Jepson (mez—Maria Aegyptiaca), Julie Simson (mez—Mulier Samaritana), Kurt Hansen (ten—Doctor Marianus), Brian Steele (bar—Pater ecstaticus), Eugene Green (b-bar—Pater profundus), Colorado MahlerFest Chorale, Colorado Mormon Chorale, Colorado Children's Chorale *(rec MahlerFest VIII, Boulder, CO, Jan 14–15, 1995)* MahlerFest 2-▲ MF8-1
Colorado String Quartet
Music of Schubert, w. Jenő Jandó (pno), Budapest PO [cnd:János Kóvacs] Laserlight ♦ 90032 [DDD]
Schubert, Franz:Rondo Vn, D.438, w. E. Verhey (vn) Vivace ▲ E 561 [DDD]
Schubert, Franz:Rondo Vn, D.438, w. E. Verhey (vn) Laserlight ▲ 15 522 [DDD]
Colorado SO
M. Alsop (cnd)
Rouse, C.:Con Trbn, w. Joseph Alessi (trbn), *(Denver, Feb 1995)* RCA Victor Red Seal ▲ 09026-68410-2 [DDD]
Rouse, C.:Gorgon, *(Denver, Nov 1995)* RCA Victor Red Seal ▲ 09026-68410-2 [DDD]
Rouse, C.:Iscariot, *(Denver, Nov 1995)* RCA Victor Red Seal ▲ 09026-68410-2 [DDD]
Columbia Baroque Ensemble
R. Craft (cnd)
Monteverdi, C.:Vespro della Beata Vergine, w. Gloria Prosper (sop), Adrienne Albert (mez), Melvin Brown (ten), Richard Levitt (ten), Archi Drake (bass), Gregg Smith Singers, Texas Boys' Choir Sony Classical ("Essential Classics" series) 2-▲ SB2K 62656
Columbia CO
A. Copland (cnd)
Copland, A.:Appalachian Spring—original version *(rec 1973)* CBS ■ MT 32736
Copland, A.:Appalachian Spring—original version *(rec 1973)* CBS ▲ MK 42431 [ADD]
I. Stern (cnd)
Haydn, J.:Con 1 Vn, w. Isaac Stern (vn), Alexander Zakin (hpd) Sony Classical 2-▲ SM2K 64528 [ADD/DDD]
Columbia Chamber SO
Z. Rozsnyai (cnd)
Bach, J.S.:Org Music (misc), w. E. P. Biggs (org), H.-J. Rotzsch (cnd), Leipzig Gewandhaus Orch—9 Organ Chorales from Cantatas 79, 129, 140, 142, 147, 207, 248; 5 Sinfonias to Cantatas 29, 31, 35, 49; Five Concerted Chorales, BWV 19, 130, 137, 250, 303; Unto us a child is born (concerto), from Christmas Cantata, BWV 142; My spirit be joyful (duet), from Easter Cantata, BWV 146; March from Cantata 207; Instrumental Trio & Sheep may safely graze from Birthday Cantata, BWV 208; In dulci jubilo (chorale prelude), from BWV 740 CBS ▲ MK 42646 [ADD]
Columbia Jazz Band
M. Tilson Thomas (cnd)
Gershwin, G.:Rhap in Blue, w. G. Gershwin (pno) [1925 piano roll] CBS ▲ MK 42516 ■ FMT 42516
Gershwin, G.:Rhap in Blue, w. G. Gershwin (pno) [1925 piano roll] CBS ▲ MK 42240 [ADD]
Columbia Jazz Combo
L. Bernstein (cnd)
Bernstein, L.:Prelude, Fugue & Riffs Cl, w. B. Goodman (cl) CBS ▲ MK 42227 ■ MYT 42227
M. Gould (cnd)
Gould, M.:Derivations, w. B. Goodman (cl) CBS ▲ MK 42227 ■ MT 42227
I. Stravinsky (cnd)
Stravinsky, I.:Ebony Con, w. B. Goodman (cl) CBS ▲ MK 42227 ■ MT 42227
Columbia String Orch
I. Stern (cnd)
Haydn, J.:Con 1 Vn, w. Isaac Stern (vn) *(rec 11/12/47; mono)* CBS 4-▲ M4K 42003 (m/s) [ADD]
Columbia String Quartet
Lewis, P.T.:Music of, w. J. Ferrell (vn), J. Avery (pno), S. Schick (perc), Peter Tod Lewis (elec), Center for New Music Ensemble—Bricolage (1979); Gestes (1973); Manestar (1970); ...of bells...and time (1967); Signs & Circuits—String Quartet No. 2 (1969) *(rec 1978–82)* CRI ▲ CD 619 [ADD]
Columbia SO
A Grand Night for Singing, w. Sherrill Milnes (bar), Mormon Tabernacle Choir CBS ■ MT 35170
Mendelssohn, F.:Music of, New York PO, Philadelphia Orch CBS ▲ MLK 39452 ■ MT 39452
L. Bernstein (cnd)
Bach, J.S.:Con 1 Hpd, w. G. Gould (pno) *(rec 1957)* CBS ▲ MYK 38524 (m) [ADD] ■ MYT 38524
Gershwin, G.:Rhap in Blue, w. L. Bernstein (pno) *(rec Brooklyn, June 23, 1959)* Sony Classical ("Bernstein:The Royal Edition" series) ▲ SMK 47529 [ADD] Δ SM 47529 [ADD]

▲ = CD ♦ = Enhanced CD Δ = MD ■ = Cassette Tape □ = DCC

Columbia SO (cont.)

L. Bernstein (cnd) (cont.)

Gershwin, G.:Rhap in Blue, w. Leonard Bernstein (pno) Polskie Nagrania ▲ PNCD 150 [ADD]
Gershwin, G.:Rhap in Blue, w. L. Bernstein (pno) CBS ▲ MYK 37242 [ADD] ■ MYT 37242
Gershwin, G.:Rhap in Blue, w. L. Bernstein (pno) CBS ▲ MLK 39454 ■ PMT 39454
Gershwin, G.:Rhap in Blue, w. L. Bernstein (pno) CBS ▲ MK 42264 [ADD]
Ravel, M.:Con in G Pno, w. L. Bernstein (pno) *(rec 1958)* Sony Classical ("Bernstein:The Royal Edition" series) ▲ SMK 47571 [ADD]

A. Copland (cnd)

Copland, A.:Con Cl, w. B. Goodman (cl) CBS ▲ MK 42227 ■ MYT 42227
Copland, A.:Old American Songs, w. W. Warfield (bar) [E] CBS ▲ MK 42430 [ADD]

R. Craft (cnd)

Bach, J.S.:Cant 131, w. Loren Driscoll (ten), Robert Oliver (bass), Leonard Arner (ob) Sony Classical ("Essential Classics" series) 2–▲ SB2K 62656
Bach, J.S.:Cant 198, w. Marnie Nixon (sop), Elaine Bonazzi (mez), Nico Castel (ten), Peter Binder (bar), American Concert Choir Sony Classical ("Essential Classics" series) 2–▲ SB2K 62656

V. Golschmann (cnd)

Bach, J.S.:Cons Hpd, BWV 1052–1058, w. G. Gould (piano) [Nos. 2–5 & 7], L. Bernstein (cnd), Columbia SO [No. 1] *(rec 1957–69)* Sony Classical ("Glenn Gould Edition" series) 2–▲ SM2K 52591 [ADD]
Bach, J.S.:Con 2 Hpd, w. G. Gould (pno) *(rec 1969)* CBS 2–▲ M2K 42270 [AAD]
Bach, J.S.:Con 3 Hpd, w. G. Gould (pno) *(rec 1967)* CBS 2–▲ M2K 42270 [AAD]
Bach, J.S.:Con 4 Hpd, w. G. Gould (pno) *(rec 1969)* CBS 2–▲ M2K 42270 [AAD]
Bach, J.S.:Con 4 Hpd, w. G. Gould (pno) *(rec stereo, 1959)* CBS ▲ MYK 38524 [ADD] ■ MYT 38524
Bach, J.S.:Con 5 Hpd, w. G. Gould (pno) *(rec stereo, 1958)* CBS ▲ MYK 38524 [ADD] ■ MYT 38524
Bach, J.S.:Con 5 Hpd, w. G. Gould (pno) *(rec 1958)* CBS 2–▲ M2K 42270 [AAD]
Bach, J.S.:Con 7 Hpd, w. G. Gould (pno) *(rec 1967)* CBS 2–▲ M2K 42270 [AAD]
Beethoven, L. van:Con 1 Pno, w. G. Gould (pno) CBS 3–▲ M3K 39036

B. Herrmann (cnd)

Achron, J.:Stimmung *(rec ca. 1949)* Cambria ▲ CD 1063 [ADD]
Bennett, Robert Russell:Con Vn, w. Louis Kaufman (vn) Cambria ("Historical" series) ▲ CD 1078 [ADD]
McBride, R.:Aria & Toccata, w. Louis Kaufman (vn) Cambria ("Historical" series) ▲ CD 1078 [ADD]
Still, W.G.:Lenox Ave, w. Louis Kaufman (vn)—The Blues Cambria ("Historical" series) ▲ CD 1078 [ADD]

A. Kostelanetz (cnd)

Puccini, G.:Music of—orch sels & trans from La Bohème, Madama Butterfly, Tosca, Manon Lescaut, Gianni Schicchi CBS ■ YT 38922
Shostakovich, D.:Festive Ov Sony Classical ("Essential Classics" series) ▲ SBK 62642 ■ SBT 62642

D. Mitropoulos (cnd)

Berlioz, H.:Les Nuits d'été, w. Eleanor Steber (sop) *(rec Columbia 30th St. Studios, New York, May 19, 1954)* Sony Classical ("Masterworks Heritage" series) ▲ MHK 62356 [ADD]

J.-P. Morel (cnd)

Berlioz, H.:La Captive, w. Eleanor Steber (sop) *(rec Columbia 30th St. Studios, New York, May 19, 1954)* Sony Classical ("Masterworks Heritage" series) ▲ MHK 62356 [ADD]
Berlioz, H.:Le Jeune pâtre breton, w. Eleanor Steber (sop) *(rec Columbia 30th St. Studios, New York, May 19, 1954)* Sony Classical ("Masterworks Heritage" series) ▲ MHK 62356 [ADD]
Berlioz, H.:Zaïde, w. Eleanor Steber (sop) *(rec Columbia 30th St. Studios, New York, May 19, 1954)* Sony Classical ("Masterworks Heritage" series) ▲ MHK 62356 [ADD]
Of Gods & Demons, w. George London (b-bar), Vienna SO, Metropolitan Opera Orch, Rudolf Moralt (cnd), Kurt Adler (cnd) Sony Classical ("Masterworks Heritage" series) ▲ MHK 62758

E. Ormandy (cnd)

Mendelssohn, F.:Con 2 Pno, w. R. Serkin (pno) Sony Classical ("Essential Classics" series) ▲ SBK 46542 [ADD] ■ SBT 46542
Rossini, G.:Music of, w. Philadelphia Orch—Cancan; Largo al factotum, Cossack Dance, Tarantella [from La boutique fantasque (music of Rossini arranged by Respighi)]; Dance for six [from William Tell]; Kostelanetz [from The Barber of Seville] CBS ▲ MLK 39449 [ADD] ■ MT 39449

J. Ottley (cnd)

Make a Joyful Noise:Beloved Choruses, w. Mormon Tabernacle Choir *(rec Salt Lake City, Utah, Feb 13–14, 1980 & Feb 27–)* Sony Classical ▲ SMK 061984 [DDD] ■ SMT 061984

Z. Rozsnyai (cnd)

Helps, R.:Sym 1 *(rec Boston, Mar 1979)* CRI ("American Masters" series) ▲ CD 717 [ADD]

M. Rudolf (cnd)

Bach, J.S.:Cant 21, w. Eleanor Steber (sop)—Sighing, Weeping *(rec Columbia 30th St. Studios, New York, Sept 20, 1951)* Sony Classical ("Masterworks Heritage" series) ▲ MHK 62356 [ADD]
Bach, J.S.:Cant 68, w. Eleanor Steber (sop)—My Heart Ever Faithful *(rec Columbia 30th St. Studios, New York, Sept 20, 1951)* Sony Classical ("Masterworks Heritage" series) ▲ MHK 62356 [ADD]
Handel, G.F.:Messiah (sels), w. Eleanor Steber (sop)—I Know That My Redeemer Liveth *(rec Columbia 30th St. Studios, New York, Sept 18, 1951)* Sony Classical ("Masterworks Heritage" series) ▲ MHK 62356 [ADD]
Haydn, J.:Die Schöpfung (sels), w. Eleanor Steber (sop)—With Verdure Clad *(rec Columbia 30th St. Studios, New York, Sept 18, 1951)* Sony Classical ("Masterworks Heritage" series) ▲ MHK 62356 [ADD]
Mendelssohn, F.:Elijah (sels), w. Eleanor Steber (sop)—Hear Ye, Israel! *(rec Columbia 30th St. Studios, New York, Sept 18, 1951)* Sony Classical ("Masterworks Heritage" series) ▲ MHK 62356 [ADD]

T. Schippers (cnd)

Barber, S.:Vanessa (sels)—Intermezzo from Act II Sony Classical ("Masterworks Heritage" series) ▲ MHK 62837
Berg, A.:Wozzeck (sels)—Interlude from Act III Sony Classical ("Masterworks Heritage" series) ▲ MHK 62837
Indy, V. d':Fervaal (sels)—Introduction Sony Classical ("Masterworks Heritage" series) ▲ MHK 62837
Menotti, G.C.:Amelia al ballo (ov) Sony Classical ("Masterworks Heritage" series) ▲ MHK 62837

A. Schneider (cnd)

Mozart, W.A.:Con 14 Pno, w. R. Serkin (pno) Sony Classical 3–▲ SM3K 47207
Mozart, W.A.:Con 17 Pno, w. R. Serkin (pno) Sony Classical 3–▲ SM3K 47207

I. Stravinsky (cnd)

Stravinsky, I.:The Firebird *(rec 1961)* CBS ▲ MK 42432 [ADD]
Stravinsky, I.:The Firebird Suite CBS ■ MGT 39015
Stravinsky, I.:Fireworks *(rec 1963)* CBS ▲ MK 42432 [ADD]
Stravinsky, I.:Pétrouchka [original version] *(rec 1960)* CBS ▲ MK 42433 [ADD]
Stravinsky, I.:Pétrouchka (suite) CBS ■ MGT 39015
Stravinsky, I.:Le Sacre du printemps Orch *(rec 1960)* CBS ▲ MK 42433 [ADD]
Stravinsky, I.:Le Sacre du printemps Orch CBS ■ MGT 39015
Stravinsky, I.:Scherzo à la russe *(rec 1963)* CBS ▲ MK 42432 [ADD]
Stravinsky, I.:Scherzo fantastique *(rec 1962)* CBS ▲ MK 42432 [ADD]
Stravinsky, I.:Sym in 3 Movts *(rec 1961)* CBS ▲ MK 42434 [ADD]

G. Szell (cnd)

Mozart, W.A.:Con 18 Pno, w. R. Serkin (pno) CBS ▲ MYK 37236 [ADD] ■ MYT 37236
Mozart, W.A.:Con 18 Pno, w. R. Serkin (pno) Sony Classical 3–▲ SM3K 47207
Mozart, W.A.:Con 19 Pno, w. R. Serkin (pno) CBS ▲ MYK 37236 [ADD] ■ MYT 37236
Mozart, W.A.:Con 19 Pno, w. R. Serkin (pno) Sony Classical 3–▲ SM3K 47207
Mozart, W.A.:Con 20 Pno, w. R. Serkin (pno) Odyssey ▲ MBK 42533 ■ YT 42533
Mozart, W.A.:Con 20 Pno, w. R. Serkin (pno) Sony Classical 3–▲ SM3K 47207
Mozart, W.A.:Con 20 Pno, w. R. Serkin (pno) CBS ▲ MYK 37236 [ADD] ■ MYT 37236
Mozart, W.A.:Con 22 Pno, w. R. Casadesus (pno) Sony Classical 3–▲ SM3K 46519
Mozart, W.A.:Con 23 Pno, w. R. Casadesus (pno) Sony Classical 3–▲ SM3K 46519
Mozart, W.A.:Con 26 Pno, w. R. Casadesus (pno) Sony Classical 3–▲ SM3K 46519
Mozart, W.A.:Con 27 Pno, w. R. Casadesus (pno) Sony Classical 3–▲ SM3K 46519
Mozart, W.A.:Con 5 Vn, w. I. Stern (vn) CBS ▲ MYK 37808 [ADD] ■ MYT 37808

Columbia SO (cont.)

B. Walter (cnd)

Beethoven, L. van:Coriolan Ov Odyssey ▲ MBK 42599 [ADD]
Beethoven, L. van:Coriolan Ov *(rec Los Angeles, CA, Apr. 15, 1959)* Sony Classical ("Bruno Walter Edition, Vol. 2" series) ▲ SMK 64460 [ADD]
Beethoven, L. van:Leonore 2 *(rec American Legion Hall, Hollywood, CA, July 1, 1960)* Sony Classical ("Bruno Walter:The Edition, Vol. 4" series) ▲ SMK 64488 [ADD]
Beethoven, L. van:Music of—Adagio [from Sym. No. 4 in Bb, Op. 60]; Allegro con brio [from Sym. No. 5 in c, Op. 67]; Poco sostenuto; Vivace [both from Sym. No. 7 in A, Op. 92]; Molto vivace [from Sym. No. 9 in d, Op. 125] *(rec Los Angeles, CA, Jan. & Feb., 1958)* Sony Classical ("Bruno Walter Edition, Vol. 2" series) ▲ SMK 64465 [ADD]
Beethoven, L. van:Sym 1 *(rec 1959)* Odyssey ▲ MBK 44775 [ADD]
Beethoven, L. van:Sym 1 *(rec Los Angeles, CA, Jan. 6–8, 1958)* Sony Classical ("Bruno Walter Edition, Vol. 2" series) ▲ SMK 64460 [ADD]
Beethoven, L. van:Sym 2 *(rec Los Angeles, CA, Jan. 5–9, 1959)* Sony Classical ("Bruno Walter Edition, Vol. 2" series) ▲ SMK 64460 [ADD]
Beethoven, L. van:Sym 2 *(rec 1959)* Odyssey ▲ MBK 44775 [ADD]
Beethoven, L. van:Sym 3, "Eroica" *(rec Los Angeles, CA, Jan. 20–25, 1958)* Sony Classical ("Bruno Walter Edition, Vol. 2" series) ▲ SMK 64461 [ADD]
Beethoven, L. van:Sym 3, "Eroica" Odyssey ■ YT 33925
Beethoven, L. van:Sym 3, "Eroica" Odyssey ▲ MBK 42599 [ADD]
Beethoven, L. van:Sym 4 *(rec Los Angeles, CA, Feb. 8–10, 1958)* Sony Classical ("Bruno Walter Edition, Vol. 2" series) ▲ SMK 64462 [ADD]
Beethoven, L. van:Sym 4 *(rec 1959)* CBS ▲ MYK 37773 [ADD] ■ MYT 37773
Beethoven, L. van:Sym 5 Odyssey ■ YT 30314
Beethoven, L. van:Sym 5 *(rec Los Angeles, CA, Jan. 27–30, 1958)* Sony Classical ("Bruno Walter Edition, Vol. 2" series) ▲ SMK 64463 [ADD]
Beethoven, L. van:Sym 6, "Pastorale" *(rec Los Angeles, CA, Jan. 13–17, 1958)* Sony Classical ("Bruno Walter Edition, Vol. 2" series) ▲ SMK 64462 [ADD]
Beethoven, L. van:Sym 6, "Pastorale" CBS ▲ MYK 36720 ■ MYT 36720
Beethoven, L. van:Sym 7 *(rec Los Angeles, CA, Feb. 1–3, 1958)* Sony Classical ("Bruno Walter Edition, Vol. 2" series) ▲ SMK 64463 [ADD]
Beethoven, L. van:Sym 8 *(rec Los Angeles, CA, Jan. 8–Feb. 12, 1958)* Sony Classical ("Bruno Walter Edition, Vol. 2" series) ▲ SMK 64461 [ADD]
Beethoven, L. van:Sym 9, "Choral Sym", w. Emilia Cundari (sop), Nell Rankin (mez), Albert Da Costa (ten), William Wilderman (bass), Westminster Sym Choir *(rec American Legion Hall, Los Angeles, CA, Apr. 6, 1954)* Sony Classical ("Bruno Walter Edition, Vol. 2" series) ▲ SMK 64464 [ADD]
Brahms, J.:Academic Festival Ov Sony Classical ("Bruno Walter:The Edition" series) ▲ SMK 64470
Brahms, J.:Academic Festival Ov Odyssey ■ YT 32225
Brahms, J.:Alto Rhap, w. Mildred Miller (mez), Occidental College Concert Choir *(rec Jan. 11, 1961)* Sony Classical ("Bruno Walter Edition, Vol. 2" series) ▲ SMK 64469 [ADD]
Brahms, J.:Con Vn & Vc, "Double Con", w. Zino Francescatti (vn), Pierre Fournier (vc) Sony Classical ("Bruno Walter:The Edition" series) ▲ SMK 64479
Brahms, J.:Con Vn & Vc, "Double Con", w. Z. Francescatti (vn), P. Fournier (vc) CBS ▲ MYK 37237 [ADD] ■ MYT 37237
Brahms, J.:Con Vn & Vc, "Double Con", w. Z. Francescatti (vn), P. Fournier (vc) CBS ▲ MK 42024
Brahms, J.:Sym 1 Sony Classical ("Bruno Walter:The Edition" series) ▲ SMK 64470
Brahms, J.:Sym 1 *(rec 1959)* Odyssey ▲ MBK 44827 [ADD]
Brahms, J.:Sym 2 Sony Classical ("Bruno Walter:The Edition" series) ▲ SMK 64471
Brahms, J.:Sym 3 CBS ▲ MK 42022
Brahms, J.:Sym 3 Odyssey ■ YT 32225
Brahms, J.:Sym 3 Sony Classical ("Bruno Walter:The Edition" series) ▲ SMK 64471
Brahms, J.:Sym 4 Sony Classical ("Bruno Walter:The Edition" series) ▲ SMK 64472
Brahms, J.:Sym 4 *(rec 1959)* Odyssey ▲ MBK 44776 [ADD]
Brahms, J.:Tragic Ov Sony Classical ("Bruno Walter:The Edition" series) ▲ SMK 64472
Brahms, J.:Tragic Ov CBS ▲ MYK 37237 [ADD] ■ MYT 37237
Brahms, J.:Tragic Ov *(rec 1960)* Odyssey ▲ MBK 44776 [ADD]
Brahms, J.:Vars on a Theme by Haydn Sony Classical ("Bruno Walter:The Edition" series) ▲ SMK 64470
Brahms, J.:Vars on a Theme by Haydn CBS ▲ MK 42022
Bruckner, A.:Sym 4, "Romantic" *(rec American Legion Hall, Hollywood, CA, Feb 13, 15, 17 & 25, 1960)* Sony Classical ("Bruno Walter:The Edition, Vol. 4" series) ▲ SMK 64481 [ADD]
Bruckner, A.:Sym 7 *(rec American Legion Hall, Hollywood, CA)* Sony Classical ("Bruno Walter:The Edition, Vol. 4" series) ▲ SMK 64482 [ADD]
Bruckner, A.:Sym 7 Odyssey 2–▲ MB2K 45669
Bruckner, A.:Sym 9 Odyssey ▲ MBK 44825 [ADD]
Bruckner, A.:Sym 9 *(rec American Legion Hall, Hollywood, CA, Nov 16 & 18, 1959)* Sony Classical ("Bruno Walter:The Edition, Vol. 4" series) ▲ SMK 64483 [ADD]
Dvořák, A.:Sym 8 *(rec American Legion Hall, Hollywood, CA, Feb 8 & 12, 1961)* Sony Classical ("Bruno Walter:The Edition, Vol. 4" series) ▲ SMK 64484 [ADD]
Dvořák, A.:Sym 8 CBS ▲ MK 42038
Dvořák, A.:Sym 9, "From the New World" CBS ▲ MK 42039
Dvořák, A.:Sym 9, "From the New World" Odyssey ■ YT 30045
Dvořák, A.:Sym 9, "From the New World" *(rec American Legion Hall, Hollywood, CA, Feb 12, 14, 16 & 20, 1959)* Sony Classical ("Bruno Walter:The Edition, Vol. 4" series) ▲ SMK 64484 [ADD]
Haydn, J.:Sym 88 Odyssey ▲ MBK 44777 [ADD] ■ YT 35932
Haydn, J.:Sym 88 *(rec American Legion Hall, Hollywood, CA, Mar 2, 4, 6 & 8, 1961)* Sony Classical ("Bruno Walter:The Edition, Vol. 4" series) ▲ SMK 64485 [ADD]
Haydn, J.:Sym 100, "Military" Odyssey ▲ MBK 44777 [ADD] ■ YT 35932
Haydn, J.:Sym 100, "Military" *(rec American Legion Hall, Hollywood, CA, Mar 2, 4, 6 & 8, 1961)* Sony Classical ("Bruno Walter:The Edition, Vol. 4" series) ▲ SMK 64485 [ADD]
Mahler, G.:Sym 1 CBS ▲ MYK 37235 [ADD] ■ MYT 37235
Mozart, W.A.:Con 3 Vn, w. Z. Francescatti (vn) *(rec 1958; from CBS Masterwork)* Sony Masterworks ("Portrait" series) ▲ MPK 52526 [ADD]
Mozart, W.A.:Con 3 Vn, w. Zino Francescatti (vn) *(rec Hollywood, CA, Dec. 10–17, 1958)* Sony Classical ("Bruno Walter Edition, Vol. 2" series) ▲ SMK 64468 [ADD]
Mozart, W.A.:Con 4 Vn, w. Zino Francescatti (vn) *(rec Hollywood, CA, Dec. 10–17, 1958)* Sony Classical ("Bruno Walter Edition, Vol. 2" series) ▲ SMK 64468 [ADD]
Mozart, W.A.:Kleine Nachtmusik CBS ▲ MYK 37774 [AAD] ■ MYT 37774
Mozart, W.A.:Kleine Nachtmusik *(rec New York City, Dec. 2–30, 1954)* Sony Classical ("Bruno Walter Edition, Vol. 2" series) ▲ SMK 64468 [ADD]
Mozart, W.A.:Maurerische Trauermusik CBS ▲ MYK 37774 [AAD] ■ MYT 37774
Mozart, W.A.:Music of—3 German Dances; Masonic Funeral Music; Minuets; Ovs *(rec 30th Street Studios, New York, Dec 2, 8, 29 & 30, 1954)* Sony Classical ("Bruno Walter:The Edition, Vol. 4" series) ▲ SMK 64486 [ADD]
Mozart, W.A.:Ovs—Impresario, Così fan tutte, Le nozze di Figaro, Die Zauberflöte CBS ▲ MYK 37774 ■ MYT 37774
Mozart, W.A.:Syms (misc)—Nos. 35, 36, 38, 39, 40 & 41 Odyssey 2–▲ MB2K 45676
Mozart, W.A.:Sym 25 Sony Classical ("Bruno Walter:The Edition" series) ▲ SMK 64473
Mozart, W.A.:Sym 28 Sony Classical ("Bruno Walter:The Edition" series) ▲ SMK 64473
Mozart, W.A.:Sym 29 Sony Classical ("Bruno Walter:The Edition" series) ▲ SMK 64473
Mozart, W.A.:Sym 35 *(rec 1959)* Odyssey ▲ MBK 44778 [ADD]
Mozart, W.A.:Sym 36 CBS ▲ MYK 38473 [ADD] ■ MYT 38473
Mozart, W.A.:Sym 38 CBS ▲ MYK 38473 [ADD] ■ MYT 38473
Mozart, W.A.:Sym 39 *(rec 1960)* Odyssey ▲ MBK 44778 [ADD]
Schubert, Franz:Rosamunde (sels) Sony Classical ("Bruno Walter:The Edition" series) ▲ SMK 64478
Schubert, Franz:Sym 5 *(rec American Legion Hall, Hollywood, CA, Feb 26 & 29 & Mar 3, 1960)* Sony Classical ("Bruno Walter:The Edition, Vol. 4" series) ▲ SMK 64487 [ADD]
Schubert, Franz:Sym 8 Odyssey ■ YT 30314

ORCH. & ENS.

Columbia SO (cont.)
B. Walter (cnd) (cont.)
Schubert, Franz:Sym 9 *(rec 1959)* — Odyssey ▲ MBK 44828 [ADD]
Schubert, Franz:Sym 9 — Sony Classical ("Bruno Walter:The Edition" series) ▲ SMK 64478
Schumann, R.:Con Pno, w. Eugene Istomin (pno) *(rec American Legion Hall, Hollywood, CA, Jan 20 & 25, 1960)* — Sony Classical ("Bruno Walter:The Edition, Vol. 4" series) ▲ SMK 64489 [ADD]
Schumann, R.:Con Pno, w. E. Istomin (pno) — CBS ▲ MK 42024
Strauss (II), Joh.:Music of—Ovs. to Die Fledermaus & Der Zigeunerbaron; An der schönen, blauen Donau; Kaiser-Walzer; Wiener Blut *(rec 1956)* — Sony Masterworks ("Portrait" series) ▲ MPK 47682 [ADD]
Wagner, R.:Lohengrin (preludes)—Act 1 — CBS ▲ MK 42050
Wagner, R.:Die Meistersinger von Nürnberg (prelude/act 1) — CBS ▲ MK 42050
Wagner, R.:Ovs, Preludes & Orch Sels—Fliegende Holländer — CBS ▲ MK 42050
Wagner, R.:Tannhäuser (ov & venusberg), w. Occidental Collegiate Chorus [G] — CBS ▲ MK 42050

Columbia Univ Group for Contemporary Music
H. Sollberger (cnd)
Chou Wen-Chung:Pien — CRI ▲ CD 691 [ADD]
Chou Wen-Chung:Yü ko — CRI ▲ CD 691 [ADD]

Columbia Wind Ensemble
L. Bernstein (cnd)
Bernstein Conducts Bernstein:The Theatre Works, Vol. 1, w. New York PO, various soloists — Sony Classical 3-▲ SM3K 47154

Columbus Orch
R. Cellini (cnd)
Leoncavallo, R.:Pagliacci, w. V. de los Angeles (sop), J. Björling (ten), R. Merrill (bar), L. Warren (bar), Robert Shaw Chorale — EMI Classics ▲ ZDC 49503

Columbus PO
I. Solomon (cnd)
Beethoven, L. van:Con 4 Pno, w. A. Schnabel (pno) *(rec live 1947)* — Pearl 3-▲ PEA 9063 [AAD]

Columbus SO
C. Badea (cnd)
Mennin, P.:Folk Ov — New World ▲ NW 371-2 [DDD]
Mennin, P.:Sym 8 — New World ▲ NW 371-2 [DDD]
Mennin, P.:Sym 9 — New World ▲ NW 371-2 [DDD]
Sessions, R.:Rhap — New World ▲ NW 345-2 [DDD]
Sessions, R.:Sym 4 — New World ▲ NW 345-2 [DDD]
Sessions, R.:Sym 5 — New World ▲ NW 345-2 [DDD]

Combattimento Consort Amsterdam
J. W. de Vriend (cnd)
Hellendaal, P.:Concerti grossi — NM Classics ▲ NM 92019
Van Wassenaer, U.:Concerti Armonici — NM Classics ▲ NM 92030
Vivaldi, A.:Cons Vn, Op. 8/1–4, "The Four Seasons", w. J. van Zweden (vn) — Fidelio ▲ FID 8841 [DDD]

Compania
A. Molino (cnd)
Petrassi, G.:Beatitudes, w. G. Kiefer (bar) — Stradivarius ▲ STR 33347
Petrassi, G.:Grand septuor Cl, w. E. Tedesco (cl) — Stradivarius ▲ STR 33347
Petrassi, G.:Sestina d'autunno — Stradivarius ▲ STR 33347
Petrassi, G.:Son da camera Hpd, w. G. Hollmann (hpd) — Stradivarius ▲ STR 33347

Compañia Musical de las Americas
J. Cabré (cnd)
Les Chemins du Baroque [The Paths of the Baroque], w. Elyma Vocal Ensemble, Elyma Instrumental Ensemble, Cordoba Children's Choir Garrado, Maîtrise National de Versailles, La Grande Ecurie et la Chambre du Roy [cnd:Jean-Claude Malgoire], La Fenice, et al. — K617 ("First 4 volumes of K617" series) ▲ 7042
Les Chemins du Baroque [The Paths of the Baroque], Vol. 3:Mexico:Messe de l'Assomption de la Vierge, w. La Fenice — K617 ▲ 7024 [DDD]
J. Malgoire (cnd)
Les Chemins du Baroque [The Paths of the Baroque], Vol. 2:Mexico – Versailles:Vepres de l'Assomption, w. Versaille National Masters, La Grande Ecurie et la Chambre du Roy — K617 ▲ 7026 [DDD]

Composers Ensemble
Mary Wiegold's Songbook, w. Mary Wiegold (sop) — NMC ▲ NMCD 003 [DDD]
S. Bainbridge (cnd)
Bainbridge, S.:Concertante in Moto Perpetuo — Continuum ▲ CCD 1020

Composers Orch
G. Kulesha (cnd)
Buczynski, W.:Fant on Themes of the Past, w. Joseph Macerollo (acc) *(rec Glenn Gould Studio, CBC Toronto, Mar 17, 1994 & Mar 13 & 2)* — CBC ▲ MVCD 1096 [DDD]
Camilleri, C.:Con Acc, w. Joseph Macerollo (acc) *(rec Glenn Gould Studio, CBC Toronto, Mar 17, 1994 & Mar 13 & 2)* — CBC ▲ MVCD 1096 [DDD]

Composers String Quartet
Babbitt, M.:Qt 5 Strs — Music & Arts ▲ CD 606 [DDD]
Brahms, J.:Qnt Cl, w. E. Daniels (cl) — Reference ▲ RR 40CD [DDD]
Carter, E.:Qt 4 Strs — Music & Arts ▲ CD 606 [DDD]
del Tredici, D.:I Hear an Army, w. P. Bryn-Julson (sop) [E] — CRI ■ ACS 6004
del Tredici, D.:I Hear an Army, w. Phyllis Bryn-Julson (sop) — CRI ("American Masters" series) ▲ CD 689 [DDD]
del Tredici, D.:Scherzo [E] — CRI ■ ACS 6004
Powell, Mel:Qt Strs — Music & Arts ▲ CD 606 [DDD]
Weber, C.M. von:Qnt Cl, w. E. Daniels (cl) — Reference ▲ RR 40CD [DDD]

Con Sordino Chamber Group [Bjarne Hansen (vn), Carl Sjöberg (vn), Søren Friis (vc), Robert Farver-Sonne (db), Inke Kesseler (pno)]
Nordic Salon Music — Classico ▲ CLASSCD 133

Concentus Bestiales
J. Reynolds (cnd)
Saint-Saëns, C.:Carnival of the Animals, w. Peter Lockwood (pno), Julian Reynolds (pno) *(rec Utrecht, Apr 1996)* — Globe ▲ GLO 5152 [DDD]

Concentus Hungaricus
Mozart, W.A.:Con 7 Pnos, w. J. Jandó (pno), D. Várjon (pno), M. Antal (pno) [arr. Mozart for 2 pianos & orch.] *(rec Jan. 7–10, 1991)* — Naxos ▲ 8.550210 [DDD]
Mozart, W.A.:Con 10 Pnos, w. J. Jandó (pno), M. Antal (pno) — Naxos ▲ 8.550206 [DDD]
Vivaldi, A.:Cons Bn—in e, R.484 *(rec Municipal Assembly Hall, Budapest, Apr. 20–May 2, 1988)* — Lydian ▲ 18032 [DDD]
Vivaldi, A.:Cons Fl (misc)—in F, R.433 (Op. 10/1) [La Tempesta di Mare]; in D, R.248 (Op. 10/3) [Il Gardellino]; in F, R.434 (Op. 10/5) *(rec Municipal Assembly Hall, Budapest, Apr. 20–May 2, 1988)* — Lydian ▲ 18032 [DDD]
Vivaldi, A.:Cons Ob—in d, R.454 (Op. 8/9) *(rec Municipal Assembly Hall, Budapest, Apr. 20–May 2, 1988)* — Lydian ▲ 18032 [DDD]
Vivaldi, A.:Cons Tpt—in g [arr Jean Thilde]; in g [trans from Con for Vn, R.324 (Op. 6/1)] *(rec Municipal Assembly Hall, Budapest, Apr. 20–May 2, 1988)* — Lydian ▲ 18032 [DDD]
Vivaldi, A.:Music of, w. Capella Istropolitana, Dall'Arco CO, Budapest Strings—selections from The Four Seasons; Flautino Con. in C; Flute Con. in F; Flute Con. in a, RV.108; Con. in B♭ for 2 Trumpets; Concerti, Op. 3/4, 8, 10 & 11; Oboe Con., Op. 8/9; Violin Con., Op. 8/5 & 12; Lute Con. in D; Il Gardellino — Naxos ▲ 8.551105 [DDD]
M. Antal (cnd)
Mozart, W.A.:Con 5 Pno, w. Jenö Jandó (pno) *(rec Jan. 4–10, 1991)* — Naxos ▲ 8.550209 [DDD]
Mozart, W.A.:Con 6 Pno, w. Jenö Jandó (pno) *(rec June & Oct. 1990)* — Naxos ▲ 8.550208 [DDD]
Mozart, W.A.:Con 8 Pno, w. Jenö Jandó (pno) *(rec June & Oct. 1990)* — Naxos ▲ 8.550208 [DDD]
Mozart, W.A.:Con 10 for 2 Pnos, w. J. Jandó (pno), D. Várjon (pno) *(rec Jan. 7–10, 1991)* — Naxos ▲ 8.550210 [DDD]

Concentus Hungaricus (cont.)
M. Antal (cnd) (cont.)
Mozart, W.A.:Con 15 Pno, w. J. Jandó (pno) *(rec Jan. 7–10, 1991)* — Naxos ▲ 8.550210 [DDD]
Mozart, W.A.:Con 16 Pno, w. J. Jandó (pno) *(rec June 29–July 1, 1990)* — Naxos ▲ 8.550207 [DDD]
Mozart, W.A.:Con 17 Pno, w. J. Jandó (pno) — Naxos ▲ 8.550205 [DDD]
Mozart, W.A.:Con 18 Pno, w. J. Jandó (pno) *(rec June & Oct. 1990)* — Naxos ▲ 8.550208 [DDD]
Mozart, W.A.:Con 18 Pno, w. J. Jandó (pno) *(rec Sept.–Oct. 1989)* — Naxos ▲ 8.550205 [DDD]
Mozart, W.A.:Con 19 Pno, w. J. Jandó (pno) *(rec June & Oct. 1990)* — Naxos ▲ 8.550208 [DDD]
Mozart, W.A.:Con 22 Pno, w. J. Jandó (pno) — Naxos ▲ 8.550206 [DDD]
Mozart, W.A.:Con 25 Pno, w. Jenö Jandó (pno) *(rec June 29–July 1, 1990)* — Naxos ▲ 8.550207 [DDD]
Mozart, W.A.:Con 26 Pno, w. J. Jandó (pno) *(rec Jan. 4–10, 1991)* — Naxos ▲ 8.550209 [DDD]
Mozart, W.A.:Rondo Pno Orch, K.382, w. J. Jandó (pno) *(rec Jan. 4–10, 1991)* — Naxos ▲ 8.550209 [DDD]
Mozart, W.A.:Rondo Pno Orch, K.386, w. Jenö Jandó (pno) *(rec Oct. 20, 1990)* — Naxos ▲ 8.550207 [DDD]
I. Hegyi (cnd)
Mozart, W.A.:Cons 1–4 Pno, w. J. Jandó (pno) — Naxos ▲ 8.550212 [DDD]
A. Ligeti (cnd)
Mozart, W.A.:Con 9 Pno, w. J. Jandó (pno) *(rec July 1989)* — Naxos ▲ 8.550203 [DDD]
Mozart, W.A.:Con 12 Pno, w. J. Jandó (pno) *(rec June 1989)* — Naxos ▲ 8.550202 [DDD]
Mozart, W.A.:Con 13 Pno, w. J. Jandó (pno) *(rec May 1989)* — Naxos ▲ 8.550201 [DDD]
Mozart, W.A.:Con 20 Pno, w. J. Jandó (pno) *(rec May 1989)* — Naxos ▲ 8.550434 [DDD]
Mozart, W.A.:Con 20 Pno, w. J. Jandó (pno) *(rec May 1989)* — Naxos ▲ 8.550201 [DDD]
Mozart, W.A.:Con 21 Pno, w. J. Jandó *(rec June 1989)* — Naxos ▲ 8.550434 [DDD]
Mozart, W.A.:Con 21 Pno, w. J. Jandó *(rec June 1989)* — Naxos ▲ 8.550202 [DDD]
Mozart, W.A.:Con 27 Pno, w. J. Jandó (pno) *(rec June 1989)* — Naxos ▲ 8.550203 [DDD]

Concentus Hungaricus [Péter Popa (vn), Ildikó Hegyi (vn), György Konrád (va), István Ella (org)]
Locatelli, P.:Concerti grossi—Nos. 1 in F, 2 in c, 3 in B♭, 4 in e, 5 in D, 6 in c — Hungaroton ("Classic" series) ▲ HCD 31531 [DDD]

Concentus Musicus Patavinus
G. Toffano (cnd)
Instrumental Music of Renaissance Venice — Bongiovanni ▲ GB 5018-2 [DDD]

Concentus Musicus Soloists
N. Harnoncourt (cnd)
Naudot, J.-C.:Con Rcr, w. F. Brüggen (rcr), J. Schröder (vn)—No. 5 in G — Teldec ▲ 92180

Concert Arban
Great Heroic Pieces, w. François-Henri Houbart (org) — Pierre Verany ("Favourites" series) ▲ 730015 [DDD]

Concert Arban Brass Quintet
Brass & Organ at the Church of the Madeleine, w. François-Henri Houbart (org), Francis Petit (perc) — Pierre Verany ▲ 785096 [DDD]

Concert Arts Strings
F. Slatkin (cnd)
Debussy, C.:Danses sacrée et profane, w. Ann Mason Stockton (hp) — Testament ▲ TESSBT 1053 (m) [ADD]

Concert Arts Symphonic Band
USA — EMI Classics ▲ CDC 47422

Concert Arts SO
E. Leinsdorf (cnd)
Portraits in Sound — EMI Classics ("FDS Series" series) ▲ CDM 65205
Rimsky-Korsakov, N.:Golden Cockerel (suite) — EMI Classics ("Full Dimensional Sound" series) ▲ CDM 65424
Rimsky-Korsakov, N.:Scheherazade — EMI Classics ("Full Dimensional Sound" series) ▲ CDM 65424
Strauss, R.:Die Frau ohne Schatten (sels), w. Philharmonia Orch—Interludes — EMI Classics ▲ CDM 65613
Strauss, R.:Till Eulenspiegels lustige Streiche, w. Philharmonia Orch — EMI Classics ▲ CDM 65613
Wagner, R.:Tannhäuser (ov & venusberg) — EMI Classics ("FDS" series) ▲ CDM 65208
D. Milhaud (cnd)
Milhaud, D.:Saudades do Brasil — EMI Classics ▲ CDC 54604
Milhaud, D.:Suite provençale — EMI Classics ▲ CDC 54604

Concert des Nations
J. Savall (cnd)
Arriaga, J.C.:Los esclavos felices (ov) — Astrée ▲ E 8532
Arriaga, J.C.:Sym in D — Astrée ▲ E 8532
Bach, J.S.:Brandenburg Cons, w. La Capella Reial de Catalunya — Astrée ▲ E 8737
Charpentier, M.-A.:Salve regina à 3 voix pareilles, w. Gérard Lesne (ct), John Elves (ten), Josep Cabré (bar) — Astrée ▲ E 8552 [DDD]
Handel, G.F.:Royal Fireworks Music — Astrée ▲ E 8512
Handel, G.F.:Water Music (comp) — Astrée ▲ E 8512
Haydn, J.:The Seven Last Words of Christ on the Cross [orchestral version] — Astrée ▲ E 8739
Marais, M.:Alcione (sels)—complete suites — Astrée ▲ E 8525
Martin Y Soler, V.:Una Cosa rara, w. M. A. Peters (sop), M. Figueras (sop), G. Fabuel (sop), E. Palacio (ten), F. Belaza-Leoz (bar), S. Palatchi (bass), F. Garrigosa (bass), I. Fresán (sgr), La Capella Reial de Catalunya [I] *(rec 1991)* — Astrée 3-▲ E 8760 [DDD]
Mozart, W.A.:Maurerische Trauermusik — Astrée ▲ E 8759

Le Concert Français
Corelli, A.:Concerti grossi, Op. 6—Nos. 3,8 & 10; No. 5 arr. into Sonata XII; Nos. 1 & 2 arr. into Sonata IV; Nos. 2,4 & 12 arr. into Sonata in F — Opus 111 ▲ OPS 54-9118 [DDD]
Mozart, W.A.:Con Pno, K.107, w. P. Hantaï (hpd) — Opus 111 ▲ OPS 30-9003
P. Hantaï (cnd)
Bach, J.S.:Con Fl, Vn & Hpd, w. Marc Hantaï (fl), François Fernandez (vn), Pierre Hantaï (hpd) — Astrée ▲ E 8523
Bach, J.S.:Con 1 Hpd, w. Pierre Hantaï (hpd) — Astrée ▲ E 8523
Bach, J.S.:Con 3 Hpd, w. Pierre Hantaï (hpd) — Astrée ▲ E 8523
Maskes & Fantazies, w. Sébastien Marc (rcr) *(rec 1992)* — Astrée ▲ E 8504 [DDD]
Telemann, G.P.:Music of, w. Sébastien Marq (rcr)—Trio in A for Rcr, Hpd & Bc; Con in F for Rcr, Hn & Bc; Fant in A for Rcr; Trio Son in F for Rcr, Vl & Bc; Trio Son in a for Rcr, Vn & Bc; Trio Son in B♭ for Rcr, Hpd & Bc; Son in C for Rcr & Bc; Fant in F [originally C] for Rcr; Trio Son in a for Rcr, Ob & Bc — Astrée ▲ E 8554

Concert Players Orch
G. Fagan (cnd)
Handel, G.F.:Messiah, w. Leslie Fagan (sop), Janis Taylor (mez), Mark Dubois (ten), Gary Relyea (b-bar), Gerald Fagan Singers, London Fanshawe Symphonic Chorus — Doremi 2-▲ 9306 [DDD]

Concert Royal
Rameau, J.P.:Le Berger fidèle, w. Christine Brandes (sop), Ann Monoyios (sop), Howard Crook (ten), Nat Wilson (b-bar) — Newport Classic ▲ NPT 85555
Rameau, J.P.:La Danse — Newport Classic ▲ NPT 85555
J. Richman (cnd)
Clérambault, L.N.:La Musette, w. A. Monoyios (sop) [F] — Elektra/Nonesuch ▲ 71371-2 ■ 71371-4
Marais, M.:Suites VI & Hpd—Suite No. 2 in D — Elektra/Nonesuch ▲ 71371-2-J ■ 71371-4
Rameau, J.P.:L'Impatience, w. Ann Monoyios (sop) [F] — Elektra/Nonesuch ▲ 71371-2 ■ 71371-4
Rameau, J.P.:Pièces de clavecin en concert—Suite No. 5 — Elektra/Nonesuch ▲ 71371-2 ■ 71371-4

Concert Spirituel Orch
H. Niquet (cnd)
Boismortier, J.B. de:Motets, w. Concert Spirituel Vocal Ensemble—Motet à grand choeur; Motet à voix seule mêlés de symphonies — Adda ▲ ADD 581255 [DDD]

Concert Spirituel Orch (cont.)
H. Niquet (cnd) (cont.)
Campra, A.:Messe de Requiem, w. Véronique Gens (sop), Anne Gotkovski (sop), Jean-Paul Fouchécourt (alt), Joseph Cornwell (ten), Peter Harvey (bar), Concert Spirituel Vocal Ensemble — Adda ▲ ADD 241952 [DDD]
Campra, A.:Motets, w. Véronique Gens (sop), Anne Gotkovski (sop), Jean-Paul Fouchécourt (alt), Joseph Cornwell (ten), Peter Harvey (bar), Concert Spirituel Vocal Ensemble—Benedictus Dominus — Adda ▲ ADD 241952 [DDD]
Campra, A.:Motets, w. Véronique Gens (sop), Anne Gotkovsky (sop), Jean-Paul Fauchecourt (ct), Hervé Lamy (ten), Peter Harvey (bass), Concert Spirituel Vocal Ensemble—2 Noster Refugium; Cantate Domino; De Profundis — Adda ▲ ADD 243912
Campra, A.:Motets, w. Véronique Gens (sop), Anne Gotkovski (sop), Jean-Paul Fouchécourt (alt), Douglas Nasrawi (ten), Peter Harvey (bar), Marcos Loureiro de Sá (bar), Kevin Mallon (vn), Concert Spirituel Vocal Ensemble—Te Deum; Notus in Judea Deus; Deus in Nomine Tuo — Adda ▲ ADD 241942 [DDD]
Gilles, J.:Sacred Music, w. Concert Spirituel Vocal Ensemble—Motet a St. Jean Baptiste; Lamentation du mercredi soir; Lamentation du jeudi soir; Lamentation du vendredi soir — Adda ▲ ADD 242322
Rossini, G.:La cambiale di matrimonio — Adda ▲ ADD 581290 [DDD]

Concertante Trio
Bartók, B.:Mikrokosmos [arr. for double bass, cello & guitar]—5 pieces *(rec 1/90)* — GM ▲ GM2035CD
Couperin, F.:Pièces en Concert *(rec 1/90)* — GM ▲ GM2035CD
Schubert, Franz:Nocturne Pno — Vox Box 2-▲ CDX 5033 [ADD]
Schubert, Franz:Trio Pno, D.28 — Vox Box 2-▲ CDX 5033 [ADD]
Schubert, Franz:Trio 1 Pno — Vox Box 2-▲ CDX 5033 [ADD]
Schubert, Franz:Trio 2 Pno — Vox Box 2-▲ CDX 5033 [ADD]
Trio Concertant — GM Recordings ▲ GM2035CD
Villa-Lobos, H.:Bachiana brasileira 5 [double bass-cello-guitar arr.] — GM ▲ GM2035CD

(Royal) Concertgebouw CO
H. Christophers (cnd)
Vivaldi, A.:Cons Fl (misc), w. J. Stinton (fl)—RV.440 — Collins Classics ▲ COL 1324 [DDD]
Vivaldi, A.:Cons Fl, Op. 10, w. J. Stinton (fl) — Collins Classics ▲ COL 1324 [DDD]
V. Negri (cnd)
Vivaldi, A.:Sacred Choral Music, w. M. Marshall (sop), J. Kowalski (ct), N. van der Meel (ten)—Deus tuorum militum, RV.612; Laudate pueri Dominum, RV.600; Sanctorum meritis, RV.620; Stabat mater, RV.621 [L] — Philips ▲ 432091-2 [DDD]
S. Preston (cnd)
Handel, G.F.:Royal Fireworks Music — London ▲ 430717-2 [DDD]
A. Rifkin (cnd)
Handel, G.F.:Cons (16) Org, w. P. Hurford (org)—Op. 4/1-6, 13 & 14 — London ("Serenata" series) 2-▲ 430569-2

(Royal) Concertgebouw Orch
V. Ashkenazy (cnd)
Rachmaninoff, S.:The Isle of the Dead — London ▲ 430733-2 [DDD]
Rachmaninoff, S.:Symphonic Dances — London ▲ 430733-2 [DDD]
Rachmaninoff, S.:Sym 2 — London ▲ 400081-2 [DDD]
E. van Beinum (cnd)
Bach, J.S.:Con 1 Hpd, w. D. Lipatti (hpd) *(rec live Oct 2, 1947)* — Jecklin-Disco ▲ JD 541-2
Debussy, C.:Orchestral Music, w. George Pieterson (cl), Vera Badings (hp)—Berceuse héroïque; Danses for Harp & Orch.; Images; Jeux; Marche écossaise; La mer; Nocturnes; Prélude à l'après-midi d'un faune; Première rapsodie for Clarinet & Orch. — Philips 2-▲ 438742-2
Flothuis, M.:Symfonische muziek — Donemus ▲ CV 26
Mozart, W.A.:Con Cl, w. de Wilde (cl) — Philips ■ 411174-4
Mozart, W.A.:Con Fl Hp, w. H. Barwahser (fl), Berghout (hp) — Philips ■ 411174-4
Stravinsky, I.:Le Sacre du printemps Orch *(rec 1946)* — Beulah ▲ 2PD11 [ADD]
L. Bernstein (cnd)
Beethoven, L. van:Missa Solemnis, w. E. Moser (sop), H. Schwarz (mez), A. Kollo (ten), K. Moll (bass), Hilversum Chorus [L] — Deutsche Grammophon 2-▲ 413780-2 [ADD]
Mahler, G.:Des Knaben Wunderhorn, w. L. Popp (sop), A. Schmidt (bar) [G] — Deutsche Grammophon ▲ 427302-2 [DDD]
Mahler, G.:Syms, w. J. Blegen (sop), B. Hendricks (sop), M. Price (sop), G. Zeumer (sop), H. Wittek (trb), A. Baltsa (mez), C. Ludwig (mez), K. Riegel (ten), H. Prey (bar), A. Schmidt (bar), J. Van Dam (b-bar), New York PO, Vienna PO, Westminster Choir, New York Choral Artists, Brooklyn Boys' Choir, Vienna Boys' Choir, Vienna State Opera Chorus, Vienna Singverein — Deutsche Grammophon 13-▲ 435162-2 [DDD]
Mahler, G.:Sym 1 — Deutsche Grammophon ▲ 427303-2 [DDD]
Mahler, G.:Sym 4, w. H. Wittek (trb) [G] — Deutsche Grammophon ▲ 423607-2 [DDD]
Mahler, G.:Sym 9 — Deutsche Grammophon 2-▲ 419208-2 [DDD]
Schubert, Franz:Sym 5 — Deutsche Grammophon ▲ 427645-2 [DDD]
Schubert, Franz:Sym 8 — Deutsche Grammophon ▲ 427645-2 [DDD]
Schubert, Franz:Sym 9 — Deutsche Grammophon ▲ 427646-2 [DDD]
P. Boulez (cnd)
Schoenberg, A.:Moses und Aaron, w. David Pittman-Jennings (nar), Gabriele Fontana (sop—Young Girl), Yvonne Naef (cta—Sick Woman), John Graham-Hall (ten—Young Man/Naked Youth), Pår Lindskog (ten—Youth), Chris Merritt (ten—Aaron), Siegfried Lorenz (bar—Another Man), Michael Devlin (b-bar—Ephraimite), László Polgár (bass—Priest), Winfried Maczewski (cnd), Netherlands Opera Chorus, Zaans Youth Choir, Waterland Music School *(rec Concertgebouw, Amsterdam, Oct 1995)* — Deutsche Grammophon 2-▲ 449 174-2 [DDD]
R. Chailly (cnd)
Berg, A.:Son Pno [orchd Verbey] — Donemus ▲ CV 31
Brahms, J.:Sym 4 — London ▲ 433151-2 [DDD]
Bruckner, A.:Sym 2 *(rec Oct. 1991)* — London ▲ 436154-2 [DDD]
Bruckner, A.:Sym 5 — London ▲ 433819-2
Debussy, C.:Khamma *(rec Grotezaal, Concertgebouw, Amsterdam, Dec 14, 1994)* — London ▲ 443934-2 [DDD]
Diepenbrock, A.:The Birds (Ov) *(rec live, Concertgebouw Amsterdam, Oct 5, 1989)* — Donemus ▲ CV 50 [DDD]
Diepenbrock, A.:Electra [arr Eduard Reeser, 1952; rev. 1992] *(rec live, Concertgebouw Amsterdam, Mar 18, 1993)* — Donemus ▲ CV 50 [DDD]
Diepenbrock, A.:Hymnen an die Nacht (2), w. Arleen Augér (sop)—Gehoben ist der Stein *(rec live, Concertgebouw Amsterdam, Oct 18, 1990)* — Donemus ▲ CV 50 [DDD]
Diepenbrock, A.:Im grossen Schweigen, w. Håkan Hagegård (bar) — London 2-▲ 444446-2
Dvořák, A.:Sym 9, "From the New World" — London ▲ 421016-2 □ 421016-5
Escher, R.:Con Str Orch — NM Classics ▲ NM 92048
Escher, R.:Musique pour l'espirit en deuil — NM Classics ▲ NM 92048
Hindemith, P.:Kammermusik (comp), w. R. Brautigam (pno), L. Harrell (vc), K. Kulka (vn), K. Kashkashian (va), N. Blume (va d'amore), L. van Doeselaar (org)—No. 1 for Small Orchestra, Op. 24/1 (1922); No. 2 (Piano Concerto) for Piano & 12 Instruments, Op. 36/1 (1924); No. 3 (Cello Concerto), foe Cello & 10 Instruments, Op. 36/2 (1925); No. 4 (Violin Concerto) for Violin & Large Orchestra, Op. 36/3 (1925); No. 5 (Viola Concerto) for Viola & Large Chamber Orchestra, Op. 36/4 (1927); No. 6 (Viola d'amore Concerto) for Viola d'amore & Chamber Orchestra, Op. 46/1 (1927); No. 7 (Organ Concerto) for Organ & chamber Orchestra, Op. 46/2 (1927) — London 2-▲ 433816-2 [DDD]
Keulen, G. van:Armonia — Donemus ▲ CV 33
Keulen, G. van:Tympan — Donemus ▲ CV 33
Mahler, G.:Sym 7 — London 2-▲ 444446-2
Messiaen, O.:Turangalîla-sym, w. T. Harada (pno) J.-Y. Thibaudet (ondes Martenot) *(rec March 1992)* — London ▲ 436626-2 [DDD]
Mosolov, A.:Foundry — London ▲ 436640-2
Prokofiev, S.:Sym 3 — London ▲ 436640-2
Ravel, M.:Daphnis et Chloé, w. Jacques Zoon (fl), Martin Wright (cnd), Netherlands Radio Chorus *(rec Grotezaal, Concertgebouw, Amsterdam, Feb 17 & 18, 1994)* — London ▲ 443934-2 [DDD]

(Royal) Concertgebouw Orch (cont.)
R. Chailly (cnd) (cont.)
Schat, P.:The Heavens — NM Classics ▲ NM 92033
Schnittke, A.:Con grosso 3 — London ▲ 430698-2 [DDD]
Schnittke, A.:Sym 5 — London ▲ 430698-2 [DDD]
Schoenberg, A.:Chamber Sym 1 — London ▲ 436467-2 [DDD]
Schoenberg, A.:Pieces Orch, Op. 16 [1949 revised version] — London ▲ 433151-2 [DDD]
Schumann, R.:Sym 1 — London □ 425608-5
Schumann, R.:Sym 4 — London □ 425608-5
Shostakovich, D.:Con 1 Pno, w. R. Brautigam (pno), P. Masseurs (tpt) — London ▲ 433702-2 [DDD]
Shostakovich, D.:Suite 1 Jazz Orch — London ▲ 433702-2 [DDD]
Shostakovich, D.:Suite 2 Jazz Orch — London ▲ 433702-2 [DDD]
Shostakovich, D.:Tahiti Trot — London ▲ 433702-2 [DDD]
Stravinsky, I.:Pétrouchka — London ▲ 443774-2 [DDD]
Stravinsky, I.:Pulcinella Suite — London ▲ 443774-2 [DDD]
Varèse, E.:Arcana — London ▲ 436640-2
Wagner, R.:Ovs, Preludes & Orch Sels—Die Meistersinger von Nürnberg [Prelude]; Die Walküre [Ride of the Valkyries]; Götterdämmerung [Dawn & Siegfried's Rhine Journey; Siegfried's Funeral March]; Tannhäuser [Ov.; Bacchanal]; Lohengrin [Prelude to Act III] *(rec Grotezaal, Concertgebouw, Amsterdam, Feb 1995)* — London ▲ 448155-2 [DDD]
Webern, A.:Im Sommerwind — London ▲ 436467-2 [DDD]
Webern, A.:Passacaglia — London ▲ 436467-2 [DDD]
Zemlinsky, A. von:Lyric Sym, w. Alessandra Marc (sop), Hakan Hagegard (bar) — London ("Entartete Musik" series) ▲ 443569-2 [DDD]
Zemlinsky, A. von:Symphonische Gesänge, w. Willard White (b-bar) — London ("Entartete Musik" series) ▲ 443569-2 [DDD]
M.-W. Chung (cnd)
Prokofiev, S.:Romeo & Juliet (sels), sels. unknown — Deutsche Grammophon ▲ 439870-2
C. Davis (cnd)
Beethoven, L. van:Con Vn, Op. 61, w. A. Grumiaux (vn) — Philips ▲ 420348-2 [ADD]
Berlioz, H.:Sym fantastique — Philips ▲ 411425-2 [ADD]
Dvořák, A.:Con Vc, w. H. Schiff (vc) — Philips ("Solo" series) ▲ 442401-2
Dvořák, A.:Sym 7 — Philips ▲ 420890-2 [ADD]
Dvořák, A.:Sym 7 — Philips 2-▲ 438347-2
Dvořák, A.:Sym 8 — Philips ▲ 420890-2 [ADD]
Dvořák, A.:Sym 8 — Philips 2-▲ 438347-2
Dvořák, A.:Sym 9, "From the New World" — Philips 2-▲ 438347-2
Haydn, J.:Syms 93-104, "The Salomon (or London) Syms"—Syms. Nos. 95, 96, 98, 102, 103 & 104 — Philips ("Duo" series) 2-▲ 442611-2
Haydn, J.:Syms 93-104, "The Salomon (or London) Syms"—Syms. Nos. 93, 94, 97, 99, 100 & 101 — Philips ("Duo" series) 2-▲ 442614-2
C. Davis, B. Haitink (cnd)
Bartók, B.:Con Orch, w. London SO, BBC SO — Philips 2-▲ 438812-2
Bartók, B.:Cons Pno (comp), w. S. Kovacevich (pno), London SO, BBC SO — Philips 2-▲ 438812-2
Bartók, B.:Con 1 Vn, w. H. Szehng (vn), London SO, BBC SO — Philips 2-▲ 438812-2
A. Dorati (cnd)
Dvořák, A.:Sym 9, "From the New World" — Philips ("Solo" series) ▲ 442401-2
Tchaikovsky, P.:The Nutcracker, w. St. Bavo Cathedral Boys' Choir — Philips ("Duo" series) 2-▲ 442562-2
Tchaikovsky, P.:Nutcracker Suite — Philips ■ 426177-4
Tchaikovsky, P.:Nutcracker Suite 2 — Philips ■ 426177-4
Tchaikovsky, P.:Sleeping Beauty — Philips ("Duo" series) 2-▲ 446166-2
Tchaikovsky, P.:Sleeping Beauty (sels), w. St. Bavo Cathedral Boys' Choir — Philips ("Duo" series) 2-▲ 442562-2
C. Dutoit (cnd)
Lalo, E.:Sym espagnole, w. Sarah Chang (vn) *(rec Concertgebouw, Amsterdam, Jan. 4-8, 1995)* — EMI Classics ▲ CDC 55292 [DDD]
C.P. Flor (cnd)
Shostakovich, D.:Sym 10 — RCA Red Seal ▲ 09026-60448-2 [DDD]
W. Furtwängler (cnd)
Beethoven, L. van:Leonore 1 *(rec live July 13, 1950)* — Music & Arts ▲ CD 2001 [AAD]
Brahms, J.:Sym 1 *(rec 1950)* — Music & Arts 2-▲ CD 289 (m) [AAD]
C. M. Giulini (cnd)
Debussy, C.:La Mer — Sony Classical ▲ SK 66832
Debussy, C.:Prélude à l'après-midi d'un faune — Sony Classical ▲ SK 66832
Dvořák, A.:Sym 7 *(rec Feb. 10-12, 1993)* — Sony Classical 2-▲ S2K 58946 [DDD]
Dvořák, A.:Sym 8 — Sony Classical ▲ SK 46670
Dvořák, A.:Sym 9, "From the New World" *(rec Feb. 10-12, 1993)* — Sony Classical 2-▲ S2K 58946 [DDD]
Mussorgsky, M.:Pictures at an Exhibition — Sony Classical ▲ SK 45935 [DDD]
Ravel, M.:Ma mère l'oye Orch — Sony Classical ▲ SK 66832
Ravel, M.:Ma mère l'oye Orch — Sony Classical ▲ SK 46670
Ravel, M.:Pavane pour une infante défunte — Sony Classical ▲ SK 66832
Stravinsky, I.:The Firebird Suite [1919 version] — Sony Classical ▲ SK 45935 [DDD]
Verdi, G.:Falstaff, w. M. Freni (sop), I. Ligabue (sop), L. Alva (ten), R. Capecchi (bar), F. Corena (bass), Netherlands Chamber Choir [I] *(rec live, The Hague 6/20/63)* — Verona 2-▲ 27095/96
B. Haitink (cnd)
Beethoven, L. van:Cons Pno (comp), w. M. Perahia (pno) — CBS 3-▲ M3K 44575 [DDD]
Beethoven, L. van:Con 1 Pno, w. M. Perahia (pno) [w. newly discovered cadenza] — CBS ▲ MK 42177 [DDD]
Beethoven, L. van:Con 2 Pno, w. M. Perahia (pno) — CBS ▲ MK 42177 [DDD]
Beethoven, L. van:Con 3 Pno, w. M. Perahia (pno) — CBS ▲ MK 39814 [DDD]
Beethoven, L. van:Con 4 Pno, w. M. Perahia (pno) — CBS ▲ MK 39814 [DDD]
Beethoven, L. van:Con 5 Pno, "Emperor", w. M. Perahia (pno) — CBS ▲ MK 42330 [DDD] ■ MT 42330 (D)
Beethoven, L. van:Con Vn, Op. 61, w. H. Szeryng (vn) — Philips ("Solo" series) ▲ 442398-2
Beethoven, L. van:Con Vn, Op. 61, w. H. Krebbers (vn) — Philips ("Duo" series) 2-▲ 442580-2
Beethoven, L. van:Romances Vn, w. Henryk Szeryng (vn) — Philips ▲ 446521-2
Beethoven, L. van:Romances Vn, w. H. Szeryng (vn) — Philips ("Solo" series) ▲ 442398-2
Beethoven, L. van:Romances Vn, w. A. Grumiaux (vn) — Philips ("Duo" series) 2-▲ 442577-2
Beethoven, L. van:Syms (comp), w. B. , C. Watkinson (contralto), P. Schreier (tenor)(te—[R. Holl (bass) in No. 9] — Philips 5-▲ 442073-2
Beethoven, L. van:Sym 5 — Philips ("Digital Classics" series) ▲ 420540-2 [DDD]
Beethoven, L. van:Sym 7 — Philips ("Digital Classics" series) ▲ 420540-2 [DDD]
Bizet, G.:Jeux d'enfants — Philips ▲ 416437-2 [ADD]
Bizet, G.:Sym 1 — Philips ▲ 416437-2 [ADD]
Brahms, J.:Academic Festival Ov — Philips 2-▲ 438320-2
Brahms, J.:Con 1 Pno, w. C. Arrau (pno) — Philips 2-▲ 438320-2
Brahms, J.:Con 1 Pno, w. V. Ashkenazy (pno) — London ▲ 410009-2 [DDD]
Brahms, J.:Con 2 Pno, w. C. Arrau (pno) — Philips 2-▲ 438320-2
Brahms, J.:Con Vn, w. Henryk Szeryng (vn) — Philips ("Solo" series) ▲ 446194-2
Brahms, J.:Con Vn, w. H. Szeryng (vn) — Philips ▲ 416438-2 [ADD]
Brahms, J.:Con Vn & Vc, "Double Con", w. Henryk Szeryng (vn), Janos Starker (vc) — Philips ("Solo" series) ▲ 446194-2
Brahms, J.:Hungarian Dances Orch — Philips 4-▲ 442068-2
Brahms, J.:Ovs — Philips 4-▲ 442068-2
Brahms, J.:Serenade 1 Orch — Philips 4-▲ 442068-2
Brahms, J.:Serenade 2 Orch — Philips 4-▲ 442068-2
Brahms, J.:Syms (comp) — Philips 4-▲ 442068-2
Brahms, J.:Tragic Ov — Philips 2-▲ 438320-2

ORCH. & ENS.

(Royal) Concertgebouw Orch (cont.)
B. Haitink (cnd) (cont.)
Brahms, J.:Vars on a Theme by Haydn Philips 2-▲ 438320-2
Brahms, J.:Vars on a Theme by Haydn Philips 4-▲ 442068-2
Bruch, M.:Con 1 Vn, w. I. Perlman (vn) EMI Classics ▲ CDC 47074 [DDD]
Bruckner, A.:Syms (comp) Philips 9-▲ 442040-2
Bruckner, A.:Sym 0 Philips 9-▲ 442040-2
Debussy, C.:Danses sacrée et profane Philips ▲ 416437-2 [ADD]
Henkemans, H.:Tre aspetti d'amore, w. NOS Radio Chorus Donemus ▲ CV 14
Ketting, O.:Symphony for Saxs, w. Netherlands Saxophone Quartet Donemus ▲ CV 21
Keuris, T.:Movements Donemus ▲ CV 30
Mahler, G.:Das Lied von der Erde, w. J. Baker (mez), J. King (ten) Philips ("Silver Line" series) ▲ 432279-2 [ADD]
Mahler, G.:Syms, w. E. Ameling (sop), H. Harper (mez), M. Forrester (cta), H. Prey (bar) Philips 10-▲ 442050-2
Mahler, G.:Sym 4, w. R. Alexander (sop) [G] Philips ▲ 412119-2 [DDD]
Mahler, G.:Sym 4, w. E. Ameling (sop) Philips ("Solo" series) ▲ 442394-2
Mahler, G.:Sym 8, w. Hanneke van Bork (sop), Ileana Cotrubas (sop), Heather Harper (sop), Brigit Finnila (mez), Marianne Dieleman (cta), William Cochran (ten), Hermann Prey (bar), Hans Sotin (bass) Philips ("Solo" series) ▲ 446195-2
Martin, F.:Con Vc, w. Jean Decroos (vc) *(rec live, Radio Hilversum, Dec 9, 1970)* Preludio ▲ PRL 2147 [ADD]
Martin, F.:Les Quatre éléments *(rec live, Radio Hilversum, Dec 9, 1970)* Preludio ▲ PRL 2147 [ADD]
Mendelssohn, F.:Con in e Vn & Orch, Op. 64, w. I. Perlman (vn) EMI Classics ▲ CDC 47074 [DDD]
Rachmaninoff, S.:Cons Pno (comp), w. V. Ashkenazy (pno) London 2-▲ 421590-2 [DDD]
Rachmaninoff, S.:Con 2 Pno, w. Vladimir Ashkenazy (pno) London ▲ 414475-2 [DDD] ■ 414475-4 □ 414475-5
Rachmaninoff, S.:Con 3 Pno, w. Vladimir Ashkenazy (pno) London ▲ 417239-2 [DDD]
Rachmaninoff, S.:Con 4 Pno, w. Vladimir Ashkenazy (pno) London ▲ 414475-2 [DDD] ■ 414475-4 □ 414475-5
Ravel, M.:Orchestral Music—Alborada del gracioso; Boléro; Daphnis et Chloé, Suite No. 2; Ma Mère l'Oye; Menuet antique; Pavane pour une infante défunte; Rhapsodie espagnole; Le tombeau de Couperin; La valse; Valses nobles et sentimentales Philips 2-▲ 438745-2
Schumann, R.:Genoveva (ov) Philips 2-▲ 442079-2
Schumann, R.:Manfred Ov Philips 2-▲ 442079-2
Schumann, R.:Syms (comp) Philips 2-▲ 442079-2
Shostakovich, D.:From Jewish Folk Poetry, w. E. Söderström (sop), O. Wenkel (cta), R. Karczykowski (ten) London ▲ 417581-2 [DDD/ADD]
Shostakovich, D.:Poems of Marina Tsvetayeva, Op. 143a, w. J. Varady (sop) London ▲ 417514-2 [DDD]
Shostakovich, D.:Sym 5 London ▲ 410017-2 [DDD]
Shostakovich, D.:Sym 13 London ▲ 417261-2 [DDD]
Shostakovich, D.:Sym 14, w. J. Varady (sop), D. Fischer-Dieskau (bar), O. Wenkel (cta) London ▲ 417514-2 [DDD]
Shostakovich, D.:Sym 15 London ▲ 417581-2 [DDD/ADD]
Strauss, R.:Eine Alpensinfonie Philips ▲ 416156-2 [DDD]
Tchaikovsky, P.:Francesca da Rimini Philips 6-▲ 442061-2
Tchaikovsky, P.:Marche slave Philips ("Concert Classics" series) ▲ 422469-2 [ADD]
Tchaikovsky, P.:Ov 1812 Philips 6-▲ 442061-2
Tchaikovsky, P.:Ov 1812 Philips ("Concert Classics" series) ▲ 422469-2 [ADD]
Tchaikovsky, P.:Romeo & Juliet Philips 6-▲ 442061-2
Tchaikovsky, P.:The Storm Philips 6-▲ 442061-2
Tchaikovsky, P.:Syms (comp) Philips 6-▲ 442061-2

N. Harnoncourt (cnd)
Haydn, J.:Sym 68 Teldec ▲ 9031-74859-2
Haydn, J.:Sym 93 Teldec ▲ 9031-74859-2
Haydn, J.:Sym 95 Teldec ▲ 9031-73148-2 [DDD]
Haydn, J.:Sym 96, "Miracle" Teldec ▲ 77315
Haydn, J.:Sym 97 Teldec ▲ 77315
Haydn, J.:Sym 98 Teldec ▲ 2292-46331-2 [DDD]
Haydn, J.:Sym 99 Teldec ▲ 2292-46331-2 [DDD]
Haydn, J.:Sym 100, "Military" Teldec ▲ 9031-74859-2
Haydn, J.:Sym 103, "Drum Roll" Teldec ▲ 2292-43526-2
Haydn, J.:Sym 104, "London" Teldec ▲ 2292-43526-2
Mozart, W.A.:Con 23 Pno, w. F. Gulda (pno) Teldec ▲ 2292-42997-2
Mozart, W.A.:Con 23 Pno, w. F. Gulda (pno) Teldec ▲ 92150
Mozart, W.A.:Con 26 Pno, w. F. Gulda (pno) Teldec ▲ 92150
Mozart, W.A.:Con 26 Pno, w. F. Gulda (pno) Teldec ▲ 2292-42997-2
Mozart, W.A.:Così fan tutte (sels), w. C. Margiono (sop), van der Walt (sop), D. Ziegler (mez), G. Cachemaille (bar)—sels. Teldec ▲ 9031-76455-2
Mozart, W.A.:Don Giovanni, w. E. Gruberova (sop), B. Bonney (sop), R. Alexander (sop), T. Hampson (bar) [I] Teldec 3-▲ 2292-44184-2 [DDD]
Mozart, W.A.:Nozze di Figaro, w. C. Margiono (sop), B. Bonney (sop), I. Rey (sop), A. Murray (mez, P.-L. Lang (mez), P. Langridge (ten), C. Späth (ten), T. Hampson (bar), K. Moll (bass), A. Scharinger (bass), K. Langan (bass), Netherlands Opera Chorus *(rec Amsterdam, May 1993)* Teldec 3-▲ 90861-2 [DDD]
Mozart, W.A.:Sym 35 Teldec ("Digital Experience" series) ▲ 9031-77595-2 [DDD] ■ 9031-77595-4
Mozart, W.A.:Sym 36 Teldec ("Digital Experience" series) ▲ 9031-77595-2 [DDD] ■ 9031-77595-4
Mozart, W.A.:Sym 38 Teldec ("Digital Experience" series) ▲ 9031-77596-2 [DDD] ■ 9031-77596-4
Mozart, W.A.:Sym 39 Teldec ("Digital Experience" series) ▲ 9031-77596-2 [DDD] ■ 9031-77596-4
Schubert, Franz:Syms (comp) Teldec 4-▲ 91184-2
Strauss (II), Joh.:Die Fledermaus (sels), w. E. Gruberova (sop)—Klänge der Heimat Teldec ▲ 450993691-2 [DDD]
Strauss (II), Joh.:Die Fledermaus (sels), w. E. Gruberova (sop), B. Bonney (sop), M. Lipovšek (mez), W. Kmentt (ten), W. Hollweg (ten), J. Protschka (ten), C. Boesch (bar), A. Scharinger (bass), Netherlands Opera Chorus Teldec ▲ 42427-2
Strauss (II), Joh.:Music of—waltzes & polkas (An der schönen, blauen Donau; etc.) Teldec ("Digital Experience" series) ▲ 9031-74786-2 AW [DDD] ■ 9031-74786-4

E. Inbal, I. Markevitch, B. Haitink (cnd)
Tchaikovsky, P.:Orch Music, w. Frankfurt RSO—Fatum, Op. 77; Francesca da Rimini, Op. 32; Hamlet, Op. 67a; The Tempest, Op. 18; The Storm, Op. 76; The Voyevode, Op. 78; Romeo & Juliet; Ov. 1812 Philips ("Duo" series) 2-▲ 442586-2

M. Jansons (cnd)
Berlioz, H.:Le Carnaval romain EMI Classics ▲ CDC 54479
Berlioz, H.:Sym fantastique EMI Classics ▲ CDC 54479

E. Jochum (cnd)
Beethoven, L. van:Egmont (ov) Theorema ▲ TH 121217

N. Järvi (cnd)
Prokofiev, S.:Cons Pno (comp), w. B. Berman (pno), H. Gutiérrez (pno) Chandos 2-▲ CHAN 8938 [DDD]
Prokofiev, S.:Con 1 Pno, w. B. Berman (pno) Chandos ▲ CHAN 8791 [DDD]
Prokofiev, S.:Con 2 Pno, w. H. Gutiérrez (pno) Chandos ▲ CHAN 8889 [DDD]
Prokofiev, S.:Con 3 Pno, w. H. Gutiérrez (pno) Chandos ▲ CHAN 8889 [DDD]
Prokofiev, S.:Con 4 Pno, w. B. Berman (pno) Chandos ▲ CHAN 8791 [DDD]
Prokofiev, S.:Con 5 Pno, w. B. Berman (pno) Chandos ▲ CHAN 8791 [DDD]

(Royal) Concertgebouw Orch (cont.)
N. Järvi (cnd) (cont.)
Rachmaninoff, S.:Rhapsody on a Theme of Paganini, w. Bella Davidovich (pno) Philips ▲ 410052-2 [DDD]
Reger, M.:Tondichtungen nach Arnold Böcklin Chandos ▲ CHAN 8794 [DDD]
Reger, M.:Vars & Fugue on a Theme of of J. A. Hiller Chandos ▲ CHAN 8794 [DDD]
Saint-Saëns, C.:Con 2 Pno, w. B. Davidovich (pno) Philips ▲ 410052-2 [DDD]
Stravinsky, I.:Jeu de cartes Chandos ▲ CHAN 9014 [DDD]
Stravinsky, I.:Orpheus Chandos ▲ CHAN 9014 [DDD]

H. von Karajan (cnd)
Brahms, J.:Sym 1 Grammofon 2000 ▲ GRM 78663

E. Kleiber (cnd)
Beethoven, L. van:Sym 7 *(rec 1950)* Theorema 2-▲ TH 121211/212

O. Klemperer (cnd)
Bach, J.S.:Brandenburg Con 1 *(rec 1957)* Legend ▲ LGD 103 [ADD]
Bach, J.S.:Cant 202, "Wedding Cant", w. Elisabeth Schwarzkopf (sop) *(rec Amsterdam, Feb 16, 1957)* Bella Voce 2-▲ 107.201 [AAD]
Bach, J.S.:Cant 202, "Wedding Cant", w. E. Schwarzkopf (sop) *(rec 1957)* Legend ▲ LGD 103 [ADD]
Bach, J.S.:Cant 202, "Wedding Cant", w. Elisabeth Schwarzkopf (sop) *(rec live, 1957)* As Disc ▲ ASD 2504 (m)
Bartók, B.:Con Va, w. W. Primrose (va) *(rec live, Jan.10, 1951)* Music & Arts ▲ CD 752-1 (m) [AAD]
Bartók, B.:Con Va, w. W. Primrose (va) *(rec live, Jan. 10, 1951)* Archipon ▲ ARC 101 (m) [ADD]
Beethoven, L. van:Ah, perfido!, w. G. Brouwenstijn (sop) *(rec live April 26, 1951)* Music & Arts ▲ CD 752-1 (m) [AAD]
Beethoven, L. van:Ah, perfido!, w. Gré Brouwenstijn (sop) *(rec Amsterdam, Apr 26, 1951)* Bella Voce 2-▲ 107.201 [AAD]
Beethoven, L. van:Sym 6, "Pastorale" *(rec live, Amsterdam, 1957)* Enterprise ("Palladio" series) ▲ ENTPD 4208 [ADD]
Beethoven, L. van:Sym 6, "Pastorale" *(rec 1956–57)* Music & Arts ▲ CD 246 [ADD]
Beethoven, L. van:Sym 7 *(rec Apr. 26, 1951)* Archipon ▲ ARC 109 [ADD]
Beethoven, L. van:Sym 8 *(rec 1956–57)* Music & Arts ▲ CD 246 [ADD]
Beethoven, L. van:Sym 9, "Choral Sym" [G] *(rec 1956)* Music & Arts ▲ CD 242
Brahms, J.:Vars on a Theme by Haydn *(rec live, 1957)* Music & Arts ▲ CD 247 (m)
Bruckner, A.:Sym 6 *(rec live, 1961)* Music & Arts ▲ CD 247 (m)
Falla, M. de:Noches en los jardines de España, w. W. Andriessen (pno) *(rec live March 29, 1951)* Music & Arts ▲ CD 752-1 (m) [AAD]
Janácek, L.:Sinfonietta *(rec live, Jan. 10, 1951)* Archipon ▲ ARC 101 (m) [ADD]
Janácek, L.:Sinfonietta *(rec live, Jan. 11, 1951)* Music & Arts ▲ CD 752-1 (m) [AAD]
Klemperer, O.:Sym 1 *(rec live, 6/22/61)* Memories 2-▲ HR 4248/49 (m) [ADD]
Mahler, G.:Lieder eines fahrenden Gesellen, w. H. Schey (bar) *(rec Nov. 24, 1948)* Archipon ▲ ARC 109 [ADD]
Mahler, G.:Sym 2, w. J. Vincent (sop), K. Ferrier (cta) [G] *(rec 7/12/51)* Verona 2-▲ 27062/63 (m) [AAD]
Mahler, G.:Sym 2, w. J. Vincent (sop), K. Ferrier (cta)—abridged version of the 4th movt., "Urlicht," from the above rec'g Verona ▲ 27076 (m) [AAD]
Mendelssohn, F.:Die Hebriden *(rec live 2/21/57)* Memories 2-▲ HR 4248/49 (m) [ADD]
Mendelssohn, F.:A Midsummer Night's Dream (ov) *(rec live 11/3/55)* Memories 2-▲ HR 4248/49 (m) [ADD]
Mozart, W.A.:Con 22 Pno, w. A. Fischer (pno) *(rec live July 12, 1956)* Memories 2-▲ HR 4248/49 (m) [ADD]
Mozart, W.A.:Sym 25 *(rec Jan. 18, 1951)* Archipon ▲ ARC 109 [ADD]
Schoenberg, A.:Verklärte Nacht *(rec live July 7, 1955)* Archipon ▲ ARC 101 (m) [ADD]
Schoenberg, A.:Verklärte Nacht *(rec live 7/7/55)* Memories 2-▲ HR 4248/49 (m) [ADD]
Schubert, Franz:Sym 4 *(rec live 2/20/57)* Memories 2-▲ HR 4248/49 (m) [ADD]
Schumann, R.:Sym 4 *(rec 1957)* Legend ▲ LGD 103 [ADD]
Strauss, R.:Till Eulenspiegels lustige Streiche *(rec live Sept. 7, 1957)* Music & Arts ▲ CD 751-1 (m) [AAD]

K. Kondrashin (cnd)
Rachmaninoff, S.:Symphonic Dances *(rec 1976)* Emergo ▲ EC 3962
Tchaikovsky, P.:Suite 3 *(rec 1974)* Emergo ▲ EC 3962

A. Lazarev (cnd)
Baby Dance:A Toddler's Jump on the Classics, w. Bolshoi SO, Cleveland Orch, English Baroque Orch, J. E. Gardiner (cnd), T. Koopman (cnd), N. Harnoncourt (cnd), R. Leppard (cnd) Erato ▲ 96887-2 ■ 96887-4 ■ 97328-4 (blis

W. Mengelberg (cnd)
Bach, J.S.:Con for 2 Vns *(rec 1935–42)* Pearl ▲ PEA 9154 [ADD]
Bach, J.S.:St. Matthew Passion (sels) Archive Documents ("The Mengelberg Edition" series) ▲ ADCD 109
Bach, J.S.:Suite 2 Orch Grammofono 2000 3-▲ GRM 78637
Beethoven, L. van:Egmont (ov) Grammofono 2000 3-▲ GRM 78637
Beethoven, L. van:Leonore 3 Grammofono 2000 3-▲ GRM 78637
Beethoven, L. van:Ovs—Coriolan; Leonore 1 InSync ■ C 4129 (m)
Beethoven, L. van:Sym 5 *(rec May 4, 1937)* Teldec ("Historic" series) ▲ 95515-2 [ADD]
Beethoven, L. van:Sym 8 *(rec Nov. 9, 1938)* Teldec ("Historic" series) ▲ 95515-2 [ADD]
Beethoven, L. van:Sym 9, "Choral Sym", w. To de Sluys (sop), Suze Luger (cta), Louis van Tulder (ten), Willem Ravelli (bass), Toonkunst Chorus *(rec 1938)* Music & Arts ▲ CD 918
Beethoven, L. van:Sym 9, "Choral Sym", w. *(chorus unknown)* Archive Documents ("The Mengelberg Edition" series) ▲ ADCD 113
Berlioz, H.:La Damnation de Faust (sels)—3 exerpts *(rec 1935–42)* Pearl ▲ PEA 9154 [ADD]
Borodin, A.:In the Steppes of Central Asia Archive Documents ("The Mengelberg Edition" series) ▲ ADCD 108
Borodin, A.:In the Steppes of Central Asia *(rec 1935–42)* Pearl ▲ PEA 9154 [ADD]
Brahms, J.:Academic Festival Ov Grammofono 2000 3-▲ GRM 78637
Brahms, J.:Sym 3 Archive Documents ("The Mengelberg Edition" series) ▲ ADCD 107
Brahms, J.:Sym 3 *(rec 1932)* GSE Claremont 2-▲ GSE 785048/49
The Complete Columbia Recordings, Vol. 1 Pearl 3-▲ PEA 9018
Debussy, C.:Prélude à l'après-midi d'un faune Archive Documents ("The Mengelberg Edition" series) ▲ ADCD 107
Franck, C.:Psyché et Eros Archive Documents ("The Mengelberg Edition" series) ▲ ADCD 107
Franck, C.:Sym in d *(rec Amsterdam, 1940)* Arkadia ▲ HP 627 [ADD]
Gluck, C.W.:Alceste (ov) *(rec 1935)* Koch Legacy ▲ 3-7011-2 (m) [DDD] ■ 3-7011-4 (m)
Grieg, E.:Peer Gynt Suite 1 Archive Documents ("The Mengelberg Edition" series) ▲ ADCD 108
Kodály, Z.:Háry János (suite) Archive Documents ("The Mengelberg Edition" series) ▲ ADCD 115
Kodály, Z.:Vars on a Hungarian Folk Song Archive Documents ("The Mengelberg Edition" series) ▲ ADCD 115
Liszt, F.:Les Préludes Archive Documents ("The Mengelberg Edition" series) ▲ ADCD 107
Liszt, F.:Les Préludes Grammofono 2000 3-▲ GRM 78637
Mozart, W.A.:Exsultate, w. *(soloists unknown)* Archive Documents ("The Mengelberg Edition" series) ▲ ADCD 109
Mozart, W.A.:Kleine Nachtmusik *(rec 1935–42)* Pearl ▲ PEA 9154 [ADD]
Overtures InSync ■ C 4129 (m)
Puccini, G.:Madama Butterfly (sels), w. Grace Moore (sop)—Un bel dí Archive Documents ("The Mengelberg Edition" series) ▲ ADCD 109
Rachmaninoff, S.:Con 2 Pno, w. W. Gieseking (pno) *(rec 1940)* Music & Arts ▲ CD 250 (m)
Rachmaninoff, S.:Con 3 Pno, w. Walter Gieseking (pno) *(rec 1940)* Music & Arts ▲ CD 250 (m)
Ravel, M.:Daphnis et Chloé (suite 2) Archive Documents ("The Mengelberg Edition" series) ▲ ADCD 115
Schubert, Franz:Rosamunde (sels), w. Betty Van den Bosch (sop)—Lieder & Arias Archive Documents ("The Mengelberg Edition" series) ▲ ADCD 109
Schubert, Franz:Sym 8 *(rec 1935–42)* Pearl ▲ PEA 9154 [ADD]

(Royal) Concertgebouw Orch (cont.)
W. Mengelberg (cnd) (cont.)
Tchaikovsky, P.:Ov 1812 *(rec Apr. 22, 1941)* Teldec (Historic) ▲ 93673
Tchaikovsky, P.:Ov 1812 Grammofono 2000 3–▲ GRM 78637
Tchaikovsky, P.:Romeo & Juliet *(rec 1931)* GSE Claremont 2–▲ GSE 785048/49
Tchaikovsky, P.:Romeo & Juliet *(rec 1930)* Music & Arts 2–▲ CD 809 [DDD]
Tchaikovsky, P.:Romeo & Juliet *(rec 1929–30)* LYS ▲ LYS 132
Tchaikovsky, P.:Serenade Strs *(rec 1928)* Music & Arts 2–▲ CD 809 [DDD]
Tchaikovsky, P.:Sym 4 *(rec 1929)* Music & Arts 2–▲ CD 809 [DDD]
Tchaikovsky, P.:Sym 4 *(rec 1929)* GSE Claremont 2–▲ GSE 785048/49
Tchaikovsky, P.:Sym 4 *(rec.1929–30)* LYS ▲ LYS 132
Tchaikovsky, P.:Sym 5 *(rec 1928)* InSync ■ C 4138
Tchaikovsky, P.:Sym 5 *(rec 1928)* Music & Arts 2–▲ CD 809 [DDD]
Tchaikovsky, P.:Sym 5 *(rec 1928)* GSE Claremont 2–▲ GSE 785048/49
Tchaikovsky, P.:Sym 6 *(rec 1937)* Music & Arts 2–▲ CD 809 [DDD]
Tchaikovsky, P.:Sym 6 Grammofono 2000 3–▲ GRM 78637
Tchaikovsky, P.:Sym 6 *(rec Apr. 22, 1941)* Teldec (Historic) ▲ 93673
Tchaikovsky, P.:Sym 6 Archive Documents ("The Mengelberg Edition" series) ▲ ADCD 108
Wagner, R.:Lohengrin (preludes)—Act 1 Grammofono 2000 3–▲ GRM 78637
Wagner, R.:Tannhäuser (ov) Grammofono 2000 3–▲ GRM 78637
Wagner, R.:Tannhäuser (ov) *(rec Amsterdam, 1926)* Iron Needle ▲ IN 1325 [ADD]
Weber, C.M. von:Der Freischütz (ov) Grammofono 2000 3–▲ GRM 78637
Weber, C.M. von:Oberon (sels), w. Ruth Horna (sop)—Ozean du ungeheuer
Archive Documents ("The Mengelberg Edition" series) ▲ ADCD 109
Weber, C.M. von:Oberon (ov) Grammofono 2000 3–▲ GRM 78637
Weber, C.M. von:Ovs—Oberon In Sync ■ C 4129 (m)
Willem Mengelberg & the Concertgebouw Orchestra:The Complete Columbia Recordings, Vol. 2 *(rec 1926–32)* Pearl 3–▲ PEA 9070 [AAD]
D. Mitropoulos (cnd)
Bach, J.S.:Con 1 Hpd, w. G. Gould (pno) *(rec live, Salzburg, Oct 10, 1958)*
Memories 2–▲ HR 4415/16 (m) [ADD]
P. Monteux (cnd)
Ravel, M.:Daphnis et Chloé *(rec June 23, 1955)* Music & Arts ▲ CD 812 [AAD]
Ravel, M.:Shéhérazade Mez, w. V. de los Angeles (sop) *(rec Nov. 20, 1953)*
Music & Arts ▲ CD 812 [AAD]
A. Panufnik (cnd)
Panufnik, A.:Arbor Cosmica Elektra/Nonesuch ▲ 79228–2 ■ 79228–4
N. Rescigno (cnd)
At the Concertgebouw Amsterdam, w. Maria Callas (sop) *(rec July 1950)* Verona ▲ 2706 [AAD]
K. Sanderling (cnd)
Beethoven, L. van:Con 3 Pno, w. Mitsuko Uchida (pno) Philips ▲ 446082–2
Beethoven, L. van:Con 4 Pno, w. Mitsuko Uchida (pno) [live recording] Philips ▲ 446082–2
W. Sawallisch (cnd)
Beethoven, L. van:Sym 2 EMI Classics ▲ CDC 54502
Beethoven, L. van:Sym 3, "Eroica" EMI Classics ▲ CDC 54501
Beethoven, L. van:Sym 4 EMI Classics ▲ CDC 54503
Beethoven, L. van:Sym 5 EMI Classics ▲ CDC 54504
Beethoven, L. van:Sym 6, "Pastorale" EMI Classics ▲ CDC 54504
Beethoven, L. van:Sym 7 EMI Classics ▲ CDC 54503
Beethoven, L. van:Sym 8 EMI Classics ▲ CDC 54502
Beethoven, L. van:Sym 9, "Choral Sym", w. M. Price (sop), M. Lipovsk (alt), P. Seifert (ten), J.–H. Rootering (bass), Düsseldorf Municipal Choral Society EMI Classics ▲ CDC 54505
C. Schuricht (cnd)
Mahler, G.:Das Lied von der Erde, w. Kerstin Thorborg (alt), Carl Martin Öhman (ten) *(rec live, Amsterdam, Oct 5, 1939)* Minerva ▲ MN A30 (m) [ADD]
Mahler, G.:Das Lied von der Erde, w. K. Thorborg (mez), C. Martin Öhmann (ten) *(rec live, Amsterdam, Oct. 5, 1939)* Archipon ▲ ARCH 3.1 (m) [ADD]
Mahler, G.:Das Lied von der Erde, w. Kerstin Thorborg (mez) Archiphon ▲ ARCH 3.1
Verdi, G.:Requiem Mass, w. I. Auez (sop), L. Fischer (cta), L. van Tulder (ten), H. Schey (bar), Amsterdam Toonkunst Choir *(rec live, Amsterdam, Nov. 2, 1939)*
Archipon 2–▲ ARC 3.2/3 (m) [ADD]
G. Solti (cnd)
Mahler, G.:Das Lied von der Erde, w. M. Lipovšek (mez), T. Moser (ten) *(rec live Dec. 1992)*
London ▲ 440314–2
Shostakovich, D.:Sym 1 London ▲ 436469–2 [DDD]
Stravinsky, I.:Le Sacre du printemps Orch London ▲ 436469–2 [DDD]
G. Szell (cnd)
Mozart, W.A.:Con 9 Pno, w. Rudolf Firkusny (pno)
Sony Classical ("Festspiel Dokumente:Salzburger Festspiele" series) ▲ SMK 68445
Mozart, W.A.:Sym 41
Sony Classical ("Festspiel Dokumente:Salzburger Festspiele" series) ▲ SMK 68445
M. Tilson Thomas (cnd)
Ives, C.:Orchestral Set 2 CBS ▲ MK 37823 [DDD]
Ives, C.:Sym 2 Sony Classical SK 46440 [DDD]
Ives, C.:Sym 3 Sony Classical ▲ SK 46440 [DDD]
Ives, C.:Sym 3 CBS ▲ MK 37823 [DDD]
L. Vis (cnd)
Escher, R.:Sinf in Memoriam Maurice Ravel—Largo Donemus ▲ CV 22
H. Vonk (cnd)
Henkemans, H.:Elégies for 4 Fls Donemus ▲ CV 14
B. Walter (cnd)
Brahms, J.:Con 1 Pno, w. Vladimir Horowitz (pno) *(rec live, Feb. 20, 1936)* As Disc ▲ ASD 2400 (m)
Busoni, F.:Con Vn, w. Adolf Busch (vn) *(rec Mar. 12, 1936)* Music & Arts ▲ CD 861 [AAD]
(Royal) Concertgebouw Orch members
C. de Wolff (cnd)
Bach, J.S.:St. John Passion, w. B. Schlick (sop), K. Ishii (ten), M. van Egmond (b–bar), Holland Bach Choir [G] Sound 3–▲ CD 3488/90
Il Concertino
Telemann, G.P.:Chamber Music—Sonata in B♭ for Oboe & Continuo, TWV 41:B6; Sonata in d for Treble Recorder & Continuo, TWV 41:d4; Two Sonatas for Treble Recorder, Oboe & Continuo (in c, TWV 42:c2 & in F, TWV 7:41); Sonata in e for Viol & Continuo, TWV 41:e5; Solo in C for Harpsichord, TWV 32:3 Kontrapunkt ▲ 32041 [DDD]
Concertiva Trio
Giocattoli di Musica Barocca Supraphon ▲ SUP 112157 [DDD]
Concerto Amsterdam
Vivaldi, A.:Music of, w. Philharmonia Baroque Orch, Boston Museum Trio, Clemencic Consort, Bologna I Filarmonici—sels. from Flute Concerto, RV.427 & 440; Four Seasons—Autumn; String Concerto, RV.129 & 152; Serenata a Tre, RV.690; Sonata, RV.2 *(rec 1970–86)*
Harmonia Mundi Plus ▲ HMP 390810
F. Brüggen (cnd)
Telemann, G.P.:Con Va, w. P. Doctor (va) Teldec ▲ 77620–2 [ADD]
J. Jürgens (cnd)
Bach, J.S.:Cant 27, w. R. Hansmann (sop), H. Watts (cta), K. Equiluz (ten), M. Van Egmond (b–bar), Monteverdi Choir London Teldec (Das alte Werke) ▲ 93687
Bach, J.S.:Cant 158, w. R. Hansmann (sop), H. Watts (cta), K. Equiluz (ten), M. Van Egmond (b–bar), Monteverdi Choir London Teldec ("Das alte Werke" series) ▲ 93687
Bach, J.S.:Cant 198, w. R. Hansmann (sop), H. Watts (cta), M. Van Egmond (b–bar), Monteverdi Choir London Teldec (Das alte Werke) ▲ 93687
J. Schröder (cnd)
Danzi, F.:Con Hn, w. Hermann Baumann (hn) *(rec 1969)* Teldec ▲ TEL SEL 12324 [ADD]

Concerto Amsterdam (cont.)
J. Schröder (cnd) (cont.)
Haydn, J.:Con 1 Hn, w. Hermann Baumann (hn) *(rec 1969)* Teldec ▲ TEL SEL 12324 [ADD]
Mozart, L.:Con 2 Hns, w. H. Baumann (hn), M. Cakar (hn) Acanta ▲ 43278
Mozart, L.:Sym in G, "Sinf da caccia", w. H. Baumann (hn) Acanta ▲ 43278
A Musical Grand Tour, w. Capella Savaria [cnd:Pál Németh], Ensemble 415 [cnd:Chiara Banchini], Philharmonia Baroque [cnd:Nicholas McGegan], et al. Harmonia Mundi ▲ HMUK 986001
Pokorny, F.X.:Con Hns, w. H. Baumann (hn), C. Kohler (hn) Acanta ▲ 43278
Rosetti, F.A.:Con Hn, w. H. Baumann (hn)—Con. in F Acanta ▲ 43278
Rosetti, F.A.:Cons Hn, w. Hermann Baumann (hn)—in d *(rec 1969)* Teldec ▲ TEL SEL 12324 [ADD]
Witt, F.:Con Hns, w. H. Baumann (hn), M. Cakar (hn)—in F Acanta ▲ 43278
Concerto Armonico
Albinoni, T.:Cons à 5 Obs, Op. 9—Book 1 *(rec Budapest, Hungary, Jan 1992)*
Arts Music ▲ 47132–2 [DDD]
Bach, C.P.E.:Cons Hpd & Strs, w. Miklós Spányi (hpd) *(rec Angyalföld Reformed Church, Dec 15–17, 1994)* BIS ▲ CD 707 [DDD]
Bach, C.P.E.:Kbd Music, w. Miklós Spányi (hpd) [period instrs]—Cons in G, A & F, H.406, 410 & 415 *(rec Angyalföld Reformed Church, Budapest, Hungary, Nov 17–19, 1994)* BIS ▲ CD 708 [DDD]
Concerto Armonico Budapest
E. Kollár (cnd)
Caldara, A.:Stabat Mater, w. I. Verebics (sop), É. Lax (mez), G. Kállay (ten), B. Szilágyi (bar), Monteverdi Chamber Choir [L] Hungaroton ▲ HCD 31273 [DDD]
P. Szüts (cnd)
Bach, C.P.E.:Cons Hpd & Strs, w. Miklós Spányi (hpd)—in g, H.409; in A, H.411; in D, H.421 *(rec Angyalföld Reformed Church, Budapest, Hungary, Oct 29–30, 1995)* BIS ▲ CD 767 [DDD]
Bach, C.P.E.:Cons Hpd & Strs, w. M. Spányi (hpd)—in d, H.427 (W.23); in c, H.441 (W.31); in F, H.443 (W.33) [period instrs] Hungaroton ▲ HCD 31159 [DDD]
Concerto Avenna
A. Mysinski (cnd)
Górecki & Friends:Polish Chamber Music Elysium ▲ GRK 703 [DDD]
Concerto Cologne
Arriaga, J.C.:Sym in D *(rec Feb & Apr 1993)* Capriccio ▲ 10 488 [DDD]
Durante, F.:Con per quartetto—Concerti Nos. 1–5 & 8 [period instrs] Capriccio ▲ CD 10 371
Dussek, J.L.:Con Pno Op. 22, w. Andreas Staier (pno) *(rec German Radio, Cologne, Nov 24–28, 1992)* Capriccio ▲ 10 444 [DDD]
Dussek, J.L.:Con Pno Op. 49, w. Andreas Staier (pno) *(rec German Radio, Cologne, Nov 24–28, 1992)* Capriccio ▲ 10 444 [DDD]
Kraus, J.M.:Syms Capriccio Δ 7039 □ 70396
Locatelli, P.:Concerti grossi—Nos. 3 & 12 *(rec Kempen, Mar. 25–28, 1994)*
Teldec ▲ 94551–2 [DDD]
Locatelli, P.:Cons for 4 Vns—Nos. 4 & 6 *(rec Kempen, Mar. 25–28, 1994)*
Teldec ▲ 94551–2 [DDD]
Locatelli, P.:Introduttioni teatrali & Concerti—Con. in E♭ *(rec Kempen, Mar. 25–28, 1994)*
Teldec ▲ 94551–2 [DDD]
Locatelli, P.:Introduttioni teatrali & Concerti, w. Werner Ehrhardt (vn)—No. 4
Pierre Verany ▲ PV 787093 [DDD]
Mendelssohn, F.:Sinf 8 *(rec Cologne, July 1994)* Teldec ▲ 94565–2 [DDD]
Mendelssohn, F.:Sinf 9 *(rec Cologne, July 1994)* Teldec ▲ 94565–2 [DDD]
Mendelssohn, F.:Sinf 10 *(rec Cologne, July 1994)* Teldec ▲ 94565–2 [DDD]
Moreno, F.J.:Sym *(rec Feb. & Apr. 1993)* Capriccio ▲ 10 488 [DDD]
Mozart, W.A.:Con Cl, w. P.–A.Taillard (b cl) Capriccio Δ 70375
Mozart, W.A.:Con Fl Hp, w. M. Sandhoff (fl), S. Kwast (hp) Capriccio Δ 70375
Mozart, W.A.:Con Ob, K.314, w. M. Niesemann (ob) Capriccio Δ 70375
Nonó, J.:Sym *(rec Feb. & Apr. 1993)* Capriccio ▲ 10 488 [DDD]
Pons, J.:Sym in G *(rec Feb. & Apr. 1993)* Capriccio ▲ 10 488 [DDD]
Vivaldi, A.:Cons Diverse Instrs—RV.158, 162, 441, 545, 565, 566, 585
Capriccio ▲ CD 10233 ■ CAS 27233 (CrO2)
Vivaldi, A.:Cons Rcr, w. Martin Sandhoff (rcr), Cordula Breuer (rcr) LaserLight ▲ 14036 [DDD]
Vivaldi, A.:Cons Rcr, w. Breuer (rcr) LaserLight ▲ 15634 [DDD]
W. Ehrhardt (cnd)
Sammartini, G.B.:Sinf in A Pierre Verany ▲ PV 787093 [DDD]
Vivaldi, A.:Cons Fl (misc), w. C. Mendoze (rcr)—RV.433, 439, 434
Pierre Verany ▲ PV 787093 [DDD]
Vivaldi, A.:Cons Orch—in b Pierre Verany ▲ PV 787093 [DDD]
R. Jacobs (cnd)
Graun, K.H.:Cesare e Cleopatra, w. Janet Williams (sop), Debora Beronesi (sop), Lynne Dawson (sop), Curtis Rayam (ten), Berlin State Opera Chorus members Serenissima 3–▲ SER 360171 [DDD]
Graun, K.H.:Cesare e Cleopatra, w. Janet Williams (sop), Lynne Dawson (sop), Iris Vermillion (mez), Robert Gambill (ten) Harmonia Mundi France 3–▲ HMC 901561.63
Handel, G.F.:Giulio Cesare in Egitto, w. Barbara Schlick (sop), Jennifer Larmore (mez), Marianne Rørholm (mez), Bernarda Fink (cta), Derek Lee Ragin (ct), Dominique Visse (ct), Oliver Lallouette (bass), Furio Zanasi (bass) [period instrs] Harmonia Mundi France 3–▲ HMC 901385/87
Handel, G.F.:Giulio Cesare in Egitto (sels), w. Barbara Schlick (sop), Jennifer Larmore (mez), Marianne Rørholm (mez), Bernarda Fink (cta), Derek Lee Ragin (ct) Harmonia Mundi France ▲ HMC 901458
R. Otto (cnd)
Bach, J.S.:Christmas Oratorio, w. Ruth Ziesak (sop), Monica Groop (alt), Christoph Pregardien (ten), Klaus Mertens (bass), Frankfurt Vocal Ensemble *(rec Festeburgkirche Frankfurt, Jan 9–16, 1991 & May 12–1)* Capriccio 2–▲ 60025–2 [DDD]
Concerto Copenhagen
A. Manze (cnd)
Agrell, J.:Con Fl, w. M. Bania (fl) *(rec Aug 1992)* Chandos ("Chaconne" series) ▲ CHAN 0535 [DDD]
Hasse, J.A.:Con Fl, w. Irene Spranger (fl) *(rec Aug. 8–10, 1992)*
Chandos ("Chaconne" series) ▲ CHAN 0535 [DDD]
Scheibe, J.A.:Con Fl in A, w. M. Bania (fl) *(rec Aug. 8–10, 1992)*
Chandos ("Chaconne" series) ▲ CHAN 0535 [DDD]
Scheibe, J.A.:Con Fl in D, w. I. Spranger (fl) *(rec Aug. 8–10, 1992)*
Chandos ("Chaconne" series) ▲ CHAN 0535 [DDD]
Scheibe, J.A.:Sinf à 16 Chandos ("Chaconne" series) ▲ CHAN 0550 [DDD]
Concerto delle Viole
R. Gini (cnd)
De Vitae Fugacitate:Lamentos, Cantatas & Arias, w. Claudio Cavina (ct/alt), R. Bertini (sop), R. Balconi (ct) *(rec Aug. 1992)* Glossa ▲ GCD 920901 [DDD]
Concerto di Viole
M. Zöbeley (cnd)
Lassus, O. de:Madrigals, w. Cornetti con Crema, Group for Early Music—Il grave dell'età; Vedi l'aurora; Più volte un bel desio; Come pianta; Ben sono i prema tuoi; Canzon, la doglia; Che giova posseder; Così cor mio; Veggio se al vero; Arse la fiamma; Chi è fermato; Chi non sa; Per aspro mar; Ecco che pur vi lasso; Deh lascia anima; Tanto è quel bene; Hor ch'a l'albergo; Prendi l'aurata lira; O fugace dolcezza; Signor, le colpe mie Ars Musici ▲ 1099 [DDD]
Concerto Ensemble
Berteau, M.:Trio (Son Sesta) *(rec 11/90)* Tactus ▲ TC 680001
Cirri, G.B.:Son Prima *(rec 11/90)* Tactus ▲ TC 680001
Cirri, G.B.:Son Terza *(rec 11/90)* Tactus ▲ TC 680001
Martini, G.B.:Son Vc & Hpd Tactus ▲ TC 680001
R. Gini (cnd)
Jommelli, N.:Agonia di Cristo [I] *(rec 5/91)* Nuova Era ("Ancient Music" series) ▲ 7030 [DDD]
Monteverdi, C.:Ballo delle ingrate [I] Tactus ▲ TC 561304 [DDD]
Monteverdi, C.:Madrigals—from Madrigals, Book Seven—Se i languidi miei sguardi (Lettera amorosa) & Se pur destina (Partenza amorosa); from Book Eight—Il lamento della ninfa [I]
Tactus ▲ TC 561302 [DDD]

ORCH. & ENS.

Concerto Ensemble (cont.)
R. Gini (cnd) (cont.)
Monteverdi, C.:Sacred Vocal Music—11 hymns, antiphons & motets by Monteverdi (with 5 intonazioni for organ by Andrea & Giovanni Gabrieli placed throughout the program)—Cantate Domino canticum novum (1615); Ego flos campi; Salve, o Regina (1624); Ecce sacrum paratum convivium; Ego dormio, et cor meum vigilat; O quam pulchra es, amica mea; Salve, Regina; Currite, populi, psallite tympanis (1625); Exulta, filia Sion (1629); Venite, videte (1645); Laudate Dominum, omnes gentes (1651) Tactus ▲ TC 561304
Pergolesi, G.B.:Cants da camera, w. A. R. de Simone (sop) *(rec Feb. 25–28, 1991)* Tactus ▲ TC 711601
Vivaldi, A.:Cants, w. A. Ruffini (sop), C. Calvi (cta)—(5 Cantatas) "Fonte del pianto," RV.656; "Sorge vermiglia in ciel," RV.667; "Lungi dal vago volto," RV.680; "Perfidissimo cor, iniquo fato," RV.674; "Piango, gemo, sospiro e peno," RV.675 [I] Nuova Era ("Ancient Music" series) ▲ 6859 [DDD]

Concerto Ensemble [Christina Miatello (sop), Claudio Cavina (alt), Laura Alvini (pno), Roberto Gini (kbd/cnd)]
Durante, F.:Duetti da camera (12)—Andate o miei sospiri; Son io barbara donna; Qualor tento scoprire; Alme voi che provaste; Metilde, alma mia; Oh quante volte, oh quante; Metilde, mio tesoro; Fiero, acerbo destin; La vezzosa Celinda; Amor, Metilde è morta; Dormono l'aure estive; Al fin m'ucciderete Tactus ▲ TC 680401

Concerto Italiano
Festa Italiana, w. Barbara Schlick (sop), Fabio Biondi (vn), Pascal Monteilhet (va), Maurizio Naddeo (vc), Rinaldo Alessandrini (hpd), Europa Galante Opus 111 5-▲ 2001
R. Alessandrini (cnd)
Banchieri, A.:Festino nella sera del giovedi grasso avanti cena Opus 111 ▲ OPS 30-137
Frescobaldi, G.:Arie musicali per cantarsi, w. G. Banditelli (mez), R. Bertini (sop), C. Cavina (alt), G. Maletto (ten), S. Naglia (ten), S. Foresti (bass) Opus 111 2-▲ OPS 30-105/106
Frescobaldi, G.:Madrigali (19)—Fortunata per me, felice aurora; Se la doglia e'l martire; Ahi, bella si, ma cruda mia nemica; Da qual sfera del ciel fra noi discese; Perchè spess'a veder la vostra luce; "Amor", ti chiama il mondo; Tu pur mi fuggi ancora; S'a la gelata mia, timida lingua; Vezzosissima Filli; Perchè fuggi tra salci; Giunt'è pur Lidia il mio; Ecco l'hora ecco ch'io; Lidia, ti lasso, ahi lasso; S'io miro in te, m'uccidi; Amor mio, perchè pianti; Lasso, io languisco e moro; Cor mio, chi mi t'invola; So ch'aveste in lasciarmi; Qui dunque, ohime, qui, dove; Se lontana voi sete; Come perder poss'io Opus 111 ▲ OPS 30-133
Lassus, O. de:Choral Music—Allala, pia calia; Saccio 'na cosa; Lucia, celu, ahi, ahi, biscania; S'io ve dico ca sete la chiù bella; Ecco la nimph 'Ebrayca chiamata; Parch'hai lasciato; Io ti vorria contar la pena mia; Hai, Lucia, bona cosa io dic'a tia; Chichilichi? Cucurucu !; Oh Lucia, miau, miau; Ad altrc le voi dare ste passate; Tutto lo di mi dici:canta, cantal; Cathalina, apra finestra; Turro 'l di piango; Matona, mia cara; S'io fusse ciaul'; Ogni giorno m'han ditt'a chi favlli; O belle fusal; Madonna mia, pietà Opus 111 ▲ OPS 30-94
Marenzio, L.:Madrigals—Book 1 (1585) Opus 111 ▲ OPS 30-117
Monteverdi, C.:Madrigals—19 selections from Books 1–4 [I] Tactus ▲ TC 561303 [DDD]
Monteverdi, C.:Madrigals (book 2) Opus 111 ▲ OPS 30-111
Monteverdi, C.:Madrigals (book 4) *(rec May 1993)* Opus 111 ▲ OPS 3081 [DDD]
Monteverdi, C.:Madrigals (book 6) Arcana ▲ ACA 66 [DDD]
Monteverdi, C.:Sacred Vocal Music—In II. Vesperis in Festis B. Mariae V. [from Vespers]; Dixit Dominus [from Psalmus 109]; Laudatae Pueri [from Psalmus 112]; Laetatus sum [from Psalmus 121]; Nisi Dominus [from Psalmus 126]; Lauda Jerusalem [from Psalmus 147]; Magnificat secondo; O quam pulchra es; Domine in furore tuo; Ego flos campi; Adoramus te; Laudate Dominum; Ego dormio, et cor meum vigilat; Cantate Dominum Opus 111 ▲ OPS 30-150
Palestrina, G.:Il Primo libro de madrigali—1596 edition *(rec Dec. 4–7 1992)* Tactus ▲ TC 521601 [DDD]
Scarlatti, A.:Cain, the First Murder, w. F. Bondi (sgr), L'Europa Galante Opus 111 2-▲ OPS 30-75/76
Scarlatti, A.:Cants Opus 111 ▲ 30-156
Striggio, A.:Il cicalamento delle donne al bucato e la caccia Opus 111 ▲ OPS 30-137
Vivaldi, A.:Cons & Sinfs [period instrs]—6 concerti—Op. 3, Nos. 2 & 8; Op. 12, No. 3; RV.154, RV.302 & RV.367 Tactus ▲ TC 672201 [DDD]

Concerto Palatino
Castello, D.:Sonate concertate in stil moderno—7 selections from Books 1 & 2 Accent ▲ 9058 [DDD]
Cavalli, P.F.:Vespero della beata Vergine Maria, w. Barbara Borden (sop), Emily van Evera (sop), Markus Brutscher (ten), Mark Padmore (ten), Rodrigo del Pozo (ten), Gerd Türk (ten), Harry van der Kamp (bass), Peter Zimpel (sgr), Bruce Dickey (sackbut), Charles Toet (sackbut), Schola Cantorum Basiliensis Harmonia Mundi France ("Documenta" series) 2-▲ HMC 905219/20
Early Music of the Netherlands, Vol. 1 (1400–1600), w. Gesualdo Consort, Ensemble Tragicomedia *(rec Dec. 1988)* Emergo ▲ EC 3987 [DDD]
North Italian Music for Cornetts & Trombones, 1580–1650 Accent ▲ 8861 [DDD]
Scarani, G.:Son concertate—6 selections Accent ▲ 9058 [DDD]
Sonate Concertate in Stil Moderno Accent ▲ 9058 [DDD]
K. Junghänel (cnd)
Monteverdi, C.:Vespro della Beata Vergine, w. Konrad Junghänel (lt), Cantus Cologne *(rec Sept 8–12, 1994)* Deutsche Harmonia Mundi 2-▲ 05472-77332-2 [DDD]
Rosenmüller, J.:Vespro della Beata Vergine, w. Cantus Cologne Harmonia Mundi 2-▲ HMC 901611.12
E. van Nevel (cnd)
Lassus, O. de:Patrocinium musicus cantionum, w. *(soloists unknown)*, Currende Vocal Ensemble Accent ▲ 8855

Concerto Rococo [J.-P. Brosse (hpd), N. Mazzoleni (vn), R. Crisafulli (vn), E. Balsa (vc)]
Schobert, J.:Music of—Quartets for Harpsichord & Strings No. 1 in E♭ "April", No. 2 in f "May", No. 3 in g "June"; Sonata for Harpsichord & Strings Pierre Verany ▲ PV.792031 [DDD]

Concerto Rotterdam
H. Friesen (cnd)
Albinoni, T.:Con Tpt, Op. 7/3, w. E. Carroll (tpt) *(rec Apr 26–27, 1988)* Erasmus ▲ WVH 005 [DDD]
Baldassare, P.:Son 1 Tpt, w. E. Carroll (tpt) *(rec Apr. 26–27, 1988)* Erasmus ▲ WVH 005 [DDD]
Franceschini, P.:Son à 7, w. E. Carroll (tp), A. van Zon *(rec Apr. 26–27, 1988)* Erasmus ▲ WVH 005 [DDD]
Mozart, L.:Con for 2 Hns, w. Michael Holtzel (hn), Herman Jeurissen (hn) MD + G ▲ MDG 3210085
Mozart, L.:Sinf da camera MD + G ▲ MDG 3210085
Mozart, L.:Sinf pastorella, w. *(soloist unknown)* MD + G ▲ MDG 3210085
Mozart, L.:Sym for 4 Hns, w. *(soloists unknown)* MD + G ▲ MDG 3210085
Torelli, G.:Con Tpt, w. E. Carroll (tpt) *(rec Apr. 26–27, 1988)* Erasmus ▲ WVH 005 [DDD]
Vivaldi, A.:Con Ob, RV.451, w. E. Carroll (tpt) [arr. for trumpet] *(rec Apr. 26–27, 1988)* Erasmus ▲ WVH 005 [DDD]
Vivaldi, A.:Con for 2 Tpts, w. E. Carroll (tpt), A. van Zon (tpt) *(rec Apr. 26–27, 1988)* Erasmus ▲ WVH 005 [DDD]

Concerto Soave [Jean-Marc Aymes (org/hpd), Sylvie Moquet (va/vc), Christina Pluhar (hp/thb/gtr/tripla), Matthias Spaeter (archlt)]
Angels, w. Ensemble Convivencia, Ensemble Lucidarum, Ensemble Venance Fortunat, La Fenice, Iberian Lyric Ensemble L'Empreinte Digitale ▲ ED 13050
Giancelli, B.:Tastegiati, w. Maria-Cristina Kiehr (sop) L'Empreinte Digitale ▲ ED 13048
Marini, B.:Sons, Syms & Retornelli, w. Maria-Cristina Kiehr (sop)—Sinf secondo tuono L'Empreinte Digitale ▲ ED 13048
Merula, T.:Music of, w. Maria-Cristina Kiehr (sop)—Cappriccio cromatico; Canzon L'Empreinte Digitale ▲ ED 13048
Strozzi, B.:Sacred Music, w. Maria-Cristina Kiehr (sop)—Salve Regina; Erat Petrus; Mater Anna; Nascente Maria; Hodie oritur; Salve Sancta caro; O Maria L'Empreinte Digitale ▲ ED 13048

Concerto Soloists Instrumental Ensemble
M. Korn (cnd)
Respighi, O.:Lauda per la Natività del Signore, w. Valente (sop), M. Forrester (cta), Gordon (ten), Philadelphia Singers RCA Red Seal ▲ 7787-2-RC [DDD] ■ 7787-4-RC (CrO2)

Concerts de Paris SO
W. Goehr (cnd)
Dvořák, A.:Con Vn, w. R. Odnoposoff (vn) *(rec June 5–6, 1957)* Doron ▲ DRC 4002 [ADD]
Glazunov, A.:Con Vn, w. R. Odnoposoff (vn) *(rec June 5–6, 1957)* Doron ▲ DRC 4002 [ADD]

Les Concerts du Monde
K. Clark (cnd)
Movies Go Baroque *(rec June 7–9, 1993)* Telarc ▲ CD 80336 [DDD] ■ CS 30336

Concerts Straram Orch
P. Gaubert (cnd)
Ravel, M.:Daphnis et Chloé (suite 2) *(rec 1928–30)* VAI Audio ▲ VAIA 1074
P. Gaubert, W. Straram (cnd)
Ravel, M.:Daphnis et Chloé (suite 2) *(rec ca. 1928/30)* InSync ■ C 4134 (m)
W. Straram (cnd)
Debussy, C.:Prélude à l'après-midi d'un faune *(rec 1928–30)* VAI Audio ▲ VAIA 1074
Ibert, J.:Escales *(rec 1928–30)* VAI Audio ▲ VAIA 1074
Ravel, M.:Alborada del gracioso *(rec 1928–30)* VAI Audio ▲ VAIA 1074
Roussel, A.:Le Festin de l'araignée *(rec ca. 1928/30)* InSync ■ C 4134 (m)
Roussel, A.:Le Festin de l'araignée *(rec 1928–30)* VAI Audio ▲ VAIA 1074

Concierto Montilla Orch
E. Estella (cnd)
Carrion, M.R.:La Tempestad, w. L. Huarte (sop), D. Perez (sop), A. Kraus (ten), F. Kraus (bar), R. Alonso (bass), S. Ramalle (bass), Concierto Montilla Chorus Montilla ▲ MON 3011 [ADD]

Concilium Musicum Vienna
Dittersdorf, K.D. von:Notturno Vn [period instrs] Koch Schwann ▲ CD 310 063 [DDD]
Fusz, J.:Notturno [period instrs] Koch Schwann ▲ CD 310 063 [DDD]
Haydn, M.:Notturno [period instrs] Koch Schwann ▲ CD 310 063 [DDD]
Mozart, F.X.W.:Qt Pno Koch Schwann ▲ CD 310085 [DDD]
Mozart, L.:Divert 2 Vns Koch Schwann ▲ CD 310085 [DDD]
Pleyel, I.:Notturno Ob [period instrs] Koch Schwann ▲ CD 310 063 [DDD]
P. Angerer (cnd)
Haydn, M.:Qnts Strs—in F, P.108; in G, P.109; in F, P.110 Koch Schwann ▲ CD 310 084 [DDD]
Mozart, L.:Sym in G, "Sinf burlesca" Koch Schwann ▲ CD 310085 [DDD]
Mozart, W.A.:Church Sons, w. E. Ullmann (org) MD + G ▲ L 3298 [DDD]
Mozart, W.A.:Divert Hns Bn, K.205 Koch Schwann ▲ SCH 310085 [DDD]
Mozart, W.A.:March Hns, K.290 Koch Schwann ▲ CD 310085 [DDD]

Concilium Musicum Vienna [Luigi Palmisano (fl), Paul Angerer (vn), Cristoph Angerer (va), Umberto Ferriani (vc), Tiziana Canfori (hpd)]
Bach, J.C.F.:Qts (6) Fl *(rec Ortisei's Palazzo dei Congressi, Bolzano, Italy, June 1984)* Dynamic ▲ CDS 31 [ADD]

Concord String Quartet [Mark Sokol (vn), Andrew Jennings (vn), John Kochanowski (va), Norman Fischer (vc)]
Bassett, L.:Sxt Vns, w. John Graham (va), Gilbert Kalish (pno) *(rec Baltimore, MD, May 19, 1975* CRI ▲ CD 677 [ADD]
Ives, C.:Qts 1 & 2 Strs Elektra/Nonesuch ■ 71306-4

Concordia
All the King's Men, w. I Fagiolini Metronome ▲ MET CD 1012 [DDD]

Concordia Orch
M. Alsop (cnd)
Gershwin, G.:Blue Monday Blues, w. A. Burton (sop), G. Hopkins (ten), W. Sharp (bar), A. Woodley (b-bar), J. J. Offenbach (b-bar) EMI Classics ▲ CDC 54851
Gershwin, G.:Con Pno, w. L. Stifelman (pno) EMI Classics ▲ CDC 54851
Johnson, J.P.:Orchestral Music—Victory Stride; Harlem Sym.; Con. Jazz a Mine for Piano & Orch. [w. L. Stifelman]; American Symphonic Suite; Drums (symphonic poem) MusicMasters ▲ 01612-67140-2 [DDD]
Johnson, J.P.:Orchestral Music—Victory Stride; Harlem Sym.; Con. Jazz a Mine for Piano & Orch. [w. Leslie Stifelman (piano)]; American Symphonic Suite; Drums (symphonic poem) MusicMasters ■ 01612-67140-4
Levant, O.:Caprice EMI Classics ▲ CDC 54851
O'Connor, M.:Con Fid, w. Mark O'Connor (vn) *(rec John Harms Center for the Arts, Englewood, NJ, Oct. 1994)* Warner Bros. ▲ 45846-2

Conjunto Iberico Octet
Villa-Lobos, H.:Bachiana brasileira 5, w. C. McFadden (sop) Canal Grande ▲ CG 9323 [DDD]
E. Arizcuren (cnd)
de Pablo, L.:Ritornello Channel Classics ▲ CG 9428
Halffter, C.:Fandango Channel Classics ▲ CG 9428
Marco, Tomas:Miro Channel Classics ▲ CG 9428
Turina, J.L.:Divertiento Vcs Channel Classics ▲ CG 9428

Connecticut Early Music Festival Ensemble
I. Kipnis (cnd)
Vivaldi, A.:Cons Fl (misc), w. J. Solum (fl), I. Kipnis (hpd) [period instrs]—Concerto in D, RV.428, "Il Gardellino" Chesky ▲ CD 78 [DDD]
Vivaldi, A.:Con Hpd, RV.780, w. I. Kipnis (hpd) [period instrs] Chesky ▲ CD 78 [DDD]
Vivaldi, A.:Cons Vn, Op. 8/1–4, "The Four Seasons", w. J.-M. Schwarz (vn), I. Kipnis (hpd) [period instrs] Chesky ▲ CD 78 [DDD]

Conniff Orch
H. Mancini (cnd)
Mancini, H.:Film Music, w. A. Williams (sgr), J. Mathis (sgr), L. Albright (sgr), B. Hackett (sgr), B. Greco (sgr), C. Byrd (sgr), P. Page (sgr). Costa Orch, Mancini Orch—sels from Breakfast at Tiffany's; Peter Gunn; Mr. Lucky & others Columbia/Legacy ▲ CK 66505

Conrad Instrumental Ensemble
Praetorius, M.:Terpsichore Elektra/Nonesuch ■ 71128-4
Schein, J.H.:Banchetto musicale—Nos. 1 & 2 Elektra/Nonesuch ■ 71128-4

Conserto Vago [Marino Lagomarsino (vn), Doron David Sherwin (cornetto), Ernest Braucher (vn), P. Tognon (instr), Marco Vitali (vc), Ero Maria Barbero (clvd), Massimo Lonardi (archlt)]
Marini, B.:Arfetti musicali *(rec Palazzo Giustiniani, Genova, Feb. 1–4, 1994)* Arkadia-Akademia ▲ 142 [DDD]

Conserto Vago [Marino Lagomarsino (vn), Ernest Brauchner (vn), Marco Vitali (vc), Ero Maria Barbero (clvd), Massimo Lonardi (archlt)]
Uccellini, M.:Sonate, arie et correnti *(rec St Bartolomeo di Cavasco Church, Genova, Feb 24–27, 1995)* Agorá ▲ 019 [DDD]

Consilium Musicum
P. Angerer (cnd)
Old German Christmas Songs, w. Ernst Haefliger (ten) Claves ▲ CD 8408 [DDD]

Consort Fontegara [Andrea Carmagnola (fl), Salvatore dell'Atti (fl), Ugo Galasso (fl), Marco Di Manno (fl), Donato Sansone (fl), Gabriela Soltz (fl), Stefano Cuturello (vn), Nanneke Schaap (vl), Sofia Martignoni (vl), Stefano Lorenzetti (hpd/org)]
R. Clemencic (cnd)
Gabrieli, G.:Canzoni et sonate (21) *(rec July 1995)* Tactus ▲ 550701 [DDD]

Consort of London
R. Haydon Clark (cnd)
Bach, J.S.:Con Vn & Ob, w. J. Fröhlich (vn), J. Girdwood (ob) Collins Quest ▲ 30182 [DDD]
Bach, J.S.:Suites Orch, BWV 1066-1069 Collins Quest ▲ COL 3009 [DDD]
Bizet, G.:L'Arlésienne, w. Consort of Voices Collins Classics ▲ 11412 [DDD]
Bizet, G.:Jeux d'enfants Collins Classics ▲ 11412 [DDD]
Corelli, A.:Con grosso, Op. 6/8, "Christmas Con" Collins Quest ▲ 30182 [DDD]
Haydn, J.:Ovs Collins Classics ▲ 10512 [DDD]
Haydn, J.:Sym 49, "La Passione" Collins Classics ▲ 10512 [DDD]

136

▲ = CD ♦ = Enhanced CD Δ = MD ■ = Cassette Tape □ = DCC

Consort of London (cont.)
R. Haydon Clark (cnd) (cont.)
Haydn, J.:Sym 100, "Military" Collins Classics ▲ 10512 [DDD]
Schubert, Franz:Octet Ww, D.803 Collins Classics ▲ COL 1375 [DDD]
Vaughan Williams, R.:Con Ob, w. J. Girdwood (ob) Collins Classics ▲ 11402 [DDD]
Vaughan Williams, R.:Fant on Greensleeves Collins Classics ▲ 11402 [DDD]
Vaughan Williams, R.:Fant on a Theme by Thomas Tallis Collins Classics ▲ 11402 [DDD]
Vaughan Williams, R.:The Lark Ascending, w. D. Juritz (vn) Collins Classics ▲ 11402 [DDD]
Consort of Musicke
Grabbe, J.:Il Primo libro de madrigali MD + G ▲ MDG 3100220
Monteverdi, C.:Madrigals (book 2), w. E. Kirby (sop) Virgin Classics ▲ CDC 59282
Monteverdi, C.:Madrigals (book 3), w. E. Kirby (sop) Virgin Classics ▲ CDC 59283
Pallavicino, B.:Madrigals—6th Book of Madrigals for 4 Voices Musica Oscura ▲ OSC 70976 [DDD]
Ward, J.:Music of Musica Oscura ▲ OSC 70981 [DDD]
Ward, J.:Sacred Music Musica Oscura ▲ OSC 70982 [DDD]
A. Rooley (cnd)
Bringing Light to the Unknown, w. Emma Kirkby (sop), Evelyn Tubb (sop), et al. Musica Oscura ▲ OSC 280826 [DDD]
Concerto Delle Donne Deutsche Harmonia Mundi ▲ 77154-2-RC [DDD]
Dowland, J.:The Third and Last Booke of Songs or Ayres L'Oiseau-Lyre ▲ 430284-2 [ADD]
Gerusalemme Liberata Musica Oscura ("The Monteverdi Circle" series) ▲ MOS 70990
Gesualdo, D.C.:Madrigali, Book 5 L'Oiseau-Lyre ▲ 410128-2 [DDD]
Greene, M.:Kbd Works Musica Oscura ("The Handel Circle" series) ▲ MOS 70978
Greene, M.:Songs, w. Emma Kirkby (sop), Lars Ulrik Mortensen (hpd) Musica Oscura ("The Handel Circle" series) ▲ MOS 70978
Guarini, G.B.:Cor mio, deh non languire Musica Oscura ("The Monteverdi Circle" series) ▲ MOS 70989
India, S. d':Madrigals Book 1 Musica Oscura ("The Monteverdi Circle" series) ▲ MOS 70985
Lamento d'Arianna *(rec 1983–84)* Editio Classica 2-▲ 77115-2-RG [ADD]
Lawes, H.:Psalms, Ayres & Dialogues [E] Hyperion ▲ CDA 66135
Lawes, W.:Choral Music—Psalms, Songs & Elegies Musica Oscura ("The English Explorers" series) ▲ MOS 70972
Marenzio, L.:Baci soavi e cari Musica Oscura ("Monteverdi Circle" series) ▲ MOS 70992
Marini, B.:Concerto terzo delle musiche da camera Musica Oscura ("Monteverdi Circle" series) ▲ MOS 70994
Monteverdi, C.:Ballo delle ingrate, w. Evelyn Tubb (sop), Emma Kirkby (sop), Barbara Nichols (sop), Maria Ewing (sop) [I] Virgin Classics ▲ 59606 [DDD]
Monteverdi, C.:Combattimento, w. E. Kirkby (sop), P. Agnew (ct), J. King (ten) [I] Virgin Classics ▲ 59606 [DDD]
Monteverdi, C.:Madrigals (book 4) Musica Oscura ("Monteverdi Circle" series) ▲ MOS 70995
Monteverdi, C.:Madrigals (book 6) [I] Virgin Classics ▲ 59605 [DDD]
Monteverdi, C.:Madrigals—Book 8, 1638—"Madrigals of War" [I] Virgin Classics ▲ 59620 [DDD]
Monteverdi, C.:Madrigals, Book 8, 1638—"Madrigals of Love" [I] Virgin Classics ▲ 59621 [DDD]
Monteverdi, C.:Volgendo il ciel, w. E. Kirkby (sop), S. LeBlanc (sop), M. Nichols (mez), P. Agnew (ct), Alan Ewing (bass) [I] Virgin Classics ▲ 59606 [DDD]
Notari, A.:Prime musiche nuove Musica Oscura ("The Monteverdi Circle" series) ▲ MOS 70983
Pallavicino, B.:Madrigals—6th Book of Madrigals for 5 Voices Musica Oscura ("The Monteverdi Circle" series) ▲ MOS 70976
Porter, W.:Madrigals & Ayres Musica Oscura ("Monteverdi Circle" series) ▲ MOS 70993
Ravenscroft:There Were 3 Ravens Virgin Classics ▲ CDC 59035
Rore, C. de:Il quinto libro di madrigali Musica Oscura ("Monteverdi Circle" series) ▲ MOS 70991
Schütz, H.:Il primo libro de madrigali [I] Editio Classica ▲ 77118-2-RG [DDD]
Stradella, A.:L'anime del purgatorio, w. Emma Kirkby (sop), Evelyn Tubb (sop), David Thomas (bass), Richard Wistreich (bass) Musica Oscura ("Favola in Musica" series) ▲ MOS 70984
Ward, J.:Anthems Musica Oscura ("The Fanshawe Circle" series) ▲ MOS 70982
Ward, J.:Fants Musica Oscura ("The Fanshawe Circle" series) ▲ MOS 70981
Ward, J.:Madrigals Musica Oscura ("The Fanshawe Circle" series) ▲ MOS 70981
Ward, J.:Psalms Musica Oscura ("The Fanshawe Circle" series) ▲ MOS 70982
Wert, G. de:Il settimo libro de madrigali Virgin Classics ▲ CDC 59161
Consort of Six
Dowland, J.:Consort Music Harmonia Mundi France 2-▲ HMC 90244, HMC 90245
Consort of Viols
A. Deller (cnd)
William Byrd & His Age, w. Schola Cantorum Basiliensis, August Wenzinger (cnd) *(rec Friends' Meeting House, Edgware Road, London, Feb 1956)* Vanguard Classics ▲ OVC 8101 [ADD]
Consort of Viols [Eduard Melkus (vl), Alice Hoffner (vl), Gustav Leonhardt (b-vl), Nicholas Harnoncourt (b-vl)]
N. Harnoncourt (cnd)
Elizabethan & Jacobean Music - Airs & Instrumental Music of England, w. Deller Consort, Consort of Viols [Desmond Dupré (lt), Gustav Leonhardt (hpd), Alfred Deller (ct)] Vanguard Classics ▲ OVC 8102 [ADD]
Consortium Classicum
Bach, Joh. Christian:Sinf (6) Ww MD + G ▲ L 3434 [DDD]
Beethoven, L. van:Allegro & Minuet CPO ▲ 999162-2 [DDD]
Beethoven, L. van:Duos Cl—No. 1 CPO ▲ 999162-2 [DDD]
Beethoven, L. van:Duos Cl—No. 2 *(rec 1993–94)* CPO ▲ 999437-2 [DDD]
Beethoven, L. van:Fidelio (sels)—excerpts [arr W. Sedlak for 2 ob, 2 cl, 2 hn, 2 bn & db (1814)] *(rec 1993–94)* CPO ▲ 999437-2 [DDD]
Beethoven, L. van:Septet Strs MD + G ▲ MDG 3010594 [DDD]
Beethoven, L. van:Septet Strs CPO ▲ 999162-2 [DDD]
Beethoven, L. van:Sxt Hns, Op. 81b MD + G ▲ MDG 3010594 [DDD]
Beethoven, L. van:Vars on "La ci direm la mano," from Mozart's *Don Giovanni* *(rec 1993–94)* CPO ▲ 999437-2 [DDD]
Berwald, F.:Qt Pno, Cl, Hn & Bn Koch Schwann ▲ CD 310056 [DDD]
Berwald, F.:Qnt Pno Koch Schwann ▲ CD 310056 [DDD]
Berwald, F.:Septet Vn, "Grand Septet" Koch Schwann ▲ CD 310056 [DDD]
Bruch, M.:Septet, Op. posth. Orfeo ▲ 167881 [DDD]
Busoni, F.:Intro & Elegie, w. D. Klöcker (cl) Orfeo ▲ 213901 [DDD]
Cartellieri, A.:Viennese Wind Divert CPO ▲ CPO 999140 [DDD]
Chamber Music with Harp Koch Schwann ▲ SCH 310001 [DDD]
Czerny, C.:Grande Sérénade Concertante, w. Claudius Tanski (pno) MD + G ("Gold" series) ▲ MDG 3010518 [DDD]
Czerny, C.:Nonet, w. Claudius Tanski (pno) MD + G ("Gold" series) ▲ MDG 3010518 [DDD]
Dvořák, A.:Serenade Ww MD + G ▲ L 3416 [DDD]
Farrenc, J.-L.:Nonet Divox ▲ CDX 29205 [DDD]
Gragnani, F.:Qt for 2 Gtrs Koch Schwann ▲ CD 310006 [DDD]
Hartmann, E.:Serenade MD + G ▲ L 3416 [DDD]
Haydn, J.:Arrangements Wind Ensemble—Der Ritter Roland Suite; Der Jahrzeiten Suite; Octet in C Claves ▲ 50-9515
Haydn, J.:Qts Cl, w. Dieter Klöcker (cl) MD + G ▲ L 3315 [DDD]
Haydn, J.:Qts Ob, w. Gernot Schmalfuss (ob) MD + G ▲ L 3314 [DDD]
Hoffmeister, F.A.:Serenades CPO ▲ CPO 999107 [DDD]
Hummel, J.N.:Concertino Pno MD + G ▲ L 3440 [DDD]
Hummel, J.N.:Grand Serenades 1 & 2 Koch Schwann ▲ CD 310006 [DDD]
Hummel, J.N.:Music of—Sextet in F for Winds MD + G ▲ L 3440 [DDD]
Hummel, J.N.:Parthia MD + G ▲ L 3440 [DDD]
Hummel, J.N.:Serenade 2 MD + G ▲ L 3440 [DDD]
Kreutzer, C.:Grand Septet Orfeo ▲ 167881 [DDD]
Krommer, F.:Qts (6) Cl, w. D. Klöcker (cl) CPO 2-▲ CPO 999141 [DDD]
Lachner, F.P.:Nonet Orfeo ▲ 382951
Lachner, F.P.:Septet Winds & Strs Orfeo ▲ 382951

Consortium Classicum (cont.)
MD & G Portraits:Consortium Classicum MD + G ▲ MDG 3493 [DDD]
Mendelssohn, F.:Ov, Op. 24 MD + G ▲ L 3416 [DDD]
Mozart, W.A.:Divert—K.213, 240, 252, 270 EMI Classics 2-▲ CDFB 69392
Mozart, W.A.:Don Giovanni, w. Gernot Schmalfub (ob), Christian Hartmann (ob), Dieter Klöcker (cl), Waldemar Wandel (cl), Sara Willis (hn), Christian Auer (hn), Karl-Otto Hartmann (bn), Eberhard Buschmann (bn), Jürgen Normann (db) Bayer ▲ BR 100 135 [DDD]
Mozart, W.A.:Music of—Serenade in E♭ [spurious]; Sextet, K.439b [spurious] MD + G ▲ MDG 3010496
Mozart, W.A.:Oct in E♭ MD + G ▲ MDG 3010495 [DDD]
Mozart, W.A.:Octet MD + G ▲ MDG 3010496
Mozart, W.A.:Qt Ob, K.370, w. G. Schmalfuss (ob) MD + G ▲ L 3314 [DDD]
Mozart, W.A.:Serenade Ww, K.361 EMI Classics 2-▲ CDFB 69392
Mozart, W.A.:Serenade Ww, K.375 EMI Classics 2-▲ CDFB 69392
Mozart, W.A.:Serenade Ww, K.388 EMI Classics 2-▲ CDFB 69392
Mozart, W.A.:Sym 36—[trans possibly Mozart or Hummel for oct] MD + G ▲ MDG 3010495 [DDD]
Mozart, W.A.:Theme & Vars MD + G ▲ MDG 3010495 [DDD]
Müller, I.:Trio Cl Koch Schwann ▲ CD 310001 [DDD]
Pfitzner, H.:Qnt Pno Orfeo ▲ 281931 [DDD]
Pfitzner, H.:Sxt Cl Orfeo ▲ 281931 [DDD]
Reicha, A.:Qnt Fl MD + G ▲ MDG 3010501 [DDD]
Reicha, A.:Qnt Ob MD + G ▲ MDG 3010501 [DDD]
Ries, F.:Sextet Hp Koch Schwann ▲ CD 310001 [DDD]
Riotte, J.P.:Notturno Koch Schwann ▲ CD 310001 [DDD]
Rossini, G.:Andante con variazioni Hp Koch Schwann ▲ CD 310001 [DDD]
Rossini, G.:Ovs [19th cent. wind ensemble arrs.]—Barber of Seville, Cenerentola, Gazza ladra, L'inganno felice, Italiana in Algeri, Otello, Scala di seta, Tancredi; plus a wind version of "The Lost Chord" MD + G ▲ L 3393 [DDD]
Rossini, G.:Qts Fl MD + G ▲ L 3207 [DDD]
Rudolph [Archduke Of Austria]:Septet in e Orfeo ▲ 182891 [DDD]
Salzburg Serenades Koch Schwann ▲ SCH 310002 [DDD]
Spohr, L.:Fant & Vars on a Theme of Danzi, w. D. Klöcker (cl) Orfeo ▲ 213901 [DDD]
Spohr, L.:Notturno, w. D. Klöcker (cl)—Andante & Variations Orfeo ▲ 213901 [DDD]
Stamitz, C.:Octets & Partitas CPO ▲ CPO 999081-2 [DDD]
Weber, J.M.:Septet Cl Orfeo ▲ 182891 [DDD]
Weigl, J.:Concertino Hp Koch Schwann ▲ CD 310001 [DDD]
W.-D. Hauschild (cnd)
Devienne, F.:Sinf concertante Cls Koch Schwann ▲ 3-1074-2 [DDD]
Devienne, F.:Sinf concertante 4 Fl Koch Schwann ▲ 3-1074-2 [DDD]
Devienne, F.:Sinf concertante 1 Hn Koch Schwann ▲ 3-1074-2 [DDD]
D. Klöcker (cnd)
Reicha, A.:Octet Ob Orfeo ▲ 282921 [DDD]
Spohr, L.:Nonet Strs Orfeo ▲ 155871 [DDD]
Spohr, L.:Notturno Orfeo ▲ 155871 [DDD]
D. Loöcker (cnd)
Blanc, A.:Septet Orfeo ▲ 282921 [DDD]
Consortium Classicum [W. Dünschede (fl), D. Klöcker (cl), K. Wallendorf (hn), K. O. Hartmann (bn)]
Boccherini, L.:Qts Fl, Cl, Hn & Bn—in D, G.262/1; in F, G.262/2; in C, G.262/3; in E♭, G.263/1; in F, G.263/2; in B, G.263/3 Orfeo ▲ 322941 [DDD]
Consortium Classicum Soloists
A. Tamayo (cnd)
Weber, C.M. von:Music of, w. D. Klöcker (cl), Slovak RSO Bratislava—Concertino in C for Oboe & Winds; Romanza Siciliana for Flute & Orch.; Romanze Appassionata for Bassoon & Orch.; Divert. for Clarinet & Orch.; Andante & Rondo Ungarese for Bassoon & Orch., Op. 35; Concertino, Op. 45 Novalis ▲ 150100
Consortium Hafniense
The King of Denmark's Delight *(rec June 16–17, 1988)* Danacord ▲ DACOCD 307 [DDD]
Consortium Musicum
W. Gönnenwein (cnd)
Bach, J.S.:St. John Passion (sels), w. Brigitte Fassbaender (cta), South German Madrigal Choir—Es ist vollbracht; Ruht wohl, ihr heiligen Gebeine *(rec Eglise de Schwaigern, Oct. 1969)* EMI Classics ▲ CDK 65334 [ADD]
Bach, J.S.:St. Matthew Passion (sels), w. Theo Altmeyer (ten), South German Madrigal Choir—Ich will bei meinem Jesu wachen; Kommt, ihr Töchter *(rec Eglise de Schwaigern, May & Jun. 1968)* EMI Classics ▲ CDK 65334 [ADD]
M. Munih (cnd)
Dvořák, A.:Stabat Mater, w. A. Pusar-Jerik (sop), E. N. Houska (mez), J. Reja (ten), F. Petrusanec (bass), Consortium Musicum Chorus [L] Vivace 2-▲ 140141 [ADD/DDD]
Constitution Brass
Austin, E.:Music of, w. Jeananne Albee (pno), Jerome Reed (pno), Mary Lou Rylands (vc), Ursula Trede-Boettcher (hpd), Markus Lücke (cl), Sibylle Dotzauer (pno), Gerald Kegelmann (cnd), Heidelberg State Music School Chamber Choir—To Begin for Brass Qnt; Klavier Double for Pno & Tape; Circling for Vc & Pno; Lighthouse I for solo Hpd; Gathering Threads for solo Cl; Zodiac Suite for Pno; An Die Nachgeborenen [To Those Born Later] Capstone ▲ CPS 8625
Austin, E.:To Begin Capstone ▲ CPS 8625
Contemporain Duo [Henri Bok (b cl/a sax), Miguel Bernar (perc)]
Ford, A.:The Art of Puffing *(rec Studio 227 ABC Sydney, Sept 1993)* Tall Poppies ▲ TP 053 [DDD]
Contemporano Ensemble
M. Ceccanti (cnd)
Berio, L.:Différences *(rec live, Museo Pecci, Prato, Italy, Mar 21, 1992)* Arts Music ▲ 447135-2 [DDD]
Bussotti, S.:Nascosto for Pierre Boulez *(rec live, Museo Pecci, Prato, Italy, Mar 21, 1992)* Arts Music ▲ 447135-2 [DDD]
Sciarrino, S.:Introduzione all'oscuro *(rec live, Museo Pecci, Prato, Italy, Mar 21, 1992)* Arts Music ▲ 447135-2 [DDD]
Xenakis, I.:Waarg *(rec live, Museo Pecci, Prato, Italy, Mar 21, 1992)* Arts Music ▲ 447135-2 [DDD]
P. Leiner (cnd)
Stravinsky, I.:L'Histoire du soldat, w. H. Schimmelpfennig (nar), A. Szerda (the Devil), M. Hoffmann (the Soldier) Bayer ▲ 100207 [DDD]
Contemporary Chamber Ensemble
A. Weisberg (cnd)
Babbitt, M.:All Set Elektra/Nonesuch ▲ 792222 J
Crumb, G.:Ancient Voices of Children, w. J. DeGaetani (mez), Dash (sgr)—[Sp] Elektra/Nonesuch ▲ 79149-2 [AAD]
Milhaud, D.:La Création du monde Elektra/Nonesuch ▲ 71281-2 [ADD]
Rochberg, G.:Serenata d'estate Elektra/Nonesuch ▲ 79222-2-J
Schoenberg, A.:Pierrot lunaire, w. J. DeGaetani (speaker) [G] Elektra/Nonesuch ■ 71251-4
Schoenberg, A.:Pierrot lunaire, w. J. DeGaetani (speaker) [G] Elektra/Nonesuch ▲ 79237-2-ZK
Schwartz, C.:Mother! Mother!, w. Clark Terry (tpt), Zoot Sims (sax) Pablo Today ■ 52312-115
Shifrin, S.:Satires of Circumstance, w. J. DeGaetani (mez) Elektra/Nonesuch ▲ 79222-2-J
Varèse, E.:Ecuatorial Elektra/Nonesuch ▲ 71269-2
Varèse, E.:Intégrales Elektra/Nonesuch ▲ 71269-2
Varèse, E.:Octandre Elektra/Nonesuch ▲ 71269-2
Varèse, E.:Offrandes, w. J. DeGaetani (mez) Elektra/Nonesuch ▲ 71269-2
Weill, K.:Kleine Dreigroschenmusik Elektra/Nonesuch ▲ 71281-2 [ADD]
Wernick, R.:Kaddish-Requiem, w. J. DeGaetani (mez) Elektra/Nonesuch ▲ 79222-2-J
Wolpe, S.:Qt Tpt Elektra/Nonesuch ▲ 79222-2-J

Contemporary Chamber Ensemble [Susan Palma (fl), George Haas (ob), Susan Jolles (hp), David Starobin (gtr), Gilbert Kalish (pno), Kenneth Hosley (perc), Joseph Passaro (perc)]
Ung, C.:Mohori, w. Barbara Martin (sop) *(rec National Edison Hotel, Feb 24, 1976)* CRI ▲ CRI 710 [DDD/ADD]
Contemporary Chamber Players [Paul Lustig Dunkel (fl), Arthur Bloom (cl), Donald MacCourt (bn), Jeanne Benjamin (vn), Jacob Glick (va), Michael Rudiakov (vc), Gilbert Kalish (pno)]
Berger, A.:Septet *(rec Rutgers Presbyterian Church, New York City)* New World ▲ 80308-2
Carter, E.:Double Con, w. P. Jacobs (hpd), G. Kalish (pno) Elektra/Nonesuch ▲ 79183-2
Contemporary Music Group
D. Speer (cnd)
Veerhoff, C.:Con Vn, w. R. Ricci (vn) One-Eleven ▲ URS 91080 [ADD]
Continuum Chamber Ensemble [David Gresham (cl), Renée Jolles (vn), Joel Sachs (pno)]
J. Sachs (cnd)
Baley, V.:Chamber Music, w. New Juillard Ensemble—Con No. 1 [chamber version]; Dreamtime Suite No. 1 [trio version]; Orpheus Singing for Ob & Str Qt; Duo Concertante for Vc & Pno Cambria ▲ CD 1087
Baley, V.:Dreamtime Suite 1 *(rec Juilliard School, NYC, Apr 22, June 21, July 12)* Cambria ▲ CD 1087
Continuum Chamber Ensemble [J. Rosenfeld (fl), D. Gresham (cl), C. Seltzer (pno), M. Steinberg (vn), M. Kitsopoulos (vc)]
T. Léon (cnd)
Léon, T.:Parajota Delaté *(rec June 4, 1993)* CRI ▲ CD 662 [DDD]
Continuum Chamber Ensemble [J. Rosenfeld (fl), R. Kelley (tpt), M. Butler (ob), D. Gresham (cl), S. Heineman (bn), D. Grabois (hn), E. Charlston (perc), C. Seltzer (pno), M. Steinberg (vn), S. Canin (vn), N. Katz (va), M. Kitsopoulos (vc), V. Kioulaphides (db)]
Léon, T.:Indigena *(rec June 4, 1993)* CRI ▲ CD 662 [DDD]
Continuum Chamber Ensemble [Renée Jolles (vn), Serena Canin (vn), Liuh-Wen Ting (va), Dorothy Lawson (vc)]
Baley, V.:Orpheus Singing, w. Stephen Caplan (ob) *(rec Juilliard School, NYC, Apr 22, June 21, July 12)* Cambria ▲ CD 1087
Continuum Percussion Quartet
Bazelon, I.:Fourscore New World ▲ NW 382-2 [AAD]
Cage, J.:Third Construction New World ▲ NW 382-2 [AAD]
Continuum Percussion Quartet New World ▲ 80382-2 [AAD]
Kurtz, E.:Logo I, w. R. Nunemaker (cl), D. Nale (pno) New World ▲ NW 382-2 [AAD]
Rouse, C.:Ku-Ka-Ilimoku New World ▲ NW 382-2 [AAD]
Verplanck, J.:Petite Suite New World ▲ NW 382-2 [AAD]
R. Brown (cnd)
Harrison, L.:Con Vn, w. Janna Lower (vn), David Colson (perc) New World ▲ NW 382-2 [AAD]
Contrabass Quartet
What a Wonderful Contrabass World!, w. New Colophonium Bass Quartet, Berlin PO Camerata ▲ 32CM 60
Contrasts Instrumental Ensemble
Bruch, M.:Trios Cl, Va & Pno, Op. 83 Arcobaleno ▲ SBCD 1512
Bruch, M.:Trio Pno Arcobaleno ▲ SBCD 1512
Contrechamps Ensemble
G. Bernasconi (cnd)
Jarrell, M.:Eco Accord ▲ ACD 204232 [DDD]
Jarrell, M.:Modifications Accord ▲ ACD 204232 [DDD]
Jarrell, M.:Trace-Ecart Accord ▲ ACD 204232 [DDD]
Jarrell, M.:Trei II Accord ▲ ACD 204232 [DDD]
H. Holliger (cnd)
Holliger, H.:Glühende Rätsel, w. Hedwig Fassbender (mez) Accord ▲ ACD 201922 [DDD]
Holliger, H.:Qnt Pno & Winds Accord ▲ ACD 201922 [DDD]
Contrechamps Ensemble members
Holliger, H.:Lieder ohne Worte Accord ▲ ACD 201922 [DDD]
Holliger, H.:(t)air(e) Accord ▲ ACD 201922 [DDD]
Convivencia Ensemble
Angels, w. Concerto Soave, Ensemble Lucidarum, Ensemble Venance Fortunat, La Fenice, Iberian Lyric Ensemble L'Empreinte Digitale ▲ ED 13050
Convivium Musicum
S. Berger (cnd)
Tugend und Untugend:German Secular Songs & Instrumental Music from the Time of Luther, w. Villanella Ensemble *(rec School of Music & Musicology, Gothenburg)* Naxos ▲ 8.553352 [DDD]
Convivium Musicum Vindobonense
G. Kramer (cnd)
Leopold I:Missa pro defunctis, w. Maria Treu Basilica Chorus Preiser ▲ 90067 [ADD]
Werner, G.J.:Requiem, w. Maria Treu Basilica Chorus Preiser ▲ 90067 [ADD]
Conway-Aschbrenner Duo
Pinkham, D.:Holland Waltzes Redwood ▲ ESCD 45
Copenhagen CO
J. Moriarty (cnd)
Haydn, M.:Con in C Tpt, w. Armando Ghitalla (tpt) *(rec 1969)* Crystal ▲ CD 760
Copenhagen Collegium Musicum
M. Schønwandt (cnd)
Beethoven, L. van:Con 1 Pno, w. E. Westenholz (pno) BIS ▲ CD 429 [DDD]
Beethoven, L. van:Con 2 Pno, w. E. Westenholz (pno) BIS ▲ CD 349
Beethoven, L. van:Con 3 Pno, w. E. Westenholz (pno) BIS ▲ CD 429 [DDD]
Beethoven, L. van:Con 4 Pno, w. E. Westenholz (pno) BIS ▲ CD 349
Gade, N.W.:Sym 1 Marco Polo ▲ DCCD 9201
Gade, N.W.:Sym 2 Marco Polo ▲ DCCD 9201
Gade, N.W.:Sym 4 Marco Polo ▲ DCCD 9202
Gade, N.W.:Sym 6 Marco Polo ▲ DCCD 9202
Gade, N.W.:Sym 7 Marco Polo ▲ DCCD 9301
Gade, N.W.:Sym 8 Marco Polo ▲ DCCD 9301
Mozart, W.A.:Con 20 Pno, w. Elisabeth Westenholz (pno) BIS ▲ CD 283 [DDD]
Mozart, W.A.:Con 23 Pno, w. E. Westenholz (pno) BIS ▲ CD 283 [DDD]
Mozart, W.A.:Con 3 Vn, w. Kim Sjøgren (vn) BIS ▲ CD 282 [DDD]
Mozart, W.A.:Con 5 Vn, w. Kim Sjøgren (vn) BIS ▲ CD 282 [DDD]
Ruders, P.:Con 2 Vn, w. Rebecca Hirsch (vn) *(rec Odd Fellow Palaeet, Copenhagen, Feb. 2, 1992)* Marco Polo ("dacapo" series) ▲ DC 9308 [DDD]
Copenhagen Contemporary Players [Elisabeth Zeuthen Schneider (vn), Annette Slaato (va), Niels Ullner (vc), Poul Rosenbaum (pno)]
Schwartz, E.:Dream Music with Vars Capstone ▲ CPS 863300
Copenhagen Opera Orch
J. Frandsen (cnd)
Nielsen, C.:Con Cl, w. L. Cahuzac (cl) *(rec Nov. 3 & 4, 1947)* Clarinet Classics ▲ CC 0002
Copenhagen PO
H. N. Bihlmaier (cnd)
Wagner, R.:Wesendonck Songs, w. E. Meyer-Topsoe (sop) Kontrapunkt ▲ KPT 32156 [DDD]
H.N. Bihlmaier (cnd)
Strauss, R.:4 Last Songs, w. E. Meyer-Topsoe (sop) Kontrapunkt ▲ KPT 32156 [DDD]
M. Horvat (cnd)
Rachmaninoff, S.:Con 3 Pno, w. David Helfgott (pno) *(rec live, Tivoli Concert Hall, Copenhagen, Nov 2, 1995)* RCA Red Seal ▲ 7432-140378-2 [DDD]
O. Kamu (cnd)
Bentzon, N.V.:Pezzi sinfonici *(rec Tivoli Concert Hall, Copenhagen, Oct 29, 1993)* Classico ▲ 129

Copenhagen PO (cont.)
O. Kamu (cnd) (cont.)
Shostakovich, D.:The Bolt (sels)—Bureaucrat; Coachman's Dance *(rec Tivoli Concert Hall, Copenhagen, Feb 7, 1995)* Classico ▲ 129
Szymanowski, K.:Sym 2 *(rec Tivoli Concert Hall, Copenhagen, Jan 19, 1994)* Classico ▲ 129
O. Vänskä (cnd)
Jersild, J.:Con Hp, w. Sonja Gislinge (hp) Paula ▲ PACD 75 [DAD]
Copenhagen String Quartet [Tutter Givskov (vn), Mogens Lydolph (vn), Mogens Bruun (va), Asger Lund Christiansen (vc)]
Gade, N.W.:Qt in F Strs *(rec Copenhagen, 1963 & 1968)* Marco Polo/Dacapo ▲ 8.224015 [ADD]
Gade, N.W.:Qt in e Strs *(rec Copenhagen, 1963 & 1968)* Marco Polo/Dacapo ▲ 8.224015 [ADD]
Gade, N.W.:Qt Strs, Op. 63 *(rec Copenhagen, 1963 & 1968)* Marco Polo/Dacapo ▲ 8.224015 [ADD]
Horneman, C.F.E.:Qt 2 Strs *(rec Copenhagen, 1969)* Marco Polo/Dacapo ▲ 8.224016 [AAD]
Kuhlau, F.:Qt Strs *(rec Copenhagen, 1969)* Marco Polo/Dacapo ▲ 8.224016 [AAD]
Rosenberg, H.:Qt 12 Strs Caprice ▲ CAP 21352 [AAD]
Stenhammar, W.:Qt 2 Strs Caprice ▲ CAP 21337 [AAD]
Tchaikovsky, P.:Qt 1 Strs Vox Box 3-▲ CD3X 3024 [ADD]
Tchaikovsky, P.:Qt 2 Strs Vox Box 3-▲ CD3X 3024 [ADD]
Tchaikovsky, P.:Qt 3 Strs Vox Box 3-▲ CD3X 3024 [ADD]
Tchaikovsky, P.:Souvenir de Florence Vox Box 3-▲ CD3X 3024 [ADD]
Copenhagen Trio [S. Elbæk (vn), T. S. Hermansen (vc), M. Mogensen (pno)]
Brahms, J.:Trios (3) Pno Kontrapunkt 2-▲ 32090/91
Fauré, G.:Trio *(rec Mar. & Apr. 1993)* Kontrapunkt ▲ KPT 32158 [DDD]
Gade, N.W.:Novelettes, Op. 29 Kontrapunkt ▲ 32077 [DDD]
Gade, N.W.:Trio in B♭ Pno Kontrapunkt ▲ 32077 [DDD]
Gade, N.W.:Trio Pno, Op. 42 Kontrapunkt ▲ 32077 [DDD]
Lange-Müller, P.E.:Trio Pno Kontrapunkt ▲ KPT 32208
Mendelssohn, F.:Trio 1 Pno Kontrapunkt ▲ 32105 [DDD]
Mendelssohn, F.:Trio 2 Pno Kontrapunkt ▲ 32105 [DDD]
Ravel, M.:Berceuse sur le nom de Gabriel Fauré *(rec Mar. & Apr. 1993)* Kontrapunkt ▲ KPT 32158 [DDD]
Ravel, M.:Trio Pno *(rec Mar. & Apr. 1993)* Kontrapunkt ▲ KPT 32158 [DDD]
Schumann, R.:Trios Pno (comp) Kontrapunkt 2-▲ KPT 32167 [DDD]
Copenhagen Wind Quintet [Lena Bust Nielsen (fl), Lars Algot Sørensen (ob), Tore Othmar Poulsen (cl), Leif Lind (hn), Karen Lassen (bn)]
Schmidt, O.:Qnt Winds *(rec Mariot, France, 1994-95)* Marco Polo/Dacapo ▲ 8.224035 [DDD]
Coral Ridge Orch
R. McMurrin (cnd)
Bish, D.:A Sym of Hymns, w. Sung Sook Lee (sop), D. Bish (org), D. James Kennedy (nar), Coral Ridge Chorus [E] VQR Digital ▲ QR 2041 [DDD]
Cordon Orch
M. Best (cnd)
Berlioz, H.:L'Enfance du Christ, w. Jean Rigby (mez), John Aler (ten), Gerald Finley (ten), Alastair Miles (bar), Gwynne Howell (bass), Corydon Singers, St. Paul's Cathedral Choir Hyperion 2-▲ CDA 66991/2
Core Ensemble [Andrew Mark (vc), Hugh Hinton (pno), Michael Parola (perc)]
Martino, D.:Jazz Set *(rec Houghton Chapel, Wellesley College & WGBH Studios, Boston, MA, June & Sept 1995)* New World ▲ 80518-2
Corelli CO
T. Pál (cnd)
Cimarosa, D.:Il Maestro di cappella, w. J. Gregor (bass) [I] Hungaroton ▲ HCD 12573 [DDD]
Telemann, G.P.:Der Schulmeister, w. J. Gregor (bass), Schola Hungarica Boys' Chorus [G] Hungaroton ▲ HCD 12573 [DDD]
Cornetti con Crema
M. Zöbeley (cnd)
Lassus, O. de:Madrigals, w. Concerto di Viole, Group for Early Music—Il grave dell'età; Vedi l'aurora; Più volte un bel desio; Come pianta; Ben sono i prema tuoi; Canzon, la doglia; Che giova posseder; Così cor mio; Veggio se al vero; Arse la fiamma; Chi è fermato; Chi non sa; Per aspro mar; Ecco che pur vi lasso; Deh lascia anima; Tanto è quel bene; Hor ch'a l'albergo; Prendi l'aurata lira; O fugace dolcezza; Signor, le colpe mie Ars Musici ▲ 1099 [DDD]
Corona
W. Christie (cnd)
Bach, C.P.E.:Die Israeliten in der Wüste, w. L. Lootens (sop), B. Schlick (sop), H. Meens (ten), S. Barcoe (sgr), Cappella Coloniensis Musique d'Abord ▲ HMA 1901321
Coronation Orch
E. Bullock (cnd)
Vaughan Williams, R.:Festival Te Deum, w. Coronation Choir *(rec Westminster Abbey, at the Coronation of King George VI & Queen Elizabeth, 5/12/37)* Pearl ▲ GEMMCD 9342 (m) [AAD]
Il Cortegiano [I. Grzesivkiewicz (sop), A. Zanotti (sop), M. Mariotti (bar), G. Ugolini (nar), P. Battistelli (s fl), S. Nicoletti (s sax), S. Vagnini (org/hpd//t fl), M. Rovinelli (perc)]
Vagnini, S.:Nicolaus (oratorio) Bongiovanni ▲ GB 5539
Corydon Orch
M. Best (cnd)
Beethoven, L. van:Ah, perfido!, w. Janice Watson (sop)—aria only Hyperion ▲ CDA 66830
Beethoven, L. van:Mass, Op. 86, w. Janice Watson (sop), Jean Rigby (mez), John Mark Ainsley (ten), Gwynne Howell (bass), Corydon Singers Hyperion ▲ CDA 66830
Beethoven, L. van:Ne' giorni tuoi felici, w. Janice Watson (sop), John Mark Ainsley (ten) Hyperion ▲ CDA 66830
Beethoven, L. van:Tremate, empi, tremate, w. Janice Watson (sop), Gwynne Howell (bass) Hyperion ▲ CDA 66830
Bruckner, A.:Choral Music, w. Corydon Singers—Aequalis 1 & 2; Libera me; Masses 1-3; Psalm 150; Te Deum Hyperion 3-▲ 44071/3
Bruckner, A.:Mass 1, w. Corydon Singers Hyperion ▲ CDA 66650
Bruckner, A.:Te Deum, w. *(soloist unknown)*, Corydon Singers Hyperion ▲ CDA 66650
Cherubini, L.:Funeral March, w. Corydon Singers Hyperion ▲ CDA 66805
Cherubini, L.:Requiem Mass in c, w. Corydon Singers Hyperion ▲ CDA 66805
Finzi, G.:Dies natalis, w. John Mark Ainsley (ten) Hyperion ▲ CDA 66876
Finzi, G.:Intimations of Immortality, w. John Mark Ainsley (ten), Corydon Singers Hyperion ▲ CDA 66876
Vaughan Williams, R.:Hugh the Dover, w. R. Evans (sop), S. Walker (mez), B. Bottone (ter), N. Jenkins (ten), A. Opie (bar), R. Van Allan (bass), Corydon Singers, New London Children's Choir Hyperion 2-▲ CDA 66901/02
Vaughan Williams, R.:Sacred Songs, w. J. Howarth (sop), J.M. Ainsley (ten), T. Allen (bar), Corydon Singers—Towards the Unknown Region; Dona nobis pacem; O Clap your hands; Lord, Thou hast been our refuge; 4 Hymns Hyperion ▲ CDA 66655 [DDD]
Villa-Lobos, H.:Choral Music, w. Corydon Singers—Missa Sao Sebastiao; Magnificat Alleluia; Bendita Sabedoria; Ave Maria; Pater noster; Cor dulce, cor amabile; Panis angelicus; Praesepe; Sub tuum Hyperion ▲ CDA 66638
Costa Orch
H. Mancini (cnd)
Mancini, H.:Film Music, w. A. Williams (sgr), J. Mathis (sgr), L. Albright (sgr), B. Hackett (sgr), B. Greco (sgr), C. Byrd (sgr), P. Page (sgr). Conniff Orch, Mancini Orch—sels from Breakfast at Tiffany's; Peter Gunn; Mr. Lucky & others Columbia/Legacy ▲ CK 66505
Coull String Quartet [R. Coull (vn), P. Gallaway (vn), D. Curtis (va), J. Todd (vc)]
Bassoon Bon-Bons, w. Daniel Smith (bn), Royal PO [cnd:Ettore Stratta], English CO [cnd:Philip Ledger], Roger Vignoles (pno) ASV ▲ ASV 2052 [DDD]
Bridge, F.:Idylls (3) Str Qt Hyperion ▲ CDA 66718
Bridge, F.:Qnt Pno, w. A. Schiller (pno) ASV ▲ ASV 678 [DDD]
Dvořák, A.:Qt 10 Strs Hyperion ▲ CDA 66679

Coull String Quartet (cont.)
Dvořák, A.:Qnt Strs, Op. 77, w. P. Buckoke (db) Hyperion ▲ CDA 66679
Elgar, E.:Qt Strs Hyperion ▲ CDA 66718
Elgar, E.:Qnt Pno Strs, w. A. Schiller (pno) ASV ▲ ASV 678 [DDD]
Gurney, I.:The Western Playland, w. G. Trew (bar), R. Vignoles (pno) [E] Meridian ▲ CDE84185
Haydn, J.:Qts Strs, Op. 33, "Russian Qts" CRD 2–▲ CRD 34956
Jacob, G.:Suite Bn, w. Daniel Smith (bn) ASV ▲ ASV 613
Mendelssohn, F.:Capriccio Str Qt Hyperion ▲ CDA 66615
Mendelssohn, F.:Fugue Str Qt Hyperion ▲ CDA 66615
Mendelssohn, F.:Pieces Str Qt, Op. 81—Andante & Scherzo Hyperion ▲ CDA 66397
Mendelssohn, F.:Qts Strs (comp)—Nos. 4, 6 & in E♭ Hyperion ▲ CDA 66579
Mendelssohn, F.:Qts Strs (comp) Hyperion 3–▲ CDS 44051/3
Mendelssohn, F.:Qt in E♭ Strs Hyperion 3–▲ CDS 44051/3
Mendelssohn, F.:Qt 1 Strs Hyperion ▲ CDA 66397
Mendelssohn, F.:Qt 2 Strs Hyperion ▲ CDA 66397
Mendelssohn, F.:Qt 3 Strs Hyperion ▲ CDA 66615
Mendelssohn, F.:Qt 4 Strs Hyperion ▲ CDA 66615
Onslow, G.:Qt Strs, Op. 46/1 ASV ▲ ASV 808 [DDD]
Onslow, G.:Qt Strs, Op. 56 ASV ▲ ASV 808 [DDD]
Onslow, G.:Songs—variation on "God Save the King" ASV ▲ ASV 808 [DDD]
Prokofiev, S.:Ov on Hebrew Themes, w. A. Malsbury (cl), D. Petit (pno) Hyperion ▲ CDA 66573
Prokofiev, S.:Qt 1 Strs Hyperion ▲ CDA 66573
Prokofiev, S.:Qt 2 Strs Hyperion ▲ CDA 66573
Reicha, A.:Qnt Bn, w. Daniel Smith (bn) ASV ▲ ASV 613
Simpson, R.:Qt 10 Strs Hyperion ▲ CDA 66225 [DDD]
Simpson, R.:Qt 11 Strs Hyperion ▲ CDA 66225 [DDD]
Simpson, R.:Qt 12 Strs Hyperion ▲ CDA 66503
Simpson, R.:Qnt Strs, w. R. Bigley (va) Hyperion ▲ CDA 66503
Walton, W.:Qt Strs Hyperion ▲ CDA 66718

Coull String Quartet members
Danzi, F.:Qts Bn, Op. 40, w. Daniel Smith (bn)—No. 3 in B♭ ASV ▲ ASV 613 [DDD]

Couperin Ensemble
Couperin, F.:Nouveaux Concerts, "Les Goûts-réunis"—Nos. 5, 8, 9, 11 & 14 *(rec 3/91)* Claves ▲ CD 9117 [DDD]

CPE Bach CO
Bach, J.S.:Con Fl, Vn & Hpd Philips ▲ 434918–2
Bach, J.S.:Con 2 for 3 Hpds Philips ▲ 434918–2

H. Haenchen (cnd)
Bach, C.P.E.:Cons Fl, w. E. Haupt (fl)—in d LaserLight ▲ 14036 [DDD]
Bach, C.P.E.:Cons Fl, w. E. Haupt (fl)—in d, H.425 (W.22); in a, H.431 (W.166); in A, H.438 (W.168) Capriccio ▲ 10104
Bach, C.P.E.:Cons Fl, w. E. Haupt (fl)—W.169 LaserLight ▲ 15634 [DDD]
Bach, C.P.E.:Cons Fl, w. E. Haupt (fl)—in B♭, H.435 (W.167) & in G, H.445 (W.169) Capriccio ▲ 10105
Bach, C.P.E.:Cons Org, H.444, w. R. Münch (org) Capriccio ▲ 10135
Bach, C.P.E.:Magnificat, w. V. Hruba-Freiberger (sop), B. Bornemann (alt), P. Schreier (ten), O. Bär (bar), Berlin Radio Chorus Berlin Classics ▲ BER 1011 [DDD]
Bach, C.P.E.:Sinfs Orch—H.649–50, 653–54, 656 (W. 174–75, 178–79, 181) Berlin Classics ▲ BER 1096 [DDD]
Bach, C.P.E.:Sinfs, H.657–662, "Hamburg Syms" Capriccio ▲ 10106
Bach, C.P.E.:Sinf Strs, H.648 Berlin Classics ▲ BER 1011 [DDD]
Bach, J.S.:Cant 35, w. Jochen Kowalski (alt) Berlin Classics ▲ BER 1132 [ADD]
Bach, J.S.:Cant 49, w. Jochen Kowalski (alt) Berlin Classics ▲ BER 1132 [ADD]
Bach, J.S.:Cant 169, w. Jochen Kowalski (alt) Berlin Classics ▲ BER 1132 [ADD]
Bach, W.F.:Orchestral Music Berlin Classics ▲ BER 1098 [DDD]
Beethoven, L. van:Qt 11 Strs, "Quartetto serioso" [orchd. Mahler] Berlin Classics ▲ BER 1064 [DDD]
Concert at the Prussian Court Berlin Classics ▲ BER 1040 [DDD]
Ferlendis, G.:Con 1 Ob, w. B. Glaetzner (ob) Capriccio ▲ 10087 [DDD]
Haydn, J.:Sym 22, "Der Philosoph" Berlin Classics ▲ BER 1109 [DDD]
Haydn, J.:Sym 26, "Lamentatione" Berlin Classics ▲ BER 1013 [DDD]
Haydn, J.:Sym 31, "Hornsignal" Berlin Classics ▲ BER 1028 [DDD]
Haydn, J.:Sym 43, "Mercury" Berlin Classics ▲ BER 1014 [DDD]
Haydn, J.:Sym 44, "Trauer" Berlin Classics ▲ BER 1013 [DDD]
Haydn, J.:Sym 45, "Farewell" Berlin Classics ▲ BER 1014 [DDD]
Haydn, J.:Sym 48, "Maria Theresia" Berlin Classics ▲ BER 1024 [DDD]
Haydn, J.:Sym 49, "La Passione" Berlin Classics ▲ BER 1013 [DDD]
Haydn, J.:Sym 53, "L'Impériale" Berlin Classics ▲ BER 1024 [DDD]
Haydn, J.:Sym 55, "Der Schulmeister" Berlin Classics ▲ BER 1109 [DDD]
Haydn, J.:Sym 59, "Fire" Berlin Classics ▲ BER 1014 [DDD]
Haydn, J.:Sym 60, "Il Distratto" Berlin Classics ▲ BER 1027 [DDD]
Haydn, J.:Sym 64, "Tempora mutantur" Berlin Classics ▲ BER 1109 [DDD]
Haydn, J.:Sym 73, "La Chasse" Berlin Classics ▲ BER 1028 [DDD]
Haydn, J.:Sym 82, "The Bear" Berlin Classics ▲ BER 1028 [DDD]
Haydn, J.:Sym 85, "La Reine de France" Berlin Classics ▲ BER 1024 [DDD]
Haydn, J.:Sym 94, "Surprise Sym" Berlin Classics ▲ BER 1027 [DDD]
Haydn, J.:Sym 103, "Drum Roll" Berlin Classics ▲ BER 1027 [DDD]
Locatelli, P.:Cons for 4 Vns Berlin Classics ▲ BER 1133 [DDD]
Mozart, W.A.:Andante Fl, K.315/285a, w. W. Tast (fl) LaserLight ▲ 15 875 [DDD]
Mozart, W.A.:Arias, w. C. Oelze (sop)—concert arias Berlin Classics ▲ BER 1094 [DDD]
Mozart, W.A.:Cons Fl, w. W. Tast (fl) LaserLight ▲ 14 037 [DDD]
Mozart, W.A.:Cons Fl, w. W. Tast (fl) LaserLight ▲ 15 873 [DDD]
Mozart, W.A.:Con Ob, K.314, w. B. Glaetzner (ob) Capriccio ▲ 10087 [DDD]
Mozart, W.A.:Con Ob, K.314, w. B. Glaetzner (ob) LaserLight ▲ 15 875 [DDD]
Mozart, W.A.:Concertone Vns, w. Thorsten Rosenbusch (vn), Erich Kruger (va) Berlin Classics ▲ BER 2003
Mozart, W.A.:Concertone Vns, w. Werner Tast (fl), Katharina Hanstedt (hp) Berlin Classics ▲ BER 2004
Mozart, W.A.:Sinf concertante Ob, K.Anh.9, w. Andreas Lorenz (ob), Sebastian Weigle (hn), Eckart Konigstedt (bn), Klaus Kirbach (hpd) Berlin Classics ▲ BER 2004
Mozart, W.A.:Sinf concertante Vn, K.364, w. Thorsten Rosenbusch (vn), Christian Trompler (va) Berlin Classics ▲ BER 2003 [DDD]
Pergolesi, G.B.:Salve regina in c, w. J. Kowalski (alt), R. Alpemann (org) *(rec Apr. 1994)* Berlin Classics ▲ BER 1047–2 [DDD]
Pergolesi, G.B.:Stabat mater, w. D. Naseband (trb), J. Kowalski (alt), R. Alpemann (org) *(rec Apr. 1992)* Berlin Classics ▲ BER 1047–2 [DDD]
Rosetti, F.A.:Cons Ob, w. B. Glaetzner (ob)—Con. in F Capriccio ▲ 10087 [DDD]
Schubert, Franz:Qt 14 Strs [orchd. Mahler] Berlin Classics ▲ BER 1064 [DDD]

P. Schreier (cnd)
Bach, J.S.:Brandenburg Cons Philips ▲ 434918–2
Flute Concertos from Sansoucci, w. Patrick Gallois (fl) Deutsche Grammophon ▲ 439895–2
Mozart, W.A.:Complete Mozart Edition, w. Barbara Hendricks (sop), H.-P. Blochwitz (ten) Philips 2–▲ 422528–2 [ADD]

Cracow Chamber Players
Penderecki, K.:Sinfonietta, w. R. Kabara (vn), E. Szczepanska (va), D. Imietowski (vc) Vienna Modern Masters ▲ VMM 3023 [DDD]

Cracow Garrison Military Band
Marsz, Marsz Polonia, w. Polish Air Force Band, Polish Army Band, Polish Navy Band, Pomeranian Military District Band, Silesian Military District Band, Warsaw Military District Band Polskie Nagrania Edition ▲ ECD 064 [DDD]

Cracow PO

D. Amos (cnd)
Creston, P.:Corinthians XIII Koch International Classics ▲ KIC 7036–2 [DDD]
Creston, P.:Sym 2 Koch International Classics ▲ KIC 7036–2 [DDD]
Creston, P.:Walt Whitman Koch International Classics ▲ KIC 7036–2 [DDD]
Dello Joio, N.:Air Power Koch International Classics ▲ KIC 7020–2 [DDD] ■ 3–7020–4 (D)
Gould, M.:Holocaust Suite Koch International Classics ▲ KIC 7020–2 [DDD] ■ 3–7020–4 (D)

R. Bader (cnd)
Bacewicz, G.:Con Orch Koch Schwann ▲ SCH 311432 [DDD]
Bacewicz, G.:Sym 3 Koch Schwann ▲ SCH 311432 [DDD]
Górecki, H.-M.:Choros I Koch Schwann ▲ SCH 310412 [DDD]
Górecki, H.-M.:Stücke im alten Stil (3) Koch Schwann ▲ SCH 310412 [DDD]
Górecki, H.-M.:Sym 1, "1959" Koch Schwann ▲ SCH 310412 [DDD]
Liatoshinsky, B.:Sym 4 CPO ▲ CPO 999183 [DDD]
Liatoshinsky, B.:Sym 5 CPO ▲ CPO 999183 [DDD]
Nicolai, O.:Te Deum, w. Bozena Betley (sop), Zofie Kilanowicz (sop), Katarztna Suska (cta), Henryk Grychnik (ten), Czeslaw Galka (bar), Jerzy Gruszczynski (bass), Cracow Phil Chorus Koch Schwann ▲ SCH CD 310872
Paderewski, I.J.:Con Pno, w. K. Radziwonowicz (pno) *(rec 1991)* Koch Schwann ▲ 3–1145–2 [DDD]
Paderewski, I.J.:Fant polonaise, w. R. Smendzianka (pno) *(rec 1991)* Koch Schwann ▲ 3–1145–2 [DDD]
Suppé, F. von:Requiem, w. Aleksandra Baranska (sop), Katarzyna Suska (cta), Jerzy Knetig (ten), Andrjez Hiolski (bass), Cracow Phil Chorus Koch Schwann ▲ SCH CD 312482
Weill, K.:Sym 1 Koch Schwann ▲ CD 311147 [DDD]
Weill, K.:Sym 2 Koch Schwann ▲ CD 311147 [DDD]
Wetz, R.:Sym 1 CPO ▲ CPO 999272 [DDD]

H. Czyz (cnd)
Penderecki, K.:The Passion & Death of Our Lord Jesus Christ According to St. Luke, w. Leszek Herdegen (nar), Stefania Woytowicz (sop), Andrzej Hiolski (bar), Bernard Ladysz (bass), Cracow Phil Boys' Chorus, Cracow Phil Mixed Choir Polskie Nagrania 2–▲ PNCD 017 A/B
Penderecki, K.:Polymorphia Polskie Nagrania 2–▲ PNCD 017 A/B

G. Levine (cnd)
Shostakovich, D.:Con 1 Pno, w. G. Ohlsson (pno), M. Murphy (tpt) Arabesque ▲ Z 6610
Shostakovich, D.:The Golden Age (suite) Arabesque ▲ Z 6610
Shostakovich, D.:Sym 1 Arabesque ▲ Z 6610

Cracow Polish Radio-TV Orch

J. Krenz (cnd)
Moniuszko, S.:Haunted Manor, w. Bozena Betley-Siradzka (sop—Hanna), Anna Witkowska (sop—Marta/Stara Niewiasta), Wiera Baniewicz (mez—Jadwiga), Aleksandra Imalska (mez—Czesnikowa), Kazimierz Dluha (Grzes), Zdzislaw Nikodem (ten—Damazy), Wieslaw Ochman (ten—Stefan), Andrzej Hiolski (bar—Miecznik), Florian Skulski (bar—Maciej), Leonard Mróz (bass—Zbigniew), Andrzej Saciuk (bass—Skoluba), Cracow Polish Radio-TV Chorus *(rec Cracovia, 1978)* Agorá Music ("Phoenix" series) 3–▲ 509 [ADD]

Cracow Polish Radio-TV SO
Warren, E.R.:Suite, w. S. Kawalla Cambria ▲ CD 1042 [DDD]
Warren, E.R.:Sym in 1 Movt, w. S. Kawalla Cambria ▲ CD 1042 [DDD]

J.M. Florencio (cnd)
Jaffe, D.A.:Whoop for Your Life! Vienna Modern Masters ▲ VMM 3024 [DDD]

J.M. Florencio, Jr. (cnd)
Iannaccone, A.:Night Rivers Vienna Modern Masters ▲ VMM 3019 [DDD]

S. Kawalla (cnd)
Constantinides, D.:Midnight Fant Vienna Modern Masters ▲ VMM 3003 [DDD]
Fortuin, H.:Extremeties Vienna Modern Masters ▲ VMM 3003 [DDD]
Jazwinski, B.:Stryga Vienna Modern Masters ▲ VMM 3002 [DDD]
Jones, R.E.:Brangwyn Ov Vienna Modern Masters ▲ VMM 3001 [DDD]
Warren, E.R.:Along the Western Shore Cambria ▲ CD 1042 [DDD]
Warren, E.R.:The Crystal Lake Cambria ▲ CD 1042 [DDD]
Warren, E.R.:Good Morning, America!, w. E. Zimbalist, Jr. (nar), Cracow Polish Radio-TV Chorus [E] Cambria ▲ CD 1042 [DDD]
Warren, E.R.:The Legend of King Arthur:A Choral Sym, w. L. Vincent (ten), T. Hampson (bar) [E] Cambria ▲ CD 1043 [DDD]

J. Wyttenbach (cnd)
Scelsi, G.:Choral Music, w. Cracow Radio-TV Chorus—Aion; Pfhat; Konx-om-pax; Quattro pezzi per Orchestra; Anahit; Uaxuctum; Hurqualia; Hymnos; Chukrum Accord 3–▲ ACD 201692 [DDD]

Cracow RSO

B. Ferden (cnd)
Warren, E.R.:Abram in Egypt, w. Thomas Hampson (bar), Cracow Radio Chorus *(rec Church of the Bernardines, Cracow, Poland, June 21–24, 1993)* Cambria ▲ CD 1095 [DDD]
Warren, E.R.:The Harp Weaver, w. Thomas Hampson (bar), Cracow Radio Chorus *(rec Church of the Bernardines, Cracow, Poland, June 21–24, 1993)* Cambria ▲ CD 1095 [DDD]
Warren, E.R.:Singing Earth, w. Thomas Hampson (bar) *(rec Church of the Bernardines, Cracow, Poland, June 21–24, 1993)* Cambria ▲ CD 1095 [DDD]
Warren, E.R.:The Sleeping Beauty, w. Maria Venuti (mez—Princess), Thomas Hampson (bar—Prince), Gerd Nienstedt (b-bar—King), David Lutz (pno), Cracow Radio Chorus *(rec Church of the Bernardines, Cracow, Poland, June 21–24, 1993)* Cambria ▲ CD 1095 [DDD]

A. Froelicher (cnd)
Mieg, P.:Combray Gallo ▲ CD 681 [DDD]
Mieg, P.:Rondeau symphonique Gallo ▲ CD 681 [DDD]
Mieg, P.:Sinf Gallo ▲ CD 681 [DDD]

M. Mitsumoto (cnd)
Arnaud, L.:Bugler's Dream *(rec Krakow, Poland, Sept. 20–22, 1993)* Cambria ▲ CMB 1074 [DDD]
Arnaud, L.:In Memoriam, w. Kazimierz Moszynski (fl) *(rec Krakow, Poland, Sept. 20–22, 1993)* Cambria ▲ CMB 1074 [DDD]
Arnaud, L.:Latin American Scenario *(rec Krakow, Poland, Sept. 20–22, 1993)* Cambria ▲ CMB 1074 [DDD]
Arnaud, L.:Midinette, w. Andrzej Godeck (cl) *(rec Krakow, Poland, Sept. 20–22, 1993)* Cambria ▲ CMB 1074 [DDD]
Arnaud, L.:Symphonie Française *(rec Krakow, Poland, Sept. 20–22, 1993)* Cambria ▲ CMB 1074 [DDD]
Arnaud, L.:Well Tempered Oboist, w. Gregorz Stec (ob) *(rec Krakow, Poland, Sept. 20–22, 1993)* Cambria ▲ CMB 1074 [DDD]

J. Semkow (cnd)
Mussorgsky, M.:Boris Godunov, w. N. Gedda (ten—Dmitri), M. Talvela (bass—Boris), Cracow Radio Chorus EMI Classics ▲ CDCC 54377

A. Wit (cnd)
Szymanowski, K.:Harnasie EMI Classics ▲ CDM 65307

Cracow Radio-TV Polonaise Orch

J. Wyttenbach (cnd)
Scelsi, G.:Chukrim Accord ▲ ACD 201112 [DDD]
Scelsi, G.:Hurqualia Accord ▲ ACD 201112 [DDD]
Scelsi, G.:Hymnos Accord ▲ ACD 201112 [DDD]

Crafoord String Quartet [Wille Sundling (vn), Gert Crafoord (vn), Lars Johnsson (va), Lars-Olof Bergström (vc)]
Bäck, S.-E.:Qt 2 Strs Caprice ▲ CAP 21490
Eliasson, A.:Disegno Str Qt Caprice ▲ CAP 21402 [AAD]

Craiova PO

M. Cichirdan (cnd)
Briquet, M.:Offrande au Rhône Gallo ▲ CD 592 [AAD]

ORCH. & ENS.

Craiova PO (cont.)
M. Cichirdan (cnd) (cont.)
Briquet, M.:Pieces (4) Orch Gallo ▲ CD 592 [AAD]
Briquet, M.:Prelude Strs Gallo ▲ CD 592 [AAD]
Briquet, M.:Suite Orch Gallo ▲ CD 592 [AAD]
Gerber, R.:Con Bn, w. K. Walker (bn) Gallo ▲ CD 620 [AAD]
Gerber, R.:Con in A CO Gallo ▲ CD 580 [AAD]
Gerber, R.:Con in E♭ CO Gallo ▲ CD 580 [AAD]
Gerber, R.:Con for 2 Pnos, w. M. Ungereanu (pno), S. Petrescu (pno) Gallo ▲ CD 580 [AAD]
Gerber, R.:Orch Music—Aucassin et Nicolette; L'Hommage à Ronsard; Petit concert; Suites française Nos. 1 & 2 Gallo ▲ CD 620 [AAD]
Mozart, W.A.:Con Pno, K.107, w. Y. Mitsui (hpd) Gallo ▲ CD 662 [ADD‡DDD]
Mozart, W.A.:Sym 24 Gallo ▲ CD 601 [AAD]
Mozart, W.A.:Sym 33 Gallo ▲ CD 601 [AAD]
Mozart, W.A.:Vars Pno, K.265, w. Y. Mitsui (hpd) Gallo ▲ CD 662 [ADD‡DDD]
Paul Falentin, w. Paul Falentin (tpt) Gallo ▲ CD 576 [AAD]
Reichel, B.:Intrada Gallo ▲ CD 619 [ADD]
Reichel, B.:Pièce concertante, w. R. Meylan (fl) Gallo ▲ CD 619 [ADD]
Reichel, B.:Suite de danses Gallo ▲ CD 619 [ADD]
Salieri, A.:Con Fl, w. G. Costea (fl), F. Ionoaia (ob) Gallo ▲ CD 601 [AAD]
Salieri, A.:Sinf CO Gallo ▲ CD 601 [AAD]
Crawford Trio [Jan Čap (pno), Adrian Petcu (vn), Iosef Calef (vc)]
* Martin, P.:Trio 1 Pno Altarus ▲ CD 9011
Cremona Musica Insieme Group
P. Antonini (cnd)
Eisler, H.:Palmström, w. Karen Ott (sop) Nuova Era ("Icarus" series) ▲ NUO 7242
Schoenberg, A.:Pierrot lunaire, w. Karen Ott (sop) Nuova Era ▲ NUO 7242
Crescent String Quartet
Aderholt, S.:Qt Strs *(rec 1981)* Leonarda ▲ LE 336
Beach, A.M.C.:Qt Strs *(rec 1981)* Leonarda ▲ LE 336
Schonthal, R.:Qt Strs *(rec 1981)* Leonarda ▲ LE 336
Vellère, L.:Qt 3 Strs *(rec 1981)* Leonarda ▲ LE 336
Cristofori Trio [Szilvia Elek (pno), Péter Szüts (vn), Balázs Máté (vc)]
Bach, C.P.E.:Trio Sons (misc)—in G, H.523; in C, H.524; in C, H.526; in A, H.527; in e, H.529; in F, H.533 *(rec Protestant Church of Tordas, Hungary, Sept 6–9, 1995)* Hungaroton ▲ HCD 31619 [DDD]
Haydn, J.:Trios Pno, Vn & Vc [period instrs]—No. 25 in C, H.XV/27; No. 1 in G, H.XV/5; No. 4 in B♭, H.XV/8; No. 9 in e, H.XV/12 Hungaroton ▲ HCD 31482 [DDD]
Crofut Consort
Bartók, B.:Music of, w. J. Baird (sop), Boston Univ Women's Chorus—various works based upon Rumanian, Ruthenian, Bulgarian & Hungarian folksongs, lullabies, & dances Albany ▲ TROY 046 [DDD]
Kodály, Z.:Songs, w. J. Baird (sop), Boston Univ Women's Chorus—Ave Maria; The Gypsy; Evening Song Albany ▲ TROY 046 [DDD]
Crommelynck Duo [Patrick Crommelynck (pno), Taeko Crommelynck (pno)]
Brahms, J.:Hungarian Dances Pno 4–Hands [piano 4–hands] Claves ▲ CD 8710 [ADD]
Brahms, J.:Liebeslieder Waltzes Pno 4–Hands Claves ▲ CD 8711 [ADD]
Brahms, J.:Neue Liebeslieder Waltzes—65a Claves ▲ CD 8711 [ADD]
Brahms, J.:Souvenir de la Russie Claves ▲ CD 8711 [ADD]
Brahms, J.:Sym 1 [composer's arr. piano duet] Claves ▲ CD 9012 [DDD]
Brahms, J.:Sym 4 [composer's piano duet arr.] Claves ▲ CD 9012 [DDD]
Brahms, J.:Vars on a Theme of Robert Schumann, Op. 23 Claves ▲ CD 8711 [ADD]
Brahms, J.:Waltzes Pno, Op. 39 [piano duet versions] Claves ▲ CD 8710 [ADD]
Debussy, C.:Épigraphes antiques Claves ▲ CD 8508 [DDD]
Debussy, C.:Marche écossaise sur un thème populaire Claves ▲ CD 8508 [DDD]
Debussy, C.:La Mer [1905 piano duet version] Claves ▲ CD 8508 [DDD]
Debussy, C.:Petite suite Claves ▲ CD 8508 [DDD]
Duo Crommelynck *(rec Mar. 1992)* Claves ▲ CD 9214 [DDD]
Dvořák, A.:Slavonic Dances (comp) [piano 4–hands] Claves ▲ CD 9107 [DDD]
Dvořák, A.:Sym 9, "From the New World" *(rec Dec. 1992)* Claves ▲ CD 9316 [DDD]
Mozart, W.A.:Con 7 Pnos, w. B. Giuranna (pno), Padua & Venice CO Claves ▲ CD 9022 [DDD]
Mozart, W.A.:Fugue Pnos, K.426 Claves ▲ CD 9022 [DDD]
Mozart, W.A.:Pno Music (misc)—40 fragments & unfinished works for piano, 2 pianos & piano 4–hands Claves ▲ CD 9109 [DDD]
Schubert, Franz:Grande marche funèbre *(rec Salle de la Fondation Tibor Varga, Sion, Feb. 6–9, 1994)* Claves ▲ CD 9413 [DDD]
Schubert, Franz:Rondo Pno, D.608 Claves ▲ CD 8901 [DDD]
Schubert, Franz:Son Pno 4–Hands, D.812 Claves ▲ CD 8901 [DDD]
Schubert, Franz:Vars on an Original Theme Pno 4–Hands Claves ▲ CD 8901 [DDD]
Smetana, B.:The Moldau *(rec Dec. 1992)* Claves ▲ CD 9316 [DDD]
Strauss (II), Joh.:Waltzes [arr. for piano duet]—An der schönen, blauen Donau, Op. 314; Frühlingsstimmen, Op. 410; G'schichten aus dem Wiener Wald, Op. 325; Morgenblätter, Op. 279; Wein, Weib und Gesang, Op. 333; Wiener Blut, Op. 354; Wo die Zitronen blühn, Op. 364 Claves ▲ CD 8915 [DDD]
Tchaikovsky, P.:Russian Folk Songs Claves ▲ CD 8805 [DDD]
Tchaikovsky, P.:Sym 6 [arr piano 4–hands] Claves ▲ CD 8805 [DDD]
B. Giuranna (cnd)
Mozart, W.A.:Con 10 Pnos, w. Padua & Venice CO Claves ▲ CD 9022 [DDD]
Crystal CO
D. Amos (cnd)
Biggs, J.:Songs of Laughter, Love, & Tears, w. J. Mack (ten) [E] *(rec Feb. 16, 1992)* Crystal ▲ CD501
A. Endo (cnd)
Foss, L.:Con Ob, w. B. Gassman (ob), Los Angeles PO members [string quintet version] Crystal ▲ CD871
Heussenstamm, G.:Set for Double Reeds, w. Los Angeles PO members Crystal ▲ CD871
Music for Double–Reed Ensemble, w. Los Angeles PO members, Bert Gassman (ob) Crystal ▲ CD871
Pillin, B.:Pieces (3) for Double–Reed Septet, w. Los Angeles PO members Crystal ▲ CD871
E. Gold (cnd)
Hovhaness, A.:Armenian Rhap 1 Crystal ■ C 800
Hovhaness, A.:Avak, the Healer, w. Marni Nixon (sop), Thomas Stevens (tpt) Crystal ■ C 800
Hovhaness, A.:Avak, the Healer, w. Marni Nixon (sop), Thomas Stevens (tpt) Crystal ▲ CD 806
Hovhaness, A.:Prayer of St. Gregory, w. T. Stevens (tpt) Crystal ■ C 800
S. Weiss (cnd)
Haydn, J.:Con Org, Vn & Strs, H.XVIII/6, w. Jeanne Weiss (pno), Sidney Weiss (vn) Crystal ▲ CD 511 ■ C 511
Mendelssohn, F.:Con in d Vn, Pno & Strs, w. S. Weiss (vn), J. Weiss (pno) Crystal ▲ CD 511 ■ C 511
CSSR State PO
P. Breiner (cnd)
Christmas Goes Baroque *(rec May 1989)* Naxos ▲ 8.550307 [DDD]
CSSR State PO Košice
P. Breiner (cnd)
Romantic French Music For Guitar & Orchestra, w. Gerald Garcia (gtr) Naxos ▲ 8.550480 [DDD]
O. Dohnányi (cnd)
Strauss (II), Joh.:Orchestral Music—Warschauer–Polka, Op. 84; Wellen und Wogen, Op. 141; Caroussel–Marsch, Op. 133; Carmelien–Polka, Op. 248; Myrthen–Kränze, Op. 154; Nordstern–Quadrille, Op. 153; Bluette–Polka, Op. 271; Concurrenzen, Op. 267; Chansonetten–Quadrille, Op. 259; Ballsträusschen, Op. 380; Kuss–Walzer, Op. 400 Marco Polo ▲ 8.223206 [DDD]

CSSR State PO Košice (cont.)
O. Dohnányi (cnd) (cont.)
Strauss (II), Joh.:Orchestral Music—Heiligenstädter Rendezvous–Polka, Op. 78; Nachtfalter, Op. 157; Quadrille sur des airs françaises, Op. 290; Musen–Polka, Op. 147; Wiener Chronik, Op. 268; Russische Marsch–Fantaisie, Op. 353; Elisen–Polka, Op. 151; Kennst du mich?, Op. 381; Hesperus–Polka, Op. 249; Italienischer Walzer, Op. 407; Pariser Polka, Op. 382 Marco Polo ▲ 8.223205 [DDD]
R. Edlinger (cnd)
Alfvén, H.:Swedish Rhap 1, "Midsommarvaka" *(rec Oct 1988)* Naxos ▲ 8.550090 [DDD]
Grieg, E.:Lyric Suite, Op. 54 *(rec Oct. 1988)* Naxos ▲ 8.550090 [DDD]
Grieg, E.:Norwegian Dances, Op. 35 *(rec Oct. 1988)* Naxos ▲ 8.550090 [DDD]
Grieg, E.:Symphonic Dances—No. 3 *(rec Oct. 1988)* Naxos ▲ 8.550090 [DDD]
Raff, J.:Italian Suite Marco Polo ▲ 8.223194
Raff, J.:Thüringer Suite Marco Polo ▲ 8.223194
Sibelius, J.:Karelia Ov *(rec Oct. 1988)* Naxos ▲ 8.550090 [DDD]
Strauss (II), Joh.:Orchestral Music—Hopser–Polka, Op. 28; Serailtänze, Op. 5; Austria–Marsch, Op. 20; Veilchen–Polka, Op. 132; Knallkügerin, Op. 140; Motor–Quadrille, Op. 129; Bürgerball–Polka, Op. 145; Dividenden–Walzer, Op. 252; Verbrüderungs–Marsch, Op. 287; Im Krapfenwaldl, Op. 336; O schöner Mai!, Op. 375 Marco Polo ▲ 8.223204 [DDD]
Svendsen, J.:Norwegian Artists' Carnival *(rec Oct. 1988)* Naxos ▲ 8.550090 [DDD]
A. Leaper (cnd)
Bantock, G.:Hebridean Sym Marco Polo ▲ 8.223274
Bantock, G.:Old English Suite Marco Polo ▲ 8.223274
Bantock, G.:Russian Scenes Marco Polo ▲ 8.223274
U. Schneider (cnd)
Raff, J.:Sym 3 Marco Polo ▲ 8.223321
Raff, J.:Sym 10 Marco Polo ▲ 8.223321
R. Stankovsky (cnd)
Dvořák, A.:Rusalka (polonaise) Naxos ▲ 8.550376 [DDD]
A. Walter (cnd)
Strauss (II), Joh.:Orchestral Music—Viribus unitis March, Op. 96; Heski–Holki–Polka, Op. 80; Idyllen Waltz, Op. 95; Demi–Fortune Polka, Op. 186; Strelna Terrassen Quadrille, Op. 185; Lockvögel Waltz, Op. 118; Rokonhangok Polka, Op. 246; Gavotte der Königin, Op. 391; Jux–Brüder Waltz, Op. 208; Licht und Schatten Polka Mazurka, Op. 374; Sinnen und Minnen Waltz, Op. 435; So ängstilch sind wir nicht! Polka, Op. 413 Marco Polo ▲ 8.223224 [DDD]
Strauss (II), Joh.:Orchestral Music—Zigeunerin–Quadrille, Op. 24; Sängerfahrten (waltz), Op. 41; Ligourianer Seufzer (scherz–polka), Op. 57; Schnellpost–Polka, Op. 159; Freuden–Salven (waltz), Op. 171; La Berceuse (quadrille), Op. 194; Fürst Bariatinsky–Marsch, Op. 212; Studenten–polka, Op. 263; Motoren (waltz), Op. 265; Bürgerweisen (waltz), Op. 306; Eljen a Magyar! (schnell–polka), Op. 332; Brautschau (polka), Op. 417 Marco Polo ▲ 8.223216 [DDD]
Strauss (II), Joh.:Orchestral Music—Berglieder, Op. 18; Jux–Polka, Op. 17; Wiener Punsch–Lieder, Op. 131; Dämonen–Quadrille, Op. 19; Freudengrüss–Polka, Op. 127; Liebeslieder, Op. 114; Vergnügungszug, Op. 281; Satanella–Quadrille, Op. 123; Die Österreicher, Op. 22; Aeskulap–Polka, Op. 130; Lind–Gesänge, Op. 21; Amazonen–Polka, Op. 9 Marco Polo ▲ 8.223203 [DDD]
Strauss (II), Joh.:Orchestral Music—Geisselhiebe (polka), Op. 60; Ernte–Tänze (waltz), Op. 45; Champagner–Polka, Op. 211; Phänomene (waltz), Op. 193; Romance No. 1 (for Cello & Orchestra), Op. 243; Kinderspiele (polka française), Op. 304; Frohsinns–Spenden (waltz), Op. 73; St. Petersburg (quadrille on Russian themes), Op. 255; Vöslauer Polka, Op. 100; Grillenbanner (waltz), Op. 247; Bal champêtre (quadrille), Op. 303; Du un Du (waltz), Op. 367 Marco Polo ▲ 8.223214 [DDD]
Strauss (II), Joh.:Orchestral Music—Czechen–Polka, Op. 13; Die jungen Wiener, Op. 7; Satanella–Polka, Op. 124; Cytheren–Quadrille, Op. 6; Solonsprüche, Op. 128; Fantasieblümchen, Op. 241; Wo die Citronen blüh'n, Op. 364; Indra–Quadrille, Op. 122; Tik–Tak–Polka, Op. 365; Vermählungs–Toaste, Op. 136; Neue Pizzicato–Polka, Op. 449; Kaiser Franz Joseph I Rettungs–Jubel–Märsch, Op. 126 Marco Polo ▲ 8.223202 [DDD]
Strauss (II), Joh.:Orchestral Music—Studenten–Marsch, Op. 56; Lava–Ströme (waltz), Op. 74; Alliance–Marsch, Op. 158; Leopoldstädter (polka), Op. 168; Grossfürstin Aexandra (waltz), Op. 181; Patronessen (waltz), Op. 264; Invitation a la Polka–Mazur, Op. 277; Die Publizisten (waltz), Op. 321; Stadt und Land (polka mazur), Op. 322; Cagliostro Quadrille, Op. 369; Entweder–oder! Schnell–Polka, Op. 403; Rathausball–Tänze (waltz), Op. 438 Marco Polo ▲ 8.223218 [DDD]
Strauss (II), Joh.:Orchestral Music—Fest–Quadrille, Op. 44; Die Gemüthlichen (Waltz), Op. 70; Harmonie–Polka, Op. 106; Ella–Polka, Op. 160; Aurora–Polka, Op. 165; Man lebt nur einmal!, Op. 167; Krönungs–Marsch, Op. 183; Neues Leben (polka), Op. 278; Hofball–Tänze (waltz), Op. 298; Stürmich in Lieb' und Tanz (schnellpolka), Op. 393; Wiener Frauen (waltz), Op. 423 Marco Polo ▲ 8.223212 [DDD]
Strauss (II), Joh.:Orchestral Music—Klänge aus der Walachei (waltz), Op. 50; Revolutions–Marsch, Op. 54; Herrmann–Polka, Op. 91; Haute–volée Polka, Op. 155; Glossen–Walzer, Op. 163; Handels–Elite–Quadrille, Op. 166; Patrioten–Polka, Op. 274; Aus den Bergen (Waltz), Op. 292; L'Africaine (Quadrille), Op. 299; Waldine (polka mazurka), Op. 385; Donauweibchen (Waltz), Op. 427; Frisch heran! (Schnellpolka) Marco Polo ▲ 8.223211 [DDD]
Strauss (II), Joh.:Orchestral Music—Gunstwerber, Op. 4; Herzenslust, Op. 3; Phönix–Schwingen, Op. 125; Debut–Quadrille, Op. 2; Zehner–Polka, Op. 121; Klangfuguren, Op. 251; Maskenzug–Polka, Op. 240; Nocturne–Quadrille, Op. 120; Freut euch des Lebens, Op. 340; Fledermaus–Polka, Op. 362; Bei uns z'Haus, Op. 361; Veilchen, Op. 256 Marco Polo ▲ 8.223201 [DDD]
Strauss (II), Joh.:Orchestral Music—Patrioten–Marsch, Op. 8; Fidelen–Polka, Op. 26; Die Belagerung von Rochelle (Quadrille), Op. 31; Die Zillerthaler (Waltz), Op. 30; Tanzi–Bari–Polka, Op. 134; Sirenen (Waltz), Op. 164; Thermen (Waltz), Op. 245; Neue Melodien–Quadrille (on themes from Italian operas), Op. 254; Demolirer–Polka, Op. 269; Egyptian March, Op. 335; Nur Fort! (polka schnell), Op. 383; Was sich liebt, neckt sich (polka française), Op. 399 Marco Polo ▲ 8.223213 [DDD]
J. Wildner (cnd)
Strauss (II), Joh.:Orchestral Music—Deutschmeister–Jubiläumsmarsch, Op. 470; Rhadamantus–Klänge Waltz, Op. 94; Maria Taglioni Polka, Op. 173; Wien, mein Sinn! Waltz, Op. 192; Le beau monde Quadrille, Op. 192; Vibrationen Waltz, Op. 204; Die Pariserin Polka, Op. 238; Telegramme Waltz, Op. 318; Indigo Quadrille, Op. 344; Glücklich ist, wer vergisst Polka Mazurka, Op. 368; Gross–Wien Waltz, Op. 440; Rasch in der Tat! Polka, Op. 409 Marco Polo ▲ 8.223223 [DDD]
Les Cuivres Francais
A. Moglia (cnd)
Mozart, L.:Con Hn, w. Thierry Caens (tpt), Alain Moglia (vn), Toulouse National CO Pierre Verany ▲ PVY 730070
Mozart, L.:Serenade Tpt, w. Thierry Caens (tpt), Alain Moglia (vn), Toulouse National CO Pierre Verany ▲ PVY 730070
Cummings Ensemble
Cummings, C.:Music of—Photo–Op:Life in the Political Fast Lane; Insertions About Love, War & Death; The American Way (From a New Opera About Vietnam) [E] *(rec 1990)* CRI ▲ CD 627 [DDD]
Cummings String Trio
Beethoven, L. van:Trios Strs, Op. 9 Unicorn–Kanchana ▲ UKCD 2081
Currende Instrumental Ensemble
E. van Nevel (cnd)
Carissimi, G.:Oratorios, w. Currende Vocal Ensemble—Ezechia, Jephte & Vanitas Vanitatum [L] Accent ▲ 9059 [DDD]
Cererols, J.:Missa pro defunctis, w. Guillemette Laurens (mez) *(rec May 1994)* Accent ▲ 94106 [DDD]
Currents New Music Ensemble
Blank, A.:Polymorphics *(rec Richmond, VA, Aug 10–11, 1993)* Centaur ▲ CRC 2248 [DDD]
Cohen, F.:Three for Emily *(rec Richmond, VA, Sept 6–11, 1993)* Centaur ▲ CRC 2248 [DDD]
Cohen, F.:Trio Ww *(rec Richmond, VA, Sept 6–11, 1993)* Centaur ▲ CRC 2248 [DDD]
Davidovsky, M.:Biblical Songs *(rec Richmond, VA, Sept 6–11, 1993)* Centaur ▲ CRC 2248 [DDD]
Feigin, J.:Poems (4) of Linda Pastan *(rec Richmond, VA, Sept 6–11, 1993)* Centaur ▲ CRC 2248 [DDD]

▲ = CD ♦ = Enhanced CD Δ = MD ■ = Cassette Tape □ = DCC

Curtis Institute of Music SO
A. Previn (cnd)
Previn, A.:Reflections — EMI Classics ▲ CDC 55371
Rorem, N.:Con Pno Left Hand, w. G. Graffman (pno) — New World ▲ 80445-2
Vaughan Williams, R.:Fant on a Theme by Thomas Tallis — EMI Classics ▲ CDC 55371
Vaughan Williams, R.:Sym 5 — EMI Classics ▲ CDC 55371
Curtis Institute Student Orch
F. Reiner (cnd)
Brahms, J.:Academic Festival Ov — VAI Audio 2-▲ VAIA/IPA 1020 (m) [ADD]
Hoffmann, Giovanni:Chromaticon, w. J. Hofmann (pno) — VAI Audio 2-▲ VAIA/IPA 1020 (m) [ADD]
Rubinstein, A.:Con 4 Pno, w. J. Hofmann (pno) *(rec live Nov. 28, 1937)* — VAI Audio 2-▲ VAIA/IPA 1020 (m) [ADD]

CWS Glasgow Band
H. Snell (cnd)
Flower of Scotland — Doyen ▲ CD 005 [DDD]
Les Cyclopes [Laura Johnson (vn), Manfred Kramer (vn), Guido Balestracci (vl), Brian Feehan (thb/gtr), Bibiane Lapointe (hpd), Thierry Maeder (org)]
Reincken, J.A.:Hortus musicus — Pierre Verany ▲ PVY 796052 [DDD]
Cygnus Ensemble
Kupferman, M.:Summer Music — Soundspells ▲ SP 103
Czech Brass Orch
P. Urbanek (cnd)
Sousa, J.P.:Marches & Dances — Elektra/Nonesuch ▲ 71266-2 [ADD]
Czech CO
J. Vlach (cnd)
Mozart, W.A.:Divert Str Qt, K.136 — Supraphon Collection ▲ 11 0614-2 [ADD]
Mozart, W.A.:Kleine Nachtmusik — Supraphon Collection ▲ 110614-2 [ADD]
Tchaikovsky, P.:Serenade Strs — Supraphon Collection ▲ 11 0614-2 [ADD]
Czech Chamber Soloists
L. Svárovský (cnd)
Dittersdorf, K.D. von:Con Vn, w. Bohumil Kotmel (vn) *(rec 1992)* — Panton ▲ PAN 811144
Dittersdorf, K.D. von:Sinfonia Concertante, w. Ladislav Kyselak (va), Miloslav Jelinek (db) *(rec 1992)* — Panton ▲ PAN 811146
Hummel, J.N.:Con in E Tpt, w. Jaroslav Halíř (tpt) *(rec Stadion-Hall, Brno, Mar 12, 1995)* — Panton ▲ 811368-2 [DDD]
Mysliveček, J.:Qnts Strs *(rec Studio II, Czech Radio, Brno, Mar 6-8, 1992)* — Panton ▲ PAN 811399 [DDD]
Czech Nonet
Berwald, F.:Septet Vn, "Grand Septet" — Supraphon ▲ SUP 111270 [DDD]
Hába, A.:Nonets—No. 1 in 12-note system, Op. 40; No. 2 in 7-note system, Op. 41; No. 3, Op. 82; No. 4, Op. 97 — Supraphon ▲ SUP 0018 [DDD]
Hába, A.:Nonets—Opp. 40/1 & 94/4 *(rec 1978 & 1992)* — Praga ▲ PR 255 005
Martinů, B.:Mazurka-Nokturno *(rec Nov 1995-Jan 1996)* — Praga ▲ PR 250097
Martinů, B.:Nonet Wws & Pno *(rec Nov 1995-Jan 1996)* — Praga ▲ PR 250097
Martinů, B.:Qt Cl, Hn, Vc & Side Drum, w. Vlastimil Mareš (cl) *(rec Nov 1995-Jan 1996)* — Praga ▲ PR 250097
Martinů, B.:Qt Ob & Pno Trio, w. Milan Langer (pno) *(rec Nov 1995-Jan 1996)* — Praga ▲ PR 250097
Mozart, W.A.:Adagio E Hn, w. Jiří Krejčí (E hn) *(rec Prague, 1995)* — Praga ▲ PR 250095
Mozart, W.A.:Divert Ob, K.251, w. Jiří Krejčí (ob), Vladimíra Klánská (hn) *(rec Prague, 1995)* — Praga ▲ PR 250095
Mozart, W.A.:Qt Ob, K.370, w. Jiří Krejčí (ob) *(rec Prague, 1995)* — Praga ▲ PR 250095
Spohr, L.:Nonet Strs — Supraphon ▲ SUP 111270 [DDD]
Czech Nonet members
Schubert, Franz:Nonet Ww, w. Czech Soloists — Praga ▲ PR 250087
Schubert, Franz:Octet Ww, D.803 — Praga ▲ PR 250087
Czech Phil CO
D. Geringas (cnd)
Haydn, J.:Con 1 Vc, w. David Geringas (vc) *(rec Domovina Studio, Prague, Nov 19-21, 1993)* — Canyon Classics ▲ 242
Haydn, J.:Con 2 Vc, w. David Geringas (vc) *(rec Domovina Studio, Prague, Nov 19-21, 1993)* — Canyon Classics ▲ 242
Haydn, J.:Sym 13, w. David Geringas (vc) [andante] *(rec Domovina Studio, Prague, Nov 19-21, 1993)* — Canyon Classics ▲ 242
J. Hnyk (cnd)
Mozart, L.:Toy Sym — Canyon Classics ▲ 3689
Mozart, W.A.:Contradances, K.462, w. Miroslav Kejmar (psthn) — Canyon Classics ▲ 3652
Mozart, W.A.:Serenade Vn, K.250, w. Josef Kroft (vn) — Canyon Classics ▲ 3689
Mozart, W.A.:Serenade Ww, K.320, w. Miroslav Kejmar (psthn) — Canyon Classics ▲ 3652
V. Válek (cnd)
Mozart, W.A.:Andante Fl, w. Jiří Válek (fl) *(rec House of Artists, Prague, Feb 1-3, 1996)* — Canyon Classics 2-▲ 336
Mozart, W.A.:Cons Fl, w. Jiří Válek (fl) *(rec House of Artists, Prague, Feb 1-3, 1996)* — Canyon Classics 2-▲ 336
Mozart, W.A.:Con Fl Hp, w. Jiří Válek (fl), Hana Müllerová-Jouzová (hp) *(rec House of Artists, Prague, Feb 1-3, 1996)* — Canyon Classics 2-▲ 336
Czech PO
Dvořák, A.:Suite, Op. 98b, "American" — Supraphon ▲ SUP 111996
Famous Opera Overtures — Supraphon Collection ▲ SUP 110640 [ADD]
Janácek, L.:The Excursions of Mr. Brouček, w. Jana Jonaová (sop), Libuše Márová (mez), Vilém Přibyl (ten), Richard Novák (bass), Czech Phil Chorus — Supraphon 2-▲ SUP 112153 [AAD]
Martinů, B.:Con grosso — Supraphon ▲ SUP 111996
Music From the Heart of Europe, w. Lubomir Brabec (gtr), Josef Suk (vn), Rudolf Firkušný (pno), Vaclav Neumann (cnd), Jiří Belohlávek (cnd), Panocha Quartet, Prague CO, Prague Musica Antiqua, et al. — Supraphon ▲ SUP 0063 [DDD]
Smetana, B.:The Bartered Bride (ov) — Supraphon ▲ SUP 111996
Stokowski Encores, w. London SO, New Philharmonia, Royal PO — London ("Weekend Classics" series) ▲ 433876-2 LC [ADD]
Suk, J.:The Ripening — Supraphon ▲ SUP 111996
G. Albrecht (cnd)
Brahms, J.:Sym 1 — Supraphon ("Czech PO Centennial" series) ▲ SUP 111995
Bruckner, A.:Sym 4, "Romantic" *(rec House of Artists, Prague, Apr 22-24, 1995)* — Canyon Classics ▲ 329
Bruckner, A.:Sym 7 *(rec House of Artists, Prague, Apr 24-26, 1995)* — Canyon Classics ▲ 330
Bruckner, A.:Sym 8 *(rec House of Artists, Prague, Apr 6-11, 1994)* — Canyon Classics ▲ CD 227
Dvořák, A.:Armida, w. Joanna Borowska (sop—Armida), Monika Brychtová (sgr—Siren), Wieslaw Ochman (ten—Rinald), Richard Sporka (ten—Dudo), Jan Markvart (bar—Sven), Pavel Daniluk (bass—King), George Fortune (bass—Ismen), Zdenek Harvánek (bass—Ubald), Miloslav Podskalský (bass—Peter), Milan Bürger (sgr—Gernand), Roman Janál (sgr—Muezzin/Hlasatel), Vratislav Kříz (sgr—Gottfried), Vladimír Nacházel (sgr—Roger), Prague Chamber Choir *(rec 1995)* — Orfeo 2-▲ 404962 [DDD]
Dvořák, A.:Carnival — Supraphon ("Czech PO Centennial" series) ▲ SUP 111995
Dvořák, A.:Dmitrij, w. *(soloists unknown)*, Czech Phil Chorus [Cz] *(rec 1989)* — Supraphon 3-▲ 11 1259-2 [DDD]
Dvořák, A.:Husitská *(rec House of Artists, Prague, Apr 27-29, 1995)* — Canyon Classics ▲ CD 293
Dvořák, A.:In Nature's Realm — Supraphon ("Czech PO Centennial" series) ▲ SUP 111995
Dvořák, A.:Kate & the Devil (sels)—Ballet *(rec House of Artists, Prague, Dec 31, 1995)* — Canyon Classics 2-▲ 323

Czech PO (cont.)
G. Albrecht (cnd) (cont.)
Dvořák, A.:Kate & the Devil (ov) *(rec House of Artists, Prague, Dec 31, 1995)* — Canyon Classics 2-▲ 323
Dvořák, A.:Legends, Op. 59 *(rec House of Artists, Prague, Apr 27-29, 1995)* — Canyon Classics ▲ CD 293
Dvořák, A.:Othello *(rec House of Artists, Prague, Jan 4-7, 1996)* — Canyon Classics 2-▲ 322
Dvořák, A.:Othello — Supraphon ("Czech PO Centennial" series) ▲ SUP 111995
Dvořák, A.:Sym 9, "From the New World" *(rec House of Artists, Prague, Jan 4-7, 1996)* — Canyon Classics 2-▲ 322
Fibich, Z.:Sym 3 *(rec Dvořák-Saal des Rudolfinums Prag, June 2, 1993)* — Orfeo ▲ 350951 [DDD]
Fibich, Z.:The Tempest (ov) *(rec Dvořák-Saal des Rudolfinums Prag, Jan 12, 1995)* — Orfeo ▲ 350951 [DDD]
Fibich, Z.:Toman & the Wood Nymph *(rec Dvořák-Saal des Rudolfinums Prag, Jan 12, 1995)* — Orfeo ▲ 350951 [DDD]
Fučík, J.:Marches & Waltzes—The Last Salute, Op. 150 [dramatic march]; Winter Storm [waltz]; Triumphal Hungarian March from Attila, Op. 211; Marinarella-Ov *(rec House of Artists, Prague, Dec 31, 1994)* — Canyon Classics ▲ CD 258
Fučík, J.:Marches & Waltzes—Arrival of the Gladiators, Op. 68 *(rec House of Artists, Prague, Dec 31, 1995)* — Canyon Classics 2-▲ 323
Fučík, J.:Marinarella *(rec House of Artists, Prague, Dec 31, 1995)* — Canyon Classics 2-▲ 323
Fučík, J.:Miramare *(rec House of Artists, Prague, Dec 31, 1995)* — Canyon Classics 2-▲ 323
Haas, P.:Study [comp. & rev. Lubomír Peduzzi] *(rec May 3-4 & June 2-3, 1993)* — Orfeo ▲ 337941 [DDD]
Janácek, L.:Fate, w. Lívia Ághová (sop—Míla), Ludmila Nováková (sop—Frl. Stuhlá/Součková), Marta Benačková (cta—Mílas Mother), Štefan Margita (ten—Dr. Suda/Hrázda), Peter Straka (ten—Zivny), Ivan Kusnjer (bar—Konečny/Verva), Peter Mikuláš (bass—Lhotsky), Prague Chamber Choir *(rec 1995)* — Orfeo ▲ 384 951 [DDD]
Klein, G.:Partita Strs *(rec May 3-4 & June 2-3, 1993)* — Orfeo ▲ 337941 [DDD]
Nedbal, O.:From Fairy Tale (sels) *(rec House of Artists, Prague, Dec 31, 1995)* — Canyon Classics 2-▲ 323
Nedbal, O.:Miss Butterfly *(rec House of Artists, Prague, Dec 31, 1994)* — Canyon Classics ▲ CD 258
Nedbal, O.:Nightingale's Waltz, w. Radomír Pivoda (fl), Bohumil Kotmel (vn) *(rec House of Artists, Prague, Dec 31, 1995)* — Canyon Classics 2-▲ 323
Nedbal, O.:Scherzo caprice *(rec House of Artists, Prague, Dec 31, 1994)* — Canyon Classics ▲ CD 258
Nedbal, O.:Stupid Simon (sels)—Krakowiak, No. 2; Valse triste, No. 4; Polonaise, No. 6 *(rec House of Artists, Prague, Dec 31, 1995)* — Canyon Classics 2-▲ 323
Schubert, Franz:Sym 8 *(rec House of Artists, Prague)* — Canyon Classics ▲ CD 287
Schubert, Franz:Sym 9 *(rec House of Artists, Prague)* — Canyon Classics ▲ CD 287
Schulhoff, E.:Sym 2 *(rec May 3-4 & June 2-3, 1993)* — Orfeo ▲ 337941 [DDD]
Ullmann, V.:Con Pno, w. Igor Ardašev (pno) *(rec live, 1994-95)* — Orfeo ("Musica Rediviva" series) ▲ 366951 [DDD]
Ullmann, V.:Don Quixote [orchd Bernhard Wulff, 1994] *(rec live, 1994-95)* — Orfeo ("Musica Rediviva" series) ▲ 366951 [DDD]
Ullmann, V.:Sym 2 *(rec May 3-4 & June 2-3, 1993)* — Orfeo ▲ 337941 [DDD]
Ullmann, V.:Die Weise von Liebe und Tod, w. Erika Pluhar (nar) [orchd Henning Brauel, 1994] *(rec live, 1994-95)* — Orfeo ("Musica Rediviva" series) ▲ 366951 [DDD]
Weinberger, J.:Czech Songs & Dances—Nos. 1 [Bodhumil Kotmel (vn)], 3 & 6 *(rec House of Artists, Prague, Dec 31, 1995)* — Canyon Classics 2-▲ 323
Weinberger, J.:Orchestral Music—Vivo; Andantino; Allegretto [all from 6 Czech Songs & Dances]; Polka; Fuga [both from Svanda Bag-piper] *(rec House of Artists, Prague, Dec 31, 1994)* — Canyon Classics ▲ CD 258

A. Almeida (cnd)
Dukas, P.:L'Apprenti sorcier — Supraphon Collection ▲ 11 0646-2 [ADD]
P. Altrichter (cnd)
Dvořák, A.:Suite, Op. 98b, "American" *(rec Feb 1996)* — Supraphon ▲ SUP 3178
Shostakovich, D.:Con 2 Vn, w. Bohumil Kotmel (vn) *(rec Feb 1996)* — Supraphon ▲ SUP 3178
K. Ančerl (cnd)
Bartók, B.:Con Orch — Sound ▲ CD 3439
Bartók, B.:Con 3 Pno, w. E. Bernathova (pno) *(rec 1961-63)* — Supraphon ▲ SUP 11 1957 [AAD]
Bartók, B.:Con Va, w. Jaroslav Karlovsky (va) — Supraphon ▲ SUP 111956 [AAD]
Bartók, B.:Con 2 Vn, w. A. Gertler (vn) — Supraphon Collection ▲ 11 0632-2 [ADD]
Bartók, B.:Con 2 Vn, w. André Gertler (vn) — Supraphon ▲ SUP 111956 [AAD]
Bartók, B.:The Wooden Prince *(rec 1961-63)* — Supraphon ▲ SUP 11 1957 [AAD]
Beethoven, L. van:Con 1 Pno, w. Sviatoslav Richter (pno) — Prelude ▲ PRE 2157 [ADD]
Beethoven, L. van:Con 3 Pno, w. Sviatoslav Richter (pno) — Prelude ▲ PRE 2157 [ADD]
Beethoven, L. van:Leonore 3 *(rec 1962)* — Supraphon ▲ 11 0572-2 [AAD]
Beethoven, L. van:Romances Vn, w. David Oistrakh (vn) — Supraphon ▲ SUP 3005
Beethoven, L. van:Sym 1 — Supraphon ("Czech Philharmonic" series) ▲ SUP 111937 [AAD]
Beethoven, L. van:Sym 5 — Supraphon ("Czech Philharmonic" series) ▲ SUP 111937 [AAD]
Berlioz, H.:Le Carnaval romain *(rec 1964)* — Supraphon ▲ 11 0572-2 [AAD]
Berlioz, H.:Le Carnaval romain — Supraphon ("Czech Philharmonic" series) ▲ SUP 111938 [AAD]
Bloch, E.:Schelomo, w. A. Navarra (vc) *(rec 1964)* — Supraphon ("Great Artists" series) ▲ 11 1002-2 [AAD]
Bloch, E.:Schelomo, w. A. Navarra (vc) *(rec Feb. 7-9, 1964)* — Supraphon ("Collection" series) ▲ 11 0674-2 [ADD]
Bloch, E.:Schelomo, w. André Navarra (vc) — Supraphon ▲ SUP 111940 [AAD]
Borodin, A.:In the Steppes of Central Asia *(rec 1965)* — Supraphon Collection ▲ 11 0602-2 [ADD]
Borodin, A.:In the Steppes of Central Asia — Supraphon ("Czech Philharmonic" series) ▲ SUP 111938 [AAD]
Brahms, J.:Sym 1 — Supraphon ("Czech Philharmonic" series) ▲ SUP 111941 [AAD]
Brahms, J.:Tragic Ov — Supraphon ("Czech Philharmonic" series) ▲ SUP 111941 [AAD]
Britten, B.:The Young Person's Guide to the Orchestra, w. E. Shilling (nar) *(rec 1963)* — Supraphon ▲ 11 1945-2 [AAD]
Bruch, M.:Con 1 Vn, w. J. Suk (vn) — Supraphon Collection ▲ 11 0639-2 [ADD]
Dvořák, A.:Carnival *(rec 1966)* — Supraphon ▲ CD 111926 [AAD]
Dvořák, A.:Carnival — Supraphon Collection ▲ 11 0605-2 [ADD]
Dvořák, A.:Con Vn, w. J. Suk (vn) — Vivace 3-▲ E 325 [ADD/DDD]
Dvořák, A.:Con Vn, w. J. Suk (vn) — Supraphon Collection ▲ 11 0601-2 [ADD]
Dvořák, A.:Con Vn, w. Josef Suk (vn) *(rec live, July 30, 1963)* — Orfeo d'or ("Festspiel Dokumente" series) ▲ 395951
Dvořák, A.:Con Vn, w. Josef Suk (vn) — Supraphon ("Czech Philharmonic Series") ▲ SUP 111928 [ADD]
Dvořák, A.:Husitská *(rec 1966)* — Supraphon ▲ CD 111926 [AAD]
Dvořák, A.:Husitská — Supraphon Collection ▲ 11 0605-2 [ADD]
Dvořák, A.:In Nature's Realm — Supraphon Collection ▲ 11 0605-2 [ADD]
Dvořák, A.:In Nature's Realm — Supraphon ▲ SUP 111927 [AAD]
Dvořák, A.:My Home — Supraphon Collection ▲ 11 0605-2 [ADD]
Dvořák, A.:My Home *(rec 1966)* — Supraphon ▲ CD 111926 [AAD]
Dvořák, A.:Othello — Supraphon Collection ▲ 11 0605-2 [ADD]
Dvořák, A.:Othello — Supraphon ▲ SUP 111927 [AAD]
Dvořák, A.:Requiem Mass, w. Maria Stader (sop), Sieglinde Wagner (cta), Ernst Haefliger (ten), Kim Borg (b-bar), Czech Chorus — Deutsche Grammophon ("Double" series) 2-▲ 437377-2
Dvořák, A.:Romance Vn, w. Josef Suk (vn) — Supraphon ("Czech Philharmonic Series") ▲ SUP 111928 [ADD]
Dvořák, A.:Romance Vn, w. J. Suk (vn) — Vivace 3-▲ E 325 [ADD/DDD]
Dvořák, A.:Sym 6 *(rec 1966)* — Supraphon ▲ CD 111926 [AAD]
Dvořák, A.:Sym 8 *(rec Nov. 1960)* — Praga ▲ PR 254 006
Dvořák, A.:Sym 9, "From the New World" — Ermitage ▲ ERM 142 [ADD]
Dvořák, A.:Sym 9, "From the New World" — Supraphon ▲ SUP 111927 [AAD]

ORCH. & ENS.

Czech PO (cont.)
K. Ančerl (cnd) (cont.)
Dvořák, A.:Sym 9, "From the New World" *(rec live, July 30, 1963)* Orfeo d'or ("Festspiel Dokumente" series) ▲ 395951
Glinka, M.:Russlan & Ludmilla (ov) Supraphon ("Czech Philharmonic" series) ▲ SUP 111938 [AAD]
Hartmann, K.A.:Con funèbre, w. André Gertler (vn) Supraphon ▲ SUP 111955 [AAD]
Hindemith, P.:Con Vc, w. P. Tortelier (vc) Supraphon ▲ SUP 111955 [AAD]
Hindemith, P.:Con Vn, w. A. Gertler (vn) Supraphon ▲ SUP 111955 [AAD]
Janácek, L.:Sinfonietta Supraphon ("Czech Philharmonic" series) ▲ SUP 111929 [AAD]
Janácek, L.:Slavonic Mass, w. *(sloists unknown)*, Czech Phil Chorus Supraphon Collection ▲ 110609
Janácek, L.:Slavonic Mass, w. *(soloists unknown)*, Czech Phil Chorus [Cz] *(rec 1960–66)* Supraphon ▲ SUP 11 1930 [AAD]
Janácek, L.:Taras Bulba Supraphon Collection ▲ 110609
Janácek, L.:Taras Bulba Supraphon ("Czech Philharmonic" series) ▲ SUP 111929 [AAD]
Kabeláč, M.:Hamlet Improvisation *(rec 1966)* Praga ▲ PR 255000
Kabeláč, M.:Hamlet Improvisation *(rec 1961–66)* Supraphon ▲ SUP 11 1930 [AAD]
Kabeláč, M.:Mystery of Time *(rec 1961–66)* Supraphon ▲ SUP 11 1930 [AAD]
Kabeláč, M.:Passacaglia *(rec 1961–66)* Supraphon ▲ SUP 11 1930 [ADD]
Kabeláč, M.:Sym 5, w. L. Domanínská (sop) *(rec 1961)* Praga ▲ PR 255000
Kabeláč, M.:Sym 5, w. L. Domanínská (sop), Czech Phil Women's Chorus *(rec live)* Panton ▲ 81 1102
Lalo, E.:Sym espagnole, w. Ida Haendel (vn) Supraphon ("Czech Philharmonic" series) ▲ SUP 111936 [AAD]
Liszt, F.:Con 1 Pno, w. Sviatoslav Richter (pno) Multisonic ▲ 31 0335
Liszt, F.:Con 1 Pno, w. S. Richter (pno) *(rec ca. 1954)* Multisonic ("Prague Spring Collection" series) ▲ 31 0038–2 [ADD]
Liszt, F.:Les Préludes Supraphon ▲ 11 0572–2 [AAD]
Liszt, F.:Les Préludes Supraphon ("Czech Philharmonic" series) ▲ SUP 111938 [AAD]
Mahler, G.:Sym 1 Supraphon ("Czech Philharmonic Series") ▲ SUP 111953 [ADD]
Mahler, G.:Sym 9 Supraphon ("Czech Philharmonic Series") ▲ SUP 111954 [ADD]
Martinů, B.:Bouquet, w. Czech Phil Chorus, Kühn Children's Chorus *(rec 1955–56)* Supraphon ▲ SUP 11 1932 [AAD]
Martinů, B.:Bouquet, w. Libuše Domanínská (sop), Soňa Červená (alt), Lubomír Havlák (ten), Ladislav Mráz (bass), Czech Phil Chorus *(rec 1967)* Praga ("Karel Ancerl Edition" series) ▲ PR 254061
Martinů, B.:Con grosso *(rec live, ca. 1963/64)* Multisonic ("Prague Spring Collection" series) ▲ 31 0150–2
Martinů, B.:Con 3 Pno, w. Josef Paleníček (pno) Supraphon ("Czech Philharmonic" series) ▲ SUP 111929 [AAD]
Martinů, B.:Memorial to Lidice Supraphon ▲ SUP 0177 [AAD]
Martinů, B.:Sym 1 *(rec ca. 1963)* Multisonic ("Prague Spring Collection" series) 2–▲ 31 0023–2 [ADD]
Martinů, B.:Sym 3 *(rec ca. 1966)* Multisonic ("Prague Spring Collection" series) 2–▲ 31 0023–2 [ADD]
Martinů, B.:Sym 3 *(rec 1966)* Praga ("Karel Ancerl Edition" series) ▲ PR 254061
Martinů, B.:Sym 5 *(rec ca. 1962)* Multisonic ("Prague Spring Collection" series) 2–▲ 31 0023–2 [ADD]
Martinů, B.:Sym 6 *(rec 1955–56)* Supraphon ▲ SUP 11 1932 [ADD]
Mendelssohn, F.:Con in e Vn & Orch, Op. 64, w. J. Suk (vn) Supraphon Collection ▲ 11 0639–2 [ADD]
Mozart, W.A.:Con Bn, w. K. Bidlo (bn) *(rec 1952–1966)* Supraphon ▲ CD 111935 [AAD]
Mozart, W.A.:Con Hn, K.447, w. M. Štefek (hn) *(rec 1952–1966)* Supraphon ▲ CD 111935 [AAD]
Mozart, W.A.:Con 23 Pno, w. H. Czerny–Stefanska (pno) *(rec 1952–1966)* Supraphon ▲ CD 111935 [AAD]
Mozart, W.A.:Con 3 Vn, w. David Oistrakh (vn) Supraphon ("Czech Philharmonic" series) ▲ SUP 111936 [AAD]
Mozart, W.A.:Con 5 Vn, w. W. Schneiderhan (vn) *(rec live 1966)* Multisonic ("Prague Spring Collection" series) ▲ 31 0079–2 [ADD]
Mozart, W.A.:Zauberflöte (sels)—Ov. *(rec 1952–1966)* Supraphon ▲ CD 111935 [AAD]
Mussorgsky, M.:Night *(rec 1965–1968)* Supraphon ▲ CD 111943 [AAD]
Mussorgsky, M.:Pictures at an Exhibition Ermitage ▲ ERM 142 [ADD]
Mussorgsky, M.:Pictures at an Exhibition *(rec 1965–1968)* Supraphon ▲ CD 111943 [AAD]
Mussorgsky, M.:Pictures at an Exhibition *(rec 1968)* Supraphon Collection ▲ 11 0602–2 [ADD]
Prokofiev, S.:Con 1 Pno, w. I. Moravec (pno) Praga ▲ PR 254004
Prokofiev, S.:Peter & the Wolf, w. E. Shilling (nar) *(rec 1963)* Supraphon ▲ 11 1945–2 [AAD]
Prokofiev, S.:Scythian Suite Praga ▲ PR 254004
Prokofiev, S.:Sym 1 Praga ▲ PR 254004
Prokofiev, S.:Sym–Con Vc, w. Andre Navarra (vc) Supraphon ("Czech Philharmonic Series") ▲ SUP 111950 [ADD]
Prokofiev, S.:They Are 7, w. J. Kachel (ten), Czech Phil Chorus Praga ▲ PR 254004
Ravel, M.:Tzigane, w. Ida Haendel (vn) Supraphon ("Czech Philharmonic" series) ▲ SUP 111936 [AAD]
Respighi, O.:Adagio con variazioni Vc Orch, w. A. Navarra (vc) *(rec 1965)* Supraphon ("Great Artists" series) ▲ 11 1002–2 [AAD]
Respighi, O.:Adagio con variazioni Vc Orch, w. André Navarra (vc) Supraphon ▲ SUP 111940 [AAD]
Rimsky–Korsakov, N.:Capriccio espagnol *(rec 1964)* Supraphon Collection ▲ 11 0602–2 [ADD]
Rimsky–Korsakov, N.:Capriccio espagnol *(rec 1965–1968)* Supraphon ▲ CD 111943 [AAD]
Roussel, A.:Bacchus et Ariane (suite 2) *(rec live ca. 1963/64)* Multisonic ("Prague Spring Collection" series) ▲ 31 0150–2
Schumann, R.:Con Vc, w. André Navarra (vc) ASV ▲ SUP 111940 [AAD]
Schumann, R.:Con Vc, w. André Navarra (vc) Supraphon ▲ SUP 111940 [AAD]
Schumann, R.:Con Vc, w. A. Navarra (vc) *(rec 1964)* Supraphon ("Great Artists" series) ▲ 11 1002–2 [AAD]
Shostakovich, D.:Con 1 Vc, w. M. Sádlo (vc) *(rec June 6–8, 1968)* Supraphon ("Collection" series) ▲ 11 0676–2 [ADD]
Shostakovich, D.:Sym 1 *(rec 1961–64)* Supraphon ▲ SUP 11 1951 [AAD]
Shostakovich, D.:Sym 5 *(rec 1961–64)* Supraphon ▲ SUP 11 1951 [AAD]
Shostakovich, D.:Sym 5 *(rec live 1961)* Praga 2–▲ PR 254002.03
Shostakovich, D.:Sym 5, w. M. Sádlo (vc) *(rec Nov. 11–14, 1961)* Supraphon ("Collection" series) ▲ 11 0676–2 [ADD]
Shostakovich, D.:Sym 7 *(rec live 1967)* Praga 2–▲ PR 254002.03
Shostakovich, D.:Sym 7 *(rec 1957)* Supraphon ▲ 11 1952–2 (m) [AAD]
Shostakovich, D.:Sym 9 *(rec live 1966)* Praga 2–▲ PR 254002.03
Smetana, B.:The Bartered Bride (orch sels)—Ov. Ermitage ▲ ERM 142 [ADD]
Smetana, B.:The Bartered Bride (ov) *(rec live, July 30, 1963)* Orfeo d'or ("Festspiel Dokumente" series) ▲ 395951
Smetana, B.:Má Vlast Supraphon 2–▲ SUP 111492 [DDD]
Strauss, R.:Till Eulenspiegels lustige Streiche Supraphon ("Czech Philharmonic" series) ▲ SUP 111938 [AAD]
Strauss, R.:Till Eulenspiegels lustige Streiche Supraphon ▲ 11 0572–2 [AAD]
Stravinsky, I.:Pétrouchka [1947 version] *(rec 1962)* Supraphon ▲ 11 1945–2 [AAD]
Suk, J.:Fant Vn, w. J. Suk (vn) *(rec 1965)* Supraphon Collection ▲ 11 0601–2 [ADD]
Suk, J.:Fant Vn, w. Josef Suk (vn) Supraphon ("Czech Philharmonic Series") ▲ SUP 111928 [ADD]
Suk, J.:The Ripening *(rec live ca. 1963/64)* Multisonic (Prague Spring Collection) ▲ 31 0150–2
Suk, J.:The Ripening *(rec live)* Panton ▲ 81 1102–2
Tchaikovsky, P.:Con 1 Pno, w. S. Richter (pno) *(rec 1953)* Supraphon ("Great Artists" series) ▲ 11 0268–2 (m) [AAD]
Tchaikovsky, P.:Con 1 Pno, w. S. Richter (pno) *(rec 1954)* Music & Arts ▲ CD 776 [AAD]
Tchaikovsky, P.:Con 1 Pno, w. Sviatoslav Richter (pno) Supraphon 3–▲ SUP 0546 [AAD]
Tchaikovsky, P.:Con 1 Pno, w. D. Baloghova (pno) Supraphon ▲ SUP 111944 [AAD]
Tchaikovsky, P.:Ov 1812 *(rec 1965)* Supraphon Collection ▲ 11 0602–2 [ADD]
Tchaikovsky, P.:Ov 1812 Supraphon ("Czech Philharmonic" series) ▲ SUP 111938 [AAD]
Weber, C.M. von:Invitation to the Dance Orch Supraphon ▲ 11 0572–2 [AAD]

Czech PO (cont.)
K. Ančerl (cnd) (cont.)
Weber, C.M. von:Invitation to the Dance Orch Supraphon ("Czech Philharmonic" series) ▲ SUP 111938 [AAD]

N. Anosov (cnd)
Sibelius, J.:Con Vn, w. Julian Sikovetsky (vn), (original 1903/04 version) Supraphon ▲ SUP 3005

J. Barbirolli (cnd)
Franck, C.:Sym in d *(rec 1962)* Supraphon ("Collection" series) ▲ 11 0613–2 [ADD]

S. Baudo (cnd)
Debussy, C.:Pelléas et Mélisande (orch version) Supraphon ▲ 11 1269–2 [DDD]
Fauré, G.:Pelléas et Mélisande (suite) *(rec live, Dvořák Hall of the House of Artists, Prague 4/13–14/89)* Supraphon ▲ 11 0973–2 [DDD]
Honegger, A.:Jeanne d'Arc au bûcher, w. C. Château (sop), A.M. Rodde (sop), H. Brachet (mez), P. Proenza (ten), Z. Jankovsky (ten), F. Loup (bass), Czech Chorus *(rec 1974)* Supraphon 2–▲ 11 0557–2 [AAD]
Honegger, A.:Mouvement symphonique 3 Supraphon 2–▲ 11 1566–2 [DDD]
Honegger, A.:Mouvement symphonique 3 Supraphon 2–▲ 11 0132 [DDD]
Honegger, A.:Pacific 231 Supraphon 2–▲ 11 1566–2 [DDD]
Honegger, A.:Le Roi David, w. Christiane Eda–Pierre (sop), Martha Senn (mez), Tibere Raffalli (ten), D. Mesguich (nar), A. Gaillard (nar), Czech Chorus [F] Supraphon 2–▲ 11 0132 [DDD]
Honegger, A.:Sym 1 Supraphon 2–▲ 11 1566–2 [DDD]
Honegger, A.:Sym 2 Supraphon 2–▲ 11 1566–2 [DDD]
Honegger, A.:Sym 3 Supraphon ▲ SUP 0177 [AAD]
Honegger, A.:Sym 3 Supraphon 2–▲ 11 1566–2 [DDD]
Honegger, A.:Sym 4 Supraphon 2–▲ 11 1566–2 [DDD]
Honegger, A.:Sym 5 Supraphon 2–▲ 11 1566–2 [DDD]
Honegger, A.:La Tempête (prelude) Supraphon 2–▲ 11 0132 [DDD]
Honegger, A.:La Tempête (prelude) Supraphon 2–▲ 11 1566–2 [DDD]
Prokofiev, S.:Sym 5 *(rec Prague, 1976)* Praga ▲ PR 250 079
Ravel, M.:Alborada del gracioso Vivace 2–▲ G 212 [DDD/ADD]
Ravel, M.:Alborada del gracioso Sound ▲ CD 3441
Ravel, M.:Boléro Sound ▲ CD 3441
Ravel, M.:Boléro Vivace 2–▲ G 212 [DDD/ADD]
Ravel, M.:Daphnis et Chloé (suite 1) Vivace 2–▲ G 212 [DDD/ADD]
Ravel, M.:Daphnis et Chloé (suite 2), w. Czech Phil Chorus Sound ▲ CD 3441
Ravel, M.:La Valse Sound ▲ CD 3441
Ravel, M.:La Valse Vivace 2–▲ G 212 [DDD/ADD]
Schoenberg, A.:Pelleas und Melisande *(rec live, Dvořák Hall of the House of Artists, Prague, Apr. 13 & 14, 1989)* Supraphon ▲ 11 0973–2 [DDD]
Sibelius, J.:Pelléas et Mélisande Supraphon ▲ 11 1269–2 [DDD]

J. Belohlávek (cnd)
Bartók, B.:Con 3 Pno, w. Boris Krajny (pno) Panton ▲ PAN 811216
Bartók, B.:Divert Panton ▲ PAN 811214
Brahms, J.:Academic Festival Ov Supraphon ▲ SUP 111990
Brahms, J.:Con 1 Pno, w. Ivan Moravec (pno) Supraphon ▲ SUP 111993
Brahms, J.:Con 2 Pno, w. Ivan Moravec (pno) Supraphon ▲ SUP 111993
Brahms, J.:Serenade 1 Orch Supraphon ▲ SUP 111823 [AAD]
Brahms, J.:Serenade 2 Orch Supraphon ▲ SUP 111823 [AAD]
Brahms, J.:Sym 1 Supraphon ▲ SUP 111989
Brahms, J.:Sym 2 Supraphon ▲ 11 0967–2 [DDD]
Brahms, J.:Sym 2 Supraphon ▲ SUP 111990
Brahms, J.:Sym 3 Supraphon ▲ SUP 111991
Brahms, J.:Sym 4 Supraphon ▲ SUP 111991
Brahms, J.:Tragic Ov Supraphon ▲ SUP 111990
Brahms, J.:Vars on a Theme by Haydn Supraphon ▲ SUP 111989
Brahms, J.:Vars on a Theme by Haydn Supraphon ▲ 11 0967–2 [DDD]
Dvořák, A.:Biblical Songs, Op. 99, w. Dagmar Peckova (mez)—Nos. 1–5 *(rec House of Artists, Prague, Jan 4–7, 1996)* Canyon Classics 2–▲ 322
Dvořák, A.:Carnival Supraphon ▲ 11 0960–2 [DDD]
Dvořák, A.:Carnival Supraphon ("Czech Philharmonic" series) ▲ 11 1987 [DDD]
Dvořák, A.:Con Pno, w. I. Moravec (pno) *(rec June 26–29, 1982)* Supraphon ("Collection" series) ▲ 11 0675–2 [ADD]
Dvořák, A.:Con Vn, w. Václav Hudeček (vn) Supraphon ▲ SUP 3187
Dvořák, A.:Con Vn, w. Václav Hudecek (vn) Panton ▲ PAN 810855
Dvořák, A.:The Golden Spinning Wheel Chandos ▲ CHAN 9048 [DDD]
Dvořák, A.:Mazurek, w. Václav Hudeček (vn) Supraphon ▲ SUP 3187
Dvořák, A.:The Noon Witch Chandos ▲ CHAN 9475
Dvořák, A.:Notturno Chandos ▲ CHAN 9391 [DDD]
Dvořák, A.:Psalm 149, w. Prague Phil Chorus [Cz] Chandos 2–▲ CHAN 8985/86 [DDD]
Dvořák, A.:Romance Vn, w. Václav Hudeček (vn) Panton ▲ PAN 810855
Dvořák, A.:Romance Vn, w. Václav Hudeček (vn) Supraphon ▲ SUP 3187
Dvořák, A.:Scherzo Capriccioso Chandos ▲ CHAN 9475
Dvořák, A.:Slavonic Rhaps, Op. 45—No. 3 *(rec House of Artists, Prague, Jan 4–7, 1996)* Canyon Classics 2–▲ 322
Dvořák, A.:Stabat Mater, w. L. Aghová (sop), M. Schiml (sop), A. Baldin (ten), L. Vele (bass), Prague Phil Chorus [L] Chandos 2–▲ CHAN 8985/86 [DDD]
Dvořák, A.:Symphonic Vars Supraphon ("Czech Philharmonic" series) ▲ 11 1987 [DDD]
Dvořák, A.:Sym 5 Chandos ▲ CHAN 9475
Dvořák, A.:Sym 6 Chandos ▲ CHAN 9170 [DDD]
Dvořák, A.:Sym 7 Chandos ▲ CHAN 9391 [DDD]
Dvořák, A.:Sym 8 Chandos ▲ CHAN 9048 [DDD]
Dvořák, A.:Sym 9, "From the New World" Supraphon ▲ 11 0960–2 [DDD]
Dvořák, A.:Sym 9, "From the New World" Supraphon ("Czech Philharmonic" series) ▲ 11 1987 [DDD]
Dvořák, A.:The Water Goblin Chandos ▲ CHAN 9391 [DDD]
Dvořák, A.:The Wild Dove Chandos ▲ CHAN 9170 [DDD]
Hindemith, P.:Concert Music Brass & Strs Chandos ▲ CHAN 9457
Hindemith, P.:Con Fl, Ob, Cl, Bn, Hp Chandos ▲ CHAN 9457
Hindemith, P.:Mathis der Maler (sym) Chandos ▲ CHAN 9457
Janácek, L.:The Cunning Little Vixen (suite) [arr Václav Talich; rev Václav Smetáček] Chandos ▲ CHAN 9080 [DDD]
Janácek, L.:The Fiddler's Child Chandos ▲ CHAN 9080 [DDD]
Janácek, L.:Jealousy Chandos ▲ CHAN 9080 [DDD]
Janácek, L.:Sinfonietta Chandos ▲ CHAN 8897 [DDD]
Janácek, L.:Taras Bulba Chandos ▲ CHAN 9080 [DDD]
Korte, O.:Con grosso, w. Miroslav Kejmar (tpt), Zdenek Šedivý (tpt), Josef Hála (pno) *(rec House of Artists, Prague, Dec. 2–4, 1987)* Panton ▲ PAN 811257 [DDD]
Krček, J.:Sym 2, w. Radovan Lukavsky (nar), Pavel Kühn (cnd), Kühn Chorus Supraphon ▲ SUP CD 3195
Mahler, G.:Lieder eines fahrenden Gesellen, w. Ivan Kusnjer (bar) Supraphon ▲ SUP 3026
Marco, Tomas:Sym 5 Col Legno ▲ AU 31812
Martinů, B.:Concertino Vc, Ww, Pno & Perc, w. R. Wallfisch (vc) Chandos ▲ CHAN 9015 [DDD]
Martinů, B.:Con 1 Vc, w. R. Wallfisch (vc) [1955 version] Chandos ▲ CHAN 9015 [DDD]
Martinů, B.:Con 2 Vc, w. R. Wallfisch (vc) Chandos ▲ CHAN 9015 [DDD]
Martinů, B.:Con 2 Pno, w. Rudolf Firkusny (pno) Supraphon ▲ SUP 111988
Martinů, B.:Double Con Pno Timp Chandos ▲ CHAN 8950 [DDD]
Martinů, B.:Estampes Supraphon ▲ SUP 111988
Martinů, B.:Parables Supraphon ▲ SUP 111988
Martinů, B.:Ricercari Supraphon ▲ SUP 111988
Martinů, B.:Sym 1 Chandos ▲ CHAN 8950 [DDD]
Martinů, B.:Sym 6 Supraphon ▲ SUP 3026

142 ▲ = CD ♦ = Enhanced CD Δ = MD ■ = Cassette Tape □ = DCC

Czech PO (cont.)

J. Belohlávek (cnd) (cont.)
Martinů, B.:Sym 6 — Chandos ▲ CHAN 8897 [DDD]
Mozart, W.A.:Con 3 Vn, w. Cenek Pavlik (vn)—Adagio — Special Music Co. ("Classics of the Heart" series) ▲ SCD 5197
Mozart, W.A.:Con 3 Vn, w. Cenek Pavlík (vn) — Panton ▲ PAN 811207
Mozart, W.A.:Con 5 Vn, w. Cenek Pavlík (vn) — Panton ▲ PAN 811207
Prokofiev, S.:Con 3 Pno, w. Boris Krajny (pno) — Panton ▲ PAN 811216
Smetana, B.:Má Vlast *(rec live at the 1988 Prague Spring festival)* — Supraphon ▲ 11 0957–2 [DDD]
Smetana, B.:Má Vlast — Supraphon ▲ SUP 111986
Suk, J.:Asrael — Chandos ▲ CHAN 9042 [DDD]
Suk, J.:Fairy Tale — Chandos ▲ CHAN 9063 [DDD]
Suk, J.:Fantastické scherzo — Chandos ▲ CHAN 8897 [DDD]
Suk, J.:Serenade Strs — Chandos ▲ CHAN 9063 [DDD]
Tchaikovsky, P.:Con 1 Pno, w. I. Ardašev (pno) *(rec 3/89)* — Supraphon ▲ 110952–2 [DDD]
Zelenka, J.D.:Missa Gratias agimus tibi, w. J. Jonášová (sop), M. Mrázová (cta), V. Dolezal (ten), P. Mikuláš (bass), Czech Phil Chorus [L] — Supraphon ▲ 11 0816–2 [DDD]

Z. Chalabala (cnd)
Dvořák, A.:Symphonic Poems, Opp. 107–111 (comp) *(rec 1961)* — Supraphon ▲ SUP CD 3056
Dvořák, A.:The Water Goblin — Supraphonet ▲ 11 1106–2 [AAD]

A. Copland (cnd)
Bohemian Marches, Polkas & Waltzes, Vols. 1 & 2, w. Václav Neumann (cnd) — Orfeo 2–▲ C 107101, C 107201 [DDD]
Gala Concert From Prague — Orfeo ▲ CD 180891 [DDD] ■ MC 180891 (D)
Little Pearls of Czech Classics — Supraphon Collection ▲ SUP 110624 [ADD]
Tribute to Václav Neumann Collection

G. Delogu (cnd)
Mendelssohn, F.:Die Hebriden — Supraphon Collection ▲ 11 0623–2 [ADD]
Mendelssohn, F.:Sym 4 — Supraphon Collection ▲ 11 0623–2 [ADD]
Mendelssohn, F.:Sym 5 — Supraphon Collection ▲ 11 0623–2 [ADD]
Stravinsky, I.:Jeu de cartes *(rec Jan. 1, 1979)* — Praga ▲ PR 250054

C. von Dohnányi (cnd)
Stravinsky, I.:The Firebird *(rec May 18, 1983)* — Praga ▲ PR 250054

J. Ferencsik (cnd)
Bartók, B.:Con 1 Vn, w. J. Suk (vn) *(rec live, Prague, 2/23/79)* — Supraphon ▲ 11 0706–2 [ADD]
Beethoven, L. van:Die Weihe des Hauses (ov) *(rec 1961)* — Supraphonet ▲ 11 1120–2 [AAD]

D. Fischer-Dieskau (cnd)
Berlioz, H.:Harold in Italy, w. J. Suk (va) *(rec 1976)* — Supraphon ▲ 11 0708–2 [ADD]

J. Fournet (cnd)
Franck, C.:Le Chasseur maudit — Supraphon ("Collection" series) ▲ 11 0613–2 [ADD]
Franck, C.:Les Djinns, w. F. Maxián (pno) — Supraphon ("Collection" series) ▲ 11 0613–2 [ADD]

B. Gregor (cnd)
Dvořák, A.:Carnival — Supraphon 2–▲ 11 0526–2 [DDD]
Dvořák, A.:The Golden Spinning Wheel — Supraphon 2–▲ 11 0526–2 [DDD]
Dvořák, A.:In Nature's Realm — Supraphon 2–▲ 11 0526–2 [DDD]
Dvořák, A.:The Noon Witch — Supraphon 2–▲ 11 0526–2 [DDD]
Dvořák, A.:Othello — Supraphon 2–▲ 11 0526–2 [DDD]
Dvořák, A.:The Water Goblin — Supraphon 2–▲ 11 0526–2 [DDD]
Dvořák, A.:The Wild Dove — Supraphon 2–▲ 11 0526–2 [DDD]
Zemlinsky, A. von:Lyric Sym, w. K. Armstrong (sop), I. Kusnjer (bar) — Supraphon ▲ 11 0395–2 [DDD]

L. Izquierdo (cnd)
Sanabria, J.J.F.:Music of, w. Grand Canary PO—Atlantica; Elan; Sinf Urbana — Col Legno ▲ AU 31850

F. Jílek (cnd)
Berlioz, H.:Harold in Italy, w. Lubomír Malý (va) *(rec 1981)* — Supraphon ▲ SUP CD 3095
Janácek, L.:Amarus, w. Vera Soukupová (mez), Vilém Přibyl (ten), Josef Veselka (cnd), Prague Phil Chorus *(rec Czech Raio Broadcast, 1974)* — Praga ▲ PR 250100
Janácek, L.:The Cunning Little Vixen (suite) [arr František Jílek] *(rec Czech Raio Broadcast, 1988)* — Praga ▲ PR 250100

E. Kleiber (cnd)
Great Recordings, w. Berlin PO, Berlin State Opera Orch, Mediaeval Ensemble — Preiser ▲ PRE 90229 [AAD]

P. Kletzki (cnd)
Beethoven, L. van:Coriolan Ov — Vivace ▲ E 574 [ADD]
Beethoven, L. van:Egmont (ov) — Vivace ▲ E 574 [ADD]
Beethoven, L. van:Sym 1 *(rec 1968)* — Supraphon Collection ▲ 11 0619–2 [ADD]
Beethoven, L. van:Sym 3, "Eroica" *(rec Feb. 17–21, 1967)* — Supraphon ("Collection" series) ▲ 11 0678–2 [ADD]
Beethoven, L. van:Sym 5 *(rec 1967)* — Supraphon Collection ▲ 11 0619–2 [ADD]

K. Kobayashi (cnd)
Sibelius, J.:Finlandia *(rec House of Artists, Prague, Feb 22–25, 1995)* — Canyon Classics ▲ 277
Sibelius, J.:The Swan of Tuonela *(rec House of Artists, Praguo, Fob 22–25, 1995)* — Canyon Classics ▲ 277
Sibelius, J.:Sym 2 *(rec House of Artists, Prague, Feb 22–25, 1995)* — Canyon Classics ▲ 277

K. Kondrashin (cnd)
Brahms, J.:Con 2 Pno, w. S. Richter (pno) *(rec ca. 1950)* — Multisonic ("Prague Spring Collection" series) 2–▲ 31 0020–2 [ADD]
Brahms, J.:Con 2 Pno, w. Sviatoslav Richter (pno) — Multisonic ▲ 31 0335

B. Kotmel (cnd)
Martinů, B.:Field Mass, w. I. Kusnjer (bar), M. Kejmar (tpt), Czech Phil Chorus [Cz] — Chandos ▲ CHAN 9138 [DDD]
Martinů, B.:Memorial to Lidice — Chandos ▲ CHAN 9138 [DDD]
Martinů, B.:Sym 4 — Chandos ▲ CHAN 9138 [DDD]

Z. Košler (cnd)
Bartók, B.:Con 2 Vn, w. Shizuka Ishikawa (vn) *(rec live, Czech Radio broadcasts, 1980)* — Praga ▲ PR 250099
Berlioz, H.:Sym fantastique *(rec 1984)* — Supraphon ▲ SUP 3059
Bořkovec, P.:Sinfonietta 2 *(rec Dvořák Hall, House of Artists, Prague, Nov 1971)* — Panton ("Protokol XX" series) ▲ PAN 811366 [ADD]
Bořkovec, P.:Start *(rec Dvořák Hall, House of Artists, Prague, Feb, Mar & June 1973)* — Panton ("Protokol XX" series) ▲ PAN 811366 [ADD]
Bořkovec, P.:Sym 3 *(rec Dvořák Hall, House of Artists, Prague, Feb, Mar & June 1973)* — Panton ("Protokol XX" series) ▲ PAN 811366 [ADD]
Dvořák, A.:Arias & Scenes, w. Miroslav Kopp (ten), Czech Chorus—from The King of Charcoal Burner, The Stubborn L — Panton ▲ PAN 811189
Dvořák, A.:The Jacobin (sels), w. Eva Randová (mez)—Julia's lullaby [Act 3, Scene 5] *(rec Dvořák Hall of Rudolfinum Prague, Sept. 4–6, 1989)* — Panton ▲ PAN 811241 [DDD]
Dvořák, A.:Kate & the Devil (sels), w. Eva Randová (mez)—The Princess [Act 3, Scene 1] *(rec Dvořák Hall of Rudolfinum Prague, Sept. 4–6, 1989)* — Panton ▲ PAN 811241 [DDD]
Dvořák, A.:Rusalka (sels), w. Eva Randová (mez)—The Witch [Act 3]; Finale; The Strange Princess; The Prince & the Water Sprite [Act 2] *(rec Dvořák Hall of Rudolfinum Prague, Sept. 4–6, 1989)* — Panton ▲ PAN 811241 [DDD]
Dvořák, A.:St Ludmilla, w. Eva Randová (mez)—Entrance, Svatava's recitative & aria *(rec Dvořák Hall of Rudolfinum Prague, Sept. 4–6, 1989)* — Panton ▲ PAN 811241 [DDD]
Dvořák, A.:Stabat Mater, w. Eva Randová (mez) *(rec Dvořák Hall of Rudolfinum Prague, Sept. 4–6, 1989)* — Panton ▲ PAN 811241 [DDD]
Dvořák, A.:Sym 7 — Supraphonet ▲ 11 1106–2 [AAD]
Dvořák, A.:Sym 9, "From the New World" — Panton ▲ PAN 811001
Dvořák, A.:Vanda (sels), w. Eva Randová (mez), Kühn Chorus—Homena, priests & priestesses of the God of Darkness [Act 3, Scene 3]; Bozena, pagan Grand Priest & the people [Act 4, Scene 1] *(rec Dvořák Hall of Rudolfinum Prague, Sept. 4–6, 1989)* — Panton ▲ PAN 811241 [DDD]

Czech PO (cont.)

Z. Košler (cnd) (cont.)
Martinů, B.:Con 1 Vc, w. Josef Chuchro (vc) — Supraphon ▲ SUP CD 3093
Novák, V.:Storm, w. Jarmila Zilková (sop), Jarmila Smycková (sop), Frantisek Livora (ten), Czech Phil Chorus — Supraphon ▲ SUP CD 3088
Prokofiev, S.:Syms (comp) — Supraphon 4–▲ SUP 0091
Roussel, A.:Evocations, w. Marie Mrázová (cta), Zdenek Svehla (ten), Jindřich Jindrák (bar), Czech Phil Chorus — Supraphon ▲ SUP 111823 [AAD]
Schoenberg, A.:Die glückliche Hand, w. Antonin Švorc (bar) *(rec 1981)* — Praga ▲ PR 250082
Schulhoff, E.:Con Str Qt, w. Talich String Quartet — Panton ▲ PAN 811225
Schulhoff, E.:Double Con Fl, w. *(soloists unknown)* — Panton ▲ PAN 811308
Schulhoff, E.:Ogelala — Panton ▲ PAN 811308
Shostakovich, D.:Sym 9 — Praga ▲ PR 250085
Smetana, B.:The Bartered Bride, w. G. Benačková (sop), P. Dvorsky (ten), R. Novak (bass), Czech Phil Chorus [Cz] — Supraphon 3–▲ 10 3511–2 [DDD]
Smetana, B.:The Bartered Bride (orch sels), w. Gabriela Benačková (sop), Peter Dvorsky (ten), Miroslav Kopp (ten), Czech Phil Chorus — Supraphon ▲ SUP 112251 [DDD]
Smetana, B.:Má Vlast *(rec May 12, 1992)* — Emergo ▲ EC 3988
Strauss, R.:Eine Alpensinfonie — Supraphon ▲ SUP 0005 [DDD]

J. Krombholc (cnd)
Dvořák, A.:The Spectre's Bride, Op. 110, w. Czech Phil Chorus *(rec 1961)* — Supraphon 2–▲ SUP 111982 [DDD]
Novák, V.:Storm, w. Maria Tauberová (sop), Drahomíra Tikalová (sop), Beno Blachut (ten), Ladislav Mráz (bar), Czech Phil Chorus *(rec 1956)* — Supraphon 2–▲ SUP 111982 (m) [DDD]

R. Kubelík (cnd)
Dvořák, A.:Con Pno, w. R. Firkusny (pno) *(rec ca. 1944)* — Multisonic (Prague Spring Collection) ▲ 31 0019–2 [ADD]
Dvořák, A.:Sym 8 *(rec ca. 1946)* — Multisonic (Prague Spring Collection) ▲ 31 0019–2 [ADD]
Dvořák, A.:Sym 9, "From the New World" *(rec Oct. 11, 1991)* — Denon ▲ CO 79728 [DDD]
Foerster, J.B.:Sym 4 — Supraphon ▲ SUP 111912
Mozart, W.A.:Sym 38 *(rec Oct. 11, 1991)* — Denon ▲ CO 79728 [DDD]
Smetana, B.:Hakon Jarl — Supraphon ▲ SUP 111911
Smetana, B.:Má Vlast *(rec 1990)* — Supraphon ▲ SUP 111208 [DDD]
Smetana, B.:Má Vlast — Supraphon 3–▲ SUP 0546 [AAD]
Smetana, B.:Má Vlast *(rec live, Prague, May 12, 1990)* — Supraphon ▲ SUP 111910
Smetana, B.:Richard III — Supraphon ▲ SUP 111911
Smetana, B.:Wallenstein's Camp — Supraphon ▲ SUP 111911
Suk, J.:Legend of the Dead Victors — Supraphon ▲ SUP 111911
Suk, J.:Meditation on the Old Czech Hymn "St. Wenceslas" — Supraphon ▲ SUP 111911
Suk, J.:Toward a New Life — Supraphon ▲ SUP 111911

G. Lehel (cnd)
Bartók, B.:Con Orch — Praga ▲ PR 254047

E. Leinsdorf (cnd)
Brahms, J.:Sym 4 *(rec ca. 1966)* — Multisonic ("Prague Spring Collection" series) 2–▲ 31 0020–2 [ADD]

C. Mackerras (cnd)
Janácek, L.:Amarus, w. Kvetoslava Nemeckova (sop), Leo Marian Vodicka (ten), Vaclav Zitek (bar), Jan Hora (org), Lubomír Mátl (cnd), Czech Phil Chorus *(rec 1984)* — Supraphon ▲ SUP CD 3045
Janácek, L.:Slavonic Mass, w. Elisabeth Söderström (sop), Drahomira Drobkova (cta), František Livora (ten), Richard Novák (bass), Czech Phil Chorus — Supraphon ▲ SUP 103575 [DDD]

S. Macura (cnd)
Martinů, B.:Double Con Pno Timp — Panton ▲ PAN 811204

K. Masur (cnd)
Beethoven, L. van:Con Vn, Vc & Pno, "Triple Con", w. Suk Trio *(rec 1973)* — Supraphon ▲ 11 0707–2 [ADD]

L. von Matačič (cnd)
Beethoven, L. van:Sym 9, "Choral Sym", w. Gabriela Benackova-Cápova (sop), Vera Soukupova (alt), Vilem Pribyl (ten), Karel Prusa (bass) — Praga ▲ PR 250076

J. Meylan (cnd)
Beethoven, L. van:Sym 1 *(rec 1963)* — Supraphonet ▲ 11 1120–2 [AAD]
Beethoven, L. van:Sym 8 *(rec 1963)* — Supraphonet ▲ 11 1120–2 [AAD]

D. Milhaud (cnd)
Milhaud, D.:Music for Prague *(rec live 1966)* — Multisonic ("Prague Spring Collection" series) ▲ 31 0022–2 [ADD]
Milhaud, D.:Sym 10 *(rec 1966)* — Multisonic ("Prague Spring Collection" series) ▲ 31 0022–2 [ADD]

E. Mravinsky (cnd)
Khachaturian, A.:Con Pno, w. L. Oborin (pno) — Praga ▲ 250017
Shostakovich, D.:Con 1 Vn, w. D. Oistrakh (vn) — Praga ▲ PR 250052

C. Munch (cnd)
Honegger, A.:Sym 2 *(rec ca. 1957)* — Multisonic ("Prague Spring Collection" series) ▲ 31 0022–2 [ADD]

J. Nelson (cnd)
Górecki, H.-M.:Beatus Vir, w. N. Storjev (bass), Prague Phil Chorus — Argo ▲ 436835–2 [DDD]
Górecki, H.-M.:Old Polish Music — Argo ▲ 436835–2 [DDD]

V. Neumann (cnd)
Beethoven, L. van:Con 1 Pno, w. R. Sherman (pno) — Pro Arte ▲ CDD 259 [DDD]
Beethoven, L. van:Con 2 Pno, w. R. Sherman (pno) — Pro Arte ▲ CDD 260 [DDD]
Beethoven, L. van:Con 3 Pno, w. R. Sherman (pno) — Pro Arte ▲ CDD 260 [DDD]
Beethoven, L. van:Con 3 Pno, w. I. Moravec (pno) — Supraphon ("Tribute to Václav Neumann" Collection) ▲ 11 0719–2 [ADD/DDD]
Beethoven, L. van:Con 4 Pno, w. R. Sherman (pno) — Pro Arte ▲ CDD 259 [DDD]
Beethoven, L. van:Con 5 Pno, "Emperor", w. R. Sherman (pno) — Pro Arte ▲ CDD 261 [DDD]
Beethoven, L. van:Fidelio (ov) — Panton ▲ PAN 811213
Beethoven, L. van:Ovs—Egmont; Ruins of Athens; King Stephen; Consecration of the House; Coriolan; Creatures of Prometheus; Fidelio; Leonore Nos. 1–3; Name-Day *(rec House of Artists, Prague, Feb–Apr 1994)* — Canyon Classics 2–▲ CD 249
Beethoven, L. van:Sym 5 — Supraphon ("Tribute to Václav Neumann" Collection) ▲ 11 0719–2 [ADD/DDD]
Beethoven, L. van:Sym 9, "Choral Sym", w. Czech Phil Chorus — Supraphon 3–▲ SUP 0546 [AAD]
Berg, A.:Con Vn, w. J. Suk (vn) *(rec 1980)* — Supraphon ▲ 11 0706–2 [ADD]
Bizet, G.:Carmen (sels)—Ovs to Acts 1, 2 & 3 — Panton ▲ PAN 811213
Dvořák, A.:Con Vc, w. A. May (vc) — Supraphon ▲ SUP 11 1544 [DDD]
Dvořák, A.:Con Vc, w. M. Sádlo (vc) — Supraphon Collection ▲ 11 0631–2 [ADD]
Dvořák, A.:Con Vc, w. Josef Chuchro (vc) — Supraphon ▲ SUP CD 3093
Dvořák, A.:Con Vc & Pno, w. M. Sádlo (vc) — Supraphon Collection ▲ 11 0631–2 [ADD]
Dvořák, A.:Con Pno, w. R. Firkusny (pno) — RCA Red Seal ▲ 09026-60781–2
Dvořák, A.:Kate & the Devil (ov) — Panton ▲ PAN 811213
Dvořák, A.:Rondo, w. Michal Kanka (vc) *(rec Ostrava, 1992)* — Praga ▲ CMX 350101
Dvořák, A.:Rondo, w. A. May (vc) — Supraphon ▲ SUP 11 1544 [DDD]
Dvořák, A.:Rusalka, w. G. Benáčkova (sop), V. Soukupová (mez), W. Ochman (ten), R. Novák (bass), Prague Phil Chorus [Cz] — Supraphon 3–▲ 10 3641 [DDD]
Dvořák, A.:Rusalka, w. G. Benáčkova (sop), V. Soukupová (mez), W. Ochman (ten), R. Novák (bass), Prague Phil Chorus [Cz] — Supraphon Collection ▲ 11 0617–2 [DDD]
Dvořák, A.:Rusalka (sels), w. Gabriela Benačková (sop), Vera Soukupová (mez), Richard Novák (bass), Czech Chorus — Supraphon ▲ SUP 112252 [DDD]
Dvořák, A.:Scherzo Capriccioso — Supraphon Collection ▲ 11 0629–2 [ADD]
Dvořák, A.:Silent Woods, w. Michal Kanka (vc) *(rec Ostrava, 1992)* — Praga ▲ CMX 350101
Dvořák, A.:Silent Woods, w. A. May (vc) — Supraphon ▲ SUP 11 1544 [DDD]
Dvořák, A.:Slavonic Dances (comp) *(rec Prague, Oct. 23–29, 1993)* — Canyon Classics ▲ 3615 [DDD]
Dvořák, A.:Slavonic Dances (comp) *(rec 1985)* — Supraphon ▲ SUP 111959 [DDD]

ORCH. & ENS.

Czech PO (cont.)

V. Neumann (cnd) (cont.)

Dvořák, A.:Symphonic Poems, Opp. 107-111 (comp) Supraphon ▲ SUP 0199
Dvořák, A.:Symphonic Vars *(rec House of Artists, Prague, Jan 4-7, 1995)* Canyon Classics ▲ CD 273
Dvořák, A.:Sym 1, "The Bells of Zlonice" *(rec 1987)* Supraphon 2-▲ 111003-2 [DDD]
Dvořák, A.:Sym 2 *(rec 10/87)* Supraphon 2-▲ 111003-2 [DDD]
Dvořák, A.:Sym 3 *(rec 3/85)* Supraphon 2-▲ 111003-2 [DDD]
Dvořák, A.:Sym 4 *(rec 1984)* Supraphon 2-▲ 11 1005-2 [DDD]
Dvořák, A.:Sym 5 *(rec 1982)* Supraphon 2-▲ 11 1005-2 [DDD]
Dvořák, A.:Sym 6 *(rec 1982)* Supraphon 2-▲ 11 1005-2 [DDD]
Dvořák, A.:Sym 7 Supraphon 2-▲ 11 0559-2 [DDD]
Dvořák, A.:Sym 7 *(rec early 1980's)* Supraphon ▲ SUP 111960 [DDD]
Dvořák, A.:Sym 7 *(rec Nov. 12-13, 1991)* Canyon Classics ▲ 3681 [DDD]
Dvořák, A.:Sym 8 Supraphon 2-▲ 11 0559-2 [DDD]
Dvořák, A.:Sym 8 Supraphon ("Collection" series) ▲ 11 0675-2 [ADD]
Dvořák, A.:Sym 8 *(rec early 1980's)* Supraphon ▲ SUP 111960 [DDD]
Dvořák, A.:Sym 9, "From the New World" *(rec House of Artists, Prague, Jan 4-7, 1995)* Canyon Classics ▲ CD 273
Dvořák, A.:Sym 9, "From the New World" *(rec live, Czech Radio broadcasts, Prague, 1971)* Praga ▲ CMX 350101
Dvořák, A.:Sym 9, "From the New World" Supraphon 2-▲ 11 0559-2 [DDD]
Dvořák, A.:Sym 9, "From the New World" *(rec 1972)* Supraphon ▲ SUP 112249 [AAD]
Dvořák, A.:Sym 9, "From the New World" Supraphon Collection ▲ 11 0629-2 [ADD]
Eben, Petr:Vox clamantis, w. R. Lukavsky (tpt) Panton ▲ 81 1141-2911
Feld, J.:Frescoes (3) *(rec 1964)* Praga ▲ PR 255001
Feld, J.:Sym 1 *(rec 1964)* Praga ▲ PR 255001
Fučík, J.:Marches & Waltzes—Entrance of the gladiators; Mississippi River; Attila; Triglav *(marches)*; Winterstürme; Donausagen; Traumideale *(waltzes)* Orfeo ▲ 147861 [DDD]
Fučík, J.:Marinarella Orfeo ▲ 147861 [DDD]
Glinka, M.:Russian & Ludmilla (ov) Panton ▲ PAN 811213
Havelka, S.:Music of, w. Brigita Sulcova (sop), Anna Barova (cta), Vladimir Dolezal (ten), Richard Novak (bass), Prague Phil Chorus—Epistola de M. Hieronymi De Praga Supplicio Panton ▲ PAN 810966
Janácek, L.:Capriccio, w. R. Firkusny (pno) RCA Red Seal ▲ 09026-60781-2
Janácek, L.:Concertino Pno, w. R. Firkusny (pno) RCA Red Seal ▲ 09026-60781-2
Janácek, L.:Con Vn, w. Josef Suk (vn) Supraphon ▲ SUP 111965 [DDD]
Janácek, L.:The Cunning Little Vixen, w. G. Benačková (sop—Goldskin), M. Hajóssyová (sop—Cunning Little Vixen), R. Novák (bass—Forester), Czech Phil Chorus, Kühn Children's Chorus [Cz] *(rec 1979-80)* Supraphon 2-▲ 10 3471-2 [AAD]
Janácek, L.:From the House of the Dead, w. M. Jirglova (sop), V. Pribyl (ten), J. Horacek (bass), R. Novák (bass), Czech Phil Chorus [Cz] Supraphon 2-▲ SUP 10 2941 [AAD]
Janácek, L.:From the House of the Dead (suite) [arr Václav Neumann] *(rec Czech Raio Broadcast, 1979)* Praga ▲ PR 250100
Janácek, L.:Schluck und Jau Supraphon ▲ SUP 111965 [DDD]
Janácek, L.:Sinfonietta Supraphon ▲ SUP 111965 [DDD]
Janácek, L.:Slavonic Mass, w. Gabriela Benacková (sop), Vera Soukupová (cta), Frantisek Livora (ten), Karel Pruss (bass), Czech Phil Chorus Panton ▲ PAN 811217
Janácek, L.:Taras Bulba Supraphon ▲ SUP 111965 [DDD]
Kabeláč, M.:Metamorphoses II of the Chorale, w. *(pianist unknown)* Panton ▲ 30CM 347
Mahler, G.:Das Lied von der Erde, w. C. Ludwig (mez), T. Moser (ten) *(rec 1983)* Praga ▲ PR 254052
Mahler, G.:Songs from Rückert, w. K. Berman (bass)—3 songs [G] *(rec Oct. 10-12, 1977)* Supraphon 2-▲ 11 1978-2
Mahler, G.:Sym 1 *(rec Oct. 3-8, 1979)* Supraphon ▲ 11 1970-2 [AAD]
Mahler, G.:Sym 1 Canyon Classics ▲ 3679
Mahler, G.:Sym 2, w. G. Benačková (sop), E. Randova (mez), Czech Phil Chorus *(rec June 11-16, 1980)* Supraphon ▲ 11 1971-2 [AAD]
Mahler, G.:Sym 3, w. C. Ludwig (mez), Czech Phil Chorus *(rec Dec. 16-19, 1981)* Supraphon 3-▲ 11 1972-2 [DDD]
Mahler, G.:Sym 3, w. Marta Benačková (alt), Czech Phil Children's Choir, Prague Chamber Choir *(rec House of Artists, Prague, Aug-Sept 1994)* Canyon Classics 2-▲ CD 256
Mahler, G.:Sym 4, w. M. Hajóssyová (sop) [G] *(rec 1980)* Supraphon ▲ 11 1975-2 [AAD]
Mahler, G.:Sym 4, w. Pamela Coburn (sop) *(rec House of Artists, Prague, Nov 22-27, 1993)* Canyon Classics ▲ CD 240
Mahler, G.:Sym 5 Supraphon ▲ SUP 11 1976 [AAD]
Mahler, G.:Sym 5 *(rec 1993)* Emergo ("Corneille" series) ▲ EC 3972
Mahler, G.:Sym 5, w. Zdenek Tylsar (hn), Miroslav Kejmar (tpt) *(rec House of Artists, Prague, Mar 1993)* Canyon Classics ▲ 3616
Mahler, G.:Sym 6 *(rec 1979)* Supraphon ▲ SUP 111977 [AAD]
Mahler, G.:Sym 6 *(rec House of Artists, Prague, Jan 23-26, 1995)* Canyon Classics 2-▲ CD 304
Mahler, G.:Sym 8, w. Czech Phil Chorus *(rec Feb. 10-14, 1982)* Supraphon 3-▲ 11 1972-2 [DDD]
Mahler, G.:Sym 9 *(rec House of Artists, Prague, Aug 21-28, 1995)* Canyon Classics ▲ CD 305
Mahler, G.:Sym 9 Supraphon ▲ SUP 111980 [DDD]
Mahler, G.:Sym 10 *(rec Feb. 27, 1976)* Supraphon ▲ 11 1970-2 [AAD]
Martinů, B.:Ariadne, w. C. Lindsley (sop), V. Dolezal (ten), R. Novák (ten), N. Phillips (bar), Czech Phil Chorus [Cz] Supraphon ▲ 10 4395-2 [DDD]
Martinů, B.:Con 1 Vn, w. Josef Suk (vn) Supraphon ▲ SUP 111969 [AAD]
Martinů, B.:Con 1 Vn, w. J. Suk (vn) Supraphon ▲ 11 0702-2 [ADD]
Martinů, B.:Con 2 Vn, w. Josef Suk (vn) Supraphon ▲ SUP 111969 [AAD]
Martinů, B.:Con 2 Vn, w. J. Suk (vn) Supraphon ▲ 11 0702-2 [ADD]
Martinů, B.:Field Mass, w. Václav Zítek (bar), Czech Phil Chorus Panton ▲ PAN 811217
Martinů, B.:Rhap-Con Va, w. Josef Suk (va) Supraphon ▲ SUP 111969 [AAD]
Martinů, B.:Syms (6) *(rec 1976-77)* Supraphon 3-▲ 11 0382-2 [ADD]
Martinů, B.:Syms (6) Supraphon ▲ SUP 111966 [AAD]
Mozart, W.A.:Con Bn, w. F. Herman (bn) Supraphon Collection ▲ 11 0636-2 [ADD]
Mozart, W.A.:Con Fl, K.313, w. J. Válek (fl) Supraphon Collection ▲ 11 0636-2 [ADD]
Mozart, W.A.:Con Ob, K.314, w. J. Mihule (ob) Supraphon Collection ▲ 11 0636-2 [ADD]
Mozart, W.A.:Don Giovanni (ov) Panton ▲ PAN 811213
Mozart, W.A.:Sinf concertante Vn, K.364, w. Josef Suk (vn/va) Panton ▲ PAN 811206
Ostrčil, O.:Way of the Cross Supraphon ▲ SUP 111964 [DDD]
Rossini, G.:Il barbiere di Siviglia (ov) Panton ▲ PAN 811213
Schoenberg, A.:Erwartung, w. Olga Pilarczyk (sop) *(rec 1964)* Praga ▲ PR 250082
Schoenberg, A.:Pieces Orch, Op. 16 *(rec 1964)* Praga ▲ PR 250082
Schoenberg, A.:A Survivor from Warsaw, w. Czech Phil Chorus Supraphon ▲ SUP 0177 [AAD]
Smetana, B.:Hakon Jarl Supraphon ▲ SUP 0198
Smetana, B.:The Kiss (ov) Panton ▲ PAN 811213
Smetana, B.:Libuše (ov) Panton ▲ PAN 811213
Smetana, B.:Má Vlast Supraphon ▲ SUP 111958 [AAD]
Smetana, B.:Má Vlast Denon/PCM Digital ▲ DEN 8095 [DDD]
Smetana, B.:Má Vlast Panton ▲ PAN 811050
Smetana, B.:The Moldau *(rec 1975)* Supraphon ▲ SUP 112249 [AAD]
Smetana, B.:Richard III Supraphon ▲ SUP 0198
Smetana, B.:Wallenstein's Camp Supraphon ▲ SUP 0198
Stravinsky, I.:Sym in C, USSR Radio-TV SO *(rec Prague, 1970)* Praga ▲ PR 250 063
Suk, J.:Asrael Supraphon ▲ 11 0278 [DDD]
Suk, J.:Asrael Supraphon 2-▲ SUP 111962 [DDD]
Suk, J.:Epilogue, w. Zora Jehličková (sop), Iván Kusnjer (bar), Ján Galla (bass) Supraphon 2-▲ SUP 111962 [DDD]
Suk, J.:Epilogue, w. Z. Jehličková (sop), I. Kusnjer (bar), J. Galla (bass), Czech Phil Chorus [Cz] Supraphon ▲ 11 0116-2 [DDD]
Suk, J.:The Ripening Supraphon 2-▲ SUP 111962 [DDD]
Suk, J.:The Ripening Supraphon ▲ 103640-2 [DDD]

Czech PO (cont.)

V. Neumann (cnd) (cont.)

Suk, J.:Sym in E Supraphon ▲ SUP 111964 [DDD]
Zemlinsky, A. von:Songs (misc), w. H. Fassbender (mez)—6 Gesänge, Op. 13 [G] Supraphon ▲ SUP 11 1811 [DDD]
Zemlinsky, A. von:Vars & Fugue on a Theme by Johann Adam Hiller Supraphon ▲ SUP 11 1811 [DDD]

D. Oistrakh (cnd)

Prokofiev, S.:Romeo & Juliet (sels), w. Václav Hudeček (vn) *(rec live, Prague Spring Festival, May 20, 1972)* Supraphon ▲ SUP 0216
Tchaikovsky, P.:Con Vn, w. Václav Hudeček (vn) *(rec live, Prague Spring Festival, May 20, 1972)* Supraphon ▲ SUP 0216

A. Pedrotti (cnd)

Brahms, J.:Con Vn, w. D. Oistrakh (vn) *(rec ca. 1961)* Multisonic ("Prague Spring Collection" series) 2-▲ 31 0020-2 [ADD]
Respighi, O.:La Boutique fantastique *(rec Sept. 20-24, 1971)* Supraphon ("Collection" series) ▲ 11 0683-2 [ADD]
Schumann, R.:Sym 3 *(rec Dvořák Hall, Jan 14, 1971)* Praga ▲ PR 250096

L. Pešek (cnd)

Bartók, B.:Con 1 Vn, w. Josef Suk (vn) *(rec live, Czech Radio broadcasts, 1985)* Praga ▲ PR 250099
Debussy, C.:Images Orch Supraphon ▲ 11 0396-2 [DDD]
Debussy, C.:La Mer Supraphon ▲ 11 0396-2 [DDD]
Dvořák, A.:Con Vn, w. C. Tetzlaff (vn) Virgin Classics ▲ CDC 45022
Dvořák, A.:Czech Suite Virgin Classics ▲ 59522 [DDD]
Dvořák, A.:In Nature's Realm Virgin Classics ▲ 59536 [DDD]
Dvořák, A.:Othello Virgin Classics ▲ 59016 [DDD]
Dvořák, A.:Sym 4 Virgin Classics ▲ 59016 [DDD]
Dvořák, A.:Sym 5 Virgin Classics ▲ 59522 [DDD]
Dvořák, A.:Sym 6 Virgin Classics ▲ 59536 [DDD]
Eben, Petr:Con 2 Org, "Symphonia gregoriana", w. K. Klugarova (org), Czech Phil Chorus [Cz] Panton ▲ 81 1141-2911
Fišer, L.:Con for 2 Pnos, w. Frantisek Maxian (pno), Garrick Ohlsson (pno) Supraphon ▲ SUP 0035 [DDD]
Kabeláč, M.:Sym in F Supraphon ▲ SUP 0035 [DDD]
Kopelent, M.:Il Canto degli Augei, w. *(sop unknown)* Supraphon ▲ SUP 0035 [DDD]
Lalo, E.:Sym espagnole, w. C. Tetzlaff (vn) Virgin Classics ▲ CDC 45022
Mahler, G.:Sym 9 Virgin Classics ▲ CDC 59635
Mahler, G.:Sym 10 Virgin Classics ▲ CDC 59635
Martinů, B.:Con Ob *(rec live, 1992-94)* Supraphon ▲ SUP 0180 [DDD]
Martinů, B.:Con 2 Pno, w. Rudolf Firkušný (pno) RCA Red Seal ▲ 09026-61934-2
Martinů, B.:Con 3 Pno, w. Rudolf Firkušny (pno) RCA Red Seal ▲ 09026-61934-2
Martinů, B.:Con 4 Pno, w. Rudolf Firkušny (pno) RCA Red Seal ▲ 09026-61934-2
Mozart, W.A.:Sinf concertante Ob, K.Anh.9 *(rec live, 1992-94)* Supraphon ▲ SUP 0180 [DDD]
Ravel, M.:Boléro Supraphon ▲ 10 3633-2 [DDD]
Ravel, M.:Daphnis et Chloé (suite 1) Supraphon ▲ 10 3633-2 [DDD]
Ravel, M.:Daphnis et Chloé (suite 2), w. Kühn Chorus Supraphon ▲ 10 3633-2 [DDD]
Scriabin, A.:Con Pno, w. Garrick Ohlsson (pno) *(rec Dvořák Hall, 1986)* Supraphon ▲ SUP 104149
Scriabin, A.:Rêverie *(rec Dvořák Hall, 1986)* Supraphon ▲ SUP 104149
Scriabin, A.:Sym 4 *(rec Dvořák Hall, 1986)* Supraphon ▲ SUP 104149
Smetana, B.:Festive Sym *(rec live, 1992-94)* Supraphon ▲ SUP 0180 [DDD]
Smetana, B.:The Moldau Interchord ▲ INT 892.934 [AAD]
Suk, J.:Fairy Tale Supraphon ▲ 10 3389 [DDD]
Suk, J.:Praga Supraphon ▲ SUP 111823 [AAD]
Suk, J.:Praga Supraphon ▲ 10 3389 [DDD]
Suk, J.:A Summer Tale Supraphon ▲ SUP 111823 [AAD]

G. Rozhdestvensky (cnd)

Martinů, B.:Partita (Suite 1) *(rec Dvořák Hall of Prague's House of Artists, Nov. 25, 1971)* Panton ▲ 81 1122-2
Shostakovich, D.:Ballet Suite 5 *(rec Jan. 1983)* Praga ▲ PR 250053
Stravinsky, I.:Sym in 3 Movts, USSR Radio-TV SO *(rec Prague, 1983)* Praga ▲ PR 250 063
Stravinsky, I.:Sym of Psalms, USSR Radio-TV SO *(rec Prague, 1977)* Praga ▲ PR 250 063

K. Sanderling (cnd)

Beethoven, L. van:Cons Pno (comp), w. E. Gilels (pno) *(rec Nov. 19, 1958)* Multisonic ("Prague Spring Collection" series) 3-▲ 31 0106-2 [ADD]

W. Sawallisch (cnd)

Dvořák, A.:In Nature's Realm *(rec live, Czech Radio broadcasts, Prague, 1971)* Praga ▲ CMX 350101
Dvořák, A.:Requiem Mass, w. G. Benačková (sop), B. Fassbaender (mez), T. Moser (ten), J.-H. Rootering (bass), Czech Chorus [L] Supraphon 2-▲ 10 4241 [DDD]
Dvořák, A.:Stabat Mater, w. G. Benačková (sop), O. Wenkel (cta), P. Dvorsky (ten), J.-H. Rootering (bass), Czech Phil Chorus [L] Supraphon 2-▲ 10 3561-2 [DDD]
Mozart, W.A.:Sym 38 Eurodisc 2-▲ 69253-2 [ADD]
Mozart, W.A.:Sym 39 Eurodisc 2-▲ 69253-2 [ADD]
Mozart, W.A.:Sym 40 Eurodisc 2-▲ 69253-2 [ADD]
Mozart, W.A.:Sym 41 Eurodisc 2-▲ 69253-2 [ADD]

H. Scherchen (cnd)

Mozart, W.A.:Serenade Ww, K.361—movts. 5 & 6 *(rec live 1951)* Multisonic ("Prague Spring Collection" series) ▲ 31 0077-2 [ADD]
Mozart, W.A.:Serenata notturna *(rec live 1951)* Multisonic ("Prague Spring Collection" series) ▲ 31 0077-2 [ADD]
Mozart, W.A.:Sym 29 *(rec live 1951)* Multisonic ("Prague Spring Collection" series) ▲ 31 0077-2 [ADD]

G. Sébastian (cnd)

Dvořák, A.:Con Vc, w. P. Fournier (vc) *(rec live, Prague 1949)* Melodram ▲ CDM 18037 [ADD]

V. Smetáček (cnd)

Boismortier, J.B. de:From Shakespeare Suite Campion ▲ 1319 [ADD/DDD]
Borodin, A.:Prince Igor (Polovtsian dances), w. Czech Phil Chorus Supraphon Collection ▲ 11 0622-2 [ADD]
Borodin, A.:Sym 2 Supraphon Collection ▲ 11 0612-2 [ADD]
Dvořák, A.:Biblical Songs, Op. 99, *(soloists unknown)* Supraphon ▲ SUP 111821 [AAD]
Dvořák, A.:Con Pno, w. S. Richter (pno) *(rec live, Prague 1964)* Melodram ▲ MEL 18029 (m) [AAD]
Dvořák, A.:Mass, *(soloists unknown)* Supraphon ▲ SUP 111821 [AAD]
Dvořák, A.:Te Deum, *(soloists unknown)* Supraphon ▲ SUP 111821 [AAD]
Foerster, J.B.:Cyrano de Bergerac Supraphon ▲ SUP 3041
Mozart, W.A.:Con Bn, w. Bidlo Karel (bn) Supraphon ▲ SUP 3053
Smetana, B.:Má Vlast Supraphon ▲ SUP 111981 [DDD]

R. Stankovsky (cnd)

Rubinstein, A.:Sym 4 Marco Polo ▲ 8.223319

L. Stokowski (cnd)

Scriabin, A.:Sym 4 *(rec Prague, June 1972)* London ("Phase 4 Stereo" series) ▲ 443898-2 [ADD]

F. Stupka (cnd)

Dvořák, A.:Carnival Supraphon ("Czech Philharmonic" series) ▲ SUP 111909 [AAD]
Novák, V.:In the Tatras Supraphon ("Czech Philharmonic" series) ▲ SUP 111909 [AAD]
Tchaikovsky, P.:Sym 6 Supraphon ("Czech Philharmonic" series) ▲ SUP 111909 [AAD]

L. Svárovský (cnd)

Dvořák, A.:Stabat Mater, w. Eva Jenisova (sop), Hana Stolfova-Bandova (cta), Vladimir Dolezal (ten), Jiri Sulzenka (bass), Petr Fiala (cnd), Brno Czech Phil Chorus Supraphon 2-▲ SUP CD 3093

H. Swarowsky (cnd)

Mahler, G.:Sym 4, w. G. Lorenz (sop) [G] *(rec 1972)* Supraphon Collection ▲ 11 0625-2 [ADD]

▲ = CD ♦ = Enhanced CD Δ = MD ■ = Cassette Tape □ = DCC

Czech PO (cont.)

H. Swarowsky (cnd) (cont.)

Wagner, R.:Lohengrin, w. Leonore Kirchstein (sop—Elsa von Brabant), Ruth Hesse (mez—Ortrud), Herbert Schachtschneider (ten—Lohengrin), Hans Helm (bar—Der Heerrufer des Königs), Otto von Rohr (bass—Heinrich der Vogler), Heinz Imdahl (sgr—Friedrich von Telramund), Prague National Theater Orch, Vienna State Opera Chorus *(rec Aug 1968)* Weltbild Classics 3–▲ 703835 [ADD]

Wagner, R.:Der Ring des Nibelungen, w. Liselotte Becker-Egner (sop—Woglinde/Ortlinde/Wellgunde), Angelika Berger (sop—Wellgunde/Waltraute), Siw Ericsdotter (sop—Norn 3), Heidemaria Ferch (sop—Freia/Gerhilde), Bella Jasper (sop—Helmwige/Waldvogel/Woglinde), Ditha Sommer (sop—Sieglinde/Gutrune), Ursula Boese (mez—Erda), Ruth Hesse (mez—Fricka), Nadezda Kniplová (mez—Brünnhilde), Margit Kobeck (mez—Schwertleite/Norn 2), Hilde Rosner (mez—Flosshilde/Siegrunde), Erica Schubert (mez—Grimgerde/Flosshilde), Ingrid Göritz (cta—Rossweisse/Norn 1), Herbert Doussant (ten—Froh), Herold Kraus (ten—Mime), Gerald McKee (ten—Siegmund/Siegfried), Fritz Uhl (ten—Loge), Rudolf Knoll (bar—Gunther/Donner), Rolf Polke (bass-bar—Wotan/Wanderer), Rolf Kühne (bass—Alberich), Takao Okamura (bass—Fafner), Otto von Rohr (bass—Hagen/Fasolt/Hunding), Prague National Theater Orch *(rec June 3 & 5, July 26–31, A)* Weltbild Classics 14–▲ 703769 [ADD]

G. Szell (cnd)

Beethoven, L. van:Egmont (ov) Sony Classical ("Festspiel Dokumente:Salzburger Festspiele" series) ▲ SMK 68447
Beethoven, L. van:Sym 3, "Eroica" Sony Classical ("Festspiel Dokumente:Salzburger Festspiele" series) ▲ SMK 68447
Dvořák, A.:Con Vc, w. Pablo Casals (vc) Dutton Laboratories ▲ DUT 5002
Dvořák, A.:Con Vc, w. P. Casals (vc) *(rec 1937)* EMI Classics (Great Recordings of the Century) ▲ CDH 63498 (m) [ADD]
Dvořák, A.:Con Vc, w. P. Casals (vc) *(rec 1937)* Pearl ▲ PEA 9349 (m) [AAD]
Dvořák, A.:Con Vc, w. P. Casals (vc) Pearl 4–▲ PEAS 9935 (m) [AAD]
Dvořák, A.:Sym 9, "From the New World" Dutton Laboratories ▲ DUT 5002

V. Talich (cnd)

Bach, J.S.:Con 1 Hpd, w. Richter (pno) *(rec live, Prague 1954)* Melodram ▲ MEL 18029 (m) [AAD]
Bach, J.S.:Con 8 Hpd, w. S. Richter (pno) *(rec 1954–55)* Supraphon ▲ SUP 11 1906 [AAD]
Dvořák, A.:Carnival Music & Arts ▲ CD 658 (m) [AAD]
Dvořák, A.:Carnival Supraphon ▲ SUP 11 1898 [AAD]
Dvořák, A.:Con Vc, w. Mstislav Rostropovich (vc) Supraphon 3–▲ SUP 0546 [AAD]
Dvořák, A.:Con Vc, w. M. Rostropovich (vc) Supraphon ▲ SUP 111901 [AAD]
Dvořák, A.:Con Pno, w. M. Rostropovich (pno) Supraphon ▲ SUP 111901 [AAD]
Dvořák, A.:The Golden Spinning Wheel *(rec 1949–51)* Supraphon ▲ SUP 11 1900 [ADD]
Dvořák, A.:In Nature's Realm Supraphon ▲ SUP 11 1898 [AAD]
Dvořák, A.:The Noon Witch Panton ▲ PAN 811100
Dvořák, A.:The Noon Witch *(rec 1949–51)* Supraphon ▲ SUP 11 1900 [ADD]
Dvořák, A.:Othello Supraphon ▲ SUP 11 1898 [AAD]
Dvořák, A.:Slavonic Dances (comp) *(rec 1935 from the original 78)* Music & Arts ▲ CD 658 (m) [AAD]
Dvořák, A.:Slavonic Dances (comp) *(rec 1950)* Supraphon ▲ SUP 111897 [AAD]
Dvořák, A.:Stabat Mater, w. Drahomira Tikalova (sop), Marta Krasova (cta), Beno Blachut (ten), Karel Kalas (bass), Czech Phil Chorus *(rec 1952)* Supraphon 2–▲ SUP 111902 [ADD]
Dvořák, A.:Sym 6 *(rec 1938 for HMV)* Koch Legacy ▲ 3–7060–2
Dvořák, A.:Sym 7 *(rec 1938 for HMV)* Koch Legacy ▲ 3–7007–2 (m) [ADD] ■ 3–7007–4 (m)
Dvořák, A.:Sym 8 *(rec 1954)* Supraphon Collection ▲ 11 0627–2 (m) [ADD]
Dvořák, A.:Sym 8 Supraphon ▲ SUP 11 1898 [AAD]
Dvořák, A.:Sym 8 *(rec 1935 for HMV)* Koch Legacy ▲ 3–7007–2 (m) [ADD] ■ 3–7007–4 (m)
Dvořák, A.:Sym 9, "From the New World" *(rec 1951–54)* Supraphon ▲ SUP 111899 [AAD]
Dvořák, A.:The Water Goblin *(rec 1949–51)* Supraphon ▲ SUP 11 1900 [ADD]
Dvořák, A.:The Water Goblin Panton ▲ PAN 811100
Dvořák, A.:The Wild Dove Panton ▲ PAN 811100
Dvořák, A.:Zigeunermelodien, Op. 55 *(rec 1949–51)* Supraphon ▲ SUP 11 1900 [ADD]
Handel, G.F.:Cons (3) Ob, w. F. Hanták (ob)—No. 3 *(rec 1954–55)* Supraphon ▲ SUP 11 1906 [AAD]
Janácek, L.:The Cunning Little Vixen (suite) [arr Václav Talich; rev Václav Smetáček] Supraphon ▲ SUP 111905 [AAD]
Janácek, L.:Taras Bulba Supraphon ▲ SUP 111905 [AAD]
Mozart, W.A.:Con Cl, w. V. Riha (cl) *(rec 1954)* Supraphon ▲ SUP 11 1907 [AAD]
Mozart, W.A.:Con 4 Vn, w. J. Novak (vn) *(rec 1954–55)* Supraphon ▲ SUP 11 1906 [AAD]
Mozart, W.A.:Serenade Ww, K.361—movts. 1–4 *(rec live 1954)* Multisonic ("Prague Spring Collection" series) ▲ 31 0078–2 [ADD]
Mozart, W.A.:Serenade Ww, K.388 *(rec 1954)* Multisonic ("Prague Spring Collection" series) ▲ 31 0078 [ADD]
Mozart, W.A.:Sym 33—movts. 1–4 *(rec live 1954)* Multisonic ("Prague Spring Collection" series) ▲ 31 0078–2 [ADD]
Mozart, W.A.:Sym 38—movts. 1–4 *(rec live 1954)* Multisonic ("Prague Spring Collection" series) ▲ 31 0078–2 [ADD]
Mozart, W.A.:Sym 39 *(rec 1953–55)* Supraphon ▲ SUP 11 0969 [DDD]
Novák, V.:Slovak Suite Supraphon ▲ SUP 111905 [AAD]
Smetana, B.:From Bohemian Fields & Groves *(rec 1954)* Supraphon Collection ▲ 11 0627–2 (m) [ADD]
Smetana, B.:Má Vlast *(rec 1929)* Koch Legacy ▲ 3–7032–2 ■ 3–7032–4
Smetana, B.:Má Vlast *(rec 1954)* Supraphon ▲ SUP 111896 [AAD]
Smetana, B.:The Moldau *(rec 1954)* Supraphon Collection ▲ 11 0627–2 (m) [ADD]
Suk, J.:Asrael *(rec 1952)* Supraphon 2–▲ SUP 111902 [ADD]
Suk, J.:Fairy Tale *(rec 1949)* Supraphon ▲ SUP 11 1904 [AAD]
Suk, J.:The Ripening *(rec 1956)* Supraphon ▲ SUP 11 1904 [AAD]
Suk, J.:Serenade Strs *(rec 1938 for HMV)* Koch Legacy ▲ 3–7060–2
Suk, J.:Serenade Strs *(rec 1951–54)* Supraphon ▲ SUP 111899 [AAD]
Tchaikovsky, P.:Sym 6 *(rec 1953–1955)* Supraphon ▲ SUP 11 0969 [DDD]

F. Vajnar (cnd)

Beethoven, L. van:Ah, perfido!, w. E. Depoltová (sop) [I] *(rec 1978)* Supraphonet ▲ 11 1118–2 [AAD]
Beethoven, L. van:Ovs—Coriolan, Egmont, König Stephen, Leonore No. 3, Die Ruinen von Athen *(rec 1978 & 1981)* Supraphonet ▲ 11 1118–2 [AAD]

J. Vlach (cnd)

Mozart, W.A.:Con 23 Pno, w. I. Moravec (pno) *(rec 1974)* Supraphon ("Great Artists" series) ▲ 11 0271–2 [AAD]
Mozart, W.A.:Con 25 Pno, w. I. Moravec (pno) *(rec 1973)* Supraphon ("Great Artists" series) ▲ 11 0271–2 [AAD]

V. Válek (cnd)

Bartók, B.:Con Orch Panton ▲ PAN 811214

C. Zecchi (cnd)

Berlioz, H.:Sym fantastique *(rec 1959)* Supraphonet ▲ 11 1103–2 [AAD]

K. Šejna (cnd)

Dvořák, A.:The Cunning Peasant (ov) Supraphon ("Czech PO Centennial" series) ▲ SUP 111914
Dvořák, A.:Husitská Supraphon ("Czech PO Centennial" series) ▲ SUP 111923
Dvořák, A.:In Nature's Realm Supraphon ("Czech Philharmonic" series) ▲ SUP 111915 [AAD]
Dvořák, A.:Legends, Op. 59 Supraphon ("Czech PO Centennial" series) ▲ SUP 111919
Dvořák, A.:Scherzo Capriccioso Supraphon ("Czech Philharmonic" series) ▲ SUP 111915 [AAD]
Dvořák, A.:Slavonic Dances (comp) *(rec 1959)* Supraphon ("Czech Philharmonic Series") ▲ SUP 111916 [ADD]
Dvořák, A.:Slavonic Rhaps, Op. 45 *(rec 1952–53)* Supraphon ("Czech Philharmonic Series") ▲ SUP 111917 [ADD]
Dvořák, A.:Suite, Op. 98b, "American" Supraphon ▲ SUP 111924
Dvořák, A.:Symphonic Vars Supraphon ("Czech PO Centennial" series) ▲ SUP 111919

Czech PO (cont.)

K. Šejna (cnd) (cont.)

Dvořák, A.:Sym 5 *(rec 1952–53)* Supraphon ("Czech Philharmonic Series") ▲ SUP 111917 [ADD]
Dvořák, A.:Sym 6 *(rec 1951)* Supraphon ("Czech Philharmonic Series") ▲ SUP 111918 [ADD]
Dvořák, A.:Sym 7 *(rec 1951)* Supraphon ("Czech Philharmonic Series") ▲ SUP 111918 [ADD]
Fibich, Z.:At Twilight Supraphon ("Czech Philharmonic" series) ▲ SUP 111920 [AAD]
Fibich, Z.:Christmas Day Supraphon ("Czech PO Centennial" series) ▲ SUP 111922
Fibich, Z.:The Romance of Spring, w. Czech Phil Chorus Supraphon ("Czech Philharmonic" series) ▲ SUP 111920 [AAD]
Fibich, Z.:Sym 1 Supraphon ("Czech Philharmonic" series) ▲ SUP 111920 [AAD]
Fibich, Z.:Sym 2 Supraphon ("Czech Philharmonic" series) ▲ SUP 111921 [AAD]
Fibich, Z.:Sym 3 Supraphon ("Czech Philharmonic" series) ▲ SUP 111921 [AAD]
Fibich, Z.:The Water Goblin Supraphon ("Czech PO Centennial" series) ▲ SUP 111922
Martinů, B.:Double Con Pno Timp Supraphon ▲ SUP 111924
Martinů, B.:Sym 3 Supraphon ▲ SUP 111924
Novák, V.:Eternal Longing Supraphon ("Czech PO Centennial" series) ▲ SUP 111922
Novák, V.:In the Tatras *(rec Feb. 1966)* Supraphon ("Collection" series) ▲ 11 0682–2 [ADD]
Novák, V.:In the Tatras Supraphon ("Czech PO Centennial" series) ▲ SUP 111922
Novák, V.:Pan [arr orch] *(rec Feb. 1966)* Supraphon ("Collection" series) ▲ 11 0682–2 [ADD]
Skroup, F.:The Tinker (ov) Supraphon ("Czech PO Centennial" series) ▲ SUP 111914
Smetana, B.:Festive Ov Supraphon ("Czech PO Centennial" series) ▲ SUP 111914
Smetana, B.:Hakon Jarl Supraphon ("Czech Philharmonic" series) ▲ SUP 111915 [AAD]
Smetana, B.:Má Vlast Supraphon ▲ SUP 111913
Smetana, B.:Richard III Supraphon ("Czech Philharmonic" series) ▲ SUP 111915 [AAD]
Smetana, B.:Triumph Sym Supraphon ("Czech PO Centennial" series) ▲ SUP 111914
Smetana, B.:Wallenstein's Camp Supraphon ("Czech Philharmonic" series) ▲ SUP 111915 [AAD]
Suk, J.:Meditation on the Old Czech Hymn "St. Wenceslas" Supraphon ("Czech PO Centennial" series) ▲ SUP 111923
Suk, J.:A Summer Tale Supraphon ("Czech PO Centennial" series) ▲ SUP 111923

Czech PO members

M. Fischer-Dieskau (cnd)

Doráti, A.:Jesus oder Barabbas?, w. W. Quadflieg (nar), New Berlin CO, Berlin HDK Chamber Choir [G] *(rec live 1992)* BIS ▲ CD 578 [DDD]

Czech PO Soloists

V. Talich (cnd)

Mozart, W.A.:Sinf concertante Ob, K.Anh.9 *(rec 1949)* Supraphon ▲ SUP 11 1907 [AAD]

Czech PO Wind Ensemble

Beethoven, L. van:Octet, Op. 103 Supraphon Collection ▲ 11 0638–2 [ADD]
Beethoven, L. van:Qnt Pno, Ob, Cl, Hn & Bn, w. Z. Jílek (pno) Supraphon Collection ▲ 11 0638–2 [ADD]
Beethoven, L. van:Sxt Winds, Op. 71 Supraphon Collection ▲ 11 0638–2 [ADD]

Czech RSO

The Dance Collection, w. Ondrej Lenard (cnd), Keith Clark (cnd), Stephen Gunzenhauser (cnd), Kenneth Jean (cnd), Barry Wordsworth (cnd), Adrian Leaper (cnd), Johannes Wildner (cnd), Slovak RSO, Slovak PO, Royal PO, Slovak State PO, CRS SO, Thalia-Schrammeln Quartet *(rec Czechoslovak Radio Concert Hall, Bratislava, Feb 1–4, 1988)* Naxos 4–▲ 8.504015 [DDD]

Z. Chen (cnd)

Griffes, C.T.:Poem Fl, w. K. Bryan (fl) Premier ▲ PRCD 1026 [DDD]
Ibert, J.:Con Fl, w. K. Bryan (fl) Premier ▲ PRCD 1026 [DDD]
Nielsen, C.:Con Fl, w. K. Bryan (fl) Premier ▲ PRCD 1026 [DDD]
Perry, W.:Summer Nocturne, w. K. Bryan (fl) Premier ▲ PRCD 1026 [DDD]

M. Halász (cnd)

Beethoven, L. van:Sym 3, "Eroica" *(rec Czechoslovak Radio Concert Hall, Bratislava, Mar 1988)* Naxos 4–▲ 8.504012 [DDD]

O. Lenárd (cnd)

Moyzes, A.:Dances from Gemer Marco Polo ▲ 8.223278 [DDD]
Moyzes, A.:Dances from Hron Marco Polo ▲ 8.223278 [DDD]
Moyzes, A.:Down the Váh Marco Polo ▲ 8.223278 [DDD]
Tchaikovsky, P.:Con 1 Pno, w. Joseph Banowetz (pno) *(rec Czechoslovak Radio Concert Hall, Bratislava, May 29–June 1, 1988)* Naxos 4–▲ 8.504011 [DDD]
Tchaikovsky, P.:Eugene Onegin (sels), w. Joseph Banowetz (pno)—Polonaise; Waltz *(rec Czechoslovak Radio Concert Hall, Bratislava, May 29–June 1, 1988)* Naxos 4–▲ 8.504011 [DDD]
Tchaikovsky, P.:Sleeping Beauty (sels) Naxos ▲ 8.550079 [DDD]
Tchaikovsky, P.:The Tempest, w. Joseph Banowetz (pno) *(rec Czechoslovak Radio Concert Hall, Bratislava, May 29–June 1, 1988)* Naxos 4–▲ 8.504011 [DDD]

V. Válek (cnd)

Funk, E.:Con Vc, "Homage to Jaqueline DuPré", w. Olga Ogranovitch (vc) *(rec 1994)* MMC ▲ MMC 2033 [DDD]
Funk, E.:Con Ob, w. Martin Schuring (ob) *(rec 1994)* MMC ▲ MMC 2033 [DDD]
Funk, E.:Lidice *(rec 1994)* MMC ▲ MMC 2033 [DDD]
Funk, E.:Sym 1, "Emily" *(rec 1994)* MMC ▲ MMC 2033 [DDD]

Czech Radio-TV Orch

E. Brizio (cnd)

Generali, P.:Sacred Music, w. Leila Bersiani (sop), Valentina di Cola (sop), Emanuela Deffai (mez), Sella Salvati (cta), Paolo Macedonio (ten), Roberto Bencivenga (ten), Carlo Lepore (bass), Czech Radio-TV Chorus—Magnificat; Domine ad Adjuvandum; Virgam Virtutis; Ecce Virgo; Ave Maria Messe Pastorale; Te Deum *(rec FHS Studios, Prague, 1995)* Studio SM ▲ 2517 [DDD]

Czech Soloists

Schubert, Franz:Nonet Ww, w. Czech Nonet members Praga ▲ PR 250087

Czech State PO

P. Breiner (cnd)

Albéniz, I.:Gtr Music, w. G. Garcia (gtr)—Asturias; Zamba Granadina [orchd Breiner] Naxos ▲ 8.550220 [DDD]
Falla, M. de:Gtr Music, w. G. Garcia (gtr)—Aragonesa [arr guitar & orchestra Breiner] Naxos ▲ 8.550220 [DDD]
Granados, E.:Pno Music (misc), w. G. Garcia (gtr), P. Breiner (pno) [arranged by cond. for guitar & orch.]—Spanish Dances Nos. 2,6,8 & 11; Zapateado Naxos ▲ 8.550220 [DDD]
Rodrigo, J.:Concierto de Aranjuez, w. G. Garcia (gtr) Naxos ▲ 8.550220 [DDD]

F. Jílek (cnd)

Janácek, L.:Orchestral Music (complete) Supraphon 3–▲ SUP 111834 [DDD]

A. Leaper (cnd)

Cowen, F.H.:The Butterfly's Ball Marco Polo ▲ 8.223273 [DDD]
Cowen, F.H.:Indian Rhap Marco Polo ▲ 8.223273 [DDD]
Cowen, F.H.:Sym 3, "Scandinavian" Marco Polo ▲ 8.223273 [DDD]

Y. Menuhin (cnd)

Dvořák, A.:Serenade Strs *(rec Nov. 26–29, 1992)* Supraphon ▲ SUP 111837 [DDD]
Martinů, B.:Concertino Pno, Vn, Vc & Strs *(rec Nov. 26–29, 1992)* Supraphon ▲ SUP 111837 [DDD]
Saint-Saëns, C.:La Muse et la poète *(rec Nov. 26–29, 1992)* Supraphon ▲ SUP 111837 [DDD]
Smetana, B.:The Bartered Bride (ov) *(rec Nov. 26–29, 1992)* Supraphon ▲ SUP 111837 [DDD]

A. Mogrelia (cnd)

Prokofiev, S.:Romeo & Juliet (sels) *(rec Nov. 20–29, 1989)* Naxos ▲ 8.550380 [DDD]

J. Serebrier (cnd)

Chadwick, G.W.:Melpomene *(rec Stadion Hall, Brno, Czech Republic, Apr. 2–5, 1995)* Reference ▲ RR 64 [DDD]
Chadwick, G.W.:Symphonic Sketches *(rec Stadion Hall, Brno, Czech Republic, Apr. 2–5, 1995)* Reference ▲ RR 64 [DDD]
Chadwick, G.W.:Tam O'Shanter *(rec Stadion Hall, Brno, Czech Republic, Apr. 2–5, 1995)* Reference ▲ RR 64 [DDD]

Czech State PO (cont.)
J. Serebrier (cnd) (cont.)
Janácek, L.:Lachian Dances *(rec Stadion Hall, Brno, Czech Republic, Apr. 2–5, 1995)* Reference ▲ RR 65 [DDD]
Janácek, L.:Sinfonietta *(rec Stadion Hall, Brno, Czech Republic, Apr. 2–5, 1995)* Reference ▲ RR 65 [DDD]
Janácek, L.:Taras Bulba *(rec Stadion Hall, Brno, Czech Republic, Apr. 2–5, 1995)* Reference ▲ RR 65 [DDD]
Tchaikovsky, P.:Music of, w. Michael Guttman (vn), Royal PO—Waltzes [from Sleeping Beauty; Eugene Onegin; Swan Lake; Nutcracker (Waltz of the Flowers)]; Marches [from Nutcracker; Coronation March for Alexander III; Solennelle; Marche Slave, Op. 31]; Méditation in d, Op. 42/1; Mélodie in Eb, Op. 42/3; Elegy in G for Strs; Andante Cantabile, Op. 11 IMG/Pickwick ▲ PIC IMG 1617
L. Svárovsky (cnd)
Tomasi, H.:Con Tpt, w. Jaroslav Halíř (tpt) *(rec Stadion-Hall, Brno, Mar 2 & 3, 1995)* Panton ▲ 811368-2 [DDD]
I. Yinon (cnd)
Schulhoff, E.:Con Str Qt, Kyndel String Quartet Koch Schwann ▲ SCH 315432 [DDD]
Schulhoff, E.:Festive Prelude Koch Schwann ▲ SCH 314372 [DDD]
Schulhoff, E.:Suite CO Koch Schwann ▲ SCH 314372 [DDD]
Schulhoff, E.:Sym 1 Koch Schwann ▲ SCH 314372 [DDD]
Schulhoff, E.:Sym 2 Koch Schwann ▲ SCH 315432 [DDD]
Schulhoff, E.:Sym 3 Koch Schwann ▲ SCH 315432 [DDD]
Czech SO
U.J. Flury (cnd)
Flury, R.:Con 1 Pno, w. Margaret Singer (pno) *(rec Filmové Studio, Prague, Apr 22–23, 1994)* Gallo ▲ CD 865 [DDD]
Flury, R.:Con 2 Pno, w. Margaret Singer (pno) *(rec Filmové Studio, Prague, Apr 22–23, 1994)* Gallo ▲ CD 865 [DDD]
Flury, R.:Con 1 Vn, w. Ulrich Lehmann (vn) *(rec Filmové Studio, Prague, May 21, 1993)* Gallo ▲ CD 865 [DDD]
O. Lenárd (cnd)
Tchaikovsky, P.:Sym 6 Naxos ▲ 8.5500097 [DDD]
Czech–Slovak RSO
The Dance Collection, w. Ondrej Lenard (cnd), Keith Clark (cnd), Stephen Gunzenhauser (cnd), Kenneth Jean (cnd), Barry Wordsworth (cnd), Adrian Leaper (cnd), Johannes Wildner (cnd), Czech RSO, Slovak RSO, Slovak PO, Royal PO, Slovak State PO, CRS SO, Thalia-Schrammeln Quartet *(rec Czechoslovak Radio Concert Hall, Bratislava, Feb 1–4, 1988)* Naxos 4–▲ 8.504015 [DDD]
A. Bramall (cnd)
Russian Festival Naxos ▲ 8.550085 [DDD]
K. Clark (cnd)
Spanish Festival Naxos ▲ 8.550086 [DDD]
S. Gunzenhauser (cnd)
Copland, A.:Appalachian Spring Naxos ▲ 8.550282 [DDD]
Copland, A.:Billy the Kid Naxos ▲ 8.550282 [DDD]
Copland, A.:Fanfare for the Common Man Naxos ▲ 8.550282 [DDD]
Copland, A.:Rodeo Naxos ▲ 8.550282 [DDD]
Saint-Saëns, C.:Le Rouet d'Omphale Naxos ▲ 8.550138 [DDD]
Saint-Saëns, C.:Samson et Dalila (Bacchanale) Naxos ▲ 8.550138 [DDD]
Saint-Saëns, C.:Sym 3 Naxos ▲ 8.550138 [DDD]
R. Hayman (cnd)
Famous Overtures, w. Polish National Radio Orch *(rec Polish Radio, Katowice, Aug 27–Sept 1, 1990; May)* Naxos 4–▲ 8.504013 [DDD]
Gershwin, G.:Con Pno, w. K. Selby (pno) *(rec 6/89)* Naxos ▲ 8.550295 [DDD]
Gershwin, G.:Rhap in Blue, w. K. Selby (pno) *(rec 6/89)* Naxos ▲ 8.550295 [DDD]
A. L. Jean (cnd)
Chinese Orchestral Music Marco Polo ▲ 8.223408 [DDD]
Chinese Orchestral Music II Marco Polo ▲ 8.223412 [DDD]
K. Jean (cnd)
Butterfly Lovers, w. Takako Nishizaki (vn) Marco Polo ▲ 8.223350
K. C. Lenárd (cnd)
French Festival Naxos ▲ 8.550088 [DDD]
O. Lenárd (cnd)
Battle Music *(rec 1989)* Naxos ▲ 8.550230 [DDD]
Glazunov, A.:Scènes de ballet Marco Polo ▲ 8.223136 [DDD]
Glazunov, A.:The Seasons Naxos ▲ 8.550079 [DDD]
Glazunov, A.:The Seasons Marco Polo ▲ 8.223136 [DDD]
Invitation to the Dance Naxos ▲ 8.550081 [DDD]
Opera Intermezzi & Preludes *(rec 1989)* Naxos ▲ 8.550240 [DDD]
Tchaikovsky, P.:The Nutcracker (sels) *(rec 1989)* Naxos ▲ 8.550515 [DDD]
Tchaikovsky, P.:The Tempest *(rec 1988)* Naxos ▲ 8.550137 [DDD]
Verdi, G.:Ovs & Preludes—Aïda—Prelude, Triumphant March & Ballet Music; Forza del destino—Overture; Rigoletto—Prelude; Traviata—Preludes to Acts I & II Naxos ▲ 8.550091 [DDD]
Verdi, G.:I vespri siciliani (sels)—ballet music Naxos ▲ 8.550091 [DDD]
O. Lenárd, A. Walter (cnd)
Strauss (II), Joh.:Music of, w. Czech–Slovak State Radio PO—9 selections Naxos ▲ 8.550340 [DDD]
Strauss (II), Joh.:Music of, w. Czech–Slovak State Radio PO, Polish State PO—9 selections Naxos ▲ 8.550339 [DDD]
Strauss (II), Joh.:Music of, w. Czech–Slovak State Radio PO, Polish State PO—9 sels. Naxos ▲ 8.550337 [DDD]
Strauss (II), Joh.:Music of, w. Polish State PO—9 selections Naxos ▲ 8.550338 [DDD]
U. Mund (cnd)
Wagner, R.:Der Ring des Nibelungen (orch sels)—Rheingold *(Entry of the Gods into Valhalla)*, Walküre *(Ride of the Valkyries, Wotan's Farewell & Magic Fire Music)*, Siegfried *(Forest Murmurs)*, Götterdämmerung *(Siegfried's Death & Funeral March; Siegfried's Rhine Journey)* Naxos ▲ 8.550211 [DDD]
K. Schermerhorn (cnd)
Sibelius, J.:Finlandia Naxos ▲ 8.550103 [DDD]
Sibelius, J.:Karelia Suite Naxos ▲ 8.550103 [DDD]
Sibelius, J.:Pohjola's Daughter Naxos ▲ 8.550103 [DDD]
Sibelius, J.:Valse triste Naxos ▲ 8.550103 [DDD]
J. Wildner (cnd)
Gretchaninoff, A.:Sym 2, "Pastoral" Marco Polo ▲ 8.223163
Czech–Slovak RSO Bratislava
Beethoven, L van:Music of, w. J. Jandó (pno), et al., Slovak PO, Capella Istropolitana—Egmont & Fidelio Ovs.; Für Elise; sels. from Pno Son. 8 & 14; Sym. 3, 5 & 6; Pno Con. 4 & 5; Vn Con. Naxos ▲ 8.551101 [DDD] Δ 7.551101 [DDD]
M. Adriano (cnd)
Bliss, A.:Film Music—from Baraza; Christopher Columbus; Men of Two Worlds; Seven Waves away Marco Polo ▲ 8.223315
Honegger, A.:Film Music—Napoléon [orchestral suite, original version] (1926–7); Les Misérables [orchestral suite] (1934); Mermoz [two suites] (1934); La Roue [overture] (1922) Marco Polo ▲ 8.223134 [DDD]
Honegger, A.:Les Misérables [complete score] Marco Polo ▲ 8.223181
Ibert, J.:Film Music—from Don Quixote; Golgotha; Macbeth Marco Polo ▲ 8.223287
Respighi, O.:Aretusa, w. F. Subrata (mez) [I] Marco Polo ▲ 8.223347 [DDD]
Respighi, O.:Liriche dal Poema paradisiaco di Gabriele d'Annunzio, w. F. Subrata (mez) [arr. by Adriano for voice, harp, keyboards & strings] [I] Marco Polo ▲ 8.223347 [DDD]
Respighi, O.:La Pentola magica *(rec Nov. 4–9, 1991)* Marco Polo ▲ 8.223346 [DDD]
Respighi, O.:Scherzo veneziano *(rec Nov. 4–9, 1991)* Marco Polo ▲ 8.223346 [DDD]
Respighi, O.:La Sensitiva, w. F. Subrata (mez) [I] Marco Polo ▲ 8.223347 [DDD]

Czech–Slovak RSO Bratislava (cont.)
M. Adriano (cnd) (cont.)
Respighi, O.:Sèvres de la vieille France *(rec Nov. 4–9, 1991)* Marco Polo ▲ 8.223346 [DDD]
Respighi, O.:Il Tramonto, w. F. Subrata (mez) [I] Marco Polo ▲ 8.223347 [DDD]
Waxman, F.:Rebecca Marco Polo ▲ 8.223399
R. Bernas (cnd)
Cresswell, L.:Con Vc, w. R. Jablonsky (vc) Continuum ▲ CCD 1033
Cresswell, L.:A Modern Ecstacy, w. P. Boylan (sop), N. Leeson-Williams (b-bar) *(rec 4/91)* Continuum ▲ CCD 1033
M. Dittrich (cnd)
Salieri, A.:La Locandiera—Les Denaïdes; La Grotta de Trofonio, et al. Marco Polo ▲ 8.223381
O. Dohnányi (cnd)
Liszt, F.:Cons Pno, w. J. Banowetz (pno) *(rec 11/88)* Naxos ▲ 8.550187 [DDD]
Liszt, F.:Totentanz, w. J. Banowetz (pno) *(rec 11/88)* Naxos ▲ 8.550187 [DDD]
Rubinstein, A.:Concertstück, w. J. Banowetz (pno) Marco Polo ▲ 8.223190
Rubinstein, A.:Fant Pno, w. J. Banowetz (pno) Marco Polo ▲ 8.223190
R. Duarte (cnd)
Villa-Lobos, H.:Amazonas Marco Polo ▲ 8.223357
A. Eschwé (cnd)
Strauss (II), Joh.:Orchestral Music—Freiheits-Lieder (waltz), Op. 52; Kaiser Franz Joseph Marsch, Op. 67; Windsor-Klänge, Op. 104; Melodien-Quadrille, Op. 112; Armenball-Polka, Op. 176; s'gibt nur a Kaiserstadt, s'gibt nur ein Wien (polka-schnell), Op. 291; Bürgersinn (waltz), Op. 295; Feenmärchen (waltz), Op. 312; Fest-Polonaise, Op. 352; Liebchen, schwing dich (polka mazurka), Op. 394; Violetta (polka française), Op. 404; Adelen-Walzer, Op. 424 Marco Polo ▲ 8.223217 [DDD]
M. Fischer-Dieskau (cnd)
Humperdinck, E.:Incidental Music—Die Marketenderin—Prelude; Merchant of Venice—Love Scene; Sleeping Beauty—Tone Pictures *(rec 5/91)* Marco Polo ▲ 8.2233369 [DDD]
Humperdinck, E.:Moorish Rhap *(rec 5/91)* Marco Polo ▲ 8.2233369 [DDD]
S. Gunzenhauser (cnd)
Borodin, A.:Sym 1 *(rec Feb. 1989)* Naxos ▲ 8.550238 [DDD]
Borodin, A.:Sym 2 *(rec Feb. 1989)* Naxos ▲ 8.550238 [DDD]
Borodin, A.:Sym 3 *(rec Feb. 1989)* Naxos ▲ 8.550238 [DDD]
Orff, C.:Carmina burana, w. E. Jenisová (sop), V. Dolezal (ten), I. Kusnjer (bar), Slovak Phil Chorus Naxos ▲ 8.550196 [DDD] Δ 7.550196 [DDD]
M. Halász (cnd)
Famous Tenor Arias, w. Thomas Harper (ten), Slovak Phil Chorus Naxos ▲ 8.550497 [DDD] Δ 7.550497 [DDD]
W. Humburg (cnd)
Favorite Soprano Arias, w. Luba Organosova (sop) *(rec 1990–91)* Naxos ▲ 8.550605 [DDD]
Puccini, G.:La Bohème (sels), w. Luba Orgonasova (sop—Mimi), Carmen Gonzales (sop—Musetta), Jonathan Welch (ten—Rudolfo), Fabio Previati (bar—Marcello), Boaz Senator (bar—Schaunard), Ivan Urbas (bass—Colline), Jiri Sulzenko (bass—Alcindoro), Bratislava Children's Choir, Slovak Phil Chorus *(rec Concert Hall, Czecho-Slovak Radio, Bratislava, Apr. 23–May 4, 1990)* Naxos ▲ 8.553151 [DDD]
K. Jean (cnd)
Albéniz, I.:Iberia Suite *(rec Sept 1988)* Naxos ▲ 8.550174 [DDD]
Falla, M. de:El amor brujo (ritual fire dance) Naxos ▲ 8.550174 [DDD]
Falla, M. de:El sombrero de tres picos (sels)—Suites 1 & 2 *(rec 9/88)* Naxos ▲ 8.550174 [DDD]
Falla, M. de:La vida breve (interlude & dance 1)—Suites 1 & 2 *(rec 9/88)* Naxos ▲ 8.550174 [DDD]
Ravel, M.:Boléro Naxos ▲ 8.550173 [DDD]
Ravel, M.:Daphnis et Chloé (suite 1) Naxos ▲ 8.550173 [DDD]
Ravel, M.:Daphnis et Chloé (suite 2) *(rec June 1990)* Naxos ▲ 8.550424 [DDD]
Ravel, M.:Ma mère l'oye Orch Naxos ▲ 8.550173 [DDD]
Ravel, M.:Pavane pour une infante défunte *(rec June 1990)* Naxos ▲ 8.550424 [DDD]
Ravel, M.:Rapsodie espagnole *(rec 1989)* Naxos ▲ 8.550327 [DDD]
Ravel, M.:Rapsodie espagnole *(rec Sept. 1988)* Naxos ▲ 8.550424 [DDD]
Ravel, M.:La Valse *(rec June 1990)* Naxos ▲ 8.550424 [DDD]
Ravel, M.:Valses nobles et sentimentales Naxos ▲ 8.550173 [DDD]
Xin Huguang:Gada Meilin Marco Polo ▲ 8.223408 [DDD]
D. Johanos (cnd)
Rimsky-Korsakov, N.:Golden Cockerel (suite) *(rec Feb. 15–18, 1991)* Naxos ▲ 8.550486 [DDD]
Rimsky-Korsakov, N.:Mlada (suite) *(rec Feb. 15–18, 1991)* Naxos ▲ 8.550486 [DDD]
Rimsky-Korsakov, N.:Snow Maiden (suite) *(rec Feb. 15–18, 1991)* Naxos ▲ 8.550486 [DDD]
A. Leaper (cnd)
Curzon, F.:Orchestral Music—The Boulevardier (Characteristic Intermezzo); Punchinello (Miniature Overture); Spanish Suite:In Malaga; Dance of an Ostracized Imp; Saltarello for Piano & Orchestra; Capricante (Spanish Caprice); Galavant; Pasquinade; Simonetta (Serenade); Cascade (Waltz); La Peineta; Robin Hood Suite; Bravada (Paso Doble) Marco Polo (British Light Music) ▲ 8.223425 [DDD]
Delius, F.:Brigg Fair:An English Rhapsody *(rec 1/89)* Naxos ▲ 8.550229 [DDD]
Delius, F.:In a Summer Garden *(rec 1/89)* Naxos ▲ 8.550229 [DDD]
Elgar, E.:Enigma Vars *(rec 1/89)* Naxos ▲ 8.550229 [DDD]
Elgar, E.:Pomp & Circumstance Marches—Nos. 1 & 4 *(rec 1/89)* Naxos ▲ 8.550229 [DDD]
Elgar, E.:Salut d'amour—Nos. 1 & 4 *(rec 1/89)* Naxos ▲ 8.550229 [DDD]
Farnon, R.:Music of—A la Claire Fontaine; Colditz March; Derby Day; Gateway to the West; How Beautiful is Night; In a Calm; Jumping Bean; Lake in the Woods; Little Manhattan Playboy; Miss Molly; Melody Fair; Peanut Polka; Pictures in the Fire; Portrait of a Flirt; A Star is Born; State Occasion; Westminster Waltz *(rec 3/91)* Marco Polo (British Light Music) ▲ 8.223401 [DDD]
German, E.:The Conqueror (sels)—Berceuse *(rec Sept. 14–19, 1991)* Marco Polo ▲ 8.223419 [DDD]
German, E.:Gipsy Suite *(rec Sept. 14–19, 1991)* Marco Polo ▲ 8.223419 [DDD]
German, E.:Henry VIII (3 dances) *(rec Sept. 14–19, 1991)* Marco Polo ▲ 8.223419 [DDD]
German, E.:Merrie England (sels) *(rec Sept. 14–19, 1991)* Marco Polo ▲ 8.223419 [DDD]
German, E.:Nell Gwyn (sels) *(rec Sept. 14–19, 1991)* Marco Polo ▲ 8.223419 [DDD]
German, E.:Romeo & Juliet *(rec Sept. 14–19, 1991)* Marco Polo ▲ 8.223419 [DDD]
German, E.:Tom Jones (sels)—Sophia's Waltz *(rec Sept. 14–19, 1991)* Marco Polo ▲ 8.223419 [DDD]
Halvorsen, J.:Air Norvegien Naxos ▲ 8.550329 [DDD]
Halvorsen, J.:Norwegian Dances, w. *(soloist unknown)* Naxos ▲ 8.550329 [DDD]
Holbrooke, J.:Byron, w. Slovak Phil Chorus *(rec Jan. 6–13, 1992)* Marco Polo ▲ 8.223446 [DDD]
Holbrooke, J.:Orchestral Works—The Bells:Prelude, Op. 50; Bronwen:Overture; The Raven, Op. 25; Ulalume, Op. 35 *(rec Jan. 6–13, 1992)* Marco Polo ▲ 8.223446 [DDD]
Holst, G.:The Planets Naxos ▲ 8.550193 [DDD]
Holst, G.:Suite de Ballet Naxos ▲ 8.550193 [DDD]
Ketèlbey, A.W.:Music of, w. Slovak Phil Chorus—In a Monastery Garden; "The Adventurers" Ov.; Chal Romano; Suite Romantique; Caprice Pianistique; The Clock and the Dresden Figures; Cockney Suite; In the Moonlight; Wedgwood Blue; Bells across the Meadow; The Phantom Melody; In a Persian Market *(rec Jan. 13–18, 1992)* Marco Polo ▲ 8.223442 [DDD]
Kodály, Z.:Galanta Dances *(rec May 29–30, 1991)* Naxos ▲ 8.550520 [DDD]
Kodály, Z.:Marosszék Dances *(rec Mar. 18–19, 1991)* Naxos ▲ 8.550520 [DDD]
Kodály, Z.:Vars on a Hungarian Folk Song *(rec Apr. 12–17, 1991)* Naxos ▲ 8.550520 [DDD]
Quilter, R.:Music of—A Children's Ov.; Where the Rainbow Ends (suite); As You Like It (suite); Country Pieces; The Rake (suite); 3 English Dances *(rec Jan. 1992)* Marco Polo ▲ 8.223444 [DDD]
Sibelius, J.:Con Vn, w. Dong-Suk Kang (vn), (original 1903/04 version) *(rec 1989 & 1991)* Naxos ▲ 8.553233 [DDD]
Sibelius, J.:Con Vn, w. D.-S. Kang (vn) Naxos ▲ 8.550329 [DDD]
Sinding, C.:Légende, w. Dong-Suk Kang (vn) Naxos ▲ 8.550329 [DDD]
Svendsen, J.:Romance Vn, w. Dong-Suk Kang (vn) Naxos ▲ 8.550329 [DDD]
Wood, Haydn:Orchestral Music—Apollo Overture; Brown Bird Singing; Joyousness Waltz; London Cameos; Mannin Veen; Rhapsody Mylecharane; Seafarer; Serenade to Youth; Sketch of a Dandy Marco Polo (British Light Music) ▲ 8.223402 [DDD]

▲ = CD ♦ = Enhanced CD Δ = MD ■ = Cassette Tape □ = DCC

Czech–Slovak RSO Bratislava (cont.)
A. Leaper, K. Jean (cnd)
Chen, Q.:Dagger Dance — Marco Polo ▲ 8.223408
Chen, Q.:Drum & Song — Marco Polo ▲ 8.223408
Chen, Q.:Fant on a Xinjian Folk Song — Marco Polo ▲ 8.223408
Ding, S.:Xinjiang Dances — Marco Polo ▲ 8.223408 [DDD]
O. Lenárd (cnd)
Britten, B.:The Young Person's Guide to the Orchestra *(rec 11/89)* — Naxos ▲ 8.550499 [DDD]
Prokofiev, S.:Peter & the Wolf, w. J. Nicholas (nar) — Naxos ▲ 8.550499 [DDD]
Saint-Saëns, C.:Carnival of the Animals, w. M. Lapsansky (pno), P. Toperczer (pno) — Naxos ▲ 8.550499 [DDD]
Tchaikovsky, P.:Con 1 Pno, w. J. Banowetz (pno) *(rec 1988)* — Naxos ▲ 8.550137 [DDD]
Tchaikovsky, P.:Eugene Onegin (sels)—Waltz & Polonaise *(rec 1988)* — Naxos ▲ 8.550137 [DDD]
A. Rahbari (cnd)
Bizet, G.:Carmen, w. D. Palade (sop), G. Alperyn (mez), G. Lamberti (ten), A. Titus (bar), et al., Slovak Phil Chorus, Bratislava Children's Choir [F] — Naxos 3-▲ 8.660005/07 [DDD]
Bizet, G.:Carmen (sels), w. D. Palade (sop—Micaëla), A. Liebeck (sop—Frasquita), G. Alperyn (mez—Carmen), D. Schaechter (mez—Mercédès), G. Lamberti (ten—Don José), M. Dvorsky (ten—Remandado), J. Durco (ten—Cancairo), A. Titus (bar—Escamillo), V. Chmelo (bar—Morales), D. Rigosa (bass—Zuniga), Slovak Phil Chorus, Bratislava Children's Choir *(rec July 1990)* — Naxos ▲ 8.550727 [DDD]
Brahms, J.:Ein Deutsches Requiem, w. M. Gauci (sop), E. Tumagian (bar), Slovak Phil Chorus *(rec June 1992)* — Naxos ▲ 8.550213 [DDD]
Duets & Arias from Italian Operas, w. G. Aragall (ten), E. Tumagian (bar) — Naxos ▲ 8.550684 [DDD]
Puccini, G.:Madama Butterfly, w. M. Gauci (sop), N. Boschkowá (mez), A. Michalková (mez), Y. Ramiro (ten), Slovak Phil Chorus [I] — Naxos 2-▲ 8.660015/16 [DDD]
Puccini, G.:Tosca, w. N. Miricioiu (sop), G. Lamberti (ten), S. Carroli (bar), Slovak Phil Chorus [I] — Naxos 2-▲ 8.660001/02 [DDD]
Puccini, G.:Tosca (sels), w. Nelly Miricioiu (sop—Tosca), Giorgio Lamberti (ten—Cavaradossi), Miroslav Dvorsky (ten—Spoletta), Silvano Carroli (bar—Baron Scarpia), Jozef Spaček (bar—Sacristan), Jan Durco (bass—Sciarrone), Stanislav Benačka (bass—Gaoler), Slovak Phil Chorus *(rec Concert Hall of the Slovak Radio, Bratislava, Apr. 7-14, 1990)* — Naxos ▲ 8.553153 [DDD]
Verdi, G.:Rigoletto, w. A. Ferrarini (sop), Y. Ramiro (ten), E. Tumagian (bar), J. Spaček (bar), Slovak Phil Chorus [I] — Naxos 2-▲ 8.660013/14 [DDD]
Verdi, G.:La traviata, w. R. Braga (mez), R. Krause (ten), Y. Ramiro (ten), Slovak Phil Chorus [I] — Naxos 2-▲ 8.660011/12 [DDD]
Verdi, G.:La traviata (sels), w. Monika Krause (sop), Ivica Neshybová (sop), Rannveig Braga (mez), Yordy Ramiro (ten), Gerog Tichy (bar), Ladislav Neshyba (bass), Jozef Spaček (bass), Jan Rozehnal (cnd), Slovak Phil Chorus—Prelude act I; Libiam ne'lieti calici; Un dì, felice; È strano! Ah, fors'e lui; Follie!...sempre libera; Lunge da lei...de'miei bollenti spiriti; O Mio rimorosol; Pura si come un angelo...Dite alla giovine; Dammi tu forza; Di Provenza il mar; Noi siamo zingarelle; Prelude act III; Teneste la promessa...Addio del passato; Signora! Che t'accade?; Ah, Violetta! *(rec Bratislava Concert Hall, Dec 1990)* — Naxos ▲ 8.553041 [DDD]
L. Rajter (cnd)
Zemlinsky, A. von:Das gläserne Herz — Marco Polo ▲ 8.223166
Zemlinsky, A. von:Sym 1 — Marco Polo ▲ 8.223166
K. Schermerhorn (cnd)
Sibelius, J.:4 Legends from the Kalevalá—Swan of Tuonela & Return of Lemminkäinen — Naxos ▲ 8.550103 [DDD]
G. Schmalfuss (cnd)
Clarinet & Orchestra, w. Dieter Klöcker (cl), Micheal Heitzler (cl) *(rec Jan. 1990)* — Marco Polo ▲ 8.223431 [DDD]
L. Slovák (cnd)
Shostakovich, D.:Sym 1 *(rec Nov. 20-25, 1985)* — Naxos ▲ 8.550623 [DDD]
Shostakovich, D.:Sym 2, w. Slovak Phil Chorus *(rec Jan. 10, 1990)* — Naxos ▲ 8.550624 [DDD]
Shostakovich, D.:Sym 3, w. Slovak Phil Chorus *(rec Nov. 20-26, 1990)* — Naxos ▲ 8.550623 [DDD]
Shostakovich, D.:Sym 4 *(rec May 23-June 1, 1988)* — Naxos ▲ 8.550625 [DDD]
Shostakovich, D.:Sym 5 *(rec Feb. 12-18, 1987)* — Naxos ▲ 8.550632 [DDD]
Shostakovich, D.:Sym 6 *(rec Dec. 3-12, 1988)* — Naxos ▲ 8.550626 [DDD]
Shostakovich, D.:Sym 7 *(rec Jan. 1-Feb. 5, 1989)* — Naxos ▲ 8.550627 [DDD]
Shostakovich, D.:Sym 8 *(rec Dec. 2-12, 1988)* — Naxos ▲ 8.550628 [DDD]
Shostakovich, D.:Sym 9 *(rec Jan. 7-11, 1988)* — Naxos ▲ 8.550632 [DDD]
Shostakovich, D.:Sym 10 *(rec June 20-26, 1989)* — Naxos ▲ 8.550633 [DDD]
Shostakovich, D.:Sym 11 *(rec Apr. 25-May 4, 1988)* — Naxos ▲ 8.550629 [DDD]
Shostakovich, D.:Sym 12 *(rec Feb. 5-12, 1989)* — Naxos ▲ 8.550626 [DDD]
Shostakovich, D.:Sym 13, w. P. Mikuláš (bass), Slovak Phil Chorus — Naxos ▲ 8.550630 [DDD]
Shostakovich, D.:Sym 14, w. M. Hajóssyová (sop), P. Mikuláš (bass) *(rec Feb. 22-Mar. 4, 1991)* — Naxos ▲ 8.550631 [ADD]
Shostakovich, D.:Sym 15 *(rec Feb. 5-12, 1989)* — Naxos ▲ 8.550624 [DDD]
R. Stankovsky (cnd)
Cui, C.:Le Flibustier (prelude) *(rec Jan. 20-23, 1993)* — Marco Polo ▲ 8.223400 [DDD]
Cui, C.:Suite 2 *(rec Jan. 20-23, 1993)* — Marco Polo ▲ 8.223400 [DDD]
Cui, C.:Suite 4 *(rec Jan. 20-23, 1993)* — Marco Polo ▲ 8.223400 [DDD]
Miaskovsky, N.:Silence — Marco Polo ▲ 8.223302
Miaskovsky, N.:Sym 6, w. Slovak Opera Chorus—4th movt. [L] — Marco Polo ▲ 8.223301 [DDD]
Miaskovsky, N.:Sym 12 — Marco Polo ▲ 8.223302
P. Steinberg (cnd)
Berlioz, H.:Sym fantastique — Naxos ▲ 8.550093 [DDD]
E. Tomlinson (cnd)
Tomlinson, E.:Music of, w. Slovak RSO Bratislava—Second Suite of English Folk Dances (1977); Silverthorn Suite; Cinderella Waltz; English Overture; Fairy Coach; Gaelic Lullaby; Hornpipe; Kielder Water; Little Serenade; Nautical Interlude; Nocturne; Sweet & Dainty — Marco Polo (British Light Music) ▲ 8.223413 [DDD]
A. Walter (cnd)
Strauss (II), Joh.:Orchestral Music—Alexander-Quadrille, Op. 33; Die Jovialen (waltz), Op. 34; Scherz-Polka, Op. 72; La Viennoise (polka mazur), Op. 144; Bijouterie-Quadrille, Op. 169; Libellen-Walzer, Op. 180; Bijoux-Polka, Op. 242; Wahlstimmen (waltz), Op. 250; Lob der Frauen (polka mazur), Op. 315; Jubelfest-Marsch, Op. 396; Kaiser-Jubiläum (waltz), Op. 434 — Marco Polo ▲ 8.223215 [DDD]
J. Wildner (cnd)
Strauss (II), Joh.:Choral Music, w. Vienna Men's Choral Association—An der schönen, blauen Donau Waltz, Op. 314; Aufs Korn March, Op. 478; Bei uns z'Haus Waltz, Op. 361; Burschenwanderung Polka, Op. 389; Gross Wien Waltz, Op. 440; Hoch Osterreich! March, Op. 371; Myrthenblüten Waltz, Op. 395; Neu Wien Waltz, Op. 342; 's gibt nur a Kaiserstadt Polka, Op. 291; Sängerlust Polka, Op. 328; Wein, Weib und Gesang Waltz, Op. 333 [G] — Marco Polo ▲ 8.223250 [DDD]
Strauss (II), Joh.:Die Fledermaus (sels), w. Ariane Calix (sop—Ida), Gabriele Fontana (sop—Rosalinde), Brigitte Karwautz (sop—Adele), Rohangiz Yachmi-Caucig (cta—Orlofsky), John Dickie (ten—Eisenstein), Josef Hopferwieser (ten—Alfred), Erich Wessner (ten—Dr. Blind), Andrea Martin (bar—Falke), Alfred Werner (bar—Frank), Bratislava City Chorus—Ov.; [Act I] Täubchen, das entflattert ist...; Ach, ich darf nicht hin zu dir; Nein, mit solchen Advokaten; Komm mit mir zum Souper; So muss allein ich bleiben; Trinke, Liebchen, trinke schnell; [Act II] Ein Souper heut' uns winkt; Ich lade gern mir Gäste ein; Mein Herr Marquis, ein Mann wie Sie; Dieser Anstand, so manierlich; Klänge der Heimat; Im Feuerstrom der Reben; Marianka komm und tanz me hier; [Act III] Entr'acte; Spiel' ich die Unschuld vom Lande; O Fledermaus, o Fledermaus *(rec Slovak Radio Concert Hall, Bratislava)* — Naxos ▲ 8.553171 [DDD]

Czech–Slovak RSO Prague
E. Fischer (cnd)
Fennelly, B.:In Wildness Is the Preservation of the World *(rec 1977)* — New World ▲ 80448-2
D. Johanos (cnd)
Glière, R.:Sym 3, "Il'ya Muromets" *(rec Feb. 11-14, 1991)* — Naxos ▲ 8.550858 [DDD]

Czech–Slovak RSO Prague (cont.)
R. Stankovsky (cnd)
Miaskovsky, N.:Sym 8 — Marco Polo ▲ 8.223297

Czech–Slovak Republic SO
O. Dohnányi (cnd)
Liszt, F.:Con 1 Pno, w. Joseph Banowetz (pno) *(rec Concert Hall, Czechoslovak Radio, Bratislava, Nov. 1988)* — Naxos ▲ 8.553267 [DDD]

Czech–Slovak State PO
S. Gunzenhauser (cnd)
Dvořák, A.:Sym 2 *(rec 5/90)* — Naxos ▲ 8.550267 [DDD]
A. Mogrelia (cnd)
Tchaikovsky, P.:Sleeping Beauty (suite) — Naxos 3-▲ 8.550490/92 [DDD]
U. Schneider (cnd)
Raff, J.:Sym 8 — Marco Polo ▲ 8.223362 [DDD]
Raff, J.:Sym 9 — Marco Polo ▲ 8.223362 [DDD]
R. Seifried (cnd)
Beethoven, L. van:Con 5 Pno, "Emperor", w. E. Chuprik (pno) — Lydian ▲ LYD 18122
Tchaikovsky, P.:Con 1 Pno, w. E. Chuprik (pno) — Lydian ▲ LYD 18122
R. Stankovsky (cnd)
Chopin, F.:Andante Spianato & Grande Polonaise, w. I. Biret (pno) — Naxos ▲ 8.550368 [DDD]
Chopin, F.:Con 1 Pno, w. I. Biret (pno) — Naxos ▲ 8.550368 [DDD]
Chopin, F.:Con 2 Pno, w. I. Biret (pno) *(rec 11/90 & 6/91)* — Naxos ▲ 8.550369 [DDD]
Chopin, F.:Krakowiak, w. I. Biret (pno) *(rec 11/90 & 6/91)* — Naxos ▲ 8.550369 [DDD]
Chopin, F.:Vars on Mozart's *La ci darem la mano*, w. I. Biret (pno) *(rec 11/90 & 6/91)* — Naxos ▲ 8.550369 [DDD]
Rubinstein, A.:Con 3 Pno, w. J. Banowetz (pno) — Marco Polo ▲ 8.223382 [DDD]
Rubinstein, A.:Con 4 Pno, w. J. Banowetz (pno) — Marco Polo ▲ 8.223382 [DDD]
Smetana, B.:Orchestral Music—selections from *The Brandenburgers in Bohemia, Dalibor, Libuše, The Two Widows, The Kiss, The Secret, The Devil's Wall, Olrich & Bózena* — Marco Polo ▲ 8.223326
A. Walter (cnd)
Furtwängler, W.:Sym 1 — Marco Polo ▲ 8.223295
Offenbach, J.:Ovs—La belle Hélène; Orpheus in the Underworld — Naxos ▲ 8.550468 [DDD]
Rubinstein, A.:Con 1 Pno, w. J. Banowetz (pno) *(rec March 3-7, 1992)* — Marco Polo ▲ 8.223456 [DDD]
Rubinstein, A.:Con 2 Pno, w. J. Banowetz (pno) *(rec March 3-7, 1992)* — Marco Polo ▲ 8.223456 [DDD]
Schillings, M. von:Con Vn, w. E. Rózsa (vn) — Marco Polo ▲ 8.223324 [DDD]
Schillings, M. von:Das Erntefest — Marco Polo ▲ 8.223324 [DDD]
Schillings, M. von:Symphonic Prologue to King Oedipus by Sophocles — Marco Polo ▲ 8.223324 [DDD]
Spohr, L.:Sym 1 — Marco Polo ▲ 8.223363 [DDD]
Spohr, L.:Sym 3 *(rec Nov 12-16, 1991)* — Marco Polo ▲ 8.223439 [DDD]
Spohr, L.:Sym 5 — Marco Polo ▲ 8.223363 [DDD]
Spohr, L.:Sym 6 *(rec Nov 12-16, 1991)* — Marco Polo ▲ 8.223439 [DDD]
Spohr, L.:Sym 9 *(rec Nov 12-16, 1991)* — Marco Polo ▲ 8.223439 [DDD]
Strauss (II), Joh.:Orchestral Music—Freiwillige vor! (march); Einheitsklänge (waltz); Spleen (polka-mazurka), Op. 197; Telegraphische Depeschen (waltz), Op. 195; Concordia (polka-mazurka), Op. 206; Tête-à-tête (quadrille), Op. 109; Lebenswecker (waltz), Op. 232; Unter Donner und Blitz (polka), Op. 324; Illustrationen (waltz), Op. 331; Pappacoda (French polka), Op. 412; Frisch ins Feld! (march), Op. 398 *(rec Apr. 29-May 6, 1991)* — Marco Polo ▲ 8.223228 [DDD]
Strauss (II), Joh.:Orchestral Music—Fest-Marsch, Op. 49; Luisen Sympathie-Klänge (waltz), Op. 81; Alexandrinen-Polka, Op. 198; Paroxysmen (waltz), Op. 189; Kammerball-Polka, Op. 230; Attaque-Quadrille, Op. 76; Reiseabenteuer (waltz), Op. 227; Par force! (polka), Op. 38; Kriegsabenteuer (polka), Op. 419; Perpetuum mobile-Musikalischer Scherz, Op. 257; Klug Gretelein (waltz), Op. 462 *(rec Jan. 7-11, 1991)* — Marco Polo ▲ 8.223230 [DDD]
Strauss (II), Joh.:Orchestral Music—Brünner-Nationalgarde-Marsch, Op. 58; Orakel-Sprüche (waltz), Op. 90; Une bagatelle (polka-mazurka), Op. 187; Volkssänger (waltz), Op. 119; Waldmeister-Quadrille, Op. 468; Deutsche Walzer, Op. 220; Secunden Polka française, Op. 258; Tausend und eine Nacht (waltz), Op. 346; Die Bajadere (polka), Op. 351; Schatz-Walzer, Op. 418; Der lustige Krieg (march), Op. 397 *(rec Nov. 2-7, 1990)* — Marco Polo ▲ 8.223229 [DDD]
Strauss (II), Joh.:Orchestral Music—Dorfgeschichten (Walzer im Ländlerstyle), Op. 47; Selaadon-Quadrille, Op. 48; Electro-Magnetische Polka, Op. 110; Novellen (waltz), Op. 146; tudententlust (waltz), Op. 285; Episode (polka française), Op. 296; Le Premier Jour de Bonheur, Opéra de D.F.E. Auber (quadrille), Op. 327; Hoch Österreich! Marsch, Op. 371; Rosen aus dem Süden (waltz), Op. 388; Burschenwanderung (polka française), Op. 389; Seid Umschlungern, Millionen (waltz), Op. 443 — Marco Polo ▲ 8.223219 [DDD]
Strauss (II), Joh.:Orchestral Music—Aurora-Ball-Tänze, Op. 87; Kaiser-Jäger-Marsch, Op. 93; Erhöhte Pulse (waltz), Op. 175; Herzel-Polka, Op. 188; Dinorah-Quadrille (after themes from Meyerbeer's opera *Die Wallfahrt nach Ploërmel*), Op. 224; Schwärmereien (concert waltz), Op. 253; Flugschriften (waltz), Op. 300; Ein Herz, ein Sinn (polka-mazurka), Op. 323; Fata Morgana (polka-mazurka), Op. 330; Slovianka-Qadrille (after Russian melodies), Op. 338; Auf zum Tanze! (schnell polka), Op. 436; Mrchen aus dem Orient (waltz), Op. 444 — Marco Polo ▲ 8.223220 [DDD]
Strauss (II), Joh.:Ovs—Die Fledermaus; Eine Nacht in Venedig; Der Zigeunerbaron — Naxos ▲ 8.550468 [DDD]
Suppé, F. von:Ovs—Fair Galatea; Light Cavalry; Morning, Noon & Night in Vienna — Naxos ▲ 8.550468 [DDD]
Waldteufel, E.:Waltzes, Polkas & Galops—Zig-zag Polka, Op. 248; Les Fleurs (waltz), Op. 190; Par-ci, par-là (polka), Op. 239; Solitude (waltz), Op. 174; Fleurs et baisers (waltz); Toujours fidèle (waltz), Op. 169; L'Esprit français (polka), Op. 182; Toujours ou jamais (waltz), Op. 156; Hébé (waltz), Op. 228 *(rec House of Arts in Košice, Dec 13, 1991)* — Marco Polo ▲ 8.223450 [DDD]
J. Wildner (cnd)
Strauss (II), Joh.:Orchestral Music—Johannis-Käferin (waltz), Op. 82; Ottinger Reiter-Marsch, Op. 83; Sans-Souci (polka), Op. 178; Cycloiden (waltz), Op. 207; Orpheus-Quadrille, Op. 236; Patronessen (polka française), Op. 286; Tändelei (polka-mazurka), Op. 310; Figaro Polka, Op. 320; Geschichten aus dem Wienerwald (waltz), Op. 325; Rotunde-Quadrille, Op. 360 — Marco Polo ▲ 8.223221 [DDD]
Strauss (II), Joh.:Orchestral Music—Aus der Heimat, Op. 347; Carnevals-Spektakel-Quadrille, Op. 152; Controversen Waltz, Op. 191; Immer heiterer, Op. 235; L'Inconnue, Op. 182; Klipp-Klapp Galopp, Op. 466; Maxing-Tänze, Op. 79; Nachtigall Polka, Op. 222; Ninetta Waltz, Op. 445; Persischer Marsch, Op. 289 — Marco Polo ▲ 8.223222 [DDD]
Strauss (II), Joh.:Orchestral Music—Bonbon Polka, Op. 213; Explosions Polka, Op. 43; Frauen-Käferln Waltz, Op. 99; Grossfürsten March, Op. 107; Ins Zentrum! Waltz, Op. 387; Krönungslieder Waltz, Op. 184; Künstler Quadrille, Op. 201; Lustger Rath Polka, Op. 350; Mutig voran! Polka, Op. 432; Le Papillon Polka-Mazurka, Op. 174; Promenade Quadrille, Op. 98; Spiralen Waltz, Op. 209 — Marco Polo ▲ 8.223225 [DDD]
Weber, C.M. von:Con 1 Cl, w. E. Ottensamer (cl) *(rec 2/90)* — Naxos ▲ 8.550378 [DDD]
Weber, C.M. von:Con 2 Cl, w. E. Ottensamer (cl) *(rec 2/90)* — Naxos ▲ 8.550378 [DDD]
W.-S. Yip (cnd)
Tcherepnin, A.:Romantic Ov — Marco Polo ▲ 8.223380 [DDD]
Tcherepnin, A.:Russian Dances — Marco Polo ▲ 8.223380 [DDD]
Tcherepnin, A.:Suite Orch — Marco Polo ▲ 8.223380 [DDD]
Tcherepnin, A.:Sym 4 — Marco Polo ▲ 8.223380 [DDD]

Czech–Slovak State Radio PO
Lenárd, Walter (cnd)
Strauss (II), Joh.:Music of, w. Czech-Slovak RSO, Polish State PO—9 sels — Naxos ▲ 8.550339 [DDD]
Strauss (II), Joh.:Music of, w. Czech-Slovak RSO—9 sels — Naxos ▲ 8.550340 [DDD]
Strauss (II), Joh.:Music of, w. Czech-Slovak RSO, Polish State PO—9 sels. — Naxos ▲ 8.550337 [DDD]

Czech–Slovak State SO
A. Walter (cnd)
Furtwängler, W.:Con Pno, w. D. Lively (pno) — Marco Polo ▲ 8.223333

ORCH. & ENS.

Da Capo Chamber Players
Carter, E.:Canon for 4 GM ▲ 2020CD
Carter, E.:Enchanted Preludes GM ▲ 2020CD
Carter, E.:Esprit rude/esprit doux GM ▲ 2020CD
Carter, E.:Pastoral E Hn GM ▲ 2020CD
Perle, G.:Lyric Piece Vc GM ▲ 2020CD
Perle, G.:Son a 4 Fl GM ▲ 2020CD
Perle, G.:Son Vc GM ▲ 2020CD
Ran, S.:Con da Camera II Bridge ▲ BCD 9052 [DDD]
Ran, S.:East Wind Bridge ▲ BCD 9052 [DDD]
Ran, S.:Inscriptions Bridge ▲ BCD 9052 [DDD]
Ran, S.:Mirage Bridge ▲ BCD 9052 [DDD]
Ran, S.:Private Game Bridge ▲ BCD 9052 [DDD]
Ran, S.:To an Actor Bridge ▲ BCD 9052 [DDD]
Schoenberg, A.:Pierrot lunaire, w. L. Shelton (sop)—2 complete performances:in German & in Andrew Porter's English translation Bridge ▲ BCD 9032 [DDD]
Tower, J.:Music of—music for fl, cl, vn, vc, pno & perc ensemble:Amazon (1977); Breakfast Rhythms (1974); Noon Dance (1982); Petroushkates (1980) CRI ▲ CD 582 [DDD]

O. Knussen (cnd)
Schoenberg, A.:Herzgewächse, w. L. Shelton (sop) Bridge ▲ BCD 9032 [DDD]

Da Sonar Ensemble [Chantal Rémillard, Christine Moran, Margaret Little, Susie Napper, Sylvain Bergeron, Réjean Poirier]
A Tre Violini *(rec Feb. 1993)* Ummus ▲ UMM 304

La Dada [Han Tol (rcr), D. Mings (baroque bn), P. Ayrton (hpd)]
Italian Music for Virtuosi *(rec Mar. 1993)* Globe ▲ GLO 5099 [DDD]

Daedalus Ensemble
El Cancionero de la Catedral de Segovia Accent ▲ 9176 [DDD]
Il Cantar Moderno Accent ▲ 9068 [DDD]
O vergin santa non m'abbandonare *(rec Sept. 1992)* Accent ▲ 9289 [DDD]

Dall'Arco CO
Vivaldi, A.:Music of, w. Capella Istropolitana, Concentus Hungaricus, Budapest Strings—selections from The Four Seasons; Flautino Con. in C; Flute Con. in F; Flute Con. in a, RV.108; Con. in B♭ for 2 Trumpets; Concerti, Op. 3/4, 8, 10 & 11; Oboe Con., Op. 8/9; Violin Con., Op. 8/5 & 12; Lute Con. in D; Il Gardellino Naxos ▲ 8.551105 [DDD]

J. M. Händler (cnd)
Bach, C.P.E.:Con Vc, H.432, w. J. Berger (vc) ebs ▲ ebs 6069 [DDD]
Bach, C.P.E.:Con Vc, H.436, w. J. Berger (vc) ebs ▲ ebs 6069 [DDD]
Bach, C.P.E.:Con Vc, H.439, w. J. Berger (vc) ebs ▲ ebs 6069 [DDD]
Wagenseil, G.C.:Con in C Vc, w. Reiner Hocmuth (vc) Thorofon ▲ CTH 2068 [DDD]
Wagenseil, G.C.:Con in A Vc, w. Reiner Hocmuth (vc) Thorofon ▲ CTH 2068 [DDD]

I. Parkányi (cnd)
Vivaldi, A.:Cons Diverse Instrs—in D for Lt & Strs, R.93; in B♭ for Ob, Vn, Strs & Bc, R.548; in d for Vl, Lt, Strs & Bc, R.540; in g for Vn, Strs & Bc, R.317; Con grosso in C, R.558 *(rec Budapest, Dec. 21–30, 1987)* Lydian ▲ 18030 [DDD]
Vivaldi, A.:Cons Fl (misc)—in a, R.108; in F, R.434 [Op. 10/5]; in C for 2 Fls, R.533; in C, R.443; in C, R.444; in a, R.445 *(rec Mafilm Studio, Budapest, Dec. 21–20, 1987)* Lydian ▲ 18031 [DDD]

Dallas Brass Quintet
Brass Bonanza, w. Annapolis Brass Quintet, Berlin Brass Quintet, Metropolitan Brass Quintet, New York Brass Quintet, 1–5 Brass Quintet, St. Louis Brass Quintet Crystal ▲ CD 200 [ADD/DDD]
Hovhaness, A.:Dances Brass Qnt Crystal ▲ CD 200 [ADD]

Dallas CO

R. Neal (cnd)
Beethoven, L. van:Sxt Hns, Op. 81b, w. G. Hustis (hn), D. Battey (hn) Crystal ▲ CD 512
Hertel, J.W.:Con à 6, w. R. Giangiulio (tpt), R. Barr (ob) Crystal ▲ CD 512
Mozart, L.:Con Hn, w. G. Hustis (hn) Crystal ▲ CD 512
Treasures for Horn & Trumpet, w. Gregory Hustis (hn), Richard Giangiulio (tpt) *(rec 11/88)* Crystal ▲ CD 512

Dallas Chamber Players [E. Barr (ob), G. Hustis (hn), S. Sargon (pno)]
Reinecke, C.:Trio Ob Klavier ▲ KCD 11050 [DDD]
Reinecke, C.:Trio Pno, Op. 264 Klavier ▲ KCD 11050 [DDD]
Reinecke, C.:Trio Pno, Op. 274 Klavier ▲ KCD 11050 [DDD]

Dallas Civic Opera Orch

N. Rescigno (cnd)
Delibes, L.:Lakmé, w. M. Spacagna (sop—Ellen), R. Welting (sop—Lakmé), A. Kraus (ten—Gérald), D. Holloway (bar—Frédéric), P. Plishka (bass—Nilakantha) *(rec Nov. 1980)* Ornamenti 2– ▲ FE 108 [ADD]
Donizetti, G.:Lucrezia Borgia, w. L. Gencer (sop), T. Troyanos (mez), J. Carreras (ten), Dallas Civic Opera Chorus *(rec 1973)* Melodram 2–▲ MLO 270109 [ADD]
Verdi, G.:La traviata (sels), w. M. Caballé (sop)—4 arias from Acts 1 & 3 [I] *(rec live 11/13/65)* Melodram 2–▲ MEL 27047 [AAD]

Dallas SO

A. Dorati (cnd)
Bartók, B.:Con 1 Vn, w. Y. Menuhin (vn) RCA Gold Seal ▲ 09026-61395-2
Liszt, F.:Con 1 Pno, w. A. Rubinstein (pno) *(rec 1952)* RCA Gold Seal ▲ 60046–2–RG (m/s) [ADD]

W. Hendl (cnd)
Rózsa, M.:Con Vn, w. J. Heifetz (vn) RCA Gold Seal ▲ 7963–2–RG [ADD]

D. Johanos (cnd)
Copland, A.:Billy the Kid (suite) *(rec 1967)* Vox Box 2–▲ CDX 5035 [ADD]
Copland, A.:Fanfare for the Common Man *(rec 1967)* Vox Box 2–▲ CDX 5035 [ADD]
Copland, A.:Fanfare for the Common Man Analogue Productions ▲ CAPC 004
Copland, A.:Rodeo *(rec 1967)* Vox Box 2–▲ CDX 5035 [ADD]
Copland, A.:Rodeo Analogue Productions ▲ CAPC 004
Ives, C.:Holidays Analogue Productions ▲ CAPC 004
Ives, C.:Holidays *(rec 1967)* Vox Box 2–▲ CDX 5035 [ADD]
Rachmaninoff, S.:Symphonic Dances *(rec 1967)* Vox Box 2–▲ CDX 5035 [ADD]
Rachmaninoff, S.:Symphonic Dances Analogue Productions ▲ CAPC 006
Rachmaninoff, S.:Vocalise [arr. orch.] Analogue Productions ▲ CAPC 006
Rachmaninoff, S.:Vocalise *(rec 1967)* Vox Box 2–▲ CDX 5035 [ADD]
Scriabin, A.:Sym 4 Allegretto ▲ ACD 8170 [ADD] ■ ACS 8170
Scriabin, A.:Sym 5 Allegretto ▲ ACD 8170 [ADD] ■ ACS 8170

A. Litton (cnd)
Gershwin, G.:Porgy & Bess (sels), w. Cynthia Clarey (sop—Serena), Cynthia Haymon (sop—Bess), Damon Evans (ten—Sportin' Life), Gordon Hawkins (bar—Porgy), Andrew Litton (pno), Dallas Sym Chorus—Intro/Jasbo Brown; Summertime; A Woman Is a Sometime Thing; Gone, Gone, Gone; My Man's Gone Now; Leavin' for the Promise' Lan'; Oh I Got Plenty O' Nuttin'; Bess, You Is My Woman Now; Oh, I Can't Sit Down; I Ain't Got No Shame; It Ain't Necessarily So; Shame on All You Sinners; I Loves You, Porgy; Hurricane; There's a Boat Dat's Leavin' Soon for New York; Act 3, Scene 3 Orchestral Intro; Good Mornin', Sistuh; Oh Lawd, I'm on My Way! [concert suite arr A. Litton] *(rec Eugene McDermott Hall, Dallas, May 1995)* Dorian ▲ DOR 90223 [DDD]
Griffes, C.T.:The White Peacock *(rec Eugene McDermott Hall, Morton H. Meyerson Symphony Center, Dallas, TX, May 1995)* Dorian ▲ DOR 90224 [DDD]
Hovhaness, A.:Sym 2 *(rec Eugene McDermott Hall, Morton H. Meyerson Symphony Center, Dallas, TX, May 1995)* Dorian ▲ DOR 90224 [DDD]
Ives, C.:Three Places in New England *(rec Eugene McDermott Hall, Morton H. Meyerson Symphony Center, Dallas, TX, May 1995)* Dorian ▲ DOR 90224 [DDD]
Korngold, E.W.:Con Vn, w. Ulrike-Anima Mathé (vn) *(rec Eugene McDermott Hall, Morton H. Meyerson Sym Center, Dallas, TX, Nov. 1994)* Dorian ▲ DOR 90216 [DDD]

Dallas SO (cont.)

A. Litton (cnd) (cont.)
Korngold, E.W.:Sinfonietta *(rec Eugene McDermott Hall, Morton H. Meyerson Sym Center, Dallas, TX, Nov. 1994)* Dorian ▲ DOR 90216 [DDD]
Liszt, F.:Con 1 Pno, w. André Watts (pno) *(rec Meyerson Symphony Center, Dallas, Texas, July 9–10, 1995)* Telarc ▲ CD 80429 [DDD]
Liszt, F.:Con 2 Pno, w. André Watts (pno) *(rec Meyerson Symphony Center, Dallas, Texas, July 9–10, 1995)* Telarc ▲ CD 80429 [DDD]
Macdowell, E.:Con 2 Pno, w. André Watts (pno) *(rec Meyerson Symphony Center, Dallas, Texas, July 9–10, 1995)* Telarc ▲ CD 80429 [DDD]
Mahler, G.:Sym 5 *(rec live, Sept. 1993)* Dorian ▲ DOR 90193
Piston, W.:The Incredible Flutist (suite) *(rec Eugene McDermott Hall, Morton H. Meyerson Symphony Center, Dallas, TX, May 1995)* Dorian ▲ DOR 90224 [DDD]
Schuman, W.:New England Triptych *(rec Eugene McDermott Hall, Morton H. Meyerson Symphony Center, Dallas, TX, May 1995)* Dorian ▲ DOR 90224 [DDD]
Tchaikovsky, P.:Moscow, w. Svetlana Furdui (mez), Vassily Gerello (bar), Dallas Sym Chorus *(rec McDermott Hall, Meyerson Center, Dallas, TX, Nov 16–18, 1995)* Delos ("Virtual Reality Recording" series) ▲ DE 3196 [DDD]
Tchaikovsky, P.:Ov 1812 *(rec McDermott Hall, Meyerson Center, Dallas, TX, Nov 16–18, 1995)* Delos ("Virtual Reality Recording" series) ▲ DE 3196 [DDD]
Tchaikovsky, P.:Sleeping Beauty (sels)—9 sels [arr Litton] *(rec McDermott Hall, Meyerson Center, Dallas, TX, Nov 16–18, 1995)* Delos ("Virtual Reality Recording" series) ▲ DE 3196 [DDD]
Tchaikovsky, P.:The Voyevoda, Op. 78 *(rec McDermott Hall, Meyerson Center, Dallas, TX, Nov 16–18, 1995)* Delos ("Virtual Reality Recording" series) ▲ DE 3196 [DDD]

E. Mata (cnd)
Albéniz, I.:Iberia Suite Pro Arte ▲ CDS 581 [DDD]
Beethoven, L. van:Ovs *(rec Sept. 1989)* Pro Arte 2–▲ CDD 479 [DDD]
Bernstein, L.:On the Waterfront (sym suite) *(rec 1 & 4/92)* Dorian ▲ DOR 90170 [DDD]
Brahms, J.:Con 1 Pno, w. I. Moravec (pno) Dorian ▲ DOR 90172
Chausson, E.:Sym in B♭ *(rec Jan. 1993)* Dorian ▲ DOR 90181 [DDD]
Copland, A.:Billy the Kid (suite) *(rec 1 & 4/92)* Dorian ▲ DOR 90170 [DDD]
Copland, A.:Danzón Cubano EMI Classics (American Composer Series) ▲ CDM 64303
Copland, A.:El salón México EMI Classics (American Composer Series) ▲ CDM 64303
Copland, A.:Sym 3 EMI Classics (American Composer Series) ▲ CDM 64304
Copland, A.:Sym 3—Finale EMI Classics ▲ CDC 54282
Debussy, C.:Ibéria Telarc ▲ CD 80055 [DDD]
Dukas, P.:L'Apprenti sorcier RCA Victrola ▲ 7727–2 RV [DDD] ■ 7727–4–RV (CrO2)
Enescu, G.:Romanian Rhap 1 RCA Victrola ▲ 7727–2–RV [DDD] ■ 7727–4–RV (CrO2)
Falla, M. de:El sombrero de tres picos (sels), w. L. Ambriz (sop) Pro Arte ▲ CDS 581 [DDD]
Gershwin, G.:An American in Paris RCA Victrola ▲ 7726–2–RV [DDD] ■ 7726–4–RV (CrO2)
Gershwin, G.:Cuban Ov RCA Victrola ▲ 7726–2–RV [DDD] ■ 7726–4–RV (CrO2)
Gershwin, G.:Porgy & Bess (symphonic picture) RCA Victrola ▲ 7726–2–RV [DDD] ■ 7726–4–RV (CrO2)
Grieg, E.:Symphonic Dances *(rec 9/89)* Pro Arte ▲ CDD 477 [DDD]
Harris, R.:Sym 3 *(rec 1 & 4/92)* Dorian ▲ DOR 90170 [DDD]
Holst, G.:The Planets Pro Arte ▲ CDD 542 [DDD]
Ibert, J.:Divert Orch *(rec Jan. 1993)* Dorian ▲ DOR 90181 [DDD]
Ibert, J.:Escales *(rec Jan. 1993)* Dorian ▲ DOR 90181 [DDD]
Jongen, J.:Symphonie Concertante, w. J. Guillou (org) *(rec Jan. 1994)* Dorian ▲ DOR 90200 [DDD]
Kodály, Z.:Háry János (suite) Pro Arte ▲ CDD 403 [DDD]
Mahler, G.:Sym 2, w. S. McNair (sop), J. van Nes (cta), Dallas Sym Chorus [G] *(rec 9/89)* Pro Arte 2–▲ CDD 479 [DDD]
Mussorgsky, M.:Night RCA Victrola ▲ 7727–2–RV [DDD] ■ 7727–4–RV
Mussorgsky, M.:Pictures at an Exhibition RCA Victrola ▲ 7729–2–RV [DDD] ■ 7729–4–RV
Prokofiev, S.:Alexander Nevsky, w. M. Paunova (cta), Dallas Sym Chorus *(rec 1992)* Dorian ▲ DOR 90169 [DDD]
Prokofiev, S.:Lt Kijé Suite Pro Arte ▲ CDD 403 [DDD]
Prokofiev, S.:Scythian Suite *(rec 1991)* Dorian ▲ DOR 90156 [DDD]
Rachmaninoff, S.:Con 2 Pno, w. V. Viardo (pno) Pro Arte ▲ CDD 442
Rachmaninoff, S.:Symphonic Dances *(rec 10/88)* Pro Arte ▲ CDD 477 [DDD]
Ravel, M.:Alborada del gracioso RCA Silver Seal ▲ 60485–2–RV [DDD] ■ 60485–4–RV (CrO2)
Ravel, M.:Boléro RCA Silver Seal ▲ 60485–2–RV [DDD] ■ 60485–4–RV (CrO2)
Ravel, M.:Rapsodie espagnole RCA Silver Seal ▲ 60485–2–RV [DDD] ■ 60485–4–RV (CrO2)
Ravel, M.:Le Tombeau de Couperin RCA Silver Seal ▲ 60485–2–RV [DDD] ■ 60485–4–RV (CrO2)
Ravel, M.:La Valse RCA Silver Seal ▲ 60485–2–RV [DDD] ■ 60485–4–RV (CrO2)
Ravel, M.:La Valse RCA Victrola ▲ 7729–2–RV [DDD] ■ 7729–4–RV3 (CrO2)
Ravel, M.:Valses nobles et sentimentales RCA Victrola ▲ 7729–2–RV [DDD] ■ 7729–4–RV3 (CrO2)
Respighi, O.:Brazilian Impressions Dorian ▲ DOR 90182 [DDD]
Respighi, O.:The Pines of Rome Dorian ▲ DOR 90182 [DDD]
Rimsky-Korsakov, N.:Capriccio espagnol Telarc ▲ CD 80055 [DDD]
Saint-Saëns, C.:Sym 3, w. J. Guillou (org) *(rec Jan. 1994)* Dorian ▲ DOR 90200 [DDD]
Schumann, R.:Con Pno, w. I. Moravec (pno) Dorian ▲ DOR 90172
Shostakovich, D.:Sym 7 Dorian ▲ DOR 90161 [DDD]
Shostakovich, D.:Sym 9 *(rec 1992)* Dorian ▲ DOR 90169 [DDD]
Sibelius, J.:Sym 2 Pro Arte ▲ CDD 320 [DDD]
Strauss, R.:Till Eulenspiegels lustige Streiche Pro Arte ▲ CDD 403 [DDD]
Stravinsky, I.:Divert Orch Pro Arte ▲ CDS 596 [DDD]
Stravinsky, I.:Fireworks Pro Arte ▲ CDS 587 [DDD]
Stravinsky, I.:Pétrouchka Pro Arte ▲ CDS 596 [DDD]
Stravinsky, I.:Le Sacre du printemps Orch *(rec 1991)* Dorian ▲ DOR 90156 [DDD]
Tchaikovsky, P.:Capriccio italien RCA Victrola ▲ 7727–2–RV [DDD] ■ 7727–4–RV (CrO2)
Tchaikovsky, P.:Festival Coronation March Pro Arte ▲ CDS 539 [DDD]
Tchaikovsky, P.:Ov 1812 Pro Arte ▲ CDS 539 [DDD]
Tchaikovsky, P.:Romeo & Juliet Pro Arte ▲ CDS 539 [DDD]
Turina, J.:Danzas fantásticas—No. 3, "Orgia" Telarc ▲ CD 80055 [DDD]

N. Rescigno (cnd)
Cherubini, L.:Médée, w. M. Callas (sop), T. Berganza (mez), J. Vickers (ten), N. Zaccaria (bass) *(rec live, Dallas Civic Opera, State Fair Music Hall 11/6/58)* Melodram 2–▲ MEL 26016

Dallas SO Trumpet Section
Linek, J.:Intradas, w. G. Hustis (hn), D. Battey (hn), D. Howard (timp) Crystal ▲ CD234
Music for Ceremony & Celebration, w. Richard Giangiulio (tpt), Paul Riedo (org) Crystal ▲ CD234

Dallas Tryptych Players [Deborah Baron (fl), Thomas Demer (va), Susan Dederich-Pejovich (hp)]
Beethoven, L. van:Serenade Fl, Op. 25 *(rec Church of Transfiguration, Dallas, TX)* Klavier ▲ KCD 11055 [DDD]
Mathias, W.:Zodiac Trio *(rec Church of Transfiguration, Dallas, TX)* Klavier ▲ KCD 11055 [DDD]
Ravel, M.:Sonatine en Trio *(rec Church of Transfiguration, Dallas, TX)* Klavier ▲ KCD 11055 [DDD]
Salzedo, C.:Sonatine en Trio *(rec Church of Transfiguration, Dallas, TX)* Klavier ▲ KCD 11055 [DDD]

Dallas Wind Sym

H. Dunn (cnd)
The Brass & the Band, w. Chicago Chamber Brass Crystal ▲ CD 431 [DDD] ■ C 431 (D)
Fiestal Reference ▲ RR 38CD [DDD]
Gould, M.:Santa Fe Saga Reference ▲ RR 38CD [DDD]
Holst, G.:Hammersmith Reference ▲ RR 39CD [DDD]
Holst, G.:A Moorside Suite Reference ▲ RR 39CD [DDD]
Holst, G.:Suites Band Reference ▲ RR 39CD [DDD]
Nixon, R.:Fiesta del Pacifico Reference ▲ RR 38CD [DDD]
Perkins, F.:Fandango Reference ▲ RR 38CD [DDD]
Reed, H.O.:La Fiesta Mexicana Reference ▲ RR 38CD [DDD]
Williams, C.:Symphonic Dance 3 Reference ▲ RR 38CD [DDD]

▲ = CD ♦ = Enhanced CD Δ = MD ■ = Cassette Tape □ = DCC

Dallas Wind Sym (cont.)
F. Fennell (cnd)
Albéniz, I.:Iberia Suite—Feast Day in Seville [arr. for winds Lucien Cailliet] *(rec June 18–19, 1992)* Reference ▲ RR 52CD [DDD]
Dello Joio, N.:Variants on a Medieval Tune *(rec June 18–19, 1992)* Reference ▲ RR 52CD [DDD]
Fennell Favorites! Reference ▲ RR 43CD [DDD]
Giannini, V.:Sym 3 *(rec June 18–19, 1992)* Reference ▲ RR 52CD [DDD]
Grieg, E.:Funeral March in Memory of Rikard Nordraak *(rec June 18–19, 1992)* Reference ▲ RR 52CD [DDD]
Nelhybel, V.:Trittico *(rec June 18–19, 1992)* Reference ▲ RR 52CD [DDD]
Pomp & Pipes, w. Riedo, Paul (org) *(rec July 26–27, 1993)* Reference ▲ RR 58 [DDD]
J. Junkin (cnd)
Arnold, M.:Music of—4 Scottish Dances, Op. 59; Overseas, Op. 70; Little Suite No. 1, Op. 80; Tam O'Shanter, Op. 51; Water Music, Op. 82; The Padstow Lifeboat, Op. 94; Little Suite No. 2, Op. 93; Fanfare for Louis; English Dances [Book 1], Op. 27; H.R.H. The Duke of Cambridge, Op. 60 *(rec Meyerson Symphony Center, Dallas, TX, June 17–18, 1995)* Reference ▲ RR 66 [DDD]
T. Seelig (cnd)
Bernstein, L.:Candide (sels), w. Turtle Creek Chorale—Make Our Garden Grow *(rec June 20–21, 1992)* Reference ▲ RR 49
Copland, A.:Old American Songs (set 1), w. Turtle Creek Chorale—Simple Gifts; The Promise of Living *(rec June 20–21, 1992)* Reference ▲ RR 49
Copland, A.:The Tender Land (sels), w. Turtle Creek Chorale—Simple Gifts; The Promise of Living *(rec June 20–21, 1992)* Reference ▲ RR 49
Hanson, H.:Song of Democracy, w. Turtle Creek Chorale *(rec June 20–21, 1992)* Reference ▲ RR 49
Nelson, R.:Behold Man, w. Turtle Creek Chorale *(rec June 20–21, 1992)* Reference ▲ RR 49
Thompson, R.:Choral Music, w. Turtle Creek Chorale—Pasture & Stopping by Woods on a Snowy Evening (from *Frostiana*); Allelujah *(rec June 20–21, 1992)* Reference ▲ RR 49
Thompson, R.:The Testament of Freedom, w. Turtle Creek Chorale *(rec June 20–21, 1992)* Reference ▲ RR 49

Dana Brass Quintet
Calvert, M.:Suite from the Monteregian Hills Dana Recording Project ▲ DRP 6 [DDD]
Etler, A.:Qnt Brass Dana Recording Project ▲ DRP 6 [DDD]
Hutchison, W.:Apocalypse V Dana Recording Project ▲ DRP 6 [DDD]
Koetsier, J.:Qnt Brass Dana Recording Project ▲ DRP 6 [DDD]
Nichols, G.:Nightmare Dana Recording Project ▲ DRP 6 [DDD]

Danceries
Satie, E.:Songs—Chanson médiévale; La divade "Empire"; Je te veux; Tendrement; La belle excentrique; Trois mélodies sans paroles; Gymnopédies; Ludions; Trois petites pièces montées; Chanson médiévale [F] Denon ▲ CO 1289 [DDD]

Danel String Quartet [Marc Danel (vn), Gilles Millet (vn), Juliette Danel (va), Guy Danel (vc)]
de Clerck, P.:Pianokwintet, w. Jean-Marie Bardèche (pno) *(rec Ravenstein Hall, May & June 1994)* Megadisc ▲ 7866
de Clerck, P.:Sferen *(rec Ravenstein Hall, May & June 1994)* Megadisc ▲ 7866
de Clerck, P.:A Stringtrio *(rec Ravenstein Hall, May & June 1994)* Megadisc ▲ 7866
Goeyvaerts, K.:For Str Qt Megadisc ▲ MDC 7853
Goeyvaerts, K.:The Seven Seals Megadisc ▲ MDC 7853

Daniel String Quartet [B. Shamir (vn), M. Furman (vn), I. Shimon (va), Z. Maschkowski (vc)]
Franck, C.:Qnt Pno, w. D. Wayenberg (pno) *(rec Rotterdam, May 28, 1985)* Erasmus ▲ WHV 001 [DDD]
Gounod, C.:Qt 3 Strs Arcobaleno ▲ SBCD 7800
Lalo, E.:Qt Strs, Op. 45 Arcobaleno ▲ SBCD 7800
Saint-Saëns, C.:Carnival of the Animals, w. D. Wayenberg (vn), H. Oudenaarden (vn), J. Hagen (fl), H. de Fraaf (cl), H. Krul (db), W. Vos (xyl), M. Dekkers (acc) *(rec Rotterdam, May 28, 1985)* Erasmus ▲ WHV 001 [DDD]
Thomas, A.:Qt Strs Arcobaleno ▲ SBCD 7800

Danish Accordion Ensemble
Werner, S.E.:Tie-Break *(rec Studio 39, Copenhagen, Aug. 1986)* Marco Polo ("dacapo" series) ▲ 8.224006 [DDD]

Danish Chamber Players
Martinů, B.:Chamber Music 1 Kontrapunkt ▲ KPT 32227
Martinů, B.:Nonet Ww, Strs & Db Kontrapunkt ▲ KPT 32227
Martinů, B.:La Revue de Cuisine Kontrapunkt ▲ KPT 32227
Martinů, B.:Les Rondes Kontrapunkt ▲ KPT 32227
S. A. Johansen (cnd)
Buck, O.:Landscapes (4) Marco Polo/Dacapo ▲ 8.224034 [DDD]

Danish Concert Band
Band Solos, w. Royal Danish Brass Rondo Grammofon ▲ RCD 8324
Concert Band Music *(rec 1990)* Rondo Grammofon ▲ RCD 8331 [DDD]
J.M. Jensen (cnd)
Bernstein, L.:Divert *(rec Brøndby Strand Church, 1994)* Rondo Grammofon ▲ RCD 8346
Horovitz, J.:Concertino Classico, w. Ole Andersen (tpt), Ketil Christensen (tpt) Rondo Grammofon ▲ RCD 8340
Hyldgaard, S.:Lydian Moods Rondo Grammofon ▲ RCD 8340
Hyldgaard, S.:Maximum Overdrive Rondo Grammofon ▲ RCD 8340
Keller, J.:In the Beginning Rondo Grammofon ▲ RCD 8340
Keller, J.:Silver Wedding March Rondo Grammofon ▲ RCD 8340
Martinussen, L.:Dialogue, w. Ole Andersen (tpt), Ketil Christensen (tpt) Rondo Grammofon ▲ RCD 8340
Meij, J. de:Sym 1 *(rec Brøndby Strand Church, 1994)* Rondo Grammofon ▲ RCD 8346
Norby, E.:Canzoni Rondo Grammofon ▲ RCD 8340
Norby, E.:Dances Rondo Grammofon ▲ RCD 8340
Plog, A.:Miniatures Tuba, w. Jens Bjørn-Larsen (tuba) Rondo Grammofon ▲ RCD 8340
Trombone Concepts *(rec Brønby Strand Church, 1994)* Rondo Grammofon ▲ RCD 8349

Danish Duo [Johannes Soe Hansen (vn), Frank Jarlsfelt (pno)]
Lange-Müller, P.E.:Fant Pieces Classico ▲ CLASSCD 118
Nielsen, C.:Son 1 Vn Classico ▲ CLASSCD 118
Nielsen, C.:Son 2 Vn Classico ▲ CLASSCD 118

Danish Guitar Duo [Søren Bødker Madsen (gtr), Morten Skott (gtr)]
Dørge, P.:Struthio Camelus Point ▲ PCD 5120 [DDD]
Frandsen, J.:Twilight Point ▲ PCD 5120 [DDD]
Nielsen, S.:Barcarole Gtr [trans. from Romantiske Klaverstykker (1974)] Point ▲ PCD 5120 [DDD]
Siegel, W.:Canons Gtr Point ▲ PCD 5120 [DDD]

Danish National Orch
S. Ehrling (cnd)
Nielsen, C.:Sym 3, w. S. Burghardt (sop), R. Bassett (bar) *(rec live, Kennedy Center, 5/19/84)* Audiofon ▲ CD 72025

Danish National RSO
H. Blomstedt (cnd)
Nielsen, C.:Songs—Bohemian-Danish Folk Tune EMI Classics ▲ CDM 65306
Nielsen, C.:Sym 1 EMI Classics ▲ CDM 65306
Nielsen, C.:Sym 2 EMI Classics ▲ CDM 65306
Nielsen, C.:Sym 3 EMI Classics ▲ CDM 65415
Nielsen, C.:Sym 4 EMI Classics ▲ CDM 65415
Nørgård, P.:Luna *(rec Danish Radio Concert Hall, 1968)* Marco Polo/Dacapo ▲ 8.224041 [AAD]
Nørholm, I.:Con Vn, w. L. Hansen (vn) BIS ▲ CD 80 [AAD]
F. Busch (cnd)
Beethoven, L. van:Sym 9, "Choral Sym", w. Kerstin Lindberg-Torlind (sop), Else Jena (mez), Erik Sjöberg (ten), Holger Byrding (bass), Danish National Radio Choir Arlecchino ARL

Danish National RSO (cont.)
F. Busch (cnd) (cont.)
Brahms, J.:Alto Rhap, w. K. Ferrier (cta), Danish National Radio Choir [G] *(rec 10/6/49)* Danacord ▲ DACOCD 301 (m)
Mozart, W.A.:Contradances, K.609 *(rec 1934)* Legend 2-▲ LGD 132 [ADD]
Mozart, W.A.:German Dances, K.571 *(rec 1934)* Legend 2-▲ LGD 132 [ADD]
Mozart, W.A.:Kleine Nachtmusik *(rec 1934)* Legend 2-▲ LGD 132 [ADD]
M. Caridis (cnd)
Ibert, J.:Con Fl, w. P. Birkelund (fl) Canzone ▲ CAN 33008 [ADD]
Skalkottas, N.:The Return of Odysseus *(rec live, 9/19/79)* Koch Schwann ▲ CD 311110 [ADD]
S. Celibidache (cnd)
Berlioz, H.:Sym fantastique *(rec live, 1970)* Enterprise ("Documents" series) ▲ ENTLV 965 [ADD]
Debussy, C.:La Mer Originals ▲ ORI 860
Dvořák, A.:Slavonic Dances (sels)—Op. 46/1, 2, 3, 5 & 8 *(rec live, 1970)* Enterprise ("Documents" series) ▲ ENTLV 965 [ADD]
T. Dausgaard (cnd)
Hartmann, J.P.E.:Sym 1 *(rec Danish Radio Concert Hall, Apr–May 1996)* Marco Polo/Dacapo ▲ 8.224042 [DDD]
Hartmann, J.P.E.:Sym 2 *(rec Danish Radio Concert Hall, Apr–May 1996)* Marco Polo/Dacapo ▲ 8.224042 [DDD]
J. Ferencsik (cnd)
Holmboe, V.:Con Vc, w. E. B. Bengtsson (vc) BIS ▲ CD 78 [AAD/DDD]
J. Frandsen (cnd)
Kuhlau, F.:Elverhøj, w. Bodil Gøbel (sop), Gurli Plesner (cta), Mogens Schmidt Johansen (bar), Danish National Radio Choir *(rec Danish Radio Concert Hall, Aug 1974)* Marco Polo/Dacapo ▲ 8.224053 [AAD]
Langgaard, R.:The Music of the Spheres Danacord 2-▲ DACOCD 340/41
Langgaard, R.:Sym 4 *(rec live, 4/2/81)* Danacord 2-▲ DACOCD 340/341 [ADD]
Langgaard, R.:Sym 6 *(rec live, 12/9/77)* Danacord 2-▲ DACOCD 340/341 [ADD]
Norby, E.:Regnbueslangen BIS ▲ CD 79 [AAD]
J. Galway (cnd)
Nielsen, C.:Con Fl, w. James Galway (fl) *(rec Danish Radio Concert Hall, Copenhagen, Mar 17, 1985)* RCA Red Seal ▲ 07863-56359-2 [ADD]
L. Gardelli (cnd)
Nielsen, T.:Passacaglia *(rec live, Nov 24, 1983)* Point ▲ PCD 5089
H. Graf (cnd)
Holten, B.:Con Cl, w. J. Schou (cl) Chandos ▲ CHAN 9272 [DDD]
O.A. Hughes (cnd)
Koppel, H.D.:Moses, w. Elisabeth Meyer-Topsøe (sop), Kirsten Dolberg (mez), Kurt Westi (ten), Michael Kristensen (ten), Per Høyer (bar), Christian Christiansen (bass), Jesper Groww Jørgensen (cnd), Danish National Radio Choir *(rec Danish Radio Concert Hall, Mar 1996)* Marco Polo/Dacapo ▲ 8.224046 [DDD]
N. Järvi (cnd)
Arensky, A.:Suite 2 for 2 Pnos, "Silhouettes" [orchd] Chandos ▲ CHAN 8898 [DDD]
Honegger, A.:Pacific 231 Chandos ▲ CHAN 9176 [DDD]
Honegger, A.:Sym 3 Chandos ▲ CHAN 9176 [DDD]
Honegger, A.:Sym 5 Chandos ▲ CHAN 9176 [DDD]
Langgaard, R.:Sym 4 Chandos ▲ CHAN 9064 [DDD]
Langgaard, R.:Sym 5 Chandos ▲ CHAN 9064 [DDD]
Langgaard, R.:Sym 6 Chandos ▲ CHAN 9064 [DDD]
Nielsen, C.:Saul & David, w. T. Kiberg (sop), A. Gjevang (mez), P. Lindroos (ten), K. Westi (ten), C. Christiansen (bass), A. Haugland (bass), J. Klint (bass), Danish National Radio Choir [Da] Chandos 2-▲ CHAN 8911/12 [DDD]
Scriabin, A.:Sym 3 Chandos ▲ CHAN 8898 [DDD]
T. Jensen (cnd)
Nielsen, C.:Sym 1 Dutton Laboratories ▲ DUT 2502 [ADD]
Nielsen, C.:Sym 5 Dutton Laboratories ▲ DUT 2502 [ADD]
D. Kitayenko (cnd)
Gade, N.W.:Echoes of Ossian Chandos ▲ CHAN 9075 [DDD]
Gade, N.W.:Echoes of Ossian Chandos ▲ CHAN 9422
Gade, N.W.:Elverskud, w. E. Johansson (sop), A. Gjevang (cta), P. Elming (ten), Danish National Radio Chamber Choir [Da] Chandos ▲ CHAN 9075 [DDD]
Gade, N.W.:Hamlet (ov) Chandos ▲ CHAN 9422
Gade, N.W.:Sym 1 Chandos ▲ CHAN 9422
Prokofiev, S.:Alexander Nevsky, w. L. Schemtchuk (mez), Danish National Radio Choir [R] Chandos ▲ CHAN 9001 [DDD]
Prokofiev, S.:Romeo & Juliet Chandos 2-▲ CHAN 9322/23 [DDD]
Prokofiev, S.:Scythian Suite Chandos ▲ CHAN 9001 [DDD]
Rachmaninoff, S.:The Bells, w. E. Ustinova (sop), K. Westi (ten), J. Hynninen (bar), Danish National Radio Choir Chandos ▲ CHAN 8966 [DDD]
Rachmaninoff, S.:Spring, w. J. Hynninen (bar), Danish National Radio Choir Chandos ▲ CHAN 8966 [DDD]
Stravinsky, I.:Le Chant du rossignol Chandos ▲ CHAN 8967 [DDD]
Stravinsky, I.:Fireworks Chandos ▲ CHAN 9198 [DDD]
Stravinsky, I.:Pétrouchka Chandos ▲ CHAN 9198 [DDD]
Stravinsky, I.:Scherzo à la russe Chandos ▲ CHAN 9198 [DDD]
Stravinsky, I.:Scherzo fantastique Chandos ▲ CHAN 9198 [DDD]
O. Knussen (cnd)
Nørgård, P.:Voyage *(rec Oct. 31, 1986)* Marco Polo ▲ DCCD 9001
R. Kubelik (cnd)
Nielsen, C.:Sym 5 EMI Classics ▲ CDM 65182
G. Kuhn (cnd)
Schumann, R.:Der Rose Pilgerfahrt, w. Danish National Radio Choir Chandos ▲ CHAN 9350 [DDD]
J. Latham-König (cnd)
Nørgård, P.:Twilight *(rec live 9/82)* Marco Polo/Dacapo ▲ DCCD 8901 [ADD]
Nørgård, P.:Twilight, w. Tom Nyobe (conga) *(rec Danish Radio Concert Hall, 1982)* Marco Polo/Dacapo ▲ 8.224041 [AAD]
Nørholm, I.:Sym 5 Kontrapunkt ▲ 32005 [ADD/DDD]
C. Mackerras (cnd)
Janácek, L.:Slavonic Mass, w. T. Kiberg (sop), R. Stene (cta), P. Svensson (ten), U. Cold (bass), Danish National Radio Choir, Copenhagen Boys' Choir Chandos ▲ CHAN 9310 [DDD]
Kodály, Z.:Psalmus hungaricus, w. P. Svensson (ten), Danish National Radio Choir, Copenhagen Boys' Choir Chandos ▲ CHAN 9310 [DDD]
J. Nelson (cnd)
Tarp, S.E.:Te Deum, w. Danish National Radio Choir *(rec Sept. 14, 1988)* Marco Polo ▲ DCCD 9005 [DDD]
J. Panula (cnd)
Gudmunsen-Holmgreen, P.:Triptykon, w. G. Mortensen (perc) BIS ▲ CD 256 [AAD/DDD]
G. Rozhdestvensky (cnd)
Lumbye, H.C.:Music of—Champagne Galop (1845); Queen Louise Waltz (1868); Lady of St. Petersburg Polka (1848); Copenhagen Railway Galop (1871); Amelie Waltz (1846); Britta Polka (1864); Dream Pictures Fantasie (1846) Chandos ▲ CHAN 9209 [DDD]
Nielsen, C.:Aladdin, w. M. Ejsing (cta), G. Paevatalu (bar), Danish National Radio Chamber Choir Chandos ▲ CHAN 9135 [DDD]
Nielsen, C.:Orch Music—Helios Ov., Op. 17; Symphonic Rhap.; Saga-drøm, Op. 39; En aften paa Giske; Paraphrase on Naermer Gud til dig for Wind Orch.; Bøhmisk-dansk folketone for String Orch.; Rhapsodic Ov.; Pan & Syrinx, Op. 49 Chandos ▲ CHAN 9287 [DDD]
K. Sanderling (cnd)
Beethoven, L. van:Con 5 Pno, "Emperor", w. H. Richter-Haaser (pno) *(rec live, October 1980)* Kontrapunkt 2-▲ 32020/21 [ADD]

ORCH. & ENS.

Danish National RSO (cont.)
K. Sanderling (cnd) (cont.)
Brahms, J.:Con 1 Pno, w. H. Richter-Haaser (pno) *(rec live, March 1979)* Kontrapunkt 2-▲ 32020/21 [ADD]
O. Schmidt (cnd)
Bentzon, N.V.:Feature on René Descartes BIS ▲ CD 79 [AAD]
Colding-Jorgensen, H.:To Love Music BIS ▲ CD 79 [AAD]
Koppel, H.D.:Con Vc, w. E. Bløndal Bengtsson (vc) BIS ▲ CD 80 [AAD]
Langgaard, R.:Sym 10 *(rec live, 8/28/77)* Danacord ▲ DACOCD 302
Schmidt, O.:Sym Fant & Fugue Acc, w. Mogens Ellegaard (acc) Point ▲ PCD 5073 [DDD]
Tarp, S.E.:Sym 7 *(rec Sept. 5, 1986)* Marco Polo ▲ DCCD 9005 [DDD]
M. Schønwandt (cnd)
Heise, P.:King & Marshall, w. P. Elming (ten), A. Haugland (bass), C. Christiansen (bass), Danish National Choir Chandos 3-▲ CHAN 9143 [DDD]
Horneman, C.F.E.:Music of, w. Guido Paevatalu (bar), Danish National Choir—Gurre; Helteliv; Alladin Ov. Chandos ▲ CHAN 9373 [DDD]
Kuhlau, F.:Lulu, w. T. Kiberg (sop), A. Frellesvig (sgr), K. von Binzer (ten), R. Saarman (ten), U. Cold (bass), E. Harbo (sgr), Danish National Radio Choir [Da] Kontrapunkt 3-▲ 32009/11 [DDD]
Langgaard, R.:Sym 14, w. Danish National Radio Choir *(rec 1979)* Danacord ▲ DACOCD 302
Nielsen, C.:Con Cl, w. N. Thomsen (cl) Chandos ▲ CHAN 8894 [DDD]
Nielsen, C.:Con Fl, w. T. L. Christiansen (fl) Chandos ▲ CHAN 8894 [DDD]
Nielsen, C.:Con Vn, w. K. Sjogren (vn) Chandos ▲ CHAN 8894 [DDD]
Nørholm, I.:Symphonic Fant Kontrapunkt ▲ 32005 [ADD/DDD]
Schoenberg, A.:Con Pno, w. Amalie Malling (pno) Chandos ▲ CHAN 9375 [DDD]
Schumann, R.:Con Pno, w. Amalie Malling (pno) Chandos ▲ CHAN 9375 [DDD]
Tarp, S.E.:Battle of Jericho *(rec Nov. 14, 1990)* Marco Polo ▲ DCCD 9005 [DDD]
Tarp, S.E.:Con Pno, w. P. Salo (pno) *(rec Sept. 7, 1990)* Marco Polo ▲ DCCD 9005 [DDD]
L. Segerstam (cnd)
Beethoven, L. van:Qt 11 Strs, "Quartetto serioso" [orchd. Mahler] Chandos 2-▲ CHAN 9266/67 [DDD]
Gudmunsen-Holmgreen, P.:Sym 3, "Antiphony" Marco Polo/Dacapo ▲ DCCD 9010 [DDD]
Langgaard, R.:From the Deep Chandos ▲ CHAN 9249 [DDD]
Langgaard, R.:Sym 1 Chandos ▲ CHAN 9249 [DDD]
Mahler, G.:Blumine Chandos ▲ CHAN 9242 [DDD]
Mahler, G.:Sym 1 Chandos ▲ CHAN 9242 [DDD]
Mahler, G.:Sym 2, w. Tina Kiberg (sop), Kirsten Dolberg (alt), Danish National Radio Choir Chandos 2-▲ CHAN 9266/67 [DDD]
Mahler, G.:Sym 3, w. A. Gjevang (mez), Danish National Radio Choir [G] Chandos 2-▲ CHAN 8970/71 [DDD]
Mahler, G.:Sym 5 Chandos ▲ CHAN 9403 [DDD]
Mahler, G.:Sym 6 Chandos 2-▲ CHAN 8956/57 [DDD]
Mahler, G.:Sym 7 Chandos 3-▲ CHAN 9057/59 [DDD]
Mahler, G.:Sym 8, w. Majken Bjerno (sop), Henriette Bonde-Hansen (sop), Inga Nielsen (sop), Kirsten Dolberg (alt), Anne Gjevang (alt), Raimo Sirkiä (ten), Jorma Hynninen (bar), Carsten Stabell (bass), Copenhagen Boys' Choir, Berlin Phil Choir, Danish National Radio Choir Chandos 2-▲ CHAN 9305/06 [DDD]
Mahler, G.:Sym 9 Chandos 3-▲ CHAN 9057/59 [DDD]
Mahler, G.:Sym 10 Chandos 2-▲ CHAN 9305/06
Mahler, G.:Totenfeier Chandos 2-▲ CHAN 8956/57 [DDD]
Nielsen, C.:Choral Music, w. Danish National Radio Choir Chandos ▲ CHAN 8853 [DDD]
Nielsen, C.:Hymnus Amoris, w. I. Nielsen (sop), A. Elkrog (ten), P. Elming (ten), P. Høyer (bar), J. Ditlevsen (bass), Copenhagen Boys' Choir, Danish National Radio Choir [L] Chandos ▲ CHAN 8853 [DDD]
Nielsen, C.:Sleep, w. Danish National Radio Choir [Da] Chandos ▲ CHAN 8853 [DDD]
Nielsen, C.:Springtime, w. I. Nielsen (sop), P. Gronlund (ten), S. Byriel (b-bar), Danish National Radio Choir, Danish National Radio Children's Choir [Da] Chandos ▲ CHAN 8853 [DDD]
Nørgård, P.:Sym 1 *(rec Danish Radio Concert Hall, Aug 31-Sept 2 & 5, 1995)* Chandos ▲ CHAN 9450
Nørgård, P.:Sym 2 *(rec Danish Radio Concert Hall, Aug 31-Sept 2 & 5, 1995)* Chandos ▲ CHAN 9450
Rasmussen, K.A.:A Sym in Time Marco Polo/Dacapo ▲ DCCD 9010 [DDD]
Ruders, P.:Music of—Gong; Symphony; Tundra; Saledes Saaes Johannes Chandos ▲ CHAN 9179 [DDD]
Schnittke, A.:Con 1 Vc, w. T. Thedéen (vc) BIS ▲ CD 507 [DDD]
Schnittke, A.:Con 1 Vc, w. Torleff Thedéen (vc) BIS ("BIS Twins" series) 2-▲ CD 437/507
Segerstam, L.:Monumental Thoughts *(rec live, Tivoli, Copenhagen, May 7, 1989)* BIS ▲ CD 583 [DDD]
Segerstam, L.:Nocturne *(rec Sept. 7, 1992)* BIS ▲ CD 584 [DDD]
Segerstam, L.:Sym 18 Ondine ▲ ODE CD 877
Segerstam, L.:Thoughts 1989 *(rec live, Helsinki Festival, Sept. 5, 1989)* BIS ▲ CD 583 [DDD]
Segerstam, L.:Thoughts 1990, w. Kontra String Quartet *(rec live, Copenhagen Nov. 15, 1990)* BIS ▲ CD 583 [DDD]
Sibelius, J.:Finlandia Chandos ▲ CHAN 9020 [DDD]
Sibelius, J.:In Memoriam Chandos ("7000" series) 4-▲ CHAN 7054
Sibelius, J.:Karelia Ov Chandos ▲ CHAN 9107 [DDD]
Sibelius, J.:Kullervo, w. Siole Isokoski (sop), Raimo Laukka (bar), Danish National Radio Choir Chandos ▲ CHAN 9393 [DDD]
Sibelius, J.:Pelléas et Mélisande (suite) Chandos ▲ CHAN 9483
Sibelius, J.:Pohjola's Daughter Chandos ▲ CHAN 8965 [DDD]
Sibelius, J.:En Saga Chandos ▲ CHAN 8965 [DDD]
Sibelius, J.:Scene with Cranes Chandos ▲ CHAN 9083 [DDD]
Sibelius, J.:Scènes historiques Chandos ▲ CHAN 9483
Sibelius, J.:Syms (comp) Chandos ("7000" series) 4-▲ CHAN 7054
Sibelius, J.:Sym 1 Chandos ▲ CHAN 9107 [DDD]
Sibelius, J.:Sym 2 Chandos ▲ CHAN 9020 [DDD]
Sibelius, J.:Sym 3 Chandos ▲ CHAN 9083 [DDD]
Sibelius, J.:Sym 4 Chandos ▲ CHAN 8943 [DDD]
Sibelius, J.:Sym 5 Chandos ▲ CHAN 9055 [DDD]
Sibelius, J.:Sym 6 Chandos ▲ CHAN 8965 [DDD]
Sibelius, J.:Sym 7 Chandos ▲ CHAN 9055 [DDD]
Sibelius, J.:Tapiola Chandos ▲ CHAN 9083 [DDD]
Sibelius, J.:The Tempest (sels)—Suite No. 1 Chandos ▲ CHAN 8943 [DDD]
Sibelius, J.:The Tempest (sels)—Suite No. 1, Op. 109/2 Chandos ("7000" series) 4-▲ CHAN 7054
Sibelius, J.:Valse triste Chandos ▲ CHAN 9055 [DDD]
Sørensen, B.:Con Vn, w. Rebecca Hirsch (vn) *(rec live, Danish Radio Concert Hall, 1992 & 1994)* Marco Polo/Dacapo ▲ 8.224039 [DDD]
Sørensen, B.:The Echoing Garden, w. Åsa Bäverstam (sop), Martyn Hill (ten), Danish National Radio Choir *(rec live, Danish Radio Concert Hall, 1992 & 1994)* Marco Polo/Dacapo ▲ 8.224039 [DDD]
Tómasson, H.:Afsprengi Music from Iceland ▲ ITM 707
E. Tuxen (cnd)
Jolivet, A.:Con Fl, w. P. Birkelund (fl) Canzone ▲ CAN 33008 [ADD]
Nielsen, C.:Con Fl, w. P. Birkelund (fl) Canzone ▲ CAN 33008 [ADD]
Nielsen, C.:Helios Dutton Laboratories ▲ DUT 2502 [ADD]
T. Vatôs (cnd)
Nørholm, I.:Shadow Kontrapunkt ▲ 32005 [ADD/DDD]
T. Vetö (cnd)
Nørgård, P.:Sym 3, w. Danish National Radio Choir *(rec live 10/14/82)* Marco Polo/Dacapo ▲ DCCD 8901 [ADD]

Danish National RSO (cont.)
T. Vetö (cnd) (cont.)
Nørgård, P.:Sym 3, w. Hedwig Rummel (alt), Danish National Radio Choir *(rec live, Danish Radio Concert Hall, 1982)* Marco Polo/Dacapo ▲ 8.224041 [AAD]
Danish Radio Concert Orch
J. Hye-Knudsen (cnd)
Gluck, C.W.:Alceste (sels), w. K. Flagstad (sop), Danish National Radio Choir—five arias & scenes *(rec live 4/14/57)* Melodram 2-▲ MEL 26514 (m) [AAD]
D. Kitayenko (cnd)
Mussorgsky, M.:Boris Godunov, w. A. Haugland (bass—Boris, Pimen & Varlaam), Danish National Radio Choir [concert version based on Mussorgsky's original 1868-69 version] [R] *(rec live 2/27/86)* Kontrapunkt 2-▲ 32036/37 [DDD]
H. Koivula (cnd)
Holmboe, V.:Chamber Con 1, w. Anne Øland (pno) *(rec Danish Radio Studio 2, June & Sept 1996)* Marco Polo/Dacapo ▲ 8.224038 [DDD]
Holmboe, V.:Chamber Con 2, w. Eva Østergaard (fl), Mikkel Futtrup (vn) *(rec Danish Radio Studio 2, June & Sept 1996)* Marco Polo/Dacapo ▲ 8.224038 [DDD]
Holmboe, V.:Chamber Con 3, w. Niels Thomsen (cl) *(rec Danish Radio Studio 2, June & Sept 1996)* Marco Polo/Dacapo ▲ 8.224038 [DDD]
Danish String Quartet
Brahms, J.:Qts Strs (comp) Kontrapunkt 2-▲ 32033/34 [DDD]
Gubaidulina, S.:Qt 1 Strs CPO ▲ CPO 999064 [DDD]
Gubaidulina, S.:Qt 2 Strs CPO ▲ CPO 999064 [DDD]
Gubaidulina, S.:Qt 3 Strs CPO ▲ CPO 999064 [DDD]
Nielsen, C.:Movts Kontrapunkt ▲ KPT 32150 [DDD]
Nielsen, C.:Qts Strs Kontrapunkt ▲ KPT 32150 [DDD]
Nørholm, I.:Qts Strs—No. 3, Op. 35 (1966); No. 4, Op. 38 (1966); No. 7, Op. 94 (1985); No. 8, Op. 107 (1988) Kontrapunkt ▲ 32049 [DDD]
Danish String Quartet members
Gubaidulina, S.:Trio Strs CPO ▲ CPO 999064 [DDD]
Danish SO
O. Knussen (cnd)
Ruders, P.:Thus Saw Saint John Point ▲ PCD 5084 [AAD]
M. Schönwandt (cnd)
Ruders, P.:Manhattan Abstraction Point ▲ PCD 5084 [AAD]
Danish Trio [Jens Schou (cl), Svend Winsløv (vc), Rosalind Bevan (pno)]
Brahms, J.:Trio Cl Paula (Denmark) ▲ CD 52
Gudmunsen-Holmgreen, P.:Mirror Pieces *(rec Dec 1987)* Paula ▲ PACD 57 [AAD]
Højsgaard, E.:Fantasistykker *(rec Dec 1987)* Paula ▲ PACD 57 [AAD]
Lorentzen, B.:Mambo *(rec Dec 1987)* Paula ▲ PACD 57 [AAD]
Ruders, P.:TATTOO for THREE *(rec Dec 1987)* Paula ▲ PACD 57 [AAD]
Zemlinsky, A. von:Trio Cl Paula (Denmark) ▲ CD 52
Danish Wind Octet [H. Goldschmidt (ob), K. Sjöblom (ob), L. Morgan (cl), J. Helmuth Madsen (cl), T. Aadne (hn), P. Castillo (hn), A. Trige (bn), S. Haugland (bn)]
Christiansen, A.L.:Octet Winds *(rec Copenhagen, Jan. 20, Mar. 20 & Apr. 1)* Marco Polo/Dacapo ▲ 8.224002 [DDD]
Graugaard, L.:Summerscapes (7) *(rec Copenhagen, Jan. 20, Mar. 20 & Apr. 1)* Marco Polo/Dacapo ▲ 8.224002 [DDD]
Koppel, H.D.:Music for Wind Octet *(rec Copenhagen, Jan. 20, Mar. 20 & Apr. 1)* Marco Polo/Dacapo ▲ 8.224002 [DDD]
Mozart, W.A.:Divert Obs, K.213 Rondo Grammofon ▲ RCD 8335
Mozart, W.A.:Divert Obs, K.252 Rondo Grammophon ▲ RCD 8336
Mozart, W.A.:Serenade Ww, K.375 Rondo Grammophon ▲ RCD 8336
Mozart, W.A.:Serenade Ww, K.375 Rondo Grammofon ▲ RCD 8335
Mozart, W.A.:Serenade Ww, K.388 Rondo Grammophon ▲ RCD 8336
Mozart, W.A.:Serenade Ww, K.388 Rondo Grammofon ▲ RCD 8335
Schultz, S.S.:Divert Ww *(rec Copenhagen, Jan. 20, Mar. 20 & Apr. 1)* Marco Polo/Dacapo ▲ 8.224002 [DDD]
Werner, S.E.:Catch *(rec Copenhagen, Jan. 20, Mar. 20 & Apr. 1)* Marco Polo/Dacapo ▲ 8.224002 [DDD]
Danish Wind Octet members
Mozart, W.A.:Divert Obs, K.213 Rondo Grammophon ▲ RCD 8336
Gerald Danovitch Saxophone Quartet
Françaix, J.:Petit Quatuor CBC ("Musica Viva" series) ▲ MVCD 1018 [DDD]
The Gerald Danovitch Saxophone Quartet Musica Viva ▲ MVCD 1018 [DDD]
Danserye Ensemble
Music from the Time of the Catholic Kings of Spain (1450-1550) Preiser ▲ PRE 90028 [AAD]
Danske Strings members
Leppard, Linde (cnd)
Vivaldi, A.:Music of, w. Wim Ten Have (va), Anthony Bailes (lt), Raymond Leppard (hpd), Hans-Martin Linde (fl/rcr), English CO, Prague CO—Concertino in D, RV.121; Cons. in f, RV.156; in G, RV.435 [Op. 10/4]; in D, RV.429; in F, RV.434 [Op. 10/5]; in D, RV.93; in d, RV.540; Son. in E♭, RV.130 [Al Santo Sepolcro] Classics for Pleasure ▲ CDCFP 4656 [ADD]
Dantchenko Moscow Stanislavsky Music Theater Orch
G. Zhemchuzhin (cnd)
Kabalevsky, D.:Colas Breugnon (ov), w. N. Isakova (sop), V. Kayevchenko (sop), L. Boldin (bar), N. Gutorovich (bar), G. Dudarev (bass), E. Maksimenko (sgr), Dantchenko Moscow Stanislavsky Music Theater Chorus Olympia 2-▲ OLY 291 [ADD]
Danubius Quartet
Korngold, E.W.:Qnt Pno, w. I. Prunyi (pno) Marco Polo ▲ 8.223385
Korngold, E.W.:Son Vn, w. A. Kiss (vn), I. Prunyi (pno) Marco Polo ▲ 8.223385
Mozart, W.A.:Qts Cl, w. J. Balogh (cl)—No. 2 in E♭ from K.380 *(rec Sept. 25, 1991)* Naxos ▲ 8.550390 [DDD]
Mozart, W.A.:Qnt Cl, K.581, w. J. Balogh (cl) *(rec Sept. 23-25, 1991)* Naxos ▲ 8.550390 [DDD]
Danubius Quartet [J. Balogh (cl), A. Miklós (vn), C. Bodolai (va), I. Ribli (vc)]
Mozart, W.A.:Qts Cl—K.378 & 496 *(rec Sept. 25-27, 1992)* Naxos ▲ 8.550439 [DDD]
Danubius Quartet [M. Szabó (vn), A. Miklós (vn), Á. Apró (va), I. Ribli (vc)]
Boccherini, L.:Qnts Gtr & Strs, w. Z. Tokos (gtr)—Qnts., G.451 & 453; Qnt. G.275 [w. György Éder (cello)] *(rec August 1992)* Naxos ▲ 8.550731 [DDD]
Boccherini, L.:Qnts Gtr & Strs, w. Z. Tokos (gtr)—in D, G.448, G.449 & in G, G.450 *(rec Aug. 1-4, 1991)* Naxos ▲ 8.550552 [DDD]
Brahms, J.:Qnt Cl, w. J. Balogh (cl), C. Onczay (vc) *(rec Oct. 16-18, 1991)* Naxos ▲ 8.550391 [DDD]
Spohr, L.:Qnts Strs, Op. 33, w. S. Papp (va) Marco Polo ▲ 8.223597 [DDD]
Villa-Lobos, H.:Qt 3 Strs Marco Polo ▲ 8.223393
Villa-Lobos, H.:Qt 4 Strs *(rec Apr. 18 & 19, 1991)* Marco Polo ▲ 8.223391 [DDD]
Villa-Lobos, H.:Qt 6 Strs *(rec May 20-23, 1991)* Marco Polo ▲ 8.223391 [DDD]
Villa-Lobos, H.:Qt 10 Strs Marco Polo ▲ 8.223393
Villa-Lobos, H.:Qt 14 Strs *(rec Apr. 22-25, 1991)* Marco Polo ▲ 8.223391 [DDD]
Villa-Lobos, H.:Qt 15 Strs Marco Polo ▲ 8.223393
Danubius Quartet members
Mozart, W.A.:Qnt Cl Bas Hn, K.580b, w. B. Kovács (cl), J. Balogh (bas hn) [completed Franz Beyer] *(rec Sept. 23-25, 1991)* Naxos ▲ 8.550390 [DDD]
Darmstadt CO
W. Seeliger (cnd)
Telemann, G.P.:St. Matthew Passion, w. M. Zedelius (sop), A. Browner (alt), H.P. Blochwitz (ten), W. Schmidt (bar), A. Scharinger (bass), Darmstadt Concert Choir Christophorus ▲ 77149 [DDD]
Darmstadt International Chamber Ensemble
B. Maderna (cnd)
Ligeti, G.:Aventures, w. Charlent (sgr), Cahn (sgr), Pearson (sgr) Wergo ▲ WER 60045-50 [ADD]

▲ = CD ♦ = Enhanced CD Δ = MD ▀ = Cassette Tape □ = DCC

Darmstadt International Chamber Ensemble (cont.)
B. Maderna (cnd) (cont.)
Ligeti, G.:Nouvelles aventures, w. Charlent (sgr), Cahn (sgr), Pearson (sgr) Wergo ▲ WER 60045-50 [ADD]
Dartington Ensemble
Martinů, B.:Madrigals Ob Hyperion ▲ CDA 66133
Martinů, B.:Madrigal Son Hyperion ▲ CDA 66133
Martinů, B.:Madrigal Stanzas Hyperion ▲ CDA 66133
Martinů, B.:Madrigals Vn Hyperion ▲ CDA 66133
Martinů, B.:Nonet Ww, Strs & Db Hyperion ▲ CDA 66084
Martinů, B.:La Revue de Cuisine Hyperion ▲ CDA 66084
Martinů, B.:Trio Fl Hyperion ▲ CDA 66084
Datura Trombone Quartet
Beethoven, L. van:Equale, WoO 30 Ars Musici ▲ AM 1154 [DDD]
Bruckner, A.:Motets, w. Robin Gritton (cnd), North German Radio Chorus—Ecce Sacerdos Magnus Ars Musici ▲ AM 1154 [DDD]
Candotto, S.:Missa brevis, w. Robin Gritton (cnd), North German Radio Chorus Ars Musici ▲ AM 1154 [DDD]
Krol, B.:Von Werden und Vergehen, w. Robin Gritton (cnd), North German Radio Chorus Ars Musici ▲ AM 1154 [DDD]
Purcell, H.:Music for the Funeral of Queen Mary, w. Robin Gritton (cnd), North German Radio Chorus Ars Musici ▲ AM 1154 [DDD]
Stravinsky, I.:In memoriam Dylan Thomas, w. Robert Chafin (ten), Robin Gritton (cnd), North German Radio Chorus Ars Musici ▲ AM 1154 [DDD]
Datura Trombone Quartet [U. Schrodl (trbn), S. Geiger (trbn), O. Siefert (trbn), V. Stoll (trbn)]
Barockmusik für Posaunen und Gesang, w. A. Scharinger (db), C. Weigel (baroque vc), T. Strauss (org), J. Gagelmann (perc), R. Haeger (perc) Ars Musici ▲ AM 1094 [DDD]
Davydov SO
K. Krimets (cnd)
Davïdov, K.Y.:Con 1 Vc, w. Marina Tarasova (vc) Olympia ▲ OLY 571 [DDD]
Davïdov, K.Y.:Con 2 Vc, w. Marina Tarasova (vc) Olympia ▲ OLY 571 [DDD]
Deakin Piano Trio [C. Dubois (pno), R. Deakin (vn), C. Dubois (vc)]
Parry, H.:Trio 2 Pno Meridian ▲ MER 84225
Parry, H.:Trio 3 Pno Meridian ▲ MER 84225
Debrecen College Cantus
The Chants of the Reformation in Hungary, w. Dezső Karasszon (org) Hungaroton ▲ HCD 12665 [DDD]
Debussy String Quartet
Webern, A.:Bagatelles Str Qt Harmonia Mundi ▲ HMN 911586
Webern, A.:Movts Str Qt Harmonia Mundi ▲ HMN 911586
Webern, A.:Qt Strs (1905) Harmonia Mundi ▲ HMN 911586
Webern, A.:Qt Strs, Op. 28 Harmonia Mundi ▲ HMN 911586
Webern, A.:Rondo Harmonia Mundi ▲ HMN 911586
Webern, A.:Slow Movt Harmonia Mundi ▲ HMN 911586
Debussy Trio
Mercier (cnd)
Marcland, P.:Music of, w. Nouvel PO, Ensemble InterContemporain, Michel Tranchant (cnd), French Vocal Group—Versets; Paroles; Failles; Mètres; Variants *(rec 1978–84)* Chamade ▲ CHCD 5636 [DDD]
Debussy Trio [A. Wiegand (fl), K. Greene (va), M. Dickstein (hp)]
Bach, Jan:Eisteddfod–Vars on a Welsh Harp Tune Sierra Classical 2–▲ SXCD 5005
Bondon, J.:Le Soleil Multicolore Sierra Classical ▲ SXCD 5001 [DDD] ■ OXMC 5001 (D)
Davenport, D.:The Celestial Harmony Sierra Classical 2–▲ SXCD 5005
Debussy, C.:Son Fl *(rec Claremont, CA, July, 1991)* Sierra Classical ▲ SXCD 5002
Frank, A.:The Way You Hear It Is the Way You Sing It Sierra Classical 2–▲ SXCD 5005
Graun, J.G.:Trio Sons—in F Sierra Classical ▲ SXCD 5004
Hagen, D.:Hp Trio Sierra Classical ▲ OXCD 5001 [DDD]; ■ OXMC 5001 (D)
Kibbe, M.:Trio Hp, Va, & Fl Sierra Classical ▲ OXCD 5001 [DDD] ■ OXMC 5001 (D)
Leclair, J.–M.:Trio Sons, w. S. Erdody (vc)—in D, Op. 2/8 *(rec July 1992)* Sierra Classical ▲ SXCD 5004
Locatelli, P.:Sons Fl, Op. 2, w. S. Erdody (vc)—No. 2 in B *(rec July 1992)* Sierra Classical ▲ SXCD 5004
Locatelli, P.:Trio 2 Fl, Va & Hp Sierra Classical ▲ SXC 5004
Mathias, W.:Zodiac Trio Sierra Classical ▲ OXCD 5001 [DDD] ■ OXMC 5001 (D)
Mays, L.:Twelve Days in the Shadow of a Miracle Sierra Classical 2–▲ SXCD 5005
Mendoza, V.:Trio Music 5/90 *(rec Claremont, CA, July 1991)* Sierra Classical ▲ OXCD 5002
Neil, R.:Kumbosora Sierra Classical 2–▲ SXC 5005
Ravel, M.:Sonatine Pno [trans. Salzedo] *(rec Claremont, CA, July, 1991)* Sierra Classical ▲ OXCD 5002
Telemann, G.P.:Trio Sons, w. S. Erdody (vc)—in g, g & b *(rec July 1992)* Sierra Classical ▲ SXCD 5004
Zeisl, E.:Arrowhead Trio Harmonia Mundi USA ▲ HMU 907044
L. Leighton Smith (cnd)
Thomas, A.R.:Triple Concerto ...night's midsummer blaze, w. Louisville Orch *(rec Robert Whitney Hall, Louisville, KY, Nov 18, 1993)* Louisville Orchestra ("First Edition Recordings" series) ▲ LCD010 [ADD]
Decca String Orch
E. Ansermet (cnd)
Handel, G.F.:Concerti grossi, Op. 6, w. L. Heward (bc) *(rec London, England, Sept 1929)* Koch International Classics ▲ KIC 7708
Robert DeCormier Ensemble
R. DeCormier
Christmas Eve, w. Robert DeCormier Singers Arabesque ▲ Z 6527
The First Nowell, w. Robert DeCormier Singers Arabesque ▲ Z 6526
The Man on the Flying Trapeze:A Celebration of an Era, w. Robert DeCormier Singers Arabesque ▲ Z 6588
Oh! You Beautiful Doll, w. Robert DeCormier Singers *(rec SUNY/Purchase Performing Arts Center, Feb 5–7, 1996)* Arabesque ▲ Z6675 [DDD]
A Victorian Christmas, w. Robert DeCormier Singers Arabesque ▲ Z 6525
Degenhardt–Kent Duo
Brown, E.:Corroboree, w. J. Zahl (pno) Mode ▲ 19
Crumb, G.:Celestial Mechanics (Makrokosmos IV) Mode ▲ 19
Crumb, G.:Zeitgeist Mode ▲ 19
Dekany String Quartet [Béla Dekany (vn), Jacques Hartog (vn), Erwin Schiffer (va), George Schiffer (vc)]
Haydn, J.:Qts Strs, Op. 1—Nos. 1, 2 *(rec 1964)* Vox Box 2–▲ CDX 5113
Haydn, J.:Qts Strs, Op. 20, "Sun Qts" *(rec 1964)* Vox Box 2–▲ CDX 5113
Delitiae Musicae Instrumental Ensemble
M. Longhini (cnd)
Verdelot, P.:Missa Philomena, w. Delitiae Musicae Vocal Ensemble Stradivarius ▲ STV 33405 [DDD]
Delius String Quartet [Nurit Pacht (vn), Josefina Vargera (vn), Nokuthula Ngwenyama (va), Brent Samuel (vc)]
Luther, J.M.:Qt Strs Vienna Modern Masters ▲ VMM 2015 [DDD]
Delmé String Quartet [G. Solodchin (vn), J. Trusler (vn), J. Underwood (va), R. Bailey (vc)]
Beautiful Dreamer (& other Parlour Favorites), w. Luxon, Benjamin (bar), David Willison (pno), et al. Omega Classics ▲ OCD 3005 [DDD]
Bliss, A.:Qts (2) Strs Hyperion ▲ CDA 66178 [DDD]
Brahms, J.:Qnt Cl, w. K. Puddy (cl) IMP Classics ▲ PCD 883 [DDD]
Bridge, F.:An Irish Melody Chandos ▲ CHAN 8426 [DDD]
Bridge, F.:Old English Songs (2) Chandos ▲ CHAN 8426 [DDD]

Delmé String Quartet (cont.)
Bridge, F.:Qt 2 Strs Chandos ▲ CHAN 8426 [DDD]
Bridge, F.:Sir Roger de Coverley Chandos ▲ CHAN 8426 [DDD]
Dvořák, A.:Qt 12 Strs, "America" IMP Classics ▲ PCD 883 [DDD]
Hamilton, I.:Qt 3 Symposium ▲ 1121
Hummel, J.N.:Qts Strs Hyperion ▲ CDA 66568
Simpson, R.:Qt 1 Strs Hyperion ▲ CDA 66419 [DDD]
Simpson, R.:Qt 2 Strs Hyperion ▲ CDA 66386 [DDD]
Simpson, R.:Qt 3 Strs Hyperion ▲ CDA 66376 [DDD]
Simpson, R.:Qt 4 Strs Hyperion ▲ CDA 66419 [DDD]
Simpson, R.:Qt 5 Strs Hyperion ▲ CDA 66386 [DDD]
Simpson, R.:Qt 6 Strs Hyperion ▲ CDA 66376 [DDD]
Simpson, R.:Qt 7 Strs Hyperion ▲ CDA 66117 [DDD]
Simpson, R.:Qt 8 Strs Hyperion ▲ CDA 66117 [DDD]
Simpson, R.:Qt 9 Strs Hyperion ▲ CDA 66127 [DDD]
Simpson, R.:Trio Strs Hyperion ▲ CDA 66376 [DDD]
A Ticket To Heaven (& other Parlour Favorites), w. Luxon, Benjamin (bar), David Willison (pno), et al. Omega Classics ▲ OCD 3006 [DDD]
Delmé String Quartet members
Britten, B.:Phantasy Qt, w. Sarah Francis (ob) Hyperion ▲ CDA 66776
Denis Clavier String Quartet [Denis Clavier (vn), Marie France Razafimbadà (vn), Florian Wallez (va), Claire Breteau (vc)]
Gouvy, T.:Qt 5 Strs *(rec l'Auditorium Tibor Varga à Sion, July 27 – Aug 1, 1995)* K617 ▲ 7054 [DDD]
Gouvy, T.:Qnt Pno, w. Dimitris Saroglou (pno) *(rec l'Auditorium Tibor Varga à Sion, July 27 – Aug 1, 1995)* K617 ▲ 7054 [DDD]
Denmark Concentus Musicus
A. Mathiesen (cnd)
Widmann, E.:Dances & Galliards *(rec Sept. 1965)* Elektra/Nonesuch ■ N5-71064
Denver Brass
K. Singleton (cnd)
Elegant Classics for Brass *(rec Bethany Lutheran Church, Englewood, CO, June 17–19, 1991)* Centaur ▲ CRC 2261 [DDD]
Denver SO
P. Entremont (cnd)
Berlioz, H.:Ovs—Carnaval romain Pro Arte ▲ CDS 541 [DDD]
Chabrier, E.:España Pro Arte ▲ CDS 541 [DDD]
Chabrier, E.:Joyeuse marche Pro Arte ▲ CDS 541 [DDD]
Debussy, C.:Prélude à l'après–midi d'un faune Pro Arte ▲ CDD 361 [DDD]
Debussy, C.:Printemps (suite) Pro Arte ▲ CDD 361 [DDD]
Dukas, P.:L'Apprenti sorcier Pro Arte ▲ CDS 541 [DDD]
Mussorgsky, M.:Pictures at an Exhibition Pro Arte ▲ CDS 544
Ravel, M.:Alborada del gracioso Pro Arte ▲ CDD 361 [DDD]
Ravel, M.:Boléro Pro Arte ▲ CDD 361 [DDD]
Ravel, M.:Rapsodie espagnole Pro Arte ▲ CDD 361 [DDD]
Vivé la Liberte Pro Arte ▲ CDS 541 [DDD]
B. Priestman (cnd)
Ginastera, A.:Milena, w. Phyllis Curtin (sop) Phoenix ▲ PHCD 107 [AAD]
Denver Sym Pops
N. Wayland (cnd)
Gershwin, G.:An American in Paris Pro Arte ▲ CDS 574 [DDD]
Gershwin, G.:An American in Paris Pro Arte ▲ CDD 352 [DDD]
Gershwin, G.:Music of—Swanee; Strike Up The Band Overture Pro Arte ▲ CDD 352 [DDD]
Gershwin, G.:Music of—Swanee; Strike Up The Band Overture Pro Arte ▲ CDS 574 [DDD]
Gershwin, G.:Rhap in Blue, w. G. Gershwin (pno) [1925 piano roll] Pro Arte ▲ CDS 574 [DDD]
Gershwin, G.:Rhap in Blue, w. G. Gershwin (pno) [1925 piano roll] Pro Arte ▲ CDD 352 [DDD]
DePaul Univ Jazz Ensemble
Bernstein, L.:Prelude, Fugue & Riffs Cl, w. J. B. Yeh (cl) *(rec May 1–3, 1993)* Reference ▲ RR 55 CD [DDD]
Gould, M.:Derivations, w. J.B. Yeh (cl) *(rec May 1–3, 1993)* Reference ▲ RR 55 CD [DDD]
Shaw, A.:Con Cl, w. J.B. Yeh *(rec May 1–3, 1993)* Reference ▲ RR 55 CD [DDD]
DePaul Univ Wind Ensemble
Stravinsky, I.:Ebony Con, w. J. B. Yeh (cl) *(rec May 1–3, 1993)* Reference ▲ RR 55 CD [DDD]
J. B. Yeh (cnd)
Babin, V.:Hillandale Waltzes [orchd. Dennis Nygren for wind ensemble, 1990] *(rec May 1–3, 1993)* Reference ▲ RR 55 CD [DDD]
Des Moines SO
J. Giunta (cnd)
Gershwin, G.:Con Pno, w. E. Wild (pno) Chesky ▲ CD 98 [DDD]
Wild, E.:Variations on an American Theme, w. E. Wild (pno) Chesky ▲ CD 98 [DDD]
Paul Desenne Ensemble
Desenne, P.:Botella al Guaire *(rec Caracas, Jan. & Feb. 1992)* Dorian Discovery ▲ DIS 80129 [DDD]
Desenne, P.:Coplas del Mangle *(rec Caracas, Jan. & Feb. 1992)* Dorian Discovery ▲ DIS 80129 [DDD]
Desenne, P.:Pizzi–Guasa Galeonica *(rec Caracas, Jan. & Feb. 1992)* Dorian Discovery ▲ DIS 80129 [DDD]
Desenne, P.:Pizzi–Quitiplas *(rec Caracas, Jan. & Feb. 1992)* Dorian Discovery ▲ DIS 80129 [DDD]
Desenne, P.:Quinteto de la Culbera *(rec Caracas, Jan. & Feb. 1992)* Dorian Discovery ▲ DIS 80129 [DDD]
Desenne, P.:Quniteto del Pajaro *(rec Caracas, Jan. & Feb. 1992)* Dorian Discovery ▲ DIS 80129 [DDD]
Desford Colliery Caterpillar Band
Lloyd Webber, A.:Music of—sels. from Cats; Phantom of the Opera; Song & Dance; Aspects of Love; Evita; Sunset Boulevard; Jesus Christ Superstar; Joseph & the Amazing Technicolor Dreamcoat; The Requiem; Friends for Life Koch Schwann ▲ SCH 340472 [DDD]; ■ SCH 340474
J. Watson (cnd)
Simpson, R.:Brass Band Music—Energy; The Four Temperaments; Introduction & Allegro on a Bass by Max Reger; Volcano; Vortex Hyperion ▲ CDA 66449
Il Desiderio [Silvia Piccollo (sop), Giuseppe Zambon (ct), Massimo Lonadi (lt), Serbio Balestracci (rcr), Gaetano Nasillo (vl)]
Willaert, A.:Madrigals—Quanto sia liet'il giorno; Quando amor i begli occhi; Donna leggiandra e bella; Madonna qual certezza; Con lagrime, et sospir; Fuggi, fuggi cor mio; Igno soave ove il mio foco; Amor se d'hor in hor; Donna che sete tra le belle bella; Se mai provasti donna; Afflitti spirti miei; Ben che'l misero cor; Madonna il tuo bel viso; Divini occhi sereni; Si lieta e grata morte; Vita de la mia vita; Gloriar mi poss'io donne; Piove da gli occhi; Con l'angelico riso; Si'io pensasse madonna; Madonna io sol vorrei; Madonna per voi ardo Stradivarius ▲ STV 33325 [DDD]
Detmold Hornists
Höltzel, M.:Music for Rügheim Hunt MD + G ("Gold" series) ▲ MDG 3240143 [DDD]
Horn Quartets MD + G ▲ L 3324 [DDD]
Hubertusmesse MD + G ▲ MDG CD 3240098
St. Hubert's Mass MD + G ▲ L 3098 [DDD]
Detmold Wind Ensemble
J. Michaels (cnd)
Weill, K.:Con Vn, w. S. Lautenbacher (vn) *(rec ca. 1973)* Vox Box 2–▲ CDX 5043 [ADD]

Detroit Chamber Winds
H.R. Reynolds (cnd)
Ives, C.:Orchestral Music—March III; Anne Street; Calcium Light Night; Holiday Quick Step; 5 Songs for Brass Quintet; Fugue in Four Keys; The Unanswered Question; Remembrance; Evening; Mists; The Circus Band; Romanzo di Central Park; Scherzo (All the way around and back); Scherzo (Over the pavements); Gyp the Blood; Adagio Sostenuto; Tone Roads Nos. 1 & 3; March II; The Seer; Luck and Work; Like A Sick Eagle; Hallowe'en Koch International Classics ▲ KIC 7182 [DDD]
Stravinsky, I.:Con Pno Ww, w. James Tocco (pno) Koch International Classics ▲ KIC 7211
Stravinsky, I.:Octet Koch International Classics ▲ KIC 7211
Stravinsky, I.:Pno-Rag-Music, w. James Tocco (pno) Koch International Classics ▲ KIC 7211
Stravinsky, I.:Septet Cl Koch International Classics ▲ KIC 7211
Stravinsky, I.:Syms Ww Koch International Classics ▲ KIC 7211
Stravinsky, I.:Tango Koch International Classics ▲ KIC 7211
Detroit SO
A. Dorati (cnd)
Copland, A.:Appalachian Spring London ("Jubilee" series) ▲ 430705-2 [DDD]
Copland, A.:Dance Sym *(rec United Artists Auditorium, Detroit, MI, May 1981)* London 2-▲ 448261-2 [DDD]
Copland, A.:Rodeo *(rec United Artists Auditorium, Detroit, MI, May 1981)* London 2-▲ 448261-2 [DDD]
Copland, A.:Rodeo London ("Jubilee" series) ▲ 430705-2 [DDD]
Copland, A.:El salón México *(rec United Artists Auditorium, Detroit, MI, May 1981)* London 2-▲ 448261-2 [DDD]
Copland, A.:El salón México London ("Jubilee" series) ▲ 430705-2 [DDD]
Gershwin, G.:Porgy & Bess (symphonic picture) London ("Jubilee" series) ▲ 430712-2 [DDD]
Grofé, F.:Grand Canyon Suite London ("Jubilee" series) ▲ 430712-2 [DDD]
Strauss, R.:Die ägyptische Helena, w. G. Jones (sop), M. Kastu (ten), B. Hendricks (sop), W. White (bass), C. Rayam (ten), B. Finnilä (mez) London ("Grand Opera" series) 2-▲ 430381-2 [AAD]
Tchaikovsky, P.:Marche slave London ▲ 417742-2 [ADD]
Tchaikovsky, P.:Ov 1812 London ▲ 417742-2 [ADD]
N. Järvi (cnd)
Barber, S.:Essays 1-3 *(rec 11/91)* Chandos ▲ CHAN 9053 [DDD]
Barber, S.:Medea's Meditation & Dance of Vengeance *(rec Jan. 16, 1994)* Chandos ▲ CHAN 9253 [DDD]
Barber, S.:Music for a Scene from Shelley *(rec Apr. 24-25, 1993)* Chandos ▲ CHAN 9253 [DDD]
Barber, S.:The School for Scandal Chandos ▲ CHAN 8958 [DDD]
Barber, S.:Sym 1 Chandos ▲ CHAN 8958 [DDD]
Barber, S.:Vanessa (sels)—Intermezzo; Under the Willow Tree *(rec Apr. 24-25, 1993)* Chandos ▲ CHAN 9253 [DDD]
Beach, A.M.C.:Sym in e, "Gaelic Sym" Chandos ▲ CHAN 8958 [DDD]
Chadwick, G.W.:Melpomene Chandos ("American" series) ▲ CHAN 9439
Chadwick, G.W.:Rip Van Winkle Chandos ("American" series) ▲ CHAN 9439
Chadwick, G.W.:Symphonic Sketches Chandos ▲ CHAN 9334 [DDD]
Chadwick, G.W.:Sym 2 Chandos ▲ CHAN 9334 [DDD]
Chadwick, G.W.:Sym 3 *(rec Apr. 24-25, 1993)* Chandos ▲ CHAN 9253 [DDD]
Chadwick, G.W.:Tam O'Shanter Chandos ("American" series) ▲ CHAN 9439
Copland, A.:Sym 3 Chandos ("American" series) ▲ CHAN 9474
Creston, P.:Sym 2 Chandos ▲ CHAN 9390 [DDD]
Dawson, W.L.:Negro Folk Sym Chandos ▲ CHAN 9226 [DDD]
Debussy, C.:La Mer *(rec Detroit SO Hall, Jan 11 & 12, 1992)* Chandos ▲ CHAN 7031
Ellington, D.:Harlem Chandos ▲ CHAN 9226 [DDD]
Ellington, D.:The River (suite) *(rec Sept. 29, Oct. 3, 1992)* Chandos ▲ CHAN 9154 [DDD]
Encore! Chandos ▲ CHAN 9227 [DDD]
Fibich, Z.:Sym 1 Chandos ▲ CHAN 9230
Fibich, Z.:Sym 2 Chandos ▲ CHAN 9328 [DDD]
Fibich, Z.:Sym 3 Chandos ▲ CHAN 9328 [DDD]
Harris, R.:Sym 3 Chandos ("American" series) ▲ CHAN 9474
Ives, C.:Sym 1 *(rec 11/91)* Chandos ▲ CHAN 9053 [DDD]
Ives, C.:Sym 2 Chandos ▲ CHAN 9390 [DDD]
Milhaud, D.:Suite provençale *(rec Detroit SO Hall, Jan 11 & 12, 1992)* Chandos ▲ CHAN 7031
Milhaud, D.:Suite provençale Chandos ▲ CHAN 9072 [DDD]
A Night in Tunisia, A Week in Detroit, w. Turtle Island String Quartet Chandos ("New Direction" series) ▲ CHAN 9331 [DDD]
Rachmaninoff, S.:Trio élégiaque 2, w. A. Kogosowski (pno) [orchd. A. Kogosowski] Chandos ▲ CHAN 9261 [DDD]
Rachmaninoff, S.:Variations on a Theme by Corelli, w. A. Kogosowski (pno) Chandos ▲ CHAN 9261 [DDD]
Rachmaninoff, S.:Vocalise Chandos ▲ CHAN 9261 [DDD]
Ravel, M.:Boléro *(rec Detroit SO Hall, May 11 & 12, 1991)* Chandos ▲ CHAN 7031
Ravel, M.:La Valse Chandos ▲ CHAN 8996 [DDD]
Ravel, M.:La Valse *(rec Detroit SO Hall, May 11 & 12, 1991)* Chandos ▲ CHAN 7031
Roussel, A.:Bacchus et Ariane (suite 2) Chandos ▲ CHAN 7007 [DDD]
Roussel, A.:Sinfonietta Strs Chandos ▲ CHAN 7007 [DDD]
Roussel, A.:Sym 3 Chandos ▲ CHAN 7007 [DDD]
Roussel, A.:Sym 3 Chandos ▲ CHAN 8996 [DDD]
Roussel, A.:Sym 4 Chandos ▲ CHAN 9072 [DDD]
Roussel, A.:Sym 4 Chandos ▲ CHAN 7007 [DDD]
Schmidt, F.:Sym 1 Chandos ▲ CHAN 9357 [DDD]
Smetana, B.:Má Vlast—Vysehrad & Vlatava movements Chandos ▲ CHAN 9230
Smetana, B.:Má Vlast Chandos ▲ CHAN 9366 [DDD]
Still, W.G.:Sym 1 *(rec Sept. 29, Oct. 3, 1992)* Chandos ▲ CHAN 9154 [DDD]
Still, W.G.:Sym 2 Chandos ▲ CHAN 9226 [DDD]
Strauss, R.:Symphonic Interludes Chandos ▲ CHAN 9357 [DDD]
Tchaikovsky, P.:Francesca da Rimini Chandos ▲ CHAN 9419
Tchaikovsky, P.:The Snow Maiden, w. Irina Mishura-Lekhtman (mez), Vladimir Grishko (ten), Univ Musical Society Choral Union Chandos ▲ CHAN 9324 [DDD]
Tchaikovsky, P.:Suite 2 *(rec Detroit SO Hall, Detroit, MI, Mar 10-12, 1995)* Chandos ▲ CHAN 9454
Tchaikovsky, P.:Suite 3 Chandos ▲ CHAN 9419
Tchaikovsky, P.:The Tempest *(rec Detroit SO Hall, Detroit, MI, Nov 12 & 13, 1994)* Chandos ▲ CHAN 9454
Thompson, R.:Sym 2 Chandos ("American" series) ▲ CHAN 9439
P. Paray (cnd)
Auber, D.-F.:Ovs—The Bronze Horse; Fra Diavolo; Masaniello Mercury Living Presence ▲ 434309-2 [ADD]
Berlioz, H.:La Damnation de Faust (sels)—Marche hongroise Mercury Living Presence ▲ 434328-2 [ADD]
Berlioz, H.:Ovs—Carnaval romain; Le Corsaire Mercury Living Presence ▲ 434328-2 [ADD]
Berlioz, H.:Sym fantastique Mercury Living Presence ▲ 434328-2 [ADD]
Berlioz, H.:Les Troyens (sels)—Trojan March Mercury Living Presence ▲ 434328-2 [ADD]
Bizet, G.:L'Arlésienne (suites) Mercury Living Presence ▲ 434321-2 [ADD]
Bizet, G.:Carmen (suite 1) Mercury Living Presence ▲ 434321-2 [ADD]
Bizet, G.:Patrie Mercury Living Presence ▲ 434321-2 [ADD]
Chabrier, E.:Bourée fantasque Mercury Living Presence ▲ 434303-2 [ADD]
Chabrier, E.:España Mercury Living Presence ▲ 434303-2 [ADD]
Chabrier, E.:Gwendoline (ov) Mercury Living Presence ▲ 434303-2 [ADD]
Chabrier, E.:Joyeuse marche Mercury Living Presence ▲ 434303-2 [ADD]
Chabrier, E.:Le Roi malgré lui (sels)—Danse slave & Fête polonaise Mercury Living Presence ▲ 434303-2 [ADD]

Detroit SO (cont.)
P. Paray (cnd) (cont.)
Chabrier, E.:Suite pastorale Mercury Living Presence ▲ 434303-2 [ADD]
Debussy, C.:Ibéria *(rec Detroit, Dec. 3 & 4, 1955)* Mercury Living Presence ▲ 434343-2
Debussy, C.:Nocturnes, w. Detroit Sym Chorus Mercury Living Presence ▲ 434306-2 [ADD]
Debussy, C.:Petite suite Mercury Living Presence ▲ 434306-2 [ADD]
Debussy, C.:Prélude à l'après-midi d'un faune *(rec Detroit, Dec. 3 & 4, 1955)* Mercury Living Presence ▲ 434343-2
Dvořák, A.:Sym 9, "From the New World" Mercury Living Presence ▲ 434317-2 [ADD]
French Opera Highlights Mercury Living Presence ▲ 432014-2 [ADD]
Ibert, J.:Escales Mercury Living Presence ▲ 432003-2 [ADD]
Liszt, F.:Mephisto Waltz 1 Orch Mercury Living Presence ▲ 434336-2
Marches & Overtures à la Française Mercury Living Presence ▲ 434332-2
Paray, P.:Mass for the 500th Anniversary of the Death of Joan of Arc, w. *(soloists unknown)*, Detroit Sym Chorus Mercury Living Presence ▲ 432719-2 [ADD]
Ravel, M.:Alborada del gracioso Mercury Living Presence ▲ 432003-2 [ADD]
Ravel, M.:Boléro Mercury Living Presence ▲ 434306-2 [ADD]
Ravel, M.:Daphnis et Chloé (suite 2) Mercury Living Presence ▲ 434306-2 [ADD]
Ravel, M.:Ma mère l'oye Orch *(rec Detroit, Mar. 19, 1957)* Mercury Living Presence ▲ 434343-2
Ravel, M.:Pavane pour une infante défunte Mercury Living Presence ▲ 432003-2
Ravel, M.:Rapsodie espagnole Mercury Living Presence ▲ 432003-2 [ADD]
Ravel, M.:Le Tombeau de Couperin Mercury Living Presence ▲ 432003-2
Ravel, M.:La Valse Mercury Living Presence ▲ 432003-2 [ADD]
Ravel, M.:Valses nobles et sentimentales Mercury Living Presence ▲ 434306-2 [ADD]
Roussel, A.:Suite Mercury Living Presence ▲ 434303-2 [ADD]
Saint-Saëns, C.:Danse macabre Mercury Living Presence ▲ 434336-2
Saint-Saëns, C.:Sym 3, w. M. Dupré (org) Mercury Living Presence ▲ 432719-2 [ADD]
Schmitt, F.:La tragédie de Salomé (sels) Mercury Living Presence ▲ 434336-2
Sibelius, J.:Sym 2 Mercury Living Presence ▲ 434317-2 [ADD]
Strauss, R.:Salome (dance) Mercury Living Presence ▲ 434336-2
Suppé, F. von:Ovs—The Beautiful Galatea; Boccaccio; Light Cavalry; Morning, Noon & Night in Vienna; Pique Dame; Poet & Peasant Mercury Living Presence ▲ 434309-2 [ADD]
Wagner, R.:Ovs, Preludes & Orch Sels—Der fliegende Holländer:Ov; Die Meistersinger:Suite; Die Walküre:Wotan's Farewell & Magic Fire Music; Rienzi:Ov; Götterdämmerung:Dawn & Siegfried's Rhine Journey; Tristan und Isolde:Prelude to Act III; Siegfried Idyll Mercury Living Presence ▲ 434383-2
Weber, C.M. von:Invitation to the Dance Orch Mercury Living Presence ▲ 434336-2
Deutsche Opera Orch
K. Böhm (cnd)
Berg, A.:Lulu, w. E. Lear (sop—Lulu), P. Johnson (mez—Countess Geschwitz), D. Grobe (ten—Alwa), Fischer-Dieskau (bar—Dr. Schön), German Opera Chorus [G] *(rec 1968)* Deutsche Grammophon 3-▲ 435705-2 [ADD]
Berg, A.:Wozzeck, w. E. Lear (sop—Marie), F. Wunderlich (ten—Andres), G. Stoltze (ten—The Captain), D. Fischer-Dieskau (bar—Wozzeck), German Opera Chorus [G] *(rec 1965)* Deutsche Grammophon 3-▲ 435705-2 [ADD]
H. Hollreiser (cnd)
Strauss, R.:Arias, w. C. Ludwig (mez), W. Berry (b-bar), German Opera Chorus—two of Ariadne's solo arias from Ariadne auf Naxos, duets from Elektra, Frau ohne Schatten, Rosenkavalier [G] *(rec Berlin, 1963-64)* Tessitura ▲ 0049-2 [ADD]
Wagner, R.:Götterdämmerung (immolation scene), w. C. Ludwig (mez) [G] *(rec studio, Berlin, ca. 1963/64)* Tessitura ▲ 0049-2 [ADD]
E. Jochum (cnd)
Wagner, R.:Die Meistersinger von Nürnberg, w. C. Ligendza (sop), C. Ludwig (mez), P. Domingo (ten), R. Laubenthal (ten), D. Fischer-Dieskau (bar), R. Hermann (bar), P. Lagger (bass), German Opera Chorus Deutsche Grammophon ("Domingo Edition" series) ▲ 435406-2
Wagner, R.:Die Meistersinger von Nürnberg, w. C. Ligendza (sop), C. Ludwig (mez), P. Domingo (ten), R. Laubenthal (ten), D. Fischer-Dieskau (bar), R. Hermann (bar), P. Lagger (bass), German Opera Chorus [G] Deutsche Grammophon 4-▲ 415278-2 [ADD]
G.L. Jochum (cnd)
Orff, C.:Carmina burana, w. G. Janowitz (sop), G. Stolze (ten), D. Fischer-Dieskau (bar), German Opera Chorus [G, L] Deutsche Grammophon ("Galleria" series) ▲ 423886-2 [ADD]
P. Van Kempen (cnd)
Brahms, J.:Con Vn, w. Gioconda de Vito (vn) *(rec live, Berlin, 1941)* Arkadia ▲ 623 [ADD]
G. Sinopoli (cnd)
Verdi, G.:Nabucco, w. G. Dimitrova (sop), L. V. Terrani (mez), P. Domingo (ten), P. Cappuccilli (bar), E. Nesterenko (bass), German Opera Chorus [I] Deutsche Grammophon 2-▲ 410512-2 [DDD]
C. Thielemann (cnd)
Strauss, E.:Songs, w. R. Kollo (ten)—"Verführung," Op. 33/1 [G] EMI Classics ▲ CDC 54776
Strauss, R.:4 Last Songs, w. R. Kollo (ten)—Im Abendroth [G] EMI Classics ▲ CDC 54776
Strauss, R.:Songs, w. R. Kollo (ten)—Verführung, Op. 33/1 [G] EMI Classics ▲ CDC 54776
Wagner, R.:Arias & Scenes, w. R. Kollo (ten)—from Tristan und Isolde *(Dünkt dich das?)*, Die Walküre (w. Ingride Haubold [soprano]) *(Ein Schwert verheiss mir der Vater; Die Männer Sippe; Winterstrme wiche dem Wonnemond)* [G] EMI Classics ▲ CDC 54776
Wagner, R.:Tristan und Isolde (sels), w. R. Kollo (ten)—Act 3 (Wesendonck Lieder) [G] EMI Classics ▲ CDC 54776
Wagner, R.:Die Walküre (act 1/scene 3), w. I. Haubold (sop), R. Kollo (ten) [G] EMI Classics ▲ CDC 54776
Diagonales Brass & Percussion Ensemble
R. Bosc (cnd)
Bernstein, L.:Music of, w. Montpelier Brass Quintet—West Side Story Suite [arr. Bosc]; Dance Suite; Elegy for Mippy [I & II]; Fanfare for Bima; Waltz for Mippy III; Rondo for Lifey; Anniversary for Aaron Copland Agora Music ▲ 007
Copland, A.:Fanfare for the Common Man, w. Montpelier Brass Quintet Agora Music ▲ 007
Copland, A.:Inaugural Fanfare, w. Montpelier Brass Quintet Agora Music ▲ 007
Dialogos Duo [Joaquim Abreu (perc), Carlos Tarcha (perc)]
Alvares, E.:Pocema *(rec Studio Cardan, Sao Paolo, 1994)* GHA ▲ 126.033
Cerqueira, F.:Sketches (7) to Frighten Guido d'Arezzo *(rec Studio Cardan, Sao Paolo, 1994)* GHA ▲ 126.033
Csekö, L.C.:Volume em sombras *(rec Studio Cardan, Sao Paolo, 1994)* GHA ▲ 126.033
Mannis, J.A.:Reflexos *(rec Studio Cardan, Sao Paolo, 1994)* GHA ▲ 126.033
Menezes, F.:A dialética da praia *(rec Studio Cardan, Sao Paolo, 1994)* GHA ▲ 126.033
Seincman, E.:A dança do Dibuk *(rec Studio Cardan, Sao Paolo, 1994)* GHA ▲ 126.033
Dianopolis Bulgarian CO
M. Harth-Bedoya (cnd)
Martin Y Soler, V.:Il Tutore Burlato, w. Liliana Marzano (sop—Menica), Maria Angeles Peters (sop—Violante), Juan Diego Florez (ten—Anselmo), Ernesto Palacio (ten—Il Cavaliere), Marcello Lippi (bar—Pippo), Giancarlo Tosi (bass—Don Fabrizio), Michela Forgione (hpd) *(rec VI Festival Internazionale di Gerace nella Chiesa di San Francesco, Aug 16, 1994)* Bongiovanni 2-▲ GB 2175/76-2 [DDD]
Diaz Trio [David Kim (vn), Roberto Diaz (va), Andres Diaz (vc)]
Seasons Remembered 2, w. Judith Lynn Stillman (pno), Toby Appel (va), John Deak (db), Eliot Porter (db), Lutz Rath (vc), Fenwick Smith (fl), Ruth Waterman (vn) North Star ▲ 9837-40052-2 ■ 9837-40052-4
Diaz-Shames-Diaz Trio
Bach, J.S.:Con Ob, BWV 1053, w. W. Rapier (ob), T. Dimitriades *(rec live in concert, Oct 1, 1989)* Boston Records ▲ BR 1001 ■ BR 1001 CT
Bach, J.S.:Con Ob d'amore, w. W. Rapier (ob d'amore), T. Dimitriades *(rec live in concert, Oct 1, 1989)* Boston Records ▲ BR 1001 ■ BR 1001 CT
Finzi, G.:Bagatelles, Op. 23, w. W. Rapier (ob), T. Dimitriades (str) *(rec live 10/1/89)* Boston Records ▲ BR 1001 ■ BR 1001 CT

▲ = CD ♦ = Enhanced CD Δ = MD ■ = Cassette Tape ◻ = DCC

Diaz-Shames-Diaz Trio (cont.)
Mozart, W.A.:Qt Ob, K.370, w. W. Rapier (ob) *(rec live in concert, Oct. 1, 1989)* Boston Records ▲ BR 1001 ■ BR 1001 CT

Dies Caniculares Festival Orch
P. Borin (cnd)
Eirlksdottlr, Karolina:Someone I Have Seen (act 2), w. Ingegerd Nilsson (sop) Music from Iceland ▲ ITM 701 [ADD]

Dinosaur Annex Music Ensemble
Sirota, R.:7 Picassos *(rec WGBH, Boston)* Capstone ▲ CPS 8616 [DDD]
D. Hoose (cnd)
Sims, E.:Come Away, w. J. Felty (mez) [E] CRI ▲ CD 578 [DDD]

Discantus
Musica Humana, w. Françoise Atlan (mez), John Fleagle (ten/hp), Crawford Young (lt), Anonymous 4, Ensemble Discantus, Ensemble Gilles Binchois, Ensemble Organum, Gothic Voices, Greece Byzantine Choir, Hilliard Ensemble, Musica Nova, et al. L'Empreinte Digitale ▲ ED 13047
B. Lesne (cnd)
Campus Stellae Opus 111 ▲ OPS 30-102

Dithyrambos
E. Ghent (cnd)
Ghent, E.:Five Brass Voices Capstone ▲ CPS 8609 CD

Divertimenti String Quartet
Dyson, G.:Rhaps (3) Hyperion ▲ CDA 66139
Howells, H.:Qt 3 Strs Hyperion ▲ CDA 66139

Il Divertimento [Mathias Spaeter (archlt), Claire Giardelli (vc), Mirella Giardelli (hpd)]
Handel, G.F.:Cants, w. Isabelle Poulenard (sop), Jean-Louis Comoretto (ct)—Menzognere speranze; Vedendo amor; Figli del mesto cor; Lungi dal mio bel nume Astrée ▲ E 8577
Handel, G.F.:Duets for Various Voices, w. Isabelle Poulenard (sop), Jean-Louis Comoretto (ct)—No, di voi non vo' fidarmi; Troppo curda, troppo fiera; Tanti strali al sen mi scocchi Astrée ▲ E 8577

Divertimento Ensemble
S. Gorli (cnd)
Maderna, B.:Satyricon Salabert ▲ SCD 9101
Togni, C.:Rondeaux per 10, w. Dorothy Dorow (sop) Stradivarius ▲ STV DTM 90002 [ADD]

Divertimento Salzburg
Haydn, J.:Concertino Org, w. Martin Haselböck (org) Orfeo ▲ 310941 [DDD]
Haydn, J.:Con Org & Strs, H.XVIII/2, w. Franz Haselböck (org) [period instrs] Orfeo ▲ 158871 [DDD]
Haydn, J.:Con Org, Vn & Strs, H.XVIII/6, w. Franz Haselböck (org) Orfeo ▲ 310941 [DDD]
Haydn, J.:Con Org, Vns & Bass Instrument, H.XVIII/7, w. Franz Haselböck (org) [period instrs] Orfeo ▲ 158871 [DDD]
Haydn, J.:Con Org, Vns & Bass Instrument, H.XVIII/8, w. Franz Haselböck (org) [period instrs] Orfeo ▲ 158871 [DDD]
Haydn, J.:Divert for 2 E Hns, Hns, Vns & Bns, H.II/16, w. Annegret Diedrichsen (vn) [arr fl, ob, 2 vns, vc, bn & db] Orfeo ▲ 310941 [DDD]
Haydn, J.:Divert Fl, Ob, Vns, Vc, Bn & Db, H.II/11, "Der Geburtstag", w. Annegret Diedrichsen (vn) Orfeo ▲ 310941 [DDD]
Haydn, J.:Divert for 2 Hns, Vns, Va & Db, H.II/22 Orfeo ▲ 310941 [DDD]
Mozart, W.A.:Qnt Cl, K.581 [period instrs] *(rec Studio Salzburg, 1980)* Claves ▲ CD 508007 [ADD]
Mozart, W.A.:Qnt Cl, K.580b [period instrs] *(rec Studio Salzburg, 1980)* Claves ▲ CD 508007 [ADD]
Mozart, W.A.:Rondo Basset Hn, K.581a [period instrs] *(rec Studio Salzburg, 1980)* Claves ▲ CD 508007 [ADD]

Divertimento Trio
Beethoven, L. van:Trios Strs, Op. 9 Arcobaleno ▲ SBCD 8500 [DDD]
Beethoven, L. van:Trios Strs, Op. 9 Masters of Art ▲ AAOC-9384

La Dolcezza Ensemble
K. Eichhorn (cnd)
Bach, J.S.:Nun Komm, der Heiden Heiland, BWV 61, w. Capella Cantorum *(rec Berlin-Wilmersdorf, Aug 8-10, 1995)* Capriccio ▲ 10721 [DDD]
Erlebach, P.H.:Lobe, lobe den Herrn, w. Berlin Baroque Trumpet Ensemble, Capella Cantorum *(rec Berlin-Wilmersdorf, Aug 8-10, 1995)* Capriccio ▲ 10721 [DDD]
Krieger, J.P.:Gloria in excelsis deo, w. Berlin Baroque Trumpet Ensemble, Capella Cantorum *(rec Berlin-Wilmersdorf, Aug 8-10, 1995)* Capriccio ▲ 10721 [DDD]
Krieger, J.P.:Magnificat, w. Berlin Baroque Trumpet Ensemble, Capella Cantorum *(rec Berlin-Wilmersdorf, Aug 8-10, 1995)* Capriccio ▲ 10721 [DDD]
Zachow, F.W.:Danksaget dem Vater, w. Capella Cantorum *(rec Berlin-Wilmersdorf, Aug 8-10, 1995)* Capriccio ▲ 10721 [DDD]
Zachow, F.W.:Preiset mit mir den Herren, w. Capella Cantorum *(rec Berlin-Wilmersdorf, Aug 8-10, 1995)* Capriccio ▲ 10721 [DDD]
Zachow, F.W.:Von Himmel kam der Engel Schar, w. Berlin Baroque Trumpet Ensemble, Capella Cantorum *(rec Berlin-Wilmersdorf, Aug 8-10, 1995)* Capriccio ▲ 10721 [DDD]

Dolezal String Quartet members
Vranicky, P.:Qts Fl, Op. 28, w. Loïc Poulain (fl) Adda ▲ ADD 581300 [DDD]

Dolezalovo String Quartet [Jiří Fišer (vn), Vladimír Kučera (vn), Karel Dolezal (va), Petr Hejny (vc)]
Janácek, L.:Qt 1 Strs *(rec Blessed Virgin Mary Angelic Church, Prague, June 1992)* Arta ▲ 0034 [DDD]
Janácek, L.:Qt 2 Strs *(rec Blessed Virgin Mary Angelic Church, Prague, June 1992)* Arta ▲ 0034 [DDD]

Dolezil String Quartet
Janácek, L.:Qt 1 Strs Accord ▲ ACD 220312 [DDD]

Dolmetsch-Schoenfeld Ensemble [Carl Dolmetsch (rcr), Alice Schoenfeld (vn), Eleonore Schoenfeld (vc), Joseph Saxby (hpd)]
Berkeley, L.:Concertino Orion ■ OC 9104
Cooke, A.:Son Rcr Orion ■ OC 9104

Domaine Musical Orch
P. Boulez (cnd)
Messiaen, O.:Couleurs de la cité céleste, w. Yvonne Loriod (pno), Strasbourg Instrumental Percussion Group Sony Classical ("Pierre Boulez Edition" series) ▲ SMK 68332
Stravinsky, I.:Syms Ww, New York PO Sony Classical ("Pierre Boulez Edition" series) ▲ SMK 68332
J.-P. Salanne (cnd)
Boulanger, L.:Pie Jesu, w. Antoine Brouquet (sop) Adès ▲ ADE 204782 [DDD]
Fauré, G.:Requiem, w. Antoine Brouquet (sop), Jean-Marie Fremeau (bar), Tarbes Midi-Pyrénées Régional Choir Adès ▲ ADE 204782 [DDD]
Franck, C.:Messe solennelle, w. *(soloists unknown)*, Henri Duparc Chorus—Domine non secundum Cypres ▲ 2610
Franck, C.:Les Sept paroles du Christ sur la croix, w. *(soloists unknown)*, Henri Duparc Chorus Cypres ▲ 2610

Domus Chamber Ensemble
Brahms, J.:Qt 1 Pno Virgin Classics ▲ CDC 59248
Brahms, J.:Qt 2 Pno Virgin Classics ▲ 59144 [DDD]
Brahms, J.:Qt 3 Pno Virgin Classics ▲ CDC 59248
Chamber Music Sampler, w. Chi-Chi Nwanoky (db), et al. Virgin Classics 2-▲ CDC 59092
Dohnányi, E. von:Serenade Virgin Classics ▲ CDC 45015
Dvořák, A.:Bagatelles, Op. 47 Virgin Classics ▲ CDC 59245
Fauré, G.:Qt 1 Pno Hyperion ▲ CDA 66166 [DDD]
Fauré, G.:Qt 2 Pno Hyperion ▲ CDA 66166 [DDD]
Kodály, Z.:Trio for 2 Vns & Va Virgin Classics ▲ CDC 45015
Lekeu, G.:Qt Pno, Vn, Va & Vc Ricercar ▲ RIS 104091 [DDD]
Mahler, G.:Qt Pno [1 movt] Virgin Classics ▲ 59144 [DDD]
Martinů, B.:Madrigals Vn Virgin Classics ▲ CDC 45015
Martinů, B.:Qt 1 Pno Virgin Classics ▲ CDC 59245

Domus Chamber Ensemble (cont.)
Martinů, B.:Trio 2 Vn Virgin Classics ▲ CDC 45015
Mendelssohn, F.:Qt 1 Pno Virgin Classics ▲ CDC 59628
Mendelssohn, F.:Qt 3 Pno Virgin Classics ▲ CDC 59628
Mozart, W.A.:Qts Pno Virgin Classics ▲ 59063 [DDD]
Mozart, W.A.:Trio Cl, K.498, w. R. Hosford (cl) Virgin Classics ▲ 59063 [DDD]
Suk, J.:Qt Pno Virgin Classics ▲ CDC 59245
Weir, J.:Chamber Music, w. William Howard (pno), Susan Tomes (pno), Petra Casen (hpd), Schubert Ensemble—Distance & Enchantment; The Bagpiper's Trio; I Broke Off a Golden Branch; El Rey de Francia; The Art of Touching the Keyboard; The King of France; Ardnamurchan Point Collins Classics ▲ COL 1453

Domus String Quartet
Fauré, G.:Qnts Pno & Strs, Opp. 89 & 115, w. Anthony Marwood (vc) Hyperion ▲ CDA 66766

Don Milani Cultural Association Orch
F. Ghiglione (cnd)
Marcello, B.:Il pianto e il riso delle quattro stagioni, w. S. Piccollo (sop-Primavera), A. Carmignani (ct-Estate), M. Beasley (ten-Autunno), R. Franceschetto (bass-Inverno), G. B. Trofello Schola Cantorum *(rec Mar. 29, 1992)* Bongiovanni 2-▲ GB 2159/60 [DDD]

Donizetti Ensemble
Amendola, F.:Ricercari, w. D. Patumi (db), A. Frederico (elecs/pno), A. Flore (voc), G. Lanzini (cl), L. Ciolfi (vn), C. Cavalieri (vn), C. Sanzo (vc), O. Mangiavacchi (perc) Bongiovanni ▲ GB 5519 [DDD]

Doppeltes Wind Quintet
H. Hennig (cnd)
Stravinsky, I.:Babel, w. North German Radio PO, Hanover Boys' Choir [E & G; 2 versions] *(rec Jan. 5-6, 1993)* Calig ▲ CAL 50918 [DDD]

Dorian Wind Quintet
Adolphe, B.:Night Journey Summit ▲ DCD 117 [DDD]
Dejong, C.:Vars on the Spanish La Folia Summit ▲ DCD117 [DDD]
Hoiby, L.:Sextet Wind Qnt & Pno Summit ▲ DCD117 [DDD]
Perle, G.:Qnts Ww New World ▲ NW 359-2 [DDD]
Schifrin, L.:La Nouvelle Orléans Summit ▲ DCD117 [DDD]
Tower, J.:Island Prelude Summit ▲ DCD117 [DDD]
Winds:20th Century Music for Woodwinds, w. New York Philomusica Chamber Ensemble, et al. Vox Box 2-▲ CDX 5083 [ADD]

Dorsey Orch
T. Dorsey (cnd)
Gershwin, G.:Girl Crazy Sandy Hook ▲ CSH 2114

Double Edge [Edmund Niemann (pno), Nurit Tilles (pno)]
Messiaen, O.:Visions de l'Amen New Albion ▲ NA 045
Reich, S.:Pno Phase Elektra/Nonesuch ▲ 79169-2 [DDD] ■ 79169-4 (D)
Tower, J.:Stepping Stones *(rec American Academy of Arts & Letters, New York City, Sept. 26-28, 1994)* New World ▲ 80470-2

Double Image members [David Carhart (pno), Erica Dearing (vn), Joanna Borrett (vc)]
Schumann, C.:Trio Pno Meridian ▲ MER 84312 [DDD]

Double Image members [Erica Dearing (vn), David Carhart (pno)]
Schumann, C.:Romances Vn Meridian ▲ MER 84312 [DDD]

Double Image members [Kym Amps (sop), David Carhart (pno)]
Schumann, C.:Songs—6 Lieder aus Jucunde, Op. 23/1-6; Er ist gekommen in Sturm und Regen, Op. 12/2; Liebst du um Schönheit, Op. 12/4; Warum willst du and're fragen, Op. 12/11 Meridian ▲ MER 84312 [DDD]

Double Reed Ensemble
I. Pederson (cnd)
A Baroque Celebration, w. New York Chamber Music *(rec June 1993)* Dorian ▲ DOR 90189 [DDD]

Douce Mémoire Ensemble
D. Raisin-Dadre (cnd)
Fricassées Lyonnaises Astrée ▲ E 8567
Pierre Attaingnant, Chansons Nouvelles & Danceries Astrée ▲ E 8545

Dowland Consort
Holborne, A.:Instrumental Consort Music, w. J. Lindberg (fl)—34 "Galliards, Almains & Other Short Airs" BIS ▲ CD 469 [DDD]
J. Lindberg (cnd)
Dowland, J.:Lachrimae, or Seaven Teares BIS ▲ CD 315 [DDD]
Heavenly Noise:English Music for Mixed Consort from the Golden Age BIS ▲ CD 451 [DDD]

Downshire Players of London
The Art of James Bowman, w. J. Bowman (ct), Crispian Steel-Perkins (nat tpt), King's Consort, Music's Re-creation Meridian ▲ MER 84332
P. Ash (cnd)
Howells, H.:Songs, w. J. Bowman (ct)—2 songs—Full Moon; O my deir hert [E] *(rec 1988)* Meridian ▲ CDE 84150
Ridout, A.:Songs Ct, w. J. Bowman (ct) [E]—5 songs—Epitaph for Amy; For Infants, Time is Like a Humming Shell; Our Youth-Time Passes Down a Colonnade; Prism of Life; To Travel Like a Bird Meridian ▲ CDE 84158
Steptoe, R.:Elegy on the Death of Cock Robin, w. J. Bowman (ct) [E] Meridian ▲ CDE 84158
Vaughan Williams, R.:Songs, w. J. Bowman (ct)—Ah! Sunflower; Cruelty Has a Human Heart; Divine Image; Eternity; How Can the Tree But Wither; Infant Joy; The Lamb; The Lawyer; Linden Lea; London; Piper; Poison Tree; Searching for Lambs; Sheperd; Sky Above the Roof [E] *(rec 1988)* Meridian ▲ CDE 84158
Warlock, P.:Songs Ct, w. J. Bowman (ct)—(3) Love for Love; My Own Country; Sleep [E] Meridian ▲ CDE 84158

Drei Narzissen
Schneider, U.P.:Studien *(rec Nov. 28, 1990)* Grammont ▲ CTSP 34-2 [ADD]

Dresden Baroque Soloists
P. Schreier (cnd)
Vivaldi, A.:Cons Fl (misc), w. E. Haupt (fl)—RV.104, 106, 108, 428, 433, 443 & 441 Berlin Classics ▲ BER 1002 [DDD]

Dresden Capella Fidicinia
H. Grüss (cnd)
Schütz, H.:Die Auferstehung unsres Herren Jesu Christi, w. Peter Schreier (ten), Dresden Church Choir Berlin Classics ▲ BER 9205
R. Mauersberger (cnd)
Schütz, H.:Choral Music, w. Dresden Church Choir *(rec 1970)* Berlin Classics ▲ BER 9187

Dresden Capella Sagittariana
D. Knothe (cnd)
Schütz, H.:Meine Seele erhebt den Herren [G] Capriccio ▲ CDC 10050 [DDD]
Schütz, H.:Psalms—SWV.482-488 [G] Capriccio ▲ CDC 10049 [DDD]
Schütz, H.:Psalms—SWV.489-493 [G] Capriccio ▲ CDC 10050 [DDD]

Dresden CO
M. Scherzer (cnd)
Katzer, G.:Con Vn MD + G ▲ L 3451 [DDD]

Dresden Instrumental Ensemble
R. Mauersberger (cnd)
Schütz, H.:Musicalische Exequien, w. Dresden Church Choir Berlin Classics ("Eterna" series) ▲ BER 2037 [ADD]

Dresden PO
Bruch, M.:Das Lied von der Glocke, w. Ute Selbig (sop), Elisabeth Graf (alt), Matthias Bleidorn (ten), André Eckert *(rec Kreuzkirche Dresden, Jun 24, 1995)* Thorofon 2-▲ DCTH 2291/2 [DDD]
Classics Go to the Movies Vol. 1, w. Hungarian State Opera Orch, Vienna Strauss Orch, Jenő Jandó (pno), Plovdiv PO, New Leipzig Bach Collegium Musicum, Budapest SO LaserLight ▲ 15 641

Dresden PO (cont.)
Classics Go to the Movies Vol. 2, w. Budapest Festival Orch, Bulgarian TV–Radio SO, Bela Kovaks, Franz Liszt CO, Bruno Lazzaretti, Berlin RSO, Hungarian State Orch LaserLight ▲ 15 642
125 Years of the Dresden Philharmonic, w. Paul Van Kempen (cnd), Carl Schuricht (cnd), Heinz Bongartz (cnd), Horst Förster (cnd), Kurt Masur (cnd), Günther Herbig (cnd), Herbert Kegel (cnd), Jörg Peter Weigle (cnd), Michel Plasson (cnd) *(rec 1938–94)* Berlin Classics 9–▲ BER 9142 [ADD/DDD]

H. Bongartz (cnd)
Brahms, J.:Serenade 2 Orch Berlin Classics ▲ BER 9019 [ADD]
Dvořák, A.:Sym 7 Berlin Classics ▲ BER 9019 [ADD]
Reger, M.:Vars & Fugue on a Theme by Mozart Berlin Classics ▲ BER 2177 [ADD]

M. Flämig (cnd)
Bach, J.S.:Masses, BWV 233–36, "Lutheran Masses", w. Renate Krahmer (sop), Annelies Burmeister (alt), Peter Schreier (ten), Theo Adam (bass) Berlin Classics 2–▲ BER 9130
Mendelssohn, F.:Vom Himmel hoch, w. Ute Selbig (sop), Egbert Junghanns (bar), Dresden Kreuz Choir *(rec Dresden, Mar & Apr 1987)* Capriccio ▲ 10216 [DDD]
Saint-Saëns, C.:Oratorio de Noël, w. Ute Selbig (sop), Elisabeth Wilke (mez), Annette Markert (cta), Armin Ude (ten), Egbert Junghans (bar), Jutta Zoff (hp), Michael–Christfield Winkler (org), Dresden Kreuz Choir *(rec Dresden, Mar & Apr 1987)* Capriccio ▲ 10216 [DDD]

G. Herbig (cnd)
Haydn, J.:Sym 95 Berlin Classics ▲ BER 9104 [ADD]
Reger, M.:Con Pno, w. Amadeus Webersinke (pno) Berlin Classics ▲ BER 9104 [ADD]

H. Kegel (cnd)
Beethoven, L. van:Con Vn, Vc & Pno, "Triple Con", w. C. Funke (vn), J. Timm (vc), Rösel (pno) Capriccio ▲ 10150 [DDD]
Beethoven, L. van:Coriolan Ov Laserlight ▲ 15 523 [DDD]
Beethoven, L. van:Coriolan Ov Capriccio ▲ 10 914 [DDD]
Beethoven, L. van:Coriolan Ov Capriccio ▲ CDC 10005 [DDD]
Beethoven, L. van:Egmont (ov) Capriccio ▲ 10 913 [DDD]
Beethoven, L. van:Fant Pno, Op. 80, "Choral Fant", w. P. Rösel (pno), Leipzig Radio Chorus [G] Capriccio ▲ 10150 [DDD]
Beethoven, L. van:Leonore 2 Laserlight ▲ 15 523 [DDD]
Beethoven, L. van:Syms (comp) LaserLight 10–♦ 33001 [DDD]
Beethoven, L. van:Syms (comp), w. Leipzig Radio Chorus, Berlin Radio Chorus Capriccio 7–▲ 10 455
Beethoven, L. van:Syms (comp)—No. 3 Capriccio ▲ CDC 10002 [DDD]
Beethoven, L. van:Syms (comp)—Nos. 4, 9 Capriccio 2–▲ CDC 10006 [DDD]
Beethoven, L. van:Syms (comp)—No. 7 Capriccio ▲ CDC 10005 [DDD]
Beethoven, L. van:Syms (comp)—No. 6 Capriccio ▲ CDC 10004 [DDD]
Beethoven, L. van:Syms (comp)—Nos. 5, 8 Capriccio ▲ CDC 10003 [DDD]
Beethoven, L. van:Syms (comp) Capriccio 7–▲ CDC 10000 [DDD]
Beethoven, L. van:Syms (comp) LaserLight 5–▲ 15 947 [DDD]
Beethoven, L. van:Syms (comp)—Nos. 1, 2 Capriccio ▲ CDC 10001 [DDD]
Beethoven, L. van:Sym No. 1 Laserlight ♦ 90003 [DDD]
Beethoven, L. van:Sym 1 Capriccio ▲ 10 451 [DDD]
Beethoven, L. van:Sym 2 Laserlight ♦ 90004 [DDD]
Beethoven, L. van:Sym 2 Capriccio ▲ 10 452 [DDD]
Beethoven, L. van:Sym 3, "Eroica" Laserlight ♦ 90005 [DDD]
Beethoven, L. van:Sym 3, "Eroica" Capriccio ▲ 10 451 [DDD]
Beethoven, L. van:Sym 3, "Eroica" Capriccio ▲ 10 913 [DDD]
Beethoven, L. van:Sym 4 Laserlight ♦ 90006 [DDD]
Beethoven, L. van:Sym 4 Capriccio ▲ 10 453 [DDD]
Beethoven, L. van:Sym 5 Laserlight ♦ 90007 [DDD]
Beethoven, L. van:Sym 5 Capriccio ▲ 10 453 [DDD]
Beethoven, L. van:Sym 6, "Pastorale" Laserlight ♦ 90008 [DDD]
Beethoven, L. van:Sym 6, "Pastorale" Laserlight ▲ 15 825 [DDD]
Beethoven, L. van:Sym 6, "Pastorale" Capriccio ▲ 10 453 [DDD]
Beethoven, L. van:Sym 7 Laserlight ♦ 90009 [DDD]
Beethoven, L. van:Sym 7 Capriccio ▲ 10 452 [DDD]
Beethoven, L. van:Sym 8 Laserlight ♦ 90010 [DDD]
Beethoven, L. van:Sym 8 Capriccio ▲ 10 453 [DDD]
Beethoven, L. van:Sym 9, "Choral Sym" Laserlight ♦ 90011 [DDD]
Beethoven, L. van:Sym 9, "Choral Sym", w. A. Hargan (sop), U. Walther (cta), E. Büchner (ten), K. Kováts (bass) Capriccio ▲ 10 453 [DDD]
Blacher, B.:Concertante Musik Berlin Classics ▲ BER 9015 [ADD]
Blacher, B.:Con 2 Pno, w. Gerty Herzog (pno) Berlin Classics ▲ BER 9015 [ADD]
Blacher, B.:Vars on a Theme by Niccolò Paganini Berlin Classics ▲ BER 9015 [ADD]
Dessau, P.:Sonatine Pno, w. Siegfried Stöckigt (pno) Berlin Classics ▲ BER 9181
Dvořák, A.:Biblical Songs, Op. 99, w. Theo Adam (bass) Berlin Classics ▲ BER 9168
Hindemith, P.:Con Tpt, Bn & Strs, w. Ludwig Güttler (tpt), Eckard Königstedt (bn) Berlin Classics 2–▲ BER 9054
Hindemith, P.:Mathis der Maler (sym) Berlin Classics 2–▲ BER 9054
Hindemith, P.:Nobilissima visione Berlin Classics 2–▲ BER 9054
Hindemith, P.:Symphonia serena Berlin Classics 2–▲ BER 9054
Hindemith, P.:Sym in E♭ for Concert Band Berlin Classics 2–▲ BER 9054
Mahler, G.:Sym 1 *(rec 1979)* Berlin Classics ▲ BER 9038 [ADD]
Martin, F.:Monologe (6) aus "Jedermann", w. Theo Adam (bass) Berlin Classics ▲ BER 9168
Stravinsky, I.:Capriccio, w. Peter Rösel (pno) *(rec 1978 or 1981)* Berlin Classics ▲ BER 2044 [ADD]
Stravinsky, I.:Le Chant du rossignol *(rec 1978 or 1981)* Berlin Classics ▲ BER 2044 [ADD]
Stravinsky, I.:Pulcinella Suite *(rec 1978 or 1981)* Berlin Classics ▲ BER 2044 [ADD]

K. Masur (cnd)
Gershwin, G.:Con Pno, w. Siegfried Stöckigt (pno) Berlin Classics ("Masur Edition" series) ▲ BER 9158
Gershwin, G.:Rhap in Blue, w. Kurt Hiltawsky (cl), Siegfried Stöckigt (pno) Berlin Classics ("Masur Edition" series) ▲ BER 9158
Grieg, E.:Con Pno, Op. 16, w. Annerose Schmidt (pno) Berlin Classics ▲ BER CD 9152
Haydn, J.:Sym 102 Berlin Classics ▲ BER CD 9154
The Masur Edition:Selected Recordings, w. Leipzig Opera House Orch Berlin Classics 9–▲ BER 9150 [ADD]
Mozart, W.A.:Con 12 Pno, w. Annerose Schmidt (pno) *(rec 1970)* Berlin Classics ▲ BER CD 9154
Mozart, W.A.:Con 18 Pno, w. Annerose Schmidt (pno) Berlin Classics 2–▲ BER 9251
Mozart, W.A.:Con 20 Pno, w. Annerose Schmidt (pno) Berlin Classics 2–▲ BER 9251
Mozart, W.A.:Con 21 Pno, w. Annerose Schmidt (pno) Berlin Classics 2–▲ BER 9251
Mozart, W.A.:Con 27 Pno, w. Annerose Schmidt (pno) Berlin Classics 2–▲ BER 9251
Prokofiev, S.:Sym 1 Berlin Classics ▲ BER CD 9153
Prokofiev, S.:Sym 1 Berlin Classics ▲ BER 2061 [ADD]
Ravel, M.:Con Pno (left hand), w. Siegfried Rapp (pno) Berlin Classics ("Masur Edition" series) ▲ BER 9158
Shostakovich, D.:Con 1 Vn, w. Gustav Schmahl (vn) Berlin Classics ▲ BER CD 9153
Tchaikovsky, P.:Sym 2 Berlin Classics ▲ BER CD 9152
Tchaikovsky, P.:Sym 2 Berlin Classics ▲ BER 2061 [ADD]

M. Plasson (cnd)
Borodin, A.:Sym 1 Berlin Classics ▲ BER 1092 [DDD]
Borodin, A.:Sym 2 Berlin Classics ▲ BER 1092 [DDD]
Liszt, F.:Ce qu'on entend sur la montagne Berlin Classics ▲ BER 1126 [DDD]
Liszt, F.:Con 1 Pno, w. Nelson Freire (pno) Berlin Classics ▲ BER 1130 [DDD]
Liszt, F.:Con 2 Pno, w. Nelson Freire (pno) Berlin Classics ▲ BER 1130 [DDD]
Liszt, F.:Festklänge Berlin Classics ▲ BER 1126 [DDD]
Liszt, F.:Mazeppa Orch Berlin Classics ▲ BER 1093 [DDD]
Liszt, F.:Orpheus Berlin Classics ▲ BER 1093 [DDD]
Liszt, F.:Les Préludes Berlin Classics ▲ BER 1093 [DDD]

Dresden PO (cont.)
M. Plasson (cnd) (cont.)
Liszt, F.:Prometheus Berlin Classics ▲ BER 1126 [DDD]
Liszt, F.:Tasso—Lamento e Trionfo Berlin Classics ▲ BER 1093 [DDD]
Liszt, F.:Totentanz, w. Nelson Freire (pno) Berlin Classics ▲ BER 1130 [DDD]

J.-P. Weigle (cnd)
Mozart, W.A.:Con Hn, K.412, w. S. Weigle (hn) LaserLight ▲ 15 874
Mozart, W.A.:Cons Hn, w. S. Weigle (hn)—No. 1 [Rondo]; Nos. 2–4 LaserLight ▲ 15 874
Mozart, W.A.:Con Movt Hn, K.370b, w. S. Weigle (hn) LaserLight ▲ 15 874
Mozart, W.A.:Con Movt Hn, K.494a, w. S. Weigle (hn) LaserLight ▲ 15 874
Mozart, W.A.:Rondo Hn, K.371, w. S. Weigle (hn) LaserLight ▲ 15 874
Reger, M.:Tondichtungen nach Arnold Böcklin Capriccio ▲ CD 10 307 [DDD]

Dresden PO Instrumental Group
R. Mauersberger (cnd)
Schütz, H.:Music of, w. Dresden Church Choir Berlin Classics 2–▲ BER 2109 [ADD]

Dresden Piano Trio
Martinů, B.:Trio 1 Pno Berlin Classics ▲ BER 1101 [DDD]
Ravel, M.:Trio Pno Berlin Classics ▲ BER 1101 [DDD]

Dresden Staatskapelle
Vivaldi, A.:Music of, w. Salvatore Accardo (vn), Frederico Agostini (vn), Heinz Holliger (ob), Ida Levin (vn), Aurele Nicolet (fl), Massimo Paris (va d'amore), Angel Romero (gtr), Celedonio Romero (gtr), Celine Romero (gtr), Henryk Szeryng (vn), Pinchas Zukerman (vn), Academy of St. Martin in the Fields, English CO, I Musici, Naples Weekly International Soloists, St. Paul CO—The Four Seasons [Winter]; Con in D for Gtr [Largo]; Con in D for Fl, "Il gardellino" [Cantabile]; Con in C for Diverse Insts [Andante molto]; Con in g for Strs [Andante molto]; Con in D for 2 Vns & 2 Vcs [Largo]; Con in g for Ob, Vn, Ww & Strs [Larghetto]; Con in a for Gtr, "L'estro armonico" [Largo]; Con in F for 3 Vns [Andante]; Con in F for Fl [Largo]; Con in d for Va D'Amore [Largo]; Con in E for Vn & Strs, "Il riposo" [Allegro]; Con in G for Ob, Bn & Strs [Largo]; Con in B♭ for Vn & Strs [Largo]; Con in A for Gtr & Strs [Larghetto]; Con in E for Vn & Strs, "L'amoroso" [Allegro]; Con in G for Fl [Largo]; Con in A for Vn [Larghetto]; Con in c for Vn & Strs, "Il sospetto" [Andante]; Con in a for 2 Obs & Strs [Largo]; Con in g for Orch [Largo non molto]; Con in a for Vn [Largo]; Con in C for Ob [Adagio]; Con in g for Fl, "La notte" [Largo] Philips ▲ 454051–2 ■ 454 051–4

P. Berglund (cnd)
Dvořák, A.:Scherzo Capriccioso EMI Classics ("Doublefforte" series) 2–▲ CDFB 68649
Dvořák, A.:Slavonic Rhaps, Op. 45—No. 3 in a♭ EMI Classics ("Doublefforte" series) 2–▲ CDFB 68649
Grieg, E.:Old Norwegian Romance EMI Classics ("Doublefforte" series) 2–▲ CDFB 68649
Smetana, B.:Má Vlast EMI Classics ("Doublefforte" series) 2–▲ CDFB 68649

H. Blomstedt (cnd)
Beethoven, L. van:Leonore (opera), w. Helen Donath (sop), Edda Moser (sop), Eberhard Büchner (ten), Richard Cassilly (ten), Theo Adam (b–bar), Hermann Christian Polster (bass), Karl Ridderbusch (bass), Leipzig Radio Chorus Berlin Classics ▲ BER 1140
Beethoven, L. van:Syms (comp), w. Helena Doese (sop), Marga Schiml (alt), Peter Schreier (ten), Theo Adam (bass), Dresden State Opera Chorus, Leipzig Radio Choir *(rec Lukaskirche, Dresden, 1975–80)* Berlin Classics 5–▲ 0021942BC [ADD]
Beethoven, L. van:Syms (comp), w. Marga Schiml (sop), Peter Schreier (ten), Theo Adam (b–bar), Helena Doese (sgr), Dresden State Opera Chorus *(rec late 1970's–early 1980's)* Berlin Classics 5–▲ BER 2194 [DDD]
Beethoven, L. van:Sym 1 *(rec 1975–1980)* Berlin Classics ▲ BER 2195
Beethoven, L. van:Sym 2 *(rec 1975–1980)* Berlin Classics ▲ BER 2196
Beethoven, L. van:Sym 3, "Eroica" *(rec 1975–1980)* Berlin Classics ▲ BER 2195
Beethoven, L. van:Sym 4 *(rec 1975–1980)* Berlin Classics ▲ BER 2196
Beethoven, L. van:Sym 5 *(rec 1975–1980)* Berlin Classics ▲ BER 2197
Beethoven, L. van:Sym 6, "Pastorale" *(rec 1975–1980)* Berlin Classics ▲ BER 2197
Beethoven, L. van:Sym 7 *(rec 1975–1980)* Berlin Classics ▲ BER 2198
Beethoven, L. van:Sym 8 *(rec 1975–1980)* Berlin Classics ▲ BER 2198
Beethoven, L. van:Sym 9, "Choral Sym", w. Dresden State Chorus [soloists Edith Wiens, Ute Walther, Reiner Goldberg, Karl–Heinz Stryczek] Capriccio ▲ CDC 10060 [DDD]
Beethoven, L. van:Sym 9, "Choral Sym" *(rec 1975–1980)* Berlin Classics ▲ BER 2199
Beethoven, L. van:Sym 9, "Choral Sym", w. Dresden State Chorus [soloists Edith Wiens, Ute Walther, Reiner Goldberg, Karl–Heinz Stryczek] LaserLight ▲ 15 826 [DDD]
Beethoven, L. van:Sym 9, "Choral Sym", w. E. Wiens (sop), U. Walther (cta), R. Goldberg (ten), K.–H. Stryczek (bass), Dresden State Opera Chorus, Dresden Sym Chorus—final chorus Capriccio ▲ 10 914 [DDD]
Dvořák, A.:Sym 8 Berlin Classics ▲ BER 9024 [ADD]
Reger, M.:Con Vn, w. Manfred Scherzer (vn) Berlin Classics ▲ BER 9124
Schubert, Franz:Sym 1 Berlin Classics ▲ BER 9263
Schubert, Franz:Sym 2 Berlin Classics ▲ BER 9263
Schubert, Franz:Sym 3 Berlin Classics ▲ BER 9266
Schubert, Franz:Sym 4 Berlin Classics ▲ BER 9266
Schubert, Franz:Sym 6 Berlin Classics ▲ BER 9024 [ADD]
Strauss, R.:Also sprach Zarathustra Denon ▲ CO 2259 [DDD]
Strauss, R.:Don Juan Denon ▲ CO 2259 [DDD]
Strauss, R.:Metamorphosen Denon ▲ CO 73801 [DDD]
Strauss, R.:Till Eulenspiegels lustige Streiche Denon ▲ CO 73801 [DDD]
Strauss, R.:Tod und Verklärung Denon ▲ CO 73801 [DDD]
Weber, C.M. von:Con 1 Pno, w. P. Rösel (pno) Berlin Classics ▲ BER 1058 [DDD]
Weber, C.M. von:Con 2 Pno, w. P. Rösel (pno) Berlin Classics ▲ BER 1058 [DDD]
Weber, C.M. von:Konzertstück Pno, w. P. Rösel (pno) Berlin Classics ▲ BER 1058 [DDD]

K. Böhm (cnd)
Beethoven, L. van:Fidelio (sels)—Ov. Deutsche Grammophon ("Double" series) 2–▲ 437928–2
Beethoven, L. van:Leonore 3 Deutsche Grammophon ("Double" series) 2–▲ 437928–2
Strauss, R.:Eine Alpensinfonie Deutsche Grammophon ("The Originals" series) ▲ 447 454–2
Strauss, R.:Elektra, w. I. Borkh (sop), M. Schech (sop), J. Madeira (mez), D. Fischer–Dieskau (bar) [G] *(rec 1961)* Deutsche Grammophon 2–▲ 445329–2
Strauss, R.:Till Eulenspiegels lustige Streiche Deutsche Grammophon ("The Originals" series) ▲ 447 454–2

C. Davis (cnd)
Beethoven, L. van:Cons Pno (comp), w. C. Arrau (pno) Philips 3–▲ 422149–2 [DDD]
Beethoven, L. van:Con 5 Pno, "Emperor", w. C. Arrau (pno) Philips ▲ 416215–2 [DDD] □ 416215–5
Beethoven, L. van:Egmont (ov) Philips ▲ 434120–2 [DDD]
Beethoven, L. van:Sym 3, "Eroica" Philips ▲ 434120–2 [DDD]
Humperdinck, E.:Hänsel und Gretel, w. E. Gruberova (sop), G. Jones (sop), B. Bonney (sop), C. Oelze (sop), A. Murray (mez), C. Ludwig (mez), F. Grundheber (bar) Philips 2–▲ 438013–2
Mozart, W.A.:Complete Mozart Edition, w. M. Price (sop), L. Serra (sop), R. Tear (ten), P. Schreier (ten), T. Adam (b–bar), K. Moll (bass), Dresden State Chorus Philips 3–▲ 422543–2 [ADD]
Mozart, W.A.:Zauberflöte, w. M. Price (sop—Pamina), L. Serra (sop—Queen of the Night), M. Venuti (sop—Papagena), M. McLaughlin (sop—1st Lady), A. Murray (mez—2nd Lady), H. Schwarz (cta—3rd Lady), F. Höher (trb—1st Boy), M. Diedrich (trb—2nd Boy), F. Klos (trb—3rd Boy), P. Schreier (ten—Tamino), R. Tear (ten—Monostatos), R. Goldberg (ten—1st Armoured Man), K. Moll (bass—Sarastro), H. Rech (bass—2nd Armoured Man), Leipzig Radio Chorus Philips ("Duo" series) 2–▲ 442568–2
Weber, C.M. von:Der Freischütz (sels), w. K. Mattila (sop), E. Lind (sop), F. Araiza (ten), K. Moll (bass) Philips ▲ 438497–2

B. Haitink (cnd)
Beethoven, L. van:Fidelio, w. J. Norman (sop), P. Coburn (sop), R. Goldberg (ten), H.–P. Blochwitz (ten), K. Möll (bass), Dresden State Chorus Philips ▲ 438496–2
Beethoven, L. van:Fidelio, w. J. Norman (sop), P. Coburn (sop), R. Goldberg (ten), H.–P. Blochwitz (ten), A. Schmidt (bar), E. Wlaschiha (bass), K. Moll (bass), Dresden State Chorus [G] Philips 2–▲ 426308–2 [DDD]

▲ = CD ♦ = Enhanced CD Δ = MD ■ = Cassette Tape □ = DCC

Dresden Staatskapelle (cont.)
B. Haitink (cnd) (cont.)
Strauss, R.:Der Rosenkavalier, w. K. Te Kanawa (sop), B. Hendricks (sop), A. S. von Otter (mez) EMI Classics 3-▲ CDCC 54259
Strauss, R.:Der Rosenkavalier (sels), w. B. Hendricks (sop), K. Te Kanawa (sop), A. S. von Otter (mez), R. Leech (ten), K. Rydl (bass), Dresden State Opera Chorus EMI Classics ▲ ZDC 54493
N. Harnoncourt (cnd)
Mozart, W.A.:March Orch, K.249 Teldec ▲ 2292-43040-2
Mozart, W.A.:Marches Orch, K.335 Teldec ▲ 92149
Mozart, W.A.:Serenade Vn, K.250 Teldec ▲ 2292-43040-2
Mozart, W.A.:Serenade Ww, K.320 Teldec ▲ 92149
M. Janowski (cnd)
Rimsky-Korsakov, N.:Mozart & Salieri, w. P. Schreier (ten), T. Adam (b-bar) [G] Berlin Classics ("Eterna" series) ▲ BER 2089 [ADD]
Wagner, R.:Der Ring des Nibelungen (sels), w. Jessye Norman (sop), Lucia Popp (sop), René Kollo (ten), Siegfried Jerusalem (ten), Kurt Moll (bass), Matti Salminen (bass) RCA Victor ▲ 09026-68084-2; ■ 09026-68084-4
Weber, C.M. von:Euryanthe, w. Jessye Norman (sop), Rita Hunter (sop), Nicolai Gedda (ten), Tom Krause (bar), Leipzig Radio Chorus Berlin Classics 3-▲ BER 1108 [ADD]
E. Jochum (cnd)
Bruckner, A.:Sym 9 EMI Classics ▲ CDE 67768
Haydn, J.:Sym 94, "Surprise Sym" Philips ("Concert Classics" series) ▲ 422973-2 [ADD]
H. von Karajan (cnd)
Bartók, B.:Con 3 Pno, w. Geza Anda (pno) *(rec live, 1972)* AS Disc ▲ ASD 2508
Wagner, R.:Die Meistersinger von Nürnberg, w. H. Donath (sop), R. Hesse (mez), A. Kollo (ten), P. Schreier (ten), T. Adam (b-bar), R. Evans (bass), K. Ridderbusch (bass), Dresden State Chorus, Leipzig Radio Chorus [G] EMI Classics 4-▲ CDCD 49683 [ADD]
R. Kempe (cnd)
Britten, B.:Sinf da requiem *(rec 1976)* Berlin Classics ▲ BER 1097 [ADD]
Strauss, R.:Eine Alpensinfonie EMI Classics 3-▲ CDZC 64350
Strauss, R.:Also sprach Zarathustra EMI Classics 3-▲ CDZC 64346
Strauss, R.:Aus italien EMI Classics 3-▲ CDZC 64350
Strauss, R.:Der Bürger als Edelmann (suite) EMI Classics 3-▲ CDZC 64346
Strauss, R.:Burleske, w. M. Frager (pno) EMI Classics 3-▲ CDZC 64342
Strauss, R.:Con 1 Hn, w. P. Damm (hn) EMI Classics 3-▲ CDZC 64342
Strauss, R.:Con 2 Hn, w. P. Damm (hn) EMI Classics 3-▲ CDZC 64342
Strauss, R.:Con Ob, w. M. Clement (ob) EMI Classics 3-▲ CDZC 64342
Strauss, R.:Con Vn, w. U. Hoelscher (vn) EMI Classics 3-▲ CDZC 64346
Strauss, R.:Don Juan EMI Classics 3-▲ CDZC 64342
Strauss, R.:Don Quixote EMI Classics 3-▲ CDZC 64350
Strauss, R.:Duet-Concertino, w. M. Weise (cl), W. Liebscher (bn) EMI Classics 3-▲ CDZC 64342
Strauss, R.:Ein Heldenleben EMI Classics 3-▲ CDZC 64342
Strauss, R.:Macbeth EMI Classics 3-▲ CDZC 64350
Strauss, R.:Metamorphosen EMI Classics 3-▲ CDZC 64350
Strauss, R.:Orchestral Music (comp)—Horn Concerti 1 & 2 (Peter Damm—horn); Oboe Concerto in D (Manfred Clement—oboe); Duett-Concertino (Manfred Weise—clarinet & Wolfgang Liebscher—bassoon); Burleske (Malcolm Frager—piano); Panathenäenug; Parergon zur Symphonia domestica (Peter Rösel—piano); Till Eulenspiegels lustige Streiche; Don Juan; Ein Heldenleben EMI Classics 3-▲ CDZC 64342
Strauss, R.:Orchestral Music (comp)—Violin Concerto (Ulf Hoelscher—violin); Symphonia domestica; Also sprach Zarathustra; Tod und Verklärung; Der Rosenkavalier (waltzes); Salome (Dance of the Seven Veils); Der Bürger als Edelmann Suite; Schlagobers (waltz); Josephs-Legende (sels.) EMI Classics 3-▲ CDZC 64346
Strauss, R.:Orchestral Music (comp)—Metamorphosen; Eine Alpensinfonie; Aus italien; Macbeth; Don Quixote; Tanzsuite EMI Classics 3-▲ CDZC 64350
Strauss, R.:Panathenäenzug, w. P. Rösel (pno) EMI Classics 3-▲ CDZC 64342
Strauss, R.:Parergon zur Symphonia domestica, w. P. Rösel (pno) EMI Classics 3-▲ CDZC 64342
Strauss, R.:Salome (dance) EMI Classics 3-▲ CDZC 64346
Strauss, R.:Symphonia domestica EMI Classics 3-▲ CDZC 64346
Strauss, R.:Tanzsuite EMI Classics 3-▲ CDZC 64350
Strauss, R.:Till Eulenspiegels lustige Streiche EMI Classics 3-▲ CDZC 64342
Strauss, R.:Tod und Verklärung EMI Classics 3-▲ CDZC 64346
Stravinsky, I.:The Firebird Suite [1919 version] *(rec 1976)* Berlin Classics ▲ BER 1097 [ADD]
F. Konwitschny (cnd)
Beethoven, L. van:Sym 3, "Eroica" *(rec Dresden, Germany, Nov, 1954)* Berlin Classics ▲ BER 9039
Brahms, J.:Con 1 Pno, w. Wilhelm Kempff (pno) Deutsche Grammophon ("Double" series) 2-▲ 437374-2
Brahms, J.:Con Vn, w. David Oistrach (vn) Deutsche Grammophon ("The Originals" series) 2-▲ 447427-2
Shostakovich, D.:Sym 11 *(rec 1960)* Berlin Classics ("Documents" series) 2-▲ BER 9042 [ADD]
Tchaikovsky, P.:Con Vn, w. David Oistrach (vn) Deutsche Grammophon ("The Originals" series) 2-▲ 447427-2
B. G. Kuhn (cnd)
Weber, C.M. von:Ovs—Der Freischütz; Oberon; Preciosa; Abu Hassan; Euryanthe; Jubel-Overture; Der Beherrscher der Geister Capriccio ▲ CDC 10052 [DDD]
J. Levine (cnd)
Dvořák, A.:Sym 8 *(rec Dresden, Dec 1990 & Nov 1994)* Deutsche Grammophon ▲ 447 754-2 [DDD]
Dvořák, A.:Sym 9, "From the New World" *(rec Dresden, Dec 1990 & Nov 1994)* Deutsche Grammophon ▲ 447 754-2 [DDD]
S. Ozawa (cnd)
Strauss, R.:Salome, w. J. Norman (sop), K. Witt (mez), A. Markert (cta), W. Raffeiner (ten), R. Leech (ten), J. Morris (bass) Philips 2-▲ 432153-2
K. Sanderling (cnd)
Brahms, J.:Syms (comp) Eurodisc 3-▲ 69220-2-RV [ADD]
Brahms, J.:Tragic Ov Eurodisc 3-▲ 69220-2-RV [ADD]
Brahms, J.:Vars on a Theme by Haydn Eurodisc 3-▲ 69220-2-RV [ADD]
H. Schmidt-Isserstedt (cnd)
Mozart, W.A.:Idomeneo, w. A. Rothenberger (sop), E. Moser (sop), N. Gedda (ten), A. Dallapozza (ten), P. Schreier (ten), T. Adam (b-bar), Leipzig Radio Chorus EMI Classics ("Studio" series) 3-▲ CDMC 63990
P. Schreier (cnd)
Mozart, W.A.:Missa, K.317, w. E. Mathis (sop), J. Rappé (ten), H. P. Blochwitz (ten), T. Quasthoff (bar), Leipzig Radio Chorus Philips ▲ 426275-2
G. Sinopoli (cnd)
Bruckner, A.:Sym 4, "Romantic" Deutsche Grammophon ▲ 423677-2 [DDD]
Schubert, Franz:Sym 9 Deutsche Grammophon ▲ 437689-2 [DDD]
Strauss, R.:4 Last Songs, w. C. Studer (sop) Deutsche Grammophon ▲ 439865-2
Wagner, R.:Tristan und Isolde (prelude & liebestod), w. C. Studer (sop) Deutsche Grammophon ▲ 439865-2
Wagner, R.:Wesendonck Songs, w. C. Studer (sop) Deutsche Grammophon ▲ 439865-2
O. Suitner (cnd)
Bizet, G.:Sym 1 *(rec 1972)* Berlin Classics ▲ BER 9040 [ADD]
Humperdinck, E.:Hänsel und Gretel, w. G. Schöter (sop), I. Springer (mez), P. Schrier (ten), T. Adam (bar), Dresden Kreuz Choir Berlin Classics ("Eterna" series) 2-▲ BER 2007 [ADD]
Mozart, W.A.:Nozze di Figaro, w. Anneliese Rothenberger (sop), Hilde Gueden (sop), Edith Mathis (sop), Peter Schreier (ten), Walter Berry (bar), Hermann Prey (bar) Berlin Classics 3-▲ BER 2096 [ADD]
Mozart, W.A.:Nozze di Figaro (sels), w. Hilde Gueden (sop), Anneliese Rothenberger (sop), Hermann Prey (bar), Walter Berry (bass) Berlin Classics ▲ BER 9079 [ADD]

Dresden Staatskapelle (cont.)
O. Suitner (cnd) (cont.)
Mozart, W.A.:Zauberflöte, w. H. Donath (sop), S. Geszty (sop), P. Schreier (ten), G. Leib (bass), T. Adam (bass) [I] RCA Gold Seal 3-▲ 6511-2 [ADD]
Strauss, R.:Salome, w. Christel Goltz (sop), Helmut Melchert (ten), Ernst Gutstein (bar), Siw Ericsdotter (sgr) *(rec 1963)* Berlin Classics 2-▲ BER 9101 [ADD]
Suppé, F. von:Ovs—Die schöne Galathee; Dichter und Bauer; Banditenstreiche:Leichte Kavallerie; Flotte Bursche; Pique Dame Berlin Classics ▲ BER 2153 [ADD]
Weber, C.M. von:Sym 1 *(rec 1972)* Berlin Classics ▲ BER 9040 [ADD]
G. Szell (cnd)
Bruckner, A.:Sym 3, "Wagner" Sony Classical ("Festspiel Dokumente:Salzburger Festspiele" series) ▲ SMK 68448
J. Tate (cnd)
Beethoven, L. van:Sym 7 Berlin Classics ▲ BER 1095 [DDD]
Beethoven, L. van:Die Weihe des Hauses (ov) Berlin Classics ▲ BER 1095 [DDD]
Offenbach, J.:Les Contes d'Hoffmann, w. J. Norman (sop), E. Lind (sop), C. Studer (sop), A. Sofie von Otter (mez), F. Araiza (ten), S. Ramey (bass) Philips ▲ 438502-2
Offenbach, J.:Les Contes d'Hoffmann, w. J. Norman (sop), C. Studer (sop), E. Lind (sop), A. S. von Otter (mez), F. Araiza (ten), S. Ramey (bass) Philips 3-▲ 422374-2 [DDD]
Schubert, Franz:Sym 9 Berlin Classics ▲ BER 1083 [DDD]
H. Vonk (cnd)
Beethoven, L. van:Cons Pno (comp), w. C. Zacharias (pno) EMI Classics ▲ ZDMC 63937
Mozart, W.A.:Ovs—Die Zauberflöte; Le nozze di Figaro; Ascanio in Alba; Idomeneo; Der Schauspieldirektor; Così fan tutte; Die Entführung aus dem Serail; La finta giardiniera; Lucio Silla; La clemenza di Tito; Don Giovanni Capriccio ▲ 10070 [DDD]
Mozart, W.A.:Ovs—Die Zauberflöte; Le nozze di Figaro; Ascanio in Alba; Idomeneo; Der Schauspieldirektor; Così fan tutte; Die Entführung aus dem Serail; La finta giardiniera; Lucio Silla; La clemenza di Tito; Don Giovanni LaserLight ▲ 15 885 [DDD]
Strauss, R.:Der Rosenkavalier (sels), w. A. Pusar-Jeric (sop), M. Stejskal (sop), A. Jahns (mez), U. Walther (cta), R. Haunstein (bar), T. Adam (b-bar), Dresden State Chorus [G] *(rec live 2/85)* Denon ▲ CO 8010 [DDD]
Tchaikovsky, P.:Eugene Onegin (sels)—Waltz & Polonaise Capriccio 2-▲ CDC 10071/72 [DDD]
Tchaikovsky, P.:The Nutcracker Capriccio 2-▲ CDC 10071/72
Tchaikovsky, P.:Nutcracker Suite Capriccio ▲ 10 923 [DDD]

Dresden State Opera Orch
K. Böhm (cnd)
Bizet, G.:Carmen, w. E. Weidlich (sop), E. Höngen (cta), T. Ralf (ten), J. Herrmann (bar), K. Böhme (bass), Dresden State Opera Chorus *(rec Dec. 4 & 5, 1942)* Preiser 2-▲ 90152 (m)
W. Boskovsky (cnd)
Schubert, Franz:Rosamunde, w. Ileana Cotrubas (sop), Leipzig Radio Chorus Berlin Classics ▲ BER 9004 [ADD]
Schubert, Franz:Die Zauberharfe (ov) Berlin Classics ▲ BER 9004 [ADD]
H. Hollreiser (cnd)
Wagner, R.:Rienzi, der Letzte der Tribunen, w. S. Wennberg (sop), Martin (sop), A. Kollo (ten), P. Schreier (ten), T. Adam (b-bar), Dresden State Opera Chorus [G] EMI Classics ("Studio" series) 3-▲ CDMB 63980
C. Kleiber (cnd)
Wagner, R.:Tristan und Isolde, w. M. Price (sop), B. Fassbaender (mez), A. Kollo (ten), D. Fischer-Dieskau (bar), K. Moll (bass) [G] Deutsche Grammophon 4-▲ 413315-2 [DDD]
O. Suitner (cnd)
Mozart, W.A.:Entführung, w. Rosemarie Ronisch (sop), Jutta Vulpius (sop), Rolf Apreck (ten), Jurgen Forster (ten), Arnold van Mill (bass), Dresden State Opera Chorus Berlin Classics 2-▲ BER 9116

Dresden State Orch
Mad About Angels, w. Cheryl Studer (sop), Christa Ludwig (mez), Anne Sofie von Otter (mez), José Carreras (ten), New York PO [cnd:Leonard Bernstein], English Baroque Soloists [cnd:John Eliot Gardiner], Philharmonia Orch, Philharmonia Chorus [cnd:Carlo Maria Giulini] Deutsche Grammophon ▲ 449113-2 ■ 449113-4
Magical Strings Capriccio ▲ CDC 10065
Overtures & Intermezzi Philips ("Digital Classics" series) ▲ 412235-2
Tchaikovsky, P.:Eugene Onegin (sels), w. Alexandrina Pendachanska (sop), Nicolai Ghiaurov (bass), Lyubomir Diakovski (sgr), Niko Isakov (sgr), Bulgarian National Chorus—Intro; Peasant's Chorus & Dance; Scene & Aria of Olga; Scene & Quartet; Letter Scene; plus others Laserlight ▲ 14210 [DDD]
C. Abbado (cnd)
Brahms, J.:Vars on a Theme by Haydn Deutsche Grammophon ▲ 431594-2 [ADD]
K. Ančerl (cnd)
Mozart, W.A.:Sym 36 Berlin Classics ▲ BER 9051
Mozart, W.A.:Sym 38 Berlin Classics ▲ BER 9051
G. Bertini (cnd)
Rossini, G.:L'italiana in Algeri, w. L. V. Terrani (mez), U. Benelli (ten), S. Bruscantini (bar), A. Mariotti (bass) [I] Acanta 2-▲ CD 42308 [DDD]
H. Blomstedt (cnd)
Weber, C.M. von:Con 1 Cl, w. Sabine Meyer (cl) *(rec Lukaskirche, Dresden, Sept. 9-13, 1985)* EMI Classics ▲ CDC 55155 [DDD]
K. Böhm (cnd)
Beethoven, L. van:Con 5 Pno, "Emperor", w. Edwin Fischer (pno) Pearl ▲ PEA 9218
Brahms, J.:Sym 4 Dutton Laboratories ▲ DUT 5006 [ADD]
Bruckner, A.:Sym 4, "Romantic" Memories ▲ MEM 3001
Bruckner, A.:Sym 4, "Romantic" Dutton Laboratories ▲ DUT 5007 [ADD]
H. Bongartz (cnd)
Reger, M.:Tondichtungen nach Arnold Böcklin Berlin Classics ▲ BER 2177 [ADD]
H. Kegel (cnd)
Mussorgsky, M.:Boris Godunov (sels), w. Hanne-Lore Kuhse (sop), Peter Schreier (ten), Martin Ritzmann (ten), Theo Adam (b-bar), Leipzig Radio Chorus Berlin Classics ▲ BER 2032 [ADD]
K. Kondrashin (cnd)
Prokofiev, S.:Sym 1 Berlin Classics ▲ BER 9051
L. Ludwig (cnd)
Mahler, G.:Sym 4, w. A. Schlemm (mez) *(rec 1957)* Berlin Classics ("Dokumente" series) ▲ BER 2119 [ADD]
R. Mauersberger (cnd)
Bach, J.S.:Mass in b, BWV 232, w. Maria Stader (sop), Sieglinde Wagner (mez), Ernst Haefliger (ten), Theo Adam (b-bar), Dresden Kreuz Choir *(rec 1958)* Berlin Classics ▲ BER 9171
F. Molinari-Pradelli (cnd)
Verdi, G.:Rigoletto, w. M. Rinaldi (sop), V. Cortez (mez), F. Bonisolli (ten), R. Panerai (bar), B. Rundgren (b-bar), Dresden State Chorus [I] Acanta 2-▲ CD 41474 [DDD]
G. Patanè (cnd)
Verdi, G.:La forza del destino, w. G. Bumbry (sop—Leonora), H. Dernesch (sop—Preziosilla), N. Gedda (ten—Alvaro), H. Prey (bar—Don Carlos), G. Frick (bass—Pater Guardian), S. Vogel (bass—Marchese), Dresden State Opera Chorus *(rec Aug. 1965)* Berlin Classics ("Eterna" series) ▲ BER 2025-2 [ADD]

Dresden State Orch members
L. Bernstein (cnd)
Beethoven, L. van:Sym 9, "Choral Sym", w. Bavarian RSO members, Dresden State Orch members, Kirov Theatre Orch members, London SO members, New York PO members, Orch de Paris members, Bavarian Radio Chorus, Berlin Radio Chorus, Dresden Philharmonie Children's Chorus [G] *(rec live, Schauspielhaus, East Berlin, 12/25/89)* Deutsche Grammophon ▲ 429861-2 [DDD] ■ 429861-4

Dresden State SO
H. Vonk (cnd)
Mozart, W.A.:Con Cl, w. Sabine Meyer (cl) *(rec Lukaskirche, Dresden, June 6-8, 1990)* EMI Classics ▲ CDC 55155 [DDD]

ORCH. & ENS.

Dresden Trio
Beethoven, L. van:Trio 6 Pno, "Archduke" Berlin Classics ▲ BER 1022 [DDD]
Brahms, J.:Trio 1 Pno Berlin Classics ▲ BER 1022 [DDD]
M. Fischer-Dieskau (cnd)
Martinů, B.:Concertino Pno, Vn, Vc & Strs, New Berlin CO *(rec live 1992)* BIS ▲ CD 578 [DDD]
Dresden Wind Collegium members
Hell brennt ein Licht [Bright Burns a Light], w. Carl Maria von Weber School for Music Soloists [cnd:G. Schwarze], Prohlis Church Choir Dresden, Dresden Church Choirs members Christophorus ▲ 77165 [DDD]
Dreseden Capella Sagittariana
D. Knothe (cnd)
Schütz, H.:Schwannengesang, w. J. Kowalski (alt), W. Marschall (ten), Berlin Soloists, Berlin Radio Children's Choir Berlin Classics 2-▲ BER 1071 [DDD]
Drottningholm Baroque Ensemble
Babell, W.:Con Fl, w. P. Evison (fl) BIS ▲ CD 249 [DDD]
Bach, J.S.:Mass in b, BWV 232, w. C. Högman (sop), M. Groop (mez), H. Crook (ten), P. Salomaa (bass), Mikaeli Chamber Choir Proprius 2-▲ PRCD 9070/71
Bach, J.S.:Suite 2 Orch, w. P. Evison (fl) BIS ▲ CD 249 [DDD]
Boccherini, L.:Qnts Gtr & Strs, w. J. Lindberg (gtr)—in d, G.445; in E, G.446; in B♭, G.447 [all rec Apr. 20–22, 1992]; in D, G.448 [rec Dec. 13, 1992]; in D, G.449; in G, G.450 [both rec Nov. 10–11, 1992] BIS 2-▲ CD 597/98 [DDD]
Haydn, J.:Music for Lt & Strs, w. Jacob Lindberg (lt) BIS ▲ CD 360
Heinichen, J.D.:Con à 8, Musica Dolce BIS ▲ CD 8
Mozart, W.A.:Diverts Str Qt, K.136–138 BIS ▲ CD 506 [DDD]
Mozart, W.A.:Kleine Nachtmusik BIS ▲ CD 506 [DDD] ∆ MD 506
Purcell, H.:Anthems, w. Stockholm Chamber Choir—O, Sing unto the Lord; Lord, How long wilt thou be angry?; O God, thou art my God; Blow up the trumpet in Sion; Praise the Lord, O Jerusalem; O god, thou hast cast us out; My heart is inditing Proprius ▲ PRCD 9062
Roman, J.H.:Golovin Music Caprice ▲ CAP 21325 [DDD]
Roman, J.H.:The Sweedish Mass, w. H. Martinpelto (sop), A.-S. von Otter (sop), M. Samuelsson (bar), Adolf Fredrik Bach Choir Proprius ▲ PRCD 9920
Sammartini, G.:Cons Rcr, w. C. Pehrsson (rcr)—in F BIS ▲ CD 210
Scarlatti, A.:Son Fl, w. C. Pehrsson (a rcr) BIS ▲ CD 8
Telemann, G.P.:Con in F Rcr Bn, w. C. Pehrsson (rcr), M. McCraw (bn) *(rec May 27–28, 1984)* BIS ▲ CD 617 [DDD]
Telemann, G.P.:Con in F Rcr Bn, w. C. Pehrsson (rcr), M. McCraw (bn) BIS ▲ CD 271 [DDD]
Telemann, G.P.:Con Rcr, Fl, w. C. Pehrsson (rcr), P. Evison (fl) *(rec Apr. 8–9, 1983)* BIS ▲ CD 617 [DDD]
Telemann, G.P.:Con Rcr, Fl, w. C. Pehrsson (rcr), P. Evison (fl) BIS ▲ CD 249 [DDD]
Telemann, G.P.:Con in C Rcr, w. C. Pehrsson (rcr) BIS ▲ CD 271 [DDD]
Telemann, G.P.:Con in F Rcr, w. C. Pehrsson (rcr) BIS ▲ CD 8
Telemann, G.P.:Con in a for Rcr, Vl, w. C. Pehrsson (rcr), O. Larsson (vc) *(rec Apr. 13, 1993)* BIS ▲ CD 617 [DDD]
Telemann, G.P.:Con in a for 2 Rcrs, w. C. Pehrsson (rcr), D. Laurin (rcr) *(rec May 31, 1993)* BIS ▲ CD 617 [DDD]
Telemann, G.P.:Con in B♭ for 2 Rcrs, w. C. Pehrsson (rcr), A.-Per Johsson (rcr) BIS ▲ CD 220 [AAD]
Telemann, G.P.:Con in B♭ for 2 Rcrs, w. C. Pehrsson (rcr), D. Laurin (rcr) *(rec May 31, 1993)* BIS ▲ CD 617 [DDD]
Telemann, G.P.:Con in B♭ for 2 Rcrs, w. C. Pehrsson (rcr), A.-Per Johsson (rcr) BIS ▲ CD 8
Telemann, G.P.:Suite in a Fl, w. C. Pehrsson (rcr) BIS ▲ CD 210
Vivaldi, A.:Cons Bn, w. M. McCraw (bn)—RV.485 BIS ▲ CD 271 [DDD]
Vivaldi, A.:Cons Rcr, w. Claas Pehrsson (rcr)—R. 428 BIS ▲ CD 210
Vivaldi, A.:Con Va d'amore Lt, w. J. Lindberg (lt), M. Huggett (vn) BIS ▲ CD 290 [DDD]
Vivaldi, A.:Cons Vn, Op. 8/1–4, "The Four Seasons", w. N.-E. Sparf (vn) BIS ▲ CD 275 [DDD] ∆ MD 275
E. Ericson (cnd)
Roman, J.H.:Bröllopsmusik, w. C. Högmann (sop), P. Mattei (b-bar), N.-E. Sparf (vn) *(rec 1992)* Musica Sveciae ▲ MSCD 413 [DDD]
Roman, J.H.:Funeral Music for Frederik I, w. C. Högmann (sop), Eric Ericson Chamber Choir *(rec 1992)* Musica Sveciae ▲ MSCD 413 [DDD]
Roman, J.H.:Jubilate, w. C. Högmann (sop), P. Mattei (b-bar), Eric Ericson Chamber Choir *(rec 1992)* Musica Sveciae ▲ MSCD 413 [DDD]
Roman, J.H.:Te Deum, w. S. Rydén (sop), P.-E. Lindskog (ten), Eric Ericson Chamber Choir *(rec 1992)* Musica Sveciae ▲ MSCD 413 [DDD]
J. Lindberg (cnd)
Vivaldi, A.:Con Lt, w. N.-E. Sparf (vn), T. Galli (va) BIS ▲ CD 290 [DDD]
A. Öhrwall (cnd)
Handel, G.F.:Concerti grossi, Op. 6—No. 6 BIS ▲ CD 322 [DDD]
Handel, G.F.:Dixit Dominus, w. Hillevi Martinpelto (sop), Anne Sofie von Otter (mez), Stockholm Bach Choir [L] BIS ▲ CD 322 [DDD]
S. Parkman (cnd)
Kraus, J.M.:Funeral Music for Gustav III, w. C. Högman (sop), H. Martinpelto (sop), C.-H. Ahnsjö (ten), T. Lander (bass), Uppsala Univ Chamber Choir Musica Sveciae ▲ MSCD 416 [DDD]
J. Schröder (cnd)
Roman, J.H.:Sinfs, w. J. Schröder (vn)—Nos. 3 in E, 9 in G, 10 in F, 11 in B♭, 15 in G, 22 in e, 24 in D & 30 in g Musica Sveciae ▲ MSCD 418 [DDD]
T. Schuback (cnd)
Haeffner, J.C.F.:Electra, w. Hillevi Martinpelto (sop), Helle Hinz (sop), Peter Mattei (bar), Mikael Samuelson (bar), Swedish Radio Choir Caprice 2-▲ CAP 22030
Haeffner, J.C.F.:Electra (sels), w. H. Martinpelto (sop), G. Hoffstedt (sop), S. Dahlberg (ten), P.-A. Wahlgren (bar)—3 recitatives & arias [Sw] *(rec 1989–90)* Musica Sveciae ▲ MSCD 426 [DDD]
Naumann, J.G.:Arias, w. G. Hoffstedt (sop), H. Martinpelto (sop), S. Dahlberg (ten), P. A. Wahlgren (bar)—sels. from Amphion & Cora och Alonzo [Sw] Musica Sveciae ▲ MSCD 426 [DDD]
Uttini, F.A.B.:Thetis och Pelée (sels), w. H. Martinpelto (sop), G. Hoffstedt (sop), S. Dahlberg (ten), P.-A. Wahlgren (bar) [Sw] Musica Sveciae ▲ MSCD 426 [DDD]
N.-E. Sparf (cnd)
Fasch, J.F.:Con Tpt, 2 Obs & Strs, w. Niklas Eklund (baroque tpt) [period instrs] *(rec Petruskyrkan, Stockholm, Sweden, Aug 8–11, 1995)* Naxos ▲ 8.553531 [DDD]
Handel, G.F.:Suite Tpt & Org, w. Niklas Eklund (baroque tpt) *(rec Petruskyrkan, Stockholm, Sweden, Aug 8–11, 1995)* Naxos ▲ 8.553531 [DDD]
Molter, J.M.:Con 1 Tpt, w. Niklas Eklund (tpt) *(rec Petruskyrkan, Stockholm, Sweden, Aug 8–11, 1995)* Naxos ▲ 8.553531 [DDD]
Mozart, L.:Con Tpt, w. Niklas Eklund (tpt) *(rec Petruskyrkan, Stockholm, Sweden, Aug 8–11, 1995)* Naxos ▲ 8.553531 [DDD]
Purcell, H.:Son Tpt, w. Niklas Eklund (baroque tpt) *(rec Petruskyrkan, Stockholm, Sweden, Aug 8–11, 1995)* Naxos ▲ 8.553531 [DDD]
Telemann, G.P.:Con Tpt Strs in D, w. Niklas Eklund (tpt) *(rec Petruskyrkan, Stockholm, Sweden, Aug 8–11, 1995)* Naxos ▲ 8.553531 [DDD]
Torelli, G.:Son Tpt, G.1, w. Niklas Eklund (tpt) *(rec Petruskyrkan, Stockholm, Sweden, Aug 8–11, 1995)* Naxos ▲ 8.553531 [DDD]
Drottningholm CO
L. Gardelli (cnd)
Chiarini, P.:Sinf for 2 Vns Swedish Society ▲ SCD 1029
Pergolesi, G.B.:Il maestro di musica, w. E. Söderström (sop) Swedish Society ▲ SCD 1029
S. Westerberg (cnd)
Roman, J.H.:Drottningholmsmusiquen Swedish Society ▲ SCD 1019
Roman, J.H.:Sinfs—Nos. 3, 16 & 20 Swedish Society ▲ SCD 1019
Drottningholm Court Theater Orch
A. Östman (cnd)
Mozart, W.A.:Nozze di Figaro, w. A. Augér (sop), B. Bonney (sop), A. Nafé (mez), H. Hagegard (bar), P. Salomaa (bass), Drottingholm Court Thea Chorus [I] L'Oiseau-Lyre 3-▲ 421333-2 [DDD]
Mozart, W.A.:Zauberflöte, w. B. Bonney (sop—Pamina), S. Jo (sop—Queen of the Night), K. Streit (ten—Tamino), G. Cachemaille (b-bar—Papageno), K. Sigmundsson (bass—Sarastro), Drottingholm Court Thea Chorus L'Oiseau-Lyre 2-▲ 440085-2 [DDD]
Dubuffet String Quartet
Vivaldi, A.:Cons Vn, Op. 8/1–4, "The Four Seasons", w. Jerome Franke (vn), Karine Garibova (vn), Pasquale Laurino (vn), Olga Miliaeva (va), Roza Borisova (vc), Mika Hennessy (db), Melanie Panush (ham dlc), Stanislav Venglevski (bayan), Mike Kashou (arabic tabla), Daryl Stuermer (gtr), Ed Palaucek (celtic fid), Gary Bottoni (highland pipe) *(rec July–Sept 1995)* EarthBeat! ▲ 35270-2 [DDD]
Duchemin Quartet
Giordani, T.:Qt 1 Vn Analekta ▲ CLCD 2005
Haydn, J.:Trios Pno, Vn & Vc—H.XVI/30 Analekta ▲ CLCD 2005
Mendelssohn, F.:Trio 1 Pno Analekta ▲ CLCD 2005
Duehlmeier-Gritton Duo
Gershwin, G.:Con Pno—2nd movt *(rec David Gardner Hall, University of Utah, Aug 16, 1994)* Centaur ▲ 2249 [DDD]
Gershwin, G.:"I Got Rhythm" Vars *(rec David Gardner Hall, University of Utah, Aug 16, 1994)* Centaur ▲ 2249 [DDD]
Gershwin, G.:Porgy & Bess (sels)—It Ain't Necessarily So [w. David Power (bar)]; Summertime [w. JoAnn Ottley (sop)] *(rec David Gardner Hall, University of Utah, Aug 16, 1994)* Centaur ▲ 2249 [DDD]
Gershwin, G.:Songs, w. JoAnn Ottley (sop), David Power (bar)—Fascinatin' Rhythm *(rec David Gardner Hall, University of Utah, Aug 16, 1994)* Centaur ▲ 2249 [DDD]
Grainger, P.:Fant on Gershwin's *Porgy & Bess* *(rec David Gardner Hall, University of Utah, Aug 16, 1994)* Centaur ▲ 2249 [DDD]
Duett Konzertant [Albert Aigner (gtr), Dieter Kreidler (gtr)]
Courtly & Gallant Music for 2 Guitars:16th–18th Centuries CPO ▲ CPO 999133 [ADD]
Music for 2 Guitars:17th–19th CPO ▲ CPO 999126 [DDD]
Dufay Collective
A Dance in the Garden of Mirth:Medieval Instrumental Music Chandos ("New Direction" series) ▲ CHAN 9320 [DDD]
A L'Estampida:Medieval Dance Music Continuum ▲ CCD 1042
Johnny, Cock Thy Beaver *(rec Forde Abbey, Sept 7–9, 1995)* Chandos ▲ CHAN 9446
Miri It Is:Songs & Instrumental Music from Medieval England Chandos ▲ CHN 9396
Duffy String Quartet
Duffy String Quartet, w. M. G. Bellocchio (pno), Ensemble Nuove Sincronie Stradavarius ▲ SIP 1011
Duke Ellington Orch
D. Ellington (cnd)
Ellington, D.:Music of—Creole Rhap; Reminiscing in Tempo Claremont ▲ CDGSE 785065
Duke String Quartet [Louisa Fuller (vn), Rick Koster (vn), John Metcalfe (va), Ivan McCready (vc)]
Barber, S.:Qt Strs Collins Classics ▲ CCS 1386 [DDD]
Bärmann, H.J.:Qnt 3 Cl, w. V. Soames (cl) Clarinet Classics ▲ CC 0003
Dvořák, A.:Qt 12 Strs, "America" Collins Classics ▲ CCS 1386 [DDD]
Ives, C.:Choral Music, w. Chrisopher Hughes (org), S. Cleobury (cnd), New London Orch members, BBC Singers—Psalms 54, 67, 90 & 135; Easter Carol; Crossing the Bar; The Celestial Country Collins Classics ▲ COL 1479
Pärt, A.:Fratres I Collins ▲ COL 1475
Schnittke, A.:Qt 2 Strs Collins Classics ▲ COL 1450
Tchaikovsky, P.:Qt 1 Strs Collins Classics ▲ COL 1450
Tüür, E.-S.:Qt Strs Collins ▲ COL 1475
Vasks, P.:Qt 2 Strs Collins ▲ COL 1475
Volans, K.:Dancers on a Plane Collins Classics ▲ COL 1417
Volans, K.:Movt Str Qt Collins Classics ▲ COL 1417
Volans, K.:Qt 4 Strs Collins Classics ▲ COL 1417
Volans, K.:Qt 5 Strs Collins Classics ▲ COL 1417
Volans, K.:The Ramanujan Notebooks Collins Classics ▲ COL 1417
Weber, C.M. von:Qnt Cl, w. V. Soames (cl) Clarinet Classics ▲ CC 0003
H. Christophers (cnd)
Tavener, J.:Music of, w. The Sixteen Orch—2 Hymns to the Mother of God; The Lamb; The Tiger; Ikon of Light; Today the Virgin; Eonia Collins Classics ▲ COL 1405 [DDD]
Dunsmuir Piano Quartet [Justin Blasdale (pno), Ronald Copes (vn), Roxann Jacobson (va), Jennifer Culp (vc)]
Hartke, S.:The King of the Sun *(rec Notre Dame Chapel, Belmont, CA, Oct. 2–3, 1994)* New World ▲ 80461-2
Sleeper, T.:Qt Pno MMC ("Chamber Music" series) ▲ MMC 2010
Duo di Basso [Frantisek Host (vc), Jiří Hudec (db)]
Barrière, J.:Son Vc & Db *(rec St. Jan Hus Church, Jilove, Oct 13–16, 1994)* Canyon Classics ▲ 331
Benda, F.:Son Vc *(rec St. Jan Hus Church, Jilove, Oct 13–16, 1994)* Canyon Classics ▲ 331
Gemrot, J.:Invention 2 *(rec St. Jan Hus Church, Jilove, Oct 13–16, 1994)* Canyon Classics ▲ 331
Lukáš, Z.:Duo di Basso *(rec St. Jan Hus Church, Jilove, Oct 13–16, 1994)* Canyon Classics ▲ 331
Pleyel, I.:Theme & Var *(rec St. Jan Hus Church, Jilove, Oct 13–16, 1994)* Canyon Classics ▲ 331
Rossini, G.:Duet Vc *(rec St. Jan Hus Church, Jilove, Oct 13–16, 1994)* Canyon Classics ▲ 331
Duodecima [Lars Karlsson (gtr), Michael Ljung (gtr)]
Duarte, J.:Vars on a French Nursery Song *(rec Dec. 1981–Mar. 1982)* Opus 3 ▲ OP 8201 [AAD]
Petit, P.:Toccata Gtrs *(rec Dec. 1981–Mar. 1982)* Opus 3 ▲ OP 8201 [AAD]
Santórsola, G.:Son a duo Gtrs *(rec Dec. 1981–Mar. 1982)* Opus 3 ▲ OP 8201 [AAD]
Sor, F.:Fant Gtrs *(rec Dec. 1981–Mar. 1982)* Opus 3 ▲ OP 8201 [AAD]
Duodena Cantitans
Mirabile Mysterium, w. Capella Rudolphina Supraphon ▲ SUP 0192
P. Danek (cnd)
Music From the Time of Prince Rudolf II, w. Michael Consort, Capella Rudolphina Supraphon ▲ SUP 112176 [DDD]
Dussek Piano Trio [Michael Dussek (pno), Peter Tanfield (vn), Margaret Powell (vc)]
Bridge, F.:Miniatures Meridian ▲ MER 84290 [DDD]
Bridge, F.:Phantasie Trio Meridian ▲ MER 84290 [DDD]
Bridge, F.:Trio 2 Pno Meridian ▲ MER 84290 [DDD]
Haydn, J.:Trios Pno, Vn & Vc—H.XV/25, 27–29 Meridian ▲ MER 84242 [DDD]
Düsseldorf CO
S. Köhler (cnd)
Weill, K.:Der Jasager, w. *(soloists unknown)* Polydor ▲ 839727-2 (m) ■ 839727-4 (m)
Düsseldorf Classical PO
F. Merz (cnd)
Schumann, R.:Ovs—(4) Ebs 3-▲ 6088
Schumann, R.:Syms (comp) Ebs 3-▲ 6088
Düsseldorf SO
H. Schmidt (cnd)
Weill, K.:Berlin Requiem, w. J. Wagner (ten), W. Holzmair (bar), Düsseldorf Sym Chorus [G] Koch Schwann ▲ CD 314 050 [DDD]
Dutch Radio PO
E. de Waart (cnd)
Schreker, F.:Die Gezeichneten, w. M. Schmiege (mez), W. Cochran (ten), S. Cowan (bar), W. Oosterkamp (bass), Dutch Radio Phil Chorus Marco Polo 3-▲ 8.223328/30

156

▲ = CD ♦ = Enhanced CD ∆ = MD ■ = Cassette Tape □ = DCC

Dutch RSO
J. Fournet (cnd)
Berlioz, H.:Choral Music, w. G. Garino (tenor), R. van der Meer (bass), L. Visser (bass), Dutch Radio Chorus—Le cinq mai, Op. 6; L'impériale, Op. 26; La mort d'Orphée; La révolution grecque, scène héroïque — Denon ▲ CO 72886 [DDD]
Dutch Royal Military Band
P. Kuijpers (cnd)
Bilik, J.H.:Sym — Ottavo ▲ OTR C18924 [DDD]
de Meij, J.:Sym 1, "The Lord of the Rings" — Ottavo ▲ OTR C18924 [DDD]
Dvořák CO
Vranicky, P.:Sym, Op. 58, w. B. Gregor — Supraphon ▲ 110956
P. Altrichter (cnd)
Reicha, A.:Sinfonie — Panton ▲ 81 1027
Reicha, A.:Sym à petit Orch — Panton ▲ 81 1026
Reicha, A.:Sym in f — Panton ▲ 81 1026
Reicha, A.:Sym 3 — Panton ▲ 81 1027
J. Belohlávek (cnd)
Mozart, W.A.:Sinf concertante Ob, K.Anh.9, w. Jan Adamus (ob), Frantisek Bláha (cl), Svatopluk Cech (bn), Zdenek Divoky (hn) — Panton ▲ PAN 811206
B. Gregor (cnd)
Vranicky, P.:Sym in c — Supraphon ▲ 110956
Vranicky, P.:Sym, Op. 11 — Supraphon ▲ CD 111332 [DDD]
Vranicky, P.:Sym, Op. 36 — Supraphon ▲ CD 111332 [DDD]
M. Homolka (cnd)
Nedbal, O.:Andersen — Supraphon ▲ SUP 111413 [DDD]
Nedbal, O.:From Fairy Tale — Supraphon ▲ SUP 111413 [DDD]
Nedbal, O.:Legend of Honza — Supraphon ▲ SUP 111414 [DDD]
Nedbal, O.:Princezna Hyacinta — Supraphon ▲ SUP 111414 [DDD]
L. Mátl (cnd)
Reicha, A.:Der neue Psalm, w. Magdaléna Hajóssyová (sop), Anna Barová (mez), Andreas Schmidt (bar), Karel Průša (bass), Czech Phil Chorus — Panton ▲ PAN 810758 [DDD]
Reicha, A.:Requiem, w. V. Hrubá-Freiberger (sop), A. Barová (mez), V. Dolezal (ten), L. Vele (bass), Czech Phil Chorus [L] — Supraphon ▲ 11 0332-2 [DDD]
L. Pešek (cnd)
Barsanti, F.:Con grosso, w. Z. Tylšar (hn), B. Tylšar (hn) — Supraphon ▲ 103907-2 [DDD]
Beethoven, L. van:Sxt Hns, Op. 81b, w. Z. Tylšar (hn), B. Tylšar (hn) — Supraphon ▲ 103907-2 [DDD]
Handel, G.F.:Con for 2 Vns & 2 Hns, w. P. Mareš (vn), J. Opsitos (vn), B. Tylšar (F hn), Z. Tylšar (F hn) — Supraphon ▲ 103907-2 [DDD]
Linek, J.:Con Org — Supraphon ▲ SUP 111007 [AAD]
Linek, J.:Sinf Pastoralis in D — Supraphon ▲ SUP 111007 [AAD]
Mozart, W.A.:Musikalischer Spass, w. Z. Tylšar (hn), B. Tylšar (hn) — Supraphon ▲ 103907-2 [DDD]
Myslivecek, J.:Cons Vn, w. Shizuka Ishikawa (vn)—in C, E, F & A — Supraphon ▲ SUP 0016 [DDD]
Myslivecek, J.:Cons Vn, w. Shizuka Ishikawa (vn)—4 cons — Supraphon ▲ SUP CD 3259
Ryba, J.J.:Czech Christmas Mass, w. Richard Novak (ten), Kühn Chamber Choir — Supraphon ▲ SUP 111007 [AAD]
F. Vajnar (cnd)
Dittersdorf, K.D. von:Concertino Va, w. L. Maly (va), F. Pasta (db) — Supraphon ▲ CD 110951 [DDD]
Dittersdorf, K.D. von:Con Db, w. F. Pasta (db) — Supraphon ▲ CD 110951 [DDD]
Dittersdorf, K.D. von:Con Va, w. L. Maly (va) — Supraphon ▲ CD 110951 [DDD]
V. Válek (cnd)
Richter, F.X.:Cons Fl, w. Jirí Válek (fl)—in E & D — Supraphon ▲ SUP 111872 [DDD]
Stamitz, C.:Cons Fl, w. Jirí Válek (fl)—in D & G — Supraphon ▲ SUP 111872 [DDD]
Stamitz, J.W.A.:Cons Org, w. A. Veselá (org) *(rec 1982)* — Supraphon Collection ▲ 11 0633-2 [ADD]
Stamitz, J.W.A.:Cons Org, w. Alena Veselá (org), Frantisek Xaver Thuri (hpd) — Supraphon ("Mannheim" series) ▲ SUP CD 3094
P. Škvor (cnd)
Haydn, J.:Con 1 Vc, w. Frantisek Host (vc) — Panton ▲ PAN 810829
Haydn, J.:Con 2 Vc, w. Frantisek Host (vc) — Panton ▲ PAN 810829
Antonín Dvořák Trio [František Maly (pno), Jiří Hurník (vn), Daniel Veis (vc)]
Smetana, B.:Trio Pno *(rec Martinů Hall, Lichtenstein Palace, Prague, June 12–14, 1995)* — Panton ▲ 811427-2 [DDD]
Suk, J.:Elegie *(rec Martinů Hall, Lichtenstein Palace, Prague, June 12–14, 1995)* — Panton ▲ 811427-2 [DDD]
Suk, J.:Trio Pno *(rec Martinů Hall, Lichtenstein Palace, Prague, June 12–14, 1995)* — Panton ▲ 811427-2 [DDD]
DZO CO
S. Behrend (cnd)
Concert Music of the 20th Century *(rec Jan. 4–6, 1989)* — Pro Viva ▲ ISPV 156 [DDD]
Eaken Piano Trio [Gloria Whitney (pno), John Eaken (vn), Nancy Baun (vc)]
Haydn, J.:Trios Pno, Vn & Vc—H.XV/24, 25, 27, 28 *(rec Market Square Church, Harrisburg, PA, June 2–6, 1992)* — WEB ▲ 28714 CD [DDD]
Haydn, J.:Trios Pno, Vn & Vc—H.XV/24, 25, 27, 28 *(rec Market Square Church, Harrisburg, PA, June 2–6, 1992)* — Web ▲ 28714 CD [DDD] F
Early Music Ensemble
J. Renz (cnd)
Christesmas in Anglia — Elektra/Nonesuch ■ N5-71369
Earplay [Janet Kutulas (fl), Peter Josheff (cl), Joseph Edelberg (vn), Roxann Jacobson (va), Robin Bonnell (vc), Karen Rosenak (pno), Andrew Lewis (perc)]
G. Thomson (cnd)
Festinger, R.:Septet *(rec Knuth Hall, San Francisco State Univ, Nov 25, 1994)* — Centaur ▲ CRC 2274 [DDD]
Earplay members [Janet Kutulas (fl), Peter Josheff (cl), Joseph Edelberg (vn), Karen Rosenak (pno)]
Peterson, W.:Labyrinth *(rec Knuth Hall, San Francisco State Univ, Nov 25, 1994)* — Centaur ▲ CRC 2274 [DDD]
Earplay members [Janet Kutulas (fl), Peter Josheff (cl), Joseph Edelberg (vn), Robin Bonnell (vc), Karen Rosenak (pno)]
Vayo, D.:Poem *(rec Knuth Hall, San Francisco State Univ, Nov 25, 1994)* — Centaur ▲ CRC 2274 [DDD]
Earplay members [Janet Kutulas (fl), Peter Josheff (cl), Joseph Edelberg (vn), Robin Bonnell (vc)]
Frank, A.:Points of Departure *(rec Knuth Hall, San Francisco State Univ, Nov 25, 1994)* — Centaur ▲ CRC 2274 [DDD]
Earplay members [Janet Kutulas (fl), Peter Josheff (cl)]
Carter, E.:Esprit rude/esprit doux *(rec Knuth Hall, San Francisco State Univ, Nov 25, 1994)* — Centaur ▲ CRC 2274 [DDD]
Earplay members [Peter Josheff (cl), George Thomson (va), Karen Rosenak (pno)]
G. Thomson (cnd)
Mamlok, U.:Rhap Cl, Va & Pno *(rec Knuth Hall, San Francisco State Univ, Nov 25, 1994)* — Centaur ▲ CRC 2274 [DDD]
Earplay members [Peter Josheff (cl), Joseph Edelberg (vn), Karen Rosenak (pno)]
Moretto, G.:Silenciosamente *(rec Knuth Hall, San Francisco State Univ, Nov 25, 1994)* — Centaur ▲ CRC 2274 [DDD]
East Coast Saxophone Quartet [Dale W. Underwood (s sax), Charlie Young (a sax), Timothy Roberts (t sax), Audrey Cupples (b sax)]
Americana Suite *(rec Omega Studios, Rockville, MD, Sept 1994)* — Open Loop ▲ 025 [DDD]

East of England Orch
M. Nabarro (cnd)
Coates, E.:Four Centuries — ASV ("White Line" series) ▲ ASV 2075
Coates, E.:From the Countryside *(rec May 1992)* — ASV ("White Line" series) ▲ WHL 2069 [DDD]
Coates, E.:The Jester at the Wedding — ASV ("White Line" series) ▲ ASV 2075 [DDD]
Coates, E.:Men of Trent *(rec May 1992)* — ASV ("White Line" series) ▲ WHL 2069 [DDD]
Coates, E.:Snow White & the 7 Dwarfs — ASV ("White Line" series) ▲ ASV 2075 [DDD]
Curzon, F.:Robin Hood *(rec May 1992)* — ASV ("White Line" series) ▲ WHL 2069 [DDD]
Goodwin, R.:City of Lincoln March *(rec May 1992)* — ASV ("White Line" series) ▲ WHL 2069 [DDD]
Korngold, E.W.:The Adventures of Robin Hood (suite) *(rec May 1992)* — ASV ("White Line" series) ▲ WHL 2069 [DDD]
Matthews, D.:Sym 4 *(rec Sept. 1993)* — Collins Classics ▲ 2008-2 [DDD]
Nabarro, M.:Lincoln Green *(rec May 1992)* — ASV ("White Line" series) ▲ WHL 2069 [DDD]
Eastern Brass Quintet
Classical Brass — Klavier ▲ KCD 11025 [ADD]
Eastern Connecticut SO
P. Phillips (cnd)
Hodkinson, S.:Chansons de Jadis, w. R. Fleming (mez) [E] — Centaur ▲ CRC 2073 [DDD]
Hodkinson, S.:Missa brevis, w. Univ of Connecticut Concert Choir [L] — Centaur ▲ CRC 2073 [DDD]
Eastern Netherlands Orch
G. Bellini (cnd)
Cimarosa, D.:Il Matrimonio segreto, w. Susan Patterson (sop—Carolina), Janet Williams (mez—Elisetta), Gloria Banditelli (cta—Fidalma), William Matteuzzi (ten—Paolino), Alfonso Antoniozzi (bass—Geronimo), Petteri Salomaa (bass—Count Robinson), Hans Ludwig Hirsch (pno) *(rec Muziekcentrum Enschede, Holland, Aug 26–Sept 8, 1991)* — Arts 3-▲ 471172 [DDD]
Donizetti, G.:Linda di Chamounix, w. Mariella Devia (sop—Linda), Sonia Ganassi (mez—Pierotto), Francesca Provvisionato (mez—Maddalena), Luca Canonici (ten—Carlo), Alfonso Antoniozzi (bass—Il Marchese di Boisfleury), Petteri Salomaa (bass—Antonio), Boguslaw Fiksinski (sgr—L'intendente), Donato Di Stefano (sgr—Il Prefetto), Andrew Wise (cnd), National Reisopera Choir *(rec Muziekcentrum Enschede, Holland, June 24–July 2, 1992)* — Arts Music 3-▲ 47151-2 [DDD]
Eastman Brass Quintet
F. Holland (cnd)
Renaissance Brass Music, w. Paris Instrumental Ensemble — Allegretto ▲ ACD 8154 [ADD] ■ ACS 8154
Eastman Chamber Ensemble
D. Effron (cnd)
Berlioz, H.:Les Nuits d'été, w. J. DeGaetani (mez) [F] — Bridge ▲ BCD 9017 [DDD] ■ BCS 9017 (D)
Mahler, G.:Des Knaben Wunderhorn, w. J. DeGaetani (mez) [G] — Bridge ▲ BCD 9017 [DDD] ■ BCS 9017 (D)
Mahler, G.:Songs from Rückert, w. J. DeGaetani (mez) [G] — Bridge ▲ BCD 9017 [DDD] ■ BCS 9017 (D)
Eastman Jazz Ensemble
R. Wright (cnd)
La Montaine, J.:Incantation — Fredonia Discs ▲ FDCD 12
Eastman Musica Nova Ensemble
S. Hodkinson (cnd)
Albert, S.:Into Eclipse, w. Stephen Oosting (ten) *(rec Eastman Theater, Mar 26, 1983)* — Albany ▲ TROY 192 [ADD]
Rouse, C.:Mitternachtlieder, w. Leslie Guinn (b-bar) *(rec Eastman Theater, Nov 29, 1983)* — Albany ▲ TROY 192 [ADD]
D. Neuen (cnd)
Rouse, C.:Madrigals, w. Graduate Chamber Singers *(rec Eastman Theater, Feb 22, 1984)* — Albany ▲ TROY 192 [ADD]
P. Phillips (cnd)
Hodkinson, S.:The Edge of the Olde One, w. Thomas Stacy (E hn) — New World ▲ 80489-2
Hodkinson, S.:The Edge of the Olde One, w. T. Stacy (E hn) — Grenadilla ■ GSC 1054
Eastman Percussion Ensemble
J. Beck (cnd)
Lewis, R.H.:Combinazioni II *(rec Eastman School of Music, May 19, 1975)* — Albany ▲ TROY 166 [ADD/DDD]
Eastman Percussion Ensemble members [David Mancini (perc), Ernest Muzquiz (perc), Steven Richards (perc), Bradley Stouffer (perc), Gordon Stout (perc)]
Harrison, L.:Con Vn, w. Carroll Glenn (vn) *(rec 1972)* — Vox Box ("The American Composers" series) 2-▲ CDX 5158
Eastman Philharmonia
D. Effron (cnd)
Corigliano, J.:Pied Piper Fant, w. J. Galway (fl) — RCA Red Seal ▲ 6602-2-RC [DDD]
Corigliano, J.:Voyage Fl, w. J. Galway (fl) — RCA Red Seal ▲ 6602-2-RC [DDD]
Eastman Quartet
Brahms, J.:Qts Pno (comp) *(rec 1968)* — Vox Box 2-▲ CDX 5052 [ADD]
Eastman Rochester Pops
F. Fennell (cnd)
Frederick Fennell Conducts Carousel Waltz & Other Orchestral Favorites, w. London Pops Orch — Mercury Living Presence ▲ 434256-2
Eastman Trio [Zvi Zeitlin (vn), Robert Sylvester (vc), Barry Snyder (pno)]
Arensky, A.:Trio 1 Pno — Vox Box 3-▲ CD3X 3021 [ADD]
Glinka, M.:Trio pathétique — Vox Box 3-▲ CD3X 3021 [ADD]
Rachmaninoff, S.:Trio élégiaque 2 — Vox Box 3-▲ CD3X 3021 [ADD]
Rimsky-Korsakov, N.:Trio Vn — Vox Box 3-▲ CD3X 3021 [ADD]
Tchaikovsky, P.:Trio Pno — Vox Box 3-▲ CD3X 3021 [ADD]
Tchaikovsky, P.:Trio Pno — Vox Box 3-▲ CD3X 3024 [ADD]
Eastman Wind Ensemble
F. Fennell (cnd)
Ballet for Band/Wagner for Band — Mercury Living Presence ▲ 434322-2 [ADD]
British & American Band Classics — Mercury Living Presence ▲ 432009-2
The Civil War:Its Music & Sounds — Philips ("Living Presence" series) 2-▲ 432591-2
Gould, M.:West Point Sym — Mercury Living Presence ▲ 434320-2 [ADD]
Gounod, C.:Faust (ballet music) — Mercury Living Presence ▲ 434322-2 [ADD]
Grainger, P.:Lincolnshire Posy — Mercury Living Presence ▲ 432754-2 [ADD]
Hands across the Sea:Marches from around the World — Mercury Living Presence ▲ 434334-2
Holst, G.:Hammersmith—Prelude only — Mercury Living Presence ▲ 432009-2 [ADD]
Jacob, G.:William Byrd Suite — Mercury Living Presence ▲ 432009-2
Khachaturian, A.:Armenian Dances — Mercury Living Presence ▲ 432754-2 [ADD]
Respighi, O.:La Boutique fantastique — Mercury Living Presence ▲ 434322-2 [ADD]
Rogers, B.:Japanese Dances — Mercury Living Presence ▲ 432754-2 [ADD]
Screamers (Circus Marches) & March Time — Mercury Living Presence ▲ 432019-2 [ADD]
Sousa, J.P.:Marches & Dances—24 favorite marches — Mercury Living Presence ▲ 434300-2 [ADD]
Sullivan, A.:Pineapple Poll [arr Frederick Fennell] — Mercury Living Presence ▲ 434322-2 [ADD]
20th Century Works for Wind Band — Mercury Living Presence ▲ 432754-2 [ADD]
Walton, W.:Crown Imperial — Mercury Living Presence ▲ 432009-2 [ADD]
D. Hunsberger (cnd)
Benson, W.:The Leaves Are Falling — Centaur ▲ CRC 2014 [AAD]
Brandt, H.:Angels & Devils, w. B. Boyd (fl) — Centaur ▲ CRC 2014 [AAD]
Copland, A.:Quiet City, w. W. Marsalis (tpt), P. Koch (E hn) — CBS ▲ MK 44916 [DDD] ■ MT 44916 (D)
Hanson, H.:Dies Natalis Band — Centaur ▲ CRC 2014 [AAD]
Hindemith, P.:Konzertmusik Band — CBS ▲ MK 44916 [DDD] ■ MT 44916 (D)
Homespun America, w. DeCormier (cnd), Eastman Chorale — Vox Box 2-▲ CDX 5088 [ADD]
Husa, K.:Music for Prague 1968 — CBS ▲ MK 44916 [DDD] ■ MT 44916 (D)

ORCH. & ENS.

Eastman Wind Ensemble (cont.)
D. Hunsberger (cnd) (cont.)
Sousa, J.P.:Marches & Dances—Anchor and star; Comrades of the legion; Corcoran cadets; El capitan; Hail to the spirit of liberty; High school cadets; Jack tar; King cotton; Liberty bell; The loyal legion; Semper fidelis; Stars and stripes forever; The Thunderer; Washington Post Kem-Disc ▲ 1004 [DDD]
Vaughan Williams, R.:Toccata marziale CBS ▲ MK 44916 [DDD] ■ MT 44916 (D)
Vaughan Williams, R.:Vars Brass Band CBS ▲ MK 44916 [DDD] ■ MT 44916 (D)
A. C. Roller (cnd)
Giannini, V.:Sym 3 Mercury Living Presence ▲ 434320-2 [ADD]
Hovhaness, A.:Sym 4 Mercury Living Presence ▲ 434320-2 [ADD]
Eastman-Dryden Orch
D. Hunsberger (cnd)
Friml, R.:Songs, w. Teresa Ringholz (sop) Arabesque ▲ Z 6562
Herbert, V.:Music of Arabesque ▲ Z 6547 [DDD]
Herbert, V.:Music of Arabesque ▲ Z 6561 [DDD]
Herbert, V.:Music of Arabesque ▲ Z 6529 [DDD]
Romberg, S.:Music of (operetta sels), w. T. Ringholz (sop)—selections from The New Moon, Maytime, Desert Song, etc. [E] Arabesque ▲ Z 6540 [DDD]
Eastman-Rochester Orch
H. Hanson (cnd)
Barber, S.:Capricorn Con, w. Eastman-Rochester Orch Soloists Mercury Living Presence ▲ 434307-2 [ADD]
Barber, S.:Medea Mercury Living Presence ▲ 432016-2 [ADD]
Bergsma, W.:Gold & the Señor Commandante Mercury Living Presence ▲ 434307-2 [ADD]
Bloch, E.:Con grosso 1 Mercury Living Presence ▲ 432718-2 [ADD]
Bloch, E.:Con grosso 2 Mercury Living Presence ▲ 432718-2 [ADD]
Bloch, E.:Schelomo, w. G. Miquelle (vc) Mercury Living Presence ▲ 432718-2 [ADD]
Carpenter, J.A.:Adventures in a Perambulator Mercury Living Presence ▲ 434319-2 [ADD]
Chadwick, G.W.:Symphonic Sketches *(rec Jan. 1956)* Mercury Living Presence ▲ 434337-2
Fiesta in Hi-Fi *(rec mid-late 1950s)* Mercury Living Presence ▲ 434324-2 [ADD]
Gershwin, G.:Con Pno, w. Eugene List (pno) Mercury Living Presence ▲ 434341-2
Gershwin, G.:Cuban Ov Mercury Living Presence ▲ 434341-2
Gershwin, G.:Rhap in Blue, w. Eugene List (pno) Mercury Living Presence ▲ 434341-2
Ginastera, A.:Ov to the Creole "Faust" Mercury Living Presence ▲ 434324-2 [ADD]
Gould, M.:Fall River Legend (suite) Mercury Living Presence ▲ 432016-2 [ADD]
Gould, M.:Spirituals Orch Mercury Living Presence ▲ 432016-2 [ADD]
Griffes, C.T.:Poem Fl, w. J. Mariano (fl) Mercury Living Presence ▲ 434307-2 [ADD]
Grofé, F.:Grand Canyon Suite Mercury Living Presence ▲ 434355-2
Grofé, F.:Mississippi Suite Mercury Living Presence ▲ 434355-2
Hanson, H.:Elegy in Memory of Serge Koussevitsky Mercury Living Presence ▲ 434302-2 [ADD]
Hanson, H.:Lament for Beowulf, w. Eastman-Rochester Chorus Mercury Living Presence ▲ 434302-2 [ADD]
Hanson, H.:Merry Mount (suite) *(rec 1940)* Biddulph ▲ WHL 038
Hanson, H.:Song of Democracy, w. Eastman School of Music Chorus Mercury Living Presence ▲ 432008-2 [ADD]
Hanson, H.:Sym 1, "Nordic" Mercury Living Presence ▲ 432008-2 [ADD]
Hanson, H.:Sym 1, "Nordic" *(rec 1942)* Biddulph ▲ WHL 038
Hanson, H.:Sym 2, "Romantic" Mercury Living Presence ▲ 432008-2 [ADD]
Hanson, H.:Sym 2, "Romantic" *(rec 1939)* Biddulph ▲ WHL 038
Hanson, H.:Sym 3 Mercury Living Presence ▲ 434302-2 [ADD]
Herbert, V.:Con 2 Vc, w. Georges Miquelle (vc) Mercury Living Presence ▲ 434355-2
Ives, C.:Sym 3 Mercury Living Presence ▲ 432755-2 [ADD]
Ives, C.:Three Places in New England Mercury Living Presence ▲ 432755-2 [ADD]
Macdowell, E.:Suite *(rec May 1961)* Mercury Living Presence ▲ 434337-2
McPhee, C.:Tabuh-Tabuhan Mercury Living Presence ▲ 434310-2 [ADD]
Mennin, P.:Sym 5 Mercury Living Presence ▲ 432755-2 [ADD]
Mitchell, L.C.:KY Mountain Mercury Living Presence ▲ 434324-2 [ADD]
Moore, D.:The Pageant of P.T. Barnum for Orchestra (1924) Mercury Living Presence ▲ 434319-2 [ADD]
Music for Quiet Listening Mercury Living Presence ▲ 434347-2
Peter, J.F.:Sinf *(rec May 1957)* Mercury Living Presence ▲ 434337-2
Phillips, B.:Sels from McGuffey's Reader Mercury Living Presence ▲ 434319-2 [ADD]
Piston, W.:The Incredible Flutist Mercury Living Presence ▲ 434307-2 [ADD]
Riegger, W.:Sym 3 CRI ▲ CD 572 [ADD]
Rogers, B.:Once Upon A Time Mercury Living Presence ▲ 434319-2 [ADD]
Schuman, W.:New England Triptych Mercury Living Presence ▲ 432755-2 [ADD]
Sessions, R.:The Black Maskers (suite) Mercury Living Presence ▲ 434310-2 [ADD]
Siegmeister, E.:Theater Set Premier ("Composer" series) ▲ PRCD 1010 [ADD]
Sousa, J.P.:Stars & Stripes Forever Mercury Living Presence ▲ 434341-2
Eastman-Rochester Orch Soloists
Barber, S.:Capricorn Con, w. Eastman-Rochester Orch Mercury Living Presence ▲ 434307-2 [ADD]
Eastman-Rochester Pops Orch
F. Fennell (cnd)
Anderson, L.:Music of—23 compositions Mercury Living Presence ▲ 432013-2 [ADD]
Grainger, P.:Music of—Country Gardens; Shepherd's Hey; Colonial Song; Children's March; The Immovable Do; Mock Morris; Handel in the Strand; Irish Tune from County Derry; Spoon River; My Robin Is to the Greenwood Gone; Molly on the Shore *(rec May 3 & 4, 1959)* Mercury Living Presence ▲ 434330-2
Hi-Fi la Española & Popovers Mercury Living Presence ▲ 434349-2
Ebony Band
W. Herbers (cnd)
Schulhoff, E.:Bartipanu—Suite; 3 Tangos Channel Classics ▲ CCS 6994 [DDD]
Echos Muse [Paul Elliot (ten), Janet Humberger (voc/hpd), Wendy Gillespie (bowed instrs), Margriet Tindemans (rcr/vn/vl), David Tayler (lt)]
Dowland, J.:Songs—19 songs—Come away, come sweet love; Flow my teares; Fortune my foe; Flow not so fast yee fountaines; Sorrow stay; Thinkst thou thenby thy fayning; Away with these selfe loving lads; Lady if you so spight me; I saw my lady weep; Weepe you no more sad fountaines; A shepherd in a shade; Sweet stay awhile; Say love if ever thou didst find; The lowest trees have tops; Now cease my wandring eies; Come heavy sleep; From silent night; In darknesse let mee dwell; Now O now I needs must part Koch International Classics ▲ KIC 7170-2 [DDD]
Eclair Salon Orch
Plaisir d'amour, w. Jochen Kowalski (ct) Capriccio Δ 70324
L'École d'Orphée
Handel, G.F.:Sons Fl—Op. 1, Nos. 1a in e, 1b in e, 5 in G & 9 in b; Son in D, HWV 378 CRD ▲ 3373 [ADD]
Handel, G.F.:Sons Fl, "Halle Sons" CRD ▲ 3373 [ADD]
Handel, G.F.:Sons Ob—in Bb, HWV 357; in F, HWV 363a; in c, HWV 366 CRD ▲ 3374 [ADD]
Handel, G.F.:Sons Rcr—7 Sons (HWV 358, 360, 362, 365, 367a, 369, 377); Trio Sonata in F, HWV 405 CRD ▲ 3378 [ADD]
Handel, G.F.:Sons Vn—in d, HWV 359a; in A, HWV 361; in G, HWV 364a; in D, HWV 371; Violin movt in a, HWV 408; Violin movt (Allegro) in c, HWV 412 CRD ▲ 3374 [ADD]
Handel, G.F.:Trio Sons—Trio Sonatas for Two Violins & Continuo—5 Trio Sonatas (in c, Op. 2, No. 1a; in F, g & e, HWV 392-394; in C, HWV 403); Sinfonia in Bb, HWV 338 CRD ▲ 3377 [ADD]
L'École d'Orphée [John Holloway (vn), Micaela Comberti (vn), S. Preston (fl), P. Pickett (rcr), et al.]
Handel, G.F.:Chamber Music CRD ▲ 3377 [ADD]
Handel, G.F.:Chamber Music CRD ▲ 3376 [ADD]
Handel, G.F.:Chamber Music CRD ■ 3375 [ADD]
Handel, G.F.:Chamber Music CRD ■ 3374 [ADD]
Handel, G.F.:Chamber Music CRD ■ 3373 [ADD]
L'École d'Orphée (cont.)
Handel, G.F.:Chamber Music CRD ▲ 3378 [ADD]
L'École d'Orphée [John Holloway (vn), Micaela Comberti (vn), Susan Sheppard (vc), Lucy Carolan (hpd)]
Handel, G.F.:Trio Sons—Op. 2/1-6 [4 for 2 Vns & Cont; one each for Fl, Vn & Cont & Rcr, Vn & Cont] CRD ▲ 3375 [ADD]
Handel, G.F.:Trio Sons—Trio Sonatas Op. 5, Nos. 1-7 CRD ▲ 3376 [ADD]
École Normale de Musique Orch
A. Cortot (cnd)
Bach, J.S.:Brandenburg Cons *(rec May- June 1932)* Koch Historic 2-▲ 7705-2 [ADD]
Ecuador National SO
A. Manzano (cnd)
Schumann, R.:Con Pno, w. Regina Shamvill (pno) *(rec live, Sucre National Theater, Quito, Ecuador, May 20, 1994)* Gallo ▲ CD 859 [DDD]
Schumann, R.:Manfred Ov *(rec live, Sucre National Theater, Quito, Ecuador, May 20, 1994)* Gallo ▲ CD 859 [DDD]
Éder String Quartet
Haydn, J.:Qts Strs, Op. 76, "Erdödy Qts"—Nos. 2, 3 & 4 Teldec ("Digital Experience" series) ▲ 9031-77602-2 [DDD] ■ 9031-77602-4
Mozart, W.A.:Qt 1 Strs *(rec Nov. 12-17, 1990)* Naxos ▲ 8.550541 [DDD]
Mozart, W.A.:Qt 2 Strs *(rec Nov. 12-17, 1990)* Naxos ▲ 8.550541 [DDD]
Mozart, W.A.:Qt 3 Strs *(rec Apr. 16-22, 1991)* Naxos ▲ 8.550542 [DDD]
Mozart, W.A.:Qt 4 Strs *(rec Nov. 12-17, 1990)* Naxos ▲ 8.550541 [DDD]
Mozart, W.A.:Qt 5 Strs *(rec Apr. 16-22, 1991)* Naxos ▲ 8.550542 [DDD]
Mozart, W.A.:Qt 6 Strs *(rec Apr. 16-22, 1991)* Naxos ▲ 8.550542 [DDD]
Mozart, W.A.:Qt 14 Strs *(rec Nov. 12-17, 1990)* Naxos ▲ 8.550541 [DDD]
Mozart, W.A.:Qt 17 Strs *(rec Apr. 16-22, 1991)* Naxos ▲ 8.550542 [DDD]
Mozart, W.A.:Qnts Strs, w. János Fehérvári (va)—K. 174 & 515 *(rec Unitarian Church, Budapest, Dec. 2-5, 1993)* Naxos ▲ 8.553103 [DDD]
Shostakovich, D.:Qt 1 Strs *(rec Unitarian Church, Budapest, Feb. 14-17, 1994)* Naxos ▲ 8.550973 [DDD]
Shostakovich, D.:Qt 8 Strs *(rec Unitarian Church, Budapest, Feb. 14-17, 1994)* Naxos ▲ 8.550973 [DDD]
Shostakovich, D.:Qt 9 Strs *(rec Unitarian Church, Budapest, Feb. 14-17, 1994)* Naxos ▲ 8.550973 [DDD]
Éder String Quartet [János Selmeczi (vn), Péter Szüts (vn), Sándor Papp (va), György Éder (vc)]
Mozart, W.A.:Qts Strs (comp)—Nos. 12, 13, & 21 *(rec Unitarian Church, Budapest, Oct. 12-15, 1992)* Naxos ▲ 8.550545 [DDD]
Mozart, W.A.:Qts Strs (comp)—Nos. 10,11, & 15 *(rec Unitarian Church, Budapest, Nov. 15-18, 1992)* Naxos ▲ 8.550546 [DDD]
Mozart, W.A.:Qnts Strs—K.170, K.171, K.421 *(rec Unitarian Church, Budapest, Dec. 2-5, 1993)* Naxos ▲ 8.550546 [DDD]
Mozart, W.A.:Qnts Strs—K.499, K.590, K.546 *(rec Unitarian Church, Budapest, Apr. 5-9, 1993)* Naxos ▲ 8.550547 [DDD]
Shostakovich, D.:Qts Strs (comp)—No. 2 in A, Op. 68; No. 12 in Db, Op. 133 *(rec Unitarian Church, Budapest, Mar 28-31, 1995)* Naxos ▲ 8.550975 [DDD]
Shostakovich, D.:Qts Strs (comp)—No. 4, in D, Op. 83; No. 6 in G, Op. 101; No. 7 in f#, Op. 108 *(rec Dec. 1-4, 1993)* Naxos ▲ 8.550972 [DDD]
Éder String Quartet [Pál Éder (vn), Erika Tóth (vn), Zoltán Tóth (va), György Éder (vc)]
Mozart, W.A.:Qt 1 Strs *(rec Sashalom Reformed Church, Budapest, Nov 12-17, 1990)* Naxos 4-▲ 8.504006 [DDD]
Mozart, W.A.:Qt 2 Strs *(rec Sashalom Reformed Church, Budapest, Nov 12-17, 1990)* Naxos 4-▲ 8.504006 [DDD]
Mozart, W.A.:Qt 4 Strs *(rec Sashalom Reformed Church, Budapest, Nov 12-17, 1990)* Naxos 4-▲ 8.504006 [DDD]
Mozart, W.A.:Qt 14 Strs *(rec Sashalom Reformed Church, Budapest, Nov 12-17, 1990)* Naxos 4-▲ 8.504006 [DDD]
Edinburgh String Quartet
Tippett, M.:Qts Strs—No. 1 in A EMI Classics 2-▲ ZDMB 63522
Edmonton SO
U. Mayer (cnd)
Borodin, A.:Prince Igor (ov) CBC ("SM 5000" series) ▲ SMCD 5069 [DDD]
Britten, B.:Canadian Carnival CBC ("SM 5000" series) ▲ SMCD 5123 [DDD]
Britten, B.:Peter Grimes (4 sea interludes) CBC ("SM 5000" series) ▲ SMCD 5123 [DDD]
Canadian & Russian Overtures CBC Records ("SM 5000" series) ▲ SMCD 5069 [DDD]
Forsyth, M.:Atayoskewin CBC ("SM 5000" series) ▲ SMCD 5059 [DDD]
Forsyth, M.:Jubilee Ov CBC ("SM 5000" series) ▲ SMCD 5069 [DDD]
Freedman, H.:Oiseaux Exotiques CBC ("SM 5000" series) ▲ SMCD 5059 [DDD]
Glinka, M.:Russian & Ludmilla (ov) CBC ("SM 5000" series) ▲ SMCD 5069 [DDD]
Great Orchestral Marches CBC Records ("SM 5000" series) ▲ SMCD 5093 [DDD] ■ SMC 5093 (D)
Great Tenor Arias, w. Ermanno Mauro CBC Records ("SM 5000" series) ▲ SMCD 5046 [DDD]
Kabalevsky, D.:Colas Breugnon (ov) CBC ("SM 5000" series) ▲ SMCD 5069 [DDD]
Morawetz, O.:Ov to a Fairy Tale CBC ("SM 5000" series) ▲ SMCD 5069 [DDD]
Ridout, G.:Fall Fair CBC ("SM 5000" series) ▲ SMCD 5069 [DDD]
Shostakovich, D.:Festive Ov CBC ("SM 5000" series) ▲ SMCD 5069 [DDD]
Verdi, G.:Arias, w. L. Quilico (bar) [I] CBC ("SM 5000" series) ▲ SMCD 5043 [DDD]
Willan, H.:Sym 2 CBC ("SM 5000" series) ▲ SMCD 5123 [DDD]
Edmonton Wind Ensemble
H. Pinchin (cnd)
Concert in the Park CBC Records ("SM 5000" series) ▲ SMCD 5079 [DDD] ■ SMC 5079 (D)
Edwards Jazz Quartet
Fascinating Rhythm, w. Simone Rebello (perc), Brittania Building Society Brass Band [cnd:Howard Snell], Stewart Death (pno) Doyen ▲ CD 024 [DDD]
EIAR Orch
D. Amfitheatrof (cnd)
Borodin, A.:Prince Igor (ov) *(rec 1937)* Label "X" ▲ LXCD 8 [ADD]
V. Gui (cnd)
Bellini, V.:Norma, w. G. Cigna (sop), E. Stignani (mez), G. Breviario (ten), EIAR Chorus [I] *(rec 1936 for Cetra)* Pearl 2-▲ PEAS 9422 (m) [AAD]
Bellini, V.:Norma, w. Gina Cigna (sop—Norma), Ebe Stignani (sop—Adalgisa), Adriana Perris (mez—Clotilde), Giovanni Breviario (ten—Pollione), Emilio Renzi (ten—Flavio), Tancredi Pasero (bass—Oroveso), Achille Consoli (cnd), EIAR Chorus *(rec Aug/Sept 1937)* Arkadia ("The 78's" series) 2-▲ 78010 [ADD]
G. Marinuzzi (cnd)
Verdi, G.:La forza del destino, w. Maria Caniglia (sop), Ebe Stignani (mez), Galliano Masini (ten), Carlo Tagliabue (bar), Tancredi Pasero (bass), EIAR Chorus *(rec 1941)* Grammofono 2000 ▲ GRM 78567 (m)
U. Tansini (cnd)
Donizetti, G.:Lucia di Lammermoor, w. Lina Pagliughi (sop—Lucia), Maria Vinciguerra (mez—Alisa), Armando Giannotti (ten—Normanno), Muzio Giovannoli (ten—Lord Arturo), Giovanni Malipiero (ten—Edgardo), Giuseppe Manacchini (bar—Lord Enrico), Luciano Neroni (bass—Raimondo), EIAR Chorus *(rec Turin, 1942)* Melodram 2-▲ IMC 202004 [ADD]
Donizetti, G.:Lucia di Lammermoor, w. Lina Pagliughi (sop—Lucia), Maria Vinciguerra (mez—Alisa), Armando Giannotti (ten—Normanno), Muzio Giovagnoli (ten—Arturo), Giovanni Malipiero (ten—Edgardo), Giuseppe Manacchini (bar—Enrico), Luciano Neroni (bass—Raimondo), EIAR Chorus *(rec 1938)* Bongiovanni ("Il mito dell'opera" series) 2-▲ GB 1122-2 [DDD]
The Early Operatic Recordings 1940-43, w. Ferruccio Tagliavini (ten) Centaur ▲ CRC 2164

▲ = CD ♦ = Enhanced CD Δ = MD ■ = Cassette Tape □ = DCC

Eighteenth Century Ensemble
J. Litton (cnd)
Handel, G.F.:Dixit Dominus, w. *(soloists unknown)*, American Boychoir, Albemarle Consort of Voices MusicMasters ▲ 01612-67084-2 [DDD]
Vivaldi, A.:Dixit Dominus, w. American Boychoir, Albemarle Consort of Voices MusicMasters ▲ 01612-67084-2 [DDD]
Eimer Trio
Bartók, B.:Contrasts Dynamic ▲ CD 60 [DDD]
Keuris, T.:Muzick Dynamic ▲ CD 60 [DDD]
Khachaturian, A.:Trio Cl Dynamic ▲ CD 60 [DDD]
Stravinsky, I.:L'Histoire du soldat Suite Vn Dynamic ▲ CD 60 [DDD]
Eindhovens Instrumental Ensemble
A. Clement (cnd)
Honegger, A.:Le Roi David, w. Bernard Kruysen (bar), Hanke De Hoogh (nar), Sasja Hunnego (nar), Eindhovens Chamber Choir [orig version] Emergo ▲ 3974
Eireann Radio-TV SO
D. Atherton (cnd)
Donizetti, G.:Il giovedì grasso, w. J. Gomez (sop), J. Peters (mez), J. Hughes (mez), U. Benelli (bar), B. Donlan (bar), F. Davià (bass), E. Esparza (sgr) [I] *(rec live, 1970)* Foyer ▲ FOY 2036 [AAD]
Donizetti, G.:Il giovedì grasso, w. J. Gomez (sop), J. Hughes (mez), J. Peters (mez), U. Benelli (bar), B. Donlan (bar), F. Davià (bass), E. Esparza (sgr), M. Williams (sgr) [I] *(rec live, 1970)* Memories ▲ HR 4482 [ADD]
Ekaterinburg PO
S. Caldwell (cnd)
Shostakovich, D.:Con 1 Vc, w. William de Rosa (vc) Audiofon ▲ CD 72060
Shostakovich, D.:Con 1 Pno, w. Valentina Lisitsa (pno), Viatcheslav Chtchennikov (tpt) Audiofon ▲ CD 72060
Bengt Eklund's Baroque Ensemble
E. H. Tarr (cnd)
Courtly Trumpet Ensemble Music, w. George Kent (org) *(rec 1980)* BIS ▲ CD 217 [AAD]
Electric Phoenix
Bruce, N.:Vocal Music—The Dream of the Other Dreamers (1987); Eight Ghosts (1989); The Plague (rock opera, a commentary on the work of the Fourth Horseman) (1983–84) Mode ▲ 20
Shapiro, G.:Phoenix Neuma ▲ 450-75 [DDD]
Wishart, P.:Vox Virgin Classics ▲ CDC 59204
Electronic Ensemble
Jarre, M.:The Mosquito Coast, w. Byron Lee's Dragonaires Fantasy ▲ FSC 21005 ■ FSP 52105
Electronics Instrumental Ensemble
L. Vis (cnd)
Schat, P.:To You, w. Lucia Meeuwsen (sop) Donemus ▲ CV 19
Les Éléments
Josquin Desprez:Chansons & Motets, w. Clément Janequin Ensemble—20 songs for 1-6 voices & instruments, 5 works for viols, 2 selections for solo lute [F] Harmonia Mundi France ▲ HMC 901279
Telemann, G.P.:Cons (misc), w. J. Ogg (hpd)—Con. a 9 in E for Piccolo, Flute, Oboe d'amore, Strings & Continuo *(rec June 1993)* Globe ▲ GLO 5104 [DDD]
Telemann, G.P.:Con in E Fl, Ob d'amore *(rec June 1993)* Globe ▲ GLO 5104 [DDD]
Telemann, G.P.:Cons for 2 Fls, w. J. Ogg (hpd)—(1) in D *(rec June 1993)* Globe ▲ GLO 5104 [DDD]
Telemann, G.P.:Con in F Rcr Bn, w. J. Ogg (hpd) *(rec June 1993)* Globe ▲ GLO 5104 [DDD]
Telemann, G.P.:Ov in e *(rec June 1993)* Globe ▲ GLO 5104 [DDD]
A. Stuurop (cnd)
Bach, Joh. Christian:Cons Hpd, T.298/1, w. Jacques Ogg (hpd)—Nos. 2 & 5 *(rec Utrecht, 1995)* Globe ▲ GLO 5139 [DDD]
Bach, Joh. Christian:Con Hpd, T.301/4, w. Jacques Ogg (hpd) *(rec Utrecht, 1995)* Globe ▲ GLO 5139 [DDD]
D. Visse (cnd)
Le Jeune, C.:Chansons & VI Fantasias, w. Clément Janequin Ensemble—Que je porte d'envie; Je ne m'lève icy me plain; Susanne un jour; Le chant de l'Alouette; Quell'eau quel air; Seconde Fantasie; Je voulu baiser ma rebelle; Je suis déshéritée; Troisième Fantaisie; Allons, allons gay; Debat la nostre trill' en may; Mais qui es-tu Musique d'Abord ▲ HMA 1901182
Les Éléments [Rachel Platt (sop), Rachel Podger (baroque vn), Mark Levy (vl), James Johnstone (hpd)]
Clérambault, L.N.:Cants, w. Rachel Brown (baroque fl) Meridian ▲ MER 84272 [DDD]
Les Éléments [Rachel Podger (baroque vn), Mark Levy (vl), James Johnstone (hpd)]
Clérambault, L.N.:Instrumental Music, w. Rachel Brown (baroque fl) Meridian ▲ MER 84272 [DDD]
Elizabethan Consort of Viols
Byrd, W.:Consort Music Duo ▲ 89027 [DDD]
Byrd, W.:Songs, w. Jean Collingsworth (sop) Duo ▲ 89027 [DDD]
Elson-Swarthout Duo [Margret Elson (pno), Elizabeth Swarthout (pno)]
20th Century American 4-Hand Piano Music Laurel ▲ LR 859 [DDD]
Elyma Ensemble
Latin American Villancicos & Motets from the 1600s Symphonia ▲ SYM 91S05 [DDD]
Musique à la Cité des Rois, w. Cantores de Córdoba Boys' Choir *(rec June 30–July 2, 1993)* K617 ▲ 7035
G. Garrido (cnd)
Baroque Music at the Royal Audience of Charcas, w. Capella Cisplatina, Luis Berger Ensemble [cnd:Emma Sanchez], Cordoba Children's Choir *(rec Apr 19–24, 1996)* K617 ▲ 7064 [DDD]
Zipoli, D.:Choral Music, w. Cristina Garcia Banegas (org), Buenos Aires Affetti Ensemble, Cordoba Children's Chorus—Misa brevis; O gloriosa virgunum; Sacris solemnis; Tantum ergo; Letania I in c; Letania II in f; Ave maris stella; Zoipaqui; Deus in adjutorium; Dixit Dominus K617 ▲ 7036
Elyma Ensemble Soloists
Zipoli, D.:Dell'offese a vendicarmi chiamo all'armi, w. D. Ferran (org) [organ at Monticello in Corsica] K617 ▲ 7037
Zipoli, D.:Mia bella Irene, w. D. Ferran (org) [organ at Monticello in Corsica] K617 ▲ 7037
Zipoli, D.:Son Vn, w. D. Ferran (org) [organ at Monticello in Corsica] K617 ▲ 7037
Elyma Instrumental Ensemble
G. Garrido (cnd)
Les Chemins du Baroque (The Paths of the Baroque), w. Elyma Vocal Ensemble, Cordoba Children's Choir Garrado, Compañia Musical de las Americas, Maîtrise National de Versailles, La Grande Ecurie et la Chambre du Roy [cnd:Jean-Claude Malgoire], Compañia Musical de las Americas, La Fenice [cnd:Josep Cabré] K617 ("First 4 volumes of K617" series) ▲ 7042
Les Chemins du Baroque (The Paths of the Baroque), Vol. 1:Lima-Plata Jesuit Missions, w. Elyma Vocal Ensemble, Cordoba Children's Choir K617 ▲ 7025 [DDD]
Elyséen Quartet
Brahms, J.:Qts Pno (comp) Arion 2-▲ ARN 268205
Elyséen String Quartet [Anne-Claude Villars (vn), Catherine Giardelli (vn), Simone Feyrabend (va), Claire Giardelli (vc)]
Furtwängler, W.:Qnt Pno, w. Daniele Bellik (pno) Bayer ▲ 100269 [ADD]
Elysian Wind Quintet
Holst, G.:Qnt Winds Chandos ▲ CHAN 9077 [DDD]
Jacob, G.:Sextet Pno & Wind Qnt, w. A. Goldstone (pno) Chandos ▲ CHAN 9077 [DDD]
Elysian Wind Quintet members
Holst, G.:Qnt Pno, Ob, Cl, Hn & Bn, w. A. Goldstone (pno) Chandos ▲ CHAN 9077 [DDD]
Emerson String Quartet
Barber, S.:Qt Strs Deutsche Grammophon ▲ 435864-2 [DDD]
Barber, S.:Songs, w. C. Studer (sop), T. Hampson (b-bar), J. Browning (pno) Deutsche Grammophon 2-▲ 435867-2 [DDD]
Bartók, B.:Qt Strs (comp) Deutsche Grammophon 2-▲ 423657-2 [DDD]

Emerson String Quartet (cont.)
Beethoven, L. van:Qt 11 Strs, "Quartetto serioso" Deutsche Grammophon ▲ 423398-2 [DDD]
Beethoven, L. van:Qt 16 Strs Deutsche Grammophon ▲ 429224-2 [DDD]
Borodin, A.:Qt 2 Strs Deutsche Grammophon ▲ 427618-2 [DDD]
Borodin, A.:Qt 2 Strs BOMR 4-▲ 21-7526 [DDD] 3-■ 11-7525 (D)
Brahms, J.:Qt 1 Strs Deutsche Grammophon ▲ 431650-2 [DDD]
Cowell, H.:Qt Euphometric New World ▲ 80453-2
Debussy, C.:Qt Strs Deutsche Grammophon ▲ 427320-2 [DDD]
Debussy, C.:Qt Strs Deutsche Grammophon ("Masters" series) ▲ 445509-2
Dvořák, A.:Qt 12 Strs, "America" Deutsche Grammophon ▲ 429723-2 [DDD]
Dvořák, A.:Qnt Pno, Op. 81, w. M. Pressler (pno) Deutsche Grammophor. ▲ 439868-2
The Great Romantic Quartets BOMR 4-▲ 21-7526 [DDD] 3-■ 11-7525 (D)
Harris, R.:Qt 2 Strs, "3 Vars on a Theme" New World ▲ 80453-2
Imbrie, A.W.:Qt 4 Strs New World ▲ 80453-2
Ives, C.:Qts 1 & 2 Strs Deutsche Grammophon ▲ 435864-2 [DDD]
Ives, C.:Scherzo Str Qt Deutsche Grammophon ▲ 435864-2 [DDD]
Mozart, W.A.:Qt 14 Strs Deutsche Grammophon ▲ 439861-2
Mozart, W.A.:Qt 15 Strs Deutsche Grammophon ▲ 439861-2
Mozart, W.A.:Qt 17 Strs Deutsche Grammophon ▲ 427657-2 [DDD]
Mozart, W.A.:Qt 19 Strs Deutsche Grammophon ▲ 427657-2 [DDD]
Prokofiev, S.:Qt 1 Strs Deutsche Grammophon ▲ 431772-2 [DDD]
Prokofiev, S.:Qt 2 Strs Deutsche Grammophon ▲ 431772-2 [DDD]
Prokofiev, S.:Son solo Vn, Op. 115 Deutsche Grammophon ▲ 431772-2 [DDD]
Ravel, M.:Qt Strs Deutsche Grammophon ▲ 427320-2 [DDD]
Ravel, M.:Qt Strs Deutsche Grammophon ("Masters" series) ▲ 445509-2
Schubert, Franz:Qt 14 Strs Deutsche Grammophon ▲ 423398-2 [DDD]
Schubert, Franz:Qt 15 Strs Deutsche Grammophon ▲ 429224-2 [DDD]
Schubert, Franz:Qnt Strs, D.956, w. M. Rostropovich (vc) Deutsche Grammophon ▲ 431792-2 [DDD] ☐ 431792-5
Schuller, G.:Qt 2 Strs New World ▲ 80453-2
Schumann, R.:Qts Strs, Op. 41—No. 3 BOMR 4-▲ 21-7526 3-■ 11-7525
Schumann, R.:Qts Strs, Op. 41—No. 3 Deutsche Grammophon ▲ 431650-2 [DDD]
Shepherd, A.:Triptych, w. B. Norden (sop) New World ▲ 80453-2
Smetana, B.:Qt 1 Strs Deutsche Grammophon ▲ 429723-2 [DDD]
Tchaikovsky, P.:Qt 1 Strs Deutsche Grammophon ▲ 427618-2 [DDD]
Tchaikovsky, P.:Qt 1 Strs BOMR 4-▲ 21-7526 3-■ 11-7525
Webern, A.:Music of—Slow Movt. for Str Qt.; 5 Movts., Op. 5; 3 Pieces for Str Qt.; Qts. for Strs, 1905 & Op. 28; 6 Bagatelles, Op. 9; Rondo; Trio for Strs, Op. 20; Movt. for Str Trio Deutsche Grammophon ▲ 445828-2
Emerson String Quartet members
Dvořák, A.:Qts Pno Strs, Opp. 23 & 87, w. M. Pressler (pno)—in E♭ Deutsche Grammophon ▲ 439868-2
Mozart, W.A.:Qts Fl, w. C. Wincenc (fl) Deutsche Grammophon ▲ 431770-2 [DDD]
Mozart, W.A.:Rondo Fl Str Trio, w. C. Wincenc (fl) Deutsche Grammophon ▲ 431770-2 [DDD]
Emilia Romagna Toscanini SO
Live in Concert, w. June Anderson (sop) *(rec 11/24/84)* Bongiovanni ▲ GB 2504-2
E. Buckley (cnd)
Luciano Pavarotti in Concert, w. Luciano Pavarotti (ten) CBS ▲ MK 44816 [DDD] ■ MT 44816 (D)
F. Luisi (cnd)
Salieri, A.:La Locandiera, w. A. Ruffini (sop), G. Sarti (bar), O. Di Credico (ten), P. Guarnera (bar) [I] *(rec live 1989)* Nuova Era 2-▲ 6888/89 [DDD]
G. Micheli (cnd)
Donizetti, G.:I pazzi per progetto, w. S. Rigacci (sop), A. Cicogna (mez), G. Polidori (bar), G. Sarti (bar), V. M. Brunetti (bass), E. Fissore (bass), L. Monreale (bass) [I] *(rec live, 12/88)* Bongiovanni ▲ GB 2070 [DDD]
B. Rigacci (cnd)
Donizetti, G.:Betly, w. S. Rigacci (sop), M. Comencini (ten), R. Scaltriti (bar), Lugo Teatro Comunale Rossini Chorus *(rec live, 6/90)* Bongiovanni 2-▲ GB 2091/92 [DDD]
Donizetti, G.:Le Convenienze Teatrali, w. M.A. Peters (sop), A. Cicogna (mez), S. Tedesco (ten), R. Scaltriti (bar), Lugo Teatro Comunale Rossini Chorus [I] *(rec live, 6/90)* Bongiovanni 2-▲ GB 2091/92 [DDD]
Emory Wind Ensemble
S. Everett (cnd)
Messiaen, O.:Et exspecto resurrectionem mortuorum ACA Digital Recording ▲ CM 20024
Empire Brass Quintet [R. Smedvig (tpt), J. Curnow (tpt), E. Ruske (hn), R. Douglas Wright (trbn), K. Amis (tuba)]
Braggin' in Brass Telarc ▲ CD 80249 [DDD] ■ CS 30249 (D)
Class Brass:Classical Favorites for Brass Telarc ▲ CD 80220 [DDD] ■ CS 30220 (D)
Class Brass II:On the Edge Telarc ▲ CD 80305 ■ CS 30305
DDD Christmas, w. Kathleen Battle (sop), Florence Quivar (mez), Taverner Consort, Taverner Choir, Taverner Players, New York Choral Artists, Toronto Mendelssohn Choir, King's Singers Angel ▲ CDM 63666
Empire Brass on Broadway Telarc ▲ CD 80303 [DDD] ■ CS 30303 (D)
Joy to the World, w. Nancy Allen (hp) Angel ▲ CDC 49097
Music for Organ, Brass & Percussion, w. Michael Murray (org) Telarc ▲ CD 80218 [DDD] ■ CS-30218 (D)
Passage, 138 B.C.–A.D. 1611, w. Laurie Monahan (sgr), M. Collver (sgr), Pete Maunu (acoustic/elec/12string gtr), Doug Lunn (fretless bass), D. Goldblatt (syn), K. Wortman (elec/acoustic perc) *(rec Lenox, MA & Los Angeles, CA May 27–29 & June 28–July)* Telarc ▲ CD 80355 [DDD]
Romantic Brass:Music of France & Spain Telarc ▲ CD 80301 [DDD] ■ CS 30301 (D)
Royal Brass:Music from the Renaissance & Baroque Telarc ▲ CD 80257 [DDD] ■ CS 30257 (D)
Empire Brass Quintet [R. Smedvig (tpt), J. Curnow (tpt), E. Ruske (hn), S. Hartman (trbn), J. S. Pilafian (tuba)]
Bach, J.S.:Music of, w. Douglas Major (org) EMI Classics ▲ CDC 47395-2 [DDD] ■ 4DS 37353
Bernstein, L.:Mass (sels)—In nomine patris/De profundis; Simple song; Sanctus Telarc ▲ CD 80159 [DDD] ■ CS 30159 (D)
Bernstein, L.:West Side Story (sels)—America; Something's coming; Maria; Tonight; Somewhere Telarc ▲ CD 80159 [DDD] ■ CS 30159 (D)
Gabrieli, G.:Canzoni Telarc ▲ CD 80204 [DDD]
Gershwin, G.:Porgy & Bess (sels)—I got plenty o' nuttin'; Summertime; My man's gone now; Bess, you is my woman; It ain't necessarily so Telarc ▲ CD 80159 [DDD] ■ CS 30159 (D)
Mozart, W.A.:Music of—Impresario:Ov, K.486; Ov & Chor der Janischaren (Allegro & Allegro vivace) [from Die Entführung aus dem Serail, K.384]; Rondo alla Turka [from Son 11, K.331]; Contradanse, K.101; Die Schlittenfahrt [from 3 German Dances, K.605]; Adagio in B♭, K.411; Son. in C, K.545; Ov. to Le nozze di Figaro, K.492; Kyrie from Requiem, K.626; Rondo from Qnt. in E♭ for Horn & Strings, K.407; March in C, K.408; Alleluia from Exsultate, Jubilate, K.165; Eine kleine, K.525 *(rec Apr. 13–15, 1993)* Telarc ▲ CD 80332 [DDD] ■ CS 80332
Tilson Thomas, M.:Street Song Telarc ▲ CD 80159 [DDD] ■ CS 30159 (D)
Empire Brass Quintet [Rolf Smedvig (tpt), Mark Inouye (tpt), Luiz Garcia (hn), Scott A. Hartman (trbn), Kenneth Amis (tuba)]
An Empire Brass Christmas, w. Laurie Monohan (sgr), Kurt Wortman (perc), Brian Jones (perc) Telarc ▲ CD 80416 [DDD]
Empire Saxophone Quartet
Escape to the Center Open Loop ▲ 032 [DDD]
Endellion String Quartet
Barber, S.:Dover Beach, w. Thomas Allen (bar) Virgin Classics ▲ CDC 45033
Barber, S.:Qt Strs Virgin Classics ▲ CDC 45033
Bartók, B.:Qt 4 Strs Virgin Classics ▲ CDC 59629
Bartók, B.:Qt 6 Strs Virgin Classics ▲ CDC 59629

ORCH. & ENS.

Endellion String Quartet (cont.)
Beach, A.M.C.:Qnt Pno, w. Martin Roscoe (pno) ASV ▲ ASV 932 [DDD]
Bridge, F.:Qt 3 Strs Virgin Classics ▲ CDC 59026
Haydn, J.:Qts Strs, Op. 74 Virgin Classics ("Ultraviolet" series) ▲ CUV 61127
Vaughan Williams, R.:Merciless Beauty EMI Classics ▲ CDM 64730
Walton, W.:Qt Strs Virgin Classics ▲ CDC 59026
R. Hickox (cnd)
Martinů, B.:Con Str Qt, City of London Sinfonia Virgin Classics ▲ 59575 [DDD]
Endellion String Quartet members
Clarke, R.:Trio Pno, w. Martin Roscoe (pno) ASV ▲ ASV 932 [DDD]
Endres String Quartet
Mozart, W.A.:Qnt Cl, K.581, w. J. Michaels (cl) Vivace 3–▲ E 319 [DDD]
Mozart, W.A.:Qnt Cl, K.581, w. J. Michaels (cl) Allegretto ▲ ACD 8013 [ADD] ■ ACS 8013
Schubert, Franz:Qnt Pno, D.667, w. R. Reinhardt (pno) Allegretto ▲ ACD 8054 [ADD] ■ ACS 8054
Endymion Ensemble
Dohnányi, E. von:Sextet ASV ▲ ASV 943 [DDD]
Fibich, Z.:Qnt Pno ASV ▲ ASV 943 [DDD]
G. Burgon (cnd)
Burgon, G.:The Fall of Lucifer, w. J. Bowman (ct), R. Covey-Crump (ten), D. Thomas (bass), M. Greenall (cnd), Elysian Singers London Silva Classics ▲ SIL 6002 [DDD]
Burgon, G.:Naring the Upper Air, w. J. Bowman (ct) Silva Classics ▲ SIL 6002 [DDD]
Enesco String Quartet [Constantin Bogdenas (vn), Florin Szigeti (vn), Liviu Stanese (va), Dorel Fodoreanu (vc)]
Brahms, J.:Qnt Cl, w. U. Zimmerman (cl) Intaglio ▲ ING 763 [ADD]
Debussy, C.:Qt Strs Forlane ▲ FRL 16521 [DDD]
Dvořák, A.:Qt 12 Strs, "America" Forlane ▲ FRL 16538
Enescu, G.:Qts Strs, Op. 22—No. 2 Forlane ▲ FRL 16538
Janácek, L.:Qt 2 Strs Forlane ▲ FRL 16538
Mozart, W.A.:Qnt Cl, K.581, w. U. Zimmerman (cl) Intaglio ▲ ING 763 [ADD]
Ravel, M.:Qt Strs Forlane ▲ FRL 16521 [DDD]
Enescu State PO
H. Andreescu (cnd)
Rubinstein, A.:Dmitry Donskoy (orchestral suite) Marco Polo ▲ 8.223320
Rubinstein, A.:Faust Marco Polo ▲ 8.223320
Rubinstein, A.:Sym 5 Marco Polo ▲ 8.223320
England SO
V. Dunn (cnd)
Sullivan, A.:The Tempest, City of Birmingham SO Klavier ▲ KCD 11033
England Virtuosi
A. Davidson (cnd)
Bach, J.S.:Brandenburg Cons Classics for Pleasure ("Silver Doubles" series) 2–▲ CFP CDCFP 4769 [ADD]
Bach, J.S.:Cons Vn (comp), w. Hugh Bean (vn) Classics for Pleasure ("Silver Doubles" series) 2–▲ CFP CDCFP 4769 [ADD]
Bach, J.S.:Con for 2 Vns, w. Hugh Bean (vn), Kenneth Sillito (vn) Classics for Pleasure ("Silver Doubles" series) 2–▲ CFP CDCFP 4769 [ADD]
English Bach Baroque Orch
M. Corboz (cnd)
Cavalli, P.F.:Ercole armante, w. Felicity Palmer (sop—Jole), Yvonne Minton (mez—Giunone), Patricia Miller (sgr—Dejanira), Ulrik Cold (bass), English Bach Festival Chorus Erato 3–▲ ERA SEL 12980 [ADD]
N. McGegan (cnd)
Rameau, J.P.:La Princesse de navarre, w. English Bach Festival Singers Erato ▲ ERA SEL 12986 [ADD]
English Bach Festival Baroque Orch
C. Farncombe (cnd)
Rameau, J.P.:Castor et Pollux, w. P. Jeffes (ten), P. Huttenlocher (bar), English Bach Festival Singers Erato 2–▲ 95311-2
English Bach Festival Orch
L. Bernstein (cnd)
Stravinsky, I.:Mass, w. Trinity Boys' Choir, English Bach Fest Chorus [L] Deutsche Grammophon ("20th Century Classics" series) ▲ 423251-2 [ADD]
Stravinsky, I.:Les Noces, w. A. Mory (sop), P. Parker (mez), J. Mitchinson (ten), P. Hudson (bass), M. Argerich (pno), H. Francesch (pno), K. Zimerman (pno), C. Katsaris (pno), English Bach Festival Chorus [R] Deutsche Grammophon ("20th Century Classics" series) ▲ 423251-2 [ADD]
J.-C. Malgoire (cnd)
Vivaldi, A.:Stabat Mater, w. H. Watts (cta) [L] *(rec 1977)* Sony Classical ("Essential Classics" series) ▲ SBK 48282 [AAD] ■ SBT 48282
English Baroque Orch
Baby Dance:A Toddler's Jump on the Classics, w. Bolshoi SO, Cleveland Orch, Royal Concertgebouw Orch, A. Lazarev (cnd), J. E. Gardiner (cnd), T. Koopman (cnd), N. Harnoncourt (cnd), R. Leppard (cnd) Erato ▲ 96887-2 ■ 96887-4 ■ 97328-4 (blis
English Baroque Soloists
J. E. Gardiner (cnd)
Bach, J.S.:Cant 36, w. N. Argenta (sop), R. Lang (mez), A. Rolfe Johnson (ten), O. Bär (bar), Monteverdi Choir London Archiv ▲ 437327-2
Bach, J.S.:Cant 50, w. Monteverdi Choir London Erato 2–▲ 2292-45979-2
Bach, J.S.:Cant 51, w. E. Kirkby (sop) [G] Philips ▲ 411458-2 [DDD]
Bach, J.S.:Cant 61, w. N. Argenta (sop), R. Lang (mez), A. Rolfe Johnson (ten), O. Bär (bar), Monteverdi Choir London Archiv ▲ 437327-2 [DDD]
Bach, J.S.:Cant 62, w. N. Argenta (sop), R. Lang (mez), A. Rolfe Johnson (ten), O. Bär (bar), Monteverdi Choir London Archiv ▲ 437327-2 [DDD]
Bach, J.S.:Cant 106, "Actus tragicus", w. N. Argenta (sop), M. Chance (ct), A. Rolfe Johnson (ten), S. Varcoe (b-bar), Monteverdi Choir London [G] Archiv ▲ 429782-2 [DDD]
Bach, J.S.:Cant 118, w. Monteverdi Choir London [G] Archiv ▲ 429782-2 [DDD]
Bach, J.S.:Cant 118, w. Monteverdi Choir London Erato 2–▲ 2292-45979-2
Bach, J.S.:Cant 131, w. W. Kendall (ten), S. Varcoe (b-bar), Monteverdi Choir London Erato ▲ 2292-45988-2
Bach, J.S.:Cant 140, w. R. Holton (sop), A. Rolfe Johnson (ten), S. Varcoe (b-bar), Monteverdi Choir London [G] Archiv ▲ 431809-2 [DDD]
Bach, J.S.:Cant 147, w. R. Holton (sop), M. Chance (ct), A. Rolfe Johnson (ten), S. Varcoe (b-bar), Monteverdi Choir London [G] Archiv ▲ 431809-2 [DDD]
Bach, J.S.:Cant 198, w. N. Argenta (sop), M. Chance (ct), A. Rolfe Johnson (ten), S. Varcoe (b-bar), Monteverdi Choir London [G] Archiv ▲ 429782-2 [DDD]
Bach, J.S.:Christmas Oratorio, w. N. Argenta (sop), A. S. von Otter (mez), H.-P. Blochwitz (ten), O. Bär (bar), Monteverdi Choir London [G] Archiv 2–▲ 423232-2 [DDD]
Bach, J.S.:Christmas Oratorio (sels), w. Monteverdi Choir London—arias & choruses Archiv ("3D Baroque" series) ▲ 431703-2 [DDD]
Bach, J.S.:Christmas Oratorio (sels), w. N. Argenta (sop), A. S. von Otter (mez), H.-P. Blochwitz (ten), O. Bär (bar), Monteverdi Choir London [G] Archiv ▲ 427653-2 [DDD]
Bach, J.S.:Magnificat, BWV 243, w. E. Kirkby (sop) et al., Monteverdi Choir London [L] Philips ("Digital Classics" series) ▲ 411458-2 [DDD]
Bach, J.S.:Mass in b, BWV 232, w. Monteverdi Choir London [L] Archiv 2–▲ 415514-2 [DDD]
Bach, J.S.:Motets, BWV 225-30, w. Monteverdi Choir London Erato 2–▲ 2292-45979-2
Bach, J.S.:St. John Passion, w. Monteverdi Choir London [G] Archiv 2–▲ 419324-2 [DDD]
Bach, J.S.:St. John Passion (sels), w. Monteverdi Choir London—arias & choruses Archiv ("3D Baroque" series) ▲ 431703-2 [DDD]
Bach, J.S.:St. Matthew Passion, w. B. Bonney (sop), A. Monoyios (sop), A. S. von Otter (mez), M. Chance (ct), H. Crook (ten), A. Rolfe Johnson (ten), O. Bär (bar), A. Schmidt (bar), C. Hauptmann (bass), Monteverdi Choir London [G] Archiv 3–▲ 427648-2 [DDD]

English Baroque Soloists (cont.)
J. E. Gardiner (cnd) (cont.)
Beethoven, L. van:Missa Solemnis, w. C. Margiono (sop), C. Robbin (mez), W. Kendall (ten), A. Miles (bass), Monteverdi Choir London [L] Archiv ▲ 429779-2 [DDD] ◻ 429779-5
Campra, A.:Messe de Requiem, w. J. Nelson (mez), C. Harris (trb), J.-C. Orliac (ten), S. Roberts (bar), Monteverdi Choir London Erato ▲ 2292-45993-2
Couperin, F.:L'Apothéose de Lully Erato (Musifrance) ▲ 2292-45011-2 ZK [DDD]
Couperin, F.:Dans le goût théatral Erato (Musifrance) ▲ 2292-45011-2 ZK [DDD]
Couperin, F.:Le Parnasse, L'apothéose de Corelli Erato (Musifrance) ▲ 2292-45011-2 ZK [DDD]
Gluck, C.W.:Don Juan, ou le festin de Pierre Erato ▲ 2292-45980-2
Gluck, C.W.:Orfeo ed Euridice, w. S. McNair (sop), C. Sieden (sop), D.L. Ragin (ct), Monteverdi Choir London Philips ▲ 434093-2
Handel, G.F.:Acis & Galatea, w. N. Burrowes (sop), M. Hill (ten), A. R. Johnson (ten), W. White (bass) [E] Archiv ▲ 423406-2 [ADD]
Handel, G.F.:L'Allegro, Il Penseroso ed il Moderato, w. Michael Ginn (trb), Patrizia Kwella (sop), Marie McLaughlin (sop), Monteverdi Choir London Erato 2–▲ 2292-45377-2 ZA
Handel, G.F.:Concerti grossi, Op. 3 Erato ▲ 2292-45981-2
Handel, G.F.:Coronation Anthems (4) for George II, w. Monteverdi Choir London—Zadok the Priest; The King Shall Rejoice Philips ▲ 432110-2
Handel, G.F.:Israel in Egypt, w. Ruth Holton (sop), Elisabeth Friday (sgr), Michael Chance (alt), Philip Salmon (ten), Paul Tindall (sgr), Monteverdi Choir London Philips ▲ 432110-2
Handel, G.F.:Laudate pueri Dominum, w. Sylvia McNair (sop), Monteverdi Choir London [G] Philips ▲ 434920-2
Handel, G.F.:Messiah, w. Saul Quirke (trb), Margaret Marshall (sop), Catherine Robbin (mez), Charles Brett (ct), Anthony Rolfe Johnson (ten), Robert Hale (b-bar), Monteverdi Choir London [E] Philips 3–▲ 411041-2 [DDD]
Handel, G.F.:Messiah, w. Saul Quirke (trb), Margaret Marshall (sop), Catherine Robbin (mez), Charles Brett (ct), Anthony Rolfe Johnson (ten), Robert Hale (b-bar), Monteverdi Choir London [E] Philips ▲ 412267-2 [DDD]
Handel, G.F.:Saul, w. D. Brown (sop), L. Dawson (sop), D. L. Ragin (ct), J. M. Ainsley (ten), A. Miles (bar), Monteverdi Choir London Philips 3–▲ 426265-2 3PH [DDD]
Handel, G.F.:Semele, w. Norma Burrowes (sop), Patrizia Kwella (sop), Elizabeth Priday (sop), Catherine Denley (mez), Della Jones (mez), Timothy Penrose (alt), Anthony Rolfe-Johnson (ct), Maldwyn Davies (ten), Robert Lloyd (b-bar), David Thomas (bass), Monteverdi Choir London Erato 2–▲ 2292-45982-2
Handel, G.F.:Solomon, w. Nancy Argenta (sop), Barbara Hendricks (sop), Carolyn Watkinson (cta), Anthony Rolfe Johnson (ct), Monteverdi Choir London [E] Philips 2–▲ 412612-2 [DDD]
Handel, G.F.:Water Music (suites)—Suite Nos. 1, 2 & 3 Philips ▲ 434122-2 [DDD]
Haydn, J.:Die Jahreszeiten, w. Barbara Bonney (sop), Anthony Rolfe Johnson (ct), Andreas Schmidt (bar), Monteverdi Choir London [period instrs] Archiv 2–▲ 431818-2 [DDD]
Haydn, J.:Die Jahreszeiten (sels), w. Barbara Bonney (sop), Anthony Rolfe Johnson (ten), Andreas Schmidt (bar), Monteverdi Choir London—arias & choruses Archiv ▲ 447282-2
Haydn, J.:Die Schöpfung, w. Donna Brown (sop), Sylvia McNair (sop), Michael Schade (ten), Gerald Finley (bar), Rodney Gilfry (bar), Monteverdi Choir London Archiv ▲ 449 217-2
Mad About Angels, w. Cheryl Studer (sop), Christa Ludwig (mez), Anne Sofie von Otter (mez), José Carreras (ten), New York PO [cnd:Leonard Bernstein], Philharmonia Orch, Philharmonia Chorus [cnd:Carlo Maria Giulini] Deutsche Grammophon ▲ 449113-2 ■ 449113-4
Monteverdi, C.:Incoronazione, w. Constanze Backes (sop—Valletto), Catherine Bott (sop—Drusilla/Pallade/La Virtù), Dana Hanchard (sop—Nerone), Sylvia McNair (sop—Poppea), Marinella Pennicchi (sop—Amore/Damigella), Annie Sofie von Otter (mez—Ottavia/Venere/La Fortuna), Julian Clarkson (alt—Littore/Mercurio), Bernarda Fink (cta—Arnalta), Roberto Balconi (ct—Nutrice), Michael Chance (ct—Ottone), Nigel Robson (ten—Liberto/Soldato Secondo), Mark Tucker (ten—Lucano/Soldato Primo), Francesco Ellero d'Artegna (bass—Seneca) *(rec Queen Elizabeth Hall, South Bank Ctr, London, Dec 1993)* Archiv 3–▲ 447088-2
Monteverdi, C.:Orfeo, w. His Majesties Sagbutts & Cornetts, Monteverdi Choir London Archiv 2–▲ 419250-2 [DDD]
Monteverdi, C.:Vespro della Beata Vergine, w. A. Monoyios (sop), M. Pennicchi (sop), M. Chance (ct), G. Tucker (ten), N. Robson (ten), S. Naglia (ten), B. Terfel (b-bar), A. Miles (bass), His Majesties Sagbutts & Cornetts, Monteverdi Choir London Archiv 2–▲ 429565-2 [DDD]
Mozart, W.A.:Clemenza di Tito (sels), w. Anne Sofie von Otter (mez—Sesto), Leslie Schatzberger (bas cl)—Parto, ma tu ben mio *(rec Queen Elizabeth Hall, South Bank Ctr, London, June 1990)* Archiv ▲ 449938-2 [DDD]
Mozart, W.A.:Cons Pno, w. M. Bilson (pno)—Nos. 1-6, 8, 9 & 11-27; No. 7 [w. R. Levin & M. Tan]; No. 10 [w. R. Levin] Deutsche Grammophon 9–▲ 431211-2 [DDD]
Mozart, W.A.:Con 9 Pno, w. Malcolm Bilson (pno) Archiv ▲ 447291-2
Mozart, W.A.:Con 17 Pno, w. Malcolm Bilson (pno) Archiv ▲ 447291-2
Mozart, W.A.:Con 20 Pno, w. Malcolm Bilson (pno) Archiv ▲ 419609-2 [DDD]
Mozart, W.A.:Con 21 Pno, w. Malcolm Bilson (pno) Archiv ▲ 419609-2 [DDD]
Mozart, W.A.:Con 22 Pno, w. Malcolm Bilson (pno) Deutsche Grammophon ▲ 447283-2
Mozart, W.A.:Con 26 Pno, w. Malcolm Bilson (pno) Deutsche Grammophon ▲ 447283-2
Mozart, W.A.:Così fan tutte, w. A. Roocroft (sop), E. James (mez), R. Gilfrey (bar), C. Feller (bass) Archiv 3–▲ 437829-2 [DDD]
Mozart, W.A.:Don Giovanni, w. Charlotte Margiono (sop—Donna Elvira), Luba Orgonasova (sop—Donna Anna), Eirian James (mez—Zerlina), Julian Clarkson (alt—Masetto), Christoph Prégardien (ten—Don Ottavio), Rodney Gilfry (bar—Don Giovanni), Ildebrando d'Arcangelo (bass—Leporello), Andrea Silvestrelli (bass—Il Commendatore), Monteverdi Choir London Deutsche Grammophon ("4D Audio" series) 3–▲ 445870-2
Mozart, W.A.:Entführung, w. L. Orgonasova (sop), C. Sieden (sop), S. Olsen (ten), Uwe Peper (ten), C. Hauptmann (bass), Hans-Peter Minetti (nar), Monteverdi Choir London [G] Deutsche Grammophon 2–▲ 435857-2
Mozart, W.A.:Exsultate, w. S. McNair (sop), Monteverdi Choir London [G] Philips ▲ 434920-2
Mozart, W.A.:Idomeneo, w. Sylvia McNair (sop), Hillevi Martinpelto (sop), Anne Sophie von Otter (mez), Anthony Rolfe Johnson (ten), Monteverdi Choir London Archiv 3–▲ 431674-2 [DDD]
Mozart, W.A.:Idomeneo (ov) *(rec Queen Elizabeth Hall, South Bank Ctr, London, June 1990)* Archiv ▲ 449938-2 [DDD]
Mozart, W.A.:Missa, K.427, w. S. McNair (sop), D. Montague (mez), A. Rolfe Johnson (ten), C. Hauptmann (bass), Monteverdi Choir London [newly revised version, ed. Gardiner] [L] Philips ▲ 420210-2 [DDD]
Mozart, W.A.:Nozze di Figaro, w. A. Hagley (sop), H. Martinpelto (sop), R. Gilfrey (bar), B. Terfel (b-bar), Monteverdi Choir London [G] Archiv 3–▲ 439871-2 [DDD]
Mozart, W.A.:Requiem, w. Barbara Bonney (sop), Anne Sophie von Otter (mez), Hans-Peter Blochwitz (ten), Willard White (bass), Monteverdi Choir London [L] Philips ▲ 420197-2 [DDD]
Mozart, W.A.:Rondo Pno Orch, K.382, w. Malcolm Bilson (pno) Archiv ▲ 447291-2
Mozart, W.A.:Sym 38 Philips ▲ 426283-2 [DDD]
Mozart, W.A.:Sym 39 Philips ▲ 426283-2 [DDD]
Mozart, W.A.:Sym 40 Philips ▲ 426315-2 [DDD] ◻ 426315-5
Mozart, W.A.:Sym 41 Philips ▲ 426315-2 [DDD] ◻ 426315-5
Mozart, W.A.:Thamos, w. A. Miles (bass), Monteverdi Choir London Archiv ▲ 437556-2 [DDD]
Mozart, W.A.:Zauberflöte, w. Constanze Backes (sop—Papagena), Christiane Oelze (sop—Pamina), Susan Roberts (sop—First Lady), Cyndia Sieden (sop—Queen of the Night), Carola Guber (cta—Second Lady), Maria Jonas (cta—Third Lady), Andreas Dieterich (trb—First Boy), Jan Andreas Mendel (trb—Second Boy), Florian Wöller (trb—Third Boy), Uwe Peper (ten—Monostatos), Nicolas Robertson (ten—First Man in Armor), Michael Schade (ten—Tamino), Gerald Finley (bar—Papageno), Noel Mann (bass—Second Man in Armour), Harry Peeters (bass—Sarastro), Detlef Roth (bass—Speaker/First Priest), Robert Burt (speaker—Third Priest), Robert Johnston (speaker—Second Priest), Wolfgang Knauer (speaker—Fourth Priest), Douglas Welbat (speaker—Second Priest), Monteverdi Choir London *(rec Forum am Schlosspark, Ludwigsburg, July 1995)* Archiv 2–▲ 449166-2

160
▲ = CD ♦ = Enhanced CD Δ = MD ■ = Cassette Tape ◻ = DCC

English Baroque Soloists (cont.)

J. E. Gardiner (cnd) (cont.)

Purcell, H.:Dido & Aeneas, w. Ruth Holton (sop—Belinda), Elisabeth Priday (sop—2nd Woman), Donna Deam (sop—1st Witch), Shauna Beesley (sop—2nd Witch), Teresa Shaw (mez—Sorceress), Carolyn Watkinson (cta—Dido), Jonathan Peter Kenny (alt—Spirit), Paul Tindall (ten—Sailor), George Mosley (bass—Aeneas), Monteverdi Choir London *(rec Saint George's, Bristol, UK, July 12-14, 1990)* Philips ▲ 432114-2

Purcell, H.:The Fairy Queen, w. Monteverdi Choir London [E] Archiv 2-▲ 419221-2 [DDD]

Purcell, H.:Hail, Bright Cecilia, w. J. Smith (sop), B. Gordon (alt), A. Stafford (alt), P. Elliot (ten), S. Varcoe (bar), D. Thomas (bass), Monteverdi Choir London Erato ("Gardiner Purcell Collection" series) ▲ 96554-2

Purcell, H.:The Indian Queen, w. Monteverdi Choir London Erato ("Gardiner Purcell Collection" series) ▲ 96551-2

Purcell, H.:King Arthur, w. Gillian Fisher (sop), E. Priday (sop), Gill Ross (sop), J. Smith (sop), A. Stafford (alt), P. Elliot (ten), S. Varcoe (bar), Monteverdi Choir London Erato ("Gardiner Purcell Collection" series) 2-▲ 96552-2

Purcell, H.:King Arthur, w. J. Smith (sop), G. Fisher (sop), E. Priday (sop), G. Ross (sop), A. Stafford (alt), P. Elliott (ten), S. Varcoe (bar), Monteverdi Choir London Erato 2-▲ 2292-45211-2 ZA

Purcell, H.:King Arthur (sels), w. J. Smith (sop), G. Fisher (sop), E. Priday (sop), G. Ross (sop), Monteverdi Choir Erato ▲ 45919-2

Purcell, H.:Welcome to All the Pleasures, w. Ruth Holton (sop), Nicola Jenkin (sop), Michael Chance (alt), Paul Tindall (ten), George Mosly (bass), Monteverdi Choir London *(rec Saint George's, Bristol, UK, July 12-14, 1990)* Philips ▲ 432114-2

Schütz, H.:Motets (misc), w. Monteverdi Choir—Freue dich des Weibes, SWV.453; Ist nicht Ephraim mein teurer Sohn, SWV.40; Saul, Saul, was verfolgst du mich, SWV.415; Auf dem Gebirge, SWV.396 [G] Archiv ▲ 423405-2 [DDD]

Schütz, H.:Musicalische Exequien, w. Monteverdi Choir [G] Archiv ▲ 423405-2 [DDD]

English Baroque Soloists members

J. E. Gardiner (cnd)

Carissimi, G.:Oratorios, w. His Majesties Sagbutts & Cornetts, Monteverdi Choir London—Jepthe, Jonas & Judicum extremum Erato ▲ 2292-45466-2 ZK [DDD]

English Brass Ensemble

P. Archibald (cnd)

Grieg, E.:Elegaic Melodies, Op. 34 [arr for brass ensemble] ASV Quicksilva ▲ ASQ 6181

Grieg, E.:Lyric Pieces—Opp. 12, 43, 54, 68 & 71 [arr for brass ensemble] ASV Quicksilva ▲ ASQ 6181

Grieg, E.:Norwegian Dances, Op. 35 [arr for brass ensemble] ASV Quicksilva ▲ ASQ 6181

Grieg, E.:Peer Gynt (sels)—Solvejg's Song [arr for brass ensemble] ASV Quicksilva ▲ ASQ 6181

Grieg, E.:Poetic Tone-Pictures, Op. 3 [arr for brass ensemble] ASV Quicksilva ▲ ASQ 6181

English CO

Albinoni, T.:Adagio Org, w. I. Watson (org), J.L. Garcia (vn), M. Eade (vn) Virgin Classics ▲ CDZ 59656

Albinoni, T.:Cons Obs, w. N. Black (ob), J. L. Garcia (vn), M. Eade (vn)—in d Virgin Classics ▲ CDZ 59656

Bach, J.S.:Con 1 Hpd, w. K. Gilbert (hpd) Novalis ▲ 150034 [DDD]

Bach, J.S.:Con 2 Hpd, w. K. Gilbert (hpd) Novalis ▲ 150034 [DDD]

Bach, J.S.:Con 4 Hpd, w. K. Gilbert (hpd) Novalis ▲ 150034 [DDD]

Bach, J.S.:Con 5 Hpd, w. K. Gilbert (hpd) Novalis ▲ 150034 [DDD]

Barry Tuckwell, w. Barry Tuckwell (hn), Academy of St. Martin in the Fields [cnd:Neville Marriner] EMI Classics ("Doublefforte" series) 2-▲ CDFB 69395

Britten, B.:Our Hunting Fathers, w. P. Bryn-Julson (soprano), S. Bedford [E] *(rec 1990)* Collins Classics ▲ 11922 [DDD]

Britten, B.:Owen Wingrave, w. S. Fisher (Miss Wingrave), J. Vyvyan (Mrs. Julian), H. Harper (Mrs. Coyle), J. Baker (Kate), P. Pears (Sir P. Wingrave; Narrator), B. Luxon (Owen Wingrave), J. Shirley-Quirk (Coyle), B. Britten, Wandworth School Boys' Choir London 2-▲ 433200-2

Canciones Españoles, w. José Carreras (ten), Martin Katz (pno) Philips ("Spanish" series) ▲ 432825-2 FM [ADD]

Corelli, A.:Concerti grossi, Op. 6, w. M. Eade (vn), J.L. Garcia (vn), W. Bennett (fl), N. Black (ob), I. Watson (hpd/org)—No. 2 in F Virgin Classics ▲ CDZ 59656

Duruflé, M.:Requiem, w. Murray, Allen, Best, Corydon Singers [L] Hyperion ▲ CDA 66191 [DDD]

Fauré, G.:Requiem, w. Arleen Augér (sop), Benjamin Luxon (bar), John Butt (org), King's College Choir Cambridge Classics for Pleasure ("Eminence" series) ▲ CDEMX 2166 [DDD]

Giuliani, M.:Con 1 Gtr, w. J. Williams (gtr) Sony Classical ("Essential Classics" series) ▲ SBK 48168 ■ SBT 48168

Giuliani, M.:Con 1 Gtr, w. J. Williams (gtr) CBS 2-▲ M2K 44791 [ADD/DDD]

Mad About Love, w. Cheryl Studer (sop), Kiri Te Kanawa (sop), José Carreras (ten), Jerry Hadley (ten), Philharmonia Orch [cnd:Giuseppe Sinopoli], Bastille Opera Orch [cnd:Myung-Whun Chung], Boston SO [cnd:Seiji Ozawa], Vienna PO Deutsche Grammophon ▲ 449112-2 ■ 449112-4

Mozart, W.A.:Con Cl, w. Richard Stoltzman (cl) RCA Victor ▲ 09026-68024-2; ■ 09026-68024-2

Mozart, W.A.:Con Cl, w. R. Stoltzman (cl) RCA Red Seal ▲ 60723-2 [DDD] ■ 60723-4 (CrO2)

Mozart, W.A.:Con 7 Pnos, w. M. Perahia (pno), R. Lupu (pno) [arr. Mozart for 2 pianos & orch.] Sony Classical ▲ SK 44915

Mozart, W.A.:Con 10 Pnos, w. M. Perahia (pno), R. Lupu (pno) Sony Classical ▲ SK 44915

Mozart, W.A.:Rondo Pno Orch, K.386, w. Murray Perahia (pno) Sony Classical 12-▲ SX12K 46441

Mozart, W.A.:Rondo Pno Orch, K.386, w. Murray Perahia (pno) CBS ▲ MK 39224 [DDD]

Musical Moments in the Garden, w. Academy of St. Martin in the Fields, Bournemouth SO, Hollywood Bowl SO, Toulouse Orch, Philharmonia Orch, Toulouse CO, L. Auriacombe (cnd), T. Beecham (cnd), C. Davis (cnd), R. Hickox (cnd), N. Marriner (cnd), M. Plasson (cnd), M. Sargent (cnd Angel ▲ CDM 65203 ■ EG 65203

Paisiello, G.:Cons Hpd, w. M. Monetti (pno)—Nos. 1, 5, 7 & 8 ASV ▲ ASV 873 [DDD]

Paisiello, G.:Cons Hpd, w. M. Monetti (pno)—Nos. 2, 3, 4 & 6 ASV ▲ ASV 872 [DDD]

Pergolesi, G.B.:Con Fl, w. W. Bennett (fl) Virgin Classics ▲ CDZ 59656

Spohr, L.:Vars in B♭ on a Theme from *Alruna*, w. T. King (cl), J. Judd (pno) Hyperion ▲ CDA 66300 [DDD]

Vivaldi, A.:Con Lt, w. J. Williams (gtr) CBS 2-▲ M2K 44791 [ADD/DDD]

Vivaldi, A.:Con Lt, w. J. Williams (gtr) Sony Classical ("Essential Classics" series) ▲ SBK 48168 ■ SBT 48168

Vivaldi, A.:Con in A Mand, w. John Williams (gtr) CBS 2-▲ M2K 44791 [ADD/DDD]

Vivaldi, A.:Cons Vn (misc), w. José-Luis Garcia (vn) ASV ("Quicksilva" series) ▲ ASQ 6148 [DDD]

Vivaldi, A.:Cons Vn, Op. 8/1-4, "The Four Seasons", w. José-Luis Garcia (vn) ASV ("Quicksilva" series) ▲ ASQ 6148 [DDD]

Vivaldi, A.:Music of, w. Salvatore Accardo (va) Frederico Agostini (vn), Heinz Holliger (ob), Ida Levin (vn), Aurele Nicolet (fl), Massimo Paris (va d'amore), Angel Romero (gtr), Celedonio Romero (gtr), Celine Romero (gtr), Henryk Szeryng (vn), Pinchas Zukerman (vn), Academy of St. Martin in the Fields, I Musici, Naples Weekly International Soloists, St. Paul CO, Dresden Staatskapelle—The Four Seasons [Winter]; Con in D for Gtr [Largo]; Con in D for Fl, "Il gardellino" [Cantabile]; Con in C for Diverse Insts [Andante molto]; Con in g for Strs [Andante molto]; Con in D for 2 Vns & 2 Vcs [Largo]; Con in g for Ob, Vn, Ww & Strs [Larghetto]; Con in a for Gtr, "L'estro armonico" [Largo]; Con in F for 3 Vns [Andante]; Con in F for Fl [Largo]; Con in d for Va D'Amore [Largo]; Con in E for Vn & Strs, "Il riposo" [Allegro]; Con in G for Ob, Bn & Strs [Largo]; Con in B♭ for Vn & Strs [Largo]; Con in A for Gtr & Strs [Larghetto]; Con in E for Vn & Strs, "L'amoroso" [Allegro]; Con in G for Fl [Largo]; Con in A for Vn [Larghetto]; Con in c for Vn & Strs, "Il sospetto" [Andante]; Con in a for 2 Obs & Strs [Largo]; Con in g for Orch [Largo non molto]; Con in a for Vn [Largo]; Con in C for Ob [Adagio]; Con in g for Fl, "La notte" [Largo] Philips ▲ 454051-2 ■ 454 051-4

S. Accardo (cnd)

Bach, J.S.:Cons Vn (comp), w. A.-S. Mutter (vn) EMI Classics ▲ CDC 47005-2 [DDD]

Bach, J.S.:Con 1 Vn, w. S. Accardo (vn) EMI Classics 3-▲ CDMC 69878

Bach, J.S.:Con for 2 Vns, w. A.-S. Mutter (vn), S. Accardo (vn) EMI Classics ▲ CDC 47005-2 [DDD]

Haydn, J.:Con Org, Vn & Strs, H.XVIII/6, w. Bruno Canino (hpd), Salvatore Accardo (vn) Philips 2-▲ 438797-2

Haydn, J.:Con 1 Vn, w. Salvatore Accardo (vn) Philips 2-▲ 438797-2

English CO (cont.)

S. Accardo (cnd) (cont.)

Haydn, J.:Con 3 Vn, w. Salvatore Accardo (vn) Philips 2-▲ 438797-2

Haydn, J.:Con 4 Vn, w. Salvatore Accardo (vn) Philips 2-▲ 438797-2

Mozart, W.A.:Con 2 Vn, w. A.-S. Mutter (vn) EMI Classics 3-▲ CDMC 69878

Mozart, W.A.:Con 3 Vn, w. A.S. Mutter (vn) EMI Classics 3-▲ CDMC 69878

P. Angerer (cnd)

Galuppi, B.:Concerti a quattro—Nos. 1-4 *(rec St. Mary's Parish Church, London, Apr 1983)* Claves ▲ CD 508306 [DDD]

Galuppi, B.:Sinf *(rec St. Mary's Parish Church, London, Apr 1983)* Claves ▲ CD 508306 [DDD]

Galuppi, B.:Sinf della Serenata *(rec St. Mary's Parish Church, London, Apr 1983)* Claves ▲ CD 508306 [DDD]

Galuppi, B.:Sons (6) Hpd, w. Jörg Ewald Dähler (hpd)—Son in F *(rec St. Mary's Parish Church, London, Apr 1983)* Claves ▲ CD 508306 [DDD]

V. Ashkenazy (cnd)

Mozart, W.A.:Con 10 Pnos, w. V. Ashkenazy (pno), D. Barenboim (pno) London ▲ 421036-2 [ADD]

J. Barbirolli (cnd)

Purcell, H.:Dido & Aeneas, w. Victoria de los Angeles (sop—Dido), Heather Harper (sop—Belinda), Patricia Johnson (mez—Sorceress), Peter Glossup (bar—Aeneas), Ambrosian Singers EMI Classics 2-▲ ZDM 65664

Purcell, H.:Dido & Aeneas (sels), w. Victoria de los Angeles (sop—Dido), Heather Harper (sop—Belinda), Sibyl Michelow (sop), Elizabeth Robson (sop), Derek Simpson (vc), Colin Tilney (hpd), Ambrosian Singers—Ov.; Shake the Cloud; Ah! Ah! Belinda; When Monarchs Unite; But Ere We This Perform; But Death, Alas! I Cannot Shun...When I am Laid in Earth; With Drooping Wings *(rec Abbey Road Studio 1, London, Aug. 1965)* EMI Classics ▲ CDK 65341 [ADD]

D. Barenboim (cnd)

Bach, J.S.:Cons Vn (comp), w. I. Perlman (vn) EMI Classics ▲ CDC 47856-2

Bach, J.S.:Con Vn, BWV 1058, w. P. Zukerman (vn) EMI Classics ▲ CDC 47856-2

Bach, J.S.:Con for 2 Vns, w. I. Perlman (vn), P. Zukerman (vn) EMI Classics ▲ CDC 47856-2

Bartók, B.:Divert EMI Classics ▲ CDM 65079

Boccherini, L.:Con Vc, G.482, w. J. Du Pré (vc) EMI Classics ▲ CDC 47840

Elgar, E.:Romance Bn, w. M. Gatt (bn) Sony Classical (Essential Classics) ▲ SBK 53510 [ADD] ■ SBT 53510

Guitar Concertos, w. J. Williams (gtr) Odyssey 2-▲ MB2K 45610

Haydn, J.:Con 1 Vc, w. Jacqueline Du Pré (vc) EMI Classics ▲ CDC 47614

Haydn, J.:Con 1 Vc, w. Jacqueline Du Pré (vc) EMI Classics ▲ CDC 47840

Hindemith, P.:Trauermusik EMI Classics ▲ CDM 65079

Mozart, W.A.:Cons Pno, w. D. Barenboim (pno) EMI Classics 10-▲ CDZJ 62825

Mozart, W.A.:Con 14 Pno, w. D. Barenboim (pno) EMI Classics ("Studio" series) ▲ CDM 69124 [ADD]

Mozart, W.A.:Con 15 Pno, w. D. Barenboim (pno) EMI Classics ("Studio" series) ▲ CDM 69124 [ADD]

Mozart, W.A.:Con 16 Pno, w. D. Barenboim (pno) EMI Classics ("Studio" series) ▲ CDM 69124 [ADD]

Mozart, W.A.:Nozze di Figaro, w. H. Harper (sop), J. Blegen (sop), T. Berganza (mez), D. Fischer-Dieskau (bar), G. Evans (bar), John Aldis Choir [I] EMI Classics ("Studio" series) 3-▲ CDMC 63646 [ADD]

Mozart, W.A.:Sinf concertante Vn, K.364, w. I. Stern (vn), P. Zukerman (va) *(rec 1971)* CBS 4-▲ M4K 42003 (m/s) [ADD]

Rodrigo, J.:Concierto de Aranjuez, w. J. Williams (gtr) CBS ▲ MK 33208

Schoenberg, A.:Verklärte Nacht EMI Classics ▲ CDM 65079

Strauss, R.:Con Ob, w. Neil Black (ob) Sony Classical ("Essential Classics" series) ▲ SBK 62652 ■ SBT 62652

Villa-Lobos, H.:Con Gtr, w. J. Williams (gtr) CBS 2-▲ M2K 44791 [ADD/DDD]

Villa-Lobos, H.:Con Gtr, w. J. Williams (gtr) CBS ▲ MK 33208

S. Bedford (cnd)

Berkeley, L.:Mont Juic Collins Classics ▲ 10312 [DDD]

Britten, B.:Chanson françaises (4), w. Heather Harper (sop) IMP ("BBC Radio Classics" series) ▲ IMP 5691582

Britten, B.:Con Pno, w. J. MacGregor (pno) *(rec 10/89)* Collins Classics ▲ 13012 [DDD]

Britten, B.:Con Pno, w. J. MacGregor (pno)—[standard 1945 revised version, plus the original 3rd movement] Collins Classics ▲ 11022 [DDD]

Britten, B.:Con Vn, w. L. McAslan (vn) *(rec 10/89)* Collins Classics ▲ 13012 [DDD]

Britten, B.:Death in Venice, w. J. Bowman (ct), P. Pears (ten), J. Shirley-Quirk (bar), English Opera Group Chorus [E] London 2-▲ 425669-2 [ADD]

Britten, B.:Death in Venice (suite) Chandos ▲ CHAN 8363 [DDD]

Britten, B.:Johnson over Jordan *(rec 1990)* Collins Classics ▲ 11922 [DDD]

Britten, B.:Sym Vc, w. R. Wallfisch (vc) Chandos ▲ CHAN 8363 [DDD]

Bridge, F.:Berceuse IMP ("BBC Radio Classics" series) ▲ IMP 5691582

The Concerto Collection, w. Stinton, Jennifer (fl), Philharmonia Orch [cnd:Tamás Vásáry] Collins Classics 2-▲ COL 7005 [DDD]

Saxton, R.:Music to Celebrate the Resurrection of Christ Collins Classics ▲ 11022 [DDD]

Shostakovich, D.:Sym 1 *(rec 1990)* Collins Classics ▲ 11922 [DDD]

Walton, W.:Spitfire Prelude & Fugue ASV Quicksilva ▲ ASQ 6093 [DDD]

L. Bernstein (cnd)

Vivaldi, A.:Music of, w. John Williams (cnd), J.-C. Malgoire (cnd), New York PO, La Grande Écurie et la Chambre du Roy—sels. from The Four Seasons, Mandolin Concerto in C, 2-Mandolin Concerto in G, Guitar Concerto in D, etc. CBS ▲ MLK 45810 ■ MLT 45810

M. Best (cnd)

Britten, B.:St. Nicolas, w. A. Rolfe-Johnson (ten), Corydon Singers Hyperion ▲ CDA 66333

Bruckner, A.:Psalm 112, w. Corydon Singers Hyperion ▲ CDA 66245 [DDD]

Bruckner, A.:Psalm 114, w. Corydon Singers Hyperion ▲ CDA 66245 [DDD]

Bruckner, A.:Requiem, w. J. Rodgers (sop), C. Denley (mez), M. Davies (ten), M. George (bass), Corydon Singers Hyperion ▲ CDA 66245 [DDD]

Fauré, G.:Requiem, w. I. Poulenard (sop), M. George (bass), Corydon Singers [1893 version] Hyperion ▲ CDA 66292

Vaughan Williams, R.:Fant on Christmas Carols, w. T. Allen (bar), Corydon Singers [E] Hyperion ▲ CDA 66420 [DDD]

Vaughan Williams, R.:Flos Campi, w. N. Imai (va), Corydon Singers Hyperion ▲ CDA 66420 [DDD]

Vaughan Williams, R.:Mystical Songs, w. T. Allen (bar), Corydon Singers [E] Hyperion ▲ CDA 66420 [DDD]

Vaughan Williams, R.:Serenade to Music, w. Corydon Singers [E] Hyperion ▲ CDA 66420 [DDD]

H. Blake (cnd)

Blake, H.:Con Cl, w. T. King (cl) Hyperion ▲ CDA 66215 [DDD]

I. Bolton (cnd)

Arnold, M.:Con 1 Cl, w. Emma Johnson (cl) ASV ▲ ASV 922 [DDD]

Arnold, M.:Con 2 Cl, w. Emma Johnson (cl) ASV ▲ ASV 922 [DDD]

Arnold, M.:Divert Fl, w. Emma Johnson (cl) ASV ▲ ASV 922 [DDD]

Arnold, M.:Fants solo Instrs, w. Emma Johnson (cl)—for solo Cl ASV ▲ ASV 922 [DDD]

Arnold, M.:Shanties, w. Emma Johnson (cl) ASV ▲ ASV 922 [DDD]

Arnold, M.:Sonatina Cl, w. Emma Johnson (cl) ASV ▲ ASV 922 [DDD]

A. Bonavera (cnd)

Martucci, G.:La canzone dei ricordi, w. C. Madalin (mez) Hyperion ▲ CDA 66290 [DDD]

Martucci, G.:Notturno Hyperion ▲ CDA 66290 [DDD]

Respighi, O.:Il Tramonto, w. C. Madalin (mez) [I] Hyperion ▲ CDA 66290 [DDD]

R. Bonynge (cnd)

Adam, A.:Le Corsaire London 2-▲ 430286-2 [DDD]

Auber, D.-F.:Le Domino noir, w. Sumi Jo (sop), Doris Lamprecht (sop), Martine Olmeda (sop), Isabelle Vernet (sop), Jocelyne Taillon (mez), Bruce Ford (ten), Patrick Power (ten), Gilles Cachemaille (bar), Jules Bastin (bass), London Voices London 2-▲ 440646-2

Auber, D.-F.:Gustave III (ballet), w. London Voices London 2-▲ 440646-2

Ballet Gala London 2-▲ 421818-2 LH2 [DDD]

Carnaval:French Arias, w. Sumi Jo (sop) London ▲ 440679-2 [DDD]

ORCH. & ENS.

English CO (cont.)
R. Bonynge (cnd) (cont.)
Donizetti, G.:L'elisir d'amore, w. J. Sutherland (sop), L. Pavarotti (ten), D. Cossa (bar), S. Malas (bass) [I] London 2-▲ 414461-2 [ADD]
Handel, G.F.:Messiah, w. Joan Sutherland (sop), Huguette Tourangeau (mez), Werner Krenn (ten), Tom Krause (bar), Ambrosian Singers [E] London ("Serenata" series) 2-▲ 433740-2 [ADD]
Lehár, F.:Das Land des Lächelns, w. Nancy Gustafson (sop—Lisa), Naomi Itami (sop—Mi), Lynton Atkinson (ten—Gustl), Jerry Hadley (ten—Prince Sou Chong) *(rec EMI Abbey Road, Studio One, London, England; Aug 2–25, 1995)* Telarc ▲ CD-80419 [DDD]
Lehár, F.:Der Zarewitsch, w. Nancy Gustafson (sop—Sonia), Naomi Itami (sop—Mascha), Lynton Atkinson (ten—Ivan), Jerry Hadley (ten—the Czarevitch), Jeffrey Carl (bar—Grand Duke/Soldier) *(rec EMI Abbey Road, Studio One, London, England; Aug 25–27, 1995)* Telarc ▲ CD-80395 [DDD]
B. Britten (cnd)
Bach, J.S.:Brandenburg Con 3 London ▲ 452485-2 ■ 452 485-4
Britten, B.:Albert Herring, w. S. Fisher (sop), A. Cantelo (sop), S. Rex (mez), P. Pears (ten), J. Noble (bar), O. Brannigan (bass) [E] London 2-▲ 421849-2 [ADD]
Britten, B.:Les Illuminations, w. P. Pears (ten) [F] London ▲ 417153-2 [ADD]
Britten, B.:Phaedra, w. J. Baker (mez) London 2-▲ 425666-2 [ADD]
Britten, B.:The Rape of Lucretia, w. H. Harper (sop), J. Baker (mez), P. Pears (ten), B. Drake (bar), B. Luxon (bar), J. Shirley-Quirk (bar) London 2-▲ 425666-2 [ADD]
Haydn, J.:Con 1 Vc, w. Mstislav Rostropovich (vc) London ("Serenata" series) ▲ 430633-2 [ADD]
Mozart, W.A.:Con 22 Pno, w. S. Richter (pno) *(rec 1967)* Music & Arts ▲ CD 761 [AAD]
Mozart, W.A.:Con 22 Pno, w. S. Richter (pno) *(rec live, Aldeburgh, 1967)* Memories 2-▲ HR 4366/67 (m) [ADD]
Mozart, W.A.:Con 27 Pno, w. S. Richter (pno) *(rec 1967)* Music & Arts ▲ CD 761 [AAD]
Mozart, W.A.:Con 27 Pno, w. S. Richter (pno) *(rec 1965)* Historical Performers ▲ HPS 7 [ADD]
Mozart, W.A.:Serenata notturna London ("Double Decca" series) 2-▲ 444323-2
Mozart, W.A.:Sym 25 London ("Double Decca" series) 2-▲ 444323-2
Mozart, W.A.:Sym 29 London ("Double Decca" series) 2-▲ 444323-2
Mozart, W.A.:Sym 38 London ("Double Decca" series) 2-▲ 444323-2
Mozart, W.A.:Sym 40 London ("Double Decca" series) 2-▲ 444323-2
S. Cleobury (cnd)
Fauré, G.:Requiem, w. A. Murray (mez), O. Bär (bar), King's College Choir Cambridge EMI Classics ▲ CDC 49880
Mozart, W.A.:Missa, K.317, w. L. Marshall (sop), A. Murray (mez), R. Covey-Crump (ten), D. Wilson-Johnson (bar), King's College Choir Cambridge [L] Argo ▲ 411904-2 [DDD]
Mozart, W.A.:Missa solemnis, K.337, w. L. Marshall (sop), A. Murray (mez), R. Covey-Crump (ten), D. Wilson-Johnson (bar) [L] Argo ▲ 411904-2 [DDD]
E. Colomer (cnd)
Debussy, C.:Danses sacrée et profane Virgin Classics ▲ CDZ 59695
J. E. Dähler (cnd)
Mozart, W.A.:Arias, w. Ernst Haefliger (ten)—Un'aura amorosa; Il mio tesoro; Dalla sua pace; Misero! Ò sogno, ò son desto?; Ich baue ganz auf deine Stärke; Dies Bildnis ist bezaubernd schön; Se all'Impero; Torna la pace; Per pietà, non ricercate *(rec St. Jude's Church, London, Apr 1983)* Claves ▲ CD 508305 [DDD]
A. Davis (cnd)
Bach, C.P.E.:Con Vc, H.439, w. M. Haimovitz (vc) Deutsche Grammophon ▲ 429219-2 [DDD]
Boccherini, L.:Con Vc, G.482, w. M. Haimovitz (vc) Deutsche Grammophon ▲ 429219-2 [DDD]
Haydn, J.:Con 1 Vc, w. Matt Haimovitz (vc) Deutsche Grammophon ▲ 429219-2 [DDD]
C. Davis (cnd)
America, w. King's Singers EMI Classics ▲ CDC 49701
Copland, A.:Old American Songs, w. Marilyn Horne (mez)—Set 1, Nos. 3–5; Set 2, Nos. 4 & 5 *(rec Walthamstow Assembly Hall, London, Aug 1985)* London 2-▲ 448261-2 [DDD]
Mozart, W.A.:Con 9 Pno, w. A. de Larrocha (pno) RCA Red Seal ▲ 60825-2 [DDD] ■ 60825-4 (CrO2) □ 60825-5
Mozart, W.A.:Con 20 Pno, w. Alicia de Larrocha (pno) *(rec Abbey Road Studio No. 1, London, Oct 3, 7 & 8, 1993)* RCA Red Seal ▲ 09026-68399-2 [DDD]
Mozart, W.A.:Con 21 Pno, w. A. de Larrocha (pno) RCA Red Seal ▲ 60825-2 [DDD] ■ 60825-4 (CrO2) □ 60825-5
Mozart, W.A.:Con 22 Pno, w. A. de Larrocha (pno) RCA Red Seal ▲ 09026-61698-2
Mozart, W.A.:Con 23 Pno, w. A. de Larrocha (pno) RCA Red Seal ▲ 09026-60989-2 [DDD] ■ 09026-60989-4 (D)
Mozart, W.A.:Con 24 Pno, w. A. de Larrocha (pno) RCA Red Seal ▲ 09026-60989-2 [DDD] ■ 09026-60989-4 (D)
Mozart, W.A.:Con 25 Pno, w. Alicia de Larrocha (pno) *(rec Abbey Road Studio No. 1, London, Oct 3, 7 & 8, 1993)* RCA Red Seal ▲ 09026-68399-2 [DDD]
Mozart, W.A.:Con 26 Pno, w. A. de Larrocha (pno) RCA Red Seal ▲ 09026-61698-2
O. Dohnányi (cnd)
Glinka, M.:Russlan & Ludmilla (ov) *(rec St. Silas Church, London, Dec 1994)* Novalis ▲ 150119 [DDD]
Khachaturian, A.:Gayane (sels) *(rec St. Silas Church, London, Dec 1994)* Novalis ▲ 150119 [DDD]
Rimsky-Korsakov, N.:Golden Cockerel (sels), w. Paul Barritt (vn)—Hymn to the Sun *(rec St. Silas Church, London, Dec 1994)* Novalis ▲ 150119 [DDD]
Rimsky-Korsakov, N.:Russian Easter Festival *(rec St. Silas Church, London, Dec 1994)* Novalis ▲ 150119 [DDD]
Rimsky-Korsakov, N.:The Tale of Tsar Saltan (orch sels)—Flight of the Bumble-Bee *(rec St. Silas Church, London, Dec 1994)* Novalis ▲ 150119 [DDD]
Tchaikovsky, P.:Characteristic Dances *(rec St. Silas Church, London, Dec 1994)* Novalis ▲ 150119 [DDD]
Tchaikovsky, P.:The Nutcracker (sels)—Ov. miniature *(rec St. Silas Church, London, Dec 1994)* Novalis ▲ 150119 [DDD]
Tchaikovsky, P.:Romeo & Juliet *(rec St. Silas Church, London, Dec 1994)* Novalis ▲ 150119 [DDD]
J. Falletta (cnd)
Ran, S.:Fant Movts, w. Nina Flyer (vc) Koch International Classics ▲ KIC 7280 [DDD]
P. Fournillier (cnd)
Mozart, W.A.:Andante Fl, w. Philippe Racine (fl) Novalis ▲ 150131 [DDD]
Mozart, W.A.:Cons Fl, w. Philippe Racine (fl)—No. 1 Novalis ▲ 150131 [DDD]
Mozart, W.A.:Rondo Vn, K.373, w. Philippe Racine (fl) [arr for fl & orch] Novalis ▲ 150131 [DDD]
Stamitz, C.:Con Fl, Op. 29, w. Philippe Racine (fl) Novalis ▲ 150131 [DDD]
Stamitz, C.:Con Fl in D, w. Philippe Racine (fl) Novalis ▲ 150131 [DDD]
A. Francis (cnd)
Mozart, W.A.:Con Cl, w. T. King (cl) Meridian ▲ CDE 84022
Spohr, L.:Con 4 Cl, w. T. King (cl) Meridian ▲ CDE 84022
D. Fraser (cnd)
Baroque Brass RCA Victor ▲ 09026-61541-2 ■ 09026-61541-4
World Anthems RCA Victor ▲ 09026-61344-2 [DDD] ■ 09026-61344-4 (CrO2)
J.-L. Garcia (cnd)
Haydn, J.:Con 1 Vc, w. Yo-Yo Ma (vc) CBS ▲ MK 36674 ■ MT 36674
Haydn, J.:Con 2 Vc, w. Yo-Yo Ma (vc) CBS 2-▲ M2K 44562 [ADD/DDD] 2-■ M2T 44562 (D)
Haydn, J.:Con 2 Vc, w. Yo-Yo Ma (vc) CBS ▲ MK 39310 ■ MT 39310
Haydn, J.:Con 2 Vc, w. Yo-Yo Ma (vc) CBS ▲ MK 36674 ■ MT 36674
Mozart, W.A.:Con Cl, w. J. Valdepeñas (cl) Summit ▲ DCD 131 [DDD]
Mozart, W.A.:Con Hn, K.447, w. F. Rizner (hn) Summit ▲ DCD 131 [DDD]
Mozart, W.A.:Con Hn, K.495, w. F. Rizner (hn) Summit ▲ DCD 131 [DDD]
L.A. Garcia-Navarro (cnd)
Rodrigo, J.:Fant para un gentilhombre, w. N. Yepes (gtr) Deutsche Grammophon ▲ 415349-2 [ADD]
D. Garforth (cnd)
Bridge, F.:Suite Str Orch Chandos ▲ CHAN 8390 [DDD]
Ireland, J.:A Downland Suite Chandos ▲ CHAN 8390 [DDD]
Ireland, J.:Elegaic Meditation Chandos ▲ CHAN 8390 [DDD]

English CO (cont.)
D. Garforth (cnd) (cont.)
Ireland, J.:The Holy Boy Chandos ▲ CHAN 8390 [DDD]
A. Gibson (cnd)
Beethoven, L. van:Con Vn, Vc & Pno, "Triple Con", w. Kalichstein-Laredo-Robinson Trio Chandos ("Collect" series) ▲ CHAN 6501 [DDD]
Mozart, W.A.:Concertone Vns, w. Norbert Brainin (vn), Peter Schidlof (va) Chandos ▲ CHAN 8315 [DDD]
Mozart, W.A.:Sinf concertante Vn, K.364, w. N. Brainin (vn), P. Schidlof (va) Chandos ▲ CHAN 8315 [DDD]
Stravinsky, I.:Danses concertantes Chandos ▲ CHAN 8325 [DDD]
Stravinsky, I.:Pulcinella Suite Chandos ▲ CHAN 8325 [DDD]
S. Gonley (cnd)
Paisiello, G.:Cons Hpd, w. Mariaclara Monetti (pno)—8 Cons (complete) ASV 2-▲ ASV 229
P.-L. Graf (cnd)
Saint-Saëns, C.:Con 1 Vc, w. Claude Starck (vc) *(rec EMI Studio London, 1975)* Claves ▲ CD 50501 [ADD]
Spohr, L.:Con 1 Vn Hp, w. Hansheinz Schneeberger (vn), Ursula Holliger (hp) *(rec EMI Studio London, 1970)* Claves ▲ CD 50208 [ADD]
H. Griffiths (cnd)
Fritz, G.:Con Vn, w. J. Lohmann (vn) Novalis ▲ 150099 [DDD]
Fritz, G.:Sym 1 Novalis ▲ 150099 [DDD]
Reindl, C.:Sinf concertante, w. J.-L. Garcia (vn) Novalis ▲ 150031 [DDD]
Scherrer, N.:Sym 5 Novalis ▲ 150099 [DDD]
Schoeck, O.:Concerto quasi una fantasia, w. U. Hoelscher (vn) Novalis ▲ 150070 [DDD]
Schoeck, O.:Serenade Novalis ▲ 150070 [DDD]
Schoeck, O.:Suite Strs Novalis ▲ 150070 [DDD]
Stalder, J.F.X.D.:Con Fl, w. W. Bennett (fl) Novalis ▲ 150031 [DDD]
Stalder, J.F.X.D.:Sym in G Novalis ▲ 150031 [DDD]
C. Groves (cnd)
Bärmann, H.J.:Qnt 3 Cl, w. E. Johnson (cl)—Adagio ASV ▲ ASV 559
Castelnuovo-Tedesco, M.:Con 1 Gtr, w. J. Williams (gtr) CBS 2-▲ M2K 44791 [ADD/DDD]
Crusell, B.H.:Con 2 Cl, w. E. Johnson (cl) ASV ▲ ASV 784
Crusell, B.H.:Con 2 Cl, w. E. Johnson (cl) ASV ▲ ASV 559
Rodrigo, J.:Concierto de Aranjuez, w. J. Williams (gtr) CBS ▲ MYK 36717
Rodrigo, J.:Fant para un gentilhombre, w. J. Williams (gtr) Sony Classical ("Essential Classics" series) ▲ SBK 48168 ■ SBT 48168
Rossini, G.:Intro, Theme & Vars Cl, w. E. Johnson (cl) ASV ▲ ASV 559
Weber, C.M. von:Concertino Cl, w. E. Johnson (cl) ASV ▲ ASV 559
Williams, G.:Music of, w. Anthony Camden (ob), Snell (cnd), London SO, Royal PO—Fant on Welsh Nursery Tunes; Sea Sketches; Penillion; Carillions Ob; Con for Tpt Lyrita ▲ SRCD 323
G. Guest (cnd)
Mozart, W.A.:Requiem, w. Y. Kenny (sop), S. Walker (mez), W. Kendall (ten), D. Wilson-Johnson (bar), St. John's College Choir Cambridge [L] Chandos ▲ CHAN 8574 [DDD]
L. Hager (cnd)
Mendelssohn, F.:Sinfs Strs—No. 9 in c *(rec All Saints' Church, London, May 1995)* Novalis ▲ 150121 [DDD]
Mendelssohn, F.:Sym 3 *(rec All Saints' Church, London, May 1995)* Novalis ▲ 150121 [DDD]
Mozart, W.A.:Ovs—(12) Bastien et Bastienne; Betulia liberata; Clemenza di Tito; Così fan tutte; Don Giovanni; Finta semplice; Idomeneo; Lucia Silla; Mitridate, re di Ponto; Le nozze di Figaro; Der Schauspieldirektor; Die Zauberflöte Novalis ▲ 150041 [DDD]
Sssmayr, F.X.:Con Movt Bas Cl, w. T. King (b cl) Hyperion ▲ CDA 66504
Tausch, F.W.:Con 1 for 2 Cls, w. T. King (cl), N. Bucknall (cl) Hyperion ▲ CDA 66504
A. Halstead (cnd)
Six Trumpet Concertos, w. Crispian Steele-Perkins (tpt) IMP Classics ("Masters" series) ▲ PCD 821 [DDD]
W.-D. Hauschild (cnd)
Eybler, J.L.E. von:Con Cl, w. D. Klöcker (cl) Novalis ▲ 150061 [DDD]
Mozart, W.A.:Con Cl, w. D. Klöcker (cl) Novalis ▲ 150061 [DDD]
Sssmayr, F.X.:Con Cl, w. D. Klöcker (cl) Novalis ▲ 150061 [DDD]
E. Heath (cnd)
Beethoven, L. van:Con Vn, Vc & Pno, "Triple Con", Zingara Trio IMP ("Classics" series) ▲ IMP 6700912
Boccherini, L.:Con Vc, G.480, w. Felix Schmidt (vc) IMP ("Classics" series) ▲ IMP 6700912
L. Heger (cnd)
Tausch, F.W.:Concertante 2, w. T. King (cl), N. Bucknall (cl) Hyperion ▲ CDA 66504
H. Holliger (cnd)
Krommer, F.:Concertino Fl, Op. 65, w. P.-L. Graf (fl) Claves ▲ CD 8203 [DDD]
Krommer, F.:Con Fl, Op. 30, w. P.-L. Graf (fl) Claves ▲ CD 8203 [DDD]
Krommer, F.:Con Ob, Op. 52, w. P.-L. Graf (fl) Claves ▲ CD 8203 [DDD]
I. Holst (cnd)
Holst, G.:Psalms 86 & 148, w. I. Partridge (ten), R. Downes (org), Purcell Singers—Psalm 86 EMI Classics ▲ CDC 49784
T. Indermühle (cnd)
Telemann, G.P.:Con in A Ob d'amore, w. Thomas Indermühle (ob) Novalis ▲ 150126 [DDD]
Telemann, G.P.:Con in G Ob d'amore, w. Thomas Indermühle (ob) Novalis ▲ 150126 [DDD]
Telemann, G.P.:Cons Ob Orch, w. Thomas Indermühle (ob)—No. 16 in c; No. 17 in D; No. 18 in d; No. 20 in e Novalis ▲ 150126 [DDD]
I. Jackson (cnd)
Ginastera, A.:Con Hp, w. A. Hobson Pilot (hp) Koch International Classics ▲ KIC 7261 [DDD]
Mathias, W.:Con Hp, w. A. Hobson Pilot (hp) Koch International Classics ▲ KIC 7261 [DDD]
J. Judd (cnd)
Heinze, G.A.:Konzertstück Cl, w. Thea King (cl) Hyperion ▲ CDA 66300 [DDD]
O. Kamu (cnd)
Arnold, M.:Con Rcr, w. Michala Petri (rcr) *(rec Hit Factory, London, Sept. 21–23, 1992)* RCA Red Seal ▲ 09026-62543-2 [DDD]
Christiansen, A.L.:Dance Suite, w. Michala Petri (rcr) *(rec Hit Factory, London, Sept. 21–23, 1992)* RCA Red Seal ▲ 09026-62543-2 [DDD]
Holmboe, V.:Con Rcr, w. Michala Petri (rcr) *(rec Hit Factory, London, Sept. 21–23, 1992)* RCA Red Seal ▲ 09026-62543-2 [DDD]
Koppel, T.:Moonchild's Dream, w. Michala Petri (rcr) *(rec Hit Factory, London, Sept. 21–23, 1992)* RCA Red Seal ▲ 09026-62543-2 [DDD]
Kulesha, G.:Con Rcr, w. Michala Petri (rcr) *(rec Hit Factory, London, Sept. 21–23, 1992)* RCA Red Seal ▲ 09026-62543-2 [DDD]
N. Kennedy (cnd)
Vivaldi, A.:Cons Vn, Op. 8/1–4, "The Four Seasons", w. N. Kennedy (vn) EMI Classics ▲ CDC 49557 [DDD] ■ 4DS 49557 (D)
B. Klee (cnd)
Mozart, W.A.:Ave verum corpus, w. Tallis Chamber Choir [L] Novalis ▲ 150064 [DDD]
Mozart, W.A.:Cons Fl, w. K. Zoeller (fl) Deutsche Grammophon ▲ 429815-2 [ADD]
Mozart, W.A.:Exsultate, w. E. Mathis (sop) [L] Novalis ▲ 150064 [DDD]
Mozart, W.A.:Sacred Music, w. E. Mathis (sop), Tallis Chamber Choir—Inter notos mulierum, K.72; Regina coeli, K.276; Laudate dominus from Vesperae solennes de confessore, K.339; Laudamus te (soprano aria) from Missa in c, K.427; Benedictus (soprano aria) from Missa brevis in Bb, K.275 [L] Novalis ▲ 150064 [DDD]
Mozart, W.A.:Schuldigkeit (sels), w. E. Mathis (sop)—Sinf. & 2 arias [G] Novalis ▲ 150064 [DDD]
P. Ledger (cnd)
Bach, Joh. Christian:Con Bn, w. Daniel Smith (bn) ASV Quicksilva ▲ ASQ 6177
Bach, Joh. Christian:Con Bn, w. D. Smith (vc) ASV ▲ ASV 681 [DDD]
Bach, J.S.:Brandenburg Con 1 IMP ▲ IMP 2006

▲ = CD ♦ = Enhanced CD Δ = MD ■ = Cassette Tape □ = DCC

English CO (cont.)

P. Ledger (cnd) (cont.)

Bach, J.S.:Brandenburg Con 2 IMP ▲ IMP 2006
Bach, J.S.:Brandenburg Con 3 IMP ▲ IMP 2006
Bach, J.S.:Brandenburg Con 4 IMP ▲ IMP 2009
Bach, J.S.:Brandenburg Con 5 IMP ▲ IMP 2009
Bach, J.S.:Brandenburg Con 6 IMP ▲ IMP 2009
Bach, J.S.:Suites Orch, BWV 1066–1069—Nos. 1, 2, & 3 Virgin Classics ▲ CDZ 59640
Bassoon Bon-Bons, w. Daniel Smith (bn), Royal PO [cnd:Ettore Stratta], Coull String Quartet, Roger Vignoles (pno) ASV ▲ ASV 2052 [DDD]
Graupner, C.:Con Bn, w. D. Smith (vc) ASV ▲ ASV 681 [DDD]
Graupner, C.:Con Bn, w. Daniel Smith (bn) ASV Quicksilva ▲ ASQ 6177
Handel, G.F.:Ode for St. Cecilia's Day, w. Jill Gomez (sop), Robert Tear (ten), King's College Choir Cambridge [E] ASV ▲ ASV 512 [DDD]
Hargrave, H.:Con 4 Bn, w. Daniel Smith (bn) ASV Quicksilva ▲ ASQ 6177
Hargrave, H.:Con 4 Bn, w. Daniel Smith (bn) ASV ▲ ASV 681 [DDD]
Hertel, J.W.:Con Bn, w. D. Smith (vc) ASV ▲ ASV 681 [DDD]
Hertel, J.W.:Con Bn, w. Daniel Smith (bn) ASV Quicksilva ▲ ASQ 6177
Vivaldi, A.:Cons Bn, w. D. Smith (bn)—Concerti RV.469, 470, 474, 476, 487, 494 ASV ▲ ASV 571 [DDD]
Vivaldi, A.:Cons Bn, w. D. Smith (bn)—Concerti RV.466, 467, 486, 491, 499, 500 ASV ▲ ASV 565 [DDD]
Vivaldi, A.:Cons Bn, w. Daniel Smith (bn)—Nos. 4, 10, 12, 15, 18, 22, 25, 28 [RV 474, 500, 499, 487, 467, 486, 491, 466] ASV ▲ ASV CD 971
Vivaldi, A.:Cons Bn, w. Daniel Smith (bn)—No. 26 in C, R.479 ASV Quicksilva ▲ ASQ 6177

R. Leppard (cnd)

Albinoni, T.:Sinf (6) e con (6) à 5, Op. 2—Nos. 3 in A & 6 in g *(rec Abbey Road Studios, London, Dec. 1969)* EMI Classics ▲ CDK 65337 [ADD]
Bach, C.P.E.:Cons Fl, w. Aurele Nicolet (fl), Zinman (cnd), Netherlands CO—in a, W.166; in B♭, W.167; in A, W.168; in G, W.169 Philips ("Classics" series) 2–▲ 442592–2
Bach, C.P.E.:Con Ob, H.466, w. Heinz Holliger (ob), Netherlands CO Philips ("Classics" series) 2–▲ 442592–2
Bach, C.P.E.:Con Ob, H.468, w. Heinz Holliger (ob), Netherlands CO Philips ("Classics" series) 2–▲ 442592–2
Bach, C.P.E.:Hp Music, w. Ursula Holliger (hp), Netherlands CO—Son. in g, W.139 Philips ("Classics" series) 2–▲ 442592–2
Bach, C.P.E.:Son Ob, H.549, w. Heinz Holliger (ob), Rama Jucker (vc), Netherlands CO Philips ("Classics" series) 2–▲ 442592–2
Bach, J.S.:Brandenburg Cons—Nos. 1–3 Philips ("Silver Line" series) ■ 420345–4
Bach, J.S.:Brandenburg Con 1 Philips ("Solo" series) ▲ 442386–2
Bach, J.S.:Brandenburg Con 2 Philips ("Solo" series) ▲ 442386–2
Bach, J.S.:Brandenburg Con 3 Philips ("Solo" series) ▲ 442386–2
Bach, J.S.:Brandenburg Con 4 Philips ("Solo" series) ▲ 442387–2
Bach, J.S.:Brandenburg Con 5 Philips ("Solo" series) ▲ 442387–2
Bach, J.S.:Brandenburg Con 6 Philips ("Solo" series) ▲ 442387–2
Bach, J.S.:Con Fl, Vn & Hpd, w. *(soloists unknown)* Philips ("Solo" series) ▲ 442387–2
Bach, J.S.:Cons Vn (comp), w. A. Grumiaux (vn) Philips ("Solo" series) ▲ 442386–2
Biber, H. von:Son in A Tpts, w. W. Marsalis (tpt) CBS ▲ MK 42478 [DDD] ■ MT 42478
Devienne, F.:Con 2 Fl, w. Peter-Lukas Graf (fl) *(rec EMI Studio London, 1975)* Claves ▲ CD 50501 [ADD]
Fasch, J.F.:Con Tpt & 2 Obs, w. Wynton Marsalis (tpt) *(rec St. Giles Church, Cripplegate, London, England, Feb. 17 & 19–23, 1993)* Sony Classical ▲ SK 57497 [DDD]; ■ ST 57497
Fasch, J.F.:Con Tpt & 2 Obs, w. W. Marsalis (tpt) CBS ▲ MK 39061 [DDD] ■ IMT 39061 (D)
Great Baroque Favorites, w. Grande Ecurie [cnd:Jean-Claude Malgoire], Philharmonia Virtuosi [cnd:Richard Kapp], et al. CBS ▲ MYK 38482 ■ MYT 38482
Handel, G.F.:Arias, w. E. Gruberova (sop), W. Marsalis (tpt), "Eternal Source of Light Divine," from *Birthday Ode for Queen Anne* & "Let the Bright Seraphim," from *Samson* [E] CBS ▲ MK 39061 [DDD]; ■ IMT 39061 (D)
Handel, G.F.:Concerti grossi, Op. 6 Philips 3–▲ 426465–2 [ADD]
Handel, G.F.:Con grosso in C, "Alexanderfest" Philips ▲ 426082–2 [ADD]
Handel, G.F.:Cons (3) Ob, w. H. Holliger (ob) Philips ▲ 426082–2 [ADD]
Handel, G.F.:Music of, w. Pauline Tinsley (sop), James Bowman (ct), Anthony Rolfe-Johnson (ten), David Wilson-Johnson (ten), Simon Preston (org), London Phil Chorus—Zadok the Priest; Eternal Source of Light Divine; Tamerlano Ov; Dead March [from Saul]; When the Ear Heard Her; She Delivered the Poor That Cried; Their Bodies Are Buried in Peace; Glory Be to the Father; As It Was in the Beginning; Con a Due Cori in B♭; Waft Her Angels to the Skies; Con in g for Org, Op. 7/5; Hallelujah Chorus [from The Messiah] IMP ("BBC Radio Classics" series) ▲ IMP 5691522
Handel, G.F.:Royal Fireworks Music Philips ▲ 420354–2 [ADD]
Handel, G.F.:Royal Fireworks Music Philips ("Solo" series) ▲ 442388–2
Handel, G.F.:Salve Regina, w. Janet Baker (mez), Helen Watts (cta), Robert Tear (ten), Benjamin Luxon (bar), John Shirley-Quirk (bar), London Voices Erato 3–▲ 2292–45994–2
Handel, G.F.:Water Music (suites)—Nos. 1–3 Philips ("Solo" series) ▲ 442388–2
Haydn, J.:Con Tpt, w. Wynton Marsalis (tpt) *(rec St. Giles Church, London, Feb. 17–23, 1993)* Sony Classical ("Front Line" series) ▲ SK 57497 [DDD]; ■ ST 57497
Haydn, M.:Con Tpt, Hns & Strs, w. Wynton Marsalis (tpt) CBS ▲ MK 42478 [DDD] ■ MT 42478
Hummel, J.N.:Con in E♭ Tpt, S.49, w. Wynton Marsalis (tpt) *(rec St. Giles Church, London, Feb. 17–23, 1993)* Sony Classical ("Front Line" series) ▲ SK 57497 [DDD]; ■ ST 57497
Ibert, J.:Con Fl, w. Peter-Lukas Graf (fl) *(rec EMI Studio London, 1975)* Claves ▲ CD 50501 [ADD]
Molter, J.M.:Con 2 Tpt, w. W. Marsalis (tpt) CBS ▲ MK 39061 [DDD] ■ IMT 39061 (D)
Mozart, L.:Con Tpt, w. Wynton Marsalis (tpt) *(rec St. Giles Church, Cripplegate, London, England, Feb. 17 & 19–23, 1993)* Sony Classical ▲ SK 57497 [DDD]; ■ ST 57497
Mozart, W.A.:Adagio Vn, K.261, w. Cho-Liang Lin (vn) CBS ▲ MK 42364 [DDD]
Mozart, W.A.:Andante Fl, K.315/285a, w. S. Milan (fl) Chandos ▲ CHAN 8613 [DDD]
Mozart, W.A.:Con Cl, w. Emma Johnson (cl) ASV ▲ ASV 532
Mozart, W.A.:Cons Fl, w. S. Milan (fl) Chandos ▲ CHAN 8613 [DDD]
Mozart, W.A.:Con Fl, Hp, w. William Bennett (fl), Osian Ellis (hp) ASV ▲ ASV 532
Mozart, W.A.:Con 1 Vn, w. Cho-Liang Lin (vn) CBS ▲ MK 44503 [DDD]
Mozart, W.A.:Con 2 Vn, w. C. Lin (vn) Sony Classical ▲ SK 44913 [DDD]
Mozart, W.A.:Con 3 Vn, w. Cho-Liang Lin (vn) CBS ▲ MK 42364 [DDD]
Mozart, W.A.:Con 4 Vn, w. Cho-Liang Lin (vn) CBS ▲ MK 44503 [DDD]
Mozart, W.A.:Con 5 Vn, w. Cho-Liang Lin (vn) CBS ▲ MK 42364 [DDD]
Mozart, W.A.:Con 7 Vn, w. C.-L. Lin (vn) Sony Classical ▲ SK 44913 [DDD]
Mozart, W.A.:Concertone Vns, w. Cho-Liang Lin (vn), J. Laredo (vn) Sony Classical ▲ SK 47693
Mozart, W.A.:Rondo Vn, K.269, w. Cho-Liang Lin (vn) CBS ▲ MK 44503 [DDD]
Mozart, W.A.:Rondo Vn, K.373, w. S. Milan (fl) Chandos ▲ CHAN 8613 [DDD]
Mozart, W.A.:Rondo Vn, K.373, w. C-L. Lin (vn) Sony Classical ▲ SK 44913 [DDD]
Mozart, W.A.:Sinf concertante Vn, K.364, w. Cho-Liang Lin (vn), J. Laredo (va) Sony Classical ▲ SK 47693
Pachelbel, J.:Canon CBS ▲ MYK 38482 ■ MYT 38482
Pachelbel, J.:Canon, w. W. Marsalis (tpt) [arranged by R. Leppard for 3 Trumpets & Strings] CBS ▲ MK 42478 [DDD] ■ MT 42478
Pachelbel's Canon in D & Other Baroque Favorites CBS ▲ MDK 44650 [DDD] ■ MDT 44650 (D)
Purcell, H.:Dido & Aeneas, w. J. Norman (sop), M. McLaughlin (sop), T. Allen (bar), Ambrosian Singers [E] Philips ▲ 416299–2 [DDD]
Purcell, H.:Music of—17 instrumental sels. from *The Gordian Knot Unty'd* & *The Old Bachelor* CBS ▲ MDK 44644 [DDD] ■ MDT 44644 (D)
Purcell, H.:Music of—9 instrumental sels. from *Abdelazer* CBS ▲ MDK 44650 [DDD] ■ MDT 44650 (D)
Purcell, H.:Music of, w. E. Gruberova (sop), W. Marsalis (tpt)—sels. from *The Indian Queen, King Arthur* & *Come Ye Sons of Art* CBS ▲ MK 39061 [DDD] ■ IMT 39061 (D)

English CO (cont.)

R. Leppard (cnd) (cont.)

Purcell, H.:Son Tpt, w. J. Wilbraham (tpt) CBS ▲ MDK 44644 [DDD] ■ MDT 44644 (D)
Rameau, J.P.:Les Fêtes d'Hébé, w. Ursula Connors (sop), Ambrosian Singers EMI Classics ("Baroque" series) ▲ CDK 65732
Scarlatti, A.:Non so qual più m'ingombra, w. Janet Baker (mez) EMI Classics ("Baroque" series) ▲ CDK 65735
Scarlatti, D.:Salve regina Sop, w. Janet Baker (mez) EMI Classics ("Baroque" series) ▲ CDK 65735
Telemann, G.P.:Con for 3 Tpts, w. W. Marsalis (tpt) CBS ▲ MK 42478 [DDD] ■ MT 42478 (D)
Torelli, G.:Sons à 5 Tpts, w. W. Marsalis (tpt)—2 sons for Tpt & Strs CBS ▲ MK 39061 [DDD] ■ IMT 39061 (D)
Vivaldi, A.:Con for 2 Tpts, w. W. Marsalis (tpt) CBS ▲ MK 42478 [DDD] ■ MT 42478 (D)
Vivaldi, A.:Music of, w. Wim Ten Have (va), Anthony Bailes (lt), Raymond Leppard (hpd), Hans-Martin Linde (fl/rcr), Linde (cnd), Prague CO, Danske Strings members—Concertino in D, RV.121; Cons. in f, RV.156; in G, RV.435 [Op. 10/4]; in D, RV.429; in F, RV.434 [Op. 10/5]; in D, RV.93; in d, RV.540; Son. in E♭, RV.130 [Al Santo Sepolcro] Classics for Pleasure ▲ CDCFP 4656 [ADD]

G. Levine (cnd)

Britten, B.:Les Illuminations, w. E. Söderström (sop) Arabesque ▲ Z 6603
Britten, B.:Simple Sym Arabesque ▲ Z 6603
Britten, B.:Vars on a Theme of Frank Bridge Arabesque ▲ Z 6603

J. Levine (cnd)

The Bells of St. Genevieve & Other Baroque Favorites, w. James Galway (fl), Vladimir Spivakov (vn), Pinchas Zukerman (vn), Canadian Brass, et al. RCA Victor ▲ 09026–61002–2 [DDD] ■ 09026–61002–4 (CrO2) □ 09026–61002–5

A. Litton (cnd)

Bottesini, G.:Andante Sostenuto Strs ASV ▲ ASV 563 [DDD]
Bottesini, G.:Gran Con Db, w. T. Martin (db) ASV ▲ ASV 563 [DDD]
Debussy, C.:Arabesques (2), w. B. Marsalis (sax)—No. 1, orchd. Michel Colombier CBS ▲ MK 42122
Debussy, C.:L'Isle joyeuse, w. B. Marsalis (sax) [orchd. Michel Colombier] CBS ▲ MK 42122
Fauré, G.:Pavane Orch, w. W. Marsalis (sax) CBS ▲ MK 42122
Fauré, G.:Sicilienne, w. W. Marsalis (sax) CBS ▲ MK 42122
Lutoslawski, W.:Dance Preludes Cl, Hp, Pno, Perc & Strs, w. T. King (cl) Hyperion ▲ CDA 66215 [DDD]
Rachmaninoff, S.:Vocalise, w. Branford Marsalis (sax) CBS ▲ MK 42122
Ravel, M.:Pièce en forme de Habanera, w. Branford Marsalis (sax) CBS ▲ MK 42122
Rietz, J.:Con Cl, w. T. King (cl) Hyperion ▲ CDA 66300 [DDD]
Romances for Saxophone, w. Branford Marsalis (s sax) CBS ▲ MK 42122 ■ PMT 42122
Satie, E.:Gymnopédies, w. B. Marsalis (sax)—No. 3 CBS ▲ MK 42122
Seiber, M.:Concertino Cl, w. T. King (cl) Hyperion ▲ CDA 66215 [DDD]
Solère, E.:Sinf concertante Cls, w. T. King (cl), G. Dobrée (cl) Hyperion ▲ CDA 66300 [DDD]
Villa-Lobos, H.:Bachiana brasileira 5, w. B. Marsalis (sax) [arr. by Michel Colombier] CBS ▲ MK 42122

P. Maag (cnd)

Mozart, W.A.:Adagio Vn, K.261, w. J. Bell (vn) London ▲ 436376–2 [DDD]
Mozart, W.A.:Con 3 Vn, w. J. Bell (vn) London ▲ 436376–2 [DDD]
Mozart, W.A.:Con 5 Vn, w. J. Bell (vn) London ▲ 436376–2 [DDD]
Mozart, W.A.:Rondo Vn, K.373, w. J. Bell (vn) London ▲ 436376–2 [DDD]

L. Maazel (cnd)

Lloyd Webber, A.:Requiem for Soloists, Orch & Chorus, w. Sarah Brightman (sop), Paul Miles-Kingston (trb), Placido Domingo (ten), Winchester Cathedral Choir [L] EMI Classics ▲ CDC 47146 [DDD] ■ 4DS 38218 (D)
Lloyd Webber, A.:Requiem for Soloists, Orch & Chorus, w. Sarah Brightman (sop), Paul Miles-Kingston (trb), Placido Domingo (ten), Winchester Cathedral Choir *(rec Studio 1, Abbey Road, London, Dec 20–22, 1984)* London ▲ 448616–2 ■ 48616
Mozart, W.A.:Cassation, K.63 Klavier ▲ KCD 11046 [ADD]
Mozart, W.A.:Cassation, K.99/63a, w. L. Maazel (vn) Klavier ▲ KCD 11046
Mozart, W.A.:Cassation, K.100/62a Klavier ▲ KCD 11046 [ADD]
Mozart, W.A.:Con 3 Vn, w. L. Maazel (vn) Klavier ▲ KCD 11046
Mozart, W.A.:Con 5 Vn, w. L. Maazel (vn) Klavier ▲ KCD 11046 [ADD]

C. Mackerras (cnd)

Beethoven, L. van:Con 2 Pno, w. Mikhail Kazakevich (pno) Conifer Classics ▲ 75605–51237–2 [DDD]
Beethoven, L. van:Con 4 Pno, w. Mikhail Kazakevich (pno) Conifer Classics ▲ 75605–51237–2 [DDD]
Dvořák, A.:Serenade Strs Classics for Pleasure ▲ CDCFP 4597 [DDD]
Handel, G.F.:Messiah, w. Elisabeth Harwood (sop), Janet Baker (mez), Paul Esswood (ct), Robert Tear (ten), Raimund Herincx (bass), Ambrosian Singers [E] Angel ("Studio" series) 2–▲ CDMB 62748 [ADD]
Handel, G.F.:Messiah, w. Elisabeth Harwood (sop), Janet Baker (mez), Paul Esswood (ct), Robert Tear (ten), Raimund Herincx (bass), Ambrosian Singers [E] Angel ("Studio" series) ▲ CDM 69040
Handel, G.F.:Messiah (sels)—Rejoice Greatly [aria; w. Elizabeth Harwood (sop)]; He was Despised [aria; w. Janet Baker (mez)]; The Trumpet Shall Sound [aria; w. Raimund Herincx (bass)]; Hallelujah; Amen [both choruses; w. Ambrosian Singers] *(rec Kingsway Hall, London, June & Aug. 1966)* EMI Classics ▲ CDK 65336 [ADD]
Handel, G.F.:Music of—Fireworks Cons. 1 in F & 2 in D; Con. grosso, Op. 3 [No. 1]; Ov. [from Rinaldo]; Einzug der Königin von Saba [from Solomon]; Sin. pastorale [from Ariodante]; Traummusik [from Alcina]; Ov. & Pastoral Sym. [from Messiah]; Ombra mai fù [from Xerxes]; Ov. [from Acis & Galathea]; Totenmarsch [from Saul]; Symphonie für vier Hörner [from Julius Caesar]; March [from Scipione] *(rec London, Dec. 1994)* Novalis ▲ 150108 [DDD]
Maurice André Trumpet Masterpieces, w. Maurice André (tpt), Munich CO [cnd:Hans Stadlmair], Zurich Collegium Musicum Orch [cnd:Paul Sacher], Munich Bach Orch [cnd:Karl Richter] Deutsche Grammophon ("Double" series) 2–▲ 413853–2
Mozart, W.A.:Sym 32 ASV Quicksilva ▲ QS 6071 [DDD]
Mozart, W.A.:Sym 35 ASV Quicksilva ▲ QS 6071 [DDD]
Mozart, W.A.:Sym 39 ASV Quicksilva ▲ QS 6071 [DDD]
Telemann, G.P.:Con Tpt Strs in D, w. M. André (tpt) Deutsche Grammophon ("Musikfest" series) ▲ 413256–4 [AAD] ■ 413256–4
Walton, W.:Belshazzar's Feast, w. Stephen Roberts (bar), Richard Cooke (cnd), John Pritchard (cnd), BBC Singers, BBC Sym Chorus, London Phil Choir IMP ("BBC Radio Classics" series) ▲ IMP 5691612
Walton, W.:Henry V (film suite) IMP ("BBC Radio Classics" series) ▲ IMP 5691612
Walton, W.:Passacaglia Orch IMP ("BBC Radio Classics" series) ▲ IMP 5691612
Walton, W.:Siesta IMP ("BBC Radio Classics" series) ▲ IMP 5691612
Walton, W.:Touch Her Soft Lips & Part IMP ("BBC Radio Classics" series) ▲ IMP 5691612
Walton, W.:The Wise Virgins IMP ("BBC Radio Classics" series) ▲ IMP 5691612

G. Malcolm (cnd)

Bach, J.S.:Con 1 Hpd, w. A. Schiff (pno) Denon ▲ 7236 [DDD]
Bach, J.S.:Con 4 Hpd, w. A. Schiff (pno) Denon ▲ 7236 [DDD]
Bach, J.S.:Con 5 Hpd, w. A. Schiff (pno) Denon ▲ 7236 [DDD]
Trumpet Concertos, w. André Bernard (tpt), Helmut Hunger (tpt), Venice Soloists [cnd:Claudio Scimone] Sony Classical ("Essential Classics" series) ▲ SBK 47663 ■ SBT 47663

I. Marin (cnd)

Rossini, G.:Il Signor Bruschino, w. K. Battle (sop), F. Lopardo (ten), C. Desderi (bar), S. Ramey (bass) Deutsche Grammophon ▲ 435865–2

A. Melville (cnd)

Boughton, R.:The Immortal Hour, w. A. Dawson (sop), D. Wilson-Johnson (bar), R. Kennedy (bass), Geoffrey Mitchell Choir [E] Hyperion 2–▲ CDA 66101/02 [DDD]

Y. Menuhin (cnd)

Elgar, E.:Chanson de matin Arabesque ▲ Z 6563 [DDD]
Elgar, E.:Chanson de nuit Arabesque ▲ Z 6563 [DDD]
Elgar, E.:Characteristic Pieces, Op. 10—Mazurka Arabesque ▲ Z 6563 [DDD]
Elgar, E.:Elegy Strs Arabesque ▲ Z 6563 [DDD]
Elgar, E.:Intro & Allegro Arabesque ▲ Z 6563 [DDD]

English CO (cont.)

Y. Menuhin (cnd) (cont.)

Elgar, E.:Salut d'amour — Arabesque ▲ Z 6563 [DDD]
Elgar, E.:Serenade Strs — Arabesque ▲ Z 6563 [DDD]
Haydn, J.:Con 1 Vc, w. Robert Cohen (vc) — Start Classics ▲ SCD 13
Mozart, W.A.:Cons Fl, w. S. Coles (fl) — Virgin Classics ▲ 59075 [DDD]
Mozart, W.A.:Con Fl Hp, w. S. Coles (fl), N. Yoshino (hp) — Virgo ▲ CDZ 61108 [DDD]
Mozart, W.A.:Con Fl Hp, w. S. Coles (fl), N. Yoshino (hp) — Virgin Classics ▲ 59075 [DDD]
Schubert, Franz:Adagio & Rondo concertante Vn, w. Jose-Luis Garcia (vn) [in A] — Start Classics ▲ SCD 13
Vaughan Williams, R.:Fant on Greensleeves — Arabesque ▲ Z 6568
Vaughan Williams, R.:Fant on a Theme by Thomas Tallis — Arabesque ▲ Z 6568
Vaughan Williams, R.:The Lark Ascending, w. J.-L. Garcia (vn) — Arabesque ▲ Z 6568
Vaughan Williams, R.:Variants of "Dives & Lazarus" — Arabesque ▲ Z 6568
Vivaldi, A.:Cons Vn, Op. 8/1-4, "The Four Seasons", w. Jose-Luis Garcia (vn), Maurice Hasson (vn), Manoug Parikian (vn), Daniel Phillips (vn) [each movt. w. different vn soloist] — Start Classics ▲ SCD 13

M. Neary (cnd)

Adeste Fideles! Christmas Down the Ages, w. Emma Kirkby (sop), Westminster Abbey Consort, Westminster Abbey Ensemble, Westminster Abbey Choir — Sony Classical ▲ SK 62688 ■ ST 62688
Tavener, J.:Little Requiem for Father Malachy Lynch, w. Westminster Abbey Choir *(rec Westminster Abbey, Oct 6, 1994)* — Sony Classical ▲ SK 66613 [DDD]

V. Negri (cnd)

Vivaldi, A.:Gloria, RV.589, w. Alldis Chorus — Philips ▲ 420648-2 [ADD]
Vivaldi, A.:Lauda Jerusalem, w. Alldis Chorus — Philips ▲ 420648-2 [ADD]
Vivaldi, A.:Sacred Choral Music, w. John Alldis Choir—Lauda Jerusalem, RV.609; Introduzione al Gloria, RV.642; Gloria, RV.589; Laudate pueri, RV.602; Laudate Dominum, RV.606 [L] — Philips ▲ 420648-2 [ADD]

J. Nelson (cnd)

Handel, G.F.:Semele, w. Kathleen Battle (sop), Sylvia McNair (sop), Marylin Horne (mez), Michael Chance (ct), John Aler (ten), Samuel Ramey (bass), Ambrosian Opera Chorus — Deutsche Grammophon 3-▲ 435782-2 –

A. Newman

In Gabriel's Garden, w. Wynton Marsalis (tpt) *(rec St. Giles Church, Cripplegate, London, June 19-23 & 25, 1995)* — Sony Classical ▲ SK 66244 [DDD]

P. Olefsky (cnd)

Boccherini, L.:Con Vc, G.482, w. P. Olefsky (vc) — Amatius Classics ▲ ACCD 1001 [DDD]
Tchaikovsky, P.:Vars on a Rococo Theme, w. H. Zheng (vc) — Amatius Classics ▲ ACCD 1002 [DDD]
Vivaldi, A.:Cons Vc, w. P. Olefsky (vc)—3 Concerti—in a, c (RV.401) & D — Amatius Classics ▲ ACCD 1001 [DDD]
Vivaldi, A.:Con for 2 Vcs, w. P. Olefsky (vc), H. Zheng (vc) — Amatius Classics ▲ ACCD 1001 [DDD]

S. Ozawa (cnd)

Sarasate, P. de:Zigeunerweisen, w. A.-S. Mutter (vn), French National Orch — EMI Classics 3-▲ CDMC 69878

J.-F. Paillard (cnd)

Basic 100 Vol. 44 — RCA Victor ▲ 09026-62564-2 ■ 09026-62564-4
Basic 100 Vol. 73 — RCA Victor ▲ 09026-68364-2 ■ 09026-68364-4
The Best of Mozart, w. Boston SO [cnd:E. Leinsdorf], Chicago SO [cnd:F. Reiner], et al. — Victrola ("Victrola Best of" series) ▲ 60773-2-RV [ADD] ■ 60773-4-RV
The Best of Vivaldi — Victrola ("Victrola Best of" series) ▲ 60776-2-RV [ADD] ■ 60776-4-RV
Haydn, J.:Sym 94, "Surprise Sym" — RCA Victor ▲ 09026-62564-2 ■ 09026-62564-4 (CrO2)
Haydn, J.:Sym 100, "Military" — RCA Victor ▲ 09026-62564-2 ■ 09026-62564-4 (CrO2)
Haydn, J.:Sym 101, "Clock" — RCA Victor ▲ 09026-62564-2 ■ 09026-62564-4 (CrO2)
Mozart, W.A.:Sym 35 — RCA ("Basic 100" series) ▲ 09026-68264-2 ■ 09026-68364-4
Mozart, W.A.:Sym 35 — RCA Silver Seal ▲ 60539-2 [ADD] ■ 60539-4
Mozart, W.A.:Sym 36 — RCA ("Basic 100" series) ▲ 09026-68264-2 ■ 09026-68364-4
Mozart, W.A.:Sym 40 — RCA Silver Seal ▲ 60539-2 [ADD] ■ 60539-4
Mozart, W.A.:Sym 41 — RCA Silver Seal ▲ 60539-2 [ADD] ■ 60539-4

A. Pay (cnd)

Krommer, F.:Con Cl, w. T. Friedli (cl) — Claves ▲ CD 8602 [DDD]
Krommer, F.:Con for 2 Cls, Op. 35, w. T. Friedli (cl), A. Pay (cl) — Claves ▲ CD 8602 [DDD]
Krommer, F.:Con Fl, Op. 86, w. T. Friedli (cl) — Claves ▲ CD 8602 [DDD]
Mozart, W.A.:Con Cl, w. Joan Enric Lluna (hn) — Cala ▲ CAL 88010 [DDD]

M. Perahia (cnd)

Mozart, W.A.:Con Pno, K.107, w. Murray Perahia (pno) — CBS ▲ MK 39222 [DDD]
Mozart, W.A.:Cons Pno, w. M. Perahia (pno)—Nos. 1-6, 8, 9 & 11-27 — Sony Classical 12-▲ SX12K 46441
Mozart, W.A.:Cons 1-4 Pno, w. Murray Perahia (pno) — CBS ▲ MK 39225 [DDD]
Mozart, W.A.:Con 5 Pno, w. Murray Perahia (pno) — CBS ▲ MK 37267 [DDD]
Mozart, W.A.:Con 6 Pno, w. Murray Perahia (pno) — CBS ▲ MK 39223
Mozart, W.A.:Con 9 Pno, w. Murray Perahia (pno) — CBS ▲ MK 34562 [AAD]
Mozart, W.A.:Con 10 Pnos, w. Murray Perahia (pno) — CBS ▲ MK 42243 [AAD]
Mozart, W.A.:Con 12 Pno, w. Murray Perahia (pno) — CBS ▲ MK 42243 [AAD]
Mozart, W.A.:Con 13 Pno, w. Murray Perahia (pno) — CBS ▲ MK 39223
Mozart, W.A.:Con 14 Pno, w. Murray Perahia (pno) — CBS ▲ MK 42243 [AAD]
Mozart, W.A.:Con 15 Pno, w. Murray Perahia (pno) — CBS ▲ MK 37824 [DDD]
Mozart, W.A.:Con 16 Pno, w. Murray Perahia (pno) — CBS ▲ MK 37824 [DDD]
Mozart, W.A.:Con 17 Pno, w. Murray Perahia (pno) — CBS ▲ MK 36686 [DDD]
Mozart, W.A.:Con 18 Pno, w. Murray Perahia (pno) — CBS ▲ MK 39064 [DDD]
Mozart, W.A.:Con 18 Pno, w. Murray Perahia (pno) — CBS ▲ MK 36686 [DDD]
Mozart, W.A.:Con 19 Pno, w. Murray Perahia (pno) — CBS ▲ MK 39064 [DDD]
Mozart, W.A.:Con 20 Pno, w. Murray Perahia (pno) — CBS ▲ MK 42241 [AAD]
Mozart, W.A.:Con 21 Pno, w. Murray Perahia (pno) — CBS ▲ MK 34562 [AAD]
Mozart, W.A.:Con 22 Pno, w. Murray Perahia (pno) — CBS ▲ MK 42242 [AAD]
Mozart, W.A.:Con 23 Pno, w. Murray Perahia (pno) — CBS ▲ MK 39064 [DDD]
Mozart, W.A.:Con 24 Pno, w. Murray Perahia (pno) — CBS ▲ MK 42242 [AAD]
Mozart, W.A.:Con 25 Pno, w. Murray Perahia (pno) — CBS ▲ MK 37267 [DDD]
Mozart, W.A.:Con 26 Pno, w. Murray Perahia (pno) — CBS ▲ MK 39224 [DDD]
Mozart, W.A.:Con 27 Pno, w. Murray Perahia (pno) — CBS ▲ MK 42241 [AAD]
Mozart, W.A.:Rondo Pno Orch, K.382, w. M. Perahia (pno) — Sony Classical 12-▲ SX12K 46441
Mozart, W.A.:Rondo Pno Orch, K.382, w. M. Perahia (pno) — CBS ▲ MK 42448 [AAD/DDD]
Mozart, W.A.:Rondo Pno Orch, K.382, w. M. Perahia (pno) — CBS ▲ MK 39224 [DDD]
Schroeter, J.S.:Con Pno, Op. 3/3 — CBS ▲ MK 39222 [DDD]

L. Pesek (cnd)

Vocal Music Sampler, w. Augér, Arleen (sop), et al. — Virgin Classics 2-▲ CDC 59098

T. Pinnock (cnd)

Handel, G.F.:Cons (16) Org, w. S. Preston (org)—Nos. 2, 9-11 & 13 — Archiv ("3D Baroque" series) ▲ 431708-2 [DDD]
Handel, G.F.:Cons for 2 Wind Choirs, "Concerti a due cori", w. *(soloist unknown)*—Nos. 2 & 3 — Archiv ▲ 415129-2 [DDD]
Handel, G.F.:Cons for 2 Wind Choirs, "Concerti a due cori" — Deutsche Grammophon ▲ 447280-2
Handel, G.F.:Coronation Anthems (4) for George II, w. Westminster Abbey Choir — Deutsche Grammophon ▲ 447280-2
Handel, G.F.:Messiah, w. Arleen Augér (sop), Anne Sofie von Otter (mez), Michael Chance (ct), Howard Crook (ten), John Tomlinson (bass), English Concert Choir [E] — Archiv 2-▲ 423630-2 [DDD]
Handel, G.F.:Messiah (sels), w. Arleen Augér (sop), Anne Sofia von Otter (mez), Michael Chance (ct), Paul Crook (ten), John Tomlinson (bass), English Concert Choir [E] — Archiv ▲ 427664-2 [DDD] ■ 427664-4
Handel, G.F.:Ode for St. Cecilia's Day, w. Felicity Lott (sop), Anthony Rolfe Johnson (ten), English Concert Choir [E] — Archiv ▲ 419220-2 [DDD]

English CO (cont.)

T. Pinnock (cnd) (cont.)

Handel, G.F.:Ovs—Alceste; Belshazzar; Saul; Samson; Arrival of the Queen of Sheba — Deutsche Grammophon ▲ 447279-2
Handel, G.F.:Ovs—Alceste; Agrippina; Pastor fido; Saul, Acts 1 & 2; Teseo; Samson — Archiv ▲ 419219-2 [DDD]
Handel, G.F.:Royal Fireworks Music — Deutsche Grammophon ▲ 447279-2
Handel, G.F.:Royal Fireworks Music — Archiv ▲ 415129-2 [DDD]
Handel, G.F.:Water Music (comp) — Deutsche Grammophon ▲ 410525-2 [DDD] ■ 410525-4 □ 410525-5
Haydn, J.:Con 1 Vn, w. Simon Standage (vn) — Archiv ▲ 427316-2 [DDD]
Haydn, J.:Mass 11, "Nelsonmesse", "Imperial Mass", "Coronation Mass", w. Felicity Lott (sop), Carolyn Watkinson (cta), Maldwyn Davies (ten), David Wilson-Johnson (bar) [L] — Archiv ▲ 423097-2 [DDD]
Haydn, J.:Stabat Mater, w. English Concert Choir [L] — Archiv ▲ 429733-2 [DDD]
Haydn, J.:Te Deum [L] — Archiv ▲ 423097-2 [DDD]
Mozart, W.A.:Exsultate, w. Barbara Bonney (sop), English Concert Choir — Archive ▲ 445353-2
Mozart, W.A.:Missa, K.317, w. Barbara Bonney (sop), Catherine Wyn-Rogers (cta), Jamie MacDougall (ten), Stephen Gadd (bass), English Concert Choir — Archive ▲ 445353-2
Mozart, W.A.:Vesperae solennes, w. Barbara Bonney (sop), Catherine Wyn-Rogers (cta), Jamie MacDougall (ten), Stephen Gadd (bass), English Concert Choir — Archive ▲ 445353-2
Vivaldi, A.:Cons Diverse Instrs—8 concerti—2 mandolins; oboe & violin; bassoon; 2 & 4 violins — Archiv ("3D Baroque" series) ▲ 431710-2 [DDD]
Vivaldi, A.:Cons Diverse Instrs—R. 558 — Archiv ▲ 415674-2 [DDD]
Vivaldi, A.:Con for 2 Mands, w. J. Tyler (mand), R. Jeffrey (mand) — Archiv ▲ 415674-2 [DDD]
Vivaldi, A.:Cons Ob, w. D. Reichenberg (ob)—R.461 — Archiv ▲ 415674-2 [DDD]
Vivaldi, A.:Cons Ob, w. D. Reichenberg (ob), S. Standage (vn)—R.548 — Archiv ▲ 415674-2 [DDD]
Vivaldi, A.:Cons Orch—R.151 — Archiv ▲ 415674-2 [DDD]
Vivaldi, A.:Con Va d'amore Lt — Archiv ▲ 419615-2 [DDD]
Vivaldi, A.:Cons Vn (misc)—R.271, "L'amoroso" — Archiv ▲ 419615-2 [DDD]
Vivaldi, A.:Cons Vn, Op. 3/1-12, "L'estro armonico", w. S. Standage (vn) — Archiv 2-▲ 423094-2 [DDD]
Vivaldi, A.:Cons Vn, Op. 4, "La stravaganza", w. S. Standage (vn) — Archiv 2-▲ 429753-2 [DDD]
Vivaldi, A.:Cons Vn, Op. 8/1-4, "The Four Seasons", w. S. Standage (vn) — Archiv ▲ 400045-2 [DDD]
Vivaldi, A.:Cons Vn, Op. 8/1-4, "The Four Seasons", w. S. Standage (vn) — CRD ▲ 3325
Vivaldi, A.:Cons for 2 Vns, w. S. Standage (vn), E. Wilcock (vn)—R.516 — Archiv ▲ 415674-2 [DDD]
Vivaldi, A.:Gloria, RV.589, w. N. Argenta (sop), I. Attrot (sop), C. Denley (mez), English Concert Choir — Archiv ▲ 423386-2 [DDD]

M. Pollini (cnd)

Mozart, W.A.:Con 19 Pno, w. M. Pollini (pno) — Exclusive ▲ EXL 35 [AAD]
Mozart, W.A.:Con 24 Pno, w. M. Pollini (pno) — Exclusive ▲ EXL 35 [AAD]

S. Preston (cnd)

Bach, J.S.:Con in E Fl, w. P. Racine (fl) — Novalis ▲ 150088 [DDD]
Bach, J.S.:Con in g Fl, w. P. Racine (fl) — Novalis ▲ 150088 [DDD]
Bach, J.S.:Cons (3) Ob, w. T. Indermühle (ob) *(rec May 1991)* — Novalis ▲ 150077 [DDD]
Bach, J.S.:Con Ob d'amore, w. P. Racine (fl) — Novalis ▲ 150088 [DDD]
Bach, J.S.:Suites Orch, BWV 1066-1069, w. P. Racine (fl) — Novalis ▲ 150088 [DDD]
Handel, G.F.:Israel in Egypt, w. Elizabeth Gale (sop), James Bowman (alt), Ian Partridge (ten), Tom McDonnell (bar), Alan Watt (bass), Watson (sgr), Christ Church Cathedral Choir Oxford — London ("Jubilee" series) 2-▲ 421602-2 [ADD]
Handel, G.F.:Israel in Egypt, w. Elizabeth Gale (sop), Lillian Watson (sop), James Bowman (alt), Ian Partridge (ten), Tom McDonnell (bass), Alan Watt (bass), Christ Church Cathedral Choir Oxford *(rec Chapel of Merton College, Oxford, 1975)* — London 2-▲ 443470-2 [ADD]
Trumpet Concertos, w. Läubin, Hannes (tpt), Wolfgang Läubin (tpt), Bernhard Läubin (tpt) — Deutsche Grammophon ▲ 431817-2 GH [DDD]

W. Prossnitz (cnd)

Ringger, R.U.:Music of, w. Tallis Chamber Choir—Gioia; Con Slancio; Cuando el Fuego Se Está Apagando...; Addio!; Odelette; Les Insaisissables; Dommage Que...; Mestizia Sospesa; A Moment of Sunrise — Tudor ▲ TUD 7036 [DDD]

J.-P. Rampal (cnd)

Bolling, C.:Suite Jazz Pno, w. Bolling (pno) — CBS ▲ MK 37798

K. Redel (cnd)

Haydn, J.:Con Hpd, Vns & Bass Instrument, H.XVIII/9, w. Oliver Roberti (hpd) — Pierre Verany ▲ PVY 793111 [DDD]
Haydn, J.:Con Org, Vns & Bass Instrument, H.XVIII/5, w. Oliver Roberti (hpd) — Pierre Verany ▲ PVY 793111 [DDD]
Haydn, J.:Con Org, Vn & Strs, H.XVIII/6, w. Oliver Roberti (hpd), Maciej Rakowski (vn) — Pierre Verany ▲ PVY 793111 [DDD]
Haydn, J.:Divert Kbd & Strs, H.XIV/8, w. Oliver Roberti (pno) — Pierre Verany ▲ PVY 793111 [DDD]

E. Ricci (cnd)

Zarzuelas, w. José Carreras (ten), I. Rey (sop) — Erato ▲ 95789-2 ■ 95789-4

A. Ros-Marbá (cnd)

Sings Zarzuelas, w. José Carreras (ten) — Koch International ▲ KOC 321948 [AAD]

M. Rostropovich (cnd)

Schnittke, A.:Quasi una son, w. M. Lubotsky (vn) *(rec Aug. 12-15, 1992)* — Sony Classical ▲ SK 53271 [DDD]

J. Rudel (cnd)

Pure Domingo, w. Plácido Domingo (ten), Madrid SO [cnd:Manuel Moreno-Buendia], Munich RSO [cnd:Eugene Kohn], National PO [cnd:Eugene Kohn], New Philharmonia Orch [cnds:Bruno Bartoletti, Riccardo Muti], Philharmonia Orch [cnd:James Levine] — Angel ▲ CDC 55616 [DDD/ADD]
Vienna, City of My Dreams, w. Plácido Domingo (ten), Ambrosian Singers — EMI Classics ▲ CDC 47398

J.-P. Saraste (cnd)

Beethoven, L. van:Con Vn, Vc & Pno, "Triple Con", w. Frank Peter Zimmermann (vn), Robert Cohen (vc), Wolfgang Manz (pno) — Classics for Pleasure ("Silver Doubles" series) 2-▲ CFP CDCFP 4775 [ADD/DDD]

A. Schneider (cnd)

Bach, J.S.:Con 2 Vn, w. I. Stern (vn) — CBS ▲ MYK 38487 [ADD] ■ MYT 38487
Bach, J.S.:Con 2 Vn, w. I. Stern (vn) — CBS ▲ MK 42258
Classical Ecstasy—Classics for a New Age, w. Chicago SO [cnd:Georg Solti], London PO [cnd:Leonard Slatkin], Philadelphia Orch [cnd:James Levine], Philharmonia Orch [cnds:Andrew Litton, Henry Lewis], RCA Italiana Opera Orch [cnd:Francesco Molinari-Pradelli], RCA Victor SO — RCA Gold Seal ▲ 74321-23041-2 [ADD/DDD]
Mozart, W.A.:Adagio Vn, K.261, w. I. Stern (vn) — CBS 2-▲ M2K 42494 [ADD]
Mozart, W.A.:Con Bn, w. R. Stoltzman (cl) [trans. Stoltzman] — RCA Gold Seal ▲ 60379-2-RG [ADD] ■ 60379-4-RG
Mozart, W.A.:Con Cl, w. R. Stoltzman (cl) — RCA Gold Seal ▲ 60379-2-RG [ADD] ■ 60379-4-RG
Mozart, W.A.:Con 17 Pno, w. R. Serkin (pno) — RCA Silver Seal ▲ 60790-2 [ADD] ■ 60790-4
Mozart, W.A.:Con 18 Pno, w. P. Serkin (pno) — RCA Silver Seal ▲ 60790-2 [ADD] ■ 60790-4
Mozart, W.A.:Con 4 Vn, w. I. Stern (vn) — CBS ▲ MYK 37808 [ADD] ■ MYT 37808
Mozart, W.A.:Serenade Vn, K.250, w. I. Stern (vn)—Rondeau — CBS 2-▲ M2K 42494 [ADD]

U. Schneider (cnd)

Mozart, W.A.:Rondo Vn, K.373, w. I. Stern (vn) — CBS 2-▲ M2K 42494 [ADD]

G. Schwarz (cnd)

Crusell, B.H.:Con 3 Cl, w. E. Johnson (cl) — ASV ▲ ASV 784

J. Sedares (cnd)

Beethoven, L. van:Cons Pno (comp), w. Gustavo Romero (pno) — Koch International Classics 3-▲ KIC 7317 [DDD]

J. Serebrier (cnd)

Falla, M. de:Con Hpd, w. J. Soriano (pno) — ASV ▲ ASV 775
Falla, M. de:Noches en los jardines de España, w. J. Soriano (pno) — ASV ▲ ASV 775
Turina, J.:La oracion del torero — ASV ▲ ASV 775

164

▲ = CD ♦ = Enhanced CD Δ = MD ■ = Cassette Tape □ = DCC

English CO (cont.)
J. Serebrier (cnd) (cont.)
Turina, J.:Rapsodia sinfónica, w. J. Soriano (pno) ASV ▲ ASV 775
G. Simon (cnd)
Barber, S.:Con Vc, w. R. Wallfisch (vc) Chandos ▲ CHAN 8322 [DDD]
Jacob, G.:Con Bn, w. R. Thompson (bn) Chandos ▲ CHAN 9278 [DDD]
Mozart, W.A.:Con Cl, w. D. Glazer (cl) LaserLight ▲ 15 875 [DDD]
Shostakovich, D.:Con 1 Vc, w. R. Wallfisch (vc) Chandos ▲ CHAN 8322 [DDD]
Tchaikovsky, P.:Pezzo capriccioso, w. R. Wallfisch (vc) Chandos ("Collect" series) ▲ CHAN 6552 [DDD]
Tchaikovsky, P.:Songs, w. R. Wallfisch (vc)—Was I not a blade of grass?, Op. 47/7; Christ had a garden, Op. 54/5 [orchd. Tchaikovsky] Chandos ("Collect" series) ▲ CHAN 6552 [DDD]
D. Sitkovetsky (cnd)
Mozart, W.A.:Cons Vn, w. Dmitri Sitkovetsky (vn)—Nos. 4–5 Novalis ▲ 150007 [DDD]
J. Snashall (cnd)
Starer, R.:Con Va, w. Melvin Berger (va) *(rec 1965)* Vox Box ("The American Composers" series) 2–▲ CDX 5158
G. Solti (cnd)
Mozart, W.A.:Con 7 Pnos, w. D. Barenboim (pno), A. Schiff (pno), G. Solti (pno) London ▲ 430232–2 [DDD]
Mozart, W.A.:Con 10 Pnos, w. *(soloists unknown)* London ▲ 430232–2 [DDD]
Mozart, W.A.:Con 20 Pno, w. G. Solti (pno) London ▲ 430232–2 [DDD]
J. Somary (cnd)
Arensky, A.:Vars on a Theme of Tchaikovsky *(rec Conway Hall, London, 1972)* Vanguard Classics ▲ SVC 37 [AAD]
Bach, J.S.:St. Matthew Passion, w. E. Ameling (sop), B. Finnilä (cta), E. Haefliger (ten), S. McCoy (ten), B. Luxon (bar), B. McDaniel (bar), Ambrosian Singers *(rec 1977)* Vanguard Classics 3–▲ OVC 4060/62 [ADD]
Bach, J.S.:St. Matthew Passion (sels), w. E. Ameling (sop), B. Finnilä (cta), E. Haefliger (ten), S. McCoy (ten), B. Luxon (bar), B. McDaniel (bar), Ambrosian Singers Vanguard Classics ▲ OVC 4063 [ADD]
Borodin, A.:Nocturne Str Orch *(rec Conway Hall, London, 1973)* Vanguard Classics ▲ SVC 37 [AAD]
Britten, B.:Simple Sym *(rec Conway Hall, London, 1973)* Vanguard Classics ▲ SVC 45 [AAD]
Britten, B.:The Young Person's Guide to the Orchestra *(rec Conway Hall, London, 1974)* Vanguard Classics 2–▲ OVC 8096/97 [ADD]
Grieg, E.:Elegaic Melodies, Op. 34—Last Spring, Op. 34/2 *(rec Conway Hall, London, 1973)* Vanguard Classics ▲ SVC 45 [AAD]
Grieg, E.:Holberg Suite *(rec Conway Hall, London, 1973)* Vanguard Classics ▲ SVC 45 [AAD]
Handel, G.F.:Judas Maccabaeus, w. Heather Harper (sop), Helen Watts (cta), Alexander Young (ten), John Shirley–Quirk (bass), Amor Artis Chorale [E] *(rec 1979)* Vanguard Classics 2–▲ OVC 4071/72 [ADD]
Handel, G.F.:Judas Maccabaeus (sels), w. Heather Harper (sop), Helen Watts (cta), Alexander Young (ten), John Shirley–Quirk (bar), Amor Artis Chorale Vanguard Classics ▲ OVC 4073 [ADD]
Handel, G.F.:Messiah, w. Margaret Price (sop), Yvonne Minton (mez), Alexander Young (ten), Justino Diaz (bass), Amor Artis Chorale [E] *(rec 1970)* Vanguard Classics ▲ OVC 4020 [ADD]
Handel, G.F.:Messiah, w. Margaret Price (sop), Yvonne Minton (mez), Alexander Young (ten), Justino Diaz (bass), Amor Artis Chorale [E] *(rec 1970)* Vanguard Classics 2–▲ OVC 4018/19 [ADD]
Handel, G.F.:Royal Fireworks Music Vanguard Classics ▲ OVC 4017 [ADD]
Handel, G.F.:Royal Fireworks Music, w. Derek Wickens (ob), Alan Civil (hn), John Wilbraham (tpt), Harold Lester (hpd) *(rec Conway Hall, London, 1973)* Vanguard Classics ▲ SVC 47 [AAD]
Handel, G.F.:Theodora, w. H. Harper (sop), M. Lehane (mez), M. Forrester (cta), A. Young (ten), J. Lawrenson (bar), Amor Artis Chorale [E] *(rec 1968)* Vanguard Classics 2–▲ OVC 4074/5 [ADD]
Handel, G.F.:Water Music (comp), w. Derek Wickens (ob), Alan Civil (hn), John Wilbraham (tpt), Harold Lester (hpd) *(rec Conway Hall, London, 1973)* Vanguard Classics ▲ SVC 47 [AAD]
Handel, G.F.:Water Music (suites) Vanguard Classics ▲ OVC 4017 [ADD]
Prokofiev, S.:Sym 1 *(rec Conway Hall, London, 1972)* Vanguard Classics ▲ SVC 37 [AAD]
Solid Gold Baroque, w. Leopold Stokowski Orch [cnd:Leopold Stokowski], I Solisti Zagreb [cnd:Janigro], et al. Vanguard Classics ▲ OVC 4021 [ADD]
Tchaikovsky, P.:Serenade Strs *(rec Conway Hall, London, 1972)* Vanguard Classics ▲ SVC 37 [AAD]
Wirén, D.:Serenade Strs *(rec Conway Hall, London, 1973)* Vanguard Classics ▲ SVC 45 [AAD]
S. Stone (cnd)
Mendelssohn, Fanny:Das Jahr (sels), w. Jennifer Eley (pno) *(rec Roslyn Hill Chapel, London)* Koch International Classics ▲ KIC 7197
Mendelssohn, F.:Con in e Pno, w. Jennifer Eley (pno) *(rec Roslyn Hill Chapel, London)* Koch International Classics ▲ KIC 7197
Schumann, C.:Pno Music, w. Jennifer Eley (pno)—Sonata (newly discovered) *(rec Roslyn Hill Chapel, London)* Koch International Classics ▲ KIC 7197
Schumann, R.:Konzertsatz Pno, w. Jennifer Eley (pno) *(rec Roslyn Hill Chapel, London)* Koch International Classics ▲ KIC 7197
V. Sutej (cnd)
The Pleasure of Love, w. José Carreras (ten) Philips ▲ 434926–2
G. Szell (cnd)
Mozart, W.A.:Concertone Vns, w. Isaac Stern (vn), Pinchas Zukerman (vn) Sony Classical 3–▲ SM3K 66475
H. Szeryng (cnd)
Bach, J.S.:Con for 2 Vns, w. H. Szeryng (vn), J.–L. Garcia (vn) *(rec live, Queen Elizabeth Hall, London Feb 26, 1972)* Intaglio ▲ INCD 7201 [ADD]
Mozart, W.A.:Con 3 Vn, w. Henryk Szeryng (vn) *(rec live, Queen Elizabeth Hall, London, Feb. 26, 1972)* Intaglio ▲ INCD 7201 [ADD]
J. Tate (cnd)
Bax, A.:Pieces (3) Orch EMI Classics ▲ CDM 64200
Beethoven, L. van:Missa Solemnis, w. C. Vaness (sop), W. Meier (mez), H.–P. Blochwitz (ten), H. Tschammer (bass), Tallis Chamber Choir [L] EMI Classics ▲ CDC 49950 [DDD]
Bridge, F.:Suite Str Orch EMI Classics ▲ CDM 64200
Bruch, M.:Con 1 Vn, w. N. Kennedy (vn) EMI Classics ▲ CDC 49663 [DDD]
Butterworth, G.:Bredon Hill & Other Songs EMI Classics ▲ CDM 64200
Canteloube, J.:Songs of Auvergne, w. K. Te Kanawa (sop) London ▲ 411730–2
Canteloube, J.:Songs of Auvergne, w. Kiri Te Kanawa (sop)—series 1–5 *(rec Kingsway Hall, London, Aug 16–19, 1982 & Sept 26)* London ("Double Decker" series) 2–▲ 444995–2 [DDD]
Haydn, J.:Con Tpt, w. Ole Edvard Antonsen (tpt) EMI Classics ▲ CDC 54897
Haydn, J.:Sym 93 EMI Classics ▲ CDD 64285
Haydn, J.:Sym 94, "Surprise Sym" Royal Classics ▲ ROY 6443
Haydn, J.:Sym 94, "Surprise Sym" EMI Classics ▲ CDD 64286
Haydn, J.:Sym 95 EMI Classics ▲ CDD 64286
Haydn, J.:Sym 96, "Miracle" EMI Classics ▲ CDD 64285
Haydn, J.:Sym 96, "Miracle" Royal Classics ▲ ROY 6443
Haydn, J.:Sym 97 EMI Classics ▲ CDD 64286
Haydn, J.:Sym 98 EMI Classics ▲ CDD 64285
Haydn, J.:Sym 104, "London" Royal Classics ▲ ROY 6443
Hummel, J.N.:Con in E♭ Tpt, S.49, w. O.E. Antonsen (tpt) EMI Classics ▲ CDC 54897
Mendelssohn, F.:Con in e Vn & Orch, Op. 64, w. N. Kennedy (vn) EMI Classics ▲ CDC 49663 [DDD]
Moeran, E.J.:Rhap 1 EMI Classics ▲ CDM 64200
Moeran, E.J.:Rhap 2 EMI Classics ▲ CDM 64200
Mozart, W.A.:Arias, w. Kiri Te Kanawa (sop)—from Die Entführung aus dem Serail; Mitridate, Re di Ponto; Don Giovanni; concert arias, K.369 & K.505 [G,I] Philips ▲ 420950–2 [DDD]
Mozart, W.A.:Cons Hn, w. R. Vlatkovic (hn) EMI Classics ▲ CDM 64851
Mozart, W.A.:Cons Pno, w. M. Uchida (pno) Philips 9–▲ 438207–2
Mozart, W.A.:Con 5 Pno, w. M. Uchida (pno) Philips ▲ 432082–2 [DDD]
Mozart, W.A.:Con 6 Pno, w. M. Uchida (pno) Philips ▲ 432082–2 [DDD]
Mozart, W.A.:Con 8 Pno, w. M. Uchida (pno) Philips ▲ 432086–2 [DDD]
Mozart, W.A.:Con 9 Pno, w. M. Uchida (pno) Philips ▲ 432086–2 [DDD]
Mozart, W.A.:Con 11 Pno, w. M. Uchida (pno) Philips ("Digital Classics" series) ▲ 422458–2 [DDD]

English CO (cont.)
J. Tate (cnd) (cont.)
Mozart, W.A.:Con 12 Pno, w. Mitsuko Uchida (pno) Philips ("Digital Classics" series) ▲ 422458–2 [DDD]
Mozart, W.A.:Con 13 Pno, w. M. Uchida (pno) Philips ▲ 422359–2 [DDD]
Mozart, W.A.:Con 14 Pno, w. M. Uchida (pno) Philips ▲ 422359–2 [DDD]
Mozart, W.A.:Con 15 Pno, w. M. Uchida (pno) Philips ▲ 426305–2 [DDD]
Mozart, W.A.:Con 16 Pno, w. M. Uchida (pno) Philips ▲ 426305–2 [DDD]
Mozart, W.A.:Con 17 Pno, w. M. Uchida (pno) Philips ▲ 422592–2 [DDD]
Mozart, W.A.:Con 18 Pno, w. M. Uchida (pno) Philips ▲ 422348–2 [DDD]
Mozart, W.A.:Con 19 Pno, w. M. Uchida (pno) Philips ▲ 422348–2 [DDD]
Mozart, W.A.:Con 20 Pno, w. Mitsuko Uchida (pno) Philips ("Insignia" series) ▲ 434164–2 [DDD]
Mozart, W.A.:Con 20 Pno, w. Mitsuko Uchida (pno) Philips ▲ 416381–2 [DDD] □ 416381–5
Mozart, W.A.:Con 21 Pno, w. M. Uchida (pno) Philips ▲ 416381–2 [DDD] □ 416381–5
Mozart, W.A.:Con 22 Pno, w. M. Uchida (pno) Philips ▲ 420187–2 [DDD]
Mozart, W.A.:Con 23 Pno, w. M. Uchida (pno) Philips ("Insignia" series) ▲ 434164–2 [DDD]
Mozart, W.A.:Con 23 Pno, w. M. Uchida (pno) Philips ▲ 420187–2 [DDD]
Mozart, W.A.:Con 24 Pno, w. M. Uchida (pno) Philips ▲ 422331–2 [DDD]
Mozart, W.A.:Con 25 Pno, w. M. Uchida (pno) Philips ▲ 422331–2 [DDD]
Mozart, W.A.:Con 26 Pno, w. M. Uchida (pno) Philips ("Digital Classics" series) ▲ 420951–2 [DDD]
Mozart, W.A.:Con 27 Pno, w. M. Uchida (pno) Philips ("Digital Classics" series) ▲ 420951–2 [DDD]
Mozart, W.A.:Rondo Hn, K.371, w. R. Vlatkovic (hn) EMI Classics ▲ CDM 64851
Mozart, W.A.:Rondo Pno Orch, K.382, w. M. Uchida (pno) Philips ▲ 432082–2 [DDD]
Mozart, W.A.:Syms (comp) EMI Classics ("Studio" series) 6–▲ CDC 63857
Neruda, J.B.G.:Con Tpt, w. O.E. Antonsen (tpt) EMI Classics ▲ CDC 54897
Schubert, Franz:Rondo Vn, D.438, w. N. Kennedy (vn) EMI Classics ▲ CDC 49663 [DDD]
Strauss, R.:Con 1 Hn, w. R. Vlatkovic (hn) EMI Classics ▲ CDM 64851
Tartini, G.:Con Tpt, w. O.E. Antonsen (tpt) EMI Classics ▲ CDC 54897
Telemann, G.P.:Con Tpt Strs in D, w. O.E. Antonsen (tpt) EMI Classics ▲ CDC 54897
B. Thomson (cnd)
Hummel, J.N.:Con Pno, Op. 85, w. S. Hough (pno) Chandos ▲ CHAN 8507 [DDD]
Hummel, J.N.:Con Pno, Op. 89, w. S. Hough (pno) Chandos ▲ CHAN 8507 [DDD]
M. Tilson Thomas (cnd)
Beethoven, L. van:Sym 1 CBS ▲ MDK 44905 [DDD]
Beethoven, L. van:Sym 2 CBS ▲ MDK 44905 [DDD]
Beethoven, L. van:Sym 7 CBS ▲ MDK 44789 [DDD]
Beethoven, L. van:Sym 8 CBS ▲ MDK 44789 [DDD]
Beethoven, L. van:Sym 9, "Choral Sym", w. Tallis Chamber Choir [G] CBS ▲ MDK 44646 [DDD]
Y. P. Tortelier (cnd)
Canteloube, J.:Songs of Auvergne, w. A. Augér (sop) Virgin Classics ("Ultraviolet" series) ▲ CUV 61120
Crusell, B.H.:Intro, Theme & Vars on a Swedish Air, w. E. Johnson (cl) ASV ▲ ASV 585 [DDD]
Debussy, C.:Première rapsodie, w. E. Johnson (cl) ASV ▲ ASV 585 [DDD]
Tartini, G.:Concertino Cl, w. Emma Johnson (cl) ASV ▲ ASV 585 [DDD]
Weber, C.M. von:Con 1 Cl, w. Emma Johnson (cl) ASV ▲ ASV 585 [DDD]
B. Tuckwell (cnd)
Mozart, W.A.:Cons Hn, w. B. Tuckwell (hn) London ▲ 410284–2 [DDD]
M. Viotti (cnd)
Donizetti, G.:Arias, w. Ramon Vargas (ten)—includes arias from Anna Bolena; Don Pasquale; Lucia di Lammermoor; Linda di Chamounix; L'Elisir d'amore; Le duc d'Alba Claves ▲ 50–9202
Donizetti, G.:L'elisir d'amore, w. M. Devia (sop), B. Pratico (bar), P. Spagnoli (bar), Tallis Chamber Choir Erato 2–▲ 4509–91701–2
Haydn, J.:Arianna a Naxos, w. Teresa Berganza (mez) [18th cent. orchestral arr. by Sigismund Ritter von Neukomm] [I] Claves ▲ CD 9016 [DDD]
Monteverdi, C.:Lamento d'Arianna, w. T. Berganza (mez) [orchestral arr. by Claudio Gallico] [I] Claves ▲ CD 9016 [DDD]
Monteverdi, C.:Lamento d'Arianna, w. Teresa Berganza (mez) Claves ▲ 50–9016
Respighi, O.:Con all'antica, w. I. Turban (vn) Claves ▲ CD 9017 [DDD]
Respighi, O.:Pastorale Vn, w. I. Turban (vn) Claves ▲ CD 9017 [DDD]
Rossini, G.:Arias, w. R. Vargas (ten)—arias from Barbiere di Siviglia, Donna del Lago, Italiana in Algeri, Occasione fa il Ladro [I] Claves ▲ CD 9202 [DDD]
Rossini, G.:La cambiale di matrimonio, w. A. Rossi (sop), M. Comencini (ten), B. de Simone (bar), B. Praticò (bar) [I] Claves 8–▲ CD 9200 [DDD]
Rossini, G.:La cambiale di matrimonio, w. Alessandra Rossi (sop), Maurizio Comencini (ten), Bruno Praticò (bar), Bruno De Simone (bar), Valeria Baiano (bass), Francesco Facini (bass) Claves ▲ 50–9101
Rossini, G.:Giovanna d'Arco, w. Teresa Berganza (mez) Claves ▲ 50–9016
Rossini, G.:L'inganno felice, w. A. Felle (sop), I. Zennaro (ten), F. Previati (bar), N. de Carolis (b–bar), D. Serraiocco (b–bar) [I] Claves 8–▲ CD 9200 [DDD]
Rossini, G.:L'inganno felice, w. Amelia Felle (sop), Iorio Zennaro (ten), Fabio Previati (bar), Natalo de Carolis (b–bar), Danilo Serraiocco (bass) Claves ▲ 50–9211
Rossini, G.:L'occassione fa il ladro, w. Maria Bayo (sop), Francesca Provvisionato (mez), Fulvio Massa (ten), Iorio Zennaro (ten), Fabio Previati (bar), Natale de Carolis (b–bar) Claves 2–▲ 50–9208/9
Rossini, G.:L'occassione fa il ladro, w. M. Bayo (sop), F. Provvisionato (mez), F. Massa (ten), I. Zennaro (ten), F. Previati (bar), N. de Carolis (b–bar), [I] Claves 8–▲ CD 9200 [DDD]
Rossini, G.:La scala di seta, w. Teresa Ringholz (sop), Francesca Provvisionata (mez), Fulvio Massa (ten), Ramon Vargas (ten), Alessandro Corbelli (bar), Natale de Carolis (b–bar) Claves 2–▲ 9219/20
Vivaldi, A.:Cants, w. Teresa Berganza (mez)—"Piango, gemo, sospiro", RV.675 Claves ▲ 50–9016 [DDD]
E. de Waart (cnd)
Haydn, J.:Con 1 Vc, w. Christine Walevska (vc) Philips 2–▲ 438797–2
Haydn, J.:Con 2 Vc, w. Christine Walevska (vc) Philips 2–▲ 438797–2
I. Watson (cnd)
Vivaldi, A.:Cons Vn, Op. 3/1–12, "L'estro armonico", w. J.L. Garcia (vn), M. Eade (vn), I. Watson (hpd) Virgin Classics ▲ CDZ 59656
D. Willcocks (cnd)
Charpentier, M.–A.:Messe de minuit pour Noël, w. I. Partridge (ten), King's College Choir Cambridge EMI Classics ▲ CDM 63135
D. Zinman (cnd)
Busoni, F.:Concertino Cl, w. P. Meyer (cl) *(rec Mar. 27–29, 1992)* Denon ▲ CO 75289 [DDD]
Copland, A.:Con Cl, w. P. Meyer (cl) *(rec Mar. 27–29, 1992)* Denon ▲ CO 75289 [DDD]
Mozart, W.A.:Con Cl, w. P. Meyer (cl) *(rec Mar. 27–29, 1992)* Denon ▲ CO 75289 [DDD]
P. Zukerman (cnd)
Bach, C.P.E.:Con Vc, H.439, w. Lynn Harrell (vc) EMI Classics ("Baroque" series) ▲ CDK 65733
Bach, J.S.:Cons Vn (comp), w. P. Zukerman (vn) RCA Red Seal ▲ 60718–2–RC [DDD] ■ 60718–4–RC (CrO2) □ 09026–60718–5
Bach, J.S.:Cons Vn (comp), w. P. Zukerman (vn) *(rec 1971)* Sony Classical ("Essential Classics" series) ▲ SBK 48273 [ADD] ■ SBT 48273
Bach, J.S.:Cons Vn (comp), w. P. Zukerman (vn) CBS ■ MGT 39798
Bach, J.S.:Con Vn, BWV 1058, w. P. Zukerman (vn) RCA Red Seal ▲ 60718–2–RC [DDD] ■ 60718–4–RC (CrO2) □ 09026–60718–5
Bach, J.S.:Con for 2 Vns, w. P. Zukerman (vn), J.–L. Garcia (vn) RCA Red Seal ▲ 60718–2–RC [DDD] ■ 60718–4–RC (CrO2) □ 09026–60718–5
Mozart, W.A.:Cons Fl, w. Eugenia Zukerman (fl) *(rec London, June 22–24, 1977)* Sony Classical ("Essential Classics" series) ▲ SBK 62424 [ADD] ■ SBT 62424
Vivaldi, A.:Cons Vc, w. L. Harrell (vc)—RV.413 & 417 EMI Classics ▲ CDM 64326
Vivaldi, A.:Cons Vn (misc), w. Pinchas Zukerman (vn) RCA Red Seal ▲ 09026–68433–2
Vivaldi, A.:Cons Vn, Op. 8/1–12, "Il cimento dell'armonia e dell'inventione", w. P. Zukerman (vn)—Nos. 5–12 Sony Classical ("Essential Classics" series) ▲ SBK 53513 ■ SBT 53513
Vivaldi, A.:Cons Vn, Op. 8/1–4, "The Four Seasons", w. P. Zukerman (vn) CBS ▲ MYK 38478 [ADD] ■ MYT 38478

ORCH. & ENS.

English CO (cont.)
P. Zukerman (cnd) (cont.)
Vivaldi, A.:Cons for 2 Vns, w. P. Zukerman (vn), K. Sillito (vn)—(2) in a, RV.522; in d, RV.565 *(rec 1971)* Sony Classical ("Essential Classics" series) ▲ SBK 48273 [ADD] ■ SBT 48273
English CO Brass [Fred Mills (tpt), Ronald Romm (tpt), David Ohnanian (hn), Eugene Watts (trbn), Charles Daellenbach (tuba)]
Baroque Brass:Basic 100, Vol. 34, w. Canadian Brass RCA Victor ▲ 09026–61854–2 ■ 09026–61854–4 (CrO2)
English CO Wind Ensemble
Beethoven, L. van:Qnt Pno, Ob, Cl, Hn & Bn, w. M. Perahia (pno) CBS ▲ MK 42099 [DDD]
Bush, G.:Air & Round–O, "Hommage to Matthew Locke", w. G. Bush (pno) Chandos ▲ CHAN 8819 [DDD]
Bush, G.:Dialogue Ob, w. G. Bush (pno) Chandos ▲ CHAN 8819 [DDD]
Bush, G.:Qnt Ww, w. G. Bush (pno) Chandos ▲ CHAN 8819 [DDD]
Bush, G.:Trio Ob, Bn & Pno, w. G. Bush (pno) Chandos ▲ CHAN 8819 [DDD]
Dvořák, A.:Serenade Ww Classics for Pleasure ▲ CDCFP 4597 [DDD]
Mozart, W.A.:Qnt Pno, K.452, w. Murray Perahia (pno) CBS ▲ MK 42099 [DDD]
G. Simon (cnd)
Andriessen, J.:Concertino Bn, w. R. Thompson (bn) Chandos ▲ CHAN 9278 [DDD]
J. Tate (cnd)
Mozart, W.A.:Qnt Pno, K.452, w. M. Uchida (pno) Philips ▲ 422592–2 [DDD]
English Concert
Mad About Angels, w. Cheryl Studer (sop), Christa Ludwig (mez), Anne Sofie von Otter (mez), José Carreras (ten), New York PO [cnd:Leonard Bernstein], English Baroque Soloists [cnd:John Eliot Gardiner], Philharmonia Orch, Philharmonia Chorus [cnd:Carlo Maria Giulini] Deutsche Grammophon ▲ 449113–2 ■ 449113–4
T. Pinnock (cnd)
Albinoni, T.:Cons à 5 Obs, Op. 9—No. 2 Archiv ▲ 415518–2 [DDD]
Avison, C.:Concerti grossi (12)—No. 9 Archiv ▲ 415518–2 [DDD]
Bach, C.P.E.:Con Ob, H.468, w. P. Goodwin (ob) Archiv ▲ 431821–2 [DDD]
Bach, J.S.:Brandenburg Cons—Nos. 4–6 Archiv ▲ 410501–2 [DDD] ■ 410501–4
Bach, J.S.:Brandenburg Cons—Nos. 1–3 Archiv ▲ 410500–2 [DDD] ■ 410500–4
Bach, J.S.:Brandenburg Cons Archiv 3–▲ 423492–2 [ADD]
Bach, J.S.:Con Fl, Vn & Hpd, w. L. Beznosiuk (fl), S. Standage (vn), T. Pinnock (hpd) Archiv ▲ 413731–2 [DDD]
Bach, J.S.:Con 1 Hpd Archiv ▲ 415991–2 [ADD]
Bach, J.S.:Con 2 Hpd Archiv ▲ 415991–2 [ADD]
Bach, J.S.:Con 3 Hpd Archiv ▲ 415991–2 [ADD]
Bach, J.S.:Con 4 Hpd Archiv ▲ 415992–2 [ADD] ■ 415992–4
Bach, J.S.:Con 5 Hpd Archiv ▲ 415992–2 [ADD]
Bach, J.S.:Con 6 Hpd Archiv ▲ 415992–2 [ADD]
Bach, J.S.:Con 7 Hpd Archiv ▲ 415992–2 [ADD]
Bach, J.S.:Con Ob d'amore, w. D. Reichenberg (ob d'amore) Archiv ▲ 413731–2 [DDD]
Bach, J.S.:Con Vn & Ob, w. S. Standage (vn), D. Reichenberg (ob) Archiv ▲ 413731–2 [DDD]
Bach, J.S.:Suites Orch, BWV 1066–1069 Archiv 3–▲ 423492–2 [ADD]
Best of Baroque, Vol. 1 Archiv ▲ 419410–2 AH [DDD/ADD]
Best of Baroque, Vol. 2 Archiv ▲ 423197–2 AH [DDD]
Boyce, W.:Syms, Op. 2 Archiv ▲ 419631–2 [DDD]
Corelli, A.:Concerti grossi, Op. 6—Nos. 1, 3, 7, 8, 11 & 12 Archiv ("3D Baroque" series) ▲ 431706–2 [DDD]
Corelli, A.:Concerti grossi, Op. 6—comp. Archiv 2–▲ 423626–2 [DDD]
Corelli, A.:Trio Sons (misc)—Op. 1/1,3,7,9,11,12; Op. 2/4,6,9,12 Archiv (Archiv) ▲ 419614–2 [DDD]
Handel, G.F.:Acis & Galatea [arr Mozart], w. B. Bonney (sop), J. MacDougall (ten), M. Schäfer (ten), J. Tomlinson (bass), English Concert Choir London 2–▲ 425792–2
Handel, G.F.:Con grosso in C, "Alexanderfest" Deutsche Grammophon ▲ 447279–2
Haydn, J.:Con Hpd, Obs, Hns & Strs, H.XVIII/11, w. Trevor Pinnock (hpd) Archiv ▲ 431678–2 [DDD]
Haydn, J.:Con Ob, w. Paul Goodwin (ob) Archiv ▲ 431678–2 [DDD]
Haydn, J.:Con Tpt, w. Mark Bennett (tpt) Archiv ▲ 431678–2 [DDD]
Haydn, J.:Con 3 Vn, w. Simon Standage (vn) Archiv ▲ 427316–2 [DDD]
Haydn, J.:Con 4 Vn, w. Simon Standage (vn) Archiv ▲ 427316–2 [DDD]
Haydn, J.:Sym 6, "Le Matin" Archiv ▲ 423098–2 [DDD]
Haydn, J.:Sym 7, "Le Midi" Archiv ▲ 423098–2 [DDD]
Haydn, J.:Sym 8, "Le Soir" Archiv ▲ 423098–2 [DDD]
Haydn, J.:Sym 41 Archiv ▲ 429399–2 [DDD]
Haydn, J.:Sym 42 Archiv ▲ 447281–2
Haydn, J.:Sym 43, "Mercury" Archiv ▲ 429400–2 [DDD]
Haydn, J.:Sym 45, "Farewell" Archiv ▲ 429757–2 [DDD]
Haydn, J.:Sym 45, "Farewell" Archiv ▲ 447281–2
Haydn, J.:Sym 46 Archiv ▲ 447281–2
Haydn, J.:Sym 47 Archiv ▲ 429757–2 [DDD]
Haydn, J.:Sym 48, "Maria Theresia" Archiv ▲ 429399–2 [DDD]
Haydn, J.:Sym 50 Archiv ▲ 429757–2 [DDD]
Haydn, J.:Sym 51 Archiv ▲ 429400–2 [DDD]
Haydn, J.:Sym 52 Archiv ▲ 429400–2 [DDD]
Haydn, J.:Sym 65 Archiv ▲ 429399–2 [DDD]
Lebrun, L.A.:Con 1 Ob, w. P. Goodwin (ob) Archiv ▲ 431821–2 [DDD]
Mozart, W.A.:Con Ob, K.314, w. P. Goodwin (ob) Archiv ▲ 431821–2 [DDD]
Mozart, W.A.:Sym 25 Archiv ▲ 431679–2 [DDD]
Mozart, W.A.:Sym 26 Archiv ▲ 431679–2 [DDD]
Mozart, W.A.:Sym 29 Archiv ▲ 431679–2 [DDD]
Pachelbel, J.:Canon Archiv ▲ 415518–2 [DDD]
Purcell, H.:Chacony Archiv ▲ 415518–2 [DDD]
Purcell, H.:Dido & Aeneas, w. L. Dawson (sop), A. S. von Otter (mez), N. Rogers (ten), S. Varcoe (bar), *(chorus unknown)* [E] Archiv ▲ 427624–2 [DDD]
Purcell, H.:King Arthur, w. N. Argenta (sop), J. Gooding (sop), L. Perillo (sop), J. MacDougall (ten), M. Tucker (ten), G. Finley (bar), B. Bannatyne–Scott (bass), *(chorus unknown)* Archiv 2–▲ 435490–2 [DDD]
Purcell, H.:Odes & Welcome Songs (misc), w. J. Smith (sop), E. Priday (sop), K. Amps (sop), M. Chance (ct), Wilson (sgr), J. M. Ainsley (ten), S. Richardson (bar), *(chorus unknown)*—Come ye Sons of Art; Welcome to All the Pleasures; Of Old, When Heroes Thought it Base Archiv ▲ 427663–2 [DDD]
Scarlatti, A.:Dixit Dominus, w. N. Argenta (sop), I. Attrot (sop), C. Denley (mez), English Chorale Archiv ▲ 423386–2 [DDD]
Telemann, G.P.:Cons Tpts, w. Mark Bennett (tpt), Michael Harrison (tpt), Nicholas Thompson (tpt), Paul Goodwin (ob), Lorraine Wood (ob)—in D *(rec Henry Wood Hall, London, Mar 1993)* Archiv Produktion ▲ 439893–2 [DDD]
Telemann, G.P.:Ovs—in g, TWV 55:g4; in d, TWV 55:D1 *(rec Henry Wood Hall, London, Mar 1993)* Archiv Produktion ▲ 439893–2 [DDD]
Vivaldi, A.:Cons Diverse Instrs—in C for Ob; in F for Bn; in C for Rcr; in g for Strs; in B♭ for Strs; in g for Vn, 2 Rcrs & 2 Obs; in G for 2 Vns & 2 Vcs Deutsche Grammophon ("4D Audio" series) ▲ 445839–2
English Concert Winds
Mozart, W.A.:Don Giovanni (Ov) [arr Triebensee for winds] Hyperion ▲ 66887
Mozart, W.A.:Nozze di Figaro (ov) [arr Vent for winds] Hyperion ▲ 66887
Mozart, W.A.:Serenade Winds, K.375 Hyperion ▲ 66887
Mozart, W.A.:Serenade Winds, K.388 Hyperion ▲ 66887
Mozart, W.A.:Zauberflöte (ov) [arr Heidenreich for winds] Hyperion ▲ 66887

English Consort of Viols
T. Penrose (cnd)
Thomas Tomkins & His Contemporaries, w. Eric Lynn Kelley (org) *(rec Honrath, Aug. 28–30, 1990)* Musicaphon ▲ 56815 [DDD]
English Fantasy [Fiona Huggett (trb vl), Angela Voss (trb vl/ten vl), Pamela Cresswell (ten vl), Rosemary Thorndycraft (ten vl/b vl), Imogen Seth–Smith (trb vl/b vl), Reiko Ichise (b vl)]
Lupo, T.:Fantasias a 3—Aire; Altre parole; Ardi et Gela; Ardo, si; Io Moriro; pavan No.28 ASV ▲ ASV 149
English Guitar Quartet
Baroque Guitar Quartets Saydisc ▲ CD SDL 386 [DDD]
Borodin, A.:Nocturne Str Orch [arr Roland Gallery] Saydisc ▲ CD SDL 379 [DDD]
Chopin, F.:Mazurkas—Opp. 50/3, 56/3 & 59/2 [arr. Roland Gallery] Saydisc ▲ CD SDL 379 [DDD]
Mendelssohn, F.:Lieder ohne Worte Pno—Opp. 30/1, 53/3, 67/5, & 102, Nos. 2 & 3 [arr Roland Gallery] Saydisc ▲ CD SDL 379 [DDD]
Schubert, Franz:Son Arpeggione [arr Roland Gallery] Saydisc ▲ CD SDL 379 [DDD]
Spanish Guitar Quartets *(rec Apr. 1992)* Saydisc ▲ CD SDL 399 [DDD]
English National Opera Orch
S. Edwards (cnd)
Weir, J.:Blond Eckbert, w. Anne–Marie Owens (mez), Nicholas Folwell (bar), Nerys Jones (sgr), Christopher Ventris (sgr) Collins Classics ▲ COL 1461
P. Robinson (cnd)
Sullivan, A.:The Mikado (sels), w. L. Garrett (sop), J. Rigby (mez), S. Bullock (sop), F. Palmer (sop/mez), B. Bottone (ten), R. Angas (bass), E. Idle (bar), R. Van Allan (bass), M. Richardson (bar), English Opera Group Chorus [E] MCA Classics ▲ MCAD 6215 [DDD]; ■ MCAC 6215 (D)
G. Simon (cnd)
The London Viola Sound, w. 48 Violas of Academy of St. Martin in the Fields, BBC SO, London PO *(rec Colosseum, Watford, UK, Jan 24, 1995)* Cala ▲ CACD 106 [DDD]
English Northern Philharmonia
P. Daniel (cnd)
Rodgers, R.:Music of, w. Bryn Terfel (bass–bar)—Oh, What a Beautiful Mornin'; The Surrey with the Fringe on Top [both from Oklahoma!]; It Might as Well Be Spring [from State Fair]; Some Enchanted Evening; Bali Ha'i; Younger than Springtime; This Nearly Was Mine [all from South Pacific]; There Is Nothin' Like a Dame [from South Pacific; w. Stephen Briggs (ten), Keith Mills (ten), Maurice Bowen (bass), Stephen Dowson (bass), Chorus of Opera North]; If I Loved You; Soliloquy [both from Carousel]; June Is Bustin' Out All Over; You'll Never Walk Alone [both from Carousel; w. Chorus of Opera North]; Something Wonderful; I Have Dreamed [both from The King & I]; So Far; A Fellow Needs a Girl; Come Home [all from Allegro]; What a Lovely Day for a Wedding [from Allegro; w. Keith Mills (ten), Chorus of Opera North]; No Other Love [from Me & Juliet], Edelweiss [from The Sound of Music] *(rec Main Hall, Albert Halls, Bolton, Oct 1995)* Deutsche Grammophon ▲ 449163–2 [DDD]
Walton, W.:Con Va, w. Lars Anders Tomter (va) *(rec Leeds Town Hall, Apr 5 & 6, 1995)* Naxos ▲ 8.553402 [DDD]
Walton, W.:Johannesburg Festival Ov *(rec Leeds Town Hall, Apr 5 & 6, 1995)* Naxos ▲ 8.553402 [DDD]
Walton, W.:Sym 2 *(rec Leeds Town Hall, Apr 5 & 6, 1995)* Naxos ▲ 8.553402 [DDD]
R. Hickox (cnd)
Walton, W.:Troilus & Cressida, w. Judith Howarth (sop—Cressida), Arthur Davies (ten—Troilus), Nigel Robson (ten—Pandarus), Brian Cookson (ten—3rd Watchman), Peter Bodenham (ten—Priest), Keith Mills (ten—Soldier), Alan Opie (bar—Diomede), James Thornton (bar—Antenor), Clive Bayley (bass—Calkas), David Owen–Lewis (bass—Horaste), Opera North Chorus Chandos 2–▲ CHAN 9370/71 [DDD]
D. Lloyd–Jones (cnd)
Bliss, A.:Con Vc, w. Tim Hugh (vc) *(rec Leeds Town Hall, England, July 10–11, 1995)* Naxos ▲ 8.553383 [DDD]
Bliss, A.:Music for Strs *(rec Leeds Town Hall, England, July 10–11, 1995)* Naxos ▲ 8.553383 [DDD]
Bliss, A.:Studies (2) *(rec Leeds Town Hall, England, July 10–11, 1995)* Naxos ▲ 8.553383 [DDD]
Elgar, E.:Froissart Hyperion ▲ CDA 66515 [DDD]
Lambert, C.:Aubade héroïque Hyperion ▲ CDA 66565 [DDD]
Lambert, C.:The Rio Grande, w. S. Burgess (mez), J. Gibbons (pno) [E] Hyperion ▲ CDA 66565 [DDD]
Lambert, C.:Summer's Last Will & Testament, w. W. Shimell (bar) [E] Hyperion ▲ CDA 66565 [DDD]
Macfarren, G.:Chevy Chace (concert overture) (1836) Hyperion ▲ CDA 66515 [DDD]
Mackenzie, A.:Brittania Hyperion ▲ CDA 66515 [DDD]
Parry, H.:Ov to an Unwritten Tragedy Hyperion ▲ CDA 66515 [DDD]
Pierson, H.:Romeo & Juliet Hyperion ▲ CDA 66515 [DDD]
Rimsky–Korsakov, N.:Con Pno, w. M. Binns (pno) Hyperion ▲ CDA 66640
Sullivan, A.:Macbeth (concert ov) Hyperion ▲ CDA 66515 [DDD]
D. Lloyd–Korsakov (cnd)
Balakirev, M.:Con 1 Pno, w. M. Binns, (pno) Hyperion ▲ CDA 66640
Balakirev, M.:Con 2 Pno, w. M. Binns, (pno) Hyperion ▲ CDA 66640
M. Tippett (cnd)
Tippett, M.:The Midsummer Marriage (dances), w. A. Hodgson (cta), Opera North Chorus [E] Nimbus ▲ NI 5217 [DDD]
Tippett, M.:Praeludium Nimbus ▲ NI 5217 [DDD]
Tippett, M.:Suite in D Nimbus ▲ NI 5217 [DDD]
English Northern PO
P. Daniel (cnd)
Blake, H.:Con Vn, "The Leeds", w. C. Edinger (vn) ASV ▲ ASV 905 [DDD]
Blake, H.:A Month in the Country ASV ▲ ASV 905 [DDD]
Blake, H.:Sinfonietta ASV ▲ ASV 905 [DDD]
English Opera Group Orch
B. Britten (cnd)
Britten, B.:The Rape of Lucretia (sels), w. Joan Cross (sop—Female Chorus), Kathleen Ferrier (cta—Lucretia), Peter Pears (ten—Male Chorus), Otakar Kraus (sgr—Tarquinius) *(rec Oct 5, 1946)* Music & Arts ▲ CD 901 [ADD]
Britten, B.:The Turn of the Screw, w. O. Dyer (sop), J. Vyvyan (sop), A. Mandikian (mez), D. Hemmings (trb), G. Cross (ten), P. Pears (ten) [E] London ▲ 425672–2 (m) [ADD]
English Piano Trio [Timothy Ravenscroft (pno), Jane Faulkner (vn), Mark Sheridan (vc)]
Beethoven, L. van:Songs, w. Ann Mackay (sop)—The Sweetest Lad Was Jamie; O, How Can I Be Blithe & Glad; Cease Your Funning; Jeanie's Distress; Faithfu' Johnie; Dim, Dim is My Eye; Oh! Thou Art the Lad of My Heart, Willy [all Scottish Folk Songs] Meridian ▲ MER 84253 [DDD]
Beethoven, L. van:Trio 3 Pno Meridian ▲ MER 84253 [DDD]
Beethoven, L. van:Trio 7 Pno Meridian ▲ MER 84253 [DDD]
English Sinfonia
J. Farrer (cnd)
Berkeley, L.:Serenade IMP Masters ▲ IMPMCD 60 [DDD]
Britten, B.:Vars on a Theme of Frank Bridge IMP Masters ▲ IMPMCD 60 [DDD]
Holst, G.:St. Paul's Suite IMP Masters ▲ IMPMCD 60 [DDD]
Tippett, M.:Little Music IMP Masters ▲ IMPMCD 60 [DDD]
C. Groves (cnd)
Haydn, J.:Sym 92, "Oxford" IMP ("Classics" series) ▲ IMP 6700352
Haydn, J.:Sym 92, "Oxford" *(rec 9/88)* IMP Classics ▲ PCD 916 [DDD]
Haydn, J.:Sym 104, "London" *(rec 9/88)* IMP Classics ▲ PCD 916 [DDD]
Haydn, J.:Sym 104, "London" IMP ("Classics" series) ▲ IMP 6700352
The Heart of the Symphony, w. London SO [cnd:B. Tuckwell, G. Rozhdestvensky], Royal PO [cnd:Y. Menuhin] Pickwick ("The Orchid" series) ▲ PICORCD 11011
Mozart, W.A.:Music of—Syms. 25, 27–29, 31–34 & 38; Ovs. to La finta giardineira & Le nozze di Figaro; Sinf. concertante, K.297b IMP Classics 4–▲ BOXD 9 [DDD]
Mozart, W.A.:Ovs—La finta giardiniera; Le nozze di Figaro IMP Classics ▲ PCD 939 [DDD]
Mozart, W.A.:Sinf concertante Ob, K.Anh.9 IMP Classics ▲ PCD 939 [DDD]

▲ = CD ♦ = Enhanced CD Δ = MD ■ = Cassette Tape □ = DCC

English Sinfonia (cont.)

C. Groves (cnd) (cont.)

Mozart, W.A.:Sym 25 — IMP Classics ▲ PCD 939 [DDD]
Mozart, W.A.:Sym 27 — IMP Classics ▲ PCD 933 [DDD]
Mozart, W.A.:Sym 28 — IMP Classics ▲ PCD 933 [DDD]
Mozart, W.A.:Sym 29 — IMP Classics ▲ PCD 922 [DDD]
Mozart, W.A.:Sym 31 — IMP Classics ▲ PCD 892 [DDD]
Mozart, W.A.:Sym 32 — IMP Classics ▲ PCD 922 [DDD]
Mozart, W.A.:Sym 33 — IMP Classics ▲ PCD 922 [DDD]
Mozart, W.A.:Sym 34 — IMP Classics ▲ PCD 933 [DDD]
Mozart, W.A.:Sym 38 — IMP Classics ▲ PCD 892 [DDD]
Schubert, Franz:Ovs—Der Häusliche Krieg; In the Italian Style; Der Teufel als Hydraulicus — IMP Classics ▲ PCD 967 [DDD]
Schubert, Franz:Ovs—Overture in D, "In the Italian Style"; Der Teufels Lustschloss *(rec 10/90)* — IMP Classics ▲ PCD 944 [DDD]
Schubert, Franz:Ovs—Overture—Die Zwillingsbruder — IMP Classics ▲ IMP PCD 968 [DDD]
Schubert, Franz:Rosamunde — IMP ("IMP Classics" series) ▲ IMP 6700872
Schubert, Franz:Sym 2—Overture—Die Zwillingsbruder — IMP Classics ▲ IMP PCD 968 [DDD]
Schubert, Franz:Sym 3 — IMP Classics ▲ PCD 967 [DDD]
Schubert, Franz:Sym 6—Overture—Die Zwillingsbruder — IMP Classics ▲ IMP PCD 968 [DDD]
Schubert, Franz:Sym 8 — IMP ("Concert Classics" series) ▲ IMP PCD 1101
Schubert, Franz:Sym 8 — IMP ("IMP Classics" series) ▲ IMP 6700872
Schubert, Franz:Sym 9 — IMP Classics ▲ PCD 943 [DDD]
30th Anniversary Sampler (1962–92) — IMP Classics ▲ PCDS 11 [DDD]

English String Orch

W. Boughton (cnd)

Albinoni, T.:Adagio Org *(rec Great Hall, Univ of Birmingham, May 3–4, 1985)* — Nimbus ▲ NI 7019 [DDD]
Arensky, A.:Vars on a Theme of Tchaikovsky *(rec Great Hall, Univ of Birmingham, Aug 24–25, 1991)* — Nimbus ▲ NI 7020 [DDD]
Barber, S.:Adagio Strs — Nimbus ▲ NI 7007 [DDD]
Barber, S.:Con Vn, w. Hu Kun (vn) *(rec 7/2/91)* — Nimbus ▲ NI 5329 [DDD]
Bernstein, L.:Serenade, w. Hu Kun (vn) *(rec 7/2/91)* — Nimbus ▲ NI 5329 [DDD]
Boccherini, L.:Con in D Vc, w. A. Michejew (vc) — Nimbus ▲ NI 5035
Boyce, W.:Syms, Op. 2 — Nimbus ▲ NI 5345 [DDD]
Britten, B.:Les Illuminations, w. J. Hadley (ten) — Nimbus ▲ 5234–2 [DDD]
Britten, B.:Lachrymae, w. R. Best (va) — Nimbus ▲ NI 5025
Britten, B.:Nocturne, w. J. Hadley (ten) — Nimbus ▲ 5234–2 [DDD]
Britten, B.:Prelude & Fugue Strs — Nimbus ▲ NI 5025
Britten, B.:Serenade, Op. 31, w. J. Hadley (ten), A. Halstead (hn) — Nimbus ▲ 5234–2 [DDD]
Britten, B.:Simple Sym — Nimbus ▲ NI 5025
Britten, B.:Vars on a Theme of Frank Bridge — Nimbus 4–▲ NI 5210/13 [DDD]
Britten, B.:Vars on a Theme of Frank Bridge — Nimbus ▲ NI 5025
Bridge, F.:An Irish Melody — Nimbus ▲ NI 5366
Bridge, F.:Sir Roger de Coverley — Nimbus ▲ NI 5366
Bridge, F.:Suite Str Orch — Nimbus ▲ NI 5068 [DDD]
Bridge, F.:Suite Str Orch — Nimbus 4–▲ NI 5210/13 [DDD]
Bridge, F.:There Is a Willow Grows Aslant a Brook — Nimbus ▲ NI 5366
Butterworth, G.:The Banks of Green Willow — Nimbus ▲ NI 5068 [DDD]
Butterworth, G.:The Banks of Green Willow — Nimbus 4–▲ NI 5210/13 [DDD]
Butterworth, G.:English Idylls — Nimbus ▲ NI 5068 [DDD]
Butterworth, G.:A Shropshire Lad — Nimbus ▲ NI 5068 [DDD]
Butterworth, G.:A Shropshire Lad — Nimbus ▲ NI 1407 [DDD]
Butterworth, G.:A Shropshire Lad — Nimbus 4–▲ NI 5210/13 [DDD]
Delius, F.:Florida — Nimbus ▲ NI 5208 [DDD]
Delius, F.:Summer Evening — Nimbus 4–▲ NI 5210/13 [DDD]
Delius, F.:Summer Evening — Nimbus ▲ NI 5208 [DDD]
Dvořák, A.:Romance Vn, w. Rima Sushanskaya (vn) — IMP ("Concert Classics" series) ▲ IMP PCD 1103
Dvořák, A.:Serenade Strs — Nimbus ▲ NI 5016
Elgar, E.:Bavarian Dances (3) — Nimbus ▲ NI 5136 [DDD]
Elgar, E.:Chanson de matin — Nimbus ▲ NI 5008
Elgar, E.:Chanson de nuit — Nimbus ▲ NI 5008
Elgar, E.:Cockaigne — Nimbus 4–▲ NI 5210/13 [DDD]
Elgar, E.:Cockaigne — Nimbus ▲ NI 5206 [DDD]
Elgar, E.:Elegy Strs — Nimbus ▲ NI 5008
Elgar, E.:Enigma Vars — Nimbus ▲ NI 5206 [DDD]
Elgar, E.:Froissart — Nimbus ▲ NI 5206 [DDD]
Elgar, E.:Intro & Allegro — Nimbus ▲ NI 5008
Elgar, E.:Intro & Allegro — Nimbus 4–▲ NI 5210/13 [DDD]
Elgar, E.:Pomp & Circumstance Marches — Nimbus ▲ NI 5136 [DDD]
Elgar, E.:Serenade Strs — Nimbus ▲ NI 5008
Elgar, E.:Sospiri — Nimbus ▲ NI 5008
Elgar, E.:Sospiri — Nimbus 4–▲ NI 5210/13 [DDD]
Elgar, E.:Suite Strs — Nimbus ▲ NI 5008
Elgar, E.:The Wand of Youth Suites—Op. 1b — Nimbus ▲ NI 5136 [DDD]
Finzi, G.:Con Cl, w. A. Hacker (cl) — Nimbus ▲ NI 5101 [DDD]
Finzi, G.:Con Cl, w. A. Hacker (cl) — Nimbus 4–▲ NI 5210/13 [DDD]
Finzi, G.:Ecologue, w. M. Jones (pno) — Nimbus ▲ NI 5366
Finzi, G.:Love's Labours Lost — Nimbus 4–▲ NI 5210/13 [DDD]
Finzi, G.:Love's Labours Lost — Nimbus ▲ NI 5101 [DDD]
Finzi, G.:Prelude — Nimbus ▲ NI 5101 [DDD]
Finzi, G.:Romance — Nimbus ▲ NI 5101 [DDD]
Grieg, E.:Holberg Suite *(rec Great Hall, Univ of Birmingham, May 3–4, 1985)* — Nimbus ▲ NI 7019 [DDD]
Haydn, J.:Con 1 Vc, w. Alexander Michejew (vc) — Nimbus ▲ NI 5035
Haydn, J.:Con 2 Vc, w. Alexander Michejew (vc) — Nimbus ▲ NI 5035
Holst, G.:St. Paul's Suite *(rec Great Hall, Univ of Birmingham, May 3–4, 1985)* — Nimbus ▲ NI 7019 [DDD]
Holst, G.:St. Paul's Suite — Nimbus 4–▲ NI 5210/13 [DDD]
Ireland, J.:A Downland Suite—Minuet [arr Ireland for Str Orch] *(rec Great Hall, Univ of Birmingham, Aug 24–25, 1991)* — Nimbus ▲ NI 7020 [DDD]
Maw, N.:Life Studies I–VIII *(rec Concert Hall of the Nimbus Foundation, Wyastone Leys, Monmouth, Nov 7–8, 1995)* — Nimbus ▲ NI 5471 [DDD]
Maw, N.:Son Notturna, w. Raphael Wallfisch (vc) *(rec Concert Hall of the Nimbus Foundation, Wyastone Leys, Monmouth, Nov 7–8, 1995)* — Nimbus ▲ NI 5471 [DDD]
Mendelssohn, F.:Sinfs Strs — Nimbus 3–▲ NI 5141, NI 5142, NI 5143 [DDD]
Orchestral Favorites, Vol. 1 — Nimbus ▲ NI 5032 [DDD]
Orchestral Favorites, Vol. 2 — Nimbus ▲ NI 5347 [DDD]
Parry, H.:An English Suite — Nimbus ▲ NI 5366
Parry, H.:Lady Radnor's Suite — Nimbus 4–▲ NI 5210/13 [DDD]
Parry, H.:Lady Radnor's Suite — Nimbus ▲ NI 5068 [DDD]
Respighi, O.:Ancient Airs & Dances—Suite No. 3 *(rec Great Hall, Univ of Birmingham, Aug 24–25, 1991)* — Nimbus ▲ NI 7020 [DDD]
Rule Britannia, w. Wallace, John (tpt), Edmund Barha (ten), Wallace Collection, Leeds Festival Chorus — Nimbus ▲ NI 5155 [DDD]
Schoenberg, A.:Verklärte Nacht — Nimbus ▲ NI 5151 [DDD]
Sibelius, J.:Andante festivo — Nimbus ▲ NI 5169 [DDD]
Sibelius, J.:Pelléas et Mélisande—orchestral suite — Nimbus ▲ NI 5169 [DDD]
Sibelius, J.:Rakastava Strs — Nimbus ▲ NI 5169 [DDD]
Sibelius, J.:Romance Strs — Nimbus ▲ NI 5169 [DDD]

English String Orch (cont.)

W. Boughton (cnd) (cont.)

Sibelius, J.:Suite champêtre — Nimbus ▲ NI 5169 [DDD]
Sibelius, J.:Suite mignonne — Nimbus ▲ NI 5169 [DDD]
Sibelius, J.:Valse triste — Nimbus ▲ NI 5169 [DDD]
The Spirit of Christmas Present, w. Kansas City Chorale [cnd:Charles Bruffy], BBC Welsh Chorus [cnd:John Hugh Thomas], Huw Tregelles Williams (org), Welsh Guards Fanfare Trumpeters, Christ Church Cathedral Choir [cnd:Stephen Darlington], Gulbenkian Orch [cnd:Michel Swierczewski] — Nimbus ▲ NI 7034 [DDD]
The Spirit of England — Nimbus 4–▲ NI 5210/13 [DDD]
Strauss, R.:Metamorphosen — Nimbus ▲ NI 5151 [DDD]
Stravinsky, I.:Apollon musagète — Nimbus ▲ NI 5097 [DDD]
String Classics — Nimbus ▲ NI 1403 [DDD]
Tchaikovsky, P.:Andante cantabile *(rec Great Hall, Univ of Birmingham, Aug 24–25, 1991)* — Nimbus ▲ NI 7020 [DDD]
Tchaikovsky, P.:Serenade Strs — Nimbus ▲ NI 5016
Telemann, G.P.:Cons Tpt, w. J. Wallace (tpt)—Concerto in D for Trumpet & Strings; 2 Concerti in D for Trumpet & Orchestra; Concerti in E♭ for 2 Trumpets & Strings & in D for 3 Trumpets & Orchestra; Suite in D for Trumpet & Strings; Overture in D for 2 Trumpets & Orchestra; Sinfonia in F for Trumpet, Recorder, 3 Trombones & Orchestra — Nimbus ▲ NI 5189 [DDD]
Tippett, M.:Con Double Str Orch *(rec June 27–29, 1987)* — Nimbus ▲ NI 7026 [DDD]
Tippett, M.:Fant Concertante on a Theme of Corelli *(rec Great Hall, Birmingham Univ., May 18–19, 1991)* — Nimbus ▲ NI 7026 [DDD]
Tippett, M.:Little Music *(rec Great Hall, Birmingham Univ., May 18–19, 1991)* — Nimbus ▲ NI 7026 [DDD]
Vaughan Williams, R.:Con Ob, w. M. Bourgue (ob) — Nimbus 4–▲ NI 5210/13 [DDD]
Vaughan Williams, R.:Con Ob, w. M. Bourgue (ob) — Nimbus ▲ NI 5019
Vaughan Williams, R.:Con grosso — Nimbus ▲ NI 5019
Vaughan Williams, R.:Fant on Greensleeves — Nimbus ▲ NI 7007 [DDD]
Vaughan Williams, R.:Fant on Greensleeves — Nimbus ▲ NI 5019
Vaughan Williams, R.:Fant on Greensleeves — Nimbus 4–▲ NI 5210/13 [DDD]
Vaughan Williams, R.:Fant on a Theme by Thomas Tallis — Nimbus ▲ NI 5019
Vaughan Williams, R.:Fant on a Theme by Thomas Tallis — Nimbus 4–▲ NI 5210/13 [DDD]
Vaughan Williams, R.:Fant on a Theme by Thomas Tallis — Nimbus ▲ NI 7007 [DDD]
Vaughan Williams, R.:Fant on a Theme by Thomas Tallis — Nimbus ▲ NI 1407 [DDD]
Vaughan Williams, R.:The Lark Ascending — Nimbus 4–▲ NI 5210/13 [DDD]
Vaughan Williams, R.:The Lark Ascending — Nimbus ▲ NI 5208 [DDD]
Vaughan Williams, R.:Orch Music—The Wasps:Ov.; The Lark Arscending; Fant. on Greensleeves; Con. for Oboe; Fant. on a Theme by Thomas Tallis; Five Vars. of Dives & Lazarus *(rec 1985 & 1989)* — Nimbus ▲ NI 7013 [DDD]
Vaughan Williams, R.:Variants of "Dives & Lazarus" — Nimbus ▲ NI 5019
Vaughan Williams, R.:The Wasps (ov) — Nimbus ▲ NI 5208 [DDD]
Walton, W.:Pieces Strs *(rec Great Hall, Univ of Birmingham, Aug 24–25, 1991)* — Nimbus ▲ NI 7020 [DDD]
Warlock, P.:Capriol Suite — Nimbus 4–▲ NI 5210/13 [DDD]
Warlock, P.:Capriol Suite *(rec Great Hall, Univ of Birmingham, May 3–4, 1985)* — Nimbus ▲ NI 7019 [DDD]
Wirén, D.:Serenade Strs *(rec Great Hall, Univ of Birmingham, Aug 24–25, 1991)* — Nimbus ▲ NI 7020 [DDD]

S. Darlington (cnd)

Vaughan Williams, R.:Flos Campi, w. R. Best (va), Christ Church Cathedral Choir Oxford — Nimbus ▲ NI 5166 [DDD]
Vaughan Williams, R.:O Clap Your Hands, w. Christ Church Cathedral Choir Oxford — Nimbus ▲ NI 5166 [DDD]
Vaughan Williams, R.:The Old 100th Psalm Tune, w. Christ Church Cathedral Choir Oxford — Nimbus ▲ NI 5166 [DDD]
Vaughan Williams, R.:An Oxford Elegy, w. Jack May (nar), Christ Church Cathedral Choir Oxford — Nimbus ▲ NI 5166 [DDD]
Vaughan Williams, R.:Te Deum, w. Christ Church Cathedral Choir Oxford — Nimbus ▲ NI 5166 [DDD]

Y. Menuhin (cnd)

Bartók, B.:Divert — Nimbus ▲ NI 5086 [DDD]
Bartók, B.:Music for Strs, Perc & Cel — Nimbus ▲ NI 5086 [DDD]
Prokofiev, S.:Con 1 Vn, w. H. Kun (vn) — Nimbus ▲ NI 5192 [DDD]
Prokofiev, S.:Peter & the Wolf, w. C. Lee (nar) — Nimbus ▲ NI 5192 [DDD]
Prokofiev, S.:Sym 1 — Nimbus ▲ NI 5192 [DDD]

English String Quartet

Bax, A.:Qt 1 Strs — Chandos ▲ CHAN 8391 [DDD]
Bax, A.:Qnt Hp & Strs, w. Kanga (hp) — Chandos ▲ CHAN 8391 [DDD]
Haydn, J.:Qts Strs, Op. 9—in E♭, Op. 9/2 — Meridian ▲ ECD 84117
Haydn, J.:Qt Strs, Op. 42 — Meridian ▲ ECD 84117
Haydn, J.:Qt Strs, Op. 103 — Meridian ▲ ECD 84117
Mendelssohn, F.:Qt 4 Strs *(rec 1988)* — Meridian ▲ CDE 84152
Mendelssohn, F.:Qt 5 Strs *(rec 1988)* — Meridian ▲ CDE 84152
Rubbra, E.:Qt 2 Strs *(rec May 1992)* — Tremula ▲ TREM 102–2
Schubert, Franz:Qt 4 Strs — Meridian ▲ CDE 84194
Schubert, Franz:Qt 8 Strs — Meridian ▲ CDE 84194
Schubert, Franz:Qt 11 Strs — Meridian ▲ CDE 84194
Tate, P.:Qt Strs *(rec May 1992)* — Tremula ▲ TREM 102–2
Walton, W.:Qt Pno, w. Robin McCabe (pno) — Meridian ▲ CDE 84139
Walton, W.:Qt Strs — Meridian ▲ CDE 84139
Wishart, P.:Qt Strs *(rec May 1992)* — Tremula ▲ TREM 102–2

English String Quartet members

Bax, A.:Qt Pno Strs, w. J. McCabe (pno) — Chandos ▲ CHAN 8391 [DDD]

English SO

R. Bonynge (cnd)

Ballet Gala:The Art of the Prima Ballerina — London ▲ 433861–2 LM [ADD]

W. Boughton (cnd)

Bach, Joh. Christian:Sinfs, Op. 18 *(rec Mar 20 & 30 & Apr 1, 1992)* — Nimbus ▲ NI 5403 [DDD]
Britten, B.:Gloriana (courtly dances) — Nimbus ▲ NI 5295 [DDD]
Britten, B.:Peter Grimes (4 sea interludes) — Nimbus ▲ NI 5295 [DDD]
Britten, B.:Peter Grimes (4 sea interludes) *(rec Apr. 11 & 12, 1991)* — Nimbus ▲ NI 7017 [DDD]
Britten, B.:Simple Sym *(rec Mar. 30 & 31, 1985)* — Nimbus ▲ NI 7017 [DDD]
Britten, B.:Suite on English Folk Tunes — Nimbus ▲ NI 5295 [DDD]
Britten, B.:Vars on a Theme of Frank Bridge *(rec Mar. 30 & 31, 1985)* — Nimbus ▲ NI 7017 [DDD]
Britten, B.:The Young Person's Guide to the Orchestra *(rec Apr. 11 & 12, 1991)* — Nimbus ▲ NI 7017 [DDD]
Britten, B.:The Young Person's Guide to the Orchestra — Nimbus ▲ NI 5295 [DDD]
Copland, A.:Appalachian Spring—original 1944 13-instrument chamber version — Nimbus ▲ NI 5246 [DDD]
Copland, A.:Appalachian Spring (suite) — Nimbus ▲ NI 4002 [ADD/DDD]
Copland, A.:Fanfare for the Common Man — Nimbus ▲ NI 4002 [ADD/DDD]
Copland, A.:Fanfare for the Common Man — Nimbus ▲ NI 5246 [DDD]
Copland, A.:Nonet — Nimbus ▲ NI 5246 [DDD]
Copland, A.:Quiet City, w. John Wallace (tpt), Paul Arden Taylor (E hn) — Nimbus ▲ NI 5246 [DDD]
Copland, A.:Quiet City, w. John Wallace (tpt), Paul Arden Taylor (E hn) — Nimbus ▲ NI 4002 [ADD/DDD]
Copland, A.:Rodeo — Nimbus ▲ NI 4002 [ADD/DDD]
Copland, A.:Rodeo — Nimbus ▲ NI 5246 [DDD]
Elgar, E.:Chanson de matin *(rec Symphony Hall, Birmingham, June 8 & 9, 1995)* — Nimbus ("Orchestral Favorites Vol. VI" series) ▲ NI 7029 [DDD]

ORCH. & ENS.

English SO (cont.)
W. Boughton (cnd) (cont.)
Elgar, E.:Chanson de nuit *(rec Symphony Hall, Birmingham, June 8 & 9, 1995)* Nimbus ("Orchestral Favorites Vol. VI" series) ▲ NI 7029 [DDD]
Elgar, E.:Dream Children *(rec Symphony Hall, Birmingham, June 8 & 9, 1995)* Nimbus ("Orchestral Favorites Vol. VI" series) ▲ NI 7029 [DDD]
Elgar, E.:Music of—Pomp & Circumstance No. 1, Op. 39 *(rec June 18–19, 1983)*; Cockaigne, Op. 40 *(rec July 28–30, 1989)*; Elegy, Op. 58 *(rec July 3–4, 1983)*; Intro. & Allegro, Op. 47 (w. Solo Quartet [J. Davis (violin), P. Joubert (violin), H. Roberts (viola), Sylvia Knussen (cello)]) *(rec July 3–4, 1983)*; Sospiri, Op. 70 (w. A. Partington [organ], R. Johnston [harp]) *(rec July 3–4, 1983)*; Enigma Vars., Op. 36 *(rec July 28–30, 1989)* Nimbus ▲ NI 7015 [DDD]
Elgar, E.:Nursery Suite *(rec Symphony Hall, Birmingham, June 8 & 9, 1995)* Nimbus ("Orchestral Favorites Vol. VI" series) ▲ NI 7029 [DDD]
Pachelbel, J.:Canon Nimbus ▲ NI 7007 [DDD]
Pachelbel, J.:Canon *(rec Great Hall, Univ of Birmingham, May 3–4, 1985)* Nimbus ▲ NI 7019 [DDD]
Parry, H.:From Death to Life Nimbus ▲ NI 5296 [DDD]
Parry, H.:Sym 1 Nimbus ▲ NI 5296 [DDD]
Shostakovich, D.:Chamber Sym, Op. 110a *(rec 11/90)* Nimbus ▲ NI 5308 [DDD]
Shostakovich, D.:Con 1 Pno, w. M. Jones (pno), G. Ashton (tpt) *(rec 11/90)* Nimbus ▲ NI 5308 [DDD]
Shostakovich, D.:Con 2 Pno, w. M. Jones (pno) *(rec 11/90)* Nimbus ▲ NI 5308 [DDD]
D. Parry (cnd)
Pacini, G.:Maria Tudor, w. M. Hill Smith (sop), P. Walker (sop), K. Lewis (ten), C. Blades (bar) *(rec 1983)* Italian Opera Rarities ▲ IOR 7714 [ADD]
J. Tobin (cnd)
Handel, G.F.:Messiah, w. Oliver Johnston (trb), Rae Woodland (sop), Norma Proctor (cta), Paul Esswood (ct), Stephen Roberts (bar), London Choral Society [Handel's original orchestration] [E] *(rec 1976)* Protone ■ CSPR 166/67
P. Zukerman (cnd)
Haydn, J.:Con 2 Vc, w. Ralph Kirshbaum (vc) RCA Red Seal ▲ 09026–62696–2
Haydn, J.:Sinf concertante, w. Ralph Kirshbaum (vc), Pinchas Zukerman (vn) RCA Red Seal ▲ 09026–62696–2
Haydn, J.:Sym 6, "Le Matin" RCA Red Seal ▲ 09026–62696–2
Ensemble Barocco Padovano Sans Souci
Boccherini, L.:Arias, w. Cristina Miatello (sop), L'Arte dell'Arco—Se non ti moro allato; Numi se giusti siete; Mi dona, mi rende quell'alma pietosa; Di giudice severo; Per quel paterno amplesso; Tornate sereni; Caro, son tua cosi; Deh respirar lasciatemi *(rec Armonia Ca' Bianca Hall, Apr 12–14, 1995)* Dynamic ▲ CD 123 [DDD]
Echoes of Love:18th Century Italian Cantatas, w. L. Serafini (sop), E. Lax (alt) *(rec Apr. 1993)* Dynamic ▲ CDS 106 [DDD]
Ensemble Barocco Padovano Sans Souci [Giuseppe Nalin (baroque ob), Alessandro Bares (baroque vn), Mario Folena (transverse fl), Giuliano Furlanetto (transverse fl), Paolo Tognon (baroque bn), Terrell Stone (thb), Carlo Zanardi (baroque vc), Aldo fiorentin (hpd)]
Telemann, G.P.:Harmonischer Gottes-Dienst, w. Janet Perry (sop) [period instrs]—Mit Sünden beleidigte Heiland; Ertrage nur das Joch der Mängel; Endlich wird die Stunde schlagen; Ach-Gott!; Deines neuen Bundesgnade; Jammerton *(rec Armonia Ca' Bianca Hall, July 19–21, 1995)* Dynamic ▲ CDS 146 [DDD]
Ensemble Barocco Padovano Sans Souci [Giuseppe Nalin (ob), Angela Nardo (vn), Roberto Lea (vn), Carlo Zanardi (vc), Pierluigi Polato (thb), Aldo Fiorentin (hpd)]
Caldara, A.:La costanza vince il rigore, w. Sylva Pozzer (sop), Stefano Abarello (alt) *(rec Carrara Santo Stefano Church, Padua, May 3–7, 1996)* Dynamic ▲ CD 166 [DDD]
Caldara, A.:La lode premiata, w. Sylva Pozzer (sop), Stefano Abarello (alt) *(rec Carrara Santo Stefano Church, Padua, May 3–7, 1996)* Dynamic ▲ CD 166 [DDD]
Ensemble Cello x 12
Baumann, H.:Vars on a Theme of Schubert Thorofon ▲ CTH 2256
Ensemble Cello x 12 members
Baumann, H.:Verses Thorofon ▲ CTH 2256
Ensemble Concerto
Cervetto, G.:Sons Vc—Sonata Prima for 3 Cellos in a; Sonata Sesta for 3 Cellos in c *(rec 11/90)* Tactus ▲ TC 680001
Ensemble de la Paix
Melchite Sacred Chant, w. Marie Keyrouz (sop) Harmonia Mundi France ▲ HMC 901497 ■ HMC 401497
Traditional Maronite Chant, w. Marie Keyrouz (sop) Harmonia Mundi France ▲ HMC 901350
Ensemble de Musique Ancienne Polyphonia Antiqua
Y. Esquieu (cnd)
Ultreia! *(rec 7/82)* Pierre Verany ▲ 790042 [ADD]
Ensemble de Tambours Provençaux
J. Cohen (cnd)
Gilles, J.:Mess des morts, w. A. Azema (sop), J. Nirouët (alt), W. Hite (ten), P. Mason (bar), Boston Camerata, Aix-en-Provence Festival Chorus Erato ▲ 2292–45989–2
Ensemble dell'Anima Eterna
Early Music of the Netherlands, 1600–1700, w. Currende Vocal Ensemble, Jos van Immerseel (kbd) Emergo ▲ 3986
Ensemble for 18th Century Music
E. Hashimoto (cnd)
Bach, C.P.E.:Sinfs, H.657–662, "Hamburg Syms", w. Eiji Hashimoto (hpd)—H.659 in C *(rec Corbett Auditorium, College-Conservatory of Music, Univ. of Cincinnati)* Klavier ▲ KCD 11054 [DDD]
Bach, C.P.E.:Sinfs, H.663–666, w. Eiji Hashimoto (hpd)—H.663 in D *(rec Corbett Auditorium, College-Conservatory of Music, Univ. of Cincinnati)* Klavier ▲ KCD 11054 [DDD]
Bach, Joh. Christian:Sinfs, Op. 6, w. Eiji Hashimoto (hpd)—Nos. 3 in E♭ & 6 in g *(rec Corbett Auditorium, College-Conservatory of Music, Univ. of Cincinnati)* Klavier ▲ KCD 11054 [DDD]
Bach, J.C.F.:Sinf, HW.I/3, w. Eiji Hashimoto (hpd) *(rec Corbett Auditorium, College-Conservatory of Music, Univ. of Cincinnati)* Klavier ▲ KCD 11054 [DDD]
Bach, W.F.:Sinf in d, w. Eiji Hashimoto (hpd) *(rec Corbett Auditorium, College-Conservatory of Music, Univ. of Cincinnati)* Klavier ▲ KCD 11054 [DDD]
Boccherini, L.:Syms—No. 6 in d, Op. 12/4; No. 8 in A, Op. 12/6; No. 26 in c, Op. 41 *(rec Corbett Auditorium, Univ of Cincinnati, College-Conservatory of Music)* Klavier ▲ KCD 11062 [DDD]
Ensemble 415
Bach, J.S.:Music of, w. R. Jacobs (ct), G. Murray (org), La Chapelle Royale Orch, Collegium Vocale—sels from Cants 35, 78 & 82, St. John Passion, St. Matthew Passion, & The Well-tempered Clavier; Chorale Prelude, BWV 622; Fl Son, BWV 1034; Toccata & Fugue in d *(rec 1969–88)* Harmonia Mundi Plus ▲ HMP 390801
Boccherini, L.:Qnts Strs—Qnt Op. 31/4 [G.328] Harmonia Mundi France ▲ HMC 901378
Boccherini, L.:Stabat Mater, w. A. Mellon (sop) Harmonia Mundi France ▲ HMC 901378
Corelli, A.:Concerti grossi, Op. 6 Harmonia Mundi France 2–▲ HMC 901406/07
Schütz, H.:Music of, w. René Jacobs (cnd), Concerto Vocale—Italian Madrigals; 'Nativity' excerpts; Sacred Concerts Harmonia Mundi ("Great Baroque Composers" series) 3–▲ HMX 390873.75
Vivaldi, A.:Trio Sons 2 Vns & Bc—in d, "La Follia," RV.63 (Op. 1, No. 12); in d, RV.64 (Op. 1, No. 8); in F, RV.68; in F, RV.70; in G, RV.71; in E♭, RV.77 Harmonia Mundi France ▲ HMC 901366
C. Banchini (cnd)
Bach, J.S.:Cant 35, w. R. Jacobs (ct) [G] Harmonia Mundi France ▲ HMC 901273 [DDD]
Bach, J.S.:Cant 53, w. R. Jacobs (alt) [G] Harmonia Mundi France ▲ HMC 901273 [DDD]
Bach, J.S.:Cant 82, w. R. Jacobs (ct) [G] Harmonia Mundi France ▲ HMC 901273 [DDD]
Boccherini, L.:Qnts Db, G.337–339 Harmonia Mundi ("Suite" series) ▲ HMT 7901334
Muffat, G.:Armonico tributo Harmonia Mundi France ▲ HMC 901581
A Musical Grand Tour, w. Concerto Amsterdam [cnd:Jaap Schröder], Capella Savaria [cnd:Pál Németh], Philharmonia Baroque [cnd:Nicholas McGegan], et al. Harmonia Mundi ▲ HMUK 986001
Sammartini, G.B.:Qnt Strs Musique d'Abord ▲ HMA 1901245 [DDD]
Sammartini, G.B.:Sinf in D Musique d'Abord ▲ HMA 1901245 [DDD]

Ensemble 415 (cont.)
C. Banchini (cnd) (cont.)
Sammartini, G.B.:Sinf in G Musique d'Abord ▲ HMA 1901245 [DDD]
Sammartini, G.:Cons grossi, Op. 5—in e & g Musique d'Abord ▲ HMA 1901245 [DDD]
Sammartini, G.:Cons Rcr, w. C. Steinmann (rcr)—in F Musique d'Abord ▲ HMA 1901245 [DDD]
R. Jacobs (cnd)
Bach, J.S.:Music of, w. Concerto Vocale—Excerpts from Cants & Passions; Toccata & Fugue in d; excerpts from Well-Tempered Clavier Harmonia Mundi ("Great Baroque Composers" series) 3–▲ HMX 390873.75
D. Mintner (cnd)
Handel, G.F.:Music of, w. Lorraine Hunt (sop), Kenneth Gilbert (hpd), et al., Philharmonia Baroque Orch, Concerto Vocale—sels. from Duetto "Tanti strali"; Flavio; Giulio Cesare; Harpsichord Suite No. 5; Nisi Dominus; Susanna; Water Music *(rec 1976–79)* Harmonia Mundi Plus ▲ HMP 390804
Ensemble 415 [C. Banchini (vn), E. Gatti (vn), E. Moreno (va), W. ten Have (va), R. Dieltiens (vc), H. Ter Brugge (vc)]
Boccherini, L.:Sextet Strs, G.454–459—Nos. 1, 2 & 5 Harmonia Mundi France ▲ HMC 901478
Ensemble 415 [Chiara Banchini (vn), Enrico Gatti (vn), Emilio Moreno (va), Irmgard Schaller (va), Käthi Gohl (vc)]
Mozart, W.A.:Qnt Strs, K.516 Harmonia Mundi France ▲ HMC 901512
Ensemble from the East
Musiana 95:Electroacoustic Music from Denmark & Japan, w. Trio Sparnaay/Kooistra/Abe, Hanne Andersen, Sofia Asunción Claro, Mari Kimura (hp/vn), Thomas Sandberg, Harry Sparnaay (b cl) Classico ▲ CLASSCD 139 [DDD]
Ensemble Instrumental
P. Nahon (cnd)
Essyad, A.:Le Collier des ruses, w. C. Bonnet (sop), F. Gonzalez (sop), V. Reinbold (mez) K617 2–▲ 7051
Ensemble InterContemporain
Cohen, Denis:Music of—Transmutations; Jeux; Il sogno di Dedalo Adès ▲ ADE 203652 [DDD]
P. Boulez (cnd)
Berg, A.:Chamber Con, w. Daniel Barenboim (pno), Pinchas Zukerman (vn) Deutsche Grammophon ("The Originals" series) ▲ 447405–2
Berio, L.:Chemins II Sony Classical ▲ SK 45862 [DDD]
Berio, L.:Chemins IV Sony Classical ▲ SK 45862 [DDD]
Berio, L.:Corale, "On Sequenza VIII" Sony Classical ▲ SK 45862 [DDD]
Berio, L.:Points on the Curve to Find... Sony Classical ▲ SK 45862 [DDD]
Berio, L.:Il Ritorno Degli Snovidenia Sony Classical ▲ SK 45862 [DDD]
Birtwistle, H.:Distances (5) Deutsche Grammophon ▲ 439910–2
Birtwistle, H.:Secret Theatre Deutsche Grammophon ▲ 439910–2
Birtwistle, H.:Settings (3) of Celan, w. Christine Whittlesey (sop) Deutsche Grammophon ▲ 439910–2
Birtwistle, H.:Tragoedia Deutsche Grammophon ▲ 439910–2
Boulez, P.:Derive Erato ▲ 2292–45648–2 [DDD]
Boulez, P.:Eclat Sony Classical ▲ SMK 45839 [DDD]
Boulez, P.:e.e. cummings ist der Dichter, w. BBC Singers Erato ▲ 2292–45648–2 [DDD]
Boulez, P.:...explosante-fixe... Deutsche Grammophon ▲ 445833–2
Boulez, P.:Mémoriale, w. S. Cherrier (fl) Erato ▲ 2292–45648–2 [DDD]
Boulez, P.:Multiples Sony Classical ▲ SMK 45839 [DDD]
Boulez, P.:Notations Pno, w. Pierre-Laurent Aimard (pno) Deutsche Grammophon ▲ 445833–2
Boulez, P.:Structures, w. Pierre-Laurent Aimard (pno)—Book II Deutsche Grammophon ▲ 445833–2
Ligeti, G.:Con Vc, w. J.-G. Queyras (vc) Deutsche Grammophon ▲ 439808–2
Ligeti, G.:Con Pno, w. P.-L. Aimard (pno) Deutsche Grammophon ▲ 439808–2
Ligeti, G.:Con Vn, w. S. Gawriloff (vn) Deutsche Grammophon ▲ 439808–2
Messiaen, O.:Couleurs de la cité céleste, w. Yvonne Loriod (pno) Montaigne ▲ MO 781111
Messiaen, O.:Haïkaï, w. Yvonne Loriod (pno) Montaigne ▲ MO 781111
Messiaen, O.:Oiseaux exotiques, w. Yvonne Loriod (pno) Montaigne ▲ MO 781111
Messiaen, O.:Un Vitrail et des oiseaux, w. Yvonne Loriod (pno) Montaigne ▲ MO 781111
Passport to the 20th Century Montaigne ▲ MO 780518
Ravel, M.:Chansons madécasses, w. J. Norman (sop) [F] CBS ▲ MK 39023
Ravel, M.:Don Quichotte à Dulcinée, w. J. Van Dam (b-bar) [F] CBS ▲ MK 39023
Ravel, M.:Mélodies populaires grecques, w. J. Van Dam (b-bar) [F] CBS ▲ MK 39023
Schoenberg, A.:Gurrelieder, w. J. Norman (sop)—Lied der Waldtaube *(rec Sept. 15, 1979)* Sony Classical ▲ SMK 48466 [ADD]
Schoenberg, A.:Die Jakobsleiter, w. BBC SO, BBC Singers Sony Classical ▲ SMK 48462 [ADD]
Schoenberg, A.:Moses und Aaron, w. R. Cassilly (ten), G. Reich (nar), BBC SO, BBC Singers *(rec Nov. 30–Dec. 06, 1974)* Sony Classical 2–▲ SM2K 48456 [ADD]
Schoenberg, A.:Ode to Napoleon, w. D. Wilson-Johnson (speaker), BBC SO *(rec Mar. 31, 1980)* Sony Classical ▲ SMK 48463 [ADD]
Schoenberg, A.:Pieces CO Sony Classical ▲ SMK 48465
Schoenberg, A.:Pieces Orch, Op. 16, BBC SO *(rec Sept. 23, 1976)* Sony Classical ▲ SMK 48463 [ADD]
Schoenberg, A.:Serenade Cl, w. J. Shirley-Quirk (bar), BBC SO *(rec Apr. 10, 1979)* Sony Classical ▲ SMK 48463 [ADD]
Schoenberg, A.:Suite Ww *(rec June 14. 1982)* Sony Classical ▲ SMK 48465
Schoenberg, A.:Verklärte Nacht *(rec June 14. 1982)* Sony Classical ▲ SMK 48465
Stravinsky, I.:Con CO Deutsche Grammophon ("The Originals" series) ▲ 447405–2
Stravinsky, I.:Ebony Con, w. M. Arrignan (cl) Deutsche Grammophon ("The Originals" series) ▲ 447405–2
Stravinsky, I.:Instr Miniatures Deutsche Grammophon ("The Originals" series) ▲ 447405–2
Stravinsky, I.:Suites Orch Sony Classical (Pierre Boulez Edition) ▲ SK 45843
Varèse, E.:Déserts Sony Classical ("Pierre Boulez Edition" series) ▲ SMK 68334
Varèse, E.:Ecuatorial Sony Classical ("Pierre Boulez Edition" series) ▲ SMK 68334
Varèse, E.:Hyperprism Sony Classical ("Pierre Boulez Edition" series) ▲ SMK 68334
Zappa, F.:Dupree's Paradise *(rec Paris, Jan. 10 & 11, 1984)* Rykodisc ▲ RCD 10542
Zappa, F.:Music of—The Perfect Stranger & other chamber works Barking Pumpkin/Capitol ▲ D21Z 74242 ■ D41H 74242
Zappa, F.:Naval Aviation in Art? *(rec Paris, Jan. 10 & 11, 1984)* Rykodisc ▲ RCD 10542
Zappa, F.:The Perfect Stranger *(rec Paris, Jan. 10 & 11, 1984)* Rykodisc ▲ RCD 10542
P. Eötvös (cnd)
Lancino, T.:Aloni, w. Les Petits Chanteurs de Paris Wergo ▲ WER 2032–2
Lindberg, M.:Music of—UR; Corrente; Duo Concertante; Joy Adès ▲ ADE 203582 [DDD]
Reynolds, R.:Archipelago Neuma 2–▲ 450–91 [DDD]
Ruders, P.:Corpus Cum Figuris Point ▲ PCD 5084 [AAD]
Mercier (cnd)
Marcland, P.:Music of, w. Nouvel PO, Debussy Trio, Michel Tranchant (cnd), French Vocal Group—Versets; Paroles; Failles; Mètres; Variants *(rec 1978–84)* Chamade ▲ CHCD 5636 [DDD]
D. Robertson (cnd)
Reynolds, R.:Odyssey, w. Marie Kobayashi (mez), Phillip Larson (b-bar) Neuma 2–▲ 450–91 [DDD]
M. Tabachnik (cnd)
Tabachnik, M.:Le Pacte des Onzes, w. R. Landry (sop), New London Chamber Choir [F] *(rec March 30, 1987)* Grammont ▲ CTSP 26–2 [ADD]
A. Tamayo (cnd)
Kolb, B.:Soundings CRI ▲ CD 576 [ADD]
H. Zender (cnd)
Dallapiccola, L.:Choral Music, w. Julie Moffat (sop), James Wood (cnd), New London Chamber Choir—Canti di Prigionia; Cinque Frammenti di Saffo; Due Liriche di Anacreonte; Sex Carmina Alcaei; Tempus Destruendi; Tempus Aedificandi; Due Cori di Michelangelo Buonarroti il Giovane Erato ▲ ERA 98509 [DDD]
Ensemble Lyrique Ibérique
Romances Judéo-Espagnoles L'Empreinte Digitale ▲ ED 13017

▲ = CD ♦ = Enhanced CD Δ = MD ■ = Cassette Tape □ = DCC

Ensemble M

E. Decou (cnd)

Griffes, C.T.:The Kairn of Koridwen — Koch International Classics ▲ KIC 7216 [DDD]

Ensemble Modern

Kagel, M.:Exotica — Koch Schwann ▲ SCH 313912 [DDD]
Stäbler, G.:im Spalier... — Koch Schwann ▲ SCH 311402 [DDD]
Stäbler, G.:Den Müllfahren von San Francisco — Koch Schwann ▲ SCH 311402 [DDD]
Stäbler, G.:Nachbeben und davor — Koch Schwann ▲ SCH 311402 [DDD]
Stäbler, G.:Warnung mit Liebeslied — Koch Schwann ▲ SCH 311402 [DDD]
Zappa, F.:Civilization Phaze III, w. Frank Zappa (elec) *(rec Apostolic Studio, NYC, Utility Muffin Research Kitchen, Hollywood & Joe's Garage, North Hollywood, 1967 & 1991–92)* — Barking Pumpkin 2–▲ UMRK 01
Zappa, F.:Music of—Intro; Dog Breath Vars.; Uncle Meat; Outrage at Valdez; Times Beach II; III Revised; The Girl in the Magnesium Dress; De-Bop Tango; Ruth Is Sleeping; None of the Above; Pentagon Afternoon; Questi cazzi di piccione; Time Beach III; Good Gathering in Post-Industrial American, 1992; Welcome to the United States; Pound for a Brown; Exercise #4; Get Whitey; G-Spot Tornado — Rykodisc ▲ RCD 40560

E. Bour (cnd)

Rihm, W.:umsungen, w. D. Fischer-Dieskau (bar) — Ars Musici ▲ 0825 [DDD]
Ruzicka, P.:Der die Gesänge zerschlug, w. D. Fischer-Dieskau (bar) — Ars Musici ▲ 0825 [DDD]

P. Eötvös (cnd)

Kurtág, G.:Messages of the Late Miss R.V. Troussova, w. R. Hardy (sop) *(rec June 14–16, 1990)* — Sony Classical ▲ SK 53290 [DDD]
Kurtág, G.:Quasi una fantasia, w. H. Kretzschmar (pno) *(rec June 14–16, 1990)* — Sony Classical ▲ SK 53290 [DDD]
Ligeti, G.:Con Vc, w. M. Perényi (vc) *(rec Aug. 2–3, 1990)* — Sony Classical ▲ SK 58945 [DDD]
Ligeti, G.:Con for 13 Instrs *(rec Apr. 8–9, 1992)* — Sony Classical ▲ SK 58945 [DDD]
Ligeti, G.:Con Pno, w. U. Wiget (pno) *(rec Aug. 4–5, 1990)* — Sony Classical ▲ SK 58945 [DDD]

H. K. Gruber (cnd)

Antheil, G.:Music of, w. Martyn Hill (ten), Jagdish Mistry (vn), Hermann Kretzschmar (pno)—Printemps I; Ballet mécanique; Fighting the Waves; A Jazz Symphony; Lithuanian Night; Jazz Sonata; Concerto for CO; Son 1 Vn; Printemps II *(rec Frankfurt, Germany, June 27–30 & Dec 20–23, 1)* — RCA Red Seal ▲ 09026-68066-2 [DDD]
Weill, K.:Songs, w. R. Hardy (sop), H. Gruber (sgr)—Berlin im Licht; Slow Fox and Algi-Song; Klopslied; Ach, wär mein Lieb ein brünnlein Kalt; Frauentanz, Op. 10; Bastille Musik; Ol-Musik; Suite panaméenne; Cowboy Song; Captain Valentine's Song; Die stille Stadt — Largo ▲ 5114 [DDD]

H. W. Henze (cnd)

Henze, H.-W.:An eine Äolsharfe, w. David Tanenbaum (gtr) — Ars Musici ▲ 0859
Henze, H.-W.:Le Miracle de la rose, w. Hans Deinzer (cl) — Ars Musici ▲ 0859

H. Holliger (cnd)

Holliger, H.:Scardanelli-Zyklus, w. A. Nicolet (fl), London Voices — ECM New Series 2–▲ 78118-21472-2 [DDD]

I. Metzmacher (cnd)

Cage, J.:Dances (16) Fl — RCA Red Seal ▲ 09026-61574-2
Cage, J.:Sixteen Dances — RCA Red Seal ▲ 09026-61574-2
Henze, H.-W.:Requiem, w. U. Wiget (pno), H. Hardenberger (tpt) *(rec Sept. 11, 1993)* — Sony Classical ▲ SK 58972 [DDD]
Ives, C.:Orchestral Music—Tone roads No. 1; From the Steeples and the Mountains; Tone roads No. 3; Adagio sostenuto (at sea); Mists; The rainbow (so may it be!); The pond (Remembrance); The gong on the hook and ladder (firemen's parade on Main Street); All the way around and back; Over the pavements; Sunrise — EMI Classics ▲ CDC 54552 [DDD]
Ives, C.:Set 1 — EMI Classics ▲ CDC 54552 [DDD]
Ives, C.:Set 2—Nos. 1 & 2 — EMI Classics ▲ CDC 54552 [DDD]
Ives, C.:Set Theatre or Chamber Orch — EMI Classics ▲ CDC 54552 [DDD]
Ives, C.:Songs, w. H. Herford (bar)—General W. Booth enters into heaven; On the antipodes; The Bells of Yale (Battell Chimes or Chapel Chimes); Aeschylus and Sophocles; Sunrise — EMI Classics ▲ CDC 54552 [DDD]
Mason, B.:Realistic Virelais, w. C. Whittlesey (sop) — Bridge ▲ BCD 9045 [DDD]
Mason, B.:Self-Reverential Songs, w. C. Whittlesey (sop) — Bridge ▲ BCD 9045 [DDD]
Nancarrow, C.:Piece 2 *(rec Studio I, Hessian Radio, Frankfurt, Feb 18–22 & Apr 14, 1992)* — RCA Red Seal ▲ 09026-61180-2 [DDD]
Nancarrow, C.:Sarabande *(rec Studio I, Hessian Radio, Frankfurt, Feb 18–22 & Apr 14, 1992)* — RCA Red Seal ▲ 09026-61180-2 [DDD]
Nancarrow, C.:Studies—Nos. 1, 2, 3c, 5, 6, 7, 9, 12, 14, 18, 19 [arr. Yvar Mikhashoff] *(rec Studio I, Hessian Radio, Frankfurt, Feb 18–22 & Apr 14, 1992)* — RCA Red Seal ▲ 09026-61180-2 [DDD]
Nancarrow, C.:Tango [arr. Yvar Mikhashoff] *(rec Studio I, Hessian Radio, Frankfurt, Feb 18–22 & Apr 14, 1992)* — RCA Red Seal ▲ 09026-61180-2 [DDD]
Nancarrow, C.:Toccata Vn [arr. Yvar Mikhashoff] *(rec Studio I, Hessian Radio, Frankfurt, Feb 18–22 & Apr 14, 1992)* — RCA Red Seal ▲ 09026-61180-2 [DDD]
Nancarrow, C.:Trio Cl *(rec Studio I, Hessian Radio, Frankfurt, Feb 18–22 & Apr 14, 1992)* — RCA Red Seal ▲ 09026-61180-2 [DDD]

P. Rundel (cnd)

Goebbels, H.:Befreiung, w. C. Anders (spkr) *(rec May 1992)* — ECM New Series ("New" series) ▲ 78118-21483-2 [DDD]
Goebbels, H.:Herakles 2 *(rec May 1992)* — ECM New Series ("New" series) ▲ 78118-21483-2 [DDD]
Goebbels, H.:La Jalousie (Noises from a Novel), w. F. Ollu (nar) *(rec May 1992)* — ECM New Series ("New" series) ▲ 78118-21483-2 [DDD]
Goebbels, H.:Red Run *(rec May 1992)* — ECM New Series ("New" series) ▲ 78118-21483-2 [DDD]

H. Zender (cnd)

Fervers, A.:Einfarbig Gebündelt — Accord ▲ ACD 205552 [DDD]
Schubert, Franz:Winterreise, w. Hans Peter Blochwitz (ten) [arr. Zender] *(rec Hessian Radio, Aug. 1–5, 1994)* — RCA Red Seal ▲ 09026-68067-2 [DDD]
Zimmermann, B.A.:Antiphonen, w. Tabea Zimmermann (va) *(rec Frankfurt, May 1–4 & Oct 24–25, 1992)* — RCA Red Seal ▲ 09026-61181-2 [DDD]
Zimmermann, B.A.:Omnia tempus habent, w. Julie Moffat (sop) *(rec Frankfurt, May 1–4 & Oct 24–25, 1992)* — RCA Red Seal ▲ 09026-61181-2 [DDD]

Ensemble 9

Dresher, P.:Casa Vecchia, w. Yuki Morimoto *(rec Vienna, 1994)* — Starkland ▲ ST 204

Ensemble 1971

O.G. Blarr (cnd)

Stravinsky, I.:Cant Sop, w. R. Yakar (sop), M. LeCocq (ten) [E] — Koch Schwann ▲ CD 313 050 [ADD]
Stravinsky, I.:Choral Music, w. John Alldis (cnd), John Alldis Choir—eleven various a cappella & vocal-instrumental works, sung in English, Latin & Russian:Introitus T.S. Eliot in memoriam (1965); Pater noster (1926); Ave Maria (1934); Credo (1932); Elegy for J.F.K. (1964); In memoriam Dylan Thomas (1954); Tres sacrae cantiones di Gesualdo (1960); Anthem (1962); Pastorale — Koch Schwann ▲ CD 313 050 [ADD]

Ensemble of the Fourteenth Century

J. G. Griffiths (cnd)

The Music of the 14th Century, Vol. 1:Two Gentlemen of Verona — Move ▲ MD 3091 [DDD]
The Music of the 14th Century, Vol. 2:Every Delight & Fair Pleasure — Move ▲ MD 3092 [DDD]

Ensemble Sax

Escribano, M.:Jondo — RNE/Spanish National Radio ▲ M3/12 [ADD]

Ensemble 13

Rihm, W.:Music for 3 — CPO ▲ CPO 999050-2 [DDD]

M. Reichert (cnd)

Cage, J.:Thirteen — CPO ▲ CPO 999227 [DDD]
Rihm, W.:Kein Firmament — CPO ▲ CPO 999134-2 [DDD]
Rihm, W.:Sine Nomine — CPO ▲ CPO 999134-2 [DDD]

Ensemble 21

A. Weisberg (cnd)

Messiaen, O.:Et expecto resurrectionem mortuorum — Summit ▲ DCD 122 [DDD]
Revueltas, S.:Homenaje a Federico García Lorca — Summit ▲ DCD 122 [DDD]
Ruggles, C.:Angels — Summit ▲ DCD 122 [DDD]
Tower, J.:Breakfast Rhythms, w. R. Spring (cl) — Summit ▲ DCD 124 [DDD]

Ensemble 2E2M

P. Méfano (cnd)

Barraqué, J.:Con Cl, w. Rémi Lerner (cl) — Musique d'Abord ▲ HMA 1905199
Barraqué, J.:Le temps restitué, w. Anne Bartelloni (mez) — Musique d'Abord ▲ HMA 1905199
Donatoni, F.:Alamari — Accord ▲ ACD 242122 [DDD]
Donatoni, F.:Ave — Accord ▲ ACD 242122 [DDD]
Donatoni, F.:Flag — Accord ▲ ACD 242122 [DDD]
Donatoni, F.:Music of—Lumen; De près; L'ultima sera; Fili; Le ruisseau su 'escalier; Feria; Still — Adda ▲ ADD 581143 [DDD]
Donatoni, F.:Nidi — Accord ▲ ACD 242122 [DDD]
Donatoni, F.:Toy — Accord ▲ ACD 242122 [DDD]
Kagel, M.:Music of, w. Lyon Orch, Lyon National Chorus—Vox Humana?; Finale; Fürst Igor, Stravinsky — Accord ▲ ACD 201262 [DDD]
Milhaud, D.:Ani maamin, un chant perdu et retrouvé, w. Sharon Cooper (sop—la Voix), Anna Parus (mez), Bernard Freyd (nar—Isaac), Michel Hermon (nar—le Récitant), Michael Lonsdale (nar—Abraham), Jean Négroni (nar—Jacob), Madrigal de Bordeaux — Arion ▲ ARN 68275 [DDD]
Solbiati, A.:Nel Deserto — Adda ▲ ADD 581237 [DDD]
Yun, I.:Con Fl, w. Pierre-Yves Artaud (fl) — Adda ▲ ADD 581166 [DDD]
Yun, I.:Octet Cl — Adda ▲ ADD 581166 [DDD]

Eos Ensemble

Cage, J.:Credo in Us *(rec New York City, July 1996)* — Catalyst ▲ 09026-68751-2 [DDD]
Cage, J.:The Seasons *(rec New York City, July 1996)* — Catalyst ▲ 09026-68751-2 [DDD]
Feldman, Morton:Ixion *(rec New York City, July 1996)* — Catalyst ▲ 09026-68751-2 [DDD]
Haieff, A.:Princess Zondilda & Her Entourage *(rec New York City, July 1996)* — Catalyst ▲ 09026-68751-2 [DDD]
Harrison, L.:The Open Road *(rec New York City, July 1996)* — Catalyst ▲ 09026-68751-2 [DDD]

J. Sheffer (cnd)

Bowles, P.:Con for 2 Pnos, w. Alan Feinberg (pno), Leslie Stifelman (pno) *(rec Manhattan Center Studios, New York, Sept 22 & 23, 1995)* — Catalyst ▲ 09026-68409-2 [DDD]
Bowles, P.:Pastorela (sels) *(rec Manhattan Center Studios, New York, Sept 22 & 23, 1995)* — Catalyst ▲ 09026-68409-2 [DDD]
Bowles, P.:Secret Words, w. Kurt Ollmann (bar) *(rec Manhattan Center Studios, New York, Sept 22 & 23, 1995)* — Catalyst ▲ 09026-68409-2 [DDD]
Bowles, P.:Suite *(rec Manhattan Center Studios, New York, Sept 22 & 23, 1995)* — Catalyst ▲ 09026-68409-2 [DDD]
Bowles, P.:The Wind Remains, w. Lucy Schaufer (mez), Carl Halvorson (ten) *(rec Manhattan Center Studios, New York, Sept 22 & 23, 1995)* — Catalyst ▲ 09026-68409-2 [DDD]

Episteme

W. H. Curry (cnd)

Davis, A.:X, The Life & Times of Malcolm X, w. Priscilla Baskerville (sop), Hilda Harris (mez), Thomas J. Young (ten), Eugene Perry (bar—Malcolm), Herbert Perry (bass), Orch of St. Luke [E] — Gramavision 2–▲ R2-79470 [DDD]

Epsilon Brass Ensemble

Musique Française pour quintette de cuivres et harmonie, w. Republican Guard Orch of Harmony [cnd:Roger Boutry] — Forlane ▲ FOR 16646 [DDD]

Equale Brass

Arnold, M.:Qnt Brass — Nimbus ▲ NIM 5004
Bartók, B.:For Children [arr. Christopher Sears]—5 sels. — Nimbus ▲ NI 5004
Couperin, F.:Pièces de clavecin (sels)—3 selections, arr. by John Wallace — Nimbus ▲ NI 5004
Poulenc, F.:Pno Music (misc) [arr. for brass by John Jenkins]—4 pieces — Nimbus ▲ NI 5004
Warlock, P.:Capriol Suite — Nimbus ▲ NI 5004

Erasmus Quartet

Finzi, A.:Qt Strs — Nuova Era ▲ NUO 7249

Erato String Quartet [E. Haudenschild (vn), A. Adámska (vn), H. Haudenschild (va), E. Kostyák (vc)]

Glass, Paul:Qt 1 Strs *(rec Schweizer Radio DRS 2, June 27, 1991)* — Grammont ▲ CTSP 43 [AAD]
Honegger, A.:Qts Strs — Ermitage ▲ ERM 411
Scherchen, H.:Qt Strs — Relief ▲ CR 900013

De Ereprijs Orch

W. Megens (cnd)

Meijering, Chiel:St. Louis Blues, w. Andrea van Beek (sop), Francine van der Heijden (sop), Jeanette Huizinga (mez), Rein Kolpa (ten), Willem-Jan van Deuveren (ten), John Vredevoldt (ten), Gérard Bernts (bar) [I] *(rec Schouwburg Arnhem, Mar 10, 1995)* — Donemus 2–▲ neos 01–02

Ivan Ericson String Quartet

The String Quartet in Sweden:A Cavalcade of Its History, w. Barkel String Quartet, Stockholm String Quartet, Garaguly String Quartet, Kyndel String Quartet, Grünfarb String Quartet, Skåne String Quartet, Hälsingborg String Quartet, Göteborg String Quartet, Galli Stri *(rec before 1951)* — Caprice 5–▲ CAP 21506 [AAD/ADD]

Erkel CO

Bach, C.P.E.:Con Ob, H.466, w. J. Kiss (ob) *(rec Oct 28–Nov 1, 1991)* — Naxos ▲ 8.550556 [DDD]
Bach, C.P.E.:Con Ob, H.468, w. J. Kiss (ob) *(rec Oct 28–Nov 1, 1991)* — Naxos ▲ 8.550556 [DDD]
Bach, C.P.E.:Son Fl, H.562, w. J. Kiss (ob) [arr for ob] *(rec Oct 28–Nov 1, 1991)* — Naxos ▲ 8.550556 [DDD]
Bach, J.S.:Ov Fl, BWV 1067, w. Laurel Zucker (fl) *(rec Hungaroton Classic Studio)* — Cantilena ▲ C 660092 [DDD]
Marcello, A.:Cons Ob, w. J. Kiss (ob) *(rec Oct. 28–Nov. 1, 1991)* — Naxos ▲ 8.550556 [DDD]
Molter, J.M.:Cons Cl, w. László Horváth (cl)—Nos. 1–5 *(rec 1990)* — Hungaroton ▲ HCD 31370 [DDD]
Mozart, W.A.:Sons Org, w. J. Sebestyén (org), *(cnd unknown) (rec Feb. 15–18, 1991)* — Naxos ▲ 8.550512 [DDD]
Telemann, G.P.:Suite in a Fl, w. Laurel Zucker (fl) *(rec Hungaroton Classic Studio)* — Cantilena ▲ C 660092 [DDD]
Telemann, G.P.:Suite in a Fl, w. Laurel Zucker (fl) *(rec Hungaroton Classic Studio, Budapest)* — Cantilena ▲ 66011-2 [DDD]

Eroica Trio [Adela Peña (pno), Sara Sant'Ambrogio (vn), Erika Nickrenz(vc)]

Dvořák, A.:Slavonic Dances (sels)—Op. 46/2 *(rec Aug. 1992)* — Strings in the Mountains ▲ STM 921
Dvořák, A.:Trio 4 Pno, "Dumky" *(rec Aug. 1992)* — Strings in the Mountains ▲ STM 921
Lalo, E.:Trio 1 Pno *(rec Aug. 1992)* — Strings in the Mountains ▲ STM 921

Erwartung Ensemble

Lecocq, C.:Songs, w. Michèle Lagrange (sop)—Le renard et les raisins; Le corbeau et le renard; La gernouille qui veut se faire plus grosse que le boeuf; Le loup et l'agneau; La cigale et la fourmi; Le savetier et le financier; La chauve-souris et les deux belettes — Accord ▲ ACD 205222 [DDD]
Offenbach, J.:Songs, w. Michèle Lagrange (sop)—Le berger et la mer; La laitière et le pot au lait; Le corbeau et le renard; La cigale et la fourmi; Le rat de ville et le rat des champs; Le savetier et le financier — Accord ▲ ACD 205222 [DDD]
Saint-Saëns, C.:Songs, w. M. Lagrange (sop)—La cigale et la fourmi — Accord ▲ ACD 205222 [DDD]

B. Desgraupes (cnd)

Clásicos de las Américas, w. Margot Pares-Reyna (sop), Marcel Quillevéré (ten), Jesús Castro Balbi (gtr), Noël Lee (pno), Georges Rabol (pno), Jazzogène Orch [cnd:Jean-Luc Fillon] — Opus 111 6–▲ 2000
Escaich, T.:Antiennes oubliées — Chamade ▲ CHCD 5638 [DDD]
Honegger, A.:Poésies, w. Florence Katz (mez) *(rec L'Opéra Comique, Paris, Dec 1989 & May 1990)* — Marco Polo ▲ 8.223788 [DDD]
Ibert, J.:Capriccio — Adda ▲ ADD 581263 [DDD]

ORCH. & ENS.

Erwartung Ensemble (cont.)
B. Desgraupes (cnd) (cont.)
Ibert, J.:Concertino da camera, w. Daniel Gremelle (a sax) — Adda ▲ ADD 581263 [DDD]
Ibert, J.:Con Vc, w. Sonia Wieder-Atherton (vc) — Adda ▲ ADD 581263 [DDD]
Ibert, J.:Le Jardinier de Samos (suite) — Adda ▲ ADD 581263 [DDD]
Ibert, J.:Pièces brèves — Adda ▲ ADD 581263 [DDD]
Jolivet, A.:Ballet des étoiles — Adda ▲ ADD 581171 [DDD]
Jolivet, A.:Poèmes pour l'enfant — Adda ▲ ADD 581171 [DDD]
Jolivet, A.:Suite delphique — Adda ▲ ADD 581171 [DDD]
Jolivet, A.:Suite liturgique — Adda ▲ ADD 581171 [DDD]
Milhaud, D.:Machines agricoles, w. Florence Katz (sop) *(rec L'Opéra Comique, Paris, Dec 1989 & May 1990)* — Marco Polo ▲ 8.223788 [DDD]
Esbjerg Ensemble
Barber, S.:Summer Music — Kontrapunkt ▲ 32002 [DDD]
Cage, J.:Music for Ww — Kontrapunkt ▲ 32002 [DDD]
Fine, I.:Partita Ww — Kontrapunkt ▲ 32002 [DDD]
Knussen, O.:Little Fants — Kontrapunkt ▲ 32002 [DDD]
Nielsen, C.:Qnt Ww — Kontrapunkt ▲ 32002 [DDD]
F. Vistisen (cnd)
Nielsen, T.:Opera Fragments — Point ▲ PCD 5089
Espoo CO
J. Lamminmäki (cnd)
Sibelius, J.:Humoresques, w. L. Kavakos (vn) *(rec May–June 1989)* — Finlandia ▲ 4509-95859-2 [DDD]
Sibelius, J.:Pelléas et Mélisande, w. L. Kavakos (vn)—Suite *(rec May–June 1989)* — Finlandia ▲ 4509-95859-2 [DDD]
P. Pohjola (cnd)
Rautavaara, E.:Children's Mass, w. E. Pohjola (cnd), Tapiola Children's Choir *(rec Nov. 25, 1977)* — BIS ▲ CD 66 [AAD]
Esprit Orch
A. Pauk (cnd)
Aitken, R.:Berceuse (For Those Who Sleep Before Us), w. Robert Aitken (fl) *(rec Studioasis, Toronto, Apr 10–11, 1995)* — CBC ("SM 5000" series) ▲ SM5 5154 [DDD]
Anhalt, I.:Sparkskraps *(rec Mar. 12 & 13, 1992)* — CBC ("SM 5000" series) ▲ SMCD 5132 [DDD]
Chan Ka Nin:Ecstasy — CBC ("SM 5000" series) ▲ SMCD 5101 [DDD]
Cherney, B.:Into the Distant Stillness... — CBC ("SM 5000" series) ▲ SMCD 5101 [DDD]
Dusatko, T.:Traces of Becoming — CBC ("SM 5000" series) ▲ SMCD 5101 [DDD]
The Esprit Orchestra [of Toronto]:Play Orchestral Works by Canadian Composers — CBC Records ("SM 5000" series) ▲ SMCD 5101 [DDD]
Freedman, H.:Graphic IV, "Town" *(rec Mar. 12 & 13, 1992)* — CBC ("SM 5000" series) ▲ SMCD 5132 [DDD]
Freedman, H.:Touchings, Nexus *(rec Studioasis, Toronto, Apr 10–11, 1995)* — CBC ("SM 5000" series) ▲ SM5 5154 [DDD]
Harman, C.P.:Iridescence *(rec Mar. 12 & 13, 1992)* — CBC ("SM 5000" series) ▲ SMCD 5132 [DDD]
Louie, A.:Music for Heaven & Earth *(rec Studioasis, Toronto, Apr 10–11, 1995)* — CBC ("SM 5000" series) ▲ SM5 5154 [DDD]
McPhee, C.:Nocturne *(rec Studioasis, Toronto, Apr 10–11, 1995)* — CBC ("SM 5000" series) ▲ SM5 5154 [DDD]
Pauk, A.:Cosmos *(rec Mar. 12 & 13, 1992)* — CBC ("SM 5000" series) ▲ SMCD 5132 [DDD]
Pauk, A.:Echo Spirit Isle — CBC ("SM 5000" series) ▲ SMCD 5101 [DDD]
Schafer, R.M.:Dream Rainbow Dream Thunder — CBC ("SM 5000" series) ▲ SMCD 5101 [DDD]
Schafer, R.M.:Scorpius *(rec Mar. 12 & 13, 1992)* — CBC ("SM 5000" series) ▲ SMCD 5132 [DDD]
Essen CO
G. Knüsel (cnd)
Romberg, A.:Der Lied von der Glocke, w. M. Friesenhausen (sop), R. Naber (alt), H. Hopfner (ten), K. Ridderbusch (bass), Duisburg State Concert Chorus — Calig ▲ CAL 50942
Essential Music
Russell, W.:Music of—Prelude, Chorale & Fugue (1932; rev. 1985); 4 Dance Movements (1933; rev. 1990); 3 Cuban Pieces (1935); Trumpet Con. (1937; rev. 1990); Chicago Scketches (1940); March Suite (1936; rev. 1984); Obou Badagri [a ballet based on voodoo rites] (1933); Made in America (1936; rev. 1990) — Mode ▲ 34
Essex String Quartet
Samuel, G.:Qt 2 Strs *(rec Corbett Auditorium, College-Conservatory of Music, Univ. of Cincinnati, OH, Feb 21, 1994)* — Centaur ▲ CRC 2238 [DDD]
Essex Winds Woodwind Quintet [Jean-François Rompré (fl), Geralyn Giovannetti (ob), Blake Stephenson (cl), Anne Marie Monaco (hn), Leslie Magowan (bn)]
Forsyth, M.:Qnt Ww *(rec Banff Centre Recording Studio, Alberta & L.A. East Studios, Salt Lake City, 1992 & 1993)* — Centrediscs ▲ CMC 5595 [DDD]
Freedman, H.:Qnt Ww *(rec Banff Centre Recording Studio, Alberta & L.A. East Studios, Salt Lake City, 1992 & 1993)* — Centrediscs ▲ CMC 5595 [DDD]
Hétu, J.:Qnt Winds *(rec Banff Centre Recording Studio, Alberta & L.A. East Studios, Salt Lake City, 1992 & 1993)* — Centrediscs ▲ CMC 5595 [DDD]
Kenins, T.:Vars on a Theme of Schubert *(rec Banff Centre Recording Studio, Alberta & L.A. East Studios, Salt Lake City, 1992 & 1993)* — Centrediscs ▲ CMC 5595 [DDD]
Estampie
A Chantar:Songs of Women—Courtly Love in the Middle Ages — Christophorus ▲ CD 74583 [DDD]
Crusaders In Nomine Domini — Christophorus ▲ 77183
With Dances & Delight:16th Century Music from England & Abroad — Meridian ▲ 84170
Estampie [M. Popp (ud/fl/shawm/fid), E. Schwindl (portative/organistum/hurdy-gurdy/bells), J. Bengen (perc/santouri), A. Gürke (fid), M.-K. Melnitzky (hp), T. Schlierf (fid/shawm)]
M. Popp (cnd)
Popp, M.:Ludus Danielis, w. T. Schlierf (spkr), A. Veljanov (spkr), P. Pöppel (sgr), S. Hausen (sgr) *(rec Jan. 1–10, 1993)* — Christophorus ▲ 77144 [DDD]
Esterházy Orch
D. Blum (cnd)
Haydn, J.:Sym 60, "Il Distratto" *(rec 1963)* — Vanguard Classics ("Everyman" series) ▲ OVC 5000 [ADD]
Haydn, J.:Sym 70 *(rec 1966)* — Vanguard Classics ("Everyman" series) ▲ OVC 5000 [ADD]
Haydn, J.:Sym 81 *(rec 1965)* — Vanguard Classics ("Everyman" series) ▲ OVC 5000 [ADD]
Nicolaus Esterházy Sinfonia
K. Berkes (cnd)
Krommer, F.:Con Cl, w. Kálmán Berkes (cl) *(rec Scottish Church, Budapest, July 14–17, 1994)* — Naxos ▲ 8.553178 [DDD]
Krommer, F.:Cons for 2 Cls, w. Kálmán Berkes (cl)—Op. 35 [w. Kaori Tsutsui (cl)]; Op. 91 [w. Tomoko Takashima (cl)] *(rec Scottish Church, Budapest, July 14–17, 1994)* — Naxos ▲ 8.553178 [DDD]
P. Breiner (cnd)
Christmas Goes Baroque II *(rec May 16–19, 1993)* — Naxos ▲ 8.550670 [DDD]
B. Drahos (cnd)
Beethoven, L. van:Ovs—The Consecration of the House, Op. 124 (Die Weihe des Hauses); Name-Day Celebration, Op. 115 (Namensfeier); Leonora, No. 1, Op. 138; Leonora, No. 2, Op. 72; King Stephen, Op. 117 (König Stephen); Music for a Knightly Ballet, WoO1 (Musik zu einem Ritterballett); Trauermarsch (Funeral March) for Leonore Prohaska, Wo0 96/4; Triumphmarsch (Triumphal March) for Tarpeja, WoO 2a *(rec Phoenix Studio, Italian Institute, Budapest, May 4–8, 1995)* — Naxos ▲ 8.553431 [DDD]
Beethoven, L. van:Sym 1 *(rec Italian Institute, Budapest, June 17–20, 1995)* — Naxos ▲ 8.223474 [DDD]
Beethoven, L. van:Sym 6, "Pastorale" *(rec Italian Institute, Budapest, June 17–20, 1995)* — Naxos ▲ 8.223474 [DDD]
Haydn, J.:Syms (comp)—Nos. 97 & 98 *(rec Italian Institute, Budapest, June 6–9, 1994)* — Naxos ▲ 8.550780 [DDD]

Nicolaus Esterházy Sinfonia (cont.)
B. Drahos (cnd) (cont.)
Haydn, J.:Sym 64, "Tempora mutantur" *(rec Budapest, 1993)* — Naxos ▲ 8.550770 [DDD]
Haydn, J.:Sym 69, "Laudon" *(rec May 1993)* — Naxos ▲ 8.550769 [DDD]
Haydn, J.:Sym 72 *(rec Italian Institute, Budapest, June 10–13, 1994)* — Naxos ▲ 8.550797 [DDD]
Haydn, J.:Sym 84, "In Nomine Domini" *(rec Budapest, 1993)* — Naxos ▲ 8.550770 [DDD]
Haydn, J.:Sym 89 *(rec May 1993)* — Naxos ▲ 8.550769 [DDD]
Haydn, J.:Sym 90 *(rec Budapest, 1993)* — Naxos ▲ 8.550770 [DDD]
Haydn, J.:Sym 91 *(rec May 1993)* — Naxos ▲ 8.550769 [DDD]
Haydn, J.:Sym 93 *(rec Italian Institute, Budapest, June 10–13, 1994)* — Naxos ▲ 8.550797 [DDD]
Haydn, J.:Sym 95 *(rec Italian Institute, Budapest, June 10–13, 1994)* — Naxos ▲ 8.550797 [DDD]
Esterházy String Quartet
Boccherini, L.:Qts Strs, G.195–200 — Teldec ("Das alte Werke" series) 2-▲ 95988-2
Willey, J.:Qt 4 Strs — CRI ▲ CD 562 [DDD]
Willey, J.:Qt 5 Strs — CRI ▲ CD 562 [DDD]
Estonian Opera Orch
E. Klas (cnd)
Coloratura Arias, w. Dilbèr (sop) — Ondine ▲ ODE 768 [DDD]
P. Lilje (cnd)
Tubin, E.:Barbara von Tisenhusen, w. H. Raamat (sop), M. Jõgeva (mez), A. Kollo (ten), I. Kuusk (ten), V. Puura (bar), T. Sild (bar), H. Miilberg (bass), U. Kreen (bass) [Estonian] — Ondine 2-▲ ODE 776-2D [DDD]
P. Mägi (cnd)
Tubin, E.:The Parson of Reigi, w. M. Eensalu (sop), Kempe (ten), Maiste (bar), Estonia Opera Company Chorus — Ondine 2-▲ ODE 783-2D [DDD]
Estonian State SO
N. Järvi (cnd)
Tobias, R.:Des Jonah Sendung, w. Pille Lill (sop), Urve Tauts (mez), Peter Svensson (ten), Raimo Laukka (bar), Mati Palm (bass), Ines Maidre (org), Oratorio Choir, Estonian Phil Chamber Choir, Tallinn Boys' Choir *(rec Estonia Concert Hall, Tallinn, Estonia, June 23–29, 1995)* — BIS 2-▲ CD 731/732 [DDD]
A. Volmer (cnd)
Beethoven, L. van:Con Vn, Op. 61, w. Mark Lubotsky (vn) [1st movt cadenza by A. Schnittke] *(rec Tallinn, Estonia, Mar 1996)* — Globe ▲ GLO 5155 [DDD]
Beethoven, L. van:Romances Vn, w. Mark Lubotsky (vn) *(rec Tallinn, Estonia, Mar 1996)* — Globe ▲ GLO 5155 [DDD]
Raid, K.:Sym 2 — Koch International Classics ▲ KIC 7291 [DDD]
Tubin, E.:Elegy Strs — Koch International Classics ▲ KIC 7291 [DDD]
Tubin, E.:Sym 11 — Koch International Classics ▲ KIC 7291 [DDD]
Estonian SO
N. Järvi (cnd)
Dvořák, A.:Con Vc, w. D. Shafran (vc) *(rec 1978)* — Multisonic (Russian Treasure) ▲ 31 0180
E. Klas (cnd)
Opera Arias, w. Jorma Hynninen (bar) — Ondine ▲ ODE 731 [DDD]
P. Lilje (cnd)
Englund, S.E.:Sym 1 — Ondine ▲ ODE 751-2 [DDD]
Englund, S.E.:Sym 2 — Ondine ▲ ODE 751-2 [DDD]
L'Estro Armonico
Felder, A.:Ballade, w. Felder (vc) — Gallo ▲ CD 493
Valmond, J.:Con Vn, w. Valmond (vn) — Gallo ▲ CD 493
D. Solomons (cnd)
Haydn, J.:Sym 42 — CBS 3-▲ M3K 39685 [DDD]
Haydn, J.:Sym 45, "Farewell" — CBS 3-▲ M3K 39685 [DDD]
Haydn, J.:Sym 46 — CBS 3-▲ M3K 39685 [DDD]
Haydn, J.:Sym 47 — CBS 3-▲ M3K 39685 [DDD]
Haydn, J.:Sym 51 — CBS 3-▲ M3K 39685 [DDD]
Haydn, J.:Sym 65 — CBS 3-▲ M3K 39685 [DDD]
Eufonia
A. de Marchi (cnd)
Jommelli, N.:La Passione di Gesù Cristo, w. Debora Beronesi (sop), Anke Herrmann (sgr), Jeffrey Francis (ten), Maurizio Picconi (sgr), Berlin Baroque Academy, Sigismondo D'India *(rec Mar 31–Apr 4, 1996)* — K617 2-▲ 7063 [DDD]
Euler String Quartet [Mariann Häberli (vn), Gerd Uwe Klein (vn), Daniel Corti (va), David Lauri (vc)]
Streiff, P.:Wandelne Gänge *(rec Apr. 27, 1991)* — Jecklin ▲ JS 283-2 [ADD]
Wehrli, W.:Qt Strs, Op. 8 *(rec 1992)* — Jecklin ▲ JS 301-2 [ADD]
Wehrli, W.:Qt Strs, Op. 8 *(rec 1992)* — Jecklin ▲ VMM 3027 [ADD]
Wehrli, W.:Qt Strs, Op. 37 *(rec 1992)* — Jecklin ▲ JS 301-2 [ADD]
Europa Galante
Boccherini, L.:Qnts Strs—Quintets in D & g; Quintet from Op. 11, "Bird Sanctuary" — Opus 111 ▲ OPS 3082
Festa Italiana, w. Barbara Schlick (sop), Fabio Biondi (vn), Pascal Monteilhet (va), Maurizio Naddeo (vc), Rinaldo Alessandrini (hpd), Concerto Italiano — Opus 111 5-▲ 2001
Vivaldi, A.:Cons Vn, Op. 8/1–4, "The Four Seasons", w. F. Biondi (vn) — Opus 111 ▲ OPS 56-9120
R. Alessandrini (cnd)
Scarlatti, A.:Cain, the First Murder, w. F. Bondi (sgr), Concerto Italiano — Opus 111 2-▲ OPS 30-75/76
F. Biondi (cnd)
Boccherini, L.:Trios Vn, G.107–112 [period instrs] — Opus 111 ▲ OPS 41-9105
Corelli, A.:Concerti grossi, Op. 6—Vol. II, Nos. 7–12 — Opus 111 ▲ OPS 30155
Corelli, A.:Concerti grossi, Op. 6 — Opus 111 ▲ OPS 30-147
Handel, G.F.:Poro, Rè dell'Indie, w. Rossana Bertini (sop), Gloria Banditelli (cta), Bernarda Fink (cta), Gérard Lesne (ct) — Opus 111 3-▲ OPS 30-113/15
Leo, L.:Salve Regina, w. Barbara Schlick (sop) — Opus 111 ▲ OPS 30-88
Pergolesi, G.B.:Salve regina in a, w. B. Schlick (sop) — Opus 111 ▲ OPS 30-88
Pergolesi, G.B.:Salve regina in d, w. B. Schlick (sop) — Opus 111 ▲ OPS 30-88
Pergolesi, G.B.:Sons—Sons. in B♭ & G — Opus 111 ▲ OPS 30-88
Scarlatti, A.:Humanità e Lucifero, w. Rossana Bertini (sop), Massimo Crispi (ten) — Opus 111 ▲ OPS 30-129
Scarlatti, A.:Santa Maria Maddalena de'pazzi, w. R. Bertini (sop), Sylvia Piccollo (sop), G. Bandittelli (mez) — Opus 111 ▲ OPS 30-96
Vivaldi, A.:Cons Vc, w. M. Naddeo (vc)—RV.407 *(rec Apr. 1993)* — Opus 111 ▲ OPS 3086 [DDD]
Vivaldi, A.:Con for 2 Vcs, w. M. Naddeo (vc), A. Fantinuoli (vc) *(rec Apr. 1993)* — Opus 111 ▲ OPS 3086 [DDD]
Vivaldi, A.:Cons Diverse Instrs—RV 133; 281; 286; 407; 511; 531; 541 — Opus 111 ▲ OPS 30861
Vivaldi, A.:Cons Orch—7 Concerti for Strings—RV.129,130,169,202,517,547 & 761 — Opus 111 ▲ OPS 30-9004
Vivaldi, A.:Cons Orch—RV.133 *(rec Apr. 1993)* — Opus 111 ▲ OPS 3086 [DDD]
Vivaldi, A.:Cons Vn (misc), w. F. Biondi (vn)—RV.281 & 286 *(rec Apr. 1993)* — Opus 111 ▲ OPS 3086 [DDD]
Vivaldi, A.:Cons Vn Org, w. F. Biondi (vn), R. Alessandrini (org)—RV.541 *(rec Apr. 1993)* — Opus 111 ▲ OPS 3086 [DDD]
Vivaldi, A.:Cons for 2 Vns, w. F. Biondi (vn), F. Cipriani (vn)—RV.511 *(rec Apr. 1993)* — Opus 111 ▲ OPS 3086 [DDD]
F. Galante (cnd)
Locatelli, P.:Concerti grossi—Nos. 2, 5 & 12 — Opus 111 ▲ OPS 30-104
Locatelli, P.:Il pianto d'Arianna — Opus 111 ▲ OPS 30-104
Locatelli, P.:Sinf funebre composta per l'esequie della sua donna — Opus 111 ▲ OPS 30-104
Europa Galante [Fabio Biondi (vn), Maurizio Naddeo (vc), Rinaldo Alessandrini (hpd)]
Vivaldi, A.:Sons Vn—RV 5, 15, 26, 28, 34; plus Sarabande in C — Opus 111 ▲ OPS 30154
European Baroque Soloists
Telemann, G.P.:Canonic Sons [arr. for flute & oboe] *(rec 8/90)* — Denon ▲ CO 77614 [DDD]

European Baroque Soloists (cont.)
Telemann, G.P.:Con in G Fl, Ob d'amore *(rec 8/90)* Denon ▲ CO 77614 [DDD]
Telemann, G.P.:Qt Bn—Nos. 1-6 & Quartet in d from Tafelmusik II *(rec 8/90)* Denon ▲ CO 77613 [DDD]
Telemann, G.P.:Suite in b Fl [arr. for flute, oboe, bassoon & basson cont.] *(rec 8/90)* Denon ▲ CO 77614-2 [DDD]
G. Schmidt-Gaden (cnd)
Mozart, W.A.:Ave verum corpus, w. Tölz Boys' Choir [L] Sony Classical ("Vivarte" series) ▲ SK 46493
Mozart, W.A.:Inter natos mulierum, w. Tölz Boys' Choir [L] Sony Classical ("Vivarte" series) ▲ SK 46493
Mozart, W.A.:Missa [longa], K.262, w. Tölz Boys' Choir [L] Sony Classical ("Vivarte" series) ▲ SK 46493
Mozart, W.A.:Regina coeli, K.276, w. Tölz Boys' Choir [L] Sony Classical ("Vivarte" series) ▲ SK 46493
Mozart, W.A.:Te Deum, w. Tölz Boys' Choir [L] Sony Classical ("Vivarte" series) ▲ SK 46493
Mozart, W.A.:Venite populi, w. Tölz Boys' Choir [L] Sony Classical ("Vivarte" series) ▲ SK 46493
European Brass Quintet
Brass Meets Brass Pavane ▲ ADW 7294 [DDD]
European Chamber Opera Orch
D. Hinnells (cnd)
Verdi, G.:Il trovatore, w. S. Bisatt (sop), G. Quinn (bar), European Chamber Chorus ASV 2-▲ ASV 225 [DDD]
European CO Per Musica
J. Reynolds (cnd)
Rossini, G.:Vars Cl, w. F. van den Brink (cl) *(rec Aug. 1986)* Globe ▲ GLO 6014 [DDD]
Rossini, G.:Vars Obbligato Instruments, w. F. van den Brink (cl) *(rec Aug. 1986)* Globe ▲ GLO 6014 [DDD]
European Community Baroque Orch
Biber, H. von:Battalia, w. M. Huggett (vn) *(rec Nov. 1991)* Channel Classics ▲ CCS 4392 [DDD]
Vivaldi, A.:Cons Vn (misc), w. M. Huggett (vn)—"Il Grosso Mogul" Concerto, Op. 7 *(rec Nov. 1991)* Channel Classics ▲ CCS 4392 [DDD]
R. Goodman (cnd)
Corbett, W.:Le Bizzarie universali, w. A. Manze (vn), R. Goodman (vn)—9 concerti Channel Classics ▲ CCS 1391 [DDD]
Hellendaal, P.:Concerti grossi, w. Roy Goodman (vn), A. Manze (vn)—complete Channel Classics ▲ CCS 3492 [DDD]
M. Huggett (cnd)
Farina, C.:Capriccio *(rec Nov. 1991)* Channel Classics ▲ CCS 4392 [DDD]
Muffat, G.:Armonico tributo—Son 2 only *(rec Nov. 1991)* Channel Classics ▲ CCS 4392 [DDD]
Schmelzer, J.H.:Balletto a 4, "Fencing School" *(rec Nov. 1991)* Channel Classics ▲ CCS 4392 [DDD]
Schmelzer, J.H.:Polish Bagpipes *(rec Nov. 1991)* Channel Classics ▲ CCS 4392 [DDD]
European Community CO
E. Aadland (cnd)
Albinoni, T.:Cons Obs—in G for 2 Obs, Op. 9/6 IMP ("Classics" series) ▲ IMP 6700222
Albinoni, T.:Cons à 5 Obs, Op. 9—No. 6 *(rec Apr & Oct 1991)* IMP Classics ▲ PCD 993 [DDD]
Bach, J.S.:Con 1 Hpd, w. O. Maione (pno) *(rec Oct 1990)* IMP Classics ▲ PCD 964 [DDD]
Barber, S.:Adagio Strs *(rec July 1991)* IMP Classics ▲ PCD 1001 [DDD]
Barber, S.:Adagio Strs IMP ▲ IMP 2044
Bartók, B.:Romanian Folk Dances Pno IMP ▲ IMP 2044
Bartók, B.:Romanian Folk Dances Pno *(rec July 1991)* IMP Classics ▲ PCD 1001 [DDD]
Britten, B.:Simple Sym *(rec July 1991)* IMP Classics ▲ PCD 1001 [DDD]
Handel, G.F.:Cants, w. A. Mackay (sop)—"Agrippna condotta a morire," HWV 110 [I] ASV ▲ ASV 766
Handel, G.F.:Ovs—Flavio; Rinaldo ASV ▲ ASV 766
Handel, G.F.:Silete Venti, w. Ann Mackay (sop) [L] ASV ▲ ASV 766
Haydn, J.:Con Org & Strs, H.XVIII/2, w. G. D'Atri (pno) *(rec 8/90)* IMP Classics ▲ PCD 964 [DDD]
Haydn, J.:Sym 28 *(rec 11/89)* IMP Classics ▲ PCD 978 [DDD]
Haydn, J.:Sym 34 *(rec 11/89)* IMP Classics ▲ PCD 978 [DDD]
Haydn, J.:Sym 43, "Mercury" *(rec 11/89)* IMP Classics ▲ PCD 978 [DDD]
Hindemith, P.:Stücke (5) Chamber Ensemble *(rec July 1991)* IMP Classics ▲ PCD 1001 [DDD]
Hindemith, P.:Stücke (5) Str Orch IMP ▲ IMP 2044
Mozart, W.A.:Andante Fl, K.315/285a, w. Giampaolo Pretto (fl) *(rec Rosslyn Hill Chapel, London, Apr 16–19, 1992)* IMP ("Classics" series) ▲ IMP PCD 1107
Mozart, W.A.:Con Bn, w. Sergio Azzolini (bn) IMP ▲ IMP 2047
Mozart, W.A.:Con Bn, w. S. Azzolini (bn) IMP Classics ▲ IMPCD 1054 [DDD]
Mozart, W.A.:Con Cl, w. M. Carulli (cl) IMP Classics ▲ IMPCD 1054 [DDD]
Mozart, W.A.:Con Cl, w. Michele Carulli (cl) IMP ▲ IMP 2047
Mozart, W.A.:Cons Fl, w. Giampaolo Pretto (fl) *(rec Rosslyn Hill Chapel, London, Apr 16–19, 1992)* IMP ("Classics" series) ▲ IMP PCD 1107
Mozart, W.A.:Con Ob, K.314, w. A. Baccini (ob) IMP Classics ▲ IMPCD 1054 [DDD]
Mozart, W.A.:Con Ob, K.314, w. Alessandro Baccini (ob) IMP ▲ IMP 2047
Mozart, W.A.:Con 8 Pno, w. P. Bruni (pno) IMP Classics ▲ PCD 964 [DDD]
Mozart, W.A.:Rondo Fl, K.Anh.184, w. Giampaolo Pretto (fl) *(rec Rosslyn Hill Chapel, London, Apr 16–19, 1992)* IMP ("Classics" series) ▲ IMP PCD 1107
Puccini, G.:Crisantemi IMP ▲ IMP 2044
Puccini, G.:Crisantemi [arr for str orch] *(rec July 1991)* IMP Classics ▲ PCD 1001 [DDD]
Telemann, G.P.:Cons (misc)—Concerto for 2 Horns in D; Concerto for 2 Violas in G IMP Classics ▲ PCD 993 [DDD]
Telemann, G.P.:Con 2 Hns in D IMP ("Classics" series) ▲ IMP 6700222
Telemann, G.P.:Con 2 Vas IMP ("Classics" series) ▲ IMP 6700222
Vivaldi, A.:Cons Diverse Instrs—in C for Pic & Strs, R.444; in d for 2 Obs & Strs, R.535; in D for Fl, Op. 10/3; in D for Gtr & Strs, R.93; in G for Vc & Strs, R.413; in a for Bn & Strs, R.498 IMP ("IMP Classics" series) ▲ IMP 6700882
Vivaldi, A.:Cons Diverse Instrs—5 Concerti—RV.98 (oboe, flute & bassoon); RV.129, 409 (cello & bassoon); RV.540 (viola & guitar); RV.580 (4 violins) IMP Classics ▲ PCD 993 [DDD]
Vivaldi, A.:Cons Diverse Instrs, w. James Johnstone (hpd)—in e for 4 Vns, R.580; for Va & Gtr, R.540; for Vc & Bn, R.409; Il Madrigalesco, R.129; La Tempesta di Mare, R.98 IMP ("Classics" series) ▲ IMP 6700222
Warlock, P.:Capriol Suite IMP ▲ IMP 2044
European Community Youth Orch
J. Judd (cnd)
Shostakovich, D.:Sym 4 *(rec live 1988)* Nuova Era ▲ 6734 [DDD]
European Concerts Orch
P. Crispini (cnd)
Poulenc, F.:Con for 2 Pnos, w. Brigitte Meyer (pno), Alexandre Rabinovitch (pno) Doron ▲ DRC 3022 [DDD]
Poulenc, F.:Gloria Sop, w. Brigette Fournier (sop), Evoe Choir Doron ▲ DRC 3022 [DDD]
Poulenc, F.:Litanies à la vierge noire, w. Evoe Choir Doron ▲ DRC 3022 [DDD]
European SO
A. Dorati (cnd)
Beethoven, L. van:Missa Solemnis, w. T. Kiberg (sop), R. Lang (cta), W. Cochran (ten), M. Krutikov (bass), Univ of Maryland Chorus [L] *(rec live, Berlin Philharmonie, 7/3/88)* BIS 2-▲ CD 406/07 [DDD]
European Winds
G. Brand (cnd)
Franck, C.:Chorals Org, M.38–40 [arr. P. Grainger]—Choral No. 2 Albany ▲ TROY 120 [DDD]
Holst, G.:A Fugal Con, w. J. Harvan (fl), M. Sintal (ob) Albany ▲ TROY 120 [DDD]
Holst, G.:Hammersmith Albany ▲ TROY 120 [DDD]
Ireland, J.:A Downland Suite [arr. Ray Steadman-Allen] Albany ▲ TROY 120 [DDD]
Jacob, G.:Sym AD 78 Albany ▲ TROY 120 [DDD]

Euterpe String Quartet
Enescu, G.:Oct Strs, w. Voces String Quartet Marco Polo ▲ 8.223147
Événements du Neuf
L. Vaillancourt (cnd)
Geugeon, D.:Voix intimes, w. Marie-Danielle Parent (sop), Yolande Parent (sop) *(rec Ottawa, 1983 & 1984)* Centrediscs ▲ CMC 5194 [DDD]
Evergreen Club Gamelan
Duggan, M.:Evocation—Gentle Rain Falling CBC ("Musica Viva" series) ▲ MVCD 1057 [DDD]
Ex Aqueo Trio
Dvořák, A.:Trio 4 Pno, "Dumky" Berlin Classics ▲ BER 2001
Franck, C.:Trios concertants Berlin Classics ▲ BER 2001
Ex Cathedra Baroque Orch
Lalande, M.-R. de:Cantate Domino...quia mirabilia, w. Ex Cathedra Choir ASV ("Gaudeamus" series) ▲ ASV 141 [DDD]
Lalande, M.-R. de:De profundis Orch & Chorus, w. Ex Cathedra Choir ASV ("Gaudeamus" series) ▲ ASV 141 [DDD]
Lalande, M.-R. de:Regina coeli, w. Ex Cathedra Choir ASV ("Gaudeamus" series) ▲ ASV 141 [DDD]
J. Skidmore (cnd)
Sanctus:Baroque Music for the Nativity, w. Ex Cathedra Chamber Choir ASV/Gaudeamus ▲ ASV CD 166
Ex Novo Ensemble
Busoni, F.:Albumblatt Fl Dynamic ▲ CD 81 [DDD]
Busoni, F.:Con Pno, Op. 17 Dynamic ▲ CD 81 [DDD]
Busoni, F.:Divert Fl—[Kurt Weill's flute & piano trans.] Dynamic ▲ CD 81 [DDD]
Busoni, F.:Kleine Suite Vc Dynamic ▲ CD 81 [DDD]
Busoni, F.:Solo Dramatique Cl Dynamic ▲ CD 81 [DDD]
Busoni, F.:Suite Cl Dynamic ▲ CD 81 [DDD]
Casella, A.:Serenata Stradivarius ▲ STR 33312 [DDD]
Donizetti, G.:Chamber Music—Largo in g for Cello & Piano; Flute Son. in C; Violin Son. in F; Studio for Clarinet; Trios in D & E♭ for Violin, Cello & Piano; Trio in F for Flute, Bassoon & Piano; Variations in B♭ for Violin & Piano *(rec 1/82)* Giulia ▲ GS 201018 [DDD]
Martucci, G.:Qnt Pno, w. A. Orvieto (pno) *(rec Dec. 1992)* Dynamic ▲ CD 99 [DDD]
Pizzetti, I.:Trio Pno Stradivarius ▲ STR 33312 [DDD]
Respighi, O.:Qnt Pno, w. A. Orvieto (pno) *(rec Dec. 1992)* Dynamic ▲ CD 99 [DDD]
Respighi, O.:Qnt Ww *(rec Dec. 1992)* Dynamic ▲ CD 99 [DDD]
Rota, N.:Trio Fl Stradivarius ▲ STR 33312 [DDD]
Wolf-Ferrari, E.:Qnt Pno Dynamic ▲ CD 54 [DDD]
Wolf-Ferrari, E.:Sinfonia da camera Dynamic ▲ CD 54 [DDD]
Ex Novo Ensemble members
Rossini, G.:Fant Cl *(rec 1/91)* Giulia ▲ GS 201001 [DDD]
Rossini, G.:Péchés de vieillesse (sels)—Un Mot à Paganini for Violin & Piano; Une larme, Thème et Variations for Cello & Piano *(rec 1/91)* Giulia ▲ GS 201001 [DDD]
Rossini, G.:Serenade Fl *(rec 1/91)* Giulia ▲ GS 201001 [DDD]
Rossini, G.:Theme & Vars Fl *(rec 1/91)* Giulia ▲ GS 201001 [DDD]
Rossini, G.:Theme, Variations & Polacca di Giovacchino Giovacchini *(rec 1/91)* Giulia ▲ GS 201001 [DDD]
Extempore String Ensemble
G. Weigand (cnd)
Byrd, W.:Consort Music—Galliard Meridian ▲ MER 84256
Dowland, J.:Consort Music—John Langton's Pavan & the King of Denmark's Galliard; The Earl of Essex his Galliard Meridian ▲ MER 84256
Holborne, A.:Instrumental Consort Music—Holborne's Almain; The Countess of Pembroke's Paradise; Nowell's Galliard; The Honie Suckle & the Faerie Round; Pavan & Galliard; The Quadro Pavan & Galliard; Muy Linda; Galliard; Heres Patemus; Heigh Ho Holiday; The Wanton Meridian ▲ MER 84256
Philips, P.:Consort Music—Pavana Dolorosa Meridian ▲ MER 84256
Extempore String Ensemble [Robin Jeffrey (thb/lt), Sally Owen (spinet/vl), Rosemary Thorndycraft (vl), William Thorp (vn), George Weigand (lt/mandore/discant mandore/archcittern)]
Byrd, W.:Kbd Music—Monsieur's Alman; The Earl of Salisbury's Pavan; Mr. Byrd's Galliard; Coranto; The Queen's Alman; Pavan & Galliard; Lavolta; The Earl of Oxford's March *(rec Rosalyn Hill Chapel, London, Jan 23–24, 1987)* Musicaphon ▲ M 56805 [DDD]
Dowland, J.:Galliards—Queen Elizabeth's *(rec Rosalyn Hill Chapel, London, Jan 23–24, 1987)* Musicaphon ▲ M 56805 [DDD]
Holborne, A.:Instrumental Consort Music—The Queen's Galliard *(rec Rosalyn Hill Chapel, London, Jan 23–24, 1987)* Musicaphon ▲ M 56805 [DDD]
Morley, T.:Music of—The Lord Sowches Maske *(rec Rosalyn Hill Chapel, London, Jan 23–24, 1987)* Musicaphon ▲ M 56805 [DDD]
Sermisy, C. de:Chansons—Jouissance Vous Donneray *(rec Rosalyn Hill Chapel, London, Jan 23–24, 1987)* Musicaphon ▲ M 56805 [DDD]
Extension Works
Carl, R.:Time/Memory/Shadow Neuma ▲ 450-81
FA Ensemble
Fénelon, P.:Mythologie I:La colère D'Achille *(rec 1993)* Thésis ▲ THC 82057 [DDD]
Fénelon, P.:Mythologie II:Orion *(rec 1993)* Thésis ▲ THC 82057 [DDD]
Fénelon, P.:Mythologie III:Hélios *(rec 1993)* Thésis ▲ THC 82057 [DDD]
Fénelon, P.:Mythologie IV:Ulysse *(rec 1993)* Thésis ▲ THC 82057 [DDD]
D. My (cnd)
Pesson, G.:Music of, w. Donatienne Michel-Dansac (sop), Sandra Roulx (mez), Stuart Patterson (ten), Paul-Alexandre Dubois (bar), Pascal Sausy (bar), Florence Millet (pno), Paris String Quartet—Le gel, par jeu for Fl, Cl, Hn, Bass Mar, Vn & Vc; Qt for Strs; Non Sapremo Mai di Questo Mi for Fl, Vn & Pno; 5 Poèmes de Sandro Penna for Bar, B Cl, Hn, Vn & Vc; La lumière n'a pas de bras pour nous porter for Amplified Pno; La vita è come l'albero di natale for Vn & Pno; Nocturnes en quatuor for Cl, Pno, Vn & Vc; Les chants faëz for Pno & 10 Instrs; Sur-le-champ for 4 Voices & 9 Instrs [from a text by Pierre Alferi] Accord ▲ ACD 204682 [DDD]
Failoni CO
M. Antal (cnd)
Bach, J.S.:Cant 51, w. I. Kertesi (sop), J. Pászthy (sop), J. Nemeth (mez), J. Mukk (ten), I. Gáti (bass), Hungarian Radio Chorus Naxos ▲ 8.550643 [DDD]
Bach, J.S.:Cant 80, w. I. Kertesi (sop), J. Nemeth (alt), J. Mukk (ten), I. Gáti (bass), Hungarian Radio Chorus *(rec Jan 1992)* Naxos ▲ 8.550642 [DDD]
Bach, J.S.:Cant 147, w. I. Kertesi (sop), J. Nemeth (alt), J. Mukk (ten), I. Gáti (bass), Hungarian Radio Chorus *(rec Jan 1992)* Naxos ▲ 8.550642 [DDD]
Bach, J.S.:Cant 208, "Hunting Cant", w. I. Kertesi (sop), J. Pászthy (sop), J. Nemeth (mez), J. Mukk (ten), I. Gáti (bass), Hungarian Radio Chorus Naxos ▲ 8.550643 [DDD]
Bach, J.S.:Cant 211, "Coffee Cant", w. I. Kertesi (sop), J. Mukk (ten), I. Gáti (bass) *(rec 1992)* Naxos ▲ 8.550641 [DDD]
Bach, J.S.:Cant 212, "Peasant Cant", w. I. Kertesi (sop), J. Mukk (ten), I. Gáti (bass) *(rec 1992)* Naxos ▲ 8.550641 [DDD]
W. Humburg (cnd)
Rossini, G.:Il barbiere di Siviglia, w. I. Kertesi (sop—Berta), S. Ganassi (mez—Rosina), R. Vargas (ten—Almaviva), A. Romero (bar—Dr. Bartolo), R. Servile (bar—Figaro), F. de Grandis (bass—Basilio), K. Sárkány (bass—Fiorello), A. Déri (pno), B. Sztankovits (gtr), Hungarian Radio Chorus *(rec Nov. 16–28, 1992)* Naxos 3-▲ 8.660027/29 [DDD]
Nagy, Morandi (cnd)
Vivaldi, A.:Cons Ob, w. S. Schilli (ob), G. Kósa (hpd), J. Kis Domonkos (vc)—RV 447, 451, 455, 457, 461 & 463 *(rec Apr. 1993)* Naxos ▲ 8.550860 [DDD]

ORCH. & ENS.

Failoni CO (cont.)
Nagy, Morandi (cnd) (cont.)
Vivaldi, A.:Cons Ob, w. S. Schilli (ob), D. Jonas (ob), G. Thomas (hpd), G. Kósa (hpd), J. Kis Domonkos (vc)—RV 450, 452, 453, 454, 534, 535 & 536 *(rec Dec. 1992)* Naxos ▲ 8.550859 [DDD]
G. Oberfrank (cnd)
Donizetti, G.:Qts Strs [arr. Tamás Benedek as Sinfonias]—Qts. in A, D & d *(rec Sept. 26–30, 1992)* Marco Polo ▲ 8.223577 [DDD]
Failoni Orch
H. Gmür (cnd)
Dittersdorf, K.D. von:Syms (Metamorphoses)—No. 4 in F; No. 5 in A; No. 6 in D *(rec Festetich Castle, Budapest, Apr, 1995)* Naxos ▲ 8.553369 [DDD]
Dittersdorf, K.D. von:Syms (Metamorphoses)—No. 1 in C; No. 2 in D; No. 3 in G *(rec Festetich Castle, Budapest, Apr, 1995)* Naxos ▲ 8.553368 [DDD]
M. Halász (cnd)
Schubert, Franz:Sym 3 *(rec Italian Institute, Budapest, Mar. 1994)* Naxos ▲ 8.553094 [DDD]
Schubert, Franz:Sym 9 *(rec Italian Institute, Budapest, Mar 1994)* Naxos 4–▲ 8.504012 [DDD]
Fairer Sax
Diversions with the Fairer Sax Saydisc ▲ CDSDL 365 [DDD] ■ CSDL 365 (D)
Dubois, P.–M.:Qt Sax Saydisc ▲ CD SDL 365 [DDD] ■ CSDL 365 (D)
Gardner, J.:Qt Sax Saydisc ▲ CD SDL 365 [DDD] ■ CSDL 365 (D)
Harvey, P.:Robert Burns Suite Saydisc ▲ CD SDL 365 [DDD] ■ CSDL 365 (D)
Patterson, P.:Diversions Saydisc ▲ CD SDL 365 [DDD] ■ CSDL 365 (D)
Fairfield Orch
T. Crawford (cnd)
Jarrett, K.:Adagio Ob ECM New Series ▲ 78118–21450–2
Jarrett, K.:Bridge of Light ECM New Series ▲ 78118–21450–2
Jarrett, K.:Elegy Vn & Str Orch ECM New Series ▲ 78118–21450–2
Jarrett, K.:Son Vn, w. K. Jarrett (pno) ECM New Series ▲ 78118–21450–2
J. Welsh (cnd)
Sowerby, L.:Con Org, w. David Mulbury (org) *(rec St. Bartholomew's Church, New York City, May 3–5, 1994)* Marco Polo ▲ 8.223725 [DDD]
Sowerby, L.:Festival Musick, w. Carl Albach (tpt), Susan Radcliff (tpt), Jeffrey Caswell (trbn), Tom Hutchinson (trbn), Dan Haskins (timp), David Mulbury (org) *(rec St. Bartholomew's Church, New York City, May 5, 1994)* Marco Polo ▲ 8.223725 [DDD]
Sowerby, L.:Medieval Poem, w. David Craighead (org) *(rec St. Bartholomew's Church, New York City, May 3–5, 1994)* Marco Polo ▲ 8.223725 [DDD]
Manuel de Falla Orch
N. Rescigno (cnd)
Alfredo Kraus, w. Alfredo Kraus (ten) *(rec Spain, 1975)* Bongiovanni ▲ GB 534
Alfredo Kraus, w. Alfredo Kraus (ten) Bongiovanni ▲ GB 535–2 [ADD]
Alfredo Kraus, w. Alfredo Kraus (ten) Bongiovanni ▲ GB 536–2 [ADD]
Granada, w. Alfredo Kraus (ten) *(rec 1960s)* Bongiovanni ▲ GB 533–2 [ADD]
Falla Trio
Albéniz, I.:Suite española (sels)—Aragon [arr. for 3 guitars] Concord Concerto ■ CC 2011 C (D)
Boyce, W.:Syms, Op. 2—No. 1 [arr for gtrs] Concord Concerto ■ CC 2011–C (D)
Corea, C.:Spain Concord Concerto ■ CC 2011–C (D)
Falla, M. de:El amor brujo (sels)—sels. [arr. for 3 guitars] Concord Concerto ■ CC 2011–C (D)
Falla Trio [Terry Graves (gtr), Dusan Bogdanovic (gtr), Kenton Youngstrom (gtr)]
Falla Guitar Trio Concord Concerto ▲ CCD 42013 [DDD] ■ CC 2013–C (D)
Falu Woodwind Quintet
A. Loguin (cnd)
Blomdahl, K.–B.:Chamber Con, w. Kerstin Jansson (pno), Kroumata (perc), Omnibus Chamber Winds Caprice ▲ CAP 21355 [DDD]
Eliasson, A.:Sotto il segno del sole, Kroumata Percussion Ensemble, Omnibus Chamber Winds Caprice ▲ CAP 21355 [DDD]
Messiaen, O.:Oiseaux exotiques, w. Kerstin Jansson (pno), Kroumata Percussion Ensemble, Omnibus Chamber Winds Caprice ▲ CAP 21355 [DDD]
Fanfare Trumpeters of the Royal Military School of Music
D. Willcocks (cnd)
Family Carols, w. Bach Choir, Graham Ashton Brass Ensemble, John Scott (org) Chandos ▲ CHAN 8973 [DDD]
Fanfare Trumpeters of the Scots Guards
L. Johnson (cnd)
Johnson, Laurie:Music of, w. W. Davies (org), London PO, London Jazz Orch, London Studio SO, Coldstream Guards Regimental Band, London Brass Chorale—Royal Tour (suite); Symphony (Synthesis) for Combined Jazz & Symphony Orchestras (1969); Three Paintings by Lautrec; The Wind In the Willows (1985) *(rec 1969–82)* Unicorn–Kanchana ▲ UKCD 2057 [DDD/ADD]
Far East Side Band [J. K. Hwang (5 str elec vn/elec processing/bird whistles), S.–W. Park (kayagum/ajang/sgr), Y. Tsuji (perc/shakuhachi/sgr)]
Hwang, J.K.:Caverns *(rec New York, Feb. 28, 1993)* New World ▲ 80458–2
Hwang, J.K.:Early Hour Vision *(rec New York, Feb. 28, 1993)* New World ▲ 80458–2
Hwang, J.K.:Memories & Ice *(rec New York, Feb. 28, 1993)* New World ▲ 80458–2
Hwang, J.K.:Palmistry *(rec New York, Feb. 28, 1993)* New World ▲ 80458–2
Hwang, J.K.:Still Water *(rec New York, Feb. 28, 1993)* New World ▲ 80458–2
Robert Farnon Orch
Love Is..., w. José Carreras (ten) Philips ▲ 412270–2 [DDD]
R. Farnon (cnd)
Farnon, R.:Prelude & Dance, w. T. Reilly (hmc) Chandos ▲ CHAN 9248 [DDD]
Farnon, R.:Prelude & Dance, w. T. Reilly (hmc) Chandos ▲ CHAN 9248 [DDD]
Fauré Quintet Rome
Fauré, G.:Qnts Pno & Strs, Opp. 89 & 115 Claves ▲ CD 8603 [DDD]
Fauré Trio [Ottavio Minola (pno), Silvano Minella (vn), Sergio Bonfanti (vc)]
Clementi, M.:Son Pno, Fl & Vc, WoO 6 *(rec Dynamic's, Genova, Italy, 1980)* Dynamic ▲ CDS 19 [ADD]
Clementi, M.:Sons Pno, Fl & Vc, Op. 29/2 & 3 *(rec Dynamic's, Genova, Italy, 1980)* Dynamic ▲ CDS 32 [ADD]
Clementi, M.:Sons Pno, Vn & Vc, Op. 27 *(rec Dynamic's, Genova, Italy, 1980)* Dynamic ▲ CDS 19 [ADD]
Clementi, M.:Sons Pno, Vn & Vc, Op. 29/1 *(rec Dynamic's, Genova, Italy, 1980)* Dynamic ▲ CDS 32 [ADD]
Clementi, M.:Sons Pno, Vn & Vc, Op. 35 *(rec Dynamic's, Genova, Italy, 1980)* Dynamic ▲ CDS 32 [ADD]
Favori Duo [Frank Armbruster (gtr), Barbara Gräsle (gtr)]
Mertz, K.J.:Gtr Music—Deutsche Weise; Der Ball; Ständchen; Am Grabe der Geliebten; Ich denke Dein; Trauermarsch; Tarantelle; Vespergang; Mazurka; Wasserfahrt am Traunsee; Barcarola; Unruhe; Impromptu Tacet ▲ 42
Federal Music Society members
J. Baldoon (cnd)
Bray, J.:The Indian Princess [ed & arr Victor Fell Yellin] New World ▲ 80232–2
Music of the Federal Era New World ▲ 80299–2
Taylor, R.:The Ethiop [ed & arr Victor Fell Yellin] New World ▲ 80232–2
I Fegi Armonici
A. Curtis (cnd)
Gesualdo, D.C.:Madrigals, w. Elena Cecchi Fedi (sop), Roberta Invernizzi (sop), Daniela Del Monaco (cta), Roberto Balconi (ct), Gian Paolo Fagotto (ten), Giuseppe Zambon (ten), Giovanni Dagnino (bass)—Book 6 [Se la Mia Morte Brami; Beltà Poi Che T'Assenti; Tu Piangi O Fille Mia; Resta di Darmi Noia; Chiaro Risplender Suole; others] Symphonia ▲ SYM 94133

La Fenice Ensemble
Gabrieli, G.:Sacred Music, w. E. P. Biggs (org), Edward Tarr Brass Ensemble, Gregg Smith Singers, Texas Boys' Choir—Deus, in nomine tuo; Beata es, virgo Maria; Juilemus singuli; Deus, Deus meus, ad te de luce vigilo; O quam suavis est; Kyrie; Sanctus; Benedictus; Cantate Domino; Domine, exaudi orationem meam; Hodie completi sunt; Magnificat; Surrexit Christus; Nunc dimittis; Jubilate Deo; Intonatio *(rec San Marco, Venice, Sept 14–22, 1967)* Sony Classical ("Essential Classics" series) ▲ SBK 62426 [ADD] ■ SBT 62426
P. Cao (cnd)
Lassus, O. de:Aurora lucis rutilat, w. Ricercar Consort, Namur Chamber Choir *(rec St. Lambert à Mozet, Nov 1994)* Ricercar ▲ 155141
Lassus, O. de:Motets, w. Ricercar Consort, Namur Chamber Choir—Omnes de saba; Da pacem Domine; Timor et tremor; Tui sunt coeli; Surge propera amica mea; Aurora lucis rutilat *(rec St. Lambert à Mozet, Nov 1994)* Ricercar ▲ 155141
Lassus, O. de:Vinum bonum, w. Ricercar Consort, Namur Chamber Choir *(rec St. Lambert à Mozet, Nov 1994)* Ricercar ▲ 155141
La Fenice Ensemble [Jean Tubery (cnt/muet/rcr), Christina Pluhar (triple hp), Matthias Spaeter (archit), Jean–Marc Aymes (org/hpd)]
Lassus, O. de:Motets, w. Françoise Fauche (bass),—Haec quae ter triplici; Suzanne un jour; Susana un jour; Suzanne un giur; Bonjour mon coeu; Bonn jour mon cueur; Mr Buctons galiard; Et d'où venez vous, Madame Lucette Ricercar ▲ 152137
Palestrina, G.:Motets, w. Françoise Fauche (bass)—Io son ferito, ahi lasso; Vestiva i colli; Io son ferito; Ricercar noni toni; Pulchra es amica mea; Vestiva i colli; Pulchra es amica mea Ricercar ▲ 152137
Schein, J.H.:Opella Nova II, w. Cantus Cologne—Mach dich auf, werde Licht, Zion; Magnificat; Warum betrübst du dich, mein Herz; Vater unser, der du bist im Himmel *(rec St. Osdag Church, Mandelsloh, Feb 13–16, 1995)* Deutsche Harmonia Mundi ▲ 05472–77359–2 [DDD]
F. Lasserre (cnd)
Cavalli, P.F.:Vespero della beata Vergine Maria, w. Jean Tubery (hn), Akademia Pierre Verany 2–▲ PVY 796042 [DDD]
Fernseh SO
V. Fedoseyev (cnd)
Tchaikovsky, P.:Eugene Onegin, w. Lidiya Chernikh (sop), Tamara Sinyavskaya (mez), Alexander Vedernikov (bass), Alexander Fedin (sgr), Yuri Mazurok (sgr), USSR SO, Moscow SO Audiophile Classics ("Legacy Collection" series) 2–▲ 101.751
Ferrara Ensemble
Forse che si, forse che no:15th Century Dance Music *(rec Oct. 1989)* Fonti Musicali ▲ FMD 182 [DDD]
Ferro String Quartet [Jonas Lindgård (vn), George Kentros (vn), Magnus Wassenius (va), Kristina Lindgård (vc)]
Wirén, D.:Qt 2 Strs Caprice ▲ CAP 21413
Wirén, D.:Qt 5 Strs Caprice ▲ CAP 21413
Les Festes Galante
Corrette, M.:Carillon ajouté pour la fin de la messe *(rec 1986)* Jecklin–Disco ▲ JD 616–2 [ADD]
Corrette, M.:Cons Comiques—No. 25, Les Sauvages et La Furstemberg *(rec 1986)* Jecklin–Disco ▲ JD 616–2 [ADD]
Corrette, M.:Fants Musette, Op. 6—No. 6 *(rec 1986)* Jecklin–Disco ▲ JD 616–2 [ADD]
Corrette, M.:Malbrough *(rec 1986)* Jecklin–Disco ▲ JD 616–2 [ADD]
Corrette, M.:La Naissance de la Musette *(rec 1986)* Jecklin–Disco ▲ JD 616–2 [ADD]
Corrette, M.:Sons—Op. 25, No. 4 *(rec 1986)* Jecklin–Disco ▲ JD 616–2 [ADD]
Corrette, M.:Les Voyages du berger fortuné aux Indes orientales *(rec 1986)* Jecklin–Disco ▲ JD 616–2 [ADD]
Festetics String Quartet [István Kertész (vn), Erika Petőfi (vn), Péter Ligeti (va), Reszö Pertorini (vc)]
Haydn, J.:Qts Strs, Op. 17 Arcana 2–▲ ACA 912 [DDD]
Haydn, J.:Qts Strs, Op. 64, "Tost Qts" Musique d'Abord 2–▲ HMA 1903040.41
Haydn, J.:Qts Strs, Op. 71 Arcana 2–▲ ACA 918
Haydn, J.:Qts Strs, Op. 71 Arcana ▲ ACA 95
Haydn, J.:Qts Strs, Op. 74 Arcana 2–▲ ACA 918
Haydn, J.:Qts Strs, Op. 74 [period instr] Arcana ▲ ACA 96
Haydn, J.:Qts Strs, Op. 77, "Lobkowitz Qts" [period instrs] Musique d'Abord ▲ HMA 1903001
Haydn, J.:Qt Strs, Op. 103 [period instrs] Musique d'Abord ▲ HMA 1903001
Haydn, J.:The Seven Last Words of Christ on the Cross [period instrs] Musique d'Abord ▲ HMA 1903043
Mozart, W.A.:Qts Pno, w. P. Badura–Skoda (pno) Arcana ▲ ACA 7 [DDD]
Mozart, W.A.:Qts Pno, w. Paul Badura–Skoda (pno) Arcana 3–▲ ACA 903 [DDD]
Mozart, W.A.:Qt 20 Strs Arcana ▲ CD 8 [DDD]
Mozart, W.A.:Qt 20 Strs Arcana 3–▲ ACA 903 [DDD]
Mozart, W.A.:Qt 21 Strs Arcana 3–▲ ACA 903 [DDD]
Mozart, W.A.:Qt 22 Strs Arcana 3–▲ ACA 903 [DDD]
Mozart, W.A.:Qt 22 Strs Arcana ▲ CD 8 [DDD]
Mozart, W.A.:Qt 23 Strs Arcana 3–▲ ACA 903 [DDD]
Schubert, Franz:Qt 4 Strs [period instrs] Arcana ▲ ACA 48
Schubert, Franz:Qt 13 Strs [period instrs] Arcana ▲ ACA 48
Festival CO
R. Dufallo (cnd)
del Tredici, D.:Syzygy, w. P. Bryn–Julson (sop) [E] CRI ■ ACS 6004
del Tredici, D.:Syzygy, w. Phyllis Bryn–Julson (sop) CRI ("American Masters" series) ▲ CD 689 [DDD]
Festival of the Sound Ensemble
J. Campbell (cnd)
Saint–Saëns, C.:Carnival of the Animals, w. J. Anagnoson (pno), L. Kinton (pno) *(rec Glenn Gould Studio, CBC Toronto, Mar. 26–27, 1994)* CBC ("Musica Viva" series) ▲ MVV 1089 [DDD]
Festival Orch
E. Stratta (cnd)
Gershwin, G.:Ovs—Girl Crazy overture Kem–Disc ▲ 1008 [DDD]
Gershwin, G.:Porgy & Bess (sels), w. C. Lindsey (sop), B. Matthews (bar)—ten songs, most in concert arrs. by Robert Russell Bennett Kem–Disc ▲ 1008 [DDD]
Gershwin, G.:Rhap in Blue, w. E. Stratta (pno) Kem–Disc ▲ 1008 [DDD]
Festival Sinfonietta
E. Chakarov (cnd)
Mozart, W.A.:Con 17 Pno, w. M. Frager (pno) Vivace ▲ E 515 [ADD]
Mozart, W.A.:Con 20 Pno, w. H. Czerny–Stefanska (pno) Vivace 2–▲ G 217 [ADD]
Mozart, W.A.:Con 23 Pno, w. M. Frager (pno) Vivace 2–▲ G 217 [ADD]
Festival SO
Schubert, Franz:Rosamunde (sels)—ballet music Critics Choice 2–▲ CCD 946 [DDD]
M. Perriere (cnd)
Poulenc, F.:Con for 2 Pnos, w. J. R. Crossan (pno), J. Nesleny (pno) Janus ■ JAN 1104 (CrO2)
Festspiel Orch members
A. Kulling (cnd)
Fun at the Festspielhaus, w. Bayreuth Chorus Campion ▲ RRCD 1328 [ADD]
Fête Rustique
Sammartini, G.:Sons 2 Fls, w. Giorgio Matteoli (fl), Tommaso Rossi (fl) *(rec Jungle Studios, Milan, June 25–26, 1995)* Agora Musica ▲ AG 020 [DDD]
Fevoré Trio
Lansky, P.:As If Centaur ▲ CRC 2110 [DDD]
FFB Orch
F. Fox (cnd)
Lehár, F.:Schön ist die Welt (sels), w. Renate Holm (sop), Rudolf Schock (ten), Gunther Arndt Chorus Emperor Operetta ▲ KO 86344

172 ▲ = CD ♦ = Enhanced CD Δ = MD ■ = Cassette Tape □ = DCC

FFB Orch (cont.)
W. Schmidt-Boelcke (cnd)
Lehár, F.:Paganini (sels), w. Melitta Muszely (sop), Rudolf Schock (ten), Siegfried Borries (vn), Gunther Arndt Chorus Emperor Operetta ▲ KO 86343
I Fiamminghi CO
Boccherini, L.:Qnts Strs, w. R. Werthen (vc)—in C, G.324 (Op. 30/6) Koch Schwann ▲ CD 311184 [ADD/DDD]
R. Werthen (cnd)
Albinoni, T.:Adagio Org Koch Schwann ▲ CD 311184 [ADD/DDD]
Bellini, V.:Con in E♭ Ob, w. J. van den Hauwe (ob) Koch Schwann ▲ SCH 310822 [DDD]
Cimarosa, D.:Con for 2 Fls, w. J. van den Hauwe (ob) [trans. for solo oboe & orch.] Koch Schwann ▲ SCH 310822 [DDD]
Corelli, A.:Concerti grossi, Op. 6, w. J. van den Hauwe (ob)—[arr. Barbirolli] Koch Schwann ▲ SCH 310822
Corigliano, J.:Campagne di Ravello *(rec Belgium, July 19–21, 1995)* Telarc ▲ CD 80421 [DDD]
Corigliano, J.:Creations (2), w. Ian McKellen (nar) *(rec Belgium, July 19–21, 1995)* Telarc ▲ CD 80421 [DDD]
Corigliano, J.:Elegy *(rec Belgium, July 19–21, 1995)* Telarc ▲ CD 80421 [DDD]
Corigliano, J.:Promenade Ov *(rec Belgium, July 19–21, 1995)* Telarc ▲ CD 80421 [DDD]
Corigliano, J.:To Music *(rec Belgium, July 19–21, 1995)* Telarc ▲ CD 80421 [DDD]
Corigliano, J.:Voyage Fl, w. Paul Edmund-Davies (fl) *(rec Belgium, July 19–21, 1995)* Telarc ▲ CD 80421 [DDD]
Elgar, E.:Serenade Strs Koch Schwann ▲ CD 311184 [ADD/DDD]
Françaix, J.:Theme & Vars Cl, w. Eduard Brunner (cl) Koch Schwann ▲ SCH 310262
Górecki, H.-M.:Kleines Requiem für eine Polka, w. Mireille Gleizes (pno) *(rec Abbey Bonne Espérance, Vellereille-les-Brayeux, Belgium; July 17–19, 1995)* Telarc ▲ CD-80417 [DDD]
Górecki, H.-M.:Stücke im alten Stil (3) *(rec Abbey Bonne Espérance, Vellereille-les-Brayeux, Belgium; July 17–19, 1995)* Telarc ▲ CD-80417 [DDD]
Hovhaness, A.:Alleluia & Fugue *(rec Basilica of Bonne Espérance, Vellereille-les-Brayeux, Belgium, Aug. 18–20, 1994)* Telarc ▲ CD 80392 [DDD]
Hovhaness, A.:Con 7 Orch *(rec Basilica of Bonne Espérance, Vellereille-les-Brayeux, Belgium, Aug. 18–20, 1994)* Telarc ▲ CD 80392 [DDD]
Hovhaness, A.:Prayer of St. Gregory, w. Benny Wiame (tpt) *(rec Basilica of Bonne Espérance, Vellereille-les-Brayeux, Belgium, Aug. 18–20, 1994)* Telarc ▲ CD 80392 [DDD]
Hovhaness, A.:Prelude & Quadruple Fugue *(rec Basilica of Bonne Espérance, Vellereille-les-Brayeux, Belgium, Aug. 18–20, 1994)* Telarc ▲ CD 80392 [DDD]
Hovhaness, A.:Sym 6 *(rec Basilica of Bonne Espérance, Vellereille-les-Brayeux, Belgium, Aug. 18–20, 1994)* Telarc ▲ CD 80392 [DDD]
Hovhaness, A.:Tzaikerk, w. Paul Edmund-Davies (fl), Arnold Kobyliansky (vn), Randy Max (timp) *(rec Basilica of Bonne Espérance, Vellereille-les-Brayeux, Belgium, Aug. 18–20, 1994)* Telarc ▲ CD 80392 [DDD]
Marcello, A.:Con Ob Bass Cl, w. J. van den Hauwe (ob) Koch Schwann ▲ SCH 310822 [DDD]
Mihalovici, M.:Nocturne, w. Eduard Brunner (cl) Koch Schwann ▲ SCH 310262
Pachelbel, J.:Canon Koch Schwann ▲ CD 311184 [ADD/DDD]
Pärt, A.:Music of—Fratres for Strs & Perc; Fratres for Vn, Strs & Perc; Cantus in Memory of Benjamin Britten; Fratres for Wind Octet & Perc; Fratres for 8 Vc; Summa for Strs; Fratres for Str Qt; Festina Lente for Strs & Hp; Fratres for Vc & Pno *(rec Basilica of Bonne Espérance, Vellereille-les-Brayeux, Belgium, Aug. 18–20, 1994)* Telarc ▲ CD 80387 [DDD]
Rivier, J.:Con Cl, w. Eduard Brunner (cl) Koch Schwann ▲ SCH 310262
Vivaldi, A.:Con Ob, RV.456, w. J. van den Hauwe (ob) Koch Schwann ▲ SCH 310822 [DDD]
Vivaldi, A.:Cons Vn, Op. 8/1–12, "Il cimento dell'armonia e dell'inventione"—Nos. 4 & 5 Koch Schwann ▲ CD 311184 [ADD/DDD]
Fiati Virtuosi
De la Renaissance au Baroque Analekta ▲ ATM 29728
Fiato del '900 Quintet
Bizet, G.:Jeux d'enfants [trans. for woodwinds] Fonè ▲ 90F24
Quintetto a Fiato del '900 *(rec March 1990)* Fonè ▲ 90F24CD
Ravel, M.:Le Tombeau de Couperin [trans. for woodwinds] Fonè ▲ 90F24
Fiddle Fever
Foster, S.C.:Songs, w. T. Hampson (bar) EMI Classics ▲ CDC 54621 ■ 4DS 54621
Fidelio
Bizet, G.:Carmen (sels) *(rec 1991)* Gallo ▲ CD 674 [DAD]
Bizet, G.:Jeux d'enfants *(rec 1991)* Gallo ▲ CD 674 [DAD]
Gounod, C.:Petite Sym *(rec 1991)* Gallo ▲ CD 674 [DAD]
Indy, V. d':Chanson et Danses *(rec 1991)* Gallo ▲ CD 674 [DAD]
Fidelio [Lois Martin (va), Harry Clark (vc), Sanda Schuldmann (pno)]
Kaminsky, L.:And Trouble Came:An African AIDS Diary, w. Mark Lamos (nar) CRI ▲ CD 729 [DDD]
Arthur Fiedler's Sinfonietta
A. Fiedler (cnd)
Arthur Fiedler's Sinfonietta RCA Gold Seal ▲ 09026-62571-2
Fiesole Trio
Beethoven, L. van:Trio 4 Pno, "Ghost" *(rec 1989–90)* Fonè ▲ 90F21 [DDD]
Schubert, Franz:Qnt Pno, D.667, w. P. Farulli (vla), F. Petracchi (db) Fonè ▲ 90F21 [DDD]
I Filarmonici
A. Ephrikian (cnd)
Vivaldi, A.:Cons Orch—6 Concerti for Strings in c, RV.120; in D, RV.123; in D, RV.124; in d, RV.129; in g, RV.152; in g, RV.155 Musique d'Abord ▲ HMA 1901012 [ADD]
A. Martini (cnd)
Vivaldi, A.:Cons Vn, Op. 4, "La stravaganza"—Nos. 1–6 *(rec Sala del Morone, Verona, Italy, Feb 1995)* Tactus ▲ TC 672226 [DDD]
Vivaldi, A.:Cons Vn, Op. 4, "La stravaganza"—Nos. 7–12 *(rec Sala del Morone, Verona, Italy, Feb 1995)* Tactus ▲ TC 672227 [DDD]
I Filarmonici [Alberto Martini (vn), Lorenzo Corbolini (vc), Emanuela Marcante (org), Elena Talò (vn)]
Vivaldi, A.:Cons Fl, Op. 10 *(rec Nov 1994)* Tactus ▲ TC 672236 [DDD]
Vivaldi, A.:Cons Vn, Op. 8/1–12, "Il cimento dell'armonia e dell'inventione"—Nos. 1–6 *(rec Sala del Morone, Verona, Italia, Nov 1995)* Tactus ▲ TC 672232 [DDD]
Vivaldi, A.:Cons Vn, Op. 8/1–12, "Il cimento dell'armonia e dell'inventione"—Nos. 7–12 *(rec Sala del Morone, Verona, Italia, Nov 1994)* Tactus ▲ TC 672233 [DDD]
Vivaldi, A.:Sons Vn, Op. 5 Tactus ▲ TC 672228 [DDD]
Vivaldi, A.:Sons for 2 Vns, Op. 1—Nos. 1–6 *(rec 1995)* Tactus ▲ TC 672220 [DDD]
Vivaldi, A.:Sons for 2 Vns, Op. 1—Nos. 7–12 *(rec 1995)* Tactus ▲ TC 672221 [DDD]
Fine Arts Brass Ensemble [Bryan Allen (tpt), Andy Culshaw (tpt), Stephen Roberts (hn), Simon Hogg (trbn), Richard Sandland (tuba)]
Best of the Fine Arts Brass Ensemble Doyen ▲ CD 010 [DDD]
The Lighter Side of the Fine Arts Brass Ensemble Saydisc ▲ CDSDL 381 [DDD]
Fine Arts Brass Quintet
Bach, J.S.:The Art of the Fugue Centaur ▲ CRC 2035 [DDD]
Fine Arts CO
M. Margolis (cnd)
Kox, H.:L'Allegria, w. L. Meeuwsen (sop) [I] *(rec 1987)* Attacca ▲ Babel 9262-1 [ADD/DDD]
Fine Arts String Quartet
Babbitt, M.:Qt 3 Strs *(rec 1972)* Music & Arts ▲ CD 707-1 [AAD]
Wuorinen, C.:Qt 1 Strs *(rec ca. 1971/72)* Music & Arts ▲ CD 707-1 [AAD]
Fine Arts String Quartet [Efim Boico (vn), Ralph Evans (vn), Jerry Horner (va), Wolfgang Laufer (vc)]
Shostakovich, D.:Qt 3 Strs Adès ▲ ADE 141612 [DDD]
Shostakovich, D.:Qt 7 Strs Adès ▲ ADE 141612 [DDD]
Shostakovich, D.:Qt 11 Strs Adès ▲ ADE 141612 [DDD]
Fine Arts String Quartet [Leonard Sorkin (vn), Abram Loft (vn), Gerald Stanick (va), George Sopkin (vc)]
Adler, S.:Qt 6 Voc & Strs, w. J. DeGaetani (mez) CRI ▲ CD 608 [ADD]
Beethoven, L. van:Qts Strs (comp)—Op. 18 Everest 2-▲ EVC 9051/52 [AAD]
Beethoven, L. van:Qts Strs (comp)—Opp. 59, 74, 95 Everest 3-▲ EVC 9053/55 [AAD]
Beethoven, L. van:Qts Strs (comp)—Opp. 127, 130–133, 135 Everest 3-▲ EVC 9056/58 [AAD]
Husa, K.:Qt 2 Strs Phoenix ▲ PHCD 113 [AAD]
Husa, K.:Qt 3 Strs Phoenix ▲ PHCD 113 [AAD]
Fine Arts String Quartet [Leonard Sorkin (vn), Abram Loft (vn), Irving Ilmer (va), George Sopkin (vc)]
Brahms, J.:Qnt Cl, w. Reginald Kell (cl) Boston Skyline ▲ BSD 135 [AAD]
Mozart, W.A.:Qnt Cl, K.581, w. Reginald Kell (cl) Boston Skyline ▲ BSD 135 [AAD]
Wuorinen, C.:Qt 1 Strs Music & Arts ▲ CD 932
Fine Arts String Quartet members [Leonard Sorkin (vn), Irving Ilmer (va), George Sopkin (vc)]
Mozart, W.A.:Qts Fl, w. Samuel Baron (fl) Boston Skyline ▲ BSD 142 [AAD]
Fine Instruments Orch
C. Halaris (cnd)
Akritika:Odes of the Byzantine Empire Border-Guards Orata 2-▲ AKR 001
Akritika, Vol. 2:Odes of the Byzantine Empire Border-Guards Orata 2-▲ AKR 002
Byzantine Maistores:Complete Works of the Greatest Byzantine Composers, Vol. 1 Orata 3-▲ CRYS 001
Byzantine Secular Classical Music Orata 3-▲ 1
Byzantine Secular Classical Music, Vol. 2 Orata 3-▲ 2
Byzantine Secular Classical Music, Vol. 3 Orata 3-▲ 3
Pandora:Music of the Post-Byzantine High Society, Vol. 1 Orata ▲ PAN 001
Sympotika:Secular Music of Byzantine Banquets, Vol. 1 Orata ▲ SYM 001
Finlandia Sinfonietta
Haydn, J.:Concertino Hpd, w. Ralf Gothóni (pno) Ondine ▲ ODE 732-2 [DDD]
Haydn, J.:Con Hpd, Obs, Hns & Strs, H.XVIII/11, w. Ralf Gothóni (pno) Ondine ▲ ODE 732-2 [DDD]
P. Helasvuo (cnd)
Sibelius, J.:Impromptu Strs Finlandia ▲ 4509-95855-2 [DDD]
Sibelius, J.:Kuolema—sels. Finlandia ▲ 4509-95855-2 [DDD]
Sibelius, J.:Presto Finlandia ▲ 4509-95855-2 [DDD]
Sibelius, J.:Romance Strs Finlandia ▲ 4509-95855-2 [DDD]
Sibelius, J.:Suite caractéristique Finlandia ▲ 4509-95855-2 [DDD]
Sibelius, J.:Suite champêtre Finlandia ▲ 4509-95855-2 [DDD]
Sibelius, J.:Suite mignonne Finlandia ▲ 4509-95855-2 [DDD]
Sibelius, J.:Valse triste Finlandia ▲ 4509-95844-2 [ADD/DDD]
O. Kamu (cnd)
Sibelius, J.:Pelléas et Mélisande Finlandia ▲ 4509-95844-2 [ADD/DDD]
Finnish National Opera Orch
E. Klas (cnd)
Sibelius, J.:Choral Music, w. Finnish National Opera Chorus—Impromptu for female choir & orchestra, Op. 19 (1902; rev. 1910); Snöfrid for mixed choir & orchestra, Op. 29 (1900); Laulu Lemminkäiselle [Song to Lemminkainen] for male choir & orchestra, Op. 31/1 (1896); Oma maa [Homeland] for mixed choir & orchestra, Op. 92 (1918); Maan virsi [Song to the Earth], cantata for mixed choir & orchestra, Op. 95 (1920); Väinön virsi [Väinö's Song], cantata for mixed choir & orchestra, Op. 110 (1926) [Fin] Ondine ▲ ODE 754-2 [DDD]
Sibelius, J.:Finlandia, w. Finnish National Opera Chorus [composer's version from the 1930s for orchestra with male voice choir; text by V.A. Koskenniemi] [Fin] Ondine ▲ ODE 754-2 [DDD]
U. Söderblom (cnd)
Bergman, E.:The Singing Tree, w. K. Hannula (sop), C. Hellekant (cta), P. Lindroos (ten), P. Salomaa (bass), S. Tiilikainen (bar), M. Wallén (bass), Dominante Chamber Choir, Tapiola Chamber Choir Ondine 2-▲ ODE 794-2D [DDD]
Sallinen, A.:Kullervo, w. G. Saarinen (pno), J. Silvasti (ten), J. Hynninen (bar), M. Salminen (bass), Finnish National Opera Chorus [Fin] Ondine 3-▲ ODE 780-3T [DDD]
Finnish National Opera Orch members
T. Tuomela (cnd)
Saariaho, K.:Maa Ondine ▲ ODE 791-2 [DDD]
Finnish RSO
Segerstam, L.:Flowerbouquette No. 43e Ondine ▲ ODE CD 877
P. Berglund (cnd)
Sibelius, J.:Sym 4 *(rec 1968)* Finlandia ▲ 4509-95843-2 [AAD]
Sibelius, J.:Tapiola *(rec 1968)* Finlandia ▲ 4509-95843-2 [AAD]
Sibelius, J.:Tapiola Finlandia ▲ 4509-95844-2 [ADD/DDD]
N.-E. Fougstedt (cnd)
Sibelius, J.:Con Vn, w. D. Oistrakh (vn) *(rec live 1954)* Ondine ▲ ODE 809 [ADD]
T. Hannikainen (cnd)
Berg, A.:Con Vn, w. Oleg Kagan (vn) *(rec Bregenzer Festspiele, Aug. 11, 1985)* Live Classics ("Kagan Edition" series) ▲ 143
Sibelius, J.:Con Vn, w. Oleg Kagan (vn) *(rec Sibelius Competition, Helsinki, Dec. 8, 1965)* Live Classics ("Kagan Edition" series) ▲ 143
N. Järvi (cnd)
Mussorgsky, M.:Songs & Dances, w. M. Talvela (bass) [orch. arr. by Aho] BIS ▲ CD 325
O. Kamu (cnd)
Sallinen, A.:Sym 1 BIS ▲ CD 41 [AAD]
Sallinen, A.:Sym 3 BIS ▲ CD 41 [AAD]
S. Oramo (cnd)
Kaipainen, J.:Con Ob, w. Helen Jahren (ob) Ondine ▲ ODE 855
Kaipainen, J.:Sisyphus Dreams Ondine ▲ ODE 855
Kaipainen, J.:Sym 2 Ondine ▲ ODE 855
Klami, U.:The Cobblers on the Health Ov Ondine ▲ ODE 859 [DDD]
Klami, U.:In the Belly of Vipunen, w. Petri Lindroos (bar), Polytech Men's Choir Ondine ▲ ODE 859 [DDD]
Klami, U.:Karelian Market Place Ondine ▲ ODE 859 [DDD]
Klami, U.:Karelian Rhap Ondine ▲ ODE 859 [DDD]
Klami, U.:Lemminkäinen Ondine ▲ ODE 859 [DDD]
Merikanto, A.:Con 2 Vc, w. Jan-Erik Gustafsson (vc) Ondine ▲ ODE 861 [DDD]
Prokofiev, S.:Sym-Con Vc, w. Jan-Erik Gustafsson (vc) Ondine ▲ ODE 861 [DDD]
Villa-Lobos, H.:Con Gtr, w. Timo Korhonen (gtr) Ondine ▲ ODE 837 [DDD]
Villa-Lobos, H.:Intro to Chôros, w. Timo Korhonen (gtr) Ondine ▲ ODE 837 [DDD]
E.-P. Salonen (cnd)
Rautavaara, E.:Regular Sets of Elements in a Semiregular Situation Ondine ▲ ODE 867
J.-P. Saraste (cnd)
Agopov, V.:Con Vc, "Tres Viae", w. A. Noras (vc) *(rec May 1988)* Finlandia ▲ 4509-95866-2 [DDD]
Bartók, B.:Rhap 1 Vc, w. A. Noras (vc) *(rec May 25–27, 1992)* Finlandia ▲ 4509-95872-2 [DDD]
Bergman, E.:Sub luna Ondine ▲ ODE 867
Crusell, B.H.:Intro, Theme & Vars on a Swedish Air, w. K. Kojo (cl) Finlandia ▲ 4509-95873-2 [DDD]
Debussy, C.:Jeux Virgin Classics ▲ CDC 45018
Debussy, C.:Khamma Virgin Classics ▲ CDC 45018
Debussy, C.:Prélude à l'après-midi d'un faune Virgin Classics ▲ CDC 45018
Debussy, C.:Première rapsodie, w. K. Kriikku (cl) Ondine ▲ ODE 778-2 [DDD]
Debussy, C.:Printemps (suite) Virgin Classics ▲ CDC 45018
Dutilleux, H.:Con Vc, "Tout un Monde Lointain", w. A. Noras (vc) *(rec Aug. 1991)* Finlandia ▲ 4509-95866-2 [DDD]
Englund, S.E.:Con Cl, w. K. Kojo (cl) Finlandia ▲ 4509-95873-2 [DDD]
Hämeenniemi, E.:Con Vn, w. Hannele Segerstam (vn) Ondine ▲ ODE 835 [DDD]
Hämeenniemi, E.:Sym 1 Ondine ▲ ODE 835 [DDD]

Finnish RSO (cont.)
J.–P. Saraste (cnd) (cont.)
Hämeenniemi, E.:Sym 2 — Ondine ▲ ODE 835 [DDD]
Heininen, P.:Adagio — Ondine ▲ ODE 867
Ibert, J.:Con Fl, w. P. Alanko (fl) — Ondine ▲ ODE 802 [DDD]
Mahler, G.:Sym 5 — Virgin Classics ▲ 59046 [DDD]
Merikanto, A.:Juha, w. Eeva-Liisa Saarinen (mez), Raimo Sirkiä (ten), Jorma Hynninen (bar) — Ondine 2-▲ ODE 872
Nielsen, C.:Con Cl, w. K. Kojo (cl) — Finlandia ▲ 4509-95873-2 [DDD]
Nielsen, C.:Con Fl, w. P. Alanko (fl) — Ondine ▲ ODE 802 [DDD]
Raitio, V.:Orch Music—Swans, Op. 15 (1919); Fantasia estatica, Op. 21 (1921); Antigone, Op. 23 (1921–2; Fantasia poetica, Op. 25 (1923); The Column Fountain [ballet music in two scenes] (1929) — Ondine ▲ ODE 790-2 [DDD]
Saint-Saëns, C.:Con 1 Vc, w. A. Noras (vc) *(rec Feb. 28–March 1, 1990)* — Finlandia ▲ 4509-95872-2 [DDD]
Sibelius, J.:Aallottaret — RCA Red Seal ▲ 60401-2-RC [DDD]
Sibelius, J.:The Bard — RCA Red Seal ▲ 60401-2-RC [DDD]
Sibelius, J.:Belshazzar's Feast (suite) — RCA Red Seal ▲ 09026-60434-2
Sibelius, J.:Con Vn, w. J. Swensen (vn) — RCA Red Seal ▲ 09026-60444-2
Sibelius, J.:Finlandia — RCA Red Seal ▲ 7765-2-RC [DDD]
Sibelius, J.:4 Legends from the Kalevalá—Lemminkäinen Suite — RCA Red Seal ▲ 09026-60575-2
Sibelius, J.:Humoresques, w. J. Swensen (vn) — RCA Red Seal ▲ 09026-60444-2
Sibelius, J.:Karelia Ov — RCA Red Seal ▲ 7765-2-RC [DDD]
Sibelius, J.:Karelia Suite — RCA Red Seal ▲ 7765-2-RC [DDD]
Sibelius, J.:King Christian II (suite) — RCA Red Seal ▲ 09026-60434-2
Sibelius, J.:Night Ride & Sunrise — RCA Red Seal ▲ 7919-2-RC [DDD]
Sibelius, J.:Pieces Vn, w. A. Noras (vc) *(rec May 25–27, 1992)* — Finlandia ▲ 4509-95872-2 [DDD]
Sibelius, J.:Pohjola's Daughter — RCA Red Seal ▲ 60401-2-RC [DDD]
Sibelius, J.:Scene with Cranes — RCA Red Seal ▲ 7919-2-RC [DDD]
Sibelius, J.:Serenades Vn, w. J. Swensen (vn) — RCA Red Seal ▲ 09026-60444-2
Sibelius, J.:Sym 1 — RCA Red Seal ▲ 7765-2-RC [DDD]
Sibelius, J.:Sym 2 — RCA Red Seal ▲ 7919-2-RC [DDD]
Sibelius, J.:Sym 3 — RCA Red Seal ▲ 09026-60434-2
Sibelius, J.:Sym 4 — RCA Red Seal ▲ 60401-2-RC [DDD]
Sibelius, J.:Sym 6 — RCA Red Seal ▲ 60157-2-RC [DDD]
Sibelius, J.:Sym 7 — RCA Red Seal ▲ 09026-60575-2
Sibelius, J.:The Tempest, w. R. Viljakainen (sop), M. Groop (mez), J. Silvasti (ten), J. Hynninen (bar), S. Tiilikainen (bar), Finnish Opera Festival Chorus — Ondine ▲ ODE 813 [DDD]
Sibelius, J.:Valse triste — RCA Red Seal ▲ 7919-2-RC [DDD]
Tchaikovsky, P.:Vars on a Rococo Theme, w. A. Noras (vc) *(rec May 25–27, 1992)* — Finlandia ▲ 4509-95872-2 [DDD]
Tiensuu, J.:Con Cl, w. K. Kriikku (cl) — Ondine ▲ ODE 778-2 [DDD]

L. Segerstam (cnd)
Bergman, E.:Birds in the Morning, w. M. Helasvuo (fl) — Finlandia ▲ 4509-95861-2 [DDD]
Bergman, E.:Con Vn, w. Hannele Segerstam (vn) — BIS ▲ CD 326
Englund, S.E.:Con Fl, w. M. Helasvuo (fl) — Finlandia ▲ 4509-95861-2 [DDD]
Hauta-Aho, T.:Fant Tpt, w. Jouko Harjanne (tpt) *(rec Nov. 1989 & Dec. 1990)* — Finlandia ▲ 4509-95863-2 [DDD]
Linkola, J.:Con Tpt, w. J. Harjanne (tpt) *(rec Nov. 1989 & Dec. 1990)* — Finlandia ▲ 4509-95863-2 [DDD]
Meriläinen, U.:Visions & Whispers, w. M. Helasvuo (fl) — Finlandia ▲ 4509-95861-2 [DDD]
Mussorgsky, M.:Night — BIS ▲ CD 325
Mussorgsky, M.:Pictures at an Exhibition [1922 arr. by Funtek] — BIS ▲ CD 325
Nordgren, P.H.:Con 2 Vn, w. H. Segerstam (vn) — BIS ▲ CD 326
Segerstam, L.:Con 2 Tpt, w. J. Harjanne (tpt) *(rec Nov. 1989 & Dec. 1990)* — Finlandia ▲ 4509-95863-2 [DDD]
Segerstam, L.:Con 1 Vn, w. H. Segerstam (vn) — BIS ▲ CD 326
Segerstam, L.:Impressions of Nordic Nature 4 — Ondine ▲ ODE CD 877
Segerstam, L.:Sym 11 — BIS ▲ CD 483 [DDD]
Segerstam, L.:Sym 14, w. M. Samuelson (bar) — BIS ▲ CD 483 [DDD]
Vuori, H.:Kri — Ondine ▲ ODE 867
Wessman, H.:Con Tpt, w. J. Harjanne (tpt) *(rec Nov. 1989 & Dec. 1990)* — Finlandia ▲ 4509-95863-2 [DDD]

U. Söderblom (cnd)
Heininen, P.:Sym 3 — Ondine ▲ ODE 722-2 [ADD]

W. Strickland (cnd)
Ives, C.:Holidays, w. Iceland SO, Tokyo PO, Finnish RSO, Göteborg SO, Iceland Sym Chorus [E] — CRI ■ ACS 6014

Finnish-Estonian Baroque Orch
P. Helasvuo (cnd)
Blak, K.:Con Db, w. Björn Malinquist (db) *(rec Nordic House, Tórshavn, June 1994)* — Tutl ▲ FKT 8

Finzi Wind Ensemble
P. Spicer (cnd)
Bliss, A.:Choral Music, w. A. Lumsden (org), Finzi Singers—Shield of Faith for Chorus & Organ (1975); The world is charged with the grandeur of God for Chorus, Winds & Brass (1969); [a cappella works]—Birthday Song for a Royal Child (1959); River Music (1967); Mar Portugues (1973) [E] — Chandos ▲ CHAN 8980 [DDD]

Fiori Musicali
Desmarets, H.:Sacred Music, w. Barbara Schlick (sop), Mieke Van der Sluis (sop), Harry Geraerts (ct), New College Choir Oxford—Deux grands motets lorrains; Mystères de notre seigneur Jésus-Christ — Erato ▲ ERA SEL 98529 [ADD]

T. Albert (cnd)
Keiser, R.:Masagniello furioso, w. *(soloists unknown)* — CPO 2-▲ CPO 999110 [DDD]

P. Rapson (cnd)
Vivaldi, A.:Arias, w. K. Eckersley (sop), P. Rapson (hpd)—from La fida Ninfa:Alma oppressa; La Griselda:Agitata da due venti [I] — Meridian ▲ CDE 84195
Vivaldi, A.:Cons Vn, Op. 8/1–4, "The Four Seasons", w. E. Wallfisch (vn), P. Rapson (hpd) — Meridian ▲ CDE 84195
Vivaldi, A.:L'incoronazione di Dario, w. P. Rapson (hpd)—Sinf. — Meridian ▲ CDE 84195
Vivaldi, A.:Motets, w. K. Eckersley (sop), P. Rapson (hpd)—In furore [I] — Meridian ▲ CDE 84195

Fires of London
Carter, E.:Triple Duo — Elektra/Nonesuch ■ 79110-4 (D)

P. M. Davies (cnd)
Davies, P.M.:Miss Donnithorne's Maggot, w. M. Thomas (cta) *(rec digital rec'g)* — Unicorn-Kanchana ▲ DKP CD 9052 [ADD/DDD]
Davies, P.M.:Songs (8) for a Mad King, w. J. Eastman (bar) *(rec analog rec'g)* — Unicorn-Kanchana ▲ DKP CD 9052 [ADD/DDD]

Firestone Orch
Live Performances 1945–1959, w. Leonard Warren (bar) — Memories 2-▲ MEM 4460 (m) [ADD]

First Avenue
Two Suns — Newport Classic ▲ NCD 60062 [DDD]

1st Battalion Argyll & Sutherland Highlanders Pipes & Drums
Royal Regiments on Parade, w. 1st Battalion Princess of Wales' Royal Regiment Band, Queen's Division Massed Bands, et al. — Bandleader ▲ BND 5111 [DDD]

1st Battalion Princess of Wales' Royal Regiment Band
Royal Regiments on Parade, w. 1st Battalion Argyll & Sutherland Highlanders Pipes & Drums, Queen's Division Massed Bands, et al. — Bandleader ▲ BND 5111 [DDD]

Edwin Fischer CO
E. Fischer (cnd)
Bach, J.S.:Brandenburg Con 2 *(rec Berlin, 1941)* — Koch Historic ▲ 7701-2 [AAD]

Edwin Fischer CO (cont.)
E. Fischer (cnd) (cont.)
Bach, J.S.:Das wohltemperierte Klavier—Fugue No. 20 in a, BWV 865 [orch. Fischer] *(rec Berlin, Feb 20, 1939)* — Koch Historic ▲ 7701-2 [AAD]
Beethoven, L. van:Grosse Fuge Str Qt *(rec Berlin ca. 1939/41)* — Koch Historic ▲ 7701-2 [AAD]

Fitzwilliam Ensemble
Falconieri, A.:Music of—Battaglia de Barabaso yerno de Satanas; Folias echa para mi Señora Doña...; Fant echa para el muy reverendo Padre Falla; Vita del l'alma; Passacalle; Corriente dicha la cuella; Bella clori; Virtu de lumi; Sinf la buon'hota; Come fugace; Cotrente detta l'avellina; O mia vita; Hoggi la dea del cielo; Gioiosa fant; La suave melodia y su corrente; Corriente dicha la mota; Bayle de los dichos diabolos; Il Rosso Brando; Filli cara; Armilla ingrata; Sinf quarta; La Borga; Al dolce mormorar; Fant detta la Portia; L'eroica — Astrée ▲ E 8551
Marais, M.:Pièces en trio — Valois ▲ V 4638

Fitzwilliam Ensemble [Jean-Pierre Nicolas (rec), Paul Dombrecht (ob), Enrico Gatti (vn), Bruno Cocset (vc), Michèle Dévérité (hpd)]
Telemann, G.P.:Trio Sons—in a for Rec, Vn & Cont; in c for Rec, Ob & Cont; in g for Ob, Vn & Cont; in d for Rec, Vn & Cont — Astrée ▲ E 8561

Fitzwilliam Ensemble [Jean-Pierre Nicolas (rec), Paul Dombrecht (ob), Enrico Gatti (vn), Michèle Dévérité (hpd)]
Telemann, G.P.:Con in a for Rcr, Ob — Astrée ▲ E 8561

Fitzwilliam Ensemble members [Bruno Cocset (vc), Michèle Dévérité (hpd)]
Telemann, G.P.:Son in D Vc — Astrée ▲ E 8561

Fitzwilliam String Quartet
Schumann, R.:Qnt Pno, w. R. Burnett (pno) [period instrs] — Amon Ra ▲ CD-SAR 54 [DDD]

Fitzwilliam String Quartet members
Schumann, R.:Qt Pno, Op. 47, w. R. Burnett (pno) [period instrs] — Amon Ra ▲ CD-SAR 54 [DDD]

Flanders CO Sinfonia
D. Vermeulen (cnd)
Britten, B.:Simple Sym — Eufoda ▲ 1138 [DDD]
Elgar, E.:Music of—Introduction & Allegro, Op. 47; Elegy, Op. 56; Mazurka, Op. 10; Serenade in e, Op. 20; Allegro piacevole; Larghetto; Allegretto; Salut d'amour, Op. 12; Chanson de nuit, Op. 15/1 & 2; Spanish Lady Suite; Country Dance; Berlesco; Adagio; Sarabande; Bourée — Eufoda ▲ EUF 1180 [DDD]
Ferlendis, G.:Con 1 Ob, w. J. Van den Hauwe (ob) — Eufoda ▲ 1154 [DDD]
Grieg, E.:Elegaic Melodies, Op. 34 — Eufoda ▲ 1134 [DDD]
Grieg, E.:Holberg Suite — Eufoda ▲ 1134 [DDD]
Grieg, E.:Lyric Pieces—Op. 68/5, "Cradle Song" — Eufoda ▲ 1134 [DDD]
Grieg, E.:Melodies, Op. 53 — Eufoda ▲ 1134 [DDD]
Grieg, E.:Nordic Melodies, Op. 63 — Eufoda ▲ 1134 [DDD]
Hummel, J.N.:Vars Ob, w. J. van den Hauwe (ob) — Eufoda ▲ 1154 [DDD]
Kersters, W.:Music of—Drie bagatellen — Eufoda ▲ 1138 [DDD]
Krommer, F.:Con Ob, Op. 52, w. J. van den Hauwe (ob) — Eufoda ▲ 1154 [DDD]
Lebrun, L.A.:Con 1 Ob, w. Joris van den Hauwe (ob) — Eufoda ▲ 1154 [DDD]
Suk, J.:Serenade Strs — Eufoda ▲ 1138 [DDD]
Turina, J.:La oracion del torero — Eufoda ▲ 1138 [DDD]
Van Der Roost, J.:Music of—Lento e mesto–Allegro con brio — Eufoda ▲ 1138 [DDD]

Flanders Recorder Quartet [Bart Spanhove (rcr), Geert Van Gele (rcr), Joris Van Goethem (rcr), Paul Van Loey (rcr)]
Geysen, F.:Digitaal-Analoog-Identiek *(rec Studio Steurbaut, Gent, Sept–Oct 1991)* — René Gailly ▲ 92004 [DDD]
Geysen, F.:Langs Hoeken en Kanten *(rec Studio Steurbaut, Gent, Sept–Oct 1991)* — René Gailly ▲ 92004 [DDD]
Pieters, P.:3 for 4 *(rec Studio Steurbaut, Gent, Sept–Oct 1991)* — René Gailly ▲ 92004 [DDD]
Swerts, P.:Novellettes *(rec Studio Steurbaut, Gent, Sept–Oct 1991)* — René Gailly ▲ 92004 [DDD]
Van Landeghem, J.:Birds *(rec Studio Steurbaut, Gent, Sept–Oct 1991)* — René Gailly ▲ 92004 [DDD]
Vivaldi, A.:Cons Vn, Op. 8/1–4, "The Four Seasons", w. Marion Verbruggen (rcr) [arr for rcrs] — Harmonia Mundi France ▲ HMU 907153

Flanders Royal PO
G. Neuhold (cnd)
Berlioz, H.:La Damnation de Faust, w. J. Larmor (mez—Marguerite), K. Olsen (ten—Faust), D. Wilson-Johnson (bar—Méphistophélès), H. Claessens (bar—Brander), Düsseldorf Municipal Choral Society — Bayer 2-▲ 500017/18 [DDD]

Flandria Baroque Soloists
Baroque Trumpet Concertos, w. William Forman (tpt) — Vivace ▲ E 557 [DDD]

Flautarte Quartet [Mauro Scappini (fl), Luca Torciani (vn), Emanuele Beschi (va), Claudio Giacomazzi (vc)]
Paisiello, G.:Qts Fl — Stradivarius ▲ STV SIP 24 [DDD]

Flonzaley String Quartet
Brahms, J.:Qt 3 Strs *(rec March 1, 2 & 6, 1928)* — Biddulph 2-▲ LAB 072/73 [ADD]
Brahms, J.:Qnt Pno, w. H. Bauer (pno) *(rec Dec. 21 & 23, 1925)* — Biddulph 2-▲ LAB 072/73 [ADD]
Mendelssohn, F.:Qt 1 Strs *(rec Dec. 19, 1928)* — Biddulph 2-▲ LAB 072/73 [ADD]
Schubert, Franz:Qt 15 Strs *(rec Dec. 19–20, 1929)* — Biddulph 2-▲ LAB 072/73 [ADD]
Schumann, R.:Qts Strs, Op. 41—No. 1 *(rec Dec. 22–23, 1927)* — Biddulph 2-▲ LAB 072/73 [ADD]
Schumann, R.:Qnt Pno, w. O. Gabrilowitsch (pno) *(rec Dec. 21, 1927)* — Biddulph 2-▲ LAB 072/73 [ADD]
Schumann, R.:Qnt Pno, w. O. Gabrilowitsch (pno) [abridged version] *(rec 1923–4)* — VAI Audio ▲ VAIA/IPA 1018 (m) [ADD]

Flora Danica
Leclair, J.-M.:Sons Vn (Books 1–4) [transverse flute, viol & harpsichord]—Op. 2/3,5&11; Op. 9/2&7 — Kontrapunkt ▲ 32006 [DDD]

Florence Maggio Musicale Orch
C. Abbado (cnd)
Rossini, G.:La Cenerentola, w. Teresa Berganza (mez), Luigi Alva (ten), Renato Capecchi (bar), Paolo Montarsolo (bass), Florence Maggio Musicale Chorus *(rec Florence, May 1971)* — Memories 2-▲ MEM 4283 [ADD]

M. Arena (cnd)
Opera Choruses, w. Florence Maggio Musicale Chorus — Acanta ▲ CD 43540

B. Bartoletti (cnd)
Boito, A.:Mefistofele, w. Daniela Dessi (sop), Alberto Cupido (ten), Samuel Ramey (bass), Florence Maggio Musicale Chorus *(rec live, 1989)* — Serenissima 2-▲ SER 360114
Puccini, G.:Il trittico, w. M. Freni (sop), E. Souljois (sop), G. Giacomini (ten), R. Alagna (ten), J. Pons (bar), L. Nucci (bar), Florence Maggio Musicale Chorus — London 3-▲ 436261-2 [DDD]

F. Capuana (cnd)
Bellini, V.:Il pirata, w. M. Caballé (sop), F. Labò (ten), P. Cappuccilli (bar), Florence Maggio Musicale Chorus [I] *(rec live, Florence 1967)* — Memories 2-▲ HR 4186/87 [ADD]
Bellini, V.:Il pirata, w. M. Caballé (sop), F. Labò (ten), P. Cappuccilli (bar), Florence Maggio Musicale Chorus [I] *(rec live, Florence 1967)* — Melodram 2-▲ MEL 27015

C. F. Cillario
Jottini & Volpi, w. Maria Jottini (sop), Giacomo Lauri Volpi (ten) *(rec Martini & Rossi Concert, 1957)* — Incontri Memorabili ▲ CDMR 5021

A. Erede (cnd)
Mascagni, P.:Cavalleria rusticana, w. R. Tebaldi (sop), J. Bjoerling (ten), Florence Maggio Musicale Chorus *(rec Sept. 1957)* — London ("Historic" series) ▲ 425985-2 [ADD]

G. Gavazzeni (cnd)
Donizetti, G.:L'elisir d'amore, w. R. Scotto (sop), C. Bergonzi (ten), P. Cava (ten), G. Taddei (bar), Florence Maggio Musicale Chorus *(rec live 1967)* — Memories 2-▲ HR 4129/30 (s)

V. Gui (cnd)
Cherubini, L.:Médée, w. M. Callas (sop), F. Barbieri (mez), M. Petri (bar), Florence Maggio Musicale Chorus [I] *(rec 1953)* — Arkadia 2-▲ 516 (m) [AAD]

▲ = CD ♦ = Enhanced CD Δ = MD ■ = Cassette Tape □ = DCC

Florence Maggio Musicale Orch (cont.)
V. Gui (cnd) (cont.)
Spontini, G.:Agnes von Hohensaufen, w. L. Udovick (sop), D. Dow (sop), F. Corelli (ten), A. Colzani (bar), G. Guelfi (bar), Florence Maggio Musicale Chorus [I] *(rec live 5/9/54)* Melodram 2-▲ MEL 27055 (m) [AAD]
Spontini, G.:La vestale, w. R. Scotto (sop), O. Dominguez (mez), F. Tagliavini (ten), M. Picchi (ten), Florence Maggio Musicale Chorus [I] *(rec live 5/5/70)* Melodram ("Connaisseur" series) 2-▲ CDM 27512 [ADD]

E. Kleiber (cnd)
Verdi, G.:I vespri siciliani, w. Maria Callas (sop), Boris Christoff (bass), Giorgio Kokolios (sgr), Florence Maggio Musicale Chorus *(rec live, Florence, May 26, 1951)* Enterprise ("Documents" series) 3-▲ ENT LV 996

Z. Mehta (cnd)
Mozart, W.A.:Nozze di Figaro, w. L. Cherici (sop), K. Mattila (sop), M. McLaughlin (sop), M. Bacelli (mez), N. Curiel (mez), U. Benelli (ten), L. Gallo (bar), A. Nosotti (bass), M. Pertusi (bass), G. Tadeo (bass), Florence Maggio Musicale Chorus Sony Classical ▲ SK 53286
Verdi, G.:La traviata, w. K. Te Kanawa (sop), A. Kraus (ten), D. Hvorostovsky (bar), Florence Maggio Musicale Chorus [I] Philips 2-▲ 438238-2
Verdi, G.:Il trovatore, w. Antonella Banaudi (sop—Leonora), Barbara Frittoli (sop—Ines), Shirley Verrett (mez—Azucena), Enrico Facini (ten—Un messo), Piero de Palma (ten—Ruiz), Luciano Pavarotti (ten—Marico), Leo Nucci (bar—Il Conte di Luna), Roberto Scaltriti (bar—Un vecchio zingaro), Francesco Ellero d'Artegna (bass—Ferrando), Florence Maggio Musicale Chorus *(rec Maggio Musicale Fiorentino Community Theater, June 18–July 2, 1990)* London 2-▲ 430694-2

D. Mitropoulos (cnd)
Mozart, W.A.:Con 20 Pno, w. A. Benedetti Michelangeli (pno) *(rec live, June 17, 1953)* Arkadia 3-▲ 552 (m) [ADD]
Verdi, G.:Ernani, w. A. Cerquetti (sop), M. Del Monaco (ten), E. Bastianni (bar), B. Christoff (bass) [I] *(rec live 6/14/57)* Melodram 2-▲ MEL 27016
Verdi, G.:Ernani (sels), w. Mario del Monaco (ten), Florence Maggio Musicale Chorus—Merc, diletti amici..Come rugiada al cespite; Dell'esilio nel dolore...O tu che l'alma adora *(rec Firenze, June 14, 1957)* Melodram ▲ CDI 104006 [ADD]
Verdi, G.:La forza del destino (sels), w. Mario del Monaco (ten), Florence Maggio Musicale Chorus—La vita è inferno all'infelice; O tu che in seno agli angeli *(rec Firenze, June 14, 1953)* Melodram ▲ CDI 104006 [ADD]

F. Molinari-Pradelli (cnd)
Donizetti, G.:Maria Stuarda, w. L. Gencer (sop), S. Verrett (mez), F. Tagliavini (ten), Florence Maggio Musicale Chorus *(rec 1967)* Memories 2-▲ MEM 4504 [AAD]
Donizetti, G.:Maria Stuarda (sels), w. L. Gencer (sop), S. Verrett (mez), F. Tagliavini (ten), Florence Maggio Musicale Chorus, 11 arias from Acts 2 & 3 [I] *(rec 5/2/67)* Myto 2-▲ 2 MCD 91137 [ADD]

R. Muti (cnd)
Bellini, V.:Norma, w. Jane Eaglen (sop—Norma), Eva Mei (sop—Adalgisa), Vincenzo La Scola (ten—Pollione), Dmitri Kavrakos (bass—Oroveso), Florence Maggio Musicale Chorus *(rec live, Alighieri Theater, Florence, July 1994)* EMI Classics 2-▲ CDCC 55471
Leoncavallo, R.:Pagliacci, w. Mietta Sighele (sop), Richard Tucker (ten), Kari Murmela (bar), Walter Alberti (bar), Florence Maggio Musicale Chorus *(rec Florence , 1971)* Memories ▲ MEM 4576 [ADD]
Mozart, W.A.:Con 24 Pno, w. S. Richter (pno) Memories ▲ HR 4218 (m) [ADD]
Rossini, G.:Stabat Mater, w. Robert Gambill (ten)—Cujus animam gementem EMI Classics ("Encore" series) ▲ CDE 68308 [ADD/DDD]

J. Perlea (cnd)
Tchaikovsky, P.:Mazeppa, w. M. Olivero (sop), M. Radev (mez), D. Poleri (ten), E. Bastianini (bar), B. Christoff (bass), Florence Maggio Musicale Chorus [I] *(rec live 6/6/54)* Melodram 2-▲ MEL 27070 (m) [AAD]

J. Pritchard (cnd)
Verdi, G.:La traviata, w. J. Sutherland (sop), C. Bergonzi (ten), R. Merrill (bar), Florence Maggio Musicale Chorus [I] London 2-▲ 411877-2 [ADD]
Verdi, G.:La traviata (sels), w. J. Sutherland (sop), C. Bergonzi (ten), R. Merrill (bar) London ▲ 421325-2 [ADD]

B. Rigacci (cnd)
Donizetti, G.:Don Pasquale, w. R. Scotto (sop), L. Alva (ten), W. Alberti (bar), F. Corena (bass), Florence Maggio Musicale Chorus [I] *(rec live, Florence 3/1/67)* Claque 2-▲ CLQ 2011 (m)

N. Sanzogno (cnd)
Meyerbeer, G.:Roberto il Diavolo, w. R. Scotto (sop), G. Merighi (sgr), B. Christoff (bass), Florence Maggio Musicale Chorus [I] *(rec live, 4/7/68)* Arkadia 3-▲ 549 (m) [ADD]
Meyerbeer, G.:Roberto il Diavolo, w. R. Scotto (sop), G. Merighi (sgr), B. Christoff (bass), Florence Maggio Musicale Chorus [I] *(rec live 4/7/68)* Melodram 3-▲ MEL 37024

T. Schippers (cnd)
Verdi, G.:Il trovatore, w. M. Caballé (sop), G. Tucker (ten), M. Zanasi (bar), Florence Maggio Musicale Chorus *(rec 1968)* Memories ▲ MEM 4521 [ADD]
Verdi, G.:Il trovatore, w. M. Caballé (sop), G. Tucker (ten), M. Zanasi (bar), Florence Maggio Musicale Chorus [I] *(rec live 1968)* Melodram 2-▲ MEL 27035

T. Serafin (cnd)
Donizetti, G.:Lucia di Lammermoor, w. M. Callas (sop), G. di Stefano (ten), T. Gobbi (bar), R. Arie (bass) [I] EMI Classics (Studio) 2-▲ CDMB 69980 (m) [ADD]
Verdi, G.:Aroldo, w. A. Stella (sop), G. Penno (ten), A. Protti (bar), F. Novelli (bar), Florence Maggio Musicale Chorus [I] *(rec live 6/3/53)* Melodram 2-▲ MEL 27014 (m) [AAD]
Verdi, G.:La traviata (sels), w. R. Tebaldi (sop), N. Filacuridi (ten), U. Savarese (bar), Florence Maggio Musicale Chorus *(rec live, Florence 1956)* Melodram ▲ MEL 15006

A. Votto (cnd)
Puccini, G.:La Bohème (sels), w. R. Scotto (sop), G. Poggi (ten), T. Gobbi (bar), Maneguzzer (sgr) IMP Collectors Series ▲ IMPX 9024 [AAD]
Verdi, G.:Don Carlos, w. Anita Cerquetti (sop), Cesare Siepi (b-bar), Ettore Bastianini (bar), Gianni Barbieri (bass), Florence Maggio Musicale Chorus Melodram 3-▲ CDM 370104
Verdi, G.:Don Carlos, w. A. Cerquetti (sop), F. Barbieri (mez), A. LoForese (ten), E. Bastianini (bar), C. Siepi (b-bar), G. Neri (bass), Florence Maggio Musicale Chorus *(rec July 16, 1956)* Melodram 3-▲ MLO 670104 [ADD]

M. Wolf-Ferrari (cnd)
Cimarosa, D.:Il Matrimonio segreto, w. Alda Noni (sop), Giulietta Simionato (mez), Riccardo Cassinelli (ten), Cesare Valletti (ten), Sesto Bruscantini (bar), Rovero (sgr) *(rec 1950)* Cetra Classic 2-▲ CDO 32

Florence Teatro Comunale Orch
C. Abbado (cnd)
Rossini, G.:L'italiana in Algeri, w. T. Berganza (sop), L. Zannini (mez), U. Benelli (ten), E. Dara (bar), A. Romero (bar), P. Montarsolo (bass), Florence Teatro Comunale Chorus *(rec 1973)* Great Opera Performances ▲ GOP 740

B. Bartoletti (cnd)
Verdi, G.:Attila, w. M. Roberti (sop—Odabella), G. Limarilli (tenor—Foresto), G. Guelfi (baritone—Ezio), B. Christoff (bass—Attila), Florence Teatro Comunale Chorus *(rec Jan. 12, 1962)* Myto 2-▲ MCD 93589 [DDD]

G. Gavazzeni (cnd)
Donizetti, G.:L'elisir d'amore, w. Renata Scotto (sop), Carlo Bergonzi (ten), Giuseppe Taddei (bar), Carlo Cava (bass), Florence Teatro Comunale Chorus *(rec June 1967)* Pantheon 2-▲ PHE 6612 (m)

E. Ghiglia (cnd)
Bellini, V.:Il pirata, w. Montserrat Caballé (sop—Imogene), Flora Raffanelli (sop—Adele), Flaviano Labó (ten—Gualtiero), Giuseppe Baratti (ten—Itulbo), Piero Cappuccilli (bar—Ernesto), Florence Teatro Comunale Chorus *(rec live, Florence, 1967)* Melodram 2-▲ IMC 205002 [ADD]

E. Kleiber (cnd)
Verdi, G.:I vespri siciliani, w. M. Callas (sop), Kokolios-Bardi (sgr), E. Mascherini (bar), Florence Teatro Comunale Chorus [I] *(rec live 5/26/51)* Melodram 3-▲ MEL 36020 (m)

Florence Teatro Comunale Orch (cont.)
E. Kleiber (cnd) (cont.)
Verdi, G.:I vespri siciliani, w. Maria Callas (sop—Duchess), Giorgio Kokolios Bardi (ten—Arrigo), Gino Sarri (ten—Danieli), Enzo Mascherini (bar—Guido di Monforte), Boris Christoff (bass—Giovanni da Procida), Mario Forsini (bass—Count Vaudemont), Bruneo Carmassi (bass—Bethune), Florence Teatro Comunale Chorus *(rec live, Florence, 1951)* Melodram 3-▲ IMC 303016 [ADD]

R. Muti (cnd)
Bellini, V.:Norma, w. Margherita Rinaldi (sop—Adalgisa), Renata Scotto (sop—Norma), Giuseppina Arista (mez—Clotilde), Ermanno Mauro (ten—Pollione), Giancarlo Turati (ten—Flavio), Agostino Ferrin (bass—Oroveso), Florence Teatro Comunale Chorus *(rec Florence, Dec 19, 1978)* Legato Classics 2-▲ LCD 203-2
Leoncavallo, R.:Pagliacci, w. M. Sighele (sop), R. Tucker (ten), E. Lorenzi (ten), K. Nurmela (bar), Florence Teatro Comunale Chorus *(rec live, Florence, 1971)* Foyer ▲ FOY 2050 [AAD]
Verdi, G.:Un ballo in maschera, w. C. Deutekom (sop), G. Tucker (ten), R. Bruson (bar), Florence Teatro Comunale Chorus *(rec live, Florence 1972)* Foyer 2-▲ FOY 2047 [AAD]
Verdi, G.:Il trovatore, w. Fiorenza Cossotto (mez), Carlos Cossutta (ten), Agistino Ferrin (bass), Florence Teatro Comunale Chorus *(rec live, 1978)* Serenissima 2-▲ SER 306101 [ADD]

T. Serafin (cnd)
Rossini, G.:Armida, w. L. Albanese (sop), M. Callas (sop), M. Filippeschi (ten), G. Raimondi (ten), Florence Teatro Comunale Chorus [I] *(rec live, Florence, 4/26/52)* Melodram 2-▲ MEL 26024

E. Tieri (cnd)
Verdi, G.:Un ballo in maschera, w. A. Cerquetti (sop), E. Stignani (mez), G. Poggi (ten), E. Bastianini (bar), Florence Teatro Comunale Chorus [I] *(rec live 1/6/57)* Standing Room Only 2-▲ SRO 804-2 (m) [ADD]

Florestan Trio [Susan Tomes (pno), Anthony Marwood (vn), Richard Lester (vc)]
Dvořák, A.:Trio 3 Pno Hyperion ▲ 66895
Dvořák, A.:Trio 4 Pno, "Dumky" Hyperion ▲ 66895

Florida Musica Nova
R. Burrichter (cnd)
White, J.:Music of the Open Road Opus One ▲ CD 167 [DDD]

Florida PO
J. Judd (cnd)
Mahler, G.:Blumine Harmonia Mundi USA ▲ HMU 907118 [DDD]
Mahler, G.:Sym 1 Harmonia Mundi USA ▲ HMU 907118 [DDD]
Walton, W.:Capriccio burlesco Harmonia Mundi USA ▲ HMU 907070
Walton, W.:Con Vn, w. A. Rosand (vn) Harmonia Mundi USA ▲ HMU 907070
Walton, W.:Henry V (film suite) Harmonia Mundi USA ▲ HMU 907070
Walton, W.:Spitfire Prelude & Fugue Harmonia Mundi USA ▲ HMU 907070

Florida State Univ Band
J. Croft (cnd)
Fillmore, H.:Marches—Americans We; Bull Trombone; Crosley March; Dusty Trombone; The Footlifter; His Excellency; King Karl King; His Honor; The Klaxon; Lassus Trombone; March Lord Baltimore; Men of Ohio; Miami March; Miss Trombone; National City Press Club; Noble Men; Sally Trombone; Shoutin' Liza Tombone *(rec 10/90)* Pro Arte ▲ CDD 545 [DDD]

Florida String Quartet [P. Wolfe, A. Brooker, Y. Vasilaki, C. Pegis]
Stravinsky, S.S.:Qts Strs *(rec May 1992)* Centaur ▲ CRC 2141 [DDD]

Florida Symphonic Pops Orch
M. Azzolina (cnd)
A Bride's Book, w. Lyn Larsen (org) Pro Arte ▲ CDS 564 [DDD]
Wedding Day, w. Lyn Larsen (org), St. Louis Brass Pro Arte ▲ CDD 569 [DDD]

Florilegium
Styles, w. Pieter Wispelwey (vc), Paul Komen (pno), Lois Shapiro (pno) Channel Classics ▲ CCS 395

Flute Exchange
Thow, J.:Breath of the Sun Music & Arts ▲ CD 915

Flute Force
Flute Force CRI ▲ CRI 581 [DDD]
Newman, Anthony:Chamber Music, w. M. Mills (pno), P.J. Bacchus (fl), Y. Waldman (vn), D. Wan, Laurentian String Quartet—Qnt for Piano & Strings, "Easter"; Qt for 4 Flutes; Introduction & Toccata for Flute & Piano; Vars & Toccata for Violin Newport Classic ▲ NCD 60032 [DDD]

Flute Force [Sheryl Henze (fl), Gretchen Pusch (fl), Rie Schmidt (fl), Wendy Stern (fl)]
Barber, S.:Adagio Strs [arr Rie Schmidt] *(rec Queens College, NY, Sept 1993)* VAI Audio ▲ VAIA 1133 [DDD]
Bozza, E.:Jour d'été à la montagne *(rec Queens College, NY, Sept 1993)* VAI Audio ▲ VAIA 1133 [DDD]
Debussy, C.:La Fille aux cheveaux de lin Pno [arr Rie Schmidt] *(rec Queens College, NY, Sept 1993)* VAI Audio ▲ VAIA 1133 [DDD]
Debussy, C.:Rêverie [arr Rie Schmidt] *(rec Queens College, NY, Sept 1993)* VAI Audio ▲ VAIA 1133 [DDD]
Handel, G.F.:Semele, w. Julius Baker (fl)—Where'er you walk [arr Cooper] *(rec Queens College, NY, Sept 1993)* VAI Audio ▲ VAIA 1133 [DDD]
Ravel, M.:Daphnis et Chloé (suite 2), w. Julius Baker (fl) [arr Rie Schmidt] *(rec Queens College, NY, Sept 1993)* VAI Audio ▲ VAIA 1133 [DDD]
Reicha, A.:Qt for 4 Fls *(rec Queens College, NY, Sept 1993)* VAI Audio ▲ VAIA 1133 [DDD]
Sollberger, H.:Grand Qt CRI ▲ CD 581 [DDD]
Stravinsky, I.:Pastorale [arr Wilkins & Gearhart] *(rec Queens College, NY, Sept 1993)* VAI Audio ▲ VAIA 1133 [DDD]

Fodor Quintet
Foerster, J.B.:Qnt Ww Ottavo ▲ OTT 69031 [DDD]
Janácek, L.:Youth, w. H. Sparnaay (b cl) Ottavo ▲ OTT 69031 [DDD]
Reicha, A.:Adagio E Hn Ottavo ▲ OTT 69031 [DDD]
Reicha, A.:Andantes E Hn Ottavo ▲ OTT 69031 [DDD]
Reicha, J.:Adagio E Hn Ottavo ▲ OTT 69031 [DDD]
Reicha, J.:Andantes E Hn Ottavo ▲ OTT 69031 [DDD]

Foerster Woodwind Quintet
Husa, K.:Serenade CRI ■ C 261
Janácek, L.:Youth, w. Josef Horák (b cl) Panton ▲ PAN 811203

K. Husa (cnd)
Husa, K.:Serenade, Prague SO *(rec 1970)* CRI ▲ CD 592 [ADD]

Folger Consort
Benet, J.:Madrigals—The Hunt is Up Folger Consort ■ BDCD1 9001C
Byrd, W.:Consort Music—My Mistress Had a Little Dog; Barley-Break; Fant in 5 Parts; My Lord of Oxenford's Maske Folger Consort ■ BDCD1 9001C
Dowland, J.:Consort Music—The King of Denmark's Galliard; Now, Oh Now, I Needs Must Part; Sir John Souch His Galliard; M. Thomas Collier His Galliard; M. Nicholas Gryffith His Galliard; Dear, If You Change; The Earl of Essex Galliard; Daphne Was Not So Chaste; M. Giles Hobies Galliard; Fine Knacks for Ladies; M. Buctons Galliard *(rec live, Folger's Great Hall, Feb 9, 1986)* Folger Consort ■ BDCD1 9001C
Hume, T.:The First Part of Ayres—The Spirit of Gambo Folger Consort ■ BDCD1 9001C
Morley, T.:Madrigals & Songs—O Mistress Mine; La couranto Folger Consort ■ BDCD1 9001C
Wilbye, J.:Madrigals—Ne riminiscaris Folger Consort ■ BDCD1 9001C

Folger Consort [R. Eisenstein, C. Kendall, S. Reiss]
Carmina Burana & Other Spirited Songs from the German Middle Ages, w. M. Bleeke, T. Chancey Folger Consort ▲ BDCD1 8901 [DAD]
Dance Songs of Renaissance England, w. M. Bleeke, T. Chancey, W. Gillespie, M. Springfels, B. Wissick *(rec Jan. 24, 1988)* Folger Consort ▲ BDCD1 9004 [DDD]
A Distant Mirror:Music of the 14th Century & Shakespeare's Music Delos ▲ DE 1003 [AAD]
Divisions on an Ayre:Lute Songs & Instrumental Music circa 1600, w. W. Sharp (bar) Folger Consort ▲ BDCD1 9005 [DDD]
Of Kindly Lust & Love's Inspiring:Pastoral Music from Italy to Elizabethan England Folger Consort ▲ BDCD1 9308

Folios Guitar Duo [Neil Anderson (gtr), William Buonocore (gtr)]
Folios Guitar Duo *(rec Jan. 16 & 17, 1992)* Centaur ▲ CRC 2181 [DDD]
Folkwang CO
Sibelius, J.:Adagio Vn, w. Pekka Dauppinen (vn) Koch Schwann ▲ SCH 317862
Sibelius, J.:Suite Vn Strs, w. Pekka Dauppinen (vn) Koch Schwann ▲ SCH 317862
H. Dressel (cnd)
Beethoven, L. van:Con Vn, Vc & Pno, "Triple Con", w. H. Szeryng (pno), J. Starker (vc), L. Grychtolowna (pno) Philips ("Duo" series) 2-▲ 442580-2
R. Maxym (cnd)
Wolf-Ferrari, E.:Concertino E hn, w. O. Zoboli (ob) Koch Schwann ▲ CD 310113 [DDD]
Wolf-Ferrari, E.:Idillio-Concertino, w. O. Zoboli (ob) Koch Schwann ▲ CD 310113 [DDD]
Folkwang Guitar Duo [Carsten Linck (gtr), Volker Niehusmann (gtr)]
Bad Boy Signum ▲ SIG X70-00 [DDD]
Works for 2 Guitars from the Renaissance & Baroque Signum ▲ X 49-00 [DDD]
La Follia Ensemble
Damaré, E.:Music of, w. Jean-Louis Beaumadier (petite fl), Christophe Poiget (vn), Marc Giradot, (ophicleide/tuba), Circe Wind Quintet—La Capricieuse, Op. 270; Feux follets, Op. 378; Les Échos des bois, Op. 220; Le Merle blanc, Op. 161; Tarentelle, Op. 391; L'Oiseau et les roses, Op. 153; Le Tourbillon, Op. 212; L'Alouette, Op. 172; Pizzicato, Op. 426; La Danse des grillons, Op. 380 *(rec 1996)* Calliope ▲ CAL 9869 [DDD]
Music in Austria before Mozart:Late 17th-Early 18th Century *(rec 1992)* VTL-The Vital Sound ▲ VTLCLAS001 [DDD]
M. de la Fuente (cnd)
Boccherini, L.:Stabat Mater, w. T. Hert (sop), K. Oshita (sop), J.-C. Orilac (ten)—2nd version—Op. 61 [L] *(rec 1979)* Arion ▲ ARN 68164 [ADD]
C. Poiget (cnd)
Vivaldi, A.:Cons Tpt, w. F. Presle (tpt)—in a, RV.461; in d, RV.454; in D, RV.453; in C, RV.447; in a, RV.463; in C, RV.450 Chamade ▲ 5616 [DDD]
Föllinger-Hedberg String Quartet
The String Quartet in Sweden:A Cavalcade of Its History, w. Barkel String Quartet, Stockholm String Quartet, Garaguly String Quartet, Kyndel String Quartet, Ivan Ericson String Quartet, Grünfarb String Quartet, Skûne String Quartet, Hälsingborg String Quartet, Göteborg String Quartet, Galli String Quartet *(rec before 1951)* Caprice 5-▲ CAP 21506 [AAD/ADD]
Il Fondamento
Hasse, J.A.:Miserere in e, w. Greta de Reyghere (sop), Dina Grossberger (mez), Ian Honeyman (ten), D Snellincks (bass) Opus 111 ▲ OPS 3080
Hasse, J.A.:Requiem, w. Greta de Reyghere (sop), Dina Grossberger (mez), Ian Honeyman (ten), D. Snellincks (bass) Opus 111 ▲ OPS 3080
P. Dombrecht (cnd)
Telemann, G.P.:Musique de Table—Set 3, Nos. 1-6 Accent ▲ 78643
Fonte di Musica CO
W. Kohlhaussen (cnd)
Stamitz, A.:Con 8 Vn, w. W. Kohlhaussen (vn) Ars Produktion ▲ FCD 368307
Stamitz, C.:Qt Orch Ars Produktion ▲ FCD 368307
Stamitz, J.W.A.:Sinfs—Sinf. in G Ars Produktion ▲ FCD 368307
Zach, J.:Music of—Symphonies Nos. 3-5; Sym. No. 2 in D for 12 Violins & Basso Continuo *(rec 2/90)* Ars Produktion ▲ FCD 368314 [DDD]
Zach, J.:Music of—Symphonies Nos. 1 & 2; Sonata a tre stromenti in D; Sym. No. 1 in G for 12 Violins & Basso Continuo *(rec 2/90)* Ars Produktion ▲ FCD 368313 [DDD]
La Fontegara Amsterdam
Boismortier, J.B. de:Sons, Op. 7 [rcr trio w continuo]—Sonata Nos. 3 & 5 Globe ▲ GLO 5033 [DDD]
Boismortier, J.B. de:Sons, Op. 34 [rcr trio w continuo] Globe ▲ GLO 5033 [DDD]
La Fontegara Amsterdam [Saskia Coolen (rcr), Peter Holtslag (rcr), Hans Tol (rcr)]
Common Grounds *(rec Utrecht, Dec. 1993)* Globe ▲ GLO 5112 [DDD]
17th Century Italian Recorder Music Globe ▲ GLO 5065 [DDD]
La Fontegara Consort
Il Giardino dell'Amore:Instrumental Music in Europe from the Medieval & Renaissance Periods Bongiovanni ▲ GB 5532 [DDD]
Fontenay Trio
Beethoven, L. van:Trios Pno (comp) Teldec 3-▲ 73281
Debussy, C.:Trio Pno Teldec ▲ 2292-44937-2 ZK
Dvořák, A.:Trios Pno, Opp. 21, 26, 65, 90 Teldec 2-▲ 9031-76458-2
Fauré, G.:Trio Teldec ▲ 2292-44937-2 ZK
Mendelssohn, F.:Trio 1 Pno Teldec ▲ 2292-44947-2 [DDD]
Mendelssohn, F.:Trio 2 Pno Teldec ▲ 2292-44947-2 [DDD]
Messiaen, O.:Quatuor pour la fin du temps, w. E. Brunner (cl) Teldec ▲ 9031-73239-2 ZK [DDD]
Mozart, W.A.:Trio Pno, K.496 Teldec 2-▲ 2292-46439-2
Mozart, W.A.:Trio Pno, K.502 Teldec 2-▲ 2292-46439-2
Mozart, W.A.:Trio Pno, K.542 Teldec 2-▲ 2292-46439-2
Mozart, W.A.:Trio Pno, K.548 Teldec 2-▲ 2292-46439-2
Mozart, W.A.:Trio Pno, K.564 Teldec 2-▲ 2292-46439-2
Ravel, M.:Trio Pno Teldec ▲ 2292-44937-2 ZK
E. Inbal (cnd)
Beethoven, L. van:Con Vn, Vc & Pno, "Triple Con", Philharmonia Orch Teldec ▲ 2292-46441-2 ZK
Beethoven, L. van:Con Vn, Vc & Pno, "Triple Con", Philharmonia Orch Teldec ("M Line" series) ▲ 97447-2
Fort Worth Chamber Ensemble
A Ceremony of Carols, w. G. Bragg (cnd), Gregg Smith Singers, Dorothy Shaw Hand Bell Choir, Texas Boys Choir Allegretto ▲ ACD 8407 [ADD]
Fort Worth CO
T. Seelig (cnd)
Brahms, J.:Alto Rhap, w. Melanie Sonnenberg (mez), Turtle Creek Chorale *(rec Meyerson Symphony Center, Dallas, June 15-16, 1995)* Reference ▲ RR 67 [DDD]
Bruckner, A.:Choral Music, w. Fort Worth Sym Brass, Turtle Creek Chorale—Das deutsche Lied; Ave Maria; Abendzauber [w. Timothy Jenkins (ten)] *(rec Meyerson Symphony Center, Dallas, June 15-16, 1995)* Reference ▲ RR 67 [DDD]
Schubert, Franz:Choral Part-Songs, w. Melanie Sonnenberg (mez), Turtle Creek Chorale—Ständchen *(rec Meyerson Symphony Center, Dallas, June 15-16, 1995)* Reference ▲ RR 67 [DDD]
Strauss, R.:Die Tageszeiten, w. Turtle Creek Chorale *(rec Meyerson Symphony Center, Dallas, June 15-16, 1995)* Reference ▲ RR 67 [DDD]
Fort Worth Sym Brass
Bruckner, A.:Choral Music, w. Fort Worth CO, Turtle Creek Chorale—Das deutsche Lied; Ave Maria; Abendzauber [w. Timothy Jenkins (ten)] *(rec Meyerson Symphony Center, Dallas, June 15-16, 1995)* Reference ▲ RR 67 [DDD]
Mendelssohn, F.:An die Künstler, w. Turtle Creek Chorale *(rec Meyerson Symphony Center, Dallas, June 15-16, 1995)* Reference ▲ RR 67 [DDD]
40 Cellos of the London PO
G. Simon (cnd)
Balcombe, R.:Greensleeves Suite, Royal PO, BBC SO, Philharmonia Orch *(rec All Hallows Church, London, Jan 18 & Apr 2, 1993)* Cala ▲ CACD 104 [DDD]
Bernstein, L.:West Side Story (sels), Royal PO, BBC SO, Philharmonia Orch—Tonight [arr. Balcombe] *(rec All Hallows Church, London, Jan 18 & Apr 2, 1993)* Cala ▲ CACD 104 [DDD]
Casals, P.:Sardana, Royal PO, BBC SO, Philharmonia Orch *(rec All Hallows Church, London, Jan 18 & Apr 2, 1993)* Cala ▲ CACD 104 [DDD]
Rachmaninoff, S.:Vocalise, BBC SO, Philharmonia Orch, Royal PO [arr. Balcombe] *(rec All Hallows Church, London, Jan 18 & Apr 2, 1993)* Cala ▲ CACD 104 [DDD]
Saint-Saëns, C.:Le Cygne, Royal PO, BBC SO, Philharmonia Orch [arr. Balcombe] *(rec All Hallows Church, London, Jan 18 & Apr 2, 1993)* Cala ▲ CACD 104 [DDD]

48 Violas of Academy of St. Martin in the Fields
The London Viola Sound, w. BBC SO, English National Opera Orch, London PO *(rec Colosseum, Watford, UK, Jan 24, 1995)* Cala ▲ CACD 106 [DDD]
Four in Hand Grosmont Handbell Ringers
Ringing Clear:The Art of Handbell Ringing, w. Sound in Brass Handbells, Launton Handbell Ringers, Change Ringing Handbell Group Saydisc ▲ CDSDL 333 [AAD]
Four Nations Ensemble [Andrew Appel (hpd), Ryan Brown (vn), Loretta O'Sullivan (vc)]
Schobert, J.:Sons Hpd, Op. 16 ASV ▲ ASV CD 156
Francesco Trio [Nathan Schwartz (pno), M. Watanabe (vn), Bonnie Hampton (vc)]
Harbison, J.:Trio Pno, Vn & Vc Music & Arts ▲ CD 756 [DDD]
Imbrie, A.W.:Trio 2 Pno Music & Arts ▲ CD 756 [DDD]
Powell, Mel:Trio Pno Music & Arts ▲ CD 756 [DDD]
Shifrin, S.:Trio Pno Music & Arts ▲ CD 756 [DDD]
Thow, J.:Qt Cl, w. Gary Gray (cl) Music & Arts ▲ CD 915
Franciscan Quartet
Smart, G.:Music of, w. B. Theurer (tpt), M. Smart (sop), G. Smart (pno)—Trumpeter Swan; Fanfare, Invocation & Alleluia Capstone ▲ CPS 8612 CD [DDD]
César Franck Ensemble
Franck, C.:Qt Strs Koch Schwann ▲ CD 310532 [DDD]
Franck, C.:Qnt Pno Koch Schwann ▲ CD 310552 [DDD]
Franck, C.:Son Vn Koch Schwann ▲ CD 310552 [DDD]
Frankenland State SO
M. Loy (cnd)
Lortzing, A.:Hans Sachs, w. M. Weindl (sop), K. Schmitt-Walter (bar) *(rec 1950)* Memories 2-▲ MEM 4550 [ADD]
Sauvina, Kloss (cnd)
Rózsa, M.:Film Music DRG ▲ CDSBL 13101
Frankfurt Baroque Orch
J.E. Martini (cnd)
Bach, J.S.:Cant 102, w. Frankfurt Kantorei EDA ▲ EDA 002-2 [DDD]
Bach, J.S.:Christmas Oratorio, w. Frankfurt Kantorei EDA ▲ EDA 002-2 [DDD]
Bach, J.S.:St. John Passion, w. Frankfurt Kantorei EDA ▲ EDA 002-2 [DDD]
Handel, G.F.:Solomon, w. Frankfurt Kantorei EDA ▲ EDA 002-2 [DDD]
Monteverdi, C.:Vespro della Beata Vergine, w. Frankfurt Kantorei EDA ▲ EDA 002-2 [DDD]
Mozart, W.A.:Missa, K.427, w. Frankfurt Kantorei EDA ▲ EDA 002-2 [DDD]
Frankfurt Contra Bass Quartet
Quattro Contra Bassi MD + G ▲ MDG CD 6030634
Frankfurt on the Oder PO
N. Athinãos (cnd)
Rheinberger, J.:Die 7 Raben—Ov. Signum ▲ X 50-00 [DDD]
Rheinberger, J.:Wallenstein Signum ▲ X 50-00 [DDD]
A. Walter (cnd)
Furtwängler, W.:Geisterchor, w. Frankfurt on the Oder Phil Chorus *(rec Konzarthalle C.P.E. Bach, Frankfurt on the Oder, June 22-25 1993)* Marco Polo ▲ 8.223546 [DDD]
Furtwängler, W.:Religiöser Hymnus, w. *(sop unknown)*, Guido Pikal (ten), Frankfurt on the Oder Phil Chorus *(rec Konzarthalle C.P.E. Bach, Frankfurt on the Oder, June 22-25 1993)* Marco Polo ▲ 8.223546 [DDD]
Furtwängler, W.:Songs, w. Guido Pikal (ten), Alfred Walter (pno), Frankfurt on the Oder Phil Chorus—Der traurige Jäger; Der Schatzgräber; Geduld; Auf dem See; Du sendest, Freund, mir Lieder; Erinnerung; Das Vaterland; Möwenflug; Lied; Erinnerung; Der Soldat *(rec Maison de la Radio Bruxelles, Oct. 7-8, 1993)* Marco Polo ▲ 8.223546 [DDD]
Furtwängler, W.:Te Deum, w. Frankfurt on the Oder Phil Chorus *(rec Konzarthalle C.P.E. Bach, Frankfurt on the Oder, June 22-25 1993)* Marco Polo ▲ 8.223546 [DDD]
Frankfurt on the Oder State Orch
N. Athinãos (cnd)
Czerny, C.:Con Pno 4-Hnds, w. Liu Xiao Ming (pno), Horst Göbel (pno) *(rec Frankfurt, June 24-28, 1996)* Signum ▲ X 78-00 [DDD]
Czerny, C.:Sym 2 *(rec Frankfurt, June 24-28, 1996)* Signum ▲ X 78-00 [DDD]
Frankfurt on the Oder SO
Blacher, B.:Con Vn, w. K. Blacher (vn) Signum ▲ X 40-00 [DDD]
Blacher, B.:Poème Signum ▲ X 40-00 [DDD]
Blacher, B.:Sym Signum ▲ X 40-00 [DDD]
Frankfurt Opera House & Museum Orch
M. Gielen (cnd)
Mahler, G.:Sym 8, w. Frankfurt Opera House & Museum Choruses *(rec 1981)* Sony Classical ("Essential Classics" series) ▲ SBK 48281 [ADD] ■ SBT 48281
Frankfurt RSO
Breezes from the Orient, w. Berlin RSO, various cnds
Breezes from the Orient Vol. 1, w. Berlin RSO, various cnds Capriccio ▲ 10 379 [DDD]
Breezes from the Orient Vol. 2, w. Berlin RSO, various cnds Capriccio ▲ 10 380 [DDD]
Breezes from the Orient Vol. 3, w. Berlin RSO, various cnds Capriccio ▲ 10 381 [DDD]
Breezes from the Orient Vol. 4, w. Berlin RSO, various cnds Capriccio 2-▲ 10 403/04
Ernest Tomlinson, w. Berlin RSO, various cnds Marco Polo ("British Light Music" series) ▲ 8.223413 [DDD]
Haydn Wood, w. Berlin RSO, various cnds Marco Polo ("British Light Music" series) ▲ 8.223402 [DDD]
Robert Farnon, w. Berlin RSO, various cnds Marco Polo ("British Light Music" series) ▲ 8.223401 [DDD]
W.A. Albert (cnd)
Hindemith, P.:Concert Music Pno, Brass & Hps CPO ▲ CPO 999138 [DDD]
Hindemith, P.:Con Cl CPO ▲ CPO 999142 [DDD]
Hindemith, P.:Con Fl, Ob, Cl, Bn, Hp CPO ▲ CPO 999142 [DDD]
Hindemith, P.:Con Hn CPO ▲ CPO 999142 [DDD]
Hindemith, P.:Con Pno, w. S. Mauser (pno) CPO ▲ CPO 999078-2 [DDD]
Hindemith, P.:Con Tpt, Bn & Strs CPO ▲ CPO 999142 [DDD]
Hindemith, P.:Der Dämon CPO ▲ CPO 999220 [DDD]
Hindemith, P.:The Four Temperaments, w. Sigfreid Mauser (pno) CPO ▲ CPO 999078-2 [DDD]
Hindemith, P.:Hérodiade [2 versions] CPO ▲ CPO 999220 [DDD]
Hindemith, P.:Kammermusik 2, w. S. Mauser (pno) CPO ▲ CPO 999138 [DDD]
G. Albrecht (cnd)
Zemlinsky, A. von:Der Traumgörge, w. P. Coburn (sop), J. Martin (sop), G. M. Ronge (sop), B. Calm (mez), P. Haage (ten), H. Kruse (ten), J. Protschka (ten), H. Welker (bar), M. Blasius (bass), V. von Halem (bass) [G] Capriccio 2-▲ CD 10241/2 [DDD]
A. Francis (cnd)
Dohnányi, E. von:American Rhap *(rec HR Studio 1, Dec 13, 1995)* CPO ▲ CPO 999308-2 [DDD]
Dohnányi, E. von:Con 1 Vn, w. Ulf Wallin (vn) *(rec HR Studio 1, Nov 28-Dec 2, 1995)* CPO ▲ CPO 999308-2 [DDD]
E. Inbal (cnd)
Berlioz, H.:L'Enfance du Christ, w. M. Zimmermann (mez), J. Aler (ten), E. Wilm Schulte (bass), S. Dean (bass), P. Kang (bass), Cologne Radio Chorus [F] Denon 2-▲ CO 76863/4 [DDD]
Berlioz, H.:Harold in Italy, w. Y. Bashmet (va) Denon ▲ CO 73207 [DDD]
Berlioz, H.:Lélio, "Le retourà la vie" Denon 2-▲ CO 73218/19 [DDD]
Berlioz, H.:Requiem, "Grande Messe des Morts", w. K. Lewis (ten), Frankfurt Kantorei Denon 2-▲ CO 73205/06 [DDD]
Berlioz, H.:Roméo et Juliette, w. N. Denize (mez), V. Cole (ten), R. Lloyd (bass), Frankfurt Radio Chorus Denon 2-▲ CO 73210/11 [DDD]
Berlioz, H.:Sym fantastique Denon 2-▲ CO 73218/19 [DDD]
Berlioz, H.:Sym fantastique Denon ▲ CO 73208 [DDD]

▲ = CD ♦ = Enhanced CD Δ = MD ■ = Cassette Tape □ = DCC

Frankfurt RSO (cont.)
E. Inbal (cnd) (cont.)
Bruckner, A.:Syms (comp)—Nos. 1-9 Teldec 10-▲ 2292-46068-2 XP [DDD]
Bruckner, A.:Sym 0 Teldec ▲ 2292-46330-2 [DDD]
Bruckner, A.:Sym 3, "Wagner" Teldec ▲ 4509-91445-2
Bruckner, A.:Sym 4, "Romantic" [original 1874 version]
Teldec ("Digital Experience" series) ▲ 9031-77597-2 AW [DDD]
Bruckner, A.:Sym 7 [original version] Teldec ▲ 2292-43259 ZK [DDD]
Bruckner, A.:Sym 9 Teldec ▲ 4509-91446-2 ■ 4509-91446-4
Mahler, G.:Lied von der Erde, w. *(soloists unknown)* Denon 15-▲ DEN 75216
Mahler, G.:Das Lied von der Erde, w. J. Van Nes (cta), P. Schreier (ten) [G] Denon ▲ CO 72605 [DDD]
Mahler, G.:Syms (comp) [includes Deryck Cooke's 1st edition (2nd performing version) of Sym 10]
Denon 15-▲ DEN 75216
Mahler, G.:Sym 1 Denon ▲ 7537 [DDD]
Mahler, G.:Sym 3, w. D. Soffel (mez), Frankfurt Radio Chorus [G] Denon 2-▲ 7828/29 [DDD]
Mahler, G.:Sym 4, w. N. Donath (sop) [G] Denon ▲ 7952 [DDD]
Mahler, G.:Sym 5 Denon ▲ CO 1088 [DDD]
Mahler, G.:Sym 6 Denon 2-▲ CO 1327/28 [DDD]
Mahler, G.:Sym 7 Denon 2-▲ CO 1553/54 [DDD]
Mahler, G.:Sym 8, w. *(chorus unknown) [G,L]* Denon 2-▲ CO 1564/65 [DDD]
Mahler, G.:Sym 9 Denon 2-▲ CO 1566/67 [DDD]
Mahler, G.:Sym 10—Adagio Denon 2-▲ CO 1566/67 [DDD]
Mahler, G.:Sym 10 Denon ▲ CO 75129 [DDD]
Puccini, G.:Mass, w. K. Lõvaas (sop), W. Hollweg (ten), B. McDaniel (bar), West German Radio Chorus
Philips ("Collector" series) ▲ 434170-2 [ADD]
Rachmaninoff, S.:Con 2 Pno, w. W. Haas (pno) Philips ("Concert Classics" series) ▲ 422465-2
Schoenberg, A.:Chamber Sym 1 Denon ▲ DEN 78843 [DDD]
Schoenberg, A.:Die Jakobsleiter, w. Barbara Kilduff (sop—Seele 1), Jadwiga Rappé (cta—Sterbende), Wilfried Gahmlich (ten—Aufrührerischer), Cornelius Hauptmann (ten—Gabriel), Keith Lewis (ten—Berfener), Kurt Azesberger (bar—Mönch), Barbara Fuchs (sgr—Seele 2), Matteo de Monti (sgr—Ringender), Bjorn Waag (sgr—Auserwählter), Robin Gritton (cnd), Berlin Radio Chorus *(rec Alte Oper, Frankfurt, Sept 6-9, 1994)* Denon ▲ CO 78977 [DDD]
Schoenberg, A.:Verklärte Nacht *(rec Alte Oper, Frankfurt, Jan 11-13, 1995)*
Denon ▲ CO 78822 [DDD]
Schumann, R.:Sym 2 Denon ▲ DEN 78843 [DDD]
Schumann, R.:Sym 3 *(rec Alte Oper, Frankfurt, Jan 11-13, 1995)* Denon ▲ CO 78822 [DDD]
Scriabin, A.:Sym 1, w. *(chorus unknown)* Philips ("Duo" series) 2-▲ 454 271-2
Scriabin, A.:Sym 2 Philips ("Duo" series) 2-▲ 454 271-2
Scriabin, A.:Sym 3 Philips ("Duo" series) 2-▲ 454 271-2
Scriabin, A.:Sym 4 Philips ("Duo" series) 2-▲ 454 271-2
Shostakovich, D.:Sym 5 Denon ▲ CO 74175 [DDD]
Tchaikovsky, P.:Con 1 Pno, w. W. Haas (pno) Philips ("Concert Classics" series) ▲ 422465-2
Tchaikovsky, P.:Sym 6 Denon ▲ CO 77715 [DDD]
Wagner, R.:Tristan und Isolde (prelude & liebestod) Denon ▲ CO 77715-2 [DDD]
Webern, A.:Con Fl *(rec Sendesaal, Hessischer Radio, Sept 3-5, 1994)* Denon ▲ CO 78977 [DDD]
Webern, A.:Im Sommerwind Denon ▲ DEN 78843 [DDD]
Webern, A.:Pieces Orch, Op. 6 *(rec Alte Oper, Frankfurt, Sept 6-9, 1994)*
Denon ▲ CO 78977 [DDD]
Webern, A.:Pieces Orch, Op. 10 *(rec Sendesaal HR, Frankfurt, Jan 3-6, 1995)*
Denon ▲ CO 78822 [DDD]
Inbal, Markevitch, Haitink (cnd)
Tchaikovsky, P.:Orch Music, Royal Concertgebouw Orch—Fatum, Op. 77; Francesca da Rimini, Op. 32; Hamlet, Op. 67a; The Tempest, Op. 18; The Storm, Op. 76; The Voyevode, Op. 78; Romeo & Juliet; Ov. 1812 Philips ("Duo" series) 2-▲ 442586-2
E. Mata (cnd)
Falla, M. de:Noches en los jardines de España, w. T. Joselson (pno) Olympia ▲ OCD 351 [DDD]
Orbón, J.:Partita 4, w. T. Joselson (pno) Olympia ▲ OCD 351 [DDD]
C. Schuricht (cnd)
Bach, J.S.:Suite 2 Orch, w. *(soloist unknown)* Theorema ▲ TH 121222 [DDD]
Bach, J.S.:Suite 3 Orch Theorema ▲ TH 121222 [DDD]
Brahms, J.:Sym 1 *(rec live 1965)* Melodram ▲ CDM 18045 [ADD]
L. Stokowski (cnd)
Messiaen, O.:Hymne au Saint Sacrement *(rec 1955)* Music & Arts ▲ CD 770 [AAD]
R. Tschupp (cnd)
Suter, R.:Die Ballade von des Cortez Leuten, w. P. Schweiger (spkr), Frankfurt Music School Chorus
Jecklin ▲ JD 690
M. Viotti (cnd)
Franchetti, A.:Cristoforo Colombo, w. R. Ragatzu (sop—Isabella), G. Pasino (mez—Annacoana), M. Berti (ten—Ferdinand), R. Bruson (bar—Cristoforo Colombo), R. Scandiuzzi (bass—Don Roldano Ximenes), Frankfurt Radio Chorus [I] *(rec live, Alte Oper Frankfurt, 8/30 & 9/2 1991)*
Koch Schwann 3-▲ CD 3-1030-2 [DDD]
Mozart, W.A.:Entführung, w. S. Greenburg (sop), J. Thames (sop), J. van der Schaaf (ten), W. Gahmlich (ten), K. Rydl (bass), Trissenaar (sgr), Bamberg Sym Chorus Capriccio 2-▲ 10 403/04
Mozart, W.A.:Entführung, w. S. Greenberg (sop), J. Thames (sop), J. Van Der Schaaf (ten), W. Gahmlich (ten), K. Rydl (bass), Bamberg Sym Chorus LaserLight ▲ 14117 [DDD]
L. Vis (cnd)
Cage, J.:Qts I-VIII *(rec live, Sendesaal Hessischer Radio, Nov. 6, 1992)* Hat Hut ▲ CD 6168 [ADD]
Cage, J.:Sixty-Eight *(rec live, Sendesaal Hessischer Radio, Nov. 6, 1992)* Hat Hut ▲ CD 6168 [ADD]
Frankfurt Renaissance Ensemble
Ave Regina Coelorum, w. Isaak Ensemble Heidelberg Bayer ▲ 100082 [DDD]
Frankfurt State Orch
N. Athinãos (cnd)
Dessau, P.:Symphonic Adaptation Signum ▲ X65-00 [DDD]
Dessau, P.:Sym 1 Signum ▲ X65-00 [DDD]
Dessau, P.:Les Voix, w. Ksenija Lukic (sop), Horst Göbel (pno) Signum ▲ X65-00 [DDD]
Lalo, E.:Con Pno, w. David Gross (pno) Signum ▲ X66-00 [DDD]
Lalo, E.:Romance-sérénade, w. Juri Toschmakow (vn) Signum ▲ X66-00 [DDD]
Lalo, E.:Scherzo Signum ▲ X66-00 [DDD]
Lalo, E.:Sym in g Signum ▲ X66-00 [DDD]
Freiburg Bach Orch
H.M. Beuerle (cnd)
Brahms, J.:Ein Deutsches Requiem, w. Christiane Oelze (sop), Kevin McMillan (bar), Freiburg Bach Choir
Ars Musici ▲ 1057 [DDD]
Freiburg Baroque Orch
Biber, H. von:Sons (misc)—Nos. 1 & 12 a otto, 4, 6-8 & 10 a cinque *(rec Maria Minor Church, Utrecht, Nov 21-23 & May 2-5, 1995)* Deutsche Harmonia Mundi ▲ 05472-77348-2 [DDD]
Schmelzer, J.H.:Sons Instrs—a tre in b for Vn, Org & Vle; a due in a for Vn & Bc; a due in d for Vn & Bc; Lamento in b for Vn, Org & Bc [sopra la morte Ferdinandi a tre]; Lamento a tre in B♭; Harmonia a cinque in B♭ *(rec Maria Minor Church, Utrecht, Nov 21-23 & May 2-5, 1995)*
Deutsche Harmonia Mundi ▲ 05472-77348-2 [DDD]
G. von der Goltz (cnd)
Handel, G.F.:Cants, w. N. Argenta (sop), M. Chance (ct)—Il duello amoroso, HWV 82 *(rec Jan 1993)*
Deutsche Harmonia Mundi ▲ 05472-77295-2 [DDD]
Handel, G.F.:Concerti grossi, Op. 6—No. 6 in g *(rec Jan 1993)*
Deutsche Harmonia Mundi ▲ 05472-77295-2 [DDD]
Pisendel, J.G.:Con a 8 *(rec Maria Minor Church, Utrecht, Sept. 29-Oct. 3, 1994)*
Deutsche Harmonia Mundi ▲ 05472-77339-2 [DDD]
Pisendel, J.G.:Cons Vn, w. Gottfried von der Goltz (vn)—in D *(rec Maria Minor Church, Utrecht, Sept. 29-Oct. 3, 1994)* Deutsche Harmonia Mundi ▲ 05472-77339-2 [DDD]

Freiburg Baroque Orch (cont.)
G. von der Goltz (cnd) (cont.)
Pisendel, J.G.:Son Ob, w. Ku Ebbinge (ob) *(rec Maria Minor Church, Utrecht, Sept. 29-Oct. 3, 1994)*
Deutsche Harmonia Mundi ▲ 05472-77339-2 [DDD]
Purcell, H.:The Prophetess (sels), w. Nancy Argenta (sop), Michael Chance (ct)—Ov; Dance; If Music Be the Food (song); Dance of the Bacchanals; Tpt tune; Prelude; Oh How Happy (song); Hornpipe; Dance of the Furies; 1st Music; Lost es My Quiet (duet); Prelude; Let the Soldiers Rejoice (song); Act Tune; Chaconne; 2nd Music; Paspe; Chair Dance *(rec Jan 1993)*
Deutsche Harmonia Mundi ▲ 05472-77295-2 [DDD]
Telemann, G.P.:Cons (misc)—Con. a 7 Deutsche Harmonia Mundi ▲ 05472-77321-2
Telemann, G.P.:Don Quichotte (suite) Deutsche Harmonia Mundi ▲ 05472-77321-2
Telemann, G.P.:Ovs—in D & F Deutsche Harmonia Mundi ▲ 05472-77321-2
Zavateri, L.G.:Cons Strs (comp), w. Gottfried von der Goltz (vn)—Nos. 2, 4, 6 & 8 also require an obligatto vn *(rec Festsaal des Maximilian-Parks, Hamm, Germany, 1995)*
Deutsche Harmonia Mundi 2-▲ 05472-77352-2 [DDD]
Zelenka, J.D.:Hipocondrie à 7 *(rec Maria Minor Church, Utrecht, Sept. 29-Oct. 3, 1994)*
Deutsche Harmonia Mundi ▲ 05472-77339-2 [DDD]
Zelenka, J.D.:Simphonie *(rec Maria Minor Church, Utrecht, Sept. 29-Oct. 3, 1994)*
Deutsche Harmonia Mundi ▲ 05472-77339-2 [DDD]
T. Hengelbrock (cnd)
Bach, C.P.E.:Con Hpd & Strs, H.474, w. A. Staier (hpd) Deutsche Harmonia Mundi ▲ 77187-2 [DDD]
Bach, C.P.E.:Con Ob, H.468, w. H.-P. Westermann (ob) Deutsche Harmonia Mundi ▲ 77187-2 [DDD]
Bach, C.P.E.:Sinfs, H.657-662, "Hamburg Syms"—H.660-662
Deutsche Harmonia Mundi ▲ 77187-2 [DDD]
Locatelli, P.:Introduttioni teatrali & Concerti Deutsche Harmonia Mundi ▲ 05472-77207-2
N. McGegan (cnd)
Handel, G.F.:Ariodante, w. J. Gondek (sop), L. Saffer (sop), L. Hunt (mez), Jennifer Lane (mez), J. Lindemann (ten), R. Müller (ten), N. Cavallier (bass), Ralf Popken (cnd), Wilhelmshaven Vocal Ensemble [172-page libretto w. production photos] Harmonia Mundi France 3-▲ HMC 907146.48
Handel, G.F.:Giustino, w. Juliana Gondek (sop), Dawn Kotoski (sop), Dorothea Röschmann (sop), Jennifer Lane (mez), Michael Chance (alt), Drew Minter (alt), Mark Padmore (ten), Dean Ely (sgr)
Harmonia Mundi France 3-▲ HMU 907130.32
Handel, G.F.:Ottone, Rè di Germania, w. Julianna Gondek (sop), Lisa Saffer (sop), Patricia Spence (mez), Drew Minter (alt), R. Popken (alt), Michael Dean (b-bar) *(rec June 9-12, 1992)*
Harmonia Mundi USA 3-▲ HMU 907073/75
Handel, G.F.:Radamisto, w. Monika Frimmer (sop), Juliana Gondek (sop), Dana Hanchard (sop), Lisa Saffer (sop), R. Popken (cta), Michael Dean (b-bar), Nicholas Cavallier (bass)
Harmonia Mundi USA 3-▲ HMU 907111/13
Freiburg Baroque Soloists
R. Hug (cnd)
Albrechtsberger, J.G.:Missa assumptionis beatae Mariae Virginis, w. F. Schmitt-Bohn (sop), J. Köble (alt), C. Elsner (ten), U. Rausch (bass) Ars Musici ▲ 0972-2 [DDD]
Haydn, M.:Missa Sancti Hieronymi, w. Florian Schmitt-Bohn (sop), Joachim Köble (alt), Christian Elsner (ten), Ulrich Rausch (bass) Ars Musici ▲ 0972-2 [DDD]
Freiburg Baroque Soloists (G. Maatz (fl), G. Theis (ob/ob d'amore), B. de Quervain (ob d'amore), T. Shirao (va), M. Schwamberger (vc), M. Scholz (bn), G. Bach (hpd))
Bach, J.S.:Trio Sons (misc)—Son. in C [reconstr. R. Gerlach from BWV 1027 & 1039 for flute, viola & continuo]; Son. in b [reconstr. W. Hindermann from BWV 36, 92, 104, 178 for 2 oboes d'amore & continuo]; Son. in g, BWV 1030b [comp. R. Meylan for oboe & harpsichord]; Son. in g [reconstr. W. Hindermann from BWV 76 & 528 for oboe, viola & continuo] Entrée ▲ 0053 [ADD]
Freiburg CO
H. Froitzheim (cnd)
Mozart, W.A.:Missa brevis, K.275, w. *(soloist unknown)* Entrée ▲ 0043
Schubert, Franz:Mass 2, w. *(soloists unknown)* Entrée ▲ 0043
Freiburg Musique de Landwehr
Balissat, J.:Incantation et Sacrifice, w. H. Klopfenstein, A. Zapf Grammont ▲ CTSP 17-2 [ADD]
French Ars Antiqua
Music of the Middle Ages, Vol. 7, w. Russell Oberlin (ct), Charles Bressler (ten), R. Price (ten), G. Meyers (bar), M. Blackman (vl), P. Wolfe (org) Lyrichord ▲ LYR 8007 [ADD]
French Brass
Alla Francese Pierre Verany ▲ 793041 [DDD]
French CO Soloists
Mozart, W.A.:Qts Fl, w. Luc Urbain (fl) Approche ▲ 6625
French Concerts Orch
J.-J. DuBois (cnd)
Franck, C.:Symphonic Vars, w. D. Bar-Illan (pno) Audiofon ▲ CD 72006
Franck, C.:Symphonic Vars, w. D. Bar-Illan (pno) InSync ■ C 4161
Liszt, F.:Con 1 Pno, w. David Bar-Illan (pno) Audiofon ▲ 72030
Saint-Saëns, C.:Con 2 Pno, w. D. Bar-Illan (pno) InSync ■ C 4161
Saint-Saëns, C.:Con 2 Pno, w. D. Bar-Illan (pno) Audiofon ▲ CD 72006
Tchaikovsky, P.:Con 2 Pno, w. D. Bar-Illan Audiofon ▲ CD 72030
Tchaikovsky, P.:Con 2 Pno, w. David Bar-Illan (pno) Audiofon ▲ CD 72065
French Flute Orch
H. Radulescu (cnd)
Radulescu, H.:Music of, w. Pierre-Yves Artaud (fl)—Dizzy Divinity I; Byzantine Prayer; Frenetico il Longing di Amare; Capricorn's Nostalgic Crickets II Adda ▲ ADD 581298 [DDD]
French Instrumental Ensemble
Albinoni's Adagio Forlane ▲ FOR 16527 [DDD]
Bach, J.S.:Con 1 Vn, w. Philip Bride (vn) *(rec Nov 5 & 6, 1988)* Pierre Verany ▲ PVY 730020 [DDD]
Bach, J.S.:Con 2 Vn, w. Philip Bride (vn) *(rec Nov 5 & 6, 1988)* Pierre Verany ▲ PVY 730020 [DDD]
Bach, J.S.:Con Vn & Ob, w. Philip Bride (vn), Daniel Arrignon (ob) *(rec Nov 5 & 6, 1988)*
Pierre Verany ▲ PVY 730020 [DDD]
Bach, J.S.:Con for 2 Vns, w. Philip Bride (vn), Christian Crenne (vn) *(rec Nov 5 & 6, 1988)*
Pierre Verany ▲ PVY 730020 [DDD]
Barber, S.:Adagio Strs *(rec 9/89)* Pierre Verany ▲ PV.789121 [DDD]
Britten, B.:Simple Sym *(rec 9/89)* Pierre Verany ▲ PV.789121 [DDD]
Hindemith, P.:Trauermusik *(rec 9/89)* Pierre Verany ▲ PV.789121 [DDD]
Landowski, M.:Preludes Vn *(rec 9/89)* Pierre Verany ▲ PV.789121 [DDD]
Stravinsky, I.:Con Str *(rec 9/89)* Pierre Verany ▲ PV.789121 [DDD]
K. Redel (cnd)
Mozart, W.A.:Concertone Vns, w. Philip Bride (vn), Christian Crenne (vn) *(rec Apr. 9 & 10, 1990)*
Pierre Verany ▲ PVY 730024 [DDD]
Mozart, W.A.:Sinf concertante Vn, K.364, w. Philip Bride (vn), Serge Soufflard (va) *(rec Apr. 9 & 10, 1990)* Pierre Verany ▲ PVY 730024 [DDD]
J.-P. Wallez (cnd)
Haydn, J.:Con 1 Vc, w. Aleth Lamasse (vc) Forlane ▲ FRL 40 [AAD]
Haydn, J.:Con 2 Vc, w. Aleth Lamasse (vc) Forlane ▲ FRL 40 [AAD]
French Isles National Orch
J. Mercier (cnd)
Schmitt, F.:Salammbô, w. French Army Chorus Adès ▲ ADE 203592 [DDD]
French National Orch String Sextet
Bruckner, A.:Qnt Strs Quantum ▲ QM 6895 [DDD] ■ QM 1990 (D)
Schoenberg, A.:Verklärte Nacht Quantum ▲ QM 6895 [DDD] ■ QM 1990 (D)
French National Orch
Vivaldi, A.:Cons Pic, w. J.-L. Beaumadier (fl), J.-P. Rampal (fl)—RV.443, 444, 445
Calliope ▲ CAL 9630
M. Andreae (cnd)
Ohana, M.:Anneau du Tamarit, w. A. Meunier (vc) *(rec 1990)*
Erato ("Musifrance" series) ▲ 2292-45503-2 [ADD/DDD]

ORCH. & ENS.

French National Orch (cont.)
P. Argento (cnd)
Falla, M. de:El amor brujo (sels), w. T. Berganza (mez) *(rec live, Paris 2/21/57)* Memories 2-▲ HR 4464/65 [ADD]
L. Bernstein (cnd)
Berlioz, H.:Harold in Italy, w. D. McInnes (va) EMI Classics ▲ CDM 64745
Berlioz, H.:Requiem, "Grande Messe des Morts", w. S. Burrows (ten) [L] Sony Classical 2-▲ SM2K 47526 [ADD]
Berlioz, H.:Sym fantastique EMI Classics ▲ CDM 64630
Bloch, E.:Schelomo, w. M. Rostropovich (vc) EMI Classics ▲ CDC 49307 [ADD]
Franck, C.:Sym in d Deutsche Grammophon ("Digital Midprice" series) ▲ 445512-2
Milhaud, D.:Le Boeuf sur le toit EMI Classics ▲ CDC 47845
Ravel, M.:Alborada del gracioso *(rec Paris, Oct. 1, 1975)* Sony Classical ("Bernstein:The Royal Edition" series) Δ SM 47603 [ADD]
Ravel, M.:Boléro *(rec Paris, Oct. 1, 1975)* Sony Classical ("Bernstein:The Royal Edition" series) Δ SM 47603 [ADD]
Ravel, M.:La Valse *(rec Paris, Oct. 1, 1975)* Sony Classical ("Bernstein:The Royal Edition" series) Δ SM 47603 [ADD]
Roussel, A.:Sym 3 *(rec 1981)* Deutsche Grammophon ("Digital Midprice" series) ▲ 445512-2
Schumann, R.:Con Vc, w. M. Rostropovich (vc) EMI Classics ▲ CDC 49307 [ADD]
P. Boulez (cnd)
Stravinsky, I.:Le Sacre du printemps Orch Fonit Cetra ("Fortissimo" series) ▲ FCT CDE 3008
Stravinsky, I.:Le Sacre du printemps Orch Elektra/Nonesuch ■ 71093-4
Stravinsky, I.:Studies Orch Elektra/Nonesuch ■ 71093-4
A. Cluytens (cnd)
Beethoven, L. van:Con 4 Pno, w. Clara Haskil (pno) *(rec Dec. 8, 1955)* Music & Arts ▲ CD 863 [ADD]
Franck, C.:Symphonic Vars, w. W. Gieseking (pno) *(rec live, Paris, 7/18/55)* Arkadia ▲ 588 [ADD]
Mozart, W.A.:Con 24 Pno, w. Clara Haskil (pno) *(rec Dec. 8, 1955)* Music & Arts ▲ CD 863 [ADD]
Shostakovich, D.:Con 1 Pno, w. D. Shostakovich (pno), L. Vaillant (tpt) EMI Classics ▲ CDC 54606
Shostakovich, D.:Con 2 Pno, w. D. Shostakovich (pno) EMI Classics ▲ CDC 54606
Shostakovich, D.:Preludes & Fugues Pno, w. D. Shostakovich (pno) EMI Classics ▲ CDC 54606
J. Conlon (cnd)
Martinů, B.:Con Str Qt, w. Brandis String Quartet Erato ▲ 2292-45499-2 ZK
Martinů, B.:Double Con Pno, Tim, w. J.-F. Heisser (pno), A. Planès (pno), J. Camosi (perc) Erato ▲ 2292-45499-2 ZK
Martinů, B.:Les Fresques de Piero della Francesca Erato ▲ 2292-45794-2 ZK
Martinů, B.:Ricercari, w. Brandis String Quartet Erato ▲ 2292-45499-2 ZK
Martinů, B.:Sinfonietta Pno, w. J.-F. Heisser (pno) Erato ▲ 2292-45794-2 ZK
Martinů, B.:Toccata e due canzoni Erato ▲ 2292-45794-2 ZK
P. Hindemith (cnd)
Hindemith, P.:The Four Temperaments, w. Clara Haskil (pno) *(rec Montreux, 1957)* Music & Arts ▲ CD 864 [ADD]
Mozart, W.A.:Con 20 Pno, w. Clara Haskil (pno) *(rec Montreux, 1957)* Music & Arts ▲ CD 864 [ADD]
E. Inbal (cnd)
Ravel, M.:Alborada del gracioso Denon ▲ CO 1797 [DDD]
Ravel, M.:Boléro Denon ▲ CO 1797 [DDD]
Ravel, M.:Daphins et Chloé, w. French National Chorus Denon ▲ CO 1796 [DDD]
Ravel, M.:Menuet antique Denon ▲ CO 1797 [DDD]
Ravel, M.:Orchestral Music, w. French National Chorus Denon/PCM Digital 4-▲ DEN 75001 [DDD]
Ravel, M.:Rapsodie espagnole Denon ▲ CO 1797 [DDD]
Ravel, M.:La Valse Denon ▲ CO 1797 [DDD]
L. Maazel (cnd)
Bizet, G.:Carmen, w. F. Esham (sop), J. Migenes-Johnson (sop), P. Domingo (ten), R. Raimondi (bass), French Radio Chorus [F] Erato 3-▲ 2292-45207-2 ZB [DDD]
Bizet, G.:Carmen, w. F. Esham (sop), J. Migenes-Johnson (sop), P. Domingo (ten), R. Raimondi (bass) [F] Erato ▲ 2292-45209-2 AW [DDD] ■ 2292-45209-4 AG (D)
Britten, B.:The Young Person's Guide to the Orchestra, w. Clunes (nar) [E] Deutsche Grammophon ("Musikfest" series) ▲ 415921-2 [ADD] ■ 415921-4
Dutilleux, H.:L'Arbre de songes, w. I. Stern (vn) CBS ▲ MK 42449 [DDD]
Holst, G.:The Planets CBS ▲ MDK 44781 [DDD]
Holst, G.:The Planets Sony Classical ("Essential Classics" series) ▲ SBK 62400 ■ SBT 62400
Prokofiev, S.:Lt Kijé Suite CBS ▲ MDK 44784 [DDD]
Prokofiev, S.:Peter & the Wolf, w. L. Maazel (nar) [E] Deutsche Grammophon ▲ 415921-2 [ADD] ■ 415921-4
Prokofiev, S.:Sym 1 CBS ▲ MDK 44785 [DDD]
Prokofiev, S.:Sym 1 CBS ▲ MDK 44901 [DDD]
Ravel, M.:Boléro CBS ▲ MDK 44781 [DDD]
Ravel, M.:Boléro CBS ▲ MDK 44901 [DDD]
Ravel, M.:La Valse CBS ▲ MDK 44901 [DDD]
Saint-Saëns, C.:Con 1 Vc, w. Yo-Yo Ma (vc) CBS ▲ MK 35848 [DDD]
Saint-Saëns, C.:Con 1 Vc, w. Yo-Yo Ma (vc) CBS 2-▲ M2K 44562 [ADD/DDD] 2-■ M2T 44562 (D)
J. Martinon (cnd)
Ibert, J.:Escales EMI Classics ▲ CDM 64276
Ibert, J.:Ouverture de fête EMI Classics ▲ CDM 64276
Ibert, J.:Tropismes pour des amours imaginaires EMI Classics ▲ CDM 64276
Khachaturian, A.:Con Vn, w. J.-P. Rampal (fl) CBS ▲ MK 44665 [ADD]
J. Mercier (cnd)
Bruneau, A.:Lazare, w. Françoise Pollet (sop), Mary Saint-Palais (sop), Sylvie Sullé (mez), Jean-Luc Viala (ten), Laurent Naouri (b-bar), Maîtrise de Paris, Vittoria French Regional Choir Adès ▲ ADE 204512
Bruneau, A.:Requiem, w. Françoise Pollet (sop), Mary Saint-Palais (sop), Sylvie Sullé (mez), Jean-Luc Viala (ten), Laurent Naouri (b-bar), Maîtrise de Paris, Vittoria French Regional Choir Adès ▲ ADE 204512
S. Ozawa (cnd)
Bach, J.S.:Con for 2 Vns, w. A.-S. Mutter (vn), S. Accardo (vn) EMI Classics 3-▲ CDMC 69878
Bizet, G.:Carmen, w. J. Norman (sop), M. Freni (sop), N. Shicoff (ten), S. Estes (bass), French Radio Chorus [F] Philips ▲ 426040-2 [DDD] ■ 426040-4 ◻ 426040-5
Bizet, G.:Carmen, w. J. Norman (sop), M. Freni (sop), N. Shicoff (ten), S. Estes (bass), French Radio Chorus [F] Philips 3-▲ 422366-2 [DDD]
Bizet, G.:Carmen (suite 1) EMI Classics ("Studio DDD" series) ▲ CDD 63898 [DDD]
Bizet, G.:Patrie EMI Classics ("Studio DDD" series) ▲ CDD 63898 [DDD]
Bizet, G.:Sym 1 EMI Classics ("Studio DDD" series) ▲ CDD 63898 [DDD]
Lalo, E.:Sym espagnole, w. Anne-Sophie Mutter (vn) EMI Classics 3-▲ CDMC 69878
Lalo, E.:Sym espagnole, w. Anne-Sophie Mutter (vn) EMI Classics ▲ CDC 47318 [DDD]
Offenbach, J.:Les Contes d'Hoffmann, w. E. Gruberova (sop), C. Eder (mez), P. Domingo (ten), M. Sénéchal (ten), Schmidt (sgr), G. Bacquier (bar), J. Morris (bass), J. Diaz (bass), French Radio Chorus [F] Deutsche Grammophon 2-▲ 427682-2 [DDD]
Offenbach, J.:Les Contes d'Hoffmann (sels), w. Edita Gruberova (sop—Giulietta), Plácido Domingo (ten—Hoffmann)—Malheureux, tu ne comprends done pas Deutsche Grammophon ▲ 447270-2 [DDD] ■ 447 270-4
Sarasate, P. de:Zigeunerweisen, w. A.-S. Mutter (vn), English CO EMI Classics 3-▲ CDMC 69878
Sarasate, P. de:Zigeunerweisen, w. A.-S. Mutter (vn) EMI Classics ▲ CDC 47318 [DDD]
Z. Peskó (cnd)
Zinsstag, G.:Innanzi, w. G. Lauridon (bar) [F] *(rec Sept. 15, 1982)* Grammont ▲ CTSP 36-2 [ADD]
J.-C. Petit (cnd)
Petit, J.-C.:Le Hussard sur le toit Travelling ▲ K 1016 ■ 5101
G. Prêtre (cnd)
Landowski, M.:Sym 1 Erato ("Musifrance" series) ▲ 2292-45018-2 ZK [DDD]
Landowski, M.:Sym 3 Erato ("Musifrance" series) ▲ 2292-45018-2 ZK [DDD]

French National Orch (cont.)
G. Prêtre (cnd) (cont.)
Landowski, M.:Sym 4 Erato ("Musifrance" series) ▲ 2292-45018-2 ZK [DDD]
Poulenc, F.:La Voix humaine, w. J. Migenes-Johnson (sop) [F] *(rec 1990)* Erato ▲ 2292-45651-2 [DDD]
Roussel, A.:Bacchus et Ariane (suite 2) EMI Classics ▲ CDM 64690
J.-P. Rampal (cnd)
Vivaldi, A.:Cons Rcr, w. J.-L. Beaumadier (pic)—RV.108 Calliope ▲ CAL 9630
M. Rosenthal (cnd)
Satie, E.:Parade Adès ▲ ADE 203842 [AAD]
Satie, E.:Socrate, w. Denise Monteil (sop)—La mort de Socrate Adès ▲ ADE 203842 [AAD]
H. Scherchen (cnd)
Mahler, G.:Sym 5 *(rec 1965)* Musique d'Abord ▲ HMA 1905179 [AAD]
C. Schuricht (cnd)
Beethoven, L. van:Sym 1 *(rec live, 1965)* Originals ▲ ORI 862
Brahms, J.:Sym 4 *(rec live 3/24/59)* Melodram ▲ CDM 18048 [ADD]
Schubert, Franz:Sym 8 *(rec live, 1963)* Originals ▲ ORI 862
Schumann, R.:Manfred Ov *(rec live 5/14/63)* Melodram ▲ CDM 18045 [ADD]
S. Skrowaczewski (cnd)
Ohana, M.:Livre des Prodiges *(rec 1984)* Erato ("Musifrance" series) ▲ 2292-45503-2 [ADD/DDD]
J. Tate (cnd)
Berg, A.:Lulu, w. P. Wise (sop—Lulu), B. Fassbaender (mez—Countess Geschwitz), H. Hotter (b-bar—Schigolch)—Act 3 [G] *(rec live 9 & 10/91)* EMI Classics 3-▲ CDCC 54622 [DDD]
H. Villa-Lobos (cnd)
Villa-Lobos, H.:Bachiana brasileira 1 EMI Classics ("Great Recordings of the Century" series) ▲ CDH 61015 (m)
Villa-Lobos, H.:Bachiana brasileira 2 EMI Classics ("Great Recordings of the Century" series) ▲ CDH 61015 (m)
Villa-Lobos, H.:Bachiana brasileira 5, w. V. de los Angeles (sop) EMI Classics ("Great Recordings of the Century" series) ▲ CDH 61015 (m)
Villa-Lobos, H.:Bachiana brasileira 9 EMI Classics ("Great Recordings of the Century" series) ▲ CDH 61015 (m)
B. Walter (cnd)
Mozart, W.A.:Sym 36 Fonit Cetra ("Fortissimo" series) ▲ FCT CDE 3010
French National Radio Orch
Mussorgsky, M.:Songs (comp), w. B. Christoff (bass), Alexandre Labinsky (pno), Gerald Moore (pno) EMI Classics ("Great Recordings of the Century" series) 3-▲ CHS 63025 (m) [ADD]
French National RSO
T. Beecham (cnd)
Berlioz, H.:Sym fantastique *(rec 1957)* EMI Classics ▲ CDM7 64032-2 (m)
Bizet, G.:Sym 1 EMI Classics ▲ CDC 47794 [ADD]
E. Bour (cnd)
Ravel, M.:L'Enfant et les sortilèges, w. French National Radio Chorus Testament ▲ TESSBT 1044 [ADD]
A. Cluytens (cnd)
Shostakovich, D.:Sym 11 *(rec 1958)* Testament ▲ SBT 1099
J. Gressier (cnd)
Auber, D.-F.:Le Domino noir, w. J. Micheau (sop), J. Peyron (ten), G. Rey (bar), French Radio Lyric Chorus Melodram 2-▲ MLO 270110 [ADD]
I. Kertész (cnd)
Mahler, G.:Songs from Rückert, w. S. Jurinac (sop)—omitting Ich atmet' einen Linden Duft [G] *(rec live, Frankfurt, 3/25/62)* Melodram 3-▲ CDM 37091 [ADD]
O. Klemperer (cnd)
Brahms, J.:Con Vn, w. D. Oistrakh (vn) EMI Classics ▲ CDM 64632
P. Kletzki (cnd)
Brahms, J.:Con Vn & Vc, "Double Con", w. A. Busch (vn), H. Busch (vc) *(rec live, Strasbourg Festival 1949)* Melodram ▲ CDM 18040 [ADD]
J.-M. Leconte (cnd)
Khachaturian, A.:Con Vn, w. L. Kaufman (vn) *(rec 1955)* Cambria ▲ CD 1063 [ADD]
J. Martinon (cnd)
Debussy, C.:Children's Corner EMI Classics ▲ CDM 69589
Debussy, C.:Danse Pno, "Tarantelle styrienne" EMI Classics ▲ CDM 69668
Debussy, C.:Danses sacrée et profane EMI Classics ▲ CDM 69589
Debussy, C.:Fant Pno EMI Classics ▲ CDM 69668
Debussy, C.:La Mer EMI Classics ▲ CDM 69587
Debussy, C.:Nocturnes EMI Classics ▲ CDM 69587
Debussy, C.:Petite suite EMI Classics ▲ CDM 69589
Debussy, C.:Prélude à l'après-midi d'un faune EMI Classics ▲ CDM 69587
Debussy, C.:Première rapsodie, w. G. Dangain (cl) EMI Classics ▲ CDM 69668
Debussy, C.:Rapsodie, w. J.-M. Londeix (sax) EMI Classics ▲ CDM 69668
Prokofiev, S.:Chout (suite) *(rec 1971)* Vox Box 2-▲ CDX 5054 [ADD]
Prokofiev, S.:Ov on Hebrew Themes Vox Box 2-▲ CDX 5001 [ADD]
Prokofiev, S.:Russian Ov Vox Box 2-▲ CDX 5001 [ADD]
Prokofiev, S.:Sym 1 Vox Box 2-▲ CDX 5001 [ADD]
Prokofiev, S.:Sym 2 *(rec 1971)* Vox Box 2-▲ CDX 5054 [ADD]
Prokofiev, S.:Sym 3 *(rec 1971)* Vox Box 2-▲ CDX 5054 [ADD]
Prokofiev, S.:Sym 5 Vox Box 2-▲ CDX 5001 [ADD]
Prokofiev, S.:Sym 6 *(rec 1971)* Vox Box 2-▲ CDX 5054 [ADD]
Prokofiev, S.:Sym 7 Vox Box 2-▲ CDX 5001 [ADD]
D. Milhaud (cnd)
Milhaud, D.:Sym 4 Erato ▲ 2292-45841-2 AW
Milhaud, D.:Sym 8 Erato ▲ 2292-45841-2 AW
C. Munch (cnd)
Debussy, C.:Ibéria—Le parfums de la nuit; Le matin d'un jour de fête *(rec 1968)* FNAC Music (Via Classique) ▲ 642303
Debussy, C.:La Mer *(rec 1968)* FNAC Music (Via Classique) ▲ 642303
Debussy, C.:Nocturnes, w. French National Radio Chorus—Nuages & Fêtes *(rec 1968)* FNAC Music (Via Classique) ▲ 642303
Debussy, C.:Prélude à l'après-midi d'un faune *(rec 1968)* FNAC Music (Via Classique) ▲ 642303
G. Prêtre (cnd)
Poulenc, F.:Con Org, w. M. Duruflé (org) EMI Classics ▲ CDC 47723 [ADD]
Poulenc, F.:Gloria Sop, w. R. Carteri (sop), French National Radio Chorus [L] EMI Classics ▲ CDC 47723 [ADD]
L. Stokowski (cnd)
Debussy, C.:Nocturnes EMI Classics ("Full Dimensional Sound" series) ▲ CDM 65422
Ibert, J.:Escales EMI Classics ("Full Dimensional Sound" series) ▲ CDM 65422
Ravel, M.:Alborada del gracioso EMI Classics ("Full Dimensional Sound" series) ▲ CDM 65423
G. Tzipine (cnd)
Bizet, G.:Ivan IV (sels), w. J. Micheau (sop), H. Legay (ten), M. Sénéchal (ten), M. Roux (bar), French Radio Chorus [F] EMI Classics ("Studio" series) 2-▲ CDMB 69704 [ADD]
French Oratorio Orch
J.-P. Lore (cnd)
Berlioz, H.:Requiem, "Grande Messe des Morts", w. Guy Touvron Brass Ensemble, French Oratorio Choir *(rec Dec. 7-13, 1987)* Esoldun 2-▲ MOS 1001 [DDD]
Berlioz, H.:Resurrexit, w. Guy Touvron Brass Ensemble, French Oratorio Choir *(rec June 10, 1987)* Esoldun 2-▲ MOS 1001 [DDD]
Massenet, J.:Eve, w. Michèle Command (sop), Carolyn Sebron (mez), Hervé Lamy (ten), Jean-Philippe Courtis (bass), French Oratorio Choir Erol 3-▲ 94002-04
Massenet, J.:Marie-Magdeleine, w. Michèle Command (sop), Carolyn Sebron (mez), Hervé Lamy (ten), Jean-Philippe Courtis (bass), French Oratorio Choir Erol 3-▲ 94002-04

178 ▲ = CD ♦ = Enhanced CD Δ = MD ■ = Cassette Tape ◻ = DCC

French Oratorio Orch (cont.)
J.-P. Lore (cnd) (cont.)
Massenet, J.:Méditation from *Thaïs*, w. French Oratorio Choir — Erol 3-▲ 94002-04
Schubert, Ferdinand:Requiem, w. D. Degos (trb), K. Markus (ten), R. Soyer (bass), J. Galard (org), J.-P. Lore Vocal Ensemble, Petits Chanteurs de Notre Dame de la Joie *(rec Nov. 9-11, 1980 & Jan. 25)* — Esoldun ▲ MOS 1003 [ADD]
Schubert, Franz:Requiem, w. D. Degos (trb), K. Markus (ten), R. Soyer (bass), J. Galard (org), J.-P. Lore Vocal Ensemble, Petits Chanteurs de Notre Dame de la Joie *(rec Nov. 9-11, 1980 & Jan. 25)* — Esoldun ▲ MOS 1003 [ADD]

French Piano Trio
Brahms, J.:Trio 2 Pno *(rec Jan. 1988)* — Quantum ▲ QM 6894 [DDD] ■ QM 1989
Mendelssohn, F.:Trio 1 Pno *(rec Jan. 1988)* — Quantum ▲ QM 6894 [DDD] ■ QM 1989

French Polyphonic Ensemble
C. Ravier
Renaissance, w. Collegium Vocale [cnd:P. Herreweghe], Hesperion XX [cnd:J. Savall] — Astrée 3-▲ 8608

French Radio Lyric Orch
T. Aubin (cnd)
Messager, A.:La Basoche, w. *(unknown radio chorus)* — Musidisc 2-▲ MUS 202572 [AAD]
M. Cariven (cnd)
Audran, E.:La Poupée, w. French Radio Lyric Chorus — Musidisc 2-▲ MUS 202402 [AAD]
R. Ellis (cnd)
Lecocq, C.:Le Petite mariée — Musidisc 2-▲ MUS 201962 [AAD]
Messager, A.:Les Dragons de l'impératrice (sels), w. French Radio Lyric Chorus — Musidisc 2-▲ MUS 202092 [AAD]
H. Gallois (cnd)
Gounod, C.:Philémon et Baucis, w. Anne-Marie Rodde (sop), Jean-Claude Orliac (ten), Pierre Néquecaur (bar), Félix Giband (bass) — Musidisc 2-▲ MUS 202342 [AAD]
A. Girard (cnd)
Delibes, L.:Le Roi l'a dit, w. *(unknown radio chorus)* — Musidisc 2-▲ MUS 202392 [AAD]
J. Gressier (cnd)
Messager, A.:Monsieur Beaucaire, w. French Radio Lyric Chorus — Musidisc 2-▲ MUS 202412 [AAD]
D. Lloyd-Jones (cnd)
Massenet, J.:Hérodiade, w. Nadine Denize (mez), Ernst Blanc (bar), French Radio Chorus *(rec Paris, Dec 5, 1974)* — Agorá ("Phoenix" series) 2-▲ 514

French Radio PO
M. Janowski (cnd)
Roussel, A.:Syms *(rec Salle Olivier Messiaen, Radio France, Sept 23 & 24, 1993 & Sept)* — RCA Red Seal 2-▲ 09026-62511-2 [DDD]
Saint-Saëns, C.:Carnival of the Animals, w. G. Pekinel (pno), S. Pekinel (pno) — Teldec ▲ 2292-46155-2 [DDD]

French Radio PO Soloists
Poulenc, F.:Chamber Music, w. Jean-Pierre Armengaud (pno)—Son for Vn & Pno; Son for Ob & Pno; Elegy for Hn & Pno; Son for 2 Cls; Son for Vc & Pno; Sxt for Pno, Fl, Ob, Cl, Bn & Hn; Son for Fl & Pno; Trio for Pno, Ob & Bn; Son for Cl & Pno; Villanelle for Pic & Pno; Son for Cl & Bn; Son for Hn, Tpt & Trbn — Accord 2-▲ ACD 202022 [DDD]

French Radio-TV Orch
H. Scherchen (cnd)
Beethoven, L. van:Sym 6, "Pastorale" — Stradivarius ▲ STV 13592 [AAD]
Schoenberg, A.:Vars Orch — Stradivarius ▲ STV 13592 [AAD]

French Radio-TV PO
G. Schuller (cnd)
Sessions, R.:Con Vn, w. Paul Zukofsky (vn) — CRI ▲ CD 676 [ADD]

French Soloists
J.-C. Hartemann (cnd)
Bach, J.S.:Con 1 Hpd, w. Michèle Boegner (pno) — Calliope ▲ CAL 6629 [ADD]
Bach, J.S.:Con 5 Hpd, w. Michèle Boegner (pno) — Calliope ▲ CAL 6629 [ADD]
Vivaldi, A.:Cons Vn, Op. 8/1-4, "The Four Seasons", w. Hervé Le Floch (vn) — Calliope ▲ CAL 6629 [ADD]

French String Trio [G. Jarry (vn), S. Collot (va), M. Tournus (vc)]
Hoffmann, E.T.A.:Qnt Hp, w. Marielle Nordmann (hp) — Koch Schwann ▲ SCH 313392 [ADD/DDD]
Onslow, G.:Qt Strs, Op. 8/1, w. Y. Caracilly (vn) *(rec 1978)* — Koch Treasure ▲ 316232 [ADD]
Onslow, G.:Qnt Strs, Op. 78/1, w. Y. Caracilly (vn), B. Pasquier (va) *(rec 1978)* — Koch Treasure ▲ 316232 [ADD]

French SO
L. Petitgirard (cnd)
Petitgirard, L.:Le Marathon *(rec Dec. 4, 1992)* — Orchestre Symphonique France ▲ OSF 49013 [DDD]

Frescoes of Kiev
A. Bondarenko (cnd)
Stetsenko, K.:The Divine Liturgy of St. J. Chrysostom, w. A. Bondarenko (vn) — Erasmus ▲ WVH 120 [DDD]

Fresk String Quartet
Rosenberg, H.:Qt 4 Strs — Caprice ▲ CAP 21353 [AAD/DDD]
Rosenberg, H.:Qt 10 Strs — Caprice ▲ CAP 21380 [DDD]
Stenhammar, W.:Qt 1 Strs — Caprice ▲ CAP 21337 [AAD]

Fretwork
Byrd, W.:Consort Music — Virgin Classics ▲ CDC 45031
Byrd, W.:Consort Music—6 Fantasias; Pavan & Galliard in 6 parts; Browning in 5 parts; La Volta & Pavana Bray for solo lute — Virgin Classics ▲ 59539 [DDD]
Byrd, W.:Consort Music—In Nomines à 5, VdGS Nos. 1-5 — Virgin Classics ▲ 59586 [DDD]
Byrd, W.:Songs, w. Sophie Yates (virs), Robert Hollingworth (cnd), I Fagiolini—Attollite port; Triumph with pleasant melody; O Lord, how vain; All in a Garden Green; Domine secundum actum meum; Truth at the first; Who likes to love; Wolsey's Wilde; Da mihi auxilium; Farewell, false love; O Mistrys Myne; Miserere mihi, Domine; My mind to me a kingdom is; La volta; Ad Dominum cum tribularer — Chandos ("Chaconne" series) ▲ CHAN 0578 [DDD]
Byrd, W.:Songs, w. Michael Chance (ct), Christopher Wilson (lt)—If women could be fair; Lullaby, my sweet little baby; Ah silly soul; Ye sacred muses — Virgin Classics ▲ 59586 [DDD]
Dowland, J.:Lachrimae, or Seaven Teares — Virgin Classics ▲ 59539 [DDD]
Dowland, J.:Lachrimae, or Seaven Teares, w. C. Wilson (lt) — EMI Classics ▲ CDC 45005
Dowland, J.:Lachrimae, or Seaven Teares (sels)—14 dances for instrumental consort — Virgin Classics ▲ 59586 [DDD]
Dowland, J.:Songs, w. Michael Chance (ct), Christopher Wilson (lt)—Goe nightly cares, the enemy to rest; Lasso vita mia, mi fu morire — Virgin Classics ▲ 59586 [DDD]
English Viol Music — Virgin Classics ("Veritas Edition" series) ▲ CDM 61173
Gibbons, O.:The Cryes of London, w. P. Nicholson (org), Red Byrd—Cries & Fancies; Fantasias, In Nomines — Virgin Classics ▲ CDC 59191
Gibbons, O.:Instrumental & Vocal Music, w. Richard Marlow (cnd), Trinity College Choir Cambridge—Hosanna to the Son of David; O Lord, I lift my heart; O all true, faithful hearts; This is the Record of John; Lift up your heads; Almighty & everlasting God — Conifer Classics ▲ 75605-51231-2 [DDD]
Gibbons, O.:Instrumental & Vocal Music—instrumental Fantasias & In Nomines, plus *The Cries of London* — Veritas ▲ VC 7 90849-2 [DDD] ■ VC 7 90849-4 (D)
Heart's Ease — Virgin Classics ▲ CDC 59667 [DDD]
In Nomine — Amon Ra ▲ CDSAR 29 [DDD]
Lawes, W.:Consort Setts, w. Paul Nicholson (org)—Consort Setss à 5—in c & F; Consort Setts à 6—in c & F; Divisions for two bass viols & organ in g; Airs for three lyra viols — Virgin Classics ▲ 59021 [DDD]
Music for Viols, w. C. Wilson (lt), P. Nicholson (kbd), M. Chance (alt) — Virgin Classics ▲ CDZ 59691
Purcell, H.:Fants — Virgin Classics ▲ CDC 45062

Fricsay SO
T. Pál (cnd)
Górecki, H.-M.:Beatus Vir, w. T. Altorjay (bar), Bartók Chorus — Stradivarius ▲ STR 33324 [DDD]
Górecki, H.-M.:Beatus Vir, w. Tamás Altorjay (bar), Bartók Chorus — Stradivarius ▲ STV 33324 [DDD]
Górecki, H.-M.:Sym 2, "Copernican Sym", w. Emese Soós (sop), Tamás Altorjay (bar) — Stradivarius ▲ STV 33324 [DDD]
Górecki, H.-M.:Sym 2, "Copernican Sym", w. E. Soós (sop), T. Altorjay (bar), Bartók Chorus — Stradivarius ▲ STR 33324 [DDD]

Friends of Apollo
Bach, J.S.:Cant 211, "Coffee Cant", w. L. Dawson (sop), N. Robertson (ten), S. Adler (bar) [G] — Meridian ▲ ECD 84110
Bach, J.S.:Cant 212, "Peasant Cant", w. L. Dawson (sop), S. Adler (bar) [G] — Meridian ▲ ECD 84110

Friend-Solomon-Hugh Trio
Shostakovich, D.:Trio 2 Pno — Altarus ▲ CD 9052
Shostakovich, D.:Trio 2 Pno — Altarus ▲ CD 9033
Tchaikovsky, P.:Trio Pno — Altarus ▲ CD 9052
Tchaikovsky, P.:Trio Pno — Altarus ▲ CD 9033

Louis de Froment CO
Vivaldi, A.:Cons Fl (misc), w. J.-P. Rampal (fl)—RV.90 — Allegretto ▲ ACD 8036 [ADD] ■ ACS 8036

Frosinone Licinio Refice Conservatory SO
R. Tigani (cnd)
Fioravanti, V.:Le cantatrici villane, w. G. Manci (sop—Agata), M. Mauro (sop—Nunziella), M. A. Peters (sop—Rosa), F. Sovilla (mez—Giannetta), E. Palacio (ten—Carlino), G. Gatti (bar—Don Bucefalo), D. Serraiocco (bass—Don Marco) *(rec Oct. 22, 23 & 25, 1992; [])* — Bongiovanni 2-▲ GB 2135/36 [DDD]

Frösunda Wind Quintet [L. Hagström (fl), S. Fagéus (ob), K. Andersson (cl), L. Økermark (bn), B. Johansson (hn)]
Arnold, M.:Shanties *(rec Mar 16-18, 1979)* — BIS ▲ CD 136 [AAD]
Farkas, F.:Antique Hungarian Dances *(rec Mar 16-18, 1979)* — BIS ▲ CD 136 [AAD]
Ibert, J.:Pièces brèves *(rec Mar 16-18, 1979)* — BIS ▲ CD 136 [AAD]
Nielsen, C.:Qnt Ww *(rec Mar 16-18, 1979)* — BIS ▲ CD 136 [AAD]

Frydén String Quartet
Berwald, F.:Qt 2 Strs — Caprice ▲ CAP 21334 [AAD]
Berwald, F.:Qt 3 Strs — Caprice ▲ CAP 21334 [AAD]

Il Fuggilotio
Cirri, G.B.:Sons Fls, Op. 9 — Stradivarius ▲ STV 33358 [DDD]

Furman Civic Wind Ensemble
J. Carmichael (cnd)
Contemporary Music Festival, w. National Festival Orch — CRS ▲ CRS 9052
J. C. Carmichael (cnd)
Hindemith, P.:Kleine Kammermusik, Mostly Modern Chamber Players — CRS ▲ 9051
Krenek, E.:Marsche, Mostly Modern Chamber Players — CRS ▲ 9051
Pepping, E.:Little Serenade, Mostly Modern Chamber Players — CRS ▲ 9051
Toch, E.:Spiel, Mostly Modern Chamber Players — CRS ▲ 9051

Gabrieli Consort
P. McCreesh (cnd)
Barbarino, B.:Music of, w. Gabrieli Players—Audi, dulcis amica mea; Ardens est cor meum *(rec Suola Grande di San Rocco, Venice, Aug 1995)* — Archiv ▲ 449 180-2 [DDD]
Gabrieli, G.:Music of, w. Gabrieli Players—Toccata; In ecclesiis; Son 19; Suscipe, clementissime Deus; Canzona 14; Buccinate in neomenia tuba; Intonazione del nono tono; Domine Deus meus; Son 21 con tre violini; Timor et tremor; Intonazione duodecimo tono; Jubilate Deo; Son 18; Misericordia tua, Domine; Son 20; Magnificat *(rec Suola Grande di San Rocco, Venice, Aug 1995)* — Archiv ▲ 449 180-2 [DDD]
Gabrieli, G.:Music of, w. Gabrieli Players [L] ceremonial music by Andrea & Giovanni Gabrieli, sequenced in this recording to take the form of a Coronation Mass, such as would have attended the installation of Doge Marino Grimani in 1595 — Virgin Classics ▲ 59006 [DDD]
Morales, C. de:Mass for the Feast, w. Gabrieli Players — Archiv ▲ 449143-2
Venetian Vespers, w. Gabrieli Players — Archiv ▲ 437552-2
Victoria, T.L. de:Officium defunctorum — Archiv ▲ 447095-2

Gabrieli Festival Orch
E. Appia (cnd)
Gabrieli, G.:Music of, w. R. Clemenic (rcr), A. Heiller (hpd), H. Tachezi (pno), Gabrieli Festival Chorus—Processional & Ceremonial Music from Sacrae Symphoniae [1597, 1615] & Concerti [1587]; originally released as Bach Guild BGS 5004)—Sancta et immaculata virginitas; O magnum mysterium; Nunc dimittis; Angelus ad pastores; O Jesu mi dulcissime; Exaudi Deus; Hodie completi sunt; O Domine Jesu Christe; Canzona Quarti Toni a 15 (ricercar); Inclina Domine *(rec Vienna, Feb. 1958)* — Vanguard Classics ("The Bach Guild" series) ▲ OVC 2007 [ADD]

Gabrieli Players
P. McCreesh (cnd)
Barbarino, B.:Music of, w. Gabrieli Consort—Audi, dulcis amica mea; Ardens est cor meum *(rec Suola Grande di San Rocco, Venice, Aug 1995)* — Archiv ▲ 449 180-2 [DDD]
Gabrieli, G.:Music of, w. Gabrieli Consort [L] ceremonial music by Andrea & Giovanni Gabrieli, sequenced in this recording to take the form of a Coronation Mass, such as would have attended the installation of Doge Marino Grimani in 1595 — Virgin Classics ▲ 59006 [DDD]
Gabrieli, G.:Music of, w. Gabrieli Consort—Toccata; In ecclesiis; Son 19; Suscipe, clementissime Deus; Canzona 14; Buccinate in neomenia tuba; Intonazione del nono tono; Domine Deus meus; Son 21 con tre violini; Timor et tremor; Intonazione duodecimo tono; Jubilate Deo; Son 18; Misericordia tua, Domine; Son 20; Magnificat *(rec Suola Grande di San Rocco, Venice, Aug 1995)* — Archiv ▲ 449 180-2 [DDD]
Morales, C. de:Mass for the Feast, w. Gabrieli Consort — Archiv ▲ 449143-2
Palestrina, G.:Missa "Hodi Christus", w. *(soloists unknown)*—Missa, "Hodid Christus natus est" — Archiv ▲ 437833-2
Venetian Vespers, w. Gabrieli Consort — Archiv ▲ 437552-2

Gabrieli String Quartet
Brahms, J.:Qts Strs (comp) — Chandos ▲ CHAN 8562 [DDD]
Brahms, J.:Qnt Cl, w. T. King (cl) — Hyperion ▲ CDA 66107
Dohnányi, E. von:Qt 2 Strs — Chandos ▲ CHAN 8718 [DDD]
Dohnányi, E. von:Qnt 1 Pno, w. W. Manz (pno) — Chandos ▲ CHAN 8718 [DDD]
Elgar, E.:Qt Strs — Chandos ▲ CHAN 8474 [DDD]
Haydn, J.:Qts Strs, Op. 54—No. 2 — Chandos ▲ CHAN 8531 [DDD]
Haydn, J.:Qts Strs, Op. 64, "Tost Qts"—No. 5 — Chandos ▲ CHAN 8531 [DDD]
Mozart, W.A.:Qt Ob, K.370, w. D. Boyd (ob) — IMP Classics ▲ PCD 810 [DDD]
Mozart, W.A.:Qnt Cl, K.581, w. K. Puddy (cl) — IMP Classics ▲ PCD 810 [DDD]
Sibelius, J.:Qt Strs, Op. 56 — Chandos ▲ CHAN 8742 [DDD]
Sibelius, J.:Qnt Pno, w. A. Gladstone (pno) — Chandos ▲ CHAN 8742 [DDD]
Walton, W.:Qt Strs — Chandos ▲ CHAN 8474 [DDD]

Gaggini String Quartet [Jenny Spanoghe (vn), Bart Lemmens (vn), Béatrice Derolez (va), Rigo Messens (vc)]
Brahms, J.:Qt 3 Strs — Cypres ▲ CYP 2616
Hindemith, P.:Die junge Magd, w. Lucienne Van Deyck (mez), Marc Grauwels (fl), Ronald Van Spaendonck (cl) — Syrinx ▲ 95101
Hindemith, P.:Qt 1 Strs — Cypres ▲ CYP 2616

Galanterie Trio [J. Schneiderman (lt), J. von Einem (vn), M. Chatfield (vc)]
Haydn, J.:Qts Strs, Op. 1—No. 6, Cassation in C [arr. for Lute/Guitar, Violin & Cello; not authentic] *(rec Apr. 1-3, 1991)* — AudioQuest ▲ AQCD 1005
Kohaut, K.:Trio Lt, Vn & Vc *(rec Apr. 1-3, 1991)* — Audioquest ▲ AQCD 1005
Kropffganss, J.I.:Son Lt, Vn & Vc *(rec Apr. 1-3, 1991)* — Audioquest ▲ AQCD 1005

Galicia SO

V.P. Pérez (cnd)

Sorozábal, P.:La Tabernera del Puerto, w. María Bayo (sop), Plácido Domingo (ten), Juan Pons (bar) Auvidis Valois ("Zarzuela Collection" series) ▲ V 4766

Galilei Ensemble

P. Beier (cnd)

Marini, B.:Music of, w. Emanuela Galli (sop) Stradivarius ▲ STV 33446 [DDD]

Galimir String Quartet

Debussy, C.:Qt Strs Vanguard Classics ▲ OVC 4049 [DDD]

Ravel, M.:Qt Strs Vanguard Classics ▲ OVC 4049 [DDD]

Galli String Quartet

The String Quartet in Sweden:A Cavalcade of Its History, w. Barkel String Quartet, Stockholm String Quartet, Garaguly String Quartet, Kyndel String Quartet, Ivan Ericson String Quartet, Grünfarb String Quartet, Skůne String Quartet, Hälsingborg String Quartet, Göteborg String Quartet *(rec before 1951)* Caprice 5–▲ CAP 21506 [AAD/ADD]

Galliard Brass Ensemble

Carols for Brass MusicMasters ▲ 01612–67175–2

La Gamba Freiburg

E. Weber (cnd)

Reusner, Esaias:Suites Lt—Suite in a Ars Musici ▲ AM 1096 [DDD]

Scheidt, S.:Instr Music—Canzona a 5 & Continuo, "O Nachbar Roland"; Suite in C a 4 & Continuo; Canzon a 5 & Continuo, "Bergamasca"; Passamezzo for Keyboard Ars Musici ▲ AM 1096 [DDD]

Schein, J.H.:Suites Instrs—Suite in d Ars Musici ▲ AM 1096 [DDD]

Schop, J.:Suite Instrs—Suite in a Ars Musici ▲ AM 1096 [DDD]

Sweelinck, J.P.:More Palatino Ars Musici ▲ AM 1096 [DDD]

Gamelan Pacifica

Giteck, J.:Home (Revisited), w. Philandros New Albion ▲ NA 054

Trance Gong ¿What Next? ▲ WN 0016

Gamelan Son of Lion members

Rolnick, N.B.:Elec Music, w. N. B. Rolnick (elec)—Balkanization (for MIDI performance system); Macedonian AirDrumming (for MIDI & AirDrums); ReRebong (for gamelan instruments & real-time digital processing); Sanctus (computer generated tape) Bridge ▲ BCD 9030 [DDD]

Gamerith Consort

Dittersdorf, K.D. von:Cons (5) Hpd [period instrs]—in A Divertimento ▲ DIV 31004

Haydn, J.:Trios Pno, Vn & Vc [period instrs]—in E♭, H.XV/22 & in A, H.XV/9 Divertimento ▲ DIV 31004

Pleyel, I.:Trios Pno [period instrs]—in C Divertimento ▲ DIV 31004

Ganassi Consort Cologne

17th Century Italian Recorder Music MD + G ▲ L 3301 [DDD]

Gangster Band [Zeena Parkins (elec hp/sampler/pno), Sara Parkins (vn), Maggie Parkins (vc/sgr), Jim Pugliese (perc/vib), Mark Stuart (vc/gtr/ mand), Carsten Dane (sgr), Matthias Brietenbach (sgr), Andy Haas (didjeridu)]

Parkins, Z.:Music of—Maul:Benya Krik; Zero Hour; Wie Sieben Meilen Miesen Dirach; Betrayer; Torrid Zone; Dough; Weaponistic Charms; Italyid; No Thing; Simcha; Chase; Hod; Blue Mirror:Ice Pick; The Dasher; Red; 2Gun; Abaddabbah; Phrases; Nails Tzadik ▲ TZA CD 7109 [DDD]

Garaguly String Quartet

The String Quartet in Sweden:A Cavalcade of Its History, w. Barkel String Quartet, Stockholm String Quartet, Kyndel String Quartet, Ivan Ericson String Quartet, Grünfarb String Quartet, Skůne String Quartet, Hälsingborg String Quartet, Göteborg String Quartet, Galli String Quartet *(rec before 1951)* Caprice 5–▲ CAP 21506 [AAD/ADD]

Garau–Millet Guitar Duo

Garau–Millet Guitar Duo Pyramid ▲ PYR 13508 [DDD]

García Trio

Ben–Haim, P.:Vars on a Hebrew Melody Caprice ▲ CAP 21348 [DDD]

Linde, B.:Son a tre Pno, Vn & Vc Caprice ▲ CAP 21348 [DDD]

Shostakovich, D.:Trio 2 Pno Caprice ▲ CAP 21348 [DDD]

Turina, J.:Trio 2 Pno Caprice ▲ CAP 21348 [DDD]

Geringas Baryton Trio [David Geringas (baryton), Vladimir Mendelssohn (va), Emil Klein (vc)]

Haydn, J.:Trios (125) Baryton, Va & Vc—4 Trios—H.XI/5 in A, 96 in b, 97 in D & 113 in D CPO ▲ CPO 999094–2 [DDD]

Peter Garland Ensemble [Lynn Case (vn), Rosalind Simpson (hp), Lynne Lawlor (perc), Landon Young (perc)]

Garland, P.:Old Men of the Fiesta ¿What Next? ▲ WN 0008 [DDD] ■ F

Screen Themes '93:The Best Film Scores of 1993 Discovery ▲ 77009–2 ■ 77009–4

Gaspero da Salò Orch

A. Orizio (cnd)

Chopin, F.:Con 1 Pno, w. M. Argerich (pno) *(rec live, Brescia 6/6/67)* Arkadia ▲ 574 [ADD]

Chopin, F.:Con 1 Pno, w. M. Argerich (pno) *(rec live 6/67)* Fonè ▲ 91F03 [ADD]

Chopin, F.:Con 2 Pno, w. A. Weissenberg (pno) *(rec live 6/67)* Fonè ▲ 91F05 [ADD]

Chopin, F.:Grand Fant on Polish Airs, w. A. Weissenberg (pno) *(rec live 6/67)* Fonè ▲ 91F05 [ADD]

Chopin, F.:Krakowiak, w. A. Weissenberg (pno) *(rec live 6/67)* Fonè ▲ 91F05 [ADD]

Chopin, F.:Vars on Mozart's *La ci darem la mano*, w. A. Weissenberg (pno) *(rec live 6/67)* Fonè ▲ 91F05 [ADD]

Gate 5 Ensemble

Partch, H.:Plectra & Percussion Dances (sels), w. Lynn Ludlow (spkr)—Ring Around the Moon *(rec International House, KPFA–Berkeley, Nov 19, 1953)* Innova 4–▲ 401

H. Partch (cnd)

Partch, H.:And on the 7th Day, Petals Fell In Petaluma CRI ■ ACS 6001

Partch, H.:And on the 7th Day, Petals Fell In Petaluma *(rec 1967, stereo)* CRI ▲ CD 7000 (m/s) [AAD]

Partch, H.:Castor & Pollux CRI ■ ACS 6001

Partch, H.:Castor & Pollux *(rec 1953, mono)* CRI ▲ CD 7000 (m/s) [AAD]

Partch, H.:Cloud Chaber Music CRI ■ ACS 6001

Partch, H.:The Letter CRI ■ ACS 6001

Gaudeamus String Quartet [Jos Verkoeyen (vn), Jan Wittenberg (vn), Hans Neuburger (va), Max Werner (vc)]

Pijper, W.:Qt 4 Strs Donemus ▲ CV 1

Pijper, W.:Qt 5 Strs Donemus ▲ CV 1

Straesser, J.:Sightseeing V *(rec July 2, 1974)* Donemus ▲ CV 44

Gaudier Ensemble

Beethoven, L. van:Septet Strs Hyperion ▲ CDA 66513

Beethoven, L. van:Sxt Winds, Op. 71 Hyperion ▲ CDA 66513

Berwald, F.:Qt Pno, Cl, Hn & Bn Hyperion ▲ CDA 66834

Berwald, F.:Septet Vn, "Grand Septet" Hyperion ▲ CDA 66834

Berwald, F.:Trio 2 Hyperion ▲ CDA 66834

Dvořák, A.:Qnt Pno, Op. 81 Hyperion ▲ CDA 66796

Dvořák, A.:Qnt Strs, Op. 77 Hyperion ▲ CDA 66796

Spohr, L.:Nonet Strs Hyperion ▲ CDA 66699 [DDD]

Spohr, L.:Octet Strs Hyperion ▲ CDA 66699 [DDD]

Gävelborg SO

M. Liljefors (cnd)

Hägg, J.A.:Amerikanische Festklänge *(rec Sweden, Jan 11–12, 1996)* Sterling ▲ 1007 [DDD]

Hägg, J.A.:Concert Ov 1 *(rec Sweden, Jan 11–12, 1996)* Sterling ▲ 1007 [DDD]

Hägg, J.A.:Concert Ov 2 *(rec Sweden, Jan 11–12, 1996)* Sterling ▲ 1007 [DDD]

Liljefors, R.:Con Pno, w. Irène Mannheimer (pno) *(rec Concert Hall of the Royal Swedish Academy of Music, Stockholm, May 15 & June 6, 1995)* Sterling ▲ 1017 [DDD]

Liljefors, R.:Sym in E♭ *(rec Concert Hall of the Royal Swedish Academy of Music, Stockholm, May 15 & June 6, 1995)* Sterling ▲ 1017 [DDD]

Gävelborg SO (cont.)

M. Liljefors (cnd) (cont.)

Lindblad, A.F.:Sym 2 *(rec Gävle, Jan 12 & 14, 1996)* Sterling ▲ 1005 [ADD/DDD]

Olsson, O.:Sym *(rec Gävle, May 22–24, 1996)* Sterling ▲ 1020 [DDD]

G. W. Nilson (cnd)

Hägg, J.A.:Nordische Sym *(rec Sweden, Oct 13, 1981)* Sterling ▲ 1007 [ADD]

Gdansk SO

W. Michniewski (cnd)

Paderewski, I.J.:Con Pno, w. Waldemar Malicki (pno) Accord ▲ ACD 201732 [DDD]

Paderewski, I.J.:Fant polonaise, w. Waldemar Malicki (pno) Accord ▲ ACD 201732 [DDD]

J. Przybylski (cnd)

Devienne, F.:Cons Fl (comp), w. Claudi Arimany (fl)—Nos. 2, 4, 5 & 7 Aura Classics ▲ AU 32002

Gelato Quartet [Peter de Sotto (ten/vn), Cynthia Steljes (ob/E hn), Claudio Vena (va/acc), George Meanwell (vc/gtr/mand)]

Rustic Chivalry Marquis Classics ▲ MAR 601

Gelland Duo [Cecilia Gelland (vn), Martin Gelland (vn)]

Acker, D.:Cantus Gemellus Vienna Modern Masters ▲ VMM 2013 [DDD]

Gemini Ensemble

E. Howarth (cnd)

Lumsdaine, D.:Aria for Edward John Eyre, w. J. Manning (sop), J. Baddeley (nar), J. Rye (nar) NM Classics ▲ NMCD 007 [DDD]

Geminiani Duo [Helmut Schaarschmidt (ob), Bernhard Hebb (gtr)]

Music for Oboe & Guitar Entrée ▲ CHE 0040–2 [ADD]

Geminiani Ensemble

Concertante Baroque Music Christophorus ▲ CD 74590 [DDD]

Gene DiNovi Trio

After Hours, w. J. Campbell (fl), S. Lemelin (pno) Marquis Classics ▲ MAR 153 [DDD]

General Motors SO

Joseph Schmidt, w. J. Schmidt (ten), Berlin RSO [cnd:Rudolf Hindemith, Bruno Seidler–Winkler, Hermann Scherchen, Fritz Stiedry, Max von Schillings], unknown orchestra [cnd:Idris Lewis], General Motors SO, General Motors Sym Chorus [cnd:Erno Rapee, José Iturbi, Oscar Straus] Koch Schwann ▲ SCH 312572 [ADD]

Geneva Baroque Duo [Jonathan Rubin (lt), Sharyn Rubin (b vl)]

Geneva Baroque Duo *(rec Dec. 1987)* Gallo ▲ CD 540 [DDD]

Geneva Collegium Academicum

R. Dunand (cnd)

Martin, F.:Die Weise von Liebe und Tod des Cornets Christoph Rilke, w. P. Huttenlocher (bar) *(rec Oct. 8, 1984)* Gallo ▲ CD 725 [ADD]

J. Guyonnet (cnd)

Guyonnet, J.:La Cantate interrompue, w. F. Rochaix (nar), S. Stenhammar (sop), S. Seban (pno), G. Calame (pno), E. Séjourne (perc), P. Geiss, E. Tarr (tpt), B. Nilsson (tpt), H. Ries (trbn), H. Rückert (trbn), J.–M. Collet [F] *(rec Nov. 15, 1986)* Grammont ▲ CTSP 30–2

Geneva Elans Orch Ensemble

P. Crispini (cnd)

Rossini, G.:Stabat Mater, w. O. Liani (sop), J. Jaques (mez), M. Zamfir (ten), T. Krause (bar), Geneva Elans Vocal Ensemble [L] Gallo ▲ CD 487

Geneva Percussion Ensemble

Gaudibert, E.:Feuillages Jecklin ▲ JS 304–2 [DDD]

Orff, C.:Carmina burana, w. Brigitte Fournier (sop), Peter Sigrist (ten), Michel Brodard (bar), Jean–Jacques Balet (pno), Mayumi Kameda (pno) [version for 2 pnos & perc] Cascavelle ▲ CVL 1009 [DDD]

G. Bernasconi (cnd)

Menozzi, S.:Quand les Ténèbres viendront... Jecklin ▲ JS 304–2 [DDD]

Ott, Daniel:zampugn Jecklin ▲ JS 304–2 [DDD]

Geneva RSO

G. Rivoli (cnd)

Chausson, E.:Poème Vn, w. R. Odnoposoff (vn) *(rec Mar. 10, 1960)* Doron ▲ DRC 4004 [ADD]

Saint–Saëns, C.:Introduction & Rondo capriccioso, w. R. Odnoposoff (vn) *(rec Mar. 10, 1960)* Doron ▲ DRC 4004 [ADD]

Sarasate, P. de:Zigeunerweisen, w. R. Odnoposoff (vn) *(rec Mar. 10, 1960)* Doron ▲ DRC 4004 [ADD]

Geneva SO

C. Liang–Sheng (cnd)

Mendelssohn, F.:Psalm 42, w. Y. Perrin (sop), M. Schwartz (mez), O. Dufour (ten), C. Traube (ten), P. Huttenlocher (bar), C. Ossola (bass), M. Hutin (bass), Geneva Univ Chorus Gallo ▲ CD 635 [AAD]

Mendelssohn, F.:Psalm 95, w. Y. Perrin (sop), M. Schwartz (mez), O. Dufour (ten), C. Traube (ten), P. Huttenlocher (bar), C. Ossola (bass), M. Hutin (bass), Geneva Univ Chorus Gallo ▲ CD 635 [AAD]

Mendelssohn, F.:Psalm 115, w. Y. Perrin (sop), M. Schwartz (mez), O. Dufour (ten), C. Traube (ten), P. Huttenlocher (bar), C. Ossola (bass), M. Hutin (bass), Geneva Univ Chorus Gallo ▲ CD 635 [AAD]

Genoa CO

A. Plotino (cnd)

Bellini, V.:Arias, w. Marco Lazzara (alt)—Questa è la valle...Quando incise su quel marmo *(rec Dec 4, 1995)* Bongiovanni ▲ GB 2521 [DDD]

Gluck, C.W.:Orfeo ed Euridice (sels), w. Marco Lazzara (alt)—Ove trascorsi...Che farò senza Euridice *(rec Dec 4, 1995)* Bongiovanni ▲ GB 2521 [DDD]

Handel, G.F.:Arias, w. Marco Lazzara (alt)—Va tacito e nascosto [from Giulio Cesare in Egitto]; Venti, turbini, prestate [from Rinaldo]; O Thou That Tellest Good Tidings to Zion [from Messiah] *(rec Dec 4, 1995)* Bongiovanni ▲ GB 2521 [DDD]

Paganini, N.:Tarantella Vn, w. F. Mezzena (vn) Dynamic ▲ CD 27 [ADD]

Pergolesi, G.B.:Stabat Mater (sels), w. Marco Lazzara (alt)—Fac ut portem *(rec Dec 4, 1995)* Bongiovanni ▲ GB 2521 [DDD]

Rossini, G.:Tancredi (sels), w. Marco Lazzara (alt)—O patria...Di tanti palpiti *(rec Dec 4, 1995)* Bongiovanni ▲ GB 2521 [DDD]

Genoa Teatro Carlo Felice Orch

P. Olmi (cnd)

Rossini, G.:The Siege of Corinth, w. L. Serra (sop), M. Comencini (ten), D. Raffanti (ten), A. Caforio (bass), M. Lippi (bass), Genoa Teatro Carlo Felice Chorus, Prague Phil Choir *(rec June 2 & 14, 1992)* Nuova Era 3–▲ 7140/42 [DDD]

Genoa Teatro Comunale Orch

M.. Bernart (cnd)

Donizetti, G.:Torquato Tasso, w. A. D'Auria (sop), L. Serra (sop), N. Ciliento (mez), E. Palacio (ten), R. Coviello (bar), S. Alaimo (bass–bar), A. Riva (bass), Genoa Teatro Comunale Chorus [I] *(rec live 10/16/85)* Bongiovanni 3–▲ GB 2028/30 [DDD]

D. Oren (cnd)

Puccini, G.:Turandot, w. G. Dimitrova (sop), C. Gasdia (sop), N. Martinucci (ten), R. Scandiuzzi (bass), Genoa Teatro Comunale Chorus [I] *(rec live, 1/20–27/89)* Nuova Era 2–▲ 6786/87 [DDD]

Puccini, G.:Turandot (sels), w. G. Dimitrova (sop), C. Gasdia (sop), N. Martinucci (ten), R. Scandiuzzi (bass), Genoa Teatro Comunale Chorus [I] Nuova Era ▲ 6871 [DDD]

M. Wolf–Ferrari (cnd)

Puccini, G.:La Bohème, w. M. Freni (sop), M. Adani (sop), L. Pavarotti (ten), L. Saccomani (bar), Genoa Teatro Comunale Chorus [I] *(rec live 4/12/69)* Verona 2–▲ 27079/80

Puccini, G.:La Bohème, w. M. Freni (sop), M. Adani (sop), L. Pavarotti (ten), L. Saccomani (bar), Genoa Teatro Comunale Chorus *(rec live, Apr 12, 1969)* Melodram 2–▲ MEL 27031 [AAD]

Georgia Woodwind Quintet [Ronald Wain (fl), Dwight Manning (ob), Theodore Jahn (cl), William Davis (bn), Jean Martin (hn)]

McKinley, T.L.:Bagatelles *(rec 1994 & 1995)* ACA Digital Recording ▲ CM 20032

Macy, C.:Twigs *(rec 1994 & 1995)* ACA Digital Recording ▲ CM 20032

Sieg, J.:Suite Ww Qnt *(rec 1994 & 1995)* ACA Digital Recording ▲ CM 20032

Vayo, D.:Qnt Winds *(rec 1994 & 1995)* ACA Digital Recording ▲ CM 20032

Georgian CO

Nassidse, S.:Con Vn, w. Liana Issakadze (vn), Eldar Issakadze (vc) Orfeo ▲ 304921 [DDD]

Taktakishvili, O.:Con 2 Vn, w. L. Issakadze (vn) Orfeo ▲ 304921 [DDD]

Tchaikovsky, P.:Sérénade mélancolique, w. L. Issakadze (vn) *(rec Sept. 26–28, 1992)* Orfeo ▲ 307921 [DDD]

Tchaikovsky, P.:Valse-Scherzo Vn, w. L. Issakadze (vn) *(rec Sept. 26–28, 1992)* Orfeo ▲ 307921 [DDD]

L. Issakadze (cnd)

Gabunija, N.:Sinf Gioconda Orfeo ▲ 304921 [DDD]

Tchaikovsky, P.:Souvenir de Florence *(rec Sept. 26–28, 1992)* Orfeo ▲ 307921 [DDD]

Tchaikovsky, P.:Souvenir d'un lieu cher *(rec Sept. 26–28, 1992)* Orfeo ▲ 307921 [DDD]

Zinzadse, S.:Phantasie Vn Orfeo ▲ 304921 [DDD]

Georgian Festival Orch

V. Kahi (cnd)

Ravel, M.:Alborada del gracioso Infinity Digital ▲ QK 57236 [DDD]

Ravel, M.:Rapsodie espagnole Infinity Digital ▲ QK 57236 [DDD]

Tchaikovsky, P.:Capriccio italien Infinity Digital ▲ QK 61978 [DDD]

Tchaikovsky, P.:Marche slave Infinity Digital ▲ QK 57242 [DDD]

Tchaikovsky, P.:Marche slave Infinity Digital ▲ QK 61978 [DDD]

Tchaikovsky, P.:Ov 1812 Infinity Digital ▲ QK 61978 [DDD]

Tchaikovsky, P.:Romeo & Juliet Infinity Digital ▲ QK 61978 [DDD]

Tchaikovsky, P.:Romeo & Juliet Infinity Digital ▲ QK 64292 [DDD]

Tchaikovsky, P.:Swan Lake (sels)—Tempo di valse; Pas de trois; Pas de deux; Tempo di polacca; Andante; Allegro moderato; Moderato assai quasi andante; Danses des cygnes; Danse hongroise; Danse espagnole; Danse napolitaine; Tempo di mazurka; Scène finale Infinity Digital ▲ QK 69273 [DDD]

J. Mardjani (cnd)

Berlioz, H.:Sym fantastique Infinity Digital ▲ QK 66170 [DDD]

Debussy, C.:Nocturnes, w. Tbilisi Festival Choir Infinity Digital ▲ QK 66307 [DDD]

Holst, G.:The Planets Infinity Digital ▲ QK 57258 [DDD]

Liszt, F.:Fant on Hungarian Folk Tunes, w. Elisso Bolkvadze (pno) Infinity Digital ▲ QK 57260 [DDD]

Mussorgsky, M.:Khovanshchina (orch sels) Infinity Digital ▲ QK 57233 [DDD]

Mussorgsky, M.:Night Infinity Digital ▲ QK 57233 [DDD]

Mussorgsky, M.:Pictures at an Exhibition Infinity Digital ▲ QK 57233 [DDD]

Ravel, M.:Boléro Infinity Digital ▲ QK 57236 [DDD]

Ravel, M.:Pavane pour une infante défunte Infinity Digital ▲ QK 57236 [DDD]

Ravel, M.:La Valse Infinity Digital ▲ QK 57236 [DDD]

Rimsky-Korsakov, N.:Capriccio espagnol Infinity Digital ▲ QK 66170 [DDD]

Schubert, Franz:Ovs—Rosamunde Infinity Digital ▲ QK 66574 [DDD]

Schubert, Franz:Sym 9 Infinity Digital ▲ QK 66574 [DDD]

Stravinsky, I.:The Firebird Suite Infinity Digital ▲ QK 66307 [DDD]

Stravinsky, I.:Pétrouchka Infinity Digital ▲ QK 66727 [DDD]

Tchaikovsky, P.:Capriccio italien Infinity Digital ▲ QK 66728 [DDD]

Tchaikovsky, P.:Sym 4 Infinity Digital ▲ QK 64292 [DDD]

Tchaikovsky, P.:Sym 5 Infinity Digital ▲ QK 57242 [DDD]

Tchaikovsky, P.:Sym 6 Infinity Digital ▲ QK 66728 [DDD]

Georgian State String Quartet [Konstantin Vardeli (vn), Tamaz Batiashvili (vn), Nodar Zhvania (va), Otar Chubinishvili (vc)]

Nasidze, S.I.:Qt 5 Strs Sony Classical ("St Petersburg Classics" series) ▲ SMK 66363

Shostakovich, D.:Qt 2 Strs *(rec 1976 & 1981)* Praga ▲ PR 254 042

Tsintsadze, S.:Miniatures Sony Classical ("St Petersburg Classics" series) ▲ SMK 66363

Tsintsadze, S.:Qt 6 Strs Sony Classical ("St Petersburg Classics" series) ▲ SMK 66363

German Bach Soloists

Bach, J.S.:Music of, w. Leonhardt Consort Pro Arte ▲ CDM 801

Classics Go to the Movies, Vol. 4, w. Budapest SO, Budapest PO, Salzburg Mozarteum Orch, Christian Altenburger, Ernst Mayer-Schieming, Sofia National Opera Orch LaserLight ▲ 15 644

Mozart, W.A.:Complete Mozart Edition, w. Daniel Chorzempa (org), Helmut Winschermann (ob) Philips 2–▲ 422521–2 [ADD]

Mozart, W.A.:Music of, w. N. Marriner (cnd), Minnesota Orch—Con 4 Vn; Haffner Serenade; Eine kleine Nachtmusik; etc. Pro Arte ▲ CDM 807 ■ PCD 807

W. Gönnenwein (cnd)

Bach, J.S.:Magnificat, BWV 243, w. Helen Donath (sop), Gundula Bernát-Klein (sop), Birgit Finnilä (alt), Peter Schreier (ten), Barry McDaniel (bass), South German Madrigal Choir [E♭ version] *(rec Stuttgart Radio, 1966)* Bayer ▲ 100081 [ADD]

G. Weinberger (cnd)

Bach, J.S.:Motets, BWV 225–30 *(rec Sept 28–30, 1995)* Calig ▲ CAL 50960 [DDD]

H. Winschermann (cnd)

Bach, J.S.:Brandenburg Con 1 LaserLight ♦ 90013 [DDD]

Bach, J.S.:Brandenburg Con 2 LaserLight ♦ 90013 [DDD]

Bach, J.S.:Brandenburg Con 3 LaserLight ♦ 90013 [DDD]

Bach, J.S.:Brandenburg Con 4 LaserLight ♦ 90014 [DDD]

Bach, J.S.:Brandenburg Con 5 LaserLight ♦ 90014 [DDD]

Bach, J.S.:Brandenburg Con 6 LaserLight ♦ 90014 [DDD]

Bach, J.S.:Con 7 Hpd, w. George Malcolm (hpd) *(rec 1967)* Musicaphon ▲ 51356 [AAD]

Bach, J.S.:Con Ob, BWV 1053, w. Helmut Winschermann (ob) *(rec Münster zu Heilsbronn, 1965)* Musicaphon ▲ 51351 [AAD]

Bach, J.S.:Con Vn & Ob, w. Georg Friedrich Hendel (vn), Helmut Winschermann (ob) Musicaphon ▲ 51357 [AAD]

Bach:Suites Nos. 1 & 2 in C & b for Orchestra Laserlight ♦ 90034 [CD-ROM]

Baroque Treasures, Vol. 2:Bach LaserLight ▲ 15657 [DDD]

Baroque Treasures, Vol. 5:Bach LaserLight ▲ 15660 [DDD]

Baroque Treasures, Vol. 8:Bach LaserLight ▲ 15663 [DDD]

Brandenburg Concertos 1–3, BWV 1046–48 Laserlight ♦ 90013 [DDD]

Brandenburg Concertos 4–6, BWV 1049–51 Laserlight ♦ 90014 [DDD]

Mozart, W.A.:Cons Vn, w. C. Altenburger (vn)—sels. from Cons. 3 & 5 for Violin LaserLight ▲ 15 650 [DDD]

Mozart, W.A.:Con 3 Vn, w. C. Altenburger (vn) LaserLight ▲ 15 525 [DDD]

Mozart, W.A.:Con 3 Vn, w. C. Altenburger (vn) LaserLight ▲ 15 879 [DDD]

Mozart, W.A.:Con 4 Vn, w. C. Altenburger (vn) LaserLight ▲ 15 879 [DDD]

Mozart, W.A.:Con 4 Vn, w. C. Altenburger (vn) LaserLight ▲ 15 650 [DDD]

Mozart, W.A.:Con 4 Vn, w. C. Altenburger (vn) Laserlight ▲ 15 525 [DDD]

Mozart, W.A.:Con 5 Vn, w. C. Altenburger (vn) LaserLight ▲ 15 880 [DDD]

Mozart, W.A.:Con 5 Vn, w. C. Altenburger (vn) Laserlight ▲ 15 525 [DDD]

Mozart, W.A.:Sinf concertante Vn, K.364, w. C. Altenburger (va), W. Christ (va) LaserLight ▲ 15 880 [DDD]

Mozart, W.A.:Sinf concertante Vn, K.364, w. C. Altenburger (va), W. Christ (va) LaserLight ▲ 15 650 [DDD]

German Chamber Academy Orch

J. Goritzki (cnd)

Haydn, M.:Syms—in D, P. 42; in D, P. 21; in F, P. 22; in D, P. 23 [w. Julia Becker (vn), Christian Wetzel (E hn)] *(rec Zeughaus Neuss, Apr 5–8, 1995)* CPO ▲ CPO 999179–2 [DDD]

Heiden, B.:Concertino Str Orch Capriccio ▲ CD 10565 [DDD]

Piazzolla, A.:Con Band, w. Lothar Hensel (band) Capriccio ▲ CD 10565 [DDD]

Rota, N.:Con Strs Capriccio ▲ CD 10565 [DDD]

Waxman, F.:Sinfonietta Timp Capriccio ▲ CD 10565 [DDD]

German CO

A. Delfs (cnd)

Schulhoff, E.:Con Pno, w. Aleksandar Madzar (pno) *(rec Freie Waldorfschule, Bremen, Oct 1994)* London ▲ 444819–2 [DDD]

Schulhoff, E.:Double Con Fl, w. Bettina Wild (fl), Aleksandar Madzar (pno) *(rec Freie Waldorfschule, Bremen, Oct 1994)* London ▲ 444819–2 [DDD]

Schulhoff, E.:Con Str Qt, w. Hawthorne String Quartet *(rec Freie Waldorfschule, Bremen, Oct 1994)* London ▲ 444819–2 [DDD]

M. Pletnev (cnd)

Mozart, W.A.:Con 23 Pno, w. M. Pletnev (pno) Virgin Classics ▲ CDC 59280

Mozart, W.A.:Con 24 Pno, w. M. Pletnev (pno) Virgin Classics ▲ CDC 59280

German Chamber PO

Beethoven, L. van:Grosse Fuge Str Qt Berlin Classics ▲ BER 1105 [DDD]

Beethoven, L. van:Septet Strs Berlin Classics ▲ BER 1105 [DDD]

Gubaidulina, S.:Concordanza Berlin Classics ▲ BER 1113 [DDD]

Gubaidulina, S.:Meditation on a Bach Chorale Berlin Classics ▲ BER 1113 [DDD]

Gubaidulina, S.:The Seven Last Words Berlin Classics ▲ BER 1113 [DDD]

Lourié, A.:Con da camera, w. G. Kremer (vn) Deutsche Grammophon ▲ 437788–2

Lourié, A.:A Little Chamber Music Deutsche Grammophon ▲ 437788–2

Lourié, A.:Little Gidding, w. K. Riegel (ten) Deutsche Grammophon ▲ 437788–2

F. Bernius (cnd)

Schubert, Franz:Mass 6, w. Stuttgart Chamber Choir Berlin Classics ▲ BER 1165

M. Pletnev (cnd)

Mozart, W.A.:Con 9 Pno, w. Mikhail Pletnev (pno) Virgin Classics ▲ CDC 45130

Mozart, W.A.:Con 20 Pno, w. Mikhail Pletnev (pno) Virgin Classics ▲ CDC 45130

J.-P. Saraste (cnd)

Bach, J.S.:Con 3 Hpd, w. Olli Mustonen (pno) London ▲ 443118–2

Beethoven, L. van:Con 6 Pno, w. Olli Mustonen (pno) London ▲ 443118–2

H. Schiff (cnd)

Beethoven, L. van:Sym 1 Berlin Classics ▲ BER 1035 [DDD]

Beethoven, L. van:Sym 2 Berlin Classics ▲ BER 1121

Beethoven, L. van:Sym 3, "Eroica" Berlin Classics ▲ BER 1121

Beethoven, L. van:Sym 4 Berlin Classics ▲ BER 1035 [DDD]

M. Venzago (cnd)

Schoenberg, A.:Chamber Sym 1 Virgin Classics ▲ CDC 59018

Schoenberg, A.:Suite Strs Virgin Classics ▲ CDC 59018

Schoenberg, A.:Verklärte Nacht Virgin Classics ▲ CDC 59018

T. Zehetmair (cnd)

Hartmann, K.A.:Con funèbre Teldec ▲ 2292–46449–2

German Chamber PO Winds

C. Tetzlaff (cnd)

Hindemith, P.:Septet Winds & Tpt Virgin Classics ▲ CDC 45056

Toch, E.:Pieces Ww Virgin Classics ▲ CDC 45056

Weill, K.:Con Vn, w. Christian Tetzlaff (vn) Virgin Classics ▲ CDC 45056

German Horn Ensemble

Wagner, R.:Lohengrin (sels)—Fantasy [trans for horn by Karl Stiegler] Koch Schwann ▲ SCH 315942 [DDD]

Wagner, R.:Parsifal (sels)—Fant [trans for horn by Holger Fransman] Koch Schwann ▲ SCH 315942 [DDD]

Wagner, R.:Tannhäuser (sels)—Fantasy [trans for horn by Hans Hombusch] Koch Schwann ▲ SCH 315942 [DDD]

Wagner, R.:Tristan und Isolde (sels)—Fantasy [trans for horn by Hermann Jeurissen] Koch Schwann ▲ SCH 315942 [DDD]

German Large RSO

Rudolf Moralt, Max Schönherr, Anton Paulik (cnds)

Max Lorenz:Recital, 1933–1957, w. M. Lorenz (ten), Maria Reining (sop), Berlin RSO [cnd:Artur Rother], Bayreuth Festival Orch [cnd:Heinz Tietjen, Richard Strauss], Hessen RSO [cnd:Kurt Schröder], Brenda Lewis (sop), Eberhard Wächter, Wolfgang Zimmer (bar) *(rec 1933–57)* Myto ▲ MCD 934.88

German Music School Orch

J.-P. Weigle (cnd)

Elgar, E.:Intro & Allegro Ars Musici ▲ 1128

Janácek, L.:Idyll Ars Musici ▲ 1128

Shostakovich, D.:Con 1 Pno, w. Veronika Reznikovskaja (pno), Falk Maertens (tpt) Ars Musici ▲ 1128

Suk, J.:Serenade Strs Ars Musici ▲ 1128

German Opera Orch

German String Trio

Fiala, J.:Qts Ob, w. L. Lencses (ob)—in F & E♭ Capriccio ▲ 10423 [DDD]

Krommer, F.:Qts Ob, w. L. Lencses (ob)—in C & F Capriccio ▲ 10423 [DDD]

German String Trio [Hans Kalafusz (vn), Christian Hedrich (va), Reiner Ginzel (vc)]

Erdmann, D.:Trio *(rec Mar 23, 1982)* Thorofon ▲ CTH 2284 [ADD/DDD]

German String Trio [Hans Kalafusz (vn), Jürgen Weber (va), Reiner Ginzel (vc)]

Meyer, K.:Trio Strs *(rec Munich, 1995)* Pro Viva ▲ ISPV 176 CD [DDD]

German SO

M. Janowski (cnd)

Weber, C.M. von:Der Freischütz, w. R. Ziesack (sop), S. Sweet (sop), A. Schmidt (bar), M. Hölle (bass), Berlin Radio Chorus RCA Red Seal 2–▲ 09026–62538–2

K. Seibel (cnd)

Korngold, E.W.:Der Ring des Polykrates, w. Beate Bilandzija (sop—Laura), Kirsten Blanck (sop—Lieschen), Endrik Wottrich (ten—Wilhelm), Jürgen Sacher (ten—Florian), Dietrich Henschel (bar—Peter) *(rec Jesus Christ Church, Dahlem, Sept 19–25, 1995)* CPO ▲ CPO 999402–2 [DDD]

M. Trojahn (cnd)

Pettersson, G.A.:Sym 6 CPO ▲ CPO 999124 [DDD]

L. Zagrosek (cnd)

Goldschmidt, B.:Der gewaltige Hahnrei, w. R. Alexander (sop), M. Posselt (sop), H. Lawrence (sop), R. Wörle (ten), M. Kraus (ten), M. Petzold (ten), C. Otelli (bar), Berlin Radio Chorus London ▲ 440850–2 [DDD]

Goldschmidt, B.:Mediterranean Songs, w. R. Alexander (sop), M. Posselt (sop), H. Lawrence (sop), R. Wörle (ten), M. Kraus (ten), M. Petzold (ten), C. Otelli (bar), Berlin Radio Chorus London ▲ 440850–2 [DDD]

H.E. Zimmer (cnd)

Eisler, H.:Kammersinfonie *(rec Jesus Christ Church, Berlin–Dahlem, Oct 1993 & 1994)* Capriccio ▲ 10500 [DDD]

Eisler, H.:Kleine Sinf *(rec Jesus Christ Church, Berlin–Dahlem, Oct 1993 & 1994)* Capriccio ▲ 10500 [DDD]

Eisler, H.:Orchesterstücke (5) *(rec Jesus Christ Church, Berlin–Dahlem, Oct 1993 & 1994)* Capriccio ▲ 10500 [DDD]

Eisler, H.:Stücke (3) Orch *(rec Jesus Christ Church, Berlin–Dahlem, Oct 1993 & 1994)* Capriccio ▲ 10500 [DDD]

Eisler, H.:Sturm-Suite *(rec Jesus Christ Church, Berlin–Dahlem, Oct 1993 & 1994)* Capriccio ▲ 10500 [DDD]

German Wind PO

F. Bernius (cnd)

Bruckner, A.:Mass 2, w. Stuttgart Chamber Choir Sony Classical ▲ SK 48037

German Wind Soloists

Lachner, F.P.:Octet Marco Polo ▲ 8.223356 [DDD]

Schubert, Franz:Minuet & Finale Marco Polo ▲ 8.223356 [DDD]

Weber, C.M. von:Adagio & Rondo Cls Marco Polo ▲ 8.223356 [DDD]

German Youth PO
R. Barshaï (cnd)
Shostakovich, D.:Sym 7, w. Moscow PO members *(rec live, Leipzig Gewandhaus, 6/22/91)* BIS ▲ CD 515 [DDD]
H. Holliger (cnd)
Lutoslawski, W.:Chain 1 Polskie Nagrania ▲ PNCD 044 [AAD]
Lutoslawski, W.:Novelette Polskie Nagrania ▲ PNCD 043 [AAD]
J. Maksymiuk (cnd)
Bloch, A.:Oratario, w. Polish CO Pro Viva ▲ ISPV 172
Bloch, A.:Twelve Time Layers, w. Polish CO Pro Viva ▲ ISPV 172
George Gershwin Festival Orch
M. Charry (cnd)
Gershwin, G.:Con Pno, w. A. Zizzo (pno) *(rec 6/90)* Pro Arte/Fanfare ▲ CDD 514 [DDD]
Gershwin, G.:Cuban Ov *(rec 6/90)* Pro Arte/Fanfare ▲ CDD 514 [DDD]
Gershwin, G.:Rhap in Blue, w. A. Zizzo (pno) *(rec 6/90)* Pro Arte/Fanfare ▲ CDD 514 [DDD]
Gervasio Duo [Carmen Schultz (baroque mand), Jürgen Thiergärtner (baroque gtr)]
Baroque Mandolin & Guitar CPO ▲ CPO 999226 [DDD]
Classical Mandolin & Guitar CPO ▲ CPO 999291 [DDD]
Gesualdo Consort
Early Music of the Netherlands, Vol. 1 (1400–1600), w. Ensemble Tragicomedia, Concerto Palatino members *(rec Dec. 1988)* Emergo ▲ EC 3987 [DDD]
Gewandhaus Orch—see Leipzig Gewandhaus Orch
Gewandhaus String Quartet
Beethoven, L. van:Sxt Hns, Op. 81b, w. H. Baumann (hn) Philips ▲ 426440–2
Berg, A.:Qt Strs Berlin Classics ▲ BER 1065 [DDD]
Dittersdorf, K.D. von:Qts (6) Strs Berlin Classics 2–▲ BER 9261
Haydn, J.:Divert Hn, Vn & Vc, H.IV/5 Philips ▲ 426440–2
Haydn, M.:Romance, w. Hermann Baumann (hn) Philips ▲ 426440–2
Mozart, W.A.:Qnt Hn, K.407, w. H. Baumann (hn) Philips ▲ 426440–2
Reicha, A.:Qnt Hn, w. H. Baumann (hn) Philips ▲ 426440–2
Schoenberg, A.:Qt 2 Strs Berlin Classics ▲ BER 1065 [DDD]
Webern, A.:Bagatelles Str Qt Berlin Classics ▲ BER 1065 [DDD]
Ghent Collegium Vocale Orch
P. Herreweghe (cnd)
Bach, J.S.:Christmas Oratorio, w. B. Schlick (sop), M. Chance (ct), H. Crook (ten), P. Kooy (bass), Ghent Collegium Vocale [G] Virgin Classics (Veritas) 2–▲ ZDCB 59530–2 [DDD]
Bach, J.S.:Masses, BWV 233–36, "Lutheran Masses", w. A. Mellon (sop), G. Lesne (alto), C. Prégardien (ten), P. Kooy (bass), Ghent Collegium Vocale—BWV 233 & 236 Virgin Classics ▲ CDC 59634
Bach, J.S.:Masses, BWV 233–36, "Lutheran Masses", w. A. Mellon (sop), G. Lesne (alto), C. Prégardien (ten), P. Kooy (bass), Ghent Collegium Vocale—BWV 234 & 235 Virgin Classics ▲ CDC 59587
Bach, J.S.:St. Matthew Passion (sels), w. A. Mellon (sop), G. Lesne (alto), C. Prégardien (ten), P. Kooy (bass), Ghent Collegium Vocale Virgin Classics ▲ CDC 59587
Il Giardino Armonico Ensemble
Christmas Concertos Teldec ▲ 2292–46013–2 ZK
Vivaldi, A.:Cons Diverse Instrs, w. Christophe Coin (vc)—in g, RV.531; in F, RV.544; in F, RV.551; in D, RV.564; in A, RV.552; in C, RV.561 Teldec ("Das alte Werk" series) ▲ 94552–2
Vivaldi, A.:Cons Diverse Instrs Teldec ▲ 9031–73269–2
Vivaldi, A.:Cons Diverse Instrs Teldec ▲ 9031–73268–2
Vivaldi, A.:Cons Diverse Instrs Teldec ▲ 9031–73267–2
Vivaldi, A.:Cons Diverse Instrs Teldec ▲ 9031–74727–2
Vivaldi, A.:Cons Diverse Instrs—6 concerti—RV.86, 98, 101, 103, 105, 107 Nuova Era ("Ancient Music" series) ▲ 6731 [DDD]
Vivaldi, A.:Cons Vn, Op. 8/1–12, "Il cimento dell'armonia e dell'inventione"—Nos. 1–4, 9 (RV.454 for Ob) & 11 Teldec ▲ 4509–97671–2
G. Antonini (cnd)
Vivaldi, A.:Cons Diverse Instrs Teldec ▲ 91182–2
Gioccarpa [Elisabeth Colard (hp), Janet Paulus (hp)]
From the Sea to the Land Pierre Verany ▲ PVY 796091
Gioia della Musica
M. Brown (cnd)
Handel, G.F.:Messiah, w. Ruth Holton (sop), Vanessa Williamson (mez), James Griffett (ten), Lawrence Albert (bass), U. Walser (tpt), Bmensky Akademicky Sbor Allegro 2–▲ ALGDPCD 1068 [DDD]
Handel, G.F.:Messiah (sels), w. Ruth Holton (sop), Vanessa Williamson (mez), James Griffett (ten), L. Albert (bass), Bmensky Akademicky Sbor Allegro ▲ ALG PCD 1078 [DDD]
Giovane Quartetto Italiano [Alessandro Simoncini (vn), Luigi Mazza (vn), Demetrio Comuzzi (va), Luca Simoncini (vc)]
Haydn, J.:Qts Strs, Op. 76, "Erdödy Qts" *(rec Milan, 1990)* Claves 2–▲ CD 9401/2 [DDD]
Martucci, G.:Qnt Pno, w. M. Borciani (pno) Claves ▲ CD 9210 [DDD]
Giovane Quartetto Italiano members
Martucci, G.:Trio 1 Pno, w. M. Borciani (pno) Claves ▲ CD 9210 [DDD]
I Giovani di Nuova Cameristica
D. Ferrari (cnd)
Sammartini, G.B.:Syms (comp)—Early Syms. (20) Nuova Era 3–▲ NUO 7206 [DDD]
I Giovani Musici Italiani
F. Ayo (cnd)
Tartini, G.:Cons Vn (misc), w. Felix Ayo (vn)—in C, D.12; in F, D.67; in G, D.78; *(rec Rome, Italy, Apr 1–3, 1996)* Dynamic ▲ CDS 163 [DDD]
Giovanile Ambrosiano Ensemble
I. Lo Vetere (cnd)
Traetta, T.:Litanies, w. S. Krasteva (sop), I. Aramayo Sandivari (sgr), A. De Lucia (sgr), R. Gierlach (bar) Bongiovanni ▲ GB 2127 [DDD]
Traetta, T.:Ov in D Bongiovanni ▲ GB 2127 [DDD]
Traetta, T.:Stabat Mater, w. S. Krasteva (sop), I. Aramayo Sandivari (sgr), A. De Lucia (sgr), R. Gierlach (bar), Piacenza Polifonico Farnesiano Chorus Bongiovanni ▲ GB 2127 [DDD]
Mauro Giuliani Trio
Matiegka, W.T.:Serenade Trio Bongiovanni ▲ GB 5048
Molino, F.:Trio Fl, Op. 45 Bongiovanni ▲ GB 5048
Rossini, G.:La gazza ladra (ov) Bongiovanni ▲ GB 5048
Schubert, Franz:Qt 15 Strs Bongiovanni ▲ GB 5048
Gjertrud's Gipsy Orch
Jiddischkeit:A Concert in the Jewish Spirit, w. Kahan, Bente (sgr) Victoria ▲ VCD 19064
Gjovik Sinfonietta
Baekkelund (cnd)
Egge, K.:Con 2 Pno, w. Eva Knardahl (pno) Norway Music ▲ BD 7026
Olsen, S.:Village Songs, w. Atle Sponberg (vn) Norway Music ▲ BD 7026
Suk, J.:Serenade Strs Norway Music ▲ BD 7026
Philip Glass Ensemble
Glass, Philip:La Belle et la Bête Elektra/Nonesuch 2–▲ 79347–2
Glass, Philip:Dances (5), w. P. Glass (org), M. Riesman (org) CBS 2–▲ M2K 44765 [ADD]
Glass, Philip:Einstein on the Beach CBS 4–▲ M4K 38875 [DDD]
Glass, Philip:Einstein on the Beach, w. G. Fulkerson (vn) Elektra/Nonesuch ▲ 79323–2 ■ 79323–4
Glass, Philip:Glassworks CBS ▲ MK 37265 ■ PMT 37265
Glass, Philip:Hydrogen Jukebox Elektra/Nonesuch ▲ 79286–2 ■ 79286–4
Glass, Philip:The Photographer, w. P. Zukovsky (vn) CBS ▲ MK 37849 ■ PMT 37849
Glass, Philip:Satyagraha CBS 3–▲ M3K 39672 [DDD]
Glass, Philip:Songs from Liquid Days CBS ▲ MK 39564 [DDD] ■ IMT 39564 (D)
Glass, Philip:Songs from the Trilogy, w. M. Vargas (sop), L. Childs (spkr), P. Esswood, D. Perry (ten) CBS ▲ MK 45580 ■ FMT 45580
Philip Glass Ensemble (cont.)
Glass, Philip:1000 Airplanes on the Roof Virgin ▲ V21Y 86106
M. Riesman (cnd)
Glass, Philip:Glasspieces CBS ▲ MK 39539 [AAD] ■ PMT 39539
Glass, Philip:In the Upper Room CBS ▲ MK 39539 [AAD] ■ PMT 39539
Philip Glass Ensemble [L. Bielawa (voc), M. Riesman (kbds), J. Gibson (sop sax/fl), P. Glass, M. Goldray (kbd), R. Peck (alt/ten sax), A. Sterman (fl/sop sax)]
Glass, Philip:Music in 12 Pts Elektra/Nonesuch ▲ 79324–2 ■ 79324–4
Glazunov String Quartet
Kabalevsky, D.:Qt 1 Strs Olympia ▲ OLY 293 [DDD]
Kabalevsky, D.:Qt 2 Strs Olympia ▲ OLY 293 [DDD]
Tishchenko, B.:Qt 3 Strs Olympia ▲ OLY 548
Tishchenko, B.:Qt 5 Strs Olympia ▲ OLY 548
Glinka String Quartet
Shostakovich, D.:Qt 3 Strs Praga ▲ PR 254054
Shostakovich, D.:Qt 14 Strs Praga ▲ PR 254 043
Gloriae Dei Brass Ensemble
Myers, G.:God's Trbn, w. Christine Helfrich (sop), Gordon Myers (bar), Richard Cragg (sgr), Matthew Gillis (sgr), Timothy Pehta (sgr), Paul Norman (sgr), Wendy Catlin (sgr) Katherine Mary Hamilton (sgr), Sharon Hunter (sgr) Paraclete ▲ CDGD 017 [DDD]; ■ GDC 017
Sowerby, L.:Festival Musick, w. J. E. Jordan (org) Paraclete 2–▲ GCCD 016
Gloriae Dei Ringers
R. Pugsley (cnd)
Hear Them Ring!:The Bells of Christmas Paraclete ▲ GDCD 019
Glorian Duo [Donna Milanovich (fl), Wendy Herner Lucas (hp)]
Diamond, D.:Concert Piece Fl Delos ▲ DE 3189 [DDD]
Sounds of the Seine Delos ▲ DE 3143 [DDD]
Glyndebourne Festival Orch
F. Busch (cnd)
Mozart, W.A.:Così fan tutte, w. I. Souez (sop), L. Helletsgrüber (sop), I. Eisinger (sop), H. Nash (ten), W. Domgraf-Fassbüander (bar), J. Brownlee (bar), Glyndebourne Festival Chorus [I] *(rec 1935)* Pearl 3–▲ PEAS 9406 (m) [AAD]
Mozart, W.A.:Così fan tutte, w. Irene Eisinger (sop—Despina), Luise Helletsgruber (sop—Dorabella), Ina Souez (sop—Fiordiligi), Heddle Nash (ten—Ferrando), John Brownlee (bass—Don Alfonso), Willi Domgraf-Fassbaender (bass—Guglielmo), Glyndebourne Festival Chorus *(rec June 25–28, 1935)* Arkadia ("The 78's" series) 2–▲ 78011 [ADD]
Mozart, W.A.:Così fan tutte (sels), w. S. Jurinac (sop), A. Noni (sop), B. Thebom (mez), R. Lewis (ten), E. Kunz (bar), M. Borriello (bar) *(rec Glyndebourne Festival, 1950)* Testament ▲ TES SBT 1040 [ADD]
Mozart, W.A.:Don Giovanni, w. I. Souez (sop), L. Helletsgrüber (sop), A. Mildmay (sop), K. von Pataky (ten), J. Brownlee (bar), R. Henderson (bar), T. Franklin (bar), S. Baccaloni (bass), Glyndebourne Festival Chorus [I] *(rec 1936, orig. issued by HMV)* Pearl 3–▲ PEAS 9369 (m) [AAD]
Mozart, W.A.:Nozze di Figaro, w. Luise Helletsgrüber (sop), Audrey Mildmay (sop), Aulikki Rautawaara (sop), Willi Domgraf-Fassbaender (bar), Roy Henderson (bar), Glyndebourne Festival Chorus *(rec 1934)* Grammofono 2000 2–▲ GRM 78624
Mozart, W.A.:Nozze di Figaro, w. Aulikki Rautawaara (sop), Audrey Mildmay (sop), Constance Willis (mez), John Heddle Nash (ten), Roy Henderson (bar), Willi Domgraf-Fassbaender (bar), Glyndebourne Festival Chorus [I] *(rec 1934–35)* Pearl 2–▲ PEAS 9375 (m) [AAD]
Mozart, W.A.:Nozze di Figaro, w. Aulikki Rautawaara (sop), Audrey Mildmay (sop), Constance Willis (mez), John Heddle Nash (ten), Roy Henderson (bar), Willi Domgraf-Fassbaender (bar) *(rec 1934)* Legend 2–▲ LGD 132 [ADD]
Mozart, W.A.:Nozze di Figaro (sels), w. Luise Helletsgrüber (sop), Audrey Mildmay (sop), Aulikki Rautawaara (sop), Constance Willis (mez), John Heddle Nash (ten), Willi Domgraf-Fassbaender (bar), Roy Henderson (bar), Norman Allin (bass) Pearl ▲ PEA CD 9230
V. Gui (cnd)
Mozart, W.A.:Nozze di Figaro, w. S. Jurinac (sop), G. Sciutti (sop), R. Stevens (mez), M. Sinclair (cta), D. McCoshan (ten), H. Counod (ten), G. Griffith (bar), S. Bruscantini (b–bar), F. Calabrese (bass), Glyndebourne Festival Chorus Classics for Pleasure ▲ CDCFP 4724 [ADD]
Rossini, G.:La Cenerentola, w. A. Noni (sop), F. Cadoni (mez), M. de Gabarain (mez), H. Alan (bass), Glyndebourne Festival Chorus *(rec 1955)* EMI Classics 2–▲ CDMB 64183
Rossini, G.:Le Comte Ory, w. J. Sinclair (sop), M. Sinclair (cta), J. Oncina (ten), M. Roux (bar), Glyndebourne Festival Chorus *(rec 1956)* EMI Classics 2–▲ CDMB 64180
J. Pritchard (cnd)
Busoni, F.:Arlecchino or Die Fenster, w. E. Malbin (sop), M. Dickie (ten), G. Evans (bar), I. Wallace (bar), F. Ollendorf (bass), Glyndebourne Festival Chorus EMI Classics ▲ CDMB 65284
Göbel Trio Berlin [H. Maile (vn), R. Forest (vc), H. Göbel (pno)]
Goetz, H.:Chamber Music—Pno Trio in g, Op. 1; 3 Easy Pieces for Vn & Pno, Op. 2; w. assisting artists Lois Landsverk (va), Akira Akahioshi (db) *(Qt in E for Pno, Vn, Va & Vc, Op. 6; Qnt in c for Pno, Vn, Va, Vc & Db, Op. 16)*, Kauro Konno (2nd pno) *(Son in g for Pno Duet, Op. 17)* CPO 2–▲ CPO 999086–2 [DDD]
Rheinberger, J.:Trio 1 Vn Thorofon ▲ CTH 2101 [DDD]
Rheinberger, J.:Trio 1 Vn *(rec 1991)* Thorofon 6–▲ BCTH 2161/6
Rheinberger, J.:Trio 2 Vn *(rec 1991)* Thorofon 6–▲ BCTH 2161/6
Rheinberger, J.:Trio 2 Vn Thorofon ▲ CTH 2061 [DDD]
Rheinberger, J.:Trio 3 Vn Thorofon ▲ CTH 2101 [DDD]
Rheinberger, J.:Trio 3 Vn *(rec 1991)* Thorofon 6–▲ BCTH 2161/6
Goldberg Ensemble
W. Conway (cnd)
Haydn, J.:Con 1 Vc, w. William Conway (vc) Meridian ▲ CDE 84177
M. Layfield (cnd)
Haydn, J.:Con Org, Vn & Strs, H.XVIII/6, w. David Francis (hpd), Malcolm Layfield (vn) Meridian ▲ CDE 84177
Haydn, J.:Con 1 Vn, w. Malcolm Layfield (vn) Meridian ▲ CDE 84177
Mendelssohn, F.:Pieces Str Qt, Op. 81 Meridian ▲ CDE 84193
Mendelssohn, F.:Sinf 6 Meridian ▲ CDE 84193
Mendelssohn, F.:Sinf 7 Meridian ▲ CDE 84193
Mozart, W.A.:Con 12 Pno, w. A. Jordao (pno) Meridian ▲ 84166
Mozart, W.A.:Con 13 Pno, w. A. Jordao (pno) Meridian ▲ 84166
Mozart, W.A.:Con 14 Pno, w. A. Jordao (pno) Meridian ▲ 84166
Schubert, Franz:German Dances Strs, D.90 Meridian ▲ CDE 84178
Schubert, Franz:Qt 14 Strs [Mahler's arr. for string orchestra] Meridian ▲ CDE 84178
Golders Orch
Y. Talmi (cnd)
Brahms, J.:Chorale Preludes, Op. 122—Nos. 7 & 8 [orchd. Erich Leinsdorf] Ottavo ▲ OTR C98402 [DDD]
Brahms, J.:Ernste Gesänge, w. R. Holl (bass) [orchd. Erich Leinsdorf] [G] Ottavo ▲ OTR C98402 [DDD]
Mahler, G.:Blumine Ottavo ▲ OTR C98402 [DDD]
Mahler, G.:Songs from Rückert, w. J. Van Nes (cta) [G] Ottavo ▲ OTR C98402 [DDD]
Goldman Band
R.F. Cox (cnd)
The Golden Age of the American March New World ▲ 80266–2 [AAD]
Golub/Kaplan/Carr Trio [David Golub (pno), Mark Kaplan (vn), Colin Carr (vc)]
Debussy, C.:Trio Pno Arabesque ▲ ARA 6643 [DDD]
Fauré, G.:Trio Arabesque ▲ ARA 6643 [DDD]
Saint-Saëns, C.:Trio 1 Pno Arabesque ▲ ARA 6643 [DDD]
Smetana, B.:Trio Pno *(rec SUNY Purchase Recital Hall, Nov 1–3, 1994)* Arabesque ▲ ARA 6661 [DDD]
Tchaikovsky, P.:Trio Pno *(rec SUNY Purchase Recital Hall, Nov 1–3, 1994)* Arabesque ▲ ARA 6661 [DDD]

▲ = CD ♦ = Enhanced CD Δ = MD ■ = Cassette Tape □ = DCC

Gosteleradio String Quartet [Sergei Ryabov (vn), Alexander Semyannikov (vn), Andrei Kevorkov (va), Genrich Elesin (vc)]
Glinka, M.:Qt 2 Strs Allegretto ▲ ACD 8178 [DDD] ■ ACS 8178
Miaskovsky, N.:Qt 13 Strs Allegretto ▲ ACD 8178 [DDD] ■ ACS 8178

Gothenburg Brass Band
B. Gray (cnd)
Mozart, W.A.:Zauberflöte (sels), w. *(chorus & soloists unknown)* [arr Gray] Imogena ▲ IGC 45

Gothenburg CO
T. Schubeck (cnd)
Grieg, E.:The Mountain Thrall, w. Knut Skram (b-bar) *(rec Gothenburg Concert Hall, Sweden, Mar 21–23, 1976)* BIS ▲ CD 43 [AAD]

Gothenburg String Quartet
The String Quartet in Sweden:A Cavalcade of Its History, w. Barkel String Quartet, Stockholm String Quartet, Garaguly String Quartet, Kyndel String Quartet, Ivan Ericson String Quartet, Grünfarb String Quartet, Skûne String Quartet, Hälsingborg String Quartet, Galli String Quartet *(rec before 1951)* Caprice 5-▲ CAP 21506 [AAD/ADD]

Gothenburg SO
Mad About Love, w. Cheryl Studer (sop), Kiri Te Kanawa (sop), José Carreras (ten), Jerry Hadley (ten), Philharmonia Orch [cnd:Giuseppe Sinopoli], Bastille Opera Orch [cnd:Myung-Whun Chung], Boston SO [cnd:Seiji Ozawa], Vienna PO Deutsche Grammophon ▲ 449112-2 ■ 449112-4
Másson, A.:Con Mar, w. Roger Carlsson (mar) Intim Musik ▲ INT 19 [DDD]
Nørgård, P.:For a Change, w. Roger Carlsson (perc) Intim Musik ▲ INT 19 [DDD]
Sallinen, A.:Sym 2, w. Roger Carlsson (mar) Intim Musik ▲ INT 19 [DDD]

V. Ashkenazy (cnd)
Kabalevsky, D.:Con 2 Vc, w. Mats Lidström (vc) *(rec Gothenburg Concert Hall, Sweden, 1995)* BIS ▲ CD 719 [DDD]
Khachaturian, A.:Con Vc, w. Mats Lidström (vc) *(rec Gothenburg Concert Hall, Sweden, 1995)* BIS ▲ CD 719 [DDD]

M.-W. Chung (cnd)
Dvořák, A.:Sym 7 BIS ▲ CD 452 [DDD]
Dvořák, A.:Sym 8 BIS ▲ CD 452 [DDD]
Nielsen, C.:Aladdin BIS ▲ CD 247 [DDD]
Nielsen, C.:Con Cl, w. O. Schill (cl) BIS ▲ CD 616 [DDD]
Nielsen, C.:Con Cl, w. O. Schill (cl) BIS ▲ CD 321 [DDD]
Nielsen, C.:Con Cl BIS 4-▲ CD 614/16 [DDD]
Nielsen, C.:Con Fl BIS 4-▲ CD 614/16 [DDD]
Nielsen, C.:Con Fl, w. P. Gallois (fl) BIS ▲ CD 454 [DDD]
Nielsen, C.:Con Fl, w. P. Gallois (fl) BIS ▲ CD 616 [DDD]
Nielsen, C.:Con Vn, w. D. S. Kang (vn) BIS ▲ CD 616 [DDD]
Nielsen, C.:Con Vn BIS 4-▲ CD 614/16 [DDD]
Nielsen, C.:Con Vn, w. D. S. Kang (vn) BIS ▲ CD 370
Nielsen, C.:Imaginary Trip BIS ▲ CD 454 [DDD]
Nielsen, C.:Maskarade—Overture BIS ▲ CD 321 [DDD]
Nielsen, C.:Syms (comp), *(N. Järvi conducts Syms. 4 & 6)* BIS 4-▲ CD 614/16 [DDD]
Nielsen, C.:Sym 1 BIS ▲ CD 454 [DDD]
Nielsen, C.:Sym 2 BIS ▲ CD 247 [DDD]
Nielsen, C.:Sym 3 BIS ▲ CD 321 [DDD]
Nielsen, C.:Sym 5 BIS ▲ CD 370

S. Ehrling (cnd)
Rosenberg, H.:Sym 4, w. Håkan Hagegård (bar), Rilke Ensemble members, Pro Musica Chamber Choir, Swedish Radio Chorus Caprice ▲ CAP 21429 [DDD]

N. Grevillius (cnd)
Alfvén, H.:Songs, w. Jussi Björling (ten)—Skogen sover; Jag längtar dig *(rec Concert Hall, Göteborg, Aug 5, 1960)* Myto ▲ MCD 953130
Puccini, G.:Manon Lescaut (sels), w. Jussi Björling (ten)—Donna non vidi mai *(rec Concert Hall, Göteborg, Aug 5, 1960)* Myto ▲ MCD 953130
Sibelius, J.:Songs, w. Jussi Björling (ten)—Säv, säv, susa; Svarta rosor *(rec Concert Hall, Göteborg, Aug 5, 1960)* Myto ▲ MCD 953130
Tchaikovsky, P.:Eugene Onegin (sels), w. Jussi Björling (ten)—Kuda, kuda *(rec Concert Hall, Göteborg, Aug 5, 1960)* Myto ▲ MCD 953130
Wagner, R.:Lohengrin (sels), w. Jussi Björling (ten)—In fernem Land *(rec Concert Hall, Göteborg, Aug 5, 1960)* Myto ▲ MCD 953130

N. Järvi (cnd)
Borodin, A.:In the Steppes of Central Asia Deutsche Grammophon 2-▲ 435757-2 [DDD]
Borodin, A.:Nocturne Str Orch Deutsche Grammophon 2-▲ 435757-2 [DDD]
Borodin, A.:Petite Suite Deutsche Grammophon 2-▲ 435757-2 [DDD]
Borodin, A.:Prince Igor (ov) Deutsche Grammophon 2-▲ 435757-2 [DDD]
Borodin, A.:Prince Igor (dance of the Polovtsian maidens) Deutsche Grammophon 2-▲ 435757-2 [DDD]
Borodin, A.:Prince Igor (Polovtsian dances) Deutsche Grammophon 2-▲ 435757-2 [DDD]
Borodin, A.:Prince Igor (Polovtsian dances) Deutsche Grammophon ▲ 429984-2 [DDD]
Borodin, A.:Sym 1 Deutsche Grammophon 2-▲ 435757-2 [DDD]
Borodin, A.:Sym 2 Deutsche Grammophon 2-▲ 435757-2 [DDD]
Borodin, A.:Sym 3 Deutsche Grammophon 2-▲ 435757-2 [DDD]
Dvořák, A.:Con Vc, w. F. Helmerson (vc) BIS ▲ CD 245 [DDD]
Dvořák, A.:Silent Woods, w. F. Helmerson (vc) BIS ▲ CD 245 [DDD]
Grieg, E.:Con Pno, Op. 16, w. L. Zilbernstein (pno) Archiv ▲ 437549-2
Grieg, E.:Holberg Suite Deutsche Grammophon ▲ 437520-2
Grieg, E.:In Autumn Archiv ▲ 437549-2
Grieg, E.:Lyric Suite, Op. 54 Deutsche Grammophon ("3D Classics" series) ▲ 427807-2D [DDD]
Grieg, E.:Lyric Suite, Op. 54 Archiv ▲ 437549-2
Grieg, E.:Norwegian Dances, Op. 35 Deutsche Grammophon ▲ 419431-2 [DDD]
Grieg, E.:Peer Gynt, w. B. Bonney (sop), M. Eklöf (mez), K. M. Sandve (ten), U. Malmberg (bar), Gothenburg Sym Chorus [N] Deutsche Grammophon 2-▲ 423079-2 [DDD]
Grieg, E.:Peer Gynt Suites, Opp. 46 & 55 Deutsche Grammophon ("3D Classics" series) ▲ 427807-2 [DDD]
Grieg, E.:Sigurd Jorsalfar, w. B. Bonney (sop), M. Eklöf (mez), K. M. Sandve (ten), U. Malmberg (bar), Gothenburg Sym Chorus [N] Deutsche Grammophon 2-▲ 423079-2 [DDD]
Grieg, E.:Sigurd Jorsalfar (suite) Deutsche Grammophon ("3D Classics" series) ▲ 427807-2 [DDD]
Grieg, E.:Symphonic Dances Deutsche Grammophon ▲ 419431-2 [DDD]
Mussorgsky, M.:Songs & Dances, w. B. Fassbaender (mez) Deutsche Grammophon ▲ 437785-2 [DDD]
Nielsen, C.:Syms (comp) Deutsche Grammophon ▲ 437507-2 [DDD]
Nielsen, C.:Sym 4 *(rec Sept. 8–9, 1990)* BIS ▲ CD 600 [DDD]
Nielsen, C.:Sym 6 *(rec March 9, 1992)* BIS ▲ CD 600 [DDD]
Orchestral Selections Deutsche Grammophon ("3D Classics" series) ▲ 429494-2 GDC [DDD]
Prokofiev, S.:The Fiery Angel, w. N. Secunde (sop), R. Engert-Ely (mez), H. Zednik (ten), S. Lorenz (bar), K. Moll (bass), Gothenburg Sym Chorus [R] Deutsche Grammophon 2-▲ 431669-2 [DDD]
Rimsky-Korsakov, N.:Antar Deutsche Grammophon 2-▲ 423604-2 [DDD]
Rimsky-Korsakov, N.:Capriccio espagnol Deutsche Grammophon 2-▲ 423604-2 [DDD]
Rimsky-Korsakov, N.:Russian Easter Festival Deutsche Grammophon 2-▲ 423604-2 [DDD]
Rimsky-Korsakov, N.:Russian Easter Festival Deutsche Grammophon ▲ 429984-2 [DDD]
Rimsky-Korsakov, N.:Sym 1 Deutsche Grammophon 2-▲ 423604-2 [DDD]
Rimsky-Korsakov, N.:Sym 3 Deutsche Grammophon 2-▲ 423604-2 [DDD]
Schnittke, A.:Pianissimo BIS ▲ CD 427 [DDD]
Schnittke, A.:Sym 5 BIS ▲ CD 427 [DDD]
Shostakovich, D.:The Golden Age (suite) Deutsche Grammophon ▲ 431688-2 [DDD]
Shostakovich, D.:Hamlet (incidental) Deutsche Grammophon ▲ 431688-2 [DDD]
Shostakovich, D.:October Deutsche Grammophon ▲ 427616-2 [DDD]

Gothenburg SO (cont.)
N. Järvi (cnd) (cont.)
Shostakovich, D.:Ov on Russian & Khirgiz Folk Themes Deutsche Grammophon ▲ 427616-2 [DDD]
Shostakovich, D.:Sym 12 Deutsche Grammophon ▲ 431688-2 [DDD]
Shostakovich, D.:Sym 14, w. L. Kazarnovskaya (sop), S. Leiferkus (bar) Deutsche Grammophon ▲ 437785-2
Shostakovich, D.:Sym 15 Deutsche Grammophon ▲ 427616-2 [DDD]
Sibelius, J.:Aallottaret BIS ▲ CD 263 [DDD]
Sibelius, J.:Andante festivo BIS ▲ CD 472 [DDD]
Sibelius, J.:Andante festivo BIS ▲ CD 222 [DDD]
Sibelius, J.:Autrefois BIS ▲ CD 384 [DDD]
Sibelius, J.:The Bard BIS ▲ CD 384 [DDD]
Sibelius, J.:Belshazzar's Feast (suite) BIS ▲ CD 359
Sibelius, J.:Canzonetta *(rec Feb. 4, 1984)* BIS ▲ CD 610 [DDD]
Sibelius, J.:Canzonetta BIS ▲ CD 263 [DDD]
Sibelius, J.:Cassazione BIS ▲ CD 448 [DDD]
Sibelius, J.:Choral Music, w. Gothenburg Male Choir—Sandels, Op. 28; Have you courage?, Op. 31/2; War Song of Tyrtaeus, Op. 31/3; The Origin of Fire, Op. 32; March of the Finnish Cavalry, Op. 91/1; Academic March BIS ▲ CD 314
Sibelius, J.:Con Vn, w. S. Marcovici, (vn) BIS ▲ CD 372 [DDD]
Sibelius, J.:Dance Intermezzo *(rec 1986)* BIS ▲ CD 610 [DDD]
Sibelius, J.:4 Legends from the Kalevalá BIS ▲ CD 294 [DDD]
Sibelius, J.:Humoresques, w. Dong-Suk Kang (vn) BIS ▲ CD 472 [DDD]
Sibelius, J.:Impromptu Pno BIS ▲ CD 312 [DDD]
Sibelius, J.:Impromptu Strs BIS ▲ CD 312
Sibelius, J.:In Memoriam BIS ▲ CD 372 [DDD]
Sibelius, J.:Karelia Ov BIS ▲ CD 222 [DDD]
Sibelius, J.:Karelia Suite *(rec May 7, 1983)* BIS ▲ CD 610 [DDD]
Sibelius, J.:Karelia Suite BIS ▲ CD 250 [DDD]
Sibelius, J.:King Christian II (suite) BIS ▲ CD 228 [DDD]
Sibelius, J.:Kullervo, w. K. Mattila (sop), J. Hynninen (bar), Laulun Ystävät Male Choir [Fin] BIS ▲ CD 313
Sibelius, J.:Kuolema BIS ▲ CD 311 [DDD]
Sibelius, J.:Lemminkäinen's Return *(rec Feb. 4–5, 1985)* BIS ▲ CD 610 [DDD]
Sibelius, J.:The Maiden in the Tower, w. M. A. Häggander (sop), E. Hagegard (ten), J. Hynninen (bar), T. Kruse (cta), Gothenburg Chorus [Fin] BIS ▲ CD 250 [DDD]
Sibelius, J.:Menuetto BIS ▲ CD 372 [DDD]
Sibelius, J.:Night Ride & Sunrise BIS ▲ CD 311 [DDD]
Sibelius, J.:Ov in a BIS ▲ CD 372 [DDD]
Sibelius, J.:Ov in E BIS ▲ CD 472 [DDD]
Sibelius, J.:Pelléas et Mélisande BIS ▲ CD 237 [DDD]
Sibelius, J.:Pieces Vn, w. D.-S. Kang (vn) BIS ▲ CD 472 [DDD]
Sibelius, J.:Pohjola's Daughter *(rec Aug. 22–23, 1985)* BIS ▲ CD 610 [DDD]
Sibelius, J.:Pohjola's Daughter BIS ▲ CD 312 [DDD]
Sibelius, J.:Preludio BIS ▲ CD 448 [DDD]
Sibelius, J.:Presto BIS ▲ CD 372 [DDD]
Sibelius, J.:Rakastava Strs *(rec Feb. 6, 1985)* BIS ▲ CD 610 [DDD]
Sibelius, J.:Rakastava Strs BIS ▲ CD 312 [DDD]
Sibelius, J.:Romance Strs BIS ▲ CD 252 [DDD]
Sibelius, J.:Scaramouche BIS ▲ CD 502 [DDD]
Sibelius, J.:Scènes historiques BIS ▲ CD 295 [DDD]
Sibelius, J.:Serenades Vn, w. D.-S. Kang (vn) BIS ▲ CD 472 [DDD]
Sibelius, J.:Die Sprache der Vögel BIS ▲ CD 502 [DDD]
Sibelius, J.:Spring Song BIS ▲ CD 384 [DDD]
Sibelius, J.:Suite caractéristique BIS ▲ CD 384 [DDD]
Sibelius, J.:Suite champêtre BIS ▲ CD 384 [DDD]
Sibelius, J.:Suite mignonne BIS ▲ CD 384 [DDD]
Sibelius, J.:The Swan of Tuonela *(rec Sept. 3, 1982)* BIS ▲ CD 610 [DDD]
Sibelius, J.:Swanwhite (suite) BIS ▲ CD 359
Sibelius, J.:Syms (comp), w. K. Mattila (sop), J. Hynninen (bar), Laulun Ystävät Male Choir BIS 4-▲ CD 622/24 [ADD]
Sibelius, J.:Sym 1 BIS ▲ CD 221 [DDD]
Sibelius, J.:Sym 2 BIS ▲ CD 252 [DDD]
Sibelius, J.:Sym 3 BIS ▲ CD 228 [DDD]
Sibelius, J.:Sym 4 BIS ▲ CD 263 [DDD]
Sibelius, J.:Sym 5 BIS ▲ CD 222 [DDD]
Sibelius, J.:Sym 6 BIS ▲ CD 237 [DDD]
Sibelius, J.:Sym 7 BIS ▲ CD 311 [DDD]
Sibelius, J.:Tapiola BIS ▲ CD 312 [DDD]
Sibelius, J.:The Tempest (sels) BIS ▲ CD 448 [DDD]
Sibelius, J.:Tiera BIS ▲ CD 448 [DDD]
Sibelius, J.:Valse chevaleresque BIS ▲ CD 384 [DDD]
Sibelius, J.:Valse lyrique BIS ▲ CD 384 [DDD]
Sibelius, J.:Valse triste *(rec Sept. 3, 1982)* BIS ▲ CD 610 [DDD]
Stenhammar, W.:Chitra BIS ▲ CD 476 [DDD]
Stenhammar, W.:Con 2 Pno, w. C. Ortiz (pno) BIS ▲ CD 476 [DDD]
Stenhammar, W.:Excelsior! BIS ▲ CD 251 [DDD]
Stenhammar, W.:Lodolezzi Sings BIS ▲ CD 438 [DDD]
Stenhammar, W.:Mellanspel BIS ▲ CD 438 [DDD]
Stenhammar, W.:Mid-Winter, w. Gothenburg Sym Chorus [Sw] BIS ▲ CD 438 [DDD]
Svendsen, J.:Sym 1 BIS ▲ CD 347
Svendsen, J.:Sym 2 BIS ▲ CD 347
Tchaikovsky, P.:Mazeppa, w. Galina Gorchakoova (sop), Larissa Dyadkova (mez), Sergei Larin (ten), Sergei Leiferkus (bar), Anatoly Kotscherga (bass), Stockholm Royal Opera Chorus Deutsche Grammophon 3-▲ 439906-2
Tchaikovsky, P.:Ov 1812 Deutsche Grammophon ▲ 429984-2 [DDD] □ 429984-5
Tubin, E.:Ballade Vn, w. G. Garcia (vn) BIS ▲ CD 337 [DDD]
Tubin, E.:Concertino Pno, w. M. Pöntinen (pno) BIS ▲ CD 401 [DDD]
Tubin, E.:Con Db, w. H. Ehrén (db) BIS ▲ CD 337 [DDD]
Tubin, E.:Con 1 Vn, w. M. Lubotsky (vn) BIS ▲ CD 286 [DDD]
Tubin, E.:Estonian Dance Suite, w. M. Lubotsky (vn) BIS ▲ CD 286 [DDD]
Tubin, E.:Prélude solennel BIS ▲ CD 286 [DDD]
Tubin, E.:Sinfonietta on Estonian Motifs BIS ▲ CD 401 [DDD]
Tubin, E.:Sym 7 BIS ▲ CD 401 [DDD]

O. Kamu (cnd)
Franck, C.:Les Djinns, w. K. Aberg (pno) *(rec May 31, 1979)* BIS ▲ CD 137 [AAD]
Franck, C.:Symphonic Vars, w. K. Aberg (pno) *(rec May 31, 1979)* BIS ▲ CD 137 [AAD]
Grieg, E.:In Autumn BIS ▲ CD 200 [DDD]
Grieg, E.:In Autumn BIS ("BIS Twins" series) 2-▲ CD 200/619
Grieg, E.:Sym BIS ▲ CD 200 [DDD]
Grieg, E.:Sym BIS ("BIS Twins" series) 2-▲ CD 200/619

G. Oskamp (cnd)
Atterberg, K.:Con Hn, w. A. Linder (hn) Caprice ▲ CAP 21364 [DDD]

J. Panula (cnd)
Sibelius, J.:Luonnotar, w. M. A. Häggander (sop) [Fin] BIS ▲ CD 270 [DDD]
Sibelius, J.:The Rapid-Shooter's Brides, w. J. Hynninen (bar) [Fin] BIS ▲ CD 270 [DDD]
Sibelius, J.:Songs, w. M. A. Häggander (sop), J. Hynninen (bar), (for solo voice & orchestra) [Fin, Sw] BIS ▲ CD 270 [DDD]
Wiklund, A.:Con 1 Pno, w. I. Edgren (pno) Caprice ▲ CAP 21363 [AAD]
Wiklund, A.:Summer Night & Sunrise Caprice ▲ CAP 21363 [AAD]

Gothenburg SO (cont.)
W. Strickland (cnd)
Carpenter, J.A.:Concertino Pno Orch, w. Marjorie Mitchell (pno) *(rec 1963)* Citadel ▲ CTD 88118 [ADD]
Carpenter, J.A.:Concertino Pno Orch, w. S. Mitchell (pno) CRI ■ C 180
Ives, C.:Fourth of July CRI ■ C 180
Ives, C.:Holidays, w. Iceland SO, Tokyo PO, Finnish RSO, Iceland Sym Chorus [E] CRI ■ ACS 6014
Piston, W.:Concertino Pno, w. M. Mitchell (pno) CRI ■ C 180
T. Svedlund (cnd)
Alfvén, H.:Bergakungen, w. Göran Marcusson (fl)—Shepherd-girl's dance Intim Musik ▲ INT 18 [DDD]
Atterberg, K.:Music of, w. Göran Marcusson (fl)—Adagio amoros Intim Musik ▲ INT 18 [DDD]
Berwald, F.:Konsertstycke Bn, w. Anders Engström (bn) Intim Musik ▲ INT 15 [DDD]
Brendler, E.:Divertissement Bn, w. Anders Engström (bn) Intim Musik ▲ INT 15 [DDD]
Crusell, B.H.:Concertino Bn, w. Anders Engström (bn) Intim Musik ▲ INT 15 [DDD]
Fernström, J.:Concertino Bn, w. Anders Engström (bn) Intim Musik ▲ INT 15 [DDD]
Frumerie, G. de:Pastoral Suite, w. Göran Marcusson (fl) Intim Musik ▲ INT 18 [DDD]
Nystroem, G.:Partita Fl, w. Göran Marcusson (fl) Intim Musik ▲ INT 18 [DDD]
Peterson-Berger, W.:Music of, w. Göran Marcusson (fl)—Sommarsång; Till Rosorna; Gratulation; Lawn Tennis; Frösö kyrka; Rentrée Intim Musik ▲ INT 18 [DDD]
Gothenburg Wind Quintet [S. Schön (fl), W. Lindgren (ob), S. Pettersson (cl), E. Schleiffer (bn), A. Linder (hn)]
Carlstedt, J.:Qnt Winds *(rec May 5–6, 1975)* BIS ▲ CD 24 [AAD]
Holmboe, V.:Notturno *(rec May 5–6, 1975)* BIS ▲ CD 24 [AAD]
Mortensen, F.:Qnt Ww *(rec May 5–6, 1975)* BIS ▲ CD 24 [AAD]
Poulenc, F.:Sxt Pno, w. E. Knardahl (pno) *(rec June 6, 1976)* BIS ▲ CD 24 [AAD]
Salmenhaara, E.:Qnt Ww *(rec May 5–6, 1975)* BIS ▲ CD 24 [AAD]
Gotland String Quartet
Rosenberg, H.:Moments musicaux Caprice ▲ CAP 21353 [AAD/DDD]
Rosenberg, H.:Qt 6 Strs Caprice ▲ CAP 21352 [AAD]
Gottfried Reiche Consort Hamburg
English Renaissance & Baroque Music Ambitus ▲ AMB 97865 [DDD]
Claude Goudimel Ensemble
C. Morel (cnd)
Goudimel, C.:Sacred Music—Psaumes 13, 104, 114, 115, 128, 130, 137, 163; Cantique de Siméon; Par le désert de mes peines *(rec Chapelle de la Maison d'Education de la Légion d'Honneur, Saint-Denis, France, Apr. 11–13, 1994)* Naxos ▲ 8.553025 [DDD]
L'Estocart, P. de:Pseaumes de David—Nos. 25 & 33 *(rec Chapelle de la Maison d'Education de la Légion d'Honneur, Saint-Denis, France, Apr. 11–13, 1994)* Naxos ▲ 8.553025 [DDD]
Sweelinck, J.P.:Psalms of David—No. 107 *(rec Chapelle de la Maison d'Education de la Légion d'Honneur, Saint-Denis, France, Apr. 11–13, 1994)* Naxos ▲ 8.553025 [DDD]
Morton Gould Orch
M. Gould (cnd)
Copland, A.:Billy the Kid (suite) *(rec 1957)* RCA Living Stereo ▲ 09026-61667-2; ■ 09026-61667-4
Copland, A.:Rodeo *(rec 1957)* RCA Living Stereo ▲ 09026-61667-2; ■ 09026-61667-4
Gershwin, G.:"I Got Rhythm" Vars, w. O. Levant (pno) *(rec 1949)* CBS ▲ MK 42514 (m) [ADD] ■ FMT 42514 (m)
Gershwin, G.:"I Got Rhythm" Vars, w. O. Levant (pno) *(rec 1949)* Sony Masterworks ("Portrait" series) ▲ MPK 47681 [ADD]
Gershwin, G.:Second Rhap, w. O. Levant (pno) *(rec 1949)* CBS ▲ MK 42514 (m) [ADD] ■ FMT 42514 (m)
Gershwin, G.:Second Rhap, w. O. Levant (pno) *(rec 1949)* Sony Masterworks ("Portrait" series) ▲ MPK 47681 [ADD]
Gould, M.:Fall River Legend (suite) *(rec 1960)* RCA Living Stereo ▲ 09026-61505-2; ■ 09026-61505-4
Gould, M.:Fall River Legend (suite) RCA Red Seal ▲ 09026-61651-2
Gould, M.:Interplay Pno, w. *(pianist unknown)* RCA Red Seal ▲ 09026-61651-2
Gould, M.:Latin American Symphonette (sels) *(rec 1960)* RCA Living Stereo ▲ 09026-61505-2; ■ 09026-61505-4
Gould, M.:Latin American Symphonette (sels)—Tango & Guaracha RCA Red Seal ▲ 09026-61651-2
Grofé, F.:Grand Canyon Suite *(rec 1960)* RCA Living Stereo ▲ 09026-61667-2; ■ 09026-61667-4
Les Goûts-Réünis [Mikael Helasvuo (baroque fl), Kati Hämäläinen (hpd), Timo Juntura (vl)]
Les Goûts-Réünis Ondine ▲ ODE 721 [DDD]
Gradiva Ensemble
Leçons de ténèbres et raga de la nuit avancée, w. Véronique Dietschy (sop), Alain Zaepffel (ct), Sulochana Brahaspati (voc) K617 ▲ 7017 [DDD]
Granada City Orch
J. de Udaeta (cnd)
Turina, J.:Danzas fantásticas *(rec Centro Cultural Manuel de Falla, Granada, Jan. 28–31, 1993 & Jan. 1)* Claves ▲ CD 9310 [DDD]
Turina, J.:Danzas gitanes, Op. 55 Claves ▲ CD 9215 [DDD]
Turina, J.:Evangelio *(rec Centro Cultural Manuel de Falla, Granada, Jan. 28–31, 1993 & Jan. 1)* Claves ▲ CD 9310 [DDD]
Turina, J.:Fantasía sobre—Prelude *(rec Centro Cultural Manuel de Falla, Granada, Jan. 28–31, 1993 & Jan. 1)* Claves ▲ CD 9310 [DDD]
Turina, J.:Navidad *(rec Centro Cultural Manuel de Falla, Granada, Jan. 28–31, 1993 & Jan. 1)* Claves ▲ CD 9310 [DDD]
Turina, J.:La oracion del torero Claves ▲ CD 9215 [DDD]
Turina, J.:Primavera Sevillana *(rec Centro Cultural Manuel de Falla, Granada, Jan. 28–31, 1993 & Jan. 1)* Claves ▲ CD 9310 [DDD]
Turina, J.:Rapsodia sinfónica, w. R. Requejo (pno) Claves ▲ CD 9215 [DDD]
Turina, J.:Serenata Str Qt Claves ▲ CD 9215 [DDD]
Turina, J.:Theme & Vars, Op. 100, w. G. Dall'Olio (hp) Claves ▲ CD 9215 [DDD]
Grand Canary PO
L. Izquierdo (cnd)
Sanabria, J.J.F.:Music of, w. Czech PO—Atlantica; Elan; Sinf Urbana Col Legno ▲ AU 31850
A. Leaper (cnd)
Górecki, H.-M.:Sym 3, "Sym of Sorrowful Songs", w. Doreen de Feis (sop) *(rec Iglesia de San Francisco, Telde, Gran Canaria, Apr 11, 1995)* RCA Gold Seal ▲ 09026-68387-2 [DDD]
Grand Duo Concertant
Le Spleen de Paris Jecklin ▲ JS 272-2 [ADD]
Grand Hotel Orch
Music for a Grand Hotel, w. Max Jaffa Trio, Max Jaffa (vn), Jean Grayston (cta) Valentine ▲ VALD 8057 [DDD]
Grand Rapids SO
C. Comet (cnd)
Erb, D.:Con Cl, w. Richard Stoltzman (cl) *(rec DeVos Hall, Grand Rapids, MI, May 22, 1994)* Koss Classics ▲ KC 3002 [DDD]
Erb, D.:Con Trbn, w. Ava Ordman (trbn) *(rec DeVos Hall, Grand Rapids, MI, May 22, 1994)* Koss Classics ▲ KC 3002 [DDD]
Erb, D.:Con Vn, w. Miriam Fried (vn) *(rec DeVos Hall, Grand Rapids, MI, Apr. 18, 1993)* Koss Classics ▲ KC 3002 [DDD]
Ott, David:Sym 2 Koss Classics ▲ KC 3301 [DDD]
Ott, David:Sym 3 Koss Classics ▲ KC 3301 [DDD]

La Grande Écurie et la Chambre du Roy
Music at the Time of Beaumarchais, w. Montserrat Figueras (sop), Lawrence Monteyro (sop), Raphel Oleg (vn), Miguel da Silva (va), Christophe Coin (vc), Marc Coppey (vc), José Miguel Moreno (gtr), Paul Badura-Skoda (pno), Philippe Cassard (pno), Eric Le Sage (pno), Bob Van Asperen (hpd) Valois ▲ V 4767
J.-C. Malgoire (cnd)
Albinoni, T.:Adagio Org Odyssey ■ YT 34605
Albinoni, T.:Adagio Org CBS ▲ MYK 38482 ■ MYT 38482
Bach, J.S.:The Art of the Fugue K617 2-▲ 7040/41
Campra, A.:Messe de Requiem, w. D. Visse (ct), G. Ragon (ten), P. Harvey (bar), Les Pages de la Chapelle *(rec Nov. 4–6, 1992)* FNAC Music ▲ 592223 [DDD]
Campra, A.:Misere, w. D. Visse (ct), G. Ragon (ten), P. Harvey (bar), Les Pages de la Chapelle *(rec Nov. 4–6, 1992)* FNAC Music ▲ 592223 [DDD]
Campra, A.:Tancrède, w. C. Alliot-Lugaz (sop), D. Evangelatos (cta), G. Reinhart (bar), F. le Roux (bar), P.-Y. le Maigat (bass-bar), Dubose (sgr) Erato (Musifrance) 2-▲ 2292-45001-2 ZA [DDD]
Charpentier, M.-A.:Te Deum in C [L] Sony Classical (Essential Classics) ▲ SBK 46344 [ADD] ■ SBT 46344
Les Chemins du Baroque (The Paths of the Baroque), w. G. Garrido (cnd), Elyma Vocal Ensemble, Elyma Instrumental Ensemble, Cordoba Children's Choir Garrado, Compañia Musical de las Americas, Maîtrise National de Versailles, Compañia Musical de las Americas, La Fenice [cnd:Josep Cabré], Ense K617 ("First 4 volumes of K617" series) ▲ 7042
Les Chemins du Baroque (The Paths of the Baroque), Vol. 2:Mexico - Versailles:Vepres de l'Assomption, w. Compañia Musical de las Americas, Versaille National Masters K617 ▲ 7026 [DDD]
Dances of the Court & Villages Odyssey ■ YT 34617
Gabrieli, A.:Aria della battaglia Odyssey ■ YT 34605
Gabrieli, G.:Canzoni—Nos. 5, 8 Odyssey ■ YT 34605
Gottschalk, L.M.:Orfeo ed Euridice (sels), w. James Bowman (ct)—Act 2, scene 2, "Les Champs-Elysées" [w. Namur Chamber Choir]; Act 3, scene 1, "Che farò senza Euridice? Astrée ▲ E 8552 [DDD]
Handel, G.F.:Concerti grossi, Op. 3 Odyssey 3-▲ MB3K 45824
Handel, G.F.:Concerti grossi, Op. 6 Odyssey 3-▲ MB3K 45824
Handel, G.F.:Giulio Cesare in Egitto, w. Lynne Dawson (sop), Eirian James (mez), Guillemette Laurens (mez), James Bowman (alt), Dominique Visse (alt), Nicolas Rivenq (bar) Astrée 3-▲ E 8558
Handel, G.F.:Messiah (sels), w. Worcester Cathedral Choir—choruses [E] CBS ▲ MDK 44787 [DDD]; ■ MDT 44787 (D)
Handel, G.F.:Rinaldo, w. Sophie Boulin (sop—Donna), Ileana Cotrubas (sop—Almirena), Marie-Françoise Jacquelin (sop—Sirene), Nicole Leport (sop—Sirene), Jeanette Scovotti (sop—Armida), Carolyn Watkinson (cta—Rinaldo), Charles Brett (ct—Eustazio), Paul Esswood (ct—Goffredo), Armand Arapian (ten—Mago Christiano/Araldo), Ulrik Cold (bass—Argante) *(rec Paris, 1977)* Sony Classical 3-▲ SM3K 34592
Handel, G.F.:Royal Fireworks Music CBS ▲ MDK 44655 [DDD]; ■ MDT 44655 (D)
Handel, G.F.:Royal Fireworks Music *(rec 1985)* Sony Classical ("Essential Classics" series) ▲ SBK 48285 [DDD]; ■ SBT 48285 (D)
Handel, G.F.:Serse, w. Barbara Hendricks (sop—Romilda), Anne-Marie Rodde (sop—Atalanta), Carolyn Watkinson (cta—Xerxes), Otrun Wenkel (cta—Amastre), Paul Esswood (ct—Arsamene), Ulrich Studer (bar—Elviro), Ulrik Cold (bass—Ariodate) *(rec Paris, 1979)* Sony Classical 3-▲ SM3K 36941
Handel, G.F.:Tamerlano, w. Isabelle Poulenard (sop—Irene), Mieke van der Sluis (sop—Asteria), René Jacobs (alt—Andronico), Henri Ledroit (ct—Tamerlano), John Elwes (ten—Bajazet), Gregory Reinhart (bass—Leone) *(rec 1983)* Sony Classical 3-▲ SM3K 37893
Handel, G.F.:Water Music (comp) CBS ▲ MDK 44655 [DDD]; ■ MDT 44655 (D)
Handel, G.F.:Water Music (comp) *(rec 1983)* Sony Classical ("Essential Classics" series) ▲ SBK 48285 [DDD]; ■ SBT 48285 (D)
Mozart, L.:Sinf pastorella, w. Michel Garcin-Marrou (alphn) Sony Classical ("Essential Classics" series) ▲ SBK 62639 ■ SBT 62639
Mozart, W.A.:Church Sons—K.278, 329 & 336 CBS ▲ MDK 44904 [DDD]
Mozart, W.A.:Così fan tutte, w. Sophie Marin-Degor (sop—Despina), Laura Polverelli (mez—Dorabella), Sophie Fournier (sgr—Fiordiligi), Nicolas Revenq (bar—Guglielmo), Patrick Donnelly (bass—Don Alfonso), Simon Edwards (sgr—Ferrando) Astrée 8-▲ E 8606
Mozart, W.A.:Don Giovanni, w. Danielle Borst (sop—Donna Anna), Véronique Gens (sop—Donna Elvira), Sophie Marin-Degor (sop—Zerlina), Huub Claessens (bar—Leporello), Nicolas Revenq (bar—Don Giovanni), Patrick Donnelly (bass—Commendatore), Simon Edwards (sgr—Don Ottavio) Astrée 8-▲ E 8606
Mozart, W.A.:Nozze di Figaro, w. Danielle Borst (sop—Countess Almaviva), Claudine Le Coz (sop—Marcellina), Sophie Marin-Degor (sop—Suzanna), Laura Polverelli (mez—Cherubino), Valérie Lecoq (sgr—Barberina), Philippe Cantor (ten—Antonio), Stuart Patterson (ten—Dons Basile & Curzio), Huub Claessens (bar—Figaro), Nicolas Revenq (bar—Count Almaviva), Patrick Donnelly (bass—Bartolo) Astrée 8-▲ E 8606
Mozart, W.A.:Requiem, w. Colette Alliot-Lugaz (sop), Dominique Vissé (ct), Martyn Hill (ten), G. Reinhart (bar), Nord-Pas-de-Calais Choir [L] CBS ▲ MDK 44904 [DDD]
Mozart, W.A.:Requiem, w. *(soloists unknown)* [L] Sony Classical ("Essential Classics" series) ▲ SBK 46344 [ADD] ■ SBT 46344
Pergolesi, G.B.:Stabat mater, w. Isabelle Poulenard (sop), Jean-Louis Comoretto (ct) Astrée ▲ E 8556
Rameau, J.P.:Les Paladins, w. A. Michael (sop), G. Raphanel (sop), B. Brewer (ten), D. Nasrawi (ten), G. Reinhart (bar), N. Rivenq (bar), Sagittarius Vocal Ensemble [F] Pierre Verany 2-▲ PV.790121/22 [DDD]
Vivaldi, A.:Beatus vir (Psalm 111), w. M. Burgess (sop), J. Chamonin (sop), C. Watkinson (cta), Raphaël Passaquet Vocal Ensemble *(rec 1976)* Sony Classical ("Essential Classics" series) ▲ SBK 48280 [ADD] ■ SBT 48280
Vivaldi, A.:Cons Pic—RV.443 Odyssey ■ YT 34605
Vivaldi, A.:Cons Vn, Op. 8/1–4, "The Four Seasons", w. J. Holloway (vn) Sony Classical ("Essential Classics" series) ▲ SBK 47662 ■ SBT 47662
Vivaldi, A.:Dixit Dominus, w. James Bowman (ct)—De torrente Astrée ▲ E 8552 [DDD]
Vivaldi, A.:Gloria, RV.589, w. M. Burgess (sop), Jocelyne Chamonine (sop), Carolyn Watkinson (cta), Raphaël Passaquet Vocal Ensemble *(rec 1976)* Sony Classical ("Essential Classics" series) ▲ SBK 48280 [ADD] ■ SBT 48280
Vivaldi, A.:Montezuma (sels), w. Dominique Visse (ct)—Gl'oltraggidella sorte Astrée ▲ E 8552 [DDD]
Vivaldi, A.:Music of, w. John Williams (cnd), L. Bernstein (cnd), New York PO, English CO—sels. from The Four Seasons, Mandolin Concerto in C, 2-Mandolin Concerto in G, Guitar Concerto in D, etc. CBS ▲ MLK 45810 ■ MLT 45810
Vivaldi, A.:Nisi Dominus, w. James Bowman (ct)—Sicut erat, Amen Astrée ▲ E 8552 [DDD]
Grande Orchestre Symphonique
P. Monteux (cnd)
Stravinsky, I.:Le Sacre du printemps Orch *(rec Paris, 1929)* Pearl ▲ GEMMCD 9329 (m) [AAD]
I. Stravinsky (cnd)
Stravinsky, I.:The Firebird Suite *(rec Paris, 11/8–10/28)* Pearl ▲ GEMMCD 9334 (m) [AAD]
Stravinsky, I.:Le Sacre du printemps Orch *(rec Paris, 5/7–10/29)* Pearl ▲ GEMMCD 9334 (m) [AAD]
Graunke SO
F. Allers (cnd)
Strauss (II), Joh.:Eine Nacht in Venedig (sels), w. Christine Gorner (sop), Rita Streich (sop), Cesare Curzi (ten), Nicolai Gedda (ten), Christian Oppleberg (bar), Graunke Chorus Emperor Operetta ▲ KO 86345
K. Graunke (cnd)
Friedhofer, H.:Private Parts Facet ▲ FCD 8105 [AAD]
Friedhofer, H.:Richthofen & Brown Facet ▲ FCD 8105 [AAD]
W. Mattes (cnd)
Lehár, F.:Giuditta (sels), w. Anneliese Rothenberger (sop), Nicolai Gedda (ten), Munich Theater Gartnerplatz Chorus Emperor Operetta ▲ KO 86342

184
▲ = CD ♦ = Enhanced CD Δ = MD ■ = Cassette Tape □ = DCC

Graunke SO (cont.)
W. Mattes (cnd) (cont.)
Lehár, F.:Das Land des Lächelns (sels), w. Renate Holm (sop), Anneliese Rothenberger (sop), Nicolai Gedda (ten), Bavarian Radio Chorus — Emperor Operetta ▲ KO 86341
Lehár, F.:Die lustige Witwe (sels), w. Erika Koth (sop), Anneliese Rothenberger (sop), Nicolai Gedda (ten), Robert Ilosfalvy (ten), Bavarian Radio Chorus — Emperor Operetta ▲ KO 86343
Lehár, F.:Operetta Arias, w. Nicolai Gedda (ten)—sels from Das Land des Lächelns; Frasquita; Friederike; Giuditta; Der Zarewitsch; Schön ist der Welt; Die lustige Witwe; Der Graf von Luxembourg — Emperor Operetta ▲ KO 86354
Strauss (II), Joh.:Wiener Blut (sels), w. Christine Gorner (sop), Anneliese Rothenberger (sop), Nicolai Gedda (ten), Munich Theater Gartnerplatz Chorus — Emperor Operetta ▲ KO 86345
C. Michalski (cnd)
Fall, L.:Die Dollarprinzessin (sels), w. Sari Barabas (sop), Christine Gorner (sop), Harry Friedauer (ten), Heinz Hoppe (ten), Botho Lucas Chorus — Emperor Operetta ▲ KO 86353
Fall, L.:Der fidele Bauer (sels), w. Sonja Knittel (sop), Brigette Fassbaender (mez), Heinz Hoppe (ten), Fritz Wunderlich (ten), Benno Kusche (bass), Rudolf Lamy Singers — Emperor Operetta ▲ KO 86353
Fall, L.:Der liebe Augustin (sels), w. Sari Barabas (sop), Christine Gorner (sop), Heinz Hoppe (ten), Benno Kusche (b-bar), Rudolf Lamy Singers — Emperor Operetta ▲ KO 86352
Fall, L.:Die Rose von Stambul (sels), w. Christine Gorner (sop), Melita Muszely (sop), Fritz Wunderlich (ten) — Emperor Operetta ▲ KO 86353
Lehár, F.:Zigeunerliebe (sels), w. Sari Barabas (sop), Christine Gorner (sop), Harry Friedauer (ten), Heinz Hoppe (ten), Rudolf Lamy Singers — Emperor Operetta ▲ KO 86342
H. Salter (cnd)
Salter, H.J.:Wichita Town *(rec 1959)* — Citadel ▲ STC 77108 [ADD]
W. Schubert (cnd)
Dostal, N.:Clivia (sels), w. Sari Barabas (sop), Heinz Hoppe (ten), Bavarian Radio Chorus — Emperor Operetta ▲ KO 86352

Graz SO
B. Aprea (cnd)
Rossini, G.:La pietra del paragone, w. Tiziana Carraro (sop—Fulvia), Elisabetta Gutierrez (mez—Baronessa Aspasia), Sara Mingardo (cta—Clarice), William Matteuzzi (ten—Giocondo), Marco Camastra (bar—Pacuvio), Pietro Spagnoli (bar—Conte Asdrubale), Gioacchino Zarrelli (bar—Fabrizio), Josè Fardilha (bass—Macrobio), Sluk Chamber Chorus Bratislava *(rec 1993)* — Bongiovanni 2-▲ GB 2179/80 [DDD]
M. Carraro (cnd)
Rossini, G.:Demetrio e Polibio, w. Christine Weidinger (sop—Lisinga), Sara Mingardo (cta—Siveno), Anna Laura Longo (sgr—Olmira), Dalmacio Gonzales (ten—Demetrio/Eumene), Giorgio Surjan (bass—Polibio), Martino Fullone (sgr—Onao), Bratislava Chamber Chorus *(rec live, Martina Franca Opera Festival, Italy, July 27, 1992)* — Dynamic 2-▲ CDS 171/1-2 [DDD]

Great American Main Street Band
Joplin, S.:Treemonisha (suite) — EMI Classics ▲ CDC 54131
Under the Big Top — Angel ▲ CDC 54728
M. G. Pilafian (cnd)
Silks & Rags:A Turn-of-the-Century Band Concert — Angel ▲ CDC 54131

Great Britain National Youth Orch
S. Rattle (cnd)
Stravinsky, I.:Le Sacre du printemps *(rec ca. 1987?)* — ASV Quicksilva ▲ QS 6031 [ADD]
C. Seaman (cnd)
Bach, J.S.:Fant & Fugue Org, BWV 537 [orchd Elgar] — IMP ("Classics" series) ▲ IMP 6700302
Elgar, E.:Enigma Vars — IMP Classics ▲ IMPPCD 1080 [DDD]
Elgar, E.:Falstaff — IMP ("Classics" series) ▲ IMP 6700302
Elgar, E.:Intro & Allegro — IMP ("Classics" series) ▲ IMP 6700302
Strauss, R.:Symphonia domestica — IMP Classics ▲ IMPPCD 1080 [DDD]

Great Consort
Gaudeamus Early Music Sampler, w. His Majesties Sagbutts & Cornetts, Rasumovsky String Quartet, Trio Sonnerie, Cappella Nova, Cardinall's Musick, Clerks' Group, Ex Cathedra, Gentlemen of the Chappell, Gonville & Caius College Choir Cambridge, et al. — ASV/Gaudeamus ▲ ASV 1002

Great Lakes Brass
Make We Joy!:Music for Christmas, w. Exultate Chamber Singers [cnd:John Tuttle], Ian Sadler (org) *(rec St. Thomas' Church, Toronto)* — Exultate Chamber Singers ▲ ECS 02

Great Lakes CO
R. Rosenberg (cnd)
Britten, B.:Lachrymae, w. Y. Schotten (va) — Crystal ▲ CD 635
Shulman, A.:Theme & Vars, w. Y. Schotten (va) — Crystal ▲ CD 635

Greate Consort
Lawes, W.:Royall Consort Suites, w. Monica Huggett (vn)—Nos. 1, 3, 6, 7 & 9 — ASV ("Gaudeamus" series) ▲ ASV 146 [DDD]

Greater Hoople Area Off-Season Philharmonic
Schickele, P.:Music of—1712 Overture; Bach Portrait; Capriccio *La Pucelle de New Orleans*; Minuet Militaire; Prelude to *Einstein on the Fritz*; The Preachers of Crimetheus — Telarc ▲ CD 80210 [DDD] ■ CS 30210 (D)
N. Wayland (cnd)
Schickele, P.:Music of, w. Okay Chorale—Oedipus Tex; Classical Rap; Knock, Knock; Birthday Ode to 'Big Daddy' Bach — Telarc ▲ CD 80239 [DDD] ■ CS 30239 (D)

Philip Green Pops Concert Orch
P. Green (cnd)
Arias & Entrechats — Alanna ▲ ALA 5558

Greene String Quartet
The String Machine — Virgin Classics ▲ CDC 59120

Grenadier Guards Band
Music from the 1994 Royal Tournament, w. Coldstream Guards Band, Irish Guards Band, Life Guards Band, Welsh Guards Band, et al. — Bandleader ▲ BND 5094 [DDD]
Sousa, J.P.:Marches & Dances—Stars & Stripes; Invincible Eagle; High School Cadets; Picadore; Semper Fidelis; El Capitan; Manhattan Beach; King Cotton; Washington Post; Liberty Bell; etc. — London ("Weekend Classics" series) ▲ 430211-2 [AAD] ■ 430211-4
Stirring Marches of the U.S. Services — London ("Weekend Classics" series) ▲ 433681-2 LC ■ 433681-4 LC
R. Bashford (cnd)
Sousa, J.P.:Marches & Dances — London ("Phase 4 Stereo" series) ▲ 448 957-2
C. Gerhardt (cnd)
Newman, Alfred:Film Music, w. National PO London, Ambrosian Singers — RCA ▲ 0184-2-RG [ADD] ■ 0184-4-RG
P. E. Hills (cnd)
Sousa, J.P.:Marches & Dances—Star & Stripes Forever; Hands Across the Sea; Power & Glory; Belle of Chicago; Fairest of Fair; plus others — Teldec ▲ 96061-2
When the Guards Are on Parade — Bandleader ▲ BND 5104 [DDD]
L. Stokowski (cnd)
Tchaikovsky, P.:Ov 1812, w. Royal PO, Royal Liverpool Phil Choir, Welsh National Opera Chorus *(rec Kingsway Hall, London, England, June 16, 1969)* — London ("Phase 4 Stereo" series) ▲ 443896-2 [ADD]
S.A. Watts (cnd)
On Stage — Bandleader ▲ BND 5032 [DDD]

Grenoble Instrumental Ensemble
S. Cardon (cnd)
Messiaen, O.:Petites liturgies (3) de la Présence Divine, w. Grenoble Vocal Ensemble — Forlane 2-▲ FOR 16504/05 [AAD/DDD]
K. Redel (cnd)
Bach, J.S.:Con 1 Hpd, w. Abdel Rahman El Bacha (pno) — Forlane ▲ FRL 16537 [DDD]
Bach, J.S.:Con 4 Hpd, w. Abdel Rahman El Bacha (pno) — Forlane ▲ FRL 16537 [DDD]
Bach, J.S.:Con 5 Hpd, w. Abdel Rahman El Bacha (pno) — Forlane ▲ FRL 16537 [DDD]

Grenoble Instrumental Ensemble (cont.)
K. Redel (cnd) (cont.)
Vivaldi, A.:Cons Mand, w. C. Schneider (mand), D. Meyer (mand)—Concerti in C & D for Mandolin & Strings; Concerto in G for 2 Mandolins & Strings; Concerto in C for 2 Mandolins & Orchestra — Forlane ▲ FOR 16548 [AAD]
M. Tardue (cnd)
Lemeland, A.:L'Automne et sens envols d'etourneaux, w. J.-L. Homs (E hn), Sabine Chefson (hp) — Skarbo ▲ SKR 3913 [DDD]
Lemeland, A.:Con grosso, w. C. Roubichou (fl) — Skarbo ▲ SKR 3913 [DDD]
Lemeland, A.:Con Va, w. F. Jeandet (va) *(rec 9/90)* — Quantum ▲ QM 6902 [DDD]
Lemeland, A.:Con 2 Vn, w. E. Plasson (vn) *(rec 9/90)* — Quantum ▲ QM 6902 [DDD]
Lemeland, A.:Élégie à la mémoire de Samuel Barber *(rec 9/90)* — Quantum ▲ QM 6902 [DDD]
Lemeland, A.:L'Hiver qui vent, w. *(not advised of chorus)* — Skarbo ▲ SKR 3913 [DDD]
Lemeland, A.:Hommage à Jean Rivier — Skarbo ▲ SKR 3913 [DDD]
Lemeland, A.:Sym 5 *(rec 9/90)* — Quantum ▲ QM 6902 [DDD]

Grenoble Instrumental String Ensemble
Lemeland, A.:Con Hp, w. S. Chefson (hp) — Skarbo ▲ SKR 2338 [DDD]
Lemeland, A.:Élégie à la mémoire de Samuel Barber — Skarbo ▲ SKR 2338 [DDD]
Lemeland, A.:Omaha:Chant pour les soldats morts, w. C. Farley (sop) — Skarbo ▲ SKR 2338 [DDD]

Griffin Music Ensemble [P. Friedland (fl), G. Itzkoff (vn), H. Yenney (vn), S. Woolweaver (va), A. Mark (vc), J. Orleans (db), V. Crumb (hp), J. Fischer (perc)]
J. McPhee (cnd)
Gandolfi, M.:Caution to the Wind *(rec 1993)* — CRI ▲ CD 661 [DDD]
S. Mosko (cnd)
Babbitt, M.:Consortini — GM ▲ GM2032CD
Bauer, R.:Along the Way — GM ▲ GM2032CD

Griffith Univ Ensemble
S. Savage (cnd)
Ford, A.:Sacred Places, w. Gerald English (ten) *(rec live, Basil Jones Theater, Queensland Conservatorium of Music, Brisbane, Sept 1993)* — Tall Poppies ▲ TP 053 [DDD]
Ford, A.:Whispers, w. Gerald English (ten) *(rec live, Basil Jones Theater, Queensland Conservatorium of Music, Brisbane, Sept 1993)* — Tall Poppies ▲ TP 053 [DDD]

Griller String Quartet
Mozart, W.A.:Adagio & Fugue Strs *(rec 1959)* — Vanguard Classics ▲ OVC 8024 [ADD]
Mozart, W.A.:Qnts Strs, w. W. Primrose (va)—K.516 & 593 *(rec 1959)* — Vanguard Classics ▲ OVC 8024 [ADD]
Mozart, W.A.:Qnts Strs, w. W. Primrose (va)—K.406, 515 & 614 *(rec 1959)* — Vanguard Classics ▲ OVC 8025 [ADD]

Grimethorpe Colliery Band
M. Arnold (cnd)
Arnold, M.:Dances — Conifer Classics ▲ 74321-2D16848-2D2
Arnold, M.:Fants—for Brass Band, Op. 113a (1974) — Conifer Classics ▲ 74321-2D16848-2D2
Arnold, M.:The Padstow Lifeboat — Conifer Classics ▲ 74321-2D16848-2D2
G. Cutt (cnd)
Wilby, P.:Flight, w. Mark Walters (flgl) *(rec Dec 1993)* — Doyen ▲ CD 029 [DDD]
Wilby, P.:Masquerade *(rec Dec 1993)* — Doyen ▲ CD 029 [DDD]
Wilby, P.:Partita Band, "Postcards from Home"—Towers & Chimneys; Lord of the Dance; Sunday Afternoon:Pastorale; Coronation Day Parade *(rec Dec 1993)* — Doyen ▲ CD 029 [DDD]
E. Howarth (cnd)
Saint-Saëns, C.:Samson et Delila (sels)—Softly Awakes My Heart [arr G. Langford for brass band] — Doyen ▲ CD 013 [DDD]
Strauss (II), Joh.:Die Fledermaus (sels)—The Bat [arr A. Winter for brass band] — Doyen ▲ CD 013 [DDD]
Verdi, G.:La forza del destino (sels)—Overture [arr F. Wright for brass band] — Doyen ▲ CD 013 [DDD]
Verdi, G.:La traviata (sels)—1 sel [arr J. Greenwood for brass band] — Doyen ▲ CD 013 [DDD]
Wagner, R.:Tannhäuser (sels)—Grand March [arr J. Greenwood for brass band] — Doyen ▲ CD 013 [DDD]
Wagner, R.:Die Walküre (sels)—Grand Selection [30 minute arr by A. Owen for brass band] — Doyen ▲ CD 013 [DDD]
P. Parkes (cnd)
French Bonbons — Chandos ("Brass" series) ▲ CHAN 4542
F. Renton (cnd)
Paganini Variations for Brass Band *(rec BBC Studio 7, Oct 1991)* — Doyen ▲ CD 015 [DDD]
Wilby, P.:The New Jerusalem *(rec Dec 1993)* — Doyen ▲ CD 029 [DDD]
Wilby, P.:Paganini Vars *(rec Dec 1993)* — Doyen ▲ CD 029 [DDD]

Groningen Guitar Duo [Remco de Haan (gtr), Erik Westerhof (gtr)]
Albéniz, I.:Gtr Music—Bajo la palmero from Cantos de España, Op. 232; Castilla from Suite española; Tango española from España, Op. 165 [arr. for 2 gtrs] — Ottavo ▲ OTR C48710 [DDD]
Debussy, C.:Petite suite — Ottavo ▲ OTR C49135 [DDD]
Duo Recital — Ottavo ▲ 118818 [DDD]
Falla, M. de:Gtr Music—Danza del molinero (from El sombrero de tres picos); Danza española No. 1 (from La vida breve) [arr. Groningen] — Ottavo ▲ OTR C48710 [DDD]
Granados, E.:Danzas españolas (10) [arr. by performers]—Nos. 1–4,6 & 11 — Ottavo ▲ OTR C48710 [DDD]
Jolivet, A.:Sérénade for 2 Gtrs — Ottavo ▲ OTR C49135 [DDD]
Rêverie — Ottavo ▲ 49135 [DDD]
Rodrigo, J.:Tonadilla — Ottavo ▲ OTR C48710 [DDD]
Satie, E.:Gnossiennes Pno — Ottavo ▲ OTR C49135 [DDD]
Sor, F.:Duos Gtr—3 Duos, Op. 55, Nos. 1–3 *(rec 12/89)* — Ottavo ▲ OTR C128925 [DDD]
Sor, F.:Fants Gtr—4 Fantasies, Op. 34, 41, 54 & 63 *(rec 12/89)* — Ottavo ▲ OTR C128925 [DDD]

Groot Omroep Orch
F. Vernizzi (cnd)
Puccini, G.:Manon Lescaut, w. Magda Olivero (sop—Manon), Tine Appelman (mez—Singer), Umberto Borso (ten—Chevalier), Mario Carlin (ten—Edmondo/Dancing Master/Lamplighter), Ferdinando Lidonni (bar—Lescaut), Giovanni Foiani (bass—Geronte/Sergeant/Captain), Joop Ruivenkamp (bass—Innkeeper), Groot Omroep Choir *(rec Amsterdam, Oct 31, 1964)* — Bella Voce 2-▲ BLV 107.221 [AAD]

Groot Radio PO
J. Fournet (cnd)
Bizet, G.:Les Pêcheurs de perles (sels), w. Erna Spoorenberg (sop), Alain Vanzo (ten), Groot Chorus *(rec Amsterdam, 1963)* — Bella Voce 2-▲ 107.208
Gounod, C.:Roméo et Juliette, w. Erna Spoorenberg (sop), Alain Vanzo (ten), Groot Chorus *(rec Amsterdam, Jan 1966)* — Bella Voce 2-▲ 107.208

Group for Contemporary Music
Harvey, J.:Qt 1 Strs *(rec Apr. 22–23, 1991)* — Koch International Classics ▲ KIC 7121-2 [DDD]
Martino, D.:Divert from the Other Side — Koch International Classics ▲ KIC 7245 [DDD]
Martino, D.:Notturno — Koch International Classics ▲ KIC 7245 [DDD]
Martino, D.:Quodlibets — Koch International Classics ▲ KIC 7245 [DDD]
Schoenberg, A.:Pieces Orch, Op. 16 [arr Webern for 2 pianos] — Koch International Classics ▲ KIC 7315
Wolpe, S.:The Man from Midian — Koch International Classics ▲ KIC 7315
A. Brehm (cnd)
Bland, E.:Piece, w. Speculum Musicae members — Cambria ▲ CD 1026
M. Pratt (cnd)
Westergaard, P.:Ariel Music, w. Maria Tegzes (sop) — CRI ▲ CD 696 [DDD]
D. Shulman (cnd)
Babbitt, M.:Groupwise — CRI ▲ CD 521
H. Sollberger (cnd)
Babbitt, M.:An Elizabethan Sextette [E] — CRI ▲ CD 521
Carter, E.:Syringa, w. J. DeGaetani (mez), T. Paul (bar), Speculum Musicae *(rec 5/81)* — CRI ▲ CD 610 [ADD]

ORCH. & ENS.

Group for Contemporary Music (cont.)
H. Sollberger (cnd) (cont.)
Carter, E.:Syringa, w. J. DeGaetani (mez), T. Paul (bar), Speculum Musicae [E] *(rec 5/81)* CRI ■ ACS 6003
Ekizian, M.:Octoechos, w. A. Cawelti (sop) [E] New World ▲ 80425-2 [DDD]
Karchin, L.:Capriccio, w. B. Hudson (vn) [E] New World ▲ 80425-2 [DDD]
Karchin, L.:Songs of John Keats, w. A. Cawelti (sop) [E] New World ▲ 80425-2 [DDD]
Martino, D.:Triple Con, w. Anand Devendra (cl), Dennis Smylie (cl), Leslie Thimmig (cl) *(rec Dec 1978)* Albany ▲ TROY 168 [DDD]
Westergaard, P.:Mr. & Mrs. Discobbolos, w. Valerie Lamoree (sop), Jack Litten (ten) CRI ▲ CD 696 [ADD]
C. Wuorinen (cnd)
Wuorinen, C.:Chamber Con Vc, w. Fred Sherry (vc) Music & Arts ▲ CD 801 [ADD]
Group for Contemporary Music members
Wolpe, S.:Qt Strs Koch International Classics ▲ KIC 7315
Wolpe, S.:Second Piece Vn Koch International Classics ▲ KIC 7315
C. Wuorinen (cnd)
Wuorinen, C.:Arabia felix Music & Arts ▲ CD 800 [ADD]
Group for Contemporary Music String Quartet [B. Hudson (vn), C. Zeavin (vn), L. Martin (va), J. Gordon (vc)]
Feldman, Morton:Qt Strs *(rec Jan. 11 & 12, 1993)* Koch International Classics ▲ KIC 7251-2 [DDD]
Peterson, W.:Qt 1 Strs *(rec Apr. 22-23, 1991)* Koch International Classics ▲ KIC 7121-2 [DDD]
Roussakis, N.:Ephemeris *(rec 1981)* CRI ▲ CD 624 [ADD/DDD]
Sessions, R.:Canons "To the Memory of Igor Stravinsky" Str Qt Koch International Classics ▲ KIC 7113-2 [DDD]
Sessions, R.:Pieces Vc Koch International Classics ▲ KIC 7113-2 [DDD]
Sessions, R.:Qt 1 Strs Koch International Classics ▲ KIC 7113-2 [DDD]
Sessions, R.:Qnt Strs Koch International Classics ▲ KIC 7113-2 [DDD]
Wuorinen, C.:Qt 2 Strs *(rec Apr. 22-23, 1991)* Koch International Classics ▲ KIC 7121-2 [DDD]
Group for Early Music
M. Zöbeley (cnd)
Josquin Desprez:Motets—Stabat mater; Inviolata, integra et casta es; Ave Maria Ars Musici ▲ AM 1133-2 [DDD]
Lassus, O. de:Madrigals, Concerto di Viole, Cornetti con Crema—Il grave dell'età; Vedi l'aurora; Più volte un bel desio; Come pianta; Ben sono i prema tuoi; Canzon, la doglia; Che giova posseder; Così cor mio; Veggio se al vero; Arse la fiamma; Chi è fermato; Chi non sa; Per aspro mar; Ecco che pur vi lasso; Deh lascia anima; Tanto è quel bene; Hor ch'a l'albergo; Prendi l'aurata lira; O fugace dolcezza; Signor, le colpe mie Ars Musici ▲ 1099 [DDD]
Senfl, L.:Motets—Ave rosa sine spinis; Mater digna Dei; Ave Maria Ars Musici ▲ AM 1133-2 [DDD]
Group for New Music
Krása, H.:Anna's Song, w. Prague Sym Youth Chorus Koch International Classics ▲ KIC 7151
Krása, H.:Brundibár, w. Prague Sym Youth Chorus Koch International Classics ▲ KIC 7151
Krása, H.:Passacaglia & Fugue Koch International Classics ▲ KIC 7151
Krása, H.:Songs, w. Prague Sym Youth Chorus Koch International Classics ▲ KIC 7151
Krása, H.:Theme & Vars Str Qt Koch International Classics ▲ KIC 7151
Group for New Music members
Ullmann, V.:Qt 3 Strs Koch International Classics ▲ KIC 7109-2 [DDD]
Group 180
Melis, L.:Etude for 3 Mirrors Hungaroton ▲ HCD 12545
Rzewski, F.:Coming Together—Attica [E] Hungaroton ▲ HCD 12545
Szemző, T.:Water-Wonder Hungaroton ▲ HCD 12545
Grubenklang Orch [Phil Minton (sgr), Radu Malfatti (trbn), Roberto Ottaviano (sax), Dieter Manderscheid (db), Achim Krämer (dr), Horst Grabosch (trumpet), Michael Riessler (cl), Phil Wachsmann (vn), Thomas Witzmann (vib)]
G. Gräwe (cnd)
Gräwe, G.:East Coker, w. Georg Gräwe (pno) *(rec Cologne, Dec. 2, 1988 & May 7, 198)* Hat Hut ▲ hat ART CD 6028 [ADD]
Gräwe, G.:Lookin' for Work, w. Georg Gräwe (pno) *(rec Cologne, Dec. 2, 1988 & May 7, 198)* Hat Hut ▲ hat ART CD 6028 [ADD]
Gräwe, G.:Vars, w. Georg Gräwe (pno) *(rec Cologne, Dec. 2, 1988 & May 7, 198)* Hat Hut ▲ hat ART CD 6028 [ADD]
Gruber & Maklar Guitar Duo
Absil, J.:Suite 2 Gtrs Signum ▲ SIG X68-00 [DDD]
Aubert, L.:Improvisation Signum ▲ SIG X68-00 [DDD]
Bogdanovic, D.:Son Fant Signum ▲ SIG X68-00 [DDD]
Bons, J.:Attacca Signum ▲ SIG X68-00 [DDD]
Jolivet, A.:Sérénade for 2 Gtrs Signum ▲ SIG X68-00 [DDD]
Smith Brindle, R.:Chaconne & Interludes Signum ▲ SIG X68-00 [DDD]
Grudgionz Festival Orch
G.-F. Masini (cnd)
Puccini, G.:Turnadot (sels), w. Luciano Pavarotti (ten), Grudgionz Festival Chorus—Nessun dorma *(rec live, Apr. 23, 1964)* RCA Gold Seal ▲ 09026-68014-2 [ADD]
Grudgionz Opera Theater Orch
Puccini, G.:Turandot (sels), w. Luciano Pavarotti (ten), Grudgionz Opera Theater Chorus—Nessun dorma *(rec Grudgionz, Apr 23, 1964)* Goldies ▲ GLD 63202 [ADD]
Grumiaux Ensemble
Mozart, W.A.:Complete Mozart Edition Philips 3-▲ 422511-2 [ADD]
Grumiaux Piano Trio [P. Koch (vn), L. Dewez (vc), L. Devos (pno)]
Arensky, A.:Trio 1 Pno Ricercar ▲ RIC 131117 [DDD]
Smetana, B.:Trio Pno Ricercar ▲ RIC 131117 [DDD]
Grumiaux Trio
Mozart, W.A.:Complete Mozart Edition, w. Academy of St. Martin in the Fields Chamber Ensemble Philips 2-▲ 422513-2 [ADD]
Schubert, Franz:Qnt Pno, D.667, w. I. Haebler (pno), J. Cazauran (db) Philips ▲ 422838-2 [ADD]
Schubert, Franz:Trio Strs, D.471 Philips ▲ 422838-2 [ADD]
Schubert, Franz:Trio Strs, D.471 Philips 2-▲ 438700-2
Schubert, Franz:Trio Strs, D.581 Philips 2-▲ 438700-2
Schubert, Franz:Trio Strs, D.581 Philips ▲ 422838-2 [ADD]
Grünfarb String Quartet
The String Quartet in Sweden:A Cavalcade of Its History, w. Barkel String Quartet, Stockholm String Quartet, Garaguly String Quartet, Kyndel String Quartet, Ivan Ericson String Quartet, Skůne String Quartet, Hälsingborg String Quartet, Göteborg String Quartet, Galli String Quartet *(rec before 1951)* Caprice 5-▲ CAP 21506 [AAD/ADD]
Grupo Cosmos [Antonia Rodriguez (fl), Carlos Galán (pno)]
Santos, A.:Son Fl RNE/Spanish National Radio ▲ M3/12 [ADD]
Gruppo di Improvvisazione Nuova consonanza
E. Morricone (cnd)
Morricone, E.:Occhi Point ▲ PRCD 122
Gruppo Musica Insieme
A. Brizzi (cnd)
Scelsi, G.:Music of, w. Michiko Hirayama (sop), Maurizio Ben Omar (gtr/perc), Federico Mondelci (sax), Nuovo Ensemble Italiano—Pranam I for Voice, 12 Instrs & Band; Ko-Tha [3 danses de Shiva] for Gtr; I presagi for 11 Instruments; Riti [I funerali di Alessandro Magno]; Trio for 3 Percussionists; Manto per quattro for Voice, Fl, Trbn & Vc; Kya for Sax & 7 Instruments; Entretiens avec Giacento Scelsi Memoire Vive ▲ CD 262009 [ADD/DDD]
A. Molino (cnd)
Donatoni, F.:Music of—For Grilly; Lied; Lumen; Ash; Arpege Stradivarius ▲ STR 33315 [DDD]
Donatoni, F.:L'Ultima sera, w. L. Castellani (sop) Stradivarius ▲ STR 33315 [DDD]

Gryphon Piano Trio [Annalee Patipatanakoon (vn), Roman Borys (vc), Jamie Parker (pno)]
Haydn, J.:Trios Pno, Vn & Vc—Trios, H.XV:18, 19, 25 & 27 *(rec Quebec, June 1996)* Analekta Fleur de Lys ▲ FL 23014 [DDD]
G-String Quartet
Piazzolla, A.:Music of—Michelangelo '70; Milonga for 3; Butcher's Death; Marejadilla; Tango appasionado; La Camorra II; Milonga del Angel; Fugo 9; Verona del '79; Coral [all arr str qt] Koch Schwann ▲ SCH CD 364232
Guarneri String Quartet [Arnold Steinhardt (vn), John Dalley (vn), Michael Tree (va), David Soyer (vc)]
Beethoven, L. van:Grosse Fuge Str Qt *(rec live, Brighton Festival 1970)* Arkadia 2-▲ 589 [ADD]
Beethoven, L. van:Grosse Fuge Str Qt Philips ▲ 422059-2 [DDD]
Beethoven, L. van:Grosse Fuge Str Qt RCA Gold Seal 3-▲ 60458-2-RG [ADD]
Beethoven, L. van:Qts Strs (comp)—Nos. 1-6, Op. 18 RCA Gold Seal 3-▲ 60456-2-RG [ADD]
Beethoven, L. van:Qts Strs (comp)—Nos. 7-11, Opp. 59, 74, 95 RCA Gold Seal 3-▲ 60457-2-RG [ADD]
Beethoven, L. van:Qts Strs (comp)—Nos. 12-16, Opp. 127, 130-132 & 135) RCA Gold Seal 3-▲ 60458-2-RG [ADD]
Beethoven, L. van:Qt 1 Strs Philips 3-▲ 434115-2
Beethoven, L. van:Qt 2 Strs Philips 3-▲ 434115-2
Beethoven, L. van:Qt 3 Strs Philips 3-▲ 434115-2
Beethoven, L. van:Qt 4 Strs Philips 3-▲ 434115-2
Beethoven, L. van:Qt 5 Strs Philips 3-▲ 434115-2
Beethoven, L. van:Qt 6 Strs Philips 3-▲ 434115-2
Beethoven, L. van:Qt 7 Strs Philips 2-▲ 432980-2
Beethoven, L. van:Qt 8 Strs Philips 2-▲ 432980-2
Beethoven, L. van:Qt 9 Strs Philips 2-▲ 432980-2
Beethoven, L. van:Qt 10 Strs, "Harp" Philips ▲ 422341-2 [DDD]
Beethoven, L. van:Qt 11 Strs, "Quartetto serioso" Philips ▲ 422388-2 [DDD]
Beethoven, L. van:Qt 12 Strs Philips ▲ 420926-2 [DDD] ■ 420926-4
Beethoven, L. van:Qt 13 Strs Philips ▲ 422059-2 [DDD]
Beethoven, L. van:Qt 14 Strs Philips ▲ 422341-2 [DDD]
Beethoven, L. van:Qt 15 Strs Philips ▲ 422388-2 [DDD]
Beethoven, L. van:Qt 16 Strs Philips ▲ 420926-2 [DDD] ■ 420926-4
Debussy, C.:Qt Strs RCA Silver Seal ▲ 09026-60909-2 ■ 09026-60909-4
Dvořák, A.:Qt 12 Strs, "America" RCA Gold Seal ▲ 6263-2-RG [ADD] ■ 6263-4-RG (CrO2)
Dvořák, A.:Qt 12 Strs, "America" Philips ▲ 420803-2 [DDD]
Dvořák, A.:Qnt Pno, Op. 81, w. A. Rubinstein (pno) RCA Gold Seal ▲ 6263-2-RG [ADD] ■ 6263-4-RG (CrO2)
Grieg, E.:Qt Strs, Op. 27 Philips ▲ 426286-2 [DDD]
Mozart, W.A.:Qt 14 Strs Philips ▲ 426240-2 [DDD]
Mozart, W.A.:Qt 15 Strs Philips ▲ 426240-2 [DDD]
Mozart, W.A.:Qnts Strs—K.515 [w. I. Kavafian (vn)] & K.614 [w. K. Kaskashian (vn] RCA Red Seal ▲ 7772-2 [DDD]
Mozart, W.A.:Qnts Strs—K.406 [w. K. Kashkashian (vn)] & K.593 [w. S. Tenonbom (vn)] RCA Red Seal ▲ 7771-2 [DDD]
Mozart, W.A.:Qnts Strs—K.174 [w. I. Kavafian (vn)] & 516 [w. S. Tenonbom (vn)] *(rec in public performance at the Metropolitan Museum of Art, New York)* RCA Red Seal ▲ 7770-2 [DDD] ■ 7770-4 (CrO2)
Ravel, M.:Qt Strs RCA Silver Seal ▲ 09026-60909-2 ■ 09026-60909-4
Schubert, Franz:Qnt Strs, D.956, w. B. Greenhouse (vc) Philips ▲ 432108-2
Sibelius, J.:Qt Strs, Op. 56 Philips ▲ 426286-2 [DDD]
Smetana, B.:Qt 1 Strs Philips ▲ 420803-2 [DDD]
Guarneri String Quartet members
Brahms, J.:Qt 1 Pno, w. A. Rubinstein (pno) RCA Gold Seal ▲ 5677-2-RG [ADD] ■ 5677-4-RG (CrO2)
Brahms, J.:Qt 3 Pno, w. A. Rubinstein (pno) RCA Gold Seal ▲ 5677-2-RG [ADD] ■ 5677-4-RG (CrO2)
Dvořák, A.:Qts Pno Strs, Opp. 23 & 87, w. A. Rubinstein (pno)—Op. 87 RCA Red Seal ▲ 6256-2-RC [ADD]
Fauré, G.:Qt 1 Pno, w. A. Rubinstein (pno) RCA Red Seal ▲ 6256-2-RC [ADD]
Mozart, W.A.:Qts Pno, w. A. Rubinstein (pno) RCA Gold Seal ▲ 60406-2 [ADD] ■ 60406-4 (CrO2)
Guarneri Trio Prague [I. Klánský (pno), C. Pavlík (vn), M. Jerie (vc)]
Brahms, J.:Trios (3) Pno Ottavo ▲ OTT 29134 [DDD]
Brahms, J.:Trio 1 Pno Supraphon ▲ SUP 11 2139 [DDD]
Dvořák, A.:Trio 4 Pno, "Dumky" Supraphon ▲ 11 1561-2 [DDD]
Mendelssohn, F.:Trio 1 Pno Supraphon ▲ SUP 11 2139 [DDD]
Reicha, A.:Trios concertants Pno—Nos 1-3 in E♭, d & C *(rec 1995)* Supraphon ▲ SUP 3024
Smetana, B.:Trio Pno Supraphon ▲ 11 1561-2 [DDD]
Smetana, B.:Trio Pno Supraphon ▲ SUP 11 1515 [DDD]
Guarneri Trio Prague members
Brahms, J.:Trio Cl, w. G. Pieterson (cl) Ottavo ▲ OTT 29134 [DDD]
Brahms, J.:Trio Hn, w. J. Slagter (hn) Ottavo ▲ OTT 29134 [DDD]
Guarneri Trio Prague members [C. Pavlík (vn), I. Klánský (pno)]
Smetana, B.:Fant sur un air bohémien Supraphon ▲ SUP 11 1515 [DDD]
Smetana, B.:From the Homeland Supraphon ▲ SUP 11 1515 [DDD]
Guidantus Ensemble
Couperin, F.:Pièces de clavecin (sels)—Le Rossignol; Les Ondes; Le Moucheron Stradivarius ▲ STV 80001 [DDD]
Vivaldi, A.:Cons Vn, Op. 8/1-4, "The Four Seasons" Stradivarius ▲ STV 80001 [DDD]
Guido d'Arezzo Orch
R. Clemencic (cnd)
Salieri, A.:Axur, Re d'Ormus, w. A. Martin (bar), E. Mei (sop), C. Rayam (ten), E. Nova (bass), A. Vespasiani (mez), M. Valenti (sop), Guido d'Arezzo Chorus [I] *(rec live 1989)* Nuova Era 3-▲ 6852/54 [DDD]
Guild Piano Trio [Janet Orenstein (vn), Brooks Whitehouse (vc), Patricia Tao (pno)]
Silver, S.:To the Spirit Unconquered *(rec American Academy of Arts & Letters, New York, Apr 23, 1994)* CRI ▲ CD 708 [DDD]
Guildford String Orch
B. Rose (cnd)
Vaughan Williams, R.:Fant on Christmas Carols, w. J. Barrow (bar), Guildford Cathedral Choir [2 Christmas Carol choral arr. Vaughan Williams]—And all in the morning & Wassail Song EMI Classics (Studio) ▲ CDM 64131 2 [ADD]
Guildhall Chamber Ensemble
D. Angus (cnd)
Britten, B.:Curlew River, w. Hugo Ticciati (trb), Mark Milhofer (ten), Mark Evans (bar), Gwynn Hughes Jones (bar), Matthew Hargreaves (bass) Koch Schwann ▲ SCH 313972
Guildhall String Ensemble
Albinoni, T.:Cons Obs, w. M. Messiter (ob) RCA Red Seal ▲ 60224-2-RC [DDD] ■ 60224-4-RC (CrO2)
Albinoni, T.:Cons à 5 Obs, Op. 9, w. M. Messiter (ob)—No. 2 RCA Red Seal ▲ 60224-2 [DDD] ■ 60224-4 (CrO2)
Bach, J.S.:Con Ob, BWV 1056, w. M. Messiter (ob) RCA Red Seal ▲ 60224-2-RC [DDD] ■ 60224-4-RC (CrO2)
Classical Ecstasy—Classics for a New Age, w. Chicago SO [cnd:Georg Solti], English CO [cnd:Alexander Schneider], London PO [cnd:Leonard Slatkin], Philadelphia Orch [cnd:James Levine], Philharmonia Orch [cnds:Andrew Litton, Henry Lewis], RCA Italiana Opera Orch [cnd:Francesco Molinari-Pradelli] RCA Gold Seal ▲ 74321-23041-2 [ADD/DDD]

Guildhall String Ensemble (cont.)
Corelli, A.:Concerti grossi, Op. 6—Nos. 1-12 RCA Red Seal 2-▲ 09026-60071-2
RCA Red Seal ▲ 60437-2-RC [DDD] ■ 60437-4-RC
Grieg, E.:Elegaic Melodies, Op. 34 RCA Red Seal ▲ 60439-2-RC [DDD]
Grieg, E.:Holberg Suite RCA Red Seal ▲ 60439-2-RC [DDD]
Handel, G.F.:Cons (3) Ob, w. M. Messiter (ob)—No. 3 in g
RCA Red Seal ▲ 60224-2-RC [DDD]; ■ 60224-4-RC (CrO2)
Marcello, A.:Con Ob & Strs, w. M. Messiter (ob)
RCA Red Seal ▲ 60224-2-RC [DDD] ■ 60224-4-RC (CrO2)
Nielsen, C.:Little Suite RCA Red Seal ▲ 60439-2-RC [DDD]
Sibelius, J.:Romance Strs RCA Red Seal ▲ 60439-2-RC [DDD]
Vivaldi, A.:Cons Ob, w. M. Messiter (ob)—in C, R.447 & in d, R.454
RCA Red Seal ▲ 60224-2-RC [DDD] ■ 60224-4-RC (CrO2)
Wirén, D.:Serenade Strs RCA Red Seal ▲ 60439-2-RC [DDD]
R. Salter (cnd)
English Music for Clarinet & String Orchestra, w. R. Stoltzman (cl)
Finzi, G.:Con Cl, w. R. Stoltzman (cl) RCA Red Seal ▲ 60437-2-RC [DDD]; ■ 60437-4-RC (CrO2)
Guillaume de Machaut Ensemble
Machaut, G. de:Music of—Felix Virgo [motet]; Comment qu'a moy lointeinne [virelay]; Bone pastor guillerme [motet]; Ma fin est mon commencement [rondeau]; Le remede de fortune; Pour quoy me bat mes maris [chanson et motet]; Honte, Paour, Doubtance [ballade instrumentale]; Sanz cuer-amis dolens-dame par vous [triple ballade]; Quant je suis mis au retour [virelay]; Quant en moy-amour et biaute [motet]; Hoquet David; Deploration sur la mort de machaut [double ballade d'andrieu]; Le veoir dit Adès 2-▲ ADE 203712 [ADD]
Guitar Symphonietta
L. Brouwer (cnd)
Angelo, N. d':Suite barocca Giulia ▲ GS 201006 [DDD]
Brouwer, L.:Acerca del cielo, el ayre y la sonrisa Giulia ▲ GS 201006 [DDD]
Brouwer, L.:Paisaje cubano con rumba Giulia ▲ GS 201006 [DDD]
Gunma SO
L. Kektjiang (cnd)
Chu, W.:Harvest Scenes *(rec Shibukawa Public Hall, Gumma Prefecture, Japan, May 24 & 25, 1981)* Marco Polo ("Chinese Music" series) ▲ 8.223920 [DDD]
Du, M.:The Mermaid (ballet suite) *(rec Shibukawa Public Hall, Gumma Prefecture, Japan, May 24 & 25, 1981)* Marco Polo ("Chinese Music" series) ▲ 8.223920 [DDD]
H. Shek (cnd)
Zi, H.:Three Wishes for a Rose, w. Takako Nishizaki (vn) [arr Akira Nishimura]
Camerata ("After Hours Classics" series) ▲ 20 CM 423 [DDD]
K. Toyoda (cnd)
Albrechtsberger, J.G.:Concertino Tpt, w. Pierre Thibaud (tpt) *(rec Tone-Numata Public Hall, Japan, Sept 8-9, 1981)* Camerata ▲ 32CM 168 [DDD]
Haydn, J.:Con Tpt, w. Pierre Thibaud (tpt) *(rec Tone-Numata Public Hall, Japan, Sept 8-9, 1981)* Camerata ▲ 32CM 168 [DDD]
Jolivet, A.:Concertino Tpt, w. Pierre Thibaud (tpt), Henriette Puig-Roget (pno) *(rec Tone-Numata Public Hall, Japan, Sept 8-9, 1981)* Camerata ▲ 32CM 168 [DDD]
Mercadante, S.:Con in B♭ Cl, Op. 101, w. Karl Leister (cl) *(rec Gunma Music Center, Takasaki, Japan, Apr 1980)* Camerata 2-▲ 25 CM 323/4 [DDD]
Mozart, W.A.:Con Cl, w. Karl Leister (cl) *(rec Gunma Music Center, Takasaki, Japan, Apr 1980)* Camerata 2-▲ 25 CM 323/4 [DDD]
Weber, C.M. von:Con 1 Cl, w. Karl Leister (cl) Camerata 2-▲ 25 CM71-2 [DDD]
Weber, C.M. von:Con 2 Cl, w. Karl Leister (cl) Camerata 2-▲ 25CM71-2 [DDD]
Weber, C.M. von:Divert Cl, w. Karl Leister (cl) Camerata 2-▲ 25 CM71-2 [DDD]
A. Wit (cnd)
Weber, C.M. von:Concertino Cl, w. Karl Leister (cl) *(rec Maebashi Shimin Bunka Kaikan, Japan, June 1986)* Camerata 2-▲ 25 CM 323/4 [DDD]
Weber, C.M. von:Concertino Cl, w. Karl Leister (cl) Camerata 2-▲ 25 CM71-2 [DDD]
Weber, C.M. von:Con 1 Cl, w. Karl Leister (cl) *(rec Honjo Bunka Kaikan, Japan, June 1982)* Camerata 2-▲ 25 CM 323/4 [DDD]
Weber, C.M. von:Con 2 Cl, w. Karl Leister (cl) *(rec Honjo Bunka Kaikan, Japan, June 1982)* Camerata 2-▲ 25 CM 323/4 [DDD]
Weber, C.M. von:Divert Cl, w. Karl Leister (cl) *(rec Maebashi Shimin Bunka Kaikan, Japan, June 1986)* Camerata 2-▲ 25 CM 323/4 [DDD]
H. Yazaki (cnd)
Castelnuovo-Tedesco, M.:Con 1 Gtr, w. Ichiro Suzuki (gtr) *(rec Shibukawa Shimin-kaikan, May 2, 1980)* Camerata ▲ 25CM 413 [AAD]
Gürzenich Orch
J. Conlon (cnd)
Zemlinsky, A. von:Der Geburtstag der Infantin, w. Soile Isokoski (sop), Iride Martinez (sgr), Andrew Collis (sgr), David Kuebler (ten), Juanita Lascarro (sgr), Machiko Obata (sgr), Anne Schwanewilms (sgr), Natalie Karl (sgr), Martina Rüping (sgr), Franfurter Kantorei (sgr), Cologne PO *(rec Cologne, Feb 1996)* EMI Classics 2-▲ CDCB 56208
Zemlinsky, A. von:Die Seejungfrau, w. Cologne PO EMI Classics ▲ CDC 55515
Zemlinsky, A. von:Sinfonietta, w. Cologne PO EMI Classics ▲ CDC 55515
J. Pritchard (cnd)
Humperdinck, E.:Hänsel und Gretel, w. I. Cotrubas (sop), E. Söderström (sop), F. von Stade (mez), C. Ludwig (mez), S. Nimsgern (b-bar) [G] CBS 2-▲ M2K 35898 [ADD]
Ludwig Güttler Brass Ensemble
Music from the Time of Schütz Berlin Classics ▲ BER 1173
Ludwig Güttler Wind Ensemble
All the World Praise God Capriccio ▲ CDC 10068 [DDD]
Dresden, City of Music Capriccio ▲ 10 395 [DDD]
Music for Winds Berlin Classics ▲ BER 1090 [DDD]
Györ PO
E. Lukács (cnd)
Haydn, M.:Con Fl, P.54, w. Imre Kovács (fl) White Label ▲ HRC 107 [ADD]
J. Sándor (cnd)
Strauss (I), Joh.:Radetzky March White Label ▲ HRC 054
Strauss (II), Joh.:Music of—waltzes & polkas White Label ▲ HRC 054
Haddens [Frances Roots Hadden (pno), R. Hadden (pno)]
Adventures in Music-Making:A Fresh Look at the Greats Cambria ▲ CD 1065 [DDD]
Haffner String Quartet
Warlock, P.:The Curlew, w. James Griffelt (ten) ASV ("Quicksilva" series) ▲ ASQ 6143 [DDD]
Warlock, P.:Songs Ten, w. James Griffelt (ten) ASV ("Quicksilva" series) ▲ ASQ 6143 [DDD]
Haffner Wind Ensemble
N. Daniel (cnd)
Alwyn, W.:Chamber Music—Son for Cl; Divert for Fl; Crépuscule for Hp; Son for Ob; Son for Fl; Son Impromptu for Vn & Va Chandos ▲ CHAN 9197 [DDD]
Alwyn, W.:Con Fl Chandos ▲ CHAN 9152 [DDD]
Alwyn, W.:Naiades Chandos ▲ CHAN 9152 [DDD]
Alwyn, W.:Suite Ob Chandos ▲ CHAN 9152 [DDD]
Alwyn, W.:Trio Fl Chandos ▲ CHAN 9152 [DDD]
R. Hickox (cnd)
Strauss, R.:Sonatina 2 Chandos ▲ CHAN 9286 [DDD]
Hagen PO
M. Halász (cnd)
Schreker, F.:Der ferne Klang, w. E. Grigorescu (sop), T. Harper (ten), Hagen Phil Chorus [G]
Marco Polo 2-▲ 8.223270/271 [DDD]

Hagen PO (cont.)
G. Markson (cnd)
Weber, C.M. von:Peter Schmoll und seine Nachbarn, w. A. Pfeffer (sop—Minnette), J. Schmidt (ten—Martin Schmoll), S. Basa (ten—Karl Pirkner), H.-J. Schöpflin (ten—Niklas), R. Busching (bar—Peter Schmoll), H.J. Porcher (bass—Hans Bast) [G] *(rec Feb. 1-5, 1993)*
Marco Polo 2-▲ 8.223592/93 [DDD]
Hagen String Quartet
Beethoven, L. van:Qt 16 Strs Deutsche Grammophon ▲ 431814-2 [DDD]
Brahms, J.:Qnt Pno, w. P. Gulda (pno) Deutsche Grammophon ▲ 437804-2
Debussy, C.:Qt Strs Deutsche Grammophon ▲ 437836-2
Haydn, J.:Qts Strs, Op. 1—No. 1 only Deutsche Grammophon ▲ 423622-2 [DDD]
Haydn, J.:Qts Strs, Op. 64, "Tost Qts"—No. 5 Deutsche Grammophon ▲ 423622-2 [DDD]
Haydn, J.:Qts Strs, Op. 74—No. 3 Deutsche Grammophon ▲ 423622-2 [DDD]
Janácek, L.:Qt 1 Strs Deutsche Grammophon ▲ 427669-2 [DDD]
Janácek, L.:Qt 2 Strs Deutsche Grammophon ▲ 427669-2 [DDD]
Ligeti, G.:Qt 1 Strs Deutsche Grammophon ▲ 431686-2 [DDD]
Lutoslawski, W.:Petite Suite Deutsche Grammophon ▲ 431686-2 [DDD]
Ravel, M.:Qt Strs Deutsche Grammophon ▲ 437836-2
Schnittke, A.:Canon in memoriam Igor Stravinsky Deutsche Grammophon ▲ 431686-2 [DDD]
Schoenberg, A.:Chamber Sym 1, w. P. Gulda (pno) [arr. Webern] Deutsche Grammophon ▲ 437804-2
Schubert, Franz:Qt 14 Strs Deutsche Grammophon ▲ 431814-2 [DDD]
Schubert, Franz:Qnt Pno, D.667, w. A. Schiff (pno), A. Posch (db) London ▲ 411975-2 [DDD]
Webern, A.:Qt Strs, Op. 28 Deutsche Grammophon ▲ 437836-2
Wolf, H.:Italian Serenade Deutsche Grammophon ▲ 427669-2 [DDD]
The Hague Percussion Group
Cage, J.:First Construction Globe ▲ GLO 5086 [DDD]
Cage, J.:Qt for 4 Perc Globe ▲ GLO 5072 [DDD]
Donatoni, F.:Omar Globe ▲ GLO 5086 [DDD]
Ford, R.:Star Globe ▲ GLO 5086 [DDD]
Ford, R.:Trarre Globe ▲ GLO 5066 [DDD]
Ford, R.:Wanne mine eyhnen misten Globe ▲ GLO 5072 [DDD]
Huber, N.A.:Clash Music Globe ▲ GLO 5086 [DDD]
Ishii, M.:Thirteen Drums Globe ▲ GLO 5066 [DDD]
Kondo, J.:Under the Umbrella Globe ▲ GLO 5086 [DDD]
Reich, S.:Drumming, Part III Globe ▲ GLO 5086 [DDD]
Smith, P.:Mare - a'440" Globe ▲ GLO 5072 [DDD]
Tsubonoh, K.:Fantom Fire Globe ▲ GLO 5072 [DDD]
Wagenaar, D.:Music of, w. Gerard Bouwhuis (pno), Cees van Zeeland (pno), Netherlands Wind Ensemble—La Volta; Stadium; Solenne; Liederen; Metrum Donemus ▲ CV 29
Xenakis, I.:Okho Globe ▲ GLO 5066 [DDD]
R. de Leeuw (cnd)
Andriessen, L.:De Tijd, w. Schoenberg Ensemble, Netherlands Chamber Choir
Elektra/Nonesuch ▲ 79291-2 ■ 79291-4
Messiaen, O.:Des Canyons aux étoiles, w. Asko Ensemble, Schoenberg Ensemble
Montaigne 2-▲ MO 782035
The Hague PO
P. Boulez (cnd)
Handel, G.F.:Water Music (comp) Elektra/Nonesuch ■ 71127-4
E. Bour (cnd)
Ruyneman, D.:Hiëroglyphen Olympia ▲ OCD 504 [AAD]
T. Koopman (cnd)
Rosier, N.-C.:Son in C Ob Olympia ▲ OCD 500 [AAD]
W. van Otterloo (cnd)
Badings, H.:Con Vns, w. H. Krebbers (vn), T. Olof (vn) Donemus ▲ CV 26
Dresden, S.:Dansflitsen Donemus ▲ CV 26
Orthel, L.:Sym 2 Donemus ▲ CV 26
Porcelijn (cnd)
Loevendie, T.:Orchestral Music, w. Netherlands Ballet Orch—Orbits; Incantations; Flexio; Naima Suite Donemus ▲ CV 24
E. Spanjaard (cnd)
de Leeuw, T.:Haiku II, w. E. Vink (sop) Donemus ▲ CV 23
de Leeuw, T.:Résonances Donemus ▲ CV 23
J. van Steen (cnd)
Wagemans, P.J.:Rosebud, w. Royal Conservatory Choir members Donemus ▲ CV 28
H. Vonk (cnd)
Wagemans, P.J.:Alla marcia, w. Tjeerd Oostendorp (tuba) Donemus ▲ CV 56 [DDD]
Zweers, B.:Sym 3 Olympia ▲ OCD 503 [AAD]
The Hague Residentie Orch—see Residentie Orch The Hague
Haifa SO
S. Sperber (cnd)
Fleischer, T.:Oratorio 1492-1992, w. Rinat & Israel Mandolin Ensemble, Israel National Choir
Vienna Modern Masters ▲ VMM 3013 [DDD]
William Hall Orch
W. Hall (cnd)
Britten, B.:War Requiem, w. Jeanine Altmeyer (sop), Douglas Lawrence (ten), Michael Sells (bar), Ladd Thomas (org), William Hall Chorale, Columbus Boys' Choir Klavier ▲ KCD 11017 [ADD]
Hallé Brass
E. Gregson (cnd)
Gregson, E.:Music of, w. Northern Trombone Quartet, RNCM Brass Ensemble—Fanfare for Europe; Equale Dances; Susie's Fanfare; Son for 4 Trbns; Fanfare for the North; Qnt for Brass; Flourish for the Theatre; Flourish for an Occasion; Dance Episodes (3); Festival Fanfare Doyen ▲ CD 038 [DDD]
Hallé Collegium Instrumentale
A. Marasch (cnd)
Bach, C.P.E.:Con Hpd & Strs, H.427, w. Werner Bärtschi (pno) *(rec Waldenburg, Switzerland, Apr-May, 1995)* Jecklin ▲ JD 701-2 [DDD]
Bach, C.P.E.:Con Hpd & Strs, H.430, w. Werner Bärtschi (pno) *(rec Waldenburg, Switzerland, Apr-May, 1995)* Jecklin ▲ JD 701-2 [DDD]
Bach, C.P.E.:Con Hpd & Strs, H.443, w. Werner Bärtschi (pno) *(rec Waldenburg, Switzerland, Apr-May, 1995)* Jecklin ▲ JD 701-2 [DDD]
Halle Handel Festival Orch
V. Hempfling (cnd)
Eben, Petr:Con 2 Org, "Symphonia gregoriana", w. P. Wisskirchen (org) Motette ▲ CD 40151 [DDD]
H.-T. Margraf (cnd)
Handel, G.F.:Imeneo, w. Sylvia Geszty (sop), Renate Krahmer (sop), Hans-Joachim Rotzsch (ten), Günther Leib (bass), Siegfried Vogel (bass), Leipzig Radio Chorus *(rec 1966)*
Berlin Classics ▲ BER 9110
Hallé Orch
J. Barbirolli (cnd)
Bizet, G.:L'Arlésienne—selections Dutton Laboratories ▲ DUT CDSJB 1002 [ADD]
Bruckner, A.:Sym 8 *(rec live, July 20, 1970)* Arkadia ▲ 717 [ADD]
Debussy, C.:Prélude à l'après-midi d'un faune Dutton Laboratories ▲ DUT CDSJB 1002 [ADD]
Delius, F.:Music of, w. Robert Tear (ten), London SO, Ambrosian Singers—Brigg Fair; In a Summer Garden; On Hearing the First Cuckoo in Spring; Summer Night on the River; A Song before Sunrise; Intermezzo & Serenade [from Hassan]; La Calinda; Late Swallows; Intermezzo [from Fennimore & Gerda]; The Walk to Paradise Garden; Prelude [from Irmelin]; A Song of Summer; Appalachia; rehearsal of Appalachia EMI Classics ▲ ZDMB 65119
Dvořák, A.:Legends, Op. 59—Nos. 4, 6 & 7 EMI Classics ▲ CDM 64193
Dvořák, A.:Scherzo Capriccioso EMI Classics ▲ CDM 64193
Dvořák, A.:Sym 8 EMI Classics ▲ CDM 64193

ORCH. & ENS.

Hallé Orch (cont.)

J. Barbirolli (cnd) (cont.)

Elgar, E.:Con Vc, w. A. Navarra (vc) EMI Classics (Phoenixa) ▲ CDM 63955
Elgar, E.:Elegy Strs EMI Classics (Phoenixa) ▲ CDM 63955
Elgar, E.:Intro & Allegro EMI Classics (Phoenixa) ▲ CDM 63955
Elgar, E.:Sea Pictures, w. K. Meyer (mez) [E] *(rec live 7/24/70)* Intaglio ▲ INCD 701-1 [ADD]
Elgar, E.:Sym 1 *(rec live 7/24/70)* Intaglio ▲ INCD 701-1 [ADD]
Elgar, E.:Sym 2 EMI Classics ▲ CDM 64724-2
Fauré, G.:Pelléas et Mélisande (suite) Dutton Laboratories ▲ DUT CDSJB 1002 [ADD]
Grieg, E.:Lyric Pieces EMI Classics ▲ CDE 67773
Grieg, E.:Peer Gynt EMI Classics ▲ CDE 67773
Ibert, J.:Divert Orch Dutton Laboratories ▲ DUT CDSJB 1002 [ADD]
Mahler, G.:Kindertotenlieder, w. J. Baker (mez) [G] EMI Classics ▲ CDC 47793 [ADD]
Mahler, G.:Kindertotenlieder, w. J. Baker (mez) EMI Classics ▲ CDZB 62707
Mahler, G.:Lieder eines fahrenden Gesellen, w. J. Baker (mez) EMI Classics ▲ CDZB 62707
Mahler, G.:Lieder eines fahrenden Gesellen, w. J. Baker (mez) [G] EMI Classics ▲ CDC 47793 [ADD]
Mozart, W.A.:Nozze di Figaro (ov) Dutton Laboratories ▲ DUT 1004 [ADD]
Saint-Saëns, C.:Carnival of the Animals, w. W. Landauer (pno), M. Rawicz (pno) Dutton Laboratories ▲ DUT CDSJB 1002 [ADD]
Schoenberg, A.:Pelleas und Melisande *(rec live, Royal Festival Hall, London, April 1968)* Intaglio ▲ INCD 7171 [ADD]
Strauss, R.:Die Liebe der Danae (sels)—symphonic fragments Dutton Laboratories ▲ DUT 1004 [ADD]
Strauss, R.:Der Rosenkavalier (suite) Dutton Laboratories ▲ DUT 1004 [ADD]
Vaughan Williams, R.:Sym 2 EMI Classics ▲ CDM 65109
Vaughan Williams, R.:Sym 5 Dutton Laboratories ▲ DUT CDAX 8011 [ADD]
Verdi, G.:La traviata (sels)—Preludes to Acts 1 & 2 Dutton Laboratories ▲ DUT 1004 [ADD]
Wagner, R.:Lohengrin (preludes)—Acts 1 & 3 Dutton Laboratories ▲ DUT 1004 [ADD]
Weber, C.M. von:Euryanthe (ov) Dutton Laboratories ▲ DUT 1004 [ADD]
Weber, C.M. von:Der Freischütz (ov) Dutton Laboratories ▲ DUT 1004 [ADD]

B. Connor (cnd)

Roylance, D.:Battle of the Atlantic Suite, w. L. Garret (sop), Hallé State Chorus Conifer Classics ▲ 74321-15008-2

L. Foster (cnd)

Rachmaninoff, S.:Con 2 Pno, w. J.-B. Pommier (pno) Virgin Classics ▲ DCD 59297 [DDD]
Tchaikovsky, P.:Con 1 Pno, w. J.-B. Pommier (pno) Virgin Classics ▲ CDC 59297 [DDD]

M. Handford (cnd)

Orff, C.:Carmina burana, w. S. Armstrong (sop), P. Hall (ten), B. Rayner Cook (bar), Hallé State Chorus Classics for Pleasure ▲ CDCFP 9005 [ADD]

V. Handley (cnd)

Delius, F.:Brigg Fair:An English Rhapsody Classics for Pleasure ▲ CDCFP 4568 [DDD]
Delius, F.:Eventyr Classics for Pleasure ▲ CDCFP 4568 [DDD]
Delius, F.:In a Summer Garden Classics for Pleasure ▲ CDCFP 4568 [DDD]
Delius, F.:A Song of Summer Classics for Pleasure ▲ CDCFP 4568 [DDD]

H. Harty (cnd)

Berlioz, H.:La Damnation de Faust (sels)—Marche hongroise & Danse des sylphes *(rec 1928)* Pearl ▲ PEA 9485 (m)
Brahms, J.:Con Vn, w. J. Szigeti (vn) *(rec 1928 for Columbia)* Pearl ▲ PEA 9345 (m) [AAD]
Brahms, J.:Con Vn, w. J. Szigeti (vn) *(rec 1928–1937)* Music & Arts 2-▲ CD 813 [AAD]
Elgar, E.:Dream Children *(rec March 1932)* Pearl ▲ PEA 9087 [ADD]
Tchaikovsky, P.:Con 1 Pno, w. Solomon (pno) *(rec 1930 for Columbia Records)* Pearl ▲ GEMMCD 9478 (m) [AAD]

L. Heward (cnd)

Borodin, A.:Prince Igor (ov) *(rec Houldsworth Hall, Manchester, Jan. 15, 1942)* Dutton Laboratories ▲ CDAX 8010 [ADD]
Borodin, A.:Sym 2 *(rec Houldsworth Hall, Manchester, June 23 & 24, 1943)* Dutton Laboratories ▲ CDAX 8010 [ADD]
Ireland, J.:Con Pno, w. E. Joyce (pno) *(rec Jan. 14, 1942)* Dutton Laboratories ▲ CDAX 8001 [ADD]
Liadov, A.:Kikimora *(rec Houldsworth Hall, Manchester, Mar. 5, 1942)* Dutton Laboratories ▲ CDAX 8010 [ADD]
Moeran, E.J.:Sym *(rec Nov. 25–26 & Dec. 1, 1942)* Dutton Laboratories ▲ CDAX 8001 [ADD]
Shostakovich, D.:Con 1 Pno, w. Eileen Joyce (pno), Arthur Lockwood (tpt) *(rec Houldsworth Hall, Manchester, Oct. 24, 1941)* Dutton Laboratories ▲ CDAX 8010 [ADD]
Tchaikovsky, P.:Sleeping Beauty (sels)—waltz *(rec Houldsworth Hall, Manchester, July 29, 1941)* Dutton Laboratories ▲ CDAX 8010 [ADD]

J. Horenstein (cnd)

Nielsen, C.:Sym 6 Intaglio ▲ ING 738 [ADD]

J. Judd (cnd)

Elgar, E.:Sym 1 IMP ▲ PCD 2019

C. Lambert (cnd)

Lambert, C.:The Rio Grande, w. A.H. Whitehead (alt), Hamilton Harty (pno), St. Michaels' Singers Claremont ▲ CDGSE 785065
Tchaikovsky, P.:Sym 4 *(rec Oct. 8 & 9, 1942)* Dutton Laboratories ▲ CDLX 7006 [ADD]

J. Loughran (cnd)

Berlioz, H.:La Damnation de Faust (sels) Classics for Pleasure ▲ CDCFP 9011 [ADD]
Brahms, J.:Con 1 Pno, w. J. Lill (pno) ASV Quicksilva ▲ ASQ 6083 [DDD]
Brahms, J.:Con 2 Pno, w. J. Lill (pno) ASV Quicksilva ▲ ASQ 6088 [DDD]
Chabrier, E.:España Classics for Pleasure ▲ CDCFP 9011 [ADD]
Chabrier, E.:Joyeuse marche Classics for Pleasure ▲ CDCFP 9011 [ADD]
Dukas, P.:L'Apprenti sorcier Classics for Pleasure ▲ CDCFP 9011 [ADD]
Elgar, E.:Sym 1 ASV Quicksilva ▲ QS 6082 [ADD/DDD]
Elgar, E.:Sym 2 ASV Quicksilva ▲ ASQ 6087 [ADD/DDD]
Holst, G.:The Planets Classics for Pleasure ▲ CDCFP 4243 [ADD]

K. Nagano (cnd)

Prokofiev, S.:Con 2 Vn, w. Vladim Repin (vn) *(rec Paris 1995)* Erato ▲ 10696-2 [DDD]
Shostakovich, D.:Con 1 Vn, w. Vladim Repin (vn) *(rec Paris 1995)* Erato ▲ 10696-2 [DDD]

S. Skrowaczewski (cnd)

Brahms, J.:Academic Festival Ov IMP ▲ PCD 2014
Brahms, J.:Academic Festival Ov IMP Classics 4-▲ BOXD 3 [DDD]
Brahms, J.:Hungarian Dances Orch IMP Classics 4-▲ BOXD 3 [DDD]
Brahms, J.:Hungarian Dances Orch—Nos. 1, 3 & 10 *(rec 11/87)* IMP Classics ▲ PCD 897 [DDD]
Brahms, J.:Syms (comp) IMP Classics 4-▲ BOXD 3 [DDD]
Brahms, J.:Sym 1 IMP ▲ PCD 2014
Brahms, J.:Sym 2 IMP Classics ▲ PCD 857 [DDD]
Brahms, J.:Sym 3 IMP ("Classic" series) ▲ IMP 2039
Brahms, J.:Sym 4 IMP Classics ▲ PCD 897 [DDD]
Brahms, J.:Tragic Ov IMP Classics 4-▲ BOXD 3 [DDD]
Brahms, J.:Tragic Ov IMP Classics ▲ PCD 857 [DDD]
Brahms, J.:Vars on a Theme by Haydn IMP ("Classic" series) ▲ IMP 2039
Brahms, J.:Vars on a Theme by Haydn IMP Classics 4-▲ BOXD 3 [DDD]
Bruckner, A.:Sym 4, "Romantic" IMP Classics ▲ IMPPCD 1059 [DDD]
Mahler, G.:Sym 4, w. A. Hargan (sop) [G] IMP Classics ▲ PCD 972 [DDD]
Popular Overtures, w. London SO, Barry Tuckwell (cnd), Royal PO [cnd:Kazuhiro Koizumi] Pickwick ("The Orchid" series) ▲ PICORCD 11003
Shostakovich, D.:Sym 5 IMP Classics ▲ PCD 940 [DDD]
Shostakovich, D.:Sym 10 *(rec Albert Hall Bolton, Nov 23–24, 1990)* IMP ▲ IMP 2043
Shostakovich, D.:Sym 10 *(rec 11/90)* IMP Classics ▲ PCD 955 [DDD]

Hallé Orch (cont.)

B. Thomson (cnd)

Strauss (II), Joh.:Waltzes—On the Beautiful Blue Danube, Op. 314; Artist's Life, Op. 316; Wine, Women & Song, Op. 333; Accelerations, Op. 234; Vienna Blood, Op. 354; Voices of Spring, Op. 410; Tales from the Vienna Woods, Op. 325; Emperor, Op. 437 Classics for Pleasure ▲ CDCFP 9015 [DDD]

D. C. Hall's New Concert & Quadrille Band

Grand Concert! *(rec Sept 20–21, 1991)* Dorian Discovery ▲ DIS 80108 [DDD]

Hamburg Academy Orch

E. Lampson (cnd)

Schnittke, A.:Canon Vn, w. M. Lubotsky (vn) *(rec June 11–12, 1991)* Sony Classical ▲ SK 53357 [DDD]

Hamburg Camerata Accademica

J. Jürgens (cnd)

Monteverdi, C.:Vespro della Beata Vergine, w. Monteverdi Choir London [L] Ambitus 2-▲ 383826-2 [DDD]

Hamburg das neue werk Ensemble

D. Cichewiecz (cnd)

Coates, G.:Time Frozen *(rec North German Radio Studio 10, Hamburg, Aug 14–25, 1995)* Musicaphon ▲ M 55706 [DDD]
Glanert, D.:Son 2, "Gestalt" *(rec North German Radio Studio 10, Hamburg, Aug 14–25, 1995)* Musicaphon ▲ M 55706 [DDD]
Kelterborn, R.:Ensemble-Buch II, w. Irène Friedli (mez) *(rec North German Radio Studio 10, Hamburg, Aug 14–25, 1995)* Musicaphon ▲ M 55706 [DDD]
Ruzicka, P.:Satyagraha:Approach & Departure *(rec North German Radio Studio 10, Hamburg, Aug 14–25, 1995)* Musicaphon ▲ M 55706 [DDD]

Hamburg PO

Pfitzner, H.:Con Pno, w. Walter Gieseking (pno) Music & Arts ▲ CD 925

G. Albrecht (cnd)

Reger, M.:Orchestral Songs, w. D. Fischer-Dieskau (bar), Monteverdi Choir London, St. Michael's Choir—Der Einsiedler, Op. 144a; Hymnus der Liebe, Op. 136; Requiem, Op. 144b; An die Hoffnung, Op. 124 [G] Orfeo ▲ 209901 [DDD]
Zemlinsky, A. von:Das gläserne Herz Capriccio ▲ 10448 [DDD]
Zemlinsky, A. von:Der König Kandaules (sels), w. F. Grundheber (bar)—Prelude & Gyge's Monologue Capriccio ▲ 10448 [DDD]
Zemlinsky, A. von:Symphonische Gesänge, w. F. Grundheber (bar) Capriccio ▲ 10448 [DDD]

C. Eschenbach (cnd)

Bach, J.S.:Con 1 for 2 Hpds, w. J. Frantz (pno), C. Eschenbach (pno) Deutsche Grammophon ▲ 415655-2 [DDD]
Bach, J.S.:Con 2 for 2 Hpds, w. J. Frantz (pno), C. Eschenbach (pno) Deutsche Grammophon ▲ 415655-2 [DDD]
Bach, J.S.:Con 1 for 3 Hpds, w. J. Frantz (pno), C. Eschenbach (pno), G. Oppitz (pno) Deutsche Grammophon ▲ 415655-2 [DDD]
Bach, J.S.:Con for 4 Hpds, w. J. Frantz (pno), C. Eschenbach (pno), G. Oppitz (pno), H. Schmidt (pno) Deutsche Grammophon ▲ 415655-2 [DDD]

W. Furtwängler (cnd)

Beethoven, L. van:Leonore 2 *(rec Hamburg, June 9, 1947)* Music & Arts 2-▲ CD 869 [ADD]
Strauss, R.:Tod und Verklärung *(rec June 9, 1947)* Music & Arts ▲ CD 829 [AAD]

Hamburg RSO

H.-J. Walther (cnd)

Tchaikovsky, P.:Sleeping Beauty (suite) PWK Classics ▲ PWK 1130 [AAD]
Tchaikovsky, P.:Swan Lake (suite) PWK Classics ▲ PWK 1130 [AAD]

Hamburg Scherbaum Baroque Ensemble

Vivaldi, A.:Con for 2 Tpts, w. A. Scherbaum (tpt), Rudolf Haubold (tpt) Deutsche Grammophon ("Musikfest" series) ▲ 413256-2 ▮ 413256-4

Hamburg State Opera Orch

G. Albrecht (cnd)

Schreker, F.:Der Schatzgräber, w. G. Schnaut (sop), J. Protschka (ten), H. Helm (bar), H. Stamm (bass), Hamburg State Opera Chorus [G] *(rec live 5/89)* Capriccio 2-▲ 60010-2 [DDD]

K. Böhm (cnd)

Strauss, R.:Salome, w. G. Jones (sop), M. Dunn (mez), D. Fischer-Dieskau (bar) *(rec live, 1970)* Deutsche Grammophon 2-▲ 445319-2 [ADD]

S. Gyártó (cnd)

Romberg, S.:The Student Prince (operetta), w. C. Jeffreys (sop), E. Geisen (ten), D. Honig (b-bar), Hamburg State Opera Chorus [G] Bayer ▲ 150004

Hamburg State PO

W. A. Albert (cnd)

Wagner, S.:Glück *(rec Hamburg Music Hall)* CPO ▲ CPO 999 366-2 [DDD]
Wagner, S.:Sehnsucht *(rec Hamburg Music Hall)* CPO ▲ CPO 999 366-2 [DDD]
Wagner, S.:Und wenn die Welt voll Teufel wär *(rec Hamburg Music Hall)* CPO ▲ CPO 999 366-2 [DDD]

G. Albrecht (cnd)

Beethoven, L. van:Egmont (incidental music), w. R. Ziesak (sop), U. Tukur (sgr) [G] Orfeo ▲ 288921 [DDD]
Beethoven, L. van:Leonore 2—Leonore Overture No. 2 Orfeo ▲ 288921 [DDD]
Dessau, P.:Haggada, w. Sabine Ritterbusch (sop), Renate Spingler (sop), Yvi Jänicke (alt), Peter Galliard (ten—Rabbi Tarfon/Jude/ten solo), Gabriel Sadé (ten—Pharaoh), Jochen Schmeckenbechier (bar—Rabbi Jehoschua), Bernd Weikl (bar—Moses), Matthias Hölle (bass—Speaker/Rabbi Akiwa), Alfred Muff (bass—Father/Rabbi Eleasar), Johann Tilli (bass—Rabbi Elieser/bass solo), Berlin Carl Maria Von Weber Men's Choir, Hamburg Alsterspatzen, North German Radio Chorus [G] *(rec Musikhalle, Hamburg, Sept 4 & 5, 1994)* Capriccio 2-▲ 10590/91 [DDD]
Dvořák, A.:The Spectre's Bride, Op. 69, w. L. Aghova (sop), J. Protschka (ten), I. Kusnjer (bar), Prague Phil Chorus [Cz] *(rec live 1991)* Orfeo ▲ 259921 [DDD]
Liebermann, R.:Medea, w. Françoise Pollet (sop—Medea), Yvi Jänicke (cta—Chalkiope), Zdena Furmančoková (sgr—Syrinx), Dagmar Hesse (sgr—Aiglaia), Hanne Krogen (sgr—Kore), Michaela Lucas (sgr—Oinone), Renate Spingler (sgr—Silene), Jochen Kowalski (ct—Kreon), Aage Haugland (bass—Jason), Hamburg State Opera Chorus *(rec live, Hamburg, Germany, Sept 24, 1995)* Musiques Suisses ▲ 6126 [DDD]
Mendelssohn, Fanny:Io d'amor, oh Dio, mi moro, w. H. Kwon (sop) Capriccio ▲ 10449 [DDD]
Mendelssohn, F.:Infelice, w. H. Kwon (sop) Capriccio ▲ 10449 [DDD]
Mendelssohn, F.:Sym 4 Capriccio ▲ 10449 [DDD]
Pettersson, G.A.:Sym 7 CPO ▲ CPO 999190 [ADD]
Pettersson, G.A.:Sym 8 *(rec live, Musikhall, Hamburg, May 16, 1994)* Orfeo ▲ 377941 [DDD]
Schnittke, A.:Historia von D. Johann Fausten, w. Hanna Schwarz (mez—Fair Helen), Arno Raunig (alt—Mephostophiles), Eberhard Büchner (ten—Old Man), Jürgen Freier (bar—Dr. Johann Faustus), Jonathan Barreto-Ramos (sgr—Student), Jürgen Fersch (sgr—Student), Eberhard Lorenz (sgr—Erzähler), Christoph Johannes Wendel (sgr—Student), Hamburg State Opera Chorus *(rec live, Hamburg, Germany)* RCA Red Seal 2-▲ 09026-68413-2
Schumann, R.:Genoveva, w. J. Faulkner (sop—Genoveva), R. Behle (sop—Margaretha), K. Lewis (ten—Golo), A. Titus (bar—Siegfried), H. Stamm (bass—Hidulfus, Caspar), J. Tilli (bass—Balthasar), Hamburg State Opera Chorus [G] *(rec 1992)* Orfeo 2-▲ 289932 [DDD]
Spohr, L.:Jessonda, w. J. Varady (sop), R. Behle (sop), T. Moser (ten), D. Fischer-Dieskau (bar), K. Moll (bass), Hamburg State Opera Chorus [G] Orfeo 2-▲ 240912 [DDD]

L. Ludwig (cnd)

Handel, G.F.:Royal Fireworks Music Allegretto ▲ ACD 8042 [ADD] ▮ ACS 8042

I. Metzmacher (cnd)

Rihm, W.:Die Eroberung von Mexico, w. R. Behle (sop), R. Salter (bar), Hamburg State Opera Chorus [G] *(rec live Feb. 9, 1992)* CPO 2-▲ CPO 999185-2 [DDD]

▲ = CD ♦ = Enhanced CD Δ = MD ▮ = Cassette Tape ☐ = DCC

Hamburg String Quartet
Ruzicka, P.:Chamber Music, w. Matthias Lorenz (vc), Carol Tainton (pno) MD + G ▲ MDG 6250549
Hamburg SO
Kalkbrenner, F.:Con 1 Pno, w. H. Kann (vn), H. Beissel (pno) Preiser ▲ 90167 [ADD]
M. A. (cnd) (cnd)
Woyrsch, F.:Symphonic Prologue to Dante's *Divine Comedy* MD + G ▲ MDG 3010501 [DDD]
Woyrsch, F.:Sym 1 MD + G ▲ MDG 3010501 [DDD]
H. Beissel (cnd)
Chopin, F.:Andante Spianato & Grande Polonaise, w. A. Simon (pno) Vox Box 2-▲ CDX 5002 [ADD]
Chopin, F.:Con 1 Pno, w. A. Simon (pno) Vox Box 2-▲ CDX 5002 [ADD]
Chopin, F.:Con 2 Pno, w. A. Simon (pno) Vox Box 2-▲ CDX 5002 [ADD]
Chopin, F.:Grand Fant on Polish Airs, w. A. Simon (pno) Vox Box 2-▲ CDX 5002 [ADD]
Chopin, F.:Krakowiak, w. A. Simon (pno) Vox Box 2-▲ CDX 5002 [ADD]
Chopin, F.:Vars on Mozart's *La ci darem la mano*, w. A. Simon (pno) Vox Box 2-▲ CDX 5002 [ADD]
Hummel, J.N.:Con Pno, Op. 110, w. H. Kann (pno) *(rec 1973)* Vox Box 2-▲ CDX 5064 [ADD]
Kalkbrenner, F.:Con 1 Pno, w. H. Kann (pno) *(rec 1973)* Vox Box 2-▲ CDX 5064 [ADD]
H. Drewanz (cnd)
Scriabin, A.:Con Pno, w. M. Ponti (pno) Allegretto ▲ ACD 8170 [ADD] ■ ACS 8170
A. Grüber (cnd)
Lutoslawski, W.:Trauermusik Vox Box 2-▲ CDX 5133
Schreker, F.:Der Geburtstag der Infantin *(rec ca. 1973)* Vox Box 2-▲ CDX 5043 [ADD]
R. Kapp (cnd)
Raff, J.:Con Pno, w. M. Ponti (pno) *(rec 1973)* Vox Box 2-▲ CDX 5067 [ADD]
Rimsky-Korsakov, N.:Con Pno, w. M. Ponti (pno) Vox Box 2-▲ CDX 5082 [ADD]
C. Schuricht (cnd)
Beethoven, L. van:Missa Solemnis, w. M. Stader (sop), E. Cavalti (mez), E. Haefliger (ten), H. Rehfuss (bass), St. Hedwig's Cathedral Choir *(rec Sept. 15, 1957)* Archipon 2-▲ ARCH 2.1CD (m) [ADD]
A. Springer (cnd)
Mendelssohn, F.:Ovs—Hebrides; The Fair Melusine; Calm Sea & Prosperous Voyage Allegretto ▲ ACD 8145 [ADD] ■ ACS 8145
Tchaikovsky, P.:Serenade Strs Vox Box 3-▲ CD3X 3024 [ADD]
Hamilton College Orch
M. Matsuo (cnd)
Matsuo, M.:Hirai V, w. E. Michael Richards (cl), Kazuko Tanosaki (pno) Opus One ▲ CD 156
Hamilton PO
B. Brott (cnd)
Gershwin, G.:Porgy & Bess (suite), "Catfish Row Suite" CBC ("SM 5000" series) ▲ SMCD 5111 [DDD]
Gershwin, G.:Rhap in Blue, w. W. Tritt (pno) CBC ("SM 5000" series) ▲ SMCD 5111 [DDD]
Gershwin, G.:Second Rhap, w. W. Tritt (pno) CBC ("SM 5000" series) ▲ SMCD 5111 [DDD]
Hammersmith Lyric Theater Orch
A. Reynolds (cnd)
Dibdin, C.:Lionel & Clarissa (sels), w. O. Groves (sgr), W. Temple (sgr) *(rec 1925 for HMV)* Pearl ▲ PEA 9917 (m) [AAD]
Hampton String Quartet
Carol of the Drum, w. Chieftains, Emily Mitchell (hp), Richard Stoltzman (cl), Michala Petri (rcr), James Galway (fl), Royal PO, Boys' Choir of Harlem RCA Victor ▲ 09026-61839-2 ■ 09026-61839-4
What If Mozart Wrote Born to Be Wild RCA Red Seal ▲ 7803-2-RC [DDD] ■ 7803-4-RC (CrO2)
What If Mozart Wrote I Saw Mommy Kissing Santa Claus RCA Victor ▲ 60120-2-RC [DDD] ■ 60120-4-RC (CrO2)
What If Mozart Wrote Roll over Beethoven RCA Red Seal ▲ 6675-2-RC [DDD] ■ 6675-4-RC9
Hampton-Schwartz Duo [Bonnie Hampton (vc), Nathan Schwartz (pno)]
Armer, E.:Recollections & Revel Music & Arts ▲ CD 903 [DDD]
Hindemith, P.:Son Vc & Pno, Op. 11/3 Music & Arts ▲ CD 903 [DDD]
Milhaud, D.:Son Vc Music & Arts ▲ CD 903 [DDD]
Shifrin, S.:Son Vc Music & Arts ▲ CD 903 [DDD]
Turok, P.:Son Vc Music & Arts ▲ CD 903 [DDD]
Handel & Haydn Society Orch
C. Hogwood (cnd)
Handel, G.F.:Concerti grossi, Op. 3 L'Oiseau-Lyre ▲ 421729-2 [DDD]
Handel, G.F.:Concerti grossi, Op. 6 L'Oiseau-Lyre ▲ 436845-2 [DDD]
Händel Collegium
N. Schutze (cnd)
Schultze, N.:Das kalte Herz, w. Grit van Jüten (sop), Elisabeth Steiner (mez), Heinz Kruse (ten), Detelf Zywietz (sgr), Cologne RSO Koch Schwann 2-▲ SCH 318002 [DDD]
Handel Festival Orch
Live at the Crystal Palace, w. National Brass Band Festival Massed Bands, Festival of English Church Music Massed Choir, Handel Festival Choir, National Union of School Orch, Salvation Army Congress Massed Bands, Non-Conformist Union Festival Choir Beulah ▲ 1 PD 1
A. Dorati (cnd)
Handel, G.F.:Messiah (sels) Pro Arte ▲ CDD 283
G. Simon (cnd)
Handel, G.F.:Choruses, w. Howard Univ Chorus—choruses from 12 oratorios [E] Arabesque ▲ Z 6538 [DDD]
Hannaford Street Silver Band
Holst, G.:A Moorside Suite CBC ("SM 5000" series) ▲ SMCD 5103 [DDD] ■ SMC 5103 (D)
Vaughan Williams, R.:English Folk Song Suite CBC ("SM 5000" series) ▲ SMCD 5103 [DDD] ■ SMC 5103 (D)
S. Chenette (cnd)
Canadian Impressions, w. Curtis Metcalf CBC Records ("SM 5000" series) ▲ SMCD 5136 [DDD]
The Hannaford Street Silver Band CBC Records ("SM 5000" series) ▲ SMCD 5103 [DDD] ■ SMC 5103 (D)
Hanover Band
Beethoven, L. van:Con 1 Pno, w. M. Verney (pno) Nimbus ▲ Ni 5003
Beethoven, L. van:Con 3 Pno, w. M. Verney (pno) [period instrs] Nimbus ▲ NI 5031 [DDD]
Beethoven, L. van:Die Geschöpfe des Prometheus (ov) [period instrs] Nimbus ▲ NI 5007
S. Darlington (cnd)
Vivaldi, A.:Gloria (& Intro), RV.588, w. P. Kwella (sop), E. Priday (sop), C. Wyn-Rogers (alt), A. Carwood (ten), Christ Church Cathedral Choir Oxford Nimbus ▲ NI 5278 [DDD]
Vivaldi, A.:Gloria, RV.589, w. P. Kwella (sop), E. Priday (sop), C. Wyn-Rogers (alt), A. Carwood (ten), Christ Church Cathedral Choir Oxford Nimbus ▲ NI 5278 [DDD]
R. Goodman (cnd)
Bach, J.S.:Cant 54, w. Nathalie Stutzmann (cta), Roy Goodman (vn) *(rec Watford Town Hall, Hertfordshire, U.K, Jan 31–Feb 3, 1994)* RCA Red Seal ▲ 09026-62655-2 [DDD]
Bach, J.S.:Cant 82, w. Nathalie Stutzmann (cta), Anthony Robson (ob), Roy Goodman (org) *(rec Watford Town Hall, Hertfordshire, U.K, Jan 31–Feb 3, 1994)* RCA Red Seal ▲ 09026-62655-2 [DDD]
Bach, J.S.:Cant 170, w. Nathalie Stutzmann (cta), Anthony Robson (ob), Roy Goodman (org), Alistair Ross (org) *(rec Watford Town Hall, Hertfordshire, U.K, Jan 31–Feb 3, 1994)* RCA Red Seal ▲ 09026-62655-2 [DDD]
Beethoven & the Philharmonic Nimbus 2-▲ NI 5138/39 [DDD]
Beethoven, L. van:Con Vn, Op. 61, w. S. Chase (vn) [period instrs] *(rec Blackheath Concert Halls, London, Feb 27-29, 1992)* Cala ▲ CACD 1013 [DDD]
Beethoven, L. van:Coriolan Ov [period instrs] Nimbus ▲ NI 5122 [DDD]
Beethoven, L. van:Egmont (ov) [period instrs] Nimbus ▲ NI 5007
Beethoven, L. van:Egmont (ov) [period instrs] Nimbus ▲ NI 1404 [DDD]
Beethoven, L. van:Fidelio (ov) [period instrs] Nimbus ▲ NI 5149 [DDD]
Beethoven, L. van:Die Geschöpfe des Prometheus (ov) [period instrs] Nimbus ▲ NI 1404 [DDD]
Beethoven, L. van:König Stephen (ov) [period instrs] Nimbus ▲ NI 5130 [DDD]
Beethoven, L. van:Leonore 2 [period instrs] Nimbus ▲ NI 5149 [DDD]

Hanover Band (cont.)
R. Goodman (cnd) (cont.)
Beethoven, L. van:Romances Vn, w. S. Chase (vn) [period instrs] *(rec Blackheath Concert Halls, London, Feb 27-29, 1992)* Cala ▲ CACD 1013 [DDD]
Beethoven, L. van:Die Ruinen von Athen (ov) [period instrs] Nimbus ▲ NI 5130 [DDD]
Beethoven, L. van:Syms (comp), w. R. Goodman [period instrs] Nimbus 5-▲ NI 5144/48 [DDD]
Beethoven, L. van:Sym 1 [period instrs] Nimbus ▲ NI 5003
Beethoven, L. van:Sym 2 [period instrs] Nimbus ▲ NI 5031 [DDD]
Beethoven, L. van:Sym 3, "Eroica" *(rec London, Nov. 23–24, 1987)* Nimbus ▲ NI 7018 [DDD]
Beethoven, L. van:Sym 3, "Eroica" [period instrs] Nimbus ▲ NI 5122 [DDD]
Beethoven, L. van:Sym 4 *(rec London, Feb. 9, 1988)* Nimbus ▲ NI 7018 [DDD]
Beethoven, L. van:Sym 4 [period instrs] Nimbus ▲ NI 5130 [DDD]
Beethoven, L. van:Sym 5 [period instrs] Nimbus ▲ NI 5007
Beethoven, L. van:Sym 6, "Pastorale" Nimbus ▲ NI 5099 [DDD]
Beethoven, L. van:Sym 7 [period instrs] Nimbus ▲ NI 5149 [DDD]
Beethoven, L. van:Sym 8 [period instrs] Nimbus ▲ NI 5130 [DDD]
Beethoven, L. van:Sym 9, "Choral Sym", w. Oslo Cathedral Choir [period instrs] [G] Nimbus ▲ NI 5134 [DDD]
Beethoven, L. van:Die Weihe des Hauses (ov) [period instrs] Nimbus ▲ NI 1404 [DDD]
Beethoven, L. van:Die Weihe des Hauses (ov) [period instrs] Nimbus ▲ NI 5099 [DDD]
Chopin, F.:Con 1 Pno, w. C. Kite (pno) *(rec 5/90)* Nimbus ▲ NI 5291 [DDD]
Handel, G.F.:Arias, w. N. Stutzmann (cta)—arias from Aci, Galatea e Polifemo, Floridante, Giulio Cesare in Egitto, Orlando, Partenope, Radamisto, Rinaldo [I] RCA Red Seal ▲ 09026-61205-2
Haydn, J.:Con 1 Hn, w. Anthony Halstead (hn) Nimbus ▲ NI 5190 [DDD]
Haydn, J.:Con 1 Hn, w. Anthony Halstead (hn) Nimbus 3-▲ NI 1789
Haydn, J.:Ovs *(rec Windsor Castle)* Hyperion ▲ CDA 66528
Haydn, J.:Ov to Salomon's opera *Windsor Castle* Hyperion ▲ CDA 66528
Haydn, J.:Syms (comp)—Nos. 82–84 Hyperion ▲ CDA 66527
Haydn, J.:Syms (comp)—Nos. 48–50 Hyperion ▲ CDA 66531
Haydn, J.:Syms (comp)—Nos. 45–47 Hyperion ▲ CDA 66522
Haydn, J.:Syms (comp)—Syms. 85, 86 & 87 Hyperion ▲ CDA 66535
Haydn, J.:Syms (comp)—Nos. 90–92 Hyperion ▲ CDA 66521
Haydn, J.:Syms (comp)—Nos. 6–8 Hyperion ▲ CDA 66523
Haydn, J.:Syms (comp)—Symphonies Nos. 70–72 Hyperion ▲ CDA 66526
Haydn, J.:Syms (comp)—Nos. 9–12 Hyperion ▲ CDA 66529
Haydn, J.:Syms (comp)—Nos. 42–44 Hyperion ▲ CDA 66530
Haydn, J.:Syms (comp)—Nos. 1–5 Hyperion ▲ CDA 66524
Haydn, J.:Syms (comp)—Nos. 76–78 Hyperion ▲ CDA 66525
Haydn, J.:Syms (comp)—Nos. 101 & 102 Hyperion ▲ CDA 66528
Haydn, J.:Syms (comp)—Symphonies Nos. 73–75 Hyperion ▲ CDA 66520
Haydn, J.:Sym 13 Hyperion ▲ CDA 66534
Haydn, J.:Sym 14 Hyperion ▲ CDA 66534
Haydn, J.:Sym 15 Hyperion ▲ CDA 66534
Haydn, J.:Sym 16 Hyperion ▲ CDA 66534
Haydn, J.:Sym 22, "Der Philosoph" Hyperion ("Haydn Edition" series) ▲ CDA 66536
Haydn, J.:Sym 23 Hyperion ("Haydn Edition" series) ▲ CDA 66536
Haydn, J.:Sym 24 Hyperion ("Haydn Edition" series) ▲ CDA 66536
Haydn, J.:Sym 25 Hyperion ("Haydn Edition" series) ▲ CDA 66536
Haydn, J.:Sym 31, "Hornsignal" Nimbus 3-▲ NI 1789
Haydn, J.:Sym 31, "Hornsignal" Nimbus ▲ NI 5190 [DDD]
Haydn, J.:Sym 93 Hyperion ▲ CDA 66532
Haydn, J.:Sym 94, "Surprise Sym" Nimbus 3-▲ NI 1789
Haydn, J.:Sym 94, "Surprise Sym" Hyperion ▲ CDA 66532
Haydn, J.:Sym 94, "Surprise Sym" [period instrs] Nimbus ▲ NI 5126 [DDD]
Haydn, J.:Sym 94, "Surprise Sym" *(rec All Saints', Tooting, Dec. 8-9, 1987)* Nimbus ▲ NI 7024 [DDD]
Haydn, J.:Sym 95 [period instrs] Nimbus ▲ NI 5126 [DDD]
Haydn, J.:Sym 95 Hyperion ▲ CDA 66532
Haydn, J.:Sym 95 Nimbus 3-▲ NI 1789
Haydn, J.:Sym 100, "Military" *(rec All Saints', Tooting, Dec. 8–9, 1987)* Nimbus ▲ NI 7024 [DDD]
Haydn, J.:Sym 100, "Military" Nimbus 3-▲ NI 1789
Haydn, J.:Sym 101, "Clock" Hyperion ▲ CDA 66528
Haydn, J.:Sym 102 Hyperion ▲ CDA 66528
Haydn, J.:Sym 104, "London" *(rec All Saints', Tooting, Dec. 8-9, 1987)* Nimbus ▲ NI 7024 [DDD]
Haydn, J.:Sym 104, "London" [period instrs] Nimbus ▲ NI 5096 [DDD]
Haydn, J.:Sym 104, "London" Nimbus 3-▲ NI 1789
Haydn, M.:Con 2 Hn, w. A. Halstead (nat hn) Nimbus ▲ NI 5190 [DDD]
Haydn, M.:Con 2 Hn, w. Anthony Halstead (hn) Nimbus 3-▲ NI 1789
Martinů, B.:Sym 1 [period instrs] RCA Red Seal 2-▲ 09026-61931-2
Martinů, B.:Sym 2 [period instrs] RCA Red Seal 2-▲ 09026-61931-2
Martinů, B.:Sym 3 [period instrs] RCA Red Seal 2-▲ 09026-61931-2
Martinů, B.:Sym 4 [period instrs] RCA Red Seal 2-▲ 09026-61931-2
Mendelssohn, F.:Con 1 Pno, w. C. Kite (pno) Nimbus ▲ NI 5158 [DDD]
Mendelssohn, F.:Con in e Vn & Orch, Op. 64, w. B. Hudson (vn) Nimbus ▲ NI 5158 [DDD]
Mendelssohn, F.:Die Hebriden Nimbus ▲ NI 5318 [DDD]
Mendelssohn, F.:Meeresstille Nimbus ▲ NI 5318 [DDD]
Mendelssohn, F.:Sinfs Strs [includes fragment known as No. 13] *(rec Rosslyn Hill Chapel, London, Nov 18–20, 1992 & Mar 1–3)* RCA Red Seal 3-▲ 09026-68069-2 [DDD]
Mendelssohn, F.:Sym 3 Nimbus ▲ NI 5318 [DDD]
Mendelssohn, F.:Sym 4 Nimbus ▲ NI 5158 [DDD]
Mozart, L.:Toy Sym Nimbus ▲ NI 1789
Mozart, L.:Toy Sym [period instrs] Nimbus ▲ NI 5126 [DDD]
Mozart, W.A.:Con Cl, w. C. Lawson (b cl) [period instrs] Nimbus ▲ NI 5228-2 [DDD]
Mozart, W.A.:Con Cl, w. C. Lawson (b cl) [period instrs] Nimbus 4-▲ NI 1791 [DDD]
Mozart, W.A.:Con Cl, w. Colin Lawson (cl) *(rec All Saints', Tooting, London, Dec. 1989)* Nimbus ▲ NI 7023 [DDD]
Mozart, W.A.:Cons Hn, w. A. Halstead (hn) [period instrs] Nimbus 4-▲ NI 1791 [DDD]
Mozart, W.A.:Cons Hn, w. A. Halstead (hn) [period instrs] Nimbus ▲ NI 5104 [DDD]
Mozart, W.A.:Con Hn, K.495, w. Anthony Halstead (hn) *(rec All Saints', Tooting, London, July 1987)* Nimbus ▲ NI 7023 [DDD]
Mozart, W.A.:Con Movt Hn, K.494a, w. A. Halstead (hn) [period instruments] Nimbus ▲ NI 5104 [DDD]
Mozart, W.A.:Con Movt Hn, K.494a, w. A. Halstead (hn) [period instrs] Nimbus 4-▲ NI 1791 [DDD]
Mozart, W.A.:Con 20 Pno, w. C. Kite (pno) [period instrs] Nimbus ▲ NI 5259 [DDD]
Mozart, W.A.:Con 20 Pno, w. C. Kite (pno) [period instrs] Nimbus 4-▲ NI 1791 [DDD]
Mozart, W.A.:Con 3 Vn, w. S. Chase (vn) [period instrs] *(rec Blackheath Concert Halls, London, May 18–20, 1992)* Cala 2-▲ CACD 1014 [DDD]
Mozart, W.A.:Con 5 Vn, w. S. Chase (vn) [period instrs] *(rec Blackheath Concert Halls, London, May 18–20, 1992)* Cala 2-▲ CACD 1014 [DDD]
Mozart, W.A.:Kleine Nachtmusik [period instrs] Nimbus ▲ NI 5228-2 [DDD]
Mozart, W.A.:Kleine Nachtmusik [period instrs] Nimbus 4-▲ NI 1791 [DDD]
Mozart, W.A.:Kleine Nachtmusik *(rec All Saints', Tooting, London, Dec. 1989)* Nimbus ▲ NI 7023 [DDD]
Mozart, W.A.:Music of, w. Gundula Janowitz (sop), Julia Bernheimer (mez), Martyn Hill (ten), David Thomas (bass), Anthony Halstead (hn), Colin Lawson (b cl), Christopher Kite (pno)—Cons for Hn, K.412, 417, 447, 494a & 495; Sym No. 40; Con for Cl; Eine kleine Nachtmusik; Requiem; Sym No. 41; Con No. 20 for Pno; Serenata Notturna Nimbus 4-▲ NI 1791 [DDD]
Mozart, W.A.:Requiem, w. G. Janowitz (sop), J. Bernheimer (mez), M. Hill (ten), D. Thomas (bass), Hanover Chorus [period instruments; H.C. Robbins Landon edition] Nimbus 4-▲ NI 1791 [DDD]

ORCH. & ENS.

Hanover Band (cont.)
R. Goodman (cnd) (cont.)
Mozart, W.A.:Requiem, w. G. Janowitz (sop), J. Bernheimer (mez), M. Hill (ten), D. Thomas (bass), Hanover Chorus [period instruments; H.C. Robbins Landon's edition; L] Nimbus ▲ NI 5241-2 [DDD]
Mozart, W.A.:Serenata notturna [period instrs] Nimbus ▲ NI 5259 [DDD]
Mozart, W.A.:Serenata notturna [period instrs] Nimbus 4-▲ NI 1791 [DDD]
Mozart, W.A.:Sinf concertante Vn, K.364, w. S. Chase (vn), R. Chase (va) [period instrs] *(rec Blackheath Concert Halls, London, May 18-20, 1992)* Cala 2-▲ CACD 1014 [DDD]
Mozart, W.A.:Sym 40 [period instrs] Nimbus ▲ 35228-2 [DDD]
Mozart, W.A.:Sym 40 [period instrs] Nimbus 4-▲ NI 1791 [DDD]
Mozart, W.A.:Sym 41 [period instrs] Nimbus ▲ NI 5259 [DDD]
Mozart, W.A.:Sym 41 [period instrs] Nimbus 4-▲ NI 1791 [DDD]
Pergolesi, w. Nathalie Stutzmann (cta), Elizabeth Norberg-Schulz (sop) RCA Red Seal ▲ 09026-61215-2
Rossini, G.:Ovs—La Scala di seta; L'Italiana in Algeri; Il Barbiere di Sivigla; La Gazza ladra; Semiramide; Le Siège de Corinth; Guillaume Tell; [period instr] *(rec Abbey Road Studios, London, Nov 6-8, 1994)* RCA Red Seal ▲ 09026-68139-2 [DDD]
Schubert, Franz:Ovs—Overture in C "In the Italian Style," D.591 Nimbus ▲ NI 5172 [DDD]
Schubert, Franz:Ovs—Overture in D, "In The Italian Style" Nimbus ▲ NI 5198 [DDD]
Schubert, Franz:Rosamunde [period instrs] Nimbus ▲ NI 5274 [DDD]
Schubert, Franz:Syms (comp) [period instrs] Nimbus 4-▲ NI 5270/73 [DDD]
Schubert, Franz:Sym 1 [period instrs] Nimbus ▲ NI 5198 [DDD]
Schubert, Franz:Sym 2 [period instrs] Nimbus ▲ NI 5252 [DDD]
Schubert, Franz:Sym 3 Nimbus ▲ NI 5172 [DDD]
Schubert, Franz:Sym 4 [period instrs] Nimbus ▲ NI 5198 [DDD]
Schubert, Franz:Sym 6 [period instrs] Nimbus ▲ NI 5252 [DDD]
Schubert, Franz:Sym 8 [period instrs] Nimbus ▲ NI 5274 [DDD]
Schubert, Franz:Sym 9 [period instrs] Nimbus ▲ NI 5222 [DDD]
Weber, C.M. von:Concertino Hn, w. A. Halstead (nat hn) [period instrs] Nimbus ▲ NI 5180 [DDD]
Weber, C.M. von:Invitation to the Dance Orch Nimbus ▲ NI 5154 [DDD]
Weber, C.M. von:Konzertstück Pno, w. C. Kite (pno) *(rec 5/90)* Nimbus ▲ NI 5291 [DDD]
Weber, C.M. von:Ovs [period instrs]—Peter Schmoll; Oberon; Euryanthe; Abu Hassan; Der Freischütz; Ruler of the Spirits Nimbus ▲ NI 5154 [DDD]
Weber, C.M. von:Sym 1 [period instrs] Nimbus ▲ NI 5180 [DDD]
Weber, C.M. von:Sym 2 [period instrs] Nimbus ▲ NI 5180 [DDD]

A. Halstead (cnd)
Abel, C.F.:Syms, Op. 10 CPO ▲ CPO 999214 [DDD]
Bach, Joh. Christian:Con Bn, w. Jeremy Ward (bn) *(rec Rosslyn Hill Chapel, London, Mar-Apr 1995)* CPO ▲ CPO 999347-2 [DDD]
Bach, Joh. Christian:Con 2 Fl, w. Rachel Brown (fl) *(rec Rosslyn Hill Chapel, London, Mar-Apr 1995)* CPO ▲ CPO 999347-2 [DDD]
Bach, Joh. Christian:Cons Hpd, T.292/1, w. Anthony Halstead (hpd) CPO ▲ CPO 999299
Bach, Joh. Christian:Con 2 Ob, w. Anthony Robson (ob) *(rec Rosslyn Hill Chapel, London, Mar-Apr 1995)* CPO ▲ CPO 999347-2 [DDD]
Bach, Joh. Christian:Ovs—to the operas Artaserse; Gli Uccellatori; Alessandro nell'Indie; La Giulia; Il Tutore e la pupilla; Catone in Utica; La Cascina; La Calamita de cuori CPO ▲ CPO 999129 [DDD]
Bach, Joh. Christian:Sinf concertante, T.284/1, w. Graham Cracknell (vn), Anna McDonald (vn), Angela East (vc) *(rec Rosslyn Hill Chapel, London, Dec 1995)* CPO ▲ CPO 999348-2 [DDD]
Bach, Joh. Christian:Sinf concertante, T.284/6, w. Graham Cracknell (vn), Anna McDonald (vn), Anthony Robson (ob) *(rec Rosslyn Hill Chapel, London, Dec 1995)* CPO ▲ CPO 999348-2 [DDD]
Bach, Joh. Christian:Sinf concertante, T.288/4, w. Graham Cracknell (vn), Anna McDonald (vn), Angela East (vc) *(rec Rosslyn Hill Chapel, London, Dec 1995)* CPO ▲ CPO 999348-2 [DDD]
Bach, Joh. Christian:Sinfs Obs, Op. 3 CPO ▲ CPO 999268 [DDD]
Bach, Joh. Christian:Sinfs, Op. 6 CPO ▲ CPO 999298 [DDD]
Vivaldi, A.:Cons Diverse Instrs, w. Anthony Halstead (hpd/org)—for Ob, RV.463; for Strs & Bc, RV.129 & 156; for Vn, RV.308; for Fl, RV.439; for 4 Vns & Vc, RV.580 Classics for Pleasure ("Eminence" series) ▲ CDEMX 2210 [DDD]

E. Higginbottom (cnd)
Mozart, W.A.:Litaniae Lauretanae, K.195, w. New College Choir Oxford *(rec July 1992)* K617 ▲ 7028 [DDD]
Mozart, W.A.:Vesperae de Dominica, w. New College Choir Oxford *(rec July 1992)* K617 ▲ 7028 [DDD]

T. Kvam (cnd)
Beethoven, L. van:Missa Solemnis, w. M. Hirsti (sop), C. Watkinson (cta), A. Murgatroyd (ten), M. George (bass), Oslo Cathedral Choir [period instrs] [L] Nimbus ▲ NI 5109 [DDD]

Hanover Chamber Academy
Wegrzyn (cnd)
Haydn, M.:Missa Sancti Aloysii, w. Erdmann (sgr), Pieweck (sgr) Ars Musici ▲ 1113

Hanover CO
H. Hennig (cnd)
Vierne, L.:Messe solennelle, w. C. Guber (mez), P. Sefcik (bar), T. Götting (org), Hanover Youth Choir Ars Musici ▲ AM 1098-2 [DDD]

Hanover North German Radio PO
W.A. Albert (cnd)
Goetz, H.:Con 1 Pno, w. Volker Banfield (pno) CPO ▲ CPO 999098 [DDD]
Goetz, H.:Con 2 Pno, w. Volker Banfield (pno) CPO ▲ CPO 999098 [DDD]

P. Kogan (cnd)
Tchaikovsky, P.:Con Vn, w. Robert Chen (vn) Berlin Classics ▲ BER 1169
Tchaikovsky, P.:Sérénade mélancolique, w. Robert Chen (vn) Berlin Classics ▲ BER 1169
Tchaikovsky, P.:Souvenir d'un lieu cher, w. Robert Chen (vn) Berlin Classics ▲ BER 1169

G. Schuller (cnd)
Schuller, G.:Of Reminiscences & Reflections *(rec North German Radio Studio, Hannover, Germany, Nov. 21-22, 1994)* New World ▲ 80492-2
Schuller, G.:The Past is the Present *(rec North German Radio Studio, Hannover, Germany, Nov. 21-22, 1994)* New World ▲ 80492-2

T. Ukigaya (cnd)
Krenek, E.:Sym 2 CPO ▲ CPO 999255

Hanover North German Radio SO
M. Tabachnik (cnd)
Tabachnik, M.:Cosmogonie pour une Rose *(rec Jan. 31, 1983)* Grammont ▲ CTSP 26-2 [ADD]

Hanover Radio PO
B. Klee (cnd)
Killmayer, W.:Songs, w. Peter Schreier (ten) Wergo 2-▲ WER 6245 2

T. Ukigaya (cnd)
Krenek, E.:Sym 1 CPO ▲ CPO 999359
Krenek, E.:Sym 5 CPO ▲ CPO 999359

Harmonia Ensemble
Lambert, C.:Con Pno, w. G. Grazioli (pno) *(rec 1/89)* Giulia ▲ GS 201009 [DDD]

D. Bouture (cnd)
Bartók, B.:Divert Koch Schwann ▲ SCH 313602 [DDD]
Bartók, B.:For Children—10 pieces [arr. for strings] Koch Schwann ▲ SCH 313602 [DDD]
Lajtha, L.:Sinfonietta Koch Schwann ▲ SCH 313602 [DDD]

G. Grazioli (cnd)
Bax, A.:Nonet Fl *(rec 1/89)* Giulia ▲ GS 201009 [DDD]
Rieti, V.:Serenata Vn, w. C. Feige (vn) Giulia ▲ GS 201009 [DDD]

Harmonia Ensemble [Orio Odori (cl), Damiano Puliti (vc), Alessandra Garosi (pno)]
Rota, N.:Film Music—Buongiorno Nino; Amarcord; The Godfather; 8 1/2; Nightwalker; Il Valzer del Gattopardo; Pavana; In Fine; Rocco e I Suoi Fratelli; Cantilena; La passerella di 8 1/2; La strada Iris ▲ 015 [DDD]

Harmonia Nova Orch
J.-P. Wallez (cnd)
Loussier, J.:Lumières, w. Déborah Rees (sop), James Bowman (ct), André Arpino (perc), Patrick Marco Vocal Ensemble *(rec Studio de Miraval, 1957)* Media 7 ▲ CD 707 [DDD]

Harmonia Nova Orch Ensemble
D. Bouture (cnd)
Bach, J.S.:Suite 1 Orch *(rec Feb 1988)* Gallo ▲ CD 542 [DDD]
Lalande, M.-R. de:Syms des Noël—No.1 *(rec Feb. 1988)* Gallo ▲ CD 542 [DDD]
Mozart, W.A.:Adagio & Fugue Strs *(rec Feb. 1988)* Gallo ▲ CD 542 [DDD]
Purcell, H.:Abdelazer, or The Moor's Revenge *(rec Feb. 1988)* Gallo ▲ CD 542 [DDD]

F. Bouture (cnd)
Vivaldi, A.:Sinf, RV.169 *(rec Feb. 1988)* Gallo ▲ CD 542 [DDD]

Landowski, Tzipine (cnd)
Landowski, M.:Music of, w. Nadine Sautereau (sop), Jean-Christophe Benoit (bar), Xavier Depraz (bass), Michel Bouquet (spkr), Gilbert Audin (bn), Evelyne Aïello, Didier Bouture, Ludovic Chevalier, Laurent Decker, Françoise Deslogères, Colonne Association des Concerts Orch, Boulogne-Billancourt Orch Conservatory, Paris Conservatory Société des Concerts Orch, L'Itinéraire Ensemble—Con Bn; Con pour ondes Martenot; Femme sans passé; Hauts de Hurlevent; Horologe; Mouvement; Notes de Nuit; Souvenir d'un jardin d'enfance; Ventriloque Chamade 3-▲ 5639/40/41 [AAD/DDD]

M. Piquemal (cnd)
Schubert, Franz:Mass 2, w. M. Pares-Reyna (sop), Fletcher (sgr), P. Fourcade (bass), Michel Piquemal Vocal Ensemble [L] Gallo ▲ CD 584 [DDD]
Schubert, Franz:Mass 4, w. M. Pares-Reyna (sop), N. Stutzmann (alt), Fletcher (ten), P. Fourcade (bass), Michel Piquemal Vocal Ensemble [L] Gallo ▲ CD 584 [DDD]
Schubert, Franz:Tantum ergo, D.739, w. Michel Piquemal Vocal Ensemble [L] Gallo ▲ CD 584 [DDD]

Harmonie Ensemble/New York
Salute to France Music & Arts ▲ MUA 649 [DDD]

S. Richman (cnd)
Beethoven, L. van:Fidelio (ov) Music & Arts ▲ CD 797 [DDD]
Dvořák, A.:Serenade Strs [arr Nicholas Ingman for cl, bn, 2 vn, va, bass & pno per Dvořák's original instrumentation] *(rec Madison Avenue Presbyterian Church, NYC, Feb 27, 1994)* Music & Arts ▲ MUA CD 926
Dvořák, A.:Serenade Ww Music & Arts ▲ CD 691-1 [DDD]
Dvořák, A.:Slavonic Dances (sels) [wind arr. Clements of Op. 72, No. 7 Music & Arts ▲ CD 691-1 [DDD]
Foster, S.C.:Old Folks at Home, w. Arthur Woodley (b-bar), Collegiate Chorale [arr Dvořák 1894] Music & Arts ▲ MUA CD 926
Hahn, R.:Le Bal de Béatrice d'Este Music & Arts ▲ CD 649 [DDD]
Ibert, J.:Con Vc, w. J. Kreger (vc) Music & Arts ▲ CD 649 [DDD]
Ibert, J.:Suite symphonique, "Paris" Music & Arts ▲ CD 649 [DDD]
Krommer, F.:Con for 2 Hns, w. S. Brubaker (hn), C. Kavalovski (hn) Music & Arts ▲ CD 691-1 [DDD]
Milhaud, D.:Chamber Sym 5 Music & Arts ▲ CD 649 [DDD]
Mozart, W.A.:Ovs—Entfürung aus dem Serail Music & Arts ▲ CD 797 [DDD]
Mysliveček, J.:Octet 2 Ww Music & Arts ▲ CD 691-1 [DDD]
Poulenc, F.:Aubade Pno, w. R. Votapek (pno) Music & Arts ▲ CD 649 [DDD]
Rossini, G.:Ovs—Il barbiere di Siviglia; Guilaume Tell; Semiramide Music & Arts ▲ CD 797 [DDD]
Weber, C.M. von:Ovs—Der Freischütz Music & Arts ▲ CD 797 [DDD]

W. Traphagan (cnd)
Rossini, G.:Zelmira (sels) [trans for wind octet & db] *(rec Houghton Memorial Chapel, Wellesley College, Wellesley, MA, July 11, 18 & 19, 1994)* Titanic ▲ TI 224

Harp Consort
A. Lawrence-King (cnd)
Purcell, H.:Musick's Hand-maid, w. Ellen Hargis (sop), Ian Honeyman (ten), Rodrigo del Pozo (ten), Harry van der Kamp (bass), Paul O'Dette (thb/cittern/lt), Andrew Lawrence-King (hps/org/hpd) Astrée ▲ E 8564
Ruiz de Ribayaz, L.:Luz Y norte, w. Andrew Lawrence-King (hp/psaltery/org/hpd)—Spanish Dances *(rec Valkkoog, Sept 1994)* Deutsche Harmonia Mundi ▲ 05472-77340-2 [DDD]

Harrington String Quartet
Bresnick, M.:Qt 3 Strs *(rec Canyon, TX, May 21, 1994)* CRI ▲ CD 682 [DDD]

Hartford CO
F. Mahler (cnd)
Purcell, H.:Abdelazer, or The Moor's Revenge *(rec 1960)* Vanguard Classics ▲ OVC 4044 [ADD]
Purcell, H.:The Gordian Knot Unty'd *(rec 1960)* Vanguard Classics ▲ OVC 4044 [ADD]
Purcell, H.:The Married Beau, or The Curious Impertinent *(rec 1960)* Vanguard Classics ▲ OVC 4044 [ADD]
Purcell, H.:The Virtuous Wife, or Good Luck at Last *(rec 1960)* Vanguard Classics ▲ OVC 4044 [ADD]

Hartford Opera Orch
A. Guadagno (cnd)
Verdi, G.:Don Carlos, w. R. Kabaivanska (sop), O. Dominguez (mez), F. Corelli (ten), L. Quilico (bar), N. Ghiaurov (bass), N. Ghiuselev (bass) *(rec live 1966)* Melodram 2-▲ MEL 27511

Hartford SO
F. Mahler (cnd)
Bloch, E.:Jewish Poems *(rec 1960)* Vanguard Classics ▲ OVC 4046 [ADD]

Hartley Piano Trio [Caroline Clemmow (pno), Jacqueline Hartley (vn), Lionel Handy (vc)]
Beach, A.M.C.:Trio Pno Gamut Classics ▲ GAM 536 [DDD]
Beethoven, L. van:Sym 2 [trans. for piano trio] Gamut ▲ GAM 542 [DDD]
Beethoven, L. van:Trio 5 Pno Gamut ▲ GAM 542 [DDD]
Bloch, E.:Nocturnes (3) Gamut Classics ▲ GAM 536 [DDD]
Copland, A.:Vitebsk:Study on a Jewish Theme Gamut Classics ▲ GAM 536 [DDD]
Cowell, H.:Combinations (4) Gamut Classics ▲ GAM 536 [DDD]
Cowell, H.:Trio in 9 Short Movements Gamut Classics ▲ GAM 536 [DDD]
Dvořák, A.:Trio 2 Pno *(rec 1/91)* Gamut Classics ▲ GAM CD 523 [DDD]
Fibich, Z.:Trio Vn *(rec 1/91)* Gamut Classics ▲ GAM CD 523 [DDD]
Ives, C.:Trio Pno Gamut Classics ▲ GAM 536 [DDD]
Martinů, B.:Bergerettes Gamut Classics ▲ GAMCD 523 [DDD]
Spohr, L.:Trio 2 Pno *(rec St Martin's Church, East Woodhay, Oct 13-14, 1994)* Naxos ▲ 8.553205 [DDD]
Spohr, L.:Trio 4 Pno *(rec St Martin's Church, East Woodhay, Oct 13-14, 1994)* Naxos ▲ 8.553205 [DDD]

Fred Hartley Quintet
R. Noble (cnd)
Mayerl, W.J.:Music of, w. Raie Da Costa (pno), Billy Mayerl (pno), New Mayfair Orch—Marigold; Pianolettes (6); Pno Exaggerations (4); 4 aces Suite; plus others Happy Days Nostalgia ▲ CDHD 205

Hartt Contemporary Players
D. Jackson (cnd)
Singer, L.:Sensazione II Opus One ▲ CD 160

Hartt Jazz Ensemble
D. Mattran (cnd)
Kupferman, M.:Con Vc & Jazz Band, w. David Wells (vc) Soundspells ▲ SP 111 [ADD]

Hartt Percussion Ensemble
A. Lepak (cnd)
Diez, C.:Naggareth RNE/Spanish National Radio ▲ M3/12 [ADD]

Harvard Univ Wind Ensemble
All American Trombone, w. Ronald Barron (trbn), Fredrik Wanger (pno), Atlantic Brass Quintet *(rec Sanders Theater, Harvard Univ; Sym Hall, Boston; Morse Auditorium, Boston Univ, Nov 7, Dec 8-9, 1995)* Boston Brass ▲ BB 1003

Harvard–Radcliffe Orch
J. Yannatos (cnd)
Copland, A.:Con Cl, w. D. Schneider (cl) AFKA ▲ SK 509
Ginastera, A.:Con Hp, w. G.V. Benet (hp) AFKA ▲ SK 509
Yannatos, J.:Ritual Images—A Fant AFKA ▲ SK 509
Hausmusik [M. Huggett (vn), P. Beznosiuk (vn), R. Chase (va), S. Whistler (va), R. Lester (vc)]
Beethoven, L. van:Qnt Strs, Op. 29 [period instrs] EMI Classics ▲ CDC 54656
Beethoven, L. van:Septet Strs [period instrs] EMI Classics ▲ CDC 54656
Mozart, W.A.:Qnt Strs, K.515 EMI Classics ▲ CDC 54482
Mozart, W.A.:Qnt Strs, K.593 EMI Classics ▲ CDC 54858
Mozart, W.A.:Qnt Strs, K.614 EMI Classics ▲ CDC 54858
Schubert, Franz:Octet Ww, D.803 EMI Classics ▲ CDC 54118 [DDD]
Hauts-de-Seine Plectrum Ensemble
C. Parmentier (cnd)
Bellini, V.:I Puritani (sels) [arr. for mands] Pierre Verany ▲ PVY 795042
Donizetti, G.:Lucia di Lammermoor (sels) [arr. for mands] Pierre Verany ▲ PVY 795042
Verdi, G.:Rigoletto (sels) [arr. for mands] Pierre Verany ▲ PVY 795042
Verdi, G.:La traviata (sels) [arr. for mands] Pierre Verany ▲ PVY 795042
Verdi, G.:Il trovatore (sels) [arr. for mands] Pierre Verany ▲ PVY 795042
Hawthorn Band–Australia's Champions
K. MacDonald (cnd)
Colonial Brass Walsingham Classics ▲ WAL 9000 [DDD]
Hawthorne String Quartet [Ronan Lefkowitz (vn), Si-Jing Huang (vn), Mark Ludwig (va), Sato Knudsen (vc)]
Coleridge-Taylor, S.:Qnt Cl & Strs, w. H. Wright (cl) *(rec 9/90)* Koch International Classics ▲ KIC 7056–2 [DDD]
Haas, P.:Qt 2, "Z opicich hor" London ▲ 440853–2 [DDD]
Haas, P.:Qt 3 London ▲ 440853–2 [DDD]
Klein, G.:Fant & Fugue Channel Classics ▲ CCS 1691 [DDD]
Klein, G.:Qt 2 Strs Channel Classics ▲ CCS 1691 [DDD]
Klein, G.:Trio Strs Channel Classics ▲ CCS 1691 [DDD]
Krása, H.:Qt Strs London ▲ 440853–2 [DDD]
Schulhoff, E.:Qt 1 Strs—Presto con fuoco; Allegretto con moto e con malinconia; Allegro giocoso alla slovacca; Andante molto sostenuto *(rec May 1992)* Northeastern ▲ NR 248–CD
Ullmann, V.:Qt 3 Strs Channel Classics ▲ CCS 1691 [DDD]
A. Delfs (cnd)
Schulhoff, E.:Con Str Qt, w. German CO *(rec Freie Waldorfschule, Bremen, Oct 1994)* London ▲ 444819–2 [DDD]
Hawthorne Trio [Susan Doering (vn), Michael Murray (vc), David Belcher (pno)]
Dankner, S.:Trio Vn Albany ▲ TROY 144 [DDD]
Hayashi Duo
Fauré, G.:Trio, w. M. Fornaciari (vn) Fonè ▲ 86F 05–11
Grieg, E.:Son Vc Fonè ▲ 87F 01–13 [DDD]
Martinů, B.:Vars on a Theme by Rossini Fonè ▲ 87F 01–13 [DDD]
Martinů, B.:Vars on a Slovak folksong Fonè ▲ 87F 01–13 [DDD]
Ravel, M.:Trio Pno, w. M. Fornaciari (vn) Fonè ▲ 86F 05–11 [DDD]
Haydn Baryton Trio [John Hsu (baryton), David Miller (va), Loretta O'Sullivan (vc)]
Haydn, J.:Trios (125) Baryton, Va & Vc—Nos. 50, 52, 57, 59, 67 & 107 *(rec Troy Savings Bank Music Hall, Troy, NY, Sept & Oct 1995)* Dorian ▲ DOR 90233 [DDD]
Haydn Philharmonia
E. Rojatti (cnd)
Respighi, O.:La Boutique fantastique—sels. Nuova Era ▲ 6876 [DDD]
Respighi, O.:Suite Fl, w. F. Fabbrizzi (fl) Nuova Era ▲ 6876 [DDD]
Respighi, O.:Suite Strs Nuova Era ▲ 6876 [DDD]
Haydn Philharmonia Soloists
Rossini, G.:Sons Str Qt Nuova Era 2–▲ 7100/01 [DDD]
Haydn PO Soloists
Caprioli, A.:Dialogue, w. F. Serafini (db) *(rec 1987)* Pro Viva ▲ ISPV 148 CD [ADD]
Haydn Sinfonietta Vienna
M. Huss (cnd)
Haydn, J.:Diverts Str Qt—H:II/20–22 Koch Schwann ▲ SCH 312742 [DDD]
Haydn String Quartet Budapest [János Horváth (vn), Lajos Földesi (vn), Anfrás Rudolf (va), Gábor Magyar (vc)]
Borodin, A.:Qt 1 Strs *(rec Unitarian Church, Budapest, Oct. 25–28, 1993)* Naxos ▲ 8.550850 [DDD]
Borodin, A.:Qt 2 Strs *(rec Unitarian Church, Budapest, Oct. 25–28, 1993)* Naxos ▲ 8.550850 [DDD]
Grétry, A.–E.–M.:Qt Strs, Op. 3 Koch Schwann ▲ CD 310158 [DDD]
Spohr, L.:Qnts Strs (comp), w. Sándor Papp (va)—No. 5, Op. 106 & No. 6, Op. 129 *(rec Unitarian Church, Budapest, Sept 6–10, 1993)* Marco Polo ▲ 8.223598 [DDD]
Haydn Trio Vienna
Dvořák, A.:Trio 3 Pno Arabesque ▲ ARA 6646 [DDD]
Dvořák, A.:Trio 4 Pno, "Dumky" Arabesque ▲ ARA 6646 [DDD]
Encores from Vienna Arabesque ▲ ARA 6657
Haydn–Héritage Ensemble
Campra, A.:Motets, w. H. Bouman (hpd)—O Jesu amantissime; Immensus es Domine; Quis ego Domine [L] REM ▲ 311110 XCD [DDD]
Morin, J.–B.:Motet pour le Saint-Sacrement, w. H. Bouman (sop) [L] REM ▲ 311110 XCD [DDD]
H. Bouman (cnd)
Bernier, N.:Benedicam Dominum [L] REM ▲ 311110 XCD [DDD]
Richard Hayman SO
R. Hayman (cnd)
I Love You Truly Naxos ▲ 8.990019 [DDD]
Anderson, L.:Music of—20 sels *(rec June 1989)* Naxos ▲ 8.990011 [DDD]
World Famous Marches *(rec 4/89)* Naxos ▲ 8.990010 [DDD]
Hedos Ensemble
Montéclair, M.P. de:Concerts Suites, w. B. Böhm (fl)—Nos. 1–4 CPO ▲ CPO 999213 [DDD]
Hedos Ensemble [Hartmut Hein (bar), Bernhard Böhm (rcr/trns fl/bgp/Rauschpfeife), Jürgen Hübscher (renaissance lt/vih/perc), Michael Spengler (vl)]
Renaissance Love Songs from Germany, Spain, England & Italy *(rec St. Laurentius Church, Meeder/Coburg, July 16–20, 1995)* CPO ▲ CPO 999388–2 [DDD]
Heiligenberg Baroque Orch
R. G. Frieberger (cnd)
Buxtehude, D.:Cants, Collegium Musicum Plagense—Alles, was ihr tut; Befiehl dem Engel, dass er komm; Ich habe List abzuscheiden; Jesu, meine Freud Christophorus ▲ CD 74588
Schein, J.H.:Cants, Collegium Musicum Plagense—An Wasserflüssen Babylon Christophorus ▲ CD 74588
Tunder, F.:Cants, w. Collegium Musicum Plagense—"Wachet auf", ruft uns die Stimme Christophorus ▲ CD 74588
Weckmann, J.:Cants, w. Collegium Musicum Plagense—Wenn der Herr die Gefangnen zu Zion erlösen wird Christophorus ▲ CD 74588
Heldon [R. Pinhas (syns/gtr), Gilbert Artman (drs), G. Grunblat (syns/gtr), Patrick Gauthier (syns/pno), Coco Roussel (perc), Gerard Prevost (bass), Alain Bellaïche (bass), Michel Ettori (gtr), Philibert Rossi (mellotron)]
Heldon I/III:Electronique Guerilla/It's Always Rock 'n' Roll Cuneiform 2–▲ Rune 51/52
Heldon II:Allez Teia Cuneiform ▲ Rune 37X
Heldon IV:Agneta Nilsson Cuneiform ▲ Rune 60
Heldon 6:Interface Cuneiform ▲ Rune 43X
Stand by Cuneiform ▲ Rune 53

Helicon [Jaap Schröder (vn), Stanley Ritchie (vn), Linda Quan (vn)]
A. Fuller (cnd)
Vivaldi/Bach Reference ▲ RR 23CD [DDD]
Hêlios Percussion Quartet
Cage, J.:Amores, w. I. Berteletti (prepared pno) Wergo ▲ WER 6203–2 [DDD]
Cage, J.:First Construction, w. I. Berteletti (prepared pno), P. Chaignon (additional perc) Wergo ▲ WER 6203–2 [DDD]
Cage, J.:Imaginary Landscape 2 Wergo ▲ WER 6203–2 [DDD]
Cage, J.:Second Construction Wergo ▲ WER 6203–2 [DDD]
Cage, J.:She Is Asleep, w. M. Viard (voice), I. Berteletti (prepared pno) Wergo ▲ WER 6203–2 [DDD]
Cage, J.:Third Construction Wergo ▲ WER 6203–2 [DDD]
Helsingborg SO
P. Auguin (cnd)
Chaminade, C.:Concertino Fl, w. M. Wiesler (fl) *(rec 6/91)* BIS ▲ CD 529 [DDD]
Françaix, J.:Con Fl, w. M. Wiesler (fl) *(rec 6/91)* BIS ▲ CD 529 [DDD]
Ibert, J.:Con Fl, w. M. Wiesler (fl) *(rec 6/91)* BIS ▲ CD 529 [DDD]
Mouquet, J.:Flûte, w. M. Wiesler (fl) *(rec 6/91)* BIS ▲ CD 529 [DDD]
H. Farberman (cnd)
Shchedrin, R.:Carmen, Kroumata Percussion Ensemble BIS ▲ CD 382 [DDD]
Shchedrin, R.:Carmen, Kroumata Percussion Ensemble BIS ("BIS Twins" series) 2–▲ CD 232/382 [DDD]
H.–P. Frank (cnd)
Alfvén, H.:A District Fairytale *(rec Nov 29, 1982)* Sterling ▲ CDS 1012 [ADD]
Elgar, E.:Sea Pictures, w. R. Lang (mez) [E] *(rec 1991)* BIS ▲ CD 530 [DDD]
Hallén, A.:Rhap 2, "Swedish Rhap" *(rec 5/87)* Musica Sveciae ▲ MSCD 621 [DDD]
Hallén, A.:Toteninsel *(rec 6/87)* Musica Sveciae ▲ MSCD 621 [DDD]
Haydn, M.:Syms—in B♭, P.18; in C, P.31; Symphony in D; Symphony in E♭ BIS ▲ CD 481 [DDD]
Larsson, L.–E.:Sym 1 BIS ▲ CD 426 [DDD]
Larsson, L.–E.:Sym 2 BIS ▲ CD 426 [DDD]
Norman, L.:Anthony Musica Sveciae ▲ MSCD 512 [DDD]
Norman, L.:Concert Ov Musica Sveciae ▲ MSCD 512 [DDD]
Norman, L.:Qt in a Strs—Andante Sostenuto e Cantabile Musica Sveciae ▲ MSCD 512 [DDD]
Norman, L.:Sym 2 Musica Sveciae ▲ MSCD 512 [DDD]
Nystroem, G.:Songs at the Sea, w. R. Lang (mez) [Sw] *(rec 1991)* BIS ▲ CD 530 [DDD]
Söderman, A.:Marshal Stig's Daughters, w. Mikaeli Chamber Choir, Helsingborgs Concert Choir, Medlemmar Concert Choir [Sw] Musica Sveciae ▲ MSCD 513
Wagner, R.:Wesendonck Songs, w. R. Lang (cta) [G] *(rec 1991)* BIS ▲ CD 530 [DDD]
S. Frykberg (cnd)
Larsson, L.–E.:God in Disguise, w. B. Nordin (sop), H. Hagegård (bar), Jonsson (nar), Helsingborg Sym Chorus [Sw] BIS ▲ CD 96 [AAD]
Larsson, L.–E.:Sym 3 BIS ▲ CD 96 [AAD]
O. Kamu (cnd)
Berwald, F.:Con Pno, w. Niklas Sivelöv (pno) *(rec Helsingborg Concert Hall, Helsingborg, Sweden, May 15–21 & May 30 – June)* Naxos ▲ 8.553052 [DDD]
Berwald, F.:Estrella de Soria (ov) *(rec Helsingborg Concert Hall, Helsingborg, Sweden, May 15–21, 1995)* Naxos ▲ 8.553051 [DDD]
Berwald, F.:Sym 1, "Sinfonie Sérieuse" *(rec Helsingborg Concert Hall, Helsingborg, Sweden, May 15–21, 1995)* Naxos ▲ 8.553051 [DDD]
Berwald, F.:Sym 2, "Sinfonie capricieuse" *(rec Helsingborg Concert Hall, Helsingborg, Sweden, May 15–21, 1995)* Naxos ▲ 8.553051 [DDD]
Berwald, F.:Sym 3, "Sinfonie singulière" *(rec Helsingborg Concert Hall, Helsingborg, Sweden, May 15–21 & May 30 – June)* Naxos ▲ 8.553052 [DDD]
Berwald, F.:Sym 4, "Sinfonie naïve" *(rec Helsingborg Concert Hall, Helsingborg, Sweden, May 15–21 & May 30 – June)* Naxos ▲ 8.553052 [DDD]
Britten, B.:Con Pno, w. Ralf Gothoni (pno) Ondine ▲ ODE 825 [DDD]
Britten, B.:Matinées musicale Ondine ▲ ODE 825 [DDD]
Britten, B.:Soirées musicales Ondine ▲ ODE 825 [DDD]
Schubert, Franz:Sym 5 *(rec Concert House, Helsingborg, Sweden, Mar. 29–Apr. 1993)* Calle Classics ▲ CLCCD 3907 [DDD]
Schubert, Franz:Sym 6 *(rec Concert House, Helsingborg, Sweden, Mar. 29–Apr. 1993)* Calle Classics ▲ CLCCD 3907 [DDD]
S. Westerberg (cnd)
Berwald, F.:Estrella de Soria (sels), w. L. Nordin (sop), K. Dalayman (sgr), S. Smith (sgr), A. Lorentzson (sgr), C. Sköld (sgr), Malmö Chamber Choir Musica Sveciae ▲ MSV 523 [DDD]
Blomdahl, K.–B.:Concert Ov MAP ▲ MAPCD 9024
Blomdahl, K.–B.:Con grosso MAP ▲ MAPCD 9024
Blomdahl, K.–B.:Con Vn, w. O. Rudner (vn) MAP ▲ MAPCD 9024
Blomdahl, K.–B.:Preludio & Allegro MAP ▲ MAPCD 9024
Blomdahl, K.–B.:Sym 2 MAP ▲ MAPCD 9024
Helsinki CO
J. Barbirolli (cnd)
Mozart, W.A.:Kleine Nachtmusik *(rec 1928)* Koch Legacy ▲ 370772
Sibelius, J.:Con Vn, w. I. Szeryng (vn) *(rec live Royal Festival Hall, London)* Intaglio ▲ INCD 7201 [ADD]
J.–P. Saraste (cnd)
Benda, F.:Con in e Fl & Orch, w. M. Helasvuo (fl) BIS ▲ CD 268 [DDD]
Stamitz, C.:Con Fl, Op. 29, w. M. Helasvuo (fl) BIS ▲ CD 268 [DDD]
L. Segerstam (cnd)
Rautavaara, E.:The Fiddlers *(rec Dec. 21, 1974)* BIS ▲ CD 66 [AAD]
Segerstam, L.:Divert Vns, w. J. Rahkonen (vn), H. Louhivuori (vn), E. Kamu (va), V. Höylä (vc) BIS ▲ CD 84 [AAD]
Helsinki Festival Orch
J. Mikael (cnd)
Sibelius, J.:Con Vn, w. R. Ricci (vn) One–Eleven ▲ URS 91070 [ADD]
Helsinki PO
T. Beecham (cnd)
Sibelius, J.:Sym 7 *(rec live 1954)* Ondine ▲ ODE 809 [ADD]
Sibelius, J.:Tapiola *(rec live 1954)* Ondine ▲ ODE 809 [ADD]
P. Berglund (cnd)
Sallinen, A.:Chorali BIS ▲ CD 41 [AAD]
Sibelius, J.:Aallottaret EMI Classics 2–▲ CDFB 68646
Sibelius, J.:Finlandia EMI Classics 2–▲ CDFB 68646
Sibelius, J.:Kullervo, w. E.–L. Saarinen (mez), J. Hynninen (bar), Helsinki Univ Male Choir, Helsinki State Academy Male Choir EMI Classics ▲ CDM 65080
Sibelius, J.:Sym 1 EMI Classics ("Doubleforte" series) 2–▲ CDFB 68643
Sibelius, J.:Sym 2 EMI Classics ("Doubleforte" series) 2–▲ CDFB 68643
Sibelius, J.:Sym 3 EMI Classics ("Doubleforte" series) 2–▲ CDFB 68643
Sibelius, J.:Sym 4 EMI Classics ("Doubleforte" series) 2–▲ CDFB 68643
Sibelius, J.:Sym 5 EMI Classics 2–▲ CDFB 68646
Sibelius, J.:Sym 6 EMI Classics 2–▲ CDFB 68646
Sibelius, J.:Sym 7 EMI Classics 2–▲ CDFB 68646
Sibelius, J.:Tapiola EMI Classics 2–▲ CDFB 68646
Sibelius, J.:Tapiola EMI Classics ▲ CDM 65176
S. Comissiona (cnd)
Hommage à Sibelius Ondine ▲ ODE 767 [DDD]
Scandinavian Rhapsody, w. L. Segerstam (cnd) Ondine ▲ ODE 824 [DDD]
Tempest:Classic Storm Scenes Pro Arte ▲ CDS 580 [DDD]

ORCH. & ENS.

Helsinki PO (cont.)
J. DePreist (cnd)
Kancheli, G.:Sym 1 Ondine ▲ ODE 829 [DDD]
Kancheli, G.:Sym 4 Ondine ▲ ODE 829 [DDD]
Kancheli, G.:Sym 5 Ondine ▲ ODE 829 [DDD]
Shostakovich, D.:Chamber Sym, Op. 110a Ondine ▲ ODE 817 [DDD]
Shostakovich, D.:Festive Ov Delos ▲ DE 3089 [DDD]
Shostakovich, D.:Sym 5 Ondine ▲ ODE 817 [DDD]
Shostakovich, D.:Sym 9 Ondine ▲ ODE 846
Shostakovich, D.:Sym 10 Delos ▲ DE 3089 [DDD]
Shostakovich, D.:Sym 11 Delos ▲ DCD 3080 [DDD]
Shostakovich, D.:Sym 12 Ondine ▲ ODE 846
J. Fürst (cnd)
Kodály, Z.:Galanta Dances Kontrapunkt 2-▲ KPT 32153 [DDD]
Kodály, Z.:Háry János (suite) Kontrapunkt 2-▲ KPT 32153 [DDD]
Kodály, Z.:Marosszék Dances Kontrapunkt 2-▲ KPT 32153 [DDD]
Kodály, Z.:Summer Evening Kontrapunkt 2-▲ KPT 32153 [DDD]
Kodály, Z.:Sym in C Kontrapunkt 2-▲ KPT 32153 [DDD]
Kodály, Z.:Vars on a Hungarian Folk Song Kontrapunkt 2-▲ KPT 32153 [DDD]
R. Kajanus (cnd)
Sibelius, J.:March of the Finnish Jaeger Battalion *(rec 1928)* Koch Legacy ▲ 3-7133-2 H1
O. Kamu (cnd)
Sallinen, A.:The Iron Age, w. Helsinki Music Institute Choir Ondine ▲ ODE 844 [DDD]
Sallinen, A.:Songs of Life & Death, w. Jorma Hynninen (bar), Helsinki Music Institute Choir Ondine ▲ ODE 844 [DDD]
Sibelius, J.:Con Vn, w. M. Fried (vn) *(rec Oct. 9–10 1987)* Finlandia ▲ 4509-95856-2 [DDD]
Sibelius, J.:Karelia Suite Finlandia ▲ 4509-95844-2 [ADD/DDD]
Sibelius, J.:Karelia Suite, w. M. Fried (vn) *(rec Oct. 9–10 1987)* Finlandia ▲ 4509-95856-2 [DDD]
J. Panula (cnd)
Sibelius, J.:Lemminkäinen's Return—No. 1 *(rec 1968)* Finlandia ▲ 4509-95843-2 [AAD]
Sibelius, J.:Sym 4 Finlandia ▲ 4509-95842-2 [AAD]
Sibelius, J.:Sym 5 Finlandia ▲ 4509-95842-2 [AAD]
M. Pommer (cnd)
Rautavaara, E.:Con Vc, w. M. Ylönen (vc) Ondine ▲ ODE 819 [DDD]
Rautavaara, E.:Sym 6 Ondine ▲ ODE 819 [DDD]
L. Segerstam (cnd)
Rautavaara, E.:Con Org, w. Kari Jussila (org) *(rec Finlandia Hall, Oct 1995)* Ondine ▲ ODE 869-2 [DDD]
Rautavaara, E.:Sym 7 *(rec Finlandia Hall, Aug 1995)* Ondine ▲ ODE 869-2 [DDD]
Sibelius, J.:Belshazzar's Feast (suite) Ondine ▲ ODE 878
Sibelius, J.:Con Vn, w. Pekka Kuusisto (vn) Ondine ▲ ODE 878
Sibelius, J.:4 Legends from the Kalevalá Ondine ▲ ODE 852
Sibelius, J.:Karelia Suite Ondine ▲ ODE 878
Sibelius, J.:Tapiola Ondine ▲ ODE 852
U. Söderblom (cnd)
Kokkonen, J.:Requiem (in memoriam Maija Kokkonen), w. Satu Vihavainen (sop), Jorma Hynninen (bar), Academic Choral Society Finlandia ▲ FIN 53353 [DDD]
Helsinki RSO
O. Kamu (cnd)
Sibelius, J.:Karelia Suite Deutsche Grammophon ("Resonance" series) ▲ 427204-2 [AAD]
Sibelius, J.:The Swan of Tuonela Deutsche Grammophon ("Resonance" series) ▲ 427204-2 [AAD]
Helsinki SO
J. Barbirolli (cnd)
Sibelius, J.:Sym 7 *(rec live at Royal Festival Hall, London)* Intaglio ▲ INCD 7171 [ADD]
Helsinki Wind Quintet [Mikael Helasvuo (fl), Jouko Teikari (ob), Reino Simola (cl), Kari Alanne (hn), Juhani Tapaninen (bn)]
Kokkonen, J.:Qnt Winds *(rec Sibelius Academy, Helsinki, Finland, June 27–28, 1974)* BIS ▲ CD 11 [AAD]
Segerstam, L.:A Nnnnoooowwws *(rec Sibelius Acad., Helsinki, Finland, June 27–28, 1974)* BIS ▲ CD 20 [AAD]
Segerstam, L.:A Nnnnoooowwws *(rec Sibelius Academy, Helsinki, Finland, June 27–28, 1974)* BIS ▲ CD 11 [AAD]
Henry Trio
Burgan, P.:Music of, w. Liliane Mazeron (sop), Clara Novakova (fl), Michel Arrignon (cl), Alain Jacquon (pno)—Jeux de femmes [6 Erotic Poems of Verlaine]; Rondes Nocturnes; Bavardage; Berceuse Maguelone ▲ 350.529
Lalo, E.:Trios Pno Pierre Verany ▲ PVY 794031 [DDD]
Herald Trumpeters
S. V. Hays (cnd)
The Queen's Birthday Salute, w. Royal Artillery Band *(rec live, Hyde Park, London, June 13, 1957)* Vanguard Classics ▲ SVC 51 [AAD]
Heritage CO
C. Peacock (cnd)
Vieuxtemps, H.:Con 1 Vn, w. P. Rosenthal (vn) *(rec Salt Lake City, Nov. 13 & 14, 1992)* Biddulph ▲ LAW 011 [DDD]
Vieuxtemps, H.:Fant appassionata, w. P. Rosenthal (vn) *(rec Salt Lake City, Nov. 13 & 14, 1992)* Biddulph ▲ LAW 011 [DDD]
Woody Herman's Thundering Herd
Ebony, w. Richard Stoltzman (cl) RCA Red Seal ▲ 6486-2-RC [DDD]
Stravinsky, I.:Ebony Con, w. R. Stoltzman (cl) RCA Red Seal ▲ 09026-61360-2 [DDD]
Herning Town Trio
Risgaard, C.:Trio 1 Pno Classico ▲ CLASSCD 120
Risgaard, C.:Trio 2 Pno Classico ▲ CLASSCD 120
Hertz Trio
Archer, V.:Trio 2 Pno Unical ▲ UC-CD 9102 [DDD]
Contant, A.:Trio Vn CBC ("Musica Viva" series) ▲ MVCD 1042 [DDD]
Hertz Trio Musica Viva ▲ MVCD 1042 [DDD]
Hummel, J.N.:Trio Vn, Vc & Pno, Op. 12 CBC ("Musica Viva" series) ▲ MVCD 1042 [DDD]
Rubbra, E.:Trio in 1 Movt CBC ("Musica Viva" series) ▲ MVCD 1042 [DDD]
Schumann, C.:Trio Pno Unical ▲ UC-CD 9102 [DDD]
Shostakovich, D.:Trio 1 Pno Unical ▲ UC-CD 9102 [DDD]
Storace, S.:Son 3 Vn Unical ▲ UC-CD 9102 [DDD]
Hesperus
Babell, W.:Con Fl, w. S. Reiss (rcr) Golden Apple ▲ GACD 7550 [DDD] ■ GAC 7550
Graupner, C.:Con Rcr, w. S. Reiss (rcr) Golden Apple ▲ GACD 7550 [DDD] ■ GAC 7550
Naudot, J.-C.:Con Rcr, w. S. Reiss (rcr)—No. 2 in C Golden Apple ▲ GACD 7550 [DDD] ■ GAC 7550
Telemann, G.P.:Con in C Rcr, w. S. Reiss (rcr) Golden Apple ▲ GACD 7550 [DDD] ■ GAC 7550
Vivaldi, A.:Cons Rcr, w. S. Reiss (rcr)—RV.428, 444 Golden Apple ▲ GACD 7550 [DDD] ■ GAC 7550
S. Reiss (cnd)
Spain in the New World Golden Apple ▲ GACD 7552 [DDD] ■ GAC 7552
Myra Hess Trio
Brahms, J.:Trio 2 Pno APR 2-▲ APR 7012 [AAD]
Mozart, W.A.:Con 21 Pno APR 2-▲ APR 7012 [AAD]
Schubert, Franz:Rosamunde (sels) APR 2-▲ APR 7012 [AAD]
Schubert, Franz:Trio 1 Pno APR 2-▲ APR 7012 [AAD]
Hesse Bach Collegium
W. Wehnert (cnd)
Zelenka, J.D.:Missa votiva, w. C. Hampe (sop), E. Graf (cta), J. Duske (ten), J. Gebhardt (bass), Marburg Bach Choir [L] Thorofon ▲ CTH 2172 [DDD]
Hesse RSO
Max Lorenz:Recital, 1933–1957, w. Lorenz, Max (ten), Maria Reining (sop), Berlin RSO [cnd:Artur Rother], Bayreuth Festival Orch [cnd:Heinz Tietjen, Richard Strauss], German Large RSO [cnd:Rudolf Moralt, Max Schönherr, Anton Paulik], Hessen RSO [cnd:Kurt Schröder], Brenda Lewis (sop), Eberhard Wächter (ten), Wolfgang Zimmer (bar) *(rec 1933–57)* Myto ▲ MCD 934.88
M. Gielen (cnd)
Ligeti, G.:Requiem, w. Lillana Poli (sop), Barbro Ericson (mez), Hesse Radio Chorus [L] Wergo ▲ WER 60045-50 [ADD]
C.M. Giulini (cnd)
Mendelssohn, F.:Con in e Vn & Orch, Op. 64, w. A. Grumiaux (vn) Originals ▲ ORISH 818 [ADD]
H. Scherchen (cnd)
Schoenberg, A.:Con Pno, w. E. Steuermann (pno) *(rec 1954)* Arkadia ▲ 768 [ADD]
K. Schröder (cnd)
Strauss, R.:Salome, w. I. Borkh (sop—Salome), M. Klose (mez—Herodias), C. Ludwig (mez—Page), M. Lorenz (ten—Herodes), F. Fehringer (ten—Narraboth), F. Frantz (bar—Jokanaan) *(rec 1952)* Myto 2-▲ 93592
Verdi, G.:I vespri siciliani, w. M. Cunitz (sop), H. Roswaenge (ten), H. Schlusnus (bar), O. von Rohr (bass), Hesse Radio Chorus *(rec 1951)* Myto 2-▲ MCD 93279
C. Schuricht (cnd)
Mahler, G.:Sym 2, w. M. Puetz (sop), M. Höffgen (cta), Hesse Radio Chorus, Frankfurt Singakademie Choir *(rec 1960)* Originals 2-▲ ORISH 819 [ADD]
D. Van Vactor (cnd)
Van Vactor, D.:Recitativo & Salterello CRI ("American Masters" series) ▲ CD 702 [ADD]
Van Vactor, D.:Sinf breve CRI ("American Masters" series) ▲ CD 702 [ADD]
Van Vactor, D.:Sym 1 CRI ("American Masters" series) ▲ CD 702 [ADD]
Van Vactor, D.:Sym 3 CRI ("American Masters" series) ▲ CD 702 [ADD]
Het Trio [Harrie Starreveld (fl), Harry Sparnaay (b cl), René Eckhardt (pno)]
de Leeuw, T.:Trio NM Classics ▲ NM 92020
Ketting, O.:Summer NM Classics ▲ NM 92022
Ketting, P.:Trio Son NM Classics ▲ NM 92022
Ringing the Changes Attacca ▲ 9161-4 [DDD]
Rokus van Roosendael, J.:Kaida NM Classics ▲ NM 92022
Rossini, G.:Qts Fl, w. Carlos Bruncel (fl)—Sons 1 in G, 2 in A, 4 in B & 6 in D; Divert Eufoda ▲ EUF 1139
Smit, S.:A Tempo Rubato NM Classics ▲ NM 92022
Straesser, J.:Son a Tre NM Classics ▲ NM 92022
Verbey, T.:Contractie Donemus ▲ CV 31
Heutling String Quartet
Reger, M.:Qnt Cl, w. Franz Klein (cl) Koch Schwann ▲ SCH 318092
Stephen Hill Orch
D. Pippin (cnd)
Porter, C.:Nymph Errant, w. K. Ballard (sgr), E. Belcourt (sgr), *(other sgrs unknown)*, Stephen Hill Singers Angel ▲ CDC 54079
Hill/Wiltschinsky Guitar Duo [Robin Hill (gtr), Peter Wiltschinsky (gtr)]
Hill & Wiltschinsky Guitar Duo IMP ("Classics" series) ▲ IMP 6700612
Danza! ASV ▲ ASV 2094 [DDD]
Hilversum NOS Radio Orch
J. Stulen (cnd)
Weiner, S.:Con Va, w. S. Weiner (va) *(rec 1987)* Koch Schwann ▲ SCH 313372 [ADD/DDD]
Hilversum RSO
K. Bakels (cnd)
Mascagni, P.:Nerone, w. R. Didonè (sop), D. Di Domenico (ten), S. Cowan (bar), M. Dirks (bar), Harry Peeters (bass), Shapero (sgr), Strow-Piccolo (sgr), Tcholakov (sgr), Hilversum Chorus [I] Bongiovanni 2-▲ GB 2052/53 [DDD]
R. de Leeuw (cnd)
Messiaen, O.:La Transfiguration de Notre Seigneur Jésus-Christ, w. Ludwig van Gijsegem (ten), Yvonne Loriod (pno), BRT Choir Montaigne 2-▲ MO 782040
K. Montgomery (cnd)
Marez Oyens, T. de:Sinf Testimonial, w. Hilversum Radio Chorus Donemus ▲ CV 8702 [AAD]
L. Stokowski (cnd)
Prokofiev, S.:Alexander Nevsky, w. *(mez unknown)* *(rec 1951–70)* Music & Arts ▲ CD 831 [ADD]
J. Stulen (cnd)
Marez Oyens, T. de:Litany Donemus ▲ CV 8702 [AAD]
Hindar String Quartet
Jacob, G.:Divert Hmc, w. T. Reilly (hmc) *(rec 1972)* Chandos ▲ CHAN 8802 [AAD]
Moody, J.:Qnt Hmc, w. T. Reilly (hmc) *(rec 1972)* Chandos ▲ CHAN 8802 [AAD]
Hindar String Quartet members
Mozart, W.A.:Qt Ob, K.370, w. Brynjar Hoff (ob) Norway Music ▲ LCD 1004
Hiroshima SO
H. Kuroiwa (cnd)
Sukegawa, T.:The Eternal Morning Vienna Modern Masters ▲ VMM 3006 [DDD]
His Majesties Sagbutts & Cornetts
For His Majestys Sagbutts & Cornetts:English Music from Henry VIII to Charles II Hyperion ▲ CDA 66894
Gaudeamus Early Music Sampler, w. Great Consort, Rasumovsky String Quartet, Trio Sonnerie, Cappella Nova, Cardinall's Musick, Clerks' Group, Ex Cathedra, Gentlemen of the Chappell, Gonville & Caius College Choir Cambridge, et al. ASV/Gaudeamus ▲ ASV 1002
Music from 17th Century Germany, w. Richard Wistreich (bass), Alistair Ross (org) Meridian ▲ 84096
J. E. Gardiner (cnd)
Carissimi, G.:Oratorios, w. English Baroque Soloists members, Monteverdi Choir London—Jepthe, Jonas & Judicum extremum Erato ▲ 2292-45466-2 ZK [DDD]
Monteverdi, C.:Orfeo, w. English Baroque Soloists, Monteverdi Choir London Archiv 2-▲ 419250-2 [DDD]
Monteverdi, C.:Vespro della Beata Vergine, w. A. Monoyios (sop), M. Pennicchi (sop), M. Chance (ct), G. Tucker (ten), N. Robson (ten), S. Naglia (ten), B. Terfel (b-bar), A. Miles (bass), English Baroque Soloists, Monteverdi Choir London Archiv 2-▲ 429565-2 [DDD]
J. O'Donnell (cnd)
Lassus, O. de:Bell'Amfitrit'altera, w. J. West (cnd), Westminster Cathedral Choir Hyperion ▲ CDA 66688
J. Skidmore (cnd)
Lassus, O. de:Sacred Music, w. Ex Cathedra Choir—Sgimus tibi a3; Ave verum corpus a6; Bicinia 3, 9 & 14; Bone Jesu a8; Christus resurgens a5; Justorum animae a5; Laudent Deum a4; Musica De donum a6; Quam pulchra es a6; Salve regina a6; Tristis est anima mea a5; Tui Sunt coeli a8; Vide homo a7; Vinum bonum a8 ASV ("Guadeamus" series) ▲ ASV 150
J. West (cnd)
Erbach, C.:Sacred Music, w. J. O'Donnell (org), Westminster Cathedral Choir—Sacredotes Dei; Canzona decundi toni; Alleluia, Hic est sacredos; Fantasia sub elevatione; Toccata octavi toni [frag.]; Post-communion; Posuisti Domine; La Paglia Hyperion ▲ CDA 66688
Hassler, H.L.:Sacred Music, w. J. O'Donnell (org), Westminster Cathedral Choir—Canzon duodecimi toni; Cantate Dominio canticum novum; Toccata in G; Canzon noni toni; O sacrum convivium; Domine Dominus noster Hyperion ▲ CDA 66688
HM Life Guards Concert Band
C. Reeves (cnd)
The Royal Salute Sony Classical ▲ SK 48473
HM Royal Marines Band Corps of Drums
Heming (cnd)
Portsmouth, w. Norman Gibbs (bgl) Bandleader ▲ BND 5020 [DDD]

▲ = CD ♦ = Enhanced CD Δ = MD ■ = Cassette Tape □ = DCC

HM Royal Marines Band
G.A. Hoskins (cnd)
Globe & Laurel — Bandleader ▲ BND 5023 [DDD]
J. R. Mason (cnd)
Alford, K.:Music of—(2 fantasias) A Musical Switch; The Lightning Switch; (18 marches) Colonel Bogey; The Great Little Army; H.M. Jollies; On the Quarter Deck; The Thin Red Line; Voice of the Guns; The Standard of St. George; Cavalry of the Clouds; The Middy; Holyrood; Army of the Nile; Dunedin; The Vanished Army; Old Panama; Eagle Squadron; By Land & Sea; The Vedette; The Mad Major *(rec early 1970s)* — Chandos ("Collect" series) ▲ CHAN 6584 [ADD]
Hoketus Ensemble
Andriessen, L.:Hoketus — Donemus ▲ CV 20
Holland Italian Opera Orch
P. Mascagni (cnd)
Mascagni, P.:Cavalleria rusticana, w. L. Bruna Rasa (sop), M. Meloni (mez), R. Gallo Toscani (mez), A. Melandri (ten), A. Poli (bar), Italian d'Olanda Opera Chorus [I] *(rec live at the Royal Theatre in the Hague, 11/7/38)* — Bongiovanni ▲ GB 1050 (m) [AAD]
Hollywood Bowl Orch
J. Mauceri (cnd)
Adams, J.:Nixon in China (sels) *(rec Culver City, CA, Sept 1992)* — Philips ▲ 438663-2 [DDD]
Always & Forever:Movies' Greatest Love Songs *(rec Hollywood, CA, Aug 9 & Sept 5, 1995)* — Philips ▲ 446681-2 [DDD]
Arlen, H.:Music of—Free & Easy (blues opera suite):medley of Any Place I Hang My Hat Is Home; I Had Myself a True Love; One for My Baby (& One for the Road) — Philips ▲ 446404-2
Berlin, I.:Songs, w. P. LuPone (sgr)—There's No Business Like Show Business; Heat Wave; No Strings; Let Yourself Go; Steppin' Out with My Baby; Hostess with the Mostes'; Best Thing for You; Lonely Heart; Always; I Got Lost in His Arms; Doin' What Comes Natur'lly; Count Your Blessings Instead of Sheep *(rec Culver City, CA, July 1994)* — Philips ▲ 446406-2 [DDD]
Bernstein, L.:West Side Story (symphonic dances) *(rec Culver City, CA, Sept 1992)* — Philips ▲ 438663-2 [DDD]
Bliss, A.:Things to Come (sels)—Main Title:War Montage; Pestilence:Happy March; The Building of the New World; Attack on the Moon Gun; Epilogue [ed Mauceri] *(rec Hollywood, CA)* — Philips ▲ 446403-2 [DDD]
Debussy, C.:Prélude à l'après-midi d'un faune, w. L. DiTullio (fl) *(rec Culver City, CA, Sept 1992)* — Philips ▲ 438867-2 [DDD]
Ellington, D.:Harlem *(rec Culver City, CA, Sept 1992)* — Philips ▲ 438663-2 [DDD]
Gershwin, G.:An American in Paris *(rec Culver City, CA, Sept 1992)* — Philips ▲ 438663-2 [DDD]
Gershwin, G.:Music of—Delicious; Shall We Dance; A Damsel in Distress; The Goldwyn Follies; The Shocking Miss Pilgrim *(rec Culver City, CA, July 1991)* — Philips ▲ 434 274-2 [DDD]
The Gershwins in Hollywood, w. Gregory Hines, Patti Austin — Philips ▲ 434274-2 [DDD]
The Great Waltz *(rec Sony Studios, Culver City, CA, Jan 1993)* — Philips ▲ 438685-2 [DDD]
Grieg, E.:Peer Gynt (sels)—Morning Mood *(rec Culver City, CA, Sept 1992)* — Philips ▲ 438867-2 [DDD]
Herrmann, B.:The Day the Earth Stood Still—Outer Space *(rec Hollywood, CA)* — Philips ▲ 446403-2 [DDD]
Herrmann, B.:North by Northwest (sels)—Conversation Piece *(rec Hollywood, CA, Aug 9 & Sept 5, 1995)* — Philips ▲ 446681-2 [DDD]
Herrmann, B.:Snows of Kilimanjaro—The Memory Waltz *(rec Sony Studios, Culver City, CA, Jan 1993)* — Philips ▲ 438685-2 [DDD]
Herrmann, B.:Vertigo (sels)—Prelude & Scene d'Amour *(rec Culver City, CA, Sept 1993)* — Philips ▲ 442425-2 [DDD]
Hollywood Dreams *(rec Culver City, CA, Feb 1991)* — Philips ▲ 432109-2 [DDD]
Hollywood Nightmares *(rec Culver City, CA, Sept 1993)* — Philips ▲ 442425-2 [DDD]
Journey to the Stars:A Sci-Fi Fantasy Adventure *(rec Hollywood, CA)* — Philips ▲ 446403-2
Kern, J.:Show Boat (sels)—scenario for orch including Old Man River; Can't Help Lovin' Dat Man; You Are Love; Why Do I Love You? — Philips ▲ 446404-2
Korngold, E.W.:The Adventures of Robin Hood (sels)—Fanfare; Love Scene Battle; Victory & Epilogue *(rec Culver City, CA, Feb 1991)* — Philips ▲ 432109-2 [DDD]
Korngold, E.W.:Escape Me Never (sels)—Love for Love *(rec Hollywood, CA, Aug 9 & Sept 5, 1995)* — Philips ▲ 446681-2 [DDD]
Korngold, E.W.:The Prince and the Pauper (sels)—Flirtation *(rec Sony Studios, Culver City, CA, Jan 1993)* — Philips ▲ 438685-2 [DDD]
Ligeti, G.:Atmosphères *(rec Hollywood, CA)* — Philips ▲ 446403-2 [DDD]
Loewe, F.:Gigi (sels)—Main Title; Fountain Scene; Chez Maxim Waltz *(rec Sony Studios, Culver City, CA, Jan 1993)* — Philips ▲ 438685-2 [DDD]
Newman, Alfred:How to Marry a Millionaire:Ov *(rec Culver City, CA, Feb 1991)* — Philips ▲ 432109-2 [DDD]
Newman, Alfred:Twentieth Century-Fox Fanfare *(rec Culver City, CA, Feb 1991)* — Philips ▲ 432109-2 [DDD]
Newman, Alfred:Wuthering Heights (sels)—Cathie's Theme *(rec Hollywood, CA, Aug 9 & Sept 5, 1995)* — Philips ▲ 446681-2 [DDD]
Nielsen, C.:Helios *(rec Culver City, CA, Sept 1992)* — Philips ▲ 438867-2 [DDD]
Opening Night:The Overtures of Rodgers & Hammerstein — Philips ▲ 434932-2 [DDD] ■ 434932-4 (D)
Ravel, M.:Daphnis et Chloé (sels)—Dawn *(rec Culver City, CA, Sept 1992)* — Philips ▲ 438867-2 [DDD]
Rodgers, R.:Carousel (sels)—Heaven Effect; Carousel Waltz *(rec Culver City, CA, Feb 1991)* — Philips ▲ 432109-2 [DDD]
Rodgers, R.:Carousel (sels)—suite including June Is Bustin' Out All Over; When the Children Are Asleep; Blow High,Blow Low; If I Loved You; A Real Nice Clambake; Stonecutter Cut It on Stone; What's the Use of Wond'rin'; You'll Never Walk Alone — Philips ▲ 446404-2
Rodgers, R.:The King & I, w. J. Andrews (sgr—Anna Leonowens), L. Salonga (sgr—Tuptim), B. Kingsley (sgr—The King), P. Bryson (sgr—Lun Tha), M. Horne (mez—Lady Thiang), M. Liufau (sgr—Prince Chulalongkorn), E. Kingsley (sgr—Louis Leonowens), R. Moore (sgr—Sir Edward Ramsay), M. Sheen (sgr—The Kralahome), Los Angeles Master Chorale *(rec Culver City, CA, Apr 1992)* — Philips ▲ 438007-2 [DDD]
Rodgers, R.:Ovs—Oklahoma!; Carousel; State Fair; Allegro; South Pacific; The King & I; Me & Juliet; Pipe Dream; Cinderella; Flower Drum Song; The Sound of Music *(rec Sony Studios, Culver City, CA, Jan 1993)* — Philips ▲ 434932-2 [DDD]
Rodgers, R.:Slaughter on 10th Avenue — Philips ▲ 446404-2
Rózsa, M.:Madame Bovary (sels)—Waltz *(rec Sony Studios, Culver City, CA, Jan 1993)* — Philips ▲ 438685-2 [DDD]
Rózsa, M.:Spellbound *(rec Culver City, CA, Sept 1993)* — Philips ▲ 442425-2 [DDD]
Rózsa, M.:The Thief of Bagdad—Eternal Love *(rec Hollywood, CA, Aug 9 & Sept 5, 1995)* — Philips ▲ 446681-2 [DDD]
Schoenberg, A.:Gurrelieder—Sunrise *(rec Culver City, CA, Sept 1992)* — Philips ▲ 438867-2 [DDD]
Songs of the Earth — Philips ▲ 438867-2
Steiner, M.:Gone with the Wind (sels)—Main Title *(rec Culver City, CA, Feb 1991)* — Philips ▲ 432109-2 [DDD]
Steiner, M.:Jezebel (sels)—Waltz *(rec Sony Studios, Culver City, CA, Jan 1993)* — Philips ▲ 438685-2 [DDD]
Steiner, M.:King Kong (sels)—Ov *(rec Culver City, CA, Sept 1993)* — Philips ▲ 442425-2 [DDD]
Steiner, M.:Now, Voyager (sels) *(rec Hollywood, CA, Aug 9 & Sept 5, 1995)* — Philips ▲ 446681-2 [DDD]
Wagner, R.:Tristan und Isolde (sels)—Love Night & Transfiguration [trans Stokowski] *(rec Culver City, CA, Sept 1992)* — Philips ▲ 438867-2 [DDD]
Waxman, F.:The Bride of Frankenstein (sels)—Creation of the Female Monster; The Tower Explodes *(rec Hollywood, CA)* — Philips ▲ 446403-2 [DDD]

Hollywood Bowl Orch (cont.)
J. Mauceri (cnd) (cont.)
Waxman, F.:Dr. Jekyll & Mr. Hyde (suite) *(rec Culver City, CA, Sept 1993)* — Philips ▲ 442425-2 [DDD]
Waxman, F.:Hotel Berlin (sels)—Cafe Waltzes *(rec Sony Studios, Culver City, CA, Jan 1993)* — Philips ▲ 438685-2 [DDD]
Waxman, F.:Night unto Night (sels), w. B. Dukov (elec vn)—Dusk *(rec Culver City, CA, Sept 1992)* — Philips ▲ 438867-2 [DDD]
Waxman, F.:Peyton Place (sels) *(rec Hollywood, CA, Aug 9 & Sept 5, 1995)* — Philips ▲ 446681-2 [DDD]
Waxman, F.:A Place in the Sun (suite) *(rec Culver City, CA, Feb 1991)* — Philips ▲ 432109-2 [DDD]
Waxman, F.:Sunset Boulevard *(rec Culver City, CA, Sept 1993)* — Philips ▲ 442425-2 [DDD]
Weill, K.:Songs—medley of Mack the Knife; Surabaya Johnny; Bilbao Song; J'Attends un Navire; Train to Johannesburg; Lost in the Stars; My Ship; September Song — Philips ▲ 446404-2
Williams, John:Dracula (sels)—Night Journeys *(rec Culver City, CA, Sept 1993)* — Philips ▲ 442425-2 [DDD]
Williams, John:E.T. (sels)—The Flying Theme *(rec Culver City, CA, Feb 1991)* — Philips ▲ 432109-2 [DDD]
Williams, John:Jurassic Park (sels)—Main Title *(rec Culver City, CA, Sept 1993)* — Philips ▲ 442425-2 [DDD]
Williams, John:Star Wars (sels)—Throne Room & Finale *(rec Hollywood, CA)* — Philips ▲ 446403-2 [DDD]
Williams, John:The Witches of Eastwick (sels)—The Devil's Dance *(rec Hollywood, CA)* — Philips ▲ 446403-2 [DDD]
Hollywood Bowl Pops Orch
C. Dragon (cnd)
Romberg, S.:Music of (orchestral sels) — EMI Classics ("Studio" series) ▲ CDM 69053
Hollywood Bowl SO
Musical Moments in the Garden, w. Academy of St. Martin in the Fields, Bournemouth SO, English CO, Toulouse Orch, Philharmonia Orch, Toulouse CO, L. Auriacombe (cnd), T. Beecham (cnd), C. Davis (cnd), R. Hickox (cnd), N. Marriner (cnd), M. Plasson (cnd), M. Sargent (cnd) — Angel ▲ CDM 65203 ■ EG 65203
C. Dragon (cnd)
The Music of Christmas — Angel ▲ CDM 66087
A. Newman (cnd)
Herrmann, B.:The Egyptian — Varése Sarabande ▲ ■ VSC 5258
C.D. Newman (cnd)
The Orchestra Sings:Great Operatic Themes for Orchestra, w. Capitol SO — Angel ▲ CDM 65430 ■ EG 65430
E. Ormandy (cnd)
Hollywood Bowl Orchestra *(rec live, Hollywood Bowl, 8/27/47)* — Melodram ▲ CDM 16512 (m) [AAD]
Mario Lanza & Frances Yeend, w. Mario Lanza (ten), Frances Yeend (sop) *(rec live at the Hollywood Bowl, 8/27/47)* — Melodram ▲ CDM 16512 (m) [AAD]
F. Slatkin (cnd)
Gershwin, G.:An American in Paris — Classics for Pleasure ("Eminence" series) ▲ CDEMX 2175
Gershwin, G.:Porgy & Bess (symphonic picture) — Classics for Pleasure ("Eminence" series) ▲ CDEMX 2175
Gershwin, G.:Rhap in Blue, w. Leonard Pennario (pno) — Classics for Pleasure ("Eminence" series) ▲ CDEMX 2175
L. Stokowski (cnd)
Tchaikovsky, P.:Sym 6 — Cala ▲ CAL CACD 506
Thomson, V.:The Plow That Broke the Plains *(rec Aug 30, 1946)* — RCA Gold Seal ▲ 09026-68163-2 [ADD]
Hollywood CO
L. Schifrin (cnd)
Saint-Saëns, C.:Carnival of the Animals, w. M. Golabek (nar), R. Golabek (nar), F. Savage (nar), C. Heston (nar), J. E. Jones (nar), B. White (nar), L. Redgrave (nar), W. Shatner (nar), J. Rivers (nar), T. Danson (nar), L. Tomlin (nar), D. Raffin (nar), A. Hepburn (nar), D. Moore (nar), W. Matthau (nar), J. Smith (nar) — Dove Audio ▲ DOV 30700
Hollywood String Quartet
Beethoven, L. van:Grosse Fuge Str Qt *(rec 1958)* — Testament 3-▲ SBT 3082
Beethoven, L. van:Qt 12 Strs *(rec 1958)* — Testament 3-▲ SBT 3082
Beethoven, L. van:Qt 13 Strs *(rec 1958)* — Testament 3-▲ SBT 3082
Beethoven, L. van:Qt 14 Strs *(rec 1958)* — Testament 3-▲ SBT 3082
Beethoven, L. van:Qt 15 Strs *(rec 1958)* — Testament 3-▲ SBT 3082
Beethoven, L. van:Qt 16 Strs *(rec 1958)* — Testament 3-▲ SBT 3082
Borodin, A.:Qt 2 Strs — Testament ▲ SBT 1061 [ADD]
Dvořák, A.:Qt 12 Strs, "America" *(rec 1955)* — Testament ▲ SBT 1072
Glazunov, A.:Novelettes, Op. 15 — Testament ▲ SBT 1061 [ADD]
Kodály, Z.:Qt Strs, Op. 10 *(rec 1959)* — Testament ▲ SBT 1072
Smetana, B.:Qt 1 Strs *(rec 1956)* — Testament ▲ SBT 1072
Tchaikovsky, P.:Qt 1 Strs — Testament ▲ SBT 1061 [ADD]
Hollywood String Quartet [Felix Slatkin (vn), Paul Shure (vn), Alvin Dinkin (va), Eleanor Aller (vc)]
Schumann, R.:Qnt Pno, w. Victor Aller (pno) *(rec Melrose Studio, Hollywood, May 13–16, 1955)* — Testament 3-▲ SBT 3063 (m) [ADD]
Hollywood String Quartet [Felix Slatkin (vn), Paul Shure (vn), Paul Robyn (va), Eleanor Aller (vc)]
Brahms, J.:Qt 2 Strs *(rec Melrose Studio, Hollywood, Jan 28–30, 1952)* — Testament 3-▲ SBT 3063 (m) [ADD]
Creston, P.:Qt Strs — Testament ▲ TESSBT 1053 (m) [ADD]
Dohnányi, E. von:Qt 3 Strs *(rec Jan 1955)* — Testament ▲ SBT 1081
Franck, C.:Qnt Pno, w. Victor Aller (pno) *(rec 1953)* — Testament ▲ SBT 1077
Haydn, J.:Qts Strs, Op. 76, "Erdödy Qts"—No. 2 in d, "Fifths" *(rec Royal Festival Hall, London, Sept 8, 1957)* — Testament ▲ SBT 1085
Hindemith, P.:Qt 3 Strs — Testament ▲ TESSBT 1052 (m) [ADD]
Hummel, J.N.:Qt 2 Strs *(rec Melrose Studio, Apr 22–23, 1955)* — Testament ▲ SBT 1085
Mozart, W.A.:Qt 17 Strs *(rec Royal Festival Hall, London, Sept 8, 1957)* — Testament ▲ SBT 1085
Prokofiev, S.:Qt 2 Strs — Testament ▲ TESSBT 1052 (m) [ADD]
Ravel, M.:Intro & Allegro, w. Ann Mason Stockton (hp), Arthur Gleghorn (fl), Mitchell Lurie (cl) — Testament ▲ TESSBT 1053 (m) [ADD]
Schubert, Franz:Qt 14 Strs *(rec Dec 1955)* — Testament ▲ SBT 1081
Schumann, R.:Qnt Pno, w. Victor Aller (pno) *(rec 1955)* — Testament 3-▲ SBT 3063
Shostakovich, D.:Qnt Pno, w. Victor Aller (pno) *(rec 1952)* — Testament ▲ SBT 1077
Turina, J.:La oracion del torero [arr str qt by composer] — Testament ▲ TESSBT 1053 (m) [ADD]
Villa-Lobos, H.:Qt 6 Strs — Testament ▲ TESSBT 1053 (m) [ADD]
Walton, W.:Qt Strs — Testament ▲ TESSBT 1052 (m) [ADD]
Wolf, H.:Italian Serenade *(rec Dec 1953)* — Testament ▲ SBT 1081
Hollywood String Quartet members [Felix Slatkin (vn), Alvin Dinkin (va), Eleanor Aller (vc)]
Brahms, J.:Qts Pno (comp), w. Victor Aller (pno) *(rec Studio A, Capitol Tower, Hollywood & Melrose Studio, Hollywood, Jan–June 1956)* — Testament 3-▲ SBT 3063 (m) [ADD]
Brahms, J.:Qnt Pno, w. Victor Aller (pno) *(rec Hollywood, Mar 30–31, 1954)* — Testament 3-▲ SBT 3063 (m) [ADD]
Holmby String Quartet
Gold, E.:Music of, w. H. Dilworth (sop), G. Nestor (gtr), F. Benedetti (gtr), R. Gianattosio (pno)—Sonata for Piano (1980); Songs of Love & Parting (1963); Quartet No. 1 for Strings (1948) *(rec 1983 & 1990)* — Cambria ▲ CD 1062 [DDD/ADD]
Holst Orch
H.D. Wetton (cnd)
Bliss, A.:Pastoral, w. S. Minty (mez), Holst Singers [E] — Hyperion ▲ CDA 66175

Holst Orch (cont.)
H.D. Wetton (cnd) (cont.)
Britten, B.:Gloriana (choral dances), w. M. Hill (ten), Holst Singers [ver. for tenor, harp & chorus] Hyperion ▲ CDA 66175
Holst, G.:Choral Hymns from the Rig-Veda, w. Holst Singers Hyperion ▲ CDA 66175
Holzbläser CO
Christmas Concert, w. Simon Dach, Collegium Tubicense Ulm, Ulmer Brass Ensemble, Holzbläser Ensemble Christophorus ▲ CD 74585
Holzbläser Ensemble
Christmas Concert, w. Simon Dach, Collegium Tubicense Ulm, Ulmer Brass Ensemble, Holzbläser CO Christophorus ▲ CD 74585
L'Homme Armé
Musica a Firenze:The Time of Lorenzo the Magnificent *(rec Apr. 1990)* Christophorus ▲ CHR 77132 [DDD]
L'Homme Armé [Eva Tognetti (sop), Gianna Grazzini (sop), Nino Marini (ten), Renato Baldassini (bar), Marcello Vargetto (bass), Gian Luca Lastraioli (lt/thb/gtr), Andrea Perugi (hpd), Bettina Hoffman (vl), Poalo Casu (perc)]
F. Lombardo (cnd)
Banchieri, A.:Barca di Venetia per Padova *(rec S. Francisco Poverino Church, Florence, Italy, Mar 1992)* Arts ▲ 472582 [DDD]
Banchieri, A.:Il zabione musicale *(rec S. Francisco Poverino Church, Florence, Italy, Mar 1992)* Arts ▲ 472582 [DDD]
Hong Kong PO
A. Almeida (cnd)
Glazunov, A.:From Darkness to Light Marco Polo ▲ 8.220444 [DDD]
Glazunov, A.:Intermezzo romantico Marco Polo ▲ 8.220445 [DDD]
Glazunov, A.:Intro & Salome's Dance Marco Polo ▲ 8.220445 [DDD]
Glazunov, A.:Karelian Legend Marco Polo ▲ 8.220444 [DDD]
Glazunov, A.:March on a Russian Theme Marco Polo ▲ 8.220444 [DDD]
Glazunov, A.:Oriental Rhap Marco Polo ▲ 8.220444 [DDD]
Glazunov, A.:Ov 2 on Greek Themes Marco Polo ▲ 8.220445 [DDD]
Glazunov, A.:The Song of Destiny Marco Polo ▲ 8.220445 [DDD]
K. Jean (cnd)
Du, M.:Festival Ov *(rec Tsuen Wan Town Hall, 1988)* Marco Polo ("Chinese Composers" series) ▲ 8.223939 [DDD]
Du, M.:The Great Wall Sym *(rec Tsuen Wan Town Hall, 1988)* Marco Polo ("Chinese Composers" series) ▲ 8.223939 [DDD]
Massenet, J.:Cendrillon (orchestral suite) Marco Polo ▲ 8.223354
Massenet, J.:Esclarmonde (orchestral suite) Marco Polo ▲ 8.223354
Massenet, J.:Suite 1 Marco Polo ▲ 8.223354
V. Kojian (cnd)
Wagner, R.:Marches—American Centennial March; Imperial March Marco Polo ▲ 8.220114 [DDD]
Wagner, R.:Ovs, Preludes & Orch Sels—Polonia Over.; Rule Britannia Over. Marco Polo ▲ 8.220114 [DDD]
K. Schermerhorn (cnd)
Chan, W.W.:Sym 3—Part III *(rec Lyric Theatre of the Hong Kong Academy for Performing Arts, June 28, 1986)* Marco Polo ("Chinese Contemporary" series) ▲ 8.223915 [DDD]
Cui, C.:In modo populari (Suite No. 3) Marco Polo ▲ 8.220308 [DDD]
Cui, C.:Suite concertante, w. T. Nishizaki (vn) Marco Polo ▲ 8.220308 [DDD]
Cui, C.:Suite miniature 1 Marco Polo ▲ 8.220308 [DDD]
Huang, A.:Con Pno, w. Joseph Banowetz (pno)—Allegro only *(rec Lyric Theatre of the Hong Kong Academy for Performing Arts, June 28, 1986)* Marco Polo ("Chinese Contemporary" series) ▲ 8.223915 [DDD]
Qu, X.:Mong Dong, w. Michael Rippon (bar), *(other soloists unknown) (rec Lyric Theatre of the Hong Kong Academy for Performing Arts, June 28, 1986)* Marco Polo ("Chinese Contemporary" series) ▲ 8.223915 [DDD]
Strauss, R.:Interludio *(rec March 31–Apr. 3, 1985)* Marco Polo ▲ 8.220323 [DDD]
Strauss, R.:Sym in d *(rec March 31–Apr. 3, 1985)* Marco Polo ▲ 8.220323 [DDD]
Strauss, R.:Der Zweikampf *(rec March 31–Apr. 3, 1985)* Marco Polo ▲ 8.220323 [DDD]
Tan, D.:Intermezzo *(rec Lyric Theatre of the Hong Kong Academy for Performing Arts, June 28, 1986)* Marco Polo ("Chinese Contemporary" series) ▲ 8.223915 [DDD]
Villa-Lobos, H.:Chôro 9 *(rec March 31–Apr. 3, 1985)* Marco Polo ▲ 8.220322 [DDD]
Ye, X.:Moon over the West River *(rec Lyric Theatre of the Hong Kong Academy for Performing Arts, June 28, 1986)* Marco Polo ("Chinese Contemporary" series) ▲ 8.223915 [DDD]
Y. W. Sie (cnd)
Chen, G.:Wang Zhaojun Con, w. Takako Nishizaki (vn), Lam Fung (pipa) *(rec Shatin Town Hall, Hong Kong, June 23, 1987)* Marco Polo ("Chinese Composers" series) ▲ 8.223908 [DDD]
Chen, P.:Fant on Cantonese Themes, w. Wong On Yuen (gaohu) *(rec Tsuen Wan Town Hall, May 25–28, 1987)* Marco Polo ("Chinese Composers" series) ▲ 8.223927 [DDD]
Chen, P.:Pieces (5) Erhu, w. Wong On Yuen (erhu)—Colourful Clouds Chasing the Moon; Scenes from Tibet; Morning-Star Lily in Flower; Song of Tong Mountain; Song of the Horse-head Fiddle *(rec Tsuen Wan Town Hall, May 25–28, 1987)* Marco Polo ("Chinese Composers" series) ▲ 8.223927 [DDD]
J. Tang (cnd)
Tang, J.:Sym 3—Andante sostenuto & Allegro only *(rec Lyric Theatre of the Hong Kong Academy for Performing Arts, June 28, 1986)* Marco Polo ("Chinese Contemporary" series) ▲ 8.223915 [DDD]
Honolulu SO
D. Johanos (cnd)
Welcher, D.:Con Cl, w. B. Jackson (cl) *(rec Jan. 10, 1992)* Marco Polo ▲ 8.223457 [DDD]
Welcher, D.:Haleakala:How Maui Snared the Sun, w. R. Chamberlain (nar), A. McCutchan (nar) *(rec Jan. 10, 1992)* Marco Polo ▲ 8.223457 [DDD]
Welcher, D.:Prairie Light:3 Texas Watercolors of Georgia O'Keefe *(rec Jan. 10, 1992)* Marco Polo ▲ 8.223457 [DDD]
Hopkins Center Orch
M. di Bonaventura (cnd)
Ginastera, A.:Con Vn, w. S. Accardo (vn) *(rec live 1968)* Dynamic ▲ CDS 110 [ADD]
Horowitz-Gurt Piano Duo
Iannaccone, A.:Inventions Redwood ▲ ESCD 45
Horsholm Percussion & Marimba Ensemble
O. Pedersen (cnd)
Horsholm Percussion & Marimba Ensemble Danacord ▲ DACOCD 329
Hotteterre Quartet
Marais, M.:Suites for Chamber Ensemble Teldec 2-▲ 77617-2
Household Cavalry Bands
The Horse Guard Bandleader ▲ BND 7005 [DDD]
Houston Grand Opera Orch
W. Holmquist (cnd)
Moran, R.:Dracula Diary Catalyst ▲ 09026-62638-2
G. Schuller (cnd)
Joplin, S.:Treemonisha, w. Houston Grand Opera Chorus *(rec 1975)* Deutsche Grammophon 2-▲ 435709-2 [ADD]
Houston Sym Chamber Players
Schoenberg, A.:Qnt Fl Koch International Classics ▲ KIC 7337
Webern, A.:Con Fl, w. Christoph Eschenbach (pno) Koch International Classics ▲ KIC 7337
Houston SO
S. Comissiona (cnd)
Dvořák, A.:Carnival *(rec 5/87)* Pro Arte ▲ CDS 3432 [DDD]
Dvořák, A.:Slavonic Dances (sels)—Op. 46 *(rec May 1987)* Pro Arte ▲ CDS 3432 [DDD]
Franck, C.:Sym in d *(rec 4/82)* Vanguard Classics ▲ OVC 4014 [DDD]
Mendelssohn, F.:Music of, w. J. Silverstein (vn), Utah SO—Violin Concerto in e, Op. 64; Midsummer Night's Dream (overture); etc. Pro Arte ▲ CDM 815 ■ PCD 815

Houston SO (cont.)
S. Comissiona (cnd) (cont.)
Picker, T.:Sym 2, w. L. Mitchell (sop) Elektra/Nonesuch ▲ 79246-2-ZK
Sabre Dance Pro Arte ▲ CDD 250
Saint-Saëns, C.:Sym 3 *(rec 1980)* Vanguard Classics ▲ OVC 4014 [DDD]
Schumann, R.:Syms (comp)—Nos. 1 & 4 Pro Arte ▲ CDD 393
Schumann, R.:Syms (comp)—Nos. 2 & 3 Pro Arte ▲ CDD 394
Tchaikovsky, P.:Music of, London Royal Promenade Orch—Capriccio italien; The Nutcracker (selections); Overture 1812; etc. Pro Arte ▲ CDM 809 ■ PCD 809
Tchaikovsky, P.:Waltzes—from Swan Lake, Sleeping Beauty, Nutcracker, Serenade Op. 48, Symphony No. 5, Eugene Onegin Pro Arte ▲ CDD 251
C. Eschenbach (cnd)
Brahms, J.:Academic Festival Ov Virgin Classics 2-▲ CUVB 61226
Brahms, J.:Academic Festival Ov Virgin Classics ▲ CDC 59223
Brahms, J.:Alto Rhap, w. D. Vejzovic (mez) EMI Classics ▲ CDC 45006
Brahms, J.:Alto Rhap, w. Dunja Vejzovic (mez), Houston Sym Male Chorus Virgin Classics 2-▲ CUVB 61226
Brahms, J.:Sym 1 Virgin Classics 2-▲ CUVB 61226
Brahms, J.:Sym 1 Virgin Classics ▲ CDC 59223
Brahms, J.:Sym 3 Virgin Classics 2-▲ CUVB 61226
Brahms, J.:Sym 3 EMI Classics ▲ CDC 45006
Bruckner, A.:Sym 2 Koch Schwann ▲ KIC CD 7391
Dvořák, A.:Sym 9, "From the New World" Virgin Classics ▲ CDC 59053
Mozart, W.A.:Con Bn, w. Benjamin Kamins (bn) *(rec Stude Concert Hall, Shephard School of Music, Rice Univ, July 12–16, 1993)* IMP ("Masters" series) ▲ IMP MCD 91
Mozart, W.A.:Con Cl, w. David Peck (cl) *(rec Stude Concert Hall, Shephard School of Music, Rice Univ, July 12–16, 1993)* IMP ("Masters" series) ▲ IMP MCD 91
Mozart, W.A.:Music of—Con. in A for Clarinet, K.622; Cons. (4) for Horn, K. 412, 417, 447 & 495; Con. in C for Oboe, K.314; Con. in B♭ for Bassoon, K.191 IMP Masters 3-▲ IMPTCD 77 [DDD]
Picker, T.:The Encantadas, w. J. Gielgud (spkr) [E] Virgin Classics ▲ 59007 [DDD]
Picker, T.:Old & Lost Rivers, w. C. Eschenbach (pno) [2 versions:orch. & solo piano] Virgin Classics ▲ 59007 [DDD]
Picker, T.:Romances & Interludes, w. R. Atherholt (ob) Virgin Classics ▲ 59007 [DDD]
Schoenberg, A.:Pelleas und Melisande Koch International Classics ▲ KIC 7316 [DDD]
Strauss, R.:4 Last Songs, w. Renée Fleming (sop) *(rec Jones Hall, Houston, TX, Mar 14 & 20, 1995)* RCA Red Seal ▲ 09026-68539-2 [DDD]
Strauss, R.:Der Rosenkavalier (suite), w. Renée Fleming (sop) *(rec Jones Hall, Houston, TX, May 8, 1995)* RCA Red Seal ▲ 09026-68539-2 [DDD]
Strauss, R.:Songs, w. Renée Fleming (sop)—Befreit, Op. 39/4; Muttertändelei, Op. 43/2; Wiegenlied, Op. 41/1; Waldseligkeit, Op. 49/1; Cäcilie, Op. 27/2 *(rec Jones Hall, Houston, TX, May 8, 1995)* RCA Red Seal ▲ 09026-68539-2 [DDD]
Tchaikovsky, P.:Francesca da Rimini Virgin Classics ▲ CDC 59053
Webern, A.:Passacaglia Koch International Classics ▲ KIC 7316 [DDD]
S. Jones (cnd)
Cooper, P.:Sym 4, "Landscape" CRI ▲ CD 579 [ADD]
Cooper, P.:Sym 4, "Landscape" CRI ■ C 347
Jones, S.:Elegy CRI ▲ CD 579 [ADD]
Jones, S.:Elegy CRI ■ C 347
Jones, S.:Let Us Now Praise Famous Men CRI ■ C 347
Jones, S.:Let Us Now Praise Famous Men CRI ▲ CD 579 [ADD]
L. Stokowski (cnd)
Bartók, B.:Con Orch Everest ▲ EVC 9008 [AAD]
Brahms, J.:Sym 3 *(rec Civic Center, Houston)* Everest ▲ EVC 9016 [AAD]
Canning, T.:Fant on Hymn Tune by Justin Morgan Everest ▲ EVC 9004 [AAD]
Glière, R.:Sym 3, "Il'ya Muromets" EMI Classics ▲ CDM 65074
Loeffler, C.M.:A Pagan Poem EMI Classics ▲ CDM 65074
Orff, C.:Carmina burana, w. Houston Chorale *(rec 1955)* EMI Classics ("FDS" series) ▲ CDM 65207
Scriabin, A.:Sym 4 Everest ▲ EVC 9037 [AAD]
Shostakovich, D.:Sym 11 *(rec 1958)* EMI Classics ("FDS" series) ▲ CDM 65206
Stravinsky, I.:The Firebird Suite, w. Houston Chorale EMI Classics (FDS Series) ▲ CDM 65207
Wagner, R.:Parsifal (sels)—The Good Friday Spell; Parsifal Act III Synthesis [arr. Stokowski] *(rec Civic Center, Houston, TX)* Everest ▲ EVC 9024 [AAD]
Wagner, R.:Die Walküre (sels)—Wotan's Farewell; Magic Fire Music [both arr. Stokowski] *(rec Civic Center, Houston, TX)* Everest ▲ EVC 9024 [AAD]
HR Brass
Bach, J.S.:Brandenburg Con 3 Capriccio ▲ 10 361 [DDD]
Barber, S.:Mutations from Bach Capriccio ▲ 10 361 [DDD]
Carter, E.:A Fant on Purcell's *Fantasia upon One Note* Capriccio ▲ 10 361 [DDD]
Copland, A.:Fanfare for the Common Man Capriccio ▲ 10 361 [DDD]
Handel, G.F.:Royal Fireworks Music Capriccio ▲ 10 361 [DDD]
L. Köhler (cnd)
HR Brass Capriccio ▲ 10 361 [DDD]
E. Tarr (cnd)
Frescobaldi, G.:Canzonas Instr Ensemble—L'Ambitiosa *(rec Ilbenstadt, Basilika, Nov 1992)* Capriccio ▲ 10599 [DDD]
Gabrieli, G.:Music of—Raveri-Sammlung; Symphoniae Sacrae I & II *(rec Ilbenstadt, Basilika, Nov 1992)* Capriccio ▲ 10599 [DDD]
Guami, G.:Canzonas—No. 25; "L'Accorta" *(rec Ilbenstadt, Basilika, Nov 1992)* Capriccio ▲ 10599 [DDD]
Gussago, C.:Canzonas—La Bottaga *(rec Ilbenstadt, Basilika, Nov 1992)* Capriccio ▲ 10599 [DDD]
Lappi, P.:Canzonas—No. 26, "La Negrona" *(rec Ilbenstadt, Basilika, Nov 1992)* Capriccio ▲ 10599 [DDD]
Massaino, T.:Canzonas—No. 33 *(rec Ilbenstadt, Basilika, Nov 1992)* Capriccio ▲ 10599 [DDD]
J. Whigham (cnd)
Bernstein, L.:West Side Story (sels) Capriccio ▲ 10429 [DDD]
Gershwin, G.:Music of—Strike up the Band; Fascinatin' Rhythm; Foggy Day; I Got Rhythm; The Man I Love Capriccio ▲ 10429 [DDD]
Gershwin, G.:Porgy & Bess (sels) Capriccio ▲ 10429 [DDD]
Hradec Kralove PO
J.-L. Leger (cnd)
Onslow, G.:Sym 2 Ligia Digital ▲ 0301036
Onslow, G.:Sym 4 Ligia Digital ▲ 0301036
Hudson River String Trio [Sheila Reinhold (vn), Jennie Hansen (va), David Calhoun (vc)]
Schubert, Franz:Trio Strs, D.471 Epiphany ▲ EP 7
Hudson Valley Philharmonic String Quartet
L. Botstein (cnd)
Kupferman, M.:A Little Ivory Con, w. K. Hayami (pno), Hudson Valley Wind Quintet Soundspells ▲ SP 101
Hudson Valley Wind Quintet
Kupferman, M.:A Little Ivory Con, w. K. Hayami (pno), Hudson Valley Philharmonic String Quartet Soundspells ▲ SP 101
Huelgas Ensemble
Brumel, A.:Et ecce terrae motus, "Earthquake Mass" Sony Classical (Vivarte) ▲ SK 46348
Canções, Vilancicos e Motetes Portugueses Sony Classical ("Vivarte" series) ▲ SK 66288
Codex las Huelgas *(rec Oct. 9–11, 1992)* Sony Classical ▲ SK 53341 [DDD]
La Dissection d'un homme armé Sony Classical ("Vivarte" series) ▲ SK 45860
Febus Avant! Music at the Court of Gaston Febus, 1331-1391 Sony Classical ("Vivarte" series) ▲ SK 48195 [DDD]
Gabrieli, G.:Exaudi me Domine Sony Classical ("Vivarte" series) ▲ SK 66261
Gallus, J.:Missa super "Sancta Maria" Sony Classical ("Vivarte" series) ▲ SK 64305

▲ = CD ♦ = Enhanced CD Δ = MD ■ = Cassette Tape □ = DCC

Huelgas Ensemble (cont.)
Gallus, J.:Opus Musicum — Sony Classical ("Vivarte" series) ▲ SK 64305
Gombert, N.:Chansons—Je prens congie; Tous les regretz — Sony Classical ("Vivarte" series) ▲ SK 48249 [DDD]
Gombert, N.:Sacred Choral Music—Magnificat secundi toni; Mass for Six Voices; 2 Motets (In te domine speravi; edia vita); Regina coeli [L] — Sony Classical ("Vivarte" series) ▲ SK 48249 [DDD]
In Morte di Madonna Laura:Madrigal Cycle after Texts of Petrarca, 1307–1374 — Sony Classical ("Vivarte" series) ▲ SK 45942
Italia mia:Musical Imagination of the Renaissance — Sony Classical ("Vivarte" series) ▲ SK 48065
Le Jeune, C.:Le Printemps — Sony Classical ("Vivarte" series) ▲ SK68259
Josquin Desprez:Qui habitat in adjutorio Altissimi — Sony Classical ("Vivarte" series) ▲ SK 66261
Lassus, O. de:Lagrime di San Pietro *(rec Mar. 5–8, 1993)* — Sony Classical ▲ SK 53373 [DDD]
Manchicourt, P. de:Laudate Dominum — Sony Classical ("Vivarte" series) ▲ SK 66261
Matteo Flecha:Las Ensaladas — Sony Classical ("Vivarte" series) ▲ SK 46699
Music from the Court of King Janus at Nicosia *(rec Belgium, June 16–18, 1993)* — Sony Classical ("Vivarte" series) ▲ SK 53976 [DDD]
Ockeghem, J.:Deo gratias — Sony Classical ("Vivarte" series) ▲ SK 66261
Pipelare, M.:Missa "L'Homme armé" *(rec Belgium, Apr 24–26, 1995)* — Sony Classical ▲ SK 68258 [DDD]
Pipelare, M.:Motets—Memorare Mater Christi; Salve Regina *(rec Belgium, Apr 24–26, 1995)* — Sony Classical ▲ SK 68258 [DDD]
Pipelare, M.:Secular Songs—Vray dieu d'amours; Een Vrouelic wesen; Fors seulement *(rec Belgium, Apr 24–26, 1995)* — Sony Classical ▲ SK 68258 [DDD]
Porta, C.:Masses—Sanctus; Agnus Dei [both from Missa Ducalis] — Sony Classical ("Vivarte" series) ▲ SK 66261
Praetorius, M.:Magnificat [L] — Sony Classical ("Vivarte" series) ▲ SK 48039
Praetorius, M.:Music of—Aus tiefer Not; Der Tag vertreibt; Venite Exultemus; Maria Magdalena; Peccavi Fateor; Psalm 116 — Sony Classical ("Vivarte" series) ▲ SK 48039
Rebelo, J.S.:Psalmi tum vesperarum, tum completarum, item Magnificat, Lamentationes, et Miserere — Sony Classical ▲ SK 53115
Striggio, A.:Ecce beatam lucem — Sony Classical ("Vivarte" series) ▲ SK 66261
Tallis, T.:Spem in allem — Sony Classical ("Vivarte" series) ▲ SK 66261
Tears of Lisbon, w. Beatriz de Conceição, António Rocha — Sony Classical ▲ SK 62256

Hugo Wolf String Quartet
Boccherini, L.:Qnts Gtr & Strs, w. Walter Abt (gtr)—Nos. 1, 4 & 9 *(rec Munich, Apr.–June 1994)* — Calig ▲ CAL 50936 [DDD]

Hungarian Army Central Wind Orch
Geiger (cnd)
Marches from the Hungarian History — Hungaroton ▲ HCD 31447 [DDD]

Hungarian CO
V. Tátrai (cnd)
Bartók, B.:Divert *(rec 1964)* — Hungaroton 3–▲ HCD 31509/11 [ADD]
Haydn, J.:Sym 6, "Le Matin" — White Label ▲ HRC 101 [ADD]
Haydn, J.:Sym 7, "Le Midi" — White Label ▲ HRC 101 [ADD]
Haydn, J.:Sym 8, "Le Soir" — White Label ▲ HRC 101 [ADD]
Haydn, J.:Sym 39 — White Label ▲ HRC 141 [ADD]
Haydn, J.:Sym 47 — White Label ▲ HRC 141 [ADD]
Haydn, J.:Sym 54 — White Label ▲ HRC 141 [ADD]
Lajtha, L.:Sinfonietta — Hungaroton ▲ HCD 31452 [ADD]
Mozart, W.A.:Sinf concertante Ob, K.Anh.9, Hungarian Wind Ensemble — White Label ▲ HRC 159 [ADD]
Mozart, W.A.:Sym 33 — White Label ▲ HRC 151 [ADD]
Mozart, W.A.:Sym 40 — White Label ▲ HRC 151 [ADD]

Hungarian National PO
T. Ferenc (cnd)
Bartók, B.:Con Orch — IMP ("Classics" series) ▲ IMP 6700712
Bartók, B.:Kossuth — IMP ("Classics" series) ▲ IMP 6700712
Bartók, B.:The Miraculous Mandarin (suite) — IMP ("Classics" series) ▲ IMP 6700712
Bartók, B.:Suite 1 Orch — IMP Classics ▲ IMP PCD 1028 [DDD]
Bartók, B.:Suite 2 Orch — IMP Classics ▲ IMP PCD 1028 [DDD]

Hungarian Operetta Orch
L. Kovács (cnd)
Kálmán, I.:Gräfin Mariza (sels), w. Ingrid Kirtesi (sop), Zsuzsa Csonka (sop), János Berkes (ten)—Komm mit nach Varasadin *(rec Budapest, Oct 1995)* — Naxos ▲ 8.550941 [DDD]
Kálmán, I.:Gräfin Mariza (sels), w. Ingrid Kirtesi (sop), Zsuzsa Csonka (sop), János Berkes (ten)—Auftrittsleid Mariza; Komm Zigány; Grüss mir die süssen *(rec Budapest, Jan 1996)* — Naxos ▲ 8.550943 [DDD]
Lehár, F.:Operetta Arias, w. Ingrid Kirtesi (sop), Zsuzsa Csonka (sop), János Berkes (ten)—Freunde, das Leben ist lebenswert!; Meine Lippen, sie küssen si heiss [both from Giuditta]; O Mädchen, mein Mädchen [from Friederike]; Dein ist mein ganzes Herz; Wer hat die Liebe uns ins Herz gesenkt?; Immer nur lächeln; Von Apfelblüten einen Kranz [all from Das Land des Lächlens]; Lippen schweigen [from Die lustige Witwe] *(rec Budapest, Oct 1995)* — Naxos ▲ 8.550941 [DDD]
Lehár, F.:Paganini (sels), w. Ingrid Kirtesi (sop), Zsuzsa Csonka (sop), János Berkes (ten)—Liebe, du Himmel auf Erden *(rec Budapest, Jan 1996)* — Naxos ▲ 8.550943 [DDD]
Stolz, R.:Arias, w. Ingrid Kirtesi (sop), Zsuzsa Csonka (sop), János Berkes (ten)—Ich liebe dich! [from Zauber der Bohème]; Zwei gerzen im Dreiviertaltakt; Du sollst der Kaiser meiner Seele sein [both from Der Favorit]; Adieu, mein kleiner Gardeoffizer [from Das Lied ist aus] *(rec Budapest, Jan 1996)* — Naxos ▲ 8.550943 [DDD]
Strauss (II), Joh.:Arias, w. Ingrid Kirtesi (sop), Zsuzsa Csonka (sop), János Berkes (ten)—Ov; Wer uns getraut; Als flotter Geist [both from Der Zigeunerbaron]; Frühlingstimmen (waltz); Komm in die Gondel [from Eine Nacht in Venedig] *(rec Budapest, Oct 1995)* — Naxos ▲ 8.550941 [DDD]
Strauss (II), Joh.:Arias, w. Ingrid Kirtesi (sop), Zsuzsa Csonka (sop), János Berkes (ten)—Ov; Klänge der Heimat; Trinke Liebchen! Trinke schnell!; Mein Herr Marquis [all from Die Fledermaus]; Laguenwaltzer [from Eine Nacht in Venedig] *(rec Budapest, Jan 1996)* — Naxos ▲ 8.550943 [DDD]
Zeller, C.A.:Vogelhändler (sels), w. Ingrid Kirtesi (sop), Zsuzsa Csonka (sop), János Berkes (ten)—Wie mein Ahn'l zwanzig Jahr' *(rec Budapest, Jan 1996)* — Naxos ▲ 8.550943 [DDD]

Hungarian Philharmonia
T. Hlasek (cnd)
Bartók, B.:Con 2 Vn, w. R. Ricci (vn) — One–Eleven ▲ URS 91030 [ADD]
Paganini, N.:Con 4 Vn, w. R. Ricci (vn), Piero Mordini (vn) — One–Eleven ▲ URS 91030 [ADD]

Hungarian PO
J. Ferencsik (cnd)
Beethoven, L. van:Sym 1 — Laserlight ▲ 15 904
Beethoven, L. van:Sym 2 — Laserlight ▲ 15 903
Beethoven, L. van:Sym 3, "Eroica" — Laserlight ▲ 15 902
Beethoven, L. van:Sym 4 — Laserlight ▲ 15 901
Beethoven, L. van:Sym 5 — Laserlight ▲ 15 901
Beethoven, L. van:Sym 6, "Pastorale" — Laserlight ▲ 15 903
Beethoven, L. van:Sym 7 — Laserlight ▲ 15 904
Beethoven, L. van:Sym 8 — Laserlight ▲ 15 902
Beethoven, L. van:Sym 9, "Choral Sym", w. E. Andor (sop), H. Szirmay (cta), G. Korondy (ten), S. Solyom–Nagy (bar), Budapest Phil Chorus — Laserlight ▲ 15 905
J. Sándor (cnd)
Brahms, J.:Hungarian Dances Orch — LaserLight ▲ 15501 [DDD]

Hungarian Quintet members
Beethoven, L. van:Qnt Pno, Ob, Cl, Hn & Bn, w. A. Brendel (pno) — Allegretto ▲ ACD 8150 [ADD] ■ ACS 8150
Mozart, W.A.:Qnt Pno, K.452, w. A. Brendel (pno) — Allegretto ▲ ACD 8150 [ADD] ■ ACS 8150

Hungarian RSO
E. Boncompagni (cnd)
Donizetti, G.:Anna Bolena, w. Edita Gruberová (sop), Delores Ziegler (mez), Stefano Palatchi (bass), Hungarian Radio Chorus — Nightingale Classics 3–▲ NIG 70565
J. Ferencsik (cnd)
Kodály, Z.:Missa Brevis, w. Hungarian Radio Chorus [L] — Hungaroton ▲ HCD 11397
G. Lehel (cnd)
Kodály, Z.:Galanta Dances — Hungaroton ▲ HCD 12252
Kodály, Z.:Marosszék Dances — Hungaroton ▲ HCD 12252
Kodály, Z.:Vars on a Hungarian Folk Song — Hungaroton ▲ HCD 12252

Hungarian Radio–TV SO
M. Pace (cnd)
Mascagni, P.:Amica, w. Katia Ricciarelli (sop), Monica Minarelli (sgr), Elia Padovan (sgr), Fabio Armiliato (sgr), Walter Donati (sgr), Hungarian Radio–TV Chorus *(rec Budapest, Nov 1995)* — Kicco Classic 2–▲ KC 00296 [DDD]
G. Patanè (cnd)
Giordano, U.:Fedora, w. V. Kincses (sop), E. Martón (sop), J. Carreras (ten), J. Gregor (bass), Hungarian Radio–TV Chorus [I] — CBS 2–▲ M2K 42181 [DDD]
Tamás (cnd)
Kálmán, I.:Die Csárdásfürstin (sels), w. Erzsébet (sgr), György (sgr), Hanna (sgr), Róbert (sgr), Hungarian Radio–TV Chorus — Hungaroton ▲ HCD 16780 [AAD]

Hungarian State Folk Ensemble Orch
L. Berki (cnd)
Csámpai, I.:In Memory of Bihari, w. Hungarian State Folk Ensemble Chorus *(rec 1969)* — Hungaroton ▲ HCD 18008 [AAD]
Gulyás, L.:Bottle Dance, w. Hungarian State Folk Ensemble Chorus *(rec 1969)* — Hungaroton ▲ HCD 18008 [AAD]
Gulyás, L.:Music from Szék, w. Hungarian State Folk Ensemble Chorus *(rec 1969)* — Hungaroton ▲ HCD 18008 [AAD]
R. Lantos (cnd)
Csenki, I.:Gypsy Dances of Hungary, w. Márta Szobek (sgr), Hungarian State Folk Ensemble Chorus *(rec 1969)* — Hungaroton ▲ HCD 18008 [AAD]
Gulyás, L.:Triple Jumping Dance, w. Erzsébet Varga (sgr), Hungarian State Folk Ensemble Chorus *(rec 1969)* — Hungaroton ▲ HCD 18008 [AAD]
Maros, R.:Wedding at Ecser, w. Hungarian State Folk Ensemble Chorus *(rec 1969)* — Hungaroton ▲ HCD 18008 [AAD]
M. Pászti (cnd)
Gulyás, L.:An Evening in the Spinning Room, w. Hungarian State Folk Ensemble Chorus *(rec 1969)* — Hungaroton ▲ HCD 18008 [AAD]
Kodály, Z.:Kálló Double Dance, w. Hungarian State Folk Ensemble Chorus *(rec 1969)* — Hungaroton ▲ HCD 18008 [AAD]

Hungarian State Opera CO
Baroque Trumpet Concertos, w. Ede Inhoff (tpt) — Lydian ▲ LYD 18109 [DDD]

Hungarian State Opera Orch
Classics Go to the Movies Vol. 1, w. Vienna Strauss Orch, Jenő Jandó (pno), Plovdiv PO, Dresden PO, New Leipzig Bach Collegium Musicum, Budapest SO — LaserLight ▲ 15 641
Gounod, C.:Faust (sels), w. Alexandrina Pendachanska (sop—Margarethe), Giuseppe Sabbatini (ten—Faust), György Melis (bar—Valentin), Nicolai Ghiaurov (bass—Méphistophélès), Nikola Ghiuselev (bass—Méphistophélès), Berlin RSO, Vienna SO, Bulgarian RSO, Sofia SO, Bulgarian National Chorus, Bulgarian National Chorus Radio Choir—Intro; Vien ou bière; O sainte médaille...Avant de quitter ces lieux; Le veau d'or [all from Act 2]; Quel trouble inconnu me pénètre!...Salut! demeure chaste et pure; Je voudrais bien savoir...Il était un roi de Thule; Un bouquet!...O Dieu! que de bijoux [both from Act 3]; Gloire immortelle de nos aieux; Vous qui faites l'endormie [both from Act 4]; Intermezzo; Walpurgis Night [both from Act 5] — Laserlight ▲ 14209 [DDD]
Vivaldi, A.:Cons Vc, w. György Kertész (vc)—Nos. 1 in c, R.401; 4 in a, R.422; 7 in d, R.406; 8 in C, R.398; 9 in b, R.424; 11 in F, R.412; 12 in G, R.413 *(rec Festetich Castle, Budapest, June 1991)* — Lydian ▲ 18120 [DDD]
J. Ferencsik (cnd)
Kodály, Z.:Háry János, w. Takács (sgr), S. Sólyom–Nagy (bar), J. Gregor (bass) [Hun] — Hungaroton 2–▲ HCD 12837/38
Puccini, G.:Gianni Schicchi, w. M. Kalmár (sop), C. Melis (sop) [I] — Hungaroton ▲ HCD 12541 [DDD]
I. Fischer (cnd)
Ballet Music from Operas, w. Hungarian State Orch, Württemberg State Orch [cnd:J. Ferencsik] — White Label ▲ HRC 058
L. Gardelli (cnd)
Puccini, G.:Suor angelica, w. I. Tokody (sop), Barlay (sgr), B. Póka (bar), Hungarian State Opera Chorus [I] — Hungaroton ▲ HCD 12490
V. Komor (cnd)
Verdi, G.:Un ballo in maschera (sels), w. Alexander Svéd (bar)—Alla vita che t'arride, Alzati!...ERi tu, che macchiavi *(rec June 7, 1954)* — Hungaroton ("Great Hungarian Voices" series) ▲ HCD 31614 [ADD]
A. Kóródi (cnd)
Szokolay, S.:Blood Wedding, w. E. Házy (sop), O. Szönyi (sop), E. Komlóssy (cta), Faragó (sgr), Hungarian State Opera Chorus [Hun] — Hungaroton 2–▲ HCD 11262/63 [ADD]
A. Kóródi, F. Molinari–Pradelli (cnds)
Verdi, G.:Rigoletto (sels), w. Mária Gyurkovics (sop), Olga Szönyi (mez), Ernő Kenéz (ten), János Fodor (bar), Alexander Svéd (bar), József Bódy (bass)—Pari siamo!; Figlial Mio padre! A te dappresso; Cortigianil Vil' razza dannata; Tutte le feste al tempio...Ah! solo per me!; Chi è mai... *(rec 1955–56)* — Hungaroton ("Great Hungarian Voices" series) ▲ HCD 31614 [ADD]
J. Kovács (cnd)
Erkel, F.:Hunyadi László, w. M. Kalmár (sop), S. Sass (sop), D. Gulyás (ten), A. Molnar (ten), I. Gáti (bar), S. Sólyom–Nagy (bar), Hungarian State Opera Chorus [Hun] — Hungaroton 3–▲ HCD 12581/83 [DDD]
E. Lukács (cnd)
Gluck, C.W.:Orfeo ed Euridice, w. V. Kincses (sop), M. Zempleni (sop), J. Hamari (mez), Hungarian State Opera Chorus — LaserLight ▲ 14113 [DDD]
Kacsóh, P.:János Vitéz, w. Mária Gyurkovics (sop), Anna Zentai (sop—Iluska), Tivadar Bilicsi (sgr), Hilda Gobbi (sgr), Sándor Pethes (sgr—Bartolo), Róbert Ilosfalvy (ten—Kukorica), György Melis (bar—Bagó), György Radnai (bar—Strázsamester), László Domahidy (bass—Csősz), Hungarian Radio–TV Chorus *(rec Budapest, 1961)* — Classical Diamonds 2–▲ CLD 4011–12 [AAD]
Puccini, G.:Arias, w. Ilona Tokody (sop), Juan Pons (bar)—O mio babbino caro [from Gianni Schicchi] *(rec live, Franz Liszt Music Academy, Budapest, Hungary, June 4, 1994)* — VAI Audio ▲ VAIA 1089
Tosti, P.F.:songs, w. Ilona Tokody (sop), Juan Pons (bar)—'A Vucchella *(rec live, Franz Liszt Music Academy, Budapest, Hungary, June 4, 1994)* — VAI Audio ▲ VAIA 1089
Verdi, G.:arias, w. Ilona Tokody (sop), Juan Pons (bar)—Favella il Doge ad Amelia Grimaldi? [duet from Simon Boccanegra]; Di Provenza il mar; Un dì, quando le veneri...Dite alla giovine [both from La Traviata]; Pace, pace, mio Dio! [from La Forza del Destino]; Udiste? Come albeggi, la scure al figlio [duet from Il Trovatore]; Cortigiani, vil razza dannata; Mio padre! Dio! mia Gilda...Tutte le feste [both from Rigoletto]; Ciel! Mio padre! [from Aida] *(rec live, Franz Liszt Music Academy, Budapest, Hungary, June 4, 1994)* — VAI Audio ▲ VAIA 1089
A. Mihály (cnd)
Opera Arias, w. Peter Dvorský (ten) — Acanta ▲ 43335
F. Molinari–Pradelli (cnd)
Verdi, G.:Aida (sels), w. Paula Takács (sop), Alexander Svéd (bar)—Ciel! Mio padre *(rec Mar 24, 1956)* — Hungaroton ("Great Hungarian Voices" series) ▲ HCD 31614 [ADD]
Verdi, G.:Falstaff (sels), w. Alexander Svéd (bar)—L'onorel Ladri *(rec Apr 29, 1955)* — Hungaroton ("Great Hungarian Voices" series) ▲ HCD 31614 [ADD]

ORCH. & ENS.

Hungarian State Opera Orch (cont.)

P. G. Morandi (cnd)

Donizetti, G.:L'elisir d'amore, w. Alessandra Ruffini (sop—Adina), Mariangela Spotorno (sop—Gianetta), Vincenzo La Scola (ten—Nemorino), Simone Alaimo (bar—Dulcamara), Roberto Frontali (bar—Belcore), Anikó Katona (cnd), Hungarian State Opera Chorus *(rec Budapest, July 1995)* Naxos 2-▲ 8.60045-6 [DDD]

Rossini, G.:Arias, w. Ewa Podles (mez), Hungarian State Opera Chorus—Cruda sorte! Amor tiranno!; Amici, in ogni evento m'affido a voi...Pensa all patria [both from L'Italiana in Algeri]; Eccomi alfine in Babilonia...Ah! quel giorno ognor rammento [from Semiramide]; Oh patria...Di tanti palpiti [from Tancredi]; Non temer:d'un basso affto [from Maometto II]; Mura felici...Elena! oh tu, che chiamo! [from La donna del lago]; Una voce poco fa [from Il Barbiere di Siviglia]; Nacqui all'affanno, al pianto [from Cinderella] *(rec Italian Institute, Budapest, May 16–22, 1995)* Naxos ▲ 8.553543 [DDD]

Verdi, G.:Ovs & Preludes—Prelude [from Ernani]; Sinf. [from Il finto Stanislao]; Prelude to Act III [from Don Carlo]; Sinf. [from Giovanna d'Arco]; Prelude [from Rigoletto]; Ov. [from Nabucco]; Prelude [from I masnadieri]; Sinf. [from Macbeth]; Sinf. [from Battaglia di Legnano]; Prelude [from I due Foscari]; Sinf. [from La forza del destino] *(rec Italian Institute, Budapest, Jan. 10–15, 1994)* Naxos ▲ 8.550699 [DDD]

Verdi, G.:Ovs & Preludes—Aroldo (Sinfonia); Il corsaro (Prelude); Luisa Miller (Sinfonia); La traviata (Prelude & Prelude to Act 3); Alzira (Sinfonia); Un ballo in maschera (Prelude); Oberto, conte di San Bonifacio (Sinfonia); Aida (Prelude); Attila (Prelude); I vespri siciliani (Sinfonia) *(rec Italian Institute, Budapest, Mar 14–20, 1994)* Naxos 4-▲ 8.504013 [DDD]

Verdi, G.:Ovs & Preludes—Sinf. [from Aroldo]; Prelude [from Il corsaro]; Sinf. [from Luisa Miller]; Prelude & Prelude to Act III [from La traviata]; Sinf. [from Alzira]; Prelude [from Un ballo in maschera] Sinf. [from Oberto, conte di San Bonifacio]; Prelude [from Aida] Prelude [from Attila]; Sinf. [from I vespri siciliani] *(rec Italian Institute, Budapest, Mar. 14–20, 1994)* Naxos ▲ 8.553018 [DDD]

Oberfrank, Gardelli (cnd)

Verdi, G.:Arias, w. Sylvia Sass (sop), Giorgio Lamberti (ten), Kolos Kováts (bass), Budapest MÁV SO, Béla Pödör (cnd), Ferenc Sapszon (cnd), Ferenc Nagy (cnd), Hungarian People's Army Male Chorus, Hungarian Radio-TV Chorus, Hungarian State Opera Chorus—Vieni, o Levita!...Tu sul labbro [from Nabucco]; Vergini!...Il ciel per ora...Sciagurata! Hai tu creduto; Qui posa il fianco [both from I Lombardi]; Che mai vegg'io...Infelice! E tu credevi...; Vigili pure il ciel...Iddio n'ascolti [both from Ernani]; Mentre gonfiarsi l'anima [from Attila]; Studia il passo...Come dal ciel precipital [from Macbeth]; O patria, o cara patria...O tu, Palermo [from I vespri Siciliani]; A te l'estremo addio... [from Simon Boccanegra]; Ella giammai m'amò [from Don Carlo] Hungaroton ("Great Hungarian Voices" series) ▲ HCD 31650 [ADD/DDD]

G. Patanè (cnd)

Puccini, G.:Madama Butterfly, w. V. Kincses (sop), T. Tákacs (mez), P. Dvorsky (ten), L. Miller (bar), Hungarian State Opera Chorus [I] Hungaroton 2-▲ HCD 12256/57

C. Rosenkrans (cnd)

Puccini, G.:Madama Butterfly, w. Maria Spacagna (sop), Sharon Grahm (mez), Vivica Genaux (mez), Richard di Renzi (ten), Richard Markley (ten), Erich Parce (bar), James Butler (bass), Anikó Katona (cnd), Hungarian State Opera Chorus—3 versions *(rec Italian Institute, Budapest, Sept 5–21, 1995)* Vox Classics 4-▲ VOX4 7525 [DDD]

Rubányi, Molinari-Pradelli (cnd)

Verdi, G.:La forza del destino (sels), w. Róbert Ilosfalvy (ten), Alexander Svéd (bar)—Solenne in quest'ora; Urna fatale *(rec 1955)* Hungaroton ("Great Hungarian Voices" series) ▲ HCD 31614 [ADD]

J. Sándor (cnd)

Suppé, F. von:Ovs—Light cavalry; O du Mein Österreich; Fatinitza; Pique Dame; Poet & Peasant; Banditenstreiche; The Beatiful Galatea; Flötte Bursche; Ein Morgen, Ein Mittag, Ein Abend in Wien LaserLight ▲ 15 611 [DDD]

V. Vaszy (cnd)

Verdi, G.:Macbeth (sels), w. Alexander Svéd (bar)—Perfidi! All'anglo...Pietà, rispetto, amore *(rec Oct 21, 1954)* Hungaroton ("Great Hungarian Voices" series) ▲ HCD 31614 [ADD]

Hungarian State Orch

Classics Go to the Movies Vol. 2, w. Dresden PO, Budapest Festival Orch, Bulgarian TV-Radio SO, Bela Kovaks, Franz Liszt CO, Bruno Lazzaretti, Berlin RSO LaserLight ▲ 15 642

Classics Go to the Movies Vol. 3, w. Lajos Meyer, Budapest Strings, Leonhard Hokanson (pno), Carmerata Labacensis, Budapest SO, Prague Festival Orch LaserLight ▲ 15 643

Mozart, W.A.:Music of, London PO, Salzburg Mozarteum Orch—sels from Syms. 24, 29, 31, 33, 35, 36, 38, 39, 40 & 41 LaserLight ▲ 15 646 [DDD]

M. Antál (cnd)

Hubay, J.:Hejre Kati, w. F. Balogh (vn) *(rec 4/88)* Naxos ▲ 8.550142 [DDD]
Kodály, Z.:Háry János (suite) *(rec 4/88)* Naxos ▲ 8.550142 [DDD]
Liszt, F.:Hungarian Rhaps—No. 12 *(rec 1988)* Naxos ▲ 8.550327 [DDD]
Liszt, F.:Hungarian Rhaps—Nos. 14, 12 & 9 *(rec Apr. 1988)* Naxos ▲ 8.550142 [DDD]

A. Dorati (cnd)

Bartók, B.:Con Orch Hungaroton ▲ HCD 11437 [ADD]
Bartók, B.:Divert Hungaroton ▲ HCD 11437 [ADD]
Kodály, Z.:Psalmus hungaricus, w. József Simándy (ten), Budapest Chorus, Hungarian Radio-TV Children's Chorus Hungaroton ▲ HCD 31503 [ADD]
Kodály, Z.:Psalmus hungaricus, w. J. Simándy (ten), Budapest Chorus [Hun] Hungaroton ▲ HCD 11392
Liszt, F.:Christus, w. Veronika Kincses (sop), Tamara Takács (mez), Robert Nagy (ten), Sándor Sólyom-Nagy (bar), László Polgár (bass), Hungarian Radio-TV Chorus [L] Hungaroton 3-▲ HCD 12831/33 [DDD]

J. Ferencsik (cnd)

Bartók, B.:Con 3 Pno, w. D. Ránki (pno) Hungaroton ▲ HCD 31036
Beethoven, L. van:Con Vn, Op. 61, w. D. Kovács (vn) White Label ▲ HRC 147 [ADD]
Beethoven, L. van:Egmont (ov) *(rec 1974)* Classical Diamonds 6-▲ 4013-18 [ADD]
Beethoven, L. van:Syms (comp), w. Éva Andor (sop), Márta Szirmay (cta), György Korondi (ten), Sándor Sólyom-Nagy (bar), Miklós Forrai (cnd), Budapest Chorus *(rec 1969, 1971, 1974–76)* Classical Diamonds 6-▲ 4013-18 [ADD]
Beethoven, L. van:Sym 2 White Label ▲ HRC 110 [ADD]
Haydn, J.:The Seven Last Words of Christ on the Cross Hungaroton ▲ HCD 12358 [DDD]
Haydn, J.:Sym 82, "The Bear" LaserLight ▲ 14 007 [DDD]
Lajtha, L.:Sym 4 Hungaroton ▲ HCD 31452 [ADD]
Lajtha, L.:Sym 9 Hungaroton ▲ HCD 31452 [ADD]
Liszt, F.:Con 2 Pno, w. S. Richter (pno) *(rec 1961)* Music & Arts ▲ CD 760 [AAD]
Liszt, F.:Con 2 Pno, w. S. Richter (pno) *(rec live, Hungarian Festival, 9/27/61)* Intaglio ▲ INCD 707-1 [ADD]
Liszt, F.:Fant on Hungarian Folk Tunes, w. S. Richter (pno) *(rec 1961)* Music & Arts ▲ CD 760 [AAD]
Liszt, F.:Fant on Hungarian Folk Tunes, w. J. Jandó (pno) Hungaroton ▲ HCD 12721
Liszt, F.:Orpheus Hungaroton ▲ HCD 12446 [DDD]
Liszt, F.:Les Préludes Hungaroton ▲ HCD 12446 [DDD]
Liszt, F.:Requiem, w. Alfonz Bartha (ten), Sándor Palcsó (ten), Zsolt Bende (bar), Pál Kovács (bar), Hungarian People's Army Male Chorus [L] Hungaroton ▲ HCD 11267
Liszt, F.:Tasso—Lamento e Trionfo Hungaroton ▲ HCD 12446 [DDD]
Mozart, W.A.:Sym 39 White Label ▲ HRC 143 [ADD]
Mozart, W.A.:Sym 41 White Label ▲ HRC 143 [ADD]
Schubert, Franz:Sym 8 White Label ▲ HRC 152 [ADD]

A. Fischer (cnd)

Bartók, B.:Bluebeard's Castle, w. E. Martón (sop), S. Ramey (bass), Hungarian State Chorus [Hun] CBS ▲ MK 44523 [DDD]
Bartók, B.:Con 1 Pno, w. G. Sándor (pno) Sony Classical ▲ SK 45835 [DDD]
Bartók, B.:Con 2 Pno, w. G. Sándor (pno) Sony Classical ▲ SK 45835 [DDD]
Bartók, B.:Con 3 Pno, w. G. Sándor (pno) Sony Classical ▲ SK 45835 [DDD]
Dvořák, A.:Slavonic Dances (comp)—Op. 46 LaserLight ▲ 15635 [DDD]
Mendelssohn, F.:A Midsummer Night's Dream (comp), w. Magda Kalmár (sop), M. Bokor (mez) [G] White Label ▲ HRC 049 [DDD]

Hungarian State Orch (cont.)

A. Fischer (cnd) (cont.)

Schubert, Franz:Ov Pno, D.675—Die Zauberharfe, D.644 White Label ▲ HRC 104 [ADD]
Schubert, Franz:Rosamunde (sels)—intermezzi after Acts 1 & 3 White Label ▲ HRC 104 [ADD]
Tchaikovsky, P.:Marche slave LaserLight ▲ 15 620 [DDD]
Tchaikovsky, P.:Marche slave LaserLight ▲ 15 821 [DDD]

I. Fischer (cnd)

Ballet Music from Operas, w. Hungarian State Opera Orch, Württemberg State Orch [cnd:J. Ferencsik] White Label ▲ HRC 058
Mendelssohn, F.:Die Hebriden Laserlight ▲ 15 623 [DDD]
Mendelssohn, F.:Songs—Song without Words; Spring Song; Spinning Song Laserlight ▲ 15 623

M. Forrai (cnd)

Schumann, R.:Requiem, Op. 148, w. E. Andor (sop), Barlay (sgr), Korondy (sgr), J. Gregor (bass), Budapest Chorus [L] Hungaroton ▲ HCD 11809
Schumann, R.:Requiem Mignon, w. E. Andor (sop), Barlay (sgr), Korondy (sgr), J. Gregor (bass), Budapest Chorus [L] Hungaroton ▲ HCD 11809

L. Gardelli (cnd)

Respighi, O.:Belfagor, w. S. Sass (sop), T. Takács (mez), G. Lamberti (ten), L. Miller (bar), L. Polgár (bass), Hungarian State Chorus [I] Hungaroton 2-▲ HCD 12850/51 [DDD]
Respighi, O.:La Fiamma, w. I. Tokody (sop), T. Takács (mez), P. Kelen (ten), S. Sólyom-Nagy (bar), Hungarian State Chorus [I] Hungaroton 3-▲ HCD 12591/93 [DDD]
Respighi, O.:Semirama, w. E. Marton (sop), V. Kincses (sop), L. Bartolini (ten), L Miller (bar), L. Polgaar (bass), T. Clementis (bass), Hungarian Radio-TV Chorus [I] Hungaroton 2-▲ HCD 31197/98

G. Győrványi-Ráth (cnd)

Beethoven, L. van:Con 6 Pno, w. M. Szenthelyi (pno) Laserlight ▲ 15 515
Beethoven, L. van:Con 6 Pno, w. M. Szenthelyi (pno) Capriccio ▲ 10 912 [DDD]
Beethoven, L. van:Con Vn, Op. 61, w. M. Szenthelyi (vn) LaserLight ▲ 15 515 [DDD]
Beethoven, L. van:Minuets Orch, WoO 10—No. 2 in G Capriccio ▲ 10 912 [DDD]
Beethoven, L. van:Minuets Orch, WoO 10 Laserlight ▲ 15 515
Beethoven, L. van:Romances Vn, w. M. Szenthelyi (vn) Laserlight ▲ 15 515
Beethoven, L. van:Romances Vn, w. M. Szenthelyi (vn) Capriccio ▲ 10 912 [DDD]

M. Honeck (cnd)

Bruch, M.:Russian Suite Marco Polo ▲ 8.223104
Bruch, M.:Sym 3 Marco Polo ▲ 8.223104

J. Kovács (cnd)

Bartók, B.:Songs, w. J. Hamari (mez), I. Prunyi (pno)—5 Songs, Op. 15 [Sz.61] [orchd. by Zltán Kodály]; 5 Songs, Op. 16 [Sz.63]; 5 Songs [from 8 Hungarian Folksongs, Sz.64]; Songs for Voice & Orch.; 5 Songs for Voice & Orch., Sz.101 [Hun] Hungaroton ▲ HCD 31535 [DDD]

A. Ligeti (cnd)

Bartók, B.:Con 1 Vn, w. Vilmos Szabadi (vn) *(rec Budapest, Dec. 17–21, 1992 & Jan. 2)* Hungaroton ("Classic" series) ▲ HCD 31543 [DDD]
Bartók, B.:Con 2 Vn, w. Vilmos Szabadi (vn) *(rec Budapest, Dec. 17–21, 1992 & Jan. 2)* Hungaroton ("Classic" series) ▲ HCD 31543 [DDD]

E. Lukács (cnd)

Mozart, W.A.:Cons Fl, w. L. Kovács (fl) White Label ▲ HRC 107 [ADD]

E. Märzendorfer (cnd)

Strauss (II), Joh.:Eine Nacht in Venedig (sels), w. J. Scovotti (sop), E. Schary (mez), E. Steiner (mez), C. Bini (ten), F. Stricker (ten), W. Brendel (bar), Hungarian State Chorus [G] Acanta ▲ CD 43809 [DDD]

G. Németh (cnd)

Liszt, F.:Rakóczy March Hungaroton ▲ HCD 12721
Tchaikovsky, P.:Romeo & Juliet White Label ▲ HRC 059
Tchaikovsky, P.:Serenade Strs White Label ▲ HRC 059

G. Patanè (cnd)

Dvořák, A.:Sym 9, "From the New World" White Label ▲ HRC 064
Giordano, U.:Andrea Chénier, w. E. Martón (sop), J. Carreras (ten), G. Zancanaro (bar), Hungarian State Chorus [I] CBS 2-▲ M2K 42369 [DDD]
Schumann, R.:Sym 2 White Label ▲ HRC 104 [ADD]
Smetana, B.:The Moldau White Label ▲ HRC 064

T. Pál (cnd)

Dvořák, A.:Carnival LaserLight ▲ 15 824 [DDD]
Dvořák, A.:Carnival LaserLight ▲ 15 517 [DDD]
Dvořák, A.:Romance Vn, w. M. Szenthelyi (vn) LaserLight ▲ 15 517 [DDD]
Dvořák, A.:Romance Vn, w. M. Szenthelyi (vn) LaserLight ▲ 15 824 [DDD]

E. Queler (cnd)

Strauss, R.:Guntram, w. I. Tokody (sop), R. Goldberg (ten), S. Sólyom-Nágy (bar), I. Gáti (bar), Hungarian People's Army Male Chorus [G] CBS 2-▲ M2K 39737 [DDD]

C. Rosekrans (cnd)

Cilea, F.:L'Arlesiana, w. M. Spacagna (sop), E. Zilio (mez), P. Kelen (ten), B. Póka (bar), T. Clementis (bass), Hungarian State Chorus Quintana 2-▲ QUI 903067/68
Mascagni, P.:Lodoletta, w. M. Spacagna (sop), P. Kelen (ten), B. Szilágyi (bar), M. Kálmándi (bar), L. Polgár (bass), Hungarian State Choruses [I] Hungaroton 2-▲ HCD 31307/08 [DDD]

J. Sándor (cnd)

Gold & Silver, w. Budapest PO White Label ▲ HRC 065
Rimsky-Korsakov, N.:Capriccio espagnol LaserLight ▲ 15 608 [DDD]
Rimsky-Korsakov, N.:Scheherazade LaserLight ▲ 15 608 [DDD]
Weber, C.M. von:Invitation to the Dance Orch LaserLight ▲ 15635 [DDD]

A. Sebestyén (cnd)

Make Wonder:Songs from Operettas, w. Kalmár, Magda (sop), Éva Köteles (sgr), Judit Takács (sgr), Bori Szita (sgr), Budapest SO [cnd:Tamás Bródy] Hungaroton ▲ HCD 16613 [AAD]

N. Sheriff (cnd)

The Famous Cantor, w. Joseph Malovany (ten) Hungaroton ▲ HCD 18178 [DDD]

K. Stratton (cnd)

Liszt, F.:De Profundis, w. P. Thomson (pno) [Michael Maxwell version] Hungaroton ▲ HCD 31525 [DDD]
Liszt, F.:Fant on Themes from Beethoven's *Ruins of Athens*, w. P. Thomson (pno) Hungaroton ▲ HCD 31525 [DDD]
Liszt, F.:Wandererfantasie, w. P. Thomson (pno) Hungaroton ▲ HCD 31525 [DDD]

F. Szekeres (cnd)

Vivaldi, A.:Cants, w. T. Takács (mez)—RV. 684, "Cessate omai cessate" [I] Hungaroton ▲ HCD 12087
Vivaldi, A.:Juditha triumphans devicta Holofernes barbarie, w. Margit László (sop—Ábra), Zsuzsa Barlay (cta—Juditha), József Réti (ten—Servo), Zsolt Bende (bar—Holofernes), József Dene (bar—Ozias), György Czigány (cnd), Budapest Madrigal Choir, 1968 Classical Diamonds ▲ CLD 4022-23 [ADD]
Vivaldi, A.:L'Olimpiade (sels), w. M. Zempléni (sop), T. Takács (mez), Horváth (sgr), Káplán (sgr), L. Miller (bar), I. Gáti (bar), K. Kováts (bass), Budapest Madrigal Choir [I] White Label ▲ HRC 073 [ADD]

M. Tilson Thomas (cnd)

Puccini, G.:Tosca, w. E. Marton (sop), J. Carreras (ten), J. Pons (bar), Hungarian State Chorus Sony Classical 2-▲ S2K 45847
Puccini, G.:Tosca (sels), w. E. Marton (sop), B. Heja (trb), J. Carreras (ten), F. Gerdesits (ten), J. Pons (bar), J. Nemeth (bar), J. Gregor (bass), Hungarian Radio-TV Chorus *(rec Budapest, Dec. 14–22, 1988)* Sony Classical ("Opera Highlights" series) ▲ SMK 53500 [DDD]

I. Zámbó (cnd)

Liszt, F.:An die Künstler, w. A. Molnár (ten), T. Daróczi (ten), J. Molday (bar), L. Domahidy Jr. (bass), Hungarian People's Army Male Chorus [G] Hungaroton ▲ HCD 12748 [DDD]
Liszt, F.:Hungaria 1848, w. M. Temesi (sop), A. Molnár (ten), S. Sólyom-Nagy (bar), Hungarian People's Army Male Chorus—composed as a salute to the Hungarian revolution [G] Hungaroton ▲ HCD 12748 [DDD]
Liszt, F.:Hungarian Royal Hymn, w. Hungarian People's Army Male Chorus, Jeunesses Musicales Women's Chorus [Hun] Hungaroton ▲ HCD 12748 [DDD]

▲ = CD ♦ = Enhanced CD Δ = MD ■ = Cassette Tape ▯ = DCC

Hungarian State Orch (cont.)
I. Zámbó (cnd) (cont.)
Liszt, F.:Septam sacramenta, w. T. Takács (mez), J. Bándi (ten), G. Kallay (ten), K. Kaváts (bar), Zsuzsa Elekes (org), Hungarian People's Army Male Chorus, Jeunesses Musicales Women's Chorus [L] Hungaroton ▲ HCD 12748 [DDD]

Hungarian State Orch CO
Silent Night, w. Kovacs, Imre (fl), Hedy Lubik (hp), Ferenc Gergely (org), Frigyes Hidas (org), Gabor Lehotka (org), Csanyi (cnd), Szekeres (cnd), Budapest Children's Choir Madrigal Choir Hungaroton ▲ HCD 16598

Hungarian State SO
F. d' Avalos (cnd)
Liszt, F.:A Faust Sym, w. A. Necolescu (ten), Hungarian Radio Chorus IMP Classics ▲ IMP PCD 1071 [DDD]

A. Fischer (cnd)
Bartók, B.:Con Orch Nimbus ▲ 5229 2 [DDD] ■ NC 5229
Bartók, B.:Dance Suite Nimbus ▲ NI 5309 [DDD]
Bartók, B.:Hungarian Sketches Nimbus ▲ NI 5309 [DDD]
Bartók, B.:The Miraculous Mandarin (suite) Nimbus ▲ 5229 2 [DDD] ■ NC 5229
Bartók, B.:Pictures Orch Nimbus ▲ NI 5309 [DDD]
Bartók, B.:Romanian Dances—Allegro vivace Nimbus ▲ NI 5309 [DDD]
Bartók, B.:Romanian Folk Dances Pno Nimbus ▲ NI 5309 [DDD]
Kodály, Z.:Galanta Dances Nimbus ▲ NI 5284 [DDD]
Kodály, Z.:Háry János (suite) Nimbus ▲ NI 5284 [DDD]
Kodály, Z.:Vars on a Hungarian Folk Song Nimbus ▲ NI 5284 [DDD]

G. Oberfrank (cnd)
Bach, J.S.:St. Matthew Passion, w. R. Kiss (sop), I. Verebics (sop), Á. Csenki (mez), J. Németh (mez), P. Cser (ten), J. Mukk (ten), I. Gati (bar), F. Korpás (bar), P. Kőves (bass), Hungarian Festival Choir, Hungarian Radio Children's Choir [G] *(rec Feb 1993)* Naxos 3-▲ 8.550832/34 [DDD]

G. Patanè (cnd)
Boito, A.:Mefistofele, w. E. Marton (sop), P. Domingo (ten), S. Ramey (bass), Hungarian State Opera Chorus [I] *(rec Budapest, 1988)* Sony Classical 2-▲ S2K 44983 [DDD]

Hungarian String Quartet
Mozart, W.A.:Qts Strs (misc)—Nos. 14–19, "The Haydn Quartets" *(rec 1972)* Vox Box 3-▲ CD3X 3009 [ADD]

Hungarian SO
Tchaikovsky, P.:Valse-Scherzo Vn, w. M. Szenthelyi (vn) Capriccio ▲ 10 924 [DDD]
A. Fischer (cnd)
Tchaikovsky, P.:Ov 1812 Laserlight ▲ 15 524 [DDD]
Tchaikovsky, P.:Sym 6 Capriccio ▲ 10 922 [DDD]
Tchaikovsky, P.:Sym 6 Laserlight ▲ 15 524 [DDD]

Hungarian Virtuosi CO
J. Dobra (cnd)
Fauré, G.:Requiem, w. D. Karasszon (org), E. Maros (hp), Budapest SO Winds, Tomkins Vocal Ensemble Hungaroton ▲ HCD 31424 [DDD]

J.-P. Rampal (cnd)
Mozart, W.A.:Andante Fl, w. Claudi Arimany (fl) PROdigital ▲ PRO 2419 [DDD]
Mozart, W.A.:Cons Fl, w. Claudi Arimany (fl) PROdigital ▲ PRO 2419 [DDD]
Mozart, W.A.:Rondo Fl, w. Claudi Arimany (fl) PROdigital ▲ PRO 2419 [DDD]

A. von Würtzler (cnd)
Christmas with the New York Harp Ensemble, w. New York Harp Ensemble Hungaroton ▲ HCD 31331 [DDD]
Masterpieces for Harp & Orchestra, w. Sylvia Kowalczuk (hp) Hungaroton ▲ HCD 31550 [DDD]

Hungarian Wind Ensemble
V. Tátrai (cnd)
Mozart, W.A.:Serenade Ww, K.375 White Label ▲ HRC 159 [ADD]
Mozart, W.A.:Sinf concertante Ob, K.Anh.9, Hungarian CO White Label ▲ HRC 159 [ADD]

Hungarian Wind Quartet
Beethoven, L. van:Qnt Pno, Ob, Cl, Hn & Bn, w. S. Falvai (pno) White Label ▲ HRC 169 [ADD]
Mozart, W.A.:Qnt Pno, K.452, w. S. Falvai (pno) White Label ▲ HRC 169 [ADD]

Hungarica Philharmonia
Z. Roznyai (cnd)
Debussy, C.:Nocturnes—Fêtes RealTime ▲ RT 2003

Huntingdon Trio [D. Gold (fl), L. Smith (vc), R. Smith (pno)]
Czerny, C.:Fant concertante Leonarda ▲ LE 325 [DDD]
Davison, J.:Son Pastorale Capstone ▲ CPS 8615
Foote, A.:Flying Cloud & Oriental Dance Leonarda ▲ LE 325 [DDD]
Foote, A.:Poem 1 Pno Leonarda ▲ LE 325 [DDD]
Goossens, E.:Impressions (6) of a Holiday Leonarda ▲ LE 325 [DDD]
Loeb, D.:Nocturnes Leonarda ▲ LE 330 [DDD]
Martinů, B.:Trio Fl Leonarda ▲ LE 330 [DDD]
Marx, B.:Divert a Tre Leonarda ▲ LE 330 [DDD]
Rorem, N.:Trio Fl Leonarda ▲ LE 330 [DDD]

Huntingdon Trio members
Musgrave, T.:Impromptu 1 Fl Leonarda ▲ LE 325 [DDD]

Hürth Music School Orch
J. Read (cnd)
Haydn, M.:Der Traum (orchestral sels) Koch Schwann ▲ CD 316051 [ADD]

Iasi Moldova Phil CO
C. Brancusi, Ionescu-Galati (cnd)
Vivaldi, A.:Cons Bn, w. M. Nenoiu (bn),—Concerti in d, C, a, e; Concerti RV.472 & 501 Electrecord ▲ ELCD 128 [AAD]

Iasi Moldova PO
I. Baciu (cnd)
Enescu, G.:Vox maris, w. Iasi Moldova Phil Chorus Marco Polo ▲ 8.223142
Baciu, Vintila (cnd)
Caudella, E.:Con 1 Vn, w. D. Podlovski (vn) *(rec 1975 & 1983)* Electrecord ▲ ELCD 104 [AAD]
Caudella, E.:Petru Rares (sels)—Prelude *(rec 1975 & 1983)* Electrecord ▲ ELCD 104 [AAD]
Caudella, E.:Remembrances from the Carpathian Mountains *(rec 1975 & 1983)* Electrecord ▲ ELCD 104 [AAD]
Caudella, E.:Symphonic Pieces (3) *(rec 1975 & 1983)* Electrecord ▲ ELCD 104 [AAD]

Iasi Moldova PO Winds
I. Baciu (cnd)
Enescu, G.:Dectet Ww Marco Polo ▲ 8.223147

Iberian Lyric Ensemble
Angels, w. Concerto Soave, Ensemble Convivencia, Ensemble Lucidarum, Ensemble Venance Fortunat, La Fenice L'Empreinte Digitale ▲ ED 13050

Ibn Báya Ensemble
Musica Andalusi, w. Eduardo Paniagua, Omar Metiovi Sony Classical ▲ SK 62262

Icebreaker [L. Andriesson (pno), D. Lang (vc), G. Bryars (db), M. Gordon]
Andriessen, L.:De Snelheid Argo ▲ 443214–2 [DDD]
Bryars, G.:The Archangel Trip Argo ▲ 443214–2 [DDD]
Gordon, M.:Yo Shakespeare Argo ▲ 443214–2 [DDD]
Lang, D.:Slow Movement Argo ▲ 443214–2 [DDD]

Icelandic CO
J.-P. Jacquillat (cnd)
Eirlksdottlr, Karolina:Pieces (5) Music from Iceland ▲ ITM 701 [ADD]

Icelandic SO
Leifs, J.:Music of, w. Sigrídur Ella Magnúsdóttir (mez), Ólafur Vignir Albertsson (pno), Sólveig Anna Jónsdóttir (pno), Hjálmar Ragnarsson (pno), Edda Erlendsdóttir (pno), Marteinn Hunger Fridriksson (org), Hildigunnur Halldórsdóttir (vn), Gréta Gudnadóttir (vn), Gudmundur Kristmundsson (va), Sigurdur Halldórsson (vc), Richard Korn (db), Icelandic Opera Chorus, Langholts Church Graduale Choir, Hamrahlíd Choir—Icelandic Cant, Op. 13/4; Valse Lento, Op. 2/1; Icelandic Dance, Op. 11/2 [Tempo Giusto]; Requiem; Lullaby [After the Riots]; Fairy-Tale in the Wood [from Baldr, Op. 34]; Funeral March; Separation [from Elegy, Op. 53]; Galdra Loftur Ov, Op. 10; Funeral March, Op. 6; Reverie; Reunion [from Elegy, Op. 53]; Fine I, Op. 55; Andante [The Last Supper]; Preludia Organo, Op. 16/3 [In the Church]; The Tear of Stone [from Elegy, Op. 53] Music From Iceland ▲ ITM 605 [DDD]

I. Buketoff (cnd)
Rachmaninoff, S.:Con 4 Pno, w. W. Black (pno) [original 1927 version] Chandos ▲ CHAN 8987 [DDD]
Rachmaninoff, S.:Monna Vanna, w. S. McCoy (ten), S. Milnes (bar), Icelandic Opera Chorus Chandos ▲ CHAN 8987 [DDD]
Ward, R.:Qt 1 Strs [F] CRI ■ C 206

G. Emilsson (cnd)
Sveinsson, A.H.:Exploration, w. I. Jónasson (va) ITM ▲ ITM 706

J.-P. Jacquillat (cnd)
Eirlksdottlr, Karolina:Sinfonietta Music from Iceland ▲ ITM 701 [ADD]

H. Leifsson (cnd)
Thórarinsson, L.:Styr, w. Thorsteinn Gauti Sigurdsson (pno) Music from Iceland ▲ ITM 705

P.P. Pálsson (cnd)
Sveinsson, A.H.:Con Fl, w. R. Aitken (fl) ITM ▲ ITM 706
Sveinsson, A.H.:Jubilus II, w. O. Björnsson (trbn) ITM ▲ ITM 706
Tómasson, H.:Strati Music from Iceland ▲ ITM 707

P. Sakari (cnd)
Alfvén, H.:Gustav II Adolph—Elegy Chandos ▲ CHAN 9313 [DDD]
Alfvén, H.:Swedish Rhap 1, "Midsommarvaka" Chandos ▲ CHAN 9313 [DDD]
Alfvén, H.:Swedish Rhap 2, "Uppsala-rhapsodi" Chandos ▲ CHAN 9313 [DDD]
Alfvén, H.:Swedish Rhap 3, "Dalarhapsodien" Chandos ▲ CHAN 9313 [DDD]
Alfvén, H.:A Tale from the Archipelago Chandos ▲ CHAN 9313 [DDD]
Grieg, E.:Erotik Chandos ▲ CHAN 9071 [DDD]
Grieg, E.:In Autumn Chandos ▲ CHAN 9071 [DDD]
Grieg, E.:Norwegian Dances, Op. 35 Chandos ▲ CHAN 9071 [DDD]
Grieg, E.:Old Norwegian Romance Chandos ▲ CHAN 9071 [DDD]
Hallgrímsson, H.:Poemi, w. Sigrún Edvaldsdóttir (vn) Music from Iceland ▲ ITM 602 [DDD]
Jóhannsson, M.B.:Adagio Music from Iceland ▲ ITM 602 [DDD]
Klami, U.:Kalevala Suite Chandos ▲ CHAN 9268 [DDD]
Klami, U.:Karelian Rhap Chandos ▲ CHAN 9268 [DDD]
Klami, U.:Sea Pictures Chandos ▲ CHAN 9268 [DDD]
Leifs, J.:Elegy Chandos ("New Directions" series) ▲ CHN 9433
Leifs, J.:Fine I Chandos ("New Directions" series) ▲ CHN 9433
Leifs, J.:Fine II Chandos ("New Directions" series) ▲ CHN 9433
Leifs, J.:Iceland Cant, w. Icelandic Opera Chorus Chandos ("New Directions" series) ▲ CHN 9433
Leifs, J.:Iceland Ov, w. Icelandic Opera Chorus Chandos ("New Directions" series) ▲ CHN 9433
Madetoja, L.:Huvinäytelmäalku Chandos ▲ CHAN 9036 [DDD]
Madetoja, L.:Okun Fuoko (suite 1) Chandos ▲ CHAN 9036 [DDD]
Madetoja, L.:The Ostrobothnians (suite) Chandos ▲ CHAN 9036 [DDD]
Madetoja, L.:Sym 1 Chandos ▲ CHAN 9115 [DDD]
Madetoja, L.:Sym 2 Chandos ▲ CHAN 9115 [DDD]
Madetoja, L.:Sym 3 Chandos ▲ CHAN 9036 [DDD]
Nordal, J.:Con Vc, w. Erling Blöndal Bengtsson (vc) Music from Iceland ▲ ITM 602 [DDD]
Sibelius, J.:King Christian II (incidental) Chandos ▲ CHAN 9158 [DDD]
Sibelius, J.:Pelléas et Mélisande (suite) Chandos ▲ CHAN 9158 [DDD]
Sibelius, J.:Swanwhite (suite) Chandos ▲ CHAN 9158 [DDD]
Svendsen, J.:Icelandic Melodies Chandos ▲ CHAN 9071 [DDD]
Thórarinsson, L.:Autumn Play Music from Iceland ▲ ITM 602 [DDD]
Thórarinsson, L.:För Music from Iceland ▲ ITM 705
Thórarinsson, L.:Io Music from Iceland ▲ ITM 705
Thórarinsson, L.:Mót Music from Iceland ▲ ITM 705

Sakari, Wilkinson (cnd)
Ragnarsson, H.:Music of, w. S. E. Magnúsdóttir (mez), H. Halldórsdóttir (vn), G. Gudnadóttir (vn), G. Kristmundsson (va), S. Halldórsson (vc), R. Korn (db), Ó. V. Albertsson (pno), S. A. Jónsdóttir (pno), H. Ragnarsson (pno), E. Erlendsdóttir (pno), M. H. Fridriksson (org), G. Cortes (cnd), J. Stefánsson (cnd), T. Ingólfsdóttir (cnd), Hamrahlíd Choir, Icelandic Opera Chorus, Langholts Church Graduale Choir—Meine kleine Freundin [In the Ballroom]; Lovers Duet; After the concert; Meine kleine Freundin [Annie listens to the Radio]; Lif's Theme [On the Beach]; Lif's Theme II [Night Prayer]; Composing Ov [Vars I, II & III] Music From Iceland ▲ ITM 605 [DDD]

W. Strickland (cnd)
Ives, C.:Holidays, w. Tokyo PO, Finnish RSO, Göteborg SO, Iceland Sym Chorus [E] CRI ■ ACS 6014
Ives, C.:Thanksgiving and/or Forefather's Day CRI ■ C 177

O. Vänskä (cnd)
Leifs, J.:Sym 1, "Saga Sym" BIS ▲ CD 730 [DDD]

P. Zukovsky (cnd)
Leifs, J.:Music of, w. Reykjavik Men's Choir—Geysir; Ov for Orch; 3 Images; Hekla Music from Iceland ▲ ITM 604 [DDD]

Icelandic Youth Orch
Rudhyar, D.:5 Stanzas CP2 Recordings ▲ CP2 105
Schoenberg, A.:Pelleas und Melisande CP2 Recordings ▲ CP2 105

Ictus Ensemble
Mey, T. de:Amor Constante Megadisc ▲ 7859
Mey, T. de:Con Vn Megadisc ▲ 7859
Mey, T. de:Kinok Megadisc ▲ 7859
Mey, T. de:Unknowness Megadisc ▲ 7859

Illinois CO
S. E. Squires (cnd)
Glise, A.L.:Cavatina, "At the Border" E.R.M. ▲ CCC 6659 [DDD]
Winstin, R.I.:Sym 2 E.R.M. ▲ CCC 6659 [DDD]

Illinois Performers' Workshop Ensemble [Mark Enslin (voc), Arun Chandra (gtr), Rick Burkhardt (gtr), Keith Johnson (gtr), Sarah Wiseman (vc), Lesley Olson (fl)]
Partch, H.:San Francisco II [arr. Mark Enslin] *(rec Sudwestfunk 3, Karlsruhe, Germany, Jan 24, 1990)* Innova 4-▲ 401

IMI Yorkshire Imperial Band
H. Mortimer (cnd)
The British Bandsman Centenary Concert (1987), w. Massed Bands, Black Dyke Mills Band [cnd:Maj. Peter Parkes], Besses o' the Barn Band [cnd:Roy Newsome], IMI Yorkshire Imperial Band [cnd:James Scott] Chandos Brass ▲ CHAN 4513 [DDD]

In Canto CO
G. Catalucci (cnd)
Sarro, D.N.:Coronatemi il crine, w. S. Mingard (cta) *(rec Dec. 8, 1992)* Bongiovanni ▲ GB 2147 [DDD]
Sarro, D.N.:Dorina e Nibbio, w. S. Mingardo (cta—Dorina), G. Gatti (bar—Nibbio) *(rec Dec. 8, 1992)* Bongiovanni ▲ GB 2147 [DDD]

F. Maestri (cnd)
Donizetti, G.:La bella prigioniera, w. S. Rigacci (sop), R. Franceschetto (sgr), P. Pellegrini (sgr) *(rec Apr. 1992)* Bongiovanni 2-▲ GB 2109/10 [DDD]
Donizetti, G.:Olimpiade, w. S. Rigacci (sop), D. Broganelli (sgr) *(rec May 1991)* Bongiovanni 2-▲ GB 2109/10 [DDD]

ORCH. & ENS.

In Canto CO (cont.)
F. Maestri (cnd) (cont.)
Donizetti, G.:Il Pigmalione, w. S. Rigacci (sop), P. Pellegrini (sgr) *(rec Sept. 1990)* Bongiovanni 2-▲ GB 2109/10 [DDD]
Donizetti, G.:Rita, or Le mari battu, w. U. Benelli (bar), S. Figacci (sgr), R. Franceschetto (sgr), G. Manini (sgr) *(rec Sept. 1990)* Bongiovanni 2-▲ GB 2109/10 [DDD]
Hasse, J.A.:La Contadina, w. Susanna Rigacci (sop), Romano Franceschetto (sgr) [I] *(rec Oct. 5, 1991)* Bongiovanni ▲ GB 2128 [DDD]
Haydn, J.:Lo Speziale, w. Gil Manuel Beltran (ten—Sempronio), Daniela Broganelli (sgr—Volpino), Cinzia Forte (sgr—Grilletta), Paolo Pellegrini (sgr—Mengone), Maurizio Gambini (vc), Marco Tinarelli (db), Gabriele Catalucci (hpd) *(rec 1993)* Bongiovanni 2-▲ GB 2171/72 [DDD]
Rossini, G.:L'inganno felice, w. S. Rigacci (sop—Isabella), E. Palacio (ten—Duke Bertrando), G. Gatti (bar—Batone), R. Ripesi (bass—Tarabotto), G. Casali (bass—Ormondo) *(rec Dec. 1992)* Bongiovanni 2-▲ GB 2133/34 [DDD]

In Canto di Terni Youth Orch
G. Catalucci (cnd)
Gluck, C.W.:L'Innocenza giustificata, w. B. Lucarini (sop—Flaminia), A. Ruffini (sop—Claudia), A. R. de Simone (sop—Flavio), U. Benelli (bar—Valerio) [I] *(rec live 9/90)* Bongiovanni 2-▲ GB 2111/12 [DDD]
Salieri, A.:Arlecchinata, w. U. Benelli (bar), P. Pellegrini (sgr), G. Gatti (bar) [I] *(rec live 9/90)* Bongiovanni 2-▲ GB 2111/12 [DDD]

In Nativitatem Domini Canticum
Charpentier, M.-A.:Noëls sur les instruments Erasmus ▲ WVH 174

In Nomine Players [Maxwell Ward (baroque va), Michael Mitchell (baroque va), Denis Stevens (baroque va), Desmond Dupré (vl), Dennis Nesbitt (vl), Francis Baines (b vl)]
Byrd, W.:Consort Music—Prelude & Fant. a 5; Fant. a 3; In Nomine a 5; Fant. a 6 Lyrichord ▲ LEMS 8014
Byrd, W.:Songs, w. Russell Oberlin (ct)—La Virginella; My Sweet Little Darling; What Pleasure Have Great Princes; Though Amaryllis Dance in Green; Blessed Is He That Fears the Lord; O Lord, How Long Wilt Thou Forget; The Man Is Blesst That God Doth Fear; Why Do I Use My Paper, Ink, and Pen Lyrichord ▲ LEMS 8014

Independent CO Boemia
H. Farkač (cnd)
Dvořák, A.:Notturno Start Classics ▲ SCD 501
Janáček, L.:Suite Str Orch Start Classics ▲ SCD 501
Martinů, B.:Serenade 2 Start Classics ▲ SCD 501
Mysliveček, J.:Divert Start Classics ▲ SCD 501
Stamitz, C.:Qts Strs—for Orch, Op. 4/4 Start Classics ▲ SCD 501

Indiana State Univ Symphonic Wind Ensemble
J. Boyd (cnd)
Andriessen, J.:Con grosso Sax Qt, w. Chicago Saxophone Quartet *(rec 1994)* Truemedia ▲ D 94127
Barker, W.:Capriccio Sax Qt, Chicago Saxophone Quartet *(rec 1994)* Truemedia ▲ D 94127
Linn, R.:Con S Sax, w. Paul Bro (s sax) *(rec 1994)* Truemedia ▲ D 94127
McCarthy, D.:Polarization *(rec 1994)* Truemedia ▲ D 94127

Indiana Trio [James Campbell (cl), Eli Eban (cl/E♭ cl), Howard Klug (cl/b cl)]
Defaye, J.-M.:Audition Pieces (6) Crystal ▲ CD 734
Fox, F.:Time Weaving Crystal ▲ CD 734
Kibbe, M.:Ebony Suite Crystal ▲ CD 734
Kulesha, G.:Political Implications, w. David Shea (cl) Crystal ▲ CD 734
Schickele, P.:Dances for 3 Crystal ▲ CD 734

Indiana Univ Early Music Institute
Hildegard Of Bingen:[St. Ursula & Her] 11,000 Virgins:Favus distillans Ursula Focus ▲ FOCUS 911 [DAD]
Laude:Medieval Italian Spiritual Songs Focus ▲ FOCUS 912 [AAD]

Indiana Univ Harp Ensemble
C. Colnot (cnd)
Eaton, J.:From the Cave of the Sybil:Sonority Movt, w. Carole Morgan (fl) *(rec Musical Arts Ctr, Bloomington, IN, Nov 20, 1986)* Indiana Univ School of Music ▲ 0-253-31842-4

Indiana Univ New Music Ensemble
C. Baker (cnd)
Eaton, J.:Ajax, w. G. Bradley Garvin (b-bar) *(rec Musical Arts Ctr, Bloomington, IN, Oct 19, 1989)* Indiana Univ School of Music ▲ 0-253-31842-4
C. Russell (cnd)
Fox, F.:Auras *(rec Musical Arts Ctr, Bloomington, IN, Nov 29, 1990)* Indiana Univ School of Music ▲ 0-253-32433-5
H. Sollberger (cnd)
Eaton, J.:The City of Clytæmnestra (sels), w. Nelda Nelson (sop)—Aria & Scene *(rec Musical Arts Ctr, Bloomington, IN, Apr 4, 1985)* Indiana Univ School of Music ▲ 0-253-31842-4
Fox, F.:Sonaspheres 5 *(rec Musical Arts Ctr, Bloomington, IN, Apr 11, 1985)* Indiana Univ School of Music ▲ 0-253-32433-5
Orrego-Salas, J.:Tangos *(rec Musical Arts Ctr, Bloomington, IN, Feb 3, 1984)* Indiana Univ School of Music ▲ IUSM 02

Indiana Univ SO
T. Baldner (cnd)
Orrego-Salas, J.:Con Vn, w. Franco Gulli (vn) *(rec Musical Arts Ctr, Bloomington, IN, Oct 4, 1984)* Indiana Univ School of Music ▲ IUSM 02
H. Sollberger (cnd)
Fox, F.:Januaries *(rec Musical Arts Ctr, Bloomington, IN, May 1, 1986)* Indiana Univ School of Music ▲ 0-253-32433-5

Indiana Winds
F. Fennell (cnd)
Bruch, M.:Kol Nidrei, w. Eugene Rousseau (sax) [arr Makio Kimura] *(rec St. Mark's United Methodist Church, Bloomington, Indiana, Sept 12-14, 1994)* Delos ▲ DE 3188 [DDD]
Gershwin, G.:Porgy & Bess (sels), w. Eugene Rousseau (sax)—Medley [arr. Ralph Hermann] *(rec St. Mark's United Methodist Church, Bloomington, Indiana, Sept 12-14, 1994)* Delos ▲ DE 3188 [DDD]
Heiden, B.:Diversion, w. Eugene Rousseau (sax) *(rec St. Mark's United Methodist Church, Bloomington, Indiana, Sept 12-14, 1994)* Delos ▲ DE 3188 [DDD]
Heiden, B.:Fant Concertante, w. Eugene Rousseau (sax) *(rec St. Mark's United Methodist Church, Bloomington, Indiana, Sept 12-14, 1994)* Delos ▲ DE 3188 [DDD]
Massenet, J.:Méditation from *Thaïs*, w. Eugene Rousseau (sax) [arr James Curnow] *(rec St. Mark's United Methodist Church, Bloomington, Indiana, Sept 12-14, 1994)* Delos ▲ DE 3188 [DDD]
Muczynski, R.:Con A Sax, w. Eugene Rousseau (sax) *(rec St. Mark's United Methodist Church, Bloomington, Indiana, Sept 12-14, 1994)* Delos ▲ DE 3188 [DDD]
Puccini, G.:Tosca (sels), w. Eugene Rousseau (sax)—Tosca Fant [arr Ralph Hermann] *(rec St. Mark's United Methodist Church, Bloomington, Indiana, Sept 12-14, 1994)* Delos ▲ DE 3188 [DDD]

Indianapolis Festival Orch
F. Burgomeister (cnd)
Fauré, G.:Requiem, w. W. Reguson-Wagstaffe (trb), S. Irwin (bass-bar), Christ Church Cathedral Men & Boys Choir Oxford Gothic ▲ G 49062 [DDD]
Howells, H.:Requiem, w. J. Barton (trb), P. Flight (ct), D. Honoré (ten), T. Woody (bar), Christ Church Cathedral Men & Boys Choir Oxford Gothic ▲ G 49062 [DDD]

Indianapolis SO
R. Leppard (cnd)
Beethoven, L. van:Coriolan Ov Koss Classics ▲ KC 2215
Beethoven, L. van:Qt 11 Strs, "Quartetto serioso" [orchd Mahler] Koss Classics ▲ KC 2215
Beethoven, L. van:Sym 7 Koss Classics ▲ KC 2215
Elgar, E.:Dream Children *(rec 4/91)* Koss Classics ▲ KC 1014 [DDD]
Elgar, E.:Nursery Suite *(rec 4/91)* Koss Classics ▲ KC 1014 [DDD]
Elgar, E.:The Wand of Youth Suites *(rec 4/91)* Koss Classics ▲ KC 1014 [DDD]
Encores Koss Classics ▲ KC 3303 [DDD]

Indianapolis SO (cont.)
R. Leppard (cnd) (cont.)
Schubert, Franz:Ovs—Overture in C, "In the Italian Style," D.591 *(rec 11/90)* Koss Classics ▲ KC 2221 [DDD]
Schubert, Franz:Son Pno 4-Hands, D.812 [orchd. by Raymond Leppard] *(rec 11/90)* Koss Classics ▲ KC 2221 [DDD]
Schumann, R.:Genoveva (ov) Koss Classics ▲ KC 2213
Schumann, R.:Ov, Scherzo & Finale Koss Classics ▲ KC 2213
Schumann, R.:Sym 1 Koss Classics ▲ KC 2213
Tchaikovsky, P.:Manfred Koss Classics ▲ KC 2216
Vaughan Williams, R.:Sym 7, w. D. Labelle (sop), R. Allam (nar), Indianapolis Symphonic Women's Choir Koss Classics ▲ KC 2214 [DDD]
J. Nelson (cnd)
Loeffler, C.M.:Irish Fants, w. Neil Rosenshein (ten) [E] New World ▲ NW 332-2 [DDD]
Loeffler, C.M.:La Mort de Tintagiles, w. Jennie Hansen (va d'amore) New World ▲ NW 332-2 [DDD]
Zwilich, E.T.:Celebration New World ▲ NW 336-2 [DDD]
Zwilich, E.T.:Prologue & Vars New World ▲ NW 336-2 [DDD]
Zwilich, E.T.:Sym 1 New World ▲ NW 336-2 [DDD]
I. Solomon (cnd)
Bazelon, I.:Sym 5 CRI ▮ C 287
Bazelon, I.:Sym 5 CRI ▲ CD 623 [ADD]

Ineluctable Modality
Martirano, S.:Mass New World ▲ 80210-2
E. London (cnd)
Powell, Morgan:Loneliness *(rec live, Urbana, IL, July 8, 1970)* New World ▲ 80499-2
Powell, Morgan:Old Man *(rec live, Urbana, IL, May 9, 1969)* New World ▲ 80499-2

Innsbruck CO
H.L. Hirsch (cnd)
Boieldieu, F.-A.:Con Harp, w. Claudia Antonelli (hp) *(rec ORF Landesstusio Tirol, Innsbruck, June 1983)* Arts ▲ 47285-2 [DDD]
Dittersdorf, K.D. von:Con Harp, w. Claudia Antonelli (hp) *(rec ORF Landesstusio Tirol, Innsbruck, June 1983)* Arts ▲ 47285-2 [DDD]
Handel, G.F.:Con Hp, w. Claudia Antonelli (hp) *(rec ORF Landesstusio Tirol, Innsbruck, June 1983)* Arts ▲ 47285-2 [DDD]

Innsbruck Salon Quintet [Raimund Jahn (vn), Reinhard Koll (vn), Endre Bihari (vc), Walter Rumer (db), Ernst Thienes (pno)]
Innsbruck Salon Quintet Koch Schwann ▲ SCH 310212 [DDD]

Innsbruck SO
R. Wagner (cnd)
Brahms, J.:Alto Rhap, w. Maura Moreira (cta), Innsbruck Chorus *(rec Innsbruck, 1963)* Allegretto ▲ ACD 8190
Brahms, J.:Con Vn, w. S. Lautenbacher (vn) Allegretto ▲ ACD 8142 [ADD] ▮ ACS 8142
Mahler, G.:Songs from Rückert, w. Maura Moreira (cta) *(rec Innsbruck, 1963)* Allegretto ▲ ACD 8190
Schumann, R.:Requiem Mignon, w. Christa Lehnert (sop), Edith Mathis (sop), Maura Moreira (cta), Margarete Witte-Waldbauer (alt), Robert Titze (bass), Innsbruck Chorus *(rec Innsbruck, 1963)* Allegretto ▲ ACD 8190
Wagner, R.:Wesendonck Songs, w. Maura Moreira (cta) *(rec Innsbruck, 1963)* Allegretto ▲ ACD 8190
Weber, C.M. von:Concertino Cl, w. David Glazer (cl) *(rec 1963)* Allegretto ▲ ACD 8189

Innsbruck Wind Ensemble
Music at the Salzburg Court, Vol. 2:1587-1612, w. Salzburg Bach Choir [cnd:Howard Arman] Deutsche Harmonia Mundi ▲ 77157-2-RC [DDD]

Innsbruck Woodwind Circle
H. Arman (cnd)
Biber, H. von:Sons (misc), w. Salzburg Baroque Ensemble Ars Musici ("Essence" series) ▲ AME 3022-2 [DDD]
Biber, H. von:Vesperae longiores ac breviores una cum litaniis Laurentanis, w. Kym Amps (sop), Christopher Robson (alt), Anton Rosner (ten), Albert Hartinger (bass), Salzburg Baroque Ensemble, Salzburg Bach Choir, Salzburg St. Benedict College Schola Ars Musici ("Essence" series) ▲ AME 3022-2 [DDD]

Le Institutioni Harmoniche
M. Longhini (cnd)
Monteverdi, C.:Laetaniae della Beata Vergine [L] Nuova Era ("Ancient Music" series) ▲ 7118 [DDD]

Intermodulation Chamber Ensemble
L. Tihanyi (cnd)
Tihanyi, L.:The Silence of Winds Hungaroton ▲ HCD 31352

International Festival Orch
P. Stamic (cnd)
Dvořák, A.:Slavonic Dances (sels)—Op. 72/1, 2, 7 & 8 Lydian ▲ LYD 18025 [DDD]
Dvořák, A.:Sym 9, "From the New World" Lydian ▲ LYD 18025 [DDD]
M. Weber (cnd)
Brahms, J.:Academic Festival Ov Lydian ▲ LYD 18027 [DDD]
Brahms, J.:Sym 4 Lydian ▲ LYD 18027 [DDD]

International Menuhin Music Academy
International Menuhin Music Academy, w. Nora Chastain (vn), Paul Coletti (vn), Hu-Kun (vn), Mi-Kyung Lee (vn), Alberto Lysy (vn) Arcobaleno ▲ SBCD 4700 [DDD]

International Musicians Seminar Soloists
S. Végh (cnd)
Beethoven, L. van:Grosse Fuge Str Qt [performed in concerted scoring] *(rec Cornwall, England 1987/89)* Capriccio ▲ 10 356 [DDD]
Beethoven, L. van:Qt 14 Strs [performed in concerted scoring] *(rec Cornwall, England 1987/89)* Capriccio ▲ 10 356 [DDD]

International Saxophone Ensemble
J.-M. Londeix (cnd)
Fusté-Lambezat, M.:Formes-Couleurs Quantum ▲ QM 6901 [DDD]
Lauba, C.:Le Sept Iles Quantum ▲ QM 6901 [DDD]
Rossé, F.:Spath Quantum ▲ QM 6901 [DDD]

International String Congress Orch
R. Harris (cnd)
Harris, R.:Chorale *(rec live, Greenleaf Lake, OK, 1959)* Citadel ▲ CTD 88114
Harris, R.:Con Amplified Pno, w. Johana Harris (pno), United States Air Force Academy Band members *(rec Colorado Springs, CO, 1971)* Citadel ▲ CTD 88114
Harris, R.:Prelude & Fugue *(rec live, Greenleaf Lake, OK, 1959)* Citadel ▲ CTD 88114
Harris, R.:Qnt Pno, w. Johana Harris (pno) *(rec live, San German, Puerto Rico, 1960)* Citadel ▲ CTD 88114

International String Quartet
Franck, C.:Qnt Pno, w. A. Cortot (pno) *(rec 1927)* Biddulph ▲ LAB 029 [ADD]
Ravel, M.:Qt Strs *(rec London, June 1927)* Music & Arts ▲ CD 703-1 [AAD]

International SO
R. Leibowitz (cnd)
Schumann, R.:Sym 3 *(rec 1960)* Chesky ▲ CD 96 [ADD]

Invocation [Julia Gooding (sop), Ana-Maria Rincón (sop), Charles Daniels (ten), Rufus Müller (ten), Christopher Purves (bass), Frances Kelly (hp), Timothy Roberts (pno)]
English Orpheus, Vol. 27:The Romantic Muse—English Music in the Time of Beethoven Hyperion ▲ CDA 66740

▲ = CD ♦ = Enhanced CD Δ = MD ▮ = Cassette Tape ▯ = DCC

Invocation [Julia Gooding (sop), Ana-María Rincón (sop), Rufus Müller (ten), Christopher Purves (bass), Frances Kelly (hp), Giles Roberts (kbd)]
T. Roberts (cnd)
Moore, T.:Irish Melodies—Dear harp of my country; Erin! The smile & the tear in thine eyes; How sweet the answer Echo makes; Silent! oh Moyle! be the roar of the water; Rich & rare were the gems she wore; The twisting of the rope; Joice's tune; The summer is coming; Carolan's con.; The harp that once through Tara's halls; Nanny McDermotroe; The valley lay smiling before me; Abigail Judge; Avenging & bright; The Minstrel-Boy; Lament for Owen O'Neil; 'Tis believed that this harp; Come, rest on this bosom; She is far from the land; Come o'er the sea; 'Tis the last rose of summer; Girls, have you seen George; The pretty girl milking the cows; John, heir of the glen; Love in secret; The jointure; How dear to me the hour; Fly not yet; At the mid hour of night; What the bee is to the floweret; Fill the bumper fair — Hyperion ▲ CDA 66774
Invocation [Julia Goodling (sop), Ana-Maria Rincon (sop), Charles Daniels (ten), Rufus Müller (ten), Christopher Purves (bass), F. Deuter (vn), M. Caudle (vc), Francis Kelly (Welsh hp), Timothy Roberts (hpd/cnd)]
Enchanting Harmonist:A Soirée with the Linleys of Bath — Hyperion ▲ CDA 66698
Iowa Brass Quintet
Mayer, William:Qnt Brass — CRI ■ C 291
Iowa Double Reed Consort
A Double Reed Consort, w. Wizards! *(rec Clapp Recital Hall, Univ. of Iowa, Iowa City, Jan. 1993 & May 1994)* — CRS Master ▲ CRS 9460
Irish Guards Band
Music from the 1994 Royal Tournament, w. Coldstream Guards Band, Grenadier Guards Band, Life Guards Band, Welsh Guards Band, et al. — Bandleader ▲ BND 5094 [DDD]
Irish National Film Orch
F. Trench (cnd)
Davey, S.:Twelfth Night — Silva America ▲ SSD 1067
Irish National SO
A. de Almeida (cnd)
Fauré, G.:Ballade Pno, w. F.-J. Thiollier (pno) *(rec May 10–11, 1993)* — Naxos ▲ 8.550754 [DDD]
Franck, C.:Symphonic Vars, w. F.-J. Thiollier (pno) *(rec May 10–11, 1993)* — Naxos ▲ 8.550754 [DDD]
Indy, V. d':Sym on a French Mountain Air, w. F.-J. Thiollier (pno) *(rec May 10–11, 1993)* — Naxos ▲ 8.550754 [DDD]
A. Anissimov (cnd)
Rubinstein, A.:The Demon, w. Ludmilla Andrew (sop—Nanny), Marina Mescheriakova (sop—Tamara), Alison Browner (mez—Angel), Anatoly Lochak (sgr—Demon), Richard Robson (sgr—Old Servant), Valery Serkin (sgr—Prince Sinodal), Wjacheslav Weinorowski (sgr—Messenger), Leonid Zimnenko (sgr—Prince Gudal), Gregory Rose (cnd), Wexford Festival Opera Chorus *(rec Wexford, Oct & Nov, 1994)* — Marco Polo 2-▲ 8.223781-2 [DDD]
M. Benini (cnd)
Pacini, G.:Saffo, w. Francesca Pedaci (sop—Saffo), Gemma Bertagnolli (sop—Dirce), Mariana Pentcheva (mez—Climene), Carlo Ventre (ten—Faone), Aled Hall (ten—Ippia), Roberto de Candia (bar—Alcandro), Davide Baronchelli (bass—Lisimaco), Lubomír Mátl (cnd), Wexford Festival Opera Chorus *(rec Wexford, Oct & Nov 1995)* — Marco Polo 2-▲ 8.223883-4 [DDD]
R. Bonynge (cnd)
Balfe, M.W.:The Bohemian Girl, w. N. Thomas (sop), P. Power (ten), J. Summers (bar), Ireland National Sym Chorus — Argo 2-▲ 433324-2 [DDD]
A. Constantine (cnd)
Brahms, J.:Con Vn & Vc, "Double Con", w. Ilya Kaler (vn), Maria Kliegel (vc) *(rec National Concert Hall, Dublin, May 16–17, 1994)* — Naxos ▲ 8.550938 [DDD]
Schumann, R.:Con Vc, w. Maria Kliegel (vc) *(rec National Concert Hall, Dublin, May 16–17, 1994)* — Naxos ▲ 8.550938 [DDD]
S. Gunzenhauser (cnd)
Goldmark, K.:Ländliche Hochzeit *(rec National Concert Hall, Dublin, Sept. 27–28, 1993)* — Naxos ▲ 8.550745 [DDD]
Goldmark, K.:Ovs—Im Frühling [In the Spring], Op. 36; In Italien [In Italy], Op. 49 *(rec National Concert Hall, Dublin, Sept. 27–28, 1993)* — Naxos ▲ 8.550745 [DDD]
M. Halász (cnd)
Mahler, G.:Das Lied von der Erde, w. Thomas Harper (ten), Ruxandra Donose (sgr) *(rec National Concert Hall, Dublin, Apr 11–12, 1994)* — Naxos ▲ 8.550933 [DDD]
A. Leaper (cnd)
Brian, H.:Festal Dance *(rec June 15–16, 1992)* — Marco Polo ▲ 8.223481 [DDD]
Brian, H.:In Memoriam *(rec June 15–16, 1992)* — Marco Polo ▲ 8.223481 [DDD]
Brian, H.:Sym 17 *(rec June 15–16, 1992)* — Marco Polo ▲ 8.223481 [DDD]
Brian, H.:Sym 32 *(rec June 15–16, 1992)* — Marco Polo ▲ 8.223481 [DDD]
Nielsen, C.:Sym 4 *(rec Nov. 18–19, 1992)* — Naxos ▲ 8.550743 [DDD]
Nielsen, C.:Sym 5 *(rec Nov. 18–19, 1992)* — Naxos ▲ 8.550743 [DDD]
J. Maksymiuk (cnd)
Rachmaninoff, S.:Con 3 Pno, w. Bernd Glemser (pno) *(rec National Concert Hall, Dublin, Dec. 17–18, 1992)* — Naxos ▲ 8.550666 [DDD]
Rachmaninoff, S.:Prince Rostislav, w. Bernd Glemser (pno) *(rec National Concert Hall, Dublin, Dec. 17–18, 1992)* — Naxos ▲ 8.550666 [DDD]
G. Markson (cnd)
Bloch, E.:Schelomo, w. Maria Kliegel (vc) *(rec National Concert Hall, Dublin, May 17–18, 1993)* — Naxos ▲ 8.550519 [DDD]
Bruch, M.:Kol Nidrei, w. Maria Kliegel (vc) *(rec National Concert Hall, Dublin, May 17–18, 1993)* — Naxos ▲ 8.550519 [DDD]
Tchaikovsky, P.:Pezzo capriccioso, w. M. Kliegel (vc) *(rec May 17–18, 1993)* — Naxos ▲ 8.550519 [DDD]
Tchaikovsky, P.:Vars on a Rococo Theme, w. M. Kliegel (vc) *(rec May 17–18, 1993)* — Naxos ▲ 8.550519 [DDD]
A. Penny (cnd)
Arnold, M.:Sym 9 *(rec National Concert Hall, Dublin, Sept 11 & 12, 1995)* — Naxos ▲ 8.553540 [DDD]
German, E.:Symphonic Suite—Valse Gracieuse *(rec National Concert Hall, Dublin, Mar. 29–30, 1994)* — Marco Polo ▲ 8.223726 [DDD]
German, E.:Sym 2, "Norwich" *(rec National Concert Hall, Dublin, Mar. 29–30, 1994)* — Marco Polo ▲ 8.223726 [DDD]
German, E.:Welsh Rhap *(rec National Concert Hall, Dublin, Mar. 29–30, 1994)* — Marco Polo ▲ 8.223726 [DDD]
Gibbs, C.A.:Sym 1 *(rec National Concert Hall, Dublin, July 25 & 26, 1993)* — Marco Polo ▲ 8.223553 [DDD]
Gibbs, C.A.:Sym 3, "Westmorland" *(rec National Concert Hall, Dublin, July 25 & 26, 1993)* — Marco Polo ▲ 8.223553 [DDD]
R. Saccani (cnd)
Respighi, O.:Ancient Airs & Dances *(rec National Concert Hall, Dublin, Sept 1995)* — Naxos ▲ 8.553546 [DDD]
S. Sanderling (cnd)
Tchaikovsky, P.:Suite 1 *(rec Sept. 1992)* — Naxos ▲ 8.550644 [DDD]
Tchaikovsky, P.:Suite 2 *(rec Sept. 1992)* — Naxos ▲ 8.550644 [DDD]
Tchaikovsky, P.:Suite 3 *(rec Sept. 3 & 4, 1992 & Mar.)* — Naxos ▲ 8.550728 [DDD]
Tchaikovsky, P.:Suite 4 *(rec Sept. 3 & 4, 1992 & Mar.)* — Naxos ▲ 8.550728 [DDD]
R. Seifried (cnd)
Mendelssohn, F.:Sym 1 *(rec National Concert Hall, Dublin, May 9–10, 1994)* — Naxos ▲ 8.550957 [DDD]
Mendelssohn, F.:Sym 5 *(rec National Concert Hall, Dublin, May 9–10, 1994)* — Naxos ▲ 8.550957 [DDD]

Isaak Ensemble Heidelberg
Ave Regina Coelorum, w. Frankfurt Renaissance Ensemble — Bayer ▲ 100082 [DDD]
Dufay, G.:Masses—Missa Ave Regina caelorum — Bayer ▲ 100082 [DDD]
M. Valentin (cnd)
Henry Viii:Songs, Ballads & Instrumental Pieces, w. T. Stemmler (nar)—The Isaak Ensemble plays 26 pieces, & Stemmler reads 9 of Henry's love letters to Anne Boleyn [E,F] — Bayer ▲ 100132 [DDD]
Isabella D'Este [A. Maurette (vl/rcr), C. Howald (vl/rcr), A.-C. Lehmann (vl/rcr), L. Milleret (vl), C. Roumy (rcr), N. Spieth (hpd), C. Gabrielle Madar (thb)]
du Mont, H.:Cantica Sacra (18)—Symphonia; Allemanda; Allemanda gravis — Nuova Era ("Ancient Music" series) ▲ NUO 7071 [DDD]
du Mont, H.:Motets—Symphonia; Allemanda — Nuova Era ("Ancient Music" series) ▲ NUO 7071 [DDD]
Hotteterre, J.:Première livre de pièce — Nuova Era ("Ancient Music" series) ▲ NUO 7071 [DDD]
Hotteterre, J.:Premiere suitte de Pièces à 2 dessus — Nuova Era ("Ancient Music" series) ▲ NUO 7071 [DDD]
Marais, M.:Pièces en trio — Nuova Era ("Ancient Music" series) ▲ NUO 7071 [DDD]
Morel, Jacques:Première livre—Chaconne en trio — Nuova Era ("Ancient Music" series) ▲ NUO 7071 [DDD]
Moulinié, E.:Airs de cour—2 Fantaisies — Nuova Era ("Ancient Music" series) ▲ NUO 7071 [DDD]
Isabella D'Este [Caroline Howald (vl/rcr), Celelia Knudtsen (vl/rcr), Ariane Maurette (vl/rcr), Friederike Daeublin (vl), Regina Haenni (vl), Lisette Milleret (vl), Magali Dami (rcr), Cécile Roumy (rcr), Christine-Gabrielle Madar (lt/mand), Shizuko Noiri (fl)]
Adson, J.:Instrumental Consort Music—Adsonns Maske; Williams his Love; The 2nd of the temple Antic; Ayres a 5 & 6; The Bull Masque; The 2nd of my Lord of Essex; The 1st of the Temple Anticke — Symphonia ▲ SY 93S22
Holborne, A.:Instrumental Consort Music—Heigh ho holiday; Decrevi; The Funerals; The Night-Watch; The Honie-Suckle; The Fairy-Round; Pavan; Galliard; The image of Melancholy; Pavana Ploravit; Nec invideo — Symphonia ▲ SY 93S22
Simpson, T.:Consort Music—Pavan; Galliard; Courant; Volta — Symphonia ▲ SY 93S22
Iscles Trio
Brahms, J.:Trio 2 Pno — REM ▲ REM 311222 [DDD]
Schumann, R.:Trio 2 Pno — REM ▲ REM 311222 [DDD]
Israel CO
Vivaldi, A.:Cons Vn (misc), w. Shlomo Mintz (vn)—in A, RV.763, "L'Ottavina"; in F, RV.286; in E♭, RV.261; in B♭, RV.366; in E♭, RV.260; in b, RV.387 — MusicMasters ▲ 01612-67155-2
G. Ben-Dor (cnd)
Ginastera, A.:Glosses on themes of Pablo Casals — Koch International Classics ▲ KIC 7149 [DDD]
S. Mintz (cnd)
Vivaldi, A.:Cons Vn (misc), w. Shlomo Mintz (vn)—Op. 6/1–6; Coucou, RV 335 *(rec Paris, Aug 1992 & Mar 1993)* — MusicMasters ("Classics" series) ▲ 671792
Vivaldi, A.:Cons Vn (misc), w. S. Mintz (vn)—"Anna Maria" Concertos, RV.223, 349, 248, 229, 343 & 267 — MusicMasters ▲ 1612-67120-2
Vivaldi, A.:Cons Vn (misc), w. S. Mintz (vn)—12 concerti—RV.171, 186, 199, 208, 230, 232, 249, 254, 265, 271, 310, 356 — MusicMasters 2-▲ 01612-67085-2
Vivaldi, A.:Cons Vn (misc), w. Shlomo Mintz (vn)—RV.189, 197, 215, 241, 321 & 329 *(rec Eglise du Liban, Aug 1992)* — MusicMasters ("Vivaldi Collection" series) ▲ 01612-67168-2
Vivaldi, A.:Sinfs—11 sinfonias—RV.114, 119, 121, 127, 133, 134, 136, 150, 159, 160, 164) — MusicMasters ▲ 01612-67096-2 [DDD]
Y. Talmi (cnd)
Barber, S.:Adagio Strs — Chandos ▲ CHAN 8593 [DDD]
Bloch, E.:Con grosso 1 — Chandos ▲ CHAN 8593 [DDD]
Grieg, E.:Holberg Suite — Chandos ▲ CHAN 8593 [DDD]
Puccini, G.:Crisantemi [arr for str orch] — Chandos ▲ CHAN 8593 [DDD]
A. Vardi (cnd)
Mozart, W.A.:Con 6 Pno, w. A. Vardi (pno) — PWK Classics ▲ PWK 1144 [AAD]
Mozart, W.A.:Con 21 Pno, w. A. Vardi (pno) — PWK Classics ▲ PWK 1144 [AAD]
Israel Flute Ensemble
Beethoven, L. van:Serenade Fl, Op. 25 — PWK Classics ▲ PWK 1139 [DDD]
Hoffmeister, F.A.:Qt Fl — PWK Classics ▲ PWK 1139 [DDD]
Mozart, W.A.:Qt Fl, K.285 — PWK Classics ▲ PWK 1139 [DDD]
Israel Flute Ensemble members
Schubert, Franz:Trio Strs, D.471 — PWK Classics ▲ PWK 1139 [DDD]
Israel PO
Bach, J.S.:Con Vn & Ob, w. I. Perlman (vn), R. Still (ob) — EMI Classics ▲ CDC 47073-2 [DDD]
D. Amos (cnd)
Chajes, J.:Israeli Melodies (6) — Crystal ▲ CD 508
Creston, P.:Chant of 1942 — Crystal ▲ CD 508
Creston, P.:Suite Str Orch — Crystal ▲ CD 508
Dello Joio, N.:Air — Crystal ▲ CD 508
Glazunov, A.:Chant du ménestrel, w. M. Rimon (hn) — Crystal ▲ CD 510 [DDD]
Hovhaness, A.:Armenian Rhap 2 — Crystal ▲ CD 508
Hovhaness, A.:Artik, w. Meir Rimon (hn) — Crystal ▲ CD 802
Hovhaness, A.:Celestial Fant — Crystal ▲ CD 508
Meir Rimon, w. M. Rimon (hn) — Crystal ▲ CD 510 [DDD]
Persichetti, V.:Introit Strs — Crystal ▲ CD 508
Premières of the Old & New — Crystal ▲ CD 510 [DDD]
Tchaikovsky, P.:Les Saisons, w. M. Rimon (hn)—No. 10, "Autumn Song" — Crystal ▲ CD 510 [DDD]
L. Bernstein (cnd)
Bernstein, L.:Chichester Psalms, w. Vienna Boys' Choir [He] — Deutsche Grammophon ▲ 415965-2 [ADD]
Bernstein, L.:On the Town — Deutsche Grammophon ("3D Classics" series) ▲ 427806-2 [DDD]
Bernstein, L.:Sym 1, "Jeremiah", w. C. Ludwig (mez) — Deutsche Grammophon 2-▲ 445245-2 [ADD]
Bernstein, L.:Sym 2, "Age of Anxiety", w. L. Foss (pno) — Deutsche Grammophon 2-▲ 445245-2 [ADD]
Bernstein, L.:Sym 3, "Kaddish", w. M. Caballé (sop), M. Wager (nar), *(chorus unknown)* — Deutsche Grammophon 2-▲ 445245-2 [ADD]
Bloch, E.:Schelomo, w. M. Maisky (vc) — Deutsche Grammophon ▲ 427347-2 [DDD]
Dvořák, A.:Con Vc, w. M. Maisky (vc) — Deutsche Grammophon ▲ 427347-2 [DDD]
Dvořák, A.:Slavonic Dances (sels)—3 from Op. 46 — Deutsche Grammophon ▲ 427346-2 [DDD]
Dvořák, A.:Sym 9, "From the New World" — Deutsche Grammophon ▲ 427346-2 [DDD]
Hindemith, P.:Concert Music Brass & Strs — Deutsche Grammophon ▲ 429404-2 [DDD]
Hindemith, P.:Mathis der Maler (sym) — Deutsche Grammophon ▲ 429404-2 [DDD]
Hindemith, P.:Symphonic Metamorphosis on Themes of Carl Maria von Weber — Deutsche Grammophon ▲ 429404-2 [DDD]
The Joy of Bernstein, w. New York PO, Vienna PO, Los Angeles PO — Deutsche Grammophon ▲ 445486-2
Les Chefs-d'Oeuvre du Violoncelle, w. Mstislav Rostropovich (vc), Berlin PO [cnd:Herbert von Karajan] — Deutsche Grammophon ("Double" series) 2-▲ 437952-2
Mahler, G.:Das Lied von der Erde, w. C. Ludwig (mez), R. Kollo (ten) — Sony Classical ▲ SMK 47589
Mozart, W.A.:Con 25 Pno, w. L. Bernstein (pno) — Sony Classical ▲ SMK 47519 [ADD]
Stravinsky, I.:The Firebird Suite — Deutsche Grammophon ("Digital Midprice" series) 2-▲ 445538-2 [DDD]
Stravinsky, I.:Pétrouchka — Deutsche Grammophon ("3D Classics" series) ▲ 429493-2 [DDD]
Stravinsky, I.:Pétrouchka (suite) — Deutsche Grammophon ("Digital Midprice" series) 2-▲ 445538-2 [DDD]
Stravinsky, I.:Le Sacre du printemps Orch — Deutsche Grammophon ("Digital Midprice" series) 2-▲ 445538-2 [DDD]
Stravinsky, I.:Le Sacre du printemps Orch — Deutsche Grammophon ▲ 431045-2 [DDD]
Stravinsky, I.:Le Sacre du printemps Orch — Deutsche Grammophon ("3D Classics" series) ▲ 429493-2 [DDD]

ORCH. & ENS.

Israel PO (cont.)
L. Bernstein (cnd) (cont.)
Stravinsky, I.:Scènes de ballet — Deutsche Grammophon ("Digital Midprice" series) 2-▲ 445538-2 [DDD]
Stravinsky, I.:Sym in 3 Movts — Deutsche Grammophon ("Digital Midprice" series) 2-▲ 445538-2 [DDD]
Tchaikovsky, P.:Capriccio italien — Deutsche Grammophon ▲ 431047-2 [DDD]
Tchaikovsky, P.:Ov 1812 — Deutsche Grammophon ▲ 431047-2 [DDD]
Tchaikovsky, P.:Romeo & Juliet — Deutsche Grammophon ▲ 431047-2 [DDD]
I. Kertész (cnd)
Schumann, R.:Con Pno, w. J. Katchen (pno) — IMP Collectors Series ▲ IMPX 9041 [ADD]
Z. Mehta (cnd)
Berlioz, H.:Harold in Italy, w. D. Benyamini (va) *(rec early/mid 1970s)* — PWK Classics ▲ PWK 1152 [ADD]
Brahms, J.:Syms (comp) *(rec Oct. 5–29, 1992)* — Sony Classical 4-▲ SX4K 53279 [DDD]
Brahms, J.:Tragic Ov *(rec Oct. 5–29, 1992)* — Sony Classical 4-▲ SX4K 53279 [DDD]
Brahms, J.:Vars on a Theme by Haydn *(rec Oct. 5–29, 1992)* — Sony Classical 4-▲ SX4K 53279 [DDD]
Bruch, M.:Con 2 Vn, w. I. Perlman (vn) — EMI Classics ▲ CDC 49071
Bruch, M.:Scottish Fant Vn, w. Midori (vn) *(rec F. Mann Auditorium, Tel Aviv, Israel, July 26–30, 1993)* — Sony Classical ▲ SK 58967 [DDD]; ■ ST 58967
Bruch, M.:Scottish Fant Vn, w. I. Perlman (vn) — EMI Classics ▲ CDC 49071
Bruckner, A.:Sym 0 — Sony Classical 2-▲ S2K 45864 [DDD]
Bruckner, A.:Sym 8 — Sony Classical 2-▲ S2K 45864 [DDD]
Chopin, F.:Con 1 Pno, w. M. Perahia (pno) — Sony Classical ▲ SK 44922 [DDD] ■ ST 44922 (CrO2)
Chopin, F.:Con 2 Pno, w. M. Perahia (pno) — Sony Classical ▲ SK 44922 [DDD] ■ ST 44922 (CrO2)
Fauré, G.:Pelléas et Mélisande (suite) — Sony Classical ▲ SK 45870 [DDD]
Glazunov, A.:Con Vn, w. I. Perlman (vn) — EMI Classics ▲ CDC 49814
Khachaturian, A.:Con Vn, w. I. Perlman (vn) — EMI Classics ▲ CDC 47087 [DDD]
Liszt, F.:Hungarian Rhaps—Nos. 2, 5, 6, 9, 12 & 14 — CBS ▲ MK 44926 [DDD] ■ MT 44926 (D)
Mahler, G.:Sym 1 — London ("Double Decker" series) 2-▲ 443030-2
Mahler, G.:Sym 1 *(rec ca. 1975/76)* — IMP Collectors Series ▲ IMPX 9005 [AAD]
Mahler, G.:Sym 2, w. Nancy Gustafson (sop), Florence Quivar (mez), Prague Phil Chorus *(rec Fredric R. Mann Auditorium, Tel Aviv, Jan–Feb. 1994)* — Teldec ▲ 94545-2 [DDD]
Mahler, G.:Sym 3, w. F. Quivar (cta) — Sony Classical ▲ S2K 52579
Mahler, G.:Sym 10 — Sony Classical ▲ S2K 52579
Mozart, W.A.:Andante Fl, K.315/285a, w. Jean-Pierre Rampal (fl) — CBS ▲ MK 44919 [DDD]
Mozart, W.A.:Cons Fl, w. Jean-Pierre Rampal (fl) — CBS ▲ MK 44919 [DDD]
Mozart, W.A.:Concertone Vns, w. I. Perlman (vn), P. Zukerman (vn) — Deutsche Grammophon ▲ 415486-2 [DDD]
Mozart, W.A.:Rondo Fl, K.Anh.184, w. Jean-Pierre Rampal (fl) — CBS ▲ MK 44919 [DDD]
Mozart, W.A.:Sinf concertante Vn, K.364, w. I. Perlman (vn), P. Zukerman (va) — Deutsche Grammophon ▲ 415486-2 [DDD]
Paganini, N.:Con 1 Vn, w. M. Vengerov (vn) — Teldec ▲ 9031-73266-2 ZK
Prokofiev, S.:Con 1 Pno, w. Y. Bronfman (pno) *(rec Nov. 14–25, 1991)* — Sony Classical ▲ SK 52483 [DDD]
Prokofiev, S.:Con 2 Pno, w. Y. Bronfman (pno) *(rec July 8–17, 1993)* — Sony Classical ▲ SK 58966 [DDD]
Prokofiev, S.:Con 3 Pno, w. Y. Bronfman (pno) *(rec Nov. 14–25, 1991)* — Sony Classical ▲ SK 52483 [DDD]
Prokofiev, S.:Con 4 Pno, w. Y. Bronfman (pno) *(rec July 8–17, 1993)* — Sony Classical ▲ SK 58966 [DDD]
Prokofiev, S.:Con 5 Pno, w. Y. Bronfman (pno) *(rec Nov. 14–25, 1991)* — Sony Classical ▲ SK 52483 [DDD]
Prokofiev, S.:Peter & the Wolf, w. I. Perlman (nar) — EMI Classics ▲ CDC 47067 [DDD]
Rachmaninoff, S.:Con 3 Pno, w. Vladimir Feltsman (pno) — CBS ▲ MK 44761 [DDD] ■ MT 44761 (D)
Rachmaninoff, S.:Rhapsody on a Theme of Paganini, w. Vladimir Feltsman (pno) — CBS ▲ MK 44761 [DDD] ■ MT 44761 (D)
Rimsky-Korsakov, N.:Russian Easter Festival — CBS ▲ MDK 45652 [DDD] ■ MDT 45652 (D)
Rimsky-Korsakov, N.:Scheherazade — CBS ▲ MDK 45652 [DDD] ■ MDT 45652 (D)
Saint-Saëns, C.:Carnival of the Animals, w. I. Perlman (nar), K. Labèque (pno), M. Labèque (pno) — EMI Classics ▲ CDC 47067 [DDD]
Saint-Saëns, C.:Con 3 Vn, w. J. Rachlin (vn) — Sony Classical ▲ SK 48373 [DDD]
Saint-Saëns, C.:Havanaise Vn, w. M. Vengerov (vn) — Teldec ▲ 9031-73266-2 ZK
Saint-Saëns, C.:Introduction & Rondo capriccioso, w. M. Vengerov (vn) — Teldec ▲ 9031-73266-2 ZK
Schoenberg, A.:Pelleas und Melisande — Sony Classical ▲ SK 45870 [DDD]
Shostakovich, D.:Con 1 Vn, w. I. Perlman (vn) — EMI Classics ▲ CDC 49814
Sibelius, J.:Con Vn, w. Midori (vn) *(rec F. Mann Auditorium, Tel Aviv, Israel, July 26–30, 1993)* — Sony Classical ▲ SK 58967 [DDD]; ■ ST 58967
Sibelius, J.:Pelléas et Mélisande — Sony Classical ▲ SK 45870 [DDD]
Smetana, B.:Má Vlast *(rec Oct. 18–27, 1991)* — Sony Classical ▲ SK 58944 [DDD]
Tchaikovsky, P.:Capriccio italien — Teldec ▲ 90201-2
Tchaikovsky, P.:Con Vn, w. P. Zukerman (vn) — CBS ▲ MDK 44643 [DDD] ■ MDT 44643 (D)
Tchaikovsky, P.:Con Vn, w. P. Zukerman (vn) — CBS ▲ MK 39563 [DDD]
Tchaikovsky, P.:Con Vn, w. I. Perlman (vn) — EMI Classics ▲ CDC 54108 ■ 4DS 54108
Tchaikovsky, P.:Méditation, w. I. Perlman (vn) — EMI Classics ▲ CDC 47087 [DDD]
Tchaikovsky, P.:Ov 1812 — Teldec ▲ 4509-90201-2
Tchaikovsky, P.:Swan Lake (sels)—Suite & Mazurka — Teldec ▲ 4509-90201-2
Vivaldi, A.:Cons Vn, Op. 8/1–4, "The Four Seasons", w. I. Perlman (vn) — Deutsche Grammophon ▲ 419214-2 [DDD] ■ 419214-4
Waxman, F.:Carmen Fant, w. M. Vengerov (vn) — Teldec ▲ 9031-73266-2 ZK
Wieniawski, H.:Con 2 Vn, w. J. Rachlin (vn) — Sony Classical ▲ SK 48373 [DDD]
I. Perlman (cnd)
Bach, J.S.:Con Vn, BWV 1052 — EMI Classics ▲ CDC 47073-2 [DDD]
Bach, J.S.:Con Vn, BWV 1058 — EMI Classics ▲ CDC 47073-2 [DDD]
Vivaldi, A.:Cons Vn (misc), w. I. Perlman (vn)—RV.199, 317, 347, 356 — EMI Classics ▲ CDC 47076 [DDD]
Vivaldi, A.:Cons Vn, Op. 8/1–4, "The Four Seasons", w. I. Perlman (vn) — EMI Classics ▲ CDM 64333
Vivaldi, A.:Cons Vn, Op. 8/1–4, "The Four Seasons", w. I. Perlman (vn) — EMI Classics ▲ CDC 47319 [DDD] ■ 4DS 38123 (D)
G. Solti (cnd)
Dukas, P.:L'Apprenti sorcier *(rec 1957)* — London 2-▲ 443033-2 [ADD]
Mendelssohn, F.:Sym 4 — London ("Weekend Classics" series) ▲ 433023-2 [AAD]
Respighi, O.:La Boutique fantastique — London ("Weekend Classics" series) 2-▲ 425509-2 [AAD] 2-■ 425509-4
Tchaikovsky, P.:The Nutcracker — London ("Weekend Classics" series) 2-▲ 425509-2 [AAD] 2-■ 425509-4

Israel PO members
D. Amos (cnd)
Dances Moods & Romances, w. Meir Rimon (hn) — Crystal ▲ CD513
Z. Dorman (cnd)
Mozart, W.A.:Cons Fl, w. Laurel Zucker (fl) *(rec Israel Conservatory of Music, Tel-Aviv)* — Cantilena ▲ C 660102 [DDD]
Mozart, W.A.:Cons Fl, w. Laurel Zucker (fl) *(rec Israel Conservatory, Tel-Aviv)* — Cantilena ▲ 66011-2 [DDD]
Mozart, W.A.:Qt Fl, K.Anh.171, w. Laurel Zucker (fl)—in C, K.285b *(rec Israel Conservatory of Music, Tel-Aviv)* — Cantilena ▲ C 660102 [DDD]
Z. Mehta (cnd)
Beethoven, L. van:Sym 5, Berlin PO *(rec live, Tel Aviv, 4/18/90)* — Sony Classical ▲ SK 45968
Ben-Haim, P.:Sym 1, Berlin PO—Psalm movt *(rec live, Tel Aviv, 4/18/90)* — Sony Classical ▲ SK 45968

Israel PO members (cont.)
Z. Mehta (cnd) (cont.)
Ravel, M.:La Valse, Berlin PO *(rec live in Tel Aviv, 4/18/90)* — Sony Classical ▲ SK 45968

Israel Pro Musica Orch
D. Atlas (cnd)
Dvořák, A.:Symphonic Vars — IMP ("Classics" series) ▲ IMP PCD 1112

Israel Sinfonietta
M. Rodan (cnd)
Mendelssohn, F.:Sym 1 — Olympia ▲ OCD 164 [DDD]
Poulenc, F.:Sinfonietta — Olympia ▲ OCD 164 [DDD]

Israel SO
G. Stern (cnd)
Esplá, O.:Andalusian Folksongs (5), w. Y. Pappas (mez)—Rutas; Pregon; Las 12; El pescador; Coplilla [Sp] — Meridian ▲ CDE 84134
Esplá, O.:Canciones playeras, w. Y. Pappas (mez) [Sp] — Meridian ▲ CDE 84134
Granados, E.:Canciones amatorias (7), w. Y. Pappas (mez)—Mañanica era; Llorad corazon; Mira que soy; Iban al pinar [Sp] — Meridian ▲ CDE 84134
Montsalvatge, X.:Canciones negras, w. Y. Pappas (mez) [Sp] — Meridian ▲ CDE 84134
Turina, J.:Canto a Sevilla, w. Y. Pappas (mez) [Sp] — Meridian ▲ CDE 84134

Istanbul State Opera Orch
A. D. Sinangil (cnd)
Sinangil, A.D.:Mevlâna Oratorio (sels), w. Leyla Demiris (sop), Isin Güyer (mez), Mesut Iktu (bar), Mustafa Iktu (bass), Kâmil Sekerkaran (fl), Istanbul State Opera Chorus—Récitatif I; Choral; Récitatif II; V^{5} partie — Gallo ▲ CD 836 [ADD]

Istanbul State Opera Soloists
A.D. Sinangil (cnd)
Sinangil, A.D.:Improv I — Gallo ▲ CD 836 [ADD]

Istanbul State SO
O. Züno (cnd)
Sinangil, A.D.:Sym 1 — Gallo ▲ CD 836 [ADD]

Italian Accademia Strumentale
G. Bernasconi (cnd)
Boccherini, L.:Syms—Opp. 35/1; 41; 45 *(rec Forli, Italy, Feb 1992)* — Arts ▲ 47110-2 [DDD]
Boccherini, L.:Syms—Op. 35/2, 4 & 5 *(rec Forli, Italy, Mar 1990)* — Arts ▲ 47108-2 [DDD]
Boccherini, L.:Syms—Opp. 21/3; 37/1 & 3 *(rec Forli, Italy, Sept 1991)* — Arts ▲ 47108-2 [DDD]
A. Rasi (cnd)
Farina, C.:Music of—Pavana 1; Capriccio Stravagante; Pavana III; Balletto Allemanno XXVIII; Aria Francesca XXVI; Corenta XVIII; Gagliarda VII; Pavana II; Corenta XIX; Aria Francesca XXV; Gagliarda XII; Gagliarda X; Pavana IV; Balletto Allemanno XXIX; Corenta XVI; Gagliarda IX; Gagliarda V — Stradivarius ▲ STV 33388 [DDD]
Purcell, H.:Fants Vls (comp) — Stradivarius ▲ STV 33357 [DDD]

Italian Camerata Orch
Vivaldi, A.:Cons Vn (misc), w. S. Accardo (vn) — RCA Silver Seal ▲ 60542-2 [ADD/DDD] ■ 60542-4
Vivaldi, A.:Cons Vn, Op. 8/1–4, "The Four Seasons", w. S. Accardo (vn) — RCA Silver Seal ▲ 60542-2 [ADD/DDD] ■ 60542-4
Vivaldi, A.:Cons Vn, Op. 8/1–4, "The Four Seasons", w. S. Accardo (vn) — RCA Victrola ▲ 7732-2 RV [DDD] ■ 7732-4 RV (CrO2)

Italian Femminile Ensemble
Nuttata 'e Sentimento—Neapolitan Songs, w. Ricciarelli, Katia (sop) — Kicco Classic ▲ 1695

Italian Accademia Strumentale
G. Bernasconi (cnd)
Cherubini, L.:Il Giuocatore, w. Monica Bacelli (sop), Giorgio Gatti (bar) *(rec Parma, Mar 20–22, 1989)* — Agorá Music ("Phoenix" series) ▲ 504

Italian International Opera Orch
M. de Bernart (cnd)
Donizetti, G.:Maria di Rohan (sels), w. M. Nicolesco (sop), G. Morino (ten), P. Coni (bar), Slovak Phil Chorus [I] *(rec live)* — Nuova Era 2-▲ 6732/33 [DDD]
G. Carella (cnd)
Mercadante, S.:Caritea, regina di Spagna, w. Nana Gordaze (sgr), Sonia Lee (sgr), Jacek Laszczkowski (sgr), Nicolas Rivenq (bar), Gregory Bonfatti (sgr), Ayhan Ustuk (sgr), Bratislava Camera Chorus *(rec Italy, 1995)* — Nuova Era 3-▲ NUO 7258
P. Fournillier (cnd)
Cherubini, L.:Médée, w. Jano Tamar (sop), Patrizia Ciofi (sgr), Luca Lombardo (sgr), Magali Damonte (sgr), Jean-Philippe Courtis (bass), Sluk Chamber Chorus Bratislava *(rec Martina Franca Festival, 1995)* — Nuova Era 2-▲ NUO 7253
M. Letonja (cnd)
Mascagni, P.:Messa di Gloria, w. Carlo Allemano (ten), Domenico Colaianni (bar), Bratislava Camera Chorus — Nuova Era ▲ NUO CD 7270

Italian International Orch
B. Aprea (cnd)
Mercadante, S.:Il bravo, w. J. Perry (sop), A. Tabiadon (mez), D. Di Domenico (ten), S. Bertocchi (ten), S. Antonucci (bar), Slovak Phil Chorus [I] *(rec live 7/28–31/90)* — Nuova Era 3-▲ 6971/73 [DDD]
Puccini, G.:Le Villi, w. Stefano Antonucci (bar), José Cura (sgr), Nana Gordaze (sgr) — Nuova Era ▲ NUO 7218 [DDD]
G. Carella (cnd)
Bellini, V.:La sonnambula, w. Maria Costanza Nocentini (sop), Vitalba Mosca (mez), Giuseppe Morino (ten), Giovanni Furlanetto (bar), Patrizia Ciofi (sgr), Etienne Ligot (sgr), Walter Mikus (sgr) — Nuova Era 2-▲ NUO 7215 [DDD]
C. Piantini (cnd)
Bizet, G.:Les Pêcheurs de perles, w. A. Ruffini (sop), G. Morino (ten), B. Praticò (bar), Slovak Phil Chorus [F] *(rec live 7/30–8/2/90)* — Nuova Era 2-▲ 6944/45 [DDD]
Delibes, L.:Lakmé, w. A. Ruffini (sop), S. Lazzarini (mez), G. Morino (ten), B. Praticò (bar), Bratislava Chamber Chorus [F] — Nuova Era 2-▲ 7096/97 [DDD]
F. Vizioli (cnd)
Grétry, A.-E.-M.:Denys le tyran, w. S. Donzelli (sgr), R. Franceschetto (sgr), C. Di Segni (ten), B. De Simone (bar), Ars Pulcherrima Artium Chorus [F] *(rec live, Fermo, Palazzo Sassatelli, 1989)* — Memories ▲ DR 3106 [DDD]

Italian International Orch String Quartet
M. Carraro (cnd)
Vinci, L.:Arias, w. M. A. Peters (sop)—nine soprano arias from the operas La Caduta dei Decemviri, Catone in Utica, Lo Cecato Fauzo, Didone Abbandonata, La Festa de Bacco, & Semiramide Riconosciuta [I] *(rec live, Festival Internazionale di Gerace, 1990)* — Memories ▲ DR 3109 [DDD]

Italian Lyric Orch
A. Basile (cnd)
Mascagni, P.:Cavalleria rusticana, w. G. Simionato (sop—Santuzza), F. Cadoni (mez—Lola), L. Pellogrino (cta—Lucia), A. Braschi (ten—Turiddu), C. Tagliabue (bar—Alfio), Turin Cetra Chorus *(rec Turin, 1950)* — Cetra Classic 2-▲ CDO 27 [ADD]
F. Capuana (cnd)
Giordano, U.:Andrea Chénier, w. Renata Tebaldi (sop—Maddalena), Anna di Stasio (mez—Bersi), Amalia Pini (mez—Madelon/Contessa), Mario Del Monaco (ten—Andrea Chenier), Antonio Pirino (ten—L'Incredibile/Abate), Aldo Protti (bar—Carlo Gerard), Arturo La Porta (bass/bar—Mathieu/Fleville), Silvano Pagliuca (bass/bar—Roucher/Fouquier-Tinville), Giorgio Onesti (bass—Dumas/Schmidt/Major-domo), Italian Lyric Chorus *(rec Tokyo, Oct 1, 1961)* — Legato Classics 2-▲ LCD 214-2 [ADD]

Italian Music Academy Orch
Alfredo Kraus in Concerto, w. Kraus, Alfredo (ten), Italian Music Academy Orch [cnd:Franco Mannino], Felix Ayo (vn) *(rec live Apr. 3, 1989)* — Fonit Cetra ▲ CDC 42 [DDD]

▲ = CD ♦ = Enhanced CD Δ = MD ■ = Cassette Tape □ = DCC

Italian PO

M. de Bernart (cnd)

Coccia, C.:Caterina di Guisa, w. C. Apollonio (sop), N. Ciliento (mez), M. Leonardi (ten), S. Antonucci (bar), Calabria Francesca Cilea Chorus *(rec Oct. 30 & Nov. 3, 1990)* Bongiovanni 2-▲ GB 2117/18 [DDD]

Manfroce, N.A.:Ecuba, w. A. C. Antonacci (sop), D. di Domenico (ten), F. Piccoli (ten), G. De Bellida (sgr), Italian Phil Chorus [I] *(rec live 1990)* Bongiovanni 2-▲ GB 2119/20 [DDD]

Italian Piano Quartet [Corrado Bolsi (vn), Angelo Bartoletti (va), Sandro Meo (vc), Riccardo Cecchetti (pno)]

Brahms, J.:Qts Pno (comp) Symphonia 2-▲ SYM 94D 26

Italian Solisti

Albinoni, T.:Cons à 5 Obs, Op. 7, w. H.-J. Schellenberger (ob)—No. 6 Denon ▲ CO 2301 [DDD]

Albinoni, T.:Cons à 5 Obs, Op. 9, w. H.-J. Schellenberger (ob)—No. 11 *(rec July 24–27, 1992)* Denon ▲ CO 75338 [DDD]

Albinoni, T.:Cons à 5 Obs, Op. 9, w. H.-J. Schellenberger (ob)—No. 8 Denon ▲ CO 2301 [DDD]

Barber, S.:Adagio Strs Denon ▲ CO 75040 [DDD]

Bartók, B.:Romanian Folk Dances Pno Denon ▲ CO 75040 [DDD]

Christmas Concertos *(rec Sept. 11–26, 1993)* Denon ▲ CO 78912 [DDD]

Grieg, E.:Elegaic Melodies, Op. 34 Denon ▲ CO 75040 [DDD]

Malipiero, G.F.:Sinf 6 *(rec Villa Contarini, Piazzola sul Brenta, Italy, June 19–23, 1994)* Denon ▲ DEN 78949 [DDD]

Marcello, A.:Con Ob & Strs, w. H.-J. Schellenberger (ob) Denon ▲ CO 2301 [DDD]

Morricone, E.:Esercizi *(rec Villa Contarini, Piazzola sul Brenta, Italy, June 19–23, 1994)* Denon ▲ CO 78949 [DDD]

Porena, B.:Vivaldi *(rec Villa Contarini, Piazzola sul Brenta, Italy, June 19–23, 1994)* Denon ▲ CO 78949 [DDD]

Promenade Concert Denon ▲ CO 75040 [DDD]

Rota, N.:Con Strs *(rec Villa Contarini, Piazzola sul Brenta, Italy, June 19–23, 1994)* Denon ▲ CO 78949 [DDD]

Sammartini, G.:Con in E♭ Ob, w. H.-J. Schellenberger (ob) Denon ▲ CO 2301 [DDD]

Scarlatti, D.:Sinfs Ob, w. H.-J. Schellenberger (ob)—in G, G & B♭ *(rec July 24–27, 1992)* Denon ▲ CO 75338 [DDD]

Tchaikovsky, P.:Andante cantabile Denon ▲ CO 75040 [DDD]

Turina, J.:La oracion del torero Denon ▲ CO 75040 [DDD]

Vivaldi, A.:Cons Bn, w. M. Turkovič (bn)—RV.478 in C; RV.480 in c; RV.484 in e; RV.498 in a; RV.501 in B♭, "La Notte" Denon ▲ CO 77528 [DDD]

Vivaldi, A.:Cons Ob, w. Hans-Jorg Schellenberger (ob)—RV.453, 455 Denon ▲ CO 2301 [DDD]

Vivaldi, A.:Cons Ob, w. Hans-Jorg Schellenberger (ob)—RV.454 & 447 *(rec July 24–27, 1992)* Denon ▲ CO 75338 [DDD]

Vivaldi, A.:Cons Vn (misc)—RV.163, 208, 234, 271, 277, 366 Denon ▲ CO 77885 [DDD]

Vivaldi, A.:Cons Vn, Op. 3/1–12, "L'estro armonico" Denon 2-▲ CO 72719/20 [DDD]

Vivaldi, A.:Cons Vn, Op. 4, "La stravaganza" *(rec Sept. 11–26, 1993)* Denon/PCM Digital 2-▲ CO 75889/90 [DDD]

Vivaldi, A.:Cons Vn, Op. 8/1–12, "Il cimento dell'armonia e dell'inventione"—Nos. 1–6 Denon ▲ CO 1471 [DDD]

Vivaldi, A.:Cons Vn, Op. 8/1–12, "Il cimento dell'armonia e dell'inventione"—Nos. 7–12 Denon ▲ CO 1520 [DDD]

Vivaldi, A.:Cons Vn, Op. 9, "La Cetra" *(rec 1990)* Denon 2-▲ CO 79475/76 [DDD]

Vivaldi, A.:Cons Vn, Op. 12 *(rec Villa Contarini, Pizzola sul Brenta, Italy, July 25–29, 1994)* Denon ▲ DEN 78974 [DDD]

Italian Virtuosi

A. Ballista (cnd)

Battiato, F.:Messa Arcaica, w. Akemi Sakamoto (mez), Franco Battiato (voc), Filippo Destrieri (kbd/cmpt), Carlo Guaitoli (pno), Angelo Privitera (kbd/cmpt), Filippo Maria Bressan (cnd), Athestis Chorus Hemisphere ▲ 837234-2

Italiano Octet [Angelo Persichelli (fl), Corrado Giuffredi (cl), Luca Milani (cl), Danilo Marchello (hn), Ettore Bongiovanni (hn), Rino Vernizzi (bn), Gabriele Screpis (bn), Luigi Milani (db)]

Rossini, G.:Ovs—Le Siège de Corinthe; Matilde di Shabran; Il Turco in Italia; Tancredi [all trans F. Beer for winds]; Il Barbiere di Siviglia; L'Italiana in Algeri; Ricciardo e Zoraide; Otello [all trans V. Gambaro for winds] *(rec Chiesa della Misericordia, Torino, Italy, June 1992)* Arts ▲ 47162-2 [DDD]

L'Itinéraire Ensemble

Landowski, Tzipine (cnd)

Landowski, M.:Music of, w. Nadine Sautereau (sop), Jean-Christophe Benoit (bar), Xavier Depraz (bass), Michel Bouquet (spkr), Gilbert Audin (bn), Evelyne Aïello, Didier Bouture, Ludovic Chevalier, Laurent Decker, Françoise Deslogères, Colonne Association des Concerts Orch, Boulogne-Billancourt Orch Conservatory, Paris Conservatory Société des Concerts Orch, Harmonia Nova Orch Ensemble—Con Bn; Con pour ondes Martenot; Femme sans passé; Hauts de Hurlevent; Horologe; Mouvement; Notes de Nuit; Souvenir d'un jardin d'enfance; Ventriloque Chamade 3-▲ 5639/40/41 [AAD/DDD]

Rophé, Foster (cnd)

Grisey, G.:Chamber Music, w. Gérard Caussé (va), Claude Delangle (sax)—Talea for ensemble; Prologue for Va & Ww; Anubis for Sax; Jour Contre Jour Accord ▲ ACD 201952 [DDD]

Ives Ensemble

Cage, J.:Fourteen *(rec Leeuwarden, Netherlands, Feb. 1994)* Hat Hut ("Now." series) ▲ hat ART CD 6159 [DDD]

Cage, J.:Ryoanji for 2 Vns *(rec Leeuwarden, Netherlands, Feb. 1994)* Hat Hut ("Now." series) ▲ hat ART CD 6159 [DDD]

Cage, J.:Ten *(rec Leeuwarden, Netherlands, Feb. 1994)* Hat Hut ("Now." series) ▲ hat ART CD 6159 [DDD]

Ives Ensemble members [Esther Probst (E hn), Hans Petra (cl), Marja Uyldert (cl), Erik van Deuren (b cl), Arnold Marinissen (perc)]

Cage, J.:Five² *(rec Theater Romein, Leeuwarden, the Netherlands, Jan 14–17, 1996)* Hat Art ("Hat NOW." series) 2-▲ 6192 [DDD]

Ives Ensemble members [John Snijders (pno), Josje Ter Haar (vn), Ruben Sanderse (va), Job Ter Haar (vc)]

Feldman, Morton:Pno, Vn, Va & Vc *(rec Hessen Radio Sendesaal, Frankfurt, Feb. 3–4, 1994)* Hat Hut ("Now." series) ▲ ART CD 6158 [DDD]

Ives Ensemble members [Rik Andriessen (b fl), Hans Petra (b cl), Harrie de Lange (b trbn), Job ter Haar (vc), Peter Luit (db), Ron Colbers (perc), Arnold Marinissen (perc)]

Cage, J.:Seven² *(rec Theater Romein, Leeuwarden, the Netherlands, Jan 14–17, 1996)* Hat Art ("Hat NOW." series) 2-▲ 6192 [DDD]

Ives Ensemble members [Rik Andriessen (fl), Hans Petra (cl), John Snijders (pno), Josje ter Haar (vn), Ruben Sanderse (va), Job ter Haar (vc), Arnold Marinissen (perc)]

Cage, J.:Seven *(rec Theater Romein, Leeuwarden, the Netherlands, Jan 14–17, 1996)* Hat Art ("Hat NOW." series) 2-▲ 6192 [DDD]

Ives Ensemble members [Rik Andriessen (fl), Hans Petra (cl), Marja Ulydert (cl), Erik van Deuren (b cl), Arnold Marinissen (perc)]

Cage, J.:Five⁵ *(rec Theater Romein, Leeuwarden, the Netherlands, Jan 14–17, 1996)* Hat Art ("Hat NOW." series) 2-▲ 6192 [DDD]

Richard Jackman Guitar Duo

Granados, E.:Danzas españolas (10) [trans. for guitar]—2 Dances Supraphon ▲ SUP 111845 [DDD]

Jacques Orch

Kathleen Ferrier Edition Vol. 3, w. K. Ferrier (cta), Malcolm Sargent (cnd), London SO, Boyd Neel String Orch *(rec 1946 & 1949)* London ▲ 433470-2 LM [ADD]

Max Jaffa Trio

Music for a Grand Hotel, w. Max Jaffa (vn), Jean Grayston (cta), Grand Hotel Orch Valentine ▲ VALD 8057 [DDD]

Music for a Palm Court, w. Jean Grayston (cta) Valentine ▲ VALD 8061 [DDD]

Janáček CO

Carulli, F.:Con Gtr, w. Yamashita (gtr) RCA Red Seal ▲ 5914-2-RC [DDD]

Giuliani, M.:Con 1 Gtr, w. N. Yamashita (gtr) RCA Red Seal ▲ 5914-2-RC [DDD]

Vivaldi, A.:Con Lt, w. K. Yamashita (gtr) RCA Red Seal ▲ 5914-2-RC [DDD]

Z. Dejmek (cnd)

Albinoni, T.:Cons à 5 Obs, Op. 9, w. I. Zenaty (vn)—No. 10 in F *(rec Aug 19–21, 1992)* Supraphon ▲ SUP 111568 [DDD]

Pergolesi, G.B.:Con Vn, w. I. Zenaty (vn) *(rec Aug. 19–21, 1992)* Supraphon ▲ SUP 111568 [DDD]

Torelli, G.:Con grossi, w. I. Zenaty (vn)—No. 7 in d for Violin & Orch. *(rec Aug. 19–21, 1992)* Supraphon ▲ SUP 111568 [DDD]

Vivaldi, A.:Cons Vn, Op. 4, "La stravaganza", w. I. Zenaty (vn)—Nos. 2 & 3 *(rec Aug. 19–21, 1992)* Supraphon ▲ SUP 111568 [DDD]

G. Delogu (cnd)

Vivaldi, A.:Cons Diverse Instrs, w. Václav Hudeček (cl), Jiří Stivín (va), Ludomír Brabec (pno), Prague CO—in C for 2 Rcrs, 2 Bns, 2 Vns, 2 Gtrs, Vc, Strings & Cont, RV.558; in d for Vn, Gtr, Strs & Cont, RV.540; in F for Vn, Gtr, Strs & Cont, RV.542; in a for Rcr, Strs & Cont, RV.108; in C for 2 Vns, 2 Gtrs, 2 Fls, 2 Rcrs, 2 Strs & 2 Conts, RV.565 Supraphon ▲ SUP 3023

Janáček PO

D. Burkh (cnd)

Beethoven, L. van:Con 1 Pno, w. E. Graf (pno) Centaur ▲ CRC 2175 [DDD]

Beethoven, L. van:Con 2 Pno, w. E. Graf (pno) Centaur ▲ CRC 2175 [DDD]

Dvořák, A.:Slavonic Rhaps, Op. 45 Centaur ▲ CRC 2121 [DDD]

Dvořák, A.:Suite, Op. 98b, "American" Centaur ▲ CRC 2121 [DDD]

Reger, M.:Ein romantische Suite Centaur ▲ CRC 2183

Reger, M.:Vars & Fugue on a Theme of Beethoven *(rec Sept. 1–5, 1992)* Centaur ▲ CRC 2160 [DDD]

Reger, M.:Vars & Fugue on a Theme of of J. A. Hiller *(rec Sept. 1–5, 1992)* Centaur ▲ CRC 2160 [DDD]

Reger, M.:Vars & Fugue on a Theme by Mozart Centaur ▲ CRC 2183

Schumann, C.:Con Pno, w. Elizabeth Rich (pno) *(rec Ostrava, Czech Republic, 1995)* Centaur ▲ 2283 [DDD]

Szymanowski, K.:Con 1 Vn, w. R. Zimansky (vn) Centaur ▲ CRC 2153

Szymanowski, K.:Sym 4, w. M. Wilson (pno) Centaur ▲ CRC 2153

Weber, C.M. von:Con 1 Pno, w. Elizabeth Rich (pno) *(rec Ostrava, Czech Republic, 1995)* Centaur ▲ 2283 [DDD]

Weber, C.M. von:Con 2 Pno, w. Elizabeth Rich (pno) *(rec Ostrava, Czech Republic, 1995)* Centaur ▲ 2283 [DDD]

J.E. Suben (cnd)

Bassett, L.:From a Source Evolving Opus One ▲ CD 156

Blank, A.:Concertino Opus One ▲ CD 156

Couper, M.:In Memoriam Opus One ▲ CD 156

Schubel, M.:Scherzo Opus One ▲ CD 151

Schubel, M.:Superscherzo Opus One ▲ CD 151

Janáček String Quartet

Mendelssohn, F.:Octet Strs, w. Smetana String Quartet Supraphon Collection ▲ 11 0648-2 [ADD]

Janáček String Quartet [Jirí Trávnícek (vn), Adolf Sykora (vn), Jirí Kratochivíl (va), Karel Krafka (vc)]

Dvořák, A.:Qt 12 Strs, "America" Canyon Classics ▲ 3680

Dvořák, A.:Qt 12 Strs, "America" Multisonic ▲ MUL 310346

Janácek, L.:Qt 1 Strs Canyon Classics ▲ 3680

Janácek, L.:Qt 2 Strs Multisonic ▲ MUL 310351

Novák, V.:Qt Strs, Op. 35 Multisonic ▲ MUL 310351

Smetana, B.:Qt 1 Strs Canyon Classics ▲ 3680

Smetana, B.:Qt 1 Strs Multisonic ▲ MUL 310346

Clément Janequin Ensemble

Fricasée parisienne:Renaissance French Chansons Harmonia Mundi ▲ HMA 190.1174 ■

Janequin, C.:Chansons—La chasse, et al. [F] Harmonia Mundi France ▲ HMC 901271 [DDD]

Janequin, C.:Chansons—Le Chant des Oyseauix [F] Harmonia Mundi France ▲ HMC 901099

Josquin Desprez:Chansons & Motets, Les Éléments Ensemble—20 songs for 1–6 voices & instruments, 5 works for viols, 2 selections for solo lute [F] Harmonia Mundi France ▲ HMC 901279

Lassus, O. de:Chansons & Moresche—Lucesit jam; En un chasteau; Vignon, vignette, Mais qui pourroit; Quand mon mari; Fuyons tous d'amour le jeu; Hai, Lucia; Canta Giorgia; etc. Harmonia Mundi France ▲ HMC 901391

L'Estocart, P. de:Octonaires de la vanité du monde Musique d'Abord ▲ HMA 1901110

Schütz, H.:Magnificat anima mea, w. Toulouse Saqueboutiers [L] Harmonia Mundi France ▲ HMC 901255

Schütz, H.:Music of, w. Toulouse Saqueboutiers—Die mit Trănen săen (motet), SWV.42; Anima mea & Adjuro vos (from Symphonia sacrae, Op. 6), SWV.263 & 264; Quemadmodum desiderat & Meine Seele erhebet den Herren (from Kleine geistliche Konzerte, Op. 0 & Op. 10), SWV.336 & 344; Erbarm dich mein, o Herre Gott, SWV.447; Ach Herr, du Schöpfer aller Ding (madrigal), SWV.450 [G,L] Harmonia Mundi France ▲ HMC 901255

Schütz, H.:The 7 Words of Jesus Christ on the Cross, w. Toulouse Saqueboutiers [G] Harmonia Mundi France ▲ HMC 901255

Vecchi, O.:L'Amfiparnaso Harmonia Mundi France ▲ HMC 901461

Vecchi, O.:Il convito musicale (sels) Harmonia Mundi France ▲ HMC 901461

M. Pérès (cnd)

Josquin Desprez:Missa & Plainchant, "Pange lingua", w. Organum Ensemble [L] Harmonia Mundi France ▲ HMC 901239

D. Visse (cnd)

Boni, G.:Sonnets (35) of Piere de Ronsard (book 1)—Rossignol mon mignon; Las! sans espoir; Quand je dors; Ha, bel accueil; Comment au départir Harmonia Mundi France ▲ HMC 901491

de Castro, J.:Chansons, odes, et sonetz de Pierre Ronsard—Je suis tellement langoureux; Quand tu tournes tes yeux; De peu de bien Harmonia Mundi France ▲ HMC 901491

de Monte, P.:Sonets de Piere de Ronsard mis en musique—Quand de ta lèvre; Si trop souvent; Le premier jour du mois de mai Harmonia Mundi France ▲ HMC 901491

Une Fête Chez Rabelais:Chanson & Instrumental Pieces Harmonia Mundi France ▲ HMC 901453

Janequin, C.:Missa super "La Bataille" Harmonia Mundi France ▲ HMC 901536

Janequin, C.:Missa super "L'Aveuglé dieu" Harmonia Mundi France ▲ HMC 901536

La Rue, P. de:Missa, "L'Homme armé" Harmonia Mundi ("Suite" series) ▲ HMT 7901286

La Rue, P. de:Missa pro defunctis Harmonia Mundi ("Suite" series) ▲ HMT 7901286

Le Jeune, C.:Chansons & VI Fantasias, w. Les Éléments Ensemble—Que je porte d'envie; Je ne m'lève icy me plain; Susanne un jour; Le chant de l'Alouette; Quell'eau quel air; Seconde Fantaisie; Je voulu baiser ma rebelle; Je suis déshéritée; Troisième Fantaisie; Allons, allons gay; Debat la nostre trill' en may; Mais qui es-tu Musique D'Abord ▲ HMA 1901182

Regnart, F.:Music of—Ni nuit ne jour; Dedans ce bois; Contre mon gré; Mon triste coeur; Heureux ennui; Las, toi qui es de moi; Bois Janin à moi Harmonia Mundi France ▲ HMC 901491

Ripa, A. da:Fant II Harmonia Mundi France ▲ HMC 901491

Jane's Minstrels

R. Montgomery (cnd)

Jane Manning Sings Weir, Nash, Connolly, Bauld, Elias, Payne & Gilbert, w. Jane Manning (sop) NMC ▲ NMC 25 [DDD]

Lutyens, E.:Music of, w. J. Manning (tuba)—Chamber Concerto No. 1; The Valley of Hatsu-se; 6 Tempi for 10 Instruments; Lament of Isis on the Death of Osiris; Triolet 1; Requiescat; Triolet 2 NM Classics ▲ NMCD 011 [DDD]

Janka & Jürg Piano Duo

Bartók, B.:Son for 2 Pnos, w. Gerhard Huber (perc), Siegfried Schmid (perc) Accord ▲ ACD 220372

Jánosi Ensemble
Bartók, B.:Music of—plays various Hungarian, Romanian & Ruthenian dance tunes, folk tunes & bagpipe songs used by Bartók in his two Violin Rhaps., Sonatina for Piano, Romanian Folk Dances, the 3 Hungarian Folksongs from the Cslk District, & as the tunes for two of the 15 Hungarian Peasant Songs Hungaroton ▲ HCD 18191 [ADD]
Liszt, F.:Music of—Hungarian folk tunes used by Liszt as the themes for his Hungarian Rhapsodies Nos. 3,6,8,13 & 15 Hungaroton ▲ HCD 18191 [ADD]
Rhapsody:Liszt & Bartók Sources Hungaroton ▲ HCD 18191 [ADD]

Japan Bach Collegium
M. Suzuki (cnd)
Bach, J.S.:Cant 4, w. Yumiko Kurisu (sop), Akira Tachikawa (ct), Koki Katano (ten), Peter Kooy (bass) *(rec Kobe Shoin Women's University, Japan, June – July 1995)* BIS ▲ CD 751 [DDD]
Bach, J.S.:Cants 12, w. Yumiko Kurisu (sop), Yoshikazu Mera (ct), Makoto Sakurada (ten), Peter Kooy (bass) *(rec Kobe Shoin Women's Univ, Japan, Apr 11–14, 1996)* BIS ▲ CD 791 [DDD]
Bach, J.S.:Cant 54, w. Yumiko Kurisu (sop), Yoshikazu Mera (ct), Makoto Sakurada (ten), Peter Kooy (bass) *(rec Kobe Shoin Women's Univ, Japan, Apr 11–14, 1996)* BIS ▲ CD 791 [DDD]
Bach, J.S.:Cant 71 *(rec Kobe Shoin Women's Univ, Japan, Nov 8–10, 1995)* BIS ▲ CD 781 [DDD]
Bach, J.S.:Cant 106, "Actus tragicus" *(rec Kobe Shoin Women's Univ, Japan, Nov 8–10, 1995)* BIS ▲ CD 781 [DDD]
Bach, J.S.:Cant 131 *(rec Kobe Shoin Women's Univ, Japan, Nov 8–10, 1995)* BIS ▲ CD 781 [DDD]
Bach, J.S.:Cant 150, w. Yumiko Kurisu (sop), Akira Tachikawa (ct), Koki Katano (ten), Peter Kooy (bass) *(rec Kobe Shoin Women's University, Japan, June – July 1995)* BIS ▲ CD 751 [DDD]
Bach, J.S.:Cant 162, w. Yumiko Kurisu (sop), Yoshikazu Mera (ct), Makoto Sakurada (ten), Peter Kooy (bass) *(rec Kobe Shoin Women's Univ, Japan, Apr 11–14, 1996)* BIS ▲ CD 791 [DDD]
Bach, J.S.:Cant 182, w. Yumiko Kurisu (sop), Yoshikazu Mera (ct), Makoto Sakurada (ten), Peter Kooy (bass) *(rec Kobe Shoin Women's Univ, Japan, Apr 11–14, 1996)* BIS ▲ CD 791 [DDD]
Bach, J.S.:Cant 196, w. Yumiko Kurisu (sop), Akira Tachikawa (ct), Koki Katano (ten), Peter Kooy (bass) *(rec Kobe Shoin Women's University, Japan, June – July 1995)* BIS ▲ CD 751 [DDD]

Japan PO
D. Josefowitz (cnd)
Mendelssohn, F.:Con in e Vn & Orch, Op. 64, w. I. Gitlis (vn) *(rec 1968)* FNAC Music ("Via Classique" series) ▲ 642305
Mendelssohn, F.:Ruy Blas (ov) *(rec 1968)* FNAC Music ("Via Classique" series) ▲ 642305
I. Markevitch (cnd)
Mendelssohn, F.:Sym 4 *(rec 1968)* FNAC Music ("Via Classique" series) ▲ 642305
L. Stokowski (cnd)
Tchaikovsky, P.:Sym 4 Music & Arts 2–▲ MUA CD 944
A. Watanabe (cnd)
Bartók, B.:Con Va, w. R. Hillyer (va) Albany ▲ TROY 076 [AAD]
Fine, V.:Concertante Pno, w. Reiko Honsho (pno) CRI ▲ CD 692 [ADD]
Hindemith, P.:Der Schwanendreher, w. R. Hillyer (va) Albany ▲ TROY 076 [AAD]
Kupferman, M.:Ostinato Burlesco Soundspells ▲ SP 111 [ADD]
Kupferman, M.:Vars Orch Soundspells ▲ SP 111 [ADD]
Ruggles, C.:Organum CRI ("American Masters" series) ▲ CD 715 [ADD]
Sessions, R.:Sym 1 CRI ▲ CD 573 [ADD]
Sibelius, J.:The Swan of Tuonela Denon/PCM Digital ▲ DEN 8083 [DDD]

Japan PSO
W. Strickland (cnd)
Moore, D.:Sym CRI ("American Masters" series) ▲ CD 714 [ADD]

Japanese RSO
A. Erede (cnd)
Verdi, G.:Otello (sels), w. Mario del Monaco (ten), Tito Gobbi (bar—Iago)—Esultate! L'orgoglio musulmano; Tu?! Indietro!...Ora e per sempre addio; Ah! Mille vite...Si, pel ciel; Dio! mi potevi scagliar; Niun mi tema *(rec Tokyo, Feb. 4, 1952)* Melodram ▲ CDI 104006 [ADD]

Jazz Trio
M. Tilson Thomas (cnd)
Gershwin, G.:Porgy & Bess (sels), w. S. Vaughan, Los Angeles PO [overture & song medley arr. Marty Paitch] CBS ▲ MK 42516 [ADD/DDD] ■ FMT 42516

Jazzantiqua [Keith Underwood (fl/rec), Jane Ira Bloom (sop sax), Frederic Hand (gtr/lt/vih), Michael Willens (db), Teddy Saunders (pno/synth), Joseph Passaro (perc)]
Hand, F.:Music of, w. Nancy Donaruma (vc), Donald York (synth)—Cantigas de Santa Maria; Rose Liz; Bachiaras; Tourdion; Lady Carey's Fant; Chaconne; Toby & Lynn MusicMasters ▲ 01612–65150–2

Jazzogène Big Band
J.–L. Fillon (cnd)
Gershwin, G.:Cuban Ov *(rec June 1992)* Opus 111 ▲ OPS 30–64 [DDD]
Gershwin, G.:Rhap in Blue, w. G. Rabol (pno) *(rec June 1992)* Opus 111 ▲ OPS 30–64 [DDD]

Jazzogène Orch
Clásicos de las Américas, w. Margot Pares–Reyna (sop), Marcel Quillevéré (ten), Jesús Castro Balbi (gtr), Noël Lee (pno), Georges Rabol (pno), Erwartung Ensemble [cnd:Bernard Desgraupes], Jazzogène Orch [cnd:Jean–Luc Fillon] Opus 111 6–▲ 2000

Piet Jeegers Clarinet Choir
P. Jeegers (cnd)
Bach, J.S.:Fant & Fugue Org, BWV 542 [arr. Paul Hogenboom] *(rec 1996)* World Wind ▲ PJ 960108 [DDD]
Grieg, E.:Peer Gynt Suite 1 [arr. L. Jan Coeck] *(rec 1996)* World Wind ▲ PJ 960108 [DDD]
Jonghe, M. de:Mini Caprices *(rec 1996)* World Wind ▲ PJ 960108 [DDD]
Lang, R.:Grenadilla Rhap *(rec 1996)* World Wind ▲ PJ 960108 [DDD]
Stalpers, H.:Sinf Concertante *(rec 1996)* World Wind ▲ PJ 960108 [DDD]
Van Der Roost, J.:Rikudim *(rec 1996)* World Wind ▲ PJ 960108 [DDD]

Jefferson String Quartet
CDCM Computer Music Series Vol. 8:Center for Computer Research in Music & Acoustics (CCRMA) at Stanford University Centaur ▲ CRC 2091 [DDD]

Jennings String Quartet [Masako Yanagito (vn), J. Schor (vin), J. Glick (va), M. Finckel (vc)]
Schwartz, E.:Bellagio Vars *(rec Feb. 1989)* GM ▲ GM 2041 CD

Jerusalem Music Center CO
J.–P. Rampal (cnd)
Vivaldi, A.:Cons for 2 Vns, w. J.–P. Rampal (fl), I. Stern (vn)—RV.514 CBS ▲ MK 38982
I. Stern (cnd)
Vivaldi, A.:Cons Vn, Op. 8/1–4, "The Four Seasons", w. I. Stern (vn) Odyssey ▲ MBK 42526

Jerusalem String Trio
Beethoven, L. van:Qt Pno, Op. 16, w. N. Ben–Or (pno) Meridian ▲ CDE 84154
Beethoven, L. van:Serenade Strs, Op. 8 Meridian ▲ CDE 84154
Dvořák, A.:Qts Pno Strs, Opp. 23 & 87, w. N. Ben–Or (pno)—Op. 87 Meridian ▲ CDE 84179
Fibich, Z.:Qt Pno, w. N. Ben–Or (pno) Meridian ▲ CDE 84179
Roussel, A.:Trio Strs PWK Classics ▲ PWK 1141 [DDD]
Taneyev, S.:Trios for Strings—Trio in E♭, Op, 31 & Trio in D Meridian ▲ CDE 84149

Jerusalem SO
D. Amos (cnd)
Rosner, A.:Con grosso 1 Laurel ▲ LR 849CD [ADD/DDD]
Rosner, A.:A Gentle Musicke Laurel ▲ LR 849CD [ADD/DDD]
Rosner, A.:Meditations Laurel ▲ LR 849CD [ADD/DDD]
Rosner, A.:Prelude to Act 2 of "The Chronicle of Nine" Laurel ▲ LR 849CD [ADD/DDD]
S. Comissiona (cnd)
Malipiero, G.F.:Dialogo 5, w. E. Wallfisch (va) Bayer ▲ BR 200028 [ADD]
L. Foss (cnd)
Weill, K.:Mahagonny *(rec 1975)* Vox Box 2–▲ CDX 5043 [ADD]
S. Ronly–Riklis (cnd)
Fleischer, T.:A Girl Named Limonad Vienna Modern Masters ▲ VMM 3004 [DDD]

Jeune PO
J.–J. Werner (cnd)
Chailly, J.:Solmisation Suite Quantum ▲ QM 6917 [DDD]
Dai, V.:Illustrations, w. E. Chen (sop) Quantum ▲ QM 6917 [DDD]
Ma, S.–L.:Lantern Quantum ▲ QM 6917 [DDD]
Weber, A.:Cantus Quantum ▲ QM 6917 [DDD]
Werner, J.–J.:Aulophonie Quantum ▲ QM 6917 [DDD]

Les Jeunes Solistes
R. Safir (cnd)
Rebotier, J.:Keno Ko–An Adès ▲ ADE 204472 [DDD/AAD]

Joachim Quartet Hannover
Schumann, R.:Qts Strs, Op. 41—Nos. 1 & 3 *(rec Oct. 3, 1985)* Calig ▲ CAL 50849 [DDD]

Joachim String Quartet
Reger, M.:Qt Strs, Op. 109 Koch Schwann ▲ CD 310 068 [DDD]
Reger, M.:Qt Strs, Op. 121 Koch Schwann ▲ CD 310 068 [DDD]

Joachim Trio [John Lenehan (pno), Rebecca Hirsch (vn), Caroline Dearnley (vc)]
Ravel, M.:Trio Pno *(rec Conway Hall, London, Oct. 5–7, 1993)* Naxos ▲ 8.550934 [DDD]
Schmitt, F.:Très lent *(rec Conway Hall, London, Oct. 5–7, 1993)* Naxos ▲ 8.550934 [DDD]

La Jolla SO
T. Nee (cnd)
Xenakis, I.:Aïs, w. P. Larson (bar), S. Schick (perc) Neuma ▲ 450–86 [DDD]

Philip Jones Brass Ensemble
Berkeley, M.:Music from Chaucer Chandos ▲ CHAN 8490 [DDD]
Civil, A.:Tarantango Claves ▲ CD 600 [ADD]
Copland, A.:Music of—Ceremonial Fanfare *(rec Kingsway Hall, London, 1976)* London 2–▲ 448261–2 [ADD]
Durkó, Z.:Sinfonietta Chandos ▲ CHAN 8490 [DDD]
Horovitz, J.:Music Hall Suite Claves ▲ CD 600 [ADD]
Howarth, E.:Music for Brass—Variations on The Carnival of Venice; arrangements of six popular Swiss melodies (Basle March, Berne Patrol, The Cuckoo, Lucerne Song, The Old Chalet, Zurich March) Claves ▲ CD 600 [ADD]
In Switzerland Claves ▲ CD 600 [ADD]
Jubilate:Music for the Kings & Queens of England, w. St. Peter ad Vincula Choir within the Tower of London Chapel Royal Chandos ("Collect" series) ▲ CHAN 6560 [ADD]
Koetsier, J.:Petite Suite Brass Claves ▲ CD 600 [ADD]
Lollipops Claves ▲ CD 8503 [DDD]
Lutoslawski, W.:Mini Ov Chandos ▲ CHAN 8490 [DDD]
PJBE Finale:Music Written for Philip Jones Chandos ▲ CHAN 8490 [DDD]
Previn, A.:Triolet Chandos ▲ CHAN 8490 [DDD]
Rautavaara, E.:Playgrounds for Angels Chandos ▲ CHAN 8490 [DDD]
Weekend Brass London ("Weekend Classics" series) ▲ 421633–2 LC
E. Howarth (cnd)
Sousa, J.P.:Marches & Dances London ▲ 410290–2 [DDD] ■ 410290–4
J. Rutter (cnd)
Rutter, J.:Gloria, w. Cambridge Singers [L] Collegium ▲ COLCD 100 [DDD] ■ COLC 100 (D)

Eric Jones Orch
E. Jones (cnd)
America Sings, w. Eric Jones Chorale London ("Weekend Classics" series) ▲ 433686–2 LC ■ 433686–4 LC

Geraint Jones Orch
G. Jones (cnd)
Bach, C.P.E.:Magnificat, w. Jennifer Vyvyan (sop), Helen Watts (cta), Wilfred Brown (ten), Thomas Hemsley (bass), Geraint Jones Singers EMI Classics ("Baroque" series) ▲ CDK 65737

Les Joueurs de Flute
P. Bauer (cnd)
Gasser, U.:Von der unerbittlichen Zufälligkeit des Todes, w. Arthur Schneiter (sounding stones) *(rec live, Heilig Kreuz Münster, Aug 26, 1995)* Jecklin ▲ JS 312–2 [DDD]

Les Joueurs de Flute [M. Ebner, A. Graf, D. Hunziker, B. Kunz, C. Kuster, M. Moldenhauer, A. Utagawa, J. Zurmhle]
Ensemble Les Joueuers de Flûte Jecklin ▲ JEC 688 [DDD]

Leonard Joy Orch
Bernstein, L.:On the Town, w. M. Martin (sgr), N. Walker (sgr), B. Comden (sgr), A. Green (sgr), Tutti Camarata Orch, Lynn Murray Orch, Lynn Murray Chorus MCA Classics ▲ MCAD 10280 (m) [AAD]

Jubal Trio
Thorne, F.:Nature Studies [E] CRI ▲ CD 586 [ADD]

Jubilee Orch
D.R. Davies (cnd)
Gounod, C.:Messe solennelle 3 de Pâques, w. Conservatorium Choir, St. Mary's Cathedral Choir Walsingham Classics ▲ WAL 8011 [DDD]

Juilliard Ensemble
L. Berio (cnd)
Berio, L.:Folk Songs Mez, w. Cathy Berberian (mez), London Sinfonietta RCA Gold Seal ▲ 09026–62540–2
Weill, K.:Songs, w. Cathy Berberian (mez), London Sinfonietta—3 songs [arr. Berio] RCA Gold Seal ▲ 09026–62540–2

Juilliard Orch
J. DePreist (cnd)
Persichetti, V.:Night Dances New World ▲ 80396–2 [DDD]
S. Ehrling (cnd)
Copland, A.:Connotations New World ▲ NW 368–2 [DDD]
L. Foss (cnd)
Druckman, J.:Chiaroscuro New World ▲ NW 381–2 [DDD]
C. Keene (cnd)
Diamond, D.:Sym 5 New World ▲ 80396–2 [DDD]
O.–W. Mueller (cnd)
Schuman, W.:In Praise of Shahn New World ▲ NW 368–2 [DDD]
T. Schippers (cnd)
Mercadante, S.:Il giuramento, w. P. Wells (sop), B. Wolff (mez), G. Colmagro (bar), M. Molese (sgr), Juilliard Chorus [l] *(rec live, Spoleto, 6/29/70)* Memories 2–▲ HR 4174/75 (m)
Mercadante, S.:Il giuramento, w. P. Wells (sop), B. Wolff (mez), G. Colmagro (bar), M. Molese (sgr), Juilliard Chorus [l] *(rec live, Spoleto, 6/29/70)* Myto 2–▲ 2 MCD 90632 [ADD]
G. Schwarz (cnd)
Albert, S.:Into Eclipse, w. G. Lakes (ten) [E] New World ▲ 80381–2 [DDD]
L. Slatkin (cnd)
Schwantner, J.:Aftertones of Infinity New World ▲ NW 381–2 [DDD]
P. Zukovsky (cnd)
Babbitt, M.:Relata I New World ▲ 80396–2 [DDD]
Sessions, R.:The Black Maskers (suite) New World ▲ NW 368–2 [DDD]

Juilliard Orch members
F.C. Rich (cnd)
Rich, F.C.:The Hudson Oratorio, w. Kathryn Radcliffe (sop), Rick Hamelin (ten), Harold von Geldern (bar) *(rec Church of the Epiphany, New York City, July 1996)* Albany ▲ TROY 217 [DDD]

Juilliard String Quartet [Robert Mann (vn), Joel Smirnoff (vn), Samuel Rhodes (va), Joel Krosnick (vc)]
Babbitt, M.:Qt 4 Strs CRI ▲ CD 587 [DDD]
Bach, J.S.:The Art of the Fugue Sony Classical 2–▲ S2K 45937
Barber, S.:Dover Beach, w. D. Fischer–Dieskau (bar) [E] *(rec 1967)* Sony Masterworks ("Portrait" series) ▲ MPK 46727 [ADD]

202

▲ = CD ♦ = Enhanced CD Δ = MD ■ = Cassette Tape □ = DCC

Juilliard String Quartet (cont.)
Beethoven, L. van:Grosse Fuge Str Qt CBS 3-▲ M3K 37873 [DDD]
Beethoven, L. van:Qts Strs (comp)—Opp. 59, 74 & 75 CBS 3-▲ M3K 37869 [DDD]
Beethoven, L. van:Qts Strs (comp)—Op. 18 CBS 3-▲ M3K 37868 [DDD]
Beethoven, L. van:Qts Strs (comp)—Opp. 127, 130, 131, 132 & 135 CBS 3-▲ M3K 37873 [DDD]
Brahms, J.:Qts Strs (comp) Sony Classical 2-▲ S2K 66285
Brahms, J.:Qt 1 Strs Sony Classical 2-▲ S2K 66285
Brahms, J.:Qt 2 Strs Sony Classical 2-▲ S2K 66285
Brahms, J.:Qt 3 Strs Sony Classical 2-▲ S2K 66285
Brahms, J.:Qnt Cl, w. Charles Neidich (cl) Sony Classical 2-▲ S2K 66285
Brahms, J.:Qnt 1 Strs, w. Walter Trampler (va) Sony Classical ▲ SK 68476
Brahms, J.:Qnt 2 Strs, w. Walter Trampler (va) Sony Classical ▲ SK 68476
Carter, E.:Qt 1 Strs Sony Classical 2-▲ S2K 47229
Carter, E.:Qt 2 Strs Sony Classical 2-▲ S2K 47229
Carter, E.:Qt 3 Strs Sony Classical 2-▲ S2K 47229
Carter, E.:Qt 4 Strs Sony Classical 2-▲ S2K 47229
Chausson, E.:Con Vn, Pno & Str Qt, w. I. Perlman (vn), J. Bolet (pno) CBS ▲ MK 37814 [DDD]
Debussy, C.:Qt Strs *(rec Oct. 11–12, 1989)* Sony Classical ▲ SK 52554 [DDD]
Dutilleux, H.:Ainsi la nuit *(rec May 13–15, 1992)* Sony Classical ▲ SK 52554 [DDD]
Dvořák, A.:Qt 12 Strs, "America" Sony Classical (Essential Classics) ▲ SBK 48170 ■ SBT 48170
Dvořák, A.:Qnt Pno, Op. 81, w. R. Firkusny (pno) Odyssey 2-▲ MB2K 45672
Dvořák, A.:Qnt Pno, Op. 81, w. R. Firkusny (pno) Sony Classical (Essential Classics) ▲ SBK 48170 ■ SBT 48170
Fine, I.:Qt Strs CRI ▲ CD 574 [ADD]
Haydn, J.:The Seven Last Words of Christ on the Cross, w. Benita Valente (sop), Jan DeGaetani (mez), Jon Humphrey (ten), Thomas Paul (bar) Sony Classical ▲ SK 44914 [DDD]
Hindemith, P.:Qt 3 Strs Wergo ▲ WER 6283-2
Hindemith, P.:Qt 5 Strs Wergo ▲ WER 6283-2
Kuhlau, F.:Qnts Fl, w. J.-P. Rampal (fl) CBS ▲ MK 44517 [DDD] ■ MT 44517 (D)
Lerdahl, F.:First Str Qt CRI ▲ CD 551 [DDD]
Martino, D.:Qt Strs CRI ▲ CD 551 [DDD]
Mozart, W.A.:Qts Strs (misc)—Nos. 14–19, "The Haydn Quartets" Odyssey 3-▲ MB3K 45826
Mozart, W.A.:Qnts Strs Odyssey 3-▲ MB3K 45827
Prokofiev, S.:Ov on Hebrew Themes, w. G. Feidman (cl), Y. Bronfman (pno) *(rec May 18, 1994)* Sony Classical ▲ SK 58966 [DDD]
Prokofiev, S.:Ov on Hebrew Themes, w. Giora Feidman (cl), Yefim Bronfman (pno) *(rec Richardson Auditorium, Alexander Hall, Princeton Univ, Princeton, NJ, May 18, 1994)* Sony Classical ("Greatest Hits" series) ▲ MLK 69249 [DDD] ■ LT 69
Ravel, M.:Qt Strs *(rec May 13–15, 1992)* Sony Classical ▲ SK 52554 [DDD]
Schoenberg, A.:Verklärte Nacht, w. W. Trampler (va), Yo Yo Ma (vc) [arr. for string sextet] Sony Classical ▲ SK 47690 [DDD]
Schubert, Franz:Qts Strs (comp)—Nos. 12–15 Odyssey 2-▲ MB2K 45617
Schubert, Franz:Qt 12 Strs Odyssey ▲ MBK 42602 [ADD] ■ YT 42602
Schubert, Franz:Qt 14 Strs Sony Classical ("Essential Classics" series) ▲ SBK 46343 [ADD] ■ SBT 46343
Schubert, Franz:Qt 14 Strs Odyssey ▲ MBK 42602 [ADD] ■ YT 42602
Schubert, Franz:Qnt Strs, D.956, w. B. Greenhouse (vc) CBS ▲ MK 42383 [DDD]
Sessions, R.:Qt 2 Strs CRI ▲ CD 587 [DDD]
Sibelius, J.:Qt Strs, Op. 56 Sony Classical ▲ SK 48193 [DDD]
Verdi, G.:Qt Strs Sony Classical ▲ SK 48193 [DDD]
Wolpe, S.:Qt Strs CRI ▲ CD 587 [DDD]
G. Schwarz (cnd)
Piston, W.:Con Perc, w. Seattle SO *(rec Jan. 27–28, 1992)* Delos ▲ DE 3126 [DDD]
Juilliard String Quartet members
Dvořák, A.:Bagatelles, Op. 47, w. R. Firkusny (pno) Odyssey 2-▲ MB2K 45672
Dvořák, A.:Qts Pno Strs, Opp. 23 & 87, w. R. Firkusny (pno) Odyssey 2-▲ MB2K 45672
Schoenberg, A.:Trio Strs Sony Classical ▲ SK 47690 [DDD]
Schumann, R.:Qt Pno, Op. 47, w. G. Gould (pno) Sony Classical ▲ SMK 52684
June in Buffalo CO
Felder, D.:Music of, w. Rachel Rudich (fl), American Brass Quintet, Arditti String Quartet—Journal; Canzone XXXI; November Sky; 3rd Face; 3 Lines from 20 Poems Bridge ▲ BCD 9049 [DDD]
B. Lubman (cnd)
Felder, D.:Three Lines from 20 Poems *(rec Slee Hall, SUNY, Buffalo)* Bridge ▲ BCD 9049 [DDD]
H. Sollberger (cnd)
Felder, D.:Journal *(rec Slee Hall, SUNY, Buffalo)* Bridge ▲ BCD 9049 [DDD]
Jura CO
B. Dupaquier (cnd)
Haydn, J.:Con Fl & Orch, w. Brigette Buxtorf (fl) Gallo ▲ CD 623 [DDD]
Haydn, J.:Con 1 Vn, w. Raphaëlle des Graviers (vn) Gallo ▲ CD 623 [DDD]
Haydn, J.:Divert Strs Gallo ▲ CD 623 [DDD]
Just Strings Ensemble [John Schneider (gtr), Susan Allen (hps), Gene Sterling (perc)]
Matson, S.:The Fifth Lake *(rec Ocean Way Recording, Hollywood, CA, July 14, 1996)* New Albion ▲ NA 091
Kaiserslautern Radio Orch
K. Arp (cnd)
Adam, A.:Le Postillon de Lonjumeau, w. P. Coburn (sop), R. Swensen (ten), J. Linn (bar), P. Lika (bass), Stuttgart Chamber Choir [G] Capriccio 2-▲ 60040-2 [DDD]
Kalamos Clarinet Quartet [Steven Hearn (cl), James Heffernan (cl), Pamela Helton (cl), Jean Gould (b cl)]
Beethoven, L. van:Qt 1 Strs [trans. Douglas Monroe] *(rec Odgen Hall, Hampton Univ, Hampton, VA)* Klavier ▲ KCD 11057 [DDD]
Brahms, J.:Hungarian Dances Orch—Nos. 1 & 6 [trans Chuck Willett] *(rec Odgen Hall, Hampton Univ, Hampton, VA)* Klavier ▲ KCD 11057 [DDD]
Debussy, C.:Qt Strs [trans David Jones] *(rec Odgen Hall, Hampton Univ, Hampton, VA)* Klavier ▲ KCD 11057 [DDD]
Farkas, F.:Antique Hungarian Dances *(rec Odgen Hall, Hampton Univ, Hampton, VA)* Klavier ▲ KCD 11057 [DDD]
Uhl, A.:Divert *(rec Odgen Hall, Hampton Univ, Hampton, VA)* Klavier ▲ KCD 11057 [DDD]
Kalenda Maya
Medieval & Renaissance Songs & Dances from Spain, Italy, France & Germany Simax ▲ PSC 1017 [DDD]
Norse Ballads Norway Music ▲ FXCD 82
Kalengo Percussion Ensemble
A Secret Place, w. Rebello, Simone (perc), Andrew Scott (a sax), Liz Gilliver (mar), Eryl Roberts (perc), John Melbourne (perc), Chris Bastock (perc), Richard Dyson (perc) *(rec Zion Institute, Manchester, 1995)* Doyen ▲ CD 040 [DDD]
Kalichstein-Laredo-Robinson Trio [J. Laredo (vn), S. Robinson (vc), J. Kalichstein (vc)]
Haydn, J.:Trios Pno, Vn & Vc—H.XV/12, 25, 27 & 28 *(rec Sept. 1991)* Dorian ▲ DOR 90164 [DDD]
A. Gibson (cnd)
Beethoven, L. van:Con Vn, Vc & Pno, "Triple Con", w. English CO Chandos ("Collect" series) ▲ CHAN 6501 [DDD]
Kalmar CO
M. Tippett (cnd)
Purcell, H.:Hail, Bright Cecilia, w. April Cantelo (sop), Alfred Deller (alt), Wilfred Brown (ten), Maurice Bevan (bar), Ambrosian Singers Vanguard Classics ▲ OVC 8020 [ADD]
Kalmar Läns CO
J.-O. Wedin (cnd)
Mozart, W.A.:Arias, w. Gunnel Bohman (sop)—K.272, K.369, K.374 & K.528 [I] BIS ▲ CD 299 [DDD]

Kalmar Läns CO (cont.)
J.-O. Wedin (cnd) (cont.)
Mozart, W.A.:Exsultate, w. Gunnel Bohman (sop) [L] BIS ▲ CD 299 [DDD]
Kandinsky Quartet [C. Désert (pno), P. Aïche (vn), N. Bône (va), N. Pierre (vc)]
Castillon, A.:Qt Pno *(rec 1993)* FNAC Music ▲ 592315 [DDD]
Saint-Saëns, C.:Qt Pno *(rec 1993)* FNAC Music ▲ 592315 [DDD]
Kansas City Brass
A Kansas City Christmas *(rec Country Club Christian Church, Kansas City, MO)* AMG Classic ▲ 1001 [DDD]
Kansas City Lyric Theater Orch
R. Patterson (cnd)
Beeson, J.:The Sweet Bye & Bye Citadel 2-▲ CT DOS 2000 [ADD]
Kansas City SO
W. McGlaughlin (cnd)
Davis, A.:Ghost Factory—MAPS, w. Shem Guibbory (vn) Gramavision ▲ R2-79429 [DDD]
Davis, A.:Wayang 5, w. Anhony Davis (pno) Gramavision ▲ R2-79429 [DDD]
Oldham, K.:Con Pno, w. I. Hobson (pno) *(rec Mar. 27, 1993)* Catalyst ▲ 09026-61979-2 ■ 09026-61979-4
R. Patterson (cnd)
Moore, D.:Devil & Daniel Webster, w. Joyce Guyer (sop—Mary Stone), Benjamin Bongers (ten—Walter Butler), Michael Philip Davis (ten—Simon Girty), Matthew Foerschler (ten—Miser Stephens), Darren Keith Woods (ten—Mr. Scratch), Michael Lanman (bass—Blackbeard Teach), David Soxman (bass—Clerk), Brian Steele (bass—Daniel Webster), John Stephens (bass—Jabez Stone), Andrew Stuckey (bass—King Philip), Robert Gibby Brand (actor), Cary Miller (actor), Kansas City Lyric Opera Chorus *(rec Sept 1995)* Newport Classic ▲ NPD 85585 [DDD]
Kapp Sinfonietta
E. Vardi (cnd)
Stravinsky, I.:L'Histoire du soldat, w. M. Douglas (nar), James Mitchell (nar), Alvin Epstein (nar) [E] MCA Classics 2-▲ MCAD2-9820 [AAD]
Karadar-Bertoldi Ensemble
Schubert, Franz:Adagio & Rondo concertante Vn Stradivarius ▲ STV SIP 20 [DDD]
Schubert, Franz:Qnt Pno, D.667 Stradivarius ▲ STV SIP 20 [DDD]
Schubert, Franz:Trio Pno, D.28 Stradivarius ▲ STV SIP 20 [DDD]
Katowice Polish Radio-TV Orch
A. Wit (cnd)
Kilar, W.:Choralvorspiel *(rec Katowice, 1995)* Milan ▲ 357792
Kilar, W.:Kresany *(rec Katowice, 1995)* Milan ▲ 357792
Kilar, W.:Mt. Kosceilec 1909 *(rec Katowice, 1995)* Milan ▲ 357792
Kilar, W.:Orawa *(rec Katowice, 1995)* Milan ▲ 357792
Kaunas CO
S. Frontalini (cnd)
Sammartini, G.:Con grossi, Op. 2—Nos. 1–5 *(rec Kaunas, Lithuania, June 1993)* Bongiovanni ▲ GB 5559 [DDD]
Sammartini, G.:Giuseppe St. Martini's Cons Hpd—Nos. 2 & 4 *(rec Kaunas, Lithuania, June 1993)* Bongiovanni ▲ GB 5559 [DDD]
Tartini, G.:Cons Vn (misc), w. Beatrice Antonioni (vn)—in C, D.12; in D, D.15; in G, D.78 *(rec Kaunas, Lithuania, 1993)* Bongiovanni ▲ GB 2177 [DDD]
Kavkasia [Carl Linch (ten/chonguri), Alan Gasser (ten), Stuart Gelzer (bass)]
Songs of the Caucasus *(rec May 1995)* Well-Tempered Productions ("Well-Tempered World" series) ▲ WTP 5178 [DDD]
KBS SO
V. Jordania (cnd)
Hovhaness, A.:Music of, w. Alexa Still (fl), Marvin Rosen (pno), Manhattan CO, New Zealand CO—The Prayer of St. Gregory; Elibris; Mystic Flute; Aria, Hymn & Fugue; Mountain Idylls; Gtr Sym; Adagio; Son; Fred the Cat; Aria [from Harotiun] Koch International Classics ▲ KIC 7311 [DDD]
Hovhaness, A.:Sym 39, w. M. Long (gtr)—also includes a Korean folk song "Milyang Arirang" arr. Kim Hee Jo Koch International Classics ▲ KIC 7208 [DDD]
Hovhaness, A.:Sym 46—also includes a Korean folk song "Milyang Arirang" arr. Kim Hee Jo Koch International Classics ▲ KIC 7208 [DDD]
Shostakovich, D.:The Gadfly (suite) Koch International Classics ▲ KIC 7274 [DDD]
Shostakovich, D.:Hamlet (film music) Koch International Classics ▲ KIC 7274 [DDD]
Shostakovich, D.:King Lear (incidental) Koch International Classics ▲ KIC 7274 [DDD]
Kegelstaat Trio Amsterdam [C. Brandenburg (cl), G. Berman (va), P. Verhagen (pno)]
Bruch, M.:Pieces Cl, Op. 83/1–8 Erasmus ▲ WVH 061 [DDD]
Reinecke, C.:Trio Pno, Op. 264 Erasmus ▲ WVH 061 [DDD]
Keller String Quartet [András Keller (vn), János Pilz (vn), Zoltán Gál (va), Ottó Kertész (vc)]
Debussy, C.:Qt Strs Erato ▲ 96361-2
Kurtág, G.:Aus der Ferne III *(rec Casino Zögernitz, Vienna, Nov 1995)* ECM New Series ▲ 78118-21598-2 [DDD]
Kurtág, G.:Hommage à Mihály András *(rec Casino Zögernitz, Vienna, Nov 1995)* ECM New Series ▲ 78118-21598-2 [DDD]
Kurtág, G.:Officium breve in memoriam Andreae Szervánsky *(rec Casino Zögernitz, Vienna, Nov 1995)* ECM New Series ▲ 78118-21598-2 [DDD]
Kurtág, G.:Qt Strs *(rec Casino Zögernitz, Vienna, Nov 1995)* ECM New Series ▲ 78118-21598-2 [DDD]
Ravel, M.:Qt Strs Erato ▲ 96361-2
Tchaikovsky, P.:Qt 3 Strs Erato ▲ 94819
Tchaikovsky, P.:Souvenir de Florence, w. K. Kashkashian (va), M. Perenyi (vc) Erato ▲ 94819
Keller String Quartet members
Beethoven, L. van:Qt Pno, Op. 16, w. Z. Kocsis (pno) Musique d'Abord ▲ HMA 1903020
Keller String Quartet members [András Keller (vn), János Pilz (vn), Ottó Kertész (vc)]
Kurtág, G.:Ligatura—Message to Frances-Marie (version 1), w. Miklós Perényi (vc), György Kurtág (cel) *(rec Casino Zögernitz, Vienna, Nov 1995)* ECM New Series ▲ 78118-21598-2 [DDD]
Kurtág, G.:Ligatura—Message to Frances-Marie (version 2), w. Miklós Perényi (vc), György Kurtág (cel) *(rec Casino Zögernitz, Vienna, Nov 1995)* ECM New Series ▲ 78118-21598-2 [DDD]
Kennedy Center Theater Chamber Players
Lebaron, A.:Noh Reflections, w. H. Fujiwara (vn), M. Kawasaki (va), E. Elsing (vc) Mode ▲ 30
Kennedy Center Theater Chamber Players [Jeannette Walters (sop), Penelope Fischer (pic/fl), Edward Walters (cl/b cl), Kwang-wu Kim (pno), John Beck (perc), Albert Merz (perc)]
L. Fleisher (cnd)
Lebaron, A.:The Sea & the Honeycomb *(rec Hubbard Hall, Manhattan School of Music, 1993)* Mode ▲ Mode 42
Kent/Shulman Duo [Peter Kent (vn), Amy Shulman (hp)]
51 Strings K/S Records ▲ KS 1 [AAD]
Kérylos Ensemble
A. Bélis (cnd)
Music from Ancient Greece *(rec July 4–7, 1996)* K617 ▲ 7069 [DDD]
Keystone Wind Ensemble
J. Stamp (cnd)
Camphouse, M.:A Movement for Rosa *(rec Fisher Auditorium & Waller Hall, IUP Campus, May 1994, Jan & Feb 1995)* Citadel ▲ CTD 88111 [DDD]
Diamond, D.:Ceremonial Fanfare *(rec Jan. 14–16, 1995)* Citadel ▲ CTD 88108 [DDD]
Diamond, D.:Tantivy *(rec Jan. 14–16, 1995)* Citadel ▲ CTD 88108 [DDD]
Grainger, P.:Folk Song Settings—Themes from Greenbushes [arr Larry Daehn for wind band] *(rec Fisher Auditorium & Waller Hall, IUP Campus, May 1994, Jan & Feb 1995)* Citadel ▲ CTD 88111 [DDD]
Hanson, H.:Chorale & Alleluia *(rec Fisher Auditorium & Waller Hall, IUP Campus, May 1994, Jan & Feb 1995)* Citadel ▲ CTD 88111 [DDD]
Hanson, H.:March Carillon [trans Erik Leidzen for wind band] *(rec Fisher Auditorium & Waller Hall, IUP Campus, May 1994, Jan & Feb 1995)* Citadel ▲ CTD 88111 [DDD]

ORCH. & ENS.

Keystone Wind Ensemble (cont.)
J. Stamp (cnd) (cont.)
Melillo, S.:Escape from Plato's Cave *(rec Fisher Auditorium & Waller Hall, IUP Campus, May 1994, Jan & Feb 1995)* Citadel ▲ CTD 88111 [DDD]
Persichetti, V.:Celebrations, w. IUP Chorale *(rec Fisher Auditorium & Waller Hall, IUP Campus, May 1994, Jan & Feb 1995)* Citadel ▲ CTD 88111 [DDD]
Stamp, J.:Divert in "F" *(rec Jan. 14–16, 1995)* Citadel ▲ CTD 88108 [DDD]
Tower, J.:Stepping Stones (sels)—Celebration Fanfare *(rec Jan. 14–16, 1995)* Citadel ▲ CTD 88108 [DDD]
Tull, F.:Sketches *(rec Jan. 14–16, 1995)* Citadel ▲ CTD 88108 [DDD]
Tull, F.:Vars on an Advent Hymn *(rec Fisher Auditorium & Waller Hall, IUP Campus, May 1994, Jan & Feb 1995)* Citadel ▲ CTD 88111 [DDD]
Ward, R.:Music of—Fanfare for Durham; Prairie Ov.; Night Fant.; Antiphony for Winds; Con. for Tenor, Saxophone & Band [w. J. Houlik (tenor)]; 4 Abstractions for Band; Fiesta Processional; Fant. for Brass Choir & Timpani Citadel ▲ CTD 88103 [DDD]
Washburn, R.:Sym Band *(rec Jan. 14–16, 1995)* Citadel ▲ CTD 88108 [DDD]

Kiel PO
K. Seibel (cnd)
Delius, F.:A Village Romeo & Juliet, w. Eva–Christine Reimer (sgr), Karsten Russ (sgr), Klaus Wallprecht (sgr) CPO 2–▲ CPO 999328 [DDD]
Schillings, M. von:Mona Lisa, w. Beate Bilandzija (sgr), Albert Bonnema (sgr), Klaus Wallprecht (sgr) CPO 2–▲ CPO 999303 [DDD]

Kiev CO
A. Vinokourov (cnd)
Elgar, E.:Serenade Strs *(rec 1990)* Analekta ▲ AN2–9001 [DDD] ■ AN4–9001
Grieg, E.:Holberg Suite *(rec Jan. 20–27, 1990)* Analekta ▲ AN 29002 [DDD]
Handel, G.F.:Concerti grossi, Op. 6—No. 4 in a *(rec Jan. 20–27, 1990)* Analekta ▲ AN 29002 [DDD]
Mozart, W.A.:Divert Str Qt, K.136 *(rec Jan. 20–27, 1990)* Analekta ▲ AN 29002 [DDD]
Mozart, W.A.:Kleine Nachtmusik *(rec 1990)* Analekta ▲ AN2–9001 [DDD] ■ AN4–9001
Tchaikovsky, P.:Serenade Strs *(rec 1990* Analekta ▲ AN2–9001 [DDD]

Kiev National Phil CO
A. Scharoev (cnd)
Mustafa–Zade, W.:Con Pno, w. Adilia Alieva (pno) Gallo ▲ CD 832 [DDD]

Kiev Pro Musica
R. Kapp (cnd)
Brouwer, L.:Con 3 Gtr, "Con Elegíaco", w. Ricardo Cobo (gtr) *(rec Kiev, Ukraine, Nov. 1–3, 1994)* ESS.A.Y ▲ CD 1040 [DDD]
Brouwer, L.:Con 4 Gtr, "De Toronto", w. R. Cobo (gtr) *(rec Kiev, Ukraine, Nov. 1–3, 1994)* ESS.A.Y ▲ CD 1040 [DDD]
Fasch, J.F.:Suites Orch—No. 1 in D; No. 2 in D; in B♭ *(rec Kiev, Ukraine, Oct 26–29, 1994)* ESS.A.Y ▲ ESS 1041 [DDD]
Locatelli, P.:L'arte del violino, w. Mela Tenenbaum (vn), Philharmonia Virtuosi—Nos. 1–6 *(rec Kiev, Ukraine, Oct. 1994–95)* ESS.A.Y ▲ CD 1043/44 [DDD]

Kiev SO
I. Blazhkov (cnd)
Kabalevsky, D.:Con Vn, w. Angèle Dubeau (vn) Analekta ▲ AN 28702
Kabalevsky, D.:Con Vn, w. A. Dubeau (vn) *(rec 1989)* Analekta Fleur de Lys ▲ FL 2 3036 [DDD] ■ AN4–8702
Prokofiev, S.:Cons Vn (comp), w. A. Dubeau (vn)—No. 1 *(rec 1989)* Analekta Fleur de Lys ▲ FL 2 3036 [DDD] ■ AN4–8702
Prokofiev, S.:Con 1 Vn, w. Angèle Dubeau (vn) Analekta ▲ AN 28702
Stankovich, E.:Prométhéus *(rec 1989)* Analekta ▲ AN2–8901 [DDD] ■ AN4–8901
Tchaikovsky, P.:Sérénade mélancolique, w. A. Dubeau (vn) *(rec 1989)* Analekta Fleur de Lys ▲ FL 2 3036 [DDD] ■ AN4–8702
Tchaikovsky, P.:Souvenir d'un lieu cher, w. Angèle Dubeau (vn)—Mélodie [arr vn & orch] Analekta ▲ AN 28702
Tchaikovsky, P.:Sym 6 *(rec 1989)* Analekta ▲ AN2–8901 [DDD] ■ AN4–8901

King's Consort
The Art of James Bowman, w. James Bowman (ct), Crispian Steel–Perkins (nat tpt), Downshire Players of London, Music's Re-creation Meridian ▲ MER 84332
Eternal Source of Light, w. James Bowman (ct) Meridian ▲ 84126
Purcell, H.:Anthems, w. J. Bowman (ct), R. Covey–Crump (ten), C. Daniels (ten), M. George (b–bar), New College Choir Oxford Hyperion ▲ CDA 66656
Purcell, H.:Songs, w. B. Bonney (sop), S. Gritton (sop), J. Bowman (ct), R. Covey–Crump (ten), C. Daniels (ten), M. George (bass), D. Miller (archlt/thb/baroque gtr), M. Caudle (b vl), R. King (org/hpd)—Incassum Lesbia; Gentle Shepherds, you that know the charms; I love and I must; Through mournful shades and solitary groves; The Knotting Song Hyperion ▲ CDA 66720 [DDD]
E. Higginbottom (cnd)
Lalande, M.–R. de:Confitebor tibi, Domine, w. G. Fisher (sop), O. Johnston (trb), C. Daniels (ct), A. Smith (ten), S. Varcoe (bass), Oxford New College Choir [L] Erato (Musifrance) ▲ 2292–45014–2 [DDD]
Lalande, M.–R. de:De profundis solo Voices, Orch & Chorus, w. G. Fisher (sop), O. Johnston (trb), C. Daniels (ct), A. Smith (ten), S. Varcoe (bass), New College Choir Oxford [L] Erato (Musifrance) ▲ 2292–45014–2 [DDD]
Lalande, M.–R. de:Miserere, w. G. Fisher (sop), O. Johnston (trb), C. Daniels (ct), A. Smith (ten), S. Varcoe (bass), Oxford New College Choir [L] Erato (Musifrance) ▲ 2292–45014–2 [DDD]
R. King (cnd)
Bach, J.S.:Arias, w. James Bowman (ct)—Erbarme dich; Stirb in mir Hyperion ▲ KING 3
Bach, J.S.:Cant 54, w. J. Bowman (ct) [G] Hyperion ▲ CDA 66326 [DDD]
Bach, J.S.:Cant 54, w. J. Bowman (ct) [G] Meridian ▲ CDE 84138
Bach, J.S.:Cant 169, w. J. Bowman (ct) [G] Hyperion ▲ CDA 66326 [DDD]
Bach, J.S.:Cant 170, w. J. Bowman (ct) [G] Hyperion ▲ CDA 66326 [DDD]
Bach, J.S.:Con Ob, BWV 1053, w. P. Goodwin (ob) Hyperion ▲ CDA 66267 [DDD]
Bach, J.S.:Con Ob d'amore, w. P. Goodwin (ob d'amore) Hyperion ▲ CDA 66267 [DDD]
Bach, J.S.:Trio Sons Org, BWV 525–530 [arr. for various instr] Hyperion ▲ CDA 66843
Blow, J.:Songs, w. James Bowman (ct), John Mark Ainsley (ten), Michael George (bass), Charles Pott (bass)—Sing unto the Lord, Oh ye Saints *(rec St Jude–on–the–Hill, London, Dec 20–21, 1968)* United ▲ CAL 88002 [DDD]
Buxtehude, D.:Jesu, meine Freud und Lust, w. J. Bowman (ct) [G] Meridian ▲ CDE 84126
Buxtehude, D.:Jubilate Domino, omnis terra, w. J. Bowman (ct) [G] Meridian ▲ CDE 84126
Couperin, F.:Motets, w. James Bowman (ct)—Jerusalem, convertere Hyperion ▲ KING 3
Ford, T.:Since First I Saw Your Face, w. James Bowman (ct) Hyperion ▲ KING 3
Gabrieli, G.:O magnum mysterium, w. James Bowman (ct) Hyperion ▲ KING 3
Great Baroque Arias, Part I Allegro ▲ ALG PCD 894
Handel, G.F.:Arias, w. J. Bowman (ct)—sels. from Alcina, Amadigi, Ariodante, Giulio Cesare, Giustino, Ottone, Rinaldo Hyperion ▲ CDA 66483
Handel, G.F.:Arias, w. S. Gritton (sop), J. Bowman (ct)—Yet can I hear that dulcet lay; How can I stay, when love invites; O fairest of 10 thousand fair; Great God! Who yet but darkly known; The raptur'd soul; Father of Heaven; Ov to Esther; O Lord, whose mercies numberless; What though I trace each herb; Martial Sym & Destructive War; Welcome as the dawn of day; Kind Heaven if virtue be thy care; Almighty pow'r; Tune your harps Hyperion ▲ CDA 66797
Handel, G.F.:Coronation Anthems (4) for George II—Zadok the Priest *(rec St Jude–on–the–Hill, London, Dec 20–21, 1968)* United ▲ CAL 88002 [DDD]
Handel, G.F.:Deborah, w. S. Gritton (sop), Y. Kenny (sop), C. Denley (mez), J. Bowman (alt), M. George (bass), Oxford New College Choir Hyperion 2–▲ CDA 66841 [DDD]
Handel, G.F.:Joseph & His Brethren, w. Yvonne Kenney (sop), Catherine Denley (mez), Connor Burrowes (trb), James Bowman (ct), John Mark Ainsley (ten), Michael George (bass), New College Choir Oxford, King's Consort Choir Hyperion 3–▲ CDA 67171/3

King's Consort (cont.)
R. King (cnd) (cont.)
Handel, G.F.:Music of, w. James Bowman (ct)—Almighty Power; Or la tromba; Eternal Source of Light; Thou Shalt Bring Them In; Tune Your Harps; Welcome As the Dawn of Day; Impious Mortal; Yet Can I Hear That Dulcet Lay; Crudeltà né lontananza Hyperion ▲ KING 3
Handel, G.F.:Occasional Oratorio, w. Susan Gritton (sop), Lisa Milne (sop), James Brown (ct), John Mark Ainsley (ten), Michael George (bass), New College Choir Oxford Hyperion 2–▲ CDA 66961/62
Handel, G.F.:Ottone, Rè di Germania, w. Jennifer Smith (sop—Gismonda), Catherine Denley (mez—Matilda), James Bowman (ct—Ottone), Dominique Visse (ct—Adelberto), Michael George (bass—Emireno) Hyperion 3–▲ CDA 66751/53
Handel, G.F.:Theodora (sels), w. James Bowman (ct)—As with rosy steps the morn advancing *(rec St Jude–on–the–Hill, London, Dec 20–21, 1968)* United ▲ CAL 88002 [DDD]
Hasse, J.A.:Salve Regina, w. Deborah York (sop), James Bowman (ct) Hyperion ▲ CDA 66875
Humfrey, P.:Anthems, w. James Bowman (ct), Jane Coe (vc), Robert King (org)—A Hymn to God the Father *(rec St Jude–on–the–Hill, London, Dec 20–21, 1968)* United ▲ CAL 88002 [DDD]
Mozart, W.A.:Church Sons, w. I. Watson (org) Hyperion ▲ CDA 66377 [DDD]
Pergolesi, G.B.:Salve regina in f, w. J. Bowman (ct) [L] Meridian ▲ CDE 84138
Purcell, H.:Anthems & Services, w. Tom Seligman (trb), James Bowman (ct), Ashley Stafford (ct), John Mark Ainsley (ten), Andrew Gant (ten), Michael George (bass), Charles Pott (bass)—O Sing unto the Lord; My beloved spake *(rec St Jude–on–the–Hill, London, Dec 20–21, 1968)* United ▲ CAL 88002 [DDD]
Purcell, H.:Anthems & Services, w. J. Bowman (ct), R. Covey–Crump (ten), C. Daniels (ten), S. Varcoe (bar), M. George (bass), New College Choir Oxford—My heart is inditing; The way of God is an undefiled way; Sing unto God; Behold, I bring you glad tidings; Since God so tender a regard; Early, O Lord, my fainting soul; Sleep, Adam, sleep and take thy rest; Awake, ye dead; The earth trembled; Lord not to us but to thy name; O all ye people, clap your hands Hyperion ▲ CDA 66644
Purcell, H.:Anthems & Services—I will sing thanks unto the Lord as long as I live, Z.22; Kyrie in B♭; Nicene Creed in B♭; Benedictus in B♭; I will give thanks unto the Lord, Z.23; Out of the deep have I called, Z.45 Hyperion ▲ CDA 66707
Purcell, H.:Anthems & Services—The Lord Is King, the Earth May Be Glad; O Lord Our Governor; In Guilty Night; O Lord God of Hosts; Cantate Domino; Deus misereator; The Lord Is My Light; Blessed Be the Lord My Strength; Blessed Is He Hyperion ▲ CDA 66693
Purcell, H.:Anthems & Services, w. James Bowman (ct), Charles Daniels (ten), Michael George (bass), Robert Evans (bass), New College Choir Oxford—O sing unto the Lord; O praise God in His holiness; Praise the Lord, O Jerusalem; It is a good thing to give thanks; O give thanks unto the Lord; Let mine eyes run down with tears; My beloved spake Hyperion ▲ CDA 66585
Purcell, H.:Anthems & Services—Begin the Song, & Strike the Living Lyre; Blow Up the Trumpet in Sion; Hear My Prayer, O Lord; Hosanna To the Highest; How Have I Strayed; Lord, I Can Suffer Thy Rebukes; The Lord is King, Be the People Never So Impatient; O God, Thou Hast Cast Us Out; O Lord, Our Governor; Remember Not, Lord, Our Offences; Tell Me, Some Pitying Angel; Thy Word is a Lantern Unto My Feet Hyperion ▲ CDA 66623
Purcell, H.:Anthems & Services—Awake, put on thy strength, Z.1; Praise the Lord, O my soul, O Lord my God, Z.48; O Lord, thou art my God, Z.41; Hear me, O Lord, Z.13a/b; Turn thou us, O good Lord, Z.62; Close thine eyes & sleep secure, Z.184; Lord, how long wilt thou be angry?, Z.25; Magnificat, Nunc Dimittis in B♭, Z.231 Hyperion ▲ CDA 66716
Purcell, H.:Anthems & Services, w. S. Gritton (sop), M. Kennedy (sop), E. O'Dwyer (trb), J. Goodman (trb), J. Bowman (ct), N. Short (ct), Rogers Covey–Crump (ten), C. Daniels (ten), M. Milhofer (ten), M. George (bass), R. Evans (bass)—I Was Glad When They Said unto Me (coronation & verse anthem); O Consider My Adversity; Beati omnes qui timent Dominum; In the Black Dismal Dungeon of Despair; Save Me, O God; Te Deum in B♭; Jubilant in B♭; Thy Way, O God, Is Holy Hyperion ▲ CDA 66677 [DDD]
Purcell, H.:Anthems & Services, w. James Bowman (ct), Roger Covey–Crump (ten), Michael George (bass), New College Choir Oxford—Behold, now praise the Lord; Blessed are they that fear the Lord; I will give thanks unto Thee, O Lord; My song shall be always Hyperion ▲ CDA 66609
Purcell, H.:Music for the Funeral of Queen Mary, w. S. Gritton (sop), M. Kennedy (sop), E. O'Dwyer (trb), J. Goodman (trb), J. Bowman (ct), N. Short (ct), Rogers Covey–Crump (ten), C. Daniels (ten), M. Milhofer (ten), M. George (bass), R. Evans (bass) Hyperion ▲ CDA 66677 [DDD]
Purcell, H.:Music of, w. New College Choir Oxford—When I Am Laid in Earth [w. G. Fisher (sop)]; Welcome, Welcome Glorious Morn; Oh, Fair Cedaria; Hear My Prayer, O Lord; Let Mine Eyes Run down with Tears; The Sparrow and the Gentle Dove; If Music Be the Food of Love; Rejoice in the Lord Alway; Hosanna to the Highest; Thou Knowest, Lord, the Secrets of Our Hearts; Fairest Isle, All Isles Excelling; Mark, How Readily Each Pliant String; Sound the Trumpet; She Loves and Confesses Too; O How Blest Is the Isle; Now that the Sun Hath Veiled His Light (an evening hymn); Vouchsafe, O Lord, to Keep Us This Day; With Rapture of Delight Hyperion ▲ KING 2
Purcell, H.:Odes & Welcome Songs (comp)—Fly, bold rebellion (Welcome Song for Charles II), Z.324 (1683); Sound the trumpet, beat the drum (Welcome Song for James II), Z.335 (1687); Celebrate this festival (Ode for Queen Mary's Birthday), Z.321 (1693) Hyperion ▲ CDA 66412 [DDD]
Purcell, H.:Odes & Welcome Songs (comp)—Hail, bright Cecilia! (Ode for St. Cecilia's Day, 1692); Who can from joy refrain? (Ode for the Duke of Gloucester's Birthday, 1695) Hyperion ▲ CDA 66349 [DDD]
Purcell, H.:Odes & Welcome Songs (comp)—Welcome, welcome, glorious morn (Ode for the Birthday of Queen Mary), Z.338 (1691); Great parent, hail to thee (Ode for the Centenary of Trinity College Dublin), Z.327 (1694); The summer's absence unconcerned we bear (Welcome Song for King Charles II), Z.337 (1682) Hyperion ▲ CDA 66476 [DDD]
Purcell, H.:Odes & Welcome Songs (comp), w. New College Choir Oxford [E] Hyperion 8–▲ CDS 44031/38 [DDD]
Purcell, H.:Odes & Welcome Songs (comp)—Welcome to all the pleasures (Ode for St. Cecilia's Day, 1683); Now does the glorious day appear (Ode for Queen Mary's Birthday, 1689); Arise, my Muse (Ode for Queen Mary's Birthday, 1690) Hyperion ▲ CDA 66314 [DDD]
Purcell, H.:Odes & Welcome Songs (comp)—Swifter, Isis, swifter flow (Welcome Song for Charles II); What, what shall be done in behalf of the man? (Welcome Song for the Duke of York); Of old, when heroes thought it base (Yorkshire Feast Song) Hyperion ▲ CDA 66587 [DDD]
Purcell, H.:Odes & Welcome Songs (comp)—From Those Serene & Rapturous Joys; Laudate Ceciliam; Love's Goddess Sure was Blind; Raise, Raise the Voice Hyperion ▲ CDA 66494
Purcell, H.:Songs, w. James Bowman (ct)—Britain, Thou Now Art Great; O Solitude; By Beauteous Softness Mixed; An Evening Hymn; On the Brow of Richmond Hill; Vouchsafe, O Lord Hyperion ▲ KING 3
Purcell, H.:Songs, w. B. Bonney (sop), S. Gritton (sop), J. Bowman (ct), R. Covey–Crump (ten), C. Daniels (ten), M. George (bass)—When Strephon Found; Let Us, Kind Lesbia; Corinna Is Divinely Fair; Olinda in the Shades; If Music Be the Food of Love [3rd setting]; Lovely Albina; I Came, I Saw; No, to What Purpose; Young Thrysis' Fate; She Loves Me and Confesses Too; From Silent Shade (Bess of Bedlam); O Solitude; If Pray'rs and Tears; The Fatal Hour; Sylvia, 'Tis True You're Fair; Amintor, Heedless of His Flocks; Love is Now Become a Trade; Phyllis, I Can Never Forgive It; Who Can Behold?; He Himself Courts His Own Ruin; Let Formal Lovers Still Pursue; Ask Me to Love No More; In Cloris All Soft Charms; Spite of the Godhead Hyperion ▲ CDA 66730
Purcell, H.:Songs, w. J. Bowman (ct), M. Chance (ct) [E, L] Hyperion ▲ CDA 66253 [DDD]
Scarlatti, A.:Cants, w. Deborah York (sop), James Bowman (ct), Crispian Steele–Perkins (tpt)—3 cants Hyperion ▲ CDA 66875
Scarlatti, D.:Salve Regina, w. Deborah York (sop), James Bowman (ct) Hyperion ▲ CDA 66875
Telemann, G.P.:Con in A Ob d'amore, w. P. Goodwin (ob) Hyperion ▲ CDA 66267 [DDD]
Telemann, G.P.:Cons Ob Orch, w. P. Goodwin (ob)—1—in d Hyperion ▲ CDA 66267 [DDD]
Telemann, G.P.:Musique de Table—Suite in D from Set 2 & Suite in B♭ from Set 3 Hyperion ▲ CDA 66278 [DDD]
Vivaldi, A.:Nisi Dominus, w. C. Robson (ct) [L] *(rec 4/86)* Meridian ▲ CDE 84129
Vivaldi, A.:Salve regina, RV.619, w. J. Bowman (ct) [L] Meridian ▲ CDE 84138

King's Noyse
D. Douglass (cnd)
Canzonetta:16th Century Canzoni & Instrumental Dances, w. Ellen Hargis (sop), Paul O'Dette (lt) Harmonia Mundi USA ▲ HMU 907127

▲ = CD ♦ = Enhanced CD Δ = MD ■ = Cassette Tape □ = DCC

King's Noyse (cont.)
D. Douglass (cnd) (cont.)
The King's Delight:17th Century Ballads for Voice & Violin Band
Harmonia Mundi USA ▲ HMU 907101
Mascharada
Harmonia Mundi France ▲ HMU 907165
Rosenmüller, J.:Music of, w. Ellen Hargis (sop), Paul O'Dette (thb), Mary Springfels (va)—Suite in C [from Studentenmusik]; Jubilent aethera; Son X à 5; Son VII à 4; In te, Domine, speravi; Son XI à 5; Son IV à 3; Ach Herr, strafe mich nicht in deinem Zorn; Son III à 2; Leiber Herre Gott, Wecke uns auf
Harmonia Mundi ▲ HMU 907179
Stravaganze:17th Century Italian Songs & Dances, w. Andrew Lawrence-King (hp) *(rec Campion Center, Boston, MA, Oct 17-19, 1994)*
Harmonia Mundi France ▲ HMU 907159

Kirov Opera Orch
V. Gergiev (cnd)
Borodin, A.:Prince Igor, w. Kirov Opera Chorus *(rec Mariinsky Theatre, St. Petersburg)*
Philips 3-▲ 442537-2
Glinka, M.:Russlan & Ludmilla, w. Galina Gorchakova (sop), Larissa Diadkova (cta), Irinia Bogachova (sgr), Anna Netrebko (sgr), Yuri Masurin (ten), Konstantin Pluzhnikov (ten), Mikhail Kit (bar), Gennady Bezzubenkov (bass), Vladimir Ognovenko (bass), Kirov Opera Chorus
Philips ▲ 456 248-2
Mussorgsky, M.:Khovanshchina, w. O. Borodina (mez), V. Galusin (ten), B. Minjelkiev (bass), Ohotnikav (sgr), Kirov Opera Chorus [R]
Philips 3-▲ 432147-2 [DDD]
Tchaikovsky, P.:Iolanta, w. Galina Gorchakova (sop), Nikolai Gassiev (ten), Gegam Grigorian (ten), Dmitri Hvorostovsky (bar), Nikolai Putilin (bar), Sergei Alexashkin (bass), Gennady Bezzubenkov (bass), Larissa Diadkova (sgr), Olga Korzhenskaya (sgr), Tatyana Kravtsova (sgr), Kirov Opera Chorus *(rec Mariinsky Theatre, St. Petersburg)*
Philips 2-▲ 442796-2
Tchaikovsky, P.:Queen of Spades, w. M. Gulegina (sop), O. Borodina (mez), G. Grigorian (ten), Kirov Opera Chorus
Philips ▲ 438141-2

B. Khaikin (cnd)
Mussorgsky, M.:Khovanshchina, w. Mark Reizen (bass), *(other soloists unknown)*, Kirov Opera Chorus *(rec 1947)*
Arlecchino 3-▲ ARL103/05

Kirov Orch
V. Fedotov (cnd)
Dargomyzhsky, A.:Rusalka (sels)—Slavonic Dance; Mermaid's Dance
IMP ("Masters" series) ▲ IMP 6600072
Glazunov, A.:Concert Waltz 2
IMP ("Masters" series) ▲ IMP 6600072
Glazunov, A.:Raymonda
IMP ("Masters" series) 2-▲ IMP 6600067
Glinka, M.:A Life for the Tsar (sels)
IMP ("Masters" series) ▲ IMP 6600072
Kabalevsky, D.:The Comedians—Galop
IMP ("Masters" series) ▲ IMP 6600072
Rimsky-Korsakov, N.:A May Night (sels)—Ov; Polonaise; Krakowiak; Waltz; Mazurka
IMP ("Masters" series) ▲ IMP 6600072
Rimsky-Korsakov, N.:Mlada (procession)
IMP ("Masters" series) ▲ IMP 6600072
Rimsky-Korsakov, N.:The Tale of Tsar Saltan (orch sels)—March; Flight of the Bumblebee
IMP ("Masters" series) ▲ IMP 6600072
Rubinstein, A.:The Demon (orch sels)—Dance; Women's Dance
IMP ("Masters" series) ▲ IMP 6600072

V. Gergiev (cnd)
Borodin, A.:Prince Igor (Polovtsian dances)
Philips ▲ 442011-2
Glinka, M.:Russlan & Ludmilla (ov)
Philips ▲ 442011-2
Jurassic Classics, w. Berlin PO, Vienna PO, London PO, Boston SO, A. Previn (cnd), C. Davis (cnd), N. Mariner (cnd)
Philips ▲ 442599-2 ■ 442599-4
Khachaturian, A.:Gayane (sels)—Sabre Dance
Philips ▲ 442011-2
Khachaturian, A.:Spartacus (sels)—Adagio
Philips ▲ 442011-2
Liadov, A.:Baba Yaga
Philips ▲ 442011-2
Liadov, A.:Kikimora
Philips ▲ 442011-2
Prokofiev, S.:Romeo & Juliet
Philips 2-▲ 432166-2 [DDD]
Prokofiev, S.:Romeo & Juliet (sels)—highlights
Philips ▲ 432819-2 [DDD] □ 432819-5
Prokofiev, S.:War & Peace, w. Y. Prokina (sop), O. Borodina (mez), G. Gregoriam (ten), A. Gergalov (bar), Kirov Opera Chorus [R]
Philips 3-▲ 434097-2
Rachmaninoff, S.:Sym 2
Philips ▲ 438864-2
Rimsky-Korsakov, N.:Sadko, w. Kirov Opera Chorus
Philips 3-▲ 442138-2
Shostakovich, D.:Sym 8
Philips ▲ 446062-2
Songs & Dances of Death, w. Dmitri Hvorostovsky (bar)
Philips ▲ 438872-2
Tchaikovsky, P.:Arias, w. Galina Gorchakova (sop), Kirov Opera Chorus—Letter Scene [from Eugene Onegin]; Zachem eti sl'ozy [Pique Dame]; Gde zhe ty, moj zjelannyj? [from Sorceress]; Pachudilis' mne butta galasa [from Oprichnik]
Philips ▲ 446405-2
Tchaikovsky, P.:Ov 1812
Philips ▲ 442011-2
Tchaikovsky, P.:Sleeping Beauty
Philips ▲ 434922-2
Tchaikovsky, P.:Sleeping Beauty (sels)
Philips ▲ 434930-2
Verdi, G.:Arias, w. Galina Gorchakova (sop), Kirov Opera Chorus—Madre, pietosa Vergine; Pace, pace mio dio [both from La Forza del destino]; Qui Radamès verrà—Oh patria mia [from Aida]; Tacea la notte placida—Di tale amor [from Il Trovatore]; Mia madre aveva; Piangea cantando; Ave Maria [Willow Song] [all from Otello]
Philips ▲ 446405-2

Kirov Theater Orch members
L. Bernstein (cnd)
Beethoven, L. van:Sym 9, "Choral Sym", w. Bavarian RSO members, Dresden State Orch members, London SO members, New York PO members, Orch de Paris members, Bavarian Radio Chorus, Berlin Radio Chorus, Dresden Philharmonie Children's Chorus [G] *(rec live, Schauspielhaus, East Berlin, 12/25/89)*
Deutsche Grammophon ▲ 429861-2 [DDD] ■ 429861-4

Kirschner Duo
Cimarosa, D.:Con in C Ob [arr for Fl & Gtr]
Gallo ▲ CD 696
Marcello, B.:Music of—Adagio for Fl & Gtr
Gallo ▲ CD 696
Piazzolla, A.:Histoire du tango—Bordel 1900
Gallo ▲ CD 696
Sarasate, P. de:Serenade andalouse
Gallo ▲ CD 696
Villa-Lobos, H.:Distribution de fleurs
Gallo ▲ CD 696

Kitchener-Waterloo SO
Viens, Gentille Dame:Romantic Arias for Lyric Tenor, w. DuBois, Mark (ten), Kitchener-Waterloo SO [cnd:Raffi Armenian]
CBC Records ("SM 5000" series) ▲ SMCD 5077 [DDD] ■ 4-5077 (D)

R. Armenian (cnd)
Brahms, J.:Serenade 1 Orch *(rec Centre in the Square, Kitchener, Mar. 22, 1992)*
CBC ("SM 5000" series) ▲ SM5 5145 [DDD]
Brahms, J.:Serenade 2 Orch *(rec Centre in the Square, Kitchener, Feb. 11, 1993)*
CBC ("SM 5000" series) ▲ SM5 5145 [DDD]
Chopin, F.:Andante Spianato & Grande Polonaise, w. Janina Fialkowska (pno) *(rec Centre in the Square, Kitchener, Ontario, Feb. 9 & 10, 1993)*
CBC ("SM 5000" series) ▲ SMCD 5140 [DDD]
Forsyth, M.:Con Tpt, w. J. Thompson (tpt)
CBC ("SM 5000" series) ▲ SMCD 5130 [DDD]
Hétu, J.:Con Tpt, w. G. Few (tpt)
CBC ("SM 5000" series) ▲ SMCD 5130 [DDD]
Heuberger, R.:Der Opernball (sels), w. J. Kolomyjec (sop), M. DuBois (ten)—Im chambre séparée
CBC ("SM 5000" series) ▲ SMCD 5126 [DDD]
Kálmán, I.:Die Csárdásfürstin (sels), w. J. Kolomyjec (sop), M. DuBois (ten)—Machen wir's den Schwalben nach; Tanzen möcht' ich
CBC ("SM 5000" series) ▲ SMCD 5126 [DDD]
Kálmán, I.:Gräfin Mariza, w. J. Kolomyjec (sop), M. DuBois (ten)—Komm Zigany; Csárdás
CBC ("SM 5000" series) ▲ SMCD 5126 [DDD]
Kálmán, I.:Gräfin Mariza, w. L. Boucher (sop), M. Dubois (ten)
CBC ("SM 5000" series) ▲ SMCD 5045 [DDD]
Koprowski, P.P.:Souvenirs de Pologne, w. Janina Fialkowska (pno) *(rec Centre in the Square, Kitchener, Ontario, Feb. 9 & 10, 1993)*
CBC ("SM 5000" series) ▲ SMCD 5140 [DDD]
Lavallée, C.:The Widow (sels), w. J. Kolomyjec (sop), M. DuBois (ten)—Oh! Trust My Love; Smiling Hope
CBC ("SM 5000" series) ▲ SMCD 5126 [DDD]
Lehár, F.:Das Land des Lächelns (sels), w. L. Boucher (sop), M. Dubois (ten)
CBC ("SM 5000" series) ▲ SMCD 5045 [DDD]

Kitchener-Waterloo SO (cont.)
R. Armenian (cnd) (cont.)
Lehár, F.:Das Land des Lächelns (sels), w. J. Kolomyjec (sop), M. DuBois (ten)—Dei einem Tee à deux; Dein ist mein ganzes Herz; Ich möcht' wieder einmal die Heimat seh'n
CBC ("SM 5000" series) ▲ SMCD 5126 [DDD]
Lehár, F.:Die lustige Witwe (sels), w. L. Boucher (sop), M. Dubois (ten)
CBC ("SM 5000" series) ▲ SMCD 5045 [DDD]
Mahler, G.:Kindertotenlieder, w. C. Robbin (mez) [G]
CBC ("SM 5000" series) ▲ SMCD 5098 [DDD] ■ SMC 5098 (D)
Mahler, G.:Lieder eines fahrenden Gesellen, w. C. Robbin (sop) [G]
CBC ("SM 5000" series) ▲ SMCD 5098 [DDD] ■ SMC 5098 (D)
Mahler, G.:Songs from Rückert, w. C. Robbin (mez) [G]
CBC ("SM 5000" series) ▲ SMCD 5098 [DDD] ■ SMC 5098 (D)
Matton, R.:Con for 2 Pnos, w. J. Anagnoson (pno), L. Kinton (pno)
CBC ("SM 5000" series) ▲ SMCD 5120 [DDD]
Moszkowski, M.:Con Pno, w. Janina Fialkowska (pno) *(rec Centre in the Square, Kitchener, Ontario, Feb. 9 & 10, 1993)*
CBC ("SM 5000" series) ▲ SMCD 5140 [DDD]
Nimmons, P.:Con Tpt, w. D. Warren (tpt)
CBC ("SM 5000" series) ▲ SMCD 5130 [DDD]
Poulenc, F.:Con for 2 Pnos, w. J. Anagnoson (pno), L. Kinton (pno)
CBC ("SM 5000" series) ▲ SMCD 5120 [DDD]
Strauss (II), Joh.:Music of, w. Boucher (sop), Dubois (ten)—selections from Die Fledermaus & Gypsy Baron
CBC ("SM 5000" series) ▲ SMCD 5045 [DDD]
Strauss (II), Joh.:Eine Nacht in Venedig (sels), w. J. Kolomyjec (sop), M. DuBois (ten)—Ov.; Sei mir gegrüsst, du holdes Venetia; Polka-Mazurka, Op. 415; Was mir der Zufall gab; Quadrille, Op. 416; Sie sagten meinem Liebesfleh'n; Lagunen-Walzer, Op. 411
CBC ("SM 5000" series) ▲ SMCD 5126 [DDD]
Stravinsky, I.:Danses concertantes *(rec Centre in the Square, Kitchener, May 23 & Oct 2, 1991)*
CBC ▲ 5159 [DDD]

Kithara [Shirley Rumsey (voc/lt/Renaissance gtr/cittern), J. Walters (Italianate triple hp), Susanna Pell (Renaissance b vl), W. Lyons (fls/rcr), D. Miller (thb/lt), C. Wilson (lt/Renaissance gtr/baroque gtr)]
Music Mediterranea:Music of the Italian & Spanish Renaissance
Chandos ▲ CHAN 0562 [DDD]

Kjellström String Quartet
The String Quartet in Sweden:A Cavalcade of Its History, w. Barkel String Quartet, Stockholm String Quartet, Garaguly String Quartet, Kyndel String Quartet, Ivan Ericson String Quartet, Grünfarb String Quartet, Skåne String Quartet, Hälsingborg String Quartet, Göteborg String Quartet, Galli String Quartet *(rec before 1951)*
Caprice 5-▲ CAP 21506 [AAD/ADD]

Das Klein Orchester
R. Batik (cnd)
Batik, R.:Con 1 Pno, w. Roland Batik (pno)
Camerata ▲ 30CM 347
Batik, R.:New Impressions, w. Roland Batik (pno)
Camerata ▲ 30CM 347
Schabata, W.:St. Marx, w. Roland Batik (pno)
Camerata ▲ 30CM 347

Das Kleine Konzert
Bach, J.S.:St. Matthew Passion, w. Monika Frimmer (sop), Veronika Winter (sop), Lena Susanne Norin (alt), Wilfried Jochens (ten), Christoph Prégardien (ten), Klaus Mertens (bass), Hans-Georg Wimmer (bass), Rhineland Kantorei
Capriccio 2-▲ 60 046 [DDD]
Telemann, G.P.:Auferstehung und Himmelfahrt Jesu, w. Monika Frimmer (sop), Veronika Winter (sop), Matthias Koch (alt), Nico Van der Meel (ten), Klaus Mertens (bass), Rhineland Kantorei
Capriccio ▲ CD 10596 [DDD]

H. Max (cnd)
Bach, W.F.:Cants (misc), w. B. Schlick (soprano), C. Schubert (contralto), W. Jochens (tenor), J. Schreckenberger (bass), Rheinische Kantorei—Lasset uns ablegen die Werke der Finsternis; Es ist eine Stimme eines Predigers in der Wüste
Capriccio ▲ 10 425 [DDD]
Bach, W.F.:Cants (misc), w. B. Schlick (soprano), C. Schubert (contralto), W. Jochens (tenor), J. Schreckenberger (bass), Rheinische Kantorei—Dies ist der Tag; Erzittert und fallet
Capriccio ▲ 10 426 [DDD]
Hasse, J.A.:Miserere in c Orch, w. Rhineland Kantorei, Dormagen Boys' Choir
Capriccio ▲ 10 557 [DDD]
Heinichen, J.D.:Sacred Music, w. Rhineland Kantorei, Dormagen Boys' Choir—Magnificat in A
Capriccio ▲ 10 557 [DDD]
Homilius, G.A.:Vocal Music, w. Rhineland Kantorei, Dormagen Boys' Choir—Verwundrung, Mitleid, Furcht und Schrecken
Capriccio ▲ 10 557 [DDD]
Zelenka, J.D.:Miserere in c, w. Dormagen Boys' Choir, Rhineland Kantorei
Capriccio ▲ 10 557 [DDD]

Donald Knaack Percussion Ensemble
Cage, J.:First Construction
Tomato ▲ R2-79695
Cage, J.:A Flower Voice
Tomato ▲ R2-79695
Cage, J.:Forever & Sunsmell
Tomato ▲ R2-79695
Cage, J.:Second Construction
Tomato ▲ R2-79695
Cage, J.:Third Construction
Tomato ▲ R2-79695

Kneller Hall All-Star Band
Knollor Hall:A Musical Salute to the Royal Military School of Music
Bandleader ▲ BND 5109 [DDD]

Die Knödel
Die Noodle!
Koch International Classics ▲ KOC 7923
Overcooked Tyroleans
Koch International Classics ▲ KOC 7908

Koch String Quartet
Erb, D.:Son Hpd, w. J. White (pno)
CRI ▲ CD 593 [ADD/DDD]

Kocian String Quartet
Brahms, J.:Sextet Strs, Op. 36, w. Smetana String Quartet Soloists
Denon ▲ CO 2141 [DDD]
Stravinsky, I.:L'Histoire du soldat Suite Ensemble, Boston Sym Chamber Players
Praga ▲ PR 250057

Kocian String Quartet [P. Hůla (vn), J. Odstčil (vn), Jiří Najnar (va), V. Bernášek (vc)]
Dvořák, A.:Qt 10 Strs
Denon ▲ 7235 [DDD]
Dvořák, A.:Qt 14 Strs
Denon ▲ 7235 [DDD]
Haydn, J.:Qts Strs, Op. 20, "Sun Qts"—Nos. 4-6
Orfeo ▲ 313201 [DDD]
Haydn, J.:Qts Strs, Op. 20, "Sun Qts"—in E♭, C & g, Nos. 1-3
Orfeo ▲ 313101 [DDD]
Hindemith, P.:Minimax *(rec Ernest Ansermet Studio, Geneva, Switzerland, June & Nov 1995)*
Praga 2-▲ PR 250093.94
Hindemith, P.:Ov to the "Flying Dutchman" *(rec Ernest Ansermet Studio, Geneva, Switzerland, June & Nov 1995)*
Praga 2-▲ PR 250093.94
Hindemith, P.:Qt Strs, Op. 2 *(rec Ernest Ansermet Studio, Geneva, Switzerland, June & Nov 1995)*
Praga 2-▲ PR 250093.94
Hindemith, P.:Qt 1 Strs
Praga ▲ PR 250088
Hindemith, P.:Qt 2 Strs
Praga ▲ PR 250088
Hindemith, P.:Qt 3 Strs *(rec Ernest Ansermet Studio, Geneva, Switzerland, June & Nov 1995)*
Praga 2-▲ PR 250093.94
Hindemith, P.:Qt 4 Strs *(rec Ernest Ansermet Studio, Geneva, Switzerland, June & Nov 1995)*
Praga 2-▲ PR 250093.94
Hindemith, P.:Qt 5 Strs *(rec Ernest Ansermet Studio, Geneva, Switzerland, June & Nov 1995)*
Praga 2-▲ PR 250093.94
Hindemith, P.:Qt 6 Strs
Praga ▲ PR 250088
Mozart, W.A.:Qt 16 Strs
Denon ▲ CO 8093 [DDD]
Mozart, W.A.:Qt 17 Strs
Denon ▲ CO 8093 [DDD]
Schulhoff, E.:Divert Str Qt
Supraphon ▲ SUP 112167 [DDD]
Schulhoff, E.:Pieces Str Qt
Supraphon ▲ SUP 112166 [DDD]
Schulhoff, E.:Qt 0 Strs
Supraphon ▲ SUP 112166 [DDD]
Schulhoff, E.:Qt 1 Strs
Supraphon ▲ SUP 112166 [DDD]
Schulhoff, E.:Qt 2 Strs
Supraphon ▲ SUP 112167 [DDD]
Schulhoff, E.:Sxt Strs
Supraphon ▲ SUP 112167 [DDD]
Zemlinsky, A. von:Qt 3 Strs *(rec Prague, 1995)*
Praga ▲ PR 250092

Kocian String Quartet members
Schulhoff, E.:Duo Vn
Supraphon ▲ SUP 112167 [DDD]

Kodály String Quartet [Attila Falvay (vn), Tamás Szabo (vn), Gábor Fias (va), Jnos Devich (vc)]
Bartók, B.:Qnt Pno & Strs, w. Jenő Jandó (pno) *(rec Unitarian Church, Budapest, June 27–28, 1993)* Naxos ▲ 8.550886 [DDD]
Beethoven, L. van:Qts Strs (comp)—Op. 18, Nos. 1-2 *(rec Oct. 22–25, 1991)* Naxos ▲ 8.550558 [DDD]
Beethoven, L. van:Qt 1 Strs *(rec Unitarian Church, Budapest, Oct 22–25, 1991)* Naxos 4-▲ 8.504006 [DDD]
Beethoven, L. van:Qt 2 strs *(rec Unitarian Church, Budapest, Oct 22–25, 1991)* Naxos 4-▲ 8.504006 [DDD]
Debussy, C.:Qt Strs *(rec Dec. 6–8, 1988)* Naxos ▲ 8.550249 [DDD]
Dohnányi, E. von:Qt 1 Strs Hungaroton ▲ HCD 11853 [ADD]
Dohnányi, E. von:Qt 2 Strs Hungaroton ▲ HCD 11853 [ADD]
Haydn, J.:Qts Strs, Op. 1—Nos. 5 & 6 *(rec June 12–15, 1991)* Naxos ▲ 8.550399 [DDD]
Haydn, J.:Qts Strs, Op. 2—Nos. 1 & 2 *(rec June 12–15, 1991)* Naxos ▲ 8.550399 [DDD]
Haydn, J.:Qts Strs, Op. 2—No. 4 in F; No. 6 in B♭ *(rec Sept. 16–18)* Naxos ▲ 8.550732 [DDD]
Haydn, J.:Qts Strs, Op. 9—No. 4 in d; No. 1 in C; No. 3 in G *(rec Unitarian Church, Budapest, Dec. 8–10, 1992)* Naxos ▲ 8.550786 [DDD]
Haydn, J.:Qts Strs, Op. 20, "Sun Qts"—Nos. 1-3 *(rec June 1992)* Naxos ▲ 8.550787 [DDD]
Haydn, J.:Qts Strs, Op. 9—No. 2 in E♭; No. 5 in B♭; No. 6 in A *(rec Unitarian Church, Budapest, Jan. 28–30, 1993)* Naxos ▲ 8.550701 [DDD]
Haydn, J.:Qts Strs, Op. 33, "Russian Qts"—Nos. 3,4, & 6 *(rec Unitarian Church, Budapest, Sept. 21–24, 1993)* Naxos ▲ 8.550789 [DDD]
Haydn, J.:Qts Strs, Op. 33, "Russian Qts"—Nos. 1,2, & 5 *(rec Unitarian Church, Budapest, Feb. 25–27, 1993)* Naxos ▲ 8.550788 [DDD]
Haydn, J.:Qt Strs, Op. 42 *(rec Sept. 16–18)* Naxos ▲ 8.550732 [DDD]
Haydn, J.:Qts Strs, Op. 54 *(rec 11–12/89)* Naxos ▲ 8.550395 [DDD]
Haydn, J.:Qts Strs, Op. 55 *(rec 5/90)* Naxos ▲ 8.550397 [DDD]
Haydn, J.:Qts Strs, Op. 71 *(rec 6/89)* Naxos ▲ 8.550394 [DDD]
Haydn, J.:Qts Strs, Op. 74 *(rec 10/89)* Naxos ▲ 8.550396 [DDD]
Haydn, J.:Qts Strs, Op. 76, "Erdődy Qts"—Nos. 1-3 Naxos ▲ 8.550314 [DDD]
Haydn, J.:Qts Strs, Op. 76, "Erdődy Qts"—Nos. 2-4 *(rec 6/88)* Naxos ▲ 8.550129 [DDD]
Haydn, J.:Qts Strs, Op. 76, "Erdődy Qts"—Nos. 4-6 Naxos ▲ 8.550315 [DDD]
Haydn, J.:Qt Strs, Op. 103 *(rec 6/16/89)* Naxos ▲ 8.550346 [DDD]
Haydn, J.:The Seven Last Words of Christ on the Cross Naxos ▲ 8.550346 [DDD]
Indy, V. d':Qt 1 Strs Marco Polo ▲ 8.223140 [DDD]
Indy, V. d':Qt 2 Strs Marco Polo ▲ 8.223140 [DDD]
Kodály, Z.:Qt Strs, Op. 2 Hungaroton ▲ HCD 12362 [DDD]
Kodály, Z.:Qt Strs, Op. 10 Hungaroton ▲ HCD 12362 [DDD]
Mozart, W.A.:Musikalischer Spass *(rec May 2–3 & 6–9, 1991)* Naxos ▲ 8.550437 [DDD]
Mozart, W.A.:Qt Ob, K.370, w. J. Kiss (ob) *(rec May 2–3 & 6–9, 1991)* Naxos ▲ 8.550437 [DDD]
Mozart, W.A.:Qnt Hn, K.407, w. J. Keveházi (hn) *(rec May 2–3 & 6–9, 1991)* Naxos ▲ 8.550437 [DDD]
Ravel, M.:Intro & Allegro, w. É. Maros (hp), Z. Gyöngyössy (fl), B. Kovács (cl) *(rec Dec. 6–8, 1988)* Naxos ▲ 8.550249 [DDD]
Ravel, M.:Qt Strs *(rec Dec. 6–8, 1988)* Naxos ▲ 8.550249 [DDD]
Schubert, Franz:Adagio & Rondo concertante Vn, w. I. Tóth (db), J. Jandó (pno) *(rec Dec. 2–4, 1991)* Naxos ▲ 8.550658 [DDD]
Schubert, Franz:Qt 10 Strs *(rec Unitarian Church, Budapest, May 4–7, 1994)* Naxos ▲ 8.550591 [DDD]
Schubert, Franz:Qt 12 Strs *(rec Unitarian Church, Budapest, Oct 8–11, 1991)* Naxos 4-▲ 8.504006 [DDD]
Schubert, Franz:Qt 13 Strs *(rec Unitarian Church, Budapest, May 4–7, 1994)* Naxos ▲ 8.550591 [DDD]
Schubert, Franz:Qt 14 Strs *(rec Unitarian Church, Budapest, Oct 8–11, 1991)* Naxos 4-▲ 8.504006 [DDD]
Schubert, Franz:Qnt Pno, D.667, w. J. Jandó (pno), I. Tóth (db) *(rec Dec. 2–4, 1991)* Naxos ▲ 8.550658 [DDD]
Schumann, R.:Qnt Pno, w. J. Jandó (pno) Naxos ▲ 8.550406 [DDD]

Kodály String Quartet members
Viotti, G.B.:Qts Fl, Op. 22, w. Gian-Luca Petrucci (fl) Tudor ▲ TUD 7021 [DDD]

Koeckert String Quartet [R. J. Koeckert (vn), A. Spiller (vn), F. Schessl (va), H. Stiehler (vc)]
Grieg, E.:Qt Strs, Op. 27 *(rec Apr. 25–26, 1990)* Calig ▲ CAL 50916 [DDD]
Saint-Saëns, C.:Qt 1 Strs *(rec Apr. 25–26, 1990)* Calig ▲ CAL 50916 [DDD]
Schubert, Franz:Qnt Pno, D.667, w. C. Eschenbach (pno) Deutsche Grammophon ("Resonance" series) ▲ 427215-2 [ADD]
Tchaikovsky, P.:Qt 1 Strs Calig ▲ CAL 50878 [DDD]
Tchaikovsky, P.:Qt 3 Strs Calig ▲ CAL 50878 [DDD]

Kohon String Quartet
Chadwick, G.W.:Qt 4 Strs *(rec 1969)* Vox Box 2-▲ CDX 5057 [ADD]
Foote, A.:Qt 3 Strs *(rec 1969)* Vox Box 2-▲ CDX 5057 [ADD]
Franklin, B.:Qt Strs *(rec 1969)* Vox Box 2-▲ CDX 5057 [ADD]
Loeffler, C.M.:Music for 4 Str Instruments *(rec 1969)* Vox Box 2-▲ CDX 5057 [ADD]
Mason, D.G.:Qt on Negro Themes *(rec 1969)* Vox Box 2-▲ CDX 5057 [ADD]

Kohon String Quartet [Harold Kohon (vn), Isadora Kohon (vn), Eugenie Dengel (va), W. Ted Hoyle (vc)]
American String Quartets, 1900–1950 Vox Box 2-▲ CDX 5090 [ADD]

Kohon String Quartet [Harold Kohon (vn), Isidora Kohon (vn), Eugenie Dengel (va), W. Ted Hoyle (vc)]
Penderecki, K.:Qt 1 Strs *(rec Feb 1972)* Vox Box 2-▲ CDX 5142

Kohon String Quartet [Harold Kohon (vn), Raymond Kunicki (vn), Bernard Zaslav (va), Robert Sylvester (vc)]
Weber, C.M. von:Qnt Cl, w. David Glazer (cl) *(rec 1962)* Allegretto ▲ ACD 8189

Kokkola String Quartet
Nordgren, P.H.:Qts Strs—No. 4, Op. 60 & No. 5, Op. 69 Ondine ▲ ODE 713-2 [DDD]

Kol Israël SO
M. Rodan (cnd)
Suk, J.:Fant Vn, w. P. Rybar (vn) *(rec Oct. 26, 1966)* Doron ▲ DRC 4003 [ADD]

Kolisch String Quartet
Mozart, W.A.:Qt 21 Strs Archipon ▲ ARC 108
Mozart, W.A.:Qt 23 Strs—3rd movt. Archipon ▲ ARC 108
Schubert, Franz:Qt 12 Strs Archiphon ▲ ARC 107
Schubert, Franz:Qt 13 Strs Archiphon ▲ ARC 107
Schubert, Franz:Qt 14 Strs Archiphon ▲ ARC 107
Schubert, Franz:Qt 15 Strs Archiphon ▲ ARC 107
Schubert, Franz:Qnt Pno, D.667—4th movt. Archiphon ▲ ARC 107
Schumann, R.:Qt Pno, Op. 47 Archipon ▲ ARC 108
Wolf, H.:Italian Serenade Archipon ▲ ARC 108

Kolisch String Quartet [F. Khuner, E. Lehner, B. Heifetz, R. Kolisch]
Schoenberg, A.:Qts Strs—Qts. Nos. 1, Op. 7; 2, Op. 10; 3, Op. 30; 4, Op. 37 Archipon 2-▲ ARC 103/4 (m) [ADD]

Kölner Saxophone Mafia
Peters, O.:Feu VIF, w. Kölner Saxophone Mafia, VIF Flute Quartet New Classic Colours ♦ NCC 8001 [DDD]

König Ensemble
J. Latham-König (cnd)
Weill, K.:Mahagonny, w. G. Ramm (sop), T. Schmidt (mez), H. Hiestermann (ten) Capriccio ▲ 60028 [DDD]

Kontra String Quartet [Anton Kontra (vn), Boris Samsing (vn), Peter Fabricius (va), Morten Zeuthen (vc)]
Gade, N.W.:Allegro Str Qt *(rec Torpen Kapel, Humlebaek, Denmark, May, 5–8, 1992)* BIS ▲ CD 545 [DDD]
Gade, N.W.:Andante & Allegro molto, w. Hans Nygaard (vc) *(rec Torpen Kapel, Humlebaek, Denmark, May, 5–8, 1992)* BIS ▲ CD 545 [DDD]
Gade, N.W.:Octet, w. Anne Egendal (vn), Per Lund Madsen (vn), Sune Ranmo (va), Hans Nygaard (vc) *(rec Torpen Kapel, Humlebaek, Denmark, May, 5–8, 1992)* BIS ▲ CD 545 [DDD]
Gade, N.W.:Qts Strs (comp) BIS ▲ CD 516 [DDD]
Gade, N.W.:Qt in F Strs *(rec Torpen Kapel, Humlebaek, Denmark, May, 5–8, 1992)* BIS ▲ CD 545 [DDD]
Grieg, E.:Fugue *(rec May 13, 1993)* BIS ▲ CD 543 [DDD]
Grieg, E.:Qt Strs (unfinished) *(rec Dec. 16, 1991)* BIS ▲ CD 543 [DDD]
Grieg, E.:Qt Strs, Op. 27 *(rec Nov. 18–21, 1991)* BIS ▲ CD 543 [DDD]
Heise, P.:Chamber Music, w. A. Malling (pno), M. Zeuthen (vc)—Quintet in F for Piano & Strings (1869); Cello Sonata in a (1867); 2 Fantasy Pieces for Cello & Piano Marco Polo/Dacapo ▲ DCCD 9113 [DDD]
Kodály, Z.:Gavotte for 3 Vns & Vc *(rec Apr. 7–11, 1992)* BIS ▲ CD 564 [DDD]
Kodály, Z.:Qt Strs, Op. 2 *(rec Apr. 7–11, 1992)* BIS ▲ CD 564 [DDD]
Kodály, Z.:Qt Strs, Op. 10 *(rec Apr. 7–11, 1992)* BIS ▲ CD 564 [DDD]
Langgaard, R.:Qt 2 Strs *(rec Copenhagen, 1984)* Marco Polo ("dacapo" series) 2-▲ DC 9302a/b [DDD]
Langgaard, R.:Qt 3 Strs *(rec Copenhagen, 1984)* Marco Polo ("dacapo" series) 2-▲ DC 9302a/b [DDD]
Langgaard, R.:Qt 4 Strs *(rec Copenhagen, 1984)* Marco Polo ("dacapo" series) 2-▲ DC 9302a/b [DDD]
Langgaard, R.:Qt 5 Strs *(rec Copenhagen, 1984)* Marco Polo ("dacapo" series) 2-▲ DC 9302a/b [DDD]
Langgaard, R.:Qt 6 Strs *(rec Copenhagen, 1984)* Marco Polo ("dacapo" series) 2-▲ DC 9302a/b [DDD]
Langgaard, R.:Vars Str Qt, "O Sacred Head! Now Wounded" *(rec Copenhagen, 1984)* Marco Polo ("dacapo" series) 2-▲ DC 9302a/b [DDD]
Nielsen, C.:At the Bier, w. J. Johansson (db) BIS 2-▲ CD 503/04 [DDD]
Nielsen, C.:Qts Strs, w. J. Johansson (db) BIS 2-▲ CD 503/04 [DDD]
Nielsen, C.:Qnt Strs, w. P. Naegele (va) BIS 2-▲ CD 503/04 [DDD]
Nørgård, P.:Qts Strs Kontrapunkt ▲ 32015 [DDD]
L. Segerstam (cnd)
Segerstam, L.:Thoughts 1990, w. Danish National RSO *(rec live, Copenhagen Nov. 15, 1990)* BIS ▲ CD 583 [DDD]

Kontraste Ensemble [Reiner Wehle (cl), Kathrin Rabus (vn), Christoph Marks (vc), Friederike Richter (pno)]
Messiaen, O.:Quatuor pour la fin du temps *(rec NDR Hannover, Oct 1993–June 1994)* Thorofon ▲ CTH 2232 [DDD]

Korea State SO
B.-H. Kim (cnd)
Yun, I.:Exemplum in memoriam Kwangju *(rec in Pyong-Yang, 1986–70)* CPO ▲ CPO 999047-2 [AAD]
Yun, I.:Naui Dang, Naui Minjokiyo!, w. *(soloists unknown) (rec in Pyong-Yang, 1986–70)* CPO ▲ CPO 999047-2 [AAD]

Korean PO
B.-K. Kim (cnd)
Kim, B.-K.:Festival Sym Cambria ▲ CD 1046

Korez Holy Trinity Nunnery Trio
Hymns for the Holy Week in the Russian Orthodox Church, w. Moscow Patriarchate Publishing Division Choir, Leningrad Religious Academy Student Choir Koch Schwann ▲ SCH 313073 [ADD]

Kostelanetz Orch
Carmen without Words, w. New York PO [cnd:Leonard Bernstein] CBS Masterworks ▲ MDK 46287 [AAD] ▮ MGT 46287
A. Kostelanetz (cnd)
Gershwin, G.:Con Pno, w. A. Previn (pno) *(rec 1960)* Odyssey ▲ MBK 46270 [ADD] ▮ YT 46270
Gershwin, G.:Porgy & Bess (sels)—Oh Bess, oh where's my Bess; plus 4 sels. from the *Catfish Row Suite (rec 1963)* Odyssey ▲ MBK 46270 [ADD] ▮ YT 46270
Gershwin, G.:Rhap in Blue, w. A. Previn (pno) *(rec 1960)* Odyssey ▲ MBK 46270 [ADD] ▮ YT 46270
Opera for Orchestra, Vol. 1 CBS ▮ YT 38921
Opera without Words CBS ▲ MDK 44999 ▮ MGT 44999
Shostakovich, D.:Ballet Suite 1—Galop, Music Box Waltz; Dance Sony Classical ("Essential Classics" series) ▲ SBK 62642 ▮ SBT 62642
Shostakovich, D.:Ballet Suite 2—Polka & Galop Sony Classical ("Essential Classics" series) ▲ SBK 62642 ▮ SBT 62642
Shostakovich, D.:The Golden Age—Polka Sony Classical ("Essential Classics" series) ▲ SBK 62642 ▮ SBT 62642
Shostakovich, D.:Moskva, Cheremushki (sels)—Galop & Ov Waltz Sony Classical ("Essential Classics" series) ▲ SBK 62642 ▮ SBT 62642
Shostakovich, D.:Suite from Gadfly—Barrel-Organ Waltz; Nocturne; Folk Festival; Galop & Intro Sony Classical ("Essential Classics" series) ▲ SBK 62642 ▮ SBT 62642
Stars & Stripes Forever Odyssey ▲ MBK 38918 [ADD] ▮ YT 38918

Koszalin State PO
S. Kawalla (cnd)
Eyser, E.:Anacrón Vienna Modern Masters ▲ VMM 3028 [DDD]
Fortner, J.:Concertpiece, w. M. Flaksman (vc) Vienna Modern Masters ▲ VMM 3024 [DDD]
Fortner, J.:Quadri, w. Silesian Univ Choir Vienna Modern Masters ▲ VMM 3022 [DDD]
Gallagher, J.:Threnody, w. Grazyna Janus (hp) Vienna Modern Masters ▲ VMM 3028 [DDD]
Jazwinski, B.:Sequenze Concertanti, w. G. Konowalow (vn) Vienna Modern Masters ▲ VMM 3024 [DDD]
Moss, P.:Valses Vienna Modern Masters ▲ VMM 3024 [DDD]
Music from 6 Continents, 1993 series, w. Slovak RSO [cnd:Kawalla], Pro Musica Nipponia [cnd:Norichika Iimori], Bohuslav Martinů PO [cnd:Miloš Machek] Vienna Modern Masters ▲ VMM 3017 [DDD]
Nakamura, H.:Litaniae, w. Silesian Univ Choir Vienna Modern Masters ▲ VMM 3022 [DDD]
Scott, D.:Arras:A Garden of Cinema, w. S. Girardi (mez), Silesian Univ Choir Vienna Modern Masters ▲ VMM 3022 [DDD]
Van De Vate, N.:Adagio & Rondo, w. J. Kawalla (vn) Vienna Modern Masters ▲ VMM 3025 [DDD]
Van De Vate, N.:An American Essay, w. C. Marstrand (sop), L. Hovman (alt), O. Støvring Larsen (ten), Chorus Soranus Vienna Modern Masters ▲ VMM 3025 [DDD]
Van De Vate, N.:Con Pno, w. M. Hirashima (pno) Vienna Modern Masters ▲ VMM 3025 [DDD]
Van De Vate, N.:How Fares the Night?, w. J. Kawalla (vn), Silesian Univ Choir Vienna Modern Masters ▲ VMM 3025 [DDD]
Van De Vate, N.:Vars CO Vienna Modern Masters ▲ VMM 2006 [DDD]
Van De Vate, N.:Voices for Women, w. S. Giraldi (mez), Silesian Univ Choir Vienna Modern Masters ▲ VMM 3022 [DDD]
Wolking, H.:A Luta Continua Vienna Modern Masters ▲ VMM 3028 [DDD]
Yu, J.J.-J.:Wu-Yu, w. Silesian Univ Choir Vienna Modern Masters ▲ VMM 3022 [DDD]

Kowalski String Quartet
Pâque, D.:Qts Strs—No. 2, Op. 30; No. 5, Op. 44; No. 7, Op. 96 Koch Schwann ▲ SCH 313782 [DDD]

Krakow—see Cracow

▲ = CD ♦ = Enhanced CD Δ = MD ▮ = Cassette Tape □ = DCC

Krauss Quartet
Mozart, W.A.:Qnt Cl, K.581, w. H.-D. Löchner (cl) LaserLight ▲ 15 878 [DDD]
Krautgartner Orch
K. Krautgartner (cnd)
Stravinsky, I.:Ragtime *(rec Jan. 29 to Feb. 2, 1968)*
Supraphon ("Collection" series) ▲ 11 0672-2 [ADD]

Kreisler String Orch
Schoenberg, A.:Verklärte Nacht Dolphin ▲ DOL 701
Shostakovich, D.:Chamber Sym, Op. 110a Dolphin ▲ DOL 701
Kremlin CO
M. Rachlevsky (cnd)
Elegy:Masterpieces for String Orchestra *(rec 1991–93)* Claves ▲ CD 9325 [DDD]
Lekeu, G.:Adagio Claves 2-▲ CD 9504/05 [DDD]
Miaskovsky, N.:Pieces Strs *(rec Moscow, June 1994)* Claves ▲ CD 9415 [DDD]
Miaskovsky, N.:Sinfonietta, Op. 32/2 *(rec Moscow, June 1994)* Claves ▲ CD 9415 [DDD]
Miaskovsky, N.:Sinfonietta, Op. 58 *(rec Moscow, June 1994)* Claves ▲ CD 9415 [DDD]
Rossini, G.:Sons Str Qt *(rec July 1992)* Claves ▲ CD 9222 [DDD]
Schnittke, A.:Qt 2 Strs [arr M. Rachlevsky] Claves 2-▲ CD 9504/05 [DDD]
Schoenberg, A.:Verklärte Nacht Claves ▲ CD 9412 [DDD]
Shostakovich, D.:Chamber Sym, Op. 110a Claves ▲ CD 9115 [DDD]
Shostakovich, D.:Chamber Sym, Op. 118a Claves ▲ CD 9115 [DDD]
Shostakovich, D.:Requiem Claves ▲ CD 9115 [DDD]
Shostakovich, D.:Requiem Claves 2-▲ CD 9504/05 [DDD]
Strauss, R.:Metamorphosen Claves ▲ CD 9412 [DDD]
Strauss, R.:Metamorphosen Claves 2-▲ CD 9504/05 [DDD]
Tchaikovsky, P.:Elegy Claves ▲ 50-9116
Tchaikovsky, P.:Qt in B♭ Strs [arr Rachlevsky] Claves ▲ 50-9414
Tchaikovsky, P.:Qt 1 Strs [arr Rachlevsky] Claves ▲ 50-9116
Tchaikovsky, P.:Qt 2 Strs [arr Rachlevsky] Claves ▲ 50-9414
Tchaikovsky, P.:Qt 3 Strs [arr Rachlevsky] Claves ▲ CD 9317 [DDD]
Tchaikovsky, P.:Les Saisons—Suite [arr Rachlevsky] Claves ▲ 50-9414
Tchaikovsky, P.:Serenade Strs Claves ▲ 50-9116
Tchaikovsky, P.:The Snow Maiden Claves ▲ CD 9317 [DDD]
Tchaikovsky, P.:The Snow Maiden (sels)—Melodrama Claves ▲ 50-9317
Tchaikovsky, P.:Souvenir de Florence [version for Str Orch] Claves ▲ CD 9317 [DDD]
Tchaikovsky, P.:Souvenir d'un lieu cher—Scherzo in c [arr Rachlevsky] Claves ▲ 50-9116
Webern, A.:Movts Str Qt Claves ▲ CD 9412 [DDD]
Webern, A.:Slow Movt Claves ▲ CD 9412 [DDD]
Kremlin SO
Mozart, W.A.:Sym 25 *(rec Moscow Conservatory Great Hall, Sept, 1995)*
PopeMusic ▲ PM 10082 [DDD]
Mozart, W.A.:Sym 29 *(rec Moscow Conservatory Great Hall, Sept, 1995)*
PopeMusic ▲ PM 10082 [DDD]
Mozart, W.A.:Sym 40 *(rec Moscow Conservatory Great Hall, Sept, 1995)*
PopeMusic ▲ PM 10082 [DDD]

Kreutzer String Quartet
Hallgrímsson, H.:Movements (4) Eye of the Storm ▲ EOS 5004 [DDD]
Hallgrímsson, H.:Qt 1 Strs, "From Memory" Eye of the Storm ▲ EOS 5004 [DDD]
Kronos Quartet [David Harrington (vn), John Sherba (vn), Hank Dutt (va), Joan Jeanrenaud (vc)]
Africa Elektra/Nonesuch ▲ 79275-2 ■ 79275-4
Bartók, B.:Qt 3 Strs Elektra/Nonesuch ▲ 79163-2 [DDD] ■ 79163-4 (D)
Coates, G.:Qt 1 Strs, "Protestation Qt" Pro Viva ▲ ISPV 173
Coates, G.:Qt 2 Strs, "Mobile" Pro Viva ▲ ISPV 173
Coates, G.:Qt 4 Strs Pro Viva ▲ ISPV 173
Crumb, G.:Black Angels (Images I) Elektra/Nonesuch ▲ 79242-2-P ■ 79242-4-H
Evans, B.:Music of, w. Jim Hall (b), Eddie Gomez (gtr) Landmark ▲ LAN 1510
Glass, Philip:Company Elektra/Nonesuch ▲ 79111-2 [DDD] ■ 79111-4 (D)
Glass, Philip:Qt 2 Strs, "Company" Elektra/Nonesuch ▲ 79356-2 ■ 79356-4
Glass, Philip:Qt 3 Strs, "Mishima" Elektra/Nonesuch ▲ 79356-2 ■ 79356-4
Glass, Philip:Qt 4 Strs, "Buczak" Elektra/Nonesuch ▲ 79356-2 ■ 79356-4
Glass, Philip:Qt 5 Strs Elektra/Nonesuch ▲ 79356-2 ■ 79356-4
Górecki, H.-M.:Qt 1 Strs, "Already It Is Dusk" Elektra/Nonesuch ▲ 79319-2 ■ 79319-4
Górecki, H.-M.:Qt 2 Strs, "Quasi una fant" Elektra/Nonesuch ▲ 79319-2 ■ 79319-4
Harrison, L.:Str Qt Set CRI ■ ACS 6006
Harrison, L.:Str Qt Set *(rec 1980)* CRI ▲ CD 613 [ADD]
Hassell, J.:Pano da Costa Elektra/Nonesuch ▲ 79163-2 [DDD] ■ 79163-4 (D)
Hendrix, J.:Purple Haze Elektra/Nonesuch ▲ 79111-2 [DDD] ■ 79111-4 (D)
Ives, C.:They Are There!, w. Charles Ives (voice)—using period recording apparatus, the Kronos String Quartet teams up with the composer in his voice & piano 1942 Columbia recording
Elektra/Nonesuch ▲ 79242-2-P ■ 79242-4-H
Johnston, B.:Amazing Grace Elektra/Nonesuch ▲ 79163-2 [DDD] ■ 79163-4 (D)
Kronos Quartet:The "Singles" Elektra/Nonesuch 3-▲ 79253/5-2 3-■ 79253/5-4
Lennon, J.A.:Voices *(rec 1984)* CRI ▲ CD 599 [ADD/DDD]
Martá, I.:Doom. A Sigh Elektra/Nonesuch ▲ 79242-2-P ■ 79242-4-H
Monk, T.:Music of—w. Ron Carter (db); sels unknown Landmark ▲ LAN 1505
Nancarrow, C.:Qt Strs Elektra/Nonesuch ▲ 79111-2 [DDD] ■ 79111-4 (D)
Reich, S.:Different Trains Elektra/Nonesuch ▲ 79176-2 ■ 79176-4
Riffkin S.:Purple Haze Elektra/Nonesuch ▲ 79111-2 [DDD] ■ 79111-4 (D)
Riley, T.:Cadenza on the Night Plain Gramavision 2-▲ R22Z 79444 2-■ R42J 79444
Riley, T.:G Song Gramavision 2-▲ R22Z 79444 2-■ R42J 79444
Riley, T.:Mythic Birds Gramavision 2-▲ R22Z 79444 2-■ R42J 79444
Riley, T.:Salome Dances Elektra/Nonesuch 2-▲ 79217-2 [DDD] 2-■ 79217-4 (D)
Riley, T.:Sunrise of the Planetary Dream Collector Gramavision 2-▲ R22Z 79444 2-■ R42J 79444
Rudhyar, D.:Advent *(rec 1979)* CRI ▲ CD 604 [AAD]
Rudhyar, D.:Crisis & Overcoming CRI ▲ CD 604 [AAD]
Saariaho, K.:Nymphea Ondine ▲ Ode 804 [DDD]
Sallinen, A.:Qt 3 Strs Elektra/Nonesuch ▲ 79111-2 [DDD] ■ 79111-4 (D)
Shostakovich, D.:Qt 8 Strs Elektra/Nonesuch ▲ 79242-2-P ■ 79242-4-H
Tallis, T.:Spem in alium [multi-tracked string quartet arr.]
Elektra/Nonesuch ▲ 79242-2-P ■ 79242-4-H
Volans, K.:White Man Sleeps 1 & 5 Str Qt Elektra/Nonesuch ▲ 79163-2 [DDD] ■ 79163-4 (D)
White Man Sleeps:Music of Ornette Coleman Elektra/Nonesuch ▲ 79163-2 [DDD] ■ 79163-4 (D)
Kroumata Percussion Ensemble
Cage, J.:Amores, w. R. Pilat (prepared pno) BIS ▲ CD 272 [DDD]
Cage, J.:Second Construction BIS ▲ CD 232 [DDD]
Cage, J.:Second Construction BIS ("BIS Twins" series) 2-▲ CD 232/382 [DDD]
Cowell, H.:Pulse BIS ("BIS Twins" series) 2-▲ CD 232/382 [DDD]
Cowell, H.:Pulse BIS ▲ CD 232 [DDD]
Harrison, L.:Con 1 Fl, w. Manuela Wiesler (fl) BIS ▲ CD 272 [DDD]
Hvoslef, K.:Sextet Fl & Perc, w. M. Wiesler (fl) *(rec 3/19/89)* BIS ▲ CD 512 [DDD]
Jolivet, A.:Suite en concert, w. M. Wiesler (fl) BIS ▲ CD 272 [DDD]
Lundquist, T.I.:Sisu BIS ("BIS Twins" series) 2-▲ CD 232/382 [DDD]
Lundquist, T.I.:Sisu BIS ▲ CD 232 [DDD]
Miki, M.:Mar Spiritual, w. K. Abe (mar) BIS ▲ CD 462 [DDD]
Miyoshi, A.:Rin-sai, w. K. Abe (mar) BIS ▲ CD 462 [DDD]
Nishimura, A.:Kala, w. K. Abe (mar) BIS ▲ CD 462 [DDD]
Nørgård, P.:Square and Round *(rec 5/91)* BIS ▲ CD 512 [DDD]

Kroumata Percussion Ensemble (cont.)
Orff, C.:Carmina burana, w. Lena Nordin (sop), Hans Dornbusch (ten), Peter Mattei (bar), Love Derwinger (pno), Roland Pöntinen (pno), Cecilia Rydinger Alin (cnd), Allmänna Sången, Uppsala Choir School Children's Chorus [chamber version] *(rec Uppsala Univ Hall, Uppsala, Sweden, June 9–11, 1995)* BIS ▲ CD 734 [DDD]
Play Works for Marimba & Percussion, w. Keiko Abe (perc) BIS ▲ CD 462 [DDD]
Sandström, S.-D.:Drums BIS ▲ CD 272 [DDD]
Sandström, S.-D.:Free Music, w. M. Wiesler (fl) BIS ▲ CD 512 [DDD]
Taïra, Y.:Hiérophonie V BIS ▲ CD 232 [DDD]
Taïra, Y.:Hiérophonie V BIS ("BIS Twins" series) 2-▲ CD 232/382 [DDD]
Takemitsu, T.:Rain Tree BIS ▲ CD 462 [DDD]
Wallin, R.:Stonewave *(rec 5/91)* BIS ▲ CD 512 [DDD]
H. Farberman (cnd)
Shchedrin, R.:Carmen, Helsingborg SO BIS ("BIS Twins" series) 2-▲ CD 232/382 [DDD]
Shchedrin, R.:Carmen, Helsingborg SO BIS ▲ CD 382 [DDD]
P. Järvi (cnd)
Jolivet, A.:Fl Music (comp), w. Manuela Wiesler (fl), Erica Goodman (hp), Patrik Swedrup (vn), Håkan Olsson (va), Helena Nilsson (vc), Christian Davidsson (bn), Roland Pöntinen (pno), Tapiola Sinfonietta—Alla rustica for Fl & Hp; Chant de Linos for Fl, Hp & Str Trio; Pastorales de Noël for Fl, Bn & Hp; Con for Fl & Strs; Suite en concert for Fl & 4 Perc Players; Fant-Caprice for Fl & Pno; Cabrioles for Fl & Pno *(rec Danderyd Grammar School, Sweden, Tapiola Hall, Tapiola, Finland, Gothenburg Concert Hall, Sweden & Studio 2, Radiohuset, Stockholm, Sweden)* BIS ▲ CD 739 [DDD]
A. Loguin (cnd)
Blomdahl, K.-B.:Chamber Con, w. Kerstin Jansson (pno), Kroumata (perc), Falu Woodwind Quintet, Omnibus Chamber Winds Caprice ▲ CAP 21355 [DDD]
Eliasson, A.:Sotto il segno del sole, Falu Woodwind Quintet, Omnibus Chamber Winds
Caprice ▲ CAP 21355 [DDD]
Messiaen, O.:Oiseaux exotiques, w. Kerstin Jansson (pno), Falu Woodwind Quintet, Omnibus Chamber Winds Caprice ▲ CAP 21355 [DDD]
Xenakis, I.:Pleiades BIS ▲ CD 482 [AAD/DDD]
Kroumata Percussion Ensemble [Ingvar Hallgren (perc), Jan Hellgren (perc), Anders Holdar (perc), Martin Steisner (perc)]
Cage, J.:Second Construction *(rec Gothenburg Concert Hall, Sweden, Mar 26, 1983)*
BIS ▲ CD 52 [AAD]
Kubín String Quartet [Ludek Cap (vn), Jan Niederle (vn), Pavel Vítek (va), Jiří Zedníček (vc)]
Novák, V.:Qt Strs, Op. 35 *(rec Ostrava Radio Studio, Czech Republic, June 12 & 13 & Nov. 27, 1)*
Centaur ▲ CRC 2191 [DDD]
Novák, V.:Qnt Pno, w. Jiří Skovajsa (pno) *(rec Ostrava Radio Studio, Czech Republic, June 12 & 13 & Nov. 27, 1)* Centaur ▲ CRC 2191 [DDD]
Paul Kuentz CO
P. Kuentz (cnd)
Handel, G.F.:Con Hp, w. N. Zabaleta (hp) Deutsche Grammophon ▲ 427206-2 [AAD]
La harpe du siècle:Hommage a Nicanor Zabaleta, w. Nicanor Zabaleta (hp), Berlin PO [cnd:Ernst Märzendorfer], Berlin RSO Deutsche Grammophon ("Double" series) 2-▲ 439693-2
Vivaldi, A.:Con Lt, w. N. Yepes (gtr)
Deutsche Grammophon ("Resonance" series) ▲ 429528-2 [ADD] ■ 429528-4
Vivaldi, A.:Con Mand, RV.425, w. T. Ochi (mand), S. Ochi (mand)
Deutsche Grammophon ("Resonance" series) ▲ 429528-2 [ADD] ■ 429528-4
Vivaldi, A.:Con for 2 Mands, w. T. Ochi (mand), S. Ochi (mand)
Deutsche Grammophon ("Resonance" series) ▲ 429528-2 [ADD] ■ 429528-4
Vivaldi, A.:Con Va d'amore Lt, w. M. Frasca-Colombier (vn), N. Yepes (gtr)
Deutsche Grammophon ("Resonance" series) ▲ 429528-2 [ADD] ■ 429528-4

Paul Kuentz Orch
Modern Favourites, w. Frasca-Colombier, Monique (vn), Pual Kuentz Orch [cnd:Paul Kuentz]
Pierre Verany ▲ PVY 730072
P. Kuentz (cnd)
Bach, J.S.:Magnificat, BWV 243, w. Hélène Obadia (sop), Brigitte Vinson (sop), Madeleine Jalabert (alt), Hervé Lamy (ten), Philip Langshaw (bass), Paul Kuentz Choir Pierre Verany ▲ PVY 730048
Bach, J.S.:Mass in b, BWV 232, w. Hélène Obadia (sop), Madeleine Jalbert (alt), Adrian Brand (ten), Paul Gay (bass), Eric Aubier (tpt), Paul Kuentz Choir Pierre Verany ▲ PVY 730060 [DDD]
Bach, J.S.:St. John Passion, w. Barbara Schlick (sop), Ingeborg Most (alt), Edrian Brand (ten), Alexander Stevenson (ten), Philip Langshaw (bass), Peter Lika (bass), Paul Kuentz Choir
Pierre Verany 2-▲ PVY 730051 [DDD]
Charpentier, M.-A.:Te Deum in C, w. Paul Kuentz Choir Pierre Verany ▲ PVY 730048
Handel, G.F.:Messiah (sels), w. Barbara Schlick (sop), Jean Nirouet (ct), Alexander Stevenson (ten), Philip Langshaw (bass), Paul Kuentz Choir Pierre Verany ▲ PVY 730045
Handel, G.F.:Water Music (comp) Pierre Verany ▲ PVY 730047
Mozart, W.A.:Missa, K.317, w. Mechtild Georg (sop), Barbara Schlick (sop), Alexander Stevenson (ten), Philip Langshaw (bass), Paul Kuentz Choir Pierre Verany ▲ PVY 730041
Mozart, W.A.:Zauberflöte, w. Birgit Been (sop), Nathalie Boiccy (cop), Marianne Seibel (sop), Renate Springer (sop), Elizabeth Vidal (sop), Eleanor James (mez), Salvador Guzman (ten), Herbert Hechenberger (ten), Wolfgang Newmann (ten), Klaus Häger (bass), Philip Langshaw (bass), Hans-Georg Moser (bass), Francis Bardot (cnd), Maitrise des Hauts-de-Seine members, Paul Kuentz Choirs
Pierre Verany 2-▲ PVY 730055 [DDD]
Orff, C.:Carmina burana, w. Elisabeth Vidal (sop), Alexander Stevensen (ten), André Cognet (bass), Paul Kuentz Choir, Mouez Armor Chorale, Lorient Conservatory Chorus, Notre Dame College Chorus
Pierre Verany ▲ PVY 730044
Saint-Saëns, C.:Allegro appassionato, w. J.-M. Gamard (vc) Pierre Verany ▲ PVY 730053 [DDD]
Saint-Saëns, C.:Con 1 Vc, w. J.-M. Gamard (vc) Pierre Verany ▲ PVY 730053 [DDD]
Schumann, R.:Con Vc, w. Jean-Marie Gamard (vc) Pierre Verany ▲ PVY 730053 [DDD]
Telemann, G.P.:Cons Ob d'amore, w. Gildas Prado (ob)—in A Pierre Verany ▲ PVY 730046
Telemann, G.P.:Con Rcr, Fl, w. Jean-Marc Labylle (rcr), Régis Manceau (fl)
Pierre Verany ▲ PVY 730046
Telemann, G.P.:Suite Rcr, w. Jean-Marc Labylle (rcr) Pierre Verany ▲ PVY 730046
Telemann, G.P.:Water Music Pierre Verany ▲ PVY 730046
Verdi, G.:Requiem Mass, w. Mariana Slavova (sop), Joke Kramer (mez), Alexander Stevenson (ten), Peter Lika (bass), Paul Kuentz Choir Pierre Verany 2-▲ PVY 730054 [DDD]
Vivaldi, A.:Cons Diverse Instrs, w. Sylvia Ochi (man), Takashi Ochi (man), Jean-Marc Labylle (pic), Monique Frasca-Colombier (vn), Laurence Paugam (vn)—in G for 2 Man; in C for Rcr; in B♭ for Bn [La notte]; in d for Vl; in a for Bn; in A for Vn & other Vns in echo Pierre Verany ▲ PVY 730052 [DDD]
Vivaldi, A.:Cons for 2 Vns Pierre Verany 2-▲ PVY 730071
Vivaldi, A.:Nisi Dominus, w. Jean Nirouët (alt) Pierre Verany ▲ PVY 730043
Vivaldi, A.:Stabat Mater Cta, w. Jean Nirouët (alt) Pierre Verany ▲ PVY 730043
Kuhlau Flute Quartet
Nørholm, I.:Chamber Music, w. B. Rørbeck (vn), J. Christiansen (gtr), N. Ullner (vc), P. Salo (pno/hpd), G. Sørensen (perc)—Before Silence, Op. 83; Contrast-Continuum, Op. 70; Guitar Sonata No. 2; The Orthodox Dream; So to Say, Op. 74; Turbulens-Laminar, Op. 93; Variants, Op. 19 *(rec 9/90)*
Kontrapunkt ▲ 32065 [DDD]
Reicha, A.:Fl Music—Three Romances, Op. 21; Variations in D, Op. 20 *(for two flutes)*; Trio in D, Op. 26 *(for three flutes)*; Sinfonico in D, Op. 12; Harmonique imitée, Op. 18; Quatuor in G, Op. 27 *(for four flutes)* Kontrapunkt ▲ 32045 [DDD]
Kuhmo Chamber Soloists
Franck, C.:Qnt Pno Ondine ▲ ODE 788-2 [DDD]
Franck, C.:Solo de Pno Ondine ▲ ODE 788-2 [DDD]
Kuhmo Virtuosi
Haydn, J.:Con Org, Vn & Strs, H.XVIII/6, w. Ralf Góthoni (pno), Péter Csaba (vn) Ondine ODE 810
Mendelssohn, F.:Con in d Vn, Pno & Strs, w. P. Csaba (vn), R.A. Gothoni (pno)
Ondine ▲ ODE 810 [DDD]

ORCH. & ENS.

Kuhmo Virtuosi (cont.)
P. Csaba (cnd)
Sibelius, J.:Andante festivo Ondine ▲ ODE 830 [DDD]
Sibelius, J.:Canzonetta Ondine ▲ ODE 830 [DDD]
Sibelius, J.:Humoresques—Nos. 3 & 4 Ondine ▲ ODE 830 [DDD]
Sibelius, J.:Impromptu Strs Ondine ▲ ODE 830 [DDD]
Sibelius, J.:Rakastava Strs Ondine ▲ ODE 830 [DDD]
Sibelius, J.:Romance Strs Ondine ▲ ODE 830 [DDD]
Sibelius, J.:Suite caractéristique Ondine ▲ ODE 830 [DDD]
Sibelius, J.:Suite champêtre Ondine ▲ ODE 830 [DDD]
Kuijken Consort
Telemann, G.P.:Cants Accent ▲ 77912 [DDD]
Kuijken Consort [W. Kuijken (vl), A. Pols (vl), M. Tindemans (fid), A. Glat (vl), K. Junghänel (thb)]
Buxtehude, D.:Muss der Tod denn nun doch trennen, w. R. Jacobs (ct) Accent ▲ 77912 [DDD]
Kuijken Consort [W. Kuijken (vl), A. Pols (vl), M. Tindemans (fid), A. Glat (vl), M. Aerts (vle), K. Junghänel (thb), R. Kohnen (org)]
Bach, Joh. Christoph:Ach, dass ich Wassers genug hätte, w. R. Jacobs (ct) Accent ▲ 77912 [DDD]
Kuijken Consort [W. Kuijken (vl), A. Pols (vl), M. Tindemans (fid), A. Glat (vl), R. Kohnen (org)]
Buxtehude, D.:Jubilate Domino, omnis terra, w. R. Jacobs (ct) Accent ▲ 77912 [DDD]
Kuijken String Quartet [Sigiswald Kuijken (vn), François Fernandez (vn), Marleen Thiers (va), Wieland Kuijken (vc)]
Haydn, J.:The Seven Last Words of Christ on the Cross *(rec Doopsgezinde-Kerk, Haarlem, The Netherlands, Oct. 17–20, 1994)* Denon ▲ DEN 78973 [DDD]
Mozart, W.A.:Qts Strs (misc)—Nos. 14–19, "Haydn Quartets" *(rec 1990–92)* Denon/PCM Digital 3-▲ CO 75850/52 [DDD]
Mozart, W.A.:Qnt Strs, K.515, w. Ryo Terakado (va) Denon ▲ DEN 78850 [DDD]
Mozart, W.A.:Qnt Strs, K.516, w. Ryo Terakado (va) Denon ▲ DEN 78850 [DDD]
Kungliga Hovkapellet
K. Ingebretsen (cnd)
Börtz, D.:Bacchanterna, w. Sylvia Lindenstrand (mez), Peter Mattei (bar) [soundtrack to the T.V. production] Caprice 2-▲ CAP 22028
S. Westerberg (cnd)
Berwald, F.:I Enter a Monastery Sterling ▲ CDS 1009 2 [AAD/DDD]
Kraus, J.M.:Prosperin Sterling ▲ CDS 1009 2 [AAD/DDD]
Norman, L.:Festive Ov Sterling ▲ CDS 1009 2 [AAD/DDD]
Randel, A.:The People from Värmland Sterling ▲ CDS 1009 2 [AAD/DDD]
Söderman, A.:The Devil's 1st Tentative Efforts Sterling ▲ CDS 1009 2 [AAD/DDD]
Kyndel String Quartet
Rosenberg, H.:Qt 1 Strs Caprice ▲ CAP 21352 [AAD]
The String Quartet in Sweden:A Cavalcade of Its History, w. Barkel String Quartet, Stockholm String Quartet, Garaguly String Quartet, Ivan Ericson String Quartet, Grünfarb String Quartet, Skåne String Quartet, Hälsingborg String Quartet, Göteborg String Quartet, Galli String Quartet *(rec before 1951)* Caprice 5-▲ CAP 21506 [AAD/ADD]
I. Yinon (cnd)
Schulhoff, E.:Con Str Qt, Czech State PO Koch Schwann ▲ SCH 315432 [DDD]
Labyrinto [Paolo Pandolfo (vl), Guido Balestracci (vl), Juan Manuel Quintana (vl), Alba Fresno (vl), Eduardo Eguez (thb/lt/pandora/gtr)]
Hume, T.:Captain Humes Poeticall Musicke, w. Emma Kirkby (sop) *(rec Dec 1995)* Glossa ▲ GCD 920402 [DDD]
Hume, T.:The First Part of Ayres, w. Emma Kirkby (sop) *(rec Dec 1995)* Glossa ▲ GCD 920402 [DDD]
Labyrinto Ensemble di Viole
Schmelzer, J.H.:Balletti, w. Aurora Ensemble—Nos. 3, 4, 5, 6, 8, 7 & 9 *(rec May 19–22, 1991)* Symphonia ▲ SY 91S07
Schmelzer, J.H.:Duodena selectarum sonatarum, w. Aurora Ensemble—Nos. 4, 6, 10, 11 & 12 *(rec May 19–22, 1991)* Symphonia ▲ SY 91S07
Schmelzer, J.H.:Die Fechtschule, w. Aurora Ensemble—Nos. 3, 4, 5, 6, 8, 7 & 9 *(rec May 19–22, 1991)* Symphonia ▲ SY 91S07
Schmelzer, J.H.:Sacro-profanus concentus musicus, w. Aurora Ensemble—Nos. 3, 4, 5, 6, 8, 7 & 9 *(rec May 19–22, 1991)* Symphonia ▲ SY 91S07
Schmelzer, J.H.:Serenata con altre arie; amento sopra la morte Ferdinandi III, w. Aurora Ensemble—Nos. 3, 4, 5, 6, 8, 7 & 9 *(rec May 19–22, 1991)* Symphonia ▲ SY 91S07
Lafayette String Quartet [Ann Elliott-Goldschmid (vn), Sharon Stanis (vn), Joanna Hood (va), Pamela Highbaugh Aloni (vc)]
Borodin, A.:Qt 2 Strs *(rec Troy Savings Bank Music Hall, Troy, NY, Feb. 1994)* Dorian ▲ DOR 90203 [DDD]
Dvořák, A.:Qnt Pno, Op. 5, w. Antonin Kubalek (pno) *(rec Troy Savings Bank Music Hall, Troy, NY, Apr 1995)* Dorian ▲ DOR 90221 [DDD]
Dvořák, A.:Qnt Pno, Op. 81, w. Antonin Kubalek (pno) *(rec Troy Savings Bank Music Hall, Troy, NY, Apr 1995)* Dorian ▲ DOR 90221 [DDD]
Shostakovich, D.:Preludes & Fugues Str Qt Dorian ▲ DOR 90163 [DDD]
Shostakovich, D.:Qt 3 Strs *(rec Troy Savings Bank Music Hall, Troy, NY, Feb. 1994)* Dorian ▲ DOR 90203 [DDD]
Shostakovich, D.:Qt 8 Strs Dorian ▲ DOR 90163 [DDD]
Stravinsky, I.:Pieces Str Qt *(rec Troy Savings Bank Music Hall, Troy, NY, Feb. 1994)* Dorian ▲ DOR 90203 [DDD]
Tchaikovsky, P.:Qt 1 Strs Dorian ▲ DOR 90163 [DDD]
Lahti Chamber Ensemble
O. Vänskä (cnd)
Gubaidulina, S.:Con Bn, w. H. Ahmas (bn) *(rec Aug. 16–19, 1993)* BIS ▲ CD 636 [DDD]
Gubaidulina, S.:Concordanza *(rec Aug. 16–19, 1993)* BIS ▲ CD 636 [DDD]
Gubaidulina, S.:Detto 2 Vc, w. I. Pälli (vc) *(rec Aug. 16–19, 1993)* BIS ▲ CD 636 [DDD]
Kaipainen, J.:Starlit Night, w. K. Mattila (sop) [Fin] Ondine ▲ ODE 792-2 [DDD]
Klami, U.:Rag-Time & Blues Ondine ▲ ODE 792-2 [DDD]
Meriläinen, U.:Metamorfora per 7 Ondine ▲ ODE 792-2 [DDD]
Nielsen, C.:Serenata in vano Ondine ▲ ODE 792-2 [DDD]
Strauss, R.:Till Eulenspiegels lustige Streiche [arr. by Franz Hasenöhrl for violin, double bass, clarinet, bassoon & horn] Ondine ▲ ODE 792-2 [DDD]
Lahti SO
E. Klas (cnd)
Opera Arias, w. Matti Salminen (bass) BIS ▲ CD 520 [DDD]
U. Söderblom (cnd)
Hindemith, P.:Das Marienleben, w. Karita Mattila (sop) Finlandia ▲ FIN 99403 [DDD]
Hindemith, P.:Das Marienleben, w. Karita Mattila (sop), Savonlinna Opera Festival Chorus *(rec Dec. 1987 & May 1988)* Finlandia ▲ 4509-95857-2 [DDD]
Kokkonen, J.:...durch einen Spiegel... BIS ▲ CD 528 [DDD]
Kokkonen, J.:The Hades of the Birds, w. M. Groop (mez) [Fin] BIS ▲ CD 485 [DDD]
Kokkonen, J.:Music for Str Orch BIS ▲ CD 485 [DDD]
Kokkonen, J.:Opus sonorum, w. I. Sivonen (pno) BIS ▲ CD 508 [DDD]
Kokkonen, J.:Requiem (in memoriam Maija Kokkonen), w. S. Isokoski (sop), W. Grönroos (bar), Savonlinna Opera Festival Chorus [L] BIS ▲ CD 508 [DDD]
Kokkonen, J.:Sym 1 BIS ▲ CD 485 [DDD]
Kokkonen, J.:Sym 3 BIS ▲ CD 508 [DDD]
Merikanto, A.:Genesis, w. Karita Mattila (sop), Savonlinna Opera Festival Chorus *(rec Dec. 1987 & May 1988)* Finlandia ▲ 4509-95857-2 [DDD]
Sallinen, A.:Dream Songs, w. K. Mattila (sop), Savonlinna Opera Festival Chorus *(rec Dec. 1987 & May 1988)* Finlandia ▲ 4509-95857-2 [DDD]
Sallinen, A.:Dream Songs, w. Karita Mattila (sop) Finlandia ▲ FIN 99403 [DDD]

Lahti SO (cont.)
O. Vänskä (cnd)
Aho, K.:Con Vc, w. Gary Hoffman (vc) *(rec Ristinkirkko, Lahti, Finland, Sept. 7–8, 1993)* BIS ▲ CD 706 [DDD]
Aho, K.:Con Vn, w. M. Gräsbeck (vn) BIS ▲ CD 396 [DDD]
Aho, K.:Pergamon, w. L. Paasikivi (nar), E.-L. Saarinen (nar), T. Nyman (nar), M. Lehtinen (nar), P. Pietiläinen (org) *(rec Lahti, Finland, May 23–25, 1994)* BIS ▲ CD 646 [DDD]
Aho, K.:Silence, w. M. Gräsbeck (vn) BIS ▲ CD 396 [DDD]
Aho, K.:Sym 1 BIS ▲ CD 396 [DDD]
Aho, K.:Sym 8, w. H.-O. Ericsson (org) *(rec Lahti, Finland, May 23–25, 1994)* BIS ▲ CD 646 [DDD]
Aho, K.:Sym 9, w. Christian Lindberg (trbn) *(rec Ristinkirkko, Lahti, Finland, Jan. 9, 1995)* BIS ▲ CD 706 [DDD]
Bashmakov, L.:Impressioni marine, w. Petri Alanko (pic/fl/a fl/b fl) *(rec Church of the Cross, Lahti, Finland, Aug 8–11, 1995)* BIS ▲ CD 687 [DDD]
Crusell, B.H.:Con 1 Cl, w. K. Leister (cl) BIS ▲ CD 345
Crusell, B.H.:Con 2 Cl, w. K. Leister (cl) BIS ▲ CD 345
Crusell, B.H.:Con 3 Cl, w. K. Leister (cl) BIS ▲ CD 345
Englund, S.E.:The White Reindeer BIS ▲ CD 575 [DDD]
Finlandia:A Festival of Finnish Music BIS ▲ CD 575 [DDD]
Klami, U.:Lemminkäinen *(rec Dec. 14–15, 1993)* BIS ▲ CD 656 [DDD]
Klami, U.:Song of Lake Kūjärvi, w. Esa Ruuttunen (bar) *(rec Dec. 14–15, 1993)* BIS ▲ CD 656 [DDD]
Klami, U.:Whirls (ballet suites 1 & 2) *(rec Dec. 14–15, 1993)* BIS ▲ CD 656 [DDD]
Kokkonen, J.:Con Vc, w. T. Thedéen (vc) BIS ▲ CD 468 [DDD]
Kokkonen, J.:Erekhtheion, w. S. Vihavainen (sop), W. Grönroos (bar), Academic Choral Society [Fin] BIS ▲ CD 498 [DDD]
Kokkonen, J.:Inauguratio BIS ▲ CD 498 [DDD]
Kokkonen, J.:The Last Temptations (interludes) BIS ▲ CD 498 [DDD]
Kokkonen, J.:Il Paesaggio BIS ▲ CD 528 [DDD]
Kokkonen, J.:Sinf da camera BIS ▲ CD 528 [DDD]
Kokkonen, J.:Symphonic Sketches BIS ▲ CD 468 [DDD]
Kokkonen, J.:Sym 2 BIS ▲ CD 498 [DDD]
Kokkonen, J.:Sym 4 BIS ▲ CD 468
Marttinen, T.:Con espagnole, w. Petri Alanko (fl/a fl) *(rec Church of the Cross, Lahti, Finland, Aug 8–11, 1995)* BIS ▲ CD 687 [DDD]
Marttinen, T.:Con Vn, w. Pekka Kauppinen (vn) *(rec Ristinkirkko, Church of the Cross, Lahti, Finland, Sept. 12–15, 1994)* BIS ▲ CD 701 [DDD]
Marttinen, T.:Sym 1 *(rec Ristinkirkko, Church of the Cross, Lahti, Finland, Sept. 12–15, 1994)* BIS ▲ CD 701 [DDD]
Marttinen, T.:Sym 8 *(rec Ristinkirkko, Church of the Cross, Lahti, Finland, Sept. 12–15, 1994)* BIS ▲ CD 701 [DDD]
Raitio, V.:The Swans BIS ▲ CD 575 [DDD]
Rautavaara, E.:Cantus Arcticus [utilizing the composer's taped birdsongs] BIS ▲ CD 575 [DDD]
Rautavaara, E.:Dances with the Winds, w. Petri Alanko (pic/fl/a fl/b fl) *(rec Church of the Cross, Lahti, Finland, Aug 8–11, 1995)* BIS ▲ CD 687 [DDD]
Sallinen, A.:Chamber Music II, w. Petri Alanko (a fl) *(rec Church of the Cross, Lahti, Finland, Aug 8–11, 1995)* BIS ▲ CD 687 [DDD]
Sibelius, J.:Belshazzar's Feast (incidental), w. Lilli Paasikivi (mez) *(rec Church of the Cross, Lahti, Finland, Jan 11–13, 1995)* BIS ▲ CD-735 [DDD]
Sibelius, J.:Con Vn, w. L. Kavakos (vn) BIS ▲ CD 500 [DDD]
Sibelius, J.:Con Vn, w. Leonidas Kavakos (vn), (original 1903/04 version) BIS ("BIS Twins" series) 2-▲ CD 500/581
Sibelius, J.:The Countess's Portrait *(rec Church of the Cross, Lahti, Finland, May 8, 1995)* BIS ▲ CD-735 [DDD]
Sibelius, J.:Everyman, w. Lilli Paasikivi (mez), Petri Lehto (ten), Sauli Tiilikainen (bar), Leena Saarenpää (pno), Pauli Pietiläinen (org), Lahti Chamber Choir *(rec Church of the Cross, Lahti, Finland, Jan 11–13, 1995)* BIS ▲ CD-735 [DDD]
Sibelius, J.:Finlandia BIS ▲ CD 575 [DDD]
Sibelius, J.:The Lonely Ski Trail, w. Lasse Pöysti (nar) *(rec Church of the Cross, Lahti, Finland, Jan 8–12, 1996)* BIS ▲ CD 815 [DDD]
Sibelius, J.:En Saga—original 1892 version *(rec Church of the Cross, Lahti, Finland, May 10, 1995)* BIS ▲ CD 800 [DDD]
Sibelius, J.:Suite Vn Strs, w. Dong-Suk Kang (vn) BIS ▲ CD 575 [DDD]
Sibelius, J.:Swanwhite (incidental), w. Sakari Tepponen (vn), Pauli Pietiläinen (org) *(rec Church of the Cross, Lahti, Finland, Jan 8–12, 1996)* BIS ▲ CD 815 [DDD]
Sibelius, J.:Sym 5—original 1915 version *(rec Church of the Cross, Lahti, Finland, May 11–12, 1995)* BIS ▲ CD 800 [DDD]
Sibelius, J.:The Tempest, w. Lahti Opera Chorus BIS ("BIS Twins" series) 2-▲ CD 500/581
Sibelius, J.:The Wood Nymph Nar, w. Lasse Pöysti (nar), Harri Karri (pno) *(rec Church of the Cross, Lahti, Finland, Jan 8–12, 1996)* BIS ▲ CD 815 [DDD]
Sibelius, J.:The Wood Nymph (tone poem), w. Timo Keinonen (vc) *(rec Church of the Cross, Lahti, Finland, Jan 8–12, 1996)* BIS ▲ CD 815 [DDD]
Lajtha String Quartet
Arensky, A.:Qt 1 Strs *(rec Rottenbiller Street Studio, Budapest, Jan. 16–22, 1994)* Marco Polo ▲ 8.223811 [DDD]
Arensky, A.:Qt 2 Strs *(rec Rottenbiller Street Studio, Budapest, Jan. 16–22, 1994)* Marco Polo ▲ 8.223811 [DDD]
Arensky, A.:Qnt Pno, w. Ilona Prunyi (pno) *(rec Rottenbiller Street Studio, Budapest, Jan. 16–22, 1994)* Marco Polo ▲ 8.223811 [DDD]
Goldmark, K.:Qnt Strs, Op. 9, w. L. Mezo (vc) Hungaroton ▲ HCD 31556
Goldmark, K.:Qnt Strs, Op. 30, w. L. Mezo (vc) Hungaroton ▲ HCD 31556
Lake Forest SO
P.A. McRae (cnd)
Rachmaninoff, S.:Con 3 Pno, w. Santiago Rodriguez (pno) Élan ▲ CD 82262 [DDD]
Lamoureux Concerts Orch
J.-P. Jacquillat (cnd)
Chausson, E.:Chanson perpétuelle, w. A. Esposito (sop) EMI Classics ▲ CDM 64365
Chausson, E.:Poème de l'amour et de la mer, w. V. de los Angeles (sop) EMI Classics ▲ CDM 64365
O. Klemperer (cnd)
Mendelssohn, F.:Sym 4 Enterprise ("Documents" series) ▲ ENT LV 939 [ADD]
Schubert, Franz:Sym 4 Enterprise ("Documents" series) ▲ ENT LV 939 [ADD]
I. Markevitch (cnd)
Beethoven, L. van:Coriolan Ov Theorema ▲ TH 121219
Beethoven, L. van:Fidelio (ov) Theorema ▲ TH 121219
Beethoven, L. van:Leonore 3 Theorema ▲ TH 121219
Beethoven, L. van:Sym 5 Theorema ▲ TH 121219
Beethoven, L. van:Die Weihe des Hauses (ov) Theorema ▲ TH 121219
Falla, M. de:Noches en los jardines de España, w. C. Haskil (pno) *(rec 1960)* Philips ("Spanish" series) ▲ 432829-2 [ADD]
Y. Sado (cnd)
Quand on n'a que l'amour, w. F. Pollet (sop), Bruno Fontaine (pno) Accord ▲ ACD 205522 [DDD]
Lamoureux Concerts Orch members
Chausson, E.:Con Vn, Pno & Str Qt, w. C. Ferras (vn), P. Barbizet (pno) EMI Classics ▲ CDM 64365
Lamoureux Orch
E. Bigot (cnd)
Bach, J.S.:Con 2 Vn, w. R. Ricci (vn) One-Eleven ▲ URS 50050 [ADD]
Bartók, B.:Con 2 Pno, w. A. Foldes (pno) *(rec 1948)* Jecklin-Disco ▲ JD 648-2 [ADD]
Bartók, B.:Rhap Pno, w. A. Foldes (pno) *(rec 1948)* Jecklin-Disco ▲ JD 648-2 [ADD]
Paganini, N.:Con 1 Vn, w. R. Ricci (vn) One-Eleven ▲ URS 50050 [ADD]
Ravel, M.:Tzigane, w. R. Ricci (vn) One-Eleven ▲ URS 50050 [ADD]

▲ = CD ♦ = Enhanced CD Δ = MD ▮ = Cassette Tape ▯ = DCC

Lamoureux Orch (cont.)
E. Bigot (cnd) (cont.)
Saint-Saëns, C.:Con 3 Vn, w. R. Ricci (vn) One-Eleven ▲ URS 50050 [ADD]
J. Fournet (cnd)
Bizet, G.:Les Pêcheurs de perles, w. P. Alerie (sgr), L. Simoneau (ten), X. Depraz (bass) *(rec 1953)* Philips 2-▲ 434782-2
Debussy, C.:Pelléas et Mélisande, w. J. Micheau (sop), R. Gorr (mez), C. Maurane (bar), M. Roux (bar), X. Depraz (bass) *(rec 1953* Philips 2-▲ 434783-2
J.-P. Jacquillat (cnd)
Canteloube, J.:Songs of Auvergne, w. V. de los Angeles (sop) EMI Classics (Studio) ▲ CDM 63178 [ADD]
L. Maazel (cnd)
Rimsky-Korsakov, N.:Capriccio espagnol, w. Berlin PO Deutsche Grammophon ("Double" series) 2-▲ 437946-2
Rimsky-Korsakov, N.:Golden Cockerel (suite), w. Berlin PO Deutsche Grammophon ("Double" series) 2-▲ 437946-2
Rimsky-Korsakov, N.:A May Night (ov), w. Berlin PO Deutsche Grammophon ("Double" series) 2-▲ 437946-2
Rimsky-Korsakov, N.:Russian Easter Festival, w. Berlin PO Deutsche Grammophon ("Double" series) 2-▲ 437946-2
I. Markevitch (cnd)
Auber, D.-F.:La muette de Portici (ov) Deutsche Grammophon ("The Originals" series) ▲ 447406-2
Berlioz, H.:Sym fantastique Deutsche Grammophon ("The Originals" series) ▲ 447406-2
Boulanger, L.:Du fond de l'abîme, w. Oralia Dominguez (ct), Raymond Amade (ten), J. J. Grunenwald (org), Elisabeth Brasseur Chorale *(rec Salle Pleyel, Paris)* Everest ▲ EVC 9034 [AAD]
Boulanger, L.:Psalm 24, w. J. J. Grunenwald (org), Elisabeth Brasseur Chorale *(rec Salle Pleyel, Paris)* Everest ▲ EVC 9034 [AAD]
Boulanger, L.:Psalm 129, w. Pierre Mollet (bar), Elisabeth Brasseur Chorale *(rec Salle Pleyel, Paris)* Everest ▲ EVC 9034 [AAD]
Boulanger, L.:Vieille prière bouddhique, w. Michel Sénéchal (ten), Elisabeth Brasseur Chorale *(rec Salle Pleyel, Paris)* Everest ▲ EVC 9034 [AAD]
Cherubini, L.:Anacréon (ov) Deutsche Grammophon ("The Originals" series) ▲ 447406-2
J. Martinon (cnd)
Bruch, M.:Kol Nidrei, w. P. Fournier (vc) Deutsche Grammophon ("Resonance" series) ▲ 429155-2 [ADD]
Lalo, E.:Con Vc, w. Pierre Fournier (vc) Deutsche Grammophon ("Double" series) 2-▲ 437371-2
20th Century Flute Masterpieces, w. J.-P. Rampal (fl), R. Veyron-Lacroix (hpd) Erato 2-▲ 45839-2 [ADD]
M. Ravel (cnd)
Ravel, M.:Boléro *(rec Paris, 1930)* Pearl ▲ PEA 9927 (m) [AAD]
Ravel, M.:Boléro *(rec Paris, 1930)* Music & Arts ▲ CD 703-1 [AAD]
Ravel, M.:Con in G Pno, w. M. Long (pno) *(rec 1932 for Columbia)* Pearl ▲ PEA 9927 (m) [AAD]
A. Wolff (cnd)
Ravel, M.:La Valse *(rec Paris, 1929)* Music & Arts ▲ CD 703-1 [AAD]
Lamoureux Orch members
I. Markevitch (cnd)
Boulanger, L.:Pie Jesu, w. Alain Fauqueur (boy sop), J. J. Grunenwald (org) *(rec Salle Pleyel, Paris)* Everest ▲ EVC 9034 [AAD]

Gordon Langford Trio
The King's Singers, w. King's Singers Chandos ("Collect" series) ▲ CHAN 6562 [ADD]
Lanier Trio [Cary Lewis (pno), William Preucil (vn), Dorothy Lewis (vc)]
Adler, S.:Aeolus, God of the Winds, w. Loren Kitt (cl) Gasparo ▲ GS 298 [DDD/DAD]
Dvořák, A.:Trios Pno, Opp. 21, 26, 65, 90 Gasparo 2-▲ GS 291/92
Paulus, S.:Life Motifs Gasparo ▲ GS 301 [DDD]
Paulus, S.:Music of the Night Gasparo ▲ GS 301 [DDD]
Lanier Trio members [Dorothy Lewis (vc), Cary Lewis (pno)]
Paulus, S.:Air on Seurat Gasparo ▲ GS 301 [DDD]
Paulus, S.:American Vignettes Gasparo ▲ GS 301 [DDD]
Lanier Trio members [William Preucil (va), Cary Lewis (pno)]
Paulus, S.:Seven for the Flowers Near the River Gasparo ▲ GS 301 [DDD]
Lanterly Ensemble
Luneburg 1647, w. Mona Spagele (sop), Werner Buchin (alt), Albrecht Pohl (bass) MD + G ▲ MDG CD 6050647

Laredo Instrumental Ensemble
Ramirez, A.:Misa Criolla, w. J. Carreras (ten), A. Ramirez (kbd), J. L. Ocejo (cnd), Bilbao Choral Society, Laredo Choral Salvé Philips ("Digital Classics" series) ▲ 420955-2 [DDD] □ 420955-5
Ramirez, A.:Navidad en Verano, w. J. Carreras (ten), A. Ramirez (kbd), J. L. Ocejo (cnd), Bilbao Choral Society, Laredo Choral Salvé Philips ("Digital Classics" series) ▲ 420955-2 [DDD] □ 420955-5
Ramirez, A.:Navidad nuestra, w. J. Carreras (ten), A. Ramirez (kbd). J. L. Ocejo (cnd), Bilbao Choral Society, Laredo Choral Salvé Philips ("Digital Classics" series) ▲ 420955-2 [DDD] □ 420955-5
Large Chamber Ensemble
Bryars, G.:Four Elements, w. R. Heaton ECM New Series ▲ 78118-21533-2 [DDD]
Large SO
M. Legrand (cnd)
Legrand, M.:Film Music, w. Catherine Michel (hp), Michel Legrand (hpd)—Suite for Hp & Orch [from The Umbrellas of Cherbourg]; Concertino for Hp & Orch [from The Summer of '42]; Suite for Hp, Hpd & Orch [from Le Messager]; Suite for Hp, Hpd & Orch [from Yentl] Travelling ("Movies & Music" series) ▲ K 1020

Lark String Quartet
Kernis, A.J.:Qt Strs Argo ▲ 436287-2 [DDD]
Wolfe, J.:Early That Summer Point Music ▲ 454054-2
Lark String Quartet [Eva Gruesser (vn), Jennifer Orchard (vn), Anna Kruger (va), Astrid Schween (vc)]
Borodin, A.:Qt 1 Strs *(rec State Univ. of New York, Purchase Recital Hall, Dec. 17-19, 1994)* Arabesque ▲ ARA 6658 [DDD]
Borodin, A.:Qt 2 Strs *(rec SUNY, Purchase Recital Hall, Dec. 17-19, 1994)* Arabesque ▲ ARA 6658 [DDD]
Schoenberg, A.:Qt 1 Strs *(rec SUNY, Purchase, June 10-12, 1995)* Arabesque ▲ Z 6671
Zemlinsky, A. von:Qt 4 Strs *(rec SUNY, Purchase, June 10-12, 1995)* Arabesque ▲ Z 6671
Lark String Quartet [K. Stern (vn), R. Mayforth (vn), A. Kruger (va), L. Sewell (vc)]
Phillips, Jim:Clouds III Innova ▲ MN 107
Lark Wind Quintet
Crawford, R.:Suite Wind Qnt CRI ▲ CD 658 [ADD]
La Roche String Quartet
Krása, H.:Chamber Music, w. K. Slowioczek (bar), I. Berix (cl)—String Quartet (1923); Tanz for String Trio (1943); Theme & Variations for String Quartet; Three Songs for Baritone, Clarinet, Viola & Cello (1943) Channel Classics ▲ CCS 3792 [DDD]
LaSalle String Quartet
Apostel, H.E.:Qt 1 Strs Deutsche Grammophon ("20th Century Classics" series) 2-▲ 427421-2 [DDD]
Beethoven, L. van:Qts Strs (comp)—Opp. 127, 130, 131, 132 & 135 Deutsche Grammophon ("Chamber Music" series) 3-▲ 431141-2 [ADD]
Berg, A.:Lyric Suite Deutsche Grammophon 4-▲ 419994-2 [ADD]
Berg, A.:Qt Strs Deutsche Grammophon 4-▲ 419994-2 [ADD]
Brahms, J.:Qts Strs (comp) Deutsche Grammophon 2-▲ 437128-2 [ADD]
Duggan, M.:Les Avoines folles Grammont ▲ CTSP 49-2
Duggan, M.:La Joute des lierres Grammont ▲ CTSP 49-2
Penderecki, K.:Qt 1 Strs Polskie Nagrania 2-▲ PNCD 017 A/B
Samuel, G.:Qt 1 Strs *(rec Corbett Auditorium, College-Conservatory of Music, Univ. of Cincinnati, OH, Oct 15, 1978)* Centaur ▲ CRC 2238 [DDD]

LaSalle String Quartet (cont.)
Schoenberg, A.:Ode to Napoleon, w. K. Griffiths (pno) Deutsche Grammophon ("20th Century Classics" series) ▲ 437036-2 [DDD]
Schoenberg, A.:Qts Strs Deutsche Grammophon 4-▲ 419994-2 [ADD]
Schoenberg, A.:Verklärte Nacht, w. D. McInnes (va), J. Pegis (vc) Deutsche Grammophon ▲ 423250-2 [ADD]
Webern, A.:Bagatelles Str Qt Deutsche Grammophon 4-▲ 419994-2 [ADD]
Webern, A.:Movts Str Qt Deutsche Grammophon 4-▲ 419994-2 [ADD]
Webern, A.:Qt Strs, Op. 28 Deutsche Grammophon 4-▲ 419994-2 [ADD]
Webern, A.:Qnt Pno, w. S. Litwin (pno) Deutsche Grammophon ("20th Century Classics" series) ▲ 437036-2 [DDD]
Webern, A.:Rondo Deutsche Grammophon ("20th Century Classics" series) ▲ 437036-2 [DDD]
Webern, A.:Slow Movt Deutsche Grammophon 4-▲ 419994-2 [ADD]
Wolf, H.:Qt Strs Deutsche Grammophon 2-▲ 437128-2 [ADD]
Zemlinsky, A. von:Qts Strs (comp) Deutsche Grammophon ("20th Century Classics" series) 2-▲ 427421-2 [DDD/ADD]
LaSalle String Quartet members
Schoenberg, A.:Trio Strs Deutsche Grammophon ("20th Century Classics" series) ▲ 423250-2 [ADD]
Webern, A.:Trio Strs Deutsche Grammophon ("20th Century Classics" series) ▲ 437036-2 [DDD]
Latin American String Quartet [Saúl Bitrán (vn), Arón Bitrán (vn), Javier Montiel (va), Alvaro Bitrán (vc)]
Alvarez, J.:Metro Chabacano New Albion ▲ NA 051
Garrido-Lecca, C.:Qt 2 Strs New Albion ▲ NA 051
Ginastera, A.:Qt 1 Strs Élan ▲ CD 2218 [DDD]
Ginastera, A.:Qt 2 Strs Élan ▲ 2234 [DDD]
Lavista, M.:Reflejos de la Noche Élan ▲ 2234 [DDD]
Orbón, J.:Qt Strs Élan ▲ 2234 [DDD]
Revueltas, S.:Qts Strs *(rec Apr. 1993)* New Albion ▲ NA 062
Revueltas, S.:Qts Strs—Qts. 2 & 4 Élan ▲ CD 2218 [DDD]
Sierra, R.:Memorias Tropicales New Albion ▲ NA 051
Tello, A.:Dansaq II New Albion ▲ NA 051
Vali, R.:Folk Songs Set 11B *(rec Carnegie Free Library Music Hall, Carnegie, PA, Apr. 21, 1995)* New Albion ▲ NAO 77
Villa-Lobos, H.:Qts Strs (comp)—Nos. 3, 8 & 14 *(rec Troy Savings Bank Music Hall, Troy, NY, Mar 1995)* Dorian ▲ DOR 90220 [DDD]
Villa-Lobos, H.:Qt 5 Strs Élan ▲ 2234 [DDD]
Villa-Lobos, H.:Qt 17 Strs Élan ▲ CD 2218 [DDD]
E. Diemecke (cnd)
Revueltas, S.:Music of, w. Lourdes Ambriz (sop), Jesús Suaste (bar), Camerata de las Américas, Juan D. Tercero Vocal Octet—Troka; Cuauhnáhuac; The Owl; Frogs; Duet for Duck & Canary; Why Do You Believe?; Walking; Scenes from Childhood; 4 Little Pieces; The Knifesharpener; Market; Sensemayá *(rec Mexico City, Sept 1996)* Dorian ▲ 90244 [DDD]
J. P. Izquierdo (cnd)
Vali, R.:Movts Str Qt, w. Carnegie Mellon PO *(rec Carnegie Music Hall, Carnegie, PA, Mar. 11 & 14, 1993)* New Albion ▲ NAO 77
Vali, R.:Music of, w. Alberto Almarza (fl), Alvaro Bitran (vc), Carnegie Mellon PO New Albion ▲ NA 077
E. Mata (cnd)
Orbón, J.:Con grosso, w. Simón Bolívar SO Dorian ▲ DOR 90178 [DDD]
Latvian National SO
A. Vilumanis (cnd)
Lyric, Coloratura, Dramatic, w. Inese Galante (sop) Campion ▲ 1335
D. Yablonsky (cnd)
Ivanovs, J.:Sym 2 *(rec Riga, Latvia, Feb & Mar 1995)* Marco Polo ▲ 8.223331 [DDD]
Ivanovs, J.:Sym 3 *(rec Riga, Latvia, Feb & Mar 1995)* Marco Polo ▲ 8.223331 [DDD]
Latvian Opera Orch
A. Vilumanis (cnd)
Heroines, w. Inessa Galante (sop) Campion ▲ 1338 [DDD]
Latvian Phil Trio
Vasks, P.:Episodi e canto perpetuo *(rec Riga Recording Studio, Latvia, Dec 1995)* Conifer Classics ▲ 51272 [DDD]

Launton Handbell Ringers
Ringing Clear:The Art of Handbell Ringing, w. Sound in Brass Handbells, Four in Hand Grosmont Handbell Ringers, Change Ringing Handbell Group Saydisc ▲ CDSDL 333 [AAD]
Laurentian String Quartet
Kupferman, M.:Qt Cl, w. N. Drucker (cl) Soundspells ▲ SP 102
Kupferman, M.:Qnt Pno, w. K. Hayami (pno) Soundspells ▲ SP 101
Newman, Anthony:Chamber Music, w. M. Mills (pno), P.J. Bacchus (fl), Y. Waldman (vn), D. Wan, Flute Force—Qnt for Piano & Strings, "Easter"; Qt for 4 Flutes; Introduction & Toccata for Flute & Piano; Vars & Toccata for Violin Newport Classic ▲ NCD 60032 [DDD]
Lausanne CO
M. Aeschbacher (cnd)
Strauss, R.:Con 2 Hn, w. B. Schneider (hn) Claves ▲ CD 9010 [DDD]
Strauss, R.:Con Ob, w. I. Goritzki (ob) Claves ▲ CD 9010 [DDD]
Strauss, R.:Duet-Concertino, w. T. Friedli (cl), K. Thunemann (bn) Claves ▲ CD 9010 [DDD]
J.-M. Auberson (cnd)
David, Ferdinand:Concertino Trbn, w. B. Slokar (trbn) Claves ▲ CD 8407 [DDD]
Gaudibert, E.:Gemmes *(rec Oct. 9, 1980)* Grammont ▲ CTSP 8-2 [ADD]
Schibler, A.:La Folie de Tristan, w. Audrey Michael (sop—Iseut), Arlette Chédel (mez—Brangien), Pierre-André Blaser (ten—Tristan), Philippe Huttenlocher (bar—Le roi Marc/Le pêcheur/Le portier), André Fauré (nar), William Jacques (nar), Snezana Zivojinovic (nar), Romande Instrumental Group Rockband, Swiss Romande Radio Choir *(rec live, Festival de Montreux, Sept 15, 1980)* Jecklin ▲ JD 695
Tomasi, H.:Con Trbn, w. B. Slokar (trbn) Claves ▲ CD 8407 [DDD]
Wagenseil, G.C.:Con Trbn, w. Branimir Slokar (trbn) Claves ▲ CD 8407 [DDD]
M. Corboz (cnd)
Bach, J.S.:Christmas Oratorio, w. B. Schlick (sop), C. Watkinson (cta), K. Equiluz (ten), M. Brodard (bar) Erato ▲ 2292-45865-2
Bach, J.S.:St. John Passion, w. F. Palmer (sop), B. Finnilä (cta), K. Equiluz (ten), W. Krenn (ten), P. Huttenlocher (bar), R. van der Meer (bass), Lausanne Vocal Ensemble Erato 2-▲ 2292-45406-2 FD
Bach, J.S.:St. Matthew Passion, w. M. Marshall (sop), C. Watkinson (cta), K. Equiluz (ten), G. Faulstisch (bar), P. Huttenlocher (bar), R. Johnson (bar), Lausanne Vocal Ensemble Erato 3-▲ 2292-45375-2 GX
O. Cuendet (cnd)
Benda, G.A.:Medea, w. Caroline Gautier (sgr) Accord ▲ ACD 202622
V. Desarzens (cnd)
Britten, B.:Prelude & Fugue Strs MCA Classics 2-▲ MCAD2-9813 [AAD]
Derbès, J.:Music of, w. D. Duport (pno), A. Chédel (cta)—Chant d'amour et de mort; Con for Pno; 7 mélodies; Adagio for Large Orch Grammont ▲ CTSP 46
Elgar, E.:Intro & Allegro MCA Classics 2-▲ MCAD2 9813 [AAD]
Mozart, W.A.:Con 27 Pno, w. Walter Gieseking (pno) *(rec live, 1948-1956)* Pearl ▲ PEA 9236
Perrin, J.:German Songs, w. V. Gohl (alt) *(rec Radio Lausanne, May 22, 1970)* Grammont ▲ CTSP 45 [AAD]
Zbinden, J.-F.:Con da camera Pno, w. J.-F. Zbinden (pno) Grammont ▲ CTSP 3-2 [ADD]
L. Foster (cnd)
Busoni, F.:Konzertstück Pno, w. J.-F. Antonioli (pno) Claves ▲ CD 8806 [DDD]
Enescu, G.:Chamber Sym Claves ▲ CD 8803 [DDD]
Enescu, G.:Dectet Ww Claves ▲ CD 8803 [DDD]
Enescu, G.:Intermezzi, Op. 12 Claves ▲ CD 8803 [DDD]

Lausanne CO (cont.)
L. Foster (cnd) (cont.)
Moret, N.:Pieces CO *(rec live Oct. 31, 1988)* Grammont ▲ CTSP 23-2 [ADD]
Raff, J.:Con Pno, w. J.-F. Antonioli (pno) Claves ▲ CD 8806 [DDD]
Raff, J.:Ode au printemps, w. J.-F. Antonioli (pno) Claves ▲ CD 8806 [DDD]
Rodrigo, J.:Concierto de Aranjuez, w. S. Isbin (gtr) Virgin Classics ▲ CDC 59024-2 [DDD]
Rodrigo, J.:Fant para un gentilhombre, w. S. Isbin (gtr) Virgin Classics ▲ CDC 59024 [DDD]
Vivaldi, A.:Con Lt, w. S. Isbin (gtr) [solo guitar & string orchestra arr. Emilio Pujol, edited by Sharon Isbin] Virgin Classics ▲ CDC 59024 [DDD]
A. Gerecz (cnd)
Regamey, C.:Autographe Grammont ▲ CTSP 5-2 [ADD]
Zbinden, J.-F.:Ethiopiques, w. J.-D. Henneberger (nar) Grammont ▲ CTSP 3-2 [ADD]
P.-L. Graf (cnd)
Mozart, W.A.:Con Fl Hp, w. Peter-Lukas Graf (fl), Ursula Holliger (hp) *(rec EMI Studio London, 1970)* Claves ▲ CD 50208 [ADD]
A. Jordan (cnd)
Bellini, V.:Con in E♭ Ob, w. J.-P. Goy (ob) Gallo ▲ CD 129
Benjamin, A.:Con Ob Strs, w. J.-P. Goy (ob) Gallo ▲ CD 129
Cimarosa, D.:Con in G Ob, w. Jean-Paul Goy (ob) Gallo ▲ CD 129
Dvořák, A.:Czech Suite Erato ▲ 2292-45928-2 [ADD/DDD] ■ 2292-45928-4
Dvořák, A.:Serenade Strs Erato ▲ 2292-45928-2 [ADD/DDD] ■ 2292-45928-4
Marcello, A.:Con Ob & Strs, w. J.-P. Goy (ob) Gallo ▲ CD 129
Mozart, W.A.:Andante Fl, K.315/285a, w. A. Magnin (fl) Gallo ▲ CD 368
Mozart, W.A.:Cons Fl, w. A. Magnin (fl) Gallo ▲ CD 368
Mozart, W.A.:Con 27 Pno, w. M.-J. Pires (pno) Erato ▲ 45934-2 [ADD] ■ 45934-4
Mozart, W.A.:Rondo Pno Orch, K.382, w. M.-J. Pires (pno) Erato ▲ 45934-2 [ADD] ■ 45934-4
Vivaldi, A.:Cons Ob, w. Jean-Paul Goy (ob)—RV.454 Gallo ▲ CD 129
A. Lazarev (cnd)
Shostakovich, D.:Chamber Sym, Op. 110a Virgin Classics ▲ CDC 59039
Shostakovich, D.:Sym 14, w. M. Kasrashvili (sop), M. Krutikov (bass) Virgin Classics ▲ CDC 59039
J. López-Cobos (cnd)
Beethoven, L. van:Con 5 Pno, "Emperor", w. Mihaela Ursuleasa (pno) *(rec Théatre de Vevey, Sept 1995)* Claves ▲ CD 9520 [DDD]
Bizet, G.:Jeux d'enfants Denon ▲ DEN 78764 [DDD]
Falla, M. de:El amor brujo, w. S. Aguilar (nar), A.B. Egea (nar), A. Nafe (nar) *(rec Mar. 25-27, 1992)* Denon ▲ CO 75339 [DDD]
Falla, M. de:Canciones populares españolas (7), w. T. Berganza (mez) [Sp] Claves ▲ CD 8405
Falla, M. de:Canciones populares españolas (7), w. A. Nafe (mez) *(rec Mar. 25-27, 1992)* Denon ▲ CO 75339 [DDD]
Falla, M. de:El corregidor y la molinera, w. Teresa Berganza (mez) Claves ▲ 50-8405
Falla, M. de:El sombrero de tres picos, w. T. Berganza (mez) [Sp] Claves ▲ CD 8405
Fauré, G.:Dolly Denon ▲ DEN 78764 [DDD]
Haydn, J.:Sym 22, "Der Philosoph" Denon/PCM Digital ▲ DEN 75660 [DDD]
Haydn, J.:Sym 26, "Lamentatione" *(rec La Chaux-de-Fonds, Switzerland, Feb. 8-10, 1995)* Denon ▲ DEN 78967 [DDD]
Haydn, J.:Sym 30, "Alleluja" *(rec La Chaux-de-Fonds, Switzerland, Feb. 8-10, 1995)* Denon ▲ DEN 78967 [DDD]
Haydn, J.:Sym 31, "Hornsignal" *(rec La Chaux-de-Fonds, Switzerland, Feb. 8-10, 1995)* Denon ▲ DEN 78967 [DDD]
Haydn, J.:Sym 45, "Farewell" Denon/PCM Digital ▲ DEN 75660 [DDD]
Haydn, J.:Sym 55, "Der Schulmeister" *(rec Musica Theatre, la Chaux-de Fonds, June 1-3, 1994)* Denon ▲ CO 78930 [DDD]
Haydn, J.:Sym 59, "Fire" *(rec Musica Theatre, la Chaux-de Fonds, June 1-3, 1994)* Denon ▲ CO 78930 [DDD]
Haydn, J.:Sym 60, "Il Distratto" *(rec Musica Theatre, la Chaux-de Fonds, June 1-3, 1994)* Denon ▲ CO 78930 [DDD]
Haydn, J.:Sym 82, "The Bear" *(rec May 31-June 2, 1992)* Denon ▲ CO 75356 [DDD]
Haydn, J.:Sym 83, "The Hen" *(rec May 31-June 2, 1992)* Denon ▲ CO 75356 [DDD]
Haydn, J.:Sym 85, "La Reine de France" *(rec May 31-June 2, 1992)* Denon ▲ CO 75356 [DDD]
Haydn, J.:Sym 94, "Surprise Sym" Denon/PCM Digital ▲ DEN 75660 [DDD]
Haydn, J.:Sym 103, "Drum Roll" *(rec Dec. 18-20, 1991)* Denon ▲ CO 79729 [DDD]
Honegger, A.:Pastorale d'été Virgin Classics ▲ CDC 59064
Honegger, A.:Prélude, arioso et fughette sur le nom de BACH Virgin Classics ▲ CDC 59064
Honegger, A.:Sym 2 Virgin Classics ▲ CDC 59064
Honegger, A.:Sym 4 Virgin Classics ▲ CDC 59064
Mozart, W.A.:Con 9 Pno, w. Mihaela Ursuleasa (pno) *(rec Théatre de Vevey, Sept 1995)* Claves ▲ CD 9520 [DDD]
Mozart, W.A.:Con 9 Pno, w. Kyoko Tabe (pno) *(rec Musica Théatre, La Chaux-de-Fonds, June 10-11, 1995)* Denon ▲ CO-78833 [DDD]
Mozart, W.A.:Con 24 Pno, w. Kyoko Tabe (pno) *(rec Musica Théatre, La Chaux-de-Fonds, June 10-11, 1995)* Denon ▲ CO-78833 [DDD]
Ravel, M.:Ma mère l'oye Pno Denon ▲ DEN 78764 [DDD]
Respighi, O.:Ancient Airs & Dances Telarc ▲ CD 80309 [DDD]
Respighi, O.:Trittico botticelliano Telarc ▲ CD 80309 [DDD]
Rossini, G.:Il barbiere di Siviglia, w. J. Larmore (cta), A. Corbelli (bar), R. Gimeniz (bar), H. Hagegard (bar), S. Ramey (bass), Geneva Grand Théâtre Chorus [I] Teldec 2-▲ 9031-74885-2
Rossini, G.:Il barbiere di Siviglia (sels), w. B. Frittoli (sop), J. Larmore (mez), R. Giménez (ten), Håkan Hagegård (bar), A. Corbelli (bar), S. Ramey (bass), Geneva Grand Théâtre Chorus Teldec ▲ 93693-2
Wagner, R.:Siegfried Idyll Denon ▲ DEN 78764 [DDD]
F. Martin (cnd)
Martin, F.:Ballade Pno, w. S. Benda (pno) *(rec 1971)* Jecklin-Disco ▲ JD 529-2 [ADD]
Martin, F.:Ballade Trbn (or T Sax), w. A. Rosin (trbn) [orchestrated] *(rec 1971)* Jecklin-Disco ▲ JD 529-2 [ADD]
Martin, F.:Con Hpd, w. C. Jaccottet (hpd) *(rec 1971)* Jecklin-Disco ▲ JD 529-2 [ADD]
L. von Matačić (cnd)
Beethoven, L. van:Sym 2 Denon ▲ CO 8120 [DDD]
Beethoven, L. van:Sym 6, "Pastorale" Denon ▲ CO 8119 [DDD]
Haydn, J.:Sym 82, "The Bear" Denon ▲ CO 8120 [DDD]
U. Segal (cnd)
Mozart, W.A.:Con 22 Pno, w. T. Fellner (pno) *(rec live Sept. 19, 1993)* Claves ▲ CD 9328 [DDD]
A. Zedda (cnd)
Debussy, C.:Danse Pno, "Tarantelle styrienne" Virgin Classics ("Ultraviolet" series) ▲ CUV 61206
Debussy, C.:Sarabande Virgin Classics ("Ultraviolet" series) ▲ CUV 61206
Milhaud, D.:La Création du monde Virgin Classics ("Ultraviolet" series) ▲ CUV 61206
Milhaud, D.:La Création du monde Virgo ▲ CDZ 61104
Prokofiev, S.:Sinfonietta, Op. 48 Virgin Classics ("Ultraviolet" series) ▲ CUV 61206
Prokofiev, S.:Sym 1 Virgo ▲ CDZ 61104
Prokofiev, S.:Sym 1 Virgin Classics ("Ultraviolet" series) ▲ CUV 61206
Smetana, B.:Má Vlast Virgin Classics ("Ultraviolet" series) ▲ CUV 61223
Lausanne Conservatory Ensemble
H. Klopfenstein (cnd)
Thury, F.:Mata-Hari Gallo ▲ CD 630 [AAD]
Lausanne Conservatory Orch
Bach, J.S.:Cant 172, w. Lausanne Conservatory Chorus [G] Gallo ▲ CD 630 [AAD]
Perrin, J.:Cantosenhal, w. L. Hauser (sop), S. Imbodem (bass) Gallo ▲ CD 630 [AAD]
Lausanne Instrumental Ensemble
M. Corboz (cnd)
Fauré, G.:Cantique de Jean Racine, w. M. Dami (sop), P. Harvey (bar), Lausanne Vocal Ensemble [F] *(rec Feb. 14-16, 1992)* FNAC Music ▲ 592097 [DDD]

Lausanne Instrumental Ensemble (cont.)
M. Corboz (cnd) (cont.)
Fauré, G.:Messe basse (in 3 movts), w. M. Dami (sop), Lausanne Vocal Ensemble [L] *(rec Feb. 14-16, 1992)* FNAC Music ▲ 592097 [DDD]
Fauré, G.:Motets, w. M. Dami (sop), P. Harvey (bar), Lausanne Vocal Ensemble—Maria Mater Gratiae, Op. 47; Ave verum, Op. 65/1; Tantum ergo, Op. 65/2; Tu es Petrus; Tantum ergo [L] *(rec Feb. 14-16, 1992)* FNAC Music ▲ 592097 [DDD]
Fauré, G.:Requiem, w. M. Dami (sop), P. Harvey (bar), Lausanne Vocal Ensemble [L] *(rec Feb. 14-16, 1992)* FNAC Music ▲ 592097 [DDD]
Handel, G.F.:Messiah (reorchd Mozart), w. Audrey Michael (sop), Jard van Nes (cta), Hans-Peter Blochwitz (tenor), Marcus Fink (bass), Lausanne Vocal Ensemble [G] Erato 2-▲ 2292-45497-2 [DDD]
Monteverdi, C.:Magnificat, w. Lausanne Vocal Ensemble Erato 2-▲ ERA SEL 12981 [ADD/DDD]
Monteverdi, C.:Vespro, w. Lausanne Vocal Ensemble Erato 2-▲ ERA SEL 12981 [ADD/DDD]
Lausanne String Trio
Geiser, W.:Trio Strs Grammont ▲ CTSP 21-2 [ADD]
Lausanne SO
V. Desarzens (cnd)
Schumann, R.:Con Vn, w. Peter Rybar (vn) *(rec Lausanne, 1951)* Doron ("Legendary Artists" series) ▲ DRC 4009 [ADD]
Lausanne Trio
Schubertiade:Rétrospective, w. Sine Nomine String Quartet, C. Homberger (ten), S. Kanoff (pno), C. Favre (pno), Choeur des XVI de Fribourg, et al. Gallo ▲ CD 631 [AAD]
Lausanne Vocal & Instrumental Ensemble
M. Corboz (cnd)
Mendelssohn, F.:Die erste Walpurgisnacht [G] Erato ▲ 2292-45462-2 [DDD]
Mendelssohn, F.:Kyrie [G] Erato ▲ 2292-45462-2 [DDD]
Mendelssohn, F.:O Haupt voll Blut und Wunden, w. G. Cachemaille (bar) [G] Erato ▲ 2292-45462-2 [DDD]
Lautentrio Ricardo Correa [R. Correa (lt), M. Chatton (lt), B. Wullschleger (lt)]
Adriaenssen, E.:Music of, w. M. von Annetteruel (lt)—Qts. Villanella & "Als ick u vinde"; Trio "Madonna mia pieta" Christophorus ▲ CHR 74527 [ADD]
Mudarra, A.:Music of, w. M. von Annette Gruel (lt)—Fantasia VII; "Fantasia que contrehaze la harpa en la manera de Luduvico" Christophorus ▲ CHR 74527 [ADD]
Pacoloni, G.:Music of, w. M. von Annette Gruel (lt)—La Bataglia; La Desperata Christophorus ▲ CHR 74527 [ADD]
Piccinini, A.:Intavolature, w. M. von Annette Gruel (lt)—Toccata IX; Toccata; Canzone Christophorus ▲ CHR 74527 [ADD]
Valderrábano, E. de:Music of, w. M. von Annette Gruel (lt)—"Contrapunto sobre el tenor de la baxa"; "Para discanto" Christophorus ▲ CHR 74527 [ADD]
Lautten Compagney
Jubilate Domino, w. A. Köhler (alt) Capriccio ▲ 10 478 [DDD]
Monteverdi, C.:Arias & Duets, w. M. van der Sluis (sop), A. Köhler (alt)—Sancta Maria; Ego flos campi; O bone Jesu; Laudate Dominum; Venite, venite; Fugge, fugge anima mea; Ballo delle Ingrate; Vorrei baciarti; Ed è pur dunque vero; Di far sempre gioire; Eri già tutta mia; O rosetta che rosetta/Non così tosto io miro; Quel sguardo sdegnosetto; Sinfonia; Adagiati, Poppea, Pur ti miro Capriccio ▲ 10 470 [DDD]
A. Köhler (cnd)
In Dulci Jubilo Capriccio ▲ 10490 [DDD]
Laval SO
J. Lacombe (cnd)
Chi il Bel Sogno..., w. Manon Feubel (sop) CBC Records ▲ SM5 5156 [DDD]
Lavel String Quartet
Brahms, J.:Qnt Pno, w. Mario Duchemin (pno) Analekta ▲ CLCD 2003
Dohnányi, E. von:Qt 3 Strs Analekta ▲ CLCD 2003
Louis Lavigueur Instrumental Ensemble
L. Lavigueur (cnd)
Gratton, H.:Imagerie:Christmas Pastoral, w. M. Keable (actor), S. Léonard (actor), J.-L. Millette (actor), M. Laferrière (sop), C. Rioux (mez), B. Levasseur (bar), N. Richard (b-bar), Louis Lavigueur Vocal Ensemble [F] *(rec 5/91)* CBC ("SM 5000" series) ▲ SMCD 5109 [DDD]
Leeds Philharmonic Society
M. Sargent (cnd)
Elgar, E.:The Music Makers, w. M. Thomas (cta), London SO, Huddersfield Choral Society, Royal Choral Society *(rec live, Royal Albert Hall April 29, 1965)* Intaglio ▲ INCD 7351 [ADD]
Byron Lee's Dragonaires
Jarre, M.:The Mosquito Coast, w. Electronic Ensemble Fantasy ▲ FSC 21005 ■ FSP 52105
Lehigh Valley CO
D. Spieth (cnd)
Barber, S.:Canzonetta, w. H. Lucarelli (ob) Koch International Classics ▲ KIC 7023-2 [DDD] ■ 3-7023-4 (D)
Copland, A.:Dance Panels Koch International Classics ▲ KIC 7166 [DDD]
Lipkis, L.:Scaramouche Vc & Orch, w. C. Brey (vc) Koch International Classics ▲ KIC 7166 [DDD]
Strauss, R.:Con Ob, w. H. B. Lucarelli (ob) Koch International Classics ▲ KIC 7023-2 [DDD] ■ 3-7023-4 (D)
Vaughan Williams, R.:Con Ob, w. B. Lucarelli (ob) Koch International Classics ▲ KIC 7023-2 [DDD] ■ 3-7023-4 (D)
Wolf-Ferrari, E.:Idillio-Concertino, w. B. Lucarelli (ob) Koch International Classics ▲ KIC 7023-2 [DDD] ■ 3-7023-4 (D)
Leipzig Bach Collegium
Bach, J.S.:A Musical Offering Capriccio ▲ CDC 10032 [DDD]
Bach, J.S.:Son Fl, BWV 1038 Capriccio ▲ 10166 [DDD]
Stradella, A.:Sinf alla Serenata Capriccio ▲ 10166 [DDD]
Telemann, G.P.:Trio Fl Capriccio ▲ 10166 [DDD]
L. Güttler (cnd)
Albinoni, T.:Con in D Tpt, w. L. Güttler (tpt) Capriccio ▲ 10166 [DDD]
Leipzig Capella Fidicinia
C. Eschenburg (cnd)
Bach, J.S.:Motets, BWV 225-30, w. Rostock Motet Chorus [G] Capriccio ▲ CDC 10030 [DDD]
M. Flämig (cnd)
Monteverdi, C.:Vespro, w. Dresden Kreuz Choir Berlin Classics 2-▲ BER 9204
H. Grüss (cnd)
Bach, J.S.:Anna Magdalena Bach Notebook, w. Burkhardt, Schreier, W.H. Bernstein Capriccio ▲ CDC 10031 [DDD]
Walther (I), Joh.:Wittenberg Spiritual Songbook (sels), w. P. Schreier (ten) [G] Capriccio ▲ CDC 11089
Leipzig Gewandhaus Orch
H. Abendroth (cnd)
Mozart, W.A.:Notturno, K.286, Berlin RSO, Leipzig RSO Berlin Classics 2-▲ BER 9271
H. Bongartz (cnd)
Beethoven, L. van:Con. Vn, WoO 5, w. Karl Suske (vn) Berlin Classics ▲ BER 2078 [DDD]
Beethoven, L. van:Romances Vn, w. Karl Suske (vn)—in G Berlin Classics ▲ BER 2078 [DDD]
Beethoven, L. van:Rondo Pno, WoO 6, w. Peter Rösel (pno) Berlin Classics ▲ BER 2078 [DDD]
Beethoven, L. van:Wellington's Victory, "Battle Sym" Berlin Classics ▲ BER 2078 [DDD]
Bruckner, A.:Sym 6 *(rec 1964)* Berlin Classics ▲ BER 9167
P. Dessau (cnd)
Dessau, P.:Bach-Variationen Berlin Classics ▲ BER 2182 [ADD]
Dessau, P.:In memoriam Bertolt Brecht Berlin Classics ▲ BER 2182 [ADD]
M. Janowski (cnd)
Beethoven, L. van:Con 4 Pno, w. Gerhard Oppitz (pno) *(rec 1995-96)* RCA Red Seal ▲ 0902-668417-2 [DDD]

210 ▲ = CD ♦ = Enhanced CD Δ = MD ■ = Cassette Tape □ = DCC

Leipzig Gewandhaus Orch (cont.)
M. Janowski (cnd) (cont.)
Beethoven, L. van:Con 5 Pno, "Emperor", w. Gerhard Oppitz (pno) *(rec 1995–96)* RCA Red Seal ▲ 0902-668417-2 [DDD]

F. Konwitschny (cnd)
Bach, J.S.:Cons Vn (comp) Berlin Classics ("Dokumente" series) ▲ BER 2130 [ADD]
Bach, J.S.:Con Vn, BWV 1052 Berlin Classics ("Dokumente" series) ▲ BER 2130 [ADD]
Beethoven, L. van:Fant Pno, Op. 80, "Choral Fant", w. G. Kootz (pno), Leipzig Radio Chorus Berlin Classics ▲ BER 2077 [ADD]
Beethoven, L. van:Ovs—Die Geschöpfe des Prometheus; Coriolan; Fidelio; Leonore Ovs. Nos. 1–3 *(rec 1959–1961)* Berlin Classics ("Eterna" series) 6–▲ BER 2005 [ADD]
Beethoven, L. van:Syms (comp), w. I. Wenglor (sop), U. Zollenkopf (cta), Hans Joachim Rotzsch (ten), T. Adam (bass-bar), Leipzig Radio Chorus *(rec 1959–1961)* Berlin Classics ("Eterna" series) 6–▲ BER 2005 [ADD]
Beethoven, L. van:Sym 9, "Choral Sym", w. Ingeborg Wenglor (sop), Ursula Zollenkopf (alt), Hans Jochim Rotzsch (ten), Theo Adam (bass), Leipzig Radio Chorus Polskie Nagrania Edition ▲ ECD 028
Brahms, J.:Con 2 Pno, w. E. Ney (pno) *(rec live 3/3/55)* Melodram ▲ MEL 18015 (m) [AAD]
Bruckner, A.:Sym 5 Berlin Classics 2–▲ BER 2079 [ADD]
Bruckner, A.:Sym 7 Berlin Classics ▲ BER 2079 [ADD]
Mendelssohn, F.:Con in e Vn & Orch, Op. 64, w. I. Oistrakh (vn) Berlin Classics ▲ BER 2076 [ADD]
Mendelssohn, F.:Sym 3 Berlin Classics ▲ BER 2076 [ADD]
Mozart, W.A.:Con 5 Vn, w. D. Oistrakh (vn) Berlin Classics ("Dokumente" series) ▲ BER 2131 [ADD]
Reger, M.:Vars & Fugue on a Theme of of J. A. Hiller Berlin Classics ("Eterna" series) ▲ BER 2006 [ADD]
Schumann, R.:Konzertstück Hns, w. P. Damm (hn), H. Märker (hn), W. Pilz (hn), G. Böhner (hn) *(rec 1960–61)* Berlin Classics ("Eterna" series) 3–▲ BER 2016 [ADD]
Schumann, R.:Ovs—Genoveva, Op. 81; Manfred, Op. 115 *(rec 1960–61)* Berlin Classics ("Eterna" series) 3–▲ BER 2016 [ADD]
Schumann, R.:Ov, Scherzo & Finale *(rec 1960–61)* Berlin Classics ("Eterna" series) 3–▲ BER 2016 [ADD]
Schumann, R.:Syms (comp) *(rec 1960–61)* Berlin Classics ("Eterna" series) 3–▲ BER 2016 [ADD]
Vivaldi, A.:Cons Vn, Op. 3/1–12, "L'estro armonico"—No. 8 Berlin Classics ("Dokumente" series) ▲ BER 2130 [ADD]
Wieniawski, H.:Con 2 Vn, w. I. Oistrakh (vn) Berlin Classics ("Dokumente" series) ▲ BER 2131 [ADD]

I. Markevitch (cnd)
Mussorgsky, M.:Night *(rec 1973)* Berlin Classics ▲ BER 2139 [ADD]
Mussorgsky, M.:Pictures at an Exhibition *(rec 1973)* Berlin Classics ▲ BER 2139 [ADD]

K. Masur (cnd)
Beethoven, L. van:Con 6 Pno, w. A. Webersinke (pno) Berlin Classics ▲ BER 2077 [ADD]
Beethoven, L. van:Con Vn, Vc & Pno, "Triple Con", w. Beaux Arts Trio Philips ▲ 438005–2
Beethoven, L. van:Con Vn, Vc & Pno, "Triple Con", w. U. Hoelscher (vn), H. Schiff (vc), C. Zacharias (pno) EMI Classics ▲ ZDMC 63937
Beethoven, L. van:Contredanses, WoO 14, w. N. Marriner (cnd), Academy of St. Martin in the Fields Philips 2–▲ 438706–2
Beethoven, L. van:Fant Pno, Op. 80, "Choral Fant", w. M. Pressler (pno), *(chorus unknown)* Philips ▲ 438005–2
Beethoven, L. van:German Dances, WoO 8, w. N. Marriner (cnd), Academy of St. Martin in the Fields Philips 2–▲ 438706–2
Beethoven, L. van:Minuets Orch, WoO 7, w. N. Marriner (cnd), Academy of St. Martin in the Fields Philips 2–▲ 438706–2
Beethoven, L. van:Missa Solemnis, w. Anna Tomowa-Sintow (sop), Annelies Burmeister (alt), Peter Schreier (ten), Hermann Christian Polster (bass), Gerhard Bosse (vn), Hannes Kastner (org), Leipzig Radio Chorus Berlin Classics ("Masur Edition" series) ▲ BER 9160
Beethoven, L. van:Music of, w. Berlin State Orch, Berlin CO, Suske Trio—Con for Piano in D, Op. 61; Son for Piano, Op. 14/1; Ländler; Minuets; Arias; plus others Berlin Classics 3–▲ BER 9131
Beethoven, L. van:Music of, w. R. Shaw (cnd), Atlanta SO—sels. from Syms. 3,5,6,7 & 9, Pno Con. 5; Vn Con.; Egmont Ov.; Für Elise; Turkish March; Military Marches Nos. 1 & 2 Pro Arte ▲ CDM 820 ■ PCD 820
Beethoven, L. van:Ovs—Fidelio; Leonore 1–3; Weihe des Hauses Philips ▲ 454038–2
Beethoven, L. van:Ovs, w. N. Marriner (cnd), Academy of St. Martin in the Fields Philips 2–▲ 438706–2
Beethoven, L. van:Syms (comp)—Nos 1–4 Philips 2–▲ 454032–2
Beethoven, L. van:Syms (comp)—Nos. 2 & 7 Philips ▲ 432994–2
Beethoven, L. van:Syms (comp)—Nos 5–8 Philips 2–▲ 454035–2
Beethoven, L. van:Syms (comp)—No 9 Philips 2–▲ 454038–2
Beethoven, L. van:Sym 3, "Eroica" Philips ▲ 434913–2
Beethoven, L. van:Sym 5 Philips ("Insignia" series) ▲ 434156–2 [DDD]
Beethoven, L. van:Sym 6, "Pastorale" Philips ("Insignia" series) ▲ 434156–2 [DDD]
Beethoven, L. van:Sym 8 Philips ▲ 434913–2
Beethoven, L. van:Sym 9, "Choral Sym", w. S. McNair (sop), U. Heilmann (ten), J. Van Nes (bar), B. Woikl (bar), London Radio Choir Philips ▲ 432995 2
Brahms, J.:Con 2 Pno, w. Elisabeth Leonskaja (pno) *(rec Gewandhaus, Leipzig, Jan. 1994)* Teldec ▲ 94544–2 [DDD]
Brahms, J.:Con 2 Pno, w. C. Ousset (pno) Berlin Classics ▲ BER 2161 [ADD]
Brahms, J.:Hungarian Dances Orch—Nos. 1–21 [Nos. 5 & 6 orch. Parlow; Nos. 8 & 9 orch. Schollum] Philips ▲ 411426–2 [DDD]
Bruch, M.:Con 1 Vn, w. M. Vengerov (vn) Teldec ▲ 90875–2
Bruch, M.:Swedish Dances Philips 2–▲ 420932–2 [DDD]
Bruch, M.:Syms (comp) Philips 2–▲ 420932–2 [DDD]
Cerha, F.:Baal Gesänge, w. T. Adam (bass-bar) *(rec 1984)* Berlin Classics ▲ BER 2072 [ADD]
Chabrier, E.:Larghetto, w. H. Baumann (hn) Philips ▲ 416380–2 [DDD]
Dukas, P.:Villanelle, w. H. Baumann (hn) Philips ▲ 416380–2 [DDD]
Gershwin, G.:Rhap in Blue, w. S. Stöckigt (pno) Deutsche Grammophon ("Resonance" series) ▲ 427203–2 [ADD] ■ 427203–4
Glière, R.:Con Hn, w. H. Baumann (hn) Philips ▲ 416380–2 [DDD]
Liszt, F.:Battle of the Huns EMI Classics 2–▲ CDFB 68598
Liszt, F.:Ce qu'on entend sur la montagne EMI Classics 2–▲ CDFB 68598
Liszt, F.:Dante Sym, w. Leipzig St. Thomas Church Choir EMI Classics 2–▲ CDFB 68598
Liszt, F.:A Faust Sym, w. Leipzig Radio Men's Chorus *(rec 1977–80)* EMI Classics ("Doublefforte" series) 2–▲ CDFB 68595
Liszt, F.:Festklänge EMI Classics 2–▲ CDFB 68598
Liszt, F.:Hungarian Rhaps—Nos. 2, 5, 6, 9, 12 & 14 Philips ▲ 412724–2 [DDD]
Liszt, F.:Die Ideale EMI Classics 2–▲ CDFB 68598
Liszt, F.:Mazeppa Orch EMI Classics ▲ CDM 64850
Liszt, F.:Mephisto Waltz EMI Classics ▲ CDM 64850
Liszt, F.:Orpheus EMI Classics ▲ CDM 64850
Liszt, F.:Les Préludes EMI Classics ▲ CDM 64850
Liszt, F.:Symphonic Poems (misc)—Nos. 5, 8–10 *(rec 1977–80)* EMI Classics ("Doublefforte" series) 2–▲ CDFB 68595
Liszt, F.:Tasso—Lamento e Trionfo EMI Classics ▲ CDM 64850
Liszt, F.:Von der Wiege bis zum Grabe EMI Classics 2–▲ CDFB 68598
Mahler, G.:Sym 7 Berlin Classics ("Masur Edition" series) ▲ BER 9159
Mahler, G.:Sym 7 Berlin Classics ("Eterna" series) ▲ BER 2058 [AAD]
Matthus, S.:Holofernes, w. D. Fischer-Dieskau (bar) *(rec 1981)* Berlin Classics ▲ BER 2072 [ADD]
Mendelssohn, F.:Con 1 Pno, w. C. Katsaris (pno) Teldec ("Digital Experience" series) ▲ 9031-75860–2 AW [DDD] ■ 9031-75860–4
Mendelssohn, F.:Con 1 Pno, w. C. Katsaris (pno) Teldec 4–▲ 9031-71104–2
Mendelssohn, F.:Con 2 Pno, w. C. Katsaris (pno) Teldec ("Digital Experience" series) ▲ 9031-75860–2 AW [DDD] ■ 9031-75860–4
Mendelssohn, F.:Con 2 Pno, w. C. Katsaris (pno) Teldec 4–▲ 9031-71104–2 ZB

Leipzig Gewandhaus Orch (cont.)
K. Masur (cnd) (cont.)
Mendelssohn, F.:Con in e Vn & Orch, Op. 64, w. M. Vengerov (vn) Teldec ▲ 90875–2
Mendelssohn, F.:Die erste Walpurgisnacht, w. A. Burmeister (mez), E. Büchner (ten), S. Lorenz (bar) Berlin Classics ("Eterna" series) ▲ BER 2057 [ADD]
Mendelssohn, F.:Infelice, w. A. Burmeister (mez) Berlin Classics ("Eterna" series) ▲ BER 2057 [ADD]
Mendelssohn, F.:Meeresstille Berlin Classics ("Eterna" series) ▲ BER 2057 [ADD]
Mendelssohn, F.:Ovs—Opp. 26, 32, 37, 95 & 101 Berlin Classics ▲ BER CD 9157
Mendelssohn, F.:Ov, Op. 101, w. A. Burmeister (mez), E. Büchner (ten), S. Lorenz (bar) Berlin Classics ("Eterna" series) ▲ BER 2057 [ADD]
Mendelssohn, F.:Die schöne Melusina Berlin Classics ("Eterna" series) ▲ BER 2057 [ADD]
Mendelssohn, F.:Sinfs Strs—Nos. 1–6 Berlin Classics ▲ BER 2105 [ADD]
Mendelssohn, F.:Sinfs Strs—No. 7 in d; No. 9 in C; No. 10 in b Berlin Classics ▲ BER 2106 [ADD]
Mendelssohn, F.:Sinfs Strs—No. 8 in D [2 versions] Berlin Classics ▲ BER 2107 [ADD]
Mendelssohn, F.:Sinfs Strs—No. 11 in F; No. 12 in g Berlin Classics ▲ BER 2108 [ADD]
Mendelssohn, F.:Sinf 13 Berlin Classics ▲ BER 2108 [ADD]
Mendelssohn, F.:Syms (comp) Teldec 4–▲ 9031-71104–2 ZB
Mendelssohn, F.:Syms (comp) [Sym 2 w. Celestina Casapietra (sop), Adele Stolte (sop), Peter Schreier (ten), Leipzig Radio Chorus)] Eurodisc 3–▲ 69237–2–RV [ADD]
Mendelssohn, F.:Sym 1 Teldec ▲ 2292-44933–2 ZK [DDD]
Mendelssohn, F.:Sym 2, w. B. Bonney (sop), E. Wiens (sop), P. Schreier (ten), Leipzig Gewandhaus Chorus [G] Teldec ▲ 2292-44178–2 ZK [DDD]
Mendelssohn, F.:Sym 3 Teldec ▲ 92148
Mendelssohn, F.:Sym 3 Teldec ▲ 2292-43463–2
Mendelssohn, F.:Sym 4 Teldec ▲ 92148
Mendelssohn, F.:Sym 4 Teldec ▲ 2292-43463–2
Mendelssohn, F.:Sym 5 Teldec ▲ 2292-44933–2 ZK [DDD]
Miki, M.:Music of, w. K. Mitsuhashi (shakuhachi), N. Yoshimura (koto), Y. Tanaka (shamisen), Tokyo Metropolitan SO, Tokyo PO—Jo No Kyoju; Prelude for Shakuhachi, Koto & Strings; Ha No Kyoku; Con. for Koto & Orch.; Kyu no Kyoku; Sym. for Two Worlds Camerata 2–▲ 30CM 223/24
Prokofiev, S.:Cons Pno (comp), w. M. Béroff (pno) EMI Classics 2–▲ CDZB 62542
Prokofiev, S.:Ov on Hebrew Themes EMI Classics 2–▲ CDZB 62542
Saint-Saëns, C.:Morceau de concert Hn, w. H. Baumann (hn) Philips ▲ 416380–2 [DDD]
Schubert, Franz:Rosamunde, w. Ameling (sop), Leipzig Radio Chorus [G] Philips ▲ 412432–2 [DDD]
Schumann, R.:Con Vc, w. Jürnjakob Timm (vc) Berlin Classics ▲ BER CD 9151
Schumann, R.:Genoveva, w. E. Moser (sop), P. Schreier (ten), D. Fischer-Dieskau (bar), S. Lorenz (b-bar), Berlin Radio Chorus Berlin Classics ("Eterna" series) 2–▲ BER 2056 [ADD]
Sensual Classics II, w. A. Sultanov (pno), C. Katsaris (pno), Brodsky Quartet, London SO [cnd:M. Shostakovich], New York PO [cnd:Z. Mehta], BBC SO [cnd:A. Davis], 12 Cellos of the Berlin PO [cnd:A. Jordan, E. Inbal], et al. Teldec ▲ 92014–2 ■ 92014–4
Strauss, R.:Ariadne auf Naxos, w. J. Norman (sop), J. Varady (sop), E. Gruberova (sop), P. Frey (ten), O. Bär (bar), D. Fischer-Dieskau (bar) [G] Philips 2–▲ 422084–2 [DDD]
Strauss, R.:Con 1 Hn, w. H. Baumann (hn) Philips ▲ 412237–2 [DDD]
Strauss, R.:Con 2 Hn, w. H. Baumann (hn) Philips ▲ 412237–2 [DDD]
Strauss, R.:4 Last Songs, w. J. Norman (sop) [G] Philips ▲ 411052–2 [DDD] ☐ 411052–5
Strauss, R.:Songs, w. J. Norman (sop)—Cäcilie; Morgen; Wiegenlied; Ruhe, meine Seele; Meinem kinde; Zueignung [G] Philips ▲ 411052–2 [DDD] ☐ 411052–5
Tchaikovsky, P.:Con 1 Pno, w. T. Nikolaeva (pno) Berlin Classics ("Dokumente" series) ▲ BER 2134 [ADD]
Tchaikovsky, P.:Festival Coronation March Teldec ▲ 76456–2
Tchaikovsky, P.:Romeo & Juliet Teldec ▲ 9031-76456–2
Tchaikovsky, P.:Romeo & Juliet Teldec ▲ 2292-44943–2 [DDD]
Tchaikovsky, P.:Sym 1 Teldec ▲ 2292-44939–2–ZK [DDD]
Tchaikovsky, P.:Sym 2 Teldec ▲ 2292-44943–2 [DDD]
Tchaikovsky, P.:Sym 3 Teldec ▲ 2292-46322–2 [DDD]
Tchaikovsky, P.:Sym 4 Teldec 2–▲ 95981–2
Tchaikovsky, P.:Sym 4 Teldec ▲ 2292-43203–2
Tchaikovsky, P.:Sym 5 Teldec ▲ 2292-43462–2 ZK [DDD]
Tchaikovsky, P.:Sym 5 Teldec 2–▲ 95981–2
Tchaikovsky, P.:Sym 6 Teldec ▲ 2292-43204–2
Tchaikovsky, P.:Sym 6 Teldec 2–▲ 95981–2
Tchaikovsky, P.:Vars on a Rococo Theme, w. Jürnjakob Timm (vc) Berlin Classics ▲ BER CD 9151
Weber, C.M. von:Concertino Hn, w. H. Baumann (hn) Philips ▲ 412237–2 [DDD]

R. & E. Mauersberger (cnd)
Bach, J.S.:St. Matthew Passion, w. A. Burmeister (mez), P. Schreier (ten), T. Adam (bass), Dresden Kreuz Choir, St. Thomas Chorus *(rec 1970)* Berlin Classics 3–▲ BER 2144 [ADD]

V. Neumann (cnd)
Beethoven, L. van:Fidelio (ov) Berlin Classics 2–▲ BER 9045 [ADD]
Beethoven, L. van:Leonore 3 Berlin Classics 2–▲ BER 9045 [ADD]
Dvořák, A.:Slavonic Dances (sels) Berlin Classics 2–▲ BER 2073 [ADD]
Mahler, G.:Sym 5 Berlin Classics ▲ BER 2074 [ADD]
Mahler, G.:Sym 9 Berlin Classics ▲ BER 2187 [ADD]
Smetana, B.:Má Vlast Berlin Classics 2–▲ BER 2073 [ADD]

M. Pommer (cnd)
Eisler, H.:Chamber Sym Berlin Classics ▲ BER 9228
Eisler, H.:Suite 1 Berlin Classics ▲ BER 9228
Eisler, H.:Suite 2, "Niemandslied" Berlin Classics ▲ BER 9228
Eisler, H.:Suite 3, "Kuhle Wampe" Berlin Classics ▲ BER 9228
Eisler, H.:Suite 4, "Die Jugend hat das Wort" Berlin Classics ▲ BER 9228
Eisler, H.:Variationen über ein marschartiges Thema "Der lange Marsch" Berlin Classics ▲ BER 9228

G. Ramin (cnd)
Bach, J.S.:St. Matthew Passion, w. T. Lemnitz (sop), F. Beckmann (alt), K. Erb (ten), G. Hüsch (bar), S. Schulze (bass), St. Thomas Choir, *(abridged performance)* [G] *(rec Mar 1941)* Calig 2–▲ CAL 50 859/60 (m) [AAD]

H.-J. Rotzsch (cnd)
Bach, J.S.:Cant 4, w. Helga Terner (sop), Ortrun Wenkel (cta), Peter Schreier (ten), Eberhard Büchner (ten), Leipzig St. Thomas Church Choir, Leipzig New Bach Collegium Musicum Berlin Classics ▲ BER 2067 [ADD]
Bach, J.S.:Cant 29, w. Regina Werner (sop), Heidi Riess (alt), Hans-Joachim Rotzsch (ten), Hermann Christian Polster (bass), Leipzig St. Thomas Church Choir Berlin Classics ▲ BER CD 9055
Bach, J.S.:Cant 31, w. Eberhard Büchner (ten), Siegfried Lorenz (bar), Hermann Christian Polster (bass), Lang (sgr), Termer (sgr), Weimann (sgr), St. Thomas Choir Berlin Classics ▲ BER 9025 [ADD]
Bach, J.S.:Cant 31, w. Helga Terner (sop), Ortrun Wenkel (cta), Peter Schreier (ten), Eberhard Büchner (ten), Leipzig St. Thomas Church Choir, Leipzig New Bach Collegium Musicum Berlin Classics ▲ BER 2067 [ADD]
Bach, J.S.:Cant 66, w. Eberhard Büchner (ten), Siegfried Lorenz (bar), Hermann Christian Polster (bass), Lang (sgr), Termer (sgr), Weimann (sgr), St. Thomas Choir Berlin Classics ▲ BER 9025 [ADD]
Bach, J.S.:Cant 106, "Actus tragicus", w. Eberhard Büchner (ten), Siegfried Lorenz (bar), Hermann Christian Polster (bass), Lang (sgr), Termer (sgr), Weimann (sgr), St. Thomas Choir Berlin Classics ▲ BER 9025 [ADD]
Bach, J.S.:Cant 119, w. Regina Werner (sop), Heidi Riess (alt), Hans-Joachim Rotzsch (ten), Hermann Christian Polster (bass), Leipzig St. Thomas Church Choir Berlin Classics ▲ BER CD 9055
Bach, J.S.:Cant 134, w. Helga Terner (sop), Ortrun Wenkel (cta), Peter Schreier (ten), Eberhard Büchner (ten), Leipzig New Bach Collegium Musicum, Leipzig St. Thomas Church Choir Berlin Classics ▲ BER 2067 [ADD]

Leipzig Gewandhaus Orch (cont.)

H.–J. Rotzsch (cnd) (cont.)

Bach, J.S.:Org Music (misc), w. E. P. Biggs (org), Z. Rozsnyai (cnd), Columbia Chamber SO—9 Organ Chorales from Cantatas 79, 129, 140, 142, 147, 207, 248; 5 Sinfonias to Cantatas 29, 31, 35, 49; Five Concerted Chorales, BWV 19, 130, 137, 250, 303; Unto us a child is born (concerto), from Christmas Cantata, BWV 142; My spirit be joyful (duet), from Easter Cantata, BWV 146; March from Cantata 207; Instrumental Trio & Sheep may safely graze from Birthday Cantata, BWV 208; In dulci jubilo (chorale prelude), from BWV 740 — CBS ▲ MK 42646 [ADD]

K. Sanderling (cnd)

Bruckner, A.:Sym 3, "Wagner" [1889 version] — Berlin Classics ("Eterna" series) ▲ BER 2151 [ADD]

W. Sawallisch (cnd)

Mendelssohn, F.:Elijah, w. E. Ameling (sop), A. Burmeister (mez), P. Schreier (ten), T. Adam (b–bar), Leipzig Radio Chorus [G] — Philips 2–▲ 420106–2 [AAD]
Mendelssohn, F.:Elijah, w. E. Ameling (sop), A. Burmeister (mez), P. Schreier (ten), T. Adam (b–bar), Leipzig Radio Chorus — Philips 2–▲ 438368–2

L. Stokowski (cnd)

Debussy, C.:Nocturnes, w. Leipzig Gewandhaus Chorus *(rec June 1, 1959)* — Music & Arts 2–▲ MUA 280 [AAD]
Ravel, M.:Rapsodie espagnole, w. Leipzig Gewandhaus Chorus *(rec June 1, 1959)* — Music & Arts 2–▲ MUA 280 [AAD]

K. Thomas (cnd)

Bach, J.S.:Cant 51, w. *(soloists unknown),* Leipzig St. Thomas Church Choir — Berlin Classics ▲ BER 9200
Bach, J.S.:Cant 54, w. Marga Hoffgen (sop), Hermann Prey (bass), Leipzig St. Thomas Church Choir — Berlin Classics ▲ BER CD 9202
Bach, J.S.:Cant 56, w. Marga Hoffgen (sop), Hermann Prey (bass), Leipzig St. Thomas Church Choir — Berlin Classics ▲ BER CD 9202
Bach, J.S.:Cant 59, w. *(soloists unknown),* Leipzig St. Thomas Church Choir — Berlin Classics ▲ BER 9200
Bach, J.S.:Cant 71, w. Leipzig St. Thomas Church Choir — Berlin Classics ▲ BER 9203
Bach, J.S.:Cant 82, w. Marga Hoffgen (sop), Hermann Prey (bass), Leipzig St. Thomas Church Choir — Berlin Classics ▲ BER CD 9202
Bach, J.S.:Cant 111, w. Leipzig St. Thomas Church Choir — Berlin Classics ▲ BER 9203
Bach, J.S.:Cant 140, w. Leipzig St. Thomas Church Choir — Berlin Classics ▲ BER 9203
Bach, J.S.:Magnificat, BWV 243, w. *(soloists unknown),* Leipzig St. Thomas Church Choir — Berlin Classics ▲ BER 9200

L. Zagrosek (cnd)

Eisler, H.:Deutsche Sinfonie, w. Hendrikje Wangemann (sop), Annette Markert (alt), Matthias Görne (bar), Peter Lika (bass), Gert Gütschow (speaker), Volker Schwarz (speaker), Ernst Senff Chorus *(rec Gewandhaus, Leipzig, May 1995)* — London ("Entartet Musik" series) ▲ 448389–2 [DDD]
Krenek, E.:Jonny spielt auf, w. A. Marc (sop), M. Kraus (ten), H. Kruse (ten), K. St. Hill (ten) [G] — London 2–▲ 436631–2 [DDD]
Ullmann, V.:Kaiser von Atlantis, w. C. Oelze (sop—Bubikopf), I. Vermillion (mez—The Drummer), M. Petzold (ten—A Soldier), M. Kraus (ten—Kaiser Overall), H. Lippert (ten—Harlekin), F. Mazura (bar—The Loudspeaker), W. Berry (bass—Death) — London ▲ 440854–2 [DDD]

Leipzig New Bach Collegium Musicum

Bach, J.S.:Cant 4, w. Helga Terner (sop), Ortrun Wenkel (cta), Peter Schreier (ten), Eberhard Büchner (ten), H.–J. Rotzsch (cnd), Leipzig Gewandhaus Orch, Leipzig St. Thomas Church Choir — Berlin Classics ▲ BER 2067 [ADD]
Bach, J.S.:Cant 31, w. Helga Terner (sop), Ortrun Wenkel (cta), Peter Schreier (ten), Eberhard Büchner (ten), H.–J. Rotzsch (cnd), Leipzig Gewandhaus Orch, Leipzig St. Thomas Church Choir — Berlin Classics ▲ BER 2067 [ADD]
Bach, J.S.:Cant 134, w. Helga Terner (sop), Ortrun Wenkel (cta), Peter Schreier (ten), Eberhard Büchner (ten), H.–J. Rotzsch (cnd), Leipzig Gewandhaus Orch, Leipzig St. Thomas Church Choir — Berlin Classics ▲ BER 2067 [ADD]

M. Pommer (cnd)

Bach, C.P.E.:Con Ob, H.466, w. B. Glaetzner (ob) — Capriccio ▲ 10069
Bach, C.P.E.:Con Ob, H.468, w. B. Glaetzner (ob) — Capriccio ▲ 10069
Bach, J.S.:The Art of the Fugue — Capriccio 2–▲ CDC 10026 [DDD]
Bach, J.S.:Brandenburg Cons—Nos. 4–6 — Capriccio ▲ CDC 10042 [DDD] Δ 80042 ▯ 70042
Bach, J.S.:Brandenburg Cons—Nos. 1–3 — Capriccio ▲ CDC 10041 [DDD] Δ 80041 ▯ 70041
Bach, J.S.:Brandenburg Cons—alternate versions, BWV 1046a, 1047a, 174/1, 1050a — Capriccio ▲ CDC 10025 [DDD]
Bach, J.S.:Cant 14, w. M. Frimmer (sop), E. Büchner (ten), A. Scheibner (bar), Leipzig St. Thomas Church Choir [G] — Capriccio ▲ CDC 10027
Bach, J.S.:Cant 51, w. M. Frimmer (sop), Leipzig St. Thomas Church Choir [G] — Capriccio ▲ CDC 10027 [DDD]
Bach, J.S.:Cant 55, w. P. Schreier (ten), Leipzig Univ Choir [G] — Capriccio ▲ 10151 [DDD]
Bach, J.S.:Cant 56, w. M. Lorenz (ten) [G] — Capriccio ▲ CDC 10028 [DDD]
Bach, J.S.:Cant 82, w. M. Lorenz (ten) [G] — Capriccio ▲ CDC 10028 [DDD]
Bach, J.S.:Cant 84, w. V. Hruba–Freiberger (sop), Leipzig Univ Choir [G] — Capriccio ▲ 10151 [DDD]
Bach, J.S.:Cant 84, w. Venceslava Hruba–Freiberger (sop), Peter Schreier (ten), Leipzig Univ Choir — Berlin Classics ▲ BER 1066 [DDD]
Bach, J.S.:Cant 143, w. M. Frimmer (sop), E. Büchner (ten), A. Scheibner (bar), Leipzig St. Thomas Church Choir [G] — Capriccio ▲ CDC 10027 [DDD]
Bach, J.S.:Cant 199, w. Venceslava Hruba–Freiberger (sop), Peter Schreier (ten), Leipzig Univ Choir — Berlin Classics ▲ BER 1066 [DDD]
Bach, J.S.:Cant 199, w. V. Hruba–Freiberger (sop), Leipzig Univ Choir [G] — Capriccio ▲ 10151 [DDD]
Bach, J.S.:Music of, w. L. Güttler (tpt), M. Lorenz (ten), A. Reiss (ten), P. Schreier (ten), H.–C. Polster (b–bar), Leipzig Choirs—arias, choruses & chorales — Capriccio ▲ CDC 10039 [DDD]
Bach, J.S.:Suite 1 Orch — Capriccio ▲ CDC 10011 [DDD]
Bach, J.S.:Suite 3 Orch — Capriccio ▲ CDC 10012 [DDD]
Fasch, J.F.:Con Tpt & Strs, w. L. Güttler (corno da caccia) — Capriccio ▲ CDC 10008 [DDD]
Handel, G.F.:The Choice of Hercules, w. Arleen Augér (sop), Venceslava Hruba–Freiberger (sop), Eberhard Büchner (ten), Zäppffel (sgr), Leipzig Univ Choir [E] — Capriccio ▲ CDC 10019 [DDD]
Handel, G.F.:Concerti grossi, Op. 3 — LaserLight ▲ 14 006 [DDD]
Handel, G.F.:Concerti grossi, Op. 3—No. 5 — LaserLight ▲ 15 629 [DDD]
Handel, G.F.:Concerti grossi, Op. 6—Nos. 9–12 — Capriccio ▲ CDC 10023 [DDD]
Handel, G.F.:Concerti grossi, Op. 6—Nos. 1–4 — Capriccio ▲ CDC 10021 [DDD]
Handel, G.F.:Concerti grossi, Op. 6—Nos. 5–8 — Capriccio ▲ CDC 10022 [DDD]
Heinichen, J.D.:Con Tpt, w. Ludvig Güttler (corno da caccia) — Capriccio ▲ CDC 10008 [DDD]
Molter, J.M.:Con 1 Tpt, w. Ludwig Güttler (tpt) — Capriccio ▲ CDC 10010 [DDD]
Mozart, L.:Con Tpt, w. L. Güttler (tpt)—& Anon.:Con. in E♭ — Capriccio ▲ CDC 10010 [DDD]
Music of Johann Sebastian Bach — Laserlight ♦ 90025 [DDD]
Neruda, J.B.G.:Con Tpt, w. L. Güttler (tpt) — Capriccio ▲ CDC 10008

Leipzig Opera House Orch

M. Janowski (cnd)

Beethoven, L. van:Con 1 Pno, w. Gerhard Oppitz (pno) *(rec Grand Hall of the Leipzig Opera House, Jan 26–Feb 4, 1995)* — RCA Red Seal ▲ 09026–68226–2 [DDD]
Beethoven, L. van:Con 3 Pno, w. Gerhard Oppitz (pno) *(rec Grand Hall of the Leipzig Opera House, Jan 26–Feb 4, 1995)* — RCA Red Seal ▲ 09026–68226–2 [DDD]

F. Konwitschny (cnd)

Shostakovich, D.:Sym 10 *(rec 1957)* — Berlin Classics ("Documents" series) 2–▲ BER 9042 [ADD]

K. Masur (cnd)

Brahms, J.:Con 2 Pno, w. Cécile Ousset (pno) — Accord ▲ ACD 201152 [AAD]
The Masur Edition:Selected Recordings, w. Dresden PO — Berlin Classics 9–▲ BER 9150 [ADD]
Mendelssohn, F.:Sinfs Strs [includes fragment known as No. 13] — Berlin Classics 4–▲ BER 9143 [ADD]

V. Neumann (cnd)

Gluck, C.W.:Orfeo ed Euridice, w. Ruth–Margaret Pütz (sop), Anneliese Rothenberger (sop), Grace Bumbry (mez), Leipzig Radio Chorus *(rec Leipzig, 1967)* — Berlin Classics 2–▲ BER 9033 [ADD]

Leipzig Opera House Orch (cont.)

V. Neumann (cnd) (cont.)

Mahler, G.:Sym 6 *(rec 1966)* — Berlin Classics 2–▲ BER 9045 [ADD]
Mahler, G.:Sym 7 — Berlin Classics ▲ BER 9046 [ADD]

K. Thomas (cnd)

Bach, J.S.:Motets, BWV 225–30, w. Leipzig St. Thomas Church Choir — Berlin Classics ▲ BER 9103 [ADD]

L. Zagrosek (cnd)

Hindemith, P.:Der Dämon — London ▲ 444182–2
Schreker, F.:Der Geburtstag der Infantin — London ▲ 444182–2
Schulhoff, E.:Die Mondsuchtige — London ▲ 444182–2

Leipzig RSO

H. Abendroth (cnd)

Beethoven, L. van:Sym 9, "Choral Sym", w. Anny Schlemm (sop), Diana Eustrati (cta), Gert Lutze (ten), Thomas Paul (bass) *(rec 1953)* — Arlecchino ARL
Brahms, J.:Sym 2 *(rec 1952–54)* — Arlecchino ▲ ARL127
Brahms, J.:Sym 4 *(rec 1952–54)* — Arlecchino ▲ ARL127
Bruckner, A.:Sym 4, "Romantic" *(rec 1951)* — Arlecchino ▲ ARL107
Bruckner, A.:Sym 4, "Romantic" — Berlin Classics ▲ BER CD 9277
Bruckner, A.:Sym 5 *(rec 1949)* — Arlecchino ARL
Bruckner, A.:Sym 5 — Berlin Classics ▲ BER 9280
Bruckner, A.:Sym 9 *(rec Oct. 29, 1951)* — Berlin Classics ("Dokumente" series) ▲ BER 2050 [ADD]
Humperdinck, E.:Moorish Rhap *(rec 1952)* — Arlecchino ARL
Mozart, W.A.:Notturno, K.286, Berlin RSO, Leipzig Gewandhaus Orch — Berlin Classics 2–▲ BER 9271
Mozart, W.A.:Sym 33 *(rec 1956)* — Arlecchino ARL
Mozart, W.A.:Sym 35 *(rec 1956)* — Arlecchino ARL
Mussorgsky, M.:Pictures *(rec 1952)* — Arlecchino ARL
Schubert, Franz:Sym 8 *(rec 1949–50)* — Berlin Classics ("Dokumente" series) ▲ BER 2051 [ADD]
Schubert, Franz:Sym 9 *(rec 1949–50)* — Berlin Classics ("Dokumente" series) ▲ BER 2051 [ADD]
Schumann, R.:Con Vc, w. P. Tortelier (vc) — Berlin Classics ("Dokumente" series) ▲ BER 2052 [ADD]
Schumann, R.:Sym 4 — Berlin Classics ("Dokumente" series) ▲ BER 2053 [DDD]
Sibelius, J.:Sym 2 *(rec 1949)* — Arlecchino ▲ ARL108
Strauss, R.:Don Juan — Tahra ("Abendroth Edition" series) ▲ TAH 138
Strauss, R.:Till Eulenspiegels lustige Streiche — Tahra ("Abendroth Edition" series) ▲ TAH 138
Strauss, R.:Tod und Verklärung — Tahra ("Abendroth Edition" series) ▲ TAH 138
Tchaikovsky, P.:Sym 4 — Berlin Classics ("Dokumente" series) ▲ BER 2053 [DDD]

W.–D. Hauschild (cnd)

Denisov, E.:Con Pno, w. Günter Philipp (pno) — Berlin Classics ▲ BER 9260
Ives, C.:Central Park in the Dark, w. Leipzig Radio Chorus — Berlin Classics ▲ BER 9008 [ADD]
Ives, C.:Holidays, w. Leipzig Radio Chorus — Berlin Classics ▲ BER 9008 [ADD]
Telemann, G.P.:Alster Ov — Berlin Classics ▲ BER 9262
Telemann, G.P.:Don Quichotte (suite), w. Wolf–Dieter Hauschild (hpd) — Berlin Classics ▲ BER 9262

H. Kegel (cnd)

Berg, A.:Lulu (sels), w. Hanne–Lore Kuhse (sop)—Adagio — Berlin Classics ▲ BER 9020 [ADD]
Berg, A.:Wozzeck, w. G. Schröter (mez), R. Goldberg (ten), H. Hiestermann (ten), T. Adam (b–bar) *(rec Apr. 9, 1973)* — Berlin Classics ("Eterna" series) 2–▲ BER 2068 [ADD]
Berg, A.:Wozzeck (sels), w. Hanne–Lore Kuhse (sop) — Berlin Classics ▲ BER 9020 [ADD]
Blacher, B.:A Jewish Chronicle, w. Anna Barová (cta), Vladimir Bauer (sgr), Leipzig Radio Chorus — Berlin Classics ▲ BER 9016 [ADD]
Brahms, J.:Ein Deutsches Requiem, w. M. A. Häggander (sop), M. Lorenz (ten), Leipzig Radio Chorus [G] — Capriccio ▲ 10095 [DDD]
Britten, B.:Les Illuminations, w. Peter Schreier (ten) — Berlin Classics ▲ BER 9035 [ADD]
Britten, B.:Serenade, Op. 31, w. Peter Schreier (ten), Günther Opitz (hn) — Berlin Classics ▲ BER 9035 [ADD]
Dessau, P.:Orchestermusik 2, "Meer der Stürme" — Berlin Classics ▲ BER 2182 [ADD]
Dessau, P.:Die Verurteilung des Lukullus, w. Annelies Burmeister (mez—Das Fischweib), Helmut Melchert (ten—Lukullus), Hans–Joachim Rotzsch (ten—Der Kirschbaumträger), Peter Schreier (ten—Lukullus' Cook), Boris Carmeli (bass—King), Leipzig Radio Chorus — Berlin Classics 2–▲ BER 1073 [ADD]
Hartmann, K.A.:Sym 8 — Berlin Classics ▲ BER 9048 [DDD]
Mendelssohn, F.:Con 1 Pno, w. Valentin Gheorghiu (pno) — Berlin Classics ▲ BER 9027 [ADD]
Mendelssohn, F.:Con 2 Pno, w. Valentin Gheorghiu (pno) — Berlin Classics ▲ BER 9027 [ADD]
Orff, C.:Carmina burana, w. *(soloists unknown),* Berlin Radio Chorus, Dresden Children's Choir, Leipzig Radio Chorus — Berlin Classics 2–▲ BER 2047 [ADD]
Orff, C.:Catulli Carmina, w. *(soloists unknown),* Berlin Radio Chorus, Dresden Children's Choir, Leipzig Radio Chorus — Berlin Classics 2–▲ BER 2047 [ADD]
Orff, C.:Die Kluge, w. Leipzig Radio Chorus — Berlin Classics 2–▲ BER 2104–2 [ADD]
Orff, C.:Der Mond—Ein kleines Welttheater, w. Leipzig Radio Chorus — Berlin Classics 2–▲ BER 2104–2 [ADD]
Orff, C.:Trionfo di Afrodite, w. *(soloists unknown),* Berlin Radio Chorus, Dresden Children's Choir, Leipzig Radio Chorus — Berlin Classics 2–▲ BER 2047 [ADD]
Prokofiev, S.:Betrothal in a Monastery (sels), w. A. Burmeister (mez), E. Büchner (bar), R. Süss (bar) [G] — Berlin Classics ▲ BER 2081 [ADD]
Schoenberg, A.:Moses und Aaron, w. Renate Krahmer (sop), Gisela Pohl (cta), Reiner Goldberg (ten), Werner Haseleu (nar), Leipzig Radio Chorus — Berlin Classics 2–▲ BER 1116 [ADD]
Weber, C.M. von:Kampf und Sieg, w. L. Schmidt–Glänzel (sop), E. Fleischer (cta), G. Lutze (ten), H. Krämer (bar), Leipzig Radio Chorus [G] — Forlane ▲ FOR 16572 (m) [AAD]
Webern, A.:Movts Str Qt — Berlin Classics ▲ BER 9020 [ADD]
Webern, A.:Passacaglia — Berlin Classics ▲ BER 9020 [ADD]
Webern, A.:Pieces Orch, Op. 6 — Berlin Classics ▲ BER 9020 [ADD]
Webern, A.:Pieces Orch, Op. 10 — Berlin Classics ▲ BER 9020 [ADD]
Webern, A.:Sym, Op. 21 — Berlin Classics ▲ BER 9020 [ADD]

F. Konwitschny (cnd)

Beethoven, L. van:Sym 4 — Forlane 2–▲ FOR 16674 [ADD]
Beethoven, L. van:Sym 5 — Forlane 2–▲ FOR 16674 [ADD]
Beethoven, L. van:Sym 9, "Choral Sym", w. Leipzig Radio Chorus — Forlane 2–▲ FOR 16674 [ADD]

H. Neumann (cnd)

Schumann, R.:Choral Music, w. Leipzig Radio Chorus *(rec 1978)* — Berlin Classics ▲ BER 9191

M. Pommer (cnd)

Aho, K.:Sym 5 — Ondine ▲ ODE 765–2 [DDD]
Aho, K.:Sym 7 — Ondine ▲ ODE 765–2 [DDD]
Brandmüller, T.:Con Org, w. Theo Brandenmüller (org) — MD + G ▲ MDG 6250551 [DDD]
Debussy, C.:La Mer — LaserLight ▲ 14 004 [DDD]
Debussy, C.:Nocturnes — LaserLight ▲ 14 004 [DDD]
Debussy, C.:Prélude à l'après–midi d'un faune — LaserLight ▲ 14 004 [DDD]
Kelemen, M.:Infinity — Berlin Classics ▲ BER 1144 [ADD]
Kelemen, M.:Love Song — Berlin Classics ▲ BER 1144 [ADD]
Kelemen, M.:Mageia — Berlin Classics ▲ BER 1144 [ADD]
Kelemen, M.:Mirabilia, w. Gerhard Erber (pno), Eckhard Rodger (ring modulator) — Berlin Classics ▲ BER 1144 [ADD]
Mozart, W.A.:Apollo et Hyacinthus, w. V. Hruba–Frieberger (sop), A. Raunig (alt), R. Popken (alt), J. Dickie (ten), Leipzig Radio Chorus — Berlin Classics 2–▲ BER 1010 [DDD]
Mozart, W.A.:Bastien und Bastienne, w. D. Schellenberger (sop), R. Eschrig (ten), R. Pape (bass), Leipzig Radio Chorus — Berlin Classics 2–▲ BER 1010 [DDD]

212

▲ = CD ♦ = Enhanced CD Δ = MD ▮ = Cassette Tape ▯ = DCC

Leipzig RSO (cont.)

M. Pommer (cnd) (cont.)

Mozart, W.A.:Contradances, K.101 — Berlin Classics ▲ BER 1081 [DDD]
Mozart, W.A.:Kleine Nachtmusik — Berlin Classics ▲ BER 1081 [DDD]
Mozart, W.A.:Notturno Orchs, K.286 — Berlin Classics ▲ BER 1081 [DDD]
Mozart, W.A.:Serenata notturna — Berlin Classics ▲ BER 1081 [DDD]
Rautavaara, E.:Cantus Arcticus — Catalyst ▲ 09026-62671-2
Rautavaara, E.:Cantus Arcticus, (with largely unprocessed taped birdsong) — Ondine ▲ ODE 747-2 [DDD]
Rautavaara, E.:Con 1 Pno, w. R. Gothoni (pno) — Ondine ▲ ODE 757-2 [DDD]
Rautavaara, E.:Sym 1 — Ondine ▲ ODE 740-2 [DDD]
Rautavaara, E.:Sym 2 — Ondine ▲ ODE 740-2 [DDD]
Rautavaara, E.:Sym 3 — Ondine ▲ ODE 740-2 [DDD]
Rautavaara, E.:Sym 4 — Ondine ▲ ODE 747-2 [DDD]
Rautavaara, E.:Sym 5 — Catalyst ▲ 09026-62671-2
Rautavaara, E.:Sym 5 — Ondine ▲ ODE 747-2 [DDD]
Weill, K.:Con Vn, w. W. Wächter (vn) — Ondine ▲ ODE 771-2 [DDD]
Weill, K.:Kleine Dreigroschenmusik — Ondine ▲ ODE 771-2 [DDD]
Weill, K.:Vom Tod im Wald, w. T. Möwes (bass) — Ondine ▲ ODE 771-2 [DDD]

R. Wolf (cnd)

Borck, E. von:Con Sax, w. D. Bensmann (sax) — MD + G ▲ L 3451 [DDD]

Leipzig RSO members

Kol Nidre:Sacred Music of the Synagogue, w. Gloria Seipelt(alt), Leo Roth (ten), Rudolf Wiebel (bar), Werner Buschnakowski (org), Harry Foss (org), Jewish Congregation Choir Berlin, Leipzig Synagogue Choir — EMI Classics ▲ CDM 65457

H. Neumann (cnd)

Henze, H.-W.:Voices, w. Roswitha Trexler (mez), Joachim Vogt (ten) — Berlin Classics 2-▲ BER 2180 [DDD]

Leipzig Radio Wind Orch

M. Miron (cnd)

Concertos for Clarinets & Military Band, w. Don Christensen, (cl), Cindy Christensen (cl) — Koch Schwann ▲ SCH 310672 [DDD]

Leipzig String Quartet

Adorno, T.W.:Pieces *(rec Studio 10, Funkhaus, Berlin, Sept 1995)* — CPO ▲ 999341-2 [DDD]
Adorno, T.W.:Qt Strs *(rec Studio 10, Funkhaus, Berlin, Sept 1995)* — CPO ▲ 999341-2 [DDD]
Adorno, T.W.:Studies *(rec Studio 10, Funkhaus, Berlin, Sept 1995)* — CPO ▲ 999341-2 [DDD]
Cage, J.:Qt Strs — MD + G ▲ MDG CD 6130701
Eisler, H.:Qt Strs *(rec Studio 10, Funkhaus, Berlin, Sept 1995)* — CPO ▲ 999341-2 [DDD]
Schubert, Franz:Ov Orch, D.470 [arr for string quartet] — MD + G ▲ MDG 3070602
Schubert, Franz:Ov Str Qt, D.8a — MD + G ▲ MDG 3070603
Schubert, Franz:Qt Strs, D.3 — MD + G ▲ MDG 3070603
Schubert, Franz:Qt Strs, D.18 — MD + G ▲ MDG 3070602
Schubert, Franz:Qt 13 Strs — MD + G ▲ MDG 3070602
Schubert, Franz:Qnt Strs, D.956, w. Michael Sanderling (vc) — MD + G ▲ MDG 3070603

Leipzig String Quartet [Andreas Seidel (vn), Tilman Büning (vn), Ivo Bauer (va), Matthias Moosdorf (vc)]

Schubert, Franz:Minuet in d Str Qt — MD + G ▲ MDG CD 3070604
Schubert, Franz:Minuets & Trios, D.89, w. Christian Ockert (db) — MD + G ▲ MDG CD 3070604
Schubert, Franz:Qt Strs, D.103 — MD + G ▲ MDG CD 3070605
Schubert, Franz:Qt 6 Strs — MD + G ▲ MDG CD 3070605
Schubert, Franz:Qt 10 Strs — MD + G ▲ MDG CD 3070605
Schubert, Franz:Qt 14 Strs — MD + G ▲ MDG CD 3070604

Leipzig String Quartet members

Eisler, H.:Präludium und Fugue über B-A-C-H *(rec Studio 10, Funkhaus, Berlin, Sept 1995)* — CPO ▲ 999341-2 [DDD]

Leipzig SO

O. Koch (cnd)

Boëllmann, L.:Fant dialoguée, w. Franz Hauk (org) — IMP ("Classics" series) ▲ IMP 6701092
Fétis, F.J.:Fant symphonique, w. Franz Hauk (org) — IMP ("Classics" series) ▲ IMP 6701092
Guilmant, A.:Org Music, w. Franz Hauk (org)—Allegro for Org & Orch, Op. 81; Marche fantasie sur deux chantes d'eglise for Org, Hp & Orch, Op. 44; Meditation sur le stabat mater for Org & Orch, Op. 63; Final all Schumann sur un Noël languedocien, Op. 83; Sym No. 1 for Org & Orch, Op. 42 — IMP ("Classics" series) ▲ IMP 6701092

Lemoges Baroque Ensemble

Music at the Time of Beaumarchais, w. Montserrat Figueras (sop), Lawrence Monteyro (sop), Raphel Oleg (vn), Miguel da Silva (va), Christophe Coin (vc), Marc Coppey (vc), José Miguel Moreno (gtr), Paul Badura-Skoda (pno), Philippe Cassard (pno), Éric Le Sage (pno), Bob Van Asperen (hpd), et al. — Valois ▲ V 4767

Léner String Quartet

Brahms, J.:Qnt Cl, w. C. Draper (cl) *(rec 1928 for Columbia Records)* — Pearl ▲ PEA 9903 (m) [AAD]
Mozart, W.A.:Divert Hns Strs, K.334, w. A. Brain (hn), D. Brain (hn) — EMI Classics ▲ CDM 64198
Mozart, W.A.:Qnt Cl, K.581, w. C. Draper (cl) *(rec 1928 for Columbia Records)* — Pearl ▲ PEA 9903 (m) [AAD]

Lengyel Duo [Gabriella Lengyel (vn), Atty Lengyel (pno)]

Farkas, F.:Sonatina 2 Vn — Media 7 ▲ 001 [ADD]
Hubay, J.:Son Vn — Media 7 ▲ 001 [ADD]
Kovách, A.:Son Vn — Media 7 ▲ 001 [ADD]
Veress, S.:Son 2 Vn — Media 7 ▲ 001 [ADD]

Leningrad Bell Music Ensemble

Y. Temirkanov (cnd)

Petrov, A.:Russia of Bells, w. Leningrad State Phil Academic SO *(rec Grand Hall of the Leningrad State PO)* — Russian Compact Disc ▲ RCD 26601

Leningrad Conservatory Academic SO

L. Slovák (cnd)

Bach, J.S.:Con 1 Hpd, w. G. Gould (pno) *(rec 1957)* — CBS 2-▲ M2K 42270 (m) [AAD]
Bach, J.S.:Con 1 Hpd, w. G. Gould (pno) *(rec May 18, 1957)* — Sony Classical ▲ SMK 52686 [ADD]
Beethoven, L. van:Con 2 Pno, w. G. Gould (pno) — CBS 3-▲ M3K 39036
Beethoven, L. van:Con 2 Pno, w. G. Gould (pno) *(rec May 18., 1957)* — Sony Classical ▲ SMK 52686 [ADD]

Leningrad Military Orch

Y. Temirkanov (cnd)

Tchaikovsky, P.:Music of, w. I. Perlman (vn), J. Norman (sop), Yo-Yo Ma (vc), Leningrad PO—Waltz & Polonaise from Eugene Onegin; Sérénade mélancolique, Op. 26; Valse scherzo, Op. 34; Variations on a Rococo Theme, Op. 33; Overture 1812, Op. 49; Symphony No. 6 (3rd movt.); 3 Chansons française from Op. 65, for Voice & Piano; Aria (Adieu, forêts) from The Maid of Orleans *(rec live, Leningrad)* — RCA Red Seal ▲ 60739-2-RC [DDD] ■ 09026-60739-4-RC (CrO2) □ 09026-60739-5

Leningrad PO

I. Blazhkov (cnd)

Shostakovich, D.:Sym 2, w. Leningrad Phil Choir *(rec Nov. 1, 1965)* — Russian Disc ▲ RUS 11195 [AAD]

A. Dmitriev (cnd)

Shostakovich, D.:Sym 5 *(rec live, City Halls, Glasgow, Apr 12, 1990)* — Linn ▲ CKD 004

N. Golovanov (cnd)

Borodin, A.:Sym 2 *(rec 1947)* — Multisonic ("Russian Treasures" series) ▲ 31 0188

M. Jansons (cnd)

Prokofiev, S.:Sym 5 — Chandos ▲ CHAN 8576 [DDD]
Rachmaninoff, S.:Con 2 Pno, w. M. Rudy (pno) — EMI Classics ▲ CDC 54232
Shostakovich, D.:Sym 7 — EMI Classics ▲ CDC 49494 [DDD]
Tchaikovsky, P.:Con 1 Pno, w. M. Rudy (pno) — EMI Classics ▲ CDC 54232

B. Khaikin (cnd)

Glazunov, A.:Sym 4 *(rec 1946)* — Multisonic ("Russian Treasures" series) ▲ 31 0237

Leningrad PO (cont.)

B. Khaikin (cnd) (cont.)

Rimsky-Korsakov, N.:Sym 1 *(rec 1946)* — Multisonic ("Russian Treasures" series) ▲ 31 0237

E. Mravinsky (cnd)

Bach, J.S.:Suite 2 Orch *(rec Nov 21, 1961)* — Russian Disc ("The Mravinsky Collection" series) ▲ RUS 11 167 [AAD]
Bartók, B.:Music for Strs, Perc & Cel *(rec 1965-1973)* — Enterprise ("Documents" series) 2-▲ ENTLV 917 [ADD]
Bartók, B.:Music for Strs, Perc & Cel — Melodiya ("Mravinsky Edition" series) ▲ 74321-25197-2 [ADD]
Bartók, B.:Music for Strs, Perc & Cel — Praga ▲ PR 254047
Bartók, B.:Music for Strs, Perc & Cel *(rec Oct. 12, 1970)* — Russian Disc ("The Mravinsky Collection" series) ▲ RUS 11 167 [AAD]
Beethoven, L. van:Sym 1 *(rec live)* — Erato ▲ 2292-45759-2 AW
Beethoven, L. van:Sym 1 — Audiophile Classics ("Legacy" series) ▲ 101.505 [ADD]
Beethoven, L. van:Sym 3, "Eroica" *(rec live)* — Erato ▲ 2292-45759-2 AW
Beethoven, L. van:Sym 4 *(rec between 1965 & 1973)* — Enterprise ("Documents" series) ▲ ENTLV 917 [ADD]
Beethoven, L. van:Sym 4 — Melodiya ("Mravinsky Edition" series) ▲ 74321-25196-2 [ADD]
Beethoven, L. van:Sym 4 *(rec 1972-74)* — Russian Disc ("The Mravinsky Collection" series) ▲ RUS 10901 [AAD]
Beethoven, L. van:Sym 5 *(rec live)* — Erato ▲ 2292-45760-2 AW
Beethoven, L. van:Sym 6, "Pastorale"—Allegro ma non troppo *(rec Leningrad Philharmonic Large Hall, URSS, Oct. 1982)* — Erato ▲ 94682-2
Beethoven, L. van:Sym 6, "Pastorale" *(rec live)* — Erato ▲ 2292-45761-2 AW
Beethoven, L. van:Sym 6, "Pastorale" *(rec 1962)* — Russian Disc ▲ RUS 11 159
Beethoven, L. van:Sym 7 *(rec live)* — Erato ▲ 2292-45760-2 AW
Brahms, J.:Con 2 Pno, w. S. Richter (pno) *(rec Dec. 27, 1961)* — Russian Disc ▲ RUS 11 158 [AAD]
Brahms, J.:Syms (comp) *(rec 1950, 1978, 1965 & 1973)* — Memoria 2-▲ 991.006 [ADD]
Brahms, J.:Sym 2 — Melodiya ("Mravinsky Edition" series) ▲ 74321-25190-2 [ADD]
Brahms, J.:Sym 4 *(rec 1973)* — Andromeda ▲ ANR 2531 [ADD]
Brahms, J.:Sym 4 *(rec 1961)* — Russian Disc ▲ RUS 10907 [AAD]
Bruckner, A.:Sym 9 — Melodiya ("Mravinsky Edition" series) ▲ 74321-25193-2 [ADD]
Davīdov, K.Y.:Con 2 Vc, w. Daniel Shafran (vc) *(rec Large Hall, Moscow Conservatory, May 2, 1949)* — Russian Compact Disc ▲ RDCD 10914 (m) [AAD]
Debussy, C.:Nocturnes *(rec Feb. 26, 1960)* — Russian Disc ("The Mravinsky Collection" series) ▲ RUS 11 167 [AAD]
Debussy, C.:Nocturnes *(rec 1949)* — Multisonic ▲ 31 0178 [DDD]
Debussy, C.:Prélude à l'après-midi d'un faune — Melodiya ("Mravinsky Edition" series) ▲ 74321-25197-2 [ADD]
Glazunov, A.:Raymonda (sels) *(rec 1972-74)* — Russian Disc ("The Mravinsky Collection" series) ▲ RUS 10901 [AAD]
Glazunov, A.:The Seasons — Russian Disc ▲ CD 11155 [AAD]
Glazunov, A.:Sym 5 *(rec Sept. 28, 1968)* — Russian Disc ▲ RUS11 165 [AAD]
Glinka, M.:Russlan & Ludmilla (ov) *(rec Leningrad PO Great Hall, Apr 8, 1983)* — Russian Disc ▲ RD CD 10912 [AAD]
Glinka, M.:Russlan & Ludmilla (ov) *(rec live, Royal Albert Hall, London, 1971)* — Intaglio ▲ INCD 7321 [ADD]
Glinka, M.:Russlan & Ludmilla (ov) *(rec live, Prague Festival, 1968)* — Arkadia ▲ 713 (m) [ADD]
Haydn, J.:Sym 88 — Russian Disc ▲ RUS 11 163 [AAD]
Haydn, J.:Sym 104, "London" — Russian Disc ▲ RUS 11 163 [AAD]
Hindemith, P.:Die Harmonie der Welt *(rec 1978)* — Originals ▲ ORISH 815 [ADD]
Hindemith, P.:Die Harmonie der Welt — Melodiya ("Mravinsky Edition" series) ▲ 74321-25195-2 [ADD]
Honegger, A.:Sym 3 — Melodiya ("Mravinsky Edition" series) ▲ 74321-25195-2 [ADD]
Klyuzner, B.:Sym 2 *(rec 1964)* — Russian Disc ("The Mravinsky Collection" series) ▲ RUS 11 162 [AAD]
Liadov, A.:Baba Yaga *(rec 1972-74)* — Russian Disc ("The Mravinsky Collection" series) ▲ RUS 10901 [AAD]
Liadov, A.:Baba Yaga *(rec Sept. 30, 1966)* — Russian Disc ▲ RUS 10 902 [AAD]
Liadov, A.:Baba Yaga *(rec Apr. 21, 1959)* — Russian Disc ("The Mravinsky Collection" series) ▲ RUS 10900 [AAD]
Liadov, A.:The Enchanted Lake *(rec Sept. 30, 1966)* — Russian Disc ▲ RUS 10 902 [AAD]
Liatoshinsky, B.:Sym 3 *(rec Dec. 29, 1955)* — Russian Disc ▲ RUS 10 902 [AAD]
Melodiya Sampler — Melodiya ▲ 09026-27247-2 [ADD/DDD]
Mozart, W.A.:Cons Hn, w. *(soloist unknown)*—No. 3 *(rec Leningrad, Feb.-Nov. 1961)* — Russian Disc ▲ RUS 10909 [AAD]
Mozart, W.A.:Nozze di Figaro (ov) — Melodiya ("Mravinsky Edition" series) ▲ 74321-25191-2 [ADD]
Mozart, W.A.:Ovs—Le nozze di Figaro *(rec 1965)* — Andromeda ▲ ANR 2531 [ADD]
Mozart, W.A.:Sinf concertante Ob, K.Anh.9 *(rec Leningrad, Feb.-Nov. 1961)* — Russian Disc ▲ RUS 10909 [AAD]
Mozart, W.A.:Sym 33 *(rec live)* — Erato ▲ 2292-45758-2
Mozart, W.A.:Sym 33 *(rec Leningrad, Feb.-Nov. 1961)* — Russian Disc ▲ RUS 10909 [AAD]
Mozart, W.A.:Sym 39 *(rec live)* — Erato ▲ 2292-45758-2
Mozart, W.A.:Sym 39 — Melodiya ("Mravinsky Edition" series) ▲ 74321-25191-2 [ADD]
Mozart, W.A.:Sym 40 *(rec 1972-74)* — Russian Disc ("The Mravinsky Collection" series) ▲ RUS 10901 [AAD]
Mravinsky Edition — Melodiya 10-▲ 09026-25189-2 [ADD]
Mussorgsky, M.:Khovanshchina (prelude)—Dawn o the Moscow River — Melodiya ("Mravinsky Edition" series) ▲ 74321-25191-2 [ADD]
Prokofiev, S.:Romeo & Juliet (sels)—Suite No. 2 *(rec live at the Bergen Festival, 8/14/61)* — Arkadia ▲ 713 (m) [ADD]
Prokofiev, S.:Romeo & Juliet (sels) — Melodiya ("Mravinsky Edition" series) ▲ 74321-25194-2 [ADD]
Prokofiev, S.:Romeo & Juliet (suites)—No. 2 *(rec 1973)* — Russian Disc ▲ RUS 11 180 [ADD]
Prokofiev, S.:Sym 5 *(rec Sept. 28, 1968)* — Russian Disc ▲ RUS11 165 [AAD]
Prokofiev, S.:Sym 6 *(rec Prague, 1967)* — Praga ▲ PR 250 079
Prokofiev, S.:Sym 6 *(rec Apr. 21, 1959)* — Russian Disc ("The Mravinsky Collection" series) ▲ RUS 10900 [AAD]
Prokofiev, S.:Sym 6 *(rec 1958)* — Multisonic ("Russian Treasures" series) ▲ 31 0189 [DDD]
Prokofiev, S.:Sym 6 *(rec live, Royal Albert Hall, London, 1971)* — Intaglio ▲ INCD 7321 [ADD]
Prokofiev, S.:Sym 6 *(rec live at the Prague Festival, 1968)* — Arkadia ▲ 713 (m) [ADD]
Ravel, M.:Boléro *(rec 1952)* — Multisonic ▲ 31 0178 [DDD]
Rimsky-Korsakov, N.:The Legend of the Invisible City of Kitzeh (suite) *(rec 1958)* — Multisonic ▲ 31 0178 [DDD]
Salmanov, V.:Sym 2 *(rec 1966)* — Russian Disc ▲ RUS CD 11 023 [AAD]
Schubert, Franz:Sym 8 — Melodiya ("Mravinsky Edition" series) ▲ 74321-25190-2 [ADD]
Schubert, Franz:Sym 8 *(rec Apr. 24, 1959)* — Russian Disc ("The Mravinsky Collection" series) ▲ RUS 10903 [AAD]
Schubert, Franz:Sym 8 — Audiophile Classics ("Legacy" series) ▲ 101.505 [ADD]
Scriabin, A.:Sym 4 *(rec 1949)* — Multisonic ▲ 31 0178 [DDD]
Scriabin, A.:Sym 4 *(rec Apr. 21, 1959)* — Russian Disc ("The Mravinsky Collection" series) ▲ RUS 10900 [AAD]
Shostakovich, D.:Festive Ov *(rec Apr. 21, 1955)* — Russian Disc ▲ RUS 10 902 [AAD]
Shostakovich, D.:Sym 5 *(rec Great Hall of the Moscow Conservatory, Nov 24, 1965)* — Russian Compact Disc ("The Mravinsky Collection" series) ▲ RDCD 10910 (m) [AAD]
Shostakovich, D.:Sym 5 — Audiophile Classics ("Legacy" series) ▲ 101.503 [ADD]
Shostakovich, D.:Sym 5 — Praga ▲ PR 250085
Shostakovich, D.:Sym 5 *(rec live)* — Erato ▲ 2292-45752-2 AW
Shostakovich, D.:Sym 5 *(rec 1966)* — Russian Disc ▲ RUS CD 11 023 [AAD]
Shostakovich, D.:Sym 5 *(rec live 1973)* — Russian Disc ▲ RUS 11 180 [ADD]
Shostakovich, D.:Sym 6 *(rec Great Hall of the Moscow Conservatory, Jan 27, 1972)* — Russian Compact Disc ("The Mravinsky Collection" series) ▲ RDCD 10910 (m) [AAD]
Shostakovich, D.:Sym 6 — Melodiya ("Mravinsky Edition" series) ▲ 74321-25198-2 [ADD]

Leningrad PO (cont.)
E. Mravinsky (cnd) (cont.)
Shostakovich, D.:Sym 6 *(rec May 1955 & Jan. 1962)* Praga ▲ PR 254017
Shostakovich, D.:Sym 8 Philips ▲ 422442-2 [DDD]
Shostakovich, D.:Sym 8 *(rec Large Hall of the Leningrad Philharmonic, Mar 27, 1982)* Russian Compact Disc ▲ RDCD 10917 [AAD]
Shostakovich, D.:Sym 10 Saga Classics ▲ 3366 [ADD]
Shostakovich, D.:Sym 10 *(rec June 1955)* Praga ▲ PR 250053 (m)
Shostakovich, D.:Sym 10 Melodiya ("Mravinsky Edition" series) ▲ 74321-25198-2 [ADD]
Shostakovich, D.:Sym 10 *(rec live)* Erato ▲ 2292-45753-2 AW
Shostakovich, D.:Sym 11 *(rec 1967)* Praga ▲ PR 254018
Shostakovich, D.:Sym 11 *(rec Nov. 3, 1957)* Russian Disc ▲ RUS 11157 [AAD]
Shostakovich, D.:Sym 12 *(rec live)* Erato ▲ 2292-45754-2 AW
Shostakovich, D.:Sym 12 *(rec Leningrad PO Great Hall, Apr 29, 1984)* Russian Disc ▲ RD CD 10912 [AAD]
Shostakovich, D.:Sym 12 *(rec May 1955 & Jan. 1962)* Praga ▲ PR 254017
Shostakovich, D.:Sym 15 Melodiya ("Mravinsky Edition" series) ▲ 74321-25192-2 [ADD]
Sibelius, J.:The Swan of Tuonela *(rec 1961)* Russian Disc ▲ RUS 10907 [AAD]
Sibelius, J.:The Swan of Tuonela Melodiya ("Mravinsky Edition" series) ▲ 74321-25191-2 [ADD]
Sibelius, J.:Sym 7 Melodiya ("Mravinsky Edition" series) ▲ 74321-25191-2 [ADD]
Strauss, R.:Con 1 Hn Russian Disc ▲ RUS 11 163 [AAD]
Stravinsky, I.:Agon Melodiya ("Mravinsky Edition" series) ▲ 74321-25192-2 [ADD]
Stravinsky, I.:Apollon musagète Melodiya ("Mravinsky Edition" series) ▲ 74321-25197-2 [ADD]
Stravinsky, I.:Apollon musagète *(rec Nov. 18, 1982)* Russian Disc ▲ RUS 10908 [AAD]
Stravinsky, I.:Le Baiser de la fée Russian Disc ▲ RUS 11 160 [ADD]
Stravinsky, I.:Pétrouchka *(rec 1964)* Russian Disc ("The Mravinsky Collection" series) ▲ RUS 11 162 [AAD]
Stravinsky, I.:Pétrouchka *(rec 1946)* Multisonic (Russian Treasures) ▲ 31 0189 [ADD]
Tchaikovsky, P.:Con 1 Pno, w. E. Gilels (pno) Russian Disc ▲ RUS 11170 [ADD]
Tchaikovsky, P.:Con 1 Pno, w. Pavel Serebryakov (pno) Multisonic ▲ MUL 310352
Tchaikovsky, P.:Francesca da Rimini *(rec 1948)* Russian Disc ▲ RUS 15003 [ADD]
Tchaikovsky, P.:Francesca da Rimini Russian Disc ▲ RUS 11 160 [ADD]
Tchaikovsky, P.:The Nutcracker (sels) Melodiya ("Mravinsky Edition" series) ▲ 74321-25194-2 [ADD]
Tchaikovsky, P.:Serenade Strs *(rec 1961)* Russian Disc ▲ RUS 15003 [ADD]
Tchaikovsky, P.:Sym 4 *(rec Apr. 24, 1959)* Russian Disc ("The Mravinsky Collection" series) ▲ RUS 10903 [AAD]
Tchaikovsky, P.:Sym 5 *(rec 1973)* Andromeda ▲ ANR 2523 [ADD]
Tchaikovsky, P.:Sym 5 *(rec 1956)* Deutsche Grammophon ("The Originals" series) 2-▲ 447423-2
Tchaikovsky, P.:Sym 5 *(rec between 1965 & 1973)* Enterprise (Documents) ▲ ENTLV 917 [ADD]
Tchaikovsky, P.:Sym 5 Melodiya ("Mravinsky Edition" series) ▲ 74321-25196-2 [ADD]
Tchaikovsky, P.:Sym 5 *(rec live)* Erato ▲ 2292-45755-2 AW
Tchaikovsky, P.:Sym 5 *(rec 1983)* Audiophile Classics ("Legacy Collection" series) ▲ 101.511
Tchaikovsky, P.:Sym 5 *(rec Large Hall, Moscow Conservatory, Jan 19, 1949)* Russian Compact Disc ▲ RDCD 10914 (m) [AAD]
Tchaikovsky, P.:Sym 5 *(rec Nov. 27, 1972)* Russian Disc ▲ RUS 10908 [AAD]
Tchaikovsky, P.:Sym 6 *(rec 1956)* Deutsche Grammophon ("The Originals" series) 2-▲ 447423-2
Tchaikovsky, P.:Sym 6 *(rec 1978)* Originals ▲ ORISH 815 [ADD]
Tchaikovsky, P.:Sym 6 *(rec live)* Erato ▲ 2292-45756-2 AW
Volumes 11-20 *(rec 1947-1973)* Melodiya ("Mravinsky Edition" series) 10-▲ 74321-29459-2 [ADD]
Wagner, R.:Götterdämmerung (siegfried's funeral) Melodiya ("Mravinsky Edition" series) ▲ 74321-25199-2 [ADD]
Wagner, R.:Lohengrin (preludes)—Act 1 Prelude *(rec 1980)* Audiophile Classics ("Legacy Collection" series) ▲ 101.511
Wagner, R.:Lohengrin (preludes)—Acts 1 & 3 Melodiya ("Mravinsky Edition" series) ▲ 74321-25199-2 [ADD]
Wagner, R.:Die Meistersinger von Nürnberg (preludes)—Act 1 Melodiya ("Mravinsky Edition" series) ▲ 74321-25199-2 [ADD]
Wagner, R.:Ovs, Preludes & Orch Sels—Tannhäusser:Ov.; Tristan and Isolde:Prelude; Liebestod; Lohengrin:Prelude Act 3 *(rec between 1965 & 1973)* Enterprise ("Documents" series) ▲ ENTLV 917 [ADD]
Wagner, R.:Ovs, Preludes & Orch Sels—Tannhäuser:Ov.; Lohengrin:Prelude Act III; Tristan und Isolde:Prelude; Liebestod *(rec 1965 & 1968)* Andromeda ▲ ANR 2523 [ADD]
Wagner, R.:Ovs, Preludes & Orch Sels—Tannhäuser;Ov.; Tristan und Isolde:Prelude; Liebestod; Lohengrin:Preludes to Acts 1 & 2 Russian Disc ▲ RUS 11166 [ADD]
Wagner, R.:Siegfried (sels)—Waldweben; Funeral Music Russian Disc ▲ RUS 11166 [ADD]
Wagner, R.:Tannhäuser (ov) Melodiya ("Mravinsky Edition" series) ▲ 74321-25199-2 [ADD]
Wagner, R.:Tristan und Isolde (prelude & liebestod) Melodiya ("Mravinsky Edition" series) ▲ 74321-25199-2 [ADD]
Wagner, R.:Die Walküre (ride of the valkyries) Melodiya ("Mravinsky Edition" series) ▲ 74321-25199-2 [ADD]
Wagner, R.:Die Walküre (ride of the valkyries) Russian Disc ▲ RUS 11166 [ADD]
Weber, C.M. von:Euryanthe (ov) *(rec Apr. 24, 1959)* Russian Disc ("The Mravinsky Collection" series) ▲ RUS 10903 [AAD]
Weber, C.M. von:Oberon (ov) Melodiya ("Mravinsky Edition" series) ▲ 74321-25190-2 [ADD]
Weber, C.M. von:Oberon (ov) *(rec 1961)* Russian Disc ▲ RUS 10907 [AAD]

G. Rozhdestvensky (cnd)
Prokofiev, S.:Sym 5 IMP ("BBC Radio" series) ▲ IMP 5691462
Tchaikovsky, P.:Con Vn, w. Mikhail Waiman (vn) IMP ("BBC Radio Classics" series) ▲ IMP 9134
Tchaikovsky, P.:Sym 4 IMP ("BBC Radio Classics" series) ▲ IMP 9134

K. Sanderling (cnd)
Prokofiev, S.:Sym-Con Vc, w. M. Rostropovich (vc) *(rec 1947)* Multisonic ("Russian Treasures" series) ▲ 31 0188
Szymanowski, K.:Con 1 Vn, w. David Oistrakh (vn) *(rec 1959)* Forlane ▲ FRL 16589 [AAD]
Tchaikovsky, P.:Sym 4 *(rec 1956)* Deutsche Grammophon ("The Originals" series) 2-▲ 447423-2

Y. Temirkanov (cnd)
Petrov, A.:The Creation of the World, w. Leningrad State Academy Boys' Chorus *(rec 1970)* RCA Gold Seal ▲ 74321-32044-2 [ADD]
Ravel, M.:Daphnis et Chloé (suite 2) *(rec 1970)* RCA Gold Seal ▲ 74321-32044-2 [ADD]
Shostakovich, D.:Sym 10, w. Leningrad Phil Choir *(rec Jan. 26, 1973)* Russian Disc ▲ RUS 11195 [AAD]
Stravinsky, I.:Pétrouchka *(rec 1975)* RCA Gold Seal ▲ 74321-32044-2 [ADD]
Tchaikovsky, P.:Music of, w. I. Perlman (vn), J. Norman (sop), Yo-Yo Ma (vc), Leningrad Military Orch—Waltz & Polonaise from Eugene Onegin; Sérénade mélancolique, Op. 26; Valse scherzo, Op. 34; Variations on a Rococo Theme, Op. 33; Overture 1812, Op. 49; Symphony No. 6 (3rd movt.); 3 Chansons française from Op. 65, for Voice & Piano; Aria (Adieu, forêts) from The Maid of Orleans *(rec live, Leningrad)* RCA Red Seal ▲ 60739-2-RC [DDD] ■ 09026-60739-4-RC (CrO2) □ 09026-60739-5

A. Yansons (cnd)
Shostakovich, D.:Sym 5 *(rec live, Royal Albert Hall, London, 9/13/71)* Intaglio ▲ INCD 7121 [ADD]
Tchaikovsky, P.:Sleeping Beauty (suite) *(rec live, Royal Albert Hall, London, 9/13/71)* Intaglio ▲ INCD 7121 [ADD]

Leningrad State Phil Academic SO
Y. Temirkanov (cnd)
Petrov, A.:Con Vn, w. Sergei Stadler (vn) *(rec Grand Hall of the Leningrad State PO)* Russian Compact Disc ▲ RCD 26601
Petrov, A.:The Creation of the World, w. Glinka Boys' Choir *(rec Grand Hall of the Leningrad State PO)* Russian Compact Disc ▲ RCD 26601
Petrov, A.:Russia of Bells, Leningrad Bell Music Ensemble *(rec Grand Hall of the Leningrad State PO)* Russian Compact Disc ▲ RCD 26601

Leningrad State Phil Academic SO (cont.)
E. Mravinsky (cnd)

Lenox Brass
Pinkham, D.:Christmas Cant, w. J. D. Christie (org), Boston Cecilia *(rec Dec. 1992)* Koch International Classics ▲ KIC 7180 [DDD]

Lenox String Quartet
H. Farberman (cnd)
Schoenberg, A.:Con Str Qt, w. London SO Phoenix ▲ PHCD 121 [ADD]

Lenox String Quartet members
Schoenberg, A.:Trio Strs Phoenix ▲ PHCD 121 [ADD]

Leonardo Trio [Cameron Grant (pno), Erica Kiesewetter (vn), Johnathan Spitz (vc)]
Brahms, J.:Trio in A Pno (posth) *(rec June 1991)* Partridge ▲ 1136-2 [DDD]
Cohn, J.:Trio Pno *(rec Sept. 1992)* XLNT ▲ CD 18007 [DDD]
Martinů, B.:Trio 1 Pno XLNT ▲ CD 18003 [DDD] ■ CA 18003 (CrO2)
Schumann, R.:Trio 2 Pno *(rec June 1991)* Partridge ▲ 1136-2 [DDD]
Shostakovich, D.:Trio 2 Pno XLNT ▲ CD 18003 [DDD] ■ CA 18003 (CrO2)
Smetana, B.:Trio Pno XLNT ▲ CD 18003 [DDD] ■ CA 18003 (CrO2)

Leonhardt Consort
Bach, J.S.:Cant 7, w. P. Esswood (ct), K. Equiluz (ten), M. van Egmond (b-bar), King's College Choir Cambridge [G] Teldec 2-▲ 2292-42498-2 [AAD]
Bach, J.S.:Cant 8, w. P. Esswood (ct), K. Equiluz (ten), G. Kiefer (bar), M. van Egmond (b-bar), King's College Choir Cambridge [G] Teldec 2-▲ 2292-42498-2 [AAD]
Bach, J.S.:Cant 9, w. P. Esswood (ct), K. Equiluz (ten), M. van Egmond (b-bar), King's College Choir Cambridge [G] Teldec 2-▲ 2292-42499-2 [AAD]
Bach, J.S.:Cant 10, w. P. Esswood (ct), K. Equiluz (ten), M. van Egmond (b-bar), King's College Choir Cambridge [G] Teldec 2-▲ 2292-42499-2 [AAD]
Bach, J.S.:Cant 12, w. P. Esswood (ct), K. Equiluz (ten), M. van Egmond (b-bar), King's College Choir Cambridge [G] Teldec 2-▲ 2292-42500-2 [AAD]
Bach, J.S.:Cant 13, w. P. Esswood (ct), K. Equiluz (ten), M. van Egmond (b-bar), King's College Choir Cambridge [G] Teldec 2-▲ 2292-42500-2 [AAD]
Bach, J.S.:Cant 14, w. M. van Altena (ten), M. van Egmond (b-bar), King's College Choir Cambridge [G] Teldec 2-▲ 2292-42500-2 [AAD]
Bach, J.S.:Cant 16, w. P. Esswood (ct), K. Equiluz (ten), M. van Egmond (b-bar), King's College Choir Cambridge [G] Teldec 2-▲ 2292-42500-2 [AAD]
Bach, J.S.:Cant 22, w. P. Esswood (ct), K. Equiluz (ten), M. van Egmond (b-bar), King's College Choir Cambridge [G] Teldec 2-▲ 2292-42502-2 [AAD]
Bach, J.S.:Cant 23, w. W. Gampert (trb), P. Esswood (ct), M. van Altena (ten), M. van Egmond (b-bar), King's College Choir Cambridge [G] Teldec 2-▲ 2292-42502-2 [AAD]
Bach, J.S.:Cant 40, w. R. Jacobs (ct), M. van Altena (ten), M. van Egmond (b-bar), Hanover Boys' Choir [G] Teldec 2-▲ 2292-42556-2 [AAD]
Bach, J.S.:Cant 45, w. P. Esswood (ct), K. Equiluz (ten), R. van der Meer (bass) [G] Teldec 2-▲ 2292-42559-2 [AAD]
Bach, J.S.:Cant 46, w. P. Esswood (ct), K. Equiluz (ten), R. van der Meer (bass) [G] Teldec 2-▲ 2292-42559-2 [AAD]
Bach, J.S.:Cant 52, w. S. Kronwitter (trb), Hanover Boys' Choir [G] Teldec 2-▲ 2292-42422-2 [AAD]
Bach, J.S.:Cant 90, w. P. Esswood (ct), K. Equiluz (ten), M. van Egmond (b-bar), Ghent Collegium Vocale [G] Teldec 2-▲ 2292-42578-2 [ADD]
Bach, J.S.:Cant 98, w. C. Lengert (trb), P. Esswood (ct), K. Equiluz (ten), M. van Egmond (b-bar) [G] Teldec ▲ 2292-42583-2 [ADD]
Bach, J.S.:Cant 106, "Actus tragicus", w. M. Klein (trb), R. Harten (alt), M. van Altena (ten), M. van Egmond (b-bar), Collegium Vocale, Hanover Boys' Chorus [G] Teldec ▲ 2292-42602-2
Bach, J.S.:Cant 107, w. M. Klein (trb), K. Equiluz (ten), M. van Egmond (b-bar), Collegium Vocale [G] Teldec 2-▲ 2292-42603-2
Bach, J.S.:Cant 113, w. S. Hennig (trb), D. Bratschke (trb), R. Jacobs (ct), K. Equiluz (ten), M. van Egmond (b-bar), Collegium Vocale, Hanover Boys' Chorus [G] Teldec 2-▲ 2292-42606-2
Bach, J.S.:Cant 114, w. S. Hennig (trb), R. Jacobs (ct), K. Equiluz (ten), M. van Egmond (b-bar), Collegium Vocale, Hanover Boys' Chorus [G] Teldec 2-▲ 2292-42606-2
Bach, J.S.:Cant 149 [G] Teldec 2-▲ 2292-42631-2 [DDD]
Bach, J.S.:Cant 150 [G] Teldec 2-▲ 2292-42631-2 [DDD]
Bach, J.S.:Cant 151 [G] Teldec 2-▲ 2292-42631-2 [DDD]
Bach, J.S.:Cant 157 [G] Teldec 2-▲ 2292-42633-2 [DDD]
Bach, J.S.:Cant 158 [G] Teldec 2-▲ 2292-42633-2 [DDD]
Bach, J.S.:Cant 159 [G] Teldec 2-▲ 2292-42633-2 [DDD]
Bach, J.S.:Music of, w. German Bach Soloists Pro Arte ▲ CDM 801

N. Harnoncourt (cnd)
Bach, J.S.:Cant 91, w. Vienna Concentus Musicus, G. Leonhardt (cnd) [G] Teldec 2-▲ 2292-42582-2 [ADD]
Bach, J.S.:Cant 92, w. Vienna Concentus Musicus, G. Leonhardt (cnd) [G] Teldec 2-▲ 2292-42582-2 [ADD]
Bach, J.S.:Cant 93, w. Vienna Concentus Musicus, G. Leonhardt (cnd) [G] Teldec 2-▲ 2292-42582-2 [ADD]
Bach, J.S.:Cant 94, w. Vienna Concentus Musicus, G. Leonhardt (cnd) [G] Teldec 2-▲ 2292-42582-2 [ADD]
Bach, J.S.:Cant 164, Vienna Concentus Musicus [G] Teldec 2-▲ 2292-42634-2 [DDD]
Bach, J.S.:Cant 165, Vienna Concentus Musicus [G] Teldec 2-▲ 2292-42634-2 [DDD]
Bach, J.S.:Cant 166, Vienna Concentus Musicus [G] Teldec 2-▲ 2292-42634-2 [DDD]
Bach, J.S.:Cant 167, Vienna Concentus Musicus [G] Teldec 2-▲ 2292-42634-2 [DDD]
Bach, J.S.:Cant 168, Vienna Concentus Musicus [G] Teldec 2-▲ 2292-42634-2 [DDD]
Bach, J.S.:Cant 169, Vienna Concentus Musicus [G] Teldec 2-▲ 2292-42634-2 [DDD]
Bach, J.S.:Cant 170, Vienna Concentus Musicus [G] Teldec 2-▲ 2292-42635-2 [DDD]
Bach, J.S.:Cant 171, Vienna Concentus Musicus [G] Teldec 2-▲ 2292-42635-2 [DDD]
Bach, J.S.:Cant 172, Vienna Concentus Musicus [G] Teldec 2-▲ 2292-42635-2 [DDD]
Bach, J.S.:Cant 173, Vienna Concentus Musicus [G] Teldec 2-▲ 2292-42635-2 [DDD]
Bach, J.S.:Cant 174, Vienna Concentus Musicus [G] Teldec 2-▲ 2292-42635-2 [DDD]
Bach, J.S.:Cant 175, Vienna Concentus Musicus [G] Teldec 2-▲ 2292-42428-2 [DDD]
Bach, J.S.:Cant 176, Vienna Concentus Musicus [G] Teldec 2-▲ 2292-42428-2 [DDD]
Bach, J.S.:Cant 177, Vienna Concentus Musicus [G] Teldec 2-▲ 2292-42428-2 [DDD]
Bach, J.S.:Cant 178, Vienna Concentus Musicus [G] Teldec 2-▲ 2292-42428-2 [DDD]
Bach, J.S.:Cant 179, Vienna Concentus Musicus [G] Teldec 2-▲ 2292-42428-2 [DDD]
Bach, J.S.:Cant 180, Vienna Concentus Musicus [G] Teldec 2-▲ 2292-42738-2 [DDD]
Bach, J.S.:Cant 181, Vienna Concentus Musicus [G] Teldec 2-▲ 2292-42738-2 [DDD]
Bach, J.S.:Cant 182, Vienna Concentus Musicus [G] Teldec 2-▲ 2292-42738-2 [DDD]
Bach, J.S.:Cant 183, Vienna Concentus Musicus [G] Teldec 2-▲ 2292-42738-2 [DDD]
Bach, J.S.:Cant 184, Vienna Concentus Musicus [G] Teldec 2-▲ 2292-42738-2 [DDD]
Bach, J.S.:Cant 192, Vienna Concentus Musicus [G] Teldec ▲ 2292-44193-2
Bach, J.S.:Cant 194, Vienna Concentus Musicus [G] Teldec ▲ 2292-44193-2
Bach, J.S.:Cant 195, Vienna Concentus Musicus [G] Teldec ▲ 2292-44193-2
Bach, J.S.:Cant 196, Vienna Concentus Musicus [G] Teldec 2-▲ 2292-44194-2
Bach, J.S.:Cant 197, Vienna Concentus Musicus [G] Teldec 2-▲ 2292-44194-2
Bach, J.S.:Cant 198, Vienna Concentus Musicus [G] Teldec 2-▲ 2292-44194-2
Bach, J.S.:Cant 199, Vienna Concentus Musicus [G] Teldec 2-▲ 2292-44194-2
Bach, J.S.:Music of, w. Vienna Concentus Musicus—arias and choruses from various cants. Teldec ▲ 93705-2

N. Harnoncourt, G. Leonhardt (cnds)
Bach, J.S.:Cants (misc), w. *(various soloists & guest choirs)*, Vienna Concentus Musicus—[Vol. 1] Nos. 1-14, 16-19; [Vol. 2] Nos. 20-36; [Vol. 3] 37-52, 54-60; [Vol. 4] Nos. 61-78; [Vol. 5] Nos. 79-99; [Vol. 6] Nos. 100-117; [Vol. 7] Nos. 119-137; [Vol. 8] Nos. 138-140, 143-159, 161-162; [Vol. 9] Nos. 163-182; [Vol. 10] Nos. 183-188, 192, 194-199 Teldec ("Das Alte Werk" series) 60-▲ 91765-2

Leonhardt Consort (cont.)
G. Leonhardt (cnd)
Bach, J.S.:Cant 32, w. W. Gampert (trb), M. van Egmond (b-bar), Hanover Boys' Choir [G] Teldec 2-▲ 2292-42505-2 [AAD]
Bach, J.S.:Cant 33, w. R. Jacobs (ct), M. van Altena (ten), Hanover Boys' Choir [G] Teldec 2-▲ 2292-42505-2 [AAD]
Bach, J.S.:Cant 39, w. R. Jacobs (ct), M. van Egmond (b-bar), Hanover Boys' Choir [G] Teldec 2-▲ 2292-42556-2 [AAD]
Bach, J.S.:Cant 51, w. M. Kweksilber (mez) [G] Teldec 2-▲ 2292-42422-2 [AAD]
Bach, J.S.:Cant 54, w. P. Esswood (ct) [G] Teldec 2-▲ 2292-42422-2 [AAD]
Bach, J.S.:Cant 55, w. K. Equiluz (ten), Hanover Boys' Choir [G] Teldec 2-▲ 2292-42422-2 [AAD]
Bach, J.S.:Cant 56, w. M. Schopper (bass), Hanover Boys' Choir [G] Teldec 2-▲ 2292-42422-2 [AAD]
Bach, J.S.:Cant 66, w. Ghent Collegium Vocale, Hanover Boys' Chorus [G] Teldec 2-▲ 2292-42571-2 [AAD]
Bach, J.S.:Cant 67, w. Ghent Collegium Vocale, Hanover Boys' Chorus [G] Teldec 2-▲ 2292-42571-2 [AAD]
Bach, J.S.:Cant 73, w. Ghent Collegium Vocale, Hanover Boys' Chorus [G] Teldec 2-▲ 2292-42573-2 [ADD]
Bach, J.S.:Cant 74, w. Ghent Collegium Vocale, Hanover Boys' Chorus [G] Teldec 2-▲ 2292-42573-2 [ADD]
Bach, J.S.:Cant 75, w. Ghent Collegium Vocale, Hanover Boys' Chorus [G] Teldec 2-▲ 2292-42573-2 [ADD]
Bach, J.S.:Cant 77, w. P. Esswood (ct), A. Kraus (ten), M. van Egmond (b-bar) [G] Teldec 2-▲ 2292-42576-2 [ADD]
Bach, J.S.:Cant 79, w. P. Esswood (ct), M. van Egmond (b-bar) [G] Teldec 2-▲ 2292-42576-2 [ADD]
Bach, J.S.:Cant 88, w. M. Klein (trb), P. Esswood (ct), K. Equiluz (ten) [G] Teldec 2-▲ 2292-42578-2 [ADD]
Bach, J.S.:Cant 89, w. M. Klein (trb), P. Esswood (ct), M. van Egmond (b-bar) [G] Teldec 2-▲ 2292-42578-2 [ADD]
Bach, J.S.:Cant 100, w. D. Bratschke (trb), P. Esswood (ct), K. Equiluz (ten), M. van Egmond (b-bar) [G] Teldec ▲ 2292-42584-2
Bach, J.S.:Cant 102, w. Maureen Forrester (alt), Richard Lewis (ten), Norman Farrow (b-bar), Brian Priestman (cnd), *(chorus unknown)* Vox Box 2-▲ CDX 5127 [ADD]
Bach, J.S.:Cant 103, w. P. Esswood (ct), K. Equiluz (ten), P. Huttenlocher (bar) [G] Teldec ▲ 2292-42602-2
Bach, J.S.:Cant 187, w. M. Emmermann (trb), P. Esswood (ct), M. van Egmond (b-bar), Hanover Men & Boys' Chorus, Collegium Vocale [G] Teldec 2-▲ 2292-44179-2 [DDD]
Bach, J.S.:Con 8 Hpd, w. G. Leonhardt (hpd) [reconstr. Gustav Leonhardt] Teldec 3-▲ 2292-42726-2 [ADD]
Bach, J.S.:Cons for 2 Hpds (comp), w. G. Leonhardt (hpd), E. Müller [2nd hpd, BWV 1060 & 1062], A. Uittenbosch [2nd hpd, BWV 1061] Teldec 3-▲ 2292-42726-2 [ADD]
Bach, J.S.:Cons for 3 Hpds (comp), w. G. Leonhardt (hpd), A. Uittenbosch (hpd), A. Curtis (hpd) Teldec 3-▲ 2292-42726-2 [ADD]
Bach, J.S.:Con for 4 Hpds, w. E. Müller (hpd), G. Leonhardt (hpd), J. van Wering (hpd), A. Uittenbosch (hpd) Teldec 3-▲ 2292-42726-2 [ADD]

Leonhardt Ensemble
Greatest Hits of 1750, w. Collegium Aureum, La Petite Bande, et al. Pro Arte ▲ CDM 817

Leontovych String Quartet [Yuri Mazurkevich (vn), Yuri Kharenko (vn), Boris Deviatov (va), Vladimir Panteleyev (vc)]
Schubert, Franz:Qt 14 Strs *(rec SUNY Recital Hall, Purchase, NY, Oct. 1994)* Greystone ▲ GS 527 [DDD]
Shostakovich, D.:Qnt Pno, w. R. Guralnik (pno) *(rec May 1994)* Greystone ▲ GS 521 [DDD]
Shostakovich, D.:Qt 8 Strs *(rec SUNY Recital Hall, Purchase, NY, Oct. 1994)* Greystone ▲ GS 527 [DDD]
Tchaikovsky, P.:Qt 2 Strs *(rec May 1994)* Greystone ▲ GS 521 [DDD]

Lester Roland Duo [N. Lester (pno), N. Roldan (pno)]
Music of the Americas, Lester/Roldan Duo Centaur ▲ CRC 2171

Levinson Family Trio [Gina Levinson (pno), Gary Levinson (vn), Eugene Levinson (db)]
Rachmaninoff, S.:Trio élégiaque 1 Cala Records ("New York Legends" series) ▲ CAL CACD 507 [DDD]

Liège New Music Ensemble
J.-P. Peuvion (cnd)
Pousseur, H.:Traverser la forêt, w. Christian Crahay (nar), Marianne Pousseur (sop), Peter Harvey (bar), Gerhard Sporken (cnd), Vocal Ensemble Adda ▲ ADD 581295 [DDD]
Schoenberg, A.:The Cabaret Songs, w. Yumi Nara (sop), Izumi Okubo (vn/va), Machiko Takahashi (fl/pic), Vincent Jacquemin (cl/b cl), François Deppe (vc), Brigitte Foccroulle (pno) [arr Patrick Davin for Salon Orch] Adda ▲ ADD 581273 [DDD]
Schoenberg, A.:Pierrot lunaire, w. Yumi Nara (sop), Izumi Okubo (vn/va), Machiko Takahashi (fl/pic), Vincent Jacquemin (cl/b cl), François Deppe (vc), Brigitte Foccroulle (pno) Adda ▲ ADD 581273 [DDD]

Liège PO
P. Bartholomée (cnd)
Biarent, A.:Sonnets, w. Luc Dewez (vc) *(rec Conservatoire Royal de Liège, Oct 16–19, 1995)* Cypres ▲ CYPRES 3601
Biarent, A.:Sym in d *(rec Conservatoire Royal de Liège, Oct 16–19, 1995)* Cypres ▲ CYPRES 3601
Biarent, A.:Trenmor *(rec Conservatoire Royal de Liège, Oct 16–19, 1995)* Cypres ▲ CYPRES 3601
de Greef, A.:Con 1 Pno, w. J.-C. Vanden Eynden (pno) EMI Classics ▲ CDM 65075
Franck, C.:Sym in d Ricercar In Ecco ▲ REC 8003
Lekeu, G.:Adagio Ricercar In Ecco ▲ REC 8003
Schubert, Franz:Sym 10 Ricercar In Ecco ▲ 8006
Sibelius, J.:Con Vn, w. Regis Pasquier (vn) Valois ▲ V 4746
Sibelius, J.:4 Legends from the Kalevalá Valois ▲ V 4746
Tournemire, C.:Sym 6, w. Daniel Galvez-Vallero (ten), Brussels Polyphonia Choir Valois ▲ V 4757
Van Rossum, F.:Con 1 Vn, w. P. Zazofsky (vn) *(rec Feb. 9–12, 1993)* Chamade ▲ 5615 [DDD]
Van Rossum, F.:Con 2 Vn, w. P. Zazofsky (vn) *(rec Feb. 9–12, 1993)* Chamade ▲ 5615 [DDD]
Van Rossum, F.:Epitaphe *(rec Feb. 9–12, 1993)* Chamade ▲ 5615 [DDD]

Liège SO
G. Cartigny (cnd)
Vieuxtemps, H.:Fant appassionata, w. Charles Jongen (vn) *(rec Conservatoire Royal de Musique, Liège, June 1972)* Pavane ▲ ADW 7340 [DDD]
R. Defossez (cnd)
Jongen, J.:Symphonie Concertante, w. H. Schoonbroodt (org) Koch Schwann ▲ CD 315012 [ADD]
L. Ferré (cnd)
Ferré, L.:Music of, w. Giuseppe Magani (vn), Milan SO—Le chant du hibou; Muss es sein es muss sein; Le superlatif EPM ▲ EPM 982372 [AAD]

Lieurance Woodwind Quintet
Lieurance Woodwind Quintet:Debut Recording Summit ▲ DCD 149 [DDD]

Life Guards Band
Music from the 1994 Royal Tournament, w. Coldstream Guards Band, Grenadier Guards Band, Irish Guards Band, Welsh Guards Band, et al. Bandleader ▲ BND 5094 [DDD]

Light Brigade
First Skirmish ASV ("White Line" series) ▲ ASV 2065

Light Fantastic Players
D. Shulman (cnd)
Bland, E.:Sketches Set 1 Cambria ▲ CD 1026
Wuorinen, C.:Grand Bamboula Music & Arts ▲ CD 801 [ADD]

Lille Brass Quintet
Suite de suite à suivre René Gailly ▲ CD 87039 [DDD]

Lille National Orch
J.-C. Casadesus (cnd)
Beethoven, L. van:Con Vn, Op. 61, w. Jean-Pierre Wallez (vn) Forlane ▲ FRL 54 [DDD]
Beethoven, L. van:Romances Vn, w. Jean-Pierre Wallez (vn) Forlane ▲ FRL 54 [DDD]
Berlioz, H.:Herminie, w. Michèle Lagrange (sop) Harmonia Mundi France ▲ HMC 901542
Berlioz, H.:La Mort de Cléopâtre, w. Béatrice Uria-Monzon (mez) Harmonia Mundi France ▲ HMC 901542
Berlioz, H.:La Mort de Sardanapale, w. Daniel Galvez Vallejo (ten) Harmonia Mundi France ▲ HMC 901542
Berlioz, H.:La Mort d'Orphée, w. Daniel Galvez Vallejo (ten) Harmonia Mundi France ▲ HMC 901542
Debussy, C.:La Damoiselle élue, w. M. Delünsch (sop), S. Sullé (mez), Michel Piquemal Vocal Ensemble Harmonia Mundi France ▲ HMC 901490
Debussy, C.:La Mer Harmonia Mundi France ▲ HMC 901490
Debussy, C.:Nocturnes, w. Michel Piquemal Vocal Ensemble Harmonia Mundi France ▲ HMC 901490
Honegger, A.:Le Roi David, w. Alessandra Marc (sop), Sylvie Sullé (mez), Laurence Dale (ten), D. Mesguich (nar) EMI Classics ▲ CDC 54793
Mahler, G.:Kindertotenlieder, w. J. Van Dam (b-bar) [G] Forlane ▲ FOR 16553 [DDD]
Mahler, G.:Des Knaben Wunderhorn, w. J. Van Dam (b-bar)—2 sels. Forlane ▲ FOR 16553 [DDD]
Mahler, G.:Songs from Rückert, w. J. Van Dam (b-bar) [G] Forlane ▲ FOR 16553 [DDD]
Mahler, G.:Sym 1 Forlane ▲ FRL 16643 [DDD]
Ravel, M.:Boléro Harmonia Mundi ▲ HMT 7901434
Ravel, M.:Con Pno (left hand), w. Georges Pludermacher (pno) Harmonia Mundi ▲ HMT 7901434
Ravel, M.:Con in G Pno, w. Georges Pludermacher (pno) Harmonia Mundi ▲ HMT 7901434
Ravel, M.:Daphnis et Chloé (suite 2), w. N. Denize (mez) *(rec Oct. 1979)* Harmonia Mundi Plus ▲ HMP 390064
Ravel, M.:Melodies hébraïques, w. N. Denize (mez) *(rec Oct. 1979)* Harmonia Mundi Plus ▲ HMP 390064
Ravel, M.:Pavane pour une infante défunte, w. N. Denize (mez) *(rec Oct. 1979)* Harmonia Mundi Plus ▲ HMP 390064
Ravel, M.:Shéhérazade Mez, w. N. Denize (mez) *(rec Oct. 1979)* Harmonia Mundi Plus ▲ HMP 390064
Ravel, M.:La Valse Harmonia Mundi ▲ HMT 7901434
Stravinsky, I.:The Firebird Forlane ▲ FRL 37 [DDD]
Stravinsky, I.:Pétrouchka Forlane ▲ FRL 37 [DDD]
Wagner, R.:Arias & Scenes, w. J. van Dam (b-bar)—Der fliegende Holländer:Die Frist ist um; Tannhäuser:Blick ich umher; O du mein holder Abendstern; Die Meistersinger von Nürnberg:Was duftet doch der Flieder; Wahn! Wahn! überall Wahn; Die Walküre:Leb wohl! du kühnes, herrliches Kind [G] Forlane ▲ FOR 16633 [DDD]
Wagner, R.:Ovs, Preludes & Orch Sels—Fliegende Holländer; Meistersinger Forlane ▲ FOR 16633 [DDD]
E. Stratta (cnd)
Duke, G.:Muir Woods Suite, w. George Duke (pno), Stanley Clarke (bass), Chester Thompson (dr), Paulinho Dacosta (perc) *(rec live, Montreaux Music Festival, Montreaux, Switzerland, July 12, 1993)* Warner Bros ▲ 9 46132-2 [DDD]

Limburg SO
S. Mas Conde (cnd)
Strauss, R.:Der Bürger als Edelmann (suite) Koch Schwann ▲ 3-1027-2 [DDD]
Stravinsky, I.:Pulcinella Suite Koch Schwann ▲ 3-1027-2 [DDD]
G. Oskamp (cnd)
Fauré, G.:Fant Fl, w. F. Adriaans (fl) *(rec Nov. 1992 & May 1993)* Erasmus ▲ WVH 099 [DDD]
Poulenc, F.:Con for 2 Pnos, w. *(pianists unknown)* Erasmus ▲ WVH 117
Poulenc, F.:Con for 2 Pnos, w. D. Wayenberg (pno), H. Oudenaarden (pno) *(rec Nov. 1992 & May 1993)* Erasmus ▲ WVH 099 [DDD]
Saint-Saëns, C.:Carnival of the Animals, w. D. Wayenberg (pno), H. Oudenaarden (pno) *(rec Nov. 1992 & May 1993)* Erasmus ▲ WVH 099 [DDD]

Limoges Baroque Ensemble
C. Coin (cnd)
Bach, J.S.:Cant 6, w. Barbara Schlick (sop), Andreas Scholl (ct), Christoph Prégardien (ten), Gotthold Schwarz (bass), Accentus Chamber Choir Astrée ▲ E 8555
Bach, J.S.:Cant 41, w. Barbara Schlick (sop), Andreas Scholl (ct), Christoph Prégardien (ten), Gotthold Schwarz (bass), Accentus Chamber Choir Astrée ▲ E 8555
Bach, J.S.:Cant 49, w. Barbara Schlick (sop), Andreas Scholl (alt), Christophe Prégardien (ten), Gotthold Schwarz (bass), Leipzig Concerto Vocale Astrée ▲ E 8530
Bach, J.S.:Cant 68, w. Barbara Schlick (sop), Andreas Scholl (ct), Christoph Prégardien (ten), Gotthold Schwarz (bass), Accentus Chamber Choir Astrée ▲ E 8555
Bach, J.S.:Cant 85, w. Barbara Schlick (sop), Andreas Scholl (alt), Christoph Prégardien (ten), Gotthold Schwarz (bass), Christophe Coin (piccolo vc), Leipzig Vocal Concerto Astrée ▲ E 8544
Bach, J.S.:Cant 115, w. Barbara Schlick (sop), Andreas Scholl (alt), Christophe Prégardien (ten), Gotthold Schwarz (bass), Leipzig Concerto Vocale Astrée ▲ E 8530
Bach, J.S.:Cant 175, w. Barbara Schlick (sop), Andreas Scholl (alt), Christoph Prégardien (ten), Gotthold Schwarz (bass), Christophe Coin (piccolo vc), Leipzig Vocal Concerto Astrée ▲ E 8544
Bach, J.S.:Cant 180, w. Barbara Schlick (sop), Andreas Scholl (alt), Christophe Prégardien (ten), Gotthold Schwarz (bass), Leipzig Concerto Vocale Astrée ▲ E 8530
Bach, J.S.:Cant 183, w. Barbara Schlick (sop), Andreas Scholl (alt), Christoph Prégardien (ten), Gotthold Schwarz (bass), Christophe Coin (piccolo vc), Leipzig Vocal Concerto Astrée ▲ E 8544
Bach, J.S.:Cant 199, w. Barbara Schlick (sop), Andreas Scholl (alt), Christoph Prégardien (ten), Gotthold Schwarz (bass), Christophe Coin (piccolo vc), Leipzig Vocal Concerto Astrée ▲ E 8544
Boccherini, L.:Aria accademica 14, w. M. Almajano (sop) Astrée ▲ E 8517 [DDD]
Mozart, W.A.:Con 20 Pno, w. Patrick Cohen (fortepno) Astrée ▲ E 8589
Mozart, W.A.:Con 21 Pno, w. Patrick Cohen (fortepno) Astrée ▲ E 8589
Nebra, J.:Viento, w. Marta Almajano (sop), Maite Arruabarrena (sop), Raquel Pierotti (sop), Pilar Jurado (sgr), Maria del Mar Doval (sgr) Valois ▲ V 4752
J.-M. Hasler (cnd)
Destouches, A.C.:Callirhöe (suite) Adès ▲ ADE 141782 [DDD]
Destouches, A.C.:Omphale (suite) Adès ▲ ADE 141782 [DDD]
Montéclair, M.P. de:Jephté (suite) Adès ▲ ADE 141782 [DDD]

Limoges Baroque Ensemble Soloists [Willem Jansen (hpd), Maria-Tecla Andreotti (trns fl), Irène Troi (vn), Christophe Coin (vl)]
Rameau, J.P.:L'Impatience, w. Sandrine Piau (sop) *(rec Sept 14–16, 1994)* FNAC Music ▲ CD 592333
Rameau, J.P.:Pièces de clavecin en concert—Nos. 1, 3 & 4 *(rec Sept 14–16, 1994)* FNAC Music ▲ CD 592333
Rameau, J.P.:Thétis, w. Bernard Delétré (bass) *(rec Sept 14–16, 1994)* FNAC Music ▲ CD 592333

Lincoln Center Chamber Music Society
Danielpour, R.:Qnt Pno & Strs, w. C. O'Riley (pno) Koch International Classics ▲ KIC 7100-2 [DDD]
O. Knussen (cnd)
Knussen, O.:Hums & Songs of Winnie-the-Pooh, w. L. Saffer (sop) Virgin Classics ▲ CDC 59308
Knussen, O.:Océan de terre, w. L. Shelton (sop) Virgin Classics ▲ CDC 59308
Knussen, O.:Songs without Voices Virgin Classics ▲ CDC 59308
G. Schuller (cnd)
Mozart, W.A.:Musikalischer Spass Arabesque ▲ 6617 [DDD]
Mozart, W.A.:Serenade Ww, K.361 Arabesque ▲ 6617 [DDD]
C. Wuorinen (cnd)
Wuorinen, C.:New York Notes Koch International Classics ▲ KIC 7272 [DDD]
Wuorinen, C.:Sextet Strs Koch International Classics ▲ KIC 7272 [DDD]
Wuorinen, C.:A Winter's Tale, w. P. Bryn-Julson (sop) Koch International Classics ▲ KIC 7272 [DDD]

Lincoln Center Chamber Music Society members [Joseph Silverstein (vn), Paul Neubauer (va), Fred Sherry (vc), Edgar Meyer (bass), Milan Turkovic (bn), David Shifrin (cl), Robert Routch (hn)]
Beethoven, L. van:Septet Strs *(rec Theater C, SUNY Purchase, NY, Nov 7–8, 1994)* Delos ▲ DE 3177 [DDD]
Lincoln Center Chamber Music Society members [Ransom Wilson (fl), Ani Kavafian (vn), Paul Neubauer (va)]
Beethoven, L. van:Serenade Fl, Op. 25 *(rec Theater C, SUNY Purchase, NY, Nov 7–8, 1994)* Delos ▲ DE 3177 [DDD]
Lincoln Center Jazz Orch members
R. Sadin (cnd)
Gershwin, G.:"I Got Rhythm" Vars, w. Marcus Roberts (pno), Orch of St. Luke members *(rec Masonic Grand Lodge, New York City, July 13, 1995)* Sony Classical ▲ SK 68488 [DDD]
Gershwin, G.:Rhap in Blue, w. Marcus Roberts (pno), Orch of St. Luke members *(rec Masonic Grand Lodge, New York City, June 2, 6 & 7, 1995)* Sony Classical ▲ SK 68488 [DDD]
Johnson, J.P.:Pno Music, w. Marcus Roberts (pno), Orch of St. Luke members—Yamekraw [orchd Still] *(rec Masonic Grand Lodge, New York City, June 2, 6 & 7, 1995)* Sony Classical ▲ SK 68488 [DDD]
Linde Consort
Bach, J.S.:Brandenburg Cons EMI Classics ("Studio" series) 2–▲ ZDMB 63434
Bach, J.S.:A Musical Offering EMI Classics ("Studio" series) 2–▲ ZDMB 63434
H.–M. Linde (cnd)
Bach, J.S.:Brandenburg Cons [period instrs] Virgin Classics ("Veritas Edition" series) ▲ CDMB 61154
Handel, G.F.:Concerti grossi, Op. 3 Virgin Classics ▲ CDM 61162
Mozart, W.A.:Cons Fl, w. Hans-Martin Linde (fl) [period instrs] Virgin Classics ("Veritas Edition" series) ▲ CDM 61176
Lindsay String Quartet
Beethoven, L. van:Grosse Fuge Str Qt ASV 3–▲ ASV DCS403 [DDD]
Beethoven, L. van:Qt 7 Strs ASV ▲ ASV 553 [DDD]
Beethoven, L. van:Qt 7 Strs ASV 2–▲ ASV DCS207 [DDD]
Beethoven, L. van:Qt 8 Strs ASV ▲ ASV 554 [DDD]
Beethoven, L. van:Qt 8 Strs ASV 2–▲ ASV DCS207 [DDD]
Beethoven, L. van:Qt 9 Strs ASV 2–▲ ASV DCS207 [DDD]
Beethoven, L. van:Qt 9 Strs ASV ▲ ASV 554 [DDD]
Beethoven, L. van:Qt 12 Strs ASV 3–▲ ASV DCS403 [DDD]
Beethoven, L. van:Qt 13 Strs ASV 3–▲ ASV DCS403 [DDD]
Beethoven, L. van:Qt 14 Strs ASV 3–▲ ASV DCS403 [DDD]
Beethoven, L. van:Qt 15 Strs ASV 3–▲ ASV DCS403 [DDD]
Beethoven, L. van:Qt 16 Strs ASV 3–▲ ASV DCS403 [DDD]
Bliss, A.:Qnt Cl, w. J. Hilton (cl) Chandos ▲ CHAN 8683 [DDD]
Brahms, J.:Qnt Cl, w. Michel Lethiec (cl) Lyrinx ▲ LYX 123 [DDD]
Brahms, J.:Qnt Pno, w. P. Frankl (pno) ASV ▲ ASV 728 [DDD]
Brown, C.:Fanfare to Welcome Sir Michael Tippett ASV ▲ ASV 879 [DDD]
Dvořák, A.:Bagatelles, Op. 47 [arr. for string qt.] ASV ▲ ASV 806 [DDD]
Dvořák, A.:Qt 5 Strs ASV ▲ ASV 777
Dvořák, A.:Qt 10 Strs ASV ▲ ASV 788
Dvořák, A.:Qt 12 Strs, "America" ASV ▲ ASV 797
Dvořák, A.:Qt 13 Strs ASV ▲ ASV 797
Dvořák, A.:Qt 14 Strs ASV ▲ ASV 788
Dvořák, A.:Qnt Pno, Op. 81, w. P. Frankl (pno) ASV ▲ ASV 889 [DDD]
Dvořák, A.:Qnt Strs, Op. 97, w. P. Ireland (va) ASV ▲ ASV 806 [DDD]
Dvořák, A.:Terzetto, w. P. Ireland (va) ASV ▲ ASV 806 [DDD]
Dvořák, A.:Waltzes Strs, B.105 ASV ▲ ASV 777
Haydn, J.:Qts Strs (misc)—Op. 20/2; Op. 50/1; Op. 76/2 ASV ("Quicksilva" series) ▲ ASQ 6144 [DDD]
Haydn, J.:Qts Strs, Op. 20, "Sun Qts"—No. 4 ASV ("Quicksilva" series) ▲ ASQ 6147 [DDD]
Haydn, J.:Qts Strs, Op. 20, "Sun Qts"—No. 5 ASV ("Quicksilva" series) ▲ ASQ 6146 [DDD]
Haydn, J.:Qts Strs, Op. 33, "Russian Qts"—No. 1 in b; No. 2 in E♭, "The Joke"; No. 4 in B♭ ASV ▲ ASV 937 [DDD]
Haydn, J.:Qts Strs, Op. 33, "Russian Qts"—Nos. 3, 5 & 6 ASV ▲ ASV 938
Haydn, J.:Qts Strs, Op. 33, "Russian Qts"—No. 4 ASV ("Quicksilva" series) ▲ ASQ 6146 [DDD]
Haydn, J.:Qt Strs, Op. 42 ASV ("Quicksilva" series) ▲ ASQ 6145 [DDD]
Haydn, J.:Qts Strs, Op. 50, "Prussian Qts"—No. 4 ASV ("Quicksilva" series) ▲ ASQ 6147 [DDD]
Haydn, J.:Qts Strs, Op. 54 ASV ("The Lindsays Play Haydn" series) ▲ ASV 582 [DDD]
Haydn, J.:Qts Strs, Op. 55 ASV ▲ ASV 906 [DDD]
Haydn, J.:Qts Strs, Op. 64, "Tost Qts"—No. 5 ASV ("Quicksilva" series) ▲ ASQ 6145 [DDD]
Haydn, J.:Qts Strs, Op. 71—No. 2 ASV ▲ ASQ 6146 [DDD]
Haydn, J.:Qts Strs, Op. 76, "Erdödy Qts"—No. 3 ASV ("Quicksilva" series) ▲ ASQ 6147 [DDD]
Haydn, J.:Qts Strs, Op. 76, "Erdödy Qts"—No. 5 ASV ("Quicksilva" series) ▲ ASQ 6145 [DDD]
Haydn, J.:The Seven Last Words of Christ on the Cross [string quartet version] ASV ▲ ASV 853
Martinů, B.:Qnt 2 Pno, w. P. Frankl (pno) ASV ▲ ASV 889 [DDD]
Morris, R.O.:Canzoni ricertati ASV ▲ ASV 879 [DDD]
Mozart, W.A.:Qt Ob, w. Nicholas Daniel (ob) ASV ▲ ASV CD 968
Mozart, W.A.:Qt 14 Strs ASV ▲ ASV 923 [DDD]
Mozart, W.A.:Qt 17 Strs ASV ▲ ASV CD 968
Mozart, W.A.:Qnt Hn, w. Stephen Bell (hn) ASV ▲ ASV CD 968
Mozart, W.A.:Qnt Strs, K.516, w. Patrick Ireland (va) ASV ▲ ASV 923 [DDD]
Schubert, Franz:Qt 8 Strs ASV ▲ ASV 593 [DDD]
Schubert, Franz:Qt 12 Strs ASV ▲ ASV 560 [DDD]
Schubert, Franz:Qt 13 Strs ASV ▲ ASV 593 [DDD]
Schubert, Franz:Qt 14 Strs ASV ▲ ASV 560 [DDD]
Schubert, Franz:Qt 15 Strs ASV ("The Lindsays Play Schubert" series) ▲ ASV 661 [DDD]
Schubert, Franz:Qnt Strs, D.956, w. D. Cummings (vc) ASV ▲ ASV 537 [DDD]
Schumann, R.:Qnt Pno, w. P. Frankl (pno) ASV ▲ ASV 728 [DDD]
Smetana, B.:Qt 1 Strs ASV ▲ ASV 777
Smetana, B.:Qt 2 Strs ASV ▲ ASV 777
Tippett, M.:Qts Strs ASV 2–▲ ASV 231
Tippett, M.:Qt 5 Strs ASV ▲ ASV 879 [DDD]
Weber, C.M. von:Qnt Cl, w. J. Hilton (cl) Chandos ▲ CHAN 8366 [DDD]
Wood, C.:Qt Strs ASV ▲ ASV 879 [DDD]
Linea Ensemble [U. Minkoff (pno), S. Risler (pno), W. Blank (perc), Y. Brustaux (perc)]
Bartók, B.:Son for 2 Pnos *(rec Apr. 1991)* Pyramid ▲ 13504 [DDD]
Stravinsky, I.:Le Sacre du printemps Orch *(rec Apr. 1991)* Pyramid ▲ 13504 [DDD]
LINensemble [E. Kaltof (pno), J. Ehde (vc), Schou (cl)]
Górecki, H.–M.:Lerchenmusik Kontrapunkt ▲ KPT 32175 [DDD]
Gubaidulina, S.:Punkte, Linien & Zickzack [arr for pno trio] Kontrapunkt ▲ KPT 32175 [DDD]
LINensemble [Jens Schou (cl), Christina Åstrand (vn), John Ehde (vc), Erik Kaltoft (pno)]
Messiaen, O.:Quatuor pour la fin du temps Kontrapunkt ▲ KPT 32232
LINensemble [Jens Schou (cl), John Ehde (vc), Erik Kaltoft (pno)]
Nørgård, P.:Cao Shu Kontrapunkt ▲ KPT 32211 [DDD]
Nørgård, P.:LIN Kontrapunkt ▲ KPT 32211 [DDD]
Nørgård, P.:Spell Kontrapunkt ▲ KPT 32211 [DDD]
Nørgård, P.:Trio Cl Kontrapunkt ▲ KPT 32211 [DDD]
Linhares Guitar Quartet [Dagoberto Linhares (gtr), Carla Minen (gtr), Joaquim Freire (gtr), Raymond Migy (gtr)]
Musique Pour Quatre Guitares Gallo ▲ CD 517
Linos Ensemble
Farrenc, J.–L.:Qnt, Op. 30 CPO ▲ CPO 999194 [DDD]
Linos Ensemble (cont.)
Farrenc, J.–L.:Qnt, Op. 31 CPO ▲ CPO 999194 [DDD]
Haydn, J.:Divert for 2 Obs, Hns, Vns, Vas & Db, H.II/20 Capriccio ▲ CD 10719 [DDD]
Haydn, J.:Divert Chamber Ensemble, H.II/B4 Capriccio ▲ CD 10719 [DDD]
Haydn, J.:Notturni (8)—No. 1 Capriccio ▲ CD 10719 [DDD]
Haydn, J.:Qts Strs (misc)—Qt in A Capriccio ▲ CD 10719 [DDD]
Hummel, J.N.:Septet Pno Calig ▲ CAL 50895 [DDD]
Mozart, W.A.:Entführung (winds) Capriccio ▲ 10 493 [DDD]
Mozart, W.A.:Nozze di Figaro (winds) Capriccio ▲ 10 493 [DDD]
Mozart, W.A.:Qnt Pno, K.452 Calig ▲ CAL 50895 [DDD]
Triebensee, J.:Menuetto & Vars Capriccio ▲ 10 492 [DDD]
Linz Bruckner Orch
K. Eichhorn (cnd)
Bruckner, A.:Sym 2—Adagio movt Camerata ("After Hours Classics" series) ▲ 20 CM 423 [DDD]
Bruckner, A.:Sym 7 *(rec Brucknerhaus, Linz, Apr 9–12, 1990)* Camerata ▲ 32CM 165 [DDD]
C. Escher (cnd)
Nishimura, A.:Con Vc, w. Walter Nothas (vc) Camerata ▲ 32CM 199
Nishimura, A.:Into the Lights, w. Walter Nothas (vc) Camerata ▲ 32CM 199
T. Guschlbauer (cnd)
Bruckner, A.:Sym 0 *(rec Brucknerhaus, Linz, July 6, 1981)* Camerata ▲ 25CM 257 [AAD]
M. Sieghart (cnd)
Bruckner, A.:Sym 4, "Romantic" Camerata ▲ 30CM 337 [DDD]
Helmut Lipsky Ensemble
Lipsky, H.:Images, w. A.–G. Duchemin (fl) Pavane ▲ ADW 7197
Lisbon Gulbenkian Foundation CO
F. Bollon (cnd)
Nunes, E.:Machina Mundi, w. Lisbon Gulbenkian Foundation Chorus Montaigne ▲ MO 782020 [DDD]
M. Corboz (cnd)
Bach, J.S.:Con 1 Hpd, w. M.–J. Pires (pno) Erato ▲ 92864–2
Bach, J.S.:Con 4 Hpd, w. M.–J. Pires (pno) Erato ▲ 92864–2
Bach, J.S.:Con 5 Hpd, w. M.–J. Pires (pno) Erato ▲ 92864–2
T. Guschlbauer (cnd)
Mozart, W.A.:Con 26 Pno, w. M.–J. Pires (pno) Erato ▲ 45934–2 [ADD] ■ 45934–4
Lisbon Gulbenkian Foundation Orch
Méhul, E.–N.:La chasse, w. M. Swierczewski Nimbus 2–▲ NI 5184/85 [DDD]
M. Corboz (cnd)
Beethoven, L. van:Mass, Op. 86, w. A. Michael (sop), L. Bizimeche-Eisinger (mez), M. Schaeffer (ten), M. Brodard (bar), Lisbon Gulbenkian Foundation Chorus [L] Erato ▲ 2292–45461–2 ZK [DDD]
Beethoven, L. van:Meeresstille und glückliche Fahrt, w. Lisbon Gulbenkian Foundation Chorus [G] Erato ▲ 2292–45461–2 ZK [DDD]
Bomtempo, J.D.:Messe de requiem consacrée à...Camões, w. Angela Maria Blasi (sop), Liliana Bizineche-Eisinger (mez), Reinaldo Macias (ten), Michel Brodard (bass), Lisbon Gulbenkian Foundation Chorus *(rec Gulbenkian Foundation Grand Auditorium, June 14–16, 1994)* FNAC Music ▲ 592302 [DDD]
Carvalho, J. de S.:Te Deum, w. Brigitte Fournier (sop), Naoko Okada (sop), Elisabeth Graf (cta), John Elwes (ten), Michel Brodard (bar), Lisbon Gulbenkian Foundation Chorus Cascavelle ▲ CVL 1016 [DDD]
Haydn, J.:Mass 3, "Cäcilienmesse", w. Brigette Fournier (sop), Bernarda Fink (alt), Charles Daniels (ten), Marcus Fink (bass), Lisbon Gulbenkian Foundation Chorus *(rec July 1993)* FNAC Music ▲ 592309 [DDD]
Mendelssohn, F.:Hymn, Op. 96, w. *(soloists & chorus unknown)* Erato ▲ 94359–2
Mendelssohn, F.:Lauda Sion, w. Lisbon Gulbenkian Foundation Chorus Erato ▲ 94359–2
Mendelssohn, F.:Psalm 98, w. Lisbon Gulbenkian Foundation Chorus Erato ▲ 94359–2
Mendelssohn, F.:Psalm 114, w. Lisbon Gulbenkian Foundation Chorus Erato ▲ 94359–2
Mendelssohn, F.:St. Paul, w. R. Yakar (sop), B. Baileys (mez), M. Schäfer (ten), T. Hampson (bar), Lisbon Gulbenkian Foundation Chorus Erato 2–▲ 45279–2
S. Gunzenhauser (cnd)
Schumann, R.:Con Pno, w. S. Costa (pno) Naxos ▲ 8.550277 [DDD]
Schumann, R.:Intro & Allegro appassionato, Op. 92, w. S. Costa (pno) Naxos ▲ 8.550277 [DDD]
Schumann, R.:Intro & Allegro, Op. 134, w. S. Costa (pno) Naxos ▲ 8.550277 [DDD]
M. Swierczewski (cnd)
Ives, C.:Central Park in the Dark Nimbus ▲ NI 5316 [DDD]
Ives, C.:Robert Browning Ov Nimbus ▲ NI 5316 [DDD]
Ives, C.:Three Places in New England Nimbus ▲ NI 5316 [DDD]
Ives, C.:The Unanswered Question Nimbus ▲ NI 5316 [DDD]
Méhul, E.–N.:Sym 1 Nimbus 2–▲ NI 5184/85 [DDD]
Méhul, E.–N.:Sym 2 Nimbus 2–▲ NI 5184/85 [DDD]
Méhul, E.–N.:Sym 3 Nimbus 2–▲ NI 5184/85 [DDD]
Méhul, E.–N.:Sym 4 Nimbus 2–▲ NI 5184/85 [DDD]
Méhul, E.–N.:Le trésor supposé (ov) Nimbus 2–▲ NI 5184/85 [DDD]
Offenbach, J.:Dance Music—American Eagle Waltz (1876); Souvenir d'Aix-les-Bains Valses (1873); Ballet des Flocons de Neige; Ballet des Mouches Nimbus ▲ NI 5303 [DDD]
Offenbach, J.:Ovs—Orpheus in the Underworld; Le Voyage dans da Lune; Die Rheinnixen; La Grande-Duchesse de Gérolstein Nimbus ▲ NI 5303 [DDD]
The Spirit of Christmas Present, w. Kansas City Chorale [cnd:Charles Bruffy], BBC Welsh Chorus [cnd:John Hugh Thomas], Huw Tregelles Williams (org), Welsh Guards Fanfare Trumpeters, Christ Church Cathedral Choir [cnd:Stephen Darlington], et al. Nimbus ▲ NI 7034 [DDD]
Waldteufel, E.:Waltzes, Polkas & Galops—(7 waltzes) The Skaters' Waltz [Les Patineurs], Op. 183; Roses de Noël, Op. 230; Pomone, Op. 155; Les Grenadiers, Op. 207; L'Estudiantina, Op. 191; España (after Chabrier), Op. 236; Amour et Printemps; (4 polkas) Bonne bouche, Op. 163; Minuit, Op. 168; Béobile; Joyeux Paris; (2 galops) Grande Vitesse, Op. 146; Prestissimo, Op. 152 Nimbus ▲ NI 5264 [DDD]
Weill, K.:Kleine Dreigroschenmusik Nimbus ▲ NI 5283 [DDD]
Weill, K.:Sym 1 Nimbus ▲ NI 5283 [DDD]
Weill, K.:Sym 2 Nimbus ▲ NI 5283 [DDD]
Lisbon Teatro São Carlos Orch
O. de Fabritiis (cnd)
Donizetti, G.:Maria di Rohan (sels), w. R. Scotto (sop), G. Merighi (sgr), Lisbon Teatro São Carlos Chorus—1 soprano aria, "Cupo fatal mestizia" & 1 duet, "Ecco l'ora" [I] *(rec live, Lisbon 3/20/68)* Melodram (Connaisseur) 2–▲ CDM 27512 [ADD]
F. Ghione (cnd)
Verdi, G.:La traviata, w. M. Callas (sop), A. Kraus (ten), M. Sereni (bar) [I] *(rec live, Lisbon 3/27/58)* EMI Classics 2–▲ CDCB 49187
Franz Liszt Academy Orch
A. Simon (cnd)
Bach, J.S.:Con 6 Hpd, w. Z. Kocsis (pno) Vivace ▲ E 563 [ADD]
Bach, J.S.:Cons for 3 Hpds (comp), w. Z. Kocsis (pno), A. Schiff (pno), S. Falvai (pno) Vivace ▲ E 563 [ADD]
Bach, J.S.:Con for 4 Hpds, w. Z. Kocsis (pno), A. Schiff (pno), S. Falvai (pno), I. Rohmann (pno) Vivace ▲ E 563 [ADD]
Franz Liszt CO
Classics Go to the Movies Vol. 2, w. Dresden PO, Budapest Festival Orch, Bulgarian TV-Radio SO, Bela Kovaks, Bruno Lazzaretti, Berlin RSO, Hungarian State Orch LaserLight ▲ 15 642
Haydn, J.:Con Fl & Orch, w. Jean-Pierre Rampal (fl) Sony Classical ("Essential Classics" series) ▲ SBK 62649 ■ SBT 62649
Haydn, J.:Con Hpd & Strs, H.XVIII/3, w. Emmanuel Ax (hpd). Sony Classical ▲ SK 48383 [DDD]
Haydn, J.:Con Hpd & Strs, H.XVIII/4, w. Emmanuel Ax (hpd) Sony Classical ▲ SK 48383 [DDD]
Haydn, J.:Con Hpd, Obs, Hns & Strs, H.XVIII/11, w. Emanuel Ax (pno) Sony Classical ▲ SK 48383 [DDD]

▲ = CD ♦ = Enhanced CD Δ = MD ■ = Cassette Tape ☐ = DCC

Franz Liszt CO (cont.)

Haydn, J.:Con Ob, w. Pierrot Pierlot (ob)
Sony Classical ("Essential Classics" series) ▲ SBK 62649 ■ SBT 62649
Mozart, W.A.:Cons Hn, w. Dale Clevenger (hn)
Sony Classical ("Essential Classics" series) ▲ SBK 62639 ■ SBT 62639
Mozart, W.A.:Cons Hn, w. Dale Clevenger (hn)—No. 1 [natural horn]; Nos. 2–4 [valve horn]
CBS ▲ MDK 44906 [DDD] ■ MDT 44906 (D)
Mozart, W.A.:Con Movt Hn, K.494a, w. Dale Clevenger (hn)
CBS ▲ MDK 44906 [DDD] ■ MDT 44906 (D)
Mozart, W.A.:Rondo Hn, K.371, w. Dale Clevenger (hn) CBS ▲ MDK 44906 [DDD] ■ MDT 44906 (D)
Mozart, W.A.:Rondo Hn, K.371, w. Dale Clevenger (hn)
Sony Classical ("Essential Classics" series) ▲ SBK 62639 ■ SBT 62639
The Princely Trumpet, w. Edward H. Tarr (tpt) Christophorus ▲ CD 74559 [DDD]
Vivaldi, A.:Cons Fl (misc), w. J.-P. Rampal (fl)—in e, RV.430; in D, RV.783; in d, RV.541 *(rec May 10-13, 1992)* Sony Classical ▲ SK 53105 [DDD] △ SM 53105 [DDD]
Vivaldi, A.:Cons Fl, Op. 10, w. A. Marion (fl) Denon ▲ CO 1406 [DDD]

L. Gardelli (cnd)
Pergolesi, G.B.:Stabat mater, w. M. Kalmár (sop), J. Hamari (mez) [L] Hungaroton ▲ HCD 12201

M. Kocsár (cnd)
Kocsár, M.:Con—in memoriam ZH, w. F. Tarjáni (hn) Hungaroton ▲ HCD 31188 [DDD]
Kocsár, M.:Elegia, w. J. Vajda (bn) Hungaroton ▲ HCD 31188 [DDD]
Kocsár, M.:Episodi, w. P. Pongrácz (ob) Hungaroton ▲ HCD 31188 [DDD]
Kocsár, M.:Movts Cl, w. B. Kovács (vn), Z. Pertis (hpd) Hungaroton ▲ HCD 31188 [DDD]
Kocsár, M.:Sequenze Hungaroton ▲ HCD 31188 [DDD]

R. Leppard (cnd)
Mozart, W.A.:Bastien und Bastienne, w. E. Gruberova (sop), V. Cole (ten), L. Polgár (bass)
Sony Classical ▲ SK 45855

J. López-Cobos (cnd)
Trumpet Concertos, w. Maurice André (tpt), Württemberg CO [cnd:Jörg Faerber], Academy of St. Martin in the Fields [cnd:Neville Marriner], London PO [cnd:Jésus López-Cobos], Philharmonia Orch [cnd:Riccardo Muti] EMI Classics 2-▲ CDZB 69152 [ADD]

E. Lukács (cnd)
Danzi, F.:Con Bn, w. L. Hara (bn) Hungaroton ▲ HCD 31139 [DDD]
Rosetti, F.A.:Con Bn, w. L. Hara (bn) Hungaroton ▲ HCD 31139 [DDD]
Weber, C.M. von:Con Bn, w. L. Hara (bn) Hungaroton ▲ HCD 31139 [DDD]
Winter, P. von:Concertino Bn, w. L. Hara (bn) Hungaroton ▲ HCD 31139 [DDD]

J.-P. Rampal (cnd)
Danzi, F.:Concertante Fl, w. Jean-Pierre Rampal (fl), Paul Meyer (cl) *(rec Italian Institute, Budapest, Jan. 4-7, 1993)* Denon ▲ CO 78911 [DDD]
Mozart, W.A.:March Orch, K.249 *(rec Italian Institute, Budapest, Apr. 13-15, 1994)*
Sony Classical ▲ SK 66270 [DDD]
Mozart, W.A.:Serenade Vn, K.250, w. Isaac Stern (vn) *(rec Italian Institute, Budapest, Apr. 13-15, 1994)*
Sony Classical ▲ SK 66270 [DDD]
Mozart, W.A.:Sym 29 Harmonia Mundi Plus ▲ HMP 3903013
Mozart, W.A.:Sym 32 Harmonia Mundi Plus ▲ HMP 3903013
Mozart, W.A.:Sym 33 Harmonia Mundi Plus ▲ HMP 3903013
Pleyel, I.:Con in B♭ Cl, w. Paul Meyer (cl) *(rec Italian Institute, Budapest, Jan. 4-7, 1993)*
Denon ▲ CO 78911 [DDD]
Pleyel, I.:Con in C Cl, w. Paul Meyer (cl) *(rec Italian Institute, Budapest, Jan. 4-7, 1993)*
Denon ▲ CO 78911 [DDD]
Vivaldi, A.:Cons Vn, Op. 8/1-4, "The Four Seasons", w. J.-P. Rampal (fl) *(rec May 10-13, 1992)*
Sony Classical ▲ SK 53105 [DDD] △ SM 53105 [DDD]

H. Rilling (cnd)
Haydn, M.:Missa Pro Defuncto Archiepiscopo Sigismundo, w. Ibolya Verebics (sop), Judit Németh (mez), Martin Klietmann (ten), József Moldvay (bass), Hungarian Radio-TV Chorus [L]
Hungaroton ▲ HCD 31022 [DDD]
Haydn, M.:Missa Sancti Francisci, w. Ibolya Verebics (sop), Judit Németh (mez), Martin Klietmann (ten), József Moldvay (bass), Hungarian Radio-TV Chorus [L] Hungaroton ▲ HCD 31022 [DDD]

J. Rolla (cnd)
Bach, C.P.E.:Cons Vc, H.432, 436 & 439, w. M. Perényi (vc) Musique d'Abord △ HMA 1903026
Bach, J.S.:The Art of the Fugue Hungaroton 2-▲ HCD 12810/11
Bach, J.S.:Con 1 Hpd, w. C. Katsaris (pno)
Teldec ("Digital Experience" series) ▲ 9031-74779-2 AW [DDD]
Bach, J.S.:Con 3 Hpd, w. C. Katsaris (pno)
Teldec ("Digital Experience" series) ▲ 9031-74779-2 AW [DDD]
Bach, J.S.:Con 5 Hpd, w. C. Katsaris (pno)
Teldec ("Digital Experience" series) ▲ 9031-74779-2 AW [DDD]
Bach, J.S.:Con 6 Hpd, w. C. Katsaris (pno)
Teldec ("Digital Experience" series) ▲ 9031-74779-2 AW [DDD]
Bach, J.S.:Suites Orch, BWV 1066-1069 Hungaroton ▲ HCD 31018 [DDD]
Bartók, B.:Divert Hungaroton ▲ HCD 12531 [DDD]
Bartók, B.:Music for Strs, Perc & Cel Hungaroton ▲ HCD 12531 [DDD]
Carulli, F.:Con Fl, w. J.-P. Rampal (fl), A. Lagoya (gtr) CBS ▲ MK 42130 [DDD]
Concerto Barock, w. Zagreb Musici Vivace 2-▲ G 216 [DDD]
Corelli, A.:Concerti grossi, Op. 6—comp. Hungaroton 2-▲ HCD 12376/77
Corelli, A.:Con grosso, Op. 6/8, "Christmas Con" Vivace ▲ E 511
Encores White Label ▲ HRC 060
Handel, G.F.:Concerti grossi, Op. 6—Nos. 7,8,10 & 12 White Label ▲ HRC 166 [ADD]
Handel, G.F.:Water Music (comp) Hungaroton ▲ HCD 12756 [DDD]
Haydn, J.:Cassation Hns Hungaroton ▲ HCD 12802
Haydn, J.:Con 1 Vc, w. Miklós Perényi (vc) LaserLight ▲ 14 009 [DDD]
Haydn, J.:Con 2 Vc, w. Miklós Perényi (vc) LaserLight ▲ 14 009 [DDD]
Haydn, J.:Con Fl, H.VIIf/D1, w. Jean-Pierre Rampal (fl) CBS 2-▲ M2K 39772 [DDD]
Haydn, J.:Cons for 2 Lire organizzata, w. Jean-Pierre Rampal (fl), Pierre Pierlot (ob)
CBS 2-▲ M2K 39772 [DDD]
Haydn, J.:Con Ob, w. Pierre Pierlot (ob) CBS 2-▲ M2K 39772 [DDD]
Haydn, J.:Con Tpt, w. Edward H. Tarr (tpt) Christophorus ▲ CD 74557 [DDD]
Hummel, J.N.:Con in E Tpt, w. E. Tarr (tpt) Christophorus ▲ CD 74557 [DDD]
Kreutzer, C.:Vars for Chromatic Tpt, w. E. Tarr (tpt) Christophorus ▲ CD 74557 [DDD]
Liszt CO Budapest
Liszt, F.:Hungarian Rhaps—Nos. 2, 6, 9, 12, 14 & 15 *(rec 1991)*
Musique d'Abord ▲ HMA 1903046
Mendelssohn, F.:Con in a Pno, Op. posth., w. C. Katsaris (pno)
Teldec ("Digital Experience" series) ▲ 9031-75860-2 AW [DDD] ■ 9031-75860-4
Millares, A.:Fant for A♭ Tpt, w. E. Tarr (tpt) Christophorus ▲ CD 74557 [DDD]
Mozart, W.A.:Adagio & Fugue Strs Hungaroton ▲ HCD 12471 [DDD]
Mozart, W.A.:Adagio Vn, K.261, w. G. Pauk (vn) Hungaroton 3-▲ HCD 31030/32 [DDD]
Mozart, W.A.:Cons Vn, w. G. Pauk (vn)—Nos. 1-5 Hungaroton 3-▲ HCD 31030/32 [DDD]
Mozart, W.A.:Concertone Vns, w. G. Pauk (vn), J. Rolla (vn) Hungaroton 3-▲ HCD 31030/32 [DDD]
Mozart, W.A.:Divert Str Qt, K.136 LaserLight ▲ 15 647
Mozart, W.A.:Divert Str Qt, K.136 Hungaroton ▲ HCD 12471 [DDD]
Mozart, W.A.:Divert Str Qt, K.136 Vivace ▲ 549 [DDD]
Mozart, W.A.:Divert Str Qt, K.136 Sound 2-▲ CDN 115/116 [DDD]
Mozart, W.A.:Kleine Nachtmusik Hungaroton ▲ HCD 12471 [DDD]
Mozart, W.A.:Kleine Nachtmusik LaserLight ▲ 15 648 [DDD]
Mozart, W.A.:Music of, w. Vienna Mozart Ensemble [cnd:Herbert Kraus], Camerata Academica Salzburg [cnd:Sándor Végh] Laserlight ♦ 90024 [DDD]
Mozart, W.A.:Rondo Vn, K.269, w. G. Pauk (vn) Hungaroton 3-▲ HCD 31030/32 [DDD]
Mozart, W.A.:Rondo Vn, K.373, w. G. Pauk (vn) Hungaroton 3-▲ HCD 31030/32 [DDD]

Franz Liszt CO (cont.)
J. Rolla (cnd) (cont.)
Mozart, W.A.:Serenata notturna Hungaroton ▲ HCD 12471 [DDD]
Mozart, W.A.:Serenata notturna Vivace ▲ 549 [DDD]
Mozart, W.A.:Serenata notturna Sound 2-▲ CDN 115/116 [DDD]
Mozart, W.A.:Serenata notturna Vivace 3-▲ E 338-2 [ADD/DDD]
Mozart, W.A.:Sinf concertante Vn, K.364, w. G. Pauk (vn), J. Rolla (va)
Hungaroton 3-▲ HCD 31030/32 [DDD]
Neruda, J.B.G.:Con Tpt, w. E. Tarr (tpt) Christophorus ▲ CD 74557 [DDD]
Orchestral Favorites (From Vivaldi to Joplin) White Label ▲ HRC 182 [ADD]
Telemann, G.P.:Cons Fl (misc), w. J.-P. Rampal (fl)—3—in D,e,G CBS ▲ MK 42362 [DDD]
Telemann, G.P.:Con in F Rcr Bn, w. L. Czidra (rcr), J. Vajda (bn) White Label ▲ HRC 042
Telemann, G.P.:Suite in e Fl, w. J.-P. Rampal (fl) CBS ▲ MK 42362 [DDD]
Vivaldi, A.:Cons Bn, w. Janota (bn)—6 concerti White Label ▲ HRC 043
Vivaldi, A.:Cons Fl Vn, w. J.-P. Rampal (fl), I. Stern (vn)
Sony Classical ▲ SK 45867 [DDD] ■ ST 45867 (D)
Vivaldi, A.:Cons Gtr, w. J. Williams (gtr) [solo parts trans for gtr]—Vn Concerti, RV.230, R.345 & R.356; Concerto for 2 Mands (w. Ben Verdery, 2nd gtr); Concerto for Lt & 2 Vns, RV.93; Con for Va d'amore & Lt, RV.540 (w. N. Blum, va d'amore); Trio for Vn & Lt, RV.82 (w. J. Rolla, vn)
Sony Classical ▲ SK 46556 [DDD]
Vivaldi, A.:Con Lt, w. D. Benkő (lt) Hungaroton ▲ HCD 11978
Vivaldi, A.:Cons Va d'amore, w. L. Bársony (va)—5 concerti, RV.392-396 Hungaroton ▲ HCD 12162
Vivaldi, A.:Con Va d'amore Lt, w. L. Bársony (va), D. Benkő (lt) Hungaroton ▲ HCD 11978
Vivaldi, A.:Cons Vn, Op. 8/1-12, "Il cimento dell'armonia e dell'inventione"
Hungaroton 2-▲ HCD 12465/66

F. Sándor (cnd)
Handel, G.F.:Water Music (suites) Laserlight ▲ 15 502

Franz Liszt SO
P. Fournillier (cnd)
Massenet, J.:Esclarmonde, w. Denia Mazzola (sop), José Sempere (ten), Christian Tréguier (bar), Hélène Parraguin (sgr), Massenet Festival Choir *(rec live, Massenet Festival, Saint-Étienne)*
Koch Schwann 3-▲ SCH 312692 [DDD]
Massenet, J.:Grisélidis, w. Michèle Command (sop), Brigitte Desnoues (sop), Jean-Luc Viala (ten), Didier Henry (bar), Maurice Sieyes (bar), Christian Treguier (bar), Jean-Philippe Courtis (bass), Claire Larcher (sgr), Budapest Lyon Chorus Koch Schwann 2-▲ SCH 312702 [DDD]

Lithuanian CO
S. Sondeckis (cnd)
Haydn, J.:Con 1 Vc, w. Alexander Rudin (vc) Allegretto ▲ ACD 8186 [ADD] ■ ACS 8186
Haydn, J.:Con 2 Vc, w. Alexander Rudin (vc) Allegretto ▲ ACD 8186 [ADD] ■ ACS 8186
Pärt, A.:Psalom *(rec Liederhalle, Stuttgart, Sept 1995)*
ECM New Series ▲ 78118-21592-2 [DDD] ■ 78118-21592-4
Pärt, A.:Tabula rasa, w. G. Kremer (vn), T. Grindenko (vn)
ECM New Series ▲ 78118-21275-2 [DDD]; ■ 78118-21275-4
Pärt, A.:Trisagion *(rec Liederhalle, Stuttgart, Sept 1995)*
ECM New Series ▲ 78118-21592-2 [DDD] ■ 78118-21592-4

Lithuanian National PO
J. Domarkas (cnd)
Kubik, L.:Con Pno Col Legno ▲ AU 31810
Kupferman, M.:Challenger, w. L. Holkmann (mez), R. Fink (sax) Soundspells ▲ CD 104
Kupferman, M.:Jazz Sym, w. L. Holkmann (mez), R. Fink (sax) Soundspells ▲ CD 104

Lithuanian National SO
S. Frontalini (cnd)
Bottesini, G.:Music of—Piccola Preghiera; Il Nilo; Nel Deserto; Alba Sul Bosforo; Alì Babà (Ov.); Il Diavolo Della Notte; Reverie; Ero e Leandro; Andante Sostenuto; Promenade des Ombres; Margherita (Ov.) Bongiovanni ▲ GB 2141 [DDD]

T. Mikkelsen (cnd)
Grieg, E.:Con Pno, Op. 16, w. Eva Knardahl (pno) Simax ▲ PSC 1107
Grieg, E.:Lyric Pieces, w. Eva Knardahl (pno)—18 pieces Simax ▲ PSC 1107
Grieg, E.:Songs, w. P. Vollestad (bar)—The Mountain Thrall, Op. 32; A Swan, Op. 25/2; 12 Songs to Poems by A.O. Vinje, Op. 35; I Walked One Balmy Summer Eve, Op. 26/2; Henrik Wergeland, Op. 58/3; From Monte Pincio, Op Simax ▲ PSC 1076
Habbestad, K.:Moster Suite, w. Kristin Kjølberg (sop), Njål Sparbo (bar), Odd Lund (goat's hn), Oslo Phil Women's Chamber Choir Norway Music ▲ 2912
Habbestad, K.:Music of, w. *(soloists unknown)*, Oslo Phil Chorus—Moster Suite, Op. 15; 1st Mass on Norwegian Soil; Goat's Horn; Medieval Lyre; Song-Dance; Articles of Norwegian Christian Law
Norway Music ▲ 2912
Habbestad, K.:One Night on Earth, w. Njal Sparbo (bar) Norway Music 2-▲ 2911

Little Consort
Ciconia, J.:Vocal & Instrumental Consort Music Channel Classics ▲ CCS 0290 [DDD]
Fontana, G.B.:Son 10 Fl *(rec 2/91)* Channel Classics ▲ CCS 2791 [DDD]
Italian Chamber Music of the Seicento Channel Classics ▲ CCS 2791 [DDD]
Johannes Ciconia & His Time Channel Classics ▲ CCS 0290 [DDD]
Little Consort with Frans Brüggen, w. Frans Brüggen (fl) Channel Classics ▲ CCS 0390 [DDD]
Machaut, G. de:Ballades, rondeaux, virelais, motets & lais—S'onques douleureusement, "Lai de confort" [F] Channel Classics ▲ CCS 0390 [DDD]
Quagliati, P.:Music for Voice—E ver che nel partire; Io vo cantar; Felice chi vi mira [I]
Channel Classics ▲ CCS 2791 [DDD]

Little Orch Society
T. Scherman (cnd)
Busoni, F.:Divert Fl, w. J. Szigeti (vn) *(rec 1954)*
Sony Masterworks ("Portrait" series) ▲ MPK 52537 (m) [ADD]

Lituana di Vilnjus SO
S. Frontalini (cnd)
Smareglia, A.:Bianca di Cervia (sels)—Marche funèbre Bongiovanni ▲ GB 2142 [DDD]
Smareglia, A.:Cornil Schut (sels)—Preludio dall'Atto 1-3 Bongiovanni ▲ GB 2142 [DDD]
Smareglia, A.:Oceàna (sels)—Ov Bongiovanni ▲ GB 2142 [DDD]
Smareglia, A.:Preziosa (sels)—Preludio Bongiovanni ▲ GB 2142 [DDD]
Smareglia, A.:Il vassallo di Szigeth (sels)—Ov; Musiche del balletto ungherese
Bongiovanni ▲ GB 2142 [DDD]

Live Oak
The Art of Flemish Song in the Courts of Europe, w. Nancy Knowles (sop), Frank Wallace (bar/fl/vih)
Centaur ▲ CRC 2109

Liverpool PO
C. Groves (cnd)
Elgar, E.:Con Vn, w. H. Bean (vn) Classics for Pleasure ▲ CDCFP 4632 [ADD]

S. Kovacevich (cnd)
Haydn, J.:Con Tpt, w. Ian Balmain (tpt) Classics for Pleasure ▲ CDCFP 4589 [DDD]

M. Sargent (cnd)
Elgar, E.:The Dream of Gerontius, w. G. Ripley (cta), H. Nash (ten), D. Noble (bar), N. Walker (bass), Huddersfield Choral Society Testament ▲ TES SBT 2025 [ADD]
Malcolm Seargent Conducts English Music Dutton Laboratories ▲ DUT 8012 [ADD]
Mendelssohn, F.:Elijah, w. Isobel Baillie (sop), Gladys Ripley (cta), James Johnston (ten), Harold Williams (b-bar), Huddersfield Choral Society Dutton Laboratories 2-▲ DUT 2004 [ADD]

G. Weldon (cnd)
Tchaikovsky, P.:Con 2 Pno, w. Benno Moiseiwitch (pno) *(rec 1944)* APR ▲ APR 5518 [ADD]

Livorno Teatro La Gran Guardia Orch
M. Parenti (cnd)
Puccini, G.:Tosca, w. R. Tebaldi (sop—Tosca), F. Corelli (ten—Cavaradossi), A. Colzani (bar—Scarpia), P. L. Latinucci (b-bar—Sacristan), G. Beloni (bass—Angelotti), Livorno Teatro La Gran Guardia Chorus *(rec live Sept. 21, 1959)* Legato Classics 2-▲ LCD 171-2 [ADD]

ORCH. & ENS.

Ljubljana RSO
Brahms, J.:Con 1 Pno, w. D. Tomsic (pno) — Critics Choice 2-▲ CCD 944 [DDD]
Brahms, J.:Con 2 Pno, w. D. Tomsic (pno) — Critics Choice 2-▲ CCD 944 [DDD]
M. Munih (cnd)
Bizet, G.:Carmen (suites) — Stradivari Classics ▲ SCD 6026 [DDD] ■ SMC 6026 (D)
Dvořák, A.:Stabat Mater, w. A. P. Jeric (sop), E. N. Houska (mez), J. Reja (ten), F. Petrusanec (bass), Ljubljana Radio Chorus [L] — PMG (Vienna Master) ▲ CD 160104 [DDD]
Tchaikovsky, P.:Swan Lake (sels) — Stradivari Classics ▲ SCD 6026 [DDD] ■ SMC 6026 (D)
A. Nanut (cnd)
Beethoven, L. van:Con 1 Pno, w. D. Tomšič (pno) — PMG ("Vienna Master" series) ▲ CD 160220 [DDD]
Beethoven, L. van:Con 3 Pno, w. D. Tomšič (pno) — PMG ("Vienna Master" series) ▲ CD 160221 [DDD]
Beethoven, L. van:Fidelio (ov) — PMG ("Vienna Master" series) ▲ CD 160221 [DDD]
Beethoven, L. van:König Stephen (ov) — PMG ("Vienna Master" series) ▲ CD 160220 [DDD]
Beethoven, L. van:Sym 5 — Stradivari Classics ▲ SCD 6004 [DDD] ■ SMC 6004 (D)
Beethoven, L. van:Sym 5 — PMG ("Vienna Master" series) ▲ CD 160222 [DDD]
Bizet, G.:Sym 1 — Stradivari Classics ▲ SCD 6025 [DDD] ■ SMC 6025 (D)
Mendelssohn, F.:Meeresstille — Stradivari Classics ▲ SCD 6025 [DDD] ■ SMC 6025 (D)
Mendelssohn, F.:Sym 4 — Stradivari Classics ▲ SCD 6025 [DDD] ■ SMC 6025 (D)
Ravel, M.:Boléro — PMG ("Vienna Master" series) ▲ CD 160213 [DDD]
Ravel, M.:Con in G Pno, w. M. C. Lee (pno) — PMG ("Vienna Master" series) ▲ CD 160213 [DDD]
Rimsky-Korsakov, N.:Scheherazade — PMG ("Vienna Master" series) ▲ CD 160214 [DDD]
Rimsky-Korsakov, N.:Scheherazade — Stradivari Classics ▲ SCD 6001 [DDD] ■ SMC 6001 (D)
Schubert, Franz:Sym 8 — Stradivari Classics ▲ SCD 6004 [DDD] ■ SMC 6004 (D)
Schubert, Franz:Sym 8 — PMG ("Vienna Master" series) ▲ CD 160222 [DDD]
L. Petitgirard (cnd)
Petitgirard, L.:Euphonia *(rec May 25-29, 1992)* — Orchestre Symphonique France ▲ OSF 49013 [DDD]

Ljubljana SO
The Great Classics, w. Ljubljana SO [cnd:Marko Munih], Sylvia Capova (pno) — Stradivari Classics ("Treasury of Great Classics" series) 5-▲ S5D 6083 [DDD] 5-■ S5C 6083 (D)
Great Overtures,Vol. 2 — Stradivari Classics ▲ SCD 6301 [DDD] ■ SMC 6301 (D)
M. Glinka (cnd)
Mozart, W.A.:Requiem, w. Jitka Pavlová (sop), Polovecova (mez), Vorapajev (ten), Gennadi Bezzubenkov (bass), Leningrad Chorus [L] — Stradivari Classics ▲ SCD 6003 [DDD] ■ SMC 6003 (D)
M. Glinka, M. Munih, A. Nanut, A. Pitamic (cnds)
The Mozart Collection, w. Joze Banic (bn), Pietro Cavaliere (cl), Ruda Kosi (hp), Joze Falout (hn), Dubrovka Tomsic (pno) — Stradivari Classics ("Treasury of Great Classics" series) 5-▲ S5D 61000 [DDD] 5-■ S5C 61000 (D)
A.N. Munih (cnd)
Great Overtures, Vol. 1 — Stradivari Classics ▲ SCD 6300 [DDD] ■ SMC 6300 (D)
M. Munih (cnd)
Borodin, A.:In the Steppes of Central Asia — Stradivari Classics ▲ SCD 6062 [DDD] ■ SMC 6062 (D)
Chopin, F.:Con 1 Pno, w. Dubravka Tomsic (pno) — Allegretto ▲ ACD 8198
Tchaikovsky, P.:Sym 5 — PMG (Vienna Master) ▲ CD 160227 [DDD]
Tchaikovsky, P.:Sym 6 — Stradivari Classics ▲ SCD 6008 [DDD] ■ SMC 6008 (D)
A. Nanut (cnd)
Beethoven, L. van:Con 5 Pno, "Emperor", w. Dubravka Tomsic (pno) — Allegretto ▲ ACD 8193
Beethoven, L. van:Egmont (ov) — Allegretto ▲ ACD 8193
Beethoven, L. van:Sym 3, "Eroica" — Stradivari Classics ▲ SCD 6023 [DDD] ■ SMC 6023 (D)
Borodin, A.:Sym 2 — Stradivari Classics ▲ SCD 6062 [DDD] ■ SMC 6062 (D)
Dvořák, A.:Carnival — Stradivari Classics ▲ SCD 6030 [DDD] ■ SMC 6030 (D)
Glinka, M.:Russlan & Ludmilla (ov) — Stradivari Classics ▲ SCD 6030 [DDD] ■ SMC 6030
The Great Symphonies, w. Slovenian PO [cnd:Milan Horvat], Slovak PO [cnd:Libor Pešek], Royal PO [cnd:Kurt Redel] — Stradivari Classics ("Treasury of Great Classics" series) 5-▲ S5D 6082 [DDD] 5-■ S5C 6082 (D)
Handel, G.F.:Cons (16) Org, w. S. Isakovic (hpd)—1 in F — Stradivari Classics ▲ SCD 6024 [DDD] ■ SMC 6024 (D)
Handel, G.F.:Water Music (comp) — Stradivari Classics ▲ SCD 6024 [DDD] ■ SMC 6024 (D)
Mahler, G.:Sym 1 — Stradivari Classics ▲ SCD 6011 [DDD] ■ SMC 6011 (D)
Mozart, W.A.:Con 26 Pno, w. Dubravka Tomsic (pno) — Allegretto ▲ ACD 8198
Rachmaninoff, S.:Rhapsody on a Theme of Paganini, w. D. Tomšič (pno) — Vox Box 3-▲ CD3X 3020 [ADD]
Schubert, Franz:Sym 8—Andante con moto — Special Music Co. ("Classics of the Heart" series) ▲ SCD 5197
Shostakovich, D.:Sym 7 — Allegretto ▲ ACD 8197
Tchaikovsky, P.:Capriccio italien — Vox Box 3-▲ CD3X 3026 [ADD]
Tchaikovsky, P.:Ov 1812 — Stradivari Classics ▲ SCD 6062 [DDD] ■ SMC 6062 (D)
Tchaikovsky, P.:Swan Lake (suite) — Vox Box 3-▲ CD3X 3026 [ADD]
Tchaikovsky, P.:Sym 5 — Stradivari Classics ▲ SCD 6007 [DDD] ■ SMC 6007 (D)
Tchaikovsky, P.:Sym 6 — PMG (Vienna Master) ▲ CD 160228 [DDD]
Wagner, R.:Arias & Scenes, w. E. Moser (sop)—Tristan und Isolde:Love-Death; Götterdämmerung:Brünnhilde's Immolation — Stradivari Classics ▲ SCD 6064 [DDD]
Wagner, R.:Götterdämmerung (rhine journey & funeral) — Stradivari Classics ▲ SCD 6064 [DDD]
C. Nice (cnd)
Barber, S.:Sym 1 — Vox Box 2-▲ CDX 5091 [ADD]
A. von Pitamic (cnd)
Mozart, W.A.:Kleine Nachtmusik — Stradivari Classics ▲ SCD 6002 [DDD] ■ SMC 6002 (D)
Mozart, W.A.:Sym 29 — Stradivari Classics ▲ SCD 6002 [DDD] ■ SMC 6002 (D)
A. Schenck (cnd)
Grieg, E.:Peer Gynt Suites, Opp. 46 & 55 — Stradivari Classics ▲ SCD 6085 [DDD] ■ SMC 6085 (D)
Sibelius, J.:Sym 5 — Stradivari Classics ▲ SCD 6085 [DDD] ■ SMC 6085 (D)
Sibelius, J.:Valse triste — Stradivari Classics ▲ SCD 6085 [DDD] ■ SMC 6085 (D)

l'Ile de la Cité Orch
L. Jean-Baptiste (cnd)
Villette, P.:Préludes Strs — Analekta ▲ ATM 29721

Locatelli Trio
English 18th-Century Violin Sonatas *(rec Nov. 1991)* — Hyperion ▲ CDA 66583 [DDD]

Locatelli Trio [Elizabeth Wallfisch (vn), Richard Tunnicliffe (vc), Paul Nicholson (hpd)]
Albinoni, T.:Sonate da chiesa, Op. 4, w. Elizabeth Wallfisch (vn) — Hyperion 2-▲ CDA 66831/32
Albinoni, T.:Trattenimenti armonici per camera, w. Elizabeth Wallfisch (vn) — Hyperion 2-▲ CDA 66831/32
Corelli, A.:Sons Vn, Op. 5—complete, plus a second version of No. 9 in A as elaborated by 18th-cent. composer Francesco Geminiani — Hyperion 2-▲ CDA 66381/82 [DDD]
Geminiani, F.:Son Vn & Continuo — Hyperion ▲ CDA 66583 [DDD]
Giardini, F.:Son Vn, Op. 1/3 — Hyperion ▲ CDA 66583 [DDD]
Gibbs, J.:Son Vn, Op. 1/1 — Hyperion ▲ CDA 66583 [DDD]
Handel, G.F.:Sons Solo Instrs, w. Rachel Beckett (fl), Lisa Beznosiuk (rcr), Paul Goodwin (ob) — Hyperion 3-▲ CDA 66921/23
Jones, Richard:Suite Vn — Hyperion ▲ CDA 66583 [DDD]
Linley, T.:Son Vn — Hyperion ▲ CDA 66583 [DDD]
Locatelli, P.:Sons Vn, Op. 8, w. Rachel Isserlis (va) — Hyperion 2-▲ CDA 67021/22
Tartini, G.:Sons Vn & Continuo—Sonata in F, Op. 1/2; Sonata in c, Op. 1/8; Sonata in g, "Didone abbandonata," Op. 1/10; Sonata in F, Op. 1/12; Sonata in A, "Pastorale"; Sonata in D, "Sonata Autografica"; Sonata in g, "The Devil's Trill" — Hyperion ▲ CDA 66430 [DDD]
Tartini, G.:Sons Vn & Continuo—Sonata in A (B A4); Sonata in B♭ (B B1); Sonata in B♭, Op. 5/6 (B B5); Sonata in D (B D19) — Hyperion ▲ CDA 66485 [DDD]

Locke Brass Consort
Rutter, J.:Gloria, w. East London Chorus — Koch Schwann ▲ 3-1266-2 [DDD]

Locke Brass Consort (cont.)
M. Kibbelwhite (cnd)
Essentially Christmas, w. East London Chorus, A. Doyle (sop), S. Liley (ten), J. Lister (hp), P. Ayres (org) — Koch International Classics ▲ KIC 7202 [DDD]
J. Stobart (cnd)
Fanfare:British Music for Symphonic Brass Ensemble — Chandos ("Collect" series) ▲ CHAN 6573 [ADD]

Locke Consort
Baltazar, T.:Suite for 2 Vns *(rec Jan. 1993)* — Globe ▲ GLO 5058 [DDD]
Blow, J.:Ground *(rec Jan. 1993)* — Globe ▲ GLO 5058 [DDD]
Blow, J.:Trio Son *(rec Jan. 1993)* — Globe ▲ GLO 5058 [DDD]
Jenkins, J.:Lady Katherine Audley's Bells *(rec Jan. 1993)* — Globe ▲ GLO 5058 [DDD]
Jenkins, J.:Suite Strs *(rec Jan. 1993)* — Globe ▲ GLO 5058 [DDD]
Locke, M.:Suites for 2 Vns [period instrs]—Suite Nos. 3,4,5 & 6 from *The Broken Consort, Part 1 (ca. 1641)*; Suite No. 4 in F from *The Broken Consort, Part 2(ca. 1641)*; Suite No. 4 in B♭ from *The Little Consort (ca. 1651)*; Suite in g from *Tripla Concordia (1677)* — Globe ▲ GLO 5027 [DDD]
Locke, M.:Suites for 2 Vns—Tripla Concordia:Suite in G (1677) *(rec Jan. 1993)* — Globe ▲ GLO 5058 [DDD]
Purcell, H.:Music of—Pavan in g, Z.751; Pavan in B♭, Z.750 *(rec Jan. 1993)* — Globe ▲ GLO 5058 [DDD]
Purcell, H.:Sons (22) Vns—Trio in d, Z.805 *(rec Jan. 1993)* — Globe ▲ GLO 5058 [DDD]

Lódz PO
W. Czepiel (cnd)
Magin, M.:Music of, w. Milosz Magin (pno)—Stabat Mater; Musique des morts; Con No. 3 for Pno; Polish Miniatures; Sonatina; Polish Triptych; Polka *(rec 1991)* — Polskie Nagrania ▲ PNCD 129 [DDD]

Lódzkiej Phil SO
H. Czyz (cnd)
Grieg, E.:Peer Gynt Suites, Opp. 46 & 55 *(rec 1976)* — Polskie Nagrania ▲ PNCD 152 [ADD]

Loïnhdana Ensemble
Early Music at Wik — BIS ▲ CD 3 [ADD]
The Four Seasons — BIS ▲ CD 75 [ADD]
Jewels of Early Music, w. Musica Antiqua, John Elwes (ten), André Isoir (org), Pierre Bardon (org) *(rec 1982-86)* — Pierre Verany ▲ 791051 [DDD]
Woods, Women & Wine — BIS ▲ CD 120 [ADD]

Loire PO
G. Carella (cnd)
Mercadante, S.:Il giuramento, w. M. Olmeda (sop), G. Morino (ten) — Nuova Era 2-▲ NUO 7179 [DDD]
M. Soustrot (cnd)
Berlioz, H.:Rêverie et caprice, w. Constantin Serban-Ioanid (vn) — Forlane ▲ FRL 63 [DDD]
Berlioz, H.:Sym fantastique — Forlane ▲ FRL 63 [DDD]
Borodin, A.:In the Steppes of Central Asia *(rec 9/88)* — Pierre Verany ▲ PV.789051 [DDD]
Chausson, E.:Sym in B♭ *(rec 1/92)* — Pierre Verany ▲ PV.792051 [DDD]
Debussy, C.:La Mer — Forlane ▲ FRL 16554 [DDD]
Debussy, C.:Prélude à l'après-midi d'un faune — Forlane ▲ FRL 16554 [DDD]
Fauré, G.:Pelléas et Mélisande (suite) *(rec 1/92)* — Pierre Verany ▲ PV.792051 [DDD]
Fauré, G.:Pénélope (prelude) *(rec 1/92)* — Pierre Verany ▲ PV.792051 [DDD]
Les grands airs italiens, w. José Van Dam (b-bar) — Forlane ▲ FOR 16681 [DDD]
Hummel, J.N.:Con in E♭ Tpt, S.49, w. B. Soustrot (tpt) — Pierre Verany ▲ PV 788011 [DDD]
Jolivet, A.:Con 2 Tpt, w. B. Soustrot (tpt) — Pierre Verany ▲ PV 788011 [DDD]
Mussorgsky, M.:Night *(rec 9/88)* — Pierre Verany ▲ PV.789051 [DDD]
Mussorgsky, M.:Pictures at an Exhibition *(rec 9/88)* — Pierre Verany ▲ PV.789051 [DDD]
Poulenc, F.:La Baigneuse de Trouville & Discours du général — Pierre Verany ▲ PV.791011 [DDD]
Poulenc, F.:Concert champêtre Hpd, w. F.-H. Houbart (hpd) — Pierre Verany ▲ PV.791011 [DDD]
Poulenc, F.:Con Org, w. F.-H. Houbart (org) — Pierre Verany ▲ PV.791011 [DDD]
Poulenc, F.:2 marches et un intermède — Pierre Verany ▲ PV.791011 [DDD]
Ravel, M.:Daphnis et Chloé (suite 2) — Forlane ▲ FRL 16554 [DDD]
Ravel, M.:Pavane pour une infante défunte — Forlane ▲ FRL 16554 [DDD]
Stravinsky, I.:Circus Polka — Forlane ▲ FRL 16717 [DDD]
Stravinsky, I.:Con CO — Forlane ▲ FRL 16717 [DDD]
Stravinsky, I.:Le Sacre du printemps Orch — Forlane ▲ FRL 16717 [DDD]

Londerzeel Youth SO
P. Himpe (cnd)
Mascagni, P.:Cavalleria rusticana (sels) *(rec 1992)* — Bongiovanni ▲ GB 2130 [DDD]
Mascagni, P.:Davanti Santa Teresa *(rec 1992)* — Bongiovanni ▲ GB 2130 [DDD]
Mascagni, P.:Rapsodia satanica *(rec 1992)* — Bongiovanni ▲ GB 2130 [DDD]

London Astarte Orch
G. Pio (cnd)
Battiato, F.:L'Ombra della Luce, w. Franco Battiato (voc), Antonio Ballista (pno), Roger Chase (va), Filippo Destrieri (kbd/computer), Anthony Pleeth (vc), Gavin Wright (vn) — Hemisphere ▲ 837234-2
Battiato, F.:Povera Patria, w. Franco Battiato (voc), Antonio Ballista (pno), Roger Chase (va), Filippo Destrieri (kbd/computer), Anthony Pleeth (vc), Gavin Wright (vn) — Hemisphere ▲ 837234-2
Battiato, F.:Le Sacre Sinfonie del Tiempo, w. Franco Battiato (voc), Antonio Ballista (pno), Roger Chase (va), Filippo Destrieri (kbd/computer), Anthony Pleeth (vc), Gavin Wright (vn) — Hemisphere ▲ 837234-2

London Baroque
Abel, C.F.:Sons Vn, Vc & Continuo, Op. 9—No. 1 in A — Amon Ra ▲ CD-SAR 14 [DDD]
Arne, T.:Trio Sons, Op. 3—No. 2 in G — Amon Ra ▲ CD-SAR 14 [DDD]
Avison, C.:Sons, Op. 5—No. 2 in C — Amon Ra ▲ CD-SAR 14 [DDD]
Handel, G.F.:Trio Sons—Op. 2, No. 3 — Amon Ra ▲ CD-SAR 14 [DDD]
Handel, G.F.:Trio Sons—Seven Sonatas for 2 Violins & Continuo, Op. 5 — Harmonia Mundi France ▲ HMC 901389
Handel, G.F.:Trio Sons—Six Trio Sonatas, Op. 2; for 2 Violins, Cello & Harpsichord Continuo — Harmonia Mundi France ▲ HMC 901379
Marais, M.:La Gamme en forme de petit Opera — Musique d'Abord ▲ HMA 1901105
Marais, M.:Son à la Marésienne — Musique d'Abord ▲ HMA 1901105
Mozart, W.A.:Divert Ob, K.251, w. R. Canter (ob) [period instrs] — Amon Ra ▲ CD-SAR 34 [DDD]
Mozart, W.A.:Qt Ob, K.370, w. R. Canter (ob) [period instrs] — Amon Ra ▲ CD-SAR 34 [DDD]
Mozart, W.A.:Qnt Ob, K.516b, w. R. Canter (ob) [period instrs] — Amon Ra ▲ CD-SAR 34 [DDD]
Muffat, G.:Son Vn, w. C. Medlam (vc) — Musique d'Abord ▲ HMA 1901220
Stanley, J.:Cons Org, Op. 10, w. J. Toll (hpd)—Concerto No. 4 in c — Amon Ra ▲ CD-SAR 14 [DDD]
H. Hennig (cnd)
Schütz, H.:Meine Seele erhebt den Herren, w. Hanover Boys' Choir, Hilliard Ensemble — EMI Classics ("Baroque" series) ▲ CDK 65736
C. Medlam (cnd)
Bach, W.F.:Cons Hpd, w. Richard Egarr (hpd)—in D, F.41; in F, F.44; in a, F.45 — Harmonia Mundi France ▲ HMC 901558
Lawes, W.:Sons Vn — Harmonia Mundi France ▲ HMC 901493 [DDD]
Muffat, G.:Son V Strs — Musique d'Abord ▲ HMA 1901220
Schmelzer, J.H.:Sons a tre Strs — Musique d'Abord ▲ HMA 1901220

London Baroque [I. Seifert (vn), R. Gwilt (vn), C. Medlam (vc), R. Egarr (hpd)]
Bach, C.P.E.:Trio Sons (misc)—W.154-56 & 158 — Harmonia Mundi France ▲ HMC 901511

London Baroque [Lars-Ulrik Mortensen (hpd), Ingrid Seifert (vn), Richard Gwilt (vn), Charles Medlam (vc)]
Bach, Joh. Christian:Con Kbd — Musique d'abord ▲ HMA 1901395
Bach, Joh. Christian:Son Kbd, Op. 20/2 — Musique d'abord ▲ HMA 1901395
Mozart, L.:Son da Camera 4 — Musique d'abord ▲ HMA 1901395
Mozart, W.A.:Cons Pno, K.107 — Musique d'abord ▲ HMA 1901395

218
▲ = CD ♦ = Enhanced CD Δ = MD ■ = Cassette Tape ▯ = DCC

London Baroque Brass
D. Hill (cnd)
Purcell, H.:Anthems, w. D. Dunnett (org), Brandenburg Consort, Winchester Cathedral Choir—Funeral Sentences; Rejoice in the Lord Always; Jehova, Quam Multi Sunt Hostes; O God, Thou Art My God; Remember Not, Lord, Our Offences; Give Sentence with Me, O God; Hear My Prayer, O Lord; Voluntary in C; A Double Verse in G; O, I'm Sick of Life Argo ▲ 436833-2 [DDD]
Purcell, H.:Music for the Funeral of Queen Mary, w. D. Dunnett (org), Brandenburg Consort, Winchester Cathedral Choir Argo ▲ 436833-2 [DDD]
Purcell, H.:My Beloved Spake, w. D. Dunnett (org), Brandenburg Consort, Winchester Cathedral Choir Argo ▲ 436833-2 [DDD]

London Brass
Baroque & Brass Teldec ("Digital Experience" series) ▲ 9031-77604-2 AW [DDD] ■ 9031-77604-4
Christmas with London Brass Teldec ▲ 2292-46443-2 [DDD] ■ 2292-46443-4 (D)
Gabrieli in Venice Teldec ▲ 90856-2
I Got Rhythm Teldec ▲ 2292-46444-2 ZK
International Folk Songs:Around the World with London Brass Teldec ▲ 9031-73270-2 ZK
¡Viva España! Teldec ▲ 9031-76990-2 ZK
R. Harvey (cnd)
Fanfare for the Common Man, w. Aquitaine Brass ASV ▲ ASV 870 [DDD]

London Brass Chorale
L. Johnson (cnd)
Johnson, Laurie:Music of, w. W. Davies (org), London PO, London Jazz Orch, London Studio SO, Coldstream Guards Regimental Band, Fanfare Trumpeters of the Scots Guards—Royal Tour (suite); Symphony (Synthesis) for Combined Jazz & Symphony Orchestras (1969); Three Paintings by Lautrec; The Wind In the Willows (1985) *(rec 1969–82)* Unicorn-Kanchana ▲ UKCD 2057 [DDD/ADD]

London Brass Ensemble
E. Dobson, F. Harrison, D. Smithers (cnds)
Now Make We Merthe, w. Purcell Consort of Voices, All Saints Boys' Choir *(rec May 1965, Dec. 21–22, 196)* Boston Skyline ▲ BSD 121 [ADD]

London Brass Players
J. Rifkin (cnd)
Baroque Fanfares & Sonatas Elektra/Nonesuch ■ 71145-4

London Brass Quintet
Horovitz, J.:Vars on a Theme by Paganini Albany ▲ TROY 093 [DDD]

London Brass Virtuosi
D. Honeyball (cnd)
Bourgeois, D.:William & Mary Suite, w. Philharmonia Orch Hyperion ▲ CDA 66870
Elgar, E.:Sursum corda, w. Philharmonia Orch Hyperion ▲ CDA 66870
Hindemith, P.:Concert Music Brass & Strs, w. Philharmonia Orch Hyperion ▲ CDA 66870
Patterson, P.:Brussels Fanfare, w. Philharmonia Orch Hyperion ▲ CDA 66870
Patterson, P.:Eurostar Fanfare, w. Philharmonia Orch Hyperion ▲ CDA 66870
Patterson, P.:Paris Fanfare, w. Philharmonia Orch Hyperion ▲ CDA 66870
Patterson, P.:The Royal Eurostar, w. Philharmonia Orch Hyperion ▲ CDA 66870
Strauss, R.:Feierlicher Einzug der Ritter des Johanniter-Ordens, w. Philharmonia Orch Hyperion ▲ CDA 66870

London Camerata
Music for Kings & Courtiers *(rec July 19–21, 1978)* Saga Classics ▲ 3367 [ADD]
Sixteenth Century Music:The Muses' Garden for Delights Saga ▲ EC 3392

London Canada Orch
U. Mayer (cnd)
Fiala, G.:The Kurelek Suite *(rec Centre in the Square, Kitchener, Jan 19–20, 1993)* CBC ("SM 5000" series) ▲ SM5 5146 [DDD]
Hindemith, P.:Mathis der Maler (sym) *(rec Centre in the Square, Kitchener, Jan 19–20, 1993)* CBC ("SM 5000" series) ▲ SM5 5146 [DDD]
Respighi, O.:Vetrate di chiesa *(rec Centre in the Square, Kitchener, Jan 19–20, 1993)* CBC ("SM 5000" series) ▲ SM5 5146 [DDD]

London CO
Albinoni, T.:Adagio Org Virgin Classics ▲ CDM 59563-2 [DDD]
Britten, B.:Lachrymae Virgin Classics ▲ 59562 [DDD]
Britten, B.:Prelude & Fugue Strs Virgin Classics ▲ 59562 [DDD]
Britten, B.:Simple Sym Virgin Classics ▲ 59562 [DDD]
Elgar, E.:Intro & Allegro Virgin Classics ▲ 59546 [DDD]
Elgar, E.:Serenade Strs Virgin Classics ▲ 59546 [DDD]
Mozart, W.A.:Sinf concertante Ob, K.Anh.9 Virgin Classics ▲ 59545 [DDD]
Mozart, W.A.:Sinf concertante Vn, K.364 Virgin Classics ▲ 59545 [DDD]
Pachelbel, J.:Canon Virgin Classics ▲ 59563 [DDD]
Purcell, H.:Chacony [Benjamin Britten's 1965 string orchestra arr.] Virgin Classics ▲ 59562 [DDD]
Vaughan Williams, R.:Fant on Greensleeves Virgin Classics ▲ 59546 [DDD]
Vaughan Williams, R.:Fant on a Theme by Thomas Tallis Virgin Classics ▲ 59546 [DDD]
Vivaldi, A.:Cons Vn, Op. 8/1–4, "The Four Seasons" Virgin Classics ▲ 59563 [DDD]
T. McIntosh (cnd)
Arne, T.:Con 2 Org, w. T. McIntosh (org) *(rec 1980)* Allegretto ▲ ACD 8165 [DDD] ■ ACS 8165
Chilcot, T.:Con Hpd, w. T. McIntosh (hpd) *(rec 1980)* Allegretto ▲ ACD 8165 [DDD] ■ ACS 8165
Purcell, H.:Abdelazer, or The Moor's Revenge *(rec 1980)* Allegretto ▲ ACD 8165 [DDD] ■ ACS 8165
Purcell, H.:Dido & Aeneas (sels)—Suite *(rec 1980)* Allegretto ▲ ACD 8165 [DDD] ■ ACS 8165
Purcell, H.:The Fairy Queen (sels)—Suite *(rec 1980)* Allegretto ▲ ACD 8165 [DDD] ■ ACS 8165
Purcell, H.:King Arthur (sels)—Suite *(rec 1980)* Allegretto ▲ ACD 8165 [DDD] ■ ACS 8165
Purcell, H.:The Prophetess (sels)—Dance of the Furies Suite *(rec 1980)* Allegretto ▲ ACD 8165 [DDD] ■ ACS 8165
Stanley, J.:Con in c Org, w. T. McIntosh (org) *(rec 1980)* Allegretto ▲ ACD 8165 [DDD] ■ ACS 8165
J. MacMillan (cnd)
Macmillan, J.:Seven Last Words from the Cross, w. Polyphony *(rec St. John-at-Hackney, London, Sept. 28–30, 1994)* Catalyst ▲ 09026-68125-2 [DDD]; ■ 09026-68125-4
C. Warren-Green (cnd)
Adams, J.:Shaker Loops Virgin Classics ▲ CDM 59610-2 [DDD]
Britten, B.:Simple Sym Virgin Classics ("Ultraviolet" series) ▲ CUV 61269
Dvořák, A.:Serenade Strs Virgin Classics ▲ CDM 59607
Elgar, E.:Intro & Allegro Virgin Classics ("Ultraviolet" series) ▲ CUV 61126
Elgar, E.:Serenade Strs Virgin Classics ("Ultraviolet" series) ▲ CUV 61126
Glass, Philip:Company Virgin Classics ▲ 59610 [DDD]
Glass, Philip:Façades Virgin Classics ▲ 59610 [DDD]
Haydn, J.:Con 1 Hn, w. Michael Thomas (hn) Virgin Classics ("Ultraviolet" series) ▲ CUV 61235
Haydn, J.:Sym 45, "Farewell" Virgin Classics ("Ultraviolet" series) ▲ CUV 61235
Haydn, J.:Sym 94, "Surprise Sym" Virgin Classics ("Ultraviolet" series) ▲ CUV 61235
Heath, David:The Frontier Virgin Classics ▲ 59610 [DDD]
LCO
LCO 1 Virgin Classics ▲ 59545 [DDD]
LCO 2 Virgin Classics ▲ 59546 [DDD]
LCO 3 Virgin Classics ▲ 59563 [DDD]
LCO 4 Virgin Classics ▲ 59564 [DDD]
LCO 7 Virgin Classics ▲ 59609 [DDD]
LCO 8 Virgin Classics ▲ 59610 [DDD]
LCO 9:Under The Eye Of Heaven
LCO 10:Power Virgin Classics ▲ 59614 [DDD]
London Chamber Orchestra Sampler Virgin Classics 2-▲ CDC 59095
Mozart, W.A.:Con 5 Vn, w. Christopher Warren-Green (vn) Virgin Classics ("Ultraviolet" series) ▲ CUV 61132

London CO (cont.)
C. Warren-Green (cnd) (cont.)
Mozart, W.A.:Divert Str Qt, K.136 Virgin Classics ("Ultraviolet" series) ▲ CUV 61132
Mozart, W.A.:Kleine Nachtmusik Virgin Classics ("Ultraviolet" series) ▲ CUV 61132
Mozart, W.A.:Sym 29 Virgin Classics ("Ultraviolet" series) ▲ CUV 61132
Purcell, H.:Chacony [orchd. Britten] Virgin Classics ("Ultraviolet" series) ▲ CUV 61269
Reich, S.:8 Lines Virgin Classics ▲ 59610 [DDD]
Suk, J.:Serenade Strs Virgin Classics ▲ CDM 59607
Tchaikovsky, P.:Serenade Strs Virgin Classics ▲ CDM 59607
Vaughan Williams, R.:Fant on Greensleeves Virgin Classics ("Ultraviolet" series) ▲ CUV 61126
Vaughan Williams, R.:Fant on a Theme by Thomas Tallis Virgin Classics ("Ultraviolet" series) ▲ CUV 61126
Vaughan Williams, R.:The Lark Ascending, w. *(vn unknown)* Virgin Classics ("Ultraviolet" series) ▲ CUV 61126
Vaughan Williams, R.:The Lark Ascending, w. C. Warren-Green (vn) Virgin Classics ▲ 59546 [DDD]
Vivaldi, A.:Cons Bn, w. M. Alexander (bn)—RV.502 in B♭ Virgin Classics ▲ 59609 [DDD]
Vivaldi, A.:Cons Vc, w. A. Shulman (vc)—RV.401 Virgin Classics ▲ 59609 [DDD]
Vivaldi, A.:Cons Ob, w. G. Hunt (ob)—RV.447 in C Virgin Classics ▲ 59609 [DDD]
Vivaldi, A.:Con for 2 Tpts, w. G. Ruddock (tpt), G. Ashton (tpt) Virgin Classics ▲ 59609 [DDD]
Vivaldi, A.:Cons for 2 Vns, w. C. Warren-Green (vn), R. Furniss (vn)—RV.522 in a Virgin Classics ▲ 59609 [DDD]
Vivaldi, A.:Con for 3 Vns, w. C. Warren-Green (vn), A. Balanescu (vn), E. Layton (vn)—RV.551 in F Virgin Classics ▲ 59609 [DDD]
Vivaldi, A.:Cons for 4 Vns, w. C. Warren-Green (vn), R. Furniss (vn), T. Bowes (vn), B. Davison (vn)—RV.580 in b Virgin Classics ▲ 59609 [DDD]

London Chamber Players [Peter Gibbs (vn), Neville Marriner (vn), Kenneth Essex (va), Derek Simpson (vc), Anthony Baines (db), Denis Vaughan (hpd)]
A. Deller (cnd)
Monteverdi, C.:Ballo delle ingrate, w. April Cantelo (sop—Una dell' Ingrate), Eileen McLoughlin (sop—Amore), Alfred Deller (alt—Venere), David Ward (bass—Plutone), Julian Bream (lt), Desmond Dupre (vl) *(rec Walthamstow Hall, London)* Vanguard Classics ▲ OVC 8100 [ADD]

London Clarinet Consort members
Cooke, A.:Suite for 3 Cls, w. Georgina Dobrée (cl) Clarinet Classics ▲ CC 0012 [AAD]

London Classical Players
R. Norrington (cnd)
Beethoven, L. van:Coriolan Ov [period instrs] EMI Classics 6-▲ A26-49852 [DDD]
Beethoven, L. van:Egmont (ov) [period instrs] EMI Classics 6-▲ A26-49852 [DDD]
Beethoven, L. van:Die Geschöpfe des Prometheus (ov) [period instrs] EMI Classics 6-▲ A26-49852 [DDD]
Beethoven, L. van:Syms (comp) [SATB soloists in No. 9 are Yvonne Kenny, Sarah Walker, Patrick Power & Petteri Salomaa] EMI Classics 6-▲ A26-49852 [DDD]
Beethoven, L. van:Sym 9, "Choral Sym", w. Schütz Choir London [G] EMI Classics ▲ CDC 49221 [DDD]
Berlioz, H.:Sym fantastique [period instrs] EMI Classics ▲ CDC 49541 [DDD] □ 0777-7-49541-5-0
Brahms, J.:Sym 1 EMI Classics ▲ CDC 54286
Brahms, J.:Sym 2 EMI Classics ▲ CDC 54875
Brahms, J.:Sym 3 EMI Classics ▲ CDC 56118
Brahms, J.:Sym 4 EMI Classics ▲ CDC 56118
Brahms, J.:Tragic Ov EMI Classics ▲ CDC 54875
Brahms, J.:Vars on a Theme by Haydn EMI Classics ▲ CDC 54286
Haydn, J.:Ovs—Ov. to an English Opera EMI Classics ▲ CDC 55192
Haydn, J.:Sym 99 EMI Classics ▲ CDC 55192
Haydn, J.:Sym 100, "Military" EMI Classics ▲ CDC 55192
Haydn, J.:Sym 101, "Clock" EMI Classics ▲ CDC 55111
Haydn, J.:Sym 102 EMI Classics ▲ CDC 55111
Haydn, J.:Sym 103, "Drum Roll" EMI Classics ▲ CDC 55002
Haydn, J.:Sym 104, "London" EMI Classics ▲ CDC 55002
Mozart, W.A.:Ave verum corpus, w. Heinrich Schütz Choir EMI Classics ▲ CDC 54525
Mozart, W.A.:Don Giovanni, w. N. Argenta (sop), A. Halgrimson (sop), L. Dawson (sop), J. M. Ainsley (ten), G. Finley (ten), A. Miles (bar), A. Schmidt (bar), G. Yurisch (bar), Schütz Choir London EMI Classics ▲ CDCB 54859
Mozart, W.A.:Maurerische Trauermusik EMI Classics ▲ CDC 54525
Mozart, W.A.:Requiem, w. N. Argenta (sop), C. Robbin (mez), J.M. Ainsley (ten), A. Miles (bass), Schütz Choir London [L] EMI Classics ▲ CDC 54525
Mozart, W.A.:Sym 38 EMI Classics ▲ CDC 54336
Mozart, W.A.:Sym 39 EMI Classics ▲ CDC 54090
Mozart, W.A.:Sym 40 EMI Classics ▲ CDC 54336
Mozart, W.A.:Sym 41 EMI Classics ▲ CDC 54090
Mozart, W.A.:Zauberflöte, w. D. Upshaw (sop), B. Hoch (sop), A. Rolfe Johnson (ten), A. Schmidt (bar) [period instrs] EMI Classics 2-▲ CDCB 54287
Mozart, W.A.:Zauberflöte (sels), w. D. Upshaw (sop), B. Hoch (sop), A. Rolfe Johnson (ten), A. Schmidt (bar) [period instrs] EMI Classics ▲ CDC 54492
Purcell, H.:The Fairy Queen, w. Lorraine Hunt (sop), Susan Bickley (mez), Catherine Pierard (mez), Howard Crook (ten), Mark Padmore (ten), David Wilson-Johnson (bar), Richard Wistreich (bass), Schütz Choir London EMI Classics ▲ CDCB 55234
Rossini, G.:Ovs—La scala di seta; La gazza ladra; Guillaume Tell; L'italiana in Algeri; Semiramide; Il signor Bruschino; Il barbiere di Siviglia EMI Classics ▲ CDC 54091 ■ 4DS 54091 □ 0777-7-54091-5-4
Schubert, Franz:Sym 6 EMI Classics ▲ CDC 54210
Wagner, R.:Lohengrin (preludes)—Act 3 EMI Classics ▲ CDC 55479
Wagner, R.:Die Meistersinger von Nürnberg (preludes) EMI Classics ▲ CDC 55479
Wagner, R.:Parsifal (prelude) EMI Classics ▲ CDC 55479
Wagner, R.:Rienzi, der Letzte der Tribunen (ov) EMI Classics ▲ CDC 55479
Wagner, R.:Siegfried Idyll EMI Classics ▲ CDC 55479
Wagner, R.:Tristan und Isolde (prelude & liebestod), w. Jane Eaglen (sop) EMI Classics ▲ CDC 55479
Weber, C.M. von:Konzertstück Pno, w. Melvyn Tan (pno) EMI Classics ▲ CDC 55348
Weber, C.M. von:Sym 1 EMI Classics ▲ CDC 55348
Weber, C.M. von:Sym 2, w. Melvyn Tan (pno) EMI Classics ▲ CDC 55348

London Collegium Musicum
A. Previn (cnd)
Walton, W.:Belshazzar's Feast, w. B. Luxon (bar), Royal PO RPO ▲ RPO 7013 [DDD]

London Concert Orch
M. Dods (cnd)
Sullivan, A.:Music of, w. M. Studholme (sop), J. Allister (cta), E. Bohan (ten), I. Wallace (bar), English Chorale—sels. from Gondoliers; H.M.S. Pinafore; Mikado; Pirates of Penzance PWK Classics ▲ PWK 1157 [AAD]
J. Georgiadis (cnd)
Strauss (II), Joh.:Music of—Acceleration Waltz; Champagne Polka; Eljen a Magyar Polka; Kettenbrucke Waltz; Lorelei-Rheinklange Waltz; Pester Czardas; Pizzicato Polka; Radetzky March; Sperl Galop; Tritsch-Tratsch Polka; Unter Donnen und Blitz Galop; Wiener Blut Waltz PWK Classics ▲ PWK 1158 [AAD]

London Concertante Ensemble
R. Mosley (cnd)
Adoration, w. Voices of the Azusa Pacific Univ [cnd:Gary Bonner] Resmiranda ▲ RES 8000
Adoration II, w. Voices of the Azusa Pacific Univ [cnd:Gary Bonner] Resmiranda ▲ RES 8001
Adoration III, w. Voices of the Azusa Pacific Univ [cnd:Gary Bonner] Resmiranda ▲ RES 8002
Gloria, w. Voices of the Azusa Pacific Univ [cnd:Gary Bonner] Resmiranda ▲ RES 8006
How Excellent Thy Name, w. Voices of the Azusa Pacific Univ [cnd:Gary Bonner] Resmiranda ▲ RES 8016

London Cornett & Sackbutt Ensemble

N. Rogers (cnd)

Monteverdi, C.:Orfeo, w. P. Kwella (sop), E. Kirkby (sop), J. Smith (sop), N. Rogers (ten), S. Varcoe (bar), D. Thomas (bass), C. Medlam (cnd), London Baroque Chiaroscuro — EMI Classics ▲ CDMB 64947

London Divertimenti

P. Barritt (cnd)

Vivaldi, A.:Cons Fl, Op. 10, w. Judith Hall (fl) — IMP ("Classics" series) ▲ IMP 6700212

London Early Music Consort

Munrow, D.:Music of—The Art of the Netherlands — EMI Classics ▲ ZDMB 64215

P. Ledger (cnd)

Monteverdi, C.:Vespro della Beata Vergine, w. Elly Ameling (sop), Norma Burrowes (sop), Charles Brett (ct), Martyn Hill (ten), Anthony Rolfe-Johnson (ten), Robert Tear (ten), Peter Knapp (bass), John Noble (bass), Francis Grier (org/hpd), James Lancelot (org/hpd), Andrew Leach (org/hpd), King's College Choir Cambridge—Nigra sum [con.]; Laudate pueri [psalm]; Sancta Maria [son. sopra]; Magnificat *(rec Chapel of King's College, Cambridge, July & Aug. 1975)* — EMI Classics ▲ CDK 65339 [ADD]

D. Munrow (cnd)

The Art of Courtly Love *(rec 1976)* — Virgin Classics ("David Munrow Edition" series) 2-▲ ZDMB 61284
Dufay, G.:Gloria ad modum tube — Virgin Classics ("David Munrow Edition" series) ▲ CDM 61283
Dufay, G.:Missa, "Se la face ay pale" — Virgin Classics ("David Munrow Edition" series) ▲ CDM 61283
Dufay, G.:Se la face ay pale — Virgin Classics ("David Munrow Edition" series) ▲ CDM 61283
The Medieval Experience:Monks, Troubadours, Motets, Masses & Memorials — Archiv 4-▲ 449082-2
Monteverdi's Contemporaries — Virgin Classics ("David Munrow Edition" series) ▲ CDM 61288
Music of the Crusades — London ("Jubilee" series) ▲ 430264-2 LM [ADD]
Music of the Gothic Era — Archiv ▲ 415292-2 AH [ADD]
Pleasures of the Royal Court, w. Christopher Hogwood (kbd) — Elektra/Nonesuch ▲ 71326-2 [ADD]
Praetorius, M.:Motets—6 Motets — Virgin Classics ("David Munrow Edition" series) ▲ CDM 61289
Praetorius, M.:Terpsichore—10 Dances — Virgin Classics ("David Munrow Edition" series) ▲ CDM 61289
Praetorius, M.:Terpsichore — EMI Classics ("Studio" series) ▲ CDM 69024

D. Munrow, P. Ledger (cnds)

Monteverdi, C.:Vespro della Beata Vergine, w. Elly Ameling (sop), Norma Burrowes (sop), Charles Brett (ct), Robert Tear (ten), Anthony Rolfe Johnson (ten), Martyn Hill (ten), Peter Knapp (bass), John Noble (bass) — EMI Classics ("Doublefforte" series) 2-▲ CDFB 68631

London Early Music Group

J. Tyler (cnd)

O Dolce Vita Mia:Italian Music of the High Renaissance — Elektra/Nonesuch ▲ 79029-2 [DDD]

London Festival Orch

Haydn, J.:Sym 104, "London" — Quintessence ▲ CDQ 2102 [DDD]
Liszt, F.:Les Préludes — Critics Choice 2-▲ CCD 943 [DDD]
Liszt, F.:Tasso—Lamento e Trionfo — Critics Choice 2-▲ CCD 943 [DDD]
Ravel, M.:Con in G Pno, w. *(pianist & cnd unknown)* — Pro Arte ("Maxiplay" series) ▲ CDM 881 [DDD]
Tchaikovsky, P.:Sym 4 — Critics Choice 2-▲ CCD 945 [DDD]
Wagner, R.:Tristan und Isolde (orch sels)—Overture — Pro Arte ("Maxiplay" series) ▲ CDM 879 [DDD]

S. Black (cnd)

Bock, J.:Fiddler on the Roof, w. Molly Picon (sgr), Robert Merrill (bar), London Festival Chorus — London ("Phase 4 Stereo" series) ▲ 448 949-2
Gershwin, G.:Rhap in Blue, w. Stanley Black (pno) *(rec Kingsway Hall, London, Dec 1965)* — London ("Phase 4 Stereo" series) ▲ 444785-2 [ADD]
Grofé, F.:Grand Canyon Suite — London ("Phase 4 Stereo" series) ▲ 448 956-2
Ives, C.:Orchestral Set 2 — London ("Phase 4 Stereo" series) ▲ 448 956-2

R. Farnon (cnd)

Farnon, R.:Captain Horatio Hornblower *(rec 1960)* — Citadel ▲ STC 77108 [ADD]
Gershwin, G.:Porgy & Bess (symphonic picture) — London ("Weekend Classics" series) ▲ 425508-2 [AAD]
Grofé, F.:Grand Canyon Suite — London ("Weekend Classics" series) ▲ 425508-2 [AAD]

A. Gibson (cnd)

Chopin, F.:Les Sylphides — Chesky ▲ CD62 [ADD]
A Concert Tour, w. London New SO — Chesky ▲ CD62 [ADD]
Dvořák, A.:Carnival — Chesky ▲ CD62 [ADD]
Grieg, E.:Peer Gynt Suite 1 — Chesky ▲ CD62 [ADD]
Sibelius, J.:Finlandia — Chesky ▲ CD62 [ADD]
Sibelius, J.:The Swan of Tuonela — Chesky ▲ CD62 [ADD]

R. Leibowitz (cnd)

Debussy, C.:Prélude à l'après-midi d'un faune — Chesky ▲ CD57 [ADD]
Stravinsky, I.:Le Sacre du printemps Orch *(rec 1960)* — Chesky ▲ CD 42 [ADD]

A. Lizzio (cnd)

Rachmaninoff, S.:Con 2 Pno, w. D. Goldmann (pno) — Vivace ▲ 550 [ADD]
Tchaikovsky, P.:Con 1 Pno, w. D. Goldmann (pno) — Vivace ▲ 550 [ADD]
Tchaikovsky, P.:Nutcracker Suite — PMG (Vienna Master) ▲ CD 160216 [DDD]
Tchaikovsky, P.:Swan Lake (sels) — PMG (Vienna Master) ▲ CD 160216 [DDD]

N. Marriner (cnd)

Haydn, J.:Sym 100, "Military" — Quintessence ▲ CDQ 2102 [DDD]

R. Pople (cnd)

Boccherini, L.:Syms—Op. 35/1-6 — Hyperion ▲ CDA 66903
Boccherini, L.:Syms—Op. 37/1, 3 & 4; Op. 42 — Hyperion ▲ CDA 66904
Boccherini, L.:Syms—G.498 in A, G.506 in d, G.508 in A — Hyperion ▲ CDA 66236 [DDD]
Franck, C.:Symphonic Vars, w. P. Rogé (pno) — ASV ▲ ASV 769 [DDD]
Holst, G.:A Fugal Ov — ASV ▲ ASV 782
Holst, G.:The Planets — ASV ▲ ASV 782
Holst, G.:St. Paul's Suite — ASV ▲ ASV 782
Mendelssohn, F.:Sinfs Strs — Hyperion 3-▲ CDA 66561/63
Mozart, W.A.:Sinf concertante Ob, K.Anh.9 — ASV ("Quicksilva" series) ▲ ASQ 6139 [DDD]
Mozart, W.A.:Sinf concertante Vn, K.364, w. Lorraine McAslan (vn), Yuko Inoue (va) — ASV ("Quicksilva" series) ▲ ASQ 6139 [DDD]
Vaughan Williams, R.:Fant on Greensleeves — ASV ▲ ASV 779
Vaughan Williams, R.:Fant on a Theme by Thomas Tallis — ASV ▲ ASV 779
Vaughan Williams, R.:In the Fen Country — ASV ▲ ASV 779
Vaughan Williams, R.:The Lark Ascending, w. Richard Friedman (vn) — ASV ▲ ASV 779
Vaughan Williams, R.:Partita — ASV ▲ ASV 779

A.S. Redel (cnd)

Famous Overtures, Vol. 2 — PMG ("Vienna Masters" series) ▲ CD 160218 [DDD]

A. Scholz (cnd)

Bizet, G.:Carmen (suites) — PMG ("Vienna Master" series) ▲ CD 160219 [DDD]
Bruch, M.:Con 1 Vn, w. J. Brezina (vn) — PMG ("Vienna Master" series) ▲ CD 160112 [DDD]
Bruch, M.:Kol Nidrei, w. *(cellist unknown)* — PMG ("Vienna Master" series) ▲ CD 160112 [DDD]
Fučík, J.:Florentine March — PMG ("Vienna Master" series) ▲ CD 160219 [DDD]
Fučík, J.:Marinarella — PMG ("Vienna Master" series) ▲ CD 160219 [DDD]
Liszt, F.:Hungarian Rhaps—No. 5 — PMG ("Vienna Master" series) ▲ CD 160115 [DDD]
Liszt, F.:Orpheus — PMG ("Vienna Master" series) ▲ CD 160115 [DDD]
Liszt, F.:Les Préludes — PMG ("Vienna Master" series) ▲ CD 160115 [DDD]
Liszt, F.:Tasso—Lamento e Trionfo — PMG ("Vienna Master" series) ▲ CD 160115 [DDD]
Popular Concert — PMG ("Vienna Masters" series) ▲ CD 160219 [DDD]
Schmidt, F.:Notre Dame (intermezzo) — PMG ("Vienna Master" series) ▲ CD 160112 [DDD]
Suppé, F. von:Ovs—Poet & Peasant — PMG (Vienna Masters) ▲ CD 160219 [DDD]

R. Sharples (cnd)

The Opera Lover's Broadway:Great Voices Sing Broadway's Greatest Hits, w. Vienna PO [cnd:Herbert von Karajan], New Philharmonia Orch [cnd:Richard Bonynge], Roland Shaw Orch, London SO [cnd:John Mauceri], Nelson Riddle & His Orch — London ▲ 448282-2 ■ 448282-4

London Festival Orch (cont.)

V. de Stradelli (cnd)

Bizet, G.:L'Arlésienne (suites) — Vivace ▲ 559 [DDD]
Bizet, G.:L'Arlésienne (suites) — Vivace 3-▲ E 327
Bizet, G.:Carmen (suites) — Vivace 3-▲ E 327
Bizet, G.:Carmen (suites) — Vivace ▲ 559 [DDD]
Gounod, C.:Faust (ballet music) — Vivace 3-▲ E 327
Mendelssohn, F.:Sym 5 — Vivace ▲ E 521 [DDD]
Ravel, M.:Boléro — Vivace 3-▲ E 327

A. Vestri (cnd)

Mahler, G.:Sym 1 — Vivace ▲ 573 [DDD]
Mahler, G.:Sym 5 — Vivace ▲ 566 [DDD]

London Festival Orch members

Franck, C.:Qnt Pno, w. P. Rogé (pno) — ASV ▲ ASV 769 [DDD]

London Festival Players

B. Herrmann (cnd)

Milhaud, D.:Saudades do Brasil *(rec DECCA Studio No. 3, West Hampstead, London, Nov 1972)* — London ("Phase 4 Stereo" series) ▲ 443897-2 [ADD]
Satie, E.:Les Aventures de Mercure *(rec DECCA Studio No. 3, West Hampstead, London, Nov 1972)* — London ("Phase 4 Stereo" series) ▲ 443897-2 [ADD]
Satie, E.:Ballet Music, London PO—Belle excentrique; Gymnopédies 1 & 3; Mercure — London ("Weekend Classics" series) ▲ 421395-2
Satie, E.:La belle excentrique—Nos. 1 & 3 *(rec DECCA Studio No. 3, West Hampstead, London, Nov 1972)* — London ("Phase 4 Stereo" series) ▲ 443897-2 [ADD]
Satie, E.:Gymnopédies—Nos. 1 & 3 *(rec Kingsway Hall, London, England, Jan 1970)* — London ("Phase 4 Stereo" series) ▲ 443897-2 [ADD]
Satie, E.:Jack in the Box *(rec DECCA Studio No. 3, West Hampstead, London, Nov 1972)* — London ("Phase 4 Stereo" series) ▲ 443897-2 [ADD]

London Festival Recording Ensemble

Gershwin, G.:"I Got Rhythm" Vars, w. David Parkhouse (pno) *(rec DECCA Studio No. 3, West Hampstead, London, Nov 1971)* — London ("Phase 4 Stereo" series) ▲ 444785-2 [ADD]
Milhaud, D.:La Création du monde *(rec DECCA Studio No. 3, West Hampstead, London, Nov 1971)* — London ("Phase 4 Stereo" series) ▲ 444785-2 [ADD]
Stravinsky, I.:Ragtime *(rec DECCA Studio No. 3, West Hampstead, London, Nov 1971)* — London ("Phase 4 Stereo" series) ▲ 444785-2 [ADD]
Weill, K.:Kleine Dreigroschenmusik *(rec DECCA Studio No. 3, West Hampstead, London, Nov 1971)* — London ("Phase 4 Stereo" series) ▲ 444785-2 [ADD]

London Fortepiano Trio [Linda Nicholson (pno), Monica Huggett (vn), Timothy Mason (vc)]

Beethoven, L. van:Trio 2 Pno — Hyperion ▲ CDA 66197 [DDD]
Mozart, W.A.:Divert Pno, K.254 — Hyperion ▲ CDA 66093
Mozart, W.A.:Trio Pno, K.496 — Hyperion ▲ CDA 66148
Mozart, W.A.:Trio Pno, K.502 — Hyperion ▲ CDA 66125
Mozart, W.A.:Trio Pno, K.542 — Hyperion ▲ CDA 66148
Mozart, W.A.:Trio Pno, K.548 — Hyperion ▲ CDA 66093
Mozart, W.A.:Trio Pno, K.564 — Hyperion ▲ CDA 66125

London Gabrieli Brass Ensemble

Barber, S.:Mutations from Bach — Hyperion ▲ CDA 66517
Carter, E.:A Fant on Purcell's *Fantasia upon One Note* — Hyperion ▲ CDA 66517
Cowell, H.:Brass Music — Hyperion ▲ CDA 66517
From the Steeples & the Mountains — Hyperion ▲ CDA 66517
A Heralding of Battles & Ceremonies, w. London Gabrieli Chorus — Elektra/Nonesuch ■ 71414-4
Ives, C.:From the Steeples & Mountains — Hyperion ▲ CDA 66517
Ives, C.:Processional — Hyperion ▲ CDA 66517
Locke, M.:Music for His Majesty's Sackbutts & Cornets — Elektra/Nonesuch ■ 71414-4
Purcell, H.:Music for the Funeral of Queen Mary, w. London Gabrieli Chorus — Elektra/Nonesuch ■ 71414-4
Ruggles, C.:Angels — Hyperion ▲ CDA 66517
The Splendour of Baroque Brass — ASV ("Quicksilva" series) ▲ ASV 6013 [ADD]

London Handel Orch

D. Darlow (cnd)

Handel, G.F.:Aminta e Fillide, w. G. Fisher (sop), P. Kwella (sop) [I] — Hyperion ▲ CDA 66118
Handel, G.F.:The Triumph of Time & Truth, w. James Goodman (trb), Fisher (sop), Emma Kirkby (sop), Charles Brett (ct), Ian Partridge (ten), Stephen Varcoe (bar), London Handel Chorus [E] — Hyperion 2-▲ CDA 66071/72

M. Neary (cnd)

Handel, G.F.:Messiah (sels), w. Winchester Cathedral Choir [E] — ASV Quicksilva ▲ QS 6001 [DDD]

London Harpsichord Ensemble

Albinoni, T.:Cons à 5 Obs, Op. 7, w. S. Francis (ob)—Nos. 3, 6, 9 & 12 — Unicorn-Kanchana ▲ DKP CD 9088 [DDD]
Albinoni, T.:Cons à 5 Obs, Op. 9, w. S. Francis (ob)—Nos. 2, 5, 8 & 11 — Unicorn-Kanchana ▲ DKP CD 9088 [DDD]
Handel, G.F.:Cons (3) Ob, w. S. Francis (ob) — Unicorn-Kanchana ▲ DKP CD 9153
Handel, G.F.:Sons Ob, w. Sarah Francis (ob)—Malmesbury Son.; Son. in c, B♭, F & g — Unicorn-Kanchana ▲ DKP CD 9153
Telemann, G.P.:Cons (misc), w. S. Francis (ob)—Concerto in E♭; Concerto in c; Concerto in G for Oboe d'amore; Concerto in E; "Concerto gratioso" in D; Concerto in F *(rec Jan. 13-15, 1992)* — Unicorn-Kanchana ▲ DKP CD 9128 [DDD]

London Jazz Orch

L. Johnson (cnd)

Johnson, Laurie:Music of, w. W. Davies (org), London PO, London Studio SO, Coldstream Guards Regimental Band, Fanfare Trumpeters of the Scots Guards, London Brass Chorale—Royal Tour (suite); Symphony (Synthesis) for Combined Jazz & Symphony Orchestras (1969); Three Paintings by Lautrec; The Wind In the Willows (1985) *(rec 1969-82)* — Unicorn-Kanchana ▲ UKCD 2057 [DDD/ADD]

London Jupiter SO

G. Rose (cnd)

Janácek, L.:Idyll — Chandos ▲ CHAN 9195 [DDD]
Janácek, L.:On an Overgrown Path [orch. J. Burghauser] — Chandos ▲ CHAN 9195 [DDD]
Janácek, L.:Suite Str Orch — Chandos ▲ CHAN 9195 [DDD]

London Little Orch

R. Batik (cnd)

Corea, C.:Sea Journey, w. Roland Batik (pno) — Camerata ▲ 30CM 347

L. Jones (cnd)

Bach, C.P.E.:Sinfs, H.663-666 — Elektra/Nonesuch ■ 71180-4
Bach, Joh. Christian:Sinf concertante Fl, w. J. Galway (fl), D. Wickens (ob), W. Armon (vn), N. Jones (vc) — Elektra/Nonesuch ■ 71165-4
Bach, Joh. Christian:Sinfs, Op. 18—Nos. 3 & 5 — Elektra/Nonesuch ■ 71165-4

London Mozart Players

Clementi, M.:Sym 1 — Chandos ▲ CHAN 9234 [DDD]
Mendelssohn, F.:Capriccio brillante, w. H. Shelley (pno) — Chandos ▲ CHAN 9215 [DDD]
Mendelssohn, F.:Con 1 Pno, w. H. Shelley (pno) — Chandos ▲ CHAN 9215 [DDD]
Mendelssohn, F.:Con 2 Pno, w. H. Shelley (pno) — Chandos ▲ CHAN 9215 [DDD]

M. Bamert (cnd)

Baguer, C.:Sym 12 — Chandos ("Contemporaries of Mozart" series) ▲ CHAN 9456
Baguer, C.:Sym 13 — Chandos ("Contemporaries of Mozart" series) ▲ CHAN 9456
Baguer, C.:Sym 16 — Chandos ("Contemporaries of Mozart" series) ▲ CHAN 9456
Baguer, C.:Sym 18 — Chandos ("Contemporaries of Mozart" series) ▲ CHAN 9456
Field, J.:Con 1 Pno, w. Míceál O'Rourke (pno) — Chandos ▲ CHAN 9368 [DDD]
Field, J.:Con 2 Pno, w. Míceál O'Rourke (pno) — Chandos ▲ CHAN 9368 [DDD]
Field, J.:Con 3 Pno, w. Míceál O'Rourke (pno) — Chandos ▲ CHAN 9495

220 ▲ = CD ♦ = Enhanced CD Δ = MD ■ = Cassette Tape □ = DCC

London Mozart Players (cont.)

M. Bamert (cnd) (cont.)

Field, J.:Con 4 Pno, w. Miceal O'Rourke (pno) Chandos ▲ CHAN 9442
Field, J.:Con 5 Pno, "L'Incendie par l'orage", w. Míceál O'Rourke (pno) Chandos ▲ CHAN 9495
Field, J.:Con 6 Pno, w. Miceal O'Rourke (pno) Chandos ▲ CHAN 9442
Haydn, M.:Syms—in A, P.6; in B♭, P.9; in G, P.16; in E♭, P.26; in F, P.32 Chandos ▲ CHAN 9352
Krommer, F.:Sym, Op. 40 Chandos ▲ CHAN 9275 [DDD]
Krommer, F.:Sym, Op. 102 Chandos ▲ CHAN 9275 [DDD]
Stamitz, C.:Syms, Op. 13—Nos. 4 in C & 5 in C Chandos ("Contemporaries of Mozart" series) ▲ CHAN 9358 [DDD]
Stamitz, C.:Syms, Op. 24—No. 3 in F Chandos ("Contemporaries of Mozart" series) ▲ CHAN 9358 [DDD]
Stamitz, C.:Sym in D Chandos ("Contemporaries of Mozart" series) ▲ CHAN 9358 [DDD]

H. Blech (cnd)

Arias & Songs, w. Irmgard Seefried (sop), Gerald Moore (pno), Hermann von Nordberg (pno), Wilhelm Schmidt (pno) Testament ▲ SBT 1026 [ADD]

N. Cleobury (cnd)

Hummel, J.N.:Con Bn, w. Yoshiyuki Nakanishi (bn) ASV ("Quicksilva" series) ▲ ASQ 6159
Stamitz, C.:Con Bn, w. Yoshiyuki Nakanishi (bn) ASV ("Quicksilva" series) ▲ ASQ 6159
Weber, C.M. von:Andante & Rondo ungarese Bn, w. Yoshiyuki Nakanishi (bn) ASV ("Quicksilva" series) ▲ ASQ 6159
Weber, C.M. von:Con Bn, w. Yoshiyuki Nakanishi (bn) ASV ("Quicksilva" series) ▲ ASQ 6159

J. Glover (cnd)

Haydn, J.:Sym 80 ASV Living Era ("Quicksilva" series) ▲ ASQ 6156
Haydn, J.:Sym 83, "The Hen" ASV Quicksilva ▲ ASQ 6167
Haydn, J.:Sym 84, "In Nomine Domini" ASV Quicksilva ▲ ASQ 6167
Haydn, J.:Sym 87 ASV Living Era ("Quicksilva" series) ▲ ASQ 6156
Haydn, J.:Sym 88 ASV Quicksilva ▲ ASQ 6167
Haydn, J.:Sym 89 ASV Living Era ("Quicksilva" series) ▲ ASQ 6156
Hummel, J.N.:Con Bn, w. K. Walker (bn) Gallo ▲ CD 499 [DDD]
Mozart, W.A.:Arias, w. F. Lott (sop)—(5 concert arias) K.217, 383, 528, 582, 583; (2 opera arias) Mitridate, Rè di Ponto *(Lungi da te*; Zaide *(Ruhe sanft, mein holdes Leben)* [G,I] ASV ▲ ASV 683 [DDD]
Mozart, W.A.:Con Bn, w. K. Walker (bn) Gallo ▲ CD 499 [DDD]
Mozart, W.A.:Con Bn, w. Y. Nakanishi (bn) Classics for Pleasure ▲ CDCFP 4484 [DDD]
Mozart, W.A.:Con Cl, w. A. Marriner (cl) Classics for Pleasure ▲ CDCFP 4484 [DDD]
Mozart, W.A.:Con Cl, w. A. Malsbury (cl) ASV ▲ ASV 795 [DDD]
Mozart, W.A.:Con Fl, K.313, w. P. Davies (fl) ASV ▲ ASV 795 [DDD]
Mozart, W.A.:Con Ob, K.314, w. C. Nicklin (ob) ASV ▲ ASV 795 [DDD]
Mozart, W.A.:Exsultate, w. F. Lott (sop) [L] ASV ▲ ASV 683 [DDD]
Mozart, W.A.:Sym 25 ASV ▲ ASV 717 [DDD]
Mozart, W.A.:Sym 29 ASV ▲ ASV 717 [DDD]
Mozart, W.A.:Sym 33 ASV ▲ ASV 717 [DDD]
Walton, W.:Façade, w. Prunella Scales (nar), Timothy West (nar) [1951 version] [E] ASV ▲ ASV 679 [DDD/ADD]
Wolf-Ferrari, E.:Suite-concertino Bn, w. K. Walker (bn) Gallo ▲ CD 499 [DDD]

P. Ledger (cnd)

Vivaldi, A.:Cons Vc, w. P. Tortelier (vc)—RV.400, 401, 424 *(rec 11/79)* EMI ("Studio" series) ▲ CDM 769835-2 [ADD]
Vivaldi, A.:Con for 2 Vcs, w. P. Tortelier (vc), M. Tortelier (vc) *(rec 11/79)* EMI ("Studio" series) ▲ CDM 769835-2 [ADD]
Vivaldi, A.:Con Vn Vcs, w. J. F. Manzone (vn), P. Tortelier (vc), M. Tortelier (vc) *(rec 11/79)* EMI ("Studio" series) ▲ CDM 769835-2 [ADD]

H. Shelley (cnd)

Mozart, W.A.:Con 9 Pno, w. H. Shelley (pno) Chandos ▲ CHAN 9068 [DDD]
Mozart, W.A.:Con 12 Pno, w. H. Shelley (pno) Chandos ▲ CHAN 9256 [DDD]
Mozart, W.A.:Con 13 Pno, w. H. Shelley (pno) Chandos ▲ CHAN 9326 [DDD]
Mozart, W.A.:Con 14 Pno, w. H. Shelley (pno) Chandos ▲ CHAN 9137 [DDD]
Mozart, W.A.:Con 17 Pno, w. H. Shelley (pno) Chandos ▲ CHAN 9068 [DDD]
Mozart, W.A.:Con 19 Pno, w. H. Shelley (pno) Chandos ▲ CHAN 9256 [DDD]
Mozart, W.A.:Con 20 Pno, w. H. Shelley (pno) Chandos ▲ CHAN 8992 [DDD]
Mozart, W.A.:Con 21 Pno, w. H. Shelley (pno) Chandos ▲ CHAN 9404 [DDD]
Mozart, W.A.:Con 22 Pno, w. H. Shelley (pno) Chandos ▲ CHAN 9404 [DDD]
Mozart, W.A.:Con 23 Pno, w. H. Shelley (pno) Chandos ▲ CHAN 8992 [DDD]
Mozart, W.A.:Con 24 Pno, w. H. Shelley (pno) Chandos ▲ CHAN 9326 [DDD]
Mozart, W.A.:Con 27 Pno, w. H. Shelley (pno) Chandos ▲ CHAN 9137 [DDD]

London Mozart Trio

Dvořák, A.:Trio 1 Pno IMP ("Classics" series) ▲ IMP 6700132
Dvořák, A.:Trio 4 Pno, "Dumky" IMP Classics ▲ PCD 1006 [DDD]
Schubert, Franz:Trio 1 Pno IMP Classics ▲ PCD 1006 [DDD]
Schubert, Franz:Trio 2 Pno IMP ("Classics" series) ▲ IMP 6700132

London Musica Antiqua

P. Thorby (cnd)

The Field of Cloth of Gold:A Celebration in Music of the Meeting in 1520 of Henry VIII of England & François I of France Amon Ra ▲ CDSAR 51 [DDD]

London Musici

Ustvolskaya, G.:Composition 3, w. Katheryn Stott (pno) Conifer Classics ▲ 75605-51194-2
Ustvolskaya, G.:Octet Obs, w. Katheryn Stott (pno) Conifer Classics ▲ 75605-51194-2
Vivaldi, A.:Cons Diverse Instrs—Il Gardellino; La Notte; La Tempesta di mare; All Rustica Conifer Classics ▲ 74321-15909-2

S. Leiferkus (cnd)

Ustvolskaya, G.:Sym 5 Conifer Classics ▲ 75605-51194-2

R. Marlow (cnd)

Duruflé, M.:Mass, "Cum jubilo", w. Trinity College Choir Cambridge Conifer Classics ▲ 74321-2D15351-2D2
Duruflé, M.:Motets on Gregorian Chants, Op. 10, w. Trinity College Choir Cambridge Conifer Classics ▲ 74321-2D15351-2D2
Fauré, G.:Requiem, w. Trinity College Choir Cambridge Conifer Classics ▲ 74321-15351-2
Messiaen, O.:O sacrum conviviuml, w. Trinity College Choir Cambridge Conifer Classics ▲ 74321 2D15351 2D2
Stravinsky, I.:Mass Conifer Classics ▲ 75605-51232-2 [DDD]

M. Stephenson (cnd)

Arnold, M.:Con 2 Cl, w. M. Collins (cl) Conifer Classics ▲ 75605-51228-2
Arnold, M.:Con 2 Fl, w. K. Jones (fl) Conifer Classics ▲ 75605-51228-2
Arnold, M.:Con Hn, w. R. Watkins (hn) Conifer Classics ▲ 75605-51228-2
Arnold, M.:Con Pno 4-Hands, w. M. Collins (pno) Conifer Classics ▲ 75605-51228-2
Arnold, M.:Con 28 Players Conifer Classics ▲ 75605-51211-2 [DDD]
Arnold, M.:Con Va, w. Rivka Golani (va) Conifer Classics ▲ 75605-51211-2 [DDD]
Arnold, M.:Larch Trees Conifer Classics ▲ 75605-51211-2 [DDD]
Arnold, M.:Serenade Conifer Classics ▲ 75605-51211-2 [DDD]
Handel, G.F.:Messiah (sels), w. Patrizia Kwella (sop), Catherine Denley (mez), John Mark Ainsley (ten), Bryn Terfel (b-bar), London Chamber Choir Conifer Classics ▲ 74321-15354-2
Heath, David:The Celtic, w. Gerard McChrystal (sax) Silva Classics ▲ SIL 6010
McGlynn, M.:From Nowhere to Nowhere, w. Gerard McChrystal (sax) Silva Classics ▲ SIL 6010
Nyman, M.:Where the Bee Dances, w. Gerard McChrystal (sax) Silva Classics ▲ SIL 6010
Torke, M.:Con Sax, w. Gerard McChrystal (sax) Silva Classics ▲ SIL 6010
Wilson, I.:I Sleep at Waking, w. Gerard McChrystal (sax) Silva Classics ▲ SIL 6010

London Musici String Quartet

Shostakovich, D.:Qnt Pno, w. Katheryn Stott (pno) Conifer Classics ▲ 75605-51194-2

London National PO

C. Gerhardt (cnd)

Fauré, G.:Ballade Pno, w. E. Wild (pno) *(rec March 28, 1967)* Chesky ▲ CD93 [ADD]

L. Maazel (cnd)

Puccini, G.:Le Villi, w. R. Scotto (sop), P. Domingo (ten), T. Gobbi (bar), L. Nucci (bar), Ambrosian Chorus [I] CBS ▲ MK 36669 [ADD]

London New SO

R. Bonynge (cnd)

Handel, G.F.:Giulio Cesare in Egitto (sels), w. Joan Sutherland (sop), Marilyn Horne (mez) London ("Grand Opera" series) 3-▲ 433723-2 [ADD]

A. Boult (cnd)

Elgar, E.:Pomp & Circumstance Marches—No. 1 *(rec , Walthamstow Town Hall, London 7/12-15/60)* Chesky ▲ CD53 [ADD]
Liszt, F.:Les Préludes *(rec Walthamstow Town Hall, London 7/12-15/60)* Chesky ▲ CD53 [ADD]
Mendelssohn, F.:Die Hebriden *(rec Walthamstow Town Hall, London, 7/12-15/60)* Chesky ▲ CD53 [ADD]
Mussorgsky, M.:Night *(rec Walthamstow Town Hall, London 7/12-15/60)* Chesky ▲ CD53 [ADD]
Sullivan, A.:Ovs—Ov. di Ballo *(rec Walthamstow Town Hall, London 7/12-15/60)* Chesky ▲ CD53 [ADD]
Tchaikovsky, P.:Nutcracker Suite *(rec Walthamstow Town Hall, London 7/12-15/60)* Chesky ▲ CD53 [ADD]
Tchaikovsky, P.:Swan Lake (suite) *(rec London, July 21-22, 1960)* Chesky ▲ CD94 [ADD]

A. Coates (cnd)

Weber, C.M. von:Der Freischütz (sels), w. Friedrich Schorr (b-bar)—Hermit's Aria *(rec 1930)* Claremont ▲ GSE 78 50 54
Weber, C.M. von:Der Freischütz (sels), w. Friedrich Schorr (bar)—Hermit's Aria *(rec 1930)* GSE Claremont ▲ GSE 78 50 54

A. Collins (cnd)

Prokofiev, S.:Con 3 Pno, w. M. Lympany (pno) Olympia ▲ OLY 191 [AAD]
Rachmaninoff, S.:Con 3 Pno, w. M. Lympany (pno) Olympia ▲ OLY 191 [AAD]

A. Gibson (cnd)

Arnold, M.:Tam o'Shanter Classic Records ▲ LSCCD 2225
A Concert Tour, w. London Festival Orch Chesky ▲ CD62 [ADD]
Grieg, E.:Norwegian Dances, Op. 35—No. 2 Chesky ▲ CD62 [ADD]
Humperdinck, E.:Hänsel und Gretel (sels)—Witches' Ride Classic Records ▲ LSCCD 2225
Liszt, F.:Mephisto Waltz 1 Pno Classic Records ▲ LSCCD 2225
Mussorgsky, M.:Night Classic Records ▲ LSCCD 2225
Mussorgsky, M.:Pictures at an Exhibition—Gnomus Classic Records ▲ LSCCD 2225
Saint-Saëns, C.:Danse macabre Classic Records ▲ LSCCD 2225
Smetana, B.:The Moldau *(rec 7/60)* Chesky ▲ CD65 [ADD]
Strauss (II), Joh.:Music of—Tritsch-Tratsch Polka Chesky ▲ CD62 [ADD]
Suppé, F. von:Ovs—Poet & Peasant Chesky ▲ CD62 [ADD]
Tchaikovsky, P.:Ov 1812 *(rec 7/60)* Chesky ▲ CD65 [ADD]
Tchaikovsky, P.:Sym 6 *(rec 7/60)* Chesky ▲ CD65 [ADD]
Wagner, R.:Lohengrin (preludes)—Act 3 Prelude Chesky ▲ CD62 [ADD]
Weber, C.M. von:Invitation to the Dance Orch Chesky ▲ CD62 [ADD]

L. Ronald (cnd)

Saint-Saëns, C.:Con 2 Pno, w. A. De Greef (pno) Pearl ▲ PEA 9974 (m) [AAD]

M. Sargent (cnd)

Bach, J.S.:Con for 2 Vns, w. J. Heifetz (vn), E. Friedman (vn) RCA Red Seal ▲ 6778-2-RC [ADD]
Bruch, M.:Con 1 Vn, w. Jascha Heifetz (vn) *(rec Walthamstow Town Hall, London, May 14 &16, 1962)* RCA Red Seal ▲ 09026-61745-2 [ADD]
Bruch, M.:Scottish Fant Vn, w. Jascha Heifetz (vn), Osian Ellis (hp) *(rec Walthamstow Town Hall, London, May 15 & 22, 1961)* RCA Red Seal ▲ 09026-61745-2 [ADD]
Vieuxtemps, H.:Con 5 Vn, w. Jascha Heifetz (vn) *(rec Walthamstow Town Hall, London, May 15 & 22, 1961)* RCA Red Seal ▲ 09026-61745-2 [ADD]
Vieuxtemps, H.:Con 5 Vn, w. J. Heifetz (vn) RCA Red Seal ▲ 6214-2-RC [ADD]

S. Skrowaczewski (cnd)

Chopin, F.:Con 1 Pno, w. A. Rubinstein (pno) RCA Red Seal ▲ 5612-2-RC [ADD]

A. Wallenstein (cnd)

Chopin, F.:Andante Spianato & Grande Polonaise, w. A. Rubinstein (pno) RCA Gold Seal ▲ 60404-2-RG [ADD] ■ 60404-4-RG (CrO2)

London New SO Strings

A. Collins (cnd)

Elgar, E.:Intro & Allegro Beulah ▲ 1PD15 (m) [ADD]
Elgar, E.:Serenade Strs Beulah ▲ 1PD15 (m) [ADD]

London Oboe Band

P. Goodwin (cnd)

Lully, J.-B.:Le Bourgeois gentilhomme (sels), w. Marie-Ange Petit (baroque perc)—wedding music Harmonia Mundi ▲ HMU 907122
Lully, J.-B.:Cadmus et Hermione (sels), w. Marie-Ange Petit (baroque perc)—wedding music Harmonia Mundi ▲ HMU 907122
Lully, J.-B.:Les Noces de village (sels), w. Marie-Ange Petit (baroque perc)—wedding music Harmonia Mundi ▲ HMU 907122
Philidor, A.D.:Le Mariage de la couture avec la grosse Cathos (sels), w. Marie-Ange Petit (baroque perc)—wedding music Harmonia Mundi ▲ HMU 907122

London Orch Society

A. Boult (cnd)

Franck, C.:Sym in d *(rec 1960)* Chesky ▲ CD 87 [ADD]

London Palladium Orch

Friml, R.:Film Music, w. D. Vane (sop), H. Williams (bar), D. Oldham (ten)—The Vagabond King; The Blue Kitten; Rose Marie; The 3 Musketeers; The Firefly Pearl ("Flapper" series) ▲ PAST CD 9764 [AAD]

London Philharmonic Festival Orch

V. de Stradelli (cnd)

Beethoven, L. van:Sym 5 Vivace ▲ E 527 [DDD]
Beethoven, L. van:Sym 5 Vivace 3-▲ E 320 [DDD]
Classical Favourites Sound 2-▲ E 221 [DDD]
Dvořák, A.:Sym 9, "From the New World" Vivace 3-▲ E 320 [DDD]
Mendelssohn, F.:Sym 4 Vivace 3-▲ E 320 [DDD]
Mendelssohn, F.:Sym 4 Vivace ▲ E 521 [DDD]
Schubert, Franz:Sym 8 Vivace ▲ E 527 [DDD]
Schubert, Franz:Sym 8 Vivace 3-▲ E 320 [DDD]
Tchaikovsky, P.:Marche slave Vivace 3-▲ E 321 [DDD]

London PO

Academy Award Themes Pickwick ▲ PWK 037 [DDD]
Adam, A.:Giselle (sels) Quintessence ▲ CDQ 2100 [DDD]
The Age of Bel Canto, w. Joan Sutherland (sop), London SO [cnd:Richard Bonynge] London ("Opera Gala" series) ▲ 421881-2 LA [ADD]
Bel Canto, w. Battle, Kathleen (sop), Benno Campanella (cnd), Ambrosian Opera Chorus Deutsche Grammophon ▲ 435866-2 ■ 435866-4
de Luca, E.:Conquerors of the Ages, w. London Phil Chorus Alshire ▲ ALCD 41
Herrmann, B.:Moby Dick, w. John Amis (ten), Robert Bowman (ten), David Kelly (bass), Michael Rippon (bass), Aeolian Singers [E] Unicorn-Kanchana ▲ UKCD 2061
Jazz Meets the Symphony:Works of Lalo Schifrin, w. Ray Brown (db), Grady Tate (dr) Atlantic ▲ 82506-2 P ■ 82506-4 P
Mozart, W.A.:Music of, Hungarian State Orch, Salzburg Mozarteum Orch—sels from Syms. 24, 29, 31, 33, 35, 36, 38, 39, 40 & 41 LaserLight ▲ 15 646 [DDD]

ORCH. & ENS.

London PO (cont.)
Tchaikovsky, P.:Romeo & Juliet Pro Arte (Maxiplay) ▲ CDM 879 [DDD]
A. de Almeida (cnd)
Thomas, A.:Hamlet, w. J. Anderson (sop—Ophelie), D. Graves (mez—Gertrude); G. Kunde (ten—Laerte), T. Hampson (bar—Hamlet), S. Ramey (bass—Claudius), Ambrosian Singers EMI Classics 3-▲ CDCC 54820
W. Alwyn (cnd)
Alwyn, W.:Autumn Legend, w. G. Browne (E hn) Lyrita ▲ SRCD 230 [ADD]
Alwyn, W.:Con grosso 2 Lyrita ▲ SRCD 230 [ADD]
Alwyn, W.:Derby Day Lyrita ▲ SRCD 229
Alwyn, W.:Elizabethan Dances Lyrita ▲ SRCD 229
Alwyn, W.:Festival March Lyrita ▲ SRCD 229
Alwyn, W.:Lyra Angelica, w. O. Ellis (hp) Lyrita ▲ SRCD 230 [ADD]
Alwyn, W.:The Magic Island Lyrita ▲ SRCD 229
Alwyn, W.:Sinfonietta Lyrita ▲ SRCD 229
Alwyn, W.:Syms (comp)—Syms. 1 & 4 Lyrita ▲ SRCD 227
Alwyn, W.:Syms (comp)—Syms. 2, 3 & 5 Lyrita ▲ SRCD 228
M. Arnold (cnd)
Arnold, M.:Dances Lyrita ▲ SRCD 201
Arnold, M.:Ovs—Beckus the Dandipratt; Commonwealth Christmas Overture; The Fair Field; The Smoke; A Sussex Overture *(rec Oct 1991)* Reference ▲ RR 48 CD [DDD]
Arnold, M.:Sarabande & Polka Lyrita ▲ SRCD 201
Arnold, M.:Scottish Dances Everest ▲ EVC 9006 [AAD]
Arnold, M.:Scottish Dances Phoenix ▲ PHCD 102 [AAD]
Arnold, M.:Sym 3 Everest ▲ EVC 9001 [AAD]
Arnold, M.:Sym 3 Phoenix ▲ PHCD 102 [AAD]
Arnold, M.:Sym 4 Lyrita ▲ SRCD 200 [DDD]
R. Armstrong (cnd)
Operatic Arias, w. Roberto Alagna (ten) *(rec Studio 1, Abbey Road, London, Jan., Mar. & Apr. 1995)* EMI Classics ▲ CDC 55477 [DDD]
D. Atherton (cnd)
Holst, G.:Orchestral Works, w. L. MacAslan (vn), A. Baillie (vc), London SO—A Winter Idyll; Elegy in Memoriam William Morris; Indra, Symphonic Poem for Orchestra, Op. 13; A Song of the Night, Op. 19/1; Sita:Interlude from Act III, Op. 23; Invocation, Op. 19/2; The Lure; Dances from the Morning of the Year, Op. 45/2 Lyrita ▲ SRCD 209
G. Aykal (cnd)
Elgar, E.:In the South Koch Schwann ▲ CD 311002 [DDD]
Saygun, A.A.:Con Va, w. R. Günes (va) Koch Schwann ▲ CD 311002 [DDD]
M. Bamert (cnd)
Martin, F.:Ballade A Sax, w. Martin Robertson (a sax) Chandos ▲ CHAN 9380 [DDD]
Martin, F.:Ballade Vc, w. Peter Dixon (vc) Chandos ▲ CHAN 9380 [DDD]
Martin, F.:Ballade Pno, w. Roderick Elms (pno) Chandos ▲ CHAN 9380 [DDD]
Martin, F.:Ballade Trbn (or T Sax), w. Ian Bousfield (trbn) Chandos ▲ CHAN 9380 [DDD]
Martin, F.:Ballade Va, Wind, Hpd & Hp, w. Philip Dukes (va) Chandos ▲ CHAN 9380 [DDD]
Martin, F.:Con for 7 Winds Chandos ▲ CHAN 9283 [DDD]
Martin, F.:Erasmi Monumentum Chandos ▲ CHAN 9283 [DDD]
Martin, F.:Etudes Str Orch Chandos ▲ CHAN 9283 [DDD]
Martin, F.:In terra pax, w. Judith Howarth (sop), Della Jones (cta), Martyn Hill (ten), Roderick Williams (bar), Stephen Roberts (bass), Laszlo Heltay (cnd), Brighton Festival Chorus Chandos ▲ CHAN 9465
Martin, F.:Maria-Triptychon, w. Lynda Russell (sop), Duncan Riddell (vn) Chandos ▲ CHAN 9411 [DDD]
Martin, F.:Monologe (6) aus "Jedermann", w. David Wilson-Johnson (bar) Chandos ▲ CHAN 9411 [DDD]
Martin, F.:Passacaglia Orch Chandos ▲ CHAN 9312 [DDD]
Martin, F.:Les Quatre éléments Chandos ▲ CHAN 9465
Martin, F.:Der Sturm (suite) Chandos ▲ CHAN 9411 [DDD]
Martin, F.:Sym concertante Chandos ▲ CHAN 9312 [DDD]
Martin, F.:Sym Chandos ▲ CHAN 9312 [DDD]
Parry, H.:Concertstück Chandos ▲ CHAN 7006 [DDD]
Parry, H.:Concertstück Chandos ▲ CHAN 9062 [DDD]
Parry, H.:Elegy for Brahms Chandos ▲ CHAN 7006 [DDD]
Parry, H.:Elegy for Brahms Chandos ▲ CHAN 8955 [DDD]
Parry, H.:From Death to Life Chandos ▲ CHAN 7006 [DDD]
Parry, H.:From Death to Life Chandos ▲ CHAN 8955 [DDD]
Parry, H.:Invocation, w. L. Dawson (sop), A. Davies (ten), B. Rayner Cook (bar), London Phil Chorus [E] Chandos ▲ CHAN 9025 [DDD]
Parry, H.:The Lotus Eaters, w. D. Jones (mez), London Phil Chorus [E] Chandos ▲ CHAN 8990 [DDD]
Parry, H.:The Soul's Ransom, w. D. Jones (mez), D. Wilson-Johnson (bar), London Phil Chorus [E] Chandos ▲ CHAN 8990 [DDD]
Parry, H.:Symphonic Vars Chandos ▲ CHAN 8961 [DDD]
Parry, H.:Symphonic Vars Chandos 3-▲ CHAN 9120/22 [DDD]
Parry, H.:Symphonic Vars Chandos ▲ CHAN 7006 [DDD]
Parry, H.:Syms (comp) Chandos 3-▲ CHAN 9120/22 [DDD]
Parry, H.:Sym 1 Chandos ▲ CHAN 9062 [DDD]
Parry, H.:Sym 2 Chandos ▲ CHAN 8961 [DDD]
Parry, H.:Sym 3 Chandos ▲ CHAN 8896 [DDD]
Parry, H.:Sym 4 Chandos ▲ CHAN 8896 [DDD]
Parry, H.:Sym 5 Chandos ▲ CHAN 8955 [DDD]
Rawsthorne, A.:Con 1 Pno, w. G. Tozer (pno) Chandos ▲ CHAN 9125 [DDD]
Rawsthorne, A.:Con 2 Pno, w. G. Tozer (pno) Chandos ▲ CHAN 9125 [DDD]
Rawsthorne, A.:Con Pnos, w. G. Tozer (pno), T.-A. Cislowski (pno) Chandos ▲ CHAN 9125 [DDD]
J. Barbirolli (cnd)
Beethoven, L. van:Con Vn, Op. 61, w. F. Kreisler (vn) *(rec 1936 for HMV)* Biddulph 3-▲ LAB 001-3 (m) [ADD]
Beethoven, L. van:Con Vn, Op. 61, w. Fritz Kreisler (vn) Enterprise ("Sirio" series) ▲ ENT SO 53009
Beethoven, L. van:Con Vn, Op. 61, w. F. Kreisler (vn) *(rec 1936 for HMV)* Pearl 2-▲ PEAS 9362 (m) [AAD]
Brahms, J.:Con Vn, w. F. Kreisler (vn) *(rec 1936 for HMV)* Biddulph 3-▲ LAB 001-3 (m) [ADD]
Brahms, J.:Con Vn, w. F. Kreisler (vn) *(rec 1936 for HMV)* Pearl 2-▲ PEAS 9362 (m) [AAD]
Glazunov, A.:Con Vn, w. J. Heifetz (vn) *(rec 1934)* EMI Classics ("Great Recordings of the Century" series) ▲ CDH 64030
Glazunov, A.:Con Vn, w. J. Heifetz (vn) *(rec 1934)* Biddulph ▲ LAB 026 [ADD]
Glazunov, A.:Con Vn, w. Jascha Heifetz (vn) *(rec Mar 28, 1934)* Iron Needle ▲ IN 1351 [ADD]
Glazunov, A.:Con Vn, w. Jascha Heifetz (vn) *(rec 1934-40)* Pearl ▲ PEA 9157 [ADD]
Mozart, W.A.:Con 5 Vn, w. J. Heifetz (vn) *(rec Feb. 23, 1934 for HMV)* Biddulph ▲ LAB 012 [AAD]
Mozart, W.A.:Con 5 Vn, w. Jascha Heifetz (vn) *(rec 1934-40)* Pearl ▲ PEA 9157 [ADD]
Saint-Saëns, C.:Introduction & Rondo capriccioso, w. J. Heifetz (vn) *(rec EMI Studios, Abbey Road, London, Mar 18, 1935)* RCA Gold Seal 2-▲ 09026-61735-2 [ADD]
Saint-Saëns, C.:Introduction & Rondo capriccioso, w. J. Heifetz (vn) *(rec 1935)* EMI Classics ▲ CDH 64251-2 (m) [ADD]
Saint-Saëns, C.:Introduction & Rondo capriccioso, w. J. Heifetz (vn) *(rec 1935; mats 2EA 1450/1, HM)* Biddulph ▲ LAB 025 [ADD]
Schumann, R.:Con Vc, w. G. Piatigorsky (vc) *(rec 1934)* Pearl ▲ PEA 9447 (m) [AAD]
Schumann, R.:Con Vc, w. G. Piatigorsky (vc) *(rec 1934)* Music & Arts ▲ CD 674 [AAD]
Tchaikovsky, P.:Con Vn, w. J. Heifetz (vn) *(rec 1937 for HMV)* Biddulph ▲ LAB 026 [ADD]
Tchaikovsky, P.:Con Vn, w. J. Heifetz (vn) *(rec 1937 for HMV)* EMI Classics ("Great Recordings of the Century" series) ▲ CDH 64030
Tchaikovsky, P.:Con Vn, w. Jascha Heifetz (vn) *(rec 1934-40)* Pearl ▲ PEA 9157 [ADD]
Tchaikovsky, P.:Swan Lake (suite) *(rec 7/20/33)* Koch Legacy ▲ 370772

London PO (cont.)
J. Barbirolli (cnd) (cont.)
Vieuxtemps, H.:Con 4 Vn, w. Jascha Heifetz (vn) *(rec 1935-41)* Pearl ▲ PEA 9167 [ADD]
Vieuxtemps, H.:Con 4 Vn, w. J. Heifetz (vn) *(rec 3/14/35)* EMI Classics ▲ CDH 64251-2 (m) [ADD]
Vieuxtemps, H.:Con 4 Vn, w. J. Heifetz (vn) *(rec 3/14/35)* Biddulph ▲ LAB 025 [ADD]
Wieniawski, H.:Con 2 Vn, w. J. Heifetz (vn) *(rec 3/18/35)* EMI Classics ▲ CDH 64251-2 (m) [ADD]
Wieniawski, H.:Con 2 Vn, w. Jascha Heifetz (vn) *(rec 1935-41)* Pearl ▲ PEA 9167 [ADD]
Wieniawski, H.:Con 2 Vn, w. J. Heifetz (vn) *(rec 1935 for HMV)* Biddulph ▲ LAB 026 [ADD]
Wieniawski, H.:Con 2 Vn, w. J. Heifetz (vn) *(rec London, 1935 & 1937)* Grammofono 2000 ▲ GRM 78511 [ADD]
D. Barenboim (cnd)
Dvořák, A.:Con Vn, w. I. Perlman (vn) EMI Classics 3-▲ ZDMC 69881
Dvořák, A.:Con Vn, w. I. Perlman (vn) EMI Classics ▲ CDC 47168 [ADD]
Dvořák, A.:Qt 5 Strs, w. I. Perlman (vn) EMI Classics 3-▲ ZDMC 69881
Dvořák, A.:Romance Vn, w. I. Perlman (vn) EMI Classics ▲ CDC 47168 [ADD]
Elgar, E.:Cockaigne *(rec Nov. 8-10, 1973)* Sony Classical (Essential Classics) ▲ SBK 53510 [ADD]
Elgar, E.:The Crown of India (suite) *(rec 1974)* Sony Classical (Essential Classics) ▲ SBK 48265 [ADD] ■ SBT 48265
Elgar, E.:Enigma Vars CBS ▲ MYK 38483 [ADD] ■ MYT 38483
Elgar, E.:Enigma Vars *(rec 1976)* Sony Classical (Essential Classics) ▲ SBK 48265 [ADD] ■ SBT 48265
Elgar, E.:Pomp & Circumstance Marches CBS ▲ MYK 38483 [ADD] ■ MYT 38483
Elgar, E.:Pomp & Circumstance Marches *(rec 1973)* Sony Classical (Essential Classics) ▲ SBK 48265 [ADD] ■ SBT 48265
Elgar, E.:Sym 1 *(rec Nov. 8-10, 1973)* Sony Classical (Essential Classics) ▲ SBK 53510 [ADD] ■ SBT 53510
Paganini, N.:Con 6 Vn, w. I. Perlman (vn). London SO, Royal PO EMI Classics 3-▲ ZDMC 69881
E. Batiz (cnd)
Dvořák, A.:Carnival ASV Quicksilva ▲ CD QS 6006 [DDD]
Dvořák, A.:Sym 9, "From the New World" ASV Quicksilva ▲ QS 6037 [DDD]
Prokofiev, S.:Lt Kijé Suite Pickwick ▲ PIC IMG 1603 [DDD]
Prokofiev, S.:The Love for 3 Oranges (suite) Pickwick ▲ PIC IMG 1603 [DDD]
Prokofiev, S.:Sym 1 Pickwick ▲ PIC IMG 1603 [DDD]
Rodrigo, J.:Concierto de Aranjuez, w. *(soloist unknown)* EMI Classics ▲ CDE 67785
Saint-Saëns, C.:Sym 3, w. N. Rawsthorne (org) ASV ▲ ASV 665 [DDD]
Tchaikovsky, P.:Sym 6 ASV ▲ ASQ 6091 [DDD]
Turina, J.:Danzas fantásticas IMG/Pickwick ▲ PICIMG 1608 [DDD]
Turina, J.:La oracion del torero IMG/Pickwick ▲ PICIMG 1608 [DDD]
Turina, J.:La procesión del Rocio IMG/Pickwick ▲ PICIMG 1608 [DDD]
Turina, J.:Rapsodia sinfónica IMG/Pickwick ▲ PICIMG 1608 [DDD]
S. Baudo (cnd)
Debussy, C.:Jeux Classics for Pleasure ("Eminence" series) ▲ CDEMX 9502 [DDD]
Debussy, C.:La Mer Classics for Pleasure ("Eminence" series) ▲ CDEMX 9502 [DDD]
Debussy, C.:Prélude à l'après-midi d'un faune Classics for Pleasure ("Eminence" series) ▲ CDEMX 9502 [DDD]
Ravel, M.:Con Pno (left hand), w. Philip Fowke (pno) Classics for Pleasure ▲ CDCFP 4667
Ravel, M.:Con in G Pno, w. Philip Fowke (pno) Classics for Pleasure ▲ CDCFP 4667
Ravel, M.:La Valse Classics for Pleasure ▲ CDCFP 4667
T. Beecham (cnd)
Beecham Conducts Favourite Overtures, Vol. 2 *(rec between 1933 & 1940)* Dutton Laboratories ▲ DUT 7009 [ADD]
Beethoven, L. van:Sym 4 Biddulph ▲ WHL 042
Berlioz, H.:La Damnation de Faust (sels)—suite *(rec 1936-1940)* Pearl ▲ CD 9065 [AAD]
Berlioz, H.:Les Troyens (sels)—Royal Hunt & Storm; Trojan March Biddulph ▲ WHL 043
Borodin, A.:Prince Igor (ov) Biddulph ▲ WHL 043
Brahms, J.:Sym 2 *(rec Abbey Road Studio No. 1, Mar. 14 & 24, 1936)* Dutton Laboratories 2-▲ 2CDAX 2003 [ADD]
Debussy, C.:Prélude à l'après-midi d'un faune *(rec 1936-1940)* Pearl ▲ CD 9065 [AAD]
Delius, F.:Appalachia, w. BBC Sym Chorus *(rec Jan. 6, 7 & 31, 1938)* Dutton Laboratories ▲ CDLX 7011 [ADD]
Delius, F.:Koanga (sels), w. London Select Choir—Closing scene *(rec Dec. 11, 1934)* Dutton Laboratories ▲ CDLX 7011 [ADD]
Delius, F.:Music of—Paris:The Song of a Great City; Irmelin (Prelude); Eventyr; "Fennimore and Gerda" (Intermezzo); Over the Hills and Far Away [arr. Beecham] *(rec 1934-38)* The Beecham Collection ▲ BEECHAM 2 [ADD]
Dvořák, A.:Slavonic Rhaps, Op. 45—No. 3 in a♭ *(rec 1935-39)* Pearl ▲ PEA 9094 [ADD]
Franck, C.:Sym in d *(rec Abbey Road Studio No. 1, Jan. 3 & 4, 1940)* Dutton Laboratories 2-▲ 2CDAX 2003 [ADD]
Franck, C.:Sym in d *(rec 1936-1940)* Pearl ▲ CD 9065 [AAD]
Gounod, C.:Faust (ballet music)—Dance of the Nubians; Adagio [both from Act V] *(rec 1939)* Dutton Laboratories 2-▲ CDAX 2001 [ADD]
Handel, G.F.:The Great Elopement Biddulph ▲ WHL 041
Handel, G.F.:Music of, w. London SO—Arrival of the Queen of Sheba [from *Solomon, arr. Beecham*]; *The Gods Go A-Begging [Suite, arr. Beecham]*, *The Origin of Design [Suite, arr. Beecham]; Moses and the Children of Israel*, *But as for His People*, *The Lord Is a Man of War [from Israel in Egypt]*, Concerto Grosso No. 3 in e, Op. 6 [Larghetto, Polonaise], The Faithful Shepherd [Suite, arr. Beecham], Pastoral Symphony [from *The Messiah*] VAI Audio ▲ VAIA 1045 [ADD]
Haydn, J.:Sym 93 *(rec Kingsway Hall, London, Dec. 18, 1936)* Dutton Laboratories 2-▲ 2CDAX 2003 [ADD]
Haydn, J.:Sym 93 *(rec 1936 & 1939)* Pearl ▲ PEA 9064 [AAD]
Haydn, J.:Sym 97 Biddulph ▲ WHL 041
Haydn, J.:Sym 97 Dutton Laboratories ▲ DUT 7019 [ADD]
Haydn, J.:Sym 99 *(rec Kingsway Hall, London, Oct. 4, 1935 & Feb. 28, 1)* Dutton Laboratories 2-▲ 2CDAX 2003 [ADD]
Haydn, J.:Sym 99 *(rec 1936 & 1939)* Pearl ▲ PEA 9064 [AAD]
Haydn, J.:Sym 104, "London" *(rec Kingsway Hall, London, Jan. 18, Feb. 13 & July 4)* Dutton Laboratories 2-▲ 2CDAX 2003 [ADD]
Haydn, J.:Sym 104, "London" *(rec 1936 & 1939)* Pearl ▲ PEA 9064 [AAD]
Mendelssohn, F.:Con in e Vn & Orch, Op. 64, w. J. Szigeti (vn) EMI Classics ▲ CDH 64562
Mendelssohn, F.:Con in e Vn & Orch, Op. 64, w. J. Szigeti (vn) *(rec 1933 for Columbia)* Pearl ▲ PEA 9377 (m) [AAD]
Mendelssohn, F.:Sym 5 Biddulph ▲ WHL 043
Mozart, W.A.:Clemenza di Tito (sels)—Ov Biddulph ▲ WHL 041
Mozart, W.A.:Clemenza (v) Dutton Laboratories ▲ DUT 7019 [ADD]
Mozart, W.A.:Con 12 Pno, w. L. Kentner (pno) *(rec 1934-1940)* Pearl ▲ PEA 9081 [ADD]
Mozart, W.A.:Con 12 Pno, w. L. Kentner (pno) *(rec 1940)* EMI Classics ("Great Recordings of the Century" series) ▲ CDH 63820
Mozart, W.A.:Con 12 Pno, w. Louis Kentner (pno) Dutton Laboratories ▲ DUT 7019 [ADD]
Mozart, W.A.:Con 4 Vn, w. A. Szigeti (vn) *(rec Oct. 8, 1934 for Columbia)* Pearl ▲ PEA 9377 (m) [AAD]
Mozart, W.A.:Don Giovanni (sels)—Ov. *(rec 1934 & 1940)* Pearl ▲ PEA 9081 [ADD]
Mozart, W.A.:Entführung (ov) Biddulph ▲ WHL 042
Mozart, W.A.:Entführung (ov) Dutton Laboratories ▲ DUT 7019 [ADD]
Mozart, W.A.:Kleine Nachtmusik Dutton Laboratories ▲ DUT 7019 [ADD]
Mozart, W.A.:Kleine Nachtmusik Biddulph ▲ WHL 041
Mozart, W.A.:Missa, K.427—sels. *(rec 1934 & 1940)* Pearl ▲ PEA 9081 [ADD]
Mozart, W.A.:Nozze di Figaro (sels)—Ov. *(rec 1935-39)* Pearl ▲ PEA 9094 [ADD]
Mozart, W.A.:Sym 35 Dutton Laboratories ▲ DUT 5001
Mozart, W.A.:Sym 36 Dutton Laboratories ▲ DUT 5001
Mozart, W.A.:Sym 38 Dutton Laboratories ▲ DUT 5001

▲ = CD ♦ = Enhanced CD Δ = MD ■ = Cassette Tape □ = DCC

London PO (cont.)
T. Beecham (cnd) (cont.)
Offenbach, J.:Les Contes d'Hoffmann—suite *(rec 1936–1940)* Pearl ▲ CD 9065 [AAD]
Prokofiev, S.:Con 1 Vn, w. J. Szigeti (vn) EMI Classics ▲ CDH 64562
Prokofiev, S.:Con 1 Vn, w. J. Szigeti (vn) *(rec 8/25/35 for Columbia)* Pearl ▲ PEA 9377 (m) [AAD]
Rimsky-Korsakov, N.:A May Night (ov) Biddulph ▲ WHL 043
Schubert, Franz:Sym 5 Dutton Laboratories ▲ DUT 7014 [ADD]
Schubert, Franz:Sym 5 *(rec 1934 & 1940)* Pearl ▲ PEA 9081 [ADD]
Schubert, Franz:Sym 6 Dutton Laboratories ▲ DUT 7014 [ADD]
Schubert, Franz:Sym 6 Biddulph ▲ WHL 042
Schubert, Franz:Sym 8 *(rec Oct 12 & Nov 1, 1937)* Dutton Laboratories ▲ DUT 7014 [ADD]
Sibelius, J.:Con Vn, w. Jascha Heifetz (vn) *(rec 1934–40)* Pearl ▲ PEA 9157 [ADD]
Sibelius, J.:Con Vn, w. J. Heifetz (vn) *(rec 11/26 & 12/14, 1935)*
EMI Classics ("Great Recordings of the Century" series) ▲ CDH 64030
Sibelius, J.:Con Vn, w. J. Heifetz (vn) *(rec 11/26 & 12/14, 1935)* Biddulph ▲ LAB 018 [ADD]
Sibelius, J.:In Memoriam Dutton Laboratories ▲ DUT CDAX 8013 [ADD]
Sibelius, J.:In Memoriam *(rec 11/14/38 for HMV)* Koch Legacy ▲ 3-7061-2
Sibelius, J.:Lemminkäinen's Return *(rec 11/12/37 for HMV)* Koch Legacy ▲ 3-7061-2
Sibelius, J.:Pelléas et Mélisande Dutton Laboratories ▲ DUT CDAX 8013 [ADD]
Sibelius, J.:En Saga *(rec 11/14/38 & 7/7/39 for HMV)* Koch Legacy ▲ 3-7061-2
Sibelius, J.:Scènes historiques Dutton Laboratories ▲ DUT CDAX 8013 [ADD]
Sibelius, J.:Sym 4 *(rec 1937)* Koch Legacy ▲ 3-7061-2
Sibelius, J.:The Tempest (sels) Dutton Laboratories ▲ DUT CDAX 8013 [ADD]
Sibelius, J.:Valse triste *(rec 11/15/38 for HMV)* Koch Legacy ▲ 3-7061-2
Sir Thomas Beecham, w. Beecham SO *(rec 1910, 1912, 1916, 1918, 1)*
Symposium 2-▲ SYM 1096/97
Suppé, F. von:Ovs—Morning, Noon & Night in Vienna *(rec 1935–39)* Pearl ▲ PEA 9094 [ADD]
Tchaikovsky, P.:Eugene Onegin (sels)—Polonaise; Waltz Biddulph ▲ WHL 043
Wagner, R.:Der fliegende Holländer (sels)—Ov. *(rec 1935–39)* Pearl ▲ PEA 9094 [ADD]
Wagner, R.:Der fliegende Holländer (ov) Dutton Laboratories ▲ DUT 7007 [ADD]
Wagner, R.:Götterdämmerung (sels), w. Frida Leider (sop), Kerstin Thorborg (mez), Lauritz Melchior (ten), Herbert Janssen (bar), Emanuel List (bass), Maria Nezadál (sgr), Royal Opera House Chorus Covent Garden *(rec Covent Garden, London, 1936)* Preiser ▲ PRE 90266
Wagner, R.:Götterdämmerung (sels), w. F. Leider (sop), Nezadál (sop), K. Thorborg (mez), L. Melchior (ten), H. Janssen (bar), L. Weber (bass), Royal Opera House Chorus Covent Garden [G] *(rec from 1925 Polydor & 1929)* Legato Classics 2-▲ LCD 146-2 (m) [ADD]
Wagner, R.:Götterdämmerung (sels)—Hier sitz' ich zur wacht; Hoi-ho!
Dutton Laboratories ▲ DUT 7007 [ADD]
Wagner, R.:Lohengrin (preludes)—Act 3 Dutton Laboratories ▲ DUT 7007 [ADD]
Wagner, R.:Die Meistersinger von Nürnberg (sels)—Ov; Da zu dir der Heiland kam; Wach'auf; Morgenlich leuchtend Dutton Laboratories ▲ DUT 7007 [ADD]
Wagner, R.:Die Meistersinger von Nürnberg (sels)—Ov. *(rec 1935–39)* Pearl ▲ PEA 9094 [ADD]
Wagner, R.:Tannhäuser (ov) Dutton Laboratories ▲ DUT 7007 [ADD]
Weber, C.M. von:Oberon (sels)—Ov. *(rec 1935–39)* Pearl ▲ PEA 9094 [ADD]
E. van Beinum (cnd)
Elgar, E.:Cockaigne Beulah ▲ 2PD15 (m) [ADD]
Elgar, E.:Con Vc, w. Anthony Pini (vc) Beulah ▲ 2PD15 (m) [ADD]
Elgar, E.:Elegy Strs Beulah ▲ 2PD15 (m) [ADD]
Elgar, E.:The Wand of Youth Suites Beulah ▲ 2PD15 (m) [ADD]
L. Berkeley (cnd)
Berkeley, L.:Canzonetta Lyrita ▲ SRCD 226
Berkeley, L.:Divertimento Lyrita ▲ SRCD 226
Berkeley, L.:Mont Juic Lyrita ▲ SRCD 226
Berkeley, L.:Partita Lyrita ▲ SRCD 226
Berkeley, L.:Serenade Lyrita ▲ SRCD 226
Berkeley, L.:Sym 3 Lyrita ▲ SRCD 226
A. Bliss (cnd)
Bliss, A.:Con Vn, w. Alfredo Campoli (vn) Beulah ▲ 3PD10 (m) [ADD]
Bliss, A.:Theme & Cadenza, w. Alfredo Campoli (vn) Beulah ▲ 3PD10 (m) [ADD]
I. Bolton (cnd)
Brahms, J.:Con Vn, w. Xue-Wei (vn) ASV ▲ ASV 748
Mendelssohn, F.:Con in e Vn & Orch, Op. 64, w. Xue-Wei (vn) ASV ▲ ASV 748
W. Boskovsky (cnd)
Liszt, F.:Hungarian Battle March, Philharmonia Hungarica EMI Classics ▲ CDM 64627
Liszt, F.:Hungarian Rhaps (orchestral versions), Philharmonia Hungarica EMI Classics ▲ CDM 64627
Liszt, F.:Rakóczy March EMI Classics ▲ CDM 64627
A. Boult (cnd)
Beethoven, L. van:Coriolan Ov *(rec Walthamstow Hall, London, June 1956)*
Vanguard Classics 3-▲ SVC 11/13 [AAD]
Beethoven, L. van:Egmont (ov) *(rec Walthamstow Hall, London, June 1956)*
Vanguard Classics 3-▲ SVC 11/13 [AAD]
Beethoven, L. van:Fidelio (ov) *(rec Walthamstow Hall, London, June 1956)*
Vanguard Classics 3-▲ SVC 11/13 [AAD]
Beethoven, L. van:Leonore 3 *(rec Walthamstow Hall, London, June 1956)*
Vanguard Classics 3-▲ SVC 11/13 [AAD]
Beethoven, L. van:Sym 3, "Eroica" *(rec Walthamstow Hall, London, June 1956)*
Vanguard Classics 3-▲ SVC 11/13 [AAD]
Beethoven, L. van:Sym 5 *(rec Walthamstow Hall, London, June 1956)*
Vanguard Classics 3-▲ SVC 11/13 [AAD]
Beethoven, L. van:Sym 6, "Pastorale" *(rec Walthamstow Hall, London, June 1956)*
Vanguard Classics 3-▲ SVC 11/13 [AAD]
Beethoven, L. van:Sym 7 *(rec Walthamstow Hall, London, June 1956)*
Vanguard Classics 3-▲ SVC 11/13 [AAD]
Berkeley, L.:Magnificat, w. BBC Chorus, BBC Choral Society *(rec live, Royal Albert Hall, London, 1969)*
Intaglio ▲ INCD 7281 [ADD]
Brahms, J.:Academic Festival Ov EMI Classics ("Doublefforte" series) 2-▲ CDFB 68655
Brahms, J.:Alto Rhap, w. Janet Baker (mez), John Alldis Choir Male Voices
EMI Classics ("Doublefforte" series) 2-▲ CDFB 68655
Brahms, J.:Serenade 1 Orch EMI Classics ("Doublefforte" series) 2-▲ CDFB 68655
Brahms, J.:Serenade 2 Orch EMI Classics ("Doublefforte" series) 2-▲ CDFB 68655
Brahms, J.:Vars on a Theme by Haydn EMI Classics ("Doublefforte" series) 2-▲ CDFB 68655
Britten, B.:Matinées musicales EMI Classics ("Studio" series) ▲ CDM 63777 [ADD]
Britten, B.:Peter Grimes (sea interludes & passacaglia)
EMI Classics ("Studio" series) ▲ CDM 63777 [ADD]
Britten, B.:Soirées musicales EMI Classics ("Studio" series) ▲ CDM 63777 [ADD]
Britten, B.:The Young Person's Guide to the Orchestra, w. W. Boult (nar)
EMI Classics ("Studio" series) ▲ CDM 63777 [ADD]
Bruch, M.:Scottish Fant Vn, w. A. Campoli (vn) IMP Collectors Series ▲ IMPX 9031 [ADD]
Colonel Bogey:The Great Military Marches Odyssey ■ YT 60318
Elgar, E.:The Apostles, w. S. Armstrong (sop), H. Watts (cta), R. Tear (ten), J. C. Case (bar), B. Luxon (bar), C. Grant (bass), London Phil Chorus, Downe House School Choir [E]
EMI Classics ▲ CDMB 64206
Elgar, E.:Cockaigne EMI Classics (British Composers) ▲ CDM 64014
Elgar, E.:Con Vn, w. A. Campoli (vn) Beulah ▲ 1PD10
Elgar, E.:Enigma Vars Classics for Pleasure ▲ CDCFP 4022 [ADD]
Elgar, E.:Intro & Allegro Classics for Pleasure ▲ CDCFP 4022 [ADD]
Elgar, E.:The Kingdom, w. London Phil Chorus EMI Classics 2-▲ ZDMB 64209
Elgar, E.:Serenade Strs EMI Classics (British Composers) ▲ CDM 64013
Elgar, E.:Sym 1 EMI Classics (British Composers) ▲ CDM 64013
Elgar, E.:Sym 2 EMI Classics (British Composers) ▲ CDM 64014

London PO (cont.)
A. Boult (cnd) (cont.)
Handel, G.F.:Cons (16) Org, w. E. P. Biggs (org) Odyssey 3-▲ MB3K 45825
Handel, G.F.:Messiah, w. Joan Sutherland (sop), Grace Bumbry (mez), Kenneth McKeller (ten), Joseph Ward (bar) London 3-▲ 433003-2 [ADD]
Hindemith, P.:Sym in E♭ for Concert Band Everest ▲ EVC 9009 [AAD]
Holst, G.:A Choral Fant, w. J. Coster (mez), John Alldis Choir *(rec Aug. 30, 1967)*
Intaglio ▲ ING 740 [ADD]
Holst, G.:Hammersmith *(rec live, Royal Festival Hall, London, 1967)* Intaglio ▲ INCD 7281 [ADD]
Holst, G.:The Planets EMI Classics ▲ CDM 64748
Kathleen Ferrier Edition Vol. 7, w. Kathleen Ferrier(cta) *(rec 1952)* London ▲ 433474-2 LM [ADD]
Mahler, G.:Sym 1 *(rec Walthamstow Assembly Hall, London)* Everest ▲ EVC 9022 [AAD]
Mendelssohn, F.:Con in e Vn & Orch, Op. 64, w. A. Campoli (vn)
IMP Collectors Series ▲ IMPX 9031 [ADD]
Mendelssohn, F.:Con in e Vn & Orch, Op. 64, w. A. Campoli (vn) Beulah ▲ 1PD10
Rachmaninoff, S.:Rhapsody on a Theme of Paganini, w. J. Katchen (pno)
London ("Weekend Classics" series) ▲ 417880-2 [AAD] ■ 417880-4
Shostakovich, D.:Sym 6 *(rec Nov. 1958)* Everest ▲ EVC 9005 [AAD]
Tchaikovsky, P.:Marche slave Odyssey ■ YT 60238
Tchaikovsky, P.:Ov 1812 Odyssey ■ YT 60238
Tchaikovsky, P.:Romeo & Juliet Odyssey ■ YT 60238
Vaughan Williams, R.:Fant on a Theme by Thomas Tallis EMI Classics ▲ CDM 64017
Vaughan Williams, R.:Job Everest ▲ EVC 9006 [AAD]
Vaughan Williams, R.:Job *(rec Oct. 12, 1972)* Intaglio ▲ ING 741 [ADD]
Vaughan Williams, R.:On Wenlock Edge, w. R. Lewis (ten) [orch. version] *(rec Oct. 12, 1972)*
Intaglio ▲ ING 741 [ADD]
Vaughan Williams, R.:The Pilgrim's Progress, w. J. Noble (bar), London Phil Chorus [E]
EMI Classics ▲ CDMB 64212
Vaughan Williams, R.:Serenade to Music [original version, with 16 solo singers]
EMI Classics (British Composers) ▲ CDM 64022
Vaughan Williams, R.:Sym 1, w. N. Armstrong (sop), J. C. Case (bar), London Phil Chorus
EMI Classics ▲ CDM 64016
Vaughan Williams, R.:Sym 2 EMI Classics ▲ CDM 64017
Vaughan Williams, R.:Sym 5 EMI Classics ▲ CDM 64018
Vaughan Williams, R.:Sym 7 EMI Classics (British Composers) ▲ CDM 64020
Vaughan Williams, R.:Sym 8 EMI Classics (British Composers) ▲ CDM 64021
Vaughan Williams, R.:Sym 9 EMI Classics (British Composers) ▲ CDM 64021
Vaughan Williams, R.:Sym 9 Everest ▲ EVC 9001 [AAD]
Vaughan Williams, R.:The Wasps EMI Classics (British Composers) ▲ CDM 64020
Vaughan Williams, R.:The Wasps Everest ▲ EVC 9006 [AAD]
Wagner, R.:Ovs, Preludes & Orch Sels, London SO, New Philharmonia Orch—from Fliegende Holländer *(Overture)*, Götterdämmerung *(Siegfried's Rhine Journey & Funeral March)*, Lohengrin *(Preludes to Acts 1 & 3)*, Meistersinger *(Overture; Prelude to Act 3)*, Parsifal *(Good Friday Music; Preludes to Acts 1 & 3; Transformation Scene)*, Rheingold *(Entrance of the Gods)*, Siegfried *(Forest Murmurs)*, Tannhäuser *(Overture; Grand March)*, Tristan *(Preludes to Acts 1 & 3)*, Walküre *(Ride of the Valkyries)* *(rec 1971–74)* EMI Classics 2-▲ CDZB 7 62539 2 [ADD]
Walton, W.:Con Vc, w. Paul Tortelier (vc) *(rec live, Royal Festival Hall, London 1967)*
Intaglio ▲ INCD 7281 [ADD]
N. Braithwaite (cnd)
Bennett, W.S.:Adagio, w. M. Binns (pno) Lyrita ▲ SRCD 205 [DDD]
Bennett, W.S.:Caprice, w. M. Binns (pno) Lyrita ▲ SRCD 204 [DDD]
Bennett, W.S.:Con 1 Pno, w. M. Binns (pno) Lyrita ▲ SRCD 204 [DDD]
Bennett, W.S.:Con 2 Pno, w. M. Binns (pno) Lyrita ▲ SRCD 205 [DDD]
Bennett, W.S.:Con 3 Pno, w. M. Binns (pno) Lyrita ▲ SRCD 204 [DDD]
Bennett, W.S.:Con 5 Pno, w. M. Binns (pno) Lyrita ▲ SRCD 205 [DDD]
Hurlstone, W.:The Magic Mirror Lyrita ▲ SRCD 208
Hurlstone, W.:Vars on a Hungarian Air Lyrita ▲ SRCD 208
Hurlstone, W.:Vars on an Original Theme Lyrita ▲ SRCD 208
Rawsthorne, A.:Sym 2, w. Tracey Chadwell (sop) Lyrita ▲ SRCD 291
B. Cameron (cnd)
Rachmaninoff, S.:Rhapsody on a Theme of Paganini, w. Benno Moiseiwitsch (pno) *(rec Dec. 5, 1938)*
APR ▲ APR 5505 [ADD]
C.F. Cillario (cnd)
Bellini, V.:Norma, w. M. Caballé (sop), F. Cossotto (mez), P. Domingo (ten), R. Raimondi (bass), Ambrosian Opera Chorus [I] RCA Gold Seal 3-▲ 6502-2-RG [ADD]
K. Clark (cnd)
Nanes, R.:Con grosso Delfon ▲ CDR 2422 [DDD] ■ DRS 2422C (D)
Nanes, R.:Rhap Pathétique, w. E. Fodor (vn) Delfon ▲ CDR 2422 [DDD] ■ DRS 2422C (D)
Nanes, R.:Sym 1 Delfon ▲ CDR 1211 [DDD] ■ DRS 1211C (D)
Nanes, R.:Sym 2 Delfon ▲ CDR 1211 [DDD] ■ DRS 1211C (D)
Nanes, R.:Sym Strs Delfon ▲ CDR 2422 [DDD] ■ DRS 2422C (D)
F. Collura (cnd)
Friedhofer, H.:The Best Years of Our Lives Preamble ▲ PRCD 1779 [AAD]
Friedhofer, H.:The Best Years of Our Lives Varése Sarabande ▲ VSD 70470 ■ VSC 70470
M. Davies (cnd)
Vaughan Williams, R.:Riders to the Sea, w. Bach Choir EMI Classics ▲ CDM 64730
A. Davis (cnd)
Mahler, G.:Lieder eines fahrenden Gesellen, w. F. von Stade (mez)
Sony Classical ("Essential Classics" series) ▲ SBK 46535 [ADD] ■ SBT 46535
Mahler, G.:Songs from Rückert, w. F. von Stade (sop) *(rec Dec. 8–16, 1978)*
Sony Classical ("Essential Classics" series) ▲ SBK 53518 [ADD] ■ SBT 53518
Carl Davis (cnd)
Brahms, J.:Sextet Strs, Op. 18 Virgin Classics ▲ CDZ 59654
Copland, A.:Fanfare for the Common Man Virgin Classics ▲ CDZ 59654
Delius, F.:A Village Romeo & Juliet—Orch. Suite Virgin Classics ▲ CDZ 59654
Jurassic Classics, w. Berlin PO, Kirov Orch, Vienna PO, Boston SO, V. Gergiev (cnd), A. Previn (cnd), N. Marriner (cnd) Philips ▲ 442599-2 ■ 442599-4
Strauss, R.:Music of Virgin Classics ▲ CDZ 59654
E. Downes (cnd)
Gershwin, G.:Con Pno, w. R. Szidon (pno)
Deutsche Grammophon ("Resonance" series) ▲ 427203-2 [ADD] ■ 427203-4
C. Dutoit (cnd)
Paganini, N.:Con 1 Vn, w. S. Accardo (vn) Deutsche Grammophon ▲ 415378-2 [ADD]
Paganini, N.:Con 2 Vn, w. S. Accardo (vn) Deutsche Grammophon ▲ 415378-2 [ADD]
Paganini, N.:Con 3 Vn, w. S. Accardo (vn) Deutsche Grammophon ▲ 423370-2 [ADD]
Paganini, N.:Con 4 Vn, w. S. Accardo (vn) Deutsche Grammophon ▲ 423370-2 [ADD]
Paganini, N.:Con 5 Vn, w. S. Accardo (vn) Deutsche Grammophon ▲ 423578-2 [ADD]
Paganini, N.:Maestoso son sentimentale, w. S. Accardo (vn)
Deutsche Grammophon ▲ 423578-2 [ADD]
Paganini, N.:Son Vn "La Primavera", w. S. Accardo (vn) Deutsche Grammophon ▲ 423578-2 [ADD]
S. Edwards (cnd)
Tchaikovsky, P.:Eugene Onegin (sels), w. Eilene Hannan (sop)—Tatiana's Letter Scene [Act I]
Classics for Pleasure ("Eminence" series) ▲ CDEMX 2187 [DDD]
Tchaikovsky, P.:Sym 5 Classics for Pleasure ("Eminence" series) ▲ CDEMX 2187 [DDD]
H. Farberman (cnd)
Bazelon, I.:Sym 8 Leonarda ▲ LE 331 [DDD]
Erb, D.:Con Ctbn, w. G. Henegar (ctbn) Leonarda ▲ LE 331 [DDD]
Erb, D.:Con Ctbn, w. G. Henegar (ctbn) Leonarda ▲ LE 302 (CrO2)
Kramer, J.D.:Atlanta Licks, w. F. Weinstock (pno), L. Raley, P. Rehfeldt, Atlanta Chamber Players
Leonarda ▲ LE 332

London PO (cont.)
H. Farberman (cnd) (cont.)
Kramer, J.D.:Music for Pno 3, w. F. Weinstock (pno), L. Raley, P. Rehfeldt, Atlanta Chamber Players Leonarda ▲ LE 332
Kramer, J.D.:Music for Pno 5, w. F. Weinstock (pno), L. Raley, P. Rehfeldt, Atlanta Chamber Players Leonarda ▲ LE 332
Kramer, J.D.:Musica Pro Musica, w. F. Weinstock (pno), L. Raley, P. Rehfeldt, Atlanta Chamber Players Leonarda ▲ LE 332
Kramer, J.D.:Renascence, w. F. Weinstock (pno), L. Raley, P. Rehfeldt, Atlanta Chamber Players Leonarda ▲ LE 332
Lundborg, E.:Switchback Leonarda ▲ LE 331 [DDD]
Richter, M.:Blackberry Vines Leonarda ▲ LE 331 [DDD]
J. Farrer (cnd)
Tchaikovsky, P.:Romeo & Juliet ASV Quicksilva ▲ ASQ 6111 [DDD]
J. Ferencsik (cnd)
Bartók, B.:Dance Suite *(rec June 1959)* Everest ▲ EVC 9000 [AAD]
Kodály, Z.:Psalmus hungaricus, w. Raymond Nilsson (ten), London Phil Chorus Everest ▲ EVC 9008 [AAD]
D. Fischer-Dieskau (cnd)
Schumann, R.:Con Pno, w. D. Barenboim (pno) EMI Classics ▲ CDM 64626
Schumann, R.:Intro & Allegro, Op. 134, w. D. Barenboim (pno) EMI Classics ▲ CDM 64626
M. Fredman (cnd)
Bax, A.:Sym 1 Lyrita ▲ SRCD 232
P. Freeman (cnd)
Macdowell, E.:Con 1 Pno, w. D. Amato (pno) Olympia ▲ OLY 353 [DDD]
Macdowell, E.:Con 2 Pno, w. D. Amato (pno) Olympia ▲ OLY 353 [DDD]
Mendelssohn, F.:Capriccio brillante, w. A. Kuerti (pno) *(rec 10/86)* IMP Classics ▲ PCD 953
Mendelssohn, F.:Capriccio brillante, w. A. Kuerti (pno) IMP ("Concert Classics" series) ▲ IMP PCD 1097
Mendelssohn, F.:Con 1 Pno, w. A. Kuerti (pno) *(rec 10/86)* IMP Classics ▲ PCD 953
Mendelssohn, F.:Con 2 Pno, w. A. Kuerti (pno) *(rec 10/86)* IMP Classics ▲ PCD 953
W. Furtwängler (cnd)
Strauss, R.:4 Last Songs, w. K. Flagstad (sop) *(rec live, London, 1949)* Melodram 2-▲ CDM 25009 [ADD]
A. Gibson (cnd)
Dvořák, A.:Con Vc, w. C. Walevska (vc) IMP Collectors Series ▲ IMPX 9035
Tchaikovsky, P.:Vars on a Rococo Theme, w. C. Walevska (vc) IMP Collectors Series ▲ IMPX 9035
M. Gielen (cnd)
Bartók, B.:Con 2 Vn, w. C. Tetzlaff (vn) Virgin Classics ▲ CDC 59062
C.M. Giulini (cnd)
Dvořák, A.:Con Vc, w. M. Rostropovich (vc) EMI Classics ▲ CDC 49306 [ADD]
Saint-Saëns, C.:Con 1 Vc, w. M. Rostropovich (vc) EMI Classics ▲ CDC 49306 [ADD]
D. Gleeson (cnd)
Prokofiev, S.:Zdravitsa, w. London Phil Chorus, Geoffrey Mitchell Choir IMP ("Masters" series) ▲ IMP 6600122
Tchaikovsky, P.:Ode to Joy, w. London Philharmonic Choir, Geoffrey Mitchell Choir IMP ("Masters" series) ▲ IMP 6600122
Tchaikovsky, P.:Romeo & Juliet IMP ("Masters" series) ▲ IMP 6600122
J. Glover (cnd)
Headington, C.:Con Vn, w. Xue-Wei (vn) ASV ▲ ASV 780 [DDD]
Strauss, R.:Con Vn, w. Xue-Wei (vn) ASV ▲ ASV 780 [DDD]
W. Goehr (cnd)
Rachmaninoff, S.:Con 2 Pno, w. Benno Moiseiwitsch (pno) *(rec Nov. 24 & Dec. 13, 1937)* APR ▲ APR 5505 [ADD]
C. Groves (cnd)
Delius, F.:Appalachia, w. John Noble (bar), BBC Chorus, BBC Choral Society, Goldsmith's Choral Union, London Phil Choir IMP ("BBC Radio Classics" series) ▲ IMP 9133
Holst, G.:Short Festival Te Deum, w. London Sym Chorus EMI Classics ▲ CDC 49784
V. Gui (cnd)
Verdi, G.:La traviata, w. Maria Caniglia (sop), Beniamino Gigli (ten), Mario Basiola (bar), London Phil Chorus *(rec Royal Opera House, Covent Garden, May 22, 1939)* Enterprise ("The Fourties" series) 2-▲ ENT 313
Verdi, G.:La traviata, w. Maria Caniglia (sop—Violetta), Maria Huder (mez—Flora), Gladys Palmer (cta—Annina), Octave Dua (ten—Giuseppe), Beniamino Gigli (ten—Alfredo), Booth Hitchen (ten—D'Obigny), Adelio Zagonara (bar—Gastone), Aristide Baracchi (bar—Douphol), Mario Basiola (bar—Germont), Norman Walker (bass—Dr. Grenville), London Phil Chorus *(rec Royal Opera House, Covent Garden, May 22, 1939)* Minerva 2-▲ MN A28/29 (m) [ADD]
B. Haitink (cnd)
Beethoven, L. van:Con 5 Pno, "Emperor", w. A. Brendel (pno) Philips ("Insignia" series) ▲ 434148-2 [ADD]
Beethoven, L. van:Con Vn, Vc & Pno, "Triple Con", Beaux Arts Trio Philips ▲ 420231-2 [ADD]
Beethoven, L. van:Fant Pno, Op. 80, "Choral Fant", w. Alfred Brendel (pno) Philips 2-▲ 454038-2
Beethoven, L. van:Fant Pno, Op. 80, "Choral Fant", w. A. Brendel (pno), London Phil Chorus Philips ("Insignia" series) ▲ 434148-2 [ADD]
Holst, G.:The Planets Philips ("Silver Line" series) ▲ 420893-2 [ADD]
Liszt, F.:Pno Music (misc), w. Alfred Brendel (pno)—Années de pèlerinage I, II, III, Nos. 2–5; Bénédiction de Dieu; Berceuse; Cons for Pno Nos. 1 & 2; Csardas Macabre; Danse Macabre; En Rêve; Evening Bells; Fantasy & Fugue on BACH; Funerailles; Invocation; Klavierstück in F; Lugubrious Gondola Nos. 1 & 2; Mosonyis Grabgeleit; Nuages Gris; Pensée des morts; Richard Wagner Venezia; St. Francis Preaching & Walking; Schlaflos; Son in b; Unstern - Sinestre; Valse Oubliée; Vexilla Regis Prodeunt; Wagner-Liszt:Isolde's Death; Weinen, Klagen, Sorgen, Zagen Philips 25-▲ 446920-2
Liszt, F.:Symphonic Poems Philips ("Duo" series) 2-▲ 438751-2
Liszt, F.:Symphonic Poems Philips ("Duo" series) 2-▲ 438754-2
Mendelssohn, F.:Sym 3 Philips ("Silver Line" series) ▲ 420884-2 [ADD]
Mendelssohn, F.:Sym 5 Philips ("Silver Line" series) ▲ 420884-2 [ADD]
Mozart, W.A.:Così fan tutte, w. Carol Vaness (sop), Delores Ziegler (mez), C. Watson (cta), J. Aler (ten), D. Duesing (bar), C. Desderi (bar), Glyndebourne Festival Chorus EMI Classics 3-▲ CDCC 47727
Mozart, W.A.:Don Giovanni, w. C. Vaness (sop), M. Ewing (sop), E. Gale (sop), K. Lewis (ten), T. Allen (bar), R. Van Allan (bass), Glyndebourne Festival Chorus [I] EMI Classics 3-▲ CDCC 47036 [DDD]
Scriabin, A.:Con Pno, w. V. Ashkenazy (pno) *(rec 1972)* Intaglio ▲ ING 7481 [ADD]
Shostakovich, D.:The Golden Age (suite) London ▲ 421131-2 [DDD]
Shostakovich, D.:The Golden Age (suite) London ▲ 430727-2 [DDD]
Shostakovich, D.:Sym 1 London ▲ 414677-2 [DDD]
Shostakovich, D.:Sym 2 London ▲ 421131-2 [DDD]
Shostakovich, D.:Sym 3 London ▲ 421131-2 [DDD]
Shostakovich, D.:Sym 9 London ▲ 414677-2 [DDD]
Stravinsky, I.:The Firebird Philips 2-▲ 438350-2
Stravinsky, I.:Le Sacre du printemps Orch Philips 2-▲ 438350-2
Stravinsky, I.:Le Sacre du printemps Orch Philips ("Insignia" series) ▲ 434147-2 [DDD]
Vaughan Williams, R.:Fant on a Theme by Thomas Tallis EMI Classics ▲ CDC 49394 [DDD]
Vaughan Williams, R.:Sym 2 EMI Classics ▲ CDC 49394 [DDD]
Vaughan Williams, R.:Sym 7, w. N. Armstrong (sop) EMI Classics ▲ CDC 47516 [DDD]
V. Handley (cnd)
Delius, F.:Air & Dance Chandos ▲ CHAN 8330
Delius, F.:On Hearing the 1st Cuckoo Chandos ▲ CHAN 8330
Delius, F.:Orchestral Music—Intermezzo from Fennimore & Gerda; On Hearing the First Cuckoo in Spring; Summer Night on the River; A Song Before Sunrise; Sleigh Ride; Prelude from Irmelin; The Walk to the Paradise Garden; La Calinda from Koanga Classics for Pleasure ▲ CDCFP 4304 [ADD]
Delius, F.:Summer Evening Chandos ▲ CHAN 8330
Delius, F.:Summer Night on the River Chandos ▲ CHAN 8330
Elgar, E.:Con Vn, w. N. Kennedy (vn) EMI Classics ▲ CDM 63795

London PO (cont.)
V. Handley (cnd) (cont.)
Elgar, E.:Enigma Vars Classics for Pleasure ("Eminence" series) ▲ CDEMX 9503 [DDD]
Elgar, E.:Intro & Allegro Classics for Pleasure ("Eminence" series) ▲ CDEMX 9503 [DDD]
Elgar, E.:Pomp & Circumstance Marches Classics for Pleasure ▲ CDCFP 9004 [AAD]
Elgar, E.:Sea Pictures, w. B. Greevy (mez) Classics for Pleasure ▲ CDCFP 9004 [AAD]
Elgar, E.:Serenade Strs Classics for Pleasure ("Eminence" series) ▲ CDEMX 9503 [DDD]
Elgar, E.:Sym 1 Classics for Pleasure ▲ CDCFP 9018 [ADD]
Elgar, E.:Sym 2 Classics for Pleasure ▲ CDCFP 4544 [ADD]
Vaughan Williams, R.:The Lark Ascending Classics for Pleasure ("Eminence" series) ▲ CDEMX 9508 [DDD]
Vaughan Williams, R.:Serenade to Music [orch. version] Chandos ▲ CHAN 8330
Vaughan Williams, R.:Variants of "Dives & Lazarus" Classics for Pleasure ("Eminence" series) ▲ CDEMX 9508 [DDD]
Vaughan Williams, R.:The Wasps—Aristophanic Suite Classics for Pleasure ("Eminence" series) ▲ CDEMX 9508 [DDD]
Vaughan Williams, R.:The Wasps (ov) Chandos ▲ CHAN 8330
H. Harty (cnd)
Bax, A.:Ov to a Picaresque Comedy Dutton Laboratories ▲ DUT 7016 [ADD]
Berlioz, H.:Marche funèbre *(rec 1935)* Pearl ▲ PEA 9485 (m)
Berlioz, H.:Marche funèbre Dutton Laboratories ▲ DUT 7016 [ADD]
Berlioz, H.:Roméo et Juliette (sels)—Romeo's Reverie & Fête of the Capulets Dutton Laboratories ▲ DUT 7016 [ADD]
Handel, G.F.:Royal Fireworks Music—Suite Dutton Laboratories ▲ DUT 7016 [ADD]
Handel, G.F.:Water Music (suites) Dutton Laboratories ▲ DUT 7016 [ADD]
Mozart, W.A.:Sinf concertante Vn, K.364, w. A. Sammons (vn), L. Tertis (va) *(rec Apr. 30, 1933 for Columbi)* Biddulph ▲ LAB 023 [ADD]
Schubert, Franz:Marches militaires, D.733 Dutton Laboratories ▲ DUT 7016 [ADD]
Sibelius, J.:Valse triste Dutton Laboratories ▲ DUT 7016 [ADD]
Smetana, B.:The Bartered Bride (ov) Dutton Laboratories ▲ DUT 7016 [ADD]
B. Herrmann (cnd)
Herrmann, B.:Film Music—Marnie; North by Northwest; Psycho; The Trouble with Harry; Vertigo *(rec DECCA Studio No. 3, West Hampstead, London, England, Dec 1968)* London ("Phase 4 Stereo" series) ▲ 443895-2 [ADD]
Herrmann, B.:Welles Raises Kane Unicorn-Kanchana ▲ UKCD 2065
Ravel, M.:5 O'Clock Foxtrot *(rec Kingsway Hall, London, Jan 1970)* London ("Phase 4 Stereo" series) ▲ 444785-2 [ADD]
Satie, E.:Ballet Music, w. London Festival Players—Belle excentrique; Gymnopédies 1 & 3; Mercure London ("Weekend Classics" series) ▲ 421395-2
J. Horenstein (cnd)
Mahler, G.:Sym 4, w. M. Price (sop) [G] Monitor ■ 55001
E. Inbal (cnd)
Chopin, F.:Music of, w. Claudio Arrau (pno), Nikita Magaloff (pno), Rotterdam PO [cnd:David Zinman]—Con. No. 2 in f for Pno, Op. 21 [Larghetto]; Berceuse in D♭, Op. 57; Nocturnes No. 1 in b♭, Op. 9/1; No. 2 in E♭, Op. 9/2; No. 5 in F♯, Op. 15/2; No. 8 in D♭, Op. 27/2; No. 20 in c♯, Op. posth.; No. 21 in c, Op. posth.; Prelude No. 7 in A, Op. 28; Andante spianato; Prelude No. 4 in e, Op. 28; Waltz No. 9 in A♭, Op. 69/1; Con. No. 1 in e for Pno, Op. 11 [Romance] Philips ▲ 446629-2 ■ 446629-4
M. Jansons (cnd)
Rimsky-Korsakov, N.:Capriccio espagnol EMI Classics ▲ CDC 55227
Rimsky-Korsakov, N.:Scheherazade EMI Classics ▲ CDC 55227
Shostakovich, D.:Con 1 Vc, w. Truls Mork (vc) Virgin Classics ▲ CDC 45145
Shostakovich, D.:Con 2 Vc, w. Truls Mork (vc) Virgin Classics ▲ CDC 45145
Tchaikovsky, P.:The Nutcracker EMI Classics 2-▲ CDQB 54649 2-■ 4D2Q 54649
N. Järvi (cnd)
Bruckner, A.:Sym 8 [Haas edition] Chandos 2-▲ CHAN 8843/44 [DDD]
Medtner, N.:Con 1 Pno, w. G. Tozer (pno) Chandos 2-▲ CHAN 9040 [DDD]
Medtner, N.:Con 2 Pno, w. G. Tozer (pno) Chandos 2-▲ CHAN 9040 [DDD]
Medtner, N.:Con 3 Pno, w. G. Tozer (pno) Chandos 2-▲ CHAN 9040 [DDD]
Reger, M.:Vars & Fugue on a Theme of Beethoven Chandos 2-▲ CHAN 8843/44 [DDD]
Tchaikovsky, P.:Con 3 Pno, w. G. Tozer (pno) *(rec June 7 & 8, 1991)* Chandos ▲ CHAN 9130 [DDD]
Tchaikovsky, P.:Sym 7, w. G. Tozer (pno) *(rec June 7 & 8, 1991)* Chandos ▲ CHAN 9130 [DDD]
K. Jenkins (cnd)
Jenkins, K.:Music of, w. Smith String Quartet—Diamond Music (Palladio); Adiemus Variations; Passacaglia (In memoriam Evelyn Mary Hopkins:1903–1995); Qt 2 Strs Sony Classical ▲ SK 62276 ■ ST 62276
E. Jochum (cnd)
Haydn, J.:Syms 93–104, "The Salomon (or London) Syms" Deutsche Grammophon 4-▲ 437201-2 [ADD]
L. Johnson (cnd)
Johnson, Laurie:Music of, w. W. Davies (org), London Jazz Orch, London Studio SO, Coldstream Guards Regimental Band, Fanfare Trumpeters of the Scots Guards, London Brass Chorale—Royal Tour (suite); Symphony (Synthesis) for Combined Jazz & Symphony Orchestras (1969); Three Paintings by Lautrec; The Wind In the Willows (1985) *(rec 1969–82)* Unicorn-Kanchana ▲ UKCD 2057 [DDD/ADD]
O. Kamu (cnd)
Tchaikovsky, P.:Con Vn, w. N. Kennedy (vn) EMI Classics ▲ CDC 54559 [DDD] ■ 4DS 54559
M. Kibblewhite (cnd)
Bliss, A.:Investiture Antiphonal Fanfare *(rec All Hallows Church, London, Nov. 16–17, 1991 & Jan 26)* Cala ▲ CACD 1010 [DDD]
Bliss, A.:Morning Heroes, w. B. Blessed (nar), East London Chorus, Harlow Chorus, Hertfordshire Chorus *(rec All Hallows Church, London, Nov. 16–17, 1991 & Jan 26)* Cala ▲ CACD 1010 [DDD]
Bliss, A.:Prayer for St. Francis of Assisi, w. East London Chorus, Harlow Chorus, Hertfordshire Chorus *(rec All Hallows Church, London, Nov. 16–17, 1991 & Jan 26)* Cala ▲ CACD 1010 [DDD]
E. Kleiber (cnd)
Beethoven, L. van:Sym 6, "Pastorale" *(rec 1948)* Theorema 2-▲ TH 121211/212
K. Klein (cnd)
Chausson, E.:Poème Vn, w. Hideko Udagawa (vn) IMP ("Classics" series) ▲ IMP 6700312
Glazunov, A.:Con Vn, w. Hideko Udagawa (vn) IMP ("Classics" series) ▲ IMP 6700312
Gould, M.:American Ballads Albany ▲ TROY 202 [DDD]
Gould, M.:American Salute Albany ▲ TROY 202 [DDD]
Gould, M.:American Symphonette 2 Albany ▲ TROY 202 [DDD]
Gould, M.:Spirituals Strs Albany ▲ TROY 202 [DDD]
Saint-Saëns, C.:Études Pno, Op. 52, w. Hideko Udagawa (vn)—Caprice en forme de valse [trans Ysaÿe] IMP ("Classics" series) ▲ IMP 6700312
Sarasate, P. de:Spanish Dances, w. Hideko Udagawa (vn)—Romanze andaluza, Op. 22/1 IMP ("Classics" series) ▲ IMP 6700312
Tchaikovsky, P.:Souvenir d'un lieu cher, w. Hideko Udagawa (vn) IMP ("Classics" series) ▲ IMP 6700312
H. Knappertsbusch (cnd)
Wagner, R.:Lohengrin (preludes) *(rec London, 1947)* Preiser ▲ PRE 90189 [AAD]
Wagner, R.:Rienzi, der Letzte der Tribunen (ov) *(rec London, 1947)* Preiser ▲ PRE 90189 [AAD]
C. Lambert (cnd)
Liszt, F.:Fant on Hungarian Folk Tunes, w. B. Moseiwitsch (pno) *(rec 1939)* Koch Legacy ▲ 3-7035-2
Weinberger, J.:Under the Spreading Chestnut Tree Time Machine ▲ 0099
J. Latham-König (cnd)
Walton, W.:Con Va, w. N. Imai (va) Chandos ▲ CHAN 9106 [DDD]
Walton, W.:Con Vn, w. L. Mordkovitch (vn) Chandos ▲ CHAN 9073 [DDD]
Walton, W.:Façade Chandos ▲ CHAN 9148 [DDD]
Walton, W.:Pieces Vn, w. L. Mordkovitch (vn) Chandos ▲ CHAN 9073 [DDD]

224
▲ = CD ♦ = Enhanced CD Δ = MD ■ = Cassette Tape □ = DCC

London PO (cont.)

J. Latham-König (cnd) (cont.)

Walton, W.:Popular Birthday — Chandos ▲ CHAN 9148 [DDD]
Walton, W.:Portsmouth Point — Chandos ▲ CHAN 9148 [DDD]
Walton, W.:Sinf Concertante, w. E. Parkin (pno) — Chandos ▲ CHAN 9148 [DDD]
Walton, W.:Son Str Orch — Chandos ▲ CHAN 9106 [DDD]
Walton, W.:Son Vn & Orch, w. L. Mordkovitch (vn) — Chandos ▲ CHAN 9073 [DDD]
Walton, W.:Vars on a Theme by Hindemith — Chandos ▲ CHAN 9106 [DDD]

A. Lazarev (cnd)

Prokofiev, S.:Con 2 Pno, w. Nikolai Demidenko (pno) — Hyperion ▲ CDA 66858
Prokofiev, S.:Con 3 Pno, w. Nikolai Demidenko (pno) — Hyperion ▲ CDA 66858

A. Leaper (cnd)

Brahms, J.:Con Vn, w. T. Wanami (vn) — IMP Classics ▲ IMP PCD 1062 [DDD]
Schumann, R.:Con Vn, w. T. Wanami (vn) — IMP Classics ▲ IMP PCD 1062 [DDD]

P. Ledger (cnd)

Elgar, E.:Coronation March — EMI Classics 2-▲ ZDMB 64209

R. Leppard (cnd)

Bax, A.:Sym 7 — Lyrita ▲ SRCD 232
Gluck, C.W.:Orfeo ed Euridice, w. E. Gale (sop), E. Speiser (sop), J. Baker (mez) — Erato 2-▲ 2292-45864-2
Music for Imaging, w. The LIND Tapes, Strausbourg PO [cnd:Armin Jordan], et al. — Lind ■ LI 201
The Ultimate Opera Collection, w. Venice Soloists, James Conlon (cnd), Armin Jordan (cnd), Alain Lombard (cnd), Lorin Maazel (cnd), Claudio Scimone (cnd), Lyon Opera, et al. — Erato ▲ 2292-45797-2 ■ 2292-45797-4 AW

R.H. Lewis (cnd)

Lewis, R.H.:Invenzione — New World ▲ 80444-2
Lewis, R.H.:Sym 4 — New World ▲ 80444-2

A. Litton (cnd)

Ravel, M.:Boléro — Virgin Classics ▲ CDZ 59658
Rimsky-Korsakov, N.:Scheherazade — Virgin Classics ▲ CDZ 59658
Shostakovich, D.:Festive Ov — Virgin Classics ("Ultraviolet" series) ▲ CUV 61134
Shostakovich, D.:Sym 10 — Virgin Classics ("Ultraviolet" series) ▲ CUV 61134

J. López-Cobos (cnd)

Haydn, J.:Con Tpt, w. Maurice André (tpt) — EMI Classics 2-▲ CDZB 69152 [ADD]
Mendelssohn, F.:Con in e Vn & Orch, Op. 64, w. Chee-Yun (vn) — Denon ▲ CO 78913
Trumpet Concertos, w. Maurice André (tpt), Franz Liszt CO [cnd:Jésus López-Cobos], Württemberg CO [cnd:Jörg Faerber], Academy of St. Martin in the Fields [cnd:Neville Marriner], Philharmonia Orch [cnd:Riccardo Muti] — EMI Classics 2-▲ CDZB 69152 [ADD]

L. Maazel (cnd)

Scriabin, A.:Con Pno, w. V. Ashkenazy (pno) — London ▲ 417252-2 [ADD]
Scriabin, A.:Sym 5 — London ▲ 417252-2 [ADD]

Z. Mącal (cnd)

Dvořák, A.:Con Vc, w. Robert Cohen (vc) — Classics for Pleasure ("Silver Doubles" series) 2-▲ CFP CDCFP 4775 [ADD/DDD]
Tchaikovsky, P.:Vars on a Rococo Theme, w. Robert Cohen (vc) — Classics for Pleasure ("Silver Doubles" series) 2-▲ CFP CDCFP 4775 [ADD/DDD]

C. Mackerras (cnd)

Basic 100 Vol. 61, w. Ofra Harnoy (vc), Lynn Harrell (vc), James Levine (cnd), London SO — RCA Victor ▲ 09026-68086-2 ■ 09026-68086-4
Bloch, E.:Schelomo, w. O. Harnoy (vc) — RCA Red Seal ▲ 60757-2-RC [DDD] ■ 60757-4-RC
Bruch, M.:Adagio on a Celtic Theme, w. O. Harnoy (vc) — RCA Red Seal ▲ 60757-2-RC [DDD] ■ 60757-4-RC (CrO2)
Bruch, M.:Ave Maria Vc, w. O. Harnoy (vc) — RCA Red Seal ▲ 60757-2-RC [DDD] ■ 60757-4-RC (CrO2)
Bruch, M.:Canzone Vc, w. O. Harnoy (vc) — RCA Red Seal ▲ 60757-2-RC [DDD] ■ 60757-4-RC (CrO2)
Bruch, M.:Kol Nidrei, w. O. Harnoy (vc) — RCA Red Seal ▲ 60757-2-RC [DDD] ■ 60757-4-RC (CrO2)
Dvořák, A.:Symphonic Vars — Classics for Pleasure ("Eminence" series) ▲ CDEMX 2216 [DDD]
Mahler, G.:Des Knaben Wunderhorn, w. Ann Murray (mez), Thomas Allen (bar) — Virgin Classics ("Ultraviolet" series) ▲ CUV 61202
Mahler, G.:Des Knaben Wunderhorn, w. A. Murray (mez), T. Allen (bar) — Virgin Classics ▲ CDC 59037
Tchaikovsky, P.:Music of, w. O. Harnoy (vc)—Chant d'automne, Op. 37b/10; Lensky's Aria (from Eugene Onegin); Nocturne, Op. 19/4; Valse sentimentale, Op. 51/6 — RCA Red Seal ▲ 09026-60758-2 ■ 09026-60758-4 (CrO2) □ 09026-60758-5
Tchaikovsky, P.:Pezzo capriccioso, w. O. Harnoy (vc) — RCA Red Seal ▲ 09026-60758-2 ■ 09026-60758-4 (CrO2) □ 09026-60758-5
Tchaikovsky, P.:Sérénade mélancolique, w. O. Harnoy (vc) — RCA Red Seal ▲ 09026-60758-2 ■ 09026-60758-4 (CrO2) □ 09026-60758-5
Tchaikovsky, P.:Vars on a Rococo Theme, w. O. Harnoy (vc) — RCA Red Seal ▲ 09026-60758-2 ■ 09026-60758-4 (CrO2) □ 09026-60758-5
Wagner, R.:Götterdämmerung (sels), w. Rita Hunter (sop—Brünnhilde), Alberto Remedios (ten—Siegfried)—Dawn; Brünnhilde & Siegfried's Entrance; Siegfried's Rhine Journey; Siegfried's Funeral Music; Brünnhilde's Immolation [Starke Scheite schichtet mir dort] — Classics for Pleasure ▲ CDCFP 4670
Walton, W.:Sym 1 — Classics for Pleasure ("Eminence" series) ▲ CDEMX 2206

J. Maksymiuk (cnd)

Grieg, E.:Con Pno, Op. 16, w. P. Devoyon (pno) — Classics For Pleasure ▲ CDCFP4574 [DDD]
Schumann, R.:Con Pno, w. P. Devoyon (pno) — Classics For Pleasure ▲ CDCFP4574 [DDD]

N. del Mar (cnd)

Elgar, E.:Con Vc, w. R. Cohen (vc) — Classics for Pleasure ▲ CDCFP 9003 [ADD]
Elgar, E.:Con Vc, w. Robert Cohen (vc) — Classics for Pleasure 2-▲ CFP CFPSD 4775 [ADD/DDD]
Elgar, E.:Con Vc, w. Robert Cohen (vc) — Classics for Pleasure ("Silver Doubles" series) 2-▲ CFP CDCFP 4775 [ADD/DDD]
Elgar, E.:Elegy Strs, w. R. Cohen (vc) — Classics for Pleasure ▲ CDCFP 9003 [ADD]
Elgar, E.:In the South, w. R. Cohen (vc) — Classics for Pleasure ▲ CDCFP 9003 [ADD]

K. Masur (cnd)

Mussorgsky, M.:Pictures at an Exhibition — Teldec ("M Line" series) ▲ 97440-2
Mussorgsky, M.:Pictures at an Exhibition [orchd. by Sergei P. Gortchakov (1950s)] *(rec Snape Maltings Concert Hall, Dec. 1990)* — Teldec ▲ 2292-44941-2 [DDD]
Prokofiev, S.:Sym 1 — Teldec ("M Line" series) ▲ 97440-2
Prokofiev, S.:Sym 1 *(rec Snape Maltings Concert Hall, Dec. 1990)* — Teldec ▲ 2292-44941-2 [DDD]
Schnittke, A.:Con 1 Vc, w. N. Gutman (vc) — EMI Classics ▲ CDC 54443
Schumann, R.:Con Vc, w. N. Gutman (vc) — EMI Classics ▲ CDC 54443
Schumann, R.:Sym 1 — Teldec ▲ 2292-46445-2
Schumann, R.:Sym 1 — Teldec 2-▲ 95501-2
Schumann, R.:Sym 2 — Teldec ▲ 2292-46446-2 [DDD]
Schumann, R.:Sym 3 — Teldec 2-▲ 95501-2
Schumann, R.:Sym 3 — Teldec ▲ 2292-46446-2 [DDD]
Schumann, R.:Sym 4 — Teldec ▲ 2292-46445-2 [DDD]

Z. Mehta (cnd)

Berlioz, H.:Béatrice et Bénédict (ov) — Teldec ▲ 90855
Berlioz, H.:Le Carnaval romain — Teldec ▲ 90855
Berlioz, H.:Sym fantastique — Teldec ▲ 90855
Bruch, M.:Con 1 Vn, w. Pinchas Zukerman (vn) *(rec Henry Wood Hall, London, Sept 24-25, 1992)* — RCA Red Seal ▲ 09026-68046-2 [DDD]
Orff, C.:Carmina burana, w. S. Jo (sop), J. Kowalski (alt), B. Skovhus (bar), London Phil Choir, Southend Boys' Choir — Teldec ▲ 74886-2
Puccini, G.:Turandot, w. J. Sutherland (sop), M. Caballé (sop), L. Pavarotti (ten), N. Ghiaurov (bass), John Alldis Choir [I] — London 2-▲ 414274-2 [ADD]
Puccini, G.:Turandot (sels), w. J. Sutherland (sop), M. Caballé (sop), L. Pavarotti (ten), N. Ghiaurov (bass) — London ▲ 421320-2 [ADD] ■ 421320-4

London PO (cont.)

J. Mester (cnd)

Copland, A.:Fanfare for the Common Man — Koch International Classics ▲ KIC 7012-2 [DDD] ■ 3-7012-4 (D)
Rachmaninoff, S.:Suite 2 for 2 Pnos [orchd. R. Harkness] — Citadel ▲ CTD 88101 [ADD]
20 Fanfares for the Common Man — Koch International Classics ▲ KIC 7012 [DDD]

A. Mitchell (cnd)

McEwen, J.:Border Ballads — Chandos ▲ CHAN 9241 [DDD]
McEwen, J.:Hills o' Heather, w. Moary Welsh (vc) — Chandos ▲ CHAN 9345 [DDD]
McEwen, J.:Sym, "Solway" — Chandos ▲ CHAN 9345 [DDD]
McEwen, J.:Where the Wild Thyme Blows — Chandos ▲ CHAN 9345 [DDD]

P. Monteux (cnd)

Tchaikovsky, P.:Swan Lake (sels) — Philips ("Silver Line" series) ▲ 420872-2 [ADD]

E. Morricone (cnd)

Morricone, E.:Mission — Virgin ▲ V21Z 86001 ■ V41H 86001

W. Morris (cnd)

Mahler, G.:Des Knaben Wunderhorn, w. Janet Baker (mez), Geraint Evans (bar), Roland Hermann (bar), London Symphonica — IMP ▲ PCD 2020
Mahler, G.:Des Knaben Wunderhorn, w. J. Baker (mez), G. Evans (ten) [G] *(rec 1966)* — Nimbus ▲ NI 5084 [AAD]
Mahler, G.:Lieder eines fahrenden Gesellen, w. Janet Baker (mez), Geraint Evans (bar), Roland Hermann (bar), London Symphonica — IMP ▲ PCD 2020

K. Nagano (cnd)

Stravinsky, I.:Perséphone, w. A. Fournet (nar), A. Rolfe-Johnson (ten), Tiffin Boys' School Choir, London Phil Chorus [F] — Virgin Classics 2-▲ 59077 [DDD]
Stravinsky, I.:Perséphone, w. Anne Fournet (nar), Anthony Rolf-Johnson (ten) — Virgin Classics ▲ ZDMB 61249
Stravinsky, I.:Le Sacre du printemps Orch — Virgin Classics 2-▲ 59077 [DDD]
Stravinsky, I.:Le Sacre du printemps Orch — Virgin Classics ▲ ZDMB 61249

D. Nolan (cnd)

Vivaldi, A.:Cons Vn, Op. 8/1-4, "The Four Seasons", w. D. Nolan (vn) — Collins Quest ▲ 30182 [DDD]

J. Pritchard (cnd)

Mozart, W.A.:Idomeneo, w. Gundula Janowitz (sop), Enriqueta Tarres (sop), Richard Lewis (ten), Luciano Pavarotti (ten), Glyndebourne Festival Chorus [I] *(rec live at Royal Albert Hall, Aug. 17, 1964)* — Verona 2-▲ 27038/39 (m) [AAD]
Mozart, W.A.:Idomeneo, w. Gundula Janowitz (sop), Enriqueta Tarres (sop), Richard Lewis (ten), Luciano Pavarotti (ten), Glyndebourne Festival Chorus [I] *(rec live, Royal Albert Hall, London Aug. 17, 1964)* — Melodram 2-▲ MEL 27003 (m)
Mozart, W.A.:Idomeneo (sels), w. Gundula Janowitz (sop), Enriqueta Tarres (sop), David Hughes (ten), Richard Lewis (ten), Luciano Pavarotti (ten), Neilson Taylor (bar), Dennis Wicks (bass), Glyndebourne Festival Chorus — Budget ("The Greatest Voice in Opera" series) ▲ SYP 107
Puccini, G.:Arias, w. K. Te Kanawa (sop) [I] — CBS ▲ MK 37298 [DDD] ■ IMT 37298 (D)
Rawsthorne, A.:Con Pnos, w. John Ogdon (pno), Brenda Lucas (pno) — IMP ("BBC Radio Classics" series) ▲ IMP 5691762
Rawsthorne, A.:Sym 1 *(rec 1977)* — Lyrita ▲ SRCD 291

A. Rahbari (cnd)

Beethoven, L. van:Leonore 3 — Discover International ▲ DICD 920114 [DDD]

S. Rattle (cnd)

Gershwin, G.:Porgy & Bess, w. C. Haymon (sop—Bess), C. Clarey (sop—Serena), M. Simpson (sop—Maria), D. Evans (ten—Sporting Life), G. Baker (bar—Crown), W. White (bar—Porgy), Glyndebourne Festival Chorus — EMI Classics 3-▲ CDCC 49568

F. Reiner (cnd)

Wagner, R.:Tristan und Isolde, w. Kirsten Flagstad (sop), Sabine Kalter (cta), Lauritz Melchoir (ten), Emmanuel List (bass) — Enterprise ("The Radio Years" series) 3-▲ ENT 39 (m)

N. Rescigno (cnd)

Bellini, V.:I Puritani (sels), w. R. A. Swenson (sop)—O rendetemi la speme *(rec Nov. 11-19, 1993)* — EMI Classics ▲ CDC 54827 [DDD]
Bellini, V.:La sonnambula (sels), w. R. A. Swenson (sop)—A te dilette...Come per me sereno *(rec Nov. 11-19, 1993)* — EMI Classics ▲ CDC 54827 [DDD]
Donizetti, G.:Linda di Chamounix (sels), w. R. A. Swenson (sop)—Ah! tardai tropp...O luce di quest'anima *(rec Nov. 11-19, 1993)* — EMI Classics ▲ CDC 54827 [DDD]
Donizetti, G.:Lucia di Lammermoor (sels), w. R. A. Swenson (sop)—Regnava nel silenzio...Quando, rapito in estasi *(rec Nov. 11-19, 1993)* — EMI Classics ▲ CDC 54827 [DDD]
Gounod, C.:Roméo et Juliette (sels), w. R. A. Swenson (sop)—Ah! Je veux vivre *(rec Nov. 11-19, 1993)* — EMI Classics ▲ CDC 54827 [DDD]
Meyerbeer, G.:L'Africaine (sels), w. R. A. Swenson (sop)—Adieu, mon doux rivage *(rec Nov. 11-19, 1993)* — EMI Classics ▲ CDC 54827 [DDD]
Meyerbeer, G.:Dinorah (sels), w. R. A. Swenson (sop)—Ombre légère, qui suis mes pas *(rec Nov. 11-19, 1993)* — EMI Classics ▲ CDC 54827 [DDD]
Meyerbeer, G.:Les Huguenots (sels), w. R. A. Swenson (sop)—Obeau pays do la Tourainol *(roc Nov. 11-19, 1993)* — EMI Classics ▲ CDC 54827 [DDD]

K. A. Rickenbacher (cnd)

Wagner, R.:Götterdämmerung (sels) — Classics for Pleasure ▲ CDCFP 9008 [DDD]
Wagner, R.:Lohengrin (preludes)—Preludes to Acts 1 & 3 — Classics for Pleasure ▲ CDCFP 9008 [DDD]
Wagner, R.:Die Meistersinger von Nürnberg (prelude/act 1) — Classics for Pleasure ▲ CDCFP 9008 [DDD]
Wagner, R.:Ovs, Preludes & Orch Sels—orchestral sels. from Götterdämmerung, Lohengrin, Die Meistersinger von Nürnberg, Die Walküre:Ride of the Valkyries — Classics for Pleasure ▲ CDCFP 9008 [DDD]
Wagner, R.:Die Walküre (ride of the valkyries) — Classics for Pleasure ▲ CDCFP 9008 [DDD]

C. Rizzi (cnd)

Respighi, O.:Feste Romane — Teldec ("M Line" series) ▲ 97438-2
Respighi, O.:The Fountains of Rome — Teldec ("M Line" series) ▲ 97438-2
Respighi, O.:The Pines of Rome — Teldec ("M Line" series) ▲ 97438-2

L. Ronald (cnd)

Elgar, E.:Coronation Ode—Orchestral parts *(rec 1935)* — Pearl ▲ PEA 9087 [ADD]
Mendelssohn, F.:Con in e Vn & Orch, Op. 64, w. F. Kreisler (vn) *(rec 1935 HMV recording)* — Biddulph ▲ LAB 047 [ADD]
Mendelssohn, F.:Con in e Vn & Orch, Op. 64, w. F. Kreisler (vn) *(rec 1935 HMV recording)* — Pearl 2-▲ PEAS 9362 (m) [AAD]

M. Rostropovich (cnd)

Shostakovich, D.:Lady Macbeth of Mtsensk, w. G. Vishnevskaya (sop), B. Finnilă (mez), N. Gedda (ten), A. Haugland (bass), Ambrosian Opera Chorus [R] — EMI Classics 2-▲ CDCB 49955 [ADD]

J. Rudel (cnd)

French Opera Arias, w. Samuel Ramey (bass) — Philips ▲ 432080-2 PH [DDD]
Welcome to Vienna, w. Beverly Sills (sop) — EMI Classics ▲ CDM 64424

T. Sanderling (cnd)

Nanes, R.:Sym 3 — Delfon ▲ CDR 4050 [DDD] ■ KST 4050 (D)
Nanes, R.:Sym 4 — Delfon ▲ CDR 4050 [DDD] ■ KST 4050 (D)

J. Sándor (cnd)

Mozart, W.A.:Sym 41 — Laserlight ▲ 15 511 [ADD]

M. Sargent (cnd)

Beethoven, L. van:Cons Pno (comp), w. A. Schnabel (pno), London SO *(rec 1932-35)* — Pearl 3-▲ PEA 9063 [AAD]
Mozart, W.A.:Con 4 Vn, w. F. Kreisler (vn) *(rec 1939 HMV)* — Biddulph ▲ LAB 016 [ADD]

W. Sawallisch (cnd)

Brahms, J.:Academic Festival Ov — EMI Classics ▲ CDC 54523
Brahms, J.:Con 2 Pno, w. Stephen Bishop Kovacevich (pno) — EMI Classics ▲ CDC 55218
Brahms, J.:Schicksalslied, w. Ambrosian Singers — EMI Classics ▲ CDC 54359

London PO (cont.)
W. Sawallisch (cnd) (cont.)
Brahms, J.:Sym 1 EMI Classics ▲ CDC 54359
Brahms, J.:Sym 2 EMI Classics ▲ CDC 54059 [DDD] □ 777-7-54059-5-8
Brahms, J.:Sym 3 EMI Classics ▲ CDC 54523
Brahms, J.:Sym 4 EMI Classics ▲ CDC 54060 [DDD]
Brahms, J.:Tragic Ov EMI Classics ▲ CDC 54060 [DDD]
Brahms, J.:Vars on a Theme by Haydn EMI Classics ▲ CDC 54059 [DDD]
N. Sheriff (cnd)
Testimonies of War:Kriegszeugnisse, 1914–45, w.Berlin RSO [cnd:B. Goldschmidt], Poznán PO [cnd:A. Borejko], BBC Sym Chorus Largo 2-▲ 5130 [DDD]
A. Scholz (cnd)
Mozart, W.A.:Kleine Nachtmusik Sound 2-▲ CDN 115/116 [DDD]
Mozart, W.A.:Ovs—Die Entführung aus dem Serail; Le nozze di Figaro; Die Zauberflöte PMG ("Vienna Master" series) ▲ CD 160211 [DDD]
Mozart, W.A.:Ovs—Nozze di Figaro Sound 2-▲ CDN 115/116 [DDD]
Mozart, W.A.:Sym 41 Sound 2-▲ CDN 115/116 [DDD]
Mozart, W.A.:Sym 41 PMG ("Vienna Master" series) ▲ CD 160211 [DDD]
Mozart, W.A.:Zauberflöte (ov) Intersound ▲ CDS 3675
Mozart, W.A.:Zauberflöte (ov) Special Music Co. ("Classics of the Heart" series) ▲ SCD 5197
M. Shostakovich (cnd)
Prokofiev, S.:Ivan the Terrible, w. Russian State Yurlov Choir *(rec live Nov. 26, 1972)* Intaglio ▲ INCD 7371 [ADD]
L. Siegel (cnd)
Handel, G.F.:Messiah (sels), w. London Sym Chorus—Glory to God; And the Glory Laserlight ▲ 15 502 [ADD]
Mozart, W.A.:Sym 40 LaserLight ▲ 15 829 [DDD]
Mozart, W.A.:Sym 41 Laserlight ▲ 15 829 [DDD]
Tchaikovsky, P.:Romeo & Juliet LaserLight ▲ 15503 [DDD]
G. Simon (cnd)
The London Viola Sound, w. 48 Violas of Academy of St. Martin in the Fields, BBC SO, English National Opera Orch *(rec Colosseum, Watford, UK, Jan 24, 1995)* Cala ▲ CACD 106 [DDD]
Saint-Saëns, C.:Music of—La jota aragonese; Samson et Dalila; Grande fantasie (luigini); La princesse jaune:Ov.; La muse et la poète; Danse macabre; Sym. 3, "Organ" [rec Westminster Cathedral, Apr. 15, 1993] *(rec All Hallows Church, London, Jan 14–19 & Apr 2, 1993)* Cala ▲ CACD 1016 [DDD]
Saint-Saëns, C.:Music of—Parysatis; Sarabande et Rigaudon; Tarantelle for Flute, Clarinet & Orch.; Suite Algérienne:Marche militaire francaise; Africa; Ascanio:Valse finale; Messe de Requiem [rec Westminster Cathedral, Apr 15, 1993] *(rec All Hallows Church, London, Jan 14–19 & Apr 2, 1993)* Cala ▲ CACD 1015 [DDD]
L. Slatkin (cnd)
Basic 100 Vol. 62 RCA Victor ▲ 09026-68087-2 ■ 09026-68087-4
Britten, B.:Peter Grimes (sea interludes & passacaglia), w. Royal PO RCA Red Seal ▲ 09026-61226-2
Britten, B.:Purcell Realizations, w. Royal PO—Chancony RCA Red Seal ▲ 09026-61226-2
Britten, B.:Sinf da requiem, w. Royal PO RCA Red Seal ▲ 09026-61226-2
Britten, B.:The Young Person's Guide to the Orchestra, w. Royal PO RCA Red Seal ▲ 09026-61226-2
Castelnuovo-Tedesco, M.:Con 1 Gtr, w. K. Yamashita (gtr) RCA Red Seal ▲ 60355-2-RC [DDD]
Castelnuovo-Tedesco, M.:Con 2 Gtr, w. K. Yamashita (gtr) RCA Red Seal ▲ 60355-2-RC [DDD]
Castelnuovo-Tedesco, M.:Con for 2 Gtrs, w. K. Yamashita (gtr), N. Yamashita (gtr) RCA Red Seal ▲ 60355-2-RC [DDD]
Classical Ecstasy—Classics for a New Age, w. Chicago SO [cnd:Georg Solti], English CO [cnd:Alexander Schneider], Philadelphia Orch [cnd:James Levine], Philharmonia Orch [cnds:Andrew Litton, Henry Lewis], RCA Italiana Opera Orch [cnd:Francesco Molinari-Pradelli], et al. RCA Gold Seal ▲ 74321-23041-2 [ADD/DDD]
Elgar, E.:Cockaigne RCA Red Seal ▲ 09026-60073-2 [DDD]
Elgar, E.:Enigma Vars RCA Victor ▲ 09026-68087-2; ■ 09026-68087-4
Elgar, E.:Enigma Vars RCA Red Seal ▲ 09026-60073-2
Elgar, E.:Froissart RCA Red Seal ▲ 09026-60073-2
Elgar, E.:In the South RCA Red Seal ▲ 60380-2-RC [DDD] ■ 60380-4-RC (CrO2)
Elgar, E.:Intro & Allegro RCA Victor ▲ 09026-68087-2; ■ 09026-68087-4
Elgar, E.:The Kingdom, w. Y. Kenny (sop), A. Hodgson (alt), C. Gillert (ten), B. Luxon (bass), London Phil Chorus RCA Red Seal 2-▲ 07863-57862-2
Elgar, E.:Pomp & Circumstance Marches RCA Victor ▲ 09026-68087-2; ■ 09026-68087-4
Elgar, E.:Serenade Strs RCA Victor ▲ 09026-68087-2; ■ 09026-68087-4
Elgar, E.:Serenade Strs RCA Red Seal ▲ 09026-60072-2
Elgar, E.:Sym 1 RCA Red Seal ▲ 60380-2-RC [DDD] ■ 60380-4-RC (CrO2)
Elgar, E.:Sym 2 RCA Red Seal ▲ 09026-60072-2
Kabalevsky, D.:The Comedians RCA Gold Seal ▲ 09026-60968-2 ■ 09026-60968-4 (CrO2)
Khachaturian, A.:Gayane (sels)—Sabre Dance RCA Gold Seal ▲ 09026-60968-2 ■ 09026-60968-4 (CrO2)
Mussorgsky, M.:Pictures at an Exhibition RCA Gold Seal ▲ 09026-60968-2 ■ 09026-60968-4 (CrO2)
Out Classics, w. Ofra Harnoy (vc), Richard Stoltzman (cl), Peter Serkin (pno), et al. RCA Red Seal ▲ 09026-68261-2 ■ 09026-68261-4
Prokofiev, S.:Sym 1 *(rec ca. 1983/4)* RCA Gold Seal ▲ 09026-61350-2 ■ 09026-61350-4
Prokofiev, S.:Sym 1 RCA Gold Seal ▲ 09026-60968-2 ■ 09026-60968-4 (CrO2)
The Russian Album RCA Gold Seal ▲ 09026-60968-2
Stravinsky, I.:Fireworks RCA Gold Seal ▲ 09026-60968-2 ■ 09026-60968-4 (CrO2)
Walton, W.:Portsmouth Point Virgin Classics ("Ultraviolet" series) ▲ CUV 61146
Walton, W.:Sym 1 Virgin Classics ("Ultraviolet" series) ▲ CUV 61146
G. Solti (cnd)
Bartók, B.:Con 2 Vn, w. K.-W. Chung (vn) London ▲ 425015-2 [ADD/DDD]
Bizet, G.:Carmen, w. T. Troyanos (mez), K. Te Kanawa (sop), P. Domingo (ten), J. Van Dam (b-bar) [F] London 3-▲ 414489-2 [ADD]
Bizet, G.:Carmen, w. T. Troyanos (mez), K. Te Kanawa (sop), P. Domingo (ten), J. Van Dam (b-bar) [F] London ▲ 421300-2 [ADD]
Elgar, E.:Cockaigne London ("Double Decca" series) 2-▲ 443856-2
Elgar, E.:In the South London ("Double Decca" series) 2-▲ 443856-2
Elgar, E.:Pomp & Circumstance Marches—Nos. 1,4 & 5 London ("Jubilee" series) ▲ 430447-2 [ADD]
Elgar, E.:Sym 1 London ("Double Decca" series) 2-▲ 443856-2
Elgar, E.:Sym 2 London ("Double Decca" series) 2-▲ 443856-2
Haydn, J.:Sym 93 London ▲ 417620-2 [DDD]
Haydn, J.:Sym 99 London ▲ 417620-2 [DDD]
Holst, G.:The Planets London ("Jubilee" series) ▲ 430447-2
Liszt, F.:Les Préludes London ▲ 417513-2 [ADD]
Liszt, F.:Prometheus London ▲ 417513-2 [ADD]
Mozart, W.A.:Don Giovanni, w. L. Price (sop), L. Popp (sop), S. Sass (sop), S. Burrows (ten), G. Bacquier (bar), B. Weikl (bar), A. Sramek (bar), K. Moll (bass), London Opera Chorus London ("Grand Opera" series) 3-▲ 425169-2 [ADD]
Mozart, W.A.:Nozze di Figaro, w. K. Te Kanawa (sop), L. Popp (sop), F. von Stade (mez), T. Allen (bar), S. Ramey (bass), K. Moll (bass) [I] London 3-▲ 410150-2 [DDD]
Mozart, W.A.:Nozze di Figaro (sels), w. K. Te Kanawa (sop), L. Popp (sop), F. von Stade (mez), T. Allen (bar), S. Ramey (bass), K. Moll (bass) [I] London ▲ 417395-2 [DDD] □ 417395-5
Puccini, G.:La Bohème, w. M. Caballé (sop), J. Blegen (sop), P. Domingo (ten), S. Milnes (bar), R. Raimondi (bass), John Alldis Choir [I] RCA Red Seal 2-▲ RCD2-0371 2-■ ARK2-0371
Puccini, G.:La Bohème (sels), w. M. Cabballé (sop), J. Blegen (sop), P. Domingo (ten), S. Milnes (bar) RCA Victor ▲ 09026-61725-2; ■ 09026-61725-4 (CrO2)
The Solti Edition, w. Chicago SO, London SO, Vienna PO, New Philharmonia Orch, Royal Opera House Orch, CO of Europe London 25-▲ 436600-2

London PO (cont.)
G. Solti (cnd) (cont.)
Strauss, R.:Ariadne auf Naxos, w. L. Price (sop), E. Gruberova (sop), R. Kollo (ten) [G] London ("Grand Opera" series) 2-▲ 430384-2 [ADD]
L. Stokowski (cnd)
Beethoven, L. van:Sym 5 London ("Weekend Classics" series) ▲ 430218-2 [AAD]
V. de Stradelli (cnd)
Mozart, W.A.:Kleine Nachtmusik Vivace 3-▲ E 338-2 [ADD/DDD]
G. Szell (cnd)
Beethoven, L. van:Con 5 Pno, "Emperor", w. B. Moseiwitsch (pno) *(rec 1938)* Koch Legacy ▲ 3-7035-2
Brahms, J.:Con 1 Pno, w. A. Schnabel (pno) *(rec 1/9 & 12/18 1938)* Pearl ▲ PEA 9376 (m) [AAD]
J.L. Temes (cnd)
Guerra, J.F.:Los Ojos verdes Discobi ▲ DIS 2008
Llanas, A.:Con Cl, w. Salvador Vidal (cl) Discobi ▲ DIS 2008
Turina, J.:Punto de encuentro Discobi ▲ DIS 2008
K. Tennstedt (cnd)
Beethoven, L. van:Con Vn, Op. 61, w. K.-W. Chung (vn) EMI Classics ▲ CDC 54072
Beethoven, L. van:Sym 3, "Eroica" EMI Classics ▲ CDC 55186
Beethoven, L. van:Sym 6, "Pastorale" EMI Classics ("Studio DDD" series) ▲ CDD 63891 [DDD]
Beethoven, L. van:Sym 8 EMI Classics ("Studio DDD" series) ▲ CDD 63891 [DDD]
Brahms, J.:Con Vn, w. N. Kennedy (vn) EMI Classics ▲ CDC 54187 [DDD] ■ 4DS 54187
Bruch, M.:Con 1 Vn, w. K.-W. Chung (vn) EMI Classics ▲ CDC 54072
Bruckner, A.:Sym 8 EMI Classics ▲ CDM 64849
Kodály, Z.:Háry János (suite) EMI Classics ("Studio DDD" series) ▲ CDD 63900 [DDD]
Mahler, G.:Des Knaben Wunderhorn, w. L. Popp (sop), J. Baker (mez), M. Dickie (ten), D. Fischer-Dieskau (bar), B. Weikl (bar) EMI Classics ▲ CDZB 62707
Mahler, G.:Das Lied von der Erde, w. A. Baltsa (mez), K. König (ten) EMI Classics ▲ CDC 54603
Mahler, G.:Syms, w. Lucia Popp (sop)—Nos. 1–4 EMI Classics 4-▲ ZDMD 64471
Mahler, G.:Syms—Nos. 5, 9 & 10 EMI Classics 3-▲ ZDMC 64481
Mahler, G.:Syms—Nos. 6, 7 & 8 EMI Classics 4-▲ ZDMD 64476 (D)
Mahler, G.:Sym 5 *(rec live, Royal Festival Hall, 12/13/88)* EMI Classics ▲ CDC 49888 [DDD]
Mahler, G.:Sym 8, w. London Phil Chorus, Tiffin School Boys' Chorus [G,L] EMI Classics 2-▲ CDCB 47625 [DDD]
Mussorgsky, M.:Night EMI Classics ▲ CDC 55186
B. Thomson (cnd)
Bax, A.:Christmas Eve on the Mountains Chandos ▲ CHAN 8480 [DDD]
Bax, A.:Con Vc (1932), w. R. Wallfisch (vc) Chandos ▲ CHAN 8494 [DDD]
Bax, A.:Cortège Chandos ▲ CHAN 8494 [DDD]
Bax, A.:The Dance of Wild Irravel Chandos ▲ CHAN 8454 [DDD]
Bax, A.:Festival Ov Chandos ▲ CHAN 8586 [DDD]
Bax, A.:From Dusk Till Dawn Chandos ▲ CHAN 8863 [DDD]
Bax, A.:Mediterranean Chandos ("Collect" series) ▲ CHAN 6538 [ADD/DDD]
Bax, A.:Mediterranean Chandos ▲ CHAN 8494 [DDD]
Bax, A.:Morning Time, w. M. Fingerhut (pno) Chandos ▲ CHAN 8516 [DDD]
Bax, A.:Northern Ballad 3, "Prelude to a Solemn Occasion" Chandos ▲ CHAN 8494 [DDD]
Bax, A.:Nympholept Chandos ▲ CHAN 8493 [DDD]
Bax, A.:Ov to a Picaresque Comedy Chandos ▲ CHAN 8494 [DDD]
Bax, A.:Paean Chandos ▲ CHAN 8454 [DDD]
Bax, A.:Pieces Orch, "4 Sketches or 4 Irish Pieces" Chandos ▲ CHAN 8454 [DDD]
Bax, A.:Russian Suite Chandos ▲ CHAN 8669 [DDD]
Bax, A.:Saga Fragment, w. Margaret Fingerhut (pno) Chandos ▲ CHAN 8484 [DDD]
Bax, A.:Songs, w. Martyn Hill (ten), Eternity; Glamour; A Lyke-Wake; Slumber Song Chandos ▲ CHAN 8628 [DDD]
Bax, A.:Symphonic Vars, w. M. Fingerhut (pno) Chandos ▲ CHAN 8516 [DDD]
Bax, A.:Sym 1 Chandos ▲ CHAN 8480 [DDD]
Bax, A.:Sym 2 Chandos ▲ CHAN 8493 [DDD]
Bax, A.:Sym 3 Chandos ▲ CHAN 8454 [DDD]
Bax, A.:Sym 5 Chandos ▲ CHAN 8669 [DDD]
Bax, A.:Sym 6 Chandos ▲ CHAN 8586 [DDD]
Bax, A.:Sym 7 Chandos ▲ CHAN 8628 [DDD]
Bax, A.:The Truth about the Russian Dancers Chandos ▲ CHAN 8863 [DDD]
Bax, A.:Winter Legends, w. Margaret Fingerhut (pno) Chandos ▲ CHAN 8484 [DDD]
Elgar, E.:Enigma Vars *(rec All Saints' Church, Jan 18–19, 1988)* Chandos ▲ CHAN 7038
Elgar, E.:Enigma Vars Chandos ▲ CHAN 8610 [DDD]
Elgar, E.:Froissart *(rec St Jude's Church, Apr 9, 1991)* Chandos ▲ CHAN 7038
Elgar, E.:Grania & Diarmid, w. Jenny Miller (sop) Chandos ▲ CHAN 8610 [DDD]
Elgar, E.:Grania & Diarmid, w. Jenny Miller (sop) *(rec All Saints' Church, Jan 18–19, 1988)* Chandos ▲ CHAN 7038
Elgar, E.:The Music Makers, w. L. Finnie (mez), London Phil Chorus [E] Chandos ▲ CHAN 9022 [DDD]
Elgar, E.:The Sanguine Fan Chandos ▲ CHAN 8610 [DDD]
Elgar, E.:The Sanguine Fan *(rec All Saints' Church, Jan 18–19, 1988)* Chandos ▲ CHAN 7038
Elgar, E.:Sea Pictures, w. L. Finnie (mez), London Phil Chorus [E] Chandos ▲ CHAN 9022 [DDD]
Elgar, E.:Sym 1 Chandos ▲ CHAN 8451 [DDD]
Elgar, E.:Sym 2 Chandos ▲ CHAN 8452 [DDD]
Glazunov, A.:Chant du ménéstrel, w. R. Wallfisch (vc) Chandos ▲ CHAN 8579 [DDD]
Glazunov, A.:Chant du ménéstrel, w. R. Wallfisch (vc) Chandos ("Collect" series) ▲ CHAN 6552 [DDD]
Ireland, J.:Con Pno, w. E. Parkin (pno) Chandos ▲ CHAN 8461 [DDD]
Ireland, J.:Legend, w. E. Parkin (pno) Chandos ▲ CHAN 8461 [DDD]
Ireland, J.:Mai-Dun Chandos ▲ CHAN 8461 [DDD]
Kabalevsky, D.:Con 2 Vc, w. R. Wallfisch (vc) Chandos ▲ CHAN 8579 [DDD]
Khachaturian, A.:Con Vc, w. R. Wallfisch (vc) Chandos ▲ CHAN 8579 [DDD]
Saint-Saëns, C.:Con 2 Pno, w. I. Margalit (pno) Chandos ▲ CHAN 8546 [DDD]
Schumann, R.:Con Pno, w. I. Margalit (pno) Chandos ▲ CHAN 8546 [DDD]
Seascapes, w. Royal Scottish National Orch [cnd:A. Gibson], Ulster Orch [cnd:V. Handley], Bournemouth Sinfonietta [cnd:G. Hurst] Chandos ("Collect" series) ▲ CHAN 6538 [ADD/DDD]
Vaughan Williams, R.:Dona nobis pacem, w. E. Wiens (sop), B. Rayner Cook (bar), London Phil Chorus [L] Chandos ▲ CHAN 8590 [DDD]
Vaughan Williams, R.:Fant on a Theme by Thomas Tallis Chandos ▲ CHAN 8502 [DDD]
Vaughan Williams, R.:In the Fen Country Chandos ▲ CHAN 8502 [DDD]
Vaughan Williams, R.:Mystical Songs, w. B. Rayner Cook (bar), London Phil Chorus [L] Chandos ▲ CHAN 8590 [DDD]
Vaughan Williams, R.:Norfolk Rhap 1 Chandos ▲ CHAN 8502 [DDD]
Vaughan Williams, R.:Variants of "Dives & Lazarus" Chandos ▲ CHAN 8502 [DDD]
Walton, W.:Capriccio burlesco Chandos ▲ CHAN 8968 [DDD]
Walton, W.:Con Vc, w. R. Wallfisch (vc) Chandos ▲ CHAN 8959 [DDD]
Walton, W.:The First Shoot Chandos ▲ CHAN 8968 [DDD]
Walton, W.:Galop final Chandos ▲ CHAN 8968 [DDD]
Walton, W.:Improvs on an Impromptu of Benjamin Britten Chandos ▲ CHAN 8959 [DDD]
Walton, W.:Johannesburg Festival Ov Chandos ▲ CHAN 8968 [DDD]
Walton, W.:Music for Children Chandos ▲ CHAN 8968 [DDD]
Walton, W.:Partita Chandos ▲ CHAN 8959 [DDD]
Walton, W.:Portsmouth Point Chandos ▲ CHAN 8968 [DDD]
Walton, W.:Prelude Chandos ▲ CHAN 8968 [DDD]
Walton, W.:Prologo e Fant Chandos ▲ CHAN 8968 [DDD]
Walton, W.:The Quest Chandos ▲ CHAN 8871 [DDD]
Walton, W.:Scapino Chandos ▲ CHAN 8968 [DDD]
Walton, W.:Siesta Chandos ▲ CHAN 9148 [DDD]
Walton, W.:Sym 1 Chandos ▲ CHAN 8862 [DDD]
Walton, W.:Sym 2 Chandos ▲ CHAN 8772 [DDD]

▲ = CD ♦ = Enhanced CD Δ = MD ■ = Cassette Tape □ = DCC

London PO (cont.)
B. Thomson (cnd) (cont.)
Walton, W.:Troilus & Cressida (suite) Chandos ▲ CHAN 8772 [DDD]
Walton, W.:Varii Capricci Chandos ▲ CHAN 8862 [DDD]
Walton, W.:The Wise Virgins Chandos ▲ CHAN 8871 [DDD]
B. Thomson, R. Hickox (cnds)
Walton, W.:Music of, w. Academy of St. Martin in the Fields, Finzi Singers Chandos 23-▲ CHAN 9426 [DDD]
B. Walter (cnd)
Beethoven, L. van:Sym 9, "Choral Sym", w. London Phil Chorus [G] *(rec live, Royal Albert Hall, London Nov. 13, 1947)* Music & Arts ▲ CD 733 [AAD]
Corelli, A.:Con grosso, Op. 6/8, "Christmas Con" *(rec 1938–42)* Phonographe ▲ PHG CD 5028
F. von Weingartner (cnd)
Beethoven, L. van:Dances Orch—Viennese Dances *(rec 1938)* Pearl ▲ PEA 9407 (m) [AAD]
Beethoven, L. van:Die Geschöpfe des Prometheus (ov) *(rec ca. 1932/33 for Columbia)* Music Memoria ▲ 30378
Beethoven, L. van:Sym 4 *(rec ca. 1932/33 for Columbia)* Music Memoria ▲ 30378
Beethoven, L. van:Sym 5 *(rec ca. 1932/33 for Columbia)* Music Memoria ▲ 30378
F. Welser-Möst (cnd)
Bartók, B.:Dance Suite, w. London Phil Chorus EMI Classics ▲ CDC 54858
Bartók, B.:The Miraculous Mandarin, w. London Phil Chorus EMI Classics ▲ CDC 54858
Bruckner, A.:Sym 5 *(rec May & June 1993)* EMI Classics ▲ CDC 55125
Bruckner, A.:Sym 7 EMI Classics ▲ CDC 54434 ▯ 0777-7-54434-5
Kancheli, G.:Sym 3, w. David James (ct) EMI Classics ▲ CDC 55619
Kodály, Z.:Vars on a Hungarian Folk Song, w. London Phil Chorus EMI Classics ▲ CDC 54858
Lehár, F.:Die lustige Witwe, w. F. Lott (sop), E. Szmytka (sop), J. Aler (ten), T. Hampson (b-bar), D. Bogarde (nar), Glyndebourne Festival Chorus EMI Classics ▲ CDCB 55152
Mendelssohn, F.:Sym 3 EMI Classics ▲ CDC 54263
Mendelssohn, F.:Sym 4 EMI Classics ▲ CDC 54263
Mozart, W.A.:Requiem, w. F. Lott (sop), D. Jones (mez), K. Lewis (ten), W. White (bar), London Phil Chorus EMI Classics ▲ CDM 63260
Mozart, W.A.:Requiem, w. Felicity Lott (sop), Cella Jones (mez), Keith Lewis (ten), Willard White (bass), David Bell (org), London Phil Choir Classics for Pleasure ("Eminence" series) ▲ CDEMX 2150 [DDD]
Operatic Arias, w. Amanda Roocroft (sop) EMI Classics ▲ CDC 55090
Orff, C.:Carmina burana, w. B. Hendricks (sop), M. Chance (ct), J. Black (bar), London Phil Chorus, St. Alban's Cathedral Choristers [G, L] EMI Classics ▲ CDC 54054 [DDD]
Pärt, A.:Fratres I [arr Pärt for strs & perc, 1991] EMI Classics ▲ CDC 55619
Pärt, A.:Sym 3 EMI Classics ▲ CDC 55619
Schumann, R.:Sym 2 EMI Classics ▲ CDC 54898
Schumann, R.:Sym 3 EMI Classics ▲ CDC 54898
Stravinsky, I.:Oedipus Rex, w. M. Lipovsek (mez), A. Rolfe-Johnson (ten), J. Tomlinson (bass), London Phil Chorus EMI Classics ▲ CDC 54445
Stravinsky, I.:Syms Ww EMI Classics ▲ CDC 55030
D. Willcocks (cnd)
Vaughan Williams, R.:Epithalamion, w. S. Roberts (b-bar), H. Shelley (pno), Bach Choir EMI Classics ▲ CDM 64730
H. Wood (cnd)
Franck, C.:Symphonic Vars, w. Walter Gieseking (pno) *(rec London, Oct 31, 1932)* APR ▲ APR 5513 [ADD]
Liszt, F.:Con 1 Pno, w. Walter Gieseking (pno) *(rec London, Oct 31, 1932)* APR ▲ APR 5513 [ADD]
Liszt, F.:Con 1 Pno, w. Walter Gieseking (pno) *(rec London, 10/31/32 for Columbia)* The Classical Collector ▲ FDC 2008 [AAD]
Sir H. J. Wood Conducts Proms Favourites, w. Queen's Hall Orch, British SO, London SO *(rec between Nov. 1929 & March)* Dutton Laboratories ▲ DUT 8008 [ADD]
B. Wordsworth (cnd)
Foulds, J.:April–England Lyrita ▲ SRCD 212
Foulds, J.:Le Cabaret Lyrita ▲ SRCD 212
Foulds, J.:Hellas Suite Lyrita ▲ SRCD 212
Foulds, J.:Mantras (3) Lyrita ▲ SRCD 212
Foulds, J.:Pasquinade Symphonique 1 Lyrita ▲ SRCD 212
Foulds, J.:Symphonique 2 Lyrita ▲ SRCD 212
B. Wright (cnd)
Milà, L.:Tirant lo blanc Regis Tro ▲ RTAC 005 [DDD]
T. Yuasa (cnd)
Prokofiev, S.:Lt Kijé Suite Classics for Pleasure ("Eminence" series) ▲ CFP 2214 [DDD]
Rimsky-Korsakov, N.:Scheherazade Classics for Pleasure ("Eminence" series) ▲ CFP 2214 [DDD]
London PO Festival Orch
V. de Stradelli (cnd)
Rimsky-Korsakov, N.:Scheherazade Vivace ▲ E 528
Tchaikovsky, P.:Sym 6 Vivace 3-▲ E 321 [DDD]
Tchaikovsky, P.:Sym 6 Vivace ▲ 588 [DDD]
Weber, C.M. von:Ovs—Oberon Vivace ▲ E 528
London PO members
Dove (cnd)
Glyndebourne Wind Serenades, w. Orch of the Age of Enlightenment members EMI Classics ▲ CDC 54424
London Phil SO
E. Leinsdorf (cnd)
Haydn, M.:Sym in G, P.16 MCA Classics 2-▲ MCAD2-9818 (m/s)
Mozart, W.A.:Syms (comp)—Nos. 1–15 MCA Classics 2-▲ MCAD2-9808 (m) [AAD]
Mozart, W.A.:Syms (comp)—Nos. 16–26 MCA Classics 2-▲ MCAD2-9812 [AAD]
Mozart, W.A.:Syms (comp)—Nos. 36 & 38–41 MCA Classics 2-▲ MCAD2-9818 (m/s)
Mozart, W.A.:Syms (comp)—Nos. 27–35 MCA Classics 2-▲ MCAD2-9814 (m) [AAD]
A. Rodzinski (cnd)
Beethoven, L. van:Sym 5 MCA Classics 2-▲ MCAD2-9806
Tchaikovsky, P.:The Nutcracker MCA Classics 2-▲ MCAD2-9801
H. Scherchen (cnd)
Beethoven, L. van:Leonore 1 *(rec 1951, 1954 & 1960)* Enterprise ("Palladio" series) ▲ ENTPD 4175 [ADD]
Beethoven, L. van:Leonore 2 Enterprise ("Palladio" series) ▲ ENTPD 4175 [ADD]
Beethoven, L. van:Syms (comp), w. Vienna State Opera Orch—Syms. 3, 4, 6 & 7 Enterprise ("Palladio" series) ▲ ENT PD 4144 [ADD]
Beethoven, L. van:Syms (comp)—Syms. 5 & 8 Enterprise ("Palladio" series) ▲ ENTPD 4175 [ADD]
Beethoven, L. van:Sym 8 MCA Classics 2-▲ MCAD2-9802
Mahler, G.:Sym 1 MCA Classics ("Double Decker" series) 2-▲ MCAD2-99833 [AAD]
Mahler, G.:Sym 1 *(rec 1958)* Enterprise ("Palladio" series) ▲ ENTPD 4180 [ADD]
Mahler, G.:Sym 2, w. M. Coertse (sop), L. West (alt), Vienna Academy Chorus MCA Classics ("Double Decker" series) 2-▲ MCAD2-99833 [AAD]
London Philomusica Antique
G. Guest (cnd)
Bononcini, A.:Stabat Mater, w. Felicity Palmer (sop), Paul Esswood (ct), Philip Langridge (ten), Christopher Keyte (bass), John Scott (org), John Willison (vn), Chris Wellington (va), Don McVeigh (va), St. John's College Choir Cambridge *(rec 1977)* London 2-▲ 443868-2 [ADD]
Caldara, A.:Crucifixus, w. Felicity Palmer (sop), Paul Esswood (ct), Philip Langridge (ten), Christopher Keyte (bass), John Scott (org), John Willison (vn), Chris Wellington (va), Don McVeigh (va), St. John's College Choir Cambridge *(rec 1977)* London 2-▲ 443868-2 [ADD]
Lotti, A.:Crucifixus, w. Felicity Palmer (sop), Paul Esswood (ct), Philip Langridge (ten), Christopher Keyte (bass), John Scott (org), John Willison (vn), Chris Wellington (va), Don McVeigh (va), St. John's College Choir Cambridge *(rec 1977)* London 2-▲ 443868-2 [ADD]

London Pops Orch
F. Fennell (cnd)
Coates, E.:Calling All Workers *(rec July 19, 1965)* Mercury Living Presence ▲ 434330-2
Coates, E.:The Three Elizabeths *(rec July 19, 1965)* Mercury Living Presence ▲ 434330-2
Frederick Fennell Conducts Carousel Waltz & Other Orchestral Favorites, w. Eastman Rochester Pops Mercury Living Presence ▲ 434256-2
London Pro Musica
Gentil Madonna:Popular Music of the Italian Renaissance Carlton ("Musick's Monument" series) ▲ MSK 6500082
B. Thomas (cnd)
A Florentine Carnival:Festival Music for Lorenzo de Medici IMP Classics ("Masters" series) ▲ PCD 825 [DDD]
London Promenade Orch
A. Faris (cnd)
Ketèlbey, A.W.:Music of Philips ▲ 400011-2
London Royal Promenade CO
A. Dorati (cnd)
Handel, G.F.:Music of, w. N. Simpson, Smithsonian Concerto Grosso, Univ of Maryland Chorus—Royal Fireworks Music; Water Music Suite; Messiah (sels.); etc. Pro Arte ▲ CDM 810; ■ PCD 810
London Royal Promenade Orch
S. Comissiona (cnd)
Tchaikovsky, P.:Music of, w. Houston SO—Capriccio italien; The Nutcracker (selections); Overture 1812; etc. Pro Arte ▲ CDM 809 ■ PCD 809
A. Gerhardt (cnd)
Grieg, E.:Music of, w. J. Silverstein (vn), Russell Sherman (pno), Utah SO—Peer Gynt Suites 1 & 2; Holberg Suite; Piano Concerto (1st movt.) Pro Arte ▲ CDM 811; ■ PCD 811
Strauss (II), Joh.:Music of Pro Arte ▲ CDM 808
World's Greatest Overtures, w. Utah SO Pro Arte ▲ CDM 813 ■ PCD 813
London Salon Ensemble
The Palm Court:Music from the Age of Romance & Elegance Meridian ▲ 84264 [DDD]
A. Reynolds (cnd)
Music for the Theatre, w. Miranda Keys (sop), Donald Maxwell (bar) Meridian ▲ MER 84308 [DDD]
London Serenata
B. Wilde (cnd)
Purcell, H.:Music of—Suite [from Dido & Aeneas]; Chaconne [from The Fairy Queen]; Fants; In Nomines; Suite for Strs [arr Barbirolli] IMP ("Classics" series) ▲ IMP 6700032
London Sinfonietta
Lerner, A.J.:Brigadoon, w. J. McGlinn (sgr), Ambrosian Chorus [1992 studio cast] Broadway Angel ▲ CDQ 54481 ■ 4DQ 54481
J. Adams (cnd)
Adams, J.:Chamber Sym Elektra/Nonesuch ▲ 79219-2 ■ 79219-4
D. Atherton (cnd)
Revueltas, S.:Alcancias Catalyst ▲ 09026-62672-2
Revueltas, S.:Ocho X Radio [2 versions] Catalyst ▲ 09026-62672-2
Revueltas, S.:Planos Catalyst ▲ 09026-62672-2
Revueltas, S.:Toccata [2 versions] Catalyst ▲ 09026-62672-2
Tippett, M.:The Ice Break, w. H. Harper (sop), S. Sylvan (bar), D. Wilson-Johnson (bar), London Sym Chorus [E] Virgin Classics ▲ 59048 [DDD]
Tippett, M.:King Priam, w. Heather Harper (sop—Hecuba), Linda Hirst (sop—Serving Woman), Felicity Palmer (sop—Andromache), Julian Saipe (sop—Paris), Yvonne Minton (mez—Helen), Ann Murray (mez—Nurse), Kenneth Bowen (ten—Hermes), Peter Hall (ten—Young Guard), Philip Langridge (ten—Paris), Robert Tear (ten—Achilles), Thomas Allen (bar—Hector), Norman Bailey (bar—Priam), Stephen Roberts (bar—Patroclus), David Wilson-Johnson (bar—Old Man), London Sinfonietta Chorus Chandos ▲ CHAN 9406/7 [DDD]
G. Benjamin (cnd)
Benjamin, G.:Antara Nimbus ▲ NI 5167 [DDD]
Benjamin, G.:At First Light Nimbus ▲ NI 5075 [DDD]
Benjamin, G.:A Mind of Winter Nimbus ▲ NI 5075 [DDD]
Boulez, P.:Derivé Nimbus ▲ NI 5167 [DDD]
Boulez, P.:Mémoriale Nimbus ▲ NI 5167 [DDD]
Harvey, J.:Song Offerings, w. Penelope Walmsley-Clark (sop) Nimbus ▲ NI 5167 [DDD]
L. Berio (cnd)
Berio, L.:Folk Songs Mez, w. Cathy Berberian (mez), Juilliard Ensemble RCA Gold Seal ▲ 09026-62540-2
Weill, K.:Songs, w. Cathy Berberian (mez), Juilliard Ensemble—3 songs [arr. Berio] RCA Gold Seal ▲ 09026-62540-2
B. Broughton (cnd)
Rózsa, M.:Ivanhoo Intrada ▲ ITD 7055 [DDD]
R. Chailly (cnd)
Stravinsky, I.:Divert Orch London ("Enterprise" series) ▲ 433079-2 [ADD]
Stravinsky, I.:Octet London ("Enterprise" series) ▲ 433079-2 [ADD]
Stravinsky, I.:Suites Orch London ("Enterprise" series) ▲ 433079-2 [ADD]
C. Dutoit (cnd)
Saint-Saëns, C.:Carnival of the Animals, w. P. Rogé (pno), C. Ortiz (pno) London ▲ 430720-2 [DDD]
Saint-Saëns, C.:Carnival of the Animals, w. P. Rogé (pno), C. Ortiz (pno) London ▲ 414460-2 [ADD] ■ 414460-4
T. Edwards (cnd)
Messiaen, O.:O sacrum convivium!, w. London Sym Chorus Virgin Classics ▲ CDC 59051
Messiaen, O.:Petites liturgies (3) de la Présence Divine, w. London Sym Chorus Virgin Classics ▲ CDC 59051
Messiaen, O.:Rechants, w. London Sym Chorus Virgin Classics ▲ CDC 59051
H.K. Gruber (cnd)
Gruber, H.K.:Con 1 Vn, w. E. Kovacic (vn) *(rec Apr. 29, 1993)* Largo ▲ 5124 [DDD]
Gruber, H.K.:Revue—Movt 1, "Der rote Teppich wird ausgerollt [The Red Carpet Will Be Rolled Out]" *(rec Apr. 29, 1993)* Largo ▲ 5124 [DDD]
R. Hickox (cnd)
Guy, B.:After the Rain NMC ▲ NMC 13 [DDD]
Poulenc, F.:Gloria Sop, w. C. Dubosc (sop), Westminster Singers Virgin Classics ▲ CDC 59286
Poulenc, F.:Litanies à la vierge noire, w. Westminster Singers Virgin Classics ▲ CDC 59286
Poulenc, F.:Stabat mater, w. C. Dubosc (sop), Westminster Singers Virgin Classics ▲ CDC 59286
E. Howarth (cnd)
Copland, A.:Music for Movies *(rec Rosslyn Hill, London, 1980)* London 2-▲ 448261-2 [ADD]
Rodby, J.:Con Sax, w. H. Pittel (sax) Crystal ■ C500
Rodby, J.:Festivals Crystal ■ C500
Rodby, J.:Vars Crystal ■ C500
O. Knussen (cnd)
Abrahamsen, H.:Walden *(rec St John's, Smith Square, London, Dec 1984)* Paula ▲ PACD 37 [DDD]
Abrahamsen, H.:Winternacht *(rec St John's, Smith Square, London, Dec 1984)* Paula ▲ PACD 37 [DDD]
Birtwistle, H.:Melencolia I, w. A. Pay (cl), *(not advised of hp)* NM Classics ▲ NMCD 009 [DDD]
Birtwistle, H.:Meridian, w. M. King (mez), London Sinfonietta Chorus NM Classics ▲ NMCD 009 [DDD]
Birtwistle, H.:Ritual Fragment NM Classics ▲ NMCD 009 [DDD]
Britten, B.:Prelude & Fugue Strs Virgin Classics 2-▲ 59578 [DDD]
Carter, E.:Con Orch Virgin Classics ▲ CDC 59271
Carter, E.:Con Vn, w. O. Böhn (vn) Virgin Classics ▲ CDC 59271
Carter, E.:In Sleep, In Thunder, w. M. Hill (ten) [E] Elektra/Nonesuch ■ 79110-4 (D)
Carter, E.:In Sleep, In Thunder, w. Martyn Hill (ten) Wergo ▲ WER 6278-2
Carter, E.:Three Occasions Virgin Classics ▲ CDC 59271

ORCH. & ENS.

London Sinfonietta (cont.)
O. Knussen (cnd) (cont.)
Goehr, A.:Con Pno, w. Peter Serkin (pno) NMC ▲ NMC 23 [DDD]
Knussen, O.:Con Hn, w. Barry Tuckwell (hn) *(rec Henry Wood Hall & All Hollows Gospel Oak, London, Oct & Dec 1995)* Deutsche Grammophon ▲ 449 572-2 [DDD]
Knussen, O.:Flourish with Fireworks (ov) *(rec Henry Wood Hall & All Hollows Gospel Oak, London, Oct & Dec 1995)* Deutsche Grammophon ▲ 449 572-2 [DDD]
Knussen, O.:Music for a Puppet Court *(rec Henry Wood Hall & All Hollows Gospel Oak, London, Oct & Dec 1995)* Deutsche Grammophon ▲ 449 572-2 [DDD]
Knussen, O.:Organa *(rec Henry Wood Hall & All Hollows Gospel Oak, London, Oct & Dec 1995)* Deutsche Grammophon ▲ 449 572-2 [DDD]
Knussen, O.:The Way to Castle Yonder *(rec Henry Wood Hall & All Hollows Gospel Oak, London, Oct & Dec 1995)* Deutsche Grammophon ▲ 449 572-2 [DDD]
Knussen, O.:Where The Wild Things Are, w. R. Hardy (sop), M. King (mez) [E] Arabesque ▲ Z 6535 [DDD]
Knussen, O.:Whitman Settings Sop & Orch, Op. 25a, w. Lucy Shelton (sop) *(rec Henry Wood Hall & All Hollows Gospel Oak, London, Oct & Dec 1995)* Deutsche Grammophon ▲ 449 572-2 [DDD]
Matthews, C.:Broken Symmetry *(rec Henry Wood Hall, London, England, Oct 1994)* Deutsche Grammophon ▲ 447067-2 [DDD]
Matthews, C.:Son 4 Orch *(rec Henry Wood Hall, London, England, Oct 1994)* Deutsche Grammophon ▲ 447067-2 [DDD]
Ruders, P.:Compositions *(rec St Luke's, Kiddapore Ave, London, Dec 1984)* Paula ▲ PACD 37 [DDD]
Stravinsky, I.:Abraham & Isaac, w. New London Chamber Choir Deutsche Grammophon ▲ 447068-2
Stravinsky, I.:The Flood, w. New London Chamber Choir Deutsche Grammophon ▲ 447068-2
Stravinsky, I.:Requiem Canticles, w. New London Chamber Choir Deutsche Grammophon ▲ 447068-2
Stravinsky, I.:Vars Orch Deutsche Grammophon ▲ 447068-2
Takemitsu, T.:Rain Coming, w. S. Bell (fl) Virgin Classics ▲ CDC 59020
Takemitsu, T.:riverrun, w. P. Crossley (pno) Virgin Classics ▲ CDC 59020
Takemitsu, T.:Tree Line, w. G. Hulse (ob) Virgin Classics ▲ CDC 59020
Takemitsu, T.:Waterways Virgin Classics ▲ CDC 59020
Wuorinen, C.:A Reliquary for Igor Stravinsky, w. New London Chamber Choir Deutsche Grammophon ▲ 447068-2

N. Kraemer (cnd)
Vivaldi, A.:Cons Vc, w. Raphael Wallfisch (vc)—in E♭, RV.408; in g, RV.531; in G, RV.413; in c, RV.401; in a, RV.422; in C, RV.400 *(rec All Saints Church, East Finchley & Conway Hall, London, Apr., May & Sept. 1994)* Naxos ("Vivaldi Collection" series) ▲ 8.550908 [DDD]
Vivaldi, A.:Cons Vc, w. Raphael Wallfisch (vc)—in F, RV.412; in a, RV.419; in D, RV.404; in C, RV.399; in d, RV.406; in C, RV.398; in F, RV.410 *(rec Conway Hall, London, Apr. 1994)* Naxos ("Vivaldi Collection" series) ▲ 8.550907 [DDD]
Vivaldi, A.:Cons Vc, w. Raphael Wallfisch (vc)—in g, RV.416; in F, RV.411; in d, RV.405; in a, RV.420; in G, RV.414; in g, RV.417; in a, RV.421 *(rec All Saints Church, East Finchley & Conway Hall, London, Apr., May & Sept. 1994)* Naxos ("Vivaldi Collection" series) ▲ 8.550910 [DDD]
Vivaldi, A.:Cons Vc, w. Raphael Wallfisch (vc)—in B♭, RV.423; in c, RV.402; in a, RV.418; in D, RV.403; in b, RV.424; in d, RV.407; in e, RV.409 *(rec All Saints Church, East Finchley & Conway Hall, London, Apr., May & Sept. 1994)* Naxos ("Vivaldi Collection" series) ▲ 8.550909 [DDD]
Vivaldi, A.:Cons Diverse Instrs, w. Joanna Graham (bn), Ruth McDowall (cl), David Rix (ct), Deborah Davis (fl), Duke Dobing (fl), Tim Caister (hn), Stephen Stirling (hn), Christopher Hooker (ob), Helen McQueen (ob), Michael Meekes (tpt), Crispian Steele-Perkins (tpt), Nicholas Kraemer (hpd)—Cons. in F, RV.539; in C, RV.533; in D, RV.122; in C, RV.537; in C, RV.560; in F, RV.538; in G, RV.545 *(rec All Saints Church, East Finchley, Oct. 1994 & Jan. 1995)* Naxos ("Vivaldi Collection" series) ▲ 8.553204 [DDD]

R.H. Lewis (cnd)
Lewis, R.H.:Con CO *(rec 1980)* CRI ▲ CD 596 [ADD]
J. McGlinn (cnd)
Kern, J.:Music of, w. K. Te Kanawa (sop) Angel ▲ CDQ 54527 ■ 4DQ 54527
Kern, J.:Show Boat, w. F. von Stade (mez), T. Stratas (sop), J. Hadley (ten), B. Hubbard (bar), P. O'Hara (sgr), K. Burns (mez), N. Kulp (sgr), Ambrosian Chorus [original orchd Robert Russell Bennett]—also includes 45 minutes of music intended for the original performance but never included, plus music from revivals and films [1988 studio cast] Angel 3-▲ A23 49108 [DDD]
Kern, J.:Show Boat, w. P. O'Hara (sop), T. Stratas (sop), K. Burns (mez), F. von Stade (mez), D. Garrison (ten), J. Hadley (ten), B. Hubbard (bar), Ambrosian Opera Chorus, Ambrosian Singers EMI Classics 3-▲ A23 49108
Kern, J.:Show Boat, w. P. O'Hara (sop), T. Stratas (sop), K. Burns (mez), F. von Stade (mez), D. Garrison (ten), J. Hadley (ten), B. Hubbard (bar), Ambrosian Opera Chorus EMI Classics ▲ ZDC 49847
Kiri Sings Kern, w. Kiri Te Kanawa (sop) Angel ▲ CDQ 54527 ■ 4DQ 54527
The Lorelei, w. Kim Criswell (sop) Angel ▲ CDC 54802
D. Mason (cnd)
Mason, B.:Double Con, w. M. Thompson (hn), D. Purser (trbn) Bridge ▲ BCD 9045 [DDD]
D. Miller (cnd)
Torke, M.:Music of, w. M. Torke (pno)—The Yellow Pages (1985); Adjustable Wrench; Rust; Slate; Vanada Argo ▲ 430209-2 [DDD]
K. Nagano (cnd)
Torke, M.:Adjustable Wrench *(rec CBS Studio 1, London, England, Nov 9-13, 1989)* Argo ▲ 452101-2 [DDD]
S. Rattle (cnd)
Gershwin, G.:Rhap in Blue, w. P. Donohoe (pno) EMI Classics ▲ CDC 54280
E.-P. Salonen (cnd)
Hindemith, P.:Kammermusik 3, w. A. Karttunen (vc) *(rec May 8-10, 1990)* Finlandia ▲ 4509-95865-2 [DDD]
Lindberg, M.:Zona, w. A. Karttunen (vc) *(rec May 8-10, 1990)* Finlandia ▲ 4509-95865-2 [DDD]
Merikanto, A.:Concert Piece Vc, w. A. Karttunen (vc) *(rec May 8-10, 1990)* Finlandia ▲ 4509-95865-2 [DDD]
Messiaen, O.:Des Canyons aux étoiles, w. P. Crossley (pno)—sels. Sony Classical ▲ SMK 53473
Messiaen, O.:Des Canyons aux étoiles CBS 2-▲ M2K 44762 [DDD]
Messiaen, O.:Couleurs de la cité céleste CBS 2-▲ M2K 44762 [DDD]
Messiaen, O.:Oiseaux exotiques CBS 2-▲ M2K 44762 [DDD]
Stravinsky, I.:Cant Sop, w. Y. Kenny (sop), J. Aler (ten), London Sinfonietta Chorus Sony Classical ▲ SK 46667
Stravinsky, I.:Capriccio, w. P. Crossley (pno) [1949 version] Sony Classical ▲ SK 45797 [DDD]
Stravinsky, I.:Con Pno Ww, w. P. Crossley (pno) [1950 version] Sony Classical ▲ SK 45797 [DDD]
Stravinsky, I.:Movts Pno, w. P. Crossley (pno) Sony Classical ▲ SK 45797 [DDD]
Stravinsky, I.:Octet Sony Classical ▲ SK 45965
Stravinsky, I.:Pulcinella, w. Y. Kenny (sop), J. Aler (ten), J. Tomlinson (bass) Sony Classical ▲ SK 45965
Stravinsky, I.:Ragtime Sony Classical ▲ SK 45965
Stravinsky, I.:Renard, w. J. Aler (ten), N. Robson (ten), D. Wilson-Johnson (bar), J. Tomlinson (bass) Sony Classical ▲ SK 45965
Stravinsky, I.:Syms Ww [1947 version] Sony Classical ▲ SK 45797 [DDD]
Takemitsu, T.:Music of, w. J. Williams (gtr), S. Bell (fl), G. Hulse (ob)—To the Edge of Dream (for Guitar & Orchestra); Vers, L'arc-en-ciel, Palma (for Guitar & Oboe); Toward the Sea (for Alto Flute & Guitar); Folios (for solo Guitar); 12 Songs for Guitar (selections) Sony Classical ▲ SK 46720
Takemitsu, T.:Music of, w. J. Williams (gtr)—Vers, l'arc-en-ceil, Palma for Guitar, Oboe & Orch.; To the Edge of Dream for Guitar & Orch. Sony Classical ▲ SMK 53473
R. Shapey (cnd)
Shapey, R.:Rituals CRI ▲ CD 690 [ADD]
M. Tilson Thomas (cnd)
Bainbridge, S.:Con Va, w. W. Trampler (va) Continuum ▲ CCD 1020
L. Zagrosek (cnd)
Torke, M.:Music on the Floor (II) *(rec Studio 1, Hit Factory, London, England, Dec 11-13, 1992)* Argo ▲ 452101-2 [DDD]

London Sinfonietta (cont.)
D. Zinman (cnd)
Górecki, H.-M.:Sym 3, "Sym of Sorrowful Songs", w. D. Upshaw (sop) Elektra/Nonesuch ▲ 79282-2 ■ 79282-4

London Sinfonietta National PO
J. McGlinn (cnd)
Gershwin, G.:Ovs, w. New Princess Theater Orch, Ambrosian Opera Chorus—A Damsel in Distress; Girl Crazy; Of Thee I Sing; Tip-Toes; Primrose; Stiff Upper Lip; Oh, Kay! EMI Classics ("Doublefforte" series) 2-▲ CDFB 68589
Kern, J.:Songs, w. New Princess Theater Orch—The Cat and the Fiddle; The Girl from Utah; Leave It to Jane; Have a Heart; Sweet Adeline; O, Lady! Lady!; Sitting Pretty; Very Warm for May; Swing Time; Show Boat EMI Classics ("Doublefforte" series) 2-▲ CDFB 68589
Porter, C.:Songs, w. New Princess Theater Orch—Anything Goes; Can-Can; Kiss Me Kate; Gay Divorce; Night & Day EMI Classics ("Doublefforte" series) 2-▲ CDFB 68589
London String Orch
J. Barbirolli (cnd)
Arensky, A.:Vars on a Theme of Tchaikovsky EMI Classics 2-▲ CDFB 69361
L. Gardelli (cnd)
Respighi, O.:Belfagor Ov EMI Classics 2-▲ CDFB 69358
Respighi, O.:The Fountains of Rome EMI Classics 2-▲ CDFB 69358
Respighi, O.:The Pines of Rome EMI Classics 2-▲ CDFB 69358
London String Quartet
Vaughan Williams, R.:On Wenlock Edge, w. G. Elwes (ten), F.B. Kiddle (pno) [E] *(rec 1917 for Columbia)* Opal ▲ CD 9844 (m) [AAD]

London Strings
N. Marriner (cnd)
Bach, J.S.:Brandenburg Con 2, w. H.-M. Linde (fl), N. Marriner (vn), I. Kipnis (hpd) CBS ■ MGT 39802
Bach, J.S.:Brandenburg Con 5, w. H.-M. Linde (fl), N. Marriner (vn), I. Kipnis (hpd) CBS ■ MGT 39802
Bach, J.S.:Cons Hpd, BWV 1052-1058, w. I. Kipnis (hpd), Jeanne Dolmetsch (rcr), Marguerite Dolmetsch (rcr)—BWV 1057 *(rec 1967-1970)* Sony Classical 2-▲ SB2K 53243 [ADD]
Bach, J.S.:Cons Hpd, BWV 1052-1058, w. I. Kipnis (hpd)—Nos. 1-5 CBS ■ MGT 39801
Bach, J.S.:Cons Hpd, BWV 1052-1058, w. I. Kipnis (hpd) Odyssey 2-▲ MB2K 45616
Bach, J.S.:Con 8 Hpd, w. I. Kipnis (hpd) [reconstr. I. Kipnis] CBS ■ MGT 39802
Bach, J.S.:Con 8 Hpd, w. I. Kipnis (hpd), Janet Craxton (obligatto ob) *(rec 1967-1970)* Sony Classical 2-▲ SB2K 53243 [ADD]

London Studio SO
Herrmann, B.:North by Northwest Varése Sarabande ▲ VSD 47205
Herrmann, B.:North by Northwest, w. *(artists unknown)* Unicorn-Kanchana ▲ UKCD 2040
M. Viotti (cnd)
With a Song in My Heart:A Tribute to Mario Lanza, w. José Carreras (ten) Teldec ▲ 92369-2 ■ 92369-4

L. Johnson (cnd)
Herrmann, B.:North by Northwest—Suite Unicorn-Kanchana ▲ 2080
Johnson, Laurie:Music of, w. W. Davies (org), London PO, London Jazz Orch, Coldstream Guards Regimental Band, Fanfare Trumpeters of the Scots Guards, London Brass Chorale—Royal Tour (suite); Symphony (Synthesis) for Combined Jazz & Symphony Orchestras (1969); Three Paintings by Lautrec; The Wind In the Willows (1985) *(rec 1969-82)* Unicorn-Kanchana ▲ UKCD 2057 [DDD/ADD]
Tiomkin, D.:Film Music, w. John McCarthy Singers—Duel in the Sun; Giant; High Noon; Night Passage; Red River; Rio Bravo Unicorn ("Souvenir" series) ▲ UKCD 2011 [DDD]
L. Schifrin (cnd)
Shifrin, L.:Voyage of the Damned Label "X" ▲ LXCD 11 [AAD]
London Symphonica
W. Morris (cnd)
Beethoven, L. van:Con 2 Pno, w. Charles Rosen (pno) IMP ("Classics" series) ▲ IMP 6700162
Beethoven, L. van:Con 4 Pno, w. Charles Rosen (pno) IMP ("Classics" series) ▲ IMP 6700162
Debussy, C.:La Damoiselle élue, w. M. Caballé (sop) [F] IMP Classics ▲ IMP PCD 1037 [DDD]
Mahler, G.:Des Knaben Wunderhorn, w. Janet Baker (mez), Geraint Evans (bar), Roland Hermann (bar), London PO IMP ▲ PCD 2020
Mahler, G.:Lieder eines fahrenden Gesellen, w. Janet Baker (mez), Geraint Evans (bar), Roland Hermann (bar), London PO IMP ▲ PCD 2020
London Sym Brass
E. Crees (cnd)
London Symphony Brass Collins Classics ▲ COL 1288 [DDD]
London SO
Bach, J.S.:Con 1 Vn, w. I. Stern (vn) CBS ▲ MK 42258
The Broadway I Love, w. Plácido Domingo (ten) Atlantic ▲ 82350-2 ■ 82350-4
The Cinema Classics Collection, Vol. 1, w. David Buechner (pno), Angeles String Quartet, New Zealand SO, Phoenix SO Koch International Classics ▲ KIC 7604
Flute Salad, w. Laura Gilbert (fl), Alexa Still (fl), Doriot Dwyer (fl), Bradley Garner (fl), New Zealand CO Koch Schwann ▲ KIC CD 7602
Miaskovsky, N.:Con Vc, w. J. Lloyd Webber (vc), M. Shostakovich (pno) Philips ▲ 434106-2 [DDD]
Music for Ceremonial Occasions, w. Westminster Abbey Choir, D. Hill (org), Francis Jackson (org) Pickwick ("The Orchid" series) ▲ PICORCD 11016
Popular Overtures, w. Barry Tuckwell (cnd), Hallé Orch [cnd:S. Skrowaczewski], Royal PO [cnd:Kazuhiro Koizumi] Pickwick ("The Orchid" series) ▲ PICORCD 11003
Porter, C.:Anything Goes, w. F. von Stade (mez), J. McGlinn (sgr), K. Criswell (sop), C. Groenendaal (sgr), J. Gilford (sgr), Ambrosian Chorus [original 1934 Broadway version w. original orchestration by Robert Russell Bennett & Hans Spialek] Angel ▲ CDC 49848-2 [DDD]
The Prima Donna Collection Highlights, w. Leontyne Price (sop), RCA Italiana Opera Orch, Philharmonia Orch, New Philharmonia Orch RCA Gold Seal ▲ 09026-62596-2
Schnittke, A.:In Memoriam, w. M. Rostropovich (vc) Sony Classical ▲ SK 48241
Siegmeister, E.:Con Cl, w. J. Brymer (cl), E. Siegmeister (pno) *(rec 1973)* Premier ("Composer" series) ▲ PRCD 1010 [ADD]
Siegmeister, E.:Con Fl, w. P. Lloyd (fl), E. Siegmeister (pno) *(rec 1973)* Premier ("Composer" series) ▲ PRCD 1010 [ADD]
The Very Best of International Pops Vox ("Sketches" series) ▲ ACD 8772 [DDD]
The Very Best of Romantic Favorites Vox ("Sketches" series) ▲ ACD 8771 [DDD]
Wagner, R.:Der Ring des Nibelungen (sels), w. Florence Austral (sop), Frieda Leider (sop), Elsie Suddaby (sop), Göta Ljunberg (sop), Walter Widdop (ten), Horst Laubenthal (ten), Lauritz Melchoir (ten), Friedrich Schorr (bar), Rudolf Bockelmann (b-bar), Ivar Andresen (bass), Emmanuel List (bass) , K. Alwin (cnd), J. Barbirolli (cnd), L. Blech (cnd), A. Coates (cnd), L. Collingwood (cnd), R. Heger (cnd), K. Muck (cnd), et al. Pearl 7-▲ PEA 9137 [ADD]
C. Abbado (cnd)
Bartók, B.:The Miraculous Mandarin Deutsche Grammophon ("Masters" series) ▲ 445501-2 [DDD]
Bizet, G.:Carmen, w. I. Cotrubas (sop), T. Berganza (mez), P. Domingo (ten), S. Milnes (bar), Ambrosian Opera Chorus [F] Deutsche Grammophon 3-▲ 419636-2 [ADD]
Bizet, G.:Carmen (sels), w. Teresa Berganza (mez—Carmen), Plácido Domingo (ten—Don José), John McCarthy (cnd), Patrick Criswell (cnd), Ambrosian Singers, George Watson's College Boys' Chorus—C'est toi? C'est moi Deutsche Grammophon ▲ 447270-2 [ADD] ■ 447 270-4
Bizet, G.:Carmen (sels), w. I. Cotrubas (sop), T. Berganza (mez), P. Domingo (ten), S. Milnes (bar), Ambrosian Opera Chorus [F] Deutsche Grammophon ▲ 435401-2 [ADD]
Brahms, J.:Pno Music (misc), w. Alfred Brendel (pno), H. Holliger (cnd), Berlin PO—Ballades, Op. 10; Cons for Pno Nos. 1 & 2; Sxt-Vars Philips 25-▲ 446920-2
Chopin, F.:Con 1 Pno, w. Martha Argerich (pno) *(rec Walthamstow Town Hall, London, Feb 1968)* Deutsche Grammophon ("The Originals" series) ▲ 449719-2 [ADD]
Granada:The Greatest Hits of Plácido Domingo, w. Plácido Domingo (ten), Los Angeles PO [cnd:C. M. Giulini], Vienna PO [cnd:H. von Karajan], Royal Opera House Orch, Covent Garden [cnd:Z. Mehta], Philharmonia Orch [cnd:Giuseppe Sinopoli] Deutsche Grammophon ▲ 445777-2 ■ 445777-4

228
▲ = CD ♦ = Enhanced CD Δ = MD ■ = Cassette Tape □ = DCC

London SO (cont.)

C. Abbado (cnd) (cont.)

Liszt, F.:Con 1 Pno, w. Martha Argerich (pno) *(rec Walthamstow Town Hall, London, Feb 1968)* Deutsche Grammophon ("The Originals" series) ▲ 449719-2 [ADD]
Mendelssohn, F.:Sym 3 Deutsche Grammophon ("3D Classics" series) ▲ 427810-2 [DDD]
Mendelssohn, F.:Sym 4 Deutsche Grammophon ("3D Classics" series) ▲ 427810-2 [DDD]
Mendelssohn, F.:Sym 4 Deutsche Grammophon ▲ 415974-2 [DDD]
Mendelssohn, F.:Sym 5 Deutsche Grammophon ▲ 415974-2 [DDD]
Mozart, W.A.:Con 20 Pno, w. R. Serkin (pno) Deutsche Grammophon ("3D Classics" series) ▲ 431278-2 [DDD]
Mozart, W.A.:Con 21 Pno, w. Rudolf Serkin (pno) Deutsche Grammophon ("Masters" series) ▲ 445516-2
Mozart, W.A.:Con 21 Pno, w. Peter Serkin (pno) Deutsche Grammophon ("3D Classics" series) ▲ 431278-2 [DDD]
Mozart, W.A.:Con 21 Pno, w. Peter Serkin (pno) Deutsche Grammophon ▲ 410068-2 [DDD]
Mozart, W.A.:Con 22 Pno, w. R. Serkin (pno) Deutsche Grammophon ("3-D Classics" series) ▲ 429978-2 [DDD]
Mozart, W.A.:Con 23 Pno, w. P. Serkin (pno) Deutsche Grammophon ▲ 410068-2 [DDD]
Mozart, W.A.:Con 25 Pno, w. R. Serkin (pno) Deutsche Grammophon ("3-D Classics" series) ▲ 429978-2 [DDD]
Mozart, W.A.:Con 27 Pno, w. Rudolf Serkin (pno) Deutsche Grammophon ("Masters" series) ▲ 445516-2
Mozart, W.A.:Sym 40 Deutsche Grammophon ▲ 429801-2 [ADD]
Mozart, W.A.:Sym 41 Deutsche Grammophon ▲ 429801-2 [ADD]
Mussorgsky, M.:Night RCA Gold Seal ▲ 09026-61354-2 ■ 09026-61354-4
Mussorgsky, M.:Orchestral Music, w. London Sym Chorus—Triumphal March; Scherzo in B♭; Destruction of Sennacherib; Joshua Salammbô—Chorus of Priestesses; Khovanshchina—Prelude & Galitsin's Journey; Oedipus in Athens—Chorus of People in the Temple RCA Gold Seal ▲ 09026-61354-2 ■ 902
Pergolesi, G.B.:Stabat mater, w. M. Marshall (sop), L. Valentini-Terrani (mez) [L] Deutsche Grammophon ▲ 415103-2 [DDD]
Prokofiev, S.:Alexander Nevsky, w. Elena Obraztsova (mez), London Sym Chorus [R] Deutsche Grammophon 3-▲ 435151-2
Prokofiev, S.:Alexander Nevsky, w. Elena Obraztsova (mez), London Sym Chorus Deutsche Grammophon ("The Originals" series) ▲ 447419-2
Prokofiev, S.:Alexander Nevsky, w. Elena Obraztsova (mez), London Sym Chorus [R] Deutsche Grammophon ▲ 419603-2 [DDD]
Rachmaninoff, S.:Con 3 Pno, w. Berman (pno) CBS ▲ MYK 37809 [AAD] ■ MYT 37809
Ravel, M.:Alborada del gracioso Deutsche Grammophon ("Masters" series) ▲ 445519-2 [DDD]
Ravel, M.:Boléro Deutsche Grammophon ▲ 415972-2 [DDD]
Ravel, M.:Boléro Deutsche Grammophon ("Masters" series) ▲ 445519-2 [DDD]
Ravel, M.:Con Pno (left hand), w. M. Béroff (pno) Deutsche Grammophon ▲ 423665-2 [DDD]
Ravel, M.:Con in G Pno, w. M. Argerich (pno) Deutsche Grammophon ▲ 423665-2 [DDD]
Ravel, M.:Daphins et Chloé Deutsche Grammophon ("Masters" series) ▲ 445519-2 [DDD]
Ravel, M.:Fanfare Deutsche Grammophon ▲ 423665-2 [DDD]
Ravel, M.:Ma mère l'oye Orch Deutsche Grammophon ▲ 415972-2 [DDD] □ 415972-5
Ravel, M.:Menuet antique Deutsche Grammophon ▲ 423665-2 [DDD]
Ravel, M.:Pavane pour une infante défunte Deutsche Grammophon ▲ 415972-2 [DDD] □ 415972-5
Ravel, M.:Rapsodie espagnole Deutsche Grammophon ▲ 415972-2 [DDD] □ 415972-5
Ravel, M.:Le Tombeau de Couperin Deutsche Grammophon ▲ 423665-2 [DDD]
Rossini, G.:Il barbiere di Siviglia, w. T. Berganza (mez), L. Alva (ten), H. Prey (bar), P. Montarsolo (bass), London Sym Chorus [I] Deutsche Grammophon 2-▲ 415695-2 [ADD]
Rossini, G.:La Cenerentola, w. T. Berganza (mez), L. Alva (ten), R. Capecchi (bar), U. Trama (bass), London Sym Chorus [I] Deutsche Grammophon 2-▲ 423861-2 [ADD]
Rossini, G.:Ovs—Semiramide, Il barbiere di Siviglia, William Tell, Tancredi, La scala di seta, Il turco in Italia RCA Victor ▲ 09026-61554-2; ■ 09026-61554-4
Rossini, G.:Ovs—Barber of Seville; Scala di seta; Semiramide; Tancredi; Turco in Italia; William Tell RCA Victrola ▲ 7814-2-RV [ADD] ■ 7814-4-RV
Schumann, R.:Con Pno, w. A. Brendel (pno) Philips ▲ 412251-2 [ADD]
Tchaikovsky, P.:Con 1 Pno, w. Ivo Pogorelich (pno) Deutsche Grammophon ▲ 415122-2 [DDD]
Tchaikovsky, P.:Sym 4 *(rec 1972-76)* Deutsche Grammophon ("Double" series) 2-▲ 437401-2
Tchaikovsky, P.:Sym 6 *(rec 1972-76)* Deutsche Grammophon ("Double" series) 2-▲ 437401-2
Verdi, G.:Ovs & Preludes—La forza del destino, I vespri siciliani RCA Victor ▲ 09026-61554-2; ■ 09026-61554-4
Vivaldi, A.:Cons Vn, Op. 8/1-4, "The Four Seasons", w. G. Kremer (vn) Deutsche Grammophon ("Galleria" series) ▲ 431172-2 [ADD]

R. Abbado (cnd)

Hindemith, P.:Symphonic Metamorphosis on Themes of Carl Maria von Weber London ("Enterprise" series) ▲ 433081-2 [ADD]

Y. Ahronovitch (cnd)

Borodin, A.:Prince Igor (Polovtsian dances) IMP Classics ("LSO Classic Masterpieces" series) ▲ IMPPCD 804 [DDD]
Mussorgsky, M.:Night IMP Classics ("LSO Classic Masterpieces" series) ▲ IMPPCD 804 [DDD]
Prokofiev, S.:Lt Kijé Suite IMP Classics ("LSO Classic Masterpieces" series) ▲ IMPPCD 804 [DDD]
Rachmaninoff, S.:Con 1 Pno, w. T. Vásáry (pno) Deutsche Grammophon ■ 415922-2
Rachmaninoff, S.:Con 2 Pno, w. T. Vásáry (pno) Deutsche Grammophon ■ 415922-4
Shostakovich, D.:The Gadfly (suite)—folkfeast IMP Classics ("LSO Classic Masterpieces" series) ▲ IMPPCD 804 [DDD]
Tchaikovsky, P.:Marche slave IMP Classics ("LSO Classic Masterpieces" series) ▲ IMPPCD 801 [DDD]
Tchaikovsky, P.:Ov 1812 IMP ("Concert Classics" series) ▲ IMP PCD 1102
Tchaikovsky, P.:Ov 1812 IMP Classics ("LSO Classic Masterpieces" series) ▲ IMPPCD 801 [DDD]
Tchaikovsky, P.:Romeo & Juliet IMP Classics ("LSO Classic Masterpieces" series) ▲ IMPPCD 801 [DDD]

D. Amos (cnd)

Bloch, E.:Con grosso 2 Laurel ▲ LR 851CD [ADD]
Bloch, E.:Con symphonique, w. M. Yui (pno) Laurel ▲ LR 851CD [ADD]
Bloch, E.:Scherzo fantasque, w. M. Yui (pno) Laurel ▲ LR 851CD [ADD]

A. Argenta (cnd)

Chabrier, E.:España Classic Records ▲ CSCD 6006
España, w. E. Ansermet (cnd), Swiss Romande Orch London ("Weekend Classics" series) ▲ 430217-2 LC [AAD]
Granados, E.:Danzas españolas (10)—No. 5 Classic Records ▲ CSCD 6006
Moszkowski, M.:Spanische Tänze—Book I Classic Records ▲ CSCD 6006
Rimsky-Korsakov, N.:Capriccio espagnol Classic Records ▲ CSCD 6006
Tchaikovsky, P.:Con Vn, w. Alfredo Campoli (vn) Beulah ▲ 3PD10 [ADD]
Tchaikovsky, P.:Con Vn, w. A. Campoli (vn) PWK Classics ▲ PWK 1145 [AAD]

D. Atherton (cnd)

Holst, G.:Orchestral Works, w. L. MacAslan (vn), A. Baillie (vc), London PO—A Winter Idyll; Elegy in Memoriam William Morris; Indra, Symphonic Poem for Orchestra, Op. 13; A Song of the Night, Op. 19/1; Sita:Interlude from Act III, Op. 23; Invocation, Op. 19/2; The Lure; Dances from the Morning of the Year, Op. 45/2 Lyrita ▲ SRCD 209
Mathias, W.:Con Cl, w. Gervase de Peyer (cl) Lyrita ▲ SRCD 325
Mathias, W.:Con 3 Pno, w. Peter Katin (pno), New Philharmonia Orch Lyrita ▲ SRCD 325

D. Atherton, D. Willcocks (cnds)

Mathias, W.:Ave Rex, w. Janet Price (sop), Kenneth Bowen (ten), Michael Rippon (bar), Geraint Evans (b-bar), New Philharmonia Orch, Welsh National Opera Chorus, Windsor Bach Choir, St. George's Chapel Choristers Lyrita ▲ SRCD .324
Mathias, W.:Elegy for a Prince, w. Michael Rippon (bar), New Philharmonia Orch Lyrita ▲ SRCD .324
Mathias, W.:This Worlde's Joie, w. Janet Price (sop), Kenneth Bowen (ten), Michael Rippon (bar), New Philharmonia Orch, Welsh National Opera Chorus, Windsor Bach Choir, St. George's Chapel Choristers Lyrita ▲ SRCD .324

London SO (cont.)

J. Barbirolli (cnd)

Chopin, F.:Con 1 Pno, w. Artur Rubinstein (pno) *(rec London, 1931-37)* Grammofono 2000 ▲ GRM 78554
Chopin, F.:Con 1 Pno, w. A. Rubinstein (pno) *(rec 1937)* EMI Classics 2-▲ ZDHB 64491
Chopin, F.:Con 1 Pno, w. Arthur Rubinstein (pno) *(rec London, Apr 5, 1937)* Iron Needle ▲ IN 1345 (m) [ADD]
Chopin, F.:Con 2 Pno, w. Artur Rubinstein (pno) *(rec London, 1931-37)* Grammofono 2000 ▲ GRM 78554
Chopin, F.:Con 2 Pno, w. Arthur Rubinstein (pno) *(rec London, Jan 8-9, 1931)* Iron Needle ▲ IN 1345 (m) [ADD]
Chopin, F.:Con 2 Pno, w. A. Rubinstein (pno) *(rec 1937)* EMI Classics 2-▲ ZDHB 64491
Delius, F.:Music of, w. Robert Tear (ten), Hallé Orch, Ambrosian Singers—Brigg Fair; In a Summer Garden; On Hearing the First Cuckoo in Spring; Summer Night on the River; A Song before Sunrise; Intermezzo & Serenade [from Hassan]; La Calinda; Late Swallows; Intermezzo [from Fennimore & Gerda]; The Walk to Paradise Garden; Prelude [from Irmelin]; A Song of Summer; Appalachia; rehearsal of Appalachia EMI Classics ▲ ZDMB 65119
Elgar, E.:Con Vc, w. J. Du Pré (vc) EMI Classics 2-▲ ZDMB 69707
Elgar, E.:Con Vc, w. J. Du Pré (vc) EMI Classics ▲ CDC 47329
Elgar, E.:Sea Pictures, w. J. Baker (mez) EMI Classics ▲ CDC 47329
Haydn, J.:Con 1 Vc, w. Jaqueline Du Pré (vc) EMI Classics 2-▲ ZDMB 69707
Ireland, J.:A London Ov EMI Classics ▲ CDM 65109
Mozart, W.A.:Con 27 Pno, w. Artur Schnabel (pno) Enterprise ("Sirio" series) ▲ ENT SO 53006
Mozart, W.A.:Con 27 Pno, w. Artur Schnabel (pno) Enterprise ("Piano Library" series) ▲ ENT PL 210
Rimsky-Korsakov, N.:Scheherazade EMI Classics 2-▲ CDFB 69361
Saint-Saëns, C.:Havanaise Vn, w. J. Heifetz (vn) *(rec London, 1935 & 1937)* Grammofono 2000 ▲ GRM 78511 [ADD]
Saint-Saëns, C.:Havanaise Vn, w. J. Heifetz (vn) *(rec EMI Studios, Abbey Road, London, Apr 9, 1937)* RCA Gold Seal 2-▲ 09026-61735-2 [ADD]
Saint-Saëns, C.:Havanaise Vn, w. J. Heifetz (vn) *(rec 1937)* EMI Classics ▲ CDH 64251-2 (m) [ADD]
Saint-Saëns, C.:Havanaise Vn, w. J. Heifetz (vn) *(rec 1937; mats 2EA 4744/5, HM)* Biddulph ▲ LAB 025 [ADD]
Saint-Saëns, C.:Introduction & Rondo capriccioso, w. J. Heifetz (vn) *(rec London, 1935 & 1937)* Grammofono 2000 ▲ GRM 78511 [ADD]
Sarasate, P. de:Zigeunerweisen, w. Jascha Heifetz (vn) *(rec EMI Studios, Abbey Road, London, Apr 9, 1937)* RCA Gold Seal 2-▲ 09026-61735-2 [ADD]
Sarasate, P. de:Zigeunerweisen, w. J. Heifetz (vn) *(rec 1937)* EMI Classics ▲ CDH 64251-2 (m) [ADD]
Sarasate, P. de:Zigeunerweisen, w. J. Heifetz (vn) *(rec 1937 HMV recording)* Biddulph ▲ LAB 026 [ADD]
Tchaikovsky, P.:Con Vn, w. M. Elman (vn) *(rec 1929 for HMV)* Pearl ▲ GEMMCD 9388 (m) [AAD]
Vaughan Williams, R.:Sym 5 EMI Classics ▲ CDM 65110
Wagner, R.:Parsifal (sels), w. F. Leider (sop)—Act 2 *(Ich sah' das Kind) (rec 1931)* Pearl ▲ PEA 9331 (m) [AAD]
Wagner, R.:Tristan und Isolde (sels), w. F. Leider (sop), E. Marherr-Wagner (mez), L. Melchior (ten), L. Blech (cnd), A. Coates (cnd), Berlin State Opera Orch—Act 1 *(Doch nun von Tristan [Leider, Marherr-Wagner])*, Act 2 *(Isolde! Geliebter; O sink hernieder [Leider, Melchior])*, Act 3 *(Mild und leise [Leider]) [G] (rec late 1920s for HMV)* Legato Classics 2-▲ LCD 146-2 (m) [ADD]

D. Barenboim (cnd)

Paganini, N.:Con 6 Vn, w. I. Perlman (vn). London PO, Royal PO EMI Classics 3-▲ ZDMC 69881

E. Bátiz (cnd)

Albéniz, I.:Con 1 Pno, w. A. Ciccolini (pno) IMG/Pickwick ▲ PICIMG 1607
Albéniz, I.:Iberia Suite, w. A. Ciccolini (pno) IMG/Pickwick ▲ PICIMG 1607
Mozart, W.A.:Sym 31 Vivace 3-▲ E 314 [DDD]
Mozart, W.A.:Sym 31 ASV Quicksilva ▲ QS 6033 [DDD]
Mozart, W.A.:Sym 31 Vivace ▲ 602 [DDD]
Mozart, W.A.:Sym 36 Vivace 3-▲ E 314 [DDD]
Mozart, W.A.:Sym 36 Vivace ▲ 602 [DDD]
Mozart, W.A.:Sym 36 ASV Quicksilva ▲ QS 6033 [DDD]

S. Baudo (cnd)

Brahms, J.:Con Vn, w. T. Shimizu (vn) Platz ▲ PLZ 574 [DDD]
Brahms, J.:Tragic Ov, w. T. Shimizu (vn) Platz ▲ PLZ 574 [DDD]

S. Bedford (cnd)

Britten, B.:Gloriana (symphonic suite) Collins Classics ▲ 10192 [DDD]
Britten, B.:Paul Bunyan (ov) Collins Classics ▲ 11022 [DDD]
Britten, B.:Peter Grimes (sea interludes & passacaglia) Collins Classics ▲ 10192 [DDD]
Britten, B.:Sinf da requiem Collins Classics ▲ 10192 [DDD]

T. Beecham (cnd)

Delius, F.:Music of—Sea Drift; Summer Night on the River, In a Summer Garden; Brigg Fair- An English Rhapsody; On Hearing the First Cuckoo in Spring; The Walk to the Paradise Garden; La Calinda *(rec 1927-38)* The Beecham Collection ▲ BEECHAM 3 [ADD]
Handel, G.F.:Music of, London PO—Arrival of the Queen of Sheba [from *Solomon, arr. Beecham]; The Gods Go A-Begging [Suite, arr. Beecham], The Origin of Design [Suite, arr. Beecham]; Moses and the Children of Israel, But as for His People, The Lord Is a Man of War [from Israel in Egypt]*, Concerto Grosso No. 3 in e, Op. 6 [Larghetto, Polonaise], The Faithful Shepherd [Suite, arr. Beecham], Pastoral Symphony [from *The Messiah*] VAI Audio ▲ VAIA 1045 [ADD]
Sir Thomas Beecham Favourites, 1934-40 Iron Needle ▲ IN 1346 (m) [ADD]
Verdi, G.:Aida, w. Maria Caniglia (sop—Aida), Ebe Stignani (mez—Amneris), Beniamino Gigli (ten—Radamés), Armando Borgioli (bar—Amonasro), London Sym Chorus *(rec Royal Opera House, Covent Garden, May 24, 1939)* Enterprise ("The Radio Years" series) 2-▲ ENT RY 62

G. Ben-Dor (cnd)

Ginastera, A.:Variaciones concertantes Koch International Classics ▲ KIC 7149 [DDD]

A. Benjamin (cnd)

Benjamin, A.:Concertino Pno, w. Lamar Crowson (pno) *(rec Walhamstow Assembly Hall, London)* Everest ▲ EVC 9029 [AAD]
Benjamin, A.:Con quasi una fantasia, w. Lamar Crowson (pno) *(rec Walhamstow Assembly Hall, London)* Everest ▲ EVC 9029 [AAD]

L. Bernstein (cnd)

Bernstein, L.:Candide (restored), w. J. Anderson (sop), C. Ludwig (mez), D. Jones (mez), J. Hadley (ten), N. Gedda (ten), A. Green (sgr), K. Ollmann (bar), London Sym Chorus *(rec 1989)* Deutsche Grammophon ▲ 429734-2 [DDD] ■ 429734-4
Bernstein, L.:Candide (restored), w. J. Anderson (sop), C. Ludwig (mez), D. Jones (mez), J. Hadley (ten), N. Gedda (ten), A. Green (sgr), K. Ollmann (bar), London Sym Chorus Deutsche Grammophon ■ 437328-4
Haydn, J.:Mass 12, "Theresienmesse", w. Lucia Popp (sop), Rosalind Elias (mez), Robert Tear (ten), Paul Hudson (bass), London Sym Chorus [L] Sony Classical 2-▲ SM2K 47522 [ADD]
Mahler, G.:Sym 2, w. S. Armstrong (sop), J. Baker (mez), Edinburgh Festival Chorus *(rec 1974)* Sony Classical ("Bernstein:The Royal Edition" series) 2-▲ SM2K 47573 [ADD]
Mahler, G.:Sym 8, w. Leeds Festival Chorus *(rec 1966)* Sony Classical ("Bernstein:The Royal Edition" series) 3-▲ SM3K 47581 [ADD]
Stravinsky, I.:Sym of Psalms, w. English Bach Festival Chorus CBS ▲ MK 44710 [ADD]
Stravinsky, I.:Sym of Psalms, w. English Bach Festival Chorus *(rec Apr. 8, 1972)* Sony Classical ▲ SMK 47628 [ADD]

S. Black (cnd)

Khachaturian, A.:Gayane (sels) London ("Weekend Classics" series) ▲ 417062-2 [AAD]
Khachaturian, A.:Masquerade (ballet suite) London ("Weekend Classics" series) ▲ 417062-2 [AAD]
Khachaturian, A.:Spartacus (sels) London ("Weekend Classics" series) ▲ 417062-2 [AAD]

L. Blech (cnd)

Schubert, Franz:Sym 9 *(rec 1927)* Koch Legacy ▲ 3-7072-2 H1

London SO (cont.)

A. Bliss (cnd)

Bliss, A.:Adam Zero (suite) Lyrita ▲ SRCD 225 [ADD]
Bliss, A.:A Colour Sym Dutton Laboratories ▲ DUT 2501 [ADD]
Bliss, A.:Hymn To Apollo Lyrita ▲ SRCD 225 [ADD]
Bliss, A.:Intro & Allegro Dutton Laboratories ▲ DUT 2501 [ADD]
Bliss, A.:Mêlée fantasque Lyrita ▲ SRCD 225 [ADD]
Bliss, A.:Rout, w. R. Woodland (sop) Lyrita ▲ SRCD 225 [ADD]
Bliss, A.:Things to Come—suite & excerpts Dutton Laboratories ▲ DUT 2501 [ADD]
Elgar, E.:Pomp & Circumstance Marches London ("Weekend Classics" series) ▲ 417878-2 [AAD] ■ 417878-4

R. Bonynge (cnd)

The Age of Bel Canto, w. Joan Sutherland (sop), London PO London ("Opera Gala" series) ▲ 421881-2 LA [ADD]
The Age of Bel Canto, w. Joan Sutherland (sop), Marilyn Horne (mez), Richard Conrad (bar), London Sym Chorus London ("The Classic Sound" series) ▲ 448594-2
Ballet Gala:Homage to Pavlova London ▲ 433863-2 LM [ADD]
Ballet Gala:Invitation to the Dance, w. National PO London ▲ 433864-2 LM [ADD/DDD]
Ballet Gala:Pas De Deux London ▲ 433862-2 LM [ADD]
Bellini, V.:Beatrice di Tenda, w. J. Sutherland (sop), L. Pavarotti (ten), Ambrosian Opera Chorus London ("Grand Opera" series) 3-▲ 433706-2 [ADD]
Bellini, V.:Norma, w. J. Sutherland (sop), M. Horne (mez), J. Alexander (ten), R. Cross (bass), London Sym Chorus [I] London 3-▲ 425488-2 [ADD]
Bellini, V.:Norma (sels), w. J. Sutherland (sop), M. Horne (mez), J. Alexander (ten), R. Cross (bass), London Sym Chorus [I] London ("Opera Gala" series) ▲ 421886-2 [ADD]
Bellini, V.:I Puritani, w. J. Sutherland (sop), L. Pavarotti (ten), P. Cappuccilli (bar), N. Ghiaurov (bass) [I] London 3-▲ 417588-2 [ADD]
Donizetti, G.:Lucia di Lammermoor (sels), w. E. Gruberova (sop), A. Agache (ten), A. Miles (bass), Ambrosian Singers—Oh giusto cielo...Il dolce suono; Ohimè! sorge il tremendo fantasma; S'avanza Enrico; Spargi d'amore pianto Teldec ▲ 4509-93691-2 [DDD]
Gounod, C.:Faust, w. J. Sutherland (sop), F. Corelli (ten), N. Ghiaurov (bass), Ambrosian Opera Chorus [F] London ("Grand Opera" series) 3-▲ 421240-2 [AAD]
Handel, G.F.:Alcina, w. M. Freni (sop), J. Sutherland (sop), T. Berganza (mez) London ("Grand Opera" series) 3-▲ 433723-2 [ADD]
Offenbach, J.:Le Papillon *(rec Kingsway Hall, London, Jan 1972)* London ("Double Decker" series) 2-▲ 444827-2 [ADD]
Rossini, G.:Semiramide, w. J. Sutherland (sop), M. Horne (mez), J. Serge (ten), J. Rouleau (bass), S. Malas (bass), Ambrosian Singers [I] *(rec 1966)* London 3-▲ 425481-2 [ADD]
Verdi, G.:Rigoletto, w. J. Sutherland (sop), H. Tourangeau (mez), L. Pavarotti (ten), S. Milnes (bar), M. Talvela (bass), London Sym Chorus [I] London 2-▲ 414269-2 [ADD]

W. Boughton (cnd)

Dvořák, A.:Con Vc, w. A. Michejew (vc) Nimbus ▲ NI 5127 [DDD]
Saint-Saëns, C.:Con 1 Vc, w. A. Michejew (vc) Nimbus ▲ NI 5127 [DDD]

P. Boulez (cnd)

Berg, A.:Chamber Con, w. Daniel Barenboim (pno), Saschko Gawriloff (vn) Sony Classical ("Pierre Boulez Edition" series) ▲ SMK 68331
Berg, A.:Con Vn, w. Pinchas Zukerman (vn) Sony Classical ("Pierre Boulez Edition" series) ▲ SMK 68331
Berg, A.:Early Songs, w. Jessye Norman (sop) Sony Classical ▲ SK 66826
Berg, A.:Orchesterlieder (5) nach Ansichtskartentexten von Peter Altenberg, w. Jessye Norman (sop) Sony Classical ▲ SK 66826
Mahler, G.:Das Klagende Lied, w. E. Lear (sop), E. Söderström (sop), G. Hoffman (mez), S. Burrows (ten), E. Haefliger (ten), G. Nienstedt (bass), London Sym Chorus Sony Classical ("Pierre Boulez Edition" series) ▲ SK 45841

A. Boult (cnd)

Bach, J.S.:Con 2 for 2 Hpds, w. A. Schnabel (pno), K.U. Schnabel (pno) *(rec Oct 28, 1936)* Pearl ▲ PEA 9399 (m) [AAD]
Bliss, A.:Music for Strs IMP ("BBC Radio Classics" series) ▲ IMP 5691632
Brahms, J.:Tragic Ov EMI Classics ("Doublefforte" series) 2-▲ CDFB 68655
Elgar, E.:Enigma Vars EMI Classics ▲ CDM 64748
Handel, G.F.:Messiah, w. Kenneth McKellar (ten), George Malcolm (hpd), Ralph Downes (org), London Sym Chorus—And the glory of the Lord; And He shall purify; For unto us a Child is born; Glory to God in the highest; His yoke is easy; Behold the Lamb of God; Surely He hath borne our griefs; And with His stripes we are healed; All we like sheep have gone astray; All they that see Him...He trusted in God; Lift up your heads; The Lord gave the word; Their sound has gone out; Let us break the bonds asunder; Hallelujah; Since by man came death; Worthy is the Lamb...Amen London ▲ 436569-2
Handel, G.F.:Messiah (sels), w. Joan Sutherland (sop), Grace Bumbry (mez), Kenneth McKellar (ten), Joseph Ward (bar), London Sym Chorus—arias & choruses London ("Weekend Classics" series) ▲ 417879-2 [AAD] ■ 417879-4
Mendelssohn, F.:Con in e Vn & Orch, Op. 64, w. Y. Menuhin (vn) EMI Classics ▲ CDE 67767
Mozart, W.A.:Con 17 Pno, w. André Previn (pno) Royal Classics ▲ ROY 6449
Mozart, W.A.:Con 24 Pno, w. André Previn (pno) Royal Classics ▲ ROY 6449
Parry, H.:Bridal March Lyrita ▲ SRCD 220 [ADD]
Parry, H.:An English Suite Lyrita ▲ SRCD 220 [ADD]
Parry, H.:Lady Radnor's Suite Lyrita ▲ SRCD 220 [ADD]
Parry, H.:Ov to an Unwritten Tragedy Lyrita ▲ SRCD 220 [ADD]
Parry, H.:Symphonic Vars Lyrita ▲ SRCD 220 [ADD]
Vaughan Williams, R.:English Folk Song Suite EMI Classics (British Composers) ▲ CDM 64022
Vaughan Williams, R.:Fant on Greensleeves EMI Classics (British Composers) ▲ CDM 64022
Wagner, R.:Ovs, Preludes & Orch Sels, London PO, New Philharmonia Orch—from Fliegende Holländer *(Overture)*, Götterdämmerung *(Siegfried's Rhine Journey & Funeral March)*, Lohengrin *(Preludes to Acts 1 & 3)*, Meistersinger *(Overture; Prelude to Act 3)*, Parsifal *(Good Friday Music; Preludes to Acts 1 & 3; Transformation Scene)*, Rheingold *(Entrance of the Gods)*, Siegfried *(Forest Murmurs)*, Tannhäuser *(Overture; Grand March)*, Tristan *(Preludes to Acts 1 & 3)*, Walküre *(Ride of the Valkyries)* *(rec 1971–74)* EMI Classics 2-▲ CDZB 7 62539 2 [ADD]

B. Britten (cnd)

Britten, B.:Billy Budd, w. P. Pears (ten), P. Glossop (bar), J. Shirley-Quirk (bar), B. Luxon (bar), M. Langdon (bass), O. Brannigan (bass), Ambrosian Singers [E] London 3-▲ 417428-2 [ADD]
Britten, B.:A Midsummer Night's Dream, w. E. Harwood (sop), J. Veasey (mez), H. Watts (cta), A. Deller (ct), P. Pears (ten), J. Shirley-Quirk (bar), London Sym Chorus [E] London 2-▲ 425663-2 [ADD]
Britten, B.:Serenade, Op. 31, w. P. Pears (ten), B. Tuckwell (hn) [E] London ▲ 417153-2 [ADD]
Britten, B.:Simple Sym London ▲ 417509-2 [ADD]
Britten, B.:Vars on a Theme of Frank Bridge London ▲ 417509-2 [ADD]
Britten, B.:War Requiem, w. G. Vishnevskaya (sop), P. Pears (ten), D. Fischer-Dieskau (bar), London Sym Chorus [E,L] London 2-▲ 414383-2 [ADD]
Britten, B.:The Young Person's Guide to the Orchestra London ▲ 417509-2 [ADD]

B. Brott (cnd)

Davies, V.:Con 1 Pno, "Mennonite Pno Con", w. I. Baerg (pno) Campion ▲ 1304 [DDD]
Davies, V.:Good Times Campion ▲ 1304 [DDD]

Y. Butt (cnd)

Glazunov, A.:Raymonda (sels), w. Royal PO—Suite ASV ▲ ASV 904 [DDD]
Glazunov, A.:Sym 6, w. Royal PO ASV ▲ ASV 904 [DDD]
Glazunov, A.:Triumphal March, w. Royal PO ASV ▲ ASV 904 [DDD]
Liszt, F.:Ce qu'on entend sur la montagne ASV ▲ ASV 586 [DDD]
Liszt, F.:Symphonic Poems—No. 1, "Mountain Symphony" ASV Quicksilva ▲ ASQ 6169
Rimsky-Korsakov, N.:Fairy Tale ASV ▲ ASV 538 [DDD]
Rimsky-Korsakov, N.:Sym 3 ASV ▲ ASV 538 [DDD]
Saint-Saëns, C.:Phaéton ASV ▲ ASV 599 [DDD]
Saint-Saëns, C.:Suite algérienne ASV ▲ ASV 599 [DDD]

London SO (cont.)

Y. Butt (cnd) (cont.)

Saint-Saëns, C.:Sym 2 ASV ▲ ASV 599 [DDD]
Strauss, R.:Don Juan *(rec Apr. & Oct. 1990)* IMP Classics ▲ PCD 954 [DDD]
Strauss, R.:Till Eulenspiegels lustige Streiche *(rec 4 & 10 90)* IMP Classics ▲ PCD 954 [DDD]
Strauss, R.:Tod und Verklärung *(rec 4 & 10 90)* IMP Classics ▲ PCD 954 [DDD]
Tchaikovsky, P.:The Tempest ASV ▲ ASV 586 [DDD]
Tchaikovsky, P.:The Tempest ASV Quicksilva ▲ ASQ 6169

S. Caldwell (cnd)

Donizetti, G.:Don Pasquale, w. Beverly Sills (sop), Alfredo Kraus (ten), Alan Titus (bar), Donald Gramm (b-bar), Ambrosian Opera Chorus EMI Classics 2-▲ CDMB 66030

A. Ceccato (cnd)

Mendelssohn, F.:Con 1 Pno, w. J. Ogdon (pno) Klavier ■ KC 531
Mendelssohn, F.:Con 1 Pno, w. J. Ogdon (pno) Klavier ▲ KCD 11029 [ADD]
Mendelssohn, F.:Con 2 Pno, w. J. Ogdon (pno) Klavier ■ KC 531
Mendelssohn, F.:Con 2 Pno, w. J. Ogdon (pno) Klavier ▲ KCD 11029 [ADD]
Mendelssohn, F.:Rondo brilliant, w. J. OgdonJ. Ogdon (pno) Klavier ▲ KCD 11011 [ADD]
Mendelssohn, F.:Rondo brilliant, w. J. Ogdon (pno) Klavier ■ KC 531

S. Celibidache (cnd)

Debussy, C.:Ibéria Artists ▲ FED 31 [ADD]
Debussy, C.:La Mer Artists ▲ FED 31 [ADD]
Debussy, C.:Prélude à l'après-midi d'un faune Artists ▲ FED 31 [ADD]
Debussy, C.:Prélude à l'après-midi d'un faune Exclusive ▲ EXL 82 [ADD]
Fauré, G.:Requiem, w. M. McLaughlin (sop), G. Howell (bass-bar), London Sym Chorus *(rec Apr. 1982)* Exclusive ▲ EXL 52 [ADD]
Ravel, M.:Con in G Pno, w. A. Benedetti-Michelangeli (pno) *(rec 1979–82)* Exclusive 2-▲ EXL 61 [ADD]
Ravel, M.:Ma mère l'oye Orch *(rec 1979–82)* Exclusive 2-▲ EXL 61 [ADD]
Ravel, M.:Rapsodie espagnole *(rec live, 1974)* Enterprise ("Documents" series) 2-▲ LV 946/47 (m/s) [ADD]
Ravel, M.:Rapsodie espagnole *(rec 1979–82)* Exclusive 2-▲ EXL 61 [ADD]

M.-W. Chung (cnd)

Italian Opera Arias, w. Kiri Te Kanawa (sop) EMI Classics ▲ CDC 54062

A. Coates (cnd)

Albert Coates Conducts, Vol. 1:Russian Favorites *(rec 1928–32)* Koch Historic ▲ KIC 7700 [ADD]
Bach, J.S.:Mass in b, BWV 232, w. E. Schumann (sop), M. Balfour (cta), W. Widdop (ten), F. Schorr (bar), London Phil Chorus [L] *(rec Kingsway Hall, London Mar-Apr 1929)* Pearl 2-▲ PEAS 9900 (m) [AAD]
Beethoven, L. van:Sym 3, "Eroica" *(rec 1926)* Claremont ▲ GSE 78 50 55
Borodin, A.:Prince Igor (sels)—Konchakovna's cavatina, Act II *(rec Feb. 21, 1935)* Claremont ▲ GSE 785061
Borodin, A.:Sym 2 *(rec Kingsway Hall, Apr. 18, 1931 & Nov. 5 &)* Claremont ▲ GSE 785061
Dvořák, A.:Carnival *(rec 1929)* Koch Historic 2-▲ 7704-2 [ADD]
Elgar, E.:Fant & Fugue *(rec 1928)* Koch Historic 2-▲ 7704-2 [ADD]
Glinka, M.:A Life for the Tsar (sels)—Vanya's arias Claremont ▲ GSE 785061
Holst, G.:The Planets—4 sections only *(rec 1926)* Koch Historic 2-▲ 7704-2 [ADD]
Liadov, A.:Kikimora *(rec Kingsway Hall, London, Oct. 10, 1930)* Claremont ▲ GSE 785061
Liadov, A.:A Musical Snuffbox *(rec Kingsway Hall, Nov. 7, 1929)* Claremont ▲ GSE 785061
Liszt, F.:Hungarian Rhaps—No. 14 *(rec 1930)* Koch Historic 2-▲ 7704-2 [ADD]
Mozart, W.A.:Sym 41 Claremont ▲ GSE 78 50 55
Mussorgsky, M.:Night *(rec 1945)* Beulah ▲ 2PD11 [ADD]
Mussorgsky, M.:Sorochintsy Fair (orch sels)—Gopak *(rec 1945)* Beulah ▲ 2PD11 [ADD]
Ravel, M.:La Valse *(rec 1926)* Koch Historic 2-▲ 7704-2 [ADD]
Respighi, O.:The Fountains of Rome *(rec 1927–8)* Koch Historic 2-▲ 7704-2 [ADD]
Rimsky-Korsakov, N.:Snow Maiden (dance) *(rec 1945)* Beulah ▲ 2PD11 [ADD]
Strauss, R.:Don Juan *(rec 1926)* Koch Historic 2-▲ 7704-2 [ADD]
Strauss, R.:Tod und Verklärung *(rec 1928)* Koch Historic 2-▲ 7704-2 [ADD]
Tchaikovsky, P.:Romeo & Juliet *(rec 1928)* GSE Claremont ▲ GSE 78 50 51
Wagner, R.:Der Ring des Nibelungen (orch sels)—Rheingold *(Entry of the Gods into Valhalla)*, Walküre *(Magic Fire Music)*, Götterdämmerung *(Siegfried's Rhine Journey & Funeral Music)* *(rec 1926)* Koch Historic 2-▲ 7704-2 [ADD]
Wagner, R.:Tannhäuser (sels), w. Lauritz Melchior (ten), Walter Widdop (ten), Friedrich Schorr (b-bar), Edward Halland (bass), New SO—Ov; Venusberg Bacchanale; 1st Pilgrims' Chorus; Wolfram's Cavatina; Prelude; Pilgrims' Return; Rome Narration *(rec 1925–30)* Claremont ▲ GSE 78 50 54
Weber, C.M. von:Ovs—Oberon *(rec 1926)* Koch Historic 2-▲ 7704-2 [ADD]

L. Collingwood (cnd)

Dohnányi, E. von:Vars on a Nursery Song, w. E. von Dohnányi (pno) *(rec 1931 for HMV)* Koch Schwann ▲ CD 311136 (m) [ADD]
Dohnányi, E. von:Vars on a Nursery Song, w. E. von Dohnányi (pno) *(rec 1928–1937)* EMI Classics ▲ CDC 55031

A. Collins (cnd)

Delius, F.:Brigg Fair:An English Rhapsody Dutton Laboratories ▲ DUT 2503 [ADD]
Delius, F.:In a Summer Garden Dutton Laboratories ▲ DUT 2503 [ADD]
Delius, F.:On Hearing the 1st Cuckoo Dutton Laboratories ▲ DUT 2503 [ADD]
Delius, F.:Paris:The Song of a Great City Dutton Laboratories ▲ DUT 2503 [ADD]
Delius, F.:A Song of Summer Dutton Laboratories ▲ DUT 2503 [ADD]
Delius, F.:Summer Night on the River Dutton Laboratories ▲ DUT 2503 [ADD]
Elgar, E.:Falstaff Beulah ▲ 1PD15 (m) [ADD]
Sibelius, J.:Karelia Ov Beulah ▲ 1PD8
Sibelius, J.:Night Ride & Sunrise Beulah ▲ 3PD8 [ADD]
Sibelius, J.:Pelléas & Mélisande (sels)—Mélisande; Pastorle; Mélisande and the spinning wheel; Entr'acte; The Death of Mélisande Beulah ▲ 3PD8 [ADD]
Sibelius, J.:Pohjola's Daughter Beulah ▲ 3PD8 [ADD]
Sibelius, J.:Sym 1 Beulah ▲ 1PD8
Sibelius, J.:Sym 2 Beulah ▲ 2PD8 (m) [ADD]
Sibelius, J.:Sym 3 Beulah ▲ 3PD8 [ADD]
Sibelius, J.:Sym 4 Beulah ▲ 4PD8 (m) [ADD]
Sibelius, J.:Sym 5 Beulah ▲ 4PD8 (m) [ADD]
Sibelius, J.:Sym 6 Beulah ▲ 2PD8 (m) [ADD]
Sibelius, J.:Sym 7 Beulah ▲ 1PD8

S. Comissiona (cnd)

Tchaikovsky, P.:Concert Fant, w. J. Lowenthal (pno) [original version] Arabesque ▲ Z 6611
Tchaikovsky, P.:Con 1 Pno, w. J. Lowenthal (pno) [original version] Arabesque ▲ Z 6611
Tchaikovsky, P.:Con 2 Pno, w. J. Lowenthal (pno) Arabesque ▲ Z 6583
Tchaikovsky, P.:Con 3 Pno, w. J. Lowenthal (pno) Arabesque ▲ Z 6583

A. Copland (cnd)

Copland, A.:Appalachian Spring (suite) CBS ▲ MK 42430 [ADD]
Copland, A.:Appalachian Spring (suite) CBS ▲ MT 30649
Copland, A.:Billy the Kid (suite) CBS ▲ MK 42431 [ADD]
Copland, A.:Billy the Kid (suite) Everest ▲ EVC 9040 [AAD]
Copland, A.:Dance Sym *(rec 1967)* Sony Classical 2-▲ SM2K 47232 [ADD]
Copland, A.:Fanfare for the Common Man *(rec 1968)* CBS ▲ MK 42430 [ADD]
Copland, A.:Fanfare for the Common Man CBS ■ MT 30649
Copland, A.:Lincoln Portrait, w. H. Fonda (nar) [E] CBS ■ MT 30649
Copland, A.:Lincoln Portrait, w. H. Fonda (nar) CBS ▲ MK 42431 [ADD]
Copland, A.:Music of—Celebration, from Billy the Kid & Hoedown, from Rodeo CBS ▲ MLK 39443 ■ MT 39443
Copland, A.:Our Town Orch CBS ▲ MK 42429 [ADD]
Copland, A.:Rodeo CBS ▲ MK 42430 [ADD]
Copland, A.:Short Sym, "Sym 2" *(rec 1965)* Sony Classical 2-▲ SM2K 47232 [ADD]

230

▲ = CD ♦ = Enhanced CD Δ = MD ■ = Cassette Tape □ = DCC

London SO (cont.)

A. Copland (cnd) (cont.)

Copland, A.:Statements Orch *(rec Walthamstow Hall, London, Feb 1959)* Everest ▲ EVC 9039 [AAD]
Copland, A.:Statements Orch Sony Classical 2-▲ SM2K 47232 [ADD]
Copland, A.:Symphonic Ode Sony Classical 2-▲ SM2K 47232 [ADD]
Copland, A.:Sym 3 Everest ▲ EVC 9040 [AAD]

P. Coppola (cnd)

Debussy, C.:Rapsodie, w. M. Viard (sax) Pearl ▲ PEA 9348 (m) [AAD]
Prokofiev, S.:Con 3 Pno, w. S. Prokofiev (pno), & Suggestion diabolique, Op. 4/4 InSync ■ C 4148
Prokofiev, S.:Con 3 Pno, w. S. Prokofiev (pno) *(rec 1932)* Pearl ▲ PEA 9470 (m) [ADD]

R. Craft (cnd)

Schoenberg, A.:Begleitmusik zu einer Lichtspielszene Koch International Classics ▲ KIC 7263-2 [DDD]
Schoenberg, A.:Herzgewächse, w. Eileen Hulse (sop) Koch International Classics ▲ KIC 7263-2 [DDD]
Schoenberg, A.:Pieces Orch, Op. 16 Koch International Classics ▲ KIC 7263-2 [DDD]
Schoenberg, A.:A Survivor from Warsaw, w. Simon Callow (nar) Koch International Classics ▲ KIC 7263-2 [DDD]
Stravinsky, I.:Apollon musagète Koch International Classics ▲ KIC 7359
Stravinsky, I.:Le Baiser de la fée Koch Schwann ▲ KIC CD 7276
Stravinsky, I.:Orpheus Koch Schwann ▲ KIC CD 7276
Stravinsky, I.:Le Sacre du printemps Orch Koch International Classics ▲ KIC 7359

G. Crum (cnd)

Baker, M.C.:Washington Square—In the house; Catherine; The party; Townsend; In the square; The betrothal; In Dr. Sloper's study; The argument; The promise; The house at night; The square in the rain [from *Entr'acte*]; Townsend returns Summit ▲ DCD 165 [DDD]

P. Daniel (cnd)

Albéniz, I.:Iberia Suite, w. J. Williams (gtr) [3 sections arr. Steve Gray for solo gtr & orch] Sony Classical ▲ SK 48480 [DDD]

A. Davis (cnd)

Mozart, W.A.:Arias, w. K. Te Kanawa (sop)—from Die Zauberflöte, Così fan tutte, Idomeneo, Zaïde, Lucio Silla; others [G,I] Philips ▲ 411148-2 [DDD]
Strauss, R.:4 Last Songs, w. K. Te Kanawa (sop) [G] CBS ▲ MK 35140 ■ MT 35140
Strauss, R.:Songs, w. K. Te Kanawa (sop)—6 songs CBS ▲ MK 35140 ■ MT 35140
Wagner, R.:Tristan und Isolde (prelude & liebestod), w. J. Norman (sop) [G] Philips ▲ 412655-2 [ADD]
Wagner, R.:Wesendonck Songs, w. J. Norman (sop) [G] Philips ▲ 412655-2 [ADD]

Carl Davis (cnd)

Gershwin, G.:An American in Paris Collins Classics ▲ 11392 [DDD]
Gershwin, G.:Con Pno, w. J. MacGregor (pno) Collins Classics ▲ COL 1362 [DDD]
Gershwin, G.:Con Pno, w. J. MacGregor (pno) Collins Classics ▲ 11392 [DDD]
Gershwin, G.:Rhap in Blue [original Paul Whiteman Orchestra arr.] Collins Classics ▲ 11392 [DDD]
Gershwin, G.:Rhap in Blue, w. J. MacGregor (pno) Collins Classics ▲ COL 1362 [DDD]

Colin Davis (cnd)

Beethoven, L. van:Con 5 Pno, "Emperor", w. S. Bishop Kovacevich (pno) Philips ("Concert Classics" series) ▲ 422482-2 [ADD]
Beethoven, L. van:Con Pno, WoO 4, w. S. Kovecevich (pno) Philips ("Duo" series) 2-▲ 442580-2
Beethoven, L. van:Mass, Op. 86, w. A. Tomwa-Sintow (sop), P. Payne (mez), R. Tear (ten), R. Lloyd (bass), London Sym Chorus [G] Philips 2-▲ 438362-2
Beethoven, L. van:Missa Solemnis, w. A. Tomwa-Sintow (sop), P. Payne (mez), R. Tear (ten), R. Lloyd (bass), London Sym Chorus [G] Philips 2-▲ 438362-2
Beethoven, L. van:Son 30 Pno, w. S. Bishop Kovacevich (pno) Philips ("Concert Classics" series) ▲ 422482-2
Berlioz, H.:Le Carnaval romain Philips ("Duo" series) 2-▲ 442290-2
Berlioz, H.:Le Corsaire Philips ("Duo" series) 2-▲ 442290-2
Berlioz, H.:La Damnation de Faust, w. J. Veasey (mez), N. Gedda (ten), G. Bastin (bar), London Sym Chorus, Ambrosian Singers [F] Philips 2-▲ 416395-2 [ADD]
Berlioz, H.:Harold in Italy, w. N. Imai (va) Philips ▲ 416431-2 [ADD]
Berlioz, H.:Harold in Italy, w. *(soloist unknown)* Philips ("Duo" series) 2-▲ 442290-2
Berlioz, H.:Les Nuits d'été, w. J. Norman (sop) [F] Philips ▲ 412493-2 [ADD]
Berlioz, H.:Ovs—Carnaval romain; Le Corsaire; Les francs-juges; Le roi Lear; Waverley Philips ▲ 416430-2 [ADD]
Berlioz, H.:Requiem, "Grande Messe des Morts", w. R. Dowd (ten), London Sym Chorus [L] Philips 2-▲ 416283-2 [ADD]
Berlioz, H.:Sym fantastique Philips ("Duo" series) 2-▲ 442290-2
Berlioz, H.:Te Deum, w. F. Tagliavini (ten), London Sym Chorus, Wandsworth School Boys' Chorus [L] Philips ▲ 416660-2 [ADD]
Berlioz, H.:Tristia, w. Alldis Chorus [F] Philips ▲ 416431-2 [ADD]
Brahms, J.:Con 1 Pno, w. S. B. Kovacevich (pno) IMP ("Collectors" series) ▲ IMPX 9039 [ADD]
Brahms, J.:Con 2 Pno, w. S. B. Kovacevich (pno) IMP ("Collectors" series) ▲ IMPX 9040 [ADD]
Brahms, J.:Hungarian Dances Orch EMI Classics ▲ CDC 54753 ■ 4DS 54753
Britten, B.:A Midsummer Night's Dream, w. Sylvia McNair (sop—Tytania), Brian Asawa (ct—Oberon), Robert Lloyd (bass) Philips 2-▲ 454 122-2
Handel, G.F.:Messiah, w. Heather Harper (sop), Helen Watts (cta), John Wakefield (ten), John Shirley-Quirk (bar), London Sym Chorus Philips 2-▲ 438356-2
Liszt, F.:Cons Pno, w. Claudio Arrau (pno) Philips ▲ 416461-2 [ADD]
Mahler, G.:Das Lied von der Erde, w. J. Norman (sop), J. Vickers (ten) [G] Philips ▲ 411474-2 [DDD]
Mozart, W.A.:Ave verum corpus, w. London Sym Chorus Philips ▲ 412873-2 [ADD]
Mozart, W.A.:Cons Vn, w. A. Grumiaux (vn) Philips 2-▲ 438323-2
Mozart, W.A.:Exsultate, w. K. Te Kanawa (sop) [L] Philips ▲ 412873-2 [ADD]
Mozart, W.A.:Kyrie, K.341, w. K. Te Kanawa (sop), E. Bainbridge (mez), A. Davies (ten), G. Howell (bass), London Sym Chorus [L] Philips ▲ 412873-2
Mozart, W.A.:Vesperae solennes, w. K. Te Kanawa (sop), E. Bainbridge (mez), A. Davies (ten), G. Howell (bass), London Sym Chorus [L] Philips ▲ 412873-2 [ADD]
Ravel, M.:Shéhérazade Mez, w. J. Norman (sop) [F] Philips ▲ 412493-2 [ADD]
Schumann, R.:Con Pno, w. A. de Larrocha (pno) RCA Red Seal ▲ 09026-61279-2
Sibelius, J.:Sym 1 *(rec Blackheath Concert Halls, London, 1994)* RCA Red Seal ▲ 0902-668183-2 [DDD]
Sibelius, J.:Sym 2 *(rec Blackheath Concert Halls, London, Dec. 12–13, 1994)* RCA Red Seal ▲ 09026-68218-2 [DDD]
Sibelius, J.:Sym 3 RCA Red Seal ▲ 09026-61963-2
Sibelius, J.:Sym 4 *(rec Blackheath Concert Halls, London, 1994)* RCA Red Seal ▲ 0902-668183-2 [DDD]
Sibelius, J.:Sym 5 RCA Red Seal ▲ 09026-61963-2
Sibelius, J.:Sym 6 *(rec Blackheath Concert Halls, London, Dec. 12–13, 1994)* RCA Red Seal ▲ 09026-68218-2 [DDD]
Tchaikovsky, P.:Con Vn, w. S. Chang (vn) EMI Classics ▲ CDC 54753 ■ 4DS 54753

Colin Davis, B. Haitink (cnds)

Bartók, B.:Con Orch, Royal Concertgebouw Orch, BBC SO Philips 2-▲ 438812-2
Bartók, B.:Cons Pno (comp), w. S. Kovacevich (pno), Royal Concertgebouw Orch, BBC SO Philips 2-▲ 438812-2
Bartók, B.:Con 1 Vn, w. H. Szehng (vn), Royal Concertgebouw Orch, BBC SO Philips 2-▲ 438812-2

Colin Davis, I. Markevitch (cnd)

Stravinsky, I.:Music of, w. E. de Waart (cnd), Russian State SO, Netherlands Wind Ensemble, Russian State Academy Chorus—Sym. in C; Sym of Psalms; Con. for Violin & others Philips ("Duo" series) 2-▲ 442583-2

E. Dohnányi (cnd)

Dohnányi, E. von:Ruralia hungarica for Orch *(rec 1931 for HMV)* Koch Schwann ▲ CD 311136 (m) [ADD]

P. Domingo (cnd)

Bellini, V.:Norma (sels), w. A. Baltsa (mez), J. Carreras (ten), Tallis Chamber Choir—Eccolal Va, mi lascia; Va, crudele, al Dio spietato *(rec Jan.–Feb. 1991)* Sony Classical ▲ SK 53968 [DDD]

London SO (cont.)

P. Domingo (cnd) (cont.)

Bizet, G.:Carmen (sels), w. A. Baltsa (mez), J. Carreras (ten), Tallis Chamber Choir—C'est toi? C'est moi; Mais moi, Carmen, je t'aime encore? *(rec Jan.–Feb. 1991)* Sony Classical ▲ SK 53968 [DDD]
Mascagni, P.:Cavalleria rusticana (sels), w. A. Baltsa (mez), J. Carreras (ten), Tallis Chamber Choir—Tu qui, Santuzza?; La tua Santuzza [w. M. Hintermeier (mez)] *(rec Jan.–Feb. 1991)* Sony Classical ▲ SK 53968 [DDD]
Massenet, J.:Werther (sels), w. A. Baltsa (mez), J. Carreras (ten), Tallis Chamber Choir—Orchestral Intro.; Il faut nous séparer; Mais vous ne savez rien de moi; Rêvel Extasel *(rec Jan.–Feb. 1991)* Sony Classical ▲ SK 53968 [DDD]
Verdi, G.:La traviata (sels), w. A. Baltsa (mez), J. Carreras (ten), Tallis Chamber Choir—Libiamo, libiamo ne' lieti calici *(rec Jan.–Feb. 1991)* Sony Classical ▲ SK 53968 [DDD]
Verdi, G.:Il trovatore (sels), w. A. Baltsa (mez), J. Carreras (ten), Tallis Chamber Choir—Soli or siamo; Non son tuo figlio; L'usato messo Ruiz m'invia [w. J. Howard (tenor)] *(rec Jan.–Feb. 1991)* Sony Classical ▲ SK 53968 [DDD]

A. Dorati (cnd)

Auric, G.:Ov *(rec London, Aug 4–6, 1965)* Mercury Living Presence ▲ 434335-2
Bartók, B.:Bluebeard's Castle, w. O. Szönyi (sop), M. Székely (bass) Mercury Living Presence ▲ 434325-2 [ADD]
Bartók, B.:Con Orch Mercury Living Presence ▲ 432017-2 [ADD]
Bartók, B.:Music for Strs, Perc & Cel Mercury Living Presence ▲ 434357-2
Bartók, B.:The Wooden Prince Mercury Living Presence ▲ 434357-2
Beethoven, L. van:Con 4 Pno, w. G. Bachauer (pno) Mercury Living Presence ▲ 432018-2 [ADD]
Beethoven, L. van:Wellington's Victory, "Battle Sym" [cannon & musket firing under the dir. of Gerald C. Stowe by the reactivated Civil War unit, Battery B, 2nd NJ Light Artillery] Mercury Living Presence ▲ 434 360-2
Berg, A.:Lulu (suite), w. H. Pilarczyk (sop) Mercury Living Presence ▲ 432006-2 [ADD]
Berg, A.:Pieces Orch, Op. 6 Mercury Living Presence ▲ 432006-2 [ADD]
Berg, A.:Wozzeck (sels), w. H. Pilarczyk (sop)—3 sels. [G] Mercury Living Presence ▲ 434325-2 [ADD]
Borodin, A.:Prince Igor (ov) Mercury Living Presence ▲ 434373-2
Borodin, A.:Prince Igor (Polovtsian dances) Mercury Living Presence ▲ 434308-2 [ADD]
Brahms, J.:Con Vn, w. H. Szeryng (vn) Mercury Living Presence ▲ 434318-2 [ADD]
Brahms, J.:Hungarian Dances Orch Mercury Living Presence ▲ 434326-2 [ADD]
Brahms, J.:Vars on a Theme by Haydn Mercury Living Presence ▲ 434326-2 [ADD]
Bruch, M.:Kol Nidrei, w. J. Starker (vc) Mercury Living Presence ▲ 432001-2 [ADD]
Chopin, F.:Con 1 Pno, w. Gina Bachauer (pno) Mercury Living Presence ▲ 434374-2
Chopin, F.:Con 2 Pno, w. Gina Bachauer (pno) Mercury Living Presence ▲ 434374-2
Copland, A.:Appalachian Spring (suite) Mercury Living Presence ▲ 434301-2 [ADD]
Copland, A.:Billy the Kid Mercury Living Presence ▲ 434301-2 [ADD]
Dvořák, A.:Con Vc, w. J. Starker (vc) Mercury Living Presence ▲ 432001-2 [ADD]
Dvořák, A.:Sym 7 Mercury Living Presence ▲ 434312-2 [ADD]
Dvořák, A.:Sym 8 Mercury Living Presence ▲ 434312-2 [ADD]
Enescu, G.:Romanian Rhap 1 Mercury Living Presence ▲ 432015-2 [ADD]
Enescu, G.:Romanian Rhap 2 Mercury Living Presence ▲ 434326-2 [ADD]
Françaix, J.:Concertino, w. Jean Françaix (pno) *(rec London, Aug. 4–6, 1965)* Mercury Living Presence ▲ 434335-2
Henryk Szeryng, w. Henryk Szeryng (vn) Mercury Living Presence ▲ 434339-2
Khachaturian, A.:Con Vn, w. H. Szeryng (vn) Mercury Living Presence ▲ 434318-2 [ADD]
Khachaturian, A.:Gayane (sels) Mercury Living Presence ▲ 434323-2 [ADD]
Liszt, F.:Hungarian Rhaps—Nos. 2, 5, 6, 9, 12 & 14 Mercury Living Presence ▲ 432015-2 [ADD]
Milhaud, D.:Le Boeuf sur le toit *(rec London, Aug. 4–6, 1965)* Mercury Living Presence ▲ 434335-2
Mussorgsky, M.:Night Mercury Living Presence ▲ 432004-2
Prokofiev, S.:Romeo & Juliet (suites)—Suite Nos. 1 & 2 Mercury Living Presence ▲ 432004-2 [ADD]
Prokofiev, S.:Sym 5 Mercury Living Presence ▲ 432753-2 [ADD]
Rachmaninoff, S.:Con 3 Pno, w. B. Janis (pno) Mercury Living Presence ▲ 432759-2 [ADD]
Respighi, O.:Brazilian Impressions Mercury Living Presence ▲ 432007-2 [ADD]
Respighi, O.:Gli uccelli Mercury Living Presence ▲ 432007-2 [ADD]
Rimsky-Korsakov, N.:Capriccio espagnol Mercury Living Presence ▲ 434308-2 [ADD]
Rimsky-Korsakov, N.:Golden Cockerel (suite) Mercury Living Presence ▲ 434308-2 [ADD]
Rimsky-Korsakov, N.:Russian Easter Festival Mercury Living Presence ▲ 434308-2 [ADD]
Rossini, G.:Ovs, w. Minneapolis SO—ovs. to La Gazza ladra; La Scala di seta; La Cenerentola; La Barbieri di Siviglia; L'Italiana in Algeri; Il Signor Bruschino Mercury Living Presence ▲ 434345-2
Saint-Saëns, C.:Con 1 Vc, w. J. Starker (vc) Mercury Living Presence ▲ 432010-2 [ADD]
Satie, E.:Parade *(rec London, Aug. 4–6, 1965)* Mercury Living Presence ▲ 434335-2
Schoenberg, A.:Pieces Orch, Op. 16 Mercury Living Presence ▲ 432006-2 [ADD]
Sibelius, J.:Aallottaret EMI Classics ▲ CDM 65182
Sibelius, J.:Luonnotar, w. G. Jones (sop) EMI Classics ▲ CDM 65182
Sibelius, J.:Night Ride & Sunrise EMI Classics ▲ CDM 65182
Stravinsky, I.:Le Chant du rossignol Mercury Living Presence ▲ 432012-2 [ADD]
Stravinsky, I.:The Firebird Mercury Living Presence ▲ 432012-2 [ADD]
Stravinsky, I.:Fireworks Mercury Living Presence ▲ 432012-2 [ADD]
Stravinsky, I.:Scherzo fantastique Mercury Living Presence ▲ 432012-2 [ADD]
Stravinsky, I.:Studies Orch *(rec July 7, 1964)* Mercury Living Presence ▲ 434331-2
Tchaikovsky, P.:Con Vn, w. P. Zukerman (vn) *(rec 1968)* Odyssey ▲ MBK 46268 [ADD] ■ YT 46268
Tchaikovsky, P.:Eugene Onegin (sels)—Waltz & Polonaise Mercury Living Presence ▲ 434305-2 [ADD]
Tchaikovsky, P.:Marche slave Mercury Living Presence ▲ 434305-2 [ADD]
Tchaikovsky, P.:The Nutcracker *(rec ca. 1962)* Mercury Living Presence 2-▲ 432750-2 [ADD]
Tchaikovsky, P.:Romeo & Juliet *(rec Watford Town Hall, June 20, 1959)* Mercury Living Presence ▲ 434353-2
Tchaikovsky, P.:Sym 4 Mercury Living Presence ▲ 434373-2
Tchaikovsky, P.:Sym 6 *(rec Wembly Town Hall, June 17–18, 1960)* Mercury Living Presence ▲ 434353-2
Verdi, G.:Ovs & Preludes, w. Minneapolis SO—ovs. from La Forza del destino; Nabucco; I Vespri siciliani; La Traviata [Preludes to Acts 1 & 3] Mercury Living Presence ▲ 434345-2
Wagner, R.:Ovs, Preludes & Orch Sels—Ov. [from Die Meistersinger von Nürnberg]; Good Friday Spell [from Parsifal]; Preludes to Acts 1 & 3 [from Lohengrin]; Ov. & Venusberg Music [from Tristan und Isolde]; Prelude & Liebestod [from Tannhäuser] *(rec June 1959 & June 1960)* Mercury Living Presence ▲ 434342-2
Webern, A.:Pieces Orch, Op. 10 Mercury Living Presence ▲ 432006-2

E. Downes (cnd)

Walton, W.:Con Vn, w. Iona Brown (vn) IMP ("BBC Radio Classics" series) ▲ IMP 5691732

P. Dreier (cnd)

Grieg, E.:Landkjending, w. Oslo Phil Chorus Unicorn-Kanchana ▲ UKCD 2056
Grieg, E.:Olav Trygvason, w. Norwegian Soloists, Oslo Phil Chorus Unicorn-Kanchana ▲ UKCD 2056
Grieg, E.:Peer Gynt, w. C. Carlson (mez), V. Hanssen (mez), K. Bjørkøy (ten), A. Hansli (bar), Oslo Phil Chorus [N] Unicorn-Kanchana 2-▲ UKCD 2003/04 [AAD]
Grieg, E.:Peer Gynt, w. Oslo Phil Chorus—Choral scenes from Act 5 Unicorn-Kanchana ▲ UKCD 2056

S. Ehrling (cnd)

Blomdahl, K.-B.:Chamber Con Swedish Society ▲ SCD 1037
Lidholm, I.:Ritornello Swedish Society ▲ SCD 1027
Rosenberg, H.:Sym 2 Swedish Society ▲ SCD 1026

E. Elgar (cnd)

Elgar, E.:Con Vc, w. *(cellist unknown)* IMP Classics ("LSO Classic Masterpieces" series) ▲ IMPPCD 930 [DDD]
Elgar, E.:Falstaff EMI Classics 3-▲ CDCC 54560
Elgar, E.:Sym 1 *(rec electrical recording)* EMI Classics 3-▲ CDCC 54560
Elgar, E.:Sym 2 *(rec electrical recording)* EMI Classics 3-▲ CDCC 54560

ORCH. & ENS.

London SO (cont.)

E. Elgar (cnd) (cont.)

Vaughan Williams, R.:Fant on Greensleeves
IMP Classics ("LSO Classic Masterpieces" series) ▲ IMPPCD 930 [DDD]
Vaughan Williams, R.:Fant on a Theme by Thomas Tallis
IMP Classics ("LSO Classic Masterpieces" series) ▲ IMPPCD 930 [DDD]

H. Faberman (cnd)

Bazelon, I.:Spires, w. M. Murphy (tpt) Albany ▲ TROY 054 [DDD]

J. Falletta (cnd)

Moross, J.:Last Judgement *(rec Mar. 1–2, 1993)* Koch International Classics ▲ KIC 7188 [DDD]
Moross, J.:Sym 1 *(rec Mar. 1–2, 1993)* Koch International Classics ▲ KIC 7188 [DDD]
Moross, J.:Vars on Waltz *(rec Mar. 1–2, 1993)* Koch International Classics ▲ KIC 7188 [DDD]

H. Farberman (cnd)

Ahrold, F.:Poems of Sylvia Plath (3), w. D. Curry (mez) CRI ■ C 380
Bazelon, I.:Trajectories, w. W. Maximillian (pno) Albany ▲ TROY 054 [DDD]
Imbrie, A.W.:Sym 3 *(rec Feb. 23, 1973; originally)* CRI ▲ CD 632 [ADD]
Mahler, G.:Sym 1 *(rec 1979)* Vox Box 2–▲ CDX 5123
Mahler, G.:Sym 4, w. Corrine Curry (mez) *(rec 1979)* Vox Box 2–▲ CDX 5123
Schoenberg, A.:Con Str Qt, w. Lenox String Quartet Phoenix ▲ PHCD 121 [ADD]

V. Fedotov (cnd)

Beethoven, L. van:Romances Vn, w. Vanessa–Mae (vn)—in F, Op. 50
Angel ▲ CDC 55395 ■ 4DS 55395
Bruch, M.:Scottish Fant Vn, w. Vanessa–Mae (vn) [arr Vanessa–Mae]
Angel ▲ CDC 55395 ■ 4DS 55395

A. Fiedler (cnd)

Paderewski, I.J.:Con Pno, w. Earl Wild (pno) *(rec Barking Town Hall, London, England, Sept 6, 1970)*
Elan ▲ CD 2266 [ADD]

I. Fischer (cnd)

Liszt, F.:Totentanz, w. Jorge Bolet (pno) London ("Jubilee" series) ▲ 430736–2 [DDD]

J. Fiore (cnd)

From the Heart:Italian Arias & Neopolitan Songs, w. Richard Leech (ten), *(rec Studio One, EMI Abbey Road, London, Dec 14–21, 1995)* Telarc ▲ CD 80432 [DDD]

A. Fistoulari (cnd)

Delibes, L.:Sylvia Mercury Living Presence 3–▲ 434313–2 [ADD]
Khachaturian, A.:Gayane (suites)—1 & 2 *(rec Walthamstow Assembly Hall, London)*
Everest ▲ EVC 9020 [AAD]

L. Foster (cnd)

Sarasate, P. de:Zigeunerweisen, w. G. Shaham (vn) Deutsche Grammophon ▲ 431815–2 [DDD]
Wieniawski, H.:Con 1 Vn, w. G. Shaham (vn) Deutsche Grammophon ▲ 431815–2 [DDD]
Wieniawski, H.:Con 2 Vn, w. G. Shaham (vn) Deutsche Grammophon ▲ 431815–2 [DDD]
Wieniawski, H.:Légende, w. G. Shaham (vn) Deutsche Grammophon ▲ 431815–2 [DDD]

A. Francis (cnd)

Bruch, M.:Con Cl & Va, w. T. King (cl), N. Imai (va) Hyperion ▲ CDA 66022
Crusell, B.H.:Con 1 Cl, w. T. King (cl) Hyperion ▲ CDA 66708 [DDD]
Crusell, B.H.:Con 2 Cl, w. T. King (cl) Hyperion ▲ CDA 66708 [DDD]
Crusell, B.H.:Con 2 Cl, w. T. King (cl) Hyperion ▲ CDA 66088
Crusell, B.H.:Con 3 Cl, w. T. King (cl) Hyperion ▲ CDA 66708 [DDD]
Crusell, B.H.:Intro, Theme & Vars on a Swedish Air, w. T. King (cl) Hyperion ▲ CDA 66022
Donizetti, G.:Maria Padilla, w. L. McDonall (sop—Maria Padilla), D. Jones (mez—Ines Padilla), G. Clark (ten—Don Ruiz), C. du Plessis (bar—Don Pedro), Geoffrey Mitchell Choir [I] *(rec at Henry Wood Hall, London June 1980)* Opera Rara 3–▲ ORC 6
Weber, C.M. von:Con 2 Cl, w. T. King (cl) Hyperion ▲ CDA 66088

P. Freeman (cnd)

English Tuba, w. Eugene Dowling (tuba), Edward Norman (pno) Pro Arte ▲ CDD 595 [DDD]
Mozart, W.A.:Con 26 Pno, w. M. Knoll Luria (pno) Centaur ▲ CRC 2093 [DDD]
Sibelius, J.:Con Vn, w. Sergiu Schwartz (vn) *(rec Feb 1988)* Allegretto ▲ ACD 8199
Svendsen, J.:Romance Vn, w. Sergiu Schwartz (vn) *(rec Feb 1988)* Allegretto ▲ ACD 8199
Tchaikovsky, P.:Vars on a Rococo Theme, w. I. Babini (vc) Centaur ▲ CRC 2058 [DDD]
Vaughan Williams, R.:Con Bass Tuba, w. E. Dowling (tuba) Pro Arte/Fanfare ▲ CDD 595 [DDD]

L. Frémaux (cnd)

Berlioz, H.:Sym fantastique Collins Classics ▲ EC 1001–2 [DDD]
Ravel, M.:Boléro Collins Quest ▲ COL 3020 [DDD]
Ravel, M.:Daphnis et Chloé (suite 2) Collins Quest ▲ COL 3020 [DDD]
Ravel, M.:Ma mère l'oye Orch Collins Quest ▲ COL 3020 [DDD]
Ravel, M.:La Valse Collins Quest ▲ COL 3020 [DDD]

R. Frühbeck de Burgos (cnd)

Bacarisse, S.:Concertino Gtr, w. Yepes (gtr) Deutsche Grammophon ▲ 435845–2
Beethoven, L. van:Sym 5 Collins Quest ▲ COL 3002 [DDD]
Beethoven, L. van:Wellington's Victory, "Battle Sym" Collins Quest ▲ COL 3002 [DDD]
Bizet, G.:L'Arlésienne (suites) IMP Classics ("LSO Classic Masterpieces" series) ▲ IMPPCD 905 [DDD]
Bizet, G.:Carmen (suite 1) IMP Classics ("LSO Classic Masterpieces" series) ▲ IMPPCD 905 [DDD]
Debussy, C.:La Mer IMP Classics ("LSO Classic Masterpieces" series) ▲ IMPPCD 915 [DDD]
Debussy, C.:Nocturnes, w. *(chorus unknown)*
IMP Classics ("LSO Classic Masterpieces" series) ▲ IMPPCD 915 [DDD]
Debussy, C.:Prélude à l'après-midi d'un faune
IMP Classics ("LSO Classic Masterpieces" series) ▲ IMPPCD 915 [DDD]
Elgar, E.:Con Vc, w. F. Schmidt (vc) IMP Classics ▲ PCD 930 [DDD]
Fauré, G.:Ballade Pno, w. L. Lortie (pno) Chandos ▲ CHAN 8773 [DDD]
Guitarra Española:Rodrigo, Aranjuez w. Yepes, Narciso (gtr), Spanish NationalRadio–TV SO [cnd:O. Alonso] Deutsche Grammophon ▲ 435845–2
Kodály, Z.:Háry János (suite) Nimbus ▲ NI 5194 [DDD]
Ravel, M.:Con Pno (left hand), w. L. Lortie (pno) Chandos ▲ CHAN 8773 [DDD]
Ravel, M.:Con in G Pno, w. L. Lortie (pno) Chandos ▲ CHAN 8773 [DDD]
Spanish Fiesta, w. M. Conn (gtr) Xalapa SO [cnd:H. de la Fuente]
Pickwick ("The Orchid" series) ▲ PICORCD 11014
Spanish Spectacular, *(rec 6/88)* IMP Classics ▲ PCD 924
Stravinsky, I.:Le Sacre du printemps Orch Collins Quest ▲ 3033 [DDD]
Tchaikovsky, P.:Sym 5 Nimbus ▲ NI 5194 [DDD]
Vaughan Williams, R.:Fant on Greensleeves IMP Classics ▲ PCD 930 [DDD]
Vaughan Williams, R.:Fant on a Theme by Thomas Tallis IMP Classics ▲ PCD 930 [DDD]

R. Fruhbeck de Burgos, R. Williams (cnds)

Invitation to the Dance, w. F. Schmidt (vc) Pickwick ("The Orchid" series) ▲ PICORCD 11002

P. Gamba (cnd)

Beethoven, L. van:Con 3 Pno, w. J. Katchen (pno) *(rec 1963)* PWK Classics ▲ PWK 1153 [AAD]
Beethoven, L. van:Con 3 Pno, w. Julius Katchen (pno) *(rec 1958)* London 2–▲ 440839–2 [ADD]
Beethoven, L. van:Con 4 Pno, w. Julius Katchen (pno) *(rec 1963)* London 2–▲ 440839–2 [ADD]
Beethoven, L. van:Con 4 Pno, w. J. Katchen (pno) *(rec 1959)* PWK Classics ▲ PWK 1153 [AAD]
Beethoven, L. van:Con 5 Pno, "Emperor", w. Julius Katchen (pno) *(rec 1963)*
London 2–▲ 440839–2 [ADD]
Beethoven, L. van:Fant Pno, Op. 80, "Choral Fant", w. Julius Katchen (pno), London Sym Chorus *(rec 1965)* London 2–▲ 440839–2 [ADD]
Rossini, G.:Ovs—Barber; Gazza ladra; Scala di seta; Semiramide; William
London ("Weekend Classics" series) ▲ 417692–2 [AAD]

J. Georgiadis (cnd)

An Evening in Vienna IMP Classics ▲ PCD 902 [DDD]
Magic of Vienna, w. Michael Reed (cnd), Royal PO Pickwick ("The Orchid" series) ▲ PICORCD 11015
Strauss, E.:Polkas & Waltzes—Old England for ever! (polka), Op. 239; Greeting Valse, on English Airs
Chandos ▲ CHAN 8739 [DDD]
Strauss, E.:Polkas & Waltzes—Bluthenkranz Waltz, Op. 292
IMP Classics ("LSO Classic Masterpieces" series) ▲ IMPPCD 1089 [DDD]

London SO (cont.)

J. Georgiadis (cnd) (cont.)

Strauss (I), Joh.:Music of—Huldigung der Königin Victoria von Grossbritannien (waltz); Frederica–Polka; March of the Royal Horse Guards; Alice–Polka; Almacks–Quadrille; Exeter–Polka
Chandos ▲ CHAN 8739 [DDD]
Strauss (I), Joh.:Radetzky March ASV Quicksilva ▲ QS 6020 [ADD]
Strauss (I), Joh.:Radetzky March
IMP Classics ("LSO Classic Masterpieces" series) ▲ IMPPCD 856 [DDD]
Strauss (II), Joh.:Music of—7 waltzes & polkas:Czech Polka; Kaiser–Walzer; Pizzicato Polka; Rosen aus dem Süden; Sänger Lust; Wiener Blut; Wiener Bonbons ASV Quicksilva ▲ QS 6020 [ADD]
Strauss (II), Joh.:Music of—Unter Donner und Blitz (polka), Op. 324; An der schönen blauen Donau (waltz), Op. 314; Tritsch, Tratsch (polka), Op. 214; Wein, Weib und Gesand (waltz), Op. 333; Wiener Blut (waltz), Op. 354 [w. John Georgiadis (vn)]; Radetzky March, Op. 228
IMP ("Concert Classics" series) ▲ IMP PCD 1101
Strauss (II), Joh.:Music of—The Gyspy Baron Ov.; Tales from the Vienna Woods, BWV 325; Bitte schön, Op. 372; Morning Papers, Op. 279; New Pizzicato Polka, Op. 449; Snowball, Op. 471
IMP Classics ("LSO Classic Masterpieces" series) ▲ IMPPCD 1089 [DDD]
Strauss (II), Joh.:Music of—Champagne Polka, Op. 211; The Blue Danube Waltz, Op. 314; Tritsch, Tratsch Polka, Op. 214; Thunder & Lightening, Op. 324; Vienna Blood Waltz, Op.354; Kaiser Waltz, Op. 437; Where the Lemons Bloom Waltz, Op. 364; Perpetuum Mobilum, Op. 257
IMP Classics ("LSO Classic Masterpieces" series) ▲ IMPPCD 856 [DDD]
Strauss (II), Joh.:Music of—Erinnerung an Covent–Garden (waltz on English folk melodies), Op. 329; Potpourri–Quadrille Chandos ▲ CHAN 8739 [DDD]
Strauss (II), Joh.:Music of—eight waltzes, polkas & overtures—Explosions Polka, Op. 43; Windsor Echoes, Op. 104; Annen–Polka, Op. 117; Wine, Women and Song, Op. 333; Auf der Jagd, Op. 373; Roses from the South, Op. 388; Voices of Spring, Op. 410; Die Fledermaus Overture
IMP Classics ▲ PCD 902 [DDD]
Strauss (III), Joh.:Krönungs–Walzer Chandos ▲ CHAN 8739 [DDD]
Strauss, Josef:Music of—Ohne sorgen; Feuerfest ASV Quicksilva ▲ QS 6020 [ADD]
Ziehrer, C.M.:Waltzes & Other Dances—Snowball, Op. 471
IMP Classics ("LSO Classic Masterpieces" series) ▲ IMPPCD 1089 [DDD]

V. Gergiev (cnd)

Rachmaninoff, S.:Con 2 Pno, w. E. Kissin (pno) RCA Red Seal 2–▲ 60567–2–RC [DDD]

C. Gerhardt (cnd)

Holdridge, L.:Film Music—Beastmaster Suite; Music for Strs [from Johnathan Livingston Seagull]; The Journey [from Going Home]; Love Theme [from Splash]; Wizards & Warriors Ov; East of Eden Suite; Parisian Sketch [from The Hemingway Play]; Introduction & Theme [from The Great Whales]
Citadel ▲ CTD 77103 [DDD]

A. Gibson (cnd)

Berlioz, H.:La Mort de Cléopâtre, w. J. Baker (mez) EMI Classics ("Studio" series) ▲ CDM 69544
Berlioz, H.:La Mort de Cléopâtre, w. Janet Baker (sop) EMI Classics 2–▲ CDFB 68583
Berlioz, H.:Les Troyens (sels), w. J. Baker (mez)—final scenes
EMI Classics ("Studio" series) ▲ CDM 69544

P. Gibson (cnd)

Bach, J.S.:Suite 2 Orch [Polonais & Rondo]
Vox Cameo Classics ("Sketches" series) ▲ ACD 8776 [DDD] ■ ACS 8776
Beethoven, L. van:Sym 5—1st movt
Vox Cameo Classics ("Sketches" series) ▲ ACD 8776 [DDD] ■ ACS 8776
Mozart, W.A.:Con Hn, K.412, w. *(soloist unknown)*—1st movt
Vox Cameo Classics ("Sketches" series) ▲ ACD 8776 [DDD] ■ ACS 8776
Mozart, W.A.:Con 21 Pno, w. P. Gibson (pno)—2nd movt
Vox Cameo Classics ("Sketches" series) ▲ ACD 8776 [DDD] ■ ACS 8776
Mozart, W.A.:Nozze di Figaro (sels)—Ov
Vox Cameo Classics ("Sketches" series) ▲ ACD 8776 [DDD] ■ ACS 8776
Offenbach, J.:Orphée aux enfers (sels)—Ov.
Vox Cameo Classics ("Sketches" series) ▲ ACD 8773 [DDD] ■ ACS 8773
Pachelbel, J.:Canon Vox Cameo Classics ("Sketches" series) ▲ ACD 8776 [DDD] ■ ACS 8776
Rossini, G.:Guillaume Tell (sels)—Ov.
Vox Cameo Classics ("Sketches" series) ▲ ACD 8773 [DDD] ■ ACS 8773
Schubert, Franz:Sym 8—1st movt
Vox Cameo Classics ("Sketches" series) ▲ ACD 8776 [DDD] ■ ACS 8776
Suppé, F. von:Ovs—Poet & Peasant; Light Cavalry
Vox Cameo Classics ("Sketches" series) ▲ ACD 8773 [DDD] ■ ACS 8773
The Very Best of Classical Encores Vox ("Sketches" series) ▲ ACD 8774 [DDD]
Wagner, R.:Die Meistersinger von Nürnberg (sels)—Ov.
Vox Cameo Classics ("Sketches" series) ▲ ACD 8773 [DDD] ■ ACS 8773
Wagner, R.:Tannhäuser (orch sels)—Ov.
Vox Cameo Classics ("Sketches" series) ▲ ACD 8773 [DDD] ■ ACS 8773
Weber, C.M. von:Der Freischütz (sels)—Ov.
Vox Cameo Classics ("Sketches" series) ▲ ACD 8773 [DDD] ■ ACS 8773

C.M. Giulini (cnd)

Beethoven, L. van:Sym 9, "Choral Sym" EMI Classics ▲ CDE 67763

W. Goehr (cnd)

Tchaikovsky, P.:Con Vn, w. Tossy Spivakovsky (vn) *(rec Walthamstow Assembly Hall, London)*
Everest ▲ EVC 9035 [AAD]
Tchaikovsky, P.:Souvenir d'un lieu cher, w. Tossy Spivakovsky (vn)—Mélodie [arr vn & orch] *(rec Walthamstow Assembly Hall, London)* Everest ▲ EVC 9035 [AAD]

E. Goossens (cnd)

Antheil, G.:Sym 4, "1942" *(rec Walthamstow Hall, London, Mar 1959)* Everest ▲ EVC 9039 [AAD]
Berlioz, H.:Sym fantastique *(rec Walthamstow Assembly Hall, London)* Everest ▲ EVC 9017 [AAD]
Berlioz, H.:Sym fantastique—The Ball *(rec Manhattan Center, NYC or Walthamstow Assembly Hall, London)* Everest ▲ EVC 9031 [AAD]
Ginastera, A.:Estancia (suite) Everest ▲ EVC 9007 [AAD]
Hindemith, P.:Con Vn, w. Joseph Fuchs (vn) Everest ▲ EVC 9009 [AAD]
Rachmaninoff, S.:Symphonic Dances Everest ▲ EVC 9002 [AAD]
Respighi, O.:Feste Romane *(rec Walthamstow Assembly Hall, London)* Everest ▲ EVC 9018 [AAD]
Stravinsky, I.:Pétrouchka Everest ▲ EVC 9042 [AAD]
Stravinsky, I.:Le Sacre du printemps Orch Everest ▲ EVC 9002 [AAD]
Stravinsky, I.:Sym in 3 Movts Everest ▲ EVC 9042 [AAD]
Tchaikovsky, P.:Manfred *(rec Walthamstow Assembly Hall, London)* Everest ▲ EVC 9025 [AAD]
Villa–Lobos, H.:Bachiana brasileira 2—The Little Train of the Caipira (toccata)
Everst ▲ EVC 9007 [AAD]

C. Groves (cnd)

Williams, G.:Fairest of Stars, w. Janet Price (sop) Lyrita ▲ SRCD 327

C. Groves, D. Atherton (cnds)

Williams, G.:Music of, w. Anthony Camden (ob), R. Allan (tpt), H. Snell (tpt), Royal PO, English CO—Fant on Welsh Nursery Tunes; Sea Sketches; Penillion; Carillions Ob; Con for Tpt
Lyrita ▲ SRCD 323

A. Guadagno (cnd)

Ponchielli, A.:La Gioconda (sels), w. Placído Domingo (ten), Sherrill Milnes (bar)—Enzo Grimaldi, Principe di Santa Fior *(rec 1970)* RCA Gold Seal ▲ 09026–62595–2 [ADD]
Puccini, G.:La Bohème (sels), w. Plácido Domingo (ten), Sherrill Milnes (bar)—O Mimì, tu più non torni *(rec 1970)* RCA Gold Seal ▲ 09026–62595–2 [ADD]
Verdi, G.:La forza del destino (sels), w. Placído Domingo (ten), Sherrill Milnes (bar)—Solenne in quest'ora; Invano, Alvaro, tu calaste al mondo *(rec 1970)*
RCA Gold Seal ▲ 09026–62595–2 [ADD]
Verdi, G.:Otello (sels), w. Placído Domingo (ten), Sherrill Milnes (bar)—Sì, pel ciel marmoreo giurol *(rec 1970)* RCA Gold Seal ▲ 09026–62595–2 [ADD]
Verdi, G.:I vespri siciliani (sels), w. Placído Domingo (ten), Sherrill Milnes (bar)—Quando al mio sen *(rec 1970)* RCA Gold Seal ▲ 09026–62595–2 [ADD]

London SO (cont.)
V. Gui (cnd)
Verdi, G.:La traviata, w. Maria Caniglia (sop—Violetta), Baniamino Gigli (ten—Alfredo), Mario Basiola (bar—Germont), London Sym Chorus Enterprise ("The Radio Years" series) 2-▲ ENT RY 64
B. Haitink (cnd)
Vaughan Williams, R.:Sym 1, w. F. Lott (sop), J. Summers (bar), London Sym Chorus [E] EMI Classics ▲ CDC 49911 [DDD]
T. Hannikainen (cnd)
Sibelius, J.:Con Vn, w. Tossy Spivakovsky (vn) *(rec Walthamstow Assembly Hall, London)* Everest ▲ EVC 9035 [AAD]
Sibelius, J.:Tapiola *(rec Walthamstow Assembly Hall, London)* Everest ▲ EVC 9025 [AAD]
H. Harty (cnd)
Walton, W.:Sym 1 *(rec Dec. 10–11, 1935)* Dutton Laboratories ▲ CDAX 8003 [ADD]
L. Haza (cnd)
Arutiunian, A.:Con Tpt, w. A. Sandoval (tpt) [Cadenza by Timofey Dokshizer] *(rec May 27–29 & July 16, 1993)* RCA Red Seal ▲ 09026-62661-2 [DDD]
Hummel, J.N.:Con in E♭ Tpt, S.49, w. A. Sandoval (tpt) [Cadenza by Sandoval] *(rec May 27–29 & July 16, 1993)* RCA Red Seal ▲ 09026-62661-2 [DDD]
Mozart, L.:Con Tpt, w. A. Sandoval (tpt) [Cadenza by Sandoval] *(rec May 27–29 & July 16, 1993)* RCA Red Seal ▲ 09026-62661-2 [DDD]
Sandoval, A.:Con Tpt, w. A. Sandoval (tpt) [Cadenza by Timofey Dokshizer] *(rec May 27–29 & July 16, 1993)* RCA Red Seal ▲ 09026-62661-2 [DDD]
R. Heger (cnd)
Rosette Anday, w. Rosette Anday (cta), Vienna State Opera Orch [cnd:Carl Alwin], Berlin State Opera Orch [cnd:Julius Prüwer] Preiser ("Lebendige Vergangenheit" series) ▲ PRE 89046 (m) [AAD]
S. Henderson (cnd)
Prokofiev, S.:Peter & the Wolf, w. B. Lillie (nar) [E] London ■ 411650-4
Prokofiev, S.:Peter & the Wolf, w. B. Lillie (nar) [E] London ("Weekend Classics" series) ▲ 436105-2
Saint-Saëns, C.:Carnival of the Animals, w. B. Lillie (nar) [E] London ("Weekend Classics" series) ▲ 436105-2
Saint-Saëns, C.:Carnival of the Animals, w. Lillie (nar), Katchen (pno), Graffman (pno) [E] London ■ 411650-4
R. Hickox (cnd)
Alwyn, W.:Con 1 Pno, w. H. Shelley (pno) Chandos ▲ CHAN 9155 [DDD]
Alwyn, W.:Con 2 Pno, w. H. Shelley (pno) Chandos ▲ CHAN 9196
Alwyn, W.:Con Vn, w. L. Mordkovitch (vn) Chandos ▲ CHAN 9187 [DDD]
Alwyn, W.:Derby Day Chandos ▲ CHAN 9093 [DDD]
Alwyn, W.:Elizabethan Dances Chandos ▲ CHAN 8902 [DDD]
Alwyn, W.:Fanfare for a Joyful Occasion Chandos ▲ CHAN 9093 [DDD]
Alwyn, W.:Festival March Chandos ▲ CHAN 8902 [DDD]
Alwyn, W.:Film Music—Odd Man Out Suite; The History of Mr. Polly Suite; The Fallen Idol Suite; Calypso from *The Rake's Progress* [arr. or ed. C. Palmer] *(rec Jan 15–16, 1993)* Chandos ▲ CHAN 9243 [DDD]
Alwyn, W.:The Magic Island Chandos ▲ CHAN 9093 [DDD]
Alwyn, W.:Ov to a Masque Chandos ▲ CHAN 9093 [DDD]
Alwyn, W.:Sinfonietta Chandos 3-▲ CHAN 9429 [DDD]
Alwyn, W.:Sinfonietta Chandos ▲ CHAN 9196
Alwyn, W.:Syms (comp) Chandos 3-▲ CHAN 9429 [DDD]
Alwyn, W.:Sym 1 Chandos ▲ CHAN 9155 [DDD]
Alwyn, W.:Sym 2 Chandos ▲ CHAN 9093 [DDD]
Alwyn, W.:Sym 3 Chandos ▲ CHAN 9187 [DDD]
Alwyn, W.:Sym 4 Chandos ▲ CHAN 8902 [DDD]
Alwyn, W.:Sym 5, "Hydriotaphia" Chandos ▲ CHAN 9196
Arnold, M.:Film Music—The Bridge on the River Kwai (suite); Hobson's Choice (orchestral suite); The Inn of the Sixth Happiness (orchestral suite); The Sound Barrier (rhapsody), Op. 38; Whistle Down the Wind (small suite) [all titles apart from *The Sound Barrier* arr. Christopher Palmer] Chandos ▲ CHAN 9100 [DDD]
Arnold, M.:Sym 1 Chandos ▲ CHAN 9335 [DDD]
Arnold, M.:Sym 2 Chandos ▲ CHAN 9335 [DDD]
Arnold, M.:Sym 3 Chandos ▲ CHAN 9290 [DDD]
Arnold, M.:Sym 4 Chandos ▲ CHAN 9290 [DDD]
Arnold, M.:Sym 5 Chandos ▲ CHAN 9385 [DDD]
Arnold, M.:Sym 6 Chandos ▲ CHAN 9385 [DDD]
The Best of Richard Hickox, w. London Sym Chorus, Penelope Walmsley-Clark (sop), John Graham-Hall (ten), D. Maxwell (bar), Southend Boys' Choir, London Voices IMP Classics 3-▲ TCD 1073 [DDD]
Bloch, E.:Schelomo, w. S. Isserlis (vc) Virgin Classics ▲ CDC 59511 [DDD]
Brahms, J.:Ein Deutsches Requiem, w. F. Lott (sop), D. Wilson-Johnson (bar), London Sym Chorus [G] Chandos ▲ CHAN 8942 [DDD]
Britten, B.:Ballad of Heroes, w. M. Hill (ten), London Sym Chorus [E] Chandos 2-▲ CHAN 8983/84 [DDD]
Britten, B.:Sinf da requiem Chandos 2-▲ CHAN 8983/84 [DDD]
Britten, B.:Spring Sym, w. E. Gale (sop), A. Hodgson (cta), M. Hill (ten), London Sym Chorus, Southend Boys' Choir [E] Chandos ▲ CHAN 8855 [DDD]
Britten, B.:War Requiem, w. H. Harper (sop), P. Langridge (ten), J. Shirley-Quirk (bar), R. Elms (org), London Sym Chorus, St. Paul's Cathedral Choristers [E,L] Chandos 2-▲ CHAN 8983/84 [DDD]
Elgar, E.:The Apostles, w. A. Hargan (sop), A. Hodgson (cta), D. Rendall (ten), S. Roberts (bar), B. Terfel (bass-bar), R. Lloyd (bass), London Sym Chorus [E] Chandos 2-▲ CHAN 8875/76 [DDD]
Elgar, E.:The Black Knight, w. London Sym Chorus Chandos ▲ CHAN 9436
Elgar, E.:Caractacus, w. J. Howarth (sop), A. Davies (ten), S. Roberts (bar), D. Wilson-Johnson (bar), A.R. Miles (bass), London Sym Chorus [E] *(rec 1992)* Chandos 2-▲ CHAN 9156/57 [DDD]
Elgar, E.:Con Vc, w. S. Isserlis (vc) Virgin Classics ▲ CDC 59511 [DDD]
Elgar, E.:Con Vn, w. S. Accardo (vn) Collins Classics ▲ COL 1338 [DDD]
Elgar, E.:The Dream of Gerontius, w. F. Palmer (sop), A. Davies (ten), G. Howell (bass), London Sym Chorus [E] Chandos 2-▲ CHAN 8641/42 [DDD]
Elgar, E.:The Kingdom, w. M. Marshall (sop), F. Palmer (sop), Davies (ten), D. Wilson-Johnson (bar), London Sym Chorus [E] Chandos 2-▲ CHAN 8788/89 [DDD]
Elgar, E.:The Light of Life, w. J. Howarth (sop), L. Finnie (mez), A. Davies (ten), J. Shirley-Quirk (bar), London Sym Chorus Chandos ▲ CHAN 9208 [DDD]
Elgar, E.:Severn Suite Orch *(rec 1992)* Chandos 2-▲ CHAN 9156/57 [DDD]
Elgar, E.:Sospiri Chandos 2-▲ CHAN 8788/89 [DDD]
Elgar, E.:Sursum corda Chandos 2-▲ CHAN 8788/89 [DDD]
Ferguson, H.:Ballads (2), w. B. Rayner Cook (bar) [E] Chandos ▲ CHAN 9082 [DDD]
Ferguson, H.:The Dream of the Rood, w. A. Dawson (sop), London Sym Chorus [E] Chandos ▲ CHAN 9082 [DDD]
Ferguson, H.:Ov for an Occasion Chandos ▲ CHAN 9082 [DDD]
Ferguson, H.:Partita Chandos ▲ CHAN 9082 [DDD]
Golden Melodies from Opera, w. Royal PO [cnd:R. Stapelton], S. McCulloch (sop), Josephine Barstow (sop), J. Oakman (ten), Edmund Barham (ten) Pickwick ("The Orchid" series) ▲ PICORCD 11005
Great Opera Choruses IMP Classics ("LSO Classic Masterpieces" series) ▲ PCD 908 [DDD]
Holst, G.:The Cloud Messenger, w. D. Jones (mez), London Sym Chorus [E] Chandos ▲ CHAN 8901 [DDD]
Holst, G.:Egdon Heath, Homage to Hardy Chandos ▲ CHAN 9420
Holst, G.:A Fugal Ov Chandos ▲ CHAN 9420
Holst, G.:Hammersmith Chandos ▲ CHAN 9420
Holst, G.:The Hymn of Jesus, w. London Sym Chorus [E] Chandos ▲ CHAN 8901 [DDD]
Holst, G.:Orchestral Works—Capriccio; Scherzo Chandos ▲ CHAN 9420
Holst, G.:The Planets w. London Sym Chorus IMP Classics ("LSO Classic Masterpieces" series) ▲ IMPPCD 890 [DDD]

London SO (cont.)
R. Hickox (cnd) (cont.)
Holst, G.:A Somerset Rhap Chandos ▲ CHAN 9420
Howells, H.:Fant Vc & Orch, w. Moray Welsh (vc) Chandos ▲ CHAN 9410 [DDD]
Howells, H.:King's Herald Chandos ▲ CHAN 9410 [DDD]
Howells, H.:Paradise Rondel Chandos ▲ CHAN 9410 [DDD]
Howells, H.:Pastoral Rhap Chandos ▲ CHAN 9410 [DDD]
Howells, H.:Procession Chandos ▲ CHAN 9410 [DDD]
Howells, H.:Threnody, w. Moray Welsh (vc) Chandos ▲ CHAN 9410 [DDD]
Ireland, J.:Epic March Chandos ▲ CHAN 8879 [DDD]
Ireland, J.:The Forgotten Rite Chandos ▲ CHAN 8994 [DDD]
Ireland, J.:Greater Love Hath No Man, w. P. Bott (sop), B. Terfel (bass-bar), London Sym Chorus [E] Chandos ▲ CHAN 8879 [DDD]
Ireland, J.:The Holy Boy Chandos ▲ CHAN 8879 [DDD]
Ireland, J.:A London Ov Chandos ▲ CHAN 8879 [DDD]
Ireland, J.:The Overlanders Chandos ▲ CHAN 8994 [DDD]
Ireland, J.:Satyricon Chandos ▲ CHAN 8994 [DDD]
Ireland, J.:Scherzo & Cortege on Themes from Julius Caesar Chandos ▲ CHAN 8994 [DDD]
Ireland, J.:These Things shall Be, w. B. Terfel (b-bar), London Sym Chorus [E] Chandos ▲ CHAN 8879 [DDD]
Ireland, J.:Tritons Chandos ▲ CHAN 8994 [DDD]
Ireland, J.:Vexilla Regis, w. P. Bott (sop), T. Shaw (mez), J. Oxley (ten), B. Terfel (bass-bar), London Sym Chorus [L] Chandos ▲ CHAN 8879 [DDD]
Mendelssohn, F.:Elijah, w. R. Plowright (sop), L. Finnie (mez), J. Budd (trb), A. Davies (ten), J. White (bass), London Sym Chorus [E] Chandos 2-▲ CHAN 8774/75 [DDD]
Orff, C.:Carmina burana, w. *(soloists & chorus unknown)* IMP Classics ("LSO Classic Masterpieces" series) ▲ IMPPCD 855 [DDD]
Orff, C.:Carmina burana, w. P. Walmsley-Clark (sop), J. Graham-Hall (ten), D. Maxwell (bar), London Sym Chorus [G, L] IMP Classics ▲ PCD 855
Parry, H.:Blest Pair of Sirens, w. London Sym Chorus Chandos 2-▲ CHAN 8641/42 [DDD]
Parry, H.:I Was Glad, w. London Sym Chorus Chandos 2-▲ CHAN 8641/42 [DDD]
Vaughan Williams, R.:Dona nobis pacem, w. Y. Kenny (sop), B. Terfel (b-bar), London Sym Chorus, St. Paul's Cathedral Choristers EMI Classics ▲ CDC 54788
Vaughan Williams, R.:Sancta civitas, w. P. Langridge (ten), B. Terfel (b-bar), London Sym Chorus, St. Paul's Cathedral Choirsters EMI Classics ▲ CDC 54788
Verdi, G.:Requiem Mass, w. Michèle Crider (sop), Markella Hatziano (mez), Gabriel Sadé (ten), Robert Lloyd (bass), London Sym Chorus Chandos ▲ CHAN 9490
Walton, W.:Belshazzar's Feast, w. David Wilson-Johnson (bar), London Sym Chorus Classics for Pleasure ("Eminence" series) ▲ CDEMX 2225 [DDD]
Walton, W.:Con Va, w. S. Accardo (vn) Collins Classics ▲ COL 1338 [DDD]
Walton, W.:In Honour of the City of London, w. London Sym Chorus Classics for Pleasure ("Eminence" series) ▲ CDEMX 2225 [DDD]
R. Hickox, Y. Butt, J. Manceri (cnds)
Classical Masterpieces, w. Royal PO, Michael Reed (cnd), Vladimir Ashkenazy (cnd), Scottish CO [cnd:Wilfried Boettcher] Pickwick ("The Orchid" series) ▲ PICORCD 11006
P. Hindemith (cnd)
Hindemith, P.:Con Vn, w. David Oistrakh (vn) London ("Enterprise" series) ▲ 433081-2 [ADD]
J. Hirokami (cnd)
Liszt, F.:Cons Pno, w. B. Douglas (pno) RCA Red Seal ▲ 7916-2-RC [DDD] ■ 7916-4-RC (CrO2)
Liszt, F.:Cons Pno, w. B. Douglas (pno) RCA Victor ▲ 09026-62679-2 ■ 09026-62679-4
Liszt, F.:Fant on Hungarian Folk Tunes, w. B. Douglas (pno) RCA Red Seal ▲ 7916-2-RC [DDD] ■ 7916-4-RC (CrO2)
L. Holdridge (cnd)
Holdridge, L.:Albinoni, w. G. Dicterow (vn) [arr. Holdridge] *(rec St. Giles Church, Cripplegate, London, Sept. & Oct. 1973)* Citadel ▲ CTD 88104 [ADD]
Holdridge, L.:Andante *(rec St. Giles Church, Cripplegate, London, Sept. & Oct. 1973)* Citadel ▲ CTD 88104 [ADD]
Holdridge, L.:Con 2 Vn, w. G. Dicterow (vn) *(rec St. Barnabas Church, Woodside Park, London, Jan. 4 & 5, 1980)* Citadel ▲ CTD 88104 [DDD]
Holdridge, L.:Lazarus & His Beloved (suite) *(rec St. Barnabas Church, Woodside Park, London, Jan. 4 & 5, 1980)* Citadel ▲ CTD 88104 [DDD]
Holdridge, L.:Scenes of Summer *(rec St. Giles Church, Cripplegate, London, Sept. & Oct. 1973)* Citadel ▲ CTD 88104 [ADD]
Tanner, J.:Boy with Goldfish, w. L. Siu (sgr), M. Elliott (sgr), Nigel Brooks Chorale Albany ▲ TROY 053 [DDD]
G. Holst (cnd)
Holst, G.:Beni Mora *(rec 1924 for Columbia)* Pearl ▲ PEA 9417 (m) [AAD]
Holst, G.:The Planets, w. London Sym Chorus *(rec 1926 Columbia electrical)* Koch Legacy ▲ 3-7018-2 H1 (m)
Holst, G.:The Planets, w. London Sym Chorus *(rec 1922–24 for Columbia)* Pearl ▲ PEA 9417 (m) [AAD]
Holst, G.:The Planets IMP ("Golden Legacy of Recorded Sound" series) ▲ IMP GLRS 108
Holst, G.:Songs without Words—Marching Song IMP ("Golden Legacy of Recorded Sound" series) ▲ IMP GLRS 108
J. Horenstein (cnd)
Brahms, J.:Sym 1 *(rec 1962)* Chesky ▲ CD 19
Bruckner, A.:Sym 8 *(rec London 1970)* Intaglio 2-▲ INCD 7272 [ADD]
Bruckner, A.:Sym 8 *(rec 1970)* Music & Arts 4-▲ CD 785 [AAD]
Hindemith, P.:Mathis der Maler (sym) *(rec 1972)* Chandos ("Collect" series) ▲ CHAN 6549 [ADD]
Mahler, G.:Sym 3, w. N. Procter (cta), Ambrosian Singers, Wandsworth School Boys' Choir [G] Unicorn-Kanchana ("Souvenir" series) 2-▲ UKCD 2006/07 [ADD]
Mahler, G.:Sym 9 *(rec live, 1966)* Music & Arts 2-▲ CD 235
Strauss, R.:Tod und Verklärung *(rec 1970)* Chandos ("Collect" series) ▲ CHAN 6549 [ADD]
E. Inbal (cnd)
Chopin, F.:Con 1 Pno, w. C. Arrau (pno) Philips ("Insignia" series) ▲ 434145-2 [ADD]
Chopin, F.:Con 2 Pno, w. C. Arrau (pno) Philips ("Insignia" series) ▲ 434145-2 [ADD]
Chopin, F.:Music of, w. C. Arrau (pno) Philips 2-▲ 438338-2
Chopin, F.:Pno Music (misc), w. C. Arrau (pno) Philips 2-▲ 438338-2
D. Jackson (cnd)
Handel, G.F.:Messiah (sels), w. Catherine Bott (sop), Clare Henry (cta), Gareth Roberts (ten), David Stephenson (bass)—Comfort Ye, My People, Saith Your God; Every Valley Shall Be Exalted; And the Glory of the Lord Shall Be Revealed; And He Shall Purify the Sons of Levi; For unto Us a Child Is Born; Pifa; Rejoice Greatly, O Daughter of Zion; Air:He Shall Feed His Flock Like a Shepherd; Behold the Lamb of God; He Was Despised and Rejected of Men; All We Like Sheep Have Gone Astray; The Trumpet Shall Sound; Chorus:Hallelujah! For the Lord God Omnipotent Reigneth Special Music Co. ▲ SCD 5102 [DDD]
Handel, G.F.:Messiah (sels), w. Catherine Bott (sop), Clare Henry (cta), Gareth Roberts (ten), David Stephenson (bass)—Comfort Ye, My People, Saith Your God; Every Valley Shall Be Exalted; And the Glory of the Lord Shall Be Revealed; And He Shall Purify the Sons of Levi; For unto Us a Child Is Born; Pifa; Rejoice Greatly, O Daughter of Zion; Air:He Shall Feed His Flock Like a Shepherd; Behold the Lamb of God; He Was Despised and Rejected of Men; All We Like Sheep Have Gone Astray; The Trumpet Shall Sound; Chorus:Hallelujah! For the Lord God Omnipotent Reigneth Special Music Co. 2-▲ S2D 5110 [DDD]
Tchaikovsky, P.:The Nutcracker (sels)—Ov; Christmas Tree; Marche; Journey through the Snow; Waltz of the Snowflakes; Chocolate; Coffee; Tea; Trepak; Dance of the Mielitons; Mother Gigogne & the Clowns; Waltz of the Flowers; Pas de Deux; Vars 1 & 2; Coda; Finale *(rec London, 1994)* Unison ■ V 40046
M. Jarre (cnd)
Jarre, M.:Lawrence of Arabia Varèse Sarabande ▲ VSD 5263 ■ VSC 5263

ORCH. & ENS.

London SO (cont.)

N. Järvi (cnd)

Brahms, J.:Con Vn & Vc, "Double Con", w. L. Mordkovitch (vn), R. Wallfisch (vc) Chandos ▲ CHAN 8667 [DDD]
Brahms, J.:Hungarian Dances Orch Chandos ▲ CHAN 8885 [DDD]
Brahms, J.:Qt 1 Pno Chandos ▲ CHAN 8825 [DDD]
Brahms, J.:Sym 1 Chandos ▲ CHAN 8653 [DDD]
Brahms, J.:Sym 2 Chandos ▲ CHAN 8649 [DDD]
Brahms, J.:Sym 3 Chandos ▲ CHAN 8646 [DDD]
Brahms, J.:Sym 4 Chandos ▲ CHAN 8595 [DDD]
Brahms, J.:Vars & Fugue on a Theme by Handel [Edmund Rubbra's 1938 orch.] Chandos ▲ CHAN 8825 [DDD]
Bruch, M.:Con 1 Vn, w. L. Mordkovitch (vn) Chandos ▲ CHAN 8667 [DDD]
Debussy, C.:La Mer Chandos ▲ CHAN 9072 [DDD]
Kallinikov, V.:Intermezzi Chandos ▲ CHAN 8614 [DDD]
Liadov, A.:Orchestral Music—Baba-Yaga, Op. 56 (1904); The Enchanted Lake, Op. 62 (1909); Kikimora, Op. 63 (1909) [orchestral music based on Russian fairy tales] Chandos ▲ CHAN 8783 [DDD]
Rachmaninoff, S.:Sym 3 Chandos ▲ CHAN 8614 [DDD]
Rimsky-Korsakov, N.:The Little Oak Stick Chandos ▲ CHAN 8783 [DDD]
Russian Ballet Masterpieces, w. Scottish National Orch Chandos ("Collect" series) ▲ CHAN 6512 [DDD]
Russian Masterpieces, w. Scottish National Orch Chandos ("Collect" series) ▲ CHAN 6511 [DDD]
Schumann, R.:Genoveva (ov) Chandos ("Collect" series) ▲ CHAN 6548 [DDD]
Schumann, R.:Genoveva (ov) Chandos ▲ CHAN 8595 [DDD]
Schumann, R.:Julius Caesar Chandos ▲ CHAN 8649 [DDD]
Schumann, R.:Julius Caesar Chandos ("Collect" series) ▲ CHAN 6548 [DDD]
Schumann, R.:Manfred Chandos ("Collect" series) ▲ CHAN 6548 [DDD]
Schumann, R.:Manfred Ov Chandos ▲ CHAN 8653 [DDD]
Schumann, R.:Ov, Scherzo & Finale Chandos ▲ CHAN 8646 [DDD]
Schumann, R.:Ov, Scherzo & Finale Chandos ("Collect" series) ▲ CHAN 6548 [DDD]
Stravinsky, I.:The Firebird Suite Chandos ▲ CHAN 8783 [DDD]

E. Jochum (cnd)

Beethoven, L. van:Fidelio (ov) EMI Classics ▲ CDM 64633
Beethoven, L. van:Sym 6, "Pastorale" Royal Classics ▲ ROY 6427
Beethoven, L. van:Sym 8 Royal Classics ▲ ROY 6427
Beethoven, L. van:Sym 9, "Choral Sym", w. K. Te Kanawa (sop), London Sym Chorus EMI Classics ▲ CDM 64633

A. Joó (cnd)

Ravel, M.:Boléro *(rec London, Apr 1983)* Arts Music ▲ 47243 [DDD]
Ravel, M.:Daphnis et Chloé (suite 2) *(rec London, Apr 1983)* Arts Music ▲ 47243 [DDD]
Ravel, M.:Pavane pour une infante défunte *(rec London, Apr 1983)* Arts Music ▲ 47243 [DDD]
Tchaikovsky, P.:Romeo & Juliet *(rec London, Apr 1983 & June 1986)* Arts Music ▲ 47241-2 [DDD]

E. Jorda (cnd)

Falla, M. de:El sombrero de tres picos, w. B. Howitt (sop) *(rec Apr. 1960)* Everest ▲ EVC 9000 [AAD]

J. Judd (cnd)

Strauss, R.:Con Ob, w. Robin Canter (ob) IMP ("Masters" series) ▲ IMP 6600212
Strauss, R.:Con Ob, w. R. Canter (ob) IMP Masters ▲ IMPMCD 58 [DDD]
Tchaikovsky, P.:Andante cantabile IMP Classics ("LSO Classic Masterpieces" series) ▲ IMPPCD 893 [DDD]
Tchaikovsky, P.:Con 1 Pno, w. John Lill (pno) IMP ("Concert Classics" series) ▲ IMP PCD 1102
Tchaikovsky, P.:Con 1 Pno, w. John Lill (pno) IMP Classics ("LSO Classic Masterpieces" series) ▲ IMPPCD 893 [DDD]
Vaughan Williams, R.:Con Ob, w. Robin Canter (ob) IMP ("Masters" series) ▲ IMP 6600212
Vaughan Williams, R.:Con Ob, w. R. Canter (ob) IMP Masters ▲ IMPMCD 58 [DDD]
Vaughan Williams, R.:Studies in English Folk-Song, w. Robin Canter (ob) [arr Canter] IMP ("Masters" series) ▲ IMP 6600212
Vaughan Williams, R.:Studies in English Folk-Song, w. R. Canter (ob) [arr. for oboe] IMP Masters ▲ IMPMCD 58 [DDD]

J. Judd, W. Morris (cnds)

The Heart of the Piano Concerto, w. John Lill (pno), Cristina Ortiz (pno), J. L. Prats (pno), Royal PO [cnd:L. Foster, E. Bátiz] Pickwick ("The Orchid" series) ▲ PICORCD 11012

R. Kajanus (cnd)

Sibelius, J.:Belshazzar's Feast (suite) *(rec 1932)* Koch Legacy ▲ 371312
Sibelius, J.:Belshazzar's Feast (suite) *(rec 1930 & 1932)* Finlandia 3-▲ 4509-95882-2 (m) [ADD]
Sibelius, J.:Karelia Suite *(rec 1930)* Koch Legacy ▲ 371312
Sibelius, J.:Karelia Suite *(rec 1930 & 1932)* Finlandia 3-▲ 4509-95882-2 (m) [ADD]
Sibelius, J.:Pohjola's Daughter *(rec 1932)* Koch Legacy ▲ 3-7127-2 H1
Sibelius, J.:Pohjola's Daughter *(rec 1930 & 1932)* Finlandia 3-▲ 4509-95882-2 (m) [ADD]
Sibelius, J.:Sym 1 *(rec 1930 & 1932)* Finlandia 3-▲ 4509-95882-2 (m) [ADD]
Sibelius, J.:Sym 1 *(rec 1930)* Koch Legacy ▲ 3-7127-2 H1
Sibelius, J.:Sym 2 *(rec 1930 & 1932)* Finlandia 3-▲ 4509-95882-2 (m) [ADD]
Sibelius, J.:Sym 2 *(rec 1930)* Koch Legacy ▲ 371312
Sibelius, J.:Sym 3 *(rec 1930 & 1932)* Finlandia 3-▲ 4509-95882-2 (m) [ADD]
Sibelius, J.:Sym 3 *(rec 1932)* Koch Legacy ▲ 3-7133-2 H1
Sibelius, J.:Sym 5 *(rec 1932)* Koch Legacy ▲ 3-7133-2 H1
Sibelius, J.:Sym 5 *(rec 1930 & 1932)* Finlandia 3-▲ 4509-95882-2 (m) [ADD]
Sibelius, J.:Tapiola *(rec 1932)* Koch Legacy ▲ 3-7127-2 H1

G. Kaplan (cnd)

Mahler, G.:Sym 2, w. B. Valente (sop), M. Forrester (cta), London Sym Chorus MCA Classics 2-▲ MCAD 11011 [DDD]; 2-■ MCAC 11011 (D)
Mahler, G.:Sym 2, w. Benita Valente (sop), Maureen Forrester (cta), Ardwyn Singers, BBC Welsh Chorus, Cardiff Polyphonic Choir, Dyfed Choir Conifer Classics 2-▲ 75605-51277-2 [DDD]
Mahler, G.:Sym 5—Adagietto Conifer Classics 2-▲ 75605-51277-2 [DDD]

J. Kaspszyk (cnd)

Mahler, G.:Sym 1 Collins Quest ▲ COL 3005 [DDD]
Strauss, R.:Also sprach Zarathustra Collins Quest ▲ COL 3004 [DDD]
Strauss, R.:Don Juan Collins Quest ▲ COL 3004 [DDD]
Strauss, R.:Till Eulenspiegels lustige Streiche Collins Quest ▲ COL 3004 [DDD]

I. Kertész (cnd)

Brahms, J.:Serenade 1 Orch London ("Weekend Classics" series) ▲ 421628-2 [AAD]
Brahms, J.:Serenade 2 Orch London ("Weekend Classics" series) ▲ 421628-2 [AAD]
Bruckner, A.:Sym 4, "Romantic" IMP ("BBC Radio Classics" series) ▲ IMP 5691712
Gershwin, G.:Rhap in Blue, w. J. Katchen (pno) London ▲ 436570-2 (m) [ADD]
Mozart, W.A.:Con 23 Pno, w. C. Curzon (pno) London ("Weekend Classics" series) ▲ 433086-2 [AAD]
Mozart, W.A.:Con 24 Pno, w. Clifford Curzon (pno) London ("Weekend Classics" series) ▲ 433086-2 [AAD]
Respighi, O.:The Fountains of Rome London ("Weekend Classics" series) ▲ 425507-2 [AAD]
Respighi, O.:The Pines of Rome London ("Weekend Classics" series) ▲ 425507-2 [AAD]
Respighi, O.:Gli uccelli London ("Weekend Classics" series) ▲ 425507-2 [AAD]

K. Kondrashin (cnd)

Chopin, F.:Andante Spianato & Grande Polonaise, w. Sviatoslav Richter (pno) Historical Performers ▲ HP 13
Chopin, F.:Andante Spianato & Grande Polonaise, w. S. Richter (pno) *(rec live, Royal Albert Hall 1961)* Intaglio ▲ INCD 707-1 [ADD]
Chopin, F.:Pno Music (misc), w. Sviatoslav Richter (pno)—Scherzo in E, Op. 54; Polonaise Fant. No. 7, Op. 61; Waltzes No. 4, Op. 34; No. 13, Op. posth.; Etudes, Op. 25/7; Op. 10/1 & 12; Mazurkas, Op. 24/1–4 Historical Performers ▲ HP 13
Dvořák, A.:Con Pno, w. S. Richter (pno) *(rec 1961)* Intaglio ▲ ING 751 [ADD]
Liszt, F.:Cons Pno, w. Sviatoslav Richter (pno) Fonit Cetra ("Fortissimo" series) ▲ FCT CDE 3012

London SO (cont.)

K. Kondrashin (cnd) (cont.)

Liszt, F.:Cons Pno, w. S. Richter (pno) Philips ("Insignia" series) ▲ 434163-2 [ADD]
Liszt, F.:Con 1 Pno, w. Sviatoslav Richter (pno) Philips ("Solo" series) ▲ 446200-2
Liszt, F.:Con 2 Pno, w. Sviatoslav Richter (pno) Philips ("Solo" series) ▲ 446200-2
Liszt, F.:Fant on Hungarian Folk Tunes, w. Sviatoslav Richter (pno) Fonit Cetra ("Fortissimo" series) ▲ FCT CDE 3012
Liszt, F.:Son Pno, w. Sviatoslav Richter (pno) Philips ("Solo" series) ▲ 446200-2

J. Krips (cnd)

Beethoven, L. van:Syms (comp) Everest 5-▲ EVC 9010/14 [AAD]

E. Kunzel (cnd)

Davies, V.:Pulsations, w. Arthur Polson (elec vn) Campion ▲ RRCD 1339 [DDD]

L. Leighton Smith (cnd)

Bernstein, L.:Prelude, Fugue & Riffs Cl, w. R. Stoltzman (cl) RCA Red Seal ▲ 09026-61360-2 [DDD]
Copland, A.:Con Cl, w. R. Stoltzman (cl) RCA Red Seal ▲ 09026-61360-2 [DDD]
Corigliano, J.:Con Cl, w. R. Stoltzman (cl) RCA Red Seal ▲ 09026-61360-2 [DDD]

E. Leinsdorf (cnd)

Mozart, W.A.:German Dances, K.509 *(rec 1975)* Sony Classical ("Essential Classics" series) ▲ SBK 48266 [ADD] ■ SBT 48266
Mozart, W.A.:Minuet Orch, K.409 *(rec 1975)* Sony Classical ("Essential Classics" series) ▲ SBK 48266 [ADD] ■ SBT 48266
Strauss, R.:Arias, w. L. Price (sop), Boston SO, New Philharmonia Orch—selections from Ägyptische Helena *(Awakening Scene)*, Ariadne auf Naxos *(Es gibt ein Reich)*, Frau ohne Schatten *(Empress's Awakening Scene)*, Guntram *(Fass ich sie bang)*, Rosenkavalier *(Marschallin's Monologue)*, Salome *(Interlude & Final Scene)* [G] RCA Gold Seal ▲ 60398-2-RG [ADD] ■ 60398-4-RG (CrO2)
Strauss, R.:Salome, w. M. Caballé (sop), R. Resnik (mez), R. Lewis (ten), S. Milnes (bar) RCA Gold Seal 2-▲ 6644-2-RG [ADD]
Verdi, G.:Aida, w. L. Price (sop), G. Bumbry (mez), P. Domingo (ten), S. Milnes (bar), R. Raimondi (bass) [I] RCA Red Seal 3-▲ 6198-2-RC [ADD] 3-■ ARK3-2541
Verdi, G.:Aida, w. L. Price (sop), G. Bumbry (mez), P. Domingo (ten), S. Milnes (bar), R. Raimondi (bass) [I] RCA ■ RK 1237
Verdi, G.:Aida (sels), w. L. Price (sop), G. Bumbry (mez), P. Domingo (ten), S. Milnes (bar) RCA Victor ▲ 09026-62676-2 ■ 09026-62676-4

J. Levine (cnd)

Basic 100 Vol. 61, w. Ofra Harnoy (vc), Lynn Harrell (vc),Charles Mackerras (cnd), London PO RCA Victor ▲ 09026-68086-2 ■ 09026-68086-4
Chopin, F.:Con 1 Pno, w. M. Argerich (pno) Exclusive ▲ EXL 48 [AAD]
Dvořák, A.:Con Vc, w. L. Harrell (vc) RCA Gold Seal ("Papillon Collection" series) ▲ 6531-2-RG [ADD]
Dvořák, A.:Con Vc, w. Lynn Harrell (vc) RCA Victor ▲ 09026-68086-2; ■ 09026-68086-4
Rossini, G.:Il barbiere di Siviglia, w. Beverly Sills (sop), Fedora Barbieri (mez), Nicolai Gedda (ten), Renato Capecchi (bar), Sherill Milnes (bar), Ruggero Raimondi (bass), John Alldis Choir EMI Classics 2-▲ CDMB 66040
Tchaikovsky, P.:Vars on a Rococo Theme, w. Lynn Harrell (vc) RCA Victor ▲ 09026-68086-2; ■ 09026-68086-4

G. Lloyd (cnd)

Lloyd, G.:Con 4 Pno, w. K. Stott (pno) *(rec 1984)* Albany ▲ AR 004-2 [DDD] ■ AR 004-4 (D)
Lloyd, G.:Music of, w. Albany SO, BBC PO—Sym No. 9 [finale]; Sym No. 5 [rondo]; Sym No. 6 [adagio]; Her Hair [from The Transformation of that Naked Ape]; Con No. 4 for Pno [1st movt]; Sym No. 11 [lento]; Sym No. 7 [vivo] Albany ▲ TROY 075

J. Lubbock (cnd)

Manuel Barrueco Plays Lennon & McCartney, w. Manuel Barrueco (gtr), David Tanenbaum (gtr) Angel ▲ CDC 55228
Pure Barrueco, w. Manuel Barrueco (gtr), David Tanenbaum (gtr) EMI Classics ▲ CDC 55315

L. Ludwig (cnd)

Strauss, R.:Ein Heldenleben, w. Hugh Maguire (vn) *(rec Walthamstow Assembly Hall, London)* Everest ▲ EVC 9033 [AAD]

T. Ludwig (cnd)

Ludwig, T.:Sym in 2 Movements *(rec EMI Studios, Abbey Road, London, May 6, 1980)* Albany ▲ TROY 195 [DDD]

P. Maag (cnd)

Mendelssohn, F.:Die Hebriden London ("The Classic Sound" series) ▲ 443578-2
Mendelssohn, F.:A Midsummer Night's Dream (sels) London ("The Classic Sound" series) ▲ 443578-2
Mendelssohn, F.:A Midsummer Night's Dream (sels), w. Jennifer Vyvyan (sop), Marion Lowe (sop), Royal Opera House Women's Chorus Covent Garden—Op. 21; Op. 61, Nos 1, 3, 5, 7, 9, 11, 12 Classic Records ▲ CSCD 6001
Mendelssohn, F.:Ovs—Hebrides London ("Weekend Classics" series) ▲ 433023-2 [AAD]
Mendelssohn, F.:Sym 3 London ("Weekend Classics" series) ▲ 433023-2 [AAD]
Mendelssohn, F.:Sym 3 London ("The Classic Sound" series) ▲ 443578-2

L. Maazel (cnd)

Prokofiev, S.:Con 5 Pno, w. Sviatoslav Richter (pno) EMI Classics ("Doublefforte" series) 2-▲ CDFB 68637
Puccini, G.:La Rondine, w. M. Nicolesco (sop), K. Te Kanawa (sop), P. Domingo (ten), D. Rendall (ten), L. Nucci (bar), Ambrosian Opera Chorus [I] CBS 2-▲ M2K 37852 [DDD]
Puccini, G.:Il trittico, w. R. Scotto (sop), I. Cotrubas (sop), M. Horne (mez), P. Domingo (ten), T. Gobbi (bar), I. Wixell (bar), Philharmonia Orch [I] CBS 3-▲ M3K 35912 [ADD]
Schumann, R.:Pno Music (misc), w. Alfred Brendel (pno), Berlin PO—Abendleid; Adagio & Allegro; Con in a; Fant in C; Fantasiestücke; Kinderszenen; Kreisleriana; 3 Stücke in Volkston; 3 Romances; Symphonic Studies Philips 25-▲ 446920-2
Tchaikovsky, P.:Con 1 Pno, w. V. Ashkenazy (pno) London ▲ 417750-2 [ADD]

J. McCarthy (cnd)

Rossini, G.:Arias, w. R. Blake (ten), Ambrosian Singers [I] Arabesque ▲ Z 6582

N. McGegan (cnd)

Mozart, W.A.:Arias, w. R. Blake (ten)— from Clemenza di Tito *(Se all'impero)*; Così fan tutte *(Un aura amorosa)*; Don Giovanni *(Dalla sua pace; Il mio tesoro)*; Entführung aus dem Serail *(Ich baue ganze)*; Idomeneo *(Fuor del mar)*; Mitridate, Rè di Ponto *(Vado incontro; Se di lauri)*; Concert Aria, "Misero! O Sognol," K.431 [G,I] Arabesque ▲ Z 6598

J. McGlinn (cnd)

Night & Day, w. Thomas Hampson (bar), Ambrosian Chorus EMI Classics ▲ CDC 54203 [DDD] ■ 4DS 54203 (D)

C. Mackerras (cnd)

Brahms, J.:Con Vn, w. H. Udegawa Chandos ▲ CHAN 8974 [DDD]
Britten, B.:The Young Person's Guide to the Orchestra Cala ▲ CAL 1022 [DDD]
Bruch, M.:Con 1 Vn, w. H. Udegawa (vn) Chandos ▲ CHAN 8974 [DDD]
Debussy, C.:La Mer *(rec 1980)* Centaur ▲ CRC 2090 [DDD]
Dohnányi, E. von:Konzertstück, w. R. Wallfisch (vc) Chandos ▲ CHAN 8662 [DDD]
Dukas, P.:L'Apprenti sorcier Cala ▲ CAL 1022 [DDD]
Dvořák, A.:Con Vc, w. R. Wallfisch (vc) Chandos ▲ CHAN 8662 [DDD]
Kaleidoscope:An Orchestral Extravaganza *(rec Walthamstow Town Hall, outside London, July 19–23, 1961)* Mercury Living Presence ▲ 434352-2
Prokofiev, S.:Peter & the Wolf, w. Ben Kingsley (nar) Cala ▲ CAL 1022 [DDD]
Ravel, M.:Daphnis et Chloé (suite 2) *(rec 1980)* Centaur ▲ CRC 2090 [DDD]
Sibelius, J.:The Swan of Tuonela IMP Classics ("LSO Classic Masterpieces" series) ▲ IMPPCD 927 [DDD]
Sibelius, J.:Sym 2 IMP Classics ("LSO Classic Masterpieces" series) ▲ IMPPCD 927 [DDD]
Stravinsky, I.:Pétrouchka *(rec 1973)* Vanguard Classics ▲ OVC 4065
Sullivan, A.:Con Vc, w. J. Lloyd Webber (vc) EMI Classics ▲ CDM 64726
Tchaikovsky, P.:The Nutcracker Telarc 2-▲ CD 80137 [DDD] 2-■ CS 30137 (D)
Tchaikovsky, P.:The Nutcracker Telarc ▲ CD 80140 [DDD] ■ CS 30140 (D)
Vieuxtemps, H.:Con 5 Vn, w. P. Zukerman (vn) *(rec 1969)* Sony Classical ("Essential Classics" series) ▲ SBK 48274 [ADD] ■ SBT 48274

▲ = CD ♦ = Enhanced CD Δ = MD ■ = Cassette Tape □ = DCC

London SO (cont.)
C. Mackerras (cnd) (cont.)
Walton, W.:Sym 2 — Classics for Pleasure ("Eminence" series) ▲ CDEMX 2206
P.A. McRae (cnd)
Peck, R.:The Upward Stream, w. J. Houlik (ten sax) — Albany ▲ TROY 040-2 [DDD]
H. Mancini (cnd)
Mancini, H.:Lifeforce — Varèse Sarabande ▲ ■ VSC 5320
I. Marin (cnd)
Donizetti, G.:Lucia di Lammermoor, w. C. Studer (sop), P. Domingo (ten), J. Pons (bar), S. Ramey (bass) — Deutsche Grammophon 2-▲ 435309-2
Donizetti, G.:Lucia di Lammermoor (sels), w. Cheryl Studer (sop—Lucia), Plácido Domingo (ten—Edgardo)—Io di te memoria viva... Ah, Verranno a te sull'aure [Act I] — Deutsche Grammophon ▲ 447270-2 [DDD] ■ 447 270-4
Rossini, G.:Semiramide, w. C. Studer (sop), J. Larmore (mez), F. Lopardo (ten), S. Ramey (bass), Ambrosian Opera Chorus — Deutsche Grammophon ▲ 437797-2
Songs of Praise, w. Ambrosian Singers — Deutsche Grammophon ▲ 435387-2 GH [DDD]
I. Markevitch (cnd)
Stravinsky, I.:Apollon musagète — Philips 2-▲ 438350-2
Tchaikovsky, P.:Francesca da Rimini — Philips ("Two-Fers" series) 2-▲ 446148-2
Tchaikovsky, P.:Francesca da Rimini — IMP ("BBC Radio Classics" series) ▲ IMP 5691772
Tchaikovsky, P.:Sym 1 — Philips ("Two-Fers" series) 2-▲ 446148-2
Tchaikovsky, P.:Sym 2 — Philips ("Two-Fers" series) 2-▲ 446148-2
Tchaikovsky, P.:Sym 3 — Philips ("Two-Fers" series) 2-▲ 446148-2
Tchaikovsky, P.:Sym 4 — Philips 2-▲ 438335-2
Tchaikovsky, P.:Sym 5 — Philips 2-▲ 438335-2
Tchaikovsky, P.:Sym 6 — Philips 2-▲ 438335-2
N. Marriner (cnd)
Bizet, G.:L'Arlésienne (suites) — Philips ▲ 412464-2 [ADD]
Bizet, G.:Carmen (suites) — Philips ▲ 412464-2 [ADD]
E. Mata (cnd)
Basic 100 Vol. 60, w. Barbara Hendricks (sop), John Aler (ten), Håkan Hagegård (bar) — RCA Victor ▲ 09026-68085-2 ■ 09026-68085-4
Chávez, C.:Sym 1, "Sinf de Antigona" *(rec 1981)* — Vox Box 2-▲ CDX 5061 [DDD]
Chávez, C.:Sym 2, "Sinf India" *(rec 1981)* — Vox Box 2-▲ CDX 5061 [DDD]
Chávez, C.:Sym 3 *(rec 1981)* — Vox Box 2-▲ CDX 5061 [DDD]
Chávez, C.:Sym 4, "Romantic" *(rec 1981)* — Vox Box 2-▲ CDX 5061 [DDD]
Chávez, C.:Sym 5 *(rec 1981)* — Vox Box 2-▲ CDX 5061 [DDD]
Chávez, C.:Sym 6 *(rec 1981)* — Vox Box 2-▲ CDX 5061 [DDD]
Dvořák, A.:Sym 7 — Allegretto ▲ ACD 8202
Elgar, E.:Enigma Vars — Allegretto ▲ ACD 8202
Grieg, E.:Con Pno, Op. 16, w. Judit Jaimes (pno) — ASV Quicksilva ▲ ASQ 6176
Mozart, W.A.:Con Fl Hp, w. James Galway (fl), Marisa Robles (hp) — RCA Gold Seal ▲ 09026-68113-2 [ADD]
Mozart, W.A.:Con Fl Hp, w. Jame Galway (fl), Marisa Robles (hp) — RCA Victor ▲ 09026-68024-2; ■ 09026-68024-2
Mozart, W.A.:Con Fl Hp, w. James Galway (fl), M. Robles (hp) — RCA Gold Seal ▲ 6723-2 [ADD] ■ 6723-4 (CrO2)
Orff, C.:Carmina burana, w. Barbara Hendricks (sop), John Aler (ten), Håkan Hagegård (bar), London Sym Chorus — RCA Victor ▲ 09026-68085-2; ■ 09026-68085-4
M. Mathieson (cnd)
Bliss, A.:Baraza, w. Eileen Joyce (pno) — Dutton Laboratories ▲ DUT 2501 [ADD]
J. Mauceri (cnd)
The Opera Lover's Broadway:Great Voices Sing Broadway's Greatest Hits, w. Vienna PO [cnd:Herbert von Karajan], New Philharmonia Orch [cnd:Richard Bonynge], Roland Shaw Orch, Nelson Riddle & His Orch, London Festival Orch [cnd:Robert Sharples] — London ▲ 448282-2 ■ 448282-4
Rimsky-Korsakov, N.:Scheherazade — IMP Classics ("LSO Classic Masterpieces" series) ▲ IMPPCD 880 [DDD]
D. Measham (cnd)
Barber, S.:Essay 1 *(rec 1973)* — Unicorn-Kanchana ▲ UKCD 2046 [ADD]
Barber, S.:Essay 2 *(rec 1973)* — Unicorn-Kanchana ▲ UKCD 2046 [ADD]
Barber, S.:Night Flight *(rec 1973)* — Unicorn-Kanchana ▲ UKCD 2046 [ADD]
Barber, S.:Sym 1 *(rec 1973)* — Unicorn-Kanchana ▲ UKCD 2046 [ADD]
D.A. Miller (cnd)
Levin, T.:Music of—Blur; Everyday; Todd Levin; Turn; Swirl — Deutsche Grammophon ("4D Audio" series) ▲ 445847-2
P. Monteux (cnd)
Beethoven, L. van:Sym 2 — London ("Double Decker" series) 2-▲ 443479-2
Beethoven, L. van:Sym 4 — London ("Double Decker" series) 2-▲ 443479-2
Beethoven, L. van:Sym 5 — London ("Double Decker" series) 2-▲ 443479-2
Beethoven, L. van:Sym 7 — London ("Double Decker" series) 2-▲ 443479-2
Beethoven, L. van:Sym 7 *(rec 1950s)* — London ("Historic" series) ▲ 433403-2 [ADD]
Beethoven, L. van:Sym 9, "Choral Sym", w. London Sym Chorus—w. rehearsal sels. — MCA Classics 2-▲ MCAD2-9806
Berlioz, H.:La Damnation de Faust, w. Regine Crespin (sop), Andre Turp (ten), Michelle Roux (bar) *(rec live, Mar 1962)* — Music & Arts 2-▲ CD 928
Berlioz, H.:Roméo et Juliette, w. R. Resnik (mez), A. Turp (ten), J. Ward (bar), London Sym Chorus [F] — MCA Classics 2-▲ MCAD2-9805
Brahms, J.:Con 1 Pno, w. J. Katchen (pno) — London ("Double Decker" series) 2-▲ 440612-2
Brahms, J.:Con 2 Pno, w. J. Katchen (pno) — London ("Double Decker" series) 2-▲ 440612-2
Dvořák, A.:Sym 7 *(rec 1950s)* — London ("Historic" series) ▲ 433403-2 [ADD]
Elgar, E.:Enigma Vars — London ("Weekend Classics" series) ▲ 417878-2 [AAD] ■ 417878-4
Ravel, M.:Boléro — Philips ("Solo" series) ▲ 442542-2
Ravel, M.:Ma mère l'oye Orch — Philips ("Solo" series) ▲ 442542-2
Ravel, M.:Pavane pour une infante défunte — Philips ("Solo" series) ▲ 442542-2
Ravel, M.:Rapsodie espagnole — Philips ("Solo" series) ▲ 442542-2
Ravel, M.:La Valse — Philips ("Solo" series) ▲ 442542-2
Tchaikovsky, P.:Romeo & Juliet *(rec live, Grosser Konzerthaussaal,Vienna 5/31/63)* — Vanguard Classics 2-▲ OVC 8031/32 [ADD]
Tchaikovsky, P.:Sym 5 *(rec live, Grosser Konzerthaussaal, Vienna 5/31/63)* — Vanguard Classics 2-▲ OVC 8031/32 [ADD]
W. Morris (cnd)
Beethoven, L. van:Coriolan Ov — IMP Classics ("LSO Classic Masterpieces" series) ▲ IMPPCD 900 [DDD]
Beethoven, L. van:Coriolan Ov — IMP ("Concert Classics" series) ▲ IMP PCD 1099
Beethoven, L. van:Egmont (ov) — IMP Classics ("LSO Classic Masterpieces" series) ▲ PCD 912 [DDD]
Beethoven, L. van:Ovs—Egmont — IMP Classics ▲ PCD 912 [DDD]
Beethoven, L. van:Sym 1 — IMP ("LSO" series) ▲ IMP 6900012 [DDD]
Beethoven, L. van:Sym 1 *(rec 5/88)* — IMP Classics ▲ PCD 929 [DDD]
Beethoven, L. van:Sym 2 — IMP ("LSO" series) ▲ IMP 6900012 [DDD]
Beethoven, L. van:Sym 2 *(rec 5/88)* — IMP Classics ▲ PCD 929 [DDD]
Beethoven, L. van:Sym 3, "Eroica" — IMP Classics ("LSO Classic Masterpieces" series) ▲ PCD 900 [DDD]
Beethoven, L. van:Sym 4 — IMP Classics ("LSO Classic Masterpieces" series) ▲ IMPPCD 869 [DDD]
Beethoven, L. van:Sym 5 — IMP Classics ("LSO Classic Masterpieces" series) ▲ IMPPCD 869 [DDD]
Beethoven, L. van:Sym 6, "Pastorale" — IMP ("Concert Classics" series) ▲ IMP PCD 1099
Beethoven, L. van:Sym 6, "Pastorale" — IMP Classics ("LSO Classic Masterpieces" series) ▲ PCD 912 [DDD]
Beethoven, L. van:Sym 7 — IMP ("LSO" series) ▲ IMP 6900022
Beethoven, L. van:Sym 8 — IMP ("LSO" series) ▲ IMP 6900022
Beethoven, L. van:Sym 9, "Choral Sym", w. London Sym Chorus [G] — IMP Classics ▲ PCD 923 [DDD]
Beethoven, L. van:Sym 9, "Choral Sym", w. Alison Hargen (sop), Della Jones (mez), David Rendall (ten), Gwynne Howell (b-bar), London Sym Chorus — IMP ("LSO" series) ▲ IMP 6900032

London SO (cont.)
W. Morris (cnd) (cont.)
Copland, A.:Lincoln Portrait, w. M. Thatcher (nar) — EMI Classics ▲ CDC 54539-2 [DDD]
Rachmaninoff, S.:Con 2 Pno, w. David Golub (pno) — IMP Classics ("LSO Classic Masterpieces" series) ▲ IMPPCD 903 [DDD]
Rachmaninoff, S.:Rhapsody on a Theme of Paganini, w. David Golub (pno) — IMP Classics ("LSO Classic Masterpieces" series) ▲ IMPPCD 903 [DDD]
K. Nagano (cnd)
Hoddinott, A.:Noctis Equi, w. Msitslav Rostropovich (vc) — Erato ▲ 2292-45489-2 [DDD]
Honegger, A.:Con Vc, w. M. Rostropovich (vc) — Erato ▲ 2292-45489-2 [DDD]
Milhaud, D.:Con 1 Vc, w. M. Rostropovich (vc) — Erato ▲ 2292-45489-2 [DDD]
Ravel, M.:Menuet antique *(rec Paris 1995)* — Erato ▲ 98479-2 [DDD]
Ravel, M.:Rapsodie espagnole *(rec Paris 1995)* — Erato ▲ 98479-2 [DDD]
Ravel, M.:La Valse *(rec Paris 1995)* — Erato ▲ 98479-2 [DDD]
Ravel, M.:Valses nobles et sentimentales *(rec Paris 1995)* — Erato ▲ 98479-2 [DDD]
Stravinsky, I.:Syms Ww — Virgin Classics ▲ CDC 45032
Zappa, F.:Bob in Dacron *(rec Jan. 12-14, 1983)* — Rykodisc 2-▲ 10540/41
Zappa, F.:Bogus Pomp *(rec Jan. 12-14, 1983)* — Rykodisc 2-▲ 10540/41
Zappa, F.:Mo 'n Herb's Vaction *(rec Jan. 12-14, 1983)* — Rykodisc 2-▲ 10540/41
Zappa, F.:Pedro's Dowry *(rec Jan. 12-14, 1983)* — Rykodisc 2-▲ 10540/41
Zappa, F.:Sad Jane *(rec Jan. 12-14, 1983)* — Rykodisc 2-▲ 10540/41
Zappa, F.:Strictly Genteel *(rec Jan. 12-14, 1983)* — Rykodisc 2-▲ 10540/41
A. Nikisch (cnd)
Beethoven, L. van:Egmont (ov) — Symposium ▲ 1087
Mozart, W.A.:Nozze di Figaro — Symposium ▲ 1087
Weber, C.M. von:Ovs—Oberon and Freischütz — Symposium ▲ 1087
C. Ogermann (cnd)
Ogermann, C.:Elegia Pno — Mobile Fidelity ▲ MFCD 786 [DDD]
Ogermann, C.:Symphonic Dances — Mobile Fidelity ▲ MFCD 786 [DDD]
E. Ormandy (cnd)
Dvořák, A.:Sym 9, "From the New World" — Sony Classical (Essential Classics) ▲ SBK 46331 [ADD] ■ SBT 46331
S. Ozawa (cnd)
The Best of Tchaikovsky, w. Philadelphia Orch [cnd:E. Ormandy], Chicago SO [cnd:F. Reiner], J. Browning (pno), et al. — Victrola ("Victrola Best of" series) ▲ 60775-2-RV [ADD] ■ 60775-4-RV
Prokofiev, S.:Sym-Con Vc, w. M. Rostropovich (vc) — Erato ▲ 45708-2
Schnittke, A.:Con 2 Vc, w. M. Rostropovich (vc) — Sony Classical ▲ SK 48241
Tchaikovsky, P.:Con 1 Pno, w. J. Browning (pno) — RCA Silver Seal ▲ 60491-2-RV [ADD] ■ 60491-4-RV (CrO2)
Tchaikovsky, P.:Con Vn, w. E. Friedman (vn) — RCA Silver Seal ▲ 60491-2-RV [ADD] ■ 60491-4-RV (CrO2)
P. Paray (cnd)
Debussy, C.:La Mer *(rec Detroit, Dec. 3 & 4, 1955)* — Mercury Living Presence ▲ 434343-2
P. Polivnick (cnd)
Peck, R.:Peace Ov — Albany ▲ TROY 040-2 [DDD]
G. Prêtre (cnd)
Mendelssohn, F.:Con in e Vn & Orch, Op. 64, w. Uto Ughi (vn) — RCA gold Seal ("Papillon Collection" series) ▲ 6536-2-RG [ADD/DDD]
A. Previn (cnd)
Barber, S.:Adagio Strs — EMI Classics ▲ CDC 54539-2 [ADD]
Barber, S.:Con Vn, w. G. Shaham (vn) — Deutsche Grammophon ▲ 439886-2 [DDD]
Basic 100 Vol. 79 — RCA Victor ▲ 09026-68456-2 ■ 09026-68456-4
Berlioz, H.:Ovs—Franc-Juges — EMI Classics ▲ CDM 64745
Berlioz, H.:Ovs—Le Corsaire; Carnaval romain; Béatrice et Bénédict — EMI Classics ▲ CDM 64630
Britten, B.:Peter Grimes (4 sea interludes) — EMI Classics ▲ CDM 64736
Britten, B.:Spring Sym, w. S. Armstrong (sop), J. Baker (mez), R. Tear (ten), London Sym Chorus — EMI Classics ▲ CDM 64736
Chausson, E.:Poème de l'amour et de la mer, w. Janet Baker (mez) — EMI Classics ("Doublefforte" series) 2-▲ CDFB 68667
Debussy, C.:La Mer — EMI Classics ▲ CDE 67770
Duparc, H.:Songs, w. Janet Baker (mez)—5 songs — EMI Classics ("Doublefforte" series) 2-▲ CDFB 68667
Elgar, E.:Con Vc, w. Y.-Y. Ma (vc) — CBS ▲ MK 39541 [DDD]
Elgar, E.:Con Vc, w. Y.-Y. Ma (vc) — CBS 2-▲ M2K 44562 [ADD/DDD] 2-■ M2T 44562 (D)
Françaix, J.:L'Horloge de Flore, w. J. de Lancie (ob) — RCA Gold Seal ▲ 7989-2-RG [ADD]
Gershwin, G.:An American in Paris — EMI Classics ▲ CDC 47161 ■ 4AM 34760
Gershwin, G.:Con Pno, w. A. Previn (pno) — EMI Classics ▲ CDC 47161 ■ 4AM 34760
Gershwin, G.:Rhap in Blue, w. A. Previn (pno) — EMI Classics ▲ CDC 47161 ■ 4AM 34760
Holst, G.:The Planets — EMI Classics ▲ CDC 47160
Ibort, J.:Symphonio concertante, w. J. de Lancie (ob) — RCA Gold Seal ▲ 7989-2-RG [ADD]
Korngold, E.W.:Con Vn, w. G. Shaham (vn) — Deutsche Grammophon ▲ 439886-2
Korngold, E.W.:Much Ado About Nothing — Deutsche Grammophon ▲ 439886-2
Lalo, E.:Sym espagnole, w. Ithzak Perlman (vn) *(rec ca. 1966/68)* — RCA Gold Seal ▲ 07863-56520-2 ■ 07863-56520-4
Mendelssohn, F.:A Midsummer Night's Dream (comp), w. Janice Watson (sop), Delia Wallis (mez), London Sym Chorus [E] — EMI Classics ▲ CDC 47163
Mendelssohn, F.:Sym 4 — EMI Classics ▲ CDE 67775
Mozart, W.A.:Con 10 Pnos, w. A. Previn (pno), R. Lupu (pno) — EMI Classics ▲ CDM 65180
Mozart, W.A.:Con 20 Pno, w. A. Previn (pno) — EMI Classics ▲ CDM 65180
Orff, C.:Carmina burana, w. S. Armstrong (sop), G. English (ten), T. Allen (bar), London Sym Chorus, St. Clement Danes Boys' Chorus [G, L] — EMI Classics ▲ CDC 47411 ■ 4AM 34770
Ponce, M.:Concierto del sur, w. J. Williams (gtr) — CBS 2-▲ M2K 44791 [ADD/DDD]
Prokofiev, S.:Cinderella — EMI Classics ("Doublefforte" series) 2-▲ CDFB 68604
Prokofiev, S.:Cinderella (sels) *(rec 1983)* — EMI Classics ▲ CDD 64289
Prokofiev, S.:Cons Pno (comp), w. V. Ashkenazy (pno) — London 2-▲ 425570-2 [ADD]
Prokofiev, S.:Cons Vn (comp), w. K.-W. Chung (vn) — London ("Jubilee" series) ▲ 425003-2 [ADD]
Prokofiev, S.:Cons Vn (comp), w. Gil Shaham (vn) *(rec Henry Wood Hall, London, June 1995)* — Deutsche Grammophon ▲ 447758-2 [DDD]
Prokofiev, S.:Romeo & Juliet *(rec 1973)* — EMI Classics ("Doublefforte" series) 2-▲ CDFB 68607
Prokofiev, S.:Sym 1 — EMI Classics ("Doublefforte" series) 2-▲ CDFB 68604
Prokofiev, S.:Sym 5 — EMI Classics ▲ CDM 65181
Prokofiev, S.:Sym 7 — EMI Classics ▲ CDM 65181
Rachmaninoff, S.:Cons Pno (comp), w. V. Ashkenazy (pno) — London 2-▲ 425576-2 [ADD]
Rachmaninoff, S.:Cons Pno (comp), w. Vladimir Ashkenazy (pno) *(rec Kingsway Hall, London, Apr 1970 to Nov 1971)* — London 2-▲ 444839-2 [ADD]
Rachmaninoff, S.:Con 1 Pno, w. Vladimir Ashkenazy (pno) — London ("Jubilee" series) ▲ 425004-2 [ADD]
Rachmaninoff, S.:Con 2 Pno, w. V. Ashkenazy (pno) — London 2-▲ 436386-2 [ADD]
Rachmaninoff, S.:Con 2 Pno, w. Vladimir Ashkenazy (pno) — London ▲ 417702-2 [ADD]
Rachmaninoff, S.:Con 3 Pno, w. Vladimir Ashkenazy (pno) — London ▲ 417764-2 [ADD]
Rachmaninoff, S.:Con 3 Pno, w. V. Ashkenazy (pno) — London 2-▲ 436386-2 [ADD]
Rachmaninoff, S.:Con 4 Pno, w. V. Ashkenazy (pno) — London ("Jubilee" series) ▲ 425004-2 [ADD]
Rachmaninoff, S.:Rhapsody on a Theme of Paganini, w. V. Ashkenazy (pno) — London ▲ 417702-2 [ADD]
Rachmaninoff, S.:Rhapsody on a Theme of Paganini, w. V. Ashkenazy (pno) — London 2-▲ 436386-2 [ADD]
Rachmaninoff, S.:The Rock — RCA Silver Seal ▲ 60791-2-RV [ADD] ■ 60791-4-RV
Rachmaninoff, S.:The Rock — RCA Gold Seal ▲ 6801-2-RG [ADD]
Rachmaninoff, S.:Syms (comp) — EMI Classics 3-▲ ZDMC 64530 [DDD]
Rachmaninoff, S.:Sym 2 — EMI Classics ■ 4AM 34740

London SO (cont.)

A. Previn (cnd) (cont.)

Rachmaninoff, S.:Sym 2 RCA Silver Seal ▲ 60791-2-RV [ADD] ■ 60791-4-RV
Ravel, M.:Daphnis et Chloé, w. London Sym Chorus EMI Classics ("Studio DDD" series) ▲ CDD 63887 [DDD]
Ravel, M.:L'Enfant et les sortilèges, w. Arleen Augér (sop), Marilyn Richardson (sop), Jane Berbié (mez), Linda Finnie (mez), Jocelyne Taillon (mez), Davenny Wyner (mez), Philip Langridge (ten), Philippe Huttenlocher (bar), Jules Bastin (bass), Ambrosian Opera Chorus Classics for Pleasure ("Eminence" series) ▲ CFP 2241
Ravel, M.:Orchestral Music, w. I. Perlman (vn)—Bolero; Rapsodie Espagnole:Prélude à la nuit; Malaguiena, Habanera, Feria; Pavane pour une infante défunte; La valse; Alborada del gracioso; Tzigane RCA Victor ▲ 09026-61712-2; ■ 09026-61712-4
Ravel, M.:Rapsodie espagnole EMI Classics ("Studio DDD" series) ▲ CDD 63887 [DDD]
Ravel, M.:Tzigane, w. I. Perlman (vn) *(rec ca. 1966/68)* RCA Gold Seal ▲ 07863-56520-2 [ADD] ■ 07863-56520-4
Rimsky-Korsakov, N.:Scheherazade RCA Silver Seal ▲ 60487-2-RV (CrO2) ■ 60487-4-RV (CrO2)
Rimsky-Korsakov, N.:The Tale of Tsar Saltan (orch sels)—Flight of the bumble-bee & March RCA Silver Seal ▲ 60487-2-RV [DDD] ■ 60487-4-RV (CrO2)
Rodrigo, J.:Concierto de Aranjuez, w. A. Romero (gtr) EMI Classics ▲ CDC 47693 [ADD]
Rodrigo, J.:Fant para un gentilhombre, w. A. Romero (gtr) EMI Classics ▲ CDC 47693 [ADD]
Satie, E.:Gymnopédies, w. J. de Lancie (pno) [arr. for solo oboe & orchestra]—No. 1 RCA Gold Seal ▲ 7989-2-RG [ADD]
Shankar, R.:Con Sitar, w. R. Shankar (sitar) EMI Classics ("Studio" series) ▲ CDM 69121
Shostakovich, D.:Sym 5 RCA ("Basic 100" series) ▲ 09026-68456-2 ■ 09026-68456-4
Shostakovich, D.:Sym 5 RCA Gold Seal ▲ 6801-2-RG [ADD]
Shostakovich, D.:Sym 8 *(rec Abbey Road, London, 1973)* EMI Classics ▲ CDM 65521
Sibelius, J.:Con Vn, w. Kyung-Wha Chung (vn) London ("The Classic Sound" series) ▲ 425080-2
Sibelius, J.:Con Vn, w. Itzhak Perlman (vn) RCA Victor ▲ 09026-68338-2 ■ 09026-68338-4
Stravinsky, I.:Con Vn, w. K.-W. Chung (vn) London ("Jubilee" series) ▲ 425003-2 [ADD]
Tchaikovsky, P.:Con Vn, w. Kyung-Wha Chung (vn) London ("The Classic Sound" series) ▲ 425080-2
Tchaikovsky, P.:The Nutcracker (sels) EMI Classics ▲ CDM 64332
Tchaikovsky, P.:Ov 1812 EMI Classics ▲ CDC 47843
Tchaikovsky, P.:Romeo & Juliet EMI Classics ▲ CDC 47843
Tchaikovsky, P.:Sleeping Beauty EMI Classics 2-▲ CDQB 54814 ■ 4D2Q 54814
Tchaikovsky, P.:Sleeping Beauty (sels) EMI Classics ▲ CDM 64332
Tchaikovsky, P.:Swan Lake (sels) EMI Classics ▲ CDM 64332
Vaughan Williams, R.:Con accademico, w. J.O. Buswell IV (vn) RCA Gold Seal ▲ 60581-2-RG [ADD]
Vaughan Williams, R.:Con Bass Tuba, w. J. Fletcher (tuba) RCA Gold Seal ▲ 60586-2-RG [ADD]
Vaughan Williams, R.:Portraits RCA Gold Seal ▲ 60586-2-RG [ADD]
Vaughan Williams, R.:Sym 1, w. H. Harper (sop), J. Shirley-Quirk (bar), London Sym Chorus [E] RCA Gold Seal ▲ 60580-2-RG [ADD] ■ 60580-4-RG (CrO2)
Vaughan Williams, R.:Sym 2 RCA Gold Seal ▲ 60581-2-RG [ADD]
Vaughan Williams, R.:Sym 3, w. H. Harper (sop) RCA Gold Seal ▲ 60583-2-RG [ADD]
Vaughan Williams, R.:Sym 4 RCA Gold Seal ▲ 60583-2-RG [ADD]
Vaughan Williams, R.:Sym 5 RCA Gold Seal ▲ 60586-2-RG [ADD]
Vaughan Williams, R.:Sym 6 RCA Gold Seal ▲ 60588-2-RG [ADD]
Vaughan Williams, R.:Sym 7, w. H. Harper (sop) RCA Gold Seal ▲ 60590-2-RG [ADD]
Vaughan Williams, R.:Sym 8 RCA Gold Seal ▲ 60590-2-RG [ADD]
Vaughan Williams, R.:Sym 9 RCA Gold Seal ▲ 60588-2-RG [ADD]
Vaughan Williams, R.:The Wasps (ov) RCA Gold Seal ▲ 60581-2-RG [ADD]
Vaughan Williams, R.:The Wasps (ov) RCA Gold Seal ▲ 7830-2-RG [ADD]
Villa-Lobos, H.:Con Gtr, w. J. Bream (gtr) RCA Gold Seal ▲ 6525-2-RG [ADD] ■ 6525-4-RG (CrO2)
Walton, W.:Belshazzar's Feast, w. J. Shirley-Quirk (bar), London Sym Chorus *(rec 1972)* EMI Classics ▲ CDM 64723
Walton, W.:Con Vc, w. Yo-Yo Ma (vc) CBS ▲ MK 39541 [DDD]
Walton, W.:Improvs on an Impromptu of Benjamin Britten EMI Classics ▲ CDM 64723
Walton, W.:Portsmouth Point EMI Classics ▲ CDM 64723
Walton, W.:Scapino EMI Classics ▲ CDM 64723
Walton, W.:Sym 1 RCA Gold Seal ▲ 7830-2-RG [ADD]

B. Priestman (cnd)

Bliss, A.:Serenade, w. J. Shirley-Quirk (bar) Lyrita ▲ SRCD 225 [ADD]

S. Rattle (cnd)

Prokofiev, S.:Con 1 Pno, w. A. Gavrilov (pno) EMI Classics ▲ CDM 64329
Ravel, M.:Con Pno (left hand), w. A. Gavrilov (pno) EMI ▲ CDM 69026

E. van Remoortel (cnd)

Beethoven, L van:Sym 7 Allegretto ▲ ACD 8055 [ADD] ■ ACS 8055
Beethoven, L van:Sym 8 Allegretto ▲ ACD 8055 [ADD] ■ ACS 8055

C. Rizzi (cnd)

Verdi, G.:La traviata, w. E. Gruberova (sop), N. Shicoff (ten), G. Zancanaro (bar), Ambrosian Singers Teldec 2-▲ 9031-76348-2 PL
Verdi, G.:La traviata (sels), w. E. Gruberova (sop)—È stranolè strano...Ah, fors'è lui Teldec ▲ 450993691-2 [DDD]
Verdi, G.:La traviata (sels), w. E. Gruberova (sop), N. Shicoff (ten), G. Zancanaro (bar) [I] Teldec ▲ 4509-91975-2

L. Ronald (cnd)

Boccherini, L.:Con Vc, G.482, w. P. Casals (vc) Pearl 4-▲ PEAS 9935 (m) [AAD]
Boccherini, L.:Con Vc, G.482, w. P. Casals (vc) *(rec for HMV, 1936)* Pearl ▲ PEA 9349 (m) [AAD]
Bruch, M.:Con 1 Vn, w. Y. Menuhin (vn) *(rec 1931)* Biddulph ▲ LAB 031 [ADD]
Bruch, M.:Kol Nidrei, w. P. Casals (vc) *(rec 1936)* Pearl ▲ PEA 9349 (m) [AAD]
Bruch, M.:Kol Nidrei, w. P. Casals (vc) *(rec 1936)* EMI Classics ("Great Recordings of the Century" series) ▲ CDH 63498 (m) [ADD]
Bruch, M.:Kol Nidrei, w. P. Casals (vc) Pearl 4-▲ PEAS 9935 (m) [AAD]
Mozart, W.A.:Con 4 Vn, w. F. Kreisler (vn) *(rec 1924 for HMV)* Biddulph 2-▲ LAB 009-10 (m) [AAD]
Mozart, W.A.:Con 4 Vn, w. F. Kreisler (vn) *(rec 1924)* Music & Arts 2-▲ CD 290 (m) [AAD]
Mozart, W.A.:Con 4 Vn, w. F. Kreisler (vn) *(rec 1924)* Pearl 2-▲ PEA 9996 [AAD]
Schumann, R.:Con Pno, w. A. Cortot (pno) *(rec 1927 for HMV)* Biddulph ▲ LHW 003 [ADD]

M. Rostropovich (cnd)

Bruch, M.:Kol Nidrei, w. Han-Na Chang (vc) EMI Classics ▲ CDC 56126
Fauré, G.:Elégie, w. Han-Na Chang (vc) EMI Classics ▲ CDC 56126
Prokofiev, S.:Con 1 Vn, w. M. Vengerov (vn) *(rec London, May 1994)* Teldec ▲ 92256-2 [DDD]
Saint-Saëns, C.:Con 1 Vc, w. Han-Na Chang (vc) EMI Classics ▲ CDC 56126
Schnittke, A.:Con Va, w. Y. Bashmet (vn) RCA Red Seal ▲ 60446-2-RC [DDD]
Shostakovich, D.:Con 1 Vn, w. M. Vengerov (vn) *(rec London, May 1994)* Teldec ▲ 92256-2 [DDD]
Shostakovich, D.:Sym 2, w. London Voices *(rec St. Augustine's Church, London, Feb. 8 & 9, 1993)* Teldec ▲ 4509-90853-2 [DDD]
Shostakovich, D.:Sym 3, w. London Voices *(rec St. Augustine's Church, London, Feb. 8 & 9, 1993)* Teldec ▲ 4509-90853-2 [DDD]
Shostakovich, D.:Sym 10 Teldec ▲ 9031-74529-2 ZK
Shostakovich, D.:Sym 15 Teldec ▲ 9031-74560-2 ZK
Tchaikovsky, P.:Vars on a Rococo Theme, w. Han-Na Chang (vc) EMI Classics ▲ CDC 56126

G. Rozhdestvensky (cnd)

Howells, H.:Missa sabrinensis, w. Janice Watson (sop), Della Jones (cta), Martyn Hill (ten), Donald Maxwell (bar), London Sym Chorus Chandos ▲ CHAN 9348 [DDD]
Howells, H.:Stabat mater, w. Neill Archer (ten), London Sym Chorus Chandos ▲ CHAN 9314 [DDD]
Prokofiev, S.:Scythian Suite IMP ("BBC Radio" series) ▲ IMP 5691462
Rachmaninoff, S.:Sym 2 IMP Classics ("LSO Classic Masterpieces" series) ▲ IMPPCD 904 [DDD]
Respighi, O.:Adagio con variazioni Vc Orch, w. M. Rostropovich (vc) *(rec live at Carnegie Hall, 1967)* Intaglio ▲ ING 766 [ADD]
Sibelius, J.:Con Vn, w. G. Kremer (vn) RCA Gold Seal ▲ 09026-60957-2
Stravinsky, I.:The Firebird Suite Nimbus ▲ NI 5087 [DDD]

London SO (cont.)

G. Rozhdestvensky (cnd) (cont.)

Stravinsky, I.:Le Sacre du printemps Orch Nimbus ▲ NI 5087 [DDD]
Stravinsky, I.:Sym in 3 Movts Nimbus ▲ NI 5088 [DDD]
Tartini, G.:Con in A Vc, w. M. Rostropovich (vc) *(rec live, Carnegie Hall, 1967)* Intaglio ▲ ING 766 [ADD]
Tavener, J.:The Protecting Veil, w. S. Isserlis (vc) Virgin Classics ▲ 59052 [DDD]
Tchaikovsky, P.:Capriccio italien IMP Classics ("LSO Classic Masterpieces" series) ▲ IMPPCD 875 [DDD]
Tchaikovsky, P.:Marche slave IMP ("Concert Classics" series) ▲ IMP PCD 1102
Tchaikovsky, P.:Marche slave IMP Classics ▲ PCD 867 [DDD]
Tchaikovsky, P.:The Storm IMP Classics ▲ PCD 878 [DDD]
Tchaikovsky, P.:Sym 4 IMP Classics ("LSO Classic Masterpieces" series) ▲ IMPPCD 867 [DDD]
Tchaikovsky, P.:Sym 5 IMP Classics ("LSO Classic Masterpieces" series) ▲ IMPPCD 875 [DDD]
Tchaikovsky, P.:Sym 6 IMP Classics ("LSO Classic Masterpieces" series) ▲ IMPPCD 878 [DDD]
Vivaldi, A.:Cons Vc, w. M. Rostropovich (vc)—in C, G & g *(rec live, Carnegie Hall, 1967)* Intaglio ▲ ING 766 [ADD]

G. Rozhdestvensky , B. Tuckwell (cnds)

The Heart of the Symphony, w. C. Groves (cnd), English Sinfonia, Royal PO [cnd:Y. Menuhin] Pickwick ("The Orchid" series) ▲ PICORCD 11011

J. Rudel (cnd)

Boito, A.:Mefistofele, w. M. Caballé (sop), P. Domingo (ten), N. Treigle (bass), Ambrosian Opera Chorus [I] EMI Classics 2-▲ CDCB 49522 [ADD]

J. Sándor (cnd)

Mozart, W.A.:Ovs—Die Zauberflöte Laserlight ▲ 15 511 [ADD]

N. Santi (cnd)

Leoncavallo, R.:Pagliacci, w. M. Caballé (sop), P. Domingo (ten), S. Milnes (bar), John Alldis Choir RCA Gold Seal 2-▲ 09026-60865-2 [ADD]

M. Sargent (cnd)

Beethoven, L van:Cons Pno (comp), w. A. Schnabel (pno), London PO *(rec 1932-35)* Pearl 3-▲ PEA 9063 [AAD]
Chausson, E.:Poème Vn, w. E. Friedman (vn) RCA Silver Seal ▲ 09026-61210-2 ■ 09026-61210-4
Elgar, E.:Con Vn, w. J. Heifetz (vn) RCA Gold Seal ▲ 7966-2-RG (m) [ADD]
Elgar, E.:The Music Makers, w. M. Thomas (cta), Leeds Philharmonic Society, Huddersfield Choral Society, Royal Choral Society *(rec live, Royal Albert Hall April 29, 1965)* Intaglio ▲ INCD 7351 [ADD]
Kathleen Ferrier Edition Vol. 3, w. Kathleen Ferrier (cta), Boyd Neel String Orch, Jacques Orch *(rec 1946 & 1949)* London ▲ 433470-2 LM [ADD]
Mozart, W.A.:Con 21 Pno, w. Artur Schnabel (pno) Enterprise ("Piano Library" series) ▲ ENT PL 210
Mozart, W.A.:Con 21 Pno, w. Artur Schnabel (pno) Enterprise ("Sirio" series) ▲ ENT SO 53006
Mozart, W.A.:Con 5 Vn, w. J. Heifetz (vn) RCA Gold Seal ▲ 7869-2 (m/s) [ADD] ■ 7869-4 (m/s)
Prokofiev, S.:Lt Kijé Suite *(rec Walthamstow Assembly Hall, London)* Everest ▲ EVC 9019 [AAD]
Ravel, M.:Tzigane, w. E. Friedman (vn) RCA Silver Seal ▲ 09026-61210-2 ■ 09026-61210-4
Respighi, O.:The Fountains of Rome *(rec Walthamstow Assembly Hall, London)* Everest ▲ EVC 9018 [AAD]
Respighi, O.:The Pines of Rome *(rec Walthamstow Assembly Hall, London)* Everest ▲ EVC 9018 [AAD]
Saint-Saëns, C.:Havanaise Vn, w. E. Friedman (vn) RCA Silver Seal ▲ 09026-61210-2 ■ 09026-61210-4
Sarasate, P. de:Zigeunerweisen, w. E. Friedman (vn) RCA Silver Seal ▲ 09026-61210-2 ■ 09026-61210-4
Shostakovich, D.:Sym 9 *(rec Sept. 1960)* Everest ▲ EVC 9005 [AAD]
Wieniawski, H.:Légende, w. E. Friedman (vn) RCA Silver Seal ▲ 09026-61210-2 ■ 09026-61210-4

W. Sawallisch (cnd)

Beethoven, L van:Con Vn, Op. 61, w. U. Ughi (vn) RCA Gold Seal ("Papillon Collection" series) ▲ 6536-2-RG [ADD/DDD]

A. Schenck (cnd)

Barber, S.:Adagio Strs ASV ▲ ASV 534 [DDD]
Barber, S.:Con Pno, w. Tedd Joselson (pno) ASV ▲ ASV 534 [DDD]
Barber, S.:Medea's Meditation & Dance of Vengeance ASV ▲ ASV 534 [DDD]

H. Scherchen (cnd)

Berlioz, H.:Sym fantastique *(rec 1954)* Theorema ▲ TH 121153

T. Schippers (cnd)

Rossini, G.:The Siege of Corinth, w. B. Sills (sop), S. Verrett (mez), J. Diaz (bass), Ambrosian Opera Chorus [I] *(rec London, 1974)* EMI Classics 3-▲ CDMC 64335

H. Schmidt-Isserstedt (cnd)

Schubert, Franz:Sym 6 *(rec Watford Town Hall, outside London, July 1-2, 1958)* Mercury Living Presence ▲ 434354-2

A. Scholz (cnd)

Adam, A.:Ovs—Si j'étais roi PMG (Vienna Master) ▲ CD 160208 [DDD]
Beethoven, L van:Egmont (ov) PMG ("Vienna Master" series) ▲ CD 160204 [DDD]
Beethoven, L van:Sym 2 PMG ("Vienna Master" series) ▲ CD 160204 [DDD]
Bizet, G.:L'Arlésienne (suites) PMG ("Vienna Master" series) ▲ CD 160205 [DDD]
Bizet, G.:Sym 1 PMG ("Vienna Master" series) ▲ CD 160205 [DDD]
Brahms, J.:Hungarian Dances Orch PMG ("Vienna Master" series) ▲ CD 160201 [DDD]
Dvořák, A.:Slavonic Dances (sels)—Op. 46/2 PMG (Vienna Master) ▲ CD 160208 [DDD]
Gounod, C.:Faust (ballet music) PMG ("Vienna Master" series) ▲ CD 160208 [DDD]
Mendelssohn, F.:Sym 4 PMG ("Vienna Master" series) ▲ CD 160210 [DDD]
Mendelssohn, F.:Sym 5 PMG ("Vienna Master" series) ▲ CD 160210 [DDD]
Mozart, W.A.:Sym 40 Vivace 3-▲ E 320 [DDD]
Mozart, W.A.:Sym 41 Vivace 3-▲ E 320 [DDD]
Music of Beethoven, w. Sofia PO [cnd:Emil Tabakov] Laserlight ♦ 90026 [DDD]
Smetana, B.:The Moldau PMG ("Vienna Master" series) ▲ CD 160208 [DDD]

G. Schwarz (cnd)

Beethoven, L van:Con 4 Pno, w. C. Rosenberger (pno) Delos ▲ DCD 3027 [DDD]
Beethoven, L van:Die Geschöpfe des Prometheus (ov) Delos ▲ DCD 3013 [DDD]
Beethoven, L van:Sym 5 Delos ▲ DCD 3027 [DDD]
Falla, M. de:Noches en los jardines de España, w. C. Rosenberger (pno) Delos ▲ DCD 3060 [DDD]
Falla, M. de:El sombrero de tres picos, w. D. Jones (mez) [Sp] Delos ▲ DCD 3060 [DDD]

R. Schwarz (cnd)

Mahler, G.:Sym 5 *(rec Walthamstow Assembly Hall, London)* Everest ▲ EVC 9032 [AAD]

J. Sedares (cnd)

American Portraits, w. Chicago SO [cnd:A. Schenck], New York Festival of Song [cnd:Jo Ann Faletta, et al.] Koch International Classics ▲ KIC 7233 [DDD]
Bernstein, L.:Halil, w. D. A. Dwyer (fl) Koch International Classics ▲ KIC 7142-2 [DDD]
Pinkham, D.:Serenades Tpt, w. Maurice Murphy (tpt) Koch International Classics ▲ KIC 7179 [DDD]
Pinkham, D.:Son 3 Vns, w. James David Christie (org) Koch International Classics ▲ KIC 7179 [DDD]
Pinkham, D.:Sym 4 Koch International Classics ▲ KIC 7179 [DDD]
Piston, W.:Concertino Pno, w. D. Anthony Dwyer (pno) Koch International Classics ▲ KIC 7142-2 [DDD]
Zwilich, E.T.:Con Fl, w. D. Anthony Dwyer (fl) Koch International Classics ▲ KIC 7142-2 [DDD]

J. Serebrier (cnd)

Barber, S.:Souvenirs Phoenix ▲ PHCD 111 [DDD]
Menotti, G.C.:Sebastian Phoenix ▲ PHCD 101 [AAD]

M. Shostakovich (cnd)

Barber, S.:Con Vn, w. N. Salerno-Sonnenberg (vn) EMI Classics ▲ CDC 54314-2 ■ 4DS 54314-4
Rachmaninoff, S.:Con 2 Pno, w. A. Sultanov (pno) Teldec (Digital Experience) ▲ 9031-77601-2 AW [DDD] ■ 9031-77601-4

▲ = CD ♦ = Enhanced CD Δ = MD ■ = Cassette Tape □ = DCC

London SO (cont.)

M. Shostakovich (cnd) (cont.)

Sensual Classics II, w. A. Sultanov (pno), C. Katsaris (pno), Brodsky Quartet, New York PO [cnd:Z. Mehta], BBC SO [cnd:A. Davis], Leipzig Gewandhaus Orch [cnd:K. Masur], 12 Cellos of the Berlin PO [cnd:A. Jordan, E. Inbal], et al. Teldec ▲ 92014-2 ■ 92014-4
Shostakovich, D.:Con 1 Vn, w. N. Salerno-Sonnenberg (vn) EMI Classics ▲ CDC 54314 ■ 4DS 54314
Shostakovich, D.:Festive Ov Collins Classics ▲ 11082 [DDD]
Shostakovich, D.:Sym 5 Collins Classics ▲ 11082 [DDD]
Shostakovich, D.:Sym 7 Collins Classics ▲ COL 7029
Shostakovich, D.:Sym 8 *(rec 1/91)* Collins Classics ▲ 12712 [DDD]
Shostakovich, D.:Sym 10 Collins Classics ▲ 11062 [DDD]
Tchaikovsky, P.:Con 1 Pno, w. A. Sultanov (pno) Teldec ("Digital Experience" series) ▲ 9031-77601-2 AW [DDD]
Tchaikovsky, P.:Vars on a Rococo Theme, w. J. Lloyd Webber (vc) Philips ▲ 434106-2 [DDD]

L. Siegel (cnd)

Tchaikovsky, P.:Romeo & Juliet Capriccio ▲ 10 924 [DDD]

G. Simon (cnd)

Brahms, J.:Qt 1 Pno [orchd. Schoenberg] *(rec St Jude-on-the-Hill, Hampstead Garden Suburb, London, Oct 1-4, 1990)* Cala ▲ CACD 1006 [DDD]
Brahms, J.:Son 1 Cl, w. James Campbell (cl) [orchd. Berio] *(rec St Jude-on-the-Hill, Hampstead Garden Suburb, London, Oct 1-4, 1990)* Cala ▲ CACD 1006 [DDD]
Conyngham, B.:Monuments, w. Tamás Ungár (pno/syn) *(rec St Jude-on-the-Hill, Hampstead Garden Suburb, London, Apr 2-4, 1990)* Cala ▲ CACD 1008 [DDD]
Conyngham, B.:Southern Cross, w. Robert Davidovici (vn), Tamás Ungár (pno) *(rec St Jude-on-the-Hill, Hampstead Garden Suburb, London, Apr 2-4, 1990)* Cala ▲ CACD 1008 [DDD]
Downey, J.:Con Db, w. G. Karr (db) *(rec Blackheath Concert Halls, London, Feb 27-28 & Mar 1, 1991)* Cala ▲ CACD 1003 [DDD]
Downey, J.:Declamations *(rec Blackheath Concert Halls, London, Feb 27-28 & Mar 1, 1991)* Cala ▲ CACD 1003 [DDD]
Downey, J.:Discourse *(rec Blackheath Concert Halls, London, Feb 27-28 & Mar 1, 1991)* Cala ▲ CACD 1003 [DDD]
Downey, J.:The Edge of Space, w. R. Thompson (bn) Chandos ▲ CHAN 9278 [DDD]
Downey, J.:Jingalodeon *(rec Blackheath Concert Halls, London, Feb 27-28 & Mar 1, 1991)* Cala ▲ CACD 1003 [DDD]
Falla, M. de:El amor brujo, w. S. Walker (mez) [Sp] Chandos ▲ CHAN 8457 [DDD]
Falla, M. de:Noches en los jardines de España, w. M. Fingerhut (pno) Chandos ▲ CHAN 8457 [DDD]
Falla, M. de:La vida breve (interlude & dance 1) Chandos ▲ CHAN 8457 [DDD]
Holst, G.:The Planets, w. London Sym Chorus LaserLight ▲ 14010 [DDD]
Paganini, N.:Intro & Vars on "Dal tuo stellato soglio", w. G. Karr (db) LaserLight ▲ 14010 [DDD]
Smetana, B.:The Bartered Bride (ov) Chandos ▲ CHAN 8412 [DDD]
Smetana, B.:The Bartered Bride (dances) Chandos ▲ CHAN 8412 [DDD]
Smetana, B.:Qt 1 Strs [orchd. by George Szell] Chandos ▲ CHAN 8412 [DDD]
Tchaikovsky, P.:Festival Ov Chandos ▲ CHAN 9190 [DDD]
Tchaikovsky, P.:Festival Ov Chandos 2-▲ CHAN 8310/11 [DDD]
Tchaikovsky, P.:Romeo & Juliet Chandos ▲ CHAN 9191 [DDD]
Tchaikovsky, P.:Romeo & Juliet [orig. 1869 version] Chandos 2-▲ CHAN 8310/11 [DDD]
Tchaikovsky, P.:Serenade for Nikolai Rubinstein's Name-Day Chandos ▲ CHAN 9190 [DDD]
Tchaikovsky, P.:Serenade for Nikolai Rubinstein's Name-Day Chandos 2-▲ CHAN 8310/11 [DDD]
Tchaikovsky, P.:Sym 2 [orig. 1872 vers.] Chandos ▲ CHAN 8304 [DDD]
Tchaikovsky, P.:Sym 2 Chandos ▲ CHAN 9190 [DDD]

Y. Simonov (cnd)

Tchaikovsky, P.:Manfred Collins Quest ▲ COL 3001 [DDD]

S. Skrowaczewski (cnd)

Beethoven, L. van:Con 5 Pno, "Emperor", w. G. Bachauer (pno) Mercury Living Presence ▲ 432018-2 [ADD]
Berlioz, H.:Sym fantastique Chandos ▲ CHAN 8727 [DDD]
Brahms, J.:Con 2 Pno, w. G. Bachauer (pno) *(rec London, July 6 & 7, 1962)* Mercury Living Presence ▲ 434340-2
Lalo, E.:Con Vc, w. János Starker (vc) Mercury Living Presence ▲ 432010-2 [ADD]
Schumann, R.:Con Vc, w. J. Starker (vc) Mercury Living Presence ▲ 432010-2 [ADD]

L. Slatkin (cnd)

Paganini, N.:Con 1 Vn, w. M. Midori (vn) Philips ▲ 420943-2 [DDD]
Tchaikovsky, P.:Con 1 Pno, w. B. Douglas (pno) RCA Red Seal ▲ 5708-2-RC [DDD]
Tchaikovsky, P.:Sérénade mélancolique, w. Midori (vn) Philips ▲ 420943-2 [DDD]
Tchaikovsky, P.:Valse-Scherzo Vn, w. Midori (vn) Philips ▲ 420943-2 [DDD]
Williams, John:Con Fl, w. P. Lloyd (fl) Varèse Sarabande ▲ VSD 5345
Williams, John:Con Vn, w. M. Peskanov (vn) Varèse Sarabande ▲ VSD 5345

G. Solti (cnd)

Borodin, A.:Prince Igor (ov) London ("Weekend Classics" series) ▲ 417689-2
Borodin, A.:Prince Igor (Polovtsian dances) London ("Weekend Classics" series) ▲ 417689-2 [AAD]
Glinka, M.:Russlan & Ludmilla (ov) London ("Weekend Classics" series) ▲ 417689-2 [AAD]
Haydn, J.:Sym 95 London ▲ 417330-2 [DDD]
Haydn, J.:Sym 104, "London" London ▲ 417330-2 [DDD]
Mahler, G.:Sym 1 London 2-▲ 425005-2 [ADD]
Mahler, G.:Sym 2, w. H. Harper (sop), H. Watts (cta), London Sym Chorus [G] London 2-▲ 425005-2 [ADD]
Mahler, G.:Sym 3, w. H. Watts (cta), Ambrosian Chorus, Wandsworth School Boys' Choir [G] London 2-▲ 414254-2 [ADD]
Mussorgsky, M.:Khovanshchina (prelude) London ("Weekend Classics" series) ▲ 417689-2
Mussorgsky, M.:Night London ("Weekend Classics" series) ▲ 417689-2
Rachmaninoff, S.:Con 2 Pno, w. J. Katchen (pno) London ("Weekend Classics" series) ▲ 417880-2 [ADD] ■ 417880-4
The Solti Edition, w. Chicago SO, London PO, Vienna PO, New Philharmonia Orch, Royal Opera House Orch, CO of Europe London 25-▲ 436600-2

I. Stern (cnd)

Bach, J.S.:Con 1 Vn, w. I. Stern (vn) CBS ▲ MYK 38487 [ADD] ■ MYT 38487

L. Stokowski (cnd)

Bach, J.S.:Music of—Air on a G string; Chaconne; Wachet auf; Komm süsser Tod; etc. RCA Victor ▲ 09026-61267-2 [ADD] ■ 09026-61267-4 (CrO2)
Bach, J.S.:Orchestral Trans—Air on the G String; Cantata 156 (arioso); Chaconne; Come Sweet Death; Little Fugue in g; Mighty Fortress; Partita No. 3 (prelude); Sleepers Awake RCA ■ 5686-4-RV
Beethoven, L. van:Sym 9, "Choral Sym", w. Heather Harper (sop), Helem Watts (cta), Alexander Young (ten), Donald McIntyre (bass), London Sym Chorus *(rec London, Sept 23, 1967)* Music & Arts ▲ MUA CD 943
Beethoven, L. van:Sym 9, "Choral Sym", w. London Sym Chorus [soloists Harper, Watts, Young, & McIntyre] [G] London ("Weekend Classics" series) ▲ 421636-2 [AAD]
Brahms, J.:Sym 1 *(rec live, Royal Festival Hall, London 6/14/72)* Intaglio ▲ INCD 7221 [ADD]
Debussy, C.:Ibéria, w. BBC Sym Women's Chorus EMI Classics ("Full Dimensional Sound" series) ▲ CDM 65422
Glazunov, A.:Con Vn, w. S. Marcovici (vn) *(rec live, Royal Festival Hall, London, 6/14/72)* Intaglio ▲ INCD 7221 [ADD]
Handel, G.F.:Messiah (sels), w. Sheila. Armstrong (sop), Norma Proctor (cta), Kenneth Bowen (ten), John Cameron (bar), London Sym Chorus [E] London ("Weekend Classics" series) ▲ 433874-2 [ADD] ■ 433874-4
Ives, C.:Orchestral Set 2, w. London Sym Chorus *(rec June 18, 1970)* Intaglio ▲ ING 7421 [ADD]
Mahler, G.:Sym 2, w. Rae Woodland (sop), Janet Baker (mez), BBC Chorus, BBC Choral Society, Goldsmith's Choral Union, Harrow Choral Society *(rec 1963)* Music & Arts ▲ CD 885 [AAD]
Messiaen, O.:L'Ascension Orch, w. London Sym Chorus *(rec June 18, 1970)* Intaglio ▲ ING 7421 [ADD]

London SO (cont.)

L. Stokowski (cnd) (cont.)

Mussorgsky, M.:Night [arr Stokowski] *(rec Kingsway Hall, London, England, June 16, 1967)* London ("Phase 4 Stereo" series) ▲ 443896-2 [ADD]
Ravel, M.:Rapsodie espagnole EMI Classics ("Full Dimensional Sound" series) ▲ CDM 65422
Rimsky-Korsakov, N.:Scheherazade London ▲ 417753-2 [ADD]
Shostakovich, D.:Sym 5 *(rec 1964)* Music & Arts ▲ CD 765 [AAD]
Shostakovich, D.:Sym 5 IMP ("BBC Radio Classics" series) ▲ IMP 5691542
Stokowski Encores, w. Czech PO, New Philharmonia, Royal PO London ("Weekend Classics" series) ▲ 433876-2 LC [ADD]
Stravinsky, I.:The Firebird Suite *(rec Kingsway Hall, London, England, June 16, 1967)* London ("Phase 4 Stereo" series) ▲ 443898-2 [ADD]
Tchaikovsky, P.:Marche slave *(rec Kingsway Hall, London, England, June 16, 1967)* London ("Phase 4 Stereo" series) ▲ 443896-2 [ADD]
Tchaikovsky, P.:Sym 6 Music & Arts 2-▲ MUA CD 944
Wagner, R.:Die Meistersinger von Nürnberg (sels), w. Heather Harper (sop), Helem Watts (cta), Alexander Young (ten), Donald McIntyre (bass), London Sym Chorus—Suite:Prelude Act III, Dance of the Apprentices, Entrance of the Mastersingers *(rec London, Sept 23, 1967)* Music & Arts ▲ MUA CD 943

W. Susskind (cnd)

Chopin, F.:Con 2 Pno, w. Witold Malcuzynski (pno) *(rec Kingsway Hall, London, Aug. 1959)* EMI Classics 2-▲ ZDMB 68226 [ADD]
Copland, A.:Appalachian Spring Everest ▲ EVC 9003 [AAD]
Gould, M.:Spirituals Orch Everest ▲ EVC 9003 [AAD]
Prokofiev, S.:Chout (suite) *(rec Walthamstow Assembly Hall, London)* Everest ▲ EVC 9019 [AAD]

E. Svetlanov (cnd)

Chausson, E.:Poème de l'amour et de la mer, w. Janet Baker (sop) IMP ("BBC Radio Classics" series) ▲ IMP 5691742

G. Szell (cnd)

Brahms, J.:Con 1 Pno, w. Clifford Curzon (pno) London ("The Classic Sound" series) ▲ 425082-2
Franck, C.:Symphonic Vars, w. Clifford Curzon (pno) London ("The Classic Sound" series) ▲ 425082-2
Handel, G.F.:Royal Fireworks Music London ("Weekend Classics" series) ▲ 417694-2 [AAD] ■ 417694-4
Handel, G.F.:Water Music (suites) London ("Weekend Classics" series) ▲ 417694-2 [AAD] ■ 417694-4
Mahler, G.:Des Knaben Wunderhorn, w. E. Schwarzkopf (sop), D. Fischer-Dieskau (bar) EMI Classics ▲ CDC 47277
Mozart, W.A.:Arias, w. E. Schwarzkopf (sop), A. Brendel (pno)—4 Concert arias EMI Classics ▲ CDH 63702

V. Tausky (cnd)

Music You Have Loved Pickwick ("The Orchid" series) ▲ PICORCD 11017

B. Thomson (cnd)

Brahms, J.:Con 1 Pno, w. I. Margalit (pno) Chandos ▲ CHAN 8724 [DDD]
Mendelssohn, F.:Capriccio brillante, w. I. Margalit (pno) Chandos ▲ CHAN 8724 [DDD]
Vaughan Williams, R.:Con accademico, w. K. Sillito (vn) Chandos ▲ CHAN 8633 [DDD]
Vaughan Williams, R.:Con Bass Tuba, w. P. Harrild (tuba) Chandos ▲ CHAN 8740 [DDD]
Vaughan Williams, R.:Con Ob, w. D. Theodore (ob) Chandos ▲ CHAN 8594 [DDD]
Vaughan Williams, R.:Con Pno, w. H. Shelley (pno) Chandos ▲ CHAN 8941 [DDD]
Vaughan Williams, R.:Con grosso Chandos ▲ CHAN 8629 [DDD]
Vaughan Williams, R.:Fant on Greensleeves Chandos ▲ CHAN 8828 [DDD]
Vaughan Williams, R.:Hymn-Tune Preludes Chandos ▲ CHAN 8828 [DDD]
Vaughan Williams, R.:The Lark Ascending, w. M. Davis (vn) Chandos ▲ CHAN 8554 [DDD]
Vaughan Williams, R.:Orch Music—Con. grosso for Strings; Con. accademico for Violin; Con. in f for Bass Tuba; Con. in a for Oboe; Con. in C for Piano; 2 Hymn-Tune Preludes for Small Orch.; The Lark Ascending (romance) for Violin & Orch.; Partita for Double String Orch.; Toward the Unknown Region for Orch. & Chorus Chandos 2-▲ CHAN 9262 [DDD]
Vaughan Williams, R.:Partita Chandos ▲ CHAN 8828 [DDD]
Vaughan Williams, R.:Syms Chandos 5-▲ CHAN 9087/91 [DDD]
Vaughan Williams, R.:Sym 1, w. Y. Kenny (sop), B. Rayner Cook (bar), London Sym Chorus [E] Chandos ▲ CHAN 8764 [DDD]
Vaughan Williams, R.:Sym 2 Chandos ▲ CHAN 8629 [DDD]
Vaughan Williams, R.:Sym 3, w. Y. Kenny (sop) Chandos ▲ CHAN 8594 [DDD]
Vaughan Williams, R.:Sym 4 Chandos ▲ CHAN 8633 [DDD]
Vaughan Williams, R.:Sym 5 Chandos ▲ CHAN 8554 [DDD]
Vaughan Williams, R.:Sym 6 Chandos ▲ CHAN 8740 [DDD]
Vaughan Williams, R.:Sym 7, w. C. Bott (sop) [E] Chandos ▲ CHAN 8796 [DDD]
Vaughan Williams, R.:Sym 8 Chandos ▲ CHAN 8828 [DDD]
Vaughan Williams, R.:Sym 9 Chandos ▲ CHAN 8941 [DDD]
Vaughan Williams, R.:Toward the Unknown, w. London Sym Chorus [E] Chandos ▲ CHAN 8796 [DDD]

M. Tilson Thomas (cnd)

Barber, S.:Adagio Strs EMI Classics ▲ CDC 55358
Barber, S.:Knoxville:Summer of 1915, w. Barbara Hendricks (sop) EMI Classics ▲ CDC 55358
Barber, S.:Songs, w. Barbara Hendricks (sop)—Nocturne; Sure on This Shining Night EMI Classics ▲ CDC 55358
Bartók, B.:Con 2 Vn, w. K. Takezawa (vn) RCA Red Seal ▲ 09026-61675-2
Beethoven, L. van:Choral Music, w. Ambrosian Singers—Elegiac Song, Op. 118; Opferlied, Op. 121b; Bundeslied, Op. 122 CBS ▲ MK 33509 [ADD]
Beethoven, L. van:König Stephen (incidental music), w. Ambrosian Singers CBS ▲ MK 33509 [ADD]
Beethoven, L. van:Meeresstille und glückliche Fahrt, w. Ambrosian Singers CBS ▲ MK 33509 [ADD]
Bernstein, L.:Arias & Barcarolles, w. Frederica von Stade (mez), Thomas Hampson (bar) *(rec Henry Wood Hall, London, Sept 1993)* Deutsche Grammophon ▲ 439926-2 [DDD]
Bernstein, L.:A Quiet Place (suite) *(rec Henry Wood Hall, London, Sept 1993)* Deutsche Grammophon ▲ 439926-2 [DDD]
Bernstein, L.:West Side Story (symphonic dances) *(rec Henry Wood Hall, London, Sept 1993)* Deutsche Grammophon ▲ 439926-2 [DDD]
Brahms, J.:Academic Festival Ov Sony Classical ▲ SK 45932 [DDD]
Brahms, J.:Hungarian Dances Orch—Nos. 1, 3 & 10 [orch. Brahms]; Nos. 17-21 [orch. Dvořák] Sony Classical ▲ SK 47195
Brahms, J.:Serenade 1 Orch Sony Classical ▲ SK 45932 [DDD]
Brahms, J.:Serenade 2 Orch Sony Classical ▲ SK 47195
Brahms, J.:Tragic Ov Sony Classical ▲ SK 45932 [DDD]
Brahms, J.:Vars on a Theme by Haydn Sony Classical ▲ SK 47195
Chausson, E.:Poème Vn, w. N. Salerno-Sonnenberg (vn) EMI Classics ▲ CDC 54855
Copland, A.:Poems (8) of Emily Dickinson, w. Barbara Hendricks (sop) EMI Classics ▲ CDC 55358
Copland, A.:Quiet City, w. Barbara Hendricks (sop) EMI Classics ▲ CDC 55358
Debussy, C.:La Boîte à joujoux Sony Classical ▲ SK 48231 [DDD]
Debussy, C.:Jeux Sony Classical ▲ SK 48231 [DDD]
Debussy, C.:Prélude à l'après-midi d'un faune Sony Classical ▲ SK 48231 [DDD]
Janácek, L.:Sinfonietta Sony Classical ▲ SK 47182
Janácek, L.:Slavonic Mass, w. G. Benačková (sop), F. Palmer (sop), G. Lakes (ten), A. Kotcherga (bass), London Sym Chorus Sony Classical ▲ SK 47182
McLaughlin, J.:Con Gtr, w. J. McLaughlin (gtr) CBS ▲ MK 45578 [DDD]
Mahler, G.:Songs from Rückert, w. J. Baker (mez), London Sym Chorus [G] CBS 2-▲ M2K 44553 [DDD]
Mahler, G.:Sym 3, w. J. Baker (mez), London Sym Chorus [G] CBS 2-▲ M2K 44553 [DDD]
Muldowney, D.:Con Ob, w. R. Carter (ob) NM Classics ▲ NMCD 018
Prokofiev, S.:Con 1 Pno, w. V. Feltsman (pno) CBS ▲ MK 44818 [DDD]
Prokofiev, S.:Con 2 Pno, w. V. Feltsman (pno) CBS ▲ MK 44818 [DDD]
Prokofiev, S.:Sym 1 Sony Classical ▲ SK 48239
Prokofiev, S.:Sym 5 Sony Classical ▲ SK 48239

London SO (cont.)
M. Tilson Thomas (cnd) (cont.)
Prokofiev, S.:Sym 5—Allegro giocoso *(rec Abbey Road, Studio 1, London, Apr 30–May 2, 1991)* Sony Classical ("Greatest Hits" series) ▲ MLK 69249 [DDD] ■ LT 69
Ravel, M.:Boléro CBS ▲ MK 44800 [DDD]
Ravel, M.:Fanfare CBS ▲ MK 44800 [DDD]
Ravel, M.:Ma mère l'oye Orch CBS ▲ MK 44800 [DDD]
Ravel, M.:Pièce en forme de Habanera [orchestral arr. by Arthur Hoérée] CBS ▲ MK 44800 [DDD]
Ravel, M.:Rapsodie espagnole CBS ▲ MK 44800 [DDD]
Reich, S.:The 4 Sections Elektra/Nonesuch ▲ 79220-2 ■ 79220-4
Reich, S.:Movts Elektra/Nonesuch ▲ 79295-2
Strauss, R.:Also sprach Zarathustra Sony Classical ▲ SK 45970
Strauss, R.:Don Juan Sony Classical ▲ SK 45970
Strauss, R.:4 Last Songs, w. L. Popp (sop) *(rec May 21–22, 1993)* Sony Classical ▲ SK 48242 [DDD]
Strauss, R.:Songs, w. K. Mattila (sop)—Zueignung, Op. 10/1; Muttertändelei, Op. 43/2; Meinem Kinde, Op. 37/3; Die heiligen drei Könige aus Morgenlied; Frühlingsfeier, Op. 56/5 *(rec Oct. 3–4, 1991)* Sony Classical ▲ SK 48242 [DDD]
Strauss, R.:Songs, Op. 68, w. E. Gruberova (sop) *(rec Feb. 6–7, 1991)* Sony Classical ▲ SK 48242 [DDD]
Stravinsky, I.:Sym in C *(rec Sept. 13–14, 1991)* Sony Classical ▲ SK 53275 [DDD]
Stravinsky, I.:Sym in 3 Movts *(rec Sept. 14–15, 1991)* Sony Classical ▲ SK 53275 [DDD]
Stravinsky, I.:Sym of Psalms, w. London Sym Chorus *(rec Sept. 13–14, 1991)* Sony Classical ▲ SK 53275 [DDD]
Tavener, J.:The Repentant Thief, w. A. Marriner (cl) Collins Classics ▲ 20052 [DDD]
Tchaikovsky, P.:Swan Lake Sony Classical 2-▲ S2K 46592
Weill, K.:Kleine Dreigroschenmusik CBS ▲ MK 44529 [DDD]
Weill, K.:The Seven Deadly Sins, w. J. Migenes (sop), R. Tear (ten), S. Kale (ten), A. Opie (bar), R. Kennedy (bass) CBS ▲ MK 44529 [DDD]
L. Tjeknavorian (cnd)
Khachaturian, A.:Con Pno, w. A. Portugheis (pno) ASV ▲ ASV 589 [DDD]
B. Tuckwell (cnd)
Dvořák, A.:Carnival IMP ("LSO" series) ▲ IMP 6900062 [DDD]
Dvořák, A.:Carnival IMP ("Concert Classics" series) ▲ IMP PCD 1103
Dvořák, A.:Carnival IMP Classics ▲ PCD 851 [DDD]
Dvořák, A.:Sym 9, "From the New World" IMP ("Concert Classics" series) ▲ IMP PCD 1103
Dvořák, A.:Sym 9, "From the New World" IMP ("LSO" series) ▲ IMP 6900062 [DDD]
Dvořák, A.:Sym 9, "From the New World" IMP Classics ▲ PCD 851 [DDD]
Elgar, E.:Coronation March IMP Classics ▲ PCD 913 [DDD]
Elgar, E.:Enigma Vars IMP Classics ▲ PCD 913 [DDD]
Elgar, E.:Imperial March IMP Classics ▲ PCD 913 [DDD]
Elgar, E.:Pomp & Circumstance Marches IMP Classics ▲ PCD 913 [DDD]
Wagner, R.:Lohengrin (preludes)—Act 3 IMP ("LSO" series) ▲ IMP 6900102
Wagner, R.:Ovs, Preludes & Orch Sels—Rienzi Ov; Die Meistersinger Ov; Der fliegende Holländer Ov; Tannhäuser Ov IMP ("LSO" series) ▲ IMP 6900102
Wagner, R.:Ovs, Preludes & Orch Sels—Fliegende Holländer; Lohengrin, Act 3; Meistersinger; Rienzi; Tannhäuser IMP Classics ▲ PCD 860 [DDD]
Wagner, R.:Die Walküre (ride of the valkyries) IMP ("LSO" series) ▲ IMP 6900102
Wagner, R.:Die Walküre (ride of the valkyries) IMP Classics ▲ PCD 860 [DDD]
V. Tatrai (cnd)
Mozart, W.A.:Sym 40 LaserLight ▲ 15 511 [ADD]
M. Valdes (cnd)
Rossini, G.:Arias, w. R. Blake (ten), Ambrosian Singers—8 arias from Armida, Ermione, Gazza ladra, Otello, Ricciardo e Zoraide, Semiramide, Zelmira [I] Arabesque ▲ Z 6612
A. Wallenstein (cnd)
Tchaikovsky, P.:Con Vn, w. I. Perlman (vn) *(rec 1960s)* Chesky ▲ CD 12
B. Walter (cnd)
Beethoven, L. van:Coriolan Ov *(rec 1938)* Iron Needle ▲ 1302 (m) [ADD]
Beethoven, L. van:Coriolan Ov Grammofono 2000 ▲ GRM 78548 (m)
Haydn, J.:Sym 86 Grammofono 2000 ▲ GRM 78629
Schubert, Franz:Rosamunde Dutton Laboratories ▲ DUT 5003
Schubert, Franz:Sym 9 Grammofono 2000 ▲ GRM 78548 (m)
Schumann, R.:Sym 4 *(rec 1938)* Historical Performers ▲ HPS 17 [ADD]
Smetana, B.:The Bartered Bride (ov) Grammofono 2000 ▲ GRM 78548 (m)
Strauss (II), Joh.:Der Zigeunerbaron (ov) Grammofono 2000 ▲ GRM 78548 (m)
W. Walton (cnd)
Walton, W.:Con Va, w. F. Riddle (va) *(rec Dec. 6, 1937)* Dutton Laboratories ▲ CDAX 8003 [ADD]
F. von Weingartner (cnd)
Brahms, J.:Academic Festival Ov *(rec London, Feb 29, 1940)* Arkadia ▲ 629 [ADD]
Brahms, J.:Academic Festival Ov *(rec ca. 1939)* EMI Classics ("References" series) 2-▲ CDHB 64256
Brahms, J.:Syms (comp)—Nos. 1 & 2 *(rec 1939–40)* Centaur ▲ CRC 2124 (m)
Brahms, J.:Sym 4 Enterprise ("Sirio" series) ▲ ENT SO 530015
Liszt, F.:Mephisto Waltz 1 Orch *(rec London, Feb 29, 1940)* Arkadia ▲ 629 [ADD]
Liszt, F.:Les Préludes *(rec London, Feb 29, 1940)* Arkadia ▲ 629 [ADD]
D. Willcocks (cnd)
Vaughan Williams, R.:Benedictine, w. H. Harper (sop), London Sym Chorus EMI Classics ▲ CDM 64722
Vaughan Williams, R.:5 Tudor Portraits, w. H. Harper (sop), *(chorus unknown)* EMI Classics ▲ CDM 64722
Vaughan Williams, R.:Variants of "Dives & Lazarus", w. H. Harper (sop) EMI Classics ▲ CDM 64722
J. Williams (cnd)
The Hollywood Sound Sony Classical ▲ SK 62788 ■ ST 62788
Williams, John:Dracula Varèse Sarabande ▲ VSD 5250 ■ VSC 5250
Williams, John:The Empire Strikes Back Polydor ▲ 825298-2 ■ 825298-4
Williams, John:Raiders of the Lost Ark *(rec Anvil Recording Studios, Denham & EMI Abbey Road Studio No. 1, London, Feb 1981)* DCC Compact Classics ▲ DZS 090
Williams, John:Star Wars Trilogy Fox 4-▲ 07822 11012-2
R. Williams (cnd)
Berlioz, H.:Sym fantastique IMP Classics ▲ PCD 870 [DDD]
Berlioz, H.:Sym fantastique IMP ("London SO" series) ▲ IMP 5
Gershwin, G.:An American in Paris IMP ("London SO" series) ▲ IMP 7
Gershwin, G.:An American in Paris, w. Gwenneth Pryor (pno) IMP ("LSO" series) ▲ IMP 6900072
Gershwin, G.:Con Pno, w. Gwenneth Pryor (pno) IMP ("London SO" series) ▲ IMP 7
Gershwin, G.:Con Pno, w. Gwenneth Pryor (pno) IMP ("LSO" series) ▲ IMP 6900072
Gershwin, G.:Rhap in Blue, w. Gwenneth Pryor (pno) IMP ("London SO" series) ▲ IMP 7
Gershwin, G.:Rhap in Blue, w. Gwenneth Pryor (pno) IMP ("LSO" series) ▲ IMP 6900072
Mussorgsky, M.:Pictures at an Exhibition IMP Classics ▲ PCD 907 [DDD]
Ravel, M.:Boléro IMP Classics ▲ PCD 907 [DDD]
Tchaikovsky, P.:Nutcracker Suite IMP ("LSO" series) ▲ IMP 6900092
Tchaikovsky, P.:Sleeping Beauty (suite) IMP ("LSO" series) ▲ IMP 6900092
Tchaikovsky, P.:Swan Lake (suite) IMP ("LSO" series) ▲ IMP 6900092
H. Wolff (cnd)
Panufnik, A.:Con Vc, w. Mstislav Rostropovich (vc) NMC ▲ NMC 10 [DDD]
H. Wood (cnd)
Litolff, H.C.:Con Symphonique 4, w. I. Scharrer (pno) *(rec 1933)* Pearl ▲ PEA 9978 (m) [AAD]
Sir H. J. Wood Conducts Proms Favourites, w. Queen's Hall Orch, British SO, London PO *(rec between Nov. 1929 & March)* Dutton Laboratories ▲ DUT 8008 [ADD]
B. Wordsworth (cnd)
Bizet, G.:Jeux d'enfants IMP ("LSO" series) ▲ IMP 6900082

London SO (cont.)
B. Wordsworth (cnd) (cont.)
Delius, F.:Music of—Brigg Fair; La Calinda; In a Summer Garden; On Hearing the First Cuckoo in Spring; A Song Before Sunrise; Summer Evening; Summer Night On the River; A Walk to the Paradise Garden *(rec 6/91)* Collins Classics ▲ 13362 [DDD]
Ravel, M.:Ma mère l'oye Pno IMP ("LSO" series) ▲ IMP 6900082
Saint-Saëns, C.:Carnival of the Animals [chamber version] IMP ("LSO" series) ▲ IMP 6900082
D. Zinman (cnd)
Chopin, F.:Con 2 Pno, w. V. Ashkenazy (pno) London ▲ 417750-2 [ADD]
London SO members
L. Bernstein (cnd)
Beethoven, L. van:Sym 9, "Choral Sym", w. Bavarian RSO members, Dresden State Orch members, Kirov Theatre Orch members, London SO members, New York PO members, Orch de Paris members, Bavarian Radio Chorus, Berlin Radio Chorus, Dresden Philharmonie Children's Chorus [G] *(rec live, Schauspielhaus, East Berlin, 12/25/89)* Deutsche Grammophon ▲ 429861-2 [DDD] ■ 429861-4
London SO Wind & Brass Ensemble
A. Bliss (cnd)
Bliss, A.:The world is charged with the grandeur of God, w. Ambrosian Singers Lyrita ▲ SRCD 225 [ADD]
London SO Winds
D. Amos (cnd)
Persichetti, V.:Music of—Divertimento, Op. 42; Psalm, Op. 53; Pageant, Op. 59; Masquerade, Op. 102; O Cool is the Valley, Op. 118; Parable, Op. 121; O God Unseen, Op. 160 Harmonia Mundi USA ▲ HMU 907092
London Tivoli Theater Orch
Strauss, R.:Der Rosenkavalier (film version) EMI Classics ▲ CDC 54610
London Viennese Orch
J. Rothstein (cnd)
Vienna Premiere, Vol. 1 Chandos ▲ CHAN 8381 [DDD]
Vienna Premiere, Vol. 2 Chandos ▲ CHAN 8527 [DDD]
Vienna Premiere, Vol. 3 Chandos ▲ CHAN 9127 [DDD]
London Virtuosi
J. Georgiadis (cnd)
Albinoni, T.:Cons à 5 Obs, Op. 9, w. A. Camden (ob)—Nos. 2, 5, 8 & 11; Nos. 3 & 9, w. Julia Girdwood *(rec Oct 11–12, 1992)* Naxos ▲ 8.550739 [DDD]
London Vivaldi Orch
Sammartini, G.:Cons Rcr, w. R. Harvey (rcr), M. Huggett (vn)—in F ASV ("Gaudeamus" series) ▲ CDGAU 111
Vivaldi, A.:Cons Rcr, w. R. Harvey (rcr), M. Huggett (vn)—RV.441 & RV.444 ASV ("Gaudeamus" series) ▲ CDGAU 111
R. Goodman (cnd)
Vivaldi, A.:Cons Vn (misc), w. M. Huggett (vn)—RV.253, 271, 277, 353 ASV ("Gaudeamus" series) ▲ CDGAU 105
M. Huggett (cnd)
Scarlatti, A.:Sinf 3, w. R Harvey (rcr) ASV ("Gaudeamus" series) ▲ CDGAU 111
London Wind Orch
D. Wick (cnd)
Holst, G.:Hammersmith ASV Quicksilva ▲ QS 6021 [ADD]
Holst, G.:Suites Band—Suite No. 2 ASV Quicksilva ▲ QS 6051 [ADD/DDD]
Holst, G.:Suites Band ASV Quicksilva ▲ QS 6021 [ADD]
Vaughan Williams, R.:English Folk Song Suite ASV Quicksilva ▲ QS 6021 [ADD]
Vaughan Williams, R.:Toccata marziale ASV Quicksilva ▲ QS 6021 [ADD]
London Winds
G. Brand (cnd)
Bourgeois, D.:Con Trbn, w. C. Lindberg (trbn) Albany ▲ TROY 093 [DDD]
Grainger, P.:Transcriptions Orch—Bach:O Mensch, bewein dein Sünde gross, BWV 402 Albany ▲ TROY 093 [DDD]
Holst, G.:A Moorside Suite [arr. Denis Wright] Albany ▲ TROY 093 [DDD]
Ireland, J.:A Comedy Ov [arr. Ray Steadman-Allen] Albany ▲ TROY 093 [DDD]
M. Collins (cnd)
Strauss, R.:Music of—Complete music for winds including Serenade, Op. 7; Sonatina No. 1; Suite, Op. 4; Sonatina No. 2 Hyperion 2-▲ CDA 66731/32
Long Beach Opera Orch
A. Culver (cnd)
Cage, J.:Europera 3, w. Suzan Hanson (sop), Ruby Hinds (mez), Patricia McAfee (mez), Michael Lyon (ten), Richard Powell (ten), Kevin Bell (bass), Brian Pezzone (pno), Vicki Ray (pno), Hannes Geiger (record players), Joseph Giri (record players), William Houston (record players), Dren McDonald (record players), Ronda Rindone (record players), Clarice Ross (record players), Scott Fraser (tape) *(rec Center Theater, Long Beach, CA, Nov. 13, 1993)* Mode 2-▲ MODE 38/39
Cage, J.:Europera 4, w. Anne-Marie Ketchum (sop), Daisetta Kim (sop), Brian Pezzone (pno), Jerry Wheeler (victrola), Scott Fraser (tape) *(rec Center Theater, Long Beach, CA, Nov. 13, 1993)* Mode 2-▲ MODE 38/39
Long Island Chamber Ensemble
Diamond, D.:Qnt Cl, w. L. Sobol (cl) Grenadilla ■ GSC 1007
Harris, R.:Con Cl, w. P. Basquin (pno), Lawrence Sobol (cl) Grenadilla ■ GSC 1007
Husa, K.:Evocations of Slovakia Phoenix ▲ PHCD 113 [AAD]
Longy Artists Ensemble
M. Strauss (cnd)
Rieti, V.:Serenata Vn, w. J. Packer (vn) *(rec 1990)* CRI ▲ CD 601 [DDD]
Lorand Trio
Synagogue Chants, w. Lorand, Marcel (sgr/harm), Karel Handler (sgr), Jeno Kohn (sgr), Alexander Kovacs (sgr) Supraphon ▲ SUP 3073
Lorraine PO
J. Houtmann (cnd)
Baird, T.:Music of—Oboe Con.; Scenes for Cello, Harp & Orch.; Canzona; Con. Lugubre; Soloists Koch Schwann ▲ SCH 311362 [DDD]
Landowski, M.:Music of, w. J. Loriod (ondes Martenot), A. Marion (fl), F. Clidat (pno), M. Becquet (trbn)—Concerto for Ondes Martenot & Orchestra; Concerto for Flute & Strings; Concerto for Piano & Orchestra; Concertino for Trombone & Strings Koch Schwann ▲ CD 311175 [DDD]
Loewe, C.:Con Pno, w. Ewa Kupiec (pno) Koch Schwann ▲ SCH 315392 [DDD]
Loewe, C.:Sym in d Koch Schwann ▲ SCH 315392 [DDD]
Marsick, A.:Scènes de montagnes Koch Schwann ▲ CD 311198 [DDD]
Marsick, A.:La Source Koch Schwann ▲ CD 311198 [DDD]
Marsick, A.:Stèle Koch Schwann ▲ CD 311198 [DDD]
Marsick, A.:Symphonic Poems—Scènes de Montagne (1910); La Source (1908); Stèle (1902) Koch Schwann ▲ CD 311 198 [DDD]
Pierné, G.:Con Pno, w. D. Achatz (pno) BIS ▲ CD 381 [DDD]
Pierné, G.:Con Pno, w. Dag Achatz (pno) BIS ("BIS Twins" series) 2-▲ CD 375/381
Pierné, G.:Ramuntcho (suites) BIS ▲ CD 381 [DDD]
Pierné, G.:Ramuntcho (suites) BIS ("BIS Twins" series) 2-▲ CD 375/381
The Trombone, w. Armin Rosin (trbn), Michel Becquet (trbn), Berlin Trombone Quintet, Berlin RIAS Sinfonietta [cnd:Ernö Sebestyen], Southwest German CO [cnd:Vladislav Czernedki] Koch Schwann ▲ SCH 313342 [DDD]
F. Quattrocchi (cnd)
Berlioz, H.:L'Enfance du Christ (sels), w. Mariette Kemmer (sop), Claire Brua (mez), Gilles Ragon (ten), Nicolas Cavallier (bass)—Toujours ce rêve *(rec June 1994)* Maguelone ▲ 350.509 [DDD]
Gluck, C.W.:Alceste (sels), w. Mariette Kemmer (sop), Claire Brua (mez), Gilles Ragon (ten), Nicolas Cavallier (bass)—Vivre sans toi *(rec June 1994)* Maguelone ▲ 350.509 [DDD]

▲ = CD ♦ = Enhanced CD Δ = MD ■ = Cassette Tape □ = DCC

Lorraine PO (cont.)
F. Quattrocchi (cnd) (cont.)
Gounod, C.:Faust (sels), w. Mariette Kemmer (sop), Claire Brua (mez), Gilles Ragon (ten), Nicolas Cavallier (bass)—Faites lui mes aveux; La coupe du Roi de Thulé; Air des Bijoux *(rec June 1994)* Maguelone ▲ 350.509 [DDD]
Mozart, W.A.:Così fan tutte (sels), w. Mariette Kemmer (sop), Claire Brua (mez), Gilles Ragon (ten), Nicolas Cavallier (bass)—Come scoglio *(rec June 1994)* Maguelone ▲ 350.509 [DDD]
Mozart, W.A.:Nozze di Figaro (sels), w. Mariette Kemmer (sop), Claire Brua (mez), Gilles Ragon (ten), Nicolas Cavallier (bass)—Ov; Voi che Sapete *(rec June 1994)* Maguelone ▲ 350.509 [DDD]
Rossini, G.:Le Comte Ory (sels), w. Mariette Kemmer (sop), Claire Brua (mez), Gilles Ragon (ten), Nicolas Cavallier (bass)—Ov; Que les destins prospères *(rec June 1994)* Maguelone ▲ 350.509 [DDD]
B. Tetu (cnd)
Mendelssohn, F.:Athalie, w. Danielle Borst (sop), Brigitte Desnoues (sop), Carolyn Watkinson (cta), Jean-Marc Avocat (sgr), Souad Natech (sgr), Lyon National Chorus Koch Schwann ▲ SCH 314282 [DDD]
Los Angeles Brass Society
Chou Wen-Chung:Soliloquy of a Bhiksuni, w. T. Stevens (tpt), M. Peters (perc) Crystal ▲ CD 667
Reynolds, V.:Signals, w. T. Stevens (tpt), R. Bobo (tuba) Crystal ▲ CD 667
Los Angeles CO
Bach, J.S.:Music of, w. Parkening (gtr) EMI Classics ▲ CDC 47195-2
A. Almeida (cnd)
Gnattali, R.:Con brasileira 4 Concord Concerto ■ CC 2001-C
L. Almeida (cnd)
Almeida, L.:Con 1 Gtr, w. L. Almeida (gtr) Concord Concerto ■ CC 2001
Almeida, L.:Lobiana, w. L Almeida (gtr) Concord Concerto ■ CC 2001
D. Crockett (cnd)
Crockett, D.:Celestial Mechanics *(rec Brandeis-Bardin Institute, Simi Valley, CA, Sept. 29–30, 1993)* CRI ▲ CD 669 [DDD]
Hartke, S.:Wir küssen ihnen tausendmal die Hände *(rec Brandeis-Bardin Institute, Simi Valley, CA, Sept. 29–30, 1993)* CRI ▲ CD 669 [DDD]
Larsen, L.:Schoenberg, Schenker & Schillinger *(rec Brandeis-Bardin Institute, Simi Valley, CA, Sept. 29–30, 1993)* CRI ▲ CD 669 [DDD]
Steiger, R.:Woven Serenade *(rec Brandeis-Bardin Institute, Simi Valley, CA, Sept. 29–30, 1993)* CRI ▲ CD 669 [DDD]
J. DePreist (cnd)
Mozart, W.A.:Sym 4 Delos ▲ DCD 1010 [AAD]
Mozart, W.A.:Sym 5 Delos ▲ DCD 1010 [AAD]
Mozart, W.A.:Sym 29 Delos ▲ DCD 1010 [AAD]
N. Marriner (cnd)
Respighi, O.:Ancient Airs & Dances EMI Classics 2-▲ CDFB 69358
Respighi, O.:Ancient Airs & Dances EMI Classics ▲ CDC 47116
Thomson, V.:Autumn EMI Classics (American Composer Series) ▲ CDM 64306
Thomson, V.:The Plow That Broke the Plains EMI Classics (American Composer Series) ▲ CDM 64306
Thomson, V.:The River (suite) EMI Classics (American Composer Series) ▲ CDM 64307
C. Perick (cnd)
Haydn, J.:Sym 38 *(rec 1/92)* Dorian ▲ DOR 90168 [DDD]
Haydn, J.:Sym 104, "London" *(rec 1/92)* Dorian ▲ DOR 90168 [DDD]
G. Schwarz (cnd)
Barber, S.:Serenade Elektra/Nonesuch ▲ 79002-2 [DDD] ■ D1-79002 (D)
Beethoven, L. van:Sym 1 Delos ▲ DCD 3013 [DDD]
Beethoven, L. van:Sym 8 Delos ▲ DCD 3013 [DDD]
Brahms, J.:Serenade 1 Orch Elektra/Nonesuch ▲ 79065-2 [DDD]
Carter, E.:Elegy Va Elektra/Nonesuch ▲ 79002-2 [DDD] ■ D1-79002 (D)
Debussy, C.:Danses sacrée et profane, w. B. Allen (hp) EMI Classics ▲ CDC 47520 [DDD]
Diamond, D.:Rounds Elektra/Nonesuch ▲ 79002-2 [DDD] ■ D1-79002 (D)
Dvořák, A.:Serenade Strs Delos ▲ DCD 3011 [DDD]
Dvořák, A.:Silent Woods, w. D. Davis (vc) Delos ▲ DCD 3011 [DDD]
Fine, I.:Serious Song Elektra/Nonesuch ▲ 79002-2 [DDD] ■ D1-79002 (D)
Janácek, L.:Idyll Elektra/Nonesuch ▲ 79033-2 [DDD]
Janácek, L.:Youth Elektra/Nonesuch ▲ 79033-2 [DDD]
Lazarof, H.:Chamber Sym *(rec Royce Hall, Univ of CA, Los Angeles)* Laurel ▲ LR 844 [DDD]
Lazarof, H.:Sinfonietta *(rec Royce Hall, Univ of CA, Los Angeles)* Laurel ▲ LR 844 [DDD]
Mozart, W.A.:Sym 40 Delos ▲ DCD 3012 [DDD]
Mozart, W.A.:Sym 41 Delos ▲ DCD 3012 [DDD]
Prokofiev, S.:Sym 1 Delos ▲ DCD 3021 [DDD]
Shostakovich, D.:Con 1 Pno, w. C. Rosenberger (pno), S. Burns (tpt) Delos ▲ DCD 3021 [DDD]
Stravinsky, I.:L'Histoire du soldat Suite Ensemble Delos ▲ DCD 3021 [DDD]
Vivaldi, A.:Cons Vn, Op. 8/1–4, "The Four Seasons", w. E. Oliveira (vn) Delos ▲ DCD 3007 [DDD]
P. Schwarz (cnd)
Handel, G.F.:Water Music (comp) Delos ▲ DCD 3010 [DDD]
Los Angeles Guitar Quartet [William Kanengiser (gtr), Scott Tennant (gtr), Andrew York (gtr), John Dearman (gtr)]
Boccherini, L.:Fandango [arr. Jeremy Sparks for guitar quartet] *(rec Dec. 1–3 & 9, 1992)* Delos ▲ DE 3144 [DDD]
Debussy, C.:Estampes—No. 2, "La soirée dans Granada" [arr. James Smith for guitar quartet] *(rec Dec. 1–3 & 9, 1992)* Delos ▲ DE 3144 [DDD]
Falla, M. de:El amor brujo [arr. Ian Krouse, Scott Tennant & William Kanengiser for guitar quartet] *(rec Dec. 1–3 & 9, 1992)* Delos ▲ DE 3144 [DDD]
Falla, M. de:El amor brujo (sels) [arr. Kanengiser] GHA ▲ 126.034
Gabrieli, G.:Gtr Trans—trans. of Canzons VI & XI; Canon per sonar primi toni; Sonata XIII *(rec April–May 1992)* Delos ▲ DE 3132 [DDD]
Krouse, I.:Folias *(rec Dec. 1–3 & 9, 1992)* Delos ▲ DE 3144 [DDD]
Labyrinth *(rec First Congregational Church, Los Angeles, CA, Nov. 28–30, 1994 & Jan. 2)* Delos ▲ DE 3163 [DDD]
Morley, T.:Dances—Can She Excuse; Joyne Hands; My Lord of Oxenfordes Maske; Response Pavin [trans guitar quartet] *(rec April–May 1992)* Delos ▲ DE 3132 [DDD]
Recital GHA ▲ 126.016
Rimsky-Korsakov, N.:Capriccio espagnol [arr. William Kanengiser for guitar quartet] *(rec Dec. 1–3 & 9, 1992)* Delos ▲ DE 3144 [DDD]
Tchaikovsky, P.:Nutcracker Suite *(rec April–May 1992)* Delos ▲ DE 3132 [DDD]
Warlock, P.:Capriol Suite *(rec April–May 1992)* Delos ▲ DE 3132 [DDD]
Los Angeles Horn Club
Kraft, William:Games:Collage 1 Cambria ▲ CMB 1071 [DDD]
Los Angeles Horn Club [Gunther Schuller, William Kraft, Russell Garcia, George Hyde, David Raksin]
Horns! Angel ("Studio" series) ▲ CDM 63764 [ADD]
Los Angeles Mozart Orch
L. Carver (cnd)
Haydn, J.:Sym 43, "Mercury" RCM ▲ RCM 19602 [DDD]
Haydn, J.:Sym 48, "Maria Theresia" RCM ▲ RCM 19602 [DDD]
Mozart, W.A.:Sym 17 RCM ▲ RCM 19603
Mozart, W.A.:Sym 29 RCM ▲ RCM 19603
Mozart, W.A.:Sym 34 RCM ▲ RCM 19603
Los Angeles Percussion Ensemble
Kraft, William:Der Imagistes, w. E. Geer (nar), M. Kermoyan (nar) [E] *(rec 1977)* CRI ▲ CD 639 [ADD/DDD]
W. Kraft (cnd)
Harrison, L.:Con Org, w. David Craighead (org) *(rec 1977)* Crystal ▲ CD850
Harrison, L.:Con Vn, w. Eudice Shapiro (vn) *(rec 1975)* Crystal ▲ CD850

Los Angeles Philharmonic New Music Group
J. Harbison (cnd)
Harbison, J.:The Natural World, w. Janice Felty (mez) [E] New World ▲ 80395-2 [DDD]
Los Angeles PO
M. Abravanel (cnd)
Bloch, E.:Nigun, w. J. Szigeti (vn) [violin & orchestra version] Music & Arts 4-▲ CD 720-4 [AAD]
L. Bernstein (cnd)
Barber, S.:Adagio Strs Deutsche Grammophon ("3D Classics" series) ▲ 427806-2 [DDD]
Barber, S.:Adagio Strs Deutsche Grammophon ▲ 431048-2 [DDD]
Bernstein, L.:West Side Story (symphonic dances) Deutsche Grammophon ("3D Classics" series) ▲ 427806-2 [DDD]
Copland, A.:Appalachian Spring (suite) Deutsche Grammophon ▲ 431048-2 [DDD]
Gershwin, G.:Rhap in Blue, w. L. Bernstein (pno) Deutsche Grammophon ▲ 431048-2 [DDD]
Gershwin, G.:Rhap in Blue, w. L. Bernstein (pno) Deutsche Grammophon ("3D Classics" series) ▲ 427806-2 [DDD]
The Joy of Bernstein, w. New York PO, Vienna PO, Israel PO Deutsche Grammophon ▲ 445486-2
L. Foster (cnd)
Weiss, A.:American Life New World ▲ 80228-2
C.M. Giulini (cnd)
Beethoven, L. van:Sym 3, "Eroica" *(rec Shrine Auditorium, LA, Nov 1978)* Deutsche Grammophon ("The Originals" series) ▲ 447444-2 [ADD]
Beethoven, L. van:Sym 5 Deutsche Grammophon ("Digital Midprice" series) ▲ 445502-2
Chopin, F.:Con 1 Pno, w. K. Zimerman (pno) Deutsche Grammophon ▲ 415970-2 [ADD]
Chopin, F.:Con 2 Pno, w. K. Zimerman (pno) Deutsche Grammophon ▲ 415970-2 [ADD]
Granada:The Greatest Hits of Plácido Domingo, w. Plácido Domingo (ten), London SO [cnd:C. Abbado], Vienna PO [cnd:H. von Karajan], Royal Opera House Orch, Covent Garden [cnd:Z. Mehta], Philharmonia Orch [cnd:Giuseppe Sinopoli] Deutsche Grammophon ▲ 445777-2 ■ 445777-4
Schumann, R.:Manfred Ov *(rec Shrine Auditorium, LA, Dec 1980)* Deutsche Grammophon ("The Originals" series) ▲ 447444-2 [DDD]
Schumann, R.:Sym 3 Deutsche Grammophon ("Digital Midprice" series) ▲ 445502-2
O. Klemperer (cnd)
Bach, J.S.:Anna Magdalena Bach Notebook—Bist du Bei Mir, BWV 508 Grammofono 2000 ▲ GRM 78643
Bach, J.S.:Suite 3 Orch—Air Grammofono 2000 ▲ GRM 78643
Corelli, A.:La Follia, w. Joseph Szigeti (vn) Grammofono 2000 ▲ GRM 78643
Liszt, F.:Totentanz, w. Bernardo Segall (pno) Grammofono 2000 ▲ GRM 78643
Strauss (II), Joh.:Die Fledermaus (ov) Grammofono 2000 ▲ GRM 78643
Thomas, A.:Mignon (Ov) Grammofono 2000 ▲ GRM 78643
E. Leinsdorf (cnd)
Debussy, C.:L'apres-midi d'un faune Sheffield Lab ▲ SLS 10043
Debussy, C.:La Mer EMI Classics ("Full Dimensional Sound" series) ▲ CDM 65425
Debussy, C.:Prélude à l'après-midi d'un faune Sheffield Lab ▲ CD 24
Dvořák, A.:Sym 9, "From the New World" EMI Classics ▲ CDM 65612
Prokofiev, S.:Romeo & Juliet (sels) Sheffield Lab ▲ SLS 10043
Prokofiev, S.:Romeo & Juliet (sels) Sheffield Lab ▲ CD 7/8
Rachmaninoff, S.:Con 2 Pno, w. L. Pennario (pno) EMI Classics ■ 4XG 60237
Rachmaninoff, S.:Prelude Pno, Op. 3/2, w. L. Pennario (pno) EMI Classics ■ 4XG 60237
Rachmaninoff, S.:Preludes Pno, Opp 23 & 32, w. L. Pennario (pno)—in g EMI Classics ■ 4XG 60237
Ravel, M.:Daphnis et Chloé (suite 2) EMI Classics ("Full Dimensional Sound" series) ▲ CDM 65425
Strauss, R.:Tod und Verklärung EMI Classics ("Full Dimensional Sound" series) ▲ CDM 65425
Wagner, R.:Götterdämmerung (siegfried's funeral) Sheffield Lab ▲ CD 7/8
Wagner, R.:Siegfried (sels)—Waldweben (Forest Murmurs) Sheffield Lab ▲ SLS 10043
Wagner, R.:Siegfried (waldweben) Sheffield Lab ▲ CD 7/8
Wagner, R.:Tristan und Isolde (prelude & liebestod)—Prelude, concert version Sheffield Lab ▲ CD 7/8
Wagner, R.:Tristan und Isolde (prelude & liebestod) EMI Classics ("FDS" series) ▲ CDM 65208
Wagner, R.:Die Walküre (ride of the valkyries) Sheffield Lab ▲ CD 7/8
Z. Mehta (cnd)
Beethoven, L. van:Con Vn, Op. 61, w. P. Zukerman (vn) RCA Red Seal ▲ 09026-61219-2 ■ 09026-61219-4 □ 09026-61219-5
Brahms, J.:Con Vn, w. Pinchas Zukerman (vn) *(rec Dorothy Chandler Pavilion, Los Angeles, Apr 1–2, 1994)* RCA Red Seal ▲ 09026-68046-2 [DDD]
Bruch, M.:Con 1 Vn, w. P. Zukerman (vn) Odyssey ▲ MBK 44717 ■ YT 44717
Bruch, M.:Con 1 Vn, w. P. Zukerman (vn) *(rec 1977)* Sony Classical ("Essential Classics" series) ▲ SBK 48274 [ADD] ■ SBT 48274
Copland, A.:Appalachian Spring (suite) *(rec Royce Hall, Univ of California, Los Angeles, July 1976)* London 2-▲ 448261-2 [ADD]
Copland, A.:Appalachian Spring (suite) London ▲ 417716-2 [ADD]
Copland, A.:Fanfare for the Common Man London ▲ 417716-2 [ADD]
Copland, A.:Fanfare for the Common Man *(rec Royce Hall, Univ of California, Los Angeles, July 1976)* London 2-▲ 448261-2 [ADD]
Gershwin, G.:An American in Paris London ▲ 436570-2 (m) [ADD]
Kraft, William:Con for 4 Perc Soloists, w. *(soloists unknown)* Cambria ▲ CMB 1071 [DDD]
Kraft, William:Contextures I:Riot—Decade '60 Cambria ▲ CMB 1071 [DDD]
Lalo, E.:Sym espagnole, w. P. Zukerman (vn) *(rec 1977)* Sony Classical ("Essential Classics" series) ▲ SBK 48274 [ADD] ■ SBT 48274
Lalo, E.:Sym espagnole, w. P. Zukerman (vn) Odyssey ▲ MBK 44717 ■ YT 44717
Mahler, G.:Sym 3, w. Maureen Forrester (cta) London ("Double Decker" series) 2-▲ 443030-2
Mahler, G.:Sym 5 London ("Weekend Classics" series) ▲ 433877-2 [ADD]
Tchaikovsky, P.:Marche slave London ("Weekend Classics" series) ▲ 417683-2 [AAD] ■ 417683-4
Tchaikovsky, P.:Ov 1812 London ("Weekend Classics" series) ▲ 417683-2 [AAD] ■ 417683-4
Tchaikovsky, P.:Romeo & Juliet London ("Weekend Classics" series) ▲ 417683-2 [AAD] ■ 417683-4
Verdi, G.:Pezzi sacri, w. Yvonne Minton (mez), Los Angeles Master Chorale *(rec 1970)* London ("Double Decker" series) 2-▲ 444833-2 [ADD]
D.A. Miller (cnd)
Powell, Mel:Duplicates, w. A. Feinberg (pno), R. Taub (pno) Harmonia Mundi USA ▲ HMU 907096
Powell, Mel:Modules Harmonia Mundi USA ▲ HMU 907096
A. Previn (cnd)
Bartók, B.:Con Orch Telarc ▲ CD 80174 [DDD]
Dvořák, A.:Carnival Telarc ▲ CD 80238 [DDD]
Dvořák, A.:My Home Telarc ▲ CD 80173 [DDD]
Dvořák, A.:Notturno Telarc ▲ CD 80206 [DDD]
Dvořák, A.:Scherzo Capriccioso Telarc ▲ CD 80206 [DDD]
Dvořák, A.:Sym 7 Telarc ▲ CD 80173 [DDD]
Dvořák, A.:Sym 7 *(rec May 4, 1988)* Telarc ("Bravo") ▲ CD 82018 [DDD]
Dvořák, A.:Sym 8 Telarc ▲ CD 80206 [DDD]
Dvořák, A.:Sym 8 *(rec May 4, 1988)* Telarc ("Bravo") ▲ CD 82018 [DDD]
Dvořák, A.:Sym 9, "From the New World" Telarc ▲ CD 80238 [DDD]
Harbison, J.:Con Double Brass Choir New World ▲ 80395-2 [DDD]
Janácek, L.:Sinfonietta Telarc ▲ CD 80174 [DDD]
Kraft, William:Contextures II:The Final Beast, w. M. Rawcliffe (sop), J. Mack (ten), New Albion Ensemble, Pasadena Boys' Choir [E,G,Gr,L] Meet The Composer ▲ 79229-2 ■ 79229-4
Prokofiev, S.:Alexander Nevsky, w. C. Cairns (mez), Master Chorale of Orange County [R] Telarc ▲ CD 80143 [DDD]
Prokofiev, S.:Lt Kijé Suite Telarc ▲ CD 80143 [DDD]
Shapero, H.:9-Minute Ov New World ▲ NW 373-2 [DDD]
Shapero, H.:Sym Classical Orch New World ▲ NW 373-2 [DDD]
E.-P. Salonen (cnd)
Bartók, B.:Con Orch Sony Classical ▲ SK 62598

ORCH. & ENS.

Los Angeles PO (cont.)
E.-P. Salonen (cnd) (cont.)
Bartók, B.:Cons Pno (comp), w. Yefim Bronfman (pno) Sony Classical ▲ SK 66718
Bartók, B.:Music for Strs, Perc & Cel Sony Classical ▲ SK 62598
Debussy, C.:La Damoiselle élue, w. D. Upshaw (sop), P. Rasmussen (mez), Los Angeles Master Chorale Women's Voices *(rec Feb. 22, 1993)* Sony Classical ▲ SK 58952 [DDD]
Debussy, C.:Images Orch Sony Classical ▲ SK 62599
Debussy, C.:Martyre de Saint Sébastien (fragments) *(rec Feb. 22, 1993)* Sony Classical ▲ SK 58952 [DDD]
Debussy, C.:La Mer Sony Classical ▲ SK 62599
Debussy, C.:Nocturnes, w. Los Angeles Master Chorale Women's Voices *(rec Feb. 22, 1993)* Sony Classical ▲ SK 58952 [DDD]
Debussy, C.:Prélude à l'après-midi d'un faune Sony Classical ▲ SK 62599
Herrmann, B.:Film Music—Torn Curtain; Taxi Driver; North by Northwest; Marnie; The Man Who Knew Too Much; Vertigo; Fahrenheit 451; Psycho Sony Classical ▲ SK 62700 ∆ SM 62700
Lutoslawski, W.:Chantefleurs et Chantefables, w. Dawn Upshaw (sop) *(rec Los Angeles, Nov 14, 17 & 18, 1994)* Sony Classical ▲ SK 67189 [DDD]
Lutoslawski, W.:Con Pno, w. Paul Crossley (pno) *(rec Los Angeles, Nov 14, 17 & 18, 1994)* Sony Classical ▲ SK 67189 [DDD]
Lutoslawski, W.:Les Espaces du sommeil, w. John Shirley-Quirk (bar) *(rec Nov. 29–Dec. 2, 1985)* Sony Classical ▲ SK 66280 [DDD]
Lutoslawski, W.:Les Espaces du sommeil, w. John Shirley-Quirk (bar) [F] CBS 2-▲ M2K 42271 [DDD]
Lutoslawski, W.:Les Espaces du sommeil, w. John Shirley-Quirk (bar) Sony Classical ▲ SMK 53473
Lutoslawski, W.:Fanfare for Los Angeles Philharmonic *(rec Los Angeles, Nov 14, 17 & 18, 1994)* Sony Classical ▲ SK 67189 [DDD]
Lutoslawski, W.:Sym 2 *(rec Los Angeles, Nov 14, 17 & 18, 1994)* Sony Classical ▲ SK 67189 [DDD]
Lutoslawski, W.:Sym 3 *(rec Nov. 29–Dec. 2, 1985)* Sony Classical ▲ SK 66280 [DDD]
Lutoslawski, W.:Sym 3 CBS 2-▲ M2K 42271
Lutoslawski, W.:Sym 4 *(rec Nov. 15, 1993)* Sony Classical ▲ SK 66280 [DDD]
Mahler, G.:Sym 4, w. B. Hendricks (sop) [G] Sony Classical ▲ SK 48380 [DDD]
Messiaen, O.:Turangalîla-sym CBS 2-▲ M2K 42271 [DDD]
Prokofiev, S.:Cons Vn (comp), w. C.-L. Lin (vn) *(rec Los Angeles, Nov. 9–10, 1992)* Sony Classical ▲ SK 53969 [DDD]
Saariaho, K.:...à la fumée, w. P. Alanko (a fl), A. Karttunen (vc) Ondine ▲ Ode 804 [DDD]
Saariaho, K.:Du cristal Ondine ▲ Ode 804 [DDD]
Sibelius, J.:4 Legends from the Kalevalá Sony Classical ▲ SK 48067 [DDD]
Sibelius, J.:Kullervo, w. M. Rorholm (mez), J. Hynninen (bar), Helsinki Univ Chorus [Fin] Sony Classical ▲ SK 52563
Sibelius, J.:En Saga Sony Classical ▲ SK 48067 [DDD]
Stravinsky, I.:Con Vn, w. C.-L. Lin (vn) *(rec Los Angeles, Feb. 24, 1992)* Sony Classical ▲ SK 53969 [DDD]

C. Simmons (cnd)
Carpenter, J.A.:Krazy Kat New World ▲ 80228-2
Gilbert, H.F.:The Dance in Place Congo New World ▲ 80228-2
Powell, J.:Rhap nègre, w. Z. Carno (pno) New World ▲ 80228-2

L. Stokowski (cnd)
Holst, G.:The Planets, w. Roger Wagner Chorale EMI Classics ("Full Dimensional Sound" series) ▲ CDM 65423

M. Tilson Thomas (cnd)
Gershwin, G.:Porgy & Bess (sels), w. S. Vaughan, Jazz Trio [overture & song medley arr. Marty Paitch] CBS ▲ MK 42516 [ADD/DDD] ■ FMT 42516
Gershwin, G.:Rhap in Blue, w. M. Tilson Thomas (pno) CBS ▲ MK 39699 [DDD]
Gershwin, G.:Second Rhap, w. M. Tilson Thomas (pno) CBS ▲ MK 39699 [DDD]
Prokofiev, S.:Lt Kijé Suite *(rec Royce Hall, Univ of CA, Los Angeles, Dec 23, 1978)* Sony Classical ("Greatest Hits" series) ▲ MLK 69249 [ADD] ■ LT 69
Prokofiev, S.:The Love for 3 Oranges (march) *(rec Royce Hall, Univ of CA, Los Angeles, Dec 23, 1978)* Sony Classical ("Greatest Hits" series) ▲ MLK 69249 [ADD] ■ LT 69

A. Wallenstein (cnd)
Castelnuovo-Tedesco, M.:Con 2 Vn, "The Prophets", w. J. Heifetz (vn) RCA Gold Seal ▲ 7872-2-RG (m/s) [ADD]
Korngold, E.W.:Con Vn, w. J. Heifetz (vn) RCA Gold Seal ▲ 7963-2-RG [ADD]
Sinding, C.:Suite im alten Stil, w. Jascha Heifetz (vn) [orchd Sinding] *(rec Republic Studios Sound Stage 9, Hollywood, Dec 9, 1953)* RCA Gold Seal 2-▲ 09026-61740-2 (m) [ADD]
Szymanowski, K.:Sym 4, w. A. Rubinstein (pno) *(rec 1947)* RCA Gold Seal ▲ 60046-2-RG (m/s) [ADD]
Tchaikovsky, P.:Sérénade mélancolique, w. J. Heifetz (vn) RCA Gold Seal ▲ 09026-60927-2 ■ 09026-60927-4

B. Walter (cnd)
Wagner, R.:Siegfried Idyll *(rec live, 1950)* Legend ▲ LGD 119
Wagner, R.:Siegfried Idyll *(rec live, 1952)* Historical Performers ▲ HPS 27
Wagner, R.:Tristan und Isolde (prelude & liebestod), w. Margareth Harshaw (sop) *(rec live, 1950)* Legend ▲ LGD 119
Wagner, R.:Tristan und Isolde (prelude & liebestod), w. Margareth Harshaw (sop) *(rec live, 1952)* Historical Performers ▲ HPS 27
Weber, C.M. von:Invitation to the Dance Orch *(rec 1950)* Enterprise ("Palladio" series) ▲ ENTPD 4202 [ADD]

P. Zukerman (cnd)
Vivaldi, A.:Cons Vn (misc), w. P. Zukerman (vn)—Concerto in a, RV.356 *(rec 1976)* Sony Classical ("Essential Classics" series) ▲ SBK 48273 [ADD] ■ SBT 48273

Los Angeles PO members
A. Endo (cnd)
Foss, L.:Con Ob, w. B. Gassman (ob), w. Crystal CO [string quintet version] Crystal ▲ CD871
Heussenstamm, G.:Set for Double Reeds, w. Crystal CO Crystal ▲ CD871
Music for Double-Reed Ensemble, w. Crystal CO, Bert Gassman (ob) Crystal ▲ CD871
Pillin, B.:Pieces (3) for Double-Reed Septet, w. Crystal CO Crystal ▲ CD871
P. Zukerman (cnd)
Mozart, W.A.:Serenade Ww, K.388 *(rec Los Angeles, Oct 7, 1976)* Sony Classical ("Essential Classics" series) ▲ SBK 62412 [ADD] ■ SBT 62412

Los Angeles Philharmonic Trombone Ensemble
Music for All Seasons:Moravian Trombones, w. Moravian Trombone Choir of Downey Crystal ▲ CD 220

Los Angeles Piano Quartet
Schurmann, G.:Qt Pno *(rec Tuscon Winter Chamber Festival; Mar 7, 1994)* Arizona Friends of Chamber Music ▲ AFCD 19951

Los Angeles Saxophone Quartet
Bach, J.S.:The Art of the Fugue Protone ▲ PRCD 1103 ■ CSPR 143/44

Los Angeles Standard SO
B. Walter (cnd)
Dvořák, A.:Sym 9, "From the New World" Music & Arts ▲ CD 788 [AAD]
Smetana, B.:The Bartered Bride (ov) Music & Arts ▲ CD 788 [AAD]
Smetana, B.:The Moldau Music & Arts ▲ CD 788 [AAD]
Tchaikovsky, P.:Romeo & Juliet Music & Arts ▲ CD 788 [AAD]

Los Angeles String Orch
L. Holdridge (cnd)
Holdridge, L.:Ballet Fant *(rec St. Giles Church, Cripplegate, London, Sept. & Oct. 1973)* Citadel ▲ CTD 88104 [ADD]
Holdridge, L.:Grand Waltz *(rec St. Giles Church, Cripplegate, London, Sept. & Oct. 1973)* Citadel ▲ CTD 88104 [ADD]

Los Angeles String Quartet [Paul Shure (vn), Bonnie Douglas (vn), Janet Lakatos (va), Armand Kaproff (vc)]
Bernstein, C.H.:Qt Strs, "Alanal" Arcobaleno 2-▲ AAOC 93922

Louire Regional PO
M. Soustrot (cnd)
Borodin, A.:In the Steppes of Central Asia Pierre Verany ("Favourites" series) ▲ PVY 730008 [DDD]
Mussorgsky, M.:Night Pierre Verany ("Favourites" series) ▲ PVY 730008 [DDD]
Rimsky-Korsakov, N.:Scheherazade Pierre Verany ("Favourites" series) ▲ PVY 730010 [DDD]

Louisiana Museum Art Ensemble
Gade, N.W.:Novelletter, Op. 53 Classico ▲ 1001
Gade, N.W.:Novelletter, Op. 58 Classico ▲ 1001

Louisiana State Univ New Music Ensemble
D. Constantinides (cnd)
Constantinides, D.:Vocal Music, w. Cynthia Dewey (nar), Angela DeVerger (sop), Evelyn Petros (sop), Susan Faust Straley (sop), Eugenia Epperson (fl), Richard Jernigan (cl), Kelly Smith Toney (vn), Hye-Yun Chung (hp), Stephen Brown (pno), John Raush (perc)—Reflections IV for Sop, Fl, Hp & Pno; Intimations [1 Act Opera]; 4 Songs on Poems by Sappho; Mutability for Sop & Str Qt.; 4 Greek Songs Vestige ▲ 04

Louisiana State Univ New Music Ensemble [Richard Jernigan (cl), Kelly Smith Toney (vn), Hye-Yun Chung (hp), John Rausch (perc)]
Constantinides, D.:Intimations, w. Susan Faust Straley (sgr—Ellen), Cynthia Dewey (sgr—Celeste) Capstone ▲ CPS 8632

Louisiana State Univ SO
J. Yestadt (cnd)
Constantinides, D.:Antigone, w. Thomas Poole (ten) Vestige ▲ 04

Louisville Orch
Dzubay, D.:Snake Alley Louisville ▲ LCD 009 [ADD]
Hailstork, A.:An American Port of Call Louisville ▲ LCD 009 [ADD]
Schuller, G.:Soundscapes Louisville ▲ LCD 009 [ADD]
Zwilich, E.T.:Con Vn, w. Jaime Laredo (vn), Sharon Robinson (vc) Louisville ▲ LCD 009 [ADD]
A. Endo (cnd)
Kay, H.:Cakewalk Albany ▲ TROY 016 [AAD]
M. Gould (cnd)
Gould, M.:Columbia Albany 2-▲ TROY 013-14-2 [AAD]
Gould, M.:Soundings Albany 2-▲ TROY 013-14-2 [AAD]
K. Husa (cnd)
Husa, K.:Apotheosis of this Earth, w. Univ of Louisville Concert Choir Louisville ▲ LCD 005 [AAD]
Husa, K.:Monodrama Louisville ▲ LCD 005 [AAD]
L. Leighton Smith (cnd)
Bolcom, W.:Seattle Slew Orchestral Suite *(rec 9/27/90)* Louisville ▲ LCD 007 [ADD]
Bolcom, W.:Sym 1 *(rec 3/14/91)* Louisville ▲ LCD 007 [ADD]
Bolcom, W.:Sym 3 *(rec 5/1/91)* Louisville ▲ LCD 007 [ADD]
Corigliano, J.:Campagne di Ravello Louisville ▲ LCD 008 [ADD]
Corigliano, J.:Con Pno, w. J. Tocco (pno) Louisville ▲ LCD 008 [ADD]
Corigliano, J.:Gazebo Dances Band Louisville ▲ LCD 008 [ADD]
Corigliano, J.:Promenade Ov Louisville ▲ LCD 008 [ADD]
Corigliano, J.:Summer Fanfare Louisville ▲ LCD 008 [ADD]
Corigliano, J.:Voyage Strs Louisville ▲ LCD 008 [ADD]
Creston, P.:Invocation & Dance Louisville ▲ LCD 005 [AAD]
Fennelly, B.:Fant Vars *(rec 1986)* Louisville ▲ LCD 003 [AAD]
Gould, M.:Con Va, w. R. Glazer (va) Albany 2-▲ TROY 013-14-2 [AAD]
Gould, M.:Flourishes & Galop Albany 2-▲ TROY 013-14-2 [AAD]
Gould, M.:Housewarming Albany 2-▲ TROY 013-14-2 [AAD]
Gould, M.:Sym of Spirituals Albany 2-▲ TROY 013-14-2 [AAD]
Gubaidulina, S.:Pro et Contra Louisville ▲ LCD 006 [ADD]
Harris, R.:Con Vn, w. Gregory Fulkerson (vn) Albany ▲ AR 012-2 [AAD]
Hindemith, P.:Con Pno, w. L. Luvisi (pno) *(rec 1987)* Louisville ▲ LCD 002 [AAD]
Hodkinson, S.:Sinf Concertante, (same as above) Louisville ▲ LCD 001 [AAD]
Korte, K.:Sym 3 Louisville ▲ LCD 001 [AAD]
Laderman, E.:Citadel Louisville ▲ LCD 004 [AAD]
Laderman, E.:Con Vn, w. E. Oliveira (vn) Louisville ▲ LCD 004 [AAD]
Lajtha, L.:Sanctuary Louisville ▲ LCD 004 [AAD]
Léon, T.:Batá *(rec Robert Whitney Hall, Louisville, KY, Apr 26, 1993)* Louisville Orchestra ("First Edition Recordings" series) ▲ LCD010 [ADD]
Luening, O.:Kentucky Rondo Louisville ▲ LCD 006 [ADD]
Schuller, G.:Farbenspiel *(rec 1988)* Louisville ▲ LCD 003 [AAD]
Thomas, A.R.:Wind Dance *(rec Robert Whitney Hall, Louisville, KY, Nov 18, 1993)* Louisville Orchestra ("First Edition Recordings" series) ▲ LCD010 [ADD]
Tower, J.:Island Rhythms Ov Louisville ▲ LCD 006 [ADD]
Zwilich, E.T.:Sym 2 *(rec 1989)* Louisville ▲ LCD 002 [AAD]
P. Leonard (cnd)
Rorem, N.:Air Music Albany ▲ TROY 047 [AAD]
J. Mester (cnd)
Balada, L.:Guernica New World ▲ 80498-2
Balada, L.:Maria Sabina, w. Hector Cortés (nar—Executioner), Amèrica Dunham (nar—Maria Sabina), Burwell Hardy (nar—Town Crier), Guillermo Helguera (nar—Constable), Richard Spalding (cnd), Louisville Univ Chorus *(rec Feb 5, 1973)* New World ▲ 80498-2
Barber, S.:Die Natali:Chorale Preludes for Christmas *(rec 1975)* Albany ▲ TROY 021-2 [AAD]
Barber, S.:Prayers of Kierkegaard, w. G. Capone (sop), Southern Baptist Theological Seminary Chorus [E], 1977) Albany ▲ TROY 021-2 [AAD]
Becker, J.J.:Symphonia brevis, "Sym No. 3" *(rec ca. 1973)* Albany ▲ TROY 027-2 [AAD]
Bird, A.:Carneval Scene Albany ▲ TROY 030 [AAD]
Chadwick, G.W.:Euterpe Albany ▲ TROY 030 [AAD]
Converse, F.S.:Endymion's Narrative Albany ▲ TROY 030 [AAD]
Converse, F.S.:Flivver Ten Million Albany ▲ TROY 030 [AAD]
Foote, A.:Francesca da Rimini Albany ▲ TROY 030-2 [AAD]
Gould, M.:American Symphonette 2 Albany 2-▲ TROY 013-14-2 [AAD]
Harris, R.:Sym 1 Albany ▲ AR 012-2 [AAD]
Harris, R.:When Johnny Comes Marching Home (ov) Orch Albany ▲ TROY 027-2 [AAD]
Mennin, P.:Con Vc, w. J. Starker (vc) *(rec 1969)* Albany ("First Edition Encores" series) ▲ TROY 044-2 [AAD]
Persichetti, V.:Sym 8 Albany ▲ TROY 024-2 [AAD]
Piston, W.:The Incredible Flutist Albany ▲ TROY 016 [AAD]
Piston, W.:Sym 1 *(rec 1976)* Albany ("First Edition Encores" series) ▲ TROY 044-2 [AAD]
Piston, W.:Sym 7 Albany ▲ AR 011-2 [AAD]
Piston, W.:Sym 8 Albany ▲ AR 011-2 [AAD]
Rorem, N.:Con 3 Pno, w. J. Lowenthal (pno) Albany ▲ TROY 047 [AAD]
Schickele, P.:Pentangle, w. K. Albrecht (hn) Albany ▲ TROY 024-2 [AAD]
Schuman, W.:Prayer in Time of War *(rec ca. 1971/72)* Albany ▲ TROY 027-2 [AAD]
Schuman, W.:Sym 4 *(rec ca. 1968/69)* Albany ▲ TROY 027-2 [AAD]
G. Schuller (cnd)
Léon, T.:Carabâli *(rec Robert Whitney Hall, Louisville, KY, Dec 3, 1993)* Louisville Orchestra ("First Edition Recordings" series) ▲ LCD010 [ADD]
J. Sedares (cnd)
Zwilich, E.T.:Con grosso 1985 Koch International Classics ▲ KIC 7278 [DDD]
Zwilich, E.T.:Con Ob, w. John Mack (ob) Koch International Classics ▲ KIC 7278 [DDD]
Zwilich, E.T.:Sym 3 Koch International Classics ▲ KIC 7278 [DDD]

Louisville Orch (cont.)
L. Slatkin (cnd)
Dello Joio, N.:Homage to Haydn *(rec 1974)* Albany ▲ TROY 024-2 [ADD]
R. Whitney (cnd)
Creston, P.:Corinthians XIII Albany ▲ TROY 021-2 [AAD]
Harris, R.:Epilogue to Profiles in Courage:JFK Albany ▲ TROY 027-2 [ADD]
Harris, R.:Sym 5 Albany ▲ AR 012-2 [AAD]
Hovhaness, A.:Magnificat, w. Audrey Nossaman (sop), Elizabeth Johnson (cta), Thomas East (ten), Richard Dales (bar), Univ of Louisville Choir Crystal ▲ CD 808
Kurka, R.:The Good Soldier Schweik (suite) *(rec 1965)* Albany ("First Edition Encores" series) ▲ TROY 044-2 [AAD]
Piston, W.:Sym 5 Albany ▲ AR 011-2 [AAD]
Toch, E.:Jephta, Rhapsodic Poem Albany ▲ TROY 021-2 [AAD]
G. Zimmermann (cnd)
Hanlon, K.:Cumulus Nimbus *(rec 1982)* Louisville ▲ LCD 003 [AAD]
Josephs, W.:Vars on a Theme of Beethoven Louisville ▲ LCD 001 [AAD]
Lawhead, D.V.:Aleost Louisville ▲ LCD 002 [AAD]
Rorem, N.:Eagles Albany ▲ TROY 047 [AAD]

Louisville Orch
L. Leighton Smith (cnd)
Thomas, A.R.:Triple Concerto ...night's midsummer blaze, w. Debussy Trio [A. Wiegand (fl), K. Greene (va), M. Dickstein (hp)] *(rec Robert Whitney Hall, Louisville, KY, Nov 18, 1993)* Louisville Orchestra ("First Edition Recordings" series) ▲ LCD010 [ADD]

Jacques Loussier Trio
Bach, J.S.:Music of—Toccata No. 4; Sicilienne; Choral No. 1; Passacaille; Invention No. 5; Fant in c Accord ▲ ACD 500182 [AAD]

Lowbury Piano Trio
Simpson, R.:Trio Vn Hyperion ▲ CDA 66737

Lower Austria Tonkünst Orch
A.J. Hochstrasser (cnd)
Schmidt, F.:Das Buch mit sieben Siegeln, w. Hertha Töpper (mez), Anton Dermota (ten), Thomas Moser (ten), Robert Holl (bass), Graezer Concert Choir *(rec 1975)* Preiser 2-▲ PRE 93263 [ADD]
I. Karabtchevsky (cnd)
Kaufmann, D.:Der Tod des Trompeters Kirilenko, w. S. Palm (vc), Erich Auer (speaker) Vienna Modern Masters ▲ VMM 3020 [AAD]

Lower Normandy Instrumental Ensemble
G. Descrieres (cnd)
Stravinsky, I.:L'Histoire du soldat Forlane ▲ FOR 16580 [DDD]

LSI PO
W. Carlos (cnd)
Carlos, W.:Carnival of Animals:Part II, w. "Weird Al" Yankovic (original poems/nar) CBS ▲ MK 44567 [DDD]
Prokofiev, S.:Peter & the Wolf, w. "Weird Al" Yankovic (nar) [all-synthesized orchestra] CBS ▲ MK 44567 [DDD]

Luc Capouillez Brass Ensemble
T. Cunningham (cnd)
Jongen, J.:Mass, Op. 130, w. J. Hughes (org), Brussels Choral Society [L] Pavane ▲ ADW 7242 [DDD]

Lucca Teatro Comunale del Giglio Orch
N. Annovazzi (cnd)
Catalani, A.:Loreley, w. M. Colalillo (sop), M. L. Garbato (sop), P. Visconti (ten), A. Cassis (bar), Lucca Teatro Comunale del Giglio Chorus *(rec live 9/19/82)* Bongiovanni 2-▲ GB 2015/16 [ADD]
M. de Bernart (cnd)
Catalani, A.:Edmea, w. M. Sokolinska Noto (sop), M. Frusoni (ten), M. Chingari (bar), P. Lefebvre (bass), A. Nosotti (bass), G. Pasella (bass), G. del Vivo (bass), Lucca Teatro Comunale del Giglio Chorus [l] *(rec live 9/89)* Bongiovanni 2-▲ GB 2093/94 [DDD]
G. Carella (cnd)
Catalani, A.:La falce (sels)—Prologue *(rec 1985)* Bongiovanni ▲ GB 2027 [DDD]
G. Cosmi (cnd)
Boccherini, L.:Credo, w. Svetla Krasteva (sop), Fernanda Piccini (cta), Manuel Beltrand (ten), Duccio Dal Monte (bass) *(rec Dec 18, 1993)* Bongiovanni ▲ GB 2178 [DDD]
Boccherini, L.:Credo & Dixit Dominus, w. Lucca St. Cecilia Choir [L] Bongiovanni ▲ GB 2087 [DDD]
Boccherini, L.:Kyrie & Gloria, w. Svetla Krasteva (sop), Fernanda Piccini (cta), Manuel Beltrand (ten), Duccio Dal Monte (bass) *(rec Dec 18, 1993)* Bongiovanni ▲ GB 2178 [DDD]
Boccherini, L.:Scene from Ines de Castro, w. Svetla Krasteva (sop) *(rec Dec 18, 1993)* Bongiovanni ▲ GB 2178 [DDD]
Boccherini, L.:Syms—Symphony in C, G.515 Bongiovanni ▲ GB 2087 [DDD]
Boccherini, L.:Syms *(rec Dec 18, 1993)* Bongiovanni ▲ GB 2178 [DDD]
Boccherini, L.:Villacicos al nacimiento (9), w. Lucca St. Cecilia Choir [L] Bongiovanni ▲ GB 2087 [DDD]
Catalani, A.:Mass, w. C. Basto (sop), A. Cipriani (cta), M. Frusoni (ten), P. Janowski (bass) [L] *(rec 1985)* Bongiovanni ▲ GB 2027 [DDD]
Puccini, D.:Canticum simeonis, w. St. Cecilia Cappella Musicale [L] Bongiovanni ▲ GB 2047 [DDD]
Puccini, D.:Con Pno, w. M. Guerrini (pno) Bongiovanni ▲ GB 2048 [DDD]
Puccini, M.:Concertone Fl, w. Mencarelli (fl), di Girolamo (cl), G. Bodanza (tpt), Caproni (hn) Bongiovanni ▲ GB 2048 [DDD]
Puccini, M.:Kyrie, w. M. Frusoni (ten), St. Cecilia Cappella Musicale [L] Bongiovanni ▲ GB 2047 [DDD]
Puccini, M.:Magnificat, w. M. Frusoni (ten), Nenci (ten), Di Benedetto (bass), St. Cecilia Cappella Musicale [L] Bongiovanni ▲ GB 2047 [DDD]
J. Latham-König (cnd)
Catalani, A.:Dejanice, w. C. Basto (sop), M. L. Garbato (sop), O. Garaventa (ten), R. Massis (bar), C. Zardo (bass), Lucca Teatro Comunale del Giglio Chorus [l] *(rec 9/6/85)* Bongiovanni 2-▲ GB 2031/32 [DDD]
G. Zani (cnd)
Rossini, G.:Aureliano in Palmira, w. L. d' Intino (sop), N. Ciliento (mez), E. di Cesare (ten), Mazzola (sgr) [l] *(rec live, Lucca, 10/28–11/2 1991)* Nuova Era 2-▲ 7069/70 [DDD]

Lucchese CO
H. Handt (cnd)
Monteverdi, C.:Orfeo, w. Nuccia Focile (sop), Claudia Clarich (mez), Enrico Facini (ten), Paolo Coni (bar), James Loomis (bass) [orchd Respighi, 1934–35] *(rec live, VII Festival Internazionale di Marlia, 1984)* Claves ▲ CD 9419 [ADD]

Lucerne City Wind Orch
F. Schaffner (cnd)
Balissat, J.:Sym Wind Orch *(rec Kunsthaus, Lucerne, June 18, 1994)* Gallo ▲ CD 885 [DDD]
Benz, A.:The Governor of Greifensee *(rec Kunsthaus, Lucerne, June 18, 1994)* Gallo ▲ CD 885 [DDD]
Jenny, A.:Dialogues Ob, w. Edwin Küttel (ob) *(rec Radio Studio Zürich, Sept 15, 1995)* Gallo ▲ CD 885 [DDD]
Planzer, M.:Provocaliente II *(rec Kunsthaus, Lucerne, Sept 10, 1995)* Gallo ▲ CD 885 [DDD]
Wagner, R.:Kaisermarsch [arr. for winds] *(rec Kunsthaus, Lucerne, Sept 10, 1995)* Gallo ▲ CD 885 [DDD]

Lucerne Festival Orch
W. Furtwängler (cnd)
Beethoven, L. van:Con 1 Pno, w. Adrian Aeschbacher (pno) *(rec Aug. 1947)* Music & Arts ▲ CD 839 [ADD]
W. Goehr (cnd)
Barber, S.:Con Vn, w. L. Kaufman (vn) *(rec 1951)* Music & Arts ▲ CD 667 (m) [AAD]

Lucerne Festival Strings
R. Baumgartner (cnd)
Bach, J.S.:Brandenburg Cons—Nos. 1-4 RCA Silver Seal ▲ 60475-2-RV [ADD] ■ 60475-4-RV (CrO2)
Bach, J.S.:Brandenburg Cons—Nos. 5 & 6 RCA Silver Seal ▲ 60533-2-RV [ADD] ■ 60533-4-RV
Bach, J.S.:Brandenburg Con 1 RCA Victor ▲ 09026-61719-2; ■ 09026-61719-4 (CrO2)
Bach, J.S.:Brandenburg Con 2—Overture & Suite No. 2, BWV 1067 Deutsche Grammophon ("Musikfest" series) ▲ 413256-2 [ADD] ■ 413256-4
Bach, J.S.:Brandenburg Con 5 RCA Victor ▲ 09026-61719-2; ■ 09026-61719-4 (CrO2)
Bach, J.S.:Brandenburg Con 6 RCA Victor ▲ 09026-61719-2; ■ 09026-61719-4 (CrO2)
Bach, J.S.:Cons Vn (comp), w. Z. Francescatti (vn) Deutsche Grammophon ("Musikfest" series) ▲ 429151-2 [ADD]
Bach, J.S.:Con for 2 Vns, w. Z. Francescatti (vn), R. Pasquier (vn) Deutsche Grammophon ("Musikfest" series) ▲ 429151-2 [ADD]
Bach, J.S.:Jesu bleibet meine Freude RCA Silver Seal ▲ 60533-2-RV [ADD] ■ 60533-4-RV
Bach, J.S.:Suites Orch, BWV 1066–1069 Eurodisc 3-▲ 69219-2-RV [ADD]
Bach, J.S.:Suite 2 Orch RCA Silver Seal ▲ 60533-2-RV [ADD] ■ 60533-4-RV
Baroque Favorites Archiv ("Galleria" series) ▲ 431479-2 AGA
Basic 100, Vol. 22 RCA Victor ▲ 09026-61719-2 ■ 09026-61719-4
The Best of Bach, w. Virgil Fox (org) Victrola ("Victrola Best of" series) ▲ 60768-2-RV [ADD] ■ 60768-4-RV
Boccherini, L.:Con Vc, G.482, w. P. Fournier (vc) Deutsche Grammophon ("Musikfest" series) ■ 413682-4
Flury, U.J.:Concertino veneziano, w. U. J. Flury (vn) *(rec Phonag Tonstudio, Dec. 5, 1978)* Gallo ▲ CD 802 [ADD]
Eine klingende Musikgeschichte des Kantons Luzern [A Resonant Music History of Lucerne Canton], w. Sybille Tschopp (vn), Karin Krauer (va) Gallo ▲ CD 727 [ADD]
Mozart, W.A.:Andante Fl, K.315/285a, w. James Galway (fl) RCA Victor ▲ 09026-68024-2; ■ 09026-68024-2
Mozart, W.A.:Andante Fl, K.315/285a, w. J. Galway (fl) RCA Gold Seal ▲ 6723-2-RG [ADD] ■ 6723-4-RG (CrO2)
Mozart, W.A.:Con Fl, K.313, w. James Galway (fl) RCA Gold Seal ▲ 6723-2 [ADD] ■ 6723-4 (CrO2)
M. Venzago (cnd)
Mieg, P.:Triple Con, w. Gunars Larsens (vn), Wilhelm Gerlach (va), Curdin Coray (vc) *(rec 1979)* Jecklin ▲ JS 314-2 [DDD]

Lucerne SO
O. Henzold (cnd)
Haydn, J.:Con Ob, w. Diana Doherty (ob) Pan Classics ▲ 510090 [DDD]
Martinů, B.:Con Ob, w. Diana Doherty (ob) Pan Classics ▲ 510090 [DDD]
Mozart, W.A.:Con Ob, K.314, w. Diana Doherty (ob) Pan Classics ▲ 510090 [DDD]
Zimmermann, B.A.:Con Ob, w. Diana Doherty (ob) Pan Classics ▲ 510090 [DDD]

Lucidarium Ensemble
Angels, w. Concerto Soave, Ensemble Convivencia, Ensemble Venance Fortunat, La Fenice, Iberian Lyric Ensemble L'Empreinte Digitale ▲ ED 13050
Lo mio servente core L'Empreinte Digitale ▲ ED 13051

Ludwig String Quartet
Alain, J.:Music of, w. Delphine Collot (sop), Bruno Boterf (ten), Jacques Bona (bar), Françoise Gyps (fl), Laurent Decker (ob), Bruno Pazqueir (va), Philippe Muller (vc), Georges Guillard (org), Georges Guillard (cnd), St. Louis Camerata Vocal Ensemble—2 Melodies for Sop & Pno; Nuptial Song for Bar, Bass, Vc & Org; Post-Scriptum for 3 Female Voices & Pno; Canticle in Phrygian Mode for 4 Mixed-Voice, Sop & Strs; Invention for Fl, Ob & Cl; Monody for solo Fl; Prelude for Str Qnt; Adagio for Str Qnt; Funerals for Str Qnt; March of the Horiaces & the Curiaces for 2 Bugles, Drum & Org Arion ▲ ARN 68321
Chausson, E.:Mélodies (comp), w. Sandrine Piau (sop), Brigitte Balleys (mez), Jean François Gardeil (bar), Billy Eidi (pno) Timpani 2-▲ 2C 2028
Debussy, C.:Qt Strs Masters of Art ▲ AAOC 9381
Honegger, A.:Chamber Music (comp), w. D.-S. Kang (vn), P.-H. Xuereb (va), R. Wallfisch (vc), M. Arrignon (cl), A. Marion (fl), A. Haraldsdottir (fl), C. Moreaux (ob), T. Caens (tpt), M. Becquet (trbn), P. Zanlonghi (hp), P. Devoyon (pno), F. Kondo (mez)—Sonatine for Clarinet & Piano (1921–22); Rapsodie for 2 Flutes, Clarinet & Piano (1917); Danse de la Chèvre for Solo Flute (1921); Romance for Flute & Piano (1953); Petite Suite for 2 Flutes & Piano (1934); Trois Contrepoints for Piccolo, Oboe, Violin & Cello (1922); Intrada for Trumpet & Piano (1947); Hommage du trombone exprimant la tristesse de l'auteur absent for Trombone & Piano (1925); J'avais un fidèle amant for String Quartet (1929); Chanson de Ronsard & 3 Chansons de la petite Sirène for Mezzo, Flute & String Quartet (1924); Introduction et Danse for Flute, Harp & String Trio [undated]; Colloque for Flute, Celesta, Violin & Viola [undated] Timpani ▲ IC1010 [DDD]
Honegger, A.:Chamber Music (comp), w. F. Kondo (mez)—String Quartets Nos. 1–3 (1916–17; 1934–36; 1936–37); Pâques à New York (Easter in New York) for Mezzo & String Quartet (1920) Timpani ▲ IC1011 [DDD]
Honegger, A.:Pâques à New York, w. F. Kondo (mez) Timpani ▲ IC1011 [DDD]
Honegger, A.:Qts Strs Timpani ▲ IC1011 [DDD]
Ravel, M.:Qt Strs Masters of Art ▲ AAOC 9381

Ludwigsburg Festival Orch
W. Gönnenwein (cnd)
Haydn, J.:Die Jahreszeiten, w. Helen Donath (sop), A. Kraus (ten), Kurt Widmer (bass), South German Madrigal Choir [G] Vox Box 2-▲ CDX 5045 [ADD]
Haydn, J.:Die Schöpfung, w. Helen Donath (sop), Scherr (alt), Adalbert Kraus (ten),Kurt Widmer (bass), South German Madrigal Choir [G] Vox Box 2-▲ CDX 5025 [ADD]
Verdi, G.:I masnadieri, w. M. Rowland (sgr), M. Malagnini (sgr), T. Migliorini (sgr), R. Bruson (bar), M. Lanskoy (bar), C. Colombara (bass), South German Madrigal Choir Bayer 2-▲ BR 500 001/2 [DDD]

Lugano Chamber Society Instrumental Ensemble
E. Loehrer (cnd)
Monteverdi, C.:Sacred Vocal Music, w. Lugano Società Cameristica Vocal Ensemble—Magnificat (for 6 voices); Vespro della Beata Vergine; Planctus Mariae; Selva Morale e Spiritual; Cantate Domino; Parnassus Musicus Ferdinandeus di G.B. Bonometti; Ab Aeterno Ordinata Sum; Selva Morale e Spirituale; O Beatae Viae; Symbolae Diversorum Musicorum di L. Calvo; Gloria; Selva Morale e Spirituale Accord ▲ ACD 202802 [ADD]
Palestrina, G.:Sacred Music, w. Luciana Ticinelli-Fattori (sop), Maria Minetto (mez), Laerte Malaguti (bar), James Loomis (bass), Lugano Chamber Society Chorus—Vexilla Regis Prodeunt; Adoramus Te; Laudario Di Cortona Accord ▲ ACD 201562 [AAD]

Lugano Chamber Society Orch
Caldara, A.:Il gioco del quadriglio, w. Maria-Grazia Ferraccini (sop), Basia Retchitzka (sop), Elena Rizzieri (sop), Maria Minetto (cta), Minetto Chorus Dynamic ▲ CDL 140
Jommelli, N.:La Passione di Gesù Cristo, w. Arturo Sacchetti (cnd), Lugano Chamber Society Chorus Accord 2-▲ ACD 204352 [AAD]
Monteverdi, C.:Madrigals, w. Basia Retchitzka (sop), Eric Tappy (ten), Rodolfo Malacarne (ten), Laerte Malaguti (bar), James Loomis (bass), Lugano Chamber Society Chorus—8 Madrigali Guerrieri e Amorosi Accord ▲ ACD 220872
Monteverdi, C.:Music of, w. Egidio Roveda (vc), Luciano Sgrizzi (hpd), Lugano Chamber Society Chorus—Altri Canti di Marte; Le Combat de Tancrede et Clorinde; Lamento Della Ninfa; Perche T'en Fuggi, O Fillide; Hor Ch'el Ciel e la Terra Accord ▲ ACD 220882
Vecchi, O.:L'Amfiparnaso Accord ▲ ACC 149040 [AAD]

Lugano String Quartet
Boulanger, L.:Songs, w. K. Ott (sop), J. Lemaire (pno)—Elle était descendue; Elle est gravement gaie; Parfois je suis triste; Un poète disait; Au pied de mon lit; Si tout ceci n'est qu'un pauvre rêve; Nous nous aimerons tant; Vous m'avez regardé avec toute votre; Les lilas qui avaient fleuri; Deux ancolies; Par ce que j'ai souffert; Je garde une médaille d'elle; Demain fera un an; Dans l'immense tristesse; Attente; Reflets; Le retour; Pie Jesu Signum ▲ X 39-00 [ADD]
Voegelin, F.:Qt 4 Strs *(rec Aug. 12, 1991)* Jecklin ▲ JS 283-2 [ADD]

ORCH. & ENS.

Lukas Consort
V. Lukas (cnd)
Bach, J.C.F:Sinf, HW.I/3 Campion ▲ 1329 [DDD]
Haydn, J.:Divert for 2 Hns, Vns, Va & Db, H.II/22 Campion ▲ 1329 [DDD]
Neubauer, F.C.:Bataille Campion ▲ 1329 [DDD]
Neubauer, F.C.:Con Vc, w. J. Metzger (vc) Campion ▲ 1329 [DDD]
Lunaire Ensemble
Japanese Folk Melodies, w. Rampal, Jean-Pierre (fl) CBS ▲ MK 35862 [ADD] ■ MT 35862
Don Lusher Trombone Ensemble
Live Brass, w. Massed Bands, Black Dyke Mills Band, James Shepherd Versatile Brass, Solna Brass, Brighouse & Rastrick Band *(rec live at the National Brass Band Festiva, Gala Concerts 1977, 1978, 1979)* Chandos ("Collect" series) ▲ CHAN 6561 [ADD]
Luxembourg Radio Orch
L. de Froment (cnd)
Aaron Rosand, w. Aaron Rosand (vn) *(rec 1971–73)* Vox Box 2-▲ CDX 5102 [ADD]
Debussy, C.:Prélude à l'après-midi d'un faune, w. Luxembourg RSO Vox Box 2-▲ CDX 5003 [ADD]
Luxembourg RSO
P. Cao (cnd)
Albert, E. d':Con 2 Pno, w. M. Ponti (pno) *(rec 1973)* Vox Box 2-▲ CDX 5067 [ADD]
Bartók, B.:Scherzo (Burlesque), w. G. Sándor (pno) *(rec 1974)*
Vox Box ("Legends" series) 2-▲ CDX2 5506 [ADD]
Goetz, H.:Con 2 Pno, w. M. Ponti (pno) *(rec 1973)* Vox Box 2-▲ CDX 5068 [ADD]
Hill, A.:Konzertstück Pno, w. J. Rose (pno) *(rec 1973)* Vox Box 2-▲ CDX 5064 [ADD]
Medtner, N.:Con 3 Pno, w. M. Ponti (pno) *(rec 1973)* Vox Box 2-▲ CDX 5068 [ADD]
Mosonyi, M.:Con Pno, w. J. Rose (pno) *(rec 1973)* Vox Box 2-▲ CDX 5067 [ADD]
Reinecke, C.:Cons Pno, w. M. Ponti (pno)—No. 1 *(rec 1973)* Vox Box 2-▲ CDX 5065 [ADD]
Saint-Saëns, C.:Con 1 Vn, w. R. Ricci (vn) Vox Box 2-▲ CDX 5084 [ADD]
Saint-Saëns, C.:Con 2 Vn, w. R. Ricci (vn) Vox Box 2-▲ CDX 5084 [ADD]
Saint-Saëns, C.:Con 3 Vn, w. R. Ricci (vn) Vox Box 2-▲ CDX 5084 [ADD]
Saint-Saëns, C.:Havanaise Vn, w. R. Ricci (vn) Vox Box 2-▲ CDX 5084 [ADD]
Saint-Saëns, C.:Introduction & Rondo capriccioso, w. R. Ricci (vn) Vox Box 2-▲ CDX 5084 [ADD]
Schumann, R.:Con Vn, w. S. Lautenbacher (vn) Vox Box 2-▲ CDX 5027 [ADD]
Schumann, R.:Fant Vn, w. S. Lautenbacher (vn) Vox Box 2-▲ CDX 5027 [ADD]
Schumann, R.:Konzertstück Hns Vox Box 2-▲ CDX 5027 [ADD]
L. de Froment (cnd)
Constant, M.:Turner *(rec 1978)* Citadel ▲ CTD 88106 [ADD]
Daniel-Lesur, D.J.Y.:Andrea del Sarto *(rec 1978)* Citadel ▲ CTD 88106 [ADD]
Debussy, C.:Berceuse héroïque *(rec 1972)* Vox Box 2-▲ CDX 5053 [ADD]
Debussy, C.:La Boîte à joujoux *(rec 1972)* Vox Box 2-▲ CDX 5053 [ADD]
Debussy, C.:L'Enfant prodigue—Cortège et Air de Danse *(rec 1972)*
Vox Box 2- 2-▲ CDX 5053 [ADD]
Debussy, C.:Fant Pno, w. M. Dosse (pno) *(rec 1972)* Vox Box 2-▲ CDX 5053 [ADD]
Debussy, C.:Images Orch Vox Box 2-▲ CDX 5003 [ADD]
Debussy, C.:Jeux Vox Box 2-▲ CDX 5003 [ADD]
Debussy, C.:Jeux Allegretto ▲ ACD 8159 [ADD] ■ ACS 8159
Debussy, C.:Khamma Vox Box 2-▲ CDX 5003 [ADD]
Debussy, C.:Marche écossaise sur un thème populaire *(rec 1972)* Vox Box 2-▲ CDX 5053 [ADD]
Debussy, C.:Martyre de Saint Sébastian (fragments), w. J. Navadic (nar) *(rec 1972)*
Vox Box 2-▲ CDX 5053 [ADD]
Debussy, C.:La Mer Vox Box 2-▲ CDX 5003 [ADD]
Debussy, C.:Nocturnes Vox Box 2-▲ CDX 5003 [ADD]
Debussy, C.:Nocturnes Allegretto ▲ ACD 8159 [ADD] ■ ACS 8159
Debussy, C.:Orchestral Music *(rec 1972)* Vox Box 2-▲ CDX 5053 [ADD]
Debussy, C.:La Plus que lente *(rec 1972)* Vox Box 2-▲ CDX 5053 [ADD]
Debussy, C.:Prélude à l'après-midi d'un faune, w. L. de Froment, Luxembourg Radio Orch.
Vox Box 2-▲ CDX 5003 [ADD]
Debussy, C.:Prélude à l'après-midi d'un faune Allegretto ▲ ACD 8159 [ADD] ■ ACS 8159
Debussy, C.:Première rapsodie, w. S. Dangain (cl) *(rec 1972)* Vox Box 2-▲ CDX 5053 [ADD]
Debussy, C.:Printemps (suite) *(rec 1972)* Vox Box 2-▲ CDX 5053 [ADD]
Debussy, C.:Rapsodie, w. J.-M. Londeix (sax) *(rec 1972)* Vox Box 2-▲ CDX 5053 [ADD]
Debussy, C.:Le Roi Lear (sels)—Fanfare & Le Sommeil de Lear *(rec 1972)*
Vox Box 2-▲ CDX 5053 [ADD]
Debussy, C.:Triomphe de Bacchus—Fanfare & Le Sommeil de Lear *(rec 1972)*
Vox Box 2-▲ CDX 5053 [ADD]
Djabadary, H.:Con Pno, w. H. Goraieb (pno) *(rec 1980)* Quantum ▲ QM 6915
Djabadary, H.:La Melopée du serpent *(rec 1980)* Quantum ▲ QM 6915
Djabadary, H.:Tiflisiana *(rec 1980)* Quantum ▲ QM 6915
Goldmark, K.:Con 1 Vn, w. R. Ricci (vn) *(rec 1977)* Allegretto ▲ ACD 8173 [ADD] ■ ACS 8173
Mendelssohn, F.:Con 1 Pno, w. Rudolf Firkusny (pno) *(rec 1971)* Allegretto ▲ ACD 8208
Mendelssohn, F.:Con in e Vn & Orch, Op. 64, w. Aaron Rosand (vn)—Allegro molto appassionato
Special Music Co. ("Classics of the Heart" series) ▲ SCD 5197
Mendelssohn, F.:Con in e Vn & Orch, Op. 64, w. Aaron Rosand (vn) *(rec 1973)*
Allegretto ▲ ACD 8207
Mendelssohn, F.:Life & Music of, w. A. Rosand (vn)—narration with selected excerpts from Ov. [Midsummer Nights Dream], Op.21; Con. for 2 Pianos in A♭; Midsummer Night's Dream, Op. 61; Song Without Words 30, Op. 62/6; Octet, Op. 20; Hebrides Ov., Op. 26; Syms. Nos. 3 & 4; Ov [from Calm Sea and Prosperous Voyage], Op. 27; St. Paul, Op. 36; Con. No. 1 for Piano, Op. 25; Con. for Violin, Op. 64; Song without Words 23, Op. 67/4; Ov. [from *Ruy Blas*], Op. 95; On Wings of Song, Op. 34/2, plus a complete version of Con. in e for Violin & Orch., Op. 64
Vox Music Masters ("Music Masters" series) ▲ MMD 8503 [ADD] ■ MMC 8503
Messiaen, O.:Turangalîla-sym, w. Y. Loriod (pno), J. Loriod (ondes Martenot)
Forlane 2-▲ FOR 16504/05 [AAD/DDD]
Milhaud, D.:Le Boeuf sur le toit Allegretto ▲ ACD 8157 [ADD] ■ ACS 8157
Poulenc, F.:Les Biches Allegretto ▲ ACD 8157 [ADD] ■ ACS 8157
Prokofiev, S.:Cons Pno (comp), w. G. Tacchino (pno) *(rec 1972–77)* Vox Box 3-▲ CD3X 3000 [ADD]
Prokofiev, S.:Con 1 Pno, w. G. Tacchino (pno) *(rec 1972)*
Allegretto ▲ ACD 8168 [ADD] ■ ACS 8168
Prokofiev, S.:Con 2 Pno, w. G. Tacchino (pno) *(rec 1977)*
Allegretto ▲ ACD 8168 [ADD] ■ ACS 8168
Prokofiev, S.:Con 3 Pno, w. G. Tacchino (pno) *(rec 1977)*
Allegretto ▲ ACD 8168 [ADD] ■ ACS 8168
Prokofiev, S.:Cons Vn (comp), w. R. Ricci (vn) Vox Box 3-▲ CD3X 3000 [ADD]
Prokofiev, S.:Sym-Con Vc, w. L. Varga (vc) Vox Box 3-▲ CD3X 3000 [ADD]
Ravel, M.:Con Pno (left hand), w. A. Simon (pno) Vox Box 2-▲ CDX 5032 [ADD]
Ravel, M.:Con in G Pno, w. A. Simon (pno) Vox Box 2-▲ CDX 5031 [ADD]
Roussel, A.:Suite *(rec 1978)* Citadel ▲ CTD 88106 [ADD]
Saint-Saëns, C.:Allegro appassionato, w. L. Varga (vc) Vox Box 2-▲ CDX 5084 [ADD]
Saint-Saëns, C.:Caprice andalous, w. R. Ricci (vn) Vox Box 2-▲ CDX 5084 [ADD]
Saint-Saëns, C.:Con 1 Vc, w. L. Varga (vc) Vox Box 2-▲ CDX 5084 [ADD]
Saint-Saëns, C.:Henry VIII (sels)—Ballet Divertissement *(rec 1973 & 1974)*
Allegretto ▲ ACD 8171 [ADD] ■ ACS 8171
Saint-Saëns, C.:Morceau de concert Vn, w. R. Ricci (vn) Vox Box 2-▲ CDX 5084 [ADD]
Saint-Saëns, C.:Romance Vn, w. R. Ricci (vn) Vox Box 2-▲ CDX 5084 [ADD]
Saint-Saëns, C.:Sym 2 *(rec 1973 & 1974)* Allegretto ▲ ACD 8171 [ADD] ■ ACS 8171
Saint-Saëns, C.:Sym 3 *(rec 1973 & 1974)* Allegretto ▲ ACD 8171 [ADD] ■ ACS 8171
Satie, E.:Parade Allegretto ▲ ACD 8157 [ADD] ■ ACS 8157
Schumann, R.:Con Pno, w. Rudolf Firkusny (pno) *(rec 1971)* Allegretto ▲ ACD 8208
Tailleferre, G.:Ballade, w. R. Marciano (pno) Allegretto ▲ ACD 8157 [ADD] ■ ACS 8157

Luxembourg RSO (cont.)
L. de Froment (cnd) (cont.)
Tchaikovsky, P.:Con 3 Pno, w. M. Ponti (pno) Vox Box 2-▲ CDX 5024 [ADD]
Tchaikovsky, P.:Con Vn, w. A. Rosand (vn) Vox Box 3-▲ CD3X 3025 [ADD]
Tchaikovsky, P.:Con Vn, w. Aaron Rosand (vn) *(rec 1973)* Allegretto ▲ ACD 8207
Tomasi, H.:Fanfares Liturgiques *(rec 1978)* Citadel ▲ CTD 88106 [ADD]
Wissmer, P.:Con 3 Pno, w. Y. Boukoff (pno) Quantum ▲ QM 6908
Froment, Cao (cnd)
Rameau, J.P.:Les Indes Galantes (syms) Forlane ▲ FRL 42 [ADD]
L. Hager (cnd)
Brahms, J.:Alto Rhap, w. M. Lipovšek (mez) Forlane ▲ FOR 16671 [DDD]
Brian, H.:The Tigers (sels)—Symphonic Movts. Forlane 2-▲ FOR 16724 [ADD]
Foulds, J.:Mirage Forlane 2-▲ FOR 16724 [ADD]
Foulds, J.:Pasquinade Symphonique 1 Forlane 2-▲ FOR 16724 [ADD]
Foulds, J.:St. Joan Suite Forlane 2-▲ FOR 16724 [ADD]
Parry, H.:Sym 3 Forlane 2-▲ FOR 16724 [ADD]
S. Köhler (cnd)
Zimmermann, B.A.:Con Vn, w. Susanne Lautenbacher (vn) Vox Box 2-▲ CDX 5134 [ADD]
F. Martin (cnd)
Martin, F.:Con 2 Pno, w. P. Badura-Skoda (pno) *(rec 1971)* Jecklin-Disco ▲ JD 632-2 [ADD]
Martin, F.:Con Vn, w. W. Schneiderhan (vn) *(rec 1971)* Jecklin-Disco ▲ JD 632-2 [ADD]
K. Redel (cnd)
Music of Johann Strauss (II), w. Vienna Strauss Orch [cnd:Joseph Francek] Laserlight ♦ 90027 [DDD]
Vivaldi, A.:Cons Ob, w. S. Trubashnik (ob), 1 concerto—in d Forlane ▲ FOR 16548 [AAD]
R. Reinhardt (cnd)
Debussy, C.:La Mer Allegretto ▲ ACD 8041 [ADD] ■ ACS 8041
A. Springer (cnd)
Penderecki, K.:Emanations *(rec Feb 1972)* Vox Box 2-▲ CDX 5142
Penderecki, K.:Son Vc, w. Thomas Blees (vc) *(rec Feb 1972)* Vox Box 2-▲ CDX 5142
E. Stratta (cnd)
Britten, B.:Scottish Ballad, w. Joshua Pierce (pno), Dorothy Jonas (pno) Phoenix ▲ PHCD 104 [DDD]
Martinů, B.:Con 2 Pnos, w. Joshua Pierce (pno), Dorothy Jonas (pno) Phoenix ▲ PHCD 104 [DDD]
P. Wissmer (cnd)
Wissmer, P.:Alerte, puits 21! Quantum ▲ QM 6908
Luxembourg Radio-TV SO
P. Bonneau (cnd)
French Operetta Highlights, w. Jean-Pierre Wallez (cnd) Forlane ▲ FRL 3 [AAD]
P. Cao (cnd)
Brahms, J.:Academic Festival Ov Forlane ▲ FRL 14 [AAD]
Elgar, E.:Pomp & Circumstance Marches—No. 1 Forlane ▲ FRL 46 [ADD]
Strauss (II), Joh.:Ovs—La chauve-souris Forlane ▲ FRL 46 [ADD]
L. de Froment (cnd)
Auber, D.-F.:La muette de Portici (ov) Forlane ▲ FRL 27 [AAD]
Berlioz, H.:Le Carnaval romain Forlane ▲ FRL 27 [AAD]
Berlioz, H.:La Damnation de Faust (sels) Forlane ▲ FRL 28 [AAD]
Berlioz, H.:La Damnation de Faust (sels) Forlane ▲ FRL 44 [AAD]
Bizet, G.:Carmen (sels) Forlane ▲ FRL 27 [AAD]
Bizet, G.:Carmen (suite 1) Forlane ▲ FRL 28 [AAD]
Boccherini, L.:Minuetto Forlane ▲ FRL 27 [AAD]
Borodin, A.:In the Steppes of Central Asia Forlane ▲ FRL 28 [AAD]
Delibes, L.:Lakmé (sels) Forlane ▲ FRL 44 [AAD]
Delibes, L.:Le Roi l'a dit (ov) Forlane ▲ FRL 44 [AAD]
Delibes, L.:La Source, ou Naila (sels)—Intermezzo Forlane ▲ FRL 44 [AAD]
Delibes, L.:Sylvia (suite) Forlane ▲ FRL 28 [AAD]
Dukas, P.:L'Apprenti sorcier Forlane ▲ FRL 46 [ADD]
Gluck, C.W.:Orfeo ed Euridice (sels), w. Daniel Roux (fl) Forlane ▲ FRL 46 [ADD]
Gounod, C.:Faust (ballet music) Forlane ▲ FRL 28 [AAD]
Gounod, C.:Faust (ballet music) Forlane ▲ FRL 44 [AAD]
Handel, G.F.:Concerti grossi, Op. 6—No. 8 in G Forlane ▲ FRL 42 [ADD]
Handel, G.F.:Water Music (suites) Forlane ▲ FRL 42 [ADD]
Hummel, J.N.:Con in E♭ Tpt, S.49, w. Gérard Milliere (tpt) Forlane ▲ FRL 42 [ADD]
Khachaturian, A.:Gayane (sels)—Sabre Dance Forlane ▲ FRL 46 [ADD]
Lalo, E.:Le Roi d'Ys (ov) Forlane ▲ FRL 44 [AAD]
Lalo, E.:Le Roi d'Ys (ov) Forlane ▲ FRL 45 [ADD]
Liszt, F.:Les Préludes Forlane ▲ FRL 46 [ADD]
Mozart, W.A.:Sym 29 Forlane ▲ FRL 12 [AAD]
Mozart, W.A.:Sym 40 Forlane ▲ FRL 12 [AAD]
Mozart, W.A.:Sym 41 Forlane ▲ FRL 12 [AAD]
Ravel, M.:Alborada del gracioso Forlane ▲ FRL 47 [AAD]
Ravel, M.:Ma mère l'oye Orch LaserLight ▲ 14013 [DDD]
Rossini, G.:Il barbiere di Siviglia (ov) Forlane ▲ FRL 27 [AAD]
Rossini, G.:Guillaume Tell (ov) Forlane ▲ FRL 27 [AAD]
Schumann, R.:Con Pno, w. Henri Goraieb (pno) Forlane ▲ FRL 14 [AAD]
Schumann, R.:Intro & Allegro appassionato, Op. 92, w. Henri Goraieb (pno) Forlane ▲ FRL 14 [AAD]
Tchaikovsky, P.:Nutcracker Suite Forlane ▲ FRL 28 [AAD]
Tchaikovsky, P.:Romeo & Juliet Forlane ▲ FRL 28 [AAD]
Wagner, R.:Die Walküre (ride of the valkyries) Forlane ▲ FRL 46 [ADD]
Weber, C.M. von:Con 1 Cl, w. Serge Dangain (cl) Forlane ▲ FRL 9 [AAD]
Weber, C.M. von:Con 2 Cl, w. Serge Dangain (cl) Forlane ▲ FRL 9 [AAD]
Weber, C.M. von:Oberon (ov) Forlane ▲ FRL 9 [AAD]
L. Hager (cnd)
Smetana, B.:The Bartered Bride (orch sels)—Ov; Polka; Furiant; Ballet Forlane ▲ FRL 49 [DDD]
Smetana, B.:Má Vlast—The Moldau; Tabor Forlane ▲ FRL 49 [DDD]
K. Redel (cnd)
Strauss (II), Joh.:Die Fledermaus (sels)—Intro; Wenn ich jenes Täubchen wär; Brüderlein und Schwesterlein; Ach, wie wird mein Auge trübe; Mein Herr, was dächten Sie von mir; Im Feuerstrom der reben; Mein Herr Marquis; Mein schönes, grosses Vogelhaus; Trinke Liebchen; Finale
Forlane ▲ FRL 6 [AAD]
Strauss (II), Joh.:Der Zigeunerbaron (sels)—Intro; Ja das Schreiben und das Lesen; Nur keusch und rein; Wer uns getraut; Werberlied; Lied und Chor; Zigeunerlied; Entracte; Zigeunerchor; Hier die Hand es muss ja sein; Entracte und Terzett; Finale Forlane ▲ FRL 6 [AAD]
Vivaldi, A.:Cons Ob, w. Senia Trubashnik (ob)—in d Forlane ▲ FRL 16644 [AAD]
Luzern Opus Novum Ensemble
P. Siegwart (cnd)
Mäder, U.:In die Oberfläche geritzt *(rec 1996)* Jecklin ▲ JS 3072 [DDD]
Mäder, U.:Stimmenfragmente *(rec 1996)* Jecklin ▲ JS 3072 [DDD]
Mäder, U.:Vom Nesselweg her *(rec 1996)* Jecklin ▲ JS 3072 [DDD]
Lydian String Quartet [Daniel Stepner (vn), Judith Eissenberg (vn), Mary Ruth Ray (va), Rhonda Rider (vc)]
Anderson, A.:Qt Strs CRI ▲ CD 727 [DDD]
Fine, I.:Qt Strs Elektra/Nonesuch ▲ 79175-2
Hyla, L.:Qt 2 Strs *(rec Brandeis Univ, Setp 26, 1995)* New World ▲ 80491-2
Hyla, L.:Qt 3 Strs *(rec Dec. 18, 1994)* New World ▲ 80491-2
Ives, C.:Halloween, w. S. Pinkas (pno), L. Hyla (dr) Centaur ▲ CRC 2069 [DDD]
Ives, C.:Largo cantabile, w. E. Barker (db) Centaur ▲ CRC 2069 [DDD]
Ives, C.:Qts 1 & 2 Strs Centaur ▲ CRC 2069 [DDD]
Schubert, Franz:Qt 8 Strs *(rec Mar. 10–12, 1992)* Centaur ▲ CRC 2186 [DDD]
Schubert, Franz:Qt 13 Strs *(rec Mar. 10–12, 1992)* Centaur ▲ CRC 2186 [DDD]
Schubert, Franz:Songs (misc)—Der Tod und das Mädchen, Op. 7/3 Centaur ▲ CRC 2186 [DDD]
Schuman, W.:Qt 2 Strs Harmonia Mundi USA ▲ HMU 907114

242

▲ = CD ♦ = Enhanced CD Δ = MD ■ = Cassette Tape □ = DCC

Lydian String Quartet (cont.)
Schuman, W.:Qt 3 Strs — Harmonia Mundi USA ▲ HMU 907114
Schuman, W.:Qt 5 Strs — Harmonia Mundi USA ▲ HMU 907114

Lyndon Baglin Brass Ensemble
Best of Brass — Saydisc ■ CSDL 347 (D)

Lyngby–Taarbaek SO
C. Eriksson (cnd)
Gade, N.W.:Mariotta (sels) — Point ▲ PCD 5093
Gade, N.W.:Michel Angelo — Point ▲ PCD 5093
Gade, N.W.:A Summer's Day in the Country — Point ▲ PCD 5093
Horneman, C.F.E.:Music of—The Gurre Suite — Point ▲ PCD 5093

Lynn Murray Orch
Bernstein, L.:On the Town, w. M. Martin (sgr), N. Walker (sgr), B. Comden (sgr), A. Green (sgr), Tutti Camarata Orch, Leonard Joy Orch, Lynn Murray Chorus — MCA Classics ▲ MCAD 10280 (m) [AAD]

Lyon National Orch
S. Baudo (cnd)
Beethoven, L. van:Christus am Ölberg, w. M. Pick–Hieronimi (sop), J. Anderson (sop), V. von Halem (bass), Lyon National Chorus [G] — Harmonia Mundi France ▲ HMC 905181
Poulenc, F.:Litanies à la vierge noire, w. Lyon National Chorus— Salve; Stabat [F] — Harmonia Mundi France ▲ HMC 905149
Poulenc, F.:Stabat mater, w. M. Lagrange (sop), Lyon National Chorus [L] — Harmonia Mundi France ▲ HMC 905149

E. Krivine (cnd)
Chabrier, E.:Pièces pittoresques—No. 9 [Menuet pompeux; orchd. Ravel] *(rec Auditorium Maurice Ravel, Nov. 4–7, 1993)* — Denon ▲ DEN 78929 [DDD]
Debussy, C.:Danse Pno, "Tarantelle styrienne" *(rec Auditorium Maurice Ravel, Nov. 4–7, 1993)* — Denon ▲ DEN 78929 [DDD]
Debussy, C.:La Mer — Denon ▲ DEN 78774 [DDD]
Debussy, C.:Nocturnes, w. Netherlands Women's Chamber Choir — Denon ▲ DEN 78774 [DDD]
Debussy, C.:Prélude à l'après-midi d'un faune — Denon ▲ DEN 78774 [DDD]
Debussy, C.:Sarabande *(rec Auditorium Maurice Ravel, Nov. 4–7, 1993)* — Denon ▲ DEN 78929 [DDD]
Fauré, G.:Elégie, w. Anne Gastinel (vc) — Valois ▲ V 4754
Fauré, G.:Masques et bergamasques (suite) — Denon ▲ CO 77527 2 [DDD]
Fauré, G.:Requiem, w. G. Le Roi (sop), F. Le Roux (bar), Lyon National Chorus [L] — Denon ▲ CO 77527 [DDD]
Franck, C.:Psyché (sels) *(rec Mar. 20–22, 1992)* — Denon ▲ CO 75199 [DDD]
Franck, C.:Sym in d *(rec Mar. 20–22, 1992)* — Denon ▲ CO 75199 [DDD]
Lalo, E.:Con Vc, w. Anne Gastinel (vc) — Valois ▲ V 4754
Mussorgsky, M.:Pictures at an Exhibition *(rec Auditorium Maurice Ravel, Nov. 4–7, 1993)* — Denon ▲ DEN 78929 [DDD]
Saint-Saëns, C.:Con 1 Vc, w. A. Gastinel (vc) — Valois ▲ V 4754
Saint-Saëns, C.:Danse macabre — Denon ▲ CO 75024
Saint-Saëns, C.:Phaéton — Denon ▲ CO 75024
Saint-Saëns, C.:Le Rouet d'Omphale — Denon ▲ CO 75024 [DDD]
Saint-Saëns, C.:Sym 3, w. M. Matthes (org) — Denon ▲ CO 75024 [DDD]
Schumann, R.:Carnaval Pno *(rec Auditorium Maurice Ravel, Nov. 4–7, 1993)* — Denon ▲ DEN 78929 [DDD]

P. Méfano (cnd)
Kagel, M.:Music of, w. Ensemble 2E2M, Lyon National Chorus—Vox Humana?; Finale; Fürst Igor, Stravinsky — Accord ▲ ACD 201262 [DDD]

Lyon Opera Orch
The Ultimate Opera Collection, w. Venice Soloists, James Conlon (cnd), Armin Jordan (cnd), Raymond Leppard (cnd), Alain Lombard (cnd), Lorin Maazel (cnd), Claudio Scimone (cnd), London PO, et al. — Erato ▲ 2292–45797–2 ■ 2292–45797–4 AW

L. Foster (cnd)
Jessye Norman at Notre Dame, w. Jessye Norman (sop) — Philips ▲ 432731–2 PH [DDD]
Operetta Duets, w. Barbara Hendricks (sop), Gino Quilico (bar) — EMI Classics ▲ CDC 55151

J.E. Gardiner (cnd)
Berlioz, H.:L'Enfance du Christ, w. A. S. von Otter (mez), Johnson (sgr), G. Cachemaille (bar), J. Van Dam (b-bar), J. Bastin (bass), Monteverdi Choir London [F] — Erato 2–▲ 2292–45275–2 [DDD]
Berlioz, H.:Les Nuits d'été, w. D. Montague (mez), C. Robbin (mez), H. Crook (ten), G. Cachémaille (bar) [F] — Erato ("Musifrance" series) ▲ 2292–45517–2 [DDD]
Berlioz, H.:Songs, w. B. Fournier (sop), D. Montague (mez), C. Robbin (mez), H. Crook (ten), G. Cachémaille (bar)—Zaïde [Fournier]; La belle voyageuse [Montague]; La Captive [Robbin]; La mort d'Ophélie [Robbin]; Le jeune pâtre breton [Crook]; Aubade [Crook]; Le Chasseur danois [Cachémaille] [F] — Erato ("Musifrance" series) ▲ 2292–45517–2 [DDD]
Bizet, G.:Sym 1—Allegro vivo *(rec Eglise Sainte Madeleine de Pérouges, Nov. 1986)* — Erato ▲ 94682–2
Gluck, C.W.:Iphigénie en Aulide, w. L. Dawson (sop), A. S. von Otter (mez), J. Aler (ten), J. Van Dam (b-bar), Monteverdi Choir London — Erato ("Musifrance" series) 2–▲ 2292–45003–2–ZA [DDD]
Gluck, C.W.:Iphigénie en Tauride, w. D. Montague (mez), J. Aler (ten), T. Allen (bar), R. Massis (bar) [F] — Philips 2–▲ 416148–2 [DDD]
Schubert, Franz:Sym 8 — Erato ▲ 45986–2
Schubert, Franz:Sym 8—Allegro moderato *(rec Montpellier Opera, July 1987)* — Erato ▲ 94682–2
Schubert, Franz:Sym 9 — Erato ▲ 45986–2

K. Nagano (cnd)
Adams, J.:The Death of Klinghoffer, w. S. Friedman (mez), S. Sylvan (bar), J. Maddalena (bar), T. Hammons (bar), English Opera Group Chorus — Elektra/Nonesuch 2–▲ 79281–2 2–■ 79281–4
Bruch, M.:Con Cl & Va, w. P. Meyer (cl), G. Caussé (va) — Erato ▲ 2292–45483–2 ZK [DDD]
Bruch, M.:Romanze Va, w. G. Caussé (va) — Erato ▲ 2292–45483–2 ZK [DDD]
Canteloube, J.:Songs of Auvergne, w. D. Upshaw (sop) *(rec Lyon, Apr. 1–4, 1994)* — Erato ▲ 96559–2 [DDD]
Debussy, C.:La Boîte à joujoux *(rec Lyon, Aug. 1992)* — Erato ▲ 97418–2 ■ 97418–4
Delibes, L.:Coppélia (sels) *(rec June & July 1993)* — Erato ▲ 96368–2 [DDD]
Delibes, L.:Coppélia (sels), w. V. Vassiliev (vn), A. Kolodenko (va) — Erato 2–▲ 91730–2
Ibert, J.:Chansons de Don Quichotte, w. J. Van Dam (bass-bar) — Virgin Classics ▲ CDC 59236
Martin, F.:Monologe (6) aus "Jedermann", w. J. van Dam (b-bar) — Virgin Classics ▲ CDC 59236
Milhaud, D.:Le Boeuf sur le toit — Erato ("Musifrance" series) ▲ 2292–45820–2–ZK
Milhaud, D.:Con Hp, w. F. Cambreling (hp) — Erato ("Musifrance" series) ▲ 2292–45820–2–ZK
Milhaud, D.:La Création du monde — Erato ("Musifrance" series) ▲ 2292–45820–2–ZK
Poulenc, F.:Le Bal masqué, w. J. Van Dam (b-bar) — Virgin Classics ▲ CDC 59236
Poulenc, F.:Dialogues des Carmélites, w. C. Dubosc (sop), R. Yakar (sop), R. Gorr (mez), M. Dupuy (mez), J. Van Dam (b-bar) — Virgin Classics ▲ CDCB 59227
Prokofiev, S.:Peter & the Wolf, w. P. Stewart (nar) *(rec Lyon, Oct. 12–16, 1993)* — Erato ▲ 97418–2 [DDD] ■ 97418–4
Ravel, M.:Don Quichotte à Dulcinée, w. J. Van Dam (bar) — Virgin Classics ▲ CDC 59236

Lyon Wind Quintet
The Art of the Cornet, w. Thierry Caens (hn) — Arion ▲ ARN 60267

Lyra Borealis Ensemble
P. Järvi (cnd)
Kasemets, U.:The Eight Houses of the I Ching — Koch International Classics ▲ KIC 7165 [DDD]
Kasemets, U.:Palestrina on Devil's Staircase — Koch International Classics ▲ KIC 7165 [DDD]
Kasemets, U.:Requiem/Renga — Koch International Classics ▲ KIC 7165 [DDD]

Lyra Ensemble
Couperin, F.:Laetentur coeli — Koch Schwann ▲ SCH 312932 [DDD]
Couperin, F.:Leçons de ténèbres 1/2 Voices — Koch Schwann ▲ SCH 312932 [DDD]
Couperin, F.:Regina coeli laetare — Koch Schwann ▲ SCH 312932 [DDD]
Couperin, F.:Victoria:Christo resurgent — Koch Schwann ▲ SCH 312932 [DDD]

La Lyre Seraphique
Lefébure–Wély, L.J.A.:Music of, w. Sylvie de May (sop), Catherine Ravenne (alt), Xavier Bisaro (org), Vincent Genvrin (org), L'Accent Grave Vocal Ensemble—Adoremus et procidamus; Marche en mib majeur; Adoro te [alterné]; Tantum ergo; Sacris solemnis; Elévation en la mineur; Marche en ut majeur; Noël varié, offertoire pour le jour de Noël; Sanctus; O Salutaris; Pastorale en sol majeur; Agnus Dei; Communion en fa majeur; Domine salvum; Missum redemptorem; Sortie en sib majeur et Cloches — Media 7 ▲ 005 [DDD]
Lefébure–Wély, L.J.A.:Music of, w. Sylvie de May (sop), Sophie Fournier (sop), Catherine Ravenne (alt), Antoine Espagno (db), Vincent Genvrin (org), Pythagore Vocal Ensemble—Sainte cité, demeure permanente; Récit de Hautbois ou de Trompette harmonique; L'Encens divin; Offertoire [grand choeur]; Seigneur dès ma première enfance; Verset; Pleins de ferveur; Marche; Jour heureux, sainte allégresse; Esprit divin, Dieu de lumière; Andante, choeur de voix humaines; Afin d'être docile et sage; Mon fils, pour apprendre; Andante; Motet à la Sainte–Vierge; Andante; Du Roi des cieux tout célèbre la gloire; Scène pastorale; Andantino — Media 7 ▲ 004 [DDD]

Lyric Art String Quartet [Fredell Lack (vn), George Bennett (vn), Wayne Crouse (va), Marion Davies (vc)]
Hanson, H.:Qt Strs *(rec St. Luke's Methodist Church, Houston, TX, Aug 23, 1989)* — Citadel ▲ CTD 88119 [DDD]
Jacobi, F.:Qt 3 Strs — CRI ("American Masters" series) ▲ CD 703 [ADD]

Lyric String Quartet [Patricia Calnan (vn), Harriet Davies (vn), Nick Barr (va), David Daniels (vc)]
Ginastera, A.:Qts Strs (comp), w. Olivia Blackburn (sop) — ASV ▲ ASV 944
Glazunov, A.:Novelettes, Op. 15 — Meridian ▲ MER 84262 [DDD]
Glazunov, A.:Qt 5 Strs — Meridian ▲ MER 84262 [DDD]
Rimsky–Korsakov, N.:Qt on Russian Themes — Meridian ▲ MER 84293 [DDD]
Rimsky–Korsakov, N.:Qt Strs, Op. 12 — Meridian ▲ MER 84293 [DDD]
Rimsky–Korsakov, N.:Qt Strs (B–la–F) — Meridian ▲ MER 84293 [DDD]
Rimsky–Korsakov, N.:Vars on a Chorale, w. — Meridian ▲ MER 84293 [DDD]

Lysell String Quartet
Berwald, F.:Qt 1 Strs — Musica Sveciae ▲ MSV 520 [DDD]
Berwald, F.:Septet Vn, "Grand Septet" — Musica Sveciae ▲ MSV 520 [DDD]
Norman, L.:Qt Strs, Op. 42 — Musica Sveciae ▲ MSV 518 [DDD]
Rosenberg, H.:Qt 2 Strs — Caprice ▲ CAP 21354 [DDD]
Rosenberg, H.:Qt 3 Strs — Caprice ▲ CAP 21379 [DDD]
Rosenberg, H.:Qt 5 Strs — Caprice ▲ CAP 21354 [DDD]
Rosenberg, H.:Qt 8 Strs — Caprice ▲ CAP 21354 [DDD]
Rosenberg, H.:Qt 9 Strs — Caprice ▲ CAP 21379 [DDD]

Ma Non Troppo Trio
Godard, B.:Trio 1 Pno — Koch Schwann ▲ SCH 315452 [DDD]
Godard, B.:Trio 2 Pno — Koch Schwann ▲ SCH 315452 [DDD]

Maarten Altena Ensemble
Altena, M.:Music of—Punt; 88; Rails; Voices; Quotl *(rec Theater Frascati, Amsterdam, Dec 5–7, 1988)* — Hat Hut ("NOW." series) ▲ hat ART CD 6029 [DDD]
Altena, M.:Music of—Slow Motion [1993 version]; Tik; Figuur; Lento; Abcde; Slow Motion [1994 version] — Donemus ▲ CV 49 [DDD]
Carl, G.:Roscoe Blvd *(rec Theater Frascati, Amsterdam, Dec. 5–7, 1988)* — Hat Hut ("NOW." series) ▲ hat ART CD 6029 [DDD]
Hoorn, M. ten:Music of—Brokken; Admiraliteit *(rec Theater Frascati, Amsterdam, Dec. 5–7, 1988)* — Hat Hut ("NOW." series) ▲ hat ART CD 6029 [DDD]
Van Bergeijk, G.:Scène Rurale *(rec Theater Frascati, Amsterdam, Dec. 5–7, 1988* — Hat Hut ("NOW." series) ▲ hat ART CD 6029 [DDD]

Maastricht Municipal Orch
H. Heimans (cnd)
Liszt, F.:Con 1 Pno, w. Walter Gieseking (pno) — Enterprise ("The Piano Library" series) ▲ ENT PL 202

Macalester Trio
Beach, A.M.C.:Trio Pno — Vox Box 2–▲ CDX 5029 [ADD]
Chaminade, C.:Trio 1 Pno — Vox Box 2–▲ CDX 5029 [ADD]
Hovhaness, A.:Tumburu & Varuna — CRI ■ C 326
Mendelssohn, Fanny:Trio Pno — Vox Box 2–▲ CDX 5029 [ADD]
Schumann, C.:Trio Pno — Vox Box 2–▲ CDX 5029 [ADD]

McCapra String Quartet
Arnold, M.:Qt 1 Strs — Chandos ▲ CHAN 9112 [DDD]
Arnold, M.:Qt 2 Strs — Chandos ▲ CHAN 9112 [DDD]

McCormick Duo [Kim McCormick (fl), Robert McCormick (perc)]
Premiers Plus One:Flute & Percussion — HoneyRock ▲ RM 01

McGill CO
B. Brott (cnd)
Brott, A.:Arabesque Vc, w. D. Brott (vc) — Analekta ▲ ANC 9801
Brott, A.:Con Vn, w. A. Dubeau (vn) — Analekta ▲ ANC 9801
Brott, A.:Paraphrase in Polyphony — Analekta ▲ ANC 9801
Brott, A.:Seven Minuets & 6 Canons — Analekta ▲ ANC 9801

Machine for Making Sense [Jim Denley (fl/sax/sgr), Chris Mann (sgr/text), Rik Rue (samples/tape manipulation), Amanda Stewart (sgr/text), Stevie Wishart (vn/elecs/h-g/sgr)]
Machine For Making Sense:On 2nd Thoughts, w. Kimmo Vennonen (samples) — O.O. Discs ▲ OO 19 [ADD]

Urs Mächler Ensemble
Giuliani, M.:Gtr Music, w. Eros Roselli (gtr)—Gran Qnt. for Gtr & Str Qt., Op. 65; 7 Pieces for Gtr & Vn, Op. 74; Intro. & Vars. for Gtr & Str Qt., Opp. 101–103 — Nuova Era ▲ NUO 7194 [DDD]
Pleyel, I.:Qt Fl — Stradivarius ▲ SIP 28
Pleyel, I.:Qnt Fl — Stradivarius ▲ SIP 28
Pleyel, I.:Sxt Strs — Stradivarius ▲ SIP 28

McPherson Trio [May–Ling Kwok (pno), Pablo Diemecke (vn), Lawrence Skaggs (vc)]
Arensky, A.:Trio 1 Pno — Mastersound ▲ MST 33 [DDD]
Shostakovich, D.:Trio 2 Pno — Mastersound ▲ MST 33 [DDD]

Madeira Festival Orch
A. Newman (cnd)
Bach, J.S.:Suites Orch, BWV 1066–1069, w. Anthony Newman (hpd) *(rec Elite Recordings, NYC, 1981)* — Allegretto ▲ ACD 8194
Telemann, G.P.:Suite in a Fl, w. Anthony Newman (hpd) *(rec Elite Recordings, NYC, 1981)* — Allegretto ▲ ACD 8194

Madrid Atrium Musicae
G. Paniagua (cnd)
La Folia de la Spagna — Harmonia Mundi ▲ 901050
Musique Arabo–Andalouse — Harmonia Mundi ▲ HMC 90389 ■
Musique de la Grèce antique — Harmonia Mundi ("Misique d'Abord" series) ▲ HMA 190.1015
La Spagna — BIS ▲ CD 163 ▲ MD 163

Madrid CO
Canzoni Spagnole, w. Alfredo Kraus (ten) *(rec 1960s)* — Bongiovanni ▲ GB 510–2 [ADD]
Zarzuela Anthology, Vol. 2, w. Spanish National Radio Chorus — Montilla ▲ MNT 3023
E. Estella (cnd)
Lehár, F.:Eva, w. J. Granados (sop—Prunelles), A. M. Olaria (sop—Eva), A. Kraus (ten—Octavio Flaubert), L. de Cordoba (sgr—Gipsy), S. Ramalle (sgr—Dagoberto), J. Peromingo (sgr—Voisin), Spanish National Radio Chorus [Sp] — Montilla ▲ CDFM 2036

Madrid Concert Orch
Classica de España, w. National Orch of Spain, Ernesto Bitetti (gtr), Alicia de Larrocha (pno) — EMI Classics 2–▲ ZDMB 64241

Madrid Concert Orch (cont.)
J. Arámbarri (cnd)
Falla, M. de:El amor brujo, w. I. Rivadeneyra (cta) *(rec 1959)* EMI Classics 2-▲ ZDMB 64555
Guridi, J.:Music of, w. P. Bayona (pno), Spanish National Orch—Amaya; 10 Melodías; Homenaje a Walt Disney *(rec 1959)* EMI Classics ▲ CDM 64558
P. de Freitas Branco (cnd)
Falla, M. de:El retablo de maese Pedro, w. T. Tourne (sop), P. Lavigren (ten), R. Cesari (bar) EMI Classics 2-▲ ZDMB 64555
Madrid Instrumental Ensemble
C. Halffter (cnd)
Guerra, J.F.:Con Vn, w. Polina Kotliarskaya (vn) RNE/Spanish National Radio ▲ 650003 [AAD]
Madrid Radio-TV Orch
G. Rivoli (cnd)
Puccini, G.:Madama Butterfly, w. Montserrat Caballé (sop—Cio-Cio-San), Carmen Rigai (mez—Suzuki), Bernabé Martí (ten—Pinkerton), Diego Monjo (ten—Goro), Juan Rico (ten—Yamadori), Manuel Ausensi (bar—Sharpless), Jose Lemar (bass—Bonze), Antonio Leval (bass—Imperial Commissioner), Alejandro Chiara (bass—Registrar), Madrid Radio-TV Chorus *(rec Madrid, June 12, 1968)* Legato Classics 2-▲ LCD 210-2 [ADD]
Madrid SO
E. F. Arbós (cnd)
Albéniz, I.:Iberia Suite *(rec 1920s)* VAI Audio ▲ VAIA 1046
Arbós, E.F.:Noche de Arabia *(rec 1920s)* VAI Audio ▲ VAIA 1046
Bretón, T.:La Dolores (sels)—Jota *(rec 1920s)* VAI Audio ▲ VAIA 1046 F
Falla, M. de:El sombrero de tres picos (dances)—Los vecinos; Danza del molinero; Danza final *(rec 1920s)* VAI Audio ▲ VAIA 1046
Granados, E.:Danzas españolas (10)—No. 6 *(rec 1920s)* VAI Audio ▲ VAIA 1046 F
Granados, E.:Goyescas (intermezzo) *(rec 1920s)* VAI Audio ▲ VAIA 1046 F
Spanish Orchestral Favorites *(rec 1920s)* VAI Audio ▲ VAIA 1046 [ADD]
Turina, J.:Danzas fantásticas—Nos. 2 & 3 *(rec 1920s)* VAI Audio ▲ VAIA 1046
Turina, J.:La procesión del Rocío *(rec 1920s)* VAI Audio VAIA 1046
E. G. Asensio (cnd)
Abril, A.G.:Con Orch, "Hemeroscopium" *(rec live, National Music Auditorium, Madrid, Dec 10, 1994)* Marco Polo ▲ 8.223849 [DDD]
Abril, A.G.:Con Pno, w. Guillermo González (pno) *(rec live, National Music Auditorium, Madrid, Dec 10, 1994)* Marco Polo ▲ 8.223849 [DDD]
Abril, A.G.:Sons (3) Orch *(rec live, National Music Auditorium, Madrid, Dec 10, 1994)* Marco Polo ▲ 8.223849 [DDD]
M. Moreno-Buendia (cnd)
Pure Domingo, w. Plácido Domingo (ten), English CO [cnd:Julius Rudel], Munich RSO [cnd:Eugene Kohn], National PO [cnd:Eugene Kohn], New Philharmonia Orch [cnds:Bruno Bartoletti, Riccardo Muti], Philharmonia Orch [cnd:James Levine] Angel ▲ CDC 55616 [DDD/ADD]
Romanzas de Zarzuelas, w. Plácido Domingo (ten), National Zarzuela Theater Chorus EMI Classics ▲ CDC 49148 [DDD] ■ 4DS 49148 (D)
J. Olmendo (cnd)
Las mejores arias, w. Alfredo Kraus (ten) Montilla ▲ MNT 3035
M. Roa (cnd)
Penella, M.:El gato montés, w. V. Villarroel (sop), T. Berganza (mez), P. Domingo (ten), J. Pons (bar) [Sp] Deutsche Grammophon 2-▲ 435776-2 [DDD]
A. Ros-Marbá (cnd)
Bretón, T.:La Verbena de la paloma, w. Maria Bayo (sop), Raquel Pierotti (sop), Plácido Domingo (ten), Enrique Baquerizo (sgr), Rafael Castejon (sgr), Milagros Martin (sgr), Silva Tro (sgr) Valois ("Zarauela" series) ▲ V 4725
Montsalvatge, X.:Concierto breve, w. Leonel Morales (pno) *(rec live, National Music Auditorium, Madrid, Nov. 23, 1993)* Marco Polo ▲ 8.223753 [DDD]
Montsalvatge, X.:Sinf de requiem, w. Catalina Moncloa (sop) *(rec live, National Music Auditorium, Madrid, Nov. 23, 1993)* Marco Polo ▲ 8.223753 [DDD]
Moreno Torroba, F.:Luisa Fernanda, w. Verónica Villaroel (sop), Ana Rodrigo (mez), Plácido Domingo (ten), Juan Pons (bar) Valois 2-▲ V 4759
Rodrigo, J.:Zarabanda lejana y villancico *(rec live, National Music Auditorium, Madrid, Nov. 23, 1993)* Marco Polo ▲ 8.223753 [DDD]
Madrigal Chamber Ensemble
S. Kralev (cnd)
Bach, J.S.:Christmas Oratorio, w. Ludmila Hadjieva (sop), Roumiana Tzatcheva (alt), Lubomir Diacovski (ten), Plamen Hidjov (bass), E. Tabakov (cnd), Sofia CO Soloists Pentagon 3-▲ 302 [DDD]
Monteverdi, C.:Madrigals, w. V. Kazandjiev (cnd), Sofia CO Soloists, Bodra-Smyana Children's Choir—Ogni Amante e Guerrier; Si, Si Ch'io V'Amo; O Come Vaghi; O Viva Fiamma; Io Son Pur Vezzosetta Pastorella; Ardo e Scoprir; Chiomo d'Oro; Baci Soavi e Cari; Bel Pastor [Dialogo di Ninfa e Pastore] Forlane ▲ FRL 16546 [DDD/AAD]
Schütz, H.:Motets (misc), w. V. Kazandjiev (cnd), Sofia Soloists CO, Bodra-Smyana Children's Choir—Herr, Wenn ich Nur Dich Habe; Herr, Nun Lässest du Deiner in Frieden fahren Forlane ▲ FRL 16546 [DDD/AAD]
Schütz, H.:Musicalische Exequien, w. V. Kazandjiev (cnd), Sofia Soloists CO, Bodra-Smyana Children's Choir Forlane ▲ FRL 16546 [DDD/AAD]
Maelström Percussion Ensemble
Stiller, A.:A Descent into the Maelstrom MMC ▲ 2014
Stiller, A.:Music of, w. James Freeman (pno), Orch 2001—The Mouse Singer; A Periodic Table of the Elements; A Descent into the Maelstrom; Son a 3 Pulsatoribus, with Gargoyle; The Water is Wide, Daisy Bell MMC ▲ MMC 2014
Stiller, A.:Sonata a 3 pulsatoribus. MMC ▲ 2014
J. Williams (cnd)
Cage, J.:Imaginary Landscapes 1-5—w. Thomas Furminger on No. 2; Craig Bitterman & Thomas Furminger on No. 3; Eberhard Blum, Patti Cudd, Erik Oña & Amy Williams on No. 4 *(rec Slee Concert Hall, Univ. at Buffalo, NY, May 28 - June 1, 1995)* Hat Art ("Hat Now" series) ▲ 6179 [DDD]
Magdeburg PO
M. Husmann (cnd)
Eisler, H.:Film Music—5 Orchesterstücke; Scherzo; Variationen über ein marshcartiges Theme; Kammersinfonie, Op. 69 CPO ▲ CPO 999071 [DDD]
Eisler, H.:Kleine Sinf CPO ▲ CPO 999071 [DDD]
Eisler, H.:Ov zu einem Lustspiel CPO ▲ CPO 999071 [DDD]
Maggini String Quartet [Laurence Jackson (vn), David Angel (vn), Martin Outram (va), Michal Kaznowski (vc)]
Bacewicz, G.:Qt 4 Strs ASV ▲ ASV 908 [DDD]
Bridge, F.:Idylls (3) Str Qt *(rec All Saints, East Finchley, Dec 16 & 17, 1994)* Naxos ▲ 8.553718 [DDD]
Bridge, F.:An Irish Melody *(rec All Saints, East Finchley, Dec 16 & 17, 1994)* Naxos ▲ 8.553718 [DDD]
Bridge, F.:Old English Songc (2) *(rec All Saints, East Finchley, Dec 16 & 17, 1994)* Naxos ▲ 8.553718 [DDD]
Bridge, F.:Phantasie Qt *(rec All Saints, East Finchley, Dec 16 & 17, 1994)* Naxos ▲ 8.553718 [DDD]
Bridge, F.:Pieces (3) Str Qt *(rec All Saints, East Finchley, Dec 16 & 17, 1994)* Naxos ▲ 8.553718 [DDD]
Bridge, F.:Sir Roger de Coverley *(rec All Saints, East Finchley, Dec 16 & 17, 1994)* Naxos ▲ 8.553718 [DDD]
Schubert, Franz:Minuets & Trios, D.89 ASV ("Quicksilva" series) ▲ ASQ 6150 [DDD]
Schubert, Franz:Minuets & Trios, D.89 ASV ("Quicksilva" series) ▲ ASQ 6149 [DDD]
Schubert, Franz:Qt Strs, D.103 ASV ("Quicksilva" series) ▲ ASQ 6150 [DDD]
Schubert, Franz:Qt 12 Strs ASV ("Quicksilva" series) ▲ ASQ 6149 [DDD]
Schubert, Franz:Qt 14 Strs ASV ("Quicksilva" series) ▲ ASQ 6149 [DDD]

Maggini String Quartet (cont.)
Schubert, Franz:Qt 14 Strs ASV ("Quicksilva" series) ▲ ASQ 6150 [DDD]
Szymanowski, K.:Qt 1 Strs ASV ▲ ASV 908 [DDD]
Szymanowski, K.:Qt 2 Strs ASV ▲ ASV 908 [DDD]
Maggio Musicale Fiorentino—see Florence Maggio Musicale Orch
Magic Circle CO
R. E. Harrell (cnd)
Rorem, N.:A Childhood Miracle, w. Michele Couture (sop—Peony), Darcy Dunn (sgr—Violet), Madeline Tsingopoulos (sgr—Mother), Mary Cidoni (sgr—Emma), Patrick Greene (sgr—Snowman), Peter Castaldi (sgr—Father) Newport Classic ▲ NPT 85594 [DDD]
Magic Circle Ensemble
Teasin':Turn of the Century Parlor Songs & Rags, w. Julianne Baird (sop), Rudolph Palmer (pno) *(rec Mallory Room, Rutger's University, Camden, NJ, June 1995)* Helicon ▲ HE 1001
Magnificat Players
P. Cave (cnd)
Ramsey, R.:Choral Music, w. Magnificat Choir—Almighty & Everlasting God; We Humbly Beseech; Go Perjur'd Man!; When David Heard; Te Deum; Nunc Dimittis; How Are the Mighty Fallen; others ASV ("Gaudeamus" series) ▲ ASV 138 [DDD]
Mainly Mozart Orch
Bach, J.S.:Chorales, w. Elmer Iseler Singers—Jesu, joy of man's desiring; Sheep may safely graze; Praise ye, almighty God; Be glory, praise & honor; To Thee our humble praise we sing; etc. CBC ("SM 5000" series) ▲ SMCD 5042C [DDD]
Mainz Bach Orch
D. Hellmann (cnd)
Saint-Saëns, C.:Oratorio de Noël, w. V. Schweizer (sop), E. Wiens (sop), H. Jung (mez), F. Melzer (ten), K. Widmer (bass), Mainz Bach Choir *(rec 1976)* Calig ▲ CAL 50512 [AAD]
Mainz CO
The Pachelbel Canon & Other Baroque Favorites, w. Württemberg CO, various soloists Allegretto ▲ ACD 8098 [ADD] ■ ACS 8098
G. K. Faerber (cnd)
The Virtuoso French Horn, w. Württemberg CO, various soloists Allegretto ▲ ACD 8144 [ADD] ■ ACS 8144
G. Kehr (cnd)
Bach, J.S.:Brandenburg Cons *(rec 1958)* Vox Box 3-▲ CD3X 3008 [ADD]
Bach, J.S.:Brandenburg Cons—Nos. 1, 3, 4 Allegretto ▲ ACD 8046 [ADD] ■ ACS 8046
Bach, J.S.:Brandenburg Cons—Nos. 2, 5, 6 Allegretto ▲ ACD 8047 [ADD] ■ ACS 8047
Bach, J.S.:Brandenburg Con 5—No. 5 Allegretto ▲ ACD 8098 [ADD] ■ ACS 8098
Bach, J.S.:Cons for 3 Hpds (comp), w. M. Galling (hpd), H. Bilgram (hpd), F. Lehrndorfer (hpd) Vox Box 2-▲ CDX 5040
Bach, J.S.:Con for 4 Hpds, w. M. Galling (hpd), H. Bilgram (hpd), F. Lehrndorfer (hpd), K.-H. Stolze (hpd) Vox Box 2-▲ CDX 5040
Bach, J.S.:Cons Vn (comp), w. S. Lautenbacher (vn) Allegretto ▲ ACD 8057 [ADD] ■ ACS 8057
Bach, J.S.:Cons Vn (comp), w. S. Lautenbacher (vn) *(rec 1958)* Vox Box 3-▲ CD3X 3008 [ADD]
Bach, J.S.:Con for 2 Vns, w. S. Lautenbacher (vn), D. Vorholz (vn) *(rec 1958)* Vox Box 3-▲ CD3X 3008 [ADD]
Bach, J.S.:Con for 2 Vns, w. S. Lautenbacher (vn), D. Vorholz (vn) Allegretto ▲ ACD 8057 [ADD] ■ ACS 8057
Bach, J.S.:Life & Music of, w. S. Lautenbacher (vn), D. Vorholz (vn)—narration with selected excerpts from Brandenburg Cons. Nos. 2, 3, 4 & 5, BWV 1047-50; Cants. Nos. 57 & 211; Chorale Prelude, BWV 645; Con. No. 2 for Violin, BWV 1042; Inventions, BWV 785; Italian Con., BWV 971; Toccata & Fugue, BWV 565; Mass in b, BWV 232; Wohltemperierte Klavier [Bk. 1], BWV 846; St. Matthew Passion, BWV 244; St. John Passion, BWV 245; Con. for 2 Violins, BWV 1043; Passacaglia & Fugue, BWV 582; Magnificat, BWV 243; plus complete versions of Con. for 2 Violins, BWV 1043 & Con. for Violin, BWV 1042 Vox Music Masters ("Music Masters" series) ▲ MMD 8500 [ADD] ■ MMC 8500
Bach, J.S.:Suites Orch, BWV 1066-1069 Vox Box 2-▲ CDX 5040
Bach, J.S.:Suite 1 Orch Allegretto ▲ ACD 8146 [ADD] ■ ACS 8146
Handel, G.F.:Concerti grossi, Op. 3 Allegretto ▲ ACD 8148 [ADD] ■ ACS 8148
Locatelli, P.:L'arte del violino, w. S. Lautenbacher (vn) Vox Box 2-▲ CDX 5018 [ADD]
Locatelli, P.:L'arte del violino, w. S. Lautenbacher (vn) Vox Box 2-▲ CDX 5037 [ADD]
Locatelli, P.:Music of, w. Susanne Lautenbacher (vn)—Con No. 2 in c [Adagio; Allegro non troppo] Special Music Co. ("Classics of the Heart" series) ▲ SCD 5198
Mozart, W.A.:Life & Music of—narration with excerpts from Serenade, K.525; Minuet, K.1; Syms. Nos. 35, 36, 40 & 41; Sonats. Nos. 11 & 15 for Piano, K.331 & 545; Ov. [from Bastien un Bastienne], K.50; Son. for Organ, K.67; Serenade No. 13, K.361; Con. for Flute & Harp, K.299; Cons. Nos. 20 & 21 for Piano, K.466 & 467; Qnt., K.581; Con. No. 5 for Violin, K.219; Mass 14, K.427; Ov. [from Nozze di Figaro], K.492; Ov. [from Don Giovanni], K.527; Magic Flute, K.620; Qt. No. 17 for Strings, K.458; Requiem, K.626, plus a complete version of Eine Kleine Nachtmusik, K.525 Vox Music Masters ("Music Masters" series) ▲ MMD 8501 [ADD] ■ MMC 8501
Mozart, W.A.:Sym, K.Anh.214 *(rec 1965-66)* Vox Box 2-▲ CDX 5070 [ADD]
Mozart, W.A.:Sym, K.Anh.221 *(rec 1965-66)* Vox Box 2-▲ CDX 5070 [ADD]
Mozart, W.A.:Syms (comp)—in D, K.161/163; Nos. 18-25 Vox Box 2-▲ CDX 5030 [ADD]
Mozart, W.A.:Syms (comp)—Syms. 26-34 *(rec 1968)* Vox Box 2-▲ CDX 5072
Mozart, W.A.:Syms (misc)—Nos. 26-34 Vox Box 2-▲ CDX 5072
Mozart, W.A.:Syms (misc)—in E♭, K.16, in G, K.221, in B♭, K.214, in F, K.75 & in F, K.76; Nos. 4-10 *(rec 1965-66)* Vox Box 2-▲ CDX 5070 [ADD]
Mozart, W.A.:Sym 29—Andante Special Music Co. ("Classics of the Heart" series) ▲ SCD 5198
Mozart, W.A.:Sym (42), K.75 *(rec 1965-66)* Vox Box 2-▲ CDX 5070 [ADD]
Mozart, W.A.:Sym (43), K.76 *(rec 1965-66)* Vox Box 2-▲ CDX 5070 [ADD]
Pachelbel, J.:Canon Allegretto ▲ ACD 8098 [ADD] ■ ACS 8098
Pergolesi, G.B.:Stabat mater, w. M. Marshall (sop), A. Hodgson (cta) *(rec 1978)* Vox Box 2-▲ CDX 5081 [ADD]
Rinaldo di Capua:La Zingara, w. Annalisa Monkewitz (sop—Nisa), Rodolfo Malacarne (ten—Tagliaborse), Laerte Malaguti (bass—Calcante), Josef Ulsamer (vl), Kurt-Heinz Stolze (hpd) Dynamic ▲ CD 141 [ADD]
Vivaldi, A.:Con Vn Obs, RV.563, w. H. Zickler (tpt), H. Thal (tpt) Allegretto ▲ ACD 8098 [ADD] ■ ACS 8098
Mair-Davis Duo [Marilynn Mair (mand), Mark Davis (gtr)]
The Sounding Joy:Music for the Winter Holidays North Star ▲ MS0011/CD [ADD] ■ MS0011/CS
A Spanish Serenade:Romantic Impressions for Guitar & Mandolin North Star ▲ NS 0016 [DDD]
Vienna Nocturne:The Mair-Davis Duo & Friends Play Waltzes & Sonatas of the Golden Age, w. Theodore Arm (vn), Mary Lou Rylands (vc), Susan Thomas (fl) North Star ▲ NS0034 [DDD]
Make Believe Brass
18 Wild, Wacky & Winsome Works for Brass Quintet Crystal ▲ CD 432 [DDD] ■ C 432 (D)
Málaga City Orch
J. Bodmer (cnd)
Sarasate, P. de:Airs espagnols, w. Gabriel Croitoru (vn) [orchd] Regis Tro ▲ RTAC 010/1 [DDD]
Sarasate, P. de:Barcarolle vénitienne, w. Gabriel Croitoru (vn) [orchd] Regis Tro ▲ RTAC 010/3 [DDD]
Sarasate, P. de:El canto del ruiseñor, w. Gabriel Croitoru (vn) [orchd Édouard Lalo] Regis Tro ▲ RTAC 010/2 [DDD]
Sarasate, P. de:Carmen Fant, w. Gabriel Croitoru (vn) Regis Tro ▲ RTAC 010/2 [DDD]
Sarasate, P. de:Chansons russe, w. Gabriel Croitoru (vn) [orchd] Regis Tro ▲ RTAC 010/3 [DDD]
Sarasate, P. de:La Chasse, w. Gabriel Croitoru (vn) [orchd] Regis Tro ▲ RTAC 010/3 [DDD]
Sarasate, P. de:Faust Fant, w. Gabriel Croitoru (vn) [orchd] Regis Tro ▲ RTAC 010/1 [DDD]
Sarasate, P. de:Freischütz Fant, w. Gabriel Croitoru (vn) [orchd] Regis Tro ▲ RTAC 010/1 [DDD]
Sarasate, P. de:Intro & Tarantella, w. Gabriel Croitoru (vn) [orchd] Regis Tro ▲ RTAC 010/3 [DDD]
Sarasate, P. de:Intro et caprice-jota, w. Gabriel Croitoru (vn) [orchd] Regis Tro ▲ RTAC 010/3 [DDD]
Sarasate, P. de:Jota de Pablo, w. Gabriel Croitoru (vn) [orchd] Regis Tro ▲ RTAC 010/3 [DDD]
Sarasate, P. de:Jota de Pamplona, w. Gabriel Croitoru (vn) [orchd] Regis Tro ▲ RTAC 010/3 [DDD]
Sarasate, P. de:Jota de San Fermín, w. Gabriel Croitoru (vn) [orchd] Regis Tro ▲ RTAC 010/2 [DDD]

244 ▲ = CD ♦ = Enhanced CD Δ = MD ■ = Cassette Tape □ = DCC

Málaga City Orch (cont.)
J. Bodmer (cnd) (cont.)
Sarasate, P. de:Miramar, w. Gabriel Croitoru (vn) [orchd] Regis Tro ▲ RTAC 010/3 [DDD]
Sarasate, P. de:Muiñeira, w. Gabriel Croitoru (vn) [orchd] Regis Tro ▲ RTAC 010/2 [DDD]
Sarasate, P. de:Navarra, w. Gabriel Croitoru (vn), Manuel Guillén Navarro (vn) [orchd] Regis Tro ▲ RTAC 010/2 [DDD]
Sarasate, P. de:Nocturne-sérénade, w. Gabriel Croitoru (vn) Regis Tro ▲ RTAC 010/3 [DDD]
Sarasate, P. de:Peteneras, w. Gabriel Croitoru (vn) [orchd] Regis Tro ▲ RTAC 010/2 [DDD]
Sarasate, P. de:Viva Sevilla!, w. Gabriel Croitoru (vn) [orchd] Regis Tro ▲ RTAC 010/2 [DDD]
Sarasate, P. de:Zapateado, w. Gabriel Croitoru (vn) [orchd] Regis Tro ▲ RTAC 010/1 [DDD]
Sarasate, P. de:Zigeunerweisen, w. Gabriel Croitoru (vn) [orchd] Regis Tro ▲ RTAC 010/1 [DDD]
Malinova Sisters [Margarita Malinova (pno), Olga Malinova (pno)]
Barber, S.:Souvenirs Koch International Classics ▲ KIC 7213 [DDD]
Khachaturian, A.:Spartacus (sels) [duo-piano suite arr.]—Dance of the Maidens, Pastoral Scene, Adagio of Spartacus and Phrygia, Dance of the Egyptian Slave, Aegina Variation and Bacchanale Koch International Classics ▲ KIC 7172-2 [DDD]
Persichetti, V.:Con Pno 4-Hands Koch International Classics ▲ KIC 7213 [DDD]
Persichetti, V.:Serenade 8 Pno Koch International Classics ▲ KIC 7213 [DDD]
Persichetti, V.:Sons Pno—Son for 2 Pnos, Op. 13 Koch International Classics ▲ KIC 7213 [DDD]
Prokofiev, S.:Romeo & Juliet (sels) [duo-piano suite arr.]—The Young Juliet, Montagues and the Capulets, Pter Lorenzo, Mercutio, Romeo bids Juliet farewell Koch International Classics ▲ KIC 7172-2 [DDD]
Tchaikovsky, P.:Nutcracker Suite [2-piano arr.] Koch International Classics ▲ KIC 7172-2 [DDD]
Malmö Brass Ensemble
Hindemith, P.:Morgenmusik *(rec Tygelsjö Church, Sweden, June 1974)* BIS ▲ CD 159 [AAD]
Music for Brass Ensemble from the 16th-18th Centuries, w. Stockholm Philharmonic Brass Ensemble *(rec June 1974 & Nov. 22-23, 1)* BIS ▲ CD 223 [ADD/DDD]
Malmö SO
M. Atzmon (cnd)
Pettersson, G.A.:Sym 5 BIS ▲ CD 480 [DDD]
J. DePreist (cnd)
Creston, P.:Fant Trbn, w. C. Lindberg (trbn) *(rec 1993)* BIS ▲ CD 628 [DDD]
Malmö SO BIS ▲ CD 570 [DDD]
Martinů, B.:Double Con Pno, Tim BIS ▲ CD 501 [DDD]
Martinů, B.:Les Fresques de Piero della Francesca BIS ▲ CD 501 [DDD]
Martinů, B.:Rhap-Con Va, w. N. Imai (va) BIS ▲ CD 501 [DDD]
Prokofiev, S.:Lt Kijé Suite BIS ▲ CD 531 [DDD]
Prokofiev, S.:Sym 4 [1947 version] BIS ▲ CD 531 [DDD]
Sallinen, A.:Shadows *(rec Malmö Concert Hall, Sweden, March 11-June 17, 1993)* BIS ▲ CD 607 [DDD]
Sallinen, A.:Sym 4 *(rec Malmö Concert Hall, Sweden, March 11-June 17, 1993)* BIS ▲ CD 607 [DDD]
Sallinen, A.:Sym 5 *(rec Malmö Concert Hall, Sweden, March 11-June 17, 1993)* BIS ▲ CD 607 [DDD]
Schnittke, A.:Faust Cant, w. Mikael Bellini (alt), Inger Blom (cta), Louis Devos (ten), Urik Cold (bass), Malmö Sym Chorus BIS ("BIS Twins" series) 2-▲ CD 437/507
Schuller, G.:Eine kleine Posaunenmusik, w. C. Lindberg (trbn) *(rec 1993)* BIS ▲ CD 628 [DDD]
Shostakovich, D.:Con 1 Vc, w. T. Thedéen (vc) *(rec June 15-16, 1993)* BIS ▲ CD 626 [DDD]
Shostakovich, D.:Con 2 Vc, w. T. Thedéen (vc) *(rec Oct. 8-9, 1992)* BIS ▲ CD 626 [DDD]
Walker, G.:Con Trbn, w. C. Lindberg (trbn) *(rec 1993)* BIS ▲ CD 628 [DDD]
Zwilich, E.T.:Con Trbn, w. C. Lindberg (trbn) *(rec 1993)* BIS ▲ CD 628 [DDD]
V. Handley (cnd)
Nilsson, T.:Con 1 Pno, w. Hans Pålsson (pno) Caprice ▲ CAP 21417 [DDD]
J. Hirokami (cnd)
Borodin, A.:In the Steppes of Central Asia BIS ▲ CD 726
Borodin, A.:Sym 1 BIS ▲ CD 726
Borodin, A.:Sym 2 BIS ▲ CD 726
Ifukube, A.:Ballata Sinfonica BIS ▲ CD 490 [DDD]
Japanese Orchestral Music BIS ▲ CD 490 [DDD]
Otaka, A.:Image BIS ▲ CD 490 [DDD]
Ravel, M.:Con Pno (left hand), w. Yukie Nagai (pno) *(rec Malmö Concert Hall, Sweden, Jan. 28, 1994)* BIS ▲ CD 666 [DDD]
Ravel, M.:Con in G Pno, w. Yukie Nagai (pno) *(rec Malmö Concert Hall, Sweden, Jan. 11, 1991)* BIS ▲ CD 666 [DDD]
Tanaka, K.:Prismes BIS ▲ CD 490 [DDD]
Toyama, Y.:Matsura BIS ▲ CD 490 [DDD]
Wada, K.:Folkloric Dance Suite BIS ▲ CD 490 [DDD]
P. Järvi (cnd)
Gade, N.W.:Con Vn, w. Anton Kontra (vn) *(rec Malmö Concert Hall, Sweden, Aug. 23-25, 1994)* BIS ▲ CD 672 [DDD]
Nystroem, G.:Con Va, w. Nobuko Imai (va) *(rec Malmö Concert Hall, Sweden, May 14, 1994)* BIS ▲ CD 682 [DDD]
Nystroem, G.:Is havet *(rec Malmö Concert Hall, Sweden, Aug. 8-9, 1994)* BIS ▲ CD 682 [DDD]
Nystroem, G.:Sinf concertante, w. Niels Ullner (vc) *(rec Malmö Concert Hall, Sweden, Aug. 16-18, 1994)* BIS ▲ CD 682 [DDD]
Stenhammar, W.:Florez och Blanzefor, w. P. Mattei (bar) [Sw] BIS ▲ CD 550 [DDD]
Stenhammar, W.:Sentimental Romances, w. U. Wallin (vn) BIS ▲ CD 550 [DDD]
Sumera, L.:Sym 1 *(rec Malmö, Sweden, May 13-14, 1994)* BIS ▲ CD 660 [DDD]
Sumera, L.:Sym 2 *(rec Malmö, Sweden, Jan. 14, 1994)* BIS ▲ CD 660 [DDD]
Sumera, L.:Sym 3 *(rec Malmö, Sweden, Oct. 1-2, 1993)* BIS ▲ CD 660 [DDD]
O. Kamu (cnd)
Sallinen, A.:Sunrise Serenade BIS ▲ CD 511 [DDD]
Sallinen, A.:Sym 2, w. G. Mortensen (perc) BIS ▲ CD 511 [DDD]
Sallinen, A.:Sym 6 BIS ▲ CD 511 [DDD]
E. Klas (cnd)
Schnittke, A.:Con 1 Vn, w. M. Lubotsky (vn) BIS ▲ CD 487 [DDD]
Schnittke, A.:Con 2 Vn, w. M. Lubotsky (vn) BIS ▲ CD 487 [DDD]
Schnittke, A.:Con 3 Vn, w. O. Krysa (vn) BIS ▲ CD 517 [DDD]
L. Markiz (cnd)
Bloch, E.:Schelomo, w. T. Thedéen (vc) *(rec Aug. 23, 1990)* BIS ▲ CD 576 [DDD]
Bloch, E.:Sym in c# *(rec Aug. 6-7, 1992)* BIS ▲ CD 576 [DDD]
Elgar, E.:Con Vc, w. T. Thedéen (vc) BIS ▲ CD 486 [DDD]
Pettersson, G.A.:Con Va, w. N. Imai (va) BIS ▲ CD 480 [DDD]
Schnittke, A.:Con 2 Vc, w. T. Thedéen (vc) BIS ▲ CD 567 [DDD]
Schnittke, A.:Con grosso 2, w. O. Krysa (vn), T. Thedéen (vc) BIS ▲ CD 567 [DDD]
Schnittke, A.:Con Va, w. N. Imai (pno) BIS ▲ CD 447 [DDD]
Schnittke, A.:Gogol Suite BIS ▲ CD 557 [DDD]
Schumann, R.:Con Vc, w. T. Thedéen (vc) BIS ▲ CD 486 [DDD]
S. Oramo (cnd)
Bloch, E.:Con symphonique, w. *(soloist unknown)* *(rec Malmö Concert Hall, Sweden, May 30-31, 1994)* BIS ▲ CD 639 [DDD]
Bloch, E.:Con Vn, w. Oleh Krysa (vn) *(rec Malmö Concert Hall, Sweden, Apr. 23-24, 1993)* BIS ▲ CD 639 [DDD]
Bloch, E.:Poems of the Sea *(rec Malmö Concert Hall, Sweden, May 30-31, 1994)* BIS ▲ CD 639 [DDD]
O. Rudner (cnd)
Ruders, P.:The Christmas Gospel *(rec Malmö, Sweden, Oct 1994)* Bridge ▲ BCD 9057 [DDD]

Malmö SO (cont.)
S. Rybrant (cnd)
Hallén, A.:Harald der Wiking (act III, final scene), w. M. Meyerson (sgr—Berta), S. Lindström (sgr—Sigrun), A. Ljungholm (sgr—Harald), S. Sjöstedt (sgr—Sigleif), K. Jacobsson (sgr—Gudmund/Torgrim), Malmö Radio Chorus [G] *(rec 6/6/74)* Musica Sveciae ▲ MSCD 621 [AAD]
O. Schmidt (cnd)
Schmidt, O.:The Öresund Sym, w. Kari Hamnøy (sop), Anders Lundh (ten), Ars Nova *(rec Malmö Concert Hall, Sweden, Apr. 11-13, 1994)* BIS ▲ CD 672 [DDD]
L. Segerstam (cnd)
Schnittke, A.:Passacaglia BIS ("BIS Twins" series) 2-▲ CD 437/507
Schnittke, A.:Ritual BIS ("BIS Twins" series) 2-▲ CD 437/507
Schnittke, A.:Ritual BIS ▲ CD 437 [DDD]
Schnittke, A.:(K)ein Sommernachtstraum BIS ▲ CD 437 [DDD]
Schnittke, A.:(K)ein Sommernachtstraum BIS ("BIS Twins" series) 2-▲ CD 437/507
Segerstam, L.:Epitaph 6, w. Hannele Segerstam (vn), Pia Segerstam (vc) Ondine ▲ ODE CD 877
G. Stern (cnd)
Jacobsen, J.:Tuba Buffo, w. Michael Lind (tuba) Caprice ▲ CAP 21493
O. Vänskä (cnd)
Poulenc, F.:Con for 2 Pnos, w. R. Pöntinen (pno), L. Derwinger (pno) *(rec Nov. 6-7, 1992)* BIS ▲ CD 593 [DDD]
Malmö SO Chamber Ensemble
L. Markiz (cnd)
Schnittke, A.:Labyrinths BIS ▲ CD 557 [DDD]
Mammoth Gavioli Fair Organ
Bioscope Memories Saydisc ■ 318
Manchester Camerata Orch
Serenade for Susan:A Musical Tribute, w. Laurence Perkins (bn) *(rec Sept. 8, 11 & 12, 1989 &)* IMP Classics ▲ PCD 1031 [DDD]
Manchester Chamber Players [Ron Levy (pno), Laura Hamilton (vn), Ariel Rudiakov (va), Cornelia Bode (vc)]
Fauré, G.:Qt 1 Pno MCP Productions ▲ CD 841
Turina, J.:Qt Pno MCP Productions ▲ CD 841
Manchester Chamber Players [Ron Levy (pno), Laura Hamilton (vn), Cornelia Bode (vc)]
Lane, R.:Trio Pno MCP Productions ▲ CD 841
Mancini Orch
H. Mancini (cnd)
Mamma, w. Luciano Pavarotti (ten) London ▲ 411959-2 LH [DDD] ■ 411959-4 LH
Mancini, H.:Film Music, w. A. Williams (sgr), J. Mathis (sgr), L. Albright (sgr), B. Hackett (sgr), B. Greco (sgr), C. Byrd (sgr), P. Page (sgr). Costa Orch, Conniff Orch—sels from Breakfast at Tiffany's; Peter Gunn; Mr. Lucky & others Columbia/Legacy ▲ CK 66505
Volare, w. Luciano Pavarotti (ten) London ▲ 421052-2 LH [DDD] ■ 421052-4 LH (D) □ 421052-5
Wild Classics:A Celebration of Animals & Nature, w. James Galway (fl), Ofra Harnoy (vc), Martin Hoherman (vc), Emily Mitchell (hp), Michael Dussek (pno), Samuel Lipman (pno), Leo Litwin (pno), Gerhard Oppitz (pno), Isao Tomita (synths), Boston Pops Orch [cnd:Arthur Fiedler], Chicago SO [cnd:Fritz Reiner] RCA Red Seal ▲ 09026-68483-2 ■ 09026-68483-4
Mancini Pops Orch
H. Mancini (cnd)
Morricone, E.:Film Music RCA ▲ 60706-2 RC [DDD] ■ 60706-4 RC
Rota, N.:Film Music RCA ▲ 60706-2 RC [DDD] ■ 60706-4 RC
Mandel Quartet
Medieval, Renaissance & Baroque Music Hungaroton ▲ HCD 31138 [DDD]
Ungaresca:500 Years of Hungarian Music Hungaroton ▲ HCD 31429 [DDD]
Mandelring String Quartet
Goldschmidt, B.:Qt 1 Strs *(rec 1991)* Largo ▲ 5117 [DDD]
Goldschmidt, B.:Qt 2 Strs *(rec June 1990)* Largo ▲ 5115 [DDD]
Goldschmidt, B.:Qt 3 Strs *(rec June 1990)* Largo ▲ 5115 [DDD]
Onslow, G.:Qts Strs, Op. 9—(2) in g & f CPO ▲ CPO 999060 [DDD]
Onslow, G.:Qt Strs, Op. 47 CPO ▲ CPO 999060 [DDD]
Pettersson, G.A.:Con 1 Vn Str Qt, w. Ulf Hoelscher (vn) CPO ▲ CPO 999169 [DDD]
Schubert, Franz:Qt 12 Strs *(rec Tonstudio Van Geest, Heidelberg, Apr. 1988)* Lydian ▲ 18114 [DDD]
Schubert, Franz:Qt 14 Strs *(rec Tonstudio Van Geest, Heidelberg, Apr. 1988)* Lydian ▲ 18114 [DDD]
Mandelring String Quartet members
Goldschmidt, B.:Qt Cl, w. Ib Hausmann (cl) *(rec 1991)* Largo ▲ 5117 [DDD]
Pettersson, G.A.:Improvs CPO ▲ CPO 999169 [DDD]
Mandolin Orch
F. Witt (cnd)
Dreyfus, G.:Music of, w. A. Rawlins (narr), Melbourne Bassoon Quartet, J. Elton-Brown (cnd), Methodist Ladies' College Chorale—Germany Teddy (Symphony for Mandolin Orchestra); Auscapes for Women's Chorus; The Adventures of Sebastian the Fox for Narrator & Bassoon Quartet; Larino, Safe Haven (versions for 2 Oboes & English Horn & for Trumpet & Piano); Tender Mercies for Horn & Piano; There is Something of Don Quixote in All of Us for Solo Guitar Move ▲ MD 3129 [DDD]
Manfred String Quartet [Marie Bereau (vn), Luigi Vecchioni (vn), Alain Pelissier (va), Christian Wolff (vc)]
Haydn, J.:Qts Strs, Op. 76, "Erdödy Qts"—Nos. 1, 3 & 4 Pierre Verany ▲ PVY 794061 [DDD]
Prokofiev, S.:Qt 1 Strs Pierre Verany ▲ PV 791112 [DDD]
Prokofiev, S.:Qt 2 Strs Pierre Verany ▲ PV 791112 [DDD]
Schoenberg, A.:Qt 1 Strs *(rec 11/90)* Pierre Verany ▲ PV.791031 [DDD]
Schumann, R.:Qts Strs, Op. 41 Pierre Verany ▲ PVY 793051 [DDD]
Smetana, B.:Qt 1 Strs Pierre Verany ▲ PVY 795041
Smetana, B.:Qt 2 Strs Pierre Verany ▲ PVY 795041
Manhattan CO
R. A. Clark (cnd)
Amram, D.:American Dance Suite Newport Classic ▲ NPD 85546 [DDD]
Amram, D.:Con Bn, w. Kenneth Pasmanick (bn) *(rec SUNY, Oct 1993)* Newport Classics ▲ NPD 85601 [DDD]
Amram, D.:Con Vn, w. Charles Castleman (vn) *(rec SUNY, Oct 1993)* Newport Classics ▲ NPD 85601 [DDD]
Amram, D.:Honor Song for Sitting Bull, w. Nathaniel Rosen (vc) *(rec SUNY, Oct 1993)* Newport Classics ▲ NPD 85601 [DDD]
Amram, D.:Songs (3) for America, w. J. Courney (bass) Newport Classic ▲ NPD 85546 [DDD]
Amram, D.:Theme & Vars on "Red River Valley", w. J. Baker (fl) Newport Classic ▲ NPD 85546 [DDD]
Amram, D.:Travels, w. C. Gekker (tpt) Newport Classic ▲ NPD 85546 [DDD]
Argento, D.:Elizabethan Songs (6), w. Frederick Urrey (ten) Newport Classic ▲ NPD 85602 [DDD]
Argento, D.:A Waterbird Talk, w. Vern Sutton (nar) Newport Classic ▲ NPD 85602 [DDD]
Bach, C.P.E.:Sinfs, H.657-662, "Hamburg Syms"—No. 2 in B♭ *(rec St. Jean Baptiste Church, New York, Jan 1996)* Helicon Classics ▲ HE 1003
Cowell, H.:Air & Scherzo Koch International Classics ▲ KIC 7282 [DDD]
Cowell, H.:Con grosso Koch International Classics ▲ KIC 7282 [DDD]
Cowell, H.:Fiddler's Jig Koch International Classics ▲ KIC 7282 [DDD]
Cowell, H.:Hymn & Fuguing Tune 10 Koch International Classics ▲ KIC 7282 [DDD]
Cowell, H.:Music of—Adagio for Cello & Thunderstick; Air for solo Violin & Strings; American Melting Pot for Orchestra; Hymn & Fuguing Tune for String Orchestra; Old American Country Set for Orchestra; Persian Set for Piccolo, Clarinet, Tar, Drum, Piano, 3 Violins, Cello, Double Bass *(rec Feb. 11 & 12, 1993)* Koch International Classics ▲ KIC 7220 [DDD]
Frederick II:Cons (4) Fl, w. Emily Newbold (fl)—No. 4 in D *(rec St. Jean Baptiste Church, New York, Jan 1996)* Helicon Classics ▲ HE 1003

ORCH. & ENS.

Manhattan CO (cont.)

R. A. Clark (cnd) (cont.)

Frederick II:Sym 1 *(rec St. Jean Baptiste Church, New York, Jan 1996)* Helicon Classics ▲ HE 1003

Frederick II:Sym 2 *(rec St. Jean Baptiste Church, New York, Jan 1996)* Helicon Classics ▲ HE 1003

Grana, E.D.:Stones, Time & Elements:A Humanist Requiem, w. M. Brecker (sax), Magic Circle Opera Ensemble Newport Classic ▲ NPT 85573

Handel, G.F.:Ezio, w. Julianne Baird (sop—Fulvia), Jennifer Lane (mez—Onoria), D'Anna Fortunato (cta—Ezio), Raymond Pellerin (alt—Emperor), Frederick Urrey (ten—Massimo), Nathaniel Watson (bar—Varo), Johannes Somary (org) *(rec St. Jean Baptiste Church, New York, Mar. 1994)* Vox Classics 2-▲ VOX 27503 [DDD]

Handel, G.F.:Tolomeo, Rè di Egitto, w. Brenda Harris (sop—Seleuce), Andrea Matthews (sop—Elisa), Mary Ann Hart (mez—Alessandro), Jennifer Lane (mez—Tolomeo), Peter Castaldi (bar—King Araspe), Bradley Brookshire (hpd) *(rec St. Jean Baptiste Church, NY, Mar 1995)* Vox Classics 3-▲ VOX 7530

Herbert, V.:Music of, w. A. Matthews (sop) Newport Classic ▲ NPT 85572

Hovhaness, A.:Haroutiun, w. C. Gekker (tpt) Koch International Classics ▲ KIC 7221 [DDD]

Hovhaness, A.:The Holy City Koch International Classics ▲ KIC 7289 [DDD]

Hovhaness, A.:Khirmian Hairig, w. *(soloist unknown)* Koch International Classics ▲ KIC 7289 [DDD]

Hovhaness, A.:Kohar Koch International Classics ▲ KIC 7289 [DDD]

Hovhaness, A.:Mountains & Rivers Without End Koch International Classics ▲ KIC 7221 [DDD]

Hovhaness, A.:Prayer of St. Gregory, w. C. Gekker (tpt) Koch International Classics ▲ KIC 7221 [DDD]

Hovhaness, A.:Psalm & Fugue Koch International Classics ▲ KIC 7289 [DDD]

Hovhaness, A.:Return & Rebuild the Desolate Places, w. C. Gekker (tpt) Koch International Classics ▲ KIC 7221 [DDD]

Hovhaness, A.:Sym 6 Koch International Classics ▲ KIC 7221 [DDD]

Hovhaness, A.:Sym 17 Koch International Classics ▲ KIC 7289 [DDD]

Ibert, J.:Capriccio Newport Classic ▲ NPD 85531 [DDD]

Ibert, J.:Concertino da camera, w. Gary Louie (sax) Newport Classic ("Manhattan CO" series) ▲ NPD 85598 [DDD]

Ibert, J.:Con Vc, w. Nathaniel Rosen (vc) Newport Classic ("Manhattan CO" series) ▲ NPD 85598 [DDD]

Ibert, J.:Con Fl Newport Classic ▲ NPD 85531 [DDD]

Ibert, J.:Divert Orch Newport Classic ("Manhattan CO" series) ▲ NPD 85598 [DDD]

Ibert, J.:Suite élisabéthaine Newport Classic ▲ NPD 85531 [DDD]

Ibert, J.:Suite symphonique, "Paris" Newport Classic ▲ NPD 85531 [DDD]

Ibert, J.:Symphonie concertante, w. Humbert Lucarelli (ob) Newport Classic ("Manhattan CO" series) ▲ NPD 85598 [DDD]

Luening, O.:Music of—Elegy for Lonesome Ones (1937; rev. 1974); 3 Songs (1917; rev. 1926); World without People (1946); Potowatomi Legends (1980); Symphonic Fantasia No. 11 (1991); Sonority Forms II (1983) Newport Classic ▲ NPT 85543

Macdowell, E.:To a Wild Rose Koch International Classics ▲ KIC 7282 [DDD]

Persichetti, V.:The Hollow Men Koch International Classics ▲ KIC 7282 [DDD]

Soldier, D.:Ultraviolet Railroad, w. Mark Feldman (vn), Erik Frielander (vc), Neal Kirkwood (pno) Newport Classic ▲ NPD 85589 [DDD]

Soldier, D.:War Prayer, w. Dionne Freeney (alt), Jason White (ten), Wilbur Pauley (bass), Gospel Singers Newport Classic ▲ NPD 85589 [DDD]

Still, W.G.:Music of, w. Margaret Astrup (sop)—American Scene:The Southwest; From the Hearts of Women; Mother & Child; American Scene:The Far West; Citadel; Phantom Chapel; Golden Days; Serenade; American Scene:The East Newport Classics ▲ NPD 85596 [DDD]

Thompson, R.:The Testament of Freedom, w. New York Choral Society Koch International Classics ▲ KIC 7283-2 [DDD]

Verdi, G.:Arias, w. Christine Weidinger (sop)—Madre pietosa; Pace, pace, mio dio [both from La forza del destino]; Ernani, involami [from Ernani]; O patria mia [from Aida]; Act 1 Prelude; Una macchia [both from Macbeth; w. Darcy Dunn (sop), Peter Castaldi (bar)]; Act 1 Prelude; Addio del passato [both from La traviata]; Tacea la notte [from Il Trovatore; w. Mary Polis (mez)]; Morrò, ma prima in grazia [from Un ballo in maschera] Newport Classic ▲ NPD 85581 [DDD]

Wilder, A.:Music of—Carl Sandberg Suite; Air for Fl [w. E. Zukerman (fl)]; Slow Dance; Suite 2 Tenor Sax [w. G. Louie (sax)]; Air for Ob [w. H. Lucarelli (ob)]; Theme & Vars; Serenade for Winds; Air for Bn [w. K. Pasmnaick (bn)] Newport Classics ▲ NPD 85570 [DDD]

Jordania (cnd)

Hovhaness, A.:Music of, w. Alexa Still (fl), Marvin Rosen (pno), New Zealand CO, KBS SO—The Prayer of St. Gregory; Elibris; Mystic Flute; Aria, Hymn & Fugue; Mountain Idylls; Gtr Sym; Adagio; Son; Fred the Cat; Aria [from Harotiun] Koch International Classics ▲ KIC 7311 [DDD]

Manhattan Chamber Sinfonia

G. Cortese (cnd)

Nelson, M.B.:Hodeeyaada MMC ▲ MMC 2023

Manhattan Marimba Quartet

Reich, S.:6 Marimbas Elektra/Nonesuch ▲ 79138-2 ■ 79138-4

Manhattan Percussion Ensemble

G. Price (cnd)

Harrison, L.:Suite Perc CRI ■ ACS 6006

Harrison, L.:Suite Perc *(rec 1/28/65)* CRI ▲ CD 613 [ADD]

Manhattan School of Music Chamber Sinfonia

G. Cortese (cnd)

McKinley, W.T.:Con for the New World, w. Quintet of the Americas *(rec Manhattan School of Music, Jan 10 & 12, 1992)* MMC ▲ MMC 2018 [DDD]

Rechtman, I.:America, Quintet of the Americas *(rec Manhattan School of Music, Jan 10 & 12, 1992)* MMC ▲ MMC 2018 [DDD]

Manhattan School of Music Opera Orch

D. Gilbert (cnd)

Rorem, N.:Miss Julie, w. Theodora Fried (sgr—Miss Julie), Heather Sarris (sgr—Christine, the cook), Laurelyn Watson (sgr—Young Girl), David Blackburn (sgr—Mr. Niels), Mark Mulligan (sgr—Young Boy), Philip Torre (sgr—John, the valet), Judd Ernster (bass), Manhattan School of Music Opera Chorus Newport Classic 2-▲ NPT 85605 [DDD]

Manhattan String Quartet [Eric Lewis (vn), Roy Lewis (vn), John Dexter (va), Judith Glyde (vc)]

Beach, A.M.C.:Theme & Vars, w. D. Anthony Dwyer (fl) Koch International Classics ▲ KIC 7001-2 [DDD] ■ 3-7001-4 (D)

Bergsma, W.:Quintet Fl, w. D. Anthony Dwyer (fl) Koch International Classics ▲ KIC 7001-2 [DDD] ■ 3-7001-4 (D)

Collins, E.J.:Allegro Piacevole *(rec Nov. 1988)* CRI ▲ CD 644 [DDD]

Shostakovich, D.:Qts Strs (comp)—Quartets Nos. 1-3 ESS.A.Y ▲ CD 1007 [DDD]

Shostakovich, D.:Qts Strs (comp)—Quartets Nos. 4 & 5 ESS.A.Y ▲ CD 1008 [DDD]

Shostakovich, D.:Qts Strs (comp)—Nos. 6-8 ESS.A.Y ▲ CD 1009 [DDD]

Shostakovich, D.:Qts Strs (comp)—Quartets Nos. 9 & 10 ESS.A.Y ▲ CD 1010 [DDD]

Shostakovich, D.:Qts Strs (comp)—Quartets Nos. 11-13 ESS.A.Y ▲ CD 1012 [DDD]

Shostakovich, D.:Qts Strs (comp)—Quartets Nos. 14 & 15 ESS.A.Y ▲ CD 1013 [DDD]

Tovey, D.F.:Vars on a Theme by Gluck, w. D. Anthony Dwyer (fl) Koch International Classics ▲ KIC 7001-2 [DDD] ■ 3-7001-4 (D)

Weber, C.M. von:Intro, Theme & Vars Cl, w. J. Manasse (cl) XLNT ▲ CD 18004 [DDD]

Weber, C.M. von:Qnt Cl, w. J. Manasse (cl) XLNT ▲ CD 18004 [DDD]

Manitoba CO

S. Streatfeild (cnd)

Eckhardt-Gramatté, S.-C.:Con Bn, w. Vincent Ellin (bn) *(rec St. Matthews Anglican Church, Winnipeg, Manitoba, Sept. 4-9, 1994)* BIS ▲ CD 698 [DDD]

Macdonald, A.:Con Vn, w. David Stewart (vn) *(rec St. Matthews Anglican Church, Winnipeg, Manitoba, Sept. 4-9, 1994)* BIS ▲ CD 698 [DDD]

Matthews, M.:Between the Wings of the Earth *(rec St. Matthews Anglican Church, Winnipeg, Manitoba, Sept. 4-9, 1994)* BIS ▲ CD 698 [DDD]

Mannheim Ensemble

Mozart, W.A.:Diverts Bas Hns, K.Anh.229 Meridian ▲ MER 84267 [DDD]

Mannheim Kurpfälzisches CO

K.-P. Hahn (cnd)

Mozart, W.A.:Serenade Vn, K.203 Vivace 3-▲ E 338-2 [ADD/DDD]

Mannheim National Theater Orch

P. Schneider (cnd)

Rihm, W.:Die Hamletmaschine, w. Mannheim Chorus Opera [G] Wergo 2-▲ WER 6195-2

Mannheim String Quartet [Andreas Krecher (vn), Claudia Hohorst (vn), Niklas Schwarz (va), Armin Fromm (vc)]

Haydn, J.:Qts Fl—No. 5 Titanic ▲ Ti 172 [DDD]

Mozart, W.A.:Qts Fl—Qt.in C, K. 285b Titanic ▲ Ti 172 [DDD]

Mozart, W.A.:Qt Ob, K.370, w. Miyamoto (ob) Novalis ▲ 150006 [DDD]

Mozart, W.A.:Qnt Cl, K.581, w. R. Wehle (cl) Novalis ▲ 150006 [DDD]

Mozart, W.A.:Qnt Hn, K.407, w. Maria-Luise Neunecker (hn) Novalis ▲ 150006 [DDD]

Pleyel, I.:Qt Fl Titanic ▲ Ti 172 [DDD]

Reger, M.:Qt Pno, w. Claudius Tanski (pno) MD + G ▲ MDG CD 3360715

Reger, M.:Serenade, Op. 141a MD + G ▲ MDG CD 3360715

Viotti, G.B.:Qts Fl, Op. 22—No. 1 in B♭ Titanic ▲ Ti 172 [DDD]

Volkmann, R.:Qt 1 Strs CPO ▲ CPO 999115 [DDD]

Volkmann, R.:Qt 2 Strs CPO ▲ CPO 999167 [DDD]

Volkmann, R.:Qt 3 Strs CPO ▲ CPO 999237 [DDD]

Volkmann, R.:Qt 4 Strs CPO ▲ CPO 999115 [DDD]

Volkmann, R.:Qt 5 Strs CPO ▲ CPO 999167 [DDD]

Volkmann, R.:Qt 6 Strs CPO ▲ CPO 999237 [DDD]

Mans SO

J.-A. Gendille (cnd)

Fauré, G.:Allegro symphonique, w. J.-P. Ferey (pno) [arr. for Piano & Orch.] Skarbo ▲ SKR 3921 [DDD]

Franck, C.:Redémption Skarbo ▲ SKR 3931 [DDD]

Franck, C.:Symphonic Vars, w. J.-P. Ferey (pno) Skarbo ▲ SKR 3921 [DDD]

Franck, C.:Sym in d Skarbo ▲ SKR 3931 [DDD]

Harsányi, T.:L'Histoire du petit tailleur *(rec 1991)* Skarbo ▲ SKR 3911 [DDD]

Messager, A.:Sym in A Skarbo ▲ SKR 3921 [DDD]

Prokofiev, S.:Peter & the Wolf *(rec 1991)* Skarbo ▲ SKR 3911 [DDD]

Mantova Orch

V. Parisi (cnd)

Dussek, J.L.:Con Hp, w. Roberta Alessandrini (hp) *(rec Jan 1995)* Naxos ▲ 8.553622 [DDD]

Krumpholtz, J.-B.:Con 6 Hp, w. Roberta Alessandrini (hp) *(rec Jan 1995)* Naxos ▲ 8.553622 [DDD]

Mantova Orch members

Dussek, J.L.:Sons Hp, Op. 34, w. Roberta Alessandrini (hp) *(rec Jan 1995)* Naxos ▲ 8.553622 [DDD]

Wagenseil, G.C.:Con in G Hp, w. Roberta Alessandrini (hp) *(rec Jan 1995)* Naxos ▲ 8.553622 [DDD]

Mantova Teatro Sociale Orch

N. Rescigno (cnd)

Cherubini, L.:Médée, w. M. Olivero (sop), E. Baggiore (sgr), L. Ganbelli (bass), A. Lo Forese (sgr), Mantova Teatro Sociale Chorus [I] *(rec live, Mantova 1/23/71)* Myto 2-▲ 2 MCD 91136 [ADD]

Mantovani Orch

S. Black (cnd)

In a Classical Mood Bainbridge ▲ BBR 6296

A.P. Mantovani (cnd)

Gershwin, G.:Con Pno, w. J. Katchen (pno) London ▲ 436570-2 (m) [ADD]

Operetta Memories London ("Weekend Classics" series) ▲ 436568-2 LC

Strauss (II), Joh.:Waltzes—Blue Danube; Tales from the Vienna Woods; Voices of Spring; Roses from the South; Emperor Waltz; A Thousand and One Nights; Treasure Waltz; Wine, Women & Song; Village Swallows; Acceleration Waltz; Morning Papers; Du und Du London ("Weekend Classics" series) ▲ 433682-2 [ADD]

Manzanillo Original Orch

W. Naranjo (cnd)

Fabré, C.:Music of—Coge el camaron; El cinturon del taxi; Traigo la ultima; Via libre que vienne la original; Que le pasa a chacumbele; El barrendero; Acabo de llegar [all orchd W. Naranjo] *(rec Havana, Cuba)* Iris ▲ 021

Torres, A.:El Diapson *(rec Havana, Cuba)* Iris ▲ 021

Marais SO

H. Reyne (cnd)

Francoeur, F.:Syms du Festin Royal de Mgr le Comte d'Artois FNAC Music ▲ 592287 [DDD]

Lalande, M.-R. de:Syms pour les soupers du roi (comp) Harmonia Mundi France 4-▲ HMC 901337/40

Lalande, M.-R. de:Syms pour les soupers du roi (sels)—highlights Harmonia Mundi France ▲ HMC 901303

O. Schneebeli (cnd)

Charpentier, M.-A.:Psaumes de David, w. Vocal Contrepoint Ensemble Adda ▲ ADD 241972 [ADD]

Benedetto Marcello CO

L. Ferrara (cnd)

Martini, G.B.:Cons (2) Fl Strs, w. M. Mercelli (fl) Bongiovanni ▲ GB 5517 [DDD]

Marchigiana PO

A. Cavallaro (cnd)

Cimarosa, D.:Il Matrimonio segreto, w. D. Mazzuccato (sop), E. Dara (bar), B. de Simone (bar) Nuova Era ▲ NUO 7014 [DDD]

G. Kuhn (cnd)

Mozart, W.A.:Così fan tutte, w. A. C. Antonacci (sop—Fiordiligi), M. Bacelli (sop—Dorabella), L. Cherici (sop—Despina), R. Decker (ten—Ferrando), A. Dohmen (bar—Gugliemo), S. Bruscantini (bar—Don Alfonso), Marchigiana Phil Chorus [I] *(rec live, Teatro Lauro Rossi at the Festival di Macerata, Aug. 3, 1990)* Orfeo 3-▲ 243913 [DDD]

Marchigiana PO String Group

F. Maestri (cnd)

Pergolesi, G.B.:Music of—Sinf in F for Vc & Cont; Org Sons in F & G; 2 Vn Sons in G; Trio in b♭ for 2 Vns & Cont; Vn Con in B♭; Hpd Son in A; Sons in F & G Bongiovanni ▲ GB 2114 [DDD]

Mare Balticum Ensemble

Music from the Time of the Royal Swedish Flagship Kronan Kontrapunkt ▲ 32066 [DDD]

Maréll Duo [Johannes Reichert (ct), Ingo Veit (vih/lt/gtr)]

Tierra y Cielos:Spanish Music in the Old & New Worlds Bayer ▲ 100115 [DDD]

Margherita Theater Orch

M. Gusella (cnd)

Gounod, C.:Faust, w. Renata Scotto (sop—Margherita), Anna di Stasio (mez—Marta), Flaviano Labò (ten—Faust), Edoardo Gimenez (ten—Siebel), Piero Cappuccilli (bar—Valentino), Bruno Grella (bar—Wagner), Ruggero Raimondi (bass—Mefistofele), Margherita Theater Chorus *(rec Genova, 1970)* Golden Age of Opera 2-▲ GAO 170/71 [ADD]

Mariani String Quartet

Starer, R.:To Think of Time, w. Ann Keri Donaldson (sop) Albany ▲ TROY 151 [DDD]

Marimolin [Sharan Leventhal (vn), Nancy Zeltsman (mar)]

Aldridge, R. Livingston:threedance GM ▲ 2023CD [DDD] ■ 2023T

Frank, A.:Elective Affinities III *(rec Dec. 10, 1989)* GM ▲ GM 2041 CD

Mays, L.:Somewhere in Maine GM ▲ 2023CD [DDD] ■ 2023T

Rogers, A.:Shadow-Play GM ▲ 2023CD [DDD] ■ 2023T

Thimmig, L.:Bluefire Crown III GM ▲ 2023CD [DDD] ■ 2023T

Wheeler, S.:Lyric Vars GM ▲ 2023CD [DDD] ■ 2023T

York, W.:Songs from Levertov Scores, w. S. Botti (sop) *(rec May 1987)* New World ▲ 80439-2

Markevitch Ensemble

Markevitch, I.:Galop *(rec Oct. 21-22, 1993)* Largo ▲ 5127 [DDD]

▲ = CD ♦ = Enhanced CD △ = MD ■ = Cassette Tape ◻ = DCC

Marlboro Alumni
Mozart, W.A.:Serenade Ww, K.361 *(rec February 25, 1980)* Klavier ■ KC 7031
Marlboro Festival Ensemble
Boccherini, L.:Qnts Gtr & Strs—G.449 & G.451 Sony Classical ▲ SMK 47298 [ADD] ■ SMT 47298
Boccherini, L.:Qnts Strs—in A, G.308 Sony Classical ▲ SMK 47298 [ADD] ■ SMT 47298
Mendelssohn, F.:Octet Strs *(rec 1965)* Sony Classical ▲ SMK 46251 [ADD]
Mozart, W.A.:Qnt Cl, K.581, w. H. Wright (cl) *(rec 1968)* Sony Classical ▲ SMK 46252 [ADD]
Mozart, W.A.:Qnt Cl, K.581, w. H. Wright (cl) Odyssey 3-▲ MB3K 45827
Mozart, W.A.:Serenade Ww, K.361 Sony Classical ▲ SMK 46248 [ADD]
L. Moyse (cnd)
Dvorák, A.:Serenade Ww *(rec Marlboro, VT, Aug 29, 1957)*
Sony Classical ("Essential Classics" series) ▲ SBK 62412 [ADD] ■ SBT 62412
D. del Tredici (cnd)
del Tredici, D.:Night Conjure-Verse, w. M. Burgess (sop), A. Valente (ten) [E] CRI ■ ACS 6004
Marlboro Festival Ensemble members
Beethoven, L. van:Octet, Op. 103, w. Marcel Moyse (fl) *(rec Marlboro, VT, Aug 30, 1957)*
Sony Classical ("Essential Classics" series) ▲ SBK 62412 [ADD] ■ SBT 62412
Marlboro Festival Orch
P. Casals (cnd)
Bach, J.S.:Brandenburg Con 2 CBS ▲ MLK 39442 [ADD] ■ MT 39442
Beethoven, L. van:Egmont (ov) Sony Classical ▲ SMK 46247 [ADD]
Beethoven, L. van:Sym 1 Sony Classical ▲ SMK 45891 [ADD]
Beethoven, L. van:Sym 2 Sony Classical ▲ SMK 46247 [ADD]
Beethoven, L. van:Sym 4 Sony Classical ▲ SMK 46246 [ADD]
Beethoven, L. van:Sym 6, "Pastorale" Sony Classical ▲ SMK 45891 [ADD]
Beethoven, L. van:Sym 7 *(rec 1969)* Sony Classical ▲ SMK 45893 [ADD]
Beethoven, L. van:Sym 7 CBS ▲ MYK 37233 [ADD] ■ MYT 37233
Beethoven, L. van:Sym 8 *(rec 1963)* Sony Classical ▲ SMK 45893 [ADD]
Brahms, J.:Vars on a Theme by Haydn Sony Classical ▲ SMK 46247 [ADD]
Mendelssohn, F.:Sym 4 *(rec 1963)* Sony Classical ▲ SMK 46251 [ADD]
Mozart, W.A.:Kleine Nachtmusik Sony Classical ▲ SMK 47295 [ADD]
Mozart, W.A.:Serenade Ww, K.375 Sony Classical ▲ SMK 47295 [ADD]
Mozart, W.A.:Serenade Ww, K.388 Sony Classical ▲ SMK 47295 [ADD]
Schubert, Franz:Sym 5 Sony Classical ▲ SMK 46246 [ADD]
A. Schneider (cnd)
Mozart, W.A.:Con 10 Pnos, w. R. Serkin (pno), P. Serkin (pno) Sony Classical 3-▲ SM3K 47207
Mozart, W.A.:Con 10 Pnos, w. R. Serkin (pno), P. Serkin (pno) *(rec 1962)*
Sony Classical ▲ SMK 46255 [ADD]
Mozart, W.A.:Con 12 Pno, w. R. Serkin, SchneiderR. Serkin (pno) *(rec 1962)*
Sony Classical ▲ SMK 46255 [ADD]
Marlboro Festival Players
D. del Tredici (cnd)
del Tredici, D.:Night Conjure-Verse, w. Benita Valente (sop), Mary Burgess (mez)
CRI ("American Masters" series) ▲ CD 689 [DDD]
Marosensemble
M. Maros (cnd)
Maros, M.:Music of, w. Ilona Maros (sop), John-Edward Kelly (sax), J. Kangas (cnd), Ostrobothnian CO, Budapest SO, Prague Radio SO—Sym No. 1; 4 Songs [from Gitanjali]; Sinf concertante [Sym No. 3]; Con for A Sax & Orch Phono Suecia ▲ PHN 23 [DDD]
Marseille Opera Orch
M. Veltri (cnd)
Verdi, G.:Simon Boccanegra, w. Alberto Cupido (ten), Ned Barth (bar), José Van Dam (b-bar), Manfred Schenk (bass), Daniela Longhi (sgr), Dino Musio (sgr), Marseille Opera Chorus
Lyrinx 3-▲ LYX 127 [DDD]
Marsiglia Opera Orch
J. Bazire (cnd)
Magda Olivero & Flaviano Labò in Concert, w. Magda Olivero (sop), Raina Kabaivanska (sop), Flaviano Labò (ten), Gianpiero Matromei (bar), Carlo Meliciani (bar), Oliveiro de Fabritiis (cnd), La Scala Orch, Turin RAI Orch *(rec between 1969 & 1973)* Bongiovanni ▲ GB 1105 [ADD]
Marteau Quintet
Mozart, W.A.:Qnt Strs, K.174 *(rec Feb. 1989)* FSM-Adagio ▲ FCD 91101 [DDD]
Martfeld String Quartet
Donizetti, G.:Qt 13 Strs Koch Schwann ▲ SCH 313882 [DDD]
Verdi, G.:Qt Strs Koch Schwann ▲ SCH 313882 [DDD]
Martinů Piano Quartet
Lukas, Z.:Qt 2 Pno Panton ▲ PAN 811189
Martinů String Quartet
Barton, H.:Qnt Con, w. Kamil Dolezal (cl) *(rec Martínok Studio, Prague, Jan 13, 16, 17, 24 & Feb)*
Panton ▲ 811397-2 [DDD]
Feld, J.:Qt 4 Strs *(rec 1970)* Praga ▲ PR 255001
Krommer, F.:Qt Strs, Op. 5/1 Panton ▲ 81 1011-2131
Myslivecek, J.:Qt Strs Panton ▲ PAN 811011
Richter, F.X.:Qt Strs Panton ▲ 811011
Ryba, J.J.:Qt Strs Panton ▲ 811011
Bohuslav Martinů CO
F. Jilek (cnd)
Brixi, F.X.:Cons Org (comp), w. A. Veselá (org)—Concerto in G
Supraphon Collection ▲ 11 0633-2 [ADD]
Linek, J.:Con Org, w. A. Veselá (org) *(rec 1972)* Supraphon Collection ▲ 11 0633-2 [ADD]
Bohuslav Martinů Philharmonic Brass
M. A. Machek (cnd)
Van De Vate, N.:Sound Pieces, w. Percussion Ensemble Vienna Modern Masters ▲ VMM 2003 [DDD]
Bohuslav Martinů PO
M. A. Machek (cnd)
Constantinides, D.:Sym 2 Vienna Modern Masters ▲ VMM 3007 [DDD]
Husa, K.:Music for Prague 1968 Vienna Modern Masters ▲ VWW 3023 [DDD]
Loeb, D.:Fantasias on East Asian Modes Vienna Modern Masters ▲ VMM 3034 [DDD]
Martinů, B.:Memorial to Lidice Vienna Modern Masters ▲ VMM 3007 [DDD]
Music from 6 Continents, 1993 series, w. Koszalin State PO, Slovak RSO [cnd:S. Kawalla], Pro Musica Nipponia [cnd:Norichika Iimori] Vienna Modern Masters ▲ VMM 3017 [DDD]
Shaffer, S.:Catherine Wheels Vienna Modern Masters ▲ VMM 3007 [DDD]
Snyder, R.:Fant Surrounding a Theme of Bartók Vienna Modern Masters ▲ VMM 3007 [DDD]
Waggoner, A.:The Train Vienna Modern Masters ▲ VMM 3007 [DDD]
W. Stiefel (cnd)
Abert, J.J.:Columbus, w. Thomas Lom (db) Bayer ▲ BR 100160 [DDD]
Abert, J.J.:Con Db, w. Thomas Lom (db) Bayer ▲ BR 100160 [DDD]
P. Tiboris (cnd)
Beethoven, L. van:Coriolan Ov *(rec Station Hall, Brno, Czech Republic, Nov. 28, 1994)*
Elysium ▲ GRK 702 [DDD]
Beethoven, L. van:Leonore 2 [w. Mahler's *Reutschen* revisions] *(rec Station Hall, Brno, Czech Republic, Nov. 28, 1994)* Elysium ▲ GRK 702 [DDD]
Beethoven, L. van:Leonore 3 *(rec Station Hall, Brno, Czech Republic, Nov 26–28, 1994)*
Elysium ▲ GRK 710 [DDD]
Beethoven, L. van:Sym 3, "Eroica" *(rec Station Hall, Brno, Czech Republic, Nov. 28, 1994)*
Elysium ▲ GRK 702 [DDD]
Dvořák, A.:Scherzo Capriccioso *(rec Dukla Radio Studio, Brno, Czech Republic, Mar. 24–27, 1994)*
Elysium ▲ GRK 701 [DDD]

Bohuslav Martinů PO (cont.)
P. Tiboris (cnd) (cont.)
Dvořák, A.:Slavonic Rhaps, Op. 45—No. 2 in g *(rec Dukla Radio Studio, Brno, Czech Republic, Mar. 24–27, 1994)* Elysium ▲ GRK 701 [DDD]
Dvořák, A.:The Spectre's Bride, Op. 69, w. Jitka Sobehartova (sop), Jiri Kubik (ten), Jan Markvart (bar), Bratislava Philharmonic Chorus [Cz] *(rec Nov. 26–30, 1993)* Elysium ▲ GRK 700 [DDD]
Dvořák, A.:Symphonic Vars *(rec Dukla Radio Studio, Brno, Czech Republic, Mar 24–27, 1994)*
Elysium ▲ GRK 701 [DDD]
Dvořák, A.:The Water Goblin *(rec Dukla Radio Studio, Brno, Czech Republic, Mar. 24–27, 1994)*
Elysium ▲ GRK 701 [DDD]
Mascagni, P.:Silvano, w. Rachel Sparer (sop—Matilde), Lorraine DiSimone (mez—Rosa), Joseph Wolverton (ten—Silvano), Bojan Knezevic (bar—Renzo) *(rec SUNY Performing Arts Center Theatre, Purchase, NY, May 23–25, 1995)* Elysium ▲ GRK 707 [DDD]
Mozart, W.A.:Sym 40 *(rec Station Hall, Brno, Czech Republic, Nov 26–28, 1994)*
Elysium ▲ GRK 710 [DDD]
Mozart, W.A.:Sym 41 *(rec Station Hall, Brno, Czech Republic, Nov 26–28, 1994)*
Elysium ▲ GRK 710 [DDD]
J. P. Williams (cnd)
Baker, D.:Kosbro Albany ▲ TROY 104 [DDD]
Burleigh, H.T.:The Young Warrior, w. E. McCorvey (ten) Albany ▲ TROY 104 [DDD]
Hailstork, A.:Sym 1 Albany ▲ TROY 104 [DDD]
Nash, G.P.:In Memoriam:Sojourner Truth Albany ▲ TROY 104 [DDD]
Williams, Julius P.:Is It True?, w. E. McCorvey (ten) Albany ▲ TROY 104 [DDD]
Williams, Julius P.:Meditation from the Easter Celebration Albany ▲ TROY 104 [DDD]
J. Zoltek (cnd)
Armanini, M.:Con Vn, w. Toni Stanick (vn) Chroma ▲ CHR CD 10001 [DDD]
Armanini, M.:Nocturne Cl, w. Ales Pavlorek (cl) Chroma ▲ CHR CD 10001 [DDD]
Armanini, M.:Of Wind, w. Qiu Xia He (pipa) Chroma ▲ CHR CD 10001 [DDD]
Armanini, M.:Poems, w. Willy Grenzberg (bar) Chroma ▲ CHR CD 10001 [DDD]
Bohuslav Martinů Philharmonic String Quartet [Josef Vyzrálek (vn), Mrek Obdrzálek (vn), Miroslav Kašný (va), Alexander Erml (vc)]
Van De Vate, N.:Letter to a Friend's Lonliness, w. S. Girardi (mez)
Vienna Modern Masters ▲ VMM 2006 [DDD]
Bohuslav Martinů Philharmonic String Trio
Van De Vate, N.:Trio Strs Vienna Modern Masters ▲ VMM 2006 [DDD]
Steve Martland Band
S. Martland (cnd)
Martland, S.:Danceworks Catalyst ▲ 09026-62670-2 ■ 09026-62670-4
Martland, S.:Music of—Crossing the Border; Principia; American Invention; Re-mix; Shoulder to Shoulder *(rec Church Studios, London, Feb 12–13 & May 6, 1991)*
Catalyst ▲ 09026-68345-2 [DDD]
Martland, S.:Principia Catalyst ▲ 09026-62670-2 ■ 09026-62670-4
Maryland Bach Aria Group members [Deborah Greitzer (bn), Pamela Greitzer (vc), Jeanne Fryberger-Vote (hpd)]
Marcello, B.:Son 2 Vls [played on vc & bn] Crystal ▲ CD 705 [DDD]
Vivaldi, A.:Cons Bn, w. Yuval Waldman (vn), José Cueto (vn), Jennifer Rende (va), Gail Kruvand (db)—in B♭, RV.501, "La notte" Crystal ▲ CD 705 [DDD]
Maryland Bach Aria Group members [Jeff B. Silberschlag (tpt), Pamela Greitzer (vc), Jeanne Fryberger-Vote (hpd)]
Stradella, A.:Sinf alla Serenata, w. Yuval Waldman (vn), José Cueto (vn), Jennifer Rende (va), Gail Kruvand (db) Crystal ▲ CD 705 [DDD]
Torelli, G.:Son Tpt, G.1, w. Yuval Waldman (vn), José Cueto (vn), Jennifer Rende (va), Gail Kruvand (db)
Crystal ▲ CD 705 [DDD]
Maryland Bach Aria Group members [Larry E. Vote (bar), Deborah Greitzer (bn), Pamela Greitzer (vc), Jeanne Fryberger-Vote (hpd)]
Marcello, B.:Salmo Decimoquinto Crystal ▲ CD 705 [DDD]
Maryland Bach Aria Group members [Larry E. Vote (bar), Jeff B. Silberschlag (tpt), Pamela Greitzer (vc), Jeanne Fryberger-Vote (hpd)]
Bach, J.S.:Cant 20, w. Yuval Waldman (vn), José Cueto (vn), Jennifer Rende (va), Gail Kruvand (db)—Wacht auf Crystal ▲ CD 705 [DDD]
Bach, J.S.:Cant 82, w. Yuval Waldman (vn), José Cueto (vn), Jennifer Rende (va), Gail Kruvand (db) *(rec St. Peter's Church, Hale, Cheshire, Mar 14, 1994)* Naxos ▲ 8.550763 [DDD]
Bach, J.S.:Cant 110, w. Yuval Waldman (vn), José Cueto (vn), Jennifer Rende (va), Gail Kruvand (db)—Wachtet auf Crystal ▲ CD 705 [DDD]
Maryland Bach Aria Group members [Larry E. Vote (bar), Jeff Silberschlag (tpt), Deborah Greitzer (bn), Jeanne Fryberger Vote (hpd)]
The Maryland Bach Aria Group, w. oboe & string Crystal ▲ CD 704
Masada
Zorn, J.:Music of—Gevurah; Nazikin; Mahshav; Rokhev; Abidan; Sheloshim; Hath-Arob; Paran; Mahlah; Socoh; Yechido; Bikkurim; Idalah-Abal; Tannaim; Nefesh; Abidan; Mo'ed; Maskil; Mishpatim; Sansanah; Shear-Jashub; Mashav; Sheloshim; Machin; Karaim Tzadik 2-▲ TZA CD 7108-2 [DDD]
Mason-Murcie-Draper-Woodhouse-Dinsey-Tomlinson-James Septet
M. Ravel (cnd)
Ravel, M.:Intro & Allegro *(rec London, 1923)* Music & Arts ▲ CD 703-1 [AAD]
Massachusetts Wind Ensemble
Rowell (cnd)
Bestor, C.:Music of, w. Slovak RSO Bratislava—Ov. to a Romantic Comedy; Vars. for Orch; In Memoriam Bill Evans; Chaconne for Chamber Winds; 3 Portraits for Wind Octet *(rec Moyzes Hall, Bratislava, Slovakia)* Centaur ▲ CRC 2216 [DDD]
Massed Bands
Live Brass, w. Black Dyke Mills Band, James Shepherd Versatile Brass, Solna Brass, Brighouse & Rastrick Band, Don Lusher Trombone Ensemble *(rec live at the National Brass Band Festiva, Gala Concerts 1977, 1978, 1979)* Chandos ("Collect" series) ▲ CHAN 6561 [ADD]
H. Mortimer (cnd)
The British Bandsman Centenary Concert (1987), w. Black Dyke Mills Band [cnd:Maj. Peter Parkes], Besses o' the Barn Band [cnd:Roy Newsome], IMI Yorkshire Imperial Band [cnd:James Scott]
Chandos Brass ▲ CHAN 4513 [DDD]
Massed Guards Bands
O. A. Hughes (cnd)
10,000 Voices, w. G. Jones (bar), D. O'Neill (ten), A. Sammons (vn), World Choir *(rec live May 23, 1992)* EMI Classics ▲ CDC 54628-2 [DDD]
Massy CO
D. Rouits (cnd)
Bach, J.S.:Con for 2 Vas, w. P. Hadjaje (va), J. Roudin (va) *(rec Mar 1990)*
Quantum ▲ QM 6906 [DDD] ■ QM 2000
Vivaldi, A.:Cons for 2 Vas, w. P. Hadjaje (va), J. Roudin (va) *(rec 3/90)*
Quantum ▲ QM 6906 [DDD] ■ QM 2000
Masterplayers
R. Schumacher (cnd)
Cimarosa, D.:Con Hpd, w. Elzbieta Stefanska Lukowicz (hpd) Fonit Cetra ("Italia" series) ▲ FCT CDC 98
Cimarosa, D.:Sinfs Hpd, w. Elzbieta Stefanska Lukowicz (hpd)—in B♭ [L'Italiana in londra]; in D [Caio Mario]; in D [I Due Supposti Conti] Fonit Cetra ("Italia" series) ▲ FCT CDC 98
Masurian PO
P. Kantschieder (cnd)
Strauss (I), Joh.:Radetzky March RS Applausi ▲ RS 6367-151
Strauss (II), Joh.:Die Fledermaus (ov) RS Applausi ▲ RS 6367-151
Strauss (II), Joh.:Music of—Perpetuum mobile, Op. 257 (1862) RS Applausi ▲ RS 6367-151
Strauss (II), Joh.:Pizzicato-Polka RS Applausi ▲ RS 6367-151
Strauss (II), Joh.:Polkas—Im Krapfenwaldl, Op. 336 (1870); Tritsch-Tratsch-Polka, Op. 214 (1858)
RS Applausi ▲ RS 6367-151

ORCH. & ENS.

Masurian PO (cont.)
P. Kantschieder (cnd) (cont.)
Strauss (II), Joh.:Waltzes—Accellerationen, Op. 234 (1860); An der schönen, blauen Donau, Op. 314 (1867); Frühlingsstimmen, Op. 410 (1883); Künsterleben, Op. 316 (1867) RS Applausi ▲ RS 6367-151
Strauss, Josef:Music of—Sphären-Klänge, Op. 235 (1868) RS Applausi ▲ RS 6367-151
Matisse Trio [E. Piemonti (pno), P. Ghidoni (vn), A. Drufuca (vc)]
Ives, C.:Trio Pno *(rec Mar. 25-27, 1994)* Ermitage ▲ ERM 413 [DDD]
Pablo, L. de:Trio Pno *(rec Mar. 25-27, 1994)* Ermitage ▲ ERM 413 [DDD]
Solbiati, A.:Trio Pno *(rec Mar. 25-27, 1994)* Ermitage ▲ ERM 413 [DDD]
Matthews/Boie Radio Drum & Radio Baton
Vol. 15:Virtuoso in the Computer Age, 5, CDCM Computer Music Series Centaur ▲ CRC 2190
La Maurache
Bawdy Songs from the Time of Francis I & Henry IV Arion ▲ ARN 68344 [AAD]
In Praise of Wine & the Vine:Songs & Dances from Rabelais to Henri IV Arion ▲ ARN 68248 [DDD]
Mayence Brass Quartet
Brandmüller, T.:Wie Du unsern Vätern geschworen hast, w. U. Mayer-Reinach (mez), G. August (org) [G] Gallo ▲ CD 604 [AAD]
Gilboa, J.:Chagall sur la Bible, w. U. Mayer-Reinach (mez), G. August (org) Gallo ▲ CD 604 [AAD]
Vogel, W.:Evocation Gallo ▲ CD 604 [AAD]
Meaux String Quartet [Nora Carter (vn), Rebecca McFaul (vn), Sharon Neufeld (va), Rebecca Thornblade (vc)]
Moore, D.R.:Modes *(rec Oberlin Conservatory, Feb. 1991)* Opus One ▲ CD 169
Mecklenburg State Orch
I. Törzs (cnd)
Wagner, R.:Die Walküre (act 1), w. Edda Moser (sop—Sieglinde), Mark Lundberg (ten—Siegmund), Frode Olsen (bass—Hunding) *(rec Mecklenburg State Theatre, Schwerin, June 29, 1994)* Calig ▲ CAL 50943 [DDD]
Mediaeval Ensemble
W. A. Albert (cnd)
Discover New Worlds with Werner Andreas Albert CPO ▲ CPO 999310 [DDD]
L. Bernstein (cnd)
Favorite French Orchestral Spectaculars, w. New York PO CBS ▲ MYK 37769 [AAD]
M. Best (cnd)
Cantigas of Santa María of Alfonso X Nimbus ▲ NI 5081 [DDD]
Dante Troubadours Nimbus ▲ NI 5002
The Last of the Troubadours:The Art & Times of Guiraut Riquier, 1230-1292 Nimbus ▲ NI 5261 [ADD]
Songs of Chivalry Nimbus ▲ NI 5006
Thys Yool:A Medieval Christmas Nimbus ▲ NI 5137 [DDD]
E. Kleiber (cnd)
Great Recordings, w. Berlin PO, Czech PO, Berlin State Opera Orch Preiser ▲ PRE 90229 [AAD]
Medici Ensemble
Isaac, H.:Sacred Music—Natalis Domini RCM ▲ RCM 19501 [DDD]
K. Coker (cnd)
Frescobaldi, G.:Music of—Balletto; Begli Occhi Io non Provo; Canzona XXXV Detta l'Alessandrina; Oscure Selve; Canzona XIV Detta la Marina; Canzona Ultima Detta la Vittoria; Capriccio Cromatico con Ligature Contrario; Se l'Aura Spira; Canzona VIII Detta l'Ambitiosa; Vanne, O Carte Amorosa; Capriccio XI; Toccata per Spinettina Sola, Over Liuto; Occhi Che Sete; Canzona Secunda; Passacaglia RCM ▲ RCM 19401 [DDD]
Lassus, O. de:Music of—La Cortesia Voi Donne; Occhi Piangete; Audi Dulcis Amica Mea; Per Pianto Mia Came; O Lucia; Expectatio Iustorum; Fant 25; Trop Endurer; Fant 13; Las voulez vous; Fant 27; Madonna Mia Pietà; Fant Quarta; Oculus Non Vidit; Vatene Lieta Homai RCM ▲ RCM 19502 [DDD]
Medici String Quartet [Paul Robertson (vn), David Matthews (vn), Ivo-Jan van der Werff (va), Anthony Lewis (vc)]
Beethoven, L. van:Grosse Fuge Str Qt Nimbus ▲ NI 5254 [DDD]
Beethoven, L. van:Qts Strs (comp) *(rec 1988-90)* Nimbus 8-▲ NI 1785 [DDD]
Beethoven, L. van:Qts Strs (comp)—Op. 18, Nos. 1-3 Nimbus ▲ NI 5173 [DDD]
Beethoven, L. van:Qts Strs (comp)—Op. 18, Nos. 4-6 Nimbus ▲ NI 5186 [DDD]
Beethoven, L. van:Qts Strs (comp)—Op. 59, No. 1 Nimbus ▲ NI 5207 [DDD]
Beethoven, L. van:Qts Strs (comp)—Op. 59, Nos. 2 & 3 Nimbus ▲ NI 5225 [DDD]
Beethoven, L. van:Qts Strs (comp)—Op. 74 & Op. 95 Nimbus ▲ 5242-2 [DDD]
Beethoven, L. van:Qts Strs (comp)—Op. 127 & Op. 131 Nimbus ▲ NI 5279 [DDD]
Beethoven, L. van:Qts Strs (comp)—Op. 130 Nimbus ▲ NI 5254 [DDD]
Beethoven, L. van:Qts Strs (comp)—Op. 132 & Op. 135 Nimbus ▲ NI 5285 [DDD]
Beethoven, L. van:Qnt Strs, Op. 29 Nimbus ▲ NI 5207 [DDD]
Brahms, J.:Qnt Cl, w. J. Brymer (cl) Medici Quartet ▲ MQT 8001 [DDD]
Brahms, J.:Qnt Pno, w. J. Lill (pno) Medici Quartet ▲ MQT 8001 [DDD]
Debussy, C.:Qt Strs Nimbus ▲ NI 5077 [DDD]
Debussy, C.:Qt Strs *(rec Nimbus Records, Wyastone, Leys, Monmouth, Mar. 19, 1987)* Nimbus ▲ NI 5389 [DDD]
Dvořák, A.:Qt 12 Strs, "America" Medici Quartet ▲ MQT 9001 [DDD]
Elgar, E.:Music of, w. Barbara Leigh-Hunt (nar), Richard Pasco (nar), John Bingham (pno)—includes excerpts from Start of the Play; Qnt. for Pno; Qt. for Strs [slow movt.]; In the South; The Wand of Youth [suite]; Chanson de Matin; Salut d'Amour; Starlight Express; Son. for Vn; Son. for Vc; Adieu; others *(rec Gateway Studios, London)* Medici Quartet ▲ MQT 7001 [DDD]
Elgar, E.:Qt Strs Medici Quartet ▲ MQT 8001 [DDD]
Elgar, E.:Qt Strs Meridian ▲ ECD 84082
Elgar, E.:Qnt Pno Strs, w. J. Bingham (pno) Medici Quartet ▲ MQT 8001 [DDD]
Elgar, E.:Qnt Pno Strs, w. J. Bingham (pno) Meridian ▲ ECD 84082
Fauré, G.:Qt Strs Nimbus ▲ NI 5114 [DDD]
Fauré, G.:Qt Strs *(rec Jan. 9, 1988)* Nimbus ▲ NI 5379 [DDD]
Franck, C.:Qnt Pno, w. J. Bingham (pno) Nimbus ▲ NI 5114 [DDD]
Haydn, J.:Qts Strs, Op. 20, "Sun Qts" Medici Quartet 2-▲ MQT 5001 [DDD]
Janácek, L.:Qt 1 Strs *(rec Jan. 8, 1988)* Nimbus ▲ NI 5379 [DDD]
Janácek, L.:Qt 1 Strs Nimbus ▲ NI 5113 [DDD]
Janácek, L.:Qt 2 Strs *(rec Nov. 4, 1987)* Nimbus ▲ NI 5379 [DDD]
Janácek, L.:Qt 2 Strs Nimbus ▲ NI 5113 [DDD]
Mendelssohn, F.:Octet Strs, w. Alberni String Quartet Nimbus ▲ NI 5140 [DDD]
Mendelssohn, F.:Qt 2 Strs Nimbus ▲ NI 5156 [DDD]
Mozart, W.A.:Music of—sels. from Qt. No. 19 in C, K.465, "Dissonance"; Qt. No. 1 in G, K.80; Qt. No. 14 in G, K.387; Eine kleine Nachtmusik; Qt. No. 16 in E♭; Qt. No. 15 in d, K.421 Medici Quartet ▲ MQT 6005 [DDD]
Mozart, W.A.:Qt 14 Strs Medici Quartet ▲ MQT 6004 [DDD]
Mozart, W.A.:Qt 15 Strs Medici Quartet ▲ MQT 6004 [DDD]
Mozart, W.A.:Qt 16 Strs Medici Quartet ▲ MQT 6002 [DDD]
Mozart, W.A.:Qt 17 Strs Medici Quartet ▲ MQT 6003 [DDD]
Mozart, W.A.:Qt 18 Strs Medici Quartet ▲ MQT 6003 [DDD]
Mozart, W.A.:Qt 19 Strs Medici Quartet ▲ MQT 6002 [DDD]
Mozart, W.A.:Qt 20 Strs Medici Quartet ▲ MQT 6001 [DDD]
Mozart, W.A.:Qnt Cl, K.581 Medici Quartet ▲ MQT 6001 [DDD]
Ravel, M.:Qt Strs Nimbus ▲ NI 5076 [DDD]
Schubert, Franz:Qt 8 Strs Medici Quartet ▲ MQT 9002 [DDD]
Schubert, Franz:Qt 14 Strs Medici Quartet ▲ MQT 9001 [DDD]
Schubert, Franz:Qnt Strs, D.956, w. Melissa Phelps (vc) Medici Quartet ▲ MQT 9002 [DDD]
Shostakovich, D.:Movts Str Qt Nimbus ▲ NI 5140 [DDD]
Shostakovich, D.:Pieces Str Octet, Alberni String Quartet Nimbus ▲ NI 5140 [DDD]
Shostakovich, D.:Qt 8 Strs Nimbus ▲ NI 5077 [DDD]
Shostakovich, D.:Qnt Pno, w. J. Bingham (pno) Nimbus ▲ NI 5156 [DDD]

Medici String Quartet (cont.)
Smetana, B.:Qt 1 Strs *(rec Nimbus Records, Wyastone, Leys, Monmouth, Nov. 5, 1987)* Nimbus ▲ NI 5389 [DDD]
Smetana, B.:Qt 1 Strs Nimbus ▲ NI 5131 [DDD]
Smetana, B.:Qt 2 Strs Nimbus ▲ NI 5131 [DDD]
Smetana, B.:Qt 2 Strs *(rec Nimbus Records, Wyastone, Leys, Monmouth, Nov. 3, 1987)* Nimbus ▲ NI 5389 [DDD]
Strauss, R.:Sxt Strs Nimbus ▲ NI 5076 [DDD]
Tippett, M.:Crown of the Year, w. Stephen Darlington (cnd), Christ Church Cathedral Choir Oxford [E] Nimbus ▲ NI 5266 [DDD]
Vaughan Williams, R.:Phantasy Qnt, w. S. Rowland-Jones (va) Nimbus ▲ NI 5191 [DDD]
Vaughan Williams, R.:Qts Strs Nimbus ▲ NI 5191 [DDD]
G. Vass (cnd)
Delius, F.:Music of, w. Oxford Camerata—Intermezzo [from Fennimore & Gerda]; A Song Before Sunrise; 2 Aquarelles; On Hearing the 1st Cuckoo in Spring; A Summer Night on the River *(rec St. Silas Church, Chalk Farm, London, July 1993)* Medici Quartet ▲ MQT 4002
Elgar, E.:Intro & Allegro, w. Oxford Camerata *(rec St. Silas Church, Chalk Farm, London, July 1993)* Medici Quartet ▲ MQT 4002
Elgar, E.:Serenade Strs, w. Oxford Camerata *(rec St. Silas Church, Chalk Farm, London, July 1993)* Medici Quartet ▲ MQT 4002
Holst, G.:Brook Green Suite, w. Oxford Camerata *(rec St. Silas Church, Chalk Farm, London, July 1993)* Medici Quartet ▲ MQT 4002
Vaughan Williams, R.:Fant on Greensleeves, w. Oxford Camerata *(rec St. Silas Church, Chalk Farm, London, July 1993)* Medici Quartet ▲ MQT 4002
Warlock, P.:Serenade, w. Oxford Camerata *(rec St. Silas Church, Chalk Farm, London, July 1993)* Medici Quartet ▲ MQT 4002
Medieval Wind Ensemble
Medieval Christmas, w. Pro Cantione Antiqua IMP Classics ▲ PCD 844 [DDD]
Meininger Trio [Christiane Meininger (fl), Ulrike Zavelberg (vn), Christopher Arpin (pno)]
Farrenc, J.-L.:Trio Vn Bayer ▲ BR 100 266 [DDD]
Manziarly, M. de:Trio Fl, Vc & Pno Bayer ▲ BR 100 266 [DDD]
Waring, K.:Alapana Bayer ▲ BR 100 266 [DDD]
Gerhard Meinl Tuba Sextet
Tuba!:A 6 Tuba Musical Romp Angel ▲ CDC 54729 ■ 4DS 54729
Meister Consort [R. M. Meister (sop), E. Casularo (fl), J. Fresno (gtr), P. Sublet (pno)]
Giuliani, M.:Songs—5 songs, Op. 27, 39, 79, 89, 95 *(rec 1989)* Jecklin-Disco ▲ JD 624-2 [ADD]
Melbourne Academy
B. Kelly (cnd)
Förster, C.:Con Hn, w. Hector McDonald (hn) Tall Poppies ▲ TP 42 [DDD]
Haydn, J.:Con 1 Hn, w. Hector McDonald (hn) Tall Poppies ▲ TP 42 [DDD]
Telemann, G.P.:Con Hn, w. Hector McDonald (hn) Tall Poppies ▲ TP 42 [DDD]
Teyber, A.:Con Hn, w. Hector McDonald (hn) Tall Poppies ▲ TP 42 [DDD]
Melbourne Bassoon Quartet
F. Witt (cnd)
Dreyfus, G.:Music of, w. A. Rawlins (narr), Mandolin Orch, J. Elton-Brown (cnd), Methodist Ladies' College Chorale—Germany Teddy (Symphony for Mandolin Orchestra); Auscapes for Women's Chorus; The Adventures of Sebastian the Fox for Narrator & Bassoon Quartet; Larino, Safe Haven (versions for 2 Oboes & English Horn & for Trumpet & Piano); Tender Mercies for Horn & Piano; There is Something of Don Quixote in All of Us for Solo Guitar Move ▲ MD 3129 [DDD]
Melbourne Brass Ensemble
Vol. 2:Hymns for All Seasons, w. Cantus Choro *(rec St. Patrick's Cathedral, Melbourne)* Move ▲ MD 3062 [DDD]
Melbourne String Quartet
Moeran, E.J.:Qt Strs Chandos ▲ CHAN 8465 [ADD]
Melbourne SO
W.A. Albert (cnd)
Hindemith, P.:Concert Music Brass & Strs CPO ▲ CPO 999006-2 [DDD]
Hindemith, P.:Con Orch CPO ▲ CPO 999014 [DDD]
Hindemith, P.:Die Harmonie der Welt CPO ▲ CPO 999006-2 [DDD]
Hindemith, P.:Marsch über den alten CPO ▲ CPO 999014 [DDD]
Hindemith, P.:Neues vom Tage (concert ov) *(rec Oct. & Nov., 1989)* CPO ▲ CPO 999007-2
Hindemith, P.:Nusch-Nuschi Dances CPO ▲ CPO 999006-2 [DDD]
Hindemith, P.:Pittsburgh Sym CPO ▲ CPO 999014 [DDD]
Hindemith, P.:Sinfonietta CPO ▲ CPO 999014 [DDD]
Hindemith, P.:Sym in E♭ for Concert Band *(rec Oct. & Nov., 1989)* CPO ▲ CPO 999007-2
G. Dreyfus (cnd)
Dreyfus, G.:Film & TV Music, w. Queensland SO—themes & suites from Dreyfus's scores for 11 feature & documentary films & Australian TV series Move ▲ MD 3098
J. Hopkins (cnd)
Britten, B.:Con Pno, w. G. Lin (pno) *(rec 1978)* Chandos ("Collect" series) ▲ CHAN 6580 [ADD]
Copland, A.:Con Pno, w. G. Lin (pno) *(rec 1978)* Chandos ("Collect" series) ▲ CHAN 6580 [ADD]
H. Iwaki (cnd)
Bartók, B.:Con Orch Virgin Classics ▲ CDZ 61106
Bartók, B.:Con Orch Virgin Classics ▲ CDZ 59690
Bartók, B.:The Miraculous Mandarin Virgo ▲ CDZ 61106
Stravinsky, I.:Pétrouchka Virgin Classics ▲ CDZ 59690
D. Measham (cnd)
Dreyfus, G.:Sym 2 Southern Cross ▲ SCCD 1024 [AAD]
H.-H. Schönzeler (cnd)
Rubbra, E.:Sym 5 Chandos ("Collect" series) ▲ CHAN 6576 [ADD/DDD]
G. Schuller (cnd)
Smalley, R.:Diptych *(rec live)* Vox Australis ▲ VAST 015-2 [DDD]
J. Serebrier (cnd)
Holst, G.:The Planets ASV Quicksilva ▲ QS 6078 [DDD]
Ravel, M.:Boléro ASV Quicksilva ▲ QS 6078 [DDD]
Sibelius, J.:Sym 1 ASV Quicksilva ▲ CD QS 6040 [DDD]
Tchaikovsky, P.:Arias, w. C. Farley (sop), Sicilian SO—15 arias from composer's 8 major operas IMP Masters ▲ IMPMCD 64 [DDD]
Tchaikovsky, P.:Eugene Onegin (sels), w. Carole Farley (sop)—Tatiana's Letter Scene IMP ("Concert Classics" series) ▲ IMP PCD 1102
Tchaikovsky, P.:Ov 1812 ASV Quicksilva ▲ QS 6078 [DDD]
G. Simon (cnd)
Grainger, P.:Danish Folk Music Suite Koch International Classics ▲ KIC 7003 2 [DDD] ■ 3-7003-4 (D)
Grainger, P.:Hill Songs 1 & 2 Koch International Classics ▲ KIC 7003 2 [DDD] ■ 3-7003-4 (D)
Grainger, P.:Orchestral Music—Beautiful Fresh Flower [orchestrated by Peter Sculthorpe]; Colleen Dhas (1904); Irish Tune from County Derry Koch International Classics ▲ KIC 7003 2 [DDD] ■ 3-7003-4 (D)
Grainger, P.:The Warriors Koch International Classics ▲ KIC 7003 2 [DDD] ■ 3-7003-4 (D)
L. Slovák (cnd)
Dreyfus, G.:Sym 1 Southern Cross ▲ SCCD 1024 [AAD]
P. Thomas (cnd)
Addinsell, R.:Warsaw Con, w. I. Goodman (pno) Philips ("Concert Classics" series) ▲ 422471-2 [ADD]
Formosa, R.:Dedica, w. J. Crellin (ob) *(rec studio)* Vox Australis ▲ VAST 015-2 [AAD]
Gershwin, G.:Rhap in Blue, w. I. Goodman (pno) Philips ("Concert Classics" series) ▲ 422471-2 [ADD]
Litolff, H.C.:Con Symphonique 4, w. I. Goodman (pno)—Scherzo Philips ("Concert Classics" series) ▲ 422471-2

▲ = CD ♦ = Enhanced CD Δ = MD ■ = Cassette Tape □ = DCC

Melbourne Windpower
R. Runnells (cnd)
Melbourne Windpower — Move ▲ MD 3082
A Night at the Opera:Arrangements for Winds (1791–1821) — Move ▲ MD 3110 [DDD]
Meliora String Quartet
Adler, S.:Qt 3 Strs — CRI ▲ CD 608 [ADD]
Mendelssohn, F.:Octet Strs, w. Cleveland Quartet — Telarc ▲ CD 80142 [DDD]
Mellstock Band
Under the Greenwood Tree:The Carols & Dances of [Thomas] Hardy's Wessex, w. Mellstock Choir — Saydisc ▲ CDSDL 360 [DDD] ■ SDLC 360 (D)
Mélodia Brass Ensemble
P.-A. Bidaud (cnd)
The European — Gallo ▲ CD 624 [ADD]
Opera Fantasies, w. Stefan Vladar [pno] — Sony Classical ▲ SK 52564
Melos Ensemble
Janácek, L.:Concertino Pno — EMI Classics ("Matrix" series) ▲ CDM 65303
Janácek, L.:In the Mists — EMI Classics ("Matrix" series) ▲ CDM 65303
Janácek, L.:Youth — EMI Classics ("Matrix" series) ▲ CDM 65303
Mozart, W.A.:Qts Fl, w. R. Adeney (fl) — ASV Quicksilva ▲ ASQ 6099 [DDD]
Mozart, W.A.:Qts Fl — ASV Quicksilva ▲ QS 6099 [ADD]
Mozart, W.A.:Qnt Cl, K.581, w. G. de Peyer (cl) — EMI Classics ▲ CDM 63116
Nielsen, C.:Qnt Ww — EMI Classics ("Matrix" series) ▲ CDM 65303
Ravel, M.:Intro & Allegro — London ▲ 421154-2 [ADD]
Reizenstein, F.:Qnt Pno — Continuum ▲ CCD 1024
Melos String Quartet [Wilhelm Melcher (vn), Ida Bieler (vn), Hermann Voss (va), Peter Buck (vc)]
Boccherini, L.:Qnts Gtr & Strs, w. N. Yepes (gtr)—Op. 50/4, 7 & 9 — Deutsche Grammophon ("Resonance" series) ▲ 429512-2 [ADD]
Brahms, J.:Qts Strs (comp) — Deutsche Grammophon 3-▲ 423670-2 [DDD]
Brahms, J.:Qnt Cl, w. M. Portal (cl) — Harmonia Mundi France ▲ HMC 901349
Brahms, J.:Qnt 2 Strs, w. G. Caussé (va) — Harmonia Mundi France ▲ HMC 901349
Janácek, L.:Qt 1 Strs — Harmonia Mundi France ▲ HMC 901380
Janácek, L.:Qt 2 Strs — Harmonia Mundi France ▲ HMC 901380
Kelemen, M.:Sonnets *(rec Feb 17, 1988)* — BIS ▲ CD 742 [AAD]
Mendelssohn, F.:Pieces Str Qt, Op. 81 — Deutsche Grammophon 3-▲ 415883-2 [ADD]
Mendelssohn, F.:Qts Strs (comp) — Deutsche Grammophon 3-▲ 415883-2 [ADD]
Mendelssohn, F.:Qt in E♭ Strs — Deutsche Grammophon 3-▲ 415883-2 [ADD]
Mozart, W.A.:Qt 17 Strs — Deutsche Grammophon ▲ 429818-2 [ADD]
Mozart, W.A.:Qt 19 Strs — Deutsche Grammophon ▲ 429818-2 [ADD]
Schubert, Franz:Qt 12 Strs—Allegro assai movt. — Harmonia Mundi France 2-▲ HMC 901408/09
Schubert, Franz:Qt 13 Strs — Novalis ▲ 150058 [DDD]
Schubert, Franz:Qt 13 Strs — Harmonia Mundi France 2-▲ HMC 901408/09
Schubert, Franz:Qt 14 Strs — Harmonia Mundi France 2-▲ HMC 901408/09
Schubert, Franz:Qt 14 Strs — Novalis ▲ 150058 [DDD]
Schubert, Franz:Qt 15 Strs — Harmonia Mundi France 2-▲ HMC 901408/09
Schubert, Franz:Qnt Strs, D.956, w. W. Boettcher (vc) — Harmonia Mundi France ▲ HMC 901494
Schubert, Franz:Qnt Strs, D.956, w. M. Rostropovich (vc) — Deutsche Grammophon ("Galleria" series) ▲ 415373-2 [ADD]
Schumann, R.:Qts Strs, Op. 41 — Deutsche Grammophon 3-▲ 423670-2 [DDD]
Hans Memling Trio [J. Duijck (pno), D. Lippens (vn), J. van Kelst (vc)]
Bouquet, J.:Trio — Eufoda ▲ 1145 [ADD]
Debussy, C.:Trio Pno — Eufoda ▲ 1145 [ADD]
Dvořák, A.:Trio 4 Pno, "Dumky"—Op. 90 — Eufoda ▲ 1145 [ADD]
Mendelssohn Quintet
Mendelssohn, F.:Qnts Strs, Opp. 18 & 87 — Musicales Actes Sud ▲ M 210001
Mendelssohn String Quartet [Ida Levin (vn), Nicholas Mann (vn), Katherine Murdock (va), Marcy Rosen (vc)]
Antheil, G.:Qt 1 Strs — MusicMasters ▲ 01612-67094-2 [DDD]
Davidson, T.:Bleached Thread, Sister Thread — CRI ▲ CD 681 [DDD]
Picker, T.:Qt 1 Strs — Elektra/Nonesuch ▲ 79246-2-ZK
Ran, S.:Qt 1 Strs — Koch International Classics ▲ KIC 7280 [DDD]
Toch, E.:Qts Strs — Laurel ▲ LR 850CD [ADD/DAD]
Fanny Mendelssohn String Quartet [Renate Eggebrecht (vn), Mario Korunic (vn), Stefan Berg (va), Friedemann Kupsa (vc)]
Bacewicz, G.:Qt 4 Strs *(rec 1991)* — Troubadisc ▲ TROCD 04 [ADD]
Bacewicz, G.:Qt 6 Strs *(rec 1991)* — Troubadisc ▲ TROCD 04 [ADD]
Bacewicz, G.:Qt 7 Strs *(rec 1991)* — Troubadisc ▲ TROCD 04 [ADD]
Bliss, A.:Qts (2) Strs *(rec Bauer Studios, Ludwigsburg, July 23–24, 1995 & Feb 4-)* — Troubadisc ▲ TRO 01412 [DDD]
Mendelssohn, Fanny:Qt Strs *(rec 1988/89)* — Troubadisc ▲ TROCD 01408 [AAD]
Milhaud, D.:Qt 1 Strs *(rec Sept. 1994)* — Troubadisc ▲ SP 109 [DDD]
Milhaud, D.:Qt 2 Strs *(rec Sept. 1994)* — Troubadisc ▲ TROCD 01409 [DDD]
Milhaud, D.:Qt 3 Strs, w. Ulrike Sonntag (sop) *(rec Ludwigsburg, Germany, Jan. 1995)* — Troubadisc ▲ TROCD 01410 [DDD]
Milhaud, D.:Qt 4 Strs *(rec Ludwigsburg, Germany, Jan. 1995)* — Troubadisc ▲ TROCD 01410 [DDD]
Milhaud, D.:Qt 5 Strs *(rec Ludwigsburg, Germany, Jan. 1995)* — Troubadisc ▲ TROCD 01410 [DDD]
Smyth, E.:Chamber Music, w. C. Dutilly (pno)—Sonata in a for Cello & Piano, Op. 5 (1887); Sonata in a for Violin & Piano, Op. 7 (1887); String Quintet in E, Op. 1 (1883); String Quartet in e (1902/12) *(rec 1990)* — Troubadisc 2-▲ TRO CD 03 [ADD]
Tailleferre, G.:Image, w. U. Siebler (fl), D. Marshall (cl), H. Stralendorf (cel), A. Gassenhuber (pno) *(rec Dec. 1992)* — Troubadisc ▲ TRO 01406 [DDD]
Tailleferre, G.:Qt Strs *(rec Dec. 1992)* — Troubadisc ▲ TRO 01406 [DDD]
Fanny Mendelssohn String Quartet members
Mendelssohn, Fanny:Qt Pno, w. C. Dutilly (pno) *(rec 1988/89)* — Troubadisc ▲ TROCD 01408 [AAD]
Mendelssohn, Fanny:Trio Pno, w. C. Dutilly (pno) *(rec 1988/89)* — Troubadisc ▲ TROCD 01408 [AAD]
Menuhin Festival Orch
Y. Menuhin (cnd)
Boyce, W.:Syms, Op. 2 — EMI Classics ("Baroque" series) ▲ CDK 65730
Handel, G.F.:Coronation Anthems (4) for George II, w. Ambrosian Singers *(rec St. Augustine's Church, Maida Vale, London, Oct. 1969)* — EMI Classics ▲ CDK 65336 [ADD]
Handel, G.F.:Solomon (sels), w. Ambrosian Singers—From the Censer Curling Rise [chorus] *(rec St. Augustine's Church, Maida Vale, London, Oct. 1969)* — EMI Classics ▲ CDK 65336 [ADD]
Menuhin Festival Piano Quartet [F. Rieger (pno), N. Chastain (vn), P. Coletti (va), F. Goutou (vc)]
Mendelssohn, F.:Qt 2 Pno — Ars Produktion ▲ FCD 368312 [DDD]
Strauss, R.:Qt Pno — Ars Produktion ▲ FCD 368312 [DDD]
Turina, J.:Qt Pno *(rec May 25–28, 1993)* — Claves ▲ CD 9403 [DDD]
Turina, J.:Qnt Pno, w. C. Busch (vn) *(rec May 25–28, 1993)* — Claves ▲ CD 9403 [DDD]
Le Mercure Galant Baroque Orch
F. Heyerick (cnd)
Telemann, G.P.:Cants, w. Greetje Anthoni (sop), Yves Saelens (ten), Stefan Geyer (bar), Ex Tempore Vocal Ensemble—Der Tod Jesu *(rec Studio Steurbaut, Gent, June 1995)* — René Gailly ▲ 92025 [DDD]
Meridian Arts Ensemble [Jon Nelson (tpt), Wayne du Maine (tpt), Daniel Grabois (hn), Benjamin Herrington (trbn), Raymond Stewart (tuba)]
Anxiety of Influence — Channel Classics ▲ CCS 9796
Barber, S.:Gone Is the River — Channel Classics ▲ CCS 9496
Luening, O.:Divert Brass Qnt *(rec 2/11/91)* — CRI ▲ CD 600 [DDD]

Meridian Arts Ensemble (cont.)
Radzynski, J.:Take 5 — Channel Classics ▲ CCS 9496
Robles, P.:Finale Rounds — Channel Classics ▲ CCS 9496
Sampson, D.:Morning Music — Channel Classics ▲ CCS 9496
Smart Went Crazy, w. Mo Roberts (perc) *(rec Mar. 1993)* — Channel Crossings ▲ CCS 4192 [DDD]
Taxin, I.:Fanfare — Channel Classics ▲ CCS 9496
Taxin, I.:Qnt Brass — Channel Classics ▲ CCS 0490 [DDD]
Winning Artists Series *(rec Feb. 1991)* — Channel Classics ▲ CCS 2191 [DDD]
Merling Trio
Curtis-Smith, C.:Sweetgrass — Albany ▲ TROY 148 [DDD]
Curtis-Smith, C.:Trio 2 Pno — Albany ▲ TROY 148 [DDD]
Olivier Messaien Quartet
Messiaen, O.:Quatuor pour la fin du temps — Pierre Verany ▲ PVY 794012 [DDD]
Metamorphosen CO
S. Yoo (cnd)
Carter, E.:Elegy Va *(rec Campion Center, Weston, MA, Apr 1994)* — Albany ▲ TROY 194 [DDD]
Coleman, D.:Long Ago, This Radiant Day *(rec Campion Center, Weston, MA, Apr 1994)* — Albany ▲ TROY 194 [DDD]
Corigliano, J.:Voyage Strs *(rec Campion Center, Weston, MA, Apr 1994)* — Albany ▲ TROY 194 [DDD]
Fine, I.:Serious Song *(rec Campion Center, Weston, MA, Apr 1994)* — Albany ▲ TROY 194 [DDD]
Ruehr, E.:Shimmer *(rec Campion Center, Weston, MA, Apr 1994)* — Albany ▲ TROY 194 [DDD]
Zwilich, E.T.:Prologue & Vars *(rec Campion Center, Weston, MA, Apr 1994)* — Albany ▲ TROY 194 [DDD]
Metropolitan Brass Ensemble
S. Sturk (cnd)
Gottlieb, J.:Sacred Music, w. M. Stone (sop), H. Reps (mez), D. Lefkowitz (ten), H. Stahl (ten), R. Abelson (bar), R. Botton (bar), P. Newman (reader), New York Motet Choir — Premier ("Composer" series) ▲ PRCD 1018 [DDD]
Metropolitan Brass Quintet
Brass Bonanza, w. Annapolis Brass Quintet, Berlin Brass Quintet, Dallas Brass Quintet, New York Brass Quintet, 1-5 Brass Quintet, St. Louis Brass Quintet — Crystal ▲ CD 200 [ADD/DDD]
Metropolitan Opera Orch
Prokofiev, S.:Summer Day, w. M. Forrester (cta) [E] — CBC ("SM 5000" series) 2-▲ SMCD 5118-2 [DDD]
K. Adler (cnd)
Of Gods & Demons, w. George London (b-bar), Vienna SO, Columbia SO, Rudolf Moralt (cnd), Jean-Paul Moral (cnd) — Sony Classical ("Masterworks Heritage" series) ▲ MHK 62758
T. Beecham (cnd)
Offenbach, J.:Les Contes d'Hoffmann, w. Patrice Munsel (sop), Jarmila Novotná (sop), Raoul Jobin (ten), Ezio Pinza (bass), New York Metropolitan Opera Chorus *(rec Feb 26, 1944)* — Enterprise ("The Radio Years") 2-▲ ENT-19 (m)
L. Bernstein (cnd)
Bizet, G.:Carmen, w. A. Maliponte (sop), M. Horne (mez), J. McCracken (bar), T. Krause (bar), Manhattan Opera Chorus [F] *(rec 1973)* — Deutsche Grammophon 3-▲ 427440-2 [ADD]
O. Danon (cnd)
Gershwin, G.:Rhap in Blue, w. R. Lewenthal (pno) *(rec 1962)* — Chesky ▲ CD56 [ADD]
A. Grossmann (cnd)
Prokofiev, S.:Peter & the Wolf, w. M. Forrester (nar) [E] — CBC ("SM 5000" series) 2-▲ SMCD 5118-2 [DDD]
Prokofiev, S.:Sym 7 — CBC ("SM 5000" series) 2-▲ SMCD 5118-2 [DDD]
Prokofiev, S.:Winter Bonfire, w. M. Forrester (nar), Les Petits Chanteurs du Mont-Royal [E] — CBC ("SM 5000" series) 2-▲ SMCD 5118-2 [DDD]
G.A. Lavigueur (cnd)
Musical Heritage of French Canada — CBC Records ("SM 5000" series) ▲ SMCD 5090 [DDD] ■ SMC 5090 (D)
E. Leinsdorf (cnd)
Rossini, G.:Il barbiere di Siviglia, w. Roberta Peters (sop—Rosina), Margaret Roggero (mez—Berta), Cesare Valletti (ten—Count Almaviva), Calvin Marsh (bar—Fiorello/Sergeant), Robert Merrill (bar—Figaro), Fernando Corena (bass—Dr. Bartolo), Carlo Tomanelli (bass—Ambrogio), Giorgio Tozzi (bass—Don Basilio), New York Metropolitan Opera Chorus *(rec Manhattan Center, New York, Sept 1-11, 1958)* — RCA Living Stereo 3-▲ 09026-68552-2 [ADD]
Rossini, G.:Il barbiere di Siviglia, w. R. Peters (sop), C. Valletti (ten), R. Merrill (bar), G. Tozzi (bass), F. Corena (bass), New York Metropolitan Opera Chorus [I] — RCA Gold Seal 3-▲ 6505-2-RG [ADD] 2-■ 6505-4-RG (CrO2)
Rossini, G.:Il barbiere di Siviglia (sels), w. R. Peters (sop), C. Valletti (ten), R. Merrill (bar), G. Tozzi (bass), F. Corena (bass), New York Metropolitan Opera Chorus — RCA Gold Seal ▲ 60188-2-RG [ADD] ■ 60188-4-RG (CrO2)
Verdi, G.:Macbeth, w. L. Rysanek (sop), C. Bergonzi (ten), L. Warren (bar), J. Hines (bass), New York Metropolitan Opera Chorus [I] — RCA Gold Seal 2-▲ 4516-2-RG [ADD]
J. Levine (cnd)
Beethoven, L. van:Sym 3, "Eroica" — Deutsche Grammophon ▲ 439862-2 [DDD]
Donizetti, G.:L'elisir d'amore, w. K. Battle (sop), D. Upshaw (sop), L. Pavarotti (ten), E. Dara (bar), L. Nucci (bar), New York Metropolitan Opera Chorus — Deutsche Grammophon 2-▲ 429744-2 [DDD]
James Levine's 25th Anniversary Metropolitan Opera Gala, w. Ileana Cotrubas (sop), Renée Fleming (sop), Hei-Kyung Hong (sop), Karita Mattila (sop), Birgit Nilsson (sop), Ruth Ann Swenson (sop), Kiri Te Kanawa (sop), Deborah Voigt (sop), Grace Bumbry (mez), Heidi Grant Murphy (mez), Anne Sofie von Otter (mez) *(rec live, Metropolitan Opera House, New York, Apr 27, 1996)* — Deutsche Grammophon 2-▲ 449177-2 [DDD]
Live in Tokyo 1988, w. Kathleen Battle (sop), Plácido Domingo (ten) — Deutsche Grammophon ▲ 427686-2 GH [DDD] ■ 427686-4
Mozart, W.A.:Idomeneo, w. Heidi Grant-Murphy (sop—Ilia), Carol Vaness (sop—Elettra), Cecilia Bartoli (mez—Idamante), Plácido Domingo (ten—Idomeneo), Frank Lopardo (ten—High Priest), Thomas Hampson (bar—Arbace), Bryn Terfel (b-bar—The Voice), Raymond Hughes (cnd), New York Metropolitan Opera Chorus *(rec Manhattan Center Studios, New York, Mar & Apr 1994)* — Deutsche Grammophon 3-▲ 447 737-2 [DDD]
Mussorgsky, M.:Pictures at an Exhibition — Deutsche Grammophon ▲ 437531-2
Opera Arias, w. Bryn Terfel (b-bar) — Deutsche Grammophon ▲ 4458862 GH [DDD]
Puccini, G.:Manon Lescaut, w. M. Freni (sop—Manon), C. Bartoli (mez—Musici I), L. Pavarotti (ten—Des Grieux), R. Vargas (ten—Edmondo), D. Croft (ten—Lescaut), G. Taddei (bar—Geronte), New York Metropolitan Opera Chorus [I] *(rec 1992)* — London ▲ 440200-2 [DDD]
Puccini, G.:Manon Lescaut (sels), w. Montserrat Caballé (sop—Manon), Plácido Domingo (ten—Des Grieux)—Tu, tu, amore? Tu? [Act II] — Deutsche Grammophon ▲ 447270-2 [ADD] ■ 447270-4
Strauss, R.:Don Quixote, w. Jerry Grossman (vc), Raymond Gniewek (vn), Michael Ouzounian (va) *(rec Manhattan Ctr, NY, May 1995)* — Deutsche Grammophon ▲ 447762-2 [DDD]
Strauss, R.:Tod und Verklärung *(rec Manhattan Ctr, NY, May 1995)* — Deutsche Grammophon ▲ 447762-2 [DDD]
Stravinsky, I.:Le Sacre du printemps Orch — Deutsche Grammophon ▲ 437531-2
Verdi, G.:Aida, w. A. Millo (sop), D. Zajick (mez), P. Domingo (ten), J. Morris (bass), S. Ramey (bass), New York Metropolitan Opera Chorus [I] — Sony Classical 3-▲ S3K 45973 [DDD] 3-■ S3T 45973 (D)
Verdi, G.:Aida (sels), w. A. Millo (sop), D. Zajick (mez), P. Domingo (ten), J. Morris (bar), S. Ramey (bass), T. Cook (bass), New York Metropolitan Opera Chorus *(rec New York, May 18-26, 1990)* — Sony Classical ("Opera Highlights" series) ▲ SMK 53506 [DDD]
Verdi, G.:Ballet Music—music from I vespri siciliani, Macbeth, Otello & Aida *(rec Apr. 24-May 16, 1992)* — Sony Classical ▲ SK 52489 [DDD]
Verdi, G.:Don Carlos (sels), w. J. Bunnell (sop), A. Millo (sop), D. Zajick (mez), M. Sylvester (ten), V. Chernov (bar), F. Furlanetto (bass), P. Plishka (bass), New York Metropolitan Opera Chorus *(rec New York, Apr. 20-May 14, 1992)* — Sony Classical ("Opera Highlights" series) ▲ SMK 53507 [DDD]

Metropolitan Opera Orch (cont.)
J. Levine (cnd) (cont.)
Verdi, G.:Luisa Miller, w. A. Millo (sop), F. Quivar (mez), P. Domingo (ten), V. Chernov (bar), New York Metropolitan Opera Chorus Sony Classical 2-▲ S2K 48073
Verdi, G.:Luisa Miller (sels), w. A. Millo (sop), W. White (mez), F. Quivar (cta), P. Domingo (ten), V. Chernov (bar), J.-H. Rootering (bass), P. Plishka (bass), New York Metropolitan Opera Chorus *(rec New York, May 2-18, 1991)* Sony Classical ("Opera Highlights" series) ▲ SMK 53508 [DDD]
Verdi, G.:Il trovatore, w. A. Millo (sop), D. Zajick (mez), S. Kelly (cta), P. Domingo (ten), T. Willson (ten), A. Laciura (ten), J. Morris (bass), G. Bater (bass), New York Metropolitan Opera Chorus *(rec June 18, 1991)* Sony Classical 2-▲ S2K 48070 [DDD]
Wagner, R.:Götterdämmerung, w. H. Behrens (sop), C. Studer (sop), H. Schwarz (mez), R. Goldberg (ten), B. Weikl (bar), E. Wlaschiha (bar), M. Salminen (bass), New York Metropolitan Opera Chorus Deutsche Grammophon 4-▲ 429385-2 [DDD]
Wagner, R.:Ovs, Preludes & Orch Sels—selections from The Flying Dutchman, Tannhäuser, Die Meistersinger, Rienzi, Lohengrin Deutsche Grammophon ▲ 435874-2
Wagner, R.:Parsifal, w. J. Norman (sop), P. Domingo (ten), E. Wlaschiha (bar), K. Moll (bass), J. Morris (bass), J.-H. Rootering (bass), New York Metropolitan Opera Chorus Deutsche Grammophon 4-▲ 437501-2
Wagner, R.:Das Rheingold, w. B. Svendén (sop), C. Ludwig (mez), S. Jerusalem (ten), H. Zednik (ten), E. Wlaschiha (bar), J. Morris (bass) [G] Deutsche Grammophon 3-▲ 427607-2 [DDD]
Wagner, R.:Der Ring des Nibelungen Deutsche Grammophon 14-▲ 445354-2
Wagner, R.:Der Ring des Nibelungen (sels), w. J. Norman (sop), H. Behrens (sop), K. Battle (sop), J. Morris (mez), C. Ludwig (mez), R. Goldberg (ten), S. Jerusalem (ten), E. Wlaschiha (bar), M. Salminen (bass)—The Compact Ring—Ride of the Valkyries Wotan's Farewell & Magic Fire Music, Forest Murmurs, Brünnhilde's Awakening, Siegfried's Funeral Music, Brünnhilde's Immolation, & others Deutsche Grammophon ▲ 437825-2
Wagner, R.:Siegfried, w. H. Behrens (sop), B. Svenden (sop), R. Goldberg (ten), J. Morris (bass), New York Metropolitan Opera Chorus [G] Deutsche Grammophon 4-▲ 429407-2 [DDD]
D. Mitropoulos (cnd)
Barber, S.:Vanessa, w. E. Steber (sop), G. Resnik (sop), R. Elias (mez), N. Gedda (ten), G. Tozzi (bass), Metropolitan Opera Chorus [E] RCA Gold Seal ▲ 7899-2-RG [ADD]
P. Monteux (cnd)
Offenbach, J.:Les Contes d'Hoffmann, w. L. Amara (sop), R. Peters (sop), R. Stevens (mez), R. Tucker (ten), M. Singher (bar), New York Metropolitan Opera Chorus Stradivarius 2-▲ DAT 12302
E. Panizza (cnd)
Ponchielli, A.:La Gioconda, w. New York Metropolitan Opera Chorus Symposium 2-▲ SYM 1176/77
W. Pelletier (cnd)
Verdi, G.:Otello (sels), w. H. Jepson (sop), G. Martinelli (ten), N. Massue (ten), L. Tibbett (bar), New York Metropolitan Opera Chorus—eleven arias & scenes *(rec 1939)* Pearl ▲ GEMMCD 9914 (m) [AAD]
G. Sébastian (cnd)
Bizet, G.:Carmen (sels), w. Risë Stevens (sop), N. Conner (sop), R. Jobin (ten), R. Weede (bar), New York Metropolitan Opera Chorus [F] Odyssey ■ YT 32102 (m)
G. Setti (cnd)
Amelita Galli-Curci in Opera & Song, w. Amelita Galli-Curci (sop), Rosario Bourdon (cnd) Happy Days ▲ CDHD 201 [ADD]
Legendary Three Tenors, w. Enrico Caruso (ten), Beniamino Gigli (ten), John McCormack (ten), Ruggiero Leoncavallo (pno), Edwin Schneider (pno), Metropolitan Opera Chorus, Philharmonia Orch [cnd:Stanford Robinson], Philharmonia Chorus *(rec 1904-1950)* RCA Gold Seal ▲ 09026-68534-2 [ADD] ■ 09026-68534-4
F. Stiedry (cnd)
Wagner, R.:Lohengrin, w. H. Traubel (sop—Elsa), A. Varnay (sop—Ortrud), L. Melchior (ten—Lohengrin), F. Guerrera (bar—Herald), H. Janssen (bar—Telramund), D. Ernster (bass—King Heinrich), New York Metropolitan Opera Chorus *(rec live Jan. 6, 1950)* Danacord 3-▲ DACOCD 322/24 [AAD]
L. Stokowski (cnd)
Puccini, G.:Turandot, w. B. Nilsson (sop—Turnadot), A. Moffo (sop—Liù), F. Corelli (ten—Calaf), C. Anthony (ten—Pong), R. Nagy (ten—Pang), F. Guarrera (bar—Ping), B. Giaiotti (bass—Timur), New York Metropolitan Opera Chorus *(rec Mar. 4, 1961)* Datum 2-▲ DAT 12301 [ADD]
B. Walter (cnd)
Ezio Pinza, Vol. III, w. Ezio Pinza (b-bar) *(rec 1944 & 46)* Preiser ▲ PRE CD 89132

Mexican National Opera Orch
R. Cellini (cnd)
Verdi, G.:Simon Boccanegra (sels), w. Celia Garcia (sop—Maria Boccanegra), Mario Filippeschi (ten—Gabriele Adorno), Ignacio Ruffino (ten—Pietro), Leonard Warren (bar—Simon Boccanegra), Roberto Silva (bass—Jacopo Fiesco), Carlo Morelli (bass—Paolo), Mexican National Opera Chorus *(rec Palacio de las Bellas Artes, Mexico City, July 4, 1950)* Legato Classics ▲ LCD 185-1 [ADD]

Mexican Soloists
E. Mata (cnd)
Falla, M. de:Con Hpd, w. Rafael Puyana (hpd) *(rec Sala Nezahualcóyotl, Universidad Nacional Autónoma de Mexico, Mexico City, Oct. 1994)* Dorian ▲ DOR 90214 [DDD]
Falla, M. de:El retablo de maese Pedro, w. Lourdes Ambriz (sop), Julianne Baird (sop), Miguel Cortez (ten), William Alvarado (bar), Rafael Puyana (hpd) *(rec Sala Nezahualcóyotl, Universidad Nacional Autónoma de Mexico, Mexico City, Oct. 1994)* Dorian ▲ DOR 90214 [DDD]
Orbón, J.:Cantigas del rey, w. *(sop unknown)*, Rafael Puyana (hpd) *(rec Sala Nezahualcóyotl, Universidad Nacional Autónoma de Mexico, Mexico City, Oct. 1994)* Dorian ▲ DOR 90214 [DDD]
Orbón, J.:Himnus ad galli cantum, w. *(sop unknown)* *(rec Sala Nezahualcóyotl, Universidad Nacional Autónoma de Mexico, Mexico City, Oct. 1994)* Dorian ▲ DOR 90214 [DDD]

Mexican State SO
E. Bátiz (cnd)
Albéniz, I.:España [orchd] ASV ▲ ASV 888 [DDD]
Albéniz, I.:Iberia Suite ASV ▲ ASV 888 [DDD]
Borodin, A.:Prince Igor (sels)—Polovtsian Maidens; Polovtsian Dances IMG/Pickwick ▲ PICIMG 1610 [DDD]
Borodin, A.:Prince Igor (ov) ASV Quicksilva ▲ CD QS 6018 [DDD]
Borodin, A.:Prince Igor (Polovtsian dances) ASV Quicksilva ▲ CD QS 6018 [DDD]
Borodin, A.:Sym 2 ASV Quicksilva ▲ CD QS 6018 [DDD]
Chabrier, E.:España ASV Quicksilva ▲ QS 6026 [DDD]
Chávez, C.:Baile ASV ▲ ASV 927 [DDD]
Chávez, C.:Cantos de México ASV ▲ ASV 927 [DDD]
Chávez, C.:La hija de Cólquide Orch ASV ▲ ASV 927 [DDD]
Chávez, C.:Paisajes Mexicanos ASV ▲ ASV 927 [DDD]
Chávez, C.:Toccata Orch ASV ▲ ASV 927 [DDD]
Copland, A.:Fanfare for the Common Man EMI Classics (American Composer Series) ▲ CDM 64306
Debussy, C.:Prélude à l'après-midi d'un faune ASV Quicksilva ▲ QS 6026 [DDD]
Dukas, P.:L'Apprenti sorcier ASV Quicksilva ▲ QS 6026 [DDD]
Falla, M. de:El sombrero de tres picos, w. Maria Luisa Salinas (sop) IMP ▲ PCD 2028
Falla, M. de:La vida breve (interlude & dance 1) IMP ▲ PCD 2028
Jeux d'Enfants, w. Christopher Hyde-Smith (fl/pic), Emma Johnson (cl), George MacDonald (cl), Gordon Back (pno), Academy of St. Martin in the Fields [cnd:Neville Marriner], Mexico City PO, Royal PO [cnd:Enrique Bátiz], Northern Sinfonia of England, et al. ASV Quicksilva ▲ ASQ 6182
Moncayo Garcia, J.P.:Huapango ASV ▲ ASV 871 [DDD]
Ponce, M.:Balada mexicana Pno, w. Jorge Federico Osorio (pno) ASV ▲ ASV 926 [DDD]
Ponce, M.:Canto y danza de los antiguos mexicanos ASV ▲ ASV 926 [DDD]
Ponce, M.:Chapultepec ASV ▲ ASV 926 [DDD]
Ponce, M.:Con Pno, w. Jorge Federico Osorio (pno) ASV ▲ ASV 952
Ponce, M.:Con Pno, w. Jorge Federico Osorio (pno) ASV ▲ ASV 926 [DDD]
Ponce, M.:Concierto del sur, w. Alfonso Moreno (gtr) ASV ▲ ASV 952
Ponce, M.:Poema elegíaco ASV ▲ ASV 926 [DDD]
Ravel, M.:Pavane pour une infante défunte ASV Quicksilva ▲ QS 6026 [DDD]
Rodrigo, J.:Concierto de Aranjuez, w. Alfonso Moreno (gtr) ASV ▲ ASV 887 [DDD]
Rodrigo, J.:Concierto para una fiesta, w. Alfonso Moreno (gtr) ASV ▲ ASV 887 [DDD]

Mexican State SO (cont.)
E. Bátiz (cnd) (cont.)
Rodrigo, J.:Fant para un gentilhombre, w. Alfonso Moreno (gtr) ASV ▲ ASV 887 [DDD]
Rodrigo, J.:Music of—Sones en la Giralda; Palilos y panderetas; Juglares; Dos piezes caballerescas; Soleriana EMI Classics ▲ CDM 65901
Rossini, G.:Ovs—La scala di seta; Il Signor Bruschino; Il barbiere di Siviglia; Le siege de Corinthe; Il turco in Italia; L'Italiana in Algeri; Semiramide; William Tell ASV ▲ ASV 857 [DDD]
Saint-Saëns, C.:Danse macabre ASV Quicksilva ▲ QS 6026 [DDD]
Saint-Saëns, C.:Danse macabre ASV ▲ ASV 665 [DDD]
Tchaikovsky, P.:Marche slave ASV Quicksilva ▲ QS 6008 [DDD]
Tchaikovsky, P.:Ov 1812 ASV Quicksilva ▲ QS 6008 [DDD]
Tchaikovsky, P.:Romeo & Juliet ASV Quicksilva ▲ QS 6008 [DDD]
Tchaikovsky, P.:Swan Lake (sels)—Waltz from Act I ASV Quicksilva ▲ QS 6008 [DDD]
Verdi, G.:Ovs & Preludes—La forza del destino; I vespri siciliani; Aida; La traviata; Nabucco; Rigoletto; Aroldo; Un ballo in maschera; Luisa Miller ASV ▲ ASV 856 [DDD]
E. Diazmunoz (cnd)
Russian Showpieces, w. Russell Brydon (org) Pickwick ("The Orchid" series) ▲ PICORCD 11004
P. Freeman (cnd)
Wolfe, S.:Canticle CRI ▲ CD 595 [DDD]
F. Lozano (cnd)
Falla, M. de:Music of—Le tricorne [3 Danses]; Danse rituelle du feu [De l'amour sorcier]; La vie brève [Interlude & danse]; Nuits dans les jardins d'espagne Forlane ▲ FRL 47 [AAD]
Grieg, E.:Lyric Suite, Op. 54 Forlane ▲ FRL 45 [ADD]
Grieg, E.:Peer Gynt Suites, Opp. 46 & 55 Forlane ▲ FRL 45 [ADD]
Revueltas, S.:Music of—Sensemaya; Dance; Mourning; Sound [w. Arturo Reyes (tpt)]; The Night of the Mayas [Molto Sostenuto]; Night of the Jaranas [Scherzo]; Night of the Yucatan [Andante Espressivo]; Enchanted Night; Theme & Vars; Nets; The Fisherman/The Burial of the Child/Fishing Pray/Corrido; The Struggle/Return of the Fisherman with Their Dead Fellow Forlane ▲ FRL 16614 [DDD]
Sibelius, J.:Sym 2 Forlane ▲ FRL 26 [ADD]
Tchaikovsky, P.:Sym 6 Forlane ▲ FRL 16 [AAD]
L. Schifrin (cnd)
Schifrin, L.:Cantos Aztecas, w. P. Domingo (ten), N. Storojev (bass), C. Julian (sop), M. Felix (sgr), Mexico City Chorus [Sp] *(rec live 10/29/88)* Pro Arte ▲ CDD 494 [DDD]

Mexico CO Soloists Ensemble
L. S. Hernandez (cnd)
Musica para una boda Mexicana:Music for a Mexican Wedding, w. Lourdes Ambres (sop), Grace Echauri (mez), Pro Musica Chorus Spartacus ▲ 21015

Mexico City CO
B. J. Echenique (cnd)
Delgado, F.:Choral Music, w. Martha Molinar (sop), Luz Angélica Uribe (sop), Ana Paula Abitia (mez), Alfredo Mendoza (ten),Noé Colín (bass), Alfredo Mendoza (cnd), Schola Cantorum—Te Deum al Sr. Felipe de Jesús Urtext ▲ URT 2001 [DDD]
Jerusalem, I.:Choral Music, w. Martha Molinar (sop), Luz Angélica Uribe (sop), Ana Paula Abitia (mez), Alfredo Mendoza (ten),Noé Colín (bass), Alfredo Mendoza (cnd), Schola Cantorum—Magnificat a Dos Voces; Misa en Sol Mayor a 8 Voces Urtext ▲ URT 2001 [DDD]
Zyman, S.:Con Fl, w. Marisa Canales (fl) Urtext ▲ URT 1 [DDD]

Mexico City PO
E. Bátiz (cnd)
Bizet, G.:L'Arlésienne (suites) ASV Quicksilva ▲ ASQ 6134 [ADD]
Bizet, G.:Carmen (suites) ASV Quicksilva ▲ ASQ 6133 [ADD]
Bizet, G.:Jeux d'enfants, w. A. Moreno (gtr) Pickwick ▲ PIC IMG 1604 [DDD]
Bizet, G.:Jeux d'enfants ASV Quicksilva ▲ ASQ 6134 [ADD]
Bizet, G.:La Jolie fille de Perth (suite) ASV Quicksilva ▲ ASQ 6134 [ADD]
Bizet, G.:Patrie ASV Quicksilva ▲ ASQ 6133 [ADD]
Bizet, G.:Les Pêcheurs de perles (sels)—Prelude ASV Quicksilva ▲ ASQ 6133 [ADD]
Castelnuovo-Tedesco, M.:Con 1 Gtr, w. A. Moreno (gtr) Pickwick ▲ PIC IMG 1604 [DDD]
Copland, A.:Danzón Cubano EMI Classics ▲ CDM 63153
Copland, A.:Fanfare for the Common Man EMI Classics ▲ CDC 54539-2 [ADD]
Copland, A.:Fanfare for the Common Man EMI Classics ▲ CDM 63153
Copland, A.:Quiet City EMI Classics ▲ CDM 63153
Copland, A.:The Red Pony (suite) IMG/Pickwick ▲ PIC IMG 1613 [DDD]
Copland, A.:Rodeo EMI Classics ▲ CDM 63153
Copland, A.:El salón México EMI Classics ▲ CDM 63153
Fauré, G.:Berceuse Vn, w. Rodolfo Bonucci (vn) ASV ▲ ASV 686
Fauré, G.:Con Vn, w. Rodolfo Bonucci (vn) ASV ▲ ASV 686
Fauré, G.:Dolly, w. A. Moreno (gtr) Pickwick ▲ PIC IMG 1604 [DDD]
Fauré, G.:Elégie, w. Viocheslav Ponomarev (vc) ASV ▲ ASV 686
Fauré, G.:Masques et bergamasques (suite)—Ov ASV ▲ ASV 686
Fauré, G.:Pelléas et Mélisande (suite) ASV ▲ ASV 686
Fauré, G.:Shylock—Nocturne ASV ▲ ASV 686
Halffter, C.:Con Vn, w. H. Szeryng (vn) ASV ▲ ASV 871 [DDD]
Jeux d'Enfants, w. Christopher Hyde-Smith (fl/pic), Emma Johnson (cl), George MacDonald (cl), Gordon Back (pno), Academy of St. Martin in the Fields [cnd:Neville Marriner], Mexico State SO, Royal PO [cnd:Enrique Bátiz], Northern Sinfonia of England, et al. ASV Quicksilva ▲ ASQ 6182
Musica Mexicana, Vol. 5 ASV ▲ ASV 894 [DDD]
Rachmaninoff, S.:Con 2 Pno, w. J. L. Prats (pno) ASV Quicksilva ▲ ASQ 6128 [DDD]
Rachmaninoff, S.:Con 3 Pno, w. J. L. Prats (pno) IMG/Pickwick ▲ PICIMG 1605
Rachmaninoff, S.:Prince Rostislav, w. J.L. Prats (pno) IMG/Pickwick ▲ PICIMG 1605
Rachmaninoff, S.:Rhapsody on a Theme of Paganini, w. J. L. Prats (pno) ASV Quicksilva ▲ ASQ 6128 [DDD]
Rachmaninoff, S.:Vocalise [arr. orch.] IMG/Pickwick ▲ PICIMG 1605
Revueltas, S.:Caminos ASV ("Musica Mexicana" series) ▲ ASV 942
Revueltas, S.:Cuauhnahuac ASV ▲ ASV 871 [DDD]
Revueltas, S.:Musica para charlar ASV ("Musica Mexicana" series) ▲ ASV 942
Revueltas, S.:Noche de los Mayas, w. Royal PO ASV ▲ ASV 866 [DDD]
Revueltas, S.:Ventanas ASV ("Musica Mexicana" series) ▲ ASV 942
Rimsky-Korsakov, N.:Capriccio espagnol ASV Quicksilva ▲ ASQ 6089 [ADD]
Rimsky-Korsakov, N.:A May Night (ov) ASV Quicksilva ▲ ASQ 6089 [ADD]
Rimsky-Korsakov, N.:Russian Easter Festival ASV Quicksilva ▲ ASQ 6089 [ADD]
Rimsky-Korsakov, N.:Sadko Orch, Op. 5 ASV Quicksilva ▲ ASQ 6089 [ADD]
Saint-Saëns, C.:Carnival of the Animals, w. G. Salvador Sr (pno), G. Salvador Jr (pno) ASV ▲ ASV 665 [DDD]
Villa-Lobos, H.:Con Gtr, w. A. Moreno (gtr) Pickwick ▲ PIC IMG 1604 [DDD]
P. Freeman (cnd)
Saint-Saëns, C.:Danse macabre Pro Arte ▲ 575
H. de la Fuente (cnd)
Aldana, M.K.:Canto Latinoamericano Spartacus ▲ SPR 21006 [DDD]
Chávez, C.:Toccata Orch Spartacus ▲ SPR 21005 [DDD]
Duran, G.:Nepantla Spartacus ▲ SPR 21006 [DDD]
Halffter, R.:La Madrugada del panadero Spartacus ▲ SPR 21006 [DDD]
Lavalle-García, A.:Obertura Colonial Spartacus ▲ SPR 21006 [DDD]
Mabarak, J.:Sinf Spartacus ▲ SPR 21006 [DDD]
Moncayo Garcia, J.P.:Bosques Spartacus ▲ SPR 21005 [DDD]
Revueltas, S.:Homenaje a Federico García Lorca Spartacus ▲ SPR 21005 [DDD]
Revueltas, S.:Janitzio Spartacus ▲ SPR 21005 [DDD]
Revueltas, S.:Noche de los Mayas Spartacus ▲ SPR 21005 [DDD]
Revueltas, S.:Sensemayá Spartacus ▲ SPR 21005 [DDD]
Sandi, L.:Theme & Vars Spartacus ▲ SPR 21006 [DDD]

▲ = CD ♦ = Enhanced CD Δ = MD ■ = Cassette Tape □ = DCC

Mexico City PO (cont.)
F. Lozano (cnd)
Beethoven, L. van:Sym 9, "Choral Sym", w. Irma Gonzalez (sop), Oralia Dominguez (cta), Flavio Becerra (ten), Roberto Banuelas (bar), Mexico City Chorus — Forlane ▲ FRL 18 [AAD]
Mexican Music — Forlane 2-▲ FOR 16688 [ADD]
Mexico through Her Music, Vol. 1 — Spartacus ▲ 25108
Mexico through Her Music, Vol. 2 — Spartacus ▲ 25109
Moncayo Garcia, J.P.:Huapango — Spartacus ▲ 21020
Revueltas, S.:Canciones para niños, w. Irma Gonzalez (sop) — Spartacus ▲ 21020
Revueltas, S.:Janitzio — Spartacus ▲ 21020
Revueltas, S.:Redes (suite) — Spartacus ▲ 21020
Revueltas, S.:Sensemayá — Spartacus ▲ 21020

Mexico City Wind Quintet
Chávez, C.:Soli 2 — Spartacus ▲ 21018
Enriquez, M.:Pentamúsica — Spartacus ▲ 21018
Ibarra, M.:Juegos nocturnos — Spartacus ▲ 21018
Lara, A.:Aulos — Spartacus ▲ 21018
Lavista, M.:Danzas breves — Spartacus ▲ 21018

Mexico Festival Orch
E. Bátiz (cnd)
Latin American Classics, Vol. 1 *(rec Mar. 1993)* — Naxos ▲ 8.550838 [DDD]

Sabine Meyer CO
Mozart, W.A.:Serenade Ww, K.361 — EMI Classics ▲ CDC 54457

Sabine Meyer Wind Ensemble
Beethoven, L. van:Qnt Pno, Ob, Cl, Hn & Bn, w. Christian Zacharias (pno) — EMI Classics ▲ CDC 55013
Krommer, F.:Octets Winds — EMI Classics ▲ CDC 54383
Mozart, W.A.:Entführung (winds) — EMI Classics ▲ CDC 55342
Mozart, W.A.:Qnt Pno, K.452, w. Christian Zacharias (pno) — EMI Classics ▲ CDC 55013
Mozart, W.A.:Serenade Ww, K.361 *(rec Pfarrkirche Pleis, Vella, July 12–15, 1991)* — EMI Classics ▲ CDC 55155 [DDD]

Mezzena–Bonucci Trio [Bruno Mezzena (pno), Franco Mezzena (vn), Arturo Bonucci (vc)]
Martucci, G.:Trio 1 Pno *(rec Genoa, Italy, Feb 5–7, 1996)* — Dynamic ▲ CD 132 [DDD]
Martucci, G.:Trio 2 Pno *(rec Genoa, Italy, Feb 5–7, 1996)* — Dynamic ▲ CD 132 [DDD]

MGM Studio SO
D. Amfitheatrof (cnd)
Amfitheatrof, D.:The Beginning or the End (suite) *(rec 1946)* — Label "X" ▲ LXCD 8 [ADD]
M. Rózsa (cnd)
Rózsa, M.:Ben–Hur, w. MGM Studio Chorus *(rec Culver City, CA & Rome, Italy)* — Rhino 2-▲ R2 72197
A. Winograd (cnd)
Bernstein, L.:Trouble in Tahiti, w. Wolff (sgr), Atkinson (sgr) [E] — Polydor ▲ 827845–2 (m) ■ 827845–4 (m)

MGM Wind Orch
I. Solomon (cnd)
Weill, K.:Con Vn, w. A. Ajemian (vn)—& Lady In the Dark:"Dance of the Tumblers"; Lost In the Stars:"Gold" — Polydor ▲ 839727–2 (m) ■ 839727–4 (m)

Miami String Quartet
Chausson, E.:Con Vn, Pno & Str Qt, w. Aaron Rosand (vn), Seymour Lipkin (pno) — Audiofon ▲ CD 72039
Debussy, C.:Danses sacrée et profane, w. M. Klinko (hp), Lucas Drew (db) — Audiofon ▲ CD 72036
Ginastera, A.:Qt 1 Strs — Pyramid ▲ PYR 13511
Ginastera, A.:Qt 2 Strs — Pyramid ▲ PYR 13511
Ravel, M.:Intro & Allegro, w. M. Klinko (hp), C. Nield (fl), R. Hancock (cl) — Audiofon ▲ CD 72036
Thórarinsson, L.:Qt Strs — Music from Iceland ▲ ITM 705

Miami Univ Oxford String Quartet
Haines, E.:Qt 4 — CRI ■ C 188

Michael Consort
P. Danek (cnd)
Music From the Time of Prince Rudolf II, w. Duodena Cantitans, Capella Rudolphina — Supraphon ▲ SUP 112176 [DDD]

Michigan Chamber Players
M. Dickey (cnd)
Brandt, H.:Con A Sax, w. C. Leaman (a sax) — Redwood ▲ ESCD 45

Michigan State Univ Symphonic Band
K. Brion (cnd)
Grainger, P.:Symphonic Band Music—12 original works, folk music settings & arrs. of works by other composers—Molly on the Shore; Country Gardens [arr. Grainger]; The Immovable Do (or "The Cyphering C"); Colonial Song; "The Gum–Suckers" March; Tuscan Serenade [Fauré]; Chorale No. 2 [Franck]; March [J.S. Bach]; O Mensch, bewein dein' sunde gross [J.S. Bach]; Country Gardens [arr. Sousa]; Ye Banks & Braes o' Bonnie Doon; Children's March, "Over the hills & far away" — Delos ▲ DE 3101 [DDD]

Micrologus Ensemble
Landini & His Contemoraries — Opus 111 ▲ OPS 30–112

Midland–Odessa SO
T. Hohstadt (cnd)
Broughton, B.:Silverado—We'll Be Back *(rec 1988)* — Citadel ▲ STC 77108 [ADD]
Tiomkin, D.:A President's Country *(rec 1988)* — Citadel ▲ STC 77108 [ADD]

Midsummer Mozart Festival Orch
G. Cleve (cnd)
Mozart, W.A.:Con 13 Pno, w. H. Menuhin (pno) *(rec live, Berkeley, CA, July 25, 1987)* — Bainbridge ▲ BCD 6273 [DDD]
Mozart, W.A.:Ovs—Lucio Silla *(rec in public performance, Berkeley, California, July 25, 1987)* — Bainbridge ▲ BCD 6273 [DDD]

Mighty Tubadours
Mighty Tubadours Merry Christmas Album — Crystal ■ C 422
Music Performed by Tuba Quartet — Crystal ▲ CD 420
The Tubadours — Crystal ■ C 421

Milan Academy Orch
D. Eckertsen (cnd)
Corelli, A.:Life & Music of—narration with selected excerpts from Con. grosso, Op. 6/1, 8, 9 & 11; Church Son., Op. 3/1 & 3 ; Son, Op. 5/3 & 12; Son., 4/12 — Vox Music Masters (Music Masters) ▲ MMD 8510 [ADD] ■ MMC 8510

Milan Angelicum CO
C.F. Cillario (cnd)
Mozart, W.A.:Lucio Silla, w. Giulo Bertola (cnd), Milan Polyphonic Choir — Sarx 2-▲ SRX 2019

Milan Angelicum Instrumentalists
G. Petrassi (cnd)
Petrassi, G.:Coro di morti, w. Antonia Ballista (pno), Bruno Canino (pno), Milan Polyphonic Choir — Stradivarius ▲ STV DTM 90001 [ADD]

Milan CO
P. Vaglieri (cnd)
Cambini, G.M.:Cons Hpd, Op. 15/1 & 3, w. F. Redondi (pno) — Nuova Era ▲ 7059 [DDD]
Cambini, G.M.:Sinf concertante Fl & 2 Vns — Nuova Era ▲ 7059 [DDD]
Menotti, G.C.:The Telephone, w. A. V. Banks (mez), G. L. Ricci (bar) [E] — Nuova Era ▲ 7122 [DDD]
Paisiello, G.:La Serva padrona, w. A. V. Banks (mez—Serpina), G. L. Ricci (bar—Umberto) [I] — Nuova Era ▲ 7043 [DDD]

Milan Complesso Barocco
A. Ephrikian (cnd)
Carissimi, G.:Historia divitus — Rivoalto ▲ CRA 8910 [ADD]

Milan Euterpe Collegio Instrumental Ensemble
A. E. Negri (cnd)
Croce, G.:Triaca Musicale, w. Milan Collegio Vocale Euterpe — Stradivarius ▲ STR 33308 [DDD]
Pellegrini, V.:Canzone, w. Milan Euterpe Collegio Vocal Ensemble — Stradivarius ▲ STR 33308 [DDD]

Milan Giuseppe Verdi Large SO
G. Noseda (cnd)
Castelnuovo–Tedesco, M.:Con 1 Gtr, w. Emanuele Segre (gtr) *(rec live, Sala Verdi del Conservatorio, Milan, Dec 1, 2 & 4, 1994)* — Claves ▲ CD 9516 [DDD]
Rodrigo, J.:Concierto de Aranjuez, w. Emanuele Segre (gtr) *(rec live, Sala Verdi del Conservatorio, Milan, Dec 1, 2 & 4, 1994)* — Claves ▲ CD 9516 [DDD]
Villa–Lobos, H.:Con Gtr, w. Emanuele Segre (gtr) *(rec live, Sala Verdi del Conservatorio, Milan, Dec 1, 2 & 4, 1994)* — Claves ▲ CD 9516 [DDD]

Milan Italian Radio–TV Orch
F. Caracciolo (cnd)
Beethoven, L. van:Con 4 Pno, w. M. Pollini (pno) *(rec 1966)* — Arkadia ▲ 533 [AAD]
Beethoven, L. van:Con 6 Pno, w. M. Pollini (pno) *(rec 1966)* — Arkadia ▲ 533 [AAD]
H. von Karajan (cnd)
Humperdinck, E.:Hänsel und Gretel, w. Sena Jurinac (sop), Elisabeth Schwarzkopf (sop), Rita Streich (sop), Vittoria Palombini (mez), Rolando Panerai (bar), Bruna Ronshini (sgr), Milan RAI Chorus — Stradivarius 2-▲ STV 12314
G. Petrassi (cnd)
Petrassi, G.:Salmo IX, w. Milan RAI Chorus — Stradivarius ▲ STV DTM 90001 [ADD]
A. Simonetto (cnd)
Bellini, V.:I Puritani (sels), w. Maria Callas (sop), Milan Italian Radio–TV Chorus—Ah! Vieni al Tempio — Fonit Cetra ("Martini & Rossi" series) ▲ FCT CDMR 5007
Cilea, F.:Adriana Lecouvreur (sels)—Ecco il Monologo [w. Toto Gobbi (bar)]; Troppo Signori...Io Son l'Umile Ancella [w. Rosanna Carteri (sop)] — Fonit Cetra ("Martini & Rossi" series) ▲ FCT CDMR 5008
Donizetti, G.:Don Pasquale (sels), w. Rosanna Carteri (sop)—Quel Guardo il Cavaliere...So Anch'io la Virtù Magica — Fonit Cetra ("Martini & Rossi" series) ▲ FCT CDMR 5008
Mascagni, P.:Lodoletta (sels), w. Rosanna Carteri (sop)—Ah! Il Suo Nome...Flammen Perdonami — Fonit Cetra ("Martini & Rossi" series) ▲ FCT CDMR 5008
Meyerbeer, G.:L'Africaine (sels), w. Gianni Raimondi (ten), Milan Italian Radio–TV Chorus—O Pardiso — Fonit Cetra ("Martini & Rossi" series) ▲ FCT CDMR 5007
Mozart, W.A.:Nozze di Figaro (sels), w. Tito Gobbi (bar)—Aprite un Po' Quegli Occhi — Fonit Cetra ("Martini & Rossi" series) ▲ FCT CDMR 5008
Rossini, G.:Guillaume Tell (sels), w. Tito Gobbi (bar)—Resta Immobile — Fonit Cetra ("Martini & Rossi" series) ▲ FCT CDMR 5008
Rossini, G.:Semiramide (sels), w. Maria Callas (sop), Milan Italian Radio–TV Chorus—Bel Raggio Lusinghiero — Fonit Cetra ("Martini & Rossi" series) ▲ FCT CDMR 5007
Spontini, G.:La vestale (sels), w. Maria Callas (sop), Milan Italian Radio–TV Chorus—Tu Che Invoco con Orrore — Fonit Cetra ("Martini & Rossi" series) ▲ FCT CDMR 5007
Thomas, A.:Hamlet (sels), w. Maria Callas (sop), Milan Italian Radio–TV Chorus—Vi Voglio Offrire i Fiori — Fonit Cetra ("Martini & Rossi" series) ▲ FCT CDMR 5007
Thomas, A.:Mignon (sels), w. Gianni Raimondi (ten), Milan Italian Radio–TV Chorus—Ah! Non Credevi Tu — Fonit Cetra ("Martini & Rossi" series) ▲ FCT CDMR 5007
Verdi, G.:Don Carlos (sels), w. Tito Gobbi (bar)—O Carlo Ascolta — Fonit Cetra ("Martini & Rossi" series) ▲ FCT CDMR 5008
Verdi, G.:Luisa Miller (sels), w. Gianni Raimondi (ten), Milan Italian Radio–TV Chorus—Quando le Sere al Placido — Fonit Cetra ("Martini & Rossi" series) ▲ FCT CDMR 5007
Verdi, G.:Otello (sels), w. Rosanna Carteri (sop)—Mia Madre Aveva...Canzone del Salice — Fonit Cetra ("Martini & Rossi" series) ▲ FCT CDMR 5008

Milan Pomeriggi Musicali Chamber SO
E. Gracis (cnd)
Mozart, W.A.:Con 15 Pno, w. A.B. Michelangeli (pno) — EMI Classics ("Great Recordings of the Century" series) ▲ CDH 63819

Milan Quartet [Roberto Baraldi (vn), Salvatore Quaranta (vn), Maria Ronchini (va), Matteo Ronchini (vc)]
Cesarini, F.:Aubade, w. Andrea Formenti (alt sax) *(rec Sept. 1993 & Jan. 1994)* — Jecklin ▲ JS 302–2

Milan RAI Lyric Orch
Pergolesi, G.B.:La serva padrona, w. Angelica Tuccari (sop), Sesto Bruscantini (bar) — Cetra Classic ▲ CDO 33
M. Rossi (cnd)
Donizetti, G.:La fille du régiment, w. Lina Pagliughi (sop), Rina Corsi (mez), Cesare Valletti (ten), Sesto Bruscantini (bar), Eraldo Coda (bar), Milan RAI Chorus *(rec 1950)* — Cetra Classic 2-▲ CDON 38 [ADD]
A. Simonetto (cnd)
Cilea, F.:Adriana Lecouvreur, w. Carla Gavazzi (sop), Miti Truccato Pace (mez), Giacinto Prandelli (ten), Saturno Meletti (bar), Milan RAI Chorus — Fonit Cetra ("Classic Collection" series) 2-▲ FCT CDO 20
Verdi, G.:Un giorno di regno, w. Lina Pagliughi (sop), Mario Carlin (ten), Juan Oncina (ten), Sesto Bruscantini (bar), Renato Capecchi (bar), Laura Cozzi (sgr), Cristiano Dalamangas (sgr), Milan RAI Chorus *(rec 1951)* — Cetra Classic 2-▲ CDON 37 [ADD]
M. Wolf–Ferrari (cnd)
Verdi, G.:I lombardi alla prima crociata, w. Renata Broilo (sop), Maria Vitale (sop), Miriam Pirazzini (mez), Aldo Bertocci (ten), Mario Frosini (sgr), Mario Petri (bass), Bruno Franchi (sgr), Gustavo Gallo (sgr), Renato Pasquali (sgr), Milan RAI Chorus *(rec 1954)* — Cetra Classic 2-▲ CDON 41 [ADD]

Milan RAI Orch
The Best of the Original "Martini & Rossi" Concerts, w. Turin RAI Orch *(rec 1953–1960)* — Memories 2-▲ MEM 4419 (m) [ADD]
C. F. Cillario (cnd)
Donizetti, G.:Gianni di Parigi, w. L. Serra (sop), E. Zilio (mez), G. Morino (ten), E. Fissore (bar), A. Romero (bar), S. Manga (sgr), Milan RAI Chorus [I] *(rec live)* — Nuova Era 2-▲ 6752/53 [DDD]
E. Gerelli (cnd)
Cherubini, L.:Pimmalione, w. M. Adani (sop), I. Ligabue (sop), G. Carturan (mez), U. Borghi (sgr), Milan RAI Chorus [I] *(rec live 1955)* — Melodram ▲ CDM 19501 [AAD]
C. M. Giulini (cnd)
Verdi, G.:La traviata, w. R. Tebaldi (sop), G. Prandelli (ten), G. Orlandini (bar), Milan RAI Chorus *(rec live 5/28/52)* — Standing Room Only 2-▲ SRO 810–2 [ADD]
F. Mannino (cnd)
Donizetti, G.:La fille du régiment, w. A. Moffo (sop), J. Gardino (mez), G. Campora (ten), G. Fioravanti (bar), Milan RAI Chorus *(rec live Dec 2, 1960)* — Melodram 2-▲ MEL 27018 [ADD]
R. Muti (cnd)
Mendelssohn, F.:St. Paul, w. A. Giebel (sop), O. Dominguez (mez), Theo Altmeyer (ten), S. Nimsgern (b–bar), R. A. El Hage (bass), Milan RAI Chorus [G] *(rec live, Milan, 12/15/70)* — Memories 2-▲ HR 4267/68 (m) [ADD]
N. Sanzogno (cnd)
Renata Tebaldi in Concert, w. Renata Tebaldi (sop) *(rec Nov 30, 1953)* — Standing Room Only 2-▲ SRO 824–2 [ADD]
Simionato & Di Stefano, w. Giulietta Sinionato (mez), Giuseppe Di Stefano (ten), Milan RAI Chorus *(rec Nov. 26, 1956)* — Incontri Memorabili ▲ CDMR 5015
A. Simonetto (cnd)
Leoncavallo, R.:Pagliacci, w. M. Micheluzzi (sop), F. Corelli (ten), M. Carlin (ten), T. Gobbi (bar), L. Puglisi (bar), Milan RAI Chorus *(rec live 9/26/54 from RAI Milan)* — HRE ▲ 1001–1 [ADD]
Mercadante, S.:Il giuramento (sels), w. M. Vitale (sop), M. Pirazzini (mez), R. Panerai (bar), A. Berdini (bar), Milan RAI Chorus [I]—14 scenes & arias *(rec live, Milan, 4/5/51)* — Myto 2-▲ 2 MCD 90632 [ADD]
Verdi, G.:Giovanna d'Arco, w. R. Tebaldi (sop), C. Bergonzi (ten), R. Panerai (bar), Milan RAI Chorus [I] *(rec live)* — Melodram 2-▲ 27021

Milan RAI SO
Arias, w. Maria Callas (sop), Turin RAI SO, Rome RAI SO, Royal Opera House Orch Covent Garden *(rec 1949–1962)* Verona 2-▲ 27058/59 (m) [AAD]
De Cavalieri, Fineschi, Olivero, Stignani, Tassinari, w. Anna de Cavalieri (sop), Ornella Fineschi (sop), Magda Olivero (sop), Ebe Stignani (mez), Pia Tassinari (mez), Rome RAI SO *(rec 1953–58)* Incontri Memorabili ("Martini & Rossi Concerts" series) ▲ 5020

P. Argento (cnd)
Bellini, V.:I Capuleti e i Montecchi (sels), w. Giulietta Simionato (mez)—Ancor di Fiori Sparsa Fonit Cetra ("Martini & Rossi" series) ▲ FCT CDMR 5006
Bellini, V.:La sonnambula (sels), w. Ferruccio Tagliavini (ten)—L'anel ti dono Fonit Cetra ("Martini & Rossi" series) ▲ FCT CDMR 5006
Bizet, G.:Carmen (sels), w. Ferruccio Tagliavini (ten)—Il Fior Che Avevi a Me Tu Dato Nella Prigion Io l'Ho Serbato Fonit Cetra ("Martini & Rossi" series) ▲ FCT CDMR 5006
Donizetti, G.:L'elisir d'amore (sels), w. Ferruccio Tagliavini (ten)—Una Furtiva Lacrima Fonit Cetra ("Martini & Rossi" series) ▲ FCT CDMR 5006
Massenet, J.:Manon (sels), w. Ferruccio Tagliavini (ten)—En fermant les yeux, je vois Fonit Cetra ("Martini & Rossi" series) ▲ FCT CDMR 5006
Massenet, J.:Werther (sels), w. Giulietta Simionato (mez)—Oh Werther! Mio Werther! Fonit Cetra ("Martini & Rossi" series) ▲ FCT CDMR 5006
Rossini, G.:Tancredi (sels), w. Giulietta Simionato (mez)—Di Tanti Palpiti, Di Tante Pene Fonit Cetra ("Martini & Rossi" series) ▲ FCT CDMR 5006
Thomas, A.:Mignon (sels), w. Giulietta Simionato (mez)—Io Consoco un Garzoncello di Boemia Che le Guance Ha Smunte e Sparute Fonit Cetra ("Martini & Rossi" series) ▲ FCT CDMR 5006

A. Basile (cnd)
Giordano, U.:Madame Sans-Gêne, w. Magda László (sop—Caterina), Carlo Tagliabue (bar—Napoleone), Renato Berti (sgr—Despréaux), Irene Callaway (sgr—Toniotta/Carolina), Danilo Cestari (sgr—Neipperg/Vinaigre), Maria Luisa Malacchi (sgr—Giulia/Principessa Elisa), Carlo Perucci (sgr—Fouché), Danilo Vega (sgr—Lefebvre), Enzo Viaro (sgr—De Brigode/Gelsomino), Milan RAI Chorus *(rec Milan, Aug 10, 1957)* Bongiovanni 2-▲ GB 1129/30

S. Celibidache (cnd)
Brahms, J.:Sym 1 *(rec Mar. 1959)* Emozioni ▲ CDAR 2009 [ADD]
Brahms, J.:Vars on a Theme by Haydn *(rec Apr. 18, 1969)* Exclusive 3-▲ EXL 44 [ADD]
Mozart, W.A.:Sym 41 *(rec live 1960)* Memories ▲ HR 4190 (m)
Shostakovich, D.:Sym 9 *(rec live, Milan Feb. 17, 1967)* Arkadia ▲ 765 [ADD]
Sibelius, J.:Valse triste Arkadia ▲ 616
Strauss, R.:Don Quixote, w. M. Amfitheatrof (vc) *(rec 4/11/68)* Arkadia ▲ 570 [ADD]

O. de Fabritiis (cnd)
Gertrud Grob-Prandl, Ferruccio Tagliavini, w. Gertrud Grob-Prandl (sop), Ferruccio Tagliavini (ten) *(rec Dec. 24, 1953)* Incontri Memorabili ("Martini & Rossi Concerts" series) ▲ 5004
Giordano, U.:Fedora, w. Pia Tassinari (sop), Ferruccio Tagliavini (ten), Meletti (sgr), Micheluzzi (sgr), Mascolo (sgr), Jolanda Torriani (sgr), Milan RAI Chorus *(rec live, July 10, 1954)* Arkadia 2-▲ 493

L. Gardelli (cnd)
Leoncavallo, R.:Pagliacci, w. R. Moberg [sop—Nedda], J. Bjoerling [ten—Canio], E. Sundquist [bar—Tonio], Milan RAI Chorus [Sw] *(rec live, Stockholm, 12/8/54)* Legato Classics ▲ LCD 155-1 [ADD]

G. Gavazzeni (cnd)
Donizetti, G.:Anna Bolena, w. Leyla Gencer (sop), Giulieta Simionato (mez), Aldo Bertocci (ten), Plinio Clabassi (bass), Milan RAI Chorus *(rec July 11, 1958)* Agorá Music ("Phoenix" series) 2-▲ 503
Donizetti, G.:Anna Bolena, w. L. Gencer (sop), G. Simionato (mez), A. Bertocci (ten), P. Clabassi (bass), Milan RAI Chorus *(rec 1958)* Memories 2-▲ MEM 4517 [AAD]
Donizetti, G.:Anna Bolena, w. M. Callas (sop—Anna Bolena), G. Simionato (mez—Giovanna Seymour), N. Rossi-Lemeni (bass—Enrico VIII), Milan RAI Chorus *(rec May 14, 1957)* EMI Classics ▲ CDMB 64941
Verdi, G.:Ernani, w. Montserrat Caballè (sop), Bruno Prevedi (ten), Peter Glossop (bar), Boris Christoff (bass), Milan RAI Chorus *(rec Milan, Mar. 25, 1969)* Pantheon 2-▲ PHE 6634 (m)
Zandonai, R.:I cavalieri di Ekebù, w. Fiorenza Cossotto (sop), Gina Longobardo Fiordaliso (sgr), Lando Bartolini (ten), Milan RAI Chorus Fonit Cetra ("Italia" series) 2-▲ FCT CDC 93

E. Gerelli (cnd)
Cherubini, L.:Pimmalione, w. Mariella Adani (sop), Ilva Ligabue (sop), Gabriella Carturan (mez), Umberto Borghi (sgr), Milan RAI Chorus Melodram 2-▲ CDM 29501

C. M. Giulini (cnd)
Cimarosa, D.:Gli Orazii e i Curiazzi, w. G. Simionato (mez), A. Vercelli (mez), G. Del Signore (ten), T. Spataro (ten), Milan RAI Chorus [I] *(rec live 4/13/52)* Melodram 2-▲ CDM 29500 [AAD]

V. Gui (cnd)
Mascagni, P.:L'amico Fritz, w. R. Carteri (sop—Suzel), R. Corsi (mez—Beppe), C. Valletti (ten—Fritz), C. Tagliabue (bar—David), Milan RAI Chorus *(rec live, Apr. 25, 1953)* Bongiovanni 2-▲ GB 1098/99 [ADD]
Rossini, G.:La cambiale di matrimonio, w. E. Fissore (bar) *(rec 1971)* Memories ▲ MEM 4506 [AAD]

A. Janigro (cnd)
Beethoven, L. van:Con 3 Pno, w. Maurizio Pollini (pno) Fonit Cetra ("Emozioni" series) ▲ FCT CDAR 2033

H. von Karajan (cnd)
Humperdinck, E.:Hänsel und Gretel (sels), w. Sena Jurinac (sop—Hänsel), Elisabeth Schwarzkopf (sop—Gretel), Vittoria Palombini (mez—Witch), Rolando Panerai (sgr—Peter), Bruna Ronchini (sgr—Gertrude), Milan RAI Chorus—[Act 1] Suse, liebe Suse, was raschelt im Stroh; [Act 2] Ein Männlein steht im Walde ganz still und Stumm; Abends, will ich schlafen gehn; [Act 3] Wo bin ich? Wach' ich?; Und bist du dann drin...schwaps!; Die Englein haben's im Traum gesagt; Schunt, o schunt das Wunder an *(rec Milan, Dec. 25, 1954)* Legato Classics 3-▲ LCD 197-3

F. Leitner (cnd)
Wagner, R.:Lohengrin (sels), w. M. Pobbe (sop), S. Kónya (ten), A. Protti (bar) [I] *(rec live 1959)* Melodram ▲ MEL 15004 (m) [AAD]

H. Lewis (cnd)
Mahler, G.:Songs from Rückert, w. Marilyn Horne (cta), Rome RAI SO *(rec live, Apr. 30 & June 18, 1971)* Arkadia ▲ 808
Rossini, G.:Arias, w. Marilyn Horne (cta), Rome RAI SO—from Semiramide; Otello; La donna del lago; Tancredi; Cenerentola; L'Italiana in Algeri *(rec live, Apr. 30 & June 18, 1971)* Arkadia ▲ 808

B. Maderna (cnd)
Maderna, B.:Ages, w. Milan RAI Chorus *(rec live, 11/6/72)* Stradivarius ▲ STR 10061 [ADD]

B. Martinotti (cnd)
Beethoven, L. van:Con 5 Pno, "Emperor", w. E. Gilels (pno) *(rec live 4/24/70)* Melodram 2-▲ CDM 28034 [AAD]

F. Molinari-Pradelli (cnd)
Donizetti, G.:Requiem Mass, w. G. Tucci (sop), A. Lazzarini (mez), G. Sinimberghi (ten), I. Sardi (bass), F. Maero (sgr), Milan RAI Chorus [L] *(rec live, Milan 3/21/61)* Memories ▲ HR 4131 [ADD]
Mozart, W.A.:Don Giovanni, w. Leyla Gencer (sop—Donn'Elvra), Teresa Stich-Randall (mez—Donn'Anna), Sesto Bruscantini (bar—Leporello), Mario Petri (bar—Don Giovanni), Milan RAI Chorus Stradivarius 3-▲ STV DTM 12321 [ADD]

T. Petralia (cnd)
Mascagni, P.:Zanetto, w. G. Arista (mez), P. Malgarini (mez) *(rec 1969)* Memories 2-▲ MEM 4519 [AAD]

E. Piazza (cnd)
Cilea, F.:Adriana Lecouvreur (sels), w. Margherita Carosio (sop), Agostino Lazzari (ten), Milan RAI Chorus Fonit Cetra ("Martini & Rossi" series) ▲ FCT CDMR 5010
Cilea, F.:L'Arlesiana (sels), w. Margherita Carosio (sop), Agostino Lazzari (ten), Milan RAI Chorus Fonit Cetra ("Martini & Rossi" series) ▲ FCT CDMR 5010
Donizetti, G.:Don Pasquale (sels), w. Margherita Carosio (sop), Agostino Lazzari (ten), Milan RAI Chorus Fonit Cetra ("Martini & Rossi" series) ▲ FCT CDMR 5010

Milan RAI SO (cont.)
E. Piazza (cnd) (cont.)
Donizetti, G.:Lucia di Lammermoor (sels), w. Margherita Carosio (sop), Agostino Lazzari (ten), Milan RAI Chorus Fonit Cetra ("Martini & Rossi" series) ▲ FCT CDMR 5010
Giordano, U.:Il re (sels), w. Margherita Carosio (sop), Agostino Lazzari (ten), Milan RAI Chorus Fonit Cetra ("Martini & Rossi" series) ▲ FCT CDMR 5010
Mascagni, P.:Nerone (sels), w. Margherita Carosio (sop), Agostino Lazzari (ten), Milan RAI Chorus Fonit Cetra ("Martini & Rossi" series) ▲ FCT CDMR 5010
Pannain, G.:Beatrice Cenci (sels), w. Margherita Carosio (sop), Agostino Lazzari (ten), Milan RAI Chorus Fonit Cetra ("Martini & Rossi" series) ▲ FCT CDMR 5010
Verdi, G.:Nabucco (sels), w. Margherita Carosio (sop), Agostino Lazzari (ten), Milan RAI Chorus Fonit Cetra ("Martini & Rossi" series) ▲ FCT CDMR 5010
Wagner, R.:Tannhäuser (sels), w. Margherita Carosio (sop), Agostino Lazzari (ten), Milan RAI Chorus Fonit Cetra ("Martini & Rossi" series) ▲ FCT CDMR 5010

F. Previtali (cnd)
Rossini, G.:Il barbiere di Siviglia, w. R. Broilo (sop—Berta), G. Simionato (mez—Rosina), L. Infantino (ten—Almaviva), G. Taddei (bar—Figaro), C. Badioli (bass—Bartolo), A. Cassinelli (bass—Basilio), Milan RAI Chorus *(rec 1950)* Cetra Classic 2-▲ CDO 6 [AAD]
Verdi, G.:Il trovatore, w. Leyla Gencer (sop—Leonora), Laura Londi (sop—Ines), Fedora Barbieri (mez—Azucena), Mario del Monaco (ten—Manrico), Athos cesarini (ten—Ruiz), Walter Artioli (ten—Messanger) Ettore Bastianini (bar—Count Luna), Plinio Clabassi (bass—Ferrando), Sergio Liliani (bass—Gypsy), Milan RAI Chorus *(rec live, Milan, May 29, 1957)* Arkadia 2-▲ 483 [ADD]
Verdi, G.:Il trovatore (sels), w. Mario del Monaco (ten), Milan RAI Chorus—Ah! si, ben mio; Di quella pira *(rec Milan, Apr. 8, 1957)* Melodram ▲ CDI 104006 [ADD]
Verdi, G.:Il trovatore (sels), w. Leyla Gencer (sop—Leonora), Laura Londi (sop—Ines), Athos Cesarini (ten—Ruiz), Mario del Monaco (ten—Manrico), Ettore Bastianini (bar), Milan RAI Chorus *(rec Milan, May 18, 1957)* Agorá Music ("Phoenix" series) 3-▲ 510 [ADD]

A. Questa (cnd)
Ebe Stignani, Nicola Lemeni, w. Ebe Stignani (mez), Nicola Rossi Lemeni (bass) *(rec Jan. 31, 1955)* Incontri Memorabili ("Martini & Rossi Concerts" series) ▲ 5013
Paisiello, G.:Fedra, w. O. Beggiato (sop), R. Mattioli (sop), A. Tuccari (sop), L. Udovick (sop), A. Lazzari (ten), Milan RAI Chorus *(rec 1958)* Memories 2-▲ MEM 4502 [AAD]

D. Renzetti (cnd)
Donizetti, G.:La favorita, w. Gloria Scalchi (mez), Luca Canonici (ten), René Massis (bar), Giorgio Surjan (bass), Milan RAI Chorus Fonit Cetra ("Ricordi" series) 3-▲ FCT RFCD 2015

N. Sanzogno (cnd)
Cimarosa, D.:Giannina e Bernardone, w. D. De Cecco (sop), S. Jurinac (sop), G. Sciutti (sop), M. Carlin (ten), M. Boriello (bar), S. Bruscantini (bar), C. De Antoni (sgr), Milan RAI Chorus [I] *(rec live, Milan July 26, 1953)* Melodram 2-▲ CDM 29505 [ADD]
Rosanna Carteri, Antonietta Stella & Beniamino Gigli, w. Rosanna Carteri (sop), Antonietta Stella (sop), Beniamino Gigli (ten), Rome RAI SO, Rome RAI Chorus [cnd:Nino Antonellini] *(rec Milan & Sanremo, Feb. 9, 1953 & Dec. 21, 1)* Incontri memorabili ("Martini & Rossi Concert" series) ▲ CDMR 5005 [ADD]
Rossini, G.:L'italiana in Algeri, w. Teresa Berganza (mez), Alvino Misciano (ten), Sesto Bruscantini (bar), Mario Petri (sgr), Milan RAI Chorus *(rec June 28, 1957)* Pantheon 2-▲ PHE 6646 (m)
Tebaldi, Barbieri & Valletti, w. Renata Tebaldi (sop), Fedora Barbieri (mez), Cesare Valletti (ten), Turin RAI SO *(rec Martini & Rossi Concert, 1951 & 1953)* Incontri Memorabili ▲ CDMR 5012

F. Scaglia (cnd)
Leoncavallo, R.:Pagliacci (sels), w. Mario del Monaco (ten)—Recitar...Vesti la giubba *(rec Milan, May 22, 1957)* Melodram ▲ CDI 104006 [ADD]
Stella, Cossotto & Monaco, w. Antonietta Stella (sop), Fiorenza Cossotto (mez), Mario Del Monaco (ten), Rome RAI SO *(rec Martini & Rossi Concert, 1959 & 1960)* Incontri Memorabili ▲ CDMR 5031
Wagner, R.:Die Walküre (sels), w. Mario del Monaco (ten)—Ein Schwert verhiess mir der Vater; Winterstürme wichen dem Wonnemond *(rec Milan, May 22, 1957)* Melodram ▲ CDI 104006 [ADD]

H. Scherchen (cnd)
Bach, J.S.:Magnificat, BWV 243, w. L. Marimpietri (sop), N. Panni (sop), A. Reynolds (mez), P. Munteanu (ten), B. Carmeli (bass), Milan RAI Chorus [L] *(rec live, Apr 5, 1963)* Memories ▲ HR 4160 (m) [ADD]

T. Serafin (cnd)
Meyerbeer, G.:Les Huguenots, w. A. Pastori (sop), A. de Cavalieri (mez), G. Lauri-Volpi (ten), G. Taddei (bar), G. Tozzi (bass), N. Zaccaria (bass), Milan RAI Chorus *(rec 1956)* Memories 3-▲ MEM 4566 [ADD]

A. Simonetto (cnd)
Callas, Gigli, w. Maria Callas (sop), Beniamino Gigli (ten) *(rec Casino Municipale Opera Theatre, Sanremo, Dec. 27, 1954)* Incontri Memorabili ▲ CDMR 5002
Gencer & Infantino, w. Leyla Gencer (sop), Luigi Infantino (ten) *(rec Martini & Rossi Concert, 1958)* Incontri Memorabili ▲ CDMR 5017
Maria Callas & Gianni Raimondi, w. Maria Callas (sop), Gianni Raimondi (ten), Milan RAI Chorus *(rec Milan, Nov. 19, 1956)* Incontri memorabili ("Martini & Rossi Concert" series) ▲ CDMR 5007 [ADD]
Massenet, J.:Don Quichotte, w. Teresa Berganza (mez), Pina Malgarini (mez), Tommaso Frascati (ten), Carlo Badioli (bass), Boris Christoff (bass), Milan RAI Chorus Melodram 2-▲ CDM 27027
Moffo & Volpi, w. Anna Moffo (sop), Giacomo Lauri Volpi (ten), Rome RAI SO [cnd:Massimo Freccia] *(rec Martini & Rossi Concert, 1960)* Incontri Memorabili ▲ CDMR 5035
Rosanna Carteri, Tito Gobbi, w. Rosanna Carteri (sop), Tito Gobbi (bar) *(rec Dec. 24, 1956)* Incontri Memorabili ("Martini & Rossi Concerts" series) ▲ 5008
Rossini, G.:Elisabetta, regina d'Inghilterra (sels), w. M. Vitale (sop), L. Pagliughi (sop), G. Campora (ten), Pinno (sgr), Milan RAI Chorus—six arias [I] *(rec live, 4/27/53)* Myto 2-▲ 2 MCD 90530 [ADD]
Verdi, G.:Aida (sels), w. Mario del Monaco (ten)—Se quel guerrier...Celeste Aida *(rec Milan, May 22, 1957)* IMC ▲ CDI 104006 [ADD]
Verdi, G.:Giovanna d'Arco, w. Renata Tebaldi (sop), Carlo Bergonzi (ten), Rolando Panerai (bar), Milan RAI Chorus *(rec Milan, May 26, 1951)* Pantheon 2-▲ PHE 6610 (m)
Verdi, G.:Macbeth (sels), w. Mario del Monaco (ten)—O Figli miei. Ah la paterna mano *(rec Milan, May 22, 1957)* Melodram ▲ CDI 104006 [ADD]
Wagner, R.:Lohengrin (sels), w. Mario del Monaco (ten)—In frenem Land *(rec Milan, May 22, 1957)* Melodram ▲ CDI 104006 [ADD]

L. Toffolo (cnd)
Pobbe, Sciutti & Siepi, w. Marcella Pobbe (sop), Graziella Sciutti (sop), Cesare Siepi (bass), Turin RAI SO [cnd:Fulvio Vernizzi] *(rec Martini & Rossi Concert, 1959)* Incontri Memorabili ▲ CDMR 5032

F. Weissman (cnd)
Teresa Berganza, Giuseppe Taddei, w. Teresa Berganza (mez), Giuseppe Taddei (bar) *(rec Dec. 16, 1957)* Incontri Memorabili ("Martini & Rossi Concerts" series) ▲ 5025

Milan Sinfonietta
D. Ferrari (cnd)
Haydn, J.:Stabat Mater, w. R. Lampo (sop), S. Zaramella (alt), V. Martino (ten), P. Turner (bass), Concentus Musicae Antiquae Vocal Group Nuova Era ▲ NUO 7170 [DDD]

Milan Solisti [F. Fantini (vn), M. Ferraris (vn), A. Pocaterra (vc), M. I. DeCarli (org/cembalo)]
Pergolesi, G.B.:Mass in F, w. B. Retchitzka (sop), G. Ferracini (sop), M. Minetto (cta), V. Gohl (cta), C. Jauquier (ten), J. Loomis (bass), Plifonia Choir *(rec 1967)* Rivoalto ▲ RIV 8922 [ADD]

A. Ephrikian (cnd)
Marcello, B.:Cons a cinque, w. Franco Fantini (vn), Genunzio Ghetti (vc)—Nos. 1–6 Rivoalto ▲ RIV 8913 [ADD]
Marcello, B.:Sinfonie a quattro—Nos. 1–5 Rivoalto ▲ RIV 8914 [ADD]
Vivaldi, A.:Cons Vn (misc)—Cons., Op. 6/1–6 Rivoalto ▲ CRA 9006 [ADD]

Milan SO
L. Ferré (cnd)
Beethoven, L. van:Coriolan Ov EPM ▲ EPM 982372 [AAD]
Ferré, L.:Music of, w. Giuseppe Magani (vn), Liège SO—Le chant du hibou; Muss es sein es muss sein; Le superlatif EPM ▲ EPM 982372 [AAD]
Ravel, M.:Con Pno (left hand), w. Dag Achatz (pno) EPM ▲ EPM 982372 [AAD]

▲ = CD ♦ = Enhanced CD Δ = MD ▮ = Cassette Tape ▯ = DCC

Milan SO (cont.)
L. Molajoli (cnd)
Mascagni, P.:Cavalleria rusticana, w. G. Arangi–Lombardi (cta), A. Melandri (ten), G. Lulli (bar), La Scala Chorus [I] *(rec 1930 for Columbia Records)* Standing Room Only ▲ SRO 806–1 (m) [ADD]
Verdi, G.:Falstaff, w. Pia Tassinari (sop—Alice Ford), Ines Alfani Tellini (sop—Nannetta), Aurora Buades (mez—Quickly), Rita Monticone (mez—Meg Page), Roberto D'Alessio (ten—Fenton), Giuseppe Nessi (ten—Bardolfo), Emilio Venturini (ten—Dr. Caius), Emilio Ghirardini (bar—Ford), Giacomo Rimini (bar—Sir John Falstaff), Salvatore Baccaloni (bass—Pistola), La Scala Chorus *(rec La Scala Theatre, Milan, Apr. 1932)* VAI Audio 2–▲ VAIA 1098–2
Verdi, G.:Il trovatore, w. Bianca Scacciati (sop), Giuseppina Zinetti (sop), Francesco Merli (ten), Enrico Molinari (bar), La Scala Chorus *(rec live, 1930)* Melodram ▲ CDI 202002
Milan Teatro alla Scala Orch—see La Scala Orch
Milan Virtuosi
P. Santi (cnd)
Vivaldi, A.:Cons Bn, w. V. Bianchi (bn)—RV.501 Allegretto ▲ ACD 8036 [ADD] ■ ACS 8036
Vivaldi, A.:Cons for 2 Obs, w. A. Caroldi (ob), A. Alvarosi (ob)—RV.535 Allegretto ▲ ACD 8036 [ADD] ■ ACS 8036
Vivaldi, A.:Cons Obs Cls, w. A. Caroldi (ob), A. Alvarosi (ob), E. Schiani (cl), A. Gerbi (cl) Allegretto ▲ ACD 8036 [ADD] ■ ACS 8036
Milano Angelicum Orch
P. Urbini (cnd)
Mendelssohn, F.:Con in d Vn, Pno & Strs, w. Franco Gulli (vn), Enrica Cavallo (pno) Sarx ▲ SRX 2027 [ADD]
Militärmusik Burgenland Wind Ensemble
Intradas & Choral Settings for Organ & Brass, w. Haselböck, Franz (org), Militärmusik Burgenland Wind Ensemble [cnd:Rudolf Schrumpf] Hänssler Classic ▲ 98.544 [AAD]
Millar Brass Ensemble
Tomasi, H.:Fanfares Liturgiques Crystal ▲ CD 433 ■ C 433
B. Briney (cnd)
A Chicago Brass Tradition Koss Classics ▲ KC 1011 [DDD]
Franzetti, C.:Vars (5) Brass *(rec Millar Chapel, Evanston, IL, 1992)* Premier ▲ PRCD 1044 [DDD]
Millar Brass Ensemble Crystal ▲ CD 433 ■ C 433
V. Cichowicz (cnd)
Brass Surround *(rec Alice Millar Chapel, Northwestern University, Evanston, IL, May 8–10 & 12, 1995)* Delos ▲ DE 3171 [DDD]
Millière String Trio
Gossec, F.–J.:Qts Fl, Op. 14, w. P. Bocquillon (fl) Koch Schwann ▲ CD 310 081 [DDD]
Jolivet, A.:Suite Str Trio REM ▲ REM 311196 [DDD]
Martinů, B.:Qt 1 Pno, w. V. Roux (pno) Quantum ▲ QM 6910 [DDD] ■ QM 2004 (D)
Martinů, B.:Trio 2 Vn Quantum ▲ QM 6910 [DDD] ■ QM 2004 (D)
Mozart, W.A.:Qts Cl, w. D. Vidal (cl) Quantum ▲ QM 6905 [DDD] ■ QM 1999 (D)
J.–L. Petit (cnd)
Jolivet, A.:Rhapsodie à 7, w. J. Vandeville (ob), Avray CO REM ▲ REM 311196 [DDD]
Mills College Gamelan Ensemble
Harrison, L.:Double Con, w. Kenneth Goldsmith (vn), Terry King (vc) Music & Arts ▲ CD 635 [AAD]
Milton Keynes City Orch
H.D. Wetton (cnd)
Raff, J.:Sym 3 Hyperion ▲ CDA 66628
Milwaukee SO
Barber, S.:Adagio Strs Pro Arte ("Maxiplay" series) ▲ CDM 879 [DDD]
L. Foss (cnd)
American Festival Pro Arte ▲ CDD 102 [DDD]
Barber, S.:Adagio Strs Pro Arte ▲ CDD 102 [DDD]
Bernstein, L.:Candide (ov) Pro Arte ▲ CDD 102 [DDD]
Foss, L.:Ode *(rec 4/89)* Koss Classics ▲ KC 1004 [DDD]
Foss, L.:Song of Songs, w. C. Page (sop) [E] *(rec 4/89)* Koss Classics ▲ KC 1004 [DDD]
Foss, L.:With Music Strong, w. Milwaukee Sym Chorus *(rec 4/89)* Koss Classics ▲ KC 1004 [DDD]
Schuman, W.:Newsreel Pro Arte ▲ CDD 102 [DDD]
Z. Macal (cnd)
Beethoven, L. van:Sym 9, "Choral Sym", w. Milwaukee Sym Chorus [soloists:B. Valente, J. Taylor, J. F. West, P. Plishka] *(rec 7/31/89)* Koss Classics ▲ KC 1003 [DDD]
Berlioz, H.:Lélio, "Le retourà la vie", w. G. Siebert (ten), W. Diana (bar), W. Klemperer (nar) *(rec 1991)* Koss Classics ▲ KC 1017 [DDD]
Berlioz, H.:Sym fantastique Koss Classics 2–▲ KC 1012 [DDD]
Berlioz, H.:Sym fantastique *(rec 9/89)* Koss Classics ▲ KC 1005 [DDD]
Duffy, J.:Freedom Ov *(rec Uihlein Hall, Milwaukee, WI, Nov. 22, 1993)* Koss Classics ▲ KC 1022 [DDD]
Duffy, J.:Sym 1, "Utah" *(rec Uihlein Hall, Milwaukee, WI, Nov. 22, 1993)* Koss Classics ▲ KC 1022 [DDD]
Duffy, J.:Three Jewish Portraits *(rec Uihlein Hall, Milwaukee, WI, Nov. 22, 1993)* Koss Classics ▲ KC 1022 [DDD]
Duffy, J.:A Time for Remembrance:A Peace Cant, w. Cynthia Clarey (mez), James Earl Jones (nar) *(rec Uihlein Hall, Milwaukee, WI, Nov. 22, 1993)* Koss Classics ▲ KC 1022 [DDD]
Dvořák, A.:Czech Suite *(rec 1988–89)* Koss Classics ▲ KC 1002 [DDD]
Dvořák, A.:Heroic Song Koss Classics ▲ KC 1019
Dvořák, A.:Husitská *(rec 1988–89)* Koss Classics ▲ KC 1001 [DDD]
Dvořák, A.:The Noon Witch Koss Classics ▲ KC 1015 [DDD]
Dvořák, A.:Sym 3 Koss Classics ▲ KC 1019
Dvořák, A.:Sym 4 Koss Classics ▲ KC 1015 [DDD]
Dvořák, A.:Sym 6 *(rec 1988–89)* Koss Classics ▲ KC 1001 [DDD]
Dvořák, A.:Sym 7 *(rec 1/30/90)* Koss Classics ▲ KC 1009 [DDD]
Dvořák, A.:Sym 8 *(rec 1988–89)* Koss Classics ▲ KC 1002 [DDD]
Dvořák, A.:Sym 9, "From the New World" *(rec 1989–90)* Koss Classics ▲ KC 1010 [DDD]
Dvořák, A.:The Water Goblin *(rec 1989–90)* Koss Classics ▲ KC 1010 [DDD]
Dvořák, A.:The Wild Dove *(rec 1/30/90)* Koss Classics ▲ KC 1009 [DDD]
Kodály, Z.:Galanta Dances *(rec 11/89 & 2/90)* Koss Classics ▲ KC 1008 [DDD]
Kodály, Z.:Háry János (suite) *(rec 11/89 & 2/90)* Koss Classics ▲ KC 1008 [DDD]
Kodály, Z.:Vars on a Hungarian Folk Song *(rec 11/89 & 2/90)* Koss Classics ▲ KC 1008 [DDD]
Ott, David:Con for 2 Vcs, w. Daniel Laufer (vc), Wolfgang Laufer (vc) *(rec Uihlein Hall, Milwaukee, Oct 4, 1992)* Koss Classics ▲ KC 1023 [DDD]
Ott, David:Music of the Canvas *(rec Uihlein Hall, Milwaukee, Jan 23, 1994)* Koss Classics ▲ KC 1023 [DDD]
Ott, David:Water Garden *(rec Uihlein Hall, Milwaukee, Jan 23, 1994)* Koss Classics ▲ KC 1023 [DDD]
Prokofiev, S.:Alexander Nevsky, w. J. Taylor (mez), Milwaukee Sym Chorus *(rec Oct. 29, 1990)* Koss Classics ▲ KC 1016 [DDD]
Prokofiev, S.:Lt Kijé Suite, w. Milwaukee Sym Chorus *(rec Oct. 29, 1990)* Koss Classics ▲ KC 1016 [DDD]
Sierra, R.:Idilio, w. Milwaukee Sym Chorus *(rec Mar. 9, 1992)* Koss Classics ▲ KC 1021 [DDD]
Sierra, R.:A Joyous Ov *(rec Mar. 9, 1992)* Koss Classics ▲ KC 1021 [DDD]
Sierra, R.:Preámbulo *(rec Oct. 4, 1992)* Koss Classics ▲ KC 1021 [DDD]
Sierra, R.:SASIMA *(rec Nov. 16, 1991)* Koss Classics ▲ KC 1021 [DDD]
Sierra, R.:Tropicalia *(rec Nov. 16, 1991)* Koss Classics ▲ KC 1021 [DDD]
Smetana, B.:Má Vlast Telarc ▲ CD 80265 [DDD]
K. Schermerhorn (cnd)
Mayer, William:Octagon, w. W. Masselos (pno) CRI ▲ CD 584 [ADD]
Mineria SO
H. de la Fuente (cnd)
Gershwin, G.:Con Pno, w. David Syme (pno) JB Records ▲ 1006–2 ■ 1006–4

Mineria SO (cont.)
H. de la Fuente (cnd) (cont.)
Gershwin, G.:"I Got Rhythm" Vars, w. David Syme (pno) JB Records ▲ 1006–2 ■ 1006–4
Gershwin, G.:Porgy & Bess (sels), w. D. Newman (sop), A. Woodley (bar), New Philharmonia Orch, Oklahoma City Ambassors Choir IMP Classics ▲ IMPPCD 1057 [DDD]
Gershwin, G.:Rhap in Blue, w. David Syme (pno) JB Records ▲ 1006–2 ■ 1006–4
Gershwin, G.:Rhap in Blue, w. D. Syme (pno) IMP Classics ▲ IMPPCD 1057 [DDD]
Orff, C.:Carmina burana, w. Gabriela Herrera (sop), Frank Kelley (ten), Ben Holt (bar), Minería Sym Choir IMP ("Classic" series) ▲ IMP 2024
Saint–Saëns, C.:Con 1 Vc, w. C. Prieto (vc) IMP Classics ▲ IMPPCD 1084 [DDD]
Minneapolis Artists Ensemble
Hummel, J.N.:Qnt Pno, Op. 87 GM ▲ 2025CD
Ives, C.:Adagio cantabile Innova ■ MCF 002 (D)
Ives, C.:Largo cantabile Innova ■ MCF 002 (D)
Ives, C.:Scherzo Str Qt Innova ■ MCF 002 (D)
Larsen, L.:Four on the Floor Innova ■ MCF 002 (D)
Mozart, W.A.:Grande Sestetto Concertante GM ▲ 2025CD
Minneapolis Guitar Quartet [Alan Johnston (gtr), Joseph Hagedorn (gtr), O. Nicholas Raths (gtr), David Crittenden (gtr)]
Bassett, L.:Narratives Albany ▲ TROY 207 [DDD]
Brouwer, L.:Cuban Landscape with Rumba Albany ▲ TROY 207 [DDD]
Hovda, E.:Armonia Albany ▲ TROY 207 [DDD]
Kechley, D.:Voices from the Garden Albany ▲ TROY 207 [DDD]
Sekiya, N.:Tobila Albany ▲ TROY 207 [DDD]
Vandervelde, J.:Genesis V Albany ▲ TROY 207 [DDD]
Minneapolis SO
A. Dorati (cnd)
Bartók, B.:Con 2 Vn, w. Yehudi Menuhin (vn) *(rec Carnegie Hall, New York City, Feb. 17, 1957)* Mercury Living Presence ▲ 434350–2
Bartók, B.:Hungarian Sketches Mercury Living Presence ▲ 432005–2 [ADD]
Bartók, B.:Romanian Dances Mercury Living Presence ▲ 432005–2 [ADD]
Bartók, B.:Suite 2 Orch *(rec Northrop Auditorium, Minneapolis, MN, Nov. 26, 1955)* Mercury Living Presence ▲ 434350–2
Bloch, E.:Sinfonia breve Mercury Living Presence ▲ 434329–2 [ADD]
Copland, A.:Danzón Cubano Mercury Living Presence ▲ 434301–2 [ADD]
Copland, A.:Rodeo Mercury Living Presence ▲ 434329–2 [ADD]
Copland, A.:El salón México Mercury Living Presence ▲ 434301–2 [ADD]
Delibes, L.:Coppélia, ou La fille aux yeux d'émail Mercury Living Presence 3–▲ 434313–2 [ADD]
Fetler, P.:Contrasts *(rec Minneapolis, Apr. 17, 1960)* Mercury Living Presence ▲ 434335–2
Gershwin, G.:An American in Paris Mercury Living Presence ▲ 434329–2 [ADD]
Kodály, Z.:Galanta Dances Mercury Living Presence ▲ 432005–2 [ADD]
Kodály, Z.:Háry János (suite) Mercury Living Presence ▲ 432005–2
Kodály, Z.:Marosszék Dances Mercury Living Presence ▲ 432005–2 [ADD]
Mussorgsky, M.:Pictures at an Exhibition *(rec Minneapolis, Apr. 21, 1959)* Mercury Living Presence ▲ 434346–2
Prokofiev, S.:The Love for 3 Oranges (suite) Mercury Living Presence ▲ 432753–2 [ADD]
Prokofiev, S.:Scythian Suite Mercury Living Presence ▲ 432753–2 [ADD]
Rachmaninoff, S.:Con 2 Pno, w. B. Janis (pno) Mercury Living Presence ▲ 432759–2 [ADD]
Respighi, O.:The Fountains of Rome Mercury Living Presence ▲ 432007–2 [ADD]
Respighi, O.:The Pines of Rome Mercury Living Presence ▲ 432007–2 [ADD]
Rossini, G.:Ovs, w. London SO—ovs. to La Gazza ladra; La Scala di seta; La Cenerentola; La Barbieri di Siviglia; L'Italiana in Algeri; Il Signor Bruschino Mercury Living Presence ▲ 434345–2
Schuller, G.:Studies on Themes of Paul Klee Mercury Living Presence ▲ 434329–2 [ADD]
Strauss, R.:Don Juan Mercury Living Presence ▲ 434348–2
Strauss, R.:Der Rosenkavalier (suite) [arr. Dorati] Mercury Living Presence ▲ 434348–2
Strauss, R.:Till Eulenspiegels lustige Streiche Mercury Living Presence ▲ 434348–2
Strauss, R.:Tod und Verklärung Mercury Living Presence ▲ 434348–2
Stravinsky, I.:Le Sacre du printemps for Orch *(rec Nov. 15, 1959)* Mercury Living Presence ▲ 434331–2
Tchaikovsky, P.:Francesca da Rimini Mercury Living Presence ▲ 434373–2
Tchaikovsky, P.:Ov 1812, w. Univ of Minnesota Brass Band [Bronze cannon courtesy of U.S. Military Academy, West Point] Mercury Living Presence ▲ 434 360–2
Tchaikovsky, P.:Sym 5 Mercury Living Presence ▲ 434305–2 [ADD]
Verdi, G.:Ovs & Preludes, w. London SO—ovs. from La Forza del destino; Nabucco; I Vespri siciliani; La Traviata [Preludes to Acts 1 & 3] Mercury Living Presence ▲ 434345–2
D. Mitropoulos (cnd)
Beethoven, L. van:Coriolan Ov Grammofono 2000 ▲ GRM 78608 (m)
Beethoven, L. van:Coriolan Ov Grammofono 2000 4–▲ GRM 78646
Beethoven, L. van:Coriolan Ov *(rec Jan 10, 1940)* Nickson ▲ NN 1007 [ADD]
Beethoven, L. van:Leonore 3 Grammofono 2000 ▲ GRM 78608 (m)
Beethoven, L. van:Leonore 3 Grammofono 2000 4–▲ GRM 78646
Beethoven, L. van:Sym 6, "Pastorale" *(rec 1940)* Grammofono 2000 ▲ GRM 78509 [ADD]
Beethoven, L. van:Sym 6, "Pastorale" Grammofono 2000 4–▲ GRM 78646
Borodin, A.:Sym 2 Grammofono 2000 4–▲ GRM 78646
Borodin, A.:Sym 2 *(rec 1940)* Grammofono 2000 ▲ GRM 78509 [ADD]
Brahms, J.:Vars on a Theme by Haydn *(rec Apr 4, 1942)* Nickson ▲ NN 1007 [ADD]
Busoni, F.:Spanish Rhap Pno, w. E. Petri (pno) *(rec 1938)* Pearl ▲ PEA 9347 (m) [AAD]
Chausson, E.:Sym in B♭ *(rec Mar 9, 1946)* Nickson 2–▲ NN 1008/1009 (m) [ADD]
Chopin, F.:Con 1 Pno, w. Edward Kilenyi (pno) *(rec Dec 6, 1941)* Nickson 2–▲ NN 1008/1009 (m) [ADD]
Chopin, F.:Music of—Chopiniana [arr Lewitzky] Grammofono 2000 4–▲ GRM 78646
Dukas, P.:L'Apprenti sorcier Grammofono 2000 ▲ GRM 78608 (m)
Dukas, P.:L'Apprenti sorcier Grammofono 2000 4–▲ GRM 78646
Lalo, E.:Le Roi d'Ys (ov) *(rec Mar 2, 1945)* Nickson 2–▲ NN 1008/1009 (m) [ADD]
Mahler, G.:Sym 1 Grammofono 2000 4–▲ GRM 78646
Mahler, G.:Sym 1 *(rec 1940)* Theorema ▲ TH 121152
Mahler, G.:Sym 1 Sony Classical ("Masterworks Heritage" series) ▲ MHK 62342
Mahler, G.:Sym 1 *(rec Nov. 4, 1940)* Grammofono 2000 ▲ GRM 78566
Mendelssohn, F.:Sym 3 *(rec 1941–56)* Nickson ▲ NN 1010 [ADD]
Rachmaninoff, S.:The Isle of the Dead Sony Classical ("Masterworks Heritage" series) ▲ MHK 62342
Rimsky–Korsakov, N.:Golden Cockerel (suite) *(rec Mat 2, 1945)* Nickson ▲ NN 1007 [ADD]
Schumann, R.:Sym 2 Grammofono 2000 4–▲ GRM 78646
Schumann, R.:Sym 2 *(rec Dec 3, 1940)* Nickson 2–▲ NN 1008/1009 (m) [ADD]
Schumann, R.:Sym 3 *(rec Jan 20, 1947)* Nickson ▲ NN 1007 [ADD]
Skalkottas, N.:Greek Dances—Peloponnesiakos; Epirotikos; Hostianos; Kleftikos *(rec 1941–56)* Nickson ▲ NN 1010 [ADD]
Tchaikovsky, P.:Sym 2 *(rec 1941–56)* Nickson ▲ NN 1010 [ADD]
Tchaikovsky, P.:Sym 4 Grammofono 2000 ▲ GRM 78608 (m)
Tchaikovsky, P.:Sym 4 Grammofono 2000 4–▲ GRM 78646
Weber, C.M. von:Jubel–Ov *(rec Mar 11, 1946)* Nickson 2–▲ NN 1008/1009 (m) [ADD]
S. Skrowaczewski (cnd)
Ravel, M.:Alborada del gracioso Analogue Productions ▲ CAPC 007
Ravel, M.:Fanfare Analogue Productions ▲ CAPC 007
Ravel, M.:Menuet antique Analogue Productions ▲ CAPC 007
Ravel, M.:Rapsodie espagnole Analogue Productions ▲ CAPC 007
Ravel, M.:La Valse Analogue Productions ▲ CAPC 007
Schubert, Franz:Sym 9 *(rec Northrop Memorial Auditorium, Univ. of Minnesota, Nov. 26, 1961)* Mercury Living Presence ▲ 434354–2
Schumann, R.:Con Pno, w. B. Janis (pno) Mercury Living Presence ▲ 432011–2 [ADD]
Shostakovich, D.:Sym 5 Mercury Living Presence ▲ 434323–2 [ADD]

Minnesota Opera Orch

P. Brunelle (cnd)

Argento, D.:Postcard from Morocco, w. S. Roche, B. Brandt, J. Hardy, Y. Marshall, V. Sutton, B. Busse, M. Foreman — CRI 2-▲ CD 614 [ADD]

Minnesota Orch

Keillor, G.:Lake Woebegon Days–A Recital, w. G. Keillor (speaker) — Virgin Classics ▲ CDC 59583

N. Marriner (cnd)

Britten, B.:The Young Person's Guide to the Orchestra — EMI Classics ▲ CDD 64300 [DDD]
Haydn, J.:Con 1 Vn, w. Cho-Liang Lin (vn) — CBS ▲ MK 39310 ■ MT 39310
Haydn, J.:Con 1 Vn, w. Cho-Liang Lin (vn) — CBS ▲ MK 37796 [DDD]
Larsen, L.:Sym, "Water Music" — Elektra/Nonesuch ▲ 79147-2
Mozart, W.A.:Music of, German Bach Soloists—Con 4 Vn; Haffner Serenade; Eine kleine Nachtmusik; etc. — Pro Arte ▲ CDM 807 ■ PCD 807
Paulus, S.:Sym in 3 Movts — Elektra/Nonesuch ▲ 79147-2
Vieuxtemps, H.:Con 5 Vn, w. Cho-Liang Lin (vn) — CBS ▲ MK 37796 [DDD]
Wagner, R.:Ovs, Preludes & Orch Sels—Die Meistersinger; Rienzi; Der fliegende Holländer — Telarc ▲ CD 82005

D. Mitropoulos (cnd)

Beethoven, L. van:Leonore 3 — Nickson ▲ N 1006 [ADD]
Dimitri Mitropoulos Conducts, Document Two — Nickson ▲ NN 1002 [ADD]
Document Three *(rec 1940–1950)* — Nickson ▲ NN 1003 [AAD]
Document Four:Popular Concert Favorites and Encores — Nickson ▲ NN 1004 [AAD]
Document Five — Nickson ▲ NN 1005 [ADD]
Rachmaninoff, S.:The Isle of the Dead — Nickson ▲ N 1006 [ADD]
Rachmaninoff, S.:Sym 2 — Nickson ▲ N 1006 [ADD]

E. Oue (cnd)

Stravinsky, I.:Le Chant du rossignol *(rec Orchestra Hall, Minneapolis, MN, Jan 18–20, 1996)* — Reference ▲ RR 70
Stravinsky, I.:The Firebird Suite [1919 version] *(rec Orchestra Hall, Minneapolis, MN, Jan 18–20, 1996)* — Reference ▲ RR 70
Stravinsky, I.:Le Sacre du printemps Orch *(rec Orchestra Hall, Minneapolis, MN, Jan 18–20, 1996)* — Reference ▲ RR 70

S. Skrowaczewski (cnd)

Bartók, B.:Con Orch *(rec 1976–77)* — Vox Box 3-▲ CD3X 3015 [ADD]
Bartók, B.:Dance Suite *(rec 1982)* — Vox Box 3-▲ CD3X 3015 [ADD]
Bartók, B.:Divert *(rec 1976–77)* — Vox Box 3-▲ CD3X 3015 [ADD]
Bartók, B.:The Miraculous Mandarin (suite) *(rec 1976–77)* — Vox Box 3-▲ CD3X 3015 [ADD]
Bartók, B.:Music for Strs, Perc & Cel *(rec 1976–77)* — Vox Box 3-▲ CD3X 3015 [ADD]
Bartók, B.:The Wooden Prince *(rec 1976–77)* — Vox Box 3-▲ CD3X 3015 [ADD]
Beethoven, L. van:Gratulations-Menuet — Vox Box 2-▲ CDX 5099 [ADD]
Beethoven, L. van:Incidental Music—from The Consecration of the House:Ov., Op. 124; Chorus for Soprano & Chorus [w. P. Bryn-Julson (soprano), Bach Society of Minnesota]; from The Ruins of Athens:Ov., Op. 113; Turkish March, Op. 113/4; March & Chorus, Op. 114, "Schmuckt die Altare"; Tarpeja:Triumphal March, WoO 2 — Vox Box 2-▲ CDX 5099 [ADD]
Beethoven, L. van:Meeresstille und glückliche Fahrt, w. P. Bryn-Julson (sop), Minnesota Bach Society — Vox Box 2-▲ CDX 5099 [ADD]
Beethoven, L. van:Ovs—Leonore 1, 2 & 3; Fidelio; Coriolan; Egmont; Die Geschöpfe des Prometheus; König Stephen; Namensfeier; Die Weihe des Hauses — Vox Box 2-▲ CDX 5099 [ADD]
Mayer, William:Andante — Phoenix ▲ PHCD 120 [AAD]
Mayer, William:Pastels — Phoenix ▲ PHCD 120 [AAD]
Prokofiev, S.:The Love for 3 Oranges (suite) *(rec 1977)* — Vox Box 3-▲ CD3X 3016 [ADD]
Prokofiev, S.:Romeo & Juliet (sels) *(rec 1977)* — Vox Box 3-▲ CD3X 3016 [ADD]
Prokofiev, S.:Scythian Suite *(rec 1983)* — Vox Box 3-▲ CD3X 3016 [ADD]
Ravel, M.:Alborada del gracioso — Vox Box 2-▲ CDX 5031 [ADD]
Ravel, M.:Une Barque sur l'océan — Vox Box 2-▲ CDX 5032 [ADD]
Ravel, M.:Boléro — Vox Box 2-▲ CDX 5031 [ADD]
Ravel, M.:Daphnis et Chloé (suite 1) — Vox Box 2-▲ CDX 5032 [ADD]
Ravel, M.:Daphnis et Chloé (suite 2) — Vox Box 2-▲ CDX 5032 [ADD]
Ravel, M.:Fanfare — Vox Box 2-▲ CDX 5032 [ADD]
Ravel, M.:Ma mère l'oye Orch — Vox Box 2-▲ CDX 5032 [ADD]
Ravel, M.:Menuet antique — Vox Box 2-▲ CDX 5031 [ADD]
Ravel, M.:Orchestral Music — Vox Box 2-▲ CDX 5032 [ADD]
Ravel, M.:Orchestral Music — Vox Box 2-▲ CDX 5031 [ADD]
Ravel, M.:Pavane pour une infante défunte — Vox Box 2-▲ CDX 5031 [ADD]
Ravel, M.:Rapsodie espagnole — Vox Box 2-▲ CDX 5031 [ADD]
Ravel, M.:Le Tombeau de Couperin — Vox Box 2-▲ CDX 5032 [ADD]
Ravel, M.:La Valse — Vox Box 2-▲ CDX 5032 [ADD]
Ravel, M.:Valses nobles et sentimentales — Vox Box 2-▲ CDX 5031 [ADD]
Ravel, M.:Valses nobles et sentimentales [orchd.] — Analogue Productions ▲ CAPC 007
Skrowaczewski, S.:Con E Hn, w. Thomas Stacy (E hn) — Phoenix ▲ PHCD 120 [AAD]
Stravinsky, I.:The Firebird Suite *(rec 1983)* — Vox Box 3-▲ CD3X 3016 [ADD]
Stravinsky, I.:Pétrouchka *(rec 1977)* — Vox Box 3-▲ CD3X 3016 [ADD]
Stravinsky, I.:Le Sacre du printemps Orch *(rec 1977)* — Vox Box 3-▲ CD3X 3016 [ADD]

L. Slatkin (cnd)

Tchaikovsky, P.:The Nutcracker (sels) — Pro Arte ▲ CDS 582 [DDD]
Tchaikovsky, P.:Nutcracker Suite — Pro Arte ▲ CDD 184 ■ PCD 184
Tchaikovsky, P.:Swan Lake (sels) — Pro Arte ▲ CDS 582 [DDD]
Viennese Sommerfest! — Pro Arte ▲ CDG 3224 [DDD]

E. de Waart (cnd)

Bernstein, L.:On the Town—3 Dance Episodes — Virgin Classics ("Ultraviolet" series) ▲ CUV 61194
Bernstein, L.:On the Town — Virgin Classics ▲ 59619 [DDD]
Bernstein, L.:West Side Story (symphonic dances) — Virgin Classics ▲ 59619 [DDD]
Bernstein, L.:West Side Story (symphonic dances) — Virgin Classics ("Ultraviolet" series) ▲ CUV 61194
Brahms, J.:Con Vn, w. N. Salerno-Sonnenberg (vn) — EMI Classics ▲ CDC 49429 [DDD]
Bruch, M.:Con 1 Vn, w. N. Salerno-Sonnenberg (vn) — EMI Classics ▲ CDC 49429 [DDD]
Gershwin, G.:An American in Paris — Virgin Classics ("Ultraviolet" series) ▲ CUV 61194
Gershwin, G.:An American in Paris — Virgin Classics ▲ 59619 [DDD]
Gershwin, G.:Cuban Ov — Virgin Classics ▲ CDZ 59693
Gershwin, G.:Rhap in Blue, w. G. Ohlsson (pno) — Virgin Classics ▲ 59619 [DDD]
Gershwin, G.:Rhap in Blue, w. Garrick Ohlsson (pno) — Virgin Classics ("Ultraviolet" series) ▲ CUV 61194
Glazunov, A.:Scènes de ballet *(rec Jan. 18–19, 1993)* — Telarc ▲ CD 80347 [DDD]
Glazunov, A.:The Seasons *(rec Jan. 18–19, 1993)* — Telarc ▲ CD 80347 [DDD]
Mahler, G.:Sym 1 — Virgin Classics ("Ultraviolet" series) ▲ CUV 61258
Strauss, R.:Don Juan — Virgin Classics ▲ CDC 59234
Strauss, R.:Don Quixote, w. Stephen Isserlis (vc) — Virgin Classics ("Ultraviolet" series) ▲ CUV 61266
Strauss, R.:Don Quixote, w. S. Isserlis (vc) — Virgin Classics ▲ CDC 59234
Strauss, R.:Suite Wws — Virgin Classics ▲ 59066 [DDD]
Strauss, R.:Symphonia domestica — Virgin Classics ▲ 59066 [DDD]
Strauss, R.:Till Eulenspiegels lustige Streiche — Virgin Classics ▲ CDC 59234
Wuorinen, C.:Sacred Music—Mass for the Restoration of St. Luke in the Fields; A Solis Ortu; Ave Christe; Genesis — Koch International Classics ▲ KIC 7336 [DDD]

Minsk Orch

W. Keitel (cnd)

Rossini, G.:La gazetta, w. Teresa Verdera (sop), Gianpiero Ruggeri (sgr), Kasimierz Sergiel (sgr), Ezio Maria Tisi (sgr), Motet & Madrigal Posen Chamber Chorus — Deutsche Schallplatten ▲ DS 1053
Schubert, Franz:Sym 4 — Deutsche Schallplatten ▲ DS 1039
Schubert, Franz:Sym 5 — Deutsche Schallplatten ▲ DS 1039

Minsk PO

S. Frontalini (cnd)

Bossi, M.E.:Con Org, w. A. Sacchetti (org) — Bongiovanni ▲ GB 5512 [DDD]
Bossi, M.E.:Ov, Op. 1 — Bongiovanni ▲ GB 5512 [DDD]
Bossi, M.E.:Siciliana & Gigue, w. A. Sacchetti (org) — Bongiovanni ▲ GB 5512 [DDD]
Bossi, M.E.:Symphonic Fant, w. A. Sacchetti (org) — Bongiovanni ▲ GB 5512 [DDD]
Caggiano, N.:Alla Città di Ferrara — Bongiovanni ▲ GB 5032 [DDD]
Caggiano, N.:La Tomba del Busento — Bongiovanni ▲ GB 5032 [DDD]
Ponchielli, A.:Music of—Elegy for Grand Orch.; Sinfonias 1 & 2; Scena Campestre; Sinfonias from *I Lituani* & *I Promessi Sposi*; Gavotte Poudrée *(rec 9/90)* — Bongiovanni ▲ GB 2115 [DDD]

Minsk State PO

P.-D. Ponnelle (cnd)

Mahler, G.:Sym 10 *(rec June 1–7, 1994)* — Musicaphon 2-▲ M 56953 [DDD]
Shostakovich, D.:Sym 5 *(rec June 1–7, 1994)* — Musicaphon 2-▲ M 56953 [DDD]
Tchaikovsky, P.:Hamlet *(rec Minsk, July 27–30, 1993)* — Musicaphon ▲ 56951 [DDD]
Tchaikovsky, P.:Romeo & Juliet *(rec Minsk, July 27–30, 1993)* — Musicaphon ▲ 56951 [DDD]
Tchaikovsky, P.:The Tempest *(rec Minsk, July 27–30, 1993)* — Musicaphon ▲ 56951 [DDD]

Minstrelsy

Vieni o cara — Lyrichord ("Early Music" series) ▲ LEMS 8023

Mirecourt Trio

Brahms, J.:Trio 3 Pno — Music & Arts ▲ CD 706-1 [DDD]
Brahms, J.:Trio in A Pno (posth) — Music & Arts ▲ CD 706-1 [DDD]
Cowell, H.:Combinations (4) — Music & Arts ▲ CD 635 [AAD]
Cowell, H.:Trio in 9 Short Movements — Music & Arts ▲ CD 686 [DDD]
Litolff, H.C.:Trio Vn, Vc & Pno — Genesis ▲ GCD 101 [ADD]
Persichetti, V.:Parable 23 — Music & Arts ▲ CD 686 [DDD]
Reale, P.V.:Trio Vn — Music & Arts ▲ CD 635 [AAD]
Reale, P.V.:Trio 2 Vn — Music & Arts ▲ CD 686 [DDD]
Sowash, R.:Anecdotes & Reflections, w. C. Olzenak (clarinet) — Gasparo ▲ GS 285
Sowash, R.:Daweswood Suite, w. C. Olzenak (cl) — Gasparo ▲ GS 285
Sowash, R.:Pno Trios—No. 1, "Four Seasons in Bellville" (1977); No. 2, "Orientale & Galop" (1980); No. 3, "A Christmas Divertimento" (1983); No. 4 (1983; rev. 1989) — Gasparo ▲ GS 254

Mirecourt Trio [John Jensen (pno), Kenneth Goldsmith (vn), Terry King (vc)]

Chihara, P.:Elegy — Music & Arts ▲ MUA CD 934
Cowell, H.:Music of—Scenario; Wedding Anniversary Music [both w. Albert Muenzer (vn)]; Duet Vn Vc; Andante — Music & Arts ▲ MUA CD 934
Creston, P.:Trio Pno, Op. 112 — Music & Arts ▲ MUA CD 934
Luening, O.:Trio 1 Pno, Vn & Vc — Music & Arts ▲ MUA CD 934

Miró Trio

Boccherini, L.:Trios Vn, G.95-100 — Christophorus 2-▲ 77174

Mirring String Quartet

Mozart, W.A.:Diverts Str Qt, K.136-138 — LaserLight ▲ 15 861 [DDD]
Mozart, W.A.:Divert Str Qt, K.136 — Berlin Classics ▲ BER 1141 [DDD]
Mozart, W.A.:Divert Str Qt, K.137 — Berlin Classics ▲ BER 1141 [DDD]
Mozart, W.A.:Divert Str Qt, K.138 — LaserLight ▲ 15 647 [DDD]
Mozart, W.A.:Divert Str Qt, K.138 — Berlin Classics ▲ BER 1141 [DDD]
Mozart, W.A.:Qt 1 Strs — LaserLight ▲ 15 878 [DDD]
Mozart, W.A.:Qt 1 Strs — Berlin Classics ▲ BER 1141 [DDD]
Mozart, W.A.:Qt 2 Strs — Berlin Classics ▲ BER 1141 [DDD]

Miskolc SO

L. Kovács (cnd)

Khachaturian, A.:Spartacus (sels), w. Miklós Szenthelyi (vn) — Classical Diamonds ▲ 4008 [ADD]
Rimsky-Korsakov, N.:Scheherazade — Classical Diamonds ▲ 4008 [ADD]

Missouri Brass Quintet [Keith Benjamin (tpt), Jay Sollenberger (tpt), Ann Ellsworth (hn), John Leisenring (trbn), Daniel Burdick (tuba)]

Festival of Organ & Brass, w. John Obetz (org), Jon Donald (perc) *(rec RLDS Peace Temple, Independence, MO)* — RBW ▲ RBWCD 008

Missouri Quintet [Steve Geibel (fl), Dan Willett (ob), Paul Garritson (cl), Laurence Lowe (hn), Barbara Wood (bn)]

Maslanka, D.:Qnt 1 Ww *(rec Dulaney Auditorium, William Woods Univ., Fulton, MO)* — Cambria ▲ CD 1079 [DDD]
Maslanka, D.:Qnt 2 Ww *(rec Dulaney Auditorium, William Woods Univ., Fulton, MO)* — Cambria ▲ CD 1079 [DDD]

Mistral Trio

Bottesini, G.:Andante e variazione Fl — Giulia ▲ GIU 201032 [DDD]
Donizetti, G.:Trio Fl — Giulia ▲ GIU 201032 [DDD]
Pacini, G.:Divert Fl — Giulia ▲ GIU 201032 [DDD]
Ponchielli, A.:Il Convegno — Giulia ▲ GIU 201032 [DDD]

Mistry String Quartet

Bax, A.:Qt 2 Strs — Chandos ▲ CHAN 8795 [DDD]
Bax, A.:Qnt Pno & Strs, w. D. Owen Norris (pno) — Chandos ▲ CHAN 8795 [DDD]

MIT SO

D. Epstein (cnd)

Barber, S.:Con Pno, w. A. Ruskin (pno) *(rec 1976)* — Vox Box 2-▲ CDX 5069 [ADD]
Barber, S.:Con Pno, w. A. Ruskin (pno) — Vox Box 2-▲ CDX 5091 [ADD]
Hanson, H.:Con Pno, w. Eugene List (pno) — Vox Box 2-▲ CDX 5091 [ADD]
Piston, W.:The Incredible Flutist (suite) *(rec 1976)* — Vox Box ("The American Composers" series) 2-▲ CDX 5157
Ravel, M.:Con Pno (left hand), w. Adriano Jordao (pno) — MP Classics ("European" series) ▲ 3-11014
Ravel, M.:Con in G Pno, w. Adriano Jordao (pno) — MP Classics ("European" series) ▲ 3-11014

Roscoe Mitchell New Chamber Ensemble [Thomas Buckner (sgr), Roscoe Mitchell (sax/ww/perc), Joseph Kubera (pno), Vartan Manoogian (vn)]

Mitchell, R.:Music of—O the Sun Comes Up-Up-Up in the Opening; He Didn't Give Up...He Was Taken; Sound Pictures, No. 3; Alternate Express; Childe Harold's Pilgrimage Canto 1, Verses 13-15; To Styles Holloway & Bubba Barnes; Sound Pictures, No. 4; Spirits Among Stones *(rec Merkin Concert Hall & Marv Nonn Studios, Cross Plains, WI)* — Lovely Music ▲ LCD 2022 [DDD]
Mitchell, R.:NONAAH — Lovely Music ▲ LCD 2021 [AAD]
Mitchell, R.:Prelude — Lovely Music ▲ LCD 2021 [AAD]

Mobile Ensemble

Neue Schweizer Werke [New Swiss Works] *(rec 1993)* — Jecklin ▲ JS 296-2 [ADD]

Mobius [P. Johnson (pno), M. Fitzpatrick (vn), X. Bjerken (vc)]

Beethoven, L. van:Trio 4 Pno, "Ghost" — Mobius 2-▲ D 0193
Brahms, J.:Trio 1 Pno — Mobius 2-▲ D 0193
Mobius:Improvs—Trauma Center; Please, Somebody, One for the New Age...ers; Stormy Weather — Mobius 2-▲ D0193
Ravel, M.:Trio Pno — Mobius 2-▲ D 0193
Shostakovich, D.:Trio 2 Pno — Mobius 2-▲ D 0193

Moda Theater Ensemble

Frescobaldi, G.:Canzonas for Instrumental Ensemble—17 sels. — Pierre Verany ▲ PVY 793092 [DDD]

Modena Teatro Comunale Orch

L. Magiera (cnd)

Verdi, G.:La traviata (sels), w. Luciano Pavarotti (ten)—Lunge da lei...de' miei bollenti spiriti *(rec live, Feb. 7, 1965)* — RCA Gold Seal ▲ 09026-68014-2 [ADD]

▲ = CD ♦ = Enhanced CD Δ = MD ■ = Cassette Tape □ = DCC

Modena Teatro Comunale Orch (cont.)
N. Verchi (cnd)
Bellini, V.:I Puritani, w. Mirella Freni (sop—Elvira), Rita Bezzi (mez—Enrichetta), Alfredo Kraus (ten—Arturo Talbot), Augusto Pedroni (ten—Sir Bruno Robertson), Attilio d'Orazi (bar—Sir Riccardo Forth), Raffaele Arié (bass—Sir Giorgio), Bruno Cioni (bass—Lord Gualtiero Walton), Modeno Teatro Comunale Chorus *(rec Modena Teatro Comunale, Dec. 26, 1962)* Legato Classics 2-▲ LCD 195-2 [ADD]
Modern Mandolin Quartet [Mike Marshall (mand), Dana Rath (mand), Paul Binkley (mandola/gtr), John Imholz (mandocello)]
Bimstein, P.K.:The Louie Louie Vars Starkland ▲ ST 205 [DDD]
Jaffe, D.A.:Grass Valley Fire, 1988 Well-Tempered Productions ▲ WTP 5164 [DDD]
Mozart, W.A.:Music of, w. Philip Aaberg, Todd Boekelheide, Chris Botti, Henry Adam Curtis, Steve Erquiaga, Béla Fleck, Eugene Friesen, Paul McCandless, Tim Story, Richard Schönherz, Tracy Scott Silverman, Thea Suits-Silverman, ValGardena Imaginary Road ▲ 314534065-2 ■ 314534065-4
20th Century String Music of the Americas, Vol. 1:Brazil, Cuba, Argentina, USA, w. Tom Miller (triangle/pandeiro/tamborim/shaker/brake drum/surdo/bongos/steel pans) Windham Hill ▲ 01934-11135-2 ■ 01934-11135-4
Modì Quartet [G. Pianezzola (vn), E. Begnis (vn), M. Righini (va), C. Frigerio (vc)]
Paisiello, G.:Qts Strs—Nos. 2 in A, 5 in E♭, 6 in C & 8 in G *(rec Jan. 20-22, 1993)* Bongiovanni ▲ GB 5526 [DDD]
Modo Antiquo
Ghirardello da Firenze Nuova Era ▲ NUO 7151 [DDD]
F. M. Sardelli (cnd)
Vivaldi, A.:Cons Diverse Instrs—Con grosso à 10 stromenti, R.562; Con for His Royal Highness of Saxony, R.576; Con for 2 Fls, 2 Obs, Bn, 2 Vns & Strs, R.566; Con for 2 Hns & Strs, R.538; Con for 2 Hunting Hns, 2 Obs, Bn, Vn & Strs, R.569 Tactus ▲ TC 672206 [DDD]
Vivaldi, A.:Fl Music—Con in e for Fl & Strs, RV.431; Con in D for Fl & Strs, RV.783; Con in e for Fl & Strs, RV.432; Sinf in G for Fl & Strs, RV.68; Son in C for Trns Fl & Bc, RV.48; Son in g for Trns Fl & Bc, RV.51; Cant for Sop, Trns Fl & Bc, RV.678 [All'ombra di sospetto] Tactus ▲ TC 672204 [DDD]
Modo Antiquo [F. M. Sardelli (fl/trns fl), U. Galasso (fl), P. Cipriani (vn) P. Focardi (vn), B. Hoffmann (vc), P. Fanciullacci (bass vl), G. L. Lastraioli (thb), A. Clemente (hpd)]
Scarlatti, A.:Sinf di con grosso Fl—3 Cons. in a; Con. in c; Con. in D; Con. in g; Con. in C; Con. in F; Con. in A *(rec May & June 1991)* Tactus ▲ TC 661902 [DDD]
Modo Antiquo [M. Gatti (fl), F. M. Sardella (fl), P. Foccardi (vn), A. Ciccolini (vn), P. Fanciullacci (vn), F. Presutti (va), B. Hoffmann (vc), A. Santi (bn), G. L. Lastraioli (thb), A. Fedi (hpd)]
Vivaldi, A.:Cons Fl (misc)—Cons. in D, D, G & a, RV.427, 429, 436 & 440 *(rec Oct. 1993)* Tactus ▲ TC 672202 [DDD]
Modus Chamber Ensemble
C. Franzetti (cnd)
Franzetti, C.:Concertino Bass Trbn, w. David Taylor (b trbn), Lois Colin (hp), Carlos Franzetti (pno) *(rec Hip Pocket Studios, New York)* Premier ▲ PRCD 1044 [DDD]
Franzetti, C.:Con Ob, w. Blair Tindall (ob), Allison Brewster Franzetti (pno) *(rec Hip Pocket Studios, New York)* Premier ▲ PRCD 1044 [DDD]
Franzetti, C.:Images Before Dawn, w. Anthony Jackson (contrabass gtr) *(rec Hip Pocket Studios, New York)* Premier ▲ PRCD 1044 [DDD]
Franzetti, C.:Suite Fl, w. Jorge de la Vega (fl), Carlos Franzetti (pno) *(rec Hip Pocket Studios, New York)* Premier ▲ PRCD 1044 [DDD]
Moldavian National SO
S. Frontalini (cnd)
Casella, A.:Italia *(rec Chisinau, CSI, Dec 1993)* Arts ▲ 447211-2 [DDD]
Respighi, O.:La Boutique fantastique *(rec Chisinau, CSI, Dec 1993)* Arts ▲ 447211-2 [DDD]
Moldavian PO
D. Goya (cnd)
Lazarev, E.:Master & Margarita Russian Disc ▲ RUS 10016 [AAD]
A. Lascae (cnd)
Enescu, G.:Romanian Rhap 1 Ottavo ▲ OTT 49240 [DDD]
Enescu, G.:Romanian Rhap 2 Ottavo ▲ OTT 59344 [DDD]
Enescu, G.:Suite 1 Orch Ottavo ▲ OTT 49240 [DDD]
Enescu, G.:Suite 3 Orch, "Villageoise" Ottavo ▲ OTT 49240 [DDD]
Enescu, G.:Sym 3, w. Gavril Musicescu Chorus Ottavo ▲ OTT 59344 [DDD]
Moldavian Radio-TV SO
C. Florea (cnd)
Eckart, E.:Anastasis Gallo ▲ CD 841 [DDD]
Eckart, E.:Beatus Ille Gallo ▲ CD 841 [DDD]
S. Frontalini (cnd)
Donizetti, G.:Music of—orchestral highlights from *Les Martyrs, Ugo Conte di Parigi, Linda di Chamounix, Rosmonda D'Inghilterra, L'Ajo nell'imbrazzo, M. di Rohan & Fausta* Bongiovanni ▲ GB 2138
D. Pacitti (cnd)
Copland, A.:Con Cl, w. Daniel Pacitti (cl), Carlo Balzaretti (pno) Agorá ▲ 026 [DDD]
Piazzolla, A.:Contemplación y danza, w. Daniel Pacitti (cl) Agorá ▲ 026 [DDD]
Moldavian SO
S. Frontalini (cnd)
Bizet, G.:Les Pêcheurs de perles (sels)—Je crois entendre encore *(rec Dec 1992)* Bongiovanni ▲ GB 8001 [DDD]
Donizetti, G.:Arias—Favorita del rel...Spirto gentil [from La Favorita]; Ina furtiva lacrima [from L'elisir d'amore] *(rec Dec 1992)* Bongiovanni ▲ GB 8001 [DDD]
Gounod, C.:Faust (sels)—Quel trouble inconnu...Salut demeure chaste et pure *(rec Dec 1992)* Bongiovanni ▲ GB 8001 [DDD]
Ponchielli, A.:La Gioconda (sels)—Cielo e mar *(rec Dec 1992)* Bongiovanni ▲ GB 8001 [DDD]
Puccini, G.:Arias—Nessun dorma [from Turandot]; Donna non vidi mai [from Manon Lescaut]; Che gelida manina [from La Bohème]; E lucevan le stelle, Recondita armonia [from Tosca] *(rec Dec 1992)* Bongiovanni ▲ GB 8001 [DDD]
Verdi, G.:Arias—O fede negar potessi...Quando le sere al placido [from Luisa Miller]; Parmi veder le lacrime [from Rigoletto]; Forse la soglia attinse...Ma se m'è forza perderti [from Un ballo in maschera]; O figli...Ah la paterna mano [from Macbeth]; La vita è un inferno...O tu che in seno agli angeli [from La forza del destino] *(rec Dec 1992)* Bongiovanni ▲ GB 8001 [DDD]
Moldova Philharmonia
A. Lascae (cnd)
Enescu, G.:Concert Ov Ottavo ▲ OTT 69450 [DDD]
Enescu, G.:Suite 2 Orch Ottavo ▲ OTT 69449 [DDD]
Enescu, G.:Symphonie concertante, w. Godfried Hoogeveen (vc) Ottavo ▲ OTT 69449 [DDD]
Enescu, G.:Sym 2 Ottavo ▲ OTT 69450 [DDD]
Molino Trio [Bent Larsen (fl), Lars Grunth (va), Jan Sommer (gtr)]
Matiegka, W.T.:Grand Trio Fl, Va & Gtr *(rec Apr 1996)* Classico ▲ CLASSCD 154
Matiegka, W.T.:Notturno *(rec Apr 1996)* Classico ▲ CLASSCD 154
Matiegka, W.T.:Serenade in C Fl Va & Gtr *(rec Apr 1996)* Classico ▲ CLASSCD 154
Monaco PO
C. Schuricht (cnd)
Brahms, J.:Sym 3 *(rec live 5/19/63)* Melodram ▲ CDM 18047 [ADD]
Monadnock Music Festival Orch
J. Bolle (cnd)
Becker, J.J.:Con arabesque, w. Anthony de Mare (pno) Koch International Classics ▲ KIC 7207 [DDD]
Becker, J.J.:Sound Piece 1, w. Anthony de Mare (pno) Koch International Classics ▲ KIC 7207 [DDD]
Bolle, J.:Con Ob, w. Basil Reeve (ob) Gasparo ▲ GSCD 317 [DDD]
Haydn, J.:Sym 35 [period instrs] Albany ▲ TROY 018-2 [DDD]
Haydn, J.:Sym 47 [period instrs] Albany ▲ TROY 018-2 [DDD]
Haydn, J.:Sym 65 [period instrs] Albany ▲ TROY 018-2 [DDD]
Sowerby, L.:Con Hp, w. Stephen Hartman (hp) Gasparo ▲ GSCD 315 [DDD]

Monadnock Music Festival Orch (cont.)
J. Bolle (cnd) (cont.)
Sowerby, L.:Rhap Gasparo ▲ GSCD 315 [DDD]
Thomson, V.:Lord Byron, w. J. Ommerlé (sop), D. Fortunato (mez), M. Lord (ten), R. Zeller (bar), R. Johnson (bar) [E] *(rec live, Aug. 31 & Sept. 2, 1991)* Koch International Classics 2-▲ KIC 7124-2 [DDD]
Thomson, V.:Sym 2 Albany ▲ AR 017-2 [DDD]
Le Monde Classique
Mîca, F.A.:L'origine di Jaromeriz in Moravia, w. Geraldine Cassidy (sgr), Manfred Equiluz (sgr), Geraldine Geister (sgr), Michael Nowak (sgr) [Cz] Supraphon 2-▲ SUP 112192 [DDD]
Mondriaan Quartet
L. Vis (cnd)
Janssen, G.:Noach, w. Claron McFaddon (sop—Noach's Wife), Lieuwe Visser (bass—Noach), Huib Rooymans (nar), New Artis Orch, Ay-Kherel Ensemble *(rec Amsterdam, June 20-21, 1994)* Donemus 2-▲ CV 42/43
Monnaie Piano Trio [D. Blumenthal (pno), T. Adamopoulos (vn), G. Zanlonghi (vc)]
Lekeu, G.:Trio Pno, Vn & Vc Koch Schwann ▲ CD 310060 [DDD]
Montagnana Trio
Glinka, M.:Trio pathétique Facet ▲ FCD 8003 [AAD]
Indy, V. d':Trio Cl Facet ▲ FCD 8004 [AAD]
Montclaire String Quartet
Hoover, K.:Qnt Pno & Strs, "Da pacem", w. Leslie Petteys (pno) Koch International Classics ▲ KIC 7147 [DDD]
Loeffler, C.M.:Music for 4 Str Instruments Koch International Classics ▲ KIC 7147 [DDD]
Stevens, H.:Qnt Fl, w. Wendell Dobbs (vlute), Leslie Petteys (pno) Koch International Classics ▲ KIC 7147 [DDD]
Monte Carlo Opera Orch
A. de Almeida (cnd)
Donizetti, G.:Ballet Music, Philharmonia Orch Philips ("Duo" series) 2-▲ 442553-2
Rodrigo, J.:Concert-Serenade, w. C. Michel (hp) Philips ("Solo" series) ▲ 442392-2
Rodrigo, J.:Concierto de Aranjuez, w. A. Lagoya (gtr) Philips ("Solo" series) ▲ 442392-2
Rodrigo, J.:Fant para un gentilhombre, w. A. Lagoya (gtr) Philips ("Solo" series) ▲ 442392-2
Rossini, G.:Ballet Music, Philharmonia Orch Philips ("Duo" series) 2-▲ 442553-2
R. Bonynge (cnd)
Delibes, L.:Lakmé, w. J. Sutherland (sop), A. Vanzo (ten), G. Bacquier (bar) [F] London 2-▲ 425485-2 [ADD]
F. Cleva (cnd)
Catalani, A.:La Wally, w. L. Marimpietri (sop), R. Tebaldi (sop), M. del Monaco (ten), P. Cappuccilli (bar), Justino Diaz (bass), Turin Lyric Chorus [I] London 2-▲ 425417-2 [ADD]
A. Galliera (cnd)
Ravel, M.:Con Pno (left hand), w. W. Hass (pno) Philips 2-▲ 438353-2
Ravel, M.:Con in G Pno, w. W. Hass (pno) Philips 2-▲ 438353-2
L. Gardelli (cnd)
Giordano, U.:Fedora, w. M. Olivero (sop), M. del Monaco (ten), T. Gobbi (bar) London ("Grand Opera" series) 2-▲ 433033-2 [ADD]
J.E. Gardiner (cnd)
Massenet, J.:Don Quichotte (sels) Erato ▲ 45859-2
Massenet, J.:Suite 3 Erato ▲ 45859-2
Massenet, J.:Suite 4 Erato ▲ 45859-2
Massenet, J.:Suite 6 Erato ▲ 45858-2
Massenet, J.:Suite 7 Erato ▲ 45859-2
Massenet, J.:La Vierge Erato ▲ 45858-2
A. Jordan (cnd)
Debussy, C.:Première rapsodie, w. Antony Morf (cl) Erato ▲ 94679-2
I. Markevitch (cnd)
Auric, G.:Les Fâcheux Adès ▲ ADE 203762 [AAD]
Milhaud, D.:Le train bleu Adès ▲ ADE 203762 [AAD]
Poulenc, F.:Les Biches Adès 2▲ ADE 203762 [AAD]
Satie, E.:Jack in the Box Adès ▲ ADE 203762 [AAD]
Sauguet, H.:La Chatte Adès ▲ ADE 203762 [AAD]
P. Paray (cnd)
Ravel, M.:Pavane pour une infante défunte FNAC Music ▲ 642318
Ravel, M.:La Valse FNAC Music ▲ 642318
Ravel, M.:Valses nobles et sentimentales FNAC Music ▲ 642318
E. van Remoortel (cnd)
Goetz, H.:Francesca von Rimini (ov) Genesis ▲ GCD 105 [ADD]
Goetz, H.:Frühlings-Ov Genesis ▲ GCD 105 [ADD]
Goetz, H.:Sym, Op. 9 Genesis ▲ GCD 105 [ADD]
Goetz, H.:Der Widerspenstigen Zähmung (ov) Genesis ▲ GCD 105 [ADD]
Litolff, H.C.:Con Symphonique 4, w. G. Robbins (pno) Genesis ▲ GCD 101 [ADD]
Reinecke, C.:Cons Pno, w. G. Robbins (pno) Genesis ▲ GCD 102 [ADD]
N. Rescigno (cnd)
Zandonai, R.:Francesca da Rimini (sels), w. M. Olivero (sop), A. Gasparini (mez), A. Cesarini (ten), M. del Monaco (ten), V. Carbonari (bass) London ("Grand Opera" series) 2-▲ 433033-2 [ADD]
C. Scimone (cnd)
Doppler, A.F.:Con Fls, w. A. Adorjan (fl), J.-P. Rampal (fl) *(rec 1977)* Erato ▲ 2292-45836-2 [ADD]
Monte Carlo PO
French Opera Arias for Tenor, w. Rockwell Blake (ten), Monte Carlo Phil Chorus [cnd:Patrick Fournillier] EMI Classics ▲ CDC 55058
S. Cambreling (cnd)
Massenet, J.:Con Pno, w. A. Ciccolini (pno) EMI Classics ▲ CDM 64277
M. Constant (cnd)
Constant, M.:Napoléon Erato ▲ 94813
Honegger, A.:Le Chant de Nigamon Erato ▲ 2292-45862-2
Honegger, A.:Monopartita Erato ▲ 2292-45862-2
Honegger, A.:Napoléon (film music) Erato ▲ 94813
Honegger, A.:Napoléon (suite) Erato ▲ 2292-45862-2
Honegger, A.:Phèdre Erato ▲ 2292-45862-2
Honegger, A.:Prélude, fugue et postlude Erato ▲ 2292-45862-2
Honegger, A.:La Tempête (prelude) Erato ▲ 2292-45862-2
J. DePreist (cnd)
Bennett, Richard Rodney:Con Vn, w. Vadim Gluzman (vn) Koch International Classics ▲ KIC 7341
Bennett, Richard Rodney:Diversions Koch International Classics ▲ KIC 7341
Bennett, Richard Rodney:Sym 3 Koch International Classics ▲ KIC 7341
Bizet, G.:Carmen (suite 1) *(rec Casino of Monte Carlo, Monaco, June 24-27, 1996)* Delos ▲ DE 3208 [DDD]
Indy, V. d':Souvenirs Koch International Classics ▲ KIC 7280 [DDD]
Indy, V. d':Sym 2 Koch International Classics ▲ KIC 7280 [DDD]
Shchedrin, R.:Carmen *(rec Casino of Monte Carlo, Monaco, June 24-27, 1996)* Delos ▲ DE 3208 [DDD]
L. Foster (cnd)
Auber, D.-F.:Zerline (sels), w. Marilyn Horne (mez) Erato ("Recital" series) ▲ 98501-2
Cooper, P.:Con 2 Vn, w. R. Patterson (vn) CRI ▲ CD 579 [ADD]
Donizetti, G.:La favorita (sels), w. Marilyn Horne (mez) Erato ("Recital" series) ▲ 98501-2
Enescu, G.:Oedipe, w. B. Hendricks (sop), B. Fassbaender (mez), M. Lipovšek (mez), J. Taillon (mez), N. Gedda (ten), J. Aler (ten), G. Bacquier (bar), Quilico (bar), J. Van Dam (bass-bar), Orféon Donostiarra, Petits Chanteurs de Monaco [F] EMI Classics 2-▲ CDCB 54011 [DDD]
Gershwin, G.:An American in Paris Erato ("Bonsai" series) ▲ 2292-45929-2 ■ 2292-45929-4
Gershwin, G.:Con Pno, w. G. Tacchino (pno) Erato ("Bonsai" series) ▲ 2292-45929-2 ■ 2292-45929-4

Monte Carlo PO (cont.)
L. Foster (cnd) (cont.)
Gershwin, G.:Rhap in Blue, w. G. Tacchino (pno)
Erato ("Bonsai" series) ▲ 2292-45929-2 ▮ 2292-45929-4
Godard, B.:La Vivandiere (sels), w. Marilyn Horne (mez) Erato ("Recital" series) ▲ 98501-2
Gounod, C.:Sappho (sels), w. Marilyn Horne (mez) Erato ("Recital" series) ▲ 98501-2
Mendelssohn, F.:Con in d Vn & Strs, w. O. Charlier (vn) Erato ▲ 92869-2
Mendelssohn, F.:Con in e Vn & Orch, Op. 64, w. O. Charlier (vn) Erato ▲ 92869-2
Paganini, N.:Con 2 Vn, w. A. Dubach (vn) [Cadenza Dubach] *(rec Sept. 23-26, 1993)*
Claves ▲ CD 9408 [DDD]
Paganini, N.:Con 3 Vn, w. Alexandre Dubach (vn) Claves ▲ CD 9503
Paganini, N.:Con 5 Vn, w. A. Dubach (vn) [Cadenza Dubach] *(rec Sept. 23-26, 1993)*
Claves ▲ CD 9408 [DDD]
Paganini, N.:Con 6 Vn, w. Alexandre Dubach (vn) Claves ▲ CD 9503
Romantic Interlude, w. Strausbourg PO [cnd:Armin Jordan], et al. Lind ▮ LI 701
Saint-Saëns, C.:Samson et Dalila (sels), w. Marilyn Horne (mez) Erato ("Recital" series) ▲ 98501-2
Zamfir, G.:Black Waltz, w. G. Zamfir (panpipes) Philips ▲ 412221-2 [DDD]
Zamfir, G.:Con 1 Panpipes, w. G. Zamfir (panpipes) Philips ▲ 412221-2 [DDD]
Zamfir, G.:Couleurs d'automne, w. G. Zamfir (panpipes) Philips ▲ 412221-2 [DDD]
Zamfir, G.:Rhap du printemps, w. G. Zamfir (panpipes) Philips ▲ 412221-2 [DDD]
D. Garforth (cnd)
Borodin, A.:Prince Igor (sels) Arion ▲ ARN 60331
Rimsky-Korsakov, N.:Scheherazade Arion ▲ ARN 60331
A. Jordan (cnd)
Berlioz, H.:Les Nuits d'été, w. F. Pollet (sop) *(rec June 30-July 3, 1993)*
FNAC Music ▲ 592275 [DDD]
Chausson, E.:Poème de l'amour et de la mer, w. F. Pollet (sop) *(rec June 30-July 3, 1993)*
FNAC Music ▲ 592275 [DDD]
A. Myrat (cnd)
Koechlin, C.:Ballade Pno, w. B. Rigutto (pno) EMI Classics ▲ CDM 64369
Koechlin, C.:The Seven Stars Sym EMI Classics ▲ CDM 64369
P. Olmi (cnd)
Virtuoso Arias, w. Sumi Jo (sop) *(rec Auditorium de l'Orchestre Philharmonique, Monte Carlo, June 1994)* Erato ▲ 97239-2 [DDD]
P.-D. Ponnelle (cnd)
Wagner, R.:Arias & Scenes, w. M. Egel (bar)—arias & scenes from Fliegende Holländer *(Die Frist ist um)*, Das Liebesverbot *(Ja, glühend, wie des Südens Hauch...)*, Parsifal *(Wehvolles Erbe, dem ich verfallen)*, Tannhäuser *(O! du mein holder Abendstern)*, Walküre *(Leb Wohl, du Kühnes)* [G]
FSM ▲ FCD 97214 [DDD]
G. Prêtre (cnd)
Caplet, A.:Conte fantastique EMI Classics ▲ CDM 64687
Debussy, C.:La Chute de la maison Usher, w. C. Barbaux (sop), J.P. Lafont (bass)
EMI Classics ▲ CDM 64687
Poulenc, F.:Aubade Pno, w. G. Tacchino (pno) EMI Classics ▲ CDM 64714
Poulenc, F.:Con Pno, w. G. Tacchino (pno) EMI Classics ▲ CDM 64714
Poulenc, F.:Con for 2 Pnos, w. B. Ringeissen (pno), G. Tacchino (pno) EMI Classics ▲ CDM 64714
Schmitt, F.:Le palais hanté, w. C. Barbaux (sop), J.P. Lafont (bass) EMI Classics ▲ CDM 64687
N. Rescigno (cnd)
Bellini, V.:Arias, w. J. Anderson (sop)—I puritani—Son vergin vezzosa; Ah! rendetemi la speme...Qui la voce...Vien diletto; I Capuleti e i Montecchi—Eccomi in lieta vesta...Oh! quante volte; La sonnambula—Oh! se una volta...Ah! non credea mirarti...Ah! non giunge; Beatrice di Tenda—Oh! miei fideli...Ma la sola...Ah! la pena [I] EMI Classics ▲ CDC 47561 [DDD]
D. Robertson (cnd)
Lalo, E.:Namouna Valois ▲ V 4677
Saint-Saëns, C.:Andromaque Valois ▲ V 4688 [DDD]
Saint-Saëns, C.:Javotte Valois ▲ V 4688 [DDD]
Saint-Saëns, C.:Rapsodie bretonne Valois ▲ V 4688 [DDD]
Saint-Saëns, C.:Suite algérienne Valois ▲ V 4688 [DDD]
Schmitt, F.:Rêves Valois ▲ V 4687
Schmitt, F.:Symphonie concertante, w. H. Sermet (pno) Valois ▲ V 4687
M. Soustrot (cnd)
Auber, D.-F.:Fra Diavolo, w. M. Mesplé (sop—Zerline), J. Berbié (mez—Lady Pamela), N. Gedda (ten—Fra Diavolo), R. Corazza (ten—Lord Cockburn), T. Dran (ten—Lorenzo), J. Bastin (bass—Matheo), Jean LaForge Ensemble Choir EMI Classics ▲ CDCB 54810
Heroines of Romantic French Opera, w. Denyce Graves (mez) Fnac Music ▲ 592056
P. Verrot (cnd)
Herrmann, B.:Con Macabre, w. Danielle Laval (pno) *(rec Monte Carlo, July 1995)*
Travelling ("Music & Movies" series) ▲ K 1019 [DDD]
Hossein, A.:Con 3 Pno, w. Danielle Laval (pno) *(rec Monte Carlo, July 1995)*
Travelling ("Music & Movies" series) ▲ K 1019 [DDD]
Legrand, M.:Concertino Pno, w. Danielle Laval (pno) [from the film Summer of '42] *(rec Monte Carlo, July 1995)*
Travelling ("Music & Movies" series) ▲ K 1019 [DDD]
Wiener, J.:Con 1 Pno, w. Danielle Laval (pno) *(rec Monte Carlo, July 1995)*
Travelling ("Music & Movies" series) ▲ K 1019 [DDD]

Monte Carlo Pro Arte Quintet
Borodin, A.:Qnt Pno & Strs Valois ▲ V 4702 [DDD]
Shostakovich, D.:Qnt Pno Valois ▲ V 4702 [DDD]
Montepulciano Arts Center Orch
S. Sanna (cnd)
Mascagni, P.:Sì, w. Vivian (sop), A. Felle (sop), Maria Gentile (sop), M.G. Liguori (sop), Nicoletti (sgr), Comas (sgr), Montepulciano Arts Center Chorus [I] *(rec live, 7/24/87)*
Bongiovanni 2-▲ GB 2050/51 [DDD]
Claudio Monteverdi Accademia Venice
H. L. Hirsch (cnd)
Marcello, B.:Sons Fl *(rec Aria Studio, Italy, Nov 1985)* Arts ▲ 47214-2 [DDD]
Monteverdi Orch
J.E. Gardiner (cnd)
Berkeley, L.:Con Gtr, w. J. Bream (gtr) RCA ▮ ALK1-9535
Handel, G.F.:Coronation Anthems (4) for George II, w. Monteverdi Choir London—Anthem No. 1
Erato ▲ 2292-45136-2 ▮ 2292-45136-4
Handel, G.F.:Dixit Dominus, w. *(soloists unknown)*, Monteverdi Choir London
Erato ▲ 2292-45136-2 ▮ 2292-45136-4
Handel, G.F.:Israel in Egypt, w. Norma Burrowes (sop), Charles Brett (ct), Paul Elliot (ten), Monteverdi Choir London Erato 2-▲ 2292-45399-2 ZA
Handel, G.F.:The Ways of Zion Do Mourn, w. Norma Burrowes (sop), Charles Brett (ct), Paul Elliot (ten), Monteverdi Choir London Erato 2-▲ 2292-45399-2 ZA
Highlights from the Julian Bream Edition, w. Julian Bream (gtr), George Malcolm (hpd), Julian Bream Consort RCA Gold Seal ▲ 09026-61848-2
Purcell, H.:Come Ye Sons of Art, w. Monteverdi Choir London
Erato ("Gardiner Purcell Collection" series) ▲ 96553-2
Purcell, H.:Music for the Funeral of Queen Mary, w. Monteverdi Choir London
Erato ("Gardiner Purcell Collection" series) ▲ 96553-2
Purcell, H.:The Prophetess, or The History of Dioclesian, w. L. Dawson (sop), Gillian Fisher (sop), R. Covey-Crump (ten), P. Elliot (ten), S. Varcoe (bar), M. George (bass), Monteverdi Choir London
Erato ("Gardiner Purcell Collection" series) 2-▲ 96556-2
Purcell, H.:The Tempest, w. Monteverdi Choir London
Erato ("Gardiner Purcell Collection" series) ▲ 96555-2
Purcell, H.:Timon of Athens, w. L. Dawson (sop), Gillian Fisher (sop), R. Covey-Crump (ten), P. Elliot (ten), S. Varcoe (bar), M. George (bass), Monteverdi Choir London
Erato ("Gardiner Purcell Collection" series) 2-▲ 96556-2

Monteverdi Orch (cont.)
J.E. Gardiner (cnd) (cont.)
Rameau, J.P.:La Danse, w. J. Gomez (sop), A.-M. Rodde (sop), J.-C. Orliac (ten), Monteverdi Choir London Erato ▲ 45985-2
Rodrigo, J.:Concierto de Aranjuez, w. J. Bream (gtr)
RCA Victor ▲ 09026-61724-2; ▮ 09026-61724-4 (CrO2)
Rodrigo, J.:Concierto de Aranjuez, w. J. Bream (gtr)
RCA Gold Seal ▲ 6525-2-RG [ADD] ▮ 6525-4-RG (CrO2)
Rodrigo, J.:Concierto de Aranjuez, w. J. Bream (gtr) RCA ▮ ALK1-9535
W. Kelber (cnd)
Brixi, F.X.:Con 1 for 2 Tpts, w. C. Hammer (org) *(rec 1993)* Calig ▲ CAL 50927 [DDD]
Schütz, H.:Symphoniae Sacrae Calig ▲ CAL 50941
Monticello Trio
Bresnick, M.:Trio Pno CRI ▲ CD 583 [DDD]
Ives, C.:Trio Pno CRI ▲ CD 583 [DDD]
Maw, N.:Trio Pno ASV ▲ ASV 920 [DDD]
Shatin, J.:Ignoto numine CRI ▲ CD 583 [DDD]
Monticello Trio members
Maw, N.:Qt Fl, w. Judith Pearce (fl), Judith Pearce (va) ASV ▲ ASV 920 [DDD]
Montilla Orch
D. Montorio (cnd)
Coros de zarzuelas, w. Montilla Chorus Montilla ▲ MNT 3028
Montpellier Brass Quintet
R. Bosc (cnd)
Bernstein, L.:Music of, w. Diagonales Brass & Percussion Ensemble—West Side Story Suite [arr. Bosc]; Dance Suite; Elegy for Mippy [I & II]; Fanfare for Bima; Waltz for Mippy III; Rondo for Lifey; Anniversary for Aaron Copland Agora Music ▲ 007
Copland, A.:Fanfare for the Common Man, w. Diagonales Brass & Percussion Ensemble
Agora Music ▲ 007
Copland, A.:Inaugural Fanfare, w. Diagonales Brass & Percussion Ensemble Agora Music ▲ 007
Montpellier Languedoc-Roussillon PO
F. Layer (cnd)
Schumann, C.:Con Pno, w. Enrica Ciccarelli (pno)—Romanze [w. Cyrille Tricoire (vc)] *(rec Opera Berlioz, Le Corum, Montpellier, June 14-16, 1995)* Agorá ▲ 014 [DDD]
Schumann, R.:Con Pno, w. Enrica Ciccarelli (pno) *(rec Opera Berlioz, Le Corum, Montpellier, June 14-16, 1995)* Agorá ▲ 014 [DDD]
Montpellier PO
M. de Bernart (cnd)
Martucci, G.:Con 1 Pno, w. J. Swann (pno) Arkadia-Akademia ▲ 111 [DDD]
Martucci, G.:Con 2 Pno, w. J. Swann (pno) Arkadia-Akademia ▲ 111 [DDD]
G.-F. Masini (cnd)
Busoni, F.:Berceuse élégiaque Arkadia-Akademia ▲ 126 [DDD]
Busoni, F.:Indianische Fant Pno, w. J. Swann (pno) Arkadia-Akademia ▲ 126 [DDD]
Busoni, F.:Indianisches Tagebuch 2, "Gesang vom Reigen der Geister"
Arkadia-Akademia ▲ 126 [DDD]
Busoni, F.:Konzertstück Pno, w. J. Swann (pno) Arkadia-Akademia ▲ 126 [DDD]
Montreal Ancient Music Ensemble
C. Jackson (cnd)
Desmarets, H.:Motets, w. Sarah Leonard (sop), Jean-Paul Fouchécourt (ten), Norman Richard (b-bar), Les Violons du Roy—Domine ne in furore; Usquequo Domine Confitebor Tibi Domine; Lauda Jerusalem; Marche Lorraine K617 2-▲ 7053
Montreal Chamber Group [Elizabeth Dolin (vc), Carmen Picard (pno)]
Vierne, L.:Son Vc *(rec St-Paul-l'Ermite de LeGardeur Church, June 2, 1994)*
CBC ("Musica Viva" series) ▲ MVV 1085 [DDD]
Montreal Chamber Group [Jamie Parker (pno), Mercelle Mallette (vn), Anne Robert (vn), Neal Gripp (va), Elizabeth Dolin (vc)]
Vierne, L.:Qnt Pno *(rec St-Paul-l'Ermite de LeGardeur Church, June 2, 1994)*
CBC ("Musica Viva" series) ▲ MVV 1085 [DDD]
Montreal Chambristes
A. Robert (cnd)
Jolivet, A.:Rhapsodie à 7 *(rec 2/91)* CBC ("Musica Viva" series) ▲ MVCD 1049 [DDD]
Stravinsky, I.:L'Histoire du soldat, w. V. Davy (nar), J.-L. Millette (nar—Devil), J. Marchand (nar—soldier)
CBC ("Musica Viva" series) ▲ MVCD 1049 [DDD]
Montreal La Scala Orch
E. Lagac(acu)e (cnd)
La Diva, w. Natalie Choquette (sop) Isba ▲ ISCD 2070
Montreal Metropolitan Orch
M. Bélanger (cnd)
Kabalevsky, D.:Con Vn, w. A.-G. Duchemin (fl) [performer's arr. for flute] Pavane ▲ ADW 7197
W. Boudreau (cnd)
Bouchard, L.:Elan CBC ("SM 5000" series) ▲ SMCD 5106 [DDD]
Boudreau, W.:Berliner Momente CBC ("SM 5000" series) ▲ SMCD 5106 [DDD]
Cherney, B.:Transfiguration CBC ("SM 5000" series) ▲ SMCD 5106 [DDD]
Gougeon, D.:A l'Aventurel CBC ("SM 5000" series) ▲ SMCD 5106 [DDD]
Longtin, M.:Autour d'Ainola Centrediscs ▲ CMCCD 3188 [DDD]
Rea, J.:Over Time Centrediscs ▲ CMCCD 3188 [DDD]
Vivier, C.:Orion CBC ("SM 5000" series) ▲ SMCD 5106 [DDD]
Vivier, C.:Siddartha Centrediscs ▲ CMCCD 3188 [DDD]
B. Jean (cnd)
Kennan, K.W.:Night Soliloquy, w. A.-G. Duchemin (fl), M. Duchemin (pno) Pavane ▲ ADW 7197
Montreal Musica Camerata [Luis Grinhauz (vn), Myriam Pellerin (vn), Matthew Hunter (va), Léo Grinhauz (vc), Berta Rosenohl (pno)]
Piazzolla, A.:Adiós Nonino *(rec Église de la Nativité, Laprairie, Québec, May 1994)*
CBC ("Musica Viva" series) ▲ MVV 1079 [DDD]
Piazzolla, A.:Prelude, Fugue & Divertimento *(rec Église de la Nativité, Laprairie, Québec, May 1994)*
CBC ("Musica Viva" series) ▲ MVV 1079 [DDD]
Montreal Musica Camerata members
Cirigliano, J.C.:El sonido de la ciudad *(rec Église de la Nativité, Laprairie, Québec, May 1994)*
CBC ("Musica Viva" series) ▲ MVCD 1079 [DDD]
Montreal Musica Camerata members [Luis Grinhauz (vn), Myriam Pellerin (vn), Léo Grinhauz (vc), Berta Rosenohl (pno)]
Piazzolla, A.:Las cuatro estaciones porteñas [arr. Jose Bragato for vn, vc & pno] *(rec Église de la Nativité, Laprairie, Québec, May 1994)* CBC ("Musica Viva" series) ▲ MVV 1079 [DDD]
Montreal Musica Camerata members [Léo Grinhauz (vc), Berta Rosenohl (pno)]
Piazzolla, A.:The Grand Tango Vc *(rec Église de la Nativité, Laprairie, Québec, May 1994)*
CBC ("Musica Viva" series) ▲ MVV 1079 [DDD]
Montreal Musici
M. Shostakovich (cnd)
Shostakovich, D.:Con 1 Pno, w. D. Shostakovich Jr (pno), J. Thompson (tpt)
Chandos ▲ CHAN 8357 [DDD]
Shostakovich, D.:Con 2 Pno, w. D. Shostakovich Jr (pno) Chandos ▲ CHAN 8443 [DDD]
M. Storojev (cnd)
Glinka, M.:Songs, w. V. Bogachev (ten), M. Storojev (sgr) Chandos ▲ CHAN 9149 [DDD]
Rimsky-Korsakov, N.:Mozart & Salieri, w. V. Bogachev (ten) Chandos ▲ CHAN 9149 [DDD]
Rimsky-Korsakov, N.:Songs, w. V. Bogachev (ten)—The Clouds Begin to Scatter, Op. 42/3; On the Hills of Georgia, Op. 3/4 Chandos ▲ CHAN 9149 [DDD]
Y. Turovsky (cnd)
Bach, Joh. Christian:Con Vc, w. Y. Turovsky (vc) Chandos ▲ CHAN 8470 [DDD]
Bach, Joh. Christian:Sinf concertante, T.284/4, w. E. Turovsky (vn), Y. Turovsky (vc)
Chandos ▲ CHAN 8470 [DDD]

▲ = CD ♦ = Enhanced CD Δ = MD ▮ = Cassette Tape ▯ = DCC

Montreal Musici (cont.)
Y. Turovsky (cnd) (cont.)
Barber, S.:Adagio Strs — Chandos ▲ CHAN 8515 [DDD]
Bartók, B.:Divert — Chandos ▲ CHAN 8515 [DDD]
Bloch, E.:From Jewish Life, w. Y. Turovsky (vc)—Prayer [trans. A. Antonini]; Suppliation & Jewish Song [trans. P. Purich for cello & orch.] — Chandos ▲ CHAN 8800 [DDD]
Bloch, E.:Méditation hébraïque, w. Y. Turovsky (vc) [vc & orch. trans. Peter Purich] — Chandos ▲ CHAN 8800 [DDD]
Bloch, E.:Nigun, w. Y. Turovsky (vc) [vc & orch. trans. Peter Purich] — Chandos ▲ CHAN 8800 [DDD]
Boccherini, L.:Adagio & Allegro, w. Y. Turovsky (vc) — Chandos ▲ CHAN 8768 [DDD]
Boccherini, L.:Con Vc, G.482, w. Y. Turovsky (vc) — Chandos ▲ CHAN 8470 [DDD]
Boccherini, L.:Con in D Vc, w. Y. Turovsky (vc) — Chandos ▲ CHAN 8408 [DDD]
Britten, B.:Lachrymae, w. R. Golani (va) — Chandos ▲ CHAN 8817 [DDD]
Britten, B.:Simple Sym — Chandos ▲ CHAN 8817 [DDD]
Britten, B.:Vars on a Theme of Frank Bridge — Chandos ▲ CHAN 8817 [DDD]
Britten, B.:Young Apollo — Chandos ▲ CHAN 8817 [DDD]
Cassadó, G.:Con Vc, w. Y. Turovsky (vc) — Chandos ▲ CHAN 8768 [DDD]
Cherney, B.:Illuminations *(rec June 7–9, 1992)* — CBC ("SM 5000" series) ▲ SMCD 5131 [DDD]
Evangelista, J.:Airs d'Espagne — Chandos ▲ CHAN 9434
Ginastera, A.:Con Strs — Chandos ▲ CHAN 9434
Handel, G.F.:Concerti grossi, Op. 6 — Chandos 3-▲ CHAN 9004/06 [DDD]
Haydn, J.:Divert Vc & Str Orch, w. Yuli Turovsky (vc) — Chandos ▲ CHAN 8768 [DDD]
Hétu, J.:Adagio et rondo *(rec June 7–9, 1992)* — CBC ("SM 5000" series) ▲ SMCD 5131 [DDD]
Kenins, T.:Partita on Lutheran Chorales *(rec June 7–9, 1992)* — CBC ("SM 5000" series) ▲ SMCD 5131 [DDD]
Lullabies, w. Nadia Pelle (sop) — Chandos ▲ CHAN 9304 [DDD]
Mather, B.:Musique pour Rouen *(rec June 7–9, 1992)* — CBC ("SM 5000" series) ▲ SMCD 5131 [DDD]
Mozart, L.:Toy Sym — Chandos ▲ CHAN 9098 [DDD]
Mozart, W.A.:Church Sons — Chandos ▲ CHAN 8745 [DDD]
Mozart, W.A.:Con 12 Pno, w. L. Lortie (pno) — Chandos ▲ CHAN 8455 [DDD]
Mozart, W.A.:Con 14 Pno, w. L. Lortie (pno) — Chandos ▲ CHAN 8455 [DDD]
Mozart, W.A.:Con Vc, w. Y. Turovsky (vc) — Chandos ▲ CHAN 8768 [DDD]
Mozart, W.A.:Diverts Str Qt, K.136–138 — Chandos ▲ CHAN 9045 [DDD]
Mozart, W.A.:Kleine Nachtmusik — Chandos ▲ CHAN 9045 [DDD]
Mozart, W.A.:Musikalischer Spass — Chandos ▲ CHAN 9246 [DDD]
Prévost, A.:Hommage *(rec June 7–9, 1992)* — CBC ("SM 5000" series) ▲ SMCD 5131 [DDD]
Prokofiev, S.:Ov on Hebrew Themes — Chandos ▲ CHAN 8800 [DDD]
Saint-Saëns, C.:Carnival of the Animals, w. D. O. Norris (pno) — Chandos ▲ CHAN 9246 [DDD]
Saint-Saëns, C.:Wedding Cake, w. D. O. Norris (pno) — Chandos ▲ CHAN 9246 [DDD]
Schoenberg, A.:Ode to Napoleon, w. K. McMillan (bar), M.-A. Hamelin (pno) [orchestral version] [G] — Chandos ▲ CHAN 9116 [DDD]
Schoenberg, A.:Qt 2 Strs, w. N. Pelle (sop) [orchestral version] [G] — Chandos ▲ CHAN 9116 [DDD]
Schoenberg, A.:Verklärte Nacht [orchestral version] [G] — Chandos ▲ CHAN 9116 [DDD]
Schubert, Franz:German Dances Strs, D.90 — Chandos ▲ CHAN 8928 [DDD]
Schubert, Franz:Minuets & Trios, D.89 — Chandos ▲ CHAN 8547 [DDD]
Schubert, Franz:Qt 14 Strs [Gustav Mahler's 1894 arr. for string orchestra] — Chandos ▲ CHAN 8928 [DDD]
Shchedrin, R.:Carmen, w. Répercussion Ensemble — Chandos ▲ CHAN 9288 [DDD]
Shchedrin, R.:Humoresque, w. Répercussion Ensemble — Chandos ▲ CHAN 9288 [DDD]
Shchedrin, R.:In Imitation of Albéniz, w. Répercussion Ensemble — Chandos ▲ CHAN 9288 [DDD]
Shchedrin, R.:Stalin Cocktail, w. C. Perrin (hpd) — Chandos ▲ CHAN 9288 [DDD]
Shostakovich, D.:Chamber Sym, Op. 110a — Chandos ▲ CHAN 8357 [DDD]
Shostakovich, D.:From Jewish Folk Poetry, w. N. Pelle (sop), M. A. Hart (mez), R. Nolan (ten) [R] — Chandos ▲ CHAN 8800 [DDD]
Shostakovich, D.:Sym 14, w. E. Holleque (sop), N. Storojev (bass) — Chandos ▲ CHAN 8607 [DDD]
Stravinsky, I.:Con Str — Chandos ▲ CHAN 8515 [DDD]
Tartini, G.:Con in D Vc, w. Y. Turovsky (vc) — Chandos ▲ CHAN 8768 [DDD]
Tchaikovsky, P.:Album pour enfants [string orch. arr. Rostislav Dubinsky & Yuli Turovsky] — Chandos ▲ CHAN 9098 [DDD]
Tchaikovsky, P.:Souvenir de Florence — Chandos ▲ CHAN 8547 [DDD]
Tranquillity — Chandos ▲ CHAN 8573 [DDD]
Tranquillity, Vol. 2, w. Ensemble Répercussion — Chandos ("7000" series) ▲ CHAN 7058
Turina, J.:La oracion del torero — Chandos ▲ CHAN 9288 [DDD]
Villa-Lobos, H.:Bachiana brasileira 9 — Chandos ▲ CHAN 9434
Vivaldi, A.:Cons Vc, w. Y. Turovsky (vc)—RV.413, 424 — Chandos ▲ CHAN 8408 [DDD]
Vivaldi, A.:Con for 2 Vcs, w. Y. Turovsky (vc), A. Aubut (vc) — Chandos ▲ CHAN 8408 [DDD]
Vivaldi, A.:Cons Fl (misc), w. T. Hutchins (fl)—RV.433 — Chandos ▲ CHAN 8444 [DDD]
Vivaldi, A.:Cons Ob, w. T. Baskin (ob)—RV.447 — Chandos ▲ CHAN 8651 [DDD]
Vivaldi, A.:Cons Ob, w. T. Baskin (ob)—in C, RV.449 & in d, RV.454 — Chandos ▲ CHAN 8444 [DDD]
Vivaldi, A.:Cons Ob Vn, w. T. Baskin (ob), E. Turovsky (vn)—RV.548 — Chandos ▲ CHAN 8651 [DDD]
Vivaldi, A.:Cons Orch—2 concerti for strings—in d, RV.127 & in A, RV.158 — Chandos ▲ CHAN 8444 [DDD]
Vivaldi, A.:Cons Rcr, w. T. Hutchins (rcr)—Concerto in C, RV.444 — Chandos ▲ CHAN 8444 [DDD]
Vivaldi, A.:Con for 2 Tpts, w. J.Thompson (tpt), R. Early (tpt) — Chandos ▲ CHAN 8651 [DDD]
Vivaldi, A.:Cons Vn Org, w. E. Turovsky (vn), G. Soly (org)—RV.542 in F — Chandos ▲ CHAN 8651 [DDD]
Vivaldi, A.:Con for 2 Vns Vc, R.565, w. E. Turovsky (vn), E. Skerjanc (vn), A. Aubut (vc)—RV.542 in F — Chandos ▲ CHAN 8651 [DDD]
Vivaldi, A.:Con for 2 Vns Vcs, w. C. Prevost (vn), L. Hall (vn), A. Aubut (vc), B. Hurtubise (vc)—RV.542 in F — Chandos ▲ CHAN 8651 [DDD]
Wassenaer, U.W. van:Concerti Armonici — Chandos ▲ CHAN 8481 [DDD]

Montreal Sinfonietta
Pergolesi, G.B.:Salve regina in a, w. J. Anderson (sop) — London ▲ 436209-2 [DDD]
Pergolesi, G.B.:Stabat mater, w. J. Anderson (sop), C. Bartoli (mez), *(organist unknown)* — London ▲ 436209-2 [DDD]
Scarlatti, A.:Salve regina, w. J. Anderson (sop), C. Bartoli (mez) — London ▲ 436209-2 [DDD]
Stravinsky, I.:Apollon musagète — London ▲ 440327-2
Stravinsky, I.:Con CO — London ▲ 440327-2
Stravinsky, I.:Con Str — London ▲ 440327-2
Stravinsky, I.:Danses concertantes — London ▲ 440327-2

Montreal String Quartet
Brahms, J.:Qnt Pno, w. G. Gould (pno) — Sony Classical ▲ SMK 52684

Montreal SO
F.-P. Decker (cnd)
Beethoven, L. van:Con 3 Pno, w. W. Kempff (pno) — Music & Arts ▲ CD 768 [ADD]
C. Dutoit (cnd)
Bartók, B.:Con Orch — London ▲ 421443-2 [DDD]
Bartók, B.:Music for Strs, Perc & Cel — London ▲ 421443-2 [DDD]
Berlioz, H.:Harold in Italy, w. P. Zukerman (va) — London ▲ 421193-2 [DDD]
Berlioz, H.:Sym fantastique — London ▲ 414203-2 [DDD]
Berlioz, H.:Les Troyens, w. F. Pollet (sop—Dido), D. Voigt (sop—Cassandre), C. Dubosc (sop—Ascagne), H. Perraguin (cta—Anna), G. Lakes (ten—Aeneas), J.-L. Maurette (ten—Iopas), J. M. Ainsley (ten—Hylas), M. P. (ten—Panthee), G. Cross (ten—Sinon), G. Quilico (bar—Chorebe), J.-P. Courtis (b-bar—Narbal), M. Belleau (bass—Ghost of Hector), R. Schirrer (bass—Priam), Montreal Sym Chorus — London 4-▲ 443693-2 [DDD]
Bizet, G.:L'Arlésienne (suites) — London ▲ 417839-2 [DDD] ▯ 417839-5
Bizet, G.:Carmen (suites) — London ▲ 417839-2 [DDD] ▯ 417839-5
Chopin, F.:Con 1 Pno, w. J. Bolet (pno) — London ▲ 425859-2 [DDD]
Chopin, F.:Con 2 Pno, w. J. Bolet (pno) — London ▲ 425859-2 [DDD]

Montreal SO (cont.)
C. Dutoit (cnd) (cont.)
Debussy, C.:La Boîte à joujoux — London ▲ 444386-2
Debussy, C.:Children's Corner — London ▲ 444386-2
Debussy, C.:Images Orch — London ▲ 425502-2 [DDD]
Debussy, C.:Jeux — London ▲ 430240-2 [DDD] ▯ 430240-5
Debussy, C.:Martyre de Saint Sébastian (fragments) — London ▲ 430240-2 [DDD]
Debussy, C.:La Mer — London ▲ 430240-2 [DDD]
Debussy, C.:Nocturnes, w. Montreal Sym Chorus — London ▲ 425502-2 [DDD]
Debussy, C.:Pelléas et Mélisande, w. C. Alliot-Lugaz (sop), F. Golfier (sop), C. Carlson (mez), D. Henry (ten), G. Cachemaille (bar), P. Thau (bass), Montreal Sym Chorus [F] — London 2-▲ 430502-2 [DDD]
Debussy, C.:La Plus que lente — London ▲ 444386-2
Debussy, C.:Printemps (suite) — London ▲ 444386-2
Elgar, E.:Enigma Vars — London ▲ 430241-2 [DDD]
Elgar, E.:Falstaff — London ▲ 430241-2 [DDD]
Falla, M. de:El amor brujo, w. H. Tourangeau (mez) — London ▲ 430703-2 [DDD]
Falla, M. de:Noches en los jardines de España, w. A. de Larrocha (pno) — London ▲ 430703-2 [DDD]
Fauré, G.:Pavane Orch, w. Montreal Sym Chorus — London ▲ 421440-2 [DDD] ▯ 421440-5
Fauré, G.:Pelléas et Mélisande (suite) — London ▲ 421440-2 [DDD] ▯ 421440-5
Fauré, G.:Requiem, w. K. Te Kanawa (sop), S. Milnes (bar), Montreal Sym Chorus [L] — London ▲ 421440-2 [DDD] ▯ 421440-5
Franck, C.:Sym in d — London ▲ 430278-2 [DDD]
Gounod, C.:Faust (ballet music) — London ▲ 430718-2 [DDD]
Holst, G.:The Planets — London ▲ 417553-2 [DDD]
Janácek, L.:Sinfonietta, w. Montreal Sym Chorus — London ▲ 436211-2
Janácek, L.:Slavonic Mass, w. N. Troitskaya (sop), E. Randova (cta), K. Kaludov (ten), S. Leiferkas (bass), T. Trotter (org), Montreal Sym Chorus — London ▲ 436211-2
Kodály, Z.:Galanta Dances — London ▲ 444322-2
Kodály, Z.:Háry János (suite) — London ▲ 444322-2
Kodály, Z.:Marosszék Dances — London ▲ 444322-2
Kodály, Z.:Vars on a Hungarian Folk Song — London ▲ 444322-2
Lalo, E.:Sym espagnole, w. J. Bell (vn) — London ▲ 425501-2 [DDD]
Liszt, F.:Cons Pno, w. J.-Y. Thibaudet (pno) — London ▲ 433075-2 [DDD] ▯ 433075-5
Liszt, F.:Fant on Hungarian Folk Tunes, w. J.-Y. Thibaudet (pno) — London ▲ 433075-2 [DDD]
Liszt, F.:Totentanz, w. J.-Y. Thibaudet (pno) — London ▲ 433075-2 [DDD]
Mendelssohn, F.:Con in e Vn & Orch, Op. 64, w. Hye-Yun Chung (vn) — London ▲ 410011-2 [DDD]
Mendelssohn, F.:Con in e Vn & Orch, Op. 64, w. K.-W. Chung (vn) — London ("Ovation" series) ▲ 430752-2 [DDD]
Mendelssohn, F.:A Midsummer Night's Dream (sels) — London ▲ 430722-2 [DDD]
Mussorgsky, M.:Night — London ▲ 417299-2 [DDD]
Offenbach, J.:Gaîté Parisienne — London ▲ 430718-2 [DDD]
Prokofiev, S.:Alexander Nevsky, w. J. van Nes (cta), Montreal Sym Chorus — London ▲ 430506-2 [DDD]
Prokofiev, S.:Cons Vn (comp), w. J. Bell (vn) — London ▲ 440331-2
Prokofiev, S.:Lt Kijé Suite — London ▲ 430506-2 [DDD]
Prokofiev, S.:The Love for 3 Oranges (suite), w. J. Bell (vn) — London ▲ 440331-2
Prokofiev, S.:Romeo & Juliet (sels) — London ▲ 430279-2 [DDD]
Prokofiev, S.:Sym 1 — London ▲ 421813-2 [DDD]
Prokofiev, S.:Sym 5 — London ▲ 421813-2 [DDD]
Ravel, M.:Alborada del gracioso — London ▲ 410010-2 [DDD]
Ravel, M.:Daphnis et Chloé, w. Montreal Sym Chorus — London ▲ 400055-2 [DDD]
Ravel, M.:Daphnis et Chloé (suite 2) — London ▲ 430714-2 [DDD]
Ravel, M.:Ma mère l'oye Orch — London ▲ 410254-2 [DDD]
Ravel, M.:Orchestral Music—including Bolero; Concerti for piano; Daphnis et Chloé; Ma mère l'oye; Rapsodie Espagnole; La valse; etc. — London ("Jubilee" series) 4-▲ 421458-2 [DDD]
Ravel, M.:Pavane pour une infante défunte — London ▲ 430714-2 [DDD]
Ravel, M.:Pavane pour une infante défunte — London ▲ 410254-2 [DDD]
Ravel, M.:Rapsodie espagnole — London ▲ 410010-2 [DDD]
Ravel, M.:Le Tombeau de Couperin — London ▲ 410254-2 [DDD]
Ravel, M.:La Valse — London ▲ 410010-2 [DDD]
Ravel, M.:La Valse — London ▲ 430714-2 [DDD]
Ravel, M.:Valses nobles et sentimentales — London ▲ 410254-2 [DDD]
Respighi, O.:The Fountains of Rome — London ▲ 410145-2 [DDD]
Respighi, O.:The Pines of Rome — London ▲ 410145-2 [DDD]
Rodrigo, J.:Concierto de Aranjuez, w. C. Bonell (gtr) — London ▲ 430703-2 [DDD]
Rossini, G.:Ovs—Barbiere di Siviglia; Cenerentola; La gazza ladra; Italiana in algeri; Scala di seta; Semiramide; Signor Bruschino; William Tell — London ▲ 433074-2 [DDD]
Saint-Saëns, C.:Con 3 Vn, w. J. Bell (vn) — London ▲ 425501-2 [DDD]
Saint-Saëns, C.:Sym 3, w. P. Hurford (org) — London ▲ 430720-2 [DDD]
Stravinsky, I.:Le Chant du rossignol — London ▲ 417019-2 [DDD]
Stravinsky, I.:Con Vn, w. C. Juliet (vn) — London ▲ 436037-2 [DDD]
Stravinsky, I.:The Firebird — London ▲ 414409-2 [DDD]
Stravinsky, I.:Fireworks — London ▲ 414409-2 [DDD]
Stravinsky, I.:Le Sacre du printemps Orch — London ▲ 414202-2 [DDD]
Stravinsky, I.:Scherzo fantastique — London ▲ 414409-2 [DDD]
Stravinsky, I.:Syms Ww — London ▲ 414202-2 [DDD]
Szymanowski, K.:Con 1 Vn, w. C. Juliet (vn) — London ▲ 436837-2 [DDD]
Szymanowski, K.:Con 2 Vn, w. C. Juliet (vn) — London ▲ 436837-2 [DDD]
Tchaikovsky, P.:Con Vn, w. K.-W. Chung (vn) — London ▲ 430725-2 [DDD]
Tchaikovsky, P.:Con Vn, w. K.-W. Chung (vn) — London ▲ 410011-2 [DDD]
Tchaikovsky, P.:Marche slave — London ▲ 417300-2 [DDD]
Tchaikovsky, P.:The Nutcracker — London 2-▲ 440477-2
Tchaikovsky, P.:The Nutcracker (sels) — London ▲ 443555-2
Tchaikovsky, P.:Ov 1812 — London ▲ 417300-2 [DDD]
Tchaikovsky, P.:Romeo & Juliet — London ♦ 00626354440
Tchaikovsky, P.:Sleeping Beauty (sels) — London ▲ 443555-2
Tchaikovsky, P.:Swan Lake — London 2-▲ 436212-2 [DDD]
Tchaikovsky, P.:Swan Lake (sels) — London ▲ 443555-2
Tchaikovsky, P.:Sym 5 — London ♦ 00626354440

Montreal SO members
Y. Turovsky (cnd)
Shostakovich, D.:Chamber Sym, Op. 118a — Chandos ▲ CHAN 8443 [DDD]

Montreux SO
B. Mersson (cnd)
Mozart, W.A.:Con 12 Pno, w. Boris Mersson (pno) — Doron ▲ DRC 3013
Mozart, W.A.:Con 26 Pno, w. Boris Mersson (pno) — Doron ▲ DRC 3013

Montserrat Capella e Escolania
I. Segarra (cnd)
Cererols, J.:Sacred Romances, w. Barcelona Ars Musicae Ensemble, [period instrs] *(rec 1979?)* — Koch Treasure ▲ 31624-2 [ADD]
Palestrina, G.:Missa de Beata Virgine — Koch Schwann ▲ SCH 317962

Montserrat Escolania
F. Maier (cnd)
Missa Salisburgensis, w. Tolz Boys' Choir, Collegium Aureum — Deutsche Harmonia Mundi ▲ 77050-2-RC [DDD]
I. Segarra (cnd)
Casals, P.:Sacred Choral Music—Nigra sum; Tota pulchra es; Cançó a la Verge; Rosari; O vos omnes; Eucaristica; Recordare Virgo Mater; Oració a la Verge de Montserrat; Salve Regina — Koch Schwann ▲ CD 313 062 [DDD]
Casanovas, N.:Responsories de Nadal, w. G. Estrada (cnd) [L] — Koch Schwann ▲ 3-1347-2 [DDD]

Montserrat Escolania (cont.)
I. Segarra (cnd) (cont.)
Mendelssohn, F.:Motets, Op. 39, w. S. Bardolet (trb), X. Canadell (trb), J. Pieres (alt), F. Gasa (alt), M. L. Ibañez (hp), G. Estrada (org) *(rec 1978?)* Koch Treasure ▲ 31624-2 [ADD]
Sacred Choral Music Koch Schwann ▲ SCH 312562 [DDD]
Viola, A.:Choral Music, w. Antics Escolans Orch,—Missa "Alma Redemptoris Mater"; Beatus vir (Psalm 111); Laetatus sum (Psalm 121); Magnificat a 7 voces [L] Koch Schwann ▲ 3-1246-2 [DDD]
Mora Vocis
Mystery of Ancient Voices Pierre Verany ▲ 793101 [DDD]
Moragues Quintet
Barber, S.:Summer Music Valois ▲ V 4639 [DDD]
Hindemith, P.:Kleine Kammermusik Valois ▲ V 4639 [DDD]
Ligeti, G.:Bagatelles Valois ▲ V 4639 [DDD]
Mendelssohn, F.:Qnts Strs, Opp. 18 & 87 Valois ▲ V 4719
Mozart, W.A.:Adagio Cls, K.411 Valois ▲ V 4684
Mozart, W.A.:Serenade Ww, K.375 Valois ▲ V 4684
Mozart, W.A.:Serenade Ww, K.388 Valois ▲ V 4684
Stockhausen, K.:Adieu Valois ▲ V 4639 [DDD]
Villa-Lobos, H.:Qnten forme de chôros Valois ▲ V 4639 [DDD]
Moran Woodwind Quintet [J. Bailey (fl), W. McMullen (ob), E. Ginsberg (cl), G. Echols (bn), A. French (hn)]
Blumer, T.:Dance Suite Crystal ▲ CD 753 [DDD]
Blumer, T.:Quintet Ww Crystal ▲ CD 753 [DDD]
Blumer, T.:Sextet Pno, w. S. Irek (pno) Crystal ▲ CD 753 [DDD]
Moravian PO
M. Müssauer (cnd)
Bach, M.:Silhouettes *(rec Olomuc Philharmonic, Oct. 1994)* Thorofon ▲ CTH 2259 [DDD]
Dickenson-Auner, M.:Irish Sym *(rec Olomuc Philharmonic, Oct. 1994)* Thorofon ▲ CTH 2259 [DDD]
Fuchs, R.:Andante grazioso & Capriccio *(rec Philharmonie Olomouc, Oct. 1994)* Thorofon ▲ CTH 2260 [DDD]
Fuchs, R.:Des Meeres und der Liebe Wellen *(rec Philharmonie Olomouc, Oct. 1994)* Thorofon ▲ CTH 2260 [DDD]
Fuchs, R.:Sym 3 *(rec Philharmonie Olomouc, Oct. 1994)* Thorofon ▲ CTH 2260 [DDD]
Müller-Hermann, J.:Heroic Ov *(rec Olomuc Philharmonic, Oct. 1994)* Thorofon ▲ CTH 2259 [DDD]
Müller-Hermann, J.:Symphonic Fant *(rec Olomuc Philharmonic, Oct. 1994)* Thorofon ▲ CTH 2259 [DDD]
R. Silva (cnd)
Beath, B.:Indonesian Diptych Vienna Modern Masters ▲ VMM 3031 [DDD]
Davis, G.R.:The Dancing Difference Vienna Modern Masters ▲ VMM 3031 [DDD]
Fetherolf, D.:Con Vc, w. Jing Jiang (vc) Vienna Modern Masters ▲ VMM 3031 [DDD]
Ocker, M.:Gettysburg:July 1, 1863 Vienna Modern Masters ▲ VMM 3034 [DDD]
Moravian-Silesian CO
Trumpet Concertos, Vol. 3, w. Christensen, Ketil (tpt), Ole Andersen (tpt), Lars Ole Schmidt (tpt), Moravian-Silesian CO [cnd:Preben Norgaard Christensen, Pavel Vitek] Rondo Grammofon ▲ RCD 8345
Moreno-Capelli Duo
Guastavino, C.:Pno Music—Romance del plata; 3 Romances; Bailecito; Gato; Llanura; Se equivoco la paloma; La siesta; Las presencias *(rec Feb. 25-27, 1992)* Marco Polo ▲ 8.223462 [DDD]
Morhange Ensemble
Alkan, C.-V.:Cons (2) de camera, w. A. Goldstone (pno) Symposium ▲ 1062
C. Stevenson (cnd)
Alkan, C.-V.:Rondo brilliant Symposium ▲ 1062
Mormon Youth SO
H. Hanson (cnd)
Hanson, H.:Lament for Beowulf, w. Mormon Youth Chorus *(rec live, Howard Hanson Festival, Salt Lake Tabernacle, Salt Lake City, UT, Mar 11, 1972)* Citadel ▲ CTD 88116 [ADD]
Hanson, H.:Merry Mount (suite) *(rec Howard Hanson Festival, Salt Lake Tabernacle, UT, Mar 11, 1972)* Citadel ▲ CTD 88110 [ADD]
Hanson, H.:Song of Democracy, w. Mormon Youth Chorus *(rec Howard Hanson Festival, Salt Lake Tabernacle, UT, Mar 11, 1972)* Citadel ▲ CTD 88110 [ADD]
Hanson, H.:Sym 2, "Romantic" *(rec Howard Hanson Festival, Salt Lake Tabernacle, UT, Mar 11, 1972)* Citadel ▲ CTD 88110 [ADD]
Mosaïques Ensemble
Mozart, W.A.:Qnt Cl, K.581, w. W. Meyer (cl), A. Mitterer (vn) Astrée ▲ E 8736
C. Coin (cnd)
Chopin, F.:Con 2 Pno, w. J. Olejniczak (pno)—Larghetto *(rec May-June 1990)* Opus 111 ▲ OPS 43-9107 [DDD]
Mosaïques String Quartet [Erich Höbarth (vn), Andrea Bischof (vn), Anita Mitterer (va), Christophe Coin (vc)]
Beethoven, L. van:Qt 5 Strs [period instrs] Astrée ▲ E 8541
Beethoven, L. van:Qt 6 Strs [period instrs] Astrée ▲ E 8541
Boccherini, L.:Qnt Pno, G.407-412, w. P. Cohen (pno)—G.407, 408 & 411 Astrée ▲ E 8518 [DDD]
Haydn, J.:Qts Strs, Op. 33, "Russian Qts"—Nos. 2, 3 & 5 Astrée ▲ E8569
Haydn, J.:The Seven Last Words of Christ on the Cross [string quartet version] Astrée ▲ E 8742
Mozart, W.A.:Qt 14 Strs Astrée 3-▲ 8596
Mozart, W.A.:Qt 15 Strs Astrée 3-▲ 8596
Mozart, W.A.:Qt 16 Strs [period instrs] Astrée ▲ E 8747
Mozart, W.A.:Qt 16 Strs Astrée 3-▲ 8596
Mozart, W.A.:Qt 17 Strs Astrée 3-▲ 8596
Mozart, W.A.:Qt 17 Strs [period instrs] Astrée ▲ E 8747
Mozart, W.A.:Qt 18 Strs Astrée 3-▲ 8596
Mozart, W.A.:Qt 18 Strs Astrée ▲ E 8748
Mozart, W.A.:Qt 19 Strs Astrée 3-▲ 8596
Mozart, W.A.:Qt 19 Strs Astrée ▲ E 8748
Music at the Time of Beaumarchais, w. Montserrat Figueras (sop), Lawrence Monteyro (sop), Raphel Oleg (vn), Miguel da Silva (va), Christophe Coin (vc), Marc Coppey (vc), José Miguel Moreno (gtr), Paul Badura-Skoda (pno), Philippe Cassard (pno), Eric Le Sage (pno), Bob Van Asperen (hpd), et al. Valois ▲ V 4767
Schubert, Franz:Qt 10 Strs Auvidis Astrée ▲ E 8580
Schubert, Franz:Qt 13 Strs Auvidis Astrée ▲ E 8580
Moscow Ancient Music Ensemble
Berezowsky, N.:Son Vn, w. V. Felitsiant (vn) MK ▲ MKA 417119 [DDD]
V. Felitsiant (cnd)
Bortnyansky, D.:Qnt Vn, Vl MK ▲ MKA 417119 [DDD]
Bortnyansky, D.:Septet MK ▲ MKA 417119 [DDD]
Dall'Oglio, D.:Sons (7) Vn—1 Sonata MK ▲ MKA 417119 [DDD]
Moscow Ancient Music Ensemble members
Dall'Oglio, D.:Sons (7) Vn—in D Olympia ▲ OLY 549 [DDD]
Lolli, A.:Sons Vn Olympia ▲ OLY 549 [DDD]
Moscow Ancient Music Ensemble members [Oksana Korokhova (pno), Victor Felitsiant (vn), Alla Tchaplygina (vc)]
Alyabiev, A.:Trio Pno Olympia ▲ OLY 549 [DDD]
Moscow Ancient Music Ensemble members [Vera Zhuravilova (sop), Oksana Korokhova (pno)]
Alyabiev, A.:Romances (5) Olympia ▲ OLY 549 [DDD]
Moscow Bach Center Orch
S. Miassojedov (cnd)
Bach, J.S.:Cant 21—Sinfonia *(rec Moscow, June 1993)* Arts ▲ 447134-2 [DDD]
Bach, J.S.:Cant 209—Sinfonia *(rec Moscow, June 1993)* Arts ▲ 447134-2 [DDD]
Bach, J.S.:Easter Oratorio—Adagio & Sinfonia *(rec Moscow, June 1993)* Arts ▲ 447133-2 [DDD]

Moscow Bach Center Orch (cont.)
S. Miassojedov (cnd) (cont.)
Bach, J.S.:Suite 1 Orch—Nos. 1 & 2 [w. Albert Razbaum (fl)] *(rec Moscow, June 1993)* Arts ▲ 447133-2 [DDD]
Bach, J.S.:Suite 2 Orch, w. Albert Razbaum (fl) *(rec Moscow, June 1993)* Arts ▲ 447133-2 [DDD]
Bach, J.S.:Suite 3 Orch Arts ▲ 447134-2 [DDD]
Bach, J.S.:Suite 4 Orch Arts ▲ 447134-2 [DDD]
Moscow Bolshoi Theater Orch—see Bolshoi Theater Orch
Moscow Chamber Ensemble
A. Korneiev (cnd)
Popov, G.N.:Chamber Sym Olympia ▲ OLY 588 [ADD]
Moscow CO
Bortnyansky, D.:Sinf concertante, w. Nina Barshay (vn), Boris Dobrokhotov (vl), Vladimir Berlinsky (vc), Olga Erdeli (hp), Sergey Dizhur (pno) *(rec 1984)* Multisonic ("Russian Treasures" series) ▲ 31 0253
R. Barshaï (cnd)
Biber, H. von:Son a 6 Tpt, w. Timofei Dokschitzer (tpt) *(rec 1968)* RCA Gold Seal ▲ 74321-32045-2 [ADD]
Hummel, J.N.:Con in E♭ Tpt, S.49, w. Timofei Dokschitzer (tpt) *(rec 1968)* RCA Gold Seal ▲ 74321-32045-2 [ADD]
Shostakovich, D.:Sym 14, w. G. Vishnevskaya (sop), M. Reshetin (bass) *(rec Sept. 29, 1969)* Russian Disc ▲ RUS 11192 [AAD]
Telemann, G.P.:Cons Ob, w. Pierre Pierlot (ob), Evgeni Nepalov (ob), Piotr Dubrov (ob), Andrei Abramenkov (vn), Rudolf Barshai (vn), Leonid Poleess (vn)—in B♭ for 3 Obs, 3 Vns & Bc *(rec Salle Wagram, Paris, June 1964)* EMI Classics ▲ CDK 65340 [ADD]
Tippett, M.:Con Double Str Orch EMI Classics 2-▲ ZDMB 63522
Vainberg, M.:Con Fl, w. A. Korneyev (fl) Russian Disc ▲ RUS 11010 [AAD]
Vainberg, M.:Sym 7 Olympia ▲ OLY 472 [ADD]
Vainberg, M.:Sym 10 *(rec 1970)* Olympia ▲ OLY 471 [AAD]
Vivaldi, A.:Cons Vn, Op. 3/1-12, "L'estro armonico"—Nos. 10 & 11 London ("Weekend Classics" series) ▲ 433680-2 [ADD]
C. Orbelian (cnd)
Paganini, N.:Con 1 Vn, w. Ilya Grubert (vn) Chandos ▲ CHAN 9492
Paganini, N.:Con 2 Vn, w. Ilya Grubert (vn) Chandos ▲ CHAN 9492
Moscow Choral Academy Orch
Rachmaninoff, S.:Spring, w. N. Surikov (bar), A. Tchistiakov (cnd), Moscow Choral Academy Russian Season ("Russian Season" series) ▲ LDC 288069
Moscow Conservatory Orch
L. Nikolayev (cnd)
Chiang, W.-Y.:The Princess Shian-Fei Sunrise ▲ 8531
Chiang, W.-Y.:The Song of Ali Mountain Sunrise ▲ 8531
Chiang, W.-Y.:Symphonia Universalis Sunrise ▲ 8531
Moscow Conservatory Student Orch String Group
M. Terian (cnd)
Zecchi, A.:Divert Fl, w. O. Kudryachov (fl), Vera Dulova (hp) *(rec 1961)* Russian Compact Disc ("Talents of Russia" series) ▲ RCD 16204 [AAD]
Moscow Contemporary Music Ensemble
Denisov, E.:Chamber Sym 2 *(rec Mosfilm Studio, June 5-7 & 19, 1995)* Triton ▲ 17003 [DDD]
Denisov, E.:Choral Music (misc), w. Moscow Ensemble of Contemporary Music Soloists, Elena Rastvorova (cnd), New Moscow Choir—Choruses from Medea; Peaceful Light; Legends of the Subterranean Waters Russian Season ▲ RUS 288131
Denisov, E.:Pictures (3) of Paul Klee—Diana in an Autumn Wind; Senecio; Child on a Railway Platform *(rec Mosfilm Studio, June 5-7 & 19, 1995)* Triton ▲ 17003 [DDD]
Denisov, E.:Sun of the Incas, w. Natalia Zagorinskaya (sop) *(rec Mosfilm Studio, June 5-7 & 19, 1995)* Triton ▲ 17003 [DDD]
Denisov, E.:Sur la nappe d'un étang glacé *(rec Mosfilm Studio, June 5-7 & 19, 1995)* Triton ▲ 17003 [DDD]
Hindemith, P.:Octet Winds & Strs Triton ▲ 17010 [DDD]
Hindemith, P.:Qnt Cl, w. Oleg Tantzov (cl) *(rec Mosfilm Studio, Dec 1994)* Triton ▲ 17005 [DDD]
Mosolov, A.:Children's Songs, w. Natalia Zagorinskaya (sop) *(rec Mosfilm Studio, Jan 1995)* Triton ▲ 17004 [DDD]
Mosolov, A.:Newspaper, w. Natalia Zagorinskaya (sop) *(rec Mosfilm Studio, Jan 1995)* Triton ▲ 17004 [DDD]
Mosolov, A.:Qt 2 Strs *(rec Mosfilm Studio, Jan 1995)* Triton ▲ 17004 [DDD]
Prokofiev, S.:Gavotte Pno [from Sym 1] [arr Y. Kasparov] Triton ▲ 17015 [DDD]
Prokofiev, S.:The Love for 3 Oranges (march) [arr Y. Kasparov] Triton ▲ 17015 [DDD]
Prokofiev, S.:Ov on Hebrew Themes Triton ▲ 17015 [DDD]
Prokofiev, S.:Qnt Ob Triton ▲ 17015 [DDD]
Prokofiev, S.:Visions fugitives [arr Y. Kasparov] Triton ▲ 17015 [DDD]
Shostakovich, D.:Trio 1 Pno Triton ▲ 17011 [DDD]
Shostakovich, D.:Trio 2 Pno Triton ▲ 17011 [DDD]
V. Ponkin (cnd)
Artyomov, V.:Star Wind *(rec 1991)* Olympia ▲ OCD 282 [DDD]
A. Vinogradov (cnd)
Hindemith, P.:Kammermusic 2, w. Victor Yampolsky (pno) Triton ▲ 17010 [DDD]
Hindemith, P.:Kammermusik 3, w. Natalia Savinova (vc) Triton ▲ 17010 [DDD]
Mosolov, A.:Con Vn, w. Leonora Dmiterko (vn) *(rec Mosfilm Studio, Jan 1995)* Triton ▲ 17004 [DDD]
Moscow Contemporary Music Ensemble [Alexander Melnikov (vn), Natalia Sabinova (vc), Victor Yampolsky (pno), Valery Popov (bn), Sergei Ampleyev (perc)]
Shostakovich, D.:Aphorisms [arr B. Bekhterev & V. Spivakov] Triton ▲ 17011 [DDD]
Moscow Contemporary Music Ensemble members
Gagnidze, M.:Trio Bn, w. V. Popov (bn) Olympia ▲ OLY 297 [DDD]
Gubaidulina, S.:Quasi hoquetus, w. V. Popov (bn) Olympia ▲ OLY 297 [DDD]
Smirnov, D.:Son Fl Olympia ▲ OCD 282 [DDD]
Vasks, P.:Flying Bird Music *(rec 1991)* Olympia ▲ OCD 282 [DDD]
Yekimovski, V.:Double Chamber Vars Olympia ▲ OCD 282 [DDD]
V. Popov (cnd)
Kasparov, Y.:Goat's Song Olympia ▲ OLY 297 [DDD]
Shoot, V.:Trio Bn Olympia ▲ OLY 297 [DDD]
Moscow Forum Theater Orch
M. Yurovski (cnd)
Rimsky-Korsakov, N.:Christmas Eve, w. Ekaterina Koudriavtchenko (sop), Elena Zaremba (mez), Vladimir Bogtatchov (ten), Alexei Maslennikov (ten), Viatcheslav Voinarovski (ten), Viatcheslav Verestnikov (bar), Maxime Mikhailov (bass), Stanislav Souleimanov (bass), Yurloff Academic Choir Russian Season 4-▲ CMX 388054
Moscow Helikon Theater Chamber Ensemble
C. Tikhonov (cnd)
Prokofiev, S.:Maddalena, w. S. Kulikova (sgr), N. Zagorinskaya (sgr), Y. Melnikova (sgr), S. Donets (sgr), S. Yakovlev (sgr) [R] MK ▲ MKA 417056 [DDD]
Stravinsky, I.:Mavra, w. S. Kulikova (sgr), N. Zagorinskaya (sgr), Y. Melnikova (sgr), S. Donets (sgr), S. Yakovlev (bar) MK ▲ MKA 417056 [DDD]
Moscow Large RSO
N. Golovanov (cnd)
Glazunov, A.:Sym 6 *(rec 1948-50)* Arlecchino ▲ ARLA 60
Glazunov, A.:Sym 7, "Pastoral" *(rec 1948-50)* Arlecchino ▲ ARLA 60
Moscow Montpellier Soloists
Vivaldi, A.:Cons Vn (misc)—in C, R.109; in C, R.110; in C, R.117; in D, R.121; in d, R.127; in E, R.131; in F, R.136; in F, R.142; in G, R.153; in a, R.161; in B♭, R.163; in B♭, R.164; in B♭, R.166 *(rec Sept. 14-16, 1993)* Arkadia-Akademia ▲ 118 [DDD]

Moscow New Opera Orch
Y. Samoilov (cnd)
Miaskovsky, N.:Con Vc, w. Marina Tarasova (vc) — Olympia ▲ OLY 530 [DDD]
Miaskovsky, N.:Lyric Concertino — Olympia ▲ OLY 528 [DDD]
Miaskovsky, N.:Salutary Ov — Olympia ▲ OLY 528 [DDD]
Miaskovsky, N.:Serenade — Olympia ▲ OLY 528 [DDD]
Miaskovsky, N.:Sinfonietta, Op. 32/2 — Olympia ▲ OLY 528 [DDD]
Moscow New PO
V. Ponkin (cnd)
Tchaikovsky, P.:Sleeping Beauty — MK 3–▲ MKA 417117 [DDD]
Moscow Orch
M. Avetisyan (cnd)
Chopin, F.:Con 2 Pno, w. Mee–Hyun Ahn (pno) — Russian Compact Disc ▲ RCD 30005 [DDD]
Scriabin, A.:Con Pno, w. Mee–Hyun Ahn (pno) — Russian Compact Disc ▲ RCD 30005 [DDD]
R. Freisitzer (cnd)
Mozart, W.A.:Con 18 Pno, w. Basinia Schulman (pno) — Russian Compact Disc ▲ RCD 30006
Ravel, M.:Con Pno in G, w. Basinia Schulman (pno) — Russian Compact Disc ▲ RCD 30006
Schubert, Franz:Sym 1 *(rec Studio V, GDRZ, Moscow, Feb 14–18, 1995)* — Russian Compact Disc ▲ RCD 30001 [DDD]
Schubert, Franz:Sym 4 *(rec Studio V, GDRZ, Moscow, Feb 14–18, 1995)* — Russian Compact Disc ▲ RCD 30001 [DDD]
Moscow PO
Husa, K.:Con Perc — Sheffield Lab ("Salon" series) ▲ SLS 506
D. Barra (cnd)
Schnittke, A.:Con Pno, w. I. Margalit (pno) *(rec Sept. 1992)* — Koch International Classics ▲ KIC 7159 [DDD]
Shostakovich, D.:Con 1 Pno, w. I. Margalit (pno), M. Khanin (tpt) *(rec Sept. 1992)* — Koch International Classics ▲ KIC 7159 [DDD]
Shostakovich, D.:Fantastic Dances, w. I. Margalit (pno) *(rec Sept. 1992)* — Koch International Classics ▲ KIC 7159 [DDD]
M. Ermler (cnd)
Rachmaninoff, S.:Con 2 Pno, w. Eun Soo Son (pno) — Russian Disc ▲ RUS 10011 [DDD]
Rachmaninoff, S.:Sym 3 — Russian Disc ▲ RUS 10011 [DDD]
P. Freeman (cnd)
Bruch, M.:Con for 2 Pnos, w. Robert Cowan (pno), Joan Yarbrough (pno) *(rec Moscow Radio Union, Feb 28, 1994)* — Centaur ▲ CRC 2227 [DDD]
Glazunov, A.:Con Vn, w. Chin Kim (vn) *(rec Great Hall of the Moscow Radio Union, Feb. 1994)* — Intersound ▲ 3535 [DDD]
Prokofiev, S.:Con 1 Vn, w. Pablo Diemecke (vn) *(rec MoscFilm Studio Concert Hall, Moscow)* — Fanfare ▲ CDS 3479 [DDD]
A. Gauk (cnd)
Shostakovich, D.:Con 1 Pno, w. D. Shostakovich (pno) *(rec 1957)* — Russian Disc ▲ RUS 15 005 [AAD]
F. Glushchenko (cnd)
Dmitriev, G.:Con Vn, w. Oleg Kagan (vn) *(rec Large Hall, Moscow Conservatory, Oct 18, 1981)* — Russian Compact Disc ▲ RD CD 10003 [AAD]
D. Kitayenko (cnd)
Artyomov, V.:Gurian Hymn, w. Y. Smirnov (vn), T. Gridenko (vn), Y. Adjemova (vn) — Olympia ▲ OLY 515 [DDD]
Artyomov, V.:In Memoriam, w. Oleh Krista (vn) — Olympia ▲ OLY 516 [DDD]
Artyomov, V.:Lamentations, w. O. Yanchenko (org) — Olympia ▲ OLY 515 [DDD]
Artyomov, V.:Sym of Elegies — Olympia ▲ OLY 515 [DDD]
Artyomov, V.:Tristia, w. Oleh Krista (vn) — Olympia ▲ OLY 516 [DDD]
Artyomov, V.:Way to Olympus, w. Oleh Krista (vn) — Olympia ▲ OLY 516 [DDD]
Barber, S.:Essay 1 *(rec Moscow, Aug 9–18, 1986)* — Sheffield Lab ▲ CD 26
Chopin, F.:Con 1 Pno, w. Evgeny Kissin (pno) *(rec live, Grand Hall of the Moscow Conservatory, Mar 27, 1984)* — RCA Red Seal ▲ 09026–68378–2 [ADD]
Chopin, F.:Con 2 Pno, w. Evgeny Kissin (pno) *(rec live, Grand Hall of the Moscow Conservatory, Mar 27, 1984)* — RCA Red Seal ▲ 09026–68378–2 [ADD]
Copland, A.:Appalachian Spring (suite) *(rec Moscow, Aug 9–18–1986)* — Sheffield Lab ▲ CD 27
Gershwin, G.:"I Got Rhythm" Vars, w. L. Mayorga (pno) — Sheffield Lab ▲ CD 28
Gershwin, G.:Music of, w. Lincoln Mayorga (pno)—I Got Rhythms Vars for Pno & Orch; Rhap in Blue; Promenade [Walking the Dog]; 3 Preludes; 2 Waltzes in C; Rialto Ripples Rag; Impromptu in 2 Keys; Lullaby for Str Qt; Summertime [Impromptu Jam] — Sheffield Lab ▲ SLS 10044
Gershwin, G.:Promenade — Sheffield Lab ▲ CD 28
Gershwin, G.:Rhap in Blue, w. L. Mayorga (pno) — Sheffield Lab ▲ CD 28
Griffes, C.T.:The White Peacock *(rec Moscow, Aug 9–18–1986)* — Sheffield Lab ▲ CD 27
Ives, C.:The Unanswered Question *(rec Moscow, Aug 9–18–1986)* — Sheffield Lab ▲ CD 27
Piston, W.:The Incredible Flutist (suite) *(rec Moscow, Aug 9–18, 1986)* — Sheffield Lab ▲ CD 26
Prokofiev, S.:Sym 1 *(rec 1987)* — RCA Gold Seal ▲ 74321–32042–2 [ADD]
Prokofiev, S.:Sym 5 *(rec 1986)* — RCA Gold Seal ▲ 74321–32042–2 [ADD]
Shostakovich, D.:Sym 5 *(rec Dec. 30, 1966)* — Russian Disc ▲ RUS 11188 [AAD]
Tchaikovsky, P.:Con 1 Pno, w. B. Berezovsky (pno) — Teldec ▲ 2292–46010–2 [DDD]
Tchaikovsky, P.:Con Vn, w. A. Suwanai (vn) — Teldec ▲ 2292–46010–2 [DDD]
K. Kondrashin (cnd)
Beethoven, L. van:Con 1 Pno, w. S. Richter (pno) — Russian Disc ▲ CD 11041 [AAD]
Beethoven, L. van:Con 3 Pno, w. S. Richter (pno) — Russian Disc ▲ CD 11041 [AAD]
Brahms, J.:Con 2 Pno, w. V. Cliburn (pno) *(rec 1972)* — RCA Red Seal ▲ 09026–62695–2 [ADD] ■ 09026–62695–4
Prokofiev, S.:Con 2 Pno, w. V. Ashkenazy (pno) *(rec live, Royal Festival Hall, London, 9/15/63)* — Intaglio ▲ INCD 7181 [ADD]
Prokofiev, S.:Con 3 Pno, w. Byron Janis (pno) *(rec Bolshoi Hall, Tchaikovsky Conservatory, Moscow, June 8–9, 1962)* — Mercury Living Presence ▲ 434333–2
Rachmaninoff, S.:The Bells, w. Yelizaveta Shumskaya (sop), Mikhail Dovenman (ten), Alexei Bolshakov (bar), Alexander Yurlov (cnd), Russian Republican Capelle — RCA Gold Seal ▲ 74321–32046–2 [ADD]
Rachmaninoff, S.:Con 1 Pno, w. Byron Janis (pno) *(rec Bolshoi Hall, Tchaikovsky Conservatory, Moscow, June 13, 1962)* — Mercury Living Presence ▲ 434333–2
Rachmaninoff, S.:Rhapsody on a Theme of Paganini, w. V. Cliburn (pno) *(rec 1972)* — RCA Red Seal ▲ 09026–62695–2 [ADD] ■ 09026–62695–4
Rachmaninoff, S.:Symphonic Dances — RCA Gold Seal ▲ 74321–32046–2 [ADD]
Shostakovich, D.:Con 1 Vn, w. Leonid Kogan (vn) — Supraphon ▲ SUP 3005
Shostakovich, D.:Con 1 Vn, w. L. Kogan (vn) *(rec 1962)* — Russian Disc ▲ RUS 11025 [AAD]
Shostakovich, D.:Con 2 Vn, w. D. Oistrakh (vn) *(rec 1968)* — Russian Disc ▲ RUS 11025 [AAD]
Sibelius, J.:Sym 3 *(rec live, Moscow, 4/4/77)* — Globe ▲ GLO 6011 [ADD]
Sibelius, J.:Sym 5 *(rec live, Moscow, 12/7/73)* — Globe ▲ GLO 6011 [ADD]
Strauss, R.:Don Quixote, w. M. Rostropovich (vc) — Russian Disc ▲ RUS 11 009 [ADD]
Tchaikovsky, B.:Con Vc, w. M. Rostropovich (vc) *(rec Mar. 13, 1964)* — Russian Disc ▲ RUS 11 115 [AAD]
Tchaikovsky, B.:Sym 2 *(rec 1969)* — Russian Disc ▲ RUS 11063 [AAD]
Tchaikovsky, P.:The Nutcracker (sels)—7 scenes from Act 1 *(rec live, Moscow 3/29/78)* — Globe ▲ GLO 6009 [ADD]
Tchaikovsky, P.:Sym 6 *(rec live, Moscow 3/29/78)* — Globe ▲ GLO 6009 [ADD]
Vainberg, M.:Sym 5 — Russian Disc ▲ RUS 11006 [AAD]
Vainberg, M.:Sym 6, w. *(chorus unknown)* *(rec 1974)* — Olympia ▲ OLY 471 [AAD]
Villa-Lobos, H.:Bachiana brasileira 1, w. M. Rostropovich (vc) — Russian Disc ▲ RUS 11 009 [ADD]
A. Lazarev (cnd)
Prokofiev, S.:Con 3 Pno, w. T. Judd (pno) — Chandos ("Collect" series) ▲ CHAN 6509 [ADD]
Tchaikovsky, P.:Con 1 Pno, w. T. Judd (pno) — Chandos ("Collect" series) ▲ CHAN 6509 [ADD]

Moscow PO (cont.)
L. Leighton Smith (cnd)
Glazunov, A.:Concert Waltz 1 *(rec Moscow, Aug 9–18–1986)* — Sheffield Lab ▲ CD 27
Glinka, M.:Russian & Ludmilla (ov) — Sheffield Lab ▲ CD 25
Mussorgsky, M.:Khovanshchina (prelude) — Sheffield Lab ▲ CD 25
Shostakovich, D.:Festive Ov *(rec Moscow, Aug 9–18–1986)* — Sheffield Lab ▲ CD 27
Shostakovich, D.:Sym 1 *(rec Moscow, Aug 9–18, 1986)* — Sheffield Lab ▲ CD 26
Tchaikovsky, P.:Sym 5 — Sheffield Lab ▲ CD 25
J. Nott (cnd)
Berio, L.:Corale, w. Irvine Arditti (vn) *(rec Great Hall, Tchaikovsky Conservatory, Moscow, Mar 11–14, 1995)* — BIS ▲ CD 772 [DDD]
Mira Fornés, R.:Desde Tan Tien, w. Irvine Arditti (vn) *(rec Great Hall, Tchaikovsky Conservatory, Moscow, Mar 11–14, 1995)* — BIS ▲ CD 772 [DDD]
Xenakis, I.:DOX–ORKH, w. Irvine Arditti (vn) *(rec Great Hall, Tchaikovsky Conservatory, Moscow, Mar 11–14, 1995)* — BIS ▲ CD 772 [DDD]
S. Samosud (cnd)
Shostakovich, D.:Con 2 Pno, w. D. Shostakovich (pno) *(rec 1957)* — Russian Disc ▲ RUS 15 005 [AAD]
V. Sinaisky (cnd)
Brahms, J.:Con 2 Pno, w. R. Coll (pno) *(rec studio 1991)* — Russian Disc ▲ RC CD 10 013 [DDD]
Fauré, G.:Ballade Pno, w. R. Coll (pno) *(rec 1991)* — Russian Disc ▲ RC CD 10 013 [DDD]
Schnittke, A.:Con Pno, w. Oleg Volkov (pno) — Brioso ▲ BR 109
Shostakovich, D.:Con 1 Pno, w. Oleg Volkov (pno) — Brioso ▲ BR 109
J. Spiegelman (cnd)
Senator, R.:Holocaust Requiem Kaddish, w. B. Kaufman (nar), Yurloff State Choir, Yekaterinburg Children's Chorus *(rec live Oct., 1992)* — Delos ▲ DE 1032 [DDD]
Smetana, B.:The Moldau *(rec live Oct. 1992)* — Delos ▲ DE 1032 [DDD]
A. Tchistiakov (cnd)
Liszt, F.:Con 1 Pno, w. L. Kuzmin (pno) — Russian Disc ▲ RUS 10020 [DDD]
Prokofiev, S.:Con 3 Pno, w. E. Kissin (pno) — RCA Red Seal 2–▲ 60567–2–RC [DDD]
Prokofiev, S.:Con 3 Pno, w. E. Kissin (pno) — RCA Red Seal ▲ 60051–2–RC [DDD] ■ 60051–4–RC (CrO2)
Tchaikovsky, P.:Con 1 Pno, w. L. Kuzmin (pno) — Russian Disc ▲ RUS 10020 [DDD]
Y. Temirkanov (cnd)
Prokofiev, S.:Con 1 Vn, w. D. Oistrakh (vn) *(rec 1966, 1969 & 1970)* — Praga ▲ PR 250 041
A. Vedernikov (cnd)
Beethoven, L. van:Con 5 Pno, "Emperor", w. L. Kuzmin (pno) — Russian Disc ▲ RUS 10023 [DDD]
Grieg, E.:Con Pno, Op. 16, w. L. Kuzmin (pno) — Russian Disc ▲ RUS 10023 [DDD]
K. Won (cnd)
Grieg, E.:Con Pno, Op. 16, w. Enrique Graf (pno) *(rec Great Hall of Moscow Radio Union, Dec 1994)* — Intersound ▲ 3539
Liszt, F.:Son Pno, w. Enrique Graf (pno) *(rec Great Hall of Moscow Radio Union, Dec 1994)* — Intersound ▲ 3539
A. Yulov (cnd)
Shostakovich, D.:Song of the Forest, w. V. Ivanovsky (ten), I. Petrov (bass), Moscow State Boys' Choir, Yurlov Russian Choir — Russian Disc ▲ RUS 11 048 [AAD]
A. Zhuraitis (cnd)
Vainberg, M.:Con Tpt, w. T. Dokshitser (tpt) — Russian Disc ▲ RUS 11006 [AAD]
Moscow PO members
R. Barshaï (cnd)
Shostakovich, D.:Sym 7, w. German Youth PO *(rec live, Leipzig Gewandhaus, 6/22/91)* — BIS ▲ CD 515 [DDD]
Moscow PO Soloists
G. Rozhdestvensky (cnd)
Shostakovich, D.:The Golden Mountains, w. USSR Ministry of Culture SO — Russian Disc ▲ RUS 11064 [AAD]
Shostakovich, D.:New Babylon, w. USSR Ministry of Culture SO — Russian Disc ▲ RUS 11064 [AAD]
Moscow PO Strings
D. Kitayenko (cnd)
Gershwin, G.:Lullaby — Sheffield Lab ▲ CD 28
Gershwin, G.:Lullaby *(rec Moscow, Aug 9–18–1986)* — Sheffield Lab ▲ CD 27
Moscow Philharmonic SO
K. Kondrashin (cnd)
Grieg, E.:Con Pno, Op. 16, w. S. Richter (pno) — Praga ▲ PR 250 048
Moscow Radio Grand SO
V. Fedoseyev (cnd)
Borodin, A.:In the Steppes of Central Asia *(rec 9/91)* — Novalis ▲ 150079 [DDD]
Borodin, A.:Prince Igor (ov) *(rec 9/91)* — Novalis ▲ 150079 [DDD]
Borodin, A.:Prince Igor (Polovtsian dances) *(rec 9/91)* — Novalis ▲ 150079 [DDD]
Borodin, A.:Sym 2 *(rec 9/91)* — Novalis ▲ 150079 [DDD]
A. Khachaturian (cnd)
Khachaturian, A.:Con Vn, w. D. Oistrakh (vn) — Vox Box 2–▲ CDX 5120
Moscow RSO
R. Abdullayev (cnd)
Amirov, F.:Shur — Olympia 2–▲ OLY 578 [ADD/DDD]
Karayev, K.:In the Path of Thunder (suite) — Olympia ▲ OLY 491 [DDD]
Karayev, K.:Seven Beauties (suite) — Olympia ▲ OLY 491 [DDD]
G. André (cnd)
Berwald, F.:Estrella de Soria (ov) — Consonance ▲ 810011 [DDD]
N. Anosov (cnd)
Rimsky-Korsakov, N.:Capriccio espagnol, w. D. Oistrakh (vn), Bolshoi Theater Orch *(rec 1960)* — Multisonic ("Russian Treasures" series) ▲ 31 0186
Rimsky-Korsakov, N.:Scheherazade, w. Bolshoi Theater Orch *(rec 1960)* — Multisonic ("Russian Treasures" series) ▲ 31 0186
R. Barshaï (cnd)
Mahler, G.:Sym 9 *(rec April 1993)* — BIS ▲ CD 632 [DDD]
M. Ermler, A. Zhuraitis (cnds)
Rimsky-Korsakov, N.:The Maid of Pskov (sels), w. Bolshoi Theater Orch—incidental music — Multisonic ▲ MUL 310274
Rimsky-Korsakov, N.:Pan Voyevoda, w. Bolshoi Theater Orch — Multisonic ▲ MUL 310274
Rimsky-Korsakov, N.:Snow Maiden (suite), w. Bolshoi Theater Orch — Multisonic ▲ MUL 310274
V. Fedoseyev (cnd)
Alfvén, H.:Bergakungen—Shepherd-girl's Dance — Consonance ▲ 810011 [DDD]
Glinka, M.:Capriccio brillante on the Jota aragonesa, "1st Spanish Ov" — Russian Season ▲ CMX 388114
Glinka, M.:A Life for the Tsar (sels) — Russian Season ▲ CMX 388114
Glinka, M.:A Life for the Tsar (sels)—Polonaise; Krakowiak; Mazurka; Ov *(rec Large Hall, Moscow Radio, May 18–20, 1995)* — Canyon Classics ▲ CD 289
Glinka, M.:Ov in D *(rec Large Hall, Moscow Radio, May 18–20, 1995)* — Canyon Classics ▲ CD 289
Glinka, M.:Russian & Ludmilla (sels) — Russian Season ▲ CMX 388114
Glinka, M.:Russian & Ludmilla (ov) *(rec Large Hall, Moscow Radio, May 18–20, 1995)* — Canyon Classics ▲ CD 289
Glinka, M.:Souvenir d'une nuit d'été — Russian Season ▲ CMX 388114
Glinka, M.:Waltz Fant — Russian Season ▲ CMX 388114
Kraus, J.M.:Tradgedy of Olympus—Ov — Consonance ▲ 810011 [DDD]
Kuss, M.I.:Lyric Poem — Consonance ▲ 810011 [DDD]
Lidholm, I.:Kontakion — Consonance ▲ 810011 [DDD]
Mussorgsky, M.:Pictures *(rec Moscow Conservatory, Large Hall, Aug 29–31, 1993)* — Canyon Classics ▲ 206
Prokofiev, S.:Con 1 Vn, w. Julian Rachlin (vn) — Sony Classical ▲ SK 66567
Prokofiev, S.:Sym 1 *(rec Moscow Radio, Large Hall, May 19–22, 1994)* — Canyon Classics ▲ 250

ORCH. & ENS.

Moscow RSO (cont.)

V. Fedoseyev (cnd) (cont.)

Prokofiev, S.:Sym 5 *(rec Moscow Radio, Large Hall, May 19–22, 1994)* Canyon Classics ▲ 250
Sibelius, J.:Finlandia Consonance ▲ 810011 [DDD]
Sviridov, G.:The Snowstorm *(rec Large Hall, Moscow Radio, May 18–20, 1995)* Canyon Classics ▲ CD 289
Tchaikovsky, B.:Theme & Vars *(rec Moscow Conservatory, Large Hall, Aug 29–31, 1993)* Canyon Classics ▲ 206
Tchaikovsky, P.:Con Vn, w. Julian Rachlin (vn) Sony Classical ▲ SK 66567

A. Gauk (cnd)

Khachaturian, A.:Sym 1 Russian Disc ▲ RUS 11 005 [ADD]
Saint-Saëns, C.:Con 1 Vc, w. S. Knushevitsky (vc) *(rec 1946)* Multisonic ("Russian Treasures" series) ▲ 31 0254
Schumann, R.:Con Pno, w. Svyatoslav Richter (pno) Multisonic ▲ MUL 310268
Tchaikovsky, P.:Vars on a Rococo Theme, w. Sviatoslav Knushevitsky (vc) *(rec 1949)* Multisonic ("Russian Treasures" series) ▲ 31 0254

N. Golovanov (cnd)

Scriabin, A.:Con Pno, w. Heinrich Neuhaus (pno) *(rec 1950)* Multisonic ("Russian Treasures" series) ▲ 31 0254

A. Heller (cnd)

Villa-Lobos, H.:The Forest of the Amazon, w. Renee Fleming (sop) Consonance ▲ 81 0012 [DDD]

N. Iimori (cnd)

Stravinsky, I.:Le Sacre du printemps Orch *(rec 1992)* Emergo ("Corneille") ▲ EC 3969

A. Khachaturian (cnd)

Khachaturian, A.:Masquerade (ballet suite) Russian Disc ▲ RUS 11 005 [ADD]

B. Khaikin (cnd)

Liapunov, S.:Con 2 Pno, w. A. Bakhchiev (pno) Russian Disc ▲ RUS 11 024 [ADD]

A. Kovalov (cnd)

Arensky, A.:Sym 2 Multisonic ▲ MUL 310272

A. Orlov (cnd)

Sibelius, J.:Con Vn, w. G. Barinova (vn) *(rec 1947)* Multisonic ("Russian Treasures" series) ▲ 31 0238

G. Rozhdestvensky (cnd)

Bartók, B.:Con 1 Vn, w. David Oistrakh (vn) *(rec 1962)* Forlane ▲ FRL 16589 [AAD]
Glinka, M.:Russlan & Ludmilla (ov) IMP ("BBC Radio Classics" series) ▲ IMP 9139
Shostakovich, D.:Con 1 Vc, w. Natalya Shakhovskaya (vc) IMP ("BBC Radio Classics" series) ▲ IMP 5691702
Sibelius, J.:Con Vn, w. D. Oistrakh (vn) Vox Box 2–▲ CDX 5120
Tchaikovsky, P.:Manfred IMP ("BBC Radio Classics" series) ▲ IMP 5691772
Tchaikovsky, P.:Sym 6 *(rec live, Royal Albert Hall, London, August 1966)* Intaglio ▲ INCD 7261 [ADD]
Tchaikovsky, P.:Sym 6 IMP ("BBC Radio Classics" series) ▲ IMP 9139

M. Shostakovich (cnd)

Vainberg, M.:Sym 12 Russian Disc ▲ RUS 11010 [AAD]

Y. Silantiev (cnd)

Schumann, R.:Con Vc, w. Mikhail Khomitser (vc) Multisonic ▲ MUL 310272
Tchaikovsky, P.:Vars on a Rococo Theme, w. Mikhail Khomitser (vc) Multisonic ▲ MUL 310272

J. Spiegelman (cnd)

Fine, I.:Blue Towers *(rec Feb. 22–27, 1993)* Delos ▲ DE 3139 [DDD]
Fine, I.:Diversions *(rec Feb. 22–27, 1993)* Delos ▲ DE 3139 [DDD]
Fine, I.:Music for Pno *(rec Feb. 22–27, 1993)* Delos ▲ DE 3139 [DDD]
Fine, I.:Sym *(rec Feb. 22–27, 1993)* Delos ▲ DE 3139 [DDD]
Fine, I.:Toccata concertante *(rec Feb. 22–27, 1993)* Delos ▲ DE 3139 [DDD]

E. Svetlanov (cnd)

Parsadanian, B.:Sym 1 Russian Disc ▲ RUS 11 050 [ADD]
Parsadanian, B.:Sym 2 Russian Disc ▲ RUS 11 050 [ADD]

Moscow Radio-TV SO

Y. Adigezalov (cnd)

Amirov, F.:Azerbaijan Capriccio Olympia ▲ OLY 490
Amirov, F.:Gyulistan-Bayatī shirazi Olympia ▲ OLY 490
Amirov, F.:Shchur, Kyurd Ovsharī Olympia ▲ OLY 490
Amirov, F.:To the Memory of Nizami Olympia ▲ OLY 490

A. Korneiev (cnd)

Pascal, C.R.G.:Con Hp, w. Vera Dulova (hp) *(rec 1970)* Russian Compact Disc ("Talents of Russia" series) ▲ RCD 16206 [AAD]

P. Tiboris (cnd)

Taneyev, S.:Duet for Romeo & Juliet, w. S. Zambalis (sop), J. Daniecki (ten) Bridge ▲ BCD 9034 [DDD]
Taneyev, S.:Sym 4 Bridge ▲ BCD 9034 [DDD]

Moscow Religious Academy & Seminary

A. Matvey (cnd)

Marienhymnen aus Russland, w. Monastery of the Holy Trinity & St. Sergius Combined Choirs, Dormition of the BVM Church Choir at Monastery of the Virgin [cnd:H. Pjotr] Koch Schwann ▲ SHC 313047 [ADD]

Moscow Solisti Virtuosi

Bach, J.S.:Cons Vn (comp), w. V. Spivakov (vn) RCA Red Seal ▲ 09026-61582-2
Bach, J.S.:Con in d Vn, w. V. Spivakov (vn) RCA Red Seal ▲ 09026-61582-2
Bach, J.S.:Con in D Vn, w. V. Spivakov (vn) RCA Red Seal ▲ 09026-61582-2

Moscow Soloists

Britten, B.:Lachrymae, w. Y. Bashmet (va) RCA Red Seal ▲ 60464-2-RC [DDD]
Hindemith, P.:Trauermusik, w. Y. Bashmet (va) RCA Red Seal ▲ 60464-2-RC [DDD]

Y. Bashmet (cnd)

Beethoven, L. van:Qt 11 Strs, "Quartetto serioso" RCA Red Seal ▲ 09026-60988-2
Grieg, E.:Holberg Suite RCA Red Seal ▲ 60368-2-RC [DDD]
Grieg, E.:Nordic Melodies, Op. 63 RCA Red Seal ▲ 60368-2-RC [DDD]
Schnittke, A.:Canon Vn, w. Gidon Kremer (vn) EMI Classics ▲ CDC 55627
Schnittke, A.:Con for 3, w. Gidon Kremer (vn), Yuri Bashmet (va), Mstislav Rostropovich (vc) EMI Classics ▲ CDC 55627
Schnittke, A.:Trio Son RCA Red Seal ▲ 60446-2-RC [DDD]
Schubert, Franz:Qt 14 Strs RCA Red Seal ▲ 09026-60988-2
Tchaikovsky, P.:Serenade Strs RCA Red Seal ▲ 60368-2-RC [DDD]

Moscow State SO

F. Glushchenko (cnd)

Liapunov, S.:Ballada Olympia ▲ OLY 519 [DDD]
Liapunov, S.:Sym 1 Olympia ▲ OLY 519 [DDD]

I. Golovshin (cnd)

Rubinstein, A.:Con 2 Pno, w. A. Paley (pno) Russian Disc ▲ RUS 11 360 [DDD]
Rubinstein, A.:Con 4 Pno, w. A. Paley (pno) Russian Disc ▲ RUS 11 360 [DDD]
Rubinstein, A.:Feramors (ballet music) Russian Disc ▲ RUS 11 356 [DDD]
Rubinstein, A.:Sym 2 Russian Disc ▲ RUS 11 356 [DDD]

K. Kondrashin (cnd)

Brahms, J.:Con Vn, w. Eduard Grach (vn) *(rec 1961)* Rondo Grammofon ▲ RCD 16211 [AAD]
Tchaikovsky, P.:Vars on a Rococo Theme, w. Natalia Shakhovskaya (vc) *(rec 1963)* Russian Compact Disc ▲ RCD 16203 [ADD]

G. Provatorov (cnd)

Popov, G.N.:Sym 1 Olympia ▲ OLY 576

G. Rozhdestvensky (cnd)

Bartók, B.:Con 2 Vn, w. Igor Oistrakh (vn) Audiophile Classics ▲ APL 101519

Moscow String Quartet

Schnittke, A.:Qnt Pno, w. C. Orbelian (pno) Russian Disc ▲ RUS 10 031 [DDD]
Shostakovich, D.:Qnt Pno, w. C. Orbelian (pno) Russian Disc ▲ RUS 10 031 [DDD]
Tchaikovsky, P.:Qt 2 Strs Le Chant du Monde ("Russian Season" series) ▲ RUS 288 102

Moscow SO

Malipiero, G.F.:Sinf 4, w. A. de Almeida *(rec May & June 1993)* Marco Polo ▲ 8.223602 [DDD]

Adriano (cnd)

Ibert, J.:Diane de Poitiers *(rec Mosfilm Studio, Aug 1995)* Marco Polo ▲ 8.223854 [DDD]
Ibert, J.:The Triumph of Chastity *(rec Mosfilm Studio, Aug 1995)* Marco Polo ▲ 8.223854 [DDD]
Lazzari, S.:Sym in E♭ *(rec Mosfilm Studio, Aug 1995)* Marco Polo ▲ 8.223853 [DDD]
Lazzari, S.:Tableaux Maritimes *(rec Mosfilm Studio, Aug 1995)* Marco Polo ▲ 8.223853 [DDD]

A. de Almeida (cnd)

Castillo, R.:Abstracción *(rec Mosfilm Studios, Feb 1994)* Marco Polo ("Latin American Classics" series) ▲ 8.223719 [DDD]
Castillo, R.:La Doncella Ixquic *(rec Mosfilm Studios, Feb 1994)* Marco Polo ("Latin American Classics" series) ▲ 8.223719 [DDD]
Castillo, R.:Estelas de Tikal *(rec Mosfilm Studios, Feb 1994)* Marco Polo ("Latin American Classics" series) ▲ 8.223719 [DDD]
Castillo, R.:Guatemala Orch *(rec Mosfilm Studio, Moscow, Feb. 1994)* Marco Polo ("Latin American Classics" series) ▲ 8.223710 [DDD]
Castillo, R.:Guatemala Pno [orchd Rodrigo Asturias 1969] *(rec Mosfilm Studio, Moscow, Feb. 1994)* Marco Polo ("Latin American Classics" series) ▲ 8.223710 [DDD]
Castillo, R.:Instantáneas Plásticas *(rec Mosfilm Studios, Feb 1994)* Marco Polo ("Latin American Classics" series) ▲ 8.223719 [DDD]
Castillo, R.:Paál Kabá *(rec Mosfilm Studios, Feb 1994)* Marco Polo ("Latin American Classics" series) ▲ 8.223719 [DDD]
Castillo, R.:Quiché Achi *(rec Mosfilm Studios, Feb 1994)* Marco Polo ("Latin American Classics" series) ▲ 8.223719 [DDD]
Castillo, R.:Sinfonietta *(rec Mosfilm Studio, Moscow, Feb. 1994)* Marco Polo ("Latin American Classics" series) ▲ 8.223710 [DDD]
Castillo, R.:Xibalbá *(rec Mosfilm Studio, Moscow, Feb. 1994)* Marco Polo ("Latin American Classics" series) ▲ 8.223710 [DDD]
Haydn, J.:The Seven Last Words of Christ on the Cross, w. Elena Evseeva (sop), Margarita Maruna (mez), Arkady Mishenkin (ten), Boris Bezhko (bass), Stanislav Gussev (cnd), Russian State Academy Chorus *(rec Mosfilm Studio, Moscow, Jan 27–28, 1995)* SOMM ▲ SOMMCD 203 [DDD]
Malipiero, G.F.:Sinf 1 *(rec May & June 1993)* Marco Polo ▲ 8.223603 [DDD]
Malipiero, G.F.:Sinf 2 *(rec May & June 1993)* Marco Polo ▲ 8.223603 [DDD]
Malipiero, G.F.:Sinf 3 *(rec May & June 1993)* Marco Polo ▲ 8.223602 [DDD]
Malipiero, G.F.:Sinf 7 *(rec May & June 1993)* Marco Polo ▲ 8.223604 [DDD]
Malipiero, G.F.:Sinf 9 *(rec Mosfilm Studio, Moscow, Feb. 1994)* Marco Polo ▲ 8.223697 [DDD]
Malipiero, G.F.:Sinf 10 *(rec Mosfilm Studio, Moscow, Feb. 1994)* Marco Polo ▲ 8.223697 [DDD]
Malipiero, G.F.:Sin del mare *(rec May & June 1993)* Marco Polo ▲ 8.223602 [DDD]
Malipiero, G.F.:Sinfonia del silenzo e de la morte *(rec May & June 1993)* Marco Polo ▲ 8.223603 [DDD]
Malipiero, G.F.:Sinf dello zodiaco *(rec Mosfilm Studio, Moscow, Feb. 1994)* Marco Polo ▲ 8.223697 [DDD]
Malipiero, G.F.:Sinf in un tempo *(rec May & June 1993)* Marco Polo ▲ 8.223604 [DDD]
Malipiero, G.F.:Sinf per Antigenida *(rec May & June 1993)* Marco Polo ▲ 8.223604 [DDD]
Martínez-Sobral, M.:Acuarelas Chapinas *(rec Mosfilm Studio, Moscow, Feb. 1994)* Marco Polo ("Latin American Classics" series) ▲ 8.223710 [DDD]
Sauguet, H.:Sym 1 *(rec Mosfilm Studio, Moscow, Oct 1994)* Marco Polo ▲ 8.223463 [DDD]
Tansman, A.:Capriccio *(rec Mosfilm Studio, Moscow, Russia, July 1994)* Marco Polo ▲ 8.223757 [DDD]
Tansman, A.:Con Orch *(rec Mosfilm Studio, Moscow, Russia, July 1994)* Marco Polo ▲ 8.223757 [DDD]
Tansman, A.:Etudes *(rec Mosfilm Studio, Moscow, Russia, July 1994)* Marco Polo ▲ 8.223757 [DDD]
Tournemire, C.:Sym 1 *(rec Mosfilm Studio, Moscow, Apr. 1994)* Marco Polo ▲ 8.223476 [DDD]
Tournemire, C.:Sym 2 *(rec Mosfilm Studio, Moscow, Apr. & May 1994)* Marco Polo ▲ 8.223478 [DDD]
Tournemire, C.:Sym 3, w. Natalia Malina (org) *(rec Mosfilm Studios, May 1994)* Marco Polo ▲ 8.223808 [DDD]
Tournemire, C.:Sym 4 *(rec Mosfilm Studio, Moscow, Apr. & May 1994)* Marco Polo ▲ 8.223478 [DDD]
Tournemire, C.:Sym 5 *(rec Mosfilm Studio, Moscow, Apr. 1994)* Marco Polo ▲ 8.223476 [DDD]
Tournemire, C.:Sym 7 *(rec Mosfilm Studio, Moscow, Feb 1995)* Marco Polo 2–▲ 8.223877–8 [DDD]
Tournemire, C.:Sym 8 *(rec Mosfilm Studios, May 1994)* Marco Polo ▲ 8.223808 [DDD]

A. de Anissimov (cnd)

Glazunov, A.:Raymonda *(rec Mosfilm Studio, Moscow, June & July 1995)* Naxos 2–▲ 8.553503–4 [DDD]

F. Devreese (cnd)

de Greef, A.:Con 1 Pno, w. André De Groote (pno) *(rec Mosfilm Studio, Moscow, Feb 1995)* Marco Polo ("Anthology of Flemish Music" series) ▲ 8.223810 [DDD]
de Greef, A.:Con 2 Pno, w. André De Groote (pno) *(rec Mosfilm Studio, Moscow, Feb 1995)* Marco Polo ("Anthology of Flemish Music" series) ▲ 8.223810 [DDD]
Devreese, G.:In memoriam *(rec Mosfilm Studio, Moscow, June 1994)* Marco Polo ("Anthology of Flemish Music" series) ▲ 8.223739 [DDD]
Devreese, G.:Poème héroïque *(rec Mosfilm Studio, Moscow, June 1994)* Marco Polo ("Anthology of Flemish Music" series) ▲ 8.223739 [DDD]
Devreese, G.:Sym 1, "Gothique" *(rec Mosfilm Studio, Moscow, June 1994)* Marco Polo ("Anthology of Flemish Music" series) ▲ 8.223739 [DDD]
Gilson, P.:Alvar Prelude *(rec Mosfilm Studio, Moscow, June, 1994)* Marco Polo ▲ 8.223809 [DDD]
Gilson, P.:Mélodies écossaises *(rec Mosfilm Studio, Moscow, June, 1994)* Marco Polo ▲ 8.223809 [DDD]
Gilson, P.:La Mer *(rec Mosfilm Studio, Moscow, June, 1994)* Marco Polo ▲ 8.223809 [DDD]
Gilson, P.:Symphonic Ov 3 *(rec Mosfilm Studio, Moscow, June, 1994)* Marco Polo ▲ 8.223809 [DDD]
Meulemans, A.:Meinacht *(rec Mosfilm Studio, Moscow, Russia, Oct 1994)* Marco Polo ▲ 8.223776 [DDD]
Meulemans, A.:Plinius Fontein *(rec Mosfilm Studio, Moscow, Russia, Oct 1994)* Marco Polo ▲ 8.223776 [DDD]
Meulemans, A.:Sym 2 *(rec Mosfilm Studio, Moscow, Russia, Oct 1994)* Marco Polo ▲ 8.223776 [DDD]
Meulemans, A.:Sym 3 *(rec Mosfilm Studio, Moscow, Russia, Oct 1994)* Marco Polo ▲ 8.223776 [DDD]
Poot, M.:Cheerful Ov *(rec Mosfilm Studio, Moscow, Russia, Oct 1994)* Marco Polo ("Anthology of Flemish Music" series) ▲ 8.223775 [DDD]
Poot, M.:Pygmalion (ballet suite) *(rec Mosfilm Studio, Moscow, Russia, Oct 1994)* Marco Polo ("Anthology of Flemish Music" series) ▲ 8.223775 [DDD]
Poot, M.:Symphonic Allegro *(rec Mosfilm Studio, Moscow, Russia, Oct 1994)* Marco Polo ("Anthology of Flemish Music" series) ▲ 8.223775 [DDD]
Poot, M.:Sym 3 *(rec Mosfilm Studio, Jan 1995)* Marco Polo ▲ 8.223805 [DDD]
Poot, M.:Sym 5 *(rec Mosfilm Studio, Jan 1995)* Marco Polo ▲ 8.223805 [DDD]
Poot, M.:Sym 6 *(rec Mosfilm Studio, Moscow, Russia, Oct 1994)* Marco Polo ("Anthology of Flemish Music" series) ▲ 8.223775 [DDD]
Poot, M.:Sym 7 *(rec Mosfilm Studio, Jan 1995)* Marco Polo ▲ 8.223805 [DDD]
Poot, M.:Tarantella *(rec Mosfilm Studio, Jan 1995)* Marco Polo ▲ 8.223805 [DDD]
Sternefeld, D.:Mater Dolorosa—4 interludes & finale *(rec Mosfilm Studio, Oct 1995)* Marco Polo ▲ 8.223813 [DDD]
Sternefeld, D.:Rossiniazata *(rec Mosfilm Studio, Oct 1995)* Marco Polo ▲ 8.223813 [DDD]
Sternefeld, D.:Sym 1 *(rec Mosfilm Studio, Oct 1995)* Marco Polo ▲ 8.223813 [DDD]

Moscow SO (cont.)

V. Dudarova (cnd)

Levina, Z.:Con 2 Pno, w. B. Petrushansky (pno) Russian Disc ▲ RUS 11 382 [DDD]

V. Fedoseyev (cnd)

Tchaikovsky, P.:Eugene Onegin, w. Lidiya Chernikh (sop), Tamara Sinyavskaya (mez), Alexander Vedernikov (bass), Alexander Fedin (sgr), Yuri Mazurok (sgr), USSR SO, Fernseh SO Audiophile Classics ("Legacy Collection" series) 2–▲ 101.751

I. Golovshin (cnd)

Glazunov, A.:Tsar Iudeyskiy, w. Moscow Capella *(rec Mosfilm Studio, Moscow, May 1995)* Naxos ▲ 8.553575 [DDD]
Scriabin, A.:Sym Poem *(rec Mosfilm Studio, Oct 1995)* Naxos ▲ 8.553581 [DDD]
Scriabin, A.:Sym 2, w. Alexander Avramenko (vn) *(rec Mosfilm Studio, Oct 1995)* Naxos ▲ 8.553581 [DDD]

P. Kogan (cnd)

Rakhmadiev, E.:Con Vn, w. Aiman Musakodzhaeva (vn) *(rec 1990)* Consonance ▲ 81–0003 [DDD]
Rakhmadiev, E.:Dairabay *(rec 1990)* Consonance ▲ 81–0003 [DDD]
Rakhmadiev, E.:Kudasha–Duman *(rec 1990)* Consonance ▲ 81–0003 [DDD]

K. Krimets (cnd)

Glazunov, A.:Cortège solennel *(rec Mosfilm Studio, May 1995)* Naxos ▲ 8.553538 [DDD]
Glazunov, A.:From Darkness to Light *(rec Mosfilm Studio, May 1995)* Naxos ▲ 8.553538 [DDD]
Glazunov, A.:From the Middle Ages *(rec Mosfilm Studio, Moscow, May 1995)* Naxos ▲ 8.553537 [DDD]
Glazunov, A.:The Kremlin *(rec Mosfilm Studio, Moscow, May 1995)* Naxos ▲ 8.553537 [DDD]
Glazunov, A.:Lyric Poem *(rec Mosfilm Studio, Moscow, May 1995)* Naxos ▲ 8.553537 [DDD]
Glazunov, A.:March on a Russian Theme *(rec Mosfilm Studio, May 1995)* Naxos ▲ 8.553538 [DDD]
Glazunov, A.:Mazurka *(rec Mosfilm Studio, May 1995)* Naxos ▲ 8.553538 [DDD]
Glazunov, A.:Poème épique *(rec Mosfilm Studio, Moscow, May 1995)* Naxos ▲ 8.553537 [DDD]
Glazunov, A.:Slav Holiday *(rec Mosfilm Studio, May 1995)* Naxos ▲ 8.553538 [DDD]
Glazunov, A.:Stenka Razin *(rec Mosfilm Studio, May 1995)* Naxos ▲ 8.553538 [DDD]
Kupferman, M.:The Moor's Con, w. K. Hayami (pno) Soundspells ▲ CD 110 [DDD]
Kupferman, M.:Wings of the Highest Tower Soundspells ▲ CD 110 [DDD]

M. Raickovich (cnd)

Raickovich, M.:Happy Ov *(rec Mosfilm Studios, Moscow, Aug 24–25, 1993)* Mode ▲ mode 45
Raickovich, M.:Romances, w. Igor Frolov (vn) *(rec Mosfilm Studios, Moscow, Aug 24–25, 1993)* Mode ▲ mode 45
Raickovich, M.:Sym 1 *(rec Mosfilm Studios, Moscow, Aug 24–25, 1993)* Mode ▲ mode 45

H. Shek (cnd)

Tcherepnin, N.:Le pavillon d'Armide *(rec Mosfilm Studio, Moscow, Nov. 1994)* Marco Polo ▲ 8.223779 [DDD]

K. Stratton (cnd)

Arensky, A.:Vars on a Theme of Tchaikovsky Dorian Discovery ▲ DOR 80144
Dvořák, A.:Notturno Dorian Discovery ▲ DOR 80144
Dvořák, A.:Qnt Strs, Op. 77—Notturno movt *(rec Mosfilm Studio, June 1995)* Dorian Discovery ▲ DIS 80144 [DDD]
Glazunov, A.:Suite Strs Dorian Discovery ▲ DOR 80144
Kallinikov, V.:Chanson triste Dorian Discovery ▲ DOR 80144
Suk, J.:Meditation on the Old Czech Hymn "St. Wenceslas" *(rec Mosfilm Studio, June 1995)* Dorian Discovery ▲ DIS 80144 [DDD]

W.T. Stromberg (cnd)

Korngold, E.W.:Another Dawn [arr John Morgan] *(rec Mosfilm Studio, Oct 1995)* Marco Polo ▲ 8.223871 [DDD]
Korngold, E.W.:Escape Me Never (ballet) [completed & arr John Morgan] *(rec Mosfilm Studio, Oct 1995)* Marco Polo ▲ 8.223871 [DDD]
Salter, H.J.:House of Frankenstein [reconstructed & orchd John Morgan or William Stromberg] *(rec Mosfilm Studio, Moscow, Russia, Dec. 1994)* Marco Polo ▲ 8.223748 [DDD]
Salter, H.J.:The Invisible Man Returns [music reconstructed & orchd John Morgan] *(rec Mosfilm Studio, Moscow, Russia, Dec. 1994)* Marco Polo ▲ 8.223747 [DDD]
Salter, H.J.:The Wolf Man [music reconstructed & orchd John Morgan] *(rec Mosfilm Studio, Moscow, Russia, Dec. 1994)* Marco Polo ▲ 8.223747 [DDD]
Skinner, F.:Son of Frankenstein [music reconstructed & orchd John Morgan] *(rec Mosfilm Studio, Moscow, Russia, Dec. 1994)* Marco Polo ▲ 8.223747 [DDD]
Steiner, M.:The Beast with 5 Fingers [arr John Morgan] *(rec Mosfilm Studio, Oct 1995)* Marco Polo ▲ 8.223870 [DDD]
Steiner, M.:The Lost Patrol [arr John Morgan] *(rec Mosfilm Studio, Oct 1995)* Marco Polo ▲ 8.223870 [DDD]
Steiner, M.:Virginia City [arr John Morgan] *(rec Mosfilm Studio, Oct 1995)* Marco Polo ▲ 8.223870 [DDD]

D. Yablonsky (cnd)

Khachaturian, A.:Dance Suite *(rec St. Petersburg Radio, 1994)* Naxos ▲ 8.550802 [DDD]

Moscow Trio

Rachmaninoff, S.:Trio élégiaque 2 Art & Electronics ▲ AED 68008
Shostakovich, D.:Suite 1 Jazz Orch, w. N. Guerassimova (sop) Russian Season ("Russian Season" series) ▲ RUS 288088
Shostakovich, D.:Trio 1 Pno Russian Season ("Russian Season" series) ▲ RUS 288088
Shostakovich, D.:Trio 2 Pno Russian Season ("Russian Season" series) ▲ RUS 288088
Spiegelman, J.:Trio Pno Art & Electronics ▲ AED 10526 [DDD]
Sviridov, G.:Trio Pno Art & Electronics ▲ AED 10526 [DDD]
Tchaikovsky, A.:Trio Art & Electronics ▲ AED 10526 [DDD]

Moscow Virtuosi

Wild Classics:A Celebration of Animals & Nature, w. James Galway (fl), Ofra Harnoy (vc), Martin Hoherman (vc), Emily Mitchell (hp), Michael Dussek (pno), Samuel Lipman (pno), Leo Litwin (pno), Gerhard Oppitz (pno), Isao Tomita (synths), Boston Pops Orch [cnd:Arthur Fiedler], Chicago SO [cnd:Fritz Reiner] RCA Red Seal ▲ 09026–68483–2 ■ 09026–68483–4

V. Spivakov (cnd)

Bach, J.S.:Con Fl, Vn & Hpd, w. E. Duran (fl), V. Spivakov (vn), S. Bezrodny (hpd) RCA Red Seal ▲ 7991–2–RC [DDD]
Bach, J.S.:Con Vn & Ob, w. V. Spivakov (vn), A. Utkin (ob) RCA Red Seal ▲ 7991–2–RC [DDD]
Bach, J.S.:Con for 2 Vns, w. V. Spivakov (vn), A. Futer (vn) RCA Red Seal ▲ 7991–2–RC [DDD]
Bach, J.S.:Con for 3 Vns, w. V. Spivakov (vn), A. Futer (vn), B. Garlitsky (vn) RCA Red Seal ▲ 7991–2–RC [DDD]
Bach, J.S.:Suites Orch, BWV 1066–1069 RCA Red Seal ▲ 60360–2–RC [DDD]
Basic 100, Vol. 80, w. Vladimir Spivakov (vn) RCA Victor ▲ 09026–68457–2 ■ 09026–68457–4
Denisov, E.:Vars on Haydn's Canon "Death is a long sleep" RCA Red Seal ▲ 09026–68061–2
Denisov, E.:Vars on Haydn's Canon "Death is a long sleep" RCA Red Seal ▲ 09026–68061–2
Encore! *(rec Reitstadel, Neumarkt, Germany, July 25–27, 1994)* RCA Red Seal ▲ 09026–68185–2 [DDD]
Gubaidulina, S.:The Seven Last Words RCA Red Seal ▲ 09026–60466–2
Hartmann, K.A.:Con funèbre, w. Vladimir Spivakov (vn) RCA Red Seal ▲ 60370–2–RC [DDD]
Haydn, J.:Con Hpd, Obs, Hns & Strs, H.XVIII/11, w. Evgeni Kissin (pno) RCA Red Seal ▲ 7948–2–RC [DDD] ■ 7948–4–RC (CrO2)
Haydn, J.:Con 1 Vn, w. Vladimir Spivakov (vn) RCA Red Seal ▲ 7948–2–RC [DDD] ■ 7948–4–RC (CrO2)
Haydn, J.:Sinf concertante RCA Red Seal ▲ 7948–2–RC [DDD] ■ 7948–4–RC (CrO2)
Mozart, W.A.:Arias, w. Nathalie Stutzmann (cta)—Ombra felice, K.255; Io ti lascio, oh cara, addio, K.Anh.245 *(rec Reitstadel, Neumarkt, Germany, July 27–30, 1994)* RCA Red Seal ▲ 09026–68187–2 [DDD]
Mozart, W.A.:Ascanio (sels), w. Nathalie Stutzmann (cta)—Ahimè! Che veggio mai?; Al mio ben mi veggio avanti; Perchè tacer degg'io?; Cara, lontano ancora; Ah di sì nobil alma *(rec Reitstadel, Neumarkt, Germany, July 27–30, 1994)* RCA Red Seal ▲ 09026–68187–2 [DDD]

Moscow Virtuosi (cont.)

V. Spivakov (cnd) (cont.)

Mozart, W.A.:Betulia (sels), w. Nathalie Stutzmann (cta)—Prigionier che fa ritorno; Parto inerme, e non pavento *(rec Reitstadel, Neumarkt, Germany, July 27–30, 1994)* RCA Red Seal ▲ 09026–68187–2 [DDD]
Mozart, W.A.:Con 12 Pno, w. E. Kissin (pno) RCA Red Seal 2–▲ 60567–2–RC [DDD]
Mozart, W.A.:Con 12 Pno, w. E. Kissin (pno) RCA Red Seal ▲ 09026–60400–2 ■ 09026–60400–4
Mozart, W.A.:Con 20 Pno, w. E. Kissin (pno) RCA Red Seal ▲ 09026–60400–2 ■ 09026–60400–4
Mozart, W.A.:Con 2 Vn, w. V. Spivakov (vn) RCA Red Seal ▲ 09026–60152–2 [DDD]
Mozart, W.A.:Con 3 Vn, w. V. Spivakov (vn) RCA Red Seal ▲ 09026–60152–2 [DDD]
Mozart, W.A.:Con 5 Vn, w. Vladimir Spivakov (vn) RCA ("Basic 100" series) ▲ 09026–68457–2 ■ 09026–68457–4
Mozart, W.A.:Con 5 Vn, w. V. Spivakov (vn) RCA Red Seal ▲ 09026–60152–2 [DDD]
Mozart, W.A.:Concertone Vns, w. V. Spivakov (vn), B. Garlitski (vn) RCA Red Seal ▲ 09026–60467–2
Mozart, W.A.:Diverts Str Qt, K.136–138 RCA Red Seal ▲ 60066–2 [DDD]
Mozart, W.A.:Kleine Nachtmusik RCA Red Seal ▲ 60066–2 [DDD]
Mozart, W.A.:Mitridate (sels), w. Nathalie Stutzmann (cta)—Venga pur, minacci e frema; Ah, giacchè son tradito; Son reo, l'error confesso; Vadasi...Oh ciel; Già dagli occhi il velo è tolto; Va, l'error mio palesa *(rec Reitstadel, Neumarkt, Germany, July 27–30, 1994)* RCA Red Seal ▲ 09026–68187–2 [DDD]
Mozart, W.A.:Rondo Pno Orch, K.382, w. E. Kissin (pno) RCA Red Seal ▲ 09026–60400–2 ■ 09026–60400–4
Mozart, W.A.:Sinf concertante Vn, K.364, w. Vladimir Spivakov (vn) RCA ("Basic 100" series) ▲ 09026–68457–2 ■ 09026–68457–4
Mozart, W.A.:Sinf concertante Vn, K.364, w. V. Spivakov (vn), S. Mintz (va) RCA Red Seal ▲ 09026–60467–2
Mozart, W.A.:Sym 15 RCA Red Seal ▲ 60715–2 [DDD] ■ 60715–4 (CrO2)
Mozart, W.A.:Sym 24 RCA Red Seal ▲ 60715–2 [DDD] ■ 60715–4 (CrO2)
Mozart, W.A.:Sym 28 RCA Red Seal ▲ 60715–2 [DDD] ■ 60715–4 (CrO2)
Mozart, W.A.:Sym 29 RCA Red Seal ▲ 60715–2 [DDD] ■ 60715–4 (CrO2)
Pärt, A.:Cantus in Memory of Benjamin Britten RCA Red Seal ▲ 09026–68061–2
Pärt, A.:Collage on the Theme B–A–C–H RCA Red Seal ▲ 09026–68061–2
Penderecki, K.:Capriccio Vn, w. V. Spivakov (vn) RCA Red Seal ▲ 60370–2–RC [DDD]
Prokofiev, S.:Ov on Hebrew Themes RCA Red Seal ▲ 60370–2–RC [DDD]
Sammartini, G.:Cons Rcr, w. Michala Petri (rcr)—Con in F *(rec Gijon Laboral Univ Theater, Spain, June 1995)* RCA Red Seal ▲ 0902–668543–2 [DDD]
Schnittke, A.:Con Pno, w. V. Krainev (pno) RCA Red Seal ▲ 09026–60466–2
Schubert, Franz:German Dances Strs, D.90 RCA Red Seal ▲ 09026–60452–2
Schubert, Franz:Minuets & Trios, D.89 RCA Red Seal ▲ 09026–60452–2
Schubert, Franz:Sym 5 RCA Red Seal ▲ 09026–60452–2
Schubert, Franz:Sym 5 RCA Victor ▲ 09026–62678–2 ■ 09026–62678–4
Schubert, Franz:Sym 9 RCA Victor ▲ 09026–62678–2 ■ 09026–62678–4
Shchedrin, R.:Music for the City of Cöthen RCA Red Seal ▲ 09026–60466–2
Shchedrin, R.:Stalin Cocktail RCA Red Seal ▲ 09026–68061–2
Shostakovich, D.:Chamber Sym, Op. 73a [trans Milman] RCA Red Seal ▲ 09026–68061–2
Shostakovich, D.:Chamber Sym, Op. 110a RCA Red Seal ▲ 7947–2–RC [DDD]
Shostakovich, D.:Con 1 Pno, w. E. Kissin (pno), V. Kan (tpt) RCA Red Seal 2–▲ 60567–2–RC [DDD]
Shostakovich, D.:Con 1 Pno, w. E. Kissin (pno), V. Kan (tpt) RCA Red Seal ▲ 7947–2–RC [DDD]
Shostakovich, D.:Preludes Pno, Op. 34, w. E. Kissin (pno) [arr. by Viktor Poltoratsky for piano & string orchestra]—Nos. 5,6,10,13,14,17 & 24 RCA Red Seal ▲ 7947–2–RC [DDD]
Stravinsky, I.:Con Vn, w. V. Spivakov (vn) RCA Red Seal ▲ 60370–2–RC [DDD]
Tchaikovsky, P.:Album pour enfants [trans. V. Spivakov & V. Milman for string orch.] RCA Red Seal ▲ 09026–61964–2
Tchaikovsky, P.:Serenade Strs RCA Red Seal ▲ 09026–61964–2
Tchaikovsky, P.:The Snow Maiden (sels)—Melodrama RCA Red Seal ▲ 09026–61964–2
Vivaldi, A.:Cons for 2 Obs, w. A. Utkin (ob), M. Evstigneev (ob)—RV.535 RCA Red Seal ▲ 60240–2–RC [DDD]
Vivaldi, A.:Cons Orch—RV.158 in A RCA Red Seal ▲ 60240–2–RC [DDD]
Vivaldi, A.:Cons Rcr, w. Michala Petri (rcr)—Cons Op. 10, RV 433, 439, 428, 435, 434 & 437 *(rec Gijon Laboral Univ Theater, Spain, June 1995)* RCA Red Seal ▲ 0902–668543–2 [DDD]
Vivaldi, A.:Cons Vn (misc), w. V. Spivakov (vn)—(2) in e, RV.278 & in a, RV.357 RCA Red Seal ▲ 60369–2 [DDD] ■ 60369–4 (CrO2)
Vivaldi, A.:Cons Vn, Op. 8/1–4, "The Four Seasons", w. V. Spivakov (vn) RCA Red Seal ▲ 60369–2 [DDD] ■ 60369–4 (CrO2)
Vivaldi, A.:Con for 2 Vns Vc, R.565, w. V. Spivakov (vn), A. Fouter (vn), M. Milman (vc) RCA Red Seal ▲ 60240–2–RC [DDD]
Vivaldi, A.:Stabat Mater Cta, w. N. Stutzmann (cta) [L] RCA Red Seal ▲ 60240–2–RC [DDD]

Moscow Youth Orch

K. Kondrashin (cnd)

Glazunov, A.:Con Vn, w. J. Sotkovetsky (vn) *(rec 1952)* Russian Disc ▲ RUS 15 009 [AAD]
Glazunov, A.:Con Vn, w. Julian Sitkovetsky (vn) *(rec 1952)* Arlecchino ▲ ARL110
Sibelius, J.:Con Vn, w. Julian Sitkovetsky (vn) *(rec 1952)* Arlecchino ▲ ARL110

Mostly Modern Chamber Players

J. C. Carmichael (cnd)

Hindemith, P.:Kleine Kammermusik, w. Furman Civic Wind Ensemble CRS ▲ 9051
Krenek, E.:Marsche, w. Furman Civic Wind Ensemble CRS ▲ 9051
Pepping, E.:Little Serenade, w. Furman Civic Wind Ensemble CRS ▲ 9051
Toch, E.:Spiel, w. Furman Civic Wind Ensemble CRS ▲ 9051

Mostly Mozart Festival Orch

A. Schneider (cnd)

Mozart, W.A.:Andante Fl, K.315/285a, w. R. Stoltzman (cl) RCA Gold Seal ▲ 60035–2–RG [DDD]
Rossini, G.:Theme & Vars Cl, w. R. Stoltzman (cl) RCA Gold Seal ▲ 60035–2–RG [DDD]
Weber, C.M. von:Con 1 Cl, w. R. Stoltzman (cl) RCA Gold Seal ▲ 60035–2–RG [DDD]

G. Schwarz (cnd)

Bach, J.S.:Arias, w. A. Augér (sop) Delos ▲ DCD 3026 [DDD]
Handel, G.F.:Alessandro (sels), w. Judith Blegen (sop)—Lusinghe più care Sony Classical ("Essential Classics" series) ▲ SBK 62646 ■ SBT 62646
Handel, G.F.:Arias, w. A. Augér (sop) Delos ▲ DCD 3026
Handel, G.F.:Cants, w. Judith Blegen (sop)—Eternal Source of Light Divine; Let the Bright Seraphim Sony Classical ("Essential Classics" series) ▲ SBK 62646 ■ SBT 62646
Mozart, W.A.:Con Cl, w. David Shifrin (cl) Delos ▲ DCD 3020 [DDD]

P. Zukerman (cnd)

Mozart, W.A.:Exsultate, w. Judith Blegen (sop) Sony Classical ("Essential Classics" series) ▲ SBK 62646 ■ SBT 62646
Mozart, W.A.:Idomeneo (sels), w. Judith Blegen (sop)—Non temer, amato bene Sony Classical ("Essential Classics" series) ▲ SBK 62646 ■ SBT 62646
Mozart, W.A.:Rè pastore (sels), w. Judith Blegen (sop)—L'amerò, sarò costante Sony Classical ("Essential Classics" series) ▲ SBK 62646 ■ SBT 62646
Mozart, W.A.:Vorrei spiegarvi, w. Judith Blegen (sop) Sony Classical ("Essential Classics" series) ▲ SBK 62646 ■ SBT 62646
Scarlatti, A.:Su le sponde del Tebro, w. Judith Blegen (sop) Sony Classical ("Essential Classics" series) ▲ SBK 62646 ■ SBT 62646

Mother Mallard [D. Borden (kbd), E. Hargis (sampled sop), L. Thimmig (bas hn/t sax), G. Borden (gtr)]

Borden, D.:The Continuing Story of Counterpoint—Parts 5–8 Cuneiform ▲ Rune 21

Mother Mallard [D. Borden (kbd), L. Purse (kbd), E. Hargis (sop/rcr), L. Thimmig (winds), G. Borden (gtr), T. Kikta (live sound production)]

Borden, D.:The Continuing Story of Counterpoint—Parts 1–4 & 8 Cuneiform ▲ Rune 28

Mother Mallard [D. Borden (syns), E. Hargis (sgr), L. Thimmig (winds)]

Borden, D.:The Continuing Story of Counterpoint—Parts 9–12 Cuneiform ▲ Rune 16

Moyzes String Quartet [Stanislav Mucha (vn), František Török (vn), Alexander Lakatoš (va), Ján Slávik (vc)]
Bella, J.L.:Notturno Str Qt *(rec Moyzes Hall of the Slovak Philharmonic, Bratislava, June 3 & Dec 4, 1994)* Marco Polo ▲ 8.223839 [DDD]
Bella, J.L.:Qt in B♭ Strs *(rec Moyzes Hall of the Slovak Philharmonic, Bratislava, June 3 & Dec 4, 1994)* Marco Polo ▲ 8.223839 [DDD]
Bella, J.L.:Qt in e Strs *(rec Moyzes Hall of the Slovak Philharmonic, Bratislava, June 3 & Dec 4, 1994)* Marco Polo ▲ 8.223839 [DDD]
Bella, J.L.:Qt Strs, Op. 25 *(rec Moyzes Hall, Slovak Philharmonic, Bratislava, Dec. 12, 1993)* Marco Polo ▲ 8.223658 [DDD]
Bella, J.L.:Qnt Strs, w. František Magyar (va) *(rec Moyzes Hall, Slovak Philharmonic, Bratislava, Dec. 6, 1993)* Marco Polo ▲ 8.223658 [DDD]
Blak, K.:Music of—Qts. 1, "Images" & 2, Rorsia; Böhmarlands Dronning; Ariettes; [w. J. Zsapka (guitar)] Nadn; Ellnborg Tutl ▲ FKT 5
Blak, K.:Qt 3 Strs, "Undirlýsi" *(rec Útvarp Føroya, Mar 1995)* Tutl ▲ FKT 8
Dvořák, A.:Qt 12 Strs, "America" *(rec Slovak Philharmonic Moyzes Hall, Nov 11–18, 1988)* Naxos 4–▲ 8.504006 [DDD]
Dvořák, A.:Qt 12 Strs, "America" *(rec 11/88)* Naxos ▲ 8.550251 [DDD]
Dvořák, A.:Qt 14 Strs *(rec 11/88)* Naxos ▲ 8.550251 [DDD]
Dvořák, A.:Qt 14 Strs *(rec Slovak Philharmonic Moyzes Hall, Nov 11–18, 1988)* Naxos 4–▲ 8.504006 [DDD]
Mozart, W.A.:Qt 17 Strs *(rec Jan. 1988)* Naxos ▲ 8.550105 [DDD]
Mozart, W.A.:Qt 19 Strs *(rec Jan. 1988)* Naxos ▲ 8.550105 [DDD]
Smetana, B.:Qt 1 Strs Naxos ▲ 8.550379 [DDD]
Smetana, B.:Qt 2 Strs Naxos ▲ 8.550379 [DDD]

Moyzes String Quartet members
Smetana, B.:From the Homeland Naxos ▲ 8.550379 [DDD]

Mozart Academy
R. Edlinger (cnd)
Mozart, W.A.:Con Bn, w. Peter Hanzel (bn) *(rec Concert Hall of the Slovak PO, Bratislava, July 1987)* Lydian ▲ 18058 [DDD]
Mozart, W.A.:Con Cl, w. Josef Luptácik (cl) *(rec Concert Hall of the Slovak PO, Bratislava, July 1987)* Lydian ▲ 18058 [DDD]
M. Sieghart (cnd)
Mozart, W.A.:Sym 28 *(rec Koliba Studio, Bratislava, Apr. 1988)* Lydian ▲ 18033 [DDD]
Mozart, W.A.:Sym 41 *(rec Koliba Studio, Bratislava, Apr. 1988)* Lydian ▲ 18033 [DDD]

Mozart Festival Orch
Mozart, W.A.:Con 20 Pno, w. A. Giulini, A. Lizzio Vivace 3–▲ E 313 [DDD]
R. Edlinger (cnd)
Mozart, W.A.:Sym 40 PMG ("Vienna Master" series) ▲ CD 160103 [DDD]
Mozart, W.A.:Sym 41 PMG ("Vienna Master" series) ▲ CD 160103 [DDD]
D. Jerome (cnd)
Haydn, J.:Sym 23 Newport Classic ▲ NPD 85612 [DDD]
Herschel, W.:Music of, w. Richard Woodhams (ob)—Cons in C & E♭ for Ob; Chamber Sym Newport Classic ▲ NPD 85612 [DDD]
A. Lizzio (cnd)
Mozart, W.A.:Con Bn, w. K. Krommer (bn) Vivace 3–▲ E 315 [DDD]
Mozart, W.A.:Con Cl, w. J. Ostrack (cl) Vivace 3–▲ E 315 [DDD]
Mozart, W.A.:Cons Fl, w. J. Angelini (fl) Vivace 3–▲ E 315 [DDD]
Mozart, W.A.:Con Fl Hp, w. P. Janovsky (fl), R. Zanelli (hp) Vivace 3–▲ E 315 [DDD]
Mozart, W.A.:Cons Hn, w. J. Falout (hn) Vivace 3–▲ E 315 [DDD]
Mozart, W.A.:Con 20 Pno, w. A. Giulini (pno) Sound 2–▲ E 219 [DDD]
Mozart, W.A.:Con 21 Pno, w. A. Giulini (pno) Vivace 3–▲ E 323 [DDD]
Mozart, W.A.:Con 21 Pno, w. A. Giulini (pno) Vivace ▲ E 552 [DDD]
Mozart, W.A.:Con 21 Pno, w. A. Giulini (pno) Sound 2–▲ E 219 [DDD]
Mozart, W.A.:Con 21 Pno, w. A. Giulini (pno) Vivace 3–▲ E 313 [DDD]
Mozart, W.A.:Con 21 Pno, w. A. Giulini (pno) Vivace 2–▲ G 117/118 [DDD]
Mozart, W.A.:Con 23 Pno, w. A. Giulini (pno) Vivace 3–▲ E 313 [DDD]
Mozart, W.A.:Con 23 Pno, w. A. Giulini (pno) Sound 2–▲ E 219 [DDD]
Mozart, W.A.:Con 26 Pno, w. A. Giulini (pno) Vivace 3–▲ E 323 [DDD]
Mozart, W.A.:Con 26 Pno, w. A. Giulini (pno) Sound 2–▲ E 219 [DDD]
Mozart, W.A.:Con 26 Pno, w. A. Giulini (pno) Vivace ▲ E 552 [DDD]
Mozart, W.A.:Con 26 Pno, w. A. Giulini (pno) Vivace 3–▲ E 313 [DDD]
Mozart, W.A.:Con 3 Vn, w. R. Marinelli (vn) Vivace 3–▲ E 325 [ADD/DDD]
Mozart, W.A.:Con 3 Vn, w. R. Marinelli (vn) Vivace ▲ 594 [DDD]
Mozart, W.A.:Con 4 Vn, w. R. Marinelli (vn) Vivace ▲ 594 [DDD]
Mozart, W.A.:Con 4 Vn, w. R. Marinelli (vn) Vivace 3–▲ E 325 [ADD/DDD]
Mozart, W.A.:Sym 16 PMG ("Vienna Master" series) ▲ CD 160108 [DDD]
Mozart, W.A.:Sym 18 PMG ("Vienna Master" series) ▲ CD 160108 [DDD]
Mozart, W.A.:Sym 21 PMG ("Vienna Master" series) ▲ CD 160114 [DDD]
Mozart, W.A.:Sym 22 PMG ("Vienna Master" series) ▲ CD 160113 [DDD]
Mozart, W.A.:Sym 24 PMG ("Vienna Master" series) ▲ CD 160113 [DDD]
Mozart, W.A.:Sym 25 PMG ("Vienna Master" series) ▲ CD 160108 [DDD]
Mozart, W.A.:Sym 29 Vivace 3–▲ E 314 [DDD]
Mozart, W.A.:Sym 29 PMG ("Vienna Master" series) ▲ CD 160113 [DDD]
Mozart, W.A.:Sym 30 PMG ("Vienna Master" series) ▲ CD 160114 [DDD]
Mozart, W.A.:Sym 33 PMG ("Vienna Master" series) ▲ CD 160114 [DDD]
Mozart, W.A.:Sym 35 Vivace 3–▲ E 314 [DDD]
Mozart, W.A.:Sym 35 PMG ("Vienna Master" series) ▲ CD 160107 [DDD]
Mozart, W.A.:Sym 38 PMG ("Vienna Master" series) ▲ CD 160107 [DDD]
Mozart, W.A.:Sym 38 Vivace 3–▲ E 314 [DDD]
Mozart, W.A.:Sym 40 Vivace 3–▲ E 314 [DDD]
Mozart, W.A.:Sym 41 Vivace 3–▲ E 314 [DDD]
B. Walter (cnd)
Schumann, R.:Sym 4 *(rec Paris, 1928)* VAI Audio ▲ VAIA 1059
Schumann, R.:Sym 4 *(rec 1928)* Grammofono 2000 ▲ GRM 78580

Mozart Piano Quartet
Draeseke, F.:Qnt Pno, Op. 48, w. Gottfried Langenstein (hn) MD + G ▲ MDG 6150673
Schumann, R.:Qt Pno, Op. 47 MD + G ▲ MDG 6150673

Mozart Trio Stuttgart
Mozart, W.A.:Trio Cl, K.498 Vivace 3–▲ E 319 [DDD]

Mozartean Players
Mozart, W.A.:Qts Pno Harmonia Mundi USA ▲ HMU 907018
Mozart, W.A.:Trios Pno (comp)—K.496, 502, 542, 548 & 564 Harmonia Mundi USA 2–▲ HMU 907033/34
Schubert, Franz:Nocturne Pno Harmonia Mundi USA ▲ HMU 907094
S. Lubin (cnd)
Mozart, W.A.:Con 12 Pno, w. S. Lubin (pno) Arabesque ▲ Z 6552 [DDD]
Mozart, W.A.:Con 15 Pno, w. S. Lubin (pno) Arabesque ▲ Z 6552 [DDD]
Mozart, W.A.:Con 20 Pno, w. Steven Lubin (pno) Arabesque ▲ Z 6530
Mozart, W.A.:Con 23 Pno, w. Steven Lubin (pno) Arabesque ▲ Z 6530

Mozartean Players [Steven Lubin (pno), Stanley Ritchie (vn), Myron Lutzke (vc)]
Schubert, Franz:Trio 2 Pno *(rec SUNY, Puchase, June 17–20, 1992)* Harmonia Mundi France ▲ HMU 907095

Mozarteum Horn Players
H. Angerer (cnd)
Eder, H.:Intermezzi, Op. 76/1 Koch Schwann ▲ CD 310 090 [DDD]
Koetsier, J.:Concertante Music Koch Schwann ▲ CD 310 090 [DDD]

Mozarteum Horn Players (cont.)
H. Angerer (cnd) (cont.)
Krol, B.:Ballade Koch Schwann ▲ CD 310 090 [DDD]
Krol, B.:Taugenichts Suite Koch Schwann ▲ CD 310 090 [DDD]

Mozarteum Hoschschule Horn Ensemble
Born for Horn Koch Schwann ▲ SCH 315352 [DDD]

Mozarteum Orch
A. Steinlucht (cnd)
Bach, J.S.:Con 1 Vn, w. A. Schulrufer (vn) Infinity Digital ▲ QK 57217 [DDD]
Bach, J.S.:Con 2 Vn, w. A. Schulrufer (vn) Infinity Digital ▲ QK 57217 [DDD]
Bach, J.S.:Con for 2 Vns, w. A. Schulrufer (vn), V. Siorenko (vn) Infinity Digital ▲ QK 57217 [DDD]

Mozartrois [Gerard Willems (pno), Robert Ingram (vn), Georg Pedersen (vc)]
Mozart, W.A.:Divert Pno, K.254 *(rec Concert Hall of the Sydney Opera House, 1991)* Tall Poppies ▲ TP 070 [DDD]
Mozart, W.A.:Trios Pno (comp) *(rec Concert Hall of the Sydney Opera House, 1991)* Tall Poppies 2–▲ TP 070 [DDD]

Mozzafiato [Charles Neidich (cl), Ayako Oshima (cl), Dennis Godburn (bn), Michael O'Donovan (bn), William Purvis (hn), Stewart Rose (hn), Marji Danilow (db)]
Blasius, F.:Suite d'harmonie Sony Classical ("Vivarte" series) ▲ SK 68263
Castil–Blaze:Sextet 1 Ww Sony Classical ("Vivarte" series) ▲ SK 68263
Mozart, W.A.:Nozze di Figaro (winds) [arr. Georg Sartorius] Sony Classical ▲ SK 53965 [DDD]
Rossini, G.:Andante e Tema con variazioni Sony Classical ▲ SK 53965 [DDD]
Rossini, G.:Il barbiere di Siviglia (wind ensemble) [arr. Wenzel Sedlak] Sony Classical ▲ SK 53965 [DDD]
Weber, C.M. von:Music for Ww—Adagio & Rondo Sony Classical ("Vivarte" series) ▲ SK 68263
C. Neidich (cnd)
Beethoven, L. van:March Ww, WoO 29 *(rec Feb. 1–5, 1992)* Sony Classical ▲ SK 53367 [DDD]
Beethoven, L. van:Octet, Op. 103 *(rec Feb. 1–5, 1992)* Sony Classical ▲ SK 53367 [DDD]
Beethoven, L. van:Sxt Winds, Op. 71 *(rec Feb. 1–5, 1992)* Sony Classical ▲ SK 53367 [DDD]
Mozart, W.A.:Serenade Ww, K.375 *(rec American Academy of Arts & Letters, New York City, Jan 14–17, 1994)* Sony Classical ("Vivarte" series) ▲ SK 64306 [DDD]
Mozart, W.A.:Sxt Ww *(rec American Academy of Arts & Letters, New York City, Jan 14–17, 1994)* Sony Classical ("Vivarte" series) ▲ SK 64306 [DDD]
Pleyel, I.:Sxt Ww *(rec American Academy of Arts & Letters, New York City, Jan 14–17, 1994)* Sony Classical ("Vivarte" series) ▲ SK 64306 [DDD]
Schubert, Franz:Octet Ww, D.803, w. L'Archibudelli Sony Classical ("Vivarte" series) ▲ SK 66264

Mozzafiato members
Beethoven, L. van:Duos, WoO 27 *(rec Feb. 1–5, 1992)* Sony Classical ▲ SK 53367 [DDD]

Mühlfeld Ensemble
Müller, I.:Qt 2 Cl, w. V. Soames (cl) Clarinet Classics ▲ CC 0006 [ADD]

Muir String Quartet [Peter Zazofsky (vn), Bayla Keyes (vn), Steven Ansell (va), Michael Reynolds (vc)]
Beethoven, L. van:Qt 15 Strs *(rec Apr. 1993)* EcoClassics ▲ ECO 003
Beethoven, L. van:Qt 16 Strs *(rec Apr. 1993)* EcoClassics ▲ ECO 003
Brahms, J.:Qts Strs (comp)—Op. 51/1 & 2 Adda ▲ ADD 581222 [DDD]
Brahms, J.:Qnt Cl, w. M. Lurie (cl) EcoClassics ▲ ECO CD 001
Dvořák, A.:Qt 12 Strs, "America" *(rec Brooks Center for Music, Holy Cross College, June 1994)* EcoClassics ▲ ECO 004
Mozart, W.A.:Qnt Cl, K.581, w. M. Lurie (cl) *(rec Jan. 2–5, 1992)* EcoClassics ▲ ECO CD 001
Schubert, Franz:Qt 14 Strs *(rec Brooks Center for Music, Holy Cross College, June 1994)* EcoClassics ▲ ECO 004
Schumann, R.:Qts Strs (comp)—Op. 41/1 & 3 Adda ▲ ADD 581218 [DDD]
Tower, J.:Night Fields *(rec American Academy of Arts & Letters, New York City, Sept. 26–28, 1994)* New World ▲ 80470–2
Wilson, R.:Qt 3 Strs CRI ▲ CD 602 [ADD]

Munich Bach Orch
K. Richter (cnd)
Bach, J.S.:Brandenburg Cons Archiv 2–▲ 427143–2 [ADD]
Bach, J.S.:Brandenburg Cons—Nos. 2, 4, 5 Deutsche Grammophon (Musikfest) ■ 415911–4
Bach, J.S.:Cants (misc), w. Munich Bach Choir—Nos. 1, 4, 6, 12, 23, 67, 87, 92, 104, 108, 126, 158 & 182 Archiv ▲ 439374–2 [ADD]
Bach, J.S.:Cant 26, w. E. Mathis (sop), P. Schreier (ten), A. Schmidt (bar), D. Fischer–Dieskau (bar), Munich Bach Choir Archiv ▲ 427130–2 [ADD]
Bach, J.S.:Cant 56, w. D. Fischer–Dieskau (bar) [G] Archiv ▲ 427128–2 [ADD]
Bach, J.S.:Cant 67, w. P. Pears (ten), K. Engen (bass), Munich Bach Choir Teldec ▲ 9031–77614–2
Bach, J.S.:Cant 80, w. E. Mathis (sop), T. Schmidt (mez), P. Schreier (ten), D. Fischer–Dieskau (bar), Munich Bach Choir Archiv ▲ 427130–2 [ADD]
Bach, J.S.:Cant 82, w. D. Fischer–Dieskau (bar) [G] Archiv ▲ 427128–2 [ADD]
Bach, J.S.:Cant 108, w. P. Pears (ten), K. Engen (bass), Munich Bach Choir Teldec ▲ 9031–77614–2
Bach, J.S.:Cant 116, w. E. Mathis (sop), T. Schmidt (mez), P. Schreier (ten), D. Fischer–Dieskau (bar), Munich Bach Choir Archiv ▲ 427130–2 [ADD]
Bach, J.S.:Cant 127, w. P. Pears (ten), K. Engen (bass), Munich Bach Choir Teldec ▲ 9031–77614–2
Bach, J.S.:Cant 140, w. E. Mathis (sop), P. Schreier (ten), D. Fischer–Dieskau (bar), Munich Bach Choir [G] Deutsche Grammophon ("Galleria" series) ▲ 419466–2 [ADD]
Bach, J.S.:Magnificat, BWV 243, w. M. Stader (sop), H. Töpper (cta), E. Haefliger (ten), D. Fischer–Dieskau (bar), Munich Bach Choir [L] Deutsche Grammophon ("Galleria" series) ▲ 419466–2 [ADD]
Bach, J.S.:St. John Passion, w. Evelyn Lear (sop), Hertha Töpper (mez), Ernst Haefliger (ten), Hermann Prey (bar), Kieth Engen (bass), Munich Bach Choir Deutsche Grammophon ("2CD" series) 2–▲ 453 007–2
Bach, J.S.:St. Matthew Passion, w. I. Seefried (sop), A. Fahberg (sop), H. Töpper (alt), E. Haefliger (ten), D. Fischer–Dieskau (bar), K. Engen (bass), M. Proebstl (bass), Munich Bach Choir Archiv ▲ 439338–2 [ADD]
Maurice André Trumpet Masterpieces, w. Maurice André (tpt), Munich CO [cnd:Hans Stadlmair], English CO [cnd:Charles Mackerras], Zurich Collegium Musicum Orch [cnd:Paul Sacher] Deutsche Grammophon ("Double" series) 2–▲ 413853–2
H.–M. Schneidt (cnd)
Bach, J.S.:Mass in b, BWV 232, w. A. Stumphius (sop), C. Kallisch (alto), R. Wörle (ten), A. Schmidt (bass), Munich Bach Choir *(rec Mar 21, 1992)* Calig 2–▲ CAL 5029/30 [ADD]

Munich Bach Soloists
P.–D. Ponnelle (cnd)
Bach, J.S.:Cant 82, w. M. Egel (bass) FSM ▲ FCD 97213 [DDD]

Munich Bach Trumpet Ensemble
Bach Trumpet Gala, Vol. 1, w. Peter Epp (baroque tpt), Arnold Mehl (baroque tpt), Rudolf Ulrich (baroque tpt), Franz Lehrndorfer (org) Ars Musici ▲ 0869
A. Mehl (cnd)
Bach Trumpet Gala, Vol. 2 Ars Musici ▲ 1054

Munich Baroque Trio
Telemann, G.P.:Son in F Fl *(rec Nov. 19–20, 1987)* Calig ▲ CAL 50869 [DDD]
Telemann, G.P.:Trio Sons—Sons. in a, c, F, g, & h *(rec Nov. 19–20, 1987)* Calig ▲ CAL 50869 [DDD]

Munich Baryton Trio [Jörg Eggebrecht (baryton), Deinhart Goritzki (va), Willi Schmid (vc)]
Haydn, J.:Trios (125) Baryton, Va & Vc—H.XI 25, 62, 66, 95, 97 Claves ▲ CD 50609 [ADD]

Munich Bavarian RSO
H. Zender (cnd)
Huber, K.:Soliloquia, w. H. Lukomska (sop), S. Klare (mez), D. Ahlstedt (ten), B. McDaniel (bar), H. G. Ahrens (b-bar), Munich Bavarian Radio Chorus [L] *(rec Dec. 17, 1979)* Grammont ▲ CTSP 24–2 [ADD]

▲ = CD ♦ = Enhanced CD Δ = MD ■ = Cassette Tape □ = DCC

Munich Bavarian RSO (cont.)

H. Zender (cnd) (cont.)

- Huber, K.:Soliloquia, Part II:Cuius legibus rotantur poli, w. H. Lukomska (sop), S. Klare (mez), D. Ahlstedt (ten), B. McDaniel (bar), H. G. Ahrens (b-bar), Munich Bavarian Radio Chorus [L] *(rec Dec. 17, 1979)* Grammont ▲ CTSP 24–2 [ADD]

Munich Bavarian State Opera Orch

F. Allers (cnd)

- Strauss (II), Joh.:Der Zigeunerbaron (sels), w. Rita Streich (sop), Grace Bumbry (mez), Biserka Cvejic (mez), Gisela Litz (alt), Nicolai Gedda (ten), Hermann Prey (bar), Kurt Bohme (bass), Munich Bavarian State Opera Chorus Emperor Operetta ▲ KO 86346

Munich Brass

- Arnold, M.:Qnt Brass Orfeo ▲ 166881 [DDD]
- Ewald, V.:Qnt 2 Brass Orfeo ▲ 166881 [DDD]
- Gershwin, G.:Music of—An American in Paris; Rhapsody in Blue; The Man I Love; Cuban Overture; Somebody Loves Me; I Got Fascinatin' Rhythm—Medley (all arr. for brass ensemble) *(rec Mar. 30–31, June 9–12 & J)* Orfeo ▲ 306931 [DDD]
- Munich Brass Orfeo ▲ 166881 [DDD]

Munich CO

H. Stadlmair (cnd)

- Albrechtsberger, J.G.:Cons Jew's Hp, w. Mayr (jew's hp), D. Kirsch (mandora) Orfeo ▲ 035821 [DDD]
- Bach, J.S.:Cons Vn (comp), w. J.-J. Kantorow (vn) Denon ▲ CO 7096 [DDD]
- Bach, J.S.:Con for 2 Vns, w. J.-J. Kantorow (vn), S. Cenariu (vn) Denon ▲ CO 7096 [DDD]
- Benjamin, A.:Con Ob Strs, w. E. Brunner (cl) [arr for cl & strs] Tudor ▲ 728 [DDD]
- Biber, H. von:Serenade Strs, "Nightwatchman's Call" Orfeo ▲ 033821 [DDD]
- Cimarosa, D.:Con Cl, w. E. Brunner (cl) Tudor ▲ 728 [DDD]
- Danzi, F.:Concertino Cl, w. E. Brunner (cl), K. Thunemann (bn) Tudor ▲ 718 [DDD]
- Danzi, F.:Cons (4) Fl, w. A. Adorján (fl) Orfeo 2–▲ 003812 [DDD]
- Danzi, F.:Phantasie on "La ci darem la mano" from Mozart's *Don Giovanni,* w. E. Brunner (cl) Tudor ▲ 718 [DDD]
- Devienne, F.:Cons Fl (comp), w. András Adorján (fl)—Nos. 4 in G, 5 in G, 6 in D & 7 in e Tudor ▲ TUD 765 [DDD]
- Devienne, F.:Cons Fl (comp), w. A. Adorján (fl)—Concerto No. 9 in e; Concerto No. 12 in A; Concerto in G, Op. Posth. Tudor ▲ TUD 782 [DDD]
- Donizetti, G.:Concertino Cl, w. E. Brunner (cl) Tudor ▲ 728 [DDD]
- Giampieri, A.:Il Carnevale di Venezia, w. E. Brunner (cl) Tudor ▲ 728 [DDD]
- Harmonies Du Soir:Virtuoso Romantic Cello Music, w. Werner Thomas-Mifune (vc) Orfeo ▲ C 131851–A [DDD]
- Hoffmeister, F.A.:Con 2 Cl, w. Eduard Brunner (cl) Tudor ▲ TUD 7008 [DDD]
- Jommelli, N.:Sinf Dulcimer, w. K.-H. Schickhaus (dulcimer) Tudor ▲ 712 [ADD]
- Maurice André Trumpet Masterpieces, w. Maurice André (tpt), English CO [cnd:Charles Mackerras], Zurich Collegium Musicum Orch [cnd:Paul Sacher], Munich Bach Orch [cnd:Karl Richter] Deutsche Grammophon ("Double" series) 2–▲ 413853–2
- Mercadante, S.:Con in B♭ Cl, Op. 101, w. E. Brunner (cl) Tudor ▲ 728 [DDD]
- Mozart, L.:Bauernhochzeit, w. J. Engel (bgp), M. Engel (h-g) Orfeo ▲ 033821 [DDD]
- Mozart, L.:Bauernhochzeit Tudor ▲ 712 [ADD]
- Mozart, L.:Musikalische Schlittenfahrt Tudor ▲ TUD 737 [DDD]
- Mozart, L.:Syms—in D [Eisen, D.26]; Sinf da Caccia in G [Jagd-Sym] Tudor ▲ TUD 737 [DDD]
- Mozart, L.:Toy Sym Tudor ▲ TUD 737 [DDD]
- Mozart, W.A.:Andante Fl, K.315/285a, w. András Adorján (fl) Denon ▲ 7803 [DDD]
- Mozart, W.A.:Cons Fl, w. H. Linde (fl) Deutsche Grammophon ("Resonance" series) ▲ 427211–2 [ADD]
- Mozart, W.A.:Cons Fl, w. A. Adorján (fl) Denon ▲ 7803 [DDD]
- Mozart, W.A.:Con Fl Hp, w. András Adorján (fl), Susanna Mildonian (hp) Denon ▲ 7804 [DDD]
- Mozart, W.A.:Con 8 Pno, w. E. Dubourg (pno) Tudor ▲ 703 [DDD]
- Mozart, W.A.:Con 9 Pno, w. E. Dubourg (pno) Tudor ▲ 703 [DDD]
- Mozart, W.A.:Concertone Vns, w. A. Adorján (flute), J.J. Kantorow (violin) [arr. flute & violin] Denon ▲ 7804 [DDD]
- Mozart, W.A.:Rondo Fl, K.Anh.184, w. A. Adorján (fl) Denon ▲ 7804 [DDD]
- Pokorny, F.X.:Cons (2) Cl, w. Eduard Brunner (cl) Tudor ▲ TUD 7008 [DDD]
- Rossini, G.:Vars Cl, w. E. Brunner (cl) Tudor ▲ 728 [DDD]
- Salulini, P.:Con Dlc, w. K.-H. Schickhaus (dlc) Tudor ▲ 712 [ADD]
- Stadlmair, H.:Capriccio Fl Koch Schwann ▲ SCH 315872 [DDD]
- Stadlmair, H.:Essay Koch Schwann ▲ SCH 315872 [DDD]
- Stadlmair, H.:Novellettes Koch Schwann ▲ SCH 315872 [DDD]
- Stadlmair, H.:Sinf Alphn Koch Schwann ▲ SCH 315872 [DDD]
- Stamitz, C.:Con Cl Bn, w. E. Brunner (cl), K. Thunemann (bn) Tudor ▲ 718 [DDD]
- Stamitz, C.:Cons Cl, w. Eduard Brunner (cl)—in B♭ for Vn & Cl; in B♭ for Cl & Bn; No. 6 in B♭; No. 10 in B♭ Tudor ▲ TUD 7004 [DDD]
- Stamitz, C.:Con Cl, w. E. Brunner (cl) Tudor ▲ 718 [DDD]
- Stamitz, J.W.A.:Con Cl, w. Eduard Brunner (cl) Tudor ▲ TUD 7008 [DDD]

Munich Consortium Musicum

G. Ratzinger (cnd)

- Dittersdorf, K.D. von:Sacred Music, w. Hanna Farinelli (sop), Birgit Calm (alt), Heiner Hopfner (ten), Nikolaus Hillebrand (bass), Regensburg Cathedral Choir—Requiem in c; Offertorium zu Ehren des Heiligen Johann von Nepomuk; Laurentanische Litanei Ars Musici ▲ AM 1158–2 [DDD]

Munich Early Music Group

M. Zöbeley (cnd)

- Kerll, J.C.:Delectus sacrarum cantionum—14 sels Ars Musici ▲ 1166 [DDD]

Munich Monteverdi Orch

W. Kelber (cnd)

- Bach, J.S.:Cant 36, w. Silke Wenzel (sop), Reiner Schneider-Waterburg (alt), Kobie van Rensburg (ten), Christian Hilz (bass) *(rec live, Dec 1995)* Calig ▲ 50963 [DDD]
- Bach, J.S.:Cant 40, w. Silke Wenzel (sop), Reiner Schneider-Waterburg (alt), Kobie van Rensburg (ten), Christian Hilz (bass) *(rec live, Dec 1995)* Calig ▲ 50963 [DDD]
- Bach, J.S.:Cant 91, w. Silke Wenzel (sop), Reiner Schneider-Waterburg (alt), Kobie van Rensburg (ten), Christian Hilz (bass) *(rec live, Dec 1995)* Calig ▲ 50963 [DDD]
- Brixi, F.X.:Missa di Gloria, w. F. Wagner (sop), R. Schneider-Waterberg (alt), B. Hirtreiter (ten), M. Mantaj (bass), C. Hammer (org), Munich Concerto Vocale *(rec 1993)* Calig ▲ CAL 50927 [ADD]

Munich National Theater Orch

J. Horenstein (cnd)

- Mahler, G.:Kindertotenlieder, w. H. Rehkemper (bar) [G] *(rec 1928 for Polydor)* Pearl 2–▲ PEAS 9929 (m) [AAD]

N. Santi (cnd)

- Mascagni, P.:Cavalleria rusticana, w. Ruth Falcon (sop—Lola), Leonie Rysanek (sop—Santuzza), Astrid Varnay (sop—Mamma Lucia), Plácido Domingo (ten—Turiddu), Benito di Bella (bar—Alfio), Munich National Theater Chorus *(rec Munich, Dec 25, 1978)* Legato Classics ▲ LCD 202-1

Munich Parforcehorn Players

- Cantin, J.:Noces du chasseur Orfeo ▲ 034821 [DDD]
- Cantin, J.:St. Hubert's Mass Orfeo ▲ 034821 [DDD]
- Rossini, G.:Rendez-vouz de chasse Orfeo ▲ 034821 [DDD]

Munich Percussion Ensemble

H.R. Zöbeley (cnd)

- Hiller, W.:Schulamit, w. Regina Klepper (sop), Edeltraud Knabel (alt), Michael Schopper (bass), Elisabeth Woska (nar), Waltraut Mastrogiovanni-Kraxner (shofar), Munich Residenz Orch, Calw Aurelius Boys' Choir Soloists, Munich Motet Choir Wergo ▲ WER 6280–2

Munich Phil CO

M. Helmrath (cnd)

- Janácek, L.:Adagio Orfeo ▲ 283921 [DDD]
- Janácek, L.:Idyll Orfeo ▲ 283921 [DDD]
- Janácek, L.:Suite Str Orch Orfeo ▲ 283921 [DDD]

Munich PO

W.A. Albert (cnd)

- Pfitzner, H.:Con Pno, w. V. Banfield (pno) CPO ▲ CPO 999045–2 [AAD]

S. Celibidache (cnd)

- Bach, J.S.:Mass in b, BWV 232, w. B. Bonney (sop), C. Wulkopf (mez), P. Schrier (ten), A. Scharinger (bass), Munich Bach Choir Exclusive ▲ EXL 33 [ADD]
- Beethoven, L. van:Sym 9, "Choral Sym", w. H. Donath (sop), D. Soffel (mez), S. Jerusalem (ten), P. Lika (bass), Munich Phil Chorus *(rec Mar. 19, 1989)* Exclusive ▲ EXL 15 [AAD]
- Bruckner, A.:Mass 3, w. *(soloists unknown)* Exclusive ▲ EXL 37 [ADD]
- Bruckner, A.:Sym 4, "Romantic" *(rec 1978)* Exclusive 2–▲ EXL 23 [AAD]
- Bruckner, A.:Sym 9 *(rec 1981)* Exclusive 2–▲ EXL 23 [AAD]
- Hindemith, P.:Mathis der Maler (sym) Exclusive ▲ EXL 37 [ADD]
- Mahler, G.:Kindertotenlieder Topazio ▲ TOP 26049
- Mendelssohn, F.:Die Hebriden Topazio ▲ TOP 26049
- Mussorgsky, M.:Pictures at an Exhibition *(rec live 1989)* Artists ▲ FED 68 [ADD]
- Ravel, M.:Boléro Topazio ▲ TOP 26049
- Ravel, M.:Daphnis et Chloé (suite 1) *(rec 1987)* Originals ▲ ORISH 803 [ADD]
- Ravel, M.:Daphnis et Chloé (suite 1), w. Munich Phil Chorus *(rec live, Munich, 1970's)* As Disc ▲ ASD 2501
- Ravel, M.:Daphnis et Chloé (suite 2) *(rec 1987)* Originals ▲ ORISH 803 [ADD]
- Ravel, M.:Daphnis et Chloé (suite 2), w. Munich Phil Chorus *(rec live, Munich, 1970's)* As Disc ▲ ASD 2501
- Rimsky-Korsakov, N.:Scheherazade Exclusive ▲ EXL 82 [ADD]
- Strauss, R.:Don Juan *(rec live 1989)* Artists ▲ FED 68 [ADD]

S. von Hausegger (cnd)

- Bruckner, A.:Sym 9 *(rec 1938)* Preiser ▲ PRE 90148 [AAD]

O. Kabasta (cnd)

- Bruckner, A.:Sym 4, "Romantic" *(rec 1943)* Preiser ▲ PRE CD 90304
- Bruckner, A.:Sym 7 *(rec 1942)* Preiser ▲ PRE CD 90308
- Mozart, W.A.:Sym 41 *(rec 1940–43)* Preiser ▲ PRE CD 90303

R. Kempe (cnd)

- Bruckner, A.:Sym 4, "Romantic" *(rec live, 1977)* Artists ▲ FED 66 [ADD]
- Dvořák, A.:Serenade Strs Sony Classical (Essential Classics) ▲ SBK 46331 [ADD] ■ SBT 46331
- Grieg, E.:Con Pno, Op. 16, w. N. Freire (pno) *(rec 1968)* Odyssey ▲ MBK 46269 [AAD]
- Korngold, E.W.:Sym in F# *(rec 1972)* Varèse Sarabande ▲ VSD 5346
- Schumann, R.:Con Pno, w. N. Freire (pno) *(rec 1968)* Odyssey ▲ MBK 46269 [AAD]
- Tchaikovsky, P.:Con 1 Pno, w. N. Freire (pno) *(rec 1968)* Odyssey ▲ MBK 46268 [ADD] ■ YT 46268

H. Knappertsbusch (cnd)

- Beethoven, L. van:Sym 8 *(rec Ascona, 1956)* Ermitage ▲ ERM 157
- Brahms, J.:Sym 2 *(rec Ascona, 1956)* Ermitage ▲ ERM 157
- Komzák, K.:Badener Madeln *(rec live, Munich, 3/20/55)* Melodram ▲ MEL 18033 [AAD]
- Lanner, J.:Music of—Die Schönbrunner *(rec live, Munich, 3/20/55)* Melodram ▲ MEL 18033 [AAD]
- Schubert, Franz:Marche militaire, D.733/1 *(rec live, Munich, 3/20/55)* Melodram ▲ MEL 18033 [AAD]
- Strauss (II), Joh.:Music of—Aegyptische Marsch; Annen-Polka; Rosen aus dem Süden; Tausen und eine Nacht; Tales from the Vienna Woods *(rec live, Munich, 3/20/55)* Melodram ▲ MEL 18033 [AAD]
- Wagner, R.:Ovs, Preludes & Orch Sels—Ride of the Valkries [w Vienna PO]; Meistersinger:Prelude Act 1; Tannhäuser:Dresda Ov; Tristan & Isolde:Prelude & Liebestod; Lohengrin:Prelude Act 1; Parsifal:Prelude Act 1 Theorema ▲ TH 121.125
- Wagner, R.:Ovs, Preludes & Orch Sels—Fliegende Holländer; Lohengrin; Meistersinger; Parsifal; Rienzi; Tannhäuser MCA Classics 2–▲ MCAD2–9811 [AAD]
- Wagner, R.:Siegfried Idyll MCA Classics 2–▲ MCAD2–9811 [AAD]
- Wagner, R.:Tristan und Isolde (prelude & liebestod) MCA Classics 2–▲ MCAD2–9811 [AAD]
- Weber, C.M. von:Invitation to the Dance Orch *(rec live, Munich 3/20/55)* Melodram ▲ MEL 18033 [AAD]

F. Leitner (cnd)

- Handel, G.F.:Giulio Cesare in Egitto, w. Lucia Popp (sop), Christa Ludwig (mez), Fritz Wunderlich (ten), Walter Berry (bass), Bavarian Radio Chorus [G] *(rec live, Munich 7/1–5/65)* Verona 3–▲ 27035/37 [AAD]
- Handel, G.F.:Giulio Cesare in Egitto, w. Lucia Popp (sop), Christa Ludwig (mez), Fritz Wunderlich (ten), Walter Berry (bass), Bavarian Radio Chorus Melodram 3–▲ MEL 37059 [AAD]

F. Rieger (cnd)

- Brahms, J.:Con Vn, w. David Oistrakh (vn) *(rec live 1973)* Topazio ▲ TOP 26048
- Chausson, E.:Poème Vn, w. David Oistrakh (vn) *(rec live, 1971)* Topazio ▲ TOP 26048

S. Westerberg (cnd)

- Koch, E. von:Music of, w. Sigurd Rascher (a sax), Andreas Röhn (vn), Kerstin Hindart (pno), Swedish RSO—Nordiskt Capriccio; Skandinaviska Danser; Saxofonkonsert; Svensk Dansrapsodi; Karaktärer Föor Vn Och Pno Phono Suecia ▲ PHN 55 [ADD]

Munich PO members

- Baumann, H.:Autumn Music Thorofon ▲ CTH 2256
- Baumann, H.:Qt Strs Thorofon ▲ CTH 2256
- Baumann, H.:Transformations of a Baroque Subject Thorofon ▲ CTH 2256

Munich PO Soloists

- Suder, J.:Qnt Ww Calig ▲ CAL 50903 [DDD]

G. Ratzinger (cnd)

- Schubert, Franz:Duetsche Messe, w. Augsburg PO, Munich RSO, Munich Radio Orch, Regensburg Cathedral Choir Ars Musici ▲ AM 0929 [DDD]

Munich Piano Trio [M. Schfer (pno), I. Then-Bergh (vn), G. Zank (vc)]

- Franck, C.:Trios concertants—Op. 1/1 *(rec Dec. 17–19, 1986)* Calig ▲ CAL 50864 [DDD]
- Lalo, E.:Trio 3 Pno *(rec Dec. 17–19, 1986)* Calig ▲ CAL 50864 [DDD]
- Mendelssohn, F.:Trio 1 Pno *(rec June 27 & July 11–12, 198)* Calig ▲ CAL 50879 [DDD]
- Mendelssohn, F.:Trio 2 Pno *(rec June 27 & July 11–12, 198)* Calig ▲ CAL 50879 [DDD]
- Saint-Saëns, C.:Trio 1 Pno Calig ▲ CD 50843
- Saint-Saëns, C.:Trio 2 Pno Calig ▲ CD 50843
- Shostakovich, D.:Songs Sop, Op. 127, w. A. Ablaberdyeva (sop) [R] MD + G ▲ L 3334 [DDD]
- Shostakovich, D.:Trio 1 Pno MD + G ▲ L 3334 [DDD]
- Shostakovich, D.:Trio 2 Pno MD + G ▲ L 3334 [DDD]
- Turina, J.:Círculo Calig ▲ CAL 50902 [DDD]
- Turina, J.:Trio 1 Pno Calig ▲ CAL 50902 [DDD]
- Turina, J.:Trio 2 Pno Calig ▲ CAL 50902 [DDD]

Munich Pro Arte Orch

K. Redel (cnd)

- Bach, J.S.:Cons solo Hpd, BWV 972–987, w. P. Bardon (org)—BWV 972 & 975 *(rec 1980)* Pierre Verany ▲ PV.79801 [ADD]
- Bach, J.S.:Cons Org, BWV 592–597, w. P. Bardon (org)—BWV 593 & 594, 1980) Pierre Verany ▲ PV.79801 [ADD]
- Les Immortels, Vol. 1 Vanstory ▲ VSK 4001

Munich Radio Orch

J. Delacôte (cnd)

- Opera Arias, w. Samuel Ramey (bass) EMI Classics ▲ CDC 49582 [DDD]

K. Eichhorn (cnd)

- Famous Opera Arias, w. Kurt Moll (bass) Orfeo ▲ C 009821 A [DDD]

G. Ferro (cnd)

- Coloratura Arias, w. Cheryl Studer (sop) EMI Classics ▲ CDC 49961

L. Gardelli (cnd)

- Famous Opera Arias, w. Edita Gruberova (sop) Orfeo ▲ C 101841
- Famous Opera Arias, w. Lucia Aliberti (sop) Orfeo ▲ C 119841 [DDD] ■ M 119841 (D)

Munich Radio Orch (cont.)
J. Georgiadis (cnd)
In Dulci Jubilo, w. James Galway (fl), Domspatzen Boys' Choir RCA Red Seal ▲ 60736-2-RC [DDD] ■ 60736-4-RC
G. Kuhn (cnd)
Famous Opera Arias, w. Maria Dragoni (sop) Orfeo ▲ C 261921 A [DDD]
G. Patané (cnd)
Famous Opera Arias, w. Marjana Lipovšek (mez) Orfeo ▲ CD 179891 [DDD] ■ MC 179891 (D)
G. Ratzinger (cnd)
Schubert, Franz:Duetsche Messe, w. Augsburg PO, Munich RSO, Munich PO Soloists, Regensburg Cathedral Choir Ars Musici ▲ AM 0929 [DDD]
K. Redel (cnd)
Munich Radio Orch Pierre Verany ▲ PV 786104 [DDD]
P. Sommer (cnd)
Famous Opera Arias, w. Anna Tomowa-Sintow (sop) Orfeo ▲ S 106841A [DDD]
H. Wallberg (cnd)
Opera Arias, w. Agnes Baltsa (mez) Orfeo ▲ 171881 [DDD]
R. Weikert (cnd)
The Romantic Tenor, w. Francisco Araiza (ten) RCA Red Seal ▲ 09026-61163-2

Munich RSO
Mozart, W.A.:Entführung (sels), w. J. Protschka (ten)—3 sels. LaserLight ▲ 15 890 [DDD]
R. Abbado (cnd)
Bizet, G.:Carmen (sels), w. Ben Heppner (ten)—La fleur que tu m'avais jetée *(rec Residenz Herkulesaal, Munich, Sept. 27–Oct. 3, 1993 & J)* RCA Red Seal ▲ 09026-62504-2 [DDD]
Donizetti, G.:Anna Bolena (sels), w. Carol Vaness (sop), Melinda Paulsen (cta), Dennis O'Neill (ten), Anton Rosner (ten), Ambrogio Riva (bass), Bavarian Radio Chorus—Final Scene & Aria [from Act II] *(rec Studio 1, Bavaria, Apr 13–17, 1993)* RCA Red Seal ▲ 09026-61828-2 [DDD]
Donizetti, G.:Don Pasquale, w. E. Mei (sop), T. Allen (bar), Bavarian Radio Chorus RCA Red Seal 2-▲ 09026-61924-2
Giordano, U.:Andrea Chénier (sels), w. Ben Heppner (ten)—Come un bel dì di maggio; Colpito qui m'avete ov'io geloso...Un dì all'azzurro spazio *(rec Residenz Herkulesaal, Munich, Sept. 27–Oct. 3, 1993 & J)* RCA Red Seal ▲ 09026-62504-2 [DDD]
Leoncavallo, R.:La Bohème (sels), w. Ben Heppner (ten)—Musetta! O gioia della mia dimora!...Testa adorata *(rec Residenz Herkulesaal, Munich, Sept. 27–Oct. 3, 1993 & J)* RCA Red Seal ▲ 09026-62504-2 [DDD]
Massenet, J.:Le Cid (sels), w. Ben Heppner (ten)—Ah! tout est bien fini...Ô souverain ô juge, ô père *(rec Residenz Herkulesaal, Munich, Sept. 27–Oct. 3, 1993 & J)* RCA Red Seal ▲ 09026-62504-2 [DDD]
Massenet, J.:Hérodiade (sels), w. Ben Heppner (ten)—Ne pouvant réprimer...Adieu donc, vains objets *(rec Residenz Herkulesaal, Munich, Sept. 27–Oct. 3, 1993 & J)* RCA Red Seal ▲ 09026-62504-2 [DDD]
Meyerbeer, G.:L'Africaine (sels), w. Ben Heppner (ten)—Pays merveilleux...Ô Paradis *(rec Residenz Herkulesaal, Munich, Sept. 27–Oct. 3, 1993 & J)* RCA Red Seal ▲ 09026-62504-2 [DDD]
Puccini, G.:La fanciulla del West (sels), w. Ben Heppner (ten)—Ch'ella mi creda libero e lontano *(rec Residenz Herkulesaal, Munich, Sept. 27–Oct. 3, 1993 & J)* RCA Red Seal ▲ 09026-62504-2 [DDD]
Puccini, G.:Manon Lescaut (sels), w. Ben Heppner (ten)—Donna non vidi mai simile a questa! *(rec Residenz Herkulesaal, Munich, Sept. 27–Oct. 3, 1993 & J)* RCA Red Seal ▲ 09026-62504-2 [DDD]
Puccini, G.:Turandot, w. E. Marton (sop—Turandot), M. Price (sop—Liù), B. Heppner (ten—Calaf), J.-H. Rootering (bass—Timur) RCA Red Seal 2-▲ 09026-60898-2
Puccini, G.:Turandot (sels), w. Ben Heppner (ten), Bavarian Radio Chorus—Nessun dorma *(rec Residenz Herkulesaal, Munich, Sept. 27–Oct. 3, 1993 & J)* RCA Red Seal ▲ 09026-62504-2 [DDD]
Rossini, G.:Tancredi, w. Veronica Cangemi (sop—Roggiero), Eva Mei (sop—Amenaide), Vasselina Kasarova (mez—Tancredi), Melinda Paulsen (cta—Isaura), Ramón Vargas (ten—Argirio), Harry Peeters (bass—Orbazzano), Janos Maté (vn), Gottfried Greiner (vc), Ingo Nawra (db), David Syrus (hpd), Bavarian Radio Chorus *(rec Studio 1, Munich, July 17–30, 1995)* RCA Red Seal 3-▲ 09026-68349-2 [DDD]
Verdi, G.:Aida (sels), w. Ben Heppner (ten)—Se quel guerrier io fossi!...Celeste Aida *(rec Residenz Herkulesaal, Munich, Sept. 27–Oct. 3, 1993 & J)* RCA Red Seal ▲ 09026-62504-2 [DDD]
Verdi, G.:Ballet Music—Ballabile:Danza di piccolli schiavi mori [from Aida]; Le ballet de la reine "La Peregrina" [from Don Carlos]; Ballabile:Ballo I, II & III [from Macbeth]; Ballabile [from Otello]; Les quatre saisons [from Les Vêpres Siciliennes] RCA Red Seal ▲ 09026-62651-2
Verdi, G.:La forza del destino (sels), w. Ben Heppner (ten)—La vita è inferno all'infelice...Oh, tu che in seno agl'angeli [with Jürgen Musser (cl)] *(rec Residenz Herkulesaal, Munich, Sept. 27–Oct. 3, 1993 & J)* RCA Red Seal ▲ 09026-62504-2 [DDD]
Verdi, G.:Luisa Miller (sels), w. Ben Heppner (ten)—Oh! fede negar potessi..Quando le sere al placido *(rec Residenz Herkulesaal, Munich, Sept. 27–Oct. 3, 1993 & J)* RCA Red Seal ▲ 09026-62504-2 [DDD]
Verdi, G.:Macbeth (sels), w. Carol Vaness (sop), Marisca Mulder (sop), Ambrogio Riva (bass), Bavarian Radio Chorus—Grand Sleepwalking Scene [from Act IV] *(rec Studio 1, Bavaria, Apr 13–17, 1993)* RCA Red Seal ▲ 09026-61828-2 [DDD]
Verdi, G.:Otello (sels), w. Carol Vaness (sop), Melinda Paulsen (cta), Bavarian Radio Chorus—Canzone del salice; Ave Maria [both from Act IV] *(rec Studio 1, Bavaria, Apr 13–17, 1993)* RCA Red Seal ▲ 09026-61828-2 [DDD]
Verdi, G.:La traviata (sels), w. Carol Vaness (sop), Dennis O'Neill (ten), Bavarian Radio Chorus—Final Scene & Aria [from Act I] *(rec Studio 1, Bavaria, Apr 13–17, 1993)* RCA Red Seal ▲ 09026-61828-2 [DDD]
Verdi, G.:Il trovatore (sels), w. Carol Vaness (sop), Dennis O'Neill (ten), Anton Rosner (ten), Bavarian Radio Chorus—Scene, Aria & Miserere [from Act IV] *(rec Studio 1, Munich, Apr 13–17, 1993)* RCA Red Seal ▲ 09026-61828-2 [DDD]
Verdi, G.:Il trovatore (sels), w. Ben Heppner (ten)—Ah sì, ben mio; Di quella pira [with Bavarian Radio Chorus (cnd:Michael Gläser)] *(rec Residenz Herkulesaal, Munich, Sept. 27–Oct. 3, 1993 & J)* RCA Red Seal ▲ 09026-62504-2 [DDD]
R. Bibl (cnd)
Operetta Gala, w. Edita Gruberova (sop) Nightingale Classics ▲ NIG CD 100560
P. Domingo (cnd)
Strauss (II), Joh.:Die Fledermaus, w. L. Popp (sop), E. Lind (sop), A. Baltsa (mez), P. Domingo (ten), W. Brendel (bar), K. Rydl (bass), Bavarian Radio Chorus [G] EMI Classics 2-▲ CDCB 47480
K. Eichhorn (cnd)
Mozart, W.A.:Arias, w. J. Protschka (ten)—arias from Le nozze di Figaro & Mitridate, ré di Ponto LaserLight ▲ 15 889 [DDD]
Orff, C.:Der Bernauerin, w. L. Popp (sop), Ostermayer (sgr), Laubenthal (ten), H. Lippert (ten), Munich Radio Chorus [G] Orfeo 2-▲ 255912 [DDD]
Orff, C.:Die Kluge, w. L. Popp (sop), J. Van Kesteren (ten), T. Stewart (bar), F. Crass (bass), G. Frick (bass) Eurodisc 2-▲ 69069-2-RG [ADD]
Orff, C.:Der Mond—Ein kleines Welttheater, w. J. Van Kesteren (ten), T. Stewart (bar), F. Crass (bass), G. Frick (bass) Eurodisc 2-▲ 69069-2-RG [ADD]
R. Farnon (cnd)
Moody, J.:Toledo, w. Tommy Reilly (hmc) Chandos ▲ CHAN 9248 [DDD]
J. Fiore (cnd)
Donizetti, G.:Arias, w. Chris Merritt (ten)—Io trar non volio [from Caterina Cornaro]; Deserto in terra [from Don Sebastiano]; Angelo casto e bel [from Il Duca d'Alba]; Fu macchiato l'onor mio [from Poliuto] Philips ▲ 434102-2
Rossini, G.:Arias, w. Chris Merritt (ten)—La sua possente voce [from Cant. in onore del Sommo Pontefice Pio IX]; Ah! sì, per voi già sento [from Otello]; Balena in man del figlio [from Ermione]; Della cieca fortuna [from Elisabetta] Philips ▲ 434102-2

Munich RSO (cont.)
H. Fricke (cnd)
Strauss, R.:Feuersnot, w. J. Varady (sop), B. Weikl (bar), H. Berger-Tuna (bass), Bavarian Radio Chorus [G] Acanta 2-▲ 43530-1-2 [DDD]
L. Gardelli (cnd)
Bellini, V.:Arias, w. L. Aliberti (sop)—Il Pirata—Oh! s'io potessi...Col sorriso d'innocenza; I Puritani—Qui la voce sua soave; La Sonnambula—Ah! non credea mirarti [I] Orfeo ▲ 119841
Bizet, G.:Djamileh, w. L. Popp (sop), F. Bonisolli (ten) [F] Orfeo ▲ 174881 [DDD]
Bizet, G.:Roma Orfeo ▲ 184891 [DDD] ■ MC 184891 (D)
Bizet, G.:Sym 1 Orfeo ▲ 184891 [DDD] ■ MC 184891 (D)
Donizetti, G.:Arias, w. L. Aliberti (sop) [I] Orfeo ▲ 119841
Gluck, C.W.:Le Cinesi, w. K. Erickson (sop), M. Schiml (sop), A. Milcheva (mez), Moser (sgr), Munich Radio Chorus [I] Orfeo ▲ 178891 [DDD] ■ MC 178891 (D)
Verdi, G.:Alzira, w. M. Cotrubas (sop), F. Araiza (ten), R. Bruson (bar), Bavarian Radio Chorus [I] Orfeo 2-▲ 057832 [DDD]
Verdi, G.:Oberto, Conte di San Bonifacio, w. G. Dimitrova (sop), R. Baldani (mez), A. Browner (mez), C. Bergonzi (ten), R. Panerai (bar), Munich Radio Chorus [I] Orfeo ▲ 175881 [DDD]
Verdi, G.:Oberto, Conte di San Bonifacio, w. G. Dimitrova (sop), R. Baldani (mez), A. Browner (mez), C. Bergonzi (ten), R. Panerai (bar), Munich Radio Chorus [I] Orfeo 2-▲ 105842 [DDD] 3-■ A 105843 F
C. Gerhardt (cnd)
Spivakovsky, M.:Con Hmc, w. Tommy Reilly (hmc) Chandos ▲ CHAN 9248 [DDD]
L. Hager (cnd)
Gluck, C.W.:La Recontre imprévue, w. J. Kaufmann (sop—Rezia), A. Stumphius (sop—Dardané), A.-M. Rodde (sop—Amine), I. Vermillion (mez—Balkis), R. Gambill (ten—Ali), C. H. Ahnsjö (ten—Osmin), J.-H. Rootering (bass—Un Calender) Orfeo 2-▲ 242912 [DDD]
Mozart, W.A.:Arias, w. C. Vaness (sop)—(11) from Clemenza di Tito, Così fan tutte, Don Giovanni, Idomeneo, Le nozze di Figaro [I] RCA Red Seal ▲ 60562-2-RC [DDD]
F. Haider (cnd)
Bellini, V.:I Capuleti e i Montecchi (sels), w. Vesselina Kasarova (mez), Bavarian Radio Chorus—Se Romeo t'uccise un figlio RCA Red Seal ▲ 0902-668522-2 [DDD]
Donizetti, G.:Arias, w. Vesselina Kasarova (mez), Bavarian Radio Chorus—Sposa a Percy...per questa fiamma indomita [from Anna Bolena]; Fia dunque vero...O mio Fernando [from La Favorita] RCA Red Seal ▲ 0902-668522-2 [DDD]
Gluck, C.W.:Orfeo ed Euridice (sels), w. Vesselina Kasarova (mez), Bavarian Radio Chorus—Che farò senza Euridice! RCA Red Seal ▲ 0902-668522-2 [DDD]
Handel, G.F.:Rinaldo (sels), w. Vesselina Kasarova (mez), Bavarian Radio Chorus—Or la tromba in suon festante RCA Red Seal ▲ 0902-668522-2 [DDD]
Mozart, W.A.:Arias, w. Vesselina Kasarova (mez), Bavarian Radio Chorus—Voi che sapete che cosa è amor [from Le nozze di Figaro]; Batti, batti, o bel Masetto [from Don Giovanni] RCA Red Seal ▲ 0902-668522-2 [DDD]
Rossini, G.:Arias, w. Vesselina Kasarova (mez), Bavarian Radio Chorus—Nacqui all'affanno e al pianto [from La cenerentola]; Una voce poco fa [from Il barbiere di Siviglia]; Amici in ogni evento...Pensa alla patria [from L'Italiana in Algeri] RCA Red Seal ▲ 0902-668522-2 [DDD]
M. Honeck (cnd)
Strauss, R.:Arabella (sels), w. P. Coburn (sop), R. Klepper (sop), M. Borst (mez), B. Skovhus (bar), F. Hawlata (bass) Capriccio ▲ 10481 [DDD]
Strauss, R.:Ariadne auf Naxos, w. P. Coburn (sop), R. Klepper (sop), M. Borst (mez), B. Skovhus (bar), F. Hawlata (bass) Capriccio ▲ 10481 [DDD]
Strauss, R.:Capriccio (sels), w. P. Coburn (sop), R. Klepper (sop), M. Borst (mez), B. Skovhus (bar), F. Hawlata (bass) Capriccio ▲ 10481 [DDD]
Strauss, R.:Der Rosenkavalier (sels), w. P. Coburn (sop), R. Klepper (sop), M. Borst (mez), B. Skovhus (bar), F. Hawlata (bass) Capriccio ▲ 10481 [DDD]
M. Janowski (cnd)
Albert, E. d':Tiefland, w. Martón, Kollo, Weikl, Moll, Munich Radio Chorus—[G] Acanta 2-▲ 43481
Korngold, E.W.:Violanta, w. E. Martón (sop), S. Jerusalem (ten), W. Berry (bass). Bavarian Radio Chorus [G] CBS ▲ MK 35909 [ADD]
E. Kohn (cnd)
Mozart, W.A.:Arias, w. C. Vaness (sop), P. Domingo (ten)—arias from Clemenza di Tito, Così fan tutte, Don Giovanni, Entführung aus dem Serail, La finta giardineira, Idomeneo, Le nozze di Figaro, Die Zauberflöte EMI Classics ▲ CDC 54329
Pure Domingo, w. Plácido Domingo (ten), English CO [cnd:Julius Rudel], Madrid SO [cnd:Manuel Moreno-Buendia], National PO [cnd:Eugene Kohn], New Philharmonia Orch [cnds:Bruno Bartoletti, Riccardo Muti], Philharmonia Orch [cnd:James Levine] Angel ▲ CDC 55616 [DDD/ADD]
J. Kourt (cnd)
Magische Töne, w. Peter Seiffert (ten) RCA Red Seal ▲ 09026-61214-2
J. Krombholc (cnd)
Smetana, B.:The Bartered Bride, w. T. Stratas (sop), R. Kollo (ten), W. Berry (b-bar), A. Malta (bass) Eurodisc 2-▲ 7795-2-RG [ADD]
G. Kuhn (cnd)
Delibes, L.:Lakmé (sels), w. Edita Guberova (sop)—Ou va la jeune Indoue? Classics for Pleasure ("Eminence" series) ▲ CFP 2234
Donizetti, G.:Lucia di Lammermoor (sels), w. Edita Guberova (sop)—Il dolce suono-Ardon gl'incensi Classics for Pleasure ("Eminence" series) ▲ CFP 2234
Gounod, C.:Roméo et Juliette (sels), w. Edita Guberova (sop)—Ah! je veux vivre Classics for Pleasure ("Eminence" series) ▲ CFP 2234
Meyerbeer, G.:Les Huguenots (sels), w. Edita Guberova (sop)—Nobles seigneurs, salut! Classics for Pleasure ("Eminence" series) ▲ CFP 2234
Rossini, G.:Il barbiere di Siviglia (sels), w. Edita Guberova (sop)—Una voce poco fa Classics for Pleasure ("Eminence" series) ▲ CFP 2234
Rossini, G.:Semiramide (sels), w. Edita Guberova (sop)—Bel raggio lushinghier Classics for Pleasure ("Eminence" series) ▲ CFP 2234
Rossini, G.:Semiramide (sels), w. Edita Gruberová (sop)—Bel raggio lusinghier [Act. I] EMI Classics ("Encore" series) ▲ CDE 68308 [ADD/DDD]
Spontini, G.:La vestale, w. R. Plowright (sop), G. Pasino (mez), F. Araiza (ten), P. Lefèbvre (ten), A. Cauli (bar), F. de Grandis (bass), Munich Radio Chorus [F] Orfeo 2-▲ 256922 [DDD]
Thomas, A.:Hamlet (sels), w. Edita Guberova (sop)—A vos jeux, mes amis-Partagez-vous mes fleurs Classics for Pleasure ("Eminence" series) ▲ CFP 2234
F. Luisi (cnd)
Bellini, V.:I Puritani, w. Edita Gruberova (sop), Katia Lytting (mez), Justin Lavender (ten), Carlo Tuand (ten), Ettore Kim (bar), Francesco Ellero d'Artegna (bass), Dankwart Siegele (bass), Bavarian Radio Chorus Nightingale Classics 3-▲ NIG 70562
German Opera Arias, w. Thomas Hampson (bar), Pestalozzi School Children's Choir EMI Classics ▲ 55233-2
Humperdinck, E.:Königskinder, w. Dagmar Schellenberger (sop—Goose girl), Marilyn Schmiege (cta—Witch), Thomas Moser (ten—King's Son), Heinrich Weber (ten—Broommaker), Dietrich Henschel (bar—Fiddler), Andreas Kohn (bass—Woodcutter), Michael Gläser (cnd), Bavarian Radio Chorus *(rec live, Munich Herkulessaal, Mar 22–24, 1996)* Calig 3-CAL 5096870 [DDD]
Mad Scenes, w. Edita Gruberova (sop) Bavarian Radio Chorus Nightingale Classics ▲ NIG CD 110560
M. Panni (cnd)
Donizetti, G.:La fille du régiment, w. Edita Gruberová (sop), Rosa Laghezza (mez), Deon van der Walt (sgr), Philippe Fourcade (bass), François Castel (sgr), Bavarian Radio Chorus Nightingale Classics 2-▲ NIG 70566
G. Patanè (cnd)
Mascagni, P.:Iris, w. I. Tokody (sop), P. Domingo (ten), J. Pons (bar), Bavarian Radio Chorus CBS 2-▲ M2K 45526
Puccini, G.:Arias, w. E. Martón (sop), 14 arias [I] CBS ▲ MK 42167 [DDD]
Puccini, G.:Gianni Schicchi, w. H. Donath (sop), P. Seiffert (ten), R. Panerai (bar) Eurodisc ▲ 7751-2-RC [DDD]

▲ = CD ♦ = Enhanced CD Δ = MD ■ = Cassette Tape □ = DCC

Munich RSO (cont.)
G. Patanè (cnd) (cont.)
Puccini, G.:Suor angelica, w. L. Popp (sop), M. Lipovšek (mez), Munich Radio Chorus
Eurodisc ▲ 7806-2-RC [DDD]
Puccini, G.:Il tabarro, w. I. Tokody (sop), G. Lamberti (ten), S. Nimsgern (bar) [I]
Eurodisc ▲ 7775-2-RC [DDD]
G. Ratzinger (cnd)
Schubert, Franz:Duetsche Messe, w. Augsburg PO, Munich Radio Orch, Munich PO Soloists, Regensburg Cathedral Choir — Ars Musici ▲ AM 0929 [DDD]
P. Schneider (cnd)
Killmayer, W.:Yolimba, w. M. Venuti (sop—Yolimba), A. Titus (bar—Möhringer), Bavarian Radio Chorus [G] — Orfeo ▲ 257921 [DDD]
L. Slatkin (cnd)
Gounod, C.:Roméo et Juliette, w. Susan Graham (sop—Stephano), Ruth Ann Swenson (sop—Juliette), Sarah Walker (mez—Gertrude), Paul Charles Clarke (ten—Tybalt), Placido Domingo (ten—Roméo), Kurt Ollmann (bar—Mercutio), Alastair Miles (bass—Frère Laurent), David Pittman-Jennings (bass—Le Duc), Alain Vernhes (bass—Capulet), Munich Radio Chorus *(rec Studio 1, Bavarian Radio, Munich, Nov 29 – Dec 10, 1995)* — RCA Red Seal 2-▲ 09026-68440-2 [DDD]
Puccini, G.:La fanciulla del West, w. Eva Martón (sop), Dennis O'Neill (ten), Walter Planté (ten), Alain Fondary (bar) — RCA Red Seal ▲ 09026-60597-2
S. Soltesz (cnd)
Gazzaniga, G.:Don Giovanni, w. P. Coburn (sop), J. Kaufmann (sop), J. Aler (ten), R. Swensen (ten), J.-L. Chaignaud (bar), G. von Kannen (bass), A. Scharinger (bass), Munich Radio Chorus [I] — Orfeo 2-▲ 214902 [DDD]
Wolf, H.:Songs (misc), w. D. Fischer-Dieskau (bar)—5 Goethe-Lieder, 5 Mörike-Lieder, Drei Michelangelo-Lieder, & 4 more [G] *(rec in studio, 1990)* — Orfeo ▲ 219911 [DDD]
P. Steinberg (cnd)
Catalani, A.:La Wally, w. E. Marton (sop), F. Araiza (ten), A. Titus (bar), F. Ellero d'Artegna (bass), Bavarian Radio Chorus [I] — Eurodisc 2-▲ 69073-2-RC [DDD] ■ 69073-4-RC (CrO2)
Massenet, J.:Chérubin, w. D. Upshaw (sop), F. von Stade (mez), M. Anderson (cta), S. Ramey (bass), Bavarian State Opera Chorus — RCA Red Seal 2-▲ 09026-60593-2 [DDD]
H. Wallberg (cnd)
Egk, W.:Peer Gynt, w. J. Perry (sop), N. Sharp (sop), C. Wulkopf (mez), H. Hopf (ten), R. Hermann (bar), Bavarian Radio Chorus [G] — Orfeo 2-▲ 005822 [DDD]
Lehár, F.:Friederike (sels), w. Helen Donath (sop), Gabriele Fuchs (sop), Adolf Dallapozza (ten), Bavarian Radio Chorus — Emperor Operetta ▲ KO 86344
Leoncavallo, R.:La Bohème, w. Lucia Popp (sop), Alexandrina Milcheva (mez), Franco Bonisolli (ten), Bernd Weikl (bar), Bavarian Radio Chorus [I] — Orfeo 2-▲ 023822 [DDD]
Mozart, W.A.:Entführung, w. E. Gruberova (sop), F. Araiza (ten), R. Orth (bar), R. Bracht (bass) — Eurodisc 2-▲ 7792-2 [ADD]
Verdi, G.:Arias, w. B. Weikl (bar)—9 arias from Ballo in maschera, Don Carlos, Forza del destino, Macbeth, Otello, Rigoletto, Traviata, Trovatore [I] — Acanta ▲ 43327
Weinberger, J.:Schwanda der Dudelsackpfeifer, w. L. Popp (sop), G. Killebrew (mez), S. Jerusalem (ten), H. Prey (bar), S. Nimsgern (bass), Bavarian Radio Chorus [F] — CBS 3-▲ M3K 36926 [ADD]

Munich Residenz CO
R. Kammler (cnd)
Diabelli, A.:Pastoralmesse, w. Augsburg Cathedral Boys' Choir — Ars Musici ▲ AM 0967 [ADD]
Kempter, K.:Pastoralmesse, w. Augsburg Cathedral Boys' Choir — Ars Musici ▲ AM 0967 [ADD]
Schubert, Franz:Deutsche Messe, w. Alexander Seitz (trb), Robert Wörle (ten), Ulrich Streckmann (bass), Augsburg Cathedral Boys' Choir — Calig ▲ CAL 50952 [DDD]
Schubert, Franz:Mass 2, w. Alexander Seitz (trb), Robert Wörle (ten), Ulrich Streckmann (bass), Augsburg Cathedral Boys' Choir — Calig ▲ CAL 50952 [DDD]

Munich Residenz Orch
H.R. Zöbeley (cnd)
Haydn, M.:Missa in honorem Sanctae Ursulae, w. Mechthild Bach (sop), Gabriele Binder (cta), Karl-Heinz Lampe (ten), Joachim Gebhardt (bass), Munich Motet Choir — Calig ▲ CAL 50901 [DDD]
Hiller, W.:Schulamit, w. Regina Klepper (sop), Edeltraud Knabel (alt), Michael Schopper (bass), Elisabeth Woska (nar), Waltraut Mastrogiovanni-Kraxner (shofar), Munich Percussion Ensemble, Calw Aurelius Boys' Choir Soloists, Munich Motet Choir — Wergo ▲ WER 6280-2
Mozart, W.A.:Ave verum corpus, w. Munich Motet Choir — Calig ▲ CAL 50901 [DDD]
Mozart, W.A.:Missa, K.257, w. Munich Motet Choir *(rec July 17, 1988 & Nov. 3, 1)* — Calig ▲ CAL 50872 [DDD]
Mozart, W.A.:Missa solemnis, K.337, w. Munich Motet Choir *(rec July 17, 1988 & Nov. 3, 1)* — Calig ▲ CAL 50872 [DDD]
Mozart, W.A.:Regina coeli, K.276, w. Munich Motet Choir *(rec July 17, 1988 & Nov. 3, 1)* — Calig ▲ CAL 50872 [DDD]
Mozart, W.A.:Regina coeli, K.276, w. J. Banse (sop), Munich Motet Choir — Calig ▲ CAL 50901 [DDD]
Orff, C.:Carmina burana, w. *(soloists unknown)*, Munich Motet Choir — Calig 2-▲ CAL 50937/38
Orff, C.:Catulli Carmina, w. *(soloists unknown)*, Munich Motet Choir — Calig 2-▲ CAL 50937/38
Orff, C.:Dithyrambo, w. *(soloists unknown)*, Munich Motet Choir — Calig 2-▲ CAL 50937/38
Schütz, H.:Magnificat anima mea, w. Munich Residenz Motet Choir [L] — Orfeo ▲ 002811 [DDD]
Schütz, H.:Weihnachtshistorie, w. Munich Residenz Motet Choir [G] — Orfeo ▲ 002811 [DDD]

Munich Residenz Quintet
Villa-Lobos, H.:Quintette forme de chôros — Calig ▲ CAL 50840 [DDD]

Munich Residenz Quintet members
Rimsky-Korsakov, N.:Qnt Fl, w. W. Sawallisch (pno) — Calig ▲ CAL 50898 [DDD]
Rubinstein, A.:Qnt Pno, w. W. Sawallisch (pno) — Calig ▲ CAL 50898 [DDD]
Villa-Lobos, H.:Qt Fl — Calig ▲ CAL 50840 [DDD]
Villa-Lobos, H.:Trio Ob — Calig ▲ CAL 50840 [DDD]

Munich Residenz Quintet members [H. Klemeyer (fl), H. Schöneberger (cl), O. Klamand (hn), J. Peters (bn)]
Rossini, G.:Sons Str Qt—Nos. 1, 2, 4, 5, & 6 *(rec Dec. 9-10 & 12, 1985 & Ja)* — Calig ▲ CAL 50850 [DDD]

Munich Rococo Soloists
Rossini, G.:Il barbiere di Siviglia (wind ensemble)—Ov. & 13 arias & scenes [arr. Franz Trautner for Flute, Oboe, Bassoon, Cello & Harpsichord ensemble] — Koch Schwann ▲ CD 310 061 [DDD] ■ MC 210 061 (D)

Munich String Trio
Mercadante, S.:Qts Fl, w. A. Adorján (fl) — Tudor ▲ 730 [DDD]
Mozart, W.A.:Qts Pno, w. R. Gothóni (pno) — Calig ▲ CAL 50 897 [DDD]
Schubert, Franz:Adagio & Rondo concertante Vn, w. R. Gothoni (pno) — Ondine ▲ ODE 763-2 [DDD]
Schubert, Franz:Qnt Pno, D.667, w. R. Gothoni (pno), E. Laine (db) — Ondine ▲ ODE 763-2 [DDD]

Munich SO
Delibes, L.:Coppélia (suite) — Quintessence ▲ CDQ 2100 [DDD]
Delibes, L.:Sylvia—suite — Quintessence ▲ CDQ 2100 [DDD]
Ravel, M.:Boléro — Quintessence ▲ CDQ 2100 [DDD]
Stravinsky, I.:Pétrouchka, w. *(cnd unknown)* — Quintessence ▲ CDQ 2099 [DDD]
J.O. Edwards (cnd)
Lloyd Webber, A.:Music of, w. M. Friedman (sgr), C. Carter (sgr), C. Moore (sgr), J. Barrowman (sgr), L. Robertson (sgr), J. Diedrich (sgr), Grania Renihan (sgr)—Cats; Joseph & the Amazing Technicolor Dreamcoat; Phantom of the Opera; Evita; Jesus Christ Superstar; Starlight Express; Song & Dance; Aspects of Love — Koch International ▲ CD 340022 [DDD] ■ MC 340022
Yates (cnd)
Lloyd Webber, A.:Music of, w. C. Burt (sgr), Graham Bickly (sgr), J. Kelly (sgr), C. D. Carroll (sgr), National SO—Song & Dance; The Phantom of the Opera; Starlight Express; Jeeves; Jesus Christ Superstar; Aspects of Love; Cats; The Requiem Mass — Koch International ▲ KOCCD 340132 ■ KOCC 340134
H.R. Zöbeley (cnd)
Bizet, G.:Te Deum, w. Angela Maria Blasi (sop), Christian Elsner (ten), Munich Motet Choir *(rec live, Herkulessaal, Munich, Mar 13 & 17, 1996)* — Calig ▲ CAL 50956 [DDD]

Munich SO (cont.)
H.R. Zöbeley (cnd) (cont.)
Cherubini, L.:Masses, w. Monika Wiebe (sop), Helena Jungwirth (alt), Rodrigo Orrego (ten), Wolf Matthias Friedrich (bass), Munich Motet Choir—Missa Solemnis — Calig ▲ CAL 50914
Gounod, C.:Messe solennelle de St. Cécile, w. Angela Maria Blasi (sop), Christian Elsner (ten), Dietrich Henschel (bar), Munich Motet Choir *(rec live, Herkulessaal, Munich, Mar 13 & 17, 1996)* — Calig ▲ CAL 50956 [DDD]

Munich Trombone Quartet
H.-C. Rademann (cnd)
Helmschrott, R.:Cross & Freedom, w. Helmut Schatz, Nancy Gibson (sop), Frieder Aurich (ten), Matthias Weichert (bass), Manfred Ball (nar), Anett Baumann (vn), Frank Philliptsch, Linda Robbins, Gerhard Wolf, Martin Homann (perc), Robert M. Helmschrott (org), Dresden Chamber Choir — Vienna Modern Masters ▲ VMM 3027 [DDD]

Munich Trumpet Ensemble
H. R. Zöbeley (cnd)
Marches & Field Music of the Baroque & Classical Periods — Calig ▲ CAL 50844 [DDD]

Munich Violin Duo [Luis Michel (vn), Martha Carfi (vn)]
Müncher Violin Duo *(rec Dec. 16–19, 1985)* — Calig ▲ CAL 50848 [DDD]

Munich Wind Academy
Heidenreich, J.:Suite Winds — Orfeo ▲ 092841

Munich Wind Academy Soloists
A. Brezina (cnd)
Dvořák, A.:Serenade Ww — Orfeo ▲ 051831 [DDD]
Gounod, C.:Petite Sym — Orfeo ▲ 051831 [DDD]

Munich Wind Ensemble
Serenades and Ständchen, w. Munich Motet Choir — Calig ▲ CAL 50890 [DDD]
Triebensee, J.:Suite — Orfeo ■ C 063841
...und Friede auf Erden, w. Munich Motet Choir — Calig ▲ CAL 50522 [DDD]

Munich Winds
W. Sawallisch (cnd)
Strauss, R.:Sonatina 2 — Orfeo ▲ 004821

Münster SO
W. Humburg (cnd)
Corghi, A.:Divara—Wasser und Blut, w. Susanna von der Burg (sop—Divara), Suzanne McLeod (mez—Else Windscherer), Eva Lillian Thingboe (mez—Hille Feiken), Robert Schwarts (ten—Lame Man), Heinz Fitz (spkr—Bernd Knipperdollinck), Hanslutz Hildmann (spkr—Jan Matthys), Michael Holm (spkr—Bernhard Rothmann), Christopher Krieg (spkr—Jan van Leiden), Münster City Theater Chorus [G] *(rec Grosses Haus, Münster State Theater, Nov. 27–29, 1993)* — Marco Polo 2-▲ 8.223706/07 [DDD]
Zimmermann, B.A.:Ich wandte mich und sah an alles Unrecht, das geschah unter der Sonne, w. C. Bantzer (nar), W. Quadflieg (nar), S. Nimsgern (b-bar) — Stradivarius ▲ STR 33340

Münster Wind Ensemble
H.-G. Freimuth (cnd)
Haydn, M.:German Masses, w. R. van Husen (ten), M. Flöth (bass), Münster Cathedral Choir—No. 1 — Calig ▲ CAL 50824 [ADD]
Schubert, Franz:Duetsche Messe, w. R. van Husen (ten), M. Flöth (bass), Münster Cathedral Choir — Calig ▲ CAL 50824 [ADD]

Murray/Lohuis Duo [Robert Murray (vn), Ardyth Lohuis (org)]
Works for Violin & Organ, Vol. 1 — Raven ▲ OAR 200 [DDD]
Rondo:Works for Violin & Organ, Vol. 2 — Raven ▲ OAR 230 [DDD]

Muse Orch
Yamash'ta, S.:Sea & Sky, w. Sen Izumi (syn), Takashi Kokobu (syn), Stomu Yamashta (syn/perc) — Kuckuck ▲ CD 072 ■ MC 072

Music for Westchester SO
S. Landau (cnd)
Kupferman, M.:Con Vc, Tape & Orch, w. Laszlo Varga (vc) *(rec 1975)* — Vox Box ("The American Composers" series) 2-▲ CDX 5158

Music Group of London
Schubert, Franz:Octet Ww, D.803 — ASV Quicksilva ▲ ASQ 6098 [ADD]
Vaughan Williams, R.:Phantasy Qnt — EMI Classics ▲ CDM 65100
Vaughan Williams, R.:Qt 2 Strs — EMI Classics ▲ CDM 65100
Vaughan Williams, R.:Son Vn, w. H. Bean (vn) — EMI Classics ▲ CDM 65100

Music in the Mountains Festival Chamber Players
Starer, R.:Qnt Cl — Albany ▲ TROY 152 [DDD]
M. Kupferman (cnd)
Kupferman, M.:The Proscenium:...On the Demise of Gertrude, w. B. Hardgrave (sop) — Soundspells ▲ SP 107

Music of the Baroque
T. Wikman (cnd)
Telemann, G.P.:Der Tag des Gerichts, w. Patrice Michaels Bell (sop), Sandra Walker (mez), Karen Brunssen (mez), Bruce Fowler (ten), Kurt R. Hansen (ten), William Stone (bar), Douglas Anderson (bar), Baroque Music Chorus *(rec live, St. Paul's United Church of Christ, Feb 23, 1992)* — Music of the Baroque 2-▲ MB 107
Telemann, G.P.:Der Tag des Gerichts *(rec live)* — d'Note ▲ DND 1017

Music Project CO
A. Goodman (cnd)
Luening, O.:No Jerusalem But This, w. K. Sullivan (sop), Jacqueline Pierce (sop), Paul Sperry (ten), M. Moliterno (bar), P. Wilder (sgr), S. Rosser (sgr), Goodman Chamber Choir [E] *(rec 6/6/90)* — CRI ▲ CD 600 [DDD]

Music Projects London
R. Bernas (cnd)
Dillon, J.:Music of—East 11th St. NY 10003; Windows & Canopies; La femme invisible — NM Classics ▲ NMCD 004 [DDD]
R. Bernas (cnd)
Casken, J.:Golem, w. P. Rozario (sop), C. Robson (ct), A. Clarke (bar), J. Hall (bar) — Virgin Classics 2-▲ CDC 59028
Gilbert, A.:Nine or Ten Osannas — NM Classics ▲ NMCD 014 [DDD]
Hopkins, B.:Music of, w. A. Wells (sop), A. Balanescu (vn)—En attendant for Flute, Oboe, Cello & Harpsichord; 2 Pomes for Soprano, Bass Cittern; Trumpet, Harp & Viola; Penandt for Violin; Sensation for Soprano, Saxophone, Trumpet, Harp & Viola — NM Classics ▲ NMCD 014 [DDD]

Music Today Ensemble
G. Schwarz (cnd)
Kolb, B.:Chromatic Fant, w. R. Reinhardt (nar) [E] — New World ▲ 80422-2 [DDD]
Perle, G.:Concertino Pno, w. R. Goode (pno) — Elektra/Nonesuch ▲ 79108-2 [DDD]
Perle, G.:Serenade 3 Pno, w. R. Goode (pno) — Elektra/Nonesuch ▲ 79108-2 [DDD]

Musica Ad Rhenum
de Fesch, W.:Concerti Opera Quinta (6) — NM Classics ▲ NM 92054
de Fesch, W.:Con 2 for 2 Vns — NM Classics ▲ NM 92037
Groneman, A.:Con Fl & 2 Vns — NM Classics ▲ NM 92037
Groneman, A.:Con for 3 Fl & Va — NM Classics ▲ NM 92037
Hurlebusch, C.F.:Con for 2 Obs & Vn — NM Classics ▲ NM 92037
Schickhardt, J.C.:Con Fl — NM Classics ▲ NM 92037

Musica Aeterna
Bach, J.S.:Cant 209, w. Kamila Zajíčkova (sop) *(rec Moyzes Hall of the Slovak Philharmonic, Bratislava, Jan 20–23, 1993)* — Slovart ▲ SR 0003-2-131 [DDD]
Biber, H. von:Fidicinium sacro-profanum *(rec Moyzes Hall of the Slovak Philharmonic, Bratislava, Mar 6–7, 1992)* — Slovart ▲ SR 0002-2-131 [DDD]
Biber, H. von:Mensa Sonora *(rec Moyzes Hall of the Slovak Philharmonic, Bratislava, Mar 6–7, 1992)* — Slovart ▲ SR 0002-2-131 [DDD]

ORCH. & ENS.

Musica Aeterna (cont.)
Biber, H. von:Sonatae tam aris quam aulis servientes *(rec Moyzes Hall of the Slovak Philharmonic, Bratislava, Mar 6–7, 1992)* Slovart ▲ SR 0002-2-131 [DDD]
Bodino, S.:Sons, w. Peter Zajíček (vn), Miloš Valent (vn), Peter Királ (vc), Pascal Dubreuil (hpd)—Sons 1–6 *(rec Castle of Tonky, Slovakia, Apr 1994)* Slovart ▲ SR 0008-2-131 [DDD]
Graupner, C.:Ovs—in E♭ for 2 Trns Fl, 2 Vns, Va & Hpd *(rec Moyzes Hall of the Slovak Philharmonic, June 21–23, 1994)* Slovart ▲ SR 0009-2-131 [DDD]
Handel, G.F.:Cants, w. Kamila Zajíčkova (sop)—Cant HWV 97, "Crudel tiranno Amor" *(rec Moyzes Hall of the Slovak Philharmonic, Bratislava, Jan 20–23, 1993)* Slovart ▲ SR 0003-2-131 [DDD]
Stamitz, J.W.A.:Orchestral Trios Arion ▲ ARN 68322
Telemann, G.P.:Cants, w. Kamila Zajíčkova (sop)—Der Weiberorden *(rec Moyzes Hall of the Slovak Philharmonic, Bratislava, Jan 20–23, 1993)* Slovart ▲ SR 0003-2-131 [DDD]
Telemann, G.P.:Con Vns Va Hpd *(rec Moyzes Hall of the Slovak Philharmonic, June 21–23, 1994)* Slovart ▲ SR 0009-2-131 [DDD]
Telemann, G.P.:Ovs—in G for Violino concertato, 2 Obs, 2 Vns, Va & Hpd *(rec Moyzes Hall of the Slovak Philharmonic, June 21–23, 1994)* Slovart ▲ SR 0009-2-131 [DDD]

O. Schneebeli (cnd)
du Mont, H.:Motets pour la chapelle du roy, w. H. Crook (cta), H. Lamy (ten), P. Harvey (bar), Les Pages de la Chapelle *(rec Sept. 1993)* FNAC Music ▲ 592054 [DDD]

F. Waldman (cnd)
Mozart, W.A.:Con 9 Pno, w. Mieczyslaw Horszowski (pno) *(rec 1962–72)* Pearl 2-▲ PEA 9138 [ADD]
Mozart, W.A.:Con 12 Pno, w. Mieczyslaw Horszowski (pno) *(rec 1962–72)* Pearl 2-▲ PEA 9138 [ADD]
Mozart, W.A.:Con 13 Pno, w. Mieczyslaw Horszowski (pno) *(rec 1962–72)* Pearl 2-▲ PEA 9138 [ADD]
Mozart, W.A.:Con 14 Pno, w. Mieczyslaw Horszowski (pno) *(rec 1962–72)* Pearl 2-▲ PEA 9138 [ADD]
Mozart, W.A.:Con 17 Pno, w. Mieczyslaw Horszowski (pno) Pearl 2-▲ PEA 9153 [ADD]
Mozart, W.A.:Con 18 Pno, w. Mieczyslaw Horszowski (pno) Pearl 2-▲ PEA 9153 [ADD]
Mozart, W.A.:Con 19 Pno, w. Mieczyslaw Horszowski (pno) *(rec 1962–72)* Pearl 2-▲ PEA 9138 [ADD]
Mozart, W.A.:Con 20 Pno, w. Mieczyslaw Horszowski (pno) Pearl 2-▲ PEA 9153 [ADD]
Mozart, W.A.:Con 22 Pno, w. Mieczyslaw Horszowski (pno) Pearl 2-▲ PEA 9153 [ADD]
Mozart, W.A.:Fant Pno, K.475, w. Mieczyslaw Horszowski (pno) Pearl 2-▲ PEA 9153 [ADD]

P. Zajicek (cnd)
Corelli, A.:Con grosso, Op. 6/8, "Christmas Con" Slovart ▲ SR 0004
Handel, G.F.:Messiah (sels) Slovart ▲ SR 0004
Kusser, J.S.:Ovs for Theater *(rec Mar. 3–7, 1993)* K617 ▲ 7032 [DDD]
Sammartini, G.:Con grossi, Op. 2—Op. 5/6, "Christmas Concerto" Slovart ▲ SR 0004
Sperger, J.:Syms—in C, F & B♭ [period instrs] Trevak ▲ TRE 40006 [DDD]
Torelli, G.:Con grossi—No. 6, "Christmas Concerto" Slovart ▲ SR 0004

Musica Aeterna Bratislava
Benda, G.A.:Cephalus & Aurora *(rec Moyzes Hall of the Slovak Philharmonic, Apr & June 1995)* Slovart ▲ SR 0013-2-131 [DDD]
Benda, G.A.:Er ist Dahin der Frühling Meiner Blüthe *(rec Moyzes Hall of the Slovak Philharmonic, Apr & June 1995)* Slovart ▲ SR 0013-2-131 [DDD]
Benda, G.A.:Marianne *(rec Moyzes Hall of the Slovak Philharmonic, Apr & June 1995)* Slovart ▲ SR 0013-2-131 [DDD]
Benda, G.A.:Scherzi Notturni, w. Peter Zajíček (vn), Miloš Valent (vn) *(rec Moyzes Hall of the Slovak Philharmonic, Apr & June 1995)* Slovart ▲ SR 0013-2-131 [DDD]
Benda, G.A.:Sinf 1 *(rec Moyzes Hall of the Slovak Philharmonic, Apr & June 1995)* Slovart ▲ SR 0013-2-131 [DDD]
Benda, G.A.:Sinf 2 *(rec Moyzes Hall of the Slovak Philharmonic, Apr & June 1995)* Slovart ▲ SR 0013-2-131 [DDD]
Benda, G.A.:Sinf 3 *(rec Moyzes Hall of the Slovak Philharmonic, Apr & June 1995)* Slovart ▲ SR 0013-2-131 [DDD]

Musica Alta Ripa
Bach, J.S.:Con 5 Hpd, w. *(soloist unknown)* MD + G ▲ MDG CD 3090681
Bach, J.S.:Con 6 Hpd, w. *(soloist unknown)* MD + G ▲ MDG CD 3090681
Bach, J.S.:Con Hpds, BWV 1061a, w. *(soloists unknown)* [unnacompanied version of BWV 1061] MD + G ▲ MDG CD 3090681
Bach, J.S.:Con for 4 Hpds, w. Gregor Hollmann (hpd), Rudolf Innig (hpd), Bernward Lohr (hpd), Ludger Rémy (hpd) MD + G ▲ MDG CD 3090681
Concert au goût italien:Chamber Music, Paris 1740 MD + G ("Gold" series) ▲ MDG 3090503 [DDD]
Leclair, J.-M.:Trio Sons—Op. 4 MD + G ▲ L 3428 [DDD]
Müthel, J.G.:Music of—Duetto in C for 2 Harpsichords; Polonaise in G for Flute, 2 Violins, Cello & Harpsichord; Son. in D for Flute; Son. in F for Harpsichord; 2 Polonaises for 2 Violins & Cello; Con. in B♭ for Harpsichord; Con. in D for 2 Bassoons; Con. I in d for Harpsichord & 2 Bassoons MD + G ("Gold" series) ▲ MDG 3250452 [DDD]
Richter, F.X.:Con in G Fl MD + G ▲ MDG 3090508 [DDD]
Richter, F.X.:Con Ob MD + G ▲ MDG 3090508 [DDD]
Richter, F.X.:Sinf MD + G ▲ MDG 3090508 [DDD]
Richter, F.X.:Son Vns MD + G ▲ MDG 3090508 [DDD]
Richter, F.X.:Trio Fl MD + G ▲ MDG 3090508 [DDD]

Música Antigua de Albuquerque
A Rose of Swych Virtu:Reverence from the Renaissance & Middle Ages Dorian Discovery ▲ DIS 80104 [DDD]

Musica Antiqua Ensemble
Jewels of Early Music, w. Loïnhdana Ensemble, John Elwes (ten), André Isoir (org), Pierre Bardon (org) *(rec 1982–86)* Pierre Verany ▲ 791051 [DDD]

C. Mendoze (cnd)
Airs & Dances of Shakespeare's Time, w. John Elwes (ten), Stephen Stubbs (lt) Pierre Verany ▲ 787092 [DDD]
Praetorius, M.:Terpsichore, w. Christian Mendoze (rcr)—Branles de la Royne No. 7; Courante No. 4; Branles Double No. 3; Suite de Gavottes; Philou No. 6; Pavane de Spaigne No. 8; Spagnoletta No. 9; La Canarie No. 10; La bourrée; Courante No. 16; Branles de Montirande Nos. 1 & 11; Suite de Branles de Villages; Suite de Courantes; Suite de Ballets; Ballet des Bacchanales No. 19; Ballet des Matelotz No. 21; Ballet des Feus; Ballet des Cocos; Suite de Voltes Pierre Verany ▲ PVY 730067 [DDD]
Zanetti, G.:Il scolaro di Gasparo Zanetti Pierre Verany ▲ PV.792012 [DDD]

M. Uridge (cnd)
Festive Fayre:Five Centuries of Popular Song & Dance Symposium ▲ SYM 1157

Musica Antiqua Sloveniae
Tabulatura Vietoris Trevak ▲ TRE 40004 [DDD]

Musica Antiquae Collegium Varsoviense
J. Dobrzanski (cnd)
Zebrowski, M.J.:Magnificat, w. Warsaw CO [L] *(rec 1968)* Olympia ▲ OCD 317 [AAD]

Musica Bohemica
The Oldest Collections of Czech Folk Songs, w. vocal soloists Supraphon ▲ 11 1293-2 [DDD]

J. Krček (cnd)
Abbesser, F.:Stabat Mater, w. Prague Chamber Choir Panton ▲ PAN 811180
Caldara, A.:Masses, w. Prague Chamber Choir—in F Panton ▲ PAN 811180
Demantius, C.:Dances Panton ▲ PAN 811008 [DDD]
Erben, K.J.:Songs—Vek detský; Písne a říkadla výroční; Mladost, krása, radost; Láska nešťastná; Vzdory; Zerty a posmešky; Hudba a tanec; Zenení a vdávání; Písne a říkadla svatební; Písne společenské; Písne o stavích, zivnostech a jiných stránkách zivota občanského; Selské hospodářství; Písne vojenské; Vzpomínky historické; Písne rozpravné; Marnost svetská, smrt a pohreb; Písne pohrební *(rec Studio Martínek, Prague, Feb 12–17, 1995)* Panton 2-▲ 811418-2
Hammerschmidt, A.:Music of—Suites 1 & 2 Panton ▲ PAN 811008 [DDD]

Musica Bohemica (cont.)
J. Krček (cnd) (cont.)
Krček, J.:Songs of Love, w. L. Vraspír (ten), J. Fišer (vn) Panton ▲ 81 1030-2
Krček, J.:Sym 2, w. L. Vraspír (ten), *(chorus unknown)* Panton ▲ 81 1030-2
Krček, J.:Testamenti, w. J. Mihálíková (sop), L. Vraspír (ten), *(chorus unknown)* Panton ▲ 81 1030-2
Marcello, A.:Cons Ob, w. G. Krčková (ob) *(rec 1989)* Supraphon ▲ 11 1290-2 [DDD]
Michna, A.V.:The Czech Lute, w. Prague Chamber Choir Panton ▲ PAN 811040
Muffat, G.:Florilegium primum Panton ▲ PAN 811008 [DDD]
Otto, V.:Music of—Dances Panton ▲ PAN 811008 [DDD]
Pascha, E.:Prosae pastorales—9 Christmas Carols Campion ▲ 1305 [AAD/DDD]
Prustmann, I.:Miserere, w. Prague Chamber Choir Panton ▲ PAN 811180
Telemann, G.P.:Con da camera, w. G. Krčková (rcr) Supraphon ▲ 11 1290-2 [DDD]
Telemann, G.P.:Con Ob Strs, w. G. Krčková (ob) Supraphon ▲ 11 1290-2 [DDD]
Tolar, J.K.:Music of—Baletti à 4 Panton ▲ PAN 811008 [DDD]
Vivaldi, A.:Cons Ob, w. G. Krčková (rcr)—Concerto in C Supraphon ▲ 11 1290-2 [DDD]
Vivaldi, A.:Cons Rcr, w. G. Krčková (ob)—Concerto in F Supraphon ▲ 11 1290-2 [DDD]

Musica Canterey Bamberg
H. Dechant (cnd)
Venetian Music at the Habsburg Court in the 17th Century Deutsche Harmonia Mundi ▲ 77086-2-RC [DDD]

Musica Concertiva
Lotti, A.:Son Fl Supraphon ▲ SUP 3097
Lotti, A.:Trio Fl Supraphon ▲ SUP 3097
Vivaldi, A.:Cons Diverse Instrs—in g for Fl, Ob, Bn & Cont, RV. 106; in g for Fl, Ob & Bn, RV. 103; in F for Hpd Supraphon ▲ SUP 3097
Vivaldi, A.:Son Rcr Bn, RV.86 Supraphon ▲ SUP 3097

Musica da Camera
Raickovich, M.:Dream Qt *(rec Radio Novi Sad Studios, Yugoslavia, 1987)* Mode ▲ mode 45

R. King (cnd)
Albinoni, T.:Adagio Org [arr Giazotto] *(rec Henry Wood Hall, London, Sept 3–4, 1992)* Linn ▲ CKD 012
Bach, J.S.:Sinfs—Sinf to Cant 42 *(rec Henry Wood Hall, London, Sept 3–4, 1992)* Linn ▲ CKD 012
Corelli, A.:Con grosso, Op. 6/8, "Christmas Con" *(rec Henry Wood Hall, London, Sept 3–4, 1992)* Linn ▲ CKD 012
Handel, G.F.:Concerti grossi, Op. 3—No. 2 *(rec Henry Wood Hall, London, Sept 3–4, 1992)* Linn ▲ CKD 012
Pachelbel, J.:Canon *(rec Henry Wood Hall, London, Sept 3–4, 1992)* Linn ▲ CKD 012
Vivaldi, A.:Cons for 2 Vns—No. 11 *(rec Henry Wood Hall, London, Sept 3–4, 1992)* Linn ▲ CKD 012

Musica d'Oggi
L. Lanzillotta (cnd)
Petrassi, G.:Laudes creaturarum, w. R. Cucciolla (nar) Bongiovanni ▲ GB 5534 [DDD]

F. Maestri (cnd)
Petrassi, G.:Grand septuor Cl, w. C. Scarponi (cl) Bongiovanni ▲ GB 5534 [DDD]

K. Martin (cnd)
Arrigo, G.:Serenata per Andromeda, w. C. Scarponi (pno), V. de Vita (cl), A. Vismara (va) Bongiovanni ▲ GB 5511 [DDD]
Ghedini, G.F.:Concert Music, w. A. Vismara (va) Bongiovanni ▲ GB 5511 [DDD]
Rota, N.:Con Strs Bongiovanni ▲ GB 5511 [DDD]

Musica Dolce
Boismortier, J.B. de:Cons for 5 Fls, Op. 15—No. 4 in b BIS ▲ CD 8
Heinichen, J.D.:Con à 8, Drottningholm Baroque Ensemble BIS ▲ CD 8

Musica Dolce Recorder Quintet
English Consort Music BIS ▲ CD 305 [DDD]
From Byrd to Birds, w. (rec 1976 & 1990) BIS ▲ CD 57 [ADD/DDD]

Musica Domestica [Brenda Blewett (pno), Paul Wahlberg (fl), Torleif Holm (vc)]
Haydn, J.:Trios Pno, Fl & Vc *(rec Finchcocks Museum, Dec 1994)* Victoria ▲ VCD 19105

Musica Duo [Bent Larsen (fl), Jan Sommer (gtr)]
Histoire du Tango *(rec 1992)* Classico ▲ CLASSCD 101

Musica Fiata
F. Bernius (cnd)
Schütz, H.:Easter Oratorio, w. Stuttgart Baroque Orch, Stuttgart Chamber Choir Sony Classical ("Vivarte" series) ▲ SK 45943
Schütz, H.:Die Geburt unsers Herren Jesu Christi, w. Stuttgart Baroque Orch, Stuttgart Chamber Choir Sony Classical ("Vivarte" series) ▲ SK 45943
Schütz, H.:Psalmen Davids, w. Stuttgart Chamber Choir—complete 26 psalms [G] Sony Classical ("Vivarte" series) 2-▲ S2K 48042 [DDD]

H. Hennig (cnd)
Monteverdi, C.:Vespro della Beata Vergine, w. Pro Cantione Antiqua, Collegium Aureum, Hanover Boys' Choir Ars Musici 2-▲ 1000 [AAD]

R. Wilson (cnd)
Barbarino, B.:Sacred Music, w. Gerd Türk (ten)—O sacrum convivium *(rec St. Osdag Church, Mandelsloh, Germany, June 11–15, 1994)* Sony Classical ("Vivarte" series) 2-▲ S2K 66254 [DDD]
Castaldi, B.:Music of—Capriccio detto svegliatoio *(rec St. Osdag Church, Mandelsloh, Germany, June 11–15, 1994)* Sony Classical ("Vivarte" series) 2-▲ S2K 66254 [DDD]
Cima, G.P.:Son Tpt *(rec St. Osdag Church, Mandelsloh, Germany, June 11–15, 1994)* Sony Classical ("Vivarte" series) 2-▲ S2K 66254 [DDD]
Cima, G.P.:Son Vn & Tpt *(rec St. Osdag Church, Mandelsloh, Germany, June 11–15, 1994)* Sony Classical ("Vivarte" series) 2-▲ S2K 66254 [DDD]
Cima, G.P.:Son Vn & Vle *(rec St. Osdag Church, Mandelsloh, Germany, June 11–15, 1994)* Sony Classical ("Vivarte" series) 2-▲ S2K 66254 [DDD]
Gabrieli, G.:Music of, w. David Cordier (alt), Wilfried Jochens (ten), Rufus Müller (ten), Gerd Türk (ten), Harry van der Kamp (bass), La Capella Ducale—Toccata [arr Wilson]; Buccinate in neomenia tuba à 19; Canzon XVII à 12; Dulcis Jesu patris imago [Son con voce à 20]; Timor et remor à 6; Son con 3 Vns; Son XIX à 15; In ecclesiis à 14; Canzon V à 7; Jubilate Deo à 10; Son XVIII à 14; Cantate Domino à 8; Canzon primi toni à 10; Misericordia tua Domine à 12; Canzon X à 8; Toccata primi toni; Magnificat à 33 [reconstructed by Wilson]; Benedictus es Dominus à 8 *(rec St. Osdag Church, Mandelsloh, Germany, June 11–15, 1994)* Sony Classical ("Vivarte" series) 2-▲ S2K 66254 [DDD]
Grandi, A.:Sacred Music, w. David Cordier (alt), Wilfried Jochens (ten), Rufus Müller (ten), Gerd Türk (ten), Harry van der Kamp (bass), La Capella Ducale—Heu mihi [Dialogo à 4]; O quam tu pulchra es; Cantemus Domino; Salvum me fac, Deus [Basso solo] *(rec St. Osdag Church, Mandelsloh, Germany, June 11–15, 1994)* Sony Classical ("Vivarte" series) 2-▲ S2K 66254 [DDD]
Monteverdi, C.:Salve, o Regina, w. Wilfried Jochens (ten) *(rec St. Osdag Church, Mandelsloh, Germany, June 11–15, 1994)* Sony Classical ("Vivarte" series) 2-▲ S2K 66254 [DDD]

Musica Florea
M. Stryncl (cnd)
Biber, H. von:Music of—Son à 3; Son à 4; Son à 6; Laetatus Sum; Son à 6 [Die Pauern Kirchfartt Genandt]; In Sole Posuisti; Battalia; Balletti Lamentabili; Serenada à 5 Studio Matous ▲ MAT 31 [DDD]
Zelenka, J.D.:Missa sanctissimae trinitatis, w. Anna Hlavenková (sop), Magdalena Kozená (alt), Lubomir Moravec (alt), Stanislav Predota (ten), Richard Sporka (ten), Michal Pospí il (bass) Studio Matou ▲ MAT 17 [DDD]

La Musica Gioiosa Trio
Sowerby, L.:Trio Vn (1911) New World ▲ NW 365-2 [AAD]
Sowerby, L.:Trio Vn (1953) New World ▲ NW 365-2 [AAD]

Musica Holmiae [L. Frydén (baroque vn), B. Orsin (baroque vn), T. Galli (baroque va), B. Ericson (baroque vc), G. Nylén (baroque db), A. Öhrwall (hpd)]
Farina, C.:Libro della pavane, gagliarde, brand:mascherata, aria fanzesa, bolte, balletti, sonate, canzone *(rec Nov. 29, 1974)* BIS ▲ CD 134 [AAD]

▲ = CD ♦ = Enhanced CD ∆ = MD ▮ = Cassette Tape □ = DCC

Musica Holmiae [L. Frydén (baroque vn), T. Galli (baroque vn), B. Sjögren (baroque va), B. Ericson (baroque vc), G. Nylén (db), A. Öhrwall (hpd)]
Telemann, G.P.:Quadri—in B♭ *(rec June 7, 1968)* BIS ▲ CD 134 [AAD]
Musica Holmiae [L. Frydén (baroque vn), T. Galli (baroque vn), B. Sjögren (va da bracchio), B. Ericson (vl), A. Öhrwall (hpd)]
Couperin, F.:La Sultane *(rec June 7, 1968)* BIS ▲ CD 134 [AAD]
Musica Holmiae [L. Frydén (baroque vn), T. Galli (baroque vn), P. Sandklef (baroque va), B. Ericson (baroque vc), G. Nylén (db), G. Wennberg (hn), B. Sundberg (hn)]
Mozart, W.A.:Musikalischer Spass *(rec June 7, 1968)* BIS ▲ CD 134 [AAD]
Musica Humana [Rebecca Stuhr-Rommereim (baroque fl), John Stuhr-Rommereim (hpd)]
Boismortier, J.B. de:Sons Fl, Op. 91 *(rec St. Bridget's Church, Solon, IA, July 11-13, 1994)* Centaur ▲ CRC 2265 [DDD]
Musica Mensurata
Frese Nouvele! FSM ▲ 97736
Musica Nova
Musica Humana, w. Françoise Atlan (mez), John Fleagle (ten/hp), Crawford Young (lt), Anonymous 4, Ensemble Discantus, Ensemble Gilles Binchois, Ensemble Organum, Gothic Voices, Greece Byzantine Choir, Hilliard Ensemble, et al. L'Empreinte Digitale ▲ ED 13047
E. Huber-Contwig (cnd)
Widmer, E.:Pulsars *(rec May 5, 1970)* Grammont ▲ CTSP 32-2 [ADD]
Musica Pacifica [Elizabeth Blumenstock (vn), Elisabeth LeGuin (vc), Judith Linsenberg (rcr), Edward Parmentier (hpd)]
Bach, J.S.:Trio Sons Org, BWV 525-530 [arr for vn, vc, rec & hpd] Virgin Classics ▲ CDC 45192
Musica Poetica Ensemble
Quantz, J.J.:Sons Fl & Hpd [period instrs]—3 Sons. in D, e & g Thorofon ▲ CTH 2073 [DDD]
Quantz, J.J.:Trio Sons [period instrs]—in D for Flute, Bassoon & Continuo; in c & G for Flute, Oboe & Continuo; in C for Recorder, Flute & Continuo Thorofon ▲ CTH 2073 [DDD]
Musica Poetica Freiberg
H.L. Hirsch (cnd)
Pergolesi, G.B.:La serva padrona, w. Jeanne Marie Bima (sop—Serpina), Petteri Salomaa (b-bar—Uberto) *(rec Waldkirch, Germany, Nov 14-18, 1990)* Arts ▲ 47119-2 [DDD]
Musica Polyphonica
L. Devos (cnd)
Charpentier, M.-A.:Leçons de ténèbres, H. 96-110, w. Jan Caals (ten), Harry Ruyl (ten), Howard Crook (ct), Luc de Meulenaere (ct), Michel Verschaeve (bar), Kurt Widmer (bass) Erato 2-▲ ERA 96376 [DDD]
Musica Reservata
16th Century Italian & French Dance Music, w. Michael Morrow (cnd) *(rec Oct. 1970 & July 1971)* Boston Skyline ▲ BSD 123 [ADD]
Musica Sacra
Ligeti, G.:Lux Aeterna Catalyst ▲ 09026-61822-2 ■ 09026-61822-4
Messiaen, O.:O sacrum convivium! Catalyst ▲ 09026-61822-2 ■ 09026-61822-4
Moran, R.:7 Sounds Unseen Catalyst ▲ 09026-61822-2 ■ 09026-61822-4
R. Westenburg (cnd)
Handel, G.F.:Messiah (sels), w. Judith Blegen (sop), Katherine Ciesinski (mez), John Aler (ten), John Cheek (bass), Musica Sacra Chorus RCA Silver Seal ▲ 60481-2-RV [DDD]; ■ 60481-4-RV (CrO2)
Songs & Psalms of the Daisy RCA Red Seal ▲ 09026-60970-2 ■ 09026-60970-4
Musica Secreta [D. Roberts (sop), S. le Blanc (sop), M. Nichols (cta), K. Elsner (thb), J. Toll (hpd)]
Luzzaschi, L.:Madrigali Amon Ra ▲ CD-SAR 58 [DDD]
Strozzi, B.:Arias & Cants—Merce di voi; Noiosa lontonanza:Dimmi dove sei; Le tre Gratie a Venere; Gl'occhi superbi; Amor dormiglione; Begli occhi; Anima del mio core; Sete pur fastidioso; I baci; Sino alla morte; Mordeva un bianco lino; Godere e tacere; Canto di bella bocca; Libertà:Non ci lusinghi più [I] *(rec Nov. 1992)* Amon Ra ▲ CD-SAR 61 [DDD]
Musica Sonora [James Pellerite (fl), Jerry Sirucek (ob), Abraham Skernick (va), Wallace Hornibrook (pno)]
Barati, G.:Indiana Triptych *(rec Indiana Univ, 1984)* Centaur ▲ CRC 2286 [DDD]
Musica Sveciae
Larsson, L.-E.:Concertinos, w. New Stockholm CO, Stockholm Chamber Ensemble, Musica Vitae, Umea Sinfonietta—G. von Bahr (fl) *(No. 1)*, H. Jahren (ob) *(No. 2)*, M. Lethiec (cl) *(No. 3)*, K. Sonstevold (bn) *(No. 4)*, S. Hermansson (hn) *(No. 5)*, U. Agnas (tpt) *(No. 6)*, C. Lindberg (trbn) *(No. 7)*, A. Kontra (vn) *(No. 8)*, B. Andersson (va) *(No. 9)*, F. Helmerson (vc) *(No. 10)*, H. Ehren (db) *(No. 11)*, H. Palsson (pno) *(No. 12)* [these 12 neo-classical, at times Hindemithesque, 3 movt concertinos were composed to suit the performing abilities of the amateur orch] BIS 2-▲ CD 473/74 [AAD/DDD]
S. Westerberg (cnd)
Pergament, M.:Sonatina Fl Strs, w. Gunilla von Bahr (fl) *(rec Feb. 20, 1976)* BIS ▲ CD 37 [AAD]
Musica Vitae
Larsson, L.-E.:Concertinos, w. New Stockholm CO, Stockholm Chamber Ensemble, Musica Sveciae, Umea Sinfonietta—G. von Bahr (fl) *(No. 1)*, H. Jahren (ob) *(No. 2)*, M. Lethiec (cl) *(No. 3)*, K. Sonstevold (bn) *(No. 4)*, S. Hermansson (hn) *(No. 5)*, U. Agnas (tpt) *(No. 6)*, C. Lindberg (trbn) *(No. 7)*, A. Kontra (vn) *(No. 8)*, B. Andersson (va) *(No. 9)*, F. Helmerson (vc) *(No. 10)*, H. Ehren (db) *(No. 11)*, H. Palsson (pno) *(No. 12)* [these 12 neo-classical, at times Hindemithesque, 3 movt concertinos were composed to suit the performing abilities of the amateur orch] BIS 2-▲ CD 473/74 [AAD/DDD]
Nordic Music, Vols. 1 & 2 BIS ▲ CD 460 & 461 [DDD]
W. Rajski (cnd)
Carlstedt, J.:Metamorphosi BIS ▲ CD 460 [DDD]
Fernström, J.:Intimate Miniatures BIS ▲ CD 461 [DDD]
Grieg, E.:Elegaic Melodies, Op. 34 BIS ▲ CD 461 [DDD]
Larsson, L.-E.:Little Serenade BIS ▲ CD 460 [DDD]
Nielsen, C.:Little Suite BIS ▲ CD 461 [DDD]
Rautavaara, E.:The Fiddlers BIS ▲ CD 460 [DDD]
Roman, J.H.:Con grosso, w. H. Jahren (ob) BIS ▲ CD 460 [DDD]
Sallinen, A.:Some Aspects of Peltoniemi Hintrik's Funeral March BIS ▲ CD 461 [DDD]
Sibelius, J.:Romance Strs BIS ▲ CD 460 [DDD]
Sigurbjörnsson, T.:Siciliano BIS ▲ CD 461 [DDD]
J.-O. Wedin (cnd)
Sun-Flute 4, w. G. von Bahr (fl), Karin Langebo (hp) BIS ▲ CD 350 [DDD]
Musica Viva CO
Silvestrov, V.:Meditation, w. *(soloist unknown)* Olympia ▲ OLY 477 [DDD]
Silvestrov, V.:Serenade Strs Olympia ▲ OLY 477 [DDD]
Silvestrov, V.:Sym 2 Olympia ▲ OLY 477 [DDD]
Tcherepnin, A.:Con da camera, w. Olga Ivusheikova (fl), Nazar Kozhukhar (vn) Olympia ▲ OLY 584 [DDD]
Tcherepnin, A.:Pieces CO Olympia ▲ OLY 584 [DDD]
Tcherepnin, A.:Serenade Strs Olympia ▲ OLY 584 [DDD]
A. Rudin (cnd)
Mozart, W.A.:Diverts Str Qt [arr for Chamber Orch] *(rec Moscow Conservatory Great Hall, 1996)* Russian Compact Disc ▲ RCD 30201 [DDD]
Mozart, W.A.:Marches 2 Hns, w. Andrey Kuznetsov (hn), Dmitry Kuznetsov (hn) *(rec Moscow Conservatory Great Hall, 1996)* Russian Compact Disc ▲ RCD 30201 [DDD]
Mozart, W.A.:Serenata Notturna, w. Alexander Mayorov (vn), Irina Belskaya (vn), Ilya Shpiegelman (va), Sergey Kirichenko (db) *(rec Moscow Conservatory Great Hall, 1996)* Russian Compact Disc ▲ RCD 30201 [DDD]
Sviridov, G.:Music CO Olympia ▲ OLY 540 [DDD]
Sviridov, G.:Petersburg Songs Olympia ▲ OLY 540 [DDD]
Tcherepnin, A.:Rhap géorgienne, w. Alexander Rudin (vc) Olympia ▲ OLY 584 [DDD]
Musica Viva CO members
Sviridov, G.:Trio Pno Olympia ▲ OLY 540 [DDD]

Musica Viva Ensemble
Kopelent, M.:Concertino Praga ▲ PR 255003
N. Alexeiev (cnd)
Tchaikovsky, P.:Nocturne Vc, w. A. Rudin (vc) Russian Season ▲ LDC 2888082
Tchaikovsky, P.:Pezzo capriccioso, w. A. Rudin (vc) Russian Season ▲ LDC 2888082
Tchaikovsky, P.:Serenade Strs, w. A. Rudin (vc) Russian Season ▲ LDC 2888082
Tchaikovsky, P.:Vars on a Rococo Theme, w. A. Rudin (vc) Russian Season ▲ LDC 2888082
U. Zimmermann (cnd)
Zimmermann, U.:Die weisse Rose (sels), w. G. Szklarecka (sop), F. Schiller (bar) [scenes for 2 solo voices & instrumental ensemble] Berlin Classics ("Eterna" series) ▲ BER 2060 [DDD]
Musical Assembly
Couperin, F.:Les Nations Music & Arts ▲ CD 825 [DDD]
Musical Elements
D. Asia (cnd)
Bresnick, M.:Wir weben, wir weben [trans. for string sextet] *(rec Sprague Hall, Yale Univ., Oct. 7, 1985)* CRI ▲ CD 682 [DDD]
Wyner, Y.:Passage I *(rec SUNY Purchase, New York, Oct, 1985)* CRI ("American Masters" series) ▲ CD 701 [ADD]
R. Beaser (cnd)
Lerdahl, F.:Fant Etudes CRI ▲ CD 580 [ADD/DDD]
Musical Offering
Vivaldi, A.:Con Fl Ob, RV.107 Elektra/Nonesuch ▲ 79067-2 ■ 79067-4
Vivaldi, A.:Con Rcr Ob, RV.95 Elektra/Nonesuch ▲ 79067-2 ■ 79067-4
Vivaldi, A.:Cons Vn (misc)—RV.217 Elektra/Nonesuch ▲ 79067-2 ■ 79067-4
Vivaldi, A.:Sons Ob—in c, RV.53 Elektra/Nonesuch ▲ 79067-2 ■ 79067-4
Vivaldi, A.:Son Vn Vc, RV.83 Elektra/Nonesuch ▲ 79067-2 ■ 79067-4
Musicalische Compagney
Schütz, H.:Secular Music MD + G ▲ MDG 3100230
Musicatreize
R. Hayrabedian (cnd)
Ohana, M.:Avoaha, w. Contemporary Choir Opus 111 ▲ OPS 30-109
Ohana, M.:Lys de Madrigaux, w. Contemporary Choir Opus 111 ▲ OPS 30-109
Shostakovich, D.:Chamber Sym, Op. 110a Opus 111 ▲ OPS 30165
Shostakovich, D.:Sym 14, w. Marie Stéphane Bernard (sop), Lionel Peintre (bass) Opus 111 ▲ OPS 30165
Musicfest Octet
Schubert, Franz:Octet Ww, D.803 *(rec 1/91)* IMP Classics ▲ PCD 957 [DDD]
I Musici
Albinoni, T.:Adagio Org Philips ("Digital Classics" series) ▲ 410606-2 [DDD] □ 410606-5
Albinoni, T.:Adagio Org Philips ("Digital Classics" series) ▲ 420816-2 [DDD] ■ 420816-4
Albinoni, T.:Cons Obs, w. H. Holliger (ob)—6 Concertos Philips ("Insignia" series) ▲ 434157-2 [DDD]
Albinoni, T.:Cons à 5 Obs, Op. 7, w. H. Holliger (ob), M. Bourgue (ob) Philips ▲ 432115-2 [DDD]
Albinoni, T.:Cons à 5 Obs, Op. 9—Nos. 1, 4, 6, 7, 10 & 12 Philips ▲ 426080-2 [ADD]
Albinoni, T.:Cons à 5 Obs, Op. 9, w. H. Holliger (ob)—No. 8 Philips ▲ 420189-2 [DDD]
Albinoni, T.:Sinf (6) e con (6) à 5, Op. 2, w. H. Holliger (ob), K. Thunemann (bn)—Nos. 5 & 6 Philips ▲ 432115-2 [DDD]
Bach, J.S.:Brandenburg Cons Philips 2-▲ 438317-2
Bach, J.S.:Brandenburg Cons Philips 2-▲ 412790-2 [DDD] 2-■ 412790-4
Bach, J.S.:Cons Vn (comp) Philips ("Concert Classics" series) ▲ 426075-2 [ADD]
Bach, J.S.:Con Vn & Ob Philips ("Concert Classics" series) ▲ 426075-2 [ADD]
Baroque Favorites Philips ("Solo" series) ▲ 442396-2
Carulli, F.:Con Gtr, w. S. Behrend (gtr) Deutsche Grammophon (Musikfest) ■ 413664-4
Cimarosa, D.:Con in C Ob, w. H. Holliger (ob) Philips ▲ 420189-2 [DDD]
Corelli, A.:Con grossi, Op. 6/8, "Christmas Con" Philips ▲ 434110-2
Geminiani, F.:Concerti grossi (misc)—12 cons. Philips ("Duo" series) 2-▲ 438766-2
Giuliani, M.:Con 1 Gtr, w. S. Behrend (gtr) Deutsche Grammophon ("Musikfest" series) ■ 413664-4
Marcello, A.:Con Ob & Strs, w. H. Holliger (ob) Philips ▲ 420189-2 [DDD]
Mozart, W.A.:Diverts Str Qt, K.136-138 Philips ▲ 420712-2 [ADD]
Mozart, W.A.:Kleine Nachtmusik Philips ("Digital Classics" series) ▲ 410606-2 [DDD] □ 410606-5
Mozart, W.A.:Kleine Nachtmusik Philips ▲ 420712-2 [ADD]
Mozart, W.A.:Kleine Nachtmusik Philips ("Digital Classics" series) ▲ 420816-2 [DDD] ■ 420816-4
Mozart, W.A.:Serenata notturna Philips ▲ 420712-2 [ADD]
Pachelbel, J.:Canon Philips ("Digital Classics" series) ▲ 410606-2 [DDD] □ 410606-5
Sammartini, G.:Con in D Ob, w. H. Holliger (ob) Philips ▲ 420189-2 [DDD]
Scarlatti, A.:Cons Fl Philips ("Insignia" series) ▲ 434160-2 [ADD/DDD]
Scarlatti, A.:Sinf di con grosso Strs Philips ("Insignia" series) ▲ 434160-2 [ADD/DDD]
Vivaldi, A.:Cons Bn, w. K. Thunemann (bn)—RV.471 in C; RV.481 in d; RV.493 in G; RV.496 in g; RV.500 in a; RV.504 in B♭, "La Notte" Philips ▲ 432124-2 [DDD]
Vivaldi, A.:Cons Bn, w. K. Thunemann (bn)—RV.473, 483, 485, 492, 497, 503 Philips ▲ 416355-2 [DDD]
Vivaldi, A.:Cons Diverse Instrs—RV.531, 542, 544, 551, 561 Philips ▲ 422212-2 [DDD]
Vivaldi, A.:Cons Fl (misc), w. Severino Gazzelloni (fl)—includes Con in F, "La tempesta di mare"; Con in g, "La Notte"; Con in D, "Il Gardellino" Philips ("Duo" series) 2-▲ 454 256-2
Vivaldi, A.:Cons Gtr, w. P. Romero (gtr) Philips ▲ 434082-2 [DDD]
Vivaldi, A.:Cons Vn (misc), w. Felix Ayo (vn)—RV.271 Philips ▲ 416611-2 [ADD]
Vivaldi, A.:Cons Vn (misc), w. R. Michelucci (vn)—RV.362 Philips ▲ 420356-2 [ADD]
Vivaldi, A.:Cons Vn (misc) Philips ▲ 438876-2
Vivaldi, A.:Cons Vn, Op. 3/1-12, "L'estro armonico", w. Roberto Michelucci (vn) Philips ("Duo" series) 2-▲ 446169-2
Vivaldi, A.:Cons Vn, Op. 8/1-12, "Il cimento dell'armonia e dell'inventione" Philips 2-▲ 438344-2
Vivaldi, A.:Cons Vn, Op. 8/1-4, "The Four Seasons", w. Pina Carmirelli (vn) Philips ▲ 410001-2 [DDD]
Vivaldi, A.:Cons Vn, Op. 8/1-4, "The Four Seasons", w. F. Ayo (vn) Philips ▲ 416611-2 [ADD]
Vivaldi, A.:Cons Vn, Op. 8/1-4, "The Four Seasons", w. R. Michelucci (vn) Philips ▲ 420356-2 [ADD]
Vivaldi, A.:Music of, w. Salvatore Accardo (vn), Frederico Agostini (vn), Heinz Holliger (ob), Ida Levin (vn), Aurele Nicolet (fl), Massimo Paris (va d'amore), Angel Romero (gtr), Celedonio Romero (gtr), Celine Romero (gtr), Henryk Szeryng (vn), Pinchas Zukerman (vn), Academy of St. Martin in the Fields, English CO, Naples Weekly International Soloists, St. Paul CO, Dresden Staatskapelle—Four Seasons [Winter]; Con in D Gtr [Largo]; Con in D Fl, "Il gardellino" [Cantabile]; Con in C Diverse Instrs [Andante molto]; Con in g Strs [Andante molto]; Con in D for 2 Vns & 2 Vcs [Largo]; Con in g Ob, Vn, Ww & Strs [Larghetto]; Con in a Gtr, "L'estro armonico" [Largo]; Con in F for 3 Vns [Andante]; Con in F Fl [Largo]; Con in d Va D'Amore [Largo]; Con in E Vn & Strs, "Il riposo" [Allegro]; Con in G, Ob, Bn & Strs [Largo]; Con in B♭ Vn & Strs [Largo]; Con in A Gtr & Strs [Larghetto]; Con in E Vn & Strs, "L'amoroso" [Allegro]; Con in g Fl [Largo]; Con in A Vn [Larghetto]; Con in c Vn & Strs, "Il sospetto" [Andante]; Con in a 2 Obs & Strs [Largo]; Con in g Orch [Largo non molto]; Con in a Vn [Largo]; Con in C Ob [Adagio]; Con in g Fl, "La notte" [Largo] Philips ▲ 454051-2 ■ 454 051-4
F. Agostini (cnd)
Vivaldi, A.:Cons Vn, Op. 8/1-12, "Il cimento dell'armonia e dell'inventione"—Nos. 1-6 Philips ▲ 426847-2 [DDD]
S. Behrend (cnd)
Vivaldi, A.:Con Lt Deutsche Grammophon ■ 413664-4
Vivaldi, A.:Con Mand, RV.425 Deutsche Grammophon ■ 413664-4
R. Michelucci (cnd)
Vivaldi, A.:The Vivaldi Edition—Concerti (12) for various Solo Instruments & Orchestra, "L'Estro Armonico," Op. 3 Philips 2-▲ 426932-2 [ADD]
K. Thunemann (cnd)
Vivaldi, A.:Cons Ob, w. H. Holliger (ob)—RV.446, 447, 452, 454, 463, 545 Philips ("Digital Classics" series) ▲ 411480-2 [ADD]

ORCH. & ENS.

Musici Bavariae
Music for 2 Trumpets, Organ, Cello & Double Bass — Koch Schwann ▲ SCH 315038 [DDD]

Musicians' Accord
Berio, L.:O King Voice, w. Christine Schadeberg (sop) — mode ▲ mode 48 [DDD]
Kaminsky, L.:Twilight Settings — Mode ▲ 23

F. Cohen (cnd)
Feigin, J.:Music of, w. Christine Schadeberg (sop)—Ecstatic Poems of Kabir (5); Veränderungen; Poems of Linda Pastan (4); Fantasy Pieces; Poems of Wallace Stevens (4); Nexus; First Tradgedy; Echos from the Holocaust; Japanese Poems (8); Transience — North/South Recordings 2–▲ N/S R 1011 [DDD]

T. Léon (cnd)
Berio, L.:Folk Songs Sop, w. Christine Schadeberg (sop) — mode ▲ mode 48 [DDD]

S. Silver (cnd)
Silver, S.:Canto — Mode ▲ 23

Musicians' Accord [Katharine Flanders (fl/pic), Matt Sullivan (ob), Terry Szor (tpt), Michael Pugliese (perc), Margaret Kampmeier (pno/syn), Ted Mook (vc), Charles Tomlinson (db)]

C.B. Rulon (cnd)
Rulon, C.B.:Self Requiem, w. Curtis Bahn (tape) — CRI ▲ CD 729 [DDD]

Musicians' Accord members [Katherine Flanders Mukherji (fl), Sheldon Berkowitz (cl), Marshall Coid (vn), Ted Mook (vc), Margaret Kampmeier (pno)]

H. Biggs (cnd)
Berio, L.:O King Orch *(rec St. Peter's Episcopal Church, New York, Apr 3, 1995)* — Mode ▲ mode 48

Musicians' Accord members [Katherine Flanders Mukherji (fl/pic), Sheldon Berkowitz (cl), Martha Mooke (va), Ted Mook (vc), Carol Emanuel (hp), William Trigg (perc), Michael Pugliese (perc)]

T. Léon (cnd)
Berio, L.:Folk Songs Mez, w. Christine Schadeberg (sop)—Black Is the Color; I Wonder As I Wander; Loosin Yelav; Rossignolet du bois; A la femminisca; La donna ideale; Ballo; Motettu de tristura; Malurous qu'o uno fenno; Lo fiolairé; Azerbaijan Love Song *(rec St. Peter's Episcopal Church, New York, Jan 6, 1995)* — Mode ▲ mode 48

Musicians' Accord members [Sheldon Berkowitz (cl), Ted Mook (vc), Barbara Allen (hp)]
Berio, L.:Chamber Music, w. Christine Schadeberg (sop) *(rec St. Peter's Episcopal Church, New York, Apr 3, 1995)* — Mode ▲ mode 48 [DDD]

Musicians' Accord members [Susan Jolles (hp/voc), William Trigg (perc/voc), Michael Pugliese (perc/voc)]
Berio, L.:Circles, w. Christine Schadeberg (sop) *(rec Borden Hall, Manhattan School of Music, New York, June 17, 1995)* — Mode ▲ mode 48

Musicians of Swanne Alley
As I Went to Walsingham — Harmonia Mundi ▲ HMC 90.5192 ■
In the Streets & Theatres of London:Elizabethan Ballads & Theatre Music — Virgin Classics ▲ 59534 [DDD]
Morley, T.:Joyne Hands — Virgin Classics ▲ CDC 59032

Musicians of the Gamelan Si Betty
Harrison, L.:Gamelan Music, w. Berkeley Chamber Singers—Homage to Pacifica; Philemon & Baukis; Cornish Lancaran; Gending Alexander; Bubaran Robert — MusicMasters ▲ 01612-67091-2 [DDD]

Les Musiciens de Provence
Musique des Trouvères et Troubadours *(rec 1973–1981)* — Arion ▲ ARN 68064 [ADD]
Popular Elizabethan Music — Focus ▲ FOCUS 933 [AAD]

Musiciens du Louvres
Handel, G.F.:Concerti grossi, Op. 3 — Erato ▲ 94354-2

M. Minkowski (cnd)
Charpentier, M.–A.:Le Malade imaginaire, w. J. Feldman (sop), I. Poulenard (sop) — Erato (Musifrance) ▲ 2292-45002-2 ZK
Handel, G.F.:Amadigi di Gaula, w. E. Harrhy (sop—Melissa), J. Smith (sop—Oriana), P. Bertin (mez—Orgando), B. Fink (cta—Dardano), N. Stutzmann (cta—Amadigi), Louvre Choir [I] — Erato 2–▲ 2292-45490-2 [DDD]
Handel, G.F.:Teseo, w. Eirian James (mez), Della Jones (mez), Derek Lee Ragin (ct) — Erato 2–▲ 2292-45806-2 ZA
Handel, G.F.:Il Trionfo del Tempo e del Disinganno, w. Isabelle Poulenard (sop), Jennifer Smith (sop), Nathalie Stutzmann (cta), John Elwes (ten) — Erato 2–▲ 2292-45351-2 ZA
Lully, J.–B.:Phaëton, w. V. Gens (sop), J. Smith (sop), R. Yakar (sop), H. Crook (ten), J.–P. Fouchécourt (ten) — Erato 2–▲ 91737
Rameau, J.P.:Hippolyte et Aricie, w. Véronique Gens (sop), Bernarda Fink (cta), Jean–Paul Fouchécourt (ten), Laurent Naouri (bar), Russell Smythe (bar), Sagittarius Vocal Ensemble — Archiv 3–▲ 445853-2
Rameau, J.P.:Platée, w. J. Smith (sop), G. Ragon (ten), G. de Mey (ten), Françoise Herr Vocal Ensemble [F] — Erato ("Musifrance" series) 2–▲ 2292-45028-2 [DDD]
Rameau, J.P.:Le Surprises de l'Amour — Erato ("Musifrance" series) ▲ 2292-45004-2-ZK

Music's Re-Creation
The Art of James Bowman, w. James Bowman (ct), Crispian Steel–Perkins (nat tpt), Downshire Players of London, King's Consort — Meridian ▲ MER 84332
Clérambault, L.N.:Cants, w. J. Baird (sop)—Léandre et Héro; Orphée; Zephire et Flore [F] — Meridian ▲ CDE 84182
Clérambault, L.N.:Son La Magnifique — Meridian ▲ CDE 84182
Leclair, J.–M.:Deuxième recréation de musique d'une exécution facile — Meridian ▲ CDE 84114
Rameau, J.P.:Pièces de clavecin en concert—Suite No. 1 — Meridian ▲ CDE 84114
Telemann, G.P.:Cants, w. J. Baird (sop), J. Bowman (ct)—Ihr Völker, hört; Ergeuss dich zur Salbung; Erscheine, Gott, in deinem Tempel; Packe dich, gelähmter Drache — Meridian ▲ CDE 84159
Telemann, G.P.:Qts Vn—No. 2 — Meridian ▲ CDE 84114
Telemann, G.P.:Son VI in e, w. J. Dornenburg (vl) — Meridian ▲ CDE 84159

Musikfabrik NRW
Bruttger, T.:Monolith — CPO ▲ CPO 999259 [DDD]
Huber, N.A.:An Hölderlins Umnachtung — CPO ▲ CPO 999259 [DDD]
Kalitzke, J.:Salto. Trapez. Ikarus — CPO ▲ CPO 999259 [DDD]
Stäbler, G.:Traum 1/9/92 — CPO ▲ CPO 999259 [DDD]

J. Kalitzke (cnd)
Birtwistle, H.:Nenia on the Death of Orpheus, w. Rosemary Hardy (sop) — CPO ▲ CPO 999360 [DDD]
Birtwistle, H.:Ritual Fragment — CPO ▲ CPO 999360 [DDD]
Birtwistle, H.:Secret Theatre — CPO ▲ CPO 999360 [DDD]
Henze, H.–W.:Voices, w. G. Pelker (mez), F. Lang (ten) — CPO ▲ CPO 999192 [DDD]

Musikkorps des Wachtbataillons

M. Diesenroth (cnd)
Foster, S.C.:Life & Music of, w. A. Robinson (nar)—narration & selected excerpts from Old Folks at Home; Oh! Susanna; Old Black Joe; Jeanie with the Light Brown Hair; My Old Kentucky Home; Camptown Races; Massa's in De Cold, Cold Ground; Come Where My Love Lies Dreaming; Beautiful Dreamer — Vox Music Masters ("Music Masters" series) ▲ MMD 8515 [ADD] ■ MMC 8515
Sousa, J.P.:Life & Music of, w. A. Hannes (nar)—narration with selected excerpts from Stars & Stripes Forever; The Crusader; The Belle of Chicago; The Gladiator; Semper Fidelis; Washington Post; High School Cadets; The Thunderer; Hands Across the Sea; El Capitan — Vox Music Masters ("Music Masters" series) ▲ MMD 8515 [ADD] ■ MMC 8515

Musiktage Mondsee Ensemble [E. Schmid (cl), K. Thunemann (bn), R. Vlatkovic (hn), J. Panocha (vn), P. Zejfart (vn), M. Sehnoutka (va)]
Janácek, L.:Capriccio, w. A. Schiff (pno) *(rec July 21–30, 1992)* — London ▲ 440312-2 [DDD]
Janácek, L.:Concertino Pno, w. A. Schiff (pno) *(rec July 21–30, 1992)* — London ▲ 440313-2 [DDD]

Musique des Gardiens de la Paix

D. Dondeyne (cnd)
Koechlin, C.:Marche funèbre *(rec 1976)* — Skarbo ▲ SKR 3924
Koechlin, C.:Quelque chorals pour des fêtes de lein air *(rec 1976)* — Skarbo ▲ SKR 3924

Musique Oblique Ensemble
Lekeu, G.:Adagio — Harmonia Mundi France ▲ HMC 901455

Musique Oblique Ensemble (cont.)
Lekeu, G.:Poèmes — Harmonia Mundi France ▲ HMC 901455
Lekeu, G.:Qt Pno & Strs — Harmonia Mundi France ▲ HMC 901455

P. Herreweghe (cnd)
Fauré, G.:Messe basse, w. Chapelle Royale Choir [L] — Harmonia Mundi France ▲ HMC 901292
Fauré, G.:Requiem, w. A. Mellon (sop), P. Kooy (bass), Chapelle Royale Choir [1893 version] [L] — Harmonia Mundi France ▲ HMC 901292
Mahler, G.:Das Lied von der Erde, w. B. Remmert (cta), H.–P. Blochwitz (ten) [arr. Schoenberg & Riehn for chamber orch.] — Harmonia Mundi France ▲ HMC 901477
Schoenberg, A.:Chamber Sym 1 [Webern's 1923 arr. for Flute, Clarinet, Violin, Cello & Piano] *(rec 7/91)* — Harmonia Mundi France ▲ HMC 901390
Schoenberg, A.:Pierrot lunaire, w. M. Pousseur (speaker) [G] — Harmonia Mundi France ▲ HMC 901390
Weill, K.:Berlin Requiem, w. A. Laiter (ten), P. Kooy (bass), Chapelle Royale Choir [G] *(rec May 1992)* — Harmonia Mundi France ▲ HMC 901422
Weill, K.:Con Vn, w. E. Glab (vn) *(rec May 1992)* — Harmonia Mundi France ▲ HMC 901422
Weill, K.:Vom Tod im Wald, w. P. Kooy (bass) [G] *(rec May 1992)* — Harmonia Mundi France ▲ HMC 901422

Musique Principale des Troupes de Marine
Salute from France, w. C. M. A. Sorlin (cnd), C. M. Dury (cnd), S. C. M. Henot (cnd) *(rec Quartier Fesch, Versailles, France, June 26–28, 1995)* — World Wind ▲ WWM 500.013 [DDD]

Musique Vivante Ensemble

L. Berio (cnd)
Berio, L.:Laborintus II, w. Sanguineti (nar), C. Legrand (sop), J. Baucomont (sop), C. Meunier (cta), Chorale Experimentale [E,I] — Musique d'Abord ▲ HMA 190764

D. Masson (cnd)
Boulez, P.:Domaines (Parts 1 & 2), w. M. Portal (cl) — Musique d'Abord ▲ HMA 190930 [ADD]
Globokar, V.:Fluide — Harmonia Mundi France ▲ HMC 90933
Stockhausen, K.:Setzt die Segel zur Sonne — Musique d'Abord ▲ HMA 190795

M. Portal (cnd)
Globokar, V.:Ausstrahlungen — Harmonia Mundi France ▲ HMC 90933

Musiviva Trio [P. Genet, M. Jaermann, P. Dinkel]
Allesandro, R. d':Music of, w. Sine Nomine String Quartet—String Quartet No. 2, Op. 73; Trio for Piano, Violin & Cello, Op. 33; Piano Sonatas, Nos. 2 & 3 — Gallo ▲ CD 621 [DDD]
Martin, F.:Trio sur les mélodies populaires irlandaises — Gallo ▲ CD 633 [DDD]

Musketeers of the Sealed Knot
Classical Spectacular 1, w. Royal PO, Michael Reed (cnd), Scots Guards Band, Welsh Guards Band, London Choral Society — RPO Records ▲ RPO 5009 [DDD]

Nancy SO

J. Kaltenbach (cnd)
Constant, M.:Choruses & Interludes, w. Jean–Jacques Justafre (hn), Pierre–Marie Bonafosse (sax), François Moutin (b gtr), Pierre Guignon (dr), Andy Emler (pno) *(rec Salle Poirel, Nancy, Apr. 4, 1990)* — Erato ▲ 94815-2 [DDD]
Constant, M.:Concertante Sax, w. Claude Delangle (sax) *(rec Salle Poirel, Nancy, Apr. 4, 1990)* — Erato ▲ 94815-2 [DDD]
Constant, M.:Con Barrel Org, w. Pierre Charial (barrel org) *(rec Salle Poirel, Nancy, Apr. 4, 1990)* — Erato ▲ 94815-2 [DDD]
Constant, M.:Con Trbn, w. Michel Becquet (trbn) *(rec Salle Poirel, Nancy, Apr. 4, 1990)* — Erato ▲ 94815-2 [DDD]
Duparc, H.:Danse lente — Accord ▲ ACD 202832
Duparc, H.:Lénore — Accord ▲ ACD 202832
Duparc, H.:Songs, w. Françoise Pollet (sop)—Le manoir de rosemonde; Chanson triste; L'invitation au voyage; La vie antérieure; Phydilé; Au pays où se fait la guerre; Testament; La vague et la cloche — Accord ▲ ACD 202832
Rosenthal, M.:Musique de table *(rec Salle Poirel, Nancy, France, Sept 6–10, 1994)* — Marco Polo ▲ 8.223768 [DDD]
Rosenthal, M.:Les petits métiers *(rec Salle Poirel, Nancy, France, Sept 6–10, 1994)* — Marco Polo ▲ 8.223768 [DDD]
Rosenthal, M.:Songs, w. Catherine Dubosc (sop)—Poèmes (3) de Marie Roustan (1933); Poèmes (2) de Jean Cassou (1944); Prières (3) *(rec Salle Poirel, Nancy, France, Sept 6–10, 1994)* — Marco Polo ▲ 8.223768 [DDD]

M. Piquemal (cnd)
Ropartz, G.:Choral Music, w. Christian Papis (nar), Didier Henry (bar), Vincent Le Texier (b-bar), Christine Lajarrige (pno), Irène Brissot (hp), Eric Lebrun (org), French Radio Chorus Soloists, Vittoria Regional French Choir—Psaume 136; Dimanche; Nocturne; Les Vêpres sonnent; Le Miracle de Saint Nicolas *(rec Salle Poirel, Nancy, Apr. 22–24, 1994)* — Marco Polo ▲ 8.223774 [DDD]

Nantes Instrumental Ensemble

P. Colléaux (cnd)
Charpentier, M.–A.:In nativitatem Domini canticum, w. J.–L. Bindi (bass), Nantes Vocal Ensemble [L] — Arion ▲ ARN 68015 [AAD]
Charpentier, M.–A.:Messe de minuit pour Noël, w. E. Lestringant (ten), G. Ragon (ten), J.–L. Bindi (bass), Piniec (sgr) [L] — Arion ▲ ARN 68015 [AAD]
Charpentier, M.–A.:Noëls, H.531 — Arion ▲ ARN 68015 [AAD]
Charpentier, M.–A.:Noëls, H.534 — Arion ▲ ARN 68015 [AAD]

Naples Accademic Musicale Solisti

F. Trinca (cnd)
Hindemith, P.:Kammermusik 3, w. Luca Signorini (vc) — Nuova Era ▲ 7075 [DDD]

Naples Alessandro Scarlatti RAI Orch

H. Albert (cnd)
Beethoven, L. van:Con Vn, Op. 61, w. D. Oistrakh (vn) *(rec live 4/15/65)* — Melodram 2–▲ CDM 28034 [AAD]

F. Caracciolo (cnd)
Mozart, W.A.:Con 13 Pno, w. Arturo B. Michelangeli (pno) — EMI Classics ("Great Recordings of the Century" series) ▲ CDH 63819
Mozart, W.A.:Con 23 Pno, w. A. Benedetti Michelangeli (pno) — EMI Classics ("Great Recordings of the Century" series) ▲ CDH 63819

S. Celibidache (cnd)
Corelli, A.:Con grosso, Op. 6/8, "Christmas Con" *(rec live, 1959)* — Originals ▲ ORI 864
Hindemith, P.:Kammermusik 2, w. Gino Gorini (pno) *(rec live, 1959)* — Originals ▲ ORI 864
Màrgola, F.:Partita Strs *(rec live, 1959)* — Originals ▲ ORI 864
Mozart, W.A.:Kleine Nachtmusik *(rec live, 1959)* — Originals ▲ ORI 864

L. Colonna (cnd)
Rossini, G.:L'occassione fa il ladro, w. C. Fusco (sop), M. T. Pace (mez), G. Sinimberghi (ten), I. Tajo (bass), R. Gonzales (sgr) [I] *(rec live, Naples, Sept. 29, 1963)* — Arkadia ▲ 602 [ADD]

M. Pradella (cnd)
Beethoven, L. van:Con 4 Pno, w. E. Gilels (pno) *(rec live 12/18/65)* — Melodram 2–▲ CDM 28034 [AAD]
Beethoven, L. van:Con 4 Pno, w. Maurizio Pollini (pno) — Fonit Cetra ("Emozioni" series) ▲ FCT CDAR 2033

U. Rapalo (cnd)
Bach, J.S.:Cant 92, w. Elisabeth Schwarzkopf (sop) *(rec Naples, Apr 15, 1958)* — Bella Voce 2–▲ 107.201 [AAD]

N. Sanzogno (cnd)
Scarlatti, A.:La Griselda, w. M. Freni (sop), L. Alva (ten), V. Luchetti (ten), R. Panerai (bar), S. Bruscantini (bar), Naples Scarlatti Chorus [I] *(rec live 10/29/70)* — Memories 2–▲ HR 4154/55 (m) [ADD]

Naples New Scarlatti Orch

D. Moles (cnd)
Leo, L.:Amor vuol sofferenze, w. Marilena Laurenza (sop), Vitalba Mosca (mez), Piero Guarnera (bar), Domenico Colaianni (sgr), Giovanna Donadini (sgr), Marilyne Fallot (sgr), Hyun Lee (sgr) *(rec Martinafranca Festival, 1994)* — Nuova Era 3–▲ NUO 7221

▲ = CD ♦ = Enhanced CD Δ = MD ■ = Cassette Tape □ = DCC

Naples PO
T. Russell (cnd)
Dello Joio, N.:Antiphonal Fant on a Theme of Vincenzo Albrici, w. Todd Wilson (org) — D'Note Classics ▲ DND 1002
Persichetti, V.:The Hollow Men, w. David Hickman (tpt) — D'Note Classics ▲ DND 1002
Planel, R.:Con Tpt, w. David Hickman (tpt) — D'Note Classics ▲ DND 1002

Naples RAI SO
F. Caracciolo (cnd)
Piccinni, N.:La cecchina (sels), w. M. Freni (sop), I. Hollweg (sop), S. Bruscantini (bar), R. Panerai (bar)—13 arias *(rec live 11/25/69)* — Arkadia 2-▲ 596 [ADD]
Schumann, R.:Con Pno, w. Artur Rubinstein (pno) *(rec Naples, Apr. 1964)* — Emozioni ▲ ARCD 2027
M. Rossi (cnd)
Piccinni, N.:Didon, w. G. Tucci (sop), O. Mori (bass), M. Petri (bass), Naples RAI Chorus *(rec live 4/16/70)* — Arkadia 2-▲ 596 [ADD]
Rossini, G.:La Cenerentola, w. Teresa Berganza (mez), Nicola Monti (ten), Sesto Bruscantini (bar), Mario Petri (bar), Leonardo Monreale (sgr), Naples Teatro San Carlo Chorus *(rec Oct 8, 1958)* — Pantheon 2-▲ PHE 6656 (m)

Naples Solisti
A. Lizzio (cnd)
Bach, J.S.:Brandenburg Cons—Nos. 1-3 — Vivace ▲ 551 [DDD]
Bach, J.S.:Brandenburg Cons—Nos. 4-6 — Vivace ▲ 582 [DDD]
H. Zanotelli (cnd)
Handel, G.F.:Concerti grossi, Op. 6—Nos. 1-5 — Vivace ▲ 553 [ADD]

Naples String Quartet
Chausson, E.:Con Vn, Pno & Str Qt, w. S. Accardo (vn), B. Canino (pno) — Dynamic ▲ CD 44

Naples Teatro San Carlo Orch
A. Basile (cnd)
Giordano, U.:Fedora, w. R. Tebaldi (sop), Mizzetti (sgr), G. di Stefano (ten), M. Sereni (bar), Naples Teatro San Carlo Chorus [I] *(rec live, 1961)* — Legato Classics 2-▲ LCD 158-2 (m) [ADD]
V. Bellezza (cnd)
Rossini, G.:Il barbiere di Siviglia (sels), w. R. Scotto (sop), A. di Stasio (mez), A. Kraus (ten), A. Protti (bar), C. Badioli (bass), E. Campi (bass), Naples Teatro San Carlo Chorus *(rec July 26, 1958)* — Golden Age of Opera 2-▲ GAO 137/38 [ADD]
Verdi, G.:Aida (sels), w. O. Rovere (sop), E. Stignani (mez), M. Filippeschi (ten), C. Cava (bass), B. McFerrin (sgr), Naples Teatro San Carlo Chorus [I] [highlights] *(rec live, Arena Flegrea, Naples, 7/15/56)* — Golden Age of Opera ▲ GAO 130 [ADD]
K. Böhm (cnd)
Wagner, R.:Tannhäuser, w. L. Rysanek (sop), J. Lustig (sgr), M. Cordes (bar), G. Frick (bass), Naples Teatro San Carlo Chorus [G] *(rec live, Naples, 3/17/56)* — Melodram 3-▲ MEL 37073 (m) [AAD]
Wagner, R.:Tannhäuser (sels), w. R. Tebaldi (sop), H. Beirer (ten), C. Tagliabue (bar), B. Christoff (bass), Naples Teatro San Carlo Chorus—10 soprano solo, duet & ensemble arias Acts 2 & 3 [I; Hans Beirer (Tannhäuser) sings in German] *(rec live, Naples, 3/12/50)* — Standing Room Only ▲ SRO 834-1 [ADD]
G. Campanino (cnd)
Verdi, G.:Rigoletto, w. Cecilia Nunez Albanese (sop—Gilda), Wilma Borelli (cta—Maddalena), Jaime Aragall (ten—Duke of Mantua), Renato Bruson (bar—Rigoletto), Loris Gambelli (bass—Sparafucile), Naples Teatro San Carlo Chorus *(rec San Carlo Theatre, Naples, Feb. 1973)* — Golden Age of Opera 2-▲ GAO 177-78 [ADD]
F. Capuana (cnd)
Pacini, G.:Saffo, w. L. Gencer (sop), F. Mattiucci (mez), T. del Bianco (ten), L. Quilico (bar), Naples Teatro San Carlo Chorus [I] *(rec live, 4/7/67)* — Arkadia 2-▲ 541 (m) [AAD]
A. Ceccato (cnd)
Verdi, G.:La traviata, w. B. Sills (sop), M. Zotti (sop), G. Borelli (mez), A. Kraus (ten), M. Zanasi (bar), Naples Teatro San Carlo Chorus *(rec live 1/17/70)* — Melodram 2-▲ MEL 27063 (m) [AAD]
C.F. Cillario (cnd)
Donizetti, G.:Caterina Cornaro, w. L. Gencer (sop), G. Aragall (ten), R. Bruson (bar), L. Risani (sgr), Naples Teatro San Carlo Chorus *(rec live, 5/28/72)* — Myto 2-▲ 2 MCD 92153 [ADD]
Donizetti, G.:Caterina Cornaro, w. L. Gencer (sop), G. Aragall (ten), R. Bruson (bar), Naples Teatro San Carlo Chorus [I] *(rec live, Naples 5/28/72)* — Memories 2-▲ HR 4448/49 (m) [ADD]
A. Erede (cnd)
Donizetti, G.:Don Pasquale, w. Gianna D'Angelo (sop), Alfredo Kraus (ten), Renato Capecchi (bar), Fernando Corena (bass), Ugo D'Alessio (sgr), Naples Teatro San Carlo Chorus — Great Opera Performances 2-▲ GOP 763
Donizetti, G.:Don Pasquale, w. G. D'Angelo (sop), A. Kraus (ten), R. Capecchi (bar), F. Corena (bass), U. d'Alessio (sgr), Naples Teatro San Carlo Chorus [I] *(rec live in Edinburgh, 9/7/63)* — Verona 2-▲ 27023/24 (m) [AAD]
O. de Fabritiis (cnd)
Bizet, G.:Les Pêcheurs de perles, w. M. Pobbe (sop), F. Tagliavini (ten), U. Savarese (bar), C. Cava (bass), Naples Teatro San Carlo Chorus [I] *(rec live 1/4/59)* — Melodram 2-▲ MEL 27069 (m) [AAD]
Cilea, F.:Adriana Lecouvreur, w. L. Gencer (sop—Adriana), A. Lazzarini (mez—Princess), F. Ricciardi (ten—Abbot), A. Zambon (ten—Maurizio), E. Sordello (bar—Michonnet), A. Zerbini (bass—Prince), Naples Teatro San Carlo Chorus *(rec Dec. 17, 1966)* — Golden Age of Opera 2-▲ GAO 143/44 [ADD]
Massenet, J.:Werther, w. E. Ravaglia (sop), B. Casoni (mez), C. Bergonzi (ten), D. Trimarchi (bar), Naples Teatro San Carlo Chorus [I] *(rec live, Naples, 2/13/69)* — Melodram 2-▲ 27058 [AAD]
Puccini, G.:Turandot (sels), w. L. Gencer (sop), L. Udovich (sop), F. Corelli (ten), Naples Teatro San Carlo Chorus—Signore ascolta; Il nome che cercate..tu che di gel sei cinta *(rec Jan. 13, 1962)* — Golden Age of Opera 2-▲ GAO 143/44 [ADD]
Verdi, G.:Stiffelio, w. A. Gulin (sop—Lina), M. del Monaco (ten—Stiffelio), A. Marchiandi (ten—Raffaele), G. Fioravanti (bar—Stankar), J. Hecht (bass—Jorg), Naples Teatro San Carlo Chorus *(rec Dec. 26, 1972)* — Standing Room Only 2-▲ SRO 169-2
A. Gatto (cnd)
Donizetti, G.:Gemma di Vergy, w. Montserrat Caballé (sop—Gemma di Vergy), Biancamaria Casoni (mez—Ida di Greville), Giorgio Lamberti (ten—Tamas), Renato Bruson (bar—Conte di Vergy), Mario Machì (bass—Rolando), Mario Rinaudo (bass—Guido), Naples Teatro San Carlo Chorus *(rec Naples, Dec. 12, 1975)* — Myto 2-▲ 952124
M. Gielen (cnd)
Mozart, W.A.:Don Giovanni, w. M. Caballé (sop), T. Stich-Randall (mez), E. Wächter (bar), E. Kunz (bar), Naples Teatro San Carlo Chorus [I] *(rec live, Lisbon, 1960)* — Standing Room Only 2-▲ SRO 813-2 [ADD]
V. Gui (cnd)
Verdi, G.:Aida, w. A. Stella (sop), F. Barbieri (mez), F. Corelli (ten), A. Colzani (bar), M. Petri (bar), Naples Teatro San Carlo Chorus [I] *(rec live, Naples 11/2/55)* — Golden Age of Opera 2-▲ GAO 116/17 [ADD]
Verdi, G.:Nabucco, w. M. Callas (sop), G. Bechi (bar), L. Neroni (bass), Naples Teatro San Carlo Chorus [I] *(rec live 12/20/49)* — Melodram 2-▲ MEL 26029 (m) [AAD]
C.M. Giulini (cnd)
Donizetti, G.:Lucia di Lammermoor (sels), w. Christina Deutekom (sop—Lucia), Luciano Pavarotti (ten—Edgardo), Domenico Trimarchi (bar—Enrico Ashton), Silviano Pagliuca (bass—Raimondo Bidebent), Naples Teatro San Carlo Chorus — Budget ("The Greatest Voice in Opera" series) ▲ SYP 103
P. Maag (cnd)
Bizet, G.:Carmen (sels), w. Mario del Monaco (ten)—Il fior che avevi a me tu dato *(rec Naples, Dec. 14, 1960)* — Melodram ▲ CDI 104006 [ADD]
F. Molinari-Pradelli (cnd)
Donizetti, G.:Lucia di Lammermoor, w. M. Callas (sop), G. Raimondi (ten), R. Panerai (bar), A. Zerbini (bass), Naples Teatro San Carlo Chorus [I] *(rec live, 3/22/56)* — Myto ▲ 2 MCD 90319 (m) [ADD]

Naples Teatro San Carlo Orch (cont.)
F. Molinari-Pradelli (cnd) (cont.)
Verdi, G.:La forza del destino, w. R. Tebaldi (sop), O. Dominguez (mez), F. Corelli (ten), R. Capecchi (bar), E. Bastianini (bar), B. Christoff (bass), Naples Teatro San Carlo Chorus *(rec Oct. 1 1958)* — Melodram 3-▲ MLO 370102 [AAD]
Verdi, G.:La forza del destino (sels), w. R. Tebaldi (sop), F. Corelli (ten), Naples Teatro San Carlo Chorus *(rec live Mar. 15, 1958)* — Legato Classics 2-▲ LCD 171-2 [ADD]
M. Panni (cnd)
Pergolesi, G.B.:Il flaminio, w. D. Dessi (sop—Flaminio), F. Pediconi (sop—Agata), E. Zilio (mez—Giustina), M. Ferrugia (ten—Fernando), G. Sica (ten—Polidoro), V. Baiano (bass—Checa), S. Pagliuca (bass—Bastiano) *(rec Nov. 12, 1983)* — Fonit Cetra 3-▲ CDC 39 [ADD]
R. Parodi (cnd)
Leoncavallo, R.:Edipo re, w. L. Infantino (ten), G. Fioravanti (bar), G. Malaspina (bar), Naples Teatro San Carlo Chorus *(rec live, Naples, 1970)* — Italian Opera Rarities ▲ IOR 7723 [ADD]
F. Patanè (cnd)
Gounod, C.:Faust (sels), w. R. Tebaldi (sop), F. Cadoni (mez), M. Filippeschi (ten), R. Panerai (bar), I. Tajo (bass), Naples Teatro San Carlo Chorus—Act IV, Scenes 1 & 2 & Act V, Scene 2 *(rec live, 4/26/51)* — Standing Room Only 2-▲ SRO 810-2 [ADD]
F. Previtali (cnd)
Donizetti, G.:La favorita, w. S. Zanolli (sop), G. Simionato (mez), G. Raimondi (ten), M. Zanasi (bar), N. Zaccaria (bass), Naples Teatro San Carlo Chorus [I] *(rec live, Naples 5/12/63)* — Golden Age of Opera 2-▲ GAO 105/06 [ADD]
Donizetti, G.:Maria di Rohan, w. Naples Teatro San Carlo Chorus — Melodram 3-▲ CDM 37017
Verdi, G.:Ernani, w. Margherita Roberti (sop), Anna di Stasio (mez), Athos Cesarini (ten), Mario del Monaco (ten), Ettore Bastianini (bar), Mario Rinaudo (bass), Nicola Rossi-Lemeni (bass), Naples Teatro San Carlo Chorus — Melodram 2-▲ CDM 270100
A. Questa (cnd)
Verdi, G.:La traviata, w. V. Zeani (sop), G. Raimondi (ten), U. Savarese (bar), Naples Teatro San Carlo Chorus [I] *(rec live, Naples 8/11/57)* — Golden Age of Opera 2-▲ GAO 103/04 [ADD]
U. Rapalo (cnd)
Massenet, J.:Manon (sels), w. V. Zeani (sop), A. Kraus (ten)—2 tenor arias & 2 soprano-tenor duets *(rec live, Naples 2/29/64)* — Bongiovanni 2-▲ GB 550/51
Mercadante, S.:Elisa e Claudio, w. Virginia Zeani (sop), Agostino Lazzari (ten), Domenico Trimarchi (bar), Ugo Trama (bass), Fiorini (sgr), Naples Teatro San Carlo Chorus *(rec live, Naples, 1/31/71)* — Melodram 2-▲ MEL 27099 [ADD]
Verdi, G.:Rigoletto (sels), w. A. Pastori (sop), Antonioli (ten), C. Tagliabue (bar), Naples Teatro San Carlo Chorus [I] *(rec live, Naples, 1/20/56)* — The Golden Age of Opera ▲ GAO 115 [ADD]
M. Rossi (cnd)
Cilea, F.:Adriana Lecouvreur, w. Magda Olivero (sop), Giulietta Simionato (mez), Franco Corelli (ten), Ettore Bastianini (bar), Naples Teatro San Carlo Chorus *(rec Naples, Nov 28, 1959)* — Agorá Music ("Phoenix" series) 2-▲ 502
Cilea, F.:Adriana Lecouvreur, w. M. Olivero (sop), G. Simionato (mez), F. Corelli (ten), E. Bastianini (bar), Naples Teatro San Carlo Chorus [I] *(rec live 11/28/59)* — Melodram 2-▲ MEL 27009 (m) [AAD]
G. Santini (cnd)
Cilea, F.:Adriana Lecouvreur (sels), w. Renata Tebaldi (sop—Adriana), Piero de Palma (ten—Abate), Gianni Poggi (ten—Mauriczio), Giuseppe Taddei (bar—Michonnet), Augusto Romani (bass—Prince), Naples Teatro San Carlo Chorus—Del sultano Amurate...Io son l'umile ancella; Giusto Cielo! che feci in tal giorno; Salvatemi! salvatemi!...Scostatevi, profani! *(rec San Carlo Theater, Naples, Dec. 26, 1952)* — Legato Classics 2-▲ LCD 193-2 [ADD]
Verdi, G.:Aida (sels), w. A. Cerquetti (sop), E. Nicolai (mez), G. Penno (ten), G. Guelfi (bar), B. Christoff (bass), Naples Teatro San Carlo Chorus [I] [highlights] *(rec live, Naples, July 24, 1954)* — Golden Age of Opera ▲ GAO 134 [ADD]
Verdi, G.:Giovanna d'Arco, w. Renata Tebaldi (sop—Giovanna), Gino Penno (ten—Carlo VII), Luciano Della Pergola (ten—Delil), Ugo Savarese (bar—Giacomo), Ignio Ricco (bass—Talbot), Naples Teatro San Carlo Chorus *(rec San Carlo Theater, Naples, Mar. 15, 1951)* — Legato Classics 2-▲ LCD 193-2 [ADD]
Verdi, G.:La traviata (sels), w. Anna de Santis (sop—Annina), Renata Tebaldi (sop—Violetta), Giuseppe Campora (ten—Alfredo), Gerardo Gaudioso (bar—Douphol), Giuseppe Taddei (bar—Germont), Antonio Picillo (bass—Grenvil), Naples Teatro San Carlo Chorus—E strano...Ah, fors'e lui; Follie!...Sempre libera; Pero l'attendo...Amami, Alfredo; Invitato a qui seguirmi; Alfredo, Alfredo, di questo core; Teneste la promessa...Addio del passato; Ma se tornando...Ah! Gran Dio! Morir si giovine; Se una pudica vergine *(rec San Carlo Theater, Naples, Jan. 17, 1952)* — Legato Classics 2-▲ LCD 193-2 [ADD]
Wagner, R.:Lohengrin (sels), w. R. Tebaldi (sop—Elsa), E. Nicolai (mez—Ortrud), G. Penno (ten—Lohengrin), G. Guelfi (bar—Telramund), G. Neri (bass—Heinrich), Naples Teatro San Carlo Chorus—8 soprano duets/trio from Acts 1-3 [I] *(rec live, Naples, 12/26/54)* — Standing Room Only ▲ SRO 834-1 [ADD]
S. Sassano (cnd)
Rossini, G.:Il barbiere di Siviglia (sels), w. M. Resemba (sop), N. Sabatano (sop), F. do Lucio (ten), F. Novelli (bar), G. Schottler (bass), A. di Tommaso (bass), S. Valentino (bass), Naples Teatro San Carlo Chorus [I] *(rec 1918 for Phonotype)* — Standing Room Only ▲ SRO 819-1 [ADD]
T. Serafin (cnd)
Donizetti, G.:Linda di Chamounix, w. A. Stella (sop), C. Valletti (ten), R. Capecchi (bar), G. Taddei (bar), Naples Teatro San Carlo Chorus *(rec 1959)* — Andromeda ▲ ANR 2509 [ADD]
Verdi, G.:La traviata, w. Renata Tebaldi (sop—Violetta), Giacinto Prandelli (ten—Alfredo), Carlo Tagliabue (bar—Germont), Naples Teatro San Carlo Chorus *(rec Arena Flegrea, Naples, July 3, 1954)* — Golden Age of Opera 2-▲ GAO 191/192 [ADD]
Verdi, G.:Il trovatore, w. M. Callas (sop), C. Elmo (mez), G. Lauri-Volpi (ten), P. Silveri (bar), Naples Teatro San Carlo Chorus [I] *(rec live, Naples, 1/27/51)* — Melodram 2-▲ MEL 26001 (m) [AAD]
Verdi, G.:Il trovatore, w. Maria Callas (sop), Cloe Elmo (cta), Giacomo Lauri-Volpi (ten), Paolo Siveri (sgr), Naples Teatro San Carlo Chorus *(rec Theatre of San Carlo, Naples, Jan. 27, 1951)* — Pantheon 2-▲ PHE 6636 (m)

Naples Weekly International Soloists
Vivaldi, A.:Music of, w. Salvatore Accardo (vn), Frederico Agostini (vn), Heinz Holliger (ob), Ida Levin (vn), Aurele Nicolet (fl), Massimo Paris (va d'amore), Angel Romero (gtr), Celedonio Romero (gtr), Celine Romero (gtr), Henryk Szeryng (vn), Pinchas Zukerman (vn), Academy of St. Martin in the Fields, English CO, I Musici, St. Paul CO, Dresden Staatskapelle—The Four Seasons [Winter]; Con in D for Gtr [Largo]; Con in D for Fl, "Il gardellino" [Cantabile]; Con in C for Diverse Insts [Andante molto]; Con in g for Strs [Andante molto]; Con in D for 2 Vns & 2 Vcs [Largo]; Con in g for Ob, Vn, Ww & Strs [Larghetto]; Con in a for Gtr, "L'estro armonico" [Largo]; Con in F for 3 Vns [Andante]; Con in F for Fl [Largo]; Con in d for Va D'Amore [Largo]; Con in E for Vn & Strs, "Il riposo" [Allegro]; Con in G for Ob, Bn & Strs [Largo]; Con in B♭ for Vn & Strs [Largo]; Con in A for Gtr & Strs [Larghetto]; Con in E for Vn & Strs, "L'amoroso" [Allegro]; Con in G for Fl [Largo]; Con in A for Vn [Larghetto]; Con in c for Vn & Strs, "Il sospetto" [Andante]; Con in a for 2 Obs & Strs [Largo]; Con in g for Orch [Largo non molto]; Con in a for Vn [Largo]; Con in C for Ob [Adagio]; Con in g for Fl, "La notte" [Largo] — Philips ▲ 454051-2 ■ 454 051-4

Narodowej PO
W. Rowicki (cnd)
Chopin, F.:Con 1 Pno, w. Halina Czerny-Stefanska (pno) *(rec Warsaw, 1959)* — Polskie Nagrania ▲ PNCD 305
Chopin, F.:Con 2 Pno, w. Halina Czerny-Stefanska (pno) *(rec Warsaw, 1959)* — Polskie Nagrania ▲ PNCD 305

Nash Ensemble
Arensky, A.:Trio 1 Pno *(rec 1982)* — CRD ▲ 3409 [ADD]
Arnold, M.:Divert Fl — Hyperion ▲ CDA 66173
Arnold, M.:Duo Fl — Hyperion ▲ CDA 66173
Arnold, M.:Qnt Fl — Hyperion ▲ CDA 66173
Arnold, M.:Shanties — Hyperion ▲ CDA 66173
Arnold, M.:Son Fl — Hyperion ▲ CDA 66173
Arnold, M.:Sonatina Fl — Hyperion ▲ CDA 66172
Arnold, M.:Sonatina Ob — Hyperion ▲ CDA 66172

Nash Ensemble (cont.)
Arnold, M.:Sonatina Rcr — Hyperion ▲ CDA 66172
Arnold, M.:Trio Fl — Hyperion ▲ CDA 66172
Bax, A.:Elegiac Trio — Hyperion ▲ CDA 66807
Bax, A.:Nonet Fl — Hyperion ▲ CDA 66807
Bax, A.:Qnt Hp & Strs — Hyperion ▲ CDA 66807
Bax, A.:Qnt Ob — Hyperion ▲ CDA 66807
Bax, A.:Son Cl & Pno — Hyperion ▲ CDA 66807
Beethoven, L. van:Qnt Pno, Ob, Cl, Hn & Bn — CRD ▲ 3367
Beethoven, L. van:Septet Strs — Virgin Classics ▲ 59597 [DDD]
Beethoven, L. van:Trio 7 Pno [clarinet version] — Virgin Classics ▲ 59597 [DDD]
Berwald, F.:Septet Vn, "Grand Septet" — CRD ▲ 3344 [ADD]
British Music on Hyperion, w. Parley of Instruments, Roy Goodman (cnd), John Mark Ainsley (ten), Graham Johnson (pno), Salomon Quartet, BBC Scottish SO, Anthony Rolfe Johnson (ten), Royal PO, St. Paul's Cathedral Choir, Martyn Hill (ten), Suasan Gritton (sop), et al. — Hyperion ▲ HYP 15
Debussy, C.:Chansons de Bilitis (recitation) — Virgin Classics ▲ 59604 [DDD]
Dvořák, A.:Serenade Ww — CRD ▲ 3410
Dvořák, A.:Trio 4 Pno, "Dumky" — Broadway Angel ▲ CDC 59141
Fauré, G.:La bonne chanson, w. S. Walker (mez) [F] — CRD ▲ 3389 [ADD]
Fauré, G.:Qt 1 Pno — CRD ▲ 3403
Fauré, G.:Qt 2 Pno — CRD ▲ 3403
Fauré, G.:Trio — CRD ▲ 3389 [ADD]
Hummel, J.N.:Septet militaire — CRD ▲ CRD 3418
Hummel, J.N.:Septet Pno — CRD ▲ 3344 [ADD]
Hummel, J.N.:Septet Pno — CRD ▲ CRD 3418
Kreutzer, C.:Grand Septet — CRD ▲ 3390
Krommer, F.:Octet-Partita, Op. 79 — CRD ▲ 3410
Mozart, W.A.:Qnt Pno, K.452 — CRD ▲ 3367
Poulenc, F.:Le Bal masqué, w. Thomas Allen (bar) [F] — CRD ▲ 3437 [DDD]
Poulenc, F.:Le Bestiarire, w. T. Allen (bar) [F] — CRD ▲ 3437 [DDD]
Poulenc, F.:Sxt Pno — CRD ▲ 3437
Poulenc, F.:Trio Ob — CRD ▲ 3437 [DDD]
Ravel, M.:Chansons madécasses, w. S. Walker (mez) — Virgin Classics ▲ CDC 45016
Ravel, M.:Son Vn Pno — Virgin Classics ▲ CDC 45016
Ravel, M.:Trio Pno — Virgin Classics ▲ CDC 45016
Rimsky-Korsakov, N.:Qnt Fl *(rec 1982)* — CRD ▲ 3409 [ADD]
Saint-Saëns, C.:Carnival of the Animals, w. I. Brown (pno), S. Tomes (pno) — Virgin Classics ▲ 59514 [DDD]
Saint-Saëns, C.:Spt Tpt, w. I. Brown (pno), P. Archibald (tpt) — Virgin Classics ▲ 59514 [DDD]
Saint-Saëns, C.:Trio 1 Pno — Virgin Classics ▲ CDC 59514
Schoenberg, A.:Chamber Sym 1 — Virgin Classics ▲ CDC 59057
Schoenberg, A.:Ode to Napoleon — Virgin Classics ▲ CDC 59057
Schoenberg, A.:Verklärte Nacht — Virgin Classics ▲ CDC 59057
Schubert, Franz:Octet Ww, D.803 — Virgin Classics ▲ CDC 45017
Schubert, Franz:Qnt Pno, D.667 — IMP Classics ▲ PCD 868 [DDD]
Shostakovich, D.:Qnt Pno — Broadway Angel ▲ CDC 59312 [DDD]
Shostakovich, D.:Trio 2 Pno — Broadway Angel ▲ CDC 59312 [DDD]
Shostakovich, D.:Waltzes Fl — Broadway Angel ▲ CDC 59312 [DDD]
Spohr, L.:Nonet Strs — CRD ▲ 3354
Spohr, L.:Octet Strs — CRD ▲ 3354
Spohr, L.:Qnt Fl — CRD ▲ 3399
Spohr, L.:Spt Fl — CRD ▲ 3399
Weber, C.M. von:Qnt Cl — CRD ■ 4098
Weber, C.M. von:Trio Fl — CRD ■ 4098

L. Friend (cnd)
Britten, B.:Lachrymae, w. Roger Chase (va) — Hyperion ▲ CDA 66845
Britten, B.:Movt Wind Sextet — Hyperion ▲ CDA 66845
Britten, B.:Night Mail, w. Nigel Hawthorne (nar) — Hyperion ▲ CDA 66845
Britten, B.:Phaedra, w. Jean Rigby (sop) — Hyperion ▲ CDA 66845
Britten, B.:Sinfonietta — Hyperion ▲ CDA 66845
Britten, B.:The Sword in the Stone — Hyperion ▲ CDA 66845
Holt, S.:Music of—...era madrugada; Canciones; Shadow Realm; Sparrow Night — NM Classics ▲ NMCD 008 [DDD]
Lambert, C.:Con Pno, w. Ian Brown (pno) — Hyperion ▲ CDA 66754
Lambert, C.:Mr. Bear Squash-you-all-flat, w. Ian Brown (pno) — Hyperion ▲ CDA 66754
Lambert, C.:Poems by Li-Po, w. Philip Langridge (ten), Ian Brown (pno), Nigel Hawthorne (nar) — Hyperion ▲ CDA 66754
Matthews, C.:Fuga — Virgin Classics ▲ CDC 59061
Matthews, C.:Great Journey, w. D. Wilson-Johnson (bar) — Virgin Classics ▲ CDC 59061
Matthews, C.:Night's Mask, w. P. Kwella (sop) — Virgin Classics ▲ CDC 59061

S. Rattle (cnd)
Schoenberg, A.:Pierrot lunaire, w. J. Manning (speaker) [G] — Chandos ("Collect" series) ▲ CHAN 6534 [ADD]
Stravinsky, I.:Japanese Lyrics, w. J. Manning (sop) — Chandos ("Collect" series) ▲ CHAN 6535 [ADD]
Webern, A.:Con Fl — Chandos ("Collect" series) ▲ CHAN 6534 [ADD]

Nash Ensemble [F. Lloyd (pno), M. Crayford (vn), I. Brown (pno)]
Brahms, J.:Trio Hn *(rec Nov. 25-27, 1991)* — CRD ▲ CRD 3489 [DDD]

Nash Ensemble [I. Brown (pno), M. Crayford (vn), E. Layton (vn), R. Chase (va), C. van Kampen (vc)]
Brahms, J.:Qnt Pno *(rec Nov. 25-27, 1991)* — CRD ▲ CRD 3489 [DDD]

Nash Ensemble [Martin Robertson (sax), Ian Brown (pno), Christopher Van Kampen (vc)]
O. Knussen (cnd)
Turnage, M.-A.:Lament for a Hanging Man, w. Fiona Kimm (mez) — NMC ▲ NMC 24 [DDD]
Turnage, M.-A.:On All 4s — NMC ▲ NMC 24 [DDD]
Turnage, M.-A.:Release — NMC ▲ NMC 24 [DDD]
Turnage, M.-A.:Sarabande — NMC ▲ NMC 24 [DDD]

National Arts Center Canada Orch
M. Bernardi (cnd)
Mozart, W.A.:Kleine Nachtmusik — CBC ("SM 5000" series) ▲ SM5 5150 [DDD]
G. Chmura (cnd)
Haydn, J.:Sym 6, "Le Matin" — CBC ("SM 5000" series) ▲ SMCD 5085 [DDD] ■ 4-5085 (D)
Haydn, J.:Sym 7, "Le Midi" — CBC ("SM 5000" series) ▲ SMCD 5085 [DDD] ■ 4-5085 (D)
Haydn, J.:Sym 8, "Le Soir" — CBC ("SM 5000" series) ▲ SMCD 5085 [DDD] ■ 4-5085 (D)
F.-P. Decker (cnd)
Copland, A.:Con Cl, w. J. Campbell (cl) — CBC ("SM 5000" series) ▲ SMCD 5096 [DDD] ■ SMC 5096 (D)
Mozart, W.A.:Con Cl, w. J. Campbell (cl) — CBC ("SM 5000" series) ▲ SMCD 5096 [DDD] ■ SMC 5096 (D)
Weber, C.M. von:Concertino Cl, w. J. Campbell (cl) — CBC ("SM 5000" series) ▲ SMCD 5096 [DDD] ■ SMC 5096 (D)
V. Feldbrill (cnd)
Somers, H.:Lyric *(rec St. Joseph's Church, Ottawa, July 6-7, 1995)* — CBC ▲ 5162 [DDD]
Somers, H.:North Country *(rec St. Joseph's Church, Ottawa, July 6-7, 1995)* — CBC ▲ 5162 [DDD]
Somers, H.:Suite Hp, w. Jennifer Swartz (hp) *(rec St. Joseph's Church, Ottawa, July 6-7, 1995)* — CBC ▲ 5162 [DDD]
Somers, H.:Sym 1 *(rec St. Joseph's Church, Ottawa, July 6-7, 1995)* — CBC ▲ 5162 [DDD]
F. Mannino (cnd)
Mozart, W.A.:Andante Fl, K.315/285a, w. Robert Aitken (fl) — CBC ("SM 5000" series) ▲ SMCD 5076 [DDD] ■ SMC 5076 (D)

National Arts Center Canada Orch (cont.)
F. Mannino (cnd) (cont.)
Mozart, W.A.:Cons Fl, w. Robert Aitken (fl) — CBC ("SM 5000" series) ▲ SMCD 5076 [DDD] ■ SMC 5076 (D)
Mozart, W.A.:Rondo Fl, K.Anh.184, w. R. Aitken (fl) — CBC ("SM 5000" series) ▲ SMCD 5076 [DDD] ■ SMC 5076 (D)
Schubert, Franz:Sym 8 — CBC ("SM 5000" series) ▲ SMCD 5034 [DDD] ■ SMC 5034 (D)
Strauss, R.:Metamorphosen — CBC ("SM 5000" series) ▲ SMCD 5034 [DDD] ■ SMC 5034 (D)
P. Zukerman (cnd)
Haydn, J.:Con 1 Vn, w. Pinchas Zukerman (vn) — RCA Red Seal ▲ 09026-60797-2
Haydn, J.:Con 4 Vn, w. Pinchas Zukerman (vn) — RCA Red Seal ▲ 09026-60797-2
Haydn, J.:Sym 22, "Der Philosoph" — RCA Red Seal ▲ 09026-60797-2

National Brass Band Festival Massed Bands
Live at the Crystal Palace, w. Festival of English Church Music Massed Choir, Handel Festival Choir, Handel Festival Orch, National Union of School Orch, Salvation Army Congress Massed Bands, Non-Conformist Union Festival Choir — Beulah ▲ 1 PD 1

National CO
J.-C. Malgoire (cnd)
Bach, J.S.:Cons Vn (comp), w. M.-A. Nicholas (vn) — Valois ▲ V 4697
Bach, J.S.:Con for 2 Vns, w. M.-A. Nicholas (vn), A. Moglia (vn) — Valois ▲ V 4697

National Czech SO
P. Freeman (cnd)
Liszt, F.:Con 1 Pno, w. Carl Gales (pno) — Mastersound ▲ MST 223 [DDD]

National Festival Orch
Russo, J.:Fort Washington Ov — CRS ▲ CD 9052
J. Carmichael (cnd)
Contemporary Music Festival, w. Furman Civic Wind Ensemble — CRS ▲ CRS 9052
J. Russo (cnd)
Van Appledorn, M.J.:Con Brevis, w. S. Blinderman (pno) — CRS ▲ CD 9052

National Museum CO
Roman, J.H.:Suite — Proprius ▲ PRCD 9047
C. Génetay (cnd)
Agrell, J.:Sinfs—4 sinfonias, Op. 1/1 in D; Op. 1/3 in A; Op. 1/4 in B♭; Op. 1/6 in F *(rec Oct 1981)* — Musica Sveciae ▲ MSCD 412 [ADD]
Bach, J.S.:Suite 2 Orch, w. G. von Bahr (fl) — BIS ▲ CD 21
Brant, P.:Sinf in d *(rec 5/84)* — Musica Sveciae ▲ MSCD 412 [ADD]
Kraus, J.M.:Sinf in E♭ — Musica Sveciae ▲ MSCD 407 [DDD]
Naumann, J.G.:Amphion (ov) — Musica Sveciae ▲ MSCD 407 [DDD]
Naumann, J.G.:Cora (ballet music) — Musica Sveciae ▲ MSCD 407 [DDD]
Roman, J.H.:Cantatas, w. P.-M. Nilsson (sop) — Proprius ▲ PRCD 9047
Roman, J.H.:Drottningholmsmusiquen — Proprius ▲ PRCD 9047
Uttini, F.A.B.:Aline — Musica Sveciae ▲ MSCD 407 [DDD]
Uttini, F.A.B.:Thetis och Pelée (ballet music) — Musica Sveciae ▲ MSCD 407 [DDD]
Vogler, G.J.:Sinf in C — Musica Sveciae ▲ MSCD 407 [DDD]
Wesström, A.:Sinfonia in D — Musica Sveciae ▲ MSCD 412 [ADD]
Zellbell, F.S.:Sinfonia in C — Musica Sveciae ▲ MSCD 412 [ADD]

National Opera Orch
P. Freeman (cnd)
Mozart, W.A.:Don Giovanni (sels)—Ov; Madamina, il cataloge é questo; La ci darem la mano; Finch'han dal vino; Il mio tesoro intanto; Non mi dir, bell'idol mio — Intersound ▲ CDS 3675
Mozart, W.A.:Nozze di Figaro (sels)—Ov; La vendetta, oh, la vendetta; Non piu andrai; Voi che sapete; Dove sono i bei momenti; Aprite, un po'quegli occhi — Intersound ▲ CDS 3675
Puccini, G.:Tosca (sels)—Intro; Dammi I colori...Recondita armonia; Mario, Mario, son qui; Vissi d'arte; E lucevan le stelle; Presto su Mario — Intersound ▲ CDS 3674
Rossini, G.:Il barbiere di Siviglia (sels)—Ecco ridente in cielo; La ran la lera...Largo al factotum; Una voce poco fa — Intersound ▲ CDS 3674
Verdi, G.:Il trovatore (sels)—Tacea la notta; Il balen del suo sorriso; Di quella pira; Miserere; Anvil Chorus — Intersound ▲ CDS 3674

National Orch
A. Cluytens (cnd)
Chopin, F.:Con 2 Pno, w. Clara Haskil (pno) *(rec Apr 1954)* — Music & Arts ▲ CD 922
C. Munch (cnd)
Mozart, W.A.:Con 23 Pno, w. Clara Haskil (pno) *(rec Sept 1959)* — Music & Arts ▲ CD 922

National Orch Alumni Association members
Thomas, D.E.:Many Happy Returns — CRI ▲ CD 595 [DDD]
J. Barnett (cnd)
Riegger, W.:Movt Tpts, American Brass Quintet — CRI ▲ CD 572 [ADD]
Riegger, W.:Music for Brass, American Brass Quintet — CRI ▲ CD 572 [ADD]
Riegger, W.:Nonet, American Brass Quintet — CRI ▲ CD 572 [ADD]

National PO London
North, A.:2001:A Space Odyssey — Varèse Sarabande ▲ VSD 5400 ■ VSC 5400
The Spectacular World of the Classic Film Scores — RCA ▲ 2792-2-RG [ADD] ■ 2792-4-RG
K. H. Adler (cnd)
O Holy Night, w. L. Pavarotti (ten) — London ▲ 414044-2 LH [ADD] ■ 414044-4
B. Bartoletti (cnd)
Ponchielli, A.:La Gioconda, w. M. Caballé (sop), A. Baltsa (mez), L. Pavarotti (ten), S. Milnes (bar), N. Ghiaurov (bass) [I] — London 3-▲ 414349-2 [DDD]
R. Bonynge (cnd)
Ballet Gala:Invitation to the Dance, w. London SO — London ▲ 433864-2 LM [ADD/DDD]
Bellini, V.:La sonnambula, w. J. Sutherland (sop), L. Pavarotti (ten), N. Ghiaurov (bass) [I] — London 2-▲ 417424-2 [DDD]
Delibes, L.:Coppélia, ou La fille aux yeux d'émail — London 2-▲ 414502-2 [DDD] 2-■ 414502-4
Delibes, L.:Sylvia — London ("Jubilee" series) 2-▲ 425475-2 [ADD]
Donizetti, G.:Lucrezia Borgia, w. J. Sutherland (sop), M. Horne (mez), G. Aragall (ten), I. Wixell (bar) [I] — London 2-▲ 421497-2 [ADD]
Lehár, F.:Die lustige Witwe (sels), w. J. Sutherland (sop), R. Resnik (mez), W. Krenn (ten), Ambrosian Singers—overture & highlights from Acts 1 & 2 — London ("Opera Gala" series) 2-▲ 421884-2 [ADD]
Massenet, J.:Le Cid (ballet suite) — London ("Jubilee" series) 2-▲ 425475-2 [ADD]
Massenet, J.:Cigale — London ("Jubilee" series) 3-▲ 425413-2 [ADD]
Massenet, J.:Le Roi de Lahore, w. J. Sutherland (sop), L. Lima (ten), S. Milnes (bar), N. Ghiaurov (bass), London Voices — London ("Grand Opera" series) 2-▲ 433851-2 [ADD]
Meyerbeer, G.:Les Patineurs (sels) — London ("Jubilee" series) 2-▲ 425468-2 [ADD]
Offenbach, J.:Le Papillon — London ("Jubilee" series) 2-▲ 425450-2 [ADD]
Tchaikovsky, P.:The Nutcracker — London ("Jubilee" series) 2-▲ 425450-2 [ADD]
Tchaikovsky, P.:The Nutcracker *(rec Kingsway Hall, London, Apr 1974)* — London ("Double Decker" series) 2-▲ 444827-2 [ADD]
Tchaikovsky, P.:Swan Lake — London ("Jubilee" series) 3-▲ 425413-2 [ADD]
Verdi, G.:La traviata, w. J. Sutherland (sop), L. Pavarotti (ten), M. Manuguerra (bar), London Opera Chorus [I] — London ▲ 400057-2 [DDD] ■ 400057-4
Verdi, G.:La traviata, w. J. Sutherland (sop), L. Pavarotti (ten), M. Manuguerra (bar), London Opera Chorus [I] — London 2-▲ 430491-2 [DDD]
Verdi, G.:Il trovatore, w. J. Sutherland (sop), M. Horne (mez), L. Pavarotti (ten), I. Wixell (bar), N. Ghiaurov (bass) [I] — London 2-▲ 417137-2 [ADD]
Verdi, G.:Il trovatore (sels), w. J. Sutherland (sop), M. Horne (mez), L. Pavarotti (ten) — London ▲ 421310-2 [ADD]
R. Chailly (cnd)
Giordano, U.:Andrea Chénier, w. M. Caballé (sop), L. Pavarotti (ten), L. Nucci (bar) [I] — London 2-▲ 410117-2 [DDD]
Rossini, G.:Ovs — London □ 400049-5

▲ = CD ♦ = Enhanced CD Δ = MD ■ = Cassette Tape □ = DCC

National PO London (cont.)
R. Chailly (cnd) (cont.)
Rossini, G.:Il turco in Italia, w. M. Caballé (sop), E. Dara (bar), L. Nucci (bar), S. Ramey (bass), Ambrosian Opera Chorus [I] CBS 2-▲ M2K 37859 [DDD]
R. Chailly, O. de Fabritis (cnds)
Grandi Voci:Luciano Pavarotti, w. L. Pavarotti (ten) *(rec 1979)* London ▲ 440400-2 [DDD]
O. de Fabritiis (cnd)
Boito, A.:Mefistofele, w. M. Freni (sop), M. Caballé (sop), L. Pavarotti (ten), N. Ghiaurov (bass) [I] London 3-▲ 410175-2 [DDD]
G. Gacazzeni (cnd)
Mascagni, P.:Cavalleria rusticana, w. J. Varady (sop), L. Pavarotti (ten), P. Cappuccilli (bar), National Phil London Chorus [I] London 2-▲ 414590-2 [ADD]
G. Gavazzeni (cnd)
Leoncavallo, R.:Pagliacci (sels), w. J. Varady (sop), M. Freni (sop), L. Pavarotti (ten), P. Cappuccilli (bar), I. Wixell (bar) London ▲ 421870-2 [ADD]
Mascagni, P.:Cavalleria rusticana (sels), w. Julia Varady (sop), Mirella Freni (sop), Luciano Pavorotti (ten), Piero Cappuccilli (bar), Ingvar Wixel (bar) London ▲ 421870-2 [ADD]
C. Gerhardt (cnd)
Bartók, B.:Con 1 Vn, w. N. Gotkovsky (vn) Pyramid ▲ PYR 13486
Bartók, B.:Con 2 Vn, w. N. Gotkovsky (vn) Pyramid ▲ PYR 13486
Casablanca:Classic Film Scores for Humphrey Bogart RCA ▲ 0422-2-RG [ADD] ■ 0422-4-RG
God Bless America, w. L. Price (sop) RCA Gold Seal ▲ 4421-2-RG [DDD] ■ 4421-4-RG
Golden Galway, w. J. Galway RCA Gold Seal ▲ 09026-60924-2 ■ 09026-60924-4
Herrmann, B.:Film Music, w. K. Te Kanawa (sop)—On Dangerous Ground; Citizen Kane; Beneath the 12-Mile Reef; Hanover Square; White Witch Doctor RCA ▲ 0707-2-RG [ADD] ■ 0707-4-RG
Korngold, E.W.:Film Music—The Prince & the Pauper; Anthony Adverse; The Sea Wolf; Deception; Another Dawn; Of Human Bondage; The Private Lives of Elizabeth & Essex RCA ▲ 0185-2-RG [ADD] ■ 0185-4-RG
Korngold, E.W.:Film Music RCA ▲ 7890-2 RG ■ 7890-4 RG
The Magic Flute of James Galway, w. J. Galway RCA Gold Seal ▲ 09026-60918-2 ■ 09026-60918-4
Newman, Alfred:Film Music, w. Grenadier Guards Band, Ambrosian Singers RCA ▲ 0184-2-RG [ADD] ■ 0184-4-RG
Rózsa, M.:Film Music, w. Ambrosian Singers RCA ("Classic Film Scores" series) ▲ 0911-2 RG ■ 0911-4 RG
Silver Screen Classics RCA 4-▲ 60763-2-RG [ADD] 4-■ 60763-4-RG
Steiner, M.:Film Music, w. Ambrosian Singers RCA ▲ 0136-2-RG [ADD] ■ 0136-4-RG
Tchaikovsky, P.:Romeo & Juliet *(rec 1968)* Chesky ▲ CD 35 [ADD]
Themes from Academy Award Winners RCA ▲ 09026-60966-2 [ADD] ■ 09026-60966-4
Waxman, F.:Film Music—Prince Valiant; A Place in the Sun; The Bride of Frankenstein; Sunset Boulevard; Old Acquaintance; Rebecca; The Philadelphia Story; Taras Bulba RCA ▲ 0708-2-RG ■ 0708-4-RG
Williams, John:The Empire Strikes Back Varése Sarabande ▲ VSD 5353 ■ VSC 5353
Williams, John:Film Music—Star Wars; Close Encounters of the 3rd Kind RCA ▲ 2698-2 RG ■ 2698-4 RG
Williams, John:Star Wars & Return of the Jedi (sels) RCA ▲ 60767-2 ■ 60767-4
B. Herrmann (cnd)
Great British Film Music London ("Phase 4 Stereo" series) ▲ 448954-2
Herrmann, B.:The Devil & Daniel Webster Unicorn-Kanchana ▲ UKCD 2065
Herrmann, B.:The Fantasticks Unicorn-Kanchana ▲ UKCD 2063
Herrmann, B.:Film Music—The Day the Earth Stood Still; Fahrenheit 451; Gulliver's Travels; Journey to the Center of the Earth; The Seventh Voyage of Sinbad *(rec Kingsway Hall, London, England, Nov 1974; Feb 1975)* London ("Phase 4 Stereo" series) ▲ 443899-2 [ADD]
Herrmann, B.:For the Fallen Unicorn-Kanchana ▲ UKCD 2061
Herrmann, B.:Obsession Unicorn-Kanchana ▲ UKCD 2065
Herrmann, B.:Psycho—Suite Unicorn-Kanchana ▲ 2080
Herrmann, B.:Psycho Unicorn-Kanchana ("Souvenir" series) ▲ UKCD 2021
Herrmann, B.:Sym 1 Unicorn-Kanchana ▲ UKCD 2063
A. Hovhaness (cnd)
Hovhaness, A.:Sym 9 Crystal ▲ CD 802
Hovhaness, A.:Sym 24, w. Martyn Hill (ten), John Wilbraham (tpt), Sax (vn), John Alldis Choir [E] *(rec 1974)* Crystal ▲ CD 803 [ADD]
E. Kohn (cnd)
Pure Domingo, w. P. Domingo (ten), English CO [cnd:Julius Rudel], Madrid SO [cnd:Manuel Moreno-Buendia], Munich RSO [cnd:Eugene Kohn], New Philharmonia Orch [cnds:Bruno Bartoletti, Riccardo Muti], Philharmonia Orch [cnd:James Levine] Angel ▲ CDC 55616 [DDD/ADD]
Roman Heroes, w. P. Domingo (ten) EMI Classics ▲ CDC 54053
R. Leppard (cnd)
Haydn, J.:Con Tpt, w. Wynton Marsalis (tpt) CBS ▲ MK 39310 ■ MT 39310
Haydn, J.:Con Tpt, w. Wynton Marsalis (tpt) CBS ▲ MK 37846 [DDD] ■ IMT 37846 (D)
Hummel, J.N.:Con in E♭ Tpt, S.49, w. Wynton Marsalis (tpt) CBS ▲ MK 37846 [DDD] ■ IMT 37846 (D)
Mozart, L.:Con Tpt, w. W. Marsalis (tpt) CBS ▲ MK 37846 [DDD] ■ IMT 37846 (D)
J. Levine (cnd)
Verdi, G.:Otello, w. R. Scotto (sop), P. Domingo (ten), S. Milnes (bass) [I] RCA Red Seal 2-▲ RCD2-2951
A. Markowski (cnd)
Szabelski, B.:Sym 5, w. National Phil London Chorus Olympia ▲ OCD 300 [AAD]
D. Measham (cnd)
Nocturne, w. J. Galway (fl) RCA Victor ▲ RCD1-4810 ■ ARK1-4810
Shostakovich, D.:Hamlet (film music) Unicorn-Kanchana ("Souvenir" series) ▲ UKCD 2066
G. Patanè (cnd)
Leoncavallo, R.:Pagliacci, w. M. Freni (sop), L. Pavarotti (ten), I. Wixell (bar), National Phil London Chorus [I] London 2-▲ 414590-2 [ADD]
P.-D. Ponnelle (cnd)
Tchaikovsky, P.:Manfred *(rec Minsk Philharmonic, Jan. 8-12, 1994)* Musicaphon ▲ 56952 [DDD]
Tchaikovsky, P.:The Voyevoda, Op. 78 *(rec Minsk Philharmonic, Jan. 8-12, 1994)* Musicaphon ▲ 56952 [DDD]
N. Rescigno (cnd)
Puccini, G.:Tosca, w. M. Freni (sop), L. Pavarotti (ten), S. Milnes (bar) [I] London 2-▲ 414036-2 [ADD]
M. Rosenstock (cnd)
Gould, M.:Fall River Legend, w. Brock Peters (spkr)—in addition to the 47-minute performance of the complete ballet score, this disc includes a 27-minute conversation recorded on 24 October 1990 between Morton Gould & Agnes de Mille concerning the creation of the Fall River Legend ballet Albany ▲ TROY 035-2 [DDD]
G. Solti (cnd)
Puccini, G.:Tosca (sels), w. K. Te Kanawa (sop), J. Aragall (ten), L. Nucci (bar), Welsh National Opera Chorus London ▲ 421611-2 [DDD]
Verdi, G.:Un ballo in maschera, w. M. Price (sop), K. Battle (sop), C. Ludwig (mez), L. Pavarotti (ten), R. Bruson (bar), National Phil London Chorus [I] London 2-▲ 410210-2 [DDD]
Verdi, G.:Un ballo in maschera, w. M. Price (sop), K. Battle (sop), C. Ludwig (mez), L. Pavarotti (ten), R. Bruson (bar), National Phil London Chorus [I] London ▲ 425529-2 [DDD]
F. Steiner (cnd)
Steiner, M.:King Kong Label "X" ("Cinema Maestro" series) ▲ LXCD 7 [AAD]
Steiner, M.:King Kong Southern Cross ▲ SRCD 901 [DDD]
L. Stokowski (cnd)
Bizet, G.:L'Arlésienne (suites) CBS ▲ MYK 37260 [AAD] ■ MYT 37260
Bizet, G.:Carmen (suites) CBS ▲ MYK 37260 [AAD] ■ MYT 37260
Bizet, G.:Sym 1 *(rec 1977)* Sony Classical ("Essential Classics" series) ▲ SBK 48264 [ADD] ■ SBT 48264

National PO London (cont.)
L. Stokowski (cnd) (cont.)
Bizet, G.:Sym 1 *(rec 1977)* Odyssey ▲ MBK 39498 [ADD]
Mendelssohn, F.:Sym 4 *(rec 1977)* Odyssey ▲ MBK 39498 [ADD]
Rachmaninoff, S.:Sym 3 InSync ■ C 4140
Rachmaninoff, S.:Vocalise InSync ■ C 4140
L. Tjeknavorian (cnd)
Borodin, A.:In the Steppes of Central Asia RCA Silver Seal ▲ 60535-2-RV [ADD] ■ 60535-4-RV
Borodin, A.:Prince Igor (Polovtsian dances) RCA Silver Seal ▲ 60535-2-RV [ADD] ■ 60535-4-RV
Borodin, A.:Sym 2 RCA Silver Seal ▲ 60535-2-RV [ADD] ■ 60535-4-RV
B. Wordsworth (cnd)
Rhythm Song, w. E. Glennie (perc) RCA Victor ▲ 60242-2-RC [DDD]
National SO
A. Coates (cnd)
Rimsky-Korsakov, N.:Golden Cockerel (sels)—Introduction; Cortege de Noces *(rec 1945)* Beulah ▲ 2PD11 [ADD]
Tchaikovsky, P.:Romeo & Juliet *(rec 1945)* Beulah ▲ 1PD6
Tchaikovsky, P.:Sym 6 *(rec 1945)* Beulah ▲ 1PD6
H. Mitchell (cnd)
Gould, M.:Declaration (suite) RCA Red Seal ▲ 09026-61651-2
Yates (cnd)
Lloyd Webber, A.:Music of, w. C. Burt (sgr), Graham Bickly (sgr), J. Kelly (sgr), C. D. Carroll (sgr), Munich SO—Song & Dance; The Phantom of the Opera; Starlight Express; Jeeves; Jesus Christ Superstar; Aspects of Love; Cats; The Requiem Mass Koch International ▲ KOCCD 340132 ■ KOCC 340134
National SO Washington D.C.
L. Bernstein (cnd)
Bernstein, L.:Songfest, w. C. Dale (sop), R. Elias (mez), N. Williams (mez), N. Rosenshein (ten), J. Reardon (bar), D. Gramm (b-bar) [E] Deutsche Grammophon ▲ 415965-2 [ADD]
Ravel, M.:Boléro CBS ▲ MYK 36714 ■ MYT 36714
A. Dorati (cnd)
La Montaine, J.:Wilderness Journal, w. Donald Gramm (b-bar), Paul Callaway (org) *(rec live, Kennedy Center, Oct 10, 1972)* Fredonia Discs ■ FDC 11
La Montaine, J.:Wilderness Journal, w. Donald Gramm (b-bar), Paul Callaway (org) *(rec live, Kennedy Center, Oct 10, 1972)* Fredonia Discs ▲ FDCD 12
Tchaikovsky, P.:Romeo & Juliet London ▲ 417742-2 [ADD]
M. Rostropovich (cnd)
Albert, S.:Sym RiverRun Delos ▲ DCD 1016 [DDD]
Mussorgsky, M.:Boris Godunov, w. G. Vishnevskaya (sop), N. Gedda (ten), G. Raimondi (ten), Washington Oratorio Society, Choral Arts Society [R] Erato 3-▲ 2292-45418-2 ZB [DDD]
Prokofiev, S.:Con 2 Vn, w. A.-S. Mutter (vn) Erato ▲ 45708-2
Prokofiev, S.:Romeo & Juliet (sels)—Suites 1 & 2 Deutsche Grammophon ▲ 410519-2 [DDD]
Shostakovich, D.:Sym 1 Teldec ▲ 90849
Shostakovich, D.:Sym 4 Teldec ▲ 9031-76261-2 ZK
Shostakovich, D.:Sym 8 Teldec ▲ 9031-74719-2 ZK
Shostakovich, D.:Sym 9 Teldec ▲ 90849
Rostropovich:Return to Russia *(rec live, Moscow February 1990)* Sony Classical ▲ SK 45836
Tchaikovsky, P.:Con 1 Pno, w. V. Feltsman (pno) Sony Classical ▲ SK 45756 [DDD]
Tchaikovsky, P.:Con 3 Pno, w. V. Feltsman (pno) Sony Classical ▲ SK 45756 [DDD]
Tchaikovsky, P.:Sym 6 *(rec live Feb. 1990)* Sony Classical ▲ SK 45836
L. Slatkin (cnd)
Corigliano, J.:Of Rage & Remembrance, w. Michelle DeYoung (mez), Michael Accinno (boy sop), Robert Baker (ten), Michael Forest (ten), Jason Stearns (bar), James Shaffran (bar), Washington Oratorio Society Men's Chorus *(rec J. F. K. Center for the Performing Arts, Washington, D. C., Nov 9-11, 1995)* RCA Red Seal ▲ 09026-68450-2 [DDD]
Corigliano, J.:Sym 1, w. David Hardy (vc), Glenn Garlick (vc), Lambert Orkis (pno) *(rec J. F. K. Center for the Performing Arts, Washington, D. C., Nov 9-11, 1995)* RCA Red Seal ▲ 09026-68450-2 [DDD]
National SO Washington D.C. members
Christmas Music, w. Washington Choral Arts Society Empire Music ▲ CA 10102
National Union of School Orch
Live at the Crystal Palace, w. National Brass Band Festival Massed Bands, Festival of English Church Music Massed Choir, Handel Festival Choir, Handel Festival Orch, Salvation Army Congress Massed Bands, Non-Conformist Union Festival Choir Beulah ▲ 1 PD 1
National Youth Ballet Orch
N. Thompson (cnd)
Reade, P.G.:Cinderella (ballet) ASV ("White Line" series) ▲ ASV 2084 [DDD]
NBC SO
W.A. Albert (cnd)
Busoni, F.:Orchestral Music—Lustspiel Ov., Op. 38; Tanzwalzer, Op. 53; Rondo Arlecchinesco, Op. 46; Nocturne Symphonique, Op. 43; Berceuse Élégiaque, Op. 42; Gesang vom Reigen der Geister, Op. 47 CPO ▲ CPO 999161 [DDD]
F. Black (cnd)
Bach, J.S.:Brandenburg Con 5, w. Harold Samuel (pno) *(rec radio broadcast Dec 11, 1935)* Koch Legacy 2-▲ 3-7137-2
Khachaturian, A.:Con Pno, w. W. Kapell (pno) *(rec live, May 20, 1945)* VAI Audio ▲ VAIA/IPA 1027 [ADD]
G. Cantelli (cnd)
Brahms, J.:Tragic Ov *(rec live, 1951)* Legend ▲ LGD 121
Franck, C.:Sym in d *(rec Carnegie Hall, NY, Apr. 1954)* EMI Classics 2-▲ ZDMB 68217 [ADD]
Franck, C.:Sym in d *(rec 1950)* Andromeda ▲ ANR 2521 [ADD]
Ravel, M.:Boléro Fortissimo ▲ CDE 3021
Ravel, M.:Boléro Legend ▲ LGD 104 [ADD]
Ravel, M.:Pavane pour une infante défunte Legend ▲ LGD 104 [ADD]
Ravel, M.:La Valse Legend ▲ LGD 104 [ADD]
Stravinsky, I.:Le Chant du rossignol Fonit Cetra ("Fortissimo" series) ▲ FCT CDE 3008
D. Mitropoulos (cnd)
Berg, A.:Con Vn, w. J. Szigeti (vn) *(rec live 12/30/45)* Intaglio ▲ IND 706-1 [ADD]
Mozart, W.A.:Ovs—Die Zauberflöte *(rec live, Dec. 9, 1945)* Arkadia 3-▲ 552 (m) [ADD]
Rossini, G.:Il barbiere di Siviglia (sels), w. Robert Merrill (bar)—Largo al Factotum *(rec live, ca 1950)* Nickson 2-▲ NN 1008/1009 (m) [ADD]
F. Reiner (cnd)
Copland, A.:Con Cl, w. Benny Goodman (cl) *(rec 1951)* Legend ▲ LGD 122
L. Stokowski (cnd)
The Age of Living Stereo:A Tribute to John Pfeiffer, w. Boston SO [cnd:Pierre Monteux, Charles Munch], Chicago SO [cnd:Fritz Reiner], RCA SO [cnd:Kiril Kondrashin] *(rec Boston & Chicago & New York, 1953-1961)* RCA Living Stereo 2-▲ 09026-68524-2 [ADD]
Prokofiev, S.:The Love for 3 Oranges (march) Cala ▲ CAL CACD 505 [ADD]
Rimsky-Korsakov, N.:Russian Easter Festival Cala ▲ CAL CACD 505 [ADD]
Shostakovich, D.:Sym 7 *(rec 1942)* Pearl ▲ PEA 9064 [AAD]
Stravinsky, I.:The Firebird Suite Cala ▲ CACD 505 [ADD]
Tchaikovsky, P.:Humoresque [orchd. Stokowski] Cala ▲ CACD 505 [ADD]
Tchaikovsky, P.:Sym 4 Cala ▲ CACD 505 [ADD]
A. Toscanini (cnd)
Atterberg, K.:Sym 6 *(rec Nov. 21, 1943)* Dell'Arte ▲ CDDA 9019 (m)
Barber, S.:Adagio Strs RCA Gold Seal ▲ 09026-60307-2 ■ 09026-60307-4
Beethoven, L. van:Con 1 Pno, w. A. Dorfmann (pno) RCA Gold Seal ▲ 60268-2-RG ■ 60268-4-RG
Beethoven, L. van:Con 3 Pno, w. A. Rubinstein (pno) RCA Gold Seal ▲ 60261-2-RG (m) [ADD] ■ 60261-4-RG

ORCH. & ENS.

NBC SO (cont.)
A. Toscanini (cnd) (cont.)

Beethoven, L. van:Con 3 Pno, w. M. Hess (pno) *(rec live 11/24/46)* Melodram 2-▲ MEL 28031 (m) [AAD]
Beethoven, L. van:Con 4 Pno, w. R. Serkin (pno) RCA Gold Seal ▲ 60268-2-RG ■ 60268-4-RG
Beethoven, L. van:Con Vn, Op. 61, w. J. Heifetz (vn) RCA Gold Seal ▲ 60261-2-RG (m) [ADD] ■ 60261-4-RG
Beethoven, L. van:Coriolan Ov *(rec live, 11/26/44)* Melodram 2-▲ MEL 28031 (m) [AAD]
Beethoven, L. van:Coriolan Ov *(rec 1953)* Music & Arts ▲ CD 3007
Beethoven, L. van:Coriolan Ov *(rec 1939)* Grammofono 2000 ▲ GRM 78573 (m)
Beethoven, L. van:Egmont (ov) RCA Gold Seal ▲ 09026-60270-2-RG ■ 09026-60270-4-RG
Beethoven, L. van:Egmont (ov) Relief ▲ CR 1885
Beethoven, L. van:Egmont (ov) *(rec 1939)* Grammofono 2000 ▲ GRM 78573 (m)
Beethoven, L. van:Fant Pno, Op. 80, "Choral Fant", w. A. Dorfmann (pno), Westminster Choir [G] *(rec live 12/2/39)* Melodram 2-▲ MEL 28031 (m) [AAD]
Beethoven, L. van:Fant Pno, Op. 80, "Choral Fant", w. Ania Dorfmann (pno), Westminster Choir *(rec New York City, 1939)* Grammofono 2000 ▲ GRM 78524 (m)
Beethoven, L. van:Fant Pno, Op. 80, "Choral Fant", w. *(pianist & chorus unknown)* Relief ▲ CR 1893
Beethoven, L. van:Fidelio (sels), w. R. Bampton (sop)—Act 1 aria, "Abscheulicher! Wo eilst du hin?" ("The Toscanini Collection, Vol. 46") RCA Gold Seal ▲ 60280-2-RG ■ 60280-4-RG
Beethoven, L. van:Fidelio (ov) *(rec 1939)* Grammofono 2000 ▲ GRM 78573 (m)
Beethoven, L. van:Fidelio (ov) Relief ▲ CR 1861
Beethoven, L. van:Leonore 1 *(rec 1939)* Grammofono 2000 ▲ GRM 78514 [ADD]
Beethoven, L. van:Leonore 1 Relief ▲ CR 1891
Beethoven, L. van:Leonore 2 Relief ▲ CR 1891
Beethoven, L. van:Leonore 3 *(rec 1939)* Grammofono 2000 ▲ GRM 78573 (m)
Beethoven, L. van:Leonore 3 RCA Gold Seal 5-▲ 60324-2-RG (m) [ADD] 5-■ 60324-4-RG
Beethoven, L. van:Leonore 3 Relief ▲ CR 1891
Beethoven, L. van:Missa Solemnis, w. Zinka Milanov (sop), Bruna Castagna (cta), Jussi Björling (ten), Alexander Kipnis (bass), Westminster Choir *(rec 1940)* Grammofono 2000 ▲ GRM 78626
Beethoven, L. van:Missa Solemnis, w. M. Marshall (sop), N. Merriman (mez), E. Conley (ten), J. Hines (bass), Robert Shaw Chorale *(rec 1953)* RCA Gold Seal ▲ 60272-2-RG [ADD] ■ 60272-4-RG
Beethoven, L. van:Missa Solemnis, w. Z. Milanov (sop), B. Castagna (mez), J. Björling, A. Kipnis (bass), Westminster Choir [L] *(rec live 12/28/40)* Melodram 3-▲ MEL 38006
Beethoven, L. van:Ovs—Die Weihe des Hauses; Coriolan; Die Geschöpfe des Prometheus; Egmont; Leonore Nos. 2 & 3 RCA Gold Seal ▲ 60267-2-RG ■ 60267-4-RG
Beethoven, L. van:Qt 16 Strs [orch. ver.] RCA Gold Seal ▲ 09026-60267-2-RG ■ 09026-60267-4-RG
Beethoven, L. van:Qt 16 Strs [orch. arr. of the 2nd & 3rd movts. *(rec live 1/1/38)* Melodram 2-▲ MEL 28031 (m) [AAD]
Beethoven, L. van:Septet Strs Relief ▲ CR 1885
Beethoven, L. van:Septet Strs RCA Gold Seal ▲ 09026-60270-2-RG ■ 09026-60270-4-RG
Beethoven, L. van:Syms (comp)—Nos. 4 & 6 RCA Gold Seal ▲ 60254-2-RG (m) [ADD] ■ 60254-4-RG (m)
Beethoven, L. van:Syms (comp) *(rec 1939)* Relief 6-▲ CR 1894/99
Beethoven, L. van:Syms (comp)—Nos. 5 & 8 RCA Gold Seal ▲ 60255-2-RG (m) [ADD] ■ 60255-4-RG (m)
Beethoven, L. van:Syms (comp)—Nos. 1 & 3 RCA Gold Seal ▲ 60252-2-RG (m) [ADD] ■ 60252-4-RG (m)
Beethoven, L. van:Syms (comp)—Nos. 2 & 7 RCA Gold Seal ▲ 60253-2-RG (m) [ADD] ■ 60253-4-RG (m)
Beethoven, L. van:Syms (comp)—No. 9 RCA Gold Seal ▲ 60256-2-RG (m) [ADD] ■ 60256-4-RG (m)
Beethoven, L. van:Syms (comp) [soloists in No. 9:Eileen Farrell, Nan Merriman, Jan Peerce, Norman Scott,; Robert Shaw Chorale] RCA Gold Seal 5-▲ 60324-2-RG (m) [ADD] 5-■ 60324-4-RG
Beethoven, L. van:Sym 1 Relief ▲ CR 1861
Beethoven, L. van:Sym 2 Relief ▲ CR 1871
Beethoven, L. van:Sym 2 *(rec live 11/4/39)* Melodram 2-▲ MEL 28031 (m) [AAD]
Beethoven, L. van:Sym 3, "Eroica" Enterprise ("Sirio" series) ▲ ENT SO 53001
Beethoven, L. van:Sym 3, "Eroica" Relief ▲ CR 1891
Beethoven, L. van:Sym 3, "Eroica" *(rec 1939)* Grammofono 2000 ▲ BRM 78505 [ADD]
Beethoven, L. van:Sym 3, "Eroica" *(rec 1945)* Music & Arts ▲ CD 753
Beethoven, L. van:Sym 3, "Eroica" RCA Gold Seal ▲ 60271-2-RG [ADD] ■ 60271-4-RG
Beethoven, L. van:Sym 3, "Eroica" RCA Gold Seal ▲ 60269-2-RG ■ 60269-4-RG
Beethoven, L. van:Sym 4 *(rec 1939)* Grammofono 2000 ▲ GRM 78514 [ADD]
Beethoven, L. van:Sym 4 Relief ▲ CR 1861
Beethoven, L. van:Sym 5 *(rec 1945)* Music & Arts ▲ CD 753
Beethoven, L. van:Sym 5 *(rec 1939)* Grammofono 2000 ▲ BRM 78505 [ADD]
Beethoven, L. van:Sym 5 RCA Gold Seal ▲ 09026-60270-2-RG ■ 09026-60270-4-RG
Beethoven, L. van:Sym 5 Relief ▲ CR 1871
Beethoven, L. van:Sym 5 Enterprise ("Sirio" series) ▲ ENT SO 53001
Beethoven, L. van:Sym 6, "Pastorale" Relief ▲ CR 1892
Beethoven, L. van:Sym 6, "Pastorale" *(rec 1939)* Grammofono 2000 ▲ GRM 78573 (m)
Beethoven, L. van:Sym 7 *(rec 1939)* Grammofono 2000 ▲ GRM 78514 [ADD]
Beethoven, L. van:Sym 7 Relief ▲ CR 1885
Beethoven, L. van:Sym 7 *(rec live 11/10/51)* Melodram 2-▲ MEL 28031 (m) [AAD]
Beethoven, L. van:Sym 8 RCA Gold Seal ▲ 60269-2-RG ■ 60269-4-RG
Beethoven, L. van:Sym 8 Relief ▲ CR 1892
Beethoven, L. van:Sym 9, "Choral Sym", w. *(chorus unknown)* Relief ▲ CR 1893
Beethoven, L. van:Sym 9, "Choral Sym", w. Westminster Choir [soloists J. Novotna, K. Thorborg, J. Peerce, N. Moscona] *(rec Carnegie Hall, 1944)* Legato Classics ▲ LCD 136-1 (m) [ADD]
Beethoven, L. van:Sym 9, "Choral Sym", w. Jarmila Novotna (sop), Kerstin Thorborg (mez), Jan Pierce (ten), Nicola Moscona (bass), Westminster Choir *(rec 1939)* LYS ▲ LYS 128
Beethoven, L. van:Sym 9, "Choral Sym", w. Westminster Choir [soloists Bovy, Thorborg, Peerce, Pinza] *(rec 1938)* Music & Arts ▲ CD 3007
Beethoven, L. van:Sym 9, "Choral Sym", w. Jarmila Novotná (sop), Kerstin Thorborg (mez), Jan Peerce (ten), Nicola Moscona (bass), Westminster Choir *(rec New York City, 1939)* Grammofono 2000 ▲ GRM 78524 (m)
Beethoven, L. van:Die Weihe des Hauses (ov), w. M. Hess (pno) *(rec live 3/16/47)* Melodram 2-▲ MEL 28031 (m) [AAD]
Berlioz, H.:La Damnation de Faust (sels)—Racókzy March RCA Gold Seal ▲ 09026-60322-2 ■ 09026-60322-4
Berlioz, H.:Harold in Italy, w. C. Cooley (va) RCA Gold Seal ▲ 60275-2-RG ■ 60275-4-RG
Berlioz, H.:Ovs—Carnaval romain RCA Gold Seal ▲ 09026-60322-2
Berlioz, H.:Roméo et Juliette, w. *(soloists unknown)* RCA Gold Seal 2-▲ 60274-2-RG 2-■ 60274-4-RG
Berlioz, H.:Roméo et Juliette (sels)—Scherzo RCA Gold Seal ▲ 09026-60322-2
Berlioz, H.:Roméo et Juliette (sels)—Part 2 RCA Gold Seal ▲ 60275-2-RG ■ 60275-4-RG
Bizet, G.:L'Arlésienne (suites)—Suite No. 1 RCA Gold Seal 2-▲ 60274-2-RG 2-■ 60274-4-RG
Bizet, G.:Carmen (suite 1) RCA Gold Seal 2-▲ 60274-2-RG
Bizet, G.:La Jolie fille de Perth (suite) Enterprise ("Palladio" series) ▲ ENT PD 4143 [ADD]
Bizet, G.:La Jolie fille de Perth (suite) Enterprise ("The Radio Years" series) ▲ ENT 42
Boito, A.:Mefistofele (sels), w. N. Moscona (bass), Robert Shaw Chorale, Columbus Boychoir—Prologue RCA Gold Seal ▲ 60276-2-RG [ADD] ■ 60276-4-RG
Brahms, J.:Academic Festival Ov RCA Gold Seal 4-▲ 60325-2-RG (m) [ADD] 4-■ 60325-4-RG (CrO2)
Brahms, J.:Academic Festival Ov RCA Gold Seal ▲ 60257-2-RG [ADD] ■ 60257-4-RG (CrO2)
Brahms, J.:Con 2 Pno, w. V. Horowitz (pno) RCA Gold Seal ▲ 60319-2-RG ■ 60319-4-RG
Brahms, J.:Con 2 Pno, w. V. Horowitz (pno) *(rec live, Carnegie Hall)* RCA Gold Seal ▲ 60523-2-RG [ADD] ■ 60523-4-RG (CrO2)
Brahms, J.:Con 2 Pno, w. V. Horowitz (pno) *(rec live, New York 10/23/48)* Arkadia ▲ 454 [ADD]

NBC SO (cont.)
A. Toscanini (cnd) (cont.)

Brahms, J.:Con 2 Pno, w. Vladimir Horowitz (pno) Stradivarius ▲ STV 13595 [AAD]
Brahms, J.:Con Vn & Vc, "Double Con", w. M. Mischakoff (vn), F. Miller (vc) RCA Gold Seal ▲ 60259-2-RG [ADD] ■ 60259-4-RG (CrO2)
Brahms, J.:Con Vn & Vc, "Double Con", w. M. Mischakoff (vn), F. Miller (vc) RCA Gold Seal 4-▲ 60325-2-RG (m) [ADD] 4-■ 60325-4-RG (CrO2)
Brahms, J.:Gesang der Parzen, w. Robert Shaw Chorale [G] RCA Gold Seal 4-▲ 60325-2-RG (m) [ADD] 4-■ 60325-4-RG (CrO2)
Brahms, J.:Gesang der Parzen, w. Robert Shaw Chorale [G] RCA Gold Seal ▲ 60260-2-RG [ADD] ■ 60260-4-RG (CrO2)
Brahms, J.:Hungarian Dances Orch—Nos. 1, 17, 20 & 21 RCA Gold Seal ▲ 60257-2-RG [ADD] ■ 60257-4-RG (CrO2)
Brahms, J.:Hungarian Dances Orch—Nos. 1, 17, 20 & 21 RCA Gold Seal 4-▲ 60325-2-RG (m) [ADD] 4-■ 60325-4-RG (CrO2)
Brahms, J.:Serenade 1 Orch—1st & 4th movt. Dell'Arte ▲ CD DA 9022
Brahms, J.:Serenade 1 Orch—1st movt. *(rec live 10/23/48)* Melodram ▲ MEL 18011 (m) [AAD]
Brahms, J.:Serenade 2 Orch RCA Gold Seal ▲ 60277-2-RG ■ 60277-4-RG
Brahms, J.:Syms (comp) RCA Gold Seal 4-▲ 60325-2-RG (m) [ADD] 4-■ 60325-4-RG (CrO2)
Brahms, J.:Syms (comp) *(rec live in Carnegie Hall 11/3/51 [No. 1], 2/10/51)* Arkadia 2-▲ 706 (m) [ADD]
Brahms, J.:Sym 1 RCA Gold Seal ▲ 60277-2-RG ■ 60277-4-RG
Brahms, J.:Sym 1 *(rec live 5/6/40)* Melodram ▲ MEL 18011 (m) [AAD]
Brahms, J.:Sym 1 *(rec live Dec. 25, 1937)* Myto ▲ 1 MCD 89009 (m) [ADD]
Brahms, J.:Sym 1 RCA Gold Seal ▲ 60257-2-RG [ADD] ■ 60257-4-RG (CrO2)
Brahms, J.:Sym 1 Enterprise ("The Radio Years" series) ▲ ENT RY 13
Brahms, J.:Sym 2 RCA Gold Seal ▲ 60258-2-RG [ADD] ■ 60258-4-RG (CrO2)
Brahms, J.:Sym 3 RCA Gold Seal ▲ 60259-2-RG [ADD] ■ 60259-4-RG (CrO2)
Brahms, J.:Sym 4 RCA Gold Seal ▲ 60260-2-RG [ADD] ■ 60260-4-RG (CrO2)
Brahms, J.:Tragic Ov RCA Gold Seal 4-▲ 60325-2-RG (m) [ADD] 4-■ 60325-4-RG (CrO2)
Brahms, J.:Tragic Ov RCA Gold Seal ▲ 60258-2-RG [ADD] ■ 60258-4-RG (CrO2)
Brahms, J.:Vars on a Theme by Haydn RCA Gold Seal 4-▲ 60325-2-RG (m) [ADD] 4-■ 60325-4-RG (CrO2)
Brahms, J.:Vars on a Theme by Haydn RCA Gold Seal ▲ 60258-2-RG [ADD] ■ 60258-4-RG (CrO2)
Brahms, J.:Vars & Fugue on a Theme by Handel [1938 orch. Edmund Rubbra] *(rec 1/7/39)* Dell'Arte ▲ CD DA9020 (m)
Cherubini, L.:Ovs—Ali Baba; Anacreon; Medea RCA Gold Seal ▲ 60278-2-RG ■ 60278-4-RG
Cherubini, L.:Requiem Mass in c, w. Robert Shaw Chorale RCA Gold Seal ▲ 60272-2-RG [ADD] ■ 60272-4-RG (CrO2)
Cherubini, L.:Sinf in D RCA Gold Seal ▲ 60278-2-RG ■ 60278-4-RG
Cimarosa, D.:Ovs—Il matrimonio per raggiro; Il matrimonio segreto RCA Gold Seal ▲ 60278-2-RG ■ 60278-4-RG
Debussy, C.:Ibéria RCA Gold Seal ▲ 60265-2-RG [ADD] ■ 60265-4-RG (CrO2)
Debussy, C.:Ibéria Fonit Cetra ("Fortissimo" series) ▲ FCT CDE 3011
Debussy, C.:Marche écossaise sur un thème populaire Dell'Arte ▲ CDDA 9021
Debussy, C.:La Mer Fonit Cetra ("Fortissimo" series) ▲ FCT CDE 3011
Debussy, C.:La Mer RCA Gold Seal ▲ 60265-2-RG [ADD] ■ 60265-4-RG (CrO2)
Debussy, C.:Nocturnes—Nuages & Fêtes RCA Gold Seal ▲ 60265-2-RG [ADD] ■ 60265-4-RG (CrO2)
Debussy, C.:Prélude à l'après-midi d'un faune RCA Gold Seal ▲ 60265-2-RG [ADD] ■ 60265-4-RG (CrO2)
Debussy, C.:Prélude à l'après-midi d'un faune Fonit Cetra ("Fortissimo" series) ▲ FCT CDE 3011
Degeyter, P.:Internationale Relief ▲ CR 1886
Dukas, P.:L'Apprenti sorcier RCA Gold Seal ▲ 09026-60322-2 ■ 09026-60322-4
Dukas, P.:Music of—Ariane et Barbe-Bleue (sels.) Enterprise (Palladio) ▲ ENT PD 4143 [ADD]
Dvořák, A.:Con Vc, w. Edmund Kurtz (vc) Grammofono 2000 ▲ GRM 78636
Dvořák, A.:Sym 9, "From the New World" RCA Gold Seal ▲ 60279-2-RG (m) [ADD] ■ 60279-4-RG (CrO2)
Elgar, E.:Enigma Vars *(rec 1951)* Relief ▲ CR 1888
Elgar, E.:Enigma Vars RCA Gold Seal ▲ 60287-2-RG [ADD] ■ 60287-4-RG (CrO2)
Elgar, E.:Intro & Allegro *(rec 1940)* Relief ▲ CR 1888
Enescu, G.:Romanian Rhap 1 Enterprise ("The Radio Years" series) ▲ ENT 42
Final Concert:April 4, 1954 Music & Arts ▲ MUA 3008
Franck, C.:Psyché et Eros RCA Gold Seal ▲ 09026-60322-2; ■ 09026-60322-4
Franck, C.:Sym in d *(rec 1940 [1st movt.] & 1946)* RCA Gold Seal ▲ 60320-2-RG; ■ 60320-4-RG
Franck, C.:Sym in d *(rec 1946)* Dell'Arte ▲ CDDA 9021
Gershwin, G.:An American in Paris RCA Gold Seal ▲ 09026-60307-2; ■ 09026-60307-4
Gershwin, G.:An American in Paris, w. Benny Goodman (cl) Iron Needle ▲ 1306
Gershwin, G.:An American in Paris, w. Benny Goodman (cl), Earl Wild (pno) Enterprise ("The Radio Years" series) ▲ ENT RY 60
Gershwin, G.:An American in Paris *(rec Nov. 14, 1943)* Vintage Jazz Classics ▲ VJC 1034
Gershwin, G.:Con Pno, w. Oscar Levant (pno) *(rec Apr. 2, 1944)* Vintage Jazz Classics ▲ VJC 1034
Gershwin, G.:Rhap in Blue, w. Earl Wild (pno), Benny Goodman (cl) *(rec Nov. 1, 1942)* Vintage Jazz Classics ▲ VJC 1034
Gershwin, G.:Rhap in Blue, w. Benny Goodman (cl), Earl Wild (pno) Enterprise ("The Radio Years" series) ▲ ENT RY 60
Gershwin, G.:Rhap in Blue, w. Earl Wild (pno), Benny Goodman (cl) Iron Needle ▲ 1306
Glinka, M.:Capriccio brillante on the Jota aragonesa, "1st Spanish Ov" Relief ▲ CR 1886
Glinka, M.:Kamarinskaya RCA Gold Seal ▲ 09026-60323-2; ■ 09026-60323-4
Glinka, M.:Orchestral Music—Jota Aragonesa [Spanish Ov No. 1] Enterprise ("The Radio Years" series) ▲ ENT 42
Gluck, C.W.:Iphigénie en Aulide (ov) RCA Gold Seal ▲ 60280-2-RG; ■ 60280-4-RG
Gluck, C.W.:Orfeo ed Euridice (sels), w. B. Gibson (sop), N. Merriman (mez), Robert Shaw Chorale—Act 2 RCA Gold Seal ▲ 60280-2-RG; ■ 60280-4-RG
Graener, P.:Die Flöte von Sanssouci Dell'Arte ▲ CDDA 9024
Grofé, F.:Grand Canyon Suite RCA Gold Seal ▲ 09026-60307-2; ■ 09026-60307-4
Harris, R.:Sym 3 *(rec 3/16/40)* Dell'Arte ▲ CD DA9020 (m)
Haydn, J.:Qts Strs, Op. 3—Serenade [from No. 5; arr for Orch] Relief ▲ CR 1842
Haydn, J.:Sinf concertante RCA Gold Seal ▲ 60282-2-RG ■ 60282-4-RG
Haydn, J.:Sym 31, "Hornsignal" Relief ▲ CR 1842
Haydn, J.:Sym 88 RCA Gold Seal ▲ 60281-2-RG ■ 60281-4-RG
Haydn, J.:Sym 94, "Surprise Sym" RCA Gold Seal ▲ 60281-2-RG ■ 60281-4-RG
Haydn, J.:Sym 99 RCA Gold Seal ▲ 60282-2-RG ■ 60282-4-RG
Haydn, J.:Sym 101, "Clock" RCA Gold Seal ▲ 60282-2-RG ■ 60282-4-RG
Kallinikov, V.:Sym 1 Relief ▲ CR 1886
Kodály, Z.:Háry János (suite) RCA Gold Seal ▲ 60279-2-RG (m) [ADD] ■ 60279-4-RG (CrO2)
Liadov, A.:Kikimora Relief ▲ CR 1886
Liadov, A.:Kikimora RCA Gold Seal ▲ 09026-60323-2 ■ 09026-60323-4
Liszt, F.:Hungarian Rhaps—No. 2 Dell'Arte ▲ CDDA 9024
Liszt, F.:Hungarian Rhaps—No. 2 Enterprise ("The Radio Years" series) ▲ ENT 42
Liszt, F.:Orpheus Dell'Arte ▲ CDDA 9024
Liszt, F.:Von der Wiege bis zum Grabe Dell'Arte ▲ CDDA 9024
Martucci, G.:Danza *(rec live, 1938)* Grammofono 2000 ▲ GRM 78593 (m)
Martucci, G.:Notturno *(rec live, 1938)* Grammofono 2000 ▲ GRM 78593 (m)
Martucci, G.:Novelletta *(rec live, 1938)* Grammofono 2000 ▲ GRM 78593 (m)
Martucci, G.:Sym 1 *(rec live, 1938)* Grammofono 2000 ▲ GRM 78593 (m)
Massenet, J.:Suite 7 Enterprise ("Palladio" series) ▲ ENT PD 4143 [ADD]
Mendelssohn, F.:Con in e Vn & Orch, Op. 64, w. J. Heifetz (vn) *(rec live)* Melodram ▲ MEL 18013
Mendelssohn, F.:A Midsummer Night's Dream (sels)—Scherzo RCA Gold Seal ▲ 60284-2-RG [ADD] ■ 60284-4-RG (CrO2)

▲ = CD ♦ = Enhanced CD Δ = MD ■ = Cassette Tape □ = DCC

NBC SO (cont.)

A. Toscanini (cnd) (cont.)

Mendelssohn, F.:A Midsummer Night's Dream (sels)—Overture, Scherzo, Intermezzo, Nocturne, Wedding March & Finale RCA Gold Seal ▲ 09026-60283-2 ■ 09026-60283-4
Mendelssohn, F.:Octet Strs—Scherzo RCA Gold Seal ▲ 60284-2-RG [ADD] ■ 60284-4-RG (CrO2)
Mendelssohn, F.:Octet Strs [orchestral version] RCA Gold Seal ▲ 09026-60283-2 ■ 09026-60283-4
Mendelssohn, F.:Sym 4 *(rec live)* Melodram ▲ MEL 18013
Mendelssohn, F.:Sym 4 RCA Gold Seal ▲ 60284-2-RG [ADD] ■ 60284-4-RG (CrO2)
Mendelssohn, F.:Sym 5 RCA Gold Seal ▲ 60284-2-RG [ADD] ■ 60284-4-RG (CrO2)
Meyerbeer, G.:Dinorah (ov) Dell'Arte ▲ CDDA 9021
Mozart, W.A.:Con Bn, w. L. Sharrow (bn) RCA Gold Seal ▲ 09026-60286-2 ■ 09026-60286-4
Mozart, W.A.:Divert Hns Strs, K.287 RCA Gold Seal ▲ 09026-60286-2 ■ 09026-60286-4
Mozart, W.A.:Ovs—Le nozze di Figaro RCA Gold Seal ▲ 09026-60286-2 ■ 09026-60286-4
Mozart, W.A.:Sym 35 RCA Gold Seal ▲ 09026-60286-2 ■ 09026-60286-4
Mozart, W.A.:Sym 39 RCA Gold Seal ▲ 09026-60285-2 ■ 09026-60285-4
Mozart, W.A.:Sym 40 Enterprise ("The Radio Years" series) ▲ ENT RY 13
Mozart, W.A.:Sym 40 RCA Gold Seal ▲ 09026-60285-2 ■ 09026-60285-4
Mozart, W.A.:Sym 40 *(rec live Dec. 25, 1937)* Myto ▲ 1 MCD 89009 (m) [ADD]
Mozart, W.A.:Sym 40 RCA Gold Seal ▲ 60271-2 [ADD] ■ 60271-4 (CrO2)
Mozart, W.A.:Sym 40 *(rec live, Carnegie Hall, Mar. 21, 1953)* Melodram 3-▲ MEL 37040 (m) [AAD]
Mozart, W.A.:Sym 41 RCA Gold Seal ▲ 09026-60285-2 ■ 09026-60285-4
Mozart, W.A.:Sym 41 *(rec 1949)* Music & Arts ▲ CD 833 [ADD]
Mussorgsky, M.:Khovanshchina (prelude) Relief ▲ CR 1886
Mussorgsky, M.:Pictures at an Exhibition RCA Gold Seal ▲ 60287-2-RG [ADD] ■ 60287-4-RG (CrO2)
NBC SO *(rec live, 1940, 1943 & 1945)* Melodram ▲ CDM 18021 (m) [AAD]
Paganini, N.:Moto perpetuo Vn & Orch *(rec Mar. 16, 1940)* dell'Arte ▲ CDDA 9020 (m)
Prokofiev, S.:Sym 1 RCA Gold Seal ▲ 09026-60323-2 ■ 09026-60323-4
Prokofiev, S.:Sym 1 *(rec Nov. 10, 1951)* Relief ▲ CR 1887 [ADD]
Puccini, G.:La Bohème, w. L. Albanese (sop), A. McKnight (sop), J. Peerce (ten), F. Valentino (bar), NBC Sym Chorus [I] RCA Gold Seal 2-▲ 60288-2-RG [ADD] 2-■ 60288-4-RG (CrO2)
Ravel, M.:Boléro Enterprise ("The Radio Years" series) ▲ ENT 42
Ravel, M.:Boléro Enterprise ("Palladio" series) ▲ ENT PD 4143 [ADD]
Ravel, M.:Daphnis et Chloé (suite 2) RCA Gold Seal ▲ 09026-60322-2 ■ 09026-60322-4
Respighi, O.:Feste Romane RCA Gold Seal ▲ 60262-2-RG (m) [ADD] ■ 60262-4-RG (CrO2)
Respighi, O.:The Fountains of Rome RCA Gold Seal ▲ 60262-2-RG (m) [ADD] ■ 60262-4-RG (CrO2)
Respighi, O.:The Pines of Rome RCA Gold Seal ▲ 60262-2-RG (m) [ADD] ■ 60262-4-RG (CrO2)
Rieti, V.:Sym 4 Premier ▲ PRCD 1033 [ADD]
Roger-Ducasse, J.:Sarabande, w. *(chorus unknown)* *(rec 4/7/46)* dell'Arte ▲ CD DA9020 (m)
Rossini, G.:Ovs—Barbiere di Siviglia, Cenerentola, Gazza ladra, Italiana in Algeri, Semiramide, Siege of Corinth, Signor Bruschino, William Tell RCA Gold Seal ▲ 60289-2-RG ■ 60289-4-RG
Rossini, G.:Sons Str Qt, w. Vladimir Horowitz (pno)—No. 3 [arr unknown] Stradivarius ▲ STV 13595 [AAD]
Roussel, A.:Le Festin de l'araignée Dell'Arte ▲ CDDA 9021
Rubinstein, A.:Valse-Caprice Enterprise ("The Radio Years" series) ▲ ENT 42
Rubinstein, A.:Valse-Caprice Relief ▲ CR 1886
Saint-Saëns, C.:Danse macabre RCA Gold Seal ▲ 09026-60322-2 ■ 09026-60322-4
Saint-Saëns, C.:Sym 3 RCA Gold Seal ▲ 60320-2-RG ■ 60320-4-RG
Schubert, Franz:Sym 2 Dell'Arte ▲ CD DA 9022
Schubert, Franz:Sym 5 RCA Gold Seal ▲ 60291-2-RG ■ 60291-4-RG
Schubert, Franz:Sym 8 RCA Gold Seal ▲ 60290-2-RG [ADD] ■ 60290-4-RG (CrO2)
Schubert, Franz:Sym 9 RCA Gold Seal ▲ 60291-2-RG ■ 60291-4-RG
Schubert, Franz:Sym 9 RCA Gold Seal ▲ 60290-2-RG [ADD] ■ 60290-4-RG (CrO2)
Schumann, R.:Manfred Ov RCA Gold Seal ▲ 09026-60292-2 ■ 09026-60292-4
Schumann, R.:Sym 2 Dell'Arte ▲ CD DA 9022
Schumann, R.:Sym 3 RCA Gold Seal ▲ 09026-60292-2 ■ 09026-60292-4
Shostakovich, D.:Sym 1 RCA Gold Seal ▲ 09026-60323-2 ■ 09026-60323-4
Shostakovich, D.:Sym 7 *(rec broadcast 1942)* RCA Gold Seal ▲ 60293-2-RG [ADD] ■ 029
Sibelius, J.:Finlandia RCA Gold Seal ▲ 09026-60294-2 ■ 09026-60294-4
Sibelius, J.:Lemminkäinen's Return *(rec 12/7/40)* dell'Arte ▲ CDDA 9020 (m)
Sibelius, J.:Pohjola's Daughter RCA Gold Seal ▲ 09026-60294-2 ■ 09026-60294-4-RG
Sibelius, J.:En Saga Dell'Arte ▲ CDDA 9024
Sibelius, J.:The Swan of Tuonela RCA Gold Seal ▲ 09026-60294-2 ■ 09026-60294-4
Sibelius, J.:Sym 2 RCA Gold Seal ▲ 09026-60294-2 ■ 09026-60294-4
Sibelius, J.:Sym 2 *(rec 2/18/39)* Dell'Arte ▲ CDDA 9019 (m)
Sibelius, J.:Sym 4 *(rec 1940)* Music & Arts ▲ CD 755
Smetana, B.:The Moldau RCA Gold Seal ▲ 60279-2-RG (m) [ADD] ■ 60279-4-RG (CrO2)
Smith, J.S.:The Star-Spangled Banner RCA Gold Seal ▲ 09026-60307-2 ■ 09026-60307-4
Sousa, J.P.:Marches & Dances—El Capitan; The Stars and Stripes Forever RCA Gold Seal ▲ 09026-60307-2 ■ 09026-60307-4
Sousa, J.P.:Stars & Stripes Forever Dell'Arte ▲ CDDA 9024
Strauss, R.:Don Juan Music & Arts ▲ CD 754
Strauss, R.:Don Juan RCA Gold Seal ▲ 09026-60296-2 ■ 09026-60296-4
Strauss, R.:Don Quixote, w. F. Miller (vc) RCA Gold Seal ▲ 60295-2-RG (m) [ADD] ■ 60295-4-RG (CrO2)
Strauss, R.:Don Quixote, w. E. Feuermann (vc) *(rec 1938)* Music & Arts ▲ CD 613 [AAD]
Strauss, R.:Ein Heldenleben *(rec 1941)* Music & Arts ▲ CD 754
Strauss, R.:Salome (dance) RCA Gold Seal ▲ 09026-60296-2 ■ 09026-60296-4
Strauss, R.:Till Eulenspiegels lustige Streiche RCA Gold Seal ▲ 09026-60296-2 ■ 09026-60296-4
Strauss, R.:Till Eulenspiegels lustige Streiche Music & Arts ▲ CD 754
Strauss, R.:Tod und Verklärung RCA Gold Seal ▲ 60295-2-RG (m) [ADD] ■ 60295-4-RG (CrO2)
Strauss, R.:Tod und Verklärung *(rec 1938)* Music & Arts ▲ CD 613
Stravinsky, I.:Pétrouchka (sels)—Tableaux Nos. 1 & 4 from the Suite RCA Gold Seal ▲ 09026-60323-2 ■ 09026-60323-4
Tchaikovsky, P.:Con 1 Pno, w. V. Horowitz (pno) *(rec 1943 broadcast)* RCA Gold Seal ▲ 60321-2-RG ■ 60321-4-RG
Tchaikovsky, P.:Con 1 Pno, w. V. Horowitz (pno) RCA Gold Seal ▲ 60449-2-RG (m) [ADD] ■ 60449-4-RG (CrO2)
Tchaikovsky, P.:Con 1 Pno, w. V. Horowitz (pno) *(rec Carnegie Hall, 4/25/43)* RCA Gold Seal ▲ 7992-2-RG (m) [ADD] ■ 7992-4-RG (CrO2)
Tchaikovsky, P.:Con 1 Pno, w. V. Horowitz (pno) *(rec Carnegie Hall, 4/25/43)* Melodram ▲ MEL 18014
Tchaikovsky, P.:Con 1 Pno, w. V. Horowitz (pno) RCA Gold Seal ▲ 60319-2-RG ■ 60319-4-RG
Tchaikovsky, P.:Nutcracker Suite RCA Gold Seal ▲ 60297-2-RG ■ 60297-4-RG
Tchaikovsky, P.:Romeo & Juliet RCA Gold Seal ▲ 60298-2-RG [ADD] ■ 60298-4-RG (CrO2)
Tchaikovsky, P.:Romeo & Juliet *(rec live 1953)* Music & Arts ▲ CD 260
Tchaikovsky, P.:Sym 6 *(rec live 1954)* Melodram ▲ MEL 18014
Tchaikovsky, P.:Sym 6 RCA Gold Seal ▲ 60297-2-RG ■ 60297-4-RG
Thomas, A.:Ovs—Mignon RCA Gold Seal ▲ 09026-60322-2 ■ 09026-60322-4
Toscanini Conducts Music by His Contemporaries dell'Arte ▲ CD DA9020 (m)
Vaughan Williams, R.:Fant on a Theme by Thomas Tallis *(rec 1938)* Relief ▲ CR 1888
Verdi, G.:Aida, w. H. Nelli (sop), E. Gustavson (mez), G. Tucker (ten), G. Valdengo (bar), Robert Shaw Chorale [I] RCA Gold Seal 3-▲ 60251-2-RG (m) [ADD] 2-■ 60251-4-RG (CrO2)
Verdi, G.:Aida, w. H. Nelli (sop), E. Gustavson (mez), G. Tucker (ten), G. Valdengo (bar), Robert Shaw Chorale [I] RCA Gold Seal 7-▲ 60326-2-RG (m) [ADD] 6-■ 60326-4-RG (CrO2)
Verdi, G.:Arias, w. J. Peerce (ten), Westminster Choir—arias from Luisa Miller *(Oh! fede negar potessi; Quando le sere al placido)* & chorus from Nabucco *(Va pensiero sull'ali dorate)* [I] RCA Gold Seal 2-▲ 60299-2-RG (m) [ADD] 2-■ 60299-4-RG (CrO2)

NBC SO (cont.)

A. Toscanini (cnd) (cont.)

Verdi, G.:Arias, w. J. Peerce (ten), Westminster Choir—arias from Luisa Miller *(Oh! fede negar potessi; Quando le sere al placido)* & chorus from Nabucco *(Va pensiero sull'ali dorate)* RCA Gold Seal 7-▲ 60326-2-RG (m) [ADD] 6-■ 60326-4-RG (CrO2)
Verdi, G.:Inno delle nazioni, w. J. Peerce (ten), Westminster Choir RCA Gold Seal 7-▲ 60326-2-RG (m) [ADD] 6-■ 60326-4-RG (CrO2)
Verdi, G.:Inno delle nazioni, w. J. Peerce (ten), Westminster Choir RCA Gold Seal 2-▲ 60299-2-RG (m) [ADD] 2-■ 60299-4-RG (CrO2)
Verdi, G.:I lombardi alla prima crociata (sels), w. V. Della Chiesa (sop), J. Peerce (ten), N. Moscona (bass)—Act 3 Trio RCA Gold Seal ▲ 60276-2-RG [ADD] ■ 60276-4-RG (CrO2)
Verdi, G.:Otello, w. H. Nelli (sop), R. Vinay (ten), G. Valdengo (bar) [I] RCA Gold Seal 2-▲ 60302-2-RG [ADD] 2-■ 60302-4-RG (CrO2)
Verdi, G.:Ovs & Preludes—Forza del destino; Luisa Miller *(rec 11/11/52)* Legato Classics ▲ LCD 136-1 (m) [ADD]
Verdi, G.:Pezzi sacri, w. Robert Shaw Chorale—No. 4 "Te Deum" [L] RCA Gold Seal 7-▲ 60326-2-RG (m) [ADD] 6-■ 60326-4-RG (CrO2)
Verdi, G.:Pezzi sacri, w. Robert Shaw Chorale—No. 4 "Te Deum" [L] RCA Gold Seal 2-▲ 60299-2-RG (m) [ADD] 2-■ 60299-4-RG (CrO2)
Verdi, G.:Requiem Mass, w. Z. Milanov (sop), B. Castagna (cta), J. Björling (ten), N. Moscona (bass), Westminster Choir [L] *(rec 11/23/40)* Melodram 3-▲ MEL 38006
Verdi, G.:Requiem Mass, w. Zinka Milanov (sop), Bruna Castagna (mez), Jussi Björling (ten), Nicola Moscona (bass), Westminster Choir *(rec Nov 23, 1940)* Music & Arts 2-▲ CD 240
Verdi, G.:Requiem Mass, w. H. Nelli (sop), F. Barbieri (mez), G. Di Stefano (Ten), C. Siepi (b-bar), Robert Shaw Chorale [L] RCA Gold Seal 2-▲ 60299-2-RG (m) [ADD] 2-■ 60299-4-RG (CrO2)
Verdi, G.:Requiem Mass, w. Z. Milanov (sop), B. Castagna (cta), J. Björling (ten), N. Moscona (bass), Westminster Choir *(rec Mar. 4, 1938)* Legato Classics 2-▲ LCD 178-2
Verdi, G.:Rigoletto (sels), w. Nan Merriman (mez), Jan Peerce (ten), Frank Valentino (bar), Nicola Moscona (bass), G. Ribla (sgr)—Act III (complete) Enterprise ("The Radio Years" series) ▲ ENT 48
Verdi, G.:Rigoletto (sels), w. Zinka Milanov (sop), Armed Forces Radio Chorus—V'ho ingannato *(rec 1938–1944)* Minerva ▲ MN A15 [ADD]
Verdi, G.:Rigoletto (act 3), w. Nan Merriman (mez), Jan Peerce (ten), Frank Valentino (bar), Nicola Moscona (bass), G. Ribla (sgr) [I] *(rec New York, 7/25/43)* Melodram 2-▲ MEL 28022 (m) [AAD]
Verdi, G.:Rigoletto (act 4), w. Z. Milanov (sop), N. Merriman (mez), J. Peerce (ten), L. Warren (bar) RCA Gold Seal ▲ 60276-2-RG [ADD] ■ 60276-4-RG (CrO2)
Verdi, G.:Te Deum, w. Westminster Choir [L] *(rec live, New York, 12/2/45)* Melodram 2-▲ MEL 28022 (m) [AAD]
Verdi, G.:Te Deum, w. Westminster Choir *(rec Nov 23, 1940)* Music & Arts 2-▲ CD 240
Verdi, G.:La traviata, w. C. N. Albanese (sop), J. Peerce (ten), R. Merrill (bar) [I] RCA Gold Seal 2-▲ 60303-2-RG [ADD] 2-■ 60303-4-RG (CrO2)
Verdi, G.:La traviata, w. C. N. Albanese (sop), J. Peerce (ten), R. Merrill (bar) Music & Arts 2-▲ CD 271
Verdi, G.:La traviata (sels)—Acts 2 & 3 [rehearsal excerpts] Relief ▲ CR 1812
Vivaldi, A.:Cons Vn, Op. 3/1-12, "L'estro armonico"—No. 11 in d *(rec live Dec. 25, 1937)* Myto ▲ 1 MCD 89009 (m) [ADD]
Vivaldi, A.:Con for 2 Vns Vc, R.565 Enterprise ("The Radio Years" series) ▲ ENT RY 13
Wagner, R.:Eine Faust-Ov RCA Gold Seal ▲ 09026-60305-2 ■ 09026-60305-4
Wagner, R.:Götterdämmerung (sels), w. H. Traubel (sop), L. Melchior (ten)—Dawn, Rhine Journey, Death & Funeral Music; Immolation Scene RCA Gold Seal ▲ 09026-60304-2 ■ 09026-60304-4
Wagner, R.:Götterdämmerung (rhine journey) Music & Arts ▲ CD 3008
Wagner, R.:Götterdämmerung (rhine journey) RCA Gold Seal ▲ 09026-60296-2 ■ 09026-60296-4
Wagner, R.:Götterdämmerung (rhine journey & funeral) RCA Gold Seal ▲ 09026-60306-2 ■ 09026-60306-4
Wagner, R.:Lohengrin (preludes)—Act 1 Prelude RCA Gold Seal ▲ 09026-60306-2 ■ 09026-60306-4
Wagner, R.:Lohengrin (preludes)—Acts 1 & 3 RCA Gold Seal ▲ 09026-60305-2 ■ 09026-60305-4
Wagner, R.:Lohengrin (preludes)—Act 1 Prelude Music & Arts ▲ CD 3008
Wagner, R.:Die Meistersinger von Nürnberg (preludes/acts 1 & 3) RCA Gold Seal ▲ 09026-60305-2 ■ 09026-60305-4
Wagner, R.:Die Meistersinger von Nürnberg (prelude/act 1) Music & Arts ▲ CD 3008
Wagner, R.:Ovs, Preludes & Orch Sels—Ov.; Bacchanale [both from Tannhäuser]; Prelude to Act 1 [from Die Meistersinger von Nürnberg]; Dawn; Siegfried's Rhine Journey [both from Die Götterdämmerung]; Forest Murmurs [from Seigfried]; Prelude to Act 1 [from Lohengrin] *(rec New York, 1954)* Originals ▲ ORISH 829 [ADD]
Wagner, R.:Parsifal (orch sels)—Preludes to Acts 1 & 3 RCA Gold Seal ▲ 09026-60305-2 ■ 09026-60305-4-RG
Wagner, R.:Parsifal (good friday) RCA Gold Seal ▲ 09026-60305-2 ■ 09026-60305-4
Wagner, R.:Der Ring des Nibelungen (sels), w. Helen Traubel (sop), Lauritz Melchoir (ten)—Complete Scene III [from Act 1 of Die Walküre]; Dawn & Bruennhilde; Siegfried's Funeral Music; Brunnhilde Immolation [all from Götterdämmerung] *(rec 1941)* Grammofono 2000 ▲ GRM 78564
Wagner, R.:Siegfried (waldweben) RCA Gold Seal ▲ 09026-60304-2 ■ 09026-60304-4
Wagner, R.:Siegfried (waldweben) Music & Arts ▲ CD 3008
Wagner, R.:Siegfried Idyll RCA Gold Seal ▲ 60264-2-RG [ADD] ■ 60264-4-RG (CrO2)
Wagner, R.:Siegfried Idyll RCA Gold Seal ▲ 09026-60296-2 ■ 09026-60296-4
Wagner, R.:Tannhäuser (orch sels)—Overture & Bacchanale RCA Gold Seal ▲ 09026-60306-2 ■ 09026-60306-4
Wagner, R.:Tannhäuser (ov & venusberg) Music & Arts ▲ CD 3008
Wagner, R.:Tristan und Isolde (prelude & liebestod) RCA Gold Seal ▲ 60264-2-RG [ADD] ■ 60264-4-RG (CrO2)
Wagner, R.:Die Walküre (sels), w. H. Traubel (sop), L. Melchior (ten)—Act 1, Scene 3 [G] RCA Gold Seal ▲ 60264-2-RG [ADD] ■ 60264-4-RG (CrO2)
Wagner, R.:Die Walküre (act 1/scene 3), w. Rose Bampton (sop), Set Svanholm (ten), NBC Sym Chorus [G] *(rec rehearsals & performance, New York, 4/4-6/47)* Myto 2-▲ 2 MCD 90316 (m) [ADD]
Wagner, R.:Die Walküre (ride of the valkyries) RCA Gold Seal ▲ 09026-60306-2 ■ 09026-60306-4
Wagner, R.:Die Walküre (ride of the valkyries) RCA Gold Seal ▲ 60264-2-RG [ADD] ■ 60264-4-RG (CrO2)
Weber, C.M. von:Ovs—Euryanthe; Der Freischütz; Oberon RCA Gold Seal ▲ 09026-60292-2 ■ 09026-60292-4

B. Walter (cnd)

Bruckner, A.:Sym 4, "Romantic" *(rec live, 1939–40)* Pearl ▲ PEA 9131 [ADD]
Mahler, G.:Sym 1 Grammofono 2000 ▲ GRM 78595 (m)
Mozart, W.A.:Con 20 Pno, w. Bruno Walter (pno) *(rec live, New York, Mar 11, 1939)* Grammofono 2000 ▲ GRM 78622
Mozart, W.A.:Con 3 Vn, w. J. Szigeti (vn) *(rec live 1951)* Music & Arts 4-▲ CD 720-4 [AAD]
Mozart, W.A.:Divert 2 Hns, K.287 *(rec live, New York, Mar 11, 1939)* Grammofono 2000 ▲ GRM 78622
Schumann, R.:Sym 4 *(rec New York City, 1940)* Grammofono 2000 ▲ GRM 78525 (m)
Smetana, B.:The Bartered Bride (ov) *(rec live, 1939–40)* Pearl ▲ PEA 9131 [ADD]
Tchaikovsky, P.:Sym 5 *(rec New York City, 1940)* Grammofono 2000 ▲ GRM 78525 (m)
Weber, C.M. von:Oberon (ov) *(rec live, 1939–40)* Pearl ▲ PEA 9131 [ADD]

Nebraska CO

J. Levick (cnd)

Parker, H.:Con Org, w. *(organist unknown)* Albany 2-▲ TROY 124/25
Parker, H.:Hora novissima, w. A. Soranno (sop), J. Simson (mez), K. Hall (b-bar), D. Andersen (b-bar), Abendmusik Chorus, Nebraska Wesleyan Univ Choir Albany 2-▲ TROY 124/25

Boyd Neel String Orch

Vol. 3, w. Ferrier, Kathleen (cta), Malcolm Sargent (cnd), London SO, Jacques Orch *(rec 1946 & 1949)* London ▲ 433470-2 LM [ADD]

Boyd Neel String Orch (cont.)
B. Britten (cnd)
Britten, B.:Serenade, Op. 31, w. Peter Pears (ten), Dennis Brain (hn) — Pearl ▲ PEA 9177 [ADD]
Britten, B.:Serenade, Op. 31, w. P. Pears (ten) *(rec 5/25/44)* — London ("Historic" series) ▲ 425996-2 [ADD]
Britten, B.:Sonnets of Michelangelo, w. P. Pears (ten) *(rec 7/54)* — London ("Historic" series) ▲ 425996-2 [AAD]
B. Neel (cnd)
Handel, G.F.:Concerti grossi, Op. 6 *(rec 1936-38))* — Pearl 2-▲ PEA 9164 [ADD]
La Nef
The Garden of Earthly Delights *(rec Saint-Alphonse-Rodriguez church, Lanaudière, Quebec, Apr. 1993)* — Dorian ▲ DOR 80135 [DDD]
Montségur:The Tragedy of the Cathars *(rec Quebec, May 1996)* — Dorian ▲ DOR 90243 [DDD]
Music for Joan the Mad, Spain, 1479-1555 *(rec Notre-Dame de Bonsecours Church on L'Iselt-sur-mer, Quebec, Sept. 1991)* — Dorian Discovery ▲ DIS 80128 [DDD]
Negative Band
Stockhausen, K.:Kurzwellen — Finnadar ■ CS 9009
Stockhausen, K.:Setzt die Segel zur Sonne — Finnadar ■ CS 9009
Nelson Riddle Orch
Blue Skies, w. Te Kanawa, Kiri (sop) — London ▲ 414666-2 LH [DDD]
The Opera Lover's Broadway:Great Voices Sing Broadway's Greatest Hits, w. Vienna PO [cnd:Herbert von Karajan], New Philharmonia Orch [cnd:Richard Bonynge], Roland Shaw Orch, London SO [cnd:John Mauceri], London Festival Orch [cnd:Robert Sharples] — London ▲ 448282-2 ■ 448282-4
Nemiga Wind Virtuosi
A. Berin, L. Muranov (cnds)
O Sole Mio:Neapolitan Songs, w. Berle Sanford Rosenberg (ten) — Olympia ▲ OLY 371 [DDD]
Netherlands Bach Society Baroque Orch
G. Leonhardt (cnd)
Biber, H. von:Requiem à 15, w. S. Paiu (sgr), B. Lettinga (alt), H. van der Kamp (bass), Netherlands Bach Society Choir — Deutsche Harmonia Mundi ▲ 05472-77277-2
Biber, H. von:Requiem à 15, w. Marta Almajano (sop), Mieke van der Sluis (sop), John Elwes (ten), Mark Padmore (ten), Frans Huijts (bar), Harry van der Kamp (bass), Netherlands Bach Society Choir *(rec Utrecht, Germany, Oct 22-24, 1994)* — Deutsche Harmonia Mundi ▲ 05472-77344-2 [DDD]
Steffani, A.:Stabat Mater, w. Marta Almajano (sop), Mieke van der Sluis (sop), John Elwes (ten), Mark Padmore (ten), Harry van der Kamp (bass), Netherlands Bach Society Choir *(rec Utrecht, Germany, Oct 22-24, 1994)* — Deutsche Harmonia Mundi ▲ 05472-77344-2 [DDD]
Valls, F.:Scala Arentina Mass, w. S. Paiu (sop), M. van der Sluis (sop), B. Lettinga (alt), D. Cordier (ct), J. Elwes (ten), H. van der Kamp (bass), Netherlands Bach Society Choir — Deutsche Harmonia Mundi ▲ 05472-77277-2
Netherlands Ballet Orch
Vries, K. de:Music of, w. Maria Orán (sop), Ketting, Montgomery, Zinman (cnds), Rotterdam PO—Areas; Bewegingen; Follia; Discantus; Phrases — Donemus ▲ CV 25
J. Carewe (cnd)
Emmerik, I. van:Architektur der Ebene — Donemus ▲ CV 27
R. van Driesten (cnd)
Webern, A.:Bach Transcription — Koch Schwann ▲ 3-1069-2 [DDD]
Webern, A.:Im Sommerwind — Koch Schwann ▲ 3-1069-2 [DDD]
Webern, A.:Passacaglia — Koch Schwann ▲ 3-1069-2 [DDD]
Webern, A.:Pieces Orch, Op. 6 — Koch Schwann ▲ 3-1069-2 [DDD]
Webern, A.:Pieces Orch, Op. 10 — Koch Schwann ▲ 3-1069-2 [DDD]
Webern, A.:Pieces Orch, Op. posth. — Koch Schwann ▲ 3-1069-2 [DDD]
Webern, A.:Vars Orch — Koch Schwann ▲ 3-1069-2 [DDD]
Porcelijn (cnd)
Loevendie, T.:Orchestral Music, The Hague PO—Orbits; Incantations; Flexio; Naima Suite — Donemus ▲ CV 24
L. Vis (cnd)
Klein, I.:Iris, w. M. Dispa (vc) — Donemus ▲ CV 27
Roosendael, J.R. van:Tala — Donemus ▲ CV 27
Rossem, A. van:Brisk — Donemus ▲ CV 27
Wagemans, P.J.:Dreams — Donemus ▲ CV 28
H. Williams (cnd)
Andriessen, L.:Anachrony 1, w. Nico de Rooij (pno), Sepp Grotenhuis (cel), Douceline Aleven (hp), Arthur Cune (vib), Nicolette Heerema (org) *(rec Amsterdam Music Theater, Oct 3-6, 1994)* — Donemus ▲ CV 54 [DDD]
Andriessen, L.:Anachrony 2, w. Han de Vries (ob) *(rec Amsterdam Music Theater, Oct 3-6, 1994)* — Donemus ▲ CV 54 [DDD]
Andriessen, L.:Ittrospezione 3, w. Gerard Bouwhuis (pno), Sepp Grotenhuis (pno), Peter van Bergen (sax), Marjan Damsté (db) *(rec Amsterdam Music Theater, Oct 3-6, 1994)* — Donemus ▲ CV 54 [DDD]
Netherlands CO
R. Bonynge (cnd)
Handel, G.F.:Rodelinda, Regina de' Longobardi, w. Joan Sutherland (sop—Rodelinda), Margaretha Elkins (mez—Bertarido's sister), Huguette Tourangeau (mez—Bertarido), Cora Canne-Meijer (alt—Unulfo), Eric Tappy (ten—Grimoaldo), Pieter van der Berg (bass—Garibaldo) *(rec Amsterdam, June 30, 1973)* — Bella Voce 2-▲ BLV 107.206 [AAD]
S. Goldberg (cnd)
Kox, H.:Con Vc, w. A. Bylsma (vc) *(rec 1970)* — Attacca ▲ Babel 9262-1 [ADD/DDD]
J.-J. Kantorow (cnd)
Bach, Joh. Christian:Con Vn & Vc, w. J.-J. Kantorow (vn), M. Fujiwara (vc) — Denon ▲ 7867 [DDD]
Haydn, J.:Con 1 Vc, w. Mari Fujiwara (vc) — Denon ▲ 7867 [DDD]
Haydn, J.:Con 2 Vc, w. Mari Fujiwara (vc) — Denon ▲ 7867 [DDD]
Mendelssohn, F.:Con in e Vn & Orch, Op. 64, w. A. Ros-Marba (vn) — Denon ▲ CO 8123 [DDD]
D. Zinman (cnd)
Bach, C.P.E.:Cons Fl, w. Aurele Nicolet (fl), R. Leppard (cnd), English CO—in a, W.166; in Bb, W.167; in A, W.168; in G, W.169 — Philips ("Classics" series) 2-▲ 442592-2
Bach, C.P.E.:Con Ob, H.466, w. Heinz Holliger (ob), R. Leppard (cnd), English CO — Philips ("Classics" series) 2-▲ 442592-2
Bach, C.P.E.:Con Ob, H.468, w. Heinz Holliger (ob), R. Leppard (cnd), English CO — Philips ("Classics" series) 2-▲ 442592-2
Bach, C.P.E.:Hp Music, w. Ursula Holliger (hp), R. Leppard (cnd), English CO—Son. in g, W.139 — Philips ("Classics" series) 2-▲ 442592-2
Bach, C.P.E.:Son Ob, H.549, w. Heinz Holliger (ob), Rama Jucker (vc), R. Leppard (cnd), English CO — Philips ("Classics" series) 2-▲ 442592-2
A. Ros-Marbá (cnd)
Bruch, M.:Con 1 Vn, w. J.-J. Kantorow (vn) — Denon ▲ CO 8123 [DDD]
D. Zinman (cnd)
Bach, Joh. Christian:Sinfs, Op. 6 — Philips ("Duo" series) 2-▲ 442275-2
Bach, Joh. Christian:Sinfs, Op. 9 — Philips ("Duo" series) 2-▲ 442275-2
Bach, Joh. Christian:Sinfs, Op. 18 — Philips ("Duo" series) 2-▲ 442275-2
Netherlands Guitar Duo
Works for 2 Guitars — Partridge ▲ 1128-2 [DDD]
Netherlands Jeugd SO
R. Kieft (cnd)
Olthuis, K.:De Naam van de Maan, w. *(soloists unknown)*, Netherlands Jeugd Chorus — Composers' Voice 2-▲ CVCD 11/12 [DDD]
Netherlands Opera Orch
C. Bruck (cnd)
The Art of Kathleen Ferrier, w. K. Ferrier (cta), Isobel Baillie (sop), Gerald Moore (pno) — EMI Classics ("Great Recordings of the Century" series) ▲ CDH 61003 (m)

Netherlands Opera Orch (cont.)
C. Bruck (cnd) (cont.)
Gluck, C.W.:Orfeo ed Euridice, w. G. Koeman (sop), D. Duval (sop), K. Ferrier (cta), Netherlands Opera Chorus *(rec live, 1951)* — Verona 2-▲ 27016/17 (m) [AAD]
F. Molinari-Pradelli (cnd)
Verdi, G.:Un ballo in maschera, w. G. Bouwenstijn (sop), E. Ratti (sop), A. Delori (cta), G. Zampieri (ten), Netherlands Opera Chorus *(rec live 1958)* — Globe 2-▲ GLO 5109
Netherlands PO
H. Haenchen (cnd)
Brahms, J.:Sym 4 — LaserLight ▲ 14 001 [DDD]
Brahms, J.:Tragic Ov — LaserLight ▲ 14 001 [DDD]
Bruckner, A.:Sym 3, "Wagner" — LaserLight ▲ 14 002 [DDD]
Mahler, G.:Sym 6 — Laserlight 2-▲ 14 140 [DDD]
J. Kantorow (cnd)
Schubert, Franz:Con Vn, w. Emmanuel Krivine (vn) — Denon ▲ CO 1666 [DDD]
E. Krivine (cnd)
Schubert, Franz:Polonaise Vn, w. J. J. Kantorow (vn) — Denon ▲ CO 1666 [DDD]
Schubert, Franz:Rondo Vn, D.438, w. J. J. Kantorow (vn) — Denon ▲ CO 1666 [DDD]
Schumann, R.:Con Vn, w. J.-J. Kantorow (vn) — Denon ▲ CO 1666 [DDD]
L. Vis (cnd)
Massenet, J.:Thérèse, w. J. Piland (sop), H. Haskin (ten), C. van Tassel (bar), Netherlands Theater Chorus [F] — Canal Grande ▲ CG 9220 [DDD]
Netherlands Radio CO
R. de Leeuw (cnd)
de Leeuw, T.:Antigone, w. Martine Mahe (mez), Netherlands Radio Male Chamber Choir — NM Classics ▲ NM 92036
Wagemans, P.J.:Requiem — Donemus ▲ CV 56 [DDD]
D. Porcelijn (cnd)
Andriessen, H.:Music of, w. Roberta Alexander (sop), Paul Verhey (fl), Ernestine Stoop (hp)—Miroir de Peine; Magna res est amor; Fiat Domine; Vars & Fugue on a Theme by Kuhnau; Vars on a Theme by Couperin; Chromatic Vars — NM Classics ▲ NM 92023
Keuris, T.:Con 2 Vn, w. Yayoi Toda (vn) — Emergo ▲ EC 3940 [DDD]
Keuris, T.:Sym — Emergo ▲ EC 3940 [DDD]
E. Spanjaard (cnd)
Bosmans, H.:Concertino Pno, w. Ronald Brautigam (pno) *(rec Geertekerk, Utrecht, May 14, 1994)* — NM Special ▲ 92095 [DDD]
Bosmans, H.:Concertino Pno, w. Ronald Brautigan (pno) — NM Classics ▲ NM 92044
Bosmans, H.:Poème, w. Dmitri Ferschtman (vc) — NM Classics ▲ NM 92040
Bosmans, H.:Poème, w. Dmitri Ferschtman (vc) *(rec Concertgebouw Haarlem, Sept 1, 1993)* — NM Special ▲ 92095 [DDD]
de Leeuw, T.:Danses sacrees, w. David Kuyken (pno) — NM Classics ▲ NM 92044
Kox, H.:Con Vc, w. Quirine Viersen (vc) — NM Classics ▲ NM 92040
Pijper, W.:Con Vc, w. Heinrich Schiff (vc) — NM Classics ▲ NM 92040
Smit, L.:Concertino Vc, w. Peter Wispelwey (vc) — NM Classics ▲ NM 92040
Smit, L.:Con Pno, w. Ronald Brautigan (pno) — NM Classics ▲ NM 92044
Van Baaren, K.:Concertino Pno, w. David Kuyken (pno) — NM Classics ▲ NM 92044
Netherlands Radio Orch
F. Vernizzi (cnd)
Mascagni, P.:Iris, w. M. Olivero (sop), L. Ottolini (ten), R. Capecchi (bar), P. Clabassi (bass), Netherlands Radio Chorus *(rec Amsterdam, 1963)* — Great Opera Performances ▲ GPO 708
Mascagni, P.:Iris, w. M. Olivero (sop), L. Ottolini (ten), R. Capecchi (bar), P. Clabassi (bass), Netherlands Radio Chorus *(rec live, 1963)* — Verona 2-▲ 27014/15 [AAD]
Netherlands Radio PO
A. Dorati (cnd)
Prokofiev, S.:Lt Kijé Suite *(rec Hilversum, Holland, May 1974)* — London ("Phase 4 Stereo" series) ▲ 444104-2 [ADD]
J. Fournet (cnd)
Bizet, G.:Les Pêcheurs de perles, w. E. Spoorenberg (sop), A. Vanzo (ten), J. Joris (bar), G. Hoekman (bass) [F] *(rec live, 1963)* — Verona 2-▲ 2707/08 (m) [AAD]
Dukas, P.:L'Apprenti sorcier *(rec Mar. 26-27, 1992)* — Denon ▲ CO 75284 [DDD]
Dukas, P.:La péri *(rec Sept. 7, 1990)* — Denon ▲ CO 75284 [DDD]
Dukas, P.:Sym in D *(rec Aug. 30, 1991)* — Denon ▲ CO 75284 [DDD]
Henkemans, H.:Villonerie, w. B. Kruysen (bar) — Donemus ▲ CV 14
Honegger, A.:Con da camera, w. Emile Biessen (fl), Miriam Hannecart-Jakes (E hn) *(rec Hilversum Music Center, Netherlands, May & Dec 1993)* — Denon ▲ CO 78831 [DDD]
Honegger, A.:Pacific 231 *(rec Hilversum Music Center, Netherlands, May & Dec 1993)* — Denon ▲ CO 78831 [DDD]
Honegger, A.:Pastorale d'été *(rec Hilversum Music Center, Netherlands, May & Dec, 1993)* — Denon ▲ CO 78831 [DDD]
Honegger, A.:Rugby *(rec Hilversum Music Center, Netherlands, May & Dec 1993)* — Denon ▲ CO 78831 [DDD]
Honegger, A.:Sym 3 *(rec Hilversum Music Center, Netherlands, May & Dec 1993)* — Denon ▲ CO 78831 [DDD]
E. Howarth (cnd)
Keuris, T.:Concerto Vn — Donemus ▲ CV 30
S. Mercurio (cnd)
Einhorn, R.:Voices of Light, w. Susan Narucki (sop), Corrie Pronk (alt), Frank Hameleers (ten), Henk van Heijnsbergen (b-bar), Ronald Hoogeveen (vn), Harm Bakker (vl), Michael Feves (vl), Naomi Hirschfeld (vl), Martin Wright (cnd), Anonymous 4, Netherlands Radio Chorus *(rec Music Center of the Netherlands Radio & TV, Aug 23-25, 1995)* — Sony Classical ▲ SK 62006 [DDD]
Z. Peskó (cnd)
Torstensson, K.:Stick on Stick *(rec 1993)* — Donemus ▲ CV 32
D. Porcelijn (cnd)
Keulen, G. van:Scena, w. Netherlands Radio Chorus — Donemus ▲ CV 33
H. Rosbaud (cnd)
Mendelssohn, F.:Die schöne Melusina *(rec live, Avro Studios, Mar 29, 1963)* — Agorá Music ("Phoenix" series) ▲ 701 [ADD]
G. Schuller (cnd)
Henkemans, H.:Con Va, w. I. van Keulen (va) — Donemus ▲ CV 14
H. Spruit (cnd)
Beethoven, L. van:Christus am Ölberg, w. Erna Spoorenberg (sop—Seraph), Fritz Wünderlich (ten—Jesus), Hermann Schey (bass—Petrus), Groot Omroep Choir *(rec Mar 8, 1957)* — Bella Voce ▲ 7003 [AAD]
E. de Waart (cnd)
Mahler, G.:Syms—Nos. 1-9 *(rec Concertgebouw, Amsterdam, 1992-95)* — RCA Red Seal 14-▲ 74321-27601-2 [DDD]
Straesser, J.:Sym 3 *(rec Concertgebouw, Amsterdam, Feb. 20, 1993)* — Donemus ▲ CV 44
Netherlands RSO
K. Bakels (cnd)
Anrooy, P. van:Piet Hein — NM Classics ▲ 92060 [DDD]
Dopper, C.:Ciaconna gotica — NM Classics ▲ 92060 [DDD]
Dopper, C.:Zuiderzee Sym — NM Classics ▲ 92060 [DDD]
Mascagni, P.:Il piccolo Marat, w. S. Neves (sop—Mariella), C. Pfeiler (mez—Principessa di Fleury), D. Galvez-Vallejo (ten—Marat), S. Cowan (bar—Soldier), M. Dirks (bar—Il Ladro), F. Vassar (bass—L'Orco), H. Claessens (bass—Spy), Netherlands Radio Chorus *(rec Feb. 9, 1992)* — Bongiovanni 2-▲ GB 2168/69 [DDD]
Netherlands Saxophone Quartet
Pierné, G.:Intro et Vars sur une ronde populaire — Elektra/Nonesuch ■ H4-71402
Torstensson, K.:Licks & Brains I — Donemus ▲ CV 13

Netherlands Saxophone Quartet (cont.)
B. Haitink (cnd)
Ketting, O.:Symphony for Saxs, Royal Concertgebouw Orch — Donemus ▲ CV 21
D. Porcelijn (cnd)
Torstensson, K.:Licks & Brains II, Asko Ensemble — Donemus ▲ CV 13
Netherlands Soloists Ensemble
Mozart, W.A.:Music of—[Disc 1] Son. Movt. for Piano, K.312; Allegro for Violin & Piano, K.372; Andante for Cello & Piano, K.Anh.46; Son. Movt. for 2 Pianos, K.Anh.42; Son. Movt. for 2 Pianos, K.Anh.43; Son. for Violin & Piano, K.403; Andante & Allegro for Violin & Piano, K.404; Son. for Piano & Violin, K.Anh.48; Son. for Piano & Violin, K.402; Son. for Piano & Violin, K.Anh.47; Son. Movt. for Piano & Violin, K.396; Allegro for Piano 4-Hands, K.357; Qt. Movt. for 2 Violins, K.Anh.72; Frag. of Qt. for Strings, K.Anh.74; 3 Pieces for Piano Trio, K.442; [Disc 2] Qnt. Movt. for Strings, K.Anh.80; Qnt. Movt. for Strings, K.Anh.79; Allegro for Violin Viola & Cello, K.Anh.91; Qnt. or Con. Movt. for Clarinet, 2 Violins, Viola & Cello, K.Anh.88; Allegro for Violin, Viola & Cello, K.Anh.66; Allegro assai for 2 Clarinets & 3 Bassethorns, K.Anh.95; Adagio for Clarinet & 3 Bassethorns, K.Anh.94; Allegro (Qnt. Movt.) for Clarinet, Bassethorn, Violin, Viola & Cello, K.Anh.90; Qnt. for Piano, Oboe, Clarinet, Bassethorn & Bassoon, K.452a; Qt. Movt. for 2 Violins, Viola & Cello, K.Anh.68; Qnt. Movt. for 2 Violins, 2 Violas & Cello, K.Anh.81; Qnt. Movt. for 2 Violins, 2 Violas & Cello, K.82; Divert. for Violin, Viola, Double Bass & 2 Horns, K.288 *(rec 1992)* — Emergo 2-▲ EC 3992 [DDD]
Netherlands Wind Ensemble
Beethoven, L. van:Octet, Op. 103 — Chandos ▲ CHAN 9470
Beethoven, L. van:Sym 7 [arr for winds] — Chandos ▲ CHAN 9470
Mozart, W.A.:Complete Mozart Edition, w. Elly Ameling (sop), Dalton Baldwin (pno) — Philips 2-▲ 422524-2 [ADD]
Wagenaar, D.:Music of, w. Gerard Bouwhuis (pno), Cees van Zeeland (pno), The Hague Percussion Group—La Volta; Stadium; Solenne; Liederen; Metrum — Donemus ▲ CV 29
R. Dufallo (cnd)
Bernstein, L.:Prelude, Fugue & Riffs Cl, w. Harmen De Boer (cl) — Chandos ("New Direction" series) ▲ CHAN 9210 [DDD]
Bernstein, L.:West Side Story (sels)—Suite [arr. Eric Crees] — Chandos ("New Direction" series) ▲ CHAN 9210 [DDD]
Copland, A.:Fanfare for the Common Man — Chandos ("New Direction" series) ▲ CHAN 9210 [DDD]
Gershwin, G.:Rhap in Blue, w. Louis Lortie (pno) — Chandos ("New Direction" series) ▲ CHAN 9210 [DDD]
Stravinsky, I.:Ebony Con — Chandos ("New Direction" series) ▲ CHAN 9210 [DDD]
T. Fischer (cnd)
Janácek, L.:Capriccio, w. Boris Berman (pno) — Chandos ▲ CHAN 9399 [DDD]
Janácek, L.:Concertino Pno, w. Boris Berman (pno) — Chandos ▲ CHAN 9399 [DDD]
Janácek, L.:Nursery Rhymes, w. Prague Academie Muzichkych Umeni — Chandos ▲ CHAN 9399 [DDD]
Janácek, L.:Youth — Chandos ▲ CHAN 9399 [DDD]
R. de Leeuw (cnd)
Messiaen, O.:Couleurs de la cité céleste, w. Peter Donohoe (pno) — Chandos ("New Direction" series) ▲ CHAN 9301/02 [DDD]
Messiaen, O.:Et exspecto resurrectionem mortuorum — Chandos ("New Direction" series) ▲ CHAN 9301/02 [DDD]
Messiaen, O.:Haïkaï, w. Peter Donohoe (pno) — Chandos ("New Direction" series) ▲ CHAN 9301/02 [DDD]
Messiaen, O.:Oiseaux exotiques, w. Peter Donohoe (pno) — Chandos ("New Direction" series) ▲ CHAN 9301/02 [DDD]
Messiaen, O.:La Ville d'en-haut, w. Peter Donohoe (pno) — Chandos ("New Direction" series) ▲ CHAN 9301/02 [DDD]
Messiaen, O.:Un Vitrail et des oiseaux, w. Peter Donohoe (pno) — Chandos ("New Direction" series) ▲ CHAN 9301/02 [DDD]
S. Mosko (cnd)
Adams, J.:Grand Pianola Music, w. Kym Amps (sop), Ruth Holton (sop), Lyndsay Wagstaff (sop), Ellen Corver (pno), Sepp Grotenhuis (pno) — Chandos ▲ CHAN 9363 [DDD]
Adams, J.:Short Ride in a Fast Machine — Chandos ▲ CHAN 9363 [DDD]
Lang, D.:Are You Experienced?, w. David Lang (nar), Hendrik Jan Renes (tuba) — Chandos ▲ CHAN 9363 [DDD]
P. Schat (cnd)
Schat, P.:Thema, w. Han de Vries (ob) — Donemus ▲ CV 19
E. de Waart (cnd)
Strauss, R.:Also sprach Zarathustra, New PO — Philips 2-▲ 438733-2
Strauss, R.:Con Ob, w. H. Holliger (ob), New PO — Philips 2-▲ 438733-2
Strauss, R.:Der Rosenkavalier (sels), New PO—Suite & Serenades — Philips 2-▲ 438733-2
Stravinsky, I.:Music of, w. Davis, Markevitch (cnds), London SO, Russian State SO, Russian State Academy Chorus—Sym. in C; Sym of Psalms; Con. for Violin & others — Philips ("Duo" series) 2-▲ 442583-2
Netherlands Wind Ensemble members
Beethoven, L. van:Qnt Pno, Ob, Cl, Hn & Bn, w. Peter Donohoe (pno) — Chandos ▲ CHAN 9470
Netherlands Wind Quintet
Hindemith, P.:Kleine Kammermusik *(rec Oct. & Dec. 1992)* — CPO ▲ CPO 999229 [DDD]
Neuchâtelois SO
T. Loosli (cnd)
Gerber, R.:Con 2 Hp, w. Line Gaudard (hp) — Gallo ▲ CD 862 [ADD]
Gerber, R.:Le Moulin de la Galette — Gallo ▲ CD 862 [ADD]
Das Neue Orch
C. Spering (cnd)
Bach, J.S.:St. Matthew Passion, w. Cologne Chorus Musicus [arr. by Mendelssohn] — Opus 111 ▲ OPS 30-74
Handel, G.F.:Acis & Galatea, w. Cologne Chorus Musicus — Opus 111 ▲ OPS 30-74
Handel, G.F.:Acis & Galatea [arr Mozart], w. Cologne Chorus Musicus — Opus 111 2-▲ OPS 45-9109/10
Handel, G.F.:Ode for St. Cecilia's Day [arr Mozart], w. Cologne Chorus Musicus [arr. Mozart] [E] — Opus 111 ▲ OPS 30-74
Handel, G.F.:Ode for St. Cecilia's Day [arr Mozart], w. Cologne Chorus Musicus — Opus 111 2-▲ OPS 45-9109/10
Le Sueur, J.-F.:Oratorios for the Coronation of Napoléon & C. X., w. Cologne Chorus Musicus — Opus 111 ▲ OPS 30-74
Le Sueur, J.-F.:Oratorios for the Coronations of the Sovereign Princes of Christendom, w. Cologne Chorus Musicus *(rec Oct. 1992)* — Opus 111 ▲ OPS 3089 [DDD]
Mendelssohn, F.:St. Paul, w. Soile Isokoski (sop), Peter Lika (bass), Rainer Trost (sgr) — Opus 111 2-▲ OPS 30-135/136
Mendelssohn, F.:Sym 2, w. S. Isokoski (sop), M. Bach (sop), F. Lang (ten), Cologne Chorus Musicus [period instrs] — Opus 111 ▲ OPS 30-98
Romberg, A.:Der Lied von der Glocke, w. B. Schlick (sop), F. Lang (ten), P. Lika (bass), Cologne Chorus Musicus *(rec May 24-27, 1992)* — Opus 111 ▲ OPS 30-67 [DDD]
Romberg, A.:Der Lied von der Glocke, w. Cologne Chorus Musicus [G] — Opus 111 ▲ OPS 30-74
Rossini, G.:Péchés de vieillesse, w. Cologne Chorus Musicus—Album Français [F] — Opus 111 ▲ OPS 30-74
Schubert, Franz:Die Verschworenen, w. *(soloists unkown)*, Cologne Chorus Musicus — Opus 111 ▲ OPS 30-167
neues kammerTrio
Diabelli, A.:Grand Serenade in F — Koch Schwann ▲ SCH 311562 [DDD]
Diabelli, A.:Grand Serenade, Op. 66 — Koch Schwann ▲ SCH 311562 [DDD]
Diabelli, A.:Grand Serenade, Op. 95 — Koch Schwann ▲ SCH 311562 [DDD]

New Albion Ensemble
A. Previn (cnd)
Kraft, William:Contextures II:The Final Beast, w. M. Rawcliffe (sop), J. Mack (ten), Los Angeles PO, Pasadena Boys' Choir [E,G,Gr,L] — Meet The Composer ▲ 79229-2 ■ 79229-4
New Amsterdam Trio [Edith Mocsanyi, John Pintavalle, Heinrich Joachim]
Shostakovich, D.:Trio 2 Pno — Vox Box 3-▲ CD3X 3021 [ADD]
New Art Wind Quintet
Riegger, W.:Con Pno, w. H. Wingreen (pno) — CRI ▲ CD 572 [ADD]
New Artis Orch
L. Vis (cnd)
Janssen, G.:Noach, w. Claron McFaddon (sop—Noach's Wife), Lieuwe Visser (bass—Noach), Huib Rooymans (nar), Mondriaan Quartet, Ay-Kherel Ensemble *(rec Amsterdam, June 20-21, 1994)* — Donemus 2-▲ CV 42/43
New Bach Collegium Musicum
B. Glaetzner (cnd)
Hertel, J.W.:Cons Various Solo Instruments & Orch, w. B. Glaetzner (ob)—Cons. for Oboe Nos. 6-9 — Berlin Classics ▲ BER 1009 [DDD]
Mozart, W.A.:Con 17 Pno, w. C. Schornsheim (pno) — LaserLight ▲ 15 872 [DDD]
Mozart, W.A.:Con 18 Pno, w. C. Schornsheim (pno) — LaserLight ▲ 15 872 [DDD]
Mozart, W.A.:Con 19 Pno, w. C. Schornsheim (pno) — Laserlight ▲ 15 872 [DDD]
Mozart, W.A.:Divert Hns Strs, K.247 — Berlin Classics ▲ BER 1086 [DDD]
Mozart, W.A.:Divert Ob, K.251 — Berlin Classics ▲ BER 1086 [DDD]
Mozart, W.A.:March Hns, K.248 — Berlin Classics ▲ BER 1086 [DDD]
M. Pommer (cnd)
Bach, J.S.:Cant 55, w. Venceslava Hruba-Freiberger (sop), Peter Schreier (ten), Leipzig Univ Choir — Berlin Classics ▲ BER 1066 [DDD]
Handel, G.F.:Serse (sels), w. Alain Zaepffel (ct) — Laserlight ▲ 15 502
Haydn, J.:Con Tpt, w. L. Güttler (tpt) — Capriccio ▲ CDC 10010 [DDD]
Pachelbel:Canon — Laserlight ▲ 15 613
Vivaldi, A.:Cons Diverse Instrs, w. L. Mayer (mand), B. Glaetzner (ob), Güttler (tpt), Sandau (tpt), Botvay (cnd), Budapest Strings — LaserLight ▲ 15518 [DDD]
Telemann, G.P.:Con Tpt Strs in D, w. L. Güttler (tpt) — Capriccio ▲ CDC 10008 [DDD]
Vivaldi, A.:Con for 2 Tpts, w. L. Güttler (tpt), K. Sandau (tpt) — Laserlight ▲ 15 518
H.-J. Rotzsch (cnd)
Bach, J.S.:Cant 21, w. Arleen Augér (sop), Ortrun Wenkel (cta), Siegfried Jerusalem (ten), Peter Schreier (ten), Theo Adam (b-bar), Leipzig St. Thomas Church Choir — Berlin Classics ▲ BER 2175 [ADD]
Bach, J.S.:Cant 50, w. Arleen Auger (sop), Ortrun Wenkel (cta), Peter Schreier (ten), Theo Adam (b-bar), Leipzig St. Thomas Church Choir — Berlin Classics ▲ BER 2176 [ADD]
Bach, J.S.:Cant 79, w. Arleen Augér (sop), Ortrun Wenkel (cta), Peter Schreier (ten), Theo Adam (b-bar), Leipzig St. Thomas Church Choir — Berlin Classics ▲ BER 2176 [ADD]
Bach, J.S.:Cant 80, w. Arleen Augér (sop), Ortrun Wenkel (cta), Peter Schreier (ten), Theo Adam (b-bar), Leipzig St. Thomas Church Choir — Berlin Classics ▲ BER 2176 [ADD]
Bach, J.S.:Cant 137, w. Arleen Augér (sop), Ortrun Wenkel (cta), Peter Schreier (ten), Siegfried Jerusalem (ten), Theo Adam (b-bar), Leipzig St. Thomas Church Choir — Berlin Classics ▲ BER 2175 [ADD]
Bach, J.S.:Cant 192, w. Arleen Auger (sop), Ortrun Wenkel (cta), Peter Schreier (ten), Theo Adam (b-bar), Leipzig St. Thomas Church Choir — Berlin Classics ▲ BER 2176 [ADD]
New Berlin CO
M. Erxleben (cnd)
Mozart, W.A.:Adagio Vn, K.261, w. M. Erxleben (vn) — LaserLight ▲ 15 881 [DDD]
Mozart, W.A.:Con 6 Vn, w. M. Erxleben (vn) — LaserLight ▲ 15 881 [DDD]
Mozart, W.A.:Con 7 Vn, w. M. Erxleben (vn) — LaserLight ▲ 15 881 [DDD]
Mozart, W.A.:Rondo Vn, K.373, w. M. Erxleben (vn) — LaserLight ▲ 15 881 [DDD]
M. Fischer-Dieskau (cnd)
Bartók, B.:Divert *(rec live, 1992)* — BIS ▲ CD 578 [DDD]
Doráti, A.:Jesus oder Barabbas?, w. W. Quadflieg (nar), Czech PO members, Berlin HDK Chamber Choir [G] *(rec live 1992)* — BIS ▲ CD 578 [DDD]
Martinů, B.:Concertino Pno, Vn, Vc & Strs, Dresden Trio *(rec live 1992)* — BIS ▲ CD 578 [DDD]
S. Weigle (cnd)
Hartmann, K.A.:Con funèbre, w. Michael Exleben (vn) — Berlin Classics ▲ BER 1049 [DDD]
Shostakovich, D.:Con 1 Vn, w. Michael Exleben (vn) — Berlin Classics ▲ BER 1049 [DDD]
New Berlin SO
M. Erxleben (cnd)
Christmas Concertos, w. Michael Erxlaben (vn), Knut Zimmerman (vn), Hans-Peter Kirchberg (org) — Capriccio ▲ 10442 [DDD]
New Bochmann String Quartet
Janácek, L.:Qt 2 Strs *(rec Mar. 1991)* — IMP Classics ▲ PCD 985 [DDD]
Martinů, B.:Qt 2 Strs — IMP Classics ▲ PCD 985 [DDD]
New Bochmann String Quartet members
Bartók, B.:Duos (44) *(rec 3/91)* — IMP Classics ▲ PCD 985 [DDD]
New Brandenburg Collegium
A. Newman (cnd)
Schumann, R.:Con Pno, w. T. Lorango (pno) [period instruments; period Viennese piano built by Johann Baptist Streicher] — Newport Classic ▲ NPD 60034 [DDD]
New Brunswick CO
J. E. Floreen (cnd)
Hummel, J.N.:Mass in B♭, Op. 77, w. Westminster Oratorio Choir [L] — Koch International Classics ▲ KIC 7117-2 [DDD]
Hummel, J.N.:Tantum ergo, w. Westminster Oratorio Choir [L] — Koch International Classics ▲ KIC 7117-2 [DDD]
New Budapest String Quartet [András Kiss (vn), Ferenc Balogh (vn), László Bársony (va), Károly Botvay (vc)]
Atterberg, K.:Qnt Pno, w. I. Prunyi (pno) — Marco Polo ▲ 8.223405 [DDD]
Atterberg, K.:Suite 1 Orch, "Orientalisk svit" — Marco Polo ▲ 8.223405 [DDD]
Bartók, B.:Qt Strs (comp) — Hyperion 2-▲ CDD 22003
Beethoven, L. van:Qts Strs (comp)—Op. 18, Nos. 1 & 2 — Hyperion ▲ CDA 66401
Beethoven, L. van:Qts Strs (comp)—Op. 127 & Op. 135 — Hyperion ▲ CDA 66408
Beethoven, L. van:Qts Strs (comp)—Op. 18, No. 5; Op. 59, No. 1 — Hyperion ▲ CDA 66403
Borodin, A.:Qnt Pno & Strs, w. I. Prunyi (pno) — Marco Polo ▲ 8.223172 [DDD]
Borodin, A.:Qnt Vns, Va & Vcs, w. O. Kertész, Jr. (vc) — Marco Polo ▲ 8.223172 [DDD]
Brahms, J.:Qt 1 Strs — Hyperion ▲ CDA 66651
Brahms, J.:Qt 2 Strs — Hyperion ▲ CDA 66651
Brahms, J.:Qt 3 Strs — Hyperion ▲ CDA 66652
Brahms, J.:Qnt Pno, w. P. Lane (pno) — Hyperion ▲ CDA 66652
Bretón, T.:Qt in D Strs *(rec Rottenbiller Street Studio, Budapest, Dec. 18-19, 1991)* — Marco Polo ▲ 8.223745 [DDD]
Indy, V. d':Qt 3 Strs *(rec Alpha-Line Studio, Festetich Castle, Budapest, Jan 1995)* — Marco Polo ▲ 8.223691 [DDD]
Indy, V. d':Qnt Pno, w. Ilona Prunyi (pno) *(rec Alpha-Line Studio, Festetich Castle, Budapest, Oct 5-6, 1993)* — Marco Polo ▲ 8.223691 [DDD]
Kiel, F.:Qnt 1, w. I. Prunyi (pno) — Marco Polo ▲ 8.223171
Kiel, F.:Qnt 2, w. I. Prunyi (pno) — Marco Polo ▲ 8.223171
Kuhlau, F.:Qt 1 Pno, w. Ilona Prunyi (pno) *(rec Dec. 20-22, 1991)* — Marco Polo ▲ 8.223482 [DDD]
Kuhlau, F.:Qt 2 Pno, w. Ilona Prunyi (pno) *(rec Dec. 20-22, 1991)* — Marco Polo ▲ 8.223482 [DDD]
Medtner, N.:Qnt Pno, w. D. Alexeev (pno) — Hyperion ▲ CDA 66744
Spohr, L.:Qts Strs (comp)—Opp. 11, 15/1 & 27 — Marco Polo ▲ 8.223254 [DDD]

ORCH. & ENS.

New Budapest String Quartet (cont.)

Spohr, L.:Qts Strs (comp)—Op. 74/1 & 2 *(rec Rottenbiller Street Studio)* Marco Polo ▲ 8.223259 [DDD]
Spohr, L.:Qts Strs (comp)—Op. 58/1 & 2 Marco Polo ▲ 8.223256 [DDD]
Spohr, L.:Qts Strs (comp)—Opp. 84/3 & 93 Marco Polo ▲ 8.223252 [DDD]
Spohr, L.:Qts Strs (comp)—Opp. 4/1 & 2 & 15/1 Marco Polo ▲ 8.223253 [DDD]
Spohr, L.:Qts Strs (comp)—Opp. 43/11 & 12, Op. 45/1 Marco Polo ▲ 8.223257
Spohr, L.:Qts Strs (comp)—Op. 84/1 & 2 Marco Polo ▲ 8.223251 [DDD]
Spohr, L.:Qts Strs (comp)—Op. 29/1 & 2 Marco Polo ▲ 8.223255 [DDD]

New Budapest String Quartet members

Bretón, T.:Trio Pno, w. György Oravecz (pno) *(rec Rottenbiller Street Studio, Budapest, Jan. 29–30, 1992)* Marco Polo ▲ 8.223745 [DDD]
Indy, V. d':Trio 2 Pno, w. Ilona Prunyi (pno) *(rec Alpha-Line Studio, Festetich Castle, Budapest, Oct 5–6, 1993)* Marco Polo ▲ 8.223691 [DDD]

New Century CO

Shostakovich, D.:Chamber Sym, Op. 110a New Albion ▲ NA 088
Shostakovich, D.:Chamber Sym, Op. 118a New Albion ▲ NA 088
Shostakovich, D.:Pieces Str Octet New Albion ▲ NA 088

S. Canin (cnd)

Martin, F.:Etudes Str Orch *(rec St. Stephen's Church, Belvedere, CA, May 29, 1995)* New Albion ▲ NA 086

New Century Saxophone Quartet [Michael Stephenson (s sax), James Boatman (a sax), Stephen Pollack (t sax), Brad Hubbard (br sax)]

Bernstein, L.:West Side Story (sels), w. Steve Kirkman (perc) [arr J. Boatman for sax qt & perc] Channel Classics ▲ CCS 9896
Gershwin, G.:Porgy & Bess (sels), w. Steve Kirkman (perc) [arr J. Boatman for sax qt & perc] Channel Classics ▲ CCS 9896
Gould, M.:Main Street March, w. Steve Kirkman (perc) [arr J. Boatman for sax qt & perc] Channel Classics ▲ CCS 9896
Gould, M.:Main Street Waltz, w. Steve Kirkman (perc) [arr J. Boatman for sax qt & perc] Channel Classics ▲ CCS 9896
Gould, M.:Pavane, w. Steve Kirkman (perc) [arr J. Boatman for sax qt & perc] Channel Classics ▲ CCS 9896

New CO

A. Blagoeva (cnd)

Pergolesi, G.B.:Stabat mater, w. T. Gabrovska (sop), H. Angelakova (alt), Sofia Boys' Choir Gega ▲ GD 153 [DDD]

New Colophonium Bass Quartet

What a Wonderful Contrabass World!, w. Berlin PO, Contrabass Quartet Camerata ▲ 32CM 60

New Czech CO

J. Belohlávek (cnd)

Ryba, J.J.:Church Music, w. Prague Soloists Choir—Mass in C; Mass in e; Mass in B♭ Multisonic ▲ 31 0200 [DDD]

New Danish Saxophone Quartet

Contemporary Works for Saxophone Quartet Kontrapunkt ▲ 32051 [DDD]
Hansen, F.C.:À la mémoire de Dali Kontrapunkt ▲ 32051 [DDD]
Hendze, J.:The Beauty of the Beast Kontrapunkt ▲ 32051 [DDD]
Lorentzen, B.:Lines Kontrapunkt ▲ 32051 [DDD]
Nørholm, I.:Patchwork in Pink Kontrapunkt ▲ 32051 [DDD]
Roikjer, K.:Divert 6 Kontrapunkt ▲ 32051 [DDD]
Teglbjaerg, H.P.S.:Skel Kontrapunkt ▲ 32051 [DDD]

New D'Oyly Carte Opera Company Orch

Sullivan, A.:Music of—sels. from The Yoemen of the Guard; The Pirates of Penzance; HMS Pinafore; The Mikado; Iolanthe; Ruddigore; The Gondoliers Koch International Classics ▲ KIC 7203 [DDD]

New England CO

P. van Haeren (cnd)

Bach, J.S.:Con 1 for 2 Hpds, w. Alfred Genovese (ob), Andrew Kohji Taylor (vn) [orig Bach version for Ob & Vn] *(rec Campion Center, Weston, MA, Feb 1993)* Boston Records ▲ BR 1007
Barlow, W.:The Winter's Past, w. Alfred Genovese (ob) *(rec Campion Center, Weston, MA, Feb 1993)* Boston Records ▲ BR 1007
Mozart, W.A.:Con 3 Vn, w. Andrew Kohji Taylor (vn) *(rec Campion Center, Weston, MA, Feb 1993)* Boston Records ▲ BR 1007

New England Conservatory Avant-Garde Ensemble

S. Drury (cnd)

Cage, J.:Ryoanji for 4 Soloists, w. Anthony D'Amico (db), Fenwick Smith (fl), Michael Miller (ob), Petur Eiriksson (b trbn) *(rec New England Conservatory of Music, Boston, MA, Mar. 4 & 6, 1991)* Mode ▲ MODE 41

New England Conservatory Ensemble

G. Schuller (cnd)

Berg, A.:Chamber Con, w. R. Sherman (pno), R. Kollsch (vn) GM ▲ GM 2033 CD
Stravinsky, I.:Le Sacre du printemps Orch GM ▲ GM 2033 CD

New England Conservatory Jazz Big Band

J. Heiss (cnd)

Cogan, R.:Music of, w. Tamara Brooks (cnd), New England Conservatory Chorus—Gulf Coast Bound; Fierce Singleness; Events Dancing Music & Arts ▲ CD 892 [DDD]
Escot, P.:Music of, w. Tamara Brooks (cnd), New England Conservatory Chorus—Missa Triste; Mirabilis I; Jubilation Music & Arts ▲ CD 892 [DDD]

New England Conservatory Orch

L. Fleisher (cnd)

Beethoven, L. van:Con 5 Pno, "Emperor", w. Leonard Shure (pno) *(rec live, Jordan Hall, Dec 15, 1982)* Audiofon ▲ CD 72018

New England Conservatory Philharmonia

Cage, J.:Apartment House 1776, w. Walter Buckingham (sgr—Protestant), Darrell Dunn (sgr—Native American), Semenya McCord (sgr—African American), Chiam Parchi (sgr—Sephardi) *(rec New England Conservatory of Music, Boston, MA, Mar. 4 & 6, 1991)* Mode ▲ MODE 41
Cage, J.:101 *(rec New England Conservatory of Music, Boston, MA, Mar. 4 & 6, 1991)* Mode ▲ MODE 41

New England Conservatory Ragtime Ensemble

G. Schuller (cnd)

Joplin, S.:Music of EMI Classics ■ 4XS 36060

New England Conservatory Youth PO

B. Zander (cnd)

Dvořák, A.:Sym 9, "From the New World" *(rec Teatro Colon, Buenos Aires, 1995)* CPI ▲ CPI 329405 [DDD]
Elgar, E.:Enigma Vars *(rec Teatro Municipal, Santiago, Chile, June 27, 1993)* CPI ▲ CPI 329402 [DDD]
Glinka, M.:Russlan & Ludmilla (ov) *(rec Teatro Municipal, Santiago, Chile, June 27, 1993)* CPI ▲ CPI 329402 [DDD]
Tchaikovsky, P.:Con 1 Pno, w. HaeSun Paik (pno) *(rec Teatro Colon, Buenos Aires, 1995)* CPI ▲ CPI 329405 [DDD]
Tchaikovsky, P.:Sym 5 *(rec Teatro Municipal, Santiago, Chile, June 27, 1993)* CPI ▲ CPI 329402 [DDD]

New England Symphonic Ensemble

Spirituals, w. Conrad, Barbara (mez), Gregory Hopkins (cnd), Convent Avenue Concert Choir *(rec Convent Avenue Baptist Church, Harlem, NY & Fisher Hall, Santa Rosa, CA, Mar. 27, 1994 & May 23, 1)* Naxos ▲ 8.553036 [DDD]

New Ensemble

Dun, T.:Circle *(rec May 13, 1992)* CRI ▲ CD 655 [DDD]

New Ensemble (cont.)

E. Spanjaard (cnd)

Ferneyhough, B.:La Chûte d'icare Etcetera ▲ KTC 1070 [DDD]
Ferneyhough, B.:Etudes transcendentales (12) Etcetera ▲ KTC 1070 [DDD]
Ferneyhough, B.:Intermedio alla ciaccona (1986) Etcetera ▲ KTC 1070 [DDD]
Ferneyhough, B.:Mnemosyne Etcetera ▲ KTC 1070 [DDD]
Ferneyhough, B.:Superscriptio Etcetera ▲ KTC 1070 [DDD]
Gerhard, R.:Concert for 8 *(rec Tillburg, Holland, Apr 11–13, 1996)* Largo ▲ 5134 [DDD]
Gerhard, R.:Leo *(rec Vredenburg/Utrecht, Holland, Apr 26–27, 1996)* Largo ▲ 5134 [DDD]
Gerhard, R.:Libra *(rec Tillburg, Holland, Apr 11–13, 1996)* Largo ▲ 5134 [DDD]
Harvey, J.:Scena, Arditti String Quartet Montaigne ▲ MO 782034
Verbey, T.:Inversie Donemus ▲ CV 31

New European Strings

D. Sitkovetsky (cnd)

Bach, J.S.:Goldberg Vars, w. D. Sitkovetsky (vn) [arr. Sitkovetsky] Elektra/Nonesuch ▲ 79341-2 ■ 79341-4

New Events Ensemble

Escot, P.:Visione Neuma ▲ 450-81

New Finnish SO

J. Engstrom (cnd)

Sibelius, J.:Karelia Ov IMP ("Classic" series) ▲ IMP 2026
Sibelius, J.:Karelia Suite IMP ("Classic" series) ▲ IMP 2026
Sibelius, J.:King Christian II (suite) IMP ("Classic" series) ▲ IMP 2026
Sibelius, J.:En Saga IMP ("Classic" series) ▲ IMP 2026
Sibelius, J.:The Swan of Tuonela IMP ("Classic" series) ▲ IMP 2026

New Flemish SO

S. van den Broeck (cnd)

Benoit, P.:Symphonic Poem Fl, w. G. Van Riet (fl) René Gailly ▲ CD 87026 [DDD]
Fétis, F.J.:Con Fl, w. G. Van Riet (fl) René Gailly ▲ CD 87026 [DDD]
Waelput, H.:Con symphonique, w. G. Van Riet (fl) René Gailly ▲ CD 87026 [DDD]

D. Brosse (cnd)

Carron, W.:Bachianas René Gailly ▲ CD 87080 [DDD]
Coryn, R.:Due Pitture René Gailly ▲ CD 87080 [DDD]
Devreese, G.:Con 2 Vn, w. H. Raudales (vn) René Gailly ▲ CD 87080 [DDD]

P. Peire (cnd)

Britten, B.:Matinées musicales René Gailly ▲ CD 87062 [DDD]
Britten, B.:Soirées musicales René Gailly ▲ CD 87062 [DDD]
Respighi, O.:La Boutique fantastique René Gailly ▲ CD 87062 [DDD]
Respighi, O.:Rossiniana René Gailly ▲ CD 87062 [DDD]

New Friends of Music Orch

W. Goehr (cnd)

Tartini, G.:Con Vn, D.45, w. J. Szigeti (vn)—in d, D.45 *(rec 1937)* Biddulph ▲ LAB 064 [ADD]

F. Stiedry (cnd)

Bach, J.S.:Con Vn, BWV 1052, w. J. Szigeti (vn) *(rec 1940)* Biddulph ▲ LAB 064 [ADD]
Mozart, W.A.:Con 17 Pno, w. A. Schnabel (pno)—excerpt from the 2nd movt. *(rec live March 22, 1942)* Music & Arts ▲ CD 750-1 [AAD]
Mozart, W.A.:Sinf concertante Vn, K.364, w. A. Spalding (vn), W. Primrose (va) *(rec May 28, 1941)* Pearl ▲ PEA 9045 [AAD]

New Generation [O. Rios (perc), Pedro Valdés (perc), Victor Sterling (perc), Daniel Ponce (perc), Erik Charlston (perc)]

Camilo, M.:Batéy, w. P. E. Clark (sop), C.B. Rowe (sop), W. Zukof (ct), L. Bennett (ten), W. L. Lee (ten), E. Levine (bar), Puntilla (sgr) Western Wind ▲ WW 2001

New German Chamber Academy

J. Goritzki (cnd)

Boccherini, L.:Syms—Op. 21/6, G.498; Op. 35/1–3, G.509–511 CPO ▲ CPO 999175-2 [DDD]
Boccherini, L.:Syms—in D, Op. 42; in D, Op. 45; in D, G.500 CPO ▲ CPO 999178 [DDD]
Boccherini, L.:Syms—Op. 21/1–5, G.493–497 CPO ▲ CPO 999174-2 [DDD]
Boccherini, L.:Syms—in d, Op. 12/4; in B, Op. 12/5; in A Op. 12/6 CPO ▲ CPO 999173 [DDD]
Boccherini, L.:Syms—in c, Op. 7; in C, Op. 10/4; in D, G.490 CPO ▲ CPO 999084 [DDD]
Boccherini, L.:Syms—Opp. 37/3 & 4, 41 in c CPO ▲ CPO 999177 [DDD]
Boccherini, L.:Syms—Op. 12/1–3 CPO ▲ CPO 999172 [DDD]
Boccherini, L.:Syms—Op. 35/4, 5 & 6; Op. 57/1 CPO ▲ CPO 999176 [DDD]
Haydn, M.:Syms—Nos. 34, 35, 36, 37, 38, 39 *(rec Zeughaus Neuss, Apr–July 1995)* CPO ▲ CPO 999379-2 [DDD]
Pettersson, G.A.:Con 1 Str Orch CPO 2–▲ CPO 999225 [DDD]
Pettersson, G.A.:Con 2 Str Orch CPO 2–▲ CPO 999225 [DDD]
Pettersson, G.A.:Con 3 Str Orch CPO 2–▲ CPO 999225 [DDD]
Reinecke, C.:Serenade CPO ▲ CPO 999159 [DDD]
Veress, S.:Musica concertante Grammont ▲ CTSP 16-2 [ADD]
Viotti, G.B.:Con 19 Vn, w. Rainer Kussmaul (vn) CPO ▲ CPO 999324
Viotti, G.B.:Con 22 Vn, w. Rainer Kussmaul (vn) CPO ▲ CPO 999324
Volkmann, R.:Serenade 1 Strs CPO ▲ CPO 999159 [DDD]
Volkmann, R.:Serenade 2 Strs CPO ▲ CPO 999159 [DDD]
Volkmann, R.:Serenade 3 Strs CPO ▲ CPO 999159 [DDD]

New Hampshire SO

J. Bolle (cnd)

Thomson, V.:Sym 3 CRI ■ ACS 6009

New Haydn String Quartet [János Horváth (vn), Péter Sárosi (vn), György Porzsolt (va), Gábor Magyar (vc)]

Spohr, L.:Qnts Strs (comp), w. Sándor Papp (va)—No. 3 in b, Op. 69 & No. 4 in a, Op 91 *(rec Unitarian Church, Budapest, Apr 17–20, 1994)* Marco Polo ▲ 8.223599 [DDD]

New Helsinki String Quartet

Weber, C.M. von:Qnt Cl, w. Kari Kriikku (cl) Ondine ▲ ODE 820 [DDD]

New Hungarian String Quartet

Beethoven, L. van:Qt 7 Strs *(rec 1978)* Vox Box 3–▲ CD3X 3012 [ADD]
Beethoven, L. van:Qt 8 Strs *(rec 1978)* Vox Box 3–▲ CD3X 3012 [ADD]
Beethoven, L. van:Qt 8 Strs Calliope ▲ CAL 9637
Beethoven, L. van:Qt 9 Strs *(rec 1978)* Vox Box 3–▲ CD3X 3012 [ADD]
Beethoven, L. van:Qt 10 Strs, "Harp" *(rec 1978)* Vox Box 3–▲ CD3X 3012 [ADD]
Beethoven, L. van:Qt 11 Strs, "Quartetto serioso" *(rec 1978)* Vox Box 3–▲ CD3X 3012 [ADD]
Ravel, M.:Qt Strs Vox Box 2–▲ CDX 5031 [ADD]
Schubert, Franz:Qt 12 Strs Vox Box 2–▲ CDX 5022 [ADD]
Schubert, Franz:Qt 13 Strs Vox Box 2–▲ CDX 5022 [ADD]
Schubert, Franz:Qt 14 Strs Vox Box 2–▲ CDX 5022 [ADD]
Schubert, Franz:Qt 15 Strs Vox Box 2–▲ CDX 5022 [ADD]

New Irish CO

Vivaldi, A.:Cons Fl, Op. 10, w. J. Galway (fl) RCA Gold Seal ▲ 09026-61351-2 ■ 09026-61351-4

J. Fürst (cnd)

Field, J.:Cons Pno (comp), w. J. O'Conor (pno)—Nos. 1–7 Onyx 3–▲ 101/103 [AAD]
Field, J.:Cons Pno (comp), w. J. O'Conor (pno)—Nos. 6 & 7 Sound ▲ 3414

New Japan PO

M. Inoue (cnd)

Yoshimatsu, T.:Music of, w. Tokyo Flute Ensemble—Threnody to Toki; Chikap; The Age of Birds; Digital Bird Suite; 4 Pieces in Bird Shape; Random Bird Vars; Sym No. 2 Camerata 2–▲ 30CM 178/9
Yoshimatsu, T.:Threnody to Toki Camerata ("After Hours Classics" series) ▲ 20 CM 423 [DDD]

H. Iwaki (cnd)

Ikebe, S.-I.:Energeia, w. Kazuo Tomioka (s sax/a sax), Shin-ichi Iwamoto (t sax) Camerata ▲ 30CM 351 [DDD]
Ikebe, S.-I.:Sym 1 Camerata ▲ 30CM 351 [DDD]

▲ = CD ♦ = Enhanced CD Δ = MD ■ = Cassette Tape □ = DCC

New Japan PO (cont.)
H. Iwaki (cnd) (cont.)
Ikebe, S.-I.:Sym 6 Camerata ▲ 30CM 351 [DDD]
N. Otomo (cnd)
Harrison, L.:Con Pno, w. Keith Jarrett (pno) New World ▲ NW 366-2 [DDD]; ■ NW 366-4 (D)
New Jefferson Chamber Players
Thompson, R.:Qt 1 Strs *(rec Carlton College Auditorium, Northfield, MN, 1992)* Citadel ▲ CTD 88119 [DDD]
Thompson, R.:Qt 2 Strs *(rec Carlton College Auditorium, Northfield, MN, 1992)* Citadel ▲ CTD 88119 [DDD]
New Jersey Chamber Music Society
Duruflé, M.:Prélude, récitatif et vars Premier ▲ PRCD 1032
Indy, V. d':Suite Fl, Str Trio & Hp Premier ▲ PRCD 1032 [DDD]
Martin, F.:Qnt Pno Premier ▲ PRCD 1032
New Jersey Percussion Ensemble
New Jersey Percussion Ensemble, w. R. DesRoches (perc) Elektra/Nonesuch ▲ 79150-2
G. Dyke (cnd)
Biscardi, C.:Trasumanar CRI ▲ CD 565 [DDD]
P. Jarvis (cnd)
Olan, D.:Prism CRI ▲ CD 565 [AAD/DDD]
C. Wuorinen (cnd)
Wuorinen, C.:Perc Sym Elektra/Nonesuch ▲ 79150-2
Wuorinen, C.:Ringing Changes Music & Arts ▲ CD 801 [ADD]
New Jersey Percussion Ensemble members
Mazurek, R.:Encounters *(rec Merkin Hall, NYC)* Capstone ▲ CPS 8616 [DDD]
New Jersey SO
Christmas Masterpieces & Familiar Carols, w. Westminster Choir [cnd:Joseph Flummerfelt], Philadelphia Concerto Soloists members Gothic ▲ GOT 47931 ■ MC 47931
Z. Macal (cnd)
Dvořák, A.:Biblical Songs, Op. 99, w. M. Hemm (bass) *(rec Apr. 9, 1994)* Delos 2-▲ DE 3161 [DDD]
Dvořák, A.:Stabat Mater, w. K. Erickson (sop), C. Carlson (mez), J. Aler (ten), J. Cheek (bass), J. Flummerfeldt (cnd), Westminster Sym Choir *(rec Feb. 8-11, 1994)* Delos 2-▲ DE 3161 [DDD]
Glière, R.:The Red Poppy (suite), "Russian Sailors' Dance", w. Christopher Collins Lee (vn) *(rec State Theater, New Brunswick, NJ, Oct 23, 1995)* Delos ▲ DE 3178 [DDD]
Glière, R.:Sym 2 *(rec State Theater, New Brunswick, NJ, Oct 23, 1995)* Delos ▲ DE 3178 [DDD]
H. Wolff (cnd)
Harbison, J.:Con Va, w. Jamie Laredo (va) *(rec 2/91)* New World ▲ 80404-2 [DDD]
Laderman, E.:Con Double Orch *(rec 8/90)* New World ▲ 80404-2 [DDD]
New Jersey Wind Sym
A. Hovhaness (cnd)
Hovhaness, A.:Requiem & Resurrection Crystal ▲ CD805
New Juilliard Ensemble
J. Sachs (cnd)
Baley, V.:Chamber Music, w. Continuum Chamber Ensemble—Con No. 1 [chamber version]; Dreamtime Suite No. 1 [trio version]; Orpheus Singing for Ob & Str Qt; Duo Concertante for Vc & Pno Cambria ▲ CD 1087
Baley, V.:Con 1 quasi una fant, w. Tom Teh Chiu (vn) *(rec Juilliard School, NYC, Apr 22, June 21, July 12)* Cambria ▲ CD 1087
New Leipzig Bach Collegium Musicum
Classics Go to the Movies, Vol. 1, w. Hungarian State Opera Orch, Vienna Strauss Orch, Jenő Jandó (pno), Plovdiv PO, Dresden PO, Budapest SO LaserLight ▲ 15 641
New Leipzig String Quartet [Andreas Seidel (vn), Tilman Büning (vn), Ivo Bauer (va), Matthias Moosdorf (vc)]
Beethoven, L. van:Qt 14 Strs MD + G ("Gold" series) ▲ MDG 3070550 [DDD]
Blacher, B.:Variationen über eienen divergierenden c-moll Dreiklang, "Str Qt No. 5" MD + G ▲ L 3507 [DDD]
Dessau, P.:Qts (7) Strs CPO 2-▲ CPO 999002 [DDD]
Kaminski, H.:Prelude & Fugue on the name A-B-E-G-G *(rec Radio DRS 2 Studio, Zurich, Jan.-Mar. 1994)* Christophorus ▲ CHR 77148 [DDD]
Kaminski, H.:Qnt Strs, w. Karl Suske (va) *(rec Radio DRS 2 Studio, Zurich, Jan.-Mar. 1994)* Christophorus ▲ CHR 77148 [DDD]
Lutoslawski, W.:Petite Suite MD + G ▲ L 3507 [DDD]
Schoenberg, A.:Qt 1 Strs *(rec July 1992)* MD + G ▲ L 3462 [DDD]
Schubert, Franz:Qt Strs, D.2c MD + G ▲ MDG 3070601 [DDD]
Schubert, Franz:Qt 12 Strs MD + G ("Gold" series) ▲ MDG 3070550 [DDD]
Schubert, Franz:Qt 15 Strs MD + G ▲ MDG 3070601 [DDD]
New Leipzig String Quartet members
Schubert, Franz:Trio Strs, D.471 MD + G ▲ MDG 3070601 [DDD]
New London Chamber Ensemble
Stravinsky, I.:Choral Music, w. James Wood (cnd), Voronezh Chamber Choir, New London Chamber Choir—Ave Maria [1934 Slavonic version]; Pater Noster [1926 Slavonic version]; Credo [1964 Slavonic version]; The dove descending breaks the air (1962); Introitus:T.S. Eliot in memoriam (1965) Hyperion ▲ CDA 66410 [DDD]
Stravinsky, I.:Les Noces, w. James Wood (cnd), Voronezh Chamber Choir, New London Chamber Choir [R] Hyperion ▲ CDA 66410 [DDD]
New London Collective
P. Pickett (cnd)
Pilgrimage to Santiago L'Oiseau-Lyre 2-▲ 433148-2 [DDD]
New London Consort
M. Neary (cnd)
Blow, J.:Songs, w. Emma Kirby (sop), Michael Chance (ct), Westminster Abbey Choir—Whilst sullen years are past; The sullen years are past Sony Classical ▲ SK 66243
Purcell, H.:Songs, w. Emma Kirkby (sop), Michael Chance (ct), Westminster Abbey Choir—I was glad; Praise the Lord, O Jerusalem; Script for their green our groves appear; Ode for Queen Mary's Birthday; Elegy on the death of Queen Mary; The Queen's Epicedium; March; The Burial Service [composed w. Thomas Morley] Sony Classical ▲ SK 66243
Tollett, T.:Music of, w. Emma Kirby (sop), Michael Chance (ct), Westminster Abbey Choir—The Queen's Farewell (march) Sony Classical ▲ SK 66243
P. Pickett (cnd)
Bach, J.S.:Brandenburg Cons L'Oiseau-Lyre ▲ 440675-2 [DDD]
Carmina Burana, Vols. 1-4
The Feast of Fools L'Oiseau-Lyre ▲ 433194-2 OH [DDD]
Monteverdi, C.:Orfeo, w. J. M. Ainsley (ten) L'Oiseau-Lyre 2-▲ 433545-2 [DDD]
Monteverdi, C.:Vespro della Beata Vergine [L] L'Oiseau-Lyre 2-▲ 425823-2 [DDD]
Praetorius, M.:Terpsichore L'Oiseau-Lyre ▲ 414633-2 [DDD]
Sinners & Saints L'Oiseau Lyre ("Ultimate" series) ▲ 448 559-2
Susato, T.:Music of—Fanfare; Passe et medio; Bergerette Sans roch; Rondes 1, 3, 4, 5, 6, 7 & 11; Bergeret Dont vient cela; Danse de Hercules oft maticine/De Matrigale de Post/Les quatre Branles Fagot/Den Hoboeckendans; Basse Danse Mon desir; Allemaingien 1, 2, 3, 5, 6, 7 & 8; Bergerette La Brosse; Pavane La Battaille; Pavane Mille Regretz; Baillardes 2, 3, 4, 7, 9, 10, 11 & 15; Danse du Roy; Entre du Fol/La Morisque *(rec Oct. 1991)* L'Oiseau-Lyre ▲ 436131-2 [DDD]
Telemann, G.P.:Con in C Rcr, w. P. Pickett (rcr) L'Oiseau-Lyre ▲ 433043-2 [DDD]
Telemann, G.P.:Con in a for Rcr, Vl, w. P. Pickett (rcr), M. Levy (vl) L'Oiseau-Lyre ▲ 433043-2 [DDD]
Telemann, G.P.:Suite in a Fl, w. P. Pickett (rcr) L'Oiseau-Lyre ▲ 433043-2 [DDD]
New London Consort members
Mad Songs, w. Bott, Catherine (sop) L'Oiseau-Lyre ▲ 433187-2 OH [DDD]
New London Orch
R. Corp (cnd)
British Light Music Classics Hyperion ▲ CDA 66868
Milhaud, D.:Apothéose de Molière Hyperion ▲ CDA 66594 [DDD]

New London Orch (cont.)
R. Corp (cnd) (cont.)
Milhaud, D.:Le Boeuf sur le toit Hyperion ▲ CDA 66594 [DDD]
Milhaud, D.:Le Carnaval d'Aix, w. J. Gibbons (pno) Hyperion ▲ CDA 66594 [DDD]
Milhaud, D.:Le Carnaval de Londres Hyperion ▲ CDA 66594 [DDD]
Thomson, V.:Acadian Songs & Dances Hyperion ▲ CDA 66576
Thomson, V.:Fugues & Cantilenas Hyperion ▲ CDA 66576
Thomson, V.:The Plow That Broke the Plains Hyperion ▲ CDA 66576
New London Orch members
S. Cleobury (cnd)
Ives, C.:Choral Music, w. Chrisopher Hughes (org), Duke String Quartet, BBC Singers—Psalms 54, 67, 90 & 135; Easter Carol; Crossing the Bar; The Celestial Country Collins Classics ▲ COL 1479
New Mayfair Orch
R. Noble (cnd)
Mayerl, W.J.:Music of, w. Raie Da Costa (pno), Billy Mayerl (pno), Fred Hartley Quintet—Marigold; Pianolettes (6); Pno Exaggerations (4); 4 aces Suite; plus others Happy Days Nostalgia ▲ CDHD 205
New Mexico Brass Quintet
Baroque & 20th Century Works Crystal ▲ CD 563
New Mexico Brass Quintet Crystal ▲ CD 560 [DDD]
New Mozart Ensemble
Mozart, W.A.:Con 9 Pno, w. M. Tan (pno) Virgin Classics ▲ CDC 45012
Mozart, W.A.:Con 27 Pno, w. M. Tan (pno) Virgin Classics ▲ CDC 45012
New Munich Piano Trio [Hermann Lechler (pno), Adrian Lazar (vn), Gerhard Zank (vc)]
Beethoven, L. van:Songs, w. Julie Kaufmann (sop)—4 Irish Songs; 7 Welsh Songs; 8 Scottish Songs Orfeo ▲ 378951
Bernstein, L.:Anniversaries (13) Pno—8 sels Orfeo ▲ 326931 [DDD]
Bernstein, L.:Mass (sels)—3 Meditations for Cello & Piano Orfeo ▲ 326931 [DDD]
Bernstein, L.:Son Cl, w. U. Wurlitzer (cl) Orfeo ▲ 326931 [DDD]
Bernstein, L.:Trio Orfeo ▲ 326931 [DDD]
Spohr, L.:Trio 1 Pno Orfeo 2-▲ C 352952 H [DDD]
Spohr, L.:Trio 2 Pno Orfeo 2-▲ C 352952 H [DDD]
Spohr, L.:Trio 3 Pno Orfeo 2-▲ C 352952 H [DDD]
Spohr, L.:Trio 4 Pno Orfeo 2-▲ C 352952 H [DDD]
Spohr, L.:Trio 5 Pno Orfeo 2-▲ C 352952 H [DDD]
New Music Concerts
Evangelista, J.:Ô Bali, w. R. Aitken (fl), D. Aitken (fl) CBC ("Musica Viva" series) ▲ MVCD 1057 [DDD]
McPhee, C.:Suite in 6 Movts CBC ("Musica Viva" series) ▲ MVCD 1057 [DDD]
New Music Consort
Cage, J.:Second Construction New World ▲ 80405-2 [AAD]
Cage, J.:Third Construction New World ▲ 80405-2 [AAD]
Cowell, H.:Pulse New World ▲ 80405-2 [AAD]
Foss, L.:Qt Perc New World ▲ 80405-2 [AAD]
Lebaron, A.:Lamentation/Invocation, w. A. Shearer (sgr), R. Yamins (sgr), M. Shapiro (vc), N. Kellman (perc), L. Bouchard (tpt) [E] Mode ▲ 30
Wen-Chung, C.:Music of, w. Boston Musica Viva, Speculum Musicae—Windswept Peaks; Suite for Hp & Ww Qnt; Echoes from the Gorge; Yü Ko Albany ▲ TROY 155
C. Heldrich (cnd)
Lebaron, A.:Rite of the Black Sun, w. W.A. Trigg (perc), F. Cassara (zoomoozophone), P. Guerguerian (perc), M. Pugliese (perc) Mode ▲ 30
A. LeBaron (cnd)
Lebaron, A.:Con for Active Frogs, w. G. Cartwright (voc), D. Shea (voc), J. Staley (voc), W. Trigg (perc) [E] Mode ▲ 30
C. H. Shapiro (cnd)
Pulse New World ▲ 80405-2 [AAD]
New Music Consort [Judith Pearce (fl), Mary Rowell (vn), Veronica Salas (va), Madeleine Shapiro (vc), Christopher Oldfather (pno)]
C. Heldrich (cnd)
Lebaron, A.:Waltz for Qnt *(rec Honrath, Germany, 1982)* Mode ▲ Mode 42
New Music Consort [Mary Rowell (vn), Judith Pearce (a fl), Robert Ingliss (E hn), Allen Blustine (b cl), Ron Borror (trbn), Donald Hayward (b trbn), Christopher Oldfather (pno), William Trigg (perc), Frank Cassara (perc)]
Chou Wen-Chung:Yü ko Albany ▲ TROY 155 [DDD]
New Music Consort [William Trigg (perc), Paul Guerguerian (perc), Franck Cassara (perc), Michael Lipsey (instr)]
Chou Wen-Chung:Echoes from the Gorge Albany ▲ TROY 155 [DDD]
New Music Studium
A. Plotino (cnd)
Stravinsky, I.:L'Histoire du soldat, w. Laurent Manzoni (nar) *(rec Torino, Italy, Jan 1995)* Arts ▲ 473572 [DDD]
Stravinsky, I.:Octet *(rec Torino, Italy, Nov 1995)* Arts ▲ 473572 [DDD]
New Opera Theater Orch
E. Kolobov (cnd)
Glinka, M.:Russlan & Ludmilla (sels), w. New Opera Theater Chorus—Fant on Russlan & Ludmilla Russian Compact Disc ▲ RCD 22001
New Orch
C. Spering (cnd)
Cherubini, L.:Requiem Mass in c, w. Cologne Chorus Musicus Opus 111 ▲ OPS 30-116
New Orleans Musica da Camera
Satires, Desires & Excesses:Songs from the 13th Century Manuscript Centaur ▲ CRC 2145 [DDD]
New Orleans Opera Orch
K. Andersson (cnd)
Floyd, C.:Markheim, w. Norman Treigle (bass—Markheim), Audrey Schuh (sgr—Tess), Alan Crofoot (sgr—Josiah Creach), William Diard (sgr—Stranger), New Orleans Opera Chorus *(rec New Orleans, LA, Mar. 31 & Apr. 2, 1966)* VAI Audio ▲ VAIA 1107
Floyd, C.:Susannah, w. Phyllis Curtin (sop—Susannah Polk), Richard Cassilly (ten—Sam Polk), Norman Treigle (bass—Olin Blitch), Marietta Muhs Cosenza (sgr—Mrs. McLean), Marilyn Davidson (sgr—Mrs. Gleaton), Kay Long (sgr—Mrs. Hayes), Jean Young (sgr—Mrs. Ott), Alton Brim (sgr—Elder Hayes), Thomas Carter (sgr—Elder Gleaton), Jack Davis (sgr—Elder McLean), Keith Kaldenberg (sgr—Little Bat McLean), Burton Parker (sgr—Elder Ott), New Orleans Opera Chorus *(rec Mar 31, 1962)* VAI Audio 2-▲ VAIA 1115-2 [ADD]
Offenbach, J.:Les Contes d'Hoffmann, w. Beverly Sills (sop—Olympia/Giulietta/Antonia/Stella), Edith Evans (mez—Nicklausse/Mother's Voice), Michael Devlin (ten—Spalanzani), André Turp (ten—Hoffmann), Luigi Vellucci (ten—Andrès/Cochenille/Pitichinaccio/Frantz), Donald Bernard (bar—Luther/Schlemil), Norman Treigle (bass—Lindorf/Coppélius/Dapertutto/Dr. Miracle), John West (bass—Crespel), Alton Brim (sgr—Nathanaël), Rodney Hall (sgr—Hermann), New Orleans Opera Chorus *(rec Feb 27, 1964)* VAI Audio 2-▲ VAIA 1121-2 [ADD]
Verdi, G.:Il trovatore, w. M. Caballé (sop), P. Domingo (ten), E. Sordello (bar), New Orleans Opera Chorus [I] *(rec live 3/14/68)* Melodram 2-▲ MEL 27047 [AAD]
R. Cellini (cnd)
Mascagni, P.:Cavalleria rusticana, w. Zinka Milanov (sop—Santuzza), Jean Craft (mez—Lucia), Marietta Cosenza (mez—Lola), Giuseppe Gismondo (ten—Turiddu), Benjamin Rayson (bar—Alfio), New Orleans Opera Chorus *(rec live, 1963)* VAI Audio ▲ VAIA 1053
Massenet, J.:Werther, w. J. Guido (sop—Sophie), N. Rankin (sop—Charlotte), C. Valletti (ten—Werther), A. Cosenza (bar—Albert) *(rec 1956)* Golden Age of Opera 2-▲ GAO 141/42 [ADD]
Puccini, G.:La Bohème, w. Licia Albanese (sop—Mimì), Audrey Schuh (sop—Musetta), Giuseppe di Stefano (ten—Rodolfo), Arthur Cosenza (bar—Schaunard), Giuseppe Valdengo (bar—Marcello), Norman Treigle (bass—Colline), Warren Gadpaille (bass—Benoît/Alcindoro), Thomas Carter (sgr—Parpignol), Harold Crane (sgr—Custom House Official), Steve Harun (sgr—Sergeant), New Orleans Opera Chorus *(rec Nov 1959)* VAI Audio 2-▲ VAIA 1119-2 [ADD]

ORCH. & ENS.

New Orleans Opera Orch (cont.)
R. Cellini (cnd) (cont.)
Puccini, G.:Madama Butterfly, w. Dorothy Kirsten (sop—Madama Butterfly), Rosalind Nadell (mez—Suzuki), Eileen Ireland (mez—Kate), Daniele Barioni (ten—Pinkerton), Thomas Carter (ten—Goro), Arthur Cosenza (ten—Yamadori), Richard Torigi (bar—Sharpless), Rodney Hall (bass—The Bronze), Harold Crane (bass—Commissioner), New Orleans Opera Chorus *(rec live, Mar 1960)* VAI Audio 2-▲ VAIA 1054-2
Saint-Saëns, C.:Samson et Dalila, w. Risë Stevens (mez—Dalila), Ramón Vinay (ten—Samson), Thomas Carter (ten—1st Philistine), Tony Lopez (ten—Philistine Messenger), Joseph Mordino (bar—High Priest), Arthur Cosenza (bass—Abimélech), Joseph Knight (bass—2nd Philistine), Ara Berberian (bass—Old Hebrew), New Orleans Opera Chorus *(rec live, Apr 2, 1960)* VAI Audio 2-▲ VAIA 1055-2 [ADD]
Verdi, G.:Falstaff, w. Vivian Della Chiesa (sop—Alice), Audrey Schuh (sop—Nannetta), Lizabeth Pritchett (mez—Quickly), Evelyn Sachs (mez—Meg), André Turp (ten—Fenton), Virginio Assandri (ten—Caius), Luigi Vellucci (ten—Bardolfo), Leonard Warren (bar—Falstaff), Richard Torigi (bar—Ford), New Orleans Opera Chorus *(rec live, May 5, 1956)* VAI Audio 2-▲ VAIA 1056-2
W. Herbert (cnd)
Gounod, C.:Faust, w. V. de los Angeles (sop), C. Ward (sgr), M. Mayhoff (sgr), R. Tucker (ten), H. Noel (sgr), N. Moscona (bass), D. Bernard (sgr) [F] *(rec Feb. 26, 1953)* Legato Classics 2-▲ LCD 167-2 [AAD]
Puccini, G.:Madama Butterfly, w. V. de los Angeles (sop), R. Nadell (mez), B. Faulkner (sgr), W. Fredericks (sgr), J. Thresh (sgr), D. Bernard (sgr), R. Torigi (sgr), A. Cosenza (bar), New Orleans Opera Chorus *(rec live March 18, 1954)* Legato Classics 2-▲ LCD 168-2 [ADD]
New Palais Royale Orch
M. Peress (cnd)
Antheil, G.:Ballet mécanique, w. percussion ensemble MusicMasters ▲ 01612-67094-2 [DDD]
Antheil, G.:A Jazz Sym, w. percussion ensemble MusicMasters ▲ 01612-67094-2 [DDD]
New Performance Group
Giteck, J.:Breathing Songs from a Turning Sky—this composition takes the form of Naftali Bacharach's 17th-cent. poem The Sefirot as a Wheel of Light, *a series of ten meditations on particular states of enlightenment* Mode ▲ 14 ■ 14CS (CrO2)
Giteck, J.:Om Shanti, w. T. Eckert (sop) New Albion ▲ NA 054
Giteck, J.:Thunder, Like A White Bear Dancing, w. Thomasa Eckert (sop) [E] Mode ▲ 14 ■ 14CS (CrO2)
New Performance Group of the Cornish Institute [Thomasa Eckert (sop), John Duykers (ten), Rinde Eckert (ten), Paul Taub (fl), Stuart Dempster (trbn), Roger Nelson (pno), Bun Ching Lam (pno), Mathew Kocmieroski (perc), Deborah Deloria (db)]
Dresher, P.:Night Songs *(rec 1983-84)* New Albion ▲ NA 053
New Philharmonia Orch
The Little Drummer Boy:Christmas Favorites, w. M. Gould (pno), Boston Pops Orch [cnd:Arthur Fiedler], et al. RCA Victor ▲ 09026-61837-2 ■ 09026-61837-4
The Prima Donna Collection Highlights, w. L. Price (sop), RCA Italiana Opera Orch, London SO, Philharmonia Orch RCA Gold Seal ▲ 09026-62596-2
Pure Domingo, w. P. Domingo (ten), English CO [cnd:Julius Rudel], Madrid SO [cnd:Manuel Moreno-Buendia], Munich RSO [cnd:Eugene Kohn], National PO [cnd:Eugene Kohn], Philharmonia Orch [cnd:James Levine] Angel ▲ CDC 55616 [DDD/ADD]
Tchaikovsky, P.:Sleeping Beauty (suite) Quintessence ▲ CDQ 2100 [DDD]
C. Abbado (cnd)
Tchaikovsky, P.:Sym 2 Deutsche Grammophon ("Resonance" series) ▲ 429527-2 [ADD]
D. Atherton (cnd)
Mathias, W.:Ave Rex, w. Janet Price (sop), Kenneth Bowen (ten), Michael Rippon (bar), Geraint Evans (b-bar), Willcocks (cnd), London SO, Welsh National Opera Chorus, Windsor Bach Choir, St. George's Chapel Choristers Lyrita ▲ SRCD .324
Mathias, W.:Con 3 Pno, w. Peter Katin (pno), London SO Lyrita ▲ SRCD 325
Mathias, W.:Elegy for a Prince, w. Michael Rippon (bar), Willcocks (cnd), London SO Lyrita ▲ SRCD .324
Mathias, W.:This Worlde's Joie, w. Janet Price (sop), Kenneth Bowen (ten), Michael Rippon (bar), Willcocks (cnd), London SO, Welsh National Opera Chorus, Windsor Bach Choir, St. George's Chapel Choristers Lyrita ▲ SRCD .324
M. Atzmon (cnd)
Liszt, F.:Cons Pno, w. Garrick Ohlsson (pno) Royal Classics ▲ ROY 6445
Rachmaninoff, S.:Cons Pno (comp), w. Agustin Anievas (pno) EMI Classics ("Doublefforte" series) 2-▲ CDFB 68619
Rachmaninoff, S.:Con 2 Pno, w. A. Anievas (pno) EMI Classics ▲ CDE 67783
Rachmaninoff, S.:Preludes Pno, Opp 23 & 32, w. A. Anievas (pno) EMI Classics ▲ CDE 67783
J. Barbirolli (cnd)
Berlioz, H.:Les Nuits d'été, w. J. Baker (mez) EMI Classics ("Studio" series) ▲ CDM 69544
Mahler, G.:Songs from Rückert, w. J. Baker (mez) EMI Classics ▲ CDZB 62707
Mahler, G.:Songs from Rückert, w. J. Baker (mez) [G] EMI Classics ▲ CDC 47793 [ADD]
Mahler, G.:Sym 5 EMI Classics ▲ CDM 64749
Mahler, G.:Sym 6 *(rec live in London, 1/22/69)* Arkadia ▲ 726 [ADD]
Ravel, M.:Shéhérazade Mez, w. Janet Baker (mez) EMI Classics ("Doublefforte" series) 2-▲ CDFB 68667
Schoenberg, A.:Pelleas und Melisande EMI Classics ▲ CDM 65078
Strauss, R.:Metamorphosen EMI Classics ▲ CDM 65078
Verdi, G.:Otello, w. G. Jones (sop—Desdemona), A. di Stasio (mez—Emilia), J. McCracken (ten—Otello), P. de Palma (ten—Cassio), D. Fischer-Dieskau (bar—Iago), Ambrosian Opera Chorus EMI Classics ▲ CDMB 65296
D. Barenboim (cnd)
Bach, J.S.:Magnificat, BWV 243, w. L. Popp (sop), A. Pashley (sop), J. Baker (mez), R. Tear (ten), New Philharmonia Chorus EMI Classics ▲ CDM 64634-2
Bach, J.S.:Magnificat, BWV 243, w. Anne Pashley (sop), Lucia Popp (sop), Janet Baker (mez), Robert Tear (ten), Thomas Hemsley (bar), New Philharmonia Chorus *(rec All Saints, Tooting, London, May 1968)* EMI Classics ▲ CDK 65334 [ADD]
Goehr, A.:Romanze, w. Jacqueline du Pré (vc) *(rec 1968)* Intaglio ▲ ING 767 [ADD]
Schumann, R.:Con Vc, w. J. Du Pré (vc) EMI Classics ▲ CDM 64626
B. Bartoletti (cnd)
Puccini, G.:Manon Lescaut, w. M. Caballé (sop—Manon Lescaut), P. Domingo (ten—Des Grieux), R. Tear (ten—Edmondo), V. Sardinero (bar—Lescaut), N. Mangin (bass—Geronte), Ambrosian Opera Chorus EMI Classics ▲ CDMB 64852
P. Berglund (cnd)
Grieg, E.:Con Pno, Op. 16, w. J. Ogdon (pno) EMI Classics ▲ CDE 67772
R. Bonynge (cnd)
Home Sweet Home, w. J. Sutherland (sop), Ambrosian Light Opera Chorus London ▲ 425048-2 LC [ADD]
Meyerbeer, G.:Les Huguenots, w. J. Sutherland (sop), M. Arroyo (sop), H. Tourangeau (mez), A. Vrenios (ten), D. Cossa (bar), G. Bacquier (bar), N. Ghiuselev (bass), Ambrosian Opera Chorus London ("Grand Opera" series) 4-▲ 430549-2 [AAD]
The Opera Lover's Broadway:Great Voices Sing Broadway's Greatest Hits, w. Vienna PO [cnd:Herbert von Karajan], Roland Shaw Orch, London SO [cnd:John Mauceri], Nelson Riddle & His Orch, London Festival Orch [cnd:Robert Sharples] London ▲ 448282-2 ■ 448282-4
Operetta Gala, w. J. Sutherland (sop), Swiss Romande Orch, Ambrosian Light Opera Chorus London ("Opera Gala" series) ▲ 421880-2 LA [ADD]
Rossini, G.:Semiramide, w. J. Sutherland (sop), M. Horne (mez), Myers (sgr), Grant (sgr), Ambrosian Opera Chorus [I] *(rec live at the Theatre Royal, Drury Lane, 2/9/69)* Arkadia 2-▲ 579 (m) [ADD]
P. Boulez (cnd)
Debussy, C.:Jeux CBS ▲ MYK 37261 ■ MYT 37261
Debussy, C.:La Mer CBS ▲ MYK 37261 ■ MYT 37261
Debussy, C.:Orchestral Music, Cleveland Orch—La mer; Nocturnes; Printemps; Rapsodie; Prélude à l'après-midi d'un faune; Jeux; Images; Danses sacrée et profane Sony Classical ("Pierre Boulez Edition" series) 2-▲ SM2K 68327

New Philharmonia Orch (cont.)
P. Boulez (cnd) (cont.)
Debussy, C.:Prélude à l'après-midi d'un faune CBS ▲ MYK 37261 ■ MYT 37261
A. Boult (cnd)
Beethoven, L. van:Con Vn, Op. 61, w. J. Suk (vn) EMI Classics ▲ CDE 67765
Beethoven, L. van:Grosse Fuge Str Qt *(rec live, Royal Albert Hall Aug. 20, 1968)* Intaglio ▲ INCD 7361 [ADD]
Elgar, E.:Con Vn, w. Y. Menuhin (vn) EMI Classics ▲ CDM 64725
Strauss, R.:Don Quixote, w. Jacqueline Du Pré (vc) *(rec 1968)* EMI Classics ▲ CDC 55528
Vaughan Williams, R.:The Lark Ascending, w. H. Bean (vn) EMI Classics (British Composers) ▲ CDM 64022
Vaughan Williams, R.:Norfolk Rhap 1 EMI Classics (British Composers) ▲ CDM 64022
Vaughan Williams, R.:Sym 3, w. M. Price (sop) EMI Classics ▲ CDM 64018
Vaughan Williams, R.:Sym 4 EMI Classics (British Composers) ▲ CDM 64019
Vaughan Williams, R.:Sym 6 EMI Classics (British Composers) ▲ CDM 64019
Wagner, R.:Ovs, Preludes & Orch Sels, w. London SO, London PO—from Fliegende Holländer *(Overture)*, Götterdammerung *(Siegfried's Rhine Journey & Funeral March)*, Lohengrin *(Preludes to Acts 1 & 3)*, Meistersinger *(Overture; Prelude to Act 3)*, Parsifal *(Good Friday Music; Preludes to Acts 1 & 3; Transformation Scene)*, Rheingold *(Entrance of the Gods)*, Siegfried *(Forest Murmurs)*, Tannhäuser *(Overture; Grand March)*, Tristan *(Preludes to Acts 1 & 3)*, Walküre *(Ride of the Valkyries) (rec 1971-74)* EMI Classics 2-▲ CDZB 7 62539 2 [ADD]
I. Buketoff (cnd)
Tchaikovsky, P.:Ov 1812 RCA Victrola ▲ 7731-2-RV [DDD] ■ 7731-4-RV (CrO2)
A. Copland (cnd)
Copland, A.:Danzón Cubano CBS ▲ MK 42429 [ADD]
Copland, A.:Latin American Sketches *(rec 1972)* CBS ▲ MK 42429 [ADD]
Copland, A.:The Red Pony (suite) CBS ▲ MK 42429 [ADD]
Copland, A.:El salón México CBS ▲ MK 42429 [ADD]
A. Davis (cnd)
Fauré, G.:Pelléas et Mélisande (suite) Sony Classical ("Essential Classics" series) ▲ SBK 62644 ■ SBT 62644
Franck, C.:Sym in d *(rec 1975)* Odyssey ▲ MBK 46276 [AAD]
Grieg, E.:Peer Gynt Suites, Opp. 46 & 55, w. E. Söderström (sop) *(rec Apr. 9-10, 1976)* Sony Classical ▲ SBK 53257; ■ SBT 53257
Grieg, E.:Peer Gynt Suite 1 *(rec 1976)* Odyssey ▲ MBK 46275 [AAD] ■ YT 46275
C. von Dohnányi (cnd)
Dohnányi, E. von:Vars on a Nursery Song, w. E. Wild (pno) Chesky ▲ CD 13
A. Dorati (cnd)
Dvořák, A.:Sym 9, "From the New World" London ("Phase 4 Stereo" series) ▲ 448 947-2
Kodály, Z.:Háry János (suite) London ("Phase 4 Stereo" series) ▲ 448 947-2
E. Downes (cnd)
Goehr, A.:Sym in 1 Movt *(rec 1970)* Intaglio ▲ ING 767 [ADD]
Puccini, G.:Arias, w. L. Price (sop)—15 arias [I] RCA Red Seal ▲ 5999-2-RC [ADD]
A. Fistoulari (cnd)
Bruch, M.:Con 1 Vn, w. T. Wanami (vn) *(rec ca. 1977)* Chandos ("Collect" series) ▲ CHAN 6558 [ADD]
Tchaikovsky, P.:Con Vn, w. T. Wanami (vn) *(rec ca. 1977)* Chandos ("Collect" series) ▲ CHAN 6558 [ADD]
A. Francis (cnd)
Donizetti, G.:Ugo, conte di Parigi, w. E. Harrhy (sop), Y. Kenny (sop), J. Price (sop), D. Jones (mez), M. Arthur (ten), C. du Plessis (bar), Geoffrey Mitchell Choir Opera Rara 3-▲ ORC 1
M. Freccia (cnd)
Respighi, O.:The Fountains of Rome *(rec 1968)* Chesky ▲ CD 18
R. Frühbeck de Burgos (cnd)
Albéniz, I.:Suite española London ("Jubilee" series) ▲ 417786-2 [ADD]
Falla, M. de:El amor brujo (sels), w. V. de los Angeles (sop) EMI Classics ▲ CDM 64746
Falla, M. de:El amor brujo (sels) London ("Jubilee" series) ▲ 417786-2 [ADD]
Falla, M. de:Noches en los jardines de España, w. G. Soriano (pno) EMI Classics ▲ CDM 64746
Mendelssohn, F.:Elijah, w. Gwyneth Jones (sop), Janet Baker (mez), Simon Woolf (trb), Nicolai Gedda (ten), Dietrich Fischer-Dieskau (bar), New Philharmonia Chorus, Wandsworth School Boys' Choir *(rec 1968)* EMI Classics ("Doublefforte" series) 2-▲ CDFB 68601
Mozart, W.A.:Requiem, w. E. Mathis (sop), G. Bumbry (mez), G. Shirley (ten), M. Rintzler (bass), New Philharmonia Chorus Classics for Pleasure ▲ CDCFP 4399 [ADD]
Orff, C.:Carmina burana, w. L. Popp (sop), G. Unger (ten), R. Wolansky (bar), J. Noble (bar), New Philharmonia Chorus EMI Classics ▲ CDM 64328
Rachmaninoff, S.:Rhapsody on a Theme of Paganini, w. Agustin Anievas (pno) EMI Classics ("Doublefforte" series) 2-▲ CDFB 68619
Ravel, M.:Boléro EMI Classics ▲ CDM 64328
H. de la Fuente (cnd)
Gershwin, G.:Porgy & Bess (sels), w. D. Newman (sop), A. Woodley (bar), Mineria SO, Oklahoma City Ambassors Choir IMP Classics ▲ IMPPCD 1057 [DDD]
L. Gardelli (cnd)
Verdi, G.:Il corsaro, w. M. Caballé (sop), J. Norman (sop), J. Carreras (ten), Ambrosian Singers [I] Philips 2-▲ 426118-2 [ADD]
C. M. Giulini (cnd)
Falla, M. de:El sombrero de tres picos, w. V. de los Angeles (sop) EMI Classics ▲ CDM 64746
A. Guadagno (cnd)
Giordano, U.:Andrea Chénier, w. A. Gulin (sop—Maddalena), C. Bergonzi (ten—Andrea Chenier), S. Milnes (bar—Gérard), Ambrosian Chorus *(rec live, London, 2/8/70)* Myto 2-▲ 2 MCD 91750 [ADD]
Great Operatic Duets, w. M. Caballé (sop), Shirley Verrett (mez), Ambrosian Opera Chorus RCA Gold Seal ▲ 60818-2-RG [ADD]
B. Herrmann (cnd)
Kabalevsky, D.:Sym 2 Unicorn-Kanchana ("Souvenir" series) ▲ UKCD 2066
Miaskovsky, N.:Sym 21 Unicorn-Kanchana ("Souvenir" series) ▲ UKCD 2066
J. Horenstein (cnd)
Beethoven, L. van:Con Vn, Op. 61, w. E. Gruenberg (vn) *(rec Walthamstow Town Hall, London 3/31/67)* Chesky ▲ CD52 [ADD]
Mahler, G.:Sym 7 *(rec Aug. 29, 1969)* Intaglio ▲ ING 753 [AAD]
Mahler, G.:Sym 7 *(rec live, London, Aug. 8, 1969)* Music & Arts ▲ CD 727-1 [ADD]
Nielsen, C.:Sym 5 IMP ("BBC Radio" series) ▲ IMP 5691492
Tchaikovsky, P.:Sym 5 *(rec London, April 29-30, 1968)* Chesky ▲ CD94 [ADD]
E. Inbal (cnd)
Beethoven, L. van:Con 5 Pno, "Emperor", w. C. Arrau (pno) Philips ("Duo" series) 2-▲ 442580-2
Schumann, R.:Syms (comp) Philips 2-▲ 438341-2 [DDD]
O. Klemperer (cnd)
Bach, J.S.:Mass in b, BWV 232, w. A. Giebel (sop), J. Baker (mez), N. Gedda (ten), H. Prey (bar), F. Crass (bass), BBC Sym Chorus [L] EMI Classics ("Studio" series) 2-▲ ZDMB 63364-2 [ADD]
Beethoven, L. van:Cons Pno (comp), w. D. Barenboim (pno) EMI Classics ("Studio" series) 3-▲ CDMC 63360
Beethoven, L. van:Fant Pno, Op. 80, "Choral Fant", w. D. Barenboim (pno), John Alldis Choir [G] EMI Classics ("Studio" series) 3-▲ CDMC 63360 [ADD]
Beethoven, L. van:Fant Pno, Op. 80, "Choral Fant", w. D. Barenboim (pno), John Alldis Choir [G] EMI Classics ("Studio" series) 2-▲ CDMB 69538 [ADD]
Beethoven, L. van:Missa Solemnis, w. E. Söderström (sop), M. Höffgen (cta), W. Kmentt (ten), M. Talvela (bass), New Philharmonia Chorus [L] EMI Classics ("Studio" series) 2-▲ CDMB 69538 [ADD]
Bruckner, A.:Sym 6 EMI Classics ("Studio" series) ▲ CDM 63351 [ADD]
Mozart, W.A.:Con 25 Pno, w. A. Brendel (pno) *(rec live, Royal Festival Hall 1970)* Foyer ▲ FOY 2037 [AAD]

New Philharmonia Orch (cont.)

O. Klemperer (cnd) (cont.)

Mozart, W.A.:Così fan tutte, w. M. Price (sop), L. Popp (sop), Y. Minton (mez), L. Alva (ten), G. Evans (bar), H. Sotin (bass), John Alldis Choir — EMI Classics 3-▲ CDMC 63845
Mozart, W.A.:Don Giovanni, w. C. Watson (sop), C. Ludwig (mez), N. Gedda (ten), N. Ghiaurov (bass), New Philharmonia Chorus — EMI Classics 3-▲ CDMC 63841
Mozart, W.A.:Nozze di Figaro, w. E. Söderström (sop), R. Grist (sop), T. Berganza (mez), G. Evans (bar), John Alldis Choir — EMI Classics 3-▲ CDMC 63849
Mozart, W.A.:Sym 29 — EMI Classics ("Studio" series) 4-▲ CDMD 63272 [ADD]
Mozart, W.A.:Sym 33 — EMI Classics ("Studio" series) 4-▲ CDMD 63272 [ADD]
Mozart, W.A.:Sym 40 *(rec live, Royal Festival Hall, 1970)* — Foyer ▲ FOY 2037 [AAD]
Schumann, R.:Con Pno, w. A. Fischer (pno) *(rec ca. 1963)* — EMI Classics ▲ CDM 64145
Schumann, R.:Scenes from Goethe's "Faust"—Ov. — EMI Classics ("Studio" series) 2-▲ CDMB 63613 [ADD]
Schumann, R.:Syms (comp), Philharmonia Orch — EMI Classics ("Studio" series) 2-▲ CDMB 63613 [ADD]
Wagner, R.:Der fliegende Holländer, w. Anja Silja (sop—Senta), Anneliese Burmeister (mez—Mary), Ernst Kozub (ten—Erik), Gerhard Unger (ten—Steersman), Theo Adam (bass—Dutchman), Martti Talvela (bass—Daland), BBC Sym Chorus — EMI Classics 3-▲ CDCC 55179
Wagner, R.:Der fliegende Holländer, w. A. Silja (sop), E. Kozub (ten), T. Adam (b-bar), M. Talvela (bass), BBC Sym Chorus [G] — EMI Classics ("Studio" series) 3-▲ CDMC 63344 [ADD]

H. Lazarof (cnd)

Lazarof, H.:Con Fl, w. J. Galway (fl) — CRI ▲ CD 588 [ADD]

E. Leinsdorf (cnd)

Mozart, W.A.:Così fan tutte, w. L. Price (sop), J. Raskin (sop), T. Troyanos (mez), G. Shirley (ten), S. Milnes (bar), New Philharmonia Chorus [I] — RCA Gold Seal 3-▲ 6677-2 [ADD]
Puccini, G.:Il tabarro, w. L. Price (sop), P. Domingo (ten), S. Milnes (bar), John Alldis Choir — RCA Gold Seal 2-▲ 09026-60865-2 [ADD]
Strauss, R.:Arias, w. L. Price (sop). Boston SO, London SO—selections from Ägyptische Helena *(Awakening Scene)*, Ariadne auf Naxos *(Es gibt ein Reich)*, Frau ohne Schatten *(Empress's Awakening Scene)*, Guntram *(Fass ich sie bang)*, Rosenkavalier *(Marschallin's Monologue)*, Salome *(Interlude & Final Scene)* [G] — RCA Gold Seal ▲ 60398-2-RG [ADD] ■ 60398-4-RG (CrO2)
Strauss, R.:4 Last Songs, w. L. Price (sop) [G] — RCA Gold Seal ("Papillon Collection" series) ▲ 6722-2-RG [ADD]
Strauss, R.:Die Frau ohne Schatten (sels), w. L. Price (sop)—Empress's Awakening Scene [G] — RCA Gold Seal ("Papillon Collection" series) ▲ 6722-2 RG [ADD]

R. Leppard (cnd)

Boccherini, L.:Syms — Philips ▲ 438314-2
Britten, B.:The Young Person's Guide to the Orchestra — Classics for Pleasure ▲ CDCFP 185
Mozart, W.A.:Missa, K.427, w. I. Cotrubas (sop), K. Te Kanawa (sop), W. Krenn (ten), H. Sotin (bass), John Alldis Choir [L] — EMI Classics ▲ CDC 47385
Prokofiev, S.:Peter & the Wolf, w. Richard Baker (nar) — Classics for Pleasure ▲ CDCFP 185

J. López-Cobos (cnd)

Donizetti, G.:Lucia di Lammermoor, w. M. Caballé (sop), A. Murray (mez), C. H. Ahnsjö (ten), V. Bello (ten), J. Carreras (ten), V. Sardinero (bar), S. Ramey (bass), Ambrosian Opera Chorus — Philips 2-▲ 426563-2

P. Maag (cnd)

Mendelssohn, F.:Con in e Vn & Orch, Op. 64, w. E. Fodor (vn) — RCA Silver Seal ▲ 09026-60910-2 ■ 09026-60910-4

L. Maazel (cnd)

Brahms, J.:Ein Deutsches Requiem, w. I. Cotrubas (sop), H. Prey (bar), New Philharmonia Chorus [G] *(rec 1976)* — Sony Classical ▲ SK 45853 [ADD]
Massenet, J.:Thaïs, w. Beverly Sills (sop—Thaïs), Nicolai Gedda (ten—Nicias), Sherrill Milnes (bar—Athanaël), John Alldis Choir — EMI Classics 2-▲ CDMB 65479
Ravel, M.:Boléro — EMI Classics ▲ CDE 67781
Tchaikovsky, P.:Con 1 Pno, w. Emil Gilels (pno) — EMI Classics ("Doublefforte" series) 2-▲ CDFB 68637
Tchaikovsky, P.:Con 2 Pno, w. Emil Gilels (pno) — EMI Classics ("Doublefforte" series) 2-▲ CDFB 68637
Tchaikovsky, P.:Con 3 Pno, w. Emil Gilels (pno) — EMI Classics ("Doublefforte" series) 2-▲ CDFB 68637

C. Mackerras (cnd)

Mussorgsky, M.:Pictures at an Exhibition *(rec 1973)* — Vanguard Classics ▲ OVC 4065

N. del Mar (cnd)

Strauss, R.:Songs, w. Elizabeth Harwood (sop) — IMP ("BBC Radio Classics" series) ▲ IMP 9138

E. Mata (cnd)

Revueltas, S.:Homenaje a Federico García Lorca — Catalyst ▲ 09026-62672-2
Revueltas, S.:Sensemayá — Catalyst ▲ 09026-62672-2

Z. Mehta (cnd)

Puccini, G.:Tosca, w. L. Price (sop), P. Domingo (ten), S. Milnes (bar), John Alldis Choir [I] — RCA Victrola 2-▲ RCD2-0105

W. Morris (cnd)

Mahler, G.:Das Klagende Lied, w. T. Zylis-Gara (sop), A. Roynolds (mez), A. Kaposy (ten), Ambrosian Singers [G] *(rec 1967)* — Nimbus ▲ NI 5085 [AAD]
Mahler, G.:Das Klagende Lied, w. T. Zylis-Gara (sop), A. Reynolds (mez), A. Kaposy (ten), Ambrosian Singers — IMP Classics ▲ IMPCD 1053 [DDD]

C. Munch (cnd)

Bizet, G.:L'Arlésienne (suites)—sels. — London ("Weekend Classics" series) ▲ 421632-2 [AAD]
Bizet, G.:L'Arlésienne (suites) *(rec 1966)* — London 2-▲ 443033-2 [ADD]
Bizet, G.:Carmen (suites) *(rec 1966)* — London 2-▲ 443033-2 [ADD]
Bizet, G.:Carmen (suite 1) — London ("Weekend Classics" series) ▲ 421632-2 [AAD]
Bizet, G.:La Jolie fille de Perth (suite) — London ("Weekend Classics" series) ▲ 421632-2 [AAD]
Offenbach, J.:Gaîté Parisienne *(rec 1965)* — London 2-▲ 443033-2 [ADD]
Respighi, O.:The Fountains of Rome *(rec Kingsway Hall, London, England, Jan 1966)* — London ("Phase 4 Stereo" series) ▲ 444106-2 [ADD]
Respighi, O.:The Pines of Rome *(rec Kingsway Hall, London, England, Jan 1966)* — London ("Phase 4 Stereo" series) ▲ 444106-2 [ADD]

R. Muti (cnd)

Cherubini, L.:Requiem Mass in c, w. Ambrosian Singers — EMI Classics ▲ CDC 49678
Verdi, G.:Aida, w. M. Caballé (sop), F. Cossotto (mez), P. Domingo (ten), P. Cappuccilli (bar), N. Ghiaurov (bass), Royal Opera House Chorus Covent Garden [I] — EMI Classics 3-▲ CDCC 47271 [ADD]
Verdi, G.:Un ballo in maschera, w. M. Arroyo (sop), R. Grist (sop), F. Cossotto (mez), P. Domingo (ten), P. Cappuccilli (bar), Royal Opera House Chorus Covent Garden [I] — EMI Classics (Studio) 2-▲ CDMB 69576 [ADD]
Vivaldi, A.:Gloria, RV.589, w. T. Berganza (mez), L. Valentini-Terrani (mez), New Philharmonia Chorus [L] — EMI Classics ▲ CDC 47990 [ADD]
Vivaldi, A.:Magnificat, RV.611, w. T. Berganza (mez), L. Valentini-Terrani (mez), New Philharmonia Chorus [L] — EMI Classics ▲ CDC 47990 [ADD]

S. Ozawa (cnd)

Liszt, F.:Fant on Hungarian Folk Tunes, w. P. Entremont (pno) — Sony Classical ("Essential Classics" series) ▲ SBK 48167 ■ SBT 48167

J. Pritchard (cnd)

Beethoven, L. van:Romances Vn, w. Y. Menuhin (vn) — EMI Classics ▲ CDM 64324
Chopin, F.:Con 2 Pno, w. C. Rosen (pno) — Odyssey ■ YT 31529
Liszt, F.:Con 1 Pno, w. Charles Rosen (pno) — Odyssey ■ YT 31529
Liszt, F.:Con 1 Pno, w. Charles Rosen (pno) — CBS ▲ MYK 37804 [ADD] ■ MYT 37804

G. Prêtre (cnd)

Charpentier, G.:Louise, w. I. Cotrubas (sop), J. Berbié (mez), P. Domingo (ten), M. Sénéchal (ten), G. Bacqier (bar), Ambrosian Opera Chorus [F] — Sony Classical 3-▲ S3K 46429 [ADD]

J. Rudel (cnd)

Massenet, J.:Manon, w. B. Sills (sop), N. Gedda (ten), G. Souzay (bar), G. Bacquier (bar), Ambrosian Opera Chorus [F] — EMI Classics ("Studio" series) 3-▲ CDMC 69831 [ADD]

New Philharmonia Orch (cont.)

T. Schippers (cnd)

Barber, S.:Antony & Cleopatra (sels), w. L. Price (sop)—Give Me Some Music; Give Me My Robe *(rec 1953)* — RCA Gold Seal ▲ 09026-61983-2
Barber, S.:Knoxville:Summer of 1915, w. L. Price (sop) *(rec 1953)* — RCA Gold Seal ▲ 09026-61983-2

A. Scholz (cnd)

Famous Overtures, Vol. 1 — PMG ("Vienna Masters" series) ▲ CD 160217 [DDD]
Glinka, M.:Russlan & Ludmilla (ov) — PMG ("Vienna Master" series) ▲ CD 160215 [DDD]
Tchaikovsky, P.:Sleeping Beauty (sels) — PMG (Vienna Master) ▲ CD 160215 [DDD]

M. Shostakovich (cnd)

Shostakovich, D.:Con 1 Vn, w. D. Oistrakh (vn) [original Op. 77 version] *(rec live, Royal Festival Hall, London 11/20/72)* — Intaglio ▲ INCD 7241 [ADD]

G. Solti (cnd)

The Solti Edition, w. Chicago SO, London PO, London SO, Vienna PO, Royal Opera House Orch, CO of Europe — London 25-▲ 436600-2

L. Stokowski (cnd)

Beethoven, L. van:Sym 7 — London ("Weekend Classics" series) ▲ 430218-2 [AAD]
Mussorgsky, M.:Pictures at an Exhibition [symphonic trans by Stokowski] *(rec Kingsway Hall, London, England, Sept 25, 1965)* — London ("Phase 4 Stereo" series) ▲ 443898-2 [ADD]
Rimsky-Korsakov, N.:Capriccio espagnol — London ▲ 417753-2 [ADD]
Tchaikovsky, P.:Romeo & Juliet — London ("Phase 4 Stereo" series) ▲ 448 950-2
Tchaikovsky, P.:Sleeping Beauty (sels) — London ■ 410105-4
Tchaikovsky, P.:Sleeping Beauty (sels) *(rec 1965)* — London ▲ 430140-2 [AAD]
Tchaikovsky, P.:Sleeping Beauty (sels) — London ("Phase 4 Stereo" series) ▲ 448 950-2
Tchaikovsky, P.:Swan Lake (sels) — London ("Phase 4 Stereo" series) ▲ 448 950-2
Tchaikovsky, P.:Swan Lake (sels)—Suites *(rec 1965)* — London ▲ 430140-2 [AAD]
Stokowski Encores, w. Czech PO, London SO, Royal PO — London ("Weekend Classics" series) ▲ 433876-2 LC [ADD]
Vivaldi, A.:Cons Vn, Op. 8/1-4, "The Four Seasons", w. H. Bean (vn) — London ("Weekend Classics" series) ▲ 433680-2 [ADD]

A. Titov (cnd)

Grieg, E.:Con Pno, Op. 16, w. I. Uryash (pno) — Infinity Digital ▲ QK 57227 [DDD]

E. de Waart (cnd)

Beethoven, L. van:Romances Vn, w. A. Grumiaux (vn) — Philips ▲ 420348-2 [ADD]
Strauss, R.:Also sprach Zarathustra, w. Netherlands Wind Ensemble — Philips 2-▲ 438733-2
Strauss, R.:Con Ob, w. H. Holliger (ob), Netherlands Wind Ensemble — Philips 2-▲ 438733-2
Strauss, R.:Der Rosenkavalier (sels), w. Netherlands Wind Ensemble—Suite & Serenades — Philips 2-▲ 438733-2

D. Willcocks (cnd)

Fauré, G.:Pavane Orch, w. R. Chilcott (trb), J.C. Case (bar), King's College Choir Cambridge [choral ver.] — EMI ▲ CDM 64715
Fauré, G.:Requiem, w. R. Chilcott (trb), J.C. Case (bar), King's College Choir Cambridge — EMI Classics ▲ CDM 64715

New Philharmonia Strings

P. Boulez (cnd)

Boulez, P.:Livre pour cordes — Sony Classical ("Pierre Boulez Edition" series) ▲ SMK 68335

New PO

D. Fischer-Dieskau (cnd)

Schubert, Franz:Sym 5 — Royal Classics ▲ ROY 6454
Schubert, Franz:Sym 8 — Royal Classics ▲ ROY 6454

New PO members

H. Farberman (cnd)

Kupferman, M.:Libretto — Soundspells ▲ SP 112 [ADD]

New Philharmony Orch

A. Titov (cnd)

Mozart, W.A.:Sym 40 — Infinity Digital ▲ QK 57231 [DDD]
Mozart, W.A.:Sym 41 — Infinity Digital ▲ QK 57231 [DDD]
Schumann, R.:Con Pno, w. I. Uryash (pno) — Infinity Digital ▲ QK 57227 [DDD]

New Polish PO

A. Natanek (cnd)

Chopin, F.:Con 2 Pno, w. Jerzy Sterczynski (pno) *(rec Warsaw, 1994)* — Selene ▲ CD 9405.21 [DDD]
Dobrzynski, I.F.:Con Pno, w. Jerzy Sterczynski (pno) *(rec Warsaw, 1994)* — Selene ▲ CD 9405.21 [DDD]

New Prague Trio

Mendelssohn, F.:Trio 1 Pno — Supraphon ▲ SUP 11 1303 [DDD]
Mendelssohn, F.:Trio 2 Pno — Supraphon ▲ SUP 11 1303 [DDD]

New Princess Theater Orch

J. McGlinn (cnd)

Gershwin, G.:Ovs, w. London Sinfonietta National PO, Ambrosian Opera Chorus—A Damsel in Distress; Girl Crazy; Of Thee I Sing; Tip-Toes; Primrose; Stiff Upper Lip; Oh, Kay! — EMI Classics ("Doublefforte" series) 2-▲ CDFB 68589
Gershwin, G.:Songs, w. K. Te Kanawa (sop) — EMI Classics ▲ CDC 47454 [DDD]
Kern, J.:Songs, w. London Sinfonietta National PO—The Cat and the Fiddle; The Girl from Utah; Leave It to Jane; Have a Heart; Sweet Adeline; O, Lady! Lady!; Sitting Pretty; Very Warm for May; Swing Time; Show Boat — EMI Classics ("Doublefforte" series) 2-▲ CDFB 68589
Porter, C.:Songs, London Sinfonietta National PO—Anything Goes; Can-Can; Kiss Me Kate; Gay Divorce; Night & Day — EMI Classics ("Doublefforte" series) 2-▲ CDFB 68589

New Queen's Hall Orch

H. Wood (cnd)

Elgar, E.:Con Vn, w. A. Sammons (vn) *(rec 1929 for Columbia Records)* — Pearl ▲ PEA 9496 (m) [AAD]

B. Wordsworth (cnd)

Vaughan Williams, R.:Fant on Greensleeves — Argo ▲ 440116-2 [DDD]
Vaughan Williams, R.:Fant on a Theme by Thomas Tallis — Argo ▲ 440116-2 [DDD]
Vaughan Williams, R.:In the Fen Country — Argo ▲ 440116-2 [DDD]
Vaughan Williams, R.:The Lark Ascending — Argo ▲ 440116-2 [DDD]
Vaughan Williams, R.:Norfolk Rhap 1 — Argo ▲ 440116-2 [DDD]
Vaughan Williams, R.:Variants of "Dives & Lazarus" — Argo ▲ 440116-2 [DDD]
Wagner, R.:Ovs, Preludes & Orch Sels—Tienzi Ov; Tannhäuser Ov; Prelude [from Act 1, Lohengrin]; Prelude [from Act 3, Tristan und Isolde]; Die Meistersinger Ov; Prelude & Close of Act 3 [from Parsifal] — Eye of the Storm 2-▲ EOS 5001 [DDD]

New River Chamber Players

T. Pusztai (cnd)

Gryc, S.:Music of, w. New World Chamber Ensemble—The Moon's Mirror; 5 Preludes for Flute Alone; 6 Mechanicals from A Midsummer Night's Dream; Delicate Balances; 3 Excursions for Oboe; Fant. Vars. On a Theme of Bela Bartók — Opus One ▲ OO 166

New Russia Orch

D. Amos (cnd)

Flagello, N.:Andante Languido — Albany ▲ TROY 143
Flagello, N.:Serenade — Albany ▲ TROY 143
Giannini, V.:Con Grosso — Albany ▲ TROY 143
Giannini, V.:Prelude & Fugue — Albany ▲ TROY 143
Gould, M.:Harvest — Albany ▲ TROY 143

S.-C. Lü (cnd)

Markov, A.:Con Vn, w. Albert Markov (vn) — Sunrise ▲ 8532
Markov, A.:Formosa Suite, w. Albert Markov (vn) — Sunrise ▲ 8532
Markov, A.:Porgy Rhap, w. Albert Markov (vn) — Sunrise ▲ 8532

New Sadler's Wells Opera Orch
S. Phipps (cnd)
Sullivan, A.:HMS Pinafore, w. New Sadler's Wells Opera Chorus [E] MCA Classics 2-▲ MCAD2-11012
Sullivan, A.:Ruddigore, w. New Sadler's Wells Opera Chorus—premiere rec'g of the original uncut score [E] MCA Classics 2-▲ MCAD2-11010 [DDD]
New School of Music Orch
T. Brooks (cnd)
Mendelssohn, F.:Die erste Walpurgisnacht, w. Mendelssohn Club Chorus Philadelphia [G] Arabesque ▲ Z 6533
New Slovak Quintet
Goodman, J.:Montségur Suite MMC ("Chamber Music" series) ▲ MMC 2010
New Sousa Band
K. Brion (cnd)
Sousa, J.P.:Marches & Dances—13 marches—The Glory of the Yankee Navy; New York Hippodrome; Solid Men to the Front!; Sabre and Spurs; The U.S. Field Artillery March; The Pride of Pittsburgh; The Free Lance; Semper Fidelis; The Royal Welch Fusiliers; Untitled March [1930]; Nobles of the Mystic Shrine; Jack Tar; The Stars and Stripes Forever Delos ▲ DE 3102 [DDD] ■ CS 3102 (D)
Sousa, J.P.:Marches & Dances Bainbridge ■ C 6250
New Stockholm CO
Larsson, L.-E.:Concertinos, w. Stockholm Chamber Ensemble, Musica Sveciae, Musica Vitae, Umea Sinfonietta—G. von Bahr (fl) *(No. 1)*, H. Jahren (ob) *(No. 2)*, M. Lethiec (cl) *(No. 3)*, K. Sonstevold (bn) *(No. 4)*, S. Hermansson (hn) *(No. 5)*, U. Agnas (tpt) *(No. 6)*, C. Lindberg (trbn) *(No. 7)*, A. Kontra (vn) *(No. 8)*, B. Andersson (va) *(No. 9)*, F. Helmerson (vc) *(No. 10)*, H. Ehren (db) *(No. 11)*, H. Palsson (pno) *(No. 12)* [these twelve neo-classical, at times Hindemithesque, three-movement concertinos were composed to suit the performing abilities of the amateur orchestra] BIS 2-▲ CD 473/74 [AAD/DDD]
P. Berglund (cnd)
Dvořák, A.:Serenade Strs BIS ▲ CD 243 [DDD]
Tchaikovsky, P.:Serenade Strs BIS ▲ CD 243 [DDD]
P. Csaba (cnd)
Britten, B.:Les Illuminations, w. C. Högman (sop) [F] BIS ▲ CD 435 [DDD]
Britten, B.:Lachrymae, w. N.-E. Sparf (va) [F] BIS ▲ CD 435 [DDD]
Britten, B.:Vars on a Theme of Frank Bridge [F] BIS ▲ CD 435 [DDD]
O. Kamu (cnd)
Larsson, L.-E.:Concertino Trbn, w. Christian Lindberg (trbn) BIS ▲ CD 348 [DDD]
Milhaud, D.:Concertino d'hiver, w. C. Lindberg (trbn) BIS ▲ CD 348 [DDD]
Pöntinen, R.:Blue Winter, w. C. Lindberg (trbn) BIS ▲ CD 348 [DDD]
Telemann, G.P.:Con Trbn, w. C. Lindberg (trbn) BIS ▲ CD 348 [DDD]
Vivaldi, A.:Cons Vn, Op. 8/1-4, "The Four Seasons", w. C. Lindberg (trbn) [trans. for solo trbn & strs]—Winter BIS ▲ CD 348 [DDD]
L. Markiz (cnd)
Schnittke, A.:Con Ob, w. H. Jahren (ob), K. A. Lier (hp) BIS ▲ CD 377 [DDD]
Schnittke, A.:Con Pno, w. R. Pöntinen (pno) BIS ▲ CD 377 [DDD]
E.-P. Salonen (cnd)
Nielsen, C.:Little Suite CBS ▲ MK 42321 [DDD]
Strauss, R.:Duet-Concertino, w. P. Meyer (cl), K. Sonstevold (bn) CBS ▲ MK 44702 [DDD]
Strauss, R.:Metamorphosen CBS ▲ MK 44702 [DDD]
Strauss, R.:Sxt Strs CBS ▲ MK 44702 [DDD]
New SO
A. Coates (cnd)
Wagner, R.:Tannhäuser (sels), w. Lauritz Melchior (ten), Walter Widdop (ten), Friedrich Schorr (b-bar), Edward Halland (bass), London SO—Ov; Venusberg Bacchanale; 1st Pilgrims' Chorus; Wolfram's Cavatina; Prelude; Pilgrims' Return; Rome Narration *(rec 1925-30)* Claremont ▲ GSE 78 50 54
New SO of London
A. Boult (cnd)
Concert Favorites *(all rec Walthamstow Town Hall, London 7/12-15/60)* Chesky ▲ CD 53 [ADD]
I. Godfrey (cnd)
Sullivan, A.:Cox & Box, D'Oyly Carte Opera Company London 2-▲ 417355-2 [ADD]
Sullivan, A.:The Gondoliers, D'Oyly Carte Opera Company London 2-▲ 425177-2 [ADD]
Sullivan, A.:HMS Pinafore, D'Oyly Carte Opera Company—highlights London ("Weekend Classics" series) ▲ 433881-2 [ADD]
Sullivan, A.:Patience, D'Oyly Carte Opera Company London 2-▲ 425193-2 [ADD]
New Tango Sex-tet [Astor Piazolla (band), Daniel Binelli (band), Horacio Malvicino (gtr), Gerardo Gandini (pno), José Bragato (vc), Hector Console (db)]
Piazzolla, A.:Music of—Hora Cero; Tanguedia; Milonga del Angel; Camorra 3; Preludio y Fuga; Sex-tet; Luna *(rec Royal Carré Theatre, Amsterdam)* Hemisphere ▲ 7243 8 35595 2 7
New Vienna Soloists
G. Meditz (cnd)
Bottesini, G.:Con 2 Db, w. W. Harrer (db) Koch Schwann ▲ SCH 313382 [ADD/DDD]
Bottesini, G.:Con 2 Db, w. W. Harrer (db) Koch Schwann ▲ CD 311112 [DDD] ■ MC 211112 (D)
Bottesini, G.:Gran Duo Concertant, w. C. Altenburger (vn), W. Harrer (db) Koch Schwann ▲ CD 311112 [DDD] ■ MC 211112 (D)
Bottesini, G.:Introduction & Gavotte, w. W. Harrer (db) Koch Schwann ▲ CD 311112 [DDD] ■ MC 211112 (D)
Bottesini, G.:Melody in e, w. W. Harrer (db) Koch Schwann ▲ CD 311112 [DDD] ■ MC 211112 (D)
Bottesini, G.:Music for Db, w. W. Harrer (db)—Melody in e Koch Schwann ▲ SCH 313382 [ADD/DDD]
New Vlach String Quartet
Arriaga, J.C.:Qts (3) Strs Multisonic ▲ 31 0172 [DDD]
Lukas, Z.:Qt 4 Strs Panton ▲ PAN 811189
New Vlach String Quartet [Jana Vlachová (vn), Ondřej Kukal (vn), Petr Verner (va), Mikael Ericsson (vc)]
Dvořák, A.:Qt 8 Strs *(rec Prague, Mar. 9, 10 & 24, 1991)* Arta ▲ 0014 [DDD]
Dvořák, A.:Qt 9 Strs *(rec Prague, Mar. 9, 10 & 24, 1991)* Arta ▲ 0014 [DDD]
New Vlach String Quartet members
Lukas, Z.:Duets Panton ▲ PAN 811186
Lukas, Z.:Duo di Basso Panton ▲ PAN 811189
New Works Calgary Ensemble [L. Eselson (fl), L. Schlessinger (vc), J. Syer (pno)]
Lee, H.:...I, Laika... New Concert Discs ▲ NCD 0294 [DDD]
New World Basset Horn Trio [Lisa Klevit (bas hn), Eric Hoeprich (bas hn), William McColl (bas hn)]
Mozart, W.A.:Diverts Bas Hns, K.Anh.229 Harmonia Mundi France ("Musique d'abord" series) ▲ HMA 1907017
Mozart, W.A.:Duos Hns—5 duos Harmonia Mundi France ("Musique d'abord" series) ▲ HMA 1907017
Stadler, A.:Trios Bas Hns—6 trios Harmonia Mundi France ("Musique d'abord" series) ▲ HMA 1907017
New World Brass [Jeffrey Biancalana (tpt), Derek Lockhart (tpt), Gregory Miller (hn), Brian Diehl (trbn), Robert Lawless (b trbn), Edwin Diefes (tuba)]
M. Tilson Thomas (cnd)
Dahl, I.:Music for Brass *(rec Au-Rene Theatre, Broward Centre for the Performing Arts, Miami, Jan 30-31, 1994)* Argo ▲ 444459-2 [DDD]
New World Chamber Ensemble
Griffes, C.T.:Tone-Pictures, Op. 5 New World ▲ NW 273-2 [ADD]
T. Pusztai (cnd)
Gryc, S.:Music of, New River Chamber Players—The Moon's Mirror; 5 Preludes for Flute Alone; 6 Mechanicals from A Midsummer Night's Dream; Delicate Balances; 3 Excursions for Oboe; Fant. Vars. On a Theme of Bela Bartók Opus One ▲ OO 166
New World Consort
Music from the Age of Discovery Musica Viva ▲ MVCD 1044 [DDD]
New World Ensemble
Ev'ry Time I Feel the Spirit:Spirituals, w. Derek Lee Ragin (male alt), Moses Hogan (pno), Chamber Choir New Orleans, Moses Hogan (cnd), et al. Channel Classics ▲ CCS 2991 [DDD]
New World Renaissance Band
Live the Legend:Love Songs of the Renaissance Nightwatch Recording ▲ NW 1001
La Tarentule Harmonia Mundi ▲ HMC 90379 [DDD]
Villancicos Harmonia Mundi ("Musique d'Abord" series) ▲ HMA 1901025
New World String Quartet [J. Yankelev (vn), W. Patterson (vn), G. Woshakiwsky (va), R. Harbaugh (vc)]
Bloch, E.:Qt 3 Strs *(rec Jan. 1978)* Vox Box 2-▲ CDX 5071 [ADD]
Brahms, J.:Qt 1 Strs IMP Masters ▲ MCD 53 [DDD]
Brahms, J.:Qt 2 Strs IMP Masters ▲ MCD 53 [DDD]
Debussy, C.:Qt Strs *(rec 1989-90)* IMP Masters ▲ MCD 17 [DDD]
Dutilleux, H.:Ainsi la nuit *(rec 1989-90)* IMP Masters ▲ MCD 17 [DDD]
Ravel, M.:Qt Strs *(rec 1989-90)* IMP Masters ▲ MCD 17 [DDD]
Rózsa, M.:Qt 1 Strs *(rec Jan. 1978)* Vox Box 2-▲ CDX 5071 [ADD]
Stravinsky, I.:Pieces Cl *(rec Jan. 1978)* Vox Box 2-▲ CDX 5071 [ADD]
Surinach, C.:Qt Strs *(rec Jan. 1978)* Vox Box 2-▲ CDX 5071 [ADD]
Tcherepnin, A.:Qt 2 Strs *(rec Jan. 1978)* Vox Box 2-▲ CDX 5071 [ADD]
New World Symphony
Flowering of Vocal Music in America, 1767-1823, w. Susan Belling (sop), Cynthia Clarey (sop), Barbara Wallace (sop), Debra Vanderlinde (sop), D'Anna Fortunato (mez), Evelyn Petros (mez), Charles Bressler (ten), Richard Anderson (bar), James Tyeska (bar), Joseph McKee (bass), Cynthia Otis (hp), et al. New World ▲ 80467-2
E. Knight (cnd)
A Classical Christmas *(rec New York)* Unison ▲ V 20015
P. Matz (cnd)
Porter, C.:Music of, w. K. Te Kanawa (sop) Angel ▲ CDQ 55050 ■ 4DQ 55050
J. Nelson (cnd)
Schoenfield, P.:Con Tpt Argo ▲ 440212-2 [DDD]
Schoenfield, P.:Klezmer Rondos Argo ▲ 440212-2 [DDD]
Schoenfield, P.:Parables Argo ▲ 440212-2 [DDD]
M. Tilson Thomas (cnd)
Dahl, I.:Con A Sax, w. John Harle (sax) *(rec Au-Rene Theatre, Broward Centre for the Performing Arts, Miami, Jan 30-31, 1994)* Argo ▲ 444459-2 [DDD]
Dahl, I.:Hymn Pno [orchd Lawrence Morton] *(rec Au-Rene Theatre, Broward Centre for the Performing Arts, Miami, Jan 30-31, 1994)* Argo ▲ 444459-2 [DDD]
Dahl, I.:The Tower of St. Barbara *(rec Au-Rene Theatre, Broward Centre for the Performing Arts, Miami, Jan 30-31, 1994)* Argo ▲ 444459-2 [DDD]
Tangazo:Music of Latin America Argo ▲ 436737-2 [DDD]
P. Urbanek (cnd)
Dvořák, A.:Sym 9, "From the New World" (1893) Laserlight ♦ 90015 [DDD]
New York Arts Orch
A. Newman (cnd)
Newman, Anthony:Con Va, w. J. Dexter (va) Newport Classic ▲ NCD 60140 [DDD]
Newman, Anthony:Largo & Rondo, w. C. Lewis (pno) Newport Classic ▲ NCD 60140 [DDD]
Newman, Anthony:Sinf 1 Newport Classic ▲ NCD 60140 [DDD]
New York Bassoon Quartet
Brehm, A.:Colloquy & Chorale Leonarda ■ LE 302 (CrO2)
Nelhybel, V.:Concert Etudes Leonarda ■ LE 302 (CrO2)
Palmer, R.:Contrasts Leonarda ■ LE 302 (CrO2)
Schickele, P.:Last Tango in Bayreuth Leonarda ■ LE 302 (CrO2)
New York Brass Quintet
Baroque Brass Victrola ■ ALK1-9538
Brass Bonanza, w. Annapolis Brass Quintet, Berlin Brass Quintet, Dallas Brass Quintet, Metropolitan Brass Quintet, 1-5 Brass Quintet, St. Louis Brass Quintet Crystal ▲ CD 200 [ADD/DDD]
Leclerc, F.:Par Monts et par vaux Crystal ▲ CD 200 [ADD]
New York Camerata
Argosh, R.:earthsong *(rec Oct 1988)* Centaur ▲ CRC 2152 [DDD]
Beveridge, T.:Radha Sings:Songs & Dances of Celestial Love *(rec Oct. 1988)* Centaur ▲ CRC 2152 [DDD]
Cory, E.:Pas de Quatre, w. Jayn Rosenfeld (fl), Diane Bruce Sinclair (vn), Charles Forbes (vc), Meg Bachman Vas (pno) Soundspells ▲ CD 116 [DDD]
Crumb, G.:Vox balaenae *(rec Oct. 1988)* Centaur ▲ CRC 2152 [DDD]
Gibson, John:A Bao A Qu *(rec Oct. 1988)* Centaur ▲ CRC 2152 [DDD]
Haydn, J.:Trios Pno, Fl & Vc—No. 17 only *(rec 1975-79)* Vox Box 3-▲ CD3X 3014 [ADD]
White, M.:Songs from Another Time *(rec Oct. 1988)* Centaur ▲ CRC 2152 [DDD]
New York Camerata [Jayn Rosenfeld (fl), Diane Bruce Sinclair (vn), Charles Forbes (vc), Meg Bachman Vas (pno)]
Cory, E.:Pas de Quatre Soundspells ▲ CD 116 [DDD]
New York Chamber Ensemble
S. R. Radcliffe (cnd)
Copland, A.:Sextet Cl, Pno & Strs Albany ▲ TROY 175 [DDD]
Griffes, C.T.:Tone-Pictures, Op. 5 Albany ▲ TROY 175 [DDD]
Hindemith, P.:Hin und zurück, w. Jeanne Ommerlé (sop—Helene), Carl Halvorson (ten—Robert), Austin Wright Moore (ten—Sage), Richard Holmes (bar—Doctor), Robert Osborne (b-bar—Orderly) *(rec LeFrak Concert Hall, Queens College, Flushing, NY, May 30 & 31, 1994)* Albany ▲ TROY 173 [DDD]
Menotti, G.C.:The Telephone, w. Jeanne Ommerle (sop—Lucy), Richard Holmes (bar—Ben) *(rec LeFrak Concert Hall, Queens College, Flushing, NY, May 30 & 31, 1994)* Albany ▲ TROY 173 [DDD]
Moore, D.:Gallantry, w. Margaret Bishop (sop—Lola Markham), Julia Parks (mez—Announcer), Carl Halvorson (ten—Donald Hopewell), Richard Holmes (bar—Doctor Gregg) *(rec LeFrak Concert Hall, Queens College, Flushing, NY, May 30 & 31, 1994)* Albany ▲ TROY 173 [DDD]
Piston, W.:Divert Fl Albany ▲ TROY 175 [DDD]
Rochberg, G.:Music for the Magic Theater *(rec New York, Feb. 24, 1993)* New World ▲ 80462-2
Rochberg, G.:Octet:A Grand Fant *(rec Purchase, NY, Mar. 6, 1992)* New World ▲ 80462-2
Rorem, N.:Studies for 11 Albany ▲ TROY 175 [DDD]
New York Chamber Music
I. Pederson (cnd)
A Baroque Celebration, w. Double Reed Ensemble *(rec June 1993)* Dorian ▲ DOR 90189 [DDD]
New York CO
Schoenberg, A.:Con Str Qt, w. American String Quartet Elektra/Nonesuch ▲ 79145-2 [DDD]
A. Lief (cnd)
Creston, P.:Gregorian Chant *(rec 1960)* Vanguard Classics ▲ OVC 4076 [ADD]
G. Schwarz (cnd)
Made in the USA:A Showcase of American Symphonic Music, w. Seattle Chamber Symphony Delos ▲ DE 3508 [DDD]
Sheng, B.:H'un New World ▲ 80407-2 [DDD]
New York CO Solisti
A. Neale (cnd)
Schoenfield, P.:Klezmer Rondos, w. C. Wincenc (fl), D. Webster (bar) New World ▲ 80403-2 [DDD]
Schwantner, J.:A Play of Shadows, w. R. Wilson (fl) New World ▲ 80403-2 [DDD]
New York Chamber Soloists
Weisgall, H.:End of Summer, w. Charles Bressler (ten) CRI ■ C 343
New York Chamber SO
A. Panufnik (cnd)
Panufnik, A.:Sinf sacra Elektra/Nonesuch ▲ 79228-2 ■ 79228-4
G. Schwarz (cnd)
Albert, S.:TreeStone, w. L. Shelton (sop) [E] Delos ▲ DE 3059 [DDD]

New York Chamber SO (cont.)
G. Schwarz (cnd) (cont.)
Carter, E.:The Minotaur Elektra/Nonesuch ▲ 79248-2-ZK ■ 79248-4-AW
Copland, A.:Con Cl, w. D. Shifrin (cl) EMI Classics ▲ CDC 49095 [DDD]
Copland, A.:Con Cl, w. D. Shifrin (cl) EMI Classics (American Composer Series) ▲ CDM 64305
Copland, A.:Dance Panels EMI Classics (American Composer Series) ▲ CDM 64315
Copland, A.:Dance Panels EMI Classics ▲ CDC 49095 [DDD]
Copland, A.:Music for the Theatre EMI Classics ▲ CDC 49095 [DDD]
Copland, A.:Quiet City EMI Classics ▲ CDC 49095 [DDD]
Copland, A.:Quiet City EMI Classics (American Composer Series) ▲ CDM 64306
Copland, A.:Quiet City EMI Classics ▲ CDC 54282
Creston, P.:Choreografic Suite, Seattle SO *(rec Oct 6, 1991)* Delos ▲ DE 3127 [DDD]
Creston, P.:Sym 5, Seattle SO *(rec Oct 6, 1991)* Delos ▲ DE 3127 [DDD]
Creston, P.:Toccata, Seattle SO *(rec Oct 6, 1991)* Delos ▲ DE 3127 [DDD]
Diamond, D.:Con CO Delos ▲ DE 3093 [DDD]
Diamond, D.:Romeo & Juliet Delos ▲ DE 3103 [DDD]
Fine, I.:Notturno Elektra/Nonesuch ▲ 79175-2-ZK
Hanson, H.:Fant Vars on a Theme of Youth, w. Carol Rosenberger (pno) Delos ▲ DE 3092 [DDD]
Hanson, H.:Fant Vars on a Theme of Youth, w. Carol Rosenberger (pno) Delos 4-▲ DE 3150 [DDD]
Hanson, H.:Syms (comp), Seattle SO *(rec 1988–92; boxed edition of)* Delos 4-▲ DE 3150 [DDD]
Haydn, J.:Con Tpt Delos ▲ DCD 3001 [DDD]
Hummel, J.N.:Con in E♭ Tpt, S.49, w. Gerard Schwarz (tpt) Delos ▲ DCD 3001 [DDD]
Kernis, A.J.:Sym in Waves Argo ▲ 436287-2 [DDD]
Mendelssohn, F.:Con in e Vn & Orch, Op. 64, w. N. Salerno-Sonnenberg (vn) EMI Classics ▲ CDC 49276 [DDD] ■ 4DS 49276 (D)
Piston, W.:Sinfonietta Delos ▲ DE 3074 [DDD]
Saint-Saëns, C.:Havanaise Vn, w. N. Salerno-Sonnenberg (vn) EMI Classics ▲ CDC 49276 [DDD] ■ 4DS 49276 (D)
Saint-Saëns, C.:Introduction & Rondo capriccioso, w. N. Salerno-Sonnenberg (vn)—& Massenet:Thaïs—Méditation EMI Classics ▲ CDC 49276 [DDD] ■ 4DS 49276 (D)
Schubert, Franz:German Dances Pno, D.820 Delos ▲ DE 3067 [DDD]
Strauss, R.:Der Bürger als Edelmann (suite), w. New York Chamber Chorus *(rec 11/88)* Pro Arte ▲ CDD 448 [DDD]
Strauss, R.:Divert Elektra/Nonesuch ▲ 79145-2 [DDD]

New York City Ballet Orch
L. Bernstein (cnd)
Bernstein, L.:Fancy Free, w. Billie Holiday (sgr)—with jazz quintet in the Prologue MCA Classics ▲ MCAD 10280 (m) [AAD]

G. Boelzner (cnd)
Hindemith, P.:The Four Temperaments, w. Irving (pno) Elektra/Nonesuch 2-▲ 79135-2
R. Irving (cnd)
Fauré, G.:Pelléas et Mélisande (suite) Elektra/Nonesuch 2-▲ 79135-2
Fauré, G.:Shylock Elektra/Nonesuch 2-▲ 79135-2
Stravinsky, I.:Agon Elektra/Nonesuch 2-▲ 79135-2
Tchaikovsky, P.:Serenade Strs Elektra/Nonesuch 2-▲ 79135-2

New York City Free-Lance Orch
P. Zukovsky (cnd)
Schnabel, A.:Dance & Secret & Joy & Peace, w. Gregg Smith (cnd), Gregg Smith Singers *(rec BMG Studio A, New York City, Feb 1993)* CP² ▲ CP² 110 [DDD]

New York City Opera Orch
E. Buckley (cnd)
Ward, R.:The Crucible, w. P. Brooks (sop), F. Bible (mez), C. Ludgin (bar), New York City Opera Chorus [E] Albany 2-▲ TROY 025/26-2 [ADD]
J. Mauceri (cnd)
Bernstein, L.:Candide, w. E. Mills (sop), D. Eisler (ten), Lankston (sgr), New York Opera Chorus [E] *(rec 1985)* New World 2-▲ NW 340/41-2 2-■ NW 340/41-4
J. Perlea (cnd)
Donizetti, G.:Lucrezia Borgia, w. Montserrat Caballé (sop), Jane Berbié (mez), Alain Vanzo (ten), Kostas Paskalis (bar), Arnold Voketaitis (bass-bar), L. D. Clements (sgr), Adib Fazah (sgr), Mauro Lampi (sgr), Vern Shinall (sgr), Jerold Siena (sgr), William Wiederanders (sgr), New York City Chorus Great Opera Performances 2-▲ GOP 769

E. Queler (cnd)
Donizetti, G.:Parisina, w. Montserrat Caballé (sop), Jérôme Pruett (ten), Louis Quilico (bar), James Morris (bass), New York Opera Chorus *(rec live, New York 1974)* Standing Room Only 2-▲ SRO 836-2 [ADD]
Donizetti, G.:Parisina, w. Montserrat Caballé (sop), Jérôme Pruett (ten), Louis Quilico (bar), James Morris (bass), New York Opera Chorus Pantheon 2-▲ PHE 6638
Janácek, L.:Jenůfa, w. G. Beňačková (sop), L. Rysanek (sop), P. Kazaras (ten), W. Ochman (ten) [Cz] *(rec live at Carnegie Hall, Mar. 30, 1988)* BIS 2-▲ CD 449/50 [DDD]
Puccini, G.:Edgar, w. R. Scotto (sop), G. Killebrew (mez), C. Bergonzi (ten), V. Sardinero (bar), New York Schola Cantorum *(rec in concert at Carnegie Hall, 4/13/77)* CBS 2-▲ M2K 34584
J. Redel (cnd)
Handel, G.F.:Giulio Cesare in Egitto, w. Beverly Sills (sop), Maureen Forrester (cta), Fritz Wolff (ten), Spiro Malas (bass), Norman Treigle (bass), New York City Opera Chorus RCA Gold Seal 2-▲ 6182-2-RG [ADD]
J. Rudel (cnd)
Donizetti, G.:Roberto Devereux, w. B. Sills (sop), S. Marsee (mez), P. Domingo (ten), L. Quilico (bar), New York City Opera Chorus *(rec 1970)* Melodram ▲ MLO 270107 [ADD]
Massenet, J.:Manon, w. Beverly Sills (sop—Manon), Plácido Domingo (ten—Des Grieux), Nico Castel (ten—Guillot), Richard Fredricks (bar—Lescaut), Robert Hale (bar—De Brétigny), Malcom Smith (bass—Count de Grieux), New York City Opera Chorus *(rec live, New York, 1969)* Melodram 2-▲ IMC 205008 [ADD]
Massenet, J.:Manon, w. B. Sills (sop), P. Domingo (ten), R. Fredricks (bar), New York City Opera Chorus *(rec live, 1969)* Melodram 2-▲ MEL 27054
Puccini, G.:Il tabarro, w. J. Crader (sop), P. Domingo (ten), C. Ludgin (bar), New York City Opera Chorus *(rec live 1968; stereo)* Melodram ▲ 17048
Verdi, G.:Rigoletto (sels), w. José Carreras (ten), New York City Opera Chorus—Questa o quella; Ella mi fu rapital...Parmi veder le lagrime; La donna è mobile *(rec New York, Apr 26, 1973)* Goldies ▲ GLD 63203 [ADD]
Weill, K.:Silverlake [E] Elektra/Nonesuch 2-▲ 79003-2 [DDD]

New York City SO
L. Bernstein (cnd)
Blitzstein, M.:The Airborne, w. W. Scheff (bar), R. Shaw (nar), RCA Victor Chorus RCA Gold Seal ▲ 09026-62568-2

L. Stokowski (cnd)
Strauss, R.:Tod und Verklärung Cala ▲ CAL CACD 506

New York Consort of Viols [Lucy Bardo (b vl), Judith Davidoff (trb vl/b vl), Lawrence Lipnik (t vl), Rosamund Morley (trb vl/t vl)]
Byrd, W.:Consort Music, w. Louis Bagger (hpd)—Prelude & Voluntary; Fant. a 3 in C; Fant. a 3 in C; Ut re mi fa sol la; Fant. a 4 in G; Fant. a 4 in D; Prelude [from Pavana, Gagliarda Ph. Tregian]; The Maiden's Songe *(rec Leverett, MA, May 24–26 & June 23, 1993)* Lyrichord ▲ LEMS 8015 [DDD]
Byrd, W.:Songs, w. Tamara Crout (sop), Lawrence Lipnik (ct), Louis Bagger (hpd)—Rejoice unto the Lord; Delight is dead; Farewell, false love; Who made thee, Hob, forsake the plough?; My mistress had a little dog; Browning (The leaves bee greene); Ye Sacred Muses *(rec Leverett, MA, May 24–26 & June 23, 1993)* Lyrichord ▲ LEMS 8015 [DDD]

New York Early Music Ensemble
So Quick, So Hot, So Mad MusicMasters ▲ 01612-67136-2 [AAD]
F. Renz (cnd)
Istanpitta II, w. Glen Velez (perc) Lyrichord ("Early Music" series) ▲ LEMS 8022
The Play of Daniel *(rec 11/86)* Fonè ▲ 88F09-29 CD [DDD]

New York Festival of Song
J. Faletta (cnd)
American Portraits, w. Chicago SO [cnd:A. Schenck], London SO [cnd:J. Sedares] Koch International Classics ▲ KIC 7233 [DDD]

New York Festival of Song [Cyndia Sieden (sop), William Sharp (bar), Steven Blier (pno)]
Unquiet Peace:The Lied Between The Wars Koch International Classics ▲ KIC 7086 [DDD]

New York Festival of Song [Lorraine Hunt (mez), Kurt Ollmann (bar), Michael Barrett (pno)]
Schumann, R.:Songs—Kerner-Lieder (12), Op. 35; Mignon Lieder (7), Op. 98a; 4 Vocal Duets, Opp. 2/5 (Papillon), 34/3 (Unterm Fenster), 78/2 (Er und Sie) & 78/4 (Wiegenlied) Koch International Classics ▲ KIC 7068-2 [DDD]

New York Flute Club
Goeb, R.:Divertimenti (2) CRI ▲ CD 561 [DDD]
Laderman, E.:June 29th CRI ▲ CD 561 [DDD]
Luening, O.:Suite 2 Fl; Canons for 2 Fls; Trio for 3 Fls CRI ▲ CD 561 [DDD]
Sollberger, H.:Killapata/Chaskapata CRI ▲ CD 561 [DDD]
A Tribute to Otto Luening CRI ▲ CRI 561 [DDD]

New York Harp Ensemble
Albinoni, T.:Adagio Org Hungaroton ▲ HCD 12726
Christmas with the New York Harp Ensemble, w. Hungarian Virtuosi CO [cnd:A. Von Würtzler] Hungaroton ▲ HCD 31331 [DDD]

A. von Würtzler (cnd)
An Evening with the New York Harp Ensemble Hungaroton ▲ HCD 31295 [DDD]
Musical Memories Hungaroton ▲ HCD 31458 [DDD]
The New York Harp Ensemble Hungaroton ▲ HCD 12726

New York Kammermusiker Double Reed Ensemble
A Renaissance Tour of Europe Dorian ▲ DOR 90133 [DDD]

New York Metropolitan Opera Orch
E. Panizza (cnd)
Verdi, G.:Aida, w. Gina Cigna (sop), Bruna Castagna (mez), Giovanni Martinelli (ten), Ezio Pinza (bass), New York Metropolitan Opera Chorus *(rec live, Feb 6, 1937)* The Fourties 2-▲ ENT 1501
T. Schippers (cnd)
Puccini, G.:La Bohème, w. L. Albanese (sop), L. Hurley (sop), C. Bergonzi (ten), C. Harvuot (bar), M. Sereni (bar), N. Scott (bass), E. Flagello (bass), New York Metropolitan Opera Chorus *(rec Feb. 15, 1958)* Golden Age of Opera 2-▲ GAO 139/40 [ADD]
G. Szell (cnd)
Mussorgsky, M.:Boris Godunov, w. Kerstin Thorborg (mez), René Maison (ten), Alexander Kipnis (bass), New York Metropolitan Opera Chorus *(rec live, Feb 13, 1943)* The Fourties 2-▲ ENT 1505
B. Walter (cnd)
Beethoven, L. van:Fidelio (sels), w. K. Flagstad (sop)—Act 1 aria, "Abscheulicher! Wo eilst du hin?" *(rec 1940)* Memories 2-▲ HR 4456/57 [ADD]
Verdi, G.:La forza del destino, w. Stella Roman (sop), Frederick Jagel (ten), Lawrence Tibbett (bar), Salvatore Baccaloni (bass), Ezio Pinza (bass) *(rec live, Jan 23, 1943)* The Fourties 2-▲ ENT 1503

New York Musica Antiqua
M. J. Newman (cnd)
Handel, G.F.:Cons (16) Org, w. Mary Jane Newman (org)—Op. 4/2 *(rec Presbyterian Church, Mt. Kisco, NY, Aug 26–27, 1995)* Helicon ▲ HE 1006 [DDD]
Handel, G.F.:Messiah (sels), w. Voci Angeli—Worthy Is the Lamb *(rec Presbyterian Church, Mt. Kisco, NY, Aug 26–27, 1995)* Helicon ▲ HE 1006 [DDD]

New York New Music Ensemble
Rolnick, N.B.:ElectriCity O.O. Discs ▲ OO 8 [ADD]
R. Black (cnd)
Dembski, S.:Alba CRI ▲ CD 570 [DDD]
Schoenberg, A.:Pierrot lunaire, w. P. Bryn-Julson (speaker) [G] *(rec Sep. 1991)* GM ▲ GM 2030

New York New Music Ensemble members [Jeanne Kopperud (cl), James Winn (pno)]
Lewis, R.H.:Fantasiemusik II Albany ▲ TROY 166 [ADD/DDD]

New York Opera Orch
E. Queler (cnd)
Massenet, J.:Le Cid, w. G. Bumbry (mez), P. Domingo (ten), P. Plishka (bass) *(rec 1976)* CBS 2-▲ M2K 34211 [ADD]
Verdi, G.:Aroldo, w. M. Caballé (sop), G. Cecchele (ten), J. Pons (bar), Westchester Choral Society, New York Oratorio Society [I] *(rec live, Carnegie Hall 4/8/79)* CBS 2-▲ M2K 35906 [ADD]

New York Philharmonia Virtuosi
R. Kapp (cnd)
Albinoni, T.:Adagio Org CBS ▲ MK 34544 ■ MT 34544
Bach, J.S.:Jesu bleibet meine Freude CBS ▲ MK 35821 ■ MT 35821
Bach, J.S.:Music of—selections from Cantatas 140 & 207, Christmas Oratorio & Orchestral Suite No. 3 Odyssey ■ YT 44514
Bach, J.S.:Sheep May Safely Graze CBS ▲ MK 35821 ■ MT 35821
Mozart, W.A.:Serenade Vn, K.203 *(rec 1975)* Vox Box 3-▲ CD3X 3013 [ADD]
Mozart, W.A.:Serenade Vn, K.204 *(rec 1973)* Vox Box 3-▲ CD3X 3013 [ADD]
Mozart, W.A.:Serenade Vn, K.250 *(rec 1975)* Vox Box 3-▲ CD3X 3013 [ADD]
Mozart, W.A.:Serenade Ww, K.320 *(rec 1975)* Vox Box 3-▲ CD3X 3013 [ADD]
Mozart, W.A.:Serenata notturna *(rec 1975)* Vox Box 3-▲ CD3X 3013 [ADD]
Pachelbel, J.:Canon CBS ▲ MK 34544 ■ MT 34544
Piston, W.:Concertino Pno, w. Gary Steigerwalt (pno) *(rec 1976)* Vox Box ("The American Composers" series) 2-▲ CDX 5158

New York Phil Brass [Fred Mills (tpt), Ronald Romm (tpt), David Ohnanian (hn), Eugene Watts (trbn), Charles Daellenbach (tuba)]
Brass Busters, w. Canadian Brass, Boston Sym Brass RCA Victor ▲ 09026-68076-2 ■ 09026-68076-4

New York PO
Mad About Love, w. Cheryl Studer (sop), Kiri Te Kanawa (sop), José Carreras (ten), Jerry Hadley (ten), Philharmonia Orch [cnd:Giuseppe Sinopoli], Bastille Opera Orch [cnd:Myung-Whun Chung], Boston SO [cnd:Seiji Ozawa], Vienna PO, et al. Deutsche Grammophon ▲ 449112-2 ■ 449112-4
Red, White & Brass, w. Canadian Brass, Boston SO members Philips ▲ 434276-2 PH [DDD] ■ 434276-4 PH
Wagner, R.:Arias & Scenes, w. Kirsten Flagstad (sop), Lauritz Melchior (bar), Philadelphia Orch, San Francisco Opera Orch, RCA Victor SO, Ormandy, McArthur, Walter (cnds)—arias & duets from Lohengrin, Tristan & Isolde, Götterdämmerung, Parsifal & Fidelio *(rec New York City, 1939–41)* Grammofono 2000 ▲ GRM 78526 (m)
Wagner, R.:Arias & Scenes, w. K. Flagstad (sop), L. Melchior (ten), RCA Victor SO, San Francisco Opera Orch, BBC SO, Walter, MacArthur, Sargent (cnds)—selections from Götterdämering; Tristan & Isolde; Lohengrin Memories 2-▲ HR 4456/57 [ADD]
J. Barbirolli (cnd)
Debussy, C.:Ibéria Dutton Laboratories ▲ DUT 5000
Respighi, O.:The Fountains of Rome *(rec Carnegie Hall, 1/21/39)* Pearl 3-▲ PEA 9922 (m) [AAD]
Schubert, Franz:Sym 4 Dutton Laboratories ▲ DUT 5000
Schumann, R.:Con Vn, w. F. Kreisler (vn) *(rec 1938 for HMV)* Biddulph ▲ LAB 047 [ADD]
Tchaikovsky, P.:Francesca da Rimini Dutton Laboratories ▲ DUT 5000
Wagner, R.:Die Meistersinger von Nürnberg (sels)—Suite from Act 3 *(rec Carnegie Hall, Nov. 20, 1938)* Dutton Laboratories ▲ CDSJB 1001 [ADD]
Wagner, R.:Rienzi, der Letzte der Tribunen (ov) *(rec Carnegie Hall, Nov. 20, 1938)* Dutton Laboratories ▲ CDSJB 1001 [ADD]
Wagner, R.:Siegfried Idyll *(rec Carnegie Hall, Nov. 20, 1938)* Dutton Laboratories ▲ CDSJB 1001 [ADD]
Wagner, R.:Tannhäuser (sels)—Venusberg Music *(rec Carnegie Hall, Nov. 20, 1938)* Dutton Laboratories ▲ CDSJB 1001 [ADD]

ORCH. & ENS.

New York PO (cont.)
J. Barbirolli (cnd) (cont.)
Wagner, R.:Tristan und Isolde (prelude & liebestod) *(rec Carnegie Hall, Nov. 20, 1938)* Dutton Laboratories ▲ CDSJB 1001 [ADD]
D. Barenboim (cnd)
Beethoven, L. van:Con Vn, Op. 61, w. I. Stern (vn) Odyssey ▲ MBK 42613 [ADD]
Beethoven, L. van:Con Vn, Op. 61, w. I. Stern (vn) CBS ▲ MK 42256 [ADD]
T. Beecham (cnd)
Sibelius, J.:Sym 7 Dutton Laboratories ▲ DUT CDAX 8013 [ADD]
Strauss, R.:Don Quixote, w. A. Wallenstein (vc) *(rec 4/7/32)* Pearl 3–▲ PEA 9922 (m) [AAD]
L. Bernstein (cnd)
Bach, J.S.:Con Vn & Ob, w. I. Stern (vn), H. Gomberg (ob) CBS ▲ MK 42258
Bach, J.S.:Con Vn & Ob, w. I. Stern (vn), H. Gomberg (ob) CBS ■ MGT 39798
Barber, S.:Adagio Strs *(rec New York, Jan. 12, 1971)* Sony Classical ("Bernstein:The Royal Edition" series) ▲ SMK 47567 [ADD] Δ SM 47567 [ADD]
Barber, S.:Adagio Strs CBS ▲ MYK 38484 [AAD] ■ MYT 38484
Bartók, B.:Con Orch Sony Classical ▲ SMK 47510 [ADD]
Bartók, B.:Con 2 Pno, w. P. Entremont (pno) Sony Classical ▲ SMK 47511 [ADD]
Bartók, B.:Con 3 Pno, w. P. Entremont (pno) Sony Classical ▲ SMK 47511 [ADD]
Bartók, B.:Con for 2 Pnos, w. P. Entremont (pno) Sony Classical ▲ SMK 47511 [ADD]
Bartók, B.:Con 2 Vn, w. I. Stern (vn) Sony Classical ▲ SMK 47511 [ADD]
Bartók, B.:Music for Strs, Perc & Cel Sony Classical ▲ SMK 47510 [ADD]
Bartók, B.:Rhaps (2) Vn & Orch, w. I. Stern (vn) Sony Classical ▲ SMK 47511 [ADD]
Beethoven, L. van:Con 1 Pno, w. L. Bernstein (pno) Sony Classical ▲ SMK 47519 [ADD]
Beethoven, L. van:Con 3 Pno, w. R. Serkin (pno) CBS ▲ MYK 38526 [ADD] ■ MYT 38526
Beethoven, L. van:Con 3 Pno, w. R. Serkin (pno) CBS ▲ MK 42259
Beethoven, L. van:Con 3 Pno, w. R. Serkin (pno) *(rec New York, 1964)* Sony Classical ("Bernstein:The Royal Edition" series) ▲ SMK 47520 [ADD] Δ SM 47520 [ADD]
Beethoven, L. van:Con 5 Pno, "Emperor", w. R. Serkin (pno) *(rec New York, May 1, 1962)* Sony Classical ("Bernstein:The Royal Edition" series) ▲ SMK 47520 [ADD] Δ SM 47520 [ADD]
Beethoven, L. van:Con 5 Pno, "Emperor", w. R. Serkin (pno) CBS ▲ MYK 37223 ■ MYT 37223
Beethoven, L. van:Con Vn, Op. 61, w. I. Stern (vn) CBS 2–■ MGT 31418
Beethoven, L. van:Con Vn, Op. 61, w. I. Stern (vn) Sony Classical ▲ SMK 47521 [ADD]
Beethoven, L. van:Egmont (ov) *(rec New York, Feb. 12, 1970)* Sony Classical ("Bernstein:The Royal Edition" series) Δ SM 47516 [ADD]
Beethoven, L. van:Fant Pno, Op. 80, "Choral Fant", w. R. Serkin (pno), New York Phil Chorus Odyssey ■ YT 42485
Beethoven, L. van:Fant Pno, Op. 80, "Choral Fant", w. R. Serkin (pno), Westminster Choir [G] CBS ▲ MYK 38526 [ADD] ■ MYT 38526
Beethoven, L. van:Fant Pno, Op. 80, "Choral Fant", w. R. Serkin (pno), Westminster Choir Sony Classical 2–▲ SM2K 47522 [ADD]
Beethoven, L. van:Fidelio (sels)—Ov. *(rec New York, Jan. 10–31, 1967)* Sony Classical ("Bernstein:The Royal Edition" series) Δ SM 47513 [ADD]
Beethoven, L. van:Fidelio (ov) Sony Classical ▲ SMK 47518 [ADD]
Beethoven, L. van:König Stephen (ov) Sony Classical ▲ SMK 47517 [ADD]
Beethoven, L. van:Leonore 3 Sony Classical ▲ SMK 47521 [ADD]
Beethoven, L. van:Missa Solemnis, w. E. Farrell (sop), C. Smith (mez), R. Lewis (ten), K. Borg (bass), Westminster Choir [L] Sony Classical 2–▲ SM2K 47522 [ADD]
Beethoven, L. van:Sym 1 Sony Classical ▲ SMK 47514 [ADD]
Beethoven, L. van:Sym 1 CBS ▲ MYK 38469 [ADD] ■ MYT 38469
Beethoven, L. van:Sym 2 Sony Classical ▲ SMK 47515 [ADD]
Beethoven, L. van:Sym 3, "Eroica" Sony Classical ▲ SMK 47514 [ADD]
Beethoven, L. van:Sym 4 *(rec New York, May 7, 1962)* Sony Classical ("Bernstein:The Royal Edition" series) ▲ SMK 47516 [ADD] Δ SM 47516 [ADD]
Beethoven, L. van:Sym 5 CBS ■ MT 31810
Beethoven, L. van:Sym 5 *(rec New York, Sept. 25, 1961)* Sony Classical ("Bernstein:The Royal Edition" series) ▲ SMK 47516 [ADD] Δ SM 47516 [ADD]
Beethoven, L. van:Sym 5 CBS ▲ MYK 36719 ■ MYK 36719
Beethoven, L. van:Sym 6, "Pastorale" Sony Classical ▲ SMK 47517 [ADD]
Beethoven, L. van:Sym 7 Sony Classical ▲ SMK 47515 [ADD]
Beethoven, L. van:Sym 8 Sony Classical ▲ SMK 47517 [ADD]
Beethoven, L. van:Sym 9, "Choral Sym", w. M. Arroy (sop), R. Sarfaty (mez), N. di Virgilio (ten), N. Scott (bass), Juilliard Chorus *(rec New York, May 18, 1964)* Sony Classical ("Bernstein:The Royal Edition" series) Δ SM 47513 [ADD]
Beethoven, L. van:Sym 9, "Choral Sym", w. Juilliard Chorus [soloists M. Arroyo, R. Sarfaty, N. deVirglio, N. Scott] Sony Classical ▲ SMK 47518 [ADD]
Beethoven, L. van:Die Weihe des Hauses (ov) Sony Classical ▲ SMK 47521 [ADD]
Ben–Haim, P.:Sweet Psalmist of Israel Sony Classical ▲ SMK 47533 [ADD]
Berlioz, H.:La Damnation de Faust (sels)—Racózky March Sony Classical ▲ SMK 47525 [ADD]
Berlioz, H.:La Mort de Cléopâtre, w. J. Tourel (mez) Sony Classical 2–▲ SM2K 47526 [ADD]
Berlioz, H.:Ovs—Benvenuto Cellini; Carnaval romain Sony Classical ▲ SMK 47525 [ADD]
Berlioz, H.:Roméo et Juliette (sels) Sony Classical 2–▲ SM2K 47526 [ADD]
Berlioz, H.:Sym fantastique CBS ▲ MYK 38475 [ADD] ■ MYT 38475
Berlioz, H.:Sym fantastique Sony Classical ▲ SMK 47525 [ADD]
Bernstein Conducts Bernstein:The Theatre Works, Vol. 1, w. Columbia Wind Ensemble, various soloists Sony Classical 3–▲ SM3K 47154
Bernstein, L.:Candide (ov) *(rec New York, Sept. 28, 1960)* Sony Classical ("Bernstein:The Royal Edition" series) ▲ SMK 47529 [ADD] Δ SM 47529 [ADD]
Bernstein, L.:Candide (ov) CBS ▲ MLK 39448 ■ MT 39448
Bernstein, L.:Candide (ov) CBS ▲ MK 42263 [ADD]
Bernstein, L.:Chichester Psalms, w. Camerata Singers [He] CBS ▲ MK 44710 [ADD]
Bernstein, L.:Fancy Free Sony Classical ▲ SMK 47530 [ADD]
Bernstein, L.:Fancy Free CBS ▲ MLK 39448 ■ MT 39448
Bernstein, L.:On the Town Sony Classical ▲ SMK 47530 [ADD]
Bernstein, L.:On the Town CBS ▲ MK 42263 [ADD]
Bernstein, L.:On the Waterfront (sym suite) Sony Classical ▲ SMK 47530 [ADD]
Bernstein, L.:On the Waterfront (sym suite) CBS ▲ MK 42263 [ADD]
Bernstein, L.:West Side Story (ballet music) CBS ▲ MK 42263 [ADD]
Bernstein, L.:West Side Story (symphonic dances) *(rec New York, Mar. 6, 1961)* Sony Classical ("Bernstein:The Royal Edition" series) ▲ SMK 47529 [ADD] Δ SM 47529 [ADD]
Bizet, G.:L'Arlésienne (suites) Sony Classical ▲ SMK 47531 [ADD]
Bizet, G.:Carmen (suites) Sony Classical ▲ SMK 47531 [ADD]
Bizet, G.:Sym 1 Sony Classical ▲ SMK 47532 [ADD]
Bizet, G.:Sym 1 CBS ▲ MYK 36725 [ADD] ■ MYT 36725
Bloch, E.:Avodath Hakodesh, w. R. Merrill (bar) [E,He] Sony Classical ▲ SMK 47533 [ADD]
Borodin, A.:In the Steppes of Central Asia CBS ▲ MYK 37770 [AAD] ■ MYT 37770
Borodin, A.:In the Steppes of Central Asia *(rec New York City, Dec 8, 1969)* Sony Classical ("Essential Classics" series) 2–▲ SB2K 62406 [ADD]
Borodin, A.:Prince Igor (Polovtsian dances) CBS ▲ MYK 37770 [AAD] ■ MYT 37770
Borodin, A.:Prince Igor (Polovtsian dances) *(rec Jan. 21, 1963)* Sony Classical ▲ SMK 47600 [ADD]
Brahms, J.:Academic Festival Ov CBS ▲ MLK 39451
Brahms, J.:Academic Festival Ov Sony Classical ▲ SMK 47538 [ADD]
Brahms, J.:Con 2 Pno, w. A. Watts (pno) Sony Classical ▲ SMK 47539 [ADD]
Brahms, J.:Con Vn, w. Z. Francescatti (vn) Sony Classical ▲ SMK 47540 [ADD]
Brahms, J.:Hungarian Dances Orch—Nos. 5 & 6 *(rec (rec 1970 & 1965)* Sony Classical ▲ SMK 47572 [ADD]
Brahms, J.:Serenade 2 Orch Sony Classical ▲ SMK 47536 [ADD]
Brahms, J.:Sym 1 Sony Classical ▲ SMK 47536 [ADD]
Brahms, J.:Sym 2 Sony Classical ▲ SMK 47537 [ADD]
Brahms, J.:Sym 3 Sony Classical ▲ SMK 47537 [ADD]

New York PO (cont.)
L. Bernstein (cnd) (cont.)
Brahms, J.:Sym 4 Sony Classical ▲ SMK 47538 [ADD]
Brahms, J.:Tragic Ov Sony Classical ▲ SMK 47538 [ADD]
Brahms, J.:Vars on a Theme by Haydn Sony Classical ▲ SMK 47539 [ADD]
Britten, B.:Peter Grimes (sea interludes & passacaglia) Sony Classical ▲ SMK 47541 [ADD]
Britten, B.:Suite on English Folk Tunes Sony Classical ▲ SMK 47541 [ADD]
Britten, B.:The Young Person's Guide to the Orchestra Sony Classical ▲ SMK 47541 [ADD]
Bruckner, A.:Sym 9 *(rec 1962)* Sony Classical ▲ SMK 47542 [ADD]
Carmen without Words, w. Kostelanetz Orch CBS Masterworks ▲ MDK 46287 [AAD] ■ MGT 46287
Chabrier, E.:España CBS ▲ MYK 37769 [AAD] ■ MYT 37769
Chausson, E.:Poème Vn, w. Z. Francescatti (vn) *(rec 1964)* Sony Classical ▲ SMK 47548 [ADD]
Copland, A.:Appalachian Spring (suite) CBS ▲ MYK 37257 [ADD] ■ MYT 37257
Copland, A.:Appalachian Spring (suite) *(rec New York, Oct. 9, 1961)* Sony Classical ("Bernstein:The Royal Edition" series) ▲ SMK 47543 [ADD] Δ SM 47543 [ADD]
Copland, A.:Appalachian Spring (suite) CBS ▲ MK 42265 [AAD]
Copland, A.:Appalachian Spring (suite) CBS ▲ MLK 39443 ■ MT 39443
Copland, A.:Billy the Kid (suite) CBS ▲ MYK 36727 [ADD] ■ MYT 36727
Copland, A.:Billy the Kid (suite) CBS ▲ MK 42265 [AAD]
Copland, A.:Billy the Kid (suite) *(rec Boston, Oct. 20, 1959)* Sony Classical ("Bernstein:The Royal Edition" series) ▲ SMK 47543 [ADD] Δ SM 47543 [ADD]
Copland, A.:Con Cl, w. S. Drucker (cl) Deutsche Grammophon ▲ 431672–2 [DDD]
Copland, A.:Con Pno, w. A. Copland (pno) *(rec 1964)* Sony Classical 2–▲ SM2K 47232 [ADD]
Copland, A.:Connotations Deutsche Grammophon ▲ 431672–2 [DDD]
Copland, A.:Danzón Cubano CBS ▲ MYK 36727 [ADD] ■ MYT 36727
Copland, A.:Danzón Cubano CBS ▲ MYK 37257 [ADD] ■ MYT 37257
Copland, A.:Fanfare for the Common Man *(rec New York Feb. 16, 1966)* Sony Classical ("Bernstein:The Royal Edition" series) ▲ SMK 47543 [ADD] Δ SM 47543 [ADD]
Copland, A.:Fanfare for the Common Man CBS ▲ MYK 37257 [ADD] ■ MYT 37257
Copland, A.:Fanfare for the Common Man CBS ▲ MK 42265 [AAD]
Copland, A.:Music for the Theatre Deutsche Grammophon ▲ 431672–2 [DDD]
Copland, A.:Music for the Theatre Sony Classical 2–▲ SM2K 47232 [ADD]
Copland, A.:Quiet City Deutsche Grammophon ▲ 419170–2 [DDD]
Copland, A.:Rodeo *(rec New York May 2, 1960)* Sony Classical ("Bernstein:The Royal Edition" series) ▲ SMK 47543 [ADD] Δ SM 47543 [ADD]
Copland, A.:Rodeo CBS ▲ MYK 36727 [ADD] ■ MYT 36727
Copland, A.:Rodeo CBS ▲ MK 42265 [AAD]
Copland, A.:El salón México Nimbus ▲ NI 4002 [ADD/DDD]
Copland, A.:El salón México CBS ▲ MLK 39443 ■ MT 39443
Copland, A.:El salón México Deutsche Grammophon ▲ 431672–2 [DDD]
Copland, A.:El salón México CBS ▲ MYK 37257 [ADD] ■ MYT 37257
Copland, A.:Sym Org & Orch, w. E. P. Biggs (org) *(rec 1967)* Sony Classical 2–▲ SM2K 47232 [ADD]
Copland, A.:Sym 3 Deutsche Grammophon ▲ 419170–2 [DDD]
Debussy, C.:Images Orch *(rec 1958)* Sony Classical ▲ SMK 47545 [ADD]
Debussy, C.:Jeux *(rec 1960)* Sony Classical ▲ SMK 47546 [ADD]
Debussy, C.:La Mer *(rec 1961)* Sony Classical ▲ SMK 47546 [ADD]
Debussy, C.:Nocturnes—Nuages & Fêtes *(rec 1960)* Sony Classical ▲ SMK 47546 [ADD]
Debussy, C.:Prélude à l'après–midi d'un faune *(rec 1960)* Sony Classical ▲ SMK 47546 [ADD]
Debussy, C.:Prélude à l'après–midi d'un faune CBS ▲ MLK 39444 ■ MT–39444
Debussy, C.:Première rapsodie, w. S. Drucker (cl) *(rec 1961)* Sony Classical ▲ SMK 47545 [ADD]
del Tredici, D.:Tatoo Deutsche Grammophon ▲ 429231–1
Dukas, P.:L'Apprenti sorcier CBS ▲ MYK 37769 [AAD] ■ MYT 37769
Dukas, P.:L'Apprenti sorcier Sony Classical ▲ SMK 47596
Dvořák, A.:Carnival *(rec 1965)* Sony Classical ▲ SMK 47547 [ADD]
Dvořák, A.:Slavonic Dances (sels)—Op. 46, Nos. 1 & 3 *(rec 1963)* Sony Classical ▲ SMK 47547 [ADD]
Dvořák, A.:Sym 9, "From the New World" *(rec 1962)* Sony Classical ▲ SMK 47547 [ADD]
Elgar, E.:Pomp & Circumstance Marches—No. 1 *(rec New York, Oct. 26, 1967)* Sony Classical ▲ SMK 47567 [ADD] Δ SM 47567 [AD
Enescu, G.:Romanian Rhap 1 *(rec 1969)* Sony Classical ▲ SMK 47572 [ADD]
Falla, M. de:El amor brujo, w. M. Horne (mez) Odyssey ▲ MBK 44721 [ADD] ■ YT 44721
Fauré, G.:Ballade Pno, w. Casadesus (pno) *(rec 1961)* Sony Classical ▲ SMK 47548 [ADD]
Favorite French Orchestral Spectaculars, w. Mediaeval Ensemble CBS ▲ MYK 37769 [AAD]
Favorite Overtures CBS ▲ MYK 37240 [AAD]
Favorite Russian Orchestral Spectaculars CBS ▲ MYK 37770 [AAD] ■ MYT 37770
Fernandez, O.L.:Batuque *(rec 1963)* Sony Classical ("Bernstein:The Royal Edition" series) ▲ SMK 47544 [ADD]
Foss, L.:Song of Songs, w. J. Tourel (mez) [E] Sony Classical ▲ SMK 47533 [ADD]
Franck, C.:Sym in d *(rec 1959)* Sony Classical ("Bernstein:The Royal Edition" series) ▲ SMK 47548 [ADD]
Gershwin, G.:An American in Paris CBS ▲ MK 42516 [ADD/DDD] ■ FMT 42516
Gershwin, G.:An American in Paris CBS ▲ MK 42240 [ADD]
Gershwin, G.:An American in Paris *(rec New York, Dec. 21, 1958)* Sony Classical ("Bernstein:The Royal Edition" series) ▲ SMK 47529 [ADD] Δ SM 47529 [ADD]
Gershwin, G.:An American in Paris CBS ▲ MYK 37242 [ADD] ■ MYT 37242
Gershwin, G.:An American in Paris CBS ▲ MK 42264 [ADD]
Gershwin, G.:An American in Paris, w. Leonard Bernstein (pno) Polskie Nagrania ▲ PNCD 150 [ADD]
Glinka, M.:Russlan & Ludmilla (ov) CBS ▲ MYK 37770 [AAD] ■ MYT 37770
Gounod, C.:Faust (ballet music) *(rec May 20, 1967)* Sony Classical ▲ SMK 47600 [ADD]
Grieg, E.:Lyric Suite, Op. 54—No. 4, "March of the Trolls" *(rec 1970)* Sony Classical ("Bernstein:The Royal Edition" series) ▲ SMK 47549 [ADD]
Grieg, E.:Norwegian Dances, Op. 35—No. 2 *(rec 1965)* Sony Classical ("Bernstein:The Royal Edition" series) ▲ SMK 47549 [ADD]
Grieg, E.:Peer Gynt Suites, Opp. 46 & 55 CBS ▲ MYK 36718 ■ MYT 36718
Grieg, E.:Peer Gynt Suites, Opp. 46 & 55 *(rec 1967)* Sony Classical ("Bernstein:The Royal Edition" series) ▲ SMK 47549 [ADD]
Grofé, F.:Grand Canyon Suite CBS ▲ MK 42264 [ADD]
Grofé, F.:Grand Canyon Suite *(rec 1963)* Sony Classical ("Bernstein:The Royal Edition" series) ▲ SMK 47544 [ADD]
Grofé, F.:Grand Canyon Suite CBS ▲ MYK 37759 [ADD] ■ MYT 37759
Handel, G.F.:Messiah (sels), w. Adele Addison (sop), Russell Oberlin (ct), Edward Lloyd (ten), William Warfield (bar), Westminster Choir [E] CBS ▲ MYK 38481 ■ MYT 38481
Harris, R.:Sym 3 Deutsche Grammophon ▲ 419780–2 [DDD]
Haydn, J.:Mass 11, "Nelsonmesse", "Imperial Mass", "Coronation Mass", w. Judith Blegen (sop), Gwendolen Killebrew (mez), Kenneth Riegel (ten), Simon Estes (bass), Westminster Choir [L] *(rec 1976)* Sony Classical ("Bernstein:The Royal Edition" series) 2–▲ SM2K 47563 [ADD]
Haydn, J.:Mass 14, "Harmoniemesse", w. Judith Blegen (sop), Fredrica von Stade (mez), Kenneth Riegel (ten), Simon Estes (bass), Westminster Choir [L] *(rec 1966)* Sony Classical 2–▲ SM2K 47560 [ADD]
Haydn, J.:Die Schöpfung, w. Judith Raskin (sop), Alexander Young (ten), John Reardon (bar), Camerata Singers [G] *(rec 1966)* Sony Classical ("Bernstein:The Royal Edition" series) 2–▲ SM2K 47560 [ADD]
Haydn, J.:Syms 82–87, "Paris Syms" *(rec 1962–67)* Sony Classical ("Bernstein:The Royal Edition" series) 2–▲ SM2K 47550 [ADD]
Haydn, J.:Sym 88 *(rec 1963)* Sony Classical ("Bernstein:The Royal Edition" series) 2–▲ SM2K 47563 [ADD]
Haydn, J.:Sym 93 *(rec 1971)* Sony Classical ("Bernstein:The Royal Edition" series) 3–▲ SM3K 47553 [ADD]
Haydn, J.:Sym 94, "Surprise Sym" *(rec 1971)* Sony Classical ("Bernstein:The Royal Edition" series) 3–▲ SM3K 47553 [ADD]

▲ = CD ♦ = Enhanced CD Δ = MD ■ = Cassette Tape ☐ = DCC

New York PO (cont.)
L. Bernstein (cnd) (cont.)
Haydn, J.:Sym 95 *(rec 1973)*
Sony Classical ("Bernstein:The Royal Edition" series) 3-▲ SM3K 47553 [ADD]
Haydn, J.:Sym 96, "Miracle" *(rec 1973)*
Sony Classical ("Bernstein:The Royal Edition" series) 3-▲ SM3K 47553 [ADD]
Haydn, J.:Sym 97 *(rec 1975)*
Sony Classical ("Bernstein:The Royal Edition" series) 3-▲ SM3K 47553 [ADD]
Haydn, J.:Sym 98 *(rec 1975)*
Sony Classical ("Bernstein:The Royal Edition" series) 3-▲ SM3K 47553 [ADD]
Haydn, J.:Sym 99 *(rec 1970)*
Sony Classical ("Bernstein:The Royal Edition" series) 3-▲ SM3K 47553 [ADD]
Haydn, J.:Sym 100, "Military" *(rec 1970)*
Sony Classical ("Bernstein:The Royal Edition" series) 2-▲ SM2K 47557 [ADD]
Haydn, J.:Sym 101, "Clock" *(rec 1970)*
Sony Classical ("Bernstein:The Royal Edition" series) 2-▲ SM2K 47557 [ADD]
Haydn, J.:Sym 102 *(rec 1962)*
Sony Classical ("Bernstein:The Royal Edition" series) 2-▲ SM2K 47557 [ADD]
Haydn, J.:Sym 103, "Drum Roll" *(rec 1970)*
Sony Classical ("Bernstein:The Royal Edition" series) 2-▲ SM2K 47557 [ADD]
Haydn, J.:Sym 104, "London" *(rec 1958)*
Sony Classical ("Bernstein:The Royal Edition" series) 2-▲ SM2K 47557 [ADD]
Hérold, F.:Zampa (ov) CBS ▲ MYK 37240 [AAD]
Hindemith, P.:Concert Music Brass & Strs *(rec 1961)*
Sony Classical ("Bernstein:The Royal Edition" series) ▲ SMK 47566 [ADD]
Hindemith, P.:Con Vn, w. S. Drucker (vn) Sony Classical ▲ SMK 47599
Hindemith, P.:Symphonic Metamorphosis on Themes of Carl Maria von Weber *(rec 1968)*
Sony Classical ("Bernstein:The Royal Edition" series) ▲ SMK 47566 [ADD]
Hindemith, P.:Sym in E♭ for Concert Band *(rec 1967)*
Sony Classical ("Bernstein:The Royal Edition" series) ▲ SMK 47566 [ADD]
Holst, G.:The Planets CBS ▲ MYK 37226 ■ MYT 37226
Holst, G.:The Planets *(rec New York, Dec. 1971–June 1973)*
Sony Classical ("Bernstein:The Royal Edition" series) ▲ SMK 47567 [ADD] Δ SM 47567 [ADD]
Holst, G.:The Planets Sony Classical ("Essential Classics" series) ▲ SBK 62400 ■ SBT 62400
Honegger, A.:Pacific 231 Sony Classical ("Masterworks Heritage" series) ▲ MHK 62352
Honegger, A.:Rugby Sony Classical ("Masterworks Heritage" series) ▲ MHK 62352
Ives, C.:Central Park in the Dark *(rec 1962)*
Sony Classical ("Bernstein:The Royal Edition" series) ▲ SMK 47568 [ADD]
Ives, C.:Orchestral Music—Central Park in the Dark; Gong on the Hook & Ladder; Hallowe'en; Hymn for Strings; Tone Roads No. 1; Unanswered Question Deutsche Grammophon ▲ 429220-2 [DDD]
Ives, C.:Sym 2 *(rec 1958)* Sony Classical ("Bernstein:The Royal Edition" series) ▲ SMK 47568 [ADD]
Ives, C.:Sym 2 Deutsche Grammophon 429220-2 [DDD]
Ives, C.:Sym 3 *(rec 1965)* Sony Classical ("Bernstein:The Royal Edition" series) ▲ SMK 47568 [ADD]
Janáček, L.:Slavonic Mass, w. H. Pilarczyk (sop), J. Martin (mez), N. Gedda (ten), G. Gaynes (sgr), Westminster Choir *(rec 1963)*
Sony Classical ("Bernstein:The Royal Edition" series) ▲ SMK 47569 [ADD]
The Joy of Bernstein, w. Vienna PO, Los Angeles PO, Israel PO Deutsche Grammophon ▲ 445486-2
Liszt, F.:Con 1 Pno, w. André Watts (pno) *(rec 1964)*
Sony Classical ("Bernstein:The Royal Edition" series) ▲ SMK 47571 [ADD]
Liszt, F.:A Faust Sym, w. C. Bressler (ten), Choral Arts Society *(rec 1960)*
Sony Classical ("Bernstein:The Royal Edition" series) ▲ SMK 47570 [ADD]
Liszt, F.:Hungarian Rhaps—Nos. 2 & 14 *(rec 1969 & 1971)*
Sony Classical ("Bernstein:The Royal Edition" series) ▲ SMK 47572 [ADD]
Liszt, F.:Les Préludes CBS ▲ MLK 39450 ■ MT 39450
Liszt, F.:Les Préludes *(rec 1963)*
Sony Classical ("Bernstein:The Royal Edition" series) ▲ SMK 47572 [ADD]
Liszt, F.:Les Préludes CBS ▲ MYK 37772 [ADD] ■ MYT 37772
Mad About Angels, w. Cheryl Studer (sop), Christa Ludwig (mez), Anne Sofie von Otter (mez), José Carreras (ten), English Baroque Soloists [cnd:John Eliot Gardiner], Philharmonia Orch, Philharmonia Chorus [cnd:Carlo Maria Giulini], Orp Deutsche Grammophon ▲ 449113-2 ■ 449113-4
Mahler, G.:Kindertotenlieder, w. J. Tourel (mez) *(rec 1960)*
Sony Classical ("Bernstein:The Royal Edition" series) 2-▲ SM2K 47576 [ADD]
Mahler, G.:Songs, w. J. Tourel (mez)—3 Rückert Songs:Ich atmet' einen linden Duft; Ich bin der Welt abhanden gekommen; Um Mitternacht; plus Das Irdische Leben from Knaben Wunderhorn *(rec 1960)*
Sony Classical ("Bernstein:The Royal Edition" series) 2-▲ SM2K 47576 [ADD]
Mahler, G.:Syms, w. J. Blegen (sop), B. Hendricks (sop), M. Price (sop), G. Zeumer (sop), H. Wittek (trb), A. Baltsa (mez), C. Ludwig (mez), K. Riegel (ten), H. Prey (bar), A. Schmidt (bar), J. Van Dam (b-bar), Royal Concertgebouw Orch, Vienna PO, Westminster Choir, New York Choral Artists, Brooklyn Boys' Choir, Vienna Boys' Choir, Vienna State Opera Chorus, Vienna Singverein
Deutsche Grammophon 13-▲ 435162-2 [DDD]
Mahler, G.:Sym 1 *(rec 1966)*
Sony Classical ("Bernstein:The Royal Edition" series) 2-▲ SM2K 47573 [ADD]
Mahler, G.:Sym 1 CBS ▲ MK 42194
Mahler, G.:Sym 3, w. C. Ludwig (mez), Brooklyn Boys' Chorus, New York Choral Artists [G]
Deutsche Grammophon 2-▲ 427328-2 [DDD]
Mahler, G.:Sym 3, w. M. Lipton (cta), New York Phil Chorus *(rec 1961)*
Sony Classical ("Bernstein:The Royal Edition" series) 2-▲ SM2K 47576 [ADD]
Mahler, G.:Sym 4, w. R. Grist (sop) *(rec 1960)*
Sony Classical ("Bernstein:The Royal Edition" series) ▲ SMK 47579 [ADD]
Mahler, G.:Sym 5—Adagietto CBS ▲ MYK 38484 [AAD] ■ MYT 38484
Mahler, G.:Sym 5 *(rec 1963)*
Sony Classical ("Bernstein:The Royal Edition" series) ▲ SMK 47580 [ADD]
Mahler, G.:Sym 5 CBS ▲ MK 42198
Mahler, G.:Sym 6 *(rec 1967)*
Sony Classical ("Bernstein:The Royal Edition" series) 3-▲ SM3K 47581 [ADD]
Mahler, G.:Sym 7 Deutsche Grammophon 2-▲ 419211-2 [DDD]
Mahler, G.:Sym 7 *(rec 1965)*
Sony Classical ("Bernstein:The Royal Edition" series) 3-▲ SM3K 47585 [ADD]
Mahler, G.:Sym 9 *(rec 1965)*
Sony Classical ("Bernstein:The Royal Edition" series) 3-▲ SM3K 47585 [ADD]
Mahler, G.:Sym 10—Adagio *(rec 1975)*
Sony Classical ("Bernstein:The Royal Edition" series) 3-▲ SM3K 47585 [ADD]
Mendelssohn, F.:Athalie (sels), w. P. Zukerman (vn)—War March of the Priests *(rec Oct. 26, 1967)*
Sony Classical ▲ SMK 47592 [ADD]
Mendelssohn, F.:Con in e Vn & Orch, Op. 64, w. P. Zukerman (vn) *(rec Feb. 6, 1969)*
Sony Classical ▲ SMK 47592 [ADD]
Mendelssohn, F.:Die Hebriden *(rec Feb. 17, 1966)* Sony Classical ▲ SMK 47592 [ADD]
Mendelssohn, F.:Music of, Columbia SO, Philadelphia Orch CBS ▲ MLK 39452 ■ MT 39452
Mendelssohn, F.:Ruy Blas (ov) Sony Classical ▲ SMK 47591
Mendelssohn, F.:Sym 3 Sony Classical ▲ SMK 47591
Mendelssohn, F.:Sym 4 *(rec Jan. 13, 1958)* Sony Classical ▲ SMK 47592 [ADD]
Mendelssohn, F.:Sym 5 Sony Classical ▲ SMK 47591
Milhaud, D.:Choëphores, w. Vera Zorina (nar), Virginia Babikian (sop), Irene Jordan (sop), McHenry Boatwright (bar), New York Schola Cantorum
Sony Classical ("Masterworks Heritage" series) ▲ MHK 62352
Mozart, W.A.:Kleine Nachtmusik *(rec Mar. 12, 1973)*
Sony Classical ("Bernstein:The Royal Edition" series) ▲ SMK 47593 Δ SM 47593 [ADD]
Mozart, W.A.:Ovs—Le nozze di Figaro Sony Classical ▲ SMK 47601
Mozart, W.A.:Sym 36 *(rec New York, Mar. 6, 1961)*
Sony Classical ("Bernstein:The Royal Edition" series) ▲ SMK 47593 Δ SM 47593 [ADD]

New York PO (cont.)
L. Bernstein (cnd) (cont.)
Mozart, W.A.:Sym 39 *(rec New York, Mar. 27, 1961)*
Sony Classical ("Bernstein:The Royal Edition" series) ▲ SMK 47594 Δ SM 47594 [ADD]
Mozart, W.A.:Sym 40 *(rec New York, May 20, 1963)*
Sony Classical ("Bernstein:The Royal Edition" series) ▲ SMK 47593 Δ SM 47593 [ADD]
Mozart, W.A.:Sym 41 *(rec New York, Jan. 23-25, 1968)*
Sony Classical ("Bernstein:The Royal Edition" series) ▲ SMK 47594 Δ SM 47594 [ADD]
Mussorgsky, M.:Night CBS ▲ MYK 36726 ■ MYT 36726
Mussorgsky, M.:Night Sony Classical ▲ SMK 47596
Mussorgsky, M.:Pictures at an Exhibition CBS ▲ MYK 36726 ■ MYT 36726
Mussorgsky, M.:Pictures at an Exhibition *(rec New York, Oct. 14, 1958)*
Sony Classical ("Bernstein:The Royal Edition" series) ▲ SMK 47595 Δ SM 47595 [ADD]
Nicolai, O.:Lustigen Weiber (ov) Sony Classical ▲ SMK 47601
Nielsen, C.:Con Cl, w. S. Drucker (cl) *(rec 1967)* Sony Classical 4-▲ S4K 45989 [ADD]
Nielsen, C.:Con Fl, w. J. Baker (fl) Sony Classical ▲ SMK 47599
Nielsen, C.:Con Fl, w. J. Baker (fl) *(rec 1966)* Sony Classical 4-▲ S4K 45989 [ADD]
Nielsen, C.:Sym 2 *(rec 1973)* Sony Classical 4-▲ S4K 45989 [ADD]
Nielsen, C.:Sym 2 Sony Classical ▲ SMK 47597
Nielsen, C.:Sym 4 *(rec 1970)* Sony Classical 4-▲ S4K 45989 [ADD]
Nielsen, C.:Sym 4 Sony Classical ▲ SMK 47597
Nielsen, C.:Sym 5 *(rec 1962)* Sony Classical 4-▲ S4K 45989 [ADD]
Nocturne Sony Classical ▲ MLK 62617 ■ MLT 62617
Offenbach, J.:Gaîté Parisienne Sony Classical ▲ SMK 47532 [ADD]
Offenbach, J.:Orphée aux enfers (sels) CBS ▲ MYK 37769 [AAD] ■ MYT 37769
Offenbach, J.:Orphée aux enfers (sels) Sony Classical ▲ SMK 47532 [ADD]
Ponchielli, A.:La Gioconda (dance) *(rec Jan. 24, 1968)* Sony Classical ▲ SMK 47600 [ADD]
Poulenc, F.:Con for 2 Pnos, w. A. Gold (pno), R. Fizdale (pno) *(rec Dec. 23, 1961)*
Sony Classical ▲ SMK 47618 [ADD]
Poulenc, F.:Gloria Sop, w. J. Blegen (sop), Westminster Choir *(rec 1976)*
Sony Classical ("Bernstein:The Royal Edition" series) ▲ SMK 47569 [ADD]
Poulenc, F.:Gloria Sop, w. J. Blegen (sop), Westminster Choir [L] CBS ▲ MK 44710 [ADD]
Prokofiev, S.:Con 2 Vn, w. I. Stern (vn) *(rec 1957; mono)* CBS 4-▲ M4K 42003 (m/s) [ADD]
Prokofiev, S.:Music of—March from *The Love for Three Oranges*; Troika from *Lt. Kijé*
CBS ▲ MYK 36725 [ADD]
Prokofiev, S.:Peter & the Wolf Sony Classical ▲ SMK 47596
Prokofiev, S.:Peter & the Wolf, w. L. Bernstein (nar) CBS ▲ MYK 37765 ■ MYT 37765
Prokofiev, S.:Peter & the Wolf—orchestral suite CBS ▲ MLK 39446 ■ MT 39446
Prokofiev, S.:Peter & the Wolf, w. Leonard Bernstein (nar) *(rec Symphony Hall, Boston, Feb 14–15, 1992)* Sony Classical ("Greatest Hits" series) ▲ MLK 69249 [ADD] ■ LT 69
Prokofiev, S.:Sym 1 CBS ▲ MLK 39446 ■ MT 39446
Prokofiev, S.:Sym 1 CBS ▲ MYK 36725 [ADD] ■ MYT 36725
Prokofiev, S.:Sym 1 Sony Classical ▲ SKM 47602
Prokofiev, S.:Sym 5 Sony Classical ▲ SKM 47602
Rachmaninoff, S.:Con 2 Pno, w. G. Graffman (pno) *(rec May 26, 1964)*
Sony Classical ▲ SMK 47630 [ADD]
Rachmaninoff, S.:Con 2 Pno, w. P. Entremont (pno) *(rec Feb. 3, 1960)*
Sony Classical ("Essential Classics" series) ▲ SBK 53512 [ADD] ■ SBT 53512
Rachmaninoff, S.:Con 2 Pno, w. Gary Graffman (pno) CBS ▲ MYK 36722 ■ MYT 36722
Rachmaninoff, S.:Con 2 Pno, w. Gary Graffman (pno) CBS ■ MT 31813
Rachmaninoff, S.:Con 2 Pno, w. Gary Graffman (pno) CBS ▲ MLK 39437 ■ MT 39437
Rachmaninoff, S.:Con 2 Pno, w. Philippe Entremont (pno) Odyssey ▲ MBK 46271 [AAD] ■ YT 46271
Rachmaninoff, S.:Rhapsody on a Theme of Paganini, w. Gary Graffman (pno)
CBS ▲ MYK 36722 ■ MYT 36722
Rachmaninoff, S.:Rhapsody on a Theme of Paganini, w. Gary Graffman (pno) CBS ■ MT 31813
Rachmaninoff, S.:Rhapsody on a Theme of Paganini, w. Gary Graffman (pno) *(rec 1964)*
Sony Classical ("Bernstein:The Royal Edition" series) ▲ SMK 47571 [ADD]
Ravel, M.:Alborada del gracioso CBS ▲ MYK 36714 ■ MYT 36714
Ravel, M.:Daphnis et Chloé (suite 2) *(rec New York, Mar. 13, 1961)*
Sony Classical ("Bernstein:The Royal Edition" series) Δ SM 47603 [ADD]
Ravel, M.:Daphnis et Chloé (suite 2) CBS ▲ MYK 36714 ■ MYT 36714
Ravel, M.:Ma mère l'oye Orch *(rec 1965)*
Sony Classical ("Bernstein:The Royal Edition" series) ▲ SMK 47545 [ADD]
Ravel, M.:Pavane pour une infante défunte *(rec 1965)*
Sony Classical ("Bernstein:The Royal Edition" series) ▲ SMK 47545 [ADD]
Ravel, M.:Pavane pour une infante défunte CBS ▲ MYK 37769 [AAD] ■ MYT 37769
Ravel, M.:Rapsodie espagnole, w. Schola Cantorum *(rec New York, Mar. 6, 1973)*
Sony Classical ("Bernstein:The Royal Edition" series) Δ SM 47603 [ADD]
Ravel, M.:Tzigane, w. Z. Francescatti (vn) *(rec 1964)* Sony Classical ▲ SMK 47548 [ADD]
Ravel, M.:La Valse CBS ▲ MYK 36714 ■ MYT 36714
Revueltas, S.:Sensemayá *(rec 1963)*
Sony Classical ("Bernstein:The Royal Edition") ▲ SMK 47544 [ADD]
Rimsky-Korsakov, N.:Capriccio espagnol *(rec New York, May 2, 1959)*
Sony Classical ("Bernstein:The Royal Edition" series) ▲ SMK 47595 Δ SM 47595 [ADD]
Rimsky-Korsakov, N.:Capriccio espagnol CBS ▲ MYK 36728 [AAD] ■ MYT 36728
Rimsky-Korsakov, N.:Scheherazade Sony Classical ▲ SMK 47605
Rimsky-Korsakov, N.:Scheherazade CBS ▲ MYK 38476 [AAD] ■ MYT 38476
Rimsky-Korsakov, N.:Snow Maiden (dance) *(rec Mar. 21, 1967)* Sony Classical ▲ SMK 47600 [ADD]
Romantic Favorites for Strings CBS ▲ MYK 38484 [AAD]
Rorem, N.:Con Vn, w. G. Kremer (vn) Deutsche Grammophon ▲ 429231-1
Rossini, G.:Ovs—W. Tell; L'Italiana in Algeri; La gazza ladra; Il barbiere de Siviglia; La scala di seta; Semiramide Sony Classical ▲ SMK 47606
Rossini, G.:Ovs, William Tell CBS ▲ MYK 37240 [AAD] ■ MYT 37240
Roussel, A.:Sym 3 Sony Classical ▲ MHK 62352
Saint-Saëns, C.:Carnival of the Animals, w. L. Bernstein (nar) CBS ▲ MYK 37765 ■ MYT 37765
Saint-Saëns, C.:Carnival of the Animals Sony Classical ▲ SMK 47596
Saint-Saëns, C.:Con 4 Pno, w. R. Casadesus (pno) Sony Classical ▲ SMK 47608
Saint-Saëns, C.:Danse macabre CBS ▲ MYK 37769 [AAD] ■ MYT 37769
Saint-Saëns, C.:Introduction & Rondo capriccioso, w. Z. Francescatti (vn) Sony Classical ▲ SMK 47608
Saint-Saëns, C.:Samson et Dalila (Bacchanale) CBS ▲ MYK 37769 [AAD] ■ MYT 37769
Saint-Saëns, C.:Samson et Dalila (Bacchanale) *(rec May 15, 1967)*
Sony Classical ▲ SMK 47600 [ADD]
Saint-Saëns, C.:Sym 3, w. L. Raver (org) CBS ▲ MYK 37255 [AAD] ■ MYT 37255
Saint-Saëns, C.:Sym 3, w. L. Raver (org) Sony Classical ▲ SMK 47608
Schubert, Franz:Sym 5 Sony Classical ▲ SMK 47609
Schubert, Franz:Sym 8 CBS ▲ MYK 36719 ■ MYT 36719
Schubert, Franz:Sym 8 Sony Classical ▲ SMK 47610
Schubert, Franz:Sym 9 Sony Classical ▲ SMK 47610
Schuman, W.:Sym 3 Deutsche Grammophon ▲ 419780-2 [DDD]
Schumann, R.:Con Vc, w. L. Rose (vc) Sony Classical ▲ SMK 47609
Schumann, R.:Genoveva (ov) Sony Classical ▲ SMK 47609
Shostakovich, D.:Con 1 Pno, w. A. Previn (pno), W. Vacchiano (tpt) *(rec Apr. 8, 1962)*
Sony Classical ▲ SMK 47618 [ADD]
Shostakovich, D.:Con 2 Pno, w. L. Bernstein (pno) *(rec Jan. 6, 1958)*
Sony Classical ▲ SMK 47618 [ADD]
Shostakovich, D.:Sym 1 *(rec Dec. 14, 1971)*
Sony Classical ("Leonard Bernstein:The Royal Edition") ▲ SMK 47614 [ADD]
Shostakovich, D.:Sym 5 *(rec 1959)* CBS ▲ MYK 37218 ■ MYT 37218
Shostakovich, D.:Sym 5 *(rec Oct. 20, 1959)*
Sony Classical ("Leonard Bernstein:The Royal Edition") ▲ SMK 47615 [ADD]

New York PO (cont.)
L. Bernstein (cnd) (cont.)
Shostakovich, D.:Sym 5 *(rec 1979)* CBS ▲ MDK 44903 [DDD] ■ MDT 44903 (D)
Shostakovich, D.:Sym 5 *(rec 1959)* CBS ▲ MK 44711 [ADD]
Shostakovich, D.:Sym 6 *(rec Oct. 14, 1963)* SMK ("Leonard Bernstein:The Royal Edition") ▲ 47614 [ADD]
Shostakovich, D.:Sym 7 CBS ▲ MK 44855 [ADD]
Shostakovich, D.:Sym 7 *(rec Oct. 22–23, 1962)* Sony Classical ("Leonard Bernstein:The Royal Edition") ▲ SMK 47616 [ADD]
Shostakovich, D.:Sym 9 *(rec Oct. 19, 1965)* Sony Classical ▲ SMK 47615 [ADD]
Shostakovich, D.:Sym 9 CBS ▲ MK 44711 [ADD]
Shostakovich, D.:Sym 14, w. T. Kubiak (sop), I. Bushkin (bass) [R] *(rec Dec. 8, 1976)* Sony Classical ▲ SMK 47617 [ADD]
Sibelius, J.:Con Vn, w. Z. Francescatti (vn) Sony Classical ▲ SMK 47540 [ADD]
Sibelius, J.:Finlandia CBS ▲ MYK 36718 ■ MYT 36718
Sibelius, J.:Finlandia *(rec 1965)* Sony Classical ("Bernstein:The Royal Edition" series) ▲ SMK 47549 [ADD]
Sibelius, J.:Luonnotar, w. P. Curtin (sop) *(rec Oct. 19, 1965)* Sony Classical 2–▲ SM2K 47619 [ADD]
Sibelius, J.:Pohjola's Daughter *(rec May 1, 1964)* Sony Classical 2–▲ SM2K 47619 [ADD]
Sibelius, J.:Pohjola's Daughter *(rec 1964)* Sony Classical ("Essential Classics" series) ▲ SBK 48271 [ADD] ■ SBT 48271
Sibelius, J.:Pohjola's Daughter CBS ▲ MYK 38474 [ADD]
Sibelius, J.:The Swan of Tuonela *(rec 1973)* Sony Classical ("Bernstein:The Royal Edition" series) ▲ SMK 47549 [ADD]
Sibelius, J.:The Swan of Tuonela CBS ▲ MYK 36718 ■ MYT 36718
Sibelius, J.:Sym 1 *(rec Mar. 14, 1967)* Sony Classical 2–▲ SM2K 47619 [ADD]
Sibelius, J.:Sym 2 CBS ▲ MYK 38477 [ADD] ■ MYT 38477
Sibelius, J.:Sym 2 *(rec Mar. 16, 1966)* Sony Classical 2–▲ SM2K 47619 [ADD]
Sibelius, J.:Sym 3 *(rec Oct. 18, 1965)* Sony Classical 2–▲ SM2K 47619 [ADD]
Sibelius, J.:Sym 4 *(rec Feb. 1, 1966)* Sony Classical ("Leonard Bernstein:The Royal Edition") 2–▲ SM2K 47622 [ADD]
Sibelius, J.:Sym 5 *(rec Mar. 27, 1961)* Sony Classical ("Leonard Bernstein:The Royal Edition") 2–▲ SM2K 47622 [ADD]
Sibelius, J.:Sym 5 CBS ▲ MYK 38474 [ADD]
Sibelius, J.:Sym 6 *(rec May 9, 1967)* Sony Classical ("Leonard Bernstein:The Royal Edition") 2–▲ SM2K 47622 [ADD]
Sibelius, J.:Sym 7 Sony Classical ("Leonard Bernstein:The Royal Edition") 2–▲ SM2K 47622 [ADD]
Sibelius, J.:Valse triste CBS ▲ MYK 36718 ■ MYT 36718
Sibelius, J.:Valse triste *(rec 1969)* Sony Classical ("Bernstein:The Royal Edition" series) ▲ SMK 47549 [ADD]
Sibelius, J.:Valse triste CBS ▲ MLK 39447 ■ MT 39447
Smetana, B.:The Bartered Bride (ov) Sony Classical ▲ SMK 47601
Smetana, B.:The Moldau *(rec 1964)* Sony Classical ("Bernstein:The Royal Edition" series) ▲ SMK 47547 [ADD]
Strauss (I), Joh.:Radetzky March *(rec Oct. 20, 1970)* Sony Classical ▲ SMK 47626 [ADD]
Strauss (II), Joh.:Music of—An der schönen, blauen Donau; Wiener Blut; Perpetuum mobile; Tritsch-Tratsch-Polka; G'schichten aus dem Wienerwald; Kaiser-Walzer; Frühlingsstimmen; Künsterleben; Auf der Jagd; Rosen aus dem Süden *(rec between 1967 & 1975)* Sony Classical ▲ SMK 47626 [ADD]
Strauss (II), Joh.:Ovs—Die Fledermaus Sony Classical ▲ SMK 47601
Strauss (II), Joh.:Waltzes—5 waltzes CBS ▲ MYK 37771 [AAD] ■ MYT 37771
Strauss, R.:Also sprach Zarathustra *(rec Oct. 5, 1970)* Sony Classical ▲ SMK 47626 [ADD]
Strauss, R.:Don Juan *(rec Feb. 3, 1963–May 15, 1990)* Sony Classical ("Leonard Bernstein:The Royal Edition") ▲ SMK 47626 [ADD]
Strauss, R.:Don Quixote, w. L. Munroe (vc) *(rec Oct. 24, 1968)* Sony Classical ▲ SMK 47625 [ADD]
Strauss, R.:Festliches Präludium *(rec Oct. 2, 1962)* Sony Classical ▲ SMK 47625 [ADD]
Strauss, R.:Salome (dance) *(rec Oct. 12, 1965)* Sony Classical ▲ SMK 47625 [ADD]
Strauss, R.:Till Eulenspiegels lustige Streiche *(rec Apr. 20, 1959)* Sony Classical ▲ SMK 47626 [ADD]
Stravinsky, I.:Con Pno Ww, w. S. Lipkin (pno) *(rec Oct. 26, 1959)* Sony Classical ▲ SMK 47628 [ADD]
Stravinsky, I.:The Firebird Suite Sony Classical ▲ SMK 47605
Stravinsky, I.:The Firebird Suite CBS ▲ MYK 37221 ■ MYT 37221
Stravinsky, I.:Pétrouchka CBS ▲ MYK 37221 ■ MYT 37221
Stravinsky, I.:Pulcinella Suite CBS ▲ MK 44709 [ADD]
Stravinsky, I.:Pulcinella Suite *(rec Mar. 28, 1960)* Sony Classical ▲ SMK 47628 [ADD]
Stravinsky, I.:Le Sacre du printemps Orch *(rec Jan. 20, 1958)* Sony Classical ▲ SMK 47629 [ADD]
Stravinsky, I.:Le Sacre du printemps Orch CBS ▲ MK 44709 [ADD]
Suppé, F. von:Ovs—Leicte Kavallierie; Dichter und Bauer Sony Classical ▲ SMK 47606
Suppé, F. von:Ovs—Poet & Peasant CBS ▲ MYK 37240 [AAD] ■ MYT 37240
Suppé, F. von:Ovs—The Beautiful Galatea Sony Classical ▲ SMK 47532 [ADD]
Tchaikovsky, P.:Andante cantabile CBS ▲ MYK 38484 [AAD] ■ MYT 38484
Tchaikovsky, P.:Capriccio italien CBS ▲ MYK 36728 ■ MYT 36728
Tchaikovsky, P.:Con 1 Pno, w. A. Watts (pno) *(rec Mar. 12, 1973)* Sony Classical ▲ SMK 47630 [ADD]
Tchaikovsky, P.:Con Vn, w. I. Stern (vn) *(rec Mar. 3, 1975)* Sony Classical ▲ SMK 47637 [ADD]
Tchaikovsky, P.:Eugene Onegin (sels) *(rec Jan. 12, 1971)* Sony Classical ▲ SMK 47636 [ADD]
Tchaikovsky, P.:Francesca da Rimini Deutsche Grammophon ▲ 429778–2 [DDD]
Tchaikovsky, P.:Marche slave CBS ▲ MYK 36723 ■ MYT 36723
Tchaikovsky, P.:Marche slave *(rec Jan. 21, 1963)* Sony Classical ▲ SMK 47634 [ADD]
Tchaikovsky, P.:Music of, w. Ormandy (cnd), Philadelphia Orch CBS ▲ MLK 39440 [ADD] ■ MT 39440
Tchaikovsky, P.:Music of, w. Ormandy (cnd), Philadelphia Orch CBS ▲ MLK 39433 ■ MT 39433
Tchaikovsky, P.:Nutcracker Suite CBS ▲ MYK 37238 ■ MYT 37238
Tchaikovsky, P.:Ov 1812 *(rec Oct. 2, 1962)* Sony Classical ▲ SMK 47634 [ADD]
Tchaikovsky, P.:Ov 1812 CBS ▲ MLK 39433 ■ MT 39433
Tchaikovsky, P.:Romeo & Juliet Deutsche Grammophon ▲ 429234–2 [DDD]
Tchaikovsky, P.:Romeo & Juliet *(rec Jan. 28, 1957)* Sony Classical ▲ SMK 47632 [ADD]
Tchaikovsky, P.:Serenade Strs, w. I. Stern (vn) *(rec Oct. 22, 1970)* Sony Classical ▲ SMK 47637 [ADD]
Tchaikovsky, P.:Sleeping Beauty (sels) *(rec Jan. 12, 1971)* Sony Classical ▲ SMK 47636 [ADD]
Tchaikovsky, P.:Swan Lake (sels) *(rec May 13–Dec. 8, 1969)* Sony Classical ▲ SMK 47636 [ADD]
Tchaikovsky, P.:Swan Lake (sels) CBS ▲ MYK 37238 ■ MYT 37238
Tchaikovsky, P.:Sym 1 *(rec Oct. 20, 1970)* Sony Classical ▲ SMK 47631 [ADD]
Tchaikovsky, P.:Sym 2 *(rec Oct. 24, 1967)* Sony Classical ▲ SMK 47631 [ADD]
Tchaikovsky, P.:Sym 3 *(rec Feb. 10, 1970)* Sony Classical ▲ SMK 47632 [ADD]
Tchaikovsky, P.:Sym 4 Deutsche Grammophon ▲ 429778–2 [DDD]
Tchaikovsky, P.:Sym 4 *(rec Apr. 28, 1975)* Sony Classical ▲ SMK 47633 [ADD]
Tchaikovsky, P.:Sym 5 *(rec May 16, 1960)* Sony Classical ▲ SMK 47634 [ADD]
Tchaikovsky, P.:Sym 6 *(rec Feb. 11, 1964)* Sony Classical ▲ SMK 47635 [ADD]
Thomas, A.:Ovs—Mignon; Raymond CBS ▲ MYK 37240 [AAD] ■ MYT 37240
Thomas, A.:Ovs—Mignon Sony Classical ▲ SMK 47601
Vaughan Williams, R.:Fant on Greensleeves CBS ▲ MYK 38484 [AAD] ■ MYT 38484
Vaughan Williams, R.:Fant on Greensleeves *(rec Dec. 8, 1969)* Sony Classical ▲ SMK 47638 [ADD]
Vaughan Williams, R.:Fant on a Theme by Thomas Tallis CBS ▲ MYK 38484 [AAD] ■ MYT 38484
Vaughan Williams, R.:Fant on a Theme by Thomas Tallis *(rec Dec. 21, 1976)* Sony Classical ▲ SMK 47638 [ADD]
Vaughan Williams, R.:Serenade to Music *(rec Sept. 23, 1962)* Sony Classical ▲ SMK 47638 [ADD]
Vaughan Williams, R.:Sym 4 *(rec Oct. 21, 1965)* Sony Classical ▲ SMK 47638 [ADD]
Verdi, G.:Aida (sels)—ballet music *(rec Jan. 24, 1968)* Sony Classical ▲ SMK 47600 [ADD]

New York PO (cont.)
L. Bernstein (cnd) (cont.)
Villa-Lobos, H.:Bachiana brasileira 5, w. N. Davrath (sop) *(rec 1963)* Sony Classical ▲ SMK 47544 [ADD]
Vivaldi, A.:Cons Diverse Instrs, w. G. Vicari (mand), C. de Filippis (mand), J. Wummer (fl), R. Morris (fl), W. Vacchiano (tpt), N. Prager (tpt), E. Brenner (b ob), C. Stavrache (hp), A. Wurtzler (hp), J. Gorigliano (vn), L. Varga (vc)—in C, RV.558 *(rec Dec. 15, 1958)* Sony Classical ("Leonard Bernstein:The Royal Edition" series) ▲ SMK 47642 [ADD]
Vivaldi, A.:Cons Fl (misc), w. J. Wummer (fl)—in c, RV.441 *(rec Dec. 15, 1958)* Sony Classical ("Leonard Bernstein:The Royal Edition" series) ▲ SMK 47642 [ADD]
Vivaldi, A.:Cons Ob, w. H. Gomberg (ob)—in d, RV.454 *(rec Dec. 15, 1958)* Sony Classical ("Leonard Bernstein:The Royal Edition" series) ▲ SMK 47642 [ADD]
Vivaldi, A.:Music of, w. John Williams (cnd), J.-C. Malgoire (cnd), English CO, La Grande Ecurie et la Chambre du Roy—sels. from The Four Seasons, Mandolin Concerto in C, 2–Mandolin Concerto in G, Guitar Concerto in D, etc. CBS ▲ MLK 45810 ■ MLT 45810
Wagner, R.:Ovs, Preludes & Orch Sels, w. E. Farrell (sop)—Tannhäuser:Ov.; Götterdämmerung:Finale Act 3; Tristan und Isolde:Prelude Act 1 *(rec 1961 & 1967)* Sony Classical ▲ SMK 47644 [ADD]
Wagner, R.:Ovs, Preludes & Orch Sels—Der fliegende Hollander:Overture; Lohengrin:Preludes Acts 1 & 3; Die Meistersinger von Nürnberg:Prelude Act 1; Die Walküre:Fire Music & Ride of the Valkyries; Tannhäuser:Festival March *(rec 1964–68)* Sony Classical ▲ SMK 47643
Wagner, R.:Die Walküre (ride of the valkyries) CBS ▲ MLK 39438 ■ MT 39438
The World's Greatest Marches CBS 2–■ MGT 35919

P. Boulez (cnd)
Bartók, B.:Con Orch CBS ▲ MK 37259 [AAD] ■ MYT 37259
Bartók, B.:The Miraculous Mandarin Sony Classical ("Pierre Boulez Edition" series) ▲ SMK 45837
Bartók, B.:Pieces Orch, Sz.51 Sony Classical ("Pierre Boulez Edition" series) ▲ SMK 45837
Bartók, B.:Village Scenes, w. Schola Cantorum, Camerata Singers Sony Classical ("Pierre Boulez Edition" series) ▲ SMK 45837
Berg, A.:Lulu (suite), w. J. Norman (sop) Sony Classical ▲ SMK 45838 [DDD]
Berg, A.:Lyric Suite Sony Classical ▲ SMK 45838 [DDD]
Berg, A.:Der Wein, w. J. Blegen (sop) Sony Classical ▲ SMK 45838 [DDD]
Carter, E.:A Sym for 3 Orchs Sony Classical ("Pierre Boulez Edition" series) ▲ SMK 68334
Dukas, P.:La péri Sony Classical ("Pierre Boulez Edition" series) ▲ SMK 68333
Falla, M. de:Con Hpd, w. Igor Kipnis (hpd) Sony Classical ("Pierre Boulez Edition" series) ▲ SMK 68333
Falla, M. de:Con Hpd, w. I. Kipnis (hpd), P. Brook (fl), H. Gomberg (ob), S. Drucker (cl), E. Chapo (vn), L. Munroe (vc) *(rec Mar. 2, 1975)* Sony Classical ▲ SBK 53264 ■ SBT 53264
Falla, M. de:El sombrero de tres picos, w. J. DeGaetani (mez) Odyssey ▲ MBK 44721 [ADD] ■ YT 44721
Falla, M. de:El sombrero de tres picos, w. Jan DeGaetani (mez) Sony Classical ("Pierre Boulez Edition" series) ▲ SMK 68333
Handel, G.F.:Royal Fireworks Music CBS ▲ MYK 38480 [AAD]; ■ MYT 38480
Handel, G.F.:Water Music (suites) CBS ▲ MYK 38480 [AAD]; ■ MYT 38480
Ravel, M.:Orchestral Music, Cleveland Orch—including Alborada del gracioso, Boléro, Daphnis et Chloé (complete), Ma Mère l'Oye, Rapsodie espagnole, La Valses, Valses nobles et sentimentales Sony Classical 3–▲ SM3K 45842 [DDD]
Schoenberg, A.:Verklärte Nacht *(rec Sept. 24, 1973)* Sony Classical ▲ SMK 48464 [ADD]
Stravinsky, I.:Le Chant du rossignol *(rec 1975)* CBS ▲ MK 42396 [ADD]
Stravinsky, I.:Pétrouchka [original 1911 version] CBS ▲ MK 42395 [AAD]
Stravinsky, I.:Scherzo fantastique Sony Classical (Pierre Boulez Edition) ▲ SK 45843
Stravinsky, I.:Syms Ww, Domaine Musical Orch Sony Classical ("Pierre Boulez Edition" series) ▲ SMK 68332

F. Busch (cnd)
Beethoven, L. van:Con Vn, Op. 61, w. A. Busch (vn) *(rec live, New York 1942)* Melodram ▲ CDM 18040 [ADD]

G. Cantelli (cnd)
Bartók, B.:Music for Strs, Perc & Cel Stradivarius ▲ STV 13591 [AAD]
Beethoven, L. van:Con 1 Pno, w. R. Serkin (pno) *(rec live 3/29/53)* Melodram ▲ MEL 18010
Beethoven, L. van:Con 4 Pno, w. Wilhelm Backhaus (pno) *(rec live, 1956)* Legend ▲ LGD 121
Beethoven, L. van:Con 5 Pno, "Emperor", w. R. Serkin (pno) *(rec live 1954)* Melodram ▲ MEL 18010
Beethoven, L. van:Con 5 Pno, "Emperor", w. Walter Gieseking (pno) Stradivarius ▲ STV 13594 [AAD]
Brahms, J.:Alto Rhap, w. Martha Lipton (alt), Westminster Choir *(rec live, 1956)* Legend ▲ LGD 121
Brahms, J.:Sym 3 Stradivarius ▲ STV 13591 [AAD]
Debussy, C.:Martyre de Saint Sébastien (complete) Legend ▲ LGD 101 [ADD]
Debussy, C.:La Mer Legend ▲ LGD 101 [ADD]
Debussy, C.:Nocturnes Legend ▲ LGD 101 [ADD]
Gabrieli, G.:Music of—Canzona per Otto Voci Stradivarius ▲ STV 13591 [AAD]
Mendelssohn, F.:Con in e Vn & Orch, Op. 64, w. Jascha Heifetz (vn) *(rec live, Mar. 14, 1954)* As Disc ▲ ASD 2500 (m)
Mozart, W.A.:Con 21 Pno, w. Walter Gieseking (pno) *(rec 1953 & 1955)* Legend ▲ LGD 130 [ADD]
Mozart, W.A.:Divert Hns Strs, K.287 *(rec 1953 & 1955)* Legend ▲ LGD 130 [ADD]
Mozart, W.A.:Musikalischer Spass *(rec 1953 & 1955)* Legend ▲ LGD 130 [ADD]
Mussorgsky, M.:Pictures Stradivarius ▲ STV 13594 [AAD]
Ravel, M.:Daphnis et Chloé (suite 2) Legend ▲ LGD 104 [ADD]
Schubert, Franz:Sym 8 *(rec 1953)* Legend ▲ LGD 111 [ADD]
Schubert, Franz:Sym 9 *(rec 1953)* Legend ▲ LGD 111 [ADD]

A. Kostelanetz (cnd)
Gershwin, G.:Con Pno, w. O. Levant (pno) *(rec 1942)* CBS ▲ MK 42514 (m) [ADD] ■ FMT 42514 (m)
Grofé, F.:Mississippi Suite CBS ▲ MYK 37759 [ADD] ■ MYT 37759

E. Kurtz
Wieniawski, H.:Con 2 Vn, w. I. Stern (vn) *(rec Carnegie Hall, 3/27/46)* CBS 4–▲ M4K 42003 (m/s) [ADD]

K. Masur (cnd)
Beethoven, L. van:Egmont (incidental music) Teldec ▲ 9031-77313-2
Beethoven, L. van:Ovs Teldec ▲ 9031-77313-2
Beethoven, L. van:Sym 5 Teldec ▲ 9031-77313-2
Berg, A.:Lulu (suite), w. A. Réaux (sop) Teldec ▲ 95029-2
Brahms, J.:Academic Festival Ov Teldec ▲ 9031-77291-2
Brahms, J.:Sym 2 Teldec ▲ 9031-77291-2
Brahms, J.:Vars on a Theme by Haydn Teldec ▲ 9031-74007-2 ZK
Bruckner, A.:Sym 4, "Romantic" *(rec New York, Oct. 1993)* Teldec ▲ 93332-2 [DDD]
Bruckner, A.:Sym 7 Teldec ("M Line" series) ▲ 97467-2
Bruckner, A.:Sym 7 *(rec live, Avery Fisher Hall, New York 9/13/91)* Teldec ▲ 9031-73243-2 [DDD]
Dvořák, A.:Con Vc, w. Yo-Yo Ma (vc) *(rec Avery Fisher Hall, Lincoln Center for the Performing Arts, Jan 27 & 30, 1995)* Sony Classical ▲ SK 67173 [DDD]
Dvořák, A.:Slavonic Dances (sels)—Nos. 6,8 & 10 *(rec live)* Teldec ▲ 9031-73244-2 ZK
Dvořák, A.:Sym 8 Teldec ▲ 90847
Dvořák, A.:Sym 9, "From the New World" Teldec ▲ 9031-73244-2 ZK
Franck, C.:Sym in d Teldec ▲ 9031-74863-2
Herbert, V.:Con 2 Vc, w. Yo-Yo Ma (vc) *(rec Avery Fisher Hall, Lincoln Center for the Performing Arts, Jan 27 & 30, 1995)* Sony Classical ▲ SK 67173 [DDD]
Janácek, L.:Sinfonietta Teldec ▲ 90847
Mahler, G.:Sym 9 *(rec Avery Fischer Hall, New York, Apr. 1994)* Teldec ▲ 90882-2 [DDD]
Reger, M.:Vars & Fugue on a Theme by Mozart Teldec ▲ 9031-74007-2 ZK
Schuman, W.:Vars on "America" Teldec ▲ 9031-74007-2 ZK
Shostakovich, D.:Sym 13, w. Y. Yevtushenko (reciter), S. Leiferkus (bass), New York Choral Artists Men's Voices Teldec ▲ 90848
Tchaikovsky, P.:Waltzes—waltzes from Swan Lake, Sleeping Beauty, Hamlet, Eugene Onegin, Nutcracker, Syms 5 & 6, Serenade Teldec ▲ 94571-2

284
▲ = CD ♦ = Enhanced CD Δ = MD ■ = Cassette Tape □ = DCC

New York PO (cont.)
K. Masur (cnd) (cont.)
Weill, K.:The Seven Deadly Sins, w. A. Réaux (sop) Teldec ▲ 95029–2
Z. Mehta (cnd)
Bach, J.S.:Con for 2 Vns, w. I. Perlman (vn), I. Stern (vn) CBS ▲ MYK 38487 ■ MYT 38487
Bach, J.S.:Con for 2 Vns, w. Isaac Stern (vn), Itzhak Perlman (vn) Sony Classical ▲ SMK 66471
Bach, J.S.:Con for 2 Vns, w. I. Perlman (vn), I. Stern (vn) CBS ■ MGT 39798
Bach, J.S.:Con for 2 Vns, w. I. Perlman (vn), I. Stern (vn) CBS ▲ MK 36692 [DDD]
Barber, S.:Essay 3 New World ▲ NW 309–2 [ADD]
Beethoven, L. van:Coriolan Ov RCA Victor ▲ 09026–61714–2; ■ 09026–61714–4
Beethoven, L. van:Fant Pno, Op. 80, "Choral Fant", w. E. Ax (pno), New York Choral Artists RCA Silver Seal ▲ 09026–61213–2 ■ 09026–61213–4
Beethoven, L. van:Sym 3, "Eroica" CBS ▲ MK 35883 [DDD]
Beethoven, L. van:Sym 9, "Choral Sym", w. New York Choral Artists [soloists Margaret Price, Marilyn Horne, Jon Vickers, Matti Salminen] [G] RCA Silver Seal ▲ 60477–2–RV [DDD] ■ 60477–4–RV
Brahms, J.:Con 1 Pno, w. D. Barenboim (pno) Odyssey 3–▲ MB3K 45828
Brahms, J.:Con 2 Pno, w. D. Barenboim (pno) Odyssey 3–▲ MB3K 45828
Brahms, J.:Con 2 Pno, w. D. Barenboim (pno) Odyssey ▲ MBK 42608 [ADD] ■ YT 42608
Brahms, J.:Con Vn, w. I. Stern (vn) Odyssey 3–▲ MB3K 45828
Brahms, J.:Con Vn & Vc, "Double Con", w. P. Zukerman (vn), L. Harrell (vc) Odyssey 3–▲ MB3K 45828
Brahms, J.:Sym 1 Odyssey ■ YT 42486
Brahms, J.:Vars on a Theme by Haydn Odyssey ■ YT 42488
Chausson, E.:Poème Vn, w. Itzhak Perlman (vn) Deutsche Grammophon ("Masters" series) ▲ 445564–2
Chausson, E.:Poème Vn, w. I. Perlman (vn) Deutsche Grammophon ▲ 423063–2 [DDD]
Chopin, F.:Con 1 Pno, w. M. Perahia (pno) CBS ▲ MK 42400 [AAD/DDD]
Corigliano, J.:Con Cl, w. S. Drucker (cl) New World ▲ NW 309–2 [ADD]
del Tredici, D.:Steps New World ▲ 80390–2 [DDD]
Domingo at the Philharmonic, w. P. Domingo (ten), Adriana Morell (sop) CBS ▲ MK 44942 [DDD] ■ MT 44942 (D)
Druckman, J.:Prism New World ▲ NW 335–2 [DDD] ■ NW 335–4 (D)
Dvořák, A.:Carnival CBS ▲ MK 44923 [DDD] ■ MT 44923 (D); □ MM 44923
Dvořák, A.:Con Vn, w. Midori (vn) CBS ▲ MK 44923 [DDD] ■ MT 44923 (D) □ NM 44923
Dvořák, A.:Romance Vn, w. Midori (vn) CBS ▲ MK 44923 [DDD] ■ MT 44923 (D) □ NM 44923
Gershwin, G.:An American in Paris Teldec ▲ 2292–46318–2 [DDD]
Gershwin, G.:Cuban Ov Teldec ▲ 2292–46318–2 [DDD]
Gershwin, G.:Music of CBS ▲ MK 42516 [ADD/DDD] ■ FMT 42516
Gershwin, G.:Porgy & Bess (sels), w. R. Alexander (sop), G. Baker (bar), New York Choral Artists—Introduction & Summertime; A woman is a sometime thing; Overflow; Since I lose my man; The promise' lan'; I got plenty o' nuttin'; Bess, you is my woman now; O, I can't sit down; It ain't necesssarily so; There's a boat dat's leavin' soon for New York; O, Lawd I'm on my way [E] Teldec ▲ 2292–46318–2 [DDD]
Holst, G.:The Planets, w. New York Choral Artists Teldec ▲ 2292–46316–2 [DDD]
Itzhak Perlman Greatest Hits, w. I. Perlman (vn), Orch de Paris [cnd:Daniel Barenboim] Deutsche Grammophon ▲ 437737–2 GH
Mahler, G.:Sym 1 *(rec Nov. 10–25, 1980)* Sony Classical ▲ SBK 53259 ■ SBT 53259
Mahler, G.:Sym 5 Teldec ▲ 2292–46152–2 ZK [DDD]
Mozart, W.A.:Sinf concertante Vn, K.364, w. I. Stern (vn), P. Zukerman (va) CBS ▲ MK 36692 [DDD]
Mussorgsky, M.:Pictures at an Exhibition Odyssey ■ YT 44505
Paine, J.K.:As You Like It New World ▲ NW 374–2 [DDD]
Paine, J.K.:Sym 1 New World ▲ NW 374–2 [DDD]
Paine, J.K.:Sym 2 New World ▲ NW 350–2 [DDD] ■ NW 350–4 (D)
Prokofiev, S.:Cons Vn (comp), w. I. Stern (vn) CBS ▲ MK 42439 [DDD]
Ravel, M.:Tzigane, w. I. Perlman (vn) Deutsche Grammophon ▲ 423063–2 [DDD]
Ravel, M.:Tzigane, w. Itzhak Perlman (vn) *(rec Manhattan Ctr, NY, Sept 1986)* Deutsche Grammophon ("The Originals" series) ▲ 447445–2 [DDD]
Ravel, M.:La Valse Odyssey ■ YT 44505
Rochberg, G.:Con Ob, w. J. Robinson (ob) New World ▲ NW 335–2 [DDD] ■ NW 335–4 (D)
Saint-Saëns, C.:Havanaise Vn, w. I. Perlman (vn) Deutsche Grammophon ▲ 423063–2 [DDD]
Saint-Saëns, C.:Introduction & Rondo capriccioso, w. I. Perlman (vn) Deutsche Grammophon ▲ 423063–2 [DDD]
Sarasate, P. de:Carmen Fant, w. I. Perlman (vn) Deutsche Grammophon ▲ 423063–2 [DDD]
Schoenberg, A.:Gurrelieder, w. E. Martón (sop), F. Quivar (mez), G. Lakes (ten), H. Hotter (b–bar), New York Choral Artists [G] Sony Classical 2–▲ S2K 48077 [DDD]
Schuman, W.:Colloquies Hn, w. P. Myers (hn) New World ▲ NW 326–2 [DDD]
Sensual Classics II, w. A. Sultanov (pno), C. Katsaris (pno), Brodsky Quartet, London SO [cnd:M. Shostakovich], BBC SO [cnd:A. Davis], Leipzig Gewandhaus Orch [cnd:K. Masur], 12 Cellos of the Berlin PO [cnd:A. Jordan, E. Inbal], et al. Teldec ▲ 92014–2 ■ 92014–4
Sibelius, J.:Sym 2 Teldec ▲ 2292–46317–2 ZK [DDD] ■ 2292–46317–4 AW (D)
Strauss, R.:Also sprach Zarathustra CBS ▲ MDK 44910 [DDD]
Strauss, R.:Ein Heldenleben CBS ▲ MDK 45650 [DDD]
Stravinsky, I.:Pétrouchka CBS ▲ MK 35823 [DDD] ■ IMT 35823 (D)
Stravinsky, I.:Le Sacre du printemps Orch *(rec Manhattan Center, New York, Sept. 1990)* Teldec ▲ 2292–46420–2 [DDD]
Stravinsky, I.:Le Sacre du printemps Orch Odyssey ▲ MBK 42616 ■ YT 42616
Stravinsky, I.:Le Sacre du printemps Orch Sony Classical (Essential Classics) ▲ SBK 48169 ■ SBT 48169
Stravinsky, I.:Sym in 3 Movts *(rec Manhattan Center, New York, Sept. 1990)* Teldec ▲ 2292–46420–2 [DDD]
Tchaikovsky, P.:Con 1 Pno, w. E. Gilels (pno) Sony Classical ("Essential Classics" series) ▲ SBK 46339 [ADD] ■ SBT 46339
Vivaldi, A.:Con for 3 Vns, w. P. Zukerman (vn), I. Perlman (vn), I. Stern (vn) CBS ▲ MK 36692 [DDD]
Wagner, R.:Arias & Scenes, w. M. Caballé (sop) [G] CBS ▲ MK 37294
Wagner, R.:Götterdämmerung (immolation scene), w. M. Caballé (sop) [G] CBS ▲ MK 37294
Wagner, R.:Parsifal (prelude) *(rec live)* Sony Classical ▲ SK 45749
Wagner, R.:Parsifal (good friday) *(rec live)* Sony Classical ▲ SK 45749
Wagner, R.:Rienzi, der Letzte der Tribunen (ov) *(rec live)* Sony Classical ▲ SK 45749
Wagner, R.:Der Ring des Nibelungen (sels), w. M. Caballé (sop), P. Wimberger (b–bar)—Rheingold *(Entry of the Gods)*, Walküre *(Ride of the Valkyries; Magic Fire Music)* Siegfried *(Waldweben)*, Götterdämmerung *(Rhine Journey & Funeral Music; Immolation Scene)* CBS ▲ MDK 44657 [DDD] ■ MDT 44657 (D)
Wagner, R.:Tannhäuser (ov & venusberg) *(rec live)* Sony Classical ▲ SK 45749
Wagner, R.:Tristan und Isolde (prelude & liebestod), w. M. Caballé (sop) [G] CBS ▲ MK 37294
Wagner, R.:Die Walküre (act 1), w. E. Martón (sop), L. Hofmann (bass), M. Talvela (bass) [G] CBS ▲ MK 39745 [DDD]
Zwilich, E.T.:Con grosso 1985 New World ▲ NW 372–2 [DDD]
Zwilich, E.T.:Symbolon New World ▲ NW 372–2 [DDD]
Z. Mehta, D. Barenboim (cnds)
Brahms, J.:Con Vn, w. Isaac Stern (vn) Sony Classical 2–▲ SM2K 66941
Brahms, J.:Con Vn & Vc, "Double Con", w. Isaac Stern (vn), Leonard Rose (vc) Sony Classical 2–▲ SM2K 66941
W. Mengelberg (cnd)
Beethoven, L. van:Sym 3, "Eroica" Grammofono 2000 3–▲ GRM 78637
D. Mitropoulos (cnd)
Beethoven, L. van:Con 4 Pno, w. A. Rubinstein (pno) *(rec 1951–54)* Legend ▲ LGD 102 [ADD]
Beethoven, L. van:Con Vn, Op. 61, w. Z. Francescatti (vn) *(rec live 1956)* Melodram ▲ MEL 18030
Beethoven, L. van:Con Vn, Op. 61, w. Jasha Heifetz (vn) *(rec live, Feb 12, 1956)* Prelude ▲ PRE 2160 [ADD]
Beethoven, L. van:Die Geschöpfe des Prometheus (ov) *(rec 1951–1954)* Legend ▲ LGD 102 [ADD]
Beethoven, L. van:Sym 1 *(rec live 1/31/54)* Melodram ▲ MEL 18030
Beethoven, L. van:Sym 8 *(rec 1957)* Enterprise ("Documents" series) ▲ ENTLV 976 [ADD]

New York PO (cont.)
D. Mitropoulos (cnd) (cont.)
Berg, A.:Wozzeck, w. E. Farrell (sop), F. Jagel (ten), M. Harrell (bar), R. Lloyd (bass) *(rec live 1950)* Andromeda ▲ ANR 2514 [ADD]
Brahms, J.:Academic Festival Ov *(rec live, 2/9/58)* Arkadia ▲ 736 [ADD]
Brahms, J.:Con 1 Pno, w. W. Kapell (pno) *(rec live 4/12/53)* Melodram ▲ MEL 18009
Brahms, J.:Con 1 Pno, w. W. Kapell (pno) *(rec live 4/12/53)* Arkadia ▲ 736 [ADD]
Brahms, J.:Con Vn, w. Joseph Szigeti (vn) *(rec 1948)* Legend ▲ LGD 135 [ADD]
Brahms, J.:Vars on a Theme by Haydn *(rec live, 10/16/55)* Arkadia ▲ 736 [ADD]
Bruch, M.:Con 1 Vn, w. Zino Francescatti (vn) *(rec Feb 1952)* Sony Classical ("Masterworks Heritage" series) 2–▲ MH2K 62339 [ADD]
Famous Russian Music, w. Philharmonia Orch [cnd:André Cluytens] Enterprise ("Flowers" series) ▲ ENTBL 22 [ADD]
Haydn, J.:Sym 100, "Military" *(rec 1956)* Enterprise ▲ ENTLV 976 [ADD]
Liszt, F.:Les Préludes Enterprise ▲ ENT PD 4104
Mahler, G.:Sym 3, w. H. Krebs (ten) *(rec live, Carnegie Hall, 4/15/56)* Arkadia ▲ 557 [AAD]
Mahler, G.:Sym 3, w. *(soloist unknown)*, New York Phil Chorus Enterprise ("Documents" series) 2–▲ ENT LV 1000
Mahler, G.:Sym 5 *(rec 1959)* Arkadia ▲ 523 (m) [AAD]
Mahler, G.:Sym 9 *(rec 1960)* Arkadia ▲ 521 (m) [AAD]
Mendelssohn, F.:Con in e Vn & Orch, Op. 64, w. Zino Francescatti (vn) *(rec Nov 1954)* Sony Classical ("Masterworks Heritage" series) 2–▲ MH2K 62339 [ADD]
Mendelssohn, F.:Sym 3 Theorema ▲ TH 121135
Mendelssohn, F.:Sym 5 Theorema ▲ TH 121135
Mozart, W.A.:Con 3 Vn, w. Joseph Szigeti (vn) *(rec 1949)* Legend ▲ LGD 135 [ADD]
Mozart, W.A.:Con 5 Vn, w. D. Oistrakh (vn) One–Eleven ▲ URS 50140 [ADD]
Mozart, W.A.:Ovs—Die Zauberflöte [rec 1958]; Le nozze di Figaro [rec 1953]; Idomeneo [rec 1941] Enterprise ▲ ENTLV 976 [ADD]
Prokofiev, S.:Con 2 Vn, w. Zino Francescatti (vn) *(rec Oct 1952)* Sony Classical ("Masterworks Heritage" series) 2–▲ MH2K 62339 [ADD]
Prokofiev, S.:Romeo & Juliet (sels) Sony Classical ("Essential Classics" series) ▲ SBK 48169 ■ SBT 48169
Prokofiev, S.:Romeo & Juliet (suites)—No. 2 *(rec St George Hotel, Brooklyn, New York, Oct 11, 1957)* Sony Classical ("Greatest Hits" series) ▲ MLK 69249 [ADD] ■ LT 69
Saint-Saëns, C.:Con 3 Vn, w. Zino Francescatti (vn) *(rec Jan 1950)* Sony Classical ("Masterworks Heritage" series) 2–▲ MH2K 62339 [ADD]
Schoenberg, A.:Con Pno, w. G. Gould (pno) *(rec live, New York, 3/16/58)* Memories 2–▲ HR 4415/16 (m) [ADD]
Schumann, R.:Con Pno, w. M. Hess (pno), D *(rec live, Carnegie Hall, 2/10/58)* Melodram ▲ MEL 18024 (m) [AAD]
Scriabin, A.:Sym 4, w. William Vacchiano (tpt) *(rec 1953)* Theorema ▲ TH 121132
Sessions, R.:Sym 2 CRI ▲ CD 573 [ADD]
Sessions, R.:Sym 2 CRI ■ ACS 6002
Tchaikovsky, P.:Con Vn, w. Zino Francescatti (vn) *(rec Jan 1950)* Sony Classical ("Masterworks Heritage" series) 2–▲ MH2K 62339 [ADD]
Tchaikovsky, P.:Sym 4 Enterprise ▲ ENT PD 4104
E. Ormandy (cnd)
Rachmaninoff, S.:Con 3 Pno, w. V. Horowitz (pno) RCA Red Seal ▲ 09026–61564–2
S. Ozawa (cnd)
Rachmaninoff, S.:Con 3 Pno, w. A. Watts (pno) *(rec Oct. 1, 1969)* Sony Classical ("Essential Classics" series) ▲ SBK 53512 [ADD] ■ SBT 53512
F. Reiner (cnd)
Mussorgsky, M.:Boris Godunov (sels), w. Alexander Kipnis (bass) *(rec live, 1944)* Legend ▲ LGD 122
Shostakovich, D.:Sym 6 *(rec live, 1943)* Legend ▲ LGD 122
A. Rodzinski (cnd)
Beethoven, L. van:Con Vn, Op. 61, w. Jascha Heifetz (vn) *(rec live, Jan. 14, 1945)* As Disc ▲ ASD 2500 (m)
Beethoven, L. van:Con Vn, Op. 61, w. J. Heifetz (vn) *(rec 1945)* Legend ▲ LGD 123 [ADD]
Beethoven, L. van:Egmont (ov) *(rec 1946)* Legend ▲ LGD 123 [ADD]
Beethoven, L. van:Sym 5 *(rec 1944)* Legend ▲ LGD 123 [ADD]
Dvořák, A.:Con Vc, w. Leonard Rose (vc) *(rec New York, Jan 7, 1945)* Iron Needle ▲ IN 1338 (m) [ADD]
Dvořák, A.:Con Vc, w. Leonard Rose (vc) *(rec 1945)* Legend ▲ LGD 141
Franck, C.:Sym in d *(rec New York, Dec 30, 1945)* Iron Needle ▲ IN 1338 (m) [ADD]
Franck, C.:Sym in d *(rec 1945)* Legend ▲ LGD 141
Mozart, W.A.:Con 13 Pno, w. Wanda Landowska (pno) *(rec New York, 1945)* Iron Needle ▲ IN 1336 (m) [ADD]
Mozart, W.A.:Con 22 Pno, w. Wanda Landowska (pno) *(rec New York, Dec 2, 1945)* Iron Needle ▲ IN 1336 (m) [ADD]
Wagner, R.:Götterdämmerung (siegfried's funeral), w. Helen Traubel (sop), Herbert Janssen (bar), Doris Doré (sgr) *(rec Carnegie Hall, New York City, Nov 25, 1945)* Enterprise ("The Radio Years" series) ▲ ENT RY 55
Wagner, R.:Das Rheingold (sels), w. Helen Traubel (sop), Herbert Janssen (bar), Doris Doré (sgr)—Entry of the Gods into Valhalla *(rec Carnegie Hall, New York City, Nov 25, 1945)* Enterprise ("The Radio Years" series) ▲ ENT RY 55
Wagner, R.:Siegfried (waldweben), w. Helen Traubel (sop), Herbert Janssen (bar), Doris Doré (sgr) *(rec Carnegie Hall, New York City, Nov 25, 1945)* Enterprise ("The Radio Years" series) ▲ ENT RY 55
Wagner, R.:Die Walküre (act 3), w. Helen Traubel (sop), Herbert Janssen (bar), Doris Doré (sgr) *(rec Carnegie Hall, New York City, Nov 25, 1945)* Enterprise ("The Radio Years" series) ▲ ENT RY 55
V. de Sabata (cnd)
Beethoven, L. van:Sym 5 *(rec live, Carnegie Hall 1950)* Melodram ▲ MEL 18008
Brahms, J.:Con Vn, w. N. Milstein (vn) *(rec live, Carnegie Hall 1950)* Melodram ▲ MEL 18008
Wagner, R.:Götterdämmerung (immolation scene), w. E. Farrell (sop) *(rec 1951)* Arkadia ▲ 512 (m) [AAD]
Wagner, R.:Die Meistersinger von Nürnberg (prelude/act 1) Arkadia ▲ 512 (m) [AAD]
Wagner, R.:Parsifal (prelude) Arkadia ▲ 512 (m) [AAD]
Wagner, R.:Parsifal (good friday) Arkadia ▲ 512 (m) [AAD]
T. Schippers (cnd)
Barber, S.:Adagio Strs Sony Classical ("Masterworks Heritage" series) ▲ MHK 62837
Barber, S.:Adagio Strs Odyssey ■ YT 33230
Barber, S.:Andromache's Farewell, w. Martina Arroyo (sop) Sony Classical ("Masterworks Heritage" series) ▲ MHK 62837
Barber, S.:Andromache's Farewell, w. M. Arroyo (sop) [E] *(rec 1963)* Sony Masterworks ("Portrait" series) ▲ MPK 46727 [ADD]
Barber, S.:Essay 2 Odyssey ■ YT 33230
Barber, S.:Essay 2 Sony Classical ("Masterworks Heritage" series) ▲ MHK 62837
Barber, S.:Medea's Meditation & Dance of Vengeance Sony Classical ("Masterworks Heritage" series) ▲ MHK 62837
Barber, S.:Medea's Meditation & Dance of Vengeance Odyssey ■ YT 33230
Barber, S.:The School for Scandal Odyssey ■ YT 33230
Barber, S.:The School for Scandal Sony Classical ("Masterworks Heritage" series) ▲ MHK 62837
Chopin, F.:Con 2 Pno, w. A. Watts (pno) Sony Classical (Essential Classics) ▲ SBK 46336 [ADD] ■ SBT 46336
Prokofiev, S.:Alexander Nevsky, w. Westminster Choir—Song about Alexander Nevsky *(rec New York City, Feb 18, 1961)* Sony Classical ("Greatest Hits" series) ▲ MLK 69249 [ADD] ■ LT 69
Rossini, G.:Stabat Mater, w. M. Arroyo (sop), B. Wolff (mez), T. del Bianco (ten), J. Diaz (bass). Camerata Singers Sony Classical ▲ SB2K 53252
M. Similä (cnd)
Jussi Björling:In Song & Ballad, w. J. Björling (ten), Harry Ebert (pno), Bertil Bokstedt (pno), Swedish Radio Orch [cnd:Sixten Ehrling] *(rec 1940, 1942 & 1957)* Bluebell ▲ BLU 050 [ADD]

ORCHESTRAS & ENSEMBLES 285

New York PO (cont.)
G. Sinopoli (cnd)
Mussorgsky, M.:Night — Deutsche Grammophon ▲ 429785–2 [DDD]
Mussorgsky, M.:Pictures at an Exhibition — Deutsche Grammophon ▲ 429785–2 [DDD]
Paganini, N.:Con 1 Vn, w. G. Shaham (vn) — Deutsche Grammophon ▲ 429786–2 [DDD]
Ravel, M.:Valses nobles et sentimentales — Deutsche Grammophon ▲ 429785–2 [DDD]
Respighi, O.:The Fountains of Rome — Deutsche Grammophon ▲ 437534–2
Respighi, O.:The Pines of Rome — Deutsche Grammophon ▲ 437534–2
Saint-Saëns, C.:Con 3 Vn, w. G. Shaham (vn) — Deutsche Grammophon ▲ 429786–2 [DDD]
Scriabin, A.:Sym 3 — Deutsche Grammophon ▲ 427324–2 [DDD]
Scriabin, A.:Sym 4 — Deutsche Grammophon ▲ 427324–2 [DDD]
W. Steinberg (cnd)
Beethoven, L. van:Con 5 Pno, "Emperor", w. A. Benedetti Michelangeli (pno) *(rec live, New York 1/8/66)* — Memories 2–▲ HR 4368/69 (m) [ADD]
G. Szell (cnd)
Brahms, J.:Con Vn, w. Jasha Heifetz (vn) *(rec live, Dec 9, 1951)* — Prelude ▲ PRE 2160 (m) [ADD]
Y. Temirkanov (cnd)
Rimsky-Korsakov, N.:Russian Easter Festival — RCA Red Seal ▲ 09026–61173–2 ■ 09026–61173–4
Rimsky-Korsakov, N.:Scheherazade, w. G. Dicterow (vn) — RCA Red Seal ▲ 09026–61173–2 ■ 09026–61173–4
A. Toscanini (cnd)
Arturo Toscanini:The 1st Recordings, 1920–26, w. La Scala Orch — Symposium ▲ SYM 1189
Beethoven, L. van:Con Vn, Vc & Pno, "Triple Con", w. Mishel Piastro (vn), Joseph Schuster (vc), Ania Dorfman (pno) — Grammofono 2000 ▲ GRM 78636
Beethoven, L. van:Missa Solemnis, w. E. Rethberg (sop), M. Telva (mez), G. Martinelli (ten), E. Pinza (bass), Westminster Choir [L] *(rec live, New York 4/28/35)* — Melodram 2–▲ CDM 28036 [ADD]
Beethoven, L. van:Sym 5 *(rec live, Carnegie Hall 3/4 & 6/31)* — Pearl 3–▲ PEA 9922 (m) [AAD]
Beethoven, L. van:Sym 5 *(rec live, 4/9/33 Victor)* — Pearl 3–▲ PEAS 9373 (m) [AAD]
Beethoven, L. van:Sym 7 — RCA Gold Seal ▲ 60316–2–RG ■ 60316–4–RG
Brahms, J.:Vars on a Theme by Haydn — RCA Gold Seal ▲ 60317–2–RG ■ 60317–4–RG
Dukas, P.:L'Apprenti sorcier — RCA Gold Seal ▲ 60317–2–RG ■ 60317–4–RG
Gluck, C.W.:Orfeo ed Euridice (dance of the blessed spirits) — RCA Gold Seal ▲ 60318–2–RG; ■ 60318–4–RG
Haydn, J.:Sym 101, "Clock" — RCA Gold Seal ▲ 60316–2–RG ■ 60316–4–RG
Haydn, J.:Sym 101, "Clock" *(rec live, Jan 13, 1945)* — Iron Needle ▲ 1335
Mendelssohn, F.:A Midsummer Night's Dream (sels)—Scherzo — RCA Gold Seal ▲ 60316–2–RG ■ 60316–4–RG
Mendelssohn, F.:A Midsummer Night's Dream (sels)—Scherzo & Nocturne — RCA Gold Seal ▲ 60317–2–RG ■ 60317–4–RG
Mozart, W.A.:Sym 35 — RCA Gold Seal ▲ 60317–2 ■ 60317–4
Respighi, O.:The Pines of Rome *(rec live, Jan 13, 1945)* — Iron Needle ▲ 1335
Rossini, G.:Ovs—Barbiere di Siviglia; Italiana in algeri; Semiramide — RCA Gold Seal ▲ 60318–2 ■ 60318–4
Sibelius, J.:The Swan of Tuonela *(rec live, Jan 13, 1945)* — Iron Needle ▲ 1335
Verdi, G.:Ovs & Preludes—Traviata—Act I & Act III Preludes — RCA Gold Seal ▲ 60318–2 ■ 60318–4
Wagner, R.:Götterdämmerung (rhine journey & funeral) — RCA Gold Seal ▲ 60318–2 ■ 60318–4
Wagner, R.:Götterdämmerung (siegfried's funeral) *(rec live, Jan 13, 1945)* — Iron Needle ▲ 1335
Wagner, R.:Lohengrin (preludes)—Act I & Act III Preludes — RCA Gold Seal ▲ 60318–2 ■ 60318–4
Wagner, R.:Siegfried Idyll — RCA Gold Seal ▲ 60317–2–RG ■ 60317–4–RG
Weber, C.M. von:Euryanthe (ov) *(rec live, Jan 13, 1945)* — Iron Needle ▲ 1335
B. Walter (cnd)
Bach, J.S.:St. Matthew Passion, w. Nadine Conner (sop), Jean Watson (cta), William Hain (ten), Mack Harrell (bar), Herbert Janssen (bar), Lorenzo Alvary (bass), New York Phil Chorus—Part I — Minerva ▲ 20
Barber, S.:Sym 1 *(rec New York City, Jan. 23, 1945)* — Sony Classical ("Bruno Walter Edition, Vol. 2" series) ▲ SMK 64466 [ADD]
Beethoven, L. van:Con 4 Pno, w. R. Serkin (pno) *(rec 1941)* — Historical Performers ▲ HPS 15 [ADD]
Beethoven, L. van:Con 5 Pno, "Emperor", w. Rudolf Serkin (pno) *(rec New York, Dec 22, 1941)* — Sony Classical ("Bruno Walter:The Edition, Vol. 4" series) ▲ SMK 64489 [ADD]
Beethoven, L. van:Con Vn, Op. 61, w. J. Szigeti (vn) *(rec 1947)* — Sony Masterworks ("Portrait" series) ▲ MPK 52536 (m) [AAD]
Beethoven, L. van:Con Vn, Op. 61, w. C. Wicks (vn) *(rec 1950)* — Legend ▲ LGD 114 [ADD]
Beethoven, L. van:Con Vn, Vc & Pno, "Triple Con", w. John Corigliano (vn), Leonard Rose (vc), Walter Hendl (pno) — Sony Classical ("Bruno Walter:The Edition" series) ▲ SMK 64479
Beethoven, L. van:Egmont (ov) *(rec 30th Street Studios, New York, Dec 4, 1954)* — Sony Classical ("Bruno Walter:The Edition, Vol. 4" series) ▲ SMK 64488 [ADD]
Beethoven, L. van:Leonore 3 *(rec 30th Street Studios, New York, Dec 4, 1954)* — Sony Classical ("Bruno Walter:The Edition, Vol. 4" series) ▲ SMK 64487 [ADD]
Beethoven, L. van:Sym 1 *(rec 1947)* — Theorema ▲ TH 121143
Beethoven, L. van:Sym 3, "Eroica" *(rec 1949)* — Theorema ▲ TH 121143
Beethoven, L. van:Sym 7 *(rec 1947)* — Historical Performers ▲ HPS 15 [ADD]
Beethoven, L. van:Sym 8 *(rec 1938–42)* — Phonographe ▲ PHG CD 5028
Berlioz, H.:Sym fantastique — Fortissimo ▲ CDE 3021
Berlioz, H.:Sym fantastique *(rec 1954)* — Enterprise ("Palladio" series) ▲ ENTPD 4202 [ADD]
Brahms, J.:Academic Festival Ov — Theorema ▲ TH 121213
Brahms, J.:Ein Deutsches Requiem, w. Irmgard Seefried (sop), George London (bar), *(chorus unknown)* — Melodram ▲ CDM 18004
Brahms, J.:Ein Deutsches Requiem, w. Irmgard Seefried (sop), George London (bass), Westminster Cathedral Choir *(rec New York City, Dec. 20–29, 1954)* — Sony Classical ("Bruno Walter Edition, Vol. 2" series) ▲ SMK 64469 [ADD]
Brahms, J.:Hungarian Dances Orch—Nos. 1 in g; 3 in F; 10 in E; 17 in f# *(rec New York City, Feb. 12, 1951)* — Sony Classical ("Bruno Walter Edition, Vol. 2" series) ▲ SMK 64467 [ADD]
Brahms, J.:Sym 2 — Theorema ▲ TH 121213
Brahms, J.:Tragic Ov — Theorema ▲ TH 121213
Bruckner, A.:Sym 9 *(rec live, 1953)* — Enterprise ("Palladio" series) ▲ ENTPD 4209 [ADD]
Bruckner, A.:Te Deum, w. Westminster Choir — Sony Classical ("Bruno Walter:The Edition" series) ▲ SMK 64480
Chopin, F.:Con 1 Pno, w. Artur Rubinstein (pno) *(rec live, 1948)* — As Disc ▲ ASD 2401 (m)
Dvořák, A.:Slavonic Dances (sels)—Op. 46/1 *(rec New York City, Feb. 4, 1941)* — Sony Classical ("Bruno Walter Edition, Vol. 2" series) ▲ SMK 64466 [ADD]
Dvořák, A.:Sym 8 *(rec live, 1948)* — As Disc ▲ ASD 2401 (m)
Goldmark, K.:Con 1 Vn, w. Nathan Milstein (vn) — One-Eleven ▲ URS 50140
Haydn, J.:Sym 102 *(rec 30th Street Studios, New York, Feb 18, 1953)* — Sony Classical ("Bruno Walter:The Edition, Vol. 4" series) ▲ SMK 64485 [ADD]
Mahler, G.:Das Lied von der Erde, w. M. Miller (mez), E. Haefliger (ten) [G] — CBS ▲ MK 42034
Mahler, G.:Sym 2, w. E. Cundari (sop), M. Forrester (cta), Westminster Choir [G] — Odyssey ■ YT 30848
Mozart, W.A.:Con 14 Pno, w. M. Hess (pno) — Historical Performers ▲ HPS 9 [ADD]
Mozart, W.A.:Con 20 Pno, w. M. Hess (pno) — Historical Performers ▲ HPS 9 [ADD]
Mozart, W.A.:Con 22 Pno, w. Artur Schnabel (pno) — Enterprise ("The Radio Years" series) ▲ ENT RY 69
Mozart, W.A.:Con 4 Vn, w. B. Huberman (vn) *(rec 1945)* — Music & Arts ▲ CD 299 [AAD]
Mozart, W.A.:Requiem, w. Westminster Choir — Sony Classical ("Bruno Walter:The Edition" series) ▲ SMK 64480
Mozart, W.A.:Requiem, w. I. Seefried (sop), J. Tourel (mez), L. Simoneau (ten), W. Warfield (bar) *(rec 1956)* — Historical Performers ▲ HPS 12 [ADD]
Mozart, W.A.:Sinf Concertante, w. John Corigliano (vn), William Lincer (va) — Enterprise ("The Radio Years" series) ▲ ENT RY 69
Mozart, W.A.:Sym 39 — Sony Classical ("Bruno Walter:The Edition" series) ▲ SMK 64477 (m)
Mozart, W.A.:Sym 39 — Fonit Cetra ("Fortissimo" series) ▲ FCT CDE 3010
Mozart, W.A.:Sym 40 — Sony Classical ("Bruno Walter:The Edition" series) ▲ SMK 64477 (m)

New York PO (cont.)
B. Walter (cnd) (cont.)
Mozart, W.A.:Sym 41 — Sony Classical ("Bruno Walter:The Edition" series) ▲ SMK 64477 (m)
Schubert, Franz:Sym 7 *(rec St. George Hotel, Brooklyn, NY, Mar 3, 1958)* — Sony Classical ("Bruno Walter:The Edition, Vol. 4" series) ▲ SMK 64487 [ADD]
Schubert, Franz:Sym 8 *(rec St. George Hotel, Brooklyn, NY, Mar 3, 1958)* — Sony Classical ("Bruno Walter:The Edition, Vol. 4" series) ▲ SMK 64487 [ADD]
Schumann, R.:Sym 3 *(rec 1941)* — Historical Performers ▲ HPS 17 [ADD]
Schumann, R.:Sym 3 *(rec New York, Feb 4, 1941)* — Sony Classical ("Bruno Walter:The Edition, Vol. 4" series) ▲ SMK 64488 [ADD]
Smetana, B.:The Moldau *(rec New York City, Feb. 4, 1941)* — Sony Classical ("Bruno Walter Edition, Vol. 2" series) ▲ SMK 64467 [ADD]
Strauss (II), Joh.:Music of—An der schönen, blauen Donau [The Blue Danube], Op. 314; Geschichten aus dem Wienerwald [Tales from the Vienna Woods], Op. 325; Kaiser-Walzer [Emperor Waltz], Op. 437; Wiener Blut [Viennese Blood], Op. 354; Der Zigeunerbaron [The Gypsy Baron] Ov.; Die Fledermaus [The Bat] Ov. *(rec New York City, Mar. 16–22, 1956)* — Sony Classical ("Bruno Walter Edition, Vol. 2" series) ▲ SMK 64467 [ADD]
Strauss, R.:Don Juan *(rec New York City, Dec. 29, 1952)* — Sony Classical ("Bruno Walter Edition, Vol. 2" series) ▲ SMK 64466 [ADD]
Strauss, R.:Tod und Verklärung *(rec New York City, Dec. 29, 1952)* — Sony Classical ("Bruno Walter Edition, Vol. 2" series) ▲ SMK 64466 [ADD]
Tchaikovsky, P.:Con 1 Pno, w. Vladimir Horowitz (pno) *(rec live, Apr. 11, 1948)* — As Disc ▲ ASD 2400 (m)
Wagner, R.:Parsifal (prelude) — Legend ▲ LGD 119
Wagner, R.:Parsifal (prelude) *(rec live, 1952)* — Historical Performers ▲ HPS 27
A. Weisberg (cnd)
Crumb, G.:A Haunted Landscape — New World ▲ NW 326–2 [DDD]
New York PO Brass Players
Gabrieli, G.:Canzoni, w. Boston SO Brass Players, Canadian Brass—13 canzoni — CBS ▲ MK 44931 [DDD] ■ MT 44931 (D)
New York PO Ensemble
Z. Mehta (cnd)
del Tredici, D.:Haddocks' Eyes, w. C. Bloom (nar), S. Narucki (sop) — New World ▲ 80390–2 [DDD]
Zwilich, E.T.:Con Tpt, w. P. Smith (tpt) — New World ▲ NW 372–2 [DDD]
E. T. Zwilich (cnd)
Zwilich, E.T.:Double Qt — New World ▲ NW 372–2 [DDD]
New York PO members
L. Bernstein (cnd)
Beethoven, L. van:Sym 9, "Choral Sym", w. Bavarian RSO members, Dresden State Orch members, Kirov Theatre Orch members, London SO members, New York PO members, Orch de Paris members, Bavarian Radio Chorus, Berlin Radio Chorus, Dresden Philharmonie Children's Chorus [G] *(rec live, Schauspielhaus, East Berlin, 12/25/89)* — Deutsche Grammophon ▲ 429861–2 [DDD] ■ 429861–4
Vivaldi, A.:Cons Vn, Op. 8/1–4, "The Four Seasons", w. J. Corigliano (vn) [arr. Alceo Toni] *(rec Dec. 15, 1958)* — Sony Classical ("Leonard Bernstein:The Royal Edition" series) ▲ SMK 47642 [ADD]
E. Iseler (cnd)
Gabrieli, G.:Music of, w. Canadian Brass, Philadelphia Orch members — Philips ▲ 438392–2
L. Magiera (cnd)
Pavarotti in Central Park, w. L. Pavarotti, Harlem Boys Choir — London ▲ 444450–2 ■ 444450–4
G. Titner (cnd)
Beethoven, L. van:Egmont (ov), w. Boston SO, Canadian Brass — Philips ("Digital Classics" series) ▲ 426487–2 [DDD]
Beethoven, L. van:Sym 5, w. Boston SO, Canadian Brass — Philips ("Digital Classics" series) ▲ 426487–2 [DDD]
Beethoven, L. van:Wellington's Victory, "Battle Sym", w. Boston SO, Canadian Brass — Philips ("Digital Classics" series) ▲ 426487–2 [DDD]
New York Philharmonic SO
G. Cantelli (cnd)
Mozart, W.A.:Con 21 Pno, w. Walter Gieseking (pno) *(rec live, 1948–1956)* — Pearl ▲ PEA 9236
A. Kostelanetz (cnd)
Gershwin, G.:Con Pno, w. O. Levant (pno) *(rec 1942)* — Sony Masterworks ("Portrait" series) ▲ MPK 47681 [ADD]
W. Mengelberg (cnd)
Beethoven, L. van:Sym 3, "Eroica" *(rec New York, 1930)* — Iron Needle ▲ IN 1325 [ADD]
A. Rodzinski (cnd)
Mozart, W.A.:Con 23 Pno, w. A. Schnabel (pno) *(rec live, Mar. 3, 1946)* — Music & Arts ▲ CD 632 (m) [AAD]
I. Stravinsky (cnd)
Stravinsky, I.:Pno-Rag-Music, w. I. Stravinsky (pno) — IMP (Golden Legacy) ▲ IMPGLRS 107 [ADD]
Stravinsky, I.:Pulcinella Suite — IMP (Golden Legacy) ▲ IMPGLRS 107 [ADD]
Stravinsky, I.:Ragtime — IMP (Golden Legacy) ▲ IMPGLRS 107 [ADD]
Stravinsky, I.:Le Sacre du printemps Orch — IMP (Golden Legacy) ▲ IMPGLRS 107 [ADD]
G. Szell (cnd)
Mozart, W.A.:Con 20 Pno, w. A. Schnabel (pno) *(rec live Dec. 24, 1944)* — Music & Arts ▲ CD 750–1 [AAD]
A. Toscanini (cnd)
Beethoven, L. van:Sym 7 *(rec 1936 for Victor)* — Pearl 3–▲ PEAS 9373 (m) [AAD]
Brahms, J.:Vars on a Theme by Haydn *(rec 1936 for Victor)* — Pearl 3–▲ PEAS 9373 (m) [AAD]
Dukas, P.:L'Apprenti sorcier *(rec 1929 for Victor)* — Pearl 3–▲ PEAS 9373 (m) [AAD]
Gluck, C.W.:Orfeo ed Euridice (dance of the blessed spirits) *(rec 1929 for Victor)* — Pearl 3–▲ PEAS 9373 (m) [AAD]
The Great Recordings 1926–1936:Vol. 1 — Pearl 3–▲ PEA 9373 (m) [AAD]
Haydn, J.:Sym 101, "Clock" *(rec 1929 for Victor)* — Pearl 3–▲ PEAS 9373 (m) [AAD]
Mendelssohn, F.:A Midsummer Night's Dream (sels) *(rec Scherzo & Nocturne, 1926)* — Pearl 3–▲ PEAS 9373 (m) [AAD]
Mozart, W.A.:Sym 35 *(rec 1929 for Victor)* — Pearl 3–▲ PEAS 9373 (m) [AAD]
Rossini, G.:Ovs—Barber of Seville—rec 1929 for Victor; Italiana in Algeri & Semiramide—rec 1936 for Victor — Pearl 3–▲ PEAS 9373 (m) [AAD]
Verdi, G.:La traviata (sels)—Preludes to Acts 1 & 3 *(rec 1929 for Victor)* — Pearl 3–▲ GEMMCDS 9373 (m) [AAD]
Wagner, R.:Götterdämmerung (rhine journey) *(rec 1936 for Victor)* — Pearl 3–▲ PEAS 9373 (m) [AAD]
Wagner, R.:Lohengrin (preludes)—Acts 1 & 3 *(rec 1936 for Victor)* — Pearl 3–▲ PEAS 9373 (m) [AAD]
Wagner, R.:Siegfried Idyll *(rec 1936 for Victor)* — Pearl 3–▲ PEAS 9373 (m) [AAD]
B. Walter (cnd)
Beethoven, L. van:Son 9 Vn, "Kreutzer", w. Adolf Busch (vn), Rudolf Serkin (pno) — Biddulph ▲ LHW 026
New York Philomusica
R. Johnson (cnd)
Mozart, W.A.:Diverts—K.166, 188, 213, 240, 251 & 287 *(rec 1971–75)* — Vox Box 2–▲ CDX 5050 [ADD]
Mozart, W.A.:Diverts—K.113, 131, 186, 205, 253, & 289 *(rec 1971–75)* — Vox Box 2–▲ CDX 5049 [ADD]
Mozart, W.A.:Diverts—K.247, 252, 270 & 334 *(rec 1972)* — Vox Box 2–▲ CDX 5051 [ADD]
Mozart, W.A.:March Orch, K.208 *(rec 1971–75)* — Vox Box 2–▲ CDX 5050 [ADD]
New York Philomusica Chamber Ensemble
Winds:20th Century Music for Woodwinds, w. Dorian Quintet, et al. — Vox Box 2–▲ CDX 5083 [ADD]
New York Philomusica Winds
R. Johnson (cnd)
Mozart, W.A.:Serenade Ww, K.361 — Vox Box 2–▲ CDX 5014 [ADD]
Mozart, W.A.:Serenade Ww, K.375 — Vox Box 2–▲ CDX 5014 [ADD]
Mozart, W.A.:Serenade Ww, K.388 — Vox Box 2–▲ CDX 5014 [ADD]
Went, J.N.:Suites Ww—sels after *Così fan tutte* & *Le nozze di Figaro* — Vox Box 2–▲ CDX 5014 [ADD]

286
▲ = CD ♦ = Enhanced CD Δ = MD ■ = Cassette Tape □ = DCC

New York Pops Orch
S. Henderson (cnd)
Christmas in the Country — Angel ▲ CDC 54891 ■ 4DS 54891
From Berlin to Bernstein — Angel ▲ CDC 54274 [DDD]
Goes to the Movies — Angel ▲ CDC 54499 [DDD] ■ 4DS 54499 (D)
New York Pro Musica
N. Greenberg (cnd)
The Play of Daniel & the Play of Herod — MCA Classics 2-▲ MCAD2-10102 [ADD]
New York Renaissance Band
S. Logemann (cnd)
Country Capers — Arabesque ▲ Z 6520
Praetorius, M.:Terpsichore — Arabesque ▲ Z 6531
New York Sinfonietta
M. Goberman (cnd)
Vivaldi, A.:Cons Vn, Op. 8/1–4, "The Four Seasons", w. A. Bronne (vn), Monosoff (vn), Kwalwasser (va), G. Koutzen (vc) — Odyssey ■ YT 60132
New York Society Orch members
T. Crawford (cnd)
Ewazen, E.:Ballade, w. J. Russo (cl), E. Etters (hp) — CRS ▲ CD 8840
New York Solisti
R. Wilson (cnd)
Beydts, L.:Chansons pour les Oiseaux, w. Darynn Zimmer (sop) — New Albion ▲ NA 078
Delage, M.:Chants de la jungle (3), w. Darynn Zimmer (sop) — New Albion ▲ NA 078
Delage, M.:Haï-kaï, w. Darynn Zimmer (sop) *(rec American Academy of Arts & Letters, New York City)* — New Albion ▲ NA 078
Delage, M.:Poèmes désenchantés, w. Darynn Zimmer (sop) *(rec American Academy of Arts & Letters, New York City)* — New Albion ▲ NA 078
Gounod, C.:Songs, w. Darynn Zimmer (sop), Gaït Sirguey (pno)—Les Deux pigeons; Le Soir; Le Temps des roses; L'Absent; Viens! Les Gazons sont verts! *(rec American Academy of Arts & Letters, New York City)* — New Albion ▲ NA 078
Massenet, J.:Songs, w. Darynn Zimmer (sop), Gaït Sirguey (pno)—Oh! Si les fleurs avaient des yeux; Crépuscule; Souvenez-vous, vierge Marie!; C'est l'amour — New Albion ▲ NA 078
New York Solisti CO
A. Neale (cnd)
Beaser, R.:Song of the Bells, w. P. Robison (fl) — New World ▲ 80403-2 [DDD]
New York Stadium SO
C. Chávez (cnd)
Chávez, C.:Sym 1, "Sinf de Antigona" — Everest ▲ EVC 9041 [AAD]
Chávez, C.:Sym 2, "Sinf India" — Everest ▲ EVC 9041 [AAD]
Chávez, C.:Sym 4, "Romantic" — Everest ▲ EVC 9041 [AAD]
R. Poliakin (cnd)
Strauss (II), Joh.:Waltzes—Wiener Blut; Künstlerleben Waltz *(rec Manhattan Center, NYC or Walthamstow Assembly Hall, London)* — Everest ▲ EVC 9031 [AAD]
Strauss, R.:Der Rosenkavalier (waltzes) *(rec Walthamstow Assembly Hall, London)* — Everest ▲ EVC 9033 [AAD]
Strauss, R.:Der Rosenkavalier (waltzes)—waltz medley *(rec Manhattan Center, NYC or Walthamstow Assembly Hall, London)* — Everest ▲ EVC 9031 [AAD]
Weber, C.M. von:Invitation to the Dance Orch *(rec Manhattan Center, NYC or Walthamstow Assembly Hall, London)* — Everest ▲ EVC 9031 [AAD]
L. Stokowski (cnd)
Debussy, C.:Children's Corner *(rec Belock Recording Studio, Bayside, NY)* — Everest ▲ EVC 9023 [AAD]
Prokofiev, S.:Cinderella (suites) [arr. Stokowski into 1 6-movt suite] *(rec Manhattan Center, NYC)* — Everest ▲ EVC 9023 [AAD]
Prokofiev, S.:The Ugly Duckling, w. Regina Resnik (sop) *(rec Belock Recording Studio, Bayside, NY)* — Everest ▲ EVC 9023 [AAD]
Shostakovich, D.:Sym 5 — Everest ▲ EVC 9030 [AAD]
Strauss, R.:Don Juan — Everest ▲ EVC 9004 [AAD]
Strauss, R.:Salome (dance) — Everest ▲ EVC 9004 [AAD]
Strauss, R.:Till Eulenspiegels lustige Streiche — Everest ▲ EVC 9004 [AAD]
Tchaikovsky, P.:Francesca da Rimini — Dell'Arte ▲ CDDA 9006
Tchaikovsky, P.:Francesca da Rimini — Everest ▲ EVC 9037 [AAD]
Tchaikovsky, P.:Hamlet — Everest ▲ EVC 9037 [AAD]
Tchaikovsky, P.:Hamlet — Dell'Arte ▲ CDDA 9006
Villa-Lobos, H.:Bachiana brasileira 1—Modinha *(rec Manhattan Center, NYC)* — Everest ▲ EVC 9023 [AAD]
Villa-Lobos, H.:Uirapuru *(rec Manhattan Center, NYC)* — Everest ▲ EVC 9023 [AAD]
New York String Orch
V. Persichetti (cnd)
Persichetti, V.:Con E Hn, w. Thomas Stacy (E hn) — New World ▲ 80489-2
New York String Quartet
Crumb, G.:Black Angels (Images I) — CRI ■ ACS 6008
Perle, G.:Qt 7 Strs — CRI ■ ACS 6015
Zwilich, E.T.:Qt Strs *(rec Nov. 1986)* — CRI ▲ CD 621 [ADD]
New York SO
B. Walter (cnd)
Chopin, F.:Con 1 Pno, w. Artur Rubinstein (pno) *(rec 1947)* — Historical Performers ▲ HPS 29
Dvořák, A.:Sym 8 *(rec 1948)* — Historical Performers ▲ HPS 29
New York Theater Ensemble
M. Rosenstock (cnd)
North, A.:Streetcar Named Desire — Premier ▲ PRCD 1017 [ADD]
New York Theater Orch
Lloyd Webber, A.:Music of—Phantom of the Opera; Cats; Jesus Christ Superstar; Joseph and the Amazing Technicolor Dreamcoat; Evita; Aspects of Love; Starlight Express; Tell Me on a Sunday; Sunset Boulevard — Special Music Co. ▲ SCD 5127 ■ SMC 5127
The Most Popular Classics, Vol. 1 — Nesak International ▲ 10001-2
The Most Popular Classics, Vol. 2 — Nesak International ▲ 10002-2
The Most Popular Classics, Vol. 3 — Nesak International ▲ 10003-2
The Most Popular Classics, Vol. 4 — Nesak International ▲ 10004-2
New York Trumpet Ensemble
G. Schwarz (cnd)
Altenburg, J.E.:Con in C Tpts, w. G. Schwarz (tpt), 92nd St. Y Chamber SO members — Delos ▲ DCD 3002 [DDD]
Biber, H. von:Son in C for 8 Tpts & Timp, w. G. Schwarz (tpt), 92nd St. Y Chamber SO — Delos ▲ DCD 3002 [DDD]
Torelli, G.:Sons à 5 Tpts, w. G. Schwarz (tpt)—Son in G — Delos ▲ DCD 3002 [DDD]
Vivaldi, A.:Con for 2 Tpts, w. G. Schwarz (tpt), 92nd St. Y Chamber SO — Delos ▲ DCD 3002 [DDD]
New York Trumpet Ensemble [Edward Carroll (tpt), David Bilger (tpt), Jeffrey Curnow (tpt), Scott Thornburg (tpt), Kenneth Finn (bass tpt), Christopher Lamb (military dr), Lynn Bernhardt (timp/military dr)]
Handel, G.F.:Music of, w. Edward Carroll (tpt), Anthony Newman (org)—Ov; Bourrée; La Paix; La Rejouissance; Minuets I & II [all from Royal Fireworks Music]; Grand Fugues Nos. 2, 3 & 6 in G, B♭ & c [from Fugues faciles]; Martial Sym [from Belshazzar]; Tpt Ov [from Atalanta]; 2 Marches [from Floridante]; Grand March [from Rinaldo]; March in D [from Hercules]; Chorus & March [from Judas Maccabaeus]; Con in B♭ [from Select Harmony]; Suite in D [from Water Music] *(rec Rye Presbyterian Church, Rye, NY, Sept 1985)* — Allegretto ▲ ACD 8205
New York Univ New Music Ensemble
Expanding Horizons *(rec Frederick Lowe Theater, NYU)* — Capstone ▲ CPS 8630 [DDD]

New York Univ New Music Ensemble (cont.)
E. Lamneck (cnd)
Kraft, L.:Washington Square *(rec William Paterson College)* — Capstone ▲ CPS 8616 [DDD]
New York Virtuosi Chamber SO
K. Klein (cnd)
Britten, B.:Serenade, Op. 31, w. Grayson Hirst (ten), L. William Kuyper (hn) — Allegretto ▲ ACD 8203
Elgar, E.:Serenade Strs — Allegretto ▲ ACD 8203
Vaughan Williams, R.:Serenade to Music, w. New York Virtuosi Chamber Chorus — Allegretto ▲ ACD 8203
New York Woodwind Quartet
Carter, E.:Etudes (8) & a Fant — CRI ■ C 118
New York Woodwind Quintet [Samuel Baron (fl), Jerome Roth (ob), David Glazer (cl), John Barrows (hn), Arthur Weisberg (bn)]
Barber, S.:Summer Music — Boston Skyline ▲ BSD 137 [AAD]
Barrows, J.:March Ww Qnt — Boston Skyline ▲ BSD 137 [AAD]
Bresnick, M.:Just Time — New World ▲ 80413-2 [DDD]
Carter, E.:Etudes (8) & a Fant — Boston Skyline ▲ BSD 137 [AAD]
Fine, I.:Partita Ww — Boston Skyline ▲ BSD 139 [AAD]
Fine, I.:Partita Ww — Elektra/Nonesuch ▲ 79175-2-ZK
Françaix, J.:Qnt 1 Ww — Boston Skyline ▲ BSD 141 [AAD]
Hindemith, P.:Kleine Kammermusik — Boston Skyline ▲ BSD 139 [AAD]
Ibert, J.:Pièces brèves — Boston Skyline ▲ BSD 139 [AAD]
Milhaud, D.:Le Cheminée du Roi René — Boston Skyline ▲ BSD 139 [AAD]
Nielsen, C.:Qnt Ww — Boston Skyline ▲ BSD 137 [AAD]
Pierné, G.:Pastorale Ww — Boston Skyline ▲ BSD 137 [AAD]
Poulenc, F.:Sxt Pno, w. Frank Glazer (pno) — Boston Skyline ▲ BSD 141 [AAD]
Powell, Mel:Qnt Ww — New World ▲ 80413-2 [DDD]
Reicha, A.:Qnts Ww, Op. 88—Finale from Qnt No. 2 for Winds in E♭ — Boston Skyline ▲ BSD 137 [AAD]
Riegger, W.:Music of, w. Gilbert Kalish (pno)—Con Pno Ww; Tone Pictures Pno; Duos for 3 Winds; The New and Old; 3 Canons; Petite Etude; Qnt Ww, Op. 51 — Bridge ▲ 9068
Roseman, R.:Double Qnt, w. American Brass Quintet — New World ▲ 80413-2 [DDD]
Shapey, R.:Movts Ww — New World ▲ 80413-2 [DDD]
Sweelinck, J.P.:Vars on a Folk Song — Boston Skyline ▲ BSD 137 [AAD]
Van Vactor, D.:Scherzo Ww — Boston Skyline ▲ BSD 139 [AAD]
Villa-Lobos, H.:Qnt Ww — Boston Skyline ▲ BSD 139 [AAD]
Wilder, A.:Qnts Ww—Nos. 3, 4 & 6 — Boston Skyline ▲ BSD 141 [AAD]
Wilder, A.:Up Tempo — Boston Skyline ▲ BSD 139 [AAD]
New York Woodwind Quintet members [Jerome Roth (ob), Arthur Weisberg (bn)]
Villa-Lobos, H.:Duo Ob — Boston Skyline ▲ BSD 139 [AAD]
New York Woodwind Quintet members [Samuel Baron (fl), Arthur Weisberg (bn)]
Villa-Lobos, H.:Bachiana brasileira 6 — Boston Skyline ▲ BSD 139 [AAD]
New York Woodwind Soloists [Henry Schuman (ob), Ronald Roseman (ob), Robert Listokin (cl), Stanley Walden (cl), Robert Cole (bn), Loren Glickman (bn), Fred Klein (hn), Earl Chapin (hn)]
N. Jenkins (cnd)
Mozart, W.A.:Serenade Ww, K.375 — Everest ▲ EVC 9026 [AAD]
Mozart, W.A.:Serenade Ww, K.388 — Everest ▲ EVC 9026 [AAD]
New Zealand CO
Flute Salad, w. L. Gilbert (fl), Alexa Still (fl), Doriot Dwyer (fl), Bradley Garner (fl), London SO — Koch Schwann ▲ KIC CD 7602
Lilburn, D.:Diversions — Koch International Classics ▲ KIC 7260 [DDD]
Lilburn, D.:Landfall in Unknown Seas, w. Edmund Hillary (nar) — Koch International Classics ▲ KIC 7260 [DDD]
Pruden, L.:Soliloquy Strs — Koch International Classics ▲ KIC 7260 [DDD]
Watson, T.:Intro & Allegro — Koch International Classics ▲ KIC 7260 [DDD]
D. Armstrong (cnd)
Moross, J.:Con Fl, w. Alexa Still (fl) — Koch Schwann ▲ KIC CD 7367
N. Braithwaite (cnd)
Alexa Still, w. Alexa Still (fl) — Koch International Classics ▲ KIC 7063 [DDD]
Arnold, M.:Con 1 Fl, w. Alexa Still (fl) — Koch International Classics ▲ KIC 7607
Arnold, M.:Con 2 Fl, w. A. Still (fl) — Koch International Classics ▲ KIC 7140 [DDD]
Arnold, M.:Con 2 Fl, w. Alexa Still (fl) — Koch International Classics ▲ KIC 7607
Bridge, F.:Old English Songs (2) [arr. for string orch.] — Koch International Classics ▲ KIC 7139-2 [DDD]
Bridge, F.:Sir Roger de Coverley — Koch International Classics ▲ KIC 7139-2 [DDD]
Bridge, F.:Suite Str Orch — Koch International Classics ▲ KIC 7139-2 [DDD]
Bridge, F.:There Is a Willow Grows Aslant a Brook — Koch International Classics ▲ KIC 7139-2 [DDD]
Delius, F.:Son Str Orch — Koch International Classics ▲ KIC 7139-2 [DDD]
Holst, G.:Brook Green Suite — Koch International Classics ▲ KIC 7058-2 [DDD]
Holst, G.:A Fugal Con — Koch International Classics ▲ KIC 7058-2 [DDD]
Holst, G.:Lyric Movement — Koch International Classics ▲ KIC 7058-2 [DDD]
Holst, G.:Morris Dances — Koch International Classics ▲ KIC 7058-2 [DDD]
Holst, G.:St. Paul's Suite — Koch International Classics ▲ KIC 7058-2 [DDD]
Jacob, G.:Con Fl, w. A. Still (fl) — Koch International Classics ▲ KIC 7140 [DDD]
Musgrave, T.:Orfeo II, w. A. Still (fl) — Koch International Classics ▲ KIC 7140
Jordania (cnd)
Hovhaness, A.:Music of, w. Alexa Still (fl), Marvin Rosen (pno), Manhattan CO, KBS SO—The Prayer of St. Gregory; Elibris; Mystic Flute; Aria, Hymn & Fugue; Mountain Idylls; Gtr Sym; Adagio; Son; Fred the Cat; Aria [from Harotiun] — Koch International Classics ▲ KIC 7311 [DDD]
New Zealand String Quartet
Still, W.G.:Folk Suites, w. A. Still (fl), M. Steer (db), S. De Witt Smith (pno)—No. 1 — Koch International Classics ▲ KIC 7192 [DDD]
Still, W.G.:Instrumental Music, w. A. Still (fl), S. De Witt Smith (pno), M. Steer (db)—Quit Dat Fool'nish; Summerland — Koch International Classics ▲ KIC 7192 [DDD]
Still, W.G.:Music of, w. S. DeWitt Smith (pno), A. Still (fl), M. Steer (db)—Summerland; Quit dat Fool'nish; Pastorela; Folk Suite 1; Suite for Violin & Piano [Movts. I & II]; Prelude for Flute, String Qnt. & Piano *(rec May 1993)* — Koch International Classics ▲ KIC 7192 [DDD]
Still, W.G.:Preludes Fl, w. A. Still (fl), S. De Witt Smith (pno), M. Steer (db) — Koch International Classics ▲ KIC 7192 [DDD]
Still, W.G.:Suite Vn, w. M. Steer (db), S. De Witt Smith (pno) — Koch International Classics ▲ KIC 7192 [DDD]
New Zealand SO
Barber, S.:Music of, w. Alexa Still (fl), Chicago SO, San Diego CO, Atlantic Sinfonietta, Arioso Wind Quintet, Capricorn, Repertory Singers—Capricorn Con; Canzone; Fadograph of a Yestern Scene; Cave of the Heart; Adagio for Strs; Souvenirs; Hermit Songs; To Be Sung on Water; The Lovers; Summer Music — Koch International Classics ▲ KIC 7361
The Cinema Classics Collection, Vol. 1, w. David Buechner (pno), Angeles String Quartet, London SO, Phoenix SO — Koch International Classics ▲ KIC 7604
F.-P. Decker (cnd)
Hindemith, P.:Mathis der Maler (sym) *(rec Lower Hutt Town Hall, Wellington, New Zealand, Apr. 1994)* — Naxos ▲ 8.553078 [DDD]
Hindemith, P.:Nobilissima visione *(rec Lower Hutt Town Hall, Wellington, New Zealand, Apr. 1994)* — Naxos ▲ 8.553078 [DDD]
Hindemith, P.:Symphonic Metamorphosis on Themes of Carl Maria von Weber *(rec Lower Hutt Town Hall, Wellington, New Zealand, Apr. 1994)* — Naxos ▲ 8.553078 [DDD]
Reger, M.:Vars & Fugue on a Theme of of J. A. Hiller *(rec Lower Hutt Town Hall, Wellington, New Zealand, Apr. 1994)* — Naxos ▲ 8.553079 [DDD]
Reger, M.:Vars & Fugue on a Theme by Mozart *(rec Lower Hutt Town Hall, Wellington, New Zealand, Apr. 1994)* — Naxos ▲ 8.553079 [DDD]

ORCH. & ENS.

New Zealand SO (cont.)
J. Falletta (cnd)
Gould, M.:Foster Gallery Koch Schwann ▲ KIC CD 7380
Moross, J.:Beguine Koch Schwann ▲ KIC CD 7367
Moross, J.:Frankie & Johnny Koch Schwann ▲ KIC CD 7367
Moross, J.:Tall Story Koch Schwann ▲ KIC CD 7367
Ravel, M.:Ma mère l'oye suite, w. Meryl Streep (nar), Mona Golabek (pno), René Golabek (pno) [E] Koch Schwann ▲ KIC CD 7368 ■ KIC MC 4368; 7371 (Blister Pack)
M. Fredman (cnd)
Britten, B.:An American Ov *(rec Lower Hutt Town Hall, Wellington, New Zealand, July 1994)* Naxos ▲ 8.553107
Britten, B.:Peter Grimes (sea interludes & passacaglia) *(rec Lower Hutt Town Hall, Wellington, New Zealand, July 1994)* Naxos ▲ 8.553107 [DDD]
Britten, B.:Sinf da requiem *(rec Lower Hutt Town Hall, Wellington, New Zealand, July 1994)* Naxos ▲ 8.553107 [DDD]
Delius, F.:Brigg Fair:An English Rhapsody *(rec Lower Hutt Town Hall, Wellington, New Zealand, July 19–21, 1994)* Naxos ▲ 8.553001 [DDD]
Delius, F.:Eventyr *(rec Lower Hutt Town Hall, Wellington, New Zealand, July 19–21, 1994)* Naxos ▲ 8.553001 [DDD]
Delius, F.:Irmelin (prelude) *(rec Lower Hutt Town Hall, Wellington, New Zealand, July 19–21, 1994)* Naxos ▲ 8.553001 [DDD]
Delius, F.:Koanga (sels)—La Calinda *(rec Lower Hutt Town Hall, Wellington, New Zealand, July 19–21, 1994)* Naxos ▲ 8.553001 [DDD]
Delius, F.:Paris:The Song of a Great City *(rec Lower Hutt Town Hall, Wellington, New Zealand, July 19–21, 1994)* Naxos ▲ 8.553001 [DDD]
J. Hopkins (cnd)
Lilburn, D.:Sym 1 Continuum ▲ CON 1069 [DDD]
Lilburn, D.:Sym 2 Continuum ▲ CON 1069 [DDD]
Lilburn, D.:Sym 3 Continuum ▲ CON 1069 [DDD]
R. Kaufman (cnd)
Young, V.:Film Music—For Whom the Bell Tolls; The Quiet Man; Around the World in 80 Days; Samson & Delilah; Shane Koch International Classics ▲ KIC 7365
C. Lyndon-Gee (cnd)
Shostakovich, D.:The Golden Age (suite) *(rec Lower Hutt Town Hall, Wellington, New Zealand, Nov 2–4, 1994)* Naxos ▲ 8.553126 [DDD]
J.-Y. Ossonce (cnd)
Massenet, J.:Hérodiade (suite) *(rec Lower Hutt Town Hall, Wellington, New Zealand, July 1994)* Naxos ▲ 8.553124 [DDD]
Massenet, J.:Suite 1 *(rec Lower Hutt Town Hall, Wellington, New Zealand, July 1994)* Naxos ▲ 8.553124 [DDD]
Massenet, J.:Suite 2 *(rec Lower Hutt Town Hall, Wellington, New Zealand, July 1994)* Naxos ▲ 8.553124 [DDD]
Massenet, J.:Suite 3 *(rec Lower Hutt Town Hall, Wellington, New Zealand, July 1994)* Naxos ▲ 8.553124 [DDD]
Massenet, J.:Suite 4 *(rec Lower Hutt Town Hall, Wellington, New Zealand, July 1994)* Naxos ▲ 8.553125 [DDD]
Massenet, J.:Suite 5 *(rec Lower Hutt Town Hall, Wellington, New Zealand, July 1994)* Naxos ▲ 8.553125 [DDD]
Massenet, J.:Suite 6 *(rec Lower Hutt Town Hall, Wellington, New Zealand, July 1994)* Naxos ▲ 8.553125 [DDD]
Massenet, J.:Suite 7 *(rec Lower Hutt Town Hall, Wellington, New Zealand, July 1994)* Naxos ▲ 8.553125 [DDD]
A. Schenck (cnd)
Barber, S.:Adagio Strs Vox Box 2–▲ CDX 5091 [ADD]
Barber, S.:Essay 1 Vox Box 2–▲ CDX 5091 [ADD]
Barber, S.:Essay 3 Koch International Classics ▲ KIC 7010–2 [DDD] ■ 3–7010–4 (D)
Barber, S.:Fadograph of a Yestern Scene Koch International Classics ▲ KIC 7010–2 [DDD] ■ 3–7010–4 (D)
Barber, S.:Medea Koch International Classics ▲ KIC 7010–2 [DDD] ■ 3–7010–4 (D)
Barber, S.:Music for a Scene from Shelley Vox Box 2–▲ CDX 5091 [ADD]
Barber, S.:The School for Scandal Vox Box 2–▲ CDX 5091 [ADD]
Barber, S.:Souvenirs Koch International Classics ▲ KIC 7005–2 [DDD] ■ 3–7005–4 (D)
Barber, S.:Sym 2 Vox Box 2–▲ CDX 5091 [ADD]
Gould, M.:Fall River Legend *(rec Nov. 1992)* Koch International Classics ▲ KIC 7181 [DDD]
Menotti, G.C.:Amahl & the Night Visitors (orchestral sels)—Introduction, March & Shepherd's Dance Koch International Classics ▲ KIC 7005–2 [DDD] ■ 3–7005–4 (D)
Menotti, G.C.:Sebastian Koch International Classics ▲ KIC 7005–2 [DDD] ■ 3–7005–4 (D)
Thompson, R.:Sym 1 Koch International Classics ▲ KIC 7181 [DDD]
Thompson, R.:Sym 2 Koch International Classics ▲ KIC 7074–2 [DDD]
Thompson, R.:Sym 3 Koch International Classics ▲ KIC 7074–2 [DDD]
P. Scholes (cnd)
Coleman, J.:Sym 1, "Idavoll" RCA Victor ▲ 09026-62717-2 ■ 09026-62717-4
J. Sedares (cnd)
Bach, J.S.:A Musical Offering—Fugue Koch International Classics ▲ KIC 7610
Barber, S.:Adagio Strs Koch ▲ KIC 7243 [DDD]
Bloch, E.:Evocations *(rec Oct. 1993)* Koch International Classics ▲ KIC 7232 [DDD]
Bloch, E.:Jewish Poems *(rec Oct. 1993)* Koch International Classics ▲ KIC 7232 [DDD]
Bloch, E.:Two Last Poems...Maybe, w. A. Still (fl) *(rec Oct. 1993)* Koch International Classics ▲ KIC 7232 [DDD]
Dello Joio, N.:Triumph of St. Joan Sym Koch International Classics ▲ KIC 7243–2 [DDD]
Dello Joio, N.:Vars, Chaconne & Finale Koch International Classics ▲ KIC 7243–2 [DDD]
Gould, M.:Fall River Legend Koch Schwann ▲ KIC CD 7380
Herrmann, B.:Con Macabre, w. David Buechner (pno) Koch International Classics ▲ KIC 7225 [DDD]
Herrmann, B.:Currier & Ives Suite Koch International Classics ▲ KIC 7224–2 [DDD]
Herrmann, B.:The Devil & Daniel Webster Koch International Classics ▲ KIC 7224–2 [DDD]
Herrmann, B.:For the Fallen Koch International Classics ▲ KIC 7224–2 [DDD]
Herrmann, B.:Silent Noon Koch International Classics ▲ KIC 7224–2 [DDD]
North, A.:Rhap Pno, w. David Buechner (pno) [w. Tpt Obbligato] Koch International Classics ▲ KIC 7225 [DDD]
Rózsa, M.:El Cid, w. Tamra Saylor Fine (org), New Zealand Youth Choir *(rec Symphony House, Wellington, New Zealand, May 1995)* Koch International Classics ▲ KIC 7340 [DDD] ■ KIC 7340
Rózsa, M.:Con Va, w. Paul Silverthorne (va) Koch International Classics ▲ KIC 7304 [DDD]
Rózsa, M.:Hungarian Sketches *(rec Nov. 1992)* Koch International Classics ▲ KIC 7191 [DDD]
Rózsa, M.:Notturno ungherese *(rec Nov. 1992)* Koch International Classics ▲ KIC 7191 [DDD]
Rózsa, M.:Ov to Sym Concert *(rec Nov. 1992)* Koch International Classics ▲ KIC 7191 [DDD]
Rózsa, M.:Sinf concertante, w. Igor Gruppman (vn), Richard Boch (vc) Koch International Classics ▲ KIC 7304 [DDD]
Rózsa, M.:Sym, Op. 6 Koch International Classics ▲ KIC 7244 [DDD]
Rózsa, M.:Theme, Vars & Finale *(rec Nov. 1992)* Koch International Classics ▲ KIC 7191 [DDD]
Rózsa, M.:The Vintner's Daughter Koch International Classics ▲ KIC 7244 [DDD]
Stokowski, L.:Transcriptions Orch—Mussorgsky:Night on Bare Mountain; Pictures at an Exhibition; Bach:Toccata & Fugue in d Koch International Classics ▲ KIC 7344 [DDD]
Waxman, F.:The Charm Bracelet Orch Koch International Classics ▲ KIC 7225 [DDD]
Waxman, F.:Rhap Pno, w. David Buechner (pno) Koch International Classics ▲ KIC 7225 [DDD]
Webern, A.:Transcriptions—Bach:Ricercare Koch International Classics ▲ KIC 7344 [DDD]
W. Southgate (cnd)
Lilburn, D.:A Birthday Offering Continuum ▲ CON 1076 [DDD]
Lilburn, D.:Drysdale Ov Continuum ▲ CON 1076 [DDD]
Lilburn, D.:Festival Ov Continuum ▲ CON 1076 [DDD]

New Zealand SO (cont.)
W. Southgate (cnd) (cont.)
Lilburn, D.:A Song of Islands Continuum ▲ CON 1076 [DDD]
Lilburn, D.:Suite Orch Continuum ▲ CON 1076 [DDD]
H. Wallberg (cnd)
American Diva, w. A. Marc (sop) Delos ▲ DE 3108 [DDD]
K. Young (cnd)
Carr, E.:Pacific Festival Ov Continuum ▲ CON 1077 [DDD]
Carr, E.:Promenade Continuum ▲ CON 1077 [DDD]
Carr, E.:Sinfonietta Continuum ▲ CON 1077 [DDD]
Carr, E.:Sym 4 Continuum ▲ CON 1077 [DDD]
New Zurich String Quartet
Lehmann, H.U.:Qt Strs *(rec June 27, 1988)* Grammont ▲ CTS P 4–2
Looser, R.:Music of, New Zurich Quartet—Fant a quattro for String Quartet Grammont ▲ CTSP 11–2 [ADD]
Newband
Cage, J.:Haikai Mode ▲ 18
La Barbara, J.:Silent Scroll, w. J. La Barbara (sop) Mode ▲ 18
Partch, H.:Studies (2) on Ancient Greek Scales Mode ▲ 18
Wolfe, J.:Steam Point Music ▲ 454054–2
D. Drummond (cnd)
Drummond, D.:Columbus Mode ▲ 18
Drummond, D.:Incredible Time (to live & die) Mode ▲ 18
Drummond, D.:Then or Never Mode ▲ 18
Thoresen, L.:Thus Norway Music ▲ ACD 4968
Newberry Consort
M. Springfels (cnd)
Ay Amor! Harmonia Mundi ▲ HMU 907022 ■
The Golden Dream:17th Century Music from the Low Countries, w. Marion Verbruggen (rcr), Paul Odette (lt) *(rec Troy Savings Bank Music Hall, Nov 1–3. 1993)* Harmonia Mundi France ▲ HMU 907123
Musick for Severall Friends, w. Drew Minter (ct), David Douglass (vn), Kevin Mason (thb/lt) Harmonia Mundi France ("Musique d'abord" series) ▲ HMA 1907013
Secular Music of 15th Century Spain Harmonia Mundi ▲ HMU 907083
Wanderers' Voices Harmonia Mundi USA ▲ HMU 907082
Newman/Oltman Guitar Duo [Michael Newman (gtr), Laura Oltman (gtr)]
The Newman & Oltman Guitar Duo MusicMasters ▲ 7071–2–C [DDD]
Passions:Baroque & Renaissance Duets Sheffield Lab ("Audiophile Reference" series) ▲ SLS 10058
Nexus [B. Becker (perc), B. Cahn (perc), R. Engelman (perc), R. Hartenberger (perc), J. Wyre (perc)]
The Best of Nexus Nexus ▲ 10251 [AAD/DDD]
Cage, J.:Third Construction Nexus ▲ 10251 [DDD]
Green, G.H.:Novelty Music Nexus ▲ 10273 [DDD]
Nexus Now Nexus ▲ 10262 [DDD]
Origins Nexus ▲ 10295 [DDD]
Ragtime Concert, featuring xylophone soloist Bob Becker Nexus ▲ 10284 [AAD]
Reich, S.:Sextet Elektra/Nonesuch ▲ 79138–2 ■ 79138–4
The Story of Percussion in the Orchestra, w. Bill Moyers (nar), Rochester PO Nexus ▲ 10306 [DDD]
Takemitsu, T.:Rain Tree Nexus ▲ 10262 [DDD]
P. Bay (cnd)
Cahn, W.:The Birds Perc, w. Rochester PO *(rec Apr. 23, 1992)* Nexus ▲ 10317 [DDD]
Cahn, W.:Kebjar–Bali, w. Rochester PO *(rec Jan. 6, 1994)* Nexus ▲ 10317 [DDD]
Cahn, W.:Voices Perc, w. Rochester PO *(rec Jan. 6, 1994)* Nexus ▲ 10317 [DDD]
Wyre, J.:Connexus, w. Rochester PO *(rec Apr. 23, 1992)* Nexus ▲ 10317 [DDD]
A. Pauk (cnd)
Freedman, H.:Touchings, Esprit Orch *(rec Studioasis, Toronto, Apr 10–11, 1995)* CBC ("SM 5000" series) ▲ SM5 5154 [DDD]
NFB Horn Quartet
Gallay, J.–F.:Qt Hns, "Grand Quattuor" Crystal ▲ CD 241
Hindemith, P.:Son for 4 Hns Crystal ▲ CD 241
Wadenpfuhl, J.:Tectonica Crystal ▲ CD 241
NHK Chamber Soloists
R. Paternostro (cnd)
Mozart, W.A.:Clemenza (sels), w. G. Sabbatini (ten)—Ah se foss intorno al trono LaserLight ▲ 15 890 [DDD]
NHK SO
C. Chen (cnd)
Bunya, K.:Idyll of the Fields Sunrise ▲ 8510
Bunya, K.:Memorial to Chu Yuan Sunrise ▲ 8510
Bunya, K.:Sinfonietta Sunrise ▲ 8510
Bunya, K.:Sketches of the Old Capital Sunrise ▲ 8510
Koh, B.:Confucian Temple Rites *(rec Edogawa-ku Sohgoh Bunka Central Hall, Sept 6, 1984)* Sunrise ▲ 8503
Koh, B.:Formosan Dance *(rec Edogawa-ku Sohgoh Bunka Central Hall, Sept 6, 1984)* Sunrise ▲ 8503
Wut, M.–C.:Festival Sketches Sunrise ▲ 8522
Wut, M.–C.:Hillside Songs of Mi Du Sunrise ▲ 8522
Wut, M.–C.:Songs of the Provinces Sunrise ▲ 8522
O. de Fabritiis (cnd)
Donizetti, G.:La favorita (sels), w. M. Zotti (sop), F. Cossotto (mez), A. Kraus (ten), R. Raimondi (bass) *(rec Sept. 13, 1971)* Myto 2–▲ MCD 93276
T. Noda (cnd)
Noda, T.:Qt Strs Camerata ▲ 30CM 344
Noda, T.:Rhap, w. Takao Kaneko (gtr) Camerata ▲ 30CM 344
T. Otaka (cnd)
Noda, T.:Concerto Pno, w. I. Kamiya (pno) Camerata ▲ 32CM 58
W. Sawallisch (cnd)
Beethoven, L. van:Sym 5 RCA Silver Seal ▲ 60534–2–RV [ADD] ■ 60534–4–RV
Beethoven, L. van:Sym 8 RCA Silver Seal ▲ 60534–2–RV [ADD] ■ 60534–4–RV
Y. Toyama (cnd)
Chopin, F.:Con 1 Pno, w. S. Bunin (pno) *(rec live 8/86)* MK ▲ 418026
Mozart, W.A.:Con 23 Pno, w. S. Bunin (pno) *(rec live Aug. 1986)* MK ▲ 418026
Niagara Brass Ensemble
J. Tinsley (cnd)
Baroque Brass Analekta Fleur de Lys ▲ FL 23087 [DDD]
Nice Baroque Ensemble
G. Bezzina (cnd)
Bach, J.C.F.:Die Auferweckung Lazarus, w. Véronique Dietschy (sop), Consuelo Caroli (mez), John Elwes (ten), Philippe Cantor (bar), Nicole Blanchi Vocal Ensemble Adda ▲ ADD 581182 [DDD]
Corrette, M.:Cons Org, Op. 26, w. R. Saorgin (org) Musique d'Abord ▲ HMA 1905148 [ADD]
Locatelli, P.:Cons for 4 Vns, w. Gilbert Bezzina (vn) Adda ▲ ADD 581118 [DDD]
Pergolesi, G.B.:La serva padrona, w. Isabelle Poulenard (sop), Philippe Cantor (bar) Pierre Verany ▲ PVY 795111
Vivaldi, A.:Cons Vn, Op. 4, "La stravaganza", w. Gilbert Bezzina (vn)—Nos. 2, 3, 6, 7, 9 & 12 *(rec Sept 1992)* Pierre Verany ▲ PVY 730028
Vivaldi, A.:Cons Vn, Op. 4, "La stravaganza", w. G. Bezzina (vn) Pierre Verany 2–▲ PVY 793022 [DDD]
Nice PO
J. Carewe (cnd)
Debussy, C.:Pelléas et Mélisande, w. E. Manchet (sop—Mélisande), M. Walker (bar—Pelléas), Nice Opera Chorus—no texts [F] *(rec 6/88)* Pierre Verany 2–▲ PV.788093/4 [DDD]

▲ = CD ♦ = Enhanced CD Δ = MD ■ = Cassette Tape □ = DCC

Nice PO (cont.)
J. Carewe (cnd) (cont.)
Elgar, E.:Songs, w. B. Svenden (sop) [E] *(rec 7 & 11/90)* Forlane ▲ FOR 16642 [DDD]
Mahler, G.:Kindertotenlieder, w. B. Svenden (sop) [G] *(rec 7 & 11/90; no texts)* Forlane ▲ FOR 16642 [DDD]
Zemlinsky, A. von:Songs to Poems by Maurice Maeterlinck, w. B. Svenden (sop) [G] Forlane ▲ FOR 16642 [DDD]
R. Delage (cnd)
Koechlin, C.:Partita *(rec 1972)* Skarbo ▲ SKR 3924
M. Schønwandt (cnd)
Busoni, F.:Con Pno, Op. 39, w. F.-J. Thiollier (pno) Kontrapunkt ▲ 32057 [DDD]
M. Valdes (cnd)
Devienne, F.:Con 7 Fl, w. A. Marion (fl) Denon ▲ 7923 [DDD]
Ibert, J.:Con Fl, w. A. Marion (fl) Denon ▲ 7923 [DDD]
Molique, W.B.:Con Fl, w. Alain Marion (fl) Denon ▲ 7923 [DDD]
K. Weise (cnd)
Mozart, W.A.:Cons 1–4 Pno, w. H. Francesch (pno) Kontrapunkt ▲ KPT 32109 [DDD]
Mozart, W.A.:Con 9 Pno, w. Homero Francesch (pno) Kontrapunkt ▲ KPT 32209
Mozart, W.A.:Con 14 Pno, w. H. Francesch (pno) *(rec live 1991)* Kontrapunkt ▲ KPT 32139 [DDD]
Mozart, W.A.:Con 15 Pno, w. H. Francesch (pno) *(rec live 1991)* Kontrapunkt ▲ KPT 32139 [DDD]
Mozart, W.A.:Con 16 Pno, w. H. Francesch (pno) *(rec live 1991)* Kontrapunkt ▲ KPT 32139 [DDD]
Mozart, W.A.:Con 17 Pno, w. H. Francesch (pno) Kontrapunkt ▲ KPT 32159 [DDD]
Mozart, W.A.:Con 18 Pno, w. H. Francesch (pno) Kontrapunkt ▲ KPT 32159 [DDD]
Mozart, W.A.:Con 19 Pno, w. H. Franesch (pno) Kontrapunkt ▲ KPT 32179 [DDD]
Mozart, W.A.:Con 20 Pno, w. H. Franesch (pno) Kontrapunkt ▲ KPT 32179 [DDD]
Mozart, W.A.:Con 21 Pno, w. H. Francesch (pno) Kontrapunkt ▲ KPT 32189 [DDD]
Mozart, W.A.:Con 22 Pno, w. H. Francesch (pno) Kontrapunkt ▲ KPT 32189 [DDD]
Mozart, W.A.:Con 25 Pno, w. Homero Francesch (pno) Kontrapunkt ▲ KPT 32209
Strauss, R.:Don Juan Forlane ▲ FRL 16625 [DDD]
Strauss, R.:Till Eulenspiegels lustige Streiche Forlane ▲ FRL 16625 [DDD]
Les Nièces de Rameau [Florence Malgoire (vn), Alice Pierot (vn), Marianne Muller (vl), Claire Giardelli (vc), Aline Zylberajch (hpd)]
Leclair, J.-M.:Recréations de Musique Pierre Verany ▲ PVY 794011 [DDD]
Purcell, H.:Sons (22) Vns Pierre Verany ▲ PVY 795093
Carl Nielsen String Quartet
Lange-Müller, P.E.:Albumsblade Kontrapunkt ▲ KPT 32208
Nilsson-Waldeland-Knardahl Trio
Valen, F.:Trio Pno Simax ▲ PSC 3116
Nine Songs Ensemble
T. Dun (cnd)
Dun, T.:Nine Songs, w. Nine Songs Chorus [Chinese] CRI ▲ CD 603 [DDD]
92nd St. Y Chamber SO
G. Schwarz (cnd)
Beethoven, L. van:Sym 6, "Pastorale" Delos ▲ DCD 3017 [DDD]
Biber, H. von:Son in C for 8 Tpts & Timp, w. G. Schwarz (tpt), New York Trumpet Ensemble Delos ▲ DCD 3002 [DDD]
Piston, W.:Serenata Orch Delos ▲ DE 3106 [DDD]
Telemann, G.P.:Con Tpt Strs in D, w. G. Schwarz (tpt) Delos ▲ DCD 3002 [DDD]
Vivaldi, A.:Con for 2 Tpts, w. G. Schwarz (tpt), New York Trumpet Ensemble Delos ▲ DCD 3002 [DDD]
92nd St. Y Chamber SO members
Altenburg, J.E.:Con in C Tpts, w. G. Schwarz (tpt), New York Trumpet Ensemble Delos ▲ DCD 3002 [DDD]
Nomos String Quartet
Boccherini, L.:Qts Strs, G.195–200—Nos. 4–6 CPO ▲ CPO 999202
Haydn, J.:Qts Strs, Op. 50, "Prussian Qts" CPO 2-▲ CPO 999218 [DDD]
Hölszky, A.:Music of, w. Pellegrini String Quartet—Hängebrücken (Suspension Bridges); Qts. I & II; Double Qt.; Hunt the Wolves Back for Percussion; Audiowindow or Franz Liszt for Piano CPO ▲ CPO 999112 [DDD]
Reicha, A.:Qnt Bn, w. E. Hübner (bn) CPO ▲ CPO 999061-2 [DDD]
Reicha, A.:Vars Bn, w. E. Hübner (bn) CPO ▲ CPO 999061-2 [DDD]
Yun, I.:Concertino Acc, w. Mie Miki (accordion) CPO ▲ CPO 999075-2 [DDD]
Yun, I.:Qt 3 Strs CPO ▲ CPO 999075-2 [DDD]
Yun, I.:Qt 4 Strs CPO ▲ CPO 999075-2 [DDD]
Yun, I.:Tapis CPO ▲ CPO 999075-2 [DDD]
Nonpareil Wind Band
T. Foley (cnd)
Sousa, J.P.:Marches & Dances—The Stars and Stripes Forever; King Cotton; The Liberty Bell; El Capitan; The Fairest of the Fair; The Washington Post; Foshay Tower Washington Memorial; Who's Who in Navy Blue; Ancient and Honorable Artillery Company; The Presidential Polonaise; 3 other dances; 4 trumpet & drum marches EMI Classics ▲ CDC 54130 [DDD] ■ 4DS 54130
Nord Ensemble
Bach, E.:Bagatelles (5) *(rec Nordjsky Musikkonservatorium, 1992)* Paula ▲ PACD 74 [DAD]
Bentzon, N.V.:Choro Daniensis *(rec Nordjsky Musikkonservatorium, 1992)* Paula ▲ PACD 74 [DAD]
Bjerno, E.:Star Dust *(rec Nordjsky Musikkonservatorium, 1992)* Paula ▲ PACD 74 [DAD]
Christensen, M.:The Lost Poems of Princess Ateh *(rec Nordjsky Musikkonservatorium, 1992)* Paula ▲ PACD 74 [DAD]
Christensen, M.:Music of—Birds of a Midsummer Night; Snow Light; Esprit Féerique; Dreamtimes; Lost Poems of Princess Ateh; Mellem livets afgrunde [w. Charlotte Meldgaard (sop)]; Ange Silencieux Paula ▲ PACD 96 [DDD]
Christiansen, S.:In Reality *(rec Nordjsky Musikkonservatorium, 1992)* Paula ▲ PACD 74 [DAD]
Rijshøjgård, K.:Qnt *(rec Nordjsky Musikkonservatorium, 1992)* Paula ▲ PACD 74 [DAD]
Nordisk CO
Wikström, I.:Den Brottsliga Modern, w. E. Saeden (bar), M. Tretom (sop), A. Häggstam (bass) Proprius ▲ 9069
De Nordiske Spillemande
Folk Inspired Instrumentals Danacord ▲ DACOCD 388 [DDD]
Nord-Pas-de-Calais Atelier Instrumental d'Expression Contemporaine
Bacri, N.:Sextet Strs *(rec 1992)* REM ▲ REM 311180 [DDD]
Correggia, E.:Voces *(rec 1992)* REM ▲ REM 311180 [DDD]
de Pablo, L.:Parafrasis & Interlude *(rec 1992)* REM ▲ REM 311180 [DDD]
Kagel, M.:Sextet Strs *(rec 1992)* REM ▲ REM 311180 [DDD]
Nord-Pas-de-Calais AIEC String Sextet
Rimsky-Korsakov, N.:Sextet Vns REM ▲ REM 311208 [DDD]
Tchaikovsky, P.:Souvenir de Florence REM ▲ REM 311208 [DDD]
Normandy Orchestral Ensemble
J.-P. Berlingen (cnd)
Bach, J.S.:Con 1 for 2 Hpds, w. Daniel Arrignon (ob), Bernard Mathern (vn) [reconstructed for ob & vn in d] *(rec Kusatsu Concert Hall, Nov 2–3, 1991)* Camerata ▲ 32CM284 [DDD]
Mozart, W.A.:Sym 29 *(rec Kusatsu Concert Hall, Nov 2–3, 1991)* Camerata ▲ 32CM284 [DDD]
Stamitz, C.:Con Fl, Op. 29, w. C. Lardé (fl) *(rec Kusatsu Concert Hall, Nov 2–3, 1991)* Camerata ▲ 32CM284 [DDD]
Norrköping SO
H. Damgaard (cnd)
Alfvén, H.:Synnöve Solbakken *(rec Aug 31, 1973)* Sterling ▲ CDS 1012 [ADD]
S. Frykberg (cnd)
Atterberg, K.:Sym 4, "Sinf piccola" *(rec Sept. 9, 1976)* Sterling ▲ CDS 1010
J. Hirokami (cnd)
Atterberg, K.:Ballad utan ord BIS ▲ CD 553 [DDD]
Atterberg, K.:Sym 6 BIS ▲ CD 553 [DDD]

Norrköping SO (cont.)
J. Hirokami (cnd) (cont.)
Atterberg, K.:En värmlandrapsodi BIS ▲ CD 553 [DDD]
Bloch, E.:Schelomo, w. Mari Fujiwara (vc) Denon ▲ DEN 78830
Dvořák, A.:Con Vc, w. Mari Fujiwara (vc) Denon ▲ DEN 78830
Grieg, E.:Con Pno, Op. 16, w. Love Derwinger (pno) BIS ("BIS Twins" series) 2-▲ CD 200/619
Grieg, E.:Con Pno, Op. 16, w. L. Derwinger (pno) [original version] *(rec Mar. 28, 1993)* BIS ▲ CD 619
Linde, B.:Con Vn, w. U. Wallin (vn) *(rec Jan. 22 & 23, 1993)* BIS ▲ CD 621 [DDD]
Linde, B.:Pensieri sopra un cnatico vecchio *(rec Jan. 22 & 23, 1993)* BIS ▲ CD 621 [DDD]
Linde, B.:Sinf, Op. 23, w. N. Veltman (vc) *(rec Mar. 26, 1993)* BIS ▲ CD 621 [DDD]
M. Jurowski (cnd)
Rangström, T.:Dithyramb CPO ▲ CPO 999367
Rangström, T.:Intermezzo drammatico CPO ▲ CPO 999368
Rangström, T.:Spring Hymn CPO ▲ CPO 999367
Rangström, T.:Sym 1 CPO ▲ CPO 999367
Rangström, T.:Sym 2 CPO ▲ CPO 999368
G.W. Nilson (cnd)
Rosenberg, H.:Dagdrivaren, w. Rolf Leanderson (bar) *(rec Hörsalen, Norrköping, Sweden, Nov. 27, 1981)* BIS ▲ CD 55 [AAD]
J. Pnule, G. Sjökvist (cnds)
Virtuoso Percussion Music, w. R. Kuisma (mar/vib) BIS ▲ CD 149 [AAD]
L. Segerstam (cnd)
Pettersson, G.A.:Sym 3 BIS ▲ CD 680
Pettersson, G.A.:Sym 7 BIS ▲ CD 580 [DDD]
Pettersson, G.A.:Sym 11 BIS ▲ CD 580 [DDD]
Pettersson, G.A.:Sym 15 BIS ▲ CD 680
Reger, M.:Eine Ballettsuite *(rec 1993)* BIS ▲ CD 601 [DDD]
Reger, M.:Con Pno, w. Love Derwinger (pno) *(rec Louis De Geer Concert Hall, Norrköping, Dec 13–14, 1994)* BIS ▲ CD 711 [DDD]
Reger, M.:Suite im alten Stil *(rec Louis De Geer Concert Hall, Norrköping, Dec 13–14, 1994)* BIS ▲ CD 711 [DDD]
Reger, M.:Tondichtungen nach Arnold Böcklin *(rec 1993)* BIS ▲ CD 601 [DDD]
Reger, M.:Vars & Fugue on a Theme of Beethoven *(rec 1993)* BIS ▲ CD 601 [DDD]
Rott, H.:Sym in E BIS ▲ CD 563 [DDD]
Norske Blåsere
G. Oskamp (cnd)
Kox, H.:Concertino A Sax, w. J.-E. Kelly (sax) *(rec 1991)* Attacca ▲ Babel 9262-1 [ADD/DDD]
North Arkansas SO
C. Woods (cnd)
Still, W.G.:Sym 3 Cambria ▲ CD 1060 [ADD]
North Carolina SO
G. Zimmermann (cnd)
Ward, R.:Con Sax, w. J. Houlik (sax) Albany ▲ AR 001-2 [DDD] ■ AR 001-4 (D)
Ward, R.:Jubilation Ov Albany ▲ AR 001-2 [DDD] ■ AR 001-4 (D)
Ward, R.:Sonic Structure Albany ▲ AR 001-2 [DDD] ■ AR 001-4 (D)
Ward, R.:Sym 4 Albany ▲ AR 001-2 [DDD] ■ AR 001-4 (D)
North German Radio Chamber Ensemble
Moscheles, I.:Intro & Rondeau Koch Schwann ▲ SCH 311782 [DDD]
Moscheles, I.:Spt Koch Schwann ▲ SCH 311782 [DDD]
Moscheles, I.:Son Fl Koch Schwann ▲ SCH 311782 [DDD]
Moscheles, I.:Terpsichore Koch Schwann ▲ SCH 311782 [DDD]
Moscheles, I.:Vivace Koch Schwann ▲ SCH 311782 [DDD]
North German Radio PO
C. Garben (cnd)
Weill, K.:The Seven Deadly Sins, w. B. Fassbaender (mez), K.-H. Brandt (ten), H. Sojer (ten), H. Komatsu (bass), I. Urbas (bass) Harmonia Mundi France ▲ HMC 901420
H. Hennig (cnd)
Stravinsky, I.:Babel, w. Doppeltes Wind Quintet, Hanover Boys' Choir [E & G; 2 versions] *(rec Jan. 5–6, 1993)* Calig ▲ CAL 50918 [DDD]
North German RSO
Bloch, A.:For the Light Is Come, w. M. Schweigmann (nar), P. Schwarz (org), North German Radio Chorus Pro Viva ▲ ISPV 169
W. A. Albert (cnd)
Goetz, H.:Con Vn, w. G. Schneider (vn) CPO ▲ CPO 999076 [DDD]
Goetz, H.:Sym, Op. 9 CPO ▲ CPO 999076 [DDD]
Goetz, H.:Der Widerspenstigen Zähmung (ov) CPO ▲ CPO 999076 [DDD]
M. Atzmon (cnd)
Ruzicka, P.:Befragung CPO ▲ CPO 999053 [DDD]
G. Aykal (cnd)
Saygun, A.A.:Con 1 Pno, w. G. Onay (pno) Koch Schwann ▲ SCH 313502 [DDD]
Saygun, A.A.:Con 2 Pno, w. G. Onay (pno) Koch Schwann ▲ SCH 313502 [DDD]
W. Brückner-Rüggeberg (cnd)
Weber, C.M. von:Andante & Rondo ungarese Va, w. E. Wallfisch (va) Bayer ▲ BR 200028 [ADD]
Weber, C.M. von:Vars on *A Schüsserl und a Reind'rl* Va, w. E. Wallfisch (va) Bayer ▲ BR 200028 [ADD]
Weill, K.:Aufstieg und Fall der Stadt Mahagonny, w. Lotte Lenya (sop), North German Radio Chorus [G] *(rec 1956)* CBS 2-▲ M2K 37874 (m) [ADD]
C. P. Flor (cnd)
Zemlinsky, A. von:Lyric Sym, w. Luba Orgonasova (sop), Bo Skovhus (bar) *(rec Musikhalle, Hamburg, Sept 8–10, 1994)* RCA Red Seal ▲ 09026-68111-2 [DDD]
W. Furtwängler (cnd)
Brahms, J.:Sym 1 Memories ▲ MEM 4531 [AAD]
Brahms, J.:Vars on a Theme by Haydn Memories ▲ MEM 4531 [AAD]
J. E. Gardiner (cnd)
Brahms, J.:Hungarian Dances Orch Deutsche Grammophon ▲ 437506-2 [DDD]
Britten, B.:War Requiem, w. L. Orgonasova (sop), A. Rolfe-Johnson (ten), B. Skovhus (bar), Monteverdi Choir London, North German Radio Chorus, Tölz Boys' Choir Deutsche Grammophon 2-▲ 437801-2
Dvořák, A.:Czech Suite Deutsche Grammophon ▲ 437506-2 [DDD]
Dvořák, A.:Symphonic Vars Deutsche Grammophon ▲ 437506-2 [DDD]
Janácek, L.:Taras Bulba Deutsche Grammophon ▲ 445838-2
Rachmaninoff, S.:Symphonic Dances Deutsche Grammophon ▲ 445838-2
W. Goehr (cnd)
Haydn, J.:Die Jahreszeiten, w. Teresa Stich-Randall (mez), Helmut Kretschmar (ten), Erik Wenk (bass), Hamburg Chorus *(rec 1966)* FNAC Music 2-▲ 642325
H. Hollreiser (cnd)
Nicolai, O.:Mass, w. G. Resick (sop), G. Killebrew (mez), F. Lang (ten), H. C. Polster (bass), North German Radio Chorus [L] Koch Schwann ▲ CD 313052 [ADD]
H. Knappertsbusch (cnd)
Wagner, R.:Götterdämmerung (immolation scene), w. C. Ludwig (mez) [G] *(rec live 3/24/63)* Arkadia ▲ 730 [ADD]
Wagner, R.:Die Meistersinger von Nürnberg (preludes/acts 1 & 3) *(rec live, 3/24/63)* Arkadia ▲ 730 [ADD]
Wagner, R.:Siegfried Idyll *(rec live, 3/24/63)* Arkadia ▲ 730 [ADD]
Wagner, R.:Tristan und Isolde (prelude & liebestod), w. C. Ludwig (mez) [G] *(rec live, 3/24/63)* Arkadia ▲ 730 [ADD]
L. Ludwig (cnd)
Haydn, J.:Sym 94, "Surprise Sym" Allegretto ▲ ACD 8031 [ADD] ■ ACS 8031
Mozart, W.A.:Sym 41 Allegretto ▲ ACD 8031 [ADD] ■ ACS 8031

North German RSO (cont.)
B. Maderna (cnd)
Nono, L.:Composizione 1 *(rec live, Hamburg 2/10/52)* Arkadia ▲ 027 [ADD]
Nono, L.:Epitaffio 3, w. North German Radio Chorus *(rec live, Hamburg 2/16/53)* Arkadia ▲ 027 [ADD]
P. Monteux (cnd)
Beethoven, L. van:Sym 2 *(rec 1960)* FNAC Music ("Via Classique" series) ▲ 642302
Beethoven, L. van:Sym 4 *(rec 1960)* FNAC Music ("Via Classique" series) ▲ 642302
K. Penderecki (cnd)
Penderecki, K.:Polish Requiem, w. I. Haubold (sop), G. Winogrodska (mez), Z. Terzakis (ten), Smith (sgr), North German Radio Chorus [L] *(rec live, Lucerne, 1989)* Deutsche Grammophon 2-▲ 429720-2 [DDD]
Penderecki, K.:Sym 2 Wergo ▲ WER 6270-2
Penderecki, K.:Sym 4 Wergo ▲ WER 6270-2
G. Prêtre (cnd)
Verdi, G.:Arias, w. M. Callas (sop)—Tu che la vanità..., from Don Carlos [I] *(rec live 3/16/62)* Melodram 2-▲ MEL 26029 (m) [AAD]
H. Scherchen (cnd)
Schoenberg, A.:Erwartung *(rec 1959)* Arkadia ▲ 769 [ADD]
Skalkottas, N.:Con 2 Pno, w. G. Hadjinikos (pno) *(rec 1953)* Arkadia ▲ 768 [ADD]
H. Schmidt-Isserstedt (cnd)
Brahms, J.:Con Vn, w. G. Neveu (vn) Acanta ▲ CD 43314 [DDD]
Mozart, W.A.:Complete Mozart Edition, w. Jessye Norman (sop), I. Cotrubas (sop), H. Donath (sop), T. Troyanos (mez), W. Hollweg (ten), H. Prey (bar) Philips 3-▲ 422534-2 [ADD]
W. Schüchter (cnd)
Wagner, R.:Lohengrin, w. Maud Cunitz (sop—Elsa), Margarete Klose (mez—Ortrud), Rudolf Schock (ten—Lohengrin), Josef Metternich (bar—Friedrich von Telramund), Gottlob Frick (bass—King Henry), North German Radio Chorus, West German Radio Men's Chorus *(rec 1953)* EMI Classics 2-▲ CDHC 65517
I. Stravinsky (cnd)
Stravinsky, I.:Chorale Variations on the German Christmas Carol "Vom Himmel hoch da komm' ich her", w. North German Radio Chorus *(rec live, Venice 9/23/58)* Arkadia 2-▲ 766 [ADD]
Stravinsky, I.:In memoriam Dylan Thomas, w. R. Robinson (ten) *(rec live, Venice 9/23/58)* Arkadia 2-▲ 766 [ADD]
Stravinsky, I.:Oedipus Rex, w. *(artists unknown)*, North German Radio Chorus *(rec live, Venice, 9/19/58)* Arkadia 2-▲ 766 [ADD]
Stravinsky, I.:Le Sacre du printemps Orch *(rec live, Venice 9/19/58)* Arkadia 2-▲ 766 [ADD]
Stravinsky, I.:Syms Ww *(rec live, Venice, 9/23/58)* Arkadia 2-▲ 766 [ADD]
Stravinsky, I.:Threni, w. North German Radio Chorus [soloists U. Zollenkopf, J. Deroubaix, H. Luenod *[sic]*, R. Robinson, R. Oliver, C. Scharbach] *(rec live, Venice 9/23/58)* Arkadia 2-▲ 766 [ADD]
K. Tennstedt (cnd)
Beethoven, L. van:Con Vn, Op. 61, w. N. Kennedy (vn) EMI Classics ▲ CDC 54574 ■ 4DS 54574
A. Walter (cnd)
Einem, G. von:Con Vn, w. C. Edinger (vn) Marco Polo ▲ 8.223138 [DDD]
Einem, G. von:Kupelweiser Waltzes Marco Polo ▲ 8.223138 [DDD]
Mussorgsky, M.:Night [version orchd. by Gottfried von Einem] Marco Polo ▲ 8.223138 [DDD]
G. Wand (cnd)
Beethoven, L. van:Leonore 3 *(rec live, Hamburg)* RCA Red Seal ▲ 60755-2-RG [DDD] □ 09026-60755-5
Beethoven, L. van:Syms (comp) RCA Red Seal 6-▲ 60090-2-RC [DDD]
Beethoven, L. van:Syms (comp)—Nos. 2 & 4 RCA Red Seal ▲ 60058-2-RC [DDD]
Beethoven, L. van:Syms (comp)—Nos. 5 & 8 RCA Red Seal ▲ 60092-2-RC [DDD]
Beethoven, L. van:Syms (comp)—Nos. 1 & 7 RCA Red Seal ▲ 60091-2-RC [DDD]
Beethoven, L. van:Syms (comp)—No. 6 RCA Red Seal ▲ 60094-2-RC [DDD]
Beethoven, L. van:Syms (comp)—No. 9 RCA Red Seal ▲ 60095-2-RC [DDD]
Beethoven, L. van:Sym 3, "Eroica" *(rec live, Hamburg)* RCA Red Seal ▲ 60755-2-RC [DDD] □ 09026-60755-5
Beethoven, L. van:Sym 5 RCA Red Seal ▲ 09026-61930-2
Beethoven, L. van:Sym 6, "Pastorale" RCA Red Seal ▲ 09026-61930-2
Brahms, J.:Syms (comp)—Nos. 3 & 4 RCA Gold Seal ▲ 60088-2-RG [DDD]
Brahms, J.:Syms (comp) RCA Gold Seal 3-▲ 60085-2-RG [DDD]
Bruckner, A.:Sym 3, "Wagner" RCA Red Seal ▲ 09026-61374-2
Bruckner, A.:Sym 4, "Romantic" *(rec live)* RCA Red Seal ▲ 60784-2-RC [DDD]
Bruckner, A.:Sym 5 *(rec live in concert at the Schleswig-Holstein Festival)* RCA Red Seal ▲ 60361-2-RC [DDD]
Bruckner, A.:Sym 6 *(rec live, Musikhalle Humburg, May 15, 1995)* RCA Victor ▲ 09026-68452-2 [DDD]
Bruckner, A.:Sym 6 *(rec live in concert at the Schleswig-Holstein Festival)* RCA Red Seal ▲ 60061-2-RC [DDD]
Bruckner, A.:Sym 7 RCA Red Seal ▲ 09026-61398-2
Bruckner, A.:Sym 8 RCA Red Seal ▲ 09026-68047-2
Bruckner, A.:Sym 9 RCA Red Seal ▲ 09026-62650-2
Fortner, W.:Intermezzo *(rec live)* RCA Red Seal ▲ 09026-60827-2 [DDD]
Martin, F.:Petite sym concertante *(rec live)* RCA Red Seal ▲ 09026-60827-2 [DDD]
Mozart, W.A.:German Dances, K.600 RCA Red Seal ▲ 60068-2-RC [DDD]
Mozart, W.A.:Serenade Vn, K.250 RCA Red Seal ▲ 60068-2 [DDD]
Mozart, W.A.:Sym 39 RCA Red Seal ▲ 60714-2 [DDD]
Mozart, W.A.:Sym 41 RCA Red Seal ▲ 60714-2 [DDD]
Schubert, Franz:Sym 3 RCA Red Seal ▲ 09026-61876-2
Schubert, Franz:Sym 4 RCA Gold Seal ▲ 60099-2-RG [ADD]
Schubert, Franz:Sym 8 *(rec live)* RCA Red Seal ▲ 09026-60826-2
Schubert, Franz:Sym 8 RCA Gold Seal ▲ 60099-2-RG [ADD]
Schubert, Franz:Sym 9 RCA Gold Seal ▲ 60101-2-RG [ADD]
Schubert, Franz:Sym 9 *(rec live)* RCA Red Seal ▲ 09026-60978-2
Schumann, R.:Sym 2 RCA Red Seal ▲ 09026-61876-2
Schumann, R.:Sym 4 *(rec live)* RCA Red Seal ▲ 09026-60826-2
Stravinsky, I.:Con CO *(rec live)* RCA Red Seal ▲ 09026-60827-2 [DDD]
Stravinsky, I.:Pulcinella Suite RCA Red Seal ▲ 09026-61190-2
Tchaikovsky, P.:Sym 6 RCA Red Seal ▲ 09026-61190-2
Webern, A.:Pieces Orch, Op. 10 *(rec live)* RCA Red Seal ▲ 09026-60827-2 [DDD]

North German RSO members
Firsova, E.:Meditation in a Japanese Garden Koch Schwann ▲ SCH 311702 [DDD]
Firsova, E.:Suite, Op. 2 Koch Schwann ▲ SCH 311702 [DDD]
Gubaidulina, S.:Qt for 4 Fls Koch Schwann ▲ SCH 311702 [DDD]
Gubaidulina, S.:Quasi hoquetus Koch Schwann ▲ SCH 311702 [DDD]
Indy, V. d':Qt Pno Koch Schwann ▲ SCH 311 662 [DDD]
Indy, V. d':Sextet Strs Koch Schwann ▲ SCH 311 662 [DDD]
Indy, V. d':Souvenirs Koch Schwann ▲ SCH 311 662 [DDD]
Ustvolskaya, G.:Composition 1 Koch Schwann ▲ SCH 311702 [DDD]

North German SO
E. Ormandy (cnd)
Beethoven, L. van:Leonore 3 *(rec live, June 6, 1963)* Originals ▲ ORI 853
Franck, C.:Sym in d *(rec live, June 6, 1963)* Originals ▲ ORI 853
Strauss, R.:Don Juan *(rec live, June 6, 1963)* Originals ▲ ORI 853
P. Ruzicka (cnd)
Ruzicka, P.:Tallis *(rec Oct. 1994)* Thorofon ▲ CTH 2220
C. Schuricht (cnd)
Schumann, R.:Manfred Ov *(rec live, 1960)* Originals ▲ ORI 862

North Rhine-Westphalia Musikfabrik
J. Kalitzke (cnd)
Kalitzke, J.:Bericht über den Tod des Musikers Jack Tiergarten, w. Werner Eggenhofer (nar), Till Krabbe (nar), Brigitte Jäger (sop), Espen Fegran (bar) *(rec live, Apr 29, 1994)* CPO ▲ 999358-2 [DDD]

North Texas College of Music Chamber Players
E. Corporon (cnd)
Bird, A.:Marche Miniature *(rec Univ. of North Texas Concert Hall, May 8–10, 1995)* Klavier ▲ KCD 11071 [DDD]
Bird, A.:Serenade Ww *(rec Univ. of North Texas Concert Hall, May 8–10, 1995)* Klavier ▲ KCD 11071 [DDD]
Bird, A.:Suite Ww *(rec Univ. of North Texas Concert Hall, May 8–10, 1995)* Klavier ▲ KCD 11071 [DDD]
Ticheli, F.:Pacific Fanfare *(rec Univ. of North Texas Concert Hall, May 8–10, 1995)* Klavier ▲ KCD 11071 [DDD]
Tull, F.:Concertino Ob, w. Charles Veazey (ob) *(rec Univ. of North Texas Concert Hall, May 8–10, 1995)* Klavier ▲ KCD 11071 [DDD]

North Texas College of Music Wind Sym
Grainger, P.:Lincolnshire Posy Klavier ▲ KCD 11079 [DDD]
Hart, P.:Cartoon Klavier ▲ KCD 11079 [DDD]
Hindemith, P.:Symphonic Metamorphosis on Themes of Carl Maria von Weber [arr Keith Wilson for winds] Klavier ▲ KCD 11077 [DDD]
Schwantner, J.:And the Mountians Rising Nowhere, w. Adam Wodnicki (pno) Klavier ▲ KCD 11079 [DDD]
Shostakovich, D.:Folk Dances [arr H. Robert Reynolds for winds] Klavier ▲ KCD 11077 [DDD]
Shostakovich, D.:Preludes Pno, Op. 34—No. 14 [arr H. Robert Reynolds for winds] Klavier ▲ KCD 11077 [DDD]
Toch, E.:Spiel Klavier ▲ KCD 11079 [DDD]
Tributes *(rec Univ. of North Texas Concert Hall, Apr. 28–May 1, 1995)* Klavier ▲ KCD 11070 [DDD]
Whitacre, E.:Ghost Train Triptych, w. James Riggs (sax), Pavel Wlosok (pno) Klavier ▲ KCD 11077 [DDD]
Wilson, D.:Dance of the New World Klavier ▲ KCD 11079 [DDD]
D. W. Fisher (cnd)
Ito, Y.:Gloriosa, w. Jerry Bierschenk (bar) Klavier ▲ KCD 11077 [DDD]

Northern Ballet Theater Orch
J. Pryce-Jones (cnd)
Davis, C.:Christmas Carol (sels)—Nephew & Niece; Keeping Warm; Patapan & Cornhill slide; Belle & Young Scrooge; Phantoms; Dressing Dance; Deck the Hall [suite compiled by J. Longstaff] *(rec Studio 7, BBC Manchester, England, Apr 14 & 15, 1995)* Naxos ▲ 8.553495 [DDD]
Feeney, P.:Cinderella (sels)—Harvest Dance; The Woodcutter's Dance; Pas de Trois; Birds; The Red Ball; Courtly Dances; The Prince & the Drunken Father; Cinderella Prepares for the Ball; Pas de Deux & Finale [suite compiled by J. Longstaff] *(rec Studio 7, BBC Manchester, England, Apr 14 & 15, 1995)* Naxos ▲ 8.553495 [DDD]
Muldowney, D.:Brōntes (sels)—The Toy Soldiers Fantasy; The Moors; Branwell & Mrs. Robinson; Wuthering Heights; Charlotte in Brussels; Pas de Deux (Charlotte & Mr. Nichols); Epilogue *(rec Studio 7, BBC Manchester, England, Apr 14 & 15, 1995)* Naxos ▲ 8.553495 [DDD]

Northern CO
N. Ward (cnd)
Abel, C.F.:Syms, Op. 7—No. 6 in E♭ [doubtfully attr. to Mozart, K.18] *(rec New Broadcasting House Concert Hall, Manchester, Apr. 17–18, 1994)* Naxos ▲ 8.550871 [DDD]
Bach, J.S.:Magnificat, BWV 243, w. Anna Crookes (sop), Jayne Whitaker (sop), Caroline Trevor (alt), Timothy Robinson (ten), Nicholas Gedge (b-bar). Oxford Schola Cantorum *(rec St. Peter's Church, Hale, Cheshire, Dec. 2, 1993)* Naxos ▲ 8.550763 [DDD]
Beck, F.I.:Syms—in b♭; in D; in G *(rec Victoria Hall, Bolton, Jan 15–16, 1996)* Naxos ▲ 8.553790 [DDD]
Beck, F.I.:Sym 1 *(rec Victoria Hall, Bolton, Jan 15–16, 1996)* Naxos ▲ 8.553790 [DDD]
Beck, F.I.:Sym 2 *(rec Victoria Hall, Bolton, Jan 15–16, 1996)* Naxos ▲ 8.553790 [DDD]
Castelnuovo-Tedesco, M.:Con 1 Gtr, w. N. Kraft (gtr) *(rec Oct. 7–9, 1992)* Naxos ▲ 8.550729 [DDD]
Haydn, J.:Syms (comp)—Nos. 30, 55, & 63 *(rec New Broadcasting House Concert Hall, Manchester, Nov. 22, 1992 & Mar. 9, 1)* Naxos ▲ 8.550757 [DDD]
Haydn, J.:Sym 6, "Le Matin" *(rec Mar. 1993)* Naxos ▲ 8.550722 [DDD]
Haydn, J.:Sym 7, "Le Midi" *(rec Mar. 1993)* Naxos ▲ 8.550722 [DDD]
Haydn, J.:Sym 8, "Le Soir" *(rec Mar. 1993)* Naxos ▲ 8.550722 [DDD]
Haydn, J.:Sym 22, "Der Philosoph" *(rec Concert Hall of New Broadcasting House, Manchester, Oct. 27, 1992)* Naxos ▲ 8.550724 [DDD]
Haydn, J.:Sym 23 *(rec Oct. 1 & 2, 1992)* Naxos ▲ 8.550726 [DDD]
Haydn, J.:Sym 24 *(rec Oct. 1 & 2, 1992)* Naxos ▲ 8.550726 [DDD]
Haydn, J.:Sym 26, "Lamentatione" *(rec Oct. 27–28, 1992)* Naxos ▲ 8.550721 [DDD]
Haydn, J.:Sym 29 *(rec Concert Hall of New Broadcasting House, Manchester, Oct. 27, 1992)* Naxos ▲ 8.550724 [DDD]
Haydn, J.:Sym 35 *(rec Oct. 27–28, 1992)* Naxos ▲ 8.550721 [DDD]
Haydn, J.:Sym 49, "La Passione" *(rec Oct. 27–28, 1992)* Naxos ▲ 8.550721 [DDD]
Haydn, J.:Sym 60, "Il Distratto" *(rec Concert Hall of New Broadcasting House, Manchester, Mar. 9–10, 1993)* Naxos ▲ 8.550724 [DDD]
Haydn, J.:Sym 61 *(rec Oct. 1 & 2, 1992)* Naxos ▲ 8.550726 [DDD]
Mendelssohn, F.:Syms Strs—Nos. 7–9 *(rec Manchester, Mar 1995)* Naxos ▲ 8.553162 [DDD]
Mozart, L.:Syms—in B♭ [doubtfully attr. to W.A. Mozart, K.17] *(rec New Broadcasting House Concert Hall, Manchester, Apr. 17–18, 1994)* Naxos ▲ 8.550871 [DDD]
Mozart, W.A.:Sym 1 *(rec New Broadcasting House Concert Hall, Manchester, Apr. 17–18, 1994)* Naxos ▲ 8.550871 [DDD]
Mozart, W.A.:Sym 4 *(rec New Broadcasting House Concert Hall, Manchester, Apr. 17–18, 1994)* Naxos ▲ 8.550871 [DDD]
Mozart, W.A.:Sym 5 *(rec New Broadcasting House Concert Hall, Manchester, Apr. 17–18, 1994)* Naxos ▲ 8.550871 [DDD]
Mozart, W.A.:Sym 11 *(rec New Broadcasting House Concert Hall, Manchester, Nov. 22–23, 1993)* Naxos ▲ 8.550873 [DDD]
Mozart, W.A.:Sym 12 *(rec New Broadcasting House Concert Hall, Manchester, Nov. 22–23, 1993)* Naxos ▲ 8.550873 [DDD]
Mozart, W.A.:Sym 13 *(rec New Broadcasting House Concert Hall, Manchester, Nov. 22–23, 1993)* Naxos ▲ 8.550873 [DDD]
Mozart, W.A.:Sym 14 *(rec New Broadcasting House Concert Hall, Manchester, Nov. 22–23, 1993)* Naxos ▲ 8.550873 [DDD]
Mozart, W.A.:Sym 15 *(rec New Broadcasting House Concert Hall, Manchester, Jan. 14–15, 1994)* Naxos ▲ 8.550874 [DDD]
Mozart, W.A.:Sym 16 *(rec New Broadcasting House Concert Hall, Manchester, Jan. 14–15, 1994)* Naxos ▲ 8.550874 [DDD]
Mozart, W.A.:Sym 17 *(rec New Broadcasting House Concert Hall, Manchester, Jan. 14–15, 1994)* Naxos ▲ 8.550874 [DDD]
Mozart, W.A.:Sym 18 *(rec New Broadcasting House Concert Hall, Manchester, Jan. 14–15, 1994)* Naxos ▲ 8.550874 [DDD]
Rodrigo, J.:Concierto de Aranjuez, w. N. Kraft (gtr) *(rec Oct. 7–9, 1992)* Naxos ▲ 8.550729 [DDD]
Villa-Lobos, H.:Con Gtr, w. N. Kraft (gtr) *(rec Oct. 7–9, 1992)* Naxos ▲ 8.550729 [DDD]
Vivaldi, A.:Beatus vir, R.597, w. Carys-Anne Lane (sop), Jayne Whitaker (sop), Christine Swain (ob), Robert Glenton (vc), Christopher Stokes (org). Oxford Schola Cantorum *(rec St. Peter's Church, Hale, Cheshire, Mar. 14, 1994)* Naxos ▲ 8.550767 [DDD]
Vivaldi, A.:Gloria, RV.589, w. Anna Crookes (sop), Jayne Whitaker (sop), Caroline Trevor (alt), Christine Swain (ob), Robert Glenton (vc), Christopher Stokes (org), Oxford Schola Cantorum *(rec St. Peter's Church, Hale, Cheshire, Dec. 3, 1993)* Naxos ▲ 8.550767 [DDD]

▲ = CD ♦ = Enhanced CD Δ = MD ■ = Cassette Tape □ = DCC

Northern Crown Soloists Ensemble [I. Zaidenshnir (vn), R. Nirsaiapova (vn), V Samoliov (va), V. Bakulin (va), E. Palitsky (vc)]
Hummel, J.N.:Con Mand & Strs, w. V. Kruglov (mand), N. Maretsky (mand) MK ▲ MKA 417114
Kollontai, M.:Sacred Symphonies *(rec Apr 1992)* Russian Compact Disc ▲ RD CD 10004 [DDD]
Vivaldi, A.:Con Lt, w. V. Kruglov (mand), N. Maretsky (mand) MK ▲ MKA 417114
Vivaldi, A.:Con Mand, RV.425, w. V. Kruglov (mand), N. Maretsky (mand) MK ▲ MKA 417114
Vivaldi, A.:Con for 2 Mands, w. V. Kruglov (mand), N. Maretsky (mand) MK ▲ MKA 417114
Vivaldi, A.:Trio Son Vn Lt, RV. 82, w. V. Kruglov (mand), N. Maretsky (mand) MK ▲ MKA 417114
V. Katajev (cnd)
Grieg, E.:Songs, w. E. Kerechanin (sop), R. Levina (sop), A. Martynov (ten) [arr. Tishchenko] MK ▲ MKA 417124 [DDD]
Lokshin, A.:Lyrics by Francois Villon (suite) MK ▲ MKA 417124 [DDD]
Lokshin, A.:Qnt Strs MK ▲ MKA 417124 [DDD]
Lokshin, A.:Sym 5, w. V. Pochapsky (bar), *(not advised of harp)* MK ▲ MKA 417124 [DDD]
Northern Light SO
P. Whitfield (cnd)
Danova, R.:The Phantom of the Opera on Ice, w. Susannah Glanville (sop), Kathy Dooley (sop), Johnny Logan (ten), Stephen Lee Garden (ten), Mungo Jerry (bar), Nigel Paul (bar), Northern Light Choir, Russian Stars on Ice Chorus Plaza ▲ PZA 008
Northern Sinfonia of England
Jeux d'Enfants, w. Christopher Hyde-Smith (fl/pic), Emma Johnson (cl), George MacDonald (cl), Gordon Back (pno), Academy of St. Martin in the Fields [cnd:Neville Marriner], Mexico City PO, Mexico State SO, Royal PO [cnd:Enrique Bátiz], et al. ASV Quicksilva ▲ ASQ 6182
M.-W. Chung (cnd)
Dvořák, A.:Serenade Strs ASV Quicksilva ▲ QS 6002 [ADD]
Dvořák, A.:Serenade Ww ASV Quicksilva ▲ QS 6002 [ADD]
Mozart, W.A.:Sym 25 ASV Quicksilva ▲ CD QS 6009 [ADD]
Mozart, W.A.:Sym 28 ASV Quicksilva ▲ CD QS 6009 [ADD]
Mozart, W.A.:Sym 29 ASV Quicksilva ▲ CD QS 6009 [ADD]
H. Griffiths (cnd)
Eichner, E.:Con 3 Ob, w. Kurt Meier (ob) Pan Classics ▲ 510088 [DDD]
Holzbauer, I.:Con Ob, w. Kurt Meier (ob) Pan Classics ▲ 510088 [DDD]
Lebrun, L.A.:Con Ob, w. Kurt Meier (ob) Pan Classics ▲ 510088 [DDD]
Winter, P. von:Con 2 Ob, w. Kurt Meier (ob) Pan Classics ▲ 510088 [DDD]
R. Hickox (cnd)
Beethoven, L. van:Coriolan Ov ASV Quicksilva ▲ QS 6053 [DDD]
Beethoven, L. van:Die Geschöpfe des Prometheus (ov) ASV Quicksilva ▲ QS 6053 [DDD]
Beethoven, L. van:Sym 1 ASV Quicksilva ▲ QS 6066 [ADD]
Beethoven, L. van:Sym 2 ASV Quicksilva ▲ ASQ 6067 [ADD]
Beethoven, L. van:Sym 3, "Eroica" ASV Quicksilva ▲ QS 6068 [ADD]
Beethoven, L. van:Sym 4 ASV Quicksilva ▲ QS 6054 [DDD]
Beethoven, L. van:Sym 5 ASV Quicksilva ▲ QS 6054 [DDD]
Beethoven, L. van:Sym 6, "Pastorale" ASV Quicksilva ▲ QS 6053 [DDD]
Beethoven, L. van:Sym 7 ASV Quicksilva ▲ QS 6066 [ADD]
Beethoven, L. van:Sym 8 ASV Quicksilva ▲ ASQ 6067 [ADD]
Beethoven, L. van:Sym 9, "Choral Sym", w. H. Harper (sop), A. Hodgson (cta), R. Tear (ten), G. Howell (bass), London Sym Chorus members ASV Quicksilva ▲ ASQ 6069 [DDD]
Bliss, A.:Music for Strs Chandos ▲ CHAN 8886 [DDD]
Bliss, A.:Pastoral, w. D. Jones (mez), Northern Sinfonia Chorus [E] Chandos ▲ CHAN 8886 [DDD]
Delius, F.:Music of—Intermezzo [from *Fennimore and Gerda*]; Hassan; Irmelin; La Calinda [from *Koanga*]; On Hearing the First Cuckoo in Spring; Summer Night on the River; A Song Before Sunrise; Summer Evening; Air & Dance; Sleigh Ride [from *Winter Night*] EMI Classics ▲ CDM 65067
Finzi, G.:The Fall of a Leaf EMI Classics ▲ CDM 64721
Finzi, G.:New Year Music EMI Classics ▲ CDM 64721
Moeran, E.J.:Serenade EMI Classics ▲ CDM 64721
Moeran, E.J.:Sinfonietta EMI Classics ▲ CDM 64721
Mozart, W.A.:Cons Hn, w. F. Lloyd (hn) Chandos ▲ CHAN 9150 [DDD]
Mozart, W.A.:Requiem Virgin Classics ("Ultraviolet" series) ▲ CUV 61260
Mozart, W.A.:Requiem, w. Y. Kenny (sop), A. Hodgson (mez), A. Davies (ten), G. Howell (bass), London Sym Chorus Virgin Classics ▲ CDZ 59648
Mozart, W.A.:Rondo Hn, K.371, w. F. Lloyd (hn) Chandos ▲ CHAN 9150 [DDD]
Strauss, R.:Ariadne auf Naxos, w. Jard van Nes (mez)—Ov. (Andante); Dance Scene (Allegretto) Chandos ▲ CHAN 9354 [DDD]
Strauss, R.:Duet-Concertino Chandos ▲ CHAN 9354 [DDD]
Sullivan, A.:Music of, w. V. Masterson (sop), S. Armstrong (sop), R. Tear (ten), B. Luxon (bar), Alwyn (cnd), Bournemouth Sinfonietta—sels. from all operettas of Gilbert & Sullivan EMI Classics ▲ CDM 64393
Vaughan Williams, R.:Flos Campi, w. Philip Dukes (va) Chandos ▲ CHAN 9392 [DDD]
Vaughan Williams, R.:Household Music Chandos ▲ CHAN 9392 [DDD]
Vaughan Williams, R.:Riders to the Sea, w. Ingrid Attrot (sop—Nora), Lynn Dawson (sop—Cathleen), Linda Finnie (mez—Maurya), Karl Daymond (bar—Bartley) Chandos ▲ CHAN 9392 [DDD]
Wagner, R.:Siegfried Idyll Chandos ▲ CHAN 9354 [DDD]
Wagner, R.:Wesendonck Songs, w. Jard van Nes (mez) Chandos ▲ CHAN 9354 [DDD]
Walton, W.:The Bear, w. D. Jones (mez), J. Shirley-Quirk (bar), A. Opie (bass) Chandos ▲ CHAN 9245 [DDD]
G. Malcolm (cnd)
Bach, J.S.:Brandenburg Cons—Nos. 1-3 ASV Quicksilva ▲ QS 6074 [ADD]
Bach, J.S.:Brandenburg Cons—Nos. 4-6 ASV Quicksilva ▲ QS 6075 [ADD]
Handel, G.F.:Concerti grossi, Op. 3 *(rec ca. 1978)* ASV Quicksilva ▲ QS 6024 [ADD]
Handel, G.F.:Concerti grossi, Op. 6—Concerto Nos. 5-8 ASV Living Era ("Quicksilva" series) ▲ ASQ 6164
Handel, G.F.:Concerti grossi, Op. 6—Nos. 1-4 ASV ("Quicksilva" series) ▲ ASQ 6163
Handel, G.F.:Concerti grossi, Op. 6 ASV ("Quicksilva" series) ▲ ASQ 6165
N. Marriner (cnd)
Britten, B.:Folksong Arrs, w. E. Söderström (sop), R. Tear (ten)—Bonny Earl O'Moray; Oliver Cromwell; O Waly, Waly; The Plough Boy EMI Classics ▲ CDM 69522
Britten, B.:Our Hunting Fathers, w. E. Söderström (sop) EMI Classics ▲ CDM 69522
J.-B. Pommier (cnd)
Debussy, C.:Petite suite, w. J.B. Pommier (pno) Virgin Classics ▲ CDZ 59654
Fauré, G.:Masques et bergamasques (suite), w. J. B. Pommier (pno) Virgin Classics ▲ CDZ 59654
Ravel, M.:Ma mère l'oye Orch Virgin Classics ▲ CDZ 59655
Ravel, M.:Pavane pour une infante défunte Virgin Classics ▲ CDZ 59655
S. Rattle (cnd)
Stravinsky, I.:Pulcinella, w. J. Smith (sop), J. Fryatt (ten), M. King (bass) EMI Classics ▲ CDM 64739
H. Schiff (cnd)
Haydn, J.:Con 1 Vn, w. Chris Tetzlaff (vn) Virgin Classics ▲ CDC 59065
Haydn, J.:Con 3 Vn, w. Chris Tetzlaff (vn) Virgin Classics ▲ CDC 59065
Haydn, J.:Con 4 Vn, w. Chris Tetzlaff (vn) Virgin Classics ▲ CDC 59065
Mozart, W.A.:Kleine Nachtmusik Virgin Classics ▲ CDZ 59692
Mozart, W.A.:Rondo Vn, K.373, w. C. Tetzlaff (vn) Virgin Classics ▲ CDC 59065
Mozart, W.A.:Sym 29 Virgin Classics ▲ CDZ 59692
Mozart, W.A.:Sym 40 Virgin Classics ▲ CDZ 59692
Schubert, Franz:Ov Orch, D.591 Chandos ▲ CHAN 9136 [DDD]
T. Vásáry (cnd)
Chopin, F.:Con 1 Pno, w. Tamas Vasary (pno) ASV ("Quicksilva" series) ▲ ASQ 6141 [DDD]
Chopin, F.:Con 2 Pno, w. Tamas Vasary (pno) ASV ("Quicksilva" series) ▲ ASQ 6141 [DDD]
Chopin, F.:Con 2 Pno, w. T. Vásáry (pno) ASV Quicksilva ▲ QS 6003 [ADD]
Schumann, R.:Con Pno, w. T. Vásáry (pno) ASV Quicksilva ▲ QS 6003 [ADD]

Northern Sinfonia of England (cont.)
R. Zollman (cnd)
Dodgson, S.:Con Fl, w. Robert Stallman (fl) *(rec St Nicholas Hospital, Newcastle-upon-Tyne, Oct 23-24, 1992)* Biddulph ▲ LAW 013 [DDD]
Dodgson, S.:Duo Con, w. Jean-Jacques Kantorow (vn), Anthea Gifford (gtr) *(rec St Nicholas Hospital, Newcastle-upon-Tyne, Oct 23-24, 1992)* Biddulph ▲ LAW 013 [DDD]
Dodgson, S.:Last of the Leaves, w. Michael George (b-bar), John Bradbury (cl) *(rec St Nicholas Hospital, Newcastle-upon-Tyne, Oct 23-24, 1992)* Biddulph ▲ LAW 013 [DDD]
Northern Trombone Quartet
E. Gregson (cnd)
Gregson, E.:Music of, w. Hallé Brass, RNCM Brass Ensemble—Fanfare for Europe; Equale Dances; Susie's Fanfare; Son for 4 Trbns; Fanfare for the North; Qnt for Brass; Flourish for the Theatre; Flourish for an Occasion; Dance Episodes (3); Festival Fanfare Doyen ▲ CD 038 [DDD]
North/South Consonance Ensemble
M. Lifchitz (cnd)
Cordero, R.:Dodecaconcerto, w. A. M. Ketchum (sop), C. Beavon (mez) North/South Recordings ▲ NS 1003 [DDD]
Dvorak, C.:Amandla Mandelal, w. R. Rosales (sop), L. Vardaman (sop) North/South Recordings ▲ NS 1004 [DDD]
Greenberg, L.:This Man Was Your Brother, w. R. Rosales (sop), L. Vardaman (sop) North/South Recordings ▲ NS 1004 [DDD]
Greenberg, L.:La Vida Es Sueño, w. R. Rosales (sop), L. Vardaman (sop) North/South Recordings ▲ NS 1004 [DDD]
Lifchitz, M.:Of Bondage & Freedom, w. R. Rosales (sop), L. Vardaman (sop) North/South Recordings ▲ NS 1004 [DDD]
Lifchitz, M.:Yellow Ribbons, w. L. Weiss (fl), M. Lifchitz (pno)—Nos. 1 (1981) & 21 (1984) Opus One ▲ 149
Pleskow, R.:Arabesques, w. R. Rosales (sop), L. Vardaman (sop) North/South Recordings ▲ NS 1004 [DDD]
Rands, B.:...in the receding mist Sop, w. A. M. Ketchum (sop), C. Beavon (mez) North/South Recordings ▲ NS 1003 [DDD]
Saylor, B.:See You in the Morning, w. A. M. Ketchum (sop), C. Beavon (mez) North/South Recordings ▲ NS 1003 [DDD]
Vega, A. de la:Testimonial, w. A. M. Ketchum (sop), C. Beavon (mez) North/South Recordings ▲ NS 1003 [DDD]
Northwest CO Seattle
A. Francis (cnd)
Cooke, A.:Con Cl, w. T. King (cl) Hyperion ▲ CDA 66031 [DDD]
Cowell, H.:Air Vn CPO ▲ CPO 999222 [DDD]
Cowell, H.:Ensemble CPO ▲ CPO 999222 [DDD]
Cowell, H.:Fiddler's Jig CPO ▲ CPO 999222 [DDD]
Cowell, H.:Hymn & Fuguing Tunes Strs—Nos. 2, 5, 8 & 10 CPO ▲ CPO 999222 [DDD]
Cowell, H.:Vars on Thirds CPO ▲ CPO 999222 [DDD]
Frankel, B.:The Aftermath, w. *(ten unknown)* CPO ▲ CPO 999221 [DDD]
Frankel, B.:Concertante lirico CPO ▲ CPO 999221 [DDD]
Frankel, B.:Sketches, Op. 2 CPO ▲ CPO 999221 [DDD]
Frankel, B.:Solemn Speech & Discussion CPO ▲ CPO 999221 [DDD]
Frankel, B.:Youth Music CPO ▲ CPO 999221 [DDD]
Jacob, G.:Mini-Con Cl, w. T. King (cl) Hyperion ▲ CDA 66031 [DDD]
Rawsthorne, A.:Con Cl, w. T. King (cl) Hyperion ▲ CDA 66031 [DDD]
Vivaldi, A.:Sinf, RV.156, w. M. Kransberg-Talvi (vn) Ambassador ▲ ARC 1010
Northwest German Chamber Soloists
Barrock on the Rocks:Musical Amusements from Bach to the Beatles *(rec Oct. 1991)* MD + G ▲ L 3442 [DDD]
Zelenka, J.D.:Sons Obs MD + G 2-▲ MDG 6050559 [DDD]
Northwest German PO
W. A. Albert (cnd)
Korngold, E.W.:Baby-Serenade CPO ▲ CPO 999077-2 [DDD]
Korngold, E.W.:Con Vc, w. J. Berger (vc) CPO ▲ CPO 999077-2 [DDD]
Korngold, E.W.:Con Pno Left-Hand, w. S. de Groote (pno) CPO ▲ CPO 999046-2 [DDD]
Korngold, E.W.:Much Ado About Nothing CPO ▲ CPO 999046-2 [DDD]
Korngold, E.W.:Schauspiel Ouvertüre CPO ▲ CPO 999037-2 [DDD]
Korngold, E.W.:Der Schneemann, w. L. Farkas (vn)—Prelude, Serenade & Entr'acte CPO ▲ CPO 999037-2 [DDD]
Korngold, E.W.:Sinfonietta CPO ▲ CPO 999037-2 [DDD]
Korngold, E.W.:Straussiana CPO ▲ CPO 999146-2 [ADD/DDD]
Korngold, E.W.:Sursum corda CPO ▲ CPO 999046-2 [DDD]
Korngold, E.W.:Symphonic Serenade, w. J. Berger (vc) CPO ▲ CPO 999077-2 [DDD]
Korngold, E.W.:Sym in F# CPO ▲ CPO 999146-2 [ADD/DDD]
Korngold, E.W.:Theme & Vars Orch CPO ▲ CPO 999146-2 [ADD/DDD]
Rossini, G.:Petite messe solennelle, w. G. de la Cruz (sop), M. L. Gilles (cta), H. D. Saretzki (ten), H. G. Grimm (bass), Northwest German Phil Choir [orchestral version] [L] *(rec ca. 1970)* Koch Schwann ▲ 3-1345-2 [ADD]
Volkmann, R.:Con Vc, w. J. Wohlmacher (vc) CPO 2-▲ CPO 999151 [DDD]
Volkmann, R.:Ov in C CPO 2-▲ CPO 999151 [DDD]
Volkmann, R.:Ov to Richard III CPO 2-▲ CPO 999151 [DDD]
Volkmann, R.:Sym 1 CPO 2-▲ CPO 999151 [DDD]
Volkmann, R.:Sym 2 CPO 2-▲ CPO 999151 [DDD]
F. Allers (cnd)
Paganini, N.:Son large Va, w. E. Wallfisch (va) Bayer ▲ BR 200028 [ADD]
K. Bernbacher (cnd)
Halaczinsky, R.:Con Pno, w. P. Roggenkamp (pno) MD + G ▲ L 3451 [DDD]
M. Jurowski (cnd)
Banter, H.:Märchenbilder *(rec Cologne Phil Hall, Mar 1995)* Marco Polo ▲ 8.223860 [DDD]
Banter, H.:Phädra, w. Maria Kliegel (vc) *(rec Cologne Phil Hall, Mar 1995)* Marco Polo ▲ 8.223860 [DDD]
Banter, H.:Prolog 2000 *(rec Cologne Phil Hall, Mar 1995)* Marco Polo ▲ 8.223860 [DDD]
Banter, H.:Rhap Intermezzo, w. Beate Berthold (pno) *(rec Cologne Phil Hall, Mar 1995)* Marco Polo ▲ 8.223860 [DDD]
Banter, H.:Tod des Aktaeon *(rec Cologne Phil Hall, Mar 1995)* Marco Polo ▲ 8.223860 [DDD]
H. Scherchen (cnd)
Reger, M.:An die Hoffnung, w. M. Bence (cta) *(rec 1960)* CPO 2-▲ CPO 999143-2 (m) [ADD]
Reger, M.:Ein Lustspielouvertüre CPO 2-▲ CPO 999143-2 (m) [ADD]
Reger, M.:Ein romantische Suite CPO 2-▲ CPO 999143-2 (m) [ADD]
Reger, M.:Serenade Orch CPO 2-▲ CPO 999143-2 (m) [ADD]
Reger, M.:Vars & Fugue on a Theme of Beethoven CPO 2-▲ CPO 999143-2 (m) [ADD]
Reger, M.:Vars & Fugue on a Theme by Mozart CPO 2-▲ CPO 999143-2 (m) [ADD]
Northwest Sinfonia
P. Anthony (cnd)
Licht, D.:Bad Moon *(rec Bastyr Univ, Seattle)* Silva America ▲ SSD 1068
A. Hovhaness (cnd)
Hovhaness, A.:Celestial Canticle, w. Hinako Fujihara (sop), Scott Goff (fl) *(rec St Thomas Center Chapel, Bothell, WA, Jan 1995)* Crystal ▲ CD 811 [DDD]
Hovhaness, A.:Tale of the Sun Goddess Going into the Stone House (sels), w. Hinako Fujihara (sop), Scott Goff (fl)—O, Joy at the Dawn of Spring *(rec St Thomas Center Chapel, Bothell, WA, Jan 1995)* Crystal ▲ CD 811 [DDD]
G. Schwarz (cnd)
Hovhaness, A.:Sym 31 *(rec St Thomas Center Chapel, Bothell, WA, Jan 1995)* Crystal ▲ CD 811 [DDD]

Northwest Sinfonia (cont.)
G. Schwarz (cnd) (cont.)
Hovhaness, A.:Sym 49 *(rec St Thomas Center Chapel, Bothell, WA, Jan 1995)* Crystal ▲ CD 811 [DDD]

Northwest SO
A. Spain (cnd)
Bergsma, W.:Serenade, "To Await the Moon" Albany ▲ TROY 184
McKay, G.:Sym for Seattle Albany ▲ TROY 184
Short, G.:The Raven Speaks Albany ▲ TROY 184

Northwestern Univ SO
V. Yampolsky (cnd)
Rachmaninoff, S.:Symphonic Dances, *(Evanston, IL, Apr 1993)* Northwestern Univ School of Music ▲ 6702
Szymanowski, K.:Con 1 Vn, w. Gerardo Ribeiro (vn), *(Evanston, IL, Apr 1993)* Northwestern Univ School of Music ▲ 6702

Northwestern Univ Sym Wind Ensemble
J. P. Paynter (cnd)
Anderson, L.:Sleigh Ride Northwestern Univ School of Music ▲
Arnold, M.:Music of—Scottish Dances (4) [arr Paynter]; Shanties (3) [arr J. Krauklis]; English Dances (set 2) [trans J. Sudduth]; Sarabande & Polka [arr Paynter]; Tam O'Shanter [arr Paynter]; Prelude, Siciliano & Rondo [arr Paynter]; A Grand, Grand Ov [arr K. Wilson], *(Evanston, IL, Nov 1995)* Northwestern Univ School of Music ▲ 6706
Giannini, V.:Sym 3 *(rec Evanston, IL, Nov 1994)* Northwestern Univ School of Music ▲ 6704
Jager, R.:Edvard Munch (suite) *(rec Evanston, IL, Nov 1994)* Northwestern Univ School of Music ▲ 6704
McBeth, W.F.:Through Countless Halls of Air *(rec Evanston, IL, Nov 1994)* Northwestern Univ School of Music ▲ 6704
Rimsky-Korsakov, N.:The Tale of Tsar Saltan (orch sels)—Flight of the Bumblebee *(rec Evanston, IL, Nov 1994)* Northwestern Univ School of Music ▲ 6704
Toch, E.:Spiel *(rec Evanston, IL, Nov 1994)* Northwestern Univ School of Music ▲ 6704

Norwegian Broadcasting Orch
C. Eggen (cnd)
Hall, P.:Suite for Shakespeare's Julius Caesar Simax ("Norway in Music" series) ▲ PSC 3105 [DDD]
Hall, P.:Verlaine Suite Simax ("Norway in Music" series) ▲ PSC 3105 [DDD]
Kleven, A.:The Sleeping Forest Simax ("Norway in Music" series) ▲ PSC 3106 [DDD]
Valen, F.:An die Hoffnung Simax ▲ PSC 3116
Valen, F.:Con Pno, w. Geir Henning Braaten (pno) Simax ▲ PSC 3116
Valen, F.:Con Vn, w. Arve Tellefsen (vn) Simax ▲ PSC 3116
Valen, F.:Epithalamion Simax ▲ PSC 3116

Norwegian CO
The Norwegian Flute, w. P. Øien (fl), G. H. Braaten (pno) *(rec 1978 & 1980)* BIS ▲ CD 103 [AAD]
I. Brown (cnd)
Haydn, J.:Con 1 Vc, w. Truls Otterbach Mørk (vc) Virgin Classics ▲ CDC 45014
Haydn, J.:Con 2 Vc, w. Truls Otterbach Mørk (vc) Virgin Classics ▲ CDC 45014
Mozart, W.A.:Con 9 Pno, w. B. Meyer (pno) Omega ▲ OCD 1003 [DDD]
Mozart, W.A.:Con 23 Pno, w. B. Meyer (pno) Omega ▲ OCD 1003 [DDD]
Mozart, W.A.:Divert Str Qt, K.136 Omega ▲ OCD 1004 [DDD]
Mozart, W.A.:Divert Str Qt, K.138 Omega ▲ OCD 1004 [DDD]
Mozart, W.A.:Kleine Nachtmusik Omega ▲ OCD 1004 [DDD]
Mozart, W.A.:Sym 29 Omega ▲ OCD 1004 [DDD]
L. A. Tomter (cnd)
Britten, B.:Lachrymae Virgin Classics ▲ CDC 45121
Britten, B.:Prelude & Fugue Strs Virgin Classics ▲ CDC 45121
Britten, B.:Simple Sym Virgin Classics ▲ CDC 45121
Britten, B.:Vars on a Theme of Frank Bridge Virgin Classics ▲ CDC 45121
T. Tønnesen (cnd)
Blavet, M.:Con Fl, w. P. Øien (fl) *(rec Sept. 2–3, 1978)* BIS ▲ CD 118 [AAD]
Grieg, E.:Cradle Song [arr for strs] BIS ▲ CD 147
Grieg, E.:Elegaic Melodies, Op. 34 BIS ▲ CD 147
Grieg, E.:Holberg Suite BIS ▲ CD 147 Δ MD 147
Grieg, E.:Melodies, Op. 53 BIS ▲ CD 147
Grieg, E.:Nordic Melodies, Op. 63 BIS ▲ CD 147
Quantz, J.J.:Con in G Fl & Strs, w. P. Øien (fl) *(rec Sept. 2–3, 1978)* BIS ▲ CD 118 [AAD]
Tartini, G.:Con in G Fl, w. P. Øien (fl) *(rec Sept. 2–3, 1978)* BIS ▲ CD 118 [AAD]
Vivaldi, A.:Cons Fl (misc), w. P. Øien (fl) *(rec Sept. 2–3, 1978)* BIS ▲ CD 118 [AAD]

Norwegian National Opera Orch
P. Andersson (cnd)
Braein, E.F.:Anne Pedersdotter, w. K. Ekeberg (sop—Anne Pedersdotter), V. Hanssen (mez—Merete Beyer), R. Eriksen (alt—Herlofs-Marte), I. M. Brekke (alt—Bente), K. M. Sandve (ten—Martin Beyer), C. Ehrstedt (ten—Master Olaus), A. Helleland (ten—David), T. Gilje (ten—Jørund), S. A. Thorsen (bar—Master Johannes), S. Carlsen (bass—Absalon Pedersøn Beyer), T. Stensvold (bass—Master Laurentius), G. Oskarsson (bass—Jens Schelderup), Norwegian National Opera Chorus Simax 2-▲ PSC 3121

Norwegian RSO
C. Eggen (cnd)
Olsen, O.:Petite suite, w. J. M. Bratlie (pno) NKF ▲ NKFCD 50024

Norwegian Soloists
P. Dreier (cnd)
Grieg, E.:Olav Trygvason, w. London SO, Oslo Phil Chorus Unicorn-Kanchana ▲ UKCD 2056

Norwegian String Quartet
Elling, C.:Qt Strs NKF ▲ NKFCD 50021
Grieg, E.:Fugue Victoria ▲ VCD 19048 [DDD]
Grieg, E.:Qt Strs (unfinished) Victoria ▲ VCD 19048 [DDD]
Grieg, E.:Qt Strs, Op. 27 Victoria ▲ VCD 19048 [DDD]
Haug, H.:Qt 1 Strs Victoria ▲ VCD 19049 [DDD]
Holter, I.:Qts Strs NKF ▲ NKFCD 50027

Norwegian Wind Quintet
K. Andersen (cnd)
Valen, F.:Serenade Ww Simax ▲ PSC 3116

Norwegian Winds
G. Oskamp (cnd)
Dvořák, A.:Serenade Ww *(rec Sofienberg Church, 1995)* Victoria ▲ VCD 19095
Enescu, G.:Dectet Ww *(rec Sofienberg Church, 1995)* Victoria ▲ VCD 19095
Gounod, C.:Petite Sym *(rec Sofienberg Church, 1995)* Victoria ▲ VCD 19095
Mendelssohn, F.:Notturno *(rec Sofienberg Church, 1995)* Victoria ▲ VCD 19095
Strauss, R.:Serenade Ww Verdi Classics 2-▲ AU 32 165
Strauss, R.:Sonatina 1 Verdi Classics 2-▲ AU 32 165
Strauss, R.:Sonatina 2 Verdi Classics 2-▲ AU 32 165
Strauss, R.:Suite Wws Verdi Classics 2-▲ AU 32 165

Norwegian Youth SO
K. Andersen (cnd)
Haug, H.:Sym 2 Victoria ▲ VCD 19049 [DDD]

Les Nostalchics
Coffee House Music REM ▲ 311189 [DDD]

Notre Dame String Trio [Carolyn Plummer (vn), Christine Rutledge (va), Karen Buranskas (vc)]
Haimo, E.:Trio Strs *(rec Annenberg Audit., Snite Museum of Art, Univ. of Notre Dame)* Centaur ▲ CRC 2253 [DDD]

Le Nouveau Quartet
Arne, T.:Trio Sons, Op. 3 [period instrs]—Nos. 2,5,6 & 7 Amon Ra ▲ CD-SAR 42 [DDD]
Bach, C.P.E.:Trio Son Fl, H.567–71 [period instrs] Amon Ra ▲ CD-SAR 44 [DDD]

Le Nouveau Quartet (cont.)
Corrette, M.:Sons—nine sonatas—6 for Flute, Violin, Cello & Harpsichord *(Op. 14, Nos. 1–6)*, plus single sonatas for flute & harpsichord *(Op. 25, No. 4)*, cello & harpsichord *(Op. 20, No. 6)*, & for violin, cello & harpsichord *(No. 1 in d from Prototips contenant des leçons... [1754])* [period instrs] Amon Ra ▲ CD-SAR 57 [DDD]
Vivaldi, A.:Cons Diverse Instrs, w. Andrew Watts (bn)—6 concerti for various combinations of flute, violin, bassoon, cello & continuo (R.83 in c; R.84 in D; R.91 in D; R.96 in d; R.100 in F; R.106 in g) Amon Ra ▲ CD-SAR 47 [DDD]

Le Nouveau Salon
Stolz, R.:Music of, w. Cologne Salon Orch—Ein Abend mit Robert Stolz; A klane Drahrerei; Hysterie; Türkischer Marsch; Träume an der Donau; Tief berauscht mich dein Haar; Spiel auf deiner Geige; Fünf-Uhr-Tee bei Robert Stoltz; Ungeküsst sollst du nicht schlafen geh'n; Oft genügt ein Gläschen Sekt; O süsse Señorita, sag' nicht nein Ars Musici ▲ AMS 8006-2 [DDD]

Le Nouveau Trio Pasquier [Régis Pasquier (vn), Bruno Pasquier (va), Roland Pidoux (vc)]
Gossec, F.-J.:Qts Fl, Op. 14, w. Aurèle Nicolet (fl) *(rec DRS Studio, May 18–19, 1984)* Talent ▲ DOM 291050 [DDD]
Hummel, J.N.:Qt Cl, w. Michel Lethiec (cl) Talent ▲ 291037
Kreutzer, C.:Qt Cl, w. Michel Lethiec (cl) Talent ▲ 291037
Vanhal, J.B.:Qt Cl, w. Michel Lethiec (cl) Talent ▲ 291037

Le Nouvel Ensemble members
Longtin, M.:Colère:Berlin 61 Ummus ▲ UMM 105
Mather, B.:Travaux de Nuit Ummus ▲ UMM 105
Rea, J.:Kubla Khan Ummus ▲ UMM 105
Rozankovic, A.:Pas de Deux Ummus ▲ UMM 105

Le Nouvel Ensemble Moderne
L. Vaillancourt (cnd)
Benjamin, G.:At First Light Ummus ▲ UMM 102
Cherney, B.:Apparitions Ummus ▲ UMM 106
Evangelista, J.:Ô Bali Ummus ▲ UMM 104
Finsterer, M.:Ruisselant Ummus ▲ UMM 106
Gentile, A.:In un silenzio ordinato Ummus ▲ UMM 102
Gervasoni, S.:Su un arco di bianco Ummus ▲ UMM 106
Gougeon, D.:Un Train pour l'enfer, Strasbourg Percussion Ensemble *(rec Strasbourg, Sept 29, 1993)* Ummus ▲ UMM 109
Harvey, J.:Bhakti Montaigne ▲ MO 782086
Hui, M.:Speaking in Tongues *(rec live, Salle Claude-Champagne, Montréal, Nov. 1994)* Ummus ▲ UMM 108
Kolb, B.:Millefoglie New World ▲ 80422-2 [DDD]
Lang, D.:Music of, w. J. Rozen (elec tuba), D. Lang (nar), E. Niemann (pno), N. Tilles (pno), R. Schulte (vn), U. Oppens (pno)—Are You Experienced?; Orpheus Over & Under; Spud; Illumination Rounds CRI ▲ CD 625 [DDD]
Lesage, J.:Les Sensations confuses *(rec Strasbourg, Sept 29, 1993)* Ummus ▲ UMM 109
Ligeti, G.:Kammerkonzert Ummus ▲ UMM 102
Ona, E.:For Ivan Lermoliev Ummus ▲ UMM 106
Perron, A.:Exil *(rec Univ of Montreal, May 12, 1993)* Ummus ▲ UMM 109
Provost, S.:L'Adorable verrotière, w. Michel Forgues (nar), Pauline Vaillancourt (sop) *(rec Studio 12, Maison de Radio-Canada, Montreal, May 12, 1993)* Ummus ▲ UMM 109
Rimkevicius, G.:Energy, Streams & Directions *(rec live, Salle Claude-Champagne, Montréal, Nov. 1994)* Ummus ▲ UMM 108
Saariaho, K.:Lichtbogen Ummus ▲ UMM 102
Sanchez-Gutierrez, C.:Son del corazón *(rec live, Salle Claude-Champagne, Montréal, Nov. 1994)* Ummus ▲ UMM 108
Vivier, C.:Pulau Dewata Ummus ▲ UMM 104
Wolfe, J.:The Vermeer Room *(rec live, New York's "Bang On a Can Festival," ca. 1987–91)* CRI ▲ CD 628 [DDD]

Nouvel PO
A. Gatto (cnd)
Donizetti, G.:Gemma di Vergy, w. Montserrat Caballe (sop—Gemma), Anna Ringart (mez—Ida), Luis Lima (ten—Tamas), Vicente Sardinero (bar—Il Conte), Juan Pons (bar—Guido), Francois Loup (b—Rolando), Jean-Paul Kreder (cnd), French Radio Chorus *(rec live, Salle Pleyet, Paris, Apr 20, 1976)* Agorá Music ("Phoenix" series) 2-▲ 501 [ADD]
Mercier (cnd)
Marcland, P.:Music of, w. Debussy Trio, Ensemble InterContemporain, Michel Tranchant (cnd), French Vocal Group—Versets; Paroles; Failles; Mètres; Variants *(rec 1978–84)* Chamade ▲ CHCD 5636 [DDD]

Nova Ensemble [Amanda Dean (perc), Evan Pritchard (perc), David Pye (perc), Paul Tanner (perc), Tim White (perc), Allan Meyer (perc)]
Benfall, S.:Rough Cut Vox Australis ▲ VAST 0212 [ADD]
Buddle, L.:Just an Inkling for an Angklung Vox Australis ▲ VAST 0212 [ADD]
Fowler, J.:Echos from an Antique Land Vox Australis ▲ VAST 0212 [ADD]
Hille, S.:Mizu to Kori Vox Australis ▲ VAST 0212 [AAD]
Smalley, R.:Ceremony I Vox Australis ▲ VAST 0212 [ADD]
Travers, C.:Cold Air Rising Vox Australis ▲ VAST 0212 [ADD]

Nova Filarmonia Portuguesa
A. Cassuto (cnd)
Arriaga, J.C.:Sym in D MP Classics ▲ 3-11026
Bomtempo, J.D.:Sym 2 MP Classics ▲ 3-11026
Corelli, A.:Con grosso, Op. 6/8, "Christmas Con" MP Classics ("European" series) ▲ 3-11024
Haydn, J.:Sym 88 MP Classics ("European" series) ▲ 3-11027
Haydn, J.:Sym 92, "Oxford" MP Classics ("European" series) ▲ 3-11027
Haydn, J.:Sym 99 MP Classics ("European" series) ▲ 3-11027
Locatelli, P.:Concerti grossi—No. 8 MP Classics ("European" series) ▲ 3-11024
Manfredini, F.:Con grosso, Op. 3/12 MP Classics ("European" series) ▲ 3-11024
Mendelssohn, F.:Sym 1 MP Classics ("European" series) ▲ 3-11029
Mendelssohn, F.:Sym 3 MP Classics ("European" series) ▲ 3-11029
Sammartini, G.:Cons grossi, Op. 5—No. 6 in g MP Classics ("European" series) ▲ 3-11024
Torelli, G.:Pastorale per Ss Natale MP Classics ("European" series) ▲ 3-11024

Nova Scotia SO
Dreyfus, G.:Serenade CBC ("SM 5000" series) ▲ SMCD 5088 [DDD] ■ 4-5088 (D)
Grainger, P.:Music of—Colonial Song; Eastern Intermezzo; Gay But Wistful; The Gum-suckers' March; Rustic Dance CBC ("SM 5000" series) ▲ SMCD 5088 [DDD] ■ 4-5088 (D)
Lilburn, D.:Diversions CBC ("SM 5000" series) ▲ SMCD 5088 [DDD] ■ 4-5088 (D)
Mozart, W.A.:Contradances, K.609 CBC ("SM 5000" series) ▲ SMCD 5095 [DDD] ■ SMC 5095 (D)
Mozart, W.A.:Dances & Marches—Contredanse, K.534, "Das Donnerwetter"; 3 German Dances, K.605; 3 Marches, K.383, 383f & 385a; 4 Minuets [w. hurdy-gurdy], K.601; 5 German Dances & Minuets from K.463, 536, 567 & 585 CBC ("SM 5000" series) ▲ SMCD 5095 [DDD] ■ SMC 5095 (D)
Mozart, W.A.:Music of—Les petits riens, K.299b; 3 German Dances, K.605; 5 Contradances, K.609; Contradance, K.534; 3 Marches, K.383, 383f, 385a; 4 Minuets, K.601; 5 Dances, K.585, Nos. 5 & 8, K.536, No. 6, K.567, No.3, K.463, No. 1 CBC ("SM 5000" series) ▲ SMCD 5095 [DDD]
Mozart, W.A.:Petits riens (sels) CBC ("SM 5000" series) ▲ SMCD 5095 [DDD]
B. Brott (cnd)
...With Glowing Hearts CBC Records ("SM 5000" series) ▲ SMCD 5062 [DDD]
H. Cable (cnd)
Delius, F.:Con Vn, w. P. Djokic (vn) CBC ("SM 5000" series) ▲ SMCD 5134 [DDD]
Delius, F.:Music of—Irmelin; Koanga; A Village Romeo & Juliet; Fennimore & Gerda; 2 Pieces for Small Orch.; Sleigh Ride CBC ("SM 5000" series) ▲ SMCD 5134 [DDD]

▲ = CD ♦ = Enhanced CD Δ = MD ■ = Cassette Tape □ = DCC

Nova Scotia SO (cont.)
H. Cable (cnd) (cont.)
Delius, F.:Orchestral Music—Prelude [from *Irmelin*]; La Calinda [from *Koanga*]; The Walk to the Paradise Garden [from *A Village Romeo and Juliet*]; Intermezzo [from *Fennimore and Gerda*, arr. E. Fenby); Con. for Violin [w. P. Djokic]; On Hearing the First Cuckoo in Spring; Summer Night on the River; Sleigh Ride *(rec Dec. 5–6, 1991)* CBC ("SM 5000" series) ▲ SMCD 5134 [DDD]
Down under CBC Records ("SM 5000" series) ▲ SMCD 5088 [DDD] ■ 4–5088 (D)
Opportunity Knocks CBC Records ("SM 5000" series) ▲ SMCD 5112 [DDD]

G. Tintner (cnd)
Benjamin, A.:North American Square Dance
CBC ("SM 5000" series) ▲ SMCD 5088 [DDD] ■ 4–5088 (D)
Coulthard, J.:Excursion Ballet Suite CBC ("SM 5000" series) ▲ SMCD 5088 [DDD] ■ 4–5088 (D)

Novair Duo [Henri Bok (a sax/b cl), Miny Dekkers (acc)]
Meijering, Chiel:No Pain, No Gain *(rec Bloomline Studios, The Netherlands, Mar. 1995)*
Globe ▲ GLO 5138 [DDD]
Raxach, E.:Decade *(rec Bloomline Studios, The Netherlands, Mar. 1995)* Globe ▲ GLO 5138 [DDD]
Söll, B.:Landscape & Clothes *(rec Bloomline Studios, The Netherlands, Mar. 1995)*
Globe ▲ GLO 5138 [DDD]
Symonds, N.:Persuasion *(rec Bloomline Studios, The Netherlands, Mar. 1995)*
Globe ▲ GLO 5138 [DDD]
Veldhuis, J. ter:Night & Day *(rec Bloomline Studios, The Netherlands, Mar. 1995)*
Globe ▲ GLO 5138 [DDD]

Novak String Quartet
Bartók, B.:Qt Strs (comp) *(rec 1965)* Philips ("Duo" series) 2–▲ 442284–2

Novak Trio
Schulhoff, E.:Divertissement Ob Supraphon ▲ SUP 112170 [DDD]

Noventa Trio [K.-A. Kolly (pno), A. Friedrich (vn), D. Riniker (vc)]
Brahms, J.:Trios (3) Pno Tudor ▲ TUD 796 [DDD]

Novsak Trio
Fiala, J.:Qts Ob, w. Simon Fuchs (ob) Tudor ▲ TUD 7022 [DDD]
Krommer, F.:Qts Ob, w. Simon Fuchs (ob) Tudor ▲ TUD 7022 [DDD]
Mozart, W.A.:Trio Vn, K.563 *(rec 1989)* Jecklin–Disco ▲ JS 269–2 [DDD]
Ries, F.:Qnt Fl, w. W. Bennett (fl), M. Kosi (va) *(rec 1990)* Jecklin–Disco ▲ JD 633–2 [DDD]
Rolla, A.:Trio Concertante 3 *(rec 1989)* Jecklin–Disco ▲ JS 269–2 [DDD]
Romberg, A.:Qnts Fl, w. W. Bennett (fl), M. Kosi (va)—Op. 21/4–5 *(rec 1990)*
Jecklin–Disco ▲ JD 633–2 [DDD]

Novus Brass Quartet
Frescobaldi, G.:Canzonas, Caprici & Ricercari, w. U. Duetschler (positive org)—19 sels.
Claves ▲ CD 9104 [DDD]

NSO RSO members
W. Mony (cnd)
Zaidel-Rudolph, J.:Tempus Fugit, w. PACT Orch members Claremont ▲ GSE 1532

Nunc Contemporary Music Ensemble
Glanert, D.:Graffiti Signum ▲ X61–00 [DDD]
Meijering, Cord:November Signum ▲ X61–00 [DDD]
Müller-Hornbach, G.:Songs Sop Signum ▲ X61–00 [DDD]
Riehm, R.:Lamento Signum ▲ X61–00 [DDD]
Scelsi, G.:Ko-Tha I Signum ▲ X61–00 [DDD]
Stahmer, K.H.:König Wiedehopf Signum ▲ X61–00 [DDD]
Yun, I.:Gagok Signum ▲ X61–00 [DDD]

Nuova Duo [Timothy McAllister (sax), Kevin Class (pno)]
Bolcom, W.:Lilith *(rec Brookwood Studios & Solid Sound, Inc., Ann Arbor, Michigan, July 1994 & May 1995)* Centaur ▲ CRC 2280 [DDD]
Lennon, J.A.:Distances Within Me *(rec Brookwood Studios & Solid Sound, Inc., Ann Arbor, Michigan, July 1994 & May 1995)* Centaur ▲ CRC 2280 [DDD]
Platti, G.B.:Music of—in G [trans Eugene Rousseau] *(rec Brookwood Studios & Solid Sound, Inc., Ann Arbor, Michigan, July 1994 & May 1995)* Centaur ▲ CRC 2280 [DDD]
Prokofiev, S.:Visions fugitives [arr Howard Harrison] *(rec Brookwood Studios & Solid Sound, Inc., Ann Arbor, Michigan, July 1994 & May 1995)* Centaur ▲ CRC 2280 [DDD]
Ravel, M.:Pièce en forme de Habanera *(rec Brookwood Studios & Solid Sound, Inc., Ann Arbor, Michigan, July 1994 & May 1995)* Centaur ▲ CRC 2280 [DDD]
Rogers, R.:Lessons of the Sky *(rec Brookwood Studios & Solid Sound, Inc., Ann Arbor, Michigan, July 1994 & May 1995)* Centaur ▲ CRC 2280 [DDD]

Nuove Sincronie Ensemble
Duffy String Quartet with M. G. Bellocchio & the Ensemble Nuove Sincronie, w. Duffy String Quartet, M. G. Bellocchio (cnd) Stradavarius ▲ SIP 1011

Nuovo Ensemble Italiano
A. Brizzi (cnd)
Scelsi, G.:Music of, w. Michiko Hirayama (sop), Maurizio Ben Omar (gtr/perc), Federico Mondelci (sax), Gruppo Musica Insieme—Pranam I for Voice, 12 Instrs & Band; Ko-Tha [3 danses de Shiva] for Gtr; I presagi for 11 Instruments; Riti (I funerali di Alessandro Magno); Trio for 3 Percussionists; Manto per quattro for Voice, Fl, Trbn & Vc; Kya for Sax & 7 Instruments; Entretiens avec Giacento Scelsi
Memoire Vive ▲ CD 262009 [ADD/DDD]

Nuovo Quartetto Modigliani
Respighi, O.:Qnt Pno, w. M. Palumbo (pno) *(rec July 1992)* Nuova Era ▲ NUO 7159 [DDD]

Nuovo Quartetto Modigliani members
Respighi, O.:Pieces Vn, w. Massimo Palumbo (pno) *(rec July 1992)* Nuova Era ▲ NUO 7159 [DDD]
Respighi, O.:Son Vn, w. Massimo Palumbo (pno) *(rec July 1992)* Nuova Era ▲ NUO 7159 [DDD]

Nuovo Trio Faure
Clementi, M.:Sons Pno, Fl & Vc, Op. 21 Dynamic ▲ CD 93 CD 93
Clementi, M.:Sons Pno, Fl & Vc, Op. 22 Dynamic ▲ CD 93 CD 93

Nuremberg Ars Nova Ensemble
W. Heider (cnd)
Stahmer, K.H.:Music of, w. *(soloists unknown)*—I Can Fly; Dreamscape; Commentaries; Rotations; plus others Thorofon ▲ CTH 2210

Nuremberg SO
A. Cox (cnd)
Prokofiev, S.:Con 2 Pno, w. J. Bolet (pno) Genesis ▲ GCD 104 [ADD]
Prokofiev, S.:Con 3 Pno, w. J. Bolet (pno) Genesis ▲ GCD 104 [ADD]

Z. Dešky (cnd)
Rheinberger, J.:Con Pno, w. A. Ruiz (pno) Genesis ▲ GCD 106 [DDD]
Rubinstein, A.:Con 5 Pno, w. A. Ruiz (pno) Genesis ▲ GCD 103 [ADD]
Sgambati, G.:Con Pno, w. A. Ruiz (pno) Genesis ▲ GCD 106 [DDD]

R. Kaufman (cnd)
Holdridge, L.:Elegy Varèse Sarabande ▲ VSD 5329 [DDD]
Holdridge, L.:Film Music—main themes from Beauty & the Beast, East of Eden, & 16 Days of Glory
Varèse Sarabande ▲ VSD 5329 [DDD]
Holdridge, L.:El Pueblo de Sol Varèse Sarabande ▲ VSD 5329 [DDD]
Holdridge, L.:Scenes of Summer Varèse Sarabande ▲ VSD 5329 [DDD]
Rózsa, M.:Con Va, w. M. Newman (va) Varèse Sarabande ▲ VSD 5329 [DDD]

P.-D. Ponnelle (cnd)
Martin, F.:Monologe (6) aus "Jedermann", w. M. Egel (bar) FSM ▲ FCD 97213 [DDD]

G. Schmöhe (cnd)
Buechner, M.:Elizabeth, w. S. Anthony (sop), J. McLean (ten) [G] Nord–Disc 2–▲ NORD 2026 [DDD]
Buechner, M.:Elizabeth (sels)—Suite 2 (w. S. Anthony (soprano) & J. McLean (tenor)]; Pas de deux; The Well-Wishers Nord–Disc ▲ NORD 2032 [DDD]
Buechner, M.:The Old Swedes Church Nord–Disc ▲ NORD 2030 [DDD]
Buechner, M.:The Old Swedes Church Nord–Disc ▲ NORD 2026 [DDD]
Buechner, M.:Phantomgreen (sels)—Suite 2 Nord–Disc ▲ NORD 2032 [DDD]

Nuremberg Wind Soloists
M. Wiemann (cnd)
Christmas in the Erz Mountains, w. Helmuth Stapff Group Entrée ▲ 0066

Michael Nyman Band
M. Nyman (cnd)
Nyman, M.:And They Do TER Limited ▲ CDTER 1123 [DDD] ■ CSTER 1123 (D)
Nyman, M.:Carrington *(rec Abbey Road Studios, London, Nov 10–11, 1994)* Argo ▲ 444873–2
Nyman, M.:MGV Argo ▲ 443382–2 [DDD]
Nyman, M.:Michael Nyman Songbook, w. Ute Lemper (sop) [E,F,G] London ▲ 425227–2 [DDD]
Nyman, M.:Music of—sels. from his film scores:The Cook, The Thief, His Wife and Her Lover; The Draughtsman's Contract; Drowning By Numbers; Prospero's Books; Water Dances; A Zed and Two Noughts Argo ▲ 436820–2 [DDD]
Nyman, M.:Prospero's Books, w. S. Leonard (sop), U. Lemper (sop), D. Conway (sgr), M. Angel (ten)
London ▲ 425224–2 [DDD]

Oakland SO
G. Samuel (cnd)
Brandt, H.:Kingdom Come, w. Henry Brandt (org), Oakland Youth Orch Phoenix ▲ PHCD 127
Lazarof, H.:Con 1 Vc, w. L. Lesser (vc) CRI ▲ CD 631

Oakland Univ Wind Sym
J. Dawson (cnd)
All-American Trombone, w. D. Smith (trbn) Coronet ▲ COR 400–7 ■ LPC 4007
Pryor, A.:Trbn & Band Music, w. D. Smith (trbn) Coronet ▲ COR 400–7 ■ LPC 4007

Oakland Youth Orch
R. Hughes (cnd)
Harrison, L.:Pacifika Rondo Phoenix ▲ PHCD 118 [AAD]

G. Samuel (cnd)
Brandt, H.:Kingdom Come, w. Henry Brandt (org), Oakland SO Phoenix ▲ PHCD 127

Oakwood Chamber Players
Koykkar, J.:Chamber Music, w. Present Music—Continuum (1982); Circumstance (1983); Modus Operandum (1984); A Three Point Perspective (1986); Expressed in Units (1989)
Northeastern ▲ NR 246–CD

Oberlin Baroque Ensemble
R. Kapp (cnd)
Masterpieces of the French Baroque, w. Philharmonia Virtuosi Vox Box 3–▲ CD3X 3006 [ADD]

Oberlin Baroque Ensemble [A. Wenzinger (vl), D. Ornstein (hpd), J. Weaver (hpd)]
Marais, M.:Music of—Sonnerie de Ste. Geneviève (1723); Suite in D (1711); Feste champêtre (1717); Tambourin (1717); Allamande la Singulière & l'Arabesque (1717); Suite for 3 Viols in G (1717)
Gasparo Gallante ▲ GG 1002 [AAD]

Oberlin CO
M. Singher (cnd)
Daugherty, M.:Mxyzptlk, w. J. Bogorad (fl), S. Y. Lee (fl) Opus One ▲ 138

Oberlin Contemporary Chamber Ensemble
Asia, D.:Miles Mix Albany ▲ TROY 106 [DDD]
Asia, D.:Rivalries Albany ▲ TROY 106 [DDD]

Oberlin Contemporary Music Ensemble
L. Rachleff (cnd)
Daugherty, M.:Blue Like an Orange Opus One ▲ 138
Daugherty, M.:Snap! Opus One ▲ 138

Oberlin Musical Union Orch
D. Moe (cnd)
Verdi, G.:Requiem Mass, w. James (sgr), Shafer (sgr), Farina (sgr), Crawford (sgr) [L]
Bainbridge 2–▲ BCD 2103 [DDD]

Oberlin Percussion Group
Holmes, R.:Circle Son Opus One ▲ CD 162

M. Rosen (cnd)
White, J.:Introit, Illusions, Ritual & Dance, w. Andro Toth (vc) Opus One ▲ CD 167 [DDD]

Oberlin Trio [J. Schwartz (pno), S. Clapp (vn), A. Toth (vc)]
Debussy, C.:Trio Pno Analekta ▲ CLCD 2004
Loeillet, J.-B.:Sons Various Instruments, Op. 2—No. 2 Analekta ▲ CLCD 2004

Oberlin Wind Ensemble
R. Ponto (cnd)
Miller, E.J.:Fant-Con in 3 Movts A Sax, w. H. Smith (sax) Opus One ▲ CD 154
Miller, E.J.:Going Home, w. H. Smith Opus One ▲ CD 154
Miller, E.J.:Seven Sides of a Crystal, w. H. Smith (sax) Opus One ▲ CD 154

L. Rachleff (cnd)
Miller, E.J.:Beyond the Wheel, w. G. Fulkerson (vn) Opus One ▲ 138

Octagon
Banks, B.:Forest Echoes Albany ▲ TROY 133 [DDD]
Doe, K.:Crazy Jay Blue Albany ▲ TROY 133 [DDD]
Doe, K.:Solstice Fragments Albany ▲ TROY 130 [DDD]
Harrison, E.:La Cité du globe captif Albany ▲ TROY 130 [DDD]
Jelliffe, A.:The Chinese Teapot Teaches Patience Albany ▲ TROY 130 [DDD]
Jespersen, E.:Totem Albany ▲ TROY 133 [DDD]
Kothman, K.:G-R-K Albany ▲ TROY 130 [DDD]
Mateus-Vasquez, C.A.:A Song Cycle Albany ▲ TROY 130 [DDD]
Melbinger, T.:A Lullaby Albany ▲ TROY 133 [DDD]
Octagon, Vol. 1 Albany ▲ TROY 130 [DDD]
Pereira, D.:Archery Albany ▲ TROY 133 [DDD]
Santore, J.:Divert Albany ▲ TROY 130 [DDD]
Sawyer, E.:Columbine Albany ▲ TROY 133 [DDD]

M. Turkovic (cnd)
Mozart, W.A.:Serenade Ww, K.361 *(rec Grosser Musikvereinssaal, Oct 14, 1988)*
Camerata ▲ 32CM 91

Octagon members
Vogl, J.:Duo Va Albany ▲ TROY 133 [DDD]

Octophorus
B. Kuijken (cnd)
Mozart, W.A.:Serenade Ww, K.361 Accent ▲ 68642

L'Octuor De Violoncelles
Stolet, J.:Simple Requests Cambria ▲ CD 1088

Odense SO
P. Guth (cnd)
Lumbye, H.C.:Music of—includes Velocipedes Galop; Memories from Vienna Valse; Indian War Dance; Britta Polka; King Christian IX March of Honor; Welcome Mazurka; Pegasus Galop
Unicorn-Kanchana ▲ DKP CD 9143

E. Serov (cnd)
Nielsen, C.:Amor (ov) Kontrapunkt ▲ KPT 32178 [DDD]
Nielsen, C.:Andante Tranquillo Kontrapunkt ▲ KPT 32203
Nielsen, C.:At the Bier [orchd.] Kontrapunkt ▲ KPT 32193 [DDD]
Nielsen, C.:Helios Kontrapunkt ▲ KPT 32157 [DDD]
Nielsen, C.:Maskarade (suite) Kontrapunkt ▲ KPT 32203
Nielsen, C.:Pan & Syrinx Kontrapunkt ▲ KPT 32193 [DDD]
Nielsen, C.:Saga-Dream Kontrapunkt ▲ KPT 32193 [DDD]
Nielsen, C.:Saul & David (sels)—Suite Kontrapunkt ▲ KPT 32157 [DDD]
Nielsen, C.:Scherzo Kontrapunkt ▲ KPT 32203
Nielsen, C.:Sleep Kontrapunkt ▲ KPT 32178 [DDD]
Nielsen, C.:Sym 1 Kontrapunkt ▲ KPT 32157 [DDD]
Nielsen, C.:Sym 2 Kontrapunkt ▲ KPT 32178 [DDD]

Odense SO (cont.)
E. Serov (cnd) (cont.)
Nielsen, C.:Sym 3, w. Eva Hess Thaysen (sop), Lars Thodberg Bertelsen (bar) Kontrapunkt ▲ KPT 32203
Nielsen, C.:Sym 4 Kontrapunkt ▲ KPT 32193 [DDD]
Nørholm, I.:Sym 2, w. A. Nyborg (nar) Kontrapunkt ▲ KPT 32182 [DDD]
Nørholm, I.:Sym 4, w. Danish National Radio Choir Kontrapunkt ▲ KPT 32212
Nørholm, I.:Sym 5 Kontrapunkt ▲ KPT 32212
Nørholm, I.:Sym 6 Kontrapunkt ▲ KPT 32162 [DDD]
Nørholm, I.:Sym 8 Kontrapunkt ▲ KPT 32162 [DDD]
T. Vetö (cnd)
Nielsen, C.:Aladdin Unicorn–Kanchana ▲ DKPCD 9054
Nielsen, C.:Springtime, w. Inga Nielsen (sop), Kim von Binzer (ten), Jørgen Klint (bass), Lille MUKO, St. Klemens School Children's Choir Unicorn–Kanchana ▲ DKPCD 9054
Syberg, F.:Adagio Strs Kontrapunkt ▲ 32088 [DDD]
Syberg, F.:Sinfonietta Kontrapunkt ▲ 32088 [DDD]
Syberg, F.:Sym Kontrapunkt ▲ 32088 [DDD]
Odessa PO
H. Earle (cnd)
Kolessa, M.:Sym 1 ASV ▲ ASV 963 [DDD]
Skoryk, M.:Carpathian Con ASV ▲ ASV 963 [DDD]
Skoryk, M.:Hutsul Tryptich ASV ▲ ASV 963 [DDD]
Odhecaton
15th & 16th Century Music from Areas along the Rhine River FSM ▲ 97217 [DDD]
In Gottes Namen fahren wir [In God's Name We Go] FSM ▲ 97208
Ohio State Univ Concert Band
K. Brion (cnd)
Hovhaness, A.:The Flowering Peach *(rec Ohio State Univ., Nov. 21–23, 1993 & Jan. 1 1994)* Delos ▲ DE 3158 [DDD]
Hovhaness, A.:Sym 20 *(rec Ohio State Univ., Nov. 21–23, 1993 & Jan. 1, 1994)* Delos ▲ DE 3158 [DDD]
Hovhaness, A.:Sym 29, w. C. Lindberg (trbn) *(rec Ohio State Univ., Nov. 21–23, 1993 & Jan. 1, 1994)* Delos ▲ DE 3158 [DDD]
Hovhaness, A.:Sym 53 *(rec Ohio State Univ., Nov. 21–23, 1993 & Jan. 1, 1994)* Delos ▲ DE 3158 [DDD]
Ohio State Univ New Music Ensemble
C. Kirchhoff (cnd)
Schwartz, E.:Chamber Con IV CRI ▲ CD 598 [ADD]
Igor Oistrakh Trio [Igor Oistrakh (vn), Valen Oistrakh (vn), N. Zertsalova (pno)]
Bach, J.S.:Trio Son for 2 Vns Art & Electronics ▲ AED 68022 [DDD]
Moszkowski, M.:Suite 2 Vns Art & Electronics ▲ AED 68022 [DDD]
Shostakovich, D.:Trio 2 Pno Praga ▲ PR 254054
Ysaÿe, E.:Amitié [arr for 2 vns & pno] Art & Electronics ▲ AED 68022 [DDD]
Okada Percussion Ensemble
Miyoshi, A.:Music of, w. Mikio Hoshido (gtr)—Constellation Noire for Gtr & Str Qt; Protase de Loin a Rien for 2 Gtrs; 5 Poems for Gtr; Epitase for Gtr on IXTACCHIHUATL Camerata ▲ 32CM 105
Oklahoma City SO
G. F. Harrison (cnd)
La Montaine, J.:Con Pno, w. Karen Keys (pno) *(rec 1962)* Citadel ▲ CTD 88118 [ADD]
La Montaine, J.:Con Pno, w. Karen Keys (pno) CRI ■ C 189
Oklahoma Woodwind Quintet
A Christmas Delight *(rec 1st Christian Church, Norman, Oklahoma, June 7–8, 1990)* Integra Classic ▲ ICD 801
Old Fairfield Academy Orch
T. Crawford (cnd)
Mozart, W.A.:Con Bn, w. Dennis Godburn (bn) MusicMasters ▲ 01612-67157-2 [DDD]
Mozart, W.A.:Con Cl, w. Eric Hoeprich (b cl) MusicMasters ▲ 01612-67157-2 [DDD]
Mozart, W.A.:Con Ob, w. Marc Schachman (ob) MusicMasters ▲ 01612-67157-2 [DDD]
Mozart, W.A.:Cons 1–4 Pno, w. M. Bilson (pno) [period instrs] MusicMasters ▲ 01612-67095-2
Old Fairfield Academy Orch members [Charles Neidich (cl), Dennis Godburn (bn), R.J. Kelley (hn), Linda Quan (vn), David Miller (va), Myron Lutzke (vc), Michael Willens (db)]
Beethoven, L. van:Septet Strs *(rec American Academy & Institute of Arts & Letters, New York City, Mar. 3–5, 1993)* MusicMasters ▲ 01612-67123-2 [DDD]
Old Fairfield Academy Orch members [R.J. Kelley (hn), Alex Cook (hn), Linda Quan (vn), Daryll Kubian (vn), David Miller (va), Myron Lutzke (vc)]
Beethoven, L. van:Sxt Hns, Op. 81b *(rec American Academy & Institute of Arts & Letters, New York City, Mar. 3–5, 1993)* MusicMasters ▲ 01612-67123-2 [DDD]
Old South Brass
R. Voisin (cnd)
The Old Brass Organ & Timpani, w. Frederick MacArthur (org) Pro Organo ▲ POCD 7051 [DDD]
Olewsky Trio
Brahms, J.:Trio Hn [composer's alternative vc–vn–pno version] Amatius Classics 2–▲ ACCD 1003 [DDD]
Brahms, J.:Trios (3) Pno Amatius Classics 2–▲ ACCD 1003 [DDD]
John Oliver Orch
Ives, C.:The Celestial Country, w. John Oliver Chorale [E] Northeastern ▲ NR 226 CD [DDD]
Loeffler, C.M.:Psalm CXXXVII (By the rivers of Babylon), w. John Oliver Chorale [E] Northeastern ▲ NR 226 CD [DDD]
Olsztyn State PO
D. Fanal (cnd)
Wissmer, P.:Con Gtr, w. P. Rayer (gtr) Quantum ▲ QM 6936 [DDD]
Wissmer, P.:Con 2 Vn, w. P. Rayer (vn) Quantum ▲ QM 6936 [DDD]
Wissmer, P.:Con 3 Vn, w. A. Milian (vn) Quantum ▲ QM 6935 [DDD]
Wissmer, P.:Stele Quantum ▲ QM 6935 [DDD]
Wissmer, P.:Sym 7 Quantum ▲ QM 6935 [DDD]
Omnibus Chamber Winds
A. Loguin (cnd)
Blomdahl, K.–B.:Chamber Con, w. Kerstin Jansson (pno), Kroumata (perc), Falu Woodwind Quintet Caprice ▲ CAP 21355 [DDD]
Eliasson, A.:Sotto il segno del sole, w. Kroumata Percussion Ensemble, Falu Woodwind Quintet Caprice ▲ CAP 21355 [DDD]
Messiaen, O.:Oiseaux exotiques, w. Kerstin Jansson (pno), Falu Woodwind Quintet, Kroumata Percussion Ensemble Caprice ▲ CAP 21355 [DDD]
Omnibus Wind Ensemble
Ravel, M.:Boléro [arr Lars–Erik Lidström] *(rec June 1994–June 1995)* Opus 3 ▲ OP 19403 [AAD]
Zappa, F.:Music of—Inca Roads; How Could I Be Such a Fool; The Black Page No. 2; Igor's Boogie [all arr Per–Erik Adamsson]; Revised Music for a Low Budget Orch; No. 7; Be-Bop Tango; Alien Orifice; Brown Shoes Don't Make It; Peaches En Regalia [all arr Lars–Erik Lidström]; Let's Make the Water Turn Black; Sinister Footwear [2nd movt] [both arr Gunnar Persson]; Dog Breath Vars; Uncle Meat [both arr Leif Halldén] *(rec June 1994–June 1995)* Opus 3 ▲ OP 19403 [AAD]
Omroep Orch
E. Downes (cnd)
Verdi, G.:Ernani (sels), w. Felicia Weathers (sop—Elvira), Delia Wallis (mez—Giovanna), Placido Domingo (ten—Ernani), Wynford Evans (ten—Don Riccardo), Piero Francia (bar—Don Carlo), Agostino Ferrin (bass—Don Ruy Gomex de Silva), Robert Holl (bass—Iago), Omroep Chorus *(rec Amsterdam, Jan 15, 1972)* Bella Voce ▲ BLV 107.004 [AAD]
G. van Keulen (cnd)
Keulen, G. van:Con Vn, w. Vera Beths (vn) Donemus ▲ CV 33
Ondine String Quartet
Trimble, L.:Qt 1 Strs Opus One ▲ 150

Ondriček String Quartet
Dvořák, A.:Qnt Pno, Op. 81, w. František Maxian (pno) Praga ▲ PR 250078
1–5 Brass Quintet
Brass Bonanza, w. Annapolis Brass Quintet, Berlin Brass Quintet, Dallas Brass Quintet, Metropolitan Brass Quintet, New York Brass Quintet, St. Louis Brass Quintet Crystal ▲ CD 200 [ADD/DDD]
Dutton, B.:Carnival of Venice Crystal ▲ CD 200 [ADD]
Ongarese Duo [Ildikó Hajdu (vn), György Déri (vc)]
Haydn, J.:Vn Solos *(rec Hungaroton Classic Studio)* Hungaroton ▲ HCD 31474 [DDD]
OP & PO Orch
C. Halaris (cnd)
Anthology of Byzantine Secular Music Orata ▲ ANT 2
Corpus of Greek Music Orata 9–▲ COL 9
Hellenic Elegies Orata ▲ ORM4012
Medieval Greek Songs, Vol. 1 Orata ▲ ORMS 1
Pandora:Music of the Post–Byzantine High Society, Vol. III Orata ▲ PAN 3 [DDD]
Opera Nova Ensemble
J. Henneberger (cnd)
Keller, M.:Gesänge IV, w. Martina Bovet (sop) *(rec June 1994–Apr 1995)* Jecklin ▲ JEC 310 [DDD]
Opera Restor'd
P. Holman (cnd)
Dibdin, C.:Operas—The Brickdust Man (1772); The Grenadier (1773); The Ephesian Matron or The Widow's Tears (1769) [E] *(rec Mar. & April 1992)* Hyperion ▲ CDA 66608 [DDD]
Lampe, J.F.:Con Fl, "The Cukoo Con" Hyperion ▲ CDA 66759
Lampe, J.F.:Pyramus & Thisbe, w. Susan Bisatt (sop), Mark Padmore (ten) Hyperion ▲ CDA 66759
Operetta Orch
Marszalek (cnd)
Lehár, F.:Das Land des Lächelns (sels), w. I. Hallstein (sop), Renate Holm (sop), Heinz Hoppe (ten), Alexander (sgr), Operetta Chorus [G] Acanta ▲ CD 43494 [DDD]
Lehár, F.:Die lustige Witwe (sels), w. I. Hallstein (sop), L. Popp (sop), H. Hoppe (ten), Alexander (bar), B. Kusche (bar), Operetta Chorus [G] Acanta ▲ CD 43455 [DDD]
Ophir Trio [C. Touboul (pno), A. Czifra (vn), Z. Maschkowski (vc)]
Arensky, A.:Trio 1 Pno Erasmus ▲ WVH 015 [DDD]
Lalo, E.:Trio 1 Pno Erasmus ▲ WVH 015 [DDD]
Opus 8 Trio [Michael Hauber (pno), Eckhard Fischer (vn), Mario de Secondi (vc)]
Tchaikovsky, P.:Trio Pno Tacet ▲ 37
Opus 95 Ensemble
J. Komives (cnd)
Bizet, G.:L'Arlésienne (sels) REM ▲ REM 311264 [DDD]
Komives, J.:La Valse du moulin lointain REM ▲ REM 311264 [DDD]
Lehár, F.:Music of—Or et argent REM ▲ REM 311264 [DDD]
Liszt, F.:Hungarian Rhaps—No. 10 REM ▲ REM 311264 [DDD]
Liszt, F.:Son Pno, w. Karoly Moscari (pno)—orig version for pno & version for 15 instruments REM ▲ REM 311265 [DDD]
Strauss (II), Joh.:Waltzes—Le beau danube bleu REM ▲ REM 311264 [DDD]
Verdi, G.:Aida (sels) REM ▲ REM 311264 [DDD]
Weber, C.M. von:Invitation to the Dance Pno REM ▲ REM 311264 [DDD]
Oradea PO
E. Acél (cnd)
Constantinescu, P.:Byzantine Vars, w. G. Szabó (vc) *(rec 1983)* Olympia ▲ OCD 415 [AAD]
Haydn, M.:Con Org, w. Ectarina Botár (hpd), Alexandru Iosif Thurzo (va) Olympia ("Explorer" series) ▲ OCD 406 [AAD]
Haydn, M.:Con Vn, P.53, w. G. Ille (vn) Olympia ("Explorer" series) ▲ OCD 406 [AAD]
Ibert, J.:Con Fl, w. N. Buchman (fl) *(rec 4/91)* Olympia ▲ OCD 420 [DDD]
Nielsen, C.:Con Fl, w. N. Buchman (fl) *(rec 4/91)* Olympia ▲ OCD 420 [DDD]
Partos, O.:Visions, w. N. Buchman (fl) *(rec 4/91)* Olympia ▲ OCD 420 [DDD]
M. Ratiu (cnd)
Dittersdorf, K.D. von:Syms in C & D Olympia (Explorer) ▲ OCD 405 [AAD]
R. Rimbu (cnd)
Dittersdorf, K.D. von:Sym in D Olympia ▲ OLY 426 [DDD]
Dittersdorf, K.D. von:Sym in A, "5 Nations" Olympia ▲ OLY 426 [DDD]
Dittersdorf, K.D. von:Sym in E Olympia ▲ OLY 426 [DDD]
Dittersdorf, K.D. von:Sym in E♭ Olympia ▲ OLY 426 [DDD]
Dittersdorf, K.D. von:Sym in e Olympia ▲ OLY 426 [DDD]
Haydn, M.:Syms—Syms., P.12, 32, 43 & 44 Olympia ▲ OLY 435 [DDD]
Pichl, V.:Music of—Sym. No. 5 in B♭, Op. 1; Sym. in D, "Mars"; Sym. in D, Op. 17; Symphonie Concertante in D, Op. 6 Olympia ▲ OLY 434 [DDD]
Orches Trio [Noriko Shirato (vn), Walther Giger (gtr), Fumio Shirato (db)]
Maggini, E.:Torso IV *(rec RTSI, Rete 2, Dec 1993)* Jecklin ▲ JS 311–2 [DDD]
Orch del'Arte
L. Korkhin (cnd)
Mozart, W.A.:Con 3 Vn, w. A. Stang (vn) Infinity Digital ▲ 64331 [DDD]
Orch dell'Angelicum
L. Rosado (cnd)
Paganini, N.:Con 5 Vn, w. F. Gulli (vn) *(rec 1963)* Dynamic ▲ CD 30U [AAD]
Orch Giovanile In Canto
G. Catalucci (cnd)
Morlacchi, F.:Nuovo barbiere, w. A. Ruffini (sop), G. Gatti (sop), M. Comencini (ten), A. Tomicich (bass), R. Franceschetto (sgr) [I] *(rec live 9/9/89)* Bongiovanni 2–▲ GB 2085/86 [DDD]
Morlacchi, F.:Poeta, w. C. Pastorello (sgr), P. Pellegrini (sgr) [I] Bongiovanni ▲ GB 2129 [DDD]
Orch Giovanile Italiana
K. Penderecki (cnd)
Penderecki, K.:Con Vn, w. S. Accardo (vn) *(rec live 1987)* Nuova Era ▲ 6705 [DDD]
Shostakovich, D.:Sym 6 *(rec live 1987)* Nuova Era ▲ 6705 [DDD]
Orch National
L. Bernstein (cnd)
Milhaud, D.:La Création du monde EMI Classics ▲ CDC 47845
Milhaud, D.:Saudades do Brasil—4 selections EMI Classics ▲ CDC 47845
L. Maazel (cnd)
Lalo, E.:Con Vc, w. Yo–Yo Ma (vc) CBS ▲ MK 35848 [DDD]
Vivaldi, A.:Cons Vn, Op. 8/1–4, "The Four Seasons", w. L. Maazel (vn) CBS ▲ MK 39008 [DDD]
Orch New England
J. Sinclair (cnd)
Ives, C.:Orchestral Music—Calcium Light Night; "Country Band" March; Largo Cantabile (Hymn); Postlude in F; Set for Theatre Orchestra; Set of Four Ragtime Dances; Three Places in New England; Yale–Princeton Football Game Koch International Classics ▲ KIC 7025–2 [DDD] ■ 3–7025–4 (D)
Ives, C.:Three Places in New England Koch International Classics ▲ KIC 7025–2 [DDD] ■ 3–7025–4 (D)
Orch of Our Time
J. Thome (cnd)
Berio, L.:Surabaya Johnny, w. Johanna Albrecht (mez) Vox Box 2–▲ CDX 5144
Boulez, P.:Eclat Vox Box 2–▲ CDX 5144
Boulez, P.:Improvisations sur Mallarmé I & II, w. Valarie Lamoree (sop)—No. 2 Vox Box 2–▲ CDX 5144
Crumb, G.:Night Music I, w. Jan De Gaetani (mez) Vox Box 2–▲ CDX 5144
Dallapiccola, L.:Concerto per la Notte di Natale dell'Anno, w. Valarie Lamoree (sop) Vox Box 2–▲ CDX 5144
Dallapiccola, L.:Parole di San Paolo, w. Benita Valente (mez) Vox Box 2–▲ CDX 5144
Dlugoszewski, L.:Fire Fragile Flight Vox Box 2–▲ CDX 5144

294 ▲ = CD ♦ = Enhanced CD Δ = MD ■ = Cassette Tape □ = DCC

Orch of Our Time (cont.)
J. Thome (cnd) (cont.)
Schoenberg, A.:Pierrot lunaire, w. Maureen McNalley (nar), Dwight Peltzer (pno), Eric Rosenblith (vn/va), Chris Finckel (vc), Sue Ann Kahn (fl), Anand Devendra (cl/b cl) — Vox Box 2-▲ CDX 5144
Thomson, V.:4 Saints in 3 Acts [E] — Elektra/Nonesuch 2-▲ 79035-2 [DDD]

Orch of St. John's Smith Square
J. Lubbock (cnd)
Chausson, E.:Poème Vn, w. M. Hasson (vn) — ASV Quicksilva ▲ QS 6051 [ADD/DDD]
Delius, F.:On Hearing the 1st Cuckoo — ASV Quicksilva ▲ QS 6051 [ADD/DDD]
Tchaikovsky, P.:Serenade Strs — ASV Quicksilva ▲ CD QS 6027 [DDD]

Orch of St. Luke's
Vivaldi, A.:Con Mand, RV.425, w. E. Fisk (gtr) *(rec July 27 & Aug. 4, 1992)* — MusicMasters ▲ 01612-67097-2 [DDD]
Vivaldi, A.:Con for 2 Mands, w. E. Fisk (gtr), F. Hand (gtr) *(rec July 27 & Aug. 4, 1992)* — MusicMasters ▲ 01612-67097-2 [DDD]
Vivaldi, A.:Con Va d'amore Lt, w. L. Schulman (vn), E. Fisk (gtr) *(rec July 27 & Aug. 4, 1992)* — MusicMasters ▲ 01612-67097-2 [DDD]
Vivaldi, A.:Cons Vn, Op. 8/1-4, "The Four Seasons", w. N. Salerno-Sonnenberg (vn) — EMI Classics ▲ CDC 49767 [DDD] ■ 4DS 49767 (D)
J. Adams (cnd)
Adams, J.:Fearful Symmetries — Elektra/Nonesuch ▲ 79218-2 [DDD] ■ 79218-4 (D)
Adams, J.:Wound Dresser, w. S. Sylvan (bar) — Elektra/Nonesuch ▲ 79218-2 [DDD] ■ 79218-4 (D)
R. Craft (cnd)
Stravinsky, I.:Abraham & Isaac, w. Stephen Varcoe (bar) — MusicMasters ▲ 01612-67158-2
Stravinsky, I.:Apollon musagète — MusicMasters 2-▲ 01612-67078-2
Stravinsky, I.:Cant Sop, w. Catherine Ciesinski (mez), Jon Humphries (ten), Gregg Smith Singers — MusicMasters ▲ 01612-67158-2
Stravinsky, I.:Capriccio, w. Mark Wait (pno) — MusicMasters ▲ 01612-67158-2
Stravinsky, I.:Choral Music, w. Gregg Smith Singers—Russian Peasant Choruses; Russian Sacred Choruses — MusicMasters ▲ 01612-67086-2
Stravinsky, I.:Concertino Instruments — MusicMasters ▲ 01612-67103-2
Stravinsky, I.:L'Histoire du soldat, w. Catherine Ciesinski (mez), Jon Humphries (ten), David Evitts (bar), Mark Wait (pno), Gregg Smith Singers — MusicMasters ▲ 01612-67152-2
Stravinsky, I.:In memoriam Dylan Thomas, w. Jon Humphries (ten) — MusicMasters ▲ 01612-67158-2
Stravinsky, I.:King of the Stars, w. Gregg Smith Singers — MusicMasters ▲ 01612-67103-2
Stravinsky, I.:Music of—Greeting Prelude; The Star-Spangled Banner; Dumbarton Oaks Concerto; Instrumental Miniatures; Circus Polka; Scherzo à la russe; Scènes de ballet; Balanchine-Stravinsky Chorale; Agon; Von Himmel hoch — MusicMasters ▲ 01612-67113-2 [DDD]
Stravinsky, I.:Les Noces, w. Gregg Smith Singers — MusicMasters ▲ 01612-67086-2
Stravinsky, I.:Norwegian Moods — MusicMasters ▲ 01612-67110-2
Stravinsky, I.:Octet — MusicMasters ▲ 01612-67103-2
Stravinsky, I.:Ode — MusicMasters ▲ 01612-67110-2
Stravinsky, I.:Oedipus Rex, w. P. Newman (nar) — MusicMasters 2-▲ 01612-67078-2
Stravinsky, I.:Perséphone, w. I. Jacob (nar), J. Aler (ten), Gregg Smith Singers, Newark Boys' Chorus — MusicMasters ▲ 01612-67103-2
Stravinsky, I.:Pulcinella Suite — MusicMasters ▲ 01612-67086-2
Stravinsky, I.:Ragtime — MusicMasters ▲ 01612-67110-2
Stravinsky, I.:Renard — MusicMasters ▲ 01612-67110-2
Stravinsky, I.:Le Sacre du printemps Orch — MusicMasters 2-▲ 01612-67078-2
Stravinsky, I.:Septet Cl — MusicMasters ▲ 01612-67158-2
Stravinsky, I.:Songs—3 Songs from William Shakespeare — MusicMasters ▲ 01612-67158-2
Stravinsky, I.:Sym in C — MusicMasters ▲ 01612-67086-2
Stravinsky, I.:Sym in 3 Movts — MusicMasters 2-▲ 01612-67078-2
Stravinsky, I.:Syms Ww — MusicMasters ▲ 01612-67103-2
W. H. Curry (cnd)
Davis, A.:X, The Life & Times of Malcolm X, w. Priscilla Baskerville (sop), Hilda Harris (mez), Thomas J. Young (ten), Eugene Perry (bar—Malcolm), Herbert Perry (bass), Episteme [E] — Gramavision 2-▲ R2-79470 [DDD]
D. R. Davies (cnd)
Bach, J.C.F.:Sinfs, HW.I/1-4 — MusicMasters ▲ 7062-2-C [DDD]
Copland, A.:Con Cl, w. W. Blount (cl) — MusicMasters ▲ 7005-2-C [DDD]
Copland, A.:Dance Panels — MusicMasters ▲ 01612-67101-2
Copland, A.:Music for Movies — MusicMasters ▲ 7005-2-C [DDD]
Copland, A.:Music for the Theatre — MusicMasters ▲ 7005-2-C [DDD]
Copland, A.:Old American Songs, w. B. Hubbard (bar) [E] — EMI Classics ▲ CDC 54282
Copland, A.:Poems (8) of Emily Dickinson, w. H. Schneiderman (mez) — MusicMasters ▲ 01612-67101-2
Copland, A.:Quiet City — MusicMasters ▲ 7005-2-C [DDD]
Copland, A.:Short Sym, "Sym 2" — MusicMasters ▲ 01612-67101-2
V. Feltsman (cnd)
Bach, J.S.:Cons Hpd, BWV 1052-1058, w. Vladimir Feltsman (pno)—BWV 1055, 1056 & 1058 *(rec American Academy & Institution of Arts & Letters, July 12-14, 1993)* — MusicMasters ▲ 01612-67143-2 [DDD]
Bach, J.S.:Con 1 Hpd, w. V. Feltsman (pno) *(rec July 12-14, 1993)* — MusicMasters ▲ 01612-67132-2 [DDD]
Bach, J.S.:Con 2 Hpd, w. V. Feltsman (pno) *(rec July 12-14, 1993)* — MusicMasters ▲ 01612-67132-2 [DDD]
E. Fischer (cnd)
Bach, J.S.:Con 3 Hpd, w. V. Feltsman (pno) *(rec July 12-14, 1993)* — MusicMasters ▲ 01612-67132-2 [DDD]
E. Fisk (cnd)
Vivaldi, A.:Con Lt *(rec July 27 & Aug. 4, 1992)* — MusicMasters ▲ 01612-67097-2 [DDD]
C. Mackerras (cnd)
Handel, G.F.:Water Music (comp) — Telarc ▲ CD 80279 [DDD]
Haydn, J.:Sym 31, "Hornsignal" — Telarc ▲ CD 80156 [DDD]
Haydn, J.:Sym 45, "Farewell" — Telarc ▲ CD 80156 [DDD]
Haydn, J.:Sym 100, "Military" — Telarc ▲ CD 80282 [DDD]
Haydn, J.:Sym 101, "Clock" — Telarc ▲ CD 80311 [DDD]
Haydn, J.:Sym 103, "Drum Roll" — Telarc ▲ CD 80282 [DDD]
Haydn, J.:Sym 104, "London" — Telarc ▲ CD 80311 [DDD]
B. H. Moyse (cnd)
Bach, J.S.:Cant 140, w. H. Schellenberg (sop), J. Humphrey (ten), S. Sylvan (bar) — MusicMasters ▲ 7059-2-C [DDD]
Bach, J.S.:Magnificat, BWV 243, w. M. A. Kruger (sop), H. Schellenberg (sop), M. Westbrook-Geha (mez), I. Humphrey (ten), S. Sylvan (bar) — MusicMasters ▲ 7059-2-C [DDD]
J. Nelson (cnd)
Baroque Duet, w. K. Battle (sop), Wynton Marsalis (tpt), Anthony Newman (hpd/org) — Sony Classical ▲ SK 46672 Δ SM 46672 ■ ST 46672
R. Norrington (cnd)
Rossini, G.:Music of, w. M. Fortuna (sop), M. Lerner (sop), D. Voigt (sop), M. Horne (mez), K. Kuhlmann (mez), F. von Stade (mez), R. Blake (ten), C. Estep (ten), C. Merritt (ten), T. Hampson (b-bar), H. Runey (b-bar), J. Opalach (bass), S. Ramey (bass), New York Concert Chorale — EMI Classics ▲ CDC 54643
A. Previn (cnd)
Barber, S.:Knoxville:Summer of 1915, w. Kathleen Battle (sop) — Deutsche Grammophon ▲ 437787-2 ■ 437 787-4
Gershwin, G.:Porgy & Bess (sels), w. Kathleen Battle (sop)—Summertime; I Loves You, Porgy — Deutsche Grammophon ▲ 437787-2 ■ 437 787-4
Mozart, W.A.:Con 10 Pnos, w. A. de Larrocha (pno), A. Previn (pno) *(rec Manhattan Center Studios, New York City, July 26-27, 1993)* — RCA Red Seal ▲ 68044-2

Orch of St. Luke's (cont.)
A. Previn (cnd) (cont.)
Previn, A.:Honey & Rue, w. Kathleen Battle (sop), Chris Gekker (tpt), James Pugh (trbn), Rufus Reid (bass), Grady Tate (dr) — Deutsche Grammophon ▲ 437787-2 ■ 437 787-4
D. Robertson (cnd)
In the Spirit:Sacred Music for Christmas, w. J. Norman (sop), American Boys Choir, Riverside Church Choir, St. Barnabas Adult Choir, St. Thomas Men & Boys Choir — Philips ▲ 454640-2 ■ 454640-4
J. Rudel (cnd)
Haydn, J.:The Seven Last Words of Christ on the Cross — MusicMasters ▲ 7050-2-C
Weill, K.:Con Vn, w. N. Tanaka (vn) — MusicMasters ▲ 7007-2-C [DDD]
Weill, K.:Kleine Dreigroschenmusik — MusicMasters ▲ 7007-2-C [DDD]
G. Schuller (cnd)
Gershwin, G.:Music of, w. Russell Sherman (pno), E. Kunzel (cnd), Rochester Pops Orch—American in Paris; Con in F; Rhap in Blue; etc. — Pro Arte ▲ CDM 814; ■ PCD 814
L. Slatkin (cnd)
A Christmas Celebration, w. K. Battle (sop), New York Choral Artists, Harlem Boys Choir — EMI Classics ▲ CDC 47587
M. Tilson Thomas (cnd)
Beethoven, L. van:Contredanses, WoO 14 — Sony Classical ▲ MLK 62369 [ADD/DDD]
Beethoven, L. van:Contredanses, WoO 14 — CBS ▲ MDK 45651 [DDD]
Beethoven, L. van:Sym 3, "Eroica" — CBS ▲ MDK 45651 [DDD]
Gershwin, G.:Let 'Em Eat Cake, w. J. Gilford McGovern (ten), L. Kert (sgr), New York Choral Artists [E] — CBS 2-▲ M2K 42522 [DDD]
Gershwin, G.:Of Thee I Sing, w. J. Gilford McGovern (ten), L. Kert (sgr), New York Choral Artists [E] — CBS 2-▲ M2K 42522 [DDD]
E. de Waart (cnd)
Adams, J.:Nixon in China, w. S. Sylvan (bar) *(other soloists unknown)* [E] — Elektra/Nonesuch 3-▲ 79177-2 2-■ 79177-4
Adams, J.:Nixon in China (sels), w. S. Sylvan (bar) *(other soloists unknown)* [E] — Elektra/Nonesuch ▲ 79193-2 ■ 79193-4
C. Wuorinen (cnd)
Wuorinen, C.:Five, w. F. Sherry (vc) *(rec Feb. 9, 1990)* — Koch International Classics ▲ KIC 7110-2 [DDD]
D. Zinman (cnd)
Barber, S.:Knoxville:Summer of 1915, w. D. Upshaw (sop) — Elektra/Nonesuch ▲ 79187-2 ■ 79187-4
Harbison, J.:Mirabai Songs, w. Dawn Upshaw (sop) — Elektra/Nonesuch ▲ 79187-2 ■ 79187-4
Menotti, G.C.:The Old Maid & the Thief, w. D. Upshaw (sop)—Act 1, Scene 6, "What a curse for a woman is a timid man" — Elektra/Nonesuch ▲ 79187-2 ■ 79187-4
Stravinsky, I.:The Rake's Progress, w. D. Upshaw (sop)—Act 1, Scene 3, "No word from Tom" — Elektra/Nonesuch ▲ 79187-2 ■ 79187-4

Orch of St. Luke's members
C. Mackerras (cnd)
Mozart, W.A.:Serenade Ww, K.361 *(rec July 1-2, 1993)* — Telarc ▲ CD 80359 [DDD]
R. Sadin (cnd)
Gershwin, G.:"I Got Rhythm" Vars, w. Marcus Roberts (pno), Lincoln Center Jazz Orch members *(rec Masonic Grand Lodge, New York City, July 13, 1995)* — Sony Classical ▲ SK 68488 [DDD]
Gershwin, G.:Rhap in Blue, w. Marcus Roberts (pno), Lincoln Center Jazz Orch members *(rec Masonic Grand Lodge, New York City, June 2, 6 & 7, 1995)* — Sony Classical ▲ SK 68488 [DDD]
Johnson, J.P.:Pno Music, w. Marcus Roberts (pno), Lincoln Center Jazz Orch members—Yamekraw [orchd Still] *(rec Masonic Grand Lodge, New York City, June 2, 6 & 7, 1995)* — Sony Classical ▲ SK 68488 [DDD]

Orch of the Age of Enlightenment
Bach, C.P.E.:Sinfs, H.657-662, "Hamburg Syms", w. Gustav Leonhardt (hpd)—No. 5, H.661 [period instrs] — Virgin Classics ("Veritas Edition" series) ▲ CDM 61182
Bach, C.P.E.:Sinfs, H.663-666, w. Gustav Leonhardt (hpd) [period instrs] — Virgin Classics ("Veritas Edition" series) ▲ CDM 61182
Bach, J.S.:Con 2 for 3 Hpds, w. E. Wallfisch (vn) [trans. for violin & strings] — Virgin Classics ▲ CDC 59319
Bach, J.S.:Cons Vn (comp), w. E. Wallfisch (vn) — Virgin Classics ▲ CDC 59319
Bach, J.S.:Con for 2 Vns, w. E. Wallfisch (vn), *(2nd vn unknown)* — Virgin Classics ▲ CDC 59319
Haydn, J.:Con 1 Vn, w. Elizabeth Wallfisch (vn) — Virgin Classics ▲ CDC 59266
Haydn, J.:Con 4 Vn, w. Elizabeth Wallfisch (vn) — Virgin Classics ▲ CDC 59266
Weber, C.M. von:Concertino Cl, w. A. Pay (cl) — Virgin Classics ▲ 59002 [DDD]
Weber, C.M. von:Con 1 Cl, w. A. Pay (cl) — Virgin Classics ▲ 59002 [DDD]
Weber, C.M. von:Con 2 Cl, w. A. Pay (cl) — Virgin Classics ▲ 59002 [DDD]
M. Elder (cnd)
Bellini, V.:Bianca e Fernando (sels), w. Jane Eaglen (sop)—Sorgi, o padre, e la figlia rimira *(rec Abbey Road Studio, June 16-23, 1996)* — Sony Classical ▲ SK 62032 [DDD]
Bellini, V.:Norma (sels), w. Jane Eaglen (sop)—Casta diva *(rec Abbey Road Studio, Sept 8-10, 1995)* — Sony Classical ▲ SK 62032 [DDD]
Bellini, V.:Il pirata (sels), w. Jane Eaglen (sop)—Col sorriso d'innocenza *(rec Abbey Road Studio, Sept 8-10, 1995; June 16-23, 1996)* — Sony Classical ▲ SK 62032 [DDD]
P. Herreweghe (cnd)
Bach, C.P.E.:Auferstehung und Himmelfahrt Jesu, w. H. Martinpelto (sop), C. Prégardien (ten), P. Harvey (bass), Collegium Vocale — Virgin Classics ▲ CDC 59069
M. Huggett (cnd)
Mozart, W.A.:Con 1 Vn, w. M. Huggett (vn) — Virgin Classics ▲ CDC 45010
Mozart, W.A.:Con 2 Vn, w. M. Huggett (vn) — Virgin Classics ▲ CDC 45010
Mozart, W.A.:Con 5 Vn, w. M. Huggett (vn) — Virgin Classics ▲ CDC 45010
Telemann, G.P.:Con in F Rcr, B Vl, w. M. Verbruggen (rcr), S. Cunningham (vl) *(rec Nov. 2-4, 1992)* — Harmonia Mundi USA ▲ HMU 907093
Telemann, G.P.:Con in a for Rcr, Vl, w. M. Verbruggen (rcr), S. Cunningham (vl) *(rec Nov. 2-4, 1992)* — Harmonia Mundi USA ▲ HMU 907093
Telemann, G.P.:Suite Rcr, w. M. Verbruggen (rcr) *(rec Nov. 2-4, 1992)* — Harmonia Mundi USA ▲ HMU 907093
Telemann, G.P.:Suite Vl, w. S. Cunningham (vl) *(rec Nov. 2-4, 1992)* — Harmonia Mundi USA ▲ HMU 907093
S. Kuijken (cnd)
Haydn, J.:Sym 82, "The Bear" — Virgin Classics ▲ 59537 [DDD]
Haydn, J.:Sym 83, "The Hen" — Virgin Classics ▲ 59537 [DDD]
Haydn, J.:Sym 84, "In Nomine Domini" — Virgin Classics ▲ 59537 [DDD]
Haydn, J.:Sym 85, "La Reine de France" — Virgin Classics ▲ 59557 [DDD]
Haydn, J.:Sym 86 — Virgin Classics ▲ 59557 [DDD]
Haydn, J.:Sym 87 — Virgin Classics ▲ 59557 [DDD]
G. Leonhardt (cnd)
Bach, C.P.E.:Cons Vc, H.432, 436 & 439, w. A. Bylsma (vc) — Virgin Classics ▲ CDC 59541-2 [DDD]
Bach, J.S.:Cant 205, w. M. van der Sluis (sop), R. Jacobs (ct), C. Prégardien (ten), D. Thomas (bass) [G] — Philips ▲ 432161-2 [DDD]
Bach, J.S.:Cant 214, w. M. van der Sluis (sop), R. Jacobs (ct), C. Prégardien (ten), D. Thomas (bass) [G] — Philips ▲ 432161-2 [DDD]
Purcell, H.:Odes & Welcome Songs (misc), w. H. Cook (ten), J. Bowman (ct), C. Robson (ct), D. Wilson-Johnson (bar), G. Leonhardt (hpd) — Virgin Classics ▲ CDC 59243
Rameau, J.P.:Les Paladins (ballet suite) — Philips ▲ 432968-2 [DDD]
C. Mackerras (cnd)
Beethoven, L. van:Con Vn, Op. 61, w. Monica Huggett (vn) — Classics for Pleasure ("Eminence" series) ▲ CDEMX 2217 [DDD]
Handel, G.F.:Alcina (sels), w. A. Murray (mez) — Forlane ▲ FRL 16738 [DDD]
Handel, G.F.:Ariodante (sels), w. A. Murray (mez) — Forlane ▲ FRL 16738 [DDD]
Handel, G.F.:Giulio Cesare in Egitto (sels), w. Ann Murray (mez) — Forlane ▲ FRL 16738 [DDD]
Handel, G.F.:Serse (sels), w. Ann Murray (mez) — Forlane ▲ FRL 16738 [DDD]

Orch of the Age of Enlightenment (cont.)
C. Mackerras (cnd) (cont.)
Mendelssohn, F.:Con in e Vn & Orch, Op. 64, w. Monica Huggett (vn) Classics for Pleasure ("Eminence" series) ▲ CDEMX 2217 [DDD]
Mendelssohn, F.:A Midsummer Night's Dream (sels)—Overture Virgin Classics ▲ CDC 59135
Mendelssohn, F.:A Midsummer Night's Dream (sels) [period instrs] Virgin Classics ("Veritas Edition" series) ▲ CDM 61183
Mendelssohn, F.:Sym 4 Virgin Classics ▲ CDC 59135
Mendelssohn, F.:Sym 4 [period instrs] Virgin Classics ("Veritas Edition" series) ▲ CDM 61183
Schubert, Franz:Rosamunde Virgin Classics ▲ CDM 61305
Schubert, Franz:Sym 5 Virgin Classics ▲ CDC 59273
Schubert, Franz:Sym 5 Virgin Classics ▲ CDM 61305
Schubert, Franz:Sym 8 Virgin Classics ▲ CDC 59273
Schubert, Franz:Sym 8 [completed by Brian Newbould] Virgin Classics ▲ CDM 61305
Schubert, Franz:Sym 9 [period instr] Virgin Classics ▲ CDM 61245
C. Mackintosh (cnd)
Bach, J.S.:Brandenburg Cons, w. C. Mackintosh (vn/pic) Virgin Classics 2-▲ CDCB 59152
Vivaldi, A.:Cons Va d'amore, w. Catherine Mackintosh (va d'amore) [period instr]—in D, RV.392; in d, RV.395; in d, RV.393; in a, RV.397; in d, RV.394; in A, RV.396 Hyperion ▲ CDA 66795
E. Wallfisch (cnd)
Bach, J.S.:Con Fl, Vn & Hpd, w. Lisa Beznosiuk (fl), Elizabeth Wallfisch (vn), Paul Nicholson (hpd) Virgin Classics ▲ CD 45190
Bach, J.S.:Con Ob, BWV 1053, w. Anthony Robson (ob d'amore) [arr Anthony Robson] Virgin Classics ▲ CD 45190
Bach, J.S.:Con Ob, BWV 1059, w. Anthony Robson (ob) [arr Anthony Robson] Virgin Classics ▲ CD 45190
Bach, J.S.:Con Ob d'amore, w. A. Robson (ob d'amore) Virgin Classics ▲ CDC 45095
Bach, J.S.:Con Vn, BWV 1052, w. E. Wallfisch (vn) Virgin Classics ▲ CDC 45095
Bach, J.S.:Con Vn, BWV 1058, w. E. Wallfisch (vn) Virgin Classics ▲ CDC 45095
Bach, J.S.:Con Vn & Ob, w. E. Wallfisch (vn), A. Robson (ob) Virgin Classics ▲ CDC 45095
Bach, J.S.:Sinfs—BWV 12 & 21 Virgin Classics ▲ CD 45190
Haydn, J.:Sinf concertante Virgin Classics ▲ CDC 59266
B. Weil (cnd)
Schubert, Franz:Deutsche Messe, w. Vienna Boys' Choir *(rec Austria, May 16–19, 1993)* Sony Classical ▲ SK 53984 [DDD]
Schubert, Franz:Mass 1, w. Alexander Nader (sop), Thomas Puchegger (sop), Georg Leskovich (alto), Jörg Hering (ten), Kurt Azesberger (ten), Harry van der Kamp (bass), Arno Hartmann (org), Vienna Boys' Choir *(rec Vienna, Austria, Sept 1995)* Sony Classical ("Vivarte" series) ▲ SK 68247 [DDD]
Schubert, Franz:Mass 2, w. Thomas Puchegger (sop), Jörg Hering (ten), Harry van der Kamp (bass), Arno Hartmann (org), Vienna Boys' Choir *(rec Vienna, Austria, Sept 1995)* Sony Classical ("Vivarte" series) ▲ SK 68247 [DDD]
Schubert, Franz:Mass 3, w. Alexander Nader (sop), Thomas Puchegger (sop), Belá Fischer (alt), Georg Leskovich (alt), Jörg Hering (ten), Harry Van der Kamp (bass), Arno Hartmann (org), Chorus Viennensis, Vienna Boys' Choir Sony Classical ("Vivarte" series) ▲ SK 68248
Schubert, Franz:Mass 4, w. Alexander Nader (sop), Thomas Puchegger (sop), Belá Fischer (alt), Georg Leskovich (alt), Jörg Hering (ten), Harry Van der Kamp (bass), Arno Hartmann (org), Chorus Viennensis, Vienna Boys' Choir Sony Classical ("Vivarte" series) ▲ SK 68248
Schubert, Franz:Mass 5, w. Vienna Boys' Choir *(rec Austria, May 16–19, 1993)* Sony Classical ▲ SK 53984 [DDD]
Schubert, Franz:Mass 6, w. Benjamin Schmidinger (sop), Albin Lenzer (alt), Kurt Azesberger (ten), Jörg Hering (ten), Harry van der Kamp (bass), Vienna Boys' Choir Sony Classical ▲ SK 66255

Orch of the Age of Enlightenment members
Dove (cnd)
Glyndebourne Wind Serenades, w. London PO members EMI Classics ▲ CDC 54424

Orch of the Americas
P. Freeman (cnd)
Bernstein, L.:Candide (ov) *(rec 2 & 6/91)* Pro Arte/Fanfare ▲ CDS 3413 [DDD]
Copland, A.:Fanfare for the Common Man *(rec 2 & 6/91)* Pro Arte/Fanfare ▲ CDS 3413 [DDD]
Crockett, D.:Melting Voices *(rec 2 & 6/91)* Pro Arte/Fanfare ▲ CDS 3413
Forsyth, M.:ukuZALWA *(rec 2 & 6/91)* Pro Arte/Fanfare ▲ CDS 3413 [DDD]
Lieuwen, P.:Angelfire Pro Arte/Fanfare ▲ CDS 3413 [DDD]
Locklair, D.:Creation's Seeing Order Pro Arte/Fanfare ▲ CDS 3413 [DDD]
H. de la Fuente (cnd)
Ginastera, A.:Con Vn, w. Ruggiero Ricci (vn) One-Eleven ▲ EPR 94020
Ginastera, A.:Con Vn, w. R. Ricci (vn) One-Eleven ▲ URS 91020 [ADD]
Paganini, N.:Con 1 Vn, w. Ruggiero Ricci (vn) One-Eleven ▲ EPR 94020
Paganini, N.:Con 1 Vn, w. R. Ricci (vn) One-Eleven ▲ URS 91020 [ADD]

Orch of the 18th Century
F. Brüggen (cnd)
Bach, J.S.:Mass in b, BWV 232, w. J. Smith (sop), M. Chance (ct), N. van der Meel (ten), H. van der Kamp (bass), Netherlands Chamber Choir [L] *(rec live)* Philips ("Digital Classics" series) 2-▲ 426238-2 [DDD]
Bach, J.S.:St. John Passion, w. Netherlands Chamber Choir Philips ▲ 434905-2
Beethoven, L. van:Coriolan Ov Philips 5-▲ 442156-2
Beethoven, L. van:Coriolan Ov Philips ▲ 434087-2 [DDD]
Beethoven, L. van:Egmont (ov) Philips 5-▲ 442156-2
Beethoven, L. van:Egmont (ov) Philips ▲ 434087-2 [DDD]
Beethoven, L. van:Syms (comp), w. Lynne Dawson (sop), Jard Van Nes (cta), Anthony Rolfe Johnson (ten), Eike Wilm Schulte (bass), Lisbon Gulbenkian Foundation Chorus [on Sym. 9] Philips 5-▲ 442156-2
Beethoven, L. van:Sym 5 Philips ▲ 434087-2 [DDD]
Haydn, J.:Sym 98 Philips ▲ 434921-2
Haydn, J.:Sym 99 Philips ▲ 434077-2 [DDD]
Haydn, J.:Sym 100, "Military" Philips ▲ 434096-2 [DDD]
Haydn, J.:Sym 101, "Clock" Philips ▲ 422240-2 [DDD] □ 422240-5
Haydn, J.:Sym 102 Philips ▲ 434077-2 [DDD]
Haydn, J.:Sym 103, "Drum Roll" Philips ▲ 422240-2 [DDD] □ 422240-5
Haydn, J.:Sym 104, "London" Philips ▲ 434096-2 [DDD]
Mozart, W.A.:Con Cl, w. E. Hoeprich (b cl) Philips ▲ 420242-2 [DDD]
Schubert, Franz:Sym 9 Deutsche Grammophon ▲ 439006-2

Orch of the Golden Age
R. Glenton (cnd)
Purcell, H.:Odes & Welcome Songs (misc), w. Jeni Bern (sop), Susan Bisatt (sop), William Purefoy (ct), Christopher Robson (ct), Ian Honeyman (ten), Thomas Guthrie (bass), Golden Age Choir—The noise of foreign wars (fragment) [ed. by Bruce Wood] *(rec Manchester Grammar School, England, May 13 & 14, 1995)* Naxos ▲ 8.553444 [DDD]
Purcell, H.:Raise, Raise the Voice, w. Jeni Bern (sop), Susan Bisatt (sop), William Purefoy (ct), Christopher Robson (ct), Ian Honeyman (ten), Thomas Guthrie (bass), Golden Age Choir *(rec Manchester Grammar School, England, May 13 & 14, 1995)* Naxos ▲ 8.553444 [DDD]
Purcell, H.:Son Tpt, w. David Staff (tpt) *(rec Manchester Grammar School, England, May 13 & 14, 1995)* Naxos ▲ 8.553444 [DDD]
Purcell, H.:Te Deum & Jubilate, w. Jeni Bern (sop), Susan Bisatt (sop), William Purefoy (ct), Christopher Robson (ct), Ian Honeyman (ten), Thomas Guthrie (bass), David Staff (tpt), Golden Age Choir *(rec Manchester Grammar School, England, May 13 & 14, 1995)* Naxos ▲ 8.553444 [DDD]
Purcell, H.:Welcome to All the Pleasures, w. Jeni Bern (sop), Susan Bisatt (sop), William Purefoy (ct), Christopher Robson (ct), Ian Honeyman (ten), Thomas Guthrie (bass), Golden Age Choir *(rec Manchester Grammar School, England, May 13 & 14, 1995)* Naxos ▲ 8.553444 [DDD]

Orch of the 20th Century
A. Weisberg (cnd)
Wolpe, S.:Sym CRI ▲ CD 676 [ADD]

Orch 2001
Stiller, A.:Music of, w. James Freeman (pno), Maelström Percussion Ensemble—The Mouse Singer; A Periodic Table of the Elements; A Descent into the Maelstrom; Son a 3 Pulsatoribus, with Gargoyle; The Water is Wide, Daisy Bell MMC ▲ MMC 2014
J. Freeman (cnd)
Finko, D.:Con Va, w. Michael Strauss (va) *(rec Lang Concert Hall, Swarthmore College)* CRI ▲ CD 723 [DDD]
Levinson, G.:Black Magic/White Magic, w. C. Beavon (mez) CRI ▲ CD 642 [DDD]
Schwantner, J.:Distant Runes & Incantations, w. Charles Abramovic (pno) *(rec Lang Concert Hall, Swarthmore College)* CRI ▲ CD 723 [DDD]
Stiller, A.:A Periodic Table of the Elements MMC ▲ 2014
Whitman, T.:Aubade *(rec Lang Concert Hall, Swarthmore College)* CRI ▲ CD 723 [DDD]

Orch 2001 members
Stiller, A.:The Mouse Singer MMC ▲ 2014

Orch de Cadaques
E. Colomer (cnd)
Rodrigo, J.:Concierto de Aranjuez, w. P. de Lucia (gtr) Verve ▲ 314-510301-2

Orchestre de Chambre 13
J.-P. Lecaudey (cnd)
Barber, S.:Adagio Strs Pavane ▲ ADW 7361 [DDD]
Bartók, B.:Romanian Folk Dances Pno Pavane ▲ ADW 7361 [DDD]
Britten, B.:Simple Sym Pavane ▲ ADW 7361 [DDD]
Lekeu, G.:Adagio Pavane ▲ ADW 7361 [DDD]

Orchestre de la Cité
M. Piquemal (cnd)
Poulenc, F.:Gloria Sop, w. Danielle Borst (sop), Vittoria d'Ile Choir *(rec Paris, Oct 1992)* Naxos ▲ 8.553176 [DDD]
Poulenc, F.:Litanies à la vierge noire, w. Vittoria d'Ile Choir *(rec Paris, Oct 1992)* Naxos ▲ 8.553176 [DDD]
Poulenc, F.:Stabat mater, w. Danielle Borst (sop), Vittoria d'Ile Choir *(rec Paris, Oct 1992)* Naxos ▲ 8.553176 [DDD]

Orchestre de Paris
Fauré, G.:Pavane Orch, w. S. Armstrong (sop), D. Fischer-Dieskau (bar), Edinburgh Festival Chorus EMI Classics ▲ CDM 64634
Fauré, G.:Requiem, w. S. Armstrong (sop), D. Fischer-Dieskau (bar), Edinburgh Festival Chorus EMI Classics ▲ CDM 64634
D. Barenboim (cnd)
Berlioz, H.:Rêverie et caprice, w. Itzhak Perlman (vn) Deutsche Grammophon ("Digital Midprice" series) ▲ 445549-2
Berlioz, H.:Les Troyens (sels)—Royal Hunt & Storm; March of the Trojans *(rec Feb 27, 1967)* Sony Classical ▲ SBK 53255 ■ SBT 53255
Bizet, G.:L'Arlésienne (suites) EMI Classics ▲ CDM 64869
Bizet, G.:Carmen (suites) EMI Classics ▲ CDM 64869
Bizet, G.:Jeux d'enfants EMI Classics ▲ CDM 64869
Bizet, G.:La Jolie fille de Perth (suite) EMI Classics ▲ CDM 64869
Bizet, G.:Patrie EMI Classics ▲ 7CDM 64869
Boulez, P.:Notations 1–4 Orch Erato ▲ 2292-45493-2 [DDD]
Boulez, P.:Rituel Erato ▲ 2292-45493-2 [DDD]
Debussy, C.:Orchestral Music—Nocturnes; Images; Prélude à l'après-midi d'un Faune; La Damoiselle élue; Printemps; Le Martyre de Saint Sébastien; Trois ballades de François Villon [w. Barbar Hendricks (soprano), Jocelyne Taillon (mezzo-soprano), Dietrich Fischer-Dieskau (baritone)] Deutsche Grammophon 2-▲ 437934-2 [DDD/ADD]
Denisov, E.:Sym Erato ▲ 2292-45600-2-ZK [DDD]
Itzhak Perlman Greatest Hits, w. Itzhak Perlman (vn), New York PO [cnd:Zubin Mehta] Deutsche Grammophon ▲ 437737-2 GH
Lalo, E.:Sym espagnole, w. Itzhak Perlman (vn) Deutsche Grammophon ("Digital Midprice" series) ▲ 445549-2
Lalo, E.:Sym espagnole, w. I. Perlman (vn) Deutsche Grammophon ("3D Classics" series) ▲ 429977-2 [DDD]
Mahler, G.:Kindertotenlieder, w. W. Meier (mez) [G] Erato ▲ 2292-45417-2 ZK [DDD]
Mozart, W.A.:Requiem, w. K. Battle (sop), A. Murray (mez), D. Rendall (ten), M. Salminen (bass), Paris Opera Chorus [L] EMI Classics ▲ CDC 47342 [DDD]
Saint-Saëns, C.:Con 3 Vn, w. I. Perlman (vn) Deutsche Grammophon ("3-D Classics" series) ▲ 429977-2 [DDD]
Saint-Saëns, C.:Con 3 Vn, w. I. Perlman (vn) Deutsche Grammophon ("Digital Midprice" series) ▲ 445549-2
Saint-Saëns, C.:Con 3 Vn, w. I. Perlman (vn) Deutsche Grammophon ▲ 410526-2 [DDD]
Saint-Saëns, C.:Samson et Dalila, w. E. Obraztsova (mez), P. Domingo (ten), R. Bruson (bar), R. Lloyd (b-bar) Deutsche Grammophon 2-▲ 413297-2 [ADD]
Wagner, R.:Wesendonck Songs, w. W. Meier (mez) [G] Erato ▲ 2292-45417-2 ZK [DDD]
Wieniawski, H.:Con 2 Vn, w. I. Perlman (vn) Deutsche Grammophon ▲ 410526-2 [DDD]
Wolf, H.:Mörike-Lieder (sels), w. W. Meier (mez)—(3) In der Frühe; Denk'es, o Seelel; Wo find'ich Trost [G] Erato ▲ 2292-45417-2 ZK [DDD]
S. Baudo (cnd)
Saint-Saëns, C.:Cons Pno (comp), w. A. Ciccolini (pno) EMI Classics ("Studio" series) 2-▲ CDMB 69443 [ADD]
S. Bychkov (cnd)
Adagio, w. Mischa Maisky (vc) Deutsche Grammophon ▲ 435781-2 GH [DDD]
Berlioz, H.:Sym fantastique Philips ▲ 438939-2
Bizet, G.:L'Arlésienne (suites) *(rec Paris, May 22–23, 1993)* Philips ▲ 442128-2
Bizet, G.:Carmen (suites) *(rec Paris, May 22–23, 1993)* Philips ▲ 442128-2
Bizet, G.:Sym 1 Philips ▲ 432096-2 [DDD] □ 432096-5
Dutilleux, H.:Métaboles (5) Philips ▲ 438008-2
Dutilleux, H.:Sym 2, "Le Double" Philips ▲ 438008-2
Dutilleux, H.:Timbres, espace, mouvement avec interlude Philips ▲ 438008-2
Franck, C.:Sym in d Philips ▲ 432096-2 [DDD] □ 432096-5
Honegger, A.:Pacific 231 Philips ▲ 432993-2
Mascagni, P.:Cavalleria rusticana, w. J. Norman (sop), M. Senn (mez), R. Laghezza (mez), G. Giacomini (ten), D. Hvorostovsky (bar) Philips ▲ 432105-2 [DDD]
Milhaud, D.:Le Boeuf sur le toit Philips ▲ 432993-2
Poulenc, F.:Les Biches Philips ▲ 432993-2
Prokofiev, S.:Alexander Nevsky, w. M. Lipovšek (cta) Philips ▲ 434070-2
Prokofiev, S.:Cinderella (suites), w. M. Lipovšek (cta)—No. 1 Philips ▲ 434070-2
Ravel, M.:Boléro Philips ▲ 438209-2
Ravel, M.:Daphnis et Chloé (suite 2) Philips ▲ 438209-2
Ravel, M.:Pavane pour une infante défunte Philips ▲ 438209-2
Ravel, M.:Rapsodie espagnole Philips ▲ 438209-2
Ravel, M.:La Valse Philips ▲ 438209-2
Tchaikovsky, P.:Eugene Onegin, w. N. Focile (sop), I. Arkhipova (mez), S. Walker (mez), F. Egerton (ten), D. Hvorostovsky (bar) Philips 2-▲ 438235-2
P. Capolongo (cnd)
Villa-Lobos, H.:Bachiana brasileira 2 EMI Classics ▲ CDC 47357 [ADD]
Villa-Lobos, H.:Bachiana brasileira 5, w. Mady Mesplé (sop) [Port] EMI Classics ▲ CDC 47357 [ADD]
Villa-Lobos, H.:Bachiana brasileira 6 EMI Classics ▲ CDC 47357 [ADD]
Villa-Lobos, H.:Bachiana brasileira 9 EMI Classics ▲ CDC 47357 [ADD]
J. Conlon (cnd)
Puccini, G.:Madama Butterfly, w. Ying Huang (sop), Richard Troxell (ten)—Original Motion Picture Soundtrack based on the opera by Puccini Sony Classical ▲ S2K 69258

▲ = CD ♦ = Enhanced CD Δ = MD ■ = Cassette Tape □ = DCC

Orchestre de Paris (cont.)
J. Conlon (cnd) (cont.)
Puccini, G.:Madama Butterfly (sels), w. Ying Huang (sop—Cio-Cio-San), Constance Hauman (mez—Kate Pinkerton), Ning Liang (mez—Suzuki), Richard Troxell (ten—B. F. Pinkerton), Richard Cowan (sgr—Sharpless), Jing Ma Fan (sgr—Goro), Christopheren Nomura (sgr—Prince Yamadori)—Dovunque al Mondo; B. F. Pinkerton Giù; Bimba, Bimba, Non Piangere; Ah! Vien! Sei Mia!; Un Bel Dí; Ora a Noi; Petali d'Ogni Fior; Coro a Bocca Chiusa; Prelude; Io So Che Alle Sue Pene; Ah! Son Vil!; E Sia! A Lui Devo Obbedir; Butterfly! *(rec Olivier Messiaen Auditorium, Paris, 1996)* Sony Classical ▲ SK 61972 [DDD]
P. Dervaux (cnd)
Satie, E.:Les Aventures de Mercure, w. Paris Opera Chorus Virgin Classics 2-▲ CDZB 62877
Satie, E.:Geneviéve de Brabant, w. A. Guiot (sop), M. Mesplé (sop), D. Millet (sop), A. Esposito (sop), J.C. Benoit (bar), A. Ciccolini (pno), Paris Opera Chorus Virgin Classics 2-▲ CDZB 62877
Satie, E.:Socrate, w. A. Guiot (sop), M. Mesplé (sop), D. Millet (sop), A. Esposito (sop), J. C. Benoit (bar), Paris Opera Chorus Virgin Classics 2-▲ CDZB 62877
H. von Karajan (cnd)
Franck, C.:Sym in d EMI Classics ▲ CDM 64747
L. Maazel (cnd)
Bartók, B.:Con 2 Pno, w. Sviatoslav Richter (pno) EMI Classics ("Doublefforte" series) 2-▲ CDFB 68637
J. Martinon (cnd)
Chausson, E.:Poème Vn, w. I. Perlman (vn) EMI Classics ▲ CDC 47725
Ravel, M.:Orchestral Music—Boléro; Ma mère l'oye; Alborada del gracioso; Rapsodie espagnole; Ov de Féerie; La Valse; Le Tombeau de Couperin; Menuet antique; Pavane pour une infante défunte; Valses nobles et sentimentales EMI Classics ("Doublefforte" series) 2-▲ CDFB 68610
Ravel, M.:Tzigane, w. I. Perlman (vn) EMI Classics ▲ CDC 47725
Saint-Saëns, C.:Havanaise Vn, w. I. Perlman (vn) EMI Classics ▲ CDC 47725
Saint-Saëns, C.:Introduction & Rondo capriccioso, w. I. Perlman (vn) EMI Classics ▲ CDC 47725
S. Ozawa (cnd)
Stravinsky, I.:Pno Music, w. M. Béroff (pno) EMI Classics 2-▲ CDZB 67276
G. Prêtre (cnd)
Berlioz, H.:La Damnation de Faust, w. Janet Baker (mez), Nicolai Gedda (ten), Gabriel Bacquier (bar), Paris Opera Chorus EMI Classics 2-▲ CDFB 68583
Gounod, C.:Faust (sels), w. M. Freni (sop), P. Domingo (ten), T. Allen (bar), N. Ghiaurov (bass), Paris Opera Chorus EMI Classics ▲ ZDM 63090
Massenet, J.:Werther, w. V. De los Angeles (sop), M. Mesplé (sop), N. Gedda (ten), Paris Chorus [F] EMI Classics ("Studio" series) 2-▲ CDMB 63973
Puccini, G.:Tosca (sels), w. M. Callas (sop), R. Scotto (sop), C. Bergonzi (ten), A. Kraus (ten), T. Gobbi (bar) EMI Classics ▲ ZDM 63087
M. Rostropovich (cnd)
Tchaikovsky, P.:Iolanta, w. G. Vishnevskaya (sop), N. Gedda (ten), W. Groenroos (bar) Erato 2-▲ 45793-2
G. Solti (cnd)
Liszt, F.:Mephisto Waltz 1 Orch London ▲ 417513-2 [ADD]
Liszt, F.:Tasso—Lamento e Trionfo London ▲ 417513-2 [ADD]
Orchestre de Paris members
L. Bernstein (cnd)
Beethoven, L. van:Sym 9, "Choral Sym", w. Bavarian RSO members, Dresden State Orch members, Kirov Theatre Orch members, London SO members, New York PO members, Bavarian Radio Chorus, Berlin Radio Chorus, Dresden Philharmonie Children's Chorus [G] *(rec live, Schauspielhaus, East Berlin, 12/25/89)* Deutsche Grammophon ▲ 429861-2 [DDD] ■ 429861-4
Orchestre de Paris Soloists
K. Husa (cnd)
Husa, K.:Fants Orch Phoenix ▲ PHCD 128
Husa, K.:Fants Orch— Nocturne CRI ■ C 261
Husa, K.:Fants Orch Grenadilla ■ GSC 1054
Orchestre Révolutionnaire et Romantique
J. E. Gardiner (cnd)
Beethoven, L. van:Ah, perfido!, w. C. Margiono (sop), Monteverdi Choir London Archiv ▲ 435391-2 [DDD]
Beethoven, L. van:Con 5 Pno, "Emperor", w. Robert Levin (pno) Archiv ▲ 447771-2
Beethoven, L. van:Fant Pno, Op. 80, "Choral Fant", w. Robert Levin (pno), Monteverdi Choir London Archiv ▲ 447771-2
Beethoven, L. van:Mass, Op. 86, w. C. Margiono (sop), C. Robbin (mez), W. Kendall (ten), A. Miles (bass), Monteverdi Choir London [period instrs] Archiv ▲ 435391-2 [DDD]
Beethoven, L. van:Meeresstille und glückliche Fahrt, w. Monteverdi Choir London [period instrs] Archiv ▲ 435391-2 [DDD]
Beethoven, L. van:Syms (comp) Archiv ▲ 439900-2 [DDD]
Beethoven, L. van:Sym 3, "Eroica" Archiv ▲ 445944-2 [DDD]
Beethoven, L. van:Sym 5 Archiv ▲ 445944-2 [DDD]
Beethoven, L. van:Sym 9, "Choral Sym", w. Luba Orgonasova (sop), Anne Sofie von Otter (mez), Anthony Rolfe Johnson (ten), Gilles Cachemaille (b-bar) [period instrs] *(rec All Saints' Church, London, Oct 1992)* Archiv ▲ 447074-2 [DDD]
Berlioz, H.:Harold in Italy, w. Gérard Caussé (va) Philips ▲ 446676-2
Berlioz, H.:Messe solennelle Sop, w. Donna Brown (sop), Jean-Luc Viala (ten), Gilles Cachemaille (bar), Monteverdi Choir London Philips ▲ 442137-2 ■ 442137-4 □ 442137-5
Berlioz, H.:Sym fantastique Philips ▲ 434402-2 [DDD]
Berlioz, H.:Tristia, w. Monteverdi Choir London Philips ▲ 446676-2
Brahms, J.:Ein Deutsches Requiem, w. C. Margiono (sop), R. Gilfry (bar), Monteverdi Choir London [period instrs] Philips ▲ 432140-2 [DDD] □ 432140-5
Debussy, C.:Chansons (3) de Charles d'Orléans, w. Monteverdi Choir London Philips ▲ 438149-2
Fauré, G.:Les Djinns, w. Monteverdi Choir London Philips ▲ 438149-2
Fauré, G.:Madrigal, w. Monteverdi Choir London Philips ▲ 438149-2
Fauré, G.:Requiem, w. *(soloists unknown)*, Monteverdi Choir London Philips ▲ 438149-2
Ravel, M.:Chansons, w. Monteverdi Choir London Philips ▲ 438149-2
Verdi, G.:Requiem Mass, w. Donna Brown (sop), Luba Orgonasova (sop), Anne Sofie von Otter (mez), Luca Canonici (ten), Alastair Miles (bass), Monteverdi Choir London Philips 2-▲ 442142-2
Orchid Series Collection
Vol. 1, w. Orchid Series Collection Pickwick ("The Orchid" series) 3-▲ PICBOXMD 51
Vol. 2, w. Orchid Series Collection Pickwick ("The Orchid" series) 3-▲ PICBOXMD 52
Vol. 3, w. Orchid Series Collection Pickwick ("The Orchid" series) 3-▲ PICBOXMD 53
Vol. 4, w. Orchid Series Collection Pickwick ("The Orchid" series) 3-▲ PICBOXMD 54
Örebro CO
L. Hedwall (cnd)
Wirén, D.:Music for Str Orch Swedish Society ▲ SCD 1035
Wirén, D.:Serenade Strs Swedish Society ▲ SCD 1035
Wirén, D.:Sym 4 Swedish Society ▲ SCD 1035
T. Svedlund (cnd)
Söderlundh, L.B.:Allegro Concertante, w. Jeffrey Lee (vn), Kerstin Svensson (vn) Intim Musik ▲ INT 36
Söderlundh, L.B.:Christina-Music Intim Musik ▲ INT 36
Söderlundh, L.B.:Concertino Ob, w. Mûrtin Larsson (ob) Intim Musik ▲ INT 36
Söderlundh, L.B.:Folk Waltzes Intim Musik ▲ INT 36
Söderlundh, L.B.:Suite from Haväng, w. Mats Widlund (pno) Intim Musik ▲ INT 36
Örebro SO
G.W. Nilson (cnd)
Aulin, T.:Mäster Olaf *(rec 1987)* Sterling ▲ CDS 1011 [DDD]
Rangström, T.:Dithyramb *(rec 1987)* Sterling ▲ CDS 1011 [DDD]
Oregon Bach Festival CO
H. Rilling (cnd)
Bach, J.S.:Suite 1 Orch, w. C. Wincenc (fl) Hänssler Classic ▲ HAN 98984 [DDD]

Oregon Bach Festival CO (cont.)
H. Rilling (cnd) (cont.)
Bach, J.S.:Suite 3 Orch Hänssler Classic ▲ 98978 [DDD]
Oregon Bach Festival Orch
Dvořák, A.:Stabat Mater, w. Marina Shaguch (sop), Ingeborg Danz (alt), James Taylor (ten), Thomas Quasthoff (bass), Oregon Bach Festival Choir *(rec Silva Concert Hall, Hult Center for the Performing Arts, Eugene, Oregon, July 8-11, 1995)* Hänssler Classic ("Exclusive" series) 2-▲ CD 98.935 [DDD]
Oregon SO
J. DePreist (cnd)
Dello Joio, N.:Meditations on Ecclesiastes Koch International Classics ▲ KIC 7156-2 [DDD]
Flagello, N.:Passion of Martin Luther King, w. Raymond Bazemore (bass), Portland Symphonic Choir Koch International Classics ▲ KIC 7293-2 [DDD]
Lo Presti, R.:The Masks Koch International Classics ▲ KIC 7156-2 [DDD]
Lutoslawski, W.:Con Orch Delos ▲ DCD 3070 [DDD]
Menotti, G.C.:Apocalypse Koch International Classics ▲ KIC 7156-2 [DDD]
Rachmaninoff, S.:Études-tableaux, Opp. 33 & 39 [arr. Respighi]—Op. 39, No. 2 Delos ▲ DCD 3071 [DDD]
Rachmaninoff, S.:Sym 2 Delos ▲ DCD 3071 [DDD]
Rachmaninoff, S.:Vocalise Delos ▲ DCD 3071 [DDD]
Respighi, O.:Feste Romane Delos ▲ DCD 3070 [DDD]
Schwantner, J.:New Morning for the World, w. Raymond Bazemore (nar) Koch International Classics ▲ KIC 7293-2 [DDD]
Strauss, R.:Don Juan Delos ▲ DCD 3070 [DDD]
Tchaikovsky, P.:Ov 1812 Delos ▲ DCD 3081 [DDD]
Tchaikovsky, P.:The Tempest Delos ▲ DCD 3081 [DDD]
ORF SO
L. Gardelli (cnd)
Berlioz, H.:Roméo et Juliette, w. B. Fassbaender (mez), N. Gedda (ten), J. Shirley-Quirk (bar), Vienna State Opera Chorus [F] Orfeo 2-▲ 087842 [DDD]
Verdi, G.:La battaglia di Legnano, w. K. Ricciarelli (sop), J. Carreras (ten), M. Manuguerra (bar), N. Ghiuselev (bass), ORTF Choir Philips 2-▲ 422435-2 [ADD]
R. Giovanetti (cnd)
Thomas, A.:Hamlet, w. Alexandrina Pendachanska (sop), Viorica Cortez (mez), Boje Skovhus (bar), Arnold Schoenberg Choir *(rec live, 1994)* Serenissima 3-▲ SER 360147
L. Segerstam (cnd)
Segerstam, L.:Con 1 Pno, w. R. Keuschnig (pno) Kontrapunkt ▲ KPT 32184 [DDD]
Segerstam, L.:Con-Fant Vn, w. H. Segerstam (vn), R. Keuschnig (pno) Kontrapunkt ▲ KPT 32184 [DDD]
Segerstam, L.:Sym 1—No. 34 Kontrapunkt ▲ KPT 32184 [DDD]
C. Stanischeff (cnd)
Pelinka, W.:Sinfonietta with Chorale Vienna Modern Masters ▲ VMM 3028 [DDD]
P. Steinberg (cnd)
Berlioz, H.:Les Nuits d'été, w. Vesselina Kasarova (mez) *(rec Vienna Concert House, June 12-24, 1994)* RCA Red Seal ▲ 09026-68008-2 [DDD]
Chausson, E.:Poème de l'amour et de la mer, w. Vesselina Kasarova (mez) *(rec Vienna Concert House, June 12-24, 1994)* RCA Red Seal ▲ 09026-68008-2 [DDD]
Ravel, M.:Shéhérazade Mez, w. Vesselina Kasarova (mez) *(rec Vienna Concert House, June 12-24, 1994)* RCA Red Seal ▲ 09026-68008-2 [DDD]
Orfeo Trio [H. Tröndle (pno), S. Hewig-Tröscher (vn), B. Tluck (vc)]
Chopin, F.:Trio Pno Calig ▲ CAL 50880 [DDD]
Suder, J.:Qt Pno, w. E. Tluck (va) Calig ▲ CAL 50880 [DDD]
Orféon Donostiarra
R. Burgos (cnd)
Falla, M. de:La vida breve, w. V. de los Angeles (sop), F. Cossutta (mez), I. Rivadeneyra (mez), Spanish National Orch [Sp] EMI Classics ▲ CDM 69590 [ADD]
L. Foster (cnd)
Enescu, G.:Oedipe, w. B. Hendricks (sop), B. Fassbaender (mez), M. Lipovšek (mez), J. Taillon (mez), N. Gedda (ten), J. Aler (ten), G. Bacquier (bar), Quilico (bar), J. Van Dam (bass-bar), Monte Carlo PO, Petits Chanteurs de Monaco [F] EMI Classics 2-▲ CDCB 54011 [DDD]
M. Plasson (cnd)
Gounod, C.:Mors et vita, w. B. Hendricks (sop), N. Denize (mez), J. Aler (ten), J. Van Dam (b-bar), Toulouse Capitole Orch [F] *(rec 1/92)* EMI Classics 2-▲ CDCB 54459
Orff, C.:Carmina burana, w. Natalie Dessay (sop), Gérard Lesne (ct), Thomas Hampson (bar), Toulouse Capitole Orch, Midi-Pyrénées Children's Choir *(rec Halle-aux-Grains, Toulouse, Dec. 2, 4 & 6, 1994)* EMI Classics ▲ CDC 55392 [DDD]
Ropartz, G.:Sym 3, w. F. Pollet (sop), N. Stutzmann (cta), T. Dran (ten), F. Vassar (b-bar), Toulouse Capitole Orch EMI Classics ▲ CDM 64689-2
Orford String Quartet
Duets:Ofra Harnoy & Friends, w. Ofra Harnoy (vc), Michael Dussek (pno), Maureen Forrester (cta), Andrew Davis (pno), Jeanne Baxtresser (fl), Catherine Wilson (pno), Paul Brodie (sax), Shauna Rolston (vc), Armin Strings, Canadian Piano Trio, Adele Armin (vn) Mastersound ▲ MCT 30 [DDD]
An Evening with Ofra Harnoy, w. Harnoy, Ofra (vc) Pro Arte ▲ CDD 418 [DDD]
Ofra Harnoy & Friends, w. Harnoy, Ofra (vc), J. Baxtresser (fl), M. Forrester (cta), P. Brodie (sax), M. Dussek (pno), et al. Pro Arte ▲ CDD 552 [DDD]
Orford String Quartet [A. Dawes (vn), K. Perkins (vn), T. Helmer (va), D. Brott (vc)]
Beethoven, L. van:Qts Strs (comp)—Op. 18/2, Op. 130 Delos ▲ DCD 3032 [DDD]
Beethoven, L. van:Qts Strs (comp)—Op. 59/2, Op. 95 Delos ▲ DCD 3034 [DDD]
Beethoven, L. van:Qts Strs (comp)—Op. 18, No. 3 & Op. 131 Delos ▲ DE 3036 [DDD]
Beethoven, L. van:Qts Strs (comp)—Op. 59/3, Op. 74 Delos ▲ DCD 3035 [DDD]
Beethoven, L. van:Qts Strs (comp)—Op. 18/1, Op. 127 Delos ▲ DCD 3031 [DDD]
Beethoven, L. van:Qts Strs (comp)—Op. 18/5, Op. 59/1 Delos ▲ DCD 3033 [DDD]
Beethoven, L. van:Qt 3 Strs Delos ▲ DE 3036 [DDD]
Beethoven, L. van:Qt 14 Strs Delos ▲ DE 3036 [DDD]
Houdy, P.:Qnt Hp, w. J. Loman (hp) Centrediscs 2-▲ CMCCD 41/4292 [DDD]
Luedeke, R.:The Moon in the Labyrinth, w. J. Loman (hp) Centrediscs 2-▲ CMCCD 41/4292 [DDD]
Mozart, W.A.:Qt 14 Strs CBC ("SM 5000" series) 2-▲ SMCD 5040-2 [DDD]
Mozart, W.A.:Qt 15 Strs CBC ("SM 5000" series) 2-▲ SMCD 5040-2 [DDD]
Mozart, W.A.:Qt 17 Strs CBC ("SM 5000" series) 2-▲ SMCD 5040-2 [DDD]
Mozart, W.A.:Qt 19 Strs CBC ("SM 5000" series) 2-▲ SMCD 5040-2 [DDD]
Mozart, W.A.:Qnt Cl, K.581, w. J. Campbell (cl) CBC ("Musica Viva" series) ▲ MVCD 1032 [DDD]
Schafer, R.M.:The Crown of Ariadne, w. J. Loman (hp) Centrediscs 2-▲ CMCCD 41/4292 [DDD]
Schafer, R.M.:Theseus, w. J. Loman (hp) Centrediscs 2-▲ CMCCD 41/4292 [DDD]
Schubert, Franz:Qnt Strs, D.956, w. Ofra Harnoy (vc) Pro Arte ▲ CDD 418 [DDD]
Weber, C.M. von:Qnt Cl, w. J. Campbell (cl) CBC ("Musica Viva" series) ▲ MVCD 1032 [DDD]
Orford String Quartet members
Mozart, W.A.:Qts Pno, w. J. Coop (pno) Skylark ▲ 9002 CD [DDD]
Organum Ensemble
Musica Humana, w. Françoise Atlan (mez), John Fleagle (ten/hp), Crawford Young (lt), Anonymous 4, Ensemble Discantus, Ensemble Gilles Binchois, Gothic Voices, Greece Byzantine Choir, Hilliard Ensemble, Musica Nova, et al. L'Empreinte Digitale ▲ ED 13047
Palestrina, G.:Sacred Music, w. P. Herreweghe (cnd), Royal Chapel European Vocal Ensemble—Missa Viri Galilaei; Motet Viri Galilaei; Magnificat Primi Toni [L] Harmonia Mundi France ▲ HMC 901388
M. Pérès (cnd)
Ambrosian Chant at the Church of Milan Harmonia Mundi France ▲ HMC 901295
Campra, A.:Mass for Christmas Day, w. M. Pérès (org), Versailles Boys' Choir Harmonia Mundi France ▲ HMC 901480
Carmina Burana:The Passion Play Harmonia Mundi France ▲ HMC 901323/24
Chants de la Cathedrale de Benevento (7th-11th cents.) Harmonia Mundi ▲ HMC 901476
Chants de L'Église de Rome *(rec 6/91)* Harmonia Mundi ▲ HMC 901382

Organum Ensemble (cont.)
M. Pérès (cnd) (cont.)
Chants de L'Église Milanaise — Harmonia Mundi ▲ 901295
Cistercian Chant of the 12th Century — Harmonia Mundi ▲ HMC 901392
The Gradual of Eleanor of Brittany — Harmonia Mundi France ▲ HMC 901403
Josquin Desprez:Missa & Plainchant, "Pange lingua", w. Janequin Ensemble, Organum Ensemble [L] — Harmonia Mundi France ▲ HMC 901239
Laudario di Cortona — Harmonia Mundi France ▲ HMC 901582
Machaut, G. de:Messe Nostre Dame — Harmonia Mundi ▲ HMC 901590
Mass for Christmas Day — Harmonia Mundi ▲ HMA 1901148
Mass of St. Marcellus:Adoration of the Cross — Harmonia Mundi France ▲ HMC 901382
Mozarabic Chant — Harmonia Mundi France ▲ HMC 901519
The Notre Dame School (12th century) — Musique d'Abord ▲ HMA 1901148
Notre-Dame School:Mass for the Nativity of the Virgin — Harmonia Mundi France ▲ HMC 901538
Ockeghem, J.:Requiem, w. Les Pages de la Chapelle — Harmonia Mundi France ▲ HMC 901441
Old Roman Chant of the 7th-8th Centuries, Byzantine period — Harmonia Mundi ▲ 901218
Plain Chant:Cathedrale d'Auxerre, 18th Cent. — Harmonia Mundi France ▲ HMC 901319
Play of the Pilgrims to Emmaus — Harmonia Mundi France ▲ HMC 901347
Signature — Harmonia Mundi France ▲ HMX 290023 [DDD]
Tournai Mass — Suite ▲ HMT 7901353
12th Century Polyphony From Aquitiaine — Harmonia Mundi France ▲ HMC 901134

Oriol Ensemble
C. Grube (cnd)
Herzogenberg, H. von:Die Geburt Christi, w. R. Schudel (sop), A. Eggers (cta), P. Maus (ten), E. Schramm (bass), *(various choruses)* [G] — Hänssler Classic 2-▲ 98.574 [AAD]

Orion String Quartet
Mustonen, O.:Toccata, w. O. Mustonen (pno), E. Laine (db) — Finlandia ▲ 4509-95860-2 [DDD]

Orkest van het Oosten
G. Bellini (cnd)
Verdi, G.:Music of, w. Andrew Wise (cnd), National Reisopera Choir—Sinf [from I Vespri Siciliani]; Vedi! le fosche...Chi del gitano i giorni abbella; Or co' dadi...Squilli, echeggi la tromba guerriera [both from Il Trovatore]; Va pensiero, sull'ali dorate; Sinf [both from Nabucco]; Sinf [from La forza del destino]; O Signore, dal tetto natio [from I Lombardi alla prima crociata]; Patria oppressa [from Macbeth]; Si ridesti il Leon di Castiglia [from Ernani]; Sinf [from Aida] *(rec Enschede, Holland, June 18-21, 1990)* — Arts Music ▲ 447107-2 [DDD]

Orlando Consort
Philippe de Vitry & the Ars Nova:14th Century Motets — Amon Ra ▲ CDSAR 49 [DDD]
Vitry, P. de:Motets & Chansons — Amon Ra ▲ CD-SAR 49 [DDD]
Worcester Fragments:English Sacred Music of the Late Middle Ages, *(rec March 1992)* — Amon Ra ▲ CDSAR 59 [DDD]
D. Greig (cnd)
Dunstable, J.:Sacred Music, w. Robert Harre Jones (ct), Charles Daniels (ten), Angus Smith (ten)—Missa Rex Seculorum; Ave Maris Stella; Gloria in Canon; O Crux Gloriosa; Descendi in Ortum Meum; Speciosa Facta Es; Sub Tuam Portectionem; Veni Sancte Spiritus; Albanus Roseo Rutilat; Specialis Virgo; Preco Preheminencie; Salve Regina — Metronome ▲ 1009

Orlando Gibbons Viol Ensemble [Kaori Uemura (vl), Anne-Marie Lasla (bass vl), Sylvie Moquet (vl), Jérôme Hantaï (vl)]
Locke, M.:Consort of Fower Parts *(rec Temple de Fénin, Switzerland)* — Alphée 2-▲ 9506045 [DDD]
Locke, M.:Flatt Consort, 'for my cousin Kemble' *(rec Temple de Fénin, Switzerland)* — Alphée 2-▲ 9506045 [DDD]

Orlando String Quartet [A. Engegard (vn), H. Oberdorfer (vn), F. Erblich (va), S. Metz (vc)]
Dvořák, A.:Qt 12 Strs, "America" — Ottavo ▲ OTR C69028 [DDD]
Grieg, E.:Qt Strs, Op. 27 *(rec May 24-25, 1993)* — Emergo ▲ EC 3980 [DDD]
Haydn, J.:Qts Strs, Op. 64, "Tost Qts"—Nos. 4-6 — Emergo ▲ 3953 [DDD]
Mozart, W.A.:Adagio E Hn, w. H. Holliger (E hn) — Philips ▲ 412618-2 [DDD]
Mozart, W.A.:Divert Ob, K.251, w. H. Holliger (ob), H. Baumann (hn) — Philips ▲ 412618-2 [DDD]
Mozart, W.A.:Qt Ob, K.370, w. H. Holliger (ob) — Philips ▲ 412618-2 [DDD]
Mozart, W.A.:Qt 16 Strs — Emergo ▲ EC 3964
Mozart, W.A.:Qt 17 Strs — Emergo ▲ EC 3964
Mozart, W.A.:Qnts Strs, w. N. Imai (va)—K.516 & K.614 — BIS ▲ CD 432 [DDD]
Mozart, W.A.:Qnts Strs, w. N. Imai (va)—K.174 in B♭ & K.406 in c — BIS ▲ CD 433 [DDD]
Mozart, W.A.:Qnts Strs, w. N. Imai (va)—K.515 & K.593 — BIS ▲ CD 431 [DDD]
Schumann, R.:Qts Strs, Op. 41—No. 1 in a *(rec May 24-25, 1993)* — Emergo ▲ EC 3980 [DDD]
Smetana, B.:Qt 1 Strs — Ottavo ▲ OTR C69028 [DDD]

Orphée Piano & Wind Quintet [Yoshie Kaminaga (pno), Atsushi Ichinohe (fl), Yasuhiro Yamamoto (ob), Shuhei Isobe (cl), Yuichi Tomiinari (hn), Katsuhisa Ohtaki (bn)]
Fauré, G.:Pavane Orch [arr. Katsuhisa Ohtaki, 1992] *(rec Saitama, Japan, July 8-10, 1992)* — Arta ▲ 0061
Fauré, G.:Sicilienne [arr. Shuhei Isobe, 1992] *(rec Saitama, Japan, July 8-10, 1992)* — Arta ▲ 0061
Poulenc, F.:Aubade Pno [arr. Katsuhisa Ohtaki, 1990] *(rec Saitama, Japan, July 8-10, 1992)* — Arta ▲ 0061
Poulenc, F.:Sxt Pno *(rec Saitama, Japan, July 8-10, 1992)* — Arta ▲ 0061
Poulenc, F.:Suite française [arr. Katsuhisa Ohtaki, 1992] *(rec Saitama, Japan, July 8-10, 1992)* — Arta ▲ 0061
Roussel, A.:Divert *(rec Saitama, Japan, July 8-10, 1992)* — Arta ▲ 0061

Orphei Drängar
Söderman, A.:Choral Music, w. C.-H. Ahnsjö (ten), F. Alin (pno), Orphei Drängar [arr. Alfvén]—In the Gleam of the Moon — BIS ▲ CD 633 [DDD]
R. Sund (cnd)
Alfvén, H.:Choral Music, w. C.-H. Ahnsjö (ten), F. Alin (pno)—Hör I Orphei Drängar; Dawn at Sea; Papillon; Gustaf Frödings Funeral; Berceuse; Spring in Roslagen; Sweden's Flag; My Sweetheart; Serenade; Night; Evening; Lullaby; So Take My Heart; Quiet Hours; Scents of Summer; You Are Peaceful Calm; I Long for You; The Forest Sleeps; The Trial; Flowers of Joy; Värmlandsvisan; Oxberg March; Swedish Dance; Fatheads; Herdboy's Song; Andrew Was a Lively Lad; And the Maiden Joins the Ring; In Our Meadow; Mood [Sw] *(rec Feb 6-7 & Sept 4-5, 1993)* — BIS ▲ CD 633 [DDD]
Christmas Music — BIS ▲ CD 533 [DDD]

Orpheus Chamber Ensemble
Roman, J.H.:Cons (3) Vn, w. N.-E. Sparf (vn) — BIS ▲ CD 284 [DDD]
Roman, J.H.:Sinfs—Nos. 14 in D, 17 in F & 26 in A — BIS ▲ CD 284 [DDD]
K. Ek (cnd)
Olsson, O.:Te Deum, w. Täby Church Choir [L] — BIS ▲ CD 289 [DDD]

Orpheus CO
Bach, J.S.:Con 8 Hpd, w. D. Boyd (ob) — Deutsche Grammophon ▲ 429225-2 [DDD]
Bach, J.S.:Con Ob, BWV 1053, w. D. Boyd (ob) — Deutsche Grammophon ▲ 429225-2 [DDD]
Bach, J.S.:Con Ob d'amore, w. D. Boyd (ob) — Deutsche Grammophon ▲ 429225-2 [DDD]
Bartók, B.:Divert — Deutsche Grammophon ("Digital Midprice" series) ▲ 445541-2
Bartók, B.:Romanian Folk Dances Pno — Deutsche Grammophon ("Digital Midprice" series) ▲ 445541-2
Beethoven, L. van:Die Geschöpfe des Prometheus — Deutsche Grammophon ▲ 419608-2 [DDD]
Beethoven, L. van:Romances Vn, w. Gil Shaham (vn) *(rec Performing Arts Ctr, State Univ of NY, Purchase, NY, Dec 1995)* — Deutsche Grammophon ▲ 449923-2 [DDD]
Bizet, G.:Sym 1 — Deutsche Grammophon ▲ 423624-2 [DDD]
Boccherini, L.:Con Vc, G.479, w. Mischa Maisky (vc) — Deutsche Grammophon ▲ 447022-2
Boccherini, L.:Con Vc, G.480, w. Mischa Maisky (vc) — Deutsche Grammophon ▲ 447022-2
Boccherini, L.:Minuetto, w. Mischa Maisky (vc) — Deutsche Grammophon ▲ 447022-2
Bolcom, W.:Orphée-Sérénade — Deutsche Grammophon ▲ 435389-2 [DDD]
Britten, B.:Simple Sym — Deutsche Grammophon ▲ 423624-2 [DDD]
Classical Hits — Deustche Grammophon ▲ 437782-2
Copland, A.:Appalachian Spring — Deutsche Grammophon ▲ 427335-2 [DDD]
Copland, A.:Latin American Sketches — Deutsche Grammophon ▲ 427335-2 [DDD]
Copland, A.:Quiet City — Deutsche Grammophon ▲ 427335-2 [DDD]

Orpheus CO (cont.)
Copland, A.:Short Sym, "Sym 2" — Deutsche Grammophon ▲ 427335-2 [DDD]
Druckman, J.:Nor Spell Nor Charm — Deutsche Grammophon ▲ 435389-2 [DDD]
Dvořák, A.:Romance Vn, w. Gil Shaham (vn) *(rec Performing Arts Ctr, State Univ of NY, Purchase, NY, Dec 1995)* — Deutsche Grammophon ▲ 449923-2 [DDD]
Elgar, E.:Salut d'amour, w. Gil Shaham (vn) *(rec Performing Arts Ctr, State Univ of NY, Purchase, NY, Dec 1995)* — Deutsche Grammophon ▲ 449923-2 [DDD]
Gandolfi, M.:Points of Departure — Deutsche Grammophon ▲ 435389-2 [DDD]
Grieg, E.:Elegaic Melodies, Op. 34 — Deutsche Grammophon ▲ 423060-2 [DDD]
Grieg, E.:Holberg Suite — Deutsche Grammophon ▲ 423060-2 [DDD]
Gros, J.A.:Con Tpt, w. Wolfgang Basch (tpt) — Koch Schwann ▲ CD 311 071 [DDD]
Handel, G.F.:Concerti grossi, Op. 6 *(rec Performing Arts Ctr, State Univ of NY, Purchase, NY, Mar 1993, Mar & Dec 1994)* — Deutsche Grammophon 3-▲ 447733-2 [DDD]
Handel, G.F.:Royal Fireworks Music — Deutsche Grammophon ▲ 435390-2 [DDD]
Handel, G.F.:Water Music (comp) — Deutsche Grammophon ▲ 435390-2 [DDD]
Haydn, J.:Sym 22, "Der Philosoph" — Deutsche Grammophon ▲ 427337-2 [DDD]
Haydn, J.:Sym 53, "L'Impériale" — Deutsche Grammophon ▲ 439779-2
Haydn, J.:Sym 60, "Il Distratto" — Deutsche Grammophon ▲ 437783-2
Haydn, J.:Sym 63, "La Roxelane" — Deutsche Grammophon ▲ 427337-2 [DDD]
Haydn, J.:Sym 73, "La Chasse" — Deutsche Grammophon ▲ 439779-2
Haydn, J.:Sym 79 — Deutsche Grammophon ▲ 439779-2
Haydn, J.:Sym 80 — Deutsche Grammophon ▲ 427337-2 [DDD]
Haydn, J.:Sym 91 — Deutsche Grammophon ▲ 437783-2
Hertel, J.W.:Con Tpt, w. W. Basch (tpt) — Koch Schwann ▲ CD 311071 [DDD]
Hummel, J.N.:Con in E♭ Tpt, S.49, w. W. Basch (tpt) — Koch Schwann ▲ CD 311071 [DDD]
Ives, C.:Set 1 — Deutsche Grammophon ▲ 439869-2
Ives, C.:Sym 3 — Deutsche Grammophon ▲ 439869-2
Ives, C.:Three Places in New England — Deutsche Grammophon ▲ 439869-2
Ives, C.:The Unanswered Question — Deutsche Grammophon ▲ 439869-2
Kodály, Z.:Hungarian Rondo *(rec Performing Arts Center, State Univ of NY at Purchase, Dec 1994)* — Deutsche Grammophon ▲ 447109-2 [DDD]
Kodály, Z.:Summer Evening *(rec Performing Arts Center, State Univ of NY at Purchase, Dec 1994)* — Deutsche Grammophon ▲ 447109-2 [DDD]
Kreisler, F.:Vn Pieces, w. Gil Shaham (vn)—Schön Rosmarin; Liebesfreud; Liebesleid [all orchd Clark McAlister] *(rec Performing Arts Ctr, State Univ of NY, Purchase, NY, Dec 1995)* — Deutsche Grammophon ▲ 449923-2 [DDD]
Lerdahl, F.:Waves — Deutsche Grammophon ▲ 435389-2 [DDD]
Mad About Angels, w. Cheryl Studer (sop), Christa Ludwig (mez), Anne Sofie von Otter (mez), José Carreras (ten), New York PO [cnd:Leonard Bernstein], English Baroque Soloists [cnd:John Eliot Gardiner], Philharmonia Orch, Philharmonia Chorus [cnd:Carlo Maria Giulini] — Deutsche Grammophon ▲ 449113-2 ■ 449113-4
Mendelssohn, F.:Con in d Vn & Strs, w. G. Kremer (vn) — Deutsche Grammophon ▲ 427338-2 [DDD]
Mendelssohn, F.:Con in d Vn, Pno & Strs, w. G. Kremer (vn), M. Argerich (pno) — Deutsche Grammophon ▲ 427338-2 [DDD]
Mendelssohn, F.:Sinf 8 — Deutsche Grammophon ▲ 437528-2
Mendelssohn, F.:Sinf 9 — Deutsche Grammophon ▲ 437528-2
Mendelssohn, F.:Sinf 10 — Deutsche Grammophon ▲ 437528-2
Mozart, W.A.:Andante Fl, K.315/285a, w. S. Palma (fl) — Deutsche Grammophon ▲ 427677-2 [DDD]
Mozart, W.A.:Con Bn, w. F. Morelli (bn) — Deutsche Grammophon ▲ 423623-2 [DDD]
Mozart, W.A.:Con Bn, w. F. Morelli (bn) — Deutsche Grammophon 3-▲ 431665-2 [DDD]
Mozart, W.A.:Con Cl, w. C. Neidich (cl) — Deutsche Grammophon 3-▲ 431665-2 [DDD]
Mozart, W.A.:Con Cl, w. C. Neidich (cl) — Deutsche Grammophon ▲ 423377-2 [DDD] ▯ 423377-5
Mozart, W.A.:Cons Fl, w. S. Palma (fl) — Deutsche Grammophon 3-▲ 431665-2 [DDD]
Mozart, W.A.:Cons Fl, w. S. Palma (fl) — Deutsche Grammophon ▲ 427677-2 [DDD]
Mozart, W.A.:Con Fl Hp, w. S. Palma (fl), N. Allen (hp) — Deutsche Grammophon 3-▲ 431665-2 [DDD]
Mozart, W.A.:Con Fl Hp, w. S. Palma (fl), N. Allen (hp) — Deutsche Grammophon ▲ 427677-2 [DDD]
Mozart, W.A.:Cons Hn, w. D. Jolley (hn) — Deutsche Grammophon 3-▲ 431665-2 [DDD]
Mozart, W.A.:Con Hn, K.412, w. D. Jolley (hn) — Deutsche Grammophon ▲ 423377-2 [DDD] ▯ 423377-5
Mozart, W.A.:Con Hn, K.417, w. W. Purvis (hn) — Deutsche Grammophon ▲ 423623-2 [DDD]
Mozart, W.A.:Con Hn, K.447, w. W. Purvis (hn) — Deutsche Grammophon ▲ 423623-2 [DDD]
Mozart, W.A.:Con Hn, K.495, w. D. Jolley (hn) — Deutsche Grammophon ▲ 423377-2 [DDD] ▯ 423377-5
Mozart, W.A.:Con Ob, K.314, w. R. Wolfgang (ob) — Deutsche Grammophon 3-▲ 431665-2 [DDD]
Mozart, W.A.:Con Ob, K.314, w. R. Wolfgang (ob) — Deutsche Grammophon ▲ 423623-2 [DDD]
Mozart, W.A.:Con 17 Pno, w. Richard Goode (pno) — Elektra/Nonesuch ▲ 79042-2 [DDD]
Mozart, W.A.:Con 23 Pno, w. Richard Goode (pno) — Elektra/Nonesuch ▲ 79042-2 [DDD]
Mozart, W.A.:Serenade Ww, K.375 — Deutsche Grammophon ▲ 431683-2 [DDD]
Mozart, W.A.:Serenade Ww, K.388 — Deutsche Grammophon ▲ 431683-2 [DDD]
Mozart, W.A.:Sinf concertante Ob, K.Anh.9 — Deutsche Grammophon 3-▲ 431665-2 [DDD]
Mozart, W.A.:Sinf concertante Ob, K.Anh.9 — Deutsche Grammophon ▲ 429784-2 [DDD]
Mozart, W.A.:Sinf concertante Vn, K.364 — Deutsche Grammophon ▲ 429784-2 [DDD]
Orpheus CO — Deutsche Grammophon ▲ 431680-2 GH [DDD]
Orpheus Chamber Orchestra — Deutsche Grammophon ▲ 429390-2 GH [DDD]
Prokofiev, S.:Sym 1 — Deutsche Grammophon ▲ 423624-2 [DDD]
Rodrigo, J.:Concierto de Aranjuez, w. G. Söllscher (gtr) — Deutsche Grammophon ▲ 429232-2 [DDD] ▯ 429232-5
Rodrigo, J.:Fant para un gentilhombre, w. G. Söllscher (gtr) — Deutsche Grammophon ▲ 429232-2 [DDD] ▯ 429232-5
Rossini, G.:Intro, Theme & Vars Cl, w. Charles Neidich (cl) — Deutsche Grammophon ("Masters" series) ▲ 445569-2
Rossini, G.:Intro, Theme & Vars Cl, w. C. Neidich (cl) — Deutsche Grammophon ▲ 435875-2
Rossini, G.:Ovs — Deutsche Grammophon ("Masters" series) ▲ 445569-2
Sarasate, P. de:Spanish Dances, w. Gil Shaham (vn)—Romanza Andaluza, Op. 22/1 [orchd Otto Hohn] *(rec Performing Arts Ctr, State Univ of NY, Purchase, NY, Dec 1995)* — Deutsche Grammophon ▲ 449923-2 [DDD]
Schoenberg, A.:Chamber Sym 1 — Deutsche Grammophon ▲ 429233-2 [DDD]
Schoenberg, A.:Chamber Sym 2 — Deutsche Grammophon ▲ 429233-2 [DDD]
Schoenberg, A.:Verklärte Nacht — Deutsche Grammophon ▲ 429233-2 [DDD]
Sibelius, J.:Valse triste — Deutsche Grammophon ▲ 431680-2 [DDD]
Strauss, R.:Der Bürger als Edelmann (suite) — Deutsche Grammophon ▲ 435871-2
Strauss, R.:Divert — Deutsche Grammophon ▲ 435871-2
Stravinsky, I.:Con CO — Deutsche Grammophon ("Digital Midprice" series) ▲ 445541-2
Stravinsky, I.:Pulcinella Suite — Deutsche Grammophon ("Digital Midprice" series) ▲ 445541-2
Suk, J.:Serenade Strs *(rec Performing Arts Center, State Univ of NY at Purchase, Dec 1994)* — Deutsche Grammophon ▲ 447109-2 [DDD]
Tchaikovsky, P.:Serenade — Deutsche Grammophon ▲ 423060-2 [DDD]
Tchaikovsky, P.:Sérénade mélancolique, w. Gil Shaham (vn) *(rec Performing Arts Ctr, State Univ of NY, Purchase, NY, Dec 1995)* — Deutsche Grammophon ▲ 449923-2 [DDD]
Turina, J.:La oracion del torero — Deutsche Grammophon ▲ 431680-2 [DDD]
Villa-Lobos, H.:Con Gtr, w. G. Söllscher (gtr) — Deutsche Grammophon ▲ 429232-2 [DDD]
Vivaldi, A.:Cons Vc, w. Mischa Maisky (vc)—Cons RV. 401, 418, 422 [Largo] & 424 — Deutsche Grammophon ▲ 447022-2
Vivaldi, A.:Cons Fl, Op. 10, w. P. Gallois (fl) — Deutsche Grammophon ▲ 437839-2
Vivaldi, A.:Cons Vn, Op. 8/1-4, "The Four Seasons", w. Gil Shaham (vn) — Deutsche Grammophon ▲ 439933-2 ■ 439933-4
Wagner, R.:Siegfried Idyll — Deutsche Grammophon ▲ 431680-2 [DDD]
Weber, C.M. von:Concertino Cl, w. C. Neidich (cl) — Deutsche Grammophon ▲ 435875-2
Weber, C.M. von:Con 1 Cl, w. C. Neidich (cl) — Deutsche Grammophon ▲ 435875-2

▲ = CD ♦ = Enhanced CD Δ = MD ■ = Cassette Tape ▯ = DCC

Orpheus CO (cont.)
Weber, C.M. von:Con 2 Cl, w. C. Neidich (cl) Deutsche Grammophon ▲ 435875–2
Wolf, H.:Italian Serenade Deutsche Grammophon ▲ 431680–2 [DDD]

Orpheus String Quartet [Charles-André Linale (vn), Emilian Piedicuta (vn), Emile Cantor (va), Laurentiu Sbarcea (vc)]
Bartók, B.:Qt 1 Strs Channel Classics ▲ CCS 8895
Bartók, B.:Qt 3 Strs Channel Classics ▲ CCS 8895
Bartók, B.:Qt 4 Strs Channel Classics ▲ CCS 8895
Beethoven, L. van:Qt 3 Strs Channel Classics ▲ CCS 6094
Beethoven, L. van:Qt 7 Strs Channel Classics ▲ CCS 6094
Debussy, C.:Qt Strs *(rec 1/92)* Channel Classics ▲ CCS 3892 [DDD]
Dutilleux, H.:Ainsi la nuit *(rec 1/92)* Channel Classics ▲ CCS 3892 [DDD]
Ravel, M.:Qt Strs Channel Classics ▲ CCS 3892 [DDD]
Schäfer, D.:Qnt Pno, w. Jacob Bogaart (pno) NM Classics ▲ NM 92046
Schlegel, L.:Qt Pno, w. John Bingham (pno) NM Classics ▲ NM 92046

Orquesta Nova
Piazzolla, A.:La muerte del angel Chesky ▲ JD54 [DDD]
C. Franzetti (cnd)
Orquesta Nova Chesky ▲ JD54 [DDD]

Orquesta Sinfonietta
L. Rooth (cnd)
Operatic Arias, w. Salinas, Isaac (sgr) Montilla ▲ MNT 3038

Orquestra Clássica do Porto
M. Minsky (cnd)
Bomtempo, J.D.:Sinf in E♭ Koch Schwann ▲ SCH 315112
Braga Santos, J.:Con Strs Koch Schwann ▲ SCH 315102
Braga Santos, J.:Divert CO Koch Schwann ▲ SCH 315102
Braga Santos, J.:Elegia a viana da mota Koch Schwann ▲ SCH 315102
Braga Santos, J.:Sinfonietta Koch Schwann ▲ SCH 315102
Braga Santos, J.:Staccato brillante Koch Schwann ▲ SCH 315102
Carvalho, J. de S.:L'Amore industrioso (sels) Koch Schwann ▲ SCH 315112
Carvalho, J. de S.:Te Deum a due cori Koch Schwann ▲ SCH 315112
Moreira, A.L.:Sinf in D Koch Schwann ▲ SCH 315112
Portugal, M.A.:La Morte di Semiramide (sels) Koch Schwann ▲ SCH 315112

ORTF Lyric Orch
Hervé:Le Joueur de flûte Musidisc ▲ MUS 202212 [AAD]
Hervé:Le Retour d'Ulysse Musidisc ▲ MUS 202212 [AAD]
Hervé:Trombolino Musidisc ▲ MUS 202212 [AAD]
E. Bigot (cnd)
Adam, A.:Le toréador, ou l'accord parfait, w. Mady Mesplé (sop), Raymond Amade (ten), Charles Clavensy (b-bar) Musidisc ▲ MUS 201672 [AAD]
J. Brebion (cnd)
Boieldieu, F.-A.:Les Voitures versées Musidisc ▲ MUS 201522 [AAD]
Hahn, R.:O mon del inconnul, w. Christiane Château (sop), Lina Dachary (sop), Monique Stiot (mez), Michel Hamel (ten), Joseph Peyron (ten), Aimé Doniat (bar), Dominique Tirmont (bar), Philippe Gaudin (sgr), Jacques Provins (sgr) Musidisc 2-▲ MUS 202562 [AAD]
M. Cariven (cnd)
Audran, E.:Le grand mogol, w. ORTF Lyric Chorale Musidisc 2-▲ MUS 201702 [AAD]
Audran, E.:Miss Helyett, w. ORTF Lyric Chorale Musidisc 2-▲ MUS 202402 [AAD]
Bernicat, F.:François les bas-bleus, w. ORTF Lyric Chorale Musidisc 2-▲ MUS 202092 [AAD]
Lecocq, C.:Giroflé-Girofla, w. ORTF Lyric Chorale Musidisc 2-▲ MUS 201842 [AAD]
Messager, A.:Coups de roulis, w. ORTF Lyric Chorale Musidisc 2-▲ MUS 202382 [AAD]
Planquette, R.:Rip van Winkle, w. Claudine Collart (sop), Lina Dachary (sop), Freda Betti (cta), René Lenoty (ten), Joseph Peyron (ten), Charles Daguerressar (bar), Julien Giovannetti (bar), Jacques Pruvost (bar), Lucien Lovano (bass), Patrick Orladey (sgr), Joëlle Pierre (sgr), ORTF Lyric Chorale Musidisc ▲ MUS 201602 [AAD]
Terrasse, C.:Les Travaux d'Hercule, w. ORTF Lyric Chorale Musidisc 2-▲ MUS 201792 [AAD]
J. Doussard (cnd)
Lecocq, C.:Le Barbier de Trouville Musidisc ▲ MUS 201842 [AAD]
Lecocq, C.:Le Myosotis Musidisc ▲ MUS 201842 [AAD]
Lecocq, C.:Le Testament de Monsieur de Crac Musidisc ▲ MUS 201842 [AAD]
Offenbach, J.:Barbe-bleue, w. Henri Legay (ten), René Lenoty (ten), Aimé Doniat (bar), Rene Terrasson (sgr), ORTF Lyric Chorale *(rec 1967)* Memories 2-▲ MEM 4591 [ADD]
Terrasse, C.:La Fiancée du scaphandrier Musidisc 2-▲ MUS 201792 [AAD]
L. Fourestier (cnd)
Boieldieu, F.-A.:Le Calife de Bagdad, w. Christiane Eda-Pierre (sop), Jane Berbié (mez), Jeannine Collard (mez), Jean Giraudeau (ten), Jean-Paul Vaquelin (sgr), ORTF Lyric Chorale Musidisc ▲ MUS 201852 [AAD]
J. Fournet (cnd)
Inghelbrecht, D.-E.:Requiem, w. Christiane Ede-Pierre (sop), Bernard Kruyssen (bar), ORTF Choirs Studio SM ("Andre Charlin Collection" series) ▲ 2522
Inghelbrecht, D.-E.:Vézelay, w. Christiane Ede-Pierre (sop), Bernard Kruyssen (bar), ORTF Choir Studio SM ("Andre Charlin Collection" series) ▲ 2522
A. Girard (cnd)
Delibes, L.:L'Omelette à la Follembuche, w. *(unknown radio chorus)* Musidisc 2-▲ MUS 202392 [AAD]
Delibes, L.:Le Serpent à plumes, w. *(unknown radio chorus)* Musidisc 2-▲ MUS 202392 [AAD]
J. Gressier (cnd)
Ganne, L.:Hans, le joueur de flûte, w. ORTF Choirs Musidisc 2-▲ MUS 201512 [AAD]
M. Hamel (cnd)
Lecocq, C.:Le Coeur et la main, w. ORTF Lyric Chorale Musidisc 2-▲ MUS 201962 [AAD]
J.-C. Hartemann (cnd)
Gounod, C.:Le Médecin malgré lui, w. Lina Dachary (sop), Monique Stiot (mez), Michel Hamel (ten), Joseph Peyron (ten), Christophe Benoit (bar), Janine Capderou (sgr), Jean-Louis Soumagnas (sgr) Musidisc ▲ MUS 202322 [AAD]
Offenbach, J.:Le Chanson de Fortunio, w. ORTF Lyric Chorale Musidisc 2-▲ MUS 201382 [AAD]
Offenbach, J.:Madame l'archiduc, w. ORTF Lyric Chorale Musidisc 2-▲ MUS 201382 [AAD]
J.-P. Kreder (cnd)
Boieldieu, F.-A.:Jean de Paris, w. Madrigal Ensemble Musidisc ▲ MUS 201782 [AAD]
J.-M. Leconte (cnd)
Poise, F.:Les Absents Musidisc ▲ MUS 202102 [AAD]
Poise, F.:Joli Gilles Musidisc ▲ MUS 202102 [AAD]
J.-P. Marty (cnd)
Hérold, F.:Le Muletier Musidisc 2-▲ MUS 202012 [AAD]
N. Santi (cnd)
Donizetti, G.:Maria Stuarda, w. M. Caballé (sop—Maria Stuarda), R. Bezinian (mez—Anna), M. V. Menendez (mez—Elisabetta), J. Carreras (ten—Roberto), M. Mazzieri (bass—Giorgio Talbot), E. Serra (bass—Lord Gugliemo Cecil), ORTF Lyric Chorale [I] *(rec live 3/26/72)* Memories 2-▲ HR4417/18 [ADD]
Donizetti, G.:Maria Stuarda (sels), w. José Carreras (ten), Maurizio Mazzieri (bass)—Ah, rimiro il bel sembiante *(rec Paris, Mar 26, 1972)* Goldies ▲ GLD 63203 [ADD]
A. Sibert (cnd)
Hellmesberger, J.P.:Scène de bal Studio SM ▲ 12 22 62
Lehár, F.:Fantaisie sur Paganini Studio SM ▲ 12 22 62
Lehár, F.:Le Pays du sourire Studio SM ▲ 12 22 62
Strauss (I), Joh.:Music of—La Chauvre Souris; Train de plaisir; Legende de la Foret; Viennoise; Perpetuum Mobile; Valse de L'Empereur; Tik Tak Studio SM ▲ 12 22 62
Strauss (I), Joh.:Radetzky March Studio SM ▲ 12 22 62

ORTF Lyric Orch (cont.)
A. Wolff (cnd)
Adam, A.:Le Chalet, w. Denise Boursin (sop), Joseph Peyron (ten), Stanislas Staskiewicz (sgr) Musidisc ▲ MUS 201942 [AAD]
Adam, A.:Le Farfadet, w. Denise Boursin (sop), Joseph Peyron (ten), Stanislas Staskiewicz (sgr) Musidisc ▲ MUS 201942 [AAD]

ORTF National Orch
S. Celibidache (cnd)
Brahms, J.:Tragic Ov *(rec Oct. 1974)* Exclusive ▲ EXL 52 [ADD]
Dvořák, A.:Con Vc, w. Pierre Fournier (vc) *(rec live, Paris, 1974)* Arkadia ▲ 615
Ravel, M.:Alborada del gracioso *(rec live, 1974)* Enterprise ("Documents" series) 2-▲ LV 946/47 (m/s) [ADD]
Ravel, M.:Alborada del gracioso *(rec 1974)* Exclusive 2-▲ EXL 61 [ADD]
Ravel, M.:Daphnis et Chloé (suite 2), w. ORTF Choir *(rec live, 1974)* Enterprise ("Documents" series) 2-▲ LV 946/47 (m/s) [ADD]
Ravel, M.:Daphnis et Chloé (suite 2) *(rec 1974)* Exclusive 2-▲ EXL 61 [ADD]
Ravel, M.:Le Tombeau de Couperin *(rec live, 1974)* Enterprise ("Documents" series) 2-▲ LV 946/47 (m/s) [ADD]
Ravel, M.:La Valse *(rec 1974)* Exclusive 2-▲ EXL 61 [ADD]
Respighi, O.:The Pines of Rome *(rec Paris, Dec. 13, 1974)* Arkadia ▲ 487 [ADD]
J.-L. LeRoux (cnd)
Ravel, M.:Alborada del gracioso *(rec 1966)* FNAC Music ▲ 642318
Ravel, M.:Boléro *(rec 1966)* FNAC Music ▲ 642318
J. Martinon (cnd)
Saint-Saëns, C.:Syms (comp), w. Bernard Gavoty (org) EMI Classics ("Studio" series) 2-▲ CDMB 62643 [ADD]
Saint-Saëns, C.:Sym 3, w. B. Gavoty (org) EMI Classics ("Studio" series) 2-▲ CDMB 62643 [ADD]
C. Munch (cnd)
Bizet, G.:Jeux d'enfants Adès ▲ ADE 203072 [DDD]
Bizet, G.:Patrie Adès ▲ ADE 203072 [DDD]
Bizet, G.:Sym 1 Adès ▲ ADE 203072 [DDD]
Rimsky-Korsakov, N.:Golden Cockerel (sels) FNAC Music ("Via Classics" series) ▲ 642330

ORTF Orch
L. Maazel (cnd)
Mozart, W.A.:Con 9 Pno, w. S. Richter (pno) *(rec 1965)* Historical Performers ▲ HPS 7 [ADD]
J. Martinon (cnd)
Bizet, G.:Jeux d'enfants Deutsche Grammophon ("Double" series) 2-▲ 437371-2
Bizet, G.:La Jolie fille de Perth (suite) Deutsche Grammophon ("Double" series) 2-▲ 437371-2
Bizet, G.:Sym 1 Deutsche Grammophon ("Double" series) 2-▲ 437371-2
Lalo, E.:Namouna Deutsche Grammophon ("Double" series) 2-▲ 437371-2
Lalo, E.:Rapsodie norvégienne Deutsche Grammophon ("Double" series) 2-▲ 437371-2
G.-F. Masini (cnd)
Donizetti, G.:Caterina Cornaro, w. Montserrat Caballé (sop), Giacomo Aragall (ten), Gwynne Howell (bass), Ryan Edwards (sgr) *(rec Paris, Nov 25, 1973)* Agorá Music ("Phoenix" series) 2-▲ 505

ORTF PO
C. Bruck (cnd)
Brahms, J.:Con Vn, w. D. Oistrakh (vn) *(rec May 30, 1967)* Memoire Vive ▲ 262007 [ADD]

ORTF String Quartet
Tournemire, C.:Musique orante *(rec Dec. 19, 1972)* Memoire Vive ▲ 262006 [ADD]

ORTF SO
S. Celibidache (cnd)
Brahms, J.:Sym 3 *(rec 1974)* Legend ▲ LGD 109 [ADD]
M. Janowski (cnd)
Poulenc, F.:Con for 2 Pnos, w. Güher Pekinel (pno), Süher Pekinel (pno) Teldec ("M Line" series) ▲ 97445-2
Saint-Saëns, C.:Carnival of the Animals, w. G. Pekinel (pno), S. Pekinel (pno) Teldec ("M Line" series) ▲ 97445-2

Orthodox Ensemble
V. Klochkov (cnd)
Byzantine Chant Jade ▲ JAD C 060

Osaka PO
T. Asahina (cnd)
Bruckner, A.:Sym 1 *(rec Osaka Phil Hall, May 15-17, 1994)* Canyon Classics ▲ 246
Mahler, G.:Lied von der Erde, w. Naoko Ihara (alt), Makoto Hayashi (ten) *(rec Symphony Hall, Osaka, Nov 11, 1995)* Canyon Classics ▲ 326
Mahler, G.:Sym 2, w. Junko Ioka (sop), Setsuko Takemoto (mez), Hakaru Matsuoka (cnd), Yutaka Tomizawa (cnd), Musashino Chorus *(rec Suntory Hall, Tokyo, July 23, 1995)* Canyon Classics 2-▲ 335

Osiris Trio
Beethoven, L. van:Trio 1 Pno Canal Grande ▲ CG 9218 [DDD]
Novák, V.:Trio Vn Canal Grande ▲ CG 9218 [DDD]
Shostakovich, D.:Trio 2 Pno Canal Grande ▲ CG 9218 [DDD]

Oskarshamn Ensemble
J.-O. Wedin (cnd)
Bottesini, G.:Con 2 Db, w. Thorvald Fredin (db) Opus 3 ▲ OP 8502
Bottesini, G.:Elegy & Tarantella, w. Thorvald Fredin (db)—Elegy Opus 3 ▲ OP 8502
Koch, E. von:Serenade Db, w. Thorvald Fredin (db) Opus 3 ▲ OP 8502
Larsson, L.-E.:Concertinos, w. Thorvald Fredin (db)—Concertino for Db Opus 3 ▲ OP 8502

Oslo PO
K. Andersen (cnd)
Thommessen, O.A.:Through a Prism, w. Truls Mörk (vc), Kåre Nordstoga (org) Caprice ▲ CAP 21403
A. Antonini (cnd)
Dello Joio, N.:Meditations on Ecclesiastes CRI ■ ACS 6012
Moore, D.:Cotillion CRI ("American Masters" series) ▲ CD 714 [ADD]
Moore, D.:Farm Journal CRI ("American Masters" series) ▲ CD 714 [ADD]
Riegger, W.:Dance Rhythms CRI ▲ CD 572 [ADD]
Riegger, W.:Music for Orch CRI ▲ CD 572 [ADD]
G. Barati (cnd)
Binkerd, G.:Sym 2 CRI ■ C 139
Kay, U.:Sinf in E CRI ■ C 139
P. Berglund (cnd)
Rachmaninoff, S.:Con 3 Pno, w. Leif Ove Andsnes (pno) Virgin Classics ▲ CDC 45173
H. Blomstedt (cnd)
Kvandal, J.:Music of, w. Anne-Lise Berntsen (sop)—Symphonic Epos, Op. 21; Con for Fl & Strs, Op. 22; Qt No. 2 for Strs, Op. 27; Qt for Fl, Vn, Va & Vc, Op. 42; Duo for Vn & Vc, Op. 19; Son for Vn, Op. 45; Da Lontano for Alto Fl & Pno, Op. 32; Intro & Allegro for Hn & Pno, Op. 30; Aria Cadenza e Finale, Op. 24; Stevtoner, Op. 40 Norway Music 2-▲ CD 4986
I. Buketoff (cnd)
Avshalomov, J.:Taking of T'ung Kuan CRI ▲ CD 667 [ADD]
M. Caridis (cnd)
Saeverud, H.:Peer Gynt Norway Music ▲ ACD 4954
Valen, F.:Orchestral Songs, w. D. Dorow (sop)—Ave Maria, Op. 4 (1917-21); 2 chinesische Gedichte, Op. 8 (1925-27); Dearest thou now, O soul, Op. 9 (1920-28); The Dark Night of the Soul, Op. 32 (1939) Simax ▲ PSC 3115
Valen, F.:Sym Poems—Pastorale, Op. 11 (1929-30); Graveyard by the Sea, Op. 20 (1933-34); Sonetto di M.angelo, Op. 17 No. 1 (1932); Nenia, Op. 18 No. 1 (1932); Song of Thanksgiving, Op. 17 No. 2 (1932-33); The Silent Island, Op. 21 (1934); Ode to Solitude, Op. 35 (1939) Simax ▲ PSC 3115

ORCH. & ENS.

Oslo PO (cont.)
Ø. Fjeldstad (cnd)
Bezanson, P.:Rondo–Prelude CRI ■ C 159
Goodenough, F.:Elegy CRI ■ C 159
Jensen, L.I.:Japanischer Frühling, w. K. Langebo (sop) Simax ▲ PSC 3118
Jensen, L.I.:Sym in d Simax ▲ PSC 3118
Wagner, R.:Wesendonck Songs, w. K. Flagstad (sop) [G] Acanta ▲ 43189
O. Grüner–Hegge (cnd)
Jensen, L.I.:Tema con variazioni Simax ▲ PSC 3118
M. Jansons (cnd)
Dukas, P.:L'Apprenti sorcier EMI Classics ▲ CDD 64291
Dvořák, A.:Con Vc, w. T. Mørk (vc) Virgin Classics ▲ CDC 59325
Dvořák, A.:Othello EMI Classics ▲ CDC 49995 [DDD]
Dvořák, A.:Scherzo Capriccioso EMI Classics ▲ CDD 64291
Dvořák, A.:Scherzo Capriccioso EMI Classics ▲ CDC 49995 [DDD]
Dvořák, A.:Sym 5 EMI Classics ▲ CDC 49995 [DDD]
Dvořák, A.:Sym 7 EMI Classics ▲ CDC 54663
Dvořák, A.:Sym 8 EMI Classics ▲ CDC 54663
Elling, C.:Con Vn, w. A. Tellefsen (vn) NKF ▲ NKFCD 50021
Honegger, A.:Pacific 231 EMI Classics ▲ CDC 55122
Honegger, A.:Sym 2 EMI Classics ▲ CDC 55122
Honegger, A.:Sym 3 EMI Classics ▲ CDC 55122
Mahler, G.:Sym 2, w. F. Lott (sop), J. Hamari (mez), Oslo Phil Chorus
Chandos ("Collect" series) 2–▲ CHAN 6595/96 [DDD]
Mussorgsky, M.:Khovanshchina (prelude) EMI Classics ▲ CDC 49797 [DDD]
Mussorgsky, M.:Night EMI Classics ▲ CDD 64291
Mussorgsky, M.:Pictures at an Exhibition EMI Classics ▲ CDC 49797 [DDD]
Saint-Saëns, C.:Con 3 Vn, w. F. P. Zimmermann (vn) EMI Classics ▲ CDC 55184
Saint-Saëns, C.:Sym 3, w. W. Marshall (org) EMI Classics ▲ CDC 55184
Shostakovich, D.:Sym 6 EMI Classics ▲ CDC 54339
Shostakovich, D.:Sym 9 EMI Classics ▲ CDC 54339
Sibelius, J.:Andante festivo EMI Classics ▲ CDC 54804
Sibelius, J.:Finlandia EMI Classics ▲ CDC 54273
Sibelius, J.:Karelia Suite EMI Classics ▲ CDC 54273 □ 54273–5–6
Sibelius, J.:The Swan of Tuonela EMI Classics ▲ CDC 54804
Sibelius, J.:Sym 1 EMI Classics ▲ CDC 54273 □ 54273–5–6
Sibelius, J.:Sym 2 EMI Classics ▲ CDC 54804
Sibelius, J.:Valse triste EMI Classics ▲ CDC 54804
Smetana, B.:The Moldau EMI Classics ▲ CDD 64291
Smetana, B.:The Moldau EMI Classics ▲ CDC 49860 [DDD]
Stravinsky, I.:Pétrouchka (suite) [1947 version] EMI Classics ▲ CDC 54899
Stravinsky, I.:Le Sacre du printemps Orch EMI Classics ▲ CDC 54899
Tchaikovsky, P.:Ov 1812 EMI Classics ▲ CDD 64291
Tchaikovsky, P.:Syms (comp) Chandos 7–▲ CHAN 8672/78 [DDD]
Tchaikovsky, P.:Sym 1 Chandos ▲ CHAN 8402 [DDD]
Tchaikovsky, P.:Sym 2 Chandos ▲ CHAN 8460 [DDD]
Tchaikovsky, P.:Sym 3 Chandos ▲ CHAN 8463 [DDD]
Tchaikovsky, P.:Sym 4 Chandos ▲ CHAN 8361 [DDD]
Tchaikovsky, P.:Sym 5 Chandos ▲ CHAN 8351 [DDD]
Tchaikovsky, P.:Sym 6 Chandos ▲ CHAN 8446 [DDD]
Tchaikovsky, P.:Vars on a Rococo Theme, w. T. Mørk (vc) Virgin Classics ▲ CDC 59325
Wagner, R.:Ovs, Preludes & Orch Sels—sels. from Götterdämmerun; Lohengrin; Die Meistersinger; Rienzi; Tannhäuser; Tristan und Isolde; Die Walküre *(rec Aug. 1991)*
EMI Classics ▲ CDC 54583–2 [DDD]
A. B. Lipkin (cnd)
Berezowsky, N.:Christmas Festival Ov CRI ■ C 209
Dello Joio, N.:New York Profiles CRI ■ ACS 6012
Kay, U.:Fant Vars CRI ■ C 209
E.-P. Salonen (cnd)
Grieg, E.:Peer Gynt, w. B. Hendricks (sop), Oslo Phil Chorus CBS ▲ MK 44528 [DDD] □ MM 44528
J. Serebrier (cnd)
Luening, O.:Legend, w. Erik Larsen (ob) Phoenix ▲ PHCD 101 [AAD]
Luening, O.:Lyric Scene, w. Per Øien (fl) Phoenix ▲ PHCD 101 [AAD]
W. Strickland (cnd)
Becker, J.J.:Con arabesque, w. A. Kayser (pno) CRI ■ C 177
Flanagan, W.:The Lady of Tearful Regret, w. D. Larsen (sop), E. Krogh (ten) CRI ■ C 163
Ives, C.:Central Park in the Dark CRI ■ C 163
Ives, C.:Halloween CRI ■ C 163
Ives, C.:The Pond CRI ■ C 163
Jacobi, F.:Psalms, w. Guido Vecchi (vc) CRI ("American Masters" series) ▲ CD 703 [ADD]
Riegger, W.:Canon & Fugue CRI ■ C 177
Y. Talmi (cnd)
Bruckner, A.:Sym 9 Chandos ▲ CHAN 8860 [DDD]
Bruckner, A.:Sym 9 Chandos ("7000" series) 2–▲ CHAN 7051
Oslo Piano Trio
Grieg, E.:Music of, w. A. Kvalbein (vc), R. Askeland (pno), Trondheim Soloists—Intermezzo for Cello & Piano; Andante con moto in c for Violin, Cello & Piano; Sonata in a for Cello & Piano, Op. 36; Holdberg Suite (sels.); Preludium; Sarabande; Gavotte; Air; Rigaudon Victoria ▲ VCD 19071
Oslo Piano Trio [S. Nilsson, A. Kvalbein, J. H. Bratlie]
Grieg, E.:Andante con moto Victoria ▲ VCD 19079
Martin, F.:Trio sur les mélodies populaires irlandaises Victoria ▲ VCD 19079
Tchaikovsky, P.:Trio Pno Victoria ▲ VCD 19079
Oslo String Quartet
Nystedt, K.:Qt 2 Strs Simax ▲ PSC 1114
Nystedt, K.:Qt 3 Strs Simax ▲ PSC 1114
Nystedt, K.:Qt 4 Strs Simax ▲ PSC 1114
Nystedt, K.:Qt 5 Strs—Allegro grazioso Simax ▲ PSC 1114
Oslo Wind Ensemble [T. O. Andreassen (fl), L. P. Berg (ob), A. Stav (cl), J. O. Marthinsen (hn), H. P. Aasen (bn)]
Fernström, J.:Qnt Ww *(rec Oslo, Sept. 1993)* Naxos ▲ 8.553050 [DDD]
Kvandal, J.:Hymn Tunes *(rec Oslo, Sept. 1993)* Naxos ▲ 8.553050 [DDD]
Kvandal, J.:Qnt Winds *(rec Oslo, Sept. 1993)* Naxos ▲ 8.553050 [DDD]
Nielsen, C.:Qnt Ww *(rec Oslo, Sept. 1993)* Naxos ▲ 8.553050 [DDD]
Ossipov Balalaika Orch
N. Kalinin (cnd)
Vol. I:Russian Classical Music *(rec Moscow, Dec 8–11, 1992)* Claves ▲ CD 509623 [DDD]
Vol. II:Russian Folk Music *(rec Moscow, Dec 21–22, 1992)* Claves ▲ CD 509624 [DDD]
Ossipov Russian Folk Orch
Dark Eyes:Russian Folk Songs, w. Hvorostovsky, Dmitri (bar)
Philips ▲ 434080–2 PH [DDD] ■ 434080–4 PH (D)
Ostankino Radio–TV Large SO
R. Abdullayev (cnd)
Karayev, K.:In the Path of Thunder (suite) Russian Disc ▲ RUS 11067 [DDD]
Karayev, K.:Seven Beauties (suite) Russian Disc ▲ RUS 11067 [DDD]
G. Cherkasov (cnd)
Feinberg, S.:Con 3 Pno, w. Vladimir Bunin (pno) *(rec 1990)* Consonance ▲ 81–0002 [DDD]
V. Fedoseyev (cnd)
Tchaikovsky, P.:Francesca da Rimini *(rec 1990 & 1991)* Consonance ▲ 81–5000 [DDD]
Tchaikovsky, P.:Romeo & Juliet *(rec 1990 & 1991)* Consonance ▲ 81–5000 [DDD]

Ostankino Radio–TV Large SO (cont.)
V. Fedoseyev (cnd) (cont.)
Tchaikovsky, P.:The Tempest *(rec 1990 & 1991)* Consonance ▲ 81–5000 [DDD]
Tchaikovsky, P.:The Voyevoda, Op. 78 *(rec 1990 & 1991)* Consonance ▲ 81–5000 [DDD]
Ostankino SO
Sviridov, G.:Cants, w. Yurloff State Choir—Snow Is Falling Olympia ▲ OLY 520 [ADD]
Sviridov, G.:Choruses, w. Yurloff State Choir Olympia ▲ OLY 520 [ADD]
Sviridov, G.:Small Triptych Olympia ▲ OLY 520 [ADD]
Sviridov, G.:The Snowstorm Olympia ▲ OLY 520 [ADD]
Ostrava Janáček CO
Z. Dejmek (cnd)
Stamitz, C.:Con 2 Vc, w. Jan Hališka (vc) *(rec Ostrava Church Studio, June 3–11, 1986)*
Panton ▲ PAN 811307 [AAD]
L. Hlaváček (cnd)
Stamic, J.V.:Sinfs—in G, A & B Panton ("Very Famous" series) ▲ PAN 811201
Ostrava Janáček PO
O. Trhlík (cnd)
Báchorek, M.:Lidice, w. Jana Stupárkova–Majtnerová (sop), Karel Průša (bar), Osvald Albín (speaker), Jan Vlasák (speaker), Ostrava Janáček Mixed Chorus *(rec Smetana Hall of Prague's Municipal House, Feb 10 & 11, 1988)* Panton ▲ 811338–2 [AAD]
Báchorek, M.:Music of, w. Osvald Albín (nar), Otakar Brousek (nar), Jan Vlassak (nar), Brigita Šulcová (sop), Drahomíra Drobková (cta), Karel Průša (bass), Pavel Kamas (sgr), Jan Kyzlink (sgr), Jana Stuperkova–Majtnerova (sgr), Bretislav Vojkuvka (sgr), Prague SO, Ostrava Janáček Chorus, Ostrava Women's Chamber Chorus, Permoník Children's Chorus—Lidice; Stereofonietta; Hukvald Poem
Panton ▲ PAN 811338 [AAD/DDD]
Báchorek, M.:Stereofonietta, w. Brigita Šulcová (sop), Jan Kyzlink (bar)*(rec Smetana Hall of Prague's Municipal House, Feb 10 & 11, 1988)* Panton ▲ 811338–2 [AAD]
Martinů, B.:Sym 5 Panton ▲ PAN 811205
Ostrobothnian CO
Eliasson, A.:Con Hn, w. Sören Hermansson (hn) Caprice ▲ CAP 21422
Eliasson, A.:Con Vn, w. Jari Valo (vn) Caprice ▲ CAP 21422
Eliasson, A.:Desert Point Caprice ▲ CAP 21422
J. Kangas (cnd)
Boccherini, L.:Con Vc, G.480, w. S. Isserlis (vc) Virgin Classics ▲ CDC 59015
Boccherini, L.:Con Vc, G.482, w. S. Isserlis (vc) Virgin Classics ▲ CDC 59015
Heininen, P.:...Floral View with Maidens Singing Ondine ▲ ODE 722–2 [ADD]
Heiniö, M.:Hermes, w. Camilla Nylund (sop), Juhani Lagerspetz (pno) Ondine ▲ ODE 870
Mustonen, O.:Fant, w. O. Mustonen (pno) *(rec June 5, 1989, Aug. 8–9, 1)*
Finlandia ▲ 4509–95860–2 [DDD]
Nordgren, P.H.:Hate–Love, w. M. Ylönen (vc) Ondine ▲ ODE 737–2 [DDD]
Nordgren, P.H.:Sym Strs Ondine ▲ ODE 737–2 [DDD]
Nordgren, P.H.:Transe–Choral Ondine ▲ ODE 737–2 [DDD]
Rautavaara, E.:Ballad Hp Ondine ▲ ODE 836 [DDD]
Rautavaara, E.:Cantos I–II Ondine ▲ ODE 836 [DDD]
Rautavaara, E.:Cantos III Ondine ▲ ODE 836 [DDD]
Rautavaara, E.:Cantos IV Ondine ▲ ODE 836 [DDD]
Rautavaara, E.:Divert Ondine ▲ ODE 821 [DDD]
Rautavaara, E.:Epitath for Béla Bartók Ondine ▲ ODE 821 [DDD]
Rautavaara, E.:The Fiddlers Ondine ▲ ODE 821 [DDD]
Rautavaara, E.:A Finnish Myth Ondine ▲ ODE 836 [DDD]
Rautavaara, E.:Hommage à Zoltán Kodály Ondine ▲ ODE 821 [DDD]
Rautavaara, E.:Hommage à Liszt Ondine ▲ ODE 821 [DDD]
Rautavaara, E.:Ostrobothnian Polka Ondine ▲ ODE 836 [DDD]
Rautavaara, E.:Suite Ondine ▲ ODE 821 [DDD]
Kangas, Maros (cnd)
Maros, M.:Music of, w. Ilona Maros (sop), John–Edward Kelly (sax), Budapest SO, Prague Radio SO, Marosensemble—Sym No. 1; 4 Songs [from Gitanjali]; Sinf concertante [Sym No. 3]; Con for A Sax & Orch Phono Suecia ▲ PHN 23 [DDD]
Ouellet/Murray Duo [Claire Ouellet (pno), Sandra Murray (pno)]
Bartók, B.:Mikrokosmos—Rythme bulgares; Étude d'accords; Perpetuum mobile; Le court canon et son Inversion; Nouveau chant populaire hongrois; Invention chromatique; Ostinato *(rec Centre National d'Exposition de Jonquière, Nov 9–11, 1994)* CBC ("Musica Viva" series) ▲ MVCD 1094 [DDD]
Bartók, B.:The Miraculous Mandarin Pno 4–Hands *(rec Centre National d'Exposition de Jonquière, Nov 9–11, 1994)* CBC ("Musica Viva" series) ▲ MVCD 1094 [DDD]
Stravinsky, I.:Le Sacre du printemps Pno *(rec Centre National d'Exposition de Jonquière, Nov 9–11, 1994)* CBC ("Musica Viva" series) ▲ MVCD 1094 [DDD]
D'Oyly Carte Opera Company Orch
Sullivan, A.:Iolanthe [E] London 2–▲ 414145–2 [ADD]
Sullivan, A.:The Mikado [without dialogue] *(rec 1926)* Pearl ▲ PEA 9025 [AAD]
Sullivan, A.:Music of—sels. from Gondoliers, H.M.S. Pinafore, Iolanthe, Mikado, Pirates of Penzance, Trial by Jury, Yeoman of the Guard *(rec 1927–36)* Memoir Classics ▲ CDMOIR 413 [AAD]
Sullivan, A.:The Sorcerer—slightly abridged without dialogue *(rec 1933)* Pearl ▲ PEA 9025 [AAD]
I. Godfrey (cnd)
Sullivan, A.:Cox & Box, New SO of London London 2–▲ 417355–2 [ADD]
Sullivan, A.:The Gondoliers, New SO of London London 2–▲ 425177–2 [ADD]
Sullivan, A.:HMS Pinafore, New SO of London—highlights
London ("Weekend Classics" series) ▲ 433881–2 [ADD]
Sullivan, A.:The Mikado [E] *(rec 1936)* Pro Arte ▲ CDD 3416
Sullivan, A.:Patience, New SO of London London 2–▲ 425193–2 [ADD]
Sullivan, A.:The Pirates of Penzance, Royal PO London 2–▲ 425196–2 [ADD]
Sullivan, A.:Ruddigore, Royal Opera House Orch Covent Gardens London 2–▲ 417355–2 [ADD]
Sullivan, A.:The Sorcerer, Royal PO London 2–▲ 436807–2
Godfrey, Sargent (cnd)
Sullivan, A.:The Yeomen of the Guard, Royal PO, Royal Opera House Orch Covent Garden
London 2–▲ 417358–2 [ADD]
R. Nash (cnd)
Sullivan, A.:The Grand Duke, w. Royal PO London 2–▲ 436813–2 [ADD]
Sullivan, A.:The Mikado, w. Royal PO London 2–▲ 425190–2 [ADD]
Sullivan, A.:Ovs, w. Royal PO—Macbeth; Marmion London 2–▲ 436816–2
Sullivan, A.:Utopia Limited, w. Royal PO London 2–▲ 436816–2
Sullivan, A.:Victoria & Merry England (suites), w. Royal PO—No. 1 London 2–▲ 436816–2
H. Norris (cnd)
Sullivan, A.:The Gondoliers, w. W. Lawson (sop), A. Davies (ten), B. Lewis (cta), D. Oldham (ten), M. Bennett (sop), G. Baker (bar), L. Sheffield (bar), H. Lytton (bar), et al., D'Oyly Carte Opera Chorus—dialogue omitted *(rec 1927)* Pearl 2–▲ PEAS 9961 (m) [AAD]
Sullivan, A.:Trial by Jury, w. W. Lawson (sop), D. Oldham (ten), G. Baker (bar), L. Sheffield (bar), A. Hosking (bar), D'Oyly Carte Opera Chorus *(rec 1928)* Pearl 2–▲ PEAS 9961 (m) [AAD]
M. Sargent (cnd)
Sullivan, A.:HMS Pinafore [E] *(rec 1930)* Pro Arte ▲ CDD 598 (m)
Sullivan, A.:Pineapple Poll, w. Royal PO [arr Charles Mackerras] London 2–▲ 436810–2 [DDD]
Sullivan, A.:The Pirates of Penzance [E] *(rec 1929)* Pro Arte ▲ CDD 597 (m)
Sullivan, A.:Princess Ida, w. Royal PO London 2–▲ 436810–2 [ADD]
Sullivan, A.:The Yeomen of the Guard, w. D'Oyly Carte Opera Chorus [E] *(rec 1928)*
Pro Arte ▲ CDD 3417
Pacific Art Trio
Ives, C.:Trio Pno Delos ▲ DCD 1009 [AAD]
Korngold, E.W.:Trio Pno Delos ▲ DCD 1009 [AAD]
Pacific Classical Winds
Michael, D.M.:Parthias *(rec Los Angeles, 1994–95)* New World ▲ 804092 [DDD]
Michael, D.M.:Water Journey New World ▲ 804092 [DDD]

300
▲ = CD ♦ = Enhanced CD Δ = MD ■ = Cassette Tape □ = DCC

Pacific Percussion Ensemble
Kraft, William:Momentum Crystal ▲ CD 124
Kraft, William:Theme & Vars Perc Crystal ▲ CD 124
Kraft, William:Triangles Crystal ▲ CD 124
Pacific Rim Soloists
E. Shumsky (cnd)
Beale, J.:Ballade, w. E. Shumsky (va) Ambassador ▲ ARC 1011 [DDD]
Kreisler, F.:Praeludium & Allegro, w. E. Shumsky (va), *(pno unknown)* Ambassador ▲ ARC 1011 [DDD]
Pacific SO
J. Alexander (cnd)
Hopkins, J.:Songs of Eternity, w. Pacific Chorale Albany ▲ TROY 182
Paulus, S.:Voices, w. Martha Jane Weaver (mez), Frank Kelley (ten), Pacific Chorale Albany ▲ TROY 182
K. Clark (cnd)
Barber, S.:Capricorn Con Albany ▲ TROY 064 [DDD]
Barber, S.:Con Vn, w. R. Ricci (vn) Reference ▲ RR 45CD [DDD]
Barber, S.:Essay 1 Albany ▲ TROY 064 [DDD]
Copland, A.:Appalachian Spring (suite)—original chamber ensemble version Reference ▲ RR 22CD [DDD]
Copland, A.:Music for Radio Albany ▲ TROY 064 [DDD]
Copland, A.:An Outdoor Ov Reference ▲ RR 22CD [DDD]
Copland, A.:Poems (8) of Emily Dickinson, w. M. Nixon (sop) Reference ▲ RR 22CD [DDD]
Harris, R.:Sym 6, "Gettysburg Address" Albany ▲ TROY 064 [DDD]
Menotti, G.C.:Con Vn, w. R. Ricci (vn) Reference ▲ RR 45CD [DDD]
Respighi, O.:Poema autunnale, w. R. Ricci (vn) Reference ▲ RR 15CD [ADD]
Respighi, O.:Vetrate di chiesa Reference ▲ RR 15CD [ADD]
C. St. Clair (cnd)
Corigliano, J.:Con Pno, w. A. Lefevre (pno) Koch International Classics ▲ KIC 7250 [DDD]
Ticheli, F.:Radiant Voices Koch International Classics ▲ KIC 7250 [DDD]
PACT Orch members
W. Mony (cnd)
Zaidel-Rudolph, J.:Tempus Fugit, w. NSO RSO members Claremont ▲ GSE 1532
Padua & Venice CO
Mozart, W.A.:Con 7 Pnos, w. B. Giuranna (pno), Crommelynck Duo Claves ▲ CD 9022 [DDD]
B. Giuranna (cnd)
Boccherini, L.:Cons Vc (comp), w. D. Geringas (vc) Claves 3-▲ CD 8814/16 [DDD]
Mozart, W.A.:Adagio & Fugue Strs Claves ▲ CD 9022 [DDD]
Mozart, W.A.:Arias, w. Natale de Carolis (b-bar)—includes Un bacio di mano; Per questa bella mano; arias from Don Giovanni; Le nozze di Figaro; Così fan tutte; La finta semplice Claves ▲ 50-9120
Mozart, W.A.:Con 10 Pnos, w. Crommelynck Duo Claves ▲ CD 9022 [DDD]
P. Maag (cnd)
Beethoven, L. van:Syms (comp) [Sym 9 w. Amadna Halgrimson (sop), Ruthild Engert (mez), Zeger Vandersteene (ten), Friedman Kunder (bass), Filippo Bressan (cnd), Athestis Chorus] Arts 5-▲ 47370-2 [DDD]
Beethoven, L. van:Sym 1 *(rec Auditorium Modigliani, Padova, Italy, July 13-16, 1994)* Arts Music ▲ 47246-2 [DDD]
Beethoven, L. van:Sym 2 *(rec Lonigo, Vicenza, Italy, Feb 1994)* Arts ▲ 47244-2 [DDD]
Beethoven, L. van:Sym 3, "Eroica" *(rec Auditorium Modigliani, Padova, Italy, July 13-16, 1994)* Arts Music ▲ 47246-2 [DDD]
Beethoven, L. van:Sym 4 *(rec Lonigo, Vicenza, Italy, Feb 1994)* Arts ▲ 47244-2 [DDD]
Beethoven, L. van:Sym 5 *(rec Pollini Auditorium, Padova, Italy, Feb 5-6, 1995)* Arts Music ▲ 47247-2 [DDD]
Beethoven, L. van:Sym 6, "Pastorale" *(rec Pollini Auditorium, Padova, Italy, Feb 5-6, 1995)* Arts Music ▲ 47247-2 [DDD]
Beethoven, L. van:Sym 7 *(rec Auditorium Modigliani, Padova, Italy, June 1994)* Arts ▲ 47245-2 [DDD]
Beethoven, L. van:Sym 8 *(rec Auditorium Modigliani, Padova, Italy, June 1994)* Arts ▲ 47245-2 [DDD]
Beethoven, L. van:Sym 9, "Choral Sym", w. Filippo Maria Bressan (cnd), Athestis Chorus *(rec Basilica di S. Antonio, Padova, Italy, Dec 20, 1994)* Arts Music ▲ 47248-2 [DDD]
C. Martignon (cnd)
Dragonetti, D.:Con Db, w. Ubaldo Fioravanti (db) *(rec Sala San Bovo, Padova, Italy, Jan 17-19, 1995)* Dynamic ▲ CD 133 [DDD]
Padua Bach Academy CO
C. Gubert (cnd)
Vivaldi, A.:Gloria, RV.589, w. R. Invernizzi (sop), P. Vaccari (sop), R. Balconi (ct), L. Gariboldi (ten), Padua Bach Academy Chamber Chorus Rivoalto ▲ RIV 9301 [DDD]
Vivaldi, A.:Magnificat, RV.610, w. R. Invernizzi (sop), P. Vaccari (sop), R. Balconi (ct), L. Gariboldi (ten), Padua Bach Academy Chamber Chorus Rivoalto ▲ RIV 9301 [DDD]
Paganini String Quartet
Paganini, N.:Nocturnes *(rec Dynamic's Genoa, Dec 10-13, 1995)* Dynamic ▲ CD 152 [DDD]
Paganini, N.:Qts (15) Vn—Nos. 1, 9, 10, 11, 12 & 13 Dynamic 2-▲ CD 17/1-2 [ADD]
Paganini, N.:Qts (15) Vn—Nos. 3, 7 & 14 Dynamic ▲ CD 46
Paganini, N.:Qts (15) Vn—Nos. 2, 8 & 15 Dynamic ▲ CD 80 [DDD]
Paganini, N.:Qts (15) Vn—No. 7 [trans for strs] *(rec Dynamic's Genoa, Dec 10-13, 1995)* Dynamic ▲ CD 152 [DDD]
Paganini String Quartet [Bruno Pignata (vn), Gian Luca Allocco (vn), Ernest Braucher (va), Dario De Stefano (vc)]
Paganini, N.:Qts Strs *(rec Genoa, Nov. 21-25, 1994)* Dynamic ▲ CD 134 [DDD]
Paganini String Quartet [Bruno Pignata (vn), Lorenzo Lugli (va), Paola Mosca (vc), Giuseppe Briasco (gtr)]
Paganini, N.:Qts (15) Vn—complete *(rec Dynamic Studio, Genoa, Italy, Feb 1991; July 1996)* Dynamic 5-▲ 1591 [ADD/DDD]
Paganini String Quartet [Pino Briasco (vn), Bruno Pignata (vn), Ernest Braucher (va), Riccardo Agosti (vc)]
Paganini, N.:Qts (15) Vn—No. 4 in D; No. 5 in C; No. 6 in d Dynamic ▲ CD 98 [DDD]
Jean-François Paillard CO
L. Martini (cnd)
Charpentier, M.-A.:Magnificat, w. Martha Angelici (sop), Jocelyn Chamonin (sop), André Mallabrera (ct), Rémy Corazza (ten), Georges Abdoun (bar), Jacques Mars (bass), Maurice André (tpt), Marie-Claire Alain (org), French Jeunesses Musicales Chorale *(rec Paris, Mar 15, 1963)* Vanguard Classics ▲ OVC 8075 [ADD]
Charpentier, M.-A.:Te Deum, H. 146, w. Martha Angelici (sop), Jocelyn Chamonin (sop), André Mallabrera (ct), Rémy Corazza (ten), Georges Abdoun (bar), Jacques Mars (bass), Maurice André (tpt), Marie-Claire Alain (org), French Jeunesses Musicales Chorale *(rec Paris, Mar 15, 1963)* Vanguard Classics ▲ OVC 8075 [ADD]
J.-F. Paillard (cnd)
Albinoni, T.:Adagio Org RCA Red Seal ▲ 65468-2 [DDD] ■ 65468-4 (CrO2)
Boismortier, J.B. de:L'Automne, w. Gérard Souzay (bar) Erato ▲ ERA 97416 [ADD]
Campra, A.:Cants françaises, w. Gérard Souzay (bar)—Les femmes Erato ▲ ERA 97416 [ADD]
Corrette, M.:Cons Comiques, w. Georges Barboteu (hn), Michel Berges (hn), Gilbert Coursier (hn), Daniel Dubar (hn)—No. 14 for Hns & Orch [La Choisy] Erato ▲ 94801-2
Courbois, P.:Dom Quichotte, w. Gérard Souzay (bar) Erato ▲ ERA 97416 [ADD]
Fasch, J.F.:Con Tpt & 2 Obs, w. Maurice André (tpt), Jacques Chambon (ob), Pierre Pierlot (ob) *(rec 1968)* Erato ▲ 98475-2 [ADD]
Fasch, J.F.:Syms (19) *(rec 1968)* Erato ▲ 98475-2 [ADD]
French Baroque Flute Concertos, w. Jean-Pierre Rampal (fl) Erato ▲ 45834-2

Jean-François Paillard CO (cont.)
J.-F. Paillard (cnd) (cont.)
German Baroque Flute Concertos, w. Jean-Pierre Rampal (fl), Scottish CO [cnd:R. Leppard] Erato ▲ 45835-2
Handel, G.F.:Cons (16) Org, w. M. Alain (org) [Haerpfer-Ermann positive organ, Eglise des Maronites, Paris]—Nos. 1 in g, 2 in B♭, 3 in g, 4 in F, 5 in F & 6 in B♭ Boston Skyline ▲ BSD 133 [ADD]
Handel, G.F.:Royal Fireworks Music Erato ("Bonsai" series) ▲ 2292-45931-2 ■ 2292-45931-4
Handel, G.F.:Water Music (comp) Erato ("Bonsai" series) ▲ 2292-45931-2
Italian Baroque Flute Concertos, w. Jean-Pierre Rampal (fl) Erato ▲ 45833-2
Japanese Melodies, w. Lily Laskine (hp), Jacques Chambon (ob) Denon ("Repertoire" series) ▲ CO 8116 [DDD]
Mozart, W.A.:Con Cl, w. Jacques Lancelot (cl)—Adagio; Rondo Erato ▲ 94679-2
Mozart, W.A.:Con Cl, w. J. Lancelot (cl) Erato ▲ 45978-2 ■ 45978-4
Mozart, W.A.:Con Fl Hp, w. J.-P. Rampal (fl), L. Laskine (hp) *(rec 1964)* Erato ▲ 45832-2 [ADD] ■ 45832-4
Mozart, W.A.:Con Fl Hp, w. J.-P. Rampal (fl), L. Laskine (hp) Erato ▲ 45978-2 ■ 45978-4
Mozart, W.A.:Con Hn, K.495, w. Pierre del Vescovo (hn)—Romanza; Rondo Erato ▲ 94801-2
The Pachelbel Canon, Albinoni Adagio & Other Baroque Melodies RCA Red Seal ▲ 65468-2-RC [DDD] ■ 65468-4-RC
Pachelbel, J.:Canon RCA Red Seal ▲ 65468-2-RC [DDD] ■ 65468-4-RC (CrO2)
Pachelbel, J.:Canon *(rec 1968)* Erato ▲ 98475-2 [ADD]
Pachelbel, J.:Suites Strs—in B♭ & G *(rec 1968)* Erato ▲ 98475-2 [ADD]
Rameau, J.P.:Les Indes galantes, w. L. Devos (ten), J. Elwes (ten), P. Huttenlocher (bar) Erato 3-▲ 95310-2
Rameau, J.P.:Thétis, w. Gérard Souzay (bar) Erato ▲ ERA 97416 [ADD]
Rodrigo, J.:Concierto de Aranjuez, w. James Galway (fl), Kazuhito Yamashita (gtr) RCA Gold Seal ▲ 09026-68428-2 ■ 09026-68428-4
Telemann, G.P.:Con Hn, w. Georges Barboteu (hn)—Allegro; Andante; Allegro Erato ▲ 94801-2
Telemann, G.P.:Musique de Table, w. J. Chambon (ob), B. Gabel (tpt)—sels. Erato ▲ 92868-2
Palacio Bellas Artes Orch
R. Cellini (cnd)
Donizetti, G.:La favorita, w. G. Simionato (mez), G. di Stefano (ten), E. Mascherini (bar), C. Siepi (bass-bar), Rodriguez (sgr), Palacio Bellas Artes Chorus [I] *(rec live, Mexico City, 7/12/49)* Standing Room Only 2-▲ SRO 816-2 [ADD]
Verdi, G.:Rigoletto (sels), w. C. O'Connor (sop), O. Dominguez (mez), G. Di Stefano (ten), G. Valdengo (bar), I. Rufino (bass), Palacio Bellas Artes Chorus [abridged performance] *(rec live, Mexico City 6/22/48)* Golden Age of Opera 2-▲ GAO 128/29 [ADD]
O. de Fabritiis (cnd)
Verdi, G.:Aida, w. M. Callas (sop), O. Dominguez (mez), M. Del Monaco (ten), G. Taddei (bar), Palacio Bellas Artes Chorus *(rec live, Mexico City 7/3/51)* Melodram 2-▲ CDM 26015
Verdi, G.:La traviata, w. M. Callas (sop), Giron (sgr), C. Valletti (ten), G. Taddei (bar), Palacio Bellas Artes Chorus [I] *(rec live, Mexico City, 7/17/51)* Melodram 2-▲ CDM 26019 [AAD]
U. Mugnai (cnd)
Puccini, G.:Tosca, w. M. Callas (sop), M. Filippeschi (ten), R. Weede (bar), Palacio Bellas Artes Chorus [I] *(rec live, Mexico City, 6/8/50)* Standing Room Only 2-▲ SRO 820-2 [ADD]
Puccini, G.:Tosca, w. Maria Callas (sop), Mario Filippeschi (ten), Carlos Sagarminaga (ten), Robert Weede (bar), Ramon Alonso (bass), Palacio Bellas Artes Chorus Melodram 3-▲ CDM 36032
Verdi, G.:Rigoletto, w. M. Callas (sop), G. Di Stefano (ten), Campolonghi (sgr), Palacio Bellas Artes Chorus [I] *(rec live, Mexico City, 6/17/52)* Melodram 2-▲ CDM 26023
Verdi, G.:La traviata, w. M. Callas (sop), G. Di Stefano (ten), Campolonghi (bar), Palacio Bellas Artes Chorus [I] *(rec live, Mexico City, 6/3/52)* Melodram 2-▲ CDM 26021
G. Picco (cnd)
Bellini, V.:Norma, w. M. Callas (sop), G. Simionato (mez), K. Baum (ten), N. Moscona (bass), Palacio Bellas Artes Chorus *(rec live, Mexico City 5/23/50)* Melodram 2-▲ MEL 26018
Bellini, V.:I Puritani, w. M. Callas (sop), G. di Stefano (ten), Campolonghi (sgr), R. Silva (bass), Palacio Bellas Artes Chorus [I] *(rec live, Mexico City 5/29/52)* Melodram 2-▲ MEL 26027 (m) [AAD]
Donizetti, G.:Lucia di Lammermoor, w. M. Callas (sop), G. di Stefano (ten), Campolonghi (sgr), Palacio Bellas Artes Chorus [I] *(rec live, Mexico City 6/10/52)* Myto 2-▲ 2 MCD 91340 [ADD]
Donizetti, G.:Lucia di Lammermoor (sels), w. Maria Callas (sop)—Mad Scene *(rec Mexico City, June 10, 14 & 26, 1952)* Memories ▲ MEM 4581 [AAD]
Puccini, G.:Tosca, w. M. Callas (sop), G. di Stefano (ten), Campolonghi (sgr), Palacio Bellas Artes Chorus [I] *(rec live, Mexico City 1952)* Melodram 2-▲ 26028 (m) [AAD]
Puccini, G.:Tosca (sels), w. M. Callas (sop), G. di Stefano (ten), Palacio Bellas Artes Chorus—nine arias & duets [I] *(rec live, Mexico City, 7/1/52)* Standing Room Only 2-▲ SRO 820-2 [ADD]
Thomas, A.:Mignon (sels), w. G. Simionato (mez), G. Di Stefano (ten), C. Siepi (b-bar), Palacio Bellas Artes Chorus *(rec live, Mexico City, 6/28/49)* Golden Age of Opera 2-▲ GAO 128/29 [ADD]
Verdi, G.:Aida, w. M. Callas (sop), G. Simionato (mez), K. Baum (ten), R. Weede (bar), Palacio Bellas Artes Chorus *(rec live, Mexico City 5/30/50)* Melodram ▲ MLO 26009 [ADD]
Verdi, G.:Il trovatore, w. M. Callas (sop), G. Simionato (mez), K. Baum (ten), L. Warren (bar), Palacio Bellas Artes Chorus *(rec live, Mexico City 6/20/50)* Melodram 2-▲ CDM 26017
Verdi, G.:Il trovatore (sels), w. M. Callas (sop), Feuss (sgr), C. Sagarminaga (ten), K. Baum (ten), L. Warren (bar), Palacio Bellas Artes Chorus—ten selections from Acts 1 & 4 [I] *(rec live, Mexico City 6/20/50)* Myto 2-▲ 2 MCD 90213 (m) [ADD]
Palais Royal Orch
J.-P. Sarcos (cnd)
Mozart, W.A.:Requiem, w. Maîtrise des Petits Chanteurs Pavane ▲ 7336
Palermo Teatro Massimo Orch
V. Gui (cnd)
Verdi, G.:Macbeth, w. Leyla Gencer (sop), Mirto Picchi (ten), Giuseppe Taddei (bar), Ferruccio Mazzoli (bass), Palermo Teatro Massimo Chorus *(rec Palermo, Jan. 14, 1960)* Pantheon 2-▲ PHE 6604 (m)
E. Pidò (cnd)
Donizetti, G.:Anna Bolena, w. Katia Ricciarelli (sop), Doris Soffel (cta), Pietro Ballo (ten), Nicolai Ghiuselev (bass), Palermo Teatro Massimo Chorus *(rec live, 1991)* Serenissima 3-▲ SER 360111
N. Sanzogno (cnd)
Bellini, V.:La straniera, w. R. Scotto (sop), E. Zilio (mez), R. Cioni (ten), D. Trimarchi (bar), E. Campi (bass), Palermo Teatro Massimo Chorus [I] *(rec live, Palermo, 1968)* Melodram 2-▲ 27039
Bellini, V.:La straniera, w. R. Scotto (sop), E. Zilio (mez), R. Cioni (ten), D. Trimarchi (bar), E. Campi (bass), Palermo Teatro Massimo Chorus [I] *(rec live, Palermo, 1968)* Verona 2-▲ 27097/98
Rossini, G.:Elisabetta, regina d'Inghilterra, w. L. Gencer (sop), S. Geszty (sop), U. Grilli (ten), P. Bottazzo (ten), Palermo Teatro Massimo Chorus [I] *(rec live, 11/24/70)* Myto 2-▲ 2 MCD 90530 [ADD]
Verdi, G.:Otello (sels), w. Mario Del Monaco (ten—Otello), Tito Gobbi (bar—Iago) *(rec Palermo, Jan 1, 1962)* Bella Voce 2-▲ 7203 [AAD]
T. Serafin (cnd)
Verdi, G.:I vespri siciliani, w. A. Stella (sop—Elena), M. Filippeschi (ten—Arrigo), G. Taddei (bar—Monforte), B. Ladysz (bass—Procida), Palermo Teatro Massimo Chorus *(rec Jan. 18, 1957)* Golden Age of Opera 2-▲ GAO 145/46 [ADD]
Palladian Ensemble [Pamela Thorby (rcr), Rachel Podger (vn), Joanna Levine (vl/vc/vle), William Carter (thb/gtr)]
An Excess of Pleasure *(rec Rosslyn Hill Chapel, Hampstead, Nov 4-6, 1992)* Linn ▲ CKD 010
Palladian Ensemble [Pamela Thorby (rcr), Rachel Podger (vn), Susanne Heinrich (vl), William Carter (thb/gtr)]
A Choice Collection:Music of Purcell's London *(rec Fitcham Church, Leatherhead, Surrey, Mar 4-6, 1995)* Linn ▲ HON 5041
Pallas Trio [Kathrin Rabus (vn), Wolfram Geiss (vc), Rolf Plagge (pno)]
Spohr, L.:Trio 2 Pno Musicaphon ▲ M 56822 [DDD]
Spohr, L.:Trio 5 Pno Musicaphon ▲ M 56822 [DDD]
Palm Court Theater Orch
A. Godwin (cnd)
Down Peacock Alley Chandos ("Collect" series) ▲ CHAN 6569 [DDD]

Palm Court Theater Orch (cont.)
A. Godwin (cnd) (cont.)
Puttin' on the Ritz Chandos ▲ CHAN 8703 [DDD]
Salon to Swing Chandos ▲ CHAN 8856 [DDD]
Palmer CO
R. Palmer (cnd)
Haydn, J.:La Cantarina, w. Brenda Harris (sop—Gasparina), Joyce Guyer (sop—Don Ettore), D'Anna Fortunato (mez—Apollonia), Jon Garrison (ten—Don Pelagio) *(rec St. Michael's Church, New York City, Apr. 1994)* Newport Classic ▲ NPD 85595 [DDD]
Pamplona Pablo Sarasate Orch
T. Bugaj (cnd)
Sarasate, P. de:Spanish Dances, w. Ruggiero Ricci (vn)—Zapateada, Op. 23/2 One–Eleven ▲ EPR 94020
PAN Ensemble
Angeli, Music of Angels, w. William Hite (ten), Harlan B. Hokin (ten), Paul Cummings (bar), Tapestry *(rec Studio A, National Music Center, Lenox, MA, Sept 11–14, 1995)* Telarc ▲ CD 80448 [DDD]
Ars Magis Subtiliter New Albion ▲ NA 021 [DDD]
Ciconia, J.:Vocal & Instrumental Consort Music—21 secular madrigals, motets, ballate, etc. New Albion ▲ NA 048
The Island of St. Hylarion:Music of Cyprus, 1413–1422 New Albion ▲ NA 038 [DDD]
Panhandle Mystery Band
Allen, T.:Bleeder, w. Jo Harvey Allen (nar—The Woman) ¿What Next? ▲ WN 0013 F
Pannon CO
J. Petró (cnd)
Schubert, Franz:Music of—5 German Dances; 5 Minuets Hungaroton ▲ HCD 31622
Volkmann, R.:Serenades Strs (comp) Hungaroton ▲ HCD 31622
Panocha String Quartet [J. Panocha (vn), P. Zejfart (vn), M. Sehnoutka (va), J. Kulhan (vc)]
Dvořák, A.:Czech Suite Supraphon ▲ CD 111457 [DDD]
Dvořák, A.:Qt Movt Supraphon ▲ SUP 111458
Dvořák, A.:Qt 8 Strs Supraphon ▲ SUP 111456 [DDD]
Dvořák, A.:Qt 9 Strs Supraphon ▲ SUP 111456 [DDD]
Dvořák, A.:Qt 10 Strs Supraphon ▲ 11 0581–2 [DDD]
Dvořák, A.:Qt 10 Strs Supraphon ▲ CD 111457 [DDD]
Dvořák, A.:Qt 11 Strs Supraphon ▲ SUP 111458
Dvořák, A.:Qt 12 Strs, "America" Supraphon ▲ SUP 111458
Dvořák, A.:Qt 12 Strs, "America" Supraphon ▲ 11 0581–2 [DDD]
Dvořák, A.:Qt 13 Strs Supraphon ▲ 11 1459–2 [DDD]
Dvořák, A.:Qt 14 Strs Supraphon ▲ 11 1459–2 [DDD]
Dvořák, A.:Qnt Pno, Op. 5, w. J. Panenka (pno) Supraphon ▲ SUP 11 1465 [DDD]
Dvořák, A.:Qnt Pno, Op. 81, w. J. Panenka (pno) Supraphon ▲ SUP 11 1465 [DDD]
Haydn, J.:Qts Strs, Op. 33, "Russian Qts"—Nos. 1–4 Supraphon Collection ▲ 11 0634–2 [ADD]
Haydn, J.:Qts Strs, Op. 76, "Erdődy Qts"—Nos. 4–6 Supraphon ▲ 11 0362–2 [DDD]
Haydn, J.:The Seven Last Words of Christ on the Cross Supraphon ▲ SUP 111484 [DDD]
Janácek, L.:Qt 1 Strs Supraphon ▲ SUP 0215
Janácek, L.:Qt 2 Strs Supraphon ▲ SUP 0215
Martinů, B.:Qts Strs Supraphon 3–▲ SUP 110994 [AAD]
Mozart, W.A.:Qt Pno, K.478, w. Rudolf Firkušný (pno) Supraphon ▲ SUP 112242 [DDD]
Music From the Heart of Europe, w. Lubomír Brabec (gtr), Josef Suk (vn), Rudolf Firkušný (pno), Vaclav Neumann (cnd), Jiří Bělohlávek (cnd), Czech PO, Prague CO, Prague Musica Antiqua, et al. Supraphon ▲ SUP 0063 [DDD]
Schubert, Franz:Qt 10 Strs Supraphon ▲ 11 0941–2 [DDD]
Schubert, Franz:Qt 13 Strs Supraphon ▲ 11 0941–2 [DDD]
Schubert, Franz:Qt 15 Strs Supraphon ▲ SUP 11 0942 [DDD]
Smetana, B.:Qt 1 Strs Supraphon ▲ 11 1514–2 [DDD]
Smetana, B.:Qt 2 Strs Supraphon ▲ 11 1514–2 [DDD]
Pantillon Trio [Marc Pantillon (pno), Louis Pantillon (vn), Christoph Pantillon (vc)]
Pantillon, F.:Trio 1029 *(rec La Salle Musica de La Chaux-de-Fonds)* Gallo ▲ CD 884 [DDD]
Parachute Regiment Bands
The Airborne Soldier Bandleader ▲ BND 7007 [DDD]
Paragon Ensemble
D. Davies (cnd)
McGuire, E.:Songs of New Beginnings Continuum ▲ CON 1032
Norris, P.:Cello Cantata Continuum ▲ CON 1032
Wilson, T.:Chamber Sym Continuum ▲ CON 1032
Paragon Ragtime Orch
R. Benjamin (cnd)
On the Boardwalk Newport Classic ▲ MC 60039 [DDD]
The Whistler & His Dog Newport Classic ▲ NCD 60069 [DDD]
Paraiba Quintet [Yerko Pinto (vn), Ronedilk Cavalcante (vn), Samuel Espinoza (va), Nicolò Amati (vc), Xisto Medeiros (db)]
Fonseca Barbosa, L. da:Song & Challenge Nimbus ▲ NI 5483 [DDD]
Maciel, J.:The Kingdom's Stone Nimbus ▲ NI 5483 [DDD]
Madureira, A.J.:Aralume Nimbus ▲ NI 5483 [DDD]
Madureira, A.J.:Baque de Luanda Nimbus ▲ NI 5483 [DDD]
Madureira, A.J.:Sloth Nimbus ▲ NI 5483 [DDD]
Madureira, A.J.:Toada e Dobrado da Cavlhada Nimbus ▲ NI 5483 [DDD]
Madureira, A.J.:Toré Nimbus ▲ NI 5483 [DDD]
Madureira, A.J.:The Warrior Nimbus ▲ NI 5483 [DDD]
Nóbrega De Almeida, A.C.:Rasgo do Nordeste Nimbus ▲ NI 5483 [DDD]
Pereira, C.:Northeastern Pieces Nimbus ▲ NI 5483 [DDD]
Pereira, C.:Variations on a Theme from *Guerra Peixe* Nimbus ▲ NI 5483 [DDD]
Paraiba SO
E. de Carvalho (cnd)
Bartók, B.:Con Va, w. K. Elaine (va) Delos ▲ DE 1018 [DDD]
Nobre, M.:Convergências Delos ▲ DE 1017 [DDD]
Prokofiev, S.:Con 2 Vn, w. S. Yoo (vn) Delos ▲ DE 1018 [DDD]
Tchaikovsky, P.:Vars on a Rococo Theme, w. E. Lopez (vc) Delos ▲ DE 1018 [DDD]
Villa–Lobos, H.:Chôro 8, w. E. Sawyer (pno), S. Muniz (pno) Delos ▲ DE 1017 [DDD]
Villa–Lobos, H.:Fant Vc, w. J. Starker (vc) Delos ▲ DE 1017 [DDD]
Villa–Lobos, H.:Uirapurú Delos ▲ DE 1017 [DDD]
Vivaldi, A.:Con for 2 Vcs, w. J. Starker (vc), Parisot (vc)—Finale Delos ▲ DE 1018 [DDD]
Paramount Studio Orch
Rodgers, R.:Music of, w. B. Crosby (sgr), R. Vallee (sgr), J. Macdonald (sgr), A. Jolson (sgr), et al., Whiteman Orch [cnd:Whiteman], Sinatra Orch [cnd:R. Sinatra]—On Your Toes; Jumbo; Present Arms; One Dam Thing After Another; The Boys from Syracuse; Heads Up; Lido Lady; Peggy Ann; Love Me Tonight; Higher & Higher; Spring is Here; The Girl Friend; Simple Simon; Hallelujah; I'm a Bum Pearl ("Flapper" series) ▲ PAST CD 9794 [AAD]
Pardubice CO
L. Hlaváček (cnd)
Voříšek, J.V.:Sym, Op. 24 Panton ("Very Famous" series) ▲ PAN 811201
P. Škvor (cnd)
Kalabis, V.:The Fable *(rec 1991)* Praga ▲ PR 255002
Pardubice Chamber PO
P. Altrichter (cnd)
Druschetzky, G.:Con Ob, w. Jan Adamus (ob) Panton ▲ PAN 810940
Gyrowetz, A.:Sinf concertante, w. Jan Adamus (ob) Panton ▲ PAN 810940
Reicha, J.:Con Ob, w. Jan Adamus (ob) Panton ▲ PAN 810940
Pardubice Philharmonic CO
T. Bräm (cnd)
Dvořák, A.:Rondo, w. Marek Jerie (vc) Panton ▲ PAN 811005

Pardubice Philharmonic CO (cont.)
T. Bräm (cnd) (cont.)
Dvořák, A.:Silent Woods, w. Marek Jerie (vc) Panton ▲ PAN 811005
Fauré, G.:Elégie, w. Marek Jerie (vc) Panton ▲ PAN 811005
Martinů, B.:Concertino Vc, Ww, Pno & Perc, w. Marek Jerie (vc) Panton ▲ PAN 811005
Tchaikovsky, P.:Vars on a Rococo Theme, w. Marek Jerie (vc) Panton ▲ PAN 811005
Pardubice State CO
L. Hlaváček (cnd)
Linek, J.:Con Hpd, w. *[unknown soloist]* Supraphon ▲ SUP 10 4154 [DDD]
Linek, J.:Con Org, w. *[unknown soloist]* Supraphon ▲ SUP 10 4154 [DDD]
Linek, J.:Epiphany Carol Supraphon ▲ SUP 10 4154 [DDD]
Linek, J.:Intradas Supraphon ▲ SUP 10 4154 [DDD]
Linek, J.:Lullaby Supraphon ▲ SUP 10 4154 [DDD]
Linek, J.:Morning Mass Pastoral Supraphon ▲ SUP 10 4154 [DDD]
Linek, J.:Pastorela iucunda Supraphon ▲ SUP 10 4154 [DDD]
Linek, J.:Sinf Pastoralis in C Supraphon ▲ SUP 10 4154 [DDD]
Linek, J.:Sinf Pastoralis in D Supraphon ▲ SUP 10 4154 [DDD]
Parforce Horn Corps Norderstedt
Musique de chasse Novalis ▲ 150051–2 [DDD]
Parforce Horn Players Munich
Hunting Music Orfeo ▲ 034821 [DDD]
Paris Chamber Ensemble
A. Jordan (cnd)
Chausson, E.:Songs, w. Felicity Lott (sop) FNAC Music ▲ 592300
Delage, M.:Songs, w. Felicity Lott (sop) FNAC Music ▲ 592300
Harsányi, T.:Nonet *(rec Oct. 1992)* Gallo ▲ CD 729 [DDD]
Jaubert, M.:Songs, w. Felicity Lott (sop) FNAC Music ▲ 592300
Martinů, B.:Nonet Wws & Strs *(rec Oct. 1992)* Gallo ▲ CD 729 [DDD]
Schoenberg, A.:Verklärte Nacht *(rec Fondation Eugène Napoléon à Paris, July 2, 1994)* Gallo ▲ CD 827 [DDD]
Strauss, R.:Sxt Strs *(rec Fondation Eugène Napoléon à Paris, July 2, 1994)* Gallo ▲ CD 827 [DDD]
Tansman, A.:Septet *(rec Oct. 1992)* Gallo ▲ CD 729 [DDD]
Wagner, R.:Siegfried Idyll *(rec Fondation Eugène Napoléon à Paris, July 2, 1994)* Gallo ▲ CD 827 [DDD]
Paris Concerts Colonne Orch
J. Horenstein (cnd)
Ravel, M.:Con Pno (left hand), w. V. Perlemuter (pno) *(rec 1955)* Vox Box ("Legends" series) 2–▲ CDX2 5507 [ADD]
Ravel, M.:Con in G Pno, w. V. Perlemuter (pno) *(rec 1955)* Vox Box ("Legends" series) 2–▲ CDX2 5507 [ADD]
Ravel, M.:Gaspard de la nuit, w. V. Perlemuter (pno) *(rec 1955)* Vox Box ("Legends" series) 2–▲ CDX2 5507 [ADD]
Paris Conservatory Société des Concerts Orch
Bach, J.S.:Brandenburg Con 5, w. A. Cortot (pno), J. Thibaud (vn), R. Cortet (fl) *(rec May 16, 1932)* Biddulph ▲ LAB 028 [ADD]
A. Argenta (cnd)
Berlioz, H.:Sym fantastique *(rec ca. 1958)* PWK Classics ▲ PWK 1147 [AAD]
L. Auriacombe (cnd)
Satie, E.:Gymnopédies—No. 2 Virgin Classics 2–▲ CDZB 62877
P. Boulez (cnd)
Berg, A.:Pieces Orch, Op. 6, w. BBC SO Originals 2–▲ ORISH 855
Debussy, C.:Jeux, w. BBC SO, w. BBC Sym Chorus Originals 2–▲ ORISH 855
Mahler, G.:Sym 2, w. Felicity Palmer (sop/mez), Tatiana Troyanos (mez), BBC SO, BBC Sym Chorus Originals 2–▲ ORISH 855
F. Cébron (cnd)
Gaubert, P.:Orch Music VAI Audio ▲ VAIA 1075 F
A. Cluytens (cnd)
Berlioz, H.:L'Enfance du Christ, w. Victoria de los Angeles (sop), Nicolai Gedda (ten), Roger Soyer (bar), Ernest Blanc (bar), René DuClos Chorus EMI Classics ("Doublefforte" series) 2–▲ CDFB 68586
The Early Recordings, w. Jeanne–Marie Darré (pno), Colonne Concerts Orch [cnd:P. Paray] *(rec between 1922 & 1947)* VAI Audio 2–▲ VAIA/IPA 1065 (m) [ADD]
Fauré, G.:Requiem, w. V. de los Angeles (sop), D. Fischer–Dieskau (bar), Brasseur Choir [L] EMI Classics ▲ CDC 47836
Offenbach, J.:Les Contes d'Hoffmann, w. E. Schwarzkopf (sop), G. d'Angelo (sop), V. de los Angeles (sop), N. Gedda (ten), G. London (bar), E. Blanc (bar), René DuClos Chorus [F] EMI Classics ("Studio" series) 2–▲ CDMB 63222 [ADD]
Rachmaninoff, S.:Con 3 Pno, w. E. Gilels (pno) Testament ▲ TES SBT 1029 [ADD]
Ravel, M.:Alborada del gracioso EMI Classics 2–▲ CDZB 69165
Ravel, M.:Une Barque sur l'océan EMI Classics 2–▲ CDZB 69165
Ravel, M.:Boléro EMI Classics 2–▲ CDZB 69165
Ravel, M.:Ma mère l'oye Orch EMI Classics 2–▲ CDZB 69165
Ravel, M.:Menuet antique EMI Classics 2–▲ CDZB 69165
Ravel, M.:Pavane pour une infante défunte EMI Classics 2–▲ CDZB 69165
Ravel, M.:Le Tombeau de Couperin EMI Classics 2–▲ CDZB 69165
Ravel, M.:La Valse EMI Classics 2–▲ CDZB 69165
Ravel, M.:Valses nobles et sentimentales EMI Classics 2–▲ CDZB 69165
Saint–Saëns, C.:Con 2 Pno, w. E. Gilels (pno) Testament ▲ TES SBT 1029 [ADD]
G. Enescu (cnd)
Lalo, E.:Sym espagnole, w. Yehudi Menuhin (vn) *(rec 1933 HMV recording)* Biddulph ▲ LAB 046 [ADD]
R. Frübeck. de Burgos (cnd)
On Wings of Song, w. Victoria de los Angeles (sop) EMI Classics ▲ CDM 69502
P. Gaubert (cnd)
Gaubert, P.:Les Chants de la mer VAI Audio ▲ VAIA 1075 F
A. Honegger (cnd)
Honegger, A.:Con Vc, w. Maurice Marechal (vc) *(rec 1929 – 1943)* Iron Needle ▲ IN 1324 [ADD]
Honegger, A.:Con Vc, w. Maurice Marechal (vc) EMI Classics ▲ CDC 55036
Honegger, A.:Pastorale d'été, w. M. Maréchal (vc) EMI Classics ▲ CDC 55036
Landowski, Tzipine (cnd)
Landowski, M.:Music of, w. Nadine Sautereau (sop), Jean–Christophe Benoit (bar), Xavier Depraz (bass), Michel Bouquet (spkr), Gilbert Audin (bn), Evelyne Atello, Didier Bouture, Ludovic Chevalier, Laurent Decker, Françoise Deslogères, Colonne Association des Concerts Orch, Boulogne–Billancourt Orch Conservatory, L'Itinéraire Ensemble, Harmonia Nova Orch Ensemble—Con Bn; Con pour ondes Martenot; Femme sans passé; Hauts de Hurlevent; Horologe; Mouvement; Notes de Nuit; Souvenir d'un jardin d'enfance; Ventriloque Chamade 3–▲ 5639/40/41 [AAD/DDD]
R. Leibowitz (cnd)
Auber, D.–F.:Les Diamants de la couronne (ov) Chesky ▲ CD61 [ADD]
Bizet, G.:Carmen (suite 1) Chesky ▲ CD61 [ADD]
Borodin, A.:Prince Igor (ov) Chesky ▲ CD61 [ADD]
Borodin, A.:Prince Igor (Polovtsian dances) Chesky ▲ CD61 [ADD]
Dukas, P.:L'Apprenti sorcier Chesky ▲ CD61 [ADD]
An Evening of Opera *(rec Paris, June 1960)* Chesky ▲ CD61 [ADD]
Gounod, C.:Faust (ballet music) Chesky ▲ CD57 [ADD]
Gounod, C.:Funeral March of a Marionette Chesky ▲ CD57 [ADD]
Mozart, W.A.:Ovs—Le nozze di Figaro Chesky ▲ CD61 [ADD]
Offenbach, J.:Barcarolle Chesky ▲ CD61 [ADD]
Offenbach, J.:Orphée aux enfers (sels) Chesky ▲ CD57 [ADD]
Pierné, G.:March of the Little Soldiers Chesky ▲ CD57 [ADD]
A Portrait of France Chesky ▲ CD57 [ADD]
Puccini, G.:Manon Lescaut (sels)—Intermezzo Chesky ▲ CD61 [ADD]

▲ = CD ♦ = Enhanced CD Δ = MD ■ = Cassette Tape □ = DCC

Paris Conservatory Société des Concerts Orch (cont.)
R. Leibowitz (cnd) (cont.)
Ravel, M.:Boléro — Chesky ▲ CD57 [ADD]
Ravel, M.:La Valse — Chesky ▲ CD57 [ADD]
Saint-Saëns, C.:Danse macabre — Chesky ▲ CD57 [ADD]
J. Martinon (cnd)
Bizet, G.:Jeux d'enfants *(rec 1960)* — London 2-▲ 443033-2 [ADD]
Saint-Saëns, C.:Danse macabre *(rec 1960)* — London 2-▲ 443033-2 [ADD]
Saint-Saëns, C.:Le Rouet d'Omphale *(rec 1960)* — London 2-▲ 443033-2 [ADD]
C. Munch (cnd)
Bloch, E.:Con Vn, w. J. Szigeti (vn) *(rec 1939 for Columbia Records)* — Pearl ▲ PEA 9938 (m) [AAD]
Mozart, W.A.:Con 5 Vn, w. Jacques Thibaud (vn) — Biddulph ▲ LAB 114
Ravel, M.:Con Pno (left hand), w. A. Cortot (pno) *(rec 1939 for Victor)* — Pearl ▲ PEA 9491 (m) [AAD]
Saint-Saëns, C.:Con 4 Pno, w. A. Cortot (pno) *(rec 1935 for Victor)* — Pearl ▲ PEA 9491 (m) [AAD]
G. Prêtre (cnd)
Puccini, G.:Tosca, w. M. Callas (sop), C. Bergonzi (ten), T. Gobbi (bar), Paris Opera Chorus [I] — EMI Classics ("Studio" series) 2-▲ CDMB 69974 [ADD]
N. Rescigno (cnd)
Beethoven, L. van:Ah, perfido!, w. M. Callas (sop) [I] — EMI Classics ("Studio" series) 2-▲ CDMB 63625 [ADD]
Verdi, G.:Arias, w. Maria Callas (sop), Philharmonia Orch—arias from Aida, Attila, Ballo in maschera, Don Carlos, Ernani, I Lombardi, Macbeth, Nabucco, Vespri siciliani [I] — EMI Classics ▲ CDC 47730 [ADD]
Verdi, G.:Arias, w. M. Callas (sop)—arias from Aroldo, Attila, Ballo in maschera, Il corsaro, Don Carlos, Otello, Trovatore [I] — EMI Classics ▲ CDC 47943
H. Rosbaud (cnd)
Mozart, W.A.:Così fan tutte, w. M. Adani (sop), T. Stich-Randall (mez), T. Berganza (mez), L. Alva (ten), A. Cortis (ten), R. Panerai (bar), Aix-en-Provence Festival Chorus [I] *(rec live, Aix-en-Provence, July 26, 1957)* — Melodram 3-▲ MEL 37084 [AAD]
Mozart, W.A.:Entführung, w. Teresa Stich-Randall (mez), Nicolai Gedda (ten), Michel Sénéchal (ten), Carmen Prieto (sgr), Elisabeth Brasseur Chorale *(rec Aix-en-Provence Festival, France, 1954)* — Agorá ("Phoenix" series) 2-▲ 512
Schubert, Franz:Sym 9 *(rec live, Aix-en-Provence 7/15/56)* — Melodram 2-▲ MEL 26524 [ADD]
R. Wagner (cnd)
Vivaldi, A.:Gloria, RV.589, w. Andrée Esposito (sop), Solange Michel (sop), Janine Collard (cta), Roger Wagner Chorale — EMI Classics ("Baroque" series) ▲ CDK 65737
B. Walter (cnd)
Berlioz, H.:Sym fantastique — Iron Needle ▲ 1305 (m)
Berlioz, H.:Sym fantastique *(rec May 19 & 20, 1939)* — VAI Audio ▲ VAIA 1081 F
Berlioz, H.:Sym fantastique *(rec 1939)* — Grammofono 2000 ▲ GRM 78580
Handel, G.F.:Concerti grossi, Op. 6—No. 12 *(rec 1938-42)* — Phonographe ▲ PHG CD 5028
Haydn, J.:Sym 92, "Oxford" — Dutton Laboratories ▲ DUT 5003
Haydn, J.:Sym 92, "Oxford" *(rec May 7, 1938)* — VAI Audio ▲ VAIA 1081
Haydn, J.:Sym 92, "Oxford" — Grammofono 2000 ▲ GRM 78629
Haydn, J.:Sym 92, "Oxford" *(rec 1938)* — Pearl ▲ PEA 9945 (m) [AAD]
Strauss (II), Joh.:Ovs—Die Fledermaus *(rec 1938, issued as HMV DB 35)* — Pearl ▲ PEA 9945 (m) [AAD]
F. von Weingartner (cnd)
Beethoven, L. van:Con 3 Pno, w. M. Long (pno) *(rec 1939)* — Koch Legacy ▲ 3-7128-2 H1
Berlioz, H.:Les Troyens (sels)—March *(rec Paris, July 21, 1939)* — Arkadia ▲ 629 [ADD]
Liszt, F.:Cons Pno, w. E. von Sauer (pno) *(rec Dec. 1928)* — Pearl ▲ PEA 9403 (m) [AAD]
Wagner, R.:Rienzi, der Letzte der Tribunen (ov) *(rec Paris, July 21, 1939)* — Arkadia ▲ 629 [ADD]
Wagner, R.:Tannhäuser (orch sels)—Prelude, Act III *(rec Paris, May 12, 1939)* — Arkadia ▲ 629 [ADD]
Wagner, R.:Tristan und Isolde (orch sels)—Prelude, Act III *(rec Paris, May 12, 1939)* — Arkadia ▲ 629 [ADD]
A. Wolff (cnd)
Glazunov, A.:The Seasons — London ("Weekend Classics" series) ▲ 433088-2 [AAD]
Massenet, J.:Suite 4 — London ("Weekend Classics" series) ▲ 433088-2 [AAD]
Massenet, J.:Suite 7 — London ("Weekend Classics" series) ▲ 433088-2 [AAD]

Paris Duo
Massenet, J.:Songs, w. Didier Henry (bar), Angeline Pondepeyre (pno)—Madrigal; Le sentier perdu; Nuit d'Espagne; Narcisse à la fontaine; Un adieu; Si les fleurs avaient des yeux; Sérénade de Zanetto; Puisqu'elle a pris ma vie; Vous aimerez demain; Elégie; A mignonne; La lettre; A colombine; Beaux yeux que j'Aime; Gavotte de Puyjoli; Fleurs cueillies; L'improvisateur; Poème du Souvenir *(rec 1868-1907)* — Maguelone ▲ MAG 519.202 [DDD]

Paris École Normale CO
A. Cortot (cnd)
Bach, J.S.:Brandenburg Con 5, w. A. Cortot (pno), Jacques Thibaud (vn) *(rec 1930)* — Music Memoria ▲ 30321
Couperin, F.:Dans le goût théatral *(rec between May 10, 1932)* — Koch Historic 2-▲ 7705-2 [ADD]

Paris Festival Orch
J. Gardinon (cnd)
Debussy, C.:La Mer — Vivace 3-▲ E 327
Debussy, C.:La Mer — Vivace ▲ 571 [ADD]
Debussy, C.:Prélude à l'après-midi d'un faune — Vivace ▲ 571 [ADD]
Debussy, C.:Prélude à l'après-midi d'un faune — Vivace 3-▲ E 327
Ravel, M.:Alborada del gracioso — Vivace 3-▲ E 327
Ravel, M.:Intro & Allegro — Vivace ▲ 571 [ADD]
Ravel, M.:Intro & Allegro — Vivace 3-▲ E 327

Paris Harmonie Orch
J. Seurre (cnd)
Paganini, N.:Intro & Vars on "Nel cor più", w. R. Ricci (vn) — One-Eleven ▲ URS 91070 [ADD]
Tchaikovsky, P.:Con Vn, w. R. Ricci (vn) — One-Eleven ▲ URS 91070 [ADD]

Paris Harp Sextet
The Paris Harp Sextet — Quantum ▲ QM 6934 [DDD]

Paris Instrumental Ensemble
F. Holland (cnd)
Renaissance Brass Music, w. Eastman Brass Quintet — Allegretto ▲ ACD 8154 [ADD] ■ ACS 8154

Paris Instrumental Group
Roussel, A.:Chamber Music—Le marchand de sable qui passe; Impromptu for Hp; Trio for Fl, Va & Vc; 2 melodies sur des poemes de Ronsard [Rossignol, mon mignon; Ciel, aer et vens]; Elpenor [Poème radiophonique]; Divertissement for Pno & Ww Qnt; Adagio for Trio — Adda ▲ ADD 581064 [DDD]

Paris Lyon Opera Orch
G. Ferro (cnd)
Donizetti, G.:Don Pasquale, w. B. Hendricks (sop), L. Canonici (ten), G. Bacquier (bar), L. Quilico (bar), R. Schirrer (bar), Paris Lyon Opera Chorus [I] — Erato 2-▲ 2292-45487-2-ZA [DDD]
Rossini, G.:Arias, w. K. Ricciarelli (sop), Paris Lyon Opera Chorus — Virgin Classics ▲ CDC 59660
J. E. Gardiner (cnd)
Gluck, C.W.:La Recontre imprévue, w. C. Le Coz (sop), L. Dawson (sop), C. Dubosc (sop), S. Marin-Degor (sop), G. Fletcher (sgr), F. Dudziak (ten), G. de Mey (ten), J.-L. Viala (ten), G. Cachémaille (bar), J.-P. Lafont (bass), Paris Lyon Opera Chorus [F] — Erato 2-▲ 2292-45516-2 [DDD]
Messager, A.:Fortunio, w. C. Alliot-Lugaz (sop), T. Dran (ten), G. Cachémaille (bar), R. Schirrer (bar), Paris Lyon Opera Chorus — Erato 2-▲ 45983-2
R. Leppard (cnd)
Rameau, J.P.:Dardanus, w. C. Eda-Pierre (sop), F. von Stade (mez), G. Gautier (ten), R. Soyer (bar), J. Van Dam (b-bar), Paris Lyon Opera Chorus — Erato 2-▲ 95312-2
K. Nagano (cnd)
Floyd, C.:Susannah, w. C. Studer (sop—Sussanah Polk), J. Hadley (ten—Sam Polk), S. Ramey (bass—Rev. Olin Blitch), Paris Lyon Opera Chorus — Virgin Classics ▲ CDCB 45039

Paris Lyon Opera Orch (cont.)
K. Nagano (cnd) (cont.)
Prokofiev, S.:The Love for 3 Oranges (suite), w. C. Dubosc (sop), G. Gautier (ten), J.-L. Viala (ten), G. Bacquier (bar), J. Bastin (bass), Paris Lyon Opera Chorus [F] — Virgin Classics ▲ 59566 [DDD]
Strauss, R.:Salome, w. K. Huffstodt (sop), H. Jossoud (mez), J. Dupouy (ten), J.L. Viala (ten), J. van Dam (bar), Paris Lyon Opera Chorus — Virgin Classics 2-▲ CDCB 59054

Paris Lyric Orch
J. Etcheverry (cnd)
Massenet, J.:Hérodiade (sels), w. Michele Le Bris (sop—Salomé), Denise Scharley (cta—Hérodiade), Guy Chauvet (ten—Jean), Robert Massard (bar—Hérode)—Il est doux, Il est bon; Hérode, Ne me refuse pas; Jean, je le revois; Vision fugitive; Astres etincelants; Charme des jours passés; Salomé, laisse-moi t'aimer; Ne pouvant réprimer les élans de la foi; Quand nos jours s'éteindront...; Ballet — Accord ▲ ACD 204272 [AAD]

Paris Métamorphoses Ensemble
Ockeghem, J.:Requiem [L] — Arion ▲ ARN 68149 [DDD]
M. Bourbon (cnd)
Bertrand, A. de:Les Amours de Ronsard (sels) — Arion 2-▲ ARN 268230
Josquin Desprez:Missa & Plainchant, "Pange lingua" [L] *(rec 1/87)* — Arion ▲ ARN 68043 [DDD]
Josquin Desprez:Motets—Proch dolor; Plaine de dueil; Cueurs désolèz; Domine, ne in furore tuo; Déploration de la mort de Ockeghem [L] *(rec 1/87)* — Arion ▲ ARN 68043 [DDD]
Monteverdi, C.:Missa in illo tempore, w. Coeli et Terra Vocal Ensemble — Arion ▲ ARN 68292 [DDD]

Paris Mozart Festival Orch
B. Walter (cnd)
Mozart, W.A.:Zauberflöte (ov) *(rec 1928)* — Iron Needle ▲ 1317 (m) [ADD]

Paris National Orch
C. Schuricht (cnd)
Beethoven, L. van:Con 3 Pno, w. C. Arrau (pno) *(rec live, Paris 3/24/59)* — Melodram ("Connaisseur" series) 2-▲ CD 27504 (m) [AAD]
Mahler, G.:Sym 2, w. E. Selig (sop), E. Zareska (cta), Paris National Chorus [G] *(rec live, Paris 2/20/58)* — Melodram ("Connaisseur" series) 2-▲ CD 27504 (m) [AAD]

Paris Opera Orch
S. Baudo (cnd)
Honegger, A.:Le Roi David, w. Henri Doublier (nar), Jacqueline Brumaire (sop), Denise Scharley (alt), Jacques Pottier (ten), Elisabeth Brasseur Chorale — Accord ▲ ACD 200822 [AAD]
R. Benzi (cnd)
Falla, M. de:El sombrero de tres picos (dances)—The Miller's Dance & Final Dance *(rec 1964)* — Philips ("Spanish" series) ▲ 432829-2 [ADD]
P. Boulez (cnd)
Berg, A.:Lulu, w. T. Stratas (sop), Y. Minton (mez), V. Schwarz (sop), K. Riegel (ten), F. Mazura (bar)—Act 3 [G] — Deutsche Grammophon 3-▲ 415489-2 [ADD]
H. Busser (cnd)
Gounod, C.:Faust, w. M. Berthon (sop—Marguerite), C. Vezzani (ten—Faust), L. Musy (b-bar—Valentin), M. Journet (bass—Mephistofeles), Paris Opera Chorus [F] *(rec 1930)* — Music Memoria 2-▲ 30187
Gounod, C.:Faust, w. M. Berthon (sop), M. Coiffier (sop), J. Montfort (mez), C. Vezzani (ten), L. Musy (b-bar), M. Cozette (bar), M. Journet (bass), Paris Opera Chorus [F] *(rec 1930)* — Pearl 2-▲ PEA 9987 [AAD]
A. Cluytens (cnd)
D. Mitropoulos (cnd)
Famous Russian Music, w. New York PO [cnd:Dmitri Mitropoulos] — Enterprise ("Flowers" series) ▲ ENTBL 22 [ADD]
Gounod, C.:Faust, w. V. de los Angeles (sop), L. Berton (sop), R. Gorr (mez), N. Gedda (ten), E. Blanc (bar), B. Christoff (bass) [F] — Angel ("Studio" series) 3-▲ CDMC 69983 [ADD]
Gounod, C.:Faust (sels), w. Liliane Berton (sop), Victoria de los Angeles (sop), Rita Gorr (mez), Nicolai Gedda (ten), Victor Autran (bar), Ernest Blanc (bar), Boris Christoff (bass), Paris Opera Chorus — Classics for Pleasure ("Eminence" series) ▲ CDEMX 2215 [DDD]
P. Dervaux (cnd)
Poulenc, F.:Dialogues des Carmélites, w. D. Duval (sop), R. Crespin (sop), L. Berton (sop), D. Scharley (mez), R. Gorr (mez), P. Finel (ten), X. Depraz (bass) [F] — EMI Classics 2-▲ CDCB 49331 (m) [ADD]
R. Frühbeck de Burgos (cnd)
Bizet, G.:Carmen, w. M. Freni (sop), G. Bumbry (mez), J. Vickers (ten), K. Paskalis (bar), Paris Opera Chorus [opéra comique version] [F] — EMI Classics ("Studio" series) 2-▲ CDMB 63643 [ADD]
A. Giorgi (cnd)
Massenet, J.:Amadis, w. Paris Opera Chorus — Forlane 2-▲ FRL 16578 [DDD]
A. Jolivet (cnd)
Jolivet, A.:Con for Hp, w. Lily Laskine (hp) — Adès ▲ ADE 203492 [ADD]
Jolivet, A.:Con for Ondes Martenot, w. Ginette Martenot (ondes martenot) — Adès ▲ ADE 203492 [ADD]
A. Lombard (cnd)
Gounod, C.:Roméo et Juliette, w. M. Freni (sop—Juliette), F. Corelli (ten—Roméo), H. Gui (bar—Mercutio), C. Càles (bar—Capulet), X. Depraz (bass—Frère Laurent), Paris Opera Chorus — EMI Classics ▲ CDMB 65290
L. Maazel (cnd)
Mozart, W.A.:Don Giovanni, w. E. Moser (sop), K. Te Kanawa (sop), T. Berganza (mez), K. Riegel (ten), G. Raimondi (ten), J. Van Dam (b-bar), J. Macurdy (bass), Paris Opera Chorus [I] — CBS 3-▲ M3K 35192
Mozart, W.A.:Don Giovanni (sels), w. Kiri Te Kanawa (sop), Teresa Berganza (mez), José Van Dam (bass-bar), Ruggero Raimondi (bass), Paris Opera Chorus — Sony Classical ("Essential Classics" series) ▲ SBK 62663 ■ SBT 62663
Mozart, W.A.:Don Giovanni (sels), w. E. Moser (sop), K. Te Kanawa (sop), T. Berganza (mez), K. Riegel (ten), G. Raimondi (ten), J. Van Dam (b-bar), J. Macurdy (bass) — CBS ■ MT 35859
C. Mackerras (cnd)
Janácek, L.:Cappriccio, w. Mikhail Rudy (pno) — EMI Classics ▲ CDC 55585
Janácek, L.:Concertino Pno, w. Mikhail Rudy (pno) — EMI Classics ▲ CDC 55585
J.-B. Mari (cnd)
Delibes, L.:Coppélia (sels) — EMI Classics 2-▲ CDZB 67208
Delibes, L.:Sylvia—highlights — EMI Classics 2-▲ CDZB 67208
D. Milhaud (cnd)
Milhaud, D.:Les Malheurs d'Orphée (sels), w. Jacqueline Brumaire (sop), Jean Giraudeau (ten) — Adès ▲ ADE 203452 [AAD]
Milhaud, D.:Pauvre matelot (sels), w. Jacqueline Brumaire (sop), Jean Giraudeau (ten) — Adès ▲ ADE 203452 [AAD]
Milhaud, D.:Service sacré, w. Heinz Rehfuss (bar), French Radio-TV Chorus — Accord ▲ ACD 201892 [AAD]
G. Prêtre (cnd)
Bellini, V.:Norma (sels), w. M. Callas (sop), F. Cossotto (mez), G. Cecchele (ten), I. Vinco (bass), Paris Opera Chorus—sels. *(rec 1965)* — Melodram ▲ MLO 16038 [ADD]
Bizet, G.:Carmen, w. M. Callas (sop), A. Guiot (sop), N. Gedda (ten), R. Massard (bar), Paris Opera Chorus [F] — EMI Classics 2-▲ CDCB 54368
Bizet, G.:Carmen (sels), w. M. Callas (sop), A. Guiot (sop), N. Gedda (ten), R. Massard (bar) [F] — EMI Classics ▲ CDM 63075 ■ EG 63075
Bizet, G.:Les Pêcheurs de perles, w. I. Cotrubas (sop), A. Vanzo (ten), G. Sarabia (bar), R. Soyer (bass), Paris Opera Chorus — Classics for Pleasure ▲ CDCFP 4721 [ADD]
Gounod, C.:Faust, w. M. Freni (sop), P. Domingo (ten), T. Allen (bar), N. Ghiaurov (bass) [F] — EMI Classics 3-▲ CDCC 47493 [ADD]
Gounod, C.:Faust (sels), w. M. Freni (sop), P. Domingo (ten), T. Allen (bar), N. Ghiaurov (bass), Orch de Paris, Paris Opera Chorus — EMI Classics ▲ ZDM 63090
Jongen, J.:Symphonie Concertante, w. V. Fox (org) — EMI Classics ▲ CDM 65075
Saint-Saëns, C.:Samson et Dalila, w. R. Gorr (mez), J. Vickers (ten), E. Blanc (bar), René DuClos Chorus [F] — EMI Classics 2-▲ CDCB 47895
Saint-Saëns, C.:Samson et Dalila (sels), w. R. Gorr (mez), J. Vickers (ten), E. Blanc (bar) — EMI Classics ▲ ZDM 63935

ORCH. & ENS.

Paris Opera Orch (cont.)

N. Rescigno (cnd)

Puccini, G.:Tosca, w. M. Callas (sop), R. Cioni (ten), T. Gobbi (bar), Paris Opera Chorus *(rec live, Paris March 3, 1965)* Melodram 2-▲ CDM 26033 [ADD]

M. Rosenthal (cnd)

Albéniz, I.:Iberia Suite Adès ▲ ADE 202502 [AAD]
Borodin, A.:In the Steppes of Central Asia Adès ▲ ADE 204182 [AAD]
Debussy, C.:Danse Pno, "Tarantelle styrienne" Adès ▲ ADE 132832 [AAD]
Debussy, C.:Invocation, w. French Radio-TV Chorus Adès ▲ ADE 203852 AAD
Debussy, C.:Marche écossaise sur un thème populaire Adès ▲ ADE 203852 AAD
Debussy, C.:La Mer Adès ▲ ADE 203852 AAD
Debussy, C.:Nocturnes, w. French Radio-TV Chorus Adès ▲ ADE 203852 AAD
Debussy, C.:Prélude à l'après-midi d'un faune, w. Lucien Lavaillotte (fl) Adès ▲ ADE 203892 [AAD]
Debussy, C.:Le Printemps, w. French Radio-TV Chorus—Salut printemps version Adès ▲ ADE 203852 AAD
Falla, M. de:El amor brujo Adès ▲ ADE 132832 [AAD]
Falla, M. de:El amor brujo, w. A. Peris de Pruliére (mez) *(rec ca. 1953)* MCA Classics ▲ MCAD 10481 (m/s) [ADD]
Falla, M. de:Noches en los jardines de España, w. Yvonne Loriod (pno)—9 sels Adès ▲ ADE 202502 [AAD]
Falla, M. de:El sombrero de tres picos, w. Yvonne Loriod (pno) Adès ▲ ADE 202502 [AAD]
Mussorgsky, M.:Night Adès ▲ ADE 204182 [AAD]
Ravel, M.:Alborada del gracioso Adès ▲ ADE 203862 [AAD]
Ravel, M.:Daphins et Chloé, w. French Radio-TV Chorus Adès ▲ ADE 140742 [DDD]
Ravel, M.:Ma mère l'oye Orch Adès ▲ ADE 203862 [AAD]
Ravel, M.:Rapsodie espagnole Adès ▲ ADE 203862 [AAD]
Ravel, M.:La Valse Adès ▲ ADE 203862 [AAD]
Rimsky-Korsakov, N.:Russian Easter Festival Adès ▲ ADE 204182 [AAD]
Rimsky-Korsakov, N.:The Tale of Tsar Saltan (orch sels)—Flight of the Bumblebee Adès ▲ ADE 204182 [AAD]
Rosenthal, M.:Offenbachiana Adès ▲ ADE 132832 [AAD]
Tchaikovsky, P.:Capriccio italien Adès ▲ ADE 204182 [AAD]

J. Rudel (cnd)

Charpentier, G.:Louise, w. B. Sills (sop—Louise), M. Dunn (mez—Louise's Mother), N. Gedda (ten—Julien), J. Van Dam (bass-bar—Louise's Father), Paris Opera Chorus EMI Classics ▲ CDMC 65299

H. Scherchen (cnd)

Weber, C.M. von:Ovs—Euryanthe; Preciosa; Jubel; Oberon; Abu Hassan; Peter Schmoll Adès ▲ ADE 202692 [AAD]

C. Schuricht (cnd)

Mozart, W.A.:Sym 36 Adès ▲ ADE 132292
Mozart, W.A.:Sym 36 *(rec live, 1964)* Originals ▲ ORISH 823 [ADD]
Mozart, W.A.:Sym 40 Adès ▲ ADE 132292
Mozart, W.A.:Sym 40 *(rec live, 1964)* Originals ▲ ORISH 823 [ADD]

G. Sébastian (cnd)

Massenet, J.:Espada *(rec 1956)* Forlane ▲ FOR 16586 [AAD]
Meyerbeer, G.:L'Africiane—Overture; & Marche Indienne *(rec 1953)* Forlane ▲ FOR 16586 [AAD]
Meyerbeer, G.:Le Pardon de Ploërmel (ov) *(rec 1953)* Forlane ▲ FOR 16586 [AAD]
Verdi, G.:Il trovatore (sels), w. M. Callas (sop)—3 arias [I] *(rec live, Paris, 12/19/58)* Melodram 2-▲ MEL 26001 (m) [AAD]

G. Solti (cnd)

Mozart, W.A.:Nozze di Figaro, w. Mirella Freni (sop), Gundala Janowitz (sop), Jane Berbié (mez), Frederica von Stade (mez), Michel Sénéchal (ten), José Van Dam (b-bar), Kurt Moll (bass), Paris Opera Chorus *(rec live, Paris, Apr 7, 1973)* Agorá ("Phoenix" series) 3-▲ 515

M. Veltri (cnd)

Live at the Paris Opera, w. June Anderson (sop), Alfredo Kraus (ten) EMI Classics ▲ CDC 49067 [DDD]

Paris Opera Orch Soloists

Debussy, C.:Danses sacrée et profane, w. M. Klinko (hp) EMI Classics ▲ CDC 54884
Debussy, C.:Petite suite, w. M. Klinko (hp)—En bateau [arr. for flute & harp] EMI Classics ▲ CDC 54884
Debussy, C.:Son Fl, w. M. Klinko (hp) [arr. for flute & harp] EMI Classics ▲ CDC 54884
Fauré, G.:Berceuse Vn, w. M. Klinko (hp) [arr. for flute & harp] EMI Classics ▲ CDC 54884
Ibert, J.:Entracte, w. M. Klinko (hp) [fl & hp] EMI Classics ▲ CDC 54884
Ravel, M.:Intro & Allegro, w. M. Klinko (hp) EMI Classics ▲ CDC 54884
Ravel, M.:Pavane pour une infante défunte, w. M. Klinko (hp) [arr. for flute & harp] EMI Classics ▲ CDC 54884
Ravel, M.:Vocalise-étude en forme de habanera, w. M. Klinko (hp) [arr. for flute & harp] EMI Classics ▲ CDC 54884
Saint-Saëns, C.:Choral Music, w. H. Lamy (ten), J.-F. Hatton (org), F. Polgár (cnd), Neuilly St-Croix Youth Chorus—Pie Jesu; Ave Verum Adès ▲ ADE 202982

L. Frémaux (cnd)

Poulenc, F.:Le Bal masqué, w. Pierre Bernac (bar), Francis Poulenc (pno) Adès ▲ ADE 202522 [AAD]

F. Polgár (cnd)

Fauré, G.:Choral Music, w. Hervé Lamy (ten), Jean-François Hatton (org), Neuilly St-Croix Youth Chorus—Requiem, Op. 48 [1893 Version]; Salve Regina, Op. 67/1; Ave Maria, Op. 67/2; Tantum Ergo, Op. 65/2; Ave Verum, Op. 65/1; Cantique de Jean Racine, Op. 11 Adès ▲ ADE 202982

Paris Opéra-Comique Orch

G. Cloëz (cnd)

Bizet, G.:Carmen (sels), w. C. Supervia (mez), A. Vavon (sop), A. Bernadet (mez), J.-F. Delmas (b-bar), G. Micheletti (ten), A. Endreze (bar), Paris Opéra-Comique Chorus—14 arias & scenes [F] *(rec Paris, 1930)* The Classical Collector ▲ FDC 2002 (m) [AAD]
Bizet, G.:Carmen (sels), w. C. Supervia (mez), A. Vavon (sop), A. Bernadet (mez), G. Micheletti (ten), A. Endreze (bar), Paris Opéra-Comique Chorus—8 arias & scenes *(rec Paris 1930)* Nimbus ("Prima Voce" series) 2-▲ NI 7836/7 [ADD]
Puccini, G.:Tosca (sels), w. M.-C. Vallin (sop), E. di Mazzei (ten), P. Payen (bar), A. Endrèze (bar), Paris Opéra-Comique Chorus [abridged version] [F] *(rec 1932)* Music Memoria ▲ 30376

E. Cohen (cnd)

Massenet, J.:Manon, w. G. Féraldy (sop), J. Rogatchewsky (ten), L. Guénot (bass), Paris Opéra-Comique Chorus [F] *(rec 1928-29 for Columbia)* Classical Collector 2-▲ FDC 2 2001 (m) [AAD]

P. Dervaux (cnd)

Bizet, G.:Les Pêcheurs de perles, w. J. Micheau (sop), N. Gedda (ten), E. Blanc (bar), J. Mars (bar), Paris Opéra-Comique Chorus [F] EMI Classics ("Studio" series) 2-▲ CDMB 69704 [ADD]

A. Lombard (cnd)

Delibes, L.:Lakmé, w. M. Mesplé (sop), D. Millet (sop), C. Burles (ten), R. Soyer (bass), Paris Opéra-Comique Chorus EMI Classics 2-▲ CDCB 49430
Delibes, L.:Lakmé (sels), w. M. Mesplé (sop), D. Millet (sop), C. Burles (ten), R. Soyer (bass), Paris Opéra-Comique Chorus EMI Classics ▲ ZDM 63447

P. Monteux (cnd)

Massenet, J.:Manon, w. V. De los Angeles (sop), H. Legay (ten), M. Dens (bar), J. Borthayre (bass), Paris Opéra-Comique Chorus [F] EMI Classics 3-▲ CDMC 63549 (m) [ADD]

F. Rühlmann (cnd)

Gounod, C.:Roméo et Juliette, w. Yvonne Gall (sop—Juliette), Champell (sop—Stéphano), Jeanne Goulancourt (mez—Gertrude), Agustarello Affre (ten—Roméo), Edmond Tirmont (ten—Tybalt), Alexis Boyer (bar—Mercutio), Pierre Dupré (bar—Paris), Hypolite Belhomme (bar—Grégorio), Marcel Journet (bass—Frère Laurent), Henri Albers (bass—Capulet), Valermont (bass—The Duke), Paris Opéra-Comique Chorus *(rec 1912)* VAI Audio ▲ VAIA 1064-3 F

Paris Orch—see Orchestre de Paris

Paris Orchestral Ensemble

A. Jordan (cnd)

Mozart, W.A.:Con 23 Pno, w. M. Tipo (pno) EMI Classics ▲ CDC 54234
Mozart, W.A.:Con 27 Pno, w. M. Tipo (pno) EMI Classics ▲ CDC 54234
Mozart, W.A.:Zauberflöte, w. S. Jo (sop), L. Orgonasova (sop), Martina Bovet (sop), G. Winbergh (ten), H. Hagegard (bar), Romande Chamber Choir, Pro Arte Lausanne Erato 2-▲ 2292-45469-2 [DDD]

J.-P. Wallez (cnd)

Mozart, W.A.:Arias, w. J. van Dam (b-bar)—from Così fan tutte, Don Giovanni, Le nozze di Figaro, Die Zauberflöte; (2 concert arias) K. 513 & K.541 [G,I] *(rec live Nov. 22, 1986)* Forlane ▲ FOR 16562 [DDD]
Mozart, W.A.:Ovs—Così fan tutte; Le nozze di Figaro *(rec live Nov. 22, 1986)* Forlane ▲ FOR 16562 [DDD]
Vivaldi, A.:Cons Vn, Op. 8/1-4, "The Four Seasons", w. Jean-Pierre Wallez (vn) Forlane ▲ FRL 16644 [AAD]

Paris Quartet [F. Brüggen (fl), J. Shröder (vn), G. Leonhardt (vl), A. Bylsma (vc)]

Telemann, G.P.:Nouveaux quatuors en six suites, "Paris Quartets" Teldec 2-▲ 92177-2

Paris RSO

W. Mengelberg (cnd)

Dvořák, A.:Con Vc, w. Maurice Gendron (vc) *(rec live, Paris, Jan 16, 1944)* Arkadia ▲ 627 [ADD]

C. Surinach (cnd)

Albéniz, I.:Rondeña, Jerez, Lavapies Montilla ▲ MNT 3018 [ADD]
Falla, M. de:La vida breve (sels) Montilla ▲ MNT 3018 [ADD]
Turina, J.:Ritmos Montilla ▲ MNT 3018 [ADD]

Paris Saxophone Quintet

Defaye, J.-M.:Dialogue Quantum ▲ QM 6945
Naude, J.-C.:Sun, Sand, Sea, Sax Quantum ▲ QM 6945
Naulais, J.:Atout Sax Quantum ▲ QM 6945
Nicolas, M.:Tango Baroque Quantum ▲ QM 6945
Robert, L.:Flammes et Fumées Quantum ▲ QM 6945
Terranova, C.:Métamorphose Quantum ▲ QM 6945

Paris Sorbonne Orch

J. Grimbert (cnd)

Caplet, A.:Myrrha, w. Sharon Coste (sop), Marc Duguay (ten), Jean-François Lapointe (bar), Paris Sorbonne Chorus *(rec Grand Amphithéâtre of the Sorbonne)* Marco Polo ▲ 8.223755 [DDD]
Caplet, A.:Tout est lumière, w. Paris Sorbonne Chorus *(rec Grand Amphithéâtre of the Sorbonne)* Marco Polo ▲ 8.223755 [DDD]
Debussy, C.:Le Printemps, w. Paris Sorbonne Chorus *(rec Grand Amphithéâtre of the Sorbonne)* Marco Polo ▲ 8.223755 [DDD]
Ravel, M.:L'Aurore, w. Paris Sorbonne Chorus *(rec Grand Amphithéâtre of the Sorbonne)* Marco Polo ▲ 8.223755 [DDD]
Ravel, M.:Les Bayadères, w. Paris Sorbonne Chorus *(rec Grand Amphithéâtre of the Sorbonne)* Marco Polo ▲ 8.223755 [DDD]
Ravel, M.:Matinée de Provence, w. Paris Sorbonne Chorus *(rec Grand Amphithéâtre of the Sorbonne)* Marco Polo ▲ 8.223755 [DDD]
Ravel, M.:La Nuit, w. Gaëlle Le Roi (sop), Paris Sorbonne Chorus *(rec Grand Amphithéâtre of the Sorbonne)* Marco Polo ▲ 8.223755 [DDD]
Ravel, M.:Tout est lumière, w. Gaëlle Le Roi (sop), Paris Sorbonne Chorus *(rec Grand Amphithéâtre of the Sorbonne)* Marco Polo ▲ 8.223755 [DDD]

Paris String Quartet

D. My (cnd)

Pesson, G.:Music of, w. Donatienne Michel-Dansac (sop), Sandra Roulx (mez), Stuart Patterson (ten), Paul-Alexandre Dubois (bar), Pascal Sausy (bar), Florence Millet (pno), Fa Ensemble—Le gel, par jeu for Fl, Cl, Hn, Bass Mar, Vn & Vc; Qt for Strs; Non Sapremo Mai di Questo Mi for Fl, Vn & Pno; 5 Poèmes de Sandro Penna for Bar, B Cl, Hn, Vn & Vc; La lumière n'a pas de bras pour nous porter for Amplified Pno; La vita è come l'albero di natale for Vn & Pno; Nocturnes en quatuor for Cl, Pno, Vn & Vc; Les chants faëz for Pno & 10 Instrs; Sur-le-champ for 4 Voices & 9 Instrs [from a text by Pierre Alferi] Accord ▲ ACD 204682 [DDD]

Paris String Quartet [Thierry Brodard (vn), Jean-Michel Berrette (vn), Dominique Lobet (va), Jean-Philippe Martignoni (vc)]

Debussy, C.:Qt Strs Valois ▲ V 4730
Franck, C.:Qnt Pno, w. Akiko Ebi (pno) Adès ▲ ADE 204112 [DDD]
Menu, P.:Sonatine Valois ▲ V 4730
Pierné, G.:Qnt Pno, w. Akiko Ebi (pno) Adès ▲ ADE 204112 [DDD]
Ravel, M.:Qt Strs Valois ▲ V 4730
Webern, A.:Bagatelles Str Qt Accord ▲ ACD 201642 [DDD]
Webern, A.:Movts Str Qt Accord ▲ ACD 201642 [DDD]
Webern, A.:Qt Strs (1905) Accord ▲ ACD 201642 [DDD]
Webern, A.:Qt Strs, Op. 28 Accord ▲ ACD 201642 [DDD]
Webern, A.:Qnt Pno, w. Akiko Ebi (pno) Accord ▲ ACD 201642 [DDD]
Webern, A.:Rondo Accord ▲ ACD 201642 [DDD]
Webern, A.:Slow Movt Accord ▲ ACD 201642 [DDD]

Paris String Trio

Togni, C.:Trio Strs Stradivarius ▲ STV DTM 90002 [ADD]

Paris SO

G. Enescu (cnd)

Chausson, E.:Poème Vn, w. Y. Menuhin (vn) *(rec 1933)* Biddulph ▲ LAB 058 [ADD]
Mozart, W.A.:Con 3 Vn, w. Y. Menuhin (vn) *(rec 1935 for HMV)* Biddulph ▲ LAB 004 [ADD]

P. Gaubert (cnd)

Lalo, E.:Con Vc, w. Maurice Marechal (vc) *(rec 1929 - 1943)* Iron Needle ▲ IN 1324 [ADD]
Mozart, W.A.:Con 23 Pno, w. Jacques Thibaud (vn) Biddulph ▲ LAB 114

H. von Karajan (cnd)

Debussy, C.:La Mer, w. Berlin PO EMI Classics ▲ CDM 64357
Ravel, M.:Boléro EMI Classics ▲ CDM 64357

P. Monteux (cnd)

Berlioz, H.:Benvenuto Cellini (ov) Music & Arts ▲ CD 762 [AAD]
Berlioz, H.:Ovs—Benvenuto Cellini; Les Troyens *(rec 1931)* Pearl ▲ PEA 9012 [AAD]
Berlioz, H.:Sym fantastique *(rec 1931)* Pearl ▲ PEA 9012 [AAD]
Chabrier, E.:Le Roi malgré lui (sels)—Fête polonaise *(rec 1931)* Pearl ▲ PEA 9012 [AAD]
Coppola, P.:Interlude dramatique *(rec June 1931)* Pearl ▲ PEA 9012 [AAD]
Mozart, W.A.:Con 7 Vn, w. Y. Menuhin (vn) *(rec 1932 HMV recording)* Biddulph ▲ LAB 004 [ADD]
Mozart, W.A.:Con Vn, K.Anh.294a, w. Y. Menuhin (vn) *(rec 1934 HMV recording)* Biddulph ▲ LAB 004 [ADD]

P. Stoll (cnd)

Boieldieu, F.-A.:La Dame blanche, w. Michel Sénéchal (ten—Georges Brown), Aimé Doniat (bar—Dikson), Pierre Héral (bass—Mac-Irton), Adrien Legros (bass—Gaveston), Paris Sym Chorus Accord 2-▲ ACD 220862 [AAD]

H. Tomasi (cnd)

Gluck, C.W.:Orfeo ed Euridice, w. Jany Delille (sop), Germaine Féraldy (sop), Alice Raveau (cta) [1859 French version, edited by Berlioz & Saint-Saëns] *(rec Paris, 1935)* Pearl 2-▲ PEA 9169 [ADD]

Paris Wind Quintet

Ibert, J.:Pièces brèves Adès ▲ ADE 203462 [AAD]
Lemeland, A.:Musique nocturne Skarbo ▲ SKR 3901 [AAD]

Paris Wind Quintet members

Ibert, J.:Pièces en trio Adès ▲ ADE 203462 [AAD]

Paris-Bastille Wind Octet

Beethoven, L. van:Octet, Op. 103 Harmonia Mundi ▲ HMN 911583
Mozart, W.A.:Serenade Winds, K.375 Harmonia Mundi ▲ HMN 911583
Mozart, W.A.:Serenade Winds, K.388 Harmonia Mundi ▲ HMN 911583

Pariser Quartet [Gérard Scharapan (fl), Daniel Cuiller (vn), Jay Bernfeld (vl), Jocelyn Cuiller (hpd)]
Telemann, G.P.:Qts Vn—Nos. 1, 2, 8 & 12 Accord ▲ ACD 243252 [DDD]
Telemann, G.P.:Qts Vn—Nos. 1, 3 & 4; 2nd Suite Accord ▲ ACD 243272 [DDD]

Parlement de Musique
Charpentier, M.-A.:Psaumes de David, (authentic instruments) [L] *(rec 9/90)* Opus 111 ▲ OPS 30-9005 [DDD]
Charpentier, M.-A.:Quatour anni tempestatis, (authentic instruments) [L] *(rec 9/90)* Opus 111 ▲ OPS 30-9005 [DDD]
Richter, F.X.:Sons (misc), Apponyi String Quartet—in B for Pno, Vn & Vc; in G for Fl & Db; in A for Hpd, Fl & Vc; in G for Pno, Vn & Vc Adda ▲ ADD 581226 [DDD]
Scarlatti, A.:Lamentazioni par la Settimana Santa, w. N. Rime (sop), M. Lins (sop) [I] Opus 111 ▲ 30-66

M. Gester (cnd)
Bach, J.S.:Con 1 Hpd, w. A. Isoir (org) [Westenfelder Organ of Fère-en-Tardenois] *(rec Oct 1993)* Calliope ▲ CAL 9720 [DDD]
Bach, J.S.:Con 2 Hpd, w. A. Isoir (org) [Westenfelder Organ of Fère-en-Tardenois] *(rec Oct 1993)* Calliope ▲ CAL 9720 [DDD]
Bach, J.S.:Con 8 Hpd, w. A. Isoir (org) [Westenfelder Organ of Fère-en-Tardenois] *(rec Oct 1993)* Calliope ▲ CAL 9720 [DDD]
Brossard, S. de:Motets, w. N. Rime (sop), J.-P. Fouchécourt (alt/ten), I. Honeyman (ten), B. Deletré (bass)—Salve Rex Christe; Psallite Superi; Qui non diligit te; O Domine quia refugium; Templa nunc fument; Oratorio seu Dialogus Poenitentis animae cum Deo; Festis laeta sonent [L] *(rec 1992)* Opus 111 ▲ OPS 30-69 [DDD]
Capricornus, S.F.:Theatrum musicum quod per duodecim scenas seu sacras cantiones aperuit, w. D. Collot (sop), L. S. Norin (mez), K. Wessel (alt), I. Honeyman (ten), S. Schreckenberger (bass) Opus 111 ▲ OPS 30-99
Hasse, J.A.:Motets, w. Monique Zanetti (sop), Jennifer Lane (mez)—Gentes barbarae, Tartarae turbae; Alta nubes illustrata; Salva R. in A; Salva R. in G Opus 111 ▲ OPS 30-100

Parley of Instruments
Blow, J.:Music of, w. Redbyrd—Awake my lyre; Salvator mundi; Paratum cor meum; Son. in A; Poor Celadon, he sighs; Musik's the cordial of a troubled breast; Go, perjur'd man; Chloe found Amyntas lying all in tears; Ground in g; Septimnius and Acme; Gloria patri qui creavit; Diva quo tendis Hyperion ▲ CDA 66658
Bond, C.:Cons in 7 Parts Hyperion ▲ CDA 66467
Monteverdi, C.:Selva morale e spirituale (sels), w. E. Kirkby (sop), I. Partridge (ten), D. Thomas (bass) [L] Hyperion ▲ CDA 66021 [DDD]

R. Goodman (cnd)
Arne, T.:Artaxerxes, w. Catherine Bott (sop), Patricia Spence (mez), Philippa Hyde (sgr), Christopher Robson (alt), Richard Edgar-Wilson (ten), Ian Partridge (ten) Hyperion ("The English Orpheus" series) 2-▲ CDA 67051/2
Arne, T.:Songs, w. E. Kirkby (sop), R. Morton (ten) [E]—not advised of sels. Hyperion ▲ CDA 66237 [DDD]
Bach, J.S.:Cant 208, "Hunting Cant", w. E. Kirkby (sop), J. Smith (sop), S. Davies (ten), M. George (b-bar) [G] Hyperion ▲ CDA 66169
British Music on Hyperion, w. John Mark Ainsley (ten), Graham Johnson (pno), Salomon Quartet, BBC Scottish SO, Anthony Rolfe Johnson (ten), Royal PO, St. Paul's Cathedral Choir, Nash Ensemble, Martyn Hill (ten), Suasan Gritton (sop), et al. Hyperion ▲ HYP 15
Clarke, J.:Come, Come Along for a Dance & a Song, w. R. Holton (sop), C. Daniels (ten), S. Birchall (bass), Parley of Instruments Chorus Hyperion ▲ CDA 66578 [DDD]
Hall, H.:Yes, My Aminta, 'tis True, w. R. Holton (sop), S. Birchall (bass), Parley of Instruments Chorus Hyperion ▲ CDA 66578 [DDD]
Muffat, G.:Armonico tributo (5 sonatas for strings) (1682) Hyperion ▲ CDA 66032 [DDD]
Purcell, H.:Music of, Baroque Orch—sels from Dioclesian, King Arthur, The Fairy Queen, The Old Bachelor, Amphitryon, The Double Dealer, The Gordian Knot Untied, Abdelazer, Bonduca, others Hyperion 3-▲ CDA 67001/3

E. Higginbottom (cnd)
Locke, M.:Anthems, Motets & Ceremonial Music, w. Oxford New College Choir—Descende caelo cincta sororibus ("The Oxford Ode"); How doth the city sit solitary; Super flumina Babylonis; O be joyful in the Lord, all ye lands; Audi, Domine, clamantes ad te; Lord let me know mine end; Jesu auctor clementie; Be thou exalted, Lord [E,L] Hyperion ▲ CDA 66373 [DDD]

D. Hill (cnd)
Blow, J.:Anthems, w. Joseph Cornwell (ten), Stephen Varcoe (bar), Robin Blaze (sgr), Winchester Cathedral Choir Hyperion 2-▲ CDA 67031/32
Christmas Music by Michael Praetorius, w. Westminster Cathedral Choir Hyperion ▲ CDA 66200
Philips, P.:Motets, w. Winchester Cathedral Choir Hyperion ▲ CDA 66643
Praetorius, M.:Music of, w. Westminster Cathedral Choir [G, L] Hyperion ▲ CDA 66200 [DDD]
Praetorius, M.:Terpsichore—sels. Hyperion ▲ CDA 66200 [DDD]

P. Holman (cnd)
Bach, Joh. Christian:Sinf concertante, T.290/9, w. Michael Harris (cl), Colin Lawson (cl) Hyperion ▲ CDA 66896
Blow, J.:The Glorious Day Is Come, w. Suzie le Blanc (sop), Michael Chance (ct), Joseph Cornwell (ten), Richard Wistreich (bass), Playford Consort Hyperion ▲ CDA 66770
Blow, J.:Ode on the Death of Mr. Henry Purcell, w. R. Covey-Crump (ten), C. Daniels (ten) Hyperion ▲ CDA 66578 [DDD]
Brooks, J.:Con 1 Vn, w. Elizabeth Wallfisch (vn) Hyperion ▲ CDA 66865
Croft, W.:Musica sacra, w. St. Paul's Cathedral Choir—Te Deum in D; Rejoice in the Lord, O Ye Righteous (A Thanksgiving Anthem); The Burial Service; Jubilate in D *(rec Feb. 24-27, May 22, 1992)* Hyperion ▲ CDA 66606 [DDD]
Dowland, J.:Lachrimae, or Seaven Teares, w. P. O'Dette (lt)—[period instrs] Hyperion ▲ CDA 66637
Hook, J.:Con Cl, w. Colin Lawson (cl) Hyperion ▲ CDA 66896
Jenkins, J.:Consort Music—Fantasia Suites Nos. 2, 6, 8 & 10; The Six Bells; Suite in G Hyperion ▲ CDA 66604
Linley, T.:Con Vn, w. Elizabeth Wallfisch (vn) Hyperion ▲ CDA 66865
Locke, M.:Broken Consort Hyperion ▲ CDA 66727
Mahon, J.:Con 2 Cl, w. Colin Lawson (cl) Hyperion ▲ CDA 66896
Monteverdi, C.:Altri canti d'amor, w. Red Byrd Hyperion ▲ CDA 66475 [DDD]
Monteverdi, C.:Ballo delle ingrate, w. Red Byrd Hyperion ▲ CDA 66475 [DDD]
Monteverdi, C.:Combattimento, w. Red Byrd Hyperion ▲ CDA 66475 [DDD]
Monteverdi, C.:Volgendo il ciel, w. Red Byrd Hyperion ▲ CDA 66475 [DDD]
Purcell, H.:Songs, w. Red Byrd—Hark Damon, hark; How pleasant is this flowery plain; We reap all the pleasures; Hark how wild musicians sing; See where she sits; Oh! what a scene does entertain my sight; Soft notes & gently raised; If ever I more riches did desire; Pavans in g, a, A & B♭ Hyperion ▲ CDA 66750
Shaw, T.:Con Vn, w. Elizabeth Wallfisch (vn) Hyperion ▲ CDA 66865
Simpson, T.:Consort Music Hyperion ▲ CDA 66435
Wesley, S.:Con 2 Vn, w. Elizabeth Wallfisch (vn) Hyperion ▲ CDA 66865
While Shepherds Watched:Christmas Music from English Parish Churches, 1740–1830, w. Psalmody Hyperion ("English Orpheus" series) ▲ CDA 66924

Holman, Goodman (cnd)
German Consort Music 1660–1710 Hyperion ▲ CDA 66074 [DDD]
Odes on the Death of Henry Purcell, w. Baroque Orch, Baroque Choir, R. Holton (sop), R. Covey-Crump (ten), C. Daniels (ten), S. Birchall (bass) Hyperion ▲ CDA 66578 [DDD]

P. Nicholson (cnd)
Arne, T.:Favourite Cons (6), w. P. Nicholson (kbds)—each on organ, harpsichord & piano Hyperion ▲ CDA 66509
Linley, T.:Cants, w. Julia Gooding (sop)—In yonder grove; Ye nymphs of Albion's beauty-blooming isle; Daughter of Heav'n, fair art thou! Hyperion ▲ CDA 66767

Parley of Instruments (cont.)
P. Nicholson (cnd) (cont.)
Linley, T.:Theatre Music, w. Julia Gooding (sop)—Music for The Tempest; Ov. to The Duenna Hyperion ▲ CDA 66767

P. Trepte (cnd)
Amner, J.:Sacred Music, w. David Price (org), Ely Cathedral Choir—Te Deaum; I Will Sing unto the Lord As Long As I Live; Blessed Be the Lord God; O Ye Little Flock; Magnigicat; Nunc dimitis; Sing, O Heav'ns; Vars. on "O Lord in Thee"; Consider, All Ye Passers by; Hear, O Lord; O Sing unto the Lord Hyperion ▲ CDA 66768

Parley of Instruments Renaissance Violin Band
Banister, J.:Music of—Curtain Tunes; Suite of Brawles; Music for The Tempest Hyperion ▲ CDA 66667
Grabu, L.:Concert of Venus Hyperion ▲ CDA 66667
Grabu, L.:Music from "Valentinian" Hyperion ▲ CDA 66667
Locke, M.:Music of—includes Curtain Tunes; Suite of Brawles; Music for The Tempest Hyperion ▲ CDA 66667

Parma Teatro Regio Orch
A. Erede (cnd)
Verdi, G.:Il trovatore, w. Katia Ricciarelli (sop), Richard Tucker (ten), Renato Bruson (bar), Zanibelli (sgr) *(rec Parma, 1971)* Golden Age of Opera 2-▲ GAO 193/194

G. Gavazzeni (cnd)
Verdi, G.:Luisa Miller, w. Cecilia Gasdia (sop), Mazzareno Antinori (ten), Simone Alaimo (b-bar), Parma Teatro Regio Chorus *(rec live, 1981)* Serenissima 2-▲ SER 360143

G. Patanè (cnd)
Verdi, G.:Un ballo in maschera, w. Ghena Dimitrova (sop—Amelia), Isabella Stramaglia (sop—Oscar), Mirna Pecile (cta—Ulrica), Mario Carlin (ten—Un giudice), José Carreras (ten—Riccardo), Piero Cappuccilli (bar—Renato), Massimiliano Malaspina (bass—Samuel), Americo de Santis (bass—Silvano), Francesco Signor (bass—Tom), Ivan Del Manto (sgr—Un servo) *(rec Teatro Regio, Dec. 26, 1972)* Golden Age of Opera 2-▲ GAO 183/84

Il Parnaso Musicale [Y. Weichsel (rcr), D. Luisi (baroque vn), S. Scholz (baroque vn), G. Nasillo (vl), J. Zwicker (baroque vc), E. Hoetzl (hpd)]
Telemann, G.P.:Trio Sons—(6) in g for Violin, Viol & Continuo; in d & in F for Recorder, Viol & Continuo; in G & in D for 2 Violins & Continuo; in d for Recorder, Violin & Continuo *(rec Nov. 9-11, 1992)* Christophorus ▲ 77138 [DDD]

Parnassus Ensemble
Haydn, M.:Con Vn & Orch, w. Peter Sheppard (vn) Meridian ▲ CDE 84243 [DDD]
Haydn, M.:Con Vn, P.53, w. Peter Sheppard (vn) Meridian ▲ CDE 84243 [DDD]
Haydn, M.:Divert Vns, Va & Db, w. Peter Sheppard (vn) Meridian ▲ CDE 84243 [DDD]

A. Korf (cnd)
Babbitt, M.:The Head of the Bed, w. J. Bettina (sop) [E] New World ▲ 80346-2 [DDD]
Imbrie, A.W.:Campion Songs, w. Joan Peterson (sop), Nancy Wertsch (alt), Mark Bleeke (ten), Nathaniel Watson (bar) *(rec Sept. 29, 1993)* New World ▲ 80441-2
Imbrie, A.W.:Dream Sequence *(rec Holy Trinity Church, New York City, Feb. 12, 1990)* New World ▲ 80441-2
Wolpe, S.:Music of, w. Joyce Castle (mez)—Musik für Hamlet for Flute, Clarinet & Cello (1929); To the Dancemaster for Mezzo, Clarinet & Piano (1938); Drei Lieder von Bertolt Brecht for Mezzo & Piano (1943); Quartet No. 1 for Trumpet, Tenor Sax, Percussion & Piano (1950); Piece in Two Parts for Six Players (1962); Piece for Two Instrumental Units (1962); Solo Piece for Trumpet (1966); Piece for Trumpet & 7 Instruments (1971) Koch International Classics ▲ KIC 7141-2 [DDD]
Wuorinen, C.:The Winds New World ▲ 80517-2

P. Sheppard (cnd)
Haydn, M.:Sym in G Meridian ▲ CDE 84243 [DDD]

Parnassus String Ensemble
J. Rennert (cnd)
Spratling, H.:Choral Music, w. Tracey Chadwell (sop), Susan Bullock (sop), Jeffery Dyball (hp), Helen Tunstall (hp), John Hatton (org), Spratling Choir—Mass of the Holy Spirit; O Salutaris Hostia; Tantum Ergo; Sinf Str Orch; Son Hp; O Magnum Mysterium; In Paradisum *(rec St. Mary Magdelene, Paddington, May 15-17, 1988)* SOMM ▲ SOMMCD 206 [ADD]

Parnassus Trio [C. Chou (pno), W.-D. Streicher (vn), M. Gross (vc)]
Arensky, A.:Trio 1 Pno MD + G ▲ L 3247 [DDD]
Arrieu, C.:Trio Pno MD + G ▲ L 3367 [DDD]
Beethoven, L. van:Sym 2 [arr. for piano trio] MD + G ▲ L 3510 [DDD]
Beethoven, L. van:Trio 7 Pno MD + G ▲ L 3510 [DDD]
Bloch, E.:Nocturnes (3) MD + G ▲ L 3367 [DDD]
Brahms, J.:Sextet Strs, Op. 18 [arr Theodor Kirchner for pno trio] MD + G ▲ MDG 3030656
Brahms, J.:Sextet Strs, Op. 36 [arr Theodore Kirchner for Pno Trio] MD + G ▲ MDG 3030655
Brahms, J.:Trio 1 Pno [1st version, 1854] MD + G ▲ MDG CD 3030657
Brahms, J.:Trio 1 Pno MD + G ▲ MDG 3030655
Brahms, J.:Trio 2 Pno MD + G ▲ MDG 3030656
Brahms, J.:Trio 3 Pno MD + G ▲ MDG CD 3030657
Casella, A.:Sonata a Tre MD + G ▲ L 3367 [DDD]
Lalo, E.:Trio 1 Pno MD + G ▲ L 3482 [DDD]
Lalo, E.:Trio 2 Pno MD + G ▲ L 3482 [DDD]
Lalo, E.:Trio 3 Pno MD + G ▲ L 3482 [DDD]
MD & G Portraits:The Trio Parnassus MD + G ▲ MDG 3492 [DDD]
Mozart, W.A.:Trios Pno (comp) MD + G 2-▲ L 3373/74 [DDD]
Rheinberger, J.:Trio 1 Vn MD + G 2-▲ L 3419/20 [DDD]
Rheinberger, J.:Trio 2 Vn MD + G 2-▲ L 3419/20 [DDD]
Rheinberger, J.:Trio 3 Vn MD + G 2-▲ L 3419/20 [DDD]
Rheinberger, J.:Trio 4 Vn MD + G 2-▲ L 3419/20 [DDD]
Scharwenka, P.:Son Vc MD + G ▲ MDG 3030532 [DDD]
Scharwenka, P.:Trio 1 Pno MD + G ▲ MDG 3030532 [DDD]
Scharwenka, P.:Trio 2 Pno MD + G ▲ MDG 3030532 [DDD]
Smetana, B.:Trio Pno MD + G ▲ L 3247 [DDD]

Parrenin String Quartet
Fauré, G.:Qt Strs EMI Classics 2-▲ ZDMB 62548
Ibert, J.:Qt Strs Adès ▲ ADE 203462 [AAD]

Parrenin String Quartet [Jacques Parrenin (vn), Marcel Charpentier (vn), D. Marton (va), Pierre Penassou (vc)]
Fauré, G.:Qnts Pno & Strs, Opp. 89 & 115, w. V. Perlemuter (pno) *(rec May 31, 1966)* Memoire Vive ▲ 262003 [ADD]
Franck, C.:Qnt Pno, w. V. Perlemuter (pno) *(rec June 2, 1967)* Memoire Vive ▲ 262003 [ADD]

Parrenin String Quartet [Jacques Parrenin (vn), Marcel Charpentier (vn), Serge Collot (va), Pierre Penassou (vc)]
Bartók, B.:Qt Strs (comp) Ades ▲ ADE 141702 [AAD]

Partch Instrumentalists
D. Mitchell (cnd)
Partch, H.:Revelation in the Courthouse Park, w. S. Costallos (sgr—Mom & Agave), C. Durham (ten—Sonny & Pentheus), M. Kimbrough (bar—Vendor & Herdsman), E. Earle (b-bar—Hobo & Tiresias), O. Babatunde (sgr—Dion & Dionysus), C. Roos (sgr—Mayor & Cadmus), O. Williams (sgr—Korypheus), R. Young (sgr—Cop & Guard), marching band, *(chorus unknown)* [E] *(rec 10/87)* Tomato 2-▲ R2 70390 [DDD]

Parthenia Baroque
C. Brembeck (cnd)
Bernhard, C.:Geistlicher Harmonien erster Theil, w. Parthenia Vocal Christophorus 2-▲ 77177
Keiser, R.:Passions Oratorium, w. T. d'Althann (sop), P. Geitner (sop), M. Paulsen (alt), J. Elbert (ten), H. Elbert (bass), Parthenia Vocal Christophorus ▲ 77143 [DDD]

Pasadena SO
J. Mester (cnd)
Saint-Saëns, C.:Sym 3, w. Hector Olivera (org) Auracle ▲ NCAU 1001

Pasadena SO (cont.)
J. Mester (cnd) (cont.)
Strauss, R.:Also sprach Zarathustra — Auracle ▲ NCAU 1001
Pasardjik SO
B. Fidetzis (cnd)
Samaras, S.:La Martyre, w. Luigi Illica (nar), Plovdiv Anghel Boukoreshtliev Choir — Orata ▲ ORAML 156
Pasdeloup Concerts Association Orch
J. Allain (cnd)
Donizetti, G.:La favorita (sels), w. *(singers unknown)*—Un ange, une femme inconnue...; Jardins de l'Alcazar; Ainsi donc on raconte...; Pour tant d'amour ne soyez pas ingrate...; O mon Fernand; Ange si pur; Vas-t-en d'ici... — Accord ▲ ACD 204282 [AAD]
Massé, V.:Les Noces de Jeannette, w. Renée Doria (sop), Lucien Huberty (bar) — Accord ▲ ACD 201192 [AAD]
D. Amfitheatrof (cnd)
Amfitheatrof, D.:Am Panorama *(rec 1937)* — Label "X" ▲ LXCD 8 [ADD]
P. Coppola (cnd)
Berlioz, H.:La Damnation de Faust, w. M. Berthon (sop), J. de Trévi (ten), C. Panzéra (bar), St. Gervais Chorus *(rec 1930)* — Pearl ▲ PEA 9080 [ADD]
R. Leibowitz (cnd)
Offenbach, J.:Le Grande-Duchesse de Gérolstein (ov) *(rec 1958; stereo)* — Forlane ▲ FOR 16586 [AAD]
Pasdeloup Orch
P. Coppola (cnd)
Berlioz, H.:La Damnation de Faust (sels), w. M. Berthon (sop), J. de Trévi (sgr), C. Panzéra (bar), L. Morturier (sgr), St. Gervais Chorus [abridged vers] [F] *(rec 1931)* — The Classical Collector 2-▲ FDC2 2006 [AAD]
Opera Arias & Scenes, w. Marjorie Lawrence (sop) — Preiser ("Lebendige Vergangenheit" series) ▲ PRE 89011 (m) [AAD]
Pasquier Trio
Mozart, W.A.:Adagio & Rondo Glass Armonica, w. J. Rampal (fl), P. Perlot (ob) — Sony Classical ▲ SK 47230
Mozart, W.A.:Divert Hns Strs, K.334, w. J. Rampal (fl) — Sony Classical ▲ SK 47230
Mozart, W.A.:Qnt Strs, K.Anh.177, w. J. Rampal (fl) — Sony Classical ▲ SK 47230
Patterson Duo [Ronald Patterson (vn), Roxanna Patterson (va)]
Cooper, P.:Canons d'amour *(rec Digital Rendezvous, Nice, France)* — CRI ▲ CD 687 [DDD]
Cooper, P.:Chamber Music, w. Shephard String Quartet—Verses; Canons d'Amour; Qts. 5 & 6 Strings — CRI ▲ CD 687 [DDD]
Cooper, P.:Versés *(rec Digital Rendezvous, Nice, France)* — CRI ▲ CD 687 [DDD]
Pau Orch
M. Maunas (cnd)
Salles, B.:Con Db, w. B. Cazauran (db) *(rec Aug. 29–30, 1992)* — Gallo ▲ CD 753 [ADD]
Pavillon Quartet
Hindemith, P.:Son for 4 Hns *(rec Oct. & Dec. 1992)* — CPO ▲ CPO 999229 [DDD]
Pécs SO
N. Pasquet (cnd)
Lajtha, L.:Capriccio *(rec Ferenc Liszt Concert Hall, Pécs, Hungary, May 1994)* — Marco Polo ▲ 8.223668 [DDD]
M. Trautmann (cnd)
Rogister, J.:Con Va, w. Therese-Marie Gilissen (va) — Koch Schwann ▲ SCH 317182
Rogister, J.:Con Vn, w. Philippe Koch (vn) — Koch Schwann ▲ SCH 317182
Rogister, J.:Fant concertante, w. Therese-Marie Gilissen (va) — Koch Schwann ▲ SCH 317182
H. Williams (cnd)
Lickl, J.G.:Missa solemnis, w. Maria Zadori (sop), Judith Nemet (mez), Boldizsar Keönch (ten), Tamas Bator (bass), Pécs Chamber Choir — Koch Schwann ▲ SCH 312962
Lickl, J.G.:Requiem, w. Maria Zadori (sop), Judith Nemet (mez), Boldizsar Keönch (ten), Tamas Bator (bass), Pécs Chamber Choir — Koch Schwann ▲ SCH 312962
Rachmaninoff, S.:The Isle of the Dead — Hungaroton ▲ HCD 31551 [DDD]
Rachmaninoff, S.:Rhapsody on a Theme of Paganini, w. I. Prunyi (pno) — Hungaroton ▲ HCD 31551 [DDD]
Rachmaninoff, S.:Symphonic Dances, w. I. Prunyi (pno) — Hungaroton ▲ HCD 31551 [DDD]
Rózsa, M.:Con Vc, w. Peter Rejto (vc) *(rec Franz Liszt Hall, Pécs, Hungary, Sept 1995)* — Silva Classics ▲ SILKD 6011 [DDD]
Schurmann, G.:The Gardens of Exile, w. Peter Rejto (vc) *(rec Franz Liszt Hall, Pécs, Hungary, Sept 1995)* — Silva Classics ▲ SILKD 6011 [DDD]
Peder Pedersen's Big Band
Ellington, D.:Music of, w. Margareta Jalkéus (sop), Tritonus—Praise God [Introduction]; Heaven; Freedom-Suite; The Shepherd; The Majesty of God; Come Sunday; David Dances before the Lord; Almighty God; T.G.T.T.; Praise God & Dance [Final] *(rec Copenhagen, Jan 1996)* — Classico ▲ CD 142
Karl Peinkofer Percussion Ensemble [Karl Peinkofer (perc), Andreas Schumacher (perc), Hugo Dümig (perc), Ralph Harrer (perc), Hermann Holler (perc), Günther Möller (perc), Andreas Vonderthann (perc), Wilfried Hiller (perc), Carl-Amadeus Hiller (perc)]
Orff, C.:Schulwerk (complete), w. Godela Orff (nar), Marina Koppelstetter (mez), Carolin Widmann (vn), Sabina Lehrmann (vc), Markus Zahnhausen (rcr)—4 Pieces for Xylophone; 5 Little Canons; 4 Dance Pieces; Songs & Instrumental Pieces; 3 Pieces for Fl & Perc; Songs & Dances; 2 Time Change Dances for Vn & Vc; 7 Folk Dances; Music for the Night *(rec Munich, 1994–95)* — Celestial Harmonies ▲ 13104-2
Mark Pekarsky Percussion Ensemble
Artyomov, V.:Invocation, w. L. Davydova (sop) — Olympia ▲ OLY 514 [DDD]
Artyomov, V.:Perc Music—Ave atque vale; A Sonata of Meditations; Totem — Olympia ▲ OLY 514 [DDD]
Pellegrini String Quartet [Antonio Pellegrini (vn), Thomas Hofer (vn), Charlotte Geselbracht (va), Helmut Menzler (vc)]
Busoni, F.:Qt 1 Strs — CPO ▲ CPO 999264 [DDD]
Busoni, F.:Qt 2 Strs — CPO ▲ CPO 999264 [DDD]
Feldman, Morton:Qt Cl, w. Ib Hausmann (cl) *(rec Church Blumenstein, Thun, Switzerland, June 20–21, 1994)* — Hat Hut ("Now." series) ▲ ART CD 6166 [DDD]
Hartmann, K.A.:Qt 1 Strs, "Carrillon" — CPO ▲ CPO 999219 [DDD]
Hartmann, K.A.:Qt 2 Strs — CPO ▲ CPO 999219 [DDD]
Hölszky, A.:Music of, w. Nomos String Quartet—Hängebrücken (Suspension Bridges); Qts. I & II; Double Qt.; Hunt the Wolves Back for Percussion; Audiowindow or Franz Liszt for Piano — CPO ▲ CPO 999112 [DDD]
Penderecki String Quartet
Bacewicz, G.:Qt 3 Strs — United ▲ UNI 88014 [DDD]
Bacewicz, G.:Qt 3 Strs *(rec St Paul's Church, Knightsbridge, London, Nov 27, 1993)* — United ▲ CAL 88021 [DDD]
Bacewicz, G.:Qt 3 Strs — United ▲ CAL 88014
Brahms, J.:Qnt Pno, w. Lev Natochenny (pno) — Marquis Classics ▲ MAR 187
Britten, B.:Qt 3 Strs — Marquis Classics ▲ MAR 173
Lason, A.:Qt 2 Strs — United ▲ UNI 88014 [DDD]
Lason, A.:Qt 3 Strs — United ▲ CAL 88014
Penderecki, K.:Qt 1 Strs — United ▲ CAL 88014
Penderecki, K.:Qt 1 Strs — United ▲ UNI 88014 [DDD]
Penderecki, K.:Qt 2 Strs — United ▲ CAL 88014
Penderecki, K.:Qt 2 Strs — United ▲ UNI 88014 [DDD]
Penderecki, K.:Unterbrochene Gedanke — United ▲ UNI 88014 [DDD]
Penderecki, K.:Unterbrochene Gedanke — United ▲ CAL 88014
Schnittke, A.:Qnt Pno, w. Lev Natochenny (pno) — Marquis Classics ▲ MAR 183
Shostakovich, D.:Qt 3 Strs — Marquis Classics ▲ MAR 173
Shostakovich, D.:Qnt Pno, w. Lev Natochenny (pno) — Marquis Classics ▲ MAR 183

Peninsula Festival Orch
T. Johnson (cnd)
Chou Wen-Chung:Landscapes — CRI ▲ CD 691 [ADD]
Penn Contemporary Players [Arne Running (cl), Barbara Sonies (vn), Lori Barnet (vc), Lambert Orkis (pno)]
Lewis, R.H.:Combinazioni I *(rec Lang Concert Hall, Swarthmore College, Swarthmore, PN, May 11, 1978)* — Albany ▲ TROY 166 [ADD/DDD]
Pennsylvania Sinfonia Orch
A. Birney (cnd)
Newman, Anthony:Concertino Pno, w. A. Newman (pno) — Newport Classic ▲ NC 60017 [DDD] ■ NC 60017 (D)
Poulenc, F.:Con Org, w. Newman (org) — Newport Classic ▲ NC 60017 [DDD] ■ NC 60017 (D) (CrO2)
Pennsylvania Sinfonia Orch members
Falla, M. de:Con Hpd, w. A. Newman (hpd) — Newport Classic ▲ NC 60017 [DDD] ■ NC 60017 (D)
Pennsylvania Wind Quintet
Bach, Jan:Skizzen — Centaur ▲ CRC 2085 [DDD]
Berger, A.:Qt Winds *(rec Unitarian Universalist Fellowship, State College, PA, May 1992–July 1993)* — Centaur ▲ CRC 2225 [DDD]
Etler, A.:Qnt 1 Ww — Centaur ▲ CRC 2085 [DDD]
Fine, I.:Partita Ww — Centaur ▲ CRC 2085 [DDD]
Rochberg, G.:To the Dark Wood — Centaur ▲ CRC 2085 [DDD]
Schafer, R.M.:Minnelieder, w. Jan Wilson (mez) *(rec Unitarian Universalist Fellowship, State College, PA, May 1992–July 1993)* — Centaur ▲ CRC 2225 [DDD]
Stucky, S.:Serenade *(rec Unitarian Universalist Fellowship, State College, PA, May 1992–July 1993)* — Centaur ▲ CRC 2225 [DDD]
Thorne, F.:Qnt Ww *(rec Unitarian Universalist Fellowship, State College, PA, May 1992–July 1993)* — Centaur ▲ CRC 2225 [DDD]
Bach, Jan:Skizzen — Centaur ▲ CRC 2085 [DDD]
Pentaèdre Ensemble [G. Pelletier (fl), G. Plante (cl), N. Forget (ob), F. Ouellet (hn), M. Bettez (bn)]
Bozza, E.:Vars sur un thème libre — Amplitude ▲ CLCD 2020
Françaix, J.:Qnt 1 Ww — Amplitude ▲ CLCD 2020
Ibert, J.:Pièces brèves — Amplitude ▲ CLCD 2020
Milhaud, D.:Le Cheminée du Roi Rèné — Amplitude ▲ CLCD 2020
Ravel, M.:Le Tombeau de Couperin — Amplitude ▲ CLCD 2020
Pentaedre Wind Quintet
Bozza, E.:Vars sur un thème libre — Analekta ▲ CLCD 2020
Françaix, J.:Qnt 1 Ww — Analekta ▲ CLCD 2020
Ibert, J.:Pièces brèves — Analekta ▲ CLCD 2020
Milhaud, D.:Le Cheminée du Roi René — Analekta ▲ CLCD 2020
Ravel, M.:Le Tombeau de Couperin — Analekta ▲ CLCD 2020
Penumbra [Mary Jo Carlsen (vn), Thomas Parchman (cl), James Parakilas (pno)]
Schwartz, E.:A Garden for RKB — Capstone ▲ CPS 863300
Pepicelli Duo [Angelo Pepicelli (pno), Francesco Pepicelli (vc)]
Busoni, F.:Small Suite Vc — Bongiovanni ▲ GB 5035 [DDD]
Casella, A.:Notturno *(rec Dynamic Studio, Genoa, Italy, Mar 20–23, 1995)* — Dynamic ▲ CDS 135 [DDD]
Casella, A.:Son 1 Vc *(rec Dynamic Studio, Genoa, Italy, Mar 20–23, 1995)* — Dynamic ▲ CDS 135 [DDD]
Casella, A.:Son 2 Vc *(rec Dynamic Studio, Genoa, Italy, Mar 20–23, 1995)* — Dynamic ▲ CDS 135 [DDD]
Casella, A.:Tarantella *(rec Dynamic Studio, Genoa, Italy, Mar 20–23, 1995)* — Dynamic ▲ CDS 135 [DDD]
Cilea, F.:Son Vc — Bongiovanni ▲ GB 5035 [DDD]
Màrgola, F.:Son Breve No. 3 — Bongiovanni ▲ GB 5035 [DDD]
Petrassi, G.:Preludio, Aria e Finale — Bongiovanni ▲ GB 5035 [DDD]
Ken Peplowski Jazz Quartet [Ken Peplowski (cl), Ben Aronov (pno), Greg Cohen (db), Chuck Redd (dr)]
The Other Portrait, w. Peplowski, Ken (cl/t sax), Bulgarian National SO [cnd:Ljubomir Denev] — Concord Concerto ▲ CCD 42043 [DDD]
Per Musica
J. Reynolds (cnd)
Chabrier, E.:Pièces pittoresques—Menuet pompeux [orchd Ravel] *(rec Amsterdam, Nov 1985)* — Globe ▲ GLO 6034 [DDD]
Debussy, C.:Danse Pno, "Tarantelle styrienne" *(rec Amsterdam, Nov 1985)* — Globe ▲ GLO 6034 [DDD]
Debussy, C.:Sarabande *(rec Amsterdam, Nov 1985)* — Globe ▲ GLO 6034 [DDD]
Ravel, M.:Ma mère l'oye Orch *(rec Amsterdam, Nov 1985)* — Globe ▲ GLO 6034 [DDD]
Rossini, G.:Music of—selections from La Cenerentola; Il barbiere di Siviglia; Semiramide; Grande fanfare-rendez-vous de chasse *(rec Aug. 1986)* — Globe ▲ GLO 6014 [DDD]
Schumann, R.:Carnaval Pno—Préambule; Valse allemande-Paganini; Marche des Davidsbündler contre les Philistins [all orchd Ravel] *(rec Amsterdam, Nov 1985)* — Globe ▲ GLO 6034 [DDD]
Percussion All Stars
Liszt, F.:Con 1 Pno, w. Todd Crow (pno) *(rec live, Purchase Univ, Theater C, White Plains, NY, Sept 23, 1995)* — Golden String ▲ GSCD 027 [DDD]
Mozart, W.A.:Con 21 Pno, w. Todd Crow (pno) *(rec live, Purchase Univ, Theater C, White Plains, NY, Sept 23, 1995)* — Golden String ▲ GSCD 027 [DDD]
Percussion Art Quartet [Stefan Eblenkamp (perc), Gergana Fasseva (perc), Anno Kesting (perc), Markus Verna (perc)]
Percussion Art Quartet:X-Pression *(rec June 1995)* — Thorofon ▲ CTH 2290 [DDD]
Schnittke, A.:Qt Perc *(rec June 1995)* — Thorofon ▲ CTH 2290 [DDD]
Sculthorpe, P.:Sun Songs *(rec June 1995)* — Thorofon ▲ CTH 2290 [DDD]
Trythall, R.:Bolero *(rec June 1995)* — Thorofon ▲ CTH 2290 [DDD]
Weigert, A.:Stick Attack *(rec June 1995)* — Thorofon ▲ CTH 2290 [DDD]
Percussion Ensemble
M. A. Machek (cnd)
Van De Vate, N.:Sound Pieces, w. Bohuslav Martinů Philharmonic Brass — Vienna Modern Masters ▲ VMM 2003 [DDD]
Percussion Group 72
Nishimura, A.:Perc Music—Ketiak; Tala; Padma in Meditation; Legong; Con for Timp & 5 Percussionists — Camerata ▲ 30CM 89
Percussion Group The Hague
Irony — Globe ▲ GLO 5086 [DDD]
Skin Hits — Globe ▲ GLO 5066 [DDD]
The Wooden Branch — Globe ▲ GLO 5072 [DDD]
Percussive Rotterdam [Norman van Dartel (perc), Christian Leenders (perc), Hans Leenders (perc), Gerrit Nulens (perc)]
Wood, James:Spirit Festival with Lamentations, w. Robert van Sice (mar/perc) *(rec Steurbaut Sound Recording Centre, Gent, Belgium, June 26, 1993)* — mode ▲ mode 51
Wood, James:Village Burial with Fire Perc *(rec Steurbaut Sound Recording Centre, Gent, Belgium, May 19, 1993)* — mode ▲ mode 51
Performing Arts Orch
J.-L. LeRoux (cnd)
Chihara, P.:The Tempest — Reference ▲ RR 10CD [ADD]
Perihelion Ensemble
Davidson, R.:Tapestry — Vox Australis ▲ VAST 014
Sabaneyev, B.:Inner-City Counterpoints — Vox Australis ▲ VAST 014
Schultz, Andrew:Barren Grounds — Vox Australis ▲ VAST 014

▲ = CD ◆ = Enhanced CD Δ = MD ■ = Cassette Tape □ = DCC

Perihelion Ensemble [N. Sabin (cl), P. Pollett (va), Gwyn Roberts (vc), Jenni Flemming (pno/sgr/whirly instr)]
Points of Departure *(rec Nickson Room, Music Department, Univ. of Queensland, 1993)* Tall Poppies ▲ TP 43 [DDD]
Perihelion Ensemble members [Nigel Sabin (cl), Gwyn Roberts (vc), Jenni Flemming (pno)]
Schultz, Andrew:Dead Songs, w. Margaret Schindler (sop) *(rec Nickson Room, Music Dept, Univ of Queensland, Australia, Dec 1994)* Tall Poppies ▲ TP 065 [DDD]
Perihelion Ensemble members [Nigel Sabin (cl), Patricia Pollett (va), Jenni Flemming (pno)]
Schultz, Andrew:Stick Dance II *(rec Nickson Room, Music Dept, Univ of Queensland, Australia, Dec 1994)* Tall Poppies ▲ TP 065 [DDD]
Perihelion Ensemble members [Nigel Sabin (cl), Patricia Pollett (va)]
G. Roberts (cnd)
Schultz, Andrew:Mephisto, w. Sonia Croucher (fl), Karen Schaupp (gtr), Michele Walsh (vn), Belinda Kendall-Smith (bass) *(rec Nickson Room, Music Dept, Univ of Queensland, Australia, Dec 1994)* Tall Poppies ▲ TP 065 [DDD]
Perpignan Festival Orch
P. Casals (cnd)
Mozart, W.A.:Ch'io mi scordi di te, w. J. Tourel (mez), M. Horszowski (pno) *(rec Perpignan, France, July 15-16, 1951)* Sony Classical ("The Casals Edition" series) ▲ SMK 58984 [ADD]
Mozart, W.A.:Con 9 Pno, w. M. Hess (pno) *(rec live 1952)* Melodram ▲ MEL 18024 (m) [AAD]
Mozart, W.A.:Con 20 Pno, w. Yvonne Lefébure (pno) *(rec June 17, 1951)* Sony Classical ▲ SMK 66570 [ADD]
Mozart, W.A.:Con 22 Pno, w. Rudolf Serkin (pno) *(rec July 26, 1951)* Sony Classical ▲ SMK 66570 [ADD]
Mozart, W.A.:Con 27 Pno, w. M. Horszowski (pno) *(rec Perpignan, France, July 10-17, 1951)* Sony Classical ("The Casals Edition" series) ▲ SMK 58984 [ADD]
Mozart, W.A.:Con 5 Vn, w. E. Morini (vn) *(rec Perpignan, France, July 13, 1951)* Sony Classical ("The Casals Edition" series) ▲ SMK 58983 [ADD]
Mozart, W.A.:Sinf concertante Vn, K.364, w. I. Stern (vn), W. Primrose (va) *(rec Perpignan, France, July 5-8, 1951)* Sony Classical ("The Casals Edition" series) ▲ SMK 58983 [ADD]
Peru Folklore Music Group
Celli, J.:Andes O.O. Discs ▲ OO 22
Pesaro Rossini Orch
F. Ayo (cnd)
Tartini, G.:Cons Vn (misc), w. F. Ayo (vn)—Cons. in A, D.96; in d, D.45; in E *(rec Mar. 5-7, 1993)* Dynamic ▲ CDS 92 [DDD]
Tartini, G.:Sym in A *(rec Mar. 5-7, 1993)* Dynamic ▲ CDS 92 [DDD]
Peterhoff Orch
L. Korkhin (cnd)
Arensky, A.:Fant on Themes of Ryabinin Audiophile Classics ▲ 101.043
Glazunov, A.:Raymonda (sels)—Suite Audiophile Classics ▲ 101.043
Liadov, A.:Kikimora Audiophile Classics ▲ 101.043
Liadov, A.:Polonaise, Op. 49 Audiophile Classics ▲ 101.043
Music at Pavlovsk Station:The Birth of the Russian Orchestra *(rec 1991)* Opus 111 ▲ OPS 58-9204 [DDD]
Rubinstein, A.:Bal costumé—Toreador; Espagnole Audiophile Classics ▲ 101.043
Rubinstein, A.:Feramors (orchestral sels)—Dance with Torches of Brides of Kaschemir Audiophile Classics ▲ 101.043
Rubinstein, A.:Soirées à Saint-Pétersbourg Audiophile Classics ▲ 101.043
Taneyev, S.:Suite de Concert Audiophile Classics ▲ 101.043
Petersen String Quartet [Conrad Muck (vn), Gernot Süssmut (vn), Friedemann Weigle (va), Hans-Jakob Eschenburg (vc)]
Beethoven, L. van:Qt 4 Strs Capriccio ▲ 10 722 [DDD]
Beethoven, L. van:Qt 15 Strs Capriccio ▲ 10 722 [DDD]
Blacher, B.:Epitaph, "Str Qt No. 4" EDA ▲ EDA 006
Blacher, B.:Pieces (4) Str Qt, "Str Qt No. 1" EDA ▲ EDA 006
Blacher, B.:Qt 2 Strs EDA ▲ EDA 006
Blacher, B.:Qt 3 Strs EDA ▲ EDA 006
Blacher, B.:Variationen über eienen divergierenden c-moll Dreiklang, "Str Qt No. 5" EDA ▲ EDA 006
Mozart, W.A.:Qts Strs (misc)—Nos. 14-19, "The Haydn Quartets" Capriccio 3-▲ CD 10 605 [DDD]
Schulhoff, E.:Qt 1 Strs *(rec Berlin, June 6-8 & Nov 7-8, 1994)* Capriccio ▲ 10 539 [DDD]
Schulhoff, E.:Sxt Strs, w. Rainer Johannes Kimstedt (va), Michael Sanderling (vc) *(rec Berlin, June 6-8 & Nov 7-8, 1994)* Capriccio ▲ 10 539 [DDD]
La Petite Bande
Bach, J.S.:Cant 49, w. N. Argenta (sop), K. Mertens (bass), M. Ponseele (ob), S. Kuijken (vn), H. Suzuki (vc), P. Hantaï (org) Accent ▲ ACC 9395 D [DDD]
Bach, J.S.:Cant 58, w. N. Argenta (sop), K. Mertens (bass), M. Ponseele (ob), S. Kuijken (vn), H. Suzuki (vc), P. Hantaï (org) Accent ▲ ACC 9395 D [DDD]
Bach, J.S.:Cant 82, w. N. Argenta (sop), K. Mertens (bass), M. Ponseele (ob), S. Kuijken (vn), H. Suzuki (vc), P. Hantaï (org) Accent ▲ ACC 9395 D [DDD]
Bach, J.S.:Cons Vn (comp), w. S. Kuijken (vn) Editio Classica ▲ 77006-2-RG [DDD]
Bach, J.S.:Con for 2 Vns, w. S. Kuijken (vn) Editio Classica ▲ 77006-2-RG [DDD]
Greatest Hits of 1750, w. Collegium Aureum, Leonhardt Ensemble, et al. Pro Arte ▲ CDM 817
Mozart, W.A.:Con 3 Vn Denon ▲ DEN 78837
Mozart, W.A.:Sinf Concertante, K.364 Denon ▲ DEN 78837
Vivaldi, A.:Cons Vn, Op. 8/1-4, "The Four Seasons", w. S. Kuijken (vn) Pro Arte ▲ CDD 214 [DDD] ■ PCD 214
Vivaldi, A.:Music of, w. S. Kuijken (vn), F. Brüggen (rcr), St. Mary's Chamber Players—The 4 Seasons; Bn Con in E♭; Ob Con in F; etc. Pro Arte ▲ CDM 816 ■ PCD 816
S. Kuijken (cnd)
Bach, J.S.:Brandenburg Cons *(rec 1993)* Deutsche Harmonia Mundi 2-▲ 05472-77308-2 [DDD]
Bach, J.S.:Cant 21, w. G. de Reyghere (mez), C. Prégardien (ten), P. Lika (bass), Netherlands Chamber Choir [G] Veritas ▲ VC 7 90779-2 [DDD] ■ VC 7 90779-4 (D)
Bach, J.S.:Cant 21, w. G. de Reyghere (mez), R. Jacobs (alt), C. Prégardien (ten), P. Lika (bass), S. Kuijken (vn), Netherlands Chamber Choir Virgin Classics ▲ CDC 59528
Bach, J.S.:Magnificat, BWV 243, w. G. de Reyghere (sop), R. Jacobs (alt), C. Prégardien (ten), P. Lika (bass), S. Kuijken (vn), Netherlands Chamber Choir Virgin Classics ▲ CDC 59528
Bach, J.S.:Magnificat, BWV 243, w. G. de Reyghere (sop), R. Jacobs (alt), C. Prégardien (ten), P. Lika (bass), S. Kuijken (vn), Netherlands Chamber Choir [L] Veritas ▲ VC 7 90779-2 [DDD] ■ VC 7 90779-4 (D)
Bach, J.S.:Motets, BWV 225-30, w. La Petite Bande Chorus Accent ▲ 9287 [DDD]
Bach, J.S.:St. John Passion Editio Classica 2-▲ 77041-2-RG [ADD]
Bach, J.S.:Suites Orch, BWV 1066-1069 Editio Classica 2-▲ 77008-2-RG [DDD] 2-■ 77008-4-RG (CrO2)
Geminiani, F.:Concerti grossi (misc)—Op. 2, Nos. 5 & 6; Op. 3, No. 3; Op. 7, Nos. 2,5 & 6 Editio Classica ▲ 77010-2 [ADD]
Gluck, C.W.:Orfeo ed Euridice, w. M. Falewicz (sop), M. Kweksilber (sop), R. Jacobs (alt), Collegium Vocale Accent 2-▲ 48223/24 [DDD]
Handel, G.F.:Partenope, w. Krisztina Laki (sop), Helga Müller-Molinari (mez), René Jacobs (alt), John York Skinner (alt) Editio Classica 3-▲ 77109-2-RG [ADD]
Haydn, J.:Die Jahreszeiten, w. Krisztina Láki (sop), Helmut Wildhaber, Peter Lika (bass), Flanders Opera Choir Virgin Classics 2-▲ ZDCB 59268
Haydn, J.:Die Schöpfung, w. Krisztina Láki (sop), Neil Mackie (ten), Philippe Huttenlocher (bar), Ghent Collegium Vocale Accent 2-▲ ACC 58228/29
Haydn, J.:Sym 88 Virgin Classics ("Veritas" series) ▲ 59070 [DDD]
Haydn, J.:Sym 89 Virgin Classics ("Veritas" series) ▲ 59070 [DDD]
Haydn, J.:Sym 92, "Oxford" Virgin Classics ("Veritas" series) ▲ 59070 [DDD]
Haydn, J.:Sym 93 Deutsche Harmonia Mundi ▲ 05472-77275-2

La Petite Bande (cont.)
S. Kuijken (cnd) (cont.)
Haydn, J.:Sym 94, "Surprise Sym" Deutsche Harmonia Mundi ▲ 05472-77275-2
Haydn, J.:Sym 95 Deutsche Harmonia Mundi ▲ 05472-77275-2
Haydn, J.:Sym 96, "Miracle" Deutsche Harmonia Mundi ▲ 05472-77294-2 [DDD]
Haydn, J.:Sym 97 Deutsche Harmonia Mundi ▲ 05472-77294-2 [DDD]
Haydn, J.:Sym 98 Deutsche Harmonia Mundi ▲ 05472-77294-2 [DDD]
Haydn, J.:Sym 99 Deutsche Harmonia Mundi ▲ 05472-77328-2 [DDD]
Haydn, J.:Sym 100, "Military" Deutsche Harmonia Mundi ▲ 05472-77328-2 [DDD]
Haydn, J.:Sym 101, "Clock" *(rec Feb 7-11, 1994)* Deutsche Harmonia Mundi ▲ 05472-77351-2 [DDD]
Haydn, J.:Sym 102 *(rec Jan 16-20, 1995)* Deutsche Harmonia Mundi ▲ 05472-77351-2 [DDD]
Mozart, W.A.:Così fan tutte, w. S. Isokoski (sop—Fiordiligi), N. Argenta (sop—Despina), M. Groop (mez—Dorabella), M. Schäfer (ten—Ferrando), P. Vollestad (bar—Guglielmo), H. Claessens (b-bar—Don Alfonso)., La Petite Bande Chorus Accent 3-▲ ACC 9296/98
Mozart, W.A.:Requiem, w. *(soloists unknown)*, Netherlands Chamber Choir Accent ▲ 68645
Muffat, G.:Sons Chamber Ensemble Editio Classica ▲ 77074-2-RG [ADD]
Muffat, G.:Suites Editio Classica ▲ 77074-2-RG [ADD]
Rameau, J.P.:Hippolyte et Aricie (orchestral suite) Editio Classica ▲ 77009-2-RG [ADD] ■ 77009-4-RG (CrO2)
G. Leonhardt (cnd)
Bach, J.S.:Mass in b, BWV 232, w. *(soloists unknown)* Editio Classica 2-▲ 77040-2-RG [ADD] 2-■ 77040-4-RG (CrO2)
Bach, J.S.:St. Matthew Passion, w. Tölz Boys' Choir Editio Classica 3-▲ 7848-2-RC [DDD]
Campra, A.:L'Europe galante, w. M. Kweksilber (sop), R. Yakar (sop), R. Jacobs (ct), S. Nimsgern (bar) Editio Classica 2-▲ 77059-2-RG [ADD]
Lully, J.-B.:Le Bourgeois gentilhomme, w. M. Kweksilber (sop), R. Yakar (sop), R. Jacobs (ct), S. Nimsgern (bar) Editio Classica 2-▲ 77059-2-RG [ADD]
Pfeiffer Trumpet Consort [Dale Marrs (tpt), Harald Pfeiffer (tpt), Joachim Pfeiffer (tpt), Martin Pfeiffer (tpt)]
Festive Trumpet Concerti, w. Mathias Müller (timp), Peter Schumann (org) *(rec St Juliana Parish Church, Malsch, July 4-6, 1995)* Cantate ▲ C 58001 [DDD]
Pforzheim CO
P. Angerer (cnd)
Hummel, J.N.:Vars Ob, w. Branimir Slokar (alt trbn) Claves ■ C 906
Philadelphia Brass Quintet [Brian Kuszyk (tpt), Lawrence Wright (tpt), Martin Webster (hn), John Ilika (trbn), Grant Moore II (tuba)]
God Of Our Fathers, w. Mormon Tabernacle Choir CBS ■ MT 30054
Joan Lippincott & Philadelphia Brass, w. Lippincott, Joan (org) Gothic ▲ GOT 49072 [DDD]
Philadelphia Brass Ensemble
Gabrieli, G.:Sacrae symphoniae, w. Chicago Brass Ensemble, Cleveland Brass Ensemble—Canzon Septimi Toni Nos 1 & 2; Canzon Duodecimi Toni; Canzon a 12 in Echo; Canzon Quarti Toni; Canzon Primi Toni; Canzon Noni Toni; Son Octavi Toni; Son pian' e forte *(rec Philadelphia, 1968)* Sony Classical ("Masterworks Heritage" series) ▲ MHK 62353 [ADD]
Philadelphia Concerto Soloists
Moran, R.:Requiem, w. Mendelssohn Club Chorus Philadelphia *(rec Chapel of Girard College, Philadelphia & Henry Wood Hall, London)* Argo ▲ 444540-2 [DDD]
Philadelphia Concerto Soloists members
J. Flummerfelt (cnd)
Christmas Masterpieces & Familiar Carols, w. Westminster Choir, New Jersey SO Gothic ▲ GOT 47931 ■ MC 47931
Philadelphia Lyric Opera Orch
A. Guadagno (cnd)
Puccini, G.:La fanciulla del West, w. D. Kirsten (sop), F. Corelli (ten), A. Colzani (bar), Philadelphia Lyric Opera Chorus [I] *(rec live, 11/10/64)* Melodram 2-▲ MEL 27081 [AAD]
Verdi, G.:La traviata, w. M. Caballé (sop), J. Carreras (ten), N. Mitic (bar), Philadelphia Lyric Opera Chorus *(rec 1973)* Melodram 2-▲ MLO 270106 [ADD]
Philadelphia Opera Orch
C. Maresco (cnd)
Puccini, G.:Tosca, w. B. Nilsson (sop), F. Tagliavini (ten), R. Vinay (ten), Philadelphia Opera Chorus *(rec Apr. 10, 1963)* Melodram 2-▲ MLO 270112 [ADD]
J. Rudel (cnd)
Donizetti, G.:Anna Bolena, w. R. Scotto (sop—Anna Bolena), K. Ciesinski (mez—Smeton), S. Marsee (mez—Giovanna Seymour), S. Kolk (ten—Riccardo Percy), S. Ramey (bass—Enrico VIII) *(rec live, Dec. 16, 1975)* Legato Classics 2-▲ LCD 175 [ADD]
Philadelphia Orch
Anvil Chorus:Favorite Opera Choruses, w. Mormon Tabernacle Choir CBS ■ MT 07061
Great Choruses of Bach & Handel, w. Mormon Tabernacle Choir CBS ■ MXT 39102
Mangold, C.A.:Abraham, w. Monika Frimmer (sop), Georg Mechthild (mez), B Gärtner (ten), Gerd Türk (ten), Giles Cachemaille (bar), Darmstadt Concert Choir Christophorus 2-▲ 77172
Mendelssohn, F.:Music of, Columbia SO, New York PO CBS ▲ MLK 39452 ■ MT 39452
C. Dutoit (cnd)
Persichetti, V.:Con Pno, w. R. Taub (pno) New World ▲ NW 370-2 [DDD]
Rachmaninoff, S.:The Bells, w. A. Pendachanska (sop), K. Kaludov (ten), S. Leiferkus (bar) London ▲ 440355-2 [DDD]
Rachmaninoff, S.:The Rock London ▲ 440604-2 [DDD]
Rachmaninoff, S.:Russian Songs, w. *(chorus unknown)* London ▲ 440355-2 [DDD]
Rachmaninoff, S.:Spring, w. S. Leiferkus (bar), *(chorus unknown)* London ▲ 440355-2 [DDD]
Rachmaninoff, S.:Symphonic Dances London ▲ 433181-2 [DDD]
Rachmaninoff, S.:Sym 2 London ▲ 440604-2 [DDD]
Rachmaninoff, S.:Sym 3 London ▲ 433181-2 [DDD]
M. Jansons (cnd)
Mussorgsky, M.:Songs & Dances, w. Robert Lloyd (bass) EMI Classics ▲ CDC 55232
Shostakovich, D.:Sym 10 EMI Classics ▲ CDC 55232
O. Klemperer (cnd)
Bach, J.S.:Brandenburg Con 1 *(rec live, 1962)* As Disc ▲ ASD 2504
Schumann, R.:Sym 4 *(rec live, 1962)* As Disc ▲ ASD 2504
J. Levine (cnd)
Classical Ecstasy—Classics for a New Age, w. Chicago SO [cnd:Georg Solti], English CO [cnd:Alexander Schneider], London PO [cnd:Leonard Slatkin], Philharmonia Orch [cnds:Andrew Litton, Henry Lewis], RCA Italiana Opera Orch [cnd:Francesco Molinari-Pradelli] RCA Gold Seal ▲ 74321-23041-2 [ADD/DDD]
Schumann, R.:Sym 1 RCA Victor ▲ 09026-61849-2; ■ 09026-61849-4 (CrO2)
C. Munch (cnd)
Berlioz, H.:La Damnation de Faust (sels)—Menuet des follets; Ballet des sylphes; Marche hongroise *(rec Mar. 14, 1963)* Sony Classical ▲ SBK 53255 ■ SBT 53255
R. Muti (cnd)
Beethoven, L. van:Fidelio (ov) EMI Classics 6-▲ A26-49487 [DDD]
Beethoven, L. van:Leonore 3 EMI Classics 6-▲ A26-49487 [DDD]
Beethoven, L. van:Syms (comp) EMI Classics 6-▲ A26-49487 [DDD]
Beethoven, L. van:Sym 9, "Choral Sym", w. Westminster Choir [G] EMI Classics ▲ CDC 49493 [DDD] ■ 4DS 49493 (D)
Beethoven, L. van:Die Weihe des Hauses (ov) EMI Classics 6-▲ A26-49487 [DDD]
Brahms, J.:Alto Rhap, w. J. Norman (mez) Philips ("Digital Classics" series) ▲ 426253-2 [DDD] □ 426253-5
Brahms, J.:Sym 1 Philips ("Digital Classics" series) ▲ 426299-2 [DDD]
Brahms, J.:Sym 3 Philips ("Digital Classics" series) ▲ 426253-2 [DDD] □ 426253-5
Brahms, J.:Vars on a Theme by Haydn Philips ("Digital Classics" series) ▲ 426299-2 [DDD]
Chausson, E.:Poème de l'amour et de la mer, w. W. Meier (mez) EMI Classics ▲ CDC 55120
Debussy, C.:La Mer EMI Classics ▲ CDC 55120

ORCH. & ENS.

Philadelphia Orch (cont.)
R. Muti (cnd) (cont.)

Dvořák, A.:Con Vn, w. K.-W. Chung (vn) EMI Classics ▲ CDC 49858 [DDD]
Dvořák, A.:Romance Vn, w. K.-W. Chung (vn) EMI Classics ▲ CDC 49858 [DDD]
Franck, C.:Le Chasseur maudit EMI Classics ▲ CDM 64747
Franck, C.:Le Chasseur maudit Classics for Pleasure ("Eminence" series) ▲ CFP 2236
Leoncavallo, R.:Pagliacci, w. D. Dessi (sop), L. Pavarotti (ten), P. Coni (bar), J. Pons (bar) [I] Philips ▲ 438132-2
Liszt, F.:Les Préludes EMI Classics ▲ CDC 47022
Mahler, G.:Sym 1 EMI Classics ▲ CDD 64287
Mussorgsky, M.:Night Philips ▲ 432170-2 [DDD]
Mussorgsky, M.:Pictures at an Exhibition EMI Classics ▲ CDM 64516
Mussorgsky, M.:Pictures at an Exhibition Philips ▲ 432170-2 [DDD]
Persichetti, V.:Sym 5 New World ▲ NW 370-2 [DDD]
Prokofiev, S.:Romeo & Juliet (sels) EMI Classics ▲ CDC 47004 [DDD]
Prokofiev, S.:Sym 1 Philips ▲ 432992-2 [DDD]
Prokofiev, S.:Sym 3 Philips ▲ 432992-2 [DDD]
Rachmaninoff, S.:Con 2 Pno, w. A. Gavrilov (pno) EMI Classics ▲ CDC 49966
Rachmaninoff, S.:Rhapsody on a Theme of Paganini, w. A. Gavrilov (pno) EMI Classics ▲ CDC 49966
Rands, B.:Ceremonial 3 New World ▲ 803922
Rands, B.:Le tambourin (suites) New World ▲ 803922
Ravel, M.:Une Barque sur l'océan EMI Classics ▲ CDC 55120
Ravel, M.:Boléro EMI Classics ▲ CDC 47022
Respighi, O.:The Fountains of Rome EMI Classics ▲ CDC 47316 [DDD]
Respighi, O.:The Pines of Rome EMI Classics ▲ CDC 47316 [DDD]
Scriabin, A.:Sym 1, w. S. Toczyska (mez), M. Myers (ten), Philadelphia Choral Arts Society EMI Classics 3-▲ CDC 54251
Scriabin, A.:Sym 2 EMI Classics 3-▲ CDC 54251
Scriabin, A.:Sym 3 EMI Classics 3-▲ CDC 54251
Scriabin, A.:Sym 4 EMI Classics 3-▲ CDC 54251
Scriabin, A.:Sym 5 EMI Classics 3-▲ CDC 54251
Shostakovich, D.:Festive Ov EMI Classics ▲ CDC 54803
Shostakovich, D.:Sym 5 EMI Classics ▲ CDC 54803
Stravinsky, I.:Le Sacre du printemps Orch EMI Classics ▲ CDM 64516
Tchaikovsky, P.:Francesca da Rimini EMI Classics ▲ CDC 54338
Tchaikovsky, P.:Ov 1812 EMI Classics ▲ CDC 47022
Tchaikovsky, P.:Sleeping Beauty (sels) EMI Classics ▲ CDC 47075 [DDD]
Tchaikovsky, P.:Swan Lake (sels) EMI Classics ▲ CDC 47075 [DDD]
Tchaikovsky, P.:Sym 5 EMI Classics ▲ CDC 54338

E. Ormandy (cnd)

Adam, A.:Giselle (sels) Sony Classical (Essential Classics) ▲ SBK 46341 [ADD] ■ SBT 46341
Alfvén, H.:Swedish Rhap 1, "Midsommarvaka" CBS ▲ MBK 38917 ■ YT 38917
Bach, C.P.E.:Cons Hpd & Strs—in D [arr M. Steinberg for orch] *(rec Mar 17, 1957)* Sony Classical ("Masterworks Heritage" series) 2-▲ MH2K 62345 [ADD]
Bach, Joh. Christian:Sinfs, Op. 18—Nos 1 & 3 *(rec Jan & Apr 1960)* Sony Classical ("Masterworks Heritage" series) 2-▲ MH2K 62345 [ADD]
Bach, J.S.:Cant 140 [arr Ormandy] *(rec Mar 11, 1968)* Sony Classical ("Masterworks Heritage" series) 2-▲ MH2K 62345 [ADD]
Bach, J.S.:Music of Odyssey ▲ MBK 38915 [ADD] ■ YT 38915
Bach, J.S.:Passacaglia & Fugue Org [arr Ormandy for orch] *(rec Jan & Apr 1960)* Sony Classical ("Masterworks Heritage" series) 2-▲ MH2K 62345 [ADD]
Bach, J.S.:Toccata, Adagio & Fugue Org, BWV 564 [arr Ormandy for orch] *(rec Jan & Apr 1960)* Sony Classical ("Masterworks Heritage" series) 2-▲ MH2K 62345 [ADD]
Bach, J.S.:Toccata & Fugue Org, BWV 565 [arr Ormandy for orch], Jan 31, 1960) Sony Classical ("Masterworks Heritage" series) 2-▲ MH2K 62345 [ADD]
Bach, W.F.:Sinf in d *(rec Mar 17, 1957)* Sony Classical ("Masterworks Heritage" series) 2-▲ MH2K 62345 [ADD]
Balakirev, M.:Islamey [orchd] Sony Classical ("Essential Classics" series) ▲ SBK 62647 ■ SBT 62647
Bartók, B.:Con Orch *(rec 1963)* Sony Classical ("Essential Classics" series) ▲ SBK 48263 [ADD] ■ SBT 48263
Bartók, B.:Con 2 Pno, w. A. Weissenberg (pno) RCA Gold Seal ▲ 09026-61396-2
Bartók, B.:The Miraculous Mandarin (suite) *(rec 1962)* Sony Classical ("Essential Classics" series) ▲ SBK 48263 [ADD] ■ SBT 48263
Bartók, B.:The Miraculous Mandarin (suite) EMI Classics ▲ CDM 65175
Bartók, B.:Music for Strs, Perc & Cel EMI Classics ▲ CDM 65175
Bartók, B.:Pictures Orch *(rec 1963)* Sony Classical ("Essential Classics" series) ▲ SBK 48263 [ADD] ■ SBT 48263
Basic 100:Vol. 14 RCA Victor ▲ 09026-61711-2 ■ 09026-61711-4
Basic 100:Vol. 25 RCA Victor ▲ 09026-61722-2 ■ 09026-61722-4
Basic 100:Vol. 27 RCA Victor ▲ 09026-61724-2 ■ 09026-61724-4
Basic 100:Vol. 32 RCA Victor ▲ 09026-61850-2 ■ 09026-61850-4
Basic 100:Vol. 35 RCA Victor ▲ 09026-61853-2 ■ 09026-61853-4
Basic 100:Vol. 38 RCA Victor ▲ 09026-61856-2 ■ 09026-61856-4
Basic 100:Vol. 63, w.Judith Blegen (sop), Frederica von Stade (mez) RCA Victor ▲ 09026-68088-2 ■ 09026-68088-4
Beethoven, L. van:Con 1 Pno, w. R. Serkin (pno) CBS ▲ MYK 37807 [ADD]
Beethoven, L. van:Con 1 Pno, w. R. Serkin (pno) CBS ▲ MK 42259
Beethoven, L. van:Con 3 Pno, w. V. Cliburn (pno) RCA Gold Seal ▲ 09026-60419-2 [ADD] ■ 09026-60419-4
Beethoven, L. van:Con 5 Pno, "Emperor", w. L. Fleisher (pno) Sony Classical ("Essential Classics" series) ▲ SBK 46549 [ADD] ■ SBT 46549
Beethoven, L. van:Con Vn, Vc & Pno, "Triple Con", w. I. Stern (vn), L. Rose (vc), E. Istomin (pno) Sony Classical ("Essential Classics" series) 3-▲ SB3K 48397
Beethoven, L. van:Con Vn, Vc & Pno, "Triple Con", w. I. Stern (vn), L. Rose (vc), E. Istomin (pno) Sony Classical ("Essential Classics" series) ▲ SBK 46549 [ADD] ■ SBT 46549
Beethoven, L. van:Minuets Orch, WoO 10—Minuet No. 2 in G Sony Classical ▲ MLK 62369 [ADD/DDD]
Beethoven, L. van:Missa Solemnis, w. M. Arroyo (sop), M. Forrester (cta), R. Lewis (ten), C. Siepi (b-bar), Singing City Choir *(rec Mar. 29-30, 1967)* Sony Classical ("Essential Classics" series) ▲ SBK 53517 [ADD] ■ SBT 53517
Beethoven, L. van:Sym 9, "Choral Sym" [G] CBS ▲ MYK 37241 [ADD] ■ MYT 37241
Beethoven, L. van:Wellington's Victory, "Battle Sym" RCA Victrola ▲ 7731-2-RV [DDD] ■ 7731-4-RV
Berlioz, H.:Harold in Italy, w. J. de Pasquale (va) *(rec Jan. 21, 1965)* Sony Classical ▲ SBK 53255 ■ SBT 53255
Berlioz, H.:Hymne des Marseillais RCA Silver Seal ▲ 09026-61211-2
Berlioz, H.:Sym fantastique Sony Classical ("Essential Classics" series) ▲ SBK 46329 [ADD] ■ SBT 46329
The Best of Mendelssohn, w. Leipzig Gewandhaus Orch [cnd:Kurt Masur], Boston Pops Orch [cnd:Arthur Fiedler], et al. ("Victrola Best of" series)
The Best of Tchaikovsky, w. Chicago SO [cnd:F. Reiner], J. Browning (pno), London SO [cnd:S. Ozawa], et al. Victrola ("Victrola Best of" series) ▲ 60775-2-RV [ADD] ■ 60775-4-RV
The Best of Wagner, w. Robert Shaw Chorale, RCA Victor SO Victrola ("Victrola Best of" series) ▲ 60777-2-RV [ADD] ■ 60777-4-RV
Bizet, G.:L'Arlésienne (suites)—Suite No. 1, & Farandole from Suite No. 2 CBS ▲ MLK 39453 ■ MT 39453
Bizet, G.:L'Arlésienne (suites) Sony Classical ("Essential Classics" series) ▲ SBK 48159 ■ SBT 48159
Bizet, G.:L'Arlésienne (suites) RCA Victor ▲ 09026-61722-2; ■ 09026-61722-4
Bizet, G.:L'Arlésienne (suites) RCA Silver Seal ▲ 60787-2-RV [ADD] ■ 60787-4-RV
Bizet, G.:Carmen (suites) RCA Silver Seal ▲ 60787-2-RV [ADD] ■ 60787-4-RV

Philadelphia Orch (cont.)
E. Ormandy (cnd) (cont.)

Bizet, G.:Carmen (suites)—sels. from Suites 1 & 2 Sony Classical ("Essential Classics" series) ▲ SBK 48159 ■ SBT 48159
Bizet, G.:Carmen (suites) RCA Victor ▲ 09026-61722-2; ■ 09026-61722-4
Bizet, G.:Carmen (suites) Odyssey ■ YT 33923
Bloch, E.:Schelomo, w. L. Rose (vc) *(rec 1967)* Sony Classical ("Essential Classics" series) ▲ SBK 48278 [ADD] ■ SBT 48278
Blockbusters from the Movies, w. Boston Pops Orch [cnd:A. Fiedler] RCA Victor ▲ 09026-68080-2 ■ 09026-68080-4
Borodin, A.:In the Steppes of Central Asia CBS ■ MGT 42280
Borodin, A.:Nocturne Str Orch CBS ■ MGT 42280
Borodin, A.:Prince Igor (Polovtsian dances) RCA Victor ▲ 09026-68336-2 ■ 09026-68336-4
Borodin, A.:Prince Igor (Polovtsian dances) CBS ■ MGT 42280
Borodin, A.:Prince Igor (Polovtsian dances) RCA Gold Seal ("Papillon Collection" series) ▲ 6721-2-RG [ADD] ■ 6721-4-RG
Brahms, J.:Alto Rhap, w. M. Anderson (cta), Philadelphia Orch Chorus [G] *(rec 1939 for HMV)* Pearl ▲ PEA 9405 (m) [AAD]
Brahms, J.:Con 2 Pno, w. R. Serkin (pno) *(rec 1960)* Odyssey ▲ MBK 46273 [ADD] ■ YT 46273
Brahms, J.:Con Vn, w. I. Stern (vn) *(rec 1959)* CBS ▲ MK 42257 [AAD]
Brahms, J.:Con Vn, w. I. Stern (vn) Sony Classical ("Essential Classics" series) ▲ SBK 46335 [ADD] ■ SBT 46335
Brahms, J.:Con Vn, w. J. Szigeti (vn) *(rec 1945; from Columbia LP ML)* Sony Masterworks ("Portrait" series) ▲ MPK 52535 (m) [ADD]
Brahms, J.:Con Vn, w. I. Stern (vn) CBS 2-■ MGT 31418
Brahms, J.:Con Vn & Vc, "Double Con", w. Jascha Heifetz (vn), Emanuel Feuermann (vc) *(rec Dec 21, 1939)* Iron Needle ▲ IN 1351 [ADD]
Brahms, J.:Con Vn & Vc, "Double Con", w. I. Stern (vn), L. Rose (vc) Sony Classical ("Essential Classics" series) ▲ SBK 46335 [ADD] ■ SBT 46335
Brahms, J.:Hungarian Dances Orch—5 sels. Sony Classical ("Essential Classics" series) ▲ SBK 46534 [ADD] ■ SBT 46534
Brahms, J.:Songs, w. M. Anderson (cta)—Der Schmied, Op. 19/4; Dein blaues Auge, Op. 59/8; Immer leiser wird mein Schlummer, Op. 105/2 [G] *(rec 1939 for HMV)* Pearl ▲ PEA 9405 (m) [AAD]
Brahms, J.:Vars on a Theme by Haydn RCA Silver Seal ▲ 60536-2-RV [ADD] ■ 60536-4-RV
Brahms, J.:Vars on a Theme by Haydn Sony Classical ("Essential Classics" series) ▲ SBK 46534 [ADD] ■ SBT 46534
Britten, B.:The Young Person's Guide to the Orchestra Sony Classical ("Essential Classics" series) ▲ SBK 62638 ■ SBT 62638
Britten, B.:The Young Person's Guide to the Orchestra Odyssey ■ YT 34616
Bruch, M.:Con 1 Vn, w. Isaac Stern (vn), National SO Washington D.C. [cnd:M. Rostropovich] Sony Classical ▲ SMK 66830
Bruch, M.:Con 1 Vn, w. I. Stern (vn) CBS ▲ MYK 37811 [ADD] ■ MYT 37811
Bruch, M.:Con 1 Vn, w. I. Stern (vn) CBS ▲ MK 42256 [ADD]
Bruckner, A.:Sym 4, "Romantic" Sony Classical ("Essential Classics" series) ▲ SBK 47653 ■ SBT 47653
Bruckner, A.:Sym 5 Odyssey 2-▲ MB2K 45669
Bruckner, A.:Sym 5 Sony Classical ("Essential Classics" series) ▲ SBK 48160 ■ SBT 48160
Casella, A.:Paganiniana Odyssey ■ YT 31246
Chabrier, E.:España CBS ▲ MBK 38917 ■ YT 38917
Chausson, E.:Poème Vn, w. Zino Francescatti (vn) *(rec Nov 1950)* Sony Classical ("Masterworks Heritage" series) 2-▲ MH2K 62339 [ADD]
Chopin, F.:Con 1 Pno, w. E. Ax (pno) RCA Silver Seal ▲ 60789-2-RV [ADD/DDD] ■ 60789-4-RV
Chopin, F.:Con 1 Pno, w. E. Gilels (pno) Odyssey ■ YT 32369
Chopin, F.:Con 1 Pno, w. E. Gilels (pno) Sony Classical (Essential Classics) ▲ SBK 46336 [ADD] ■ SBT 46336
Chopin, F.:Con 1 Pno, w. Emmanuel Ax (pno) RCA Victor ▲ 09026-68023-2; ■ 09026-68023-4
Chopin, F.:Con 1 Pno, w. E. Gilels (pno) CBS ▲ MYK 37804 [ADD] ■ MYT 37804
Chopin, F.:Con 1 Pno, w. V. Cliburn (pno) RCA Gold Seal ▲ 7945-2-RG [ADD] ■ 7945-4-RG (CrO2)
Chopin, F.:Con 2 Pno, w. E. Ax (pno) *(rec analog)* RCA Silver Seal ▲ 60789-2-RV [ADD/DDD] ■ 60789-4-RV
Chopin, F.:Con 2 Pno, w. Emmanuel Ax (pno) RCA Victor ▲ 09026-68023-2; ■ 09026-68023-4
Chopin, F.:Con 2 Pno, w. A. Rubinstein (pno) RCA Gold Seal ▲ 60404-2-RG [ADD] ■ 60404-4-RG (CrO2)
Chopin, F.:Grand Fant on Polish Airs, w. A. Rubinstein (pno) RCA Gold Seal ▲ 60404-2-RG [ADD] ■ 60404-4-RG (CrO2)
Chopin, F.:Les Sylphides Sony Classical (Essential Classics) ▲ SBK 46551 [ADD] ■ SBT 46551
Clair De Lune:Music in a Romantic Mood Odyssey ▲ MBK 38919 [ADD] ■ YT 38919
Classical Hit Parade CBS ■ YT 38916
Classical Jukebox, w. Boston Pops Orch [cnd:A. Fiedler] RCA Victor ▲ 09026-68121-2 ■ 09026-68121-4
Classical Music for Home Improvement, w. Boston Pops Orch [cnd:A. Fiedler] RCA Victor ▲ 09026-61369-2 ■ 09026-61369-4 (CrO2)
Classics from the Crypt, w. Boston Pops Orch [cnd:A. Fiedler] RCA Victor ▲ 09026-61238-2 ■ 09026-61238-4 (CrO2)
The Complete 1937 Victor Recordings, w. Kirsten Flagstad(sop) Romophone ▲ 81023-2
Copland, A.:Billy the Kid (suite) RCA Gold Seal ▲ 6802-2-RG [ADD] ■ 6802-4-RG (CrO2)
Copland, A.:Fanfare for the Common Man CBS ▲ MLK 39443 ■ MT 39443
Copland, A.:Fanfare for the Common Man Sony Classical ("Essential Classics" series) ▲ SBK 62401 ■ SBT 62401
Copland, A.:Lincoln Portrait, w. Adlai Stevenson (nar) Sony Classical ("Essential Classics" series) ▲ SBK 62401 ■ SBT 62401
Debussy, C.:Clair de lune CBS 2-■ MGT 30950
Debussy, C.:Danse Pno, "Tarantelle styrienne" *(rec Mar. 14, 1959)* Sony Classical ▲ SBK 53256 ■ SBT 53256
Debussy, C.:Danses sacrée et profane, w. M. Costello (hp) CBS 2-■ MGT 30950
Debussy, C.:La Mer CBS 2-■ MGT 30950
Debussy, C.:La Mer RCA Victrola ▲ 60133-2-RV [ADD] ■ 60133-4-RV
Debussy, C.:La Mer *(rec Jan. 25, 1959)* Sony Classical ▲ SBK 53256 ■ SBT 53256
Debussy, C.:Nocturnes, w. Temple Univ Women's Choir *(rec Mar. 14, 1964)* Sony Classical ▲ SBK 53256 ■ SBT 53256
Debussy, C.:Nocturnes, w. Temple Univ Women's Choir CBS 2-■ MGT 30950
Debussy, C.:Prélude à l'après-midi d'un faune CBS 2-■ MGT 30950
Debussy, C.:Prélude à l'après-midi d'un faune RCA Victrola ▲ 60133-2-RV [ADD] ■ 60133-4-RV
Debussy, C.:Prélude à l'après-midi d'un faune *(rec Mar. 14, 1959)* Sony Classical ▲ SBK 53256 ■ SBT 53256
Delibes, L.:Coppélia (suite) Sony Classical (Essential Classics) ▲ SBK 46551 [ADD] ■ SBT 46551
Delibes, L.:Sylvia—suite Sony Classical (Essential Classics) ▲ SBK 46551 [ADD] ■ SBT 46551
Delius, F.:Music of—Brigg Fair; Dance Rhap No. 2; In a Summer Garden; On Hearing the 1st Cuckoo in Spring; Rhap Sony Classical ("Essential Classics" series) ▲ SBK 62645 ■ SBT 62645
Dukas, P.:L'Apprenti sorcier Sony Classical (Essential Classics) ▲ SBK 46329 [ADD] ■ SBT 46329
Dvořák, A.:Con Vc, w. L. Rose (vc) Sony Classical (Essential Classics) ▲ SBK 46337 [ADD] ■ SBT 46337
Dvořák, A.:Con Vn, w. I. Stern (vn) CBS ▲ MK 42257 [AAD]
Dvořák, A.:Con Vn, w. I. Stern (vn) Sony Classical (Essential Classics) ▲ SBK 46337 [ADD] ■ SBT 46337
Dvořák, A.:Scherzo Capriccioso RCA Silver Seal ▲ 60537-2-RV [ADD] ■ 60537-4-RV
Dvořák, A.:Sym 9, "From the New World" RCA Silver Seal ▲ 60537-2-RV [ADD] ■ 60537-4-RV
Enescu, G.:Romanian Rhap 1 CBS ▲ MBK 38917 ■ YT 38917
Everything You Wanted to Know about Classical Music, w. Boston Pops Orch [cnd:A. Fiedler] RCA Victor ▲ 09026-61239-2 ■ 09026-61239-4 (CrO2)

▲ = CD ♦ = Enhanced CD ∆ = MD ■ = Cassette Tape ☐ = DCC

Philadelphia Orch (cont.)
E. Ormandy (cnd) (cont.)
Fauré, G.:Elégie, w. L. Rose (vc) *(rec 1967)*
Sony Classical (Essential Classics) ▲ SBK 48278 [ADD] ■ SBT 48278
Fauré, G.:Pavane Orch Sony Classical ("Essential Classics" series) ▲ SBK 62644 ■ SBT 62644
Fauré, G.:Sicilienne RCA Silver Seal ▲ 09026-61211-2 ■ 09026-61211-4
Franck, C.:Symphonic Vars, w. G. Casadesus (pno) Odyssey ■ YT 31274
Gershwin, G.:An American in Paris *(rec Philadelphia, Jan 5, 1967)*
Sony Classical ("Essential Classics" series) ▲ SBK 62402 [ADD] ■ SBT 62402
Gershwin, G.:An American in Paris CBS ▲ MLK 39454 ■ PMT 39454
Gershwin, G.:An American in Paris Odyssey ■ YT 35496
Gershwin, G.:An American in Paris CBS 2-■ MGT 30073
Gershwin, G.:Con Pno, w. P. Entremont (pno) CBS 2-■ MGT 30073
Gershwin, G.:Con Pno, w. P. Entremont (pno)
Sony Classical ("Essential Classics" series) ▲ SBK 46338 [ADD] ■ SBT 46338
Gershwin, G.:Porgy & Bess (symphonic picture) *(rec Philadelphia, Jan 5, 1967)*
Sony Classical ("Essential Classics" series) ▲ SBK 62402 [ADD] ■ SBT 62402
Gershwin, G.:Porgy & Bess (symphonic picture) CBS 2-■ MGT 30073
Gershwin, G.:Rhap in Blue, w. P. Entremont (pno) CBS 2-■ MGT 30073
Gershwin, G.:Rhap in Blue, w. O. Levant (pno) *(rec 1945)*
CBS ▲ MK 42514 (m) [ADD] ■ FMT 42514 (m)
Gershwin, G.:Rhap in Blue, w. O. Levant (pno) *(rec 1945)*
Sony Masterworks ("Portrait" series) ▲ MPK 47681 [ADD]
Gershwin, G.:Rhap in Blue, w. P. Entremont (pno) Odyssey ■ YT 35496
Glière, R.:The Red Poppy (suite), "Russian Sailors' Dance"
Sony Classical ("Essential Classics" series) ▲ SBK 62647 ■ SBT 62647
Gluck, C.W.:Iphigénie en Aulide (sels)—Gavotte [arr by Thomas Frost]
Sony Classical ▲ MLK 62369 [ADD/DDD]
Grieg, E.:Con Pno, Op. 16, w. P. Entremont (pno) CBS ▲ MLK 39435 [ADD] ■ MT 39435
Grieg, E.:Con Pno, Op. 16, w. A. Rubinstein (pno) *(rec 1942)* RCA Gold Seal ▲ 09026-61883-2
Grieg, E.:Con Pno, Op. 16, w. P. Entremont (pno)
Sony Classical ("Essential Classics" series) ▲ SBK 46543 [ADD] ■ SBT 46543
Grieg, E.:Con Pno, Op. 16, w. P. Entremont (pno) CBS ▲ MYK 37805 [ADD] ■ MYT 37805
Grieg, E.:Con Pno, Op. 16, w. A. Rubinstein (pno)
RCA Gold Seal ▲ 09026-60897-2; ■ 09026-60897-4 (CrO2)
Grieg, E.:Con Pno, Op. 16, w. V. Cliburn (pno)
RCA Gold Seal ▲ 7834-2-RG [ADD] ■ 7834-4-RG (CrO2)
Grieg, E.:Elegiac Melodies, Op. 34 *(rec Oct. 18, 1967)* Sony Classical ▲ SBK 53257; ■ SBT 53257
Grieg:Greatest Hits, w. Boston Pops Orch [cnd:A. Fiedler] RCA Victor ▲ 60832-2-RG ■ 60832-4-RG
Grieg, E.:Lyric Suite, Op. 54—No. 3, March of the Trolls; No. 5, Notturno *(rec May 15, 1968)*
Sony Classical ▲ SBK 53257; ■ SBT 53257
Grieg, E.:Lyric Suite, Op. 54—Norwegian Rustic March & Nocturne Odyssey ▲ MBK 39785
Grieg, E.:Norwegian Dances, Op. 35—No. 2 *(rec Feb. 27, 1968)*
Sony Classical ▲ SBK 53257; ■ SBT 53257
Grieg, E.:Peer Gynt Suites, Opp. 46 & 55 RCA ■ ALK1-4979
Grieg, E.:Peer Gynt Suites, Opp. 46 & 55 RCA Silver Seal ▲ 60538-2-RV [ADD]
Grieg, E.:Peer Gynt Suites, Opp. 46 & 55 RCA Victor ▲ 09026-68088-2; ■ 09026-68088-4
Grieg, E.:Sigurd Jorsalfar (sels)—Homage March Odyssey ▲ MBK 39785
Grieg, E.:Sigurd Jorsalfar (suite)—No. 3, Homage March *(rec May 15, 1968)*
Sony Classical ▲ SBK 53257; ■ BT
Grofé, F.:Grand Canyon Suite CBS ■ MT 30446
Grofé, F.:Grand Canyon Suite *(rec Philadelphia, Dec 12 & 20, 1967)*
Sony Classical ("Essential Classics" series) ▲ SBK 62402 [ADD] ■ SBT 62402
Handel, G.F.:Messiah, w. Eileen Farrell (sop), Martha Lipton (cta), T. Cunningham (ten), William Warfield (bar), Mormon Tabernacle Choir [E] CBS 2-▲ M2K 00607 ■ M2T 00607
Handel, G.F.:Music of, w. Igor Kipnis (hpd), Mormon Tabernacle Choir—The Harmonious Blacksmith; See the conquering hero comes & Hallelujah Amen, from Judas Maccabaeus ("Handel's Greatest Hits")
CBS ▲ MLK 39441 ■ MT 39441
Handel, G.F.:Serse (sels)—Largo [arr by Thomas Frost] Sony Classical ▲ MLK 62369 [ADD/DDD]
Handel, G.F.:Water Music (suites) CBS ▲ MLK 39441 ■ MT 39441
Haydn, J.:Con Tpt, w. Gilbert Johnson (tpt)
Sony Classical ("Essential Classics" series) ▲ SBK 62649 ■ SBT 62649
Haydn, J.:Sinf concertante, w. John DeLancie (ob), Bernard Garfield (bn), Jacob Krachmalnick (vn), Lorne Munroe (vc) Sony Classical ("Essential Classics" series) ▲ SBK 62649 ■ SBT 62649
Hindemith, P.:Mathis der Maler (sym) *(rec Jan. 17, 1962)*
Sony Classical ▲ SBK 53258 ■ SBT 53258
Hindemith, P.:Symphonic Metamorphosis on Themes of Carl Maria von Weber
EMI Classics ▲ CDM 65175
Holst, G.:The Planets RCA Victor ▲ 09026-61270-2 [ADD] ■ 09026-61270-4 (CrO2)
Holst, G.:The Planets RCA Victor ▲ 09026-61724-2; ■ 09026-61724-4 (CrO2)
Ibert, J.:Divert Orch Sony Classical ("Essential Classics" series) ▲ SBK 62644 ■ SBT 62644
Ibert, J.:Escales Sony Classical ("Essential Classics" series) ▲ SBK 62644 ■ SBT 62644
Indy, V. d':Sym on a French Mountain Air, w. G. Casadesus (pno) Odyssey ■ YT 31274
Ippolitov-Ivanov, M.:Caucasian Sketches, Opp. 10 & 42—Procession of the Sardar
RCA Silver Seal ▲ 09026-61209-2 ■ 09026-61209-4
Ippolitov-Ivanov, M.:Caucasian Sketches (sels)—Procession of the Sardar
Sony Classical ("Essential Classics" series) ▲ SBK 62647 ■ SBT 62647
It's Good to Be the King:Musical Delights for Kings, Queens, Princes & Royalty, w. Claudio Abbado (cnd), Esa-Pekka Salonen (cnd), Michael Tilson Thomas (cnd), Canadian Brass, Chicago SO, Royal PO, Tafelmusik Sony Classical ▲ SFK 57483 ■ SFT 57483
Joy to the World RCA Gold Seal ▲ 6430-2-RG [ADD] ■ 6430-4-RG
Kabalevsky, D.:The Comedians—Comedian's Galop
Sony Classical ("Essential Classics" series) ▲ SBK 62647 ■ SBT 62647
Kabalevsky, D.:Con 1 Vc, w. Yo-Yo Ma (vc) CBS ▲ MK 37840 [DDD]
Khachaturian, A.:Gayane (suites)—Dance of the Young Maiden & Sabre Dance
Sony Classical ("Essential Classics" series) ▲ SBK 62647 ■ SBT 62647
Khachaturian, A.:Masquerade (ballet suite)—Galop
Sony Classical ("Essential Classics" series) ▲ SBK 62647 ■ SBT 62647
Kirsten Flagstad Recordings from 1935-39, w. Kirsten Flagstad (sop), San Francisco Opera Orch [cnd:Edwin McArthur], Hans Lange (cnd) Nimbus ▲ NI 7847
Kodály, Z.:Galanta Dances *(rec Philadelphia, Dec 9, 1962)*
Sony Classical ("Essential Classics" series) ▲ SBK 62404 ■ SBT 62404
Kodály, Z.:Marosszék Dances *(rec Philadelphia, Nov 15, 1962)*
Sony Classical ("Essential Classics" series) ▲ SBK 62404 ■ SBT 62404
Lalo, E.:Con Vc, w. L. Rose (vc) *(rec 1967)*
Sony Classical ("Essential Classics" series) ▲ SBK 48278 [ADD] ■ SBT 48278
Lalo, E.:Sym espagnole, w. I. Stern (vn) CBS ▲ MYK 37811 [ADD] ■ MYT-37811
Liszt, F.:Cons Pno, w. V. Cliburn (pno) RCA Gold Seal ▲ 7834-2-RG [ADD] ■ 7834-4-RG (CrO2)
Liszt, F.:Cons Pno, w. P. Entremont (pno)
Sony Classical ("Essential Classics" series) ▲ SBK 48167 ■ SBT 48167
Liszt, F.:Con 1 Pno, w. Claudio Arrau (pno) *(rec Feb 1952)*
Sony Classical ("Masterworks Heritage" series) ▲ MHK 62338 [ADD]
Liszt, F.:Fant on Hungarian Folk Tunes, w. I. Davis (pno) CBS ▲ MLK 39450 ■ MT 39450
Liszt, F.:Fant on Hungarian Folk Tunes, w. Claudio Arrau (pno) *(rec Feb 1952)*
Sony Classical ("Masterworks Heritage" series) ▲ MHK 62338 [ADD]
Liszt, F.:Hungarian Rhaps—No. 12 CBS ▲ MBK 38917 ■ YT 38917
Liszt, F.:Mephisto Waltz 1 Orch CBS ▲ MYK 37772 [ADD] ■ MYT 37772
Liszt, F.:Mephisto Waltz 1 Orch CBS ▲ MLK 39450 ■ MT 39450
Liszt, F.:Totentanz, w. Alexander Brailowsky (pno)
Sony Classical ("Essential Classics" series) ▲ SBK 48167 ■ SBT 48167

Philadelphia Orch (cont.)
E. Ormandy (cnd) (cont.)
Mahler, G.:Das Lied von der Erde, w. L. Chookasian (mez), R. Lewis (ten) *(rec Feb. 9, 1966)*
Sony Classical ("Essential Classics" series) ▲ SBK 53518 [ADD] ■ SBT 53518
Mendelssohn, F.:Capriccio brillante, w. R. Serkin (pno)
Sony Classical ("Essential Classics" series) ▲ SBK 48166 ■ SBT 48166
Mendelssohn, F.:Con 1 Pno, w. R. Serkin (pno)
Sony Classical ("Essential Classics" series) ▲ SBK 46542 [ADD] ■ SBT 46542
Mendelssohn, F.:Con in e Vn & Orch, Op. 64, w. I. Stern (vn) CBS ▲ MYK 36724 ■ MYT 36724
Mendelssohn, F.:Con in e Vn & Orch, Op. 64, w. I. Stern (vn) CBS ▲ MLK 39452 ■ MT 39452
Mendelssohn, F.:Con in e Vn & Orch, Op. 64, w. I. Stern (vn)
Sony Classical ("Essential Classics" series) ▲ SBK 46542 [ADD] ■ SBT 46542
Mendelssohn, F.:Con in e Vn & Orch, Op. 64, w. A. Spalding (vn) *(rec 12/20/41 for Victor, prev)*
Biddulph ▲ LAB 054 [ADD]
Mendelssohn, F.:A Midsummer Night's Dream (sels)
RCA Victor ▲ 09026-68088-2; ■ 09026-68088-4
Meyerbeer, G.:Les Patineurs (sels)
Sony Classical ("Essential Classics" series) ▲ SBK 46341 [ADD] ■ SBT 46341
The Mormon Tabernacle Choir Album, w. Mormon Tabernacle Choir CBS 2-■ MGT 31081
Movie Love Songs RCA Victor ▲ 09026-60965-2 [ADD]
Mozart, W.A.:Con Bn, w. Bernard Garfield (bn)
Sony Classical ("Essential Classics" series) ▲ SBK 62652 ■ SBT 62652
Mozart, W.A.:Con Ob, w. John DeLancie (ob)
Sony Classical ("Essential Classics" series) ▲ SBK 62652 ■ SBT 62652
Mozart, W.A.:Con 17 Pno, w. Sviatoslav Richter (pno) Stradivarius ▲ STV 33303
Mozart, W.A.:Con 17 Pno, w. S. Richter (pno) *(rec live, Philadelphia, Jan. 29, 1970)*
Intaglio ▲ INCD 707-1 [ADD]
Mozart, W.A.:Con 27 Pno, w. R. Serkin (pno) Sony Classical 3-▲ SM3K 47207
Mozart, W.A.:Con 27 Pno, w. R. Serkin (pno) Odyssey ▲ MBK 42533 ■ YT 42533
Mozart, W.A.:Kleine Nachtmusik CBS ▲ MLK 39436 ■ MT 39436
Music of France Victrola ▲ 09026-61211-2 ■ 09026-61211-4
Mussorgsky, M.:Khovanshchina (prelude) RCA Victor ▲ 09026-68336-2 ■ 09026-68336-4
Mussorgsky, M.:Night Sony Classical ("Essential Classics" series) ▲ SBK 46329 [ADD] ■ SBT 46329
Mussorgsky, M.:Night RCA Victor ▲ 09026-68336-2 ■ 09026-68336-4
Mussorgsky, M.:Night
RCA Gold Seal ("Papillon Collection" series) ▲ 6721-2-RG [ADD] ■ 6721-4-RG (CrO2)
Mussorgsky, M.:Night RCA Silver Seal ▲ 09026-61209-2 ■ 09026-61209-4
Mussorgsky, M.:Pictures at an Exhibition RCA Victor ▲ 09026-68336-2 ■ 09026-68336-4
Mussorgsky, M.:Pictures at an Exhibition RCA Silver Seal ▲ 09026-61209-2 ■ 09026-61209-4
Mussorgsky, M.:Pictures at an Exhibition
RCA Gold Seal ("Papillon Collection" series) ▲ 6721-2-RG [ADD] ■ 6721-4-RG (CrO2)
Mussorgsky, M.:Sorochintsy Fair (orch sels)—Hopak
Sony Classical ("Essential Classics" series) ▲ SBK 62647 ■ SBT 62647
Nielsen, C.:Helios *(rec 1967)* Sony Classical 4-▲ S4K 45989 [ADD]
Nielsen, C.:Imaginary Trip *(rec 1967)* Sony Classical 4-▲ S4K 45989 [ADD]
Nielsen, C.:Maskarade—Overture & Act II Prelude *(rec 1966)* Sony Classical 4-▲ S4K 45989 [ADD]
Nielsen, C.:Pan & Syrinx *(rec 1967)* Sony Classical 4-▲ S4K 45989 [ADD]
Nielsen, C.:Sym 1 *(rec 1967)* Sony Classical 4-▲ S4K 45989 [ADD]
Nielsen, C.:Sym 6 *(rec 1966)* Sony Classical 4-▲ S4K 45989 [ADD]
Offenbach, J.:Gaîté Parisienne *(rec 1963)*
Sony Classical ("Essential Classics" series) ▲ SBK 48279 [ADD] ■ SBT 48279
Orff, C.:Carmina burana, w. J. Harsanyi (sop), R. Petrak (ten), H. Presnell (bar), Rutgers Univ Choir
Sony Classical ("Essential Classics" series) ▲ SBK 47668 ■ SBT 47668
Paganini, N.:Con 1 Vn, w. F. Kreisler (vn) *(rec 1938 for HMV)* Pearl 2-▲ PEAS 9362 (m) [AAD]
Paganini, N.:Con 1 Vn, w. Z. Francescatti (vn)
Sony Classical ("Essential Classics" series) ▲ SBK 47661 ■ SBT 47661
Paganini, N.:Con 4 Vn, w. Z. Francescatti (vn)
Sony Classical ("Essential Classics" series) ▲ SBK 47661 ■ SBT 47661
Ponchielli, A.:La Gioconda (dance)
Sony Classical ("Essential Classics" series) ▲ SBK 48159 ■ SBT 48159
Prokofiev, S.:Cons Vn (comp), w. I. Stern (vn) CBS ▲ MYK 38525 [ADD] ■ MYT 38525
Prokofiev, S.:Lt Kijé Suite CBS ▲ MLK 39446 ■ MT 39446
Prokofiev, S.:Lt Kijé Suite Odyssey ▲ MBK 39783 [ADD]
Prokofiev, S.:The Love for 3 Oranges (suite) Odyssey ▲ MBK 39783 [ADD]
Prokofiev, S.:The Love for 3 Oranges (suite) *(rec Feb. 24, 1963)*
Sony Classical ▲ SBK 53261 ■ SBT 53261
Prokofiev, S.:Music of—March from The Love for Three Oranges Suite, Op. 33a
CBS ▲ MLK 39446 ■ MT 39446
Prokofiev, S.:Peter & the Wolf, w. David Bowie (nar)
RCA Victor ▲ 09026-60878-2 [ADD] ■ 09026-60878-4 (CrO2)
Prokofiev, S.:Peter & the Wolf, w. Cyril Ritchard (nar)
Sony Classical ("Essential Classics" series) ▲ SBK 62638 ■ SBT 62638
Prokofiev, S.:Peter & the Wolf, w. C. Ritchard (nar) Odyssey ■ YT 34616
Prokofiev, S.:Sym 1
RCA Gold Seal ("Papillon Collection" series) ▲ 6721-2-RG [ADD] ■ 6721-4-RG (CrO2)
Prokofiev, S.:Sym 1 *(rec Mar. 26, 1961)* Sony Classical ▲ SBK 53260 ■ SBT 53260
Prokofiev, S.:Sym 1 Odyssey ▲ MBK 39783 [ADD]
Prokofiev, S.:Sym 1 RCA Silver Seal ▲ 09026-61209-2 ■ 09026-61209-4
Prokofiev, S.:Sym 5 Odyssey ■ YT 30490
Prokofiev, S.:Sym 5 *(rec Mar. 14, 1957)* Sony Classical ▲ SBK 53260 ■ SBT 53260
Rachmaninoff, S.:Con 1 Pno, w. Philippe Entremont (pno)
Sony Classical ("Essential Classics" series) ▲ SBK 46541 [ADD] ■ SBT 46541
Rachmaninoff, S.:Con 1 Pno, w. Sergei Rachmaninoff (pno) RCA Red Seal ▲ 6659-2-RC (m) [ADD]
Rachmaninoff, S.:Con 3 Pno, w. S. Rachmaninoff (pno) *(rec 1940)*
RCA Red Seal ▲ 5997-2-RC (m) [ADD]
Rachmaninoff, S.:Con 4 Pno, w. P. Entremont (pno)
Sony Classical ("Essential Classics" series) ▲ SBK 46541 [ADD] ■ SBT 46541
Rachmaninoff, S.:Con 4 Pno, w. S. Rachmaninoff (pno) RCA Red Seal ▲ 6659-2 RC (m) [ADD]
Rachmaninoff, S.:Music of, w. Philippe Entremont (pno), Gary Graffman (pno)
CBS ▲ MLK 39437 ■ MT 39437
Rachmaninoff, S.:Rhapsody on a Theme of Paganini, w. Van Cliburn (pno)
RCA Gold Seal ▲ 7945-2-RG [ADD] ■ 7945-4-RG (CrO2)
Rachmaninoff, S.:Rhapsody on a Theme of Paganini, w. P. Entremont (pno)
Odyssey ▲ MBK 46271 [AAD] ■ YT 46271
Rachmaninoff, S.:Symphonic Dances Odyssey ■ YT 31246
Rachmaninoff, S.:Symphonic Dances *(rec 1960)*
Sony Classical ("Essential Classics" series) ▲ SBK 48279 [ADD] ■ SBT 48279
Rachmaninoff, S.:Syms (comp) Odyssey 2-▲ MB2K 45678
Rachmaninoff, S.:Sym 2 RCA Victor ▲ 09026-68022-2; ■ 09026-68022-4
Rachmaninoff, S.:Sym 2 RCA Victrola ▲ 60132-2 RV [ADD] ■ 60132-4 RV
Rachmaninoff, S.:Vocalise Odyssey 2-▲ MB2K 45678
Ravel, M.:Alborada del gracioso
Sony Classical ("Essential Classics" series) ▲ SBK 48163 ■ SBT 48163
Ravel, M.:Alborada del gracioso *(rec 1968)* Odyssey ▲ MBK 46274 [ADD] ■ YT 46274
Ravel, M.:Alborada del gracioso Odyssey ■ YT 33926
Ravel, M.:Boléro *(rec 1968)* Odyssey ▲ MBK 46274 [ADD] ■ YT 46274
Ravel, M.:Boléro Sony Classical ("Essential Classics" series) ▲ SBK 48163 ■ SBT 48163
Ravel, M.:Boléro Odyssey ■ YT 33926
Ravel, M.:Daphnis et Chloé (suite 2) RCA Victrola ▲ 60133-2-RV [ADD] ■ 60133-4-RV

ORCH. & ENS.

Philadelphia Orch (cont.)
E. Ormandy (cnd) (cont.)

Ravel, M.:Daphnis et Chloé (suite 2)
Sony Classical ("Essential Classics" series) ▲ SBK 47664 ■ SBT 47664
Ravel, M.:Daphnis et Chloé (suite 2) *(rec 1969)* Odyssey ▲ MBK 46274 [ADD] ■ YT 46274
Ravel, M.:Pavane pour une infante défunte *(rec 1963)* Odyssey ▲ MBK 46274 [ADD] ■ YT 46274
Ravel, M.:Rapsodie espagnole *(rec 1963)* Odyssey ▲ MBK 46274 [ADD] ■ YT 46274
Ravel, M.:Rapsodie espagnole CBS ▲ MBK 38917 ■ YT 38917
Ravel, M.:Rapsodie espagnole Sony Classical ("Essential Classics" series) ▲ SBK 48163 ■ SBT 48163
Ravel, M.:Le Tombeau de Couperin
Sony Classical ("Essential Classics" series) ▲ SBK 48163 ■ SBT 48163
Ravel, M.:Le Tombeau de Couperin Odyssey ■ YT 33926
Ravel, M.:Tzigane, w. I. Stern (vn) *(rec 1957)* CBS 4-▲ M4K 42003 (m/s) [ADD]
Ravel, M.:La Valse *(rec 1963)* Odyssey ▲ MBK 46274 [ADD] ■ YT 46274
Ravel, M.:Valses nobles et sentimentales
Sony Classical ("Essential Classics" series) ▲ SBK 48163 ■ SBT 48163
Respighi, O.:La Boutique fantastique
Sony Classical ("Essential Classics" series) ▲ SBK 46340 [ADD] ■ SBT 46340
Respighi, O.:Feste Romane RCA Victor ▲ 09026-62675-2 ■ 09026-62675-4
Respighi, O.:The Fountains of Rome CBS ▲ MYK 38485 [ADD] ■ MYT 38485
Respighi, O.:The Fountains of Rome *(rec 1957)*
Sony Classical ("Essential Classics" series) ▲ SBK 48267 [ADD] ■ SBT 48267
Respighi, O.:The Fountains of Rome RCA Silver Seal ▲ 60486-2-RV [ADD] ■ 60486-4-RV (CrO2)
Respighi, O.:The Fountains of Rome RCA Victor ▲ 09026-62675-2 ■ 09026-62675-4
Respighi, O.:The Pines of Rome *(rec 1958)*
Sony Classical ("Essential Classics" series) ▲ SBK 48267 [ADD] ■ SBT 48267
Respighi, O.:The Pines of Rome RCA Silver Seal ▲ 60486-2-RV [ADD] ■ 60486-4-RV (CrO2)
Respighi, O.:The Pines of Rome RCA Victor ▲ 09026-62675-2 ■ 09026-62675-4
Respighi, O.:The Pines of Rome CBS ▲ MYK 38485 [ADD] ■ MYT 38485
Rhapsodies Odyssey ▲ MBK 38917 [ADD]
Rimsky-Korsakov, N.:Capriccio espagnol Odyssey ▲ MBK 42248 [ADD]
Rimsky-Korsakov, N.:Capriccio espagnol
Sony Classical ("Essential Classics" series) ▲ SBK 46537 [ADD] ■ SBT 46537
Rimsky-Korsakov, N.:Golden Cockerel (sels)—Bridal Procession
RCA Silver Seal ▲ 09026-61209-2 ■ 09026-61209-4
Rimsky-Korsakov, N.:Golden Cockerel (sels)—Bridal Procession & Lamentable Death of King Dodon
Odyssey ▲ MBK 39786 [ADD]
Rimsky-Korsakov, N.:Mlada (procession) Odyssey ▲ MBK 39786 [ADD]
Rimsky-Korsakov, N.:Russian Easter Festival
Sony Classical ("Essential Classics" series) ▲ SBK 46537 [ADD] ■ SBT 46537
Rimsky-Korsakov, N.:Russian Easter Festival Odyssey ▲ MBK 42248 [ADD]
Rimsky-Korsakov, N.:Scheherazade Odyssey ▲ MBK 39786 [ADD]
Rimsky-Korsakov, N.:Scheherazade
Sony Classical ("Essential Classics" series) ▲ SBK 46537 [ADD] ■ SBT 46537
Rodrigo, J.:Concierto de Aranjuez, w. J. Williams (gtr)
Sony Classical ("Essential Classics" series) ▲ SBK 48168 ■ SBT 48168
Rossini, G.:Music of, w. Columbia SO, Cancan; Largo al factotum, Cossack Dance, Tarantella [from La boutique fantasque (music of Rossini arranged by Respighi)]; Dance for six [from William Tell]; Kostelanetz [from The Barber of Seville] CBS ▲ MLK 39449 [ADD] ■ MT 39449
Roussel, A.:Bacchus et Ariane (suite 2)
Sony Classical ("Essential Classics" series) ▲ SBK 62644 ■ SBT 62644
Saint-Saëns, C.:Carnival of the Animals, w. Claude Frank (pno), Lilian Kallir (pno)
Sony Classical ("Essential Classics" series) ▲ SBK 62638 ■ SBT 62638
Saint-Saëns, C.:Carnival of the Animals
Sony Classical ("Essential Classics" series) ▲ SBK 47655 ■ SBT 47655
Saint-Saëns, C.:Con 1 Vc, w. L. Rose (vc) *(rec 1967)*
Sony Classical ("Essential Classics" series) ▲ SBK 48276 [ADD] ■ SBT 48276
Saint-Saëns, C.:Con 2 Pno, w. P. Entremont (pno) *(rec 1964)*
Sony Classical ("Essential Classics" series) ▲ SBK 48276 [ADD] ■ SBT 48276
Saint-Saëns, C.:Con 2 Pno, w. P. Entremont (pno) CBS ▲ MYK 37805 [ADD] ■ MYT 37805
Saint-Saëns, C.:Con 4 Pno, w. P. Entremont (pno) *(rec 1961)*
Sony Classical ("Essential Classics" series) ▲ SBK 48276 [ADD] ■ SBT 48276
Saint-Saëns, C.:Danse macabre Sony Classical ("Essential Classics" series) ▲ SBK 47655 ■ SBT 47655
Saint-Saëns, C.:Introduction & Rondo capriccioso, w. I. Stern (vn) *(rec 1957)*
CBS 4-▲ M4K 42003 (m/s) [ADD]
Saint-Saëns, C.:Introduction & Rondo capriccioso, w. D. Jenson (vn)
RCA Victrola ▲ 7730-2-RV [DDD] ■ 7730-4-RV (CrO2)
Saint-Saëns, C.:Marche militaire française, w. E. P. Biggs (org)
Sony Classical ("Essential Classics" series) ▲ SBK 47655 ■ SBT 47655
Saint-Saëns, C.:Music of—Bacchanale (from Samson & Delilah); Le cygne (The Swan); Danse macabre, Op. 40; Marche militaire française (from Suite algérienne)
Odyssey ▲ MBK 38920 [ADD] ■ YT 38920
Saint-Saëns, C.:Samson et Dalila (Bacchanale)
Sony Classical ("Essential Classics" series) ▲ SBK 47655 ■ SBT 47655
Saint-Saëns, C.:Sym 3, w. E. P. Biggs (org)
Sony Classical ("Essential Classics" series) ▲ SBK 47655 ■ SBT 47655
Saint-Saëns, C.:Sym 3, w. V. Fox (org)
RCA Victor ▲ 09026-61269-2 [ADD] ■ 09026-61269-4 (CrO2)
Saint-Saëns, C.:Sym 3, w. E. P. Biggs (org) Odyssey ▲ MBK 38920 [ADD] ■ YT 38920
Saint-Saëns, C.:Sym 3, w. V. Fox (org) RCA Victrola ▲ 7737-2-RV [ADD] ■ 7737-4-RV (CrO2)
Saint-Saëns, C.:Sym 3, w. T. Murray (org) Telarc ▲ CD 80051 [DDD]
Schuman, W.:Credendum CRI ■ C 308
Schumann, R.:Con Pno, w. R. Serkin (pno)
Sony Classical ("Essential Classics" series) ▲ SBK 46543 [ADD] ■ SBT 46543
Schumann, R.:Con Pno, w. R. Serkin (pno) CBS ▲ MYK 37256 [ADD] ■ MYT 37256
Schumann, R.:Intro & Allegro appassionato, Op. 92, w. R. Serkin (pno) *(rec 1964)*
Odyssey ▲ MBK 46273 [ADD] ■ YT 46273
Schumann, R.:Intro & Allegro appassionato, Op. 92, w. R. Serkin (pno)
Sony Classical ("Essential Classics" series) ▲ SBK 46543 [ADD] ■ SBT 46543
Schumann, R.:Intro & Allegro, Op. 134, w. R. Serkin (pno) *(rec 1968)*
Sony Classical ("Essential Classics" series) ▲ SBK 48166 ■ SBT 48166
Shostakovich, D.:Con 1 Vc, w. Yo Yo Ma (vc) CBS ▲ MK 37840
Shostakovich, D.:Con 1 Vc, w. Yo Yo Ma (vc) CBS ▲ MDK 44903 [DDD] ■ MDT 44903 (D)
Shostakovich, D.:The Golden Age (suite)—Polka allegretto *(rec Apr. 13, 1966)*
Sony Classical ▲ SBK 53261 ■ SBT 53261
Shostakovich, D.:Sym 1 Sony Classical ("Essential Classics" series) ▲ SBK 62642 ■ SBT 62642
Shostakovich, D.:Sym 4 Sony Classical ("Essential Classics" series) 2-▲ SB2K 62409
Shostakovich, D.:Sym 5 *(rec Apr. 8, 1965)* Sony Classical ▲ SBK 53261 ■ SBT 53261
Shostakovich, D.:Sym 10 Sony Classical ("Essential Classics" series) 2-▲ SB2K 62409
Sibelius, J.:Con Vn, w. Isaac Stern (vn) Sony Classical ▲ SMK 66829
Sibelius, J.:Con Vn, w. D. Oistrakh (vn) *(rec 1959)*
Sony Classical ("Essential Classics" series) ▲ SBK 47659 ■ SBT 47659
Sibelius, J.:Con Vn, w. D. Jenson (vn) RCA Victrola ▲ 7730-2-RV [DDD] ■ 7730-4-RV (CrO2)
Sibelius, J.:Finlandia RCA Victor ▲ 09026-61856-2; ■ 09026-61856-4
Sibelius, J.:Finlandia CBS ▲ MLK 39447 ■ MT 39447
Sibelius, J.:Finlandia *(rec 1968)*
Sony Classical ("Essential Classics" series) ▲ SBK 48271 [ADD] ■ SBT 48271
Sibelius, J.:4 Legends from the Kalevalá EMI Classics ▲ CDM 65176
Sibelius, J.:Karelia Suite RCA ■ ALK1-4979
Sibelius, J.:Karelia Suite Odyssey ▲ MBK 39785

Philadelphia Orch (cont.)
E. Ormandy (cnd) (cont.)

Sibelius, J.:Karelia Suite *(rec 1968)*
Sony Classical ("Essential Classics" series) ▲ SBK 48271 [ADD] ■ SBT 48271
Sibelius, J.:Pohjola's Daughter RCA Silver Seal ▲ 60489-2-RV [ADD] ■ 60489-4-RV (CrO2)
Sibelius, J.:En Saga *(rec 1963)*
Sony Classical ("Essential Classics" series) ▲ SBK 48271 [ADD] ■ SBT 48271
Sibelius, J.:The Swan of Tuonela RCA Victor ▲ 09026-61856-2; ■ 09026-61856-4
Sibelius, J.:The Swan of Tuonela RCA Silver Seal ▲ 60489-2-RV [ADD] ■ 60489-4-RV (CrO2)
Sibelius, J.:The Swan of Tuonela Odyssey ▲ MBK 39785
Sibelius, J.:The Swan of Tuonela *(rec 1960)*
Sony Classical ("Essential Classics" series) ▲ SBK 48271 [ADD] ■ SBT 48271
Sibelius, J.:The Swan of Tuonela CBS ▲ MLK 39447 ■ MT 39447
Sibelius, J.:Sym 2 RCA Silver Seal ▲ 60489-2-RV [ADD] ■ 60489-4-RV (CrO2)
Sibelius, J.:Sym 2 *(rec Mar. 17, 1957)*
Sony Classical ("Essential Classics" series) ▲ SBK 53509 [ADD] ■ SBT 53509
Sibelius, J.:Sym 2 Odyssey ■ YT 30046
Sibelius, J.:Sym 2 RCA Victor ▲ 09026-61856-2; ■ 09026-61856-4
Sibelius, J.:Sym 7 *(rec May 1, 1960)*
Sony Classical ("Essential Classics" series) ▲ SBK 53509 [ADD] ■ SBT 53509
Sibelius, J.:Valse triste RCA Victor ▲ 09026-61856-2; ■ 09026-61856-4
Sibelius, J.:Valse triste Odyssey ▲ MBK 39785
Sibelius, J.:Valse triste RCA Silver Seal ▲ 60489-2-RV [ADD] ■ 60489-4-RV (CrO2)
Sibelius, J.:Valse triste *(rec 1959)*
Sony Classical ("Essential Classics" series) ▲ SBK 48271 [ADD] ■ SBT 48271
Spohr, L.:Con 8 Vn, w. A. Spalding (vn) *(rec 5/9/38)* Biddulph ▲ LAB 054 [ADD]
Strauss (II), Joh.:Music of—waltzes and polkas CBS ▲ MLK 39432 ■ MT 39432
Strauss (II), Joh.:Waltzes—Artist's Life; Blue Danube; Emperor Waltz; Morning Papers; Tales from the Vienna Woods; Treasure Waltz; Vienna Blood; Where the Citrons Bloom
RCA Silver Seal ▲ 60490-2-RV [ADD] ■ 60490-4-RV (CrO2)
Strauss, R.:Also sprach Zarathustra EMI Classics ("DDD Midline" series) ▲ CDD 64106 [DDD]
Strauss, R.:Also sprach Zarathustra RCA Silver Seal ▲ 60793-2-RV [ADD] ■ 60793-4-RV
Strauss, R.:Also sprach Zarathustra
Sony Classical ("Essential Classics" series) ▲ SBK 47656 ■ SBT 47656
Strauss, R.:Burleske, w. R. Serkin (pno) CBS ▲ MK 42261 [ADD]
Strauss, R.:Burleske, w. R. Serkin (pno) *(rec Feb. 3, 1966)*
Sony Classical ▲ SBK 53262 ■ SBT 53262
Strauss, R.:Don Juan RCA Silver Seal ▲ 60793-2-RV [ADD] ■ 60793-4-RV
Strauss, R.:Don Juan EMI Classics ("DDD Midline" series) ▲ CDD 64106 [DDD]
Strauss, R.:Don Quixote, w. E. Feuermann (vc) *(rec 1940 for Victor)* Biddulph ▲ LAB 042 [ADD]
Strauss, R.:Don Quixote, w. L. Munroe (vc)
Sony Classical ("Essential Classics" series) ▲ SBK 47656 ■ SBT 47656
Strauss, R.:Ein Heldenleben *(rec 1960)*
Sony Classical ("Essential Classics" series) ▲ SBK 48272 [ADD] ■ SBT 48272
Strauss, R.:Salome (dance) *(rec Nov. 15, 1962)*
Sony Classical ("Essential Classics" series) ▲ SBK 53511 [ADD] ■ SBT 53511
Strauss, R.:Till Eulenspiegels lustige Streiche RCA Silver Seal ▲ 60793-2-RV [ADD] ■ 60793-4-RV
Sweet Dreams CBS ▲ MDK 44998 [ADD/DDD] ■ MGT 44998
Tchaikovsky, P.:Capriccio italien
Sony Classical ("Essential Classics" series) ▲ SBK 47657 ■ SBT 47657
Tchaikovsky, P.:Capriccio italien RCA Silver Seal ▲ 60492-2-RV [ADD] ■ 60492-4-RV (CrO2)
Tchaikovsky, P.:Capriccio italien Odyssey ▲ MBK 42248 [ADD]
Tchaikovsky, P.:Con Vn, w. B. Huberman (vn) *(rec 1946)* Music & Arts ▲ CD 299 [AAD]
Tchaikovsky, P.:Con Vn, w. I. Perlman (vn) EMI Classics ▲ CDC 47106
Tchaikovsky, P.:Con Vn, w. Isaac Stern (vn) Sony Classical ▲ SMK 66829
Tchaikovsky, P.:Con Vn, w. I. Stern (vn) CBS ▲ MYK 36724 ■ MYT 36724
Tchaikovsky, P.:Con Vn, w. D. Oistrakh (vn)
Sony Classical ("Essential Classics" series) ▲ SBK 46339 [ADD] ■ SBT 46339
Tchaikovsky, P.:Eugene Onegin (sels)—Waltz & Polonaise
Sony Classical (Essential Classics) ▲ SBK 47657 ■ SBT 47657
Tchaikovsky, P.:Marche slave Sony Classical (Essential Classics) ▲ SBK 46334 [ADD] ■ SBT 46334
Tchaikovsky, P.:Marche slave RCA Silver Seal ▲ 60492-2-RV [ADD] ■ 60492-4-RV (CrO2)
Tchaikovsky, P.:Marche slave Odyssey ▲ MBK 39784 [ADD]
Tchaikovsky, P.:Marche slave Odyssey ▲ MBK 42248 [ADD]
Tchaikovsky, P.:Music of, New York PO [cnd:L. Bernstein] CBS ▲ MLK 39433 ■ MT 39433
Tchaikovsky, P.:Music of, New York PO [cnd:L. Bernstein] CBS ▲ MLK 39440 [ADD] ■ MT 39440
Tchaikovsky, P.:The Nutcracker (sels) RCA Silver Seal ▲ 60794-2-RV [ADD] ■ 60794-4-RV
Tchaikovsky, P.:The Nutcracker (sels) RCA ■ ARK1-0027
Tchaikovsky, P.:Nutcracker Suite RCA Victor ▲ 09026-61711-2; ■ 09026-61711-4
Tchaikovsky, P.:Nutcracker Suite Sony Classical (Essential Classics) ▲ SBK 46551 [ADD] ■ SBT 46551
Tchaikovsky, P.:Nutcracker Suite CBS ■ MT 06807
Tchaikovsky, P.:Ov 1812 Sony Classical (Essential Classics) ▲ SBK 46334 [ADD] ■ SBT 46334
Tchaikovsky, P.:Ov 1812 RCA Silver Seal ▲ 60492-2-RV [ADD] ■ 60492-4-RV (CrO2)
Tchaikovsky, P.:Ov 1812, w. Brass Band, Mormon Tabernacle Choir CBS ■ MT 30447
Tchaikovsky, P.:Romeo & Juliet RCA Victor ▲ 09026-61853-2; ■ 09026-61853-4 (CrO2)
Tchaikovsky, P.:Romeo & Juliet RCA Silver Seal ▲ 09026-60908-2 ■ 09026-60908-4
Tchaikovsky, P.:Serenade Strs CBS ■ MT 30447
Tchaikovsky, P.:Sérénade mélancolique, w. Isaac Stern (vn) Sony Classical ▲ SMK 66830
Tchaikovsky, P.:Sérénade mélancolique, w. I. Perlman (vn) EMI Classics ▲ CDC 47106
Tchaikovsky, P.:Sleeping Beauty (sels) RCA Victor ▲ 09026-61711-2; ■ 09026-61711-4
Tchaikovsky, P.:Sleeping Beauty (sels) RCA Silver Seal ▲ 60794-2-RV [ADD] ■ 60794-4-RV
Tchaikovsky, P.:Sleeping Beauty (sels)
Sony Classical (Essential Classics) ▲ SBK 46340 [ADD] ■ SBT 46340
Tchaikovsky, P.:Sleeping Beauty (sels) Odyssey ▲ MBK 39500 [ADD] ■ YT 39500
Tchaikovsky, P.:Sleeping Beauty (sels)
RCA Gold Seal ("Papillon Collection" series) ▲ 6537-2-RG [ADD] ■ 6537-4-RG
Tchaikovsky, P.:Souvenir d'un lieu cher, w. Isaac Stern (vn)—Méditation [arr Glazunov]
Sony Classical ▲ SMK 66830
Tchaikovsky, P.:Swan Lake (sels) Odyssey ▲ MBK 42252
Tchaikovsky, P.:Swan Lake (sels)
RCA Gold Seal ("Papillon Collection" series) ▲ 6537-2-RG [ADD] ■ 6537-4-RG
Tchaikovsky, P.:Swan Lake (sels) RCA Silver Seal ▲ 60794-2-RV [ADD] ■ 60794-4-RV
Tchaikovsky, P.:Swan Lake (sels) CBS ■ MT 06807
Tchaikovsky, P.:Swan Lake (sels) Sony Classical (Essential Classics) ▲ SBK 46341 [ADD] ■ SBT 46341
Tchaikovsky, P.:Swan Lake (suite) RCA Victor ▲ 09026-61711-2 ■ 09026-61711-4
Tchaikovsky, P.:Sym 4 Sony Classical (Essential Classics) ▲ SBK 46334 [ADD] ■ SBT 46334
Tchaikovsky, P.:Sym 5 Delos ▲ DCD 3015 [DDD]
Tchaikovsky, P.:Sym 5 RCA Victrola ▲ 7820-2-RV [ADD] ■ 7820-4-RV
Tchaikovsky, P.:Sym 5 RCA Victor ▲ 09026-61853-2; ■ 09026-61853-4 (CrO2)
Tchaikovsky, P.:Sym 5 Sony Classical (Essential Classics) ▲ SBK 46538 [ADD] ■ SBT 46538
Tchaikovsky, P.:Sym 6 Sony Classical (Essential Classics) ▲ SBK 47657 ■ SBT 47657
Tchaikovsky, P.:Sym 6 RCA Silver Seal ▲ 09026-60908-2 ■ 09026-60908-4
Tchaikovsky, P.:Sym 6 RCA Victrola ▲ 7740-2-RV [ADD] ■ 7740-4-RV (CrO2)
Tchaikovsky, P.:Sym 6 Delos ▲ DCD 3016 [DDD]
Tchaikovsky, P.:Vars on a Rococo Theme, w. L. Rose (vc) *(rec 1962)*
Sony Classical (Essential Classics) ▲ SBK 48278 [ADD] ■ SBT 48278
Tchaikovsky, P.:Waltzes—waltze from Eugene Onegin Odyssey ▲ MBK 39784
Thomson, V.:Wheat Field at Noon CRI ■ ACS 6009
The Tsar, w. André Kostelanetz (cnd), Jennie Tourel (mez), Claudio Abbado (cnd), Chicago SO, et al.
Sony Classical ("Greatest Hits" series) ▲ MLK 62683 ■ MLT 62683

▲ = CD ♦ = Enhanced CD Δ = MD ■ = Cassette Tape □ = DCC

Philadelphia Orch (cont.)
E. Ormandy (cnd) (cont.)
Vaughan Williams, R.:Fant on Greensleeves
Sony Classical ("Essential Classics" series) ▲ SBK 62645 ■ SBT 62645
Vaughan Williams, R.:Fant on Greensleeves
RCA Victor ▲ 09026-61724-2; ■ 09026-61724-4 (CrO2)
Vaughan Williams, R.:Fant on a Theme by Thomas Tallis
RCA Victor ▲ 09026-61724-2; ■ 09026-61724-4 (CrO2)
Vaughan Williams, R.:Fant on a Theme by Thomas Tallis
Sony Classical ("Essential Classics" series) ▲ SBK 62645 ■ SBT 62645
Verdi, G.:Requiem Mass, w. L. Amara (sop), M. Forrester (cta), R. Tucker (ten), G. London (bar), Westminster Choir [L] Odyssey ■ YT 35230
Verdi, G.:Requiem Mass, w. L. Price (sop), N. Merriman (mez), R. Tucker (ten), G. Tozzi (bass) *(rec live Apr. 6, 1957)* Standing Room Only ▲ SRO 842-1 [ADD]
Verdi, G.:Requiem Mass, w. L. Amara (sop), M. Forrester (cta), R. Tucker (ten), G. London (bar), Westminster Choir Sony Classical ▲ SB2K 53252
Viennese Waltzes & Polkas Sony Classical ("Essential Classics" series) ▲ SBK 48164 ■ SBT 48164
Vivaldi, A.:Cons for 2 Vns, w. D. Oistrakh (vn), I. Stern (vn) *(rec 1955–6)*
CBS 4-▲ M4K 42003 (m/s) [ADD]
Wagner, R.:Arias & Scenes, w. Kirsten Flagstad (sop), Lauritz Melchior (bar), San Francisco Opera Orch, RCA Victor SO, New York PO, McArthur (cnd), B. Walter (cnd)—arias & duets from Lohengrin, Tristan & Isolde, Götterdämmerung, Parsifal & Fidelio *(rec New York City, 1939–41)*
Grammofono 2000 ▲ GRM 78526 (m)
Wagner, R.:Lohengrin (preludes), Cleveland Orch, G. Szell (cnd)—Acts 1 & 3
Sony Classical ("Essential Classics" series) ▲ SBK 62403 ■ SBT 62403
Wagner, R.:Die Meistersinger von Nürnberg (sels)—Act 1—Prelude; Act 2—Prelude & Entrance of the Meistersingers RCA Silver Seal ▲ 60493-2-RV [ADD] ■ 60493-4-RV (CrO2)
Wagner, R.:Die Meistersinger von Nürnberg (sels)—Dance of the Apprentices; Entrance of the Meistersingers CBS 2-■ MGT 30300
Wagner, R.:Die Meistersinger von Nürnberg (prelude/act 1)—& Act 3 CBS 2-■ MGT 30300
Wagner, R.:Ovs, Préludes & Orch Sels—Tannhäuser CBS 2-■ MGT 30300
Wagner, R.:Der Ring des Nibelungen (orch sels)—Die Walküre:Ride of the Valkyries; Magic Fire Music; Siegfried:Waldweben; Das Rheingold:Invocation of Alberich; Entrance of the Gods into Valhalla; Götterdämmerung:Dawn & Siegfried's Rhine Journey; Siegfried's Funeral Music; Immolation Scene
RCA Victor ▲ 09026-61850-2; ■ 09026-61850-4 (CrO2)
Wagner, R.:Der Ring des Nibelungen (orch sels)—Rheingold *(Entry of the Gods into Valhalla)*, Walküre *(Magic Fire Music; Ride of the Valkyries)*, Siegfried *(Forest Murmers)*, Götterdämmerung *(Rhine Journey & Funeral Music; Immolation scene)* RCA Victrola ▲ 7819-2-RV [ADD] ■ 7819-4-RV
Wagner, R.:Siegfried Idyll CBS 2-■ MGT 30300
Wagner, R.:Tannhäuser (orch sels)—Ov; Fest March
Sony Classical ("Essential Classics" series) ▲ SBK 62403 ■ SBT 62403
Wagner, R.:Tannhäuser (ov & venusberg)
RCA Silver Seal ▲ 60493-2-RV [ADD] ■ 60493-4-RV (CrO2)
Wagner, R.:Tristan und Isolde (prelude & liebestod) CBS 2-■ MGT 30300
Wagner, R.:Tristan und Isolde (prelude & liebestod)
RCA Silver Seal ▲ 60493-2-RV [ADD] ■ 60493-4-RV (CrO2)
Wagner, R.:Die Walküre (magic fire) CBS 2-■ MGT 30300
Wagner, R.:Die Walküre (ride of the valkyries) CBS 2-■ MGT 30300
Walton, W.:Façade, w. Vera Zorina (nar)
Sony Classical ("Essential Classics" series) ▲ SBK 62400 ■ SBT 62400
Weber, C.M. von:Andante & Rondo ungarese Bn, w. Bernard Garfield (bn)
Sony Classical ("Essential Classics" series) ▲ SBK 62652 ■ SBT 62652
Wieniawski, H.:Con 2 Vn, w. Isaac Stern (vn) Sony Classical ▲ SMK 66830

Ormandy, Lange (cnd)
Wagner, R.:Arias & Scenes, w. Kirsten Flagstad (sop)—arias from Die Walküre; Tristan und Isolde; Tannhäuser; Lohengrin IMP ("Golden Legacy" series) ▲ IMPGLRS 105 [ADD]

Ormandy, Stokowski (cnd) (cnd)
Rachmaninoff, S.:Cons Pno (comp), w. S. Rachmaninoff (pno) RCA Gold Seal 2-▲ 61658-2
Rachmaninoff, S.:Cons Pno (comp), w. S. Rachmaninoff (pno) RCA Gold Seal 10-▲ 09026-61265-2

S. Rachmaninoff (cnd)
Rachmaninoff, S.:The Isle of the Dead RCA Gold Seal 10-▲ 09026-61265-2
Rachmaninoff, S.:The Isle of the Dead *(rec 1929)* Pearl ▲ PEA 9414 (m) [AAD]
Rachmaninoff, S.:The Isle of the Dead *(rec Apr 20, 1929)* RCA Gold Seal ▲ 09026-62532-2 [ADD]
Rachmaninoff, S.:Sym 3 RCA Gold Seal 10-▲ 09026-61265-2
Rachmaninoff, S.:Sym 3 *(rec Dec 11, 1939)* RCA Gold Seal ▲ 09026-62532-2 [ADD]
Rachmaninoff, S.:Sym 3 *(rec 1939)* Pearl ▲ PEA 9414 (m) [AAD]
Rachmaninoff, S.:Vocalise *(rec 1929)* Pearl ▲ PEA 9414 (m) [AAD]
Rachmaninoff, S.:Vocalise [orchd Rachmaninoff] *(rec Apr 20, 1929)*
RCA Gold Seal ▲ 09026-62532-2 [ADD]

W. Sawallisch (cnd)
Bruckner, A.:Sym 4, "Romantic" EMI Classics ▲ CDC 55119
Dvořák, A.:Con Vc, w. N. Gutman (vc) EMI Classics ▲ CDC 54320
Dvořák, A.:Scherzo Capriccioso EMI Classics ▲ CDC 49114 [DDD]
Dvořák, A.:Symphonic Vars EMI Classics ▲ CDC 54320
Dvořák, A.:Sym 7 EMI Classics ▲ CDC 49948 [DDD] ■ 4DS 49948 (D)
Dvořák, A.:Sym 8 EMI Classics ▲ CDC 49948 [DDD] ■ 4DS 49948 (D)
Dvořák, A.:Sym 9, "From the New World" EMI Classics ▲ CDC 49114 [DDD]
Hindemith, P.:Mathis der Maler (sym) EMI Classics ▲ CDC 55230
Hindemith, P.:Nobilissima visione EMI Classics ▲ CDC 55230
Hindemith, P.:Symphonic Metamorphosis on Themes of Carl Maria von Weber
EMI Classics ▲ CDC 55230
Paganini, N.:Con 1 Vn, w. S. Chang (vn) EMI Classics ▲ CDC 55026
Saint-Saëns, C.:Havanaise Vn, w. S. Chang (vn) EMI Classics ▲ CDC 55026
Saint-Saëns, C.:Introduction & Rondo capriccioso, w. S. Chang (vn) EMI Classics ▲ CDC 55026
Strauss, R.:Con Ob, w. Richard Woodhams (ob) EMI Classics ▲ CDC 56149
Strauss, R.:Festliches Präludium EMI Classics ▲ CDC 55185
Strauss, R.:4 Last Songs, w. Barbara Hendricks (sop), Wolfgang Sawallisch (pno)
EMI Classics ▲ CDC 55594
Strauss, R.:Ein Heldenleben, w. Richard Woodhams (ob) EMI Classics ▲ CDC 56149
Strauss, R.:Songs, w. Barbara Hendricks (sop), Wolfgang Sawallisch (pno)—Ich wollt' ein Sträusslein binden; Säusle, liebe Myrthe; Kornblumen; Mohnblumen; Epheu; Wasserrose; Die Georgine; Die Zeitlose; Allerseelen; Ruhe, meine Seele!; Cäcilie; Heimliche Aufforderung; Morgen!; Das Rosenband; Heimkehr EMI Classics ▲ CDC 55594
Strauss, R.:Symphonia domestica EMI Classics ▲ CDC 55185
Strauss, R.:Till Eulenspiegels lustige Streiche EMI Classics ▲ CDC 55185
Tchaikovsky, P.:Swan Lake EMI Classics 2-▲ CDQB 55041 2-■ 4D2Q 55041
Wagner, R.:Eine Faust-Ov EMI Classics ▲ CDC 56165
Wagner, R.:Das Liebesverbot (ov) EMI Classics ▲ CDC 56165
Wagner, R.:Rienzi, der Letzte der Tribunen (ov) EMI Classics ▲ CDC 56165
Wagner, R.:Sym in E EMI Classics ▲ CDC 56165
Wagner, R.:Wesendonck Songs, w. Marjana Lipovšek (mez) EMI Classics ▲ CDC 56165

G. Schwarz (cnd)
Rands, B.:Canti dell'eclisse, w. Thomas Paul (bass) New World ▲ 803922

G. Simon (cnd)
Respighi, O.:Brazilian Impressions Chandos ▲ CHAN 8317 [DDD]
Respighi, O.:Vetrate di chiesa Chandos ▲ CHAN 8317 [DDD]

L. Stokowski (cnd)
Bach, J.S.:Brandenburg Con 5, w. Fernando Valenti (hpd), Anshel Brusilow (vn), William Kincaid (fl) *(rec Feb 25, 1960)* Sony Classical ("Masterworks Heritage" series) 2-▲ MH2K 62345 [ADD]

Philadelphia Orch (cont.)
L. Stokowski (cnd) (cont.)
Bach, J.S.:Chorale Preludes Org—BWV 62, 177 & 437 [arr Stokowski for orch] *(rec Feb 15, 1960)*
Sony Classical ("Masterworks Heritage" series) 2-▲ MH2K 62345 [ADD]
Bach, J.S.:Toccata & Fugue Org, BWV 565 Pearl ▲ PEA 9488 (m) [AAD]
Beethoven, L. van:Sym 9, "Choral Sym", w. Agnes Davis (sop), Robert Betts (sgr), Ruth Cathcart (sgr), Eugene Lowenthal (sgr), Philadelphia Orch Chorus *(rec 1934)* Music & Arts ▲ CD 846 [ADD]
Beethoven, L. van:Sym 9, "Choral Sym", w. Agnes Davis (sop), Robert Betts (sgr), Ruth Cathcart (sgr), Eugene Lowenthal (sgr) Grammofono 2000 ▲ GRM 78577 (m)
Berlioz, H.:La Damnation de Faust (sels)—Racóczy March *(rec 1927–30)*
Grammofono 2000 ▲ GRM 78586 (m)
Bloch, E.:Schelomo, w. E. Feuermann (vc) *(rec 1940 Victor)* Biddulph ▲ LAB 042 [ADD]
Borodin, A.:Prince Igor (dance of the Polovtsian maidens) *(rec Academy of Music, Philadelphia, Apr. 5, 1937)* Dutton Laboratories ▲ CDAX 8009 [ADD]
Borodin, A.:Prince Igor (Polovtsian dances) Dutton Laboratories ▲ DUT 8009 [ADD]
Dukas, P.:L'Apprenti sorcier Pearl ▲ PEA 9488 (m) [AAD]
Dvořák, A.:Sym 9, "From the New World" Grammofono 2000 ▲ GRM 78552 (m)
Great Recordings with the Philadelphia Orchestra *(rec 1927 & 1940)*
Phonographe 2-▲ PHG CD 5025
Liadov, A.:Russian Folksongs Enterprise ("Sirio" series) ▲ ENT SO 530010
Liadov, A.:Russian Folksongs *(rec 1934)* Iron Needle ▲ 1334
Liszt, F.:Hungarian Rhaps Grammofono 2000 ▲ GRM 78552 (m)
Mussorgsky, M.:Boris Godunov (sels)—Symphonic Synthesis [arr Stokowski] *(rec Academy of Music, Philadelphia, Nov. 16, 1936)* Dutton Laboratories ▲ CDAX 8009 [ADD]
Mussorgsky, M.:Khovanshchina (orch sels)—Entr'acte to Act IV [orchd Stokowski] *(rec Academy of Music, Philadelphia, Oct. 12, 1927)* Dutton Laboratories ▲ CDAX 8009 [ADD]
Mussorgsky, M.:Khovanshchina (orch sels)—Intermezzo from Act IV
Grammofono 2000 ▲ GRM 78552 (m)
Mussorgsky, M.:Night [arr Rimsky-Korsakov & Stokowski] Dutton Laboratories ▲ DUT 8009 [ADD]
Mussorgsky, M.:Night Pearl ▲ PEA 9488 (m) [AAD]
Mussorgsky, M.:Night *(rec Academy of Music, Philadelphia, Dec. 8, 1940)*
Dutton Laboratories ▲ CDAX 8009 [ADD]
Mussorgsky, M.:Pictures at an Exhibition [ed. & orchd. Stokowski] *(rec Academy of Music, Philadelphia, Nov. 27, 1939)* Dutton Laboratories ▲ CDAX 8009 [ADD]
Philadelphia Rarities *(rec between 1929 & 1940)* Cala ("Artists" series) ▲ CACD 501 [ADD]
Rachmaninoff, S.:Con 2 Pno, w. S. Rachmaninoff (pno) *(rec 1929)*
RCA Red Seal ▲ 5997-2-RC (m) [ADD]
Rachmaninoff, S.:Con 2 Pno, w. S. Rachmaninoff (pno) IMP Classics ▲ IMPGLRS 104 [ADD]
Rachmaninoff, S.:Rhapsody on a Theme of Paganini, w. S. Rachmaninoff (pno)
RCA Gold Seal 10-▲ 09026-61265-2
Rachmaninoff, S.:Rhapsody on a Theme of Paganini, w. S. Rachmaninoff (pno)
IMP Classics ▲ IMPGLRS 104 [ADD]
Rachmaninoff, S.:Rhapsody on a Theme of Paganini, w. S. Rachmaninoff (pno)
RCA Red Seal ▲ 6659-2-RC (m) [ADD]
Rachmaninoff, S.:Rhapsody on a Theme of Paganini, w. S. Rachmaninoff (pno)
RCA Gold Seal 2-▲ 61658-2
Saint-Saëns, C.:Danse macabre Grammofono 2000 ▲ GRM 78552 (m)
Saint-Saëns, C.:Samson et Dalila (Bacchanale) *(rec 1927–30)* Grammofono 2000 ▲ GRM 78586 (m)
Schoenberg, A.:Gurrelieder, w. R. Bampton (sop), P. Althouse (ten), Fortnightly Club, Princeton Glee Club, Mendelssohn Club Philadelphia *(rec live Apr. 9, 1932)* Pearl 2-▲ PEA 9066 [AAD]
Scriabin, A.:Sym 4 *(rec live Apr. 9, 1932)* Pearl 2-▲ PEA 9066 [AAD]
Scriabin, A.:Sym 5 *(rec live Apr. 9, 1932)* Pearl 2-▲ PEA 9066 [AAD]
Shostakovich, D.:Preludes Pno, Op. 34—No. 14 *(rec 1935)* Pearl ▲ PEA 9064 [AAD]
Shostakovich, D.:Sym 1 *(rec 1933)* Pearl ▲ PEA 9064 [AAD]
Shostakovich, D.:Sym 5 *(rec 1935)* Pearl ▲ PEA 9064 [AAD]
Shostakovich, D.:Sym 5 Dutton Laboratories ▲ DUT 8017 [ADD]
Shostakovich, D.:Sym 6 Dell'Arte ▲ CD DA 9023
Shostakovich, D.:Sym 6 Dutton Laboratories ▲ DUT 8017 [ADD]
Sibelius, J.:The Swan of Tuonela *(rec 1927–30)* Grammofono 2000 ▲ GRM 78586 (m)
Sibelius, J.:Sym 4 Dell'Arte ▲ CD DA 9023
A Stokowski Fantasia Pearl ▲ [AAD]
Stokowski, L.:Transcriptions Orch—Shostakovich:Prelude in e♭
Dutton Laboratories ▲ DUT 8002 [ADD]
Stokowski, L.:Transcriptions Orch—Bach:Passacaglia & Fugue in c; Great Fugue in g; Chaconne in d; Toccata & Fugue in d; Ein feste Burg ist unser Gott; selected Chorale Preludes & shorter works *(rec between 1927 & 1940)* Pearl 2-▲ PEA 9098 [ADD]
Stravinsky, I.:The Firebird Suite Dutton Laboratories ▲ DUT 8002 [ADD]
Stravinsky, I.:Fireworks Dutton Laboratories ▲ DUT 8002 [ADD]
Stravinsky, I.:Pastorale Dutton Laboratories ▲ DUT 8002 [ADD]
Stravinsky, I.:Pétrouchka Dutton Laboratories ▲ DUT 8002 [ADD]
Stravinsky, I.:Pétrouchka (sels) RCA Gold Seal ▲ 09026-61394-2
Stravinsky, I.:Le Sacre du printemps Orch RCA Gold Seal ▲ 09026-61394-2
Stravinsky, I.:Le Sacre du printemps Orch—sels. Pearl ▲ GEMMCD 9488 (m) [AAD]
Tchaikovsky, P.:Capriccio italien *(rec 1928–29)* Pearl ▲ PEA 9120 [AAD]
Tchaikovsky, P.:Nutcracker Suite *(rec 1927–30)* Grammofono 2000 ▲ GRM 78586 (m)
Tchaikovsky, P.:Nutcracker Suite Pearl ▲ GEMMCD 9488 (m) [AAD]
Tchaikovsky, P.:Romeo & Juliet *(rec 1928–29)* Pearl ▲ PEA 9120 [AAD]
Tchaikovsky, P.:Sym 4 *(rec 1928–29)* Pearl ▲ PEA 9120 [AAD]
Wagner, R.:Lohengrin (preludes)—Preludes to Acts I & III *(rec 1927 & 1940 for Victor)*
Pearl ▲ PEA 9486 (m) [AAD]
Wagner, R.:Die Meistersinger von Nürnberg (prelude/act 1) *(rec 1936 for Victor)*
Pearl ▲ PEA 9486 (m) [AAD]
Wagner, R.:Parsifal (orch sels) [arranged by Stokowski]—Prelude to Act 1; Good Friday Spell (from Act 3); Symphonic Synthesis from Act 3 *(rec 1934–36 for Victor)* Pearl ▲ PEA 9448 (m) [AAD]
Wagner, R.:Der Ring des Nibelungen, w. A. Davis (sop), F. Jagel (ten), L. Tibbett (bar) *(rec 1933–1939)*
Pearl 2-▲ CD 9076 [AAD]
Wagner, R.:Tannhäuser (orch sels)—Overture & Venusberg Music (Paris version); Prelude to Act 3 [arranged by Stokowski] *(rec 1936–37 for Victor)* Pearl ▲ PEA 9448 (m) [AAD]
Wagner, R.:Wesendonck Songs, w. H. Traubel (sop)—3 songs only—Im Treibhaus, Schmerzen & Träume *(rec 1940 for Victor)* Pearl ▲ PEA 9486 (m) [AAD]
Weber, C.M. von:Invitation to the Dance Orch Grammofono 2000 ▲ GRM 78552 (m)

V. Thomson (cnd)
Thomson, V.:Portraits CRI ■ ACS 6009

A. Toscanini (cnd)
Berlioz, H.:Roméo et Juliette (sels)—Queen Mab Scherzo
RCA Gold Seal 4-▲ 60328-2-RG [ADD] 4-■ 60328-4-RG
Berlioz, H.:Roméo et Juliette (sels)—Queen Mab Scherzo
RCA Gold Seal ▲ 60314-2-RG [ADD] ■ 60314-4-RG
Debussy, C.:La Mer RCA Gold Seal ▲ 60311-2-RG [ADD] ■ 60311-4-RG (CrO2)
Mendelssohn, F.:A Midsummer Night's Dream (comp)
RCA Gold Seal ▲ 60314-2-RG [ADD] ■ 60314-4-RG (CrO2)
Mendelssohn, F.:A Midsummer Night's Dream (comp)
RCA Gold Seal 4-▲ 60328-2-RG [ADD] 4-■ 60328-4-RG (CrO2)
Respighi, O.:Feste Romane RCA Gold Seal ▲ 60311-2-RG [ADD] ■ 60311-4-RG (CrO2)
Respighi, O.:Feste Romane RCA Gold Seal 4-▲ 60328-2-RG [ADD] 4-■ 60328-4-RG (CrO2)
Schubert, Franz:Sym 9 RCA Gold Seal 4-▲ 60328-2-RG [ADD] 4-■ 60328-4-RG (CrO2)
Schubert, Franz:Sym 9 RCA Gold Seal ▲ 60313-2-RG [ADD] ■ 60313-4-RG (CrO2)
Strauss, R.:Tod und Verklärung RCA Gold Seal 4-▲ 60328-2-RG [ADD] 4-■ 60328-4-RG (CrO2)
Strauss, R.:Tod und Verklärung RCA Gold Seal ▲ 60312-2-RG [ADD] ■ 60312-4-RG (CrO2)
Tchaikovsky, P.:Sym 6 RCA Gold Seal ▲ 60312-2-RG [ADD] ■ 60312-4-RG (CrO2)

Philadelphia Orch (cont.)
A. Wallenstein (cnd)
Grieg, E.:Con Pno, Op. 16, w. *(pianist unknown)*
RCA Victor ▲ 09026-62677-2; ■ 09026-62677-4
D. Zinman (cnd)
Danielpour, R.:Con Vc, w. Yo-Yo Ma (vc) Sony Classical ▲ SK 66299
Kirchner, L.:Music for Vc & Orch, w. Yo-Yo Ma (vc) Sony Classical ▲ SK 66299
Rouse, C.:Con Vc, w. Yo-Yo Ma (vc) Sony Classical ▲ SK 66299
Philadelphia Orch Brass Band
E. Ormandy (cnd)
Tchaikovsky, P.:Ov 1812, w. Mormon Tabernacle Choir Odyssey ▲ MBK 39784
Tchaikovsky, P.:Romeo & Juliet, w. Mormon Tabernacle Choir Odyssey ▲ MBK 39784
Philadelphia Orch members
E. Iseler (cnd)
Gabrieli, G.:Music of, w. Canadian Brass, New York PO members Philips ▲ 438392-2
Philadelphia Rapid Transit Company Band
J.P. Sousa (cnd)
Sousa, J.P.:Marches & Dances, Sousa Band—Washington Post; Stars & Stripes Forever; 23 others
Pearl ▲ PEA 9249
Philadelphia Trio [Elizabeth Keller (pno), Barbara Sonies (vn), Deborah Reeder (vc)]
Martinů, B.:Bergerettes *(rec Curtis Hall, Curtis Institute of Music, Philadelphia, PA, May, 1994)*
Centaur ▲ CRC 2259 [DDD]
Turina, J.:Trio 1 Pno *(rec Curtis Hall, Curtis Institute of Music, Philadelphia, PA, May, 1994)*
Centaur ▲ CRC 2259 [DDD]
Turina, J.:Trio 2 Pno *(rec Curtis Hall, Curtis Institute of Music, Philadelphia, PA, May, 1994)*
Centaur ▲ CRC 2259 [DDD]
Philadelphia Youth Orch
J. Primavera (cnd)
Jongen, J.:Symphonie Concertante, w. D. M. Belcher (org)
Direct-to-Tape Recording ▲ DTR 8804CD ■ DTR 8804
Poulenc, F.:Con Org, w. B. Schultz (org) Direct-to-Tape Recording ▲ DTR 8804CD ■ DTR 8804
Philharmonia
Y. P. Tortelier (cnd)
Falla, M. de:El sombrero de tres picos, w. J. Gomez (sop) [Sp] Chandos ▲ CHAN 8904 [DDD]
Philharmonia Baroque
Vivaldi, A.:Music of, Concerto Amsterdam, Boston Museum Trio, Clemencic Consort, Bologna I Filarmonici—sels. from Flute Concerto, RV.427 & 440; Four Seasons—Autumn; String Concerto, RV.129 & 152; Serenata a Tre, RV.690; Sonata, RV.2 *(rec 1970–86)*
Harmonia Mundi Plus ▲ HMP 390810
N. McGegan (cnd)
Corelli, A.:Concerti grossi, Op. 6—Nos. 7-12 [period instrs] Harmonia Mundi USA ▲ HMU 907015
Corelli, A.:Concerti grossi, Op. 6—Nos. 1-6 [period instrs] Harmonia Mundi USA ▲ HMU 907014
Handel, G.F.:Apollo e Dafne, w. Judith Nelson (sop), David Thomas (bass)
Harmonia Mundi France ("Musique d'abord" series) ▲ HMA 1905157
Handel, G.F.:Arias, w. L. Hunt (sop)—opera & oratorio arias from Messiah, Theodora & Susanna
Harmonia Mundi USA ▲ HMU 907149 [DDD]
Handel, G.F.:Arias, w. L. Hunt (sop)—L'angue offeso; L'aure che spira; Cara speme; Dimmi, crudele Amore; La giustizia; Miriami; Ogni vento; Ombra cara; Pensieri; Qual leon; Qual nave; Svegliatevi; Vieni, o figlio [I] *(rec Oct. 1991)* Harmonia Mundi USA ▲ HMU 907056
Handel, G.F.:Arias, w. D. Thomas (bass)—17 arias from Acis & Galatea, Athaliah, Deborah, Esther, Ezio, Orlando, Sosarme, Tolomeo [composed for Italian bass Antonio Montagnana] [E,I]
Harmonia Mundi USA ▲ HMU 907016
Handel, G.F.:Arias, w. Lisa Saffer (sop—Cuzzoni), Lorraine Hunt (mez—Durastanti), Drew Minter (ct—Senesino), David Thomas (bass—Montagnana) Harmonia Mundi 4-▲ HMX 2907171.74
Handel, G.F.:Arias, w. D. Minter (ct)—11 arias & scenes from Flavio, Giulio Cesare, Orlando, Riccardo Primo, Rodelinda, Tolomeo [all composed for the alto castrato Francesco Bernardi, stage name Senesino] [I] Harmonia Mundi France ▲ HMC 905183 [ADD]
Handel, G.F.:Arias, w. L. Saffer (sop)—12 arias from Alessandro, Flavio, Giulio Cesare, Ottone, Riccardo I, Rodelinda, Scipione, Tamerlano [composed for Italian soprano Francesca Cuzzoni] [I]
Harmonia Mundi USA ▲ HMU 907036
Handel, G.F.:Clori, Tirsi e Fileno, w. J. Feldman (sop), L. Hunt (sop), D. Minter (alt) [I]
Harmonia Mundi USA ▲ HMU 907045
Handel, G.F.:Cons (3) Ob, w. Bruce Haynes (ob)—in g
Harmonia Mundi France ("Musique d'abord" series) ▲ HMA 1905157
Handel, G.F.:Judas Maccabaeus, w. Linda Saffer (sop), Patricia Spence (mez), Brian Asawa (ct), Guy de Mey (ten), Leroy Kromm (b-bar), David Thomas (bass), Univ of California at Berkeley Chamber Chorus [E] *(rec Nov. 15–18, 1992)* Harmonia Mundi USA 2-▲ HMU 907077/78
Handel, G.F.:Messiah, w. Lorraine Hunt (sop), Janet Williams (sop), Patricia Spence (mez), Drew Minter (alt), Jeffery Thomas (ten), William Parker (bar), Univ of California at Berkeley Chamber Chorus—standard version of Messiah *occupies the first sections of each of the three CDs, one part per disc. Each part is followed, after a significant pause, by alternative versions of certain sections of the preceding material, 13 altogether.* [E] Harmonia Mundi USA 3-▲ HMU 907050/52
Handel, G.F.:Messiah (sels), w. Lorraine Hunt (sop), Janet Williams (sop), Patricia Spence (mez), Drew Minter (alt), Jeffery Thomas (ten), William Parker (bar), Univ of California at Berkeley Chamber Chorus
Harmonia Mundi USA ▲ HMU 907120
Handel, G.F.:Messiah (sels), w. Lorraine Hunt (sop), Janet Williams (sop), Patricia Spence (mez), Drew Minter (alt), Jeffery Thomas (ten), William Parker (bar), Univ of California at Berkeley Chamber Chorus [E] Harmonia Mundi USA ("Nightingale" series) ▲ HMN 907601
Handel, G.F.:La Rezurrezione, w. Linda Saffer (sop), Judith Nelson (mez), Patricia Spence (mez), Jeffery Thomas (ten), Michael George (bass) [I] Harmonia Mundi USA 2-▲ HMU 907027/28
Handel, G.F.:Susanna, w. Jill Feldman (sop), Lorraine Hunt (sop), Drew Minter (alt), Jeffery Thomas (ten), William Parker (bar), David Thomas (bass), Univ of California at Berkeley Chamber Chorus [E]
Harmonia Mundi USA 3-▲ HMU 907030/32
Handel, G.F.:Susanna (sels), w. Jill Feldman (sop), Lorraine Hunt (sop), Drew Minter (alt), Jeffery Thomas (ten), William Parker (bar), David Thomas (bass), Univ of California at Berkeley Chamber Chorus [E] Harmonia Mundi USA ("Nightingale" series) ▲ HMN 907601
Handel, G.F.:Susanna (sels), w. Jill Feldman (sop), Lorraine Hunt (sop), Drew Minter (alt), Jeffrey Thomas (ten), William Parker (bar), David Thomas (bass) Harmonia Mundi France ▲ HMU 907168
Handel, G.F.:Theodora, w. Lorraine Hunt (sop—Theodora), Jennifer Lane (mez—Irene), Drew Minter (alt—Didymus), Jeffery Thomas (ten—Septimius), David Thomas (bass—Valens), Univ of California at Berkeley Chamber Chorus [period instrs] [E] *(rec 9/91)*
Harmonia Mundi USA 3-▲ HMU 907060/62 [DDD]
Handel, G.F.:Theodora (sels), w. Lorraine Hunt (sop), Jennifer Lane (mez), Drew Minter (ct), Jeffrey Thomas (ten), David Thomas (bass), Univ of California at Berkeley Chamber Chorus
Harmonia Mundi France ▲ HMU 907188
Handel, G.F.:Water Music (comp) [period instrs] Harmonia Mundi USA ▲ HMU 907010 [AAD]
Mozart, W.A.:Cons Hn, w. L. Greer (hn) Harmonia Mundi USA ▲ HMU 907012 [AAD]
Mozart, W.A.:Con 18 Pno, w. Melvyn Tan (pno) *(rec Walnut Creek Regional Center for the Arts, Feb 27–28 & Mar 2, 1995)* Harmonia Mundi France ▲ HMU 907138
Mozart, W.A.:Con 19 Pno, w. Melvyn Tan (pno) *(rec Walnut Creek Regional Center for the Arts, Feb 27–28 & Mar 2, 1995)* Harmonia Mundi France ▲ HMU 907138
Mozart, W.A.:Rondo Hn, K.371, w. L. Greer (nat hn) Harmonia Mundi USA ▲ HMU 907012 [AAD]
Mozart, W.A.:Rondo Hn, K.514 (compl'd Jeurissen), w. L. Greer (nat hn)
Harmonia Mundi USA ▲ HMU 907012 [AAD]
A Musical Grand Tour, w. Concerto Amsterdam [cnd:Jaap Schröder], Capella Savaria [cnd:Pál Németh], Ensemble 415 [cnd:Chiara Banchini], et al. Harmonia Mundi ▲ HMUK 986001
Purcell, H.:Dido & Aeneas, w. L. Hunt (sop), L. Saffer (sop), D. Deam (sop), C. Brandes (sop), R. Rainero (sop), E. Rabiner (mez), P. Elliot (ten), M. Dean (bar), Clare College Choir Cambridge
Harmonia Mundi USA ▲ HMU 907110

Philharmonia Baroque (cont.)
N. McGegan (cnd) (cont.)
Purcell, H.:The Gordian Knot Unty'd Harmonia Mundi USA ▲ HMU 907110
Rameau, J.P.:Naïs (sels) Harmonia Mundi France ▲ HMU 907121
Rameau, J.P.:Le Temple de la gloire (sels) Harmonia Mundi France ▲ HMU 907121
Vivaldi, A.:Cons Fl (misc), w. J. See (fl)—RV.427-429, 436, 438 & 440
Harmonia Mundi France ▲ HMC 905193 [DDD]
Vivaldi, A.:Cons Fl, Op. 10, w. Janet See (fl) Harmonia Mundi ▲ HMX 2905193
Vivaldi, A.:Con Fl Bn, w. M. Verbruggen (rcr), D. Godburn (bn) Harmonia Mundi USA ▲ HMU 907040
Vivaldi, A.:Con for 2 Fls, w. J. See (fl), S. Schultz (fl) Harmonia Mundi France ▲ HMC 905193 [DDD]
Vivaldi, A.:Cons Rcr, w. M. Verbruggen (rcr)—(6) in C, RV.443 & in C, RV.444 (sopranino recorder); in F, RV.433, "La Tempesta di Mare"; in F, RV.434; in G, RV.435; in c, RV.441 (alto recorder)
Harmonia Mundi USA ▲ HMU 907040
D. Mintner (cnd)
Handel, G.F.:Music of, w. Lorraine Hunt (sop), Kenneth Gilbert (hpd), et al., Ensemble 415, Concerto Vocale—sels. from Duetto "Tanti strali"; Flavio; Giulio Cesare; Harpsichord Suite No. 5; Nisi Dominus; Susanna; Water Music *(rec 1976–79)* Harmonia Mundi Plus ▲ HMP 390804
Philharmonia Bulgarica
J. Alfidi (cnd)
Gershwin, G.:Con Pno, w. B. Vodenicharov (pno) Vivace ▲ E 548 [ADD]
Gershwin, G.:Rhap in Blue, w. B. Vodenicharov (pno) Vivace ▲ E 548 [ADD]
C. Iliev (cnd)
Mozart, W.A.:Con 1 Vn, w. G. Badev (vn) Vivace 2-▲ G 217 [ADD]
Mozart, W.A.:Con 1 Vn, w. G. Badev (vn) Vivace ▲ 516
Mozart, W.A.:Con 2 Vn, w. G. Badev (vn) Vivace 2-▲ G 217 [ADD]
Mozart, W.A.:Con 2 Vn, w. G. Badev (vn) Vivace ▲ 516
D. Manolov (cnd)
Chopin, F.:Andante Spianato & Grande Polonaise, w. A. Moreira Lima (pno) Vivace 2-▲ G 218 [DDD]
Chopin, F.:Con 1 Pno, w. A. Moreira-Lima (pno) Vivace 3-▲ E 322 [DDD]
Chopin, F.:Con 1 Pno, w. A. Moreira Lima (pno) Vivace 2-▲ G 218 [DDD]
Chopin, F.:Con 1 Pno, w. A. Moreira-Lima (pno) Sound 2-▲ E 220 [DDD]
Chopin, F.:Con 2 Pno, w. A. Moreira Lima (pno) Vivace 3-▲ E 322 [DDD]
Chopin, F.:Con 2 Pno, w. A. Moreira Lima (pno) Vivace 2-▲ G 218 [DDD]
Chopin, F.:Con 2 Pno, w. A. Moreira-Lima (pno) Sound 2-▲ E 220 [DDD]
Chopin, F.:Con 2 Pno, w. A. Moreira Lima (pno) Vivace 2-▲ G 107/108 [DDD/ADD]
Chopin, F.:Grand Fant on Polish Airs, w. A. Moreira Lima (pno) Vivace 2-▲ G 218 [DDD]
Chopin, F.:Krakowiak, w. A. Moreira Lima (pno) Vivace 2-▲ G 218 [DDD]
Chopin, F.:Vars on Mozart's *La ci darem la mano*, w. A. Moreira Lima (pno) Vivace 2-▲ G 218 [DDD]
I. Stefanov (cnd)
Dvořák, A.:Sym 9, "From the New World" Vivace ▲ 512 [DDD]
Smetana, B.:The Moldau Vivace ▲ 512 [DDD]
V. Stefanov (cnd)
Brahms, J.:Con Vn, w. M. Minchev (vn) Vivace 3-▲ E 325 [ADD/DDD]
Brahms, J.:Con Vn, w. M. Minchev (vn) Vivace ▲ 586 [ADD]
Bruch, M.:Con 1 Vn, w. S. Milanova (vn) Vivace 3-▲ E 324 [ADD/DDD]
Classical Gold Vivace ▲ E 537 [ADD]
Glazunov, A.:Con Vn, w. S. Milanova (vn) Vivace 3-▲ E 324 [ADD/DDD]
Mozart, W.A.:Kleine Nachtmusik Vivace ▲ E 537 [ADD]
Philharmonia Cassovia
M. Klemens (cnd)
Brahms, J.:Sym 1 Lydian ▲ LYD 18005 [DDD]
A. Mogrelia (cnd)
Ballet Favorites Lydian ▲ LYD 18110 [DDD]
Borodin, A.:Prince Igor (Polovtsian dances) *(rec House of Arts, Kosice, Sept. 4–5, 1991)*
Lydian ▲ 18111 [DDD]
Brahms, J.:Hungarian Dances Orch Lydian ▲ LYD 18080
Liszt, F.:Hungarian Rhaps—Nos. 2 & 6 *(rec House of Arts, Kosice, Aug. 13–17, 1990)*
Lydian ▲ 18111 [DDD]
Smetana, B.:The Moldau *(rec House of Arts, Kosice, Sept. 4–5, 1991)* Lydian ▲ 18111 [DDD]
Tchaikovsky, P.:Sleeping Beauty (suite) *(rec House of Arts, Kosice, Aug. 15–17, 1990)*
Lydian ▲ 18069 [DDD]
Tchaikovsky, P.:Swan Lake (suite) *(rec House of Arts, Kosice, Aug. 15–17, 1990)*
Lydian ▲ 18069 [DDD]
R. Stankovsky (cnd)
Grieg, E.:Con Pno, Op. 16, w. Stanislav Zamborsky (pno) *(rec House of Arts, Kosice, Nov. 13–14, 1990)*
Lydian ▲ 18106 [DDD]
Rimsky-Korsakov, N.:Capriccio espagnol *(rec House of Arts, Kosice, Jan 13–14, 1992)*
Lydian ▲ 18111 [DDD]
O. Trhlík (cnd)
Chopin, F.:Con 1 Pno, w. Zuzana Paulechava (pno) *(rec House of Arts, Kosice, Jan. 31, 1990)*
Lydian ▲ 18102 [DDD]
Mozart, W.A.:Con 20 Pno, w. Peter Breiner (pno) *(rec House of Arts, Kosice, Jan. 31, 1990)*
Lydian ▲ 18102 [DDD]
A. Walter (cnd)
Bizet, G.:L'Arlésienne (suites) Lydian ▲ LYD 18073 [DDD]
Bizet, G.:Carmen (suites) Lydian ▲ LYD 18073 [DDD]
J. Wehner (cnd)
Beethoven, L. van:Sym 4 Lydian ▲ LYD 18092 [DDD]
J. Wildner (cnd)
Beethoven, L. van:Leonore 3 Lydian ▲ LYD 18020
Beethoven, L. van:Sym 7 Lydian ▲ LYD 18092 [DDD]
Brahms, J.:Sym 2 Lydian ▲ LYD 18099 [DDD]
Brahms, J.:Tragic Ov Lydian ▲ LYD 18005 [DDD]
Brahms, J.:Vars on a Theme by Haydn Lydian ▲ LYD 18099 [DDD]
Mendelssohn, F.:A Midsummer Night's Dream (sels) *(rec House of Arts, Kosice, June 13–15, 1990)*
Lydian ▲ 18070 [DDD]
Mendelssohn, F.:Sym 4 *(rec House of Arts, Kosice, June 13–15, 1990)* Lydian ▲ 18070 [DDD]
Mozart, W.A.:Così fan tutte (sels)—Ov. Lydian ▲ LYD 18020
Mozart, W.A.:Sym 38 *(rec House of Arts, Kosice, Nov. 10–11, 1990)* Lydian ▲ 18082 [DDD]
Mozart, W.A.:Sym 40 *(rec House of Arts, Kosice, Nov. 10–11, 1990)* Lydian ▲ 18082 [DDD]
Mozart, W.A.:Zauberflöte (sels)—Ov. Lydian ▲ LYD 18020
Schubert, Franz:Rosamunde (sels)—Ov; Ballet Music No. 1 *(rec House of Arts, Kosice, June 6–8, 1990)*
Lydian ▲ 18087 [DDD]
Schubert, Franz:Sym 5 *(rec House of Arts, Kosice, June 6–8, 1990)* Lydian ▲ 18087 [DDD]
Schubert, Franz:Sym 8 *(rec House of Arts, Kosice, June 6–8, 1990)* Lydian ▲ 18087 [DDD]
Schubert, Franz:Sym 9 *(rec House of the Arts, Kosice, Nov. 15–20, 1990)* Lydian ▲ 18107 [DDD]
Schumann, R.:Con Pno, w. Thomas Hlawatsch (pno) *(rec House of Arts, Kosice, Nov. 13–14, 1990)*
Lydian ▲ 18106 [DDD]
Tchaikovsky, P.:Capriccio italien *(rec House of Arts, Kosice, June 9–12, 1990)*
Lydian ▲ 18066 [DDD]
Tchaikovsky, P.:Eugene Onegin (sels)—Waltz; Polonaise *(rec House of Arts, Kosice, Aug. 27–30, 1990)*
Lydian ▲ 18105 [DDD]
Tchaikovsky, P.:Hamlet *(rec House of Arts, Kosice, June 6–8, 1990)* Lydian ▲ 18077 [DDD]
Tchaikovsky, P.:Marche slave *(rec House of Arts, Kosice, June 9–12, 1990)* Lydian ▲ 18066 [DDD]
Tchaikovsky, P.:Ov 1812 *(rec House of Arts, Kosice, June 9–12, 1990)* Lydian ▲ 18066 [DDD]
Tchaikovsky, P.:Romeo & Juliet *(rec House of Arts, Kosice, June 9–12, 1990)*
Lydian ▲ 18066 [DDD]
Tchaikovsky, P.:Sym 5 *(rec House of Arts, Kosice, Aug. 27–30, 1990)* Lydian ▲ 18105 [DDD]
Tchaikovsky, P.:Sym 6 *(rec House of Arts, Kosice, June 6–8, 1990)* Lydian ▲ 18077 [DDD]

▲ = CD ♦ = Enhanced CD Δ = MD ■ = Cassette Tape □ = DCC

Philharmonia Cassovia (cont.)
R. Zimmer (cnd)
Tchaikovsky, P.:Con Vn, w. Peter Michalica (vn) *(rec Moyzes Hall of the Slovak PO, Bratislava, Mar. 1988)* Lydian ▲ 18084 [DDD]
Philharmonia Chamber Artists
R. H. Lewis (cnd)
Lewis, R.H.:Diptychon New World ▲ 80444–2
Philharmonia da Camera
M. Hötzel (cnd)
Baroque Concert MD + G ▲ L 3185 [DDD]
Philharmonia Hungarica
W. A. Albert (cnd)
Albert, E. d':Con Vc, w. Catalin Ilea (vc) Arcobaleno ▲ AAOC 9390
Taneyev, A.:Suite 2 Marco Polo ▲ 8.223133 [DDD]
Taneyev, A.:Sym 2 Marco Polo ▲ 8.223133 [DDD]
G.A. Albrecht (cnd)
Schulhoff, E.:Sym 1 CPO ▲ CPO 999251 [DDD]
Schulhoff, E.:Sym 2 CPO ▲ CPO 999251 [DDD]
Schulhoff, E.:Sym 3 CPO ▲ CPO 999251 [DDD]
D. Atlas (cnd)
Suk, J.:Sym in E IMP ("Classics" series) ▲ IMP PCD 1112
W. Boskovsky (cnd)
Liszt, F.:Hungarian Battle March, w. London PO EMI Classics ▲ CDM 64627
Liszt, F.:Hungarian Rhaps (orchestral versions), w. London PO EMI Classics ▲ CDM 64627
A. Dorati (cnd)
Bartók, B.:Dance Suite Mercury Living Presence ▲ 432017–2 [ADD]
Bartók, B.:Mikrokosmos [arr. for orch.]—2 sels. Mercury Living Presence ▲ 432017–2 [ADD]
Bartók, B.:Portraits Mercury Living Presence ▲ 432017–2 [ADD]
Haydn, J.:Syms (comp)—Nos. 84–95 London 4–▲ 425930–2 [ADD]
Haydn, J.:Syms (comp)—Nos. 72–83 London 4–▲ 425925–2 [ADD]
Haydn, J.:Syms (comp)—Nos. 48–59 London 4–▲ 425915–2 [ADD]
Haydn, J.:Syms (comp)—Nos. 96–104 London 4–▲ 425935–2 [ADD]
Haydn, J.:Syms (comp)—Nos. 1–16 London 4–▲ 425900–2 [ADD]
Haydn, J.:Syms (comp)—Nos. 17–33 London 4–▲ 425905–2 [ADD]
Haydn, J.:Syms (comp)—Nos. 34–47 London 4–▲ 425910–2 [ADD]
Haydn, J.:Syms (comp)—Nos. 60–71 London 4–▲ 425920–2 [ADD]
Haydn, J.:Syms 82–87, "Paris Syms" London 2–▲ 448194–2
Kodály, Z.:Galanta Dances London ("Jubilee" series) ▲ 425034–2 [ADD]
Kodály, Z.:Galanta Dances London ("Double Decker" series) 2–▲ 443006–2
Kodály, Z.:Háry János (suite) London ("Double Decker" series) 2–▲ 443006–2
Kodály, Z.:Háry János (suite) London ("Jubilee" series) ▲ 425034–2 [ADD]
Kodály, Z.:Marosszék Dances London ("Jubilee" series) ▲ 425034–2 [ADD]
Kodály, Z.:Vars on a Hungarian Folk Song London ("Jubilee" series) ▲ 425034–2 [ADD]
Kodály, Z.:Vars on a Hungarian Folk Song London ("Double Decker" series) 2–▲ 443006–2
Respighi, O.:Ancient Airs & Dances Mercury Living Presence ▲ 434304–2 [ADD]
Tchaikovsky, P.:Serenade Strs Mercury Living Presence 2–▲ 432750–2 [ADD]
A. Grüber (cnd)
Weber, C.M. von:Ovs—Oberon; Freischütz; Euryanthe; Preciosa Allegretto ▲ ACD 8145 [ADD] ■ ACS 8145
R. Kapp (cnd)
Rimsky-Korsakov, N.:The Legend of the Invisible City of Kitzeh (suite) Vox Box 2–▲ CDX 5082 [ADD]
S. Köhler (cnd)
Tchaikovsky, P.:The Slippers—Introduation; Russian Dance; Dance of the Cossacks Vox Box 3–▲ CD3X 3026 [ADD]
P. Maag (cnd)
Schubert, Franz:Life & Music of—narration with selected excerpts from Rosamunde, D.797; Marche militaire, D.733; Hark, Hark, the Lark!, D.889; Mass No. 5, D.678; Mass No. 6, D.950; Son. in a, D.845; The Elf King, D.328; Syms. Nos. 2, 4, 5, 6, 8 & 9; Moments Musicaux, D.780; To Music, D.547; The Trout, D.550; Qnt. for Piano, D667; Impromptu, D.935; Octet, D.803; Qnt., D.956; Wanderer Fantasy, D.760; Qt. No. 14 for Strings, D.810; Ave Maria, D.839, plus a complete version of Sym. No. 5 in Bb, D. 485 Vox Music Masters ("Music Masters" series) ▲ MMD 8504 [ADD] ■ MMC 8504
Schubert, Franz:Sym 9 Allegretto ▲ ACD 8081 [ADD] ■ ACS 8081
O. Maga (cnd)
Borodin, A.:In the Steppes of Central Asia Allegretto ▲ ACD 8161 [ADD] ■ ACS 8161
Borodin, A.:Sym 2 Allegretto ▲ ACD 8161 [ADD] ■ ACS 8161
Henselt, A. von:Con Pno, w. M. Ponti (pno) *(rec 1968)* Vox Box 2–▲ CDX 5064 [ADD]
Moscheles, I.:Con 3 Pno, w. M. Ponti (pno) *(rec 1968)* Vox Box 2–▲ CDX 5065 [ADD]
Rubinstein, A.:Con 4 Pno, w. M. Ponti (pno) *(rec 1968)* Vox Box 2–▲ CDX 5066 [ADD]
Scharwenka, X.:Con 2 Pno, w. M. Ponti (pno) *(rec 1972)* Vox Box 2–▲ CDX 5066 [ADD]
U. Mund (cnd)
Enescu, G.:Symphonie concertante, w. Catalin Ilea (vc) Arcobaleno ▲ AAOC 9390
K. Redel (cnd)
Brahms, J.:Academic Festival Ov *(rec 9/89)* Pierre Verany ▲ PV.790012 [DDD]
Brahms, J.:Sym 4 *(rec 9/89)* Pierre Verany ▲ PV.790012 [DDD]
Brahms, J.:Tragic Ov *(rec 9/89)* Pierre Verany ▲ PV.790012 [DDD]
Z. Rozsnyai (cnd)
Chabrier, E.:España RealTime ▲ RT 2001 [DDD]
Debussy, C.:Prélude à l'après-midi d'un faune RealTime ▲ RT 2003
Digital Masterpiece Series, Vol. 1 RealTime ▲ RT 2001 [DDD]
Digital Masterpiece Series Vol. 2 RealTime ▲ RT 2003
Digital Masterpiece Series Vol. 3 RealTime ▲ RT 2004 [DDD]
Dukas, P.:L'Apprenti sorcier RealTime ▲ RT 2001
Ginastera, A.:Panambí (suite) RealTime ▲ RT 2003
Handel, G.F.:Water Music (suites) RealTime ▲ RT 2004 [DDD]
Liszt, F.:Les Préludes RealTime ▲ RT 2001 [DDD]
1959 Concert, w. Helge Roswaenge (ten), *(rec live, Grossen Musikvereinssaal, Vienna, 5/3/59)* Preiser ▲ PRE 90103 (m) [ADD]
Rimsky-Korsakov, N.:Mlada (procession) RealTime ▲ RT 2003
Smetana, B.:The Moldau RealTime ▲ RT 2004
Tchaikovsky, P.:Nutcracker Suite, sels. RealTime ▲ RT 2004
Tchaikovsky, P.:Romeo & Juliet RealTime ▲ RT 2003
H. R. Stracke (cnd)
Moszkowski, M.:Con Pno, w. M. Ponti (pno) *(rec 1969)* Vox Box 2–▲ CDX 5066 [ADD]
J. Valach (cnd)
Dvořák, A.:Sym 9, "From the New World" Forlane ▲ FRL 36 [ADD]
Fibich, Z.:Crepuscule Forlane ▲ FRL 36 [ADD]
G. Varga (cnd)
Rubinstein, A.:Sym 6 Marco Polo ▲ 8.220489 [DDD]
G. Wich (cnd)
Pfitzner, H.:Con Vn, w. Susanne Lautenbacher (vn) Vox Box 2–▲ CDX 5134 [ADD]
G. Wright (cnd)
Reznicek, E.N. von:Con Vn, w. M. Davis (vn) *(rec 1984)* Koch Schwann ▲ CD 311 128 [ADD]
Philharmonia Orch
Beethoven, L. van:Con 1 Pno, w. Walter Gieseking (pno) Theorema ▲ TH 121215
Burgon, G.:Film Music, w. L. Garrett (sop)—Brideshead Revisited; The Chronicles of Narnia; Bleak House; The Testament of Youth; Tinker, Tailor, Soldier, Spy Silva America ▲ SSD 1005 [DDD] ■ SSC 1005

Philharmonia Orch (cont.)
Classics Go to the Movies,Vol. 5, w. Hannes Käster (org), Salzburg Mozarteum Orch, Bavarian RSO, Ludovic Spiess (ten), Virginia Zeani (sop), Rumanian Opera Orch, Rumanian Radio–TV Studio Orch, Sofia PO, Budapest SO LaserLight ▲ 15 645
Collins Classics 2–▲ COL 7005 [DDD]
Haydn's Trumpet Concerto & Other Classical Concerti, w. John Wallace (tpt) Nimbus ▲ NI 7016 [DDD]
Legendary Three Tenors, w. Enrico Caruso (ten), Beniamino Gigli (ten), John McCormack (ten), Ruggiero Leoncavallo (pno), Edwin Schneider (pno), Metropolitan Opera Orch, Metropolitan Opera Chorus [cnd:Giulio Setti], Philharmonia Chorus [cnd:Stanford Robinson] *(rec 1904–1950)* RCA Gold Seal ▲ 09026–68534–2 [ADD] ■ 09026–68534–4
Mozart, W.A.:Con 7 Pnos, w. V. Ashkenazy (pno), D. Barenboim (pno), Fou Ts'ong (pno) London 2–▲ 421577–2 [ADD]
Musical Moments in the Garden, w. Academy of St. Martin in the Fields, Bournemouth SO, English CO, Hollywood Bowl SO, Toulouse Orch, Philharmonia Orch, Toulouse CO, L. Auriacombe (cnd), T. Beecham (cnd), C. Davis (cnd), R. Hickox (cnd), N. Marriner (cnd), M. Plasson (cnd), M. Sargent (cnd) Angel ▲ CDM 65203 ■ EG 65203
The Prima Donna Collection Highlights, w. Leontyne Price (sop), RCA Italiana Opera Orch, London SO, New Philharmonia Orch RCA Gold Seal ▲ 09026–62596–2
Taylor, B.J.:Wuthering Heights, w. Dave Willets (sgr), L. Garrett (sop), C. Carter (sgr), J. Sladdon (sgr), S. Campbell (sgr), Contorum Choir Silva America ▲ SSD 1008 ■ SSC 1008
Vivaldi Concerti & Baroque Trumpet Music, w. John Wallace (tpt) Nimbus ▲ NI 7012 [DDD]
Wagner, R.:Arias & Scenes, w. Kirsten Flagstad (sop)—Tannhäuser:Allmächt'ge Jungfrau! *[cond. Issay Dobrowen; rec 4/1/48]*; Siegfried:Ewig war ich *[w. Set Svanholm, tenor, cond. Georges Sebastian; rec 6/12–13/51]*; Götterdämmerung:Starke Scheite schichtet mir dort (Brünnhilde's Immolation) *[cond. Furtwängler; rec 3/26/48]*; Tristan und Isolde:Doch nun von Tristan genau will ich's vernehmen! (Isolde's Narrative and Curse) *[w. Elisabeth Höngen, mezzo, cond. Dobrowen; rec 3/31/48]*; Mild und leise (Liebestod) *[cond. Dobrowen, rec 4/1/48]* [G] EMI Classics ("Great Recordings of the Century" series) ▲ CDH 63030 (m) [ADD]
S. Accardo (cnd)
Tchaikovsky, P.:Con Vn, w. Xue-Wei (vn) ASV ▲ ASV 713 [DDD]
Tchaikovsky, P.:Sérénade mélancolique, w. Xue-Wei (vn) ASV ▲ ASV 713 [DDD]
Tchaikovsky, P.:Souvenir d'un lieu cher, w. Xue-Wei (vn)—Mélodie [arr vn & orch] ASV ▲ ASV 713 [DDD]
Tchaikovsky, P.:Valse-Scherzo Vn, w. Xue-Wei (vn) ASV ▲ ASV 713 [DDD]
O. Ackermann (cnd)
Lehár, F.:Die lustige Witwe, w. E. Schwarzkopf (sop), E. Loose (sop), N. Gedda (ten), E. Kunz (bar), A. Kraus (ten), Philharmonia Chorus [G] EMI Classics ("Studio" series) ▲ CDH 69520 (m) [ADD]
Liszt, F.:Con 1 Pno, w. Géza Anda (pno) *(rec May 1955)* Testament ▲ SBT 1071
Liszt, F.:Fant on Hungarian Folk Tunes, w. Géza Anda (pno) *(rec May 1955)* Testament ▲ SBT 1071
Schwarzkopf Sings Operetta, w. Elisabeth Schwarzkopf (sop), Philharmonia Chorus EMI Classics ▲ CDC 47284
Strauss (II), Joh.:Die Fledermaus (sels), w. Wilma Lipp (sop), Gerda Scheyer (sop), Christa Ludwig (mez), Anton Dermota (ten), Walter Berry (bar), Erich Kunz (bar), Eberhard Wachter (bar), London Phil Chorus Emperor Operetta ▲ KO 86340
Strauss, R.:Capriccio (sels), w. E. Schwarzkopf (sop)—Closing Scene [G] EMI Classics ("Great Recordings of the Century" series) ▲ CDH 61001 (m)
Strauss, R.:4 Last Songs, w. E. Schwarzkopf (sop) [G] EMI Classics ("Great Recordings of the Century" series) ▲ CDH 61001 (m)
A. de Almeida (cnd)
Donizetti, G.:Ballet Music, Monte Carlo Opera Orch Philips ("Duo" series) 2–▲ 442553–2
Offenbach, J.:Orphée aux enfers (sels) *(rec Aug. 7–9, 1987)* Philips ("Solo" series) ▲ 442403–2
Offenbach, J.:Le Voyage dans la lune (sels) *(rec Aug. 7–9, 1987)* Philips ("Solo" series) ▲ 442403–2
Rossini, G.:Ballet Music, Monte Carlo Opera Orch Philips ("Duo" series) 2–▲ 442553–2
K. Alwyn (cnd)
Bliss, A.:Conquest of the Air Silva America ▲ SSD 1011 [DDD]
Easdale, B.:The Red Shoes Ballet Silva America ▲ SIL 1028
Schurmann, G.:Attack & Celebration Silva America ▲ SSD 1011 [DDD]
Vaughan Williams, R.:Coastal Command Silva America ▲ SSD 1011 [DDD]
D. Amos (cnd)
Hovhaness, A.:Alleluia & Fugue Crystal ▲ CD 810 [DDD] ■ C 810 (D)
Hovhaness, A.:Anahid Crystal ▲ CD 810 [DDD] ■ C 810 (D)
Hovhaness, A.:And God Created Whales Crystal ▲ CD 810 [DDD] ■ C 810 (D)
Hovhaness, A.:Con 8 Orch Crystal ▲ CD 810 [DDD] ■ C 810 (D)
Hovhaness, A.:Elibris, w. C. Messiter (fl) Crystal ▲ CD 810 [DDD] ■ C 810 (D)
M. Arnold (cnd)
Arnold, M.:English Dances—Nos. 3 & 5 EMI Classics ▲ CDM 64044–2
Arnold, M.:Tam o'Shanter EMI Classics ▲ CDM 64044
V. Ashkenazy (cnd)
Beethoven, L. van:Egmont (ov) London ▲ 430721–2 [DDD]
Beethoven, L. van:Leonore 3 London ▲ 430721–2 [DDD]
Beethoven, L. van:Sym 6, "Pastorale" London ▲ 430721–2 [DDD]
Beethoven, L. van:Sym 7 London ▲ 430701–2 [DDD]
Dvořák, A.:Con Vc, w. L. Harrell (vc) London ("Jubilee" series) ▲ 430743–2 [DDD]
Mozart, W.A.:Cons Pno, w. V. Ashkenazy (pno)—Nos. 1–6, 8, 9 & 11–27 London 12–▲ 425557–2 [ADD]
Mozart, W.A.:Con 17 Pno, w. Vladimir Ashkenazy (pno) London ▲ 411947–2 [ADD]
Mozart, W.A.:Con 20 Pno, w. V. Ashkenazy (pno) London 2–▲ 436383–2 [ADD]
Mozart, W.A.:Con 21 Pno, w. V. Ashkenazy (pno) London ▲ 411947–2 [ADD]
Mozart, W.A.:Con 21 Pno, w. V. Ashkenazy (pno) London 2–▲ 436383–2 [ADD/DDD]
Mozart, W.A.:Con 22 Pno, w. V. Ashkenazy (pno) London ▲ 421036–2 [ADD]
Mozart, W.A.:Con 23 Pno, w. V. Ashkenazy (pno) London 2–▲ 436383–2 [ADD/DDD]
Mozart, W.A.:Con 25 Pno, w. V. Ashkenazy (pno) London ▲ 411810–2 [DDD]
Mozart, W.A.:Con 26 Pno, w. V. Ashkenazy (pno) London ▲ 411810–2 [DDD]
Mozart, W.A.:Con 27 Pno, w. V. Ashkenazy (pno) London 2–▲ 436383–2 [ADD/DDD]
Rimsky-Korsakov, N.:Scheherazade London ▲ 417301–2 [DDD]
Rimsky-Korsakov, N.:The Tale of Tsar Saltan Orch, Op. 57 London ▲ 417301–2 [DDD]
Sibelius, J.:Finlandia London ("Jubilee" series) ▲ 430737–2 [DDD]
Sibelius, J.:Finlandia London ▲ 417762–2 [DDD]
Sibelius, J.:Karelia Suite London ("Jubilee" series) ▲ 430737–2 [DDD]
Sibelius, J.:Karelia Suite London ▲ 417762–2 [DDD]
Sibelius, J.:En Saga London ▲ 417762–2 [DDD]
Sibelius, J.:Sym 2 London ("Jubilee" series) ▲ 430737–2 [DDD]
Sibelius, J.:Sym 4 London ("Ovation" series) ▲ 430749–2 [DDD]
Sibelius, J.:Sym 5 London ("Ovation" series) ▲ 430749–2 [DDD]
Sibelius, J.:Tapiola London ▲ 417762–2 [DDD]
F. d' Avalos (cnd)
Bruckner, A.:Sym 7 ASV ("Quicksilva" series) ▲ ASQ 6154 [DDD]
Clementi, M.:Orchestral Music (comp)—Overture in D; Sym. Nos. 2 & 4 ASV ▲ ASV 804
Clementi, M.:Orchestral Music (comp), w. P. Spada (piano)—Piano Con.; Minuetto Pastorale; 2 Symphonies, Op. 18 ASV ▲ ASV 802
Clementi, M.:Orchestral Music (comp)—Overture in C; Sym. Nos. 1 & 3 ASV ▲ ASV 803
Martucci, G.:Con 2 Pno, w. F. Caramiello (pno) ASV ▲ ASV 691 [DDD]
Martucci, G.:Orchestral Music—6 short orchestral works:Canzonetta & Gavotta, Op. 55, Nos. 1 & 2; Serenata, Minuetto & Momento musicale, Op. 57, Nos. 1–3; Giga, Op. 61, No. 3 ASV ▲ ASV 691 [DDD]
Martucci, G.:Orchestral Music—3 short orch. works:Notturno, Op. 70, No. 1; Noveletta, Op. 82; Tarantella, Op. 44 ASV ▲ ASV 675 [DDD]
Martucci, G.:Sym 1 ASV ▲ ASV 675 [DDD]
Martucci, G.:Sym 2 ASV ▲ ASV 689 [DDD]

Philharmonia Orch (cont.)
F. d' Avalos (cnd) (cont.)
Raff, J.:Abends Rhap ASV ▲ ASV 793
Raff, J.:Romeo & Juliet Ov ASV ▲ ASV 793
Raff, J.:Sym 3 ASV ▲ ASV 793
Schubert, Franz:Sym 9 ASV Quicksilva ▲ QS 6029 [DDD]
Schubert, Franz:Sym 9 Vivace ▲ 604 [DDD]
Wagner, R.:Lohengrin (preludes)—Acts 1 & 3 Preludes ASV ▲ ASV 666 [DDD]
Wagner, R.:Die Meistersinger von Nürnberg (prelude/act 1) ASV ▲ ASV 666 [DDD]
Wagner, R.:Siegfried Idyll ASV ▲ ASV 666 [DDD]
Wagner, R.:Die Walküre (sels), w. J. Tomlinson (bass)—Wotan's Farewell & Magic Fire Music [G] ASV ▲ ASV 666 [DDD]
K. Bakels (cnd)
Bruch, M.:Con 1 Vn, w. Xue-Wei (vn) ASV ▲ ASV 680 [DDD]
Saint-Saëns, C.:Con 3 Vn, w. Xue-Wei (vn) ASV ▲ ASV 680 [DDD]
M. Bamert (cnd)
Hadley, P.:The Trees So High, w. Philharmonia Chorus Chandos ▲ CHAN 9181 [DDD]
Respighi, O.:Con gregoriano, w. A. Capalletti (vn) Koch Schwann ▲ SCH 311242 [DDD]
Sainton, P.:The Island, w. Philharmonia Chorus Chandos ▲ CHAN 9181 [DDD]
J. Barbirolli (cnd)
Bax, A.:Tintagel EMI Classics ▲ CDM 65110
Elgar, E.:Cockaigne EMI Classics ▲ CDM 64511
Elgar, E.:Elegy Strs EMI Classics ▲ CDM 64724-2
Elgar, E.:Sospiri EMI Classics ▲ CDM 64724-2
Elgar, E.:Sym 1 EMI Classics ▲ CDM 64511
D. Barenboim (cnd)
Mozart, W.A.:Cons 1–4 Pno, w. V. Ashkenazy (pno) London 2-▲ 421577-2 [ADD]
Mozart, W.A.:Con 5 Pno, w. V. Ashkenazy (pno) London 2-▲ 421577-2 [ADD]
Mozart, W.A.:Con 6 Pno, w. V. Ashkenazy (pno) London 2-▲ 421577-2 [ADD]
L. Barzin (cnd)
Bruch, M.:Con 1 Vn, w. N. Milstein (vn) Classics for Pleasure ▲ CDCFP 4374 [ADD]
Mendelssohn, F.:Con in e Vn & Orch, Op. 64, w. N. Milstein (vn) Classics for Pleasure ▲ CDCFP 4374 [ADD]
E. Bátiz (cnd)
Berlioz, H.:Ovs—Le Corsaire, Op. 21; Le carnaval romain, Op. 9 IMG/Pickwick ▲ PICIMG 1606
Berlioz, H.:Sym fantastique IMG/Pickwick ▲ PICIMG 1606
Rimsky-Korsakov, N.:Scheherazade *(rec Aug. 20–21, 1992)* Naxos ▲ 8.550726 [DDD]
Rimsky-Korsakov, N.:The Tale of Tsar Saltan (orch sels)—The Tsar's Farewell & Departure; The Tsarina in a Barrel at Sea; The 3 Wonders *(rec Aug. 20–21, 1992)* Naxos ▲ 8.550726 [DDD]
T. Beecham (cnd)
Wagner, R.:Tristan und Isolde, w. Kirsten Flagstad (sop), Margarete Klose (mez), Lauritz Melchior (ten/bar), Herbert Janssen (bar), Sven Nilsson (bass), Royal Opera House Chorus Covent Garden *(rec 1937)* Grammofono 2000 3-▲ GRM 78570 (m)
R. Behr (cnd)
Tchaikovsky, P.:Eugene Onegin (sels), w. P. Domingo (ten)—Lensky's aria EMI Classics ▲ CDC 55018 ■ 4DS 55018
L. Berio (cnd)
Mahler, G.:Songs, w. T. Hampson (bar)—5 frühe Lieder; 6 frühe Lieder; Frühe Lieder [w. D. Lutz (piano)] Teldec ▲ 74002
A. Bernard (cnd)
Bach, J.S.:Cant 82, w. H. Hotter (b-bar) [G] *(rec 1950)* EMI Classics ("Great Recordings of the Century" series) ▲ CDH 63198-2 (m) [ADD]
H. Blech (cnd)
Goldmark, K.:Con 1 Vn, w. Nathan Milstein (vn) Testament ▲ TES SBT 1047
K. Böhm (cnd)
Mozart, W.A.:Così fan tutte, w. E. Schwarzkopf (sop), H. Steffek (sop), C. Ludwig (mez), A. Kraus (ten), G. Taddei (bar), W. Berry (bass), Philharmonia Chorus [I] EMI Classics ("Studio" series) 3-▲ CDMC 69330 [ADD]
I. Bolton (cnd)
Lesley Garrett:Prima Donna, w. Lesley Garrett (sop) *(rec July–Aug., 1992)* Silva America ▲ SIL 1023 [DDD] ■ SIL MC1023
W. Boughton (cnd)
Holst, G.:The Perfect Fool Nimbus ▲ NI 5117 [DDD]
Holst, G.:The Planets Nimbus ▲ NI 5117 [DDD]
Popular Operatic Overtures Nimbus ▲ NI 5120 [DDD]
Rimsky-Korsakov, N.:Russian Easter Festival Nimbus ▲ NI 5128 [DDD]
Rimsky-Korsakov, N.:Scheherazade Nimbus ▲ NI 5128 [DDD]
P. Boulez (cnd)
Bartók, B.:Con 1 Pno, w. D. Barenboim (pno) *(rec 1967)* EMI Classics ▲ CDC 54770-2
Bartók, B.:Con 3 Pno, w. D. Barenboim (pno) *(rec 1967)* EMI Classics ▲ CDC 54770-2
Debussy, C.:Orchestral Music, Cleveland Orch—Images pour orchestre; Jeux; La Mer; Nocturnes; Prélude à l'après-midi d'un faune; Printemps Odyssey 2-▲ MB2K 45620
A. Boult (cnd)
Moeran, E.J.:Sinfonietta IMP ("BBC Radio Classics" series) ▲ IMP 5691632
M. Brabbins (cnd)
Hindemith, P.:Kammermusik 5, w. Paul Cortese (va) ASV ▲ ASV 931 [DDD]
Hindemith, P.:Konzertmusik Va, w. Paul Cortese (va) ASV ▲ ASV 931 [DDD]
Hindemith, P.:Der Schwanendreher, w. Paul Cortese (va) ASV ▲ ASV 931 [DDD]
T. Bremner (cnd)
Moross, J.:Big Country Silva America ▲ SSD 1048
Y. Butt (cnd)
Goldmark, K.:Der gefesselte Prometheus ASV ▲ ASV 934 [DDD]
Goldmark, K.:In Italian ASV ▲ ASV 934 [DDD]
Goldmark, K.:Sym 2 ASV ▲ ASV 934 [DDD]
Kodály, Z.:Hungarian Rondo ASV ▲ ASV 924 [DDD]
Kodály, Z.:Summer Evening ASV ▲ ASV 924 [DDD]
Kodály, Z.:Sym in C ASV ▲ ASV 924 [DDD]
G. Cantelli (cnd)
Beethoven, L. van:Sym 5 Testament ▲ TES SBT 1034 [ADD]
Beethoven, L. van:Sym 7 *(rec Kingsway Hall, London, May 1956)* EMI Classics 2-▲ ZDMB 68217 [ADD]
Beethoven, L. van:Sym 7 *(rec 1956)* Andromeda ▲ ANR 2521 [ADD]
Dukas, P.:L'Apprenti sorcier Testament ▲ TES SBT1017 (m) [ADD]
Falla, M. de:El sombrero de tres picos (sels) Testament ▲ TES SBT1017 (m) [ADD]
Mendelssohn, F.:Sym 4 Enterprise ("Palladio" series) ▲ ENT PD 4158 [ADD]
Mendelssohn, F.:Sym 4 Testament ▲ TES SBT 1034 [ADD]
Mozart, W.A.:Musikalischer Spass *(rec Kingsway Hall, London, Aug. 1955)* EMI Classics 2-▲ ZDMB 68217 [ADD]
Mozart, W.A.:Sym 29 *(rec Kingsway Hall, London, June 1956)* EMI Classics 2-▲ ZDMB 68217 [ADD]
Ravel, M.:Daphnis et Chloé (suite 2) Testament ▲ TES SBT1017 (m) [ADD]
Ravel, M.:Pavane pour une infante défunte Testament ▲ TES SBT1017 (m) [ADD]
Rossini, G.:La gazza ladra (sels)—Ov. Testament ▲ TES SBT 1034 [ADD]
Schubert, Franz:Sym 8 *(rec Kingsway Hall, London, Aug. 1955)* EMI Classics 2-▲ ZDMB 68217 [ADD]
Schubert, Franz:Sym 8 Enterprise ("Palladio" series) ▲ ENT PD 4158 [ADD]
Tchaikovsky, P.:Romeo & Juliet *(rec 1951)* Theorema ▲ TH 121139
Wagner, R.:Siegfried Idyll Enterprise ("Palladio" series) ▲ ENT PD 4158 [ADD]
A. Davis (cnd)
Beethoven, L. van:Con Vn, Op. 61, w. O. Shumsky (vn) ASV Quicksilva ▲ QS 6080 [DDD]

Philharmonia Orch (cont.)
A. Davis (cnd) (cont.)
Beethoven, L. van:Romances Vn, w. O. Shumsky (vn)—Op. 50 ASV Quicksilva ▲ QS 6080 [DDD]
Dvořák, A.:Carnival Odyssey 2-▲ MB2K 45618
Dvořák, A.:Sym 7 Odyssey 2-▲ MB2K 45618
Dvořák, A.:Sym 7 *(rec 1979)* Odyssey ▲ MBK 46277 [ADD] ■ YT 46277
Dvořák, A.:Sym 8 *(rec 1979)* Odyssey ▲ MBK 46277 [ADD] ■ YT 46277
Dvořák, A.:Sym 8 Odyssey 2-▲ MB2K 45618
Dvořák, A.:Sym 9, "From the New World" Odyssey 2-▲ MB2K 45618
Elgar, E.:Enigma Vars CBS ▲ MDK 44788 [DDD] ■ MDT 44788 (D)
Elgar, E.:Pomp & Circumstance Marches CBS ▲ MDK 44788 [DDD] ■ MDT 44788 (D)
C. Davis (cnd)
"La Bellisima":Anna Moffo, the Debut Recordings, w. Anna Moffo (sop), La Scala Orch [cnd:A. Galliera, A. Votto] *(rec 1956–59)* EMI Classics ▲ CDM 63413
Christmas with Kiri, w. Kiri Te Kanawa (sop), London Voices London ▲ 414632-2 LH [DDD]
Tippett, M.:Con Pno, w. J. Ogdon (pno) EMI Classics 2-▲ ZDMB 63522
P. Domingo (cnd)
Tchaikovsky, P.:Ov 1812 EMI Classics ▲ CDC 55018 ■ 4DS 55018
Tchaikovsky, P.:Romeo & Juliet EMI Classics ▲ CDC 55018 ■ 4DS 55018
C. Dutoit (cnd)
Franck, C.:Symphonic Vars, w. P. Entremont (pno) *(rec 1981)* Odyssey ▲ MBK 46276 [AAD]
Poulenc, F.:Con Org, w. P. Hurford (org) *(rec Feb. 24–28, 1992)* London ▲ 436546-2
Poulenc, F.:Con Pno, w. P. Rogé (pno) *(rec Feb. 24–28, 1992)* London ▲ 436546-2
Poulenc, F.:Con for 2 Pnos, w. P. Rogé (pno), Sylviane Deferne (pno) *(rec Feb. 24–28, 1992)* London ▲ 436546-2
Saint-Saëns, C.:Danse macabre London ("Jubilee" series) ▲ 425021-2 [ADD]
Saint-Saëns, C.:Danse macabre London ▲ 414460-2 [ADD] ■ 414460-4
Saint-Saëns, C.:La Jeunesse d'Hercule London ("Jubilee" series) ▲ 425021-2 [ADD]
Saint-Saëns, C.:Marche héroïque London ("Jubilee" series) ▲ 425021-2 [ADD]
Saint-Saëns, C.:Phaéton, w. C London ▲ 414460-2 [ADD] ■ 414460-4
Saint-Saëns, C.:Phaéton London ("Jubilee" series) ▲ 425021-2 [ADD]
Saint-Saëns, C.:Le Rouet d'Omphale London ("Jubilee" series) ▲ 425021-2 [ADD]
Saint-Saëns, C.:Le Rouet d'Omphale London ▲ 414460-2 [ADD] ■ 414460-4
Tchaikovsky, P.:Con 1 Pno, w. P. Devoyon (pno) Erato ▲ 92865-2
Tchaikovsky, P.:Con Vn, w. P. Amoyal (vn) Erato ▲ 45971-2
Tchaikovsky, P.:Con Vn, w. P. Amoyal (vn) Erato ▲ 92865-2
Tchaikovsky, P.:Sérénade mélancolique, w. P. Amoyal (vn) Erato ▲ 45971-2
Tchaikovsky, P.:Valse-Scherzo Vn, w. P. Amoyal (vn) Erato ▲ 45971-2
Vieuxtemps, H.:Con 5 Vn, w. Sarah Chang (vn) *(rec Henry Wood Hall, London, Dec. 22–23, 1994)* EMI Classics ▲ CDC 55292 [DDD]
V. Fedoseyev (cnd)
Tchaikovsky, P.:Concert Fant, w. M. Pletnev (pno) Virgin Classics ▲ 59612 [DDD]
Tchaikovsky, P.:Con 1 Pno, w. M. Pletnev (pno) Virgin Classics ▲ 59612 [DDD]
Tchaikovsky, P.:Con 2 Pno, w. M. Pletnev (pno) Virgin Classics ▲ CDC 59631
Tchaikovsky, P.:Con 3 Pno, w. M. Pletnev (pno) Virgin Classics ▲ CDC 59631
E. Fischer (cnd)
Bach, J.S.:Brandenburg Con 2 EMI Classics ▲ CDH 64928
Bach, J.S.:Chromatic Fant & Fugue EMI Classics ▲ CDH 64928
Bach, J.S.:Con 2 Hpd EMI Classics ▲ CDH 64928
Bach, J.S.:Con 2 for 3 Hpds EMI Classics ▲ CDH 64928
A. Fistoulari (cnd)
Granados, E.:Goyescas (sels), w. V. de los Angeles (sop)—La maja y el ruiseñor [Sp] *(rec 3/7/50)* EMI Classics ▲ CDH 64028-2 (m) [ADD]
Turina, J.:Canto a Sevilla, w. V. De Los Angeles (sop) [Sp] *(rec 10/52 & 10/53)* EMI Classics ▲ CDH 64028-2 (m) [ADD]
C. P. Flor (cnd)
Mozart, W.A.:Ave verum corpus, w. London Voices RCA Red Seal ▲ 09026-60812-2
Mozart, W.A.:Exsultate, w. Y. Kenny (sop) RCA Red Seal ▲ 09026-60812-2
Mozart, W.A.:Missa, K.317, w. Y. Kenny (sop), K. Kuhlmann (mez), K. Lewis (ten), D. Wilson-Johnson (bar), London Voices RCA Red Seal ▲ 09026-60812-2
Prokofiev, S.:Romeo & Juliet (sels) RCA Red Seal ▲ 09026-61388-2
Weber, C.M. von:Der Freischütz (ov) *(rec Watford Town Hall, Hertfordshire, England, June 29–30, 1991 & Feb. 1)* RCA Red Seal ▲ 09026-62712-2 [DDD]
Weber, C.M. von:Sym 1 *(rec Watford Town Hall, Hertfordshire, England, June 29–30, 1991 & Feb. 1)* RCA Red Seal ▲ 09026-62712-2 [DDD]
Weber, C.M. von:Sym 2 *(rec Watford Town Hall, Hertfordshire, England, June 29–30, 1991 & Feb. 1)* RCA Red Seal ▲ 09026-62712-2 [DDD]
T. R. Forrester (cnd)
Tchaikovsky, P.:Swan Lake (sels)—Lake by Moonlight Interchord ▲ INT 892.923 [AAD]
L. Foster (cnd)
Operetta Arias, w. Barbara Hendricks (sop) EMI Classics ▲ CDC 54626
A. Francis (cnd)
Finzi, G.:Con Cl, w. T. King (cl) Hyperion ▲ CDA 66001 [AAD]
Stanford, C.V.:Con Cl, w. T. King (cl) Hyperion ▲ CDA 66001 [AAD]
P. Freeman (cnd)
Mozart, W.A.:Cons Pno, w. D. Han (pno)—Nos. 3, 13 & 24 Pro Arte/Fanfare ▲ CDS 593 [DDD]
Mozart, W.A.:Cons Pno, w. D. Han (pno)—Nos. 1, 21 & 25 Pro Arte ▲ CDS 3445
Mozart, W.A.:Cons Pno, w. D. Han (pno)—Nos. 11, 15 & 23 Pro Arte/Fanfare ▲ CDS 3434 [DDD]
L. Frémaux (cnd)
Rodrigo, J.:Concierto de Aranjuez, w. J. Williams (gtr) CBS 2-▲ M2K 44791 [ADD/DDD]
Rodrigo, J.:Concierto de Aranjuez, w. J. Williams (gtr) CBS ▲ MDK 45648 [DDD] ■ MDT 45648 (D)
Rodrigo, J.:Fant para un gentilhombre, w. J. Williams (gtr) CBS 2-▲ M2K 44791 [ADD/DDD]
Rodrigo, J.:Fant para un gentilhombre, w. J. Williams (gtr) CBS ▲ MDK 45648 [DDD] ■ MDT 45648 (D)
Walton, W.:Sym 1 Collins Classics ▲ 10312 [DDD]
W. Furtwängler (cnd)
Bartók, B.:Con 2 Vn, w. Y. Menuhin (vn) *(rec 1953)* EMI Classics ▲ CDH 69804 (m) [ADD]
Beethoven, L. van:Con 5 Pno, "Emperor", w. E. Fischer (pno) EMI Classics ▲ CDH 61005 (m)
Beethoven, L. van:Con Vn, Op. 61, w. Y. Menuhin (vn) EMI Classics (Great Recordings of the Century) ▲ CDH 69799 (m) [ADD]
Beethoven, L. van:Sym 9, "Choral Sym", w. Elisabeth Schwarzkopf (sop), Elsa Cavelti (mez), Ernst Haefliger (ten), Otto Edelmann (bass), Lucerne Festival Chorus *(rec Aug 22, 1954)* Music & Arts ▲ CD 790 [ADD]
Beethoven, L. van:Sym 9, "Choral Sym" *(rec Lucerne, 1954)* Tahra ▲ FURT 1003
Mahler, G.:Lieder eines fahrenden Gesellen, w. D. Fischer-Dieskau (bar) [G] EMI Classics ▲ CDC 47657 (m) [ADD]
Wagner, R.:Ovs, Preludes & Orch Sels, Berlin PO—orchestral excerpts from *Der fliegende Hollander; Gotterdämmerung; Lohengrin; Meistersinger von Nürnberg; Parsifal; Tannhaüser; Tristan und Isolde* & the Immolation Scene from *Götterdammerung* [w. Kirsten Flagstad (soprano)] *(rec 1938–1954)* EMI Classics ▲ CDHB 64935
Wagner, R.:Ovs, Preludes & Orch Sels, Berlin PO—Der fliegende Holländer; Tannhäuser; Lohengrin; Die Meistersinger von Nürnberg; Tristan und Isolde Historical Performers ▲ HPS 4 [ADD]
A. Galliera (cnd)
Bach, J.S.:Mass in b, BWV 232, w. E. Schwarzkopf (sop), K. Ferrier (cta) EMI Classics ▲ CDM 63655
Brahms, J.:Con Vn & Vc, "Double Con", w. David Oistrakh (vn), Pierre Fournier (vc) EMI Classics 2-▲ CDFB 69331
Chopin, F.:Con 1 Pno, w. Géza Anda (pno) *(rec London 1956)* Testament ▲ SBT 1066
Grieg, E.:Con Pno, Op. 16, w. D. Lipatti (pno) *(rec 1947)* EMI Classics ▲ CDH 63497 (m) [ADD]
Grieg, E.:Con Pno, Op. 16, w. D. Lipatti (pno) Odyssey ■ YT 60141 (m)
Mozart, W.A.:Nehmt meninen Dank, w. E. Schwarzkopf (sop) EMI Classics ▲ CDM 63655

▲ = CD ♦ = Enhanced CD Δ = MD ■ = Cassette Tape ◻ = DCC

Philharmonia Orch (cont.)

A. Galliera (cnd) (cont.)

- Rachmaninoff, S.:Con 2 Pno, w. Géza Anda (pno) Testament ▲ SBT 1064
- Rachmaninoff, S.:Preludes Pno, Opp 23 & 32, w. Géza Anda (pno)—2 Preludes Testament ▲ SBT 1064
- Rossini, G.:Il barbiere di Siviglia, w. M. Callas (sop), L. Alva (ten), T. Gobbi (bar), N. Zaccaria (bass), F. Ollendorf (bass) EMI Classics ▲ ZDM 63076
- Rossini, G.:Il barbiere di Siviglia, w. M. Callas (sop), L. Alva (ten), T. Gobbi (bar) [I] *(rec 1957)* EMI Classics 2–▲ CDCB 47634 [ADD]
- Tchaikovsky, P.:Con 1 Pno, w. Géza Anda (pno) Testament ▲ SBT 1064

L. A. Garcia–Navarro (cnd)

- Rodrigo, J.:Concierto de Aranjuez, w. N. Yepes (gtr) Deutsche Grammophon ▲ 415349–2 [ADD]

J. E. Gardiner (cnd)

- Grainger, P.:The Warriors Deutsche Grammophon ▲ 445860–2
- Holst, G.:The Planets, w. Monteverdi Choir London members Deutsche Grammophon ▲ 445860–2

A. Gibson (cnd)

- Beethoven, L. van:Con 6 Pno, w. Pietro Spada (pno) ASV ▲ ASV 911 [DDD]
- Beethoven, L. van:Fant Pno, Op. 80, "Choral Fant", w. Pietro Spada (pno) ASV ▲ ASV 911 [DDD]
- Beethoven, L. van:Rondo Pno, WoO 6, w. Pietro Spada (pno) ASV ▲ ASV 911 [DDD]

C. M. Giulini (cnd)

- Beethoven, L. van:Con Vn, Op. 61, w. I. Perlman (vn) EMI Classics ▲ CDC 47002 [DDD]
- Britten, B.:Peter Grimes (4 sea interludes) EMI Classics ("Artist Profile" series) 2–▲ CDZB 67723
- Britten, B.:The Young Person's Guide to the Orchestra EMI Classics ("The Artist Profile" series) 2–▲ CDZB 67723
- Falla, M. de:El amor brujo, w. V. de los Angeles (sop) [Sp] EMI Classics ▲ CDM 64746 CDM 64746
- Falla, M. de:El sombrero de tres picos (sels)—Suite EMI Classics ▲ CDM 64746 CDM 64746
- Fauré, G.:Requiem, w. K. Battle (sop), A. Schmidt (bar), Philharmonia Chorus [L] Deutsche Grammophon ▲ 419243–2 [DDD]
- Franck, C.:Psyché et Eros EMI Classics ("Artist Profile" series) 2–▲ CDZB 67723
- Franck, C.:Sym in d EMI Classics ("Artist Profile" series) 2–▲ CDZB 67723
- Grieg, E.:Con Pno, Op. 16, w. A. Rubinstein (pno) *(rec live Royal Festival Hall)* Intaglio ▲ INCD 7101 [ADD]
- Mad About Angels, w. Cheryl Studer (sop), Christa Ludwig (mez), Anne Sofie von Otter (mez), José Carreras (ten), New York PO [cnd:Leonard Bernstein], English Baroque Soloists [cnd:John Eliot Gardiner], Philharmonia Chorus, et al. Deutsche Grammophon ▲ 449113–2 ■ 449113–4
- Mozart, W.A.:Con 20 Pno, w. A. Rubinstein (pno) Intaglio ▲ INCD 7101 [ADD]
- Mozart, W.A.:Don Giovanni (sels), w. E. Schwarzkopf (sop), G. Sciutti (sop), J. Sutherland (sop), L. Alva (ten), E. Wächter (bar) EMI Classics ▲ ZDM 63078
- Mozart, W.A.:Nozze di Figaro, w. A. Moffo (sop), E. Schwarzkopf (sop), F. Cossotto (mez), G. Taddei (bar), E. Wächter (bar), Philharmonia Chorus [I] EMI Classics ("Studio" series) 2–▲ CDMB 63266 [ADD]
- Mozart, W.A.:Nozze di Figaro (sels), w. A. Moffo (sop), E. Schwarzkopf (sop), F. Cossotto (mez), G. Taddei (bar), E. Wächter (bar), Philharmonia Chorus—sels. EMI Classics ("Studio" series) ▲ CDM 63409
- Ravel, M.:Alborada del gracioso EMI Classics ("The Artist Profile" series) 2–▲ CDZB 67723
- Ravel, M.:Daphnis et Chloé (suite 2) EMI Classics ("The Artist Profile" series) 2–▲ CDZB 67723
- Ravel, M.:Pavane pour une infante défunte Deutsche Grammophon ▲ 419243–2 [DDD]
- Rossini, G.:La gazza ladra (ov) EMI Classics ("Encore" series) ▲ CDE 68308 [ADD/DDD]
- Rossini, G.:Ovs—Barber of Seville; La Cenerentola; La gazza ladra; L'Italiana in Algeri; Scala di seta; Semiramide; Il Signor Bruschino; William Tell EMI Classics ("Studio" series) ▲ CDM 69042
- Schumann, R.:Manfred Ov EMI Classics ("The Artist Profile" series) 2–▲ CDZB 67723
- Tchaikovsky, P.:Sym 2 EMI Classics ("The Artist Profile" series) 2–▲ CDZB 67723
- Verdi, G.:Requiem Mass, w. E. Schwarzkopf (sop), C. Ludwig (mez), N. Gedda (ten), N. Ghiaurov (bass), London Phil Choir [L] EMI Classics 2–▲ CDCB 47257 [ADD]
- Verdi, G.:quattro pezzi sacri, w. J. Baker (sop), London Phil Choir [I,L] EMI Classics 2–▲ CDCB 47257 [ADD]

Giulini, Muti (cnd)

- Rossini, G.:Ovs—Il barbiere di Siviglia; La Cenerentola; La gazza ladra; Semiramide *(rec 1958–89)* EMI Classics 2–▲ CZS 67440–2 [ADD/DDD]

F. Glushchenko (cnd)

- Chopin, F.:Con 1 Pno, w. Martino Tirimo (pno) Conifer Classics ▲ 75605–51247–2 [DDD]
- Chopin, F.:Con 2 Pno, w. Martino Tirimo (pno) Conifer Classics ▲ 75605–51247–2 [DDD]

A. Greenwood (cnd)

- Dival:A Soprano at the Movies, w. Lesley Garrett (sop) Silva America ▲ SIL 1007 [DDD] ■ SSC 1007 (D)

C. Groves (cnd)

- Britten, B.:The Young Person's Guide to the Orchestra, w. M. Flanders (nar), Royal Liverpool PO [cnd:Kurtz] EMI Classics ▲ CDM 63177
- Elgar, E.:Pomp & Circumstance Marches *(rec live in concert)* Denon ▲ CO 73534
- Elgar, E.:Salut d'amour *(rec live in concert)* Denon ▲ CO 73534
- Kabalevsky, D.:The Comedians *(rec live)* Denon ▲ CO 73534
- Saint-Saëns, C.:Carnival of the Animals *(rec live in concert)* Denon ▲ CO 73534

C. M. Guilini (cnd)

- Mozart, W.A.:Requiem, w. L. Dawson (sop), J. van Nes (cta), K. Lewis (ten), S. Estes (bass), Philharmonia Chorus [L] Sony Classical ▲ SK 45577 [DDD]

P. Hindemith (cnd)

- Hindemith, P.:Concert Music Brass & Strs EMI Classics 2–▲ ZDCB 55032
- Hindemith, P.:Con Cl, w. L. Cahuzac (cl) EMI Classics 2–▲ ZDCB 55032
- Hindemith, P.:Con Hn, w. D. Brain (hn) EMI Classics 2–▲ ZDCB 55032
- Hindemith, P.:Nobilissima visione EMI Classics 2–▲ ZDCB 55032
- Hindemith, P.:Symphonia serena EMI Classics 2–▲ ZDCB 55032

H. Holliger (cnd)

- Berg, A.:Con Vn, w. Thomas Zehetmair (vn) Teldec ("M Line" series) ▲ 97449–2
- Hartmann, K.A.:Con funèbre, w. Thomas Zehetmair (vn) Teldec ("M Line" series) ▲ 97449–2
- Janácek, L.:Con Vn, w. Thomas Zehetmair (vn) Teldec ("M Line" series) ▲ 97449–2
- Janácek, L.:Con Vn, w. T. Zehetmair (vn) Teldec ▲ 2292–46449–2 ZK

D. Honeyball (cnd)

- Bourgeois, D.:William & Mary Suite, w. London Brass Virtuosi Hyperion ▲ CDA 66870
- Elgar, E.:Sursum corda, w. London Brass Virtuosi Hyperion ▲ CDA 66870
- Hindemith, P.:Concert Music Brass & Strs, w. London Brass Virtuosi Hyperion ▲ CDA 66870
- Patterson, P.:Brussels Fanfare, w. London Brass Virtuosi Hyperion ▲ CDA 66870
- Patterson, P.:Eurostar Fanfare, w. London Brass Virtuosi Hyperion ▲ CDA 66870
- Patterson, P.:Paris Fanfare, w. London Brass Virtuosi Hyperion ▲ CDA 66870
- Patterson, P.:The Royal Eurostar, w. London Brass Virtuosi Hyperion ▲ CDA 66870
- Strauss, R.:Feierlicher Einzug der Ritter des Johanniter-Ordens, w. London Brass Virtuosi Hyperion ▲ CDA 66870

E. Howarth (cnd)

- Birtwistle, H.:Gawain's Journey Collins Classics ▲ COL 1387 [DDD]
- Birtwistle, H.:The Triumph of Time Collins Classics ▲ COL 1387 [DDD]

O. A. Hughes (cnd)

- Elgar, E.:Cockaigne ASV Quicksilva ▲ QS 6082 [ADD/DDD]
- Elgar, E.:Cockaigne ASV ("Quicksilva" series) ▲ ASQ 6162 [DDD]
- Vaughan Williams, R.:Sym 2 ASV ("Quicksilva" series) ▲ ASQ 6162 [DDD]

E. Inbal (cnd)

- Beethoven, L. van:Con Vn, Vc & Pno, "Triple Con", Fontenay Trio Teldec ("M Line" series) ▲ 97447–2
- Beethoven, L. van:Con Vn, Vc & Pno, "Triple Con", Fontenay Trio Teldec ▲ 2292–46441–2 ZK
- Brahms, J.:Con 1 Pno, w. Elisabeth Leonskaja (pno) Teldec ("M Line" series) ▲ 97450–2
- Brahms, J.:Con 2 Pno, w. C. Katsaris (pno) Teldec ("Digital Experience" series) ▲ 9031–77599–2 AW [DDD]
- Dvořák, A.:The Golden Spinning Wheel Teldec ▲ 9031–72305–2 ZK

Philharmonia Orch (cont.)

E. Inbal (cnd) (cont.)

- Dvořák, A.:Sym 7 Teldec ▲ 2292–46460–2 ZK
- Dvořák, A.:Sym 7 Teldec 2–▲ 95497–2
- Dvořák, A.:Sym 8 Teldec 2–▲ 95497–2
- Dvořák, A.:Sym 8 Teldec ▲ 9031–72305–2 ZK
- Dvořák, A.:Sym 9, "From the New World" Teldec 2–▲ 95497–2
- Dvořák, A.:Sym 9, "From the New World" Teldec ▲ 4509–91447–2
- Dvořák, A.:The Water Goblin Teldec ▲ 2292–46460–2 ZK
- Dvořák, A.:The Wild Dove Teldec ▲ 4509–91447–2
- Rachmaninoff, S.:Con 3 Pno, w. B. Berezovsky (pno) Teldec ▲ 9031–73797–2 ZK
- Stravinsky, I.:Pétrouchka Teldec 2–▲ 95496–2
- Stravinsky, I.:Le Sacre du printemps Orch Teldec 2–▲ 95496–2
- Stravinsky, I.:Le Sacre du printemps Orch Teldec ▲ 4509–91449–2
- Stravinsky, I.:Scherzo à la russe Teldec ▲ 4509–91449–2
- Stravinsky, I.:Studies Orch Teldec ▲ 4509–91449–2

M. Janowski (cnd)

- Wagner, R.:Tannhäuser (sels), w. K. Te Kanawa (sop), R. Kollo (ten), Håkan Hagegård (bar), W. Meier (mez), M. Holle (bass), Ambrosian Singers; music from film soundtrack for Meeting Venus Teldec ▲ 2292 46336–2 [DDD] ■ 2292 46336–4 □ 2292 46336–5
- Wagner, R.:Tannhäuser (sels), w. K. Te Kanawa (sop), W. Meier (mez), R. Kollo (ten), H. Hagegard (bar), Ambrosian Singers Teldec ▲ 46336–2 ■ 46336–4

M. Jansons (cnd)

- Prokofiev, S.:Con 2 Vn, w. F. P. Zimmerman (vn) EMI Classics ▲ CDC 54454
- Rachmaninoff, S.:Sym 2 Chandos ▲ CHAN 8520 [DDD]
- Sibelius, J.:Con Vn, w. F. P. Zimmerman (vn) EMI Classics ▲ CDC 54454

N. Järvi (cnd)

- Bartók, B.:Hungarian Sketches Chandos ▲ CHAN 8895 [DDD]
- Bartók, B.:The Miraculous Mandarin, w. London Voices *(rec 10/90)* Chandos ▲ CHAN 9029 [DDD]
- Bartók, B.:The Miraculous Mandarin (suite) [arr. by Järvi] Chandos ▲ CHAN 9133 [DDD]
- Bartók, B.:The Wooden Prince Chandos ▲ CHAN 8895 [DDD]
- Bartók, B.:The Wooden Prince [arr. by Järvi] Chandos ▲ CHAN 9133 [DDD]
- Chopin, F.:Con 2 Pno, w. L. Lortie (pno) Chandos ▲ CHAN 9061 [DDD]
- Hindemith, P.:Symphonic Metamorphosis on Themes of Carl Maria von Weber Chandos ▲ CHAN 8766 [DDD]
- Pärt, A.:Collage on the Theme B–A–C–H, w. *(soloists unknown)*, B. Berman (pno) Chandos ▲ CHAN 9134 [DDD]
- Pärt, A.:Credo, w. B. Berman (pno), Philharmonia Chorus Chandos ▲ CHAN 9134 [DDD]
- Pärt, A.:Festina lente Chandos ▲ CHAN 9134 [DDD]
- Pärt, A.:Fratres I Chandos ▲ CHAN 9134 [DDD]
- Pärt, A.:Summa Chandos ▲ CHAN 9134 [DDD]
- Pärt, A.:Sym 2 Chandos ▲ CHAN 9134 [DDD]
- Pärt, A.:Wenn Bach Bienen gezüchtet hätte, w. B. Berman (pno) Chandos ▲ CHAN 9134 [DDD]
- Prokofiev, S.:Cantata for the 20th Aniversary of the October Revolution, w. G. Rozhdestvensky (nar), Philharmonia Chorus Chandos ▲ CHAN 9095 [DDD]
- Prokofiev, S.:Ivan the Terrible Cta, w. L. Finnie (mez), N. Storojev (bass), Philharmonia Chorus Chandos ▲ CHAN 8977 [DDD]
- Prokofiev, S.:Russian Ov Chandos ▲ CHAN 9096 [DDD]
- Prokofiev, S.:Summer Night Chandos ▲ CHAN 9096 [DDD]
- Prokofiev, S.:The Tale of the Stone Flower—7 sels. Chandos ▲ CHAN 9095 [DDD]
- Prokofiev, S.:War & Peace (suite) Chandos ▲ CHAN 9096 [DDD]
- Rachmaninoff, S.:Aleko (sels)—Women's Dance & Men's Dance Chandos ▲ CHAN 9081 [DDD]
- Rachmaninoff, S.:Capriccio bohémien Chandos ▲ CHAN 9081 [DDD]
- Rachmaninoff, S.:Symphonic Dances Chandos ▲ CHAN 9081 [DDD]
- Schumann, R.:Con Pno, w. L. Lortie (pno) Chandos ▲ CHAN 9061 [DDD]
- Taneyev, S.:The Oresteia (ov) Chandos ▲ CHAN 8953 [DDD]
- Taneyev, S.:Sym 4 Chandos ▲ CHAN 8953 [DDD]
- Tchaikovsky, P.:Con 1 Pno, w. C. Orbelian (pno) Chandos ▲ CHAN 8777 [DDD]
- Tchaikovsky, P.:Suite 4 Chandos ▲ CHAN 8777 [DDD]
- Weber, C.M. von:Ovs—Abu Hassan; Der Beherrscher der Geister; Euryanthe; Der Freischütz; Jubel–Ouvertüre; Oberon; Peter Schmoll; Preciosa; Silvana; Turandot Overture & March Chandos ▲ CHAN 9066 [DDD]
- Weber, C.M. von:Ovs—Der Beherrscher der Geister; Euryanthe; Der Freischütz; Oberon; Turandot Overture & March Chandos ▲ CHAN 8766 [DDD]
- Weiner, L.:Hungarian Folkdance Suite, w. London Voices Chandos ▲ CHAN 9029 [DDD]

A. Joó (cnd)

- Strauss, R.:Ein Heldenleben, w. Christopher Warren-Green (vn) *(rec London, June 1984)* Arts ▲ 47240–2 [DDD]
- Strauss, R.:Der Rosenkavalier (suite), w. Christopher Warren-Green (vn) *(rec London, June 1984)* Arts ▲ 47240–2 [DDD]
- Tchaikovsky, P.:Sym 5 *(rec London, Apr 1983 & June 1986)* Arts Music ▲ 47241–2 [DDD]

H. von Karajan (cnd)

- Balakirev, M.:Sym 1 Enterprise ▲ ENTPD 4110 [ADD]
- Beethoven, L. van:Coriolan Ov EMI Classics ("Studio" series) 5–▲ CDME 63310 (m/s) [ADD]
- Beethoven, L. van:Egmont (ov)—[soloists in No. 9:Schwarzkopf, Höffgen, Haefliger, Edelmann; & Vienna Singverein] *(rec Kingsway Hall, London & Musikvereinssaal, Vienna 1951–1955)* EMI Classics ("Studio" series) 5–▲ CDME 63310 (m/s) [ADD]
- Beethoven, L. van:Syms (comp)—[soloists in No. 9:Schwarzkopf, Höffgen, Haefliger, Edelmann; & Vienna Singverein] *(rec Kingsway Hall, London & Musikvereinssaal, Vienna 1951–1955)* EMI Classics ("Studio" series) 5–▲ CDME 63310 (m/s) [ADD]
- Grieg, E.:Con Pno, Op. 16, w. W. Gieseking (pno) *(rec 1951)* Enterprise ("Palladio" series) ▲ ENT 4178 [ADD]
- Humperdinck, E.:Hänsel und Gretel, w. E. Schwarzkopf (sop), E. Grümmer (sop), A. Felbermayer (sop), M. von Ilosvay (mez), E. Schürhoff (mez), J. Metternich (bar), Loughton High School Chorus, Bancroft's School Chorus [G] *(rec 1953)* EMI Classics ("Studio" series) 2–▲ CDMB 69293 (m) [ADD]
- Mozart, W.A.:Cons Hn, w. D. Brain (hn) EMI Classics ("Great Recordings of the Century" series) ▲ CDH 61013 (m)
- Mozart, W.A.:Così fan tutte, w. E. Schwarzkopf (sop), L. Otto (sop), N. Merriman (mez), L. Simoneau (ten), R. Panerai (bar), S. Bruscantini (bar), Philharmonia Chorus [I] EMI Classics ("Studio" series) 3–▲ CDHC 69635 (m) [ADD]
- Mozart, W.A.:Così fan tutte (sels), w. Lisa Otto (sop), Elizabeth Schwarzkopf (sop), Nan Merriman (mez), Rolando Panerai (bar), Leopold Simoneau (ten), Sesto Bruscantini (bass) Classics for Pleasure ("Eminence" series) ▲ CDEMX 2211 [DDD]
- Mozart, W.A.:Sinf Concertante Vn Va *(rec London, 1953)* Testament ▲ SBT 1091
- Rossini, G.:Ovs—The Italian Girl in Algiers; Semiramide; The Barber of Seville; William Tell; The Silken Ladder; The Thieving Magpie EMI Classics ▲ CDM 63113
- Schwarzkopf & Seefried, Duets, w. Elisabeth Schwarzkopf (sop), Irmgard Seefried (sop), Gerald Moore (pno) EMI Classics ▲ CDH 69793
- Sibelius, J.:Tapiola Enterprise ▲ ENTPD 4110 [ADD]
- Strauss (II), Joh.:Die Fledermaus, w. E. Schwarzkopf (sop), R. Streich (sop), N. Gedda (ten), H. Krebs (ten), R. Christ (ten), E. Kunz (bar), K. Dönch (bar), Philharmonia Chorus [G] EMI Classics ("Studio" series) 2–▲ CDHB 69531 (m) [ADD]
- Strauss, R.:Ariadne auf Naxos, w. Elisabeth Schwarzkopf (sop—Ariadne/Prima Donna), Irmgard Seefried (sop—Zerbinetta), Rita Streich (sop—The Composer), Rudolf Schock (ten—Bacchus) EMI Classics 2–▲ CDCB 55176
- Strauss, R.:Ariadne auf Naxos, w. E. Schwarzkopf (sop), I. Seefried (sop), R. Streich (sop), L. Otto (sop), G. Hoffman (mez), R. Schock (ten), G. Unger (ten), H. Cuénod (ten), H. Prey (bar), F. Ollendorff (bass) [G] *(rec 1954)* EMI Classics ("Studio" series) 2–▲ CDMB 69296 (m) [ADD]
- Strauss, R.:4 Last Songs, w. E. Schwarzkopf (sop) EMI Classics ▲ CDM 63655

Philharmonia Orch (cont.)
H. von Karajan (cnd) (cont.)
Strauss, R.:Der Rosenkavalier, w. E. Schwarzkopf (sop), T. Stich-Randall (sop), C. Ludwig (mez), O. Edelmann (bass) [G] EMI Classics 3-▲ CDCC 49354 [ADD] 3-■ 3CDX 3970
Strauss, R.:Der Rosenkavalier, w. Elisabeth Schwarzkopf (sop), Christa Ludwig (mez), Teresa Stich-Randall (mez), Otto Edelmann (b-bar), Philharmonia Chorus *(rec 1956)* EMI Classics ▲ CDCC 56113 (m)
Strauss, R.:Der Rosenkavalier (sels), w. E. Schwarzkopf (sop), T. Stich-Randall (mez), C. Ludwig (mez), O. Edelmann (bass), Philharmonia Chorus EMI Classics ▲ ZDM 63452
J. Kaspszyk (cnd)
Franck, C.:Le Chasseur maudit *(rec 7/90)* Collins Classics ▲ 11582 [DDD]
Franck, C.:Symphonic Vars, w. S. Tanyel (pno) *(rec 9/90)* Collins Classics ▲ 11582 [DDD]
Franck, C.:Sym in d *(rec 7/90)* Collins Classics ▲ 11582 [DDD]
Mahler, G.:Blumine Collins Quest ▲ COL 3005 [DDD]
A. Khachaturian (cnd)
Khachaturian, A.:Con Vn, w. D. Oistrakh (vn) EMI Classics ▲ CDC 55035
Khachaturian, A.:Gayane (suites)—Sabre Dance; Lezghinka EMI Classics ▲ CDC 55035
Khachaturian, A.:Masquerade (ballet suite)—Nocturne EMI Classics ▲ CDC 55035
O. Klemperer (cnd)
Bach, J.S.:St. Matthew Passion, w. E. Schwarzkopf (sop), C. Ludwig (mez), N. Gedda (ten), S. Fischer-Dieskau (bar), W. Berry (bass) EMI Classics 3-▲ ZDMC 63058
Beethoven, L. van:Con Vn, Op. 61, w. Y. Menuhin (vn) EMI Classics ▲ CDM 64324
Beethoven, L. van:Coriolan Ov *(rec Vienna, 1960)* Music & Arts 5-▲ CD 886 [ADD]
Beethoven, L. van:Egmont (ov) Arkadia ▲ 757
Beethoven, L. van:Egmont (ov) *(rec Vienna, 1960)* Music & Arts 5-▲ CD 886 [ADD]
Beethoven, L. van:Fidelio, w. Ingeborg Hallstein (sop—Marzelline), Christa Ludwig (mez—Leonore/Fidelio), Gerhard Unger (ten—Jaquino), Jon Vickers (ten—Florestan), Walter Berry (bass—Pizarro), Franz Crass (bass—Don Fernando), Gottlob Frick (bass—Rocco), Philharmonia Chorus EMI Classics 2-▲ CDCB 55170
Beethoven, L. van:Fidelio, w. I. Hallstein (sop), C. Ludwig (mez), J. Vickers (ten), G. Unger (ten), W. Berry (bass), G. Frick (bass), Philharmonia Chorus [G]; w. minimal dialog EMI Classics ("Studio" series) 2-▲ CDMB 69324 [ADD]
Beethoven, L. van:Die Geschöpfe des Prometheus (ov) Arkadia ▲ 757
Beethoven, L. van:Die Geschöpfe des Prometheus (ov) *(rec Vienna, 1960)* Music & Arts 5-▲ CD 886 [ADD]
Beethoven, L. van:Leonore 1 *(rec ca. 1960)* EMI Classics ▲ CDM 64143
Beethoven, L. van:Leonore 2 *(rec 1954/55)* EMI Classics ▲ CDM 63855 (m)
Beethoven, L. van:Leonore 3 *(rec 1954/55)* EMI Classics ▲ CDM 63855 (m)
Beethoven, L. van:Ovs—Prometheus; Egmont *(rec live, 1960)* Originals ▲ ORISH 823 [ADD]
Beethoven, L. van:Syms (comp) EMI Classics 7-▲ CDZG 68057
Beethoven, L. van:Syms (comp) *(rec Vienna, 1960)* Music & Arts 5-▲ CD 886 [ADD]
Beethoven, L. van:Sym 3, "Eroica" *(rec 1954/55)* EMI Classics ▲ CDM 63855 (m)
Beethoven, L. van:Sym 4 Arkadia ▲ 757
Beethoven, L. van:Sym 5 *(rec 1955)* EMI Classics ▲ CDM 63868 (m)
Beethoven, L. van:Sym 7 *(rec 1955)* EMI Classics ▲ CDM 63868 (m)
Beethoven, L. van:Sym 8 Arkadia ▲ 757
Beethoven, L. van:Sym 9, "Choral Sym", w. W. Lipp (sop), F. Wunderlich (ten), F. Crass (bass), Vienna Singverein Arkadia ▲ 759
Berlioz, H.:Sym fantastique *(rec ca. 1964)* EMI Classics ▲ CDM 64143
Brahms, J.:Academic Festival Ov EMI Classics ("Studio" series) ▲ CDM 69651 [ADD]
Brahms, J.:Alto Rhap, w. C. Ludwig (mez), Philharmonia Chorus [G] EMI Classics ("Studio" series) ▲ CDM 69650 [ADD]
Brahms, J.:Ein Deutsches Requiem, w. E. Schwarzkopf (sop), D. Fischer-Dieskau (bar), Philharmonia Chorus [G] EMI Classics 2-▲ CDC 47238
Brahms, J.:Sym 1 EMI Classics ("Studio" series) ▲ CDM 69651 [ADD]
Brahms, J.:Sym 2 EMI Classics ("Studio" series) ▲ CDM 69650 [ADD]
Brahms, J.:Sym 3 EMI Classics ("Studio" series) ▲ CDM 69649 [ADD]
Brahms, J.:Sym 4 EMI Classics ("Studio" series) ▲ CDM 69649 [ADD]
Brahms, J.:Tragic Ov EMI Classics ("Studio" series) ▲ CDM 69651 [ADD]
Bruckner, A.:Sym 5 EMI Classics ("Studio" series) ▲ CDM 63612 [ADD]
Dvořák, A.:Sym 9, "From the New World" EMI Classics ▲ CDM 63869
Gluck, C.W.:Iphigénie en Aulide EMI Classics ▲ CDM 64143
Handel, G.F.:Messiah, w. Elisabeth Schwarzkopf (sop), Grace Hoffman (cta), Nikolai Gedda (ten), Jerome Hines (bass), Philharmonia Chorus EMI Classics 3-▲ ZDMC 63621
Liszt, F.:Con 1 Pno, w. A. Fischer (pno) *(rec ca. 1963)* EMI Classics ▲ CDM 64144
Mahler, G.:Das Lied von der Erde, w. C. Ludwig (mez), F. Wunderlich (ten) [G] EMI Classics ▲ CDC 47231
Mahler, G.:Songs, w. C. Ludwig (mez)—Ich bin der Welt abhanden gekommen; Um Mitternacht; Das irdische Leben; Ich atmet' einen Lindenduft; Wo die schönen Trompeten blasen [G] EMI Classics ("Studio" series) ▲ CDM 69499 [ADD]
Mahler, G.:Songs from Rückert, w. C. Ludwig (mez)—3 songs EMI Classics ("Studio" series) ▲ CDM 69499 [ADD]
Mahler, G.:Sym 2, w. E. Schwarzkopf (sop), H. Rössl-Majdan (mez), Philharmonia Chorus [G] EMI Classics ("Studio" series) ▲ CDM 69662 [ADD]
Mahler, G.:Sym 4, w. E. Schwarzkopf (sop) EMI Classics ▲ CDM 69667
Mahler, G.:Sym 7 *(rec ca. 1969)* EMI Classics 2-▲ CDMB 64147
Mendelssohn, F.:A Midsummer Night's Dream (comp), w. H. Harper (sop), J. Baker (mez), Philharmonia Chorus *(rec ca. 1961)* EMI Classics ▲ CDM 64144
Mendelssohn, F.:Sym 3 EMI Classics ▲ CDM 63853
Mendelssohn, F.:Sym 4 EMI Classics ▲ CDM 63853
Mozart, W.A.:Sym 25 EMI Classics ("Studio" series) 4-▲ CDMD 63272 [ADD]
Mozart, W.A.:Sym 35 EMI Classics ("Studio" series) 4-▲ CDMD 63272 [ADD]
Mozart, W.A.:Sym 36 EMI Classics ("Studio" series) 4-▲ CDMD 63272 [ADD]
Mozart, W.A.:Sym 38 EMI Classics ("Studio" series) 4-▲ CDMD 63272 [ADD]
Mozart, W.A.:Sym 39 EMI Classics ("Studio" series) 4-▲ CDMD 63272 [ADD]
Mozart, W.A.:Sym 40 EMI Classics ("Studio" series) 4-▲ CDMD 63272 [ADD]
Mozart, W.A.:Sym 41 EMI Classics ("Studio" series) 4-▲ CDMD 63272 [ADD]
Mozart, W.A.:Zauberflöte, w. Gundula Janowitz (sop—Pamina), Lucia Popp (sop—Queen of the Night), Nicolai Gedda (ten—Tamina), Walter Berry (bass—Papageno), Gottlob Frick (bass—Sarastro), Philharmonia Chorus EMI Classics 2-▲ CDCB 55173
Mozart, W.A.:Zauberflöte, w. G. Janowitz (sop), L. Popp (sop), R. Pütz (sop), N. Gedda (ten), W. Berry (bass), G. Frick (bass), Philharmonia Chorus [without dialog; G] EMI Classics ("Studio" series) 2-▲ CDMB 69971 [ADD]
Schubert, Franz:Sym 9 EMI Classics ▲ CDM 63854
Schumann, R.:Syms (comp), New Philharmonia Orch EMI Classics ("Studio" series) 2-▲ CDMB 63613 [ADD]
Strauss (II), Joh.:Ovs—Die Fledermaus *(rec ca. 1962)* EMI Classics ▲ CDM 64144
Tchaikovsky, P.:Sym 5 EMI Classics 2-▲ CDMB 63838
Tchaikovsky, P.:Sym 6 EMI Classics 2-▲ CDMB 63838
P. Kletzki (cnd)
Berg, A.:Con Vn, w. Andre Gertler (vn) Hungaroton ▲ HCD 31635
Borodin, A.:Sym 2 Testament ▲ TESSBT 1048 [ADD]
Chopin, F.:Con 1 Pno, w. M. Pollini (pno) EMI Classics ▲ CDM 64354 [ADD]
Mahler, G.:Das Lied von der Erde, w. L. Popp (sop), J. Baker (mez), M. Dickie (ten), D. Fischer-Dieskau (bar), B. Weikl (bar) EMI Classics ▲ CDZB 62707
Sibelius, J.:Sym 1 Testament ▲ TESSBT 1049 [ADD]
Sibelius, J.:Sym 3 Testament ▲ TESSBT 1049 [ADD]
Tchaikovsky, P.:Manfred Testament ▲ TESSBT 1048 [ADD]

Philharmonia Orch (cont.)
Krips (cnd)
Opera Arias, w. Maria Cebotari (sop), Vienna PO [cnd:Karajan], Vienna PO [cnd:Prohaska], et al. *(rec ca. 1934-1949)* Preiser ▲ PRE 90034 (m) [AAD]
E. Krivine (cnd)
Mozart, W.A.:Sym 25 Denon ▲ CO 76103 [DDD]
Mozart, W.A.:Sym 36 Denon ▲ CO 74176 [DDD]
Mozart, W.A.:Sym 38 Denon ▲ CO 74176 [DDD]
Mozart, W.A.:Sym 40 Denon ▲ CO 76103 [DDD]
Mussorgsky, M.:Night Denon ▲ CO 77068 [DDD]
Rimsky-Korsakov, N.:Scheherazade Denon ▲ CO 77068 [DDD]
R. Kubelik (cnd)
Beethoven, L. van:Con Vn, Op. 61, w. Ida Haendel (vn) *(rec 1951)* Testament ▲ SBT 1083
Bruch, M.:Con 1 Vn, w. Ida Haendel (vn) *(rec 1948)* Testament ▲ SBT 1083
Dvořák, A.:Sym 7 *(rec 1953)* Testament ▲ SBT 1079
Dvořák, A.:Sym 8 *(rec 1949)* Testament ▲ SBT 1079
E. Kurtz (cnd)
Mozart, W.A.:Con 1 Fl, w. Elaine Shaffer (fl) Royal Classics ▲ ROY 6450
Prokofiev, S.:Peter & the Wolf, w. M. Flanders (nar) EMI Classics ▲ CDM 63177
Saint-Saëns, C.:Carnival of the Animals, w. M. Flanders (nar) EMI Classics ▲ CDM 63177
Shostakovich, D.:The Golden Age *(rec 1956)* Testament ▲ SBT 1078
Shostakovich, D.:Sym 10 *(rec 1956)* Testament ▲ SBT 1078
C. Lambert (cnd)
Liszt, F.:Apparitions d'après Lamartine—Cave Scene; Galop [both arr Jacob] Time Machine ▲ 0099
Waldteufel, E.:Waltzes, Polkas & Galops—Sur la plage, Op. 234 Time Machine ▲ 0099
J. Lanchbery (cnd)
Ketèlbey, A.W.:Music of, w. J. Temperley (mez), V. Mdegley (ten), L. Pearson (pno), Ambrosian Singers—In a Persian Market; In a Monastery Garden; Chal Romano; In the Mystic Land of Egypt; The Clock and the Dresden Figures; Bells across the Meadows; In a Chinese Temple; In the Moonlight; Sanctuary of the Heart Classics for Pleasure ▲ CDCFP 4637 [ADD]
Tchaikovsky, P.:The Nutcracker (sels) EMI Classics (DDD Midline) ▲ CDD 64109 [DDD]
Tchaikovsky, P.:Sleeping Beauty (sels) EMI Classics (DDD Midline) ▲ CDD 64109 [DDD]
Tchaikovsky, P.:Swan Lake, w. C. Warren-Green (vn) Classics for Pleasure 2-▲ CDCFP 4727 [DDD]
Tchaikovsky, P.:Swan Lake (sels) EMI Classics (DDD Midline) ▲ CDD 64109 [DDD]
M. Legrand (cnd)
Duruflé, M.:Requiem, w. B. Bonney (sop), J. Larmore (mez), T. Hampson (b-bar), Ambrosian Singers Teldec ▲ 90879-2
Fauré, G.:Requiem, w. B. Bonney (sop), J. Larmore (mez), T. Hampson (b-bar), Ambrosian Singers Teldec ▲ 90879-2
E. Leinsdorf (cnd)
Brahms, J.:Sym 3 EMI Classics ▲ CDM 65612
Cornelius, P.:Der Barbier von Bagdad, w. E. Schwarzkopf (sop), G. Hoffman (cta), N. Gedda (ten), G. Unger (ten), O. Czerwenka (bass), Philharmonia Chorus EMI Classics ▲ CDMB 65284
Strauss, R.:Die Frau ohne Schatten (sels), Concert Arts SO—Interludes EMI Classics ▲ CDM 65613
Strauss, R.:Till Eulenspiegels lustige Streiche, Concert Arts SO EMI Classics ▲ CDM 65613
Y. Levi (cnd)
Rachmaninoff, S.:Études-tableaux, Opp. 33 & 39, w. M. Tirimo (pno) Classics for Pleasure ▲ CDCFP 9017 [DDD]
Rachmaninoff, S.:Rhapsody on a Theme of Paganini, w. M. Tirimo (pno) Classics for Pleasure ▲ CDCFP 9017 [DDD]
J. Levine (cnd)
Cilea, F.:Adriana Lecouvreur, w. R. Scotto (sop), E. Obraztsova (mez), P. Domingo (ten), S. Milnes (bar) *(rec 1977)* CBS 2-▲ M2K 34588 [ADD]
Puccini, G.:Tosca, w. R. Scotto (sop), P. Domingo (ten), R. Bruson (bar), Ambrosian Opera Chorus [I] EMI Classics 2-▲ CDCB 49364 [DDD]
Puccini, G.:Tosca (sels), w. R. Scotto (sop), P. Domingo (ten), R. Bruson (bar), Ambrosian Opera Chorus EMI Classics ▲ CDC 54324
Pure Domingo, w. Plácido Domingo (ten), English CO [cnd:Julius Rudel], Madrid SO [cnd:Manuel Moreno-Buendia], Munich RSO [cnd:Eugene Kohn], National PO [cnd:Eugene Kohn], New Philharmonia Orch [cnds:Bruno Bartoletti, Riccardo Muti] Angel ▲ CDC 55616 [DDD/ADD]
Litton, Lewis (cnd)
Classical Ecstasy—Classics for a New Age, w. Chicago SO [cnd:Georg Solti], English CO [cnd:Alexander Schneider], London PO [cnd:Leonard Slatkin], Philadelphia Orch [cnd:James Levine], RCA Italiana Opera Orch [cnd:Francesco Molinari-Pradelli], RCA RCA Gold Seal ▲ 74321-23041-2 [ADD/DDD]
G. Lloyd (cnd)
Lloyd, G.:John Socman (sels), w. J. Watson (sop), D. Montague (mez), T. Booth (ten), D. Wilson-Johnson (bar), M. Rivers (bar), M. George (bass), London Voices Albany ▲ TROY 131 [DDD]
Lloyd, G.:A Litany, w. Janice Watson (sop), Jeremy White (bar), Guildford Choral Society *(rec Watford Town Hall, Mar 24-25, 1996)* Albany ▲ TROY 200 [DDD]
J. López-Cobos (cnd)
Rossini, G.:Otello, w. F. von Stade (mez), J. Carreras (ten), S. Fisichella (ten), S. Ramey (bass), Ambrosian Opera Chorus [I] Philips 2-▲ 432456-2 [ADD]
J. Loughran (cnd)
Saint-Saëns, C.:Con 2 Pno, w. I. Biret (pno) Naxos ▲ 8.550334 [DDD]
Saint-Saëns, C.:Con 4 Pno, w. I. Biret (pno) Naxos ▲ 8.550334 [DDD]
L. Maazel (cnd)
Puccini, G.:Madama Butterfly, w. R. Scotto (sop), P. Domingo (ten), I. Wixell (bar), Ambrosian Singers [I] CBS 2-▲ M2K 35181 [AAD]
Puccini, G.:Il trittico, w. R. Scotto (sop), I. Cotrubas (sop), M. Horne (mez), P. Domingo (ten), T. Gobbi (bar), I. Wixell (bar), London SO [I] CBS 3-▲ M3K 35912 [ADD]
Ravel, M.:La Valse EMI Classics ▲ CDE 67781
Wagner, R.:Die Meistersinger von Nürnberg (prelude/act 1) CBS ▲ MK 36699
Wagner, R.:Ovs, Preludes & Orch Sels—Fliegende Holländer; Meistersinger; Rienzi; Tannhäuser Odyssey ■ YT 44507
Wagner, R.:Ovs, Preludes & Orch Sels—Fliegende Holländer; Rienzi CBS ▲ MK 36699
Wagner, R.:Tannhäuser (ov) CBS ▲ MK 36699
Z. Macal (cnd)
Franck, C.:Symphonic Vars, w. France Clidat (pno) Forlane ▲ FRL 16673 [ADD]
C. Mackerras (cnd)
Berlioz, H.:Le Jeune pâtre breton, w. Jennifer Smith (sop) IMP ("BBC Radio Classics" series) ▲ IMP 5691532
Berlioz, H.:Les Nuits d'été, w. Jennifer Smith (sop) IMP ("BBC Radio Classics" series) ▲ IMP 5691532
Christmas Album, w. Elisabeth Schwarzkopf (sop), Ambrosian Singers *(rec 1957)* EMI Classics ("Studio" series) ▲ CDM 63574 [ADD]
Sullivan, A.:Ovs—Di Ballo London 2-▲ 436813-2 [DDD]
L. Magiera (cnd)
Pavarotti in Hyde Park, w. Luciano Pavarotti (ten) *(rec live July 1991)* London ▲ 436320-2 [DDD]
N. Malko (cnd)
Borodin, A.:Prince Igor (sels)—Ov; Polovtsian Dances *(rec 1955-56)* Testament ▲ SBT 1062
Borodin, A.:Sym 3 *(rec 1955-56)* Testament ▲ SBT 1062
Glazunov, A.:Les Vendredis *(rec 1955-56)* Testament ▲ SBT 1062
Legendary Nicolai Malko Conducts the Philharmonia Orch Stradavarius 2-▲ MSC 2011/12
Liadov, A.:Russian Folksongs *(rec 1955-56)* Testament ▲ SBT 1062
Prokofiev, S.:The Love for 3 Oranges (suite) Classics for Pleasure ▲ CDCFP 4523 [ADD]
Prokofiev, S.:Sym 1 Classics for Pleasure ▲ CDCFP 4523 [ADD]
Prokofiev, S.:Sym 7 Classics for Pleasure ▲ CDCFP 4523 [ADD]
Rimsky-Korsakov, N.:The Maid of Pskov (ov) *(rec 1955-56)* Testament ▲ SBT 1062
Taneyev, S.:Suite de Concert, w. David Oistrakh (vn) EMI Classics ▲ CDM 65419

▲ = CD ♦ = Enhanced CD Δ = MD ■ = Cassette Tape □ = DCC

Philharmonia Orch (cont.)

N. del Mar (cnd)

Rubbra, E.:Resurgam — Lyrita ▲ SRCD 202 [DDD]
Rubbra, E.:Sym 3 — Lyrita ▲ SRCD 202 [DDD]
Rubbra, E.:Sym 4 — Lyrita ▲ SRCD 202 [DDD]
Rubbra, E.:A Tribute — Lyrita ▲ SRCD 202 [DDD]
Strauss, R.:Burleske, w. C. Hobson (pno) — Arabesque ▲ Z 6567 [DDD]
Strauss, R.:Parergon zur Symphonia domestica, w. C. Hobson (pno) — Arabesque ▲ Z 6567 [DDD]

I. Marin (cnd)

Bellini, V.:Arias, w. D. Hvorostovsky (bar)—Si, vincemmo [from Il Pirata]; Ah! per sempre io ti perdei [from Puritani] — Philips ▲ 434912-2
Donizetti, G.:Arias, w. D. Hvorostovsky (bar)—Vien, Leonora; A tanto amor, Leonora [both from La favorita]; Nei miei superbi gaudi [from Il duca d'Alba]; Di tua beltade immagine [from Poliuto]; Come Paride vezzoso [from L'elisir d'amore]; Bella siccome un angelo [from Don Pasquale]; O Lisbona, alfin ti miro [from Don Sebastiano]; Cruda, funesta smania [from Lucia di Lammermoor] — Philips ▲ 434912-2
Rossini, G.:Arias, w. D. Hvorostovsky (bar)—Largo al Factotum [from Il barbiere di Siviglia]; Resta immobile [from Guilaume Tell] — Philips ▲ 434912-2

I. Markevitch (cnd)

Bartók, B.:Con 3 Pno, w. Annie Fischer (pno) — EMI Classics ("Artist Profile" series) 2-▲ CDZB 68733
Beethoven, L. van:Son 14 Pno, "Moonlight Son", w. Annie Fischer (pno) — EMI Classics ("Artist Profile" series) 2-▲ CDZB 68733
Beethoven, L. van:Son 32 Pno, w. Annie Fischer (pno) — EMI Classics ("Artist Profile" series) 2-▲ CDZB 68733
Saint-Saëns, C.:Carnival of the Animals, w. Géza Anda (pno), Béla Siki (pno) *(rec Jan 1954)* — Testament ▲ SBT 1071
Schubert, Franz:Impromptus Pno (comp), w. Annie Fischer (pno) — EMI Classics ("Artist Profile" series) 2-▲ CDZB 68733
Schumann, R.:Kinderszenen, w. Annie Fischer (pno) — EMI Classics ("Artist Profile" series) 2-▲ CDZB 68733
Schumann, R.:Kreisleriana, w. Annie Fischer (pno) — EMI Classics ("Artist Profile" series) 2-▲ CDZB 68733

N. Marriner (cnd)

Addinsell, R.:Warsaw Con, w. M. Dichter (pno) — Philips ▲ 411123-2 [DDD]
Gershwin, G.:Rhap in Blue, w. M. Dichter (pno) — Philips ▲ 411123-2 [DDD]
Liszt, F.:Polonaises Pno, w. M. Dichter (pno) — Philips ▲ 411123-2 [DDD]
Mendelssohn, F.:A Midsummer Night's Dream (comp), w. A. Augér (sop), A. Murray (mez), Ambrosian Singers [E] — Philips ▲ 411106-2 [DDD]
Offenbach, J.:Ovs—La Belle Hélène; La Fille du Tambour-Major; Orphée aux enfers; Les Deux aveugles; La Grande-Duchesse de Gérolstein; La Périchole; Barbe-bleue; La Vie Parisienne — Philips ▲ 411476-2 [DDD]

E. Mata (cnd)

Rodrigo, J.:Concierto pastorale, w. James Galway (fl) — RCA Gold Seal ▲ 09026-68428-2
Rodrigo, J.:Fant para un gentilhombre, w. James Galway (fl) [arr Galway for flute & orchestra] — RCA Gold Seal ▲ 09026-68428-2

L. von Matačič (cnd)

Bruckner, A.:Ov in g — Testament ▲ TES SBT 1050 [ADD]
Bruckner, A.:Sym 1 — Testament ▲ TES SBT 1050 [ADD]
Lehár, F.:Die lustige Witwe, w. E. Schwarzkopf (sop), H. Steffek (sop), N. Gedda (ten), E. Wächter (bar), Philharmonia Chorus [G] — EMI Classics 2-▲ CDCB 47177
Strauss, R.:Arabella (sels), w. E. Schwarzkopf (sop), E. Loose (sop), J. Metternich (bar) [G] — EMI Classics ("Great Recordings of the Century" series) ▲ CDH 61001 (m)

H. Menges (cnd)

Beethoven, L. van:Con 1 Pno, w. Solomon (pno) — EMI Classics ("The Artist Profile" series) 2-▲ CDZB 67735
Beethoven, L. van:Con 3 Pno, w. Solomon (pno) — EMI Classics ("The Artist Profile" series) 2-▲ CDZB 67735
Beethoven, L. van:Son 27 Pno, w. Solomon (pno) — EMI Classics ("The Artist Profile" series) 2-▲ CDZB 67735
Grieg, E.:Con Pno, Op. 16, w. Solomon (pno) — EMI Classics ("The Artist Profile" series) 2-▲ CDZB 67735
Schumann, R.:Con Pno, w. Solomon (pno) — EMI Classics ("The Artist Profile" series) 2-▲ CDZB 67735

Y. Menuhin (cnd)

Mozart, W.A.:Con Fl Hp, w. Elaine Shaffer (fl), Marilyn Costello (hp) — Royal Classics ▲ ROY 6450
Telemann, G.P.:Suite in a Fl, w. Elaine Shaffer (fl) *(rec Abbey Road Studio 1, London, June 1963)* — EMI Classics ▲ CDK 65340 [ADD]

R. Muti (cnd)

Bach, J.S.:Con 2 Vn, w. A.-S. Mutter (vn) — EMI Classics 3-▲ CDMC 69878
Beethoven, L. van:Con 3 Pno, w. S. Richter (pno) — EMI Classics ▲ CDM 64750
Cherubini, L.:Requiem Mass in c, w. Ambrosian Chorus — EMI Classics 2-▲ CDFB 68613
Donizetti, G.:Don Pasquale, w. M. Freni (sop), G. Winbergh (ten), S. Bruscantini (bar), L. Nucci (bar), Ambrosian Opera Chorus — EMI Classics 2-▲ CDCB 47068
Donizetti, G.:Don Pasquale (sels), w. M. Freni (sop), G. Winbergh (ten), S. Bruscantini (bar), L. Nucci (bar), Ambrosian Opera Chorus — EMI Classics ▲ CDC 54490
Gluck, C.W.:Orfeo ed Euridice, w. E. Gruberova (sop), Marshall (sop), A. Baltsa (mez), Ambrosian Opera Chorus — Angel ("Studio" series) 2-▲ CDMB 63637 [DDD]
Leoncavallo, R.:Pagliacci, w. M. Caballé (sop), R. Scotto (sop), A. Varnay (mez), J. Hamari (mez), J. Carreras (ten), M. Manuguerra (bar), T. Allen (bar), K. Nurmela (bar), U. Benelli (bar), Ambrosian Opera Chorus — EMI Classics 2-▲ CDMB 63650
Leoncavallo, R.:Pagliacci (sels), w. R. Scotto (sop), J. Carreras (ten), K. Nurmela (bar), Ambrosian Opera Chorus — EMI Classics ("Studio" series) ▲ CDM 63933 ■ EG 63933
Mascagni, P.:Cavalleria rusticana (sels), w. M. Caballé (sop), J. Carreras (ten), Ambrosian Opera Chorus — EMI Classics ("Studio" series) ▲ CDM 63933 ■ EG 63933
Mozart, W.A.:Con 22 Pno, w. S. Richter (pno) — EMI Classics ▲ CDM 64750
Mozart, W.A.:Con 2 Vn, w. A.-S. Mutter (vn) — EMI Classics ▲ CDC 47011 [DDD]
Mozart, W.A.:Con 4 Vn, w. A.S. Mutter (vn) — EMI Classics ▲ CDC 47011 [DDD]
Orff, C.:Carmina burana, w. A. Augér (sop), J. Van Kesteren (ten), J. Summers (bar), Philharmonia Chorus [G, L] — EMI Classics ▲ CDC 47100
Schumann, R.:Con Vn, w. G. Kremer (vn) — EMI Classics ("Studio DDD" series) ▲ CDD 63894 [DDD]
Sibelius, J.:Con Vn, w. G. Kremer (vn) — EMI Classics ("Studio DDD" series) ▲ CDD 63894 [DDD]
Tchaikovsky, P.:Con 1 Pno, w. A. Gavrilov (pno) — EMI Classics ▲ CDM 64329
Tchaikovsky, P.:Syms (comp) — EMI Classics 5-▲ CDZE 67742
Trumpet Concertos, w. Maurice André (tpt), Franz Liszt CO [cnd:Jesus Lopez-Cobos], Württemberg CO [cnd:Jörg Faerber], Academy of St. Martin in the Fields [cnd:Neville Marriner], London PO [cnd:Jesus Lopez-Cobos] — EMI Classics 2-▲ CDZB 69152 [ADD]
Verdi, G.:Requiem Mass, w. Renata Scotto (sop), Agnes Baltsa (mez), Veriano Luchetti (ten), Evgeny Nesterenko (bass), Ambrosian Chorus — EMI Classics 2-▲ CDFB 68613

K. Nagano (cnd)

Prokofiev, S.:Con 1 Pno, w. M. Kodama (pno) — ASV ▲ ASV 786
Prokofiev, S.:Con 3 Pno, w. M. Kodama (pno) — ASV ▲ ASV 786

V. Neumann (cnd)

Brahms, J.:Sym 2 — Collins Classics ▲ 11002 [DDD]
Brahms, J.:Vars on a Theme by Haydn *(rec 12/89)* — Collins Classics ▲ 11002 [DDD]

A. Pappano (cnd)

Puccini, G.:La Bohème, w. Leontina Vaduva (sop—Mimi), Ruth Ann Swenson (sop—Musetta), Roberto Alagna (ten—Rodolfo), Simon Keenlyside (bar—Schaunard), Thomas Hampson (bar—Marcello), Samuel Ramey (bass—Colline), Enrico Fissore (bass—Benoit) — EMI Classics 2-◆ CDCB 56120

D. Parry (cnd)

Donizetti, G.:L'assedio di Calais, w. E. Harrhy (sop), D. Jones (mez), R. Serbo (ten), J. Treleaven (ten), R. Smythe (bar), Geoffrey Mitchell Choir — Opera Rara 2-▲ OR 9 [DDD]

Philharmonia Orch (cont.)

D. Parry (cnd) (cont.)

Donizetti, G.:Emilia di Liverpool, w. Y. Kenny (sop), A. Mason (sop), B. Mills (sop), C. Merritt (ten), S. Bruscantini (bar), G. Dolton (bar), C. Thornton-Holmes (bar), Geoffrey Mitchell Choir—complete opera, without dialogue — Opera Rara 3-▲ OR 8
Donizetti, G.:L'Eremitaggio di Liverpool, w. Y. Kenny (sop), A. Mason (sop), B. Mills (sop), C. Merritt (ten), S. Bruscantini (bar), G. Dolton (bar), C. Thornton-Holmes (bar), Geoffrey Mitchell Choir—complete opera, without dialogue — Opera Rara 3-▲ OR 8
Puccini, G.:Tosca, w. Jane Eaglen (sop—Floria Tosca), Charbel Michael (alt—Shepherd Boy), John Daszak (ten—Spoletta), Dennis O'Neill (ten—Mario Cavaradossi), Christopher Booth-Jones (bar—Sciarrone), Ashley Holland (bar—Jailor), Gregory Yurisich (bar—Baron Scarpia), Peter Rose (bass—Cesare Angelotti), Andrew Shore (bass—Sacristan), Geoffrey Mitchell Choir, Peter Kay Children's Chorus — Chandos ("Opera in English" series) 2-▲ CHAN 3000

L. Pešek (cnd)

Bartók, B.:Con 1 Vn, w. Dmitry Sitkovetsky (vn) — Virgin Classics ▲ CDC 45118
Bartók, B.:Con 2 Vn, w. Dmitry Sitkovetsky (vn) — Virgin Classics ▲ CDC 45118
Janácek, L.:Con Vn, w. C. Tetzlaff (vn) — Virgin Classics ▲ 59076 [DDD]
Janácek, L.:From the House of the Dead (ov) — Virgin Classics ▲ 59076 [DDD]
Janácek, L.:Sinfonietta — Virgin Classics ▲ 59076 [DDD]
Janácek, L.:Taras Bulba — Virgin Classics ▲ 59076 [DDD]
Rachmaninoff, S.:Con 1 Pno, w. M. Pletnev (pno) — Virgin Classics ▲ 59506 [DDD]
Rachmaninoff, S.:Rhapsody on a Theme of Paganini, w. Mikhail Pletnev (pno) — Virgin Classics ▲ 59506 [DDD]
Ravel, M.:Alborada del gracioso — Virgin Classics ▲ CDC 59235
Ravel, M.:Boléro — Virgin Classics ▲ CDC 59235
Ravel, M.:Pavane pour une infante défunte — Virgin Classics ▲ CDC 59235
Ravel, M.:Shéhérazade Mez, w. A. Augér (sop) — Virgin Classics ▲ CDC 59235
Ravel, M.:La Valse — Virgin Classics ▲ CDC 59235

J.-B. Pommier (cnd)

Franck, C.:Symphonic Vars, w. M. Dalberto (pno) *(rec Jan. 29–31, 1992)* — Denon ▲ CO 75258 [DDD]
Grieg, E.:Con Pno, Op. 16, w. M. Dalberto (pno) *(rec June 19, 1992)* — Denon ▲ CO 75258 [DDD]
Mozart, W.A.:Con 25 Pno, w. J.-B. Pommier (pno) *(rec Aldeburgh, Grande Bretagne, Aug. 1992)* — Erato ▲ 2292-45999-2
Mozart, W.A.:Con 26 Pno, w. J.-B. Pommier (pno) *(rec Aldeburgh, Grande Bretagne, Aug. 1992)* — Erato ▲ 2292-45999-2
Strauss, R.:Burleske, w. M. Dalberto (pno) *(rec Jan. 29–31, 1992)* — Denon ▲ CO 75258 [DDD]

Premu (cnd)

Lewis, R.H.:Music of—Atto for String Orchestra (1981); Concerto for String Orchestra, Trumpets, Keyboard & Harp (1987); Destini for Orchestra (1985); Moto for Orchestra (1980); Osservazioni II for Winds, Keyboard, Harp & Percussion (1978) — CRI ▲ CD 569 [DDD]

G. Prêtre (cnd)

Strauss, R.:Also sprach Zarathustra — RCA Victrola ▲ 7733-2-RV [DDD]

J. Pritchard (cnd)

Canteloube, J.:Songs of Auvergne, w. P. Rozario (sop) — IMP Classics ▲ PCD 938 [DDD]

S. Rattle (cnd)

Holst, G.:The Planets, w. Ambrosian Singers — Classics for Pleasure ("Eminence" series) ▲ CDEMX 9513 [DDD]
Nielsen, C.:Pan & Syrinx, w. City of Birmingham Sym Chorus — EMI Classics ▲ CDM 64737
Nielsen, C.:Sym 4, w. City of Birmingham Sym Chorus — EMI Classics ▲ CDM 64737
Shostakovich, D.:Sym 10, City of Birmingham SO — EMI Classics ▲ CDM 64870
Sibelius, J.:Sym 5, w. City of Birmingham Sym Chorus — EMI Classics (▲ CDM 64737

D. Renzetti (cnd)

Opera Arias, w. Samuel Ramey (bass), Ambrosian Opera Chorus — Philips ▲ 420184-2 PH [DDD] ■ 420184-4

N. Rescigno (cnd)

Verdi, G.:Arias, w. Maria Callas (sop), Paris Conservatory Société des Concerts Orch—arias from Aida, Attila, Ballo in maschera, Don Carlos, Ernani, I Lombardi, Macbeth, Nabucco, Vespri siciliani [I] — EMI Classics ▲ CDC 47730 [ADD]

H. Rignold (cnd)

Rachmaninoff, S.:Con 2 Pno, w. Benno Moiseiwitch (pno) — Royal Classics ▲ ROY 6451
Rachmaninoff, S.:Rhapsody on a Theme of Paganini, w. Benno Moiseiwitch (pno) — Royal Classics ▲ ROY 6451

S. Robinson (cnd)

Falla, M. de:La vida breve, w. V. de los Angeles (sop)—"Vivan los que rien!"; & "Allí está! Riyendo" [Sp] *(rec 3/14/48)* — EMI Classics ▲ CDH 64028-2 (m) [ADD]

A. Ros-Marbá (cnd)

Rodrigo, J.:Concierto de Aranjuez, w. E. Bitetti (gtr) — Classics for Pleasure ▲ CDCFP 4614 [DDD]
Rodrigo, J.:Fant para un gentilhombre, w. E. Bitetti (gtr) — Classics for Pleasure ▲ CDCFP 4614 [DDD]
Rodrigo, J.:Gtr Music, w. E. Bitetti (gtr)—En Los Trigales; Sonata a la Española — Classics for Pleasure ▲ CDCFP 4614 [DDD]

J.-P. Rouchon (cnd)

Berlioz, H.:Béatrice et Bénédict (ov) — ASV ▲ ASV 895 [DDD]
Berlioz, H.:Herminie, w. R. Plowright (sop) — ASV ▲ ASV 895 [DDD]
Berlioz, H.:La Mort de Cléopâtre, w. R. Plowright (sop) — ASV ▲ ASV 895 [DDD]
Berlioz, H.:Le Roi Lear — ASV ▲ ASV 895 [DDD]

G. Rozhdestvensky (cnd)

Shostakovich, D.:Con 1 Vn, w. David Oistrakh (vn) — IMP ("BBC Radio Classics" series) ▲ IMP 5691702

J. Rudel (cnd)

Massenet, J.:Cendrillon, w. R. Welting (sop), F. von Stade (mez), N. Gedda (ten), J. Bastin (bass), Ambrosian Opera Chorus [F] — CBS 2-▲ M2K 35194 [ADD]
Verdi, G.:Rigoletto, w. Beverly Sills (sop), Sherill Milnes (bar), Alfredo Kraus (bar), Samuel Ramy (bass), Ambrosian Opera Chorus — EMI Classics 2-▲ CDMB 724356603721

P. Sacher (cnd)

Stravinsky, I.:Con Vn, w. A.-S. Mutter (vn) — Deutsche Grammophon ▲ 423696-2 [DDD]

E.-P. Salonen (cnd)

Jolivet, A.:Concertino Tpt, w. W. Marsalis (tpt), C. Sheppard (pno) — CBS ▲ MK 42096 [DDD]
Jolivet, A.:Con 2 Tpt, w. W. Marsalis (tpt) — CBS ▲ MK 42096 [DDD]
Ligeti, G.:The Ligeti Edition, w. Phyllis Bryn-Julson (sop), Rosemary Hardy (sop), Christiane Oelze (sop), Rose Taylor (mez), Sibylle Ehlert (sgr), Omar Ebrahim (bar), Pierre-Laurent Aimard (pno), King's Singers—Vocal Works; Madrigals; Mysteries; Adventures; Songs; Nonsense Madrigals — Sony Classical ▲ SK 62311
Liszt, F.:Con 1 Pno, w. E. Ax (pno) *(rec Dec. 20–21, 1992)* — Sony Classical ▲ SK 53289 [DDD]
Liszt, F.:Con 2 Pno, w. E. Ax (pno) *(rec Dec. 20–21, 1992)* — Sony Classical ▲ SK 53289 [DDD]
Messiaen, O.:Turangalîla-sym—sels. — Sony Classical ▲ SMK 53473
Rachmaninoff, S.:Con 2 Pno, w. Yefim Bronfman (pno) — Sony Classical ▲ SK 47183
Rachmaninoff, S.:Con 3 Pno, w. Yefim Bronfman (pno) — Sony Classical ▲ SK 47183
Schoenberg, A.:Con Pno, w. E. Ax (pno) *(rec Dec. 20–21, 1992)* — Sony Classical ▲ SK 53289 [DDD]
Sibelius, J.:Pohjola's Daughter — CBS ▲ MK 42366 [DDD]
Sibelius, J.:Sym 5 — CBS ▲ MK 42366 [DDD]
Stravinsky, I.:The Firebird — CBS ▲ MK 44917 [DDD]
Stravinsky, I.:Orpheus *(rec Dec. 22, 1992)* — Sony Classical ▲ SK 53274 [DDD]
Stravinsky, I.:Pétrouchka *(rec Dec. 22, 1992)* — Sony Classical ▲ SK 53274 [DDD]
Stravinsky, I.:Le Sacre du printemps Orch—sels. — Sony Classical ▲ SMK 53473
Stravinsky, I.:Le Sacre du printemps Orch — Sony Classical ▲ SK 45796 [DDD] ▲ SM 45796 [DDD]
Stravinsky, I.:Sym in 3 Movts — Sony Classical ▲ SK 45796 [DDD]
Tomasi, H.:Con Tpt, w. W. Marsalis (tpt) — CBS ▲ MK 42096 [DDD]

K. Sanderling (cnd)

Mahler, G.:Sym 9 — Erato 2-▲ 2292-45816-2 ZA

J. Sándor (cnd)

Mendelssohn, F.:Sym 3 — LaserLight ▲ 15 822 [DDD]

ORCH. & ENS.

Philharmonia Orch (cont.)
J. Sándor (cnd) (cont.)
Mendelssohn, F.:Sym 4 LaserLight ▲ 15 822 [DDD]
Mendelssohn, F.:Sym 4 LaserLight ▲ 15526 [DDD]
M. Sargent (cnd)
Beethoven, L. van:Con Vn, Vc & Pno, "Triple Con", w. David Oistrakh (vn), Sviatoslav Knushevitzy (vc), Lev Oborin (pno) EMI Classics 2-▲ CDFB 69331
Dvořák, A.:Symphonic Vars Theorema ▲ TH 121224
Miaskovsky, N.:Con Vc, w. Mstislav Rostropovich (vc) EMI Classics ▲ CDM 65419
Mozart, W.A.:Con 3 Vn, w. David Oistrakh (vn) EMI Classics 2-▲ CDFB 69331
Prokofiev, S.:Con 2 Vn, w. David Oistrakh (vn) EMI Classics 2-▲ CDFB 69331
W. Sawallisch (cnd)
Brahms, J.:Con Vn, w. U. Ughi (vn) RCA Silver Seal ▲ 60479-2-RV [DDD] ■ 60479-4-RV (CrO2)
Bruch, M.:Con 1 Vn, w. U. Ughi (vn) RCA Silver Seal ▲ 60479-2-RV [DDD] ■ 60479-4-RV (CrO2)
Mozart, W.A.:Con 20 Pno, w. W. Sawallisch (pno) EMI Classics ▲ CDE 67764
Mozart, W.A.:Con 21 Pno, w. W. Sawallisch (pno) EMI Classics ▲ CDE 67778
Mozart, W.A.:Con 21 Pno, w. A. Fischer (pno) EMI Classics ▲ CDE 67780
Mozart, W.A.:Con 22 Pno, w. W. Sawallisch (pno) EMI Classics ▲ CDE 67778
Orff, C.:Die Kluge, w. E. Schwarzkopf (sop), R. Christ (ten), P. Kuén (ten), M. Cordes (bar), B. Kusche (bar), H. Prey (bar), G. Frick (bass), G. Wieter (bass) [G] EMI Classics ("Studio" series) 2-▲ CDMB 63712 [ADD]
Orff, C.:Der Mond—Ein kleines Welttheater, w. R. Christ (ten), P. Kuén (ten), K. Schmitt-Walter (bar), H. Graml (bar), H. Hotter (b-bar), P. Lagger (bass), Philharmonia Chorus [G] EMI Classics ("Studio" series) 2-▲ CDMB 63712 [ADD]
Strauss, R.:Capriccio, w. E. Schwarzkopf (sop), A. Moffo (sop), C. Ludwig (mez), N. Gedda (ten), D. Fischer-Dieskau (bar), E. Wächter (bar), H. Hotter (b-bar) [G] EMI Classics 2-▲ CDCB 49014 (m) [ADD]
Strauss, R.:Con 1 Hn, w. D. Brain (hn) EMI Classics ▲ CDC 47834 (m)
Strauss, R.:Con 2 Hn, w. D. Brain (hn) EMI Classics 2-▲ CDC 47834 (m)
H. Schiff (cnd)
Chopin, F.:Con 1 Pno, w. N. Demidenko (pno) Hyperion ▲ CDA 66647
Chopin, F.:Con 2 Pno, w. N. Demidenko (pno) Hyperion ▲ CDA 66647
Lutoslawski, W.:Chain 2, w. Isabelle Van Keulen (vn) Koch Schwann ▲ SCH 315232 [DDD]
Schnittke, A.:Con Va, w. Isabelle Van Keulen (va) Koch Schwann ▲ SCH 315232 [DDD]
T. Schippers (cnd)
Opera Arias & Songs, w. Eileen Farrell (sop), George Trovillo (pno) Testament ▲ SBT 1073
C. Scimone (cnd)
Handel, G.F.:Water Music (suites)—Suite No. 2 in D EMI Classics ▲ CDC 54620
Haydn, J.:Con Tpt, w. B. Black (tpt) EMI Classics ▲ CDC 54620
Hummel, J.N.:Con in E♭ Tpt, S.49, w. B. Black (tpt) EMI Classics ▲ CDC 54620
Rossini, G.:Mosè in Egitto, w. J. Anderson (sop), S. Nimsgern (b-bar), R. Raimondi (bass), Ambrosian Opera Chorus [I] Philips 2-▲ 420109-2 [ADD]
Vivaldi, A.:Con for 2 Tpts, w. B. Black (tpt) EMI Classics ▲ CDC 54620
T. Serafin (cnd)
Donizetti, G.:Lucia di Lammermoor, w. M. Callas (sop), F. Tagliavini (ten), P. Cappuccilli (bar), B. Ladysz (bass) [I] EMI Classics 2-▲ CDCB 47440
Donizetti, G.:Lucia di Lammermoor (sels), w. M. Callas (sop), R. Casellato (ten), P. Cappuccilli (bar)—highlights *(rec live, London 3/16-21/59)* EMI Classics (Studio) ▲ CDM 63934 ■ EG 63934
Puccini, G.:Arias, w. M. Callas (sop)—11 arias [I] *(rec 1954)* EMI Classics ▲ CDC 47966 [ADD]
J. Serebrier (cnd)
Hindemith, P.:Con Orch ASV ▲ ASV 945 [DDD]
Hindemith, P.:Con Vn, w. Michael Guttman (vn) ASV ▲ ASV 945 [DDD]
Hindemith, P.:Kammermusik 4, w. Michael Guttman (vn) ASV ▲ ASV 945 [DDD]
Hindemith, P.:Rag Time ASV ▲ ASV 945 [DDD]
Hindemith, P.:Symphonische Tänze ASV ▲ ASV 945 [DDD]
L. Siegel (cnd)
Tchaikovsky, P.:Sleeping Beauty (suite) Capriccio ▲ 10 923 [DDD]
C. Silvestri (cnd)
Liszt, F.:Les Préludes, w. Garrick Ohlsson (pno) Royal Classics ▲ ROY 6445
G. Simon (cnd)
Balcombe, R.:Greensleeves Suite, w. 40 Cellos of the London PO, Royal PO, BBC SO *(rec All Hallows Church, London, Jan 18 & Apr 2, 1993)* Cala ▲ CACD 104 [DDD]
Bernstein, L.:West Side Story (sels), w. 40 Cellos of the London PO, Royal PO, BBC SO—Tonight [arr. Balcombe] *(rec All Hallows Church, London, Jan 18 & Apr 2, 1993)* Cala ▲ CACD 104 [DDD]
Borodin, A.:In the Steppes of Central Asia *(rec All Hallows Church, Gospel Oak, London, Feb 21-24 & Apr 8-10, 1993)* Cala ▲ CAL 1011 [DDD]
Borodin, A.:Nocturne Vn & Orch, w. Stephanie Chase (vn) *(rec All Hallows Church, Gospel Oak, London, Feb 21-24 & Apr 8-10, 1993)* Cala ▲ CAL 1011 [DDD]
Borodin, A.:Petite Suite *(rec All Hallows Church, Gospel Oak, London, Feb 21-24 & Apr 8-10, 1993)* Cala ▲ CAL 1011 [DDD]
Casals, P.:Sardana, w. 40 Cellos of the London PO, Royal PO, BBC SO *(rec All Hallows Church, London, Jan 18 & Apr 2, 1993)* Cala ▲ CACD 104 [DDD]
Debussy, C.:Children's Corner *(rec St. Jude-on-the-Hill, Hampstead, London, Jan 2-6, 1990)* Cala ▲ CACD 1002 [DDD]
Debussy, C.:Clair de lune [orchd. André Caplet] *(rec St. Jude-on-the-Hill, Hampstead, London, Jan 2-6, 1990)* Cala ▲ CACD 1001 [DDD]
Debussy, C.:Danse Pno, "Tarantelle styrienne" *(rec St. Jude-on-the-Hill, Hampstead, London, Jan 2-6, 1990)* Cala ▲ CACD 1002 [DDD]
Debussy, C.:La Mer *(rec St. Jude-on-the-Hill, Hampstead, London, Jan 2-6, 1990)* Cala ▲ CACD 1001 [DDD]
Debussy, C.:Nocturnes, w. Philharmonia Women's Chorus *(rec St. Jude-on-the-Hill, Hampstead, London, Jan 2-6, 1990)* Cala ▲ CACD 1002 [DDD]
Debussy, C.:Petite suite *(rec St. Jude-on-the-Hill, Hampstead, London, Jan 2-6, 1990)* Cala ▲ CACD 1001 [DDD]
Debussy, C.:Première rapsodie, w. J. Campbell (cl) *(rec St. Jude-on-the-Hill, Hampstead, London, Jan 2-6, 1990)* Cala ▲ CACD 1001 [DDD]
Debussy, C.:Transcriptions Orch—Deux arabesques (H. Mouton); La cathédrale engloutie (Stokowski) *(rec St. Jude-on-the-Hill, Hampstead, London, Jan 2-6, 1990)* Cala ▲ CACD 1001 [DDD]
Debussy, C.:Transcriptions Orch—L'isle joyeuse (Bernardino Molinari); La fille aux cheveux de lin (William Gleichmann); La soirée dans Grenade (Leopold Stokowski) *(rec St. Jude-on-the-Hill, Hampstead, London, Jan 2-6, 1990)* Cala ▲ CACD 1002 [DDD]
French Ballet Music of the 1920s Chandos ▲ CHAN 8356 [DDD]
Grainger, P.:Transcriptions Orch—Debussy—Bruyères *(rec St. Jude-on-the-Hill, Hampstead, London, Jan 2-6, 1990)* Cala ▲ CACD 1002 [DDD]
Grainger, P.:Transcriptions Orch—Debussy—Pagodes (1928) *(rec St. Jude-on-the-Hill, Hampstead, London, Jan 2-6, 1990)* Cala ▲ CACD 1001 [DDD]
Mussorgsky, M.:Khovanshchina (orch sels)—Dawn on the Moscow River [Rimsky-Korsakov]; Galitsin's Journey [Stokowski] *(rec All Hallows Church, Gospel Oak, London)* Cala ▲ CACD 1012 [DDD]
Mussorgsky, M.:Night *(rec All Hallows Church, Gospel Oak, London)* Cala ▲ CACD 1012 [DDD]
Mussorgsky, M.:Pictures at an Exhibition, w. Tamás Ungár (pno) [arr Lawrence Leonard, 1977] *(rec All Hallows Church, Gospel Oak, London)* Cala ▲ CACD 1012 [DDD]
Mussorgsky, M.:Pictures from the Crimea *(rec All Hallows Church, Gospel Oak)* Cala ▲ CACD 1012 [DDD]
Mussorgsky, M.:Scherzo *(rec All Hallows Church, Gospel Oak, London)* Cala ▲ CACD 1012 [DDD]
Mussorgsky, M.:Sorochintsy Fair (orch sels)—Gopak *(rec All Hallows Church, Gospel Oak, London)* Cala ▲ CACD 1012 [DDD]
Mussorgsky, M.:Tear-Drop *(rec All Hallows Church, Gospel Oak, London)* Cala ▲ CACD 1012 [DDD]
Rachmaninoff, S.:Vocalise, BBC SO, w. 40 Cellos of the London PO, Royal PO [arr. Balcombe] *(rec All Hallows Church, London, Jan 18 & Apr 2, 1993)* Cala ▲ CACD 104 [DDD]

Philharmonia Orch (cont.)
G. Simon (cnd) (cont.)
Ravel, M.:Boléro *(rec St. Jude-on-the-Hill, Hampstead, London, Apr 16-17, 1986)* Cala ▲ CACD 1004 [DDD]
Ravel, M.:Con in G Pno, w. G. Mok (pno) *(rec St. Jude-on-the-Hill, Hampstead, London, Feb 8-12, 1991)* Cala ▲ CACD 1005 [DDD]
Ravel, M.:Daphnis et Chloé (suite 2) *(rec St. Jude-on-the-Hill, Hampstead, London, Feb 8-12, 1991)* Cala ▲ CACD 1005 [DDD]
Ravel, M.:5 O'Clock Foxtrot *(rec St. Jude-on-the-Hill, Hampstead, London, Feb 8-12, 1991)* Cala ▲ CACD 1005 [DDD]
Ravel, M.:Jeux d'eau *(rec St. Jude-on-the-Hill, Hampstead, London, Feb 8-12, 1991)* Cala ▲ CACD 1004 [DDD]
Ravel, M.:Ma mère l'oye Orch *(rec St. Jude-on-the-Hill, Hampstead, London, Feb 8-12, 1991)* Cala ▲ CACD 1004 [DDD]
Ravel, M.:Mélodies populaires grecques, w. S. Burgess (mez) [F] *(rec St. Jude-on-the-Hill, Hampstead, London, Feb 8-12, 1991)* Cala ▲ CACD 1004 [DDD]
Ravel, M.:Pavane pour une infante défunte *(rec St. Jude-on-the-Hill, Hampstead, London, Feb 8-12, 1991)* Cala ▲ CACD 1005 [DDD]
Ravel, M.:Pièce en forme de Habanera, w. H. de Vries (ob) [orchd. by Arthur Hoérée] *(rec St. Jude-on-the-Hill, Hampstead, London, Feb 8-12, 1991)* Cala ▲ CACD 1005 [DDD]
Ravel, M.:Rapsodie espagnole [orchd. by Arthur Hoérée] *(rec St. Jude-on-the-Hill, Hampstead, London, Feb 8-12, 1991)* Cala ▲ CACD 1005 [DDD]
Ravel, M.:Tzigane, w. S. Chase (vn) *(rec St. Jude-on-the-Hill, Hampstead, London, Feb 8-12, 1991)* Cala ▲ CACD 1004 [DDD]
Ravel, M.:La Vallée des cloches *(rec St. Jude-on-the-Hill, Hampstead, London, Feb 8-12, 1991)* Cala ▲ CACD 1004 [DDD]
Ravel, M.:La Valse *(rec St. Jude-on-the-Hill, Hampstead, London, Feb 8-12, 1991)* Cala ▲ CACD 1004 [DDD]
Respighi, O.:Adagio con variazioni Vc Orch, w. Alexander Baillie (vc) *(rec Goldsmith's College, London, Dec 19-22, 1990)* Cala ▲ CACD 1007 [DDD]
Respighi, O.:Ballad of the Gnomes *(rec Goldsmith's College, London, Dec 19-22, 1990)* Cala ▲ CACD 1007 [DDD]
Respighi, O.:Belkis, Queen of Sheba Chandos ▲ CHAN 8405 [DDD]
Respighi, O.:Suite Org, w. Leslie Pearson (org) *(rec Goldsmith's College, London, Dec 19-22, 1990)* Cala ▲ CACD 1007 [DDD]
Respighi, O.:Trittico botticelliano *(rec Goldsmith's College, London, Dec 19-22, 1990)* Cala ▲ CACD 1007 [DDD]
Saint-Saëns, C.:Le Cygne, w. 40 Cellos of the London PO, Royal PO, BBC SO [arr. Balcombe] *(rec All Hallows Church, London, Jan 18 & Apr 2, 1993)* Cala ▲ CACD 104 [DDD]
Stokowski, L.:Transcriptions Orch—Debussy—La cathédrale engloutie *(rec St. Jude-on-the-Hill, Hampstead, London, Jan 2-6, 1990)* Cala ▲ CACD 1001 [DDD]
Stokowski, L.:Transcriptions Orch—Debussy—La soirée dans Grenade *(rec St. Jude-on-the-Hill, Hampstead, London, Jan 2-6, 1990)* Cala ▲ CACD 1002 [DDD]
Stokowski, L.:Transcriptions Orch, w. Ian Boughton (ten), BBC Sym Men's Chorus—Borodin:Requiem *(rec All Hallows Church, Gospel Oak, London)* Cala ▲ CAL 1011 [DDD]
Y. Simonov (cnd)
Wagner, R.:Ovs, Preludes & Orch Sels—selections from Rienzi, Fliegende Holländer, Tannhäuser, Lohengrin:Prel., Meistersinger Collins Classics ▲ COL 1294 [DDD]
Wagner, R.:Parsifal (prelude) Collins Classics ▲ 12072 [DDD]
Wagner, R.:Der Ring des Nibelungen (orch sels)—selections from Walküre *(Ride of the Valkyries)*, Siegfried *(Forest Murmurs)*, & Götterdämmerung *(Siegfried's Rhine Journey & Funeral Music)* Collins Classics ▲ 12072 [DDD]
Wagner, R.:Tristan und Isolde (prelude & liebestod) Collins Classics ▲ 12072 [DDD]
G. Sinopoli (cnd)
Beethoven, L. van:Con 1 Pno, w. Martha Argerich (pno) Deutsche Grammophon ("Masters" series) ▲ 445504-2
Beethoven, L. van:Con 2 Pno, w. Martha Argerich (pno) Deutsche Grammophon ("Masters" series) ▲ 445504-2
Bruch, M.:Con 1 Vn, w. G. Shaham (vn) Deutsche Grammophon ▲ 427656-2 [DDD]
Debussy, C.:La Mer Deutsche Grammophon ▲ 427644-2 [DDD]
Elgar, E.:Con Vc Deutsche Grammophon ("Digital Midprice" series) ▲ 445511-2
Elgar, E.:Con Vc, w. M. Maisky (vc) Deutsche Grammophon ▲ 431685-2 [DDD]
Elgar, E.:Enigma Vars Deutsche Grammophon ("Digital Midprice" series) ▲ 445511-2
Elgar, E.:Pomp & Circumstance Marches—Nos. 1 & 4 Deutsche Grammophon ▲ 431663-2 [DDD]
Elgar, E.:Serenade Strs Deutsche Grammophon ("Digital Midprice" series) ▲ 445511-2
Elgar, E.:Sym 1 Deutsche Grammophon ▲ 431663-2 [DDD]
Granada:The Greatest Hits of Plácido Domingo, w. Domingo, Plácido (ten), London SO [cnd:C. Abbado], Los Angeles PO [cnd:C. M. Giulini], Vienna PO [cnd:H. von Karajan], Royal Opera House Orch, Covent Garden [cnd:Z. Mehta] Deutsche Grammophon ▲ 445777-2 ■ 445777-4
Mad About Love, w. Cheryl Studer (sop), Kiri Te Kanawa (sop), José Carreras (ten), Jerry Hadley (ten), Bastille Opera Orch [cnd:Myung-Whun Chung], Boston SO [cnd:Seiji Ozawa], Vienna PO [cnd:John Eliot Gardiner, James Levine] Deutsche Grammophon ▲ 449112-2 ■ 449112-4
Mahler, G.:Das Klagende Lied, w. C. Studer (sop), W. Meier (mez), R. Goldberg (ten), T. Allen (bar), Shin-Yuh Kai Chorus *(rec live, Japan 1990)* Deutsche Grammophon ▲ 435382-2 [DDD]
Mahler, G.:Lieder eines fahrenden Gesellen, w. B. Fassbaender (mez) [G] Deutsche Grammophon 2-▲ 415959-2 [DDD]
Mahler, G.:Sym 2, w. R. Plowright (sop), B. Fassbaender (mez), Philharmonia Chorus [G] Deutsche Grammophon 2-▲ 415959-2 [DDD]
Mahler, G.:Sym 4, w. E. Gruberova (sop) Deutsche Grammophon ▲ 437527-2
Mahler, G.:Sym 6 Deutsche Grammophon 2-▲ 423082-2 [DDD]
Mahler, G.:Sym 8, w. S. Jo (sop), C. Studer (sop), W. Meier (mez), K. Lewis (ten), T. Allen (bar), H. Sotin (bass), Philharmonia Chorus, Southend Boys' Choir [G] Deutsche Grammophon 2-▲ 435433-2
Mahler, G.:Sym 10—Adagio Deutsche Grammophon 2-▲ 423082-2 [DDD]
Mascagni, P.:Cavalleria rusticana, w. A. Baltsa (mez), S. Mentzer (mez) P. Domingo (ten), J. Pons (bar), Royal Opera House Chorus Covent Garden [I] Deutsche Grammophon ▲ 429568-2 [DDD]
Mascagni, P.:Cavalleria rusticana (sels), w. Agnes Baltsa (mez—Santuzza), Plácido Domingo (ten—Turiddu)—No, no, Turiddu Deutsche Grammophon ▲ 447270-2 [DDD] ■ 447 270-4
Mendelssohn, F.:Con in e Vn & Orch, Op. 64, w. G. Shaham (vn) Deutsche Grammophon ▲ 427656-2
Mendelssohn, F.:Sym 4 Deutsche Grammophon ("Masters" series) ▲ 445514-2
Puccini, G.:Madama Butterfly, w. M. Freni (sop), T. Berganza (mez), J. Carreras (ten), J. Pons (bar), Ambrosian Opera Chorus [I] Deutsche Grammophon 3-▲ 423567-2 [DDD]
Puccini, G.:Manon Lescaut, w. M. Freni (sop), P. Domingo (ten), R. Bruson (bar), Royal Opera House Chorus Covent Garden [I] *(rec 1984)* Deutsche Grammophon 2-▲ 413893-2 [DDD]
Puccini, G.:Tosca, w. M. Freni (sop), P. Domingo (ten), S. Ramey (bass), Royal Opera House Chorus Covent Garden [I] Deutsche Grammophon 2-▲ 431775-2 [DDD]
Puccini, G.:Tosca (sels), w. Mirella Freni (sop—Tosca), Plácido Domingo (ten—Cavaradossi)—Ah, quegli occhil - Qual occhio al mondo può star [Act I, Part II] Deutsche Grammophon ▲ 447270-2 [DDD] ■ 447270-4
Ravel, M.:Boléro Deutsche Grammophon ▲ 427644-2 [DDD]
Ravel, M.:Daphnis et Chloé (suite 2) Deutsche Grammophon ▲ 427644-2 [DDD]
Schubert, Franz:Sym 8 Deutsche Grammophon ("Masters" series) ▲ 445514-2
Sibelius, J.:Con Vn, w. G. Shaham (vn) Deutsche Grammophon ▲ 437540-2
Tchaikovsky, P.:Con Vn, w. G. Shaham (vn) Deutsche Grammophon ▲ 437540-2
Tchaikovsky, P.:Romeo & Juliet Deutsche Grammophon ▲ 429740-2 [DDD] ■ 429740-4 □ 429740-5
Tchaikovsky, P.:Sym 6 Deutsche Grammophon ▲ 429740-2 [DDD] □ 429740-5
Tchaikovsky, P.:Vars on a Rococo Theme, w. M. Maisky (vc) Deutsche Grammophon ▲ 431685-2 [DDD]

Philharmonia Orch (cont.)
G. Sinopoli (cnd) (cont.)
Wagner, R.:Tannhäuser, w. C. Studer (sop), A. Baltsa (mez), P. Domingo (ten), A. Schmidt (bar), M. Salminen (bass), Royal Opera House Chorus Covent Garden [G] — Deutsche Grammophon 3-▲ 427625-2 [DDD]
Wagner, R.:Tannhäuser, w. C. Studer (sop), A. Baltsa (mez), P. Domingo (ten), A. Schmidt (bar), M. Salminen (bass), Royal Opera House Chorus Covent Garden — Deutsche Grammophon ▲ 435405-2 [DDD]
L. Slatkin (cnd)
Dvořák, A.:Con Vn, w. U. Ughi (vn) — RCA Red Seal ▲ 60431-2-RC [DDD]
Dvořák, A.:Romance Vn, w. U. Ughi (vn) — RCA Red Seal ▲ 60431-2-RC [DDD]
Haydn, J.:Sym 94, "Surprise Sym" — RCA Red Seal ▲ 09026-62549-2
Haydn, J.:Sym 96, "Miracle", w. Hugh Bean (vn), Nicholas Whiting (vn), John Anderson (ob) *(rec Abbey Road Studio No. 1, London, Aug 1993)* — RCA Red Seal ▲ 09026-68424-2 [DDD]
Haydn, J.:Sym 98 — RCA Red Seal ▲ 09026-62549-2
Haydn, J.:Sym 102, w. Matthias Feile (vc) *(rec Abbey Road Studio No. 1, London, Apr & Oct 1994)* — RCA Red Seal ▲ 09026-68424-2 [DDD]
Haydn, J.:Sym 103, "Drum Roll" *(rec Abbey Road Studio No. 1, London, Apr & Oct 1994)* — RCA Red Seal ▲ 09026-68424-2 [DDD]
Haydn, J.:Sym 104, "London" — RCA Red Seal ▲ 09026-62549-2
Tchaikovsky, P.:Concert Fant, w. B. Douglas (pno) — RCA Red Seal ▲ 09026-61632-2
Tchaikovsky, P.:Con 1 Pno, w. B. Douglas (pno) — RCA Red Seal ▲ 09026-61632-2
Tchaikovsky, P.:Con 2 Pno, w. B. Douglas (pno) — RCA Red Seal ▲ 09026-61633-2
Tchaikovsky, P.:Con 3 Pno, w. B. Douglas (pno) — RCA Red Seal ▲ 09026-61633-2
Vaughan Williams, R.:Fant on a Theme by Thomas Tallis — RCA Red Seal ▲ 09026-61193-2
Vaughan Williams, R.:Flourish for Glorious John — RCA Red Seal ▲ 09026-61196-2
Vaughan Williams, R.:Norfolk Rhap 1 — RCA Red Seal ▲ 09026-61193-2
Vaughan Williams, R.:Sym 1, w. B. Valente (sop), T. Allen (bar), Philharmonia Chorus — RCA Red Seal ▲ 09026-61197-2
Vaughan Williams, R.:Sym 2 — RCA Red Seal ▲ 09026-61193-2
Vaughan Williams, R.:Sym 5 — RCA Red Seal ▲ 09026-60556-2 [DDD]
Vaughan Williams, R.:Sym 6 — RCA Red Seal ▲ 09026-60556-2 [DDD]
Vaughan Williams, R.:Sym 8 — RCA Red Seal ▲ 09026-61196-2
Vaughan Williams, R.:Sym 9 — RCA Red Seal ▲ 09026-61196-2
P. Spada (cnd)
Salieri, A.:Cons Pno, w. Pietro Spada (pno) — ASV ▲ ASV 955
Salieri, A.:Les Horaces (ov) — ASV ▲ ASV 955
Salieri, A.:Semiramide (ov) — ASV ▲ ASV 955
Salieri, A.:Variations on "La folia di Spagnia" — ASV ▲ ASV 955
W. Steinberg (cnd)
Strauss, R.:Don Juan — EMI Classics ▲ CDM 65610
Strauss, R.:Der Rosenkavalier (suite) — EMI Classics ▲ CDM 65610
W. Susskind (cnd)
Bruch, M.:Con 1 Vn, w. Y. Menuhin (vn) — EMI Classics ("Laser" series) 3-▲
Mozart, W.A.:Con Hn, K.417, w. Dennis Brain (hn) — EMI Classics ▲ CDM 64198
Mozart, W.A.:Con 5 Vn, w. S. Goldberg (vn) — Testament ▲ TES SBT 1028 [ADD]
Turina, J.:Poema en forma de canciones, w. V. de los Angeles (sop)—Cantares [Sp] *(rec 1949)* — EMI Classics ▲ CDH 64028-2 (m) [ADD]
Turina, J.:Saeta en forma de Salve a la Virgen de la Esperanza, w. V. De Los Angeles (sop) [Sp] *(rec 1949)* — EMI Classics ▲ CDH 64028-2 (m) [ADD]
E. Svetlanov (cnd)
Balakirev, M.:Ov on 3 Russian Themes — Hyperion ▲ CDA 66586
Balakirev, M.:Rus — Hyperion ▲ CDA 66493
Balakirev, M.:Sym 1 — Hyperion ▲ CDA 66493
Balakirev, M.:Sym 2 — Hyperion ▲ CDA 66586
Balakirev, M.:Tamara — Hyperion ▲ CDA 66586
Glazunov, A.:Concert Waltz 1 — EMI Classics 2-▲ CDFB 69361
Glazunov, A.:Concert Waltz 2 — EMI Classics 2-▲ CDFB 69361
Glazunov, A.:The Seasons — EMI Classics 2-▲ CDFB 69361
P. Thomas (cnd)
Debussy, C.:La Mer — CBS ▲ MDK 44645 [DDD] ■ MDT 44645 (D)
Debussy, C.:Nocturnes, w. Ambrosian Chorus — CBS ▲ MDK 44645 [DDD] ■ MDT 44645 (D)
Mendelssohn, F.:Con in e Vn & Orch, Op. 64, w. Cho-Liang Lin (vn) — CBS ▲ MK 39007 [DDD]
Mendelssohn, F.:Con in e Vn & Orch, Op. 64, w. Cho-Liang Lin (vn) — CBS ▲ MDK 44902 [DDD] ■ MDT 44902 (D)
Mozart, W.A.:Cons Fl, w. Judith Hall (fl) — IMP ("Classic" series) ▲ IMP 2036
Tchaikovsky, P.:The Nutcracker — CBS 2-▲ M2K 42173 [DDD]
B. Thomson (cnd)
Arnold, M.:Dances—English Dances — Chandos ▲ CHAN 8867 [DDD]
M. Tilson Thomas (cnd)
Saint-Saëns, C.:Con 3 Vn, w. C.-L. Lin (vn) — CBS ▲ MK 39007 [DDD]
Tchaikovsky, P.:The Nutcracker (sels)—Sabre Dance; Dance of the Sugar Plum Fairies; Waltz of the Flowers — Sony Classical ▲ SFK 62675 ■ SFT 62675
Tchaikovsky, P.:Nutcracker Suite — CBS ▲ MDK 45649 [DDD]
M. Torke (cnd)
Torke, M.:December *(rec The Colosseum, Watford, Jul 1, 1995)* — Argo ▲ 452101-2 [DDD]
Y. P. Tortelier (cnd)
Albéniz, I.:Iberia Suite — Chandos ▲ CHAN 8904 [DDD]
Gershwin, G.:Con Pno, w. H. Shelley (pno) — Chandos ▲ CHAN 9092 [DDD]
Gershwin, G.:Rhap in Blue, w. H. Shelley (pno) — Chandos ▲ CHAN 9092 [DDD]
Gershwin, G.:Second Rhap, w. H. Shelley (pno) — Chandos ▲ CHAN 9092 [DDD]
Respighi, O.:The Fountains of Rome — Chandos ▲ CHAN 8989 [DDD]
Respighi, O.:The Pines of Rome — Chandos ▲ CHAN 8989 [DDD]
A. Toscanini (cnd)
Brahms, J.:Syms (comp) *(rec 1952)* — Arkadia 3-▲ 524 (m) [AAD]
Brahms, J.:Tragic Ov *(rec 1952)* — Arkadia 3-▲ 524 (m) [AAD]
Brahms, J.:Vars on a Theme by Haydn *(rec 1952)* — Arkadia 3-▲ 524 (m) [AAD]
B. Tuckwell (cnd)
Mozart, W.A.:Con "0" Hn, w. B. Tuckwell (hn) *(rec July 1990)* — Collins Classics ▲ 11532 [DDD]
Mozart, W.A.:Cons Hn, w. B. Tuckwell (hn) *(rec July 1990)* — Collins Classics ▲ 11532 [DDD]
Mozart, W.A.:Con Movt Hn, K.494a, w. B. Tuckwell (hn) *(rec July 1990)* — Collins Classics ▲ 11532 [DDD]
L. Tung (cnd)
Rachmaninoff, S.:Sym 2 — ASV ▲ ASQ 6107 [DDD]
A. Vandernoot (cnd)
Mahler, G.:Kindertotenlieder, w. C. Ludwig (mez) [G] — EMI Classics ("Studio" series) ▲ CDM 69499 [ADD]
T. Vásáry (cnd)
The Concerto Collection, w. Jennifer Stinton (fl), English CO [cnd:Steuart Bedford]
Mozart, W.A.:Con Fl, K.314, w. J. Stinton (fl) — Collins Classics 2-▲ 70052 [DDD]
Mozart, W.A.:Con Fl Hp, w. J. Stinton (fl), A. Brewer (hp) — Collins Classics 2-▲ 70052 [DDD]
Rodrigo, J.:Concierto pastorale, w. J. Stinton (fl) — Collins Classics 2-▲ 70052 [DDD]
E. de Waart (cnd)
Bach, J.S.:Cons Vn (comp), w. A. Grumiaux (vn) — Philips ("Silver Line" series) ▲ 420700-2 [ADD]
Bach, J.S.:Con Vn & Ob, w. A. Grumiaux (vn), H. Holliger (ob) — Philips ("Silver Line" series) ▲ 420700-2 [ADD]
Bach, J.S.:Con for 2 Vns, w. A. Grumiaux (vn) — Philips ("Silver Line" series) ▲ 420700-2 [ADD]
W. Walton (cnd)
Walton, W.:Con Vn, w. J. Heifetz (vn) — RCA Gold Seal ▲ 7966-2-RG (m) [ADD]

Philharmonia Orch (cont.)
W. Walton (cnd) (cont.)
Walton, W.:Troilus & Cressida (sels), w. E. Schwarzkopf (sop), M. Sinclair (cta), P. Pears (ten), R. Lewis (ten)—scenes — EMI Classics ▲ ZDM 64199
G. R. Warren (cnd)
Nicolai, O.:Lustigen Weiber (ov) — Interchord ▲ INT 892.923 [AAD]
C. Warren-Green (cnd)
Fasch, J.F.:Con Tpt & Ob d'amore, w. J. Wallace (tpt) *(rec July 13-15, 1988)* — Nimbus ▲ NI 7016 [DDD]
Haydn, J.:Cons Hn, w. Michael Thompson (hn) — Nimbus ▲ NI 5010
Haydn, J.:Con for 2 Hns, w. Michael Thompson (hn), Richard Watkins (hn) — Nimbus ▲ NI 5018
Haydn, J.:Con Tpt, w. John Wallace (tpt) *(rec Dec. 19-20, 1983)* — Nimbus ▲ NI 7016 [DDD]
Haydn, J.:Con Tpt, w. John Wallace (tpt) — Nimbus ▲ NI 5010
Hummel, J.N.:Con in E♭ Tpt, S.49, w. J. Wallace (tpt) — Nimbus ▲ NI 5065 [DDD]
Hummel, J.N.:Con in E Tpt, w. J. Wallace (tpt) *(rec June 23-25, 1986)* — Nimbus ▲ NI 7016 [DDD]
Man:The Measure of All Things—Italian Baroque Trumpet Music, w. John Wallace (tpt) — Nimbus ▲ NI 5017 [DDD]
Mozart, L.:Con Hn, w. M. Thompson (hn) — Nimbus ▲ NI 5018
Neruda, J.B.G.:Con Tpt, w. J. Wallace (tpt) — Nimbus ▲ NI 5065 [DDD]
Neruda, J.B.G.:Con Tpt, w. J. Wallace (tpt) *(rec July 13-15, 1988)* — Nimbus ▲ NI 7016 [DDD]
Rosetti, F.A.:Cons Hn, w. M. Thompson (hn)—Con. in d — Nimbus ▲ NI 5018
T for Trumpeter:Trumpet Concertos & Fanfares, w. John Wallace (tpt), Wallace Collection — Nimbus ▲ NI 5065 [DDD]
Vivaldi, A.:Cons for 2 Hns, w. M. Thompson (hn), R. Watkins (hn)—RV.539 — Nimbus ▲ NI 5018
Weber, F.D.:Vars Tpt, w. J. Wallace (tpt) *(rec June 23-25, 1986)* — Nimbus ▲ NI 7016 [DDD]
Weber, F.D.:Vars Tpt, w. J. Wallace (tpt) — Nimbus ▲ NI 5065 [DDD]
G. Weldon (cnd)
Tchaikovsky, P.:Con 1 Pno, w. Benno Moiseiwitch (pno) *(rec 1944)* — APR ▲ APR 5518 [ADD]
Tchaikovsky, P.:Sleeping Beauty — Classics for Pleasure ▲ CDCFP 4458 [ADD]
W. Weller (cnd)
Mendelssohn, F.:Die Hebriden — Chandos ▲ CHAN 9099 [DDD]
Mendelssohn, F.:Sym 1 — Chandos ▲ CHAN 9099 [DDD]
Mendelssohn, F.:Sym 2, w. C. Haymon (sop), A. Hagley (sop), P. Straka (ten), Philharmonia Chorus [G] — Chandos ▲ CHAN 8995 [DDD]
Mendelssohn, F.:Sym 3 — Chandos ▲ CHAN 9032 [DDD]
Mendelssohn, F.:Sym 4 — Chandos ▲ CHAN 9032 [DDD]
Mendelssohn, F.:Sym 5 — Chandos ▲ CHAN 9099 [DDD]
I. Westrip (cnd)
Bizet, G.:Carmen (suites) — IMP Classics ▲ IMPPCD 1075 [DDD]
H. D. Wetton (cnd)
Holst, G.:The Golden Goose, w. Guildford Choral Society — Hyperion ▲ CDA 66784
Holst, G.:King Estmere, w. Guildford Choral Society — Hyperion ▲ CDA 66784
Holst, G.:The Morning of the Year, w. Guildford Choral Society — Hyperion ▲ CDA 66784
D. Willcocks (cnd)
Bennett, Richard Rodney:Spells, w. J. Manning (sop), Bach Choir [E] — Continuum ▲ CCD 1030
Walton, W.:Belshazzar's Feast, w. G. Howell (bass), Bach Choir [E] — Chandos ▲ CHAN 8760 [DDD]
Walton, W.:Coronation Te Deum, w. J. Scott (org), Bach Choir [L] — Chandos ▲ CHAN 8760 [DDD]
Walton, W.:Crown Imperial — Chandos ▲ CHAN 8998 [DDD]
Walton, W.:Fanfares—A Queen's Fanfare (1959); Anniversary Fanfare (1973) — Chandos ▲ CHAN 8998 [DDD]
Walton, W.:Gloria, w. A. Gunson (cta), N. Mackie (ten), S. Roberts (bar), Bach Choir [L] — Chandos ▲ CHAN 8760 [DDD]
Walton, W.:In Honour of the City of London, w. Bach Choir [E] — Chandos ▲ CHAN 8998 [DDD]
Walton, W.:March:A History of the English Speaking Peoples — Chandos ▲ CHAN 8998 [DDD]
Walton, W.:Orb & Sceptre — Chandos ▲ CHAN 8998 [DDD]
H. Wolff (cnd)
Bartók, B.:Con Orch — Teldec ▲ 76350
Bartók, B.:The Miraculous Mandarin (suite) — Teldec ▲ 76350
Bartók, B.:Pictures Orch — Teldec ▲ 76350
S. Wright (cnd)
Albinoni, T.:Cons à 5 Obs, Op. 7, w. John Anderson (ob)—Nos. 3 & 6 *(rec St. Jude-on-the-Hill, Hampstead, Jan. 5-6, 1989)* — Nimbus ▲ NI 7027 [DDD]
Arias for Soprano & Trumpet, w. Helen Field (sop), John Wallace (tpt) — Nimbus ▲ NI 5123 [DDD]
Benjamin, A.:Con Ob Strs, w. John Anderson (ob) *(rec St. Jude-on-the-Hill, Hampstead, Jan. 5-6, 1989)* — Nimbus ▲ NI 7027 [DDD]
Classical Trumpet Concertos, w. John Wallace (tpt) — Nimbus ▲ NI 5121 [DDD]
Françaix, J.:L'Horloge de Flore, w. J. Anderson (ob) — Nimbus ▲ NI 5330 [DDD]
Hindemith, P.:Concert Music Pno, Brass & Hps, w. J. Wallace (tpt), R. Kapil (pno), Wallace Collection — Nimbus ▲ NI 5103 [DDD]
Italian Oboe Concertos, w. John Anderson (ob) — Nimbus ▲ NI 5188 [DDD]
Marcello, A.:Cons Ob, w. John Anderson (ob)—in d *(rec St. Jude-on-the-Hill, Hampstead, Jan. 5-6, 1989)* — Nimbus ▲ NI 7027 [DDD]
Martinů, B.:Con Ob, w. J. Anderson (ob) — Nimbus ▲ NI 5330 [DDD]
Strauss, R.:Con Ob, w. J. Anderson (ob) — Nimbus ▲ NI 5330 [DDD]
Trumpet Music from the Italian Baroque, w. John Wallace (tpt), Wallace Collection — Nimbus ▲ NI 5079 [DDD]
Vivaldi, A.:Cons Ob, w. John Anderson (ob)—in F, RV.461; in D, RV.453; in F, RV.455 *(rec St. Jude-on-the-Hill, Hampstead, Jan. 5-6, 1989)* — Nimbus ▲ NI 7027 [DDD]
D. V. Yu (cnd)
Balakirev, M.:Islamey [orchd.] — IMP Masters ▲ IMP MCD 82 [DDD]
Balakirev, M.:Ov on 3 Russian Themes — IMP Masters ▲ IMP MCD 82 [DDD]
Mussorgsky, M.:Pictures at an Exhibition — IMP Masters ▲ IMP MCD 82 [DDD]
Rachmaninoff, S.:The Isle of the Dead — IMP Masters ▲ IMP MCD 82 [DDD]
Rimsky-Korsakov, N.:The Tale of Tsar Saltan (orch sels)—Flight of the Bumblebee — IMP Masters ▲ IMP MCD 82 [DDD]
T. Zehetmair (cnd)
Beethoven, L. van:Romances Vn, w. Thomas Zehetmair (vn) — Teldec ("M Line" series) ▲ 97448-2
Mozart, W.A.:Adagio Vn, K.261, w. Thomas Zehetmair (vn) — Teldec ("M Line" series) ▲ 97448-2
Mozart, W.A.:Con 1 Vn, w. T. Zehetmair (vn) — Teldec ▲ 2292-46341-2
Mozart, W.A.:Con 2 Vn, w. T. Zehetmair (vn) — Teldec ▲ 2292-46340-2 [DDD]
Mozart, W.A.:Con 3 Vn, w. T. Zehetmair (vn) — Teldec ▲ 2292-46340-2 [DDD]
Mozart, W.A.:Con 4 Vn, w. T. Zehetmair (vn) — Teldec ▲ 2292-46341-2
Mozart, W.A.:Con 5 Vn, w. T. Zehetmair (vn) — Teldec ▲ 2292-46340-2 [DDD]
Mozart, W.A.:Con 7 Vn, w. T. Zehetmair (vn) — Teldec ▲ 2292-46341-2
Mozart, W.A.:Rondo Vn, K.269, w. Thomas Zehetmair (vn) — Teldec ("M Line" series) ▲ 97448-2
Mozart, W.A.:Rondo Vn, K.373, w. Thomas Zehetmair (vn) — Teldec ("M Line" series) ▲ 97448-2
Schubert, Franz:Polonaise Vn — Teldec ("M Line" series) ▲ 97448-2
Schubert, Franz:Rondo Vn, D.438 — Teldec ("M Line" series) ▲ 97448-2

Philharmonia Orch members
C. Warren-Green (cnd)
Altenburg, J.E.:Con in C Tpts — Nimbus ▲ NI 5065 [DDD]
Weber, C.M. von:Marcia Vivace, Wallace Collection — Nimbus ▲ NI 5065 [DDD]
S. Wright (cnd)
Vačkář, D.:Jazz Con, w. John Wallace (tpt), Radoslav Kapil (pno), Wallace Collection — Nimbus ▲ NI 5103 [DDD]

Philharmonia Orch Off-stage Brass
G. Simon (cnd)
Borodin, A.:Prince Igor (sels), w. Margaret Field (sop), BBC Sym Chorus—Suite [orchd Glazunov & Rimsky-Korsakov] *(rec All Hallows Church, Gospel Oak, London)* — Cala ▲ CAL 1011 [DDD]

Philharmonia Orch Soloists
P. Spada (cnd)
Mercadante, S.:Decimini ASV ▲ ASV 936 [DDD]
Mercadante, S.:La Poesia ASV ▲ ASV 936 [DDD]
Philharmonia Pomorska
T. Ukigaya (cnd)
Louis Ferdinand, Prince:Octet Fl, w. H. Göbel (pno) Thorofon ▲ CTH 2088 [DDD]
Philharmonia Quartet
Klemperer, O.:Qt 7 Strs *(rec ca. 1970)* EMI Classics 2-▲ CDMB 64147
Philharmonia Slavonica
A. Lizzio (cnd)
Grieg, E.:Con Pno, Op. 16, w. D. Tomšic (pno) Vivace 2-▲ G 117/118 [DDD]
Grieg, E.:Con Pno, Op. 16, w. D. Tomšic (pno) Vivace 3-▲ E 322 [DDD]
Schumann, R.:Con Pno, w. D. Tomšic (pno) Vivace 3-▲ E 322 [DDD]
A. Nanut (cnd)
Beethoven, L. van:Con 1 Pno, w. D. Tomšič (pno) Vivace 3-▲ E 323 [DDD]
Beethoven, L. van:Con 3 Pno, w. D. Tomšič (pno) Vivace 3-▲ E 323 [DDD]
Philharmonia String Quartet
Mozart, W.A.:Qnt Cl, K.581, w. Karl Leister (cl) *(rec Studio Baumgarten, Vienna, Mar. 1981)* Camerata ▲ 25CM 331 [DDD]
Mozart, W.A.:Qnts Cl Bas Hn, w. Karl Leister (cl)—in B♭ *(rec Jesus Christ Church, Berlin Oct. 1988)* Camerata ▲ 25CM 331 [DDD]
Reger, M.:Qt Strs, Op. 74 Thorofon ▲ CTH 2116 [DDD]
Reger, M.:Qnt Cl, w. K. Leister (cl) Camerata 2-▲ 25CM-371-2
Philharmonia String Quartet [Daniel Stabrawa (vn), Christian Stadelmann (vn), Neithard Resa (va), Jan Diesselhorst (vc)]
Mozart, W.A.:Qt 14 Strs *(rec Waldkirche Heiligensee, Berlin, 1994)* Thorofon ▲ CTH 2214 [DDD]
Schubert, Franz:Qt 13 Strs *(rec Waldkirche Heiligensee, Berlin, 1994)* Thorofon ▲ CTH 2214 [DDD]
Philharmonia Virtuosi
R. Kapp (cnd)
Bach, J.S.:Brandenburg Cons *(rec Dec 1983)* Sony Classical ("Essential Classics") 2-▲ SB2K 53525 [DDD]
Bach, J.S.:Brandenburg Cons—Nos. 5 & 6 *(rec 1983)* Odyssey ■ YT 44514
Bach, J.S.:Brandenburg Cons ESS.A.Y 2-▲ CD 1037/38 [DDD]
Bach, J.S.:Cons Vn (comp), w. P. Peabody (vn) ESS.A.Y ▲ CD 1002 [DDD] ■ C 1002 (D)
Bach, J.S.:Con Vn & Ob, w. P. Peabody (vn), S. Taylor (ob) ESS.A.Y ▲ CD 1002 [DDD] ■ C 1002 (D)
Bach, J.S.:Con for 3 Vns, w. P. Peabody (vn), R. Rood (vn), E. Sato (vn) ESS.A.Y ▲ CD 1002 [DDD] ■ C 1002 (D)
Barber, S.:Adagio Strs CBS ▲ MK 42125 ■ MXT 42125
Baroque Trumpetissimo, w. Bilger, David (tpt), Stephen Burns (tpt), Edward Carroll (tpt), Alex Holton (tpt), Raymond Mase (tpt), Timothy Morrison (tpt), Lee Soper (tpt), Atsuko Sato (bn), Ben Harms (timp), Edward Brewer (org/hpd) ESS.A.Y ▲ ESS 1035 [DDD]
Bernstein, L.:Candide (ov) CBS ▲ MK 42125 ■ MXT 42125
Great Baroque Favorites, w. R. Leppard (cnd), English CO, Grande Ecurie [cnd:Jean-Claude Malgoire], et al. CBS ▲ MYK 38482 ■ MYT 38482
The Greatest Hits Of 1790 CBS ▲ MK 37216 [DDD]
Greatest Hits of 1720 CBS ▲ MK 34544 ■ MT 34544
Greatest Hits of 1721 CBS ▲ MK 35821 ■ MT 35821
Jewels of the Classics, w. Lisa Moore (pno) *(rec Apr. 7-9, 1993)* RCA Victor ▲ 09026-61935-2 ■ 09026-61935-4
Locatelli, P.:L'arte del violino, w. Mela Tenenbaum (vn), Kiev Pro Musica—Nos. 1-6 *(rec Kiev, Ukraine, Oct. 1994-95)* ESS.A.Y ▲ CD 1043/44 [DDD]
Martin, F.:Ballade Fl, w. R. Brown (fl) [orchestral version] ESS.A.Y ▲ CD 1014 [DDD]
Martin, F.:Con for 7 Winds ESS.A.Y ▲ CD 1014 [DDD]
Martin, F.:Petite sym concertante, w. V. Drake (hp), A. Newman (hpd), R. Hoca (pno) ESS.A.Y ▲ CD 1014 [DDD]
Masterpieces of the French Baroque, w. Oberlin Baroque Ensemble Vox Box 3-▲ CD3X 3006 [ADD]
Mozart, W.A.:Serenade Ww, K.361 ESS.A.Y ▲ CD 1020 [DDD]
Prokofiev, S.:Sym 1—Gavotta; Non troppo allegro *(rec SUNY, Purchase, Mar 17, 1985)* Sony Classical ("Greatest Hits" series) ▲ MLK 69249 [DDD] ■ LT 69
Sousa, J.P.:The Dwellers in the Western World ESS.A.Y ▲ CD 1003 [DDD] ■ C 1003 (D)
Sousa, J.P.:3 Quotations ESS.A.Y ▲ CD 1003 [DDD] ■ C 1003 (D)
Telemann, G.P.:Con Va, w. P. Peabody (vn) ESS.A.Y ▲ CD 1016
Telemann, G.P.:Cons Vn, w. P. Peabody (vn)—4 Concerti—in D, a, E & D ESS.A.Y ▲ CD 1016
Telemann, G.P.:Con in C for 2 Vns, w. P. Peabody (vn), E. Lim (vn)—4 Concerti—in D, a, E & D ESS.A.Y ▲ CD 1016
Telemann, G.P.:Suites Strs—3 Suites—in C, "Le Bouffonne"; in g, "La Changeante"; in G, "La Bizarre" ESS.A.Y ▲ CD 1017
Thomson, V.:The River (film music) ESS.A.Y ▲ CD 1005 [DDD] ■ C 1005 (D)
Vivaldi, A.:Cons Diverse Instrs—3 Concerti—RV.555, 558, 577 ESS.A.Y ▲ CD 1022 [DDD]
Vivaldi, A.:Con Gtr, RV.93, w. Peter Press (gtr) ESS.A.Y ▲ ESS 1004 [DDD]
Vivaldi, A.:Con Gtr Vl, w. Peter Press (gtr), Louise Schulman (vl) ESS.A.Y ▲ ESS 1004 [DDD]
Vivaldi, A.:Cons for 2 Hns, w. D. Smith (hn), A. Spanjer (hn)—RV.538 ESS.A.Y ▲ CD 1022 [DDD]
Vivaldi, A.:Con Mand, RV.425, w. Peter Press (mand) ESS.A.Y ▲ ESS 1004 [DDD]
Vivaldi, A.:Con Mand, RV.425, w. P. Press (gtr) ESS.A.Y ▲ CD 1004 [DDD] ■ C 1004 (D)
Vivaldi, A.:Con for 2 Mands, w. Scott Kuney (mand), Peter Press (mand) ESS.A.Y ▲ ESS 1004 [DDD]
Vivaldi, A.:Con for 2 Mands, w. P. Press (gtr), S. Kuney (gtr) ESS.A.Y ▲ CD 1004 [DDD] ■ C 1004 (D)
Vivaldi, A.:Cons Rcr, w. A. Kemp (rcr)—RV.441 ESS.A.Y ▲ CD 1022 [DDD]
Vivaldi, A.:Cons Va d'amore, w. S. Tenenbaum (va)—RV.394 ESS.A.Y ▲ CD 1022 [DDD]
Vivaldi, A.:Con Va d'amore Lt, w. L. Schulman (va), P. Press (gtr) ESS.A.Y ▲ CD 1004 [DDD] ■ C 1004 (D)
Vivaldi, A.:Cons Vn (misc), w. Mela Tenenbaum (vn)—Cons for Vn & 2 Orchs *(rec Recital Hall, Purchase College, Purchase, NY, Oct. 22 & 23, 1995)* ESS.A.Y ▲ CD 1046 [DDD]
Vivaldi, A.:Cons Vn (misc), w. P. Peabody (vn)—in A, in D, in c, in g & in G ESS.A.Y ▲ CD 1024 [DDD]
Vivaldi, A.:Cons Vn, Op. 8/1–4, "The Four Seasons", w. P. Peabody (vn) ESS.A.Y ▲ CD 1001 [DDD] ■ C 1001 (D)
Vivaldi, A.:Cons for 2 Vns, w. Paul Peabody (vn), Richard Rood (vn)—RV.522 ESS.A.Y ▲ CD 1001 [DDD] ■ C 1001 (D)
Wagner, R.:Siegfried Idyll ESS.A.Y ▲ CD 1020 [DDD]
Philharmonia Virtuosi [Mela Tenenbaum (vn), Alexandr Tenenbaum (vn), Dorothy Lawson (vc), Richard Kapp (pno)]
Boccherini, L.:Son Vn *(rec Purchase College, Purchase, NY, Aug. 13 & 14, 1995)* ESS.A.Y ▲ CD 1047 [DDD]
Handel, G.F.:Pieces (8) Vn *(rec Purchase College, Purchase, NY, Aug. 13 & 14, 1995)* ESS.A.Y ▲ CD 1047 [DDD]
Haydn, J.:Duet Vn & Vc *(rec Purchase College, Purchase, NY, Aug. 13 & 14, 1995)* ESS.A.Y ▲ CD 1047 [DDD]
Leclair, J.-M.:Son in d for 2 Vns *(rec Purchase College, Purchase, NY, Aug. 13 & 14, 1995)* ESS.A.Y ▲ CD 1047 [DDD]
Locatelli, P.:Son Vn, Op. 6 *(rec Purchase College, Purchase, NY, Aug. 13 & 14, 1995)* ESS.A.Y ▲ CD 1047 [DDD]
Locatelli, P.:Sons for 2 Vns, Op. 5—No. 1 *(rec Purchase College, Purchase, NY, Aug. 13 & 14, 1995)* ESS.A.Y ▲ CD 1047 [DDD]
Philharmonia Virtuosi members
Stravinsky, I.:Apollon musagète [original version] ESS.A.Y ▲ CD 1015 [DDD]
Tchaikovsky, P.:Souvenir de Florence ESS.A.Y ▲ CD 1015 [DDD]

Philharmonia Wind Quartet
Beethoven, L. van:Qnt Pno, Ob, Cl, Hn & Bn, w. Walter Gieseking (pno) *(rec London, 1955)* Testament ▲ SBT 1091
Mozart, W.A.:Qnt Pno Wnds, w. Walter Gieseking (pno) *(rec London, 1955)* Testament ▲ SBT 1091
Philharmonic Chamber Ensemble
Roman, J.H.:Con Vn, w. L. Berlin (vn), Stockholm Chamber Soloists Swedish Society ▲ SCD 1019
Philharmonic CO
P. Škvor (cnd)
Albinoni, T.:Con Tpt, Strs & Continuo, w. Zdenek Sedivy (tpt) Panton ▲ PAN 811023
Fasch, J.F.:Con Tpt & 2 Obs, w. Zdenek Sedivy (tpt), Frantisek Kimel (ob), Ivan Sequardt (ob) Panton ▲ PAN 811023
Telemann, G.P.:Con Tpt 2 Obs, w. Zdenek Sedivy (tpt), Frantisek Kimel (ob), Ivan Sequardt (ob) Panton ▲ PAN 811023
Telemann, G.P.:Con Tpt Strs in D, w. Zdenek Sedivy (tpt) Panton ▲ PAN 811023
Torelli, G.:Sons à 5 Tpts, w. Zdenek Sedivy (tpt)—Nos. 1 & 7 Panton ▲ PAN 811023
Veracini, F.M.:Con Tpt, w. Zdenek Sedivy (tpt) Panton ▲ PAN 811023
Philharmonic Orch
R. Muti (cnd)
Schumann, R.:Con Vn, w. Gidon Kremer (vn) EMI Classics 2-▲ CDFB 69334
W. Susskind (cnd)
Mozart, W.A.:Con 3 Vn, w. S. Goldberg (vn) Testament ▲ TES SBT 1028 [ADD]
Mozart, W.A.:Con 4 Vn, w. S. Goldberg (vn) Testament ▲ TES SBT 1028 [ADD]
Philharmonic Society Concert SO
Folklore Sinfónico I Producciones Fonograficas ▲ PFCD 0225
Folklore Sinfónico II Producciones Fonograficas ▲ PFCD 0164
Folklore Sinfónico III Producciones Fonograficas ▲ PFCD 0171
Folklore Sinfónico IV Producciones Fonograficas ▲ PFCD 0188
Folklore Sinfónico V Producciones Fonograficas ▲ PFCD 0195
Philharmonic SO
E. Kurtz (cnd)
Beethoven, L. van:Con 5 Pno, "Emperor", w. M. Hess (pno) *(rec Feb. 6, 1953)* Music & Arts 3-▲ CD 779 [AAD]
D. Mitropoulos (cnd)
Sibelius, J.:Con Vn, w. J. Heifetz (vn) *(rec Mar. 11, 1951)* Music & Arts 2-▲ CD 766 [AAD]
L. Stokowski (cnd)
Falla, M. de:Noches en los jardines de España, w. W. Kapell (pno) *(rec 1949)* Music & Arts ▲ CD 771 [AAD]
Mahler, G.:Sym 8, w. Westminster Choir *(rec live, Carnegie Hall, New York, 4/6/50)* Arkadia ▲ 761 [ADD]
Mahler, G.:Sym 8, w. Westminster Choir, P.S. 12 Boys' Choir, Schola Cantorum *(rec 1950)* Music & Arts 2-▲ MUA 280 [AAD]
Mozart, W.A.:Con 21 Pno, w. M. Hess (pno) *(rec Feb. 6, 1949)* Music & Arts 3-▲ CD 779 [AAD]
B. Walter (cnd)
Berlioz, H.:Sym fantastique *(rec 1948)* Music & Arts ▲ CD 822 [ADD]
Brahms, J.:Con 2 Pno, w. M. Hess (pno) *(rec Feb. 11, 1951)* Music & Arts 3-▲ CD 779 [AAD]
Mendelssohn, F.:A Midsummer Night's Dream (sels) *(rec 1954)* Music & Arts ▲ CD 822 [ADD]
Philharmonic Wedding Ensemble
B. Lucarelli (cnd)
Everybody's Favorite Wedding Music, Marni Nixon (sop), John Cullum (bar) Essex Entertainment ▲ ESD 7050 ■ ESC 7050
Philharmonica Hungarica Orch
Miklos Gafni Sings, w. Miklos Gafni (ten), Vienna Operetta Orch Aurora ▲ AUR 5051 [ADD]
Philidor Ensemble
Musique de Cour:Court Music of the 17th & 18th Centuries Supraphon ▲ SUP 112182 [DDD]
E. Baude-Delhommais (cnd)
Mozart, W.A.:Don Giovanni (sels)—sels unknwon [arr Vent] Supraphon ▲ SUP 3018
Mozart, W.A.:Entführung (sels)—sels unknwon [arr Vent] Supraphon ▲ SUP 3018
Carl Philipp Ensemble
Handel, G.F.:Cons (16) Org, w. G. Soly (org) Analekta Fleur de Lys ▲ FL 2 3026
Handel, G.F.:Cons (16) Org, w. D. Bédard (org) Analekta Fleur de Lys ▲ FL 2 3027
Handel, G.F.:Cons (16) Org, w. D. Laberge (org) Analekta Fleur de Lys ▲ FL 2 3028
Handel, G.F.:Cons (16) Org, w. G. Soly (org) Analekta Fleur de Lys ▲ FL 2 3029
Philomel
Telemann, G.P.:Trio Son Rcr Dorian ▲ DOR 90147 [DDD]
Vivaldi, A.:Cants, w. J. Baird (sop)—"All'ombra di sospetto," RV.678 [I] Dorian ▲ DOR 90147 [DDD]
Philomel Baroque CO
Handel, G.F.:Arias, w. J. Baird (sop)—"Tra le fiamme," "Pensieri notturni di Filli," "Alpestre monte" Dorian ▲ DOR 90147 [DDD]
Handel, G.F.:Cants, w. J. Baird (sop)—3 Italian Cantatas—"Tra le fiamme"; "Nel dolce dell'oblio"; Alpestre monte" [I] Dorian ▲ DOR 90147 [DDD]
R. Palmer (cnd)
Pergolesi, G.B.:La serva padrona, w. J. Baird (sop), J. Ostendorf (b-bar) [I] Omega ▲ OCD 1016 [DDD]
Philomusica Orch
C. Farncombe (cnd)
Handel, G.F.:Rodelinda, Regina de' Longobardi, w. Joan Sutherland (sop), Janet Baker (mez), Raimund Herincx (bar), Chandos Choir *(rec 1959)* Memories 2-▲ MEM 4577 [ADD]
Phoenix SO
The Cinema Classics Collection, Vol. 1, w. David Buechner (pno), Angeles String Quartet, London SO, New Zealand SO Koch International Classics ▲ KIC 7604
J. Sedares (cnd)
Asia, D.:Sym 2, "Celebration Sym" *(rec May 8 & 9, 1993)* New World ▲ 80447 [DDD]
Asia, D.:Sym 3 *(rec May 9, 1993)* New World ▲ 80447 [DDD]
Copland, A.:Latin American Sketches Koch International Classics ▲ KIC 7092-2 [DDD] ■ 3-7092-4 H1 (D)
Copland, A.:The Red Pony (suite) Koch International Classics ▲ KIC 7092-2 [DDD] ■ 3-7092-4 H1 (D)
Copland, A.:The Tender Land (suite) Koch International Classics ▲ KIC 7092-2 [DDD] ■ 3-7092-4 H1 (D)
Herrmann, B.:Sym 1 Koch International Classics ▲ KIC 7135-2 [DDD]
Schuman, W.:New England Triptych Koch International Classics ▲ KIC 7135-2 [DDD]
Phoenix Trio [Kay Stern (vn), Sarah Fiene (vc), Josephine Gandolfi (pno)]
Cowell, H.:Combinations (4) Koch International Classics ▲ KIC 7205 [DDD]
Cowell, H.:Trio in 9 Short Movements Koch International Classics ▲ KIC 7205 [DDD]
Piacenza SO
M. de Bernart (cnd)
Donizetti, G.:L'Esule di Roma, w. C. Gasdia (sop), E. Palacio (ten), A. Ariostini (bar), S. Alaimo (bass-bar), Paris Opéra-Comique Chorus *(rec live, 10/14/86)* Bongiovanni 2-▲ GB 2045/46 [DDD]
C. Rizzi (cnd)
Donizetti, G.:Il furioso all'isola di Santo Domingo, w. P. Antonucci (sop), L. Serra (sop), E. Tandura (mez), L. Canonici (ten), R. Coviello (bar), Picconi (sgr), Piacenza Chorus [I] *(rec live, 11/10/87)* Bongiovanni 3-▲ GB 2056/58 [DDD]
N. Sanzogno (cnd)
Giordano, U.:La Cena delle beffe, w. R. Lantieri (sop), Armiliato (sgr), M. Chingari (bar) [I] *(rec live, 12/14/88)* Bongiovanni 2-▲ GB 2068/69 [DDD]
M. Viotti (cnd)
Bellini, V.:La sonnambula, w. M. Devia (sop), L. Canonici (ten), A. Verducci (bass), Piacenza Chorus [I] *(rec live 11/88)* Nuova Era 2-▲ 6764/65 [DDD]

320 ▲ = CD ♦ = Enhanced CD Δ = MD ■ = Cassette Tape □ = DCC

Pian e Forte Ensemble
Cazzati, M.:Sons 5 Instr, Op. 35, w. G. Cassone (natural tpt)—Nos. 10 & 11 *(rec Feb. 17–20, 1992)* Nuova Era ("Ancient Music" series) ▲ NUO 7128 [DDD]
Gabrielli, D.:Son 2 Tpt, w. G. Cassone (tpt) *(rec Feb. 17–20, 1992)* Nuova Era ("Ancient Music" series) ▲ NUO 7128 [DDD]
Gabrielli, D.:Son 5 Tpt, w. G. Cassone (tpt) *(rec Feb. 17–20, 1992)* Nuova Era ("Ancient Music" series) ▲ NUO 7128 [DDD]
Giardini, F.:Chamber Music, w. Andrea Dandolo (gtr)—Sons. & Trios w. Guitar Nuova Era ("Ancient Music" series) ▲ NUO 7186 [DDD]
Jacchini, G.M.:Sons Tpt, w. G. Cassone (tpt)—Nos. 5 & 6 *(rec Feb. 17–20, 1992)* Nuova Era ("Ancient Music" series) ▲ NUO 7128 [DDD]
Melani, A.:Cants, w. E. Gambarini (sop), G. Cassone (nat tpt)—"All'armi, pensieri" & "Qual bellici, accenti" [I] Nuova Era ("Ancient Music" series) ▲ 7009 [DDD]
Mozart, W.A.:Church Sons, w. Antonio Frigé (org) *(rec St. Francis of Paola Church, Milan, Aug. 1994)* Agora Music ▲ 002
Noferi, G.B.:Chamber Music, w. Andrea Dandolo (gtr)—Sons. & Trios w. Guitar Nuova Era ("Ancient Music" series) ▲ NUO 7186 [DDD]
Scarlatti, A.:Su le sponde del Tebro, w. E. Gambarini (sop), G. Cassone (tpt) [I] Nuova Era ("Ancient Music" series) ▲ 7009 [DDD]
Stanley, J.:Cons Strs, w. A. Frigé (org) Nuova Era ("Ancient Music" series) ▲ 7019 [DDD]
Stradella, A.:Sinf alla Serenata Nuova Era ("Ancient Music" series) ▲ 7009 [DDD]
Stradella, A.:Sinf Vn Nuova Era ("Ancient Music" series) ▲ 7009 [DDD]
Telemann, G.P.:Con Tpt 2 Obs, w. G. Cassone (tpt) *(rec 4/91)* Giulia ▲ GS 201008 [DDD]
Telemann, G.P.:Con Tpt 2 Obs, w. Gabriele Cassone (tpt) *(rec Milan, Apr 1991)* Arts ▲ 47320–2 [DDD]
Telemann, G.P.:Con Tpt 2 Vns, w. Gabriele Cassone (tpt) *(rec Milan, Apr 1991)* Arts ▲ 47320–2 [DDD]
Telemann, G.P.:Con Tpt 2 Vns, w. G. Cassone (tpt) *(rec 4/91)* Giulia ▲ GS 201008 [DDD]
Telemann, G.P.:Musique de Table—Overture in D; Trio in e; Conclusion in D [all from set 2] *(rec 4/91)* Giulia ▲ GS 201008 [DDD]
Telemann, G.P.:Tafelmusic II—Ov-Suite; Trio; Conclusion *(rec Milan, Apr 1991)* Arts ▲ 47320–2 [DDD]
Torelli, G.:Sinf Tp, w. G. Cassone (tpt) *(rec Feb. 17–20, 1992)* Nuova Era ("Ancient Music" series) ▲ NUO 7128 [DDD]
Torelli, G.:Son Tpt, G.1, w. G. Cassone (tpt) *(rec Feb. 17–20, 1992)* Nuova Era ("Ancient Music" series) ▲ NUO 7128 [DDD]
Vivaldi, A.:Cons Diverse Instrs—Cons, R.94, 100, 106, 541, 542 & 554 *(rec Milan, June 1991)* Arts ▲ 47131–2 [DDD]

G. Cassone (cnd)
Grossi, A.:Sons, Op. 3, w. G. Cassone (tpt)—Nos. 10 & 11 *(rec Feb. 17–20, 1992)* Nuova Era ("Ancient Music" series) ▲ NUO 7128 [DDD]

Piano Circus
Fitkin, C.:Sextet Argo ▲ 433522–2 [DDD]
Fitkin, G.:Line Argo ▲ 436100–2 [DDD]
Fitkin, G.:Log Argo ▲ 436100–2 [DDD]
Fitkin, G.:Loud Argo ▲ 436100–2 [DDD]
Nyman, M.:1–100 for Multiple Pianos Argo ▲ 433522–2 [DDD]
Rackham, S.:Which ever way your nose bends Argo ▲ 433522–2 [DDD]
Reich, S.:6 Pianos Argo ▲ 430380–2 [DDD]
Riley, T.:In C Argo ▲ 430380–2 [DDD]
Seddon, T.:16 Argo ▲ 433522–2 [DDD]
Volans, K.:Kneeling Dance Argo ▲ 440294–2 [DDD]

Piano Circus [K. Davidson–Kelly (pno), R. Harris (pno), M. Haslam (pno), K. Heath (pno), M. Richter (pno), G. Strawson (pno)]
Lang, D.:Face So Pale Argo ▲ 440294–2 [DDD]
Moran, R.:Dances Argo ▲ 440294–2 [DDD]
Reich, S.:4 Orgs Argo ▲ 440294–2 [DDD]

Piano Circus Band
Moran, R.:Arias & Inventions, w. et. al. Argo ▲ 436128–2 [DDD]
Moran, R.:Open Veins, w. et. al. Argo ▲ 436128–2 [DDD]
Moran, R.:10 Miles Argo ▲ 436128–2 [DDD]

Daniel Piazzolla Octet
Piazzolla, A.:Music of, w. Fito Páez (sgr)—Fuga y Misterio [composed with H. Ferrer]; Romance del Diablo; Verano Porteño; Tanti Anni Prima [all arr D. Piazzolla & S. Cosentino for octet]; Violentango; Libertango; Adiós Nonino *(rec Moebio Studios, Buenos Aires, Sept–Oct 1995)* Milan ▲ 35782–2
Piazzolla, D.H.:El Diego *(rec Moebio Studios, Buenos Aires, Sept–Oct 1995)* Milan ▲ 35782–2
Piazzolla, D.H.:Lalla *(rec Moebio Studios, Buenos Aires, Sept–Oct 1995)* Milan ▲ 35782–2

Picardie Orch
P. Fournillier (cnd)
Haydn, J.:Applausus:Jubilaeum virtutis Palatium, w. Rosemary Musoleno (sop—Temperantia), Kirsten Dolberg (mez—Prudentia), Douglas Johnson (ten—Justitia), Desmond Byrne (bass—Fortitudo), Jean–Philippe Courtis (bass—Theologia), Haydn Vocal Ensemble [L] *(rec 9/91)* Opus 111 2–▲ OPS 61–9207/8 [DDD]

Piccolo Ensemble
Music in Neapolitan Theaters in the 1700's, w. Gloria Guida Borrelli (sop), Quintetto da Camera Kicco Classics ▲ 496 [DDD]

Pihtipudas Quintet
Beach, A.M.C.:Qnt Pno EDA ▲ EDA 003–2 [DDD]
Bloch, E.:Qnt 1 Pno EDA ▲ EDA 003–2 [DDD]
Borodin, A.:Qnt Pno & Strs EDA ▲ EDA 001–2 [DDD]
Bruch, M.:Qnt Pno EDA ▲ EDA 001–2 [DDD]
Elgar, E.:Qnt Pno Strs EDA ▲ EDA 004–2 [DDD]
Kuula, T.:Scherzo EDA ▲ EDA 003–2 [DDD]
Nordgren, P.H.:Qnt EDA ▲ EDA 001–2 [DDD]
Rubinstein, A.:Qnt Pno Strs *(rec Kuopio, Finland, May 1996)* EDA ▲ EDA 0102 [DDD]
Saint–Saëns, C.:Qnt Pno EDA ▲ EDA 004–2 [DDD]
Shostakovich, D.:Qnt Pno *(rec Kuopio, Finland, May 1996)* EDA ▲ EDA 0102 [DDD]
Sibelius, J.:Qnt Pno EDA 2–▲ EDA 007
Sinding, C.:Qnt Pno EDA 2–▲ EDA 007

Pilsen RSO
A. Apolin (cnd)
Mercadante, S.:Con in e Fl, Op. 57, w. Isabelle Schnöller (fl) *(rec Sept 1994)* Jecklin ▲ JEC 704 [DDD]
Mozart, W.A.:Con Fl, K.314, w. Isabelle Schnöller (fl) *(rec Sept 1994)* Jecklin ▲ JEC 704 [DDD]
Reinecke, C.:Con Fl, w. Isabelle Schnöller (fl) *(rec Sept 1994)* Jecklin ▲ JEC 704 [DDD]
J. Malát (cnd)
Kalliwoda, J.W.:Sym 5 Centaur ▲ CRC 2123
Kalliwoda, J.W.:Sym 6 Centaur ▲ CRC 2123

Pioneer Brass
Acres of Clams *(rec 1991)* Centaur ▲ CRC 2131 [DDD]

Pirasti Trio
Holst, G.:Short Trio ASV ▲ ASV 925 [DDD]
Stanford, C.V.:Trio 2 Pno ASV ▲ ASV 925 [DDD]

Pittsburgh New Music Ensemble
W. Kraft (cnd)
Kraft, William:The Sublime & the Beautiful, w. P. Sperry (ten) [E] *(rec 1984)* CRI ▲ CD 639 [ADD/DDD]

Pittsburgh New Music Ensemble (cont.)
D. Stock (cnd)
Roussakis, N.:Hymn to Apollo *(rec 1990)* CRI ▲ CD 624 [ADD/DDD]
Stock, D.:The Particle Zoo *(rec Levy Hall, Rodef Shalom Temple, Pittsburgh, Feb. 11, 1990)* Northeastern ("Contemporary" series) ▲ NR 255 [DDD]
Stock, D.:Tekiah, w. Stephen Burns (tpt) *(rec Levy Hall, Rodef Shalom Temple, Pittsburgh, Feb. 11, 1990)* Northeastern ("Contemporary" series) ▲ NR 255 [DDD]
Stock, D.:Yerusha, w. Richard Stoltzman (cl) *(rec Levy Hall, Rodef Shalom Temple, Pittsburgh, Feb. 11, 1990)* Northeastern ("Contemporary" series) ▲ NR 255 [DDD]

Pittsburgh SO
E. Leinsdorf (cnd)
Wagner, R.:Die Meistersinger von Nürnberg (prelude/act 1) EMI Classics ("FDS" series) ▲ CDM 65208
Wagner, R.:Parsifal (sels)—Prelude; Good Friday Music EMI Classics ("FDS" series) ▲ CDM 65208
Wagner, R.:Siegfried Idyll . EMI Classics ("FDS" series) ▲ CDM 65208
L. Maazel (cnd)
Balada, L.:Lament, w. Cynthia Koledo DeAlmeida (ob) *(rec Pittsburgh, May 10–12, 1996)* New World ▲ 805032 [DDD]
Balada, L.:Steel Sym New World ▲ NW 348–2 [DDD] ■ NW 348–4 (D)
Grofé, F.:Grand Canyon Suite *(rec Oct. 13, 1991)* Sony Classical ▲ SK 52491 [DDD]
Herbert, V.:Hero & Leander *(rec Sept. 30–Oct. 13, 1991)* Sony Classical ▲ SK 52491 [DDD]
Lees, B.:Con Hn, w. William Caballero (hn) *(rec Pittsburgh, May 10–12, 1996)* New World ▲ 805032 [DDD]
Prokofiev, S.:Sym–Con Vc, w. Yo–Yo Ma (vc) Sony Classical ▲ SK 48382 [DDD]
Rachmaninoff, S.:Con 2 Pno, w. H. Gutiérrez (pno) Telarc ▲ CD 80259 [DDD]
Rachmaninoff, S.:Con 3 Pno, w. H. Gutiérrez (pno) Telarc ▲ CD 80259 [DDD]
Respighi, O.:Feste Romane Sony Classical ▲ SK 66843
Respighi, O.:The Fountains of Rome Sony Classical ▲ SK 66843
Respighi, O.:The Pines of Rome Sony Classical ▲ SK 66843
Rimsky–Korsakov, N.:Antar Telarc ▲ CD 80131 [DDD]
Saint–Saëns, C.:Danse macabre Sony Classical ▲ SK 53979
Saint–Saëns, C.:Phaéton Sony Classical ▲ SK 53979
Saint–Saëns, C.:Samson et Dalila (sels)—Danse Bacchanale Sony Classical ▲ SK 53979
Saint–Saëns, C.:Sym 3, w. Anthony Newman (org) Sony Classical ▲ SK 53979
Schuman, W.:Sym 7 New World ▲ NW 348–2 [DDD] ■ NW 348–4 (D)
Sibelius, J.:Con Vn, w. J. Rachlin (vn) *(rec Sept. 26–27, 1992)* Sony Classical ▲ SK 53272 [DDD]
Sibelius, J.:Finlandia Sony Classical ▲ SK 61963
Sibelius, J.:Karelia Suite Sony Classical ▲ SK 61963
Sibelius, J.:En Saga *(rec Sept. 26–27, 1992)* Sony Classical ▲ SK 53272 [DDD]
Sibelius, J.:Serenades Vn, w. J. Rachlin (vn)—No. 2 in g *(rec Sept. 26–27, 1992)* Sony Classical ▲ SK 53272 [DDD]
Sibelius, J.:Sym 1 Sony Classical ▲ SK 52566
Sibelius, J.:Sym 2 Sony Classical ▲ SK 53268
Sibelius, J.:Sym 3 Sony Classical ▲ SK 61963
Sibelius, J.:Sym 4 Sony Classical ▲ SK 46499
Sibelius, J.:Sym 5 Sony Classical ▲ SK 46499
Sibelius, J.:Sym 6 Sony Classical ▲ SK 53268
Sibelius, J.:Sym 7 Sony Classical ▲ SK 52566
Sibelius, J.:Valse triste Sony Classical ▲ SK 61963
Tchaikovsky, P.:Sym 2 Telarc ▲ CD 80131 [DDD]
Tchaikovsky, P.:Vars on a Rococo Theme, w. Yo–Yo Ma (vc) Sony Classical ▲ SK 48382 [DDD]
Wagner, R.:Tannhäuser (without words) Sony Classical ▲ SK 47178
Wagner, R.:Die Walküre (act 1), w. S. Dunn (sop), K. König (ten), P. Meven (bass) [G] Telarc ▲ CD 80258 [DDD]
Zwilich, E.T.:Con Bn, w. Nancy Goeres (bn) *(rec Pittsburgh, May 10–12, 1996)* New World ▲ 805032 [DDD]
A. Previn (cnd)
Gershwin, G.:An American in Paris Philips ▲ 412611–2 [DDD] □ 412611-5
Gershwin, G.:Con Pno, w. A. Previn (pno) Philips ▲ 412611–2 [DDD] □ 412611-5
Gershwin, G.:Rhap in Blue, w. A. Previn (pno) Philips ▲ 412611–2 [DDD] □ 412611-5
Handel, G.F.:Ovs [arr. Elgar]—in d Philips ▲ 411047-2 [DDD]
Handel, G.F.:Royal Fireworks Music Philips ▲ 411047-2 [DDD]
Handel, G.F.:Water Music (suites) Philips ▲ 411047-2 [DDD]
Harbison, J.:Ulysses' Bow Elektra/Nonesuch ▲ 79129-2 [DDD]
Haydn, J.:Sym 94, "Surprise Sym" EMI Classics ▲ CDM 65178
Haydn, J.:Sym 96, "Miracle" EMI Classics ▲ CDM 65178
Haydn, J.:Sym 104, "London" EMI Classics ▲ CDM 65178
Korngold, E.W.:Con Vn, w. I. Perlman (vn) EMI Classics ▲ CDC 47846
Mahler, G.:Sym 4, w. E. Ameling (sop) EMI Classics ▲ CDM 65179
Offenbach, J.:Gaîté Parisienne *(rec Oct. 1–2, 1982)* Philips ("Solo" series) ▲ 442403-2
Ravel, M.:Ma mère l'oye Orch Philips ▲ 400016-2 [DDD]
Saint–Saëns, C.:Carnival of the Animals, w. V. Jennings (pno), P. Jennings (pno) Philips ▲ 400016-2 [DDD]
Sarasate, P. de:Zigeunerweisen, w. I. Perlman (vn) EMI Classics ▲ CDM 63533
Schubert, Franz:Songs (misc), w. E. Ameling (sop)—An die Musik; Ständchen EMI Classics ▲ CDM 65179
F. Reiner (cnd)
Bach, J.S.:Suite 2 Orch, w. Caratelli (fl) *(rec 1945–46)* LYS ▲ LYS 126
Bartók, B.:Hungarian Sketches—Nos. 2 & 4 *(rec Apr 1947)* Sony Classical ("Masterworks Heritage" series) ▲ MHK 062343 [ADD]
Beethoven, L. van:Sym 2 Sony Classical ("Masterworks Heritage" series) ▲ MHK 62344
Beethoven, L. van:Sym 2, w. Caratelli (fl) *(rec 1945–46)* LYS ▲ LYS 126
Brahms, J.:Con 1 Pno, w. Rudolf Serkin (pno) LYS ▲ LYS 127
Brahms, J.:Hungarian Dances Orch LYS ▲ LYS 127
Brahms, J.:Hungarian Dances Orch—Nos. 1, 5–7, 12, 13, 19 & 21 *(rec 1946)* Arlecchino ▲ ARL 131
Kabalevsky, D.:Colas Breugnon (ov) *(rec Mar 1945)* Sony Classical ("Masterworks Heritage" series) ▲ MHK 062343 [ADD]
Kodály, Z.:Galanta Dances, w. Sigurd Bockman (cl) *(rec Mar 1945)* Sony Classical ("Masterworks Heritage" series) ▲ MHK 062343 [ADD]
Mozart, W.A.:Sym 35 Sony Classical ("Masterworks Heritage" series) ▲ MHK 62344
Mozart, W.A.:Sym 40 Sony Classical ("Masterworks Heritage" series) ▲ MHK 62344
Shostakovich, D.:Sym 6 *(rec Mar 1945)* Sony Classical ("Masterworks Heritage" series) ▲ MHK 062343 [ADD]
Weiner, L.:Divert 1 Str Orch *(rec Mar 1945)* Sony Classical ("Masterworks Heritage" series) ▲ MHK 062343 [ADD]
W. Steinberg (cnd)
Beethoven, L. van:Leonore 3 MCA Classics 2–▲ MCAD2–9810 [AAD]
Beethoven, L. van:Sym 2 MCA Classics 2–▲ MCAD2–9810 [AAD]
Beethoven, L. van:Sym 4 MCA Classics 2–▲ MCAD2–9810 [AAD]
Beethoven, L. van:Sym 7 MCA Classics 2–▲ MCAD2–9810 [AAD]
Beethoven, L. van:Sym 7 EMI Classics ▲ CDM 65611
Bennett, Robert Russell:Stephen Collins Foster:A Commemoration Sym *(rec Syria Mosque, Pittsburgh; Belock Recording Studio, Bayside, NY)* Everest ▲ EVC 9027 [AAD]
Bennett, Robert Russell:A Symphonic Story of Jerome Kern *(rec Syria Mosque, Pittsburgh; Belock Recording Studio, Bayside, NY)* Everest ▲ EVC 9027 [AAD]
Brahms, J.:Syms (comp) MCA Classics 2–▲ MCAD2–9817 [AAD]
Brahms, J.:Sym 4 *(rec Syria Mosque, Pittsburgh)* Everest ▲ EVC 9016 [AAD]
Elgar, E.:Enigma Vars EMI Classics ▲ CDM 65610
Gershwin, G.:An American in Paris MCA Classics 2–▲ MCAD2-9800

ORCH. & ENS.

Pittsburgh SO (cont.)
W. Steinberg (cnd) (cont.)
Gershwin, G.:An American in Paris — Everest ▲ EVC 9003 [AAD]
Gershwin, G.:Porgy & Bess (symphonic picture) — MCA Classics 2–▲ MCAD2–9800
Mendelssohn, F.:Sym 4 — EMI Classics ▲ CDM 65611
Orchestral Masterworks — EMI Classics ("FDS Series" series) ▲ CDM 65204
Prokofiev, S.:Con 3 Pno, w. V. Ashkenazy (pno) *(rec live 11/7/69)* — Intaglio ▲ INCD 7181 [ADD]
Prokofiev, S.:The Love for 3 Oranges (suite) — EMI Classics ("Full Dimensional Sound" series) ▲ CDM 65424
Wolf, H.:Italian Serenade — EMI Classics ▲ CDM 65611
Plasma SO
I. Tomita (cnd)
Back to the Earth, w. Clamma Dale (sop), Nikolai Demidenko (pno), et al. *(rec live, NYC, 1986)* — RCA Red Seal ▲ 7717–2–RC [DDD]
Firebird — RCA Victor ▲ 60578–2–RG [ADD]
Kosmos — RCA Victor ▲ 2616–2–RG [ADD] ■ 2616–4–RG (CrO2)
Pictures at an Exhibition — RCA Victor ▲ 60576–2–RG [ADD] ■ 60576–4–RG (CrO2)
Snowflakes Are Dancing — RCA Victor ▲ 60579–2–RG [ADD] ■ 60579–4–RG (CrO2)
The Tomita Planets — RCA Victor ▲ 60518–2–RG [ADD] ■ 60518–4–RG (CrO2)
Tomita's Greatest Hits — RCA Victor ▲ 5660–2 RC ■ ARK1–3439
Plectr'Archi Quartet
Giuliani, G.F.:Qts (3) Vn — Pavane ▲ ADW 7224 [DDD]
Hoffmann, Giovanni:Qts Vn, Va, Mand & Lt — Pavane ▲ ADW 7224 [DDD]
Pleeth Cello Octet
Villa–Lobos, H.:Bachiana brasileira 5, w. J. Gomez (sop) — Hyperion ▲ CDA 66257 [DDD]
Les Pléiades Ensemble
Boucourechliev, A.:Les Archipels, w. Brigitte Sylvestre (hp), Elisabeth Chojnacka (hpd), Françoise Rieunier (org), Roland Auzet, Jean–Pierre Drouet (perc), Hakon Austbö (pno), Françoise–Frédéric Guy (pno), Claude Helffer (pno), Georges Pludermacher (pno), Ysaÿe String Quartet — Musique Francaise d'Aujourd'hui ("Collection MFA–Radio France" series) ▲ MFA 216001
Pleven PO
G. Notev (cnd)
Puccini, G.:Arias, w. Qilian Chen (sop)—Intermezzo [orch solo]; In quelle trine morbide; Sola, perduta, abbandonata [all from Manon Lescaut]; O mio babbino caro [from Gianni Schicchi]; Un bel dì vedremo; Che tua madre; Con onor muore [all from Madame Butterfly]; Signore, ascolta; Tu che di gel sei cinta [both from Turandot]; Senza mamma [from Suor Angelica]; Sì, mi chiamano; Donde lieta usci; Quando men vo [all from La bohème]; Chi il bel sogno di Doretta [from La rondine] *(rec Sofia, 1996)* — Pavane ▲ ADW 7366 [DDD]
Ploiesti PO
H. Andreescu (cnd)
Marbe, M.:Con for Daniel Kientzy & Saxes, w. D. Kientzy (sax) — Olympia ("Explorer" series) ▲ OCD 410 [AAD]
Plovdiv PO
Vol. 1, w. Classics Go to the Movies, Hungarian State Opera Orch, Vienna Strauss Orch, Jenő Jandó (pno), Dresden PO, New Leipzig Bach Collegium Musicum, Budapest SO — LaserLight ▲ 15 641
V. Ghiaurov (cnd)
Dvořák, A.:Husitská — LaserLight ▲ 14 005 [DDD]
Dvořák, A.:Sym 5 — LaserLight ▲ 14 005 [DDD]
D. Petkov (cnd)
Paganini, N.:Con 5 Vn, w. M. Minchev (vn) — Vivace ▲ E 534 [ADD]
R. Raichev (cnd)
Chabrier, E.:España — Laserlight ▲ 15 528 [DDD]
Debussy, C.:Prélude à l'après–midi d'un faune — Laserlight ▲ 15 528 [DDD]
Dukas, P.:L'Apprenti sorcier — Laserlight ▲ 15 528 [DDD]
Glinka, M.:Waltz Fant — LaserLight ▲ 15635 [DDD]
Mussorgsky, M.:Khovanshchina (orch sels)—Dance of Persian Slaves, Intermezzo—act 4 — LaserLight ▲ 14 012 [DDD]
Ravel, M.:Rapsodie espagnole — Laserlight ▲ 15 528 [DDD]
Respighi, O.:La Boutique fantastique — LaserLight ▲ 15 520 [DDD]
Rimsky–Korsakov, N.:Capriccio espagnol — Laserlight ▲ 15 528 [DDD]
Rossini, G.:Ovs—Barber of Seville, William Tell, La gazza ladra, Cenerentola, Italiana in Algeri, Cambiale di Matrimonio, Scala di seta, Semiramide — Harmonia Mundi Plus ▲ HMP 390466
Rossini, G.:Ovs—Barber of Seville; Italian Girl in Algiers; The Silken Ladder; Tancredi; Semiramis; Siege of Corinth; The Thieving Magpie — Laserlight ▲ 15 506 [DDD]
Rossini, G.:Ovs—La Cambiale di matrimonio; Le cenerentola; Matilde di Shabran; Il viaggio a Reims; Guillaume Tell; La boutique fantastique — Laserlight ▲ 15 520 [DDD]
Plymouth Festival Orch
P. Brunelle (cnd)
Argento, D.:Te Deum [Verbi Domini cum verbus populi], w. Plymouth Festival Chorus [L] — Virgin Classics ▲ CDC 59009–2 [DDD]
Argento, D.:Vars for Orch [The Mask of Night], w. M. Jette (sop) [E] — Virgin Classics ▲ CDC 59009–2 [DDD]
Plymouth Music Series Orch
Britten, B.:Paul Bunyan, w. *(soloists unknown)*, Soloists, Plymouth Music Series Chorus [E] — Virgin Classics 2–▲ 59126 [DDD]
Smyth, E.:The Boatswain's Mate, w. E. Harrhy (sop), J. Hardy (alt), D. Dressen (ten), J. Bohn (bass), Plymouth Music Series Chorus—Mrs. Water's Aria — Virgin Classics ▲ CDC 59022
Smyth, E.:The March of the Women, w. Plymouth Music Series Chorus — Virgin Classics ▲ CDC 59022
Smyth, E.:Mass in D, w. E. Harrhy (sop), J. Hardy (alt), D. Dressen (ten), J. Bohn (bass), Plymouth Music Series Chorus — Virgin Classics ▲ CDC 59022
Still, W.G.:Music of, w. William Warfield (nar), Yolanda Williams (sop), Hilda Harris (alt), Plymouth Music Series Chorus, Leigh Morris Chorale—Wailing Woman; Swanee River; And They Lynched Him on a Tree; Miss Sally's Party — Collins Classics ▲ COL 1454
Plymouth Music Series Orch Soloists
Copland, A.:The Tender Land, w. Plymouth Music Series Chorus [E] — Virgin Classics 2–▲ 59207 [DDD]
Plymouth Trio [Christina Price (sop), John Mack (ob), John Herr (kbd)]
Adler, S.:The Rocking Horse Winner — Crystal ▲ CD 640
The Plymouth Trio, w. Robert Perry (vc) *(rec 1992)* — Crystal ▲ 641
The Plymouth Trio, w. Robert Perry (vc) — Crystal ▲ CD 640
Roy, K.G.:Miracles Are Not Ceased — Crystal ▲ CD 640
Pohjola Trio
Kuula, T.:Trio Pno — BIS ▲ CD 56 [AAD]
Poliakin Orch
R. Poliakin (cnd)
Berlin, I.:Music of, w. Poliakin Chorale—Easter Parade; With You; Let's Face the Music & Dance; I've Got My Love to Keep Me Warm; What'll I Do ; Say It Isn't So; How Deep Is the Ocean?; Now It Can Be Told; The Girl That I Marry; I'm Putting All My Eggs in One Basket; The Song Is Ended *(rec Syria Mosque, Pittsburgh; Belock Recording Studio, Bayside, NY)* — Everest ▲ EVC 9027 [AAD]
Polish Air Force Band
Marsz, Marsz Polonia, w. Krakow Garrison Military Band, Polish Army Band, Polish Navy Band, Pomeranian Military District Band, Silesian Military District Band, Warsaw Military District Band — Polskie Nagrania Edition ▲ ECD 064 [DDD]
Polish Army Band
Marsz, Marsz Polonia, w. Krakow Garrison Military Band, Polish Air Force Band, Polish Navy Band, Pomeranian Military District Band, Silesian Military District Band, Warsaw Military District Band — Polskie Nagrania Edition ▲ ECD 064 [DDD]
Polish CO
J. Maksymiuk (cnd)
Bacewicz, G.:Con Str — Olympia ▲ OLY 392 [ADD]

Polish CO (cont.)
J. Maksymiuk (cnd) (cont.)
Baird, T.:Colas Breugnon, w. Konstanty Kulka (vn) [arr for violin & string orch] — EMI Classics ▲ CDM 65418
Bloch, A.:Oratario, German Youth PO — Pro Viva ▲ ISPV 172
Bloch, A.:Twelve Time Layers, German Youth PO — Pro Viva ▲ ISPV 172
Górecki, H.–M.:Stücke im alten Stil (3), w. Konstanty Kulka (vn), Polish RSO — EMI Classics ▲ CDM 65418
Lidholm, I.:Musik — Caprice ▲ CAP 21366 [AAD]
Mozart, W.A.:Con 6 Pno, w. Ewa Osinska (pno) *(rec Studio S II, Polish Radio, Warsaw, Oct 8–10, 1985)* — Polskie Nagrania ▲ PNCD 316
Mozart, W.A.:Con 16 Pno, w. Ewa Osinska (pno) *(rec Studio S II, Polish Radio, Warsaw, Oct 8–10, 1985)* — Polskie Nagrania ▲ PNCD 316
Mozart, W.A.:Con 18 Pno, w. F. Ts'ong (pno) — Vivace ▲ E 572 [ADD]
Mozart, W.A.:Con 20 Pno, w. Ewa Poblocka (pno) *(rec Concert Hall of the National Philharmonic, Warsaw, May 5–6, 1990)* — Polskie Nagrania ▲ PNCD 077 [DDD]
Mozart, W.A.:Con 21 Pno, w. Ewa Osinska (pno) *(rec Studio S II, Polish Radio, Warsaw, May 19–20, 1980)* — Polskie Nagrania ▲ PNCD 316
Mozart, W.A.:Con 23 Pno, w. Ewa Poblocka (pno) *(rec Concert Hall of the National Philharmonic, Warsaw, May 5–6, 1990)* — Polskie Nagrania ▲ PNCD 077 [DDD]
Mozart, W.A.:Con 25 Pno, w. Fou Ts'ong (pno) — Vivace ▲ E 572 [ADD]
Palester, R.:Concertino Sax, w. David Pituch (sax) *(rec Polish Radio, 1982)* — Pro Viva ▲ ISPV 175 [ADD]
Ptaszynska, M.:La Novella d'inverno *(rec Music Academy, Warsaw, Oct. 9, 1987)* — Polskie Nagrania ▲ PLN 075 [ADD]
Rossini, G.:Sons Str Qt—No. 3 — EMI Classics ("Encore" series) ▲ CDE 68308 [ADD/DDD]
Vivaldi, A.:Cons Vn, Op. 8/1–4, "The Four Seasons", w. Krzysztof Jakowicz (vn) — Classics for Pleasure ("Eminence" series) ▲ CFP 2009 [ADD]
W. Michniewski (cnd)
Fennelly, B.:Con Sax, w. David Pituch (sax) *(rec Apr 1986)* — Pro Viva ▲ ISPV 175 [ADD]
Polish Chamber PO
Strauss, R.:Con Ob, w. S. Dent (ob) — Amati ▲ 9205
Strauss, R.:Duet–Concertino, w. M. Spangenberg (cl), K. Nagel (bn) — Amati ▲ 9205
W. Rajski (cnd)
Fiala, J.:Con Ob, w. I. Goritzki (ob) — Claves ▲ CD 9018 [DDD]
Kalliwoda, J.W.:Concertino Ob, w. I. Goritzki (ob) — Claves ▲ CD 9018 [DDD]
Krommer, F.:Con Ob, Op. 37, w. I. Goritzki (ob) — Claves ▲ CD 9018 [DDD]
Martinů, B.:Con Ob, w. I. Goritzki (ob) — Claves ▲ CD 9018 [DDD]
Mozart, W.A.:Andante Fl, K.315/285a, w. I. Goritzki (ob) [arr. for oboe] *(rec Apr. 21–25, 1992)* — Claves ▲ CD 9302 [DDD]
Mozart, W.A.:Con Fl, K.313, w. I. Goritzki (ob) [arr for oboe] *(rec Apr. 21–25, 1992)* — Claves ▲ CD 9302 [DDD]
Mozart, W.A.:Con Ob, K.314, w. I. Goritzki (ob) *(rec Apr. 21–25, 1992)* — Claves ▲ CD 9302 [DDD]
E. Terwilliger (cnd)
Strauss, R.:Con 1 Hn, w. E. Terwilliger (hn) — Amati ▲ 9205
Polish National PO
K. Kord (cnd)
Kilar, W.:Requiem for Father Kolbe *(rec Katowice, 1995)* — Milan ▲ 357792
Polish National Radio Orch
R. Hayman (cnd)
Famous Overtures, w. Czech–Slovak RSOI *(rec Polish Radio, Katowice, Aug 27–Sept 1, 1990; May)* — Naxos 4–▲ 8.504013 [DDD]
K. Stryja (cnd)
The Polish Violin, w. Roman Lasocki (vn), Urszula Bozek–Musialska (pno) *(rec 1986 & 1988)* — Olympia ▲ OCD 323 [AAD]
Polish National RSO
M. Halász (cnd)
Mahler, G.:Sym 9 *(rec Apr. 1993)* — Naxos 2–▲ 8.550535/36 [DDD]
Polish National RSO Cracow
Bloch, E.:Suite Va & Pno, w. J. Kosmala (va), S. Kawalla (pno) — Centaur ▲ CRC 2094 [ADD]
F. Haider (cnd)
Strauss, R.:4 Last Songs, w. Joanna Borowska (sop) — Nightingale Classics ▲ NIG 161864
S. Heinrich (cnd)
Honegger, A.:Jeanne d'Arc au bûcher, w. *soloists unknown*, Hersfelder Festival Choir, Frankfurt Children's Choir — Koch Schwann ▲ SCH 312922 [DDD]
S. Kawalla (cnd)
Ptaszynska, M.:Con Mar, w. Keiko Abe (mar) *(rec Cracow Philharmonic, May 8–10, 1986)* — Polskie Nagrania ▲ PLN 075 [ADD]
Vaughan Williams, R.:Flos Campi, w. J. Kosmala (va), Cracow Polish Radio–TV Chorus — Centaur ▲ CRC 2094 [ADD]
Polish National RSO Katowice
Szymanowski, K.:Demeter, w. Krystyna Szostek–Radkowa (mez), Polish Radio Women's Choir *(rec Concert Hall at the National PO, Warsaw, 1982)* — Polskie Nagrania ▲ PLN 063 [ADD]
D. Amos (cnd)
Diciedue, R.:Con Vn, w. M. Lefkowitz (vn) *(rec June 1990)* — Cambria ▲ CD 1064 [DDD]
Fauré, G.:Con Vn, w. M. Lefkowitz (vn) *(rec June 1990)* — Cambria ▲ CD 1064 [DDD]
Sibelius, J.:Con Vn, w. M. Lefkowitz (vn) *(rec June 1990)* — Cambria ▲ CD 1064 [DDD]
M. Bartos (cnd)
Lecuona, E.:Rapsodia Cubana, w. Thomas Tirino (pno) — BIS ▲ CD 794 [DDD]
Lecuona, E.:Rapsodia negra, w. Thomas Tirino (pno) *(rec Centre of Culture, Katowice, Poland, Feb 27, 1993)* — BIS ▲ CD 754 [DDD]
C. von Borries (cnd)
Branca, G.:Sym 9, "L'eve future", w. Camerata Silesia Singers Ensemble *(rec Polish National RSO Concert Hall, Katowice, Poland, Oct. 1994)* — Point Music ▲ 446505–2
V. Brodsky (cnd)
Saint–Saëns, C.:Con 3 Vn, w. Andrzej Straszynski (vn) *(rec Katowice, Poland, Aug 4–8, 1988)* — Arts ▲ 4471402 [DDD]
Saint–Saëns, C.:Havanaise Vn, w. Andrzej Straszynski (vn) *(rec Katowice, Poland, Aug 4–8, 1988)* — Arts ▲ 4471402 [DDD]
Saint–Saëns, C.:Introduction & Rondo capriccioso, w. Andrzej Straszynski (vn) *(rec Katowice, Poland, Aug 4–8, 1988)* — Arts ▲ 4471402 [DDD]
D. D. Gier (cnd)
Kievman, C.:Sym 2, w. Polish Radio Chorus *(rec Katowice, Poland, June 29–July 3, 1995)* — New Albion ▲ NA 081CD
S. Gunzenhauser (cnd)
Dvořák, A.:The Golden Spinning Wheel *(rec Sept. 1–6, 1992)* — Naxos ▲ 8.550598 [DDD]
Dvořák, A.:The Noon Witch *(rec Sept. 1–6, 1992)* — Naxos ▲ 8.550598 [DDD]
Dvořák, A.:The Wild Dove *(rec Sept. 1–6, 1992)* — Naxos ▲ 8.550598 [DDD]
Paganini, N.:Con 1 Vn, w. I. Kaler (vn) *(rec Sept. 3–6, 1992)* — Naxos ▲ 8.550649 [DDD]
Paganini, N.:Con 2 Vn, w. I. Kaler (vn) *(rec Sept. 3–6, 1992)* — Naxos ▲ 8.550649 [DDD]
M. Halász (cnd)
Liszt, F.:Mazeppa Orch *(rec Apr. 2–6, 1991)* — Naxos ▲ 8.550487 [DDD]
Liszt, F.:Les Préludes *(rec Apr. 2–6, 1991)* — Naxos ▲ 8.550487 [DDD]
Liszt, F.:Prometheus *(rec Apr. 2–6, 1991)* — Naxos ▲ 8.550487 [DDD]
Liszt, F.:Tasso—Lamento e Trionfo *(rec Apr. 2–6, 1991)* — Naxos ▲ 8.550487 [DDD]
Mahler, G.:Sym 1 *(rec Polish Radio Concert Hall, Katowice, Dec. 11–14, 1993)* — Naxos ▲ 8.550522 [DDD]
Mahler, G.:Sym 7 *(rec Concert Hall of the Polish National Radio, Katowice, Nov. 28–Dec. 2, 1994)* — Naxos ▲ 8.550531 [DDD]

▲ = CD ♦ = Enhanced CD Δ = MD ■ = Cassette Tape □ = DCC

Polish National RSO Katowice (cont.)

J. Kaspszyk (cnd)
Penderecki, K.:Sym 2 Polskie Nagrania ▲ PLN 19 [AAD]
Szymanowski, K.:Concert Ov EMI Classics ▲ CDM 65082

J. Katlewicz (cnd)
Górecki, H.–M.:Stücke im alten Stil (3) *(rec 1970)* Olympia ▲ OCD 313 [AAD]
Górecki, H.–M.:Sym 3, "Sym of Sorrowful Songs", w. S. Woytowicz (sop) [Pol] *(rec 1977)* Olympia ▲ OCD 313 [AAD]

C. Kolchinsky (cnd)
Dvořák, A.:Con Vn, w. Ilya Kaler (vn) *(rec Polish Radio Concert Hall, Katowice, Mar. 28–31, 1994)* Naxos ▲ 8.550758 [DDD]
Dvořák, A.:Romance Vn, w. Ilya Kaler (vn) *(rec Polish Radio Concert Hall, Katowice, Mar. 28–31, 1994)* Naxos ▲ 8.550758 [DDD]
Glazunov, A.:Con Vn, w. Ilya Kaler (vn) *(rec Polish Radio Concert Hall, Katowice, Mar. 28–31, 1994)* Naxos ▲ 8.550758 [DDD]

J. Krenz (cnd)
Chopin, F.:Con 1 Pno, w. Artur Rubinstein (pno) *(rec Warsaw, 1966)* Prelude ▲ PRE 2165 [ADD]
Chopin, F.:Con 2 Pno, w. Artur Rubinstein (pno) *(rec Warsaw, 1966)* Prelude ▲ PRE 2165 [ADD]
Diamond, D.:Romeo & Juliet CRI ■ C 216
Hoiby, L.:Con Pno & Orch, w. John Atkins (pno) *(rec 1966)* Citadel ▲ CTD 88118 [ADD]
Lutoslawski, W.:Poems of Henri Michaux, w. Witold Lutoslawski (cnd), Polish Radio Chorus *(rec Katowice, 1964)* Polskie Nagrania ▲ PNCD 041 [AAD]
Lutoslawski, W.:Postludes—No. 1 *(rec Katowice, 1964)* Polskie Nagrania ▲ PNCD 042 [AAD]
Malawski, A.:Ov *(rec 1964)* Olympia ▲ OCD 327 [AAD]
Rozycki, L.:Ballade, w. B. Hesse–Bukowska (pno) Olympia ▲ OCD 306 [AAD]
Szabelski, B.:Orch Music—Aphorismes "9" (1962); Concerto grosso (1954); Etude (1939); Preludes (1963); Toccata (1938) Olympia ▲ OCD 300 [AAD]

Latoszewski, Rezler (cnd)
Puccini, G.:Arias, w. Maria Foltyn (sop), Franciszek Arno (ten), Warsaw Opera Orch—Mi chiamano Mimi [from Cyganeria]; Ah! que gli ochi; Vissi d'arte [both from Tosca] Polskie Nagrania ▲ PNCD 275

A. Leaper (cnd)
Elgar, E.:Cockaigne *(rec Apr. 13–16, 1991)* Naxos ▲ 8.550489 [DDD]
Elgar, E.:Con Vn *(rec Apr. 13–16, 1991)* Naxos ▲ 8.550489 [DDD]
Elgar, E.:Con Vn, w. Dong–Suk Kang (vn) *(rec 1989 & 1991)* Naxos ▲ 8.553233 [DDD]
Tchaikovsky, P.:Hamlet *(rec Concert Hall of the Polish Radio, Katowice, Sept. 7–12, 1991)* Naxos ▲ 8.553017 [DDD]
Tchaikovsky, P.:Sym 1 *(rec Sept. 7–12, 1991)* Naxos ▲ 8.550517 [DDD]
Tchaikovsky, P.:Sym 2 *(rec March 23–29, 1991)* Naxos ▲ 8.550488 [DDD]
Tchaikovsky, P.:Sym 4 *(rec March 23–29, 1991)* Naxos ▲ 8.550488 [DDD]

W. Lutoslawski (cnd)
Lutoslawski, W.:Chain 3 *(rec Katowice, 1988)* Polskie Nagrania ▲ PNCD 044 [AAD]
Lutoslawski, W.:Con Vc, w. Roman Jablonski (vc) *(rec Katowice, 1976)* Polskie Nagrania ▲ PNCD 042 [AAD]
Lutoslawski, W.:Con Orch EMI Classics ▲ CDM 65305
Lutoslawski, W.:Livre EMI Classics ▲ CDM 65305
Lutoslawski, W.:Mi–parti EMI Classics ▲ CDM 65305
Lutoslawski, W.:Mi–parti *(rec Katowice, 1976)* Polskie Nagrania ▲ PNCD 043 [AAD]
Lutoslawski, W.:Musique funèbre EMI Classics ▲ CDM 65076
Lutoslawski, W.:Symphonic Vars EMI Classics ▲ CDM 65076
Lutoslawski, W.:Sym 1 EMI Classics ▲ CDM 65076
Lutoslawski, W.:Venetian Games EMI Classics ▲ CDM 65305

W. Michniewski (cnd)
Baird, T.:Psychodrama Olympia ▲ OCD 326 [AAD]

B. Oledzki (cnd)
Schaeffer, B.:Con 3 Pno, w. Boguslaw Schaeffer (pno), Marek Choloniewski (cmpt) Pro Viva ▲ ISPV 168 [ADD]

K. Penderecki (cnd)
Penderecki, K.:Con Vn, w. Konstanty Andrzej Kulka (vn) Polskie Nagrania ▲ PLN 19 [AAD]
Penderecki, K.:Music of—Threnody for the Victims of Hiroshima; Fonogrammi; De Natura Sonoris 1 & 2; Capriccio for Violin & Orch.; Canticum Canticorum Salomonis; The Awakening of Jacob EMI Classics ▲ CDM 65077
Penderecki, K.:St. Luke Passion, w. S. van Osten (sop), S. Roberts (bar), K. Rydl (bass), E. Lubaszenko (narr), Cracow Boys Choir, Warsaw National Phil Chorus Argo ▲ 430328–2 [DDD]
Stachowski, M.:Sapphic Odes, w. Grazyna Winogrodzka (mez) *(rec Apr. 1–6, 1987)* Polskie Nagrania ▲ PLN 076 [ADD]

Rezler, Latoszewski (cnd)
Moniuszko, S.:Halka (sels), w. Maria Foltyn (sop), Franciszek Arno (ten), Warsaw Opera Orch—Gdyby rannym slonkiem; O mój malenki Polskie Nagrania ▲ PNCD 275
Verdi, G.:Arias, w. Maria Foltyn (sop), Franciszek Arno (ten), Warsaw Opera Orch—O Patria mia [from Aida]; Ma dall'arido stelo [from Bal Maskowy]; Pace, pace, mio Dio [from Moc Przeznaczenia] Polskie Nagrania ▲ PNCD 275
Wagner, R.:Lohengrin (sels), w. Maria Foltyn (sop), Franciszek Arno (ten), Warsaw Opera Orch—Einsam in truben Tagen Polskie Nagrania ▲ PNCD 275

J. Salwarowski (cnd)
Sibelius, J.:Con Vn, w. V. Brodsky (vn) ASV Quicksilva ▲ QS 6016 [DDD]

J. Semkow (cnd)
Rossini, G.:Il barbiere di Siviglia (ov) *(rec Katowice, 1971)* Polskie Nagrania ▲ PNCD 137 [ADD]
Rossini, G.:L'italiana in Algeri (ov) *(rec Katowice, 1971)* Polskie Nagrania ▲ PNCD 137 [ADD]
Szymanowski, K.:Sym 2, w. Polish Radio Chorus EMI Classics ▲ CDM 65082
Szymanowski, K.:Sym 3, w. W. Ochman (ten), Polish Radio Chorus EMI Classics ▲ CDM 65082
Szymanowski, K.:Sym 4 EMI Classics ▲ CDM 65307

A. Straszynski (cnd)
Tchaikovsky, P.:Con Vn, w. Vadim Brodsky (vn) *(rec Katowice, Poland, Aug 1988)* Arts ▲ 447144–2 [DDD]
Tchaikovsky, P.:Sérénade méloncolique, w. Vadim Brodsky (vn) *(rec Katowice, Poland, Aug 1988)* Arts ▲ 447144–2 [DDD]
Tchaikovsky, P.:Valse–Scherzo Vn, w. Vadim Brodsky (vn) *(rec Katowice, Poland, Aug 1988)* Arts ▲ 447144–2 [DDD]

W. Strickland (cnd)
Josten, W.:Sym in F CRI ▲ CD 597 [ADD]
Ruggles, C.:Men & Mountains CRI ("American Masters" series) ▲ CD 715 [ADD]
Thorne, F.:Burlesque Ov CRI ▲ CD 586 [ADD]
Thorne, F.:Rhapsodic Vars 1, w. F. Thorne (pno) CRI ▲ CD 586 [ADD]
Ward, R.:Songs for Pantheists, w. S. Stahlman (sop) [F] CRI ■ C 206

T. Strugala (cnd)
Paderewski, I.J.:Con Pno, w. P. Paleczny (pno) Olympia ▲ OLY 398 [DDD]

K. Stryja (cnd)
Bacewicz, G.:Con 7 Vn, w. R. Lasocki (vn) Olympia ▲ OCD 323 [AAD]
Meyer, K.:Con Vn, w. R. Lasocki (vn) Olympia ▲ OCD 323 [AAD]

J. E. Suben (cnd)
Cory, E.:Canyons CO Soundspells ▲ CD 116 [DDD]
Cory, E.:Canyons Orch Soundspells ▲ CD 116 [DDD]
Fennelly, B.:On Civil Disobedience *(rec 1977)* New World ▲ 80448–2
Scarmolin, A.L.:Sym 3, w. Zygmunt Tlatlik (bn) *(rec Katowice, Poland, Sept 25, 1993)* New World ▲ 80502–2
Schubel, M.:Divert Tpt, w. Anthony Perfetti (tpt), Barry David Salwen (pno) Opus One ▲ CD 171 [DDD]
Schubel, M.:Fracture/ReFractured Opus One ▲ CD 171 [DDD]

J. Wildner (cnd)
Lalo, E.:Sym espagnole, w. M. Bisengaliev (vn) *(rec Jan. 31–Feb. 3, 1992)* Naxos ▲ 8.550494 [DDD]

Polish National RSO Katowice (cont.)

J. Wildner (cnd) (cont.)
Ravel, M.:Tzigane, w. M. Bisengaliev (vn) *(rec Jan. 31–Feb. 3, 1992)* Naxos ▲ 8.550494 [DDD]
Saint–Saëns, C.:Havanaise Vn, w. M. Bisengaliev (vn) *(rec Jan. 31–Feb. 3, 1992)* Naxos ▲ 8.550494 [DDD]
Sarasate, P. de:Zigeunerweisen, w. M. Bisengaliev (vn) *(rec Jan. 31–Feb. 3, 1992)* Naxos ▲ 8.550494 [DDD]
Schumann, R.:Ovs—Ov., Scherzo & Finale, Op. 52; Genoveva, Op. 81; Bride of Messina, Op. 100; Julius Caesar, Op. 128; Hermann & Dorothea, Op. 136; Faust; Manfred, Op. 115 Naxos ▲ 8.550608 [DDD]

A. Wit (cnd)
Bloch, E.:From Jewish Life, w. J. Berger (vc)—Prayer [arr. A. Antonini for cello & orch.] ebs ▲ ebs 6070 [DDD]
Bloch, E.:Schelomo, w. J. Berger (vc) ebs ▲ ebs 6070 [DDD]
Bloch, E.:Voice in the Wilderness, w. J. Berger (vc) ebs ▲ ebs 6070 [DDD]
Brahms, J.:Con Vn, w. Karin Adam (vn) *(rec Katowice, May 21–23, 1991)* Camerata ▲ 32CM 219
Brahms, J.:Con Vn, w. R. Totenberg (vn) Titanic ▲ Ti 163 [DDD]
Bruch, M.:Adagio on a Celtic Theme, w. J. Berger (vc) ebs ▲ ebs 6060 [DDD]
Bruch, M.:Ave Maria Vc, w. J. Berger (vc) ebs ▲ ebs 6060 [DDD]
Bruch, M.:Canzone Vc, w. J. Berger (vc) ebs ▲ ebs 6060 [DDD]
Bruch, M.:Kol Nidrei, w. J. Berger (vc) ebs ▲ ebs 6060 [DDD]
Dvořák, A.:Con Vc, w. Ko Iwasaki (vc) *(rec Centre of Culture, Katowice, Nov 21–24, 1989)* Polskie Nagrania ▲ PNCD 059 [DDD]
Dvořák, A.:Con Vc, w. Ko Iwasaki (vc) *(rec 11/89)* Muza ▲ PNCD 059 [DDD]
Dvořák, A.:Con Pno, w. J. Jandó (pno) *(rec Nov. 9–13, 1993)* Naxos ▲ 8.550896 [DDD]
Dvořák, A.:Czech Suite *(rec Concert Hall of the Polish Radio, Katowice, Apr. 11–15, 1994)* Naxos ▲ 8.553005 [DDD]
Dvořák, A.:Festival March *(rec Concert Hall of the Polish Radio, Katowice, Apr. 11–15, 1994)* Naxos ▲ 8.553005 [DDD]
Dvořák, A.:Heroic Song *(rec Concert Hall of the Polish Radio, Katowice, Oct. 12–13, 1993)* Naxos ▲ 8.553005 [DDD]
Dvořák, A.:Husitská *(rec Concert Hall of the Polish Radio, Katowice, Apr. 11–15, 1994)* Naxos ▲ 8.553005 [DDD]
Dvořák, A.:The Water Goblin *(rec Nov. 9–13, 1993)* Naxos ▲ 8.550896 [DDD]
Falla, M. de:Noches en los jardines de España, w. François–Joël Thiollier (pno) *(rec Polish Radio Concert Hall, Katowice, Nov. 29–Dec. 2, 1993)* Naxos ▲ 8.550753 [DDD]
Lipinski, K.J.:Con 2 Vn, w. Roman Totenberg (vn) Titanic ▲ Ti 163 [DDD]
Lutoslawski, W.:Chain 2, w. Krzysztof Bakowski (vn) *(rec Polish Radio Concert Hall, Katowice, Dec 19–22, 1994)* Naxos ▲ 8.553202 [DDD]
Lutoslawski, W.:Con Pno, w. Piotr Paleczny (pno) *(rec Katowice, Poland, 1994–95)* Naxos ▲ 8.553169 [DDD]
Lutoslawski, W.:Funeral Music *(rec Polish Radio Concert Hall, Katowice, Dec 19–22, 1994)* Naxos ▲ 8.553202 [DDD]
Lutoslawski, W.:Interlude Orch *(rec Polish Radio Concert Hall, Katowice, Dec 19–22, 1994)* Naxos ▲ 8.553202 [DDD]
Lutoslawski, W.:Partita Vn, Orch & Obbligato Pno, w. Krzysztof Bakowski (vn) *(rec Polish Radio Concert Hall, Katowice, Dec 19–22, 1994)* Naxos ▲ 8.553202 [DDD]
Lutoslawski, W.:Petite Suite *(rec Katowice, Poland, 1994–95)* Naxos ▲ 8.553169 [DDD]
Lutoslawski, W.:Symphonic Vars *(rec Katowice, Poland, 1994–95)* Naxos ▲ 8.553169 [DDD]
Lutoslawski, W.:Sym 2 *(rec Katowice, Poland, 1994–95)* Naxos ▲ 8.553169 [DDD]
Lutoslawski, W.:Sym 3 *(rec Katowice, 1988)* Polskie Nagrania ▲ PNCD 044 [AAD]
Lutoslawski, W.:Sym 4 *(rec Polish Radio Concert Hall, Katowice, Dec 19–22, 1994)* Naxos ▲ 8.553202 [DDD]
Mahler, G.:Sym 2, w. H. Lisowska (sop), J. Rappé (ten), Cracow Polish Radio–TV Chorus *(rec Jan. 9–17, 1993)* Naxos 2–▲ 8.550523/24 [DDD]
Mahler, G.:Sym 3, w. Ewa Podles (cta), Jacek Mentel (cnd), Cracow Boys' Choir, Cracow Phil Choir *(rec Concert Hall of the Polish National Radio, Katowice, Nov 12–16, 1994)* Naxos 2–▲ 8.550525–6 [DDD]
Mahler, G.:Sym 4, w. L. Russell (sop) Naxos ▲ 8.550527 [DDD]
Mahler, G.:Sym 5 Naxos ▲ 8.550528 [DDD]
Mahler, G.:Sym 6 *(rec Dec. 15–19, 1992)* Naxos 2–▲ 8.550529/30 [DDD]
Mahler, G.:Sym 10 *(rec Concert Hall of the Polish National Radio, Katowice, Nov 12–16, 1994)* Naxos 2–▲ 8.550525–6 [DDD]
Messiaen, O.:Éclair sur l'Au–Dela... Jade ▲ JADC 099
Paderewski, I.J.:Con Pno, w. Karol Radziwonowicz (pno) *(rec Centre of Culture, Katowice, Jan 2–6, 1991)* Polskie Nagrania ▲ PNCD 105 [DDD]
Paderewski, I.J.:Fant polonaise, w. Karol Radziwonowicz (pno) *(rec Centre of Culture, Katowice, Jan 2–6, 1991)* Polskie Nagrania ▲ PNCD 105 [DDD]
Penderecki, K.:Als Jakob erwachte—Adagietto Polskie Nagrania ▲ PLN 20 [AAD]
Penderecki, K.:Con 2 Vc, w. Ivan Monighetti (vc) Polskie Nagrania ▲ PLN 20 [AAD]
Penderecki, K.:Con Va, w. Stefan Kamasa (va) Polskie Nagrania ▲ PLN 20 [AAD]
Prokofiev, S.:Con 1 Pno, w. K. W. Paik (pno) *(rec May 13–18, 1991)* Naxos ▲ 8.550566 [DDD]
Prokofiev, S.:Con 2 Pno, w. K. W. Paik (pno) *(rec May 13–18, 1991)* Naxos ▲ 8.550565 [DDD]
Prokofiev, S.:Con 3 Pno, w. K. W. Paik (pno) *(rec May 13–18, 1991)* Naxos ▲ 8.550566 [DDD]
Prokofiev, S.:Con 4 Pno, w. K. W. Paik (pno) *(rec May 13–18, 1991)* Naxos ▲ 8.550566 [DDD]
Prokofiev, S.:Con 5 Pno, w. K. W. Paik (pno) *(rec May 13–18, 1991)* Naxos ▲ 8.550565 [DDD]
Ravel, M.:Con Pno (left hand), w. François–Joël Thiollier (pno) *(rec Concert Hall of the Polish Radio in Katowice, Nov. 29–Dec. 2, 1993)* Naxos ▲ 8.550753 [DDD]
Ravel, M.:Con in G Pno, w. François–Joël Thiollier (pno) *(rec Polish Radio Concert Hall, Katowice, Nov. 29–Dec. 2, 1993)* Naxos ▲ 8.550753 [DDD]
Saint–Saëns, C.:Caprice andalous, w. D.–S. Kang (vn) *(rec May 24–26, 1993)* Naxos ▲ 8.550752 [DDD]
Saint–Saëns, C.:Con 3 Vn, w. D.–S. Kang (vn) *(rec May 24–26, 1993)* Naxos ▲ 8.550752 [DDD]
Saint–Saëns, C.:Introduction & Rondo capriccioso, w. D.–S. Kang (vn) *(rec May 24–26, 1993)* Naxos ▲ 8.550752 [DDD]
Saint–Saëns, C.:Morceau de concert Vn, w. D.–S. Kang (vn) *(rec May 24–26, 1993)* Naxos ▲ 8.550752 [DDD]
Saint–Saëns, C.:Romance Vn, w. D.–S. Kang (vn) *(rec May 24–26, 1993)* Naxos ▲ 8.550752 [DDD]
Shostakovich, D.:Con 1 Vc, w. Maria Kliegel (vc) *(rec Polish Radio Concert Hall, Katowice, Feb 27–Mar 1, 1995)* Naxos ▲ 8.550813 [DDD]
Shostakovich, D.:Con 2 Vc, w. Maria Kliegel (vc) *(rec Polish Radio Concert Hall, Katowice, Feb 27–Mar 1, 1995)* Naxos ▲ 8.550813 [DDD]
Sibelius, J.:Con Vn, w. Karin Adam (vn) *(rec Katowice, May 21–23, 1991)* Camerata ▲ 32CM 219
Smetana, B.:Má Vlast *(rec Concert Hall of the Polish Radio, Katowice, Dec. 20–22, 1993 & Jan. 2)* Naxos ▲ 8.550931 [DDD]
Stachowski, M.:Divert Strs *(rec Apr. 1–6, 1987)* Polskie Nagrania ▲ PLN 076 [ADD]
Strauss, F.:Con Hn, w. I. James (hn) ebs ▲ ebs 6063 [DDD]
Strauss, R.:Con 1 Hn, w. I. James (hn) ebs ▲ ebs 6063 [DDD]
Strauss, R.:Con 2 Hn, w. I. James (hn) ebs ▲ ebs 6063 [DDD]
Strauss, R.:Don Juan Polskie Nagrania ▲ PLN 50 [DDD]
Strauss, R.:Till Eulenspiegels lustige Streiche Polskie Nagrania ▲ PLN 50 [DDD]
Strauss, R.:Tod und Verklärung Polskie Nagrania ▲ PLN 50 [DDD]
Szymanowski, K.:Prince Potemkin *(rec May 12, 1993)* Marco Polo ("Opera Classics" series) 2–▲ 8.223339/40 [DDD]
Tchaikovsky, P.:Andante & Finale, w. Bernd Glemser (pno) *(rec Polish Radio Concert Hall, Mar 1995)* Naxos ▲ 8.550819 [DDD]
Tchaikovsky, P.:Concert Fant, w. Bernd Glemser (pno) *(rec Polish Radio Concert Hall, Katowice, Mar 20–24, 1995)* Naxos ▲ 8.550820 [DDD]
Tchaikovsky, P.:Con 1 Pno, w. Bernd Glemser (pno) *(rec Polish Radio Concert Hall, Mar 1995)* Naxos ▲ 8.550819 [DDD]

Polish National RSO Katowice (cont.)
A. Wit (cnd) (cont.)
Tchaikovsky, P.:Con 2 Pno, w. Bernd Glemser (pno) *(rec Polish Radio Concert Hall, Katowice, Mar 20–24, 1995)* Naxos ▲ 8.550820 [DDD]
Tchaikovsky, P.:Con 3 Pno, w. Bernd Glemser (pno) *(rec Polish Radio Concert Hall, Mar 1995)* Naxos ▲ 8.550819 [DDD]
Tchaikovsky, P.:Con Vn, w. V. Brodsky (vn) ASV Quicksilva ▲ QS 6016 [DDD]
Tchaikovsky, P.:Francesca da Rimini *(rec Polish Radio Concert Hall, Katowice, Mar 28–Apr 1, 1993)* Naxos 4–▲ 8.504012 [DDD]
Tchaikovsky, P.:Francesca da Rimini *(rec Mar. 28–Apr. 1, 1993)* Naxos ▲ 8.550782 [DDD]
Tchaikovsky, P.:The Storm *(rec Nov. 23–25, 1992)* Naxos ▲ 8.550716 [DDD]
Tchaikovsky, P.:Sym 3 *(rec Sept. 14–18, 1992)* Naxos ▲ 8.550518
Tchaikovsky, P.:Sym 5 *(rec Nov. 23–25, 1992)* Naxos ▲ 8.550716 [DDD]
Tchaikovsky, P.:Sym 6 *(rec Polish Radio Concert Hall, Katowice, Mar 28–Apr 1, 1993)* Naxos 4–▲ 8.504012 [DDD]
Tchaikovsky, P.:Sym 6 *(rec Mar. 28–Apr. 1, 1993)* Naxos ▲ 8.550782 [DDD]
Tchaikovsky, P.:The Tempest *(rec Concert Hall of the Polish Radio, Katowice, Sept. 14–18, 1992)* Naxos ▲ 8.553017 [DDD]
Tchaikovsky, P.:The Tempest *(rec Sept. 14–18, 1992)* Naxos ▲ 8.550518
Tchaikovsky, P.:Vars on a Rococo Theme, w. Ko Iwasaki (vc) *(rec Centre of Culture, Katowice, Nov 21–24, 1989)* Polskie Nagrania ▲ PNCD 059 [DDD]
Wieniawski, H.:Con 1 Vn, w. Marat Bisengaliev (vn) *(rec Katowice, Poland, Aug 1995)* Naxos ▲ 8.553517 [DDD]
Wieniawski, H.:Con 2 Vn, w. Marat Bisengaliev (vn) *(rec Katowice, Poland, Aug 1995)* Naxos ▲ 8.553517 [DDD]
Wieniawski, H.:Fant brilliante on Themes from Gounod's *Faust*, w. Marat Bisengaliev (vn) *(rec Katowice, Poland, Aug 1995)* Naxos ▲ 8.553517 [DDD]
B. Wodiczko (cnd)
Stravinsky, I.:Le Sacre du printemps Orch Polskie Nagrania ▲ PNCD 260
T. Wojciechowski (cnd)
Grieg, E.:Con Pno, Op. 16, w. Ewa Poblocka (pno) Conifer Classics 2–▲ 75605–51750–2 [DDD]
Grieg, E.:Elegaic Melodies, Op. 34 Conifer Classics 2–▲ 75605–51750–2 [DDD]
Grieg, E.:Holberg Suite Conifer Classics 2–▲ 75605–51750–2 [DDD]
Grieg, E.:Lyric Pieces—6 Pieces Conifer Classics 2–▲ 75605–51750–2 [DDD]
Grieg, E.:Peer Gynt—March of the Trolls; Norwegian March Conifer Classics 2–▲ 75605–51750–2 [DDD]
Grieg, E.:Peer Gynt Suites, Opp. 46 & 55 Conifer Classics 2–▲ 75605–51750–2 [DDD]
Grieg, E.:Symphonic Dances Conifer Classics 2–▲ 75605–51750–2 [DDD]

Polish National SO
J. Katlewicz (cnd)
Górecki, H.–M.:Sym 3, "Sym of Sorrowful Songs", w. Stefania Woytowicz (sop) *(rec May 1978)* Polskie Nagrania ▲ PNCD 215
J. Krenz (cnd)
Berg, A.:Con Vn, w. Henryk Szernyg (vn) *(rec Warsaw, 1958)* Prelude ▲ PRE 2148 [ADD]
Ponce, M.:Con Vn, w. Henryk Szernyg (vn) *(rec Warsaw, 1958)* Prelude ▲ PRE 2148 [ADD]
Prokofiev, S.:Con 2 Vn, w. Henryk Szernyg (vn) *(rec Warsaw, 1958)* Prelude ▲ PRE 2148 [ADD]
J. Maksymiuk (cnd)
Paderewski, I.J.:Con Pno, w. P. Paleczny (pno) Sound ▲ CD 3446
W. Rowicki (cnd)
Karlowicz, M.:Music to the White Dove *(rec 1977)* Olympia ▲ OCD 389 [AAD]
Noskowski, Z.:Morskie Oko *(rec 1977)* Olympia ▲ OCD 389 [AAD]
Noskowski, Z.:Steppe *(rec 1977)* Olympia ▲ OCD 389 [AAD]
Noskowski, Z.:Sym in c *(rec 1977)* Olympia ▲ OCD 389 [AAD]
S. Wislocki (cnd)
Lipinski, K.J.:Con 2 Vn, w. *(soloist unknown)* *(rec 1977)* Olympia ▲ OCD 389 [AAD]

Polish Navy Band
Marsz, Marsz Polonia, w. Krakow Garrison Military Band, Polish Air Force Band, Polish Army Band, Pomeranian Military District Band, Silesian Military District Band, Warsaw Military District Band Polskie Nagrania Edition ▲ ECD 064 [DDD]

Polish Radio CO
Musica Antiqua Polonica:Choral Music from Poland, w. [cnd:Wroclaw Edmund Kajdasz], Polish Radio Chorus Olympia ▲ OLY 322 [AAD]
A. Duczmal (cnd)
Suk, J.:Serenade Strs ASV Quicksilva ▲ ASQ 6094 [ADD]
Tchaikovsky, P.:Serenade Strs ASV Quicksilva ▲ ASQ 6094 [ADD]
E. Kajdasz (cnd)
Mielczewski, M.:Vesperae Dominicales, w. Wroclaw Choir [L] *(rec 1966)* Olympia ▲ OCD 317 [AAD]

Polish RSO
Alfred Orda Operatic Recital, w. Alfred Orda (bar) Symposium ▲ SYM 1117
J. Maksymiuk (cnd)
Górecki, H.–M.:Stücke im alten Stil (3), w. Konstanty Kulka (vn), Polish CO EMI Classics ▲ CDM 65418
Wicherek (cnd)
Moniuszko, S.:Songs & Arias, w. Hanna Rumowska–Machnikowska (sop), Anna Pawluk (pno), Polish Radio–TV SO, Warsaw Theatr Wielk Orch—Do Faona; Przasniczka; Mogila; Nad Rzeka; Powiedzcie Mi; Czy Powroci; Gdyby Kto Mnie Kochal Szczerze; Przepioreczka; Nawrócona; Hola Ptaszki; O, Sama Nie Wiem; Oj, Polece Ja Daleko; Jako Od Wichru Krzew Polamany; O! Jakzebym Kleczec Juz Chciala Gdyby Rannym Slonkiem; Ha! Dzieciatko Nam Umiera O Mój Malenki Polskie Nagrania ("Polskie Radio" series) ▲ PNCD 322

Polish Radio–TV Orch
Pruszak, Kamirski (cnd)
Bel Canto, w. Urszula Trawinska–Moroz (sop) Polskie Nagrania Edition ▲ ECD 063

Polish Radio–TV SO
D. Amos (cnd)
Berezowsky, N.:Fant for 2 Pnos, w. J. Pierce (pno), D. Jonas (pno) Albany ▲ TROY 112 [DDD]
Creston, P.:Con for 2 Pnos, w. D. Jonas (pno), J. Pierce (pno) Albany ▲ TROY 112 [DDD]
Poulenc, F.:Con for 2 Pnos, w. J. Pierce (pno), D. Jonas (pno) Albany ▲ TROY 112 [DDD]
J. M. Florencio (cnd)
Myers, T.:Sym 1969, w. J. M. Florêncio Vienna Modern Masters ▲ VMM 3019 [DDD]
Perron, A.:Séquences violées Vienna Modern Masters ▲ VMM 3023 [DDD]
Redmann, B.:Fiasko Vienna Modern Masters ▲ VMM 3019 [DDD]
Van De Vate, N.:Con Va, w. G. Zhislin (va) Vienna Modern Masters ▲ VMM 3023 [DDD]
Weiss, F.:Relazioni variabili Vienna Modern Masters ▲ VMM 3023 [DDD]
S. Kawalla (cnd)
Constantinides, D.:Dedications Vienna Modern Masters ▲ VMM 3004 [DDD]
Dembski, S.:Of Mere Being, w. S. Girardi (mez) Vienna Modern Masters ▲ VMM 3002 [DDD]
Penderecki, K.:Con Va Vienna Modern Masters ▲ VMM 3010 [ADD]
Penderecki, K.:Dies Irae, w. O. Szwajgier (sop), Z. Jankovski (ten), L. Mróz (bass), Polish Radio–TV Chorus [L] Vienna Modern Masters ▲ VMM 3015 [DDD]
Penderecki, K.:Threnody for the Victims of Hiroshima Vienna Modern Masters ▲ VMM 3010 [ADD]
Reichardt, J.F.:Stiller Friede, w. R. Ciecla (bar) [G] Vienna Modern Masters ▲ VMM 3003 [DDD]
Reichel, E.:Configurations Vienna Modern Masters ▲ VMM 3004 [DDD]
Schoenberg, A.:A Survivor from Warsaw, w. D. Olbrychsk (narr), Polish Radio–TV Chorus [E] Vienna Modern Masters ▲ VMM 3015 [DDD]
Tanner, J.:Aukele Vienna Modern Masters ▲ VMM 3004 [DDD]
Van De Vate, N.:Chernobyl Vienna Modern Masters ▲ VMM 3010 [ADD]
Van De Vate, N.:Con 1 Vn Vienna Modern Masters ▲ VMM 3010 [ADD]
Van De Vate, N.:Concertpiece Vc, w. Z. Lapinsky (vc) Vienna Modern Masters ▲ VMM 3008 [ADD]
Van De Vate, N.:Dark Nebulae Vienna Modern Masters ▲ VMM 3008 [ADD]
Van De Vate, N.:Distant Worlds, w. J. Mirynski (vn) Vienna Modern Masters ▲ VMM 3008 [ADD]
Van De Vate, N.:Journeys Vienna Modern Masters ▲ VMM 3008 [ADD]

Polish Radio–TV SO (cont.)
S. Kawalla (cnd) (cont.)
Van De Vate, N.:Katyn, w. Polish Radio–TV Chorus Vienna Modern Masters ▲ VMM 3015 [DDD]
Van De Vate, N.:Krakow Con, w. Polish Radio–TV Chorus Vienna Modern Masters ▲ VMM 3015 [DDD]
Wolff, J.–C.:Sym 2, w. W. Kwasny (vn) Vienna Modern Masters ▲ VMM 3001 [DDD]
Wolff, J.–C.:Sym 4 Vienna Modern Masters ▲ VMM 3002 [DDD]
Maksymiuk, Strugala, Wislocki (cnd)
Szymanowski, K.:Fragments from Poems by Jan Kasprowicz, w. Polish Radio–TV Chorus—Tryptich Koch Schwann ▲ CD 312652 [DDD]
Szymanowski, K.:Stabat Mater, w. Polish Radio–TV Chorus Koch Schwann ▲ CD 312652 [DDD]
Szymanowski, K.:Sym 3, w. Polish Radio–TV Chorus Koch Schwann ▲ CD 312652 [DDD]
J. McLeod (cnd)
McLeod, J.:Gokstad Ship, w. J. Manning (sop), M. Skoczen–Staniszewska (hp) Vienna Modern Masters ▲ VMM 3026 [DDD]
McLeod, J.:Lieder der Jugend, w. R. Gilvan (ten) Vienna Modern Masters ▲ VMM 3026 [DDD]
S. Stuligrosz (cnd)
Polish Stars Sing the Carols, w. Teresa Zylis–Gara (sop), Wieslaw Ochman (ten), Warsaw CO, Poznan State PO Men's & Boys' Choir Polskie Nagrania Edition ▲ ECD 025
Z. Szostak (cnd)
Bergsma, W.:Con Vn, w. Edward Statkiewicz (vn) *(rec 1969)* Vox Box ("The American Composers" series) 2–▲ CDX 5158
Wicherek (cnd)
Moniuszko, S.:Songs & Arias, w. Hanna Rumowska–Machnikowska (sop), Anna Pawluk (pno), Polish RSO, Warsaw Theatr Wielk Orch—Do Faona; Przasniczka; Mogila; Nad Rzeka; Powiedzcie Mi; Czy Powroci; Gdyby Kto Mnie Kochal Szczerze; Przepioreczka; Nawrócona; Hola Ptaszki; O, Sama Nie Wiem; Oj, Polece Ja Daleko; Jako Od Wichru Krzew Polamany; O! Jakzebym Kleczec Juz Chciala Gdyby Rannym Slonkiem; Ha! Dzieciatko Nam Umiera O Mój Malenki Polskie Nagrania ("Polskie Radio" series) ▲ PNCD 322

Polish Radio–TV SO Cracow
S. Kawalla (cnd)
Biggs, J.:Vars on a Theme of Shostakovich, w. B. Oberacker (pno) Vienna Modern Masters ▲ VMM 3002 [DDD]
Ocker, M.:Eclogue Vienna Modern Masters ▲ VMM 3028 [DDD]
Saunway, T.:Troktès Vienna Modern Masters ▲ VMM 3003 [DDD]
Schulze, W.:Snúningur Vienna Modern Masters ▲ VMM 3001 [DDD]
Wallach, J.:The Tiger's Tail Vienna Modern Masters ▲ VMM 3003 [DDD]

Polish State PO
O. Dohnányi (cnd)
Strauss (II), Joh.:Orchestral Music—Die Sanguiniker, Op. 27; Pepita Polka, Op. 138; Wiedersehen–Polka, Op. 142; Schallwellen, Op. 148; Erzherzog Wilhelm Genesungs–Marsch, Op. 149; Carnevals–Botschafter, Op. 270; "Un ballo in Maschera," Op. 272; Saison–Quadrille, Op. 283; Leichtes Blut, Op. 319; Cagliostro–Walzer, Op. 370; Banditen Galopp, Op. 378; Lagunen–Walzer, Op. 411 Marco Polo ▲ 8.223208 [DDD]
Strauss (II), Joh.:Orchestral Music—Zeitgeister, Op. 25; Odeon–Quadrille, Op. 29; Bachus–Polka, Op. 38; Neuhauser–Polka, Op. 137; Kron–Marsch, Op. 139; Schnee–Glöckchen Walzer, Op. 143; Ballg'schichten, Op. 150; Furioso–Polka, Op. 250; Colonnen Walzer, Op. 262; Deutscher Kriegermarsch, Op. 284; Kriegers Liebchen, Op. 379; Nordseebilder, Op. 390 Marco Polo ▲ 8.223207 [DDD]
S. Gunzenhauser (cnd)
Lachner, F.P.:Suite 1 Marco Polo ▲ 8.223195 [DDD]
Lachner, F.P.:Suite 7 Marco Polo ▲ 8.223195 [DDD]
Taneyev, S.:Sym 2 Marco Polo ▲ 8.223196
Taneyev, S.:Sym 4 Marco Polo ▲ 8.223196
Lenárd, Walter (cnd)
Strauss (II), Joh.:Music of, w. Czech–Slovak RSO—9 selections Naxos ▲ 8.550338 [DDD]
Strauss (II), Joh.:Music of, w. Czech–Slovak RSO, Czech–Slovak State Radio PO—9 selections Naxos ▲ 8.550339 [DDD]
Strauss (II), Joh.:Music of, w. Czech–Slovak RSO, Czech–Slovak State Radio PO—9 sels. Naxos ▲ 8.550337 [DDD]
K. Stryja (cnd)
Szymanowski, K.:Concert Ov Marco Polo ▲ 8.223290 [DDD]
Szymanowski, K.:Con 1 Vn, w. K. A. Kulka (vn) Marco Polo ▲ 8.223291 [DDD]
Szymanowski, K.:Con 2 Vn, w. R. Lasocki (vn) Marco Polo ▲ 8.223291 [DDD]
Szymanowski, K.:Demeter, w. A. Malewicz–Madej (cta), Polish State Phil Chorus Marco Polo ▲ 8.223293 [DDD]
Szymanowski, K.:Harnasie Marco Polo ▲ 8.223292 [DDD]
Szymanowski, K.:Litany to the Virgin Mary, w. Polish State Phil Chorus Marco Polo ▲ 8.223293 [DDD]
Szymanowski, K.:Mandragora Marco Polo ▲ 8.223292 [DDD]
Szymanowski, K.:Penthesilea, w. R. Owstoska (sop) Marco Polo ▲ 8.223293 [DDD]
Szymanowski, K.:Stabat Mater, w. J. Gadulanka (sop), K. Szostek–Radkowa (mez), A. Hlolski (bar), Polish State Phil Chorus Marco Polo ▲ 8.223293 [DDD]
Szymanowski, K.:Sym 1 Marco Polo ▲ 8.223248
Szymanowski, K.:Sym 2 Marco Polo ▲ 8.223248
Szymanowski, K.:Sym 3, w. W. Ochman (ten), Polish State Phil Chorus Marco Polo ▲ 8.223290 [DDD]
Szymanowski, K.:Sym 4, w. T. Zmudzinski (pno) Marco Polo ▲ 8.223290 [DDD]
Szymanowski, K.:Veni Creator, w. B. Zagórzanka (sop), Polish State Phil Chorus Marco Polo ▲ 8.223293 [DDD]
J. Swoboda (cnd)
Górecki, H.–M.:Sym 3, "Sym of Sorrowful Songs", w. Zofia Kilanowicz (sop) *(rec Symphony Hall, Katowice, Poland, 1993)* Vox Classics ▲ VOX 7511 [DDD]
J. Wildner (cnd)
Strauss (II), Joh.:Orchestral Music—Pester Csárdas, Op. 23; Blumenfest–Polka, Op. 111; Panacea–Klänge (Waltz), Op. 161; Diabolin–Polka, Op. 244; Lieder–Quadrille, Op. 275; Bauern–Polka, Op. 276; Morgenblätter (Waltz), Op. 279; Juristenball–Polka, Op. 280; Feuilleton (Waltz), Op. 293; Myrthenblüthen (Waltz), Op. 395 Marco Polo ▲ 8.223210 [DDD]
Strauss (II), Joh.:Orchestral Music—Albion–Polka, Op. 102; Annen–Polka, Op. 117; Nachtveilchen (Polka Mazur), Op. 170; Gedanken auf den Alpen, Op. 172; Luzifer Polka, Op. 266; Festival–Quadrille, Op. 341; Indigo–Marsch, Op. 349; Carnevalsbilder (Waltz), Op. 357; Hapsburg Hoch! (March), Op. 408; Kaiserwalzer, Op. 437 Marco Polo ▲ 8.223209 [DDD]

Polish State PO Katowice
K. Stryja (cnd)
Szymanowski, K.:King Roger, w. B. Zagòrzanka (sop), A. Malewicz–Madey (cta), H. Grychnik (ten), W. Ochman (ten), A. Hiolski (bar), L. A. Mròz (bass), Cracow Phil Boys' Chorus, Polish State Phil Chorus *(rec Apr. 7–9, 1990)* Marco Polo ("Opera Classics" series) 2–▲ 8.223339/40 [DDD]

Polychromie Ensemble
N. Andreassian (cnd)
Radulescu, H.:lubiri Adès ▲ ADE 204482 [DDD]
Radulescu, H.:Sensual Sky, w. Pierre–Yves Artaud (fl) Adès ▲ ADE 204482 [DDD]

Polyphonia Orch
B. Fairfax (cnd)
Bliss, A.:The Olympians, w. R. Woodland (sop), S. Minty (mez), T. Hemsley (bar), R. Herincx (bass), Ambrosian Singers *(rec 1972)* Intaglio 2–▲ ING 755 [ADD]
A. Hovhaness (cnd)
Hovhaness, A.:Prayer of St. Gregory, w. J. Wilbraham (tpt) Crystal ▲ CD 807
Hovhaness, A.:Sym 6 Crystal ▲ CD 807
Hovhaness, A.:Sym 25 Crystal ▲ CD 807

Polyphony
S. Layton (cnd)
Grainger, P.:Jungle Book (comp), w. John Mark Ainsley (ten), David Wilson-Johnson (bar) Hyperion ▲ CDA 66863
O Magnum Misterium:20th Century Carols & Sarum Chant Hyperion ▲ CDA 66925
J. MacMillan (cnd)
Macmillan, J.:Cantos Sagrados, w. Christopher Bowers-Broadbent (org) *(rec St. John-at-Hackney, London, Sept. 28-30, 1994)* Catalyst ▲ 09026-68125-2 [DDD]; ■ 09026-68125-4
Macmillan, J.:Seven Last Words from the Cross, w. London CO, Polyphony *(rec St. John-at-Hackney, London, Sept. 28-30, 1994)* Catalyst ▲ 09026-68125-2 [DDD]; ■ 09026-68125-4
Polyrhythmia
Fink, S.:Perc Music—Pictures for Percussion (1986); Batu Ferringhi for Solo Marimba (1987); Vibracussion for Vibraphone & Percussion Quartet (1960); Toccatina for Six Percussionists (1989); Images para Percusion (1985); Top-Kapi (1980); Conga Brasil (1974); Ostinati Machina (1984); Marcha del Tambor (1973); Ritmo (1971) Thorofon ▲ CTH 2169 [DDD]
Pomeranian Military District Band
Marsz, Marsz Polonia, w. Krakow Garrison Military Band, Polish Air Force Band, Polish Army Band, Polish Navy Band, Silesian Military District Band, Warsaw Military District Band Polskie Nagrania Edition ▲ ECD 064 [DDD]
Pomeranian PO
T. Ukigaya (cnd)
Busoni, F.:Concertino Cl, w. S. Isobe (cl) Thorofon ▲ CTH 2159 [DDD]
Hindemith, P.:Con Cl, w. S. Isobe (cl) Thorofon ▲ CTH 2159 [DDD]
Weber, C.M. von:Con 1 Cl, w. S. Isobe (cl) Thorofon ▲ CTH 2159 [DDD]
Yun, I.:Sym 1 CPO ▲ CPO 999125-2 [DDD]
Yun, I.:Sym 2 CPO ▲ CPO 999147-2 [DDD]
Yun, I.:Sym 3 CPO ▲ CPO 999125-2 [DDD]
Yun, I.:Sym 4 CPO ▲ CPO 999147-2 [DDD]
Yun, I.:Sym 5, w. R. Salter (bar) CPO ▲ CPO 999148 [DDD]
I Pomeriggi Musicali Orch
M. de Bernart (cnd)
Beethoven, L. van:Arias & Duets, w. Marisa Vitali (sop), Ernesto Palacio (ten)—Soll ein Schuh nicht drücken; O welch' ein Leben! ein ganzes Meer! [both from Die schöne Schusterin]; Primo amore piacer del ciel; Ne' giorni tuoi felici [from Olimpiade] *(rec Milano, Apr 1994)* Arcadia ▲ 153 [DDD]
Beethoven, L. van:Egmont (incidental music), w. Marisa Vitali (sop) *(rec Milano, Apr 1994)* Arcadia ▲ 153 [DDD]
Pomorska PO
Koch, Ukigaya (cnd)
Erdmann, D.:Music of, w. Detlef Bensmann (sax), Thüringen PO—Con for Sax & Orch (1989); Saxophonata (1985); Fant Colorata for Ten Sax; Con for Alt Sax & Orch; Resonanze for Sax Qt; plus others Thorofon ▲ CTH 2269
T. Ukigaya (cnd)
Blacher, B.:Con 2 Pno, w. *(soloist unknown)* *(rec 1992)* Thorofon ▲ CTH 2167 [ADD/DDD]
Blacher, B.:Vars on a Theme by Muzio Clementi *(rec 1992)* Thorofon ▲ CTH 2167 [ADD/DDD]
Karlowicz, M.:Con Vn, w. E. Zienkowski (vn) *(rec 1988-89)* Thorofon ▲ CTH 2046 [DDD]
Karlowicz, M.:Eternal Songs *(rec 1988-89)* Thorofon ▲ CTH 2046 [DDD]
Lutoslawski, W.:Chain 2, w. K. Jacowicz (vn) Thorofon ▲ CTH 2041 [DDD]
Lutoslawski, W.:Funeral Music Thorofon ▲ CTH 2041 [DDD]
Lutoslawski, W.:Petite Suite Thorofon ▲ CTH 2041 [DDD]
Lutoslawski, W.:Venetian Games Thorofon ▲ CTH 2041 [DDD]
Wagenseil, G.C.:Syms—in C; in g Thorofon ▲ CTH 2068 [DDD]
Porter String Quartet [Roy Malan (vn), Beni Shinohara (vn), Nanci Severance (va), Carolyn McIntosh (vc)]
Tailleferre, G.:Qt Strs *(rec UC, Santa Cruz, May 1992)* Helicon Classics ▲ HE 1008
Portland String Quartet [Stephen Kecskemethy (vn), Ronald Lantz (vn), Julia Adams (va), Paul Ross (vc)]
Bach, J.S.:The Art of the Fugue [1936 arr. Roy Harris & M. D. Herter Norton] Arabesque 2-▲ Z 6519-2 [DDD]
Bloch, E.:Qt 1 Strs Arabesque ▲ Z 6543 [DDD]
Bloch, E.:Qt 1 Strs Arabesque ▲ 6626 [DDD]
Bloch, E.:Qt 3 Strs Arabesque ▲ 6626 [DDD]
Bloch, E.:Qt 4 Strs Arabesque ▲ 6627 [DDD]
Bloch, E.:Qt 5 Strs Arabesque ▲ 6627 [DDD]
Bloch, E.:Qnt 1 Pno, w. P. Posnak (pno) Arabesque ▲ 6618 [DDD]
Britton, D.G.:Chinoiserie:Histoire d'un Amour Oriental, w. R. Noel (mez) [F] *(rec Dec. 1991)* Arabesque ▲ Z 6632 [DDD]
Chadwick, G.W.:Qt 1 Strs Northeastern (Classical Arts) ▲ NR 236-CD
Chadwick, G.W.:Qt 2 Strs Northeastern (Classical Arts) ▲ NR 236-CD
Chadwick, G.W.:Qt 3 Strs Northeastern (Classical Arts) ▲ NR 235-CD
Chadwick, G.W.:Qt 4 Strs Northeastern (Classical Arts) ▲ NR 234-CD
Chadwick, G.W.:Qt 5 Strs Northeastern (Classical Arts) ▲ NR 234-CD
Chadwick, G.W.:Qnt Pno, w. V. Eskin (pno) Northeastern (Classical Arts) ▲ NR 235-CD
Dvořák, A.:Qt 7 Strs *(rec Theatre C, SUNY, Purchase, Aug. 22-24, 1994)* Arabesque ▲ ARA 6660 [DDD]
Dvořák, A.:Qt 12 Strs, "America" Arabesque ▲ Z 6558 [DDD]
Dvořák, A.:Qnt Pno, Op. 81, w. Virginia Eskin (pno) *(rec Theatre C, SUNY, Purchase, Aug. 22-24, 1994)* Arabesque ▲ ARA 6660 [DDD]
Dvořák, A.:Qnt Strs, Op. 77, w. Gary Karr (db) Arabesque ▲ Z 6558 [DDD]
Kreisler, F.:Qt Strs Arabesque ▲ Z 6521 [DDD]
Levines, T.A.:Travel Journal:Books 1-3, w. T. Shimada (nar) [J] *(rec Dec. 1991 & July 1992)* Arabesque ▲ Z 6632 [DDD]
Piston, W.:Qt 1 Strs Northeastern ▲ NR 9001-CD
Piston, W.:Qt 2 Strs Northeastern ▲ NR 9001-CD
Piston, W.:Qt 3 Strs Northeastern ▲ NR 9001-CD
Piston, W.:Qt 4 Strs Northeastern ▲ NR 9002-CD
Piston, W.:Qt 5 Strs Northeastern ▲ NR 9002-CD
Piston, W.:Qnt Fl, w. D. A. Dwyer (fl) Northeastern ▲ NR 9002-CD
Piston, W.:Qnt Pno, w. L. Hokanson (pno) Northeastern ▲ NR 232-CD
Schubert, Franz:Qt 12 Strs Arabesque ▲ Z 6536 [DDD]
Schubert, Franz:Qt 14 Strs Arabesque ▲ Z 6536 [DDD]
Strauss, R.:Qt Strs Arabesque ▲ Z 6521 [DDD]
P. Posnak (cnd)
Bloch, E.:Qnt 2 Pno Arabesque ▲ 6618 [DDD]
Portland Youth PO
J. Avshalomov (cnd)
Avshalomov, A.:Con Pno, w. M. Moore CRI ▲ CD 667 [ADD]
Avshalomov, A.:Peiping Hutungs CRI ▲ CD 667 [ADD]
Avshalomov, J.:Praises from the Corners of the Earth *(rec Civic Auditorium or Arlene Schnitzer Concert Hall, Portland, OR, Feb. 25, 1984)* Albany ▲ TROY 160 [DDD]
Avshalomov, J.:Raptures on the Madrigals of Gesualdo *(rec Civic Auditorium or Arlene Schnitzer Concert Hall, Portland, OR, May 7, 1989)* Albany ▲ TROY 160 [DDD]
Avshalomov, J.:Sym of Songs *(rec Civic Auditorium or Arlene Schnitzer Concert Hall, Portland, OR, Feb. 26, 1994)* Albany ▲ TROY 160 [DDD]
Bergsma, W.:Chameleon Vars *(rec ca. 1961)* CRI ▲ CD 634 [ADD]
Bloch, E.:Suite symphonique *(rec 1976)* CRI ▲ CD 634 [ADD]
Bloch, E.:Sym Trbn, w. H. Prince (trbn) *(rec 1976)* CRI ▲ CD 634 [ADD]
Brotons, S.:Obstinacy Albany ▲ TROY 115 [DDD]
Diamond, D.:The World of Paul Klee *(rec ca. 1961)* CRI ▲ CD 634 [ADD]

Portland Youth PO (cont.)
J. Avshalomov (cnd) (cont.)
Johanson, B.:Cretan Rhap Albany ▲ TROY 115 [DDD]
Lees, B.:Prologue, Capriccio & Epilogue *(rec ca. 1961)* CRI ▲ CD 634 [ADD]
Van Buren, J.:Mementos Albany ▲ TROY 115 [DDD]
Walczyk, K.:The Delphic Suite Albany ▲ TROY 115 [DDD]
Portland Youth SO
Avshalomov, J.:Low Long, O Lord CRI ▲ CD 664 [ADD]
Avshalomov, J.:Open Sesame! Albany ▲ TROY 115 [DDD]
Avshalomov, J.:Phases of the Great Land CRI ▲ CD 664 [ADD]
Harris, R.:Elegy & Dance CRI ▲ CD 664 [ADD]
Ward, R.:Divert CRI ▲ CD 664 [ADD]
Postcards [Elliot Rosoff (elec), Henry Aronson (elec)]
Bach, J.S.:Cons Vn (comp) [arr for electronics] *(rec The Magic Shop, New York City, 1995)* Arc ▲ OC9604CD [DDD]
Bach, J.S.:Con for 2 Vns [arr for electronics] *(rec The Magic Shop, New York City, 1995)* Arc ▲ OC9604CD [DDD]
Postiglione Duo [Wolfgang Schulz (vc), Ginette Kostenbader (pno)]
Duo Postiglione *(rec Oct. 1988)* FSM ("Fono" series) ▲ 97721 [DDD]
Fauré, G.:Romance Vc *(rec 10/88)* FSM-Fono ▲ FCD 97721 [DDD]
Fauré, G.:Son 1 Vc *(rec 10/88)* FSM-Fono ▲ FCD 97721 [DDD]
Schumann, R.:Fantasiestücke Cl *(rec 10/88)* FSM-Fono ▲ FCD 97721 [DDD]
Poznan PO
A. Borejko (cnd)
Ginastera, A.:Estancia *(rec May 1993)* Largo ▲ 5122 [DDD]
Ginastera, A.:Ollantay *(rec May 1993)* Largo ▲ 5122 [DDD]
Ginastera, A.:Panambi *(rec May 1993)* Largo ▲ 5122 [DDD]
J. L. Temes (cnd)
Garrido, T.:Música diuma Discobi ▲ DIS 2011 [DDD]
Marco, Tomas:Pulsar Discobi ▲ DIS 2011 [DDD]
Marco, Tomas:Sym 1 Discobi ▲ DIS 2005
Marco, Tomas:Sym 2 Discobi ▲ DIS 2005
Marco, Tomas:Sym 3 Discobi ▲ DIS 2005
Testimonies of War:Kriegszeugnisse, 1914-45, w. London PO [cnd:N. Sheriff], Berlin RSO [cnd:B. Goldschmidt], BBC Sym Chorus Largo 2-▲ 5130 [DDD]
Turina, J.L.:Fant sobre una Fant de Alonso Mudarra Discobi ▲ DIS 2011 [DDD]
Turina, J.L.:Pentimento Discobi ▲ DIS 2011 [DDD]
Poznan Philharmonic SO
R. Czajkowski (cnd)
Baird, T.:Tomorrow, w. K. Szostek-Radkowa (mez), J. Artysz (bar), E. Pawlak (bass), J. Ostrowski (nar) [Pol] Olympia ▲ OCD 326 [AAD]
R. Satanowski (cnd)
Rozycki, L.:Anhelli Olympia ▲ OCD 306 [AAD]
Rozycki, L.:Stanczyk Olympia ▲ OCD 306 [AAD]
Poznan Polish Radio-TV CO
A. Duczmal (cnd)
Bach, C.P.E.:Cons Hpd & Strs, w. Grzegorz Olkiewicz (fl)—Con in d, H.425 (W.22) [arr fl & strs] *(rec Assembly Hall of Poznan Univ, May 18-22, 1988)* Polskie Nagrania Edition ▲ ECD 029 [DDD]
Bach, J.S.:Suite 2 Orch, w. Grzegorz Olkiewicz (fl) *(rec Assembly Hall of Poznan Univ, May 18-22, 1988)* Polskie Nagrania Edition ▲ ECD 029 [DDD]
Mercadante, S.:Cons (6) Fl (1819), w. Grzegorz Olkiewicz (fl)—in e *(rec Assembly Hall of Poznan Univ, May 18-22, 1988)* Polskie Nagrania Edition ▲ ECD 029 [DDD]
Prades Festival Orch
P. Casals (cnd)
Bach, J.S.:Brandenburg Con 5, w. E. Istomin (pno), J. Szigeti (vn), J. Wummer (cl) *(rec June 10-12, 1950)* Sony Classical ("The Casals Edition" series) ▲ SMK 58982 [ADD]
Bach, J.S.:Con 5 Hpd, w. C. Haskil (pno) *(rec June 6, 1950)* Sony Classical ("The Casals Edition" series) ▲ SMK 58982 [ADD]
Bach, J.S.:Con 1 Vn, w. I. Stern (vn) *(rec June 16, 1950)* Sony Classical ("The Casals Edition" series) ▲ SMK 58982 [ADD]
Bach, J.S.:Con Vn & Ob, w. I. Stern (vn), M. Tabuteau (ob) *(rec June 5, 1950)* Sony Classical ("The Casals Edition" series) ▲ SMK 58982
E. Ormandy (cnd)
Schumann, R.:Con Vc, w. Pablo Casals (vc) Andromeda ▲ ANR 2524
Schumann, R.:Con Vc, w. P. Casals (vc) *(rec Prades, France, May 28-29, 1953)* Sony Classical ("The Casals Edition" series) ▲ SMK 58993 [ADD]
Prague Academia Wind Quintet
Reicha, A.:Qnts Ww, Op. 88 Hyperion 2-▲ CDD 22006
Prague Brass Quintet
Carolling, w. Benačková, Gabriela (sop), Lubomír Vraspír (ten), Bambini di Praga [cnd:Jaroslav Krček], Tuma (org) Supraphon ▲ SUP 111417 [DDD]
Prague Brixi CO
J. Meier (cnd)
Meier, J.:Esquisses, w. C. Dobler (pno) Gallo ▲ CD 728 [DDD]
C. Meister (cnd)
Bloch, E.:Con grosso 1, w. C. Dobler (pno) Gallo ▲ CD 728 [DDD]
Haydn, J.:Con 1 Vn, w. Gilles Colliard (vn) *(rec Oct. 5-7, 1993)* Doron ▲ DRC 5003 [DDD]
Haydn, J.:Con 3 Vn, w. Gilles Colliard (vn) *(rec Oct. 5-7, 1993)* Doron ▲ DRC 5003 [DDD]
Haydn, J.:Con 4 Vn, w. Giles Colliard (vn) *(rec Oct. 5-7, 1993)* Doron ▲ DRC 5003 [DDD]
Vogel, W.:Hörformen II Gallo ▲ CD 728 [DDD]
Zbinden, J.-F.:Con da camera Pno, w. C. Dobler (pno) Gallo ▲ CD 728 [DDD]
Prague Castle Brass Septet
J. Sebesta (cnd)
Dances of Rudolphian Prague Multisonic ▲ MUL 310374 [DDD]
Demantius, C.:Conviviorum deliciae—Nos. 21, 28 & 29 *(rec Dvořák Hall of Rudolfinum, Prague, Apr 6-10, 1995)* Panton ▲ PAN 811442 [DDD]
Franck, M.:Newe musicalische Intraden—Nos. 1-3, 6, 20 & 23 *(rec Dvořák Hall of Rudolfinum, Prague, Apr 6-10, 1995)* Panton ▲ PAN 811442 [DDD]
Hassler, H.L.:Lustgarten neuer teutscher Gesäng, Balletti, Gaillarden und Intraden—Nos. 40-45 *(rec Dvořák Hall of Rudolfinum, Prague, Apr 6-10, 1995)* Panton ▲ PAN 811442 [DDD]
Orologio, A.:Intradae—Nos. 11, 13-15, 17 & 18 *(rec Dvořák Hall of Rudolfinum, Prague, Apr 6-10, 1995)* Panton ▲ PAN 811442 [DDD]
Otto, V.:Music of—Newe Paduanen, Galliarden, Intraden & Currenten [Nos. 32-34, 36, 39 & 43] *(rec Dvořák Hall of Rudolfinum, Prague, Apr 6-10, 1995)* Panton ▲ PAN 811442 [DDD]
Prague Chamber Ensemble [Jan Marek (vn), Rita Caplurcenko (vn), Jiri Uosek (vc), Frantisek Bilek (cl), Elena Jordanova (pno)]
Verdi, G.:arias—Va pensiero [from Nabucco]; Libiamo; Ah, fors'è lui che l'anima; Di Provenza del mar [all from La Traviata]; Celeste Aida [from Aida]; La donna è mobile; Gaultier Malte; Caro nome [all from Rigoletto] [all arr. Puklicky for chamber ensemble] Vox Classics ▲ VOX 7507 [DDD]
Prague Chamber Ensemble [Zbynek l'Adourek (vn), Jan Marek (vn), Jiri Uosek (vc), Frantisek Bilek (cl), Barbora Vachalova (hp), Elena Jordanova (pno)]
Puccini, G.:Arias—Signora ascolta; Nessun dorma [both from Turandot]; Donna non vidi mai [from Manon Lescaut]; Un bel dì [from Madama Butterfly]; Vissi d'arte; E lucevan le stelle [both from Tosca]; Si mi chiamano Mimi; Musatta's Waltz; Che gelida manina [all from La Boheme] [all arr. Puklicky for chamber ensemble] Vox Classics ▲ VOX 7507 [DDD]
Prague Chamber Harmony
Stravinsky, I.:Ebony Con, w. K. Krautgartner (cl) *(rec Jan. 29 to Feb. 2, 1968)* Supraphon ▲ 11 0672-2 [ADD]

Prague Chamber Harmony (cont.)

L. Pešek (cnd)

Stravinsky, I.:L'Histoire du soldat Suite Ensemble, w. J. Novotný (fl), K. Zlatníková, K. Krautgartner (cl) *(rec May 18–22, 1964)* Supraphon ("Collection" series) ▲ 11 0672-2 [ADD]
Stravinsky, I.:Octet, w. K. Krautgartner (cl) *(rec Feb. 12–15, 1962)* Supraphon ("Collection" series) ▲ 11 0672-2 [ADD]
Stravinsky, I.:Syms Ww *(rec Jan. 28 to Feb. 1, 1965)* Supraphon ("Collection" series) ▲ 11 0672-2 [ADD]

Prague CO

Cartellieri, A.:Cons Cl, w. Dieter Klocker (cl)—in B♭ & E♭ MD + G ▲ MDG 3010527
Castelnuovo-Tedesco, M.:Con 1 Gtr, w. Milan Zelenka (gtr) Supraphon ▲ SUP 0038
Castelnuovo-Tedesco, M.:Con 2 Gtr, w. Milan Zelenka (gtr) Supraphon ▲ SUP 0038
Dvořák, A.:Czech Suite Supraphon Collection ▲ 11 0649-2 [ADD]
Dvořák, A.:Serenade Strs [without conductor] Supraphon Collection ▲ 11 0649-2 [ADD]
Dvořák, A.:Serenade Strs *(rec Rudolfinum, Prague, June 28–July 2, 1994)* Denon ▲ CO 78919 [DDD]
Eduard Haken, w. Eduard Haken (bass), Prague National Theater Orch, Prague National Theater Chorus, Prague Smetana Theater Orch, Prague RSO Supraphon ▲ SUP 3186
Evening Tunes in Prague:Prague CO Encore *(rec Rudolfinum, Prague, June 28–July 2, 1993)* Denon ▲ CO 78926 [DDD]
Haydn, J.:Con Tpt, w. Guy Touvron (tpt) RCA Red Seal ▲ 09026-60858-2
Haydn, M.:Con in C Tpt, w. Guy Touvron (tpt) RCA Red Seal ▲ 09026-60858-2
Hummel, J.N.:Con in E♭ Tpt, S.49, w. G. Touvron (tpt) RCA Victor ▲ 09026-61857-2; ■ 09026-61857-4
Hummel, J.N.:Con in E♭ Tpt, S.49, w. G. Touvron (tpt) RCA Red Seal ▲ 09026-60858-2
Janácek, L.:Suite Str Orch *(rec Rudolfinum, Prague, June 28–July 2, 1994)* Denon ▲ CO 78919 [DDD]
Kabeláč, M.:Sym 4 Supraphon ▲ SUP 3020
Martinů, B.:Partita (Suite 1) *(rec Rudolfinum, Prague, June 28–July 2, 1994)* Denon ▲ CO 78919 [DDD]
Mozart, W.A.:Sym 38 Supraphon Collection ▲ 11 0621-2 [ADD]
Music at the Time of Beaumarchais, w. Montserrat Figueras (sop), Lawrence Monteyro (sop), Raphel Oleg (vn), Miguel da Silva (va), Christophe Coin (vc), Marc Coppey (vc), José Miguel Moreno (gtr), Paul Badura-Skoda (pno), Philippe Cassard (pno), Eric Le Sage (pno), Bob Van Asperen (hn), et al. Valois ▲ V 4767
Music From the Heart of Europe, w. Lubomir Brabec (gtr), Josef Suk (vn), Rudolf Firkušný (pno), Vaclav Neumann (cnd), Jiří Belohlávek (cnd), Panocha Quartet, Czech PO, Prague CO, Prague Musica Antiqua, et al. Supraphon ▲ SUP 0063 [DDD]
Mysliveček, J.:Con Fl, w. B. Meier (fl) Koch Schwann ▲ CD 311104 [DDD] ■ 211104 (D)
Mysliveček, J.:Sinfs—in B♭ (1762), in G & F (1764), & in F, B♭ & G (1778) Supraphon ▲ 11 0304-2 [AAD]
Neruda, J.B.G.:Con Tpt, w. G. Touvron (tpt) RCA Red Seal ▲ 09026-60858-2
Rodrigo, J.:Concierto de Aranjuez, w. L. Brabec (gtr) Supraphon ▲ 11 1563-2 [DDD]
Rodrigo, J.:Fant para un gentilhombre, w. L. Brabec (gtr) Supraphon ▲ 11 1563-2 [DDD]
Vanhal, J.B.:Con Fl, w. B. Meier (fl) Koch Schwann ▲ CD 311104 [DDD] ■ 211104 (D)
Voříšek, J.V.:Intro et rondeau brillant, w. B. Krajný, I. Pařík Supraphon ▲ 10 3868 [DDD]
Witt, F.:Con Fl, w. B. Meier (fl) Koch Schwann ▲ CD 311104 [DDD] ■ 211104 (D)

S. Accardo (cnd)

Mozart, W.A.:Concertone Vns, w. M. Batjer (vn), S. Accardo (vn) Nuova Era ▲ 6949 [DDD]
Mozart, W.A.:Sinf concertante Vn, K.364, w. S. Accardo (vn), T. Hoffman (va) Nuova Era ▲ 6949 [DDD]

P. Badura-Skoda (cnd)

Mozart, W.A.:Con 20 Pno, w. Paul Badura-Skoda (pno) Valois ▲ V 4664
Mozart, W.A.:Con 21 Pno, w. Paul Badura-Skoda (pno) *(rec 1971)* Supraphon Collection ▲ 11 0610-2 [ADD]
Mozart, W.A.:Con 21 Pno, w. Paul Badura-Skoda (pno) Valois ▲ V 4664
Mozart, W.A.:Con 23 Pno, w. P. Badura-Skoda (pno) Valois ▲ V 4687
Mozart, W.A.:Con 24 Pno, w. P. Badura-Skoda (pno) *(rec 1970)* Supraphon Collection ▲ 11 0610-2 [ADD]
Mozart, W.A.:Con 25 Pno, w. P. Badura-Skoda (pno) Valois ▲ V 4687

A. Barta (cnd)

Vivaldi, A.:Cons Vc, w. M. Kanka (vc)—RV.404, 418, 421, 422, 424 & 547 Supraphon ▲ SUP 11 2121 [DDD]
Vivaldi, A.:Con for 2 Vcs, w. M. Kanka (vc), *(2nd cellist unknown)* Supraphon ▲ SUP 11 2121 [DDD]

C. Benda (cnd)

Benda, G.A.:Medea, w. Hertha Schell (nar), Peter Uray (nar), Brigitte Quadlbauer (nar) *(rec Prague, Nov 1994)* Naxos ▲ 8.553346 [DDD]
Benda, J.G.:Con Vn, w. Christian Benda (vc) [trans for vc & strs] *(rec Prague, Nov 1994)* Naxos ▲ 8.553346 [DDD]
Stamitz, C.:Con 1 Vc, w. C. Benda (vc) *(rec Jan. 1993)* Naxos ▲ 8.550865 [DDD]
Stamitz, C.:Con 2 Vc, w. C. Benda (vc) *(rec Jan. 1993)* Naxos ▲ 8.550865 [DDD]
Stamitz, C.:Con 3 Vc, w. C. Benda (vc) *(rec Jan. 1993)* Naxos ▲ 8.550865 [DDD]

M. Bruni (cnd)

Pergolesi, G.B.:Stabat mater, w. Tynes (sop), Turner-Butler (alt), Czech Phil Chorus [L] *(rec 1968)* Supraphon Collection ▲ 11 0620-2 [ADD]

G. Delogu (cnd)

Vivaldi, A.:Cons Diverse Instrs, w. Václav Hudeček (cl), Jiří Stivín (va), Ludomír Brabec (pno), Janáček CO—in C for 2 Rcrs, 2 Bns, 2 Vns, 2 Gtrs, Vc, Strings & Cont, RV.558; in d for Vn, Gtr, Strs & Cont, RV.540; in F for Vn, Gtr, Strs & Cont, RV.542; in a for Rcr, Strs & Cont, RV.108; in C for 2 Vns, 2 Gtrs, 2 Fls, 2 Rcrs, 2 Strs & 2 Conts, RV.565 Supraphon ▲ SUP 3023

B. Gregor (cnd)

Dittersdorf, K.D. von:Syms (Metamorphoses) Supraphon 2-▲ 11 0579-2 [DDD]
Martinů, B.:Divertimento for Pno Left Hand & Orch, w. J. Panenka (pno) Supraphon ("Great Artists" series) ▲ 11 0273-2 [DDD]
Martinů, B.:Sinfonietta giocosa Pno, w. J. Panenka (pno) Supraphon ("Great Artists" series) ▲ 11 0273-2 [DDD]

L. Hlaváček (cnd)

Haydn, J.:Con 1 Vn, w. Bohuslav Matoušek (vn) Supraphonet ▲ 11 1119-2 [AAD]
Haydn, J.:Con 2 Vn, w. Bohuslav Matoušek (vn) Supraphonet ▲ 11 1119-2 [AAD]
Haydn, J.:Con 4 Vn, w. Bohuslav Matoušek (vn) *(rec 1971)* Supraphonet ▲ 11 1119-2 [AAD]
Vivaldi, A.:Cons Vn, Op. 8/1–4, "The Four Seasons", w. J. Suk (vn) *(rec Apr 13–16, 1975)* Supraphon ("Collection" series) ▲ 110685-2 [ADD]
Vivaldi, A.:Cons Vn, Op. 8/1–4, "The Four Seasons", w. J. Suk (vn) Supraphon ▲ 110281-2 [AAD]

W.-M. Kim (cnd)

Dvořák, A.:Serenade Strs Mastersound ▲ MST 219 [DDD]
Vivaldi, A.:Cons Vn, Op. 8/1–4, "The Four Seasons" Mastersound ▲ MST 219 [DDD]

J. Krips (cnd)

Dvořák, A.:Czech Suite *(rec 1968)* FNAC Music ▲ 642324
Dvořák, A.:Sym 9, "From the New World" *(rec 1968)* FNAC Music ▲ 642324

P. Kühn (cnd)

Mozart, W.A.:Masonic Music, w. Prague Phil Chorus—Masonic Cants. & Songs Supraphon ▲ SUP 112155 [DDD]
Tomášek, V.J.K.:Coronation Mass, w. Kühn Chorus Supraphon ▲ SUP 112138 [DDD]
Vranicky, A.:Missa, w. Kühn Chorus Supraphon ▲ SUP 112138 [DDD]

Leppard, Linde (cnd)

Vivaldi, A.:Music of, w. Wim Ten Have (va), Anthony Bailes (lt), Raymond Leppard (hpd), Hans-Martin Linde (fl/rcr), English CO, Danske Strings members—Concertino in D, RV.121; Cons. in f, RV.156; in G, RV.435 [Op. 10/4]; in D, RV.429; in F, RV.434 [Op. 10/5]; in D, RV.93; in d, RV.540; Son. in E♭, RV.130 [Al Santo Sepolcro] Classics for Pleasure ▲ CDCFP 4656 [ADD]

Prague CO (cont.)

C. Mackerras (cnd)

Handel, G.F.:Water Music (comp) EMI Classics ▲ CDE 67774
Mozart, W.A.:Kleine Nachtmusik Telarc ▲ CD 80108 [DDD]
Mozart, W.A.:Serenade Vn, K.250 Telarc ▲ CD 80161 [DDD]
Mozart, W.A.:Serenade Ww, K.320 Telarc ▲ CD 80108 [DDD]
Mozart, W.A.:Serenata notturna Telarc ▲ CD 80161 [DDD]
Mozart, W.A.:Syms (comp)—in D, K.81/73i, in D, K.97/73m, in D, K.95/73n; Nos. 8, 9 & 11 Telarc ▲ CD 80272 [DDD]
Mozart, W.A.:Syms (comp) Telarc 10-▲ CD 80300 [DDD]
Mozart, W.A.:Syms (comp)—in C, K.96/111b, in F, K.75; Nos. 10, 12 & 13 Telarc ▲ CD 80273 [DDD]
Mozart, W.A.:Syms (comp)—in F, K.19a; in B♭, K.45b; Nos. 1, 4, 5, 6 & 7 Telarc ▲ CD 80256 [DDD]
Mozart, W.A.:Sym 14 Telarc ▲ CD 80242 [DDD]
Mozart, W.A.:Sym 15 Telarc ▲ CD 80242 [DDD]
Mozart, W.A.:Sym 16 Telarc ▲ CD 80242 [DDD]
Mozart, W.A.:Sym 17 Telarc ▲ CD 80242 [DDD]
Mozart, W.A.:Sym 18 Telarc ▲ CD 80242 [DDD]
Mozart, W.A.:Sym 19 Telarc ▲ CD 80217 [DDD]
Mozart, W.A.:Sym 20 Telarc ▲ CD 80217 [DDD]
Mozart, W.A.:Sym 21 Telarc ▲ CD 80217 [DDD]
Mozart, W.A.:Sym 22 Telarc ▲ CD 80217 [DDD]
Mozart, W.A.:Sym 23 Telarc ▲ CD 80217 [DDD]
Mozart, W.A.:Sym 24 Telarc ▲ CD 80186 [DDD]
Mozart, W.A.:Sym 25 Telarc ▲ CD 80165 [DDD]
Mozart, W.A.:Sym 26 Telarc ▲ CD 80186 [DDD]
Mozart, W.A.:Sym 27 Telarc ▲ CD 80186 [DDD]
Mozart, W.A.:Sym 28 Telarc ▲ CD 80165 [DDD]
Mozart, W.A.:Sym 29 Telarc ▲ CD 80165 [DDD]
Mozart, W.A.:Sym 30 Telarc ▲ CD 80186 [DDD]
Mozart, W.A.:Sym 31 Telarc ▲ CD 80190 [DDD]
Mozart, W.A.:Sym 32 Telarc ▲ CD 80203 [DDD]
Mozart, W.A.:Sym 33 Telarc ▲ CD 80190 [DDD]
Mozart, W.A.:Sym 34 Telarc ▲ CD 80190 [DDD]
Mozart, W.A.:Sym 35 Telarc ▲ CD 80203 [DDD]
Mozart, W.A.:Sym 36 Telarc ▲ CD 80148 [DDD]
Mozart, W.A.:Sym 38 Telarc ▲ CD 80148 [DDD]
Mozart, W.A.:Sym 39 Telarc ▲ CD 80203 [DDD]
Mozart, W.A.:Sym 40 Telarc ▲ CD 80139 [DDD]
Mozart, W.A.:Sym 41 Telarc ▲ CD 80139 [DDD]

M. Munclinger (cnd)

Benda, F.:Con in e Fl & Orch, w. J.-P. Rampal (fl) *(rec 1956)* Supraphon ▲ 111308-2 [AAD]
Telemann, G.P.:Con Rcr, Fl, w. Jiří Stivín (rcr), Jiří Válek (fl) Supraphon ▲ SUP 3039
Telemann, G.P.:Con in a for 2 Rcrs, w. Jiří Stivín (rcr), Miloslav Klement (rcr) Supraphon ▲ SUP 3039
Telemann, G.P.:Suite Rcr, w. Jiří Stivín (rcr) Supraphon ▲ SUP 3039

V. Neumann (cnd)

Stamitz, C.:Con Fl, Op. 29, w. J.-P. Rampal (fl) *(rec 1955)* Supraphon ▲ 111308-2 [AAD]

B. Novotny (cnd)

Mozart, W.A.:Idomeneo (ballet music) Supraphon 2-▲ 11 1166-2 [DDD]

I. Pařík (cnd)

Voříšek, J.V.:Sym, Op. 24 Supraphon ▲ 10 3868 [DDD]
Voříšek, J.V.:Variazione di bravura, w. B. Krajný (pno) Supraphon ▲ 10 3868 [DDD]

Z. Peskó (cnd)

Mysliveček, J.:Belerofonte, w. C. Lindsleyová (sop), G. Mayová (sop), K. Lakiová (sop), D. Ahlstedt (ten), R. Giménéz (ten), S. Margita (ten), Czech Phil Chorus [I] *(rec 1987)* Supraphon 3-▲ 11 0006-2 [DDD]

L. Pešek (cnd)

Krommer, F.:Con Cl, w. V. Mares (cl) Supraphon ▲ SUP 111596 [DDD]
Krommer, F.:Cons for 2 Cls, w. V. Mares (cl), *(2nd clarinetist unknown)* Supraphon ▲ SUP 111596 [DDD]
Mozart, W.A.:Ovs—Don Giovanni Supraphon Collection ▲ 11 0621-2 [ADD]
Vejvanovsky, P.J.:Sons & Serenades, w. M. Kejmar (tpt), Z. Šedivý (tpt)—Serenades in A & C; Sonata a 4; Sonata a 5; Sonata Secunda a 6; Sonata Venatoria in D; Sonata Vespertina a 8 Supraphon ▲ 10 3593 [DDD]

H. Rilling (cnd)

Brixi, F.X.:Missa Interga, w. I. Verebics (sop), C. Borchers (cta), S. Weir (ten), Genhardt (bass), Kühn Chorus Supraphon ▲ 11 0092-2 [DDD]
Brixi, F.X.:Opus Patheticum de Septem Doloribus Beatae Mariae Virginis, w. I. Verebics (sop), C. Borchers (cta), S. Weir (ten), Genhardt (bass), Kühn Chorus Supraphon ▲ 11 0092-2 [DDD]

V. Smetáček (cnd)

Brahms, J.:Serenade 2 Orch Supraphon ▲ SUP 11 0048 [DDD]
Strauss, R.:Serenade Ww Supraphon ▲ SUP 11 0048 [DDD]

F. Vajnar (cnd)

Brixi, F.X.:Cons Org (comp), w. J. Hora (org)—3 Concerti—in D, C & C *(rec 1982)* Supraphon ▲ 10 3029-2 [AAD]
Fiala, J.:Con Ob, w. J. Krejčí (ob) Supraphon ▲ 10 3624-2 [DDD]
Krommer, F.:Con Ob, Op. 52, w. J. Krejčí (ob) Supraphon ▲ 10 3624-2 [DDD]
Stamitz, A.:Con Fls, w. J. Válek (fl), R. Pivoda (fl) Supraphon ▲ 11 1424-2 [DDD]
Stamitz, C.:Con 11 Cl, w. B. Zahradník (cl) Supraphon ▲ 11 1424-2 [DDD]
Stamitz, C.:Con Hn in E♭, w. Z. Tylšar (hn) Supraphon ▲ 11 1424-2 [DDD]
Zach, J.:Con Ob, w. J. Krejčí (ob) Supraphon ▲ 10 3624-2 [DDD]

J. Vlach (cnd)

Respighi, O.:Gli uccelli *(rec Feb. 4–8, 1974)* Supraphon ("Collection" series) ▲ 11 0683-2 [ADD]

O. Vlček (cnd)

Mozart, W.A.:Cons Hn, w. Z. Tylšar (hn) *(rec live Sept. 1982)* Supraphon ▲ 103619-2 [DDD]
Mozart, W.A.:Ovs—to all of Mozart's 18 completed dramatic works played in chronological order) Die Schuldigkeit des ersten Gebotes, K.35; Apollo et Hyacinthus, K.38; Bastien und Bastienne, K.50; La finta semplice, K.51; Mitridate, Rè di Ponto, K.87; Ascanio in Alba, K.111; Il sogno di Scipione, K.126; Lucio Silla, K.135; La finta giardineira, K.196; Il ré pastore, K.208; Idomeneo, K.366; Die Entführung aus dem Serail, K.384; Der Schauspieldirektor, K.486; Le nozze di Figaro, K.492; Don Giovanni, K.527; Così fan tutte, K.588; Die Zauberflöte, K.620; La clemenza di Tito, K.621 Supraphon 2-▲ 11 1166-2 [DDD]
Vivaldi, A.:Con Lt, w. L. Brabec (gtr) Supraphon ▲ 10 4126-2 [DDD]
Vivaldi, A.:Con Mand, RV.425, w. L. Brabec (gtr) Supraphon ▲ 10 4126-2 [DDD]
Vivaldi, A.:Con for 2 Mands, w. L. Brabec (gtr), M. Myslivicek (gtr) Supraphon ▲ 10 4126-2 [DDD]
Vivaldi, A.:Con Va d'amore Lt, w. L. Maly (va), L. Brabec (gtr) Supraphon ▲ 10 4126-2 [DDD]

P. Škvor (cnd)

Respighi, O.:Trittico botticelliano *(rec Feb. 4–8, 1974)* Supraphon ("Collection" series) ▲ 11 0683-2 [ADD]

Prague Chamber PO

J. Belohlávek (cnd)

Dvořák, A.:Con Vn, w. Frantisek Novotny (vn) Studio Matous ▲ MAT 31 [DDD]
Dvořák, A.:Mazurek, w. Frantisek Novotny (vn) Studio Matous ▲ MAT 31 [DDD]
Dvořák, A.:Romance Vn, w. Frantisek Novotny (vn) Studio Matous ▲ MAT 31 [DDD]
Dvořák, A.:Serenade Strs Supraphon ▲ SUP CD 3157
Mahler, G.:Kindertotenlieder, w. Dagmar Pecková (mez) Supraphon ▲ SUP 3030
Mahler, G.:Lieder eines fahrenden Gesellen, w. Dagmar Pecková (mez) Supraphon ▲ SUP 3030
Mahler, G.:Songs from Rückert, w. Dagmar Pecková (mez) Supraphon ▲ SUP 3030
Mahler, G.:Sym 5—Adagietto Supraphon ▲ SUP 3030

▲ = CD ♦ = Enhanced CD Δ = MD ■ = Cassette Tape □ = DCC

Prague Chamber PO (cont.)
J. Belohlávek (cnd) (cont.)
Stamitz, A.:Con Va, w. Jan Peruška (va) *(rec Studio Martínek, Prague)* Panton ▲ PAN 811422 [DDD]
Stamitz, C.:Con Va, w. Jan Peruška (va) *(rec Studio Martínek, Prague)* Panton ▲ PAN 811422 [DDD]
Stamitz, J.W.A.:Con Va, w. Jan Peruška (va) *(rec Studio Martínek, Prague)* Panton ▲ PAN 811422 [DDD]
Suk, J.:Serenade Strs Supraphon ▲ SUP CD 3157
T. Hanuš (cnd)
Bach, J.S.:Christmas Oratorio, w. Magdalena Kozena (mez)—also includes Air for Violin & Orchestra Lotos ▲ CD 0031 [DDD]
Mozart, W.A.:Adagio Vn, w. Josef Suk (vn) Lotos ▲ CD 0031 [DDD]
Mozart, W.A.:Kleine Nachtmusik—Allegro; Menuetto.Allegretto Lotos ▲ CD 0031 [DDD]
Mozart, W.A.:Sacred Music—Laudate Dominum Lotos ▲ CD 0031 [DDD]
Prague Chamber Soloists
Z. Lukás (cnd)
Mozart, W.A.:Arias, w. J. Jonášová (sop)—Bella mia fiamma...Resta, o cara (concert aria), K.528 [I] Supraphon Collection ▲ 11 0621–2 [ADD]
A. Mogrelia (cnd)
Bach, J.S.:Brandenburg Con 1 Lydian ▲ LYD 18119 [DDD]
Bach, J.S.:Brandenburg Con 2 Lydian ▲ LYD 18119 [DDD]
Bach, J.S.:Brandenburg Con 3 Lydian ▲ LYD 18119 [DDD]
Bach, J.S.:Brandenburg Con 4 Lydian ▲ LYD 18119 [DDD]
Handel, G.F.:Royal Fireworks Music Lydian ▲ LYD 18118 [DDD]
Handel, G.F.:Water Music (comp) Lydian ▲ LYD 18118 [DDD]
V. Neumann (cnd)
Bach, J.S.:Con 1 Hpd, w. Z. Ruzičková (hpd) *(rec 1968)* Supraphon Collection ▲ 11 0615–2 [ADD]
Bach, J.S.:Con 4 Hpd, w. Z. Ruzičková (hpd) *(rec 1966)* Supraphon Collection ▲ 11 0615–2 [ADD]
Bach, J.S.:Con 6 Hpd, w. Z. Ruzičková (hpd) *(rec 1963)* Supraphon Collection ▲ 11 0615–2 [ADD]
L. Pešek (cnd)
Kubík, L.:Con Vn Col Legno ▲ AU 31810
Prague Collegium Musicum
F. Vajnar (cnd)
Went, J.N.:Suite from *Le nozze di Figaro* Ww Supraphon ▲ 10 3426–2 [DDD]
Prague Concertino Nutturno
A. Kroper (cnd)
Mozart, W.A.:Ave verum corpus, w. E. Mirgova (sop), M. Kozená (cta), J. Griffett (ten), J. Klecker (bass) Allegro ▲ ALG PCD 1022 [DDD]
Mozart, W.A.:Requiem, w. E. Mirgova (sop), M. Kozená (cta), J. Griffett (ten), J. Klecker (bass), Brnensky Academy Choir Allegro ▲ ALG PCD 1022 [DDD]
Prague Czech SO
U. J. Flury (cnd)
Flury, R.:Die alte Truhe, w. Metelka Michal (vn) Gallo ▲ CD 860 [DDD]
Flury, R.:Pieces (6) Orch, w. Metelka Michal (vn) Gallo ▲ CD 860 [DDD]
Prague Festival Orch
Classics Go to the Movies, Vol. 3, w. Hungarian State Orch, Lajos Meyer, Budapest Strings, Leonhard Hokanson (pno), Carmerata Labacensis, Budapest SO LaserLight ▲ 15 643
P. Urbanek (cnd)
Dvořák, A.:Sym 9, "From the New World" LaserLight ♦ 90015 [DDD]
Dvořák, A.:Sym 9, "From the New World" LaserLight ▲ 15 517 [DDD]
Dvořák, A.:Sym 9, "From the New World" LaserLight ▲ 15 824 [DDD]
Mahler, G.:Sym 1 Laserlight ▲ 15 529 [DDD]
Mahler, G.:Sym 1 Laserlight ▲ 15 828 [DDD]
Mozart, L.:Toy Sym LaserLight ▲ 15 386 [DDD]
Orff, C.:Carmina burana, w. *(soloists unknown)*, Prague Festival Chorus *(rec live)* LaserLight ▲ 14 020 [DDD]
Prokofiev, S.:Peter & the Wolf, w. J. Lemmon (nar) LaserLight ▲ 15386 [DDD]
Prokofiev, S.:Peter & the Wolf, w. Jack Lemmon (nar) Laserlight ♦ 90035 [DDD]
Tchaikovsky, P.:Mélodie Laserlight ▲ 15 821
Tchaikovsky, P.:Sym 5 Laserlight ▲ 15 620 [DDD]
Tchaikovsky, P.:Sym 5 Laserlight ♦ 90019 [DDD]
Tchaikovsky, P.:Sym 6 LaserLight ▲ 15 821 [DDD]
Prague Festival Strings
D. Berkovsky (cnd)
Dvořák, A.:Serenade Strs Vivace ▲ 585 [DDD]
Dvořák, A.:Serenade Strs Vivace 3–▲ E 338–2 [ADD/DDD]
Tchaikovsky, P.:Serenade Strs Vivace 3–▲ E 338–2 [ADD/DDD]
Tchaikovsky, P.:Serenade Strs Vivace ▲ 585 [DDD]
Prague Gioio della Musica
Hallelujah, w. [cnd:Mark Brown, Andreas Kröper], Brnenský Academy Chorus Sbor, Pro Cantione Antiqua IMP Classics ("Allegro" series) ▲ ALGPCD 1094 [DDD]
Prague Guitar Quartet
Gershwin, G.:Preludes (3) Pno [arr for Gtr Qt] Panton ▲ PAN 810993
Morel, Jorge:Suite del sur Panton ▲ PAN 810993
Moreno Torroba, F.:Ráfagas Panton ▲ PAN 810993
Villa-Lobos, H.:Bachiana brasileira 1 [arr for Gtr Qt] Panton ▲ PAN 810993
Prague Guitar Quartet [Marek Veleminský (gtr), Václav Kučera (gtr), Jiří Mrhal (gtr), Martin Sauer (gtr)]
Duarte, J.:Americana *(rec Divertimento Studio, Prague, Jan–Mar 1995)* Panton ▲ PAN 811394 [DDD]
Duarte, J.:Ballade *(rec Divertimento Studio, Prague, Jan–Mar 1995)* Panton ▲ PAN 811394 [DDD]
Duarte, J.:Con democratico *(rec Divertimento Studio, Prague, Jan–Mar 1995)* Panton ▲ PAN 811394 [DDD]
Duarte, J.:Diptych 1 *(rec Divertimento Studio, Prague, Jan–Mar 1995)* Panton ▲ PAN 811394 [DDD]
Duarte, J.:Little Suite 1 *(rec Divertimento Studio, Prague, Jan–Mar 1995)* Panton ▲ PAN 811394 [DDD]
Rak, S.:Aria di Bohemia *(rec Divertimento Studio, Prague, Jan–Mar 1995)* Panton ▲ PAN 811394 [DDD]
Rak, S.:Chimeric Prelude *(rec Divertimento Studio, Prague, Jan–Mar 1995)* Panton ▲ PAN 811394 [DDD]
Rak, S.:Czech Fairy Tales *(rec Divertimento Studio, Prague, Jan–Mar 1995)* Panton ▲ PAN 811394 [DDD]
Rak, S.:Moods *(rec Divertimento Studio, Prague, Jan–Mar 1995)* Panton ▲ PAN 811394 [DDD]
Rak, S.:Rumba *(rec Divertimento Studio, Prague, Jan–Mar 1995)* Panton ▲ PAN 811394 [DDD]
Rak, S.:Taranto *(rec Divertimento Studio, Prague, Jan–Mar 1995)* Panton ▲ PAN 811394 [DDD]
Prague Madrigalists
Zelenka, J.D.:Chwalte Boha sylneho Supraphon ▲ SUP 112175 [DDD]
Zelenka, J.D.:Laetatus sum Supraphon ▲ SUP 112175 [DDD]
Zelenka, J.D.:Memento Domine David Supraphon ▲ SUP 112175 [DDD]
Zelenka, J.D.:Miserere in c Supraphon ▲ SUP 112175 [DDD]
Prague Musica Antiqua
Music From the Heart of Europe, w. Lubomir Brabec (gtr), Josef Suk (vn), Rudolf Firkušný (pno), Vaclav Neumann (cnd), Jiří Belohlávek (cnd), Panocha Quartet, Czech PO, Prague CO, Prague Musica Antiqua, et al. Supraphon ▲ SUP 0063 [DDD]
P. Klikar (cnd)
Baroque Music from the Kromeríz Archives Supraphon ▲ SUP 111416 [DDD]
Italian Music of Early Baroque Supraphon ▲ SUP 111816 [DDD]
Prague Musici
Baroque Music in France Pierre Verany ("Favourites" series) ▲ 730013 [DDD]

Prague Musici (cont.)
M. Klemens (cnd)
Reicha, J.:Con Vc, w. Miloš Sádlo (vc) [rev & cadenza by Sádlo] *(rec House of Artists, Prague, Nov. 1972)* Panton ▲ PAN 811307 [AAD]
Vranicky, A.:Con Vc, w. Miloš Sádlo (vc) [rev & cadenza by Sádlo] *(rec House of Artists, Prague, Nov. 1972)* Panton ▲ PAN 811307 [AAD]
L. Sagrestano (cnd)
Haydn, J.:Con 1 Hn, w. Joseph Brázada (hn) Accord ▲ ACD 220462 [DDD]
Haydn, J.:Con Tpt, w. Bernard Soustrot (tpt) Accord ▲ ACD 220462 [DDD]
Haydn, J.:Con Vn, Hpd & Strs, w. Václav Hudecek (vn), Martin Derungs (hpd) Accord ▲ ACD 220462 [DDD]
V. Smetáček (cnd)
Dvořák, A.:Con Vn, w. Václav Hudecek (vn) Panton ▲ PAN 811211
Prague National Orch
B. Gregor (cnd)
Janácek, L.:The Makropulos Affair, w. Libuse Prylova (sop), Helena Tattermuschová (sop), Rudolf Vanasek (ten), Ivo Zídek (ten), Prague National Theater Chorus *(rec mid 1960's)* Supraphon 2–▲ SUP 108351 [AAD]
Prague National Theater Orch
Eduard Haken, w. Eduard Haken (bass), Prague National Theater Chorus, Prague Smetana Theater Orch, Prague CO, Prague RSO Supraphon ▲ SUP 3186
Ivo Zídek Operatic Recital, w. Ivo Zídek (ten) Supraphon ▲ SUP 3189
K. Böhm (cnd)
Mozart, W.A.:Don Giovanni (sels), w. R. Grist (sop), B. Nilsson (sop), M. Arroyo (sop), P. Schreier (ten), D. Fischer-Dieskau (bar), M. Talvela (bass) IMP Collectors Series ▲ IMPX 9023 [AAD]
Z. Chalabala (cnd)
Dvořák, A.:Rusalka, w. Milada Šubrtová (sop), Ivo Zídek (ten), Eduard Haken (bass), Prague National Theater Chorus Supraphon 2–▲ SUP 0013 [AAD]
Smetana, B.:The Bartered Bride, w. Drahomira Tikalová (sop), Ivo Zídek (ten), Eduard Haken (bass), Prague National Theater Chorus Supraphon 2–▲ SUP 0040 [AAD]
Smetana, B.:The Devil's Wall, w. Milada Šubrtová (sop), Ivana Mixová (mez), Vaclav Bednář (bass), Prague National Theater Chorus *(rec Prague, 1960)* Supraphon 2–▲ SUP 112201 [AAD]
J. Chaloupka (cnd)
Dvořák, A.:King & Charcoal Burner, w. Drahonira Drobkova (cta), Viktor Koci (ten), René Tucek (bar), Dalibor Jedlicka (bass), Milan Maly (cnd), Prague National Theater Chorus [final version] *(rec 1989)* Supraphon ("Hidden Treasures from Prague" series) ▲ SUP CD 3078
O. Dohnányi (cnd)
Smetana, B.:Libuše, w. Eva Urbanová (sop), Leo Marian Vodička (ten), Prague National Theater Chorus Supraphon 2–▲ SUP 3200
B. Gregor (cnd)
Janácek, L.:The Cunning Little Vixen, w. Tattermuschova Helena (sop—Cunning Little Vixen), Eva Zikmundová (sop—The Fox), Prague National Theater Chorus *(rec 1970)* Supraphon 2–▲ SUP 3071
Janácek, L.:Jenůfa, w. Libuse Domininská (sop—Jenufa), Nadeshda Kniplová (sop—Kostelnicka), Vilém Příbyl (ten—Laca), Ivo Zidek (ten—Steva), Prague National Theater Chorus EMI Classics 2–▲ CDMB 65476
F. Jílek (cnd)
Fibich, Z.:The Bride of Messina, w. G. Benackova (sop), L. Marova (mez), I. Zidek (ten), Prague National Theater Chorus Supraphon ▲ SUP 111492 [ADD]
Smetana, B.:The 2 Widows, w. N. Sormova (sop), M. Machotková (sop), J. Zahradnicek (ten), Prague National Theater Chorus [Cz] *(rec 1975)* Supraphon 2–▲ SUP 11 2122 [AAD]
J. Jirous (cnd)
Hába, A.:Quarter-Tone, w. Prague National Theater Chorus Supraphon ▲ SUP 108258 [ADD]
Z. Košler (cnd)
Smetana, B.:Dalibor, w. Eva Urbanová (sgr), Leo Maria Vodička (ten), Iván Kusnjer (bar), Prague National Theater Chorus Supraphon 2–▲ SUP 0077 [DDD]
Smetana, B.:Libuše, w. G. Benackova (sop), V. Soupukova (sop), V. Zitek (ten), Prague National Theater Chorus Supraphon 3–▲ SUP 111276 [DDD]
Smetana, B.:The Secret, w. Daniela Šounová-Brouková (sop), Vera Soukupová (mez), Leo Marian Vodička (ten) Supraphon 2–▲ SUP 112177 [ADD]
Smetana, B.:Viola, w. Daniela Šounová-Brouková (sop), Vera Soukupová (mez), Leo Marian Vodička (ten) Supraphon ▲ SUP 112177 [ADD]
J. Krombholc (cnd)
Janácek, L.:Káťa Kabanová, w. D. Tikalová (sop), B. Blachut (ten), Prague National Theater Chorus Supraphon 2–▲ SUP 108016 [ADD]
Martinů, B.:Julietta, w. M. Tauberová (sop), I. Zidek (ten), Prague National Theater Chorus [Cz] *(rec 1964)* Supraphon 3–▲ 10 8176–2 [ADD]
Smetana, B.:Dalibor, w. N. Kniplova (mez), V. Pribyl (ten), J. Jindrak (bar), Prague National Theater Chorus [Cz] Supraphon 2–▲ 11 2185 [ADD]
J. Stych (cnd)
Live in Prague, w. Dagmar Pecková (mez), Ivan Kusjner (bar), *(rec live, Jan 17, 1996)* Supraphon ▲ SUP 3180
H. Swarowsky (cnd)
Wagner, R.:Lohengrin, w. Leonore Kirchstein (sop—Elsa von Brabant), Ruth Hesse (mez—Ortrud), Herbert Schachtschneider (ten—Lohengrin), Hans Helm (bar—Der Heerrufer des Königs), Otto von Rohr (bass—Heinrich der Vogler), Heinz Imdahl (sgr—Friedrich von Telramund), Czech PO, Vienna State Opera Chorus *(rec Aug 1968)* Weltbild Classics 3–▲ 703835 [ADD]
Wagner, R.:Der Ring des Nibelungen, w. Liselotte Becker-Egner (sop—Woglinde/Ortlinde/Wellgunde), Angelika Berger (sop—Wellgunde/Waltraute), Siw Ericsdotter (sop—Norn 3), Heidemaria Ferch (sop—Freia/Gerhilde), Bella Jasper (sop—Helmwige/Waldvogel/Woglinde), Ditha Sommer (sop—Sieglinde/Gutrune), Ursula Boese (mez—Erda), Ruth Hesse (mez—Fricka), Nadezda Kniplová (mez—Brünnhilde), Margit Kobeck (mez—Schwertleite/Norn 2), Hilde Rosner (mez—Flosshilde/Siegrunde), Erica Schubert (mez—Grimgerde/Flosshilde), Ingrid Göritz (cta—Rossweisse/Norn 1), Herbert Doussant (ten—Froh), Herold Kraus (ten—Mime), Gerald McKee (ten—Siegmund/Siegfried), Fritz Uhl (ten—Loge), Rudolf Knoll (bar—Gunther/Donner), Rolf Polke (bass-bar—Wotan/Wanderer), Rolf Kühne (bass—Alberich), Takao Okamura (bass—Fafner), Otto von Rohr (bass—Hagen/Fasolt/Hunding), Czech PO *(rec June 3 & 5, July 26–31, A)* Weltbild Classics 14–▲ 703769 [ADD]
J.H. Tichý (cnd)
Smetana, B.:The Brandenbergers in Bohemia, w. V. Soukupova (sop), A. Vetava (ten), K. Kalas (bar), Prague National Theater Chorus [G] Supraphon 2–▲ SUP 111802 [AAD]
J. Štych (cnd)
Blodek, V.:In the Well, w. Prague National Theater Chorus Supraphon ▲ SUP 0033 [ADD]
Prague Percussion Ensemble
Kabeláč, M.:Fated Dramas of Man, w. F. Maxian (pno), M. Kejmar (tpt) *(rec 1993)* Panton ▲ PAN 811143
Kabeláč, M.:Inventions *(rec 1978)* Panton ▲ PAN 811144
Kabeláč, M.:Ricercari *(rec 1993)* Panton ▲ PAN 811144
V. Neumann (cnd)
Kabeláč, M.:Sym 8, w. *(soloists unknown)*, Prague Phil Chorus Panton ▲ PAN 811105
V. Smetáček (cnd)
Fišer, L.:Crux Panton ▲ PAN 811105
Fišer, L.:Istanu, w. *(soloists unknown)* Panton ▲ PAN 811105
Fišer, L.:Lament Over the Ruined Town of Ur, w. *(soloists unknown)* Panton ▲ PAN 811124
Fišer, L.:Son Pno, w. *(soloists unknown)* Panton ▲ PAN 811143
Prague Percussion Project [Amy Lynn Barber (perc), Josef Fojta (perc), Ivan Hoznedr (perc), Jaromír Kubiček (perc), David Rehoř (perc), Pavel Skála (perc)]
Jirásek, J.:Bread & Circuses *(rec Studio FHS, Prague)* Arta ▲ 0054 [DDD]

Prague PO

Fibich, Z.:At Twilight, w. B. Kulínský *(rec Sept. 1990)* Multisonic ▲ 31 0045-2 [DDD]

Jarre, M.:Film Music—Doctor Zhivago; A Passage to India; Ryan's Daughter; Lawrence of Arabia; Ghost; Witness; Is Paris Burning?; Night of the Generals; Man Who Would Be King; Villa Rides; Fatal Attraction; El Condor; The Fixer; Jesus of Nazareth Silva America ▲ SILCD 1047 [DDD]

Williams, John:Film Music—Jurassic Park; The Empire Strikes Back; Return of the Jedi; The Cowboys; Far and Away; Indiana Jones Trilogy; Born on the 4th of July; Presumed Innocent; Star Wars; Schindler's List; plus others Silva America ▲ SILCD 1046 [DDD]

K. Alwyn (cnd)

Rózsa, M.:Film Music—Ben-Hur; King of Kings; Sodom & Gomorrah; The Golden Voyage of Sinbad; El Cid; Quo Vadis & others Silva America ▲ SSD 1056

P. Bateman (cnd)

Moross, J.:Film Music—The Adventures of Huckleberry Finn; The Sharkfighters; The Mountain Road; Rachel Rachel, The War Lord; Five Finger Exercise; Wagon Train Silva America ▲ SSD 1049

E. Brizio (cnd)

Rossini, G.:Giovanna d'Arco, w. *(soloist unknown)*, Prague Phil Chorus Studio SM 3-▲ 12 23.27

Rossini, G.:Sacred Music, w. Prague Phil Chorus—Kyrie; Credo; Gloria de Ravenne; Tantum Ergo; Kyrie; Pieces Liturgiques; Messe de Rimini; Miserere; Quoniam; Tantum Ergo Studio SM 3-▲ 12 23.27

B. Kulinsky (cnd)

Dvořák, A.:Carnival *(rec Sept. 1990)* Multisonic ▲ 31 0045-2 [DDD]

Dvořák, A.:Con Vn, w. I. Zenaty (vn) Multisonic ▲ 31 0156 [DDD]

Dvořák, A.:Humoresques, Op. 101—No. 7 [arr. V. Smetáček for orch.] *(rec Sept. 1990)* Multisonic ▲ 31 0045-2 [DDD]

Dvořák, A.:Othello Multisonic ▲ 31 0072 [DDD]

Dvořák, A.:Slavonic Dances (sels)—No. 15 in C *(rec Sept. 1990)* Multisonic ▲ 31 0045-2 [DDD]

Dvořák, A.:Songs, w. P. Dvorsky (ten)—Oh, My Shepherd Is the Lord; Song of Gladness Will I Sing Thee [from Biblical Songs, Op. 99] Multisonic ▲ 31 0003-2 [ADD]

Dvořák, A.:Sym 5 Multisonic ▲ 31 0072 [DDD]

Kozeluch, Joh. A.:Missa Pastoralis, w. S. Losová (sop), Y. Škvárová (cta), M. Švejda (ten), M. Podskalský (bass), Prague Radio Chorus Multisonic ▲ 31 0003-2 [ADD]

Smetana, B.:The Bartered Bride (ov) *(rec Sept. 1990)* Multisonic ▲ 31 0045-2 [DDD]

Smetana, B.:Má Vlast *(rec Sept. 1990)* Multisonic ▲ 31 0045-2 [DDD]

Suk, J.:Fairy Tale, w. I. Zenaty (vn) *(rec Sept. 1990)* Multisonic ▲ 31 0045-2 [DDD]

Suk, J.:Toward a New Life *(rec Sept. 1990)* Multisonic ▲ 31 0045-2 [DDD]

M. Legrand (cnd)

Legrand, M.:The Ring Silva America ▲ SSD 1072

N. Raine (cnd)

Barry, J.:Film Music—The Ipcress File; The Scarlet Letter; Cry the Beloved Country Silva America ▲ SSD 1055

Barry, J.:Film Music—Zulu; Out of Africa; Body Heat; Indecent Proposal Silva America ▲ SSD 1033 ■ SSC 1033

How the West Was Won:Classic Western Film Scores, Vol. 1 *(rec FHS Studios, Prague)* Silva America ▲ SSD 1058

D. Wadsworth (cnd)

The Longest Day:Music from the Classic War Films Silva America ▲ SILCD 1036 [DDD]

Music from the Films of Clint Eastwood Silva America ' ▲ SILCD 1031

Music from the Films of Harrison Ford Silva America ▲ SILCD 1040 [DDD]

R. White (cnd)

Coward, N.:The Grand Tour Silva Classics ▲ SIL 6007 [DDD]

Coward, N.:London Morning Silva Classics ▲ SIL 6007 [DDD]

Prague RSO

Eduard Haken, w. Eduard Haken (bass), Prague National Theater Orch, Prague National Theater Chorus, Prague Smetana Theater Orch, Prague CO Supraphon ▲ SUP 3186

H. Abendroth (cnd)

Brahms, J.:Sym 1 *(rec 1949–50)* Arlecchino ARL

Brahms, J.:Sym 3 *(rec 1949–50)* Arlecchino ARL

K. Ančerl (cnd)

Dvořák, A.:Con Vn, w. D. Oistrakh (vn) *(rec May 1950)* Praga ▲ PR 254 006

Smetana, B.:The Bartered Bride, w. *(soloists unknown)*, Prague Radio Chorus *(rec 1947)* Multisonic ("Prague Opera Collection" series) ▲ 31 0185 [ADD]

J. Belohlávek (cnd)

Kalabis, V.:Sym 3 *(rec 1972)* Praga ▲ PR 255002

Sibelius, J.:Con Vn, w. Václav Hudecek (vn) Panton ▲ PAN 811209

Tchaikovsky, P.:Con Vn, w. Václav Hudecek (vn) Panton ▲ PAN 811208

F. Dyk (cnd)

Dvořák, A.:Vanda, w. Drahomira Tikalova (sop), Stefa Petrova (mez), Beno Blachut (ten), Karel Kalas (bass), Jiri Pinkas (cnd), Prague Radio Chorus *(rec 1951)* Supraphon ("Hidden Treasures from Prague" series) 2-▲ SUP CD 3007 (m)

Skroup, F.:Columbus (sels), w. M. Subrtová (sop), B. Blachut (ten), Z. Otava (bar), Prague Radio Chorus *(rec 1962)* Multisonic ("Prague Opera Collection" series) ▲ 31 0153

V. Jiráček (cnd)

Dvořák, A.:Armida, w. *(soloists unknown)*, Prague Chorus *(rec Prague, 1956)* Multisonic ("Prague Opera Collection" series) 3-▲ 31 0246

Kangas, Maros (cnd)

Maros, M.:Music of, w. Ilona Maros (sop), John-Edward Kelly (sax), Budapest SO, Ostrobothnian CO, Marosensemble—Sym No. 1; 4 Songs [from Gitanjali]; Sinf concertante [Sym No. 3]; Con for A Sax & Orch Phono Suecia ▲ PHN 23 [DDD]

A. Klima (cnd)

Kabalevsky, D.:Con 3 Pno, w. P. Štěpán (pno) Sound ▲ 3437 [AAD]

Prokofiev, S.:Con 3 Pno, w. F. Maxián (pno) Sound ▲ 3437 [AAD]

J. Kout (cnd)

Kalabis, V.:Sym 5 *(rec 1977)* Praga ▲ PR 255002

Z. Košler (cnd)

Martinů, B.:Rhap-Con Va, w. Lubomir Maly (va) Panton ▲ PAN 811204

J. Krombholc (cnd)

Dvořák, A.:Con Vn, w. V. Příhoda (vn) *(rec ca. 1956)* Multisonic (Prague Spring Collection) ▲ 31 0039-2 [ADD]

Dvořák, A.:In Nature's Realm *(rec 1973)* Multisonic (Prague Spring Collection) ▲ 31 0155 [ADD]

Dvořák, A.:Sym 9, "From the New World" *(rec 1975)* Multisonic (Prague Spring Collection) ▲ 31 0155 [ADD]

Smetana, B.:Dalibor, w. G. Abrahamová (sop), Vilém Přibyl (ten), Prague Radio Chorus [Cz] *(rec Sept. 1977)* Praga 2-▲ PR 250050/51

Smetana, B.:Má Vlast *(rec 1973)* Multisonic ("Prague Spring Collection" series) ▲ 31 0152-2

R. Kubelik (cnd)

Khachaturian, A.:Con Vn, w. D. Oistrakh (vn) Praga ▲ 250017

C. Mackerras (cnd)

Martinů, B.:Double Con Pno, Tim Supraphon ▲ 10 3393-2 [DDD]

Martinů, B.:Les Fresques de Piero della Francesca Supraphon ▲ 10 3393-2 [DDD]

Shostakovich, D.:Con 2 Vn, w. J. Tomasek (vn) Praga ▲ PR 250052

J. Meylan (cnd)

Prokofiev, S.:Cinderella (sels)—Marred departure, Scene with the clock & Cinderella departs to the ball Supraphon Collection ▲ 11 0643-2 [ADD]

C. Munch (cnd)

Martinů, B.:Sym 6 *(rec Dvořák Hall of Prague's House of Artists, March 27, 1967)* Panton ▲ 81 1122-2

Prague RSO (cont.)

L. Pešek (cnd)

Dvořák, A.:Con Vc, w. Daniel Veis (vc) Panton ▲ PAN 811211

Mozart, W.A.:Con Cl, w. V. Mareš (cl) Suprahon Collection ▲ 11 0621-2 [ADD]

V. Smetáček (cnd)

Dvořák, A.:St Ludmilla Praga 2-▲ PR 250 059/60

Dvořák, A.:Sym 9, "From the New World" *(rec 1974)* Praga ▲ PR 250016

Mendelssohn, F.:Con in e Vn & Orch, Op. 64, w. Václav Hudecek (vn) Panton ▲ PAN 811209

Schumann, R.:Sym 1 *(rec Studio No. 1, June 17, 1971)* Praga ▲ PR 250096

F. Stupka (cnd)

Dvořák, A.:Con Vc, w. A. Navarra (vc) *(rec ca. 1951)* Multisonic (Prague Spring Collection) ▲ 31 0039-2 [ADD]

O. Trhlík (cnd)

Tchaikovsky, P.:Con 1 Pno, w. Bozena Steinerová (pno) Panton ▲ PAN 811208

F. Vajnar (cnd)

Dvořák, A.:The Cunning Peasant, w. Eva Depoltová (sop), Václav Zítek (bar), Karel Berman (bass), Prague Radio Chorus Supraphon 2-▲ SUP 0019 [DDD]

Fibich, Z.:At Twilight, w. Prague Radio Chorus Supraphon ▲ SUP 3197

Fibich, Z.:A Night at Karlstein, w. Prague Radio Chorus Supraphon ▲ SUP 3197

Fibich, Z.:The Romance of Spring, w. Nada Sormova (sop), Karel Prusa (bass), Prague Radio Chorus Supraphon ▲ SUP 3197

Fibich, Z.:Spring, w. Prague Radio Chorus Supraphon ▲ SUP 3197

Foerster, J.B.:Eva, w. Eva Depoltová (sop), Anna Barová (mez), Leo Marian Vodicka (ten), Jaroslav Soucek (bar), Prague Radio Chorus *(rec 1982)* Supraphon 2-▲ SUP 3001

P. Vronsky (cnd)

Suk, J.:Fairy Tale Panton ▲ PAN 811212

V. Válek (cnd)

Arutiunian, A.:Music of, w. W. Forman (tpt)—Trumpet Con. Supraphon ▲ 11 1409 [DDD]

Goedicke, A.:Music of, w. W. Forman (tpt)—Con Tpt Supraphon ▲ 11 1409 [DDD]

Hummel, B.:Music of, w. W. Forman (tpt)—Trumpet Con. Supraphon ▲ 11 1409 [DDD]

Lalo, E.:Con russe, w. Gérard Poulet (vn) Praga ▲ PR 250062

Lalo, E.:Sym espagnole, w. Gérard Poulet (vn) Praga ▲ PR 250062

Martinů, B.:Les Fresques de Piero della Francesca Praga ▲ PR 254050

Martinů, B.:Memorial to Lidice Praga ▲ PR 254050

Martinů, B.:Sym 6 Praga ▲ PR 254050

Saint-Saëns, C.:Suite algérienne *(rec 1987)* Supraphon ▲ 11 0971-2 [DDD]

Saint-Saëns, C.:Sym 3, w. J. Hora (org) *(rec 1986)* Supraphon ▲ 11 0971-2 [DDD]

Schulhoff, E.:Sym 1 Supraphon ▲ SUP 112160

Schulhoff, E.:Sym 2 Supraphon ▲ SUP 112160

Schulhoff, E.:Sym 3 Supraphon ▲ SUP 112161

Schulhoff, E.:Sym 5 Supraphon ▲ SUP 112161

Sibelius, J.:Karelia Suite Supraphon ▲ SUP 111268 [DDD]

Sibelius, J.:Sym 2 Supraphon ▲ SUP 111268 [DDD]

Sibelius, J.:Valse triste Supraphon ▲ SUP 111268 [DDD]

Stravinsky, I.:Pétrouchka (suite) *(rec 1992 & 1993)* Praga ▲ 250 049 [DDD]

Stravinsky, I.:Le Sacre du printemps Orch *(rec 1992 & 1993)* Praga ▲ 250 049 [DDD]

Suk, J.:Asrael Praga ▲ PR 250 018

Suk, J.:Fantastické scherzo Praga ▲ PR 250 018

Tomasi, H.:Con Tpt, w. W. Forman (tpt) Supraphon ▲ 11 1409 [DDD]

Zemlinsky, A. von:Lyric Sym, w. Jirina Markova (sop), Ivan Kusnjer (bar) *(rec live, Prague, 1993)* Praga ▲ PR 250092

Prague Rozmberk Consort

F. Pok (cnd)

Renaissance Music at Princely Courts of Europe Supraphon ▲ SUP CD 3194

Prague Sinfonietta

I. Parik (cnd)

Myslivecek, J.:Isacco figura, w. Ilona Czaková (sgr), Hye Jin Kim (sgr), Tatiana Korovina (sgr), Victoria Luchianez (sgr), Vladimir Dolezal (ten), Ivan Kusnjer (bar), Pavel Kühn (cnd), Kühn Chorus Supraphon 2-▲ SUP 3209

Prague Smetana Theater Orch

Eduard Haken, w. Eduard Haken (bass), Prague National Theater Orch, Prague National Theater Chorus, Prague CO, Prague RSO Supraphon ▲ SUP 3186

Prague String Quartet

Dvořák, A.:Qts Strs (comp) Deutsche Grammophon 9-▲ 429193-2 [DDD]

Franck, C.:Qt Strs Praga ▲ PR 250 024

Schubert, Franz:Qt 13 Strs Denon/PCM Digital ▲ DEN 8005 [DDD]

Schubert, Franz:Qt 14 Strs Denon/PCM Digital ▲ DEN 8005 [DDD]

Prague SO

P. Altrichter (cnd)

Brahms, J.:Con 1 Pno, w. L. Berman (pno) *(rec 1992)* Supraphon ▲ SUP 111832 [DDD]

Brahms, J.:Con Vn, w. P. Berman (vc) *(rec 1992)* Supraphon ▲ SUP 111832 [DDD]

Dvořák, A.:Sym 9, "From the New World" Supraphon ▲ SUP 111810 [DDD]

Haydn, J.:Sym 94, "Surprise Sym" Stradivari Classics ▲ SCD 6094 [DDD] ■ SMC 6094 (D)

Haydn, J.:Sym 100, "Military" Stradivari Classics ▲ SCD 6094 [DDD] ■ SMC 6094 (D)

Haydn, J.:Sym 104, "London" Stradivari Classics ▲ SCD 6094 [DDD] ■ SMC 6094 (D)

Janácek, L.:The Cunning Little Vixen (suite) [arr Václav Talich; rev Václav Smetáček] Supraphon ▲ SUP 111810 [DDD]

Mendelssohn, F.:Con in d Vn & Strs, w. I. Zenaty (vn) Supraphon ▲ SUP 111808 [DDD]

Mendelssohn, F.:Con in e Vn & Orch, Op. 64, w. I. Zenaty (vn) Supraphon ▲ SUP 111808 [DDD]

Suk, J.:Dramatic Ov Supraphon ▲ SUP 111825 [DDD]

Suk, J.:Legend of the Dead Victors Supraphon ▲ SUP 111825 [DDD]

Suk, J.:Meditation on the Old Czech Hymn "St. Wenceslas" Supraphon ▲ SUP 111825 [DDD]

Suk, J.:Praga Supraphon ▲ SUP 111825 [DDD]

Suk, J.:Toward a New Life Supraphon ▲ SUP 111825 [DDD]

K. Ančerl (cnd)

Mendelssohn, F.:Con in e Vn & Orch, Op. 64, w. I. Stern (vn) Multisonic ("Prague Spring Collection" series) ▲ 31 0104 [ADD]

Prokofiev, S.:Con 1 Pno, w. S. Richter (pno) *(rec 1954)* Supraphon ("Great Artists" series) ▲ 11 0268-2 (m) [AAD]

P. Argento (cnd)

Mozart, W.A.:Con 23 Pno, w. J. Katchen (pno) *(rec live 1966)* Multisonic ("Prague Spring Collection" series) ▲ 31 0079-2 [ADD]

J. Belohlávek (cnd)

Dvořák, A.:Carnival Eurodisc ▲ 69072-2-RG [DDD]

Dvořák, A.:Con Vc, w. Michaela Fukacová (vc) Panton ▲ PAN 810706

Dvořák, A.:Con Pno, w. J. Frantz (pno) *(rec live)* Eurodisc ▲ 69072-2-RG [DDD]

Dvořák, A.:Festival March *(rec 1982)* Supraphon ("Collection" series) ▲ 110664-2 [ADD]

Dvořák, A.:Polka, "For Prague Students" *(rec 1982)* Supraphon ("Collection" series) ▲ 110664-2 [ADD]

Dvořák, A.:Polonaise Orch *(rec 1982)* Supraphon ("Collection" series) ▲ 110664-2 [ADD]

Dvořák, A.:The Spectre's Bride, Op. 110, w. Eva Urbanová (sop), Ludovit Ludha (ten), Ivan Kusnjer (b-bar), Pavel Kühn (cnd), Prague Phil Chorus *(rec live, 1995)* Supraphon ▲ SUP 3091

Dvořák, A.:Waltzes (8) Orch *(rec 1982)* Supraphon ("Collection" series) ▲ 110664-2 [ADD]

Glinka, M.:Capriccio brillante on the Jota aragonesa, "1st Spanish Ov" Supraphon ("Collection" series) ▲ 11 0622-2 [ADD]

Kubík, L.:Con Grosso Col Legno ▲ AU 31810

Martinů, B.:The Butterfly That Stamped Supraphon ▲ SUP 110380 [DDD]

Martinů, B.:Echec au roi Supraphon ▲ SUP 111415 [DDD]

328

▲ = CD ♦ = Enhanced CD Δ = MD ■ = Cassette Tape □ = DCC

Prague SO (cont.)

J. Bělohlávek (cnd) (cont.)

Martinů, B.:The Epic of Gilgamesh, w. M. Machotková (sop), J. Zaradníček (ten), V. Zítek (ten), K. Průša (bass), Czech Phil Chorus — Supraphon ▲ SUP 11 1824 [ADD]
Martinů, B.:The Miracles of Mary, w. Prague Radio Chorus — Supraphon ▲ SUP 111802 [DDD]
Martinů, B.:Revolt — Supraphon ▲ SUP 111415 [DDD]
Martinů, B.:Sym 4 — Panton ▲ PAN 811205
Opera Arias, w. Eva Urbanova (sgr) — Supraphon ▲ SUP 111851 [DDD]
Ostrčil, O.:Symfonietta — Supraphon ▲ SUP 111826 [AAD]
Ostrčil, O.:Sym in A — Supraphon ▲ SUP 111826 [AAD]
Schnittke, A.:Requiem, w. Zdena Kloubová (sop), Olga Štepánová (alt), Vladimir Dolezal (ten), Kühn Chorus *(rec live, Smetana Hall, Municipal House, Prague, Dec 19, 1990)* — Panton ("60 Years of the Prague SO" series) ▲ PAN 811374 [ADD]
Slavický, K.:Sinfonietta 4, w. Brigita Šulcová (sop), Rudolf Pellar (nar), Václav Rabas (org) *(rec Dvořák Hall of Rudolfinum, Prague, Sept. 6 & 8, 1986)* — Panton ("Protokol XX" series) ▲ PAN 811142 [DDD]
Smetana, B.:The Bartered Bride (orch sels)—Overture, Polka, Furiant & Skočná — Supraphon ▲ 11 0377–2 [DDD]
Smetana, B.:From Bohemian Fields & Groves — Supraphon ▲ 11 0377–2 [DDD]
Smetana, B.:Libuše (ov) — Supraphon ▲ 11 0377–2 [DDD]
Smetana, B.:The Moldau — Supraphon ▲ 11 0377–2 [DDD]
Smetana, B.:Polkas — Supraphon ▲ SUP 0198
Smetana, B.:Prague Carnival — Supraphon ▲ SUP 0198
Smetana, B.:Triumph Sym—Scherzo movt. — Supraphon ▲ 11 0377–2 [DDD]
Suk, J.:Fantastické scherzo *(rec 1/80)* — Supraphon ("Collection" series) ▲ 110664–2 [ADD]
Tchaikovsky, P.:Con 1 Pno, w. Peter Toperczer (pno) *(rec live, Smetana Hall, Municipal House, Prague, Mar 15, 1978)* — Panton ("60 Years of the Prague SO" series) ▲ PAN 811374 [ADD]
Tchaikovsky, P.:Suite 1 — Supraphon ▲ SUP 11 0969 [DDD]
Tchaikovsky, P.:Suite 2 — Supraphon ▲ SUP 11 0969 [DDD]
Tchaikovsky, P.:Suite 3 — Supraphon ▲ SUP 11 0969 [DDD]
Tchaikovsky, P.:Suite 4 — Supraphon ▲ SUP 11 0969 [DDD]

E. Brizio (cnd)

Bellini, V.:Mass in a, w. Leila Bersiani (sop), Valentina di Cola (sop), Stella Salvati (cta), José Antonio Campo (ten), Carlo Lepore (bass), Czech Radio–TV Chorus *(rec Prague, June 1994)* — Studio SM ▲ D 2444
Bellini, V.:Salve Regina in f, w. Carlo Lepore (bass) [orchd.] *(rec Prague, June 1994)* — Studio SM ▲ D 2444
Bellini, V.:Salve Regina in a, w. Czech Radio–TV Chorus *(rec Prague, June 1994)* — Studio SM ▲ D 2444
Paisiello, G.:Gloria Patri, w. Prague Sym Chorus *(rec June 1994)* — Studio SM ▲ 12 23 89
Paisiello, G.:Missa in pastorale per il Natale per la cappella del Primo Consolo, w. Prague Sym Chorus *(rec June 1994)* — Studio SM ▲ 12 23 89
Paisiello, G.:Tantum ergo, w. Prague Sym Chorus *(rec June 1994)* — Studio SM ▲ 12 23 89
Paisiello, G.:Tecum principium, w. Prague Sym Chorus *(rec June 1994)* — Studio SM ▲ 12 23 89

G. Delogu (cnd)

Orff, C.:Carmina burana, w. Zdena Kloubová (sop), Vladimir Dolezal (ten), Ivan Kusnjer (bar), Bambini di Praga, Kühn Choir *(rec live, Prague, Dec 12, 1995)* — Supraphon ▲ SUP 3160

Z. Fekete (cnd)

Berlioz, H.:Ovs—Benvenuto Cellini; Le Corsaire *(rec 1965)* — Supraphonet ▲ 11 1116–2 [AAD]
Indy, V. d':Istar — Supraphonet ▲ 11 1116–2 [AAD]
Indy, V. d':La Mort de Wallenstein — Supraphonet ▲ 11 1116–2 [AAD]

P. Fournillier (cnd)

Massenet, J.:La Vierge, w. M. Command (sop), M. Castets (sop), M. Olmeda (sop), M. Keller (sop), P. Salmon (ten), M. Hacquard (bar), Prague Sym Chorus — Koch Schwann 2–▲ CD 313084 [DDD]

J. Hrnčíř (cnd)

Kraft, A.:Con Vc, Op 4, w. Jiří Hošek (vc) *(rec Smetana Hall of Prague's City House, Apr 11, 12 & 28, 1989)* — Panton ▲ 811024–2 [DDD]
Kraft, A.:Con Vc, "Seydel's Con", w. Jiří Hošek (vc) *(rec Smetana Hall of Prague's City House, Apr 11, 12 & 28, 1989)* — Panton ▲ 811024–2 [DDD]
Kraft, N.:Polonaise Strs, w. Jiří Hošek (vc) *(rec Smetana Hall of Prague's City House, Apr 11, 12 & 28, 1989)* — Panton ▲ 811024–2 [DDD]

K. Husa (cnd)

Husa, K.:Serenade, Foerster Woodwind Quintet *(rec 1970)* — CRI ▲ CD 592 [ADD]
Husa, K.:Sym 1 — CRI ■ C 261
Husa, K.:Sym 1 *(rec 1970)* — CRI ▲ CD 592 [ADD]

B. Kalinsky (cnd)

Suk, J.:Fant Vn, w. I. Zenaty (vn) — Multisonic ▲ 31 0156 [DDD]

R. Kapp (cnd)

Tchaikovsky, P.:Concert Fant, w. M. Ponti (pno) — Vox Box 2–▲ CDX 5024 [ADD]
Tchaikovsky, P.:Con 1 Pno, w. M. Ponti (pno) — Vox Box 2–▲ CDX 5024 [ADD]
Tchaikovsky, P.:Con 2 Pno, w. M. Ponti (pno) — Vox Box 2–▲ CDX 5024 [ADD]

A. Klima (cnd)

Prokofiev, S.:Con 3 Pno, w. P. Štěpán (pno) — Sound ▲ CD 3437

M. Konvalinka (cnd)

Dvořák, A.:Armida (ov) — Praga ▲ PR 254045
Forsyth, C.:Con Va, w. Lubomír Malý (va) *(rec Smetana Hall, Prague, Dec. 15 & 21–22, 1987)* — Panton ("Panorama" series) ▲ PAN 811306
Vaughan Williams, R.:Flos Campi, w. Lubomír Malý (va), Prague Radio Chorus *(rec Smetana Hall, Prague, Dec. 15 & 21–22, 1987)* — Panton ("Panorama" series) ▲ PAN 811306

T. Koutník (cnd)

Dvořák, A.:Hymn, "The Heirs of the White Mountain", w. *(chorus unknown)* — Praga ▲ PR 254045

Z. Košler (cnd)

Smetana, B.:Choral Music, w. Miroslav Švejda (ten), Vratislav Jahna (bar), Jaroslav Horáček (bass), Prague Radio Chorus, Czech Phil Chorus — Supraphon ▲ SUP CD 3040

R. Kubelík (cnd)

Beethoven, L. van:Con Vn, Vc & Pno, "Triple Con", w. D. Oistrakh (vn), S. Knushevitsky (vc), L. Oborin (pno) — Multisonic ("Prague Spring" Collection) ▲ 31 0104 [ADD]
Khachaturian, A.:Con Vn, w. D. Oistrakh (vn) *(rec ca. 1947)* — Multisonic ("Prague Spring Collection" series) ▲ 31 0038–2 [ADD]
Prokofiev, S.:Con 1 Vn, w. D. Oistrakh (vn) *(rec ca. 1947)* — Multisonic ("Prague Spring Collection" series) ▲ 31 0038–2 [ADD]

B. Kulínský (cnd)

Messiaen, O.:Petites liturgies (3) de la Présence Divine, w. J. Loriod (ondes Martenot), Y. Loriod (pno), Kühn Women's Chorus *(rec Dec. 5–6, 1987)* — Supraphon ▲ 11 0404–2 [DDD]

C. Mackerras (cnd)

Dvořák, A.:Con Vc, w. Ofra Harnoy (vc) *(rec Smetana Hall, Prague, Sept 24–25, 1994)* — RCA Red Seal ▲ 09026–68186–2 [DDD]
Dvořák, A.:Rondo, w. Ofra Harnoy (vc) *(rec Smetana Hall, Prague, Sept 24–25, 1994)* — RCA Red Seal ▲ 09026–68186–2 [DDD]
Dvořák, A.:Silent Woods, w. Ofra Harnoy (vc) *(rec Smetana Hall, Prague, Sept 24–25, 1994)* — RCA Red Seal ▲ 09026–68186–2 [DDD]

A. Polizzi (cnd)

Beethoven, L. van:Syms (comp), w. Budapest SO *(rec 1986 & 1990–94)* — Harmonia Mundi France 6–▲ HMX 2905225.30
Wagner, R.:Götterdämmerung (siegfried's funeral), w. Budapest SO *(rec 1986 & 1990–94)* — Harmonia Mundi France 6–▲ HMX 2905225.30

J. Rohan (cnd)

Bloch, E.:Con Vn, w. H. Bress (vn) *(rec Apr. 25–29, 1966)* — Supraphon ("Collection" series) ▲ 11 0674–2 [ADD]
Bloch, E.:Suite hébraïque, w. H. Bress (vn) *(rec Apr. 25–29, 1966)* — Supraphon ("Collection" series) ▲ 11 0674–2 [ADD]

Prague SO (cont.)

J. Rohan (cnd) (cont.)

Tchaikovsky, P.:Nutcracker Suite — Supraphon Collection ▲ 11 0643–2 [ADD]
Tchaikovsky, P.:Sleeping Beauty (suite) — Supraphon Collection ▲ 11 0643–2 [ADD]

M. Shostakovich (cnd)

Shostakovich, D.:Sym 13, w. Peter Mikuláš (bass), Pavel Kühn (cnd), Prague Phil Chorus — Supraphon ▲ SUP 0160 [DDD]

L. Slovák (cnd)

Loudová, I.:Choral *(rec Smetana Hall, Municipal House, Prague, Jan 24, 1974)* — Panton ("60 Years of the Prague SO" series) ▲ PAN 811373 [ADD]
Martinů, B.:Sym 6 *(rec Smetana Hall, Municipal House, Prague, Jan 24, 1974)* — Panton ("60 Years of the Prague SO" series) ▲ PAN 811373 [ADD]

V. Smetáček (cnd)

Bach, J.S.:Cons Vn (comp), w. J. Suk (vn) *(rec 1966)* — Supraphon Collection ▲ 11 0642–2 [ADD]
Bach, J.S.:Con for 2 Vns, w. J. Suk (vn), L. Jásek (vn) *(rec 1965)* — Supraphon Collection ▲ 11 0642–2 [ADD]
Beethoven, L. van:Con 2 Pno, w. J. Panenka (pno) *(rec Sept. 27–28, 1968)* — Supraphon ("Collection" series) ▲ 11 0678–2 [ADD]
Beethoven, L. van:Con 3 Pno, w. J. Panenka (pno) — Vivace ▲ E 574 [ADD]
Beethoven, L. van:Con 4 Pno, w. J. Panenka (pno) *(rec 6/71)* — Supraphon ▲ 110652–2 [ADD]
Berlioz, H.:Ovs—Le roi Lear *(rec 1963)* — Supraphonet ▲ 11 1103–2 [AAD]
Berlioz, H.:Rêverie et caprice, w. J. Suk (vn) *(rec 1977)* — Supraphon ▲ 11 0708–2 [ADD]
Berlioz, H.:Rêverie et caprice, w. J. Suk (vn) — Supraphon Collection ▲ 11 0639–2 [ADD]
Bizet, G.:L'Arlésienne (suites) — Supraphon Collection ▲ 11 0646–2 [ADD]
Boismortier, J.B. de:Cyrano de Bergerac Suite — Campion ▲ 1319 [ADD/DDD]
Dvořák, A.:Con Pno, w. S. Richter (pno) *(rec 1966)* — Praga ▲ PR 250016
Dvořák, A.:St Ludmilla, w. Vera Soukupová (mez), Eva Zikmundová (mez), Beno Blachut (ten), Richard Novák (bass), Czech Phil Chorus *(rec 1963)* — Supraphon 2–▲ SUP 112141 [AAD]
Dvořák, A.:Sym 6 — Praga ▲ PR 254045
Foerster, J.B.:From Shakespeare — Supraphon ▲ SUP 3041
Foerster, J.B.:Spring & Longing — Supraphon ▲ SUP 11 1822 [AAD]
Foerster, J.B.:Sym 4 — Supraphon ▲ SUP 11 1822 [AAD]
Martinů, B.:Parables — Panton ▲ PAN 811204
Mendelssohn, F.:A Midsummer Night's Dream (sels)—Overture, Op. 21; Scherzo, Notturno & Wedding March, from Op. 61 *(rec 1963)* — Supraphon Collection ▲ 11 0616–2 [ADD]
Reicha, A.:Te Deum, w. Marta Boháčová (sop), Oldřich Lindauer (ten), Karel Průša (bass), Ladislav Vachulka (org), Kühn Chorus *(rec Cathedral of the Ascension of the Virgin, Karlov, Prague, 1970)* — Panton ▲ PAN 800242 [ADD]
Small Czech Musical Gems — ▲ SUP 101429 [AAD]
Tchaikovsky, P.:Sym 1 *(rec 1961)* — Supraphon Collection ▲ 11 0612–2 [ADD]

O. Trhlík (cnd)

Báchorek, M.:Hukvald Poem, w. Drahomíra Drobková (sop), Břetislav Vojkůvka (ten), Pavel Kamas (bar), Otakar Brousek (reciter), Ostrava Female Chamber Chorus, Permoník Children's Chorus *(rec Smetana Hall of Prague's Municipal House, Feb 10 & 11, 1988)* — Panton ▲ 811338–2 [DDD]
Báchorek, M.:Music of, w. Osvald Albin (nar), Otakar Brousek (nar), Jan Vlassak (nar), Brigita Šulcová (sop), Drahomira Drobková (cta), Karel Průša (bass), Pavel Kamas (sgr), Jan Kyzlink (sgr), Jana Stuperkova–Majtnerova (sgr), Bretislav Vojkuvka (sgr), Ostrava Janáček PO, Ostrava Janáček Chorus, Ostrava Women's Chamber Chorus, Permoník Children's Chorus—Lidice; Stereofonietta; Hukvald Poem — Panton ▲ PAN 811338 [AAD/DDD]

M. Turnovsky (cnd)

Saint-Saëns, C.:Carnival of the Animals, w. P. Stepan (pno), I. Hurnik (pno) — Supraphon Collection ▲ 11 0646–2 [ADD]

V. Válek (cnd)

Fibich, Z.:The Fall of Arkona (ov) — Supraphon ▲ SUP 111823 [AAD]
Fibich, Z.:Komenský — Supraphon ▲ SUP 111823 [AAD]
Fibich, Z.:Toman & the Wood Nymph — Supraphon ▲ SUP 111823 [AAD]
Fibich, Z.:Záboj, Slavoj & Ludek — Supraphon ▲ SUP 111823 [AAD]
Smetana, B.:Ceremonial prelude — Supraphon ▲ SUP 0198
Smetana, B.:March for Shakespeare Fest — Supraphon ▲ SUP 0198
Suk, J.:Fant Vn, w. Václav Snítil (vn) — Panton ▲ PAN 811212
Suk, J.:Praga — Panton ▲ PAN 811212

P. Zukovsky (cnd)

Schnabel, A.:Sym 3 *(rec Smetana Hall, Prague, Apr 23–29, 1992)* — CP² ▲ CP² 109 [DDD]

Prague SO members

Z. Košler (cnd)

Stravinsky, I.:Les Noces, w. Prague Sym Chorus — Praga ▲ PR 250057

P. Kühn (cnd)

Martinů, B.:Hymn to St. James, w. N. Romanová (sop), D. Drobková (cta), R. Novák (ten), P. Haničinec (nar), Prague Radio Chorus [Cz] *(rec 2–3/88)* — Supraphon ▲ 11 0751–2 [DDD]

Prague Symposium Musicum

L. Vachulka (cnd)

Viadana, L. da:Sinfonie musicali a 8 [period instrs] *(rec 1981)* — Koch Treasure ▲ 31620–2 [ADD]

Prague Trumpet Players Ensemble

J. Svejkovsky (cnd)

Music from the Towers of Prague — Multisonic ▲ MUL 310069 [DDD]

Prague Virtuosi

Finger, G.:Son Tpt & Vn, w. Richard Steuart (tpt) *(rec Prague, Nov. 1994)* — Discover International ▲ DI 920244 [DDD]
Neruda, J.B.G.:Con Tpt, w. Richard Steuart (tpt) *(rec Prague, Nov. 1994)* — Discover International ▲ DI 920244 [DDD]
Vejvanovsky, P.J.:Harmonia romana, w. Oldrich Vlcek (vn) *(rec Prague, Nov. 1994)* — Discover International ▲ DI 920244 [DDD]
Vejvanovsky, P.J.:Son à 4, w. Richard Steuart (tpt) *(rec Prague, Nov. 1994)* — Discover International ▲ DI 920244 [DDD]
Vivaldi, A.:Cons for 2 Vns, w. J. Suk (vn), O. Vlček (vn)—RV.509 in c, RV.514 in d, RV.522 in a, RV.523 in a, RV.524 in B♭ — Supraphon ▲ 11 1271–2 [DDD]
Vivaldi, A.:Cons for 2 Vns, w. J. Suk (vn), O. Vlček (vn)—RV. 505, RV. 515, RV. 519, RV. 530 — Supraphon ▲ SUP 11 1819 [DDD]

T. Briccetti (cnd)

Debussy, C.:Danses sacrée et profane, w. Renie Yamahata (hp) *(rec Korunni Studios, Prague, Oct. 31–Nov. 3, 1994)* — Discover International ▲ DI 920281 [DDD]
Gaos, A.:Impressión nocturna *(rec Korunni Studios, Prague, Oct. 31–Nov. 3, 1994)* — Discover International ▲ DI 920281 [DDD]
Griffes, C.T.:Poem Fl, w. Angela Jones (fl) *(rec Korunni Studios, Prague, Oct. 31–Nov. 3, 1994)* — Discover International ▲ DI 920281 [DDD]
Ravel, M.:Intro & Allegro, w. Renie Yamahata (hp), Angela Jones (fl) *(rec Korunni Studios, Prague, Oct. 31–Nov. 3, 1994)* — Discover International ▲ DI 920281 [DDD]

G. Delogu (cnd)

Mozart, W.A.:Missa, K.317, w. Ludmila Vernerova (sop), Marta Benackova (mez), Richard Sporka (ten), Ladislav Nezhyba (bass), Prague Chamber Choir *(rec Domovina Studio, Prague, June 4–6, 1994)* — Discover International ▲ DI 920260 [DDD]
Mozart, W.A.:Vesperae solennes, w. Ludmila Vernerova (sop), Marta Benackova (mez), Richard Sporka (ten), Ladislav Nezhyba (bass), Prague Chamber Choir *(rec Domovina Studio, Prague, June 4–6, 1994)* — Discover International ▲ DI 920260 [DDD]

Prague Virtuosi (cont.)
V. Neumann (cnd)
Vanhal, J.B.:Missa Solemnis, w. Marta Filová (sop), Marta Benačková (mez), Jörg Dürmüller (ten), Jiří Sulzenko (bass), Prague Chamber Choir—Kyrie eleison, Adagio— Allegro; Christe eleison, Andante; Kyrie eleison, Allegro; Gloria, Allegro moderato; Laudamus te, Andante; Gratias agimus tibi, Allegro moderato; Domine Deus, Rex caelestis, andante; Domine Deus, Agnus Dei, Adagio; Quoniam tu solus sanctus, Allegro moderato, Cum sancto spiritu, Allegro; Credo, Allegro moderato, Et incarnatus est. Adagio; Et resurrexit, Allegro moderato; Sanctus, Adagio—Osanna, Allegro; Benedictus, Andante—Osanna, Allegro; Agnus Dei, Adagio; Dona nobis pacem, Allegro *(rec Evangelische Kirche der böhmischen Brüder, Prag, Sept 25–28, 1994)* Orfeo ▲ C 353 951 A [DDD]
I. Oistrakh (cnd)
Mozart, W.A.:Con 3 Vn, w. Vaclav Hudecek (vn) Supraphon ▲ SUP 112240 [DDD]
Mozart, W.A.:Con 4 Vn, w. Vaclav Hudecek (vn) Supraphon ▲ SUP 112240 [DDD]
Mozart, W.A.:Con 5 Vn, w. Vaclav Hudecek (vn) Supraphon ▲ SUP 112240 [DDD]
J. Rudel (cnd)
Mozart, W.A.:Kleine Nachtmusik *(rec May 23–26, 1993)* MusicMasters ▲ 01612-67141-2 [DDD]
Mozart, W.A.:Sym 35 *(rec May 23–26, 1993)* MusicMasters ▲ 01612-67141-2 [DDD]
Mozart, W.A.:Sym 40 *(rec May 23–26, 1993)* MusicMasters ▲ 01612-67141-2 [DDD]
P. Schmelzer (cnd)
Castelnuovo-Tedesco, M.:Con 1 Gtr, w. Wolfgang Weigl (gtr) Koch Schwann ▲ SCH 310392 [DDD]
Ponce, M.:Concierto del sur, w. Wolfgang Weigl (gtr) Koch Schwann ▲ SCH 310392 [DDD]
Villa-Lobos, H.:Con Gtr, w. Wolfgang Weigl (gtr) Koch Schwann ▲ SCH 310392 [DDD]
D. Sitkovetsky (cnd)
Bach, J.S.:Cons Vn (comp), w. Vaclav Hudacek (vn), Dmitry Sitkovetsky (vn) Supraphon ▲ SUP 3085
Bach, J.S.:Con Vn & Ob, w. Vaclav Hudacek (vn), Dmitry Sitkovetsky (vn) Supraphon ▲ SUP 3085
Bach, J.S.:Con for 2 Vns, w. Vaclav Hudacek (vn), Dmitry Sitkovetsky (vn) Supraphon ▲ SUP 3085
P. Tiboris (cnd)
Haydn, J.:Arianna a Naxos, w. Eleni Matos (mez) *(rec Studio Domovina, Prague, Mar 23–25, 1995)* Elysium ▲ GRK 706 [DDD]
Haydn, J.:Arias, w. Eleni Matos (mez), Jeff Prillman (ten)—L'anima del filosofo, H.XXVIII:13/3 [from Orfeo ed Euridice]; Scena di Berenice, H.XXIVa:10; Recitative & Aria of Oreste, H.XXIVa:10 [for Traetta's "Ifigenia in Tauride"] *(rec Studio Domovina, Prague, Mar 23–25, 1995)* Elysium ▲ GRK 706 [DDD]
Haydn, J.:Sym 43, "Mercury" *(rec Studio Domovina, Prague, Mar 23–25, 1995)* Elysium ▲ GRK 706 [DDD]
O. Vlček (cnd)
Donizetti, G.:Concertino Cl, w. Lucien Aubert (cl) ICN ▲ 008 [DDD]
Dvořák, A.:Mazurek, w. Ivan Zenaty (vn) *(rec Domovina Studio, Prague, Aug. 23–25, 1994)* Discover International ▲ DI 920265 [DDD]
Dvořák, A.:Romance Vn, w. Ivan Zenaty (vn) *(rec Domovina Studio, Prague, Aug. 23–25, 1994)* Discover International ▲ DI 920265 [DDD]
Elgar, E.:Serenade Strs *(rec Domovina Studio, Prague, Nov. 22–25, 1993)* Discover International ▲ DICD 920236 [DDD]
Grieg, E.:Holberg Suite *(rec Domovina Studio, Prague, Nov. 22–25, 1993)* Discover International ▲ DICD 920236 [DDD]
Handel, G.F.:Cons (16) Org, w. J. Tůma (org)—Nos 1–12 Supraphon 3-▲ SUP 11 1494 [DDD]
Mercadante, S.:Con in E♭ Cl, w. Lucien Aubert (cl) ICN ▲ 008 [DDD]
Mercadante, S.:Con in B♭ Cl, Op. 101, w. Lucien Aubert (cl) ICN ▲ 008 [DDD]
Mozart, W.A.:Divert Fls, K.187 *(rec Nov. 13–16, 1990)* Emergo ▲ EC 3983 [DDD]
Mozart, W.A.:Divert Fls, K.188 *(rec Nov. 13–16, 1990)* Emergo ▲ EC 3983 [DDD]
Mozart, W.A.:Divert Str Qt, K.138 *(rec Nov. 13–16, 1990)* Emergo ▲ EC 3983 [DDD]
Mozart, W.A.:Serenade Ww, K.388 *(rec Nov. 13–16, 1990)* Emergo ▲ EC 3983 [DDD]
Mysliveček, J.:Con in C Vn, w. Ivan Zenaty (vn) *(rec Domovina Studio, Prague, Aug. 23–25, 1994)* Discover International ▲ DI 920265 [DDD]
Respighi, O.:Ancient Airs & Dances—Suite No. 3 *(rec Domovina Studio, Prague, Nov. 22–25, 1993)* Discover International ▲ DICD 920236 [DDD]
Rossini, G.:Vars Cl, w. Lucien Aubert (cl) ICN ▲ 008 [DDD]
Roussel, A.:Sinfonietta Strs *(rec Domovina Studio, Prague, Nov. 22–25, 1993)* Discover International ▲ DICD 920236 [DDD]
Telemann, G.P.:Cons Tpt, w. J. Hasenöhrl (tpt)—Con. in D Trumpet; Son. in D for Trumpet; Con. in B for 2 Trumpets [w. J. Burian]; Con. in D for 3 Trumpets [J. Burian & U. F. Walser]; Con. in G for 4 Trumpets [J. Burian, U. F. Walser & F. Vlasák (trumpets), J. Tuma (organ), J. Kolár (oboe)] Emergo ▲ EC 3982 [DDD]
Vanhal, J.B.:Con Vn, w. Ivan Zenaty (vn) *(rec Domovina Studio, Prague, Aug. 23–25, 1994)* Discover International ▲ DI 920265 [DDD]
Vejvanovsky, P.J.:Sons & Serenades, w. Vaclav Jirovec (vc), Jan Hasenöhrl (tpt), Jiri Pribyl (trbn), Frantisek Xaver (hpd), Milan Hruby (brass), Oldrich Vlcek (vn)—Intrada; Harmonia romana; Serenada; Offertur ad duos chorus; Son à 4 be mollis; Son paschalis; Son tribus quadrantibus; Son campanarum; Serenada *(rec Lobochovice castle, July 26–28, 1992)* Discover International ▲ DI 920243 [DDD]
Vivaldi, A.:Cons Bn, w. E. Polách (bn)—Con. in B♭, RV.501 *(rec 1991)* Emergo ▲ EC 3981 [DDD]
Vivaldi, A.:Cons Ob, w. J. Kolár (ob)—Con. in F, RV.457 *(rec 1991)* Emergo ▲ EC 3981 [DDD]
Vivaldi, A.:Con Ob Bn, w. J. Kolár (ob), E. Polách (bn) *(rec 1991)* Emergo ▲ EC 3981 [DDD]
Vivaldi, A.:Cons for 2 Obs, w. J. Kolár (ob), R. Hrabé (ob), J. Hasenöhrl (tpt), F. Vlasák (tpt)—Con. in C, RV.559 *(rec 1991)* Emergo ▲ EC 3981 [DDD]
Vivaldi, A.:Cons Rcr, w. G. Krcková (ob)—Con. in a, RV.108 *(rec 1991)* Emergo ▲ EC 3981 [DDD]
Vivaldi, A.:Con for 2 Tpts, w. J. Hasenöhrl (tpt), F. Vlasák (tpt) *(rec 1991)* Emergo ▲ EC 3981 [DDD]
Prague Wind Quintet
Françaix, J.:Qnt Fl Supraphon ▲ 11 0372-2 [DDD]
Ibert, J.:Pièces brèves Supraphon ▲ 11 0372-2 [DDD]
Janácek, L.:Youth, w. P. Čáp (b cl) Supraphon ▲ 11 1354-2 [DDD]
Milhaud, D.:Le Cheminée du Roi René Supraphon ▲ 11 0372-2 [DDD]
Poulenc, F.:Sxt Pno, w. J. Hála (pno) Supraphon ▲ 11 0372-2 [DDD]
Reicha, A.:Qnts Ww, Op. 100—No. 3 in E♭ Studio Matous ▲ MAT 25 [DDD]
Prague Wind Quintet [Jan Riedlbauch (fl), Jurij Likin (ob), Vlastimil Marev (cl), Vladimira Klánská (hn), Lumír Vanek (bn)]
Reicha, A.:Qnts Ww, Op. 100—Nos. 4 & 6 Studio Matous ▲ MAT 23 [DDD]
Prague Wind Quintet members
Reicha, A.:Grand quatator concertant, w. Adam Skoumal (pno) Studio Matous ▲ MAT 25 [DDD]
Prazak String Quartet [V. Remes (vn), V. Holek (vn), J. Kluson (va), M. Kanka (vc)]
Berg, A.:Lyric Suite *(rec 1989 & 1991)* Praga ▲ PR 250 034
Crusell, B.H.:Qnt Cl, w. K. Leister (cl) Orfeo ▲ 141861 [DDD]
Dvořák, A.:Qt 14 Strs Ottavo ▲ OTT 69237 [DDD]
Dvořák, A.:Qnt Strs, Op. 77, w. H. Roelofson (db) Ottavo ▲ OTT 69237 [DDD]
Haydn, J.:Qts Strs, Op. 76, "Erdödy Qts"—Nos. 1–3 Praga ▲ PR 250069
Martinů, B.:Qt 7 Strs *(rec Nov 1995–Jan 1996)* Praga ▲ PR 250097
Mozart, W.A.:Qts Strs (misc)—Nos. 16 & 17 Nuova Era ▲ 7018 [DDD]
Mozart, W.A.:Qts Strs (misc)—Nos. 14 & 15 Nuova Era ▲ 7017 [DDD]
Mozart, W.A.:Qt 21 Strs Praga ▲ PR 250026
Mozart, W.A.:Qt 22 Strs Praga ▲ PR 250026
Mozart, W.A.:Qt 23 Strs Praga ▲ PR 250026
Mozart, W.A.:Qnt Cl, K.581, w. K. Leister (cl) Orfeo ▲ 141861 [DDD]
Mozart, W.A.:Qnt Hn, K.407, w. Vladimíra Klánská (hn) *(rec Prague, 1995)* Praga ▲ PR 250095
Schoenberg, A.:Qt in D Strs Praga ▲ PR 250056
Schoenberg, A.:Qt 1 Strs *(rec 1989 & 1991)* Praga ▲ PR 250 034
Schoenberg, A.:Qt 2 Strs, w. Christine Whittlesey (sop) Praga ▲ PR 250056
Schubert, Franz:Qt 13 Strs Praga ▲ PR 250091
Schubert, Franz:Qt 14 Strs Praga ▲ PR 250091
Prazak String Quartet members
Schoenberg, A.:Trio Strs Praga ▲ PR 250056

Premiere Ensemble
M. Wiggelsworth (cnd)
Mahler, G.:Das Lied von der Erde, w. Jean Rigby (mez), Robert Tear (ten) [arr. Schoenberg] RCA Red Seal ▲ 09026-68043-2
Premierospel Quartet
Arlen, H.:Americanegro Suite, w. J. Kaye, P. Howard (pno)—plus ten Arlen songs from stage & screen [w. J. Kaye (soprano)] Premier ▲ PRCD 1004 [DDD]
Present Music
Koykkar, J.:Chamber Music, w. Oakwood Chamber Players, w. gueat artists—Continuum (1982); Circumstance (1983); Modus Operandum (1984); A Three Point Perspective (1986); Expressed in Units (1989) Northeastern ▲ NR 246-CD
Present Music [M. Sander, D. Gangolli, D. Snipe, E. Segnitz, P. Gmeinder, D. Armstrong, K. Ince, T. Smirl]
Ince, K.:Night Passage *(rec Milwaukee, Sept. 1992 & Oct. 1993)* Northeastern ("Contemporary" series) ▲ NR 254
Present Music [M. Sander, D. Gangolli, E. Segnitz, B. Renzelman, P. Gmeinder, K. Ince, T. Smirl]
Ince, K.:Hammer Music *(rec Milwaukee, Sept. 1992 & Oct. 1993)* Northeastern ("Contemporary" series) ▲ NR 254
Present Music [S. Jutt, D. Gangolli, E. Segnitz, P. Gmeinder, K. Ince, T. Smirl]
Ince, K.:Waves of Talya *(rec Milwaukee, Sept. 1992 & Oct. 1993)* Northeastern ("Contemporary" series) ▲ NR 254
Preston's Pocket
Bach, J.S.:Trio Son for 2 Fls, BWV 1039 Amon Ra ■ CD-SAR 11 (D)
Handel, G.F.:Trio Sons—Op. 2/5 Amon Ra ■ CD-SAR 11 (D)
Paul Price Percussion Ensemble
Flagello, N.:Pno Music, w. J. Pierce (pno)—Divertimento for Piano & Percussion (1960); Electra for Piano solo, Celesta, Harp & Percussion (1966); Sonata for Piano (1962); Prelude, Ostinato & Fugue (1960); Two Waltzes (1953); Three Episodes (1957); Etude:Homage to Chopin (1941) Premier ("Composer" series) ▲ PRCD 1014 [ADD/DDD]
Prima Carezza
Extase Tudor ▲ 795 [DDD]
Prima La Musica
D. Vermeulen (cnd)
Handel, G.F.:Water Music (suites)—Suites in F, D & G, HWV 348–350 René Gailly ▲ CD 87073 [DDD]
Primavera Chamber Ensemble
Mendelssohn, F.:Octet Strs ASV ("Quicksilva" series) ▲ ASQ 6168 [DDD]
Mendelssohn, F.:Qnt 2 Strs—Op. 87 ASV ("Quicksilva" series) ▲ ASQ 6168 [DDD]
Primavera CO
P. Manley (cnd)
Debussy, C.:Danses sacrée et profane *(rec 10 & 11/90 & 9/91)* Collins Quest ▲ 30062 [DDD]
Elgar, E.:Serenade Strs *(rec 10 & 11/90 & 9/91)* Collins Quest ▲ 30062 [DDD]
Roussel, A.:Sinfonietta Strs Collins Quest ▲ 30062 [DDD]
Vaughan Williams, R.:Fant on Greensleeves Collins Quest ▲ 30062 [DDD]
Vaughan Williams, R.:Fant on a Theme by Thomas Tallis Collins Quest ▲ 30062 [DDD]
La Primavera String Ensemble
M. Broussard (cnd)
Beethoven, L. van:Qt 13 Strs [string orch. arr. Maurice Broussard] Partridge ▲ 1124-2 [DDD]
Liszt, F.:Am Grabe Richard Wagners Partridge ▲ 1124-2 [DDD]
Liszt, F.:Angelus, Prière aux Anges gardiens Partridge ▲ 1124-2 [DDD]
La Primavera String Ensemble [F. Sonnen (vn), E. Schaling (vc)]
Liszt, F.:Sätze ungarishen Charakters Partridge ▲ 1124-2 [DDD]
Primrose String Quartet
Brahms, J.:Qt 3 Strs *(rec 1941)* Biddulph 2-▲ LAB 052 [ADD]
Haydn, J.:The Seven Last Words of Christ on the Cross [string quartet version] *(rec 1940–41)* Biddulph 2-▲ LAB 052 [ADD]
Schumann, R.:Qnt Pno, w. J.-M. Sanromá (pno) *(rec 1940)* Biddulph 2-▲ LAB 052 [ADD]
Smetana, B.:Qt 1 Strs *(rec 1940)* Biddulph 2-▲ LAB 052 [ADD]
Prince of Wales Brass
Christmas Fanfare ASV ▲ ASV 2083 [DDD]
Prism CO
R. Black (cnd)
Shatin, J.:Ruah Fl, w. R. Siebert (fl) CRI ▲ CD 605 [DDD]
Prism Orch
Dembski, S.:Spectra CRI ▲ CD 570 [DDD]
Dembski, S.:Stacked Deck CRI ▲ CD 570 [DDD]
Jaffe, S.:The Rhythm of the Running Plough *(rec Dec. 15, 1988)* Bridge ▲ BCD 9047 [DDD]
Macbride, D.:Nocturnos de la Ventana, w. F. Hoffmeister (ten) [Sp] Owl ▲ OWL 34 [DDD]
Machover, T.:Nature's Breath Bridge ▲ BCD 9002 ■ BC5-7002
McKinley, W.T.:Con Fl, w. R. Stallman (fl) Owl ▲ OWL 34 [DDD]
Shore, C.:July Remembrances, w. D. Podenski (sop) [E] Owl ▲ OWL 34 [DDD]
Stravinsky, I.:Con CO Bridge ▲ BCD 9061 [DDD]
Prism Saxophone Quartet [R. Barik (s sax), M. Whitcombe (a sax), M. Levy (t sax), T. Miller (b sax)]
Dubois, P.-M.:Qt Sax Koch International Classics ▲ KIC 7024-2 [DDD]
Levy, M.:Sax Qt Music—Lament (1986); Quartet (1987); Tenor Indigo (1987) Koch International Classics ▲ KIC 7024-2 [DDD]
Peck, R.:Drastic Measures Koch International Classics ▲ KIC 7024-2 [DDD]
Singelée, J.-B.:Qt 1 Sax Koch International Classics ▲ KIC 7024-2 [DDD]
Woods, P.:Improvs Sax Qt Koch International Classics ▲ KIC 7024-2 [DDD]
Prisma Chamber Players Copenhagen
H. Farberman (cnd)
Kupferman, M.:Sym 2 Soundspells ▲ SP 112 [ADD]
Pro Arte Antiqua Prague
Otto, V.:Praha Dances—Nos. 1–6 *(rec St. Michael Church, Prague, Sept 13–19, 1994)* Canyon Classics ▲ 254
Pachelbel, J.:Canon *(rec St. Michael Church, Prague, July 28–30, 1995)* Canyon Classics ▲ CD 308
Pachelbel, J.:Suites Strs—Musical Recreation [6 suites for 2 Vns & Bc]; Suite for 5 Strs & Bc *(rec St. Michael Church, Prague, July 28–30, 1995)* Canyon Classics ▲ CD 308
Plánicky, J.A.:Opella ecclesiastica seu Ariae duodecim nova idea exornatae—Opella Prima–De amore erga Deum; Opella Quinta–De venerabili sacramento; Opella Duodecima–Funebris *(rec St. Michael Church, Prague, July 31–Aug 2, 1994)* Canyon Classics ▲ 257
Telemann, G.P.:Cons Rcr, w. Jiří Stiví (rcr)—in C Arta ▲ ARTA 0058 [DDD]
Telemann, G.P.:Cons Rcr, Vl, w. Jiří Stiví (rcr), Petr Hejný (va)—in a Arta ▲ ARTA 0058 [DDD]
Telemann, G.P.:Suite Vl, w. Petr Hejný (va) Arta ▲ ARTA 0058 [DDD]
Telemann, G.P.:Trio Sons, w. Jiří Stiví (rcr), Petr Hejný (va)—in g & F for Rcr, Vl & Bc Arta ▲ ARTA 0058 [DDD]
Tůma, F.I.A.:Partitas—in d *(rec St. Michael Church, Prague, July 31–Aug 2, 1994)* Canyon Classics ▲ 257
Tůma, F.I.A.:Sinfs—in B♭ *(rec St. Michael Church, Prague, July 31–Aug 2, 1994)* Canyon Classics ▲ 257
Tůma, F.I.A.:Sons—in e; in a [Andante] *(rec St. Michael Church, Prague, July 31–Aug 2, 1994)* Canyon Classics ▲ 257
Vejvanovsky, P.J.:Balletti *(rec St. Michael Church, Prague, July 31–Aug 1, 1994)* Canyon Classics ▲ 255
Vejvanovsky, P.J.:Harmonia romana *(rec St. Michael Church, Prague, July 31–Aug 1, 1994)* Canyon Classics ▲ 255

Pro Arte Antiqua Prague (cont.)
Vejvanovsky, P.J.:Sons & Serenades—Son Paschalis; Son Secunda; Son Laetitiae; Son Sancti Spiritus; Son a 6 in E; Son a 6 in D; Son a 5; Son a 6 Campanarum *(rec St. Michael Church, Prague, July 31–Aug 1, 1994)* Canyon Classics ▲ 255
Zelenka, J.D.:Sons Obs *(rec Jemniště Castle, Benešov, Oct 17–21, 1994)* Canyon Classics ▲ 274

Pro Arte Antiqua Prague [Jan Šimon (trb vl), Václav Návrat (s vl), Ivo Anýz (a vl), Hana Fleková (t vl), Vít Mach (vle), Aleš Bárta (hps/postivie org)]
Purcell, H.:Abdelazer, or The Moor's Revenge *(rec Evangelic Church, Korunní, Prague, Feb. 1993)* Arta ▲ 0043
Purcell, H.:The Fairy Queen (sels)—suites & incidental music *(rec Evangelic Church, Korunní, Prague, Feb. 1993)* Arta ▲ 0043
Purcell, H.:The Gordian Knot Unty'd *(rec Evangelic Church, Korunní, Prague, Feb. 1993)* Arta ▲ 0043

Pro Arte Guitar Trio
Arabesque ASV ("White Line" series) ▲ ASV 2063
Bernstein, L.:West Side Story (sels)—Suite [arr for 3 gtrs] ASV ▲ ASV 2099 ■ ASV 2099
Brazileira ASV ▲ ASV 2079 [DDD]
Gershwin, G.:Lullaby [arr for 3 gtrs] ASV ▲ ASV 2099 ■ ASV 2099
Gershwin, G.:Pno Music—Impromptu in 2 Keys; 3/4 Blues [arr for 3 gtrs] ASV ▲ ASV 2099 ■ ASV 2099
Gershwin, G.:Porgy & Bess (suite), "Catfish Row Suite" [arr for 3 gtrs] ASV ▲ ASV 2099 ■ ASV 2099
Gershwin, G.:Preludes (3) Pno [arr for 3 gtrs] ASV ▲ ASV 2099 ■ ASV 2099
Three Guitars ASV ("White Line" series) ▲ ASV 2061

Pro Arte Orch
B. Herrmann (cnd)
Herrmann, B.:Wuthering Heights, w. M. Beaton (sop—Catherine), P. Bowden (mez—Isabella), E. Bainbridge (mez—Nelly), M. Snashall (trb—Hareton), D. Bell (bar—Heathcliff), J. Kitchiner (bar—Hindley), J. Ward (bar—Edgar), M. Rippon (bass—Joseph), D. Kelly (bass—Mr. Lockwood) *(rec 1965–66)* Unicorn-Kanchana 3-▲ UKCD 2050/51/52 [ADD]
K. Redel (cnd)
Bach, J.S.:Masses, BWV 233–36, "Lutheran Masses", w. A. Giebel (sop), G. Litz (mez), H. Prey (bar), Pro Arte Chorale—BWV 233 in F Philips 2-▲ 438739-2
B. Rose (cnd)
Hely-Hutchinson, V.:Carol Sym EMI Classics ("Studio" series) ▲ CDM 64131 2 [ADD]
M. Sargent (cnd)
Sullivan, A.:The Gondoliers, w. G. Evans (bar), A. Young (ten), O. Brannigan (bass), R. Lewis (ten), Glyndebourne Festival Chorus EMI Classics 2-▲ CDMB 64394
Sullivan, A.:HMS Pinafore, w. G. Baker (bar), J. Cameron (bar), R. Lewis (ten), Glyndebourne Festival Chorus EMI Classics 2-▲ CDMB 64397
Sullivan, A.:The Mikado, w. O. Brannigan (bass), R. Lewis (ten), G. Evans (bar), I. Wallace (bass), Glyndebourne Festival Chorus EMI Classics 2-▲ CDMB 64403
Sullivan, A.:Music of, w. Glyndebourne Festival Chorus—sels. from The Mikado; The Yoemen of the Guard; Iolanthe; The Gondoliers; The Pirates of Penzance; H.M.S. Pinafore Classics for Pleasure ▲ CDCFP 4238 [ADD]
Sullivan, A.:Ovs—Ovs. to Cox and Box, The Gondoliers, HMS Pinafore, Iolanthe, The Mikado, Patience, Pirates of Penzance, Princess Ida, Ruddigore, The Sorcerer, The Yeomen of the Guard *(rec 1957–61)* Classics for Pleasure ▲ CDCFP4529 [ADD]
Sullivan, A.:Patience, w. J. Shaw (bar), T. Anthony (bass), A. Young (ten), G. Baker (bar), Glyndebourne Festival Chorus EMI Classics 2-▲ CDMB 64406
Sullivan, A.:The Pirates of Penzance, w. G. Baker (bar), J. Milligan (b-bar), J. Cameron (bar), R. Lewis (ten), Glyndebourne Festival Chorus EMI Classics 2-▲ CDMB 64409
Sullivan, A.:The Sorcerer (sels), w. G. Baker (bar), E. Morison (sop), J. Cameron (bar), R. Lewis (ten), Glyndebourne Festival Chorus EMI Classics 2-▲ CDMB 64397
Sullivan, A.:The Yeomen of the Guard, w. R. Lewis (ten), A. Young (ten), J. Cameron (bar), Glyndebourne Festival Chorus EMI Classics 2-▲ CDMB 64415

Pro Arte Piano Trio [M. Vítek (vn), P. R. Honnens (vc), E. Westenholz (pno)]
Brahms, J.:Trio 1 Pno BIS ▲ CD 98 [AAD]
Brahms, J.:Trio 2 Pno BIS ▲ CD 99 [AAD]
Brahms, J.:Trio 3 Pno BIS ▲ CD 98 [AAD]
Brahms, J.:Trio in A Pno (posth) BIS ▲ CD 99 [AAD]
Mendelssohn, F.:Trio 1 Pno *(rec May 31, 1977)* BIS ▲ CD 97 [AAD]
Smetana, B.:Trio Pno *(rec June 2, 1977)* BIS ▲ CD 97 [AAD]

Pro Arte String Quartet
Bloch, E.:In the Mountains Laurel ▲ LR 841CD [DDD]
Bloch, E.:Night Laurel ▲ LR 826CD [ADD]
Bloch, E.:Paysages Laurel ▲ LR 841CD [DDD]
Bloch, E.:Pieces (2) Str Qt Laurel ▲ LR 826CD [ADD]
Bloch, E.:Prelude Laurel ▲ LR 826CD [ADD]
Bloch, E.:Qt 1 Strs Laurel ▲ LR 826CD [ADD]
Bloch, E.:Qt 3 Strs Laurel ▲ LR 841CD [DDD]
Bloch, E.:Qt 4 Strs Laurel ▲ LR 841CD [DDD]
Bloch, E.:Qnt 1 Pno, w. H. Karp (pno) Laurel ▲ LR 848 CD [ADD]
Bloch, E.:Qnt 2 Pno, w. H. Karp (pno) Laurel ▲ LR 848 CD [ADD]
Rózsa, M.:Qt 1 Strs Laurel ▲ LR 842CD [DDD]
Rózsa, M.:Qt 2 Strs Laurel ▲ LR 842CD [DDD]
Schubert, Franz:Qt 9 Strs EMI Classics ▲ CDH 63031
Schubert, Franz:Qnt Pno, D.667, w. A. Schnabel (pno) EMI Classics ▲ CDH 63031

Pro Arte String Quartet [Alphonse Onnou (vn), Laurent Halleux (vn), Germain Prévost (va), Robert Maas (vc)]
Haydn, J.:Qts Strs (misc)—No. 6 in C, Op. 1/6; No. 27 in D, Op. 20/4; No. 28 in E♭, Op. 20/1; No. 30 in E♭, Op. 33/2 [The Joke]; No. 32 in C, Op. 33/3 [The Bird]; No. 33 in D, Op. 33/6; No. 41 in D, Op. 50/6 [The Frog]; No. 45 in A, Op. 55/1; No. 47 in B♭, Op. 55/3; No. 52 in E♭, Op. 64/6; No. 54 in B♭, Op. 71/1; No. 57 in C, Op. 74/1; No. 58 in F, Op. 74/2; No. 66 in G, Op. 77/1 *(rec Studio 3, Abbey Road, London, 1931–38)* Testament 7▲ SBT 3055/4056 (m) [ADD]
Hoffstetter, R.:Qts Strs—Nos. 4 in B♭ & 5 in F *(rec Studio 3, Abbey Road, London)* Testament 7-▲ SBT 3055/4056 (m) [ADD]

Pro Arte String Quartet [H. Herzl (vn), B. Schmidt (vn), P. Langgartner (va), B. Lübke (vc)]
Mozart, W.A.:Qt 10 Strs RCA Red Seal ▲ 09026-61809-2
Mozart, W.A.:Qt 16 Strs RCA Red Seal ▲ 09026-61809-2
Mozart, W.A.:Qt 18 Strs RCA Red Seal ▲ 09026-61809-2

Pro Arte String Quartet members
Brahms, J.:Qt 1 Pno, w. A. Rubinstein (pno) *(rec 1932)* Biddulph ▲ LAB 027 [ADD]
Mozart, W.A.:Qt Pno, K.478, w. Artur Schnabel (pno) *(rec 1934)* Iron Needle 2-▲ IN 1342/43 (m) [ADD]

Pro Arte String Trio [Alison Dolly (vn), Elizabeth Turnbull (va), Christina Shillito (vc)]
Stoll, D.:Qt Pno, w. D. Ward (pno) Meridian ▲ MER 84245 [DDD]
Stoll, D.:Trio Strs Meridian ▲ MER 84245 [DDD]

Pro Arte Wind Quintet
Françaix, J.:Qnt Fl Nimbus ▲ NI 5327 [ADD]
Ibert, J.:Pièces brèves Nimbus ▲ NI 5327 [ADD]

Pro Arte Wind Quintet members
Auric, G.:Trio Ob *(rec 1981)* Nimbus ▲ NI 5327 [ADD]

Pro Christe Orch
T. Dean (cnd)
Handel, G.F.:Messiah, w. Helen Kucharek (sop), Jennifer Smith (sop), Linda Finnie (mez), Niel Mackie (ten), Rodney Macann (b-bar), Pro Christe Choir *(rec St. Augustine's Church, Kilburn, London, 1986)* Guild 2-▲ GMDD 7112/3 [ADD]

Pro Civitate Christiana di Assisi Orch
A. Renzi (cnd)
Rota, N.:Mysterium, w. A. Tuccari (sop), C. Vozza (mez), G. Sinimberghi (ten), U. Trama (bass), Pro Civitate Christiana di Assisi Chorus *(rec live 1962)* Claves ▲ CD 9323 [DDD]

Pro Musica CO
T. Russell (cnd)
Baker, M.C.:The Flight of Aphrodite, w. Michael Davis (vn) *(rec Ohio State Univ., Weigel Hall, 1995)* Summit ▲ SMT 182 [DDD]
Baker, M.C.:Summit Con, w. David Hickman (tpt) *(rec Ohio State Univ., Weigel Hall, 1995)* Summit ▲ SMT 182 [DDD]
Paulus, S.:Voices from the Gallery, w. Janet Bookspan (nar)—The Winged Victory of Samothrace; American Gothic; The Garden of Earthly Delights; Infanta Margarita; She-Goat; Nude Descending a Staircase; The Birth of Venus; Mona Lisa; The Beggars; Cristina's World; Dance at Bougival *(rec Weigel Hall, Ohio State Univ.; Magee Audio Engineering, Los Angeles, CA)* d'Note Classics ▲ DND 1010 [DDD]
Schickele, P.:Thurber's Dogs—A Litter of Perfectly Healthy Puppies Raised on Fried Pancakes; Dog & Butterfly; He Goes with His Owner into Bars; Dog Asleep; Dog at His Master's Grave; Hunting Hounds *(rec Weigel Hall, Ohio State Univ.; Magee Audio Engineering, Los Angeles, CA)* d'Note Classics ▲ DND 1010 [DDD]

Pro Musica Nipponia
Japanese Melodies, w. Yo-Yo Ma (vc), P. Zander (hpd), M. Mamiya CBS ▲ MK 39703 ■ FMT 39703
Miki, M.:Wa, *(no cnd)* *(rec Toshi Center Hall, May & Oct. 1980)* Camerata ▲ 30CM 54 [AAD]
N. Iimori (cnd)
Music from 6 Continents, 1993 series, w. Koszalin State PO, Slovak RSO [cnd:Kawalla], Bohuslav Martinů PO [cnd:Miłoš Machek] Vienna Modern Masters ▲ VMM 3017 [DDD]
T. Tamura (cnd)
Ifukube, A.:Bintatara Camerata ▲ 32CM 290
Miki, M.:Danses concértantes *(rec Iruma Public Hall, Sept. & Nov. 1976)* Camerata ▲ 30CM 54 [AAD]
Miki, M.:Music of, w. Keiko Nosaka (koto)—Con Requiem for 20-string Koto & Japanese Instruments; Hanayagi; Autumn Fant; Sao-no-Kyoku; Tatsuta-no-Kyoku Camerata ▲ 32CM 55

Pro Musica Nova
U. Dierksen (cnd)
Ernst, S.:Triade Vienna Modern Masters ▲ VMM 2018 [DDD]

Pro Musica Orch
Gaspar Cassado Performs Cello Masterpieces, w. Gaspar Cassado (vc), Bamberg SO *(rec mid-late 1950s)* Vox Box 2-▲ CDX2 5502 [ADD]
F. Grossmann (cnd)
Mozart, W.A.:Missa, K.427, w. W. Lipp (sop), C. Ludwig (sop), M. Dickie (ten), W. Berry (bass), Vienna Oratorio Chorus [L] *(rec stereo, 1958)* Preiser ▲ 90053 [AAD]
J. Horenstein (cnd)
Bruckner, A.:Sym 8 Vox Box ("Legends" series) 2-▲ CDX2 5504 [ADD]
E. Jorda (cnd)
Mozart, W.A.:Con 20 Pno, w. L. Kraus (pno) Vox Box ("Legends" series) 2-▲ CDX2 5510 [ADD]
J. Perlea (cnd)
Dvořák, A.:Con Vc, w. G. Cassado (vc) *(rec 1950s)* Vox Box ("Legends" series) 2-▲ CDX2 5502 [ADD]
Respighi, O.:Adagio con variazioni Vc Orch, w. G. Cassado (vc) *(rec 1950s)* Vox Box ("Legends" series) 2-▲ CDX2 5502 [ADD]
Tchaikovsky, P.:Vars on a Rococo Theme, w. G. Cassado (vc) *(rec 1950s)* Vox Box ("Legends" series) 2-▲ CDX2 5502 [ADD]

Pro Musica Sacra Orch
H. Banzhaf (cnd)
Schubert, Franz:Lazarus, or Die Feier der Auferstehung, w. Antonia Fahberg (sop), Pro Musica Sacra Chorus Studio SM ▲ 2498

Progetto Musica Instrumental Ensemble
G. Monaco (cnd)
Ancina, G.:L'amorosa ero fatta spirituale, w. Progetto Musica Vocal Ensemble *(rec Santuario di Graglia, Mar. 1995)* Tactus ▲ TC 520001 [DDD]
Arascione, G.:Nuove laudi ariose della Beatissima Virgine scelte da diversi autori, w. Progetto Musica Vocal Ensemble *(rec Santuario di Graglia, Mar. 1995)* Tactus ▲ TC 520001 [DDD]
Palestrina, G.:Missa "In minoribus", w. Progetto Musica Vocal Ensemble *(rec Santuario di Graglia, Mar. 1995)* Tactus ▲ TC 520001 [DDD]
Razzi, G.:Laude spirituale, w. Progetto Musica Vocal Ensemble—Book 1 *(rec Santuario di Graglia, Mar. 1995)* Tactus ▲ TC 520001 [DDD]

Project Ars Nova Ensemble [Laurie Monahan (mez), Michael Collver (alt/symphonia), John Fleagle (ten/hp), Crawford Young (lt), Shira Kammen (vielle), R. Mealy (vielle)]
Machaut, G. de:Ballades, rondeaux, virelais, motets & lais New Albion ▲ NA 068 [DDD]
Machaut, G. de:Remede de fortune New Albion ▲ NA 068 [DDD]

Project Ars Nova Ensemble [Laurie Monahan (mez), Michael Collver (sgr), John Fleagle (sgr) Shira Kammen (vielles), Crawford Young (lt)]
Kyr, R.:Songs of the Shining Wind *(rec Campion Center, Newton, MA, Feb. 1993)* New Albion ▲ NA 075
Kyr, R.:Threefold Vision *(rec Mt. Holyoke College Chapel, South Hadley, MA, Aug. 1993)* New Albion ▲ NA 075
B. Taylor (cnd)
Kyr, R.:Unseen Rain, w. Back Bay Chorale *(rec 1st & 2nd Church, Boston, MA, Feb. 1993)* New Albion ▲ NA 075

Provence Camerata Genève
C. Delley (cnd)
Gerber, R.:Con Pno & Winds, w. Gui-Michel Caillat (pno) Gallo ▲ CD 861 [ADD]

Provence Instrumental Ensemble
C. Zaffini (cnd)
Campra, A.:Tancrède, w. C. Dussaut (sop—Herminie), A. Arapian (ten—Argant), J. Bona (bar—Tancrède), Avignon Vocal Ensemble—highlights *(rec 1986)* Pierre Verany ▲ PV.786111 [ADD]

Prunes [Frøydis Ree Werke (hn), Roger Bobo (tuba/b hn)]
Music for Horn, Tuba & Bass Horn Crystal ■ C 126

Prussian State Orch
H. von Karajan (cnd)
Beethoven, L. van:Sym 3, "Eroica" *(rec 1944)* Koch Schwann ▲ SCH 315092 [ADD]
Bruckner, A.:Sym 8 *(rec June & Sept. 1944)* Koch Schwann ▲ SCH 314482 [ADD]

Pryor Band
Trombone Solos, w. Arthur Pryor (trbn), Sousa Band *(rec 1897–1911)* Crystal ■ C 451

Purcell Quartet
Biber, H. von:Harmonia artificiosa-ariosa, w. E. Wallfisch (vn) Chandos ("Chaconne" series) 2-▲ CHAN 0575/76 [DDD]
Biber, H. von:Sonatae tam aris quam aulis servientes, w. Mark Bennett (tpt), Michael Laird (tpt), Katherine McGillvray (va), Jane Rogers (va), Tim Cronin (va) Chandos ▲ CHAN 0591
Corelli, A.:Sons Strs (comp)—Op. 1, Nos. 7–12 & Op. 2, Nos. 7–12 Chandos ("Chaconne" series) ▲ CHAN 0515 [DDD]
Corelli, A.:Sons Strs (comp)—12 Sonatas—Op. 3, Nos. 7–12 & Op. 4, Nos. 7–12 Chandos ("Chaconne" series) ▲ CHAN 0532 [DDD]
Corelli, A.:Sons Strs (comp)—12 Sonatas—Op. 1, Nos. 1–6 & Op. 2, Nos. 1–6 Chandos ("Chaconne" series) ▲ CHAN 0516 [DDD]
Corelli, A.:Sons Strs (comp)—12 Sonatas—Op. 3, Nos. 1–6 & Op. 4, Nos. 1–6 Chandos ("Chaconne" series) ▲ CHAN 0526 [DDD]
Corelli, A.:Sons Vn, Op. 5—Nos. 3, 11 & 12 Hyperion ▲ CDA 66226 [DDD]

Purcell Quartet (cont.)
Corelli, A.:Son Vn, Op. 5/12, "La Follia" Hyperion ▲ CDA 66226 [DDD]
Corelli, A.:Sons 2 Vns, Opp. 1–4 (sels)—Op. 1/9; Op. 2/4,12; Op. 3/12; Op. 4/3 Hyperion ▲ CDA 66226 [DDD]
Lawes, W.:Royall Consort Suites, w. Nigel North (thb), Paul O'Dette (thb) Chandos ("Early Music" series) 2–▲ CHAN 0584/5 [DDD]
Leclair, J.–M.:Ouvertures et sonates en trio Chandos ("Chaconne" series) ▲ CHAN 0542 [DDD]
Leclair, J.–M.:Trio Sons for 2 Vns, Op. 4 [period instrs] *(rec Sept. 3–5, 1992)* Chandos ("Chaconne" series) ▲ CHAN 0536 [DDD]
Purcell, H.:Music for 2 or 3 Vns—3 Pavans, Z.572, 749, 750 Chandos ▲ CHAN 8591 [DDD]
Purcell, H.:Music for 2 or 3 Vns, w. Risa Browder (vn/va)—Chacony in g, Z.730; Fantasia upon a Ground in D, Z.731; Pavan in A, Z.748; Pavan in g, Z.751 Chandos ▲ CHAN 8663 [DDD]
Purcell, H.:Sons (22) Vns—Sonatas, Z.804–811 (plus a Variant to two movts. of Z.809, & the Prelude in g for solo Violin, ZN.733) Chandos ▲ CHAN 8763 [DDD]
Purcell, H.:Sons (22) Vns—Sonatas, Z.797–803 Chandos ▲ CHAN 8663 [DDD]
Purcell, H.:Sons (22) Vns—Sonatas, Z.790–796 Chandos ▲ CHAN 8591 [DDD]
Vivaldi, A.:Sons Vn—in C, RV.754 & in A, RV.758 Hyperion ▲ CDA 66193
Vivaldi, A.:Sons Vn, w. Catherine Mackintosh (vn) Chandos ("Chaconne" series) ▲ CHAN 0502 [DDD]
Vivaldi, A.:Sons Vn—(2) for Solo Violin & Continuo in C, RV.2 & in c, RV.6; (5) for 2 Violins & Continuo in d,A & b, Op. 1, Nos. 8,9 & 11; in F, RV.68; in B♭, RV.77 Chandos ("Chaconne" series) ▲ CHAN 0511 [DDD]
Vivaldi, A.:Trio Sons 2 Vns & Bc—(6) in E♭, RV.65; in F, RV.70; in G, RV.71; in g, RV.72; in B♭, RV.76; in B♭, RV.78 Chandos ("Chaconne" series) ▲ CHAN 0502 [DDD]
Vivaldi, A.:Trio Sons 2 Vns & Bc—in d, "La folla," RV.63; in g, RV.74; in C, RV.60 Hyperion ▲ CDA 66193

J. Washburn (cnd)
Weisgarber, E.:Night, w. B. Pullan (bar), W. Fawcett (db), Vancouver Chamber Choir [E] Centrediscs ▲ CMCCD 3790 [DDD]

Purcell Quartet [Catherine Mackintosh (vn), Catherine Weiss (vn), Richard Boothby (vl), Robert Woolley (hpd)]
Bach, J.S.:Brandenburg Con 5, w. Steven Preston (fl), Jane Rogers (va), Jonathan Manson (vc) Chandos ("Chaconne" series) ▲ CHAN 0595
Bach, J.S.:Con 3 Hpd, w. Jane Rogers (va), Jonathan Manson (vc) Chandos ("Chaconne" series) ▲ CHAN 0595
Bach, J.S.:Con 5 Hpd, w. Jane Rogers (va), Jonathan Manson (vc) Chandos ("Chaconne" series) ▲ CHAN 0595
Bach, J.S.:Con 3 for 2 Hpds, w. Jane Rogers (va), Jonathan Manson (vc), Paul Nicholson (hpd) Chandos ("Chaconne" series) ▲ CHAN 0595

Purcell Quartet [Catherine Mackintosh (vn), Elizabeth Wallfisch (vn), Richard Boothby (vl), Robert Woolley (hpd)]
Purcell, H.:Chacony Chandos ("Chaconne" series) 2–▲ CHAN 0572/73 [DDD]
Purcell, H.:Music of—Curtain Tune [from Timon of Athens, Z.632]; Ov. in g, Z.772; Cibell for Trumpet & Strings [w. Mark Bennett (trumpot)]; A New Scotch Tune, Z.655; Sefauchi's Farewell, Z.656; A New Irish Tune, Z.646; Suite in G, Z.770; Suite No. 6 in d for Harpsichord, Z.667; Suite [from Abdelazar]; Ov. in G, Z.770; Dances [from masque in Dioclesian]; The Staircase Ov.; Ov. in d; Son. for Trumpet & Strings [w. Bennett] Chandos ("Chaconne" series) ▲ CHAN 0571 [DDD]
Purcell, H.:Sons (12) Vns, Z.790–801 Chandos ("Chaconne" series) 2–▲ CHAN 0572/73 [DDD]
Purcell, H.:Sons (10) Vns, Z.802–811 Chandos ("Chaconne" series) 2–▲ CHAN 0572/73 [DDD]
Purcell, H.:Songs, w. Catherine Bott (sop)—Hark how all things; If Music be the food of love; If love's a sweet passion; See, even Night herself is here; Thus the ever grateful Spring; Lord, what is man?, Z.192 Chandos ("Chaconne" series) ▲ CHAN 0571 [DDD]

Purcell Sinfony
C. Mackintosh (cnd)
Purcell, H.:The Indian Queen, w. Tessa Bonner (sop), Sally Bruce–Payne (alt), Steven Liley (ten), Edward Caswell (bass) *(rec St. Bartholomew's Church, Orford, Suffolk, Sept 21–23, 1994)* Linn ▲ CKD 035

Pusl String Quartet
Suder, J.:Qt 2 Strs Calig ▲ CAL 50903 [DDD]
Suder, J.:Qt 3 Strs Calig ▲ CAL 50903 [DDD]

Quanzou Troupe of String Puppets
The Festival of Happiness *(rec Geneva, Nov 23, 1995)* Gallo ▲ VDE 911 [DDD]

Quartet of London
Alwyn, W.:Qt 1 Strs Chandos ▲ CHAN 9219 [DDD]
Alwyn, W.:Qt 2 Strs, "Spring Waters" Chandos ▲ CHAN 9219 [DDD]
Alwyn, W.:Qt 3 Strs Chandos ▲ CHAN 8440 [DDD]

Quartet of London members
Alwyn, W.:Rhap Pno, w. D. Willison (pno) Chandos ▲ CHAN 8440 [DDD]
Alwyn, W.:Trio Strs Chandos ▲ CHAN 8440 [DDD]

Quartetto Academica
Bruch, M.:Qt 1 Strs Dynamic ▲ CD 29
Bruch, M.:Qt 2 Strs Dynamic ▲ CD 29

Quartetto Academica members
Mercadante, S.:Qts Fl, w. M. Ancillotti (fl)—Quartet in a Nuova Era ▲ 6901 [DDD]
Rolla, A.:Qt 3 Fl, w. M. Ancillotti (fl) Nuova Era ▲ 6901 [DDD]
Viotti, G.B.:Qts Fl, Op. 22, w. M. Ancillottj (fl)—Nos 1 & 2 Nuova Era ▲ 6901 [DDD]

Quartetto con Flauto [Václav Slivansky (fl), Ada Slivanská (vn), Lubomír Herza (vc), Renata Jelínková (hpd)]
Jirásek, J.:Katharsis *(rec Church of St. Virgin Mary, Strahov, Czech Republic)* Catalyst ▲ 09026–68331–2 [DDD/ADD]

Quartetto Italiano [Paolo Borciani (vn), Elisa Pegreffi (vn), Piero Farulli (va), Franco Rossi (vc)]
Beethoven, L. van:Qts Strs (comp)—Opp. 59, 74, 95 Philips 3–▲ 420797–2 [ADD]
Beethoven, L. van:Qts Strs (comp)—Op. 18 Philips 3–▲ 426046–2 [ADD]
Beethoven, L. van:Qts Strs (comp)—Opp. 127, 130, 131, 132, 135 Philips 4–▲ 426050–2 [ADD]
Beethoven, L. van:Qts Strs (misc)—includes No. 12 in E♭, Op. 127; No. 16 in F, Op. 135; No. 13 in B♭, Op. 130; Grosse Fugue in B♭, Op. 133 Philips ("Duo" series) 2–▲ 454 711–2
Beethoven, L. van:Qts Strs (misc)—includes No. 14 in c#, Op. 131; No. 15 in a, Op. 132 Philips ("Duo" series) 2–▲ 454 712–2
Brahms, J.:Qnt Pno, w. M. Pollini (pno) Deutsche Grammophon ▲ 419673–2 [AAD]
Debussy, C.:Qt Strs Philips ("Silver Line" series) ▲ 420894–2 [ADD] ■ 420894–4
Haydn, J.:Qts Strs, Op. 3—No. 5 *(rec live, Venice, Feb. 12, 1969)* Arkadia ("Historical Performances" series) ▲ 497
Haydn, J.:Qts Strs, Op. 33, "Russian Qts"—No. 2 Adès ▲ ADE 203422 [AAD]
Haydn, J.:Qts Strs, Op. 64, "Tost Qts"—No. 6 *(rec live, Venice, Feb. 12, 1969)* Arkadia ("Historical Performances" series) ▲ 497
Haydn, J.:Qts Strs, Op. 76, "Erdödy Qts"—Nos. 2 & 3 *(rec live, Venice, Feb. 12, 1969)* Arkadia ("Historical Performances" series) ▲ 497
Haydn, J.:Qts Strs, Op. 76, "Erdödy Qts"—No. 3 Adès ▲ ADE 203422 [AAD]
Mozart, W.A.:Complete Mozart Edition Philips 8–▲ 422512–2 [ADD]
Ravel, M.:Qt Strs Philips ("Silver Line" series) ▲ 420894–2 [ADD] ■ 420894–4
Schubert, Franz:Qt 12 Strs Philips ("Two–Fers" series) 2–▲ 446163–2
Schubert, Franz:Qt 13 Strs Philips ("Two–Fers" series) 2–▲ 446163–2
Schubert, Franz:Qt 14 Strs Philips ("Two–Fers" series) 2–▲ 446163–2
Schubert, Franz:Qt 15 Strs Philips ("Two–Fers" series) 2–▲ 446163–2

Il Quartettone CO
Bartók, B.:Music of—trans. of Bagatelles (sels.); Dances of Transylvania; For Children (sels.); Four Small Dances; Six Hungarian Folksongs; Sketches & Dirges *(rec 5 & 6/91)* Giulia ▲ GS 201013 [DDD]

La Quatrième Chambre
Couperin, F.:Les Nations Nuova Era ("Ancient Music" series) ▲ NUO 7181 [DDD]
Leclair, J.–M.:Deuxième recréation de musique d'une exécution facile Nuova Era ("Ancient Music" series) ▲ NUO 7181 [DDD]

Quatuor de cuivres Novus [P.A. Monot (tpt), P. Lehmann (tpt), J. Henry (trbn), P. Krüttli (tuba)]
Ducommun, S.:Toccata et Dialogue, w. R. Márki (org) Gallo ▲ CD 654 [DDD]

Il Quattro [Brian Reagin (vn), Stephanie Tretick (vn), Joen Vasquez (vn), Irvin Kaufman (vc)]
Dvořák, A.:Qt 12 Strs, "America" Alanna ▲ ALA 5552

I Quattro Temperamenti
Handel, G.F.:Arias, w. C. Hogman (sop)— HWV.202–210; "Hush, ye pretty warbling quire," from Acis & Galatea [E,G] BIS ▲ CD 403 [DDD]
Handel, G.F.:Cants, w. C. Hogman (sop) [I] BIS ▲ CD 403 [DDD]
Handel, G.F.:Trio Sons—Sonata in c BIS ▲ CD 403 [DDD]

Quebec Society of Contemporary Music
S. Garant (cnd)
Evangelista, J.:Clos de vie, "In memoriam Claude Vivier" *(rec Ottawa, 1983 & 1984)* Centrediscs ▲ CMC 5194 [DDD]
Rea, J.:Treppenmusik *(rec Ottawa, 1983 & 1984)* Centrediscs ▲ CMC 5194 [DDD]
Vivier, C.:Lonely Child, w. Marie–Danielle Parent (sop) *(rec Ottawa, 1983 & 1984)* Centrediscs ▲ CMC 5194 [DDD]

Quebec String Quartet
Enescu, G.:Oct Strs, w. Alcan String Quartet *(rec June 9–10, 1992)* CBC ("Musica Viva" series) ▲ MVCD 1063 [DDD]
Mendelssohn, F.:Octet Strs, Alcan String Quartet *(rec June 9–10, 1992)* CBC ("Musica Viva" series) ▲ MVCD 1063 [DDD]

Quebec SO
S. Streatfeild (cnd)
A Tribute to Pavlova CBC Records ("SM 5000" series) ▲ SMCD 5048 [DDD]
P. Verrot (cnd)
Roussel, A.:Concert Small Orch Analekta Fleur de Lys ▲ FL 2 3052
Roussel, A.:Le Festin de l'araignée Analekta Fleur de Lys ▲ FL 2 3052
Roussel, A.:Sinfonietta Strs Analekta Fleur de Lys ▲ FL 2 3052
Roussel, A.:Sym 4 Analekta Fleur de Lys ▲ FL 2 3052

Queen's Division Massed Bands
Royal Regiments on Parade, w. 1st Battalion Argyll & Sutherland Highlanders Pipes & Drums, 1st Battalion Princess of Wales' Royal Regiment Band, et al. Bandleader ▲ BND 5111 [DDD]

Queen's Hall Orch
Rich & Rare:The Voice of Margaret Sheridan, w. Margaret Sheridan (sop), Aureliano Pertile (ten), Renato Zanelli (ten), Hubert Greenslade (pno), Carlo Sabajno (cnd), La Scala Orch *(rec 1926–29)* Time Machine ▲ 0100
H. Wood (cnd)
Sir H. J. Wood Conducts Proms Favourites, w. British SO, London PO, London SO *(rec between Nov. 1929 & March)* Dutton Laboratories ▲ DUT 8008 [ADD]
Sir Henry's Themes & Variations Beulah ▲ 1 PD 3
H. J. Wood (cnd)
Vaughan Williams, R.:Fant on Greensleeves *(rec Apr. 22, 1936)* Dutton Laboratories ▲ CDAX 8004 [ADD]
Vaughan Williams, R.:Sym 2 *(rec Apr. 21–22, 1936)* Dutton Laboratories ▲ CDAX 8004 [ADD]
Vaughan Williams, R.:The Wasps (ov) *(rec Apr. 22, 1936)* Dutton Laboratories ▲ CDAX 8004 [ADD]

Queensland PO
Christmas Day, w. [cnd:Ralph Morton], Quodlibet *(rec Thomas Dixon Centre, West End, Brisbane & the Great Hall of Brisbane Grammar School, 1992–93)* Tall Poppies ▲ TP 46 [DDD]
J. Georgiadis (cnd)
Weber, C.M. von:Die drei Pintos (sels)—Entr'acte *(rec Brisbane, Feb. 20–23, 1994.)* Naxos ▲ 8.550928 [DDD]
Weber, C.M. von:Silvana (sels)—Dance of the Edelknaben; Fackel Dance *(rec Brisbane, Feb. 20–23, 1994.)* Naxos ▲ 8.550928 [DDD]
Weber, C.M. von:Sym 1 *(rec Brisbane, Feb. 20–23, 1994.)* Naxos ▲ 8.550928 [DDD]
Weber, C.M. von:Sym 2 *(rec Brisbane, Feb. 20–23, 1994)* Naxos ▲ 8.550928 [DDD]
Weber, C.M. von:Turandot, Prinzessin von China (sels)—Ov. & Marches *(rec Brisbane, Feb. 20–23, 1994.)* Naxos ▲ 8.550928 [DDD]

Queensland SO
W. A. Albert (cnd)
Frankel, B.:May Day:A Panorama CPO ▲ CPO 999240 [DDD]
Frankel, B.:Mephistopheles' Serenade *(rec ABC Ferry Road, Brisbane, 1994–95)* CPO ▲ 999242–2 [DDD]
Frankel, B.:Sym 1 CPO ▲ CPO 999240 [DDD]
Frankel, B.:Sym 4 *(rec ABC Ferry Road, Brisbane, 1994–95)* CPO ▲ 999242–2 [DDD]
Frankel, B.:Sym 5 CPO ▲ CPO 999240 [DDD]
Frankel, B.:Sym 6 *(rec ABC Ferry Road, Brisbane, 1994–95)* CPO ▲ 999242–2 [DDD]
Hindemith, P.:Cupid & Psyche CPO ▲ CPO 999004–2 [DDD]
Hindemith, P.:Lustige Sinfonietta CPO ▲ CPO 999005–2 [DDD]
Hindemith, P.:Nobilissima visione CPO ▲ CPO 999004–2 [DDD]
Hindemith, P.:Philharmonisches Konzert CPO ▲ CPO 999004–2 [DDD]
Hindemith, P.:Rag Time CPO ▲ CPO 999005–2 [DDD]
Hindemith, P.:Symphonic Metamorphosis on Themes of Carl Maria von Weber CPO ▲ CPO 999004–2 [DDD]
Hindemith, P.:Symphonische Tänze CPO ▲ CPO 999005–2 [DDD]
G. Dreyfus (cnd)
Dreyfus, G.:Film & TV Music, Melbourne SO—themes & suites from Dreyfus's scores for 11 feature & documentary films & Australian TV series Move ▲ MD 3098
M. Fredman (cnd)
Brophy, G.:Forbidden Colours *(rec live)* Vox Australis ▲ VAST 015–2 [DDD]
J. Hopkins (cnd)
Kos, B.:Con Vn, w. D. Olding (vn) *(rec live)* Vox Australis ▲ VAST 015–2 [DDD]
V. Kamirski (cnd)
Opera Arias, w. Marilyn Richardson (sop) ABC Classics ▲ 434138–2 [DDD]
T. Kuchar (cnd)
Mendelssohn, F.:Sym in D Ondine ▲ ODE 741–2 [DDD]
Mendelssohn, F.:Sym 1 Ondine ▲ ODE 741–2 [DDD]
W. Lehmann (cnd)
Hill, A.:The Lost Hunter *(rec ABC Music Centre, Ferry Road, West End, Brisbane, Australia, Feb 1–12, 1993)* Marco Polo ▲ 8.223537 [DDD]
Hill, A.:The Moon's Golden Horn *(rec ABC Music Centre, Ferry Road, West End, Brisbane, Australia, Feb 1–12, 1993)* Marco Polo ▲ 8.223537 [DDD]
Hill, A.:Sym 3 *(rec ABC Music Centre, Ferry Road, West End, Brisbane, Australia, Feb 1–12, 1993)* Marco Polo ▲ 8.223537 [DDD]
Hill, A.:Sym 7 *(rec ABC Music Centre, Ferry Road, West End, Brisbane, Australia, Feb 1–12, 1993)* Marco Polo ▲ 8.223537 [DDD]
L. Williams (cnd)
Mageau, M.J.:Furies, w. Wendy Lorenz (pno) Vienna Modern Masters ▲ VMM 3036 [DDD]

Queensland Wind Soloists
Jacob, G.:Divert Wind Octet Vox Australis ▲ VAST 008–2
Kvandal, J.:Night Music 2 Vox Australis ▲ VAST 008–2
Mysliveček, J.:Octet 2 Ww Vox Australis ▲ VAST 008–2
Rankine, P.:Music of—From Fire by Fire Vox Australis ▲ VAST 008–2

Quintessens [G. Baeckelandt, F. Heyndrickx, J. Maebe, B. Snauwaert, R. Vercruysse]
Beethoven, L. van:Qnt Pno, Ob, Cl, Hn & Bn, w. Quintessens Eufoda ▲ 1159
Lannoy, E.F. von:Qnt Pno Eufoda ▲ 1159
Poulenc, F.:Sxt Pno Eufoda ▲ 1159

▲ = CD ◆ = Enhanced CD Δ = MD ■ = Cassette Tape ☐ = DCC

Quintet of the Americas
Ballard, L.W.:Ritmo Indio—The Soul *(rec Manhattan School of Music, Jan 10 & 12, 1992)* MMC ▲ MMC 2018 [DDD]
G. Cortese (cnd)
McKinley, W.T.:Con for the New World, w. Manhattan School of Music Chamber Sinfonia *(rec Manhattan School of Music, Jan 10 & 12, 1992)* MMC ▲ MMC 2018 [DDD]
Rechtman, I.:America, w. Manhattan School of Music Chamber Sinfonia *(rec Manhattan School of Music, Jan 10 & 12, 1992)* MMC ▲ MMC 2018 [DDD]
Quintet of the Americas [Marco Granados (fl), Matthew Sullivan (ob), Christopher Jepperson (cl), Thomas Novak (bn), Barbara Oldham (hn)]
Cohn, J.:Con da Camera, w. E. Kiesewetter (vn), C. Grant (pno) *(rec Sept. 1992)* XLNT ▲ CD 18007 [DDD]
Cohn, J.:Qnt 2 Winds *(rec Sept. 1992)* XLNT ▲ CD 18007 [DDD]
Souvenirs:20 Musical Mementos from the New World XLNT ▲ CD 18008 [DDD]
Quintet of the Americas [Marco Granados (fl), Peggy Pearson (ob), Daniel Granados (cl), Thomas Novak (bn), Barbara Oldham (hn)]
Culpo, C.:Qnt Ww *(rec Vasser College, June 25–29, 1995)* CRI ▲ CD 722 [DDD]
Hyla, L.:Amnesia Breaks *(rec Vasser College, June 25–29, 1995)* CRI ▲ CD 722 [DDD]
Oliveros, P.:Portrait of the Qnt of the Americas *(rec Vassar College, June 25–29, 1995)* CRI ▲ CD 722 [DDD]
Rubin, A.:La Loba, w. Amy Rubin (pno) *(rec Vassar College, June 25–29, 1995)* CRI ▲ CD 722 [DDD]
Sharp, E.:JAG, w. Michael Lowenstern (b cl) *(rec Vassar College, June 25–29, 1995)* CRI ▲ CD 722 [DDD]
Quintette Sax of Paris
Classic Sax Quantum ▲ QM 6923
Quintetto da Camera
Music in Neapolitan Theaters in the 1700's, w. Gloria Guida Borrelli (sop), Piccolo Ensemble Kicco Classics ▲ 496 [DDD]
Quintetto Italiano
Bloch, E.:Chanty Koch Schwann ▲ SCH 312802
Casares, O.R.:Canciones Sefaradies (7) y Danza Koch Schwann ▲ SCH 312802
Casares, O.R.:L'Ultima Strada Koch Schwann ▲ SCH 312802
Gerhard, R.:Fant Gtr Qnt Koch Schwann ▲ SCH 312802
Quodlibet Musicum CO
A. O. Popa (cnd)
Haydn, M.:Con Fl, P.54, w. A. Octav Popa (cl) Olympia ("Explorer" series) ▲ OCD 406 [AAD]
Rachmaninoff Trio
Rachmaninoff, S.:Trio élégiaque 1 Centaur ▲ CRC 2059 [DDD]
Rachmaninoff, S.:Trio élégiaque 2 Centaur ▲ CRC 2059 [DDD]
Radio City Music Hall Orch
E. Rapée (cnd)
Charpentier, M.–A.:Louise (sels), w. Grace Moore (sop), Josef Schmidt (ten), Robert Weede (bar), Radio City Music Hall Chorus—Depuis le jour Enterprise ("The Radio Years" series) ▲ ENT RY 58
Leoncavallo, R.:Pagliacci (sels), w. Grace Moore (sop), Josef Schmidt (ten), Robert Weede (bar), Radio City Music Hall Chorus—Stridono lassù Enterprise ("The Radio Years" series) ▲ ENT RY 58
Massenet, J.:Manon (sels), w. Grace Moore (sop), Josef Schmidt (ten), Robert Weede (bar), Radio City Music Hall Chorus—Obéissons quand leur voix appelle [Gavotte] Enterprise ("The Radio Years" series) ▲ ENT RY 58
Puccini, G.:La Bohème (sels), w. Grace Moore (sop), Josef Schmidt (ten), Robert Weede (bar), Radio City Music Hall Chorus—Che Gelida Manina; Sì, Mi Chiamano Mimì; O Soave Fanciulla Enterprise ("The Radio Years" series) ▲ ENT RY 58
Puccini, G.:Madama Butterfly (sels), w. Grace Moore (sop), Josef Schmidt (ten), Robert Weede (bar), Radio City Music Hall Chorus—Vogliatemi Bene Enterprise ("The Radio Years" series) ▲ ENT RY 58
Puccini, G.:Tosca (sels), w. Grace Moore (sop), Josef Schmidt (ten), Robert Weede (bar), Radio City Music Hall Chorus—Recondita Armonia; Vissi d'Arte; E Lucevan le Stelle; Te Deum Enterprise ("The Radio Years" series) ▲ ENT RY 58
Radio France PO
S. Gualda (cnd)
Dao, N.–T.:Les Enfants d'Izieu, w. Sophie Boulin (sop), Eric Trémolières (ten), Christian Tréguier (bass) Musique Francaise d'Aujourd'hui ("Collection MFA–Radio France" series) ▲ MFA 216003
P. Herreweghe (cnd)
Haydn, J.:Con 1 Hn, w. Hervé Joulain (hn) Arion ▲ ARN 68311 [DDD]
M. Janowski (cnd)
Bruckner, A.:Ov in g Virgin Classics ▲ 59014 [DDD]
Bruckner, A.:Sym 4, "Romantic" [N] Virgin Classics ▲ 59014 [DDD]
Indy, V. d':Jour d'été à la montagne Erato ("Musifrance" series) ▲ 2292–45821–2–ZK
Indy, V. d':Sym on a French Mountain Air, w. C. Collard (pno) Erato ("Musifrance" series) ▲ 2292–45821–2–ZK
Lutoslawski, W.:Con Orch RCA Red Seal 2–▲ 09026–61520–2
Messiaen, O.:Un Sourire RCA Red Seal 2–▲ 09026–61520–2
Messiaen, O.:Turangalîla–sym RCA Red Seal 2–▲ 09026–61520–2
Poulenc, F.:Con for 2 Pnos, w. G. Pekinel (pno), S. Pekinel (pno) Teldec ▲ 2292–46155–2 [DDD]
Wagner, R.:Siegfried Idyll Virgo ▲ CDZ 559689
Y. Prin (cnd)
Chen, Q.:Yuan REM ▲ REM 311223 [DDD]
G. Prêtre (cnd)
Gounod, C.:Messe solennelle de St. Cécile, w. B. Hendricks (sop), L. Dale (ten), J.–P. Lafont (bass), French Radio Chorus [L] EMI Classics ▲ CDC 47094
Raglan Baroque Players
Locatelli, P.:Concerti grossi, w. Nicholas Kraemer (hpd), Elizabeth Wallfisch (vn) Hyperion 2–▲ CDA 66981/2
N. Kraemer (cnd)
Charpentier, M.–A.:Music of—Prelude [from Te Deum]; Joseph est bien marié; O nous dites, Marie; Laissez paître vos bêtes; A la venue de noël United ▲ CAL 88009 [DDD]
Couperin, F.:Dans le goût théatral United ▲ CAL 88009 [DDD]
Leclair, J.–M.:Cons Vn, Op. 7, w. Elizabeth Wallfisch (vn)—No. 2 in D United ▲ CAL 88009 [DDD]
Locatelli, P.:L'arte del violino, w. E. Wallfisch (vn) Hyperion 3–▲ CDA 66721/23
Lully, J.–B.:Carousel United ▲ CAL 88009 [DDD]
Lully, J.–B.:Trios pour le Coucher du Roy United ▲ CAL 88009 [DDD]
Rameau, J.P.:Platée (sels)—Suite [L'orage; Passepied 1 & 2; Rigaudon 1 & 2; Minuet 1 & 2; Chaconne; Tambourin] United ▲ CAL 88009 [DDD]
Vivaldi, A.:Cons Vn, Op. 8/1–12, "Il cimento dell'armonia e dell'inventione", w. M. Huggett (vn) Veritas 2–▲ VCD 7 90803–2 [DDD] 2–■ VCD 7 90803–4 (D)
Vivaldi, A.:Con Vn Vc, RV.546, w. M. Huggett (vn), T. Mason (vc) Veritas 2–▲ VCD 7 90803–2 [DDD] 2–■ VCD 7 90803–4 (D)
Vivaldi, A.:Cons for 2 Vns, w. M. Huggett (vn), E. Wallfisch (vn)—Concerto in G, RV.516 Veritas 2–▲ VCD 7 90803–2 [DDD] 2–■ VCD 7 90803–4 (D)
Konrad Ragossnig CO
Falla, M. de:Homenaje 'Le tombeau de Debussy' Allegretto ▲ ACD 8175 [ADD] ■ ACS 8175
Rallye Trompes de L'Hertogenwald
Fanfares de Venerie et de Fantaisie Ricercar ▲ RIC 137103
Ramat Gan CO
E. Inbal (cnd)
Mozart, W.A.:Adagio & Fugue Strs Adès ▲ ADE 132322 [AAD]
Mozart, W.A.:Diverts Str Qt, K.136–138 Adès ▲ ADE 132322 [AAD]
Rameau Trio
Telemann, G.P.:Sons VI Berlin Classics ▲ BER 2162

Rameau Trio (cont.)
Telemann, G.P.:Trio Sons Berlin Classics ▲ BER 2162
Paul Rans Ensemble [P. Rans, P. Malfeyt, P. Strychers, P. van Loey]
Egidius waer bestu bleven:Gruuthuse Manuscript Eufoda ▲ EUF 1170
Raphael Ensemble
Arensky, A.:Qt 2 Strs Hyperion ▲ CDA 66648
Brahms, J.:Qnt 1 Strs Hyperion ▲ CDA 66804
Brahms, J.:Qnt 2 Strs Hyperion ▲ CDA 66804
Brahms, J.:Sextet Strs, Op. 18 Hyperion ▲ CDA 66276
Brahms, J.:Sextet Strs, Op. 36 Hyperion ▲ CDA 66276
Bruckner, A.:Qnt Strs Hyperion ▲ CDA 66704
Korngold, E.W.:Sextet Strs Hyperion ▲ CDA 66425 [DDD]
Martinů, B.:Sextet Strs Hyperion ▲ CDA 66516
Schoenberg, A.:Verklärte Nacht [sextet version] Hyperion ▲ CDA 66425 [DDD]
Schubert, Franz:Qnt Strs, D.956 Hyperion ▲ CDA 66724
Schubert, Franz:Trio Strs, D.471 Hyperion ▲ CDA 66724
Schulhoff, E.:Sxt Strs Hyperion ▲ CDA 66516
Strauss, R.:Capriccio (sels)—Prelude Hyperion ▲ CDA 66704
Tchaikovsky, P.:Souvenir de Florence Hyperion ▲ CDA 66648
Raphael String Quartet
Bruckner, A.:Intermezzo Str Qnt, w. P. Pacey (va) Globe ▲ GLO 5078 [DDD]
Bruckner, A.:Qnt Strs, w. P. Pacey (va) Globe ▲ GLO 5078 [DDD]
Bruckner, A.:Rondo Str Qt Globe ▲ GLO 5078 [DDD]
Debussy, C.:Qt Strs Globe ▲ GLO 5039 [DDD]
Franck, C.:Qt Strs Globe ▲ GLO 5039 [DDD]
Keuris, T.:Qt 2 Strs Attacca ▲ 8948–5 [DDD]
Shostakovich, D.:Qt 8 Strs Attacca ▲ 8948–5 [DDD]
Shostakovich, D.:Qt 13 Strs Attacca ▲ 8948–5 [DDD]
Raphael Trio
Mendelssohn, F.:Trio 1 Pno Arcobaleno ▲ SBCD 6500 [DDD]
Mendelssohn, F.:Trio 2 Pno Arcobaleno ▲ SBCD 6500 [DDD]
Wolf–Ferrari, E.:Trio 1 Pno ASV ▲ ASV 935 [DDD]
Wolf–Ferrari, E.:Trio 2 Pno ASV ▲ ASV 935 [DDD]
Raphaele Concert Orch
Paris–Vienne Express EPM ▲ EPM 1135 [AAD]
P. Walden (cnd)
Strauss (II), Joh.:Waltzes—Kaiser Walzer; Bitte Schön; Wiener Blut; Der Vergnugungszug; Lagunenwalzer; Der Zigeunerbaron; An den schönen blauen Donau (The Blue Danube); Eljen a Magyar; Telegramme; Sperl Polka; Das Spitzentuch der Königin; Marchen aus dem Orient; Persischer Marsch; Eine Nact in Venedig; Frauenherz; G'schichten aus dem Wienerwald EPM ▲ 995062 [AAD]
Rara Ensemble [Angelica Celeghin (fl), Filippo Cianfoni (fl), Stefania Mercuri (ob), Mauro Panzieri (ob), Maurizio D'Alessandro (cl), Sergio Mondavio (cl), Claudia Galli (bn), Massimo Meloni (bn), Maurizio Aschelter (pno)]
F. di Cesare (cnd)
Setaccioli, G.:Poema lirico *(rec Audiovisivi S. Paolo–Albano Laziale, 1995)* Bongiovanni ▲ 5560 [DDD]
Rare Fruits Council [Manfredo Kraemer (vn), Pablo Valetti (vn), Rolf Lislevand (thb)]
Biber, H. von:Harmonia artificiosa–ariosa Astrée ▲ E 8572
Rascher Saxophone Quartet [Carina Rascher (sax), Harry White (sax), Bruce Weinberger (sax), Kenneth Coon (sax)]
Bach, J.S.:Cant 190—Prelude & Fugue [arr for sax qt] Cala ▲ CAL CACD 77003 [DDD]
Glazunov, A.:Qt Saxes Cala ▲ CAL CACD 77003 [DDD]
Grainger, P.:Shepherd's Hey [arr for sax qt] Cala ▲ CAL CACD 77003 [DDD]
Keuris, T.:Music for Saxs Cala ▲ CAL CACD 77003 [DDD]
Koch, E. von:Cantilena Cala ▲ CAL CACD 77003 [DDD]
Reich, S.:Manhatan Counterpoint Cala ▲ CAL CACD 77003 [DDD]
Starer, R.:Light & Shadow Cala ▲ CAL CACD 77003 [DDD]
Maurice Raskin String Quartet
Vieuxtemps, H.:Qt Strs, Op. 51 Koch Schwann ▲ SCH 317202 [DDD]
Vieuxtemps, H.:Qt Strs, Op. 52 Koch Schwann ▲ SCH 317202 [DDD]
Rasumovsky String Quartet
Gaudeamus Early Music Sampler, w. Great Consort, His Majesties Sagbutts & Cornetts, Trio Sonnerie, Cappella Nova, Cardinall's Musick, Clerks' Group, Ex Cathedra, Gentlemen of the Chappell, Gonville & Caius College Choir Cambridge, et al. ASV/Gaudeamus ▲ ASV 1002
Jadin, H.:Qts Strs, Op. 1—No. 3 [period instrs] ASV/Gaudeamus ▲ ASV 151
Jadin, H.:Qts Strs, Op. 2—No. 1 [period instrs] ASV/Gaudeamus ▲ ASV 151
Jadin, H.:Qts Strs, Op. 4—No. 1 [period instrs] ASV/Gaudeamus ▲ ASV 151
Vachon, P.:Qts Strs, Op. 5—No. 2 [period instrs] ASV/Gaudeamus ▲ ASV 151
Vachon, P.:Qts Strs, Op. 7—No. 2 [period instrs] ASV/Gaudeamus ▲ ASV 151
Raugel Orch
E. Bigot (cnd)
Charpentier, G.:Louise, w. N. Vallin (sop—Louise), C. Gaudel (sop—Irma), A. Lecouvreur (mez—Mother), G. Thill (ten—Julien), A. Pernet (bass—Father), Raugel Chorus *(rec 1936)* Nimbus (Prima Voce) ▲ NI 7829 (m) [ADD]
Maurice Ravel CO
J.–P Rouchon (cnd)
Danzi, F.:Sinf concertante, w. K. F. Schmid (cl), C. Slepicka (bn) Divertimento ▲ DIV 31008 [DDD]
Hoffmeister, F.A.:Con Cl, Bn & Orch, w. K. F. Schmid (cl), C. Slepicka (bn) Divertimento ▲ DIV 31008 [DDD]
J.–P. Rouchon (cnd)
Vogel, J.C.:Sinf concertante Cl, w. K. F. Schmid (cl), C. Slepicka (bn) Divertimento ▲ DIV 31008 [DDD]
Ravel Ensemble
Ravel, M.:Chansons madécasses, w. M. Grey (sop) [F] *(rec 1932)* InSync ■ C 4143
Ravel String Quartet [Nathalie Geoffray (vn), Reiko Kitahama (vn), Zoltan Toth (va), Jean–Michel Fonteneau (vc)]
Chausson, E.:Qt Strs Musidisc ▲ MUS 290272 [DDD]
Debussy, C.:Qt Strs Musidisc ▲ MUS 290442 [DDD]
Dutilleux, H.:Thus the Night Musidisc ▲ MUS 290442 [DDD]
Fauré, G.:Qt Strs Musidisc ▲ MUS 290442 [DDD]
Ravel, M.:Qt Strs Musidisc ▲ MUS 290272 [DDD]
Ravel Trio [Christian Crenne (vn), Manfred Stilz (vc), Chantal de Buchy (pno)]
Debussy, C.:Trio Pno Arion ▲ ARN 68018 [DDD]
Ravel, M.:Trio Pno Arion ▲ ARN 68018 [DDD]
Saint–Saëns, C.:Trio 1 Pno Arion ▲ ARN 68010 [AAD]
Saint–Saëns, C.:Trio 2 Pno Arion ▲ ARN 68010 [AAD]
Ravinia Chamber Ensemble
Vivaldi, A.:Cons Bn, w. D. Smith (bn)—5 selections Crystal ■ C 344
Ravinia Festival Ensemble
J. Levine (cnd)
Bach, J.S.:Brandenburg Con 2 RCA Gold Seal ▲ 09026–61365–2 [ADD] ■ 09026–61365–4–RG
Bach, J.S.:Brandenburg Con 5 RCA Gold Seal ▲ 09026–61365–2 [ADD] ■ 09026–61365–4–RG
Bach, J.S.:Cant 202, "Wedding Cant", w. K. Battle (sop) [G] RCA Gold Seal ▲ 09026–61365–2 [ADD] ■ 09026–61365–4–RG
Ravinia Trio [R. Schmidt (vn), P. Hörr (vc), S. Sasaki (pno)]
Schoenberg, A.:Verklärte Nacht [trans. Eduard Steuermann for piano trio 1932] *(rec Aug. 1992)* Divox ▲ CDX 29107 [DDD]
Steuermann, E.:Trio Pno *(rec Aug. 1992)* Divox ▲ CDX 29107 [DDD]
Rawlins Piano Trio [Dennis Ondrozeck (pno), David Neely (vn), Richard Rognstad (vc)]
Adler, S.:Trio 1 Pno Albany ▲ TROY 107 [DDD]

ORCH. & ENS.

Rawlins Piano Trio (cont.)
Heilman, W.C.:Suite Pno Trio Albany ▲ TROY 107 [DDD]
Heilman, W.C.:Trio Pno Albany ▲ TROY 107 [DDD]
Parker, H.:Suite Pno Albany ▲ TROY 107 [DDD]
Parker, H.:Trio Pno Albany ▲ TROY 107 [DDD]

Razumovsky Sinfonia

P. Breiner (cnd)
Granados, E.:Danzas españolas (10), w. Norbert Kraft (gtr) [arr. Peter Breiner for Gtr & Orch.] *(rec Moyzes Hall, Bratislava, Aug. 31–Sep. 2, 1994)* Naxos ▲ 8.553037 [DDD]
Granados, E.:Escenas poeticas, w. Norbert Kraft (gtr)—Berceuse; Eva y Walter; Danza de la Rosa [arr. Peter Breiner for Gtr & Orch.] *(rec Moyzes Hall, Bratislava, Aug. 31–Sep. 2, 1994)* Naxos ▲ 8.553037 [DDD]

A. Mogrelia (cnd)
Delibes, L.:Sylvia *(rec Slovak Radio Concert Hall, Bratislava, Mar 27–Apr 4, 1995)* Naxos 2–▲ 8.553338–9 [DDD]
Saint-Saëns, C.:Henry VIII (sels)—Fête populaire [ballet-divertissement from Act II] *(rec Slovak Radio Concert Hall, Bratislava, Mar 27–Apr 4, 1995)* Naxos 2–▲ 8.553338–9 [DDD]

RCA Italiana Opera Orch
The Prima Donna Collection Highlights, w. L. Price (sop), London SO, Philharmonia Orch, New Philharmonia Orch RCA Gold Seal ▲ 09026–62596–2

F. Cleva (cnd)
Verdi, G.:Luisa Miller, w. A. Moffo (sop), S. Verrett (mez), C. Bergonzi (ten), C. MacNeil (bar), G. Tozzi (bass) [I] RCA Gold Seal 2–▲ 6646–2–RG [ADD]

E. Leinsdorf (cnd)
Puccini, G.:Madama Butterfly, w. L. Price (sop), R. Elias (mez), G. Tucker (ten), P. Maero (bar) [I] RCA Red Seal 2–▲ 6160–2–RC [ADD]
Puccini, G.:Madama Butterfly (sels), w. L. Price (sop), R. Elias (mez), G. Tucker (ten), P. Maero (bar) [I] RCA ■ RK 1048
Puccini, G.:Madama Butterfly (sels), w. Leontyne Price (sop), Rosalind Elias (mez), Piero De Palma (ten), Richard Tucker (ten), Phillip Maero (bar), RCA Italiana Opera Chorus RCA Victor ▲ 09026–68089–2; ■ 09026–68089–4
Verdi, G.:Un ballo in maschera, w. L. Price (sop), C. Bergonzi (ten), R. Merrill (bar) [I] RCA Gold Seal 2–▲ 6645–2–RG [ADD]

F. Molinari-Pradelli (cnd)
Classical Ecstasy—Classics for a New Age, w. Chicago SO [cnd:Georg Solti], English CO [cnd:Alexander Schneider], London PO [cnd:Leonard Slatkin], Philadelphia Orch [cnd:James Levine], Philharmonia Orch [cnds:Andrew Litton, Henry Lewis], et al. RCA Gold Seal ▲ 74321–23041–2 [ADD/DDD]

G. Prêtre (cnd)
Donizetti, G.:Lucia di Lammermoor, w. A. Moffo (sop), C. Bergonzi (ten), M. Sereni (bar), E. Flagello (bass) [I] RCA Gold Seal 2–▲ 6504–2–RG [ADD]
Verdi, G.:La traviata, w. M. Caballé (sop), C. Bergonzi (ten), S. Milnes (bar) RCA Gold Seal 2–▲ 6180–2 RC [ADD]

T. Schippers (cnd)
Verdi, G.:Ernani, w. L. Price (sop), C. Bergonzi (ten), M. Sereni (bar), E. Flagello (bass) [I] RCA Gold Seal 2–▲ 6503–2–RG [ADD]

G. Solti (cnd)
Verdi, G.:Falstaff, w. M. Freni (sop), I. Ligabue (sop), G. Simionato (mez), R. Elias (mez), R. Krause (ten), G. Evans (bar), R. Merrill (bar), RCA Italiana Opera Chorus [I] London 2–▲ 417168–2 [ADD]
Verdi, G.:Rigoletto, w. A. Moffo (sop), R. Elias (mez), A. Kraus (ten), R. Merrill (bar), RCA Italiana Opera Chorus [I] RCA Gold Seal ▲ 60203–2–RG ■ 60203–4–RG
Verdi, G.:Rigoletto, w. A. Moffo (sop), R. Elias (mez), A. Kraus (ten), R. Merrill (bar), RCA Italiana Opera Chorus [I] RCA Gold Seal 2–▲ 6506–2–RG [ADD]

RCA SO
Jan Peerce Sings Hebrew Melodies, w. J. Peerce (ten) RCA Living Stereo ▲ 09026–61687–2 ■ 09026–61687–4

K. Kondrashin (cnd)
The Age of Living Stereo:A Tribute to John Pfeiffer, w. Boston SO [cnd:Pierre Monteux, Charles Munch], Chicago SO [cnd:Fritz Reiner], NBC SO [cnd:Leopold Stokowski] *(rec Boston & Chicago & New York, 1953–1961)* RCA Living Stereo 2–▲ 09026–68524–2 [ADD]

RCA Victor CO

L. Brouwer (cnd)
Brouwer, L.:Con 3 Gtr, "Con Elegíaco", w. J. Bream (gtr) RCA Red Seal ▲ 7718–2–RC [DDD]
Rodrigo, J.:Fant para un gentilhombre, w. J. Bream (gtr) RCA Victor ▲ 09026–61724–2; ■ 09026–61724–4 (CrO2)
Rodrigo, J.:Fant para un gentilhombre, w. J. Bream (gtr) RCA Red Seal ▲ 7718–2–RC [DDD]

RCA Victor Orch
Three Tenors of the Golden Age, w. Björling, Jussi (ten), Mario Lanza (ten), Jan Peerce (ten), John Corigliano (vn), Constantine Callinicos (pno), Frederick Schauwecker (pno), Renato Cellini (cnd), Constantine Callinicos (cnd), Erich Leinsdorf (cnd), Sylvan Levin (cnd), Maximilian Pilzer (cnd), Frieder Weissmann (cnd), Rome Opera Orch, Rome Opera Chorus, et al. RCA Gold Seal ▲ 09026–68531–2 [ADD] ■ 09026–68531–4
The Voices of Living Stereo, Vol. 2, w. Farrell, Eileen (sop), Birgit Nilsson (sop), Roberta Peters (sop), Leontyne Price (sop), Galina Vishnevskaya (sop), Rosalind Elias (mez), Shirley Verrett (mez), Marian Anderson (cta), Maureen Forrester (cta), Sergio Franchi (ten), Mario Lanza (ten), Richard Lewis (ten), Jan Pee, Alexander Dedyukhin (pno), Franz Rupp (pno), Leo Taubman (pno), George Trovillo (pno), Charles Wadsworth (pno), Boston Pops Orch [cnd:Arthur Fiedler], Boston SO [cnd:Charles Munch], Chicago SO [cnd:Fritz Reiner], RCA Victor Chorus, et al. *(rec Boston & Chicago & New York & Rome, 1957–1964)* RCA Living Stereo ▲ 09026–68167–2 [ADD]

R. Cellini
O Paradiso:Great Opera Arias, w. J. Björling (ten), Frederick Schauwecker (pno), Rome Opera Orch [cnd:Erich Leinsdorf, Jonel Perlea], Robert Shaw Chorale [cnd:Robert Shaw] *(rec 1951–1959)* RCA Gold Seal ▲ 09026–68429–2 [ADD]

P. Monteux (cnd)
The Pierre Monteux Edition, w. San Fransisco SO, Boston SO, Chicago SO RCA Gold Seal 15–▲ 09026–61893–2

RCA Victor SO
The Battle Cry of Freedom, w. Robert Shaw Chorale RCA Gold Seal ▲ 60814–2–RG [ADD] ■ 60814–4–RG
The Best of Wagner, w. Philadelphia Orch [cnd:E. Ormandy], Robert Shaw Chorale Victrola ("Victrola Best of" series) ▲ 60777–2–RV [ADD] ■ 60777–4–RV
Classical Ecstasy—Classics for a New Age, w. Chicago SO [cnd:Georg Solti], English CO [cnd:Alexander Schneider], London PO [cnd:Leonard Slatkin], Philadelphia Orch [cnd:James Levine], Philharmonia Orch [cnds:Andrew Litton, Henry Lewis], RCA Italiana Opera Orch [cnd:Francesco Molinari-Pradelli], et al. RCA Gold Seal ▲ 74321–23041–2 [ADD/DDD]
Piano Greatest Hits, w. A. Rubinstein (pno), Boston SO, Chicago SO RCA Victor ▲ 09026–62662–2 ■ 09026–62662–4

T. Beecham (cnd)
Puccini, G.:La Bohème, w. V. de los Angeles (sop), J. Bjoerling (ten), R. Merrill (bar) [I] EMI Classics 2–▲ CDCB 47235 (m) [ADD] 2–■ 4X2G 47235

R. R. Bennett (cnd)
Bernstein, L.:West Side Story (sels)—orchestral sels RCA Victor ▲ 09026–68334–2 ■ 09026–68334–4
Bernstein, L.:West Side Story (ballet music) RCA ■ ALK1–4505
Gershwin, G.:Porgy & Bess (symphonic picture) RCA ■ ALK1–4505
Gershwin, G.:Porgy & Bess (symphonic picture) RCA Victor ▲ 09026–68334–2 ■ 09026–68334–4

N. Berezowsky (cnd)
Mussorgsky, M.:Boris Godunov (sels), w. A. Kipnis (bass)—eight selections RCA Gold Seal ▲ 60522–2–RC [ADD] ■ 60522–4–RC (CrO2)

RCA Victor SO (cont.)

L. Bernstein (cnd)
Bernstein, L.:On the Town *(rec 1945)* RCA Gold Seal ▲ 09026–60915–2 ■ 09026–60915–4
Copland, A.:Billy the Kid (suite) *(rec 1949)* RCA Gold Seal ▲ 09026–60915–2 ■ 09026–60915–4 (CrO2)

R. Cellini (cnd)
Mascagni, P.:Cavalleria rusticana, w. Z. Milanov (sop), Carol Smith (sop), J. Bjöerling (ten), R. Merrill (bar), Robert Shaw Chorale [I] RCA Gold Seal ▲ 6510–2–RG [ADD]
Verdi, G.:Il trovatore, w. Z. Milanov (sop), F. Barbieri (mez), J. Björling (ten), L. Warren (bar), Robert Shaw Chorale [I] RCA Gold Seal ▲ 60191–2–RG [ADD] ■ 60191–4–RG (CrO2)
Verdi, G.:Il trovatore, w. Z. Milanov (sop), F. Barbieri (mez), J. Björling (ten), L. Warren (bar), Robert Shaw Chorale [I] RCA Gold Seal 2–▲ 6643–2–RG (m) [ADD] 2–■ CLK2–5377 (m)

O. Danon (cnd)
Gershwin, G.:Con Pno, w. R. Lewenthal (pno) *(rec 1962)* Chesky ▲ CD56 [ADD]

G. Daugherty (cnd)
Patrick, C.:Peter & the Wolf *(rec Studio 1 & LA Studios East, Salt Lake City, Utah)* RCA Gold Seal ▲ 74321–31869–2 [DDD]
Prokofiev, S.:Peter & the Wolf, w. Kirstie Alley (nar), Lloyd Bridges (nar), Ross Malinger (nar)—2 versions:1 with narration & 1 without *(rec Studio 1 & LA Studios East, Salt Lake City, Utah)* RCA Gold Seal ▲ 74321–31869–2 [DDD]

M. Freccia (cnd)
Franck, C.:Le Chasseur maudit *(rec 1968)* Chesky ▲ CD 87 [ADD]
Franck, C.:Symphonic Vars, w. E. Wild (pno) *(rec 1968)* Chesky ▲ CD 87 [ADD]
Macdowell, E.:Con 2 Pno, w. E. Wild (pno) *(rec 1967)* Chesky ▲ CD 76 [ADD]
Saint-Saëns, C.:Con 2 Pno, w. E. Wild (pno) *(rec 1967)* Chesky ▲ CD50 [ADD]

C. Gerhardt (cnd)
Strauss, R.:Der Rosenkavalier (suite) *(rec 1964)* Chesky ▲ CD 35 [ADD]

S. Henderson (cnd)
Gershwin, G.:Porgy & Bess (sels), w. H. Boatwright (sop), L. Price (sop), W. Warfield (bar), RCA Victor Chorus [E] RCA Gold Seal ▲ 5234–2–RG [ADD]

W. Hendl (cnd)
Glazunov, A.:Con Vn, w. J. Heifetz (vn) RCA Red Seal ▲ RCD1–7019
Glazunov, A.:Con Vn, w. Jascha Heifetz (vn) *(rec Santa Monica Civic Auditorium, CA, June 3 & 4, 1963)* RCA Red Seal ▲ 09026–61744–2 [ADD]

K. Kondrashin (cnd)
Tchaikovsky, P.:Con 1 Pno, w. V. Cliburn (pno) RCA Red Seal ▲ 07863–55912–2 [ADD] ■ 07863–55912–4

J. Krips (cnd)
Brahms, J.:Con 2 Pno, w. A. Rubinstein (pno) *(rec 1958)* RCA Gold Seal ▲ 09026–61442–2
Mozart, W.A.:Con 24 Pno, w. A. Rubinstein (pno) RCA Gold Seal ▲ 7968–2 [ADD]
Schumann, R.:Con Pno, w. A. Rubinstein (pno) *(rec 1958)* RCA Gold Seal ▲ 09026–61444–2

E. McArthur (cnd)
Wagner, R.:Arias & Scenes, w. Kirsten Flagstad (sop), Lauritz Melchior (ten), San Francisco Opera Orch—duets from Lohengrin; Tristan und Isolde; Götterdämmerung; Parsifal Pearl ▲ PEA 9190
Wagner, R.:Parsifal (sels), w. K. Flagstad (sop), L. Melchior (ten)—Act 2 *(Dies alles hab' ich nun geträumt [Herzenleide Scene])* RCA Gold Seal ▲ 7915–2–RG (m) [ADD] ■ 7915–4–RG (CrO2)

Ormandy, McArthur, Walter (cnd)
Wagner, R.:Arias & Scenes, w. Kirsten Flagstad (sop), Lauritz Melchior (bar), Philadelphia Orch, San Francisco Opera Orch, New York PO—arias & duets from Lohengrin, Tristan & Isolde, Götterdämmerung, Parsifal & Fidelio *(rec New York City, 1939–41)* Grammofono 2000 ▲ GRM 78526 (m)

F. Reiner (cnd)
Beethoven, L van:Con 5 Pno, "Emperor", w. V. Horowitz (pno) *(rec Carnegie Hall 1952)* RCA Gold Seal ▲ 7992–2–RG (m) [ADD] ■ 7992–4–RG
Rachmaninoff, S.:Con 3 Pno, w. Vladimir Horowitz (pno) RCA Gold Seal ▲ 7754–2–RC [ADD] ■ 7754–4–RC (CrO2)
Strauss, R.:Tod und Verklärung RCA Gold Seal ▲ 60388–2–RG [ADD]

N. Shilkret (cnd)
Gershwin, G.:An American in Paris, w. G. Gershwin (pno/cel) *(rec 2/4/29 for Victor)* Pearl 2–▲ PEAS 9483 (m) [AAD]
Gershwin, G.:An American in Paris, w. G. Gershwin (pno/cel) Pro Arte ▲ CDD 433 (m)

I. Solomon (cnd)
Bruch, M.:Con 2 Vn, w. J. Heifetz (vn) RCA Gold Seal ▲ 09026–60927–2 ■ 09026–60927–4
Chausson, E.:Poème Vn, w. J. Heifetz (vn) RCA Gold Seal ▲ 7709–2 RG [ADD] ■ 7709–4 RG6 (CrO2)
Conus, J.:Con Vn, w. J. Heifetz (vn) RCA Gold Seal ▲ 09026–60927–2 ■ 09026–60927–4
Mozart, W.A.:Sinf concertante Vn, K.364, w. J. Heifetz (vn), W. Primrose (va) RCA Red Seal ▲ 6778–2 [ADD]
Spohr, L.:Con 8 Vn, w. J. Heifetz (vn) RCA Gold Seal ▲ 7870–2–RG (m/s) [ADD]
Wieniawski, H.:Con 2 Vn, w. J. Heifetz (vn) RCA Gold Seal ▲ 09026–60927–2 ■ 09026–60927–4

P. Steinberg (cnd)
Saint-Saëns, C.:Havanaise Vn, w. J. Heifetz (vn) RCA Gold Seal ▲ 7709–2–RG [ADD] ■ 7709–4–RG (CrO2)
Saint-Saëns, C.:Introduction & Rondo capriccioso, w. J. Heifetz (vn) RCA Gold Seal ▲ 7709–2–RG [ADD] ■ 7709–4–RG (CrO2)

W. Steinberg (cnd)
Chopin, F.:Con 1 Pno, w. A. Brailowsky (pno) RCA Gold Seal ▲ 09026–61656–2 [AAD]
Sarasate, P. de:Zigeunerweisen, w. J. Heifetz (vn) RCA Gold Seal ▲ 7709–2–RG [ADD] ■ 7709–4–RG (CrO2)

L. Stokowski (cnd)
The Best of Handel, w. Boston Pops Orch [cnd:Arthur Fiedler], et al. Victrola ("Victrola Best of" series) ▲ 60771–2–RV [ADD] ■ 60771–4–RV
Enescu, G.:Romanian Rhap 1, w. Sym of the Air RCA Living Stereo ▲ 09026–61503–2
Handel, G.F.:Royal Fireworks Music RCA Victrola ▲ 7817–2–RV [ADD]; ■ 7817–4–RV
Handel, G.F.:Water Music (suites) RCA Victrola ▲ 7817–2–RV [ADD]; ■ 7817–4–RV
Liszt, F.:Hungarian Rhaps (orchestral versions), w. Sym of the Air RCA Living Stereo ▲ 09026–61503–2
Smetana, B.:The Bartered Bride (ov), w. Sym of the Air RCA Living Stereo ▲ 09026–61503–2
Smetana, B.:The Moldau, w. Sym of the Air RCA Living Stereo ▲ 09026–61503–2
Wagner, R.:Tannhäuser (orch sels), w. Sym of the Air RCA Living Stereo ▲ 09026–61503–2

D. Vorhees (cnd)
Waxman, F.:Carmen Fant, w. J. Heifetz (vn) RCA Gold Seal ▲ 7963–2–RG (m) [ADD]

A. Wallenstein (cnd)
Brahms, J.:Con Vn & Vc, "Double Con", w. J. Heifetz (vn), G. Piatigorsky (vc) RCA Red Seal ▲ 6778–2–RC [ADD]
Grieg, E.:Con Pno, Op. 16, w. A. Rubinstein (pno) RCA Gold Seal ▲ 09026–61262–2; ■ 09026–61262–4
Liszt, F.:Con 1 Pno, w. A. Rubinstein (pno) RCA Gold Seal ▲ 09026–61496–2 ■ 09026–61496–4
Liszt, F.:Con 1 Pno, w. A. Rubinstein (pno) RCA Red Seal ▲ 6255–2–RC [ADD]
Mozart, W.A.:Con 20 Pno, w. A. Rubinstein (pno) RCA Gold Seal ▲ 7967–2 [ADD] ■ 7967–4
Mozart, W.A.:Con 20 Pno, w. Artur Rubinstein (pno) RCA Victor ▲ 09026–68337–2 ■ 09026–68337–4
Mozart, W.A.:Con 21 Pno, w. A. Rubinstein (pno) RCA Gold Seal ▲ 7967–2 [ADD] ■ 7967–4
Mozart, W.A.:Con 23 Pno, w. Artur Rubinstein (pno) RCA Victor ▲ 09026–68337–2 ■ 09026–68337–4
Mozart, W.A.:Con 23 Pno, w. A. Rubinstein (pno) RCA Gold Seal ▲ 7968–2 [ADD]

Walter, MacArthur, Sargent (cnd)
Wagner, R.:Arias & Scenes, w. K. Flagstad (sop), L. Melchior (ten), New York PO, San Francisco Opera Orch, BBC SO—selections from Götterdämering; Tristan & Isolde; Lohengrin Memories 2–▲ HR 4456/57 [ADD]

▲ = CD ♦ = Enhanced CD Δ = MD ■ = Cassette Tape □ = DCC

La Real Camera [Emilio Moreno (vn), Enrico Gatti (vn), Wouter Moller (vc)]
Boccherini, L.:Trios for 2 Vns, G.113–118—Op. 54/2, 4–6 Glossa ▲ 920302
Rechérche Ensemble
Feldman, Morton:For Frank O'Hara Montaigne ▲ MO 782018
Feldman, Morton:I met Heine in the Rue Fürstenberg Montaigne ▲ MO 782018
Feldman, Morton:Routine Investigations Montaigne ▲ MO 782018
Feldman, Morton:The Va in My Life Montaigne ▲ MO 782018
Lachenmann, H.:Pno Music, w. Helmut Lachenmann (pno) Montaigne ▲ MO 782075
Lachenmann, H.:temA, w. L. Hirst (mez) Montaigne ▲ MO 782023
Lachenmann, H.:Trio fluido Montaigne ▲ MO 782023
Lachenmann, H.:Trio Strs Montaigne ▲ MO 782023
M. Foster (cnd)
Fervers, A.:Sextet Fl Accord ▲ ACD 205552 [DDD]
A. Richard (cnd)
Nono, L.:guai ai gelidi mostri, w. Susanne Otto (cta), Helena Rasker (alt), Klaus Burger (tuba/pic tpt), Stefano Scodanibbio (db) Montaigne ▲ MO 782047
Nono, L.:Omaggio a Gyorgy Kurtag Montaigne ▲ MO 782047
M. Schwartz (cnd)
Huber, K.:Music of—Auf die ruhige Nacht-Zeit; Ascensus; Transpositio ad infinitum; Schattenblätter; Fragmente aus Frühling; Des Dichters pflug Accord ▲ ACD 201652 [DDD]
Reconnaissance Chamber Ensemble
Asia, D.:Sand II, w. M. Feinsinger (mez) Albany ▲ TROY 106 [DDD]
Asia, D.:Shtay Albany ▲ TROY 106 [DDD]
Redcliffe Ensemble
Lutyens, E.:Driving out the Death *(rec BBC Studio 2, Nov 1986)* Redcliffe ▲ RR 006
Rawsthorne, A.:Qt Ob *(rec BBC Studio 2, Nov 1986)* Redcliffe ▲ RR 006
Rawsthorne, A.:Theme & Vars *(rec BBC Studio 2, July 1990)* Redcliffe ▲ RR 006
Routh, F.:Qt Ob *(rec BBC Studio 2, June 1987)* Redcliffe ▲ RR 006
Redwood Sym
E. Kujawsky (cnd)
Stravinsky, I.:L'Histoire du soldat Suite Ensemble Clarity ▲ CCD-1003
Stravinsky, I.:Les Noces, w. Magen Solomon (cnd), Oakland Sym Chorus Clarity ▲ CCD 1005
Stravinsky, I.:Pétrouchka [arr. Kujawsky] Clarity ▲ CCD-1003
Stravinsky, I.:Le Sacre du printemps Orch Clarity ▲ CCD 1005
Reger String Quartet
Pfitzner, H.:Qt 3 Strs Vox Box 2–▲ CDX 5134 [ADD]
Reggio Emilia Teatro Municipale Orch
Puccini, G.:La Bohème (sels), w. Bianco Bellisia (sop—Musetta), Alberto Pellegrini (sop—Mimi), Luciano Pavarotti (ten—Rodolfo), Walter de Ambrosis (bar—Schaunard), Vito Mattioli (bar—Marcello), Dmitri Nabokov (bass—Colline), Reggio Emilia Teatro Municipale Chorus Budget ("The Greatest Voice in Opera" series) ▲ SYP 105
F. Molinari-Pradelli (cnd)
Puccini, G.:La Bohème (sels), w. R. Mattioli (sop), P. Pellegrini (sgr), Bellesia (sgr), L. Pavarotti (ten)—sels from Pavarotti's debut performance *(rec live, Apr 29, 1961)* Melodram 2–▲ MEL 27031 [AAD]
Regina Music Box
Regina Sings Opera Bornand ■ 6
Reich Radio Königsberg Large Orch
W. Brückner-Rüggeberg (cnd)
Wagner, R.:Die Walküre (sels), w. G. Rünger (sop), E. Friedrich (sop), K. Buschmann (ten), W. Rode (bar)—Act II, Scenes 2,3 & 4 & Act III, Scenes 1,2 & 3 [G] *(rec live 2/17 & 5/1 1938)* Preiser 2–▲ 90075 (m) [AAD]
Die Reihe Ensemble
Ligeti, G.:Aventures *(rec mid-1968)* Vox Box 2–▲ CDX 5142
Ligeti, G.:Nouvelles aventures *(rec mid-1968)* Vox Box 2–▲ CDX 5142
Varèse, E.:Hyperprism *(rec Nov 1968–Mar 1969)* Vox Box 2–▲ CDX 5142
Varèse, E.:Intégrales *(rec Nov 1968–Mar 1969)* Vox Box 2–▲ CDX 5142
Varèse, E.:Ionisation *(rec Nov 1968–Mar 1969)* Vox Box 2–▲ CDX 5142
Varèse, E.:Octandre *(rec Nov 1968–Mar 1969)* Vox Box 2–▲ CDX 5142
Varèse, E.:Offrandes, w. Gertie Charlent (sop) *(rec Nov 1968–Mar 1969)* Vox Box 2–▲ CDX 5142
F. Cerha (cnd)
Debussy, C.:Chansons de Bilitis (recitation), w. M. T. Escribano (sop) Allegretto ▲ ACD 8159 [ADD] ■ ACS 8159
Reine Elisabeth Duo [Wolfgang Manz (pno), Rolf Plagge (pno)]
Debussy, C.:En blanc et noir Thorofon ▲ CTH 2297
Debussy, C.:Marche écossaise sur un thème populaire Thorofon ▲ CTH 2297
Rachmaninoff, S.:Suite 1 for 2 Pnos Thorofon ▲ CTH 2297
Rachmaninoff, S.:Suite 2 for 2 Pnos Thorofon ▲ CTH 2297
Ravel, M.:Rapsodie espagnole [arr for 2 pnos] Thorofon ▲ CTH 2297
Reineckétrio
Reinecke, C.:Trio Pno, Op. 264 *(rec June 19–22, 1993)* Bongiovanni ▲ GB 5537 [DDD]
Fritz Reiner SO
F. Reiner (cnd)
Haydn, J.:Sym 95 *(rec 1963)* RCA Gold Seal ▲ 09026-60729-2 ■ 09026-60729-4
Haydn, J.:Sym 101, "Clock" *(rec 1963)* RCA Gold Seal ▲ 09026-60729-2 ■ 09026-60729-4
Reist String Quartet
Daetwyler, J.:Rilke Songs (3), w. Ingrid Frauchiger (sop)—[G] Grammont ▲ CTSP 15-2
Relâche Ensemble [W. Hall (cl), C. Holdeman (bn), G. Klucevsek (acc), B. Noska (voc), M. Taylor (saxes), J. Tanenbaum (perc)]
Albert, T.:Devil's Rain Mode ▲ 22
Albert, T.:A Maze (With Grace) Mode ▲ 22
Ashley, R.:Outcome Inevitable O.O. Discs ▲ OO 17 [DDD]
Childs, M.E.:Parterre XI Compact Discs ▲ XI 114
Childs, M.E.:Parterre Innova ▲ MN 108
Epstein, P.A.:Songs (3) from "Home", w. B. Noska (mez) [E] Mode ▲ 22
Hovda, E.:Borealis Music O.O. Discs ▲ OO 17 [DDD]
Tenney, J.:Critical Band Mode ▲ 22
Vierk, L.V.:Timberline O.O. Discs ▲ OO 17 [DDD]
Rembrandt Chamber Players
Argento, D.:Elizabethan Songs (6), w. P. Michaels Bedi (sop) Cedille ▲ CDR 90000 011 [DDD]
Carter, E.:Son Fl Cedille ▲ CDR 90000 011 [DDD]
Falla, M. de:Con Hpd, w. Larry Combs (cl) Cedille ▲ CDR 90000 011 [DDD]
Hurník, I.:Son da camera Cedille ▲ CDR 90000 011 [DDD]
Rembrandt Trio [V. Tryon (pno), G. Kantarjian (vn), C. Bloemendal (vc)]
Arensky, A.:Trio 1 Pno Dorian ▲ DOR 90146 [DDD]
Brahms, J.:Trio 1 Pno *(rec Apr. 1991)* Dorian ▲ DOR 90160 [DDD]
Chaminade, C.:Romanza appassionata Dorian ▲ DOR 90187 [DDD]
Chaminade, C.:Sérénade espagnole Dorian ▲ DOR 90187 [DDD]
Dvořák, A.:Trio 4 Pno, "Dumky" *(rec Apr. 1991)* Dorian ▲ DOR 90160 [DDD]
Mendelssohn, F.:Trio 1 Pno Dorian ▲ DOR 90130 [DDD]
Ravel, M.:Trio Pno Dorian ▲ DOR 90187 [DDD]
Saint-Saëns, C.:Trio 1 Pno Dorian ▲ DOR 90187 [DDD]
Schubert, Franz:Trio 1 Pno Dorian ▲ DOR 90130 [DDD]
Tchaikovsky, P.:Trio Pno Dorian ▲ DOR 90146 [DDD]
Renaissance CO
L. Korchin (cnd)
A Baroque Festival Infinity Digital ▲ QK 57253 [DDD]

Renaissance CO (cont.)
L. Korkhin (cnd)
Vivaldi, A.:Cons Bn, w. O. Talipin (bn)—in a, RV.497 Infinity Digital ▲ QK 57244 [DDD]
Vivaldi, A.:Con for 2 Vcs, w. S. Raldugin (vc), Z. Zaliyailo (vc) Infinity Digital ▲ QK 57244 [DDD]
Vivaldi, A.:Con Mand, RV.425, w. T. Kostyanaia (mand) Infinity Digital ▲ QK 57244 [DDD]
Vivaldi, A.:Con for 2 Mands, w. T. Kostyanaia (mand), Alina Boguk (mand) Infinity Digital ▲ QK 57244 [DDD]
Vivaldi, A.:Cons Ob Vn, w. C. Oshinakaev (ob), A. Stang (vn)—in B♭, RV.548 Infinity Digital ▲ QK 57244 [DDD]
Vivaldi, A.:Cons for 2 Obs, w. C. Oshinakaev (ob), P. Tosenko (ob)—in a, RV.536 Infinity Digital ▲ QK 57244 [DDD]
Vivaldi, A.:Cons Vn (misc), w. A. Stang (vn) Infinity Digital ▲ QK 57217 [DDD]
Renaissance Orch
Ave Maris Stella:Music From the Cathedral of Seville Dedicated to the Virgin Mary, ca. 1470–1550 Almaviva ▲ 0115
Renaissance Players
W. Evans (cnd)
The Muses Gift Walsingham Classics ▲ WAL 8003-2 [DDD]
Renaissonics [John Tyson (rcr/pipe/tabor), Douglas Freundlich (lt), Reinmar Seidler (vc), Jacqueline Schwab (pno), James Johnston (vn/va)]
Dancel:Renaissance Dances & Improvisations *(rec Pamela Emerson's Music Room, Cambridge, MA, 1995)* Titanic ▲ TI 232 [DDD]
Renano Quintet
Borodin, A.:Qnt Vns, Va & Vcs Ars Produktion ▲ FCD 368309 [DDD]
Glazunov, A.:Qnt Strs Ars Produktion ▲ FCD 368309 [DDD]
Renn Brass Quintet
Con Eleganza, w. Southwest German RSO Bayer ▲ 100245 [DDD]
Répercussion Ensemble
Repercussion Analekta ▲ ATM 29719
Y. Turovsky (cnd)
Shchedrin, R.:Carmen, Montreal Musici Chandos ▲ CHAN 9288 [DDD]
Shchedrin, R.:Humoresque, Montreal Musici Chandos ▲ CHAN 9288 [DDD]
Shchedrin, R.:In Imitation of Albéniz, Montreal Musici, Montreal Musici Chandos ▲ CHAN 9288 [DDD]
Tranquillity, Vol. 2, w. I Musici de Montreal Chandos ("7000" series) ▲ CHAN 7058
Republican Guard Brass & Percussion
Y. Parmentier (cnd)
Liszt, F.:Requiem, w. Jacques Maresch (ten), Daniel Galvez-Vallejo (ten), Lionel Peintre (bar), Bertrand Bontoux (bass), Francois-Henri Houbart (org), French Army Chorus Adès ▲ ADE 203032
Republican Guard Orch of Harmony
In Honor of the 50th Anniversary of the End of the War, w. Armée Française Choir Socadisc ▲ 895766
R. Boutry (cnd)
Musique Française pour quintette de cuivres et harmonie, w. Epsilon Brass Ensemble Forlane ▲ FOR 16646 [DDD]
Polkas & Varied Airs, 1900, w. F. Presle (cnt/bgl) *(rec Feb. 10, 11 & 13, 1992)* Chamade ▲ 5603 [DDD]
Residentie Orch The Hague
400 Years of Dutch Music, Vol. 1 Olympia ▲ OCD 500 [AAD]
400 Years of Dutch Music, Vol. 2 Olympia ▲ OCD 501 [AAD]
400 Years of Dutch Music, Vol. 3 Olympia ▲ OCD 502 [AAD]
400 Years of Dutch Music, Vol. 4 Olympia ▲ OCD 503 [AAD]
400 Years of Dutch Music, Vol. 5 Olympia ▲ OCD 504 [AAD]
400 Years of Dutch Music, Vol. 6 Olympia ▲ OCD 505 [AAD]
C. Abbado (cnd)
Bellini, V.:I Capuleti e i Montecchi, w. M. Rinaldi (sop—Giulietta), G. Aragall (ten—Romeo), L. Pavarotti (ten—Tebaldo), N. Zaccaria (bass—Capellio), Bologna Chorus [I] *(rec live, Amsterdam 6/30/66)* Verona 2–▲ 28001/2
Bellini, V.:I Capuleti e i Montecchi, w. M. Rinaldi (sop), G. Aragall (ten), L. Pavarotti (ten), N. Zaccaria (bass), Bologna Chorus *(rec live, Amsterdam 6/30/66)* Melodram 2–▲ MEL 27001
E. Bour (cnd)
de Leeuw, T.:Mouvements rétrogrades Olympia ▲ OCD 505 [AAD]
Loevendie, T.:Turkish Folk Poems, w. D. Dorow (sop) [F] *(rec 1978–82)* Olympia ▲ OCD 506 [AAD]
Meder, Joh. Gabriel:Sym, Op. 3/1 *(rec 1982)* Olympia ▲ OCD 501 [AAD]
Wilms, J.W.:Symphonie Olympia ▲ OCD 502 [AAD]
A. Dorati (cnd)
Brahms, J.:Con Vn, w. Ginette Neveu (vn) *(rec The Hague, June 10, 1949)* Music & Arts 2–▲ CD 837 [AAD]
Fodor, C.A.:Sym 4 *(rec 1978)* Olympia ▲ OCD 501 [AAD]
R. van Driesten (cnd)
Pijper, W.:Con Pno, w. R. Brautigam (pno) Olympia ▲ OCD 504 [AAD]
C. M. Giulini (cnd)
Mozart, W.A.:Nozze di Figaro, w. E. Schwarzkopf (sop), G. Sciurri (sop), G. Taddei (bar), H. Prey (bar), Netherlands Chamber Choir [I] *(rec live, Holland Festival, 1961)* Verona 3–▲ 27092/94
N. Harnoncourt (cnd)
Hellendaal, P.:Concerti grossi—No. 1 *(rec 1975)* Olympia ▲ OCD 501 [AAD]
E. Howarth (cnd)
Martland, S.:Babi Yar *(rec Philips Concert Hall, Den Haag, Holland, Feb 18, 1989)* Catalyst ▲ 09026-68397-2 [DDD]
T. Koopman (cnd)
de Fesch, W.:Con grosso Olympia ▲ OCD 500 [AAD]
Graaf, C.E.:Sym, Op. 14/4 Olympia ▲ OCD 501 [AAD]
Hacquart, C.:Cantiones sacrae, w. *(soloists unknown)*—Canto X Olympia ▲ OCD 500 [AAD]
Hacquart, C.:Harmonia parnassia—Son 10 Olympia ▲ OCD 500 [AAD]
Lentz, J.N.:Con 2 Hpd *(rec 1982)* Olympia ▲ OCD 501 [AAD]
Mercker, M.:Instrumental Dances Olympia ▲ OCD 500 [AAD]
Schuyt, C.:Instrl Music—(4 selections) from Dodeci Padovane et Altretante Gagliarde...con due canzone..., 1611 Olympia ▲ OCD 500 [AAD]
Sweelinck, J.P.:Psalms of David, w. Netherlands Chamber Choir—Psalms 130 & 150 [F] Olympia ▲ OCD 500 [AAD]
Van Blanckenburg, Q.:Cant, w. M. von Egmond (bar) Olympia ▲ OCD 500 [AAD]
Wassenaer, U.W. van:Concerti Armonici—Concerto No. 1 Olympia ▲ OCD 500 [AAD]
F. Leitner (cnd)
Andriessen, H.:Vars & Fugue on a Theme by Kuhnau Olympia ▲ OCD 504 [AAD]
Escher, R.:Univers de Rimbaud, w. J. Giraudeau (ten) [F] *(rec 1978–82)* Olympia ▲ OCD 506 [AAD]
Van Bree, J.B.:Allegro Moderato Olympia ▲ OCD 502 [AAD]
Vermeulen, M.:Sym 3 Olympia ▲ OCD 504 [AAD]
A. Lombard (cnd)
Wagenaar, J.:Ovs—Cyrano Olympia ▲ OCD 504 [AAD]
A. Medveczky (cnd)
Van Der Horst, A.:Chorus II, w. Residentie Chorus The Hague Olympia ▲ OCD 505 [AAD]
L. Stokowski (cnd)
Tchaikovsky, P.:Romeo & Juliet *(rec 1951–70)* Music & Arts ▲ CD 831 [ADD]
L. Vis (cnd)
Janssen, G.:Dans van de Malic Matrijzen, w. G. Janssen (pno) *(rec 1978–82)* Olympia ▲ OCD 506 [AAD]
Verhey, T.:Con Fl, w. K. Verheul (fl) Olympia ▲ OCD 503 [AAD]
H. Vonk (cnd)
Diepenbrock, A.:Hymne Vn, w. E. Verhey (vn) Chandos ▲ CHAN 8821 [DDD]

Residentie Orch The Hague (cont.)
H. Vonk (cnd) (cont.)
Diepenbrock, A.:Incidental Music—The Birds:Overture [from his incidental music to Aristophanes' play] (1917); Elektra:Symphonic Suite [arr. in 1952 by Eduard Reeser from the incidental music to Sophocles' play] (1920); Maryas:Concert Suite [from his incidental music to Balthazar Verhagen's comic play depicting the Greek myth of the centaur who was flayed to death by Apollo after presuming to comete with the god in lyre-playing] (1910) Chandos ▲ CHAN 8821 [DDD]
Ketting, O.:Canzoni Olympia ▲ OCD 505 [AAD]
Laman, W.:Fleurs du Mal, w. J. van Nes (cta) [F] *(rec 1978–82)* Olympia ▲ OCD 506 [AAD]
Verhulst, J.:Sym in e Olympia ▲ OCD 502 [AAD]
H. Wallberg (cnd)
Beethoven, L. van:Sym 6, "Pastorale" Emergo ("Corneille" series) ▲ EC 3973
Residenz Quintet
Baumann, H.:Chamber Music—Divert. for Oboe, Clarinet & Bassoon; Rondo mit Mozart for Oboe, Clarinet, Horn & Bassoon; Monodie for Saxophone [w. G. Solera]; One Persucssion & 4 Winds [w. G. Quellmelz]; Con una marcetta for 2 Oboes & English Horn [w. H. Wollenweber (oboe) & G. Sirotek (English horn)]; Qnt. for Flute, Oboe, Clarinet, Horn & Bassoon *(rec June 1–3, 1993)* Thorofon ▲ CTH 2196 [DDD]
Resounding Winds Saxophone Quartet [J. Eric Wilson (sop sax), Helen Martell (alt sax), Charles Rochester Young (ten sax), Denise C. Dabney (bar sax)]
Kershner, B.:Contours, Canons & Caricatures *(rec Worthington United Methodist Church, Columbus, Ohio, Mar 14, 1993)* Vienna Modern Masters ▲ VMM 2015 [DDD]
Revels Company
J. Langstaff (cnd)
Christmas Day in the Morning:A Revels Celebration of the Winter Solstice Revels ■ CA 1087
La Reverdie [Elisabetta de'Mircovich (sgr/rebec/medieval hp/portitive org), Doron D. Sherwin (sgr/cnt/perc), C. Daffagni (lt/sgr/perc), Livia Caffagni (rcr/h-g/sgr]
Laude di Sancta Maria Arcana ▲ ACA 34 [DDD]
O Tu Chara Sciencia:Music of Medieval Thought Arcana ▲ ACA 29 [DDD]
Speculum Amoris:Lyrique de l'amour médiéval du mysticisme à l'érotisme Arcana ▲ ACA 20 [DDD]
Revolutionary Drawing Room String Quartet [Graham Cracknell (vn), Adrian Butterfield (vn), Judith Tarling (va), Angela East (vc)]
Boccherini, L.:Qts Strs, G.201–206 [period instrs] CPO ▲ CPO 999206 [DDD]
Boccherini, L.:Qt Strs, G.213 CPO ▲ CPO 999205 [DDD]
Boccherini, L.:Qt Strs, G.214 CPO ▲ CPO 999205 [DDD]
Boccherini, L.:Qt Strs, G.215 CPO ▲ CPO 999205 [DDD]
Boccherini, L.:Qts Strs, G.242–247 CPO 2-▲ CPO 999070 [DDD]
Donizetti, G.:Qts Strs—Nos. 7–9 CPO ▲ CPO 999170 [DDD]
Donizetti, G.:Qts Strs—Introduzione; No. 10 in g; No. 11 in C; No. 12 in C *(rec Heathfield Church, East Sussex, July 19–21, 1994)* CPO ▲ CPO 999279–2 [DDD]
Reykjavik CO
Pálsson, P.P.:Music of, w. S. Saemundsdóttir (sop), R. Bragadóttir (mez)—Gudis-Mana-Hasi; Crystals; Tomorro; August Sonnet; September Sonnet; Lantao; 6 Thoughtful Songs Music from Iceland ▲ ITM 807
P. Zukovsky (cnd)
Nordal, J.:Music of—Adagio; Epitafion; Concerto lirico; Twin Song [w. E. G. Sveinbjörnsson (vn), I. Jónasson (va)] Music from Iceland ▲ ITM 704 [DDD]
Reykjavik Trio
Eiriksdottir, Karolina:Trio Pno Music from Iceland ▲ ITM 701 [ADD]
Reykjavik Wind Quintet [Bernhardur Wilkinson (fl), Einar Jóhannesson (cl), Dadi Kolbeinsson (ob), Joseph Ognibene (hn), Hafsteinn Gudmundsson (bn)]
Barber, Beach & Other American Works Chandos ▲ CHAN 9174 [DDD]
French Wind Music Chandos ▲ CHAN 9362 [DDD]
Rheinland-Pfalz State PO Trombonists
Trombonissimo Bayer ▲ 100158 [DDD]
Rhenish CO
J. Corazolla (cnd)
Gluck, C.W.:Ovs, w. J. Felmlee (fl), A. Mirschel (ob), P. R. Klecka (hpd)—Euristeo; Iphigénie en Aulide; Orfeo ed Euridice; Don Juan Entrée ▲ 0064
Rhenish PO
W. A. Albert (cnd)
Méhul, E.-N.:Sym 1 Marco Polo ▲ 8.223139
Méhul, E.-N.:Sym 2 Marco Polo ▲ 8.223139
W. Balzer (cnd)
Bruch, M.:Die Loreley (ov) ebs ▲ ebs 6071 [DDD]
Bruch, M.:Romanze Va, w. R. Moog (va) ebs ▲ ebs 6071 [DDD]
Bruch, M.:Russian Suite ebs ▲ ebs 6071 [DDD]
Bruch, M.:Sym 1 ebs ▲ ebs 6071 [DDD]
S. Friedmann (cnd)
Raff, J.:Sym 1 Marco Polo ▲ 8.223165
M. Halász (cnd)
Goldmark, K.:Ovs—Pentheseilea Overture, Op. 31 *(rec Dec, 1985)* Marco Polo ▲ 8.220417 [DDD]
Goldmark, K.:Sym 2 *(rec Dec, 1985)* Marco Polo ▲ 8.220417 [DDD]
J. Lockhart (cnd)
Bruneau, A.:Orchestral Music (sels)—Prelude; Legend of Gold [from *Messidor*]; Prelude to Act 1 [from *Naïs Micoulin*]; Prelude; War; Forest; Betrothal at the Mill [from *L'Attaque du moulin*] Marco Polo ▲ 8.223498 [DDD]
Le Flem, P.:Pièces enfantines *(rec Koblenz, June 12–13, 1987)* Marco Polo ▲ 8.223655 [DDD]
Le Flem, P.:Pour les morts *(rec Koblenz, June 12–13, 1987)* Marco Polo ▲ 8.223655 [DDD]
Le Flem, P.:Sym 4 *(rec Koblenz, June 12–13, 1987)* Marco Polo ▲ 8.223655 [DDD]
G. Nopre (cnd)
Le Flem, P.:Film Music—Le grand jardinier de France [The Great Gardener of France] (1942) *(rec Koblenz, May 14, 1993)* Marco Polo ▲ 8.223655 [DDD]
A. Walter (cnd)
Reinecke, C.:King Manfred (sels) Marco Polo ▲ 8.223117 [DDD]
Reinecke, C.:Sym 1 Marco Polo ▲ 8.223117 [DDD]
Rhine Bach Collegium
Hölszky, A.:Intarsien III Koch Schwann ▲ 3-1062-2 [DDD]
The Marriage of the Hen & the Cuckoo:Program Music of the Baroque Period CPO ▲ CPO 999083 [DDD]
Rhine State PO
J. Lockhart (cnd)
Dittersdorf, K.D. von:Doctor und Apotheker, w. Hildegard Uhrmacher (sop—Leonore), Donna Woodward (sop—Rosalia), Waltraud Meier (mez—Claudia), Martin Finke (ten—Sichel), Frieder Lang (ten—Gotthold), Alois Perl (ten—Gallus), Gerhard Unger (ten—Sturmwald), Thomas Pfeiffer (bar—Police Commisioner), Wolfgang Schöne (bar—Krautmann), Harald Stamm (bass—Stössel) Bayer 2-▲ BR 100 238/39 [DDD]
K. Redel (cnd)
Schumann, R.:Sym 3 Pierre Verany ▲ PV.790011 [DDD]
Schumann, R.:Sym 4 Pierre Verany ▲ PV.790011 [DDD]
Rhineland-Palatinate State PO
W. A. Albert (cnd)
Wagner, S.:Concertino Fl, w. Andrea Lieberknecht (fl) *(rec Apr 1996)* CPO ▲ 999427-2 [DDD]
Wagner, S.:Con Vn, w. Ulf Hoelscher (vn) *(rec Apr 1996)* CPO ▲ 999427-2 [DDD]
Wagner, S.:Der Friedensengel (ov) CPO ▲ CPO 999003 [DDD]
Wagner, S.:Die heilige Linde (sels), -Prelude to Act II *(rec Apr 1996)* CPO ▲ 999427-2 [DDD]
Wagner, S.:Die heilige Linde (ov) CPO ▲ CPO 999003 [DDD]
Wagner, S.:Herzog Wildfang (ov) CPO ▲ CPO 999003 [DDD]
Wagner, S.:Der Kobold (sels)—Prelude Act III *(rec Apr 1996)* CPO ▲ 999427-2 [DDD]

Rhineland-Palatinate State PO (cont.)
W. A. Albert (cnd) (cont.)
Wagner, S.:Das Märchen vom dicken fetten Pfannkuchen, w. Dietrich Henschel (bar) *(rec Apr 1996)* CPO ▲ 999427-2 [DDD]
Wagner, S.:Music of—Prelude, Forest Scene & Waltz [all from An allem ist Hütchen Schuld]; Das Flüchlein Prelude; Ov, Intro to Act III & Devil's Waltz [all from Der Bärenhäuter] CPO ▲ CPO 999300 [DDD]
Wagner, S.:Der Schmied von Marienburg (ov) CPO ▲ CPO 999003 [DDD]
P. Davin (cnd)
Holmès, A.:Orchestral Music—Andromède; Ov. pour une comédie; Irlande; La Nuit et l'Amour; Pologne Marco Polo ▲ 8.223449
M. Jurowski (cnd)
Goldschmidt, B.:Comedy of Errors CPO ▲ CPO 999323
Goldschmidt, B.:Greek Suite CPO ▲ CPO 999323
Schulhoff, E.:Ogelala CPO ▲ CPO 999323
K. Redel (cnd)
Borodin, A.:Prince Igor (Polovtsian dances) Forlane ▲ FRL 58 [AAD]
Glinka, M.:Russlan & Ludmilla (ov) Forlane ▲ FRL 58 [AAD]
Khachaturian, A.:Gayane (sels)—Sabre Dance Forlane ▲ FRL 58 [AAD]
Mussorgsky, M.:Khovanshchina (orch sels)—Intro Forlane ▲ FRL 58 [AAD]
Rimsky-Korsakov, N.:Golden Cockerel (sels)—Hymn to the Sun Forlane ▲ FRL 58 [AAD]
Tchaikovsky, P.:The Nutcracker (sels)—Characteristic Dances Forlane ▲ FRL 58 [AAD]
Tchaikovsky, P.:The Nutcracker (sels)—Characteristic Dances Forlane ▲ FRL 16696 [ADD]
Tchaikovsky, P.:Nutcracker Suite Forlane ▲ FRL 16 [AAD]
Tchaikovsky, P.:Romeo & Juliet Forlane ▲ FRL 16696 [ADD]
Tchaikovsky, P.:Sleeping Beauty (sels)—Waltz Forlane ▲ FRL 58 [AAD]
Tchaikovsky, P.:Sleeping Beauty (sels)—waltz Forlane ▲ FRL 16 [AAD]
Tchaikovsky, P.:Sleeping Beauty (sels)—Waltz Forlane ▲ FRL 16696 [ADD]
Tchaikovsky, P.:Swan Lake (sels)—Suites & Dances Forlane ▲ FRL 58 [AAD]
Tchaikovsky, P.:Swan Lake (sels)—Suites & Dances Forlane ▲ FRL 16696 [ADD]
Viotti, G.B.:Con 22 Vn, w. L. Bobesco (vn) Talent ▲ DOM 291013 [ADD]
Viotti, G.B.:Con 23 Vn, w. L. Bobesco (vn) Talent ▲ DOM 291013 [ADD]
O. Schmidt (cnd)
Gade, N.W.:Echoes of Ossian *(rec Oct 17–20, 1995)* CPO ▲ CPO 999362-2 [DDD]
Gade, N.W.:Hamlet (ov) *(rec Oct 17–20, 1995)* CPO ▲ CPO 999362-2 [DDD]
Gade, N.W.:Holbergiana *(rec Oct 17–20, 1995)* CPO ▲ CPO 999362-2 [DDD]
Gade, N.W.:A Summer's Day in the Country *(rec Oct 17–20, 1995)* CPO ▲ CPO 999362-2 [DDD]
L. Segerstam (cnd)
Aubert, L.:Orch Music—Offrande; Cinema:Six Tableaux; Dryade; Feuille d'Images; Tombeau de Chateaubriand *(rec Feb & Dec 1989)* Marco Polo ▲ 8.223531 [DDD]
Caplet, A.:Légende Orch *(rec Pfalzbau-Hall, Ludwigshafen, Sept. 23, 1987)* Marco Polo ▲ 8.223751 [DDD]
Caplet, A.:Marche triomphale et pompière *(rec Pfalzbau-Hall, Ludwigshafen, Sept. 23, 1987)* Marco Polo ▲ 8.223751 [DDD]
Caplet, A.:Nihavend Orch *(rec Pfalzbau-Hall, Ludwigshafen, Sept. 23, 1987)* Marco Polo ▲ 8.223751 [DDD]
Debussy, C.:Children's Corner *(rec Pfalzbau-Hall, Ludwigshafen, Sept. 23, 1987)* Marco Polo ▲ 8.223751 [DDD]
Debussy, C.:Clair de lune *(rec Pfalzbau-Hall, Ludwigshafen, Sept. 23, 1987)* Marco Polo ▲ 8.223751 [DDD]
Dvořák, A.:Slavonic Dances (comp) BIS ▲ CD 425 [DDD]
Koechlin, C.:Le Buisson ardent *(rec Pfalzbau-Hall, Ludwigshafen, Germany, Sept. 4, 1985)* Marco Polo ▲ 8.223704 [DDD]
Koechlin, C.:Les Heures Persanes Orch Marco Polo ▲ 8.223504 [DDD]
Koechlin, C.:Sur les flots lointaines—contains 2 versions [1 arr. for Strs] *(rec Pfalzbau-Hall, Ludwigshafen, Germany, Apr. 10, 1987)* Marco Polo ▲ 8.223704 [DDD]
Koechlin, C.:Symphonic Pieces—Au loin *(rec Pfalzbau-Hall, Ludwigshafen, Germany, Dec. 3, 1986)* Marco Polo ▲ 8.223704 [DDD]
Rabaud, H.:Divertissement sur des chansons russes *(rec Ludwigshafen, June 21 & 22, 1990)* Marco Polo ▲ 8.223503 [DDD]
Rabaud, H.:Eclogue *(rec Ludwigshafen, June 21 & 22, 1990)* Marco Polo ▲ 8.223503 [DDD]
Rabaud, H.:Mârouf, Savetier du Caire (sels)—Dances *(rec Ludwigshafen, June 21 & 22, 1990)* Marco Polo ▲ 8.223503 [DDD]
Rabaud, H.:The Merchant of Venice (sels)—Suites Anglaise, Nos. 2 & 3 *(rec Ludwigshafen)* Marco Polo ▲ 8.223503 [DDD]
Rabaud, H.:Procession Nocturne *(rec Ludwigshafen, June 21 & 22, 1990)* Marco Polo ▲ 8.223503 [DDD]
Roger-Ducasse, J.:Au Jardin de Marguerite (sels)—Interlude *(rec Ludwigshafen, Apr. 10 & Sept. 9, 1987)* Marco Polo ▲ 8.223641 [DDD]
Roger-Ducasse, J.:Epithalame *(rec Ludwigshafen, Apr. 10 & Sept. 9, 1987)* Marco Polo ▲ 8.223641 [DDD]
Roger-Ducasse, J.:Le joli jeu de furet *(rec Ludwigshafen)* Marco Polo ▲ 8.223501 [DDD]
Roger-Ducasse, J.:Marche française *(rec Ludwigshafen)* Marco Polo ▲ 8.223501 [DDD]
Roger-Ducasse, J.:Nocturne de printemps *(rec Ludwigshafen)* Marco Polo ▲ 8.223501 [DDD]
Roger-Ducasse, J.:Orphée (sels)—3 symphonic fragments:Orpheus Invokes the God; Hymen—Torchlight Procession; Bacchanale *(rec Ludwigshafen)* Marco Polo ▲ 8.223501 [DDD]
Roger-Ducasse, J.:Petite Suite *(rec Ludwigshafen, Apr. 10 & Sept. 9 & 23, 1)* Marco Polo ▲ 8.223501 [DDD]
Roger-Ducasse, J.:Prélude d'un ballet *(rec Ludwigshafen, Apr. 10 & Sept. 9, 1987)* Marco Polo ▲ 8.223641 [DDD]
Roger-Ducasse, J.:Suite française *(rec Ludwigshafen, Apr. 10 & Sept. 9, 1987)* Marco Polo ▲ 8.223641 [DDD]
Schmitt, F.:Danse d'Abisag *(rec Philharmonie Hall, Ludwigshafen, Germany, Nov. 11, 1992)* Marco Polo ▲ 8.223689 [DDD]
Schmitt, F.:Habeyssée, w. Hannele Segerstam (vn) *(rec Philharmonie Hall, Ludwigshafen, Germany, Sept. 14, 1988)* Marco Polo ▲ 8.223689 [DDD]
Schmitt, F.:Rêves *(rec Pfalzbau-Hall, Ludwigshafen, Germany, Sept. 9, 1987)* Marco Polo ▲ 8.223689 [DDD]
Schmitt, F.:Sym 2 *(rec Pfalzbau-Hall, Ludwigshafen, Germany, Apr. 6 & 7, 1988)* Marco Polo ▲ 8.223689 [DDD]
Segerstam, L.:Con 3 Pno, w. R. Keuschnig (pno) *(rec live 2/26/89)* BIS ▲ CD 484 [DDD]
Segerstam, L.:Sym 9 Finlandia ▲ FIN 403 [ADD]
Segerstam, L.:Sym 12 Finlandia ▲ FIN 403 [ADD]
Segerstam, L.:Sym 13, w. R. Keuschnig (pno) BIS ▲ CD 484 [DDD]
Segerstam, L.:Sym 14 *(rec live 12/3/89)* BIS ▲ CD 484 [DDD]
Segerstam, L.:Sym 16 *(rec June 2–3, 1992)* BIS ▲ CD 584 [DDD]
Rhineland-Palatinate State PO Chamber Soloists
Villa-Lobos, H.:Chôro 4 Bayer ▲ BR 100117 [DDD]
Rhizome
Ballif, C.:Cendres Arion ▲ ARN 68289 [DDD]
Ballif, C.:L'Habitant du labyrinthe Arion ▲ ARN 68289 [DDD]
Ballif, C.:Timbres et postes Arion ▲ ARN 68289 [DDD]
Rhythm & Bluefield Band [David Bluefield (pno), Chris Bank (sax), Howard Arthur (gtr), Kirwan Brown (elec bass), Tom Hills (dr/perc), Brian Savage (fl), Tim Fox (tpt), Steve Cole (cl)]
Reclassified:Clazzual Sax 2 D'Blue ▲ DB 0123
Ricercar Academy
Beethoven, L. van:Qnt Ob, 3 Hns & Bn *(rec 11/90–1/91)* Ricercar ▲ RIC 92078 [DDD]
Beethoven, L. van:Romances Vn *(rec 11/90–1/91)* Ricercar ▲ RIC 92078 [DDD]
Beethoven, L. van:Sxt Winds, Op. 71 *(rec 11/90–1/91)* Ricercar ▲ RIC 92078 [DDD]
Beethoven, L. van:Trio 2 Obs, Op. 87 *(rec 11/90–1/91)* Ricercar ▲ RIC 92078 [DDD]

▲ = CD ♦ = Enhanced CD Δ = MD ■ = Cassette Tape □ = DCC

Ricercar Academy (cont.)
Beethoven, L. van:Vars on "La ci direm la mano," from Mozart's *Don Giovanni* *(rec 11/90–1/91)* Ricercar ▲ RIC 92078 [DDD]

P. Busca (cnd)
Mascharada:2 Centuries of European Dances & Instrumental Music Stradavarius ▲ STV 33381 [DDD]
La Rovattina Stradavarius ▲ STV 33380 [DDD]

M. Minkowski (cnd)
Grétry, A.-E.-M.:La Caravane du Caire, w. I. Poulenard (sop), G. de Reyghere (sop), G. Ragon (ten), G. de Mey (ten), P. Huttenlocher (bar), V. Le Téxier (bar), J. Bastin (bass), Ricercar Academy Chorus [period instrs] [F] Ricercar 2-▲ RIC 100084/85 [DDD]

D. Tabbia (cnd)
Lassus, O. de:Sacred Music, w. Insieme Vocale Datrocanto—Missa Super Je Suis Deshéritée; Lectiones Matutinae de Nativitate Christi; Lectiones Sacrae ex Libri Hiob; Stabat Mater Dolorosa Stradivarius ▲ STV 33345 [DDD]

Ricercar Consort
Biber, H. von:Requiem à 15, w. G. de Reyghere (sop), J. Feldman (sop), J. Bowman (ct), I. Honeyman (ten), M. van Egmond (bass), Erik Van Nevel (cnd), Capella Sancti Michaelis [L] *(rec 5/90)* Ricercar ▲ RIC 81063 [DDD]
Bruhns, N.:Cants, w. Jill Feldman (sop), Greta de Reyghere (sop), James Bowman (ct), Ian Honeyman (ten), Guy de Mey (ten), Max Van Egmond (bass)—Hemmt eure Tränenflut; Jauchzet dem Herren alle Welt; Wohl dem, der den Herren fürchtet; De profundis; Paratum cor meum; O werter heil'ger Geis; Zeit meines Abschieds; Erstanden ist der heilige Christ; Herr hat seinem Stuhl im Himmel bereitet; Ich liege und schlafe; Mein Herz ist bereit; Muss nicht der Mensch auf dieser Erden in Stetem Streite sein Ricercar In Ecco 2-▲ REC8001/2
Compendium of Baroque Musical Instruments Ricercar 3-▲ 93001 [DDD]
Dalla Casa, G.:Music of, w. Delphine Collot (sop)—Susane un jour Ricercar ▲ 154149
Defense de la Basse Viole contre les Enterprises du Violon et les Pretentions du Violoncelle [Defense of the Bass Viol against the Enterprise of the Violin & the Pretension of the Cello], w. P. Pierlot (b vl), François Fernandez (vn), Hidemi Suzuki (vc) Ricercar 3-▲ RIC 93005
Guide des Instruments de la Renaissance, w. La Fenice, Le Tourdion Ricercar 3-▲ 95001
Haydn, J.:Diverts for 2 Hns, Vns, Baryton, Va, Vc & B Vl, H.X/1-6 & 12—Nos. 1, 2, 4 & 6 in D, D, G & A Ricercar ▲ 67124
Jarzebski, A.:Music of, w. Delphine Collot (sop)—Susanna Videns Ricercar ▲ 154149
Lassus, O. de:Chansons & Moresche, w. Delphine Collot (sop)—Chanter je veux; Je ne veux plus que chanter; Ton nom que mon vers dira; Et d'où venez-vous, Madame Lucette; Du fond de ma pensée; Vivre sera et toujours perdurable; Il estoit une religieuse; etc. Ricercar ▲ 154149
Philips, P.:Kbd Music, w. Delphine Collot (sop)—Le Rossignuol [after Lassus] (1595); Margott laborez [after Lassus] (1605) Ricercar ▲ 154149
Purcell, H.:Sons (12) Vns, Z.790-801 Ricercar ▲ 80088 [DDD]
Purcell, H.:Sons (10) Vns, Z.802-811 *(rec Abbaye de Stavelot, Jan. 1994)* Ricercar ▲ 127140
Telemann, G.P.:Con in F Rcr, B Vl, w. F. de Roos (rcr), P. Pierlot (vl) Ricercar ▲ RIC 44021 [DDD]
Telemann, G.P.:Con in F Rcr Bn, w. F. de Roos (rcr), M. Minkowski (bn) Ricercar ▲ RIC 44021 [DDD]
Telemann, G.P.:Con in F Rcr Fl, w. F. de Roos (rcr), P. Beuckels (fl) Ricercar ▲ RIC 44021 [DDD]
Telemann, G.P.:Suite in a Fl, w. F. de Roos (rcr) Ricercar ▲ RIC 44021 [DDD]

P. Cao (cnd)
Lassus, O. de:Aurora lucis rutilat, w. La Fenice Ensemble, Namur Chamber Choir *(rec St. Lambert à Mozet, Nov 1994)* Ricercar ▲ 155141
Lassus, O. de:Motets, w. La Fenice Ensemble, Namur Chamber Choir—Omnes de saba; Da pacem Domine; Timor et tremor; Tui sunt coeli; Surge propera amica mea; Aurora lucis rutilat *(rec St. Lambert à Mozet, Nov 1994)* Ricercar ▲ 155141
Lassus, O. de:Vinum bonum, w. La Fenice Ensemble, Namur Chamber Choir *(rec St. Lambert à Mozet, Nov 1994)* Ricercar ▲ 155141

E. van Nevel (cnd)
Kerll, J.C.:Missa pro defunctis, w. G. de Reyghere (sop), J. Bowman (alt), I. Honeyman (ten), G. de Mey (ten), M. van Egmond (bass), Capella Sancti Michaelis [L] *(rec 5/90)* Ricercar ▲ RIC 81063 [DDD]

P. Pierlot (cnd)
German Baroque Chamber Music Ricercar ▲ RIC 78060 [DDD]

Ricercar Consort [Frédéric de Roos (rec), Claude Wassmer (bn), Marc Minkowski (bn), Philippe Malfeyt (thb), Philippe Pierlot (b vl), Guy Penson (hpd/org)]
Handel, G.F.:Sons Fl Ricercar In Ecco 2-▲ 8004/05
Handel, G.F.:Sons Rcr & Hpd—Op. 1/Nos. 2, 4, 5, 7, 9, 11; Son in B♭ Ricercar In Ecco 2-▲ 8004/05

Ricercar Consort [Ryo Terakado (vn), Luis-Otavio Santos (vn), Philippe Pierlot (vl), Sophie Watillon (vl), Kaori Uemura (vl), Piet Strijkers (vl), David Sinclair (vie), Siebe Henstra (org), Vincent Dumestre (thb)]

P. Pierlot (cnd)
Sebastiani, J.:St. Matthew Passion, w. Greta de Reyghere (sop), Vincent Gregoire (ct), Stéphane van Dijck (ten), Hervé Lamy (ten—Evangéliste), Max van Egmond (bass—Christ) Ricercar ▲ 160144

Ricercar Ensemble
Redolfi, M.:Underwater Music, w. Lanie Goodman (fl), Melissa Morgan (hp), Michel Redolfi (syn)—Effractions (1988); Sunny Afternoon at Bird Rock Beach (1983); Full Scale Ocean (1989) *(rec Pacific Ocean, CA & Nice, France, 1983 & 1989)* Hat Hut ("NOW." series) ▲ hat ART CD 6026 [ADD]

Richmond Sinfonia

G. Manahan (cnd)
Castelnuovo-Tedesco, M.:Con Pno, w. S. Rodriguez (pno) Élan ▲ CD 2222 [DDD]
Ginastera, A.:Variaciones concertantes Élan ▲ CD 2222 [DDD]
Surinach, C.:Concertino Pno, w. S. Rodriguez (pno) Élan ▲ CD 2222 [DDD]

Ricordanze String Quartet [Carlo de Martini (vn), Stefano Barneschi (vn), Livia Baldi (va), Caterina Dell'Agnello (vc)]
Cambini, G.M.:Qts (149) Strs—No. 1 in E♭; No. 2 in F; No. 3 in b Stradivarius ▲ STV 33327 [DDD]

Ridge String Quartet
Dvořák, A.:Qnt Pno, Op. 5, w. R. Firkusny (pno) RCA Red Seal ▲ 09026-60436-2
Dvořák, A.:Qnt Pno, Op. 81, w. R. Firkusny (pno) RCA Red Seal ▲ 09026-60436-2
Van De Vate, N.:Qt 1 Strs Vienna Modern Masters ▲ VMM CD 2001 [ADD]

Riga Musicians

S. Klava (cnd)
Bach, J.S.:Motets, BWV 225-30, w. Riga Radio Chorus Audiophile Classics ▲ 101.047
Mozart, W.A.:Alma Dei creatoris, w. Dita Paēgle (sop), Antra Bīgaca (mez), Martins Klisans (ten), Riga Radio Chorus Audiophile Classics ▲ 101.048 [DDD]
Mozart, W.A.:Ave verum corpus, w. Riga Radio Chorus Audiophile Classics ▲ 101.048 [DDD]
Mozart, W.A.:Litaniae Lauretanae, K.195, w. Dita Paēgle (sop), Antra Bīgaca (mez), Martins Klisans (ten), Janis Mārkovs (bass), Riga Radio Chorus Audiophile Classics ▲ 101.048 [DDD]
Mozart, W.A.:Misericordias Domini, w. Riga Radio Chorus Audiophile Classics ▲ 101.048 [DDD]
Mozart, W.A.:Regina coeli, K.276, w. Dita Paēgle (sop), Antra Bīgaca (mez), Martins Klisans (ten), Janis Mārkovs (bass), Riga Radio Chorus Audiophile Classics ▲ 101.048 [DDD]
Mozart, W.A.:Sancta Maria, w. Riga Radio Chorus Audiophile Classics ▲ 101.048 [DDD]
Mozart, W.A.:Te Deum, w. Riga Radio Chorus Audiophile Classics ▲ 101.048 [DDD]
Mozart, W.A.:Venite populi, w. Riga Radio Chorus Audiophile Classics ▲ 101.048 [DDD]

Riga PO

J. Aleksa (cnd)
Vasks, P.:Con Vc, w. David Geringas (vc), *(Riga, Latvia, Dec 1995)* Conifer Classics ▲ 75605-51271-2 [DDD]
Vasks, P.:Sym Strs, *(Riga, Latvia, Dec 1995)* Conifer Classics ▲ 75605-51271-2 [DDD]

K. Rusmanis (cnd)
Vasks, P.:Cantabile Conifer Classics ▲ 75605-51236-2 [DDD]
Vasks, P.:Con E Hn, w. *(soloist unknown)* Conifer Classics ▲ 75605-51236-2 [DDD]
Vasks, P.:Lauda Conifer Classics ▲ 75605-51236-2 [DDD]
Vasks, P.:Message Conifer Classics ▲ 75605-51236-2 [DDD]

Riga PO (cont.)

K. Rusmanis (cnd) (cont.)
Vasks, P.:Musica Dolorosa Conifer Classics ▲ 75605-51236-2 [DDD]

Riga String Quartet [Uldis Sprúdzs (vn), Jurijs Savkins (vn), Einars Rozevics (va), Agne Stepina (vc)]
Erdmann, D.:Sketches (4) *(rec May 15, 1995)* Thorofon ▲ CTH 2284 [ADD/DDD]

Riga Wind Quintet
Vasks, P.:Music for a Deceased Friend *(rec Riga Recording Studio, Latvia, Dec 1995)* Conifer Classics ▲ 51272 [DDD]

Rilke Ensemble
New Music for Choir, w. Ars Nova [cnd:Bo Holten] Kontrapunkt ▲ 32016 [DDD]

Rilke Ensemble members

S. Ehrling (cnd)
Rosenberg, H.:Sym 4, w. Håkan Hagegård (bar), Gothenburg SO, Pro Musica Chamber Choir, Swedish Radio Chorus Caprice ▲ CAP 21429 [DDD]

Rimsky-Korsakov String Quartet
Borodin, A.:Qt 2 Strs Ars Musici ▲ 1137
Glazunov, A.:Qt 5 Strs Ars Musici ▲ 1137

Rinat & Israel Mandolin Ensemble

S. Sperber (cnd)
Fleischer, T.:Oratorio 1492-1992, w. Haifa SO, Israel National Choir Vienna Modern Masters ▲ VMM 3013 [DDD]

Rio de Janeiro Teatro Municipale Orch

N. Rescigno (cnd)
Verdi, G.:La traviata (sels), w. L. Gencer (sop), F. Labò (ten), P. Cappuccilli (bar), Rio de Janeiro Teatro Municipale Chorus *(rec live 8/8/64)* Golden Age of Opera ▲ GAO 120 [ADD]

A. Votto (cnd)
Verdi, G.:La forza del destino (sels), w. Barbato (sop), B. Gigli (ten), E. Mascherini (bar), G. Neri (bass), Rio de Janeiro Teatro Municipale Chorus [I] *(rec live 8/16/51)* Standing Room Only ▲ SRO 807-1 (m) [ADD]

Ritz-Carlton Orch

W. Noll (cnd)
Swing Ye Noël Sony Classical ▲ SFK 62483 ■ SFT 62483

River City Brass Band
Concert in the Park River City Brass Band ▲ BB 192
Footlifters River City Brass Band ▲ BB 191
Pittsburgh on Parade River City Brass Band ▲ BB 193

D. Colwell (cnd)
Christmas!, w. Pittsburgh Mendelssohn Choir [cnd:Robert Page] *(rec Carnegie Library, July 1996)* RCBB ▲ BB 196 A [DDD]

Riverside SO

G. Rothman (cnd)
Davidovsky, M.:Divert Vc, w. F. Sherry (vc) New World ▲ NW 383-2 [DDD]
Korf, A.:Sym 2 New World ▲ NW 383-2 [DDD]
Ruders, P.:Con 1 Vn, w. Rolf Schulte (vn) *(rec SUNY, Purchase, Theater C, Nov 9, 1994)* Bridge ▲ BCD 9057 [DDD]
Wright, M.:Night Scenes New World ▲ NW 383-2 [DDD]

Roberts Wesleyan College Brass Ensemble

R. Shewan (cnd)
Bruckner, A.:Choral Music, w. T.J. Stuart (org), Roberts Wesleyan College Chorale—Ave Maria I [w. E. Stedman (soprano), J. Richardson (mezzo-soprano)]; Ave Maria II; Aequale; Afferentur regi; Aequale II; Germanenzug [w. J. Richardson (tenor), B. Clicker (tenor)]; Inveni David; Tröstrin Musik; Tota pulchra es Maria [w. C. Jones (tenor)]; Or justi meditabitur; Ave Maria III [w. A. Mosher (baritone)]; Christus factus est pro nobis; Ecce sacerdos magnus; Ave Regina coelorum; Virga Jesse floruit; Vexilla regis prodeunt; Das deutsche Lied *(rec Apr. 19–21, 1991)* Albany ▲ TROY 063 [DDD]
Harris, R.:Easter Cant, w. Ann Honeywell (org), Wesleyan College Chorale—Alleluia *(rec St. Louis Roman Catholic Church, Pittsford, NY)* Albany ▲ TROY 164 [DDD]

S. Shewan (cnd)
Shewan, S.:A Feast of Carols, w. Jill Richardson (sop), Alexander Burgess (bar), Roberts Wesleyan College Chorale Albany ▲ TROY 149 [DDD]

Roberts Wesleyan College Wind Ensemble

R. Shewan (cnd)
Shewan, S.:Of Animals & Insects:A Musical Zoo, w. Roberts Wesleyan College Chorale Albany ▲ TROY 149 [DDD]

Eric Robertson Trio
Bolling, C.:Suite 1 Fl, w. Jean Baxtresser (fl) IMP ("Classics" series) ▲ IMP 6700962

Robin Hood Dell Orch Philadelphia

F. Reiner (cnd)
Brahms, J.:Con Vn & Vc, "Double Con", w. N. Milstein (vn), G. Piatigorsky (vc) RCA Gold Seal ▲ 09026-61485-2

Marisa Robles Ensemble
Jeux d'Enfants, w. Christopher Hyde-Smith (fl/pic), Emma Johnson (cl), George MacDonald (cl), Gordon Back (pno), Academy of St. Martin in the Fields [cnd:Neville Marriner], Mexico City PO, Mexico State SO, Royal PO [cnd:Enrique Bátiz], Northern Sinfonia of England [cnd ASV Quicksilva ▲ ASQ 6182
Robertson, E.:The Namia Suite, w. M. Robles (hp), C. Hyde-Smith (fl) ASV ("White Line" series) ▲ WHL 2068 [DDD]

Rochester CO

D. Fetler (cnd)
Hanson, H.:Con Org, w. David Craighead (org), E. Malone (hp) Albany ▲ TROY 129 [ADD]
Hanson, H.:Nymphs & Satyr Albany ▲ TROY 129 [ADD]

Rochester Chamber Players
Schubert, Franz:Adagio & Rondo concertante Vn Vox Box 2-▲ CDX 5033 [ADD]
Schubert, Franz:Qnt Pno, D.667, w. Eugene List (pno) Vox Box 2-▲ CDX 5033 [ADD]

Rochester Opera Theater Orch

P. Stuart (cnd)
Stuart, P.:Kill Bear Comes Home, w. Elana Gizzi (sop—Hasty Girl), Mi-Kyung Huh (sop—Cold Feet), Therese Murray (sop—Song Bird), Cherie Pfeil (sop—1st Sister), Renia Shukis (sop—2nd Sister), Riki Connaughton (mez—4th Sister), Lucy Fee (mez—3rd Sister), David Averbach (ten—Song Leader), Mark Schmidt (ten—Kill Bear), Jason Smith (bar—Cheif Wife Hunter), Rochester Opera Theater Chorus VM ▲ DRK 154 [DDD]

Rochester PO
The Story of Percussion in the Orchestra, w. Nexus, Bill Moyers (nar) Nexus ▲ 10306 [DDD]

P. Nero (cnd)
Classic Connections, w. P. Nero (pno) Pro Arte ▲ CDS 576 [DDD]

T. Bloomfield (cnd)
Rogers, B.:Vars on a Song by Mussorgsky *(rec 1961)* Citadel ▲ CTD 88117 [ADD]

D. Effron (cnd)
Adler, S.:Con Fl, w. Bonita Boyd (fl) *(rec 1983)* Vox Classics ▲ VOX 7509

M. Elder (cnd)
Sullivan, A.:HMS Pinafore, w. D. Hays (sop), M. Rawlins (sgr), C. Freeman (ten), E. Schilling (sgr), E. Johnson (cta), Eastman Chorale members—highlights *(rec 11/89)* Pro Arte ▲ CDd 480 [DDD]
Sullivan, A.:The Mikado, w. D. Hays (sop), M. Rawlins (sgr), C. Freeman (ten), E. Schilling (sgr), E. Johnson (cta), Eastman Chorale members—highlights *(rec 11/89)* Pro Arte ▲ CDd 480 [DDD]
Sullivan, A.:The Pirates of Penzance, w. D. Hays (sgr), M. Rawlins (sgr), C. Freeman (ten), E. Schilling (sgr), E. Johnson (cta), Eastman Chorale members—highlights *(rec 11/89)* Pro Arte ▲ CDd 480 [DDD]

S. Hodkinson (cnd)
Bolcom, W.:Con Pno, w. William Bolcom (pno) *(rec 1983)* Vox Classics ▲ VOX 7509

ORCH. & ENS.

Rochester PO (cont.)
M. Palmer (cnd)
Rorem, N.:Con E Hn, w. Thomas Stacy (E hn) *(rec Eastman Theater, Rochester, NY, Oct. 8, 1994)* New World ▲ 80489-2
D. Zinman (cnd)
Dvořák, A.:Legends, Op. 59—orch. ver. Elektra/Nonesuch ▲ 79066-2 [DDD]
Mendelssohn, F.:A Midsummer Night's Dream (sels)—Ov; Scherzo; Entrance of the Fairy King; Intermezzo; Nocturne; Dance of the Artisans; Wedding March *(rec Eastman Theater, Rochester, NY, 1979 & 1980)* Vox Box 2-▲ CDX 5165
Mendelssohn, F.:Sym 3 *(rec Eastman Theater, Rochester, NY, 1979 & 1980)* Vox Box 2-▲ CDX 5165
Mendelssohn, F.:Sym 4 *(rec Eastman Theater, Rochester, NY, 1979 & 1980)* Vox Box 2-▲ CDX 5165
Mendelssohn, F.:Sym 5 *(rec Eastman Theater, Rochester, NY, 1979 & 1980)* Vox Box 2-▲ CDX 5165
Mozart, W.A.:Con 10 Pnos, w. R. Firkušný (pno), A. Weiss (pno) *(rec 1978)* Vox Box 3-▲ CD3X 3010 [ADD]
Mozart, W.A.:Con 26 Pno, w. B. Snyder (pno) *(rec 1978)* Vox Box 3-▲ CDX 3010 [ADD]
Mozart, W.A.:Missa, K.317, w. C. Bogard (sop), J. de Gaetani (mez), R. White (ten), T. Paul (bass), Roberts Wesleyan College Chorale *(rec 1978)* Allegretto ▲ ACD 8164 [ADD] ■ ACS 8164
Rochester PO
P. Bay (cnd)
Cahn, W.:The Birds, w. Nexus *(rec Apr. 23, 1992)* Nexus ▲ 10317 [DDD]
Cahn, W.:Kebjar-Bali, w. Nexus *(rec Jan. 6, 1994)* Nexus ▲ 10317 [DDD]
Cahn, W.:Voices, w. Nexus *(rec Jan. 6, 1994)* Nexus ▲ 10317 [DDD]
Wyre, J.:Connexus, w. Nexus *(rec Apr. 23, 1992)* Nexus ▲ 10317 [DDD]
Rochester Pops Orch
E. Kunzel (cnd)
Anderson, L.:Music of Pro Arte ▲ CD 264 ■ PCD 264
Rodgers, R.:Music of—Ghost Town; March of the Siamese Children; Sound of Music Medley; South Pacific Medley *(rec 1986–87)* Pro Arte ▲ CDD 275 [DDD]
Rodgers, R.:Slaughter on 10th Avenue *(rec 1986–87)* Pro Arte ▲ CDD 275 [DDD]
Kunzel, Schuller (cnd)
Gershwin, G.:Music of, w. Russell Sherman (pno), Orch of St. Luke—American in Paris; Con in F; Rhap in Blue; etc. Pro Arte ▲ CDM 814; ■ PCD 814
N. Wayland (cnd)
Anderson, L.:Music of—13 compositions *(rec June 29, 1988)* Pro Arte ▲ CDD 414 [DDD]
Rococo Trio [Niels Eje (ob), Inge Mulvad Eje (vc), Lillian Törnqvist (hp)]
Crystal Bridge Danacord ▲ DACOCD 346 [DDD]
Mozart, W.A.:Diverts [trans. for oboe, cello & harp]—K.253 & 299 *(rec Mar. 1988)* Danacord ▲ DACOCD 326 [DDD]
Mozart, W.A.:Sons Vn Pno (misc) [trans. for oboe, cello & harp]—K.28 *(rec Mar. 1988)* Danacord ▲ DACOCD 326 [DDD]
Norwegian Wood:A Classical Take on Beatles Classics RCA ▲ 09026-22488-2 ■ 09026-22488-4
Trio Rococo Plays Rococo Trios Danacord ▲ DACOCD 350 [DDD]
Rodin String Quartet
Lachner, I.:Qts Strs—in A, Op. 74; in B, Op. posth. Amati ▲ AMi 9503 [DDD]
Rogeri Trio [Yoshiko Endo (pno), Nadia Myerscough (vn), Peter Adams (vc)]
Dvořák, A.:Trio 2 Pno Meridian ▲ MER 84294 [DDD]
Smetana, B.:Trio Pno Meridian ▲ MER 84294 [DDD]
Suk, J.:Elegie Meridian ▲ MER 84294 [DDD]
Röhn Trio [A. Röhn (vn), K. Moser (vc), K. Hindart (pno)]
Brahms, J.:Trio 1 Pno Calig ▲ CAL 50932
Brahms, J.:Trio 2 Pno Calig ▲ CAL 50932
Dvořák, A.:Trio 4 Pno, "Dumky" Calig ▲ CAL 50925
Korngold, E.W.:Son Vn Calig ▲ CAL 50905 [DDD]
Korngold, E.W.:Trio Pno Calig ▲ CAL 50905 [DDD]
Smetana, B.:Trio Pno Calig ▲ CAL 50925
Taneyev, S.:Trio Pno *(rec Studio 2 of the Bavarian Radio, Sept 19, 1995)* Calig ▲ CAL 50951 [DDD]
Tchaikovsky, P.:Trio Pno *(rec Studio 2 of the Bavarian Radio, July 12–13, 1995)* Calig ▲ CAL 50951 [DDD]
Rollin' Phones
Bozza, E.:Andante & Scherzo BIS ▲ CD 466 [DDD]
Françaix, J.:Petit Quatuor BIS ▲ CD 466 [DDD]
Glazunov, A.:Qt Saxes BIS ▲ CD 466 [DDD]
Singelée, J.–B.:Qt 1 Sax BIS ▲ CD 466 [DDD]
Romande Instrumental Group Rockband
J. Auberson (cnd)
Schibler, A.:La Folie de Tristan, w. Audrey Michael (sop—Iseut), Arlette Chédel (mez—Brangien), Pierre-André Blaser (ten—Tristan), Philippe Huttenlocher (bar—Le roi Marc/Le pêcheur/Le portier), André Fauré (nar), William Jacques (nar), Snezana Zivojinovic (nar), Lausanne CO, Swiss Romande Radio Choir *(rec live, Festival de Montreux, Sept 15, 1980)* Jecklin ▲ JD 695
La Romanesca
Codax, M.:Cantigas d'amigo (7) Move ▲ MD 3044 [DDD]
Medieval Monodies Move ▲ MD 3044 [DDD]
Musica en Tiempos de Velázquez *(rec 1992)* Glossa ▲ GCD 920201 [DDD]
La Romanesca [A. Manze (baroque vn), N. North (lt/thb), J. Toll (hpd/org)]
Biber, H. von:Sons Vn & Continuo—8 Sons. *(rec East Woodhay, UK, Sept. 15–18, 1993 & Jan.)* Harmonia Mundi USA 2-▲ HMU 907134/35
Biber, H. von:Son violino solo representativa *(rec East Woodhay, UK, Sept. 15–18, 1993 & Jan.)* Harmonia Mundi USA 2-▲ HMU 907134/35
Schmelzer, J.H.:Sons Instrs Harmonia Mundi ▲ HMU 907143
Vivaldi, A.:Sons Vn, Op. 2 Harmonia Mundi USA 2-▲ HMU 907089/90
Romanesque [Hannelore Devaere (hp), Sophie Watillon (b vl), Piet Stryckers (b vl/perc), Frank Liegeois (b vl), Bert Coen (fls), Philippe Malfeyt (lt/chit/perc)]
Willaert, A.:Madrigals, w. Katelijne Van Laethem (sop)—Qual dolcezza giamai; Zoia zentil; Dessus le marché d'Arras; Allons, allons gay; Canzon di Adriano; Quante volte diss'io; Vecchie letrose; Chi la dira; Chi la dira Disminuita; Tiento IV sobre "Qui la dira"; E se per gelosia; Un giorno mi pregò; A la fontana; Cingari simo; O quando a quando havea; Joyssance vous donneray; Joyssance; Arousez vo violette; O bene mio famm'uno favore; Occhio non fu; Sempre mi ride sta Ricercar ▲ 151145
Willaert, A.:Ricercars, w. Katelijne Van Laethem (sop)—Ricercar X Ricercar ▲ 151145
Romanian National RSO
H. Andreescu (cnd)
Enescu, G.:Andantino Olympia ▲ OLY 495
Enescu, G.:Mélodies, Op. 4, w. Christina Anghelescu (vn), Romanian National Radio Chorus—No. 1 [arr for Vn & Orch] Olympia ▲ OLY 496
Enescu, G.:School Syms (4), w. Romanian National Radio Chorus—No. 1 in d Olympia ▲ OLY 496
Enescu, G.:Suite 2 Orch Olympia ▲ OLY 495
Enescu, G.:Suite 3 Orch, "Villageoise" Olympia ▲ OLY 495
Enescu, G.:Vox maris, w. Robert Nagy (ten), Romanian National Radio Chorus Olympia ▲ OLY 496
L. Baci (cnd)
Vieru, A.:Sym 5, w. Romanian Radio Chorus Olympia ▲ OCD 409 [AAD]
I. Conta (cnd)
Niculescu, S.:Concertante Sym 3, w. D. Kientzy (sax) Olympia ("Explorer" series) ▲ OCD 410 [AAD]
A. Vieru (cnd)
Vieru, A.:Con Vn Vc, w. O. Kagan (vn), N. Gutman (vc) Olympia ▲ OCD 409 [AAD]

Romanian Opera Orch
J. Bobescu (cnd)
Verdi, G.:Rigoletto, w. Victoria Draganescu (sop—Countess Ceprano), Magda Ianculescu (sop—Gilda), Dorothea Palade (mez—Maddalena), Valeria Savu (mez—Giovanna), Ion Buzea (ten—Duke of Mantua), Dimitrie Scurtu (ten—Borsa), Nicolae Herlea (bar—Rigoletto), Stefan Petrescu (bar—Marullo), Jean Banescu (bass—Count Ceprano), Nicolae Florei (bass—Monterone), Nicolae Rafael (bass—Sparafucile), Romanian Opera Chorus *(rec 1965)* Vox Box 2-▲ CDX 5162
Verdi, G.:La traviata, w. Elena Simionescu (sop—Annina), Virginia Zeani (sop—Violetta Valery), Elisabeta Neculce-Cartis (mez—Flera Bervoix), Ion Buzea (ten—Alfredo Germont), Vasile Moldoveanu (ten—Gastone/Viconte de Letorieres/Giuseppe), Teodor Panea (ten—Flora's Servant), Constantin Dumitru (bar—Commissioner/Baron Douphol), Nicolae Herlea (bar—Giorgio Germont), Valentin Loghin (bass—Marchese D'Obigny), Nicolae Rafael (bass—Doctor Grenvil), Stelian Olariu (cnd), Romanian Opera Chorus *(rec 1968)* Vox Box 2-▲ CDX 5154
M. Brediceanu (cnd)
Rossini, G.:Il barbiere di Siviglia, w. Magda Ianculescu (sop—Rosina), Maria Sandulescu (mez—Berta), Valentin Teodorian (ten—Count Almaviva), Nicolae Herlea (bar—Figaro), Stefan Petrescu (bar—Fiorello), Constantin Gabor (bass—Don Bartolo), Valentin Loghin (bass—Don Basilio), Romanian Opera Chorus *(rec 1960–61)* Vox Box 2-▲ CDX 5159
E. Massini (cnd)
Verdi, G.:Il trovatore, w. Elena Dima (sop—Leonora), Victoria Draganescu (sop—Ines), Zenaida Pally (mez—Azucena), Ion Buzea (ten—Duke of Mantua), Constantin Iliescu (ten—Ruiz), Cornel Stavru (ten—Manrico), Octav Enigarescu (bar—Count di Luna), Constantin Dumitru (bass—Ferrando), Romanian Opera Chorus *(rec 1960–61)* Vox Box 2-▲ CDX 5163
C. Petrovici (cnd)
Donizetti, G.:Lucia di Lammermoor, w. Silvia Voinea (sop—Lucia), Lucia Cicoara (mez—Alisa), Florin Georgescu (ten—Edgardo), Gabriel Nastase (ten—Arturo), Nicolae Herlea (bar—Lord Enrico), Pompei Harasteanu (bass—Raimondo), Romanian Opera Chorus *(rec 1984)* Vox Box 2-▲ CDX 5164
Puccini, G.:La Bohème, w. Elvira Cirje-Druica (sop—Musetta), Eugenia Moldoveanu (sop—Mimi), Andrei Borsos (ten—Parpignol), Constantin Gabor (ten—Alcindoro), Ludovic Spiess (ten—Rodolfo), Lucian Marinescu (bar—Schaunard), David Ohanesian (bar—Marcello), Pompei Harasteanu (bass—Benoit), Dan Zancu (bass—Colline), Romanian Opera Chorus *(rec 1982)* Vox Box 2-▲ CDX 5156
C. Trailescu (cnd)
Puccini, G.:Tosca, w. Virginia Zeani (sop—Floria Tosca), Emilia Oprea (mez—Shepherd), Nicolae Andreescu (ten—Spoletta), Corneliu Fanateanu (ten—Mario Cavaradossi), Nicolae Herlea (bar—Baron Scarpia), Gheorghe Crasnaru (bass—Cesare Angelotti), Constantin Gabor (bass—Sacristan), Pompei Harasteanu (bass—Jailer), Adrian Stefanescu (bass—Sciarrone), Romanian Opera Chorus *(rec Sept 1977)* Vox Box 2-▲ CDX 5153
Romanian Radio Orch
H. Andreescu (cnd)
Enescu, G.:Concert Ov Olympia ▲ OLY 441 [DDD]
Enescu, G.:Romanian Rhap 1 Olympia ▲ OLY 442 [DDD]
Enescu, G.:Romanian Rhap 2 Olympia ▲ OLY 442 [DDD]
Enescu, G.:School Syms (4)—No. 4 in E♭ Olympia ▲ OLY 441 [DDD]
Enescu, G.:Sym 1 Olympia ▲ OLY 441 [DDD]
Enescu, G.:Sym 2 Olympia ▲ OLY 442 [DDD]
Niyazi (cnd)
Khachaturian, A.:Con Vn, w. J. Sotkovetsky (vn) *(rec 1954)* Russian Disc ▲ RUS 15 009 [AAD]
Romanian RSO
C. Litvin (cnd)
Romanian Rhapsody, w. Cluj-Napoca PO [cnd:Emil Simon], Arad PO [cnd:Eliodor Rau] Olympia ("Explorer" series) ▲ OCD 408 [AAD]
Romanian Radio-TV Orch
I. Conta (cnd)
Constantinescu, P.:Con Hp, w. E. Gantolea (hpd) *(rec 1981)* Olympia ▲ OCD 415 [AAD]
Enescu, G.:Romanian Poem, w. Romanian Radio-TV Chorus Stradivari Classics ▲ SCD 6038 [DDD] ■ SMC 6038 (D)
Enescu, G.:Romanian Poem, w. Romanian Radio-TV Chorus Marco Polo ▲ 8.223146
Enescu, G.:Romanian Rhap 1 Stradivari Classics ▲ SCD 6038 [DDD] ■ SMC 6038 (D)
Enescu, G.:Romanian Rhap 1 Marco Polo ▲ 8.223146
Enescu, G.:Romanian Rhap 2 Stradivari Classics ▲ SCD 6038 [DDD] ■ SMC 6038 (D)
Enescu, G.:Romanian Rhap 2 Marco Polo ▲ 8.223146
Enescu, G.:Suite 1 Orch Marco Polo ▲ 8.223144
Enescu, G.:Suite 2 Orch Marco Polo ▲ 8.223144
Enescu, G.:Suite 3 Orch, "Villageoise" Marco Polo ▲ 8.223145
Enescu, G.:Symphonie concertante, w. V. Arcu (vc) Marco Polo ▲ 8.223141
C. Litvin (cnd)
Puccini, G.:Turandot, w. Teodora Lucaciu (sop—Liù), Maria Slatinaru (sop—Princess Turandot), Corneliu Finateanu (ten—Pong), George Mircea (ten—Emperor Altoum), Ludovic Speiss (ten—Prince Calaf), Valentin Teodorian (ten—Pang), Octav Enigarescu (bar—Ping), Dionisie Konya (bar—A Mandarin), Mircea Stefanescu (bar—The Prince of Persia), Nicolae Florei (bass—Timur), Romanian Radio-TV Chorus *(rec Jan 1970)* Vox Box 2-▲ CDX 5160
Verdi, G.:La forza del destino, w. Maria Nistor-Slatinaru (sop—Donna Leonora), Mihaela Mariacineanu (mez—Curra), Zenaida Pally (mez—Preziosilla), Ludovic Speiss (ten—Don Alvaro), Ion Stoian (ten—Trabucco), Nicolae Herlea (bar—Don Carlo), Nicolae Florei (bass—Padre Guardiano) Constantin Gabor (bass—Fra Melitone), Dan Musetescu (bass—An Alcalde), Mihai Panghe (bass—Marquis of Calatrava), Romanian Radio-TV Chorus *(rec Jan 1970)* Vox Box 3-▲ CD3X 3038
P. Popescu (cnd)
Bentoiu, P.:Sym 5 *(rec 1983)* Olympia ▲ OCD 416 [AAD]
C. Silvestri (cnd)
Enescu, G.:Concert Ov Marco Polo ▲ 8.223144
Romanian State Orch
H. Andreescu (cnd)
Glazunov, A.:Carnaval Marco Polo ▲ 8.220487 [DDD]
Glazunov, A.:Cortège solennel Marco Polo ▲ 8.220487 [DDD]
Glazunov, A.:Idylle & Rêverie orientale Marco Polo ▲ 8.220487 [DDD]
Glazunov, A.:Les Ruses d'amour Marco Polo ▲ 8.220485 [DDD]
Glazunov, A.:Scène dansante Marco Polo ▲ 8.220487 [DDD]
Glazunov, A.:Serenades, Opp. 7 & 11 Marco Polo ▲ 8.220487 [DDD]
Glazunov, A.:Wedding Procession Marco Polo ▲ 8.220487 [DDD]
Romanian State PO
R. Edlinger (cnd)
Gretchaninoff, A.:Sym 1 Marco Polo ▲ 8.223163
Romantic Trio
Rubinstein, A.:Trio 1 Pno Russian Disc ▲ RUS 10041 [DDD]
Rubinstein, A.:Trio 3 Pno Russian Disc ▲ RUS 10041 [DDD]
Rome CO
N. Flagello (cnd)
Britten, B.:Simple Sym *(rec Oct. 1977)* Phoenix ▲ PHCD 119 [ADD]
Flagello, N.:The Land, w. Ezio Flagello (bass) Citadel ▲ CTD 88115 [ADD/DDD]
Flagello, N.:Serenade Citadel ▲ CTD 88115 [ADD/DDD]
Flagello, N.:Sym 2, "Sym of the Winds" Citadel ▲ CTD 88115 [ADD/DDD]
Hovhaness, Diamon, Barber & Others *(rec 1977)* Citadel ▲ CTD 88107 [ADD]
Warlock, P.:Capriol Suite *(rec Oct. 1977)* Phoenix ▲ PHCD 119 [ADD]
E. Müller (cnd)
Tosti, P.F.:Songs, w. C. Bergonzi (ten) [I] Orfeo ▲ 073831 [DDD]

▲ = CD ♦ = Enhanced CD Δ = MD ■ = Cassette Tape □ = DCC

Rome CO (cont.)
V. de Sabata (cnd)
Verdi, G.:Requiem Mass (sels), w. M. Caniglia (sop), E. Stignani (mez), B. Gigli (ten), T. Pasero (bass), Rome RAI Chorus, Turin RAI Chorus—Dies irae; Sanctus; Libera me *(rec Dec. 14, 1940)* Legato Classics 2-▲ LCD 178-2

Rome Festival Orch
C. Bertolini (cnd)
Tchaikovsky, P.:Sleeping Beauty (suite) Vivace ▲ E 505 [DDD]
Tchaikovsky, P.:Swan Lake (suite) Vivace ▲ E 505 [DDD]
B. Mersson (cnd)
Chopin, F.:Con 2 Pno, w. Christian Favre (pno)—Larghetto Intercord ▲ INT 892.923 [AAD]

Rome Italian Radio-TV Orch
S. Celibidache (cnd)
Strauss, R.:4 Last Songs, w. G. Janowitz (sop) *(rec 4/12/69)* Arkadia ▲ 570 [ADD]
F. Scaglia (cnd)
Verdi, G.:Arias, w. A. Stella (sop)—arias from Ernani & Forza del destino [I] *(rec live 9/5/59)* Melodram 2-▲ MEL 27068 (m) [AAD]

Rome New Virtuosi Orch
Vivaldi, A.:Cons Vn (misc)—6 concerti RCA Victrola ▲ 7741-2-RV [DDD] ■ 7741-4-RV (CrO2)

Rome Opera CO
M. Panni (cnd)
Pergolesi, G.B.:Adriano in Siria, w. D. Dessi (sop), J. Omilian (sop), L. Mazzaria (sop), S. Anselmi (sop), G. Banditelli (cta), E. di Cesare (ten) [I] *(rec live 12/20/86)* Bongiovanni 3-▲ GB 2078/80 [DDD]

Rome Opera Orch
Puccini, G.:Il trittico, w. V. de los Angeles (sop), F. Barbieri (mez), G. Prandelli (ten), T. Gobbi (bar), *(other soloists unknown)*, Rome Opera Chorus *(rec Rome, 1950s)* EMI Classics 3-▲ CDMC 64165 (m)
Three Tenors of the Golden Age, w. J. Björling (ten), Mario Lanza (ten), Jan Peerce (ten), John Corigliano (vn), Constantine Callinicos (pno), Frederick Schauwecker (pno), RCA Victor Orch [cnd:Renato Cellini, Constantine Callinicos, Erich Leinsdorf, Sylvan Levin, Maximilian Pilzer, Frieder Weissmann], Rome Opera Orch, Rome Opera Chorus, et al. RCA Gold Seal ▲ 09026-68531-2 [ADD] ■ 09026-68531-4

N. Annovazzi (cnd)
Massenet, J.:Manon, w. V. De los Angeles (sop), F. Tagliavini (ten), A. Poli (bar), Rome Opera Chorus *(rec live 1957)* Melodram 2-▲ MEL 27082
J. Barbirolli (cnd)
Puccini, G.:Madama Butterfly, w. R. Scotto (sop), A. di Stasio (mez), C. Bergonzi (ten), R. Panerai (bar), Rome Opera Chorus [I] EMI Classics ("Studio" series) ▲ CDM 63411 ■ EG 63411
Puccini, G.:Madama Butterfly, w. R. Scotto (sop), C. Bergonzi (ten), R. Panerai (bar), Rome Opera Chorus EMI Classics 2-▲ CDMB 69654
Puccini, G.:Madama Butterfly (sels), w. R. Scotto (sop), C. Bergonzi (ten), Rome Opera Chorus EMI Classics ■ 4XS 36567

B. Bartoletti (cnd)
Ponchielli, A.:La Gioconda, w. Leyla Gencer (sop), Anna di Stasio (mez), Gianni Raimondi (ten), Ruggero Raimondi (bass), Rome Opera Chorus Melodram 3-▲ CDM 37092
A. Basile (cnd)
Verdi, G.:Il trovatore, w. L. Price (sop), R. Elias (mez), G. Tucker (ten), L. Warren (bar), G. Tozzi (bass) RCA Gold Seal 2-▲ 60560-2-RG [ADD] 2-■ 60560-4-RG (CrO2)
V. Bellezza (cnd)
Puccini, G.:La fanciulla del West (sels), w. Magda Olivero (sop—Minnie), Corinna Vozza (mez—Wowkle), Paolo Caroli (ten—Harry), Giacomo Lauri-Volpi (ten—Dick Johnson), Marco Rogani (ten—Pony Express Rider), Salvatore di Tommaso (ten—Trin), Adelio Zagonara (ten—Nick), Virgilio Ascorro (bar—Sid), Alfredo Colella (bar—Jake Wallace), Giuseppe Forgione (bar—Bello), Giancarlo Guelfi (bar—Jack Rance), Arturo la Porta (bar—Sonora), Gino Conti (bass—José Castro), Piere Passarotti (bass—Bill), Enzo Titta (bass—Larkens), Giulio Tomei (bass—Ashby), Rome Opera Chorus—Minnie, dalla mia casa son partito; Laggiù nel Soledad; Chi c'è per farmi i ricci; Oh! Mister Johnson, siete rimasto; Non so ben neppur io; Io non son che una povera fanciulla; No, Minnie, non piangete; Vorrei mettermi queste; Hallo!; Oh, se sapeste; Credo che abbiate torto; Ma ti giuro ch'io non ti lascio più; Vieni fuori!; Una parola sola!...Or son sei mesi; Che c'è di nuovo Jack?; È là; Siete pronto; Ch'ella mi creda; È Minniel...È Minnie! *(rec Rome, Mar. 30, 1957)* Golden Age of Opera ▲ GAO 180 [ADD]
Verdi, G.:Aida (sels), w. M. Callas (sop), E. Stignani (mez), M. Picchi (ten), R. De Falchi (bar), G. Neri (bass)—five arias with Callas (solo, three duets & quintet) *(rec live 10/2/50)* Melodram 2-▲ CDM 26019 [AAD]

F. Capuana (cnd)
Verdi, G.:Alzira, w. V. Zeani (sop), G. Cecchele (ten), C. MacNeil (bar), C. Cava (bass), Rome Opera Chorus [I] *(rec live 3/16/67)* Melodram 2-▲ MEL 27013 (m) [AAD]
Verdi, G.:Alzira, w. V. Zeani (sop), G. Cecchele (ten), C. MacNeil (bar), C. Cava (bass), Rome Opera Chorus [I] *(rec live, 3/16/67)* Verona 2-▲ 27042/43 (m) [AAD]
O. de Fabritiis (cnd)
Puccini, G.:Madama Butterfly, w. Toti dal Monte (sop—Madama Butterfly), Maria Huder (mez—Kate Pinkerton), Beniamino Gigli (ten—B.F. Pinkerton), Adelio Zagonara (ten—Goro), Mario Basiola (bar—Sharpless), Gino Conti (bass—Principe Yamadori), Ernesto Dominici (bass—Il Bonzo), Vittoria Paolombini (sgr—Suzuki), Giuseppe Conca (cnd), Rome Opera Chorus *(rec Aug 1939)* Arkadia 2-▲ CD 78004 (m) [ADD]
Verdi, G.:Il trovatore, w. Fedora Barbieri (mez), Franco Corelli (ten), Ettore Bastianini (bar), Agostino Ferrin (bass), Mirella Parutto (sgr), Rome Opera Chorus Stradivarius 2-▲ STV DTM 12313 [ADD]
G. Gavazzeni (cnd)
Verdi, G.:I lombardi alla prima crociata, w. R. Scotto (sop), L. Pavarotti (ten), R. Raimondi (bass), Rome Opera Chorus [I] *(rec live, Rome, 11/20/69)* Memories 2-▲ HR 4337/38 [ADD]
Verdi, G.:I lombardi alla prima crociata (sels), w. Sofia Mazzetti (sop), Luciano Pavarotti (ten)—O madre mia...La mia letizia infondere *(rec live, Nov. 20, 1969)* RCA Gold Seal ▲ 09026-68014-2 [ADD]
Verdi, G.:I masnadieri, w. I. Ligabue (sop), G. Raimondi (ten), R. Bruson (bar), B. Christoff (bass), Rome Opera Chorus [I] *(rec live, Rome, Nov. 25, 1972)* Golden Age of Opera 2-▲ GAO 135/36 [ADD]
Verdi, G.:Stiffelio, w. Gulin-Dominguez (sop), G. Limarilli (ten), G. Guelfi (bar), Rome Opera Chorus *(rec live, Rome 1964)* Melodram 2-▲ MEL 27033
Verdi, G.:I vespri siciliani, w. L. Gencer (sop), G. Limarilli (ten), G. Guelfi (bar), N. Rossi-Lemeni (bass), Rome Opera Chorus [I] *(rec live, Rome 1964)* Melodram 2-▲ MEL 27037 [ADD]
Verdi, G.:I vespri siciliani, w. Leyla Gencer (sop), Giangiacomo Guelfi (bar), Nicola Rossi-Lemeni (bass), Gastone Limarilli (sgr), Rome Opera Chorus *(rec Dec 5, 1964)* Pantheon 2-▲ PHE 6770
C. M. Giulini (cnd)
Verdi, G.:Rigoletto (sels), w. Luciano Pavarotti (ten)—La Donna è mobile Goldies ▲ GLD 63202 [ADD]
V. Gui (cnd)
Boito, A.:Mefistofele, w. Orietta Moscucci (sop—Margherita), Amalia Pini (mez—Martha), Piero de Palma (ten—Wagner), Giacinto Prandelli (ten—Faust), Boris Christoff (bass—Mefistofele), Rome Opera Chorus EMI Classics 2-▲ CDMB 65655
C. M. Guilini (cnd)
Verdi, G.:Rigoletto (sels), w. Renata Scotto (sop—Gilda), Corinna Vozza (mez—Giovanna), Bianca Vortoluzzi (cta—Maddalena), Luciano Pavarotti (ten—Duke of Mantua), Kostas Paskalis (bar—Rigoletto), Paolo Washington (bass—Sparafucile), Rome Opera Chorus Budget ("The Greatest Voice in Opera" series) ▲ SYP 104

J. Latham-König (cnd)
Donizetti, G.:Poliuto, w. E. Connell (sop), N. Martinucci (ten), R. Bruson (bar), Rome Opera Chorus [I] *(rec live, 1988)* Nuova Era 2-▲ 6776/77 [DDD]
E. Leinsdorf (cnd)
Donizetti, G.:Lucia di Lammermoor, w. Roberta Peters (sop—Lucia), Mitì Truccato Pace (mez—Alisa), Jan Peerce (ten—Edgardo), Piero de Palma (ten—Lord Arturo Bucklaw), Mario Carlin (ten—Normanno), Philip Maero (bar—Lord Enrico Ashton), Giorgio Tozzi (bass—Raimondo), Rome Opera Chorus *(rec Rome Opera House, Aug 5-14, 1957)* RCA Living Stereo 2-▲ 09026-68537-2 [ADD]
Puccini, G.:La Bohème, w. A. Moffo (sop), F. Costa (mez), G. Tucker (ten), R. Merrill (bar), G. Tozzi (bass), Rome Opera Chorus [I] RCA Gold Seal 2-▲ 3969-2-RG [ADD] 2-■ 3969-4-RG (CrO2)

Rome Opera Orch (cont.)
E. Leinsdorf (cnd) (cont.)
Puccini, G.:La Bohème (sels), w. A. Moffo (sop), F. Costa (mez), G. Tucker (ten), R. Merrill (bar), G. Tozzi (bass), Rome Opera Chorus RCA Gold Seal ▲ 60189-2-RG [ADD] ■ 60189-4-RG (CrO2)
Puccini, G.:Madama Butterfly, w. A. Moffo (sop), R. Elias (mez), C. Valletti (ten), R. Cesari (bar), Rome Opera Chorus [I] RCA Gold Seal 2-▲ 4145-2-RG [ADD]
Puccini, G.:Madama Butterfly, w. A. Moffo (sop), R. Elias (mez), C. Valletti (ten), R. Cesari (bar), Rome Opera Chorus [I] RCA Gold Seal ▲ 60202-2-RG [ADD] ■ 60202-4-RG
Puccini, G.:Tosca, w. Z. Milanov (sop), J. Björling (ten), L. Warren (bar), Rome Opera Chorus [I] RCA Gold Seal 2-▲ 4514-2-RG [ADD] 2-■ 4514-2-RG
Puccini, G.:Tosca (sels), w. Z. Milanov (sop), J. Björling (ten), L. Warren (bar), Rome Opera Chorus RCA Gold Seal ▲ 60192-2-RG [ADD] ■ 60192-4-RG (CrO2)
Puccini, G.:Turandot, w. Birgit Nilsson (sop—Turandot), Renata Tebaldi (sop—Liù), Jussi Björling (ten—Calaf), Alessio De Paolis (ten—Emperor Altoum), Piero de Palma (ten—Pang), Mario Sereni (bar—Ping), Adelio Zagonara (bar—Prince of Persia), Giorgio Tozzi (bass—Timur), Tommaso Frascati (bass—Pong), Leonardo Monreale (bass—Mandarin), Rome Opera Chorus *(rec Rome Opera House, July 3-11, 1959)* RCA Living Stereo 2-▲ 09026-62687-2 [ADD]
Puccini, G.:Turandot, w. B. Nilsson (sop), R. Tebaldi (sop), J. Bjoerling (ten), G. Tozzi (bass), Rome Opera Chorus [I] RCA Red Seal 2-▲ 5932-2-RC 3-■ AGK3-3970
E. Leinsdorf, J. Perlea (cnds)
O Paradiso:Great Opera Arias, w. J. Björling (ten), Frederick Schauwecker (pno), RCA Victor Orch [cnd:Renato Cellini], Robert Shaw Chorale [cnd:Robert Shaw] *(rec 1951-1959)* RCA Gold Seal ▲ 09026-68429-2 [ADD]
Z. Mehta (cnd)
Verdi, G.:Aida (sels), w. B. Nilsson (sop), G. Bumbry (mez), F. Corelli (ten) [I] [highlights] EMI Classics (Classics for Pleasure) ▲ CDM 64035
F. Molinari-Pradelli (cnd)
Donizetti, G.:L'elisir d'amore, w. M. Freni (sop), N. Gedda (ten), R. Capecchi (bar), M. Sereni (bar) [I] EMI Classics (Studio) 2-▲ CDMB 69897 [ADD]
Puccini, G.:Turandot, w. B. Nilsson (sop), R. Scotto (sop), F. Corelli (ten), B. Giaiotti (bass), Rome Opera Chorus [I] EMI Classics ("Studio" series) 2-▲ CDMB 69327 [ADD]
D. Oren (cnd)
Basic 100, Vol. 78, w. Raina Kabaivanska (sop), Luciano Pavarotti (ten), Ingvar Wixell (bar) RCA Victor ▲ 09026-68455-2 ■ 09026-68455-4
Puccini, G.:Tosca, w. R. Kaibaivanska (sop—Floria), L. Pavarotti (ten—Mario), I. Wixell (bar—Scarpia), F. Federici (bass—Angelotti), Rome Opera Chorus RCA Red Seal 2-▲ 09026-61806-2
Puccini, G.:Tosca, w. R. Kaibaivanska (sop—Floria), L. Pavarotti (ten—Mario), I. Wixell (bar—Scarpia), F. Federici (bass—Angelotti), Rome Opera Chorus RCA Red Seal ▲ 09026-61807-2; ■ 09026-61807-4
Puccini, G.:Tosca (sels), w. Raina Kabaivanska (sop), Luciano Pavarotti (ten), Ingvar Wixell (bar) RCA ("Basic 100" series) ▲ 09026-68455-2 ■ 09026-68455-4

A. Paoletti (cnd)
Puccini, G.:La Bohème, w. Schimenti (sop), Micheluzi (sgr), G. Lauri-Volpi (ten), G. Ciavola (bass), Rome Opera Chorus *(rec 1952)* Bongiovanni 2-▲ GB 1057/58 [ADD]
J. Perlea (cnd)
Puccini, G.:Manon Lescaut, w. L. Albanese (sop), J. Bjoerling (ten), R. Merrill (bar), Rome Opera Chorus [I] RCA Gold Seal 2-▲ 60573-2-RG [ADD]
Verdi, G.:Aida, w. Z. Milanov (sop), F. Barbieri (mez), J. Björling (ten), L. Warren (bar), B. Christoff (bass), Rome Opera Chorus [I] RCA Gold Seal 3-▲ 6652-2-RG (m) [ADD] 3-■ ALK3-5380 (m)
Verdi, G.:Aida, w. Z. Milanov (sop), F. Barbieri (mez), J. Björling (ten), L. Warren (bar), B. Christoff (bass), Rome Opera Chorus [I] RCA Gold Seal ▲ 60201-2-RG (m) [ADD] ■ 60201-4-RG (m)
Verdi, G.:Rigoletto, w. R. Peters (sop), J. Björling (ten), R. Merrill (bar), G. Tozzi (bass), Rome Opera Chorus [I] RCA Gold Seal 2-▲ 60172-2-RG [ADD] 2-■ 60172-4-RG (CrO2)
F. Previtali (cnd)
Verdi, G.:Don Carlos, w. L. Gencer (sop), F. Cossotto (mez), B. Prevedi (ten), S. Bruscantini (bar), N. Ghiaurov (bass), Rome Opera Chorus *(rec live)* Melodram 3-▲ MEL 37022
Verdi, G.:La traviata, w. A. Moffo (sop), G. Tucker (ten), R. Merrill (bar) [I] RCA Gold Seal ▲ 60204-2-RG [ADD] ■ 60204-4-RG
Verdi, G.:La traviata, w. A. Moffo (sop), G. Tucker (ten), R. Merrill (bar) [I] RCA Gold Seal 2-▲ 4144-2-RG [ADD] 2-■ 4144-4-RG

G. Santini (cnd)
Bellini, V.:Norma (sels), w. M. Callas (sop), M. Pirazzini (mez), F. Corelli (ten), P. De Palma (ten), Rome Opera Chorus [I] *(rec live 1/2/58)* Melodram ▲ MEL 16000 (m) [AAD]
Giordano, U.:Andrea Chénier, w. A. Stella (sop—Maddalena), F. Corelli (ten—Andrea Chénier), M. Sereni (bar—Carlo Gerard), Rome Opera Chorus EMI Classics ▲ CDMB 65287
Mascagni, P.:Cavalleria rusticana, w. V. De los Angeles (sop), F. Corelli (ten), Rome Opera Chorus [I] EMI Classics ("Studio" series) 2-▲ CDMB 63967
Puccini, G.:Madama Butterfly, w. V. de los Angeles (sop), M. Pirazzini (mez), J. Bjoerling (ten), M. Sereni (bar), Rome Opera Chorus [I] EMI Classics ("Studio" series) 2-▲ CDMB 63634 [ADD]
T. Schippers (cnd)
Puccini, G.:La Bohème, w. M. Freni (sop), N. Gedda (ten), M. Sereni (bar), Rome Opera Chorus [I] EMI Classics ("Studio" series) 2-▲ CDMB 69657
Puccini, G.:La Bohème (sels), w. M. Freni (sop), N. Gedda (ten), M. Sereni (bar), Rome Opera Chorus EMI Classics ("Studio" series) ▲ CDM 63932 ■ EG 63932
T. Serafin (cnd)
Italian Opera Arias, w. J. Vickers (ten) *(rec Rome, July 1961)* VAI Audio ▲ VAIA 1016 [AAD]
Verdi, G.:Un ballo in maschera, w. Maria Caniglia (sop—Amelia), Fedora Barbieri (mez—Ulrica), Beniamino Gigli (ten—Riccardo), Gino Bechi (bar—Renato), Tancredi Pasero (bass—Samuel), Blando Giusti (sgr—Un Giudice), Nicola Niccolini (sgr—Silvano), Ugo Novelli (sgr—Tom), Elda Ribetti (sgr—Oscar), Giuseppe Conca (cnd), Rome Opera Chorus *(rec 1943)* Arkadia 2-▲ CD 78005 (m) [ADD]
Verdi, G.:Un ballo in maschera, w. Maria Caniglia (sop), Fedora Barbieri (cta), Beniamino Gigli (ten), Gino Bechi (bar), Rome Opera Chorus *(rec Rome, July, 1943)* Grammofono 2000 2-▲ GRM 78556
Verdi, G.:Requiem Mass, w. Maria Caniglia (sop), Ebe Stignani (cta), Benjamino Gigli (ten), Ezio Pinza (bass), Rome Opera Chorus *(rec 1939)* Pearl ▲ PEA 9162 [ADD]
G. Solti (cnd)
Verdi, G.:Aida, w. L. Price (sop), R. Gorr (mez), J. Vickers (ten), R. Merrill (bar), G. Tozzi (bass), Rome Opera Chorus [I] London 3-▲ 417416-2 [ADD]
Verdi, G.:Aida, w. L. Price (sop), R. Gorr (mez), J. Vickers (ten), R. Merrill (bar), G. Tozzi (bass), Rome Opera Chorus [I] London ▲ 421860-2 [ADD]
S. Varviso (cnd)
Mascagni, P.:Cavalleria rusticana, w. E. Suliotis (sop), S. Malagu (mez), A. Di Stasio (mez), M. Del Monaco (ten), T. Gobbi (bar), Rome Opera Chorus [I] IMP Collectors Series ▲ IMPX 9018 [AAD]

Rome PO
Verdi, G.:Arias, w. K. Ricciarelli (sop), P. Domingo (ten)—arias & duets from Ballo in maschera, Il Corsaro, Don Carlos, Jerusalem, Giovanna d'Arco, I Masnadieri, Otello, Trovatore, I Vespri siciliani RCA Gold Seal ▲ 6534-2-RG [ADD] ■ 6534-4-RG (CrO2)
W. Perry (cnd)
Perry, W.:Film Music, w. Richard Hayman (hmc), Slovak PO, Vienna SO, Slovak Phil Chorus, Vienna Boys' Choir [scores for 6 Mark Twain films originally produced for PBS in the 1980s]—Adventures of Huckleberry Finn; The Innocents Abroad; Life on the Mississippi; The Mysterious Stranger; The Private History of a Campaign That Failed; Pudd'head Wilson Premier ▲ PRCD 1015 [DDD]

Rome Radio Orch
J. Barbirolli (cnd)
Elgar, E.:The Dream of Gerontius, w. C. Shacklock (mez), J. Vickers (ten), M. Nowkovski (bass), Rome RAI Chorus [E] *(rec live, Rome 11/20/57)* Arkadia 2-▲ 584 [ADD]
C.M. Giulini (cnd)
Live on Stage, w. L. Pavarotti (ten), Royal Opera House Covent Garden Orch, Royal Opera House Covent Garden Chorus [cnd:Carlo Felice Cillario], et al. LaserLight ▲ 15104

Rome Radio Orch (cont.)
C.M. Giulini (cnd) (cont.)
Rossini, G.:Stabat Mater, w. T. Zylis-Gara (sop), S. Verrett (mez), L. Pavarotti (ten), N. Zaccaria (bass), Rome RAI Chorus [L] *(rec live 12/22/67)* Verona 2-▲ 27060/61 (m) [AAD]
H. von Karajan (cnd)
Debussy, C.:Pelléas et Mélisande, w. E. Schwarzkopf (sop), E. Haefliger (ten), M. Roux (bar), M. Petri (bass), Rome RAI Chorus [F] *(rec live, 12/19/54)* Arkadia 2-▲ 218 (m) [ADD]
Mozart, W.A.:Zauberflöte, w. E. Schwarzkopf (sop), R. Streich (sop), A. Noni (sop), N. Gedda (ten), G. Taddei (bar), M. Petri (bass), Rome RAI Chorus [I] *(rec live, Dec. 19, 1953)* Myto 2-▲ 2 MCD 89007 (m) [ADD]
F. Molinari-Pradelli (cnd)
Verdi, G.:Simon Boccanegra, w. A. Stella (sop—Maria), C. Bergonzi (ten—Gabriele), G. Giorgetti (bar—Pietro), W. Monachesi (bar—Paolo), M. Petri (bar—Jacopo), P. Silveri (bar—Simon), Rome RAI Chorus *(rec 1951)* Cetra Classic ▲ CDO 23 [ADD]
R. Muti (cnd)
Spontini, G.:Agnes von Hohensaufen, w. M. Caballé (sop), A. Stella (sop), B. Prevedi (ten), G. Guelfi (bar), Rome RAI Chorus [I] *(rec live, 4/30/70)* Myto 2-▲ 2 MCD 90215 (m) [ADD]
Rome Radio-TV Orch
G. Gavazzeni (cnd)
Bellini, V.:Il pirata, w. M. Caballé (sop), F. Rafanelli (sop), B. Marti (ten), Baratti, P. Cappuccilli (bar), R. Raimondi (bass), Rome Radio-TV Chorus [I] *(rec Rome, 1973)* EMI Classics 2-▲ CDMB 64169
Rome Radio-TV SO
V. Gui (cnd)
Wagner, R.:Parsifal, w. M. Callas (sop), Baldelli (sgr), R. Panerai (bar), D. Lopatto (bar), B. Christoff (bass), Rome Radio-TV Chorus [I] *(rec 11/20-21/50)* Melodram 3-▲ MEL 36041 (m)
Wagner, R.:Parsifal, w. M. Callas (sop), Baldelli (sgr), R. Panerai (bar), D. Lopatto (bar), B. Christoff (bass), Rome Radio-TV Chorus [I] *(rec in concert, 11/20-21/50)* Verona 3-▲ 27085/87
M. Rossi (cnd)
Liszt, F.:Con 1 Pno, w. Arturo Benedetti Michelangeli (pno) Arkadia ▲ 507 [AAD]
Liszt, F.:Totentanz, w. A. Benedetti Michelangeli (pno) Arkadia ▲ 507 [AAD]
B. Walter (cnd)
Brahms, J.:Ein Deutsches Requiem, w. Rosanna Carteri (sop), Boris Christoff (bass), Rome Radio-TV Chorus Stradivarius 2-▲ STV DTM 12323 [ADD]
Rome RAI Orch
S. Celibidache (cnd)
Wolf, H.:Italian Serenade *(rec live, Rome, 5/11/68)* Arkadia ▲ 763 [ADD]
O. de Fabritiis (cnd)
Verdi, G.:La forza del destino (sels), w. G. Cigna (sop—Leonora), E. Ghirardini (bar—Melitone), G. Vaghi (bar—Guardiano), Rome RAI Chorus *(rec Oct. 10, 1938)* Legato Classics 2-▲ LCD 173-2 [ADD]
C. M. Giulini (cnd)
Mozart, W.A.:Don Giovanni, w. G. Janowitz (sop), S. Jurinac (sop), G. von Milivkovic (mez), A. Kraus (ten), N. Ghiaurov (bass), Rome RAI Chorus *(rec live, May 12, 1970)* Melodram 3-▲ MEL 37080
Rossini, G.:Stabat Mater, w. Teresa Zylis-Gara (sop), Shirley Verrett (mez), Luciano Pavarotti (ten), Nicola Zaccaria (bass), Rome RAI Chorus *(rec Rome, Dec. 1967)* Emozioni ▲ ARCD 2041
Rossini, G.:Stabat Mater, w. T. Zylis-Gara (sop), S. Verrett (mez), L. Pavarotti (ten), N. Zaccaria (bass), Rome RAI Chorus [L] *(rec live 12/22/67)* Melodram 2-▲ MEL 28012
L. Maazel (cnd)
Bellini, V.:I Capuleti e i Montecchi (sels), w. F. Cossotto (mez), R. Gavarini (ten), V. Tatozzi (bar), Rome RAI Chorus—2 solo tenor arias & 1 mezzo-bass duet [I] *(rec live 10/23/58)* Melodram ("Connaisseur" series) 2-▲ CDM 27509 [ADD]
B. Maderna (cnd)
Nono, L.:Epitaffio 1, w. L. Marimpietri (sop), M. Boriello (bar), Rome RAI Chorus *(rec live, Rome 1/28/61)* Arkadia ▲ 027 [ADD]
R. Muti (cnd)
Verdi, G.:Attila, w. Antonietta Stella (sop), Gianfranco Cecchele (ten), Giangiacomo Guelfi (bar), Ruggiero Raimondi (bass), Rome RAI Chorus *(rec live 1970)* Memories 2-▲ HR 4178/79 (m)
A. La Rosa Parodi (cnd)
Borodin, A.:Prince Igor, w. Kalmus (sgr), Infantino (sgr), G. Taddei (bar), B. Christoff (bass), O. Dominguez (mez), Rome RAI Chorus *(rec live 9/19/64)* Melodram 2-▲ MEL 27028 (s)
F. Previtali (cnd)
Mozart, W.A.:Nozze di Figaro, w. G. Gatti (sop), A. Noni (sop), G. Sciurri (sop), J. Gardino (mez), M.T. Pace (mez), A. Mercuriali (ten), S. Bruscantini (bar), I. Tajo (bass), F. Corena (bass) [I] *(rec 1951)* Cetra Classic 2-▲ CDO 12
Verdi, G.:Nabucco, w. C. Mancini (sop—Abigaille), G. Gatti (sop—Fenena), B. Preziosa (sop—Anna), M. Binci (ten—Ismaele), L. Francardi (ten—Abdallo), P. Silveri (bar—Nabucodonosor), A. Cassinelli (bass—Zaccaria), A. Gaggi (bass—High Priest of Baal), Rome RAI Chorus *(rec Rome, 1951)* Cetra Classic 2-▲ CDO 26 [ADD]
Verdi, G.:Rigoletto (sels), w. L. Pagliughi (sop), G. Lauri-Volpi (ten), T. Gobbi (bar), Rome RAI Chorus [highlights] *(rec 1947)* Melodram ▲ MEL 15008
A. Rodzinski (cnd)
Prokofiev, S.:Alexander Nevsky, w. I. Compañez (cta) *(rec May 22, 1958)* Stradivarius ▲ STR 10035 [ADD]
Prokofiev, S.:Sym 5 Stradivarius ▲ STV 13613 [ADD]
Scriabin, A.:Sym 3 Stradivarius ▲ STV 13613 [ADD]
Shostakovich, D.:Sym 10 Stradivarius ▲ STV 10035 [ADD]
Wagner, R.:Tannhäuser (sels), w. G. Brouwenstijn (sop), H. Wilfert (sgr), K. Liebl (ten), E. Wächter (bar), Rome RAI Chorus *(rec Nov. 21 1957)* Myto 3-▲ MCD 93277
H. Rosbaud (cnd)
Castiglioni, N.:Sequenze Stradivarius ▲ STV 10022 [ADD]
Hindemith, P.:Con Fl, Ob, Cl, Bn, Hp Stradivarius ▲ STV 10022 [ADD]
Ravel, M.:Valses nobles et sentimentales Stradivarius ▲ STV 10022 [ADD]
M. Rossi (cnd)
Verdi, G.:Luisa Miller, w. L. Kelston (sop—Luisa), M.T. Pace (mez—Federica), G. Larui-Volpi (ten—Rodolfo), S. Colombo (bar—Miller), G. Vaghi (bar—Count Walter), D. Baronti (bass—Wurm), Rome RAI Chorus *(rec 1951)* Cetra Classic 2-▲ CDO 17 [AAD]
W. Sawallisch (cnd)
Rossini, G.:Mosè in Egitto, w. Teresa Zylis-Gara (sop), Shirley Verrett (mez), Ottavio Garaventa (ten), Giampaolo Corradi (bass), Nicolai Ghiaurov (bass), Mario Petri (bass), Rome RAI Chorus *(rec live, Rome, 1968)* Italian Opera Rarities 2-▲ IOR 7724 [ADD]
T. Schippers (cnd)
Beethoven, L. van:Ah, perfidol, w. R. Crespin (sop) *(rec live 6/6/70)* Melodram 2-▲ CDM 28034 [AAD]
Rome RAI Radio-TV SO
A. Rodzinski (cnd)
Mussorgsky, M.:Khovanshchina, w. Irene Companez (cta), Herbert Handt (ten), Mirto Picchi (ten), Boris Christoff (bass), Armedeo Berdini (sgr), Giorgio Canello (sgr), Dmitri Lopatto (sgr), Michele Malaspina (sgr), Jolanda Mancini (sgr), Mario Petri (sgr), Rome RAI Chorus Stradivarius 2-▲ STV DTM 12320 [ADD]
Wagner, R.:Tannhäuser, w. Gré Brouwestijn (sop), Murray Dickie (ten), Karl Liebl (ten), Eberhard Waechter (bar), Alois Pernerstorfer (b-bar), Deszö Ernster (bass), Walter Brunelli (sgr), Peter Harrower (sgr), Rosl Schweiger (sgr), Herta Wilfert (sgr), Rome RAI Chorus Stradivarius 3-▲ STV 12318
Rome RAI SO
Arias, w. M. Callas (sop), Turin RAI SO, Milan RAI SO, Royal Opera House Orch Covent Garden *(rec 1949-1962)* Verona 2-▲ 27058/59 (m) [AAD]
De Cavalieri, Fineschi, Olivero, Stignani, Tassinari, w. A. de Cavalieri (sop), Ornella Fineschi (sop), Magda Olivero (sop), Ebe Stignani (mez), Pia Tassinari (mez), Milan RAI SO *(rec 1953-58)* Incontri Memorabili ("Martini & Rossi Concerts" series) ▲ 5020
Gatta, Moffo, Rizzieri, Christoff & Mazzolli, w. D. Gatta (sop), Anna Moffo (sop), Elena Rizzieri (sop), Boris Christoff (bass), Ferruccio Mazzoli (bass), Turin RAI SO *(rec Martini & Rossi Concert)* Incontri Memorabili ▲ CDMR 5033

Rome RAI SO (cont.)
Maria Coleva, Cesare Valletti, w. M. Coleva (sop), Cesare Valletti (ten) *(rec Dec. 4, 1961)* Incontri Memorabili ("Martini & Rossi Concerts" series) ▲ 5030
Rosanna Carteri, Antonietta Stella & Beniamino Gigli, w. R. Carteri (sop), Antonietta Stella (sop), Beniamino Gigli (ten), Rome RAI Chorus [cnd:Nino Antonellini], Milan RAI SO [cnd:Nino Sanzogno] *(rec Milan & Sanremo, Feb. 9, 1953 & Dec. 21, 1)* Incontri memorabili ("Martini & Rossi Concert" series) ▲ CDMR 5005 [ADD]
Stella, Cossotto & Monaco, w. A. Stella (sop), Fiorenza Cossotto (mez), Mario Del Monaco (ten), Ferruccio Scaglia (cnd), Milan RAI SO *(rec Martini & Rossi Concert, 1959 & 1960)* Incontri Memorabili ▲ CDMR 5031
C. Abbado (cnd)
Ravel, M.:Con in G Pno, w. M. Argerich (pno) Exclusive ▲ EXL 65 [ADD]
Ravel, M.:Con in G Pno, w. M. Argerich (pno) Enterprise ("Documents" series) ▲ ENT LV 960 [ADD]
G. Albrecht (cnd)
Massenet, J.:Thérèse, w. Agnes Baltsa (mez—Thérèse), Francisco Araiza (ten—Armand), Gino Sinimberghi (ten—Officer), George Fortune (bass—André), Giancarlo Luccardi (bass—Morel), Eftimios Michalopoulos (sgr—Officer/Municipal Officer), Giuseppe Piccillo (cnd), Rome RAI Chorus Orfeo ▲ 387961 [DDD]
M. Freccia (cnd)
Moffo & Volpi, w. A. Moffo (sop), Giacomo Lauri Volpi (ten), Milan RAI SO [cnd:Alfredo Simonetto] *(rec Martini & Rossi Concert, 1960)* Incontri Memorabili ▲ CDMR 5035
G. Gavazzeni (cnd)
Donizetti, G.:L'elisir d'amore, w. Alda Noni (sop), Cesare Valletti (ten), Sesto Bruscantini (bar), Rome RAI Chorus Fonit Cetra ("Classic Collection" series) 2-▲ FCT CDO 5
Donizetti, G.:L'elisir d'amore, w. A. Noni (sop), B. Rizzoli (sop), C. Valletti (ten), S. Bruscantini (bar), A. Poli (bar), Rome RAI Chorus *(rec 1952)* Cetra Classic ▲ CDO 5 [AAD]
C. M. Giulini (cnd)
Rossini, G.:Stabat Mater, w. Luciano Pavarotti (ten)—Cuius aninam *(rec Rome, Dec 22, 1967)* Goldies ▲ GLD 63202 [ADD]
A. Guarnieri (cnd)
Zandonai, R.:Francesca da Rimini, w. M. Caniglia (sop—Francesca), A. M. Canali (mez—Altichiara), A. Bertocci (ten—Ser Toldo Berardengo), M. Carlin (ten—Malatestino), G. Prandelli (ten—Paolo), C. Tagliabue (bar—Giovanni), E. Campi (bass—Il Giuliare/Il Torrigiano), Rome RAI Chorus *(rec 1952)* Cetra Classic ▲ CDO 22 [ADD]
H. von Karajan (cnd)
Stravinsky, I.:Oedipus Rex, w. M. Laszlò (mez—Jocasta), N. Gedda (ten—Oedipus), A. Bertocci (ten—Shepherd), M. Petri (bar—Creon & Tireseus), N. Catalani (bar—Messenger), A. Foà (speaker), Rome RAI Chorus *(rec Dec. 20, 1952)* Stradivarius ▲ DAT 12311 [ADD]
B. Leskovich (cnd)
Mussorgsky, M.:Khovanshchina, w. Mietta Sighele (sop—Emma), Elena Souliotis (sop—Susanna), Fiorenza Cossotto (mez—Marfa), Herbert Handt (ten—Scribe), Veriano Luchetti (ten—Prince Andrey Khovansky), Ludovic Spiess (ten—Prince Vasily Golitsin), Claudio Strudthoff (ten—Streshnev), Angelo Marchiandi (bar—Kuz'ka), Teodoro Rovetta (bar—1st Strel'tsi), Siegmund Nimsgern (b-bar—Shaklovity), Cesare Siepi (b-bar—Dosifey), Carlo del Bosco (bass—2nd Strel'tsi), Ubaldo Carosi (bass—Varsonofiev), Nicolai Ghiaurov (bass—Prince Ivan Khovnasky), Giovanni Sciarpeletti (bass—Pastor), Rome RAI Chorus—also includes bonus Act V [w Boris Christoff] (Rome, 1958) *(rec Rome, 1973)* Bella Voce 3-▲ BLV 107.402 [AAD]
H. Lewis (cnd)
Mahler, G.:Songs from Rückert, w. Marilyn Horne (cta), Milan RAI SO *(rec live, Apr. 30 & June 18, 1971)* Arkadia ▲ 808
Rossini, G.:Arias, w. Marilyn Horne (cta), Milan RAI SO—from Semiramide; Otello; La donna del lago; Tancredi; Cenerentola; L'Italiana in Algeri *(rec live, Apr. 30 & June 18, 1971)* Arkadia ▲ 808
L. Maazel (cnd)
Bruch, M.:Con 1 Vn, w. Leonid Kogan (vn) *(rec 1969)* Arlecchino ARL
Mendelssohn, F.:Con Vn, Op. 64, w. Leonid Kogan (vn) *(rec 1969)* Arlecchino ARL
B. Maderna (cnd)
Nono, L.:Composizione 2 *(rec live, Venice 10/1/59)* Arkadia ▲ 027 [ADD]
R. Muti (cnd)
Bellini, V.:I Puritani, w. Mirella Freni (sop), Mirelle Fiorentini (mez), Luciano Pavarotti (ten), Emilio Venturini (ten), Sesto Bruscantini (bar), Giovanni Antonini (bass), Bonaldo Giaiotti (bass), Rome RAI Chorus Melodram 2-▲ CDM 27062
Bellini, V.:I Puritani, w. Mirella Freni (sop), Luciano Pavarotti (ten), Sesto Bruscantini (b-bar), Rome RAI Chorus *(rec Rome, 1969)* Enterprise ("Palladio" series) 3-▲ ENTPD 4205 [ADD]
Bellini, V.:I Puritani, w. M. Freni (sop), L. Pavarotti (ten), S. Bruscantini (bar), B. Giaotti (bass), Rome RAI Chorus [I] *(rec live, Rome 7/8/69)* Verona 3-▲ 27029/31
Bellini, V.:I Puritani (sels), w. Mirella Freni (sop), Luciano Pavarotti (ten), Giovanni Antonini (bass), Bonaldo Giaiotti (bass), Rome RAI Chorus—A te, o cara *(rec Rome, July 8, 1969)* Goldies ▲ GLD 63202 [ADD]
Verdi, G.:Attila, w. Antonietta Stella (sop), Gianfranco Cecchele (ten), Giangiacomo Guelfi (bar), Ruggiero Raimondi (bass), Rome RAI Chorus *(rec Rome, Nov. 21, 1970)* Pantheon 2-▲ PHE 6642 (m)
F. Previtali (cnd)
Bellini, V.:I Puritani, w. Lina Pagliughi (sop), Mario Filippeschi (ten), Rolando Panerai (bar), Sesto Bruscantini (bass), Rome RAI Chorus *(rec Rome, Jan. 4 & 5, 1952)* Pantheon 2-▲ PHE 6640 (m)
Verdi, G.:La battaglia di Legnano, w. Caterina Mancini (sop), Amedeo Berdini (bar), Rolando Panerai (bar), Albino Gaggi (bass), Edmea Limberti (sgr), Manfredi Ponz de Leon (sgr), Rome RAI Chorus *(rec 1951)* Cetra Classic 2-▲ CDON 40 [ADD]
Verdi, G.:Don Carlos, w. M. Caniglia (sop—Elisabeth de Valois), G. Sciutti (sop—Page), E. Stignani (mez—Princess Eboli), M. Picchi (ten—Don Carlos), M. Ponz de L. (ten—Count of Lerma), P. Silveri (bar—Rodrigue), N. Rossi Lemeni (bass—Philip II), G. Neri (bass—Grand Inquisitor), A. Gaggi (bass—Old Monk), Rome RAI Chorus *(rec Rome, 1951)* Cetra Classic 3-▲ CDO 25 [ADD]
Verdi, G.:Ernani, w. Caterina Mancini (sop), Vittorio Pandano (ten), Gino Penno (ten), Giuseppe Taddei (bar), Giacomo Vaghi (bar), Ezio Achilli (sgr), Licia Rossini (sgr), Rome RAI Chorus Cetra Classic 2-▲ CDON 39 [ADD]
G. Prêtre (cnd)
Berlioz, H.:La Damnation de Faust, w. M. Horne (mez—Marguerite), N. Gedda (ten—Faust), R. Soyer (bass—Mephistofeles), D. Petkov (bass—Brander), Rome RAI Chorus *(rec live 1/11/69)* Arkadia 4-▲ 461 [ADD]
Berlioz, H.:Les Troyens, w. M. Horne (mez), S. Verrett (mez), N. Gedda (ten), V. Luchetti (ten), R. Massard (bar), Rome RAI Chorus *(rec live 5/30/69)* Arkadia 4-▲ 461 [ADD]
Berlioz, H.:Les Troyens, w. M. Horne (mez), S. Verrett (mez), N. Gedda (ten), V. Luchetti (ten), R. Massard (bar), Rome RAI Chorus [F] *(rec live 5/30/69)* Melodram 3-▲ MEL 37060 [AAD]
Berlioz, H.:Les Troyens (sels), w. Shirley Verrett (sop—Didon), Rome RAI Chorus *(rec live, Rome, May 30, 1969)* Arkadia ▲ 619 [ADD]
A. Rodzinski (cnd)
Scriabin, A.:Sym 3 *(rec 1958)* Stradivarius ▲ DAT 12306 [ADD]
Szymanowski, K.:Con 2 Vn, w. H. Szeryng (vn) *(rec 1958)* Stradivarius 2-▲ DAT 12306 [ADD]
G. Santini (cnd)
Catalani, A.:La Wally, w. R. Tebaldi (sop), G. Prandelli (ten), S. Majonica (bass), Rome RAI Chorus *(rec 1960)* Enterprise (Palladio) 2-▲ ENTPD 4165 [ADD]
T. Schippers (cnd)
Berlioz, H.:Te Deum Melodram ▲ CDM 28033
Dvořák, A.:Serenade Strs Melodram ▲ CDM 28033
Puccini, G.:La Bohème (sels), w. Luciano Pavarotti (ten)—Che gelida manina *(rec Rome, Nov 19, 1966)* Goldies ▲ GLD 63202 [ADD]
Ravel, M.:Alborada del gracioso Melodram ▲ CDM 28033
Ravel, M.:Shéhérazade Mez, w. *(vocalist unknown)* Melodram 2-▲ CDM 28033

▲ = CD ♦ = Enhanced CD Δ = MD ■ = Cassette Tape □ = DCC

Rome RAI SO (cont.)
T. Serafin (cnd)
Bellini, V.:Norma (sels), w. Mario del Monaco (ten), Athos Cesarini (ten)—Svanir le voci; Meco all'altar di Venere; Me protegge, me difende *(rec Rome, June 29, 1955)* Melodram ▲ CDI 104006 [ADD]
Donizetti, G.:Lucia di Lammermoor, w. Maria Callas (sop), Eugenio Fernandi (ten), Rolando Panerai (bar), Giuseppe Modesti (bass), Rome RAI Chorus *(rec live, Rome, 1957)* Enterprise ("Documents" series) 2-▲ ENTLV 973 [ADD]
J. Serebrier (cnd)
Borodin, A.:Sym 1 ASV ▲ ASV 706 [DDD]
Borodin, A.:Sym 2 ASV ▲ ASV 706 [DDD]
Borodin, A.:Sym 3 ASV ▲ ASV 706 [DDD]
A. Simonetto (cnd)
D'Angelo & Christoff, w. G. D'Angelo (sop), Boris Christoff (bass) *(rec Martini & Rossi Concert, 1961)* Incontri Memorabili ▲ CDMR 5034
Rome Solisti [Massimo Coen (vn), Mario Buffa (vn), Margot Burton (va), Maurizio Gambini (vc)]
Boccherini, L.:Qnts Fl, G.431–436, w. Gianfranco Gambini (ob)—No. 1 in G *(rec Rome, 1996)* musicaimmagine ▲ MR 10031
Bottesini, P.:Andante e Tema con variazioni, w. Monica Berni (fl), Ciro Scarponi (cl) *(rec Rome, 1996)* musicaimmagine ▲ MR 10031
Broschi, R.:Arias, w. Angelo Manzotti (sop), Maria Pia Jacoboni (clvd)—Di costanza il core armato Bongiovanni ▲ GB 5564 [DDD]
Cherubini, L.:Sons (2) Hn, w. Luciano Giuliani (hn)—No. 2 *(rec Rome, 1996)* musicaimmagine ▲ MR 10031
Donizetti, G.:Qnts Gtr, w. Bruno Battisti D'Amario (gtr)—Nos. 2, 3 & 5 *(rec Rome, 1996)* musicaimmagine ▲ MR 10031
Farinelli (Carlo Broschi):Aria for la Maestà de Ferdinando VI Re cattolico, w. Angelo Manzotti (sop), Maria Pia Jacoboni (clvd) Bongiovanni ▲ GB 5564 [DDD]
Giacomelli, G.:Merope (sels), w. Angelo Manzotti (sop), Maria Pia Jacoboni (clvd)—Quell'usignolo che innamorato canta; Sposa non mi conosci Bongiovanni ▲ GB 5564 [DDD]
Hasse, J.A.:Artaserse (sels), w. Angelo Manzotti (sop), Maria Pia Jacoboni (clvd) Bongiovanni ▲ GB 5564 [DDD]
Mercadante, S.:Qts Fl, w. Monica Berni (fl)—in a *(rec Rome, 1996)* musicaimmagine ▲ MR 10031
Salieri, G.:Adagio e Tema con variazioni, w. Ciro Scarponi (cl) *(rec Rome, 1996)* musicaimmagine ▲ MR 10031
Rome Stradivari Ensemble
M. Peca (cnd)
Handel, G.F.:Cants, w. F. Caniglia (mez)—"Il Pianto di Maria al Sepolcro di Cristo" [I] Bongiovanni ▲ GB 2100 [DDD]
Handel, G.F.:Con Fl, w. S. Gazzelloni (fl) Bongiovanni ▲ GB 2100 [DDD]
Handel, G.F.:Con for 2 Vns & Vc, w. M. Domini (vn), A. Reale (vn), N. Chirivi (vc) Bongiovanni ▲ GB 2100 [DDD]
Rome SO
N. Bonavolontà (cnd)
Verdi, G.:Luisa Miller (sels), w. Luciano Pavarotti (ten)—Oh! fede negar potessi...Quando le sere al placido *(rec live, Jan. 1, 1967)* RCA Gold Seal ▲ 09026-68014-2 [ADD]
N. Flagello (cnd)
Flagello, N.:Capriccio Vc, w. G. Koutzen (vc) Phoenix ▲ PHCD 125 [ADD]
Flagello, N.:Contemplations, w. N. Tatum (sop) Phoenix ▲ PHCD 125 [ADD]
Flagello, N.:Lautrec, w. M. Randolph (sop) Phoenix ▲ PHCD 125 [ADD]
Flagello, N.:She Walks In Beauty, w. J. Grillo (sop) Phoenix ▲ PHCD 125 [ADD]
R. Muti (cnd)
Bellini, V.:I Puritani (sels), w. Mirella Freni (sop), Luciano Pavarotti (ten), Bonaldo Giaiotti (bass), Rome Sym Chorus—A te, o cara, amor talora *(rec live, Oct. 7, 1969)* RCA Gold Seal ▲ 09026-68014-2 [ADD]
D. Savino (cnd)
Puccini without Words MCA Classics ("Double Decker" series) 2-▲ MCAD2-99834 [AAD]
Rome Teatro Reale Orch
O. de Fabritiis (cnd)
Puccini, G.:Tosca, w. Maria Caniglia (sop), Beniamino Gigli (ten), Armando Borgioli (bar), Reale Theater Chorus *(rec 1938)* Grammofono 2000 2-▲ GRM 78591 (m)
Rome Virtuosi
R. Fasano (cnd)
Bach, J.S.:Con for 4 Hpds EMI Classics ("Doubleforte" series) 2-▲ CDFB 68625
Cavalli, P.F.:Ormindo, w. E. Zilio (mez), V. Manno (ten), G. Gatti (bar), A. Rinaldi (bar) Stradivarius 2-▲ DAT 12307
Gluck, C.W.:Orfeo ed Euridice, w. A. Moffo (sop), J. Raskin (sop), S. Verrett (mez), Collegium Musicum Italicum Instrumental Ensemble, Rome Virtuosi RCA Gold Seal 2-▲ 7896-2-RG [ADD]
Leo, L.:Cons Vn—Largo EMI Classics ("Doubleforte" series) 2-▲ CDFB 68625
Marcello, A.:Cons Ob—Con in c EMI Classics ("Doubleforte" series) 2-▲ CDFB 68625
Vivaldi, A.:Cons Fl (misc), w. Pasquale Ripoli (fl)—in D, Op. 10/3, "Il gardellino" *(rec Opéra de Rome, July, 1962)* EMI Classics ▲ CDK 65338 [ADD]
Vivaldi, A.:Cons Fl, Op. 10—No. 3 EMI Classics ("Doubleforte" series) 2-▲ CDFB 68625
Vivaldi, A.:Cons Vn (misc), w. Edmondo Malanotte (vn)—in g, Op. 8/5, "La tempesta di mare" *(rec Opéra de Rome, Oct. 1959)* EMI Classics ▲ CDK 65338 [ADD]
Vivaldi, A.:Cons Vn, Op. 3/1–12, "L'estro armonico" EMI Classics 2-▲ CDFB 69374
Vivaldi, A.:Cons Vn, Op. 8/1–12, "Il cimento dell'armonia e dell'inventione"—Nos. 1–5 EMI Classics ("Doubleforte" series) 2-▲ CDFB 68625
Vivaldi, A.:Cons Vn, Op. 8/1–4, "The Four Seasons" EMI Classics ("Doubleforte" series) 2-▲ CDFB 68625
Vivaldi, A.:Cons Vn, Op. 8/1–4, "The Four Seasons", w. Luigi Ferro (vn), Guido Mozzato (vn) *(rec Abbey Road Studios, London, Mar. 1959)* EMI Classics ▲ CDK 65338 [ADD]
Vivaldi, A.:Cons for 4 Vns, w. Luigi Ferro (vn), Franco Gulli (vn), Edmondo Malanotte (vn), Angelo Stefanato (vn)—in b, Op. 3/10 *(rec Opéra de Rome, July & August, 1959)* EMI Classics ▲ CDK 65338 [ADD]
Los Romeros [Pepe Romero (gtr), Celedonio Romero (gtr), Celín Romero (gtr), Celino Romero (gtr)]
The Romeros Philips ▲ 412609-2
Spanish Guitar Favorites Philips ▲ 442781-2
La Rondinella [Alice Kosloski (alt), Paul Bensel (rec/crumhorn/perc), Howard Bass (lt/gtr), Tina Chancey (trb vl/b vl/rebec/kamenj/lyra/rec/perc)]
A Song of David:Music of the Sephardim & Renaissance Spain *(rec St. John's Episcopal Church, Ellicott City, MD, Sept. 1994 & Jan. 1995)* Dorian Discovery ▲ DIS 80130 [DDD]
Rondo Piano [Peter Maurer (pno), Stephan Schappé (pno)]
Pretty Pianos Koch Schwann ▲ SCH 310572 [DDD]
Rooke Chapel Ringers
On This Day Earth Shall Ring!, w. Rooke Chapel Choir, D'Anna Fortunato (mez), Elizabeth Etters-Asmus (hp), David Cover (org), William Payn (cnd) *(rec Rooke Chapel, Bucknell Univ, Feb & May 1995)* Albany ▲ TROY 177 [DDD]
Rosalyra String Quartet
Bartók, B.:Qt 1 Strs *(rec Minneapolis, Aug. 1992)* Boston Records ▲ BR 1003
Beethoven, L. van:Qt 7 Strs *(rec Minneapolis, Aug. 1992)* Boston Records ▲ BR 1003
Rosamunde String Quartet [Agnès Sulem-Bialobroda (vn), Thomas Tercieux (vn), Jean Sulem (va), Xavier Gagnepain (vc)]
Dutilleux, H.:Ainsi la nuit Adda ▲ ADD 581280 [DDD]
Fénelon, P.:Inventions (11) Adda ▲ ADD 581280 [DDD]
Goldmark, K.:Qt Strs, Op. 8 Berlin Classics ▲ BER 1111 [DDD]
Haydn, J.:Qts Strs, Op. 64, "Tost Qts"—No. 5 Berlin Classics ▲ BER 1127 [DDD]
Haydn, J.:Qts Strs, Op. 74—No. 3 Berlin Classics ▲ BER 1127 [DDD]

Rosamunde String Quartet (cont.)
Haydn, J.:Qts Strs, Op. 76, "Erdödy Qts"—No. 3 Berlin Classics ▲ BER 1127 [DDD]
Hersant, P.:Qt 2 Strs Adda ▲ ADD 581280 [DDD]
Schubert, Franz:Qt 13 Strs Berlin Classics ▲ BER 1111 [DDD]
Rose Consort of Viols
Byrd, W.:Consort Music, w. Red Byrd—Pavan; Galliard; Fantasia; Fantasia No. 2; Fantasia No. 3; In Nomine No. 2; In Nomine No. 5 *(rec Dorset, between Apr. & No)* Naxos ▲ 8.550604 [DDD]
Byrd, W.:Songs, w. T. Bonner (sop), Red Byrd—Susanna Fair; Rejoice unto the Lord; Have Mercy upon Me, O God; In Angel's Weed; Fair Britain Isle; Triumph with Pleasant Melody; Christ Rising Again *(rec Dorset, between Apr. & Nov. 1992)* Naxos ▲ 8.550604 [DDD]
Dowland, J.:Lachrimae, or Seaven Teares, w. Caroline Trevor (alt), J. Heringman (Renaissance lt) Amon Ra ▲ CD-SAR 55 [DDD]
Elizabethan Christmas Anthems, w. Red Byrd Amon Ra ▲ CDSAR 46 [DDD]
Gibbons, O.:Instrumental & Vocal Music, w. Red Byrd—Behold, thou hast made my days for 5 Voices & 5 Viols; Pavan for 6 Viols; Galliard for 6 Viols; Fant. No. 1 for 2 Treble Viols; I weigh not Fortune's frown for Soprano & 4 Viols [w. Tessa Bonner]; I tremble not at noise of war; I see ambition never pleased; I feign not friendship where I hate; Go from my window for 6 Viols; Dainty fine bird for Soprano & 4 Viols [w. T. Bonner]; Fair is the Rose; Fant. No. 3 for 6 Viols; Fant. No. 5 for 6 viols; Lincoln's Inn Mask; Allmaine in G; Fantasia No. 1for the Great Double Bass for Organ & 3 Viols [w. Timothy Roberts]; Galliard for 3 Viols; The silver swan for Soprano & 5 Viols [w. T. Bonner]; In Nomine for 4 Viols; Glorious and powerful God for 5 Voices & 5 Viols *(rec Forde Abbey, Dorset, Apr. 27–28, May 11–13 & 2)* Naxos ▲ 8.550603 [DDD]
Jenkins, J.:Music of—Pavan in F; Fant. in c; Divisions for 2 Basses in C; Fant. in c; Fant. in F; Newarke Seidge; Four-part ayres in d; Fant.-suite in a; Fant in c; Fant. in D; Fant. in e; Four-part ayre in g; In Nomine in g *(rec Apr. 1992)* Naxos ▲ 8.550687 [DDD]
Jenkins, J.:VI Music—Pavan in F; Divisions in C for 2 Basses; Fant. in F, "All in a Garden Green"; Newarke Seidge; 4-Part ayres in d; Fant.-suite in a; Fants. in c, c, c, D & e; 4-Part ayre in g; In Nomine in g *(rec Apr. 27–29 & May 11–13, 1)* Naxos ▲ 8.550687 [DDD]
Tomkins, T.:Instr & Voc Music, w. John Bryan (hpd), Timothy Roberts (hpd/org), Red Byrd—Pavan in F; Almain in F; In Nomine; Above the stars; Fant. XIV; Fant. I; A Fancy, for 2 to play; Ut re mi; O Lord, let me know mine end; Fant. XII; In Nomine II; Pavan & galliard, Earl Strafford; Fant. for 6 Vls; Miserere; Voluntary; Pavan in a; Galliard; Thou art my King, O God *(rec Forde Abbey, Dorset, Apr. 27–28, May 12, 25–27)* Naxos ("Early Music" series) ▲ 8.550602 [DDD]
Rosé String Quartet
Bach, J.S.:Air on the G String [string qt. version of Wilhelmj's violin–piano arr.] *(rec 1927)* Biddulph 2-▲ LAB 056/057 [ADD]
Beethoven, L. van:Qt 4 Strs *(rec 1927)* Biddulph 2-▲ LAB 056/057 [ADD]
Beethoven, L. van:Qt 10 Strs, "Harp" *(rec 1927)* Biddulph 2-▲ LAB 056/057 [ADD]
Beethoven, L. van:Qt 14 Strs *(rec 1927)* Biddulph 2-▲ LAB 056/057 [ADD]
Roseau Wind Quintet [J. Krämer (fl), J. Blank (ob), N. Nagel (cl), K. Reitmayer (hn), K. Nagel (bn)]
Danzi, F.:Qnts Ww, Op. 56—No. 1 in B *(rec 1987)* Ambitus ▲ 97877 [DDD]
Ligeti, G.:Bagatelles *(rec 1987)* Ambitus ▲ 97877 [DDD]
Schmid, H.K.:Qnt Ww *(rec 1987)* Ambitus ▲ 97877 [DDD]
Seiber, M.:Parmutazioni *(rec 1987)* Ambitus ▲ 97877 [DDD]
Rossini Ensemble
Donizetti, G.:Allegro Strs, w. A. Kiss (vn) *(rec Oct. 1991)* Naxos ▲ 8.550621 [DDD]
Rossini, G.:Sons Str Qt, w. A. Kiss (vn)—Nos. 1, 2 & 3 *(rec 1991)* Naxos ▲ 8.550621 [DDD]
Rossini, G.:Sons Str Qt, w. A. Kiss (vn)—Nos. 4, 5 & 6 *(rec Oct. 1991)* Naxos ▲ 8.550622 [DDD]
Rossini Wind Quartet [A. Griminelli (fl), C. Giuffredi (cl), R. Vernizzi (bn), D. Marchello (hn)]
Gambaro, V.:Qts (3) Ww *(rec Genoa, June 1993)* Dynamic ▲ CD 107 [DDD]
Mercadante, S.:Qts Ww *(rec Genoa, June 1993)* Dynamic ▲ CD 107 [DDD]
Rossmarin [G. Ross (sgr/lt), A. Marin (sgr/va)]
Oyez! La Nouvelle Analekta ▲ ATM 29718
Rotenbeck Trio [Heike Krugmann (gtr), Gerd Blasejewicz (gtr), Peter Lohse (gtr)]
Canción y Tango Ambitus ▲ AMB 97842 [DDD]
Roth Trio [André Previn (pno), Feri Roth (vn), Joseph Schuster (vc)]
Fauré, G.:Trio *(rec Hollywood, July 11, 1961)* Sony Classical ("Essential Classics" series) ▲ SBK 62413 [ADD] ■ SBT 62413
Rotterdam Conservatory Ensemble
O. Ketting (cnd)
Ketting, O.:Monumentum Donemus ▲ CV 21
Rotterdam Conservatory Symphonic Band
A. van Beek (cnd)
Vries, K. de:De Profundis Donemus ▲ CV 34
Wagemans, P.J.:Sym 6, w. Walter Boeyekens (cl) Donemus ▲ CV 56 [DDD]
Rotterdam PO
J. Conlon (cnd)
Mussorgsky, M.:Khovanshchina (orch sels) Erato ▲ 92870-2
Mussorgsky, M.:Pictures at an Exhibition Erato ▲ 92870-2
Weber, C.M. von:Concertino Cl, w. W. Boeykens (cl) Erato ▲ 2292-45459-2-ZK
Weber, C.M. von:Con 1 Cl, w. W. Boeykens (cl) Erato ▲ 2292-45459-2-ZK
Weber, C.M. von:Con 1 Cl, w. Walter Boykens (cl)—Rondo-allegretto *(rec Doelen, Rotterdam, Jan. 1989)* Erato ▲ 94679-2
Weber, C.M. von:Con 2 Cl, w. Walter Boykens (cl)—Alla Polacca *(rec Doelen, Rotterdam, Jan. 1989)* Erato ▲ 94679-2
Weber, C.M. von:Con 2 Cl, w. W. Boeyekens (cl) Erato ▲ 2292-45459-2-ZK
P. Daniel (cnd)
Debussy, C.:Epigraphes antiques [orchd Escher] Donemus ▲ CV 22
R. van Driesten (cnd)
Pijper, W.:Adagios Donemus ▲ CV 1
Pijper, W.:Con Pno, w. T. Bruins (pno) Donemus ▲ CV 1
Pijper, W.:Sym 2 Donemus ▲ CV 1
R. Dufallo (cnd)
Kox, H.:Con 2 Vn, w. V. Liberman (vn) *(rec 1983)* Attacca ▲ Babel 9262-1 [ADD/DDD]
J. Fournet (cnd)
Fauré, G.:Pavane Orch Philips ▲ 420707-2 [ADD]
Fauré, G.:Requiem, w. E. Ameling (sop), B. Kruysen (bar) [L] Philips ▲ 420707-2 [ADD]
V. Gergiev (cnd)
Borodin, A.:Sym 1 Philips ▲ 422996-2 [DDD]
Borodin, A.:Sym 2 Philips ▲ 422996-2 [DDD]
Ketting, Montgomery, Zinman (cnd)
Vries, K. de:Music of, w. Maria Orán (sop), Netherlands Ballet Orch—Areas; Bewegingen; Follia; Discantus; Phrases Donemus ▲ CV 25
C. Munch (cnd)
Beethoven, L. van:Sym 6, "Pastorale" FNAC Music ("Via Classics" series) ▲ 642316
M. Rostropovich (cnd)
Schnittke, A.:Life with an Idiot, w. T. Ringholz (sop), H. Haskin (ten), D. Duesing (bar), Rotterdam Vocal Ensemble *(rec Amsterdam, world premiere performance, April 13, 1992)* Sony Classical 2-▲ S2K 52495 [DDD]
G. Rozhdestvensky (cnd)
Fleischmann, B.:Rothschild's Vn, w. Marina Shaguch (sop), Larissa Diadkova (mez), Ilya Levinsky (ten), Konstantin Pluzhnikov (ten), Sergei Leiferkus (bar) *(rec Rotterdam, Netherlands, Aug 24–31, 1995)* RCA Red Seal ▲ 09026-68434-2 [DDD]
Shostakovich, D.:From Jewish Folk Poetry, w. Marina Shaguch (sop), Larissa Diadkova (mez), Konstantin Pluzhnikov (ten) *(rec Rotterdam, Netherlands, Aug 24–31, 1995)* RCA Red Seal ▲ 09026-68434-2 [DDD]
J. Tate (cnd)
Escher, R.:Hymne du grand Meaulnes Donemus ▲ CV 22

Rotterdam PO (cont.)
J. Tate (cnd) (cont.)
Mendelssohn, F.:A Midsummer Night's Dream (comp), w. L. Dawson (sop), S. Mentzer (mez), Toonkunst Chorus, Peter Hall Company EMI Classics 2-▲ CDCB 54348
E. de Waart (cnd)
de Leeuw, T.:Syms of Winds Donemus ▲ CV 23
Ketting, O.:Time Machine Donemus ▲ CV 21
Keuris, T.:Sinf for Orch Donemus ▲ CV 30
Rachmaninoff, S.:The Rock Philips ("Duo" series) 2-▲ 438724-2
Rachmaninoff, S.:Syms (comp) Philips ("Duo" series) 2-▲ 438724-2
D. Zinman (cnd)
Chopin, F.:Music of, w. Claudio Arrau (pno), Nikita Magaloff (pno), E. Inbal (cnd), London PO—Con. No. 2 in f for Pno, Op. 21 [Larghetto]; Berceuse in Db, Op. 57; Nocturnes No. 1 in bb, Op. 9/1; No. 2 in Eb, Op. 9/2; No. 5 in F#, Op. 15/2; No. 8 in Db, Op. 27/2; No. 20 in c#, Op. posth.; No. 21 in c, Op. posth.; Prelude No. 7 in A, Op. 28; Andante spianato; Prelude No. 4 in e, Op. 28; Waltz No. 9 in Ab, Op. 69/1; Con. No. 1 in e for Pno, Op. 11 [Romance] Philips ▲ 446629-2 ■ 446629-4
Chopin, F.:Les Sylphides Philips ("Duo" series) 2-▲ 438763-2
Delibes, L.:Coppélia, ou La fille aux yeux d'émail Philips ("Duo" series) 2-▲ 438763-2
Fauré, G.:Pelléas et Mélisande (suite) Philips ▲ 420707-2 [ADD]
Gounod, C.:Faust (ballet music) Philips ("Duo" series) 2-▲ 438763-2
Rimsky-Korsakov, N.:Antar Philips ("Classics" series) 2-▲ 442605-2
Rimsky-Korsakov, N.:Capriccio espagnol Philips ("Classics" series) 2-▲ 442605-2
Rimsky-Korsakov, N.:Capriccio espagnol Philips ▲ 411446-2 [DDD]
Rimsky-Korsakov, N.:Golden Cockerel (suite) Philips ▲ 411435-2 [DDD]
Rimsky-Korsakov, N.:Golden Cockerel (suite) Philips ("Classics" series) 2-▲ 442605-2
Rimsky-Korsakov, N.:A May Night (ov) Philips ▲ 411446-2 [DDD]
Rimsky-Korsakov, N.:A May Night (ov) Philips ("Classics" series) 2-▲ 442605-2
Rimsky-Korsakov, N.:Sadko Orch, Op. 5 Philips ("Classics" series) 2-▲ 442605-2
Rimsky-Korsakov, N.:Sadko Orch, Op. 5 Philips ▲ 411446-2 [DDD]
Rimsky-Korsakov, N.:Snow Maiden (suite) Philips ▲ 411446-2 [DDD]
Rimsky-Korsakov, N.:Snow Maiden (suite) Philips ("Classics" series) 2-▲ 442605-2
Rimsky-Korsakov, N.:The Tale of Tsar Saltan Orch, Op. 57 Philips ▲ 411435-2 [DDD]
Rimsky-Korsakov, N.:The Tale of Tsar Saltan Orch, Op. 57 Philips ("Classics" series) 2-▲ 442605-2

Rouen SO
F. Chaslin (cnd)
Chaynes, C.:Jocaste, w. René Boutet (ten), Jean-Marie Frémeau (bar), André Cognet (b-bar), Théâtre des Arts Chorus *(rec Rouen Theater, Rouen, France, 1993)* Chamade 2-▲ 5633/34

Rouvier-Kantorow-Müller Trio
Fauré, G.:Trio Denon ▲ CO 72508 [DDD]

Rova Saxophone Quartet
Riley, T.:Music of—The Tuning Path; Pipes of Medb; Song Announcing Dawn's Combat; The Chord of War; Ferdia's Death Chant; Chanting the Light of Foresight *(rec 1991 & 1993)* New Albion ▲ NA 064

Rowallan Consort [Mhairi Lawson (sgr), Paul Rendall (sgr), Robert Phillips (lt), William Taylor (hp)]
Notes of Joy *(rec Temple Record Studios, Scotland)* Temple ▲ COMD 2058

Royal Air Force College Band
Marching through the 20th Century Bandleader ▲ BND 5103 [DDD]
633 Squadron Chandos ▲ CHAN 6585 [ADD]

Royal Albert Hall Orch
E. Elgar (cnd)
Elgar, E.:The Dream of Gerontius (sels), w. M. Balfour (cta), S. Wilson (ten), H. Heyner (bar), Royal Choral Society [E] *(rec 1927)* Opal ▲ CD 9810 (m) [AAD]
Elgar, E.:Enigma Vars *(rec 1921)* Pearl 5-▲ PEAS 9951/55 (m) [AAD]
Elgar, E.:Sym 2 *(rec acoustic recording 1924-5)* Pearl 5-▲ PEAS 9951/55 (m) [AAD]
E. Goossens (cnd)
Bruch, M.:Con 1 Vn, w. Fritz Kreisler (vn) Grammofono 2000 ▲ GRM 78579

Royal Artillery Band
Leeds Castle Classics, w. Royal PO, Carl Davis (cnd), Brighton Festival Choir RPO Records ▲ RPO 7018 [DDD]
S. V. Hays (cnd)
The Queen's Birthday Salute, w. Herald Trumpeters *(rec live, Hyde Park, London, June 13, 1957)* Vanguard Classics ▲ SVC 51 [AAD]

Royal College of Music Brass Ensemble
Carols for Christmas, Vols. 1 & 2, w. [cnd:David Willcocks], Royal College of Music Chamber Choir Rykodisk 2-▲ RCD 10004/5

Royal College of Music Orch
S. Baudo (cnd)
Handel, G.F.:Messiah (sels)—And the Glory of the Lord; Behold a Virgin Shall Concieve; O Thou That Tellest Good Tidings to Zion; For Unto Us a Child Is Born; Glory to God; He Shall Feed His Flock Like a Shepherd; Behold the Lamb of God; Lift Up Your Head O Ye Gates; The Trumpet Shall Sound; Hallelujah! Unison ▲ V 20014 [ADD]
D. Willcocks (cnd)
Tiomkin, D.:Film Music—The Fall of the Roman Empire; A President's Country; The Guns of Navarone; Rhapsody of Steel; Wild is the Wind Unicorn ▲ UKP 9047

Royal Concert PO
P. Bateman (cnd)
Lloyd Webber, A.:Music of, w. L. Garrett (sop) Silva America ▲ SSD 1029 ■ SSC 1029

Royal Concertgebouw Orch—see Concertgebouw Orch (Royal)

Royal Consort [Mieneke van der Velden (vl), Johannes Boer (vl), Hermann Hickethier (vl), Susanne Braumann (vl)]
Jenkins, J.:VI Music—Suite in G *(rec Utrecht, Dec. 1994)* Globe ▲ GLO 5132 [DDD]
Purcell, H.:Fants Vls, Z.732-734 *(rec Utrecht, Dec. 1994)* Globe ▲ GLO 5132 [DDD]
Purcell, H.:Fants Vls, Z.735-743 *(rec Utrecht, Dec. 1994)* Globe ▲ GLO 5132 [DDD]

Royal Czech SO
W.-M. Kim (cnd)
Dvořák, A.:Carnival Mastersound ▲ MST 218 [DDD]
Dvořák, A.:Slavonic Dances (sels)—Op. 46/1, 2, 7 & 8 Mastersound ▲ MST 218 [DDD]
Dvořák, A.:Sym 9, "From the New World" Mastersound ▲ MST 218 [DDD]

Royal Danish Brass [Jonas Wiik (tpt), Niels-Jørn Jessen (tpt), Niels Vind (tpt), Thomas Jensen (tpt), Henning Hansen (hn), Ola Nilsson (hn), Torbjörn Kroon (trbn), Keld Jørgensen (trbn), Jan Mortensen (b trbn), Mogens Andresen (eup), Jens Bjørn-Larsen (tuba
Band Solos, w. Danish Concert Band Rondo Grammofon ▲ RCD 8324
Brass Ability Rondo Grammophon ▲ RCD 8344
Cascade, w. Søren Monrad (perc), Per Jensen (perc) *(rec 1996)* Rondo ▲ RCD 8352
Masterpieces for Brass & Encores!, Vol. II Rondo Grammofon ▲ RCD 8333

Royal Danish Orch
P. Berglund (cnd)
Nielsen, C.:Sym 1 RCA Red Seal ▲ 7701-2-RC [DDD]
Nielsen, C.:Sym 2 RCA Red Seal ▲ 7884-2-RC [DDD]
Nielsen, C.:Sym 3 RCA Red Seal ▲ 60427-2-RC [DDD]
Nielsen, C.:Sym 4 RCA Red Seal ▲ 7701-2-RC [DDD]
Nielsen, C.:Sym 5 RCA Red Seal ▲ 7884-2-RC [DDD]
Nielsen, C.:Sym 6 RCA Gold Seal ▲ 60427-2-RC [DDD]
L. Bernstein (cnd)
Nielsen, C.:Sym 3 *(rec 1965)* Sony Classical 4-▲ S4K 45989 [ADD]
Nielsen, C.:Sym 3 Sony Classical ▲ SMK 47598
Nielsen, C.:Sym 5 Sony Classical ▲ SMK 47598
E. Fischer (cnd)
Mozart, W.A.:Con 22 Pno, w. Edwin Fischer (pno) *(rec 1954)* Music & Arts ▲ CD 872 [ADD]

Royal Danish Orch (cont.)
E. Fischer (cnd) (cont.)
Mozart, W.A.:Con 24 Pno, w. Edwin Fischer (pno) *(rec 1954)* Music & Arts ▲ CD 872 [ADD]
Mozart, W.A.:Rondo Pno Orch, K.382, w. Edwin Fischer (pno) *(rec 1954)* Music & Arts ▲ CD 872 [ADD]
D. Garforth (cnd)
Lovenskiold, H.S.:La Sylphide Chandos ("Collect" series) ▲ CHAN 6546 [DDD]
J. Hye-Knudsen (cnd)
du Puy, E.:Youth & Folly (ov) Sterling ▲ 1018 [AAD]
Hartmann, J.P.E.:Little Kristen (ov) Sterling ▲ 1018 [AAD]
Heise, P.:King & Marshal (ov) Sterling ▲ 1018 [AAD]
Horneman, C.F.E.:Aladdin (ov) Sterling ▲ 1018 [AAD]
Kuhlau, F.:William Shakespeare (ov) Sterling ▲ 1018 [AAD]
Weyse, C.E.F.:The Sleeping-draught (ov) Sterling ▲ 1018 [AAD]
M. Schønwandt (cnd)
Weyse, C.E.F.:Sym 1 Marco Polo/Dacapo ▲ 8.224012 [DDD]
Weyse, C.E.F.:Sym 2 Marco Polo/Dacapo ▲ 8.224012 [DDD]
Weyse, C.E.F.:Sym 3 Marco Polo/Dacapo ▲ 8.224012 [DDD]
Weyse, C.E.F.:Sym 4 *(rec Copenhagen, Feb 9-11 & 22-24, 1994)* Marco Polo ("dacapo" series) ▲ 8.224013 [DDD]
Weyse, C.E.F.:Sym 5 *(rec Copenhagen, Feb 9-11 & 22-24, 1994)* Marco Polo ("dacapo" series) ▲ 8.224013 [DDD]
Weyse, C.E.F.:Sym 6 *(rec Copenhagen, Feb 9-11 & 22-24, 1994)* Marco Polo ("dacapo" series) ▲ 8.224014 [DDD]
Weyse, C.E.F.:Sym 7 *(rec Copenhagen, Feb 9-11 & 22-24, 1994)* Marco Polo ("dacapo" series) ▲ 8.224014 [DDD]

Royal Danish Radio Orch
Luening, O.:Poem in Cycles & Bells, w. Otto Luening (elec), Ussachevsky (elec) CRI ■ ACS 6011

Royal Dragoon Guards Regimental Band
R. Pennington (cnd)
Fame & Renown Bandleader ▲ BND 5110 [DDD]

Royal Engineers Orch
Showtime, w. Atherstone Choral Society Bandleader ▲ BND 5084 [DDD]

Royal Festival Opera SO
J. Hoffman (cnd)
Sarasate, P. de:Zigeunerweisen, w. R. Ricci (vn) One-Eleven ▲ URS 93020 [ADD]

Royal Flanders PO
F. Devreese (cnd)
Benoit, P.:Le Roi des Aulnes (ov) *(rec Elisabeth Hall, Antwerp, Belgium, Apr 1995)* Marco Polo ("Anthology of Flemish Music" series) ▲ 8.223827 [DDD]
Benoit, P.:Symphonic Poem Fl, w. Gaby Van Riet (fl) *(rec Elisabeth Hall, Antwerp, Belgium, Apr 1995)* Marco Polo ("Anthology of Flemish Music" series) ▲ 8.223827 [DDD]
Benoit, P.:Symphonic Poem Pno, w. Luc Devos (pno) *(rec Elisabeth Hall, Antwerp, Belgium, Apr 1995)* Marco Polo ("Anthology of Flemish Music" series) ▲ 8.223827 [DDD]
Boeck, A. de:Con Vn, w. Guido De Neve (vn) *(rec Elisabeth Hall, Antwerp, July 1994)* Marco Polo ("Anthology of Flemish Music" series) ▲ 8.223740 [DDD]
Boeck, A. de:Rhap Dahoméenne *(rec Elisabeth Hall, Antwerp, July 1994)* Marco Polo ("Anthology of Flemish Music" series) ▲ 8.223740 [DDD]
Boeck, A. de:Sym in G *(rec Elisabeth Hall, Antwerp, July 1994)* Marco Polo ("Anthology of Flemish Music" series) ▲ 8.223740 [DDD]
G. Llewellyn (cnd)
Ryelandt, J.:Agnus Dei, w. Ingrid Kapelle (sop), Lucienne van Deyck (mez), Joseph Cornwell (ten), Huub Claessens (bass), Stephan Macleod (bass), Altra Voce, Audite Nova *(rec live, Elisabeth Hall, Antwerp, Holland, Dec 9, 1994)* Marco Polo 2-▲ 8.223785/86 [DDD]
G. Neuhold (cnd)
Bruckner, A.:Sym 4, "Romantic" *(rec 7/88)* Naxos ▲ 8.550154 [DDD]
Franck, C.:Prélude, choral et fugue [orchd. Paul Pierné] *(rec 7/88)* Naxos ▲ 8.550155 [DDD]
Franck, C.:Sym in d *(rec 7/88)* Naxos ▲ 8.550155 [DDD]
G. Oskamp (cnd)
Maes, J.:Arabesque & Scherzo, w. Frank Vanhove (fl) *(rec Elisabeth Hall, Antwerp, July 1994)* Marco Polo ("Anthology of Flemish Music" series) ▲ 8.223741 [DDD]
Maes, J.:Con Va, w. Leo De Neve (va) *(rec Elisabeth Hall, Antwerp, July 1994)* Marco Polo ("Anthology of Flemish Music" series) ▲ 8.223741 [DDD]
Maes, J.:Ov concertante *(rec Elisabeth Hall, Antwerp, July 1994)* Marco Polo ("Anthology of Flemish Music" series) ▲ 8.223741 [DDD]
Maes, J.:Sym 2 *(rec Elisabeth Hall, Antwerp, July 1994)* Marco Polo ("Anthology of Flemish Music" series) ▲ 8.223741 [DDD]

Royal Flemish PO
M. Tang (cnd)
Orff, C.:Carmina burana, w. Lisa Griffith (sop), Ulrich Ress (ten), Thomas Mohr (bar), Frankfurt Figuralchor, Frankfurt Children's Choir, Frankfurt Choral Society, Goethe Academy Children's Choir *(rec Oct. 1993)* Wergo ▲ WER 6602-2 [DDD]

Royal Highland Fusiliers Regimental Band Pipes & Drums
Afore Ye Go Bandleader ▲ BND 5102 [DDD]

Royal Liverpool Orch
G. Llewellyn (cnd)
Butterworth, G.:Bredon Hill & Other Songs Argo ▲ 436401-2 [DDD]
Butterworth, G.:English Idylls Argo ▲ 436401-2 [DDD]
Butterworth, G.:A Shropshire Lad Argo ▲ 436401-2 [DDD]
Coleridge-Taylor, S.:Ballade Argo ▲ 436401-2 [DDD]
Coleridge-Taylor, S.:Symphonic Vars on an African Air Argo ▲ 436401-2 [DDD]
Maccunn, H.:Land of the Mountain & the Flood Argo ▲ 436401-2 [DDD]
M. Nyman (cnd)
Nyman, M.:Con Pno, w. K. Stott (pno) Argo ▲ 443382-2 [DDD]
L. Pešek (cnd)
Suk, J.:A Summer Tale Virgin Classics ▲ CDC 45057

Royal Liverpool PO
E. Bátiz (cnd)
Bizet, G.:Roma Alfa ▲ 1004 [DDD]
Bizet, G.:Sym 1 Alfa ▲ 1004 [DDD]
Dvořák, A.:Sym 8 ASV Quicksilva ▲ CD QS 6006 [DDD]
Dvořák, A.:Sym 8 Alfa ▲ 1001 [DDD]
Rachmaninoff, S.:The Isle of the Dead Alfa ▲ 1011 [DDD]
Rachmaninoff, S.:Symphonic Dances Alfa ▲ 1011 [DDD]
Respighi, O.:Feste Romane Alfa ▲ 1010 [DDD]
Respighi, O.:The Fountains of Rome Alfa ▲ 1010 [DDD]
Respighi, O.:The Pines of Rome Alfa ▲ 1010 [DDD]
Tchaikovsky, P.:Sym 4 Alfa ▲ 1001 [DDD]
Tchaikovsky, P.:Sym 4 ASV Quicksilva ▲ CD QS 6027 [DDD]
C. Davis (cnd)
McCartney, P.:Liverpool Oratorio, w. K. Te Kanawa (sop), S. Burgess (mez), J. Hadley (ten), W. White (bass), Royal Liverpool Phil Choir EMI Classics 2-▲ CDQB 54371 2-■ 4D2Q 54371
S. Edwards (cnd)
Tchaikovsky, P.:Francesca da Rimini Classics for Pleasure ("Eminence" series) ▲ CDEMX 2152 [DDD]
Tchaikovsky, P.:Marche slave Classics for Pleasure ("Eminence" series) ▲ CDEMX 2152 [DDD]
Tchaikovsky, P.:Ov 1812 Classics for Pleasure ("Eminence" series) ▲ CDEMX 2152 [DDD]
Tchaikovsky, P.:Romeo & Juliet Classics for Pleasure ("Eminence" series) ▲ CDEMX 2152 [DDD]
C. Groves (cnd)
Bliss, A.:Meditations on a Theme by John Blow IMP ("BBC Radio Classics" series) ▲ IMP 5691682

▲ = CD ♦ = Enhanced CD Δ = MD ■ = Cassette Tape □ = DCC

Royal Liverpool PO (cont.)

C. Groves (cnd) (cont.)

Coates, E.:Music of—London [London Every Day] (1933); London Again (1936); The Three Bears Phantasy (1926); Cinderella Phantasy (1929) Arabesque ▲ Z 8036
Delius, F.:Brigg Fair:An English Rhapsody, w. J. Shirley-Quirk (bar), Royal Liverpool Phil Choir EMI Classics ▲ ZDMB 64218
Delius, F.:Requiem, w. H. Harper (sop), T. Hemsley (bar), Royal Liverpool Phil Choir *(rec live, Liverpool 1965)* Intaglio 2-▲ INCD 702-2 [ADD]
Delius, F.:Songs of Sunset, w. J. Baker (mez), Royal Liverpool Phil Choir EMI Classics ▲ ZDMB 64218
Elgar, E.:The Light of Life, w. M. Marshall (sop), H. Watts (cta), J. Shirley-Quirk (bar), Royal Liverpool Phil Choir EMI Classics ▲ CDM 64732
Elgar, E.:The Light of Life (sels), w. M. Marshall (sop), H. Watts (cta), J. Shirley-Quirk (bass)—Meditation EMI Classics ▲ CDM 64732
Meditation Classics for Pleasure ▲ CDCFP 4515 [DDD]
Rubbra, E.:Sym 8 *(rec live, Philharmonic Hall, Liverpool, world premiere performance, 8/5/71)* Intaglio ▲ INCD 7311 [ADD]
Rule Brittania, w. A. Collins (cta), Liverpool Philharmonic Choir Classics for Pleasure ▲ CDCFP 4567 [ADD]
Sullivan, A.:Irish Sym EMI Classics ▲ CDM 64726
Sullivan, A.:Irish Sym EMI Classics 2-▲ CDMB 64406
Sullivan, A.:Ovs—Ov. di Ballo EMI Classics ▲ CDM 64726
Sullivan, A.:Ovs—In Memoriam EMI Classics 2-▲ CDMB 64409

Groves, Kurtz (cnd)

Britten, B.:The Young Person's Guide to the Orchestra, w. M. Flanders (nar), Royal Liverpool PO, Philharmonia Orch EMI Classics ▲ CDM 63177

V. Handley (cnd)

Bruch, M.:Con 1 Vn, w. T. Little (vn) Classics for Pleasure ▲ CDCFP 4566 [DDD]
Delius, F.:Con Pno, w. Piers Lane (pno) Classics for Pleasure ("Eminence" series) ▲ CFP 2239
Dvořák, A.:Con Vn, w. T. Little (vn) Classics for Pleasure ▲ CDCFP 4566 [ADD]
Finzi, G.:Con Vc, w. R. Wallfisch (vc) Chandos ▲ CHAN 8471 [DDD]
Finzi, G.:Ecologue, w. Piers Lane (pno) Classics for Pleasure ("Eminence" series) ▲ CFP 2239
Howells, H.:Hymnus Paradisi, w. J. Kennard (sop), J. M. Ainsley (ten), Royal Liverpool Phil Choir Hyperion ▲ CDA 66488
Howells, H.:Orchestral Music, w. K. Stott (pno), M. Stewart (vn)—Concerto for String Orchestra (1938); Concerto No. 2 in c for Piano & Orchestra (1925); Three Dances for Violin & Orchestra (1915) *(rec Feb. 1991 & Mar. 1992)* Hyperion ▲ CDA 66610 [DDD]
Leighton, K.:Veris gratia, w. Raphael Wallfisch (vc), George Caird (ob) Chandos ▲ CHAN 8471 [DDD]
Simpson, R.:Sym 6 Hyperion ▲ CDA 66280 [DDD]
Simpson, R.:Sym 7 Hyperion ▲ CDA 66280 [DDD]
Simpson, R.:Sym 10 Hyperion ▲ CDA 66510
Vaughan Williams, R.:Con Ob, w. Jonathan Small (ob) Classics for Pleasure ("Eminence" series) ▲ CDEMX 2179 [DDD]
Vaughan Williams, R.:Con Ob EMI Classics (Classics for Pleasure) ▲ CDM 64114
Vaughan Williams, R.:Con Pno, w. Piers Lane (pno) Classics for Pleasure ("Eminence" series) ▲ CFP 2239
Vaughan Williams, R.:English Folk Song Suite EMI Classics (Classics for Pleasure) ▲ CDM 64114
Vaughan Williams, R.:English Folk Song Suite Classics for Pleasure ("Eminence" series) ▲ CDEMX 2179 [DDD]
Vaughan Williams, R.:Fant on Greensleeves EMI Classics (Classics for Pleasure) ▲ CDM 64114
Vaughan Williams, R.:Fant on Greensleeves Classics for Pleasure ("Eminence" series) ▲ CDEMX 2179 [DDD]
Vaughan Williams, R.:Fant on a Theme by Thomas Tallis EMI Classics (Classics for Pleasure) ▲ CDM 64114
Vaughan Williams, R.:Fant on a Theme by Thomas Tallis Classics for Pleasure ("Eminence" series) ▲ CDEMX 2179 [DDD]
Vaughan Williams, R.:Flos Campi Classics for Pleasure 6-▲ CDCFP VW 1
Vaughan Williams, R.:Flos Campi, w. Christopher Balmer (va), Royal Liverpool Phil Choir Classics for Pleasure ("Eminence" series) ▲ CDEMX 9512 [DDD]
Vaughan Williams, R.:Partita Classics for Pleasure ("Eminence" series) ▲ CDEMX 2179 [DDD]
Vaughan Williams, R.:Partita EMI Classics (Classics for Pleasure) ▲ CDM 64114
Vaughan Williams, R.:Serenade to Music EMI Classics (Classics for Pleasure) ▲ CDM 64034
Vaughan Williams, R.:Serenade to Music, w. Royal Liverpool Phil Choir Classics for Pleasure ("Eminence" series) ▲ CDEMX 2173 [DDD]
Vaughan Williams, R.:Serenade to Music Classics for Pleasure 6-▲ CDCFP VW 1
Vaughan Williams, R.:Syms Classics for Pleasure 6-▲ CDCFP VW 1
Vaughan Williams, R.:Sym 1, w. Joan Rodgers (sop), William Shimell (bar) Classics for Pleasure ("Eminence" series) ▲ CDEMX 2142 [DDD]
Vaughan Williams, R.:Sym 2 Classics for Pleasure ("Eminence" series) ▲ CDEMX 2209 [DDD]
Vaughan Williams, R.:Sym 5 Classics for Pleasure ("Eminence" series) ▲ CDEMX 9512 [DDD]
Vaughan Williams, R.:Sym 7, w. Royal Liverpool Phil Choir Classics for Pleasure ("Eminence" series) ▲ CDEMX 2173 [DDD]
Vaughan Williams, R.:Sym 7 EMI Classics (Classics for Pleasure) ▲ CDM 64034
Vaughan Williams, R.:Sym 8 Classics for Pleasure ("Eminence" series) ▲ CDEMX 2209 [DDD]
Walton, W.:Sym 1 ASV Quicksilva ▲ ASQ 6093 [DDD]

R. Hickox (cnd)

Finzi, G.:Grand Fant & Toccata, w. Philip Fowke (pno) EMI Classics ▲ CDM 64720
Finzi, G.:Intimations of Immortality, w. P. Langridge (ten), Royal Liverpool Phil Choir EMI Classics ▲ CDM 64720

M. Janowski (cnd)

Brahms, J.:Academic Festival Ov ASV Quicksilva ▲ ASQ 6104 [DDD]
Brahms, J.:Sym 1 ASV Quicksilva ▲ ASQ 6101 [DDD]
Brahms, J.:Sym 2 ASV Quicksilva ▲ ASQ 6102 [DDD]
Brahms, J.:Sym 3 ASV Quicksilva ▲ ASQ 6103 [DDD]
Brahms, J.:Sym 4 ASV Quicksilva ▲ ASQ 6104 [DDD]
Brahms, J.:Vars on a Theme by Haydn ASV Quicksilva ▲ ASQ 6103 [DDD]
Schumann, R.:Sym 1 ASV Quicksilva ▲ ASQ 6073 [DDD]
Schumann, R.:Sym 2 ASV Quicksilva ▲ QS 6084 [DDD]
Schumann, R.:Sym 3 ASV Quicksilva ▲ ASQ 6073 [DDD]
Schumann, R.:Sym 4 ASV Quicksilva ▲ QS 6084 [DDD]

S. Kovacevich (cnd)

Mozart, W.A.:Cons Hn, w. C. Briggs (hn) Classics for Pleasure ▲ CDCFP 4589 [DDD]

C. Mackerras (cnd)

Beethoven, L. van:Sym 5 Classics for Pleasure ("Eminence" series) ▲ CFP 2212 [DDD]
Beethoven, L. van:Sym 7 Classics for Pleasure ("Eminence" series) ▲ CFP 2212 [DDD]
Beethoven, L. van:Sym 9, "Choral Sym", w. Joan Rodgers (sop), Della Jones (alt), Peter Bronder (ten), Bryn Terfel (bass), Royal Liverpool Phil Choir Classics for Pleasure ("Eminence" series) ▲ CFP 2186 [DDD]
Borodin, A.:Prince Igor (sels) Virgin Classics ("Ultraviolet" series) ▲ CUV 61135
Borodin, A.:Prince Igor (ov) Virgin Classics ▲ CDC 59625
Borodin, A.:Prince Igor (Polovtsian dances) Virgin Classics ▲ CDC 59625
Delius, F.:Con Vc, w. Raphael Wallfisch (vc) Classics for Pleasure ("Eminence" series) ▲ CDEMX 2185 [DDD]
Delius, F.:Double Con, w. Tasmin Little (vn), Raphael Wallfisch (vc) Classics for Pleasure ("Eminence" series) ▲ CDEMX 2185 [DDD]
Delius, F.:Paris:The Song of a Great City Classics for Pleasure ("Eminence" series) ▲ CDEMX 2185 [DDD]
Holst, G.:The Perfect Fool Virgin Classics ▲ CDZ 59645
Holst, G.:The Planets Virgin Classics ("Ultraviolet" series) ▲ CUV 61257
Holst, G.:The Planets Virgin Classics ▲ CDZ 59645
Mahler, G.:Sym 5 Classics for Pleasure ("Eminence" series) ▲ CDEMX 2164 [DDD]

Royal Liverpool PO (cont.)

C. Mackerras (cnd) (cont.)

Mussorgsky, M.:Night Virgin Classics ("Ultraviolet" series) ▲ CUV 61135
Mussorgsky, M.:Night Virgin Classics ▲ CDC 59625
Mussorgsky, M.:Pictures at an Exhibition Virgin Classics ▲ CDC 59625
Mussorgsky, M.:Pictures at an Exhibition Virgin Classics ("Ultraviolet" series) ▲ CUV 61135

L. Pešek (cnd)

Brahms, J.:Con Vn, w. R. Oleg (vn) Denon ▲ CO 79944 [DDD]
Britten, B.:Peter Grimes (sea interludes & passacaglia) Virgin Classics ▲ 59550 [DDD]
Britten, B.:Peter Grimes (sea interludes & passacaglia) Virgin Classics ("Ultraviolet" series) ▲ CUV 61195
Britten, B.:Sinf da requiem Virgin Classics ▲ 59550 [DDD]
Britten, B.:Sinf da requiem Virgin Classics ("Ultraviolet" series) ▲ CUV 61195
Britten, B.:The Young Person's Guide to the Orchestra Virgin Classics ("Ultraviolet" series) ▲ CUV 61195
Britten, B.:The Young Person's Guide to the Orchestra Virgin Classics ▲ 59550 [DDD]
Bruch, M.:Con 1 Vn, w. R. Oleg (vn) Denon ▲ CO 79944 [DDD]
Dvořák, A.:Carnival Virgin Classics ▲ CDC 59174
Dvořák, A.:Husitská Virgin Classics ▲ CDC 59285
Dvořák, A.:Romance Vn Virgin Classics ▲ CDC 59285
Dvořák, A.:Scherzo Capriccioso Virgin Classics ▲ CDC 59174
Dvořák, A.:Silent Woods Virgin Classics ▲ CDC 59285
Dvořák, A.:Suite, Op. 98b, "American" Virgin Classics ▲ 59505 [DDD]
Dvořák, A.:Sym 3 Virgin Classics ▲ CDC 59174
Dvořák, A.:Sym 7 Virgin Classics ▲ 59516 [DDD]
Dvořák, A.:Sym 8 Virgin Classics ▲ 59516 [DDD]
Dvořák, A.:Sym 9, "From the New World" Virgin Classics ▲ 59505 [DDD]
Fučík, J.:Marches & Waltzes—Die lustigen Dofschmiede; Der alte Brummbar; Entry of the Gladiators Virgin Classics ▲ CDC 59285
Prokofiev, S.:Romeo & Juliet (sels) Virgin Classics ▲ CDC 59278 [DDD]
Smetana, B.:The Bartered Bride (ov) Virgin Classics ▲ CDC 59285
Smetana, B.:The Bartered Bride (dances) Virgin Classics ▲ CDC 59285
Smetana, B.:Má Vlast Virgin Classics ▲ CDC 59285
Strauss, R.:Don Juan Virgin Classics ▲ 59623 [DDD]
Strauss, R.:Ein Heldenleben Virgin Classics ▲ 59623 [DDD]
Suk, J.:Asrael Virgin Classics ▲ CDC 59638
Suk, J.:Praga Virgin Classics ▲ CDC 59318
Suk, J.:The Ripening Virgin Classics ▲ CDC 59318

J. Pritchard (cnd)

Donizetti, G.:Emilia di Liverpool (sels), w. A. Cantelo (sop), J. Sutherland (sop), W. McAlpine (ten), D. Dowling (bar), H. Alan (bass), Liverpool Music Group Singers—13 arias from Act 1, & 4 from Act 2 [I] *(rec live, Liverpool Sept. 1957)* Myto ▲ 1 MCD 91545 [ADD]

M. Sargent (cnd)

Handel, G.F.:Messiah, w. Elsie Morison (sop), Marjorie Thomas (cta), Richard Lewis (ten), James Milligan (bass), Huddersfield Choral Society Classics for Pleasure 2-▲ CDCFP 4718 [ADD]
Handel, G.F.:Messiah (sels), w. Elsie Morison (sop), Marjorie Thomas (cta), Richard Lewis (ten), James Milligan (bass), Eric Chadwick (org), Huddersfield Choral Society Classics for Pleasure ▲ CDCFP 9007 [ADD]

L. Tjeknavorian (cnd)

Mendelssohn, F.:Ovs—Fingal's Cave Klavier ▲ KCD 11034 [DDD]

B. Wordsworth (cnd)

Berners:Fant espagnole EMI Classics ▲ CDM 65098
Berners:Nicholas Nickleby EMI Classics ▲ CDM 65098
Berners:Pieces (3) Orch EMI Classics ▲ CDM 65098
Berners:The Triumph of Neptune—Suite EMI Classics ▲ CDM 65098

Royal Marines Band

G. A. C. Hoskins (cnd)

Best of the Royal Marines EMI Classics ▲ CDM 69935
Sousa, J.P.:Marches & Dances EMI Classics ▲ CDM 64671
Sousa, J.P.:Marches & Dances EMI Classics ▲ CDM 64672

Royal Northern College of Music Brass Ensemble

E. Gregson (cnd)

Gregson, E.:Music of, w. Hallé Brass, Northern Trombone Quartet—Fanfare for Europe; Equale Dances; Susie's Fanfare; Son for 4 Trbns; Fanfare for the North; Qnt for Brass; Flourish for the Theatre; Flourish for an Occasion; Dance Episodes (3); Festival Fanfare Doyen ▲ CD 038 [DDD]

Royal Northern College of Music CO

O. Schmidt (cnd)

Schmidt, O.:Chamber Sym *(rec Mariot, France, 1994–95)* Marco Polo/Dacapo ▲ 8.224035 [DDD]
Schmidt, O.:Con Fl, w. Susan Milan (fl) *(rec Mariot, France, 1994–95)* Marco Polo/Dacapo ▲ 8.224035 [DDD]
Schmidt, O.:Hommage à Franz Liszt *(rec Mariot, France, 1994–95)* Marco Polo/Dacapo ▲ 8.224035 [DDD]

Royal Northern College of Music Wind Orch

E. Gregson (cnd)

Gregson, E.:Metamorphoses, w. Owain Bailey (fl), Karen Fotherby (cl) Doyen ▲ CD 043 [DDD]
Gregson, E.:Missa Brevis Pacem, w. James Keenan (trb), Henry Herford (bar), Manchester Boy's Choir Doyen ▲ CD 043 [DDD]
Gregson, E.:The Sword & the Crown Doyen ▲ CD 043 [DDD]

T. Reynish (cnd)

Gregson, E.:Celebration Doyen ▲ CD 043 [DDD]
Gregson, E.:Festivo Doyen ▲ CD 043 [DDD]

C. Rundell (cnd)

McLeod, J.:The Dramatic Landscape, w. A. Wilson (cl) Vienna Modern Masters ▲ VMM 3026 [DDD]

G. Woolfenden (cnd)

Woolfenden, G.:Music of—Illyrian Dances; SPQR; Suite Française; Mockbeggar Vars; Deo Gracias; Full Fathom Five [w. Nemo Brass Quintet]; Gallimaufry *(rec Zion Institute, Manchester, 1995)* Doyen ▲ CD 042 [DDD]

Royal Opera House Covent Garden Orch

Arias, w. M. Callas (sop), Turin RAI SO, Rome RAI SO, Milan RAI SO *(rec 1949–1962)* Verona 2-▲ 27058/59 (m) [AAD]
Christmas from Covent Garden, w. Royal Opera House Covent Garden Chorus *(rec All Saints' Church, Tooting, London & All Saints' Church, Petersham, Surrey, May 1989 & May 1994)* Conifer Classics ▲ 75605-55011-2 [DDD]
Puccini, G.:Tosca, w. M. Caballé (sop), J. Carreras (ten) Philips 2-▲ 438359-2
Puccini, G.:Tosca, w. M. Caballé (sop), J. Carreras (ten), I. Wixell (bar) [I] Philips 2-▲ 412885-2 [ADD]

C. Abbado (cnd)

Verdi, G.:Un ballo in maschera, w. Reri Grist (sop), Katia Ricciarelli (sop), Elizabeth Bainbridge (mez), Plácido Domingo (ten), Piero Cappuccilli (bar), Royal Opera House Covent Garden Chorus *(rec 1975)* Arkadia 2-▲ 488

J. Barbirolli (cnd)

Verdi, G.:Aida, w. Maria Callas (sop—Aida), Joan Sutherland (sop—Priestess), Giulietta Simionato (cta—Amneris), Kurt Baum (ten—Radames), Hector Thomas (ten—Messenger), Jess Walters (bar—Amonasro), Michael Langdon (bass—King), Giulio Neri (bass—Ramfis), Royal Opera House Covent Garden Chorus *(rec Covent Garden, London, June 10, 1953)* Legato Classics 2-▲ LCD 187-2

T. Beecham (cnd)

Smetana, B.:The Bartered Bride, w. H. Konetzni (sop), R. Tauber (ten), F. Krenn (bass), Royal Opera House Covent Garden Chorus [G] *(rec live, Covent Garden, 5/1/39)* Standing Room Only 2-▲ SRO 830-2 [ADD]

ORCH. & ENS.

Royal Opera House Covent Garden Orch (cont.)
T. Beecham (cnd) (cont.)
Wagner, R.:Der fliegende Holländer (sels), w. Kirsten Flagstad (sop), Tiana Lemnitz (sop), Torsten Ralf (ten), Rudolf Bockelmann (b-bar), Ludwig Weber (bass), Royal Opera House Covent Garden Chorus Memories ("Golden" series) ▲ MEM 3003
Wagner, R.:Götterdämmerung (sels), w. Kirsten Flagstad (sop), Tiana Lemnitz (sop), Torsten Ralf (ten), Rudolf Bockelmann (b-bar), Ludwig Weber (bass), Royal Opera House Covent Garden Chorus Memories ("Golden" series) ▲ MEM 3003
Wagner, R.:Lohengrin (sels), w. Kirsten Flagstad (sop), Tiana Lemnitz (sop), Torsten Ralf (ten), Rudolf Bockelmann (b-bar), Ludwig Weber (bass), Royal Opera House Covent Garden Chorus Memories ("Golden" series) ▲ MEM 3003
Wagner, R.:Die Meistersinger von Nürnberg (sels), w. Kirsten Flagstad (sop), Tiana Lemnitz (sop), Torsten Ralf (ten), Rudolf Bockelmann (b-bar), Ludwig Weber (bass), Royal Opera House Covent Garden Chorus Memories ("Golden" series) ▲ MEM 3003
Wagner, R.:Tristan und Isolde, w. K. Flagstad (sop), L. Melchior (ten), H. Janssen (bar), P. Schoeffler (b-bar), Royal Opera House Covent Garden Chorus *(rec live, Covent Garden, 6/18 & 22/37)* Melodram 3-▲ MEL 37029 (m) [AAD]
Wagner, R.:Tristan und Isolde (sels), w. Kirsten Flagstad (sop), Tiana Lemnitz (sop), Torsten Ralf (ten), Rudolf Bockelmann (b-bar), Ludwig Weber (bass), Royal Opera House Covent Garden Chorus Memories ("Golden" series) ▲ MEM 3003
V. Bellezza (cnd)
Verdi, G.:Otello (sels), w. Giovanni Zenatello (ten), C. Sabajno (cnd), La Scala Orch, Royal Opera House Covent Garden Chorus Phonographe ("Great Voices" series) ▲ PHG 5048
R. Bonynge (cnd)
Donizetti, G.:Lucia di Lammermoor (sels), w. J. Sutherland (sop), L. Pavarotti (ten), S. Milnes (bar), N. Ghiaurov (bass), Royal Opera House Covent Garden Chorus [I] London ("Opera Gala" series) ▲ 421885-2 [ADD]
P. Boulez (cnd)
Debussy, C.:Pelléas et Mélisande, w. E. Söderström (sop), Y. Minton (mez), G. Shirley (ten), D. McIntyre (bass-bar), D. Ward (bass), Royal Opera House Covent Garden Chorus Sony Classical (Pierre Boulez Edition) 3-▲ SM3K 47265
B. Britten (cnd)
Britten, B.:Billy Budd, w. P. Pears (ten), T. Uppman (bar), H. Alan (bar), G. Evans (b-bar), F. Dalberg (bass), Royal Opera House Covent Garden Chorus *(rec Dec. 1, 1951)* VAI Audio 3-▲ VAIA 1034-3 [ADD]
Britten, B.:Peter Grimes, w. C. Watson (sop), P. Pears (ten), G. Evans (bar), Royal Opera House Covent Garden Chorus [E] London 3-▲ 414577-2 [ADD]
C. F. Cillario (cnd)
Live on Stage, w. Luciano Pavarotti (ten), Rome Opera Orch [cnd:Carlo Maria Giulini], Royal Opera House Covent Garden Chorus, et al. LaserLight ▲ 15104
Puccini, G.:Tosca, w. Maria Callas (sop—Floria Tosca), Robert Bowman (ten—Spoletta), Renato Cioni (ten—Mario Cavaradossi), Eric Garrett (bar—Il Sagrestano), Tito Gobbi (bar—Scarpia), Victor Godfrey (bass—Casare Angelotti), Dennis Wicks (bass—Sciarrone), Royal Opera House Covent Garden Chorus *(rec London, 1964)* Melodram 2-▲ CDI 203003 [ADD]
Puccini, G.:Tosca, w. M. Callas (sop), R. Cioni (ten), T. Gobbi (bar), Royal Opera House Covent Garden Chorus [I] *(rec live, 1/21/64)* Verona 2-▲ 27027/28 (m) [AAD]
Puccini, G.:Tosca, w. M. Callas (sop), R. Cioni (ten), T. Gobbi (bar), Royal Opera House Covent Garden Chorus [I] *(rec live 1/21/64)* Melodram 2-▲ MEL 26011
Verdi, G.:La traviata, w. R. Scotto (sop), L. Pavarotti (ten), P. Glossop (bar), Royal Opera House Covent Garden Chorus *(rec live 1965)* Memories 2-▲ HR 4404/05 (m)
Verdi, G.:La traviata (sels), w. R. Scotto (sop), L. Pavarotti (ten), Royal Opera House Covent Garden Chorus—2 scenes [I] *(rec live, Covent Garden 3/19/65)* Verona 2-▲ 27081/82
C. Davis (cnd)
Britten, B.:Peter Grimes, w. H. Harper (sop), J. Vickers (ten), J. Summers (bar), Royal Opera House Covent Garden Chorus [E] Philips 2-▲ 432578-2 [ADD]
C. Davis (cnd)
Massenet, J.:Werther, w. F. von Stade (mez), J. Carreras (ten), T. Allen (bar), R. Lloyd (b-bar), Royal Opera House Orch Covent Garden Chorus [F] Philips 2-▲ 416654-2 [ADD]
Mozart, W.A.:Complete Mozart Edition, w. K. Te Kanawa (sop), M. Arroyo (sop), M. Freni (sop), S. Burrows (ten), I. Wixell (bar), Royal Opera House Covent Garden Chorus Philips 3-▲ 422541-2 [ADD]
Mozart, W.A.:Complete Mozart Edition, w. M. Caballé (sop), I. Cotrubas (sop), J. Baker (mez), N. Gedda (ten), Royal Opera House Covent Garden Chorus Philips 3-▲ 422542-2 [ADD]
Mozart, W.A.:Complete Mozart Edition, w. L. Popp (sop), J. Baker (mez), Y. Minton (mez), F. von Stade (mez), S. Burrows (ten), R. Lloyd (b-bar), Royal Opera House Covent Garden Chorus Philips 2-▲ 422544-2 [ADD]
Tippett, M.:The Midsummer Marriage, w. Joan Carlyle (sop—Joan), Elizabeth Harwood (sop—Beth), Elizabeth Bainbridge (mez), Helen Watts (cta—Sosostris), Stuart Burrows (ten—Jack), Alberto Remedios (ten—Mark), Stafford Dean (bass), Raimund Herincx (bass—King Fisher), Royal Opera House Covent Garden Chorus Lyrita 2-▲ SRCD 2217
Verdi, G.:Il trovatore, w. Katia Ricciarelli (sop), Stefania Toczyska (mez), José Carreras (ten), Yuri Mazurok (bar), Royal Opera House Covent Garden Chorus Philips ("Two-Fers" series) 2-▲ 446151-2
A. Dorati (cnd)
Wagner, R.:Der fliegende Holländer, w. L. Rysanek (sop), K. Liebl (ten), G. London (bar), G. Tozzi (bass), Royal Opera House Covent Garden Chorus[G] London 2-▲ 417319-2 [ADD]
E. Downes (cnd)
Puccini, G.:Arias, w. Angela Gheorghiu (sop), Nina Rautio (sop), Johan Botha (ten), Anthony Michaels-Moore (bar), Royal Opera House Covent Garden Chorus—Se come voi piccina io fossi [from Le villi]; Addio mio dolce amor [from Edgar]; Donna non vidi mai; Sola, perduta, abbandonata [both from Manon Lescaut]; Donde lieta usci [from La Bohème]; Act 1 Finale; E lucevan le stelle [both from Tosca]; Un tal baccano in chiesa; Or tutto è chiaro; Tre sbirri, una carrozza; Un bel dì [from Madama Butterfly]; Ch'ella mi creda [from La fanciulla del West]; Chi il bel sogno di Doretta [from La rondine]; Nulla, silenzio [from Il tabarro]; Senza mamma [from Suor Angelica]; O mio babbino caro [from Gianni Schicchi]; Act I Finale; Nessun dorma [both from Turandot]; Signore, acolta; Non piangere, Liù *(rec Henry Wood Hall, London, Feb 12-27 & Mar 5, 1995)* Conifer Classics ("Royal Opera House" series) ▲ 75605-55013-2 [DDD]
Verdi, G.:Aida, w. G. Jones (sop), J. Vickers (ten), Dourian (sgr), Shaw (sgr), Royal Opera House Covent Garden Chorus [I] *(rec live, Covent Garden, 1/27/68)* Melodram 2-▲ MEL 27019
M. Ermler (cnd)
Essential Russian Ballet Conifer Classics ▲ 74321-18814-2
M. Ermler, B. Wordsworth (cnds)
The Ballet Album Conifer Classics ▲ 75605-55014-2 [DDD]
L. Gardelli (cnd)
Opera Choruses, w. Royal Opera House Covent Garden Chorus EMI Classics ▲ CDM 64356
G. Gavazzeni (cnd)
Mascagni, P.:L'amico Fritz, w. M. Freni (sop), L. Pavarotti (ten), V. Sardinero (bar), Royal Opera House Covent Garden Chorus [I] EMI Classics 2-▲ CDCB 47905 [ADD]
C. M. Giulini (cnd)
Verdi, G.:Don Carlos, w. G. Brouwenstein (sop—Elisabeta di Valois), F. Barbieri (mez—Princess Eboli), J. Vickers (ten—Don Carlo), T. Gobbi (bar—Rodrigo), B. Christoff (bass—Fillipo), Royal Opera House Covent Garden Chorus *(rec 1958)* Myto 3-▲ MCD 94197
I. Godfrey (cnd)
Sullivan, A.:Ruddigore, w. D'Oyly Carte Opera Company London 2-▲ 417355-2 [ADD]
Sullivan, A.:The Yeomen of the Guard, w. M. Sargent (cnd), D'Oyly Carte Opera Company, Royal PO London 2-▲ 417358-2 [ADD]
V. Gui (cnd)
Bellini, V.:Norma, w. M. Callas (sop), J. Sutherland (sop), E. Stignani (mez), M. Picchi (ten), G. Vaghi (bass), Royal Opera House Covent Garden Chorus [I] *(rec live, Covent Garden 11/52)* Legato Classics 2-▲ LCD 130-2 (m) [AAD]

Royal Opera House Covent Garden Orch (cont.)
V. Gui (cnd) (cont.)
Bellini, V.:Norma, w. M. Callas (sop), J. Sutherland (sop), E. Stignani (mez), M. Picchi (ten), G. Vaghi (bass), Royal Opera House Covent Garden Chorus [I] *(rec live, Covent Garden 11/52)* Melodram 2-▲ MEL 26025
Bellini, V.:Norma, w. M. Callas (sop), J. Sutherland (sop), E. Stignani (mez), M. Picchi (ten), G. Vaghi (bass), Royal Opera House Covent Garden Chorus [I] *(rec live, Covent Garden 11/52)* Verona 3-▲ 27018/20 (m) [AAD]
Verdi, G.:Il trovatore, w. G. Cigna (sop—Leonora), G. Wettergren (mez—Azucena), M. Huder (mez—Ines), J. Björling (ten—Manrico), O. Dua (ten—Ruiz), C. Zambelli (ten—Ferrando), M. Basiola (bar—Count di Luna), L. Horsman (bar—Old Gypsy), Royal Opera House Covent Garden Chorus *(rec May 12, 1939)* Legato Classics 2-▲ LCD 173-2 [ADD]
B. Haitink (cnd)
Britten, B.:Peter Grimes, w. F. Lott (sop—Ellen Orford), T. Allen (ten—Captain Balstrode), A. R. Johnson (ten—Peter Grimes) Royal Opera House Covent Garden Chorus EMI Classics ▲ CDCB 54832
R. Kempe (cnd)
Puccini, G.:Madama Butterfly, w. V. de los Angeles (sop—Madama Butterfly), B. Howitt (mez—Suzuki), J. Livingston (mez—Kate), J. Lanigan (ten—Pinkerton), D. Tree (ten—Goro), D. A. (ten—Yamadori), G. Evans (bar—Sharpless), M. Langdon (bass—Bonzo), Royal Opera House Covent Garden Chorus *(rec London, May 1957)* Ornamenti 2-▲ FE 112 [ADD]
O. Klemperer (cnd)
Beethoven, L. van:Fidelio, w. S. Jurinac (sop), J. Vickers (ten), H. Hotter (b-bar), G. Frick (bass), Royal Opera House Covent Garden Chorus [G] *(rec live, Covent Garden, 3/7/61)* Melodram 2-▲ MEL 27076 (m) [AAD]
R. Kubelik (cnd)
Janácek, L.:Jenůfa (sels), w. M. Collier (sop), A. Varnay (sop), R. Cassilly (ten), J. Lanigan (ten), Royal Opera House Covent Garden Chorus—eight solo, duet & trio arias featuring Astrid Varnay [G] *(rec live at Covent Garden, Feb. 24, 1968)* Myto 2-▲ 2 MCD 90422 [ADD]
Z. Mehta (cnd)
Puccini, G.:La fanciulla del West, w. C. Neblett (sop), P. Domingo (ten), S. Milnes (bar), Royal Opera House Covent Garden Chorus [I] Deutsche Grammophon 2-▲ 419640-2 [ADD]
F. Molinari-Pradelli (cnd)
Puccini, G.:Tosca, w. R. Tebaldi (sop), F. Tagliavini (ten), T. Gobbi (bar), Royal Opera House Covent Garden Chorus [I] *(rec live at Covent Garden, 6/30/55)* Legato Classics 2-▲ LCD 157-2 (m) [ADD]
Verdi, G.:Macbeth, w. Amy Shuard (sop—Lady Macbeth), Noreen Berry (mez—Lady-in-waiting), John Dobson (ten—Malcolm), André Turp (ten—Macduff), Tito Gobbi (bar—Macbeth), Edgar Boniface (bass—Servant), Rydderch Davies (bass—Doctor), Forbes Robinson (bass—Banco), Jean Holmes (sgr—Apparition), Celia Penny (sgr—Apparition), Glynne Thomas (sgr—Apparition), Brian Wrigt (sgr—Araldo), Royal Opera House Covent Garden Chorus *(rec London, Apr 8, 1960)* Bella Voce 2-▲ 7203 [AAD]
R. Muti (cnd)
Bellini, V.:I Capuleti e i Montecchi, w. E. Guberova (sop—Giulietta), A. Baltsa (mez—Romeo), D. Raffanti (ten—Tebaldo), Royal Opera House Covent Garden Chorus EMI Classics ▲ CDMB 64846
J. Pritchard (cnd)
Donizetti, G.:L'elisir d'amore, w. I. Cotrubas (sop), L. Watson (sop), P. Domingo (ten), G. Evans (bar), I. Wixell (bar), Royal Opera House Covent Garden Chorus *(rec 1977)* CBS 2-▲ M2K 34585 [ADD]
F. Reiner (cnd)
Wagner, R.:Der fliegende Holländer (sels), w. K. Flagstad (sop), M. Lorenz (ten), H. Janssen (bar), L. Weber (bass), Royal Opera House Covent Garden Chorus [G] *(rec live, Covent Garden, 6/11/37)* Standing Room Only ▲ SRO 808-1 (m) [ADD]
Wagner, R.:Tristan und Isolde, w. K. Flagstad (sop), S. Kalter (cta), L. Melchior (ten), H. Janssen (bar), E. List (bass), Royal Opera House Covent Garden Chorus [G] *(rec live, Covent Garden May/June 1936)* VAI Audio 3-▲ VAIA 1004-3 (m) [ADD]
N. Rescigno (cnd)
Cherubini, L.:Médée, w. M. Callas (sop), F. Cossotto (mez), J. Vickers (ten), N. Zaccaria (bass), Royal Opera House Covent Garden Chorus [I] *(rec live, Covent Garden, 6/30/59)* Melodram 2-▲ MEL 26005
Verdi, G.:La traviata, w. M. Callas (sop), C. Valletti (ten), A. Zanasi (bass), Royal Opera House Covent Garden Chorus [I] *(rec live 6/20/58)* Melodram 2-▲ MEL 26007 (m)
Verdi, G.:La traviata, w. M. Callas (sop), C. Valletti (ten), A. Zanasi (bass), Royal Opera House Covent Garden Chorus [I] *(rec live 6/20/58)* Verona 2-▲ 27054/55 (m) [AAD]
H. Sandberg (cnd)
Verdi, G.:Il trovatore (sels), w. Hjördis Schymberg (sop), Kerstin Meyer (mez), Jussi Björling (ten), Olle Sivall (ten), Hugo Hasslo (bar), Royal Opera House Covent Garden Chorus—Non son tuo figlio?; Mal reggendo all'aspro assalto; Quale d'armi fragor; Ah! sì, ben mio, coll'essere; L'onda de' suoni mistici; Di quella pira l'orrendo foco; Miserere d'un'alma già vicina; Madre?...non dormi?; Se m'ami ancor; Ciel!...non m'inganna; Ti scosta... *(rec Royal Opera, Stockholm, Mar 6, 1960)* Myto ▲ MCD 953130
T. Serafin (cnd)
Bellini, V.:La sonnambula (sels), w. J. Sutherland (sop), Royal Opera House Covent Garden Chorus—seven arias & scenes [I] *(rec live, Covent Garden 1960)* Myto 2-▲ 2 MCD 90529 [ADD]
Donizetti, G.:Lucia di Lammermoor (sels), w. J. McDonald (sop), J. Sutherland (sop), M. Elkins (mez), J. Bowman (alt), J. Gibin (ten), J. Rouleau (bass), Shaw (sgr), Royal Opera House Covent Garden Chorus—3 duets from Act 1, & 3 soprano solo arias from Act 2 [I] Myto ▲ 1 MCD 91545 [ADD]
G. Solti (cnd)
Bizet, G.:Carmen, w. Kiri Te Kanawa (sop), Shirley Verrett (mez), Placido Domingo (ten), José Van Dam (b-bar), Royal Opera House Covent Garden Chorus *(rec live, London, 1973)* Arkadia 3-▲ 498
Gluck, C.W.:Orfeo ed Euridice, w. H. Donath (sop), P. Lorengar (sop), M. Horne (mez), Royal Opera House Covent Garden Chorus London 2-▲ 417410-2 [ADD]
Verdi, G.:Don Carlos, w. R. Tebaldi (sop), G. Bumbry (mez), C. Bergonzi (ten), D. Fischer-Dieskau (bar), N. Ghiaurov (bass), Royal Opera House Covent Garden Chorus [1886 5-act Italian version] [I] London 3-▲ 421114-2 [ADD]
Verdi, G.:Otello, w. Raina Kabaivanska (sop), Josephine Veasey (mez), John Lanigan (ten), Mario del Monaco (ten), Tito Gobbi (bar), Royal Opera House Covent Garden Chorus *(rec June 30, 1962)* Memories ▲ MEM 4583 [AAD]
Verdi, G.:Otello, w. Raina Kabaivanska (sop), Mario del Monaco (ten), Tito Gobbi (bar), Royal Opera House Covent Garden Chorus Pantheon 2-▲ PHE 6608
Verdi, G.:La traviata, w. Angela Gheorghiu (sop—Violetta), Leah-Marian Jones (mez—Flora Bervoix), Gillian Knight (mez—Annina), Robin Leggate (ten—Gastone), Frank Lopardo (ten—Alfredo Germont), Rodney Gibson (ten—Servo di Flora), Neil Griffiths (ten—Giuseppe), Mark Beesley (bar—Dottore Grenvile), Leo Nucci (bar—Giorgio Germont), Richard Van Allan (bass—Barone Douphol), Roderick Earle (bass—Marquese d'Obigny), Bryan Secombe (bass—Commissionario), Royal Opera House Covent Garden Chorus *(rec live, Royal Opera House, Covent Garden, Dec. 1994)* London 2-▲ 448119-2
Royal Orch
Three Tenors of the Golden Age, w. J. Björling (ten), Mario Lanza (ten), Jan Peerce (ten), John Corigliano (vn), Constantine Callinicos (pno), Frederick Schauwecker (pno), RCA Victor Orch [cnd:Renato Cellini, Constantine Callinicos, Erich Leinsdorf, Sylvan Levin, Maximilian Pilzer, Frieder Weissmann], Rome Opera Orch, Rome Opera Chorus, et al. RCA Gold Seal ▲ 09026-68531-2 [ADD] ■ 09026-68531-4
Royal Philharmonic Chamber Ensemble
J. Carney (cnd)
Borodin, A.:Qt 2 Strs Tring ▲ TRP 17 [DDD]
Dvořák, A.:Qt 12 Strs, "America" Tring ▲ TRP 17 [DDD]
Schubert, Franz:Qt 13 Strs Tring ("Royal Philharmonic Collection" series) ▲ TRP 16 [DDD]
Schubert, Franz:Qnt Pno, D.667, w. Ronan O'Hora (pno) Tring ("Royal Philharmonic Collection" series) ▲ TRP 16 [DDD]

▲ = CD ♦ = Enhanced CD △ = MD ■ = Cassette Tape □ = DCC

Royal PO Concert Orch

Lloyd Webber, A.:Music of, w. L. Garrett (sgr), Dave Willets (sgr), C. Corcoran (sgr), Gerard Casey (sgr), S. Campbell (sgr), Royal PO, Royal PO Pops Orch—sels from The Phantom of the Opera; Evita; Cats; Joseph & the Amazing Technicolor Dreamcoat; Jesus Christ Superstar; Tell Me on a Sunday; Song & Dance; Starlight Express; Sunset Boulevard Silva America 2–▲ SILCD 1044 [DDD] ■ SILMC 1044

Royal Philharmonic Concert Orch

J. Holmes (cnd)

A Soprano in Red, w. L. Garrett (sop) Silva Classics ▲ SIL 6008 ■ SIL 6008

Royal PO

Amazing Grace, w. J. Norman (sop), Dalton Baldwin (pno), Geoffrey Parsons (pno), Christopher Bowers–Broadbent (org), Alexander Gibson (cnd), Willis Patterson (cnd), Ambrosian Singers Philips ▲ 432546–2 PH [DDD] ■ 432546–4 PH

British Music on Hyperion, w. Parley of Instruments, Roy Goodman (cnd), John Mark Ainsley (ten), Graham Johnson (pno), Salomon Quartet, BBC Scottish SO, Anthony Rolfe Johnson (ten), Royal PO, St. Paul's Cathedral Choir, Nash Ensemble, Martyn Hill (ten), Suasan Gritton (sop), et al. Hyperion ▲ HYP 15

Carol of the Drum, w. Chieftains, Emily Mitchell (hp), Richard Stoltzman (cl), Michala Petri (rcr), James Galway (fl), Hampton String Quartet, Boys' Choir of Harlem RCA Victor ▲ 09026–61839–2 ■ 09026–61839–4

Classical Masterpieces, w. Michael Reed (cnd), Vladimir Ashkenazy (cnd), Scottish CO [cnd:Wilfried Boettcher], London SO, et al. Pickwick ("The Orchid" series) ▲ PICORCD 11006

Classical Spectacular, w. Michael Reed (cnd), London Choral Society, Scots Guards Band, Welsh Guards Band RPO Records 2–▲ CDRPD 9001 [DDD]

Classical Spectacular 1, w. Michael Reed (cnd), Scots Guards Band, Welsh Guards Band, Musketeers of the Sealed Knot, London Choral Society RPO Records ▲ RPO 5009 [DDD]

Classical Spectacular 2, w. Michael Reed (cnd), Gunnar Gudbjornsson (ten), J. Howard (bar), Scots Guards Band, Welsh Guards Band, London Choral Society RPO Records ▲ CDRPO 5010 [DDD]

Concert Favorites, Vol. 1, w. Frank Shipway Vivace ▲ 541

Concert Favorites, Vol. 2 Vivace ▲ 542

The Dance Collection, w. Ondrej Lenard (cnd), Keith Clark (cnd), Stephen Gunzenhauser (cnd), Kenneth Jean (cnd), Barry Wordsworth (cnd), Adrian Leaper (cnd), Johannes Wildner (cnd), Czech RSO, Slovak RSO, Slovak PO, Slovak State PO, CRS SO, Thalia–Schrammeln Quartet *(rec Czechoslovak Radio Concert Hall, Bratislava, Feb 1–4, 1988)* Naxos 4–▲ 8.504015 [DDD]

Delius, F.:An Arabesk, w. Thomas Allen (bar), Ambrosian Singers Unicorn–Kanchana ▲ UK 2076

Delius, F.:Fennimore & Gerda (intermezzo) Unicorn–Kanchana ▲ UK 2076

Delius, F.:Songs of Farewell, w. Ambrosian Singers Unicorn–Kanchana ▲ UK 2076

Donizetti, G.:Lucia di Lammermoor, w. E. Gruberová (sop), A. Kraus (ten), D. Lloyd (ten), R. Bruson (bar), Ambrosian Opera Chorus *(rec 1983)* EMI Classics ▲ CDMB 64622

It's Good to Be the King:Musical Delights for Kings, Queens, Princes & Royalty, w. Claudio Abbado (cnd), Eugene Ormandy (cnd), Esa–Pekka Salonen (cnd), Michael Tilson Thomas (cnd), Canadian Brass, Chicago SO, Philadelphia Orch, Tafelmusik Sony Classical ▲ SFK 57483 ■ SFT 57483

Leeds Castle Classics, w. Carl Davis (cnd), Brighton Festival Choir, Royal Artillery Band RPO Records ▲ RPO 7018 [DDD]

Lloyd Webber, A.:Music of, w. L. Garrett (sgr), Dave Willets (sgr), C. Corcoran (sgr), Gerard Casey (sgr), S. Campbell (sgr), Royal PO Pops Orch, Royal PO Concert Orch—sels from The Phantom of the Opera; Evita; Cats; Joseph & the Amazing Technicolor Dreamcoat; Jesus Christ Superstar; Tell Me on a Sunday; Song & Dance; Starlight Express; Sunset Boulevard Silva America 2–▲ SILCD 1044 [DDD] ■ SILMC 1044

Lloyd Webber, A.:Music of, w. J. Carreras (ten), S. Brightman (sop), P. Domingo (ten), M. Crawford (sgr)—Cats; Joseph & the Amazing Technicolor Dreamcoat; Requiem; Jesus Christ Superstar; Phantom of the Opera; Aspects of Love; Starlight Express; Evita Polydor ▲ 314 517336–2 ■ 314 517336–4

Magic of Vienna, w. Michael Reed (cnd), London SO [cnd:John Georgiadis] Pickwick ("The Orchid" series) ▲ PICORCD 11015

Wild Classics:A Celebration of Animals & Nature, w. James Galway (fl), Ofra Harnoy (vc), Martin Hoherman (vc), Emily Mitchell (hp), Michael Dussek (pno), Samuel Lipman (pno), Leo Litwin (pno), Gerhard Oppitz (pno), Isao Tomita (synths), Boston Pops Orch [cnd:Arthur Fiedler], Chicago SO [cnd:Fritz Reiner], et al. RCA Red Seal ▲ 09026–68483–2 ■ 09026–68483–4

A. de Almeida (cnd)

Canteloube, J.:Songs of Auvergne, w. F. von Stade (mez) CBS ▲ MK 37299 [DDD]

D. Amos (cnd)

Gould, M.:Dance Vars, w. J. Pierce (pno), D. Jonas (pno) Koch International Classics ▲ KIC 7002–2 [DDD] ■ 3–7002–4 (D)

Piston, W.:Con for 2 Pnos, w. D. Jonas (pno), J. Pierce (pno) Koch International Classics ▲ KIC 7002–2 [DDD] ■ 3–7002–4 (D)

E. Ansermet (cnd)

Schumann, R.:Con Pno, w. F. Davies (pno) Pearl 6–▲ PEA 99049 (m) [AAD]

V. Ashkenazy (cnd)

Beethoven, L. van:Con 3 Pno, w. V. Achkonazy (pno) *(rec live 11/89)* RPO ▲ CDRPO 7014 [DDD]
Borodin, A.:In the Steppes of Central Asia London ▲ 436651–2 [DDD]
Borodin, A.:Sym 1 London ▲ 436651–2 [DDD]
Borodin, A.:Sym 2 London ▲ 436651–2 [DDD]
Britten, B.:Serenade, Op. 31, w. M. Hill (ten), J. Bryant (hn) *(rec live, Moscow, 11/89)* RPO ▲ CDRPO 7015 [DDD]
Gershwin, G.:Con Pno, w. P. Jablonski (pno) London ▲ 430542–2 [DDD]
Glazunov, A.:The Seasons London 2–▲ 433000–2 [DDD]
Knussen, O.:Sym 3 *(rec live, Moscow, 11/89)* RPO ▲ CDRPO 7015 [DDD]
Lutoslawski, W.:Vars on a Theme of Paganini Pno & Orch, w. P. Jablonski (pno) London ▲ 436239–2 [DDD]
Mussorgsky, M.:Khovanshchina (prelude) *(rec live 11/89)* RPO ▲ CDRPO 7014 [DDD]
Rachmaninoff, S.:Rhapsody on a Theme of Paganini, w. P. Jablonski (pno) London ▲ 436239–2 [DDD]
Ravel, M.:Daphnis et Chloé (suite 2) *(rec live 11/89)* RPO ▲ CDRPO 7014 [DDD]
Shostakovich, D.:Con 1 Pno, w. P. Jablonski (pno) London ▲ 436239–2 [DDD]
Shostakovich, D.:Con 2 Pno, w. C. Ortiz (pno) London ▲ 425793–2 [DDD]
Shostakovich, D.:Con 1 Vn, w. B. Belkin (vn) London ▲ 425793–2 [DDD]
Shostakovich, D.:Festive Ov London ▲ 436762–2 [DDD]
Shostakovich, D.:Fragments London ▲ 421120–2 [DDD] □ 421120–5
Shostakovich, D.:Mournful–Triumphant Prelude *(rec Oct. 1991)* London ▲ 436763–2 [DDD]
Shostakovich, D.:Novorossik Chimes London ▲ 436762–2 [DDD]
Shostakovich, D.:Novorossik Chimes *(rec Oct. 1991)* London ▲ 436763–2 [DDD]
Shostakovich, D.:Song of the Forest, w. M. Kotliarov (ten), N. Storoyev (bass), Brighton Festival Chorus, New London Children's Choir London ▲ 436762–2 [DDD]
Shostakovich, D.:Sym 1 London ▲ 425609–2 [DDD]
Shostakovich, D.:Sym 2 London ▲ 436762–2 [DDD]
Shostakovich, D.:Sym 4 London ▲ 425693–2 [DDD]
Shostakovich, D.:Sym 5 London ▲ 421120–2 [DDD] □ 421120–5
Shostakovich, D.:Sym 6 London ▲ 425609–2 [DDD]
Shostakovich, D.:Sym 8 *(rec Apr. 1992)* London ▲ 436763–2 [DDD]
Shostakovich, D.:Sym 9 London ▲ 430227–2 [DDD]
Shostakovich, D.:Sym 15 London ▲ 430227–2 [DDD]
Strauss, R.:Con 1 Hn, w. B. Tuckwell (hn) London ▲ 430370–2 [DDD]
Strauss, R.:Con 2 Hn, w. B. Tuckwell (hn) London ▲ 430370–2 [DDD]
Tchaikovsky, P.:Elegy London ▲ 421715–2 [DDD]
Tchaikovsky, P.:The Nutcracker London 2–▲ 433000–2 [DDD]
Tchaikovsky, P.:Romeo & Juliet London ▲ 421715–2 [DDD]
Tchaikovsky, P.:Waltzes—"Waltz of the Flowers" from Nutcracker *(rec live 11/89)* RPO ▲ CDRPO 7014 [DDD]
Walton, W.:Sym 1 London ▲ 433703–2 [DDD]

Royal PO (cont.)

V. Ashkenazy (cnd) (cont.)

Walton, W.:Sym 2 *(rec live, Moscow 11/89)* RPO ▲ CDRPO 7015 [DDD]
Walton, W.:Sym 2 London ▲ 433703–2 [DDD]

D. Atlas (cnd)

Stravinsky, I.:Sym 1 IMP Classics ▲ IMPPCD 1045 [DDD]

M. Atzmon (cnd)

Addinsell, R.:Warsaw Con, w. C. Ortiz (pno) London ▲ 414348–2 [DDD]
Rachmaninoff, S.:Con 2 Pno, w. Cristina Ortiz (pno) London ▲ 414348–2 [DDD]

C. Badea (cnd)

Saint–Saëns, C.:Phaéton Telarc ▲ CD 80274 [DDD]
Saint–Saëns, C.:Sym 3, w. M. Murray (org) Telarc ▲ CD 80274 [DDD]

J. Barbirolli (cnd)

Sibelius, J.:Sym 2 Chesky ▲ CD 3

D. Barenboim (cnd)

Paganini, N.:Con 6 Vn, w. I. Perlman (vn). London SO, London PO EMI Classics 3–▲ ZDMC 69881

A. Barlow (cnd)

Delius, F.:Irmelin (prelude) ASV Quicksilva ▲ QS 6070 [DDD]
Delius, F.:On Hearing the 1st Cuckoo ASV Quicksilva ▲ QS 6070 [DDD]
Delius, F.:Summer Night on the River ASV Quicksilva ▲ QS 6070 [DDD]
Elgar, E.:Serenade Strs ASV Quicksilva ▲ QS 6070 [DDD]
Holst, G.:Brook Green Suite ASV Quicksilva ▲ QS 6070 [DDD]
Holst, G.:St. Paul's Suite ASV Quicksilva ▲ QS 6070 [DDD]
Warlock, P.:Capriol Suite ASV Quicksilva ▲ QS 6070 [DDD]
Warlock, P.:Capriol Suite ASV ("Quicksilva" series) ▲ ASQ 6143 [DDD]

E. Batiz (cnd)

Chávez, C.:Sym 2, "Sinf India" ASV ▲ ASV 866 [DDD]
Jeux d'Enfants, w. Christopher Hyde–Smith (fl/pic), Emma Johnson (cl), George MacDonald (cl), Gordon Back (pno), Academy of St. Martin in the Fields [cnd:Neville Marriner], Mexico City PO, Mexico State SO, Northern Sinfonia of England, et al. ASV Quicksilva ▲ ASQ 6182
Revueltas, S.:Noche de los Mayas, Mexico City PO ASV ▲ ASV 866 [DDD]

E. Bátiz (cnd), L. Foster (cnd)

The Heart of the Piano Concerto, w. J. Lill (pno), Cristina Ortiz (pno), J. L. Prats (pno), London SO [cnd:J. Judd, W. Morris] Pickwick ("The Orchid" series) ▲ PICORCD 11012

T. Beecham (cnd)

Basic 100, Vol. 21 RCA Victor ▲ 09026–61718–2 ■ 09026–61718–4
Beecham in Rehearsal *(rec 1951, 1956 & 1958)* EMI Classics ▲ CDM 64465–2 (m) [ADD]
Beethoven, L. van:Mass, Op. 86, w. Beecham Choral Society EMI Classics ▲ CDM 64385
Beethoven, L. van:Sym 7 *(rec in concert, 1959)* Music & Arts ▲ CD 281 [AAD]
Berlioz, H.:Harold in Italy, w. W. Primrose (va) *(rec 1951)* Sony Masterworks ("Portrait" series) ▲ MPK 47679 [ADD]
Berlioz, H.:Ovs—Le Corsaire EMI Classics ▲ CDM 63407
Berlioz, H.:Ovs—Carnaval romain; Le roi Lear *(rec 1954)* Sony Masterworks ("Portrait" series) ▲ MPK 47679 [ADD]
Bizet, G.:L'Arlésienne (suites) EMI Classics ▲ CDC 47794 [ADD]
Borodin, A.:Prince Igor (Polovtsian dances) EMI Classics ▲ CDC 47717 [ADD]
Cherubini, L.:Les Deux journées, w. J. Micheau (sop), M. Davies (ten), P. Gianotti (ten), E. Regnier (ten), C. Paul (bar), BBC Theater Chorus *(rec live, London Dec. 19, 1947)* Intaglio 2–▲ INCD 7342 [ADD]
Delius, F.:Brigg Fair:An English Rhapsody, w. E. Nørby (bar), BBC Sym Chorus *(rec 1955)* Sony Masterworks (Portrait) ▲ MPK 47680 [ADD]
Delius, F.:Con Vn, w. J. Pougnet (vn) *(rec 1946)* EMI Classics ▲ CDM 64054
Delius, F.:Dance Rhap 1 *(rec prob. the 1946 recording)* EMI Classics ▲ CDM 64054
Delius, F.:Hassan, w. L. Fry (bar), BBC Sym Chorus *(rec 1955–56)* Sony Masterworks (Portrait) ▲ MPK 47680 [ADD]
Delius, F.:Music of—Over the Hills and Far Away (fantasy overture, 1895–7; ed. Beecham); 2 Pieces (Sleigh Ride; Marche caprice) (1887–8); Brigg Fair (1907); Florida Suite (1887; rev. & ed. Beecham); Dance Rhapsody No. 2 (1916); Summer Evening (1890; ed. & arr. Beecham); 2 Pieces for Small Orchestra (On Hearing the First Cuckoo in Spring, 1912; Summer Night on the River, 1911); A Song Before Sunrise (1918); Intermezzo from Fennimore and Gerda (1909–10); Prelude to Irmelin (1890–92); Songs of Sunset (1906–7; w. Maureen Forrester [contralto], John Cameron [baritone] & The Beecham Choral Society) EMI Classics 2–▲ CDCB 47509 [ADD]
Delius, F.:North Country Sketches *(rec in concert, 1959)* Music & Arts ▲ CD 281 [AAD]
Delius, F.:On Hearing the 1st Cuckoo *(rec Dec. 19, 1927)* Dutton Laboratories ▲ CDLX 7011 [ADD]
Delius, F.:On the Heights *(rec 1946)* EMI Classics ▲ CDM 64054
Delius, F.:Sea Drift, w. *(soloist unknown)*, Beecham Choral Society EMI Classics 2–▲ ZDMB 64386
Delius, F.:Sea Drift, w. B. Boyce (bar), BBC Sym Chorus *(rec 1954)* Sony Masterworks (Portrait) ▲ MPK 47680 [ADD]
Delius, F.:A Song of the High Hills *(rec 1946)* EMI Classics ▲ CDM 64054
Delius, F.:Summer Night on the River *(rec July 12, 1928)* Dutton Laboratories ▲ CDLX 7011 [ADD]
Delius, F.:A Village Romeo & Juliet—Orch. Suite EMI Classics 2–▲ ZDMB 64386
Grieg, E.:In Autumn EMI Classics ▲ CDM 64751
Grieg, E.:Peer Gynt EMI Classics ▲ CDM 64751
Grieg, E.:Peer Gynt Suites, Opp. 46 & 55 EMI Classics ▲ CDM 64751
Grieg, E.:Symphonic Dances—No. 2 EMI Classics ▲ CDM 64751
Handel, G.F.:The Gods Go a'Begging EMI Classics ▲ CDM 63374
Handel, G.F.:Love In Bath, w. Ilse Hollweg (sop) EMI Classics ▲ CDM 63374
Handel, G.F.:Messiah, w. Jennifer Vyvyan (sop), Monica Sinclair (cta), Jon Vickers (ten), Giorgio Tozzi (bass) *(rec 1959)* RCA Gold Seal 3–▲ 09026–61266–2
Handel, G.F.:Messiah (sels), w. Jennifer Vyvyan (sop), Monica Sinclair (mez), Jon Vickers (ten), Giorgio Tozzi (bass), John McCarthy (cnd), Royal Choral Society—Ov; Comfort Ye My People; Every Valley Shall Be Exalted; And the Glory of the Lord; And He Shall Purify; O Thou That Tellest Good Tidings; For unto Us a Child is Born; Pastoral Symphony; There Were Shepherds Abiding; And the Angel Said unto Them; And Suddenly There Was; Glory to God in the Highest; He Shall Feed His Flock; Come unto Him; Behold the Lamb of God; He Was Despised; All We Like Sheep Have Gone Astray; Hallelujah!; I Know That My Redeemer Liveth; The Trumpet Shall Sound *(rec Walthamstow Town Hall, London, June–Aug 1959)* RCA Victor ▲ 09026–68159–2 [ADD]
Handel, G.F.:Messiah (sels) RCA Victor ▲ 09026–61718–2; ■ 09026–61718–4 (CrO2)
Haydn, J.:Syms 93–98 EMI Classics 2–▲ ZDMB 64389
Lollipops EMI Classics ▲ CDM 63412
Mendelssohn, F.:A Midsummer Night's Dream (ov) EMI Classics ▲ CDM 63407
Mendelssohn, F.:Die schöne Melusina EMI Classics ▲ CDM 63407
Mendelssohn, F.:Die schöne Melusina *(rec in concert, 1959)* Music & Arts ▲ CD 281 [AAD]
Mozart, W.A.:Arias, w. I. Hollweg (sop), L. Marshall (sop), L. Simoneau (ten), G. Unger (ten), G. Frick (bass), Beecham Choral Society EMI Classics 2–▲ CDHB 63715
Mozart, W.A.:Con Fl Hp, w. R. Le Roy (fl), L. Laskine (hp) *(rec 1947)* EMI Classics ("Great Recordings of the Century" series) ▲ CDH 63820
Mozart, W.A.:Con 4 Vn, w. J. Heifetz (vn) *(rec 1947)* EMI Classics ("Great Recordings of the Century" series) ▲ CDH 63820
Mozart, W.A.:Entführung, w. I. Hollweg (sop), L. Marshall (sop), L. Simoneau (ten), G. Unger (ten), G. Frick (bass), Beecham Choral Society EMI Classics 2–▲ CDHB 63715
Mozart, W.A.:Requiem, w. Elsie Morison (sop), Monica Sinclair (cta), Alexander Young (ten), Marian Nowakowski (bass), BBC Sym Chorus *(rec 1958)* Theorema ▲ TH 121151
Mozart, W.A.:Sym 35 Theorema ▲ TH 121169
Mozart, W.A.:Sym 35 *(rec live, Dec. 25, 1958)* Music & Arts ▲ CD 631 [AAD]
Mozart, W.A.:Sym 41 Theorema ▲ TH 121169
Rimsky–Korsakov, N.:Scheherazade EMI Classics ▲ CDC 47717 [ADD]
Rossini, G.:Ovs—Cambiale di Matrimonio; La gazza ladra; Semiramide EMI Classics ▲ CDM 63407
Schubert, Franz:Sym 3 EMI Classics ▲ CDM 69750
Schubert, Franz:Sym 5 EMI Classics ▲ CDM 69750

Royal PO (cont.)
T. Beecham (cnd) (cont.)
Schumann, R.:Con Pno, w. T. Beecham (pno) EMI Classics ▲ CDH 69792
Schumann, R.:Pno Music (misc)—Con. 21, "Elvira Madigan" EMI Classics ▲ CDH 69792
Suppé, F. von:Ovs—Poet & Peasant EMI Classics ▲ CDH 63407
Tchaikovsky, P.:Nutcracker Suite *(rec live, 12/25/58)* Music & Arts ▲ CD 631 [AAD]
Tchaikovsky, P.:Romeo & Juliet The Beecham Collection ▲ BEECHAM 1 [ADD]
Tchaikovsky, P.:Sym 3 The Beecham Collection ▲ BEECHAM 1 [ADD]
Wagner, R.:Die Meistersinger von Nürnberg (preludes/acts 1 & 3) EMI Classics ▲ CDM 63407
Wagner, R.:Die Meistersinger von Nürnberg (prelude/act 1) *(rec live, 11/4/59)* Music & Arts ▲ CD 631 [AAD]
Wagner, R.:Tannhäuser (ov & venusberg) *(rec live, 9/16/54)* Music & Arts ▲ CD 631 [AAD]
P. Bellugi (cnd)
Bottesini, G.:Gran Duo Concertant, w. R. Ricci (vn), F. Petracchi (db) Sony Classical ("Essential Classics" series) ▲ SBK 47661 ■ SBT 47661
Paganini, N.:Le Streghe, w. R. Ricci (vn) One–Eleven ▲ URS 93030 [ADD]
M. Benini (cnd)
My Heart's Delight, w. L. Pavarotti (ten), N. Focile (sop) *(rec 1993)* London ▲ 433260–2 Δ 433260–4 ■ 433260–4
R. Bernhardt (cnd)
Spohr, L.:Con 3 Cl, w. John Denman (cl) IMP ("Masters" series) ▲ IMP 6600082
Spohr, L.:Con 4 Cl, w. John Denman (cl) IMP ("Masters" series) ▲ IMP 6600082
Spohr, L.:Potpourri, w. John Denman (cl) IMP ("Masters" series) ▲ IMP 6600082
Spohr, L.:Vars in B♭ on a Theme from *Alruna*, w. John Denman (cl) IMP ("Masters" series) ▲ IMP 6600082
E. Bernstein (cnd)
Bernstein, E.:Genocide Intrada ▲ MAF 8007
Original Scores from the MGM Classics, w. Ambrosian Singers Chandos ("7000" series) ▲ CHAN 7053
U. Björlin (cnd)
Berwald, F.:Elfenspiel EMI Classics ("Matrix" series) ▲ CDM 65303
Berwald, F.:Music of—The Queen of Golconda [Ov.]; Serious & Joyful Fancies; Con. in D for Piano [w. M. Migdal (piano)]; Con. for Violin, Op. 2 [w. A. Tellefsen (violin)] EMI Classics ▲ CDM 65073
Berwald, F.:Sym 1, "Sinfonie Sérieuse" EMI Classics ("Matrix" series) ▲ CDM 65303
Berwald, F.:Sym 4, "Sinfonie naïve" EMI Classics ("Matrix" series) ▲ CDM 65303
I. Bolton (cnd)
Mozart, W.A.:Con 20 Pno, w. Mariaclara Monetti (pno) Royal Philharmonic Collection ▲ TRP 45 [DDD]
Mozart, W.A.:Con 27 Pno, w. Mariaclara Monetti (pno) Royal Philharmonic Collection ▲ TRP 45 [DDD]
A. Boult (cnd)
Rubbra, E.:Sym 6 *(rec live, London, 1971)* Intaglio ▲ INCD 7311 [ADD]
J. Brown (cnd)
Tavener, J.:Eternal Memory, w. Raphael Wallfisch (vc) Royal Philharmonic Collection ▲ TRP 48 [DDD]
Tavener, J.:The Protecting Veil, w. Raphael Wallfisch (vc) Royal Philharmonic Collection ▲ TRP 48 [DDD]
I. Buketoff (cnd)
Sessions, R.:Sym 3 CRI ■ ACS 6002
Sessions, R.:Sym 3 CRI ▲ CD 573 [ADD]
Y. Butt (cnd)
Elgar, E.:Coronation March ASV ▲ ASV 619 [DDD]
Elgar, E.:Froissart ASV ▲ ASV 619 [DDD]
Elgar, E.:In the South ASV ▲ ASV 619
Elgar, E.:The Light of Life (sels)—Meditation ASV ▲ ASV 619 [DDD]
Elgar, E.:Meditation ASV ▲ ASV 619
Glazunov, A.:Raymonda (sels), London SO—Suite ASV ▲ ASV 904 [DDD]
Glazunov, A.:Sym 6, London SO ASV ▲ ASV 904 [DDD]
Glazunov, A.:Triumphal March, London SO ASV ▲ ASV 904 [DDD]
Goldmark, K.:Ländliche Hochzeit ASV ▲ ASV 791
Goldmark, K.:Ovs—Sakuntala Overture, Op. 13 ASV ▲ ASV 791
Gounod, C.:Mors et vita—Judex ASV ▲ ASV 878 [DDD]
Grieg, E.:Lyric Suite, Op. 54 ASV Quicksilva ▲ ASQ 6176
Lalo, E.:Namouna (suites 1 & 2) ASV ▲ ASV 878 [DDD]
E. Bátiz (cnd)
Beethoven, L. van:Con 4 Pno, w. J. F. Osorio (pno) ASV Quicksilva ▲ ASQ 6129 [DDD]
Beethoven, L. van:Con 4 Pno, w. Jorge Federico Osorio (pno) Alfa ▲ 1003 [DDD]
Beethoven, L. van:Con 5 Pno, "Emperor", w. J. F. Osorio (pno) ASV Quicksilva ▲ ASQ 6129 [ADD]
Beethoven, L. van:Con 5 Pno, "Emperor", w. Jorge Federico Osorio (pno) Alfa ▲ 1003 [DDD]
Beethoven, L. van:Leonore 3 ASV Quicksilva ▲ QS 6076 [DDD]
Berlioz, H.:Le Carnaval romain ASV Quicksilva ▲ QS 6076 [DDD]
Berlioz, H.:Ovs—Le carnaval romain; Le corsaire ASV Quicksilva ▲ ASQ 6090 [DDD]
Berlioz, H.:Ovs—Le Corsaire ASV Quicksilva ▲ QS 6026 [DDD]
Berlioz, H.:Sym fantastique ASV Quicksilva ▲ ASQ 6090 [DDD]
Bizet, G.:Roma ASV ("Quiksilva" series) ▲ ASQ 6135 [DDD]
Brahms, J.:Academic Festival Ov ASV Quicksilva ▲ QS 6037 [DDD]
Chávez, C.:Sym 1, "Sinf de Antigona" ASV ("Musica Mexicana" series) ▲ ASV 942
Chávez, C.:Sym 4, "Romantic" ASV ("Musica Mexicana" series) ▲ ASV 942
Dohnányi, E. von:Vars on a Nursery Song, w. Jorge Luis Prats (pno) IMP ▲ IMP 2048
8 Popular Overtures ASV ("Quicksilva" series) ▲ ASV 6076 [DDD]
Franck, C.:Symphonic Vars, w. J. F. Osorio (pno) ASV Quicksilva ▲ ASQ 6092 [DDD]
Grieg, E.:Con Pno, Op. 16, w. J. L. Prats (pno) IMP Classics ▲ IMPPCD 1063 [DDD]
Grieg, E.:Con Pno, Op. 16, w. Jorge Luis Prats (pno) IMP ▲ IMP 2048
Grofé, F.:Grand Canyon Suite IMG/Pickwick ▲ PIC IMG 1613 [DDD]
Litolff, H.C.:Con Symphonique 4, w. J.L. Prats (pno)—Scherzo IMP Classics ▲ IMPPCD 1063 [DDD]
Litolff, H.C.:Con Symphonique 4—Scherzo IMP ▲ IMP 2048
Mendelssohn, F.:Die Hebriden ASV Quicksilva ▲ QS 6076 [DDD]
Mozart, W.A.:Con 18 Pno, w. J.F. Osorio (pno) ASV Quicksilva ▲ QS 6015 [DDD]
Mozart, W.A.:Con 19 Pno, w. J.F. Osorio (pno) ASV Quicksilva ▲ QS 6015 [DDD]
Mozart, W.A.:Con 24 Pno, w. J.F. Osorio (pno) ASV Quicksilva ▲ QS 6015 [DDD]
Mozart, W.A.:Ovs—Le nozze di Figaro Vivace 3–▲ E 314 [DDD]
Mozart, W.A.:Ovs—Le nozze di Figaro Vivace ▲ 602 [DDD]
Mozart, W.A.:Ovs—Le nozze di Figaro ASV Quicksilva ▲ QS 6033 [DDD]
Orchestral Lollipops RPO Records ▲ CDRPO 5006 [DDD]
Orchestral Lollipops Alfa ▲ 1005
Ponce, M.:Con Vn, w. Henryk Szeryng (vn) ASV ▲ ASV 952
Rachmaninoff, S.:The Isle of the Dead *(rec Nov. 1991)* Naxos ▲ 8.550583 [DDD]
Rachmaninoff, S.:Symphonic Dances *(rec Nov. 1991)* Naxos ▲ 8.550583 [DDD]
Ravel, M.:Con Pno (left hand), w. J. F. Osorio (pno) ASV Quicksilva ▲ ASQ 6092 [DDD]
Respighi, O.:Feste Romane Naxos ▲ 7.550539 [DDD]
Respighi, O.:The Fountains of Rome Naxos Δ 7.550539 [DDD]
Respighi, O.:The Pines of Rome Naxos Δ 7.550539 [DDD]
Saint-Saëns, C.:Wedding Cake, w. J.F. Osorio (pno) ASV Quicksilva ▲ ASQ 6092 [DDD]
Saint-Saëns, C.:Wedding Cake, w. J.F. Osorio (pno) ASV Quicksilva ▲ QS 6026 [DDD]
Saint-Saëns, C.:Wedding Cake, w. J.F. Osorio (pno) ASV ▲ ASV 665 [DDD]
Schumann, R.:Con Pno, w. J. F. Osorio (pno) ASV Quicksilva ▲ ASQ 6092 [DDD]
Shostakovich, D.:Novorossik Chimes ASV ▲ ASV 707 [DDD]
Shostakovich, D.:October ASV ▲ ASV 707 [DDD]
Shostakovich, D.:Ov on Russian & Khirgiz Folk Themes ASV ▲ ASV 707 [DDD]
Shostakovich, D.:Sym 5 ASV ▲ ASV 707 [DDD]
Sibelius, J.:Finlandia *(rec St. Barnabas Church, Mitcham, Nov 8 & 10, 1993 & Mar 17)* IMP ("Classics" series) ▲ IMP PCD 1114
Sibelius, J.:Sym 5 *(rec St. Barnabas Church, Mitcham, Nov 8 & 10, 1993 & Mar 17)* IMP ("Classics" series) ▲ IMP PCD 1114

Royal PO (cont.)
E. Bátiz (cnd) (cont.)
Sibelius, J.:Tapiola *(rec St. Barnabas Church, Mitcham, Nov 8 & 10, 1993 & Mar 17)* IMP ("Classics" series) ▲ IMP PCD 1114
Sibelius, J.:Valse triste *(rec St. Barnabas Church, Mitcham, Nov 8 & 10, 1993 & Mar 17)* IMP ("Classics" series) ▲ IMP PCD 1114
Stravinsky, I.:Circus Polka IMG/Pickwick ▲ PICIMG 1610 [DDD]
Stravinsky, I.:Fireworks IMG/Pickwick ▲ PICIMG 1610 [DDD]
Stravinsky, I.:Pétrouchka IMG/Pickwick ▲ PICIMG 1610 [DDD]
Tchaikovsky, P.:Nutcracker Suite ASV Quicksilva ▲ ASQ 6183
Tchaikovsky, P.:Nutcracker Suite Alfa ▲ 1007 [DDD]
Tchaikovsky, P.:Sleeping Beauty (sels)—waltz Alfa ▲ 1007 [DDD]
Tchaikovsky, P.:Sleeping Beauty (suite) ASV Quicksilva ▲ ASQ 6183
Tchaikovsky, P.:Swan Lake (suite) ASV Quicksilva ▲ ASQ 6183
Tchaikovsky, P.:Swan Lake (suite) ASV Quicksilva ▲ ASQ 6091 [DDD]
Tchaikovsky, P.:Sym 5 Alfa ▲ 1007 [DDD]
Villa-Lobos, H.:Bachiana brasileira 1 EMI Classics ▲ CDC 47433 [DDD]
J. Carney (cnd)
Mozart, W.A.:Con 21 Pno, w. Ronan O'Hora (pno) Royal Philharmonic Collection ▲ TRP 43 [DDD]
Mozart, W.A.:Con 23 Pno, w. Ronan O'Hora (pno) Royal Philharmonic Collection ▲ TRP 43 [DDD]
J.-C. Casadesus (cnd)
Fauré, G.:Ballade Pno, w. L. Parham (pno) RPO ▲ RPO 7023 [DDD]
Franck, C.:Les Djinns, w. L. Parham (pno) RPO ▲ RPO 7023 [DDD]
Franck, C.:Symphonic Vars, w. L. Parham (pno) RPO ▲ RPO 7023 [DDD]
Mussorgsky, M.:Pictures at an Exhibition Royal Philharmonic Collection ▲ TRP 34 [DDD]
Ravel, M.:Con in G Pno, w. L. Parham (pno) RPO ▲ RPO 7023 [DDD]
Ravel, M.:Daphnis et Chloé (suite 2) Royal Philharmonic Collection ▲ TRP 34 [DDD]
Ravel, M.:La Valse Royal Philharmonic Collection ▲ TRP 34 [DDD]
C. Chen (cnd)
Chausson, E.:Poème Vn, w. Nai-Yuan Hu (vn) *(rec St. Barnabas Church, England, Sept 22, 1986)* Sunrise ▲ 8516
Ravel, M.:Tzigane, w. Nai-Yuan Hu (vn) *(rec St. Barnabas Church, England, Sept 22, 1986)* Sunrise ▲ 8516
Saint-Saëns, C.:Introduction & Rondo capriccioso, w. Nai-Yuan Hu (vn) *(rec St. Barnabas Church, England, Sept 22, 1986)* Sunrise ▲ 8516
Sarasate, P. de:Carmen Fant, w. Nai-Yuan Hu (vn) *(rec St. Barnabas Church, England, Sept 22, 1986)* Sunrise ▲ 8516
Sarasate, P. de:Zigeunerweisen, w. Nai-Yuan Hu (vn) *(rec St. Barnabas Church, England, Sept 22, 1986)* Sunrise ▲ 8516
M.-W. Chung (cnd)
Khachaturian, A.:Con Vn, w. J. Galway (fl) RCA Red Seal ▲ 57010–2
Khachaturian, A.:Masquerade (sels), w. J. Galway (fl)—Waltz RCA Red Seal ▲ 57010–2
Khachaturian, A.:Spartacus (sels), w. J. Galway (fl)—Adagio of Spartacus & Phrygia RCA Red Seal ▲ 57010–2
R. Condie (cnd)
Handel, G.F.:Messiah (sels), w. Mormon Tabernacle Choir—choruses [E] CBS ▲ MK 32935
O. Danon (cnd)
Enescu, G.:Romanian Rhap 1 *(rec 1962)* Chesky ▲ CD56 [ADD]
Prokofiev, S.:The Love for 3 Oranges (suite) *(rec 1962)* Chesky ▲ CD56 [ADD]
T. Dausgaard (cnd)
Mozart, W.A.:Cons Hn, w. Jeffrey Bryant (hn) Tring ▲ TRP 47 [DDD]
Mozart, W.A.:Rondo Hn, K.371, w. Jeffrey Bryant (hn) Tring ▲ TRP 47 [DDD]
M. Davies (cnd)
Delius, F.:Con Vn, w. Y. Menuhin (vn) EMI Classics ▲ CDM 64725
P. M. Davies (cnd)
Davies, P.M.:Sym 6 Collins ▲ COL 1482
Davies, P.M.:Time & the Raven Collins ▲ COL 1482
Davies, P.M.:Worldes Blis Collins Classics ▲ 13902 [DDD]
C. Davis (cnd)
Mozart, W.A.:Ovs, w. Philharmonia Chorus—(9) EMI Classics ▲ CDE 67777
J. DePreist (cnd)
Hindemith, P.:The Four Temperaments, w. Carol Rosenberger (pno) Delos ▲ DCD 1006 [AAD]
Hindemith, P.:Nobilissima visione Delos ▲ DCD 1006 [AAD]
J. Delacôte (cnd)
Bizet, G.:L'Arlésienne (suites), w. Jonathan Snowden (fl) Tring ▲ TRP 49 [DDD]
Bizet, G.:Sym 1 Tring ▲ TRP 49 [DDD]
J. Dixon (cnd)
Thorne, F.:Liebesrock, w. G. Fuller (elec gtr/elec bass) CRI ▲ CD 586 [ADD]
P. Domingo (cnd)
The Magic Flute:A Night at the Opera, w. J.-P. Rampal (fl) CBS ▲ MK 42100 [DDD]
A. Dorati (cnd)
Britten, B.:The Young Person's Guide to the Orchestra, w. S. Connery (nar) IMP Collectors Series ▲ IMPX 9002 [AAD]
Britten, B.:The Young Person's Guide to the Orchestra, w. Sean Connery (nar) *(rec Kingsway Hall, London, England, Mar 1965)* London ("Phase 4 Stereo" series) ▲ 444104–2 [ADD]
Dvořák, A.:Slavonic Dances (comp) London ▲ 430735–2 [DDD]
Dvořák, A.:Suite, Op. 98b, "American" London ("Jubilee" series) ▲ 430702–2 [DDD]
Haydn, J.:Die Schöpfung, w. Helena Döse (sop—Eva), Lucia Popp (sop—Gabriel), Werner Hollweg (ten—Uriel), Benjamin Luxon (bar—Adam), Kurt Moll (bass—Raphael), Jack McCormack (db), David Strange (vc), Antál Dorati (hpd), Brighton Festival Chorus *(rec Kingsway Hall, London, Dec 1976)* London 2–▲ 443027–2 [ADD]
Orff, C.:Carmina burana, w. Norma Burrowes (sop), Louis Devos (ten), John Shirley-Quirk (bar), Brighton Festival Chorus, Southend Boys' Choir *(rec Kingsway Hall, London, Feb 1976)* London ("Phase 4 Stereo" series) ▲ 444105–2 [ADD]
Orff, C.:Carmina burana, w. N. Burrowes (sop), L. Devos (ten), J. Shirley-Quirk (bar), Brighton Festival Chorus [G,L] London ▲ 417714–2 [ADD]
Prokofiev, S.:Peter & the Wolf, w. Sean Connery (nar) IMP Collectors Series ▲ IMPX 9002 [AAD]
Prokofiev, S.:Peter & the Wolf, w. Sean Connery (nar) *(rec Kingsway Hall, London, England, Mar 1965)* London ("Phase 4 Stereo" series) ▲ 444104–2 [ADD]
Respighi, O.:Rossiniana *(rec Kingsway Hall, London, England, Apr 1976)* London ("Phase 4 Stereo" series) ▲ 444106–2 [ADD]
Strauss, R.:Salome (dance) *(rec 1962)* Chesky ▲ CD 36 [ADD]
Stravinsky, I.:The Firebird *(rec ca. 1987?)* ASV Quicksilva ▲ QS 6031 [ADD]
P. Dreier (cnd)
Norwegian Rhapsody RPO Records ▲ CDRPO 5003 [DDD]
Tveitt, G.:Con 2 Hp, w. T. Kniejski (hp) Simax ▲ PSC 3108 [DDD]
Tveitt, G.:Suite 1 Simax ▲ PSC 3108 [DDD]
Tveitt, G.:Water Sprite Simax ▲ PSC 3108 [DDD]
C. Dutoit (cnd)
Saint-Saëns, C.:Cons Pno (comp), w. P. Rogé (pno) London 2–▲ 417351–2 [ADD]
Saint-Saëns, C.:Havanaise Vn, w. H. Chung (vn) London ("Jubilee" series) ▲ 425021–2 [ADD]
Saint-Saëns, C.:Introduction & Rondo capriccioso, w. Chung (vn) London ("Jubilee" series) ▲ 425021–2 [ADD]
Tchaikovsky, P.:Con 1 Pno, w. M. Argerich (pno) Deutsche Grammophon ▲ 415062–2 [ADD]
Tchaikovsky, P.:Con 1 Pno, w. M. Argerich (pno) Deutsche Grammophon ▲ 431609–2
P. Ellis (cnd)
Copland, A.:Appalachian Spring (suite) The Royal Philharmonic Collection ▲ TRP 40 [DDD]
Copland, A.:Billy the Kid (suite) The Royal Philharmonic Collection ▲ TRP 40 [DDD]
Copland, A.:Fanfare for the Common Man The Royal Philharmonic Collection ▲ TRP 40 [DDD]
Copland, A.:Rodeo (sels)—Hoe-Down The Royal Philharmonic Collection ▲ TRP 40 [DDD]

▲ = CD ♦ = Enhanced CD Δ = MD ■ = Cassette Tape □ = DCC

Royal PO (cont.)
P. Ellis (cnd) (cont.)
Copland, A.:El salón México — The Royal Philharmonic Collection ▲ TRP 40 [DDD]
Epstein (cnd)
Perle, G.:Movts — CRI ■ ACS 6015
A. Erede (cnd)
Paganini, N.:Con 1 Vn, w. Y. Menuhin (vn) — EMI Classics ▲ CDC 47088
Paganini, N.:Con 2 Vn, w. Y. Menuhin (vn) — EMI Classics ▲ CDC 47088
Farnon, Gamley (cnd)
Farnon, R.:Music of, w. A. Brewer (hp), R. Cohen (vn)—Capt. Horatio Hornblower Suite; A la claire fontaine; Intermezzo for Harp & Strings; Lake of the Woods; A Promise of Spring; Rhapsody for Violin & Orchestra; State Occasion *(rec 1991)* — Reference ▲ RR 47CD [DDD]
J. Farrer (cnd)
Dvořák, A.:Carnival — ASV ▲ ASV 794
Dvořák, A.:In Nature's Realm — ASV ▲ ASV 794
Dvořák, A.:Othello — ASV ▲ ASV 794
Dvořák, A.:Scherzo Capriccioso — ASV ▲ ASV 794
Dvořák, A.:Symphonic Vars — ASV ▲ ASV 794
E. Fenby (cnd)
Delius, F.:Aquarelles (2) — Unicorn-Kanchana ▲ UK 2076
Delius, F.:Caprice & Elegy, w. Julian Lloyd Webber (vc) — Unicorn-Kanchana ▲ UK 2076
Delius, F.:Cynara, w. Thomas Allen (bar) — Unicorn-Kanchana ▲ UK 2076
Delius, F.:Irmelin (prelude) — Unicorn-Kanchana ("Souvenir" series) ▲ UK 2072
Delius, F.:A Late Lark, w. Anthony Rolfe-Johnson (ten) — Unicorn-Kanchana ("Souvenir" series) ▲ UK 2072
Delius, F.:Légende, w. Ralph Holmes (vn) — Unicorn-Kanchana ▲ UK 2076
Delius, F.:A Song of Summer — Unicorn-Kanchana ("Souvenir" series) ▲ UK 2072
Delius, F.:Songs, w. Felicity Lott (sop), Sarah Walker (mez), Anthony Rolfe Johnson (ten)—Orchestral Songs; Songs w. Pno [Scandinavian, French & English] — Unicorn-Kanchana ("Souvenir" series) ▲ UK 2075
A. Fischer (cnd)
Chopin, F.:Con 1 Pno, w. T. Barto (pno) *(rec Dec. 9, 1991)* — EMI Classics ▲ CDC 54648-2 [DDD]
Liszt, F.:Con 2 Pno, w. T. Barto (pno) *(rec Dec. 9, 1991)* — EMI Classics ▲ CDC 54648-2 [DDD]
A. Fistoulari (cnd)
Luigini, A.:Ballet Egyptien—Suite — Classics for Pleasure ▲ CDCFP 4637 [ADD]
Tchaikovsky, P.:Con 1 Pno, w. E. Wild (pno) — Chesky ▲ CD 13
L. Foster (cnd)
Mendelssohn, F.:Con in e Vn & Orch, Op. 64, w. I. Perlman (vn) — EMI Classics 3-▲ ZDMC 69881
Mozart, W.A.:Con Hn, K.495, w. A. Civil (hn) — IMP Collectors Series ▲ IMPX 9012
Mozart, W.A.:Ovs—Le nozze di Figaro — IMP Collectors Series ▲ IMPX 9012
Mozart, W.A.:Sym 40 *(rec ca. 1972/73)* — PWK Classics ▲ PWK 1155
Mozart, W.A.:Sym 40 — IMP Collectors Series ▲ IMPX 9012
Paganini, N.:Con 1 Vn, w. I. Perlman (vn) — EMI Classics ▲ CDC 47101
Sarasate, P. de:Carmen Fant, w. I. Perlman (vn) — EMI Classics ▲ CDC 47101
Sarasate, P. de:Carmen Fant, w. I. Perlman (vn) — EMI Classics 3-▲ ZDMC 69881
Schumann, R.:Con Pno, w. C. Ortiz (pno) — RPO Records Impact ▲ RPO 5004 [DDD]
M. Freccia (cnd)
Berlioz, H.:Sym fantastique *(rec 1962)* — Chesky ▲ CD 88 [ADD]
Berlioz, H.:Sym fantastique — Chesky ■ CC 1
P. Freeman (cnd)
Kupferman, M.:Atto — Soundspells ▲ SP 112 [ADD]
Milhaud, D.:Con for 2 Pnos, w. Robert Cowan (pno), Joan Yarbrough (pno) *(rec Henry Wood Hall, London, Sept 26, 1977)* — Centaur ▲ CRC 2227 [DDD]
L. Gardelli (cnd)
Rossini, G.:Guillaume Tell, w. M. Caballé (sop), M. Mesplé (sop), C. Burles (ten), N. Gedda (ten), G. Bacquier (bar), G. Howell (bass), Ambrosian Opera Chorus — EMI Classics 4-▲ CDMD 69951
Verdi, G.:Attila, w. C. Deutekom (sop), G. Raimondi (ten), C. Bergonzi (ten), S. Milnes (bar), Ambrosian Singers — Philips 2-▲ 426115-2
Verdi, G.:Un giorno di regno, w. J. Norman (sop), F. Cossotto (mez), J. Carreras (ten), I. Wixell (bar), V. Sardinero (bar), W. Ganzarolli (bar), P. Elvin (bass), A. Cassinelli (bass), Ambrosian Singers — Philips 2-▲ 422429-2 [ADD]
Verdi, G.:I lombardi alla prima crociata, w. C. Deutekom (sop), D. Malvisi (sop), M. Aparici (sop), P. Domingo (ten), G. Raimondi (ten), M. Lo Monaco (ten), M. Dean (b-bar), C. Grant (bass), Ambrosian Singers — Philips 2-▲ 422420-2 [ADD]
P. Geminiani (cnd)
Rodgers, R.:Carousel, w. B. Cook (sop), S. Ramey (bass), S. Brightman (sop), M. Forrester (cta), et al., Ambrosian Singers [1987 studio cast] — MCA Classics ▲ MCAD 6209 [DDD] ■ MCAC 6209
C. Gerhardt (cnd)
Ravel, M.:Boléro *(rec 1971)* — Chesky ▲ CD 35 [ADD]
C. Gibault (cnd)
Beethoven, L. van:Sym 5 — Royal Philharmonic Collection ▲ TRP 22 [DDD]
Schubert, Franz:Sym 8 — Royal Philharmonic Collection ▲ TRP 22 [DDD]
A. Gibson (cnd)
Sibelius, J.:4 Legends from the Kalevalá — Collins Quest ▲ COL 3013 [DDD]
M. Gielen (cnd)
Birtwistle, H.:Antiphonies, w. Joanna MacGregor (pno) — Collins Classics ▲ COL 1414
J. Glover (cnd)
Haydn, J.:Sym 101, "Clock" — Tring ("Royal Philharmonic Collection" series) ▲ TRP 53 [DDD]
Haydn, J.:Sym 102 — Royal Philharmonic Collection ▲ TRP 42 [DDD]
Haydn, J.:Sym 103, "Drum Roll" — Tring ("Royal Philharmonic Collection" series) ▲ TRP 53 [DDD]
Haydn, J.:Sym 104, "London" — Royal Philharmonic Collection ▲ TRP 42 [DDD]
I. Godfrey (cnd)
Sullivan, A.:The Pirates of Penzance, D'Oyly Carte Opera Company — London 2-▲ 425196-2 [ADD]
Sullivan, A.:The Pirates of Penzance (sels), w. V. Masterson (sop), D. Adams (bass), D'Oyly Carte Opera Chorus — London ("Weekend Classics" series) ▲ 436292-2
Sullivan, A.:The Sorcerer, D'Oyly Carte Opera Company — London 2-▲ 436807-2
Godfrey, Sargent (cnd)
Sullivan, A.:The Yeomen of the Guard, D'Oyly Carte Opera Company, Royal Opera House Orch Covent Garden — London 2-▲ 417358-2 [ADD]
E. Goossens (cnd)
Beethoven, L. van:Romances Vn, w. David Oistrach (vn) — Deutsche Grammophon ("The Originals" series) 2-▲ 447427-2
H. Griffiths (cnd)
Bruch, M.:Adagio appassionato, w. Tomotada Soh (vn) — Gallo ▲ CD 692
Bruch, M.:Adagio on a Celtic Theme, w. Curdin Coray (vc) — Gallo ▲ CD 692
Bruch, M.:Canzone Vc, w. Curdin Coray (vc) — Gallo ▲ CD 692
Bruch, M.:In memoriam, w. Tomotada Soh (vn) — Gallo ▲ CD 692
Bruch, M.:Kol Nidrei, w. Curdin Coray (vc) — Gallo ▲ CD 692
Bruch, M.:Romance Vn, w. Tomotada Soh (vn) — Gallo ▲ CD 692
C. Groves (cnd)
Britten, B.:Les Illuminations, w. Heather Harper (sop) — IMP ("BBC Radio Classics" series) ▲ IMP 5691582
Britten, B.:Vars on a Theme of Frank Bridge — IMP ("Classics" series) ▲ IMP 6700682
Dvořák, A.:Rondo, w. Paul Tortelier (vc) — IMP ("Masters" series) ▲ IMP 6600112 [DDD]
Dvořák, A.:Rondo, w. P. Tortelier (vc) — MCA Classics ▲ MCAD 6295 [DDD] ■ MCAC 6295 (D)
Elgar, E.:Con Vc, w. P. Tortelier (vc) — MCA Classics ▲ MCAD 6295 [DDD] ■ MCAC 6295 (D)
Elgar, E.:Con Vc, w. Paul Tortelier (vc) — IMP ("Masters" series) ▲ IMP 6600112 [DDD]
Elgar, E.:Serenade Strs — IMP ("Classics" series) ▲ IMP 6700682
Finzi, G.:Con Cl, w. E. Johnson (cl) — ASV ▲ ASV 787 [DDD]

Royal PO (cont.)
C. Groves (cnd) (cont.)
The Heart of the Symphony, w. English Sinfonia, London SO [cnd:B. Tuckwell, G. Rozhdestvensky] — Pickwick ("The Orchid" series) ▲ PICORCD 11011
Stanford, C.V.:Con Cl, w. E. Johnson (cl) — ASV ▲ ASV 787 [DDD]
Tchaikovsky, P.:Vars on a Rococo Theme, w. P. Tortelier (vc) — MCA Classics ▲ MCAD 6295 [DDD] ■ MCAC 6295 (D)
Tchaikovsky, P.:Vars on a Rococo Theme, w. Paul Tortelier (vc) — IMP ("Masters" series) ▲ IMP 6600112 [DDD]
Tippett, M.:Fant Concertante on a Theme of Corelli — IMP ("Classics" series) ▲ IMP 6700682
Vaughan Williams, R.:Fant on a Theme by Thomas Tallis — IMP ("Classics" series) ▲ IMP 6700682
V. Gui (cnd)
Rossini, G.:Il barbiere di Siviglia, w. V. de los Angeles (sop), L. Alva (ten), C. Cava (bass), I. Wallace (bass), Glyndebourne Festival Chorus *(rec 1962)* — EMI Classics 2-▲ CDMB 64162
M. A. Gómez Martínez (cnd)
Villa-Lobos, H.:Cons Pno (comp), w. C. Ortiz (pno) — London 2-▲ 430628-2 [DDD]
M. Halász (cnd)
Dvořák, A.:Con Vc, w. M. Kliegel (vc) *(rec Nov. 8-10, 1991)* — Naxos ▲ 8.550503 [DDD] △ 7.550503 [DD
Elgar, E.:Con Vc, w. M. Kliegel (vc) *(rec Nov. 8-10, 1991)* — Naxos ▲ 8.550503 [DDD] △ 7.550503 [DD
V. Handley (cnd)
Arnold, M.:A Carnival of Animals — Conifer Classics ▲ 75605-51240-2 [DDD]
Arnold, M.:Con for 2 Pnos, w. Richard Markham (pno), David Nettle (pno) — Conifer Classics ▲ 75605-51240-2 [DDD]
Arnold, M.:Fant on a Theme of J. Field — Conifer Classics ▲ 74321-16847-2
Arnold, M.:A Grand, Grand Ov — Conifer Classics ▲ 75605-51240-2 [DDD]
Arnold, M.:Sweeny Todd — Conifer Classics ▲ 74321-16847-2
Arnold, M.:Sym 1 *(rec Walthamstow Assembly Rooms, London, Sept 14-15, 1995)* — Conifer Classics ▲ 75605-51257-2 [DDD]
Arnold, M.:Sym 2 — Conifer Classics ▲ 75605-51240-2 [DDD]
Arnold, M.:Sym 5 *(rec Walthamstow Assembly Rooms, London, Sept 14-15, 1995)* — Conifer Classics ▲ 75605-51257-2 [DDD]
Arnold, M.:Sym 6 — Conifer Classics ▲ 74321-16847-2
Arnold, M.:Sym 7 — Conifer Classics ▲ 74321-15005-2
Arnold, M.:Sym 8 — Conifer Classics ▲ 74321-15005-2
Arnold, M.:Tam o'Shanter — Conifer Classics ▲ 74321-16847-2
Bantock, G.:Aphrodite in Cyprus — Hyperion ▲ CDA 66810
Bantock, G.:Dante & Beatrice — Hyperion ▲ CDA 66810
Bantock, G.:Helena Vars — Hyperion ▲ CDA 66810
Bantock, G.:Heroic Ballads (2) *(rec Aug. 1992)* — Hyperion ▲ CDA 66630 [DDD]
Bantock, G.:Pagan Sym *(rec Aug. 1992)* — Hyperion ▲ CDA 66630 [DDD]
Bantock, G.:Tone Poem 3, "Fifine at the Fair" *(rec Aug. 1992)* — Hyperion ▲ CDA 66630 [DDD]
Bax, A.:Enchanted Summer, w. A. Williams-King (sop), L. McWhirter (sop), Brighton Festival Chorus [E] — Chandos ▲ CHAN 8625 [DDD]
Bax, A.:Fatherland, w. M. Hill (ten), Brighton Festival Chorus [E] — Chandos ▲ CHAN 8625 [DDD]
Bax, A.:Northern Ballad 2 — Chandos ▲ CHAN 8464 [DDD]
Bax, A.:Spring Fire — Chandos ▲ CHAN 8464 [DDD]
Bax, A.:Symphonic Scherzo — Chandos ▲ CHAN 8464 [DDD]
Bax, A.:Walsinghame, w. L. McWhirter (sop), M. Hill (ten), Brighton Festival Chorus [E] — Chandos ▲ CHAN 8625 [DDD]
Chausson, E.:Poème Vn, w. A. Brind (vn) — Chandos ("Collect" series) ▲ CHAN 6514 [DDD]
Delius, F.:Con Vn — Unicorn-Kanchana ("Souvenir" series) ▲ UK 2072
Delius, F.:Suite Vn, w. Ralph Holmes (vn) — Unicorn-Kanchana ▲ UK 2076
Rubbra, E.:Con Va, w. Rivka Golani (va) *(rec All Saints' Church, Petersham, Surrey, Dec. 10-11, 1993)* — Conifer Classics ▲ 75605-51225-2 [DDD]
Rubbra, E.:Con Vn, w. Tasmin Little (vn) *(rec All Saints' Church, Petersham, Surrey, Dec. 10-11, 1993)* — Conifer Classics ▲ 75605-51225-2 [DDD]
Sibelius, J.:Con Vn, w. A. Brind (vn) — Chandos ("Collect" series) ▲ CHAN 6514 [DDD]
Simpson, R.:Sym 1 — Hyperion ▲ 66890
Simpson, R.:Sym 3 — Hyperion ▲ CDA 66728
Simpson, R.:Sym 5 — Hyperion ▲ CDA 66728
Simpson, R.:Sym 8 — Hyperion ▲ 66890
G. Herbig (cnd)
Beethoven, L. van:Fidelio (ov) — Royal Philharmonic Collection ▲ TRP 26 [DDD]
Beethoven, L. van:Sym 3, "Eroica" — Royal Philharmonic Collection ▲ TRP 26 [DDD]
Crusell, B.H.:Con 1 Cl, w. E. Johnson (cl) — ASV ▲ ASV 784
R. Hickox (cnd)
Bernstein, L.:Chichester Psalms, w. London Sym Chorus [He] — MCA Classics ▲ MCAD 6199 [DDD]
Fauré, G.:Requiem, w. A. Jones (trb), S. Roberts (bar), London Sym Chorus [L] — MCA Classics ▲ MCAD 6199 [DDD]
J. Hirokami (cnd)
Bruch, M.:Con 1 Vn, w. Boris Belkin (vn) *(rec All Saints Church, Tooting, London, May 3-5, 1994)* — Denon ▲ CO 78951 [DDD]
Mahler, G.:Sym 4, w. Inger Dam-Jensen (sop) *(rec Abbey Road Studio, Apr 25-26, 1995)* — Denon ▲ CO 78832 [DDD]
Sibelius, J.:Con Vn, w. Boris Belkin (vn) *(rec All Saints Church, Tooting, London, May 3-5, 1994)* — Denon ▲ CO 78951 [DDD]
Webern, A.:Im Sommerwind *(rec Abbey Road Studio, Apr 25-26, 1995)* — Denon ▲ CO 78832 [DDD]
L. Holdridge (cnd)
Lecuona, E.:Songs, w. P. Domingo (ten) — CBS ▲ MK 38828 ■ FMT 38828
J. Horenstein (cnd)
Dvořák, A.:Sym 9, "From the New World" *(rec 1962)* — Chesky ▲ CD 31 [ADD]
Rachmaninoff, S.:Cons Pno (comp), w. E. Wild (pno) — Chandos 2-▲ CHAN 8521/22 [ADD]
Rachmaninoff, S.:Con 1 Pno, w. E. Wild (pno) — Chandos ("Collect" series) ▲ CHAN 6605 [ADD]
Rachmaninoff, S.:Con 1 Pno, w. E. Wild (pno) *(rec 1965)* — Chesky ▲ CD 41 [ADD]
Rachmaninoff, S.:Con 2 Pno, w. Earl Wild (pno) — Chandos ("Collect" series) ▲ CHAN 6507 [ADD]
Rachmaninoff, S.:Con 2 Pno, w. Earl Wild (pno) *(rec 1966)* — Chesky ▲ CD 2 ■ CC 2
Rachmaninoff, S.:Con 3 Pno, w. Earl Wild (pno) — Chandos ("Collect" series) ▲ CHAN 6507 [ADD]
Rachmaninoff, S.:Con 3 Pno, w. Earl Wild (pno) *(rec 1965)* — Chesky ▲ CD 76 [ADD]
Rachmaninoff, S.:Con 4 Pno, w. E. Wild (pno) *(rec 1965)* — Chesky ▲ CD 41 [ADD]
Rachmaninoff, S.:Con 4 Pno, w. E. Wild (pno) — Chandos ("Collect" series) ▲ CHAN 6605 [ADD]
Rachmaninoff, S.:The Isle of the Dead — Chesky ▲ CD 2
Rachmaninoff, S.:Rhapsody on a Theme of Paganini, w. E. Wild (pno) *(rec 1965)* — Chesky ▲ CD 41 [ADD]
Rachmaninoff, S.:Rhapsody on a Theme of Paganini, w. E. Wild (pno) — Chandos ("Collect" series) ▲ CHAN 6605 [ADD]
Rachmaninoff, S.:Rhapsody on a Theme of Paganini, w. E. Wild (pno) — Chandos 2-▲ CHAN 8521/22 [ADD]
Schumann, R.:Con Pno, w. M. Frager (pno) *(rec , Walthamstow Town Hall, London, 2/2/67)* — Chesky ▲ CD52 [ADD]
Shostakovich, D.:Sym 1 — IMP ("BBC Radio Classics" series) ▲ IMP 5691542
Simpson, R.:Sym 3 *(rec in rehearsal, London, 5/5/66)* — Intaglio 2-▲ INCD 7272 [ADD]
Wagner, R.:Ovs, Preludes & Orch Sels—Fliegende Holländer *(rec 1962)* — Chesky ▲ CD 31 [ADD]
Wagner, R.:Siegfried Idyll *(rec 1962)* — Chesky ▲ CD 31 [ADD]
Wagner, R.:Tannhäuser (sels), w. Beecham Choral Society—Bacchanale *(rec 1962)* — Chesky ▲ CD 19
Walton, W.:Sym 1 *(rec 1971)* — Intaglio ▲ INCD 7231 [ADD]
A. Hovhaness (cnd)
Hovhaness, A.:Armenian Rhap 3 — Crystal ▲ CD 804 [ADD]
Hovhaness, A.:Fra Angelico — Crystal ▲ CD 804 [ADD]

Royal PO (cont.)
A. Hovhaness (cnd) (cont.)
Hovhaness, A.:Lady of Light, w. Patricia Clark (sop), Leslie Fyson (bar), Ambrosian Chorus
Crystal ▲ CD 806
Hovhaness, A.:Mountains & Rivers Without End — Crystal ▲ CD 804 [ADD]
Hovhaness, A.:Sym 11 — Crystal ▲ CD 801
Hovhaness, A.:Sym 21 — Crystal ▲ CD 804 [ADD]
O. A. Hughes (cnd)
Handel, G.F.:Messiah, w. Yvonne Kenny (sop), Jean Rigby (cta), Thomas Randle (ten), Willard White (bass), Royal Choral Society — IMP Classics 2-▲ IMPDPCD 1106 [DDD]
O.A. Hughes (cnd)
Prokofiev, S.:Peter & the Wolf, w. A. Rippon (nar) [E] — ASV Quicksilva ▲ CD QS 6017 [ADD]
Saint-Saëns, C.:Carnival of the Animals, w. A. Goldstone (pno), I. Brown (pno)
ASV Quicksilva ▲ CD QS 6017 [ADD]
K. Ingebretsen (cnd)
Grieg, E.:Con Pno, Op. 16, w. E. Knardahl (pno) — BIS ▲ CD 113
M. Inoue (cnd)
Mahler, G.:Sym 4, w. Y. Kenny (sop) — RPO ▲ 5007 [DDD]
D. Jackson (cnd)
Tchaikovsky, P.:The Nutcracker (sels)—Overture; March; Battle Scene:Journey through the Snow
Vox Box 3-▲ CD3X 3026 [ADD]
Tchaikovsky, P.:Nutcracker Suite — Special Music Co. 2-▲ S2D 5110 [DDD]
Tchaikovsky, P.:Sleeping Beauty (suite) — Vox Box 3-▲ CD3X 3026 [ADD]
M. Jarre (cnd)
Jarre, M.:Film Music — Columbia ▲ MK 42307
D. Joeres (cnd)
Gade, N.W.:Echoes of Ossian — IMP ("Classics" series) ▲ IMP 6700152
Mendelssohn, F.:Die Hebriden — IMP ("Classics" series) ▲ IMP 6700152
Schumann, R.:Ov, Scherzo & Finale — IMP ("Classics" series) ▲ IMP 6700152
Sterndale-Bennett, W.:The Naiads — IMP ("Classics" series) ▲ IMP 6700152
J. Judd (cnd)
Grieg, E.:Con Pno, Op. 16, w. Ronan O'Hora (pno) — Royal Philharmonic Collection ▲ TRP 24 [DDD]
Holst, G.:The Planets, w. King's College Choir Cambridge *(rec Dec. 1-2, 1991)*
Denon ▲ CO 75076 [DDD]
Tchaikovsky, P.:Con 1 Pno, w. Ronan O'Hora (pno) — Royal Philharmonic Collection ▲ TRP 23 [DDD]
R. Kempe (cnd)
Brahms, J.:Con Vn, w. Y. Menuhin (vn) — EMI Classics ▲ CDE 67766
Bruch, M.:Scottish Fant Vn, w. K.-W. Chung (vn) — London ("Jubilee" series) ▲ 425035-2 [ADD]
Respighi, O.:The Pines of Rome *(rec 1964)* — Chesky ▲ CD 18
Strauss, R.:Don Juan *(rec 1964)* — Chesky ▲ CD 88 [ADD]
O. Ketting (cnd)
Ketting, O.:For Moonlight Nights, w. A. de Quant (fl) — Donemus ▲ CV 21
O. Kielland (cnd)
Kielland, O.:Sinfonia I — Simax ▲ PSC 3120
K. Koizumi (cnd)
Popular Overtures, w. London SO, Barry Tuckwell (cnd), Hallé Orch [cnd:S. Skrowaczewski]
Pickwick ("The Orchid" series) ▲ PICORCD 11003
Tchaikovsky, P.:Manfred — RPO ▲ RPO 7020 [DDD]
Tchaikovsky, P.:Marche slave — RPO ▲ RPO 7017 [DDD]
Tchaikovsky, P.:Romeo & Juliet — RPO ▲ RPO 7004 [DDD]
Tchaikovsky, P.:Sym 5 — RPO ▲ RPO 7017 [DDD]
Tchaikovsky, P.:Sym 6 — RPO ▲ RPO 7004 [DDD]
J. Krips (cnd)
Haydn, J.:Sym 104, "London" *(rec 1962)* — Chesky ▲ CD 16
Mozart, W.A.:Sym 35 *(rec 1962)* — Chesky ▲ CD 16
E. Krivine (cnd)
Schumann, R.:Con Pno, w. B. Engerer (pno) *(rec Nov. 14-16, 1991)* — Denon ▲ CO 75290 [DDD]
Tchaikovsky, P.:Con 1 Pno, w. B. Engerer (pno) *(rec Nov. 14-16, 1991)* — Denon ▲ CO 75290 [DDD]
A. Leaper (cnd)
Borodin, A.:Prince Igor (Polovtsian dances) *(rec 1/91)* — Naxos ▲ 8.550501 [DDD]
Chabrier, E.:España *(rec 1/91)* — Naxos ▲ 8.550501 [DDD]
Mussorgsky, M.:Night *(rec 1/91)* — Naxos ▲ 8.550501 [DDD]
Ravel, M.:Boléro *(rec 1/91)* — Naxos ▲ 8.550501 [DDD]
Rimsky-Korsakov, N.:Capriccio espagnol *(rec 1/91)* — Naxos ▲ 8.550501 [DDD]
Tchaikovsky, P.:Ov 1812 — Naxos ▲ 8.550500 [DDD] ∆ 7.550500 [DDD]
Tchaikovsky, P.:Romeo & Juliet — Naxos ▲ 8.550500 [DDD] ∆ 7.550500 [DDD]
Tchaikovsky, P.:Romeo & Juliet *(rec Watford Town Hall, London, Jan. 7-10, 1991)*
Naxos ▲ 8.553017 [DDD]
R. Leibowitz (cnd)
Beethoven, L. van:Egmont (ov) — Chesky ▲ CD 6
Beethoven, L. van:Leonore 3 *(rec 1962)* — Chesky ▲ CD 17
Beethoven, L. van:Sym 2 *(rec 1961)* — Chesky ▲ CD 17
Beethoven, L. van:Sym 3, "Eroica" *(rec 1961)* — Chesky ▲ CD 74 [ADD]
Beethoven, L. van:Sym 4 *(rec 5/61)* — Chesky ▲ CD 81 [ADD]
Beethoven, L. van:Sym 5 *(rec 1961)* — Chesky ▲ CD 17
Beethoven, L. van:Sym 6, "Pastorale" *(rec 4/61)* — Chesky ▲ CD69 [ADD]
Beethoven, L. van:Sym 7 *(rec 4/61)* — Chesky ▲ CD 81 [ADD]
Beethoven, L. van:Sym 8 *(rec 4/61)* — Chesky ▲ CD69 [ADD]
Beethoven, L. van:Sym 9, "Choral Sym", w. I. Borkh (sop), R. Siewert (cta), R. Lewis (ten), L. Weber (bass), Beecham Choral Society [G] *(rec 6/61)* — Chesky ▲ CD66 [ADD]
Grieg, E.:Con Pno, Op. 16, w. E. Wild (pno) *(rec 1962)* — Chesky ▲ CD50 [ADD]
Mozart, W.A.:Sym 41 *(rec 1962)* — Chesky ▲ CD 16
Schumann, R.:Manfred Ov *(rec Jan. 9, 1962)* — Chesky ▲ CD 96 [ADD]
Wagner, R.:Tannhäuser (ov) *(rec Jan. 28, 1962)* — Chesky ▲ CD 96 [ADD]
R. Leppard (cnd)
Beethoven, L. van:Sym 9, "Choral Sym", w. Gillian Webster (sop), Catherine Wyn-Rogers (cta), Martyn Hill (ten), Robert Hayward (bar), Ambrosian Singers
Tring ("Royal Philharmonic Collection" series) ▲ TRP 51 [DDD]
G. Levine (cnd)
Beethoven, L. van:Sym 9, "Choral Sym"—Movt. 3 *(rec Apr. 7, 1994)* — Justice ▲ JR 1801 [DDD]
Bernstein, L.:Chichester Psalms, w. G. D. Rodriguez (boy alto), Rome Phil Academy Chorus, St. Peter's Basilica Cappella Giulia Chorus Vatican City *(rec Apr. 7, 1994)* — Justice ▲ JR 1801 [DDD]
Bernstein, L.:Sym 3, "Kaddish", w. R. Dreyfuss (nar) *(rec Apr. 7, 1994)* — Justice ▲ JR 1801 [DDD]
Bruch, M.:Kol Nidrei, w. L. Harrell (vc) *(rec Apr. 7, 1994)* — Justice ▲ JR 1801 [DDD]
H. Lewis (cnd)
Bizet, G.:Carmen (sels), w. M. Horne (sop), M. Molese (sgr), M. Pellegrini (sgr), G. Griffiths (bar), D. Bowman (bar), F. Egerton (ten), Royal Liverpool Phil Choir
IMP Collectors Series ▲ IMPX 9016 [AAD]
Gershwin, G.:An American in Paris — RPO ▲ RPO 5012 [DDD]
Gershwin, G.:Con Pno, w. J. Vakarelis (pno) — RPO ▲ RPO 5012 [DDD]
Meyerbeer, G.:Le Prophète, w. Renata Scotto (sop), Marilyn Horne (mez), James McCracken (ten), Jerome Hines (bass), Ambrosian Opera Chorus [F] — CBS 3-▲ M3K 34340 [ADD]
Rossini, G.:Arias, w. M. Horne (mez). Swiss Romande Orch, Ambrosian Opera Chorus [I]
London ▲ 421306-2 [ADD]
Showcase — RPO Records ▲ DSRPO 001 [DDD]
R. H. Lewis (cnd)
Lewis, R.H.:Nuances II *(rec 1977)* — CRI ▲ CD 596 [ADD]
Lewis, R.H.:Sym 2 *(rec 1974)* — CRI ▲ CD 596 [ADD]
A. Licata (cnd)
Giordano, U.:Fedora (sels)—Intermezzo — Royal Philharmonic Collection ▲ TRP 44 [DDD]

Royal PO (cont.)
A. Licata (cnd) (cont.)
Leoncavallo, R.:Pagliacci (sels)—Intermezzo — Royal Philharmonic Collection ▲ TRP 44 [DDD]
Mascagni, P.:Cavalleria rusticana (sels)—Intermezzo — Royal Philharmonic Collection ▲ TRP 44 [DDD]
Puccini, G.:Manon Lescaut (sels)—Intermezzo to Act 3 — Royal Philharmonic Collection ▲ TRP 44 [DDD]
Puccini, G.:Suor angelica (sels)—Intermezzo — Royal Philharmonic Collection ▲ TRP 44 [DDD]
Verdi, G.:Ovs & Preludes—La forza del destino Ov; Partita & Prelude to A Masked Ball; Luisa Miller Ov; Prelude to Aida; Joan of Arc Ov; I Vespri Siciliani Ov
Royal Philharmonic Collection ▲ TRP 44 [DDD]
J. Ling (cnd)
Dupré, M.:Sym, Op. 25, w. Murray (org) *(rec 1986)* — Telarc ▲ CD 80136 [DDD]
Rheinberger, J.:Con 1 Org, w. M. Murray (org) — Telarc ▲ CD 80136 [DDD]
A. B. Lipkin (cnd)
Cohn, A.:Kaddish — CRI ■ C 259
Hovhaness, A.:The Holy City — CRI ■ C 259
Rogers, B.:Apparitions — CRI ■ C 259
Still, W.G.:Festive Ov — Cambria ▲ CD 1060 [ADD]
Still, W.G.:Festive Ov — CRI ■ C 259
Travis, R.:Collage — CRI ■ C 259
A. Litton (cnd)
Elgar, E.:Enigma Vars — Virgin Classics ("Ultraviolet" series) ▲ CUV 61255
Elgar, E.:Enigma Vars — Virgin Classics ▲ CDZ 59643
Gershwin, G.:An American in Paris — RPO 2-▲ CDRPD 9002 [DDD]
Gershwin, G.:Con Pno, w. A. Litton (pno) — RPO 2-▲ CDRPD 9002 [DDD]
Gershwin, G.:Rhap in Blue, w. A. Litton (pno) — RPO 2-▲ CDRPD 9002 [DDD]
Gershwin, G.:Who Cares? — RPO 2-▲ CDRPD 9002 [DDD]
Poème, w. Joshua Bell (vn) — London ("Digital" series) ▲ 433519-2 LH [DDD] □ 433519-5
Rachmaninoff, S.:The Isle of the Dead — Virgin Classics ▲ 59547 [DDD]
Rachmaninoff, S.:Symphonic Dances — Virgin Classics ▲ 59549 [DDD]
Rachmaninoff, S.:Syms (comp) — Virgin Classics ▲ ZDMC 59279
Rachmaninoff, S.:Sym 1 — Virgin Classics ▲ ZDMC 59279
Rachmaninoff, S.:Sym 1 — Virgin Classics ▲ CDC 59547 [DDD]
Rachmaninoff, S.:Sym 2 — Virgin Classics ▲ ZDMC 59279
Rachmaninoff, S.:Sym 2 — Virgin Classics ▲ CDC 59548 [DDD]
Rachmaninoff, S.:Sym 3 — Virgin Classics ▲ CDC 59549 [DDD]
Rachmaninoff, S.:Sym 3 — Virgin Classics ▲ ZDMC 59279
Rachmaninoff, S.:Vocalise — Virgin Classics ▲ 59548 [DDD]
Rodrigo, J.:Concierto de Aranjuez, w. C. Parkening (gtr) — EMI Classics ▲ CDC 54665 ■ 4DS 54665
Rodrigo, J.:Fant para un gentilhombre, w. C. Parkening (gtr)
EMI Classics ▲ CDC 54665 ■ 4DS 54665
Walton, W.:Bagatelles Gtr, w. C. Parkening (gtr) — EMI Classics ▲ CDC 54665 ■ 4DS 54665
J. Lockhart (cnd)
Beethoven, L. van:Sym 2 — The Royal Philharmonic Collection ▲ TRP 39 [DDD]
Beethoven, L. van:Sym 8 — The Royal Philharmonic Collection ▲ TRP 39 [DDD]
Mozart, W.A.:Sym 36 — The Royal Philharmonic Collection ▲ TRP 38 [DDD]
Mozart, W.A.:Sym 39 — The Royal Philharmonic Collection ▲ TRP 38 [DDD]
Mozart, W.A.:Zauberflöte (ov) — The Royal Philharmonic Collection ▲ TRP 38 [DDD]
J. López-Cobos (cnd)
Bruch, M.:Scottish Fant Vn, w. A. A. Meyers (vn)
RCA Red Seal ▲ 09026-60942-2 ■ 09026-60942-4
Lalo, E.:Sym espagnole, w. A. Akiko Meyers (vn)
RCA Red Seal ▲ 09026-60942-2 ■ 09026-60942-4
Rachmaninoff, S.:Con 2 Pno, w. H. Grimaud (pno) — Denon/PCM Digital ▲ CO 75368 [DDD]
Ravel, M.:Con in G Pno, w. H. Grimaud (pno) — Denon/PCM Digital ▲ CO 75368 [DDD]
C. Mackerras (cnd)
Handel, G.F.:Messiah (reorchd Mozart), w. Felicity Lott (sop), Felicity Palmer (sop), Phillip Langridge (ten), Robert Lloyd (b-bar), Huddersfield Choral Society [E] — ASV ▲ ASV CD 960
Shostakovich, D.:Festive Ov — Royal Philharmonic Collection ▲ TRP 32 [DDD]
Shostakovich, D.:Sym 5 — Royal Philharmonic Collection ▲ TRP 32 [DDD]
Tchaikovsky, P.:Sleeping Beauty (sels) — Telarc ▲ CD 80151 [DDD]
Tchaikovsky, P.:Swan Lake (sels) — Telarc ▲ CD 80151 [DDD]
N. del Mar (cnd)
Delius, F.:Paris:The Song of a Great City — Unicorn-Kanchana ▲ UK 2076
Delius, F.:La Ronde se déroule — Unicorn-Kanchana ▲ UK 2076
Strauss, R.:4 Last Songs, w. Heather Harper (sop) — IMP ("BBC Radio Classics" series) ▲ IMP 9138
Y. Menuhin (cnd)
Beethoven, L. van:Sym 9, "Choral Sym", w. Brighton Festival Chorus [soloists:R. Falcon, K. McKellar-Ferguson, R. Margison] — RPO ▲ RPO 7001 [DDD]
Berlioz, H.:Le Carnaval romain — Virgo ▲ CDZ 61100
Berlioz, H.:Sym fantastique — Virgo ▲ CDZ 61100
Dvořák, A.:Serenade Strs — Royal Philharmonic Collection ▲ TRP 19 [DDD]
Dvořák, A.:Sym 8 — Royal Philharmonic Collection ▲ TRP 19 [DDD]
Elgar, E.:Cockaigne — Virgin Classics ▲ 59626 [DDD]
Elgar, E.:Cockaigne — Virgin Classics ("Ultraviolet" series) ▲ CUV 61199
Elgar, E.:Con Vn, w. D. Sitkovetsky (vn) — Virgin Classics ▲ CDC 45065
Elgar, E.:Coronation March — Virgin Classics ▲ 59626 [DDD]
Elgar, E.:Empire March — Virgin Classics ▲ 59626 [DDD]
Elgar, E.:Imperial March — Virgin Classics ▲ 59626 [DDD]
Elgar, E.:Pomp & Circumstance Marches — Virgin Classics ("Ultraviolet" series) ▲ CUV 61199
Elgar, E.:Pomp & Circumstance Marches — Virgin Classics ▲ 59626 [DDD]
Elgar, E.:Sym 2 — Virgin Classics ▲ 59627 [DDD]
Elgar, E.:Triumphal March — Virgin Classics ▲ 59626 [DDD]
Khachaturian, A.:Con Vn, w. H. Kun (vn) — Nimbus ▲ NI 5277 [DDD]
Nielsen, C.:Con Vn, w. A. Tellefsen (vn) — Virgin Classics ("Ultraviolet" series) ▲ CUV 61136
Nielsen, C.:Sym 4 — Virgin Classics ("Ultraviolet" series) ▲ CUV 61136
Orchestra Sampler — Virgin Classics 2-▲ CDC 59080
Sibelius, J.:Con Vn, w. H. Kun (vn) — Nimbus ▲ NI 5277 [DDD]
Vaughan Williams, R.:Con Pno, w. K. Broadway (pno), R. Markham (pno) — Virgo ▲ CDZ 61105
Vaughan Williams, R.:Sym 5, w. K. Broadway (pno), R. Markham (pno) — Virgo ▲ CDZ 61105
C. Munch (cnd)
Bizet, G.:Sym 1 *(rec 1963)* — Chesky ▲ CD 7
Tchaikovsky, P.:Francesca da Rimini *(rec 1963)* — Chesky ▲ CD 7
R. Nash (cnd)
Sullivan, A.:The Grand Duke, D'Oyly Carte Opera Company — London 2-▲ 436813-2 [ADD]
Sullivan, A.:Henry VIII — London 2-▲ 436813-2 [ADD]
Sullivan, A.:The Mikado, w. D'Oyly Carte Opera Chorus—highlights
London ("Weekend Classics" series) ▲ 433684-2 [ADD] ■ 433684-4
Sullivan, A.:The Mikado, D'Oyly Carte Opera Company — London 2-▲ 425190-2 [ADD]
Sullivan, A.:Ovs, D'Oyly Carte Opera Company—Macbeth; Marmion — London 2-▲ 436816-2
Sullivan, A.:Utopia Limited, D'Oyly Carte Opera Company — London 2-▲ 436816-2
Sullivan, A.:Victoria & Merry England (suites), D'Oyly Carte Opera Company—No. 1
London 2-▲ 436816-2
Sullivan, A.:The Zoo, w. D'Oyly Carte Opera Chorus — London 2-▲ 436807-2 [ADD]
D. Parry (cnd)
Meyerbeer, G.:Il crociato, w. Linda Kitchen (sop), Y. Kenny (sop), R. Platt (sop), D. Montague (mez), D. Jones (mez), B. Ford (ten), U. Benelli (bar), Geoffrey Mitchell Choir [I] *(rec CTS Studios, Wembley, London, Dec. 1990-June 1991)* — Opera Rara 4-▲ OR 10
L. Pešek (cnd)
Smetana, B.:Má Vlast — Virgin Classics ▲ CDC 59576

▲ = CD ♦ = Enhanced CD ∆ = MD ■ = Cassette Tape □ = DCC

Royal PO (cont.)

A. Previn (cnd)
Basic 100, Vol. 36 RCA Victor ▲ 09026-61854-2 ■ 09026-61854-4
Beethoven, L. van:Con 3 Pno, w. E. Ax (pno) RCA Silver Seal ▲ 60476-2-RV [DDD] ■ 60476-4-RV
Beethoven, L. van:Con 4 Pno, w. E. Ax (pno) RCA Silver Seal ▲ 60476-2-RV [DDD] ■ 60476-4-RV
Beethoven, L. van:Con 5 Pno, "Emperor", w. E. Ax (pno) RCA Victor ▲ 09026-61714-2; ■ 09026-61714-4
Beethoven, L. van:Con 5 Pno, "Emperor", w. E. Ax (pno) RCA Silver Seal ▲ 09026-61213-2 ■ 09026-61213-4
Beethoven, L. van:Coriolan Ov RCA Victrola ▲ 7748-2-RC [DDD]
Beethoven, L. van:Egmont (ov) RCA Victrola ▲ 7747-2-RC [DDD]
Beethoven, L. van:Fant Pno, Op. 80, "Choral Fant", w. A. Previn (pno), *(chorus unknown)* RCA Victor ▲ 09026-61714-2; ■ 09026-61714-4
Beethoven, L. van:Fidelio (sels)—Overture RCA Victor ▲ 09026-61720-2; ■ 09026-61720-4
Beethoven, L. van:Die Geschöpfe des Prometheus (ov) RCA Victrola ▲ 7748-2-RC [DDD]
Beethoven, L. van:Leonore 3 RCA Red Seal ▲ 7894-2-RC [DDD]
Beethoven, L. van:Sym 4 RCA Red Seal ▲ 60362-2-RC [DDD]
Beethoven, L. van:Sym 5 RCA Red Seal ▲ 7894-2-RC [DDD]
Beethoven, L. van:Sym 6, "Pastorale" RCA Victrola ▲ 7747-2-RC [DDD]
Beethoven, L. van:Sym 7 RCA Victrola ▲ 7748-2-RC [DDD]
Beethoven, L. van:Sym 7 RCA Victor ▲ 09026-61854-2 ■ 09026-61854-4
Beethoven, L. van:Sym 8 RCA Victor ▲ 09026-61854-2; ■ 09026-61854-4
Beethoven, L. van:Sym 8 RCA Red Seal ▲ 60362-2-RC [DDD]
Beethoven, L. van:Sym 9, "Choral Sym", w. Roberta Alexander (sop), Florence Quivar (cta), Gary Lakes (ten), Paul Plishka (bass) RCA Red Seal ▲ 09026-60363-2
Berlioz, H.:Ovs—Le Corsaire RPO ▲ RPO 7016 [DDD]
Berlioz, H.:Sym fantastique RPO ▲ RPO 7016 [DDD]
Brahms, J.:Academic Festival Ov Telarc ▲ CD 82006
Brahms, J.:Academic Festival Ov Telarc ▲ CD 80155 [DDD]
Brahms, J.:Con 1 Pno, w. H. Gutiérrez (pno) Telarc ▲ CD 80252 [DDD]
Brahms, J.:Con 2 Pno, w. H. Gutiérrez (pno) Telarc ▲ CD 80197 [DDD]
Brahms, J.:Ein Deutsches Requiem, w. M. Price (sop), S. Ramey (bar), Ambrosian Singers [G] Teldec ("Digital Experience" series) ▲ 9031-75862-2 AW [DDD] ■ 9031-75862-4
Brahms, J.:Sym 4 Telarc ▲ CD 82006
Brahms, J.:Sym 4 Telarc ▲ CD 80155 [DDD]
Brahms, J.:Tragic Ov Telarc ▲ CD 80252 [DDD]
Brahms, J.:Vars on a Theme by Haydn Telarc ▲ CD 80197 [DDD]
Britten, B.:Gloriana (courtly dances) Telarc ▲ CD 80126 [DDD]
Britten, B.:The Young Person's Guide to the Orchestra Telarc ▲ CD 80126 [DDD]
Chopin, F.:Con 2 Pno, w. Maria João Pires (pno) Deutsche Grammophon ▲ 437817-2
Davies, P.M.:Con Vn, w. I. Stern (vn) CBS ▲ MK 42449 [DDD]
Debussy, C.:Nocturnes EMI Classics ▲ CDE 67770
Elgar, E.:Enigma Vars Philips ▲ 416813-2 [DDD]
Elgar, E.:Pomp & Circumstance Marches Philips ▲ 416813-2 [DDD]
Holst, G.:The Planets, w. Brighton Festival Women's Chorus *(rec 4/14-15/86)* Telarc ▲ CD 80133 [DDD] ■ CS 30133 (D)
Mozart, W.A.:Arias, w. K. Battle (sop) [I] EMI Classics ▲ CDC 47355 [DDD] ■ 4DS 38297 (D)
Mozart, W.A.:Exsultate, w. Kathleen Battle (sop) [L] EMI Classics ▲ CDC 47355 [DDD] ■ 4DS 38297 (D)
Prokofiev, S.:Con 3 Pno, w. J. K. Parker (pno) Telarc ▲ CD 80124 [DDD]
Prokofiev, S.:Con 2 Vn, w. V. Mullova (vn) Philips ▲ 422364-2 [DDD]
Prokofiev, S.:Peter & the Wolf, w. A. Previn (nar) Telarc ▲ CD 80126 [DDD]
Rachmaninoff, S.:Sym 2 Telarc ▲ CD 80113 [DDD]
Rimsky-Korsakov, N.:The Tale of Tsar Saltan Orch, Op. 57 Telarc ▲ CD 80107 [DDD]
Saint-Saëns, C.:Africa, w. J. P. Collard (pno) EMI Classics ▲ CDC 49757
Saint-Saëns, C.:Allegro appassionato, w. J. P. Collard (pno) EMI Classics ▲ CDC 49757
Saint-Saëns, C.:Cons Pno (comp), w. J.-P. Collard (pno)—No. 1 in D EMI Classics ▲ CDC 49757
Saint-Saëns, C.:Con 2 Pno, w. J.-P. Collard (pno) EMI Classics ▲ CDC 47816
Saint-Saëns, C.:Con 3 Pno, w. J.-P. Collard (pno) EMI Classics ▲ CDC 49051
Saint-Saëns, C.:Con 4 Pno, w. J.-P. Collard (pno) EMI Classics ▲ CDC 47816
Saint-Saëns, C.:Con 5 Pno, w. J.-P. Collard (pno) EMI Classics ▲ CDC 49051
Saint-Saëns, C.:Rapsodie d'Auvergne, w. J.-P. Collard (pno) EMI Classics ▲ CDC 49757
Saint-Saëns, C.:Wedding Cake, w. J.-P. Collard (pno) EMI Classics ▲ CDC 49757
Shostakovich, D.:Con 1 Vn, w. V. Mullova (vn) Philips ▲ 422364-2 [DDD]
Tchaikovsky, P.:Con 1 Pno, w. S. Parker (pno) Telarc ▲ CD 80124 [DDD]
Tchaikovsky, P.:The Nutcracker EMI Classics 2-▲ CDCB 47267 [DDD] 2-■ 4D2S 47267 (D)
Tchaikovsky, P.:Sym 5 Telarc ▲ CD 80107 [DDD]
Vaughan Williams, R.:Fant on a Theme by Thomas Tallis Telarc ▲ CD 80158 [DDD]
Vaughan Williams, R.:The Lark Ascending, w. B. Griffiths (vn) Telarc ▲ CD 80138 [DDD]
Vaughan Williams, R.:Sym 2 Telarc ▲ CD 80138 [DDD]
Vaughan Williams, R.:Sym 5 Telarc ▲ CD 80158 [DDD]
Walton, W.:Belshazzar's Feast, w. B. Luxon (bar), London Collegium Musicum RPO ▲ RPO 7013 [DDD]
Walton, W.:Con Va, w. N. Kennedy (vn) EMI Classics ▲ CDC 49628 [DDD]
Walton, W.:Con Vn, w. N. Kennedy (vn) EMI Classics ▲ CDC 49628 [DDD]
Walton, W.:Crown Imperial Telarc ▲ CD 80125 [DDD]
Walton, W.:Henry V (film suite) RPO ▲ RPO 7013 [DDD]
Walton, W.:Orb & Sceptre Telarc ▲ CD 80125 [DDD]
Walton, W.:Sym 1 Telarc ▲ CD 80125 [DDD]

G. Prêtre (cnd)
Franck, C.:Psyché et Eros *(rec 1963)* Chesky ▲ CD 87 [ADD]
Ravel, M.:Daphnis et Chloé (suite 1), w. G. Gilbert (fl), Beecham Choral Society *(rec Apr. 8 & 9, 1963)* Chesky ▲ CD 101 [ADD]
Ravel, M.:Daphnis et Chloé (suite 2), w. G. Gilbert (fl), Beecham Choral Society *(rec Apr. 8 & 9, 1963)* Chesky ▲ CD 101 [ADD]

K. Redel (cnd)
Brahms, J.:Sym 2 Stradivari Classics ▲ SCD 6012 [DDD] ■ SMC 6012 (D)
Brahms, J.:Tragic Ov Stradivari Classics ▲ SCD 6012 [DDD] ■ SMC 6012 (D)
The Great Symphonies, w. Slovenian PO [cnd:Milan Horvat], Ljubljana SO [cnd:Anton Nanut], Slovak PO [cnd:Libor Pešek] Stradivari Classics ("Treasury of Great Classics" series) 5-▲ S5D 6082 [DDD] 5-■ S5C 6082

F. Reiner (cnd)
Brahms, J.:Sym 4 *(rec 1962)* Chesky ▲ CD 6

D. Revenaugh (cnd)
Busoni, F.:Con Pno, Op. 39, w. J. Ogdon (pno), male chorus EMI Classics ▲ CDH 69850

P. Robinson (cnd)
Simple Gifts, w. L. Garrett (sop) Silva Classics ▲ SIL 6004 [DDD] ■ SIL MC 6004

E. Rogers (cnd)
Ketèlbey, A.W.:Music of, w. Royal Liverpool Phil Choir—In a Monastery Garden; Wedgewood Blue; In the Mystic Land of Egypt; Bells across the Meadows; In a Chinese Temple Garden; Sanctuary of the Heart; 'Appy 'Ampstead; The Phantom Melody; In a Persian Market *(rec Kingsway Hall, London, Feb 1969)* London ("Phase 4 Stereo") ▲ 444786-2 [ADD]

W. Rowicki (cnd)
Liszt, F.:Con 2 Pno, w. J. Vakarelis (pno) RPO Records Impact ▲ 5001 [DDD]
Prokofiev, S.:Con 3 Pno, w. J. Vakarelis (pno) RPO Records Impact ▲ 5001 [DDD]

M. Rózsa (cnd)
Rózsa, M.:Time After Time Southern Cross ▲ SCCD 1014 [ADD]

G. Samuel (cnd)
Harrison, L.:Sym on G CRI ("American Masters" series) ▲ CD 715 [ADD]

Royal PO (cont.)

S. Sanderling (cnd)
Haydn, J.:Ovs—La fedelta premiata Royal Philharmonic Collection ▲ TRP 21 [DDD]
Haydn, J.:Sym 94, "Surprise Sym" Royal Philharmonic Collection ▲ TRP 21 [DDD]
Haydn, J.:Sym 100, "Military" Royal Philharmonic Collection ▲ TRP 21 [DDD]
Mendelssohn, F.:Sym 3 Royal Philharmonic Collection ▲ TRP 20 [DDD]
Mendelssohn, F.:Sym 4 Royal Philharmonic Collection ▲ TRP 20 [DDD]

N. Santi (cnd)
Verdi, G.:Arias, w. Fiorenza Cossotto (sop)—Ben Io T'Invenni...Anch'io Dischiuso un Giorno...Salga Già del Trono Aurato [from Nabucco]; Egli non Riede Ancora...Non So le Tetre Immagini [from Il Corsaro]; O Don Fatale [from Don Carlo]; Surta È la Notte...Ernani, Ernani Involami [from Ernani]; Ecco L'Orrido Campo...Ma Dall'Arido Stelo & Morrò, Ma Prima in Grazia [from Un Ballo in Maschera] Fonit Cetra ("Italia" series) ▲ FCT CDC 89

M. Sargent (cnd)
Chopin, F.:Con 1 Pno, w. E. Wild (pno) *(rec October 9 & 10, 1965)* Chesky ▲ CD93 [ADD]
Holst, G.:St. Paul's Suite EMI Classics ▲ CDC 49784
Liszt, F.:Con 1 Pno, w. E. Wild (pno) *(rec October 9 & 10, 1962)* Chesky ▲ CD93 [ADD]
Sullivan, A.:Pineapple Poll, w. D'Oyly Carte Opera Company [arr Charles Mackerras] London 2-▲ 436810-2 [DDD]
Sullivan, A.:Princess Ida, w. D'Oyly Carte Opera Company London 2-▲ 436810-2 [ADD]

A. Scholz (cnd)
Beethoven, L. van:Egmont (ov) Stradivari Classics ▲ SCD 6018 [DDD] ■ SMC 6018 (D)

J. Scott (cnd)
St. Paul's Christmas Concert RPO Records ▲ RPO 7021 [DDD]

C. Seaman (cnd)
Barber, S.:Con Vn, w. A. A. Meyers (vn) *(rec Sept. 18-20, 1988)* Canyon Classics ▲ 3699 [DDD]
Bruch, M.:Con 1 Vn, w. A. A. Meyers (vn) *(rec Sept. 18-20, 1988)* Canyon Classics ▲ 3699 [DDD]
Delius, F.:Music of—Brigg Fair; La calinda [from Koanga]; Intermezzo & Serenade [from Hassan]; A Song Before Sunrise; On Hearing the 1st Cuckoo in Spring; The Walk to the Paradise Garden; Irmelin Prelude; Over the Hills & Far Away Royal Philharmonic Collection ▲ TRP 36 [DDD]
Rachmaninoff, S.:Con 1 Pno, w. Sequeira Costa (pno) RPO ▲ RPO 7024 [DDD]
Vaughan Williams, R.:English Folk Song Suite Royal Philharmonic Collection ▲ TRP 31 [DDD]
Vaughan Williams, R.:Fant on Greensleeves Royal Philharmonic Collection ▲ TRP 31 [DDD]
Vaughan Williams, R.:Fant on a Theme by Thomas Tallis Royal Philharmonic Collection ▲ TRP 31 [DDD]
Vaughan Williams, R.:The Lark Ascending, w. *(vn unknown)* Royal Philharmonic Collection ▲ TRP 31 [DDD]
Vaughan Williams, R.:The Wasps Royal Philharmonic Collection ▲ TRP 31 [DDD]

J. Serebrier (cnd)
Bloch, E.:Baal Shem, "3 Pictures of Chassidic Life", w. Michael Guttman (vn) ASV ▲ ASV 785
Bloch, E.:Con Vn, w. Michael Guttman (vn) ASV ▲ ASV 785
Chaminade, C.:Automne, w. M. Guttman (vn) [orchd for solo vn by Paul Uy] ASV ▲ ASV 855 [DDD]
Dvořák, A.:Con Vn, w. Michael Guttman (vn) *(rec St. Barnabas Church, Mitcham, Jan 12 & Mar 4, 1994)* IMP ("Classics" series) ▲ IMP PCD 1110
Dvořák, A.:Legends, Op. 59—Nos. 1 & 3 *(rec St. Barnabas Church, Mitcham, Jan 12 & Mar 4, 1994)* IMP ("Classics" series) ▲ IMP PCD 1110
Dvořák, A.:Mazurek, w. Michael Guttman (vn) *(rec St. Barnabas Church, Mitcham, Jan 12 & Mar 4, 1994)* IMP ("Classics" series) ▲ IMP PCD 1110
Dvořák, A.:Romance Vn, w. Michael Guttman (vn) *(rec St. Barnabas Church, Mitcham, Jan 12 & Mar 4, 1994)* IMP ("Classics" series) ▲ IMP PCD 1110
Dvořák, A.:Scherzo Capriccioso *(rec St. Barnabas Church, Mitcham, Jan 12 & Mar 4, 1994)* IMP ("Classics" series) ▲ IMP PCD 1110
Fauré, G.:Ballade Pno, w. Valerie Traficante (pno) IMP ("Classics" series) ▲ IMP 6700782
Indy, V. d':Sym on a French Mountain Air, w. Valerie Traficante (pno) IMP ("Classics" series) ▲ IMP 6700782
Milhaud, D.:Concertino de printemps, w. M. Guttman (vn) ASV ▲ ASV 855 [DDD]
Rodrigo, J.:Concierto de estío, w. M. Guttman (vn) ASV ▲ ASV 855 [DDD]
Saint-Saëns, C.:Con 2 Pno, w. Valerie Traficante (pno) IMP ("Classics" series) ▲ IMP 6700782
Serebrier, J.:Momento psicológico ASV ▲ ASV 785
Serebrier, J.:Poema elegiaco ASV ▲ ASV 785
Serebrier, J.:Winter Con Vn, w. M. Guttman (vn) ASV ▲ ASV 855 [DDD]
Tchaikovsky, P.:Music of, w. Michael Guttman (vn), Czech State PO—Waltzes [from Sleeping Beauty; Eugene Onegin; Swan Lake; Nutcracker (Waltz of the Flowers)]; Marches [from Nutcracker; Coronation March for Alexander III; Solennelle; Marche Slave, Op. 31]; Méditation in d, Op. 42/1; Mélodie in Eb, Op. 42/3; Elegy in G for Strs; Andante Cantabile, Op. 11 IMG/Pickwick ▲ PIC IMG 1617
Wolf-Ferrari, E.:Orchestral Music—I gioielli della Madonna; I quattro rusteghi; La dama boba; L'amore medico; Il campiello; Il segreto di Susanna [from operas] ASV ▲ ASV 861

F. Shipway (cnd)
Massenet, J.:Méditation from *Thaïs* Special Music Co. ("Classics of the Heart" series) ▲ SCD 5197

L. Siegel (cnd)
Tchaikovsky, P.:Sleeping Beauty (sels) Stradivari Classics ▲ SCD 6017 [DDD] ■ SMC 6017 (D)

G. Simon (cnd)
Balcombe, R.:Greensleeves Suite, 40 Cellos of the London PO, BBC SO, Philharmonia Orch *(rec All Hallows Church, London, Jan 18 & Apr 2, 1993)* Cala ▲ CACD 104 [DDD]
Bernstein, L.:West Side Story (sels), 40 Cellos of the London PO, BBC SO, Philharmonia Orch—Tonight [arr. Balcombe] *(rec All Hallows Church, London, Jan 18 & Apr 2, 1993)* Cala ▲ CACD 104 [DDD]
Casals, P.:Sardana, 40 Cellos of the London PO, BBC SO, Philharmonia Orch *(rec All Hallows Church, London, Jan 18 & Apr 2, 1993)* Cala ▲ CACD 104 [DDD]
Rachmaninoff, S.:Vocalise, BBC SO, 40 Cellos of the London PO, Philharmonia Orch [arr. Balcombe] *(rec All Hallows Church, London, Jan 18 & Apr 2, 1993)* Cala ▲ CACD 104 [DDD]
Saint-Saëns, C.:Le Cygne, 40 Cellos of the London PO, BBC SO, Philharmonia Orch [arr. Balcombe] *(rec All Hallows Church, London, Jan 18 & Apr 2, 1993)* Cala ▲ CACD 104 [DDD]

Y. Simonov (cnd)
Berlioz, H.:La Damnation de Faust (sels)—Hungarian March Royal Philharmonic Collection ▲ TRP 30 [DDD]
Glinka, M.:Russlan & Ludmilla (ov) Royal Philharmonic Collection ▲ TRP 30 [DDD]
Grieg, E.:Holberg Suite The Royal Philharmonic Collection ▲ TRP 41 [DDD]
Khachaturian, A.:Gayane (sels) Royal Philharmonic Collection ▲ TRP 35 [DDD]
Khachaturian, A.:Masquerade (sels) Royal Philharmonic Collection ▲ TRP 35 [DDD]
Khachaturian, A.:Spartacus (sels) Royal Philharmonic Collection ▲ TRP 35 [DDD]
Liszt, F.:Mephisto Waltz 1 Orch Royal Philharmonic Collection ▲ TRP 30 [DDD]
Mahler, G.:Sym 1 Royal Philharmonic Collection ▲ TRP 29 [DDD]
Mozart, W.A.:Kleine Nachtmusik The Royal Philharmonic Collection ▲ TRP 41 [DDD]
Ponchielli, A.:La Gioconda (dance) Royal Philharmonic Collection ▲ TRP 30 [DDD]
Tchaikovsky, P.:Serenade Strs The Royal Philharmonic Collection ▲ TRP 41 [DDD]
Thomas, A.:Mignon (Ov) Royal Philharmonic Collection ▲ TRP 30 [DDD]
Verdi, G.:La traviata (sels)—Preludes to Acts 1 & 3 Royal Philharmonic Collection ▲ TRP 30 [DDD]
Weber, C.M. von:Invitation to the Dance Orch Royal Philharmonic Collection ▲ TRP 30 [DDD]

L. Slatkin (cnd)
Britten, B.:Peter Grimes (sea interludes & passacaglia), w. Royal PO, London PO RCA Red Seal ▲ 09026-61226-2
Britten, B.:Purcell Realizations, w. Royal PO, London PO—Chancony RCA Red Seal ▲ 09026-61226-2
Britten, B.:Sinf da requiem, London PO RCA Red Seal ▲ 09026-61226-2
Britten, B.:The Young Person's Guide to the Orchestra, London PO RCA Red Seal ▲ 09026-61226-2

Snell, Groves (cnd)
Williams, G.:Music of, w. Anthony Camden (ob), London SO, English CO—Fant on Welsh Nursery Tunes; Sea Sketches; Penillion; Carillions Ob; Con for Tpt Lyrita ▲ SRCD 323

Royal PO (cont.)

R. Stanger (cnd)

Liszt, F.:Fant on Hungarian Folk Tunes, w. E. Wild (pno) *(rec 1963)* Chesky ▲ CD50 [ADD]

R. Stapleton (cnd)

Dvorák, A.:Rusalka (sels), w. Josephine Barstow (sop)—O Silver Moon IMP ("Concert Classics" series) ▲ IMP PCD 1103

Golden Melodies from Opera, w. London SO, S. McCulloch (sop), Josephine Barstow (sop), J. Oakman (ten), Edmund Barham (ten) Pickwick ("The Orchid" series) ▲ PICORCD 11005

Opera Spectacular 2, w. Royal Opera House Chorus Covent Garden RPO Records ▲ CDRPO 7009 [DDD]

Tito Beltran, w. B. Beltran (ten), Royal PO [cnd:Robin Stapleton] Silva Classics ▲ SIL 6005 [DDD] ■ SIL 6005

L. Stokowski (cnd)

Borodin, A.:Prince Igor (Polovtsian dances), w. Royal Liverpool Phil Choir, Welsh National Opera Chorus *(rec Kingsway Hall, London, England, June 17, 1969)* London ("Phase 4 Stereo" series) ▲ 443896-2 [ADD]

Borodin, A.:Prince Igor (Polovtsian dances), w. Royal Liverpool Phil Choir [R] London ▲ 417753-2 [ADD]

Rimsky-Korsakov, N.:Scheherazade RCA Victrola ▲ 7743-2-RV [ADD] ■ 7743-4-RV3 (CrO2)

Stokowski Encores, w. Czech PO, London SO, New Philharmonia London ("Weekend Classics" series) ▲ 433876-2 LC [ADD]

Stravinsky, I.:Pastorale, w. Neville Taweel (vn), Derek Wickens (ob), Leonard Brain (E hn), Thomas Kelly (cl), John Price (bn) *(rec Kingsway Hall, London, England, June 16-17, 1969)* London ("Phase 4 Stereo" series) ▲ 443898-2 [ADD]

Tchaikovsky, P.:Ov 1812, w. Grenadier Guards Band, Royal Liverpool Phil Choir, Welsh National Opera Chorus *(rec Kingsway Hall, London, England, June 16, 1969)* London ("Phase 4 Stereo" series) ▲ 443896-2 [ADD]

Tchaikovsky, P.:Ov 1812 Music & Arts 2-▲ MUA CD 944

Wagner, R.:Die Meistersinger von Nürnberg (sels)—Dance of the Apprentices; Entry of the Masters; Act 3 Prelude RCA Victor ▲ 09026-61268-2 [ADD] ■ 09026-61268-4 (CrO2)

Wagner, R.:Rienzi, der Letzte der Tribunen (ov) RCA Victor ▲ 09026-61268-2 [ADD] ■ 09026-61268-4 (CrO2)

Wagner, R.:Tristan und Isolde (prelude & liebestod) RCA Victor ▲ 09026-61268-2 [ADD] ■ 09026-61268-4 (CrO2)

Wagner, R.:Die Walküre (magic fire) RCA ▲ 09026-61268-2 [ADD] ■ 09026-61268-4 (CrO2)

E. Stratta (cnd)

Bassoon Bon-Bons, w. D. Smith (bn), English CO [cnd:Philip Ledger], Coull String Quartet, Roger Vignoles (pno) ASV ▲ ASV 2052 [DDD]

Lloyd Webber, A.:Music of—includes music from Aspects of Love, Cats, Evita, Phantom of the Opera Teldec ▲ 9031-73742-2 ■ 9031-73742-4

Symphonic Boleros, w. Ernie Watts (sax), Sal Marquez (tpt), Clare Fischer (pno), Jorge Callandrelli (pno), Brian Monroney (gtr) Teldec ▲ 91180-2 ■ 91180-4

I. Stravinsky (cnd)

Stravinsky, I.:The Rake's Progress, w. J. Raskin (sop), A. Young (ten), J. Reardon (bar) *(rec 1964)* Sony Classical 2-▲ SM2K 46299

Y. Temirankov (cnd)

Shostakovich, D.:Con 1 Vc, w. N. Gutman (vc) RCA Red Seal ▲ 7918-2-RC [DDD]

Shostakovich, D.:Con 2 Vc, w. N. Gutman (vc) RCA Red Seal ▲ 7918-2-RC [DDD]

Y. Temirkanov (cnd)

Berlioz, H.:Ovs—Le Corsaire; Béatrice et Bénédict RCA Red Seal ▲ 09026-61203-2 [DDD]

Berlioz, H.:Sym fantastique RCA Red Seal ▲ 09026-61203-2 [DDD]

Brahms, J.:Con Vn, w. V. Spivakov (vn) RCA Red Seal ▲ 09026-61696-2

Brahms, J.:Con Vn & Vc, "Double Con", w. V. Spivakov (vn), A. Kniazev (vc) RCA Red Seal ▲ 09026-61696-2

Grieg, E.:Con Pno, Op. 16, w. D. Alexeev (pno) Classics for Pleasure ▲ CDEMX 2195 [DDD]

Khachaturian, A.:Gayane (sels) EMI Classics ▲ CDC 47348 [DDD]

Khachaturian, A.:Spartacus (sels) EMI Classics ▲ CDC 47348 [DDD]

Mussorgsky, M.:Khovanshchina (prelude) RCA Red Seal ▲ 60195-2-RC [DDD]

Mussorgsky, M.:Pictures at an Exhibition RCA Red Seal ▲ 60195-2-RC [DDD]

Mussorgsky, M.:Songs & Dances, w. S. Leiferkus (bar) RCA Red Seal ▲ 60195-2-RC [DDD]

Prokofiev, S.:Con 1 Vn, w. V. Spivakov (vn) RCA Red Seal ▲ 09026-60990-2

Rachmaninoff, S.:Con 2 Pno, w. Philip Fowke (pno) Classics for Pleasure ("Eminence" series) ▲ CFP-9509 [DDD]

Schumann, R.:Con Pno, w. D. Alexeev (pno) Classics for Pleasure ▲ CDEMX 2195 [DDD]

Stravinsky, I.:Divert Orch RCA Red Seal ▲ 60394-2-RC [DDD] ■ 60394-4-RC (CrO2)

Stravinsky, I.:The Firebird RCA Red Seal ▲ 60394-2-RC [DDD] ■ 60394-4-RC (CrO2)

Stravinsky, I.:Pulcinella Suite RCA Red Seal ▲ 60394-2-RC [DDD] ■ 60394-4-RC (CrO2)

Stravinsky, I.:Le Sacre du printemps Orch RCA Red Seal ▲ 7985-2-RC [DDD]

Tchaikovsky, P.:Con Vn, w. V. Spivakov (vn) RCA Red Seal ▲ 09026-60990-2

Tchaikovsky, P.:Eugene Onegin (sels)—Introduction, Waltz & Polonaise RCA Red Seal 2-▲ 60465-2-RC [DDD]

Tchaikovsky, P.:Music of—Syms. (complete); Swan Lake:Ballet Suite; Francesca da Rimini; Marche Slave; Fatum; Capriccio italien; Romeo and Juliet RCA Red Seal 6-▲ 09026-61821-2

Tchaikovsky, P.:The Nutcracker RCA Red Seal 2-▲ 60465-2-RC [DDD]

Tchaikovsky, P.:The Nutcracker (sels)—Ov.; March; Waltz of the Snowflakes [with Finchley Children's Music Group]; Chocolate; Coffee; Tea; Trepak; Dance of the Flutes; Dance of the Sugar-Plum Fairy; Waltz of the Flowers RCA Gold Seal ▲ 09026-68149-2 [DDD]

Tchaikovsky, P.:Sym 1—Movts 1 & 2 RCA Gold Seal ▲ 09026-68149-2 [DDD]

B. Tovey (cnd)

Falla, M. de:El amor brujo (ritual fire dance) IMP ("Classics" series) ▲ IMP 6700702

Hérold, F.:Clog Dance IMP ("Classics" series) ▲ IMP 6700702

Khachaturian, A.:Adagio IMP ("Classics" series) ▲ IMP 6700702

Massenet, J.:Le Cid (ballet suite) IMP ("Classics" series) ▲ IMP 6700702

Tchaikovsky, P.:Nutcracker Suite IMP ("Classics" series) ▲ IMP 6700702

Tchaikovsky, P.:Sleeping Beauty (suite) IMP ("Classics" series) ▲ IMP 6700702

Tchaikovsky, P.:Swan Lake (suite) IMP ("Classics" series) ▲ IMP 6700702

H. Vonk (cnd)

Beethoven, L. van:Romances Vn, w. E. Verhey (vn) Vivace 3-▲ E 324 [ADD/DDD]

Fauré, G.:Elégie, w. A. Eldredge (vc) *(rec London, Aug. 9-11, 1989)* Canyon Classics ▲ 3694 [DDD]

Glazunov, A.:Chant du ménéstrel, w. A. Eldredge (vc) *(rec London, Aug. 9-11, 1989)* Canyon Classics ▲ 3694 [DDD]

Lalo, E.:Con Vc, w. A. Eldredge (vc) *(rec London, Aug. 9-11, 1989)* Canyon Classics ▲ 3694 [DDD]

Saint-Saëns, C.:Con 1 Vc, w. A. Eldredge (vc) *(rec London, Aug. 9-11, 1989)* Canyon Classics ▲ 3694 [DDD]

E. de Waart (cnd)

Rachmaninoff, S.:Con 2 Pno, w. R. Orozco (pno) Philips 2-▲ 438383-2

Rachmaninoff, S.:Music of, w. R. Orozco (pno) Philips 2-▲ 438326-2

Rachmaninoff, S.:Rhapsody on a Theme of Paganini, w. R. Orozco (pno) Philips 2-▲ 438383-2

Rachmaninoff, S.:Sym 2 Philips 2-▲ 438383-2

Rachmaninoff, S.:Vocalise, w. Rafael Orozco (pno) Philips 2-▲ 438383-2

B. Walter (cnd)

Berlioz, H.:La Damnation de Faust (sels)—Danse des Sylphes Iron Needle ▲ 1305 (m)

Strauss, R.:Don Juan Grammofono 2000 ▲ GRM 78585

Strauss, R.:Don Juan *(rec 1926)* Iron Needle ▲ IN 1312 [ADD]

Strauss, R.:Tod und Verklärung *(rec 1924)* Iron Needle ▲ IN 1312 [ADD]

Wagner, R.:Arias & Scenes, British SO—Prelude to Act I [2 versions]; Transformation Scene [both fromParsifal]; Venusberg Music [from Tannhäuser]; Rienzi Ov; Liebestod [from Tristan & Isolde]; Preludes to Acts I & III; Dance of the Apprentices & Entrance of the Masters [all from Die Meistersinger von Nürnberg] VAI Audio ▲ VAIA 1114 [ADD]

Royal PO (cont.)

B. Walter (cnd) (cont.)

Wagner, R.:Der fliegende Holländer (ov) Iron Needle ▲ IN 1309 [ADD]

Wagner, R.:Der fliegende Holländer (ov) Grammofono 2000 ▲ GRM 78585

Wagner, R.:Götterdämmerung (rhine journey) Iron Needle ▲ IN 1309 [ADD]

Wagner, R.:Götterdämmerung (rhine journey) Grammofono 2000 ▲ GRM 78585

Wagner, R.:Lohengrin (preludes)—to Act 3 Iron Needle ▲ IN 1309 [ADD]

Wagner, R.:Lohengrin (preludes)—Prelude to Act 3 Grammofono 2000 ▲ GRM 78585

Wagner, R.:Ovs, Preludes & Orch Sels, British SO—Prelude to Act 3 [from Lohengrin]; Parsifal; Ov. [from Der fliegende Holländer]; Siegfried's Journey to the Rhine & Funeral March [from Götterdämmerung] *(rec 1925-27 & 1931)* VAI Audio ▲ VAIA 1059

Wagner, R.:Parsifal (sels)—Prelude to Act 1; Music of Change Scene; Klingsors Zaubergarten Iron Needle ▲ IN 1309 [ADD]

Wagner, R.:Parsifal (orch sels)—Klingors Zaubergarten; Prelude to Act 1 Grammofono 2000 ▲ GRM 78585

Wagner, R.:Rienzi, der Letzte der Tribunen (ov) Iron Needle ▲ IN 1309 [ADD]

Wagner, R.:Tannhäuser (ov & venusberg)—Venusberg Music Grammofono 2000 ▲ GRM 78585

Wagner, R.:Tannhäuser (ov & venusberg)—Venusberg Music Iron Needle ▲ IN 1309 [ADD]

Wagner, R.:Tristan und Isolde (prelude & liebestod)—Liebestod Grammofono 2000 ▲ GRM 78585

W. Walton (cnd)

Walton, W.:Vars on a Theme by Hindemith IMP ("BBC Radio Classics" series) ▲ IMP 5691782

F. von Weingartner (cnd)

Beethoven, L. van:Son 29 Pno, "Hammerklavier" [orch. trans. Weingartner] *(rec 3/26-31/30)* Pearl ▲ PEA 9358 (m) [AAD]

Brahms, J.:Sym 1 *(rec 1928)* Koch Legacy ▲ 3-7128-2 H1

Mendelssohn, F.:Sym 3 Enterprise ("Sirio" series) ▲ ENT SO 530015

H. D. Wetton (cnd)

Holst, G.:A Choral Fant, w. L. Dawson (sop), Guildford Choral Society Hyperion ▲ CDA 66660

Holst, G.:First Choral Sym, w. L. Dawson (sop), Guildford Choral Society Hyperion ▲ CDA 66660

B. Wordsworth (cnd)

Beethoven, L. van:Sym 1 Royal Philharmonic Collection ▲ TRP 33

Beethoven, L. van:Sym 7 Royal Philharmonic Collection ▲ TRP 33

Delius, F.:Aquarelles (2) The Royal Philharmonic Collection ▲ TRP 37 [DDD]

Elgar, E.:Intro & Allegro The Royal Philharmonic Collection ▲ TRP 37 [DDD]

Elgar, E.:Serenade Strs The Royal Philharmonic Collection ▲ TRP 37 [DDD]

Holst, G.:Brook Green Suite The Royal Philharmonic Collection ▲ TRP 37 [DDD]

Lloyd Webber, A.:Music of, w. Julian Lloyd Webber (vc)—highlights from Aspects of Love, Cats, Phantom of the Opera, Starlight Express, Jesus Christ Superstar, Evita, Requiem, Song and Dance, Joseph and His Amazing Technicolor Dreamcoat Philips ▲ 426484-2 [DDD]

Purcell, H.:Suite Strs The Royal Philharmonic Collection ▲ TRP 37 [DDD]

Walton, W.:Pieces Strs The Royal Philharmonic Collection ▲ TRP 37 [DDD]

Warlock, P.:Capriol Suite—Basse-danse; Pavanne; Tordion; Bransles; Pieds-en-l'air; Mattachins [Sword Dance] The Royal Philharmonic Collection ▲ TRP 37 [DDD]

P. Zukovsky (cnd)

Schnabel, A.:Sym 2 CP2 Recordings ▲ CP2 104

Royal PO Chamber Ensemble

J. Carney (cnd)

Haydn, J.:Qts Strs, Op. 1—No. 1 in B♭ [Hunt] Royal Philharmonic Collection ▲ TRP 28 [DDD]

Haydn, J.:Qts Strs, Op. 64, "Tost Qts"—No. 5 in D [Lark] Royal Philharmonic Collection ▲ TRP 28 [DDD]

Haydn, J.:Qts Strs, Op. 76, "Erdödy Qts"—No. 3 in C [Emperor] Royal Philharmonic Collection ▲ TRP 28 [DDD]

Royal PO Soloists

P. Freeman (cnd)

Fennimore, J.:Pno Music, w. J. Fennimore (pno)—Two Pieces from Armistice; Variations on a Theme by Beethoven; Two Rags; Foxtrot; Second Romance; Calentura de Teresa [w. J. Zayas (piano)]; Concerto Piccolo Albany ▲ TROY 113 [ADD]

Royal PO Strings

E. Stratta (cnd)

The Symphonic Tango, w. Buenos Aires Quintet Teldec ▲ 9031-76997-2 ■ 9031-76997-4

Royal PO Pops

Lloyd Webber, A.:Music of, w. L. Garrett (sgr), Dave Willets (sgr), C. Corcoran (sgr), Gerard Casey (sgr), S. Campbell (sgr), Royal PO, Royal PO Concert Orch—sels from The Phantom of the Opera; Evita; Cats; Joseph & the Amazing Technicolor Dreamcoat; Jesus Christ Superstar; Tell Me on a Sunday; Song & Dance; Starlight Express; Sunset Boulevard Silva America 2-▲ SILCD 1044 [DDD] ■ SILMC 1044

Shows Orchestral Pickwick 3-▲ PIC BOXD 50 [DDD]

J. Scott (cnd)

Europe Goes to Hollywood Denon/PCM Digital ▲ DEN 75470

Royal Scottish National Orch

Seascapes, w. Royal Scottish National Orch [cnd:A. Gibson], Ulster Orch [cnd:V. Handley], Bournemouth Sinfonietta [cnd:G. Hurst], London PO [cnd:B. Thomson] Chandos ("Collect" series) ▲ CHAN 6538 [ADD/DDD]

J. Currie (cnd)

The Holly & the Ivy, w. Royal Scottish Chorus ASV ("White Line" series) ▲ ASV 2073

The Holly & the Ivy, w. Royal Scottish Chorus ASV ▲ ASV 2073 [DDD]

A. Gibson (cnd)

Arnold, M.:Tam o'Shanter Chandos ▲ CHAN 8379 [DDD]

Berlioz, H.:Ovs—Le Corsaire Chandos ("Collect" series) ▲ CHAN 6538 [ADD/DDD]

Berlioz, H.:Ovs—Waverley Chandos ▲ CHAN 8379 [DDD]

Elgar, E.:Con Vc, w. R. Kirshbaum (vc) Chandos ("Collect" series) ▲ CHAN 6607 [DDD]

Elgar, E.:Falstaff, w. R. Kirshbaum (vc) Chandos ("Collect" series) ▲ CHAN 6607 [DDD]

Maccunn, H.:Land of the Mountain & the Flood Chandos ▲ CHAN 8379 [DDD]

Mendelssohn, F.:Die Hebriden Chandos ▲ CHAN 8379 [DDD]

Mendelssohn, F.:Die Hebriden Chandos ("Collect" series) ▲ CHAN 6538 [ADD/DDD]

Nielsen, C.:Helios Chandos ("Collect" series) ▲ CHAN 6533 [ADD]

Nielsen, C.:Sym 5 Chandos ("Collect" series) ▲ CHAN 6533 [ADD]

Rachmaninoff, S.:Sym 2 Chandos ("Collect" series) ▲ CHAN 6606 [DDD]

Sibelius, J.:Aallottaret Chandos ("Collect" series) ▲ CHAN 6538 [ADD/DDD]

Sibelius, J.:Night Ride & Sunrise Chandos ("Collect" series) ▲ CHAN 6533 [ADD]

Sibelius, J.:Spring Song Chandos ("Collect" series) ▲ CHAN 6533 [ADD]

Sibelius, J.:Syms (comp) Chandos ("Collect" series) 3-▲ CHAN 6559 [DDD]

Sibelius, J.:Sym 1 Chandos ("Collect" series) ▲ CHAN 6555 [ADD]

Sibelius, J.:Sym 2 Chandos ("Collect" series) ▲ CHAN 6556 [DDD]

Sibelius, J.:Sym 3 Chandos ("Collect" series) ▲ CHAN 6557 [DDD]

Sibelius, J.:Sym 4 Chandos ("Collect" series) ▲ CHAN 6555 [ADD]

Sibelius, J.:Sym 5 Chandos ("Collect" series) ▲ CHAN 6556 [DDD]

Sibelius, J.:Sym 6 Chandos ("Collect" series) ▲ CHAN 6557 [DDD]

Sibelius, J.:Sym 7 Chandos ("Collect" series) ▲ CHAN 6557 [DDD]

Stravinsky, I.:Sym in 3 Movts Chandos ("Collect" series) ▲ CHAN 6577 [DDD]

Verdi, G.:Ballet Music—from Macbeth, Act 3 Chandos ▲ CHAN 8379 [DDD]

N. Järvi (cnd)

Barber, S.:Adagio Strs *(rec Caird Hall, Dundee, Aug 14, 1989)* Chandos ▲ CHAN 7039

Eller, H.:Elegia *(rec Henry Wood Hall, Glasgow, Aug 1986)* Chandos ▲ CHAN 7039

Enescu, G.:Romanian Rhap 1 Chandos ▲ CHAN 8947 [DDD]

Enescu, G.:Romanian Rhap 2 Chandos ▲ CHAN 8947 [DDD]

Mahler, G.:Blumine Chandos ▲ CHAN 9308 [DDD]

Mahler, G.:Kindertotenlieder, w. L. Finnie (mez) [G] Chandos 2-▲ CHAN 9117/18 [DDD]

Mahler, G.:Lieder eines fahrenden Gesellen, w. L. Finnie (mez) [G] Chandos ▲ CHAN 8951 [DDD]

Mahler, G.:Sym 1 Chandos ▲ CHAN 9308 [DDD]

Mahler, G.:Sym 3, w. L. Finnie (mez), Royal Scottish Chorus [G] Chandos 2-▲ CHAN 9117/18 [DDD]

▲ = CD ♦ = Enhanced CD Δ = MD ■ = Cassette Tape ◻ = DCC

Royal Scottish National Orch (cont.)

N. Järvi (cnd) (cont.)

Mahler, G.:Sym 4, w. L. Finnie (mez) [G] — Chandos ▲ CHAN 8951 [DDD]
Mahler, G.:Sym 5—Adagio *(rec Caird Hall, Dundee, Oct 23–24, 1989)* — Chandos ▲ CHAN 7039
Mahler, G.:Sym 6 — Chandos ▲ CHAN 9207 [DDD]
Pärt, A.:Cantus in Memory of Benjamin Britten *(rec Henry Wood Hall, Glasgow, Aug 23–24, 1987)* — Chandos ▲ CHAN 7039
Prokofiev, S.:Romeo & Juliet (suites)—Suite No. 3 (from above) — Chandos ▲ CHAN 8508 [DDD]
Prokofiev, S.:Romeo & Juliet (suites)—Suite No. 1, (from above) — Chandos ▲ CHAN 8368 [DDD]
Prokofiev, S.:Romeo & Juliet (suites)—Suite No. 2 (from above) — Chandos ▲ CHAN 8472 [DDD]
Prokofiev, S.:Romeo & Juliet (suites)—Suite Nos. 1–3 — Chandos ▲ CHAN 8940 [DDD]
Prokofiev, S.:Syms (comp)—includes both versions of Sym. No. 4 — Chandos 4–▲ CHAN 8931/34 [DDD]
Shostakovich, D.:Ballet Suites (comp) — Chandos 2–▲ CHAN 7000/01 [DDD]
Shostakovich, D.:Festive Ov — Chandos 2–▲ CHAN 7000/01 [DDD]
Shostakovich, D.:Katerina Ismaylova (suite) — Chandos 2–▲ CHAN 7000/01 [DDD]
Strauss, R.:Eine Alpensinfonie — Chandos 2–▲ CHAN 7009/10 [DDD]
Strauss, R.:Also sprach Zarathustra — Chandos 2–▲ CHAN 7011/12
Strauss, R.:Don Juan — Chandos 2–▲ CHAN 7009/10 [DDD]
Strauss, R.:Don Quixote — Chandos 2–▲ CHAN 7011/12
Strauss, R.:Ein Heldenleben — Chandos 2–▲ CHAN 7009/10 [DDD]
Strauss, R.:Macbeth — Chandos 2–▲ CHAN 7011/12
Strauss, R.:Metamorphosen *(rec SNO Center, Glasgow)* — Chandos ▲ CHAN 7039
Strauss, R.:Songs, w. E. Hulse (sop)—6 Lieder, Op. 68 — Chandos ▲ CHAN 9166 [DDD]
Strauss, R.:Symphonia domestica — Chandos 2–▲ CHAN 7011/12
Strauss, R.:Till Eulenspiegels lustige Streiche — Chandos 2–▲ CHAN 7011/12
Strauss, R.:Tod und Verklärung — Chandos 2–▲ CHAN 7009/10 [DDD]
Stravinsky, I.:L'Histoire du soldat Suite Ensemble — Chandos ▲ CHAN 9291 [DDD]
Stravinsky, I.:Octet — Chandos ▲ CHAN 9291 [DDD]
Stravinsky, I.:Pétrouchka [1911 version] — Chandos ▲ CHAN 9291 [DDD]
Stravinsky, I.:Ragtime — Chandos ▲ CHAN 9291 [DDD]

J. MacMillan (cnd)

Macmillan, J.:Britannia *(rec Glasgow City Hall, Jan 29–31, 1995)* — RCA Red Seal ▲ 09026–68328–2 [DDD]
Macmillan, J.:Sinfonietta *(rec Glasgow City Hall, Jan 29–31, 1995)* — RCA Red Seal ▲ 09026–68328–2 [DDD]
Macmillan, J.:Sowetan Spring *(rec Glasgow City Hall, Jan 29–31, 1995)* — RCA Red Seal ▲ 09026–68328–2 [DDD]

N. Mantle (cnd)

Buechner, M.:The Liberty Bell, w. Royal Scottish Chorus *(rec Henry Wood Hall, Glasgow, Sept. 1994)* — Nord–Disc ▲ NORD 2034 [DDD] ■ NORDC 2035

A. Penny (cnd)

Parry, H.:Ov to an Unwritten Tragedy *(rec Glasgow)* — Naxos ▲ 8.553469 [DDD]
Parry, H.:Symphonic Vars *(rec Glasgow)* — Naxos ▲ 8.553469 [DDD]
Parry, H.:Sym 2 *(rec Glasgow)* — Naxos ▲ 8.553469 [DDD]

M. Stenz (cnd)

Macmillan, J.:The Berserking, w. Peter Donohoe (pno) *(rec Glasgow City Hall, Jan 29–31, 1995)* — RCA Red Seal ▲ 09026–68328–2 [DDD]

B. Thomson (cnd)

Martinů, B.:Syms (6) — Chandos 3–▲ CHAN 9103/05 [DDD]
Martinů, B.:Sym 1 — Chandos ▲ CHAN 8915 [DDD]
Martinů, B.:Sym 2 — Chandos ▲ CHAN 8916 [DDD]
Martinů, B.:Sym 5 — Chandos ▲ CHAN 8915 [DDD]
Martinů, B.:Sym 6 — Chandos ▲ CHAN 8916 [DDD]
Nielsen, C.:Syms (comp) — Chandos 3–▲ CHAN 9163
Nielsen, C.:Sym 1 — Chandos ▲ CHAN 8880 [DDD]
Nielsen, C.:Sym 2 — Chandos ▲ CHAN 8880 [DDD]
Nielsen, C.:Sym 3 — Chandos ▲ CHAN 9067 [DDD]
Nielsen, C.:Sym 4 — Chandos ▲ CHAN 9047 [DDD]
Nielsen, C.:Sym 5 — Chandos ▲ CHAN 9067 [DDD]
Nielsen, C.:Sym 6 — Chandos ▲ CHAN 9047 [DDD]
Rachmaninoff, S.:Con 1 Pno, w. H. Shelley (pno) — Chandos ▲ CHAN 9192 [DDD]
Rachmaninoff, S.:Con 2 Pno, w. H. Shelley (pno) — Chandos ▲ CHAN 9193 [DDD]
Rachmaninoff, S.:Con 3 Pno, w. H. Shelley (pno) — Chandos ▲ CHAN 9193 [DDD]
Rachmaninoff, S.:Con 4 Pno, w. H. Shelley (pno) — Chandos ▲ CHAN 9192 [DDD]
Rachmaninoff, S.:Rhapsody on a Theme of Paganini, w. H. Shelley (pno) — Chandos ▲ CHAN 9192 [DDD]

J. Varineau (cnd)

Buechner, M.:The American Civil War *(rec Dec. 28–29, 1992)* — Nord–Disc ▲ NORD 2028 [DDD] ■ Nord 2029
Buechner, M.:The Blue & the Gray — Nord–Disc ▲ NORD 2030 [DDD]
Buechner, M.:Erlkönig Orch — Nord–Disc ▲ NORD 2024 [DDD]
Buechner, M.:Erlkönig Orch—Suite 2 — Nord–Disc ▲ NORD 2032 [DDD]
Buechner, M.:Erlkönig Orch—Suite 1 — Nord–Disc ▲ NORD 2030 [DDD]
Buechner, M.:Essay I Orch — Nord–Disc ▲ NORD 2030 [DDD]
Buechner, M.:The Flight of the American Eagle — Nord–Disc ▲ NORD 2030 [DDD]

Royal Shakespeare Company

P. Brook (cnd)

Peaslee, R.:Marat/Sade, w. Glenda Jackson (actor), *(orch unknown), (this is a reissue of the 1966 New York Original Cast recording)* — Premier ▲ PRCD 1022 [ADD]
Peaslee, R.:US, w. Glenda Jackson (actor), *(orch unknown), (this is a reissue of the 1966 London Original Cast recording)* — Premier ▲ PRCD 1022 [ADD]

Royal Stockholm Orch

K. Ingebretsen (cnd)

Lidholm, I.:A Dream Play, w. Hillevi Martinpelto (sop), Håkan Hagegård (bar) — Caprice 2–▲ CAP 22029

E. Klas (cnd)

Crusell, B.H.:Den Lilla Slavinnan (sels), w. Kjell Fagéus (cl)—Aria — Opus 3 ▲ OP 8801
Frumerie, G. de:Con Cl, w. Kjell Fagéus (cl)—1st movt — Opus 3 ▲ OP 8801
Larsson, L.-E.:Hommage à Mozart, w. Kjell Fagéus (cl) — Opus 3 ▲ OP 8801
Mozart, W.A.:Con Cl, w. Kjell Fagéus (cl) — Opus 3 ▲ OP 8801

S. Köhler (cnd)

Strauss, R.:4 Last Songs, w. Britt Marie Aruhn (sop), Viktor Åslund (pno) — Bluebell ▲ BLU 062 [DDD]
Strauss, R.:Songs, w. Britt Marie Aruhn (sop), Viktor Åslund (pno)—Begegnung, AV.72; Die Nacht, Op. 10; Allerseelen, Op. 10; Wie sollten wir geheim sie halten, Op. 19; Du meines herzens Krönelein, Op. 21; Cäcilie, Op. 27; Morgen, Op. 27; Befreit, Op. 39; Wiegenlied, Op. 41; Freundliche Vision, Op. 48; Sie wissen's nicht, Op. 49; Frühlingsfeier, Op. 56; Ich wolt' ein Sträusslein binden, Op. 68; Säusle, liebe Myrthe, Op. 68; Malven, AV.304 — Bluebell ▲ BLU 062 [DDD]

Royal Stockholm PO

J. DePreist (cnd)

Gubaidulina, S.:Offertorium, w. O. Krysa (vn) — BIS ▲ CD 566 [DDD]
Saint-Saëns, C.:Danse macabre — BIS ▲ CD 555 [DDD]
Saint-Saëns, C.:Samson et Dalila (Bacchanale) — BIS ▲ CD 555 [DDD]
Saint-Saëns, C.:Sym 3, w. H. Fagius (org) — BIS ▲ CD 555 [DDD]

Ehrling, Grevillius, Larsson, Mann, Sandberg (cnd)

Rossini, G.:Il barbiere di Siviglia (sels), w. Birgit Nilsson (sop), Set Svanholm (ten), Sigurd Björling (bar), Swedish RSO—Largo al factotum — Bluebell ▲ BLU 058 [ADD]
Verdi, G.:Otello (sels), w. Birgit Nilsson (sop), Set Svanholm (ten), Sigurd Björling (bar), Swedish RSO—Desdemona real...Ora e per sempre adio...Si, pel ciel marmoreo giuro! — Bluebell ▲ BLU 058 [ADD]

Royal Stockholm PO (cont.)

Ehrling, Grevillius, Larsson, Mann, Sandberg (cnd) (cont.)

Wagner, R.:Arias & Scenes, w. Birgit Nilsson (sop), Set Svanholm (ten), Sigurd Björling (bar), Swedish RSO—Morgenlich leuchtend [from Die Meistersinger von Nürnberg]; Ein Schwert verhiess mir der Vater [from Die Walküre]; Mime hiess ein mürrischer Zwerg...Brünnhilde, heilige Braut [from Götterdämmerung] — Bluebell ▲ BLU 058 [ADD]
Weber, C.M. von:Der Freischütz (sels), w. Birgit Nilsson (sop), Set Svanholm (ten), Sigurd Björling (bar), Swedish RSO—Durch die Wälder, durch die Auen — Bluebell ▲ BLU 058 [ADD]

N. Järvi (cnd)

Alfvén, H.:Bergakungen (suite) *(rec Stockholm Concert Hall, Sweden, Dec. 18, 1992)* — BIS ▲ CD 725 [DDD]
Alfvén, H.:Swedish Rhap 1, "Midsommarvaka" *(rec Stockholm Concert Hall, Sweden, Dec. 3, 1987)* — BIS ▲ CD 725 [DDD]
Alfvén, H.:Swedish Rhap 2, "Uppsala–rhapsodi" *(rec Stockholm Concert Hall, Sweden, Feb. 11, 1988)* — BIS ▲ CD 725 [DDD]
Alfvén, H.:Swedish Rhap 3, "Dalarhapsodien" *(rec Stockholm Concert Hall, Sweden, May 25, 1989)* — BIS ▲ CD 725 [DDD]
Alfvén, H.:A Tale from the Archipelago *(rec Stockholm Concert Hall, Sweden, Oct. 4, 1990)* — BIS ▲ CD 725 [DDD]

P. Järvi (cnd)

Sibelius, J.:4 Legends from the Kalevalá — Virgin Classics ▲ CDC 45213
Sibelius, J.:Luonnotar, w. Solvieg Kringelborn (sop) — Virgin Classics ▲ CDC 45213
Sibelius, J.:Night Ride & Sunrise — Virgin Classics ▲ CDC 45213

K. Penderecki (cnd)

Penderecki, K.:Als Jakob erwachte, w. Jadwiga Gadulanka (sop), Zahos Terzakis (ten), Piotr Nowacki (bass), Stockholm Royal Theater Opera Chorus — Chandos 2–▲ CHAN 9459
Penderecki, K.:Polish Requiem, w. Jadwiga Gadulanka (sop), Zahos Terzakis (ten), Piotr Nowacki (bass), Stockholm Royal Theater Opera Chorus — Chandos 2–▲ CHAN 9459

G. Rozhdestvensky (cnd)

Berlioz, H.:Ovs—Le Corsaire — Chandos ▲ CHAN 9052 [DDD]
Berlioz, H.:Sym fantastique — Chandos ▲ CHAN 9052 [DDD]
Borodin, A.:Petite Suite — Chandos ▲ CHAN 9386 [DDD]
Borodin, A.:Prince Igor (Polovtsian dances) — Chandos ▲ CHAN 9386 [DDD]
Borodin, A.:Songs—Romance (w. L. Duadkova [mezzo-soprano]); At the Homes of Other Folk (w. T. Wallström [baritone]) — Chandos ▲ CHAN 9199 [DDD]
Borodin, A.:Sym 1 — Chandos ▲ CHAN 9199 [DDD]
Borodin, A.:Sym 2 — Chandos ▲ CHAN 9386 [DDD]
Borodin, A.:Sym 3 — Chandos ▲ CHAN 9199 [DDD]
Börtz, D.:Parodos — Chandos ▲ CHAN 9473
Börtz, D.:Sinf 1 — Chandos ▲ CHAN 9473
Börtz, D.:Sinf 7 — Chandos ▲ CHAN 9473
Börtz, D.:Strindberg Suite — Chandos ▲ CHAN 9473
Grieg, E.:Sigurd Jorsalfar (suite) — Chandos ▲ CHAN 9113 [DDD]
Grieg, E.:Songs, w. S. Kringelborn (sop)—Six Orchestral Songs (1894–5)—Solveigs Sang [Solveig's Song]; Solveigs Vuggevise [Solveig's Cradle Song]; Fra Monte Pincio [From Monte Pincio]; En Svane [A Swan]; Varen [Springtide]; Henrik Wergeland — Chandos ▲ CHAN 9113 [DDD]
Grieg, E.:Symphonic Dances — Chandos ▲ CHAN 9113 [DDD]
Gubaidulina, S.:Stufen — Chandos ▲ CHAN 9183 [DDD]
Gubaidulina, S.:Sym in 12 Movts, "Stimmen...Verstummen" — Chandos ▲ CHAN 9183 [DDD]
Lidholm, I.:Greetings from an Old World *(rec Nov. 19, 1992)* — Chandos ▲ CHAN 9231 [DDD]
Lidholm, I.:Kontakion *(rec Nov. 5 1991)* — Chandos ▲ CHAN 9231 [DDD]
Lidholm, I.:Ritornello *(rec June 10, 1993)* — Chandos ▲ CHAN 9231 [DDD]
Lidholm, I.:Toccata e canto *(rec Apr. 1, 1993)* — Chandos ▲ CHAN 9231 [DDD]
Nielsen, C.:Sym 2 — Chandos ▲ CHAN 9300 [DDD]
Nielsen, C.:Sym 2 — Chandos ▲ CHAN 9260 [DDD]
Nielsen, C.:Sym 3 — Chandos ▲ CHAN 9300 [DDD]
Nielsen, C.:Sym 4 — Chandos ▲ CHAN 9260 [DDD]
Nielsen, C.:Sym 5 — Chandos ▲ CHAN 9367 [DDD]
Nielsen, C.:Sym 6 — Chandos ▲ CHAN 9367 [DDD]
Schnittke, A.:Con grosso 6, w. Sasha Rozhdestvensky (vn), Viktoria Postnikova (pno) — Chandos ▲ CHAN 9359 [DDD]
Schnittke, A.:Sym 8 — Chandos ▲ CHAN 9359 [DDD]
Shostakovich, D.:The Bolt — Chandos 2–▲ CHAN 9343/44 [DDD]
Shostakovich, D.:The Golden Age (suite) — Chandos 2–▲ CHAN 9251 [DDD]
Shostakovich, D.:The Limpid Stream — Chandos ▲ CHAN 9423
Stenhammar, W.:Sym 3—performing the 7-page fragment of the 1st movement, the only material for the piece that was fully completed by Stenhammar — Chandos ▲ CHAN 9074 [DDD]

L. Segerstam (cnd)

Schnittke, A.:Sym 1, w. C.-A. Dominique (pno), B. Kallenberg (vn), A. Lännerholm (trbn) *(rec Oct. 14, 1992)* — BIS ▲ CD 577 [DDD]
Schnittke, A.:Sym 2, w. Malena Ernman (alt), Mikael Bellini (ct), Göran Eliasson (ten), Torkel Borelius (bass), Anders Eby (cnd), Mikaeli Chamber Choir *(rec Stockholm Concert Hall, Sweden, Feb. 24–25, 1994)* — BIS ▲ CD 667 [DDD]
Scriabin, A.:Rêverie — BIS ▲ CD 535 [DDD]
Scriabin, A.:Sym 2 — BIS ▲ CD 535 [DDD]
Scriabin, A.:Sym 4 — BIS ▲ CD 535 [DDD]
Vaughan Williams, R.:Con Bass Tuba, w. Michael Lind (tuba) — Caprice ▲ CAP 21493

Royal Swedish Opera Orch

Andersson, B.T.:Apollo Con, w. Markus Leoson (perc) — Caprice ▲ CAP 21466
Milhaud, D.:Con Mar, w. Markus Leoson (mar/vib) — Caprice ▲ CAP 21466

P. Brunelle (cnd)

Frigel, P.:Ov Orch — Virgin Classics ▲ CDC 45186
Grenser, J.F.:Sinf alla Posta Orch — Virgin Classics ▲ CDC 45186
Haeffner, J.C.F.:Ov in E♭ — Virgin Classics ▲ CDC 45186
Kraus, J.M.:Riksdagsmusiken — Virgin Classics ▲ CDC 45186
Kraus, J.M.:Soliman II, w. L. Hoel (sop), B. Ortendahl–Corin (sop), B.-O. Morgny (ten), T. Wallstrom (bass), Sweden Royal Opera Chorus — Virgin Classics ▲ 59068 [DDD]
Naumann, J.G.:Gustaf Wasa, w. Anders Andersson (ten—Gustav Wasa), Nicolai Gedda (ten—Christjern), Stockholm Royal Theater Opera Chorus — Virgin Classics ▲ CDCB 45148
Zander, J.D.:Sym in B♭ — Virgin Classics ▲ CDC 45186

Royal Swedish Orch

E. Klas (cnd)

Atterberg, K.:Suite 1 Orch, "Orientalisk svit" *(rec Sept & Oct 1987)* — Musica Sveciae ▲ MSCD 618 [DDD]

Royal Welsh Fusiliers Regimental Band

P. Goodwin (cnd)

We'll Keep a Welcome — Bandleader ▲ BND 5107 [DDD]

Rozmberk Ensemble

F. Pok (cnd)

European Danserye & Ayres — Supraphon ▲ SUP 110347 [DDD]

RTBF New SO

E. Doneux (cnd)

Beethoven, L. van:Con Vn, Op. 61, w. Lola Bobesco (vn) — Talent ▲ 2910501
Mendelssohn, F.:Con in e Vn & Orch, Op. 64, w. Lola Bobesco (vn) — Talent ▲ 2910501

RTBF SO

S. Argiris (cnd)

Menotti, G.C.:Apocalypse — Masters of Art ▲ AAOC 9377
Menotti, G.C.:Sebastian — Masters of Art ▲ AAOC 9377

B. Priestman (cnd)

Franck, C.:Ce qu'on entend sur la montagne — Koch Schwann ▲ CD 311 105

RTBF SO (cont.)
B. Priestman (cnd) (cont.)
Jongen, J.:Allegro appassionata, w. T.–M. Gilissen (va) Koch Schwann ▲ CD 315012 [ADD]
Jongen, J.:Suite Va, w. T.–M. Gilissen (va) Koch Schwann ▲ CD 315012 [ADD]
Jongen, J.:Suite Va, w. T.–M. Gilissen (va) Koch Schwann ▲ SCH 313372 [ADD/DDD]
RTE Concert Orch
P. Ó. Duinn (cnd)
Wallace, V.:Maritana, w. Majella Cullagh (sop), Lynda Lee (mez), Paul Charles Clarke (ten), Ian Caddy (bar), Damien Smith (bar), Quentin Hayes (bass), RTE Phil Choir *(rec O'Reilly Hall, Dublin, Sept 1995)* Marco Polo 2–▲ 8.223406–7 [DDD]
A. Penny (cnd)
German, E.:Richard III (ov) *(rec Taney Parish Centre, Dublin, Jan 6–7, 1994)* Marco Polo ▲ 8.223695 [DDD]
German, E.:The Seasons *(rec Taney Parish Centre, Dublin, Jan 6–7, 1994)* Marco Polo ▲ 8.223695 [DDD]
German, E.:Theme & 6 Diversions *(rec Taney Parish Centre, Dublin, Jan 6–7, 1994)* Marco Polo ▲ 8.223695 [DDD]
Joyce, A.:Orchestral Music (misc)—Dreaming; Prince of Wales [Grand March]; Songe d'automne [Dream of Autumn]; Frou–Frou [polka]; A Thousand Kisses; Caravan Suite [Caravan Camp in the Desert; Caravan Camp Attacked by Brigands; Convoy on the March]; Dreams of You; Iris [danse de ballet]; Passing of Salome; Toto [sel.]; Acushla; Bohemia; Brighton Hike; Song of the River *(rec Taney Parish Centre, Dublin, Jan. 4 & 5, 1994)* Marco Polo ▲ 8.223694 [DDD]
Sullivan, A.:Henry VIII, w. E. Lawler *(rec Apr. 13–16, 1992)* Marco Polo ▲ 8.223461 [DDD]
Sullivan, A.:The Merchant of Venice, w. E. Lawler *(rec Apr. 13–16, 1992)* Marco Polo ▲ 8.223461 [DDD]
Sullivan, A.:The Sapphire Necklace *(rec Apr. 13–16, 1992)* Marco Polo ▲ 8.223461 [DDD]
Vaughan Williams, R.:Coastal Command *(rec National Concert Hall, Dublin, Nov. 16–17, 1993)* Marco Polo ("Film Music Classics" series) ▲ 8.223665 [DDD]
Vaughan Williams, R.:49th Parallel—Prelude *(rec National Concert Hall, Dublin, Nov. 16–17, 1993)* Marco Polo ("Film Music Classics" series) ▲ 8.223665 [DDD]
Vaughan Williams, R.:Portraits *(rec National Concert Hall, Dublin, Nov. 16–17, 1993)* Marco Polo ("Film Music Classics" series) ▲ 8.223665 [DDD]
Vaughan Williams, R.:The Story of a Flemish Farm—The Flag Flutters in the Wind; Night by the Sea [Farewell to the Flag]; Dawn in the Barn [The Parting of the Lovers]; In a Belgian Café; The Major goes to face his Fate; The Dead Man's Kit; The Wanderings of the Flag *(rec National Concert Hall, Dublin, Nov. 16–17, 1993)* Marco Polo ("Film Music Classics" series) ▲ 8.223665 [DDD]
E. Tomlinson (cnd)
Miniatures *(rec National Concert Hall, Dublin, Jan. 1993)* Marco Polo ▲ 8.223522 [DDD]
RTE Sinfonietta
K. Alwyn (cnd)
Berners:Luna Park *(rec Taney Parish Ctr., Dublin, Feb 14 & 15, 1994)* Marco Polo ▲ 8.223716 [DDD]
Berners:March Pno [arr. for brass ensemble] *(rec Taney Parish Ctr., Dublin, Feb 14 & 15, 1994)* Marco Polo ▲ 8.223716 [DDD]
Berners:A Wedding Banquet, w. RTE Chamber Choir *(rec Taney Parish Ctr., Dublin, Feb 14 & 15, 1994)* Marco Polo ▲ 8.223716 [DDD]
P. Ó. Duinn (cnd)
Duff, A.:Echoes of Georgian Dublin *(rec Taney Parish Center & O'Reilly Hall, UCD, Dublin)* Marco Polo ("Irish Composer" series) ▲ 8.223804 [DDD]
Larchet, J.F.:By the Waters of Moyle *(rec Taney Parish Center & O'Reilly Hall, UCD, Dublin)* Marco Polo ("Irish Composer" series) ▲ 8.223804 [DDD]
Mendelssohn, F.:Cons 2 Pnos, w. Benjamin Frith (pno), Hugh Tinney (pno) *(rec Dublin, Oct 1995)* Naxos ▲ 8.553416 [DDD]
O'Connor, P.:Introspect *(rec Taney Parish Center & O'Reilly Hall, UCD, Dublin, Sept 28–29, 1994 &)* Marco Polo ("Irish Composer" series) ▲ 8.223804 [DDD]
Potter, A.J.:Rhap under a High Sky *(rec Taney Parish Center & O'Reilly Hall, UCD, Dublin)* Marco Polo ("Irish Composer" series) ▲ 8.223804 [DDD]
Victory, G.:Irish Pictures *(rec Taney Parish Center & O'Reilly Hall, UCD, Dublin)* Marco Polo ("Irish Composer" series) ▲ 8.223804 [DDD]
D. Lloyd-Jones (cnd)
Berners:Caprice Péruvien Marco Polo ▲ 8.223780 [DDD]
Berners:Cupid & Psyche Marco Polo ▲ 8.223780 [DDD]
Berners:Les Sirènes Marco Polo ▲ 8.223780 [DDD]
RTE SO
A. Penny (cnd)
Sullivan, A.:L'Ile Enchantée *(rec Apr. 13–16, 1992)* Marco Polo ▲ 8.223460 [DDD]
Sullivan, A.:Thespis—ballet music *(rec Apr. 13–16, 1992)* Marco Polo ▲ 8.223460 [DDD]
RTF National Orch
E. Appia (cnd)
Koechlin, C.:Poème, w. P. Van Lew (hn) *(rec 1957)* Skarbo ▲ SKR 3924
G. Szell (cnd)
Haydn, J.:Sym 92, "Oxford" Sony Classical ("Festspiel Dokumente:Salzburger Festspiele" series) ▲ SMK 68446
Mozart, W.A.:Con 5 Vn, w. Erica Morini (vn) Sony Classical ("Festspiel Dokumente:Salzburger Festspiele" series) ▲ SMK 68446
Mozart, W.A.:Sym 35 Sony Classical ("Festspiel Dokumente:Salzburger Festspiele" series) ▲ SMK 68446
RTL SO
L. Hager (cnd)
Honegger, A.:Allegretto *(rec Nov. 16–20, 1992)* Timpani ▲ 1C 1016 [DDD]
Honegger, A.:Blues *(rec Nov. 16–20, 1992)* Timpani ▲ 1C 1016 [DDD]
Honegger, A.:Fantasio *(rec Nov. 16–20, 1992)* Timpani ▲ 1C 1016 [DDD]
Honegger, A.:Largo *(rec Nov. 16–20, 1992)* Timpani ▲ 1C 1016 [DDD]
Honegger, A.:La Mort de Sainte Alméenne (interlude) *(rec Nov. 16–20, 1992)* Timpani ▲ 1C 1016 [DDD]
Honegger, A.:La Rédemption de François Villon *(rec Nov. 16–20, 1992)* Timpani ▲ 1C 1016 [DDD]
Honegger, A.:Sémiramis, w. V. Ivanov (vn), M. Kemmer (sgr), Brussels Polyphonia Choir, Namur Belgium French Community Symphonic Choir *(rec Nov. 16–20, 1992)* Timpani ▲ 1C 1016 [DDD]
Honegger, A.:Vivace *(rec Nov. 16–20, 1992)* Timpani ▲ 1C 1016 [DDD]
M. Kemmer (cnd)
Honegger, A.:La Tempête (suite), w. L. Hager (hpd) *(rec Nov. 16–20, 1992)* Timpani ▲ 1C 1016 [DDD]
RTSI Orch
B. Marinotti (cnd)
Cimarosa, D.:I Finti nobili (sels), w. C. Cadelo (sop), M.G. Ferracini (sop), R. Cassinelli (ten), R. Malacarne (ten), G. Sarti (bar)—Li sposi per accidente (Act 3) *(rec 1970)* Foyer ▲ FOY 2057 [AAD]
H. Scherchen (cnd)
Mozart, W.A.:Con 15 Pno, w. Arturo Benedetti Michelangeli (pno) *(rec live, Lugano, 1956)* As Disc ▲ ASD 2601 (m)
Schumann, R.:Con Pno, w. Arturo Benedetti Michelangeli (pno) *(rec live, Lugano, 1956)* As Disc ▲ ASD 2601 (m)
RTV SO
P. Freeman (cnd)
Liszt, F.:Totentanz, w. J. Pierce (pno) Mastersound ▲ MST 215 [DDD]
Tchaikovsky, P.:Con 1 Pno, w. J. Pierce (pno) Mastersound ▲ MST 215 [DDD]
Tchaikovsky, P.:Con 3 Pno, w. J. Pierce (pno) Mastersound ▲ MST 215 [DDD]
J. Guinjoán (cnd)
Guinjoán, J.:Trama RNE/Spanish National Radio ▲ 650003 [AAD]

Rubin String Quartet [Irmgard Zavelberg (vn), Tinta S. von Altenstadt (vn), Sylvie Altenburger (va), Ulrike Zavelberg (vc)]
Debussy, C.:Qt Strs New Classic Colours ♦ NCC 8004 [DDD]
Feldhandler, J.–C.:Nacht und Nacht New Classic Colours ♦ NCC 8004 [DDD]
Haydn, J.:Qt Strs, Op. 42 New Classic Colours ♦ NCC 8004 [DDD]
Webern, A.:Bagatelles Str Qt New Classic Colours ♦ NCC 8004 [DDD]
Artur Rubinstein PO
I. Stupel (cnd)
Boccherini, L.:Con Vc, G.482, w. E. B. Bengtsson (vc) *(rec Apr. 1993)* Danacord ▲ DACOCD 416 [DDD]
Dvořák, A.:Con Vc, w. E.B. Bengtsson (vc) Danacord ▲ DACOCD 413 [DDD]
Gardens of the World, w. A. Hepburn (nar) Conifer Classics ▲ 74321–17841–2 ■ 74321–17841–4
Gershwin, G.:An American in Paris, w. G. D. Madge (pno) *(rec Apr. 1992)* Danacord ▲ DACOCD 412 [DDD]
Gershwin, G.:Con Pno, w. G. D. Madge (pno) *(rec Apr. 1992)* Danacord ▲ DACOCD 412 [DDD]
Gershwin, G.:Rhap in Blue, w. G. D. Madge (pno) *(rec Apr. 1992)* Danacord ▲ DACOCD 412 [DDD]
Haydn, J.:Con 1 Vc, w. Erling Bløndal Bengtsson (vc) *(rec Apr. 1993)* Danacord ▲ DACOCD 416 [DDD]
Haydn, J.:Con 2 Vc, w. Erling Bløndal Bengtsson (vc) *(rec Apr. 1993)* Danacord ▲ DACOCD 416 [DDD]
Langgaard, R.:Death of a Hero *(rec Nov. 1991)* Danacord ▲ DACOCD 406 [DDD]
Langgaard, R.:Drapa *(rec May 1992)* Danacord ▲ DACOCD 405 [DDD]
Langgaard, R.:Interdikt, "At the Grave of Christopher I in Ribe" *(rec Nov. 1991)* Danacord ▲ DACOCD 406 [DDD]
Langgaard, R.:Prélude to "Antichrist" *(rec Sept. 1991)* Danacord ▲ DACOCD 410 [DDD]
Langgaard, R.:Sfinx *(rec Nov. 1991)* Danacord ▲ DACOCD 408 [DDD]
Langgaard, R.:Sym 1 *(rec Aug. 1992)* Danacord ▲ DACOCD 404
Langgaard, R.:Sym 2 *(rec May 1992)* Danacord ▲ DACOCD 405 [DDD]
Langgaard, R.:Sym 3 *(rec May 1992)* Danacord ▲ DACOCD 405 [DDD]
Langgaard, R.:Sym 4 *(rec 11/91)* Danacord ▲ DACOCD 406 [DDD]
Langgaard, R.:Sym 5 *(rec Jun. 1991)* Danacord ▲ DACOCD 407 [DDD]
Langgaard, R.:Sym 6 *(rec Nov. 1991)* Danacord ▲ DACOCD 406 [DDD]
Langgaard, R.:Sym 7 *(rec Jun. 1991)* Danacord ▲ DACOCD 407 [DDD]
Langgaard, R.:Sym 8 *(rec Jun. 1992 & Aug. 1992)* Danacord ▲ DACOCD 409 [DDD]
Langgaard, R.:Sym 9 *(rec Jun. 1991)* Danacord ▲ DACOCD 407 [DDD]
Langgaard, R.:Sym 10 *(rec Nov. 1991)* Danacord ▲ DACOCD 408 [DDD]
Langgaard, R.:Sym 11 *(rec Nov. 1991)* Danacord ▲ DACOCD 408 [DDD]
Langgaard, R.:Sym 12 *(rec Nov. 1991)* Danacord ▲ DACOCD 408 [DDD]
Langgaard, R.:Sym 13 *(rec Sept. 1991)* Danacord ▲ DACOCD 410 [DDD]
Langgaard, R.:Sym 14 *(rec June & Aug. 1992)* Danacord ▲ DACOCD 409 [DDD]
Langgaard, R.:Sym 15 *(rec June & Aug. 1992)* Danacord ▲ DACOCD 409 [DDD]
Langgaard, R.:Sym 16 *(rec Sept. 1991)* Danacord ▲ DACOCD 410 [DDD]
Medtner, N.:Con 1 Pno, w. G.D. Madge (pno) *(rec Oct. 1991)* Danacord ▲ DACOCD 401 [DDD]
Medtner, N.:Con 2 Pno, w. G.D. Madge (pno) *(rec Oct. 1991)* Danacord ▲ DACOCD 402 [DDD]
Medtner, N.:Con 3 Pno, w. G.D. Madge (pno) *(rec Oct. 1991)* Danacord ▲ DACOCD 403 [DDD]
Orff, C.:Carmina burana, w. A. M. Dahl (sop), B. Grek (ten), J. Wolanski (bass), Artur Rubinstein Phil Chorus *(rec Apr. 1991)* Danacord ▲ DACOCD 400 [DDD]
Rubinstein, A.:Con 3 Pno, w. O. Marshev (pno) Danacord ▲ DACOCD 411 [DDD]
Rubinstein, A.:Con 4 Pno, w. O. Marshev (pno) Danacord ▲ DACOCD 411 [DDD]
Schierbeck, P.:Radio Rhap *(rec Apr. 1993)* Danacord ▲ DACOCD 417 [DDD]
Schierbeck, P.:Sym, Op. 15 *(rec Apr. 1993)* Danacord ▲ DACOCD 417 [DDD]
Schumann, R.:Con Vc, w. E. B. Bengtsson (vc) Danacord ▲ DACOCD 413 [DDD]
Tchaikovsky, P.:Capriccio italien Danacord ▲ DACOCD 414
Tchaikovsky, P.:Sym 5 Danacord ▲ DACOCD 414
Il Ruggiero [Bettina Mussumeli (vn), Hedwig Raffeiner (vn), Franziska Romaner (vc), Terrell Stone (thb), Emanuela Marcante (hpd), Zeno Zaccaria (hpd)]
Scarlatti, A.:Concerti sacri, motetti, w. Ilaria Galgani (sop), Susanna Anselmi (cta), Luca Casalin (ten), Daniele Tonini (bass)—Nos. 6–10 Tactus ▲ TC 661904 [DDD]
Scarlatti, A.:Concerti sacri, motetti, w. Ilaria Galgani (sop), Susanna Anselmi (cta), Luca Casalin (ten), Daniele Tonini (bass)—Nos. 1–5 Tactus ▲ TC 661903 [DDD]
Il Ruggiero [Francesco La Bruna (vn), Bettina Mussumeli (vn), Franziska Romaner (vc), Terrell Stone (thb), Emanuela Marcante (hpd/org), Emanuela Marcante (cnd)]
Corelli, A.:Trio Sons, Op. 4 Tactus ▲ TC 650303 [DDD]
Romanian Opera Orch
Classics Go to the Movies, Vol. 5, w. Hannes Käster (org), Salzburg Mozarteum Orch, Bavarian RSO, Ludovic Spiess (ten), Virginia Zeani (sop), Rumanian Radio–TV Studio Orch, Sofia PO, Budapest SO, Philharmonia Orch LaserLight ▲ 15 645
Romanian Radio-TV Studio Orch
Classics Go to the Movies ,Vol. 5, w. Hannes Käster (org), Salzburg Mozarteum Orch, Bavarian RSO, Ludovic Spiess (ten), Virginia Zeani (sop), Rumanian Opera Orch, Sofia PO, Budapest SO, Philharmonia Orch LaserLight ▲ 15 645
Ruse PO
T. Delibozov (cnd)
Beath, B.:Lagu Lagu Manis II Vienna Modern Masters ▲ VMM 3036 [DDD]
Gallagher, J.:Persistence of Memory, w. Bogdana Peneva (vc) Vienna Modern Masters ▲ VMM 3036 [DDD]
Nuorvala, J.:Notturno urbano Vienna Modern Masters ▲ VMM 3036 [DDD]
Pelinka, W.:Diagonal Vienna Modern Masters ▲ VMM 3036 [DDD]
Russian CO
E. Blank (cnd)
Bach, J.S.:Con 1 Hpd, w. I. Heifetz (pno) Sonora ▲ SO 22564CD [DDD]
Bach, J.S.:Con 1 for 2 Hpds, w. I. Heifetz (pno), N. Zusman (pno) Sonora ▲ SO 22564CD [DDD]
V. Esipov (cnd)
Devienne, F.:Cons Fl (comp), w. Claudi Arimany (fl)—Nos. 6, 11 & 12 Aura Classics ▲ AU 32172
D. Mihailovic (cnd)
Devienne, F.:Cons Fl (comp), w. Claudi Arimany (fl)—Nos. 3, 8 & 10 Aura Classics ▲ AU 32162
Russian Federation State SO
E. Svetlanov (cnd)
Borodin, A.:In the Steppes of Central Asia *(rec June 18, 19 & 22, 1992)* Canyon Classics ▲ 3657 [DDD]
Borodin, A.:Prince Igor (Polovtsian dances) *(rec June 18, 19 & 22, 1992)* Canyon Classics ▲ 3657 [DDD]
Glinka, M.:Russlan & Ludmilla (ov) *(rec June 18, 19 & 22, 1992)* Canyon Classics ▲ 3657 [DDD]
Khachaturian, A.:Gayane (sels)—Sabre Dance *(rec June 18, 19 & 22, 1992)* Canyon Classics ▲ 3657 [DDD]
Mussorgsky, M.:Khovanshchina (prelude) *(rec June 18, 19 & 22, 1992)* Canyon Classics ▲ 3657 [DDD]
Mussorgsky, M.:Night *(rec June 18, 19 & 22, 1992)* Canyon Classics ▲ 3657 [DDD]
Rachmaninoff, S.:Music of—Syms Nos. 1–3; Capriccio bohémian; The Rock; Symphonic Dances; Price Rostislav; Vocalise; Scherzo; The Isle of the Dead Canyon Classics 4–▲ 325 [DDD]
Rimsky-Korsakov, N.:Capriccio espagnol *(rec June 18, 19 & 22, 1992)* Canyon Classics ▲ 3657 [DDD]
Tchaikovsky, P.:Capriccio italien *(rec June 17 & 22–25, 1992)* Canyon ▲ EC 3661 [DDD]
Tchaikovsky, P.:Manfred *(rec 1992)* Canyon 7–▲ EC 3630 [DDD]
Tchaikovsky, P.:Syms (comp) *(rec 1990–91)* Canyon 7–▲ EC 3630 [DDD]
Russian Festival Ensemble
M. Verhoeff (cnd)
Popular Russian Melodies, w. Ural Cossack Choir Koch Schwann ▲ SCH 314048 [DDD]

Russian Ministry of Culture SO
G. Rozhdestvensky (cnd)
Shostakovich, D.:Sym 4 — Praga ▲ PR 250090
Russian National Orch
M. Pletnev (cnd)
Liadov, A.:Baba Yaga *(rec Great Hall, Conservatory, Moscow, Apr 1994)* — Deutsche Grammophon ▲ 447084–2 [DDD]
Liadov, A.:The Enchanted Lake *(rec Great Hall, Conservatory, Moscow, Apr 1994)* — Deutsche Grammophon ▲ 447084–2 [DDD]
Liadov, A.:Kikimora *(rec Great Hall, Conservatory, Moscow, Apr 1994)* — Deutsche Grammophon ▲ 447084–2 [DDD]
Miaskovsky, N.:Con Vc, w. Mischa Maisky (vc) — Deutsche Grammophon ▲ 449 821–2
Prokofiev, S.:Sinf Concertante, w. Mischa Maisky (vc) — Deutsche Grammophon ▲ 449 821–2
Rachmaninoff, S.:The Rock — Deutsche Grammophon ▲ 439888–2
Rachmaninoff, S.:Sym 2 — Deutsche Grammophon ▲ 439888–2
Rimsky–Korsakov, N.:Golden Cockerel (suite) [arr Alexander Glazunov & Maximilian Steinberg] *(rec Great Hall, Conservatory, Moscow, Apr 1994)* — Deutsche Grammophon ▲ 447084–2 [DDD]
Russian Overtures — Deutsche Grammophon ▲ 439892–2
Tchaikovsky, P.:Manfred — Deutsche Grammophon ▲ 439891–2
Tchaikovsky, P.:Marche slave — Virgin Classics ▲ CDC 59661
Tchaikovsky, P.:Syms (comp) *(rec Moscow Conservatory Great Hall, Apr & Nov 1995)* — Deutsche Grammophon 5–▲ 449967–2 [DDD]
Tchaikovsky, P.:Sym 6 — Virgin Classics ▲ CDC 59661
Tchaikovsky, P.:The Tempest — Deutsche Grammophon ▲ 439891–2
Tcherepnin, N.:Prélude pour la princesse Lointaine *(rec Great Hall, Conservatory, Moscow, Apr 1994)* — Deutsche Grammophon ▲ 447084–2 [DDD]
Tcherepnin, N.:Le Royaume enchanté *(rec Great Hall, Conservatory, Moscow, Apr 1994)* — Deutsche Grammophon ▲ 447084–2 [DDD]

Russian Philharmonia
A. Vedernikov (cnd)
Tchaikovsky, P.:Ballet Music, w. Olga Vedernikova (vn), Alexander Dardyikin (vc), Anna Verkholanzeva (hp)—ballet suites from Swan Lake; Sleeping Beauty; Nutcracker *(rec Moscow Conservatory Large Hall, Feb 1996)* — Arts ▲ 47372–2 [DDD]
Russian PO
V. Polianski (cnd)
Tchaikovsky, P.:Choral Music, w. Russian Phil Choir—Legend — Opus 111 ▲ OPS 57–9203 [DDD]
Russian Radio Orch
I. Markevitch (cnd)
Sarasate, P. de:Intro & Tarantella, w. R. Ricci (vn) — One–Eleven ▲ URS 91070 [ADD]
Russian Radio–TV SO
A. Zhuraitis (cnd)
Jolivet, A.:Con Hp, w. Vera Dulova (hp) *(rec 1961)* — Russian Compact Disc ("Talents of Russia" series) ▲ RCD 16204 [AAD]
Russian State Brass Orch
N. Sergeyev (cnd)
Miaskovsky, N.:Sym 19 — Russian Disc ▲ RUS 11008 [AAD]
Russian State Cinema Orch
S. Skripka (cnd)
Artemyev, E.:Burnt by the Sun — Travelling ▲ K 1011
Russian State SO
Davis, Waart, Markevitch (cnd)
Stravinsky, I.:Music of, w. London SO, Netherlands Wind Ensemble, Russian State Academy Chorus—Sym. in C; Sym of Psalms; Con. for Violin & others — Philips ("Duo" series) 2–▲ 442583–2
I. Golovshin (cnd)
Balakirev, M.:Rus *(rec Mosfilm Studio, Moscow, Sept. 2–4, 1993)* — Naxos ▲ 8.550793 [DDD]
Balakirev, M.:Sym 2 *(rec Mosfilm Studio, Moscow, Apr. 15–17, 1993)* — Naxos ▲ 8.550793 [DDD]
Bruch, M.:Con 1 Vn, w. Ilya Grubert (vn) — Russian Disc ▲ RUS 10012 [DDD]
Rubinstein, A.:Don Quixote — Russian Disc ▲ RUS 11 397 [DDD]
Rubinstein, A.:Ivan the Terrible — Russian Disc ▲ RUS 11 397 [DDD]
Rubinstein, A.:Sym 4 — Russian Disc ("The A. Rubinstein Edition" series) ▲ RUS 11 357 [DDD]
Scriabin, A.:Mysterium:Prefatory Act, w. Peter Izotov (pno), Lyudmila Ermakova (cnd), Ostankino Radio Chorus *(rec Large Hall of the Moscow Conservatory, 1995)* — Triton ▲ 17001 [DDD]
Sibelius, J.:Con Vn, w. Ilya Grubert (vn) — Russian Disc ▲ RUS 10012 [DDD]
Stravinsky, I.:Sym in 3 Movts — Russian Disc ▲ RUS 11 355 [DDD]
K. Ivanov (cnd)
Rachmaninoff, S.:Con 3 Pno, w. Viktor Merzhanov (pno) — Multisonic ▲ MUL 310352
Tchaikovsky, P.:Romeo & Juliet *(rec 1959)* — Multisonic (Russian Treasures) ▲ 31 0187
Tchaikovsky, P.:The Voyevoda, Op. 78 *(rec 1959)* — Multisonic (Russian Treasures) ▲ 31 0187
P. Kogan (cnd)
Dmitriev, G.:Sym 3, "Misterioso" *(rec Large Hall, Moscow Conservatory, Nov 17, 1989)* — Russian Compact Disc ▲ RD CD 10003 [AAD]
K. Kondrashin (cnd)
Beethoven, L. van:Con Vn, Op. 61, w. Marina Kozolupova (vn) — Multisonic ▲ MUL 310268
Schumann, R.:Con Vc, w. D. Shafran (vc) *(rec 1962)* — Multisonic ("Russian Treasure" series) ▲ 31 0180
Tchaikovsky, P.:Concert Fant, w. T. Nikolayeva (pno) *(rec 1950)* — Multisonic ("Russian Treasures" series) ▲ 31 0238
E. London (cnd)
Aschaffenburg, W.:Con Ob, w. Elizaveta Zuyeva (ob) — New World ▲ 805112 [DDD]
London, E.:A Hero of Our Time — New World ▲ 805112 [DDD]
Miller, E.:Anacrusis — New World ▲ 805112 [DDD]
V. Polianski (cnd)
Gretchaninoff, A.:Liturgica Domestica for St. John Chrysostom, w. Russian State Symphonic Cappella—Great Litany; Antiphon I; Antiphon II; Glori & Unigenitus; Trisagion; Alleluia...After the Gospel; Litany of Supplication; Cherubic Hymn; After the Cherubic Hymn; Credo; Pax Hominibus; Hymn of the Blessed Virgin; Pater Noster; Laudate Deum; End of the Liturgy — Chandos ▲ CHAN 9365 [DDD]
Gretchaninoff, A.:Missa Sancti Spiritus, w. Tatiana Jeranje (cta), Russian State Symphonic Cappella — Chandos ▲ CHAN 9397 [DDD]
Gretchaninoff, A.:Snowflakes, w. Ludmila Kuznetsova (mez) [arr voice & orch] — Chandos ▲ CHAN 9397 [DDD]
Gretchaninoff, A.:Sym 1 — Chandos ▲ CHAN 9397 [DDD]
Gretchaninoff, A.:Sym 2, "Pastoral" — Chandos ▲ CHAN 9486
Schnittke, A.:In Memoriam — Chandos ▲ CHAN 9466
Schnittke, A.:Sacred Hymns, w. Russian State Symphonic Cappella — Chandos ▲ CHAN 9463
Schnittke, A.:Septet — Chandos ▲ CHAN 9466
Schnittke, A.:Sym 4, w. Russian State Symphonic Cappella — Chandos ▲ CHAN 9463
Shostakovich, D.:Sym 11 — Chandos ▲ CHAN 9476
Tchaikovsky, P.:Romeo & Juliet — Chandos ▲ CHAN 9383 [DDD]
Tchaikovsky, P.:Sym 5 — Chandos ▲ CHAN 9383 [DDD]
Tchaikovsky, P.:Sym 6 — Chandos ("New Direction" series) ▲ CHAN 9356 [DDD]
G. Rozhdestvensky (cnd)
Glazunov, A.:The King of the Jews, w. Russian State Sym Cappella — Chandos ▲ CHAN 9467
Milhaud, D.:The Bells *(rec live, Moscow, 1993)* — Olympia ▲ OLY 452 [DDD]
Milhaud, D.:Saudades do Brasil — Olympia ▲ OLY 452 [DDD]
Milhaud, D.:Sym 3 *(rec live, Moscow, 1993)* — Olympia ▲ OLY 452 [DDD]
Schnittke, A.:Music Pno — Chandos ▲ CHAN 9466
Schnittke, A.:Sym 1 *(rec live)* — Chandos ▲ CHAN 9417

Russian State SO (cont.)
I. Shpiller (cnd)
Scriabin, A.:Con Pno, w. Elena Kuznetsova (pno) *(rec Large Hall of the Moscow Conservatory, 1995)* — Triton ▲ 17001 [DDD]
E. Svetlanov (cnd)
Boiko, R.:Carpathian Rhap, w. A. Korsakov (vn) — Russian Disc ▲ RUS 11020 [AAD]
Boiko, R.:Festival Procession, w. Gostelradio Choir — Russian Disc ▲ RUS 11020 [AAD]
Boiko, R.:Gutsul Rhap, w. A. Korsakov (vn) — Russian Disc ▲ RUS 11020 [AAD]
Boiko, R.:Gypsy Rhap, w. A. Korsakov (vn) — Russian Disc ▲ RUS 11020 [AAD]
Boiko, R.:Sym 3 — Russian Disc ▲ RUS 11020 [AAD]
Boiko, R.:Volga Rhap, w. A. Korsakov (vn) — Russian Disc ▲ RUS 11020 [AAD]
Borodin, A.:Petite Suite — RCA Red Seal ▲ 09026–62505–2 [DDD]
Borodin, A.:Prince Igor (ov) — RCA Red Seal ▲ 09026–61674–2
Borodin, A.:Prince Igor (Polovtsian dances) — RCA Red Seal ▲ 09026–61674–2
Borodin, A.:Sym 1 — RCA Red Seal ▲ 09026–61674–2
Borodin, A.:Sym 2 — RCA Red Seal ▲ 09026–62505–2 [DDD]
Borodin, A.:Sym 3 — RCA Red Seal ▲ 09026–61674–2
Mahler, G.:Sym 1 — Russian Season ▲ RUS 288123
Mahler, G.:Sym 2, w. Natalia Guerassimova (sop), Olga Alexandrova (alt), Russian Radio–TV Large Academic Choir — Russian Season 2–▲ 288136.37
Mahler, G.:Sym 3, w. Olga Alexandrova (mez), Russian Academic Choir, Moscow Boys' Cappella *(rec Large Hall of the Conservatory, Moscow, Dec. 1994)* — Russian Season 2–▲ RUS 288111/12 [DDD]
Mahler, G.:Sym 4, w. Natalia Guerassimova (sop) — Russian Season ▲ RUS 288133
Mahler, G.:Sym 7 — Russian Season 2–▲ RUS 288117/18
Mahler, G.:Sym 9 — Russian Season ▲ RUS 288132
Mahler, G.:Sym 10 — Russian Season 2–▲ RUS 288117/18
Mussorgsky, M.:Boris Godunov (sels)—Intro & Polsky *(rec L'Arsenal, Metz, France, July 5–9, 1994)* — RCA Red Seal ▲ 09026–68406–2 [DDD]
Mussorgsky, M.:Intermezzo symphonique *(rec L'Arsenal, Metz, France, July 5–9, 1994)* — RCA Red Seal ▲ 09026–68406–2 [DDD]
Mussorgsky, M.:Khovanshchina (orch sels)—Dance of the Persian Women; Entr'acte; Solemn March *(rec L'Arsenal, Metz, France, July 5–9, 1994)* — RCA Red Seal ▲ 09026–68406–2 [DDD]
Mussorgsky, M.:Scherzo *(rec L'Arsenal, Metz, France, July 5–9, 1994)* — RCA Red Seal ▲ 09026–68406–2 [DDD]
Mussorgsky, M.:Sorochintsy Fair (orch sels)—Gopak No. 5; Ov; Parassia's Dumka *(rec L'Arsenal, Metz, France, July 5–9, 1994)* — RCA Red Seal ▲ 09026–68406–2 [DDD]
Mussorgsky, M.:Sunless, w. Nathalia Gerasimova (sop) *(rec L'Arsenal, Metz, France, July 5–9, 1994)* — RCA Red Seal ▲ 09026–68406–2 [DDD]
Rimsky–Korsakov, N.:Antar — RCA Red Seal ▲ 09026–62558–2
Rimsky–Korsakov, N.:Sym 1 — RCA Red Seal ▲ 09026–62558–2
Rimsky–Korsakov, N.:Sym 3 — RCA Red Seal ▲ 09026–62684–2 [DDD]
Shostakovich, D.:Festive Ov, w. Bolshoi Theater SO Brass Section *(rec Moscow, June 15–16, 1992)* — Canyon Classics ▲ 3672 [DDD]
Shostakovich, D.:Sym 5 *(rec Moscow, June 15–16, 1992)* — Canyon Classics ▲ 3672 [DDD]
Suk, J.:Asrael *(rec 1993)* — Russian Disc ▲ RUS 11011 [DDD]
Svetlanov, E.:Poem, w. I. Oistrakh (vn) *(rec 1978)* — Russian Disc ▲ RUS 11042 [AAD]
Svetlanov, E.:Sym 1 *(rec 1975)* — Russian Disc ▲ RUS 11042 [AAD]
Tchaikovsky, P.:Swan Lake — Melodiya 3–▲ 17082–2 [DDD]
A. Vedernikov (cnd)
Shostakovich, D.:Con 1 Vn, w. Maxim Fedotov (vn) — Triton ▲ 17006 [DDD]
Shostakovich, D.:Con 2 Vn, w. Maxim Fedotov (vn) — Triton ▲ 17006 [DDD]
Russian SO
V. Dudarova (cnd)
Kabalevsky, D.:Con 1 Vc, w. M. Tarasova (vc) — Olympia ▲ OLY 292 [DDD]
Kabalevsky, D.:Con 2 Vc, w. M. Tarasova (vc) — Olympia ▲ OLY 292 [DDD]
Kabalevsky, D.:Con Vn, w. Andrew Hardy (vn) — Olympia ▲ OLY 573
Kabalevsky, D.:Improvisation Vn, w. M. Tarasova (vc) — Olympia ▲ OLY 292 [DDD]
Kabalevsky, D.:Rondo Vn, w. M. Tarasova (vc) — Olympia ▲ OLY 292 [DDD]
Khachaturian, A.:Con Vc, w. Marina Tarasova (vc) — Olympia ▲ OLY 539 [DDD]
Khachaturian, A.:Con–Rhap Vc, w. Marina Tarasova (vc) — Olympia ▲ OLY 539 [DDD]
Rakov, N.:Con 1 Vn, w. Andrew Hardy (vn) — Olympia ▲ OLY 573
Shebalin, V.Y.:Con Vn, w. Andrew Hardy (vn) — Olympia ▲ OLY 573
P. Freeman (cnd)
Liszt, F.:Con 1 Pno, w. J. Pierce (pno) *(rec Moscow, Sept. 17, 1993)* — Intersound ▲ CDS 3488
Tchaikovsky, P.:Con Vn, w. Chin Kim (vn) *(rec Great Hall of the Moscow Radio Union, Sept. 1993)* — Intersound ▲ 3535 [DDD]
M. Gorenstein (cnd)
Beethoven, L. van:Con 5 Pno, "Emperor", w. Naum Starkman (pno) *(rec Moscow Conservatory Great Hall, May & June, 1995)* — PopeMusic ▲ PM 10042 [DDD]
Glazunov, A.:Con Vn, w. Ruben Aharonian (vn) — Russian Disc ▲ RUS 10039 [DDD]
Glazunov, A.:Serenade 1 — Russian Disc ▲ RUS 10039 [DDD]
Glazunov, A.:Serenade 2 — Russian Disc ▲ RUS 10039 [DDD]
Glazunov, A.:Sym 4 — Russian Disc ▲ RUS 10039 [DDD]
Khrennikov, T.:Love for Love *(rec Moscow Conservatory Great Hall, Sept 1995)* — PopeMusic ▲ PM 10072 [DDD]
Schnittke, A.:Gogol Suite *(rec Moscow Conservatory Great Hall, Sept 1995)* — PopeMusic ▲ PM 10072 [DDD]
Schnittke, A.:(K)ein Sommernachtstraum *(rec Moscow Conservatory Great Hall, Sept 1995)* — PopeMusic ▲ PM 10072 [DDD]
Shostakovich, D.:Chamber Sym, Op. 110a *(rec Moscow Conservatory Great Hall, Jan 1996)* — PopeMusic ▲ PM 10092 [DDD]
Shostakovich, D.:Sym 5 *(rec Moscow Conservatory Great Hall, Jan 1996)* — PopeMusic ▲ PM 10092 [DDD]
Tchaikovsky, P.:Francesca da Rimini *(rec Moscow Conservatory Great Hall, May & Sept 1995)* — PopeMusic ▲ PM 10062 [DDD]
Tchaikovsky, P.:Sym 6 *(rec Moscow Conservatory Great Hall, May & Sept 1995)* — PopeMusic ▲ PM 10062 [DDD]
Rutgers Univ Contemporary Chamber Ensemble
A. Weisberg (cnd)
Martino, D.:Con Ww Qnt — CRI ▲ CD 693 [ADD]
Rymour String Quartet
Asia, D.:Qt 1 Strs — Albany ▲ TROY 106 [DDD]
Saar CO
K. Ristenpart (cnd)
Bach, J.S.:Brandenburg Cons—Nos. 4–6 — Elektra/Nonesuch ■ 71419–4
Bach, J.S.:Con in g Fl, w. J.–P. Rampal (fl) — Odyssey ■ YT 32890
Bach, J.S.:Con 1 Vn, w. J.–P. Rampal (fl) — Odyssey ■ YT 32890
Telemann, G.P.:Cons Fl (misc), w. J.–P. Rampal (fl) — Odyssey ■ YT 32890
Saarbrück RSO
M.–W. Chung (cnd)
Rimsky–Korsakov, N.:The Legend of the Invisible City of Kitzeh (suite) — Koch Schwann ▲ CD 311 202 [DDD]
Shostakovich, D.:Sym 6 — Koch Schwann ▲ CD 311 202 [DDD]
D.R. Davies (cnd)
Schnittke, A.:Con Va, w. K. Kashkashian (va) — ECM New Series ▲ 78118–21471–2 [DDD]
A. Francis (cnd)
Pettersson, G.A.:Sym 3 — CPO ▲ CPO 999223 [DDD]
Pettersson, G.A.:Sym 4 — CPO ▲ CPO 999223 [DDD]

ORCH. & ENS.

Saarbrück RSO (cont.)
J. Françaix (cnd)
Françaix, J.:Con Hpd, w. E. Naoumoff (pno) *(rec 9/88)* Wergo ▲ WER 6198-2 [AAD]
M. Kagel (cnd)
Kagel, M.:Les Idées fixes Col Legno ▲ AU 31826
Kagel, M.:Music for Kbd Instrument & Orch Col Legno ▲ AU 31826
Kagel, M.:Opus 1,991 Col Legno ▲ AU 31826
G. Markson (cnd)
Schnittke, A.:Con 1 Vc, w. M. Kliegel (vc) Marco Polo ▲ 8.223334
G. Schuller (cnd)
Schuller, G.:Con Bn, w. K. Pasmanick (bn) GM ▲ GM 2044
Schuller, G.:Con 1 Hn, w. R. Todd (hn) GM ▲ GM 2044
M. Viotti (cnd)
Brandmüller, T.:Cosmic Episodes MD + G ▲ MDG 6250551 [DDD]
Paganini, N.:Con 1 Vn, w. A. Markov (vn) Erato ▲ 2292-45788-2
Paganini, N.:Con 2 Vn, w. A. Markov (vn) Erato ▲ 2292-45788-2
Schubert, Franz:Sym 1 Claves ▲ 50-9319
Schubert, Franz:Sym 2 Claves ▲ 50-9319
Schubert, Franz:Sym 4 Claves ▲ 50-9417
Schubert, Franz:Sym 5 Claves ▲ 50-9417
Schubert, Franz:Sym 8 Claves ▲ 50-9221
H. Zender (cnd)
Yun, I.:Con Fl, w. Roswitha Staege (fl) *(rec Saarbrück Radio Studio, May 1985)* Camerata ▲ 30CM 109 [AAD]

Saarbrück String Quartet
Delz, C.:Qt Str Grammont ▲ CTSP 18-2 [ADD]

Sadler's Wells Opera Orch
A. Faris (cnd)
Sullivan, A.:Iolanthe (sels), w. E. Harwood (sop), S. Bevin (ten), D. Dowling (bar), E. Shilling (bar), J. Holmes (bass), Sadler's Wells Opera Chorus Classics for Pleasure 2-▲ CDCFP 4730 [ADD]
Sullivan, A.:The Mikado, w. M. Studholme (sop), J. Wakefield (ten), C. Revill (bar), D. Dowling (bar), J. Holmes (bass), Sadler's Wells Opera Chorus Classics for Pleasure 2-▲ CDCFP 4730 [ADD]
R. Goodall (cnd)
Wagner, R.:Götterdämmerung (sels), w. M. Curphey (sop), R. Hunter (sop), A. Remedios (ten), N. Bailey (bar), C. Grant (bass), Sadler's Wells Opera Chorus—Act 3, Scenes 2 & 3 [E] Chandos ("Collect" series) ▲ CHAN 6593 [ADD]
C. Lambert (cnd)
Boyce, W.:The Prospect Before Us [arr Lambert for Orch] Time Machine ▲ 0099
W. Reid (cnd)
Lehár, F.:Die lustige Witwe (sels), w. Sadler's Wells Opera Chorus Classics for Pleasure ▲ CDCFP 4485 [ADD]

Safri Duo
Goldrush *(rec Danish Radio Concert Hall, Feb 19-23, 1996)* Chandos ▲ CHAN 9482

Safri Duo [Morten Friis (perc), Uffe Savery (perc)]
Bach, J.S.:English Suites—Nos. 2 in a & 4 in F [trans. for percussion] Chandos ("New Direction" series) ▲ CHAN 9339 [DDD]
Bach, J.S.:French Suites—No. 6 in E [trans. for percussion] Chandos ("New Direction" series) ▲ CHAN 9339 [DDD]
Barber, S.:Prayers of Kierkegaard, w. S. Skov (pno), J. Koch (pno), C. Bjørkøe (pno), La Camerata Danica ▲ DCD 8154
Britten, B.:Flower Songs, w. S. Skov (sop), J. Koch (pno), C. Bjørkøe (pno), La Camerata Danica ▲ DCD 8154
Fuzzy:Fireplay Chandos ("New Direction" series) ▲ CHAN 9330 [DDD]
Helweg, K.:America Fant—A Tribute to Leonard Bernstein Chandos ▲ CHAN 9398 [DDD]
Holmboe, V.:Songs, w. S. Skov (sop), J. Koch (pno), C. Bjørkøe (pno)—Americana Danica ▲ DCD 8154
Koppel, A.:Toccata Chandos ("New Direction" series) ▲ CHAN 9330 [DDD]
Lutoslawski, W.:Vars on a Theme of Paganini for 2 Pnos [arr. Martha Ptsazynska] Chandos ▲ CHAN 9398 [DDD]
Miki, M.:Mar Spiritual Chandos ("New Direction" series) ▲ CHAN 9330 [DDD]
Nørgård, P.:Echo Zone I-III Chandos ("New Direction" series) ▲ CHAN 9330 [DDD]
Nørholm, I.:Songs, w. S. Skov (sop), J. Koch (pno), C. Bjørkøe (pno), Camerata—Song at Sunset Danica ▲ DCD 8154
Pape, A.:CaDance Chandos ("New Direction" series) ▲ CHAN 9330 [DDD]
M. Bojesen (cnd)
Grainger, P.:Songs, w. S. Skov (sop), J. Koch (pno), C. Bjørkøe (pno), Camerata—No Nighean Dhu; O Mistress Mine; 6 Dukes Went a-Fishing; Mary Thompson; Old Irish Tune Danica ▲ DCD 8154

Saidenberg Little Sym
D. Saidenberg (cnd)
Schuman, W.:Con Pno, w. Rosalyn Tureck (pno) *(rec NY, Jan 13, 1943)* VAI Audio ▲ VAIA 1124 [ADD]

St. Andrew Camerata
L. Friedman (cnd)
17 Jewels in the Crown of the Baroque Omega Classics ▲ OCD 1002 [DDD]
Telemann, G.P.:Con Fl, Vn, Vc, w. S. Milan (fl) Omega ▲ OCD 1006 [DDD]
Telemann, G.P.:Don Quichotte (suite) Omega ▲ OCD 1006 [DDD]
Telemann, G.P.:Suite in a Fl, w. S. Milan (fl) Omega ▲ OCD 1006 [DDD]
Vivaldi, A.:Cons Bn, w. J. Graham (bn)—RV.495 Omega ▲ OCD 1012 [DDD]
Vivaldi, A.:Cons Fl (misc), w. P. Davis (fl)—RV.428, "Il Gardellino" Omega ▲ OCD 1012 [DDD]
Vivaldi, A.:Con for 2 Mands, w. P. Sparks (mand), N. Woodhouse (mand) Omega ▲ OCD 1012 [DDD]
Vivaldi, A.:Con for 2 Tpts, w. M. Bennett (tpt), A. Crowley (tpt) Omega ▲ OCD 1012 [DDD]
Vivaldi, A.:Cons for 2 Vns, w. L. Friedman (vn), R. Friedman (vn) Omega ▲ OCD 1012 [DDD]
Vivaldi, A.:Sinf, RV.149 Omega ▲ OCD 1012 [DDD]

St. Augustin Orch
F. Wolf (cnd)
Dvořák, A.:Mass, w. G. Schmid (sop), J. Bernheimer (mez), J. Reinprecht (ten), A. Sramek (bar), St. Augustin Chorus [L] *(rec 1987)* Preiser ▲ 93378 [ADD]
Haydn, J.:Mass 5, "Missa Sancti Josephi", "Grosse Orgelmesse", w. St. Augustin Chorus Preiser ▲ PRE 93347 [ADD]
Haydn, J.:Mass 6, "Nikolai-messe", "6/4-Takt-Messe", w. St. Augustin Chorus Preiser ▲ PRE 93347 [ADD]
Mozart, W.A.:Ave verum corpus, w. St. Augustin Chorus Preiser ▲ 93325
Schubert, Franz:Duetsche Messe, w. R. Hansmann (sop), M. Lipovšek (mez), J. Reinprecht (ten), L. Spitzer (pno), St. Augustin Chorus Preiser ▲ 93325
Schubert, Franz:Mass 3, w. R. Hansmann (sop), M. Lipovšek (mez), J. Reinprecht (ten), Spitzer (bass), St. Augustin Chorus Preiser ▲ 93325

St. Cecilia Academy Orch Rome
The Early Recordings (1949-1952), w. Renata Tebaldi (sop), Alberto Erede (cnd), Swiss Romande Orch London ("Historic" series) ▲ 425989-2 LM [ADD]
Vivaldi, A.:Cons Bn, w. C. Wassmer (bn) [period instrs] Pierre Verany ▲ PVY 793042 [DDD]
A. Antonini (cnd)
Riegger, W.:Romanza CRI ▲ CD 572 [ADD]
B. Bartoletti (cnd)
Verdi, G.:Un ballo in maschera, w. R. Tebaldi (sop), L. Pavarotti (ten), S. Milnes (bar), St. Cecilia Academy Chorus Rome London ▲ 440042-2
L. Bernstein (cnd)
Debussy, C.:Ibéria *(rec live, Rome June 1989)* Deutsche Grammophon ▲ 429728-2 [DDD]
Debussy, C.:La Mer *(rec live, Rome June 1989)* Deutsche Grammophon ▲ 429728-2 [DDD]
Debussy, C.:Prélude à l'après-midi d'un faune *(rec live, Rome, June 1989)* Deutsche Grammophon ▲ 429728-2 [DDD]

St. Cecilia Academy Orch Rome (cont.)
G. Cantelli (cnd)
Casella, A.:Paganiniana *(rec May, 1949)* Testament ▲ TES SBT1017 (m) [ADD]
Rossini, G.:Ovs—The Siege of Corinth *(rec May 1949)* Testament ▲ TES SBT1017 (m) [ADD]
F. Capuana (cnd)
Cilea, F.:Adriana Lecouvreur, w. R. Tebaldi (sop), M. del Monaco (ten), St. Cecilia Academy Chorus Rome London 2-▲ 430256-2 [ADD]
Puccini, G.:La fanciulla del West, w. R. Tebaldi (sop), M. del Monaco (ten), C. MacNeil (bar), G. Tozzi (bass), St. Cecilia Academy Chorus Rome [!] London 2-▲ 421595-2 [ADD]
P. Couvert (cnd)
Molter, J.M.:Cons Cl, w. J.-C. Veilhan (cl) Pierre Verany ▲ PV 792011 [DDD]
Vivaldi, A.:Cons Diverse Instrs, w. Jean-Claude Veilhan (cl)—in C, R.555; in C, R.556; in C, R.558; in C, R.560; in g, R.577; in B♭, R. 579; in C, R. 599 *(rec Paris, Jan 1996)* K617 ▲ 7062 [DDD]
A. Erede (cnd)
Puccini, G.:La Bohème, w. R. Tebaldi (sop), H. Gueden (sop), G. Prandelli (ten), G. Inghilleri (bar), F. Corena (bass), Raphäel Arié (bass), St. Cecilia Academy Chorus Rome London 2-▲ 440233-2 [ADD]
Puccini, G.:Tosca, w. Ranata Tebaldi (sop), Gian Franco Volante (trb), Piero de Palma (ten), Giuseppe Campora (ten), Enzo Mascherini (bar), Fernando Corena (bass), Dario Caselli (bass), Antonio Sacchetti (bass), St. Cecilia Academy Chorus Rome *(rec 1952)* Andromeda 2-▲ ANR 2539 [ADD]
Puccini, G.:Tosca, w. R. Tebaldi (sop), G. Campora (ten), Enzo Mascherini (bar), F. Corena (bass), St. Cecilia Academy Chorus Rome London 2-▲ 440236-2 [ADD]
Puccini, G.:Tosca, w. R. Tebaldi (sop), G. Campora (ten), Enzo Mascherini (bar), F. Corena (bass), St. Cecilia Academy Chorus Rome Enterprise 2-▲ ENTPD 4106 [DDD]
Puccini, G.:Turandot, w. I. Borkh (sop), R. Tebaldi (sop), M. del Monaco (ten), St. Cecilia Academy Chorus Rome London 2-▲ 433761-2 [ADD]
Verdi, G.:Aida, w. R. Tebaldi (sop), E. Stignani (mez), M. del Monaco (ten), A. Protti (bar), F. Corena (bass), St. Cecilia Academy Chorus Rome London 2-▲ 440239-2 [ADD]
Verdi, G.:Aida, w. Renata Tebaldi (sop—Aida), Ebe Stignani (mez—Amneris), Mario Del Monaco (ten—Radamès), Piero de Palma (ten—Messenger), Aldo Protti (bar—Amonasro), Fernando Corena (bass—King), Dario Caselli (bass—Ramfis), St. Cecilia Academy Chorus Rome *(rec 1952)* Theorema 2-▲ TH 121133/34
Verdi, G.:Otello, w. H. Gueden (sop), G. Simionato (mez), M. del Monaco (ten), A. Protti (bar), C. Siepi (b-bar), St. Cecilia Academy Chorus Rome London 2-▲ 440242-2 [ADD]
Verdi, G.:Otello, w. Renata Tebaldi (sop—Desdemona), Luisa Ribacchi (mez—Emilia), Angelo Mercuriali (ten—Roderigo), Mario del Monaco (ten—Otello), Piero de Palma (ten—Cassio), Aldo Protti (bar—Iago), Dario Caselli (bass—A Herald), Fernando Corena (bass—Lodovico), Pierluigi Martinucci (bass—Montano), St. Cecilia Academy Chorus Rome Theorema ▲ TH 121141/142
Verdi, G.:Rigoletto, w. R. Tebaldi (sop), M. del Monaco (ten), A. Protti (bar), P. de Palma (bass), F. Corena (bass), St. Cecilia Academy Chorus Rome London 2-▲ 440245-2 [ADD]
Verdi, G.:Rigoletto, w. Hilde Gueden (sop—Gilda), Piero de Palma (ten—Borsa), Luisa Ribacchi (mez—Giovanna), Giulietta Simionato (mez—Maddalena), Mario del Monaco (ten—Duca de Mantova), Aldo Protti (bar—Rigoletto), Fernando Corena (bass—Conte Monterone), Cesare Siepi (bass—Sparafucile), St. Cecilia Academy Chorus Rome Theorema ▲ TH 121179/180
L. Gardelli (cnd)
Leoncavallo, R.:Pagliacci, w. P. Lorengar (sop), R. Krause (ten), J. McCracken (ten), R. Merrill (bar), U. Benelli (bar), St. Cecilia Academy Chorus Rome [!] IMP Collectors Series ▲ IMPX 9017 [AAD]
Ponchielli, A.:La Gioconda, w. R. Tebaldi (sop), C. Bergonzi (ten), *(other soloists unknown)*, St. Cecilia Academy Chorus Rome London 3-▲ 430042-2 [ADD]
A. Guadagno (cnd)
Bizet, G.:Les Pêcheurs de perles (sels), w. Katia Ricciarelli (sop), Placído Domingo (ten)—Au fond du temple saint *(rec 1972)* RCA Gold Seal ▲ 09026-62595-2 [ADD]
Puccini, G.:Madama Butterfly (sels), w. Katia Ricciarelli (sop), Plácido Domingo (ten)—Bimba dagli occhi pieni di malia *(rec 1972)* RCA Gold Seal ▲ 09026-62595-2 [ADD]
Zandonai, R.:Francesca da Rimini (sels), w. Katia Ricciarelli (sop), Placído Domingo (ten)—Benvenuto, signore mio cognato *(rec 1972)* RCA Gold Seal ▲ 09026-62595-2 [ADD]
A. Lewis (cnd)
Handel, G.F.:Sosarme, Rè di Media, w. Margaret Ritchie (sop—Elmira), Alfred Deller (mez—Sosarme), Nancy Evans (mez—Erenice), Helen Watts (cta—Melo), John Kentish (ct—Argone), William Herbert (ten—King Haliate), Ian Wallace (bass—Altomaro), St. Anthony Singers Theorema 2-▲ TH 121194/195
L. Maazel (cnd)
Puccini, G.:Tosca, w. B. Nilsson (sop), F. Corelli (ten), D. Fischer-Dieskau (bar), St. Cecilia Academy Chorus Rome *(rec June 1966)* London ▲ 440051-2
F. Molinari-Pradelli (cnd)
Puccini, G.:Manon Lescaut, w. R. Tebaldi (sop), M. del Monaco (ten), St. Cecilia Academy Chorus Rome London 2-▲ 430253-2 [ADD]
Puccini, G.:Tosca, w. R. Tebaldi (sop), M. del Monaco (ten), St. Cecilia Academy Chorus Rome London 2-▲ 411871-2 [ADD]
Verdi, G.:La forza del destino, w. R. Tebaldi (sop), G. Simionato (mez), M. del Monaco (ten), E. Bastianini (bar), C. Siepi (b-bar), St. Cecilia Academy Chorus Rome [!] London 3-▲ 421598-2 [ADD]
Verdi, G.:La traviata, w. R. Tebaldi (sop), et al., St. Cecilia Academy Chorus Rome London 2-▲ 430250-2 [ADD]
F. Previtali (cnd)
Ponchielli, A.:La Gioconda, w. Zinka Milanov (sop—La Gioconda), Rosalind Elias (mez—Laura), Belan Amparan (cta—La Cieca), Giacomo Cottino (ten—Isepo), Giuseppe Di Stefano (ten—Enzo Grimaldo), Fernando Valentini (bar—Zuane/Un Nocchiere), Leonard Warren (bar—Barnaba), Virgilio Carbonari (bass—Un Cantore), Plinio Clabassi (bass—Alvise Badoero), St. Cecilia Academy Chorus Rome Theorema 3-▲ TH 121182/184
Verdi, G.:La forza del destino, w. Zinka Milanov (sop—Donna Leonora di Vargas), Rosalind Elias (mez—Preziosilla), Luisa Gioia (sgr—Curra), Angelo Mercuriali (ten—Trabuco), Giuseppe di Stefano (ten—Son Alvaro), Leonard Warren (bar—Don Carlos di Vargas), Giorgio Tozzi (b-bar—Padre guardiano), Dino Mantovani (bar—Fra Melitone), Paolo Washington (b-bar—Il marchese di Calatrava), Virgilio Carbonari (b-bar—un alcalde), Sergio Liviabella (sgr—un chirurgo), St. Cecilia Academy Chorus Rome [!] London ▲ 443678-2 [ADD]
Verdi, G.:La forza del destino, w. Zinka Milanov (sop), Rosalind Elias (mez), Giuseppe Di Stefano (ten), Leonard Warren (bar), Giorgio Tozzi (bass), Paolo Washington (bass), St. Cecilia Academy Chorus Rome *(rec 1959)* Theorema 3-▲ TH 121157/59
J. Pritchard (cnd)
Donizetti, G.:Lucia di Lammermoor, w. J. Sutherland (sop), R. Cioni (ten), R. Merrill (bar), C. Siepi (bass-bar), St. Cecilia Academy Chorus Rome [!] London 2-▲ 411622-2 [ADD]
N. Sanzogno (cnd)
Verdi, G.:Rigoletto, w. Joan Sutherland (sop—Gilda), Renato Cioni (ten—Duke), Cornell MacNeil (bar—Rigoletto), St. Cecilia Academy Chorus Rome London ("Double Decca" series) 2-▲ 443853-2
T. Schippers (cnd)
Verdi, G.:Macbeth, w. B. Nilsson (sop), B. Prevedi (ten), G. Taddei (bar), St. Cecilia Academy Chorus Rome London ("Grand Opera" series) 2-▲ 433039-2 [ADD]
T. Serafin (cnd)
Boito, A.:Mefistofele, w. R. Tebaldi (sop), M. del Monaco (ten), C. Siepi (bass), St. Cecilia Academy Chorus Rome *(rec 1958)* London ▲ 440054-2
Puccini, G.:La Bohème, w. R. Tebaldi (sop), G. d'Angelo (sop), C. Bergonzi (ten), E. Bastianini (bar), C. Siepi (b-bar), St. Cecilia Academy Chorus Rome [!] London 2-▲ 425534-2 [ADD]
Puccini, G.:La Bohème (sels), w. R. Tebaldi (sop), C. Bergonzi (ten), E. Bastianini (bar), C. Siepi (b-bar), St. Cecilia Academy Chorus Rome—scenes & arias London ▲ 421301-2 [ADD]
Puccini, G.:Madama Butterfly, w. R. Tebaldi (sop), F. Cossotto (mez), C. Bergonzi (ten), E. Sordello (bar), St. Cecilia Academy Chorus Rome [!] London 2-▲ 425531-2 [ADD]
Puccini, G.:Madama Butterfly (sels), w. R. Tebaldi (sop), C. Bergonzi (ten), E. Sordello (bar), St. Cecilia Academy Chorus Rome London ▲ 417733-2 [ADD]

St. Cecilia Academy Orch Rome (cont.)
T. Serafin (cnd) (cont.)
Puccini, G.:Madama Butterfly (sels), w. R. Tebaldi (sop), F. Cossotto (mez), C. Bergonzi (ten), E. Sordello (bar), St. Cecilia Academy Chorus Rome [I] London ("Opera Gala" series) ▲ 421873–2 [ADD]
G. Sinopoli (cnd)
Verdi, G.:Rigoletto, w. E. Gruberova (sop), B. Fassbaender (mez), Schicoff (ten), R. Bruson (bar), R. Lloyd (b-bar), St. Cecilia Academy Chorus Rome [I] Philips 2–▲ 412592–2 [DDD]
G. Solti (cnd)
Verdi, G.:Un ballo in maschera, w. B. Nilsson (sop), G. Simionato (mez), C. Bergonzi (ten), C. MacNeil (bar), St. Cecilia Academy Chorus Rome [I] London 2–▲ 425655–2 [ADD]
St. Cecilia CO
Paisiello, G.:Cons Hpd, w. Pietro Spada (pno)—Nos. 1, 3, 4 & 7 *(rec Roma, Italy, Mar 8–14, 1992)* Arts ▲ 741202 [DDD]
Paisiello, G.:Cons Hpd, w. Pietro Spada (pno)—Nos. 2, 5, 6 & 8 *(rec Roma, Italy, Mar 8–14, 1992)* Arts ▲ 471212 [DDD]
L. Friedman (cnd)
Paganini, N.:Con 1 Vn, w. Uto Ughi (vn) RCA ("Basic 100" series) ▲ 09026–68453–2 ■ 09026–68453–4
Paganini, N.:Con 2 Vn, w. Uto Ughi (vn) RCA ("Basic 100" series) ▲ 09026–68453–2 ■ 09026–68453–4
U. Ughi (cnd)
Paganini, N.:Con 2 Vn, w. U. Ughi (vn) RCA Red Seal ▲ 7844–2 RC [DDD]
Paganini, N.:Con 4 Vn, w. U. Ughi (vn) RCA Red Seal ▲ 7844–2 RC [DDD]
A. Vlad (cnd)
Catalani, A.:A sera, in Paganini [arr strings] *(rec Rome, Italy, Nov 1986)* Arts ▲ 47201–2 [DDD]
Catalani, A.:Scherzo-Tarantella [arr strings] *(rec Rome, Italy, Nov 1986)* Arts ▲ 47201–2 [DDD]
Pergolesi, G.B.:Music of—Olimpiade; O frate'nnammurato; Salustia; Piccola sinf; Flaminio; Sinf in F; Adriano in Siria; Sinf in B♭; Il prigionier superbo [all rev P. Spada] *(rec Roma, Italy, May 1986)* Arts ▲ 47347–2 [DDD]
Puccini, G.:Music of—Crisantemi; Minuettos I–III; Scherzo in a; Qt in D; Fugues in A, C & G *(rec Rome, Italy, Nov 1986)* Arts ▲ 47201–2 [DDD]
St. Clair Trio
Arnold, M.:Pieces (5) Vn Koch International Classics ▲ KIC 7607
Arnold, M.:Trio Pno Koch International Classics ▲ KIC 7266 [DDD]
St. Clair Trio members
Arnold, M.:Pieces (5) Vn Koch International Classics ▲ KIC 7266 [DDD]
St. Cloud State Univ Wind Ensemble
R. Hansen (cnd)
Bertrand, A.:The Creatures of Proteus Vienna Modern Masters ▲ VMM 3034 [DDD]
St. Gallen Collegium Musicum
M. Schwarz (cnd)
Bach, J.S.:Cant 29, w. Karl Raas (org)—Sinf Musiques Suisses ▲ 6125 [DDD]
Derungs, G.A.:Con da chiesa, w. Karl Raas (org), Stephan Thomas (org), Peter Schneider (vib), Adrian Schilling (timp) Musiques Suisses ▲ 6125 [DDD]
Handel, G.F.:Cons (16) Org, w. Karl Raas (org)—Con No. 13 in F for Org Musiques Suisses ▲ 6125 [DDD]
Haydn, J.:Con Org, Obs & Strs, H.XVIII/1, w. Karl Raas (org) Musiques Suisses ▲ 6125 [DDD]
Huber, P.:Con Org, w. Karl Raas (org) Musiques Suisses ▲ 6125 [DDD]
St. Gallen String Orch
Lamentationes, w. [cnd:Rudolf Lutz], Schola Cantorum Basiliensis *(rec St. Mangen Church, St. Gallen, Switzerland)* Guild ▲ GMCD 7123 [DDD]
St. Gallen SO
J. Neschling (cnd)
Castelnuovo-Tedesco, M.:Con for 2 Gtrs, w. O.Assad (gtr), S. Assad (gtr) GHA ▲ 126.018
Rodrigo, J.:Concierto madrigal, w. S. Assad (gtr), O. Assad (gtr) GHA ▲ 126.018
St. George's Canzona
J. Sothcott (cnd)
A Medieval Banquet ASV ("Quicksilva" series) ▲ ASQ 6131 [DDD]
Medieval Songs & Dances CRD ▲ CD 3421
Merry It Is While Summer Lasts CRD ▲ 3412 [ADD]
St. James' Baroque Players
I. Bolton (cnd)
Bach, J.S.:Cons Hpd, BWV 1052–1058, w. I. Bolton (hpd)—Nos. 1 & 4–6 IMP Classics ▲ PCD 864 [DDD]
Bach, J.S.:Con 1 Hpd, w. Ivor Bolton (hpd) IMP ("Classics" series) ▲ IMP 6700692
Bach, J.S.:Con 2 Hpd, w. I. Bolton (hpd) IMP Classics ▲ PCD 901 [DDD]
Bach, J.S.:Con 3 Hpd, w. I. Bolton (hpd) IMP Classics ▲ PCD 901 [DDD]
Bach, J.S.:Con 4 Hpd, w. Ivor Bolton (hpd) IMP ("Classics" series) ▲ IMP 6700692
Bach, J.S.:Con 5 Hpd, w. Ivor Bolton (hpd) IMP ("Classics" series) ▲ IMP 6700692
Bach, J.S.:Con 6 Hpd, w. Ivor Bolton (hpd) IMP ("Classics" series) ▲ IMP 6700692
Bach, J.S.:Con 7 Hpd, w. I. Bolton (hpd) IMP Classics ▲ PCD 901 [DDD]
Baroque Music of Bologna Teldec ▲ 91192–2
St. John's Episcopal Cathedral Festival Orch
D. Pearson (cnd)
Hovhaness, A.:Sacred Music, w. Eric Plutz (org), St. John's Episcopal Cathedral Boy & Girls' Choir, St. John's Episcopal Cathedral Choir—Magnificat, Op. 157; Psalm 23 [Cant from Sym No. 12, Op. 188]; A Rose Tree Blossoms, Op. 246/4; Jesus, Lover of My Soul, Op. 53b; Jesus Christ Is Risen Today, Op. 100/3b; The Lord's Prayer, Op. 35; Peace by Multiplied, Op. 259/1; O For a Shout of Sacred Joy, Op. 161; Out of the Depths, Op. 142/3; O God, Our Help in Ages Past, Op. 137 *(rec St. John's Episcopal Cathedral, Denver, Mar 6–8, 1995)* Delos ▲ DE 3176 [DDD]
St. John's Smith Square Orch
Handel, G.F.:Music of, w. Alain Zaepffel (ct)—sels. from Solomon & Xerxes LaserLight ▲ 15502 [ADD]
J. Lubbock (cnd)
Arnold, M.:Con Gtr, w. M. Conn (gtr) IMP Classics ▲ PCD 859 [DDD]
Arnold, M.:Con Gtr, w. Michael Conn (gtr) IMP ("Classic" series) ▲ IMP 2035
Bach, C.P.E.:Cons Fl, w. J. Stinton (fl)—in d, A & G Collins Classics ▲ COL 1373 [DDD]
Gounod, C.:Sym 1 ASV ▲ ASV CD 981
Gounod, C.:Sym 2 ASV ▲ ASV CD 981
Handel, G.F.:Solomon (sels) Laserlight ▲ 15 502
Haydn, J.:Sym 44, "Trauer" IMP Classics ▲ PCD 820 [DDD]
Haydn, J.:Sym 49, "La Passione" IMP Classics ▲ PCD 819 [DDD]
Mendelssohn, F.:Sym 3 ASV Quicksilva ▲ QS 6004 [ADD]
Mendelssohn, F.:Sym 4 ASV Quicksilva ▲ QS 6004 [ADD]
Mozart, W.A.:Sym 40 IMP Classics ▲ IMP PCD 820
On Hearing the First Cuckoo in Spring ASV ("Quicksilva" series) ▲ ASV 6007 [DDD]
Rodrigo, J.:Concierto de Aranjuez, w. M. Conn (gtr) IMP Classics ▲ PCD 859 [DDD]
Rodrigo, J.:Concierto de Aranjuez, w. Michael Conn (gtr) IMP ("Classic" series) ▲ IMP 2035
Schubert, Franz:Sym 5 IMP Classics ▲ PCD 819 [DDD]
Stravinsky, I.:Apollon musagète ASV ▲ ASV 618 [DDD]
Stravinsky, I.:Orpheus ASV ▲ ASV 618 [DDD]
Virtuoso Violin, w. Maurice Hasson, (vn), Ian Brown (pno) ASV ("Quicksilva" series) ▲ ASV 6034 [ADD]
Vivaldi, A.:Cons Fl, Op. 10, w. R. Stallman (fl) ASV ▲ ASV 733 [DDD]
St. Laurent Instrumental Ensemble
Children's Songs, w. [cnd:François Rauber], St. Laurent Children's Choir, Maurice André (tpt), Jean-Pierre Rampal (fl) CBS ▲ MK 39669
St. Louis Brass
M. Azzolina (cnd)
Wedding Day, w. Florida Symphonic Pops Orch, Lyn Larsen (org) Pro Arte ▲ CDD 569 [DDD]
St. Louis Brass Quintet
Arnold, M.:Qnt Brass Crystal ▲ CD 200 [DDD]
Baroque Brass Summit ▲ DCD 120 [DDD] ■ DCD 120
Brass Bonanza, w. Annapolis Brass Quintet, Berlin Brass Quintet, Dallas Brass Quintet, Metropolitan Brass Quintet, New York Brass Quintet, 1–5 Brass Quintet Crystal ▲ CD 200 [ADD/DDD]
Horovitz, J.:Music Hall Suite Crystal ▲ CD 200 [ADD]
Plog, A.:Music of, w. Thomas Bacon (nar), Summit Brass—Animal Ditties [poetry by Ogden Nash] for Narrator & Brass Ensemble (1989); Concerto for Trumpet, Brass Ensemble & Percussion (1989); Four Sketches for Brass Quintet (1989); Mini-Variations on Amazing Grace for Brass Ensemble (1987); Music for Brass Octet (1981) Summit ▲ DCD 116 [DDD]
St. Louis SO
Wild Classics:A Celebration of Animals & Nature, w. James Galway (fl), Ofra Harnoy (vc), Martin Hoherman (vc), Emily Mitchell (hp), Michael Dussek (pno), Samuel Lipman (pno), Leo Litwin (pno), Gerhard Oppitz (pno), Isao Tomita (synths), Boston Pops Orch [cnd:Arthur Fiedler], Chicago SO [cnd:Fritz Reiner] RCA Red Seal ▲ 09026–68483–2 ■ 09026–68483–4
L. Bernstein (cnd)
Bernstein, L.:Sym 1, "Jeremiah", w. Nan Merriman (sop) *(rec 1945)* RCA Red Seal ▲ 09026–61581–2
V. Golschmann (cnd)
Falla, M. de:Noches en los jardines de España, w. A. Rubinstein (pno) RCA Gold Seal ▲ 09026–61261–2
Lalo, E.:Sym espagnole, w. Nathan Milstein (vn) Testament ▲ TES SBT 1047
A. Previn (cnd)
Copland, A.:The Red Pony (suite) Sony Classical ("Essential Classics" series) ▲ SBK 62401 ■ SBT 62401
G. Schuller (cnd)
Paine, J.K.:Mass, Op. 10, w. C. Balthrop (sop), J. Blackett (cta), V. Cole (ten), J. Cheek (bass), J. Lange (org), St. Louis Sym Chorus [L] *(rec ca. mid-1970s)* New World ▲ 80262–2 [AAD]
J. Semkow (cnd)
Beethoven, L. van:Elegischer Gesang, "Sanft wie du lebtest", w. St. Louis Sym Chorus [arr. for small 4-part chorus & string ensemble] Vox Box 2–▲ CDX 5104 [ADD]
Beethoven, L. van:Fant Pno, Op. 80, "Choral Fant", w. W. Klien (pno), St. Louis Sym Chorus Vox Box 2–▲ CDX 5104 [ADD]
Beethoven, L. van:Meeresstille und glückliche Fahrt, w. St. Louis Sym Chorus Vox Box 2–▲ CDX 5104 [ADD]
Beethoven, L. van:Rondo Pno, WoO 6, w. W. Klien (pno) Vox Box 2–▲ CDX 5104 [ADD]
Wagner, R.:Ovs, Preludes & Orch Sels, w. St. Louis Sym Chorus—Rienzi:Ov.; Lohengrin:Preludes, Acts 1 & 3; Die Meistersinger von Nürnberg:Prelude; Parsifal:Good Friday Spell; Die Walküre:The Ride of the Valkyries Vox Box 2–▲ CDX 5104 [ADD]
F. Slatkin (cnd)
Shostakovich, D.:Sym 5 RCA Red Seal ▲ 5608–2–RC
l Slatkin (cnd)
Walton, W.:Belshazzar's Feast, w. T. Allen (bar) RCA Red Seal ▲ 09026–60813–2
L. Slatkin (cnd)
The American Album RCA Red Seal ▲ 60778–2–RC [DDD] ■ 60778–4–RC □ 09026–60778–5
American Portraits RCA Red Seal ▲ 09026–60983–2 [DDD] ■ 09026–60983–4
Anderson, L.:Music of—Belle of the Ball; The Phantom Regiment; The First Day of Spring; Sleigh Ride; Plink, Plank, Plunk!; Blue Tango; Forgotten Dreams; Bugler's Holiday; The Penny-Whistle Song; Clarinet Candy; Horse & Buggy; A Trumpeter's Lullaby; Fiddle Faddle; Jazz Pizzicato; Jazz Legato; The Syncopated Clock; Sandpaper Ballet; The Typwriter; The Waltzing Cat; Promenade; Saraband; Serenata; Balladette; Arietta; Home Stretch *(rec Powell Symphony Hall, St. Louis, MO)* RCA Red Seal ▲ 09026–68046–2 [DDD]
Barber, S.:Adagio Strs EMI Classics ("American Composer" series) ▲ CDM 64306
Barber, S.:Adagio Strs Telarc ▲ CD 80059 [DDD] ■ CS 30059 (D)
Barber, S.:Adagio Strs EMI Classics ▲ CDC 49463 [DDD] ■ 4DS 49463
Barber, S.:Capricorn Con, w. Jacob Berg (fl), Peter Bowman (ob), Susan Slaughter (tpt) *(rec Powell Symphony Hall, St. Louis, MO, May 7, 1995)* RCA Red Seal ▲ 09026–68283–2 [DDD]
Barber, S.:Con Vc, w. Steven Isserlis (vc) *(rec Powell Symphony Hall, St. Louis, MO, Dec 2, 1994)* RCA Red Seal ▲ 09026–68283–2 [DDD]
Barber, S.:Con Pno, w. J. Browning (pno) RCA Red Seal ▲ 60732–2–RC [DDD] ■ 60732–4–RC (CrO2)
Barber, S.:Con Vn, w. E. Oliveira (vn) EMI Classics ("American Composer" series) ▲ CDM 64305
Barber, S.:Con Vn, w. Kyoko Takezawa (vn) *(rec Powell Symphony Hall, St. Louis, MO, Apr 24, 1994)* RCA Red Seal ▲ 09026–68283–2 [DDD]
Barber, S.:Con Vn, w. E. Oliveira (vn) EMI Classics ▲ CDC 47850 [DDD]
Barber, S.:Essay 1 EMI Classics ▲ CDC 49463 [DDD] ■ 4DS 49463
Barber, S.:Essay 2 EMI Classics ▲ CDC 49463 [DDD] ■ 4DS 49463
Barber, S.:Essay 3 EMI Classics ▲ CDC 49463 [DDD] ■ 4DS 49463
Barber, S.:Medea's Meditation & Dance of Vengeance EMI Classics ▲ CDC 49463 [DDD] ■ 4DS 49463
Barber, S.:The School for Scandal EMI Classics ("American Composer" series) ▲ CDM 64303
Barber, S.:The School for Scandal EMI Classics ▲ CDC 49463 [DDD] ■ 4DS 49463
Barber, S.:Souvenirs RCA Red Seal ▲ 60732–2–RC [DDD] ■ 60732–4–RC (CrO2)
Barber, S.:Sym 1 RCA Red Seal ▲ 60732–2–RC [DDD] ■ 60732–4–RC (CrO2)
Bartók, B.:Con Va, w. J. Starker (vc) RCA Red Seal ▲ 60717–2–RC [DDD] ■ 60717–4–RC (CrO2)
Bartók, B.:Con Va, w. P. Zukerman (va) RCA Red Seal ▲ 60749–2–RC [DDD] ■ 60749–4–RC
Bartók, B.:Con 2 Vn, w. P. Zukerman (vn) RCA Red Seal ▲ 60749–2–RC [DDD] ■ 60749–4–RC
Bartók, B.:The Miraculous Mandarin RCA Red Seal ▲ 09026–61702–2
Bernstein, L.:Candide (ov) EMI Classics ("American Composer" series) ▲ CDM 64303
Bernstein, L.:On the Town EMI Classics ("American Composer" series) ▲ CDM 64303
Bernstein, L.:Songfest, w. Linda Hohenfeld (sop), Wendy White (mez), Patricia Spence (mez), Walter Plante (ten), Vernon Hartman (bar), John Cheek (bass) RCA Red Seal ▲ 09026–61581–2
Bizet, G.:Carmen (suites) Telarc ▲ CD 80048 [DDD]
Bolcom, W.:Sym 4, w. Joan Morris (sop) [E] New World ▲ NW 356–2 [DDD]
Borodin, A.:In the Steppes of Central Asia Telarc ▲ CD 80072 [DDD]
Borodin, A.:Nocturne Str Orch Telarc ▲ CD 80080 [DDD] ■ CS 30080 (D)
Brahms, J.:Academic Festival Ov RCA Red Seal ▲ 7920–2–RC [DDD]
Brahms, J.:Serenade 2 Orch RCA Red Seal ▲ 7920–2–RC [DDD]
Brahms, J.:Vars on a Theme by Haydn RCA Red Seal ▲ 7920–2–RC [DDD]
Colgrass, M.:Déjà Vu New World ▲ NW 318–2 [DDD]
Copland, A.:Appalachian Spring EMI Classics ▲ CDC 49766
Copland, A.:Billy the Kid EMI Classics ▲ CDC 47382 [DDD] ■ 4DS 37357 (D)
Copland, A.:Billy the Kid EMI Classics (American Composer Series) ▲ CDM 64315
Copland, A.:Billy the Kid (suite) EMI Classics (American Composer Series) ▲ CDM 64315
Copland, A.:Dance Sym *(rec Powell Symphony Hall, St. Louis, Feb 17 & 18, 1995)* RCA Red Seal ▲ 09026–68292–2 [DDD]
Copland, A.:Fanfare for the Common Man RCA Red Seal ▲ 09026–60983–2 [DDD] ■ 09026–60983–4 (CrO2)
Copland, A.:Grohg (sels)—Cortège macabre EMI Classics ▲ CDC 49766
Copland, A.:The Heiress (suite) *(rec Powell Symphony Hall, St. Louis, Apr 18, 1992)* RCA Red Seal ▲ 09026–61699–2 [DDD]
Copland, A.:John Henry EMI Classics ▲ CDC 54282
Copland, A.:John Henry EMI Classics (American Composer Series) ▲ CDM 64306
Copland, A.:Letter from Home EMI Classics (American Composer Series) ▲ CDM 64306
Copland, A.:Letter from Home EMI Classics ▲ CDC 49766
Copland, A.:Lincoln Portrait, w. H. Norman Schwarzkopf (nar) [E] RCA Red Seal ▲ 09026–60983–2 [DDD] ■ 09026–60983–4 (CrO2)
Copland, A.:Music for a Great City RCA Red Seal ▲ 60149–2–RC [DDD] ■ 60149–4–RC (CrO2)

St. Louis SO (cont.)
L. Slatkin (cnd) (cont.)
Copland, A.:Music for Movies *(rec Powell Symphony Hall, St. Louis, Nov 22, 1991)* RCA Red Seal ▲ 09026-61699-2 [DDD]
Copland, A.:Music for Radio *(rec Powell Symphony Hall, St. Louis, Nov 22, 1991)* RCA Red Seal ▲ 09026-61699-2 [DDD]
Copland, A.:Our Town (film music) *(rec Powell Symphony Hall, St. Louis, Nov 22, 1991)* RCA Red Seal ▲ 09026-61699-2 [DDD]
Copland, A.:The Red Pony (film music) *(rec Powell Symphony Hall, St. Louis, Apr 18, 1992)* RCA Red Seal ▲ 09026-61699-2 [DDD]
Copland, A.:Rodeo EMI Classics ▲ CDC 47382 [DDD] ■ 4DS 37357 (D)
Copland, A.:Rodeo EMI Classics (American Composer Series) ▲ CDM 64315
Copland, A.:Rodeo EMI Classics ▲ CDC 54282
Copland, A.:Short Sym, "Sym 2" *(rec Powell Symphony Hall, St. Louis, Feb 17 & 18, 1995)* RCA Red Seal ▲ 09026-68292-2 [DDD]
Copland, A.:Sym Org & Orch, w. Simon Preston (org) *(rec Christ Church Cathedral, St. Louis, Sept 21, 1993)* RCA Red Seal ▲ 09026-68292-2 [DDD]
Copland, A.:Sym 3 RCA Red Seal ▲ 60149-2-RC [DDD] ■ 60149-4-RC (CrO2)
Copland, A.:Vars Orch *(rec Powell Symphony Hall, St. Louis, May 9, 1995)* RCA Red Seal ▲ 09026-68292-2 [DDD]
Corigliano, J.:Con Pno, w. Barry Douglas (pno) *(rec Powell Symphony Hall, St. Louis, MO, Feb 11 & 13, 1994)* RCA Red Seal ▲ 09026-68100-2 [DDD]
Corigliano, J.:Elegy *(rec Powell Symphony Hall, St. Louis, MO, Apr 24, 1994)* RCA Red Seal ▲ 09026-68100-2 [DDD]
Corigliano, J.:Fant on an Ostinato *(rec Powell Symphony Hall, St. Louis, MO, May 11, 1993)* RCA Red Seal ▲ 09026-68100-2 [DDD]
Corigliano, J.:Tournaments Ov *(rec Powell Symphony Hall, St. Louis, MO, May 11, 1993)* RCA Red Seal ▲ 09026-68100-2 [DDD]
Debussy, C.:Danses sacrée et profane, w. Tietov (hp) Telarc ▲ CD 80071 [DDD]
Debussy, C.:La Mer Telarc ▲ CD 80071 [DDD]
Debussy, C.:Prélude à l'après-midi d'un faune Telarc ▲ CD 80071 [DDD]
del Tredici, D.:In Memory of a Summer Day, w. P. Bryn-Julson (sop) [E] Elektra/Nonesuch ▲ 79043-2 [DDD]
Druckman, J.:Aureole New World ▲ NW 318-2 [ADD]
Dvořák, A.:Con Vc, w. J. Starker (vc) RCA Red Seal ▲ 60717-2-RC [DDD] ■ 60717-4-RC (CrO2)
Dvořák, A.:Sym 9, "From the New World" *(rec Apr. 30, 1980)* Telarc ▲ CD 82007 [DDD]
Elgar, E.:Con Vn, w. P. Zukerman (vn) RCA Red Seal ▲ 09026-61672-2 ■ 09026-61672-4
Elgar, E.:Salut d'amour RCA Red Seal ▲ 09026-61672-2; ■ 09026-61672-4
Encore! *(rec Powell Symphony Hall, St. Louis, Jan 20, 1991 & Nov 27-29)* RCA Red Seal ▲ 09026-68511-2 [DDD]
Erb, D.:Orchestral Music, w. Lynn Harrell (vc)—Concerto for Brass & Orchestra (1987); Concerto for Cello & Orchestra (1976); Ritual Observances (1992) *(rec 1991-92)* New World ▲ 80415-2
Fauré, G.:Pavane Orch Telarc ▲ CD 80059 [DDD] ■ CS 30059 (D)
Gershwin, G.:An American in Paris *(rec 1987)* Angel ("DDD Midline" series) ▲ CDD 64084 [DDD]
Gershwin, G.:An American in Paris EMI Classics ("American Composer" series) ▲ CDM 64303
Gershwin, G.:An American in Paris Vox Box 2-▲ CDX 5007 [ADD]
Gershwin, G.:Con Pno, w. J. Siegel (pno) Vox Box 2-▲ CDX 5007 [ADD]
Gershwin, G.:Cuban Ov EMI Classics ("American Composer" series) ▲ CDM 64303
Gershwin, G.:Cuban Ov *(rec 1987)* EMI Classics ("DDD Midline" series) ▲ CDD 64084 [DDD]
Gershwin, G.:Cuban Ov Vox Box 2-▲ CDX 5007 [ADD]
Gershwin, G.:"I Got Rhythm" Vars, w. J. Siegel (pno) Vox Box 2-▲ CDX 5007 [ADD]
Gershwin, G.:Lullaby Vox Box 2-▲ CDX 5007 [ADD]
Gershwin, G.:Lullaby *(rec 1987)* EMI Classics ▲ CDD 64084 [DDD]
Gershwin, G.:Porgy & Bess (suite), "Catfish Row Suite" *(rec 1987)* Angel ("DDD Midline" series) ▲ CDD 64084 [DDD]
Gershwin, G.:Porgy & Bess (suite), "Catfish Row Suite" Vox Box 2-▲ CDX 5007 [ADD]
Gershwin, G.:Promenade Vox Box 2-▲ CDX 5007 [ADD]
Gershwin, G.:Rhap in Blue, w. J. Siegel (pno) Vox Box 2-▲ CDX 5007 [ADD]
Gershwin, G.:Second Rhap, w. J. Siegel (pno) Vox Box 2-▲ CDX 5007 [ADD]
Ginastera, A.:Popol vuh RCA Red Seal ▲ 09026-60993-2
Glière, R.:The Red Poppy (suite), "Russian Sailors' Dance" Telarc ▲ CD 80072 [DDD]
Glinka, M.:Russlan & Ludmilla (ov) Telarc ▲ CD 80072 [DDD]
Grainger, P.:Irish Tune from County Derry Telarc ▲ CD 80059 [DDD] ■ CS 30059 (D)
Grieg, E.:Peer Gynt Suites, Opp. 46 & 55 Telarc ▲ CD 80048 [DDD]
Hanson, H.:Sym 2, "Romantic" EMI Classics ▲ CDC 47850 [DDD]
Hanson, H.:Sym 2, "Romantic" EMI Classics ("American Composer" series) ▲ CDM 64304
Haydn, J.:The Representation of Chaos RCA Red Seal ▲ 09026-60993-2
Herbert, V.:American Fant RCA Red Seal ▲ 09026-60983-2 [DDD] ■ 09026-60983-4 (CrO2)
In Step RCA Red Seal ▲ 07863-57716-2 [DDD]
Ives, C.:Central Park in the Dark RCA Red Seal ▲ 09026-61222-2
Ives, C.:Fugue in 4 Keys on *The Shining Shore* RCA Red Seal ▲ 09026-61222-2
Ives, C.:March 3 RCA Red Seal ▲ 09026-61222-2
Ives, C.:Sym 3 RCA Red Seal ▲ 09026-61222-2
Ives, C.:Three Places in New England RCA Red Seal ▲ 09026-61222-2
Ives, C.:The Unanswered Question RCA Red Seal ▲ 09026-61222-2
Mahler, G.:Sym 1 Telarc ▲ CD 82004
Mahler, G.:Sym 1 Telarc ▲ CD 80066 [DDD]
Mahler, G.:Sym 2, w. K. Battle (sop), M. Forrester (cta), St. Louis Sym Chorus Telarc 2-▲ CD 80081/82 [DDD]
Mahler, G.:Sym 10 [reconstructed by Remo Mazetti Jr.] *(rec Powell Symphony Hall, St Louis, MS, Mar 10-13, 1995)* RCA Red Seal ▲ 09026-68190-2 [DDD]
Orff, C.:Carmina burana, w. S. McNair (sop), J. Aler (ten), Håkan Hagegård (bar) RCA Red Seal ▲ 09026-61673-2; ■ 09026-61673-4
Pachelbel, J.:Canon Telarc ▲ CD 80080 [DDD] ■ CS 30080 (D)
Piston, W.:The Incredible Flutist RCA Red Seal ▲ 60798-2-RC [DDD]
Piston, W.:New England Sketches RCA Red Seal ▲ 60798-2-RC [DDD]
Piston, W.:Sym 6 RCA Red Seal ▲ 60798-2-RC [DDD]
Prokofiev, S.:Alexander Nevsky, w. C. Carlson (mez), St. Louis Sym Chorus [R] Vox Box 2-▲ CDX 5021 [ADD]
Prokofiev, S.:Ivan the Terrible, w. C. Carlson (mez), S. Timberlake (bass), St. Louis Sym Chorus [R] Vox Box 2-▲ CDX 5021 [ADD]
Prokofiev, S.:Lt Kijé Suite Vox Box 2-▲ CDX 5021 [ADD]
Prokofiev, S.:Sym 5 *(rec ca. 1983/4)* RCA Gold Seal ▲ 09026-61350-2 ■ 09026-61350-4
Rachmaninoff, S.:The Bells, w. Christos (sop), Walter Planté (ten), Arnold Voketaitis (bar), St. Louis Sym Chorus *(rec 1980)* Vox Box 3-▲ CD3X 3002 [ADD]
Rachmaninoff, S.:Capriccio bohémien *(rec 1979)* Vox Box 3-▲ CD3X 3002 [ADD]
Rachmaninoff, S.:Cons Pno (comp), w. A. Simon (pno) Vox Box 2-▲ CDX 5008 [ADD]
Rachmaninoff, S.:The Isle of the Dead *(rec 1979)* Vox Box 3-▲ CD3X 3002 [ADD]
Rachmaninoff, S.:Prince Rostislav *(rec 1980)* Vox Box 3-▲ CD3X 3002 [ADD]
Rachmaninoff, S.:Rhapsody on a Theme of Paganini, w. A. Simon (pno) Vox Box 2-▲ CDX 5008 [ADD]
Rachmaninoff, S.:The Rock *(rec 1979)* Vox Box 3-▲ CD3X 3002 [ADD]
Rachmaninoff, S.:Russian Songs, w. St. Louis Sym Chorus *(rec 1980)* Vox Box 3-▲ CD3X 3002 [ADD]
Rachmaninoff, S.:Scherzo *(rec 1980)* Vox Box 3-▲ CD3X 3002 [ADD]
Rachmaninoff, S.:Spring, w. A. Voketaitis (bar), St. Louis Sym Chorus *(rec 1980)* Vox Box 3-▲ CD3X 3002 [ADD]
Rachmaninoff, S.:Symphonic Dances *(rec 1979)* Vox Box 3-▲ CD3X 3002 [ADD]
Rachmaninoff, S.:Sym in d *(rec 1980)* Vox Box 3-▲ CD3X 3002 [ADD]
Rachmaninoff, S.:Syms (comp) *(rec 1976-79)* Vox Box 2-▲ CDX 5034 [ADD]
Rachmaninoff, S.:Vocalise *(rec 1979)* Vox Box 3-▲ CD3X 3002 [ADD]

St. Louis SO (cont.)
L. Slatkin (cnd) (cont.)
Ravel, M.:Boléro Telarc ▲ CD 80052 [DDD]
Ravel, M.:Con Pno (left hand), w. A. de Larrocha (pno) RCA Red Seal ▲ 09026-60985-2
Ravel, M.:Con in G Pno, w. A. de Larrocha (pno) RCA Red Seal ▲ 09026-60985-2
Ravel, M.:Daphnis et Chloé (suite 2) Telarc ▲ CD 80052 [DDD]
Ravel, M.:Pavane pour une infante défunte Telarc ▲ CD 80052 [DDD]
Ravel, M.:Sonatine Pno, w. A. de Larrocha (pno) RCA Red Seal ▲ 09026-60985-2
Ravel, M.:Valses nobles et sentimentales, w. A. de Larrocha (pno) RCA Red Seal ▲ 09026-60985-2
Rimsky-Korsakov, N.:Russian Easter Festival Telarc ▲ CD 80072 [DDD]
Satie, E.:Gymnopédies—Nos. 1 & 3 Telarc ▲ CD 80059 [DDD] ■ CS 30059 (D)
Schuman, W.:American Festival Ov RCA Red Seal ▲ 09026-61282-2
Schuman, W.:New England Triptych RCA Red Seal ▲ 09026-61282-2
Schuman, W.:Sym 10 RCA Red Seal ▲ 09026-61282-2
Shostakovich, D.:Sym 4 RCA Red Seal ▲ 09026-60887-2
The Slatkin Years St. Louis Symphony ▲ no catalog number [ADD/DDD]
Stravinsky, I.:Le Sacre du printemps Orch RCA Red Seal ▲ 09026-60993-2
Tchaikovsky, P.:Capriccio italien RCA Red Seal ▲ 09026-60433-2
Tchaikovsky, P.:Marche slave Telarc ▲ CD 80072 [DDD]
Tchaikovsky, P.:The Nutcracker RCA Red Seal 2-▲ 09026-61704-2
Tchaikovsky, P.:The Nutcracker (sels) RCA Red Seal ▲ 09026-61224-2 ■ 09026-61224-4
Tchaikovsky, P.:Ov 1812 *(rec Powell Symphony Hall, Jan. 27, 1993)* RCA Red Seal ▲ 09026-68045-2 [DDD]
Tchaikovsky, P.:Romeo & Juliet *(rec Powell Symphony Hall, Nov. 23, 1991)* RCA Red Seal ▲ 09026-68045-2 [DDD]
Tchaikovsky, P.:Serenade Strs Telarc ▲ CD 80080 [DDD]
Tchaikovsky, P.:Sleeping Beauty RCA Red Seal ▲ 09026-61682-2
Tchaikovsky, P.:Swan Lake RCA Red Seal 2-▲ 09026-62557-2
Tchaikovsky, P.:Swan Lake (sels) RCA Red Seal ▲ 09026-61224-2 ■ 09026-61224-4
Tchaikovsky, P.:Sym 2 *(rec Powell Symphony Hall, Jan. 31, 1993)* RCA Red Seal ▲ 09026-68045-2 [DDD]
Tchaikovsky, P.:Sym 3 RCA Red Seal ▲ 09026-60433-2
Tchaikovsky, P.:Sym 5 RCA Red Seal ▲ 60425-2-RC [DDD] ■ 60425-4-RC (CrO2)
Tchaikovsky, P.:Sym 6 RCA Red Seal ▲ 09026-60438-2 ■ 09026-60438-4
Tchaikovsky, P.:The Tempest RCA Red Seal ▲ 60425-2-RC [DDD] ■ 60425-4-RC (CrO2)
Tower, J.:Island Prelude, w. P. Bowman (ob) Elektra/Nonesuch ▲ 79245-2-ZK ■ 79245-4-AW
Tower, J.:Music for Vc, w. Lynn Harrell (vc) Elektra/Nonesuch ▲ 79245-2-ZK ■ 79245-4-AW
Tower, J.:Sequoia Elektra/Nonesuch ▲ 79245-2-ZK ■ 79245-4-AW
Tower, J.:Silver Ladders Elektra/Nonesuch ▲ 79245-2-ZK ■ 79245-4-AW
Vaughan Williams, R.:Fant on Greensleeves Telarc ▲ CD 80080 [DDD] ■ CS 30080 (D)
Vaughan Williams, R.:Fant on a Theme by Thomas Tallis Telarc ▲ CD 80059 [DDD] ■ CS 30059 (D)
Walton, W.:Henry V (film suite) RCA Red Seal ▲ 09026-60813-2
Walton, W.:Partita RCA Red Seal ▲ 09026-60813-2

W. Susskind (cnd)
Dvořák, A.:Con Vc, w. Z. Nelsova (vc) Vox Box 2-▲ CDX 5015 [ADD]
Dvořák, A.:Con Pno, w. R. Firkusny (pno) Vox Box 2-▲ CDX 5015 [ADD]
Dvořák, A.:Con Vn, w. R. Ricci (vn) Vox Box 2-▲ CDX 5015 [ADD]
Dvořák, A.:Mazurek, w. R. Ricci (vn) Vox Box 2-▲ CDX 5015 [ADD]
Dvořák, A.:Romance Vn, w. R. Ricci (vn) Vox Box 2-▲ CDX 5015 [ADD]
Dvořák, A.:Rondo, w. Z. Nelsova (vc) Vox Box 2-▲ CDX 5015 [ADD]
Dvořák, A.:Silent Woods, w. Z. Nelsova (vc) Vox Box 2-▲ CDX 5015 [ADD]
Holst, G.:The Planets, w. Missouri Singers, Ronald Arnatt Chorale Vox Box 2-▲ CDX 5105 [ADD]
Smetana, B.:Má Vlast Vox Box 2-▲ CDX 5105 [ADD]

St. Louis SO members
L. Slatkin (cnd)
Bartók, B.:Con Orch RCA Red Seal ▲ 09026-61702-2
Bolcom, W.:Session I New World ▲ NW 356-2 [DDD]

St. Luke's Baroque Orch
R. Palmer (cnd)
Telemann, G.P.:Pimpinone, w. Julianne Baird (sop—Vespetta), John Ostendorf (bass—Pimpinone) Newport Classics ▲ NCD 60117 [DDD]

St. Luke's Chamber Ensemble
Hymn, w. American Boychoir, Albemarle Consort of Voices Angel ▲ CDC 55064; ■ 4DS 55064
D. R. Davies (cnd)
Copland, A.:Appalachian Spring (suite) MusicMasters ▲ 7055-2-C [DDD]
Copland, A.:Nonet MusicMasters ▲ 7055-2-C [DDD]
Copland, A.:Pieces (2) Str Qt MusicMasters ▲ 7055-2-C [DDD]
C. Wuorinen (cnd)
Wuorinen, C.:Archaeopteryx, w. D. Taylor (trbn) *(rec June 14-17, 1991)* Koch International Classics ▲ KIC 7110-2 [DDD]
Wuorinen, C.:Hyperion *(rec June 14-17, 1991)* Koch International Classics ▲ KIC 7110-2 [DDD]

St. Luke's Chamber Ensemble [Mitsuru Tsubota (vn), Mayuki Fukuhara (vn), Louise Schulman (va), Myron Lutzke (vc)]
Ewazen, E.:Qnt Tpt, w. Chris Gekker (tpt) *(rec Recital Hall, SUNY Purchase, 1993)* Well-Tempered Productions ▲ WTP 5172 [DDD]

St. Mary's Chamber Players
Vivaldi, A.:Music of, w. S. Kuijken (vn), F. Brüggen (rcr), La Petite Bande—The 4 Seasons; Bn Con in E♭; Ob Con in F; etc. Pro Arte ▲ CDM 816 ■ PCD 816
N. Marriner (cnd)
Mozart, W.A.:Con Bn, w. Miller (bn) Pro Arte ▲ CDD 195 [DDD]
Vanhal, J.B.:Con Bn, w. C. Miller (bn) Pro Arte ▲ CDD 195 [DDD]
Vivaldi, A.:Cons Bn, w. J. Miller (bn)—RV.477,483,484,504 *(rec 1/86)* Pro Arte ▲ CDD 273 [DDD]

St. Michael's Orch Munich
Weber, C.M. von:Gloria et honore, w. M. Toborsky, E. Ehret, St. Michael Chorus Munich Koch Schwann ▲ CD 313 055 [ADD]
E. Ehret (cnd)
Diabelli, A.:Pastoralmesse, w. C. Degler (sop), S. Linden (sop), S. Rauschkolb (cta), D. Clayton (ten), H. Müller (bass), Munich St. Michael Choir [L] Koch Schwann ▲ CD 313015 [ADD]
Weber, C.M. von:Missa sancta 1, w. Maria Taborsky (sop), Gerda Kink (cta), Hermann Pöllmann (ten), Hans Huber (bass), Gisela Schindler (org), St. Michael Chorus Munich Koch Schwann ▲ SCH CD 316372
Weber, C.M. von:Missa sancta 2, w. Maria Taborsky (sop), Gerda Kink (alt), Hermann Pöllmann (ten), Hans Huber (bass), Gisela Schindler (org), Munich St. Michael Choir Studio SM ▲ D 2454 [ADD]
Weber, C.M. von:In die solemnitatis, w. M. Toborsky (sop), St. Michael's Chorus Koch Schwann ▲ CD 313 055 [ADD]

St. Paul CO
Bach, J.S.:Con Vn & Ob, w. P. Zukerman (vn), R. Killmer (ob) CBS ▲ MK 37278 [DDD]
Bach, J.S.:Con for 2 Vns, w. I. Stern (vn), P. Zukerman (vn) CBS ▲ MK 37278 [DDD]

356 ▲ = CD ♦ = Enhanced CD Δ = MD ■ = Cassette Tape □ = DCC

St. Paul CO (cont.)

Vivaldi, A.:Music of, w. Salvatore Accardo (vn), Frederico Agostini (vn), Heinz Holliger (ob), Ida Levin (vn), Aurele Nicolet (fl), Massimo Paris (va d'amore), Angel Romero (gtr), Celedonio Romero (gtr), Celine Romero (gtr), Henryk Szeryng (vn), Pinchas Zukerman (vn), Academy of St. Martin in the Fields, English CO, I Musici, Naples Weekly International Soloists, Dresden Staatskapelle—The Four Seasons [Winter]; Con in D for Gtr [Largo]; Con in D for Fl, "Il gardellino" [Cantabile]; Con in C for Diverse Insts [Andante molto]; Con in g for Strs [Andante molto]; Con in D for 2 Vns & 2 Vcs [Largo]; Con in g for Ob, Vn, Ww & Strs [Larghetto]; Con in a for Gtr, "L'estro armonico" [Largo]; Con in F for 3 Vns [Andante]; Con in F for Fl [Largo]; Con in d for Va D'Amore [Largo]; Con in E for Vn & Strs, "Il riposo" [Allegro]; Con in G for Ob, Bn & Strs [Largo]; Con in B♭ for Vn & Strs [Largo]; Con in A for Gtr & Strs [Larghetto]; Con in E for Vn & Strs, "L'amoroso" [Allegro]; Con in G for Fl [Largo]; Con in A for Vn [Larghetto]; Con in c for Vn & Strs, "Il sospetto" [Andante]; Con in a for 2 Obs & Strs [Largo]; Con in g for Orch [Largo non molto]; Con in a for Vn [Largo]; Con in C for Ob [Adagio]; Con in g for Fl, "La notte" [Largo] Philips ▲ 454051-2 ■ 454 051-4

D. R. Davies (cnd)

Copland, A.:Appalachian Spring—re-release of Pro Arte CDD-140 Pro Arte ▲ CDS 3429
Copland, A.:Appalachian Spring (suite)—original version Pro Arte ▲ CDD-140 [DDD]
Copland, A.:Short Sym, "Sym 2"—re-release of Pro Arte CDD-140 Pro Arte ▲ CDS 3429
Ives, C.:Sym 3 Pro Arte ▲ CDS 3429
Ives, C.:Three Places in New England Pro Arte ▲ CDD 140 [DDD] ■ PCD 140
Rhodes, P.:Divert CRI ■ C 361

C. Hogwood (cnd)

Bizet, G.:L'Arlésienne London ▲ 430231-2 [DDD]
Corelli, A.:Concerti grossi, Op. 6, w. L. Shank (vn), R. Tecco (vn), J. Koestenbaum (vc)—No. 2 *(rec May 1992)* London ▲ 440376-2
Gallo, D.:Trio Sons (36) London ▲ 425614-2 [DDD]
Gounod, C.:Petite Sym London ▲ 430231-2 [DDD]
Gounod, C.:Sym 1 London ▲ 430231-2 [DDD]
Holst, G.:A Fugal Con, w. J. Bogorad (vn), K. Greenbank (vn), R. Tecco (vn), L. Shank (vn), J. Koestenbaum (vc) *(rec May 1992)* London ▲ 440376-2
Holst, G.:Savitri, w. R. Tecco (vn), L. Shank (vn), J. Koestenbaum (vc) *(rec May 1992)* London ▲ 440376-2
Pergolesi, G.B.:Sinf Vc London ▲ 425614-2 [DDD]
Stravinsky, I.:Con CO London ▲ 425614-2 [DDD]
Stravinsky, I.:Pulcinella London ▲ 425614-2 [DDD]
Tippett, M.:Fant Concertante on a Theme of Corelli, w. R. Tecco (vn), L. Shank (vn), J. Koestenbaum (vc) *(rec May 1992)* London ▲ 440376-2

B. McFerrin (cnd)

Mozart, W.A.:Con 20 Pno, w. Bobby McFerrin (sgr), Chick Corea (pno)—Prelude [a capella voc & pno improvisation] *(rec Donald Benson Great Hall, Bethel College, St. Paul & Masonic Grand Lodge, New York, Feb 5-7, 1996 & May 21, 1)* Sony Classical ▲ SK 62601 [DDD] ■ ST 62601
Mozart, W.A.:Con 23 Pno, w. Bobby McFerrin (sgr), Chick Corea (pno)—Prelude [a capella voc & pno improvisation] *(rec Donald Benson Great Hall, Bethel College, St. Paul & Masonic Grand Lodge, New York, Feb 5-7, 1996 & May 21, 1)* Sony Classical ▲ SK 62601 [DDD] △ SM 62601 ■ ST 62601
Mozart, W.A.:Son 2 Pno, w. Bobby McFerrin (sgr), Chick Corea (pno) [Voc & Pno improvisation based on Adagio] *(rec Donald Benson Great Hall, Bethel College, St. Paul & Masonic Grand Lodge, New York, Feb 5-7, 1996 & May 21, 1)* Sony Classical ▲ SK 62601 [DDD] ■ ST 62601
Paper Music *(rec Ordway Music Theatre, St Paul, MN, Jan 30-31 & Mar 14, 1995)* Sony Classical ▲ 7464-64600-2 [DDD]

J. Revzen (cnd)

Haydn, J.:Die Jahreszeiten, w. Arleen Auger (sop), John Aler (ten), Håkan Hågegard (bar), Minnesota Chorale [G] Koch International Classics 2-▲ KIC 7065-2 [DDD]
Haydn, J.:Die Schöpfung, w. Lynn Dawson (sop), Neil Rosenshein (ten), John Cheek (bass), Minnesota Chorale Albany 2-▲ AR 005-6-2

A. Wolff (cnd)

Haydn, J.:Sym 1 Teldec ▲ 77309-2

H. Wolff (cnd)

Bartók, B.:Divert Teldec ▲ 73134-2
Bartók, B.:Romanian Folk Dances Pno Teldec ▲ 73134-2
Bizet, G.:Sym 1 Teldec ▲ 77309-2
Christmas with Thomas Hampson, w. Thomas Hampson,(bar) Teldec ▲ 9031-73135-2 [DDD]
Copland, A.:Appalachian Spring—original 13-instrument chamber version Teldec ▲ 2292-46314-2 [DDD]
Copland, A.:Billy the Kid (suite) Teldec ▲ 77310
Copland, A.:Down a Country Lane Teldec ▲ 77310
Copland, A.:Latin American Sketches Teldec ▲ 2292-46314-2 [DDD]
Copland, A.:Music for the Theatre Teldec ▲ 2292-46314-2 [DDD]
Copland, A.:Old American Songs, w. D. Upshaw (sop), T. Hampson (bar) Teldec ▲ 77310
Copland, A.:Poems (8) of Emily Dickinson, w. D. Upshaw (sop) Teldec ▲ 77310
Copland, A.:Quiet City, w. G. Bordner (tpt), T. Tempel (E hn) Teldec ▲ 2292-46314-2 [DDD]
Corigliano, J.:Troubadours, w. Sharon Isbin (gtr) Virgin Classics ▲ CDC 55083
Dvořák, A.:Serenade Strs Teldec ▲ 2292-46315-2 [DDD]
Dvořák, A.:Serenade Strs Teldec ("M Line" series) ▲ 97446-2
Dvořák, A.:Serenade Ww Teldec ("M Line" series) ▲ 97446-2
Dvořák, A.:Serenade Ww Teldec ▲ 2292-46315-2 [DDD]
Falla, M. de:El amor brujo, w. Jennifer Larmore (mez) *(rec Ordway Music Theatre, Saint Paul, MN, Feb. 1993)* Teldec ▲ 90852-2 [DDD]
Foss, L.:American Landscapes, w. Sharon Isbin (gtr) Virgin Classics ▲ CDC 55083
Haydn, J.:Sym 82, "The Bear" Teldec ▲ 9031-174005-2 ZK
Haydn, J.:Sym 83, "The Hen" Teldec ▲ 2292-73133-2 [DDD]
Haydn, J.:Sym 84, "In Nomine Domini" Teldec ▲ 9031-74005-2 ZK
Haydn, J.:Sym 85, "La Reine de France" Teldec ▲ 2292-46313-2 [DDD]
Haydn, J.:Sym 86 Teldec ▲ 2292-46313-2 [DDD]
Haydn, J.:Sym 87 Teldec ▲ 9031-73133-2 [DDD]
Kodály, Z.:Galanta Dances Teldec ▲ 73134-2
Kodály, Z.:Marosszék Dances Teldec ▲ 73134-2
Martin, F.:Fox Trot *(rec Ordway Music Theatre, Saint Paul, MN, Feb. 1993)* Teldec ▲ 90852-2 [DDD]
Milhaud, D.:La Création du monde *(rec Ordway Music Theatre, Saint Paul, MN, Feb. 1993)* Teldec ▲ 90852-2 [DDD]
Respighi, O.:Ancient Airs & Dances—Sets 1 & 3 *(rec St. Paul, Feb. 1993 & Feb. 1994)* Teldec ▲ 91729-2 [DDD]
Respighi, O.:Trittico botticelliano *(rec St. Paul, Sept. 1993)* Teldec ▲ 91729-2 [DDD]
Respighi, O.:Gli uccelli Teldec ▲ 91729-2 [DDD]
Schwantner, J.:From Afar, w. Sharon Isbin (gtr) Virgin Classics ▲ CDC 55083
Shostakovich, D.:Con 1 Pno, w. E. Leonskaja (pno) Teldec ▲ 73282-2
Shostakovich, D.:Con 2 Pno, w. E. Leonskaja (pno) Teldec ▲ 73282-2
Shostakovich, D.:Son 2 Pno, w. E. Leonskaja (pno) Teldec ▲ 73282-2
Walton, W.:Façade (suites) *(rec Ordway Music Theatre, Saint Paul, MN, Feb. 1993)* Teldec ▲ 90852-2 [DDD]

P. Zukerman (cnd)

Bach, Joh. Christian:Sinf concertante, T.284/4, w. P. Zukerman (vn), Yo-Yo Ma (vc) CBS ▲ MK 39964
Bach, Joh. Christian:Sinf for Double Orch, Op. 18/1 CBS ▲ MK 39964
Bach, J.S.:Con 2 Vn, w. P. Zukerman (vn) Philips ▲ 416389-2 [DDD]
Bach, J.S.:Con for 2 Vns, w. Midori (vn), P. Zukerman (vn) Philips ▲ 416389-2 [DDD]
Bach, J.S.:Con for 2 Vns, w. I. Stern (vn), P. Zukerman (vn) CBS ▲ MK 42258
Baroque Music Philips ▲ 412215-2 PH [DDD]
Beethoven, L. van:Romances Vn, w. P. Zukerman (vn) Philips ▲ 420168-2 [DDD]
Boccherini, L.:Con Vc, G.482, w. Yo Yo Ma (vc) CBS ▲ MK 39964

St. Paul CO (cont.)

P. Zukerman (cnd) (cont.)

Heberle, A.:Con Rcr, w. Michala Petri (rcr) Philips ("Digital Classics" series) ▲ 420243-2
Mendelssohn, F.:Con in e Vn & Orch, Op. 64, w. P. Zukerman (vn) Philips ▲ 412212-2 [DDD]
Mendelssohn, F.:Octet Strs Philips ▲ 412212-2 [DDD]
Mozart, W.A.:Adagio Vn, K.261, w. P. Zukerman (vn) CBS ▲ MDK 44654 [DDD] ■ MDT 44654 (D)
Mozart, W.A.:Cons Hn, w. Hermann Baumann (hn) Philips ▲ 412737-2 [DDD]
Mozart, W.A.:Con 17 Pno, w. E. Ax (pno) RCA Victrola ▲ 60136-2 [DDD] ■ 60136-4 (D)
Mozart, W.A.:Con 18 Pno, w. E. Ax (pno) RCA Victrola ▲ 60136-2 [DDD] ■ 60136-4 (D)
Mozart, W.A.:Cons Vn, w. P. Zukerman (vn)—Nos. 1-3 CBS ▲ MDK 44653 [DDD] ■ MDT 44653 (D)
Mozart, W.A.:Cons Vn, w. P. Zukerman (vn)—Nos. 4 & 5 Sony Classical ("Essential Classics" series) ▲ SBK 46540 [ADD] ■ SBT 46540
Mozart, W.A.:Cons Vn, w. P. Zukerman (vn)—Nos. 4 & 5 CBS ▲ MDK 44654 [DDD] ■ MDT 44654 (D)
Mozart, W.A.:Cons Vn, w. P. Zukerman (vn)—Nos. 1-3 Sony Classical ("Essential Classics" series) ▲ SBK 46539 [ADD] ■ SBT 46539
Mozart, W.A.:Rondo Vn, K.269, w. P. Zukerman (vn) CBS ▲ MDK 44647 [DDD]
Mozart, W.A.:Rondo Vn, K.373, w. P. Zukerman (vn) CBS ▲ MDK 44654 [DDD] ■ MDT 44654 (D)
Pachelbel, J.:Canon Philips ▲ 412215-2 [DDD]
Telemann, G.P.:Con in a for Rcr, Vl, w. M. Petri (rcr), P. Zukerman (va) Philips ("Digital Classics" series) ▲ 420243-2 [DDD]
Telemann, G.P.:Con Va Philips ▲ 412215-2 [DDD]
Telemann, G.P.:Duet Rcr & Vn, w. M. Petri (rcr), P. Zukerman (vn) Philips ("Digital Classics" series) ▲ 420243-2 [DDD]
Vivaldi, A.:Cons Vn (misc), w. P. Zukerman (vn)—RV.199 Philips ▲ 416389-2 [DDD]
Vivaldi, A.:Cons Vn, Op. 8/1-4, "The Four Seasons", w. P. Zukerman (vn) CBS ▲ MK 36710 [DDD] ■ IMT 36710 (D)
Vivaldi, A.:Cons Vn, Op. 8/1-4, "The Four Seasons", w. P. Zukerman (vn) CBS ▲ MDK 44644 [DDD] ■ MDT 44644 (D)
Vivaldi, A.:Cons for 2 Vns, w. I. Stern (vn), P. Zukerman (vn)—1—in A CBS ▲ MK 37278 [DDD]

St. Paul's PO

Swack, I.:Elegy for Moss Land, w. G. Campbell (sax), Valcour String Quartet *(rec Aug. 1991)* Centaur ▲ CRC 2111 [DDD]

St. Petersburg Camerata

Hindemith, P.:Trauermusik Sony Classical ▲ SMK 48372
Shostakovich, D.:Chamber Sym, Op. 110a Sony Classical ▲ SMK 48372

S. Sondeckis (cnd)

Arensky, A.:Vars on a Theme of Tchaikovsky Sony Classical ("St Petersburg Classics" series) ▲ SMK 58976
Borodin, A.:Nocturne Str Orch *(rec St. Petersburg, June 1993)* Sony Classical ("Essential Classics" series) 2-▲ SB2K 62406 [ADD]
Haydn, J.:Sym 49, "La Passione" Sony Classical ▲ SMK 48372
Tchaikovsky, P.:Andante cantabile Sony Classical ("St Petersburg Classics" series) ▲ SMK 58976
Tchaikovsky, P.:Elegy Sony Classical ("St Petersburg Classics" series) ▲ SMK 58976
Tchaikovsky, P.:Qt 1 Strs Sony Classical ("St Petersburg Classics" series) ▲ SMK 58976
Tchaikovsky, P.:Serenade Strs Sony Classical ("St Petersburg Classics" series) ▲ SMK 58976
Tchaikovsky, P.:The Snow Maiden (sels)—Melodrama Sony Classical ("St Petersburg Classics" series) ▲ SMK 58976

St. Petersburg Cappella Orch

V. Tchernushenko (cnd)

Le Sueur, J.-F.:Sacred Music, w. *(soloists unknown)*, Guy Touvron Brass Ensemble, St. Petersburg Capella Chorus—March; Unxerunt Salomonem; Tu es Petrus *(rec La Chaise-Dieu Abbey, Aug 22 & 23, 1995)* Koch Schwann ▲ SCH 312082
Paisiello, G.:Sacred Music, w. *(soloists unknown)*, Guy Touvron Brass Ensemble, St. Petersburg Cappella—Mass; Te Deum *(rec La Chaise-Dieu Abbey, Aug 22 & 23, 1995)* Koch Schwann ▲ SCH 312082
Roze, N.:Vivat in aeternum—Vivat Rex, w. *(soloists unknown)*, St. Petersburg Capella Chorus *(rec La Chaise-Dieu Abbey, Aug 22 & 23, 1995)* Koch Schwann ▲ SCH 312082

St. Petersburg Chamber Ensemble

R. Melia (cnd)

Mirzoyan, E.:In Memory of Aram Khachaturian ASV ▲ ASV 916 [DDD]
Mirzoyan, E.:Sym Strs ASV ▲ ASV 916 [DDD]
Mirzoyan, E.:Theme & Vars ASV ▲ ASV 916 [DDD]

St. Petersburg CO

Telemann, G.P.:Cons Vn—in B Sony Classical ("Essential Classics" series) ▲ SBK 53516 ■ SBT 53516
Telemann, G.P.:Musique de Table—Suite No. 3 Sony Classical ("Essential Classics" series) ▲ SBK 53516 ■ SBT 53516
Telemann, G.P.:Suites Orch—in A Sony Classical ("Essential Classics" series) ▲ SBK 53516 ■ SBT 53516

St. Petersburg Classical Music Studio Orch

A. Titov (cnd)

Bach, J.S.:Brandenburg Con 3 Infinity Digital ▲ QK 57216 [DDD]
Bach, J.S.:Brandenburg Con 4 Infinity Digital ▲ QK 57216 [DDD]
Bach, J.S.:Brandenburg Con 6 Infinity Digital ▲ QK 57216 [DDD]
Bach, J.S.:Con 1 Hpd, w. O. Malov (pno) Infinity Digital ▲ QK 57720 [DDD]
Bach, J.S.:Con 3 Hpd, w. O. Malov (pno) Infinity Digital ▲ QK 57720 [DDD]
Bach, J.S.:Con 5 Hpd, w. O. Malov (pno) Infinity Digital ▲ QK 57720 [DDD]
Bach, J.S.:Con 1 for 2 Hpds, w. O. Malov (pno), A. Kustariova (pno) Infinity Digital ▲ QK 57720 [DDD]
Bach, J.S.:Toccatas Hpd, BWV 910-16—Nos. 1 & 2 [w. A. Kiskachi (flute)] Infinity Digital ▲ QK 64096 [DDD]
Beethoven, L. van:Con 3 Pno, w. S. Uruvayev (pno) Infinity Digital ▲ QK 57222 [DDD]
Handel, G.F.:Concerti grossi, Op. 6—No. 7 Infinity Digital ▲ QK 64096 [DDD]
Mozart, W.A.:Adagio & Fugue Strs Infinity Digital ▲ 64331 [DDD]
Mozart, W.A.:Con 19 Pno, w. S. Uruvayev (pno) Infinity Digital ▲ QK 64333 [DDD]
Mozart, W.A.:Con 23 Pno, w. V. Reznikovskaya (pno) Infinity Digital ▲ QK 57259 [DDD]
Mozart, W.A.:Con 27 Pno, w. V. Reznikovskaya (pno) Infinity Digital ▲ QK 57259 [DDD]
Mozart, W.A.:Divert Hns Strs, K.247 Infinity Digital ▲ QK 64332 [DDD]
Mozart, W.A.:Divert Str Qt, K.137 Infinity Digital ▲ QK 64332 [DDD]
Mozart, W.A.:Divert Str Qt, K.138 Infinity Digital ▲ QK 64332 [DDD]
Vivaldi, A.:Cons Vn, Op. 3/1-12, "L'estro armonico", w. V. Gluz (vn), I. Romanyuk (vn)—No. 8 in a, RV.522; No. 11 in d, RV.565 Infinity Digital ▲ QK 57243 [DDD]
Vivaldi, A.:Cons Vn, Op. 8/1-4, "The Four Seasons", w. V. Gluz (vn) Infinity Digital ▲ QK 57243 [DDD]
Vivaldi, A.:Cons Vn, Op. 8/1-4, "The Four Seasons", w. Vladislav Gluz (vn)—Winter Infinity Digital ▲ QK 69255 [DDD]
Vivaldi, A.:Cons for 2 Vns, w. V. Gluz (vn), I. Romanyuk (vn)—in G, RV.516 Infinity Digital ▲ QK 57243 [DDD]

St. Petersburg Conservatory CO

Bach, J.S.:Cant 122, w. St. Petersburg Conservatory Chorus Infinity Digital ▲ QK 57254 [DDD]
Bach, J.S.:Cant 191, w. St. Petersburg Conservatory Chorus Infinity Digital ▲ QK 57254 [DDD]
Bach, J.S.:Christmas Oratorio (sels), w. St. Petersburg Conservatory Chorus—Jauchzet, frohlocket; Ach, mein herzliebes Jesulein; Sinf.; Brich an, o schönes Morgenlicht; Ich steh' an deiner Krippen hier Infinity Digital ▲ QK 57254 [DDD]
Bach, J.S.:Christmas Oratorio (sels), w. St. Petersburg Conservatory Chamber Choir—Jauchzet, frohlocket; Ach, mein herzliebes Jesulein!; Sinf; Brich an, o schönes Morgenlicht; Ich steh'an deiner Krippen hier Infinity Digital ▲ QK 69255 [DDD]
Beethoven, L. van:Die Ruinen von Athen (ov) Infinity Digital ▲ QK 57219 [DDD]
Beethoven, L. van:Sym 3, "Eroica" Infinity Digital ▲ QK 57219 [DDD]
Dvořák, A.:Serenade Strs Infinity Digital ▲ QK 57226 [DDD]

St. Petersburg Conservatory CO (cont.)
Handel, G.F.:Messiah (sels), w. St. Petersburg Conservatory Chamber Choir—For Unto Us a Child is Born; Hallelujah! Infinity Digital ▲ QK 69255 [DDD]
Handel, G.F.:Messiah (sels), w. St. Petersburg Conservatory Chorus—Sinf.; For unto Us a Child Is Born; Pifa (pastoral sym.); He Shall Feed His Flock; Alleluia Chorus Infinity Digital ▲ QK 57254 [DDD]
Mozart, W.A.:Ave verum corpus, w. St. Petersburg Conservatory Chorus Infinity Digital ▲ QK 57254 [DDD]
Tchaikovsky, P.:Serenade Strs Infinity Digital ▲ QK 57226 [DDD]
St. Petersburg Festival Orch
S. Litkov (cnd)
Mozart, W.A.:Con 24 Pno, w. P. Osetinskaya (pno) Infinity Digital ▲ QK 64333 [DDD]
St. Petersburg Hermitage Orch
M. Liljefors (cnd)
Berwald, F.:The Dressmaker Sterling ▲ CDS 1009 2 [AAD/DDD]
Foroni, J.:Ov 3 Sterling ▲ CDS 1009 2 [AAD/DDD]
St. Petersburg New Classical Orch
A. Titov (cnd)
Beethoven, L. van:Con 1 Pno, w. Vladimir Shakin (pno) Infinity Digital ▲ QK 66723 [DDD]
Beethoven, L. van:Con 4 Pno, w. Vladimir Shakin (pno) Infinity Digital ▲ QK 66723 [DDD]
Beethoven, L. van:Music of, w. Nodar Gabunia (pno), Ekaterina Murina (pno)—Allegro con brio [from Sym No. 5]; Adagio sostenuto [from Son No. 14 for Pno]; Scherzo; Allegro vivace [both from Sym No. 3]; Adagio cantabile [from Son No. 8 for Pno]; Egmont Ov; Allegro ma non troppo [from Son No. 23 for Pno]; Adagio un poco moto; Rondo; Allegro [all from Con No. 5 for Pno]; Leonore Ov No. 3 Infinity Digital ▲ QK 61975 [DDD]
Corelli, A.:Concerti grossi, Op. 6—Nos. 1–4, 8 & 9 Infinity Digital ▲ QK 66722 [DDD]
Corelli, A.:Con grosso, Op. 6/8, "Christmas Con" Infinity Digital ▲ QK 69255 [DDD]
Rachmaninoff, S.:Con 3 Pno, w. Alexei Orlovetsky (pno) Infinity Digital ▲ QK 57260 [DDD]
Vivaldi, A.:Cons Vn, Op. 3/1–12, "L'estro armonico"—Op. 3/1; Op. 3/3 [w. Igor Romanyuk (violin)]; Op. 3/9 [w. Vladislav Gluz (violin)]; Op. 3/5 [w. V. Gluz & I. Romanyuk] Infinity Digital ▲ QK 66725 [DDD]
Vivaldi, A.:Cons for 2 Vns, w. Vladislav Gluz (vn), Igor Romanyuk (vn) Infinity Digital ▲ QK 66725 [DDD]
St. Petersburg New Philharmony Orch
Mozart, W.A.:Con 20 Pno, w. S. Uruvayev (pno) Infinity Digital ▲ QK 57232 [DDD]
Mozart, W.A.:Con 21 Pno, w. S. Uruvayev (pno) Infinity Digital ▲ QK 57232 [DDD]
S. Gorkovenko (cnd)
Tchaikovsky, P.:Sleeping Beauty (suite) Infinity Digital ▲ QK 57241 [DDD]
A. Titov (cnd)
Beethoven, L. van:Con 5 Pno, "Emperor", w. A. Sandler (pno) Infinity Digital ▲ QK 57222 [DDD]
Beethoven, L. van:Coriolan Ov Infinity Digital ▲ QK 57220 [DDD]
Beethoven, L. van:Egmont (ov) Infinity Digital ▲ QK 57219 [DDD]
Beethoven, L. van:Die Geschöpfe des Prometheus (ov) Infinity Digital ▲ QK 57220 [DDD]
Beethoven, L. van:Leonore 2 Infinity Digital ▲ QK 57220 [DDD]
Beethoven, L. van:Sym 5 Infinity Digital ▲ QK 57220 [DDD]
Dvořák, A.:Sym 9, "From the New World" Infinity Digital ▲ QK 57225 [DDD]
Mozart, W.A.:Kleine Nachtmusik Infinity Digital ▲ QK 57230
Tchaikovsky, P.:Nutcracker Suite Infinity Digital ▲ QK 57241 [DDD]
Tchaikovsky, P.:Swan Lake (sels) Infinity Digital ▲ QK 57241 [DDD]
St. Petersburg PO
P. Freeman (cnd)
Franck, C.:Symphonic Vars, w. J. Robilette (pno) *(rec 1993)* Pro Arte ▲ CDS 3491
Prokofiev, S.:Con 2 Vn, w. C. Kim (vn) Pro Arte ▲ CDS 3442
Prokofiev, S.:Son Vn, Op. 94bis, w. C. Kim (vn) [arr for vn & orch] Pro Arte ▲ CDS 3442
Schumann, R.:Con Pno, w. J. Robilette (pno) Pro Arte ▲ CDS 3464
Tchaikovsky, P.:Con 2 Pno, w. D. Han (pno) Pro Arte ▲ CDS 3441
M. Jansons (cnd)
Rachmaninoff, S.:Con 1 Pno, w. M. Rudy (pno) EMI Classics ▲ CDC 55188
Rachmaninoff, S.:Con 3 Pno, w. M. Rudy (pno) EMI Classics ▲ CDC 54880
Rachmaninoff, S.:Con 4 Pno, w. M. Rudy (pno) EMI Classics ▲ CDC 55188
Rachmaninoff, S.:Rhapsody on a Theme of Paganini, w. M. Rudy (pno) EMI Classics ▲ CDC 54880
Rachmaninoff, S.:Scherzo EMI Classics ▲ CDC 55140
Rachmaninoff, S.:Symphonic Dances EMI Classics ▲ CDC 54877
Rachmaninoff, S.:Sym 2 EMI Classics ▲ CDC 55140
Rachmaninoff, S.:Sym 3 EMI Classics ▲ CDC 54877
Rachmaninoff, S.:Vocalise EMI Classics ▲ CDC 55140
Y. Temirkanov (cnd)
Prokofiev, S.:Alexander Nevsky, w. Evgenia Gorohovskaya (mez) *(rec Philharmonia Hall, St. Petersburg, Mar 16 & 17, 1993)* RCA Red Seal ▲ 0902-668642-2 [DDD]
Prokofiev, S.:Lt Kijé Suite RCA Red Seal ▲ 09026-60984-2
Prokofiev, S.:Sym 5 RCA Red Seal ▲ 09026-60984-2
Rachmaninoff, S.:Aleko (sels)—Ov. RCA Red Seal ▲ 09026-62710-2
Rachmaninoff, S.:Rhapsody on a Theme of Paganini, w. *(pianist unknown)* RCA Red Seal ▲ 09026-62710-2
Rachmaninoff, S.:Symphonic Dances RCA Red Seal ▲ 09026-62710-2
Rachmaninoff, S.:Sym 2 RCA Red Seal ▲ 09026-61281-2
Rachmaninoff, S.:Vocalise RCA Red Seal ▲ 09026-61281-2
Shostakovich, D.:Sym 5 *(rec Large Shostakovich Hall, 1995)* RCA Red Seal ▲ 0902-668548-2 [DDD]
Shostakovich, D.:Sym 7 *(rec Large Shostakovich Hall, St. Petersburg, Russia, Jan 18–19, 1995)* RCA Red Seal ▲ 09026-62548-2 [DDD]
Shostakovich, D.:Sym 9 *(rec Large Shostakovich Hall, 1995)* RCA Red Seal ▲ 0902-668548-2 [DDD]
Sibelius, J.:Con Vn, w. Vladimir Spivakov (vn) *(rec Coventry, England & St. Petersburg, Russia)* RCA Red Seal ▲ 09026-61701-2 [DDD]
Sibelius, J.:Sym 2 *(rec Coventry, England & St. Petersburg, Russia)* RCA Red Seal ▲ 09026-61701-2 [DDD]
Tchaikovsky, P.:Sym 4 RCA Red Seal 2-▲ 09026-61377-2
Tchaikovsky, P.:Sym 5 RCA Red Seal 2-▲ 09026-61377-2
Tchaikovsky, P.:Sym 6 RCA Red Seal 2-▲ 09026-61377-2
St. Petersburg Philharmony Academic SO
A. Dmitriev (cnd)
Tchaikovsky, P.:The Snow Maiden (sels)—Melodrama; Buffoon's Dance; Entr'acte to Act IV Sony Classical ("St Petersburg Classics" series) ▲ SMK 46680
Tchaikovsky, P.:Sym 5 Sony Classical ("St Petersburg Classics" series) ▲ SMK 46680
V. Fedotov (cnd)
Rimsky-Korsakov, N.:Golden Cockerel (suite) Infinity Digital ▲ QK 57253 [DDD]
St. Petersburg Philharmony CO
V. Altschuler (cnd)
Castelnuovo-Tedesco, M.:Con 1 Gtr, w. M. Tsessos (gtr) Infinity Digital ▲ QK 64335 [DDD]
Villa-Lobos, H.:Con Gtr, w. M. Tsessos (gtr) Infinity Digital ▲ QK 64335 [DDD]
Vivaldi, A.:Cons Gtr, w. M. Tsessos (gtr) Infinity Digital ▲ QK 64335 [DDD]
St. Petersburg Phil String Quartet
Tchaikovsky, P.:Qt in B♭ Strs Audiophile Classics 2-▲ 101.252
Tchaikovsky, P.:Qt 1 Strs Audiophile Classics 2-▲ 101.252
Tchaikovsky, P.:Qt 2 Strs Audiophile Classics 2-▲ 101.252
Tchaikovsky, P.:Qt 3 Strs Audiophile Classics 2-▲ 101.252
St. Petersburg Radio-TV SO
S. Gorkovenko (cnd)
Prokofiev, S.:Peter & the Wolf Infinity Digital ▲ QK 57234 [DDD]

St. Petersburg Radio-TV SO (cont.)
S. Gorkovenko (cnd) (cont.)
Prokofiev, S.:Tales of an Old Grandmother Infinity Digital ▲ QK 57234 [DDD]
Rimsky-Korsakov, N.:Scheherazade Infinity Digital ▲ QK 57253 [DDD]
Tchaikovsky, P.:Nutcracker Suite Infinity Digital ▲ QK 69255 [DDD]
St. Petersburg Soloists
Ustvolskaya, G.:Trio Cl Megadisc ▲ 7858
M. Gantvarg (cnd)
Bach, J.S.:Con 1 Vn, w. Mikhail Gantvarg (vn) Audiophile Classics ▲ 101.021
Bach, J.S.:Con 2 Vn, w. Mikhail Gantvarg (vn) Audiophile Classics ▲ 101.021
Bach, J.S.:Con Vn & Ob, w. Mikhail Gantvarg (vn), Chanjafi Tchinakajev (ob) Audiophile Classics ▲ 101.021
Bach, J.S.:Con for 2 Vns, w. Mikhail Gantvarg (vn), Olga Martinova (vn) Audiophile Classics ▲ 101.021
O. Malov (cnd)
Ustvolskaya, G.:Composition 2 Megadisc ▲ 7858
Ustvolskaya, G.:Son 5 Pno Megadisc ▲ 7858
Ustvolskaya, G.:Sym 4 Megadisc ▲ 7858
R. Martynov (cnd)
Haydn, J.:Con 1 Vc, w. Leonid Gorokhov (vc), St. Petersburg State SO, St. Petersburg Soloists Audiophile Classics ▲ 101.023
Haydn, J.:Con 2 Vc, w. Leonid Gorokhov (vc), St. Petersburg State SO, St. Petersburg Soloists Audiophile Classics ▲ 101.023
Haydn, J.:Con 1 Vn, w. Mikhail Gantvarg (vn), St. Petersburg State SO, St. Petersburg Soloists Audiophile Classics ▲ 101.023
St. Petersburg State Academic Cappella SO
C. Croci (cnd)
Schumann, R.:Con Pno, w. Pavel Egorov (pno) Audiophile Classics ▲ 101.020 [DDD]
V. Ponkin (cnd)
Boccherini, L.:Con Vc, G.475, w. Kyrill Kravtsov (vc) Audiophile Classics ▲ 101.051
Bruch, M.:Kol Nidrei, w. Kyrill Kravtsov (vc) Audiophile Classics ▲ 101.051
Saint-Saëns, C.:Con 1 Vc, w. K. Kravtsov (vc) Audiophile Classics ▲ 101.051
Tchaikovsky, P.:Vars on a Rococo Theme, w. Kyrill Kravtsov (vc) Audiophile Classics ▲ 101.051
A. Tchernushenko (cnd)
Rachmaninoff, S.:Con 1 Pno, w. Vladimir Mischuk (pno) Audiophile Classics ▲ 101.037
Saint-Saëns, C.:Con 3 Vn, w. Alla Aranovskaya (vn) Audiophile Classics ▲ 101.042
V. Tchernushenko (cnd)
Tchaikovsky, P.:Con Vn, w. Anton Barakhovsky (vn) Audiophile Classics ▲ 101.042
St. Petersburg State SO
A. Anichanov (cnd)
Glière, R.:The Bronze Horseman (sels)—Yevgeny; Parasha; Lyric Scene; Dance Scene *(rec St. Petersburg Philharmonic Hall, Feb.–Apr. 1994)* Marco Polo ▲ 8.223675 [DDD]
Glière, R.:Gyul'sara (ov) *(rec St. Petersburg Philharmonic Hall, Feb.–Apr. 1994)* Marco Polo ▲ 8.223675 [DDD]
Glière, R.:Heroic March for the Buryiat-Mongolian ASSR *(rec St. Petersburg Philharmonic Hall, Feb.–Apr. 1994)* Marco Polo ▲ 8.223675 [DDD]
Glière, R.:The Red Poppy *(rec Concert Hall, St. Petersburg Radio, June 1994)* Naxos 2-▲ 8.553496/97 [DDD]
Glière, R.:Shakh-Senem (ov) *(rec St. Petersburg Philharmonic Hall, Feb.–Apr. 1994)* Marco Polo ▲ 8.223675 [DDD]
Khachaturian, A.:Circus *(rec St. Petersburg Radio, 1994)* Naxos ▲ 8.550802 [DDD]
Khachaturian, A.:Gayane (suites) *(rec Aug. 1–3, 1993)* Naxos ▲ 8.550800 [DDD]
Khachaturian, A.:Masquerade (ballet suite) *(rec St. Petersburg Radio, 1994)* Naxos ▲ 8.550802 [DDD]
Khachaturian, A.:Spartacus (suite 4) *(rec St. Petersburg Radio, 1994)* Naxos ▲ 8.550802 [DDD]
Liszt, F.:Con 1 Pno, w. Igor Lebedev (pno) Audiophile Classics ▲ 101.044
Liszt, F.:Con 2 Pno, w. Igor Lebedev (pno) Audiophile Classics ▲ 101.044
Liszt, F.:Totentanz, w. Igor Lebedev (pno) Audiophile Classics ▲ 101.044
Rachmaninoff, S.:Con 2 Pno, w. Alexander Svyatkin (pno) Audiophile Classics ▲ 101.037
Rachmaninoff, S.:Con 3 Pno, w. Natalia Trull (pno) Audiophile Classics ▲ 101.038
Rachmaninoff, S.:Rhapsody on a Theme of Paganini, w. Konstantin Serovatov (pno) Audiophile Classics ▲ 101.038
Rimsky-Korsakov, N.:Antar *(rec St. Petersburg Radio Studio One, St. Petersburg, Russia, June 26– July 2, 1993)* Naxos ▲ 8.550811 [DDD]
Rimsky-Korsakov, N.:Sym 1 *(rec St. Petersburg Radio Studio One, St. Petersburg, Russia, June 26– July 2, 1993)* Naxos ▲ 8.550811 [DDD]
Tchaikovsky, P.:Capriccio italien Audiophile Classics ▲ 101.032
Tchaikovsky, P.:Con 1 Pno, w. Alexander Svyatkin (pno) *(rec St. Petersburg, 1992 & 1993)* Audiophile Classics ▲ 101.024 [DDD]
Tchaikovsky, P.:Con 2 Pno, w. Alexander Svyatkin (pno) *(rec St. Petersburg, 1992 & 1993)* Audiophile Classics ▲ 101.024 [DDD]
Tchaikovsky, P.:Francesca da Rimini Audiophile Classics ▲ 101.031
Tchaikovsky, P.:Hamlet *(rec St. Petersburg, 1993)* Audiophile Classics ▲ 101.030 [DDD]
Tchaikovsky, P.:Manfred Audiophile Classics ▲ 101.034
Tchaikovsky, P.:Marche slave Audiophile Classics ▲ 101.034
Tchaikovsky, P.:Ov 1812 Audiophile Classics ▲ 101.032
Tchaikovsky, P.:Romeo & Juliet *(rec St. Petersburg, 1992 & 1993)* Audiophile Classics ▲ 101.028 [DDD]
Tchaikovsky, P.:Serenade Strs *(rec St. Petersburg, 1993)* Audiophile Classics ▲ 101.029 [DDD]
Tchaikovsky, P.:Sym 1 *(rec St. Petersburg, 1992 & 1993)* Audiophile Classics ▲ 101.028 [DDD]
Tchaikovsky, P.:Sym 2 *(rec St. Petersburg, 1993)* Audiophile Classics ▲ 101.029 [DDD]
Tchaikovsky, P.:Sym 3 *(rec St. Petersburg, 1993)* Audiophile Classics ▲ 101.030 [DDD]
Tchaikovsky, P.:Sym 4 Audiophile Classics ▲ 101.031
Tchaikovsky, P.:Sym 5 Audiophile Classics ▲ 101.032
Tchaikovsky, P.:Sym 6 Audiophile Classics ▲ 101.033
Tchaikovsky, P.:The Tempest Audiophile Classics ▲ 101.033
A. Kantorov (cnd)
Grieg, E.:Con Pno, Op. 16, w. Tatyana Zagorovskaya (pno) Audiophile Classics ▲ 101.020 [DDD]
R. Martynov (cnd)
Haydn, J.:Con 1 Vc, w. Leonid Gorokhov (vc), St. Petersburg Soloists Audiophile Classics ▲ 101.023
Haydn, J.:Con 2 Vc, w. Leonid Gorokhov (vc), St. Petersburg Soloists Audiophile Classics ▲ 101.023
Haydn, J.:Con 1 Vn, w. Mikhail Gantvarg (vn), St. Petersburg Soloists Audiophile Classics ▲ 101.023
Prokofiev, S.:Sym 1 Infinity Digital ▲ QK 57225 [DDD]
Stravinsky, I.:Apollon musagète Infinity Digital ▲ QK 66727 [DDD]
Tchaikovsky, P.:Con 3 Pno, w. Andréi Hotéev (pno) Accord ▲ ACD 202752 [DDD]
St. Petersburg String Quartet [Alla Aranovskaya (vn), Ilya Teplyakov (vn), Andrei Dogadin (va), Leonid Shukaev (vc)]
Borodin, A.:Qt 1 Strs *(rec St. Petersburg, Nov. 1993)* Sony Classical ("St. Petersburg Classics" series) ▲ SMK 64097 [DDD]
Borodin, A.:Qt 2 Strs *(rec St. Petersburg, June 1993)* Sony Classical ("St. Petersburg Classics" series) ▲ SMK 64097 [DDD]
Shostakovich, D.:Qt 1 Strs Sony Classical ▲ SMK 64584
Shostakovich, D.:Qt 2 Strs Sony Classical ▲ SMK 64584
Shostakovich, D.:Qt 3 Strs Sony Classical ("St. Petersburg Classics" series) ▲ SMK 66592
Shostakovich, D.:Qt 4 Strs Sony Classical ▲ SMK 64584
Shostakovich, D.:Qt 5 Strs Sony Classical ("St. Petersburg Classics" series) ▲ SMK 66592
Shostakovich, D.:Qt 7 Strs Sony Classical ("St. Petersburg Classics" series) ▲ SMK 66592
St. Petersburg Trio [Maria Safariants (vn), Leonid Shukayev (vc), Sergei Uryvayev (pno)]
Alyabiev, A.:Trio in E♭ Vn *(rec St. Petersburg Radio Studio, Nov 1994–Feb 1995)* Russian Disc ▲ RDCD 10054 [DDD]

St. Petersburg Trio (cont.)
Borodin, A.:Trio Pno *(rec St. Petersburg Radio Studio, Nov 1994–Feb 1995)* Russian Disc ▲ RDCD 10054 [DDD]
Rimsky-Korsakov, N.:Trio Vn *(rec St. Petersburg Radio Studio, Nov 1994–Feb 1995)* Russian Disc ▲ RDCD 10054 [DDD]

St. Petersburg TV & Broadcast Company SO
S. Gorkovenko (cnd)
Saint-Saëns, C.:Carnival of the Animals Infinity Digital ▲ QK 57234 [DDD]
Strauss (II), Joh.:Music of—Cagliostro in Wien Waltz, Op. 370; Künstlerleben Waltz, Op. 316; Wiener Blut, Op. 354; Gross Wien, Op. 440; Donauweibchen Waltz, Op. 427; An der schönen, blauen Donau, Op. 314; Frühl Infinity Digital ▲ QK 57238 [DDD]

St. Stephen's CO
L. Muti (cnd)
Johnson, H.:Letter to the World Albany ▲ TROY 111 [DDD]
Rendelman Jr., R.:Concertino T Sax, w. James Houlik (sax) Albany ▲ TROY 111 [DDD]
Ross, W.:Mosaics, w. M. Mitchell (pno) Albany ▲ TROY 111 [DDD]
Ward, R.:Concertino Strs Albany ▲ TROY 111 [DDD]

St. Thomas Moore Cathedral Orch
H. Mardirosian (cnd)
Mozart, W.A.:Missa brevis, K.194, w. M. Busching (mez), G. Tucker (ten), P. Fay (bar), C. Dill Smith (sgr), St. Thomas Moore Cathedral Chorus [L] Centaur ▲ CRC 2074 [DDD]
Mozart, W.A.:Tantum ergo, w. Carolyn Dill Smith (sop), Marianna Busching (mez), Gene Tucker (ten), Peter Fay (bar), St. Thomas Moore Cathedral Chorus [L] Centaur ▲ CRC 2074 [DDD]
Mozart, W.A.:Vesperae de Dominica, w. C. Dill Smith (sop), M. Busching (mez), G. Tucker (ten), P. Fay (bar), St. Thomas Moore Cathedral Chorus [L] Centaur ▲ CRC 2074 [DDD]

St.-Etienne Nouvel Orch
P. Fournillier (cnd)
Gounod, C.:Sappho, w. M. Command (sop), S. Coste (sop), C. Popis (ten), E. Faury (bar) Koch Schwann 2-▲ SCH 313112 [DDD]
Massenet, J.:Cléopâtre, w. B. Harries (sop), Danièle Streiff (sop), M. Olmeda (sop), J. Maurette (ten), D. Henry (bar), M. Hacquard (bar), Saint-Etienne Nouvel Chorus [F] *(rec live, Massenet Festival in Saint-Etienne 1990)* Koch Schwann 2-▲ 3-1032-2 [DDD]

Saito Kinen Orch
S. Ozawa (cnd)
Brahms, J.:Hungarian Dances Orch—Nos. 1, 3 & 10 Philips ▲ 432121-2 [DDD]
Brahms, J.:Sym 1 Philips ▲ 432121-2 [DDD]
Brahms, J.:Sym 2 Philips ▲ 434089-2 [DDD]
Brahms, J.:Sym 3 Philips ▲ 434089-2 [DDD]
Stravinsky, I.:Oedipus Rex, w. J. Norman (sop), P. Langridge (ten), P. Schreier (ten), B. Terfel (b-bar) Philips ▲ 438865-2
Takemitsu, T.:Con Va, w. N. Imai (va) Philips ▲ 432176-2 [DDD]
Takemitsu, T.:Eclipse Philips ▲ 432176-2 [DDD]
Takemitsu, T.:November Steps Philips ▲ 432176-2 [DDD]

Salieri CO
T. Pál (cnd)
Mozart, W.A.:Arias, w. E. Palacio (ten)—Miserol O sogno o son desto; Si mostra la sorte; Un aura amorosa [from Cosi fan tutte]; Dalla sua pace [from Don Giovanni]; Il mio tesoro [from Don Giovanni]; Se all'impero, amici Dei Arkadia-Akademia ▲ 138 [DDD]
Muffat, G.:Concerti grossi (12) for Chamber Orchestra (1701)—Delirium amoris; Propitia Sydera; Cor Vigilans *(rec Nov. 10–15, 1993)* Arkadia-Akademia 2-▲ 136 [DDD]
Muffat, G.:Florilegium primum (7 orchestral suites) (1695)—Gratitudo; Impatienta; Constantia *(rec Nov. 10–15, 1993)* Arkadia-Akademia 2-▲ 136 [DDD]
Pietro Metastasio's Kings & Heroes, w. Ernesto Palacio(ten), *(rec Nov. 23–24, 1993)* Arkadia-Akademia ▲ 137 [DDD]
Wagenseil, G.C.:Con in C Vc, w. G. Korosi (vc) *(rec Sept. 14–15, 1993)* Arkadia-Akademia ▲ 130
Wagenseil, G.C.:Syms à 4 parties obligées, w. G. Korosi (vc) *(rec Sept. 14–15, 1993)* Arkadia-Akademia ▲ 130

Salisburg String Quartet members
Viotti, G.B.:Qts Fl, Op. 22, w. Claudio Ferrarini (fl) Stradivarius ▲ STV 33338 [DDD]

Salomon Ensemble
T. Dausgaard (cnd)
Grieg, E.:Elegaic Melodies, Op. 34 Rondo Grammophon ▲ RCD 8342
Grieg, E.:Fugue Rondo Grammophon ▲ RCD 8342
Grieg, E.:Lyric Suite, Op. 54 Rondo Grammofon ▲ RCD 8342
Grieg, E.:Melodies, Op. 53 Rondo Grammophon ▲ RCD 8342
Grieg, E.:Norwegian Melodies, Op. 63 Rondo Grammophon ▲ RCD 8342

Salomon String Quartet
British Music on Hyperion, w. Parley of Instruments, Roy Goodman (cnd), John Mark Ainsley (ten), Graham Johnson (pno), BBC Scottish SO, Anthony Rolfe Johnson (ten), Royal PO, St. Paul's Cathedral Choir, Nash Ensemble, Martyn Hill (ten), Susan Gritton (sop), et al. Hyperion ▲ HYP 15

Salomon String Quartet [Simon Standage (vn), Micaela Comberti (vn), Trevor Jones (va), Jennifer Ward Clarke (vc)]
Abel, C.F.:Qts Strs, Op. 8—Quartet in A for Strings, Op. 8/5 [period instr] Hyperion ▲ CDA 66780
Haydn, J.:Qts Strs, Op. 33, "Russian Qts"—Nos. 1–3 Hyperion ▲ CDA 66681
Haydn, J.:Qts Strs, Op. 33, "Russian Qts"—Nos. 4–6 Hyperion ▲ CDA 66682
Haydn, J.:Qt Strs, Op. 42 Hyperion ▲ CDA 66682
Haydn, J.:Qts Strs, Op. 50, "Prussian Qts"—Nos. 4–6 Hyperion ▲ CDA 66822
Haydn, J.:Qts Strs, Op. 50, "Prussian Qts"—Nos. 1–3 Hyperion ▲ CDA 66821
Haydn, J.:Qts Strs, Op. 55 Hyperion ▲ CDA 66972
Haydn, J.:Qts Strs, Op. 64, "Tost Qts"—Nos. 1–3 Hyperion ▲ CDA 67011
Haydn, J.:Qts Strs, Op. 64, "Tost Qts"—Nos. 4–6 Hyperion ▲ CDA 67012
Haydn, J.:Qts Strs, Op. 71—Nos. 1 & 2 Hyperion ▲ CDA 66065 [AAD]
Haydn, J.:Qts Strs, Op. 71—No. 3 Hyperion ▲ CDA 66098
Haydn, J.:Qts Strs, Op. 74—Nos. 2 & 3 Hyperion ▲ CDA 66214
Haydn, J.:Qts Strs, Op. 74—No. 1 Hyperion ▲ CDA 66098
Marsh, J.:Qt Strs [period instr] Hyperion ▲ CDA 66780
Mozart, W.A.:Qts Pno, w. Richard Burnett (pno) [period instrs] Amon Ra ▲ CD-SAR 31 [DDD]
Mozart, W.A.:Qt 15 Strs Hyperion ▲ CDA 66170 [DAD]
Mozart, W.A.:Qt 19 Strs Hyperion ▲ CDA 66170 [DAD]
Mozart, W.A.:Qnt Cl, K.581, w. Alan Hacker (cl) Amon Ra ▲ CD-SAR 17 [DDD]
Mozart, W.A.:Qnts Strs, w. Simon Whistler (va) Hyperion 2-▲ CDD 22005
Shield, W.:Qts Strs, Op. 31—Quartet in c for Strings, Op. 3/6 [period instr] Hyperion ▲ CDA 66780
Webbe, S.:Vars on *Adeste Fideles* [period instr] Hyperion ▲ CDA 66780
Wesley, S.:Qt Strs [period instr] Hyperion ▲ CDA 66780

Salomon String Quartet members
Mozart, W.A.:Qnts Cl Bas Hn, w. Alan Hacker (cl), Lesley Schatzberger (bas hn) Amon Ra ▲ CD-SAR 17 [DDD]

I Salonisti
Salon Music:Intermezzo RCA Victor ▲ 09478-69298-2 [ADD]
Salon Music, Vol. 5:Serenata RCA Victor ▲ 09478-69299-2 [ADD]

Salterio Duo
A Touch of Spring:Peaceful Poetic Music for Dulcimer & Guitar Classico ▲ CLASSCD 117

Salvation Army Congress Massed Bands
Live at the Crystal Palace, w. National Brass Band Festival Massed Bands, Festival of English Church Music Massed Choir, Handel Festival Choir, Handel Festival Orch, National Union of School Orch, Non-Conformist Union Festival Choir Beulah ▲ 1 PD 1

Salzburg Baroque Ensemble
H. Arman (cnd)
Biber, H. von:Sons (misc), w. Innsbruck Woodwind Circle Ars Musici ("Essence" series) ▲ AME 3022-2 [DDD]
Biber, H. von:Vesperae longiores ac breviores una cum litaniis Laurentanis, w. Kym Amps (sop), Christopher Robson (alt), Anton Rosner (ten), Albert Hartinger (bass), Innsbruck Woodwind Circle, Salzburg Bach Choir, Salzburg St. Benedict College Schola Ars Musici ("Essence" series) ▲ AME 3022-2 [DDD]
E. Ortner (cnd)
Bach, J.S.:Mass in b, BWV 232, w. M. Venuti (sop), C. Kallisch (cta), C. Prégardien (ten), A. Scharinger (bass), Arnold Schoenberg Choir Koch Schwann 2-▲ SCH 312512 [DDD]

Salzburg Camerata
S. Végh (cnd)
Mozart, W.A.:Divert Hns Strs, K.334 Capriccio ▲ 10153 [DDD] △ 80153
Mozart, W.A.:Divert Str Qt, K.136 Capriccio ▲ 10185 [DDD] △ 70185 □ 70185
Mozart, W.A.:Divert Str Qt, K.137 Capriccio ▲ 10185 [DDD] △ 70185 □ 70185
Mozart, W.A.:Divert Str Qt, K.137 LaserLight ▲ 15 647
Mozart, W.A.:Divert Str Qt, K.138 Capriccio ▲ 10153 [DDD] △ 80153 □ 70153
Mozart, W.A.:Kleine Nachtmusik Capriccio ▲ 10185 [DDD] △ 70185 □ 70185

Salzburg Camerata Academica
Graf, Végh (cnd)
Mozart, W.A.:Dances & Marches, Salzburg Mozarteum Orch—Cassation, K.63; 4 Dances, K.101; German Dance, K.605/1; 6 Ländler, K.606; March, K.189; March, K.215; March, K.248; March, K.408/1 & 2; Die Entführung aus dem Serail:March of the Janissaries; 2 Marches, K.335; 5 Contradances, K.609; Idomeneo:Marches:Le nozze di Figaro:Marcia LaserLight ▲ 15 653 [DDD]
E. Hinreiner (cnd)
Mozart, L.:Toy Sym Koch Schwann ▲ CD 316051 [ADD]
Mozart, W.A.:Missa, K.66, w. P. Wise (sop), M. Aoyama (cta), P. Baillie (ten), H. Müller (bass), Salzburg RSO, Mozart Choir [L] *(rec May 1974)* Koch Treasure ▲ 316182 [ADD]
S. Végh (cnd)
Mozart, W.A.:Con 9 Pno, w. A. Schiff (pno) London ▲ 425466-2 [DDD]
Mozart, W.A.:Con 13 Pno, w. A. Schiff (pno) London ▲ 425466-2 [DDD]
Mozart, W.A.:Divert Fl, K.131 LaserLight ▲ 15 862 [DDD]
Mozart, W.A.:Divert Hns Bn, K.205 LaserLight ▲ 15 862 [DDD]
Mozart, W.A.:Divert Hns Strs, K.247 LaserLight ▲ 15 863 [DDD]
Mozart, W.A.:Divert Ob, K.251 LaserLight ▲ 15 863 [DDD]
Mozart, W.A.:Divert Ob, K.251 LaserLight ▲ 15 648 [DDD]
Mozart, W.A.:Divert Ww, K.113 LaserLight ▲ 15 861 [DDD]
Mozart, W.A.:Fant Mechanical Org LaserLight ▲ 15 879 [DDD]
Music of Mozart, w. Franz Liszt CO [cnd:Janos Rolla], Vienna Mozart Ensemble [cnd:Herbert Kraus] Laserlight ♦ 90024 [DDD]

Salzburg CO
Mozart, W.A.:Cassation, K.63, w. G. Hölscher (ob), S. Winiarczyk (ob), R. Schnepps (hn), H. Nerat (hn) *(rec March 28–30, 1992)* Naxos ▲ 8.550609 [DDD]
Mozart, W.A.:Cassation, K.99/63a, w. G. Hölscher (ob), S. Winiarczyk (ob), R. Schnepps (hn), H. Nerat (hn) *(rec March 28–30, 1992)* Naxos ▲ 8.550609 [DDD]
Mozart, W.A.:Cassation, K.100/62a, w. G. Hölscher (ob), S. Winiarczyk (ob), R. Schnepps (hn), H. Nerat (hn) *(rec March 28–30, 1992)* Naxos ▲ 8.550609 [DDD]
H. Nerat (cnd)
Mozart, W.A.:Serenade Vn, K.185 Naxos ▲ 8.550413 [DDD]
Mozart, W.A.:Serenade Vn, K.203 Naxos ▲ 8.550413 [DDD]

Salzburg Chamber Soloists
Mozart, W.A.:Con 5 Vn, w. Boris Belkin (vn) *(rec Mozarteum Grosse Saal, Salzburg, Feb. 21–23, 1994)* Denon ▲ CO 78918 [DDD]
Mozart, W.A.:Divert Hns Bn, K.205 *(rec Mozarteum Grosse Saal, Salzburg, Feb. 21–23, 1994)* Denon ▲ CO 78918 [DDD]
Mozart, W.A.:Sinf concertante Vn, K.364, w. Boris Belkin (vn), Lavard Skou Larsen (va) *(rec Mozarteum Grosse Saal, Salzburg, Feb. 21–23, 1994)* Denon ▲ CO 78918 [DDD]

Salzburg Hofmusik
W. Brunner (cnd)
Biber, H. von:Chi la dura la vince, w. Barbara Schlick (sop), Gerd Türk (ten), Gotthold Schwarz (bass), Xenia Meijer (sgr) CPO 3-▲ CPO 999258 [DDD]

Salzburg Mozart Players
E. Hinreiner (cnd)
Gruber, F.X.:Choral Music, w. *(chorus unknown)*—Hornmesse in D; Hochzeitsmesse in D; Stille Nacht, Heilige Nacht! (3 versions); Heiligste Nacht [G,L] Koch Schwann ▲ CD 313 014 [ADD]

Salzburg Mozarteum Camerata Academica
Brahms, J.:Rhaps Pno, Op. 79 Capriccio ▲ 10 427 [DDD]
G. Anda (cnd)
Mozart, W.A.:Cons Pno, w. G. Anda (pno)—Nos. 1–6, 8, 9 & 11–27 Deutsche Grammophon 10-▲ 429001-2 [ADD]
Mozart, W.A.:Con 6 Pno, w. Géza Anda (pno) *(rec Neues Festspielhaus, Salzburg, Apr 1962)* Deutsche Grammophon ▲ 447436-2 [ADD]
Mozart, W.A.:Con 17 Pno, w. Géza Anda (pno) *(rec Neues Festspielhaus, Salzburg, May 1961)* Deutsche Grammophon ▲ 447436-2 [ADD]
Mozart, W.A.:Con 21 Pno, w. Géza Anda (pno) *(rec Neues Festspielhaus, Salzburg, May 1961)* Deutsche Grammophon ▲ 447436-2 [ADD]
E. Hinreiner (cnd)
Mozart, W.A.:Kyrie, K.322/296a, w. Salzburg Mozarteum Chorus Studio SM ▲ 2518
Mozart, W.A.:Kyrie, K.341/368 Studio SM ▲ 2518
Mozart, W.A.:Misercordias Studio SM ▲ 2518
Mozart, W.A.:Vesperae, w. Christa Degler (sop), Margarete Kissel (alt), Desmond Clayton (ten), Hartmut Müller (bass) Studio SM ▲ 2518
S. Végh (cnd)
Bartók, B.:Divert—Allegro assai Capriccio ▲ 14 860 [DDD]
Beethoven, L. van:Qt 14 Strs—Presto Capriccio ▲ 14 860 [DDD]
Brahms, J.:Qnt 2 Strs—Adagio Capriccio ▲ 14 860 [DDD]
Haydn, J.:The Seven Last Words of Christ on the Cross—Grave e cantabile Capriccio ▲ 14 860 [DDD]
Mozart, W.A.:Con 18 Pno, w. A. Schiff (pno) London ▲ 421259-2 [DDD] □ 421259-5
Mozart, W.A.:Con 19 Pno, w. A. Schiff (pno) London ▲ 421259-2 [DDD] □ 421259-5
Mozart, W.A.:Con 20 Pno, w. A. Schiff (pno) London ▲ 430510-2 [DDD]
Mozart, W.A.:Con 21 Pno, w. A. Schiff (pno) London ▲ 430510-2 [DDD]
Mozart, W.A.:Con 22 Pno, w. A. Schiff (pno) London ▲ 425855-2 [DDD]
Mozart, W.A.:Con 23 Pno, w. A. Schiff (pno) London ▲ 425855-2 [DDD]
Mozart, W.A.:Con 27 Pno, w. A. Schiff (pno) London ▲ 421259-2 [DDD] □ 421259-5
Mozart, W.A.:Music of—Eine kleine Nachtmusik, K.525 [Allegro]; Divert in D, K.251 [Andantino]; Serenade in D, K.250, "Haffner" [Menuetto]; Cassation in G, K.63 [Finale. Allegro assai]; Divertimento in D, K.205 [Adagio]; Contredance No. 1, K.609; Minuet No. 1, K.164; Serenade No. 1 in D, K.100 [Finale. Allegro] Capriccio ▲ 14 860 [DDD]
Schoenberg, A.:Verklärte Nacht Capriccio ▲ 10 427 [DDD]
Schubert, Franz:Music of—Sym No. 6 in C, D.589 [Andante]; Sym No. 9 in C, D.944, "The Great" [Scherzo. Allegro vivace] Capriccio ▲ 14 860 [DDD]

Salzburg Mozarteum CO
E. Hinreiner (cnd)
Haydn, J.:Mass 13, "Schöpfungsmesse", w. *(soloists unknown)*, Salzburg Radio Chorus Studio SM 2-▲ 2441

Salzburg Mozarteum Orch
Vol. 4, Classics Go to the Movies, w. Budapest SO, Budapest PO, Christian Altenburger, Ernst Mayer-Schieming, German Bach Soloists, Sofia National Opera Orch — LaserLight ▲ 15 644
Vol. 5, Classics Go to the Movies, w. Hannes Käster (org), Bavarian RSO, Ludovic Spiess (ten), Virginia Zeani (sop), Rumanian Opera Orch, Rumanian Radio-TV Studio Orch, Sofia PO, Budapest SO, Philharmonia Orch — LaserLight ▲ 15 645
Mozart, W.A.:Complete Mozart Edition, w. E. Gruberova (sop), E. Mathis (sop), L. Popp (mez), F. Araiza (ten), P. Schreier (ten), W. Berry (bass) — Philips 8-▲ 422523-2 [ADD]
Mozart, W.A.:Music of, Hungarian State Orch, London PO—sels from Syms. 24, 29, 31, 33, 35, 36, 38, 39, 40 & 41 — LaserLight ▲ 15 646 [DDD]

E. Graf (cnd)
Mozart, W.A.:Sym 1 — LaserLight ▲ 15 647 [DDD]

H. Graf (cnd)
Mozart, W.A.:Dances & Marches—Marches, K.62, 189, 214, 215, 237, 248, 249, 335/1&2, 408/1-3, 445; 3 marches from Idomeneo; march from Le nozze di Figaro — LaserLight ▲ 15 886 [DDD]
Mozart, W.A.:Dances & Marches—Contredanses, K.534, 535, 587; 2 Contredanses, K.603; 6 Contredanses, K.462; 3 German Dances, K.605; 6 German Dances, K.509; 6 German Dances, K.600; 5 Minuets, K.461; 2 Quadrilles, K.463 — LaserLight ▲ 15 887 [DDD]
Mozart, W.A.:Syms (comp)—(5) No. 7 in D, K.45; in G, K.45a. "Old Lambach"; in B♭, K.45b; No. 8 in D, K.48; in F, K.76/42a — LaserLight ▲ 15 868 [DDD]
Mozart, W.A.:Syms (comp)—(6) No. 1 in E♭, K.16; in a, K.16a; No. 4 in D, K.19; in F, K.19a; No. 5 in B♭, K.22; No. 6 in F, K.43 — LaserLight ▲ 15 867 [DDD]
Mozart, W.A.:Syms (comp)—(6) No. 9 in C, K.73 (75a); No. 10 in G, K.74; in D, K.81/73l; No. 11 in D, K.84/73g; in D, K.95/73a; in F, K.75 — LaserLight ▲ 15 869 [DDD]
Mozart, W.A.:Sym 5 — LaserLight ▲ 15 647 [DDD]
Mozart, W.A.:Sym 6 — LaserLight ▲ 15 647 [DDD]
Mozart, W.A.:Sym 34 — LaserLight ▲ 15 864 [DDD]
Mozart, W.A.:Sym 35 — LaserLight ▲ 15 864 [DDD]
Mozart, W.A.:Sym 36 — LaserLight ▲ 15 864 [DDD]
Mozart, W.A.:Sym 38 — LaserLight ▲ 15 865 [DDD]
Mozart, W.A.:Sym 39 — LaserLight ▲ 15 865 [DDD]
Mozart, W.A.:Sym 40 — LaserLight ♦ 90001 [DDD]
Mozart, W.A.:Sym 40 — LaserLight ▲ 15 829 [DDD]
Mozart, W.A.:Sym 41 — LaserLight ♦ 90002 [DDD]
Mozart, W.A.:Sym 41 — LaserLight ▲ 15 866 [DDD]
Mozart, W.A.:Sym 41 — LaserLight ♦ 90001 [DDD]

Graf, Végh (cnd)
Mozart, W.A.:Dances & Marches, w. Salzburg Camerata Academica—Cassation, K.63; 4 Dances, K.101; German Dance, K.605/1; 6 Ländler, K.606; March, K.189; March, K.215; March, K.248; March, K.408/1 & 2; Die Entführung aus dem Serail:March of the Janissaries; 2 Marches, K.335; 5 Contradances, K.609; Idomeneo:Marches:Le nozze di Figaro:Marcia — LaserLight ▲ 15 653 [DDD]

L. Hager (cnd)
Mozart, W.A.:Complete Mozart Edition, w. A. Augér (sop), E. Gruberova (sop), I. Cotrubas (sop), A. Baltsa (mez), W. Hollweg (ten) — Philips 3-▲ 422529-2 [ADD]
Mozart, W.A.:Complete Mozart Edition, w. A. Augér (sop), E. Mathis (sop), A. Baltsa (mez), P. Schreier (ten) — Philips 3-▲ 422530-2 [ADD]
Mozart, W.A.:Complete Mozart Edition, w. B. Fassbaender (mez), T. Moser (ten), B. McDaniel (bar) — Philips 3-▲ 422533-2 [ADD]
Mozart, W.A.:Complete Mozart Edition, w. A. Augér (sop), E. Mathis (sop), H. Schwarz (mez), A. Rolfe Johnson (ten), Salzburg Mozarteum Chorus — Philips 2-▲ 422526-2 [ADD]
Mozart, W.A.:Complete Mozart Edition, w. A. Augér (sop), E. Mathis (sop), J. Varady (sop), H. Donath (sop), P. Schreier (ten) — Philips 3-▲ 422532-2 [ADD]
Mozart, W.A.:Complete Mozart Edition, w. E. Mathis (sop), E. Gruberova (sop), E. Moser (sop), L. Popp (mez), P. Schreier (ten) — Philips 2-▲ 422531-2 [ADD]
Mozart, W.A.:Finta semplice, w. Helen Donath (sop), Jutta-Renate Ihloff (sop), Teresa Berganza (mez), A. Rolfe Johnson (ten), Thomas Moser (ten), Robert Lloyd (b-bar), Robert Holl (bass) [I] — Orfeo 3-▲ 085843 [DDD]
Mozart, W.A.:Mitridate, w. M. Zara (sop), E. Gabry (sgr), G. Stanley (sgr) [I] *(rec live in Salzburg, Jan. 31, 1970)* — Memories 2-▲ HR 4156/57 (m) [ADD]
Mozart, W.A.:Sym 40 *(rec 1974)* — Allegretto ▲ ACD 8206
Mozart, W.A.:Sym 41 *(rec 1974)* — Allegretto ▲ ACD 8206
Mozart, W.A.:Zaide, w. J. Blegen (sop), I. Hollweg (sop), T. Moser (ten), W. Schöne (bass), R. Holl (bass) [G] — Orfeo 2-▲ 055832 [DDD]

E. Hinreiner (cnd)
Mozart, W.A.:Church Sons, w. R. Kuppelwieser (org)—K. 328 — Pro Arte ▲ CDD 471 [DDD]
Mozart, W.A.:Exsultate, w. G. Fuchs (sop) [L] — Pro Arte ▲ CDD 471 [DDD]
Mozart, W.A.:Missa, K.317, w. G. Fuchs (sop), Novak (alt), Sailer (ten), H. Müller (bass), Salzburg Mozarteum Chorus [L] — Pro Arte ▲ CDD 471 [DDD]

J. Messner (cnd)
Mozart, W.A.:Church Sons *(rec Aug 24, 1952)* — Orfeo d'or ("Festspiel Dokumente" series) ▲ 396951
Mozart, W.A.:Grabmusik, w. Maria Seebach (sop), Otto Wiener (bass), Salzburg Cathedral Choir *(rec Aug 24, 1952)* — Orfeo d'or ("Festspiel Dokumente" series) ▲ 396951

B. Paumgartner (cnd)
Mozart, W.A.:Missa, K.427, w. Annelohre Cahnbley (sop), Maria Stader (sop), George Maran (ten), Walter Raninger (bass), Salzburg Radio Chorus, Salzburg Mozarteum Chorus *(rec Aug 16, 1958)* — Orfeo d'or ("Festspiel Dokumente" series) ▲ 397951 (m)

J.-P. Rampal (cnd)
Cimarosa, D.:Con for 2 Fls, w. S. Kudo (fl), J.-P. Rampal (fl) — Sony Classical ▲ SK 45930 [DDD]
Mozart, W.A.:Concertone Vns, w. J.-P. Rampal (fl), S. Kudo (fl) — Sony Classical ▲ SK 45930 [DDD]
Stamitz, A.:Con Fls, w. J.-P. Rampal (fl), S. Kudo (fl) — Sony Classical ▲ SK 45930 [DDD]
Vivaldi, A.:Con for 2 Fls, w. J.-P. Rampal (fl), S. Kudo (fl) — Sony Classical ▲ SK 45930 [DDD]

Salzburg Mozarteum String Quartet
Mozart, W.A.:Qts Strs, K.Anh.210-213—Nos. 2 & 4 — PMG ("Vienna Master" series) ▲ CD 160226 [DDD]
Mozart, W.A.:Qts Strs, K.Anh.210-213—Nos. 1 & 3 — PMG ("Vienna Master" series) ▲ CD 160225 [DDD]
Mozart, W.A.:Qts Strs (misc)—Nos. 14-19, "The Haydn Quartets" — Vivace 3-▲ E 317 [DDD]
Mozart, W.A.:Qts Strs (misc)—Nos. 14 & 18 — Pro Arte ▲ CDD 426
Mozart, W.A.:Qts Strs (misc)—Nos. 15, 16 & 17 — Pro Arte ▲ CDD 427
Mozart, W.A.:Qt 1 Strs — Pro Arte ▲ CDD 425
Mozart, W.A.:Qt 2 Strs — Pro Arte ▲ CDD 425
Mozart, W.A.:Qt 3 Strs — Pro Arte ▲ CDD 425
Mozart, W.A.:Qt 4 Strs — Pro Arte ▲ CDD 425
Mozart, W.A.:Qt 14 Strs — PMG ("Vienna Master" series) ▲ CD 160225 [DDD]
Mozart, W.A.:Qt 15 Strs — PMG ("Vienna Master" series) ▲ CD 160225 [DDD]
Mozart, W.A.:Qt 16 Strs — PMG ("Vienna Master" series) ▲ CD 160226 [DDD]
Mozart, W.A.:Qt 17 Strs — PMG ("Vienna Master" series) ▲ CD 160226 [DDD]
Mozart, W.A.:Qt 17 Strs — Vivace ▲ 596 [DDD]
Mozart, W.A.:Qt 19 Strs — Pro Arte ▲ CDD 425
Mozart, W.A.:Qt 19 Strs — Vivace ▲ 596 [DDD]

Salzburg Orch

B. Walter (cnd)
Mozart, W.A.:Don Giovanni, w. E. Rethberg (sop), L. Helletsgruber (sop), M. Bokor (mez), D. Borgioli (ten), A. Lazzari (ten), E. Pinza (bass), Salzburg Mozarteum Chorus [I] *(rec live, Salzburg, Aug. 2, 1937)* — Melodram ("Connaisseur" series) 3-▲ CD 37506 (m) [AAD]

Salzburg Piano Trio
Granados, E.:Trio Pno — CPO ▲ CPO 999365

Salzburg Piano Trio members
Granados, E.:Danzas españolas (10)—No. 6 (Rondalla aragonesa for Cello & Piano) — CPO ▲ CPO 999365
Granados, E.:Goyescas (intermezzo) — CPO ▲ CPO 999365
Granados, E.:Madrigal — CPO ▲ CPO 999365
Granados, E.:Son Vn — CPO ▲ CPO 999365

Salzburg RSO

E. Hinreiner (cnd)
Haydn, M.:Requiem in c, w. Siglinde Damisch (sop), Gabriele Schreckenbach (mez), Chris Merritt (ten), Hans Udo Müller (pno), Gerhard Walterskirchen (org), Mozart Choir *(rec June 1981)* — Koch Treasure ▲ 31608-2 [ADD]
Mozart, W.A.:Missa, K.66, w. P. Wise (sop), M. Aoyama (cta), P. Baillie (ten), H. Müller (bass), Salzburg Camerata Academica, Mozart Choir [L] *(rec May 1974)* — Koch Treasure ▲ 316182 [ADD]

Salzburg Soloists
Glass Music from Mozart's Time, w. James, Dennis (glass hmc), Salzburg Soloists [cnd:Luz Leskowitz] — Syrinx ▲ CSR 91101 [DDD]

Salzburg String Quartet
Boccherini, L.:Minuetto — Preiser ▲ 93387 [ADD]
Haydn, J.:Qts Strs, Op. 76, "Erdődy Qts"—No. 2 — Preiser ▲ 93387 [ADD]
Mozart, W.A.:Kleine Nachtmusik, w. Rudolf Harlander (db) — Preiser ▲ 93387 [ADD]

San Cassiano Musici

B. Brookshire (cnd)
Purcell, H.:Dido & Aeneas, w. Cassandra Hoffman (sop—Belinda), Arlene Travis (sop—2nd Witch), Desirée Halac (mez—Sorceress/Spirit), Jennifer Lane (mez—Dido), Elizabeth Norman (alt), Thomas Bogdan (ten—A Sailor), Michael Brown (bar—Aeneas), Curtis Streetman (bar), Caitriona O'Leary (sgr—2nd Woman), Sarah Pillow (sgr—1st Witch) *(rec St. Ignatius of Antioch Episcopal Church, New York City, Spring 1995)* — Vox Classics ▲ VOX 7518

San Diego CO
Barber, S.:Music of, w. Alexa Still (fl), Chicago SO, Atlantic Sinfonietta, New Zealand SO, Arioso Wind Quintet, Capricorn, Repertory Singers—Capricorn Con; Canzone; Fadograph of a Yestern Scene; Cave of the Heart; Adagio for Strs; Souvenirs; Hermit Songs; To Be Sung on Water; The Lovers; Summer Music — Koch International Classics ▲ KIC 7361

D. Barra (cnd)
Arnold, M.:Con for 2 Vns, w. I. Gruppman (pno), V. Gruppman (pno) *(rec Nov 29, 1991)* — Koch International Classics ▲ KIC 7134-2 [DDD]
Arnold, M.:Serenade — Koch International Classics ▲ KIC 7607
Arnold, M.:Serenade *(rec Nov 29, 1991)* — Koch International Classics ▲ KIC 7134-2 [DDD]
Arnold, M.:Sinfoniettas 1 & 2 *(rec Nov 29, 1991)* — Koch International Classics ▲ KIC 7134-2 [DDD]
Barber, S.:Adagio Strs — Koch International Classics ▲ KIC 7206 [DDD]
Barber, S.:Capricorn Con, Arioso Wind Quintet — Koch International Classics ▲ KIC 7206 [DDD]
Barber, S.:Horizon — Koch International Classics ▲ KIC 7206 [DDD]
Barber, S.:Knoxville:Summer of 1915, w. Ruth Golden (sop) — Koch International Classics ▲ KIC 7206 [DDD]
Barber, S.:Serenade — Koch International Classics ▲ KIC 7206 [DDD]
Bloch, E.:Con grosso 1, w. S. D. Smith (pno) — Koch International Classics ▲ KIC 7196 [DDD]
Bloch, E.:Con grosso 2 — Koch International Classics ▲ KIC 7196 [DDD]
Glinka, M.:Kamarinskaya — Koch International Classics ▲ KIC 7042-2 [DDD]
Ibert, J.:Concertino da camera, w. M. Whitcombe (sax) — Koch International Classics ▲ KIC 7094-2 [DDD]
Ibert, J.:Divert Orch — Koch International Classics ▲ KIC 7094-2 [DDD]
Kabalevsky, D.:The Comedians — Koch International Classics ▲ KIC 7042-2 [DDD]
Menotti, G.C.:Cantilena e scherzo, w. M. R. Hays (hp) — Koch International Classics ▲ KIC 7215 [DDD]
Porter, Q.:Ukrainian Suite — Koch International Classics ▲ KIC 7196 [DDD]
Poulenc, F.:Sinfonietta — Koch International Classics ▲ KIC 7094-2 [DDD]
Prokofiev, S.:Summer Day — Koch International Classics ▲ KIC 7042-2 [DDD]
Respighi, O.:Poema autunnale, w. I. Gruppman (vn) — Koch International Classics ▲ KIC 7215 [DDD]
Respighi, O.:Suite Org, w. H. C. Koman (org) — Koch International Classics ▲ KIC 7215 [DDD]
Rodrigo, J.:Madrigales amatorias, w. R. Golden (sop) — Koch International Classics ▲ KIC 7160-2 [DDD]
Rodrigo, J.:Viejos aires de danza — Koch International Classics ▲ KIC 7160-2 [DDD]
Rodrigo, J.:Zarabanda lejana y villancico — Koch International Classics ▲ KIC 7160-2 [DDD]
Tchaikovsky, P.:Suite 4 — Koch International Classics ▲ KIC 7042-2 [DDD]
Turina, J.:La oracion del torero — Koch International Classics ▲ KIC 7160-2 [DDD]
Turina, J.:Rapsodia sinfónica, w. G. Romero (pno) — Koch International Classics ▲ KIC 7160-2 [DDD]

San Diego SO

P. Erös (cnd)
Wayditch, G. von:Jesus before Herod, w. Michael Best (ten—Jappeticus), Christopher Lindbloom (sgr—Philippo/Herod), Eileen Moss (sgr—Pabula), Vincent Russo (sgr—Pabo), Stephen A. Scot-Shepherd (sgr—Luke the Evangelist), Pauline Tweed (sgr—1st & 2nd girls), San Diego Master Chorale *(rec 1979)* — VAI Audio 2-▲ VAIA 1095-2 [ADD]

Y. Talmi (cnd)
Berlioz, H.:Harold in Italy, w. Rivka Golani (va) *(rec Copley Symphony Hall, San Diego, May 13-14, 1995)* — Naxos ▲ 8.553034 [DDD]
Berlioz, H.:Ovs—Les Francs-Juges, Op.3 *(rec Copley Symphony Hall, San Diego, May 13-14, 1995)* — Naxos ▲ 8.553034 [DDD]
Berlioz, H.:Ovs—Benvenuto Cellini, Op. 23; Waverly, Op. 1; Beatrice & Benedict; King Lear, Op. 4 [w. Elizabeth Green (oboe)]; Roman Carnival, Op. 9 [w. Sidney Green (horn)]; Rob Roy [w. S. Green (horn), Sheila Sterling (harp)]; Le Corsaire, Op. 21 *(rec Copley Symphony Hall, San Diego, CA, Jan. 28-30, 1994)* — Naxos ▲ 8.550999 [DDD]
Berlioz, H.:Rêverie et caprice, w. Igor Gruppman (vn) *(rec Copley Symphony Hall, San Diego, May 13-14, 1995)* — Naxos ▲ 8.553034 [DDD]
Berlioz, H.:Roméo et Juliette (sels), w. San Diego Master Chorale—Intro; Prologue [Ball at the Capulets]; Romeo Alone; Love Scene; Queen Mab Scherzo; Romeo at the tomb *(rec Copley Symphony Hall, San Diego, CA, Nov. 19-20, 1994)* — Naxos ▲ 8.553195 [DDD]
Berlioz, H.:Les Troyens (sels), w. San Diego Master Chorale—Prelude; Royal Hunt & Storm *(rec Copley Symphony Hall, San Diego, CA, Nov. 19-20, 1994)* — Naxos ▲ 8.553195 [DDD]
Glière, R.:Sym 3, "Il'ya Muromets" — Pro Arte ▲ CDS 589

San Diego SO Ensemble

H. Sollberger (cnd)
Reynolds, R.:Transfigured Wind 2, w. J. Fonville (fl) — New World ▲ NW 80401-2 [DDD]
Reynolds, R.:Whispers out of Time, w. J. Négyesy (vn), Liu (va), P. Farrell (vc), B. Turetzky (db) — New World ▲ NW 80401-2 [DDD]

San Francisco Contemporary Music Players
Harrison, L.:The Perilous Chapel — New Albion ▲ NA 055
Thow, J.:Songs, w. Stephanie Friedman (mez) — Music & Arts ▲ CD 915

S. Mosko (cnd)
Lazarof, H.:Prayers — Delos ▲ DE 3124 [DDD]

San Francisco Contemporary Music Players [Peter Wahrhaftig (tuba), William Winant (perc), Marvin Tartak (cel), Roy Malan (vn)]
Feldman, Morton:Vertical Thoughts 5, w. Joan La Barbara (sop) *(rec Fantasy Studios, Berkeley, CA, O'Henry Studios, Burbank, CA & Metamusic Productions, Los Angeles, CA, Jan 18, Aug 25-26 & Dec 1)* — New Albion ▲ NA 085

San Francisco Contemporary Music Players [Roy Malan (vn), Marvin Tartak (pno)]
Feldman, Morton:Voice, Vn & Pno, w. Joan La Barbara (sop) *(rec Fantasy Studios, Berkeley, CA, O'Henry Studios, Burbank, CA & Metamusic Productions, Los Angeles, CA, Jan 18, Aug 25-26 & Dec 1)* — New Albion ▲ NA 085

San Francisco Guitar Quartet
Biberian, G.:Waltzes (2) — Klavier ▲ KCD 11028

▲ = CD ♦ = Enhanced CD Δ = MD ▮ = Cassette Tape □ = DCC

San Francisco Guitar Quartet (cont.)
Falla, M. de:Gtr Music—The Miller Dance; Pantomime; Spanish Dance; The Magic Circle; Ritual Fire Dance Klavier ▲ KCD 11028
Falu, E.:Gtr Music—La Cuartelera; La Fronteriza Klavier ▲ KCD 11028
Moreno Torroba, F.:Gtr Music Klavier ▲ KCD 11028
Rodrigo, J.:Gtr Music—Estudiantina Klavier ▲ KCD 11028

San Francisco Guitar Quartet [J. Colgan (gtr), T. Fox (gtr), G. Stewart (gtr), L. Zemlin (gtr)]
San Francisco Guitar Quartet
The San Francisco Guitar Quartet:Spanish Music Klavier ■ KC 573

San Francisco Opera Orch
K. Böhm (cnd)
Beethoven, L. van:Fidelio, w. Judith Blegen (sop), Leonie Rysanek (sop), Jon Vickers (ten), Walter Berry (bass), John Macurdy (bass), Giorgio Tozzi (bass), San Francisco Opera Chorus Melodram 2-▲ CDM 27086
R. Bonynge (cnd)
Bellini, V.:I Puritani (sels), w. J. Sutherland (sop), D. Cole (sop), A. Kraus (ten), R. Wolansky (bar), N. Ghiuselev (bass), San Francisco Opera Chorus *(rec live, San Francisco, 9/2/66)* Golden Age of Opera ▲ GAO 133 [ADD]
V. Gergiev (cnd)
Massenet, J.:Hérodiade, w. Renée Fleming (sop—Salome), Dolora Zajick (mez—Hérodiade), Plácido Domingo (ten—Jean), Juan Pons (bar—Erode), Kenneth Cox (bass—Phanuel), San Francisco Opera Chorus Sony Classical 2-▲ S2K 66847
Massenet, J.:Hérodiade (sels), w. Renée Fleming (sop—Salomé), Dolora Zajick (mez—Hérodiade), Plácido Domingo (ten—Jean), Juan Pons (bar—Hérode), Hector Vásquez (bar—Vitellius), Kenneth Cox (bass—Phanuel), San Francisco Opera Chorus Sony Classical ▲ SK 61965
Massenet, J.:Hérodiade (sels), w. Renée Fleming (sop), Dolora Zajick (mez), Kristin Clayton (sgr), Plácido Domingo (ten), Kenneth Cox (bass), Juan Pons (bar), Hector Vásquez (sgr), San Francisco Opera Chorus—highlights *(rec San Francisco Opera, Nov 1994)* Sony Classical ▲ SK 61965
C. Mackerras (cnd)
Verdi, G.:Un ballo in maschera (sels), w. M. Arroyo (sop), L. Pavarotti (ten)—Ma dall'arido stelo...Teco io sto *(rec Nov. 5, 1971)* Golden Age of Opera 2-▲ GAO 164/65 [ADD]
E. McArthur (cnd)
Kirsten Flagstad Recordings from 1935–39, w. Kirsten Flagstad (sop), Philadelphia Orch [cnd:Eugene Ormandy], Hans Lange (cnd) Nimbus ▲ NI 7847
Wagner, R.:Arias & Scenes, w. Kirsten Flagstad (sop), Lauritz Melchior (ten), RCA Victor SO—duets from Lohengrin; Tristan und Isolde; Götterdämmerung; Parsifal Pearl ▲ PEA 9190
F. Molinari-Pradelli (cnd)
Puccini, G.:Tosca, w. Leonie Rysanek (sop), Russell Christopher (ten), Andrea Velis (ten), Clifford Harvuot (bar), Cornell MacNeil (bar), Fernando Corena (bass), Paul Plishka (bass), San Francisco Opera Chorus Melodram 2-▲ CDM 27508
Ormandy, McArthur, Walter (cnd)
Wagner, R.:Arias & Scenes, w. Kirsten Flagstad (sop), Lauritz Melchior (bar), Philadelphia Orch, RCA Victor SO, New York PO—arias & duets from Lohengrin, Tristan & Isolde, Götterdämmerung, Parsifal & Fidelio *(rec New York City, 1939–41)* Grammofono 2000 ▲ GRM 78526 (m)
Walter, MacArthur, Sargent (cnd)
Wagner, R.:Arias & Scenes, w. K. Flagstad (sop), L. Melchior (ten), New York PO, RCA Victor SO, BBC SO—selections from Götterdämering; Tristan & Isolde; Lohengrin Memories 2-▲ HR 4456/57 [ADD]

San Francisco SO
H. Blomstedt (cnd)
Bartók, B.:Con Orch London ▲ 443773-2
Bartók, B.:Kossuth London ▲ 443773-2
Brahms, J.:Alto Rhap, w. J. van Nes (mez), San Francisco Sym Chorus [G] London ▲ 430281-2 [DDD]
Brahms, J.:Begräbnisgesang, w. San Francisco Sym Chorus [G] London ▲ 430281-2 [DDD]
Brahms, J.:Ein Deutsches Requiem, w. Elizabeth Norberg-Schulz (sop), Wolfgang Holzmair (bar) London ▲ 443771-2
Brahms, J.:Gesang der Parzen, w. San Francisco Sym Chorus [G] London ▲ 430281-2 [DDD]
Brahms, J.:Nänie, w. San Francisco Sym Chorus [G] London ▲ 430281-2 [DDD]
Brahms, J.:Schicksalslied, w. San Francisco Sym Chorus [G] London ▲ 430281-2 [DDD]
Bruckner, A.:Sym 4, "Romantic" London ▲ 443327-2 [DDD]
Bruckner, A.:Sym 6 London ▲ 436129-2
Chopin, F.:Con 1 Pno, w. Olli Mustonen (pno) *(rec Davies Symphony Hall, San Francisco, May 16 & 17, 1994)* London ▲ 444518-2 [DDD]
Grieg, E.:Peer Gynt, w. M. Häggander (sop), U. Malmberg (bar), *(chorus unknown)* [N] London ▲ 425448-2 [DDD]
Grieg, E.:Peer Gynt Suites, Opp. 46 & 55 London ▲ 425857-2 [DDD]
Harbison, J.:Con Ob, w. William Bennett (ob) *(rec Oct. 8, 1993)* London ▲ 443376-2 [DDD]
Harbison, J.:Sym 2 *(rec May 27, 1993)* London ▲ 443376-2 [DDD]
Hindemith, P.:Concert Music Brass & Strs London ▲ 433809-2 [DDD]
Hindemith, P.:Mathis der Maler (sym) London ▲ 421523-2 [DDD]
Hindemith, P.:Nobilissima visione London ▲ 433809-2 [DDD]
Hindemith, P.:Der Schwanendreher, w. G. Walther (va) London ▲ 433809-2 [DDD]
Hindemith, P.:Symphonic Metamorphosis on Themes of Carl Maria von Weber London ▲ 421523-2 [DDD]
Hindemith, P.:Trauermusik London ▲ 421523-2 [DDD]
Mahler, G.:Sym 2, w. R. Ziesak (sop), C. Hellekant (mez), San Francisco Sym Chorus London ▲ 443350-2
Mendelssohn, F.:Sym 3 London ▲ 433811-2 [DDD]
Mendelssohn, F.:Sym 4 London ▲ 433811-2 [DDD]
Nielsen, C.:Aladdin—orchestral suite London ▲ 425857-2 [DDD]
Nielsen, C.:Maskarade—ov. London ▲ 425857-2 [DDD]
Nielsen, C.:Sym 1 London ▲ 425607-2 [DDD]
Nielsen, C.:Sym 2 London ▲ 430280-2 [DDD]
Nielsen, C.:Sym 3 London ▲ 430280-2 [DDD]
Nielsen, C.:Sym 4 London ▲ 421524-2 [DDD]
Nielsen, C.:Sym 5 London ▲ 421524-2 [DDD]
Nielsen, C.:Sym 6 London ▲ 425607-2 [DDD]
Orff, C.:Carmina burana, w. San Francisco Sym Chorus [G, L] London ▲ 430509-2 [DDD] □ 430509-5
Schubert, Franz:Ov Orch, D.591 London ▲ 436837-2 [DDD]
Schubert, Franz:Sym 9 London ▲ 436837-2 [DDD]
Sessions, R.:Sym 2 *(rec May 31, 1993)* London ▲ 443376-2 [DDD]
Sibelius, J.:Sym 4 London ▲ 425858-2 [DDD] □ 425858-5
Sibelius, J.:Sym 5 London ▲ 425858-2 [DDD] □ 425858-5
Strauss, R.:Eine Alpensinfonie London ▲ 421815-2 [DDD] □ 421815-5
Strauss, R.:Don Juan London ▲ 421815-2 [DDD] □ 421815-5
Strauss, R.:Ein Heldenleben *(rec Feb. 21, 24 & 25, 1992)* London ▲ 436596-2 [DDD]
Strauss, R.:Metamorphosen, w. R. Kobler (vn), D. Krehbiel (hn) *(rec Feb. 21, 24 & 25, 1992)* London ▲ 436596-2 [DDD]
Wuorinen, C.:Con 3 Pno, w. G. Ohlsson (pno) Elektra/Nonesuch ▲ 79185-2 [DDD]
Wuorinen, C.:The Golden Dance, w. G. Ohlsson (pno) Elektra/Nonesuch ▲ 79185-2 [DDD]
E. Jorda (cnd)
Cushing, C.:Cereus *(rec 1961)* Citadel ▲ CTD 88117 [ADD]
Falla, M. de:Noches en los jardines de España, w. A. Rubinstein (pno) *(rec 1957)* RCA Gold Seal ▲ 60046-2-RG (m/s) [ADD]
Imbrie, A.W.:Legend *(rec 1961)* Citadel ▲ CTD 88117 [ADD]
P. Monteux (cnd)
Bach, J.S.:Passacaglia & Fugue Org [arr for orch] RCA Gold Seal ("Pierre Monteux Edition" series) ▲ 09026-61892-2

San Francisco SO (cont.)
P. Monteux (cnd) (cont.)
Beethoven, L. van:Die Ruinen von Athen (ov) RCA Gold Seal ("Pierre Monteux Edition" series) ▲ 09026-61892-2
Beethoven, L. van:Sym 4 RCA Gold Seal ("Pierre Monteux Edition" series) ▲ 09026-61892-2
Beethoven, L. van:Sym 8 RCA Gold Seal ("Pierre Monteux Edition" series) ▲ 09026-61892-2
Berlioz, H.:Benvenuto Cellini (ov) RCA Gold Seal ("Pierre Monteux Edition" series) ▲ 09026-61894-2
Berlioz, H.:La Damnation de Faust (sels)—Rákóczy March RCA Gold Seal ("Pierre Monteux Edition" series) ▲ 09026-61894-2
Berlioz, H.:Sym fantastique RCA Gold Seal ("Pierre Monteux Edition" series) ▲ 09026-61894-2
Berlioz, H.:Les Troyens (sels)—Ov [from Act II] RCA Gold Seal ("Pierre Monteux Edition" series) ▲ 09026-61894-2
Brahms, J.:Schicksalslied, w. Marian Anderson (cta) [arr for voc & orch] RCA Gold Seal ("Pierre Monteux Edition" series) ▲ 09026-61891-2
Brahms, J.:Sym 2 RCA Gold Seal ("Pierre Monteux Edition" series) ▲ 09026-61891-2
Chabrier, E.:Le Roi malgré lui (fête polonaise) RCA Gold Seal ("Pierre Monteux Edition" series) ▲ 09026-61899-2
Chausson, E.:Poème de l'amour et de la mer, w. Gladys Swarthout (mez) RCA Gold Seal ("Pierre Monteux Edition" series) ▲ 09026-61899-2
Chausson, E.:Sym in B♭ RCA Gold Seal ("Pierre Monteux Edition" series) ▲ 09026-61899-2
Debussy, C.:La Mer RCA Gold Seal ("Pierre Monteux Edition" series) ▲ 09026-61890-2
Debussy, C.:Preludes Pno (sels), w. Y. Menuhin (vn)—sels. from Book 1:No. 8, "La Fille aux cheveux de lin" RCA Gold Seal ▲ 09026-61395-2
Elgar, E.:Salut d'amour RCA Gold Seal ▲ 09026-61395-2
Gounod, C.:Faust (ballet music) RCA Gold Seal ▲ 09026-61975-2
Highlights from the Pierre Monteux Edition, w. Chicago SO, Boston SO RCA Gold Seal ▲ 09026-61978-2
Ibert, J.:Escales RCA Gold Seal ▲ 09026-61895-2
Indy, V. d':Fervaal (sels)—Prélude RCA Gold Seal ("Pierre Monteux Edition" series) ▲ 09026-61888-2
Indy, V. d':Istar RCA Gold Seal ▲ 09026-61900-2
Indy, V. d':Sym 2 RCA Gold Seal ("Pierre Monteux Edition" series) ▲ 09026-61888-2
Indy, V. d':Sym on a French Mountain Air RCA Gold Seal ("Pierre Monteux Edition" series) ▲ 09026-61888-2
Lalo, E.:Le Roi d'Ys (ov) RCA Gold Seal ▲ 09026-61895-2
Lalo, E.:Sym espagnole, w. Yehudi Menuhin (vn) RCA Gold Seal ▲ 09026-61395-2
Liszt, F.:Les Préludes RCA Gold Seal ("Pierre Monteux Edition" series) ▲ 09026-61890-2
Mahler, G.:Kindertotenlieder, w. Marian Anderson (cta) RCA Gold Seal ("Pierre Monteux Edition" series) ▲ 09026-61891-2
The Pierre Monteux Edition, w. RCA Victor Orch, Boston SO, Chicago SO RCA Gold Seal 15-▲ 09026-61893-2
Ravel, M.:Alborada del gracioso RCA Gold Seal ▲ 09026-61895-2
Ravel, M.:Daphnis et Chloé (suite 1) RCA Gold Seal ▲ 09026-61895-2
Ravel, M.:La Valse RCA Gold Seal ▲ 09026-61895-2
Ravel, M.:Valses nobles et sentimentales RCA Gold Seal ▲ 09026-61895-2
Rimsky-Korsakov, N.:Antar RCA Gold Seal ("Pierre Monteux Edition" series) ▲ 09026-61897-2
Rimsky-Korsakov, N.:Sadko (sels) RCA Gold Seal ("Pierre Monteux Edition" series) ▲ 09026-61897-2
Rimsky-Korsakov, N.:Scheherazade RCA Gold Seal ("Pierre Monteux Edition" series) ▲ 09026-61897-2
Saint-Saëns, C.:Havanaise Vn RCA Gold Seal ("Pierre Monteux Edition" series) ▲ 09026-61890-2
Scriabin, A.:Sym 4 RCA Gold Seal ("Pierre Monteux Edition" series) ▲ 09026-61890-2
Strauss, R.:Ein Heldenleben RCA Gold Seal ("Pierre Monteux Edition" series) ▲ 09026-61889-2
Strauss, R.:Tod und Verklärung RCA Gold Seal ("Pierre Monteux Edition" series) ▲ 09026-61889-2
A. Neale (cnd)
Kernis, A.J.:Colored Field, w. Julie Ann Giacobassi (Eng hn) *(rec Davies Symphony Hall, San Francisco, May 14, 1994)* Argo ▲ 448174-2 [DDD]
S. Ozawa (cnd)
Gershwin, G.:An American in Paris Deutsche Grammophon ("Resonance" series) ▲ 427203-2 [ADD] ■ 427203-4
M. Tilson Thomas (cnd)
Copland, A.:Con Pno, w. Garrick Ohlsson (pno) *(rec Davies Symphony Hall, San Francisco, June 25, 1996)* RCA Red Seal ▲ 09026-68541-2 [DDD]
Copland, A.:Short Sym, "Sym 2" *(rec Davies Symphony Hall, San Francisco, June 25, 1996)* RCA Red Seal ▲ 09026-68541-2 [DDD]
Copland, A.:Symphonic Ode *(rec Davies Symphony Hall, San Francisco, June 25, 1996)* RCA Red Seal ▲ 09026-68541-2 [DDD]
Copland, A.:Vars Orch *(rec Davies Symphony Hall, San Francisco, June 25, 1996)* RCA Red Seal ▲ 09026-68541-2 [DDD]
Prokofiev, S.:Romeo & Juliet (sels)—Intro to Act 1; Romeo; The Street Awakens; The Quarrel; The Fight; The Duke's Command; Interlude; Nurse; Young Juliet; Arrival of the Guests; Dance of the Knights; Mercutio; Madrigal; Gavotte; Balcony Scene, Intro to Act III; Folk Dance; Dance with Mandolins; Public Merrymaking; The Meeting of Tybalt & Mercutio; The Duel; Romeo Decides to Avenge Mercutio; Finale (Death of Tybalt); Romeo & Juliet; Romeo & Juliet at Parting; Interlude; Juliet Alone; Juliet's Funeral; Juliet's Death *(rec live, Louise Davies Symphony Hall, San Francisco, Sept 20–24, 1995)* RCA Red Seal ▲ 09026-68288-2 [DDD]
E. de Waart (cnd)
Adams, J.:Harmonielehre Elektra/Nonesuch ▲ 79115-2 [DDD] ■ 79115-4
Adams, J.:Harmonium, w. San Francisco Sym Chorus [E] ECM New Series ▲ 78118-21277-2
Adams, J.:Music of—The Chairman Dances; Christian Zeal & Activity; Short Ride in a Fast Machine; Tromba Lontana; Common Tones in Simple Time Elektra/Nonesuch ▲ 79144-2 [DDD] ■ 79144-4 (D)
Adams, J.:Shaker Loops Philips ▲ 412214-2 [DDD]
Jongen, J.:Symphonie Concertante, w. Murray (org) Telarc ▲ CD 80096 [DDD]
Rachmaninoff, S.:Con 1 Pno, w. Zoltán Kocsis (pno) Philips ▲ 412881-2 [DDD]
Rachmaninoff, S.:Con 2 Pno, w. Z. Kocsis (pno) Philips ▲ 412881-2 [DDD]
Reich, S.:Vars Ww Philips ▲ 412214-2 [DDD]

San Francisco SO members
Thow, J.:Trilce Music & Arts ▲ CD 915

San Francisco War Memorial Opera House Orch
G. Patanè (cnd)
Donizetti, G.:L'elisir d'amore (sels), w. Reri Grist (sop), Luciano Pavarotti (ten), Sesto Bruscantini (bar), Ingvar Wixell (bar), Maria Ambrosio (sgr), San Francisco War Memorial Opera House Chorus *(rec live, San Francisco, 1969)* Budget ("The Greatest Voice in Opera" series) ▲ SYP 109

San Marco Musici
A. Lizzio (cnd)
Haydn, J.:Sym 6, "Le Matin" PMG ("Vienna Master" series) ▲ CD 160301 [DDD]
Haydn, J.:Sym 7, "Le Midi" PMG ("Vienna Master" series) ▲ CD 160301 [DDD]
Haydn, J.:Sym 8, "Le Soir" PMG ("Vienna Master" series) ▲ CD 160301 [DDD]
Haydn, J.:Sym 22, "Der Philosoph" PMG ("Vienna Master" series) ▲ CD 160302 [DDD]
Haydn, J.:Sym 26, "Lamentatione" PMG ("Vienna Master" series) ▲ CD 160302 [DDD]
Haydn, J.:Sym 53, "L'Impériale" PMG ("Vienna Master" series) ▲ CD 160302 [DDD]
Vivaldi, A.:Cons Vn, Op. 8/1–4, "The Four Seasons" PMG ("Vienna Master" series) ▲ CD 160109 [DDD]
Vivaldi, A.:Music of PMG ("Vienna Master" series) ▲ CD 160110 [DDD]

San Petronio Capella Musicale Orch
Barbieri, L.:Surgite pastores, w. St. Petronio Voci Bianche Chorus, Tölz Boys' Choir, Avignon Vocal Ensemble *(rec Oct. 3–5, 1991)* Tactus ▲ TC 551801
Colonna, G.P.:Magnificat, w. J. Feldman (sop), San Petronio Cappella Musicale [L] Tactus 2-▲ TC 630390 [DDD]
Colonna, G.P.:Psalms, w. San Petronio Cappella Musicale—Beatus vir; Dixit à 9; Laudate Dominum; Laudate pueri à 8 [L] Tactus 2-▲ TC 630390 [DDD]

ORCH. & ENS.

San Petronio Capella Musicale Orch (cont.)
Franceschini, P.:Sacred Music, w. Avignon Vocal Ensemble—Dixit Dominus a 8 for Trumpet & Violin; Laudate a Pueri a 6 for Trumpet & Violins *(rec Oct. 3–5, 1991)* Tactus ▲ TC 650001
Franceschini, P.:Son à 7 *(rec Oct. 3–5, 1991)* Tactus ▲ TC 650001
Gabrielli, D.:Sons (6) Tpts *(rec Oct. 3–5, 1991)* Tactus ▲ TC 650001
Monteverdi, C.:Ballo *(rec Salone da musica, Palazzo Magnagutti, Sermide)* Naxos ("Early Music" series) ▲ 8.553322 [DDD]
Monteverdi, C.:Combattimento *(rec Salone da musica, Palazzo Magnagutti, Sermide)* Naxos ("Early Music" series) ▲ 8.553322 [DDD]
Perti, G.A.:Gesù al sepolcro, w. L. M. Åkerlund (sop), M. Zanetti (sop), C. Cavina (alt), M. Cecchetti (ten), A. W. Schultze (bass) [l] Tactus ▲ TC 661601
Perti, G.A.:Messa e salmi concertati, w. Avignon Vocal Ensemble, San Petronio Voci Bianche Chorus, Tölz Boys' Choir *(rec Oct. 3–5, 1991)* Tactus ▲ TC 551801
Rota, A.:Missarum liber primus, w. Avignon Vocal Ensemble, San Petroni Voci Bianche Chorus, Tölz Boys' Choir *(rec Oct. 3–5, 1991)* Tactus ▲ TC 551801
Torelli, G.:Son à 4 for Tpts *(rec Oct. 3–5, 1991)* Tactus ▲ TC 650001
Torelli, G.:Tpt Music, w. P.-O. Lindeke (tpt), D. Staff (tpt), E. Tarr (tpt), G. Cassone (tpt)—Sinfs., G.1, 2, 8, 10, 11, 26, 29, 30, 31, 33; Sons. G.3–6, 13, 15–25; Con. G.27 Bongiovanni 3–▲ GB 5523/25
Trombetti, A.:Il primo libro de motetti accomodati per cantare e far concerti, w. St. Petronio Voci Bianche Chorus, Tölz Boys' Choir, Avignon Vocal Ensemble *(rec Oct. 3–5, 1991)* Tactus ▲ TC 551801
Vecchi, O.:L'Amfiparnaso *(rec Salone da musica, Palazzo Magnagutti, Sermide, Apr 25–28, 1995)* Naxos ("Early Music" series) ▲ 8.553312 [DDD]

S. Vartolo (cnd)
Carissimi, G.:Lamento della Regina Maria Stuarda *(rec Sept 1995)* Naxos ▲ 8.553320 [DDD]
Cesti, A.:Lamento della Madre Ebrea *(rec Sept 1995)* Naxos ▲ 8.553320 [DDD]
Giramo, P.A.:Lamento della Pazza *(rec Sept 1995)* Naxos ▲ 8.553320 [DDD]
Monteverdi, C.:Lamento d'Arianna *(rec Sept 1995)* Naxos ▲ 8.553320 [DDD]
Perti, G.A.:Liturgy for Good Friday, w. Patrizia Vaccari (sop), Maura Pederzoli (sop), Cristina Calzolari (sop), Alida Oliva (sop), Claudia Bugli (sop), Lucia Bagnoli (alt), Cinzia Meneghel (alt), Renzo Bez (alt), Alessandro Carmignani (alt), Michel van Goethem (alt), Mauro Collina (ten), Vincenzo Di Donato (ten), Paolo Fanciullacci (ten), Giovanni Caccamo (ten), Paolo Da Col (ten), Sergio Foresti (bass), Marco Scavazza (bass), Luca Ferracin (bass), Paride Montanari (bass), Liuwe Tamminga (org), Sergio Vartolo (org)—Omnes amici mei; De lamentatione Jeremiae Prophetae:Heth. Cogitavit; Velum templi; Vinea mea; De lamentatione Jeremiae Prophetae:Lamed. Matribus suis; Tamquam ad latronem; Tenebrae factae sunt; Animam meam; Tradiderunt me; Jesum tradidit; De lamentatione Jeremiae Prophetae:Aleph. Ego vir; Caligaverunt *(rec St. Petronio Basilica, Bologna, Mar 28–31, 1995)* Naxos ▲ 8.553321 [DDD]
Rossi, L.:Laments—Lamento della Regina di Svezia *(rec Sept 1995)* Naxos ▲ 8.553320 [DDD]
Strozzi, B.:Lamento del Marchese Cinq-Mars *(rec Sept 1995)* Naxos ▲ 8.553320 [DDD]

San Remo SO
Boito, A.:Mefistofele (sels), w. Marcella Pobbe (sop), Turin RAI SO *(rec Turin & San Remo, 1954–58)* Cetra Classic ▲ CDON 110
Mascagni, P.:Isabeau (sels), w. Marcella Pobbe (sop), Turin RAI SO *(rec Torino & San Remo, 1954–58)* Cetra Classic ▲ CDON 110
Mascagni, P.:Isabeau (sels), w. Marcella Pobbe (sop), Pier Miranda Ferraro (ten), Rinaldo Rosa (sgr) Cetra Classic ▲ CDON 44

Basile, Cattini, Questa, Serafin (cnd)
Puccini, G.:Arias, w. Marcella Pobbe (sop), Turin RAI SO—from Suor Angelica, La Rondine, Tosca, Turandot, Manon Lescaut, La Bohème & Gianni Schicchi *(rec Torino & San Remo, 1954–58)* Cetra Classic ▲ CDON 110

M. de Bernart (cnd)
Vivaldi, A.:Il Farnace, w. M. Dupuy (mez), K. Angeloni (mez), P. Malakova (mez), D. Dessy (mez), L. Rizzi (cta), R. Garazioti (sgr) [l] *(rec live 12/1/82)* Arkadia-Akademia 2–▲ 110 [ADD]

P. Carignani (cnd)
Ricci, L.:Crispino e la comare, w. D. Lojarro (sop), A. Lazzarini (mez), Cossutta (ten), S. Alaimo (bar), R. Coviello (bar), A. Marani (bass), R. Ristori (bass), Benori (sgr), Siclari (sgr), San Remo Sym Chorus [l] *(rec live 11/89)* Bongiovanni 2–▲ GB 2095/96 [DDD]

W. Proost (cnd)
Barber, S.:Essay 1 Gallo ▲ CD 890 [DDD]
Beethoven, L. van:Con 4 Pno, w. Adilia Alieva (pno) Gallo ▲ CD 891 [DDD]
Beethoven, L. van:Egmont (ov) Gallo ▲ CD 891 [DDD]
Bernstein, L.:Divert Gallo ▲ CD 890 [DDD]
Brahms, J.:Vars on a Theme by Haydn Gallo ▲ CD 891 [DDD]
Hanson, H.:Sym 2, "Romantic" Gallo ▲ CD 890 [DDD]
Prokofiev, S.:Con 2 Pno, w. Adilia Alieva (pno) Gallo ▲ CD 849 [DAD]
Prokofiev, S.:Ov on Hebrew Themes Gallo ▲ CD 849 [DAD]
Rachmaninoff, S.:Rhapsody on a Theme of Paganini, w. Adilia Alieva (pno) Gallo ▲ CD 849 [DAD]

C. Rizzi (cnd)
Rossini, G.:Ciro in Babilonia, w. C. Calvi (cta), E. Palacio (ten), Dessy-Ceriani (sgr), San Remo Sym Chorus [l] *(rec live 10/30/88)* Arkadia-Akademia 2–▲ 105 [DDD]

T. Serafin (cnd)
Mascagni, P.:Isabeau, w. Marcella Pobbe (sop—Isabeau), Licia Galvano (mez—Giglietta), Pier Miranda Ferraro (ten—Folco), Orazio Gualtiero (bar—Cornelius), Rinaldo Rola (bass—Re Raimondo), Amelia Bazzini (sgr—Ermyngarde), Piero Benzi (sgr—L'araldo), Renata Davini (sgr—Ermynthrude), Piero Francia (sgr—Il Cavaliere) *(rec Sanremo, Jan 13, 1962)* Bongiovanni ("Il Mito dell'Opera" series) 2–▲ GB 1135/36–2 [ADD]

San Rocco Accademia
Vivaldi, A.:Cons Vn, Op. 8/1–12, "Il cimento dell'armonia e dell'inventione", w. Enrico Casazza (vn)—Nos. 1–6 *(rec Silvelle, Treviso, Italy, Mar 1996)* Arts ▲ 473692 [DDD]

Sancoussi Ensemble Hamburg [T. Pietsch (vn), G. Hildebrandt (vn), C. Jung (vc), M. Nitz (hpd)]
Early Baroque Violin Entrée ▲ 0052 [ADD]

Sanderi Trio
Brahms, J.:Trio 1 Pno *(rec 1983)* Classic Studio Berlin ▲ CS 10608 [DDD]
Brahms, J.:Trio 2 Pno *(rec 1983)* Classic Studio Berlin ▲ CS 10608 [DDD]
Brahms, J.:Trio 3 Pno *(rec 1985)* Classic Studio Berlin ▲ CS 11008 [DDD]
Brahms, J.:Trio in A Pno (posth) *(rec 1985)* Classic Studio Berlin ▲ CS 11008 [DDD]
Tchaikovsky, P.:Trio Pno *(rec 1985)* Classic Studio Berlin ▲ CS 11208 [DDD]

Sanssouci Ensemble
Biber, H. von:Sons Vn & Continuo Ambitus ▲ 97804

Santa Cecilia CO
Vol. 76, w. Basic 100, Uto Ughi (vn), Santa Cecilia CO [cnd:Leonard Friedman] RCA Victor ▲ 09026-68453-2 ■ 09026-68453-4

Santa Fe Chamber Music Festival
Schoenberg, A.:Trio Strs Elektra/Nonesuch ■ D4-79028 (D)
Schoenberg, A.:Verklärte Nacht Elektra/Nonesuch ■ D4-79028 (D)

Santa Fe Festival Orch
Bach, C.P.E.:Con Vc, H.439, w. János Starker (vc) Delos ▲ DE 3197 [DDD]
Boccherini, L.:Con Vc, G.480, w. János Starker (vc) Delos ▲ DE 3197 [DDD]
Couperin, F.:Pièces en Concert, w. János Starker (vc) [trans. Paul Bazelaire] Delos ▲ DE 3197 [DDD]
Janson, J.-B.-A.:Cons Vc, w. János Starker (vc)—Concerto in D Delos ▲ DE 3197 [DDD]
Vivaldi, A.:Cons Vn (misc), w. János Starker (vc)—in D, RV.230 [trans. for vc] Delos ▲ DE 3197 [DDD]

Santa Fe Guitar Quintet
Argentina's Santa Fe Guitar Quintet Klavier ▲ KCD 11045 [DDD] ■ KC 7045

Santa Fe Opera Orch
R. Leppard (cnd)
Thomson, V.:The Mother of Us All [E] *(rec 1977)* New World 2–▲ NW 288/289 [AAD]

Santa Fe SO
S. Robertson (cnd)
McLaughlin, J.:Sifotheol *(rec Sweeney Center, Sante Fe, NM, Mar 27, 1988)* Ludifichord ▲ LDCD 1001

Santa Fe SO Chamber Players
McLaughlin, J.:The Flowers of Dawn, w. James Bustenid (bar), Santa Fe Sym Chamber Choir *(rec St. Francis Auditorium, Sante Fe, NM, Mar 17, 1991)* Ludifichord ▲ LDCD 1001

Santa Fe Trio [Donna McRae (sop), Frank Bowen (fl), Rita Angel (pno)]
Schmitz, A.:4 Songs from Green Lotus Man Capstone ▲ CPS 8618

Santa Monica Orch
J. Rachmilovich (cnd)
Martinů, B.:Con 2 Vn, w. L. Kaufman (vn) *(rec ca. 1946)* Cambria ▲ CD 1063 [ADD]

Sante Palumbo String Orch
S. Palumbo (cnd)
Puccini, G.:Music of—melodies from Madama Butterfly; Tosca; Turandot; La Bohème; Manon Lescaut; plus others Kicco Classic ▲ 895

Santiago Teatro Municipale Orch
A. Guadagno (cnd)
Bizet, G.:Carmen, w. Laura Bustamante (sop—Frasquita), Ximena Riveros (sop—Mercedes), Nancy Stokes (sop—Micaela), Regina Resnik (mez—Carmen), Plácido Domingo (ten—Don José), Ismildo Tedeschi (ten—Remendado), Ramon Vinay (ten—Escamillo), Juan Charles (ten/bar—Dancaire), Agustin Letelier (bar—Morles), Jorge Algorta (bass—Zuniga), Santiago Teatro Municipale Chorus *(rec Santiago Municipal Theater, Sept. 4, 1967)* Legato Classics 2–▲ LCD 194–2 [ADD]

Santo Spirito Academy Orch
S. Balestracci (cnd)
Stradella, A.:Cants, w. Cristina Miatello (sop), Gianpaolo Fagotto (ten), Antonio Abete (sgr), Roberto Balconi (sgr), Lavinia Bertotti (sgr), Roberta Giua (sgr), Santo Spirito Academy Chorus—for 5 w. vns [For Holy Christmas]; for 5 w. instruments [For the Souls in Purgatory] Stradivarius ▲ STV 33392 [DDD]

Saõ Paulo Teatro Municipale Orch
A. Belardi (cnd)
Gomes, A.C.:Il Guarany, w. Niza De Castro Tank (sop—Cecilia), Roque Lotti (ten—Ruy Bento), Manrico Patassini (ten—Pery), Paschoal Raymundo (ten—Don Alvaro), Paulo Fortes (bar—Gonzales), Juan Carlos Ortiz (b-bar—Il Cacico), Waldomiro Furlan (bass—Alonso), Josè Perrotta (bass—Don Antonio De Mariz), Saõ Paulo Teatro Municipale Chorus *(rec Studios of the Teatro Municipal, Saõ Paulo, Brazil, 1959)* Arkadia 2–▲ HP 617.2 [ADD]

Saraband Ensemble [Fadia El-Hage (voc), Belinda Sykes (voc/shawms/bagpipe), Mustafa Doğan Dikmen (voc/fl/dr), Ihsan Mehmet Özer (psaltery), Ahmed Kadri Rizeli (fid/perc), Mehmet Cemal Yesilcay (lt/perc), Vladimir Ivanoff (lt/perc)]
V. Ivanoff (cnd)
Sepharad *(rec Beirut & Istanbul & Munich, 1994)* Deutsche Harmonia Mundi ▲ 05472-77372-2 [DDD]

Sarre CO
K. Ristenpart (cnd)
Bach, J.S.:Cant 51, w. Teresa Stich-Randall (mez) Accord ▲ ACD 200042
Bach, J.S.:Cant 57, w. Jacob Staempfli (bass), Sarre Choir Accord ▲ ACD 202652 [AAD]
Bach, J.S.:Cant 82, w. Jacob Staempfli (bass), Sarre Choir Accord ▲ ACD 202652 [AAD]
Bach, J.S.:Cant 159, w. Jacob Staempfli (bass), Sarre Choir Accord ▲ ACD 202652 [AAD]
Mozart, W.A.:Exsultate, w. Teresa Stich-Randall (mez) Accord ▲ ACD 200042
Mozart, W.A.:Missa, K.317, w. Teresa Stich-Randall (sop), Bianca Maria Casoni (alt), Pietro Bottazzo (ten), Herbert Schmolzi (cnd), Sarrebrück Conservatory Choir Accord ▲ ACD 220252 [AAD]
Mozart, W.A.:Missa, K.427, w. Teresa Stich-Randall (mez) Accord ▲ ACD 200042
Mozart, W.A.:Vesperae solennes, w. Teresa Stich-Randall (sop), Bianca Maria Casoni (alt), Pietro Bottazzo (ten), Herbert Schmolzi (cnd), Sarrebrück Conservatory Choir Accord ▲ ACD 220252 [AAD]

Sarum Consort
Byrd, W.:Infelix ego, w. Andrew Mackay (cnd), Sarum Consort ASV/Quicksilva ▲ ASQ CD 6185
Byrd, W.:Mass in 5 Parts, w. Andrew Mackay (cnd), Sarum Consort ASV/Quicksilva ▲ ASQ CD 6185
Tallis, T.:The Lamentations of Jeremiah, w. Andrew Mackay (cnd), Sarum Consort ASV/Quicksilva ▲ ASQ CD 6185
Tallis, T.:O sacrum convivium, w. Andrew Mackay (cnd), Sarum Consort ASV/Quicksilva ▲ ASQ CD 6185
Tallis, T.:Sancte Deus, w. Andrew Mackay (cnd), Sarum Consort ASV/Quicksilva ▲ ASQ CD 6185

M. N. Johnson (cnd)
Buxtehude, D.:Cants, w. St. Peter's in the Great Valley Chamber Choir—Wachtet auf, BuxWV 101 [dubious]; Singet dem Herrn ein neues Lied, BuxWV 98; Quemadmodum desiderat cervus, BuxWV 92; O fröhliche Stunden, o herrliche Zeit, BuxWV 85; Jubilate Domino, omnis terra, BuxWV 64; Lobe den Herrn, meine Seele, BuxWV 71; Erfreue dich, Erdel, BuxWV 26 *(rec Church of St.-Martin-in-the-Fields, Chestnut Hill, PA, Sept 7–9 1994)* PGM ▲ PGM 102
Buxtehude, D.:Cants, w. Laura Heimes (sop), Tamara Crout Matthews (sop), Steven Richards (ct), James Russell (ten), John Alston (bass), St. Peter's in the Great Valley Chamber Choir—Wachet auf, ruft uns die Stimme!; Singet dem Herrn; Quemadmodum desiderat cervus; O fröhliche Stunden, o herrliche Zeit; Jubilate Domino omnis terra; Lobe den Herrn, meine Seele; Erfreue dich, Erdel *(rec St-Martin-in-the-Fields Church, Chestnut Hill, PA, Sept 7–9, 1994)* Pro gloria musicae ▲ PGM 102 [DDD]

Sassari SO
G. Catalucci (cnd)
Sacchini, A.:La contandina in corte, w. S. Rigacci (sop—Tancia), E. Palacio (ten—Ruggiero), G. Gatti (bar—Berto), C. Boersma (vc), M. Clavenna (db), M. T. Conti (hpd) *(rec Dec. 17–18, 1991)* Bongiovanni 2–▲ GB 2145/46 [DDD]

R. Tigani (cnd)
Respighi, O.:Adagio con variazioni Vc Orch, w. Massimiliano Agelao (vc) *(rec Rome, Oct 11–14, 1994)* Bongiovanni ▲ GB 2166 [DDD]
Respighi, O.:Con Vn, w. Vincenzo Bolognese (vn) *(rec Rome, Oct 11–14, 1994)* Bongiovanni ▲ GB 2166 [DDD]
Respighi, O.:Di Sera, w. Alberto Cesaraccio (ob), Emanuela Saba (ob) *(rec Rome, Oct 11–14, 1994)* Bongiovanni ▲ GB 2166 [DDD]
Respighi, O.:Seranata, w. Oscar Piastrelloni (vc) *(rec Rome, Oct 11–14, 1994)* Bongiovanni ▲ GB 2166 [DDD]
Respighi, O.:Gli uccelli, w. Stefano Mancini (fl), Alberto Cesaraccio (ob), Antonio Puglia (cl), Paloma Tironi (hp), Stefano Melis (cel) *(rec Rome, Oct 11–14, 1994)* Bongiovanni ▲ GB 2166 [DDD]

Sassari SO Ensemble
G. Catalucci (cnd)
Hasse, J.A.:La Serva scaltra, w. Bernadette Lucarini (sop), Giorgio Gatti (bar) [l] Bongiovanni ▲ GB 2101 [DDD]

Satu Mare PO
P. Popescu (cnd)
Puccini, G.:Madama Butterfly, w. Eugenia Moldoveanu (sop—Madama Butterfly), Mihaela Agachi (mez—Suzuki), Corina Circa (mez—Kate Pinkerton), Emil Gherman (ten—B.F. Pinkerton), Stefan Popescu (ten—Goro), Ioan Soanea (bar—The Bonze/Yakuside), Eduard Tumageanian (bar—Sharpless), Alexandru Kopeczi (bass—Prince Yamadori), Mircea Moisa (bass—Commissioner), Cluj-Napoca Phil Chorus *(rec 1979)* Vox Box 2–▲ CDX 5155

Saturday Brass Quintet
Danielpour, R.:Urban Dances Koch International Classics ▲ KIC 7100-2 [DDD]

Saulesco String Quartet
Atterberg, K.:Qt Strs Swedish Society ▲ SCD 1021
Atterberg, K.:Suite 5 Strs, "Suite barocco" Swedish Society ▲ SCD 1021
Atterberg, K.:Suite 8 Strs, "Suite pastorale in modo antico" Swedish Society ▲ SCD 1021
Wirén, D.:Qt 5 Strs Caprice ▲ CAP 21326 [DDD/AAD]

Savonlinna Opera Festival Orch

Haatanen (cnd)

Opera Scenes from Savonlinna, w. Savonlinna Opera Festival Chorus BIS 2-▲ CD 373/74 [DDD]

U. Söderblom (cnd)

Kokkonen, J.:The Last Temptations, w. Ritva Auvinen (sop), Martti Talvela (bass), Savonlinna Opera Festival Chorus Finlandia 2-▲ FIN 104 [AAD]

Sawai Koto Ensemble

Matsumura, T.:Fant Koto, w. T. Sawai (koto) Camerata ▲ 32CM 92

Nishimura, A.:A River of Time, w. T. Sawai (koto) Camerata ▲ 32CM 92

Nishimura, A.:Iris of Time, w. T. Sawai (koto) Camerata ▲ 32CM 92

Nishimura, A.:Stratums of Time, w. T. Sawai (koto) Camerata ▲ 32CM 92

Sawai, T.:Gosechi No Mai, w. T. Sawai (koto) Camerata ▲ 32CM 92

Yuasa, J.:Koto Uta Basho's 5 Haiku, w. T. Sawai (koto) Camerata ▲ 32CM 92

Saxology Saxophone Quartet

The Sax:Centenary Collection ASV ▲ ASV 2090 [DDD]

Saxon State Orch

K. Böhm (cnd)

Beethoven, L. van:Con 4 Pno, w. W. Giesking (pno) *(rec 1934)* Grammofono 2000 ▲ GRM 78506 [ADD]

Beethoven, L. van:Con 4 Pno, w. Walter Gieseking (pno) Enterprise ("The Radio Years" series) ▲ ENT RY 61

Beethoven, L. van:Con 4 Pno, w. Walter Gieseking (pno) *(rec Berlin, Jan. 3, 1939)* APR ▲ APR 5512 [ADD]

Brahms, J.:Con 2 Pno, w. Wilhelm Backhaus (pno) Enterprise ("Piano Library" series) ▲ ENT PL 213

Brahms, J.:Con 2 Pno, w. W. Backhaus (pno) *(rec Dresden 1939 from HMV 78s)* Memories 2-▲ HR 4442/43 [ADD]

Karl Böhm:The Dresden Years, 1938–1940 Enterprise ("Palladio" series) 2-▲ ENTPD 4119 [ADD]

Leoncavallo, R.:Pagliacci (sels)—Intermezzo *(rec 1938)* Iron Needle ▲ IN 1311 [ADD]

Mascagni, P.:Cavalleria rusticana (sels)—Intermezzo *(rec 1938)* Iron Needle ▲ IN 1311 [ADD]

Mozart, W.A.:Ovs—Die Entführung aus dem Serail; Le Nozze di Figaro *(rec 1939)* Iron Needle ▲ IN 1311 [ADD]

Strauss, R.:Don Juan Dutton Laboratories ▲ DUT 5007 [ADD]

Verdi, G.:Aida (sels)—Prelude *(rec 1939)* Iron Needle ▲ IN 1311 [ADD]

Verdi, G.:Otello (sels), w. Torsten Ralf (ten—Otello), Josef Hermann (ten—Iago)—Sì, pel ciel marmoreo giuro *(rec 1940)* Iron Needle ▲ IN 1311 [ADD]

Wagner, R.:Die Meistersinger von Nürnberg (sels), w. M. Teschemacher (sop), H. Jung (mez), M. Kremer (ten), T. RA. (ten), E. Fuchs (bar), H.-H. Nissen (bar), S. Nilsson (bass)—Act. 3 *(rec 1939)* Pearl 2-▲ PEA 9121 [ADD]

Wagner, R.:Ovs, Preludes & Orch Sels—Der fliegende Holländer Ov; Tannhäuser Ov; Prelude to Act II [from Lohengrin]; Prelude to Act I [from Die Meistersinger von Nürnberg] *(rec 1939)* Iron Needle ▲ IN 1311 [ADD]

Weber, C.M. von:Der Freischütz (ov) *(rec 1938)* Iron Needle ▲ IN 1311 [ADD]

K. Elmendorff (cnd)

Mozart, W.A.:Don Giovanni, w. M. Schech (sop), M. Teschemacher (sop), H. Hopf (ten), M. Ahlersmeyer (bar), K. Böhme (bass), G. Frick (bass), Dresden State Opera Chorus [G] *(rec 1943)* Berlin Classics ("Dokumente" series) 3-▲ BER 2048 [ADD]

Wagner, R.:Die Walküre (act 1), w. M. Teschemacher (sop), M. Lorenz (ten), K. Böhme (bass) [G] *(rec 9/21/44)* Preiser ▲ 90015 (m) [AAD]

Wolf, H.:Der Corregidor, w. M. Teschemacher (sop), M. Fuchs (sop), K. Erb (ten), J. Herrmann (bar), K. Böhme (b-bar), G. Hann (bass), G. Frick (bass), Saxon State Chorus *(rec 1944)* Preiser 2-▲ PRE 90182 [AAD]

R. Kempe (cnd)

Wagner, R.:Die Meistersinger von Nürnberg, w. Tiana Lemnitz (sop—Eva), Bernd Aldenhoff (ten—Walther von Stolzing), Gerhard Unger (ten—David), Ferdinand Frantz (b-bar—Hans Sachs), Kurt Boehme (bass—Veit Pogner), Heinrich Pflanzl (bass—Sixtus Beckmesser) *(rec Dresden, 1951)* Myto 4-▲ MCD 961138

La Scala Orch

"La Bellisima":Anna Moffo, the Debut Recordings, w. Anna Moffo (sop), Philharmonia Orch [cnd:C. Davis, A. Galliera, A. Votto] *(rec 1956–59)* EMI Classics ▲ CDM 63413

Five Heroines, w. Maria Callas (sop), T. Serafin (cnd), H. von Karajan (cnd), V. de Sabata (cnd), C. M. Giulini (cnd) EMI Classics 5-▲ CDME 64418

Magda Olivero & Flaviano Labò in Concert, w. Magda Olivero (sop), Flaviano Labò (ten), Jacques Bazire (cnd), Marsiglia Opera Orch, Raina Kabaivanska (sop), Gianpiero Matromei (bar), Carlo Meliciani (bar), Oliveiro de Fabritiis (cnd), Turin RAI Orch *(rec between 1969 & 1973)* Bongiovanni ▲ GB 1105 [ADD]

Opera Arias & Songs, w. Toti Dal Monte (sop) *(rec 1926–1929)* Preiser ("Lebendige Vergangenheit" series) ▲ PRE 89001 (m) [AAD]

Rich & Rare:The Voice of Margaret Sheridan, w. Margaret Sheridan (sop), Aureliano Pertile (ten), Renato Zanelli (ten), Hubert Greenslade (pno), Carlo Sabajno (cnd), Queens Hall Orch *(rec 1926–29)* Time Machine ▲ 0100

Verdi, G.:Ernani (sels), w. R. Kabaivanska (sop), P. Domingo (ten)—six solo arias & one chorus *(rec live 12/4/69)* Melodram 2-▲ MEL 27064 (m) [AAD]

Verdi, G.:I vespri siciliani (sels), w. L. Gencer (sop), G. Casellato-Lamberti (ten), La Scala Chorus—one solo soprano aria & three duets from Act 4 [I] Myto 2-▲ 2 MCD 90524 [ADD]

C. Abbado (cnd)

Bellini, V.:I Capuleti e i Montecchi, w. R. Scotto (sop), G. Aragall (ten), L. Pavarotti (ten), La Scala Chorus [I] *(rec live, La Scala, 1/8/68)* Arkadia 2-▲ 550 (m) [AAD]

Bellini, V.:I Capuleti e i Montecchi, w. R. Scotto (sop), G. Aragall (ten), L. Pavarotti (ten), A. Giacomotti (bass), A. Ferrin (bass), La Scala Chorus *(rec live 1967)* Butterfly Music 2-▲ BMC 12 [AAD]

Bellini, V.:I Capuleti e i Montecchi (sels), w. Luciano Pavarotti (ten), Gaetano Ferrin (bass), Alfredo Giacomotti (bass), La Scala Chorus—O di Cappelio generoso amici...E serbato a questo acciaro *(rec live, Nov. 20, 1969)* RCA Gold Seal ▲ 09026-68014-2 [ADD]

Gounod, C.:Roméo et Juliette (sels), w. Renata Scotto (sop—Juliet), Giacomo Aragall (ten—Romeo), Luciano Pavarotti (ten—Tebaldo), Gaetano Ferrin (bass—Capellio), Alfredo Giacomotti (bass—Lorenzo), La Scala Chorus Budget ("The Greatest Voice in Opera" series) ▲ SYP 111

Mozart, W.A.:Con 23 Pno, w. M. Pollini (pno) Exclusive ▲ EXL 64 [ADD]

Mozart, W.A.:Nozze di Figaro, w. Mirella Freni (sop), Daniela Mazzucato (sop), Teresa Berganza (mez), Mirto Picchi (ten), Hermann Prey (bar), José Van Dam (b-bar), Paolo Montarsolo (bass), La Scala Chorus *(rec live, Apr 22, 1974)* Arkadia 3-▲ 614

Verdi, G.:Aida, w. K. Ricciarelli (sop), E. Obraztsova (mez), P. Domingo (ten), L. Nucci (bar), N. Ghiaurov (bass), La Scala Chorus [I] Deutsche Grammophon ▲ 435410-2 [DDD]

Verdi, G.:Aida, w. K. Ricciarelli (sop), E. Obraztsova (mez), P. Domingo (ten), L. Nucci (bar), N. Ghiaurov (bass), La Scala Chorus [I] Deutsche Grammophon 3-▲ 410092-2 [DDD]

Verdi, G.:Arias, w. L. Pavarotti (ten) [I] CBS ▲ MK 37228 ■ MT 37228

Verdi, G.:Macbeth, w. Shirley Verrett (mez—Lady Macbeth), Plácido Domingo (ten—Macduff), Piero Cappuccilli (bar—Macbeth), Nicolai Ghiaurov (bass—Banco), La Scala Chorus Deutsche Grammophon ("The Originals" series) ▲ 449 732-2

P. Bellugi (cnd)

Donizetti, G.:Don Pasquale, w. Margherita Guglielmi (sop—Norina), Alfredo Kraus (ten—Ernesto), Rolando Panerai (bar—Malatesta), Paolo Montarsolo (bass—Don Pasquale), La Scala Chorus *(rec Jan 13, 1974)* Golden Age of Opera 2-▲ GAO 202/203 [ADD]

L. Bernstein (cnd)

Bellini, V.:La sonnambula, w. M. Callas (sop), G. Carturan (mez), C. Valletti (ten), G. Modesti (bass), La Scala Chorus [I] *(rec live, 3/5/55)* Myto 2-▲ 2 MCD 89006 (m) [ADD]

Cherubini, L.:Médée, w. M. Callas (sop), F. Barbieri (mez), G. Penno (ten), G. Modesti (bass), Nache (sgr), La Scala Chorus [I] *(rec live 12/10/53)* Melodram 2-▲ MEL 26022 (m) [AAD]

Cherubini, L.:Médée, w. M. Callas (sop), F. Barbieri (mez), G. Penno (ten), G. Modesti (bass), Nache (sgr), La Scala Chorus [I] *(rec live, Milan 12/10/53)* Verona 2-▲ 27088/89

La Scala Orch (cont.)

U. Berrettoni (cnd)

Puccini, G.:La Bohème, w. Licia Albanese (sop), Tatiana Menotti (sop), Beniamino Gigli (ten), Afro Poli (bar), La Scala Chorus *(rec Milan, 1938)* Phonographe 2-▲ PHG CD 5071

Puccini, G.:La Bohème, w. L. Albanese (sop), T. Menotti (sop), B. Gigli (ten), A. Poli (bar), La Scala Chorus [I] *(rec 1937)* EMI Classics ("Studio" series) 2-▲ CDHB 63335 (m) [ADD]

Puccini, G.:La Bohème, w. L. Albanese (sop—Mimì), T. Menotti (sop—Musetta), B. Gigli (ten—Rodolfo), N. Palai (ten—Parpignol), A. Poli (bar—Marcello), A. Baracchi (bar—Schaunard), D. Baronti (bass—Colline), C. Scattola (bass—Benoit/Alcindoro), La Scala Chorus [I] *(rec Milan, May 1938)* Nimbus 2-▲ NI 7862/63 [ADD]

Puccini, G.:La Bohème, w. Licia Albanese (sop—Mimì), Tatiana Menotti (sop—Musetta), Beniamino Gigli (ten—Rodolfo), Nello Palai (ten—Parpignol), Aristide Baracchi (bar—Schaunard), Afro Poli (bar—Marcello), Duilio Baronti (bass—Colline), Carlo Scattola (bass—Benoit/Alcindoro), Vittore Veneziani (cnd), La Scala Chorus *(rec Feb–Mar 1938)* Arkadia ("The 78's" series) 2-▲ 78009 [ADD]

G. Cantelli (cnd)

Mozart, W.A.:Così fan tutte, w. E. Schwarzkopf (sop—Fiordiligi), G. Sciurri (sop—Despina), N. Merriman (mez—Dorabella), L. Alva (ten—Ferrando), R. Panerai (bar—Guglielmo), F. Clabrese (b-bar—Don Alfonso)., La Scala Chorus *(rec Jan. 27, 1956)* Datum 2-▲ DAT 12304 [ADD]

Mozart, W.A.:Così fan tutte, w. Elisabeth Schwarzkopf (sop), Graziella Sciutti (sop), Nan Merriman (mez), Luigi Alva (ten), Rolando Panerai (bar), Franco Calabrese (bass), La Scala Chorus Stradivarius 2-▲ STV DTM 12304 [ADD]

Tchaikovsky, P.:Sym 5 *(rec 1950)* Theorema ▲ TH 121139

F. Capuana (cnd)

Boito, A.:Mefistofele, w. R. Noli (sop—Margherita), S. dall'Argine (sop—Elena), G. Poggi (ten—Faust), G. Neri (bass-Mefistofele), La Scala Chorus [I] *(rec 1952)* Preiser 2-▲ 90122 (m) [AAD]

Massenet, J.:Werther, w. D. Gatta (sop—Sofia), I. Ligabue (sop—Kaethlen), G. Simionato (mez—Charlotte), F. Tagliavini (ten—Werther), V. Pandano (ten—Schmidt), E. Campi (bass—Johann), S. Bruscantini (bass—Le Bailli), La Scala Chorus *(rec Apr. 21, 1951)* Bongiovanni 2-▲ GB 1101/02 [ADD]

R. Chailly (cnd)

Rossini, G.:Il barbiere di Siviglia, w. M. Horne (mez), E. Dara (bar), L. Nucci (bar), S. Ramey (bass). La Scala Chorus [I] CBS 3-▲ M3K 37862 [DDD]

Rossini, G.:Il barbiere di Siviglia (sels), w. M. Horne (mez), R. Pierotti (mez), P. Barbacini (ten), E. Dara (bar), L. Nucci (bar), S. Ramey (bass), S. Sammaritano (bass), La Scala Chorus *(rec Milan, Jan. 2–18, 1982)* Sony Classical ("Opera Highlights" series) ▲ SMK 53501 [DDD]

C.F. Cillario (cnd)

Donizetti, G.:Maria Stuarda, w. M. Caballé (sop), S. Verrett (mez), O. Garaventa (ten), La Scala Chorus [I] *(rec live, Milan 4/20/71)* Myto 2-▲ 2 MCD 91137 [ADD]

O. de Fabritiis (cnd)

Giordano, U.:Andrea Chénier, w. M. Caniglia (sop), G. Simionato (mez), B. Gigli (ten), G. Bechi (bar), G. Taddei (bar), I. Tajo (bass), La Scala Chorus [I] *(rec 1941, HMV DB 5423/35)* Angel ("Studio" series) 2-▲ CDHB 69996 (m) [ADD]

Giordano, U.:Andrea Chénier, w. Maria Caniglia (sop—Maddalena), Maria Huder (mez—Bersi), Vittoria Palombini (mez—Madelon), Giulietta Simionato (mez—Contessa), Beniamino Gigli (ten—Andrea), Adelio Zagonara (ten—Incroyable/Abbé), Gino Bechi (bar—Carlo), Leone Paci (bar—Mathieu), Giuseppe Taddei (b-bar—Pietro/Fouquier), Italo Tajo (b-bar—Roucher), Gino Conti (bass—Master/Schmidt), La Scala Chorus *(rec Nov 1941)* Arkadia ("The 78's" series) 2-▲ 78012 [ADD]

Franci, Lewis, Schippers (cnd)

Rossini, G.:Arias, w. Marylin Horne (mez), Turin RAI SO—sels from Semiramide, Otello, La donna del Lago, Tancredi, La Cenerentola, L'Italiana in Algeri & L'Assedio di Dorinto *(rec live, 1968–71)* Enterprise ("Documents" series) ▲ ENT LV 979 (m)

W. Furtwängler (cnd)

Wagner, R.:Der Ring des Nibelungen, w. Kirsten Flagstad (sop), Hilde Konetzni (sop), Elisabeth Höngen (cta), Max Lorenz (ten), Set Svanholm (ten), Günther Treptow (ten), Josef Hermann (bar), Ludwig Weber (bass), Ferdinand Franz (sgr), La Scala Chorus *(rec Milan, 1950)* Music & Arts 12-▲ CD 914

Wagner, R.:Der Ring des Nibelungen, w. K. Flagstad (sop), H. Konetzni (sop), E. Höngen (cta), G. Treptow (ten), S. Svanholm (ten), M. Lorenz (ten), F. Frantz (b-bar), L. Weber (bass), B. Herrmann (bass), La Scala Chorus *(rec live 1950)* Arkadia 12-▲ 351 [ADD]

A. Galliera (cnd)

Grieg, E.:Con Pno, Op. 16, w. Arturo Benedetti Michelangeli (pno) *(rec 1941)* Enterprise ("The Piano Library" series) ▲ ENT 183

G. Gavazzeni (cnd)

Catalani, A.:Loreley, w. E. Suliotis (sop), G. Talarico (ten), P. Cappuccilli (bar), La Scala Chorus *(rec 1968)* Memories 2-▲ MEM 4511 [ADD]

Donizetti, G.:Anna Bolena, w. Maria Callas (sop), Gabriella Carturan (mez), Giulietta Simionato (mez), Gianni Raimondi (ten), Plinio Clabassi (bass), Nicola Rossi Lemmeni (sgr), Luigi Rumo (sgr), La Scala Chorus Great Opera Performances 2-▲ GOP 768

Donizetti, G.:Anna Bolena, w. M. Callas (sop—Anna Bolena), G. Simionato (mez—Giovanna), G. Raimondi (ten—Percy), N. Rossi-Lemeni (bass—King), La Scala Chorus [I] *(rec live, Milan 4/14/57)* Verona 2-▲ 27090/91

Donizetti, G.:Anna Bolena, w. M. Callas (sop), G. Simionato (mez), G. Raimondi (ten), La Scala Chorus [I] *(rec live, 4/17/57)* Melodram 2-▲ MEL 26010

Giordano, U.:Fedora, w. Mirella Freni (sop—Principessa Fedora), Adelina Scarabelli (sop—Contessa Olga), Silvia Mazzoni (mez—Dimitri), Monica Minarelli (sgr—Savoiardo), Placido Domingo (ten—Conte Loris), Ernesto Gavazzi (ten—Desiré), Aldo Bottion (ten—Barone Rouvel), Alessandro Corbelli (bar—Siriex), Luigi Roni (bass—Cirillo), Silvestro Sammaritano (bass—Baroff), Alfredo Giacomotti (bass—Gretch), Ernesto Panariello (bass—Lorek), Vincenzo Alaimo (sgr—Nicola), Arnold Bosman (sgr—Boleslao), Bruno Capisani (sgr—Sergio), Renato Zanchetta (sgr—Michele), La Scala Chorus *(rec La Scala, Apr 5, 1993)* Legato 2-▲ LCD 213-2 [ADD]

Meyerbeer, G.:Les Huguenots, w. J. Sutherland (sop), F. Cossotto (mez), G. Simionato (mez), F. Corelli (ten), V. Ganzarolli (bar), N. Ghiaurov (bass), G. Tozzi (bass), La Scala Chorus [I] *(rec live 5/28/62)* Melodram 3-▲ MEL 37026 (m) [AAD]

Verdi, G.:Un ballo in maschera, w. M. Callas (sop), E. Ratti (sop), G. Simionato (mez), G. di Stefano (ten), E. Bastianini (bar), La Scala Chorus *(rec 1957)* Melodram ▲ MLO 26039 [ADD]

Verdi, G.:Un ballo in maschera, w. M. Callas (sop), E. Ratti (sop), G. Simionato (mez), G. di Stefano (ten), E. Bastianini (bar), La Scala Chorus [I] *(rec live 12/7/57)* Arkadia 2-▲ 519 (m) [ADD]

Verdi, G.:La battaglia di Legnano, w. A. Stella (sop), F. Corelli (ten), E. Bastianini (bar), La Scala Chorus [I] *(rec live 12/7/61)* Myto 2-▲ 2 MCD 89010 (m) [ADD]

Verdi, G.:La forza del destino (sels), w. I. Ligabue (sop), C. Bergonzi (ten), Meliciani (sgr), La Scala Chorus [substantial highlights] *(rec live, Milan 12/7/65)* Myto 2-▲ 2 MCD 91750 [ADD]

Verdi, G.:Nabucco, w. Gloria Lane (mez), Gianni Raimondi (ten), Giangiacomo Guelfi (bar), Nicolai Ghiaurov (bass), Elena Saliotis (sgr), La Scala Chorus *(rec La Scala Theater, Milan, Dec. 7, 1966)* Pantheon 2-▲ PHE 6757 (m)

Verdi, G.:Il trovatore, w. A. Stella (sop), M. Fiorentini (mez), F. Cossotto (mez), F. Corelli (ten), E. Bastianini (bar), I. Vinco (bass), La Scala Chorus [I] *(rec live, Milan, 12/7/62)* Claque 2-▲ CLQ 2013 (m)

Verdi, G.:Il trovatore, w. A. Stella (sop), M. Fiorentini (mez), F. Cossotto (mez), F. Corelli (ten), E. Bastianini (bar), I. Vinco (bass), La Scala Chorus *(rec live, Milan, 12/7/62)* Melodram 2-▲ MEL 27068 (m) [AAD]

Verdi, G.:Il trovatore, w. G. Tucci (sop), G. Simionato (mez), C. Bergonzi (ten), P. Cappuccilli (bar), La Scala Chorus *(rec live, Moscow 1965)* Melodram 2-▲ MEL 27008

Verdi, G.:I vespri siciliani, w. R. Scotto (sop), G. Raimondi (ten), P. Cappuccilli (bar), R. Raimondi (bass), La Scala Chorus [I] *(rec live, 12/4/70 [Acts 1–3], 12/10)* Myto 2-▲ 2 MCD 90524 [ADD]

La Scala Orch (cont.)

G. Gavazzeni (cnd) (cont.)

Zandonai, R.:Francesca da Rimini, w. Lydia Marimpietri (sop—Biancofiore), Magda Olivero (sop—Francesca), Pinuccia Perotti (sop—Samaritana), Edda Vincenzi (sop—Garsenda), Gabriella Carturan (mez—Smaragdi), Biancamaria Casoni (mez—Altichiara), Anna Maria Rota (cta—Donella), Athos Cesarini (ten—Archer), Angelo Mercuriali (ten—Ser Toldo Berardengo), Mario del Monaco (ten—Paolo), Piero de Palma (ten—Malatestino), Rinaldo Pelizzoni (ten—Prisoner), Gianpiero Malaspina (bar—Gianciotto), Dino Mantovani (bar—Jester), Enrico Campi (bass—Ostasio), Giuseppe Morresi (bass—Tower warden), La Scala Chorus *(rec La Scala Theatre, Milan, June 4, 1959)* Legato Classics 2-▲ LCD 186-2

F. Ghione (cnd)

Leoncavallo, R.:Pagliacci, w. I. Pacetti (sop—Nedda), B. Gigli (ten—Canio), G. Nessi (ten—Peppe), M. Basiola (bar—Tonio), La Scala Chorus [I] *(rec 1934)* EMI Classics ("Studio" series) ▲ CDH 63309 (m) [ADD]

Leoncavallo, R.:Pagliacci, w. I. Pacetti (sop—Nedda), B. Gigli (ten—Canio), G. Nessi (ten—Peppe), M. Basiola (bar—Tonio), La Scala Chorus [I] *(rec July 1934)* Nimbus 2-▲ NI 7843/44 [ADD]

Leoncavallo, R.:Pagliacci, w. I. Pacetti (sop—Nedda), B. Gigli (ten—Canio), G. Nessi (ten—Peppe), M. Basiola (bar—Tonio), La Scala Chorus [I] *(rec 1934 for HMV)* Music Memoria ▲ 30275

A. Giulini (cnd)

Mozart, W.A.:Con 23 Pno, w. V. Horowitz (pno) Deutsche Grammophon ▲ 423287-2 [DDD] ■ 423287-4

C. M. Giulini (cnd)

Beethoven, L. van:Con Vn, Op. 61, w. Salvatore Accardo (vn) *(rec Milan Teatro Abanella, Italy, Dec. 10–13, 1992)* Sony Classical ▲ SK 53287 [DDD]

Beethoven, L. van:Coriolan Ov Sony Classical ▲ SK 53974

Beethoven, L. van:Egmont (ov) Sony Classical ▲ SK 53974

Beethoven, L. van:Romances Vn, w. Salvatore Accardo (vn) *(rec Milan Teatro Abanella, Italy, Dec. 10–13, 1992)* Sony Classical ▲ SK 53287 [DDD]

Beethoven, L. van:Sym 1 Sony Classical ▲ SK 48236 [DDD]

Beethoven, L. van:Sym 2 *(rec Dec. 8–11, 1991)* Sony Classical ▲ SK 48238 [DDD]

Beethoven, L. van:Sym 4 Sony Classical ▲ SK 58921

Beethoven, L. van:Sym 5 Sony Classical ▲ SK 58921

Beethoven, L. van:Sym 6, "Pastorale" Sony Classical ▲ SK 53974

Beethoven, L. van:Sym 7 Sony Classical ▲ SK 48236 [DDD]

Beethoven, L. van:Sym 8 *(rec Sept. 20–22, 1992)* Sony Classical ▲ SK 48238 [DDD]

Catalani, A.:La Wally, w. R. Scotto (sop—Walter), R. Tebaldi (sop—Wally), J. Gardino (mez—Afra), M. Del Monaco (ten—Giuseppe Hagenbach), G.G. Guelfi (bar—Vincenzo Gellner), G. Tozzi (bass—Stromminger), La Scala Chorus *(rec Dec. 7, 1953)* Legato Classics 2-▲ LCD 177-2 [ADD]

Gluck, C.W.:Alceste, w. M. Callas (sop), R. Gavarini (ten), R. Panerai (bar), S. Maionica (bass), La Scala Chorus—plus "Callas Sings Gluck & Rossini" [French version] *(rec live, La Scala, 4/4/54)* Melodram 2-▲ MEL 26026

Rossini, G.:Il barbiere di Siviglia, w. M. Callas (sop), L. Alva (ten), T. Gobbi (bar), La Scala Chorus [I] *(rec live 1956)* Melodram 2-▲ MEL 26020

Verdi, G.:Arias, w. M. Callàs (sop), M. Gavazzeni (ten), G. Di Stefano (ten)—E strano...Sempre libera;—Ecco l'orrido campo...Ma dall' arido stelo Myto 2-▲ MCD 89003 (m) [ADD]

Verdi, G.:La traviata, w. M. Callas (sop), G. Di Stefano (ten), E. Bastianini (bar), La Scala Chorus [I] *(rec 1955)* EMI Classics (Studio) 2-▲ CDMB 63628 (m) [ADD]

Verdi, G.:La traviata, w. M. Callas (sop), A. Zanolli (sop), L. Mandelli (sop), G. Raimondi (ten), E. Bastianini (bar), La Scala Chorus *(rec live 1/19/56)* Myto 2-▲ MCD 89003 (m) [ADD]

Verdi, G.:La traviata, w. M. Callas (sop), G. Di Stefano (ten), E. Bastianini (bar), La Scala Chorus [I] *(rec live 5/28/55)* Arkadia 2-▲ 501 (m) [AAD]

E. Gracis (cnd)

Donizetti, G.:Lucrezia Borgia, w. M. Caballé (sop), A. M. Rota (cta), G. Raimondi (ten), E. Flagello (bass), La Scala Chorus [I] *(rec live, 3/2/70)* Myto 2-▲ 2 MCD 90423 [ADD]

Donizetti, G.:Lucrezia Borgia (sels), w. L. Gencer (sop), G. Raimondi (ten), L. Roni (bass-bar), La Scala Chorus—8 scenes & arias [I] *(rec live, 3/12/70)* Myto 2-▲ 2 MCD 90423 [ADD]

A. Guarnieri (cnd)

Massenet, J.:Manon (sels), w. M. Favero (sop), G. Di Stefano (ten), M. Borriello (bar), M. Mainardi (bar), La Scala Chorus *(rec live, Milan, 3/15/47)* Myto ▲ 1 MCD 90526 [ADD]

H. von Karajan (cnd)

Bizet, G.:Carmen (sels), w. G. Simionato (mez), G. di Stefano (ten), La Scala Chorus—14 arias [F] *(rec live, Milan, 1/18/55)* Arkadia 3-▲ 221 [ADD]

Donizetti, G.:Lucia di Lammermoor, w. M. Callas (sop), G. di Stefano (ten), G. Zampieri (ten), R. Panerai (bar), G. Modesti (bass), La Scala Chorus *(rec 1954)* Melodram 2-▲ MLO 26040 [DDD]

Donizetti, G.:Lucia di Lammermoor, w. M. Callas (sop), G. di Stefano (ten), R. Panerai (bar), La Scala Chorus [I] *(rec live, Milan 1/18/54)* Standing Room Only 2-▲ SRO 831-2 [ADD]

Leoncavallo, R.:Pagliacci, w. J. Carlyle (sop), C. Bergonzi (ten), U. Benelli (bar), R. Panerai (bar), G. Taddei (bar) [I] Deutsche Grammophon 3-▲ 419257-2 [ADD]

Leoncavallo, R.:Pagliacci, w. Joan Carlyle (sop—Nedda/Colombina), Carlo Bergonzi (ten—Canio/Pagliaccio), Franco Ricciardi (ten—Villager), Ugo Benelli (bar—Peppe/Arlecchino), Rolando Panerai (bar—Silvio), Giuseppe Taddei (bar—Tonio/Taddeo), Giuseppe Morresi (bass—Villager), La Scala Chorus *(rec La Scala, Milan, Oct 1965)* Deutsche Grammophon ("The Originals" series) ▲ 449727-2 [ADD]

Mascagni, P.:Cavalleria rusticana, w. F. Cossotto (mez), C. Bergonzi (ten), G. Guelfi (bar), La Scala Chorus [I] Deutsche Grammophon 3-▲ 419257-2 [ADD]

Mozart, W.A.:Nozze di Figaro, w. E. Schwarzkopf (sop), I. Seefried (sop), S. Jurinac (sop), L. Villa (sop), R. Panerai (bar), La Scala Chorus [I] *(rec live Feb. 4, 1954)* Melodram 3-▲ MEL 37075 [AAD]

Puccini, G.:Madama Butterfly, w. M. Callas (sop), L. Danieli (mez), N. Gedda (ten), M. Borriello (bar), La Scala Chorus [I] *(rec 1955)* EMI Classics 2-▲ CDCB 47959 (m) [ADD]

Strauss, R.:Der Rosenkavalier, w. Jarmila Barton (sop—Marianne), Lisa Della Casa (sop—Sophie), Sena Jurinac (sop—Octavian), Ilva Ligabue (sop—Orphan), Elisabeth Schwarzkopf (sop—Marschallin), Else Schürhoff (mez—Annina), Luisa Villa (mez—Milliner), Hugues Cuénod (ten—Marschallin's majordomo), Erich Majkut (ten—Valzacchi), Giuseppe Nessi (ten—Animal seller), Luciano Della Pergola (ten—Lackey/Faninal's majordomo), Antonio Pirino (ten—An Italian Singer), Gino Del Signore (ten—Lackey/Waiter), Erich Kunz (bar—Herr von Faninal), Paolo Pedani (bar—Lackey), Attilo Barbesi (bass—Lackey/Waiter), Enrico Campi (bass—Waiter), Otto Edelmann (bass—Baron Ochs), Bruno Fichtinger (bass—Notary), Franco Taino (bass—Waiter), Maria Amadini (sgr—Orphan), Pina Carrillo (sgr—Orphan), Joszi Trojan Regar (sgr—Innkeeper), La Scala Chorus *(rec La Scala Theater, Milan, Jan. 26, 1952)* Legato Classics 3-▲ LCD 197-3

Verdi, G.:Requiem Mass, w. L. Price (sop), F. Cossotto (mez), L. Pavarotti (ten), N. Ghiaurov (bass), La Scala Chorus [L] *(rec live 1/16/67)* Melodram 2-▲ MEL 28012

Verdi, G.:Requiem Mass, w. L. Price (sop), F. Cossotto (mez), L. Pavarotti (ten), N. Ghiaurov (bass), La Scala Chorus [L] *(rec live 1/16/67)* Verona 2-▲ 27060/61 (m) [AAD]

Verdi, G.:La traviata, w. M. Freni (sop), R. Righetti (mez), R. Cioni (ten), M. Sereni (bar), La Scala Chorus *(rec Milan, 1964)* Legend 2-▲ LGD 125 [ADD]

Verdi, G.:Il trovatore (sels), w. Maria Callas (sop), La Scala Chorus—selected arias *(rec Milan, 1955)* Andromeda ▲ ANR 2541 [ADD]

Wagner, R.:Die Walküre (sels), w. B. Nilsson (sop), L. Rysanek (sop), L. Suthaus (ten)—nine selections from Acts 1 & 2 *(rec live in Milan, 4/21/58)* Hunt Productions 12-▲ 12 CDKAR 223 (m) [ADD]

C. Kleiber (cnd)

Puccini, G.:La Bohème, w. M. Freni (sop), P. Dvorsky (ten), La Scala Chorus Artists 2-▲ FED 15 [ADD]

R. Kubelik (cnd)

Berlioz, H.:Les Troyens (sels), w. N. Rankin (mez), G. Simionato (mez), M. del Monaco (ten) [I] *(rec May 27, 1960)* VAI Audio ▲ VAIA 1026 [ADD]

P. Maag (cnd)

Massenet, J.:Manon, w. M. Freni (sop), L. Pavarotti (ten), R. Panerai (bar), La Scala Chorus [I] *(rec live, 6/3/69)* Verona 2-▲ 27052/53 (m) [AAD]

Massenet, J.:Manon, w. M. Freni (sop), L. Pavarotti (ten), R. Panerai (bar), La Scala Chorus [I] *(rec live, 6/3/69)* Melodram 2-▲ MEL 27046 [AAD]

La Scala Orch (cont.)

P. Maag (cnd) (cont.)

Massenet, J.:Manon (sels), w. Mirella Freni (sop), Luciano Pavarotti (ten), Franco Ricciardi (ten), Wladimiro Ganzarolli (bar), Giuseppe Morresi (bass), Antonio Zerbini (bass), Ida Farina (sgr), La Scala Chorus *(rec live, Milan, 1969)* Budget ("The Greatest Voice in Opera" series) ▲ SYP 110

L. Maazel (cnd)

Puccini, G.:La fanciulla del West, w. M. Zampieri (sop), P. Domingo (ten), J. Pons (bar), La Scala Chorus *(rec live 1991)* Sony Classical 2-▲ S2K 47189

Verdi, G.:Aida, w. M. Chiara (sop), G. Dimitrova (sop), L. Pavarotti (ten), L. Nucci (bar), P. Burchuladze (bass), La Scala Chorus [I] London 3-▲ 417439-2 [DDD] 2-■ 417439-4

Verdi, G.:Aida, w. M. Chiara (sop), G. Dimitrova (sop), L. Pavarotti (ten), L. Nucci (bar), P. Burchuladze (bass), La Scala Chorus [I] London □ 433162-5

L. Malajoli (cnd)

Opera Arias, w. Giannina Arangi-Lombardi (sop) *(rec 1928–33)* Preiser ("Lebendige Vergangenheit" series) ▲ PRE 89013 [AAD]

Puccini, G.:Madama Butterfly, w. R. Pampanini (sop), A. Granda (ten), G. Nessi (ten), G. Vanelli (bar), S. Baccaloni (bass), La Scala Chorus *(rec 1928)* Centaur 2-▲ CRC 2196/97

P. Mascagni (cnd)

Mascagni, P.:Canto del lavoro *(rec 1928)* VAI Audio ▲ VAIA 1113 [ADD]

Mascagni, P.:Cavalleria rusticana, w. L. Bruna Rasa (sop), G. Simionato (mez), B. Gigli (ten), G. Bechi (bar), La Scala Chorus [I] *(rec 1940)* EMI Classics ("Studio" series) 2-▲ CDHB 69987 (m) [ADD]

Mascagni, P.:Cavalleria rusticana, w. L.B. Rasa (sop), M. Marucucci (mez), G. Simionato (mez), B. Gigli (ten), G. Bechi (bar), La Scala Chorus *(rec 1940)* Nimbus 2-▲ NI 7843/44 [ADD]

Mascagni, P.:Cavalliera rusticana, w. Lina Bruna-Rasa (sop), Giulietta Simionato (mez), Benia Gigli (ten), Giuseppe Nessi (ten), Gino Bechi (bar), Carlo Galeffi (bar), La Scala Chorus *(rec Milan, 1940)* Phonographe 2-▲ PHG CD 5066

L. von Matačič (cnd)

Leoncavallo, R.:Pagliacci, w. Lucine Amara (sop), France Corelli (ten), Tito Gobbi (bar), La Scala Chorus [I] EMI Classics ("Studio" series) 2-▲ CDMB 63967

Puccini, G.:La fanciulla del West, w. B. Nilsson (sop), J. Gibin (ten), A. Mongelli (bar), La Scala Chorus [I] EMI Classics ("Studio" series) 2-▲ CDMB 63970

L. Molajoli (cnd)

Bizet, G.:Carmen, w. Ines Alfani Tellini (sop), Aurora d'Alessio Buades (cta), Aureliano Pertile (ten), Benvenuto Franci (bar), La Scala Chorus *(rec Milan, 1933)* Phonographie 2-▲ PHG 5013 [ADD]

Boito, A.:Mefistofele, w. Giannina Arangi-Lombardi (sop), Mafalda Favero (sop), Antonio Melandri (ten), Giuseppe Nessi (ten), Nazzareno de Angelis (bass), La Scala Chorus Grammofono 2000 2-▲ GRM 78606 (m)

Donizetti, G.:Lucia di Lammermoor, w. M. Capsir (sop—Lucia), E. de Muro Lomanto (ten—Sir Ravenswood), E. Venturini (ten—Lord Bucklaw), E. Molinari (bar—Lord Ashton), S. Baccaloni (bass—Bidebent), La Scala Chorus *(rec 1933)* Myto 2-▲ 2MCD 94299

Leoncavallo, R.:Pagliacci, w. Rosetta Pampanini (sop), Francesco Merli (ten), Giuseppe Nessi (ten), Carlo Galeffi (bar), La Scala Chorus *(rec Milan, 1930)* Phonographe 2-▲ PHG CD 5066

Mascagni, P.:Cavalleria rusticana, w. G. A. Lombardi (sop), I. Mannarini (mez), M. Castagna (mez), A. Melandri (ten), G. Lulli (bar), La Scala Chorus *(rec 1930)* Preiser ▲ 90042 (m) [AAD]

Puccini, G.:La Bohème, w. Luba Mirella (sop—Musetta), Rosetta Pampanini (sop—Mimì), Luigi Marini (ten—Rodolfo), Giuseppe Nessi (ten—Alcindoro), Aristide Baracchi (bar—Schaunard), Gino Vanelli (bar—Marcello), Salvatore Baccaloni (bass—Benoit), Tancredi Pasero (bass—Colline), La Scala Chorus Bongiovanni 2-▲ 1125/26 [ADD]

Puccini, G.:Madama Butterfly, w. Rosetta Pampanini (sop—Madama Butterfly), Conchita Velasquez (mez—Suzuki), Cesira Ferrari (mez—Kate Pinkerton), Alessandro Granda (ten—F. B. Pinkerton), Giuseppe Nessi (ten—Goro), Aristide Baracchi (bar—Il Principe Yamadori), Gino Vanelli (bar—Sharpless), Lino Bonardi (bass—Il Commissario Imperiale), Salvatore Baccaloni (bass—Lo zio Bonzo), La Scala Chorus Bongiovanni 2-▲ 1123/24 [ADD]

Puccini, G.:Manon Lescaut, w. Marla Zamboni (sop), Francesco Merli (ten), Lorenzo Conati (sgr), La Scala Chorus *(rec Milan, 1930)* Melodram 2-▲ IMC 202001

Puccini, G.:Manon Lescaut, w. Maria Zamboni (sop), Francesco Merli (ten), Lorenzo Conati (sgr), La Scala Chorus *(rec Milan, 1930)* Phonographie 2-▲ PHG 5006 [ADD]

Puccini, G.:Manon Lescaut, w. Maria Zamboni (sop—Manon), Anna Masetti-Bassi (mez—Singer), Francesco Merli (ten—Chevalier), Giuseppe Nessi (ten—Edmondo/Dancing Master/ Lamplighter), Lorenzo Conati (bar—Lescaut), Aristide Baracchi (bass—Innkeeper/Sergeant), Attilio Bordonali (bass—Geronte), Natale Villa (bass—Naval Captain), Vittore Veneziani (cnd), La Scala Chorus *(rec 1930)* Arkadia ("The 78's" series) 2-▲ 78014 [ADD]

Rossini, G.:Il barbiere di Siviglia, w. M. Capsir (sop), D. Borgioli (ten), R. Stracciari (bar), S. Baccaloni (bass), V. Bettoni (bass), La Scala Chorus *(rec 1929 for Columbia Records)* Music Memoria 2-▲ 30276/77

Rossini, G.:Il barbiere di Siviglia, w. Cesira Ferrari (mez—Berta), Mercedes Capsir (cta—Rosina), Dino Borgioli (ten—Count), Salvatore Baccaloni (bar—Bortolo), Aristide Baracchi (bar—Officer), Riccardo Stracciari (bar—Figaro), Vincenzo Bettoni (bass—Don Basilio), Attilo Bordonali (bass—Fiorello), La Scala Chorus *(rec 1930)* Arkadia ("The 78's" series) 2-▲ 78008 [ADD]

Verdi, G.:Aida, w. Giannina Arangi-Lombardi (sop—Aida), Maria Capuana (mez—Amneris), Aroldo Lindi (ten—Radames), Giuseppe Nessi (ten—Messenger), Armando Borgioli (bar—Amonasro), Salvatore Baccaloni (bass—King), Tancredi Pasero (bass—Ramfis), La Scala Chorus *(rec Nov 1928)* VAI Audio 2-▲ VAIA 1083-2

Verdi, G.:Rigoletto, w. Mercedes Capsir (sop), Dino Borgioli (ten), Riccardo Stracciari (bar), Ernesto Dominici (bass), La Scala Chorus Phonographe 2-▲ PHG 5036 [ADD]

F. Molinari-Pradelli (cnd)

Verdi, G.:Un ballo in maschera (sels), w. Margherita Guglielmi (sop), José Carreras (ten), Frederico Davià (bass), Giovanni Foiani (bass), La Scala Chorus—S'avanza il Conte...La rivedrà nell'estasi; Ma se m'è forza perderti...Ah! dessa è là! *(rec Milan, Feb 13, 1975)* Goldies ▲ GLD 63203 [ADD]

R. Muti (cnd)

Bartók, B.:2 Pictures Sony Classical ▲ SK 58949

Beethoven, L. van:Fant Pno, Op. 80, "Choral Fant", w. D. Ciani (pno), La Scala Chorus [G] *(rec live, Milan 11/5/70)* Arkadia ▲ 743 [ADD]

Boito, A.:Mefistofele, w. Michèle Crider (sop—Margherita/Elena), Eleonora Jankovic (mez—Marta/Pantalis), Ernesto Gavazzi (ten—Wagner/Nereo), Vincenza La Scola (ten—Faust), Samuel Ramey (bass—Mefistofele), La Scala Chorus *(rec live Mar 3,5 & 8, 1995, Milan)* RCA Victor 2-▲ 09026-68284-2 [DDD]

Brahms, J.:Serenade 1 Orch *(rec July 8–12, 1993)* Sony Classical ▲ SK 57973 [DDD]

Busoni, F.:Turandot (suite) *(rec Oct. 2–Dec. 14, 1992)* Sony Classical ▲ SK 53280 [DDD]

Casella, A.:Paganiniana *(rec Oct. 2–Dec. 14, 1992)* Sony Classical ▲ SK 53280 [DDD]

Cherubini, L.:Lodoïska, w. M. Devia (sop), F. Pedaci (sgr), B. Lombardo (ten), T. Moser (ten), A. Corbelli (bar), W. Shimell (bar), La Scala Chorus Sony Classical 2-▲ SM2K 47290

Elgar, E.:In the South *(rec July 8–12, 1993)* Sony Classical ▲ SK 57973 [DDD]

Gluck, C.W.:Iphigénie en Tauride, w. C. Vaness (sop—Iphigénie), S. Brunet (sop—Diane), G. Winbergh (ten—Pylade), T. Allen (bar—Oreste), G. Surian (bass—Thoas), La Scala Chorus *(rec Mar. 14–26, 1992)* Sony Classical 2-▲ S2K 52492 [DDD]

Martucci, G.:La canzone dei ricordi, w. Mirella Freni (sop) *(rec Teatro Abanella, Milan, Italy, Jan 17–22, 1995)* Sony Classical ▲ SK 64582 [DDD]

Martucci, G.:Orchestral Music—Notturno, Op. 70/1; Novelletta, Op. 82; Giga, Op. 61/3 *(rec Oct. 2–Dec. 14, 1992)* Sony Classical ▲ SK 53280 [DDD]

Pergolesi, G.B.:Lo frate 'nnamorato, w. N. Focile (sop), A. Felle (sop), B. Manca di Nissa (cta), A. Corbelli (bar), La Scala Chorus EMI Classics 3-▲ CDCC 54240

Rossini, G.:Guillaume Tell, w. C. Studer (sop), C. Merritt (ten), G. Zancanaro (bar), La Scala Chorus [I] *(rec live, 12/7/88)* Philips 4-▲ 422391-2 [DDD]

Rota, N.:Con Strs *(rec Abanella Theatre, Milan, Italy, Apr. 9–14, 1994)* Sony Classical ▲ SK 66279 [DDD]

Rota, N.:Film Music, w. Giuseppe Bodanza (tpt), Stefano Pagliani (vn)—Ballet Suite [from La Strada]; Dances [from Il Gattopardo] *(rec Abanella Theatre, Milan, Italy, Apr. 9–14, 1994)* Sony Classical ▲ SK 66279 [DDD]

▲ = CD ◆ = Enhanced CD Δ = MD ■ = Cassette Tape □ = DCC

La Scala Orch (cont.)
R. Muti (cnd) (cont.)
Spontini, G.:La vestale, w. Karen Huffstodt (sop—Julie), Denyce Graves (mez—La Grande Vestale), Patrick Raftery (ten—Cinna), Anthony Michaels-Moore (bar—Licinius), La Scala Chorus Sony Classical 3-▲ S3K 66357
Stravinsky, I.:Le Baiser de la fée—1950 rev. version Sony Classical ▲ SK 58949
Verdi, G.:Attila, w. S. Studer (sop), N. Shicoff (ten), G. Zancanaro (bar), S. Ramey (bass), La Scala Chorus [I] EMI Classics 2-▲ CDCB 49952 [DDD]
Verdi, G.:Ernani, w. M. Freni (sop), P. Domingo (ten), R. Bruson (bar), N. Ghiaurov (bass), La Scala Chorus [I] EMI Classics 3-▲ CDC 47082 [DDD]
Verdi, G.:Falstaff, w. Maureen O'Flynn (sop), Daniela Dessi (sop), Bernadette Manca di Nissa (mez), Delores Ziegler (mez), Ramon Vargas (ten), Ernesto Gavazzi (ten), Paolo Barbacini (ten), Juan Pons (bar), Roberto Frontali (bar), Luigi Roni (bass), La Scala Chorus *(rec Milan La Scala Theater, Italy, Mar. 29 & 31)* Sony Classical ▲ S2K 58961 [DDD]
Verdi, G.:Ovs & Preludes—sels from Aida; Attila; Giovanna d'Arco; I masnadieri; I vespri Siciliani; La battaglia di Legnano; La forza del destino; La traviata; Luisa Miller; Nabucco; Un ballo in maschera Sony Classical ▲ SK 68468
Verdi, G.:Rigoletto, w. Andrea Rost (sop—Gilda), Mariana Pentcheva (cta—Maddalena), Roberto Alagna (ten—Il Duca di Mantova), Renato Bruson (bar—Rigoletto), Dmitri Kavrakos (bass—Sparafucile), La Scala Chorus Sony Classical 2-▲ S2K 66314
Verdi, G.:Rigoletto (sels), w. Andrea Rost (sop), Roberto Alagna (ten), Renato Bruson (bar) Sony Classical ▲ SK 61966
Verdi, G.:La traviata, w. T. Fabbricini (sop—Violetta), A. Trevisan (mez—Annina), N. Curiel (mez—Flora), R. Alagna (ten—Alfredo), E. Cossutta (ten—Gastone), E. Gavazzi (ten—Giuseppe), O. Mori (bar—Douphol), E. Capuano (bass—d'Obigny), F. Musinu (bass—Grenvil), La Scala Chorus Sony Classical 2-▲ S2K 52486 [DDD]

G. Patanè (cnd)
Verdi, G.:Attila, w. Rita Orlandi Malaspina (sop—Odabella), Veriano Luchetti (ten—Foresto), Piero de Palma (ten—Uldino), Piero Cappuccilli (bar—Ezio), Nicolai Ghiaurov (bass—Attila), Luigi Roni (bass—Leone), La Scala Chorus *(rec Milan, May 15, 1972)* Golden Age of Opera 2-▲ GAO 187/88 [ADD]
Verdi, G.:Attila, w. Rita Orlandi Malaspina (sop—Odabella), Veriano Luchetti (ten—Foresto), Piero De Palma (ten—Uldino), Piero Cappuccilli (bar—Ezio), Nicolai Ghiaurov (bass—Attila), Luigi Roni (bass—Leone), La Scala Chorus *(rec Milan, May 12, 1975)* Myto 2-▲ MCD 961140

A. Pedrotti (cnd)
Schumann, R.:Con Pno, w. Arturo Benedetti Michelangeli (pno) Enterprise ("Piano Library" series) ▲ ENT PL 211

F.M. Pradelli (cnd)
Puccini, G.:Tosca, w. Raina Kabaivanska (sop), Plácido Domingo (ten), Zanasi (sgr) *(rec live, May 17, 1974)* Arkadia ("Historical Performances" series) 2-▲ 496

G. Prêtre (cnd)
Gounod, C.:Faust, w. M. Freni (sop), G. Raimondi (ten), N. Ghiaurov (bass), La Scala Chorus *(rec live 1967)* Melodram 3-▲ MEL 37005
Leoncavallo, R.:Pagliacci, w. T. Stratas (sop), P. Domingo (ten), J. Pons (bar), La Scala Chorus [I] Philips 2-▲ 411484-2
Leoncavallo, R.:Pagliacci, w. Teresa Stratas (sop—Nedda), Placido Domingo (ten—Canio), Juan Pons (bar—Tonio), La Scala Chorus Philips ("Duo" series) 2-▲ 454 265-2
Mascagni, P.:Cavalleria rusticana, w. Elena Obraztsova (mez—Santuzza), Placido Domingo (ten—Turridu), La Scala Chorus Philips ("Duo" series) 2-▲ 454 265-2
Mascagni, P.:Cavalleria rusticana, w. E. Obraztsova (mez), F. Barbieri (mez), P. Domingo (ten), R. Bruson (bar), La Scala Chorus [I] Philips ▲ 416137-2 [DDD]
Puccini, G.:La Bohème, w. Ileana Cotrubas (sop—Mimi), Margherita Guglielmi (sop—Musetta), José Carreras (ten—Rodolfo), Saverio Porzano (ten—Parpignol), Regolo Romani (ten—Vendor), Claudio Giombi (bar—Benoit), Gianni Maffeo (bar—Schaunard), Angelo Romero (bar—Marcello), Alfredo Giacomotti (bass—Alcindoro), Carlo Meliciani (bass—Customs Officer), Giuseppe Morresi (bass—Sergeant), Paolo Washington (bass—Colline), La Scala Chorus *(rec Washington D.C., Sept 8, 1976)* Legato Classics 2-▲ LCD 201-2
Saint-Saëns, C.:Samson et Dalila, w. Shirley Verrett (mez), Richard Cassilly (ten), Robert Massard (bar) *(rec La Scala Theatre, May 30, 1969)* Arkadia ("Historical Performances" series) 2-▲ 495

S. Ranzani (cnd)
Donizetti, G.:Lucia di Lammermoor, w. Mariella Devia (sop), Vencenzo La Scola (ten), Renato Bruson (bar), La Scala Chorus Serenissima 2-▲ SER 360153 [DDD]

M. Rossi (cnd)
Cimarosa, D.:Il Matrimonio segreto (sels), w. H. Gueden (sop), A. Noni (sop), F. Barbieri (mez), T. Schipa (ten), S. Bruscantini (bar), B. Christoff (bass)—Act I highlights [I] *(rec live, Milan March 22, 1949)* Melodram 2-▲ CDM 29505 [ADD]

C. Sabajno (cnd)
Antonio Cortis, 1891-1952, w. Antonio Cortis (ten) *(rec 1929-30 for HMV)* Preiser ("Lebendige Vergangenheit" series) ▲ PRE 89043 (m) [AAD]
Apollo Granforte, 1886-1975, w. Apollo Granforte (bar), La Scala Chorus *(rec HMV 1928-31)* Preiser ("Lebendige Vergangenheit" series) ▲ PRE 89048 (m) [AAD]
Donizetti, G.:Don Pasquale, w. Adelaide Saraceni (sop), Tito Schipa (ten), Ernesto Badini (bar), Afro Poli (bar), La Scala Chorus *(rec 1932)* Grammofono 2000 2-▲ GRM 78561 (m)
Hina Spani, w. Hina Spani (sop), Double quintet [cnd:Gino Nastrucci] *(rec 1927-1930 for HMV)* Preiser ("Lebendige Vergangenheit" series) ▲ PRE 89037 (m) [AAD]
Irene Minghini Cattaneo, w. Irene Minghini Cattaneo (mez), J. Barbiroll (cnd), *(rec for HMV 1928-1930)* Preiser ("Lebendige Vergangenheit" series) ▲ PRE 89008 (m) [AAD]
Leoncavallo, R.:Pagliacci, w. Josefina Huguet (sop—Nedda), Antonio Paoli (ten), Gaetano Pini-Corsi (ten—Beppe), Ernesto Badini (bar—Silvio), Francesco Cigada (bar—Tonio), Giuseppe Rosci (sgr—Un contadino), La Scala Chorus *(rec 1907)* Bongiovanni ▲ GB 1120-2 [ADD]
Leoncavallo, R.:Pagliacci, w. Adelaide Saraceni (sop—Nedda), Alessandro Valente (ten—Canio), Nello Palai (ten—Beppe), Apollo Granforte (bar—Tonio), Leonildo Basi (bass—Silvio), La Scala Chorus *(rec Apr, Sept 1929 & Jan 1930)* VAI Audio 2-▲ VAIA 1082-2
Mascagni, P.:Cavalleria rusticana, w. Delia Sanzio (sop—Santuzza), Mimma Pantaleoni (mez—Lola), Olga de Franco (cta—Lucia), Giovanni Breviario (ten—Turiddu), Piero Biasini (bar—Alfio), La Scala Chorus VAI Audio ▲ VAIA 1082-2
Puccini, G.:La Bohème, w. Rosina Torri (sop—Mimi), Thea Vitulli (sop—Musetta), Aristodemo Giorgini (ten—Rodolfo), Giuseppe Nessi (ten—Parpignol), Ernesto Badini (bar—Marcello), Aristide Baracchi (bar—Schaunard), Luigi Manfrini (bass—Colline), Salvatore Baccaloni (bass—Benoit/Alcindoro), La Scala Chorus *(rec 1928)* VAI Audio 2-▲ VAIA 1078-2
Puccini, G.:La Bohème, w. R. Torri (sop), T. Vitulli (sop), A. Giorgini (ten), E. Badini (bar), L. Manfrini (bass) [I] *(rec 1927)* InSync 2-■ C 4131/2 (m)
Puccini, G.:Tosca, w. C. Melis (sop—Tosca), P. Pauloi (ten—Cavarodossi), N. Palai (ten—Spoletta), A. Granforte (bar—Scarpia), G. Azzimonti (bass—Sciarrone/Angelotti), A. Gelli (bass—Sacristan), La Scala Chorus [I] *(rec Milan, Nov. 1929)* VAI Audio 2-▲ VAIA 1076-2 (m) [ADD]
Puccini, G.:Tosca, w. Carmen Melis (sop—Tosca), Nello Palai (ten—Spoletta), Piero Pauli (ten—Cavaradossi), Apollo Granforte (bar—Scarpia), Giovanni Azzimonti (bass—Angelotti/Sciarrone), Antonio Gelli (bass—Sagrestano), La Scala Chorus *(rec Nov 1929)* Arkadia 2-▲ CD 78002 (m) [ADD]
Verdi, G.:Aida, w. Dusolina Giannini (sop—Aida), Irene Minghini-Cattaneo (mez—Amneris), Giuseppe Nessi (ten—Messenger), Aureliano Pertile (ten—Radames), Giovanni Inghilleri (bar—Amonasro), Luigi Manfrini (bass—Ramfis), Guglielmo Masini (bass—King), Vittore Veneziani (cnd), La Scala Chorus *(rec 1928)* Arkadia ("The 78's" series) 2-▲ 78013 [ADD]
Verdi, G.:Aida, w. D. Giannini (sop), I. Minghini-Cattaneo (cta), A. Pertile (ten), G. Inghilleri (bar), L. Manfrini (bass), La Scala Chorus [I] *(rec 1928 for HMV)* Pearl 2-▲ CDS 9402 (m) [AAD]
Verdi, G.:Aida, w. Dusolina Giannini (sop), Irene Minghini-Cattaneo (cta), Aureliano Pertile (ten), La Scala Chorus *(rec Milan, 1928)* Phonographie 2-▲ PHG 5004 [ADD]
Verdi, G.:Otello, w. Maria Carbone (sgr), Nicola Fusati (ten), Piero Girardi (ten), Corrado Zambelli (ten), Apollo Granforte (bar), Enrico Spada (sgr), La Scala Chorus Grammofono 2000 2-▲ GRM 78651

La Scala Orch (cont.)
C. Sabajno (cnd) (cont.)
Verdi, G.:Requiem Mass, w. Maria Luisa Fanelli (sop), Irene Minghini-Cattaneo (mez), Fracno Lo Giudice (ten), E. Pinza (bass), La Scala Chorus *(rec 1927 for HMV)* Pearl ▲ GEMMCD 9374 (m) [AAD]
Verdi, G.:Rigoletto, w. Lina Pagliughi (sop), Salvatore Baccaloni (bass), Luigi Piazza (sgr), Tino Folgar (sgr), La Scala Chorus Pearl 2-▲ PEA 9180 [ADD]
Verdi, G.:Rigoletto, w. Lina Pagliughi (sop—Gilda), Linda Brambilla (mez—Contessa di Ceprano), Vera de Cristoff (cta—Maddalena), Tino Folgar (ten—Duca di Mantova), Giuseppe Nessi (ten—Borsa), Aristide Baracchi (bar—Conte di Monterone/Marullo), Luigi Piazza (bar—Rigoletto), Salvatore Baccaloni (bass—Sparafucile), Giuseppe Menni (bass—Conte di Ceprano), La Scala Chorus *(rec 1927-28)* Arkadia 2-▲ CD 78003 (m) [ADD]
Verdi, G.:Rigoletto, w. Lina Pagliughi (sop—Gilda), Linda Brambilla (mez—Countess Ceprano), Vera De Cristoff (cta—Maddalena), Tino Folgar (ten—Duke of Mantua), Giuseppe Nessi (ten—Borsa), Luigi Piazza (bar—Rigoletto), Aristide Baracchi (b-bar—Monterone/Marullo), Salvatore Baccaloni (bass—Sparafucile), Giuseppe Menni (bass—Ceprano), La Scala Chorus VAI Audio 2-▲ VAIA 1097-2
Verdi, G.:La traviata, w. Olga de Franco (sop—Flora Bervoix/Annina), Anna Rosza (sop—Violetta Valéry), Giordano Callegari (ten—Gastone), Alessandro Ziliani (ten—Alfredo Germont), Luigi Borgonovo (bar—Giorgio Germont), Arnoldo Lenzi (bar—Baron Douphol), Antonio Gelli (bass—Marquis d'Obigny/Dr. Grenvil), La Scala Chorus *(rec La Scala Theatre, Milan, Oct.-Nov. 1930)* VAI Audio 2-▲ VAIA 1108-2
Verdi, G.:La traviata, w. Olga de Franco (sop—Flora Bervoix/Annina), Anna Rosza (sop—Violetta Valery), Giordano Callegari (ten—Gastone), Alessandro Ziliani (ten—Alfredo Germont), Luigi Borgonovo (bar—Giorgio Germont), Arnoldo Lenzi (bar—Barone Douphol), Antonio Gelli (bass—Marchese d'Obigny/Dottor Grenvil), Vittore Veneziani (cnd), La Scala Chorus *(rec Oct-Nov 1930)* Arkadia 2-▲ CD 78001 (m) [ADD]
Verdi, G.:Il trovatore, w. Maria Carena (sop—Leonora), Olga De Franco (sop—Ines), Irene Minghini Cattaneo (mez—Azucena), Aureliano Pertile (ten—Manrico), Giordano Callegari (ten—Ruiz/Messenger), Apollo Granforte (bar—Count), Bruno Carmassi (bass—Ferrando), Antonio Gelli (bass—Old Gypsy), Vittore Veneziani (cnd), La Scala Chorus *(rec 1930)* Arkadia ("The 78's" series) 2-▲ 78007 [ADD]
Verdi, G.:Il trovatore, w. Maria Caniglia (sop), Aureliano Pertile (ten), Apollo Granforte (bar), La Scala Chorus *(rec Milan, Sept.-Oct. 1930)* Phonographie 2-▲ PHG 5002 [ADD]

Sabajno, Bellezza (cnd)
Verdi, G.:Otello (sels), w. Giovanni Zenatello (ten), Royal Opera House Orch Covent Garden, Royal Opera House Chorus Covent Garden Phonographe ("Great Voices" series) ▲ PHG 5048

V. de Sabata (cnd)
Beethoven, L. van:Sym 3, "Eroica"—Funeral March *(rec live, Milan, Feb. 18, 1957)* Arkadia ("Historical Performances" series) 2-▲ 604 (m)
Giordano, U.:Andrea Chénier (sels), w. R. Tebaldi (sop), F. Barbieri (mez), M. del Monaco (ten), P. Silveri (bar), La Scala Chorus—14 arias from Acts 1-3 [I] *(rec live, Milan, 3/6/49)* Myto ▲ 1 MCD 90634 [ADD]
Puccini, G.:La Bohème (sels), w. M. Carosio (sop), A. Noni (sop), G. Poggi (ten), P. Silveri (bar), La Scala Chorus—6 arias from Acts 3 & 4 [I] *(rec live, Milan, 12/7/49)* Myto ▲ 1 MCD 90634 [ADD]
Puccini, G.:Tosca, w. M. Callas (sop), G. di Stefano (ten), T. Gobbi (bar), La Scala Chorus [I] *(rec 1953)* EMI Classics 2-▲ CDCB 47174 (m) 2-■ 4AV 34047 (m)
Rossini, G.:Il barbiere di Siviglia, w. D. Gatta (sop), C. Valletti (ten), G. Bechi (bar), N. Rossi-Lemeni (bass), La Scala Chorus *(rec 1952)* Memories 2-▲ MEM 4525 [AAD]
Verdi, G.:Requiem Mass, w. Elizabeth Schwarzkopf (sop), Oralia Dominguez (mez), Giuseppe Di Stefano (ten), Cesare Siepi (b-bar), La Scala Chorus Theorema 2-▲ TH 121123/24
Verdi, G.:La traviata (sels), w. Elizabeth Schwarzkopf (sop), Oralia Dominguez (mez), Giuseppe DiStefano (ten), Cesare Siepi (b-bar), La Scala Chorus—Preludes to Acts I & III Theorema 2-▲ TH 121123/24

G. Santini (cnd)
Rossini, G.:Il barbiere di Siviglia, w. Fiorenza Cossotto (mez), Luigi Alva (ten), Sesto Bruscantini (bar), Carlo Badioli (bass), Nicolai Ghiaurov (bass), La Scala Chorus *(rec Jan 20, 1964)* Pantheon 2-▲ PHE 6644 (m)

N. Sanzogno (cnd)
Cherubini, L.:Ali Baba, ou Les Quarante voleurs, w. T. Stich-Randall (sop), A. Kraus (ten), V. Ganzarolli (bar), La Scala Chorus *(rec 1963)* Memories 2-▲ MEM 4513 [ADD]
Donizetti, G.:La fille du régiment, w. M. Freni (sop), L. Pavarotti (ten), W. Ganzarolli (bar), La Scala Chorus *(rec 1969)* Memories 2-▲ MEM 4507 [ADD]
Donizetti, G.:La fille du régiment, w. M. Freni (sop), A. di Stasio (mez), L. Pavarotti (ten), W. Ganzarolli (bar), W. Monachesi (bar), La Scala Chorus [I] *(rec live, 2/11/69)* Verona 2-▲ 27046/47 (m) [AAD]
Donizetti, G.:La fille du régiment, w. M. Freni (sop), A. di Stasio (mez), L. Pavarotti (ten), W. Ganzarolli (bar), W. Monachesi (bar), La Scala Chorus [I] *(rec live, 2/11/69)* Melodram 2-▲ MEL 27045
Donizetti, G.:La fille du régiment (sels), w. Mirella Freni (sop), Anna di Stasio (mez), Angelo Mercuriali (ten), Luciano Pavarotti (ten), Wladimiro Ganzarolli (bar), Walter Monachesi (bar), Giuseppe Morresi (bass), V. Gullino (sgr), Luisa Rezzadore (sgr), La Scala Chorus Budget ("The Greatest Voice in Opera" series) ▲ SYP 108
Donizetti, G.:Lucia di Lammermoor, w. R. Scotto (sop), G. di Stefano (ten), E. Bastianini (bar), La Scala Chorus *(rec 1959)* Enterprise (Palladio) 2-▲ ENTPD 4117 [ADD]
Gluck, C.W.:Iphigénie en Tauride, w. M. Callas (sop), F. Cossotto (mez), Albanese (sgr), La Scala Chorus [I] *(rec live 6/1/57)* Melodram 2-▲ MEL 26012 (m)
Tchaikovsky, P.:Queen of Spades (sels), w. L. Gencer (sop—Liza), A. Annaloro (ten—Hermann) [I] *(rec Feb. 2, 1960)* Arkadia 2-▲ 599 [ADD]

W. Sawallisch (cnd)
Mozart, W.A.:Entführung, w. Mariella Devia (sop), Uwe Peper (ten), Kurt Moss (sgr), La Scala Chorus *(rec live, 1994)* Serenissima 2-▲ SER 360161
Wagner, R.:Der fliegende Holländer, w. L. Rysanek (sop), A.-M. Bessel (mez), C. Heater (ten), F. Crass (bass), K. Ridderbusch (bass), La Scala Chorus [G] *(rec live, Milan 2/2/66)* Memories 2-▲ HR 4281/82 (m) [ADD]
Wagner, R.:Lohengrin, w. A. Varnay (sop), I. Bjoner (sop), J. Thomas (ten), G. Neidlinger (b-bar), Prague Phil Chorus [G] *(rec live, Milan 1965)* Melodram 3-▲ MEL 37067 [AAD]
Wagner, R.:Tannhäuser, w. S. Jurinac (sop), B. Martin (sop), H. Beirer (ten), H. Braun (bar), M. Talvela (bass), La Scala Chorus [G] *(rec live, Milan 4/13/67)* Melodram 3-▲ CDM 37091 [ADD]

T. Schippers (cnd)
Falla, M. de:Atlántida, w. T. Stratas (sop), G. Simionato (mez), R. Browne (sgr), Halley (sgr), La Scala Chorus *(rec live, Milan 6/18/62)* Memories 2-▲ HR 4464/65 [ADD]
Rossini, G.:The Siege of Corinth, w. B. Sills (sop), M. Horne (mez), F. Bonisoli (ten), J. Diaz (bass), La Scala Chorus [I] *(rec live 1969)* Melodram 2-▲ MEL 27043 [ADD]

J. Semkow (cnd)
Janácek, L.:Jenůfa, w. Magda Olivero (sop—Kostelnicka), Bruna Baglioni (mez—La vecchia Buryja), Grace Bumbry (mez—Jenufa), Renato Cioni (ten—Steva Buryja), Robleto Merolla (bar—Laca Klemen), Carlo Meliciani (sgr—Vecchio compagno), La Scala Chorus *(rec Milan, Apr 2, 1974)* Myto 2-▲ MCD 961142

T. Serafin (cnd)
Bellini, V.:Arias, w. M. Callas (sop)—La sonnambula—Compagne, teneri amici...Come per me sereno; Oh, se una volta sola...Ah, non credea mirarti [I] *(rec 1955)* EMI Classics ▲ CDC 47966 [ADD]
Bellini, V.:Norma, w. M. Callas (sop), C. Ludwig (mez), F. Corelli (ten), N. Zaccaria (bass), La Scala Chorus [I] EMI Classics ("Studio" series) 3-▲ CDMC 63000 [ADD]
Bellini, V.:Norma, w. M. Callas (sop), E. Stignani (mez), M. Filippeschi (ten), N. Rossi-Lemeni (bass), La Scala Chorus [I] EMI Classics 3-▲ CDC 47303 (m)
Bellini, V.:Norma (sels), w. M. Callas (sop), C. Ludwig (mez), F. Corelli (ten), N. Zaccaria (bass), La Scala Chorus EMI Classics ▲ ZDM 63091
Bellini, V.:I Puritani, w. M. Callas (sop), G. di Stefano (ten), R. Panerai (bar), N. Rossi-Lemeni (bass), La Scala Chorus [I] EMI Classics 2-▲ CDCB 47308 (m) [ADD]
Cherubini, L.:Médée, w. M. Callas (sop), R. Scotto (sop), M. Pirazzini (mez), M. Picchi (ten), La Scala Chorus [I] *(rec live, 1953)* EMI Classics (Studio) 2-▲ CDMB 63625 [ADD]

La Scala Orch (cont.)
T. Serafin (cnd) (cont.)
Donizetti, G.:L'elisir d'amore, w. Rosanna Carteri (sop—Adina), Luigi Angela Vercelli (mez—Gianetta), Luigi Alva (ten—Nemorino), Rolando Panerai (bar—Belcore), Giuseppe Taddei (bar—Dulcamara), La Scala Chorus EMI Classics 2-▲ CDMB 65658
Leoncavallo, R.:Pagliacci, w. M. Callas (sop), G. di Stefano (ten), T. Gobbi (bar), R. Panerai (bar) [I] EMI Classics 3-▲ CDCC 47981 [ADD]
Mascagni, P.:Cavalleria rusticana, w. M. Callas (sop), E. Ticozzi (mez), G. di Stefano (ten), R. Panerai (bar), La Scala Chorus [I] EMI Classics 3-▲ CDCC 47981 [ADD]
Puccini, G.:Manon Lescaut, w. M. Callas (sop), G. di Stefano (ten), Fioravanti (sgr), La Scala Chorus [I] EMI Classics 2-▲ CDCB 47392 (m)
Puccini, G.:Turandot, w. M. Callas (sop), E. Schwarzkopf (sop), E. Fernandi (ten), N. Zaccaria (bass), La Scala Chorus [I] *(rec 1957)* EMI Classics 2-▲ CDCB 47971 (m) [ADD]
Verdi, G.:Aida, w. M. Callas (sop), F. Barbieri (mez), G. Tucker (ten), T. Gobbi (bar), N. Zaccaria (bass), La Scala Chorus [I] EMI Classics 3-▲ CDCC 49030 [ADD]
Verdi, G.:Requiem Mass, w. Maria Caniglia (sop), Ebe Stignani (cta), Beniamino Gigli (ten), Ezio Pinza (bass), La Scala Chorus *(rec 1939)* Phonographie ▲ PHG 5012 [ADD]
Verdi, G.:Rigoletto (sels), w. Maria Callas (sop), La Scala Chorus—selected arias *(rec Milan, 1953)* Andromeda ▲ ANR 2541 [ADD]

G. Solti (cnd)
Verdi, G.:Simon Boccanegra, w. K. Te Kanawa (sop), J. Aragall (ten), L. Nucci (bar), P. Burchuladze (bass), La Scala Chorus [I] London 2-▲ 425628-2 [DDD]

A. Toscanini (cnd)
Arturo Toscanini:The 1st Recordings, 1920–26, w. New York PO Symposium ▲ SYM 1189
Boito, A.:Mefistofele (sels)—Prologue *(rec live, Milan, May 18, 1946)* Arkadia ("Historical Performances" series) 2-▲ 604 (m)
Mussorgsky, M.:Pictures at an Exhibition—selections *(rec Milan, Sept. 16, 1948)* Originals ▲ ORISH 852
Puccini, G.:Manon Lescaut (sels), w. M. Favero (sop), R. Tebaldi (sop), J. Gardino (mez), G. Malipiero (ten), G. Nessi (ten), M. Stabile (bar), T. Pasero (b-bar), C. Forti (bass), La Scala Chorus—Intermezzo; Act 3 *(rec live, Milan, May 18, 1946)* Arkadia ("Historical Performances" series) 2-▲ 604 (m)
Rossini, G.:La gazza ladra (sels)—Ov. *(rec live, Milan, May 18, 1946)* Arkadia ("Historical Performances" series) 2-▲ 604 (m)
Rossini, G.:Mosè in Egitto (sels), w. La Scala Chorus—Prayer *(rec live, Milan, May 18, 1946)* Arkadia ("Historical Performances" series) 2-▲ 604 (m)
Rossini, G.:Ovs—Scala di Seta *(rec Milan, Sept. 16, 1948)* Originals ▲ ORISH 852
Tchaikovsky, P.:Romeo & Juliet *(rec Milan, Sept. 16, 1948)* Originals ▲ ORISH 852
Verdi, G.:Nabucco (sels), w. La Scala Chorus—Ov.; Chorus of the Hebrew Slaves *(rec live, Milan, May 18, 1946)* Arkadia ("Historical Performances" series) 2-▲ 604 (m)
Verdi, G.:Otello (sels)—Ballabili [from Act III] *(rec Milan, Sept. 16, 1948)* Originals ▲ ORISH 852
Verdi, G.:Te Deum, w. La Scala Chorus *(rec live, Milan, May 18, 1946)* Arkadia ("Historical Performances" series) 2-▲ 604 (m)
Verdi, G.:I vespri siciliani (sels)—Ov. *(rec live, Milan, May 18, 1946)* Arkadia ("Historical Performances" series) 2-▲ 604 (m)

A. Votto (cnd)
Bellini, V.:Norma, w. M. Callas (sop), G. Simionato (mez), M. Del Monaco (ten), N. Zaccaria (bass), La Scala Chorus *(rec 12/7/55)* HRE 2-▲ 1007-2
Bellini, V.:Norma, w. Maria Callas (sop), Gabriella Carturan (mez), Giulietta Simionato (mez), Mario del Monaco (ten), Giuseppe Zampieri (ten), Nicola Zaccaria (bass), La Scala Chorus Melodram 2-▲ CDM 26036
Bellini, V.:La sonnambula, w. M. Callas (sop), F. Cossotto (mez), N. Monti (ten), N. Zaccaria (bass), La Scala Chorus [I] *(rec live 1957)* Verona 2-▲ 2704/05 (m) [AAD]
Bellini, V.:La sonnambula, w. M. Callas (sop), F. Cossotto (mez), N. Monti (ten), N. Zaccaria (bass), La Scala Chorus [I] *(rec live 1957)* Melodram 2-▲ MEL 26003
Bellini, V.:La sonnambula, w. M. Callas (sop), F. Cossotto (mez), N. Monti (ten), N. Zaccaria (bass), La Scala Chorus [I] *(rec live 1957)* Arkadia 2-▲ 503 (m) [AAD]
Bellini, V.:La sonnambula, w. M. Callas (sop), F. Cossotto (mez), N. Monti (ten), N. Zaccaria (bass), La Scala Chorus [I] EMI Classics 2-▲ CDCB 47377 (m)
Bellini, V.:La sonnambula, w. Maria Callas (sop), Fiorenza Cossotto (mez), Nicola Monti (ten), Franco Ricciardi (ten), Dino Mantovani (bar), Nicola Zaccaria (bass), La Scala Chorus Melodram 2-▲ CDM 26037
Bellini, V.:La sonnambula (sels), w. M. Callas (sop), F. Cossotto (mez), N. Monti (ten), N. Zaccaria (bass), La Scala Chorus, from Act 2—Oh! se una volta sola rivederio; Ah, non creda mirarti [I] *(rec live, 7/4/57)* Myto 2-▲ 2 MCD 89006 (m) [ADD]
Donizetti, G.:Poliuto, w. Maria Callas (sop), Franco Corelli (ten), Ettore Bastianini (bar), La Scala Chorus *(rec live, Milan, 1960)* Enterprise ("Documents" series) 2-▲ ENT LV 977 (m)
Donizetti, G.:Poliuto, w. M. Callas (sop), F. Corelli (ten), E. Bastianini (bar), N. Zaccaria (bass), La Scala Chorus [I] *(rec live, Milan 12/7/60)* Verona 2-▲ 28003/04
Donizetti, G.:Poliuto, w. M. Callas (sop), F. Corelli (ten), E. Bastianini (bar), N. Zaccaria (bass), La Scala Chorus [I] *(rec live, 12/7/60)* Arkadia 2-▲ 520 (m) [AAD]
Donizetti, G.:Poliuto, w. M. Callas (sop), F. Corelli (ten), E. Bastianini (bar), N. Zaccaria (bass), La Scala Chorus [I] *(rec live, 12/7/60)* Melodram 2-▲ MEL 26006
Giordano, U.:Andrea Chénier, w. M. Callas (sop), M. del Monaco (ten), A. Protti (bar), La Scala Chorus *(rec live, Milan, 1/8/55)* Melodram 2-▲ MEL 26002 [ADD]
Giordano, U.:Andrea Chénier, w. M. Callas (sop), M. del Monaco (ten), A. Protti (bar), La Scala Chorus *(rec live)* Verona 2-▲ VER 28020
Mascagni, P.:Cavalleria rusticana (sels), w. G. Simionato (mez), G. Di Stefano (ten), La Scala Chorus—Tu qui Santuzza [I] *(rec live, Milan, 5/10/55)* Standing Room Only 2-▲ SRO 816-2 [ADD]
Ponchielli, A.:La Gioconda, w. M. Callas (sop), F. Cossotto (mez), I. Companeez (cta), P. M. Ferraro (ten), P. Cappuccilli (bar), I. Vinco (bass), La Scala Chorus EMI Classics ▲ CDCC 49518
Puccini, G.:La Bohème, w. M. Callas (sop), A. Moffo (sop), G. di Stefano (ten), R. Panerai (bar), La Scala Chorus [I] *(rec 1956)* EMI Classics 2-▲ CDCB 47475 (m) [ADD]
Spontini, G.:La vestale, w. M. Callas (sop), F. Corelli (ten), E. Sordello (bar), La Scala Chorus [I] *(rec live, Milan, 12/7/54)* Melodram 2-▲ MEL 26008
Spontini, G.:La vestale, w. M. Callas (sop), N. Rossi-Lemeni (bass), F. Corelli (ten), E. Sordello (bar), V. Tatozzi (bar), N. Zaccaria (bass), La Scala Chorus Great Opera Performances ▲ GOP 741
Spontini, G.:La vestale (sels), w. M. Callas (sop), A. Corelli (bar), E. Sordello (bar), La Scala Chorus [I]—3 scenes *(rec live, Milan, 12/7/54)* Verona 2-▲ 28003/04
Verdi, G.:Aida, w. Antonietta Stella (sop—Aida), Mirella Parutto (sop—Priestess), Giulietta Simionato (mez—Amneris), Giuseppe DiStefano (ten—Radames), Giuseppe Zampiere (ten—Messenger), Giangiacomo Guelfi (bar—Amonasro), Silvio Maionica (bass—King of Egypt), Nicola Zaccaria (bass-Ramfis), La Scala Chorus *(rec Milan, Dec 7, 1956)* Legato Classics 2-▲ LCD 204-2 [ADD]
Verdi, G.:Un ballo in maschera, w. M. Callas (sop), E. Ratti (sop), F. Barbieri (mez), G. Di Stefano (ten), T. Gobbi (bar), La Scala Chorus [I] *(rec 1956)* EMI Classics 2-▲ CDCB 47498 (m)
Verdi, G.:Ernani, w. R. Kabaivanska (sop), P. Domingo (ten), N. Ghiaurov (bass), Meliciani (sgr), La Scala Chorus *(rec live 12/7/69)* Melodram 2-▲ MEL 27064 (m) [AAD]
Verdi, G.:La forza del destino, w. Leyla Gencer (sop—Leonora), Gabriella Carturan (mez—Preziosilla), Giuseppe di Stefano (ten—Don Alvaro), Aldo Protti (bar—Don Carlo), Cesare Siepi (b-bar), Franco Calabrese (bass—Marchese di Calatrava), Enrico Campi (bass—Fra Melitone), La Scala Chorus *(rec Bühnen der Stadt, Köln, July 5, 1957)* Agorá Music ("Phoenix" series) 3-▲ 510 [ADD]
Verdi, G.:La forza del destino, w. Leyla Gencer (sop), Giuseppe di Stefano (ten), Aldo Protti (bar), Cesare Siepi (bass), La Scala Chorus *(rec La Scala Theatre, Milan, July 5, 1957)* Pantheon 3-▲ PHE 6627 (m)
Verdi, G.:La forza del destino (sels), w. C. Bergonzi (ten), Meliciani (sgr)—La vita è inferno all'infelice; O tu che in seno; Invano, Alvaro [I] *(rec live 12/7/65)* Melodram 2-▲ 27058 [AAD]
Verdi, G.:Otello, w. R. Tebaldi (sop), M. del Monaco (ten), L. Warren (bar), La Scala Chorus *(rec July 1, 1954)* Melodram 2-▲ MLO 270101 [AAD]
Verdi, G.:La traviata, w. Renata Scotto (sop—Violetta Valery), Giuliana Tavolaccini (sop—Flora Bervoix), Gianni Raimondi (ten—Alfredo Germont), Ettore Bastianini (bar—Giorgio Germont), La Scala Chorus *(rec La Scala Theatre, Milan, 1963)* Deutsche Grammophon 2-▲ 439720-2 [ADD]

La Scala Orch (cont.)
A. Votto (cnd) (cont.)
Verdi, G.:La traviata (sels), w. R. Scotto (sop), G. Tavolccini (sop), A. Bonato (sop), G. Raimondi (ten), E. Bastianini (bar), La Scala Chorus IMP Collectors Series ▲ IMPX 9025 [AAD]
Verdi, G.:Il trovatore, w. M. Callas (sop), E. Stignani (mez), G. Penno (ten), C. Tagliabue (bar), La Scala Chorus [I] *(rec live 2/23/53)* Myto 2-▲ 2 MCD 90213 (m) [ADD]

La Scala Orch Soloists
R. Muti (cnd)
Vivaldi, A.:Cons Fl, Op. 10 EMI Classics ▲ CDC 55183
Vivaldi, A.:Cons Vn, Op. 8/1–12, "Il cimento dell'armonia e dell'inventione", w. G. Franzetti (vn)—Nos. 1–5 EMI Classics ▲ CDC 55183

La Scala String Trio [S. Pagliani (vn), D. Rossi (va), E. Dindo (vc)]
Eisler, H.:Präludium und Fugue über B–A–C–H *(rec Nov. 5–6, 1992)* Arcadia ▲ ARC 2001-2 [DDD]
Mozart, W.A.:Trio Vn, K.563 *(rec Nov. 1992)* Arcadia ▲ ARC 2001-2 [DDD]
Webern, A.:Movt Str Trio *(rec Nov. 1992)* Arcadia ▲ ARC 2001-2 [DDD]
Webern, A.:Piece Str Trio *(rec Nov. 5–6, 1992)* Arcadia ▲ ARC 2001

Scaligero Trio
Borodin, A.:Trio Pno Stradivarius ▲ SIP 26
Cilea, F.:Trio Vn Stradivarius ▲ SIP 26
Lalo, E.:Trio 1 Pno Stradivarius ▲ SIP 26

Scandinavian Brass Ensemble
Danielsson, C.:Suite 3 BIS ▲ CD 265 [DDD]
Holmboe, V.:Con Brass BIS ▲ CD 265 [DDD]
Madsen, T.:Divert Brass & Perc BIS ▲ CD 265 [DDD]
J. Panula (cnd)
Brass Festival BIS ▲ CD 265 [DDD]

Scandinavian Wind Quintet [M. Johansen (fl), K. Sjöblom (ob), J. Helmuth Madsen (cl), O. Nilsson (hn), P. Andersen (bn)]
Abrahamsen, H.:Walden Marco Polo/Dacapo ▲ 8.224001 [DDD]
Holmboe, V.:Notturno Marco Polo/Dacapo ▲ 8.224001 [DDD]
Nielsen, C.:Qnt Ww Marco Polo/Dacapo ▲ 8.224001 [DDD]
Nørgård, P.:Whirl's World Marco Polo/Dacapo ▲ 8.224001 [DDD]

Scapoli
R. Aghamir (cnd)
Habbestad, K.:The First Mass on Norwegian Soil Norway Music ▲ 2912
T. Mikkelsen (cnd)
Habbestad, K.:Song–Dance, w. Odd Lund (goat's hn), Åshild Watne (Medieval lyre), Oslo Phil Women's Chamber Choir Norway Music ▲ 2912

Scaramouche [Andrew Manze (vn), Caroline Balding (vn), Ulrike Wild (hpd/org), Jaap ter Linden (b vl)]
Henry Purcell & His Times:17th Century English Chamber Music *(rec Jan. 1992)* Channel Classics ▲ CCS 4792 [DDD]

Scarborough Chamber Players
Villa-Lobos, H.:Bachiana brasileira 6 Centaur ▲ CRC 2106
Scarborough Chamber Players [B. Scarpelli (sop), V. Sindelar (fl), P. Cokkinias (cl)]
Blank, A.:Poems (4)—How Happy Is the Little Stone, In This Short Life, Surgeons Must Be Very Careful, Nature Is What We See Centaur ▲ CRC 2106
Scarborough Chamber Players [M. Saunders (sop), P. Cokkinias (cl), M. Romanul (pno)]
Spohr, L.:German Songs , Op. 103 Centaur ▲ CRC 2106
Scarborough Chamber Players [M. Saunders (sop), P. Cokkinias (cl/b cl), V. Sindelar (fl/pic), M. Romanul (pno)]
Starer, R.:Songs of Youth & Age—Youth, Old Age, Day Night; Young and Old; The Life of This World; That Which We Are, We Are Centaur ▲ CRC 2106
Scarborough Chamber Players [M. Saunders (sop), V. Sindelar (fl)]
Roussel, A.:Poèmes de Ronsard—Rossignol, mon mignon, Ciel, aer, et vens Centaur ▲ CRC 2106

Alessandro Scarlatti CO
F. Caracciolo (cnd)
Paisiello, G.:La Molinara, w. Graziella Sciutti (sop), Agostino Lazzari (ten), Alvinio Misciano (ten), Sesto Bruscantini (bar), Franco Calabrese (bass), Leonardo Monreale (bass) Melodram 2-▲ CDM 29502

Scarlatti Quintet
Hindemith, P.:Kleine Kammermusik Nuova Era ▲ 7075 [DDD]

Scarponi Quintet
Fuchs, R.:Qnt Cl Nuova Era ▲ NUO CD 7252
Kornauth, E.:Qnt Cl Nuova Era ▲ NUO CD 7252

Schanzer/Speach Duo
Léon, T.:Ajiaco Avant ▲ 02

Scharoun Ensemble
H. Holliger (cnd)
Yun, I.:Distanzen *(rec live, Berlin, 10/9/88)* Arcadia ▲ ARC 1997-2 [DDD]
B. Jones (cnd)
Henze, H.-W.:Chamber Music, w. N. Jenkins (ten), T. Walker (gtr) Koch Schwann ▲ CD 310004 [DDD]

Schleswig-Holstein Festival Orch
C. Eschenbach (cnd)
Beethoven, L. van:Con 1 Pno, w. S. Richter (pno) RCA Red Seal ▲ 09026-61534-2 [DDD]

Schlierbach CO
T. Fey (cnd)
Handel, G.F.:Judas Maccabaeus, w. M. Meier-Schmid (sop), Elisabeth von Magnus (alt), Jörg Dürmüller (ten), Robert Wörle (ten), Franz-Josef Selig (bass), Munich Motet Choir [E] Christophorus 2-▲ 77128 [DDD]

Schmidt-Gaden Orch
Schubert, Franz:Duetsche Messe, w. Tölz Boys' Choir [G] Acanta ▲ CD 42409

Schnabel Piano Duo [Joan Rowland (pno), Karl Ulrich Schnabel (pno)]
Schubert, Franz:Fant Pno, D.940 Sheffield Lab ("Audiophile Reference Series") ▲ 10054-2
Schubert, Franz:Ländler Pno, D.814 Sheffield Lab ("Audiophile Reference Series") ▲ 10054-2
Schubert, Franz:Pno Music (4-hands)—Fant in f, Op. 103; 4 Polonaises in E, Opp. 61/3, 4, 6 & 75/3; Vars in A♭, Op. 35; 4 Ländler, D.814; Rondo in D, D.608 Sheffield Lab ▲ SLS 10054
Schubert, Franz:Polonaises Pno, D.599—No. 3 Sheffield Lab ("Audiophile Reference Series") ▲ 10054-2
Schubert, Franz:Polonaises Pno, D.824—Nos. 3, 4 & 6 Sheffield Lab ("Audiophile Reference Series") ▲ 10054-2
Schubert, Franz:Rondo Pno, D.608 Sheffield Lab ("Audiophile Reference Series") ▲ 10054-2
Schubert, Franz:Son Pno 4-Hands, D.812 Town Hall ▲ THCD 37
Schubert, Franz:Vars on an Original Theme Pno 4-Hands Sheffield Lab ("Audiophile Reference Series") ▲ 10054-2
Schubert, Franz:Vars on an Original Theme Pno 4-Hands Town Hall ▲ THCD 37

Alexander Schneider String Quartet
Lanner, J.:Music of CBS ▲ MK 44522 [DDD]
Strauss (I), Joh.:Radetzky March CBS ▲ MK 44522 [DDD]
Strauss (II), Joh.:Waltzes—An der schönen blauen Donau CBS ▲ MK 44522 [DDD]

Alexander Schneider String Quintet
On The Beautiful Blue Danube CBS ▲ MK 44522 [DDD]

Schneiderhan String Quartet
Beethoven, L. van:Qt 6 Strs *(rec South German Radio, Stuttgart, Mar. 20, 1949)* Orfeo d'or ▲ 402951 (m) [ADD]
Mozart, W.A.:Qt 17 Strs *(rec South German Radio, Stuttgart, Mar. 20, 1949)* Orfeo d'or ▲ 402951 (m) [ADD]
Ravel, M.:Qt Strs *(rec South German Radio, Stuttgart, Nov. 25, 1950)* Orfeo d'or ▲ 402951 (m) [ADD]

Schoenberg Ensemble

Busoni, F.:Berceuse élégiaque, w. J. van Nes (alt), J. Bröcheler (bar) Koch Schwann ▲ SCH 312632 [DDD]

Mahler, G.:Kindertotenlieder, w. J. Van Nes (alt), J. Bröcheler (bar) Koch Schwann ▲ SCH 312632 [DDD]

Mahler, G.:Lieder eines fahrenden Gesellen, w. J. Van Nes (alt), J. Bröcheler (bar) Koch Schwann ▲ SCH 312632 [DDD]

Schoenberg, A.:Phantasy Vn Philips ▲ 416306-2 [DDD]

Schoenberg, A.:Trio Strs Philips ▲ 416306-2 [DDD]

Schoenberg, A.:Verklärte Nacht Philips ▲ 416306-2 [DDD]

Webern, A.:Bagatelles Str Qt—Nos. 1 & 6 Koch Schwann ▲ CD 314005 [DDD]

R. de Leeuw (cnd)

Andriessen, L.:Mausoleum, w. David Barick (bar), Charles van Tassel (bar), Asko Ensemble Donemus ▲ CV 20

Andriessen, L.:De Tijd, w. The Hague Percussion Group, Netherlands Chamber Choir Elektra/Nonesuch ▲ 79291-2 ■ 79291-4

Górecki, H.-M.:Kleines Requiem für eine Polka Philips ▲ 442533-2

Górecki, H.-M.:Lerchenmusik Philips ▲ 442533-2

Kagel, M.:Phantasiestück Montaigne ▲ MO 782017

Kagel, M.:Stücke der Windrose Montaigne ▲ MO 782017

Messiaen, O.:Des Canyons aux étoiles, Asko Ensemble, The Hague Percussion Ensemble Montaigne 2-▲ MO 782035

Reich, S.:Tehillim [He] Elektra/Nonesuch ▲ 79295-2

Schoenberg, A.:Pierrot lunaire, w. B. Sukowa (speaker) [G] Koch Schwann ▲ CD 310 117 [DDD]

Schoenberg, A.:Suite Ww Koch Schwann ▲ CD 310 117 [DDD]

Torstensson, K.:The Last Diary, w. Palle Fuhr Jørgensen (nar), Asko Ensemble *(rec The Hague, Netherlands, Mar 6 1995)* Donemus ▲ CV 57 [DDD]

Vries, K. de:...Sub nocte per umbras... Donemus ▲ CV 34

Webern, A.:Vocal Chamber Music, w. D. Dorow (sop), Netherlands Chamber Choir—(choral songs) Entflieht auf leichten Kähnen, Op. 2 (1908 & 1914 versions); Two Songs, Op. 19 (1926); (songs for solo voice & instrumental chamber ensemble) Two Songs, Op. 8 (1910); Schmerz, immer blick' nach oben (1913); Three Songs (1913–14); Four Songs, Op. 13 (1914–18); Six Songs, Op. 14 (1917–21); Five Sacred Songs, Op. 15 (1917–22); Five Canons, Op. 16 (1923–24); Three Traditional Rhymes, Op. 17 (1924–25); Three Songs, Op. 18 (1925) [G,L] Koch Schwann ▲ CD 314005 [DDD]

Schoenberg String Quartet

Berg, A.:Lyric Suite Koch Schwann ▲ CD 310005 [DDD]

Berg, A.:Qt Strs Koch Schwann ▲ CD 310005 [DDD]

Brahms, J.:Qnt Cl, w. Pierre Woudenberg (cl) Koch Schwann ▲ SCH 311502

Chausson, E.:Con Vn, Pno & Str Qt, w. R. Kussmaul (vn), F. Meinders (pno) Koch Schwann ▲ SCH 312312 [DDD]

Dutilleux, H.:Ainsi la nuit Koch Schwann ▲ SCH 312312 [DDD]

Pijper, W.:Qts Strs Olympia ▲ OLY 457 [DDD]

Reger, M.:Qnt Cl, w. Pierre Woudenberg (cl) Koch Schwann ▲ SCH 311502

Roussel, A.:Chamber Music, w. Paul Verhey (fl/pic), Frank van den Brink (cl), Hans Roerade (ob), Jos de Lange (bn), Herre-Jan Stegenga (vc), Jet Röling (pno)—Trio for Fl, Va & Vc, Op. 40; Qt for Strs, Op. 45; Andante & Scherzo for Fl & Pno, Op. 51; Pipe for Pic & Pno; Trio for Strs, Op. 58; Music from Elpenor for Fl & Str Qt, Op. 59; Andante from an unfinished Ww Trio for Ob, Cl & Bn Olympia ▲ OLY 460 [DDD]

Schoenberg, A.:Qt 1 Strs Koch Schwann ▲ CD 310033 [DDD]

Schulhoff, E.:Pieces Str Qt Koch Schwann ▲ SCH 312332 [DDD]

Schulhoff, E.:Qt 1 Strs Koch Schwann ▲ SCH 312332 [DDD]

Schulhoff, E.:Qt 2 Strs Koch Schwann ▲ SCH 312332 [DDD]

Schulhoff, E.:Sxt Strs, w. J. E. van Regteren (va), T. Kooistra (vc) Koch Schwann ▲ SCH 312332 [DDD]

Zemlinsky, A. von:Qt 2 Strs Koch Schwann ▲ CD 310 118 [DDD]

Zemlinsky, A. von:Qt 3 Strs Koch Schwann ▲ CD 310 118 [DDD]

Schola Cantorum Basiliensis Instrumental Ensemble

R. Jacobs (cnd)

Caldara, A.:Maddalena ai Piedi di Cristo, w. Maria Cristina Kiehr (sop), Rosa Dominguez (sop), Bernarda Fink (cta), Andreas Scholl (ct), Gerd Türk (ten), Ulrich Messthaler (bass) Harmonia Mundi France 2-▲ HMC 905221.22

Gluck, C.W.:Le Cinesi, w. I. Poulenard (sop), A. S. von Otter (mez), G. Banditelli (cta), G. de Mey (ten) Editio Classica ▲ 77174-2-RG [DDD]

Zelenka, J.D.:Lamentationes Jeremiae Prophetae, w. R. Jacobs (alt), G. de Mey (ten), K. Widmer (bass) Editio Classica ▲ 77112-2-RG [ADD]

Scholars Baroque Ensemble

Purcell, H.:The Fairy Queen (orch suites) *(rec Nov. 1992)* Naxos 2-▲ 8.550660/61 [DDD]

Schönbrunn Ensemble Amsterdam

Beethoven, L. van:Serenade Fl, Op. 25 *(rec July 1992)* Globe ▲ GLO 5090 [DDD]

Beethoven, L. van:Serenade Strs, Op. 8 *(rec July 1992)* Globe ▲ GLO 5090 [DDD]

Hugot, A.:Qt Fl *(rec 8/90)* Channel Classics ▲ CCS 1290 [DDD]

Mozart, W.A.:Qts Fl *(rec 8/90)* Channel Classics ▲ CCS 1290 [DDD]

Schönbrunn Ensemble Amsterdam [Marten Root (trns fl), Frank de Bruine (ob), Johannes Leertouwer (vn), Irmgard Schaller (vn/va), Viola de Hoog (vc), Richard Myron (db)]

Haydn, J.:Diverts (misc)—in C, H.II/11; in D, H.II/D8; in G, H.II/1 *(rec Utrecht, Feb 1995)* Globe ▲ 5137 [DDD]

Haydn, M.:Diverts (misc)—in C, P.98 *(rec Utrecht, Feb 1995)* Globe ▲ 5137 [DDD]

Schubert Camerata

C.F. Sedazzari (cnd)

Angrisani, G.:Con Fl, w. Gian-Luca Petrucci (fl) *(rec live, Rome, July 27, 1995)* Bongiovanni ▲ GB 5553 [ADD]

Papa, F.:Con Fl, w. Gian-Luca Petrucci (fl) *(rec live, Rome, July 27, 1995)* Bongiovanni ▲ GB 5553 [ADD]

Prota, T.:Con Fl, w. Gian-Luca Petrucci (fl) *(rec live, Rome, July 27, 1995)* Bongiovanni ▲ GB 5553 [ADD]

Sciroli, G.:Con Fl, w. Gian-Luca Petrucci (fl) *(rec live, Rome, July 27, 1995)* Bongiovanni ▲ GB 5553 [ADD]

Servillo, M.:Con 1 Fl, w. Gian-Luca Petrucci (fl) *(rec live, Rome, July 27, 1995)* Bongiovanni ▲ GB 5553 [ADD]

Schubert Ensemble

Hummel, J.N.:Qnt Pno, Op. 87 Hyperion 2-▲ CDD 22008

Schubert, Franz:Minuet & Finale *(rec Feb. 10–14, 1992)* Naxos ▲ 8.550389 [DDD]

Schubert, Franz:Octet Ww, D.803 *(rec Feb. 10–14, 1992)* Naxos ▲ 8.550389 [DDD]

Schubert, Franz:Qnt Pno, D.667 Hyperion 2-▲ CDD 22008

Schumann, R.:Qt Pno in c Hyperion 2-▲ CDD 22008

Schumann, R.:Qt Pno, Op. 47 Hyperion ▲ CDA 66657

Schumann, R.:Qnt Pno Hyperion ▲ CDA 66657

Schumann, R.:Qnt Pno Hyperion 2-▲ CDD 22008

Weir, J.:Chamber Music, w. William Howard (pno), Susan Tomes (pno), Petra Casen (hpd), Domus Chamber Ensemble—Distance & Enchantment; The Bagpiper's Trio; I Broke Off a Golden Branch; El Rey de Francia; The Art of Touching the Keyboard; The King of France; Ardnamurchan Point Collins Classics ▲ COL 1453

Schubert Ensemble [Mayumi Seiler (vn), Ralph De Souza (vn), Douglas Paterson (va), Jane Salmon (vc), William Howard (pno)]

Dohnányi, E. von:Qnt 1 Pno Hyperion ▲ CDA 66786

Dohnányi, E. von:Qnt 2 Pno Hyperion ▲ CDA 66786

Schubert Ensemble [Mayumi Seiler (vn), Ralph De Souza (vn), Douglas Paterson (va), Jane Salmon (vc)]

Dohnányi, E. von:Serenade Hyperion ▲ CDA 66786

Franz Schubert String Quartet [Florian Zwiauer (vn), Helge Rosenkranz (vn), Hartmut Pascher (va), Vincent Stadlmair (vc)]

Dittersdorf, K.D. von:Qts (6) Strs—Nos. 2 & 6 CPO ▲ CPO 999122-2 [DDD]

Dittersdorf, K.D. von:Qts (6) Strs—Nos. 1,3,4 & 5 CPO ▲ CPO 999038-2 [DDD]

Dittersdorf, K.D. von:Qnts Strs, w. J. Berger (vc)—Nos. 3 & 6 CPO ▲ CPO 999122-2 [DDD]

Haydn, J.:Qts Strs, Op. 77, "Lobkowitz Qts" Nimbus ▲ NI 5312 [DDD]

Haydn, J.:Qt Strs, Op. 103 Nimbus ▲ NI 5312 [DDD]

Mozart, W.A.:Qt 14 Strs *(rec Nimbus Foundation Concert Hall, July 7–8, 1994)* Nimbus ▲ NI 5433 [DDD]

Mozart, W.A.:Qt 15 Strs *(rec Concert Hall of the Nimbus Foundation, Mar 18, 1994)* Nimbus 2-▲ NI 5455/6 [DDD]

Mozart, W.A.:Qt 16 Strs *(rec Concert Hall of the Nimbus Foundation, June 21, 1994)* Nimbus 2-▲ NI 5455/6 [DDD]

Mozart, W.A.:Qt 17 Strs *(rec Concert Hall of the Nimbus Foundation, Mar 21, 1994)* Nimbus 2-▲ NI 5455/6 [DDD]

Mozart, W.A.:Qt 18 Strs *(rec Nimbus Foundation Concert Hall, June 20–21, 1994)* Nimbus ▲ NI 5433 [DDD]

Mozart, W.A.:Qt 19 Strs *(rec June 22–23, 1992)* Nimbus ▲ NI 5381 [DDD]

Mozart, W.A.:Qt 20 Strs *(rec Concert Hall of the Nimbus Foundation, Mar 19, 1994)* Nimbus 2-▲ NI 5455/6 [DDD]

Mozart, W.A.:Qt 22 Strs Nimbus ▲ NI 5351

Mozart, W.A.:Qt 23 Strs *(rec Sept. 18–19, 1992)* Nimbus ▲ NI 5381 [DDD]

Pascher, H.:Qt 1 Strs Pro Viva ▲ ISPV 173

Pernes, T.:Qt 1 Strs Pro Viva ▲ ISPV 173

Pfitzner, H.:Qt 2 Strs *(rec Feb 2–5, 1993)* CPO ▲ CPO 999072-2 [DDD]

Pfitzner, H.:Qt 4 Strs *(rec Feb 2–5, 1993)* CPO ▲ CPO 999072-2 [DDD]

Przbylski, B.K.:Qt 2 Strs Pro Viva ▲ ISPV 173

Schmidt, F.:Qt Strs in A *(rec Concert Hall of the Nimbus Foundation, Apr 3–6, 1995)* Nimbus ▲ NI 5467 [DDD]

Schmidt, F.:Qt Strs in G *(rec Concert Hall of the Nimbus Foundation, Apr 3–6, 1995)* Nimbus ▲ NI 5467 [DDD]

Schubert, Franz:Qt 15 Strs GM ▲ 2018 CD [DDD]

Tchaikovsky, P.:Qt 1 Strs *(rec June 12–15, 1993)* Nimbus ▲ NI 5380 [DDD]

Tchaikovsky, P.:Qt 2 Strs *(rec Nov. 9–12, 1993)* Nimbus ▲ NI 5399 [DDD]

Tchaikovsky, P.:Qt 3 Strs *(rec June 12–15, 1993)* Nimbus ▲ NI 5380 [DDD]

Tchaikovsky, P.:Souvenir de Florence, w. J. Flieder (va), W. Schulz (vc) *(rec Nov. 9–12, 1993)* Nimbus ▲ NI 5399 [DDD]

Robert Schumann CO

M.-A. Schlingensiepen (cnd)

Weill, K.:Songs, w. W. Holzmair (bar)—Four Walt Whitman Songs (1943–47) [E] Koch Schwann ▲ CD 314 050 [DDD]

Clara Schumann Cologne Orch

E.M. Blankenburg (cnd)

Martinez, M.:Music of, w. Cologne Kurrende—Psalm Cants; In Exitu Israel; Dixit Dominus Koch Schwann ▲ SCH 317882

Schütz Academy

H. Arman (cnd)

Monteverdi, C.:Vespers, w. Susanne Ryden (sop), Irena Troupova-Wilke (sop), Detlef Bratschke (alt), Erich Mentzel (ten), Hermann Oswald (ten), Manuel Warwitz (ten), Thomas Herberich (bass), Günther Schmidt (bass) Capriccio ▲ CD 10521 [DDD]

Schelle, J.:Actus Musicus auf Weyh-Nachten, w. Mona Spägle (sop), Wilfried Jochens (ten) *(rec Dec 15–18, 1992)* Capriccio ▲ 10508 [DDD]

Schütz, H.:Weihnachtshistorie, w. Mona Spägle (sop), Wilfried Jochens (ten) *(rec Dec 15–18, 1992)* Capriccio ▲ 10508 [DDD]

Heinrich Schütz Ensemble

W. Kelber (cnd)

Schütz, H.:Die Geburt unsers Herren Jesu Christi *(rec Sept 1994)* Calig ▲ CAL 50941

Albert Schweitzer Wind Quintet

Danzi, F.:Qnts Ww, Op. 56—No. 1 CPO ▲ CPO 999180 [DDD]

Danzi, F.:Qnts Ww, Op. 67—No. 3 CPO ▲ CPO 999180 [DDD]

Danzi, F.:Qnts Ww, Op. 68—No. 2 CPO ▲ CPO 999180 [DDD]

Reicha, A.:Adagio E Hn CPO ▲ CPO 999024-2 [DDD]

Reicha, A.:Andantes E Hn—No. 1 in E♭ CPO ▲ CPO 999029-2 [DDD]

Reicha, A.:Andantes E Hn—No. 2 in F CPO ▲ CPO 999043-2 [DDD]

Reicha, A.:Qnts Ww (comp)—Quintets No. 12 in c, Op. 91/6 & No. 24 in B♭, Op. 100/6 CPO ▲ CPO 999029-2 [DDD]

Reicha, A.:Qnts Ww (comp)—Quintets No. 16 in D, Op. 99/4 & No. 17 in b, Op. 99/5 CPO ▲ CPO 999025-2 [DDD]

Reicha, A.:Qnts Ww (comp)—Quintets No. 7 in C, Op. 91/1, No. 18 in G, Op. 99/6 & No. 23 in a, Op. 100/5 CPO ▲ CPO 999027-2 [DDD]

Reicha, A.:Qnts Ww (comp)—Quintets No. 15 in A, Op. 99/3 & No. 22 in e, Op. 100, No. 4 CPO ▲ CPO 999030-2 [DDD]

Reicha, A.:Qnts Ww (comp)—Quintets No. 6 in F, Op. 88/6, No. 9 in D, Op. 91/3 & No. 21 in E♭, Op. 100/3 CPO ▲ CPO 999026-2 [DDD]

Reicha, A.:Qnts Ww (comp)—Quintets No. 2 in E♭, Op. 88/2, No. 13 in C, Op. 99, No. 1, & No. 25 in f, no opus number CPO ▲ CPO 999028-2 [DDD]

Reicha, A.:Qnts Ww (comp)—Quintets No. 10 in g, Op. 91/4 & No. 19 in F, Op. 100/1 CPO ▲ CPO 999024-2 [DDD]

Reicha, A.:Qnts Ww (comp)—Quintets No. 1 in e, Op. 88/1, No. 5 in B♭, Op. 88/5 & No. 14 in f, Op. 99/2 CPO ▲ CPO 999022-2 [DDD]

Reicha, A.:Qnts Ww (comp)—Quintets No. 8 in a, Op. 91/2 & No. 20 in d, Op. 100, No. 2 CPO ▲ CPO 999043-2 [DDD]

Reicha, A.:Qnts Ww (comp)—Quintets No. 3 in G, Op. 88/3, No. 4 in d, Op. 88/4 & No. 11 in A, Op. 91/5 CPO ▲ CPO 999023-2 [DDD]

Albert Schweitzer Wind Quintet [A. Tezlaff (fl), C. Dimigen (ob), D. Schneider (cl), S. Schurack (hn), E. Hübner (bn)]

Yun, I.:Festlicher Tanz *(rec Dec. 1991)* CPO ▲ CPO 999184 [DDD]

Yun, I.:Movt I *(rec Dec. 1991)* CPO ▲ CPO 999184 [DDD]

Yun, I.:Movt II *(rec Dec. 1991)* CPO ▲ CPO 999184 [DDD]

Yun, I.:Pezzo fantasioso *(rec Dec. 1991)* CPO ▲ CPO 999184 [DDD]

Albert Schweitzer Wind Quintet members

Pettersson, G.A.:Fuga CPO ▲ CPO 999169 [DDD]

Scots Guards Band

M. Reed (cnd)

Classical Spectacular, w. Royal PO, London Choral Society, Welsh Guards Band RPO Records 2-▲ CDRPD 9001 [DDD]

Classical Spectacular 1, w. Royal PO, Welsh Guards Band, Musketeers of the Sealed Knot, London Choral Society RPO Records ▲ RPO 5009 [DDD]

Classical Spectacular 2, w. Royal PO, Gunnar Gudbjornsson (ten), J. Howard (bar), Welsh Guards Band, London Choral Society RPO Records ▲ CDRPO 5010 [DDD]

Scott Chamber Players [L. Scott (vn), B. Scott (va), P. Scott (vc), G. S. Dugan (db), S. Patterson (pno)]

Swafford, J.:Music of—Midsummer Vars. for Piano Qnt.; They Who Hunger for Piano Qt. *(rec Nov. 1991 & Aug. 1992)* CRI ▲ CD 633 [DDD]

Scott Chamber Players [S. Patterson (pno), L. Scott (vn), B. Scott (va), P. Scott (vc)]

Gass, G.:Music of—Qt. for Piano & Strings; Trio for Strings *(rec 1988)* CRI ▲ CD 633 [DDD]

Scottish CO

Bach, J.S.:Cons Vn (comp), w. O. Shumsky (vn) Nimbus ▲ NI 5325 [DDD]

ORCH. & ENS.

Scottish CO (cont.)
Bach, J.S.:Con Vn & Ob, w. O. Shumsky (vn), R. Miller (ob) Nimbus ▲ NI 5325 [DDD]
Bach, J.S.:Con for 2 Vns, w. O. Shumsky (vn), J. Tunnell (vn) Nimbus ▲ NI 5325 [DDD]
G. Alexander (cnd)
Handel, G.F.:Water Music (comp) Chandos ▲ CHAN 8382 [DDD]
A. de Almeida (cnd)
Offenbach, J.:Music of, w. Frederica von Stade (mez)—Ov; Lettre de la Périchole; Ah! que les homes sont bêtes!; Ariette de la griserie; Entr'acte [all from La Périchole]; Chanson de la fille du tambour-major [from La Fille du tambour-major]; Amours divins [from La Belle Hélène]; Ov; Couplets de pomme; J'en prendrai un, deux, trois [all from Pomme d'api]; Couplets de l'alphabet [from Madame l'Archiduc]; Ov [from La Romance de la rose]; Rondeau et valse [from La Vie parisienne]; Couplets du berger joli [from Orphée aux enfers]; Ov; Couplets de Boulette; Couplets de la rosière [all from Barbe Bleu]; Ov; Dites-lui; Ah! que j'aime les militaires! [all from La Grande-Duchesse de Gérolstein] *(rec City Hall, Glasgow, Scotland, Dec 16-18, 1994)* RCA Red Seal ▲ 09026-68116-2 [DDD]
M. Bamert (cnd)
Holloway, R.:Con Hn, w. Barry Tuckwell (hn) Collins Classics ▲ COL 1439 [DDD]
Holloway, R.:Con Vn, w. Ernst Kovacic (vn) Collins Classics ▲ COL 1439 [DDD]
S. Bedford (cnd)
Honegger, A.:Con da camera, w. J. Stinton (fl), G. Browne (E hn) Collins Classics ▲ 12102 [DDD]
Honegger, A.:Con da camera, w. J. Stinton (fl), G. Browne (E hn) Collins Classics 2-▲ 70052 [DDD]
Ibert, J.:Con Fl, w. J. Stinton (fl), G. Browne (E hn) Collins Classics 2-▲ 70052 [DDD]
Ibert, J.:Con Fl, w. J. Stinton (fl) Collins Classics ▲ 12102 [DDD]
Nielsen, C.:Con Fl, w. J. Stinton (fl) Collins Classics ▲ 12102 [DDD]
Nielsen, C.:Con Fl, w. J. Stinton (fl) Collins Classics 2-▲ 70052 [DDD]
Poulenc, F.:Son Fl, w. J. Stinton (fl) [orchd. by Lennox Berkeley] Collins Classics ▲ 12102 [DDD]
Poulenc, F.:Son Fl, w. J. Stinton (fl) [orchd. by Lennox Berkeley] Collins Classics 2-▲ 70052 [DDD]
W. Boettcher (cnd)
Classical Masterpieces, w. Royal PO, Michael Reed (cnd), Vladimir Ashkenazy (cnd), London SO [cnd:Richard Hickox, Yondani Butt, John Manceri] Pickwick ("The Orchid" series) ▲ PICORCD 11006
Elgar, E.:Intro & Allegro IMP ▲ IMP 2042
Elgar, E.:Serenade Strs IMP ▲ IMP 2042
Vaughan Williams, R.:Fant on Greensleeves IMP ▲ IMP 2042
Vaughan Williams, R.:Fant on a Theme by Thomas Tallis IMP ▲ IMP 2042
B. Britten (cnd)
Bach, J.S.:Brandenburg Cons London ("Double Decca" series) 2-▲ 443847-2
P. Daniel (cnd)
Bennett, Richard Rodney:Con Perc, w. E. Glennie (perc) RCA Red Seal ▲ 09026-61277-2 ■ 09026-61277-4
Milhaud, D.:Con Perc, w. E. Glennie (perc) RCA Red Seal ▲ 09026-61277-2 ■ 09026-61277-4
Miyoshi, A.:Con Mar, w. E. Glennie (mar) RCA Red Seal ▲ 09026-61277-2 ■ 09026-61277-4
Rebounds:Concertos for Percussion, w. Evelyn Glennie (perc) RCA Red Seal ▲ 09026-61277-2
Rosauro, N.:Con Mar, w. E. Glennie (mar) RCA Red Seal ▲ 09026-61277-2 ■ 09026-61277-4
P. M. Davies (cnd)
Davies, P.M.:A Spell for Green Corn:The MacDonald Dances Collins Classics ▲ COL 1396 [DDD]
Davies, P.M.:Strathclyde Con 5, w. J. Clark (vn), C. Marwood (vc) Collins Classics ▲ COL 1303 [DDD]
Davies, P.M.:Strathclyde Con 6, w. D. Nicholson (fl) Collins Classics ▲ COL 1303 [DDD]
Davies, P.M.:Strathclyde Con 7, w. D. McTier (db) Collins Classics ▲ COL 1396 [DDD]
Davies, P.M.:Strathclyde Con 8, w. U. Leveaux (bn) Collins Classics ▲ COL 1396 [DDD]
Davies, P.M.:Sym 4 Collins Classics ▲ 11812 [DDD]
A. Faris (cnd)
Sullivan, A.:Ovs—Yeomen of the Guard, Princess Ida, Pirates of Penzance, Patience, HMS Pinafore, Iolanthe, The Gondoliers, The Sorcerer, Ruddigore, & Overture di ballo [concert overture] Nimbus ▲ NI 5066 [DDD]
A. Gibson (cnd)
Handel, G.F.:Cons (3) Ob, w. Robin Miller (ob) ASV/Quicksilva ▲ ASQCD 6188
Handel, G.F.:Ovs ASV/Quicksilva ▲ ASQCD 6188
Handel, G.F.:Royal Fireworks Music ASV/Quicksilva ▲ ASQCD 6188
Mozart, W.A.:Don Giovanni (sels) Classics for Pleasure ("Silver Doubles" series) 2-▲ CFP CDCFP 4739 [ADD]
Mozart, W.A.:Don Giovanni (sels), Scottish National Orch Classics for Pleasure 2-▲ CFP CFPSD 4739 [ADD]
Strauss, R.:Der Rosenkavalier (sels), Scottish National Orch Classics for Pleasure ▲ CFP CFPSD 4739 [ADD]
E. Kovacic (cnd)
Mozart, W.A.:Con 1 Vn, w. E. Kovacic (vn) *(rec Aug. 1990)* IMP Classics ▲ PCD 946 [DDD]
Mozart, W.A.:Con 3 Vn, w. E. Kovacic (vn) *(rec Aug. 1990)* IMP Classics ▲ PCD 946 [DDD]
Mozart, W.A.:Con 4 Vn, w. E. Kovacic (vn) *(rec Aug. 1990)* IMP Classics ▲ PCD 947 [DDD]
Mozart, W.A.:Con 6 Vn, w. E. Kovacic (vn) *(rec Aug. 1990)* IMP Classics ▲ PCD 947 [DDD]
Mozart, W.A.:Con 7 Vn, w. E. Kovacic (vn) IMP Classics ▲ PCD 946 [DDD]
Mozart, W.A.:Rondo Vn, K.269, w. E. Kovacic (vn) *(rec Aug. 1990)* IMP Classics ▲ PCD 947 [DDD]
Mozart, W.A.:Rondo Vn, K.373, w. E. Kovacic (vn) *(rec Aug. 1990)* IMP Classics ▲ PCD 947 [DDD]
J. Laredo (cnd)
Bach, J.S.:Cons Vn (comp), w. Jaime Laredo (vn) IMP ("Classics" series) ▲ IMP 6700402
Bach, J.S.:Con for 2 Vns, w. Jaime Laredo (vn), John Tunnell (vn) IMP ("Classics" series) ▲ IMP 6700402
Baroque Beauties, w. City of London Sinfonia [cnd:R. Hickox], E. Ritchie (sop), Bowman (ct), J. Purvis (pno) Pickwick ("The Orchid" series) ▲ PICORCD 11010
Beethoven, L. van:Con Vn, Op. 61, w. J. Laredo (vn) IMP Classics ▲ PCD 977 [DDD]
Beethoven, L. van:Con Vn, Op. 61, w. Jaime Laredo (vn) IMP ("Classics" series) ▲ IMP 6700242
Beethoven, L. van:Romances Vn, w. Jaime Laredo (vn) IMP ("Classics" series) ▲ IMP 6700242
Beethoven, L. van:Romances Vn, w. J. Laredo (vn) IMP Classics ▲ PCD 977 [DDD]
Beethoven, L. van:Romances Vn, w. Jaime Laredo (vn)—No. 1 in G IMP ("Concert Classics" series) ▲ IMP PCD 1099
Bruch, M.:Con 1 Vn, w. Jaime Laredo (vn) IMP ▲ IMP 2005
Dvořák, A.:Romance Vn, w. Jaime Laredo (vn) IMP ("Classics" series) ▲ IMP 6700292
Dvořák, A.:Serenade Strs IMP ("Classics" series) ▲ IMP 6700292
Mendelssohn, F.:Con 1 Pno, w. J. Kalichstein (pno) Nimbus ▲ NI 5112 [DDD]
Mendelssohn, F.:Con 2 Pno, w. J. Kalichstein (pno) Nimbus ▲ NI 5112 [DDD]
Mendelssohn, F.:Con in e Vn & Orch, Op. 64, w. Jaime Laredo (vn) IMP ("Concert Classics" series) ▲ IMP PCD 1097
Mendelssohn, F.:Con in e Vn & Orch, Op. 64, w. Jaime Laredo (vn) IMP ▲ IMP 2005
Mendelssohn, F.:Die Hebriden Nimbus ▲ NI 5112 [DDD]
Mendelssohn, F.:A Midsummer Night's Dream (comp), w. J. Howarth (sop), E. James (mez), Scottish Phil Singers [E] Nimbus 2-▲ NI 5041/42 [DDD]
Mendelssohn, F.:Sym 3 Nimbus ▲ NI 5067 [DDD]
Mendelssohn, F.:Sym 4 Nimbus ▲ NI 5067 [DDD]
Mendelssohn, F.:Sym 4 Nimbus ▲ NI 1408 [DDD]
Rossini, G.:Ovs—William Tell; Italiana in Algeri; Signor Bruschino; Cenerentola; Tancredi; Barber of Seville; La gazza ladra; Semiramide Nimbus ▲ NI 5078 [DDD]
Vivaldi, A.:Cons Vn, Op. 8/1-4, "The Four Seasons" IMP ▲ IMP 2000
Vivaldi, A.:Music of IMP Classics ▲ PCD 809 [DDD]
Vivaldi, A.:Music of—(5 Concerti) in C for 2 Flutes & Strings; in d for 2 Oboes & Strings; in F for 2 Horns & Strings; in C for 2 Trumpets & Strings; in C for 2 Oboes, 2 Clarinets & Strings IMP Classics ▲ PCD 811 [DDD]
Wagner, R.:Siegfried Idyll IMP ("Classics" series) ▲ IMP 6700292
R. Leppard (cnd)
Cavalli, P.F.:Music of, w. Frederica von Stade (mez)—Lamento di Cassandra; Lamento di Clori; Numi Ciechi Piodi Me Erato ▲ 98504-2

Scottish CO (cont.)
R. Leppard (cnd) (cont.)
German Baroque Flute Concertos, w. Jean-Pierre Rampal (fl), Jean-François Paillard CO [cnd:Jean-François Paillard], Scottish CO [cnd:R. Leppard] Erato ▲ 45835-2
Haydn, J.:Arias, w. T. Berganza (mez)—Aria di Giannina; Aria di Agatina; Aria di Errisena; Cantilena Pro Adventu; Cant Miseri Noil, Misera Patria; Cavatina di Alcina; Aria di Merlina; Aria di Lindora Erato ("Recital" series) ▲ 98498-2
Haydn, J.:Sym 94, "Surprise Sym"—Andante Erato ▲ 94682-2
Haydn, J.:Sym 101, "Clock"—Andante *(rec Queen's Hall, Edimbourg, Nov. 1982-Mar. 1983)* Erato ▲ 94682-2
Monteverdi, C.:Music of, w. Frederica von Stade (mez)—Lamento di Ottavia; Aria di Ottavia; Et è pur dunque vero Erato ▲ 98504-2
Mozart, W.A.:Arias, w. J. Baker (mez)—Arias di Madama Lucilla, K.582 & 583; Aria di Sesto, K.624; Recitativo & Rondo di Idamante, K.505; others Erato ("Recital" series) ▲ 98497-2
Mozart, W.A.:Così fan tutte (sels), w. Frederica von Stade (mez) Erato ▲ 98504-2
J. Ling (cnd)
Bach, J.S.:Brandenburg Con 2, w. R. Smedvig (tpt) Telarc ▲ CD 80227 [DDD]
Bach, J.S.:Suite 2 Orch, w. R. Smedvig (tpt) Telarc ▲ CD 80227 [DDD]
Bellini, V.:Con in E♭ Ob, w. R. Smedvig (tpt) Telarc ▲ CD 80232 [DDD] ■ CS 30232 (D)
Haydn, J.:Con Tpt, w. Rolf Smedvig (tpt) Telarc ▲ CD 80232 [DDD] ■ CS 30232 (D)
Hummel, J.N.:Con in E♭ Tpt, S.49, w. R. Smedvig (tpt) Telarc ▲ CD 80232 [DDD] ■ CS 30232 (D)
Mozart, L.:Con Tpt, w. R. Smedvig (tpt) Telarc ▲ CD 80227 [DDD]
Tartini, G.:Con Tpt, w. R. Smedvig (tpt) Telarc ▲ CD 80232 [DDD] ■ CS 30232 (D)
Telemann, G.P.:Con Tpt Strs in D, w. R. Smedvig (tpt) Telarc ▲ CD 80227 [DDD]
Torelli, G.:Con Tpt, w. R. Smedvig (tpt) Telarc ▲ CD 80232 [DDD] ■ CS 30232 (D)
J. MacMillan (cnd)
Macmillan, J.:Busqueda Catalyst ▲ 09026-62669-2 ■ 09026-62669-4
Macmillan, J.:Music of, w. E. Glennie (perc)—Veni, veni, Emannuel; After the Tryst; "...as others see us...": 3 Dawn Rituals; Untold Catalyst ▲ 09026-61916-2
Macmillan, J.:Visitatio Sepulchri Catalyst ▲ 09026-62669-2 ■ 09026-62669-4
C. Mackerras (cnd)
Arriaga, J.C.:Los esclavos felices (ov) Hyperion ▲ CDA 66800
Arriaga, J.C.:Sym in D Hyperion ▲ CDA 66800
Beethoven, L. van:Die Geschöpfe des Prometheus Hyperion ▲ CDA 66748
Field, J.:Con 2 Pno, w. J. O'Conor (pno) *(rec Feb. 27-28 & Mar. 1, 1993)* Telarc ▲ CD 80370 [DDD]
Field, J.:Con 3 Pno, w. J. O'Conor (pno) *(rec Feb. 27-28 & Mar. 1, 1993)* Telarc ▲ CD 80370 [DDD]
Mozart, W.A.:Cons Hn, w. E. Ruske (hn) *(rec Dec. 4-5, 1993)* Telarc ▲ 80367 [DDD]
Mozart, W.A.:Con 17 Pno, w. J. O'Conor (pno) Telarc ▲ CD 80306 [DDD]
Mozart, W.A.:Con 18 Pno, w. J. O'Conor (pno) Telarc ▲ CD 80285 [DDD]
Mozart, W.A.:Con 19 Pno, w. J. O'Conor (pno) Telarc ▲ CD 8028 [DDD]
Mozart, W.A.:Con 20 Pno, w. J. O'Conor (pno) *(rec Oct. 30-31, 1991)* Telarc ▲ CD 80308 [DDD]
Mozart, W.A.:Con 21 Pno, w. J. O'Conor (pno) Telarc ▲ CD 80219 [DDD]
Mozart, W.A.:Con 22 Pno, w. J. O'Conor (pno) *(rec Oct. 30-31, 1991)* Telarc ▲ CD 80308 [DDD]
Mozart, W.A.:Con 23 Pno, w. J. O'Conor (pno) Telarc ▲ CD 80285 [DDD]
Mozart, W.A.:Con 24 Pno, w. J. O'Conor (pno) Telarc ▲ CD 80306 [DDD]
Mozart, W.A.:Con 27 Pno, w. J. O'Conor (pno) Telarc ▲ CD 80219 [DDD]
Mozart, W.A.:Don Giovanni, w. Christine Brewer (sop—Donna Anna), Nuccia Focile (sop—Zerlina), Felicity Lott (sop—Donna Elvira), Jerry Hadley (ten—Don Ottavio), Bo Skovhus (bar—Don Giovanni), Umberto Chiummo (bass—Masetto/Il Commendatore), Alessandro Corbelli (bass—Leporello), Scottish Chamber Chorus *(rec Usher Hall, Edinburgh, Scotland, July 31- Aug 11, 1995)* Telarc 3-▲ CD 80420 [DDD]
Mozart, W.A.:Nozze di Figaro, w. Rebecca Evans (sop—Barbarina), Nuccia Focile (sop—Susanna), Suzanne Murphy (sop—Marcellina), Carol Vaness (sop—Countess Almaviva), Susanne Mentzer (mez—Cherubino), Ryland Davies (ten—Don Basilio/Don Curzio), Alessandro Corbelli (bar—Count Almaviva), Alfonso Antoniozzi (bass—Doctor Bartolo/Antonio), Alastair Miles (bass—Figaro), Scottish Chamber Chorus *(rec Usher Hall, Edingurgh, Scotland, July 31-Aug. 12, 1994)* Telarc 3-▲ CD 80388 [DDD]
Mozart, W.A.:Rondo Pno Orch, K.386, w. J. O'Conor (pno) Telarc ▲ CD 80285 [DDD]
Mozart, W.A.:Zauberflöte, w. B. Hendricks (sop—Pamina), J. Anderson (sop—Queen of the Night), U. Steinsky (sop—Papagena), J. Hadley (ten—Tamino), T. Allen (bar—Papageno), R. Lloyd (bass—Sarastro), Scottish Chamber Chorus [G] Telarc 2-▲ CD 80302 [DDD]
Voříšek, J.V.:Los esclavos felices (ov) Hyperion ▲ CDA 66800
Voříšek, J.V.:Sym in d Hyperion ▲ CDA 66800
Weber, C.M. von:Con 1 Pno, w. Nikolai Demidenko (pno) Hyperion ▲ CDA 66680
Weber, C.M. von:Con 2 Pno, w. Nikolai Demidenko (pno) Hyperion ▲ CDA 66680
Weber, C.M. von:Konzertstück Pno, w. Nikolai Demidenko (pno) Hyperion ▲ CDA 66680
G. Malcolm (cnd)
Handel, G.F.:Messiah (sels), w. Felicity Lott (sop), Linda Finnie (mez), Glenn Winslade (ten), Henry Herford (bar), Scottish Phil Singers IMP ("Classic" series) ▲ IMP 2031
J.-P. Saraste (cnd)
Barber, S.:Adagio Strs Virgin Classics ▲ CDC 59565-2 [DDD]
Barber, S.:Con Vc, w. R. Kirshbaum (vc) Virgin Classics ▲ 59565 [DDD]
Bizet, G.:Sym 1 Virgin Classics ▲ CDZ 59657
Mozart, W.A.:Sym 39 Virgin Classics ▲ CDZ 59649
Mozart, W.A.:Sym 41 Virgin Classics ▲ CDZ 59649
Ravel, M.:Ma mère l'oye Orch Virgin Classics ▲ CDZ 59657
Ravel, M.:Pavane pour une infante défunte Virgin Classics ▲ CDZ 59657
P. Schreier (cnd)
Bach, J.S.:Cant 56, w. O. Bär (bar), Scottish Chamber Chorus [G] *(rec May 1991)* EMI Classics ▲ CDC 54453-2 [DDD]
Bach, J.S.:Cant 82, w. O. Bär (bar), Scottish Chamber Chorus *(rec May 1991)* EMI Classics ▲ CDC 54453-2 [DDD]
Bach, J.S.:Cant 158, w. O. Bär (bar), Scottish Chamber Chorus *(rec 5/91)* EMI Classics ▲ CDC 54453-2 [DDD]
G. Schwarz (cnd)
Haydn, J.:Con 1 Vc, w. János Starker (vc) Delos ▲ DCD 3062
Haydn, J.:Con 2 Vc, w. János Starker (vc) Delos ▲ DE 3063 [DDD]
Haydn, J.:Con Org & Strs, H.XVIII/2, w. Carol Rosenberger (pno) Delos ▲ DCD 3061
Haydn, J.:Con Org, Vns & Bass Instrument, H.XVIII/5, w. Carol Rosenberger (pno) Delos ▲ DCD 3064 [DDD]
Haydn, J.:Sym 21 Delos ▲ DCD 3062 [DDD]
Haydn, J.:Sym 22, "Der Philosoph" Delos ▲ DCD 3061 [DDD]
Haydn, J.:Sym 51 Delos ▲ DCD 3064 [DDD]
Haydn, J.:Sym 61 Delos ▲ DE 3063 [DDD]
Haydn, J.:Sym 96, "Miracle" Delos ▲ DCD 3062 [DDD]
Haydn, J.:Sym 100, "Military" Delos ▲ DCD 3064 [DDD]
Haydn, J.:Sym 103, "Drum Roll" Delos ▲ DE 3063 [DDD]
Haydn, J.:Sym 104, "London" Delos ▲ DCD 3061 [DDD]
J. Serebrier (cnd)
Barber, S.:Canzonetta, w. Julia Girdwood (ob) Phoenix ▲ PHCD 111 [DDD]
Britten, B.:Les Illuminations, w. Carole Farley (sop) Phoenix ▲ PHCD 111 [DDD]
Britten, B.:Young Apollo Phoenix ▲ PHCD 111 [DDD]
Tchaikovsky, P.:Elegy ASV ▲ ASV 719 [DDD]
Tchaikovsky, P.:Serenade Strs ASV ▲ ASV 719 [DDD]
Tchaikovsky, P.:Sleeping Beauty (2 scenes) ASV ▲ ASV 719 [DDD]
Tchaikovsky, P.:Suite 4 ASV ▲ ASV 719 [DDD]

▲ = CD ♦ = Enhanced CD Δ = MD ■ = Cassette Tape □ = DCC

Scottish CO (cont.)

U. Steinsky (cnd)

Mozart, W.A.:Zauberflöte (sels), w. B. Hendricks (sop), J. Hadley (sop), J. Anderson (sop), T. Allen (bar), R. Lloyd (b-bar), Scottish Sym Chorus *(rec July 13–22, 1991)* Telarc ▲ CD 80345 [DDD]

Y. P. Tortelier (cnd)

Couperin, F.:Dans le goût théatral [arr. for trumpet & orch.] *(rec 6/76)* EMI (Studio) ▲ CDM 763118 [ADD]

Couperin, L.:Pièces en concert, w. P. Tortelier (vc) [arr. by Paul Bazelaire from various short Couperin works] *(rec 6/76)* EMI (Studio) ▲ CDM 763118-2 [ADD]

Mozart, W.A.:Con 4 Vn, w. O. Shumsky (vn) Nimbus ▲ NI 5009

Mozart, W.A.:Con 5 Vn, w. O. Shumsky (vn) Nimbus ▲ NI 5009

M. Veltri (cnd)

Bellini, V.:Arias, w. R. Giménez (ten)—arias from I Puritani, La Sonnambula Nimbus ▲ NI 5224 [DDD]

Donizetti, G.:Arias, w. R. Giménez (ten)—arias from Don Pasquale, Elisir d'amore, La Favorita, Fille du régiment, Lucia di Lammermoor Nimbus ▲ NI 5224 [DDD]

Rossini, G.:Arias, w. R. Giménez (ten), Scottish Chamber Chorus Nimbus ▲ NI 5106 [DDD]

Scottish CO members

L. Friend (cnd)

Stravinsky, I.:L'Histoire du soldat, w. C. Lee (nar) [E] Nimbus ▲ NI 5063 [DDD]

Scottish Early Music Consort

Burns, R.:Scottish Songs—Songs for the Scots Musical Museum; Burn's Visit to Niel Gow; George Thomson & the Inimitable Sangs of Burns Chandos ("Early Music" series) ▲ CHAN 0581 [DDD]

W. Edwards (cnd)

Mary's Music Chandos ("Chaconne" series) ▲ CHAN 0529 [DDD]

Robert Burns Chandos ▲ CHAN 8636 [DDD]

Scottish Ensemble

J. Rees (cnd)

Bach, J.S.:Brandenburg Con 1 Virgin Classics ▲ CDZ 59688-2

Bach, J.S.:Brandenburg Con 2, w. G. Ashton (tpt) Virgin Classics ▲ CDZ 59688-2

Bach, J.S.:Brandenburg Con 4 Virgin Classics ▲ CDZ 59688-2

Bach, J.S.:Con 4 Hpd, w. S. Heath (hpd) Virgin Classics ▲ CDZ 59641

Bach, J.S.:Con 2 Vn, w. J. Murdoch (vn) Virgin Classics ▲ CDZ 59641

Bach, J.S.:Con Vn, BWV 1058, w. C. Dale (vn) Virgin Classics ▲ CDZ 59641

Bach, J.S.:Con for 2 Vns, w. J. Murdoch (vn), C. Dale (vn) Virgin Classics ▲ CDZ 59641

Virgo Collections, w. Jane Murdoch (vn), C. Dale (vn), S. Heath (vc) Virgin Classics ▲ CDZ 59652

Scottish Festival Brass Bands

A. Gibson (cnd)

Walton, W.:Belshazzar's Feast, w. S. Milnes (bar), Scottish National Orch, Scottish National Chorus *(rec 1977)* Chandos ("Collect" series) ▲ CHAN 6547 [ADD/DDD]

Scottish National Orch

M. Bamert (cnd)

Copland, A.:Con Cl, w. J. Hilton (cl) Chandos ▲ CHAN 8618 [DDD]

Lutoslawski, W.:Dance Preludes Cl, Hp, Pno, Perc & Strs, w. J. Hilton (cl) Chandos ▲ CHAN 8618 [DDD]

Nielsen, C.:Con Cl, w. J. Hilton (cl) Chandos ▲ CHAN 8618 [DDD]

Schoenberg, A.:Pelleas und Melisande Chandos ▲ CHAN 8619 [DDD]

Webern, A.:Passacaglia Chandos ▲ CHAN 8619 [DDD]

R. Bonynge (cnd)

Haydn, J.:L'Anima del filosofo, or Orfeo ed Euridice, w. Joan Sutherland (sop), Nicolai Gedda (ten), Scottish National Chorus *(rec live)* Verona 2-▲ VER 28018

Haydn, J.:L'Anima del filosofo, or Orfeo ed Euridice, w. Joan Sutherland (sop), Nicolai Gedda (ten) [I] *(rec live Edinburgh International Festival, 1967)* Myto 2-▲ 2 MCD 90529 [ADD]

P. M. Davies (cnd)

Davies, P.M.:Con Tpt, w. J. Wallace (tpt) Collins Classics ▲ 11812 [DDD]

A. Gibson (cnd)

Berlioz, H.:Ovs—Le roi Lear; Rob Roy; Le Corsaire; Béatrice et Bénédict; Carnaval romain Chandos ▲ CHAN 8316 [DDD]

Bizet, G.:Jeux d'enfants Classics for Pleasure ▲ CDCFP 4086 [ADD]

Elgar, E.:Cockaigne Chandos ("Collect" series) ▲ CHAN 6570 [ADD/DDD]

Elgar, E.:Cockaigne Chandos ▲ CHAN 8429 [ADD]

Elgar, E.:Coronation Ode, w. T. Cahill (sop), A. Collins (cta), A. Rolfe Johnson (ten), G. Howell (bass), Scottish National Chorus [E] *(rec 1976)* Chandos ("Collect" series) ▲ CHAN 6574 [ADD]

Elgar, E.:The Crown of India (suite) Chandos ▲ CHAN 8429 [ADD]

Elgar, E.:The Dream of Gerontius, w. Alfreda Hodgson (cta), Robert Tear (ten), Benjamin Luxon (bar), Scottish National Chorus CRD 2-▲ 33267

Elgar, E.:Enigma Vars Chandos ("Collect" series) ▲ CHAN 6504 [ADD]

Elgar, E.:Enigma Vars Chandos ▲ CHAN 8431 [ADD]

Elgar, E.:Falstaff Chandos ▲ CHAN 8431 [ADD]

Elgar, E.:Pomp & Circumstance Marches Chandos ▲ CHAN 8429 [ADD]

Elgar, E.:Pomp & Circumstance Marches Chandos ("Collect" series) ▲ CHAN 6504 [ADD]

Elgar, E.:The Spirit of England, w. T. Cahill (sop), Scottish National Chorus [E] *(rec 1976)* Chandos ("Collect" series) ▲ CHAN 6574 [ADD]

German, E.:Welsh Rhap Classics for Pleasure ▲ CDCFP 4635 [ADD]

Harty, H.:With the Wild Geese Classics for Pleasure ▲ CDCFP 4635 [ADD]

Holst, G.:The Planets Chandos ▲ CHAN 8302 [DDD]

Maccunn, H.:Land of the Mountain & the Flood Classics for Pleasure ▲ CDCFP 4635 [ADD]

Mozart, W.A.:Don Giovanni (sels), Scottish CO Classics for Pleasure 2-▲ CFP CFPSD 4739 [ADD]

Ravel, M.:Ma mère l'oye Orch Classics for Pleasure ▲ CDCFP 4086 [ADD]

Saint-Saëns, C.:Carnival of the Animals, w. P. Katin (pno), P. Fowke (pno) Classics for Pleasure ▲ CDCFP 4086 [ADD]

Sibelius, J.:Aallottaret Chandos ("Collect" series) ▲ CHAN 6508 [ADD]

Sibelius, J.:The Bard Chandos ("Collect" series) ▲ CHAN 6586 [ADD]

Sibelius, J.:4 Legends from the Kalevalá Chandos ("Collect" series) ▲ CHAN 6586 [ADD]

Sibelius, J.:Luonnotar Chandos ("Collect" series) ▲ CHAN 6586 [ADD]

Sibelius, J.:Pohjola's Daughter Chandos ("Collect" series) ▲ CHAN 6508 [ADD]

Sibelius, J.:Rakastava Strs Chandos ("Collect" series) ▲ CHAN 6591 [ADD]

Sibelius, J.:Scènes historiques Chandos ("Collect" series) ▲ CHAN 6591 [ADD]

Sibelius, J.:The Swan of Tuonela Chandos ("Collect" series) ▲ CHAN 6508 [ADD]

Sibelius, J.:Tapiola Chandos ("Collect" series) ▲ CHAN 6508 [ADD]

Sibelius, J.:Tone Poems—The Bard, Op. 64; The Dryad, Op. 45/1; En Saga, Op. 9; Finlandia, Op. 26; Luonnotar, Op. 70; Night-Ride and Sunrise, Op. 55; The Oceanides, Op. 73; Pohjola's Daughter, Op. 49; Spring Song, Op. 16; Tapiola, Op. 112 Chandos 2-▲ CHAN 8395/96 [ADD]

Sibelius, J.:Valse lyrique Chandos ("Collect" series) ▲ CHAN 6591 [ADD]

Smyth, E.:The Wreckers (ov) Classics for Pleasure ▲ CDCFP 4635 [ADD]

Strauss, R.:Der Rosenkavalier (sels), Scottish CO Classics for Pleasure ▲ CFP CFPSD 4739 [ADD]

Strauss, R.:Der Rosenkavalier (sels) Classics for Pleasure ("Silver Doubles" series) 2-▲ CFP CDCFP 4739 [ADD]

Walton, W.:Belshazzar's Feast, w. S. Milnes (bar), Scottish Festival Brass Bands, Scottish National Chorus *(rec 1977)* Chandos ("Collect" series) ▲ CHAN 6547 [ADD/DDD]

Walton, W.:Con Vc, w. R. Kirshbaum (vc) Chandos ("Collect" series) ▲ CHAN 6547 [ADD/DDD]

Walton, W.:Coronation Te Deum, w. Scottish National Chorus *(rec 1977)* Chandos ("Collect" series) ▲ CHAN 6547 [ADD/DDD]

Walton, W.:Sym 1 Chandos ("Collect" series) ▲ CHAN 6570 [ADD/DDD]

Walton, W.:Sym 1 Chandos ▲ CHAN 8313 [DDD]

N. Järvi (cnd)

Dvořák, A.:Biblical Songs, Op. 99, w. B. Rayner Cook (bar) Chandos ▲ CHAN 8608 [DDD]

Dvořák, A.:Biblical Songs, Op. 99, w. B. Rayner Cook (bar) [Cz] Chandos ▲ CHAN 9002 [DDD]

Dvořák, A.:Carnival Chandos ▲ CHAN 9002 [DDD]

Dvořák, A.:Carnival Chandos ▲ CHAN 8575 [DDD]

Scottish National Orch (cont.)

N. Järvi (cnd) (cont.)

Dvořák, A.:The Golden Spinning Wheel Chandos ▲ CHAN 8501 [DDD]

Dvořák, A.:Heroic Song Chandos ▲ CHAN 8597 [DDD]

Dvořák, A.:My Home Chandos 2-▲ CHAN 8798/99 [DDD]

Dvořák, A.:My Home Chandos ▲ CHAN 8510 [DDD]

Dvořák, A.:The Noon Witch Chandos ▲ CHAN 8530 [DDD]

Dvořák, A.:Slavonic Dances (comp) Chandos ▲ CHAN 8406 [DDD]

Dvořák, A.:Slavonic Rhaps, Op. 45—No. 3 Chandos ▲ CHAN 8589 [DDD]

Dvořák, A.:Slavonic Rhaps, Op. 45—No. 3 Chandos ▲ CHAN 9002 [DDD]

Dvořák, A.:Symphonic Poems, Opp. 107–111 (comp) Chandos 2-▲ CHAN 8798/99 [DDD]

Dvořák, A.:Symphonic Vars Chandos ▲ CHAN 9002 [DDD]

Dvořák, A.:Symphonic Vars Chandos ▲ CHAN 8575 [DDD]

Dvořák, A.:Syms (comp) Chandos 6-▲ CHAN 9008/13 [DDD]

Dvořák, A.:Sym 1, "The Bells of Zlonice" Chandos ▲ CHAN 8597 [DDD]

Dvořák, A.:Sym 2 Chandos ▲ CHAN 8589 [DDD]

Dvořák, A.:Sym 3 Chandos ▲ CHAN 8575 [DDD]

Dvořák, A.:Sym 4 Chandos ▲ CHAN 8608 [DDD]

Dvořák, A.:Sym 5 Chandos ▲ CHAN 8552 [DDD]

Dvořák, A.:Sym 6 Chandos ▲ CHAN 8530 [DDD]

Dvořák, A.:Sym 7 Chandos ▲ CHAN 8501 [DDD]

Dvořák, A.:Sym 8 Chandos ▲ CHAN 8666 [DDD]

Dvořák, A.:Sym 9, "From the New World" Chandos ▲ CHAN 8510 [DDD]

Dvořák, A.:The Water Goblin Chandos ▲ CHAN 8552 [DDD]

Dvořák, A.:The Wild Dove Chandos ▲ CHAN 8666 [DDD]

Eller, H.:Dawn, w. J. Digney (ob) Chandos ▲ CHAN 8525 [DDD]

Eller, H.:Elegia, w. E. Pierce (hp) Chandos ▲ CHAN 8525 [DDD]

Eller, H.:Pieces (5) Str Orch Chandos ▲ CHAN 8525 [DDD]

Eller, H.:Twilight Chandos ▲ CHAN 8656 [DDD]

Glazunov, A.:Con Vn, w. O. Shumsky (vn) Chandos ▲ CHAN 8596 [DDD]

Glazunov, A.:From the Middle Ages Chandos ▲ CHAN 8804 [DDD]

Glazunov, A.:Raymonda (sels) Chandos ▲ CHAN 8447 [DDD]

Glazunov, A.:Scènes de ballet Chandos ▲ CHAN 8804 [DDD]

Glazunov, A.:The Sea Chandos ▲ CHAN 8611 [DDD]

Glazunov, A.:The Seasons Chandos ▲ CHAN 8596 [DDD]

Glazunov, A.:Spring Chandos ▲ CHAN 8611 [DDD]

Glazunov, A.:Stenka Razin Chandos ▲ CHAN 8479 [DDD]

Kabalevsky, D.:Con Vn, w. L. Mordkovitch (vn) Chandos ▲ CHAN 8918 [DDD]

Kallinikov, V.:The Cedar & the Palm Chandos ▲ CHAN 8805 [DDD]

Kallinikov, V.:Sym 1 Chandos ▲ CHAN 8611 [DDD]

Kallinikov, V.:Sym 2 Chandos ▲ CHAN 8805 [DDD]

Kallinikov, V.:Tsar Boris (ov) Chandos ▲ CHAN 8805 [DDD]

Khachaturian, A.:Con Pno, w. C. Orbelian (pno) Chandos ▲ CHAN 8542 [DDD]

Khachaturian, A.:Con Vn, w. L. Mordkovitch (vn) Chandos ▲ CHAN 8918 [DDD]

Khachaturian, A.:Gayane (sels)—four movts. from the Ballet Suite No. 1:Sabre dance; Dance of the rose maidens; Lullaby; Lezghinka Chandos ▲ CHAN 8945 [DDD]

Khachaturian, A.:Gayane (sels)—four movts. from the Ballet Suite No. 1:Sabre dance; Dance of the rose maidens; Lullaby; Lezghinka Chandos ▲ CHAN 8542 [DDD]

Khachaturian, A.:Masquerade (ballet suite) Chandos ▲ CHAN 8542 [DDD]

Khachaturian, A.:Spartacus (suites 1–3) Chandos ▲ CHAN 8927 [DDD]

Khachaturian, A.:Sym 2 [original version] Chandos ▲ CHAN 8945 [DDD]

Lemba, A.:Sym in c# Chandos ▲ CHAN 8656 [DDD]

Liadov, A.:A Musical Snuffbox Chandos ▲ CHAN 8804 [DDD]

Mahler, G.:Sym 5 Chandos ▲ CHAN 8829 [DDD]

Music from Estonia, Vols. 1 & 2

Pärt, A.:Cantus in Memory of Benjamin Britten Chandos ▲ CHAN 8656 [DDD]

Prokofiev, S.:Alexander Nevsky, w. L. Finnie (mez), Scottish National Chorus Chandos ▲ CHAN 8584 [DDD]

Prokofiev, S.:Andante, Op. 29bis Chandos ▲ CHAN 8728 [DDD]

Prokofiev, S.:Andante, Op. 50bis Chandos ▲ CHAN 8806 [DDD]

Prokofiev, S.:Autumn Chandos ▲ CHAN 8806 [DDD]

Prokofiev, S.:Chout (suite) Chandos ▲ CHAN 8729 [DDD]

Prokofiev, S.:Cinderella (sels) Chandos ▲ CHAN 8511 [DDD]

Prokofiev, S.:Cons Vn (comp), w. L. Mordkovitch (vn) Chandos ▲ CHAN 8709 [DDD]

Prokofiev, S.:Divertissement Chandos ▲ CHAN 8728 [DDD]

Prokofiev, S.:Dreams Chandos ▲ CHAN 8472 [DDD]

Prokofiev, S.:4 Portraits Chandos ▲ CHAN 8803 [DDD]

Prokofiev, S.:Lt Kijé Suite Chandos ▲ CHAN 8806 [DDD]

Prokofiev, S.:The Love for 3 Oranges (suite) Chandos ▲ CHAN 8729 [DDD]

Prokofiev, S.:Peter & the Wolf, w. L. Prokofiev (nar) Chandos ▲ CHAN 8511 [DDD]

Prokofiev, S.:The Prodigal Son Chandos ▲ CHAN 8728 [DDD]

Prokofiev, S.:Pushkin Waltzes Chandos ▲ CHAN 8472 [DDD]

Prokofiev, S.:Scythian Suite Chandos ▲ CHAN 8584 [DDD]

Prokofiev, S.:Semyon Kotko (suite) Chandos ▲ CHAN 8803 [DDD]

Prokofiev, S.:Sinfonietta, Op. 5 Chandos ▲ CHAN 8442 [DDD]

Prokofiev, S.:The Steel Step (suite) Chandos ▲ CHAN 8729 [DDD]

Prokofiev, S.:Symphonic Song Chandos ▲ CHAN 8728 [DDD]

Prokofiev, S.:Sym 1 Chandos ▲ CHAN 8400 [DDD]

Prokofiev, S.:Sym 2 Chandos ▲ CHAN 8368 [DDD]

Prokofiev, S.:Sym 3 Chandos ▲ CHAN 8401 [DDD]

Prokofiev, S.:Sym 4 [Op. 112 version] Chandos ▲ CHAN 8400 [DDD]

Prokofiev, S.:Sym 4 [Op. 47 version] Chandos ▲ CHAN 8401 [DDD]

Prokofiev, S.:Sym 5 Chandos ▲ CHAN 8450 [DDD]

Prokofiev, S.:Sym 6 Chandos ▲ CHAN 8359 [DDD]

Prokofiev, S.:Sym 7 Chandos ▲ CHAN 8442 [DDD]

Prokofiev, S.:Sym–Con Vc, w. R. Wallfisch (vc) Chandos ▲ CHAN 8508 [DDD]

Prokofiev, S.:The Tale of the Stone Flower (sels)—Prologue (The Mistress of the Copper Mountain); Wedding Suite (five dances arranged as a concert suite), Op. 126; Scene 4, No. 19 (Scene & Waltz of the Diamonds); Scene 4, No. 21 (Waltz) Chandos ▲ CHAN 8806 [DDD]

Prokofiev, S.:Waltz Suite—Nos. 2, 5, 6 Chandos ▲ CHAN 8359 [DDD]

Prokofiev, S.:Waltz Suite—Nos. 1, 3, 4 Chandos ▲ CHAN 8450 [DDD]

Rachmaninoff, S.:The Bells, w. S. Murphy (sop), K. Lewis (ten), D. Wilson-Johnson (bar), Scottish National Chorus [R] Chandos ▲ CHAN 8476 [DDD]

Rachmaninoff, S.:Vocalise, w. S. Murphy (sop) Chandos ▲ CHAN 8476 [DDD]

Raid, K.:Sym 1 Chandos ▲ CHAN 8525 [DDD]

Rimsky-Korsakov, N.:Christmas Eve (suite) Chandos 3-▲ CHAN 8327/29 [DDD]

Rimsky-Korsakov, N.:Golden Cockerel (suite) Chandos 3-▲ CHAN 8327/29 [DDD]

Rimsky-Korsakov, N.:The Legend of the Invisible City of Kitzeh (suite) Chandos 3-▲ CHAN 8327/29 [DDD]

Rimsky-Korsakov, N.:A May Night (ov) Chandos 3-▲ CHAN 8327/29 [DDD]

Rimsky-Korsakov, N.:Mlada (suite) Chandos 3-▲ CHAN 8327/29 [DDD]

Rimsky-Korsakov, N.:Scheherazade Chandos ▲ CHAN 8479 [DDD]

Rimsky-Korsakov, N.:Snow Maiden (suite) Chandos 3-▲ CHAN 8327/29 [DDD]

Rimsky-Korsakov, N.:The Tale of Tsar Saltan Orch, Op. 57 Chandos 3-▲ CHAN 8327/29 [DDD]

Russian Ballet Masterpieces, w. London SO Chandos ("Collect" series) ▲ CHAN 6512 [DDD]

Russian Dances Chandos ▲ CHAN 6598 [DDD]

Russian Masterpieces, w. London SO Chandos ("Collect" series) ▲ CHAN 6511 [DDD]

Scriabin, A.:Rêverie Chandos ▲ CHAN 8462 [DDD]

Scriabin, A.:Sym 2 Chandos ▲ CHAN 8462 [DDD]

Shostakovich, D.:Ballet Suite 1 Chandos ▲ CHAN 8730 [DDD]

Scottish National Orch (cont.)
N. Järvi (cnd) (cont.)
Shostakovich, D.:Ballet Suite 2 — Chandos ▲ CHAN 8730 [DDD]
Shostakovich, D.:Ballet Suite 3 — Chandos ▲ CHAN 8730 [DDD]
Shostakovich, D.:Ballet Suite 4 — Chandos ▲ CHAN 8630 [DDD]
Shostakovich, D.:Ballet Suite 5 — Chandos ▲ CHAN 8650 [DDD]
Shostakovich, D.:Con 1 Vn, w. L. Mordkovitch (vn) — Chandos ▲ CHAN 8820 [DDD]
Shostakovich, D.:Con 2 Vn, w. L. Mordkovitch (vn) — Chandos ▲ CHAN 8820 [DDD]
Shostakovich, D.:Festive Ov — Chandos ▲ CHAN 8587 [DDD]
Shostakovich, D.:Katerina Ismaylova (suite) — Chandos ▲ CHAN 8587 [DDD]
Shostakovich, D.:Sym 1 — Chandos ▲ CHAN 8411 [DDD]
Shostakovich, D.:Sym 4 — Chandos ▲ CHAN 8640 [DDD]
Shostakovich, D.:Sym 5 — Chandos ▲ CHAN 8650 [DDD]
Shostakovich, D.:Sym 6 — Chandos ▲ CHAN 8411 [DDD]
Shostakovich, D.:Sym 7 — Chandos ▲ CHAN 8623 [DDD]
Shostakovich, D.:Sym 8 — Chandos ▲ CHAN 8757 [DDD]
Shostakovich, D.:Sym 9 — Chandos ▲ CHAN 8587 [DDD]
Shostakovich, D.:Sym 10 — Chandos ▲ CHAN 8630 [DDD]
Shostakovich, D.:Tahiti Trot — Chandos ▲ CHAN 8587 [DDD]
Strauss, R.:Eine Alpensinfonie — Chandos ▲ CHAN 8557 [DDD]
Strauss, R.:Also sprach Zarathustra — Chandos ▲ CHAN 8538 [DDD]
Strauss, R.:Aus italien — Chandos ▲ CHAN 8744 [DDD]
Strauss, R.:Capriccio (sels), w. F. Lott (sop)—Overture, Intermezzo & Closing Scene [G] — Chandos ▲ CHAN 8758 [DDD]
Strauss, R.:Don Juan — Chandos ▲ CHAN 8538 [DDD]
Strauss, R.:Don Quixote, w. R. Wallfisch (vc) — Chandos ▲ CHAN 8631 [DDD]
Strauss, R.:4 Last Songs, w. F. Lott (sop) [G] — Chandos ▲ CHAN 8518 [DDD]
Strauss, R.:4 Last Songs, w. F. Lott (sop) [G] — Chandos ▲ CHAN 9054 [DDD]
Strauss, R.:Ein Heldenleben — Chandos ▲ CHAN 8518 [DDD]
Strauss, R.:Macbeth — Chandos ▲ CHAN 8834 [DDD]
Strauss, R.:Metamorphosen — Chandos ▲ CHAN 8734 [DDD]
Strauss, R.:Romanze Vc, w. R. Wallfisch (vc) — Chandos ▲ CHAN 8631 [DDD]
Strauss, R.:Der Rosenkavalier (suite) — Chandos ▲ CHAN 8758 [DDD]
Strauss, R.:Der Rosenkavalier (waltzes)—1st & 2nd Waltz Sequences — Chandos ▲ CHAN 8834 [DDD]
Strauss, R.:Salome (dance) — Chandos ▲ CHAN 8758 [DDD]
Strauss, R.:Songs, w. F. Lott (sop)—Drei Hymnen, Op. 71 [G] — Chandos ▲ CHAN 8734 [DDD]
Strauss, R.:Songs, w. F. Lott (sop)—Opp. 27/4, 37/3, 48/1, 88/1 [G] — Chandos ▲ CHAN 8557 [DDD]
Strauss, R.:Songs, w. F. Lott (sop)—Verführung; Winterliebe; Das Dichters Abendgang; Frühlingsfeier; Liebeshymnus; Winterweihe; Das Rosenband; Gesang der Apollopriesterin; Zueignung; Hymne an die Liebe; Rückkehr in die Heimat; Die Liebe [G] — Chandos ▲ CHAN 9159 [DDD]
Strauss, R.:Songs, w. F. Lott (sop)—Das Rosenband, Op. 36/1; Mein Auge, Op. 37/4; Befreit, Op. 39/4; Winterweihe, Op. 48/4 [G] — Chandos ▲ CHAN 8744 [DDD]
Strauss, R.:Songs, w. F. Lott (sop)—2 songs—Opp. 27/2 & 43/2 [G] — Chandos ▲ CHAN 8538 [DDD]
Strauss, R.:Songs, w. L. Finnie (mez)—Notturno, Op. 44, No. 1 [G] — Chandos ▲ CHAN 8834 [DDD]
Strauss, R.:Songs, w. F. Lott (sop)—Opp. 27/1 & 33/2 [G] — Chandos ▲ CHAN 8631 [DDD]
Strauss, R.:Songs, w. F. Lott (sop)—12 songs—Op. 27, Nos. 1,2 & 4; Op. 37, Nos. 3 & 4; Op. 39, No. 4; Op. 41, No. 1; Op. 43, No. 2; Op. 48, No. 1; Op. 49, No. 1; Op. 56, No. 6; Op. 88, No. 1 [G] — Chandos ▲ CHAN 9054 [DDD]
Strauss, R.:Songs, w. F. Lott (sop)—Opp. 10/1 & 56/6 [G] — Chandos ▲ CHAN 8572 [DDD]
Strauss, R.:Symphonia domestica — Chandos ▲ CHAN 8572 [DDD]
Strauss, R.:Till Eulenspiegels lustige Streiche — Chandos ▲ CHAN 8572 [DDD]
Strauss, R.:Tod und Verklärung — Chandos ▲ CHAN 8734 [DDD]
Taneyev, S.:Duet for Romeo & Juliet, w. S. Murphy (sop), K. Lewis (ten) [R] — Chandos ▲ CHAN 8476 [DDD]
Tchaikovsky, P.:Festival Coronation March — Chandos ▲ CHAN 8476 [DDD]
Tchaikovsky, P.:Sleeping Beauty (sels) ["Bluebird" Pas de deux, arr. for small orch. Igor Stravinsky] — Chandos ▲ CHAN 8360 [DDD]
Tobias, R.:Julius Caesar — Chandos ▲ CHAN 8656 [DDD]
Tormis, V.:Ov 2 — Chandos ▲ CHAN 8656 [DDD]

J. Serebrier (cnd)
Vivaldi, A.:Cons Vn, Op. 8/1–4, "The Four Seasons", w. M. Guttman (vn) — Pickwick ("IMG" series) ▲ PIC IMG 1602 [DDD]

B. Thomson (cnd)
Britten, B.:Chanson françaises (4), w. F. Lott (sop) [F] — Chandos ▲ CHAN 8657 [DDD]
Britten, B.:Les Illuminations, w. F. Lott (sop) [F] — Chandos ▲ CHAN 8657 [DDD]
Britten, B.:Serenade, Op. 31, w. A. Rolfe-Johnson (ten), M. Thompson (hn) [E] — Chandos ▲ CHAN 8657 [DDD]
Leighton, K.:Con Vc, w. R. Wallfisch (vc) — Chandos ▲ CHAN 8741 [DDD]
Leighton, K.:Sym 3, w. N. Mackie (ten) [E] — Chandos ▲ CHAN 8741 [DDD]
Martinů, B.:Sym 3 — Chandos ▲ CHAN 8917 [DDD]
Martinů, B.:Sym 4 — Chandos ▲ CHAN 8917 [DDD]
Rachmaninoff, S.:Cons Pno (comp), w. H. Shelley (pno) — Chandos 2-▲ CHAN 8882/83 [DDD]
Rachmaninoff, S.:Rhapsody on a Theme of Paganini, w. H. Shelley (pno) — Chandos 2-▲ CHAN 8882/83 [DDD]
Wilson, T.:Con Pno, w. D. Wilde (pno) — Chandos ▲ CHAN 8626 [DDD]
Wilson, T.:Introit, "Towards the Light..." — Chandos ▲ CHAN 8626 [DDD]

Scottish National Orch Wind Ensemble
P. Järvi (cnd)
Mozart, W.A.:Divert Obs, K.213 — Chandos ("Collect" series) ▲ CHAN 6575 [DDD]
Mozart, W.A.:Serenade Ww, K.361 — Chandos ("Collect" series) ▲ CHAN 6575 [DDD]

Scottish Opera Orch
J. Mauceri (cnd)
Blitzstein, M.:Regina, w. A. Réaux (sop), S. Greenawald (sop), K. Ciesinski (mez), S. Ramey (bass), Scottish Opera Chorus [E] — London 2-▲ 433812-2 [DDD]
Weill, K.:Street Scene, w. J. Barstow (sop), A. Réaux (sop), J. Hadley (ten), S. Ramey (bass), Scottish Opera Chorus [E] — London 2-▲ 433371-2 [DDD]

Scripps Javanese Gamelan of Univ of California
R. Feliciano (cnd)
Feliciano, R.:In Celebration of Golden Rain, w. L. Moe (org) — Opus One ▲ 155 CD

SDR SO
S. Celibidache (cnd)
Ravel, M.:Boléro *(rec 1978–80)* — Exclusive 2-▲ EXL 61 [ADD]
C. Kleiber (cnd)
Borodin, A.:Sym 2 *(rec live, 1972)* — AS Disc ▲ ASD 2510

Seattle Chamber Sym
G. Schwarz (cnd)
Made in the USA:A Showcase of American Symphonic Music, New York CO — Delos ▲ DE 3508 [DDD]

Seattle SO
Bernard Herrmann:Fahrenheit 451 — Varèse Sarabande ▲ VSD 5551
Hollywood '94 — Varèse Sarabande ▲ VSD 5531
Piston, W.:Con Perc, w. Juilliard String Quartet *(rec Jan. 27–28, 1992)* — Delos ▲ DE 3126 [DDD]
C. Eidelman (cnd)
Blood & Thunder *(rec Seattle, WA, Sept 1994)* — Varèse Sarabande ▲ VSD 5561
A. Hovhaness (cnd)
Hovhaness, A.:Sym 22 *(rec May 17 & 19, 1992)* — Delos ▲ DE 3137 [DDD]
M. Kamen (cnd)
Kamen, M.:Mr. Holland's Opus [original film score]—also includes mvmts from Beethoven's Sym 7 & Bach's Con for 3 Hpds — London ▲ 452065-2 ■ 452 065-4
M. Katims (cnd)
Rimsky-Korsakov, N.:Sadko Orch, Op. 5 — Vox Box 2-▲ CDX 5082 [ADD]

Seattle SO (cont.)
J. McNeely (cnd)
Herrmann, B.:Film Music—Fahrenheit 451; The Man in the Grey Flannel Suit; Tender is the Night & others — Varèse Sarabande ▲ VSD 5551
G. Schwarz (cnd)
Albert, S.:In Concordiam, w. I. Talvi (vn) — Delos ▲ DE 3059 [DDD]
Bach, J.S.:Orchestral Trans—"Bach Transcriptions" & Respighi — Delos ▲ DE 3098 [DDD]
Barber, S.:The School for Scandal — Delos ▲ DE 3078 [DDD]
Bartók, B.:Con Orch — Delos ▲ DE 3095 [DDD]
Bartók, B.:The Miraculous Mandarin — Delos ▲ DE 3083 [DDD]
Bernstein, L.:Arias & Barcarolles, w. Jane Bunnell (mez), Dale Duesing (bar) [E] — Delos ▲ DE 3078 [DDD]
Bloch, E.:America, w. Seattle Chorale *(rec June 1–2, 1993)* — Delos ▲ DE 3135 [DDD]
Bloch, E.:Con grosso 1 *(rec Jan. 21, 1993)* — Delos ▲ DE 3135 [DDD]
Bruch, M.:Con 2 Vn, w. Nai-Yuan Hu (vn) — Delos ▲ DE 3156 [DDD]
Copland, A.:Appalachian Spring (suite) *(rec Seattle Opera House, Nov. 22, 1994)* — Delos ▲ DE 3154 [DDD]
Copland, A.:Billy the Kid (suite) — Delos ▲ DE 3104 [DDD]
Copland, A.:Canticle of Freedom, w. Seattle Chorale [E] — Delos ▲ DE 3140 [DDD]
Copland, A.:Con Pno, w. Lorin Hollander (pno) *(rec Seattle Opera House, May 26, 1993)* — Delos ▲ DE 3154 [DDD]
Copland, A.:Fanfare for the Common Man *(rec June 1992)* — Delos ▲ DE 3140 [DDD]
Copland, A.:Lincoln Portrait, w. J. E. Jones (nar) [E] *(rec June 1992)* — Delos ▲ DE 3140 [DDD]
Copland, A.:An Outdoor Ov *(rec June 1992)* — Delos ▲ DE 3140 [DDD]
Copland, A.:Rodeo — Delos ▲ DE 3104 [DDD]
Copland, A.:Symphonic Ode *(rec Seattle Opera House, June 2, 1993)* — Delos ▲ DE 3154 [DDD]
Creston, P.:Choreografic Suite, New York Chamber SO *(rec Oct 6, 1991)* — Delos ▲ DE 3127 [DDD]
Creston, P.:Invocation & Dance *(rec 3/24/91)* — Delos ▲ DE 3114 [DDD]
Creston, P.:Out of the Cradle *(rec 9/17/91)* — Delos ▲ DE 3114 [DDD]
Creston, P.:Partita Fl, w. S. Goff (fl), I. Talvi (vn) *(rec 3/1/91)* — Delos ▲ DE 3114 [DDD]
Creston, P.:Sym 3, "3 Mysteries" *(rec 1/92)* — Delos ▲ DE 3114 [DDD]
Creston, P.:Sym 5, New York Chamber SO *(rec Oct 6, 1991)* — Delos ▲ DE 3127 [DDD]
Creston, P.:Toccata, New York Chamber SO *(rec Oct 6, 1991)* — Delos ▲ DE 3127 [DDD]
Danielpour, R.:The Awakened Heart — Delos ▲ DE 3118 [DDD]
Danielpour, R.:First Light — Delos ▲ DE 3118 [DDD]
Danielpour, R.:Sym 3, "Journey Without Distance", w. Faith Esham (sop) — Delos ▲ DE 3118 [DDD]
Debussy, C.:Hommage à Haydn [orchd Diamond] — Koch Schwann ▲ SCH 373582
Diamond, D.:Concert Piece Orch *(rec Seattle Opera House, June 2, 1993)* — Delos ▲ DE 3189 [DDD]
Diamond, D.:Con 2 Vn, w. I. Talvi (vn) *(rec Sept. 11, 1991)* — Delos ▲ DE 3119 [DDD]
Diamond, D.:Elegy in Memory of Maurice Ravel — Delos ▲ DE 3189 [DDD]
Diamond, D.:Elegy in Memory of Maurice Ravel — Koch Schwann ▲ SCH 373582
Diamond, D.:Elegy in Memory of Maurice Ravel — Delos ▲ DE 3110 [DDD]
Diamond, D.:The Enormous Room *(rec Oct. 18 & 20, 1992)* — Delos ▲ DE 3119 [DDD]
Diamond, D.:Kaddish, w. J. Starker (vc) — Delos ▲ DE 3103 [DDD]
Diamond, D.:Psalm — Delos ▲ DE 3103 [DDD]
Diamond, D.:Rounds *(rec Seattle Opera House, June 4, 1995)* — Delos ▲ DE 3189 [DDD]
Diamond, D.:Sym 1 *(rec June 8, 1992)* — Delos ▲ DE 3119 [DDD]
Diamond, D.:Sym 2 — Delos ▲ DE 3093 [DDD]
Diamond, D.:Sym 3 — Delos ▲ DE 3103 [DDD]
Diamond, D.:Sym 4 — Delos ▲ DE 3093 [DDD]
Diamond, D.:Sym 8 *(rec May 24–26, 1993)* — Delos ▲ DE 3141 [DDD]
Diamond, D.:Sym 11—Adagio assai e molto cantabile *(rec Seattle Opera House, June 4, 1995)* — Delos ▲ DE 3189 [DDD]
Diamond, D.:This Sacred Ground, w. Erich Parce (bar), Seattle Chorale, Seattle Girls' Choir, Northwest Boychoir *(rec Feb. 13, 1994)* — Delos ▲ DE 3141 [DDD]
Diamond, D.:Tom (suite) *(rec June 10, 1992)* — Delos ▲ DE 3141 [DDD]
Dohnányi, E. von:Konzertstück, w. J. Starker (vc) — Delos ▲ DE 3095 [DDD]
Drattell, D.:Con Cl, "Fire Dances", w. David Shifrin (cl) *(rec Seattle Opera House, June 17, 1994)* — Delos ▲ DE 3159 [DDD]
Drattell, D.:The Fire Within, w. Scott Goff (fl) *(rec Seattle Opera House, June 17, 1994)* — Delos ▲ DE 3159 [DDD]
Drattell, D.:Lilith *(rec Seattle Opera House, June 17, 1994)* — Delos ▲ DE 3159 [DDD]
Drattell, D.:Sorrow Is Not Melancholy *(rec Seattle Opera House, Nov 15–16, 1993)* — Delos ▲ DE 3159 [DDD]
Drattell, D.:Syzygy *(rec Seattle Opera House, Nov 15–16, 1993)* — Delos ▲ DE 3159 [DDD]
Elgar, E.:Fant & Fugue — Delos ▲ DE 3098 [DDD]
Gershwin, G.:An American in Paris—first recording of the original, uncut score, which includes about three minutes of music excised by Gershwin before the first performance — Delos ▲ DE 3078 [DDD]
Goldmark, K.:Con 1 Vn, w. Nai-Yuan Hu (vn) — Delos ▲ DE 3156 [DDD]
Gould, M.:American Symphonette 2—Pavanne *(rec Seattle Opera House, June 13, 1994)* — Delos ▲ DE 3166 [DDD]
Gould, M.:Audibon:Birds of America—Con Grosso *(rec Seattle Opera House, Nov 22, 1994)* — Delos ▲ DE 3166 [DDD]
Gould, M.:Festive Music, w. Jeffrey Silberschlag (tpt)—Interlude *(rec Seattle Opera House, June 13, 1994)* — Delos ▲ DE 3166 [DDD]
Gould, M.:Formations *(rec Seattle Opera House, Mar 28, 1995)* — Delos ▲ DE 3166 [DDD]
Gould, M.:Holocaust Suite *(rec Seattle Opera House, June 13, 1994)* — Delos ▲ DE 3166 [DDD]
Gould, M.:World War I—Prologue & Drum Waltz; Sad Song; Royal Hunt [Galop] *(rec Seattle Opera House, June 13, 1994)* — Delos ▲ DE 3166 [DDD]
Grieg, E.:Con Pno, Op. 16, w. B. Davidovich (pno) — Delos ▲ DE 3091 [DDD]
Grieg, E.:Holberg Suite — Delos ▲ DE 3091 [DDD]
Grieg, E.:Lyric Suite, Op. 54 — Delos ▲ DE 3091 [DDD]
Griffes, C.T.:Bacchanale — Delos ▲ DE 3099 [DDD]
Griffes, C.T.:The Pleasure Dome of Kubla Khan — Delos ▲ DE 3099 [DDD]
Griffes, C.T.:Poem Fl, w. S. Goff (fl) — Delos ▲ DE 3099 [DDD]
Griffes, C.T.:Tone-Pictures, Op. 5 — Delos ▲ DE 3099 [DDD]
Griffes, C.T.:The White Peacock — Delos ▲ DE 3099 [DDD]
Grofé, F.:Grand Canyon Suite — Delos ▲ DE 3104 [DDD]
Handel, G.F.:Acis & Galatea, w. D. Kotoski (sop—Galatea), D. Gordon (ten—Acis), G. Siebert (ten—Damon), J. Opalach (bass—Polyphemus), Seattle Chorale [E] — Delos 2-▲ DE 3107 [DDD]
Hanson, H.:Con Pno, w. Carol Rosenberger (pno) — Delos 4-▲ DE 3150 [DDD]
Hanson, H.:Con Pno, w. Carol Rosenberger (pno) — Delos ▲ DE 3130 [DDD]
Hanson, H.:Dies Natalis I *(rec June 6–7, 1994)* — Delos ▲ DE 3160 [DDD]
Hanson, H.:Elegy in Memory of Serge Koussevitsky — Delos 4-▲ DE 3150 [DDD]
Hanson, H.:Elegy in Memory of Serge Koussevitsky — Delos ▲ DCD 3073 [DDD]
Hanson, H.:Lament for Beowulf, w. Seattle Chorale — Delos ▲ DE 3105 [DDD]
Hanson, H.:Lament for Beowulf, w. Seattle Chorale — Delos 4-▲ DE 3150 [DDD]
Hanson, H.:Lumen in Christo, w. Seattle Chorale *(rec June 6–7, 1994)* — Delos ▲ DE 3160 [DDD]
Hanson, H.:Lux Aeterna, w. Seattle Chorale *(rec June 6–7, 1994)* — Delos ▲ DE 3160 [DDD]
Hanson, H.:Merry Mount (suite) — Delos 4-▲ DE 3150 [DDD]
Hanson, H.:Merry Mount (suite) — Delos ▲ DE 3105 [DDD]
Hanson, H.:Mosaics — Delos 4-▲ DE 3150 [DDD]
Hanson, H.:Mosaics — Delos ▲ DE 3130 [DDD]
Hanson, H.:The Mystic Trumpeter, w. James Earl Jones (nar), Seattle Chorale *(rec June 6–7, 1994)* — Delos ▲ DE 3160 [DDD]
Hanson, H.:Pastorale Ob, w. Robert Ellis (ob), Susan Jolles (hp) — Delos 4-▲ DE 3150 [DDD]
Hanson, H.:Pastorale Ob, w. Robert Ellis (ob), Susan Jolles (hp) — Delos ▲ DE 3105 [DDD]
Hanson, H.:Serenade Fl, w. Susan Jolles (hp), J. Mendenhall (fl) — Delos 4-▲ DE 3150 [DDD]
Hanson, H.:Serenade Fl, w. Susan Jolles (hp), J. Mendenhall (fl) — Delos ▲ DE 3105 [DDD]

▲ = CD ♦ = Enhanced CD Δ = MD ■ = Cassette Tape □ = DCC

Seattle SO (cont.)
G. Schwarz (cnd) (cont.)
Hanson, H.:Syms (comp), New York Chamber SO *(rec 1988–92)* Delos 4–▲ DE 3150 [DDD]
Hanson, H.:Sym 1, "Nordic" Delos ▲ DCD 3073 [DDD]
Hanson, H.:Sym 2, "Romantic" Delos ▲ DCD 3073 [DDD]
Hanson, H.:Sym 3 Delos ▲ DE 3092 [DDD]
Hanson, H.:Sym 4, "Requiem" Delos ▲ DE 3105 [DDD]
Hanson, H.:Sym 5, "Sinf Sacra" Delos ▲ DE 3130 [DDD]
Hanson, H.:Sym 6 Delos ▲ DE 3092 [DDD]
Hanson, H.:Sym 7, "A Sea Sym", w. Seattle Chorale Delos ▲ DE 3130 [DDD]
Harris, R.:American Creed *(rec June 1992)* Delos ▲ DE 3140 [DDD]
Honegger, A.:Sym 2 *(rec Apr. 17, 1992 & Feb. 8–9, 1993)* Delos ▲ DE 3121 [DDD]
Hovhaness, A.:Alleluia & Fugue *(rec Sept. 1993)* Delos ▲ DE 3157 [DDD]
Hovhaness, A.:And God Created Whales *(rec Sept. 1993)* Delos ▲ DE 3157 [DDD]
Hovhaness, A.:Celestial Fant *(rec Sept. 1993)* Delos ▲ DE 3157 [DDD]
Hovhaness, A.:Fant on Japanese Woodprints, w. Ron Johnson (mar) *(rec Seattle Opera House, June 6–7, 1994)* Delos ▲ DE 3168 [DDD]
Hovhaness, A.:Meditations on Orpheus *(rec Seattle Opera House, June 6–7, 1994)* Delos ▲ DE 3168 [DDD]
Hovhaness, A.:Prayer of St. Gregory *(rec Sept. 1993)* Delos ▲ DE 3157 [DDD]
Hovhaness, A.:Prelude & Quadruple Fugue *(rec Sept. 1993)* Delos ▲ DE 3157 [DDD]
Hovhaness, A.:Rubaiyat, w. Michael York (nar), Diane Schmidt (acc) *(rec Seattle Opera House, June 6–7, 1994)* Delos ▲ DE 3168 [DDD]
Hovhaness, A.:Sym 1 *(rec Seattle Opera House, June 6–7, 1994)* Delos ▲ DE 3168 [DDD]
Hovhaness, A.:Sym 2 *(rec Sept. 1993)* Delos ▲ DE 3157 [DDD]
Hovhaness, A.:Sym 50 *(rec May 17 & 19, 1992)* Delos ▲ DE 3137 [DDD]
Khachaturian, A.:Con Pno, w. D. Atamian (pno) *(rec Nov. 22–23, 1993)* Delos ▲ DE 3155 [DDD]
Kodály, Z.:Galanta Dances Delos ▲ DE 3083 [DDD]
Kodály, Z.:Háry János (suite) Delos ▲ DE 3083 [DDD]
Lazarof, H.:Icarus Delos ▲ DE 3069 [DDD]
Lazarof, H.:Poema Delos ▲ DE 3069 [DDD]
Lazarof, H.:Tableaux Delos ▲ DE 3069 [DDD]
Mendelssohn, F.:Sym 2, w. M. Chalker (sop), M. Rivera (sop), V. Cole (ten), Seattle Chorale *(rec Apr. 22–23, 1991)* Delos ▲ DE 3112 [DDD]
Mennin, P.:Concertato *(rec Seattle Center Opera House, Nov 21–22, 1994 & Jan 30, 1995)* Delos ▲ DE 3164 [DDD]
Mennin, P.:Sym 3 *(rec Seattle Center Opera House, Nov 21–22, 1994 & Jan 30, 1995)* Delos ▲ DE 3164 [DDD]
Mennin, P.:Sym 7 *(rec Seattle Center Opera House, Nov 21–22, 1994 & Jan 30, 1995)* Delos ▲ DE 3164 [DDD]
Mozart, W.A.:Con 21 Pno, w. Eugene Istomin (pno) *(rec St. Thomas Center, Bothell, WA, Oct 10, 1995)* Reference ▲ RR–68CD
Mozart, W.A.:Con 24 Pno, w. Eugene Istomin (pno) *(rec St. Thomas Center, Bothell, WA, Oct 10, 1995)* Reference ▲ RR–68CD
Piston, W.:Capriccio Hp, w. T. Elder Wunrow (hp) Delos ▲ DE 3106 [DDD]
Piston, W.:Fant E Hn, w. G. Danielson (E hn), T. E. Wunrow (hp) *(rec Jan. 27–28, 1992)* Delos ▲ DE 3126 [DDD]
Piston, W.:New England Sketches Delos ▲ DE 3106 [DDD]
Piston, W.:Psalm & Prayer of David, w. Seattle Chorale *(rec Jan. 27–28, 1992)* Delos ▲ DE 3126 [DDD]
Piston, W.:Suite 1 *(rec Jan. 27–28, 1992)* Delos ▲ DE 3126 [DDD]
Piston, W.:Sym 2 Delos ▲ DE 3074 [DDD]
Piston, W.:Sym 4 Delos ▲ DE 3106 [DDD]
Piston, W.:Sym 6 Delos ▲ DE 3074 [DDD]
Prokofiev, S.:Con 3 Pno, w. D. Atamian (pno) *(rec Nov. 22–23, 1993)* Delos ▲ DE 3155 [DDD]
Prokofiev, S.:Pushkin Waltzes—No. 2 Delos ▲ CD 3050 [DDD]
Prokofiev, S.:Romeo & Juliet (sels)—Suites 1 & 2 Delos ▲ CD 3050 [DDD]
Ravel, M.:Daphins et Chloé, w. Seattle Chorale Delos ▲ DE 3110 [DDD]
Ravel, M.:Menuet sur le nom d'Haydn [orchd Diamond] Koch Schwann ▲ SCH 373582
Ravel, M.:Le Tombeau de Couperin [Fugue orchd Diamond] Koch Schwann ▲ SCH 373582
Respighi, O.:Bach Transcriptions—Chorale Preludes, BWV.62, 10 & 140; Passacaglia & Fugue, BWV.582; Prelude & Fugue, BWV.532; Sonata in e for Violin & Continuo, BWV.1023 Delos ▲ DE 3098 [DDD]
Rimsky–Korsakov, N.:Russian Easter Festival Delos ▲ DCD 3054 [DDD]
Satie, E.:Gymnopédies [No. 2 orchd Diamond] Koch Schwann ▲ SCH 373582
Satie, E.:Messe des pauvres [orchd Diamond] Koch Schwann ▲ SCH 373582
Satie, E.:Pasacaille Pno [orchd Diamond] Koch Schwann ▲ SCH 373582
Schuman, W.:Judith Delos ▲ DE3115 [DDD]
Schuman, W.:New England Triptych Delos ▲ DE3115 [DDD]
Schuman, W.:Sym 5 Delos ▲ DE3115 [DDD]
Schuman, W.:Vars on "America" Delos ▲ DE3115 [DDD]
Schumann, R.:Konzertstück Hns, w. R. Bonnevie (hn), et al. Delos ▲ DE 3084 [DDD]
Schumann, R.:Orch Music—Ov., Scherzo & Finale, Op. 52; Syms.1–4; Symphonic Etudes, Op. 13; Konzertstück for 4 Hns & Orch., Op. 86 [w. Robert Bonnevie (hn), Mark Robbins (hn), David C. Knapp (hn), Scott Wilson (hn)]; Con. in a for Pno, Op. 54; Ov. to Manfred, Op. 115 *(rec Seattle Opera House, Sept. 1988–Feb. 1992)* Delos 4–▲ DE 3146 [DDD]
Schumann, R.:Ov, Scherzo & Finale Delos ▲ DE 3084 [DDD]
Strauss, R.:Also sprach Zarathustra Delos ▲ DCD 3052 [DDD]
Strauss, R.:Burleske, w. C. Rosenberger (pno) Delos ▲ DE 3109 [DDD]
Strauss, R.:Ein Heldenleben Delos ▲ DE 3094 [DDD]
Strauss, R.:Josephs–Legende (fragment) Delos ▲ DE 3082 [DDD]
Strauss, R.:Macbeth Delos ▲ DE 3094 [DDD]
Strauss, R.:Metamorphosen *(rec Apr.17, 1992 & Feb. 8–9, 1993)* Delos ▲ DE 3121 [DDD]
Strauss, R.:Der Rosenkavalier (waltzes) Delos ▲ DE 3109 [DDD]
Strauss, R.:Salome (dance) Delos ▲ DCD 3052 [DDD]
Strauss, R.:Serenade Ww Delos ▲ DE 3094 [DDD]
Strauss, R.:Symphonia domestica Delos ▲ DE 3082 [DDD]
Strauss, R.:Symphonic Fant Delos ▲ DE 3109 [DDD]
Strauss, R.:Symphonic Interludes Delos ▲ DCD 3052 [DDD]
Stravinsky, I.:Le Chant du rossignol Delos ▲ CD 3051 [DDD]
Stravinsky, I.:The Firebird Delos ▲ DE 6005 [DDD] ■ CS 6005 (D)
Stravinsky, I.:Fireworks Delos ▲ DCD 3054 [DDD]
Stravinsky, I.:Pulcinella, w. J. Graham–Hall (ten), G. Wilson (ten), J. Opalach (bass) Delos ▲ DE 3100 [DDD]
Stravinsky, I.:Le Sacre du printemps Orch Delos ▲ DE 3100 [DDD]
Stravinsky, I.:Scherzo fantastique Delos ▲ DCD 3054 [DDD]
Taylor, D.:Through the Looking Glass Delos ▲ DE 3099 [DDD]
Tchaikovsky, P.:Sym 1 *(rec June 7, 1992)* Delos ▲ DE 3087 [DDD]
Tchaikovsky, P.:Sym 2 *(rec May 25, 1993)* Delos ▲ DE 3087 [DDD]
Wagner, R.:Eine Faust–Ov *(rec Feb. 19–20, 1992)* Delos ▲ DE 3120 [DDD]
Wagner, R.:Lohengrin (sels), w. A. Marc (sop)—Elsa's Dream (Einsam in trüben Tagen), Act I [G] *(rec Feb. 19–20, 1992)* Delos ▲ DE 3120 [DDD]
Wagner, R.:Lohengrin (preludes)—Acts 1 & 3 Delos ▲ DCD 3053 [DDD]
Wagner, R.:Ovs, Preludes & Orch Sels—Der fliegende Holländer Delos ▲ DCD 3053 [DDD]
Wagner, R.:Parsifal (prelude) Delos ▲ DCD 3053 [DDD]
Wagner, R.:Parsifal (good friday) Delos ▲ DCD 3053 [DDD]
Wagner, R.:Siegfried (waldweben) *(rec Feb. 19–20, 1992)* Delos ▲ DE 3120 [DDD]
Wagner, R.:Wagner Concert—orchestral selections from Götterdämmerung, Meistersinger, Rheingold, Tannhäuser Delos ▲ DCD 3040 [DDD]

Seattle SO (cont.)
G. Schwarz (cnd) (cont.)
Wagner, R.:Die Walküre (sels)—Wotan's Farewell (Wotans Scheidegruss); Magic Fire Music (Feuerzauber) *(rec Feb. 19–20, 1992)* Delos ▲ DE 3120 [DDD]
Webern, A.:Slow Movt *(rec Apr.17, 1992 & Feb. 8–9, 1993)* Delos ▲ DE 3121 [DDD]

Seaven Teares
Dowland, J.:The First Booke of Songs or Ayres Ambitus ▲ 97821

Sebon Quartet [Karl Bernhard Sebon (fl), Günter Zorn (ob), Jörg Fadle (cl), Peter Utesch (bn)]
Erdmann, D.:Improvisation *(rec Oct 17, 1976)* Thorofon ▲ CTH 2284 [ADD/DDD]

Sedlacek String Quartet
Janácek, L.:Qt 2 Strs *(rec Panton Studios, Prague, 1992)* Panton ▲ PAN 811186
Lukas, Z.:Qt Strs *(rec Panton Studios, Prague, 1992)* Panton ▲ PAN 811186
Martinů, B.:Qt 6 Strs *(rec Panton Studios, Prague, 1992)* Panton ▲ PAN 811186
Teml, J.:Qt 2 Strs *(rec Panton Studios, Prague, 1992)* Panton ▲ PAN 811186

Segerstam String Quartet [Leif Segerstam (vn), Hannele Segerstam (vn), Mauri Pietikäinen (va), Veikko Höylä (vc)]
Segerstam, L.:Qt 6 Strs *(rec Sibelius Acad., Helsinki, Finland, Oct 23, 1974)* BIS ▲ CD 20 [AAD]
Segerstam, L.:Qt 7 Strs *(rec Studio 1, Finnish Radio House, Helsinki, Sept. 13, 1975)* BIS ▲ CD 39 [AAD]

Segovia Guitar Quartet
Bizet, G.:L'Arlésienne (suites) Ottavo ▲ OTT 79239 [DDD]
Bizet, G.:Carmen (suites) Ottavo ▲ OTT 79239 [DDD]

Seicentonovecento Ensemble
F. Colusso (cnd)
Aldrovandini, G.:Sinf Tpt, w. S. Verzari (tpt) Bongiovanni ▲ GB 10010 [DDD]
Carissimi, G.:Oratorio della Santissima Vergine, w. P. Borri (sop), A. M. Ferrante (sop), P. Pace (sop), A. Christofellis (alt), L. Petroni (ten), F. Sclaverano (ten), R. Abbondanza (bass), M. Mondelli (bass), P. Spagnoli (bass) [I] Bongiovanni ▲ GB 10011 [DDD]
Carissimi, G.:Oratorio di Daniele Profeta, w. P. Borri (sop), A. M. Ferrante (sop), P. Pace (sop), A. Christofellis (alt), L. Petroni (ten), F. Sclaverano (ten), R. Abbondanza (bass), M. Mondelli (bass), P. Spagnoli (bass) [I] Bongiovanni ▲ GB 10011 [DDD]
Gabrielli, D.:Con Tpt, w. S. Verzari (tpt) Bongiovanni ▲ GB 10010 [DDD]
Gabrielli, D.:Sons Tpt, w. S. Verzari (tpt)—Sons 4, 5, 7 & 8 Tpt Bongiovanni ▲ GB 10010 [DDD]
Mascagni, P.:Messa di gloria, w. I. Zennaro (ten), P. Spagnoli (bar) Musicaimmagine ▲ MR 10001 [DDD]
Paternoster, V.:Inzaffirio:Prayers (6) to the Virgin Mary, w. P. Pace (sop), V. Paternoster (vc) Musicaimmagine ▲ MR 10006
Torelli, G.:Tpt Music, w. S. Verzari (tpt)—Concerto; Sinfonia G.2–4 & 8; Sonata G.1 & 5–7 *(rec 9/90)* Bongiovanni ▲ GB 10008 [DDD]

Seicentonovecento Ensemble [G. del Sulli (fl), U. Maccari (cl), P. Montin (cl), A. dalle Lucche (s sax), A. Warshaw (vn), C. Tofani (vns), G. Russo (va), M. Scarpelli (vc), G. Taddei (db), E. di Filippo (perc), A. Monti (gtr)]
Monti, A.:Panjim Musicaimmagine ▲ MR 10003

Seiler CO
W. Hofmann (cnd)
Vivaldi, A.:Cons Vc, w. K. Storck (vc)—RV.401 Deutsche Grammophon ("Musikfest" series) ■ 413682–4

Sekar Jaya Gamelan Orch
Tenzer, M.:Banyuari New World ▲ 804302
Tenzer, M.:Situ Banda New World ▲ 804302
Vitale, W.:Khayalan Tiga New World ▲ 804302
Ziporyn, E.:Aneh Tapi Nyata, w. Kate Beddall (voc) New World ▲ 804302
Ziporyn, E.:Kekembangan, w. Chris Jonas (sax), Randy McKean (sax), Dan Plonsey (sax), Evan Ziporyn (sax) New World ▲ 804302

Selandia Wind Ensemble
Bentzon, J.:Racconto 3 Kontrapunkt ▲ 32032 [DDD]
Bozza, E.:Pièces pour une musique de nuit (3) Kontrapunkt ▲ 32032 [DDD]
Françaix, J.:Qt Fl Kontrapunkt ▲ 32032 [DDD]
Mozart, W.A.:Andante Mechanical Org, K.616 Kontrapunkt ▲ 32058 [DDD]
Mozart, W.A.:Qt 17 Strs [arr. Geoffrey Emerson for wind quintet] Kontrapunkt ▲ 32058 [DDD]
Pierné, G.:Pastorale Ww Kontrapunkt ▲ 32032 [DDD]
Riisager, K.:Divert Fl Kontrapunkt ▲ 32032 [DDD]
Wind Chamber Music I Kontrapunkt ▲ 32032 [DDD]

Sellers Engineering Band
All of the World's Most Beautiful Melodies!, w. Phillip McCann (cnt), Gordon Langford (cnd), Roy Newsome (cnd), Peter Parkes (cnd), Black Dyke Mills Band, Academy of St. Martin in the Fields Chamber Ensemble, Huddersfield Choral Society, Leeds Parish Church Boys Choir Chandos ("Brass" series) 5–▲ CHN 4536(5)
Legend in Brass Chandos ▲ CHAN 4531 [DDD]
A Song of Yorkshire, w. Honley Male Voice Choir, S. Lindley (org), Leeds Parish Church Choir Boys' Voices, Sellers Engineering Band Chandos Brass ▲ CHAN 4515 [DDD]
We Love a Parade Chandos ▲ CHAN 4527 [DDD]
The World of Brass Chandos Brass ▲ CHAN 4511 [DDD]
The World's Most Beautiful Melodies, Vol. 3:The Golden Cornet of Phillip McCann, w. McCann, Phillip (cnt), Simon Lindley (org) Chandos Brass ▲ CHAN 4503 [DDD]
The World's Most Beautiful Melodies, Vol. 5, w. McCann, Phillip (cnt), Huddersfield Choral Society Youth Choir, S. Lindley (org) Chandos ▲ CHAN 4532 [DDD]

S.E.M. Ensemble Orch
P. Kotik (cnd)
Cage, J.:Atlas Eclipticalis, w. J. Kubera (pno) Wergo ▲ WER 6216–2
Cage, J.:Concert Pno, w. J. Kubera (pno) Wergo ▲ WER 6216–2
Cage, J.:Winter Music, w. J. Kubera (pno) Wergo ▲ WER 6216–2

Semantics [Elliott Sharp (electric gtr/bass), Samm Bennett (perc), Ned Rothenberg (sax)]
Sato, M.:Improvs, w. Michihiro Sato (tsugaru shamisen), Bill Frisell (elec gtr), Fred Frith (elec gtr), Tenko (sgr), Mark Miller (elec bass), Nicolas Collins (elec), Christian Marclay (turntables), Steve Colemann (sax), Tom Cora (vc), Joey Baron (perc), Mark Dresser (elec bass), Gerry Hemingway (perc), Toh Ban Djan [Ikue Mori (perc), Luli Shioi (elec bass/sgr)]—23 improvisations with various accompaniment combinations *(rec Baby Monster Studio, NY, Apr. 11–16, 1988)* Hat Hut ▲ hat ART CD 6015 [ADD]

Il Seminario Musicale
Caldara, A.:Medea in Corinto, w. G. Lesne (ct) Virgin Classics ▲ CDC 59058
Vivaldi, A.:Salve regina, RV.616, w. G. Lesne (alt) Virgin Classics ▲ CDC 59232

Senario Ensemble [S. Coolen (rcr), P. Frankenberg (ob), J. Leertouwer (vn), K. Koelmans (vn), D. Mings (bn), J. Ogg (hpd), P. Rikkers (vc)]
Vivaldi, A.:Cons Rcr—Cons. in C, D, D, D, g & g, RV.87, 92, 94, 95, 103 & 105 *(rec Feb. 1994)* Globe ▲ GLO 5119 [DDD]

Sendai PO
M. Enkoji (cnd)
Nishimura, A.:Tapas, w. I. Magome (bn) Camerata ▲ 32CM 175
Yoshimatsu, T.:Unicorn Circuit, w. I. Magome (bn) Camerata ▲ 32CM 175

Senzoku Gakuen Symphonic Wind Orch
A. Reed (cnd)
Reed, A.:Armenian Dances *(rec Senzoku Gakuen Maeda Hall, Aug 2–5, 1995)* Walking Frog ▲ WFR 140 [DDD]
Reed, A.:The Music–Makers *(rec Senzoku Gakuen Maeda Hall, Aug 2–5, 1995)* Walking Frog ▲ WFR 140 [DDD]
Reed, A.:Pro Texana *(rec Senzoku Gakuen Maeda Hall, Aug 2–5, 1995)* Walking Frog ▲ WFR 140 [DDD]
Reed, A.:A Springtime Celebration *(rec Senzoku Gakuen Maeda Hall, Aug 2–5, 1995)* Walking Frog ▲ WFR 140 [DDD]

Senzoku Gakuen Symphonic Wind Orch (cont.)
A. Reed (cnd) (cont.)
Reed, A.:Sym 5 *(rec Senzoku Gakuen Maeda Hall, Aug 2–5, 1995)* Walking Frog ▲ WFR 140 [DDD]
Seoul PO
C.-D. Chung (cnd)
Kim, B.-K.:Choyop Cambria ▲ CD 1046
Sephira Ensemble Stuttgart
Isabella Leonarda:Motets, w. R. Sonnenschmidt (sop) [period instrs]—Alta del ciel regina (from Op. 14) & Veni amor, veni Jesu (from Op. 15) [L] Bayer 2-▲ 100078/79 [DDD]
Isabella Leonarda:Sons [period instrs]—Sonata duodecima for Violin & Harpsichord & Sonata seconda for 2 Violins, Viol & Organ (from Op. 16) [L] Bayer 2-▲ 100078/79 [DDD]
Strozzi, B.:Arias & Cants, w. R. Sonnenschmidt (sop)—nine soprano arias & cantatas, from Opp. 2,6,7 & 8 [period instrs] [I,L] Bayer 2-▲ 100078/79 CD [DDD]
Sequoia String Quartet
Frøydis Ree Wekre, Horn, w. Frøydis Ree Wekre (hn), Zita Carno (pno) *(rec 1980 & 1983)* Crystal ▲ CD 377
Sequoia String Quartet [Yoko Matsuda (vn), Miwako Watanabe (vn), James Dunham (va), Robert Martin (vc)]
Bartók, B.:Qt 3 Strs Delos ▲ DCD 3004 [DDD]
Britten, B.:Qt 2 Strs Music & Arts ▲ CD 740 [DDD]
Giuliani, M.:Intro, Theme, Vars & Polonaise, w. M. Newman (gtr) Sheffield Lab ("Salon" series) ▲ SLS 504 [ADD]
Prokofiev, S.:Qt 1 Strs Elektra/Nonesuch ▲ 79048-2 [DDD]
Prokofiev, S.:Qt 2 Strs Elektra/Nonesuch ▲ 79048-2 [DDD]
Ravel, M.:Qt Strs Delos ▲ DCD 3004 [DDD]
Seraphin Trio
Babadjanyan, A.:Trio Pno Entrée ▲ 0070
Roslavets, N.:Trio 3 Pno Entrée ▲ 0070
Shostakovich, D.:Trio 1 Pno Entrée ▲ 0070
Serenata of London
Elgar, E.:Serenade Strs IMP Classics ▲ PCD 861 [DDD]
Mozart, W.A.:Kleine Nachtmusik IMP Classics ▲ PCD 861 [DDD]
Mozart, W.A.:Serenata notturna IMP Classics ▲ PCD 861 [DDD]
B. Wilde (cnd)
Dvořák, A.:Notturno IMP Classics ▲ IMPPCD 1108 [DDD]
Dvořák, A.:Waltzes Strs, B.105 IMP Classics ▲ IMPPCD 1108 [DDD]
Elgar, E.:Salut d'amour IMP Classics ▲ IMPPCD 1108 [DDD]
Elgar, E.:Sospiri IMP Classics ▲ IMPPCD 1108 [DDD]
Grieg, E.:Elegaic Melodies, Op. 34 IMP Classics ▲ IMPPCD 1108 [DDD]
Grieg, E.:Holberg Suite IMP Classics ▲ PCD 861 [DDD]
Grieg, E.:Melodies, Op. 53 IMP Classics ▲ IMPPCD 1108 [DDD]
Grieg, E.:Norwegian Melodies, Op. 63 IMP Classics ▲ IMPPCD 1108 [DDD]
Nocturnal Classics, w. J. Ogdon (pno), Cristina Ortiz (pno), F. Lott (sop) Pickwick ("The Orchid" series) ▲ PICORCD 11007
Sibelius, J.:Canzonetta IMP Classics ▲ IMPPCD 1108 [DDD]
Sibelius, J.:Suite champêtre IMP Classics ▲ IMPPCD 1108 [DDD]
Tchaikovsky, P.:Elegy IMP Classics ▲ IMPPCD 1108 [DDD]
Serenissima Pro Arte Orch
B. Campanella (cnd)
Piccinni, N.:La cecchinaLa cecchina, ossia la buona figliola, w. M. A. Peters (sop), A. Ruffini (sop), G. Morino (ten), B. Praticò (bar) [I] *(rec live 1990)* Memories 3-▲ DR 3101/03 [DDD]
Sessions of London
Herrmann, B.:Night Digger:Scenario Macbre, w. T. R. Herrmann (hmc), R. Green (va d'amore) Label "X" ▲ LXCD 12 [AAD]
Sestetto Classico
Bertini, H.-J.:Sextet Pno MD + G ▲ L 3067
Hummel, J.N.:Qnt Pno, Op. 87 MD + G ▲ L 3067
Sevan PO
A. Hovhaness (cnd)
Hovhaness, A.:Sym 19 Crystal ▲ CD805
Seville Real SO
A. Ros-Marbà (cnd)
Bacarisse, S.:Fant andaluza *(rec Central Theater, Seville, July 1995)* Almaviva ("Musical Heritage of Andalusia" series) ▲ 118 [DDD]
Halffter, R.:Don Lindo de Almeria *(rec Central Theater, Seville, July 1995)* Almaviva ("Musical Heritage of Andalusia" series) ▲ 118 [DDD]
Pittaluga, G.:Romeria de los Cornudos *(rec Central Theater, Seville, July 1995)* Almaviva ("Musical Heritage of Andalusia" series) ▲ 118 [DDD]
Seymour Group
S. Challender (cnd)
Butterly, N.:The Owl, w. J. Carden (sop) Vox Australis ▲ VAST 011
D. Stanhope (cnd)
Lumsdaine, D.:Aria for Edward John Eyre, w. M. Qualfe (sop), P. Gwynne (nar), J. Tong (nar) Vox Australis ▲ VAST 011
Shakuhachi 1979
Loeb, D.:Yuukuu Vienna Modern Masters ▲ VMM 2008 [DDD]
Shanghai Chinese Folk Orch
G. Guanren (cnd)
Gu, G.:Con Erhu, "Gazing at the Moon", w. Ma Xiaohui (erhu) *(rec Shanghai, Jan 1994)* Marco Polo ("Chinese Composers" series) ▲ 8.223951 [DDD]
Gu, G.:Singapore Glimpses *(rec Shanghai, Jan 1994)* Marco Polo ("Chinese Composers" series) ▲ 8.223951 [DDD]
Gu, G.:Spring Suite *(rec Shanghai, Jan 1994)* Marco Polo ("Chinese Composers" series) ▲ 8.223951 [DDD]
Gu, G.:Torrent Qnt *(rec Shanghai, Jan 1994)* Marco Polo ("Chinese Composers" series) ▲ 8.223951 [DDD]
Shanghai Conservatory
Yuan, Xia (cnd)
The Legend of Shadi-er:Compositions for Chinese Instrument Ensembles Yellow River ▲ 82001 [DDD]
Shanghai Film Orch
T. Riley (cnd)
Riley, T.:In C Celestial Harmonies ▲ 13026-2 ■ 13026-4
Shanghai PO
C. Peng (cnd)
Ding, S.:Vars on a Chinese Folk Theme *(rec Shanghai, China, Apr 1993)* Marco Polo ("Chinese Music" series) ▲ 8.223956 [DDD]
Ding, S.:Vars on a Xinjiang Tune *(rec Shanghai, China, Apr 1993)* Marco Polo ("Chinese Music" series) ▲ 8.223956 [DDD]
Ding, S.:Xinjiang Dances *(rec Shanghai, China, Apr 1993)* Marco Polo ("Chinese Music" series) ▲ 8.223956 [DDD]
He, L.:Orchestral Works—Evening Party; Senjidma; Rebirth in the Mountains; Flute at Night in a Desolate Village; Great World; Ov. *(rec Shanghai, China, Apr 1993)* Marco Polo ("Chinese Music" series) ▲ 8.223956 [DDD]
Huang, Z.:In Memoriam *(rec Shanghai, Apr 1993)* Marco Polo ("Chinese Music" series) ▲ 8.223956 [DDD]
Huang, Z.:Metropolitan Scene Fant *(rec Shanghai, Apr 1993)* Marco Polo ("Chinese Music" series) ▲ 8.223956 [DDD]
Ma, S.:Song of the Mountain Forest *(rec Shanghai, Dec 1993)* Marco Polo ("Chinese Composer" series) ▲ 8.223950 [DDD]
Ma, S.:Sym 2 *(rec Shanghai, Dec 1993)* Marco Polo ("Chinese Composer" series) ▲ 8.223950 [DDD]

Shanghai PO (cont.)
C. Peng (cnd) (cont.)
Zhu, J.:Festival Ov *(rec Shanghai, China, Dec 1993)* Marco Polo ("Chinese Composers" series) ▲ 8.223940 [DDD]
Zhu, J.:Sketches in the Mountains of Guizhou *(rec Shanghai, China, Jan 1994)* Marco Polo ("Chinese Composers" series) ▲ 8.223941 [DDD]
Zhu, J.:Symphonic Fant, "In Memory of Martyrs for Truth" *(rec Shanghai, China, Jan 1994)* Marco Polo ("Chinese Composers" series) ▲ 8.223941 [DDD]
Zhu, J.:Sym 1 *(rec Shanghai, China, Dec 1993)* Marco Polo ("Chinese Composers" series) ▲ 8.223940 [DDD]
Zhu, J.:Sym 4, w. Yu Xunfa (bamboo fl) *(rec Shanghai, China, Jan 1994)* Marco Polo ("Chinese Composers" series) ▲ 8.223941 [DDD]
Shanghai String Quartet [Weigang Li (vn), Yiwen Jiang (vn), Honggang Li (va), James Wilson (vc)]
Beach, A.M.C.:Theme & Vars, w. Eugenia Zukerman (fl) *(rec Church of the Ascension, New York, Oct 19–22, 1994)* Delos ▲ DE 3173 [DDD]
Foote, A.:Scherzo, w. Eugenia Zukerman (fl) *(rec Church of the Ascension, New York, Oct 19–22, 1994)* Delos ▲ DE 3173 [DDD]
Ginastera, A.:Impresiones de la Puna, w. Eugenia Zukerman (fl) *(rec Church of the Ascension, New York, Oct 19–22, 1994)* Delos ▲ DE 3173 [DDD]
Grieg, E.:Qt Strs, Op. 27 Delos ▲ DE 3153 [DDD]
Hovhaness, A.:Bagatelles *(rec May 9–11, 1994)* Delos ▲ DE 3162 [DDD]
Hovhaness, A.:Qt 1 Strs *(rec May 9–11, 1994)* Delos ▲ DE 3162 [DDD]
Hovhaness, A.:Qt 2 Strs *(rec May 9–11, 1994)* Delos ▲ DE 3162 [DDD]
Hovhaness, A.:Qt 3 Strs *(rec May 9–11, 1994)* Delos ▲ DE 3162 [DDD]
Hovhaness, A.:Qt 4 Strs *(rec May 9–11, 1994)* Delos ▲ DE 3162 [DDD]
Long, Z.:Song of the Ch'in *(rec May 9–11, 1994)* Delos ▲ DE 3162 [DDD]
Mendelssohn, F.:Qt 2 Strs Delos ▲ DE 3153 [DDD]
Mozart, W.A.:Kleine Nachtmusik, w. Anthony Newman (hpd) *(rec Church of the Ascension, New York, Oct 19–22, 1994)* Delos ▲ DE 3173 [DDD]
Mozart, W.A.:Qt 22 Strs *(rec First Congregational Church of Los Angeles, June 11–13, 1995)* Delos ▲ DE 3192 [DDD]
Mozart, W.A.:Qt 23 Strs *(rec First Congregational Church of Los Angeles, June 11–13, 1995)* Delos ▲ DE 3192 [DDD]
Mozart, W.A.:Qnt Cl, K.581, w. J. Manasse (cl) *(rec Oct. 1993)* XLNT ▲ CD 18009 [DDD]
Sierra, R.:Triptico, w. D. Tanenbaum (gtr) New Albion ▲ NA 032 [ADD]
Spohr, L.:Fant & Vars on a Theme of Danzi, w. J. Manasse (cl) *(rec Oct. 1993)* XLNT ▲ CD 18009 [DDD]
Shanghai SO
V. Bond (cnd)
Bond, V.:Thinking Like a Mountain, w. Cui Wen (nar) *(rec Shanghai Music Hall)* Protone ▲ NRPR 2205 [DDD]
Sousa, J.P.:Stars & Stripes Forever *(rec Shanghai Music Hall)* Protone ▲ NRPR 2205 [DDD]
Tchaikovsky, P.:Sym 6 *(rec Shanghai Music Hall)* Protone ▲ NRPR 2205 [DDD]
X. Chen (cnd)
Tingyu, L.:Su-San Suite *(rec Shanghai Music Hall)* Protone ▲ NRPR 2205 [DDD]
Sharon String Quartet
Mozart, W.A.:Divert Hns Strs, K.334, w. Amati Ensemble Arcobaleno ▲ AAOC 9389
Spohr, L.:Nonet Strs, Amati Ensemble Arcobaleno ▲ AAOC 9389
Dorothy Shaw Bell Choir
G. Bragg (cnd)
A Ceremony of Carols, w. Gregg Smith Singers, Fort Worth Chamber Ensemble, Texas Boys Choir Allegretto ▲ ACD 8407 [ADD]
G. Smith (cnd)
A World of Folksong, w. Gregg Smith Singers, Texas Boys' Choir, Texas Little Sym *(rec Nov. 1981)* Premier ▲ PRCD 1031 [ADD]
Robert Shaw Orch
R. Shaw (cnd)
Handel, G.F.:Messiah (choruses), w. Robert Shaw Chorale RCA Gold Seal ▲ 09026-61368-2; ■ 09026-61368-4
Roland Shaw Orch
The Opera Lover's Broadway:Great Voices Sing Broadway's Greatest Hits, w. Vienna PO [cnd:Herbert von Karajan], New Philharmonia Orch [cnd:Richard Bonynge], London SO [cnd:John Mauceri], Nelson Riddle & His Orch, London Festival Orch [cnd:Robert Sharples] London ▲ 448282-2 ■ 448282-4
Sheffield Ensemble
L. Foss (cnd)
Bach, J.S.:The Art of the Fugue [orchd Malloch] *(rec 1st Presbyterian Church, Hollywood)* Sheffield Lab ▲ 10047-2
Bach, J.S.:The Art of the Fugue (sels), w. California Boys' Choir [arr. William Malloch] Sheffield Lab ▲ SLS 502
Shelburne String Quartet
Sowash, R.:Fant on "Shenandoah", w. J. Pell (gtr) Gasparo ▲ GS 236
Shelly/Egler Duo [Frances Shelly (fl), Steven Egler (org)]
The Dove Descending Summit ▲ DCD 174 [DDD]
Shephard String Quartet
Cooper, P.:Chamber Music, w. Patterson Duo—Verses; Canons d'Amour; Qts. 5 & 6 Strings CRI ▲ CD 687 [DDD]
Shepherd String Quartet [Ronald Patterson (vn), Raphael Fliegel (va), Wayne Crouse (va), Shirley Trepel (vc)]
Cooper, P.:Qt 5 Strs, "Umbrae" *(rec Houston, TX, Mar 1974)* CRI ▲ CD 687 [DDD]
Cooper, P.:Qt 6 Strs *(rec Miami, FL, July 1978)* CRI ▲ CD 687 [DDD]
James Shepherd Versatile Brass
Live Brass, w. Massed Bands, Black Dyke Mills Band, Solna Brass, Brighouse & Rastrick Band, Don Lusher Trombone Ensemble *(rec live at the National Brass Band Festiva, Gala Concerts 1977, 1978, 1979)* Chandos ("Collect" series) ▲ CHAN 6561 [ADD]
Shostakovich String Quartet [A. Shislov (vn), S. Pishchugin (vn), A. Galkovsky (va), A. Korchagin (vc)]
Borodin, A.:Qt 1 Strs Olympia ▲ OLY 538 [AAD]
Borodin, A.:Qt 2 Strs Olympia ▲ OLY 538 [AAD]
Glazunov, A.:Qt 6 Strs Olympia ▲ OLY 526 [AAD]
Glazunov, A.:Qt 7 Strs, "Hommage au passé" Olympia ▲ OLY 526 [AAD]
Shostakovich, D.:Movts Str Qt Olympia ▲ OLY 531 [ADD]
Shostakovich, D.:Qts Strs (comp)—Nos. 6, 8 & 9 Olympia ▲ OLY 532 [ADD]
Shostakovich, D.:Qts Strs (comp)—Nos. 1, 3 & 4 Olympia ▲ OLY 531 [ADD]
Shostakovich, D.:Qt 10 Strs Olympia ▲ OLY 534 [ADD]
Shostakovich, D.:Qt 11 Strs Olympia ▲ OLY 534 [ADD]
Shostakovich, D.:Qt 12 Strs Olympia ▲ OLY 535 [ADD]
Shostakovich, D.:Qt 13 Strs Olympia ▲ OLY 535 [ADD]
Shostakovich, D.:Qt 14 Strs Olympia ▲ OLY 535 [ADD]
Shostakovich, D.:Qt 15 Strs Olympia ▲ OLY 534 [ADD]
Sibelius Academy String Quartet [Seppo Tukiainen (vn), Erkki Kantola (vn), Veikko Kosonen (va), Arto Noras (vc)]
Kokkonen, J.:Qts Strs BIS ▲ CD 458 [DDD]
Kokkonen, J.:Qnt Pno, w. T. Valsta (pno) BIS ▲ CD 458 [DDD]
Shostakovich, D.:Qt 2 Strs Finlandia ▲ FIN 98996 [DDD]
Shostakovich, D.:Qt 3 Strs Finlandia ▲ FIN 98997 [DDD]
Shostakovich, D.:Qt 4 Strs Finlandia ▲ FIN 98997 [DDD]
Shostakovich, D.:Qt 6 Strs Finlandia ▲ FIN 98996 [DDD]
Sibelius, J.:Qt in a Strs Finlandia 2-▲ 4509-95851-2 [ADD/DDD]
Sibelius, J.:Qt in E♭ Strs Finlandia 2-▲ 4509-95851-2 [ADD/DDD]

Sibelius Academy String Quartet (cont.)
Sibelius, J.:Qt in E♭ Strs *(rec Dec. 1988)* Finlandia ▲ 4509-95858-2 [DDD]
Sibelius, J.:Qt Strs, Op. 4 Finlandia 2-▲ 4509-95851-2 [ADD/DDD]
Sibelius, J.:Qt Strs, Op. 56 Finlandia 2-▲ 4509-95851-2 [ADD/DDD]
Sibelius, J.:Qnt Pno, w. E. T. Tawaststjerna (pno) *(rec Jan. 1985)* Finlandia ▲ 4509-95858-2 [DDD]
Jean Sibelius String Quartet
Sallinen, A.:Qts Strs—Nos. 1-5 Ondine ▲ ODE 831 [DDD]
Sibelius, J.:Adagio & Fugue Str Qt Ondine ▲ ODE 850 [DDD]
Jean Sibelius String Quartet members
Sibelius, J.:Trio Pno (1888) Ondine ▲ ODE 850 [DDD]
Sibelius, J.:Water Drops Ondine ▲ ODE 850 [DDD]
Sibiu PO
P. Sbârcea (cnd)
Caudella, E.:Dochia, w. F. Diaconescu (ten) *(rec 1983)* Electrecord ▲ ELCD 104 [AAD]
Sicilian CO
F. Amendola (cnd)
Donizetti, G.:Rita, or Le mari battu, w. A. Scarabelli (sop), P. Ballo (ten), A. Corbelli (bar) [I] *(rec live, Palermo 6/19-20/91)* Nuova Era ▲ 7045 [DDD]
Sicilian SO
M. de Bernart (cnd)
Rota, N.:Con-soirée, w. B. Lupo (pno) Nuova Era ▲ 7063 [DDD]
Rota, N.:Sinfonia sopra una canzone d'amore Nuova Era ▲ 7063 [DDD]
G. Ferro (cnd)
Bellini, V.:I Puritani, w. K. Ricciarelli (sop), E. Jankovic (mez), C. Merritt (ten), C. Gaifa (ten), A. Riva (bass), R. Scandiuzzi (bass), Bari Teatro Petruzzelli Chorus *(rec Apr. 10, 1986)* Cetra Classic ▲ CDC 20 [ADD]
Bellini, V.:I Puritani, w. Katia Ricciarelli (sop), Eleonora Jankovic (mez), Juan Luque Carmona (ten), Carlo Gaifa (ten), Chris Merritt (ten), Roberto Scandiuzzi (bass), Bari Teatro Petruzzelli Chorus Fonit Cetra ("Digital Operas" series) 3-▲ FCT CDC 20
J. Serebrier (cnd)
Tchaikovsky, P.:Arias, w. C. Farley (sop), Melbourne SO—15 arias from composer's 8 major operas IMP Masters ▲ IMPMCD 64 [DDD]
H. Soudant (cnd)
Petrassi, G.:Con Fl, w. Mario Ancillotti (fl) Koch Schwann ▲ SCH 315242
Sierra String Quartet
Swack, I.:Qt 4 Strs Opus One ▲ 150
Sierra Wind Quintet
Carter, E.:Etudes (8) & a Fant Cambria ▲ 1091 [DDD]
Piston, W.:Qnt Ww Cambria ▲ 1091 [DDD]
Schuller, G.:Suite Ww Qnt Cambria ▲ 1091 [DDD]
Sierra Winds [Richard Soule (fl/pic), Carol Urban-Stivers (pno), Kim DeLibero (hp), Teresa Lang (vn), Rebecca Ramsey (vn), John Peskey (va), Kelly Mikkelsen (vc), Stephen Caplan (ob), Felix Viscuglia (cl/a sax), Bernard Kolle (bn)]
Still, W.G.:Music of—Miniatures; Folk Suite Nos. 2-4; Incantation & Dance; Quit dat Fool'nish; Summerland; Romance; Vignettes; Get on Board *(rec Artemus W. Ham Concert Hall, Las Vegas, Nevada)* Cambria ▲ CMB 1083 [DDD]
Sikorsi String Quartet [Christian Sikorski (vn), Uta Terjung (vn), Sebastian Wohlfahrt (va), Arnold Ilg (vc)]
Schubert, Franz:Qt 9 Strs Ars Musici ▲ AM 1152 [DDD]
Schubert, Franz:Qt 14 Strs Ars Musici ▲ AM 1152 [DDD]
Silesian Military District Band
Marsz, Marsz Polonia, w. Krakow Garrison Military Band, Polish Air Force Band, Polish Army Band, Polish Navy Band, Pomeranian Military District Band, Warsaw Military District Band Polskie Nagrania Edition ▲ ECD 064 [DDD]
Silesian PO
R. Black (cnd)
Hoose, A.:Gestures & Intimations MMC ▲ MMC 2017 [DDD]
K. Stryja (cnd)
Schumann, R.:Sym 1 *(rec Concert Hall of the Silesian PO, Katowice, Dec. 11-16, 1988)* Lydian ▲ 18055 [DDD]
Schumann, R.:Sym 3 *(rec Concert Hall of the Silesian PO, Katowice, Dec. 11-16, 1988)* Lydian ▲ 18055 [DDD]
J. Swoboda (cnd)
Briggs, R.:Tracer, w. Jeffery Jacob (pno) MMC ▲ MMC 2028 [DDD]
Farmer, P.:On Mount Pleasant MMC ▲ MMC 2028 [DDD]
George, E.:Intro & Allegro MMC ▲ MMC 2027 [DDD]
Griebling, S.:Queensmere:December 1964 MMC ▲ MMC 2027 [DDD]
McKinley, W.T.:Con 2 Pno, w. Jeffery Jacob (pno) MMC ▲ MMC 2028 [DDD]
Rossi, M.:Negru Voda MMC ▲ MMC 2028 [DDD]
R. Tomaro (cnd)
Tomaro, R.:Celestial Navigation MMC ▲ MMC 2028 [DDD]
Silesian Philharmonic SO
K. Stryja (cnd)
Haydn, J.:Sym 73, "La Chasse" *(rec Silesian Philharmonic Concert Hall, Katowice, Mar 18-20, 1989)* Polskie Nagrania ▲ PNCD 058 [DDD]
Haydn, J.:Sym 82, "The Bear" *(rec Silesian Philharmonic Concert Hall, Katowice, Mar 18-20, 1989)* Polskie Nagrania ▲ PNCD 058 [DDD]
Haydn, J.:Sym 83, "The Hen" *(rec Silesian Philharmonic Concert Hall, Katowice, Mar 18-20, 1989)* Polskie Nagrania ▲ PNCD 058 [DDD]
Silesian String Quartet
Górecki, H.-M.:Qt 1 Strs, "Already It Is Dusk" Olympia ▲ OLY 375 [DDD]
Górecki, H.-M.:Qt 2 Strs, "Quasi una fant" Olympia ▲ OLY 375 [DDD]
Penderecki, K.:Chamber Music, w. A. Romanski (cl), W. Malicki (pno)—Qts. Nos. 1 & 2 for Strings; Trio for Strings; Der unterbrochene Gedanke; Son. for Violin & Piano; Miniature, Op. 15; 3 Miniatures for Clarinet & Piano; Cadenza for Viola; Per Slava; Capriccio for Siegfried Palm; Prelude in B♭ for solo Clarinet Wergo ▲ WER 6258-2
Stravinsky, I.:Concertino Str Qt Partridge ▲ 1138-2
Stravinsky, I.:Double Canon Partridge ▲ 1138-2
Stravinsky, I.:Pieces Str Qt Partridge ▲ 1138-2
Szymanowski, K.:Qt 1 Strs Partridge ▲ 1138-2
Szymanowski, K.:Qt 2 Strs Partridge ▲ 1138-2
Silesian String Quartet members
Górecki, H.-M.:Elementi Olympia ▲ OLY 375 [DDD]
Górecki, H.-M.:Son for 2 Vns Olympia ▲ OLY 375 [DDD]
Stachowski, M.:Madrigali dell'estate, w. Olga Szwajgier (sop) *(rec Apr. 1-6, 1987)* Polskie Nagrania ▲ PLN 076 [ADD]
Simi String Quartet
Brahms, J.:Qt 2 Strs *(rec Music Centre Tbilisi, Sept 1994)* Infinity Digital ▲ QK 69283 [DDD]
Simon String Quartet
Debussy, C.:Qt Strs Pavane ▲ ADW 7288 [DDD]
Fauré, G.:Qt Strs Pavane ▲ ADW 7288 [DDD]
Ravel, M.:Qt Strs Pavane ▲ ADW 7288 [DDD]
Simple SO
Fantasies on Operatic Themes *(rec Apr. 1991)* Pierre Verany ▲ 791111 [DDD]
Ray Sinatra Orch
R. Sinatra (cnd)
The Great Mario Lanza, w. Mario Lanza (ten) Goldies ▲ GLD 63201 [ADD]

Ray Sinatra Orch (cont.)
R. Sinatra (cnd) (cont.)
Rodgers, R.:Music of, w. B. Crosby (sgr), R. Vallee (sgr), J. Macdonald (sgr), A. Jolson (sgr), et al., Whiteman Orch, Paramount Studio Orch—On Your Toes; Jumbo; Present Arms; One Dam Thing After Another; The Boys from Syracuse; Heads Up; Lido Lady; Peggy Ann; Love Me Tonight; Higher & Higher; Spring is Here; The Girl Friend; Simple Simon; Hallelujah; I'm a Bum Pearl ("Flapper" series) ▲ PAST CD 9794 [AAD]
Sine Nomine Ensemble [Andrea Budgey (sop), Holly Cluett (sop), Jay Lambie (ten), Bryan Martin (bar), Bryan Martin (lt), Randall Rosenfeld (vielle/gittern/fl/rcr), Andrea Budgey (hp/rcr/darabukka)]
A Golden Treasury of Medieval Music *(rec Valley Recordings, Littleton-on-Severn, July 1995)* Amon-Ra ("Golden Treasury" series) ▲ CD-SAR 63
Sine Nomine String Quartet
Allesandro, R. d':Music of, w. Musiviva Trio—String Quartet No. 2, Op. 73; Trio for Piano, Violin & Cello, Op. 33; Piano Sonatas, Nos. 2 & 3 Gallo ▲ CD 621 [DDD]
Schubertiade:Rétrospective, w. Lausanne Trio, C. Homberger (ten), S. Kanoff (pno), C. Favre (pno), Choeur des XVI de Fribourg, et al. Gallo ▲ CD 631 [AAD]
Sine Nomine String Quartet [P. Genet (vn), F. Gottraux (vn), N. Pache (va), M. Jaermann (vc)]
Arriaga, J.C.:Qts (3) Strs *(rec Salle de la Fondation Tibor Varga, Sion, June 6-8, 1994)* Claves ▲ CD 9501 [DDD]
Brahms, J.:Qts Strs (comp) *(rec Jan. 14-17, 1993)* Claves 2-▲ CD 9404/05 [DDD]
Dutilleux, H.:Ainsi la nuit Erato 2-▲ 91721
Dvořák, A.:Qnt Pno, Op. 81, w. Philippe Dinkel (pno) Cascavelle ▲ CVL 1018 [DDD]
Dvořák, A.:Qnt Strs, Op. 77, w. Pawquier (db) Cascavelle ▲ CVL 1018 [DDD]
Furtwängler, W.:Qnt Pno, w. F. Kerdoncuff (pno) Timpani ▲ 1C 1018 [DDD]
Perrin, J.:Qt Strs *(rec Sept 25, 1989)* Grammont ▲ CTSP 45 [AAD]
Turina, J.:Las musas de Andalucía, w. M. Bayo (sop), R. Requeno (pno) *(rec Apr. 1992)* Claves ▲ CD 9320 [DDD]
Turina, J.:Qt Strs, w. M. Bayo (sop), R. Requeno (pno) *(rec Apr. 1992)* Claves ▲ CD 9320 [DDD]
Turina, J.:Serenata Str Qt *(rec Apr. 1992)* Claves ▲ CD 9320 [DDD]
Sine Nomine Vocal & Instrumental Group
Cavalli, P.F.:Musiche sacre concernenti messa, e salmi concertati con instromenti, imni artifone e sonate Rivoalto ▲ CRR 8905 [DDD]
Sinfóuhljómsveit Aeskunnar
P. Zukovsky (cnd)
Leifs, J.:Baldur, Söngsveitin PO CP2 Recordings 2-▲ CP2 106/7
Sinfonia da Camera
I. Hobson (cnd)
Milhaud, D.:La Création du monde Arabesque ▲ Z 6569 [DDD]
Saint-Saëns, C.:Carnival of the Animals Arabesque ▲ Z 6570
Saint-Saëns, C.:Spt Tpt, w. I. Hobson (pno) Arabesque ▲ Z 6570
Stravinsky, I.:L'Histoire du soldat (sels), w. W. Warfield (bar) [E] *(rec Feb. 1992)* Arabesque ▲ Z 6644
Walton, W.:Façade, w. W. Warfield (nar) [E] *(rec Feb. 1992)* Arabesque ▲ Z 6644
Sinfonia Lahti Chamber Ensemble
Martinů, B.:Nonet Wws & Pno *(rec Järvenpää Hall, Finland, Feb 28-Mar 4, 1994)* BIS ▲ CD 653 [DDD]
Martinů, B.:Nonet Ww, Strs & Db *(rec Järvenpää Hall, Finland, Feb 28-Mar 4, 1994)* BIS ▲ CD 653 [DDD]
Martinů, B.:La Revue de Cuisine *(rec Järvenpää Hall, Finland, Feb 28-Mar 4, 1994)* BIS ▲ CD 653 [DDD]
Sinfonia Lahti Chamber Ensemble members [Eeva Heikkilä (fl), Ilkka Pälli (vc), Ilkka Sivonen (pno)]
Martinů, B.:Trio Fl *(rec Järvenpää Hall, Finland, Feb 28-Mar 4, 1994)* BIS ▲ CD 653 [DDD]
Sinfonia Lahti Wind Quintet
Kokkonen, J.:Qnt Winds BIS ▲ CD 528 [DDD]
Sinfonia Rubinstein
L. Woodside (cnd)
Handel, G.F.:Messiah (reorchd Mozart), w. Andrew Murphy (b-bar), M. Altman (sgr), J. Davidson (sgr), Peter Elvin (sgr), P. Price (sgr), New York Oratorio Society [Sinfonia Rubinstein is made up from musicians from the Lodz Philharmonic Orchestra and the Lodz Opera of Poland] [E] Koch Schwann 2-▲ SC 100308 [DDD]
Sinfonia 21
E. Downes (cnd)
Prokofiev, S.:Eugene Onegin, w. T. West (nar), K. Fuge (sop), P. im Thurn (bar), J. Walker (bass), New Company Chandos 2-▲ CHAN 9318/19 [DDD]
R. Hickox (cnd)
Respighi, O.:Ancient Airs & Dances Chandos ▲ CHAN 9415 [DDD]
Respighi, O.:Aria Chandos ▲ CHAN 9415 [DDD]
Respighi, O.:Berceuse Chandos ▲ CHAN 9415 [DDD]
Sinfonia Varsovia
E. Krivine (cnd)
Mozart, W.A.:Sym 23 Denon ▲ CO 77884 [DDD]
Mozart, W.A.:Sym 28 Denon ▲ CO 77884 [DDD]
Mozart, W.A.:Sym 35 Denon ▲ CO 77884 [DDD]
Schoenberg, A.:Verklärte Nacht *(rec Aug. 12-17, 1990)* Denon ▲ CO 79442 [DDD]
Strauss, R.:Metamorphosen *(rec Aug. 12-17, 1990)* Denon ▲ CO 79442 [DDD]
Wagner, R.:Siegfried Idyll *(rec Aug. 12-17, 1990)* Denon ▲ CO 79442 [DDD]
Y. Menuhin (cnd)
Beethoven, L. van:Syms (comp), w. Jean Glennon (sop), Dalia Schaechter (cta), Algridas Janutas (ten), Benno Schollum (bass), Kuanas State Choir Lithuania IMP ("IMG" series) 5-▲ IMP 6800025
Mozart Sampler Virgin Classics 2-▲ CDC 59104
Mozart, W.A.:Sym 40 Virgin Classics ("Ultraviolet" series) ▲ CUV 61133
Mozart, W.A.:Sym 40 Virgin Classics ▲ 59564 [DDD]
Mozart, W.A.:Sym 41 Virgin Classics ("Ultraviolet" series) ▲ CUV 61133
Mozart, W.A.:Sym 41 Virgin Classics ▲ 59564 [DDD]
W. Michniewski (cnd)
Giuliani, M.:Con 1 Gtr, w. David Russell (gtr) Polskie Nagrania ▲ PNCD 103 [DDD]
Rodrigo, J.:Concierto de Aranjuez, w. David Russell (gtr), Lidia Zabka (hn) Polskie Nagrania ▲ PNCD 103 [DDD]
M. Nowakowski (cnd)
Handel, G.F.:Alessandro, w. L. Atkinson (trb), Watson (sop), A. Terzian (mez), B. J. Rieders (cta), T. Poole (ten), D. Price (ten), Andersson (sgr) [I] *(rec live)* Koch Schwann 3-▲ CD SC 100 303 [DDD]
K. Penderecki (cnd)
Penderecki, K.:Choral Music, w. Warsaw National Phil Chorus—Benedicamus Domino; Song of Cherubin; Lacrimosa *(rec National Philharmonic Hall, Warsaw, Poland, Nov. 23, 1993)* Sony Classical ▲ SK 66284 [DDD]
Penderecki, K.:Con Fl, w. Jean-Pierre Rampal (fl) *(rec National Philharmonic Hall, Warsaw, Poland, Nov. 23, 1993)* Sony Classical ▲ SK 66284 [DDD]
Penderecki, K.:Sinfonietta *(rec National Philharmonic Hall, Warsaw, Poland, Nov. 23, 1993)* Sony Classical ▲ SK 66284 [DDD]
J.-B. Pommier (cnd)
Mozart, W.A.:Con 21 Pno, w. Jean-Bernard Pommer (pno) Virgin Classics ("Ultraviolet" series) ▲ CUV 61123
Mozart, W.A.:Con 23 Pno, w. Jean-Bernard Pommier (pno) Virgin Classics ("Ultraviolet" series) ▲ CUV 61123
M. Tang (cnd)
Chopin, F.:Con 1 Pno, w. Fou Ts'ong (pno) Collins Quest ▲ COL 3015 [DDD]
Chopin, F.:Con 2 Pno, w. Fou Ts'ong (pno) Collins Quest ▲ COL 3015 [DDD]

ENS.

Sinfonia Varsovia (cont.)
K. Teutsch (cnd)
Mozart, W.A.:Arias, w. Artur Stefanowicz (ct)—Mitridate, Rè di Ponto, K.87; Apollo et Hyacinthus, K.38; Ascanio in Alba, K.111; Ombra Felice, K.255 *(rec Polish Radio, Warsaw, Feb 1991)* Polskie Nagrania ▲ PNCD 110 [DDD]
F. Ts'ong (cnd)
Mozart, W.A.:Con 21 Pno, w. F. Ts'ong (pno) IMP Masters ▲ IMPMCD 74 [DDD]
Mozart, W.A.:Con 27 Pno, w. F. Ts'ong (pno) IMP Masters ▲ IMPMCD 74 [DDD]
Sinfonia Varsovia String Ensemble
J. Krenz (cnd)
Krauze, Z.:Aus aller Welt stammende *(rec National Philharmonic, Warsaw, Mar. 1991)* Polskie Nagrania ▲ PLN 113 [DDD]
Krauze, Z.:Sym Parisienne *(rec National Philharmonic, Warsaw, Mar. 1991)* Polskie Nagrania ▲ PLN 113 [DDD]
Krauze, Z.:Tableau Vivant *(rec National Philharmonic, Warsaw, Mar. 1991)* Polskie Nagrania ▲ PLN 113 [DDD]
Sinfonye
Codax, M.:Music of Hyperion ▲ CDA 66283 [DDD]
S. Wishart (cnd)
Bella Domna Hyperion ▲ CDA 66283 [DDD]
Gabriel's Greeting Hyperion ▲ CDA 66685
Poder á Santa Maria, w. Equidad Barés (sgr), Vivien Ellis (sgr), Paula Chateauneuf (sgr), Jim Denley (sgr) *(rec Cartuja de Santa María de Cazalla de la Sierra, Seville, Oct. 1993)* Almaviva ▲ 0105 [DDD]
The Sweet Look & the Loving Manner Hyperion ▲ CDA 66625
Singapore SO
C. Hoey (cnd)
A, K.J.:Con Vn, "Hung Hu", w. Takako Nishizaki (vn) *(rec Victoria Memorial Hall, Singapore, Jan 1981)* Marco Polo ("Chinese Music" series) ▲ 8.223902 [ADD]
Balakirev, M.:King Lear (ov) Marco Polo ▲ 8.220324
Balakirev, M.:Ov on Czech Themes Marco Polo ▲ 8.220324
Balakirev, M.:Ov on a Spanish March Theme Marco Polo ▲ 8.220324
Balakirev, M.:Suite on 4 Pieces Marco Polo ▲ 8.220324
Beethoven, L. van:Con 4 Pno, w. J. Bingham (pno) Meridian ▲ CDE 84172
Beethoven, L. van:Con 5 Pno, "Emperor", w. J. Bingham (pno) Meridian ▲ CDE 84172
Chen, G.:Fant on a Xinjiang Folk Song [orchd. Manabu Kawai] *(rec Victoria Memorial Hall, Singapore, Jan 1981)* Marco Polo ("Chinese Music" series) ▲ 8.223902 [ADD]
Du, M.:Xinjiang Dances (10), w. Takako Nishizaki (vn) *(rec Victoria Memorial Hall, Singapore, June 3–7, 1985)* Marco Polo ("Chinese Composers" series) ▲ 8.223903 [DDD]
Fu, G.C.:Celebration Dance *(rec Victoria Memorial Hall, Singapore, Jan 1981)* Marco Polo ("Chinese Music" series) ▲ 8.223902 [ADD]
Ge, Y.:The Horse Cart *(rec Victoria Memorial Hall, Singapore, Jan 1981)* Marco Polo ("Chinese Music" series) ▲ 8.223902 [ADD]
Ippolitov-Ivanov, M.:Sym 1 Marco Polo ▲ 8.220217 [DDD]
Ippolitov-Ivanov, M.:Turkish Fragments Marco Polo ▲ 8.220217 [DDD]
Ippolitov-Ivanov, M.:Turkish March Marco Polo ▲ 8.220217 [DDD]
Lachner, F.P.:Sym 1 Marco Polo ▲ 8.220360 [DDD]
Ma, K.:Shanbei Suite *(rec Victoria Memorial Hall, Singapore, Jan 1981)* Marco Polo ("Chinese Music" series) ▲ 8.223902 [ADD]
Qin, Y.C.:Happy Grassland *(rec Victoria Memorial Hall, Singapore, Jan 1981)* Marco Polo ("Chinese Music" series) ▲ 8.223902 [ADD]
Respighi, O.:Poema autunnale, w. T. Nishizaki (vn) Marco Polo ▲ 8.220152 [DDD]
Spohr, L.:Sym 2 Marco Polo ▲ 8.220360 [DDD]
Sinnhoffer String Quartet
Luening, O.:Qt 2 Strs CRI ("American Masters" series) ▲ CD 716 [ADD]
Luening, O.:Qt 3 Strs CRI ("American Masters" series) ▲ CD 716 [ADD]
Sinnhoffer String Quartet members [Ingo Sinnhoffer (vn), Roland Metzger (va), Peter Wöpke (vc)]
Strauss, R.:Music of, w. Wolfgang Sawallisch (pno)—4 Stücke *(rec Kleiner Konzertsaal, Gasteig, Munich, Oct 17, 1985)* Arts Music ▲ 447259-2 [DDD]
Strauss, R.:Qt Pno, w. Wolfgang Sawallisch (pno) *(rec Kleiner Konzertsaal, Gasteig, Munich, Oct 17, 1985)* Arts Music ▲ 447259-2 [DDD]
Sirinu [Sara Stowe (sop/org/perc), Matthew Spring (lt/h-g/lira da braccio/vl/gittern), Jon Banks (hp/sackbut/org/vl/perc), Henry Stobart (rcr/bgp/vl/shawm/pipe/tabor)]
The Cradle of the Renaissance Hyperion ▲ CDA 66814
Sirius String Quartet
Rautavaara, E.:Qt 4 Strs Catalyst ▲ 09026-62671-2
Sirius String Quartet [Mary Rowell (vn), Laura Seaton (vn), Ron Lawrence (va), Mary Wooten (vc)]
Kim, J.H.:Nong Rock, w. Jin Hi Kim (komungo) O. O. Discs ▲ 0024
The Sixteen Orch
H. Christophers (cnd)
Bach, J.S.:St. John Passion, w. P. Kwella (sop), D. James (ct), W. Kendall (ten), I. Partridge (ten), M. George (bar), D. Wilson-Johnson (b-bar), The Sixteen [G] Chandos ("Chaconne" series) 2-▲ CHAN 0507/08 [DDD]
Caldara, A.:Stabat Mater, w. The Sixteen Chorus [L] *(rec 10/91)* Collins Classics ▲ 13202 [DDD]
Cardoso, M.:Missa Regina caeli, w. The Sixteen Chorus Collins Classics ▲ COL 1407 [DDD]
Cardoso, M.:Motets, w. The Sixteen Chorus—Sitivit anima mea; Tulerunt lapides ut iacerent in eum; Non mortui qui sunt in inferno Collins Classics ▲ COL 1407 [DDD]
Handel, G.F.:Alexander's Feast (ode), w. N. Argenta (sop), I. Partridge (ten), M. George (bass), The Sixteen Chorus Collins Classics 2-▲ COL 7016 [DDD]
Handel, G.F.:Chandos Anthems (11), w. L. Dawson (sop), P. Kwella (sop), J. Bowman (alt), I. Partridge (ten), M. George (bass), The Sixteen Chandos ("Chaconne" series) 4-▲ CHAN 0554 [DDD]
Handel, G.F.:Chandos Anthems (11), w. L. Dawson (sop), I. Partridge (ten), M. George (bass), The Sixteen—Nos. 1, 2 & 3 Chandos ("Chaconne" series) ▲ CHAN 0503 [DDD]
Handel, G.F.:Chandos Anthems (11), w. L. Dawson (sop), I. Partridge (ten), The Sixteen—Anthem Nos. 4–6 [E] Chandos ("Chaconne" series) ▲ CHAN 0504 [DDD]
Handel, G.F.:Chandos Anthems (11), w. P. Kwella (sop), J. Bowman (ct), I. Partridge (ten), M. George (bass), The Sixteen—Anthem Nos. 7–9 [E] Chandos ("Chaconne" series) ▲ CHAN 0505 [DDD]
Handel, G.F.:Chandos Anthems (11), w. L. Dawson (sop), I. Partridge (ten), The Sixteen—Anthem Nos. 10 & 11 [E] Chandos ("Chaconne" series) ▲ CHAN 0509 [DDD]
Handel, G.F.:Dixit Dominus, w. Lynn Dawson (sop), Linda Russell (alt), Charles Brett (ct), Ian Partridge (ten), Michael George (bass), The Sixteen [L] Chandos ("Chaconne" series) ▲ CHAN 0517 [DDD]
Handel, G.F.:Israel in Egypt, w. The Sixteen *(rec 1990)* Collins Classics ▲ COL 7035 [DDD]
Handel, G.F.:Messiah, w. Lynn Dawson (sop), Catherine Denley (mez), David James (alt), Arthur Davies (ten), Michael George (bass), The Sixteen [20-member orchestra, 19-member chorus] [E] *(rec 1986)* Hyperion 2-▲ CDA 66251/52 [DDD]
Handel, G.F.:Nisi Dominus, w. Charles Brett (ct), Ian Partridge (ten), Michael George (bass), The Sixteen [L] Chandos ("Chaconne" series) ▲ CHAN 0517 [DDD]
Handel, G.F.:Silete Venti, w. Lynne Dawson (sop), The Sixteen [L] Chandos ("Chaconne" series) ▲ CHAN 0517 [DDD]
Lôbo, D.:Sacred Music, w. The Sixteen Collins Classics ▲ COL 1407 [DDD]
Lotti, A.:Crucifixus, w. The Sixteen Chorus [L] Collins Classics ▲ 50092 [DDD]
Purcell, H.:The Fairy Queen, w. The Sixteen Collins Classics 2-▲ 7013
Purcell, H.:Music for the Funeral of Queen Mary, w. The Sixteen Collins Classics ▲ COL 1425 [DDD]
Purcell, H.:Music of, w. The Sixteen—Funeral Sentences; 2 Elegies on the Death of Queen Mary; 2 Latin Motets Collins Classics ▲ COL 1425 [DDD]
Reich, S.:Clapping Music Collins Classics ▲ 12872 [DDD]
Tavener, J.:Music of, w. Duke String Quartet—2 Hymns to the Mother of God; The Lamb; The Tiger; Ikon of Light; Today the Virgin; Eonia Collins Classics ▲ COL 1405 [DDD]

The Sixteen Orch (cont.)
H. Christophers (cnd) (cont.)
Vivaldi, A.:Gloria, RV.589, w. The Sixteen [L] Collins Classics ▲ 13202 [DDD]
H. Stephens (cnd)
Bach, J.S.:Christmas Oratorio, w. The Sixteen Collins Classics 2-▲ COL 7028 [DDD]
Sjaellends SO
J. Frandsen (cnd)
Nielsen, C.:Con Fl, w. J.-P. Rampal (fl) CBS ▲ MK 44665 [ADD]
Skampa String Quartet
Dvořák, A.:Waltzes Pno, Op. 54—2 sels [arr. unknown] Supraphon ▲ SUP 0162 [DDD]
Haydn, J.:Qts Strs, Op. 76, "Erdődy Qts"—No. 2 Supraphon ▲ SUP CD 3156
Ravel, M.:Qt Strs Supraphon ▲ SUP CD 3156
Schubert, Franz:Qt 12 Strs Supraphon ▲ SUP CD 3156
Smetana, B.:Qt 2 Strs Supraphon ▲ SUP 0162 [DDD]
Skåne String Quartet
The String Quartet in Sweden:A Cavalcade of Its History, w. Barkel String Quartet, Stockholm String Quartet, Garaguly String Quartet, Kyndel String Quartet, Ivan Ericson String Quartet, Grünfarb String Quartet, Hälsingborg String Quartet, Göteborg String Quartet, et al. *(rec before 1951)* Caprice 5-▲ CAP 21506 [AAD/ADD]
Slaska PO
K. Stryja (cnd)
Kopelent, M.:Legend, w. Slaska-Katowice Phil Choir Praga ▲ PR 255003
Kopelent, M.:Still Life Praga ▲ PR 255003
Slokar Trombone Ensemble
Baroque Music for Trombones Claves ▲ CD 8402 [DDD]
Slovak CO
B. Warchal (cnd)
Caldara, A.:Sinfonie a 4 (12) CPO ▲ CPO 999137-2 [DDD]
Devienne, F.:Cons (4) Bn, w. E. Hübner (bn) CPO ▲ CPO 999120 [DDD]
Haydn, J.:Cons for 2 Lire organizzata, w. Lajos Lencsés (ob), Robert Dohn (fl) CPO ▲ CPO 999182 [DDD]
Haydn, J.:Notturni (8), w. Robert Dohn (fl), Lajos Lencsés (ob) CPO 2-▲ CPO 999121-2 [DDD]
Haydn, M.:Syms—in C, P.35; in C, P.2 *(rec 1991)* CPO ▲ CPO 999101-2 [DDD]
Haydn, M.:Syms—in B♭, P.51; in A, P.3; in C, P.6 *(rec 1991)* CPO ▲ CPO 999152-2 [DDD]
Haydn, M.:Syms—in B♭, P.9; in G, P.7; in D, P.41; in A, P.6 *(rec 1992)* CPO ▲ CPO 999154-2 [DDD]
Haydn, M.:Syms—in C, P.10; in G, P.16; in G, P.8 *(rec 1992)* CPO ▲ CPO 999155-2 [DDD]
Haydn, M.:Syms—in E♭, P.17; in B♭, P.18; in C, P.19 *(rec 1992)* CPO ▲ CPO 999156-2 [DDD]
Haydn, M.:Syms—in E, P.5; in D, P.38; in D, P.36; in F, P.45 *(rec 1992)* CPO ▲ CPO 999153-2 [DDD]
Haydn, M.:Sym in G *(rec 1991)* CPO ▲ CPO 999101-2 [DDD]
Kalabis, V.:Tristium *(rec 1986)* Praga ▲ PR 255002
Kohaut, K.:Sym in f Orfeo ▲ 165881 [DDD]
Mozart, L.:Syms—in A [Eisen A 1]; in D [Eisen D 18]; in D [Eisen D 26]; in F [Eisen F 2]; in F [Eisen F 6]; in G [Eisen G 5]; in G [Eisen G 7] CPO 2-▲ CPO 999144-2 [DDD]
Richter, F.X.:Cons Fl, w. R. Dohn (fl)—in D & e CPO ▲ CPO 999117 [DDD]
Richter, F.X.:Con Ob, w. R. Dohn (ob) CPO ▲ CPO 999117 [DDD]
Richter, F.X.:Syms Orfeo ▲ 165881 [DDD]
Rosetti, F.A.:Cons Ob, w. L. Lencsés (ob)—Cons. in C, D & F CPO ▲ CPO 999062-2 [DDD]
Vivaldi, A.:Cons Bn, w. F. Herman (bn)—5 concerti—RV.472, 481, 484, 497, 501 Supraphon ▲ 110109-2 [DDD]
Slovak National Orch
P. Freeman (cnd)
Dvořák, A.:Con Vn, w. Pablo Diemecke (vn) *(rec Concert Hall of Radio Bratislava, Slovakia, Dec 1994)* Intersound ▲ 3538
Slovak PO
Bartók, B.:Con Orch Quintessence ▲ CDQ 2099 [DDD]
Beethoven, L. van:Music of, w. J. Jandó (pno), et al., CSR SO Bratislava, Capella Istropolitana—Egmont & Fidelio Ovs.; Für Elise; sels. from Pno Son. 8 & 14; Sym. 3, 5 & 6; Pno Con. 4 & 5; Vn Con. Naxos ▲ 8.551101 [DDD] Δ 7.551101 [DDD]
The Dance Collection, w. Ondrej Lenard (cnd), Keith Clark (cnd), Stephen Gunzenhauser (cnd), Kenneth Jean (cnd), Barry Wordsworth (cnd), Adrian Leaper (cnd), Johannes Wildner (cnd), Czech RSO, Slovak RSO, Slovak PO, Royal PO, Slovak State PO, CRS SO, Thalia-Schrammeln Quartet *(rec Czechoslovak Radio Concert Hall, Bratislava, Feb 1–4, 1988)* Naxos 4-▲ 8.504015 [DDD]
Haydn, J.:Sym 53, "L'Impériale" Quintessence ▲ CDQ 2102 [DDD]
Liszt, F.:Cons Pno, w. S. Capova (pno) Critics Choice 2-▲ CCD 943 [DDD]
Prokofiev, S.:Con 2 Vn, w. *(vn & cnd unknown)* Pro Arte ("Maxiplay" series) ▲ CDM 882 [DDD]
Prokofiev, S.:The Love for 3 Oranges (suite) Pro Arte ("Maxiplay" series) ▲ CDM 882 [DDD]
Prokofiev, S.:Romeo & Juliet (suites) Pro Arte ("Maxiplay" series) ▲ CDM 882 [DDD]
Ravel, M.:Daphnis et Chloé Pro Arte ("Maxiplay" series) ▲ CDM 881 [DDD]
Ravel, M.:Daphnis et Chloé Pro Arte ("Maxiplay" series) ▲ CDM 879 [DDD]
Ravel, M.:La Valse Pro Arte ("Maxiplay" series) ▲ CDM 881 [DDD]
Tchaikovsky, P.:Sym 2 Critics Choice 2-▲ CCD 945 [DDD]
H. Adolph (cnd)
Rossini, G.:La gazza ladra (ov) Intersound ▲ CDS 3674
A. Bramall (cnd)
Bizet, G.:L'Arlésienne (suites) Naxos ▲ 8.550061 [DDD] Δ 7.550061 [DDD]
Bizet, G.:Carmen (suites) Naxos ▲ 8.550061 [DDD] Δ 7.550061 [DDD]
Mendelssohn, F.:A Midsummer Night's Dream (sels)—Overture, Op. 21; Scherzo & Intermezzo (from Op. 61) Naxos ▲ 8.550055 [DDD]
Mendelssohn, F.:Sym 4 Naxos ▲ 8.550055 [DDD]
Z. Bílek (cnd)
Novák, V.:Pan [arr orch] Marco Polo ▲ 8.223325 [DDD]
K. Clark (cnd)
Bruch, M.:Con 1 Vn, w. Mariko Honda (vn) *(rec Concert Hall of Slovak PO, Bratislava, May 11–16, 1988)* Lydian ▲ 18026 [DDD]
Dvořák, A.:Con Vn, w. Mariko Honda (vn) *(rec Moyzes Hall of the Slovak PO, Bratislava, Mar. 1988)* Lydian ▲ 18084 [DDD]
Mendelssohn, F.:Con in e Vn & Orch, Op. 64, w. Mariko Honda (vn) *(rec Concert Hall of Slovak PO, Bratislava, May 11–16, 1988)* Lydian ▲ 18026 [DDD]
O. Dohnányi (cnd)
Mendelssohn, F.:Die Hebriden *(rec 11/88)* Naxos ▲ 8.550222 [DDD]
Mendelssohn, F.:Meeresstille *(rec 11/88)* Naxos ▲ 8.550222 [DDD]
Mendelssohn, F.:Ruy Blas (ov) *(rec 11/88)* Naxos ▲ 8.550222 [DDD]
Mendelssohn, F.:Sym 3 *(rec 11/88)* Naxos ▲ 8.550222 [DDD]
P. Freeman (cnd)
Brahms, J.:Con 1 Pno, w. Joshua Pierce (pno) *(rec Philharmonic Hall, Bratislava, Slovakia, June 24, 1993)* Pro Arte ▲ CDS 3488 [DDD]
Liszt, F.:Con 1 Pno, w. Joshua Pierce (pno) *(rec Great Hall of the Moscow Radio Union, Sept. 17, 1993)* Pro Arte ▲ CDS 3488 [DDD]
S. Gunzenhauser (cnd)
Beethoven, L. van:Ovs—Die Weihe des Hauses, Coriolan, Die Geschöpfe des Prometheus, Egmont, Fidelio, Leonore 3, Die Ruinen von Athen Naxos ▲ 8.550072 [DDD]
Bloch, E.:Sym in c# Marco Polo ▲ 8.223103 [DDD]
Brahms, J.:Con Vn, w. T. Nishizaki (vn) *(rec 5/89)* Naxos ▲ 8.550195 [DDD]
Bruch, M.:Con 1 Vn, w. T. Nishizaki (vn) *(rec 5/89)* Naxos ▲ 8.550195 [DDD]
Dvořák, A.:The Cunning Peasant (ov) *(rec July 12–22, 1987)* Marco Polo ▲ 8.220420 [DDD]
Dvořák, A.:Legends, Op. 59—Nos. 6–10 *(rec 5/91)* Naxos ▲ 8.550267 [DDD]
Dvořák, A.:Legends, Op. 59—Nos. 1–5 *(rec 5/91)* Naxos ▲ 8.550266 [DDD]
Dvořák, A.:Symphonic Vars *(rec Mar 89)* Naxos ▲ 8.550271 [DDD] Δ 7.550271 [DD

Slovak PO (cont.)
S. Gunzenhauser (cnd) (cont.)
Dvořák, A.:Sym 3 *(rec 5/90)* Naxos ▲ 8.550268 [DDD]
Dvořák, A.:Sym 4 *(rec 2/89)* Naxos ▲ 8.550269 [DDD]
Dvořák, A.:Sym 5 *(rec 2/89)* Naxos ▲ 8.550270 [DDD]
Dvořák, A.:Sym 6 *(rec 5/90)* Naxos ▲ 8.550268 [DDD]
Dvořák, A.:Sym 7 *(rec 2/89)* Naxos ▲ 8.550270 [DDD]
Dvořák, A.:Sym 8 *(rec 2/89)* Naxos ▲ 8.550269 [DDD]
Dvořák, A.:Sym 9, "From the New World" Naxos ▲ 8.550271 [DDD] Δ 7.550271 [DD
Liadov, A.:From the Apocalypse Marco Polo ▲ 8.220348 [DDD]
Liadov, A.:Orchestral Music—Baba Yaga, Op. 56 (1905); Intermezzo No. 1 for Piano, Op. 8 (arr. Orch.) (1902); Ballade, Op. 21b (1906); Mazurka, Op. 19 (1887); Kikimora, Op. 63 (1909); Enchanted Lake, Op. 62 (1909); Nénie, Op. 67 (1914) Marco Polo ▲ 8.220348 [DDD]
Liadov, A.:Polonaise, Op. 49 Marco Polo ▲ 8.220348 [DDD]
Liadov, A.:Polonaise, Op. 55 Marco Polo ▲ 8.220348 [DDD]
Prokofiev, S.:Sym 1 Naxos ▲ 8.550237 [DDD]
Prokofiev, S.:Sym 5 Naxos ▲ 8.550237 [DDD]
Rubinstein, A.:Sym 2 Marco Polo ▲ 8.220449 [DDD]
M. Halász (cnd)
Miaskovsky, N.:Sym 7 Marco Polo ▲ 8.223113 [DDD]
Miaskovsky, N.:Sym 10 Marco Polo ▲ 8.223113 [DDD]
Rubinstein, A.:Con Vn, w. T. Nishizaki (vn) Marco Polo ▲ 8.220359 [DDD]
Rubinstein, A.:The Demon (orch sels)—ballet music & Caucasian dance Marco Polo ▲ 8.220451 [DDD]
Rubinstein, A.:Don Quixote Marco Polo ▲ 8.220359 [DDD]
Rubinstein, A.:Feramors (orchestral sels)—3 dances & bridal procession Marco Polo ▲ 8.220451 [DDD]
Rubinstein, A.:Nero (orchestral sels)—ballet music & 2 marches Marco Polo ▲ 8.220451 [DDD]
Russian Fireworks Naxos ▲ 8.550328 [DDD] Δ 7.550328 [DDD]
Schubert, Franz:Rosamunde (sels)—Ballet Music, No. 2 *(rec 6/88)* Naxos ▲ 8.550145 [DDD]
Schubert, Franz:Sym 8 Naxos ▲ 8.550145 [DDD]
Schubert, Franz:Sym 8 Naxos ▲ 8.550289 [DDD]
Tchaikovsky, P.:Swan Lake (sels) Naxos ▲ 8.550050 [DDD]
Wagner, R.:Der fliegende Holländer (sels)—Overture Naxos ▲ 8.550136 [DDD]
Wagner, R.:Lohengrin (preludes)—Prelude; Intro. to Act 3 Naxos ▲ 8.550136 [DDD]
Wagner, R.:Tannhäuser (orch sels) Naxos ▲ 8.550136 [DDD]
R. Hayman (cnd)
Gershwin, G.:An American in Paris *(rec 6/89)* Naxos ▲ 8.550295 [DDD]
Majestic Marches *(rec 4–6/89)* Naxos ▲ 8.550370 [DDD]
New Composer Series Master Musicians Collective ▲ MMC 2001
Slovak PO
J. Hopkins (cnd)
Delius, F.:Appalachia—orchestral version *(rec Dec. 7–12, 1986)* Marco Polo ▲ 8.220452 [DDD]
Delius, F.:Folkeraadet *(rec Dec. 7–12, 1986)* Marco Polo ▲ 8.220452 [DDD]
Delius, F.:On the Heights *(rec Dec. 7–12, 1986)* Marco Polo ▲ 8.220452 [DDD]
Delius, F.:Spring Morning *(rec Dec. 7–12, 1986)* Marco Polo ▲ 8.220452 [DDD]
K. Jean (cnd)
Beethoven, L. van:Con Vn, Op. 61, w. T. Nishizaki (vn) Naxos ▲ 8.550149 [DDD]
Beethoven, L. van:Romances Vn, w. T. Nishizaki (vn) Naxos ▲ 8.550149 [DDD]
Enescu, G.:Romanian Rhap 1 Naxos ▲ 8.550327 [DDD]
Enescu, G.:Romanian Rhap 2 Naxos ▲ 8.550327 [DDD]
E. Körner (cnd)
Marschner, H.A.:Hans Heiling, w. M. Hajóssyová (sop), E. Seniglova (sop), M. Eklöf (mez), K. Markus (ten), T. Mohr (bar), L. Neshyba (bass), Slovak Phil Chorus [G] Marco Polo ("Opera Rara" series) 2-▲ 8.223306/07 [DDD]
Z. Košler (cnd)
Dvořák, A.:Scherzo Capriccioso Naxos ▲ 8.550376 [DDD]
Dvořák, A.:Slavonic Dances (comp) Naxos ▲ 8.550143 [DDD]
Dvořák, A.:Slavonic Rhaps, Op. 45—No. 3 *(rec 1987)* Naxos ▲ 8.550327 [DDD]
Dvořák, A.:Slavonic Rhaps, Op. 45—No. 2 Naxos ▲ 8.550376 [DDD]
Dvořák, A.:Slavonic Rhaps, Op. 45 *(rec Sept. 1987 & March 1988)* Naxos ▲ 8.550610 [DDD]
Martinů, B.:The Epic of Gilgamesh, w. *(soloists unknown)*, Slovak Phil Chorus Marco Polo ▲ 8.223316
Mozart, W.A.:Requiem, w. M. Hajóssyová (sop), J. Horská (cta), J. Kundlák (ten), P. Mikuláš (bass), Slovak Phil Chorus Naxos ▲ 8.550235 [DDD] Δ 7.550235 [DDD]
Strauss, R.:Also sprach Zarathustra *(rec 1988–89)* Naxos ▲ 8.550182 [DDD]
Strauss, R.:Aus italien Naxos ▲ 8.550342 [DDD]
Strauss, R.:Don Juan *(rec 9/89)* Naxos ▲ 8.550250 [DDD]
Strauss, R.:Die Liebe der Danae (sym fragment) Naxos ▲ 8.550342 [DDD]
Strauss, R.:Der Rosenkavalier (waltzes)—Waltz Sequence I Naxos ▲ 8.550182 [DDD]
Strauss, R.:Der Rosenkavalier (waltzes)—Waltz Sequence 2 Naxos ▲ 8.550342 [DDD]
Strauss, R.:Salome (dance) *(rec 1988–89)* Naxos ▲ 8.550182 [DDD]
Strauss, R.:Till Eulenspiegels lustige Streiche *(rec 9/89)* Naxos ▲ 8.550250 [DDD]
Strauss, R.:Tod und Verklärung *(rec 9/89)* Naxos ▲ 8.550250 [DDD]
A. Leaper (cnd)
Sibelius, J.:En Saga *(rec 10/89)* Naxos ▲ 8.550200 [DDD]
Sibelius, J.:Sym 1 Naxos ▲ 8.550197 [DDD]
Sibelius, J.:Sym 2 Naxos ▲ 8.550198 [DDD]
Sibelius, J.:Sym 3 Naxos ▲ 8.550199 [DDD]
Sibelius, J.:Sym 4 Naxos ▲ 8.550199 [DDD]
Sibelius, J.:Sym 5 *(rec 9/90)* Naxos ▲ 8.550200 [DDD]
Sibelius, J.:Sym 6 Naxos ▲ 8.550197 [DDD]
Sibelius, J.:Sym 7 Naxos ▲ 8.550198 [DDD]
O. Lenárd (cnd)
Brian, H.:Sym 1, "Gothic", w. et al. Marco Polo 2-▲ 8.223280/281
Liszt, F.:Hungarian Rhaps—Nos 2 & 6 *(rec Concert Hall, Bratislava, Slovak Republic, June 13–16, 1995)* Sony Classical ▲ SK 62012 [DDD]
Liszt, F.:Liebesträume *(rec Concert Hall, Bratislava, Slovak Republic, June 13–16, 1995)* Sony Classical ▲ SK 62012 [DDD]
Liszt, F.:Mephisto Waltz *(rec Concert Hall, Bratislava, Slovak Republic, June 13–16, 1995)* Sony Classical ▲ SK 62012 [DDD]
Liszt, F.:Orpheus *(rec Concert Hall, Bratislava, Slovak Republic, June 13–16, 1995)* Sony Classical ▲ SK 62012 [DDD]
Liszt, F.:Les Préludes *(rec Concert Hall, Bratislava, Slovak Republic, June 13–16, 1995)* Sony Classical ▲ SK 62012 [DDD]
Strauss (II), Joh.:Music of—New Pizzicato-Polka, Op. 449; Perpetual Motion:Musical Scherzo, Op. 257 *(rec Bratislava, Slovak Republic, Feb 27–Mar 1, 1995)* Sony Classical ▲ SK 62014 [DDD]
Strauss (II), Joh.:Waltzes—Emperor Waltz, Op. 437; Roses from the South, Op. 388; Vienna Blood, Op. 354; On the Beautiful Blue Danube, Op. 314; Artist's Life, Op. 316; Tales from the Vienna Woods, Op. 325 *(rec Bratislava, Slovak Republic, Feb 27–Mar 1, 1995)* Sony Classical ▲ SK 62014 [DDD]
D. Nazareth (cnd)
Borodin, A.:In the Steppes of Central Asia Naxos ▲ 8.550051 [DDD] Δ 7.550051 [DDD]
Borodin, A.:Prince Igor (Polovtsian dances) Naxos ▲ 8.550051 [DDD] Δ 7.550051 [DDD]
Mussorgsky, M.:Night Naxos ▲ 8.550051 [DDD] Δ 7.550051 [DDD]
Mussorgsky, M.:Pictures at an Exhibition Naxos ▲ 8.550051 [DDD] 7.550051 Δ 7.550051 [DDD]
J.-P. Pepin (cnd)
Chabrier, E.:Gwendoline, w. Adriana Kohútková (sop—Gwendoline), Gérard Garino (ten—Armel), Didier Henry (bar—Harald), Czech Phil Chorus, Slovak Phil Chorus L'Empreinte Digitale 2-▲ ED 13059
W. Perry (cnd)
Böhme, O.:Con Tpt, w. A. Ghitalla (tpt) Premier ▲ PRCD 1027 [DDD]
Perry, W.:Con Tpt, w. A. Ghitalla (tpt) Premier ▲ PRCD 1027 [DDD]

Slovak PO (cont.)
W. Perry (cnd) (cont.)
Perry, W.:Film Music, w. Richard Hayman (hmc), Rome PO, Vienna SO, Slovak Phil Chorus, Vienna Boys' Choir [scores for 6 Mark Twain films originally produced for PBS in the 1980s]—Adventures of Huckleberry Finn; The Innocents Abroad; Life on the Mississippi; The Mysterious Stranger; The Private History of a Campaign That Failed; Pudd'head Wilson Premier ▲ PRCD 1015 [DDD]
Ponchielli, A.:Con Tpt, w. A. Ghitalla (tpt) Premier ▲ PRCD 1027 [DDD]
L. Pešek (cnd)
Beethoven, L. van:Sym 7 Stradivari Classics ▲ SCD 6018 [DDD] ■ SMC 6018 (D)
Dvořák, A.:Symphonic Poem *(rec March, 1986)* Marco Polo ▲ 8.220420 [DDD]
Dvořák, A.:Symphonic Poem *(rec March 1986)* Naxos ▲ 8.550610 [DDD]
Dvořák, A.:Tragic Ov *(rec March, 1986)* Marco Polo ▲ 8.220420 [DDD]
Dvořák, A.:Vanda (ov) *(rec March, 1986)* Marco Polo ▲ 8.220420 [DDD]
The Great Symphonies, w. Slovenian PO [cnd:Milan Horvat], Ljubljana SO [cnd:Anton Nanut], Royal PO [cnd:Kurt Redel] Stradivari Classics ("Treasury of Great Classics" series) 5-▲ S5D 6082 [DDD] 5-■ S5C 6082 (D)
Janácek, L.:The Danube Orch Marco Polo ▲ 8.220362 [DDD]
Janácek, L.:Moravian Dances Orch—Kozich; Kalamajka; Trojky; Silnice; Rozek Marco Polo ▲ 8.220362 [DDD]
Janácek, L.:Moravian Dances Orch Naxos ▲ 8.550376 [DDD]
Janácek, L.:Schluck und Jau Marco Polo ▲ 8.220362 [DDD]
Janácek, L.:Suite Orch, Op. 3 Marco Polo ▲ 8.220362 [DDD]
Mozart, W.A.:Kleine Nachtmusik Stradivari Classics ▲ SCD 6014 [DDD] ■ SMC 6014 (D)
Mozart, W.A.:Sym 38 Stradivari Classics ▲ SCD 6015 [DDD] ■ SMC 6015 (D)
Mozart, W.A.:Sym 40 Stradivari Classics ▲ SCD 6015 [DDD] ■ SMC 6015 (D)
Mozart, W.A.:Sym 41 Stradivari Classics ▲ SCD 6014 [DDD] ■ SMC 6014 (D)
K. Redel (cnd)
Dvořák, A.:Sym 9, "From the New World" Pierre Verany ("Favourites" series) ▲ PVY 730007 [DDD]
Dvořák, A.:Sym 9, "From the New World" Pierre Verany ▲ PV.789055 [DDD]
Smetana, B.:The Moldau *(rec 4/87)* Pierre Verany ▲ PV.789055 [DDD]
Smetana, B.:The Moldau Pierre Verany ("Favourites" series) ▲ PVY 730007 [DDD]
Waldteufel, E.:Waltzes, Polkas & Galops *(rec 5/87)* Pierre Verany ▲ PV 787101 [DDD]
B. Rezucha (cnd)
Rimsky-Korsakov, N.:Night on Mount Triglov Marco Polo ▲ 8.220438 [DDD]
Rimsky-Korsakov, N.:Pan Voyevoda Marco Polo ▲ 8.220438 [DDD]
Saint-Saëns, C.:Sym 3, w. I. Sokol (org) Vivace 3-▲ E 321 [DDD]
Tchaikovsky, P.:Capriccio italien Stradivari Classics ▲ SCD 6016 [DDD] ■ SMC 6016 (D)
Tchaikovsky, P.:Con 1 Pno, w. P. Troperczer (pno) Stradivari Classics ▲ SCD 6017 [DDD] ■ SMC 6017 (D)
Tchaikovsky, P.:Ov 1812 Stradivari Classics ▲ SCD 6016 [DDD] ■ SMC 6016 (D)
U. Schneider (cnd)
Daetwyler, J.:Con Alphn, w. J. Molnár (alphn) Marco Polo ▲ 8.223101 [DDD]
E. Seipenbusch (cnd)
Schreker, F.:Ekkehard Marco Polo ▲ 8.220392 [DDD]
Schreker, F.:Fantastic Ov Marco Polo ▲ 8.220392 [DDD]
Schreker, F.:Opera Preludes & Interludes—Preludes to Die Gezeichneten (1918) & Der Schatzgräber (1920); Interlude from Act 3 of Das Spielwerk und die Prinzessin (1912) Marco Polo ▲ 8.220392 [DDD]
Zemlinsky, A. von:Sym 2 *(rec Nov. 1985)* Marco Polo ▲ 8.220391 [DDD]
L. Slovák (cnd)
Hummel, J.N.:Con Pno, Op. 85, w. I. Palovič (pno) Koch Schwann ▲ CD 311120
B. Wordsworth (cnd)
Bax, A.:Ov, Elegy & Rondo Marco Polo ▲ 8.223102 [DDD]
Bax, A.:Sinfonietta Marco Polo ▲ 8.223102 [DDD]
Smetana, B.:The Bartered Bride (orch sels)—Overture, Polka, Furiant, Dance of the Comedians Naxos ▲ 8.550376 [DDD]
Smetana, B.:The Moldau Naxos ▲ 8.550376 [DDD]

Slovak Radio New PO
A. Rahbari (cnd)
Beethoven, L. van:Con 1 Pno, w. J. Stancul (pno) Discover International ▲ DICD 920104 [DDD]
Beethoven, L. van:Con 2 Pno, w. J. Stancul (pno) Discover International ▲ DICD 920104 [DDD]
Beethoven, L. van:Con 3 Pno, w. J. Stancul (pno) Discover International ▲ DICD 920121 [DDD]
Beethoven, L. van:Con 4 Pno, w. J. Stancul (pno) Discover International ▲ DICD 920121 [DDD]
Tchaikovsky, P.:Con 1 Pno, w. D. Lively (pno) Discover International ▲ DICD 920118 [DDD]

Slovak Radio Sym CO
T. Koutník (cnd)
Martinů, B.:Con 5 Pno, w. K. Havlokova (pno) Campion ▲ 1321 [DDD]
Z. Košler (cnd)
Martinů, B.:Con Hpd, w. Z. Ruzickova (hpd) Campion ▲ 1321 [DDD]
O. Lenárd (cnd)
Martinů, B.:Con 4 Pno, w. K. Havlokova (pno) Campion ▲ 1321 [DDD]

Slovak RSO
The Dance Collection, w. Ondrej Lenard (cnd), Keith Clark (cnd), Stephen Gunzenhauser (cnd), Kenneth Jean (cnd), Barry Wordsworth (cnd), Adrian Leaper (cnd), Johannes Wildner (cnd), Czech RSO, Slovak PO, Royal PO, Slovak State PO, CRS SO, Thalia-Schrammeln Quartet *(rec Czechoslovak Radio Concert Hall, Bratislava, Feb 1–4, 1988)* Naxos 4-▲ 8.504015 [DDD]
R. Black (cnd)
MMC Brataslava Series Master Musicians Collective ▲ MMC 2002
O. Dohnányi (cnd)
Verdi, G.:Choruses, w. Slovak Radio Chorus—from Aida, Battaglia di Legnano, Don Carlos, Ernani, Forza del destino, Macbeth, Nabucco, Otello, Traviata, Trovatore [I] Naxos ▲ 8.550241 [DDD] Δ 7.550241 [DDD]
S. Kawalla (cnd)
Music from 6 Continents, 1993 series, w. Koszalin State PO, Pro Musica Nipponia [cnd:Norichika Iimori], Bohuslav Martinů PO [cnd:Miloš Machek] Vienna Modern Masters ▲ VMM 3017 [DDD]
E. Tomlinson (cnd)
Binge, R.:Prelude:The Whispering Valley, w. S. Cápová (pno) *(rec Oct. 1992)* Marco Polo ("British Light Music" series) ▲ 8.223515 [DDD]
Binge, R.:The Watermill *(rec Oct. 1992)* Marco Polo ("British Light Music" series) ▲ 8.223515 [DDD]

Slovak RSO Bratislava
Ross, W.:Mosaics, w. Marjorie Mitchell (pno) Master Musicians Collective ▲ MMC 2020
M. Adriano (cnd)
Herrmann, B.:Jane Eyre (film music) for Orchestra *(rec Jan. 3–7, 1994)* Marco Polo ▲ 8.223535 [DDD]
Honegger, A.:Film Music—Mayerling:Suite (1936); Regain:Suites 1 & 2 (1937); Le démon de l'Himalaya (2 symphonic movts; 1935) Marco Polo ▲ 8.223467 [DDD]
Ibert, J.:La Ballade de la geôle de Reading *(rec Feb. 8–13, 1993)* Marco Polo ▲ 8.223508 [DDD]
Ibert, J.:Chant de folie, w. Slovak Phil Chorus *(rec Feb. 8–13, 1993)* Marco Polo ▲ 8.223508 [DDD]
Ibert, J.:Féerique *(rec Feb. 8–13, 1993)* Marco Polo ▲ 8.223508 [DDD]
Ibert, J.:Les Recontres *(rec Feb. 8–13, 1993)* Marco Polo ▲ 8.223508 [DDD]
Ibert, J.:Suite élisabéthaine, w. D. Kubrická (sop), Slovak Phil Chorus *(rec Feb. 8–13, 1993)* Marco Polo ▲ 8.223508 [DDD]
Khachaturian, A.:The Battle of Stalingrad (sels) Marco Polo ▲ 8.223314
Khachaturian, A.:Othello (sels) Marco Polo ▲ 8.223314

ORCH. & ENS.

Slovak RSO Bratislava (cont.)

M. Adriano (cnd) (cont.)

Respighi, O.:La bella dormente nel bosco, w. Ivana Czaková (sop—Old Woman/Green Fairy), Adriana Kohútková (sop—Blue Fairy/Nightingale), Henrietta Lednárová (sop—Frog/Spindle), Jana Valásková (sop—Princess), Dagmar Pecková (mez—Cuckoo/Cat), Denisa Slepkovská (mez—Queen/Duchess), Karol Bernáth (ten—Doctor), Guillermo Dominguez (ten—Prince April), Igor Pasek (ten—Jester), Ján Durčo (bar—Ambassador), Richard Haan (bar—King/Woodcutter), Stanislav Benačka (bass—Doctor), Anton Kúrnava (bass—Doctor), Marián Smolárik (bass—Doctor), M. Adriano (nar—Mr. Dollar Chèques), Ján Rozehnal (cnd), Slovak Phil Chorus *(rec Concert Hall of the Slovak Radio, Bratislava, June 8–20, 1994)* Marco Polo ("Opera Classics" series) ▲ 8.223742 [DDD]

Respighi, O.:La Primavera, w. Henrietta Lednárová (sop—Prima fanciulla), Jana Valásková (sop—Sirvard), Beata Geriová (mez—Seconda fanciulla), Miroslav Dvorsky (ten—Il giovine), Richard Haan (bar—L'orante), Vladimír Kubovčik (bass—Il vecchio), Vera Rasková (fl), Slovak Phil Chorus *(rec Slovak Radio Concert Hall, Bratislava)* Marco Polo ▲ 8.223595 [DDD]

F. Bauer-Theussl (cnd)

Strauss (II), Joh.:Orchestral Music—Heimats-Kinder, Op. 85 [waltz]; Hochzeits-Praeludium, Op. 469 [w. Viktor Simčisko (vn), Katrina Vavreková (hp), Imrich Szabo (org)]; Wildfeuer, Op. 313 [polka]; Wilhelminen-Quadrille, Op. 37; Irrlichter, Op. 218 [waltz]; Herzenskönigin, Op. 445 [polka]; The Herald Waltz [New York Herald]; Ninetta-Quadrille, Op. 446; Liebe und Ehe, Op. 465 [polka mazurka]; Jubilee Waltz *(rec Slovak Radio Concert Hall, Bratislava & Moyzes Hall of the Slovak PO)* Marco Polo ▲ 8.223240 [DDD]

H. Beissel (cnd)

Pfitzner, H.:Das Christelfein (ov) Marco Polo ▲ 8.223162 [DDD]
Pfitzner, H.:Con Pno, w. W. Harden (pno) Marco Polo ▲ 8.223162 [DDD]
Pfitzner, H.:Das Herz (sels)—Liebesmelodie Marco Polo ▲ 8.223162 [DDD]

R. Black (cnd)

Althans, M.:Valse Excentrique *(rec Slovak Radio & Television Studios)* MMC ▲ MMC 2009 [DDD]
Brisman, H.:Con Pno, w. Joshua Pierce (pno) *(rec Slovak Radio & TV Studios, Slovak National Republic)* MMC ▲ MMC 2016 [DDD]
Crowell, J.:Black Holes & Anti-Matters MMC ▲ MMC 2017 [DDD]
Elkana, A.:A Color in Time MMC ▲ MMC 2017 [DDD]
Erickson, E.:A Shipwrecked Landscape *(rec Slovak Radio & TV Studios, Slovak National Republic)* MMC ▲ MMC 2016 [DDD]
Kessler, M.:Con Pno, w. Helena Vesterman (pno) *(rec Slovak Radio & Television Studios)* MMC ▲ MMC 2009 [DDD]
Leclaire, D.:Haiku—Nos. 1 & 4 *(rec Slovak Radio & Television Studios)* MMC ▲ MMC 2009 [DDD]
Nytch, J.:Novas MMC ▲ MMC 2017 [DDD]
Perlongo, D.:Con Pno, w. Donna Coleman (pno) *(rec Slovak Radio & Television Studios, Slovak National Republic)* Master Musicians Collective ▲ MMC 2020 [DDD]
Rahbee, D.G.:Tapestry 1 *(rec Slovak Radio & Television Studios)* MMC ▲ MMC 2009 [DDD]
Skupinsky, G.:Wild n' Sexy, w. Solati Trio *(rec Slovak Radio & TV Studios, Slovak National Republic, June & Sept 1993)* MMC ▲ MMC 2015 [DDD]
Stango, J.:Sol' per Dirti Addio *(rec Slovak Radio & Television Studios)* MMC ▲ MMC 2009 [DDD]
Vali, R.:Persian Folk Songs, w. Wendy Kallen (sop), Slovak Radio Chorus *(rec Slovak Radio & Television Studios)* Master Muscicians Collective ▲ MMC 2021 [DDD]
Ziffrin, M.:Sym, "Letters", w. Neva Pilgrim (sop) *(rec Slovak Radio & TV Studios, Slovak National Republic, June & Sept 1993)* MMC ▲ MMC 2015 [DDD]

Black, Stankovsky (cnd)

Melloni, R.C.:Sym Pno, w. Frances Burnett (pno) Master Musicians Collective ▲ MMC 2020

G. Carpenter (cnd)

Mayerl, W.J.:Music of, w. A. Ball (pno)—Marigold; A L. Pond; 4 Aces Suite; From a Spanish Lattice; Minuet by Candlelight; Aquarium Suite; Autumn Crocus; Bats in the Belfry; Pastoral Sketches; Fireside Fusiliers; Parade of the Sandwich-Board Men; Waltz for a Lonely Heart; Busybody *(rec Oct. 1992)* Marco Polo ("British Light Music" series) ▲ 8.223514 [DDD]

Z. Chen (cnd)

Gould, M.:Con Fl, w. Keith Bryan (fl) *(rec Concert Hall of Slovak Radio, Bratislava, June 20–24, 1994)* Premier ▲ PR 1045 [DDD]
La Montaine, J.:Con Fl, w. Keith Bryan (fl) *(rec Concert Hall of Slovak Radio, Bratislava, June 20–24, 1994)* Premier ▲ PR 1045 [DDD]

J. Cohen (cnd)

Strauss (II), Joh.:Music of, w. Slovak Phil Chorus—Polka mazurka champêtre; Manhattan Waltzes; Centennial Waltzes; Enchantment Waltzes; Idylle 'Auf der Alm'; Engagement Waltzes; Farewell to America; Romance 2 Vc [w. Ivan Tvrdik (vc)]; Liebesbotschaft-Galopp; Tauben-walzer; Promenade-Abenteuer; Bauersleut'im Künstlerhaus; D'Hauptsach; Entr'acte from Fürstin Ninetta; An der schönen, blauen Donau *(rec Slovak Radio Concert Hall, Apr 1996)* Marco Polo ▲ 8.223279 [DDD]

M. Dittrich (cnd)

Strauss (II), Joh.:Orchestral Music—Wo uns're Fahne weht, Op. 473 [march]; Burschen-Lieder, Op. 55 [waltz]; Martha, Op. 46 [quadrille]; Gedankenflug, Op. 215 [waltz]; Newa, Op. 288 [polka]; Aschenbrödel [prelude to Act III]; Vivat!, Op. 103 [quadrille]; Lagunen, Op. 411 [waltz]; Shawl, Op. 343 [polka]; Traumbild I [symphonic poem] *(rec Slovak Radio Concert Hall, Bratislava, Dec. 3–6, 1993)* Marco Polo ▲ 8.223241 [DDD]
Strauss (II), Joh.:Orchestral Music—Russischer Marsch, Op. 426; Slaven-Potpourri, Op. 39; 5 Paragraphen Waltz, Op. 105; La favorite, Polka française, Op. 217; Nikolai-Quadrille, Op. 65; Abschied von St. Petersburg, Waltz, Op. 210; Der Kobold, Polka mazurka, Op. 226; Im russischen Dorfe, Op. 355 [orch. Max Schönherr]; Dolci pianti for Cello & Orch. [w. J. Sikora]; Niko-Polka, Op. 228 *(rec Apr.23–27, 1991)* Marco Polo ▲ 8.223234 [DDD]
Strauss (II), Joh.:Orchestral Music—Greetings to America Waltzes [arr. Cohen]; Marien-Quadrille, Op. 51[arr. Haklik]; Engagement Waltzes [arr. Cohen]; Probirmamsell-Polka [from Aschenbrödel]; Annika-Quadrille; Tu qui regis totum orbem (gradual) [w. Peter La Garde (tpt)]; Cagliostro-Walzer, Op. 370; Vaterländischer Marsch; Pizzicato-Polka [both collaborations w. Josef Strauss]; Robert Schumann's Widmung [orch'd. by Johann Strauss II]; Sehnsucht Romanze [Op. 259]; Pawlowsk-Polka quasi Galopp [unconfirmed; w. Slovak Phil Chorus members] *(rec Bratislava Slovak Radio Concert Hall, June 4–7, 1993)* Marco Polo ▲ 8.223246 [DDD]

O. Dohnányi (cnd)

Van Appledorn, M.J.:Rising Night after Night, w. Bratislava City Chorus Vienna Modern Masters ▲ VMM 3004 [DDD]

R. Duarte (cnd)

Villa-Lobos, H.:Dança dos mosquitos *(rec May 10–15, 1993)* Marco Polo ("Latin American Classics" series) ▲ 8.223552 [DDD]
Villa-Lobos, H.:Dança frenética *(rec May 10–15, 1993)* Marco Polo ("Latin American Classics" series) ▲ 8.223552 [DDD]
Villa-Lobos, H.:Danças características africanas *(rec May 10–15, 1993)* Marco Polo ("Latin American Classics" series) ▲ 8.223552 [DDD]
Villa-Lobos, H.:Rudá [rev R. Duarte] *(rec Slovak Radio Concert Hall, Bratislava, Feb 27–Mar 6, 1995)* Marco Polo ▲ 8.223720 [DDD]
Villa-Lobos, H.:Rudepoema [arr. for orchestra] *(rec May 10–15, 1993)* Marco Polo ("Latin American Classics" series) ▲ 8.223552 [DDD]
Villa-Lobos, H.:Sym 6 [rev R. Duarte] *(rec Slovak Radio Concert Hall, Bratislava, Feb 27–Mar 6, 1995)* Marco Polo ▲ 8.223720 [DDD]

P. Freeman (cnd)

La Montaine, J.:Con 4 Pno, w. Ramon Salvatore (pno) *(rec Bratislava, Feb 26 & 27, 1995)* Cedille ▲ CDR 90000 028 [DDD]

H. Griffiths (cnd)

Glazunov, A.:Carnaval Pan Classics ▲ CD 510084 [DDD]
Glazunov, A.:Con 1 Pno, w. Karl-Andreas Kolly (pno) Pan Classics ▲ CD 510084 [DDD]
Glazunov, A.:Con 2 Pno, w. Karl-Andreas Kolly (pno) Pan Classics ▲ CD 510084 [DDD]
Respighi, O.:Con Pno, w. Konstantin Scherbakov (pno) *(rec Concert Hall of the Slovak Radio, Bratislava, Sept. 19–22, 1994)* Naxos ▲ 8.553207 [DDD]

Slovak RSO Bratislava (cont.)

H. Griffiths (cnd) (cont.)

Respighi, O.:Fant slava, w. Konstantin Scherbakov (pno) *(rec Concert Hall of the Slovak Radio, Bratislava, Sept. 19–22, 1994)* Naxos ▲ 8.553207 [DDD]
Respighi, O.:Toccata Pno, w. Konstantin Scherbakov (pno), Ivan Tvrdík (vc) *(rec Concert Hall of the Slovak Radio, Bratislava, Sept. 19–22, 1994)* Naxos ▲ 8.553207 [DDD]

S. Gunzenhauser (cnd)

Dvořák, A.:Sym 1, "The Bells of Zlonice" *(rec 5/90)* Naxos ▲ 8.550266 [DDD]

S. Kawalla (cnd)

Axelrod, L.:Cassandra Speaks Vienna Modern Masters ▲ VMM 3012 [DDD]
Bell, L.:Sacred Syms Vienna Modern Masters ▲ VMM 3016 [DDD]
Carbon, J.:Hommage à trois Vienna Modern Masters ▲ VMM 3011 [DDD]
Constantinides, D.:Composition Vienna Modern Masters ▲ VMM 3009 [DDD]
Cronin, S.:Con Pno Vienna Modern Masters ▲ VMM 3011 [DDD]
Fortner, J.:Prelude to an Opera:The House of Atreus Vienna Modern Masters ▲ VMM 3009 [DDD]
Görsch, U.:Transformationen Vienna Modern Masters ▲ VMM 3012 [DDD]
Heard, Alan:Elegy for Our Time Vienna Modern Masters ▲ VMM 3011 [DDD]
Hobson, B.:Con Orch Vienna Modern Masters ▲ VMM 3024 [DDD]
Loeb, D.:Unkei, w. D. Loeb (shinobue) Vienna Modern Masters ▲ VMM 3006 [DDD]
Lorentzen, B.:Con Pno Vienna Modern Masters ▲ VMM 3009 [DDD]
Moravec, P.:Spiritdance Vienna Modern Masters ▲ VMM 3016 [DDD]
Nuorvala, J.:Pinta ja säe Vienna Modern Masters ▲ VMM 3012 [DDD]
Ovens, D.:Play Us a Tune Vienna Modern Masters ▲ VMM 3009 [DDD]
Schwartz, E.:Celebrations/Reflections Vienna Modern Masters ▲ VMM 3012 [DDD]
Silsbee, A.:Sanctuary Vienna Modern Masters ▲ VMM 3016 [DDD]
Tanner, J.:Fragrant Harbor Vienna Modern Masters ▲ VMM 3013 [DDD]
Tanner, J.:Suite from the Singing Snails Vienna Modern Masters ▲ VMM 3016 [DDD]
Van De Vate, N.:Adagio Vienna Modern Masters ▲ VMM 2006 [DDD]
Van De Vate, N.:Gema Jawa Vienna Modern Masters ▲ VMM 2003 [DDD]
Van De Vate, N.:Pura Besakih Vienna Modern Masters ▲ VMM 3006 [DDD]
Van De Vate, N.:Somber Songs Vienna Modern Masters ▲ VMM 3013 [DDD]
Verrando, G.:Saopirato Passo Vienna Modern Masters ▲ VMM 3009 [DDD]

O. Lenárd (cnd)

Delibes, L.:Coppélia (suite) *(rec 4/86)* Naxos ▲ 8.550080 [DDD]
Delibes, L.:Le Roi s'amuse—Air de danse *(rec 10/23/89)* Naxos ▲ 8.550080 [DDD]
Delibes, L.:La Source, ou Naila—suite *(rec 4/89)* Naxos ▲ 8.550080 [DDD]
Delibes, L.:Sylvia—suite *(rec 4/89)* Naxos ▲ 8.550080 [DDD]
Janácek, L.:Lachian Dances *(rec Feb. 1990)* Naxos ▲ 8.550411 [DDD]
Janácek, L.:Sinfonietta *(rec Feb. 1990)* Naxos ▲ 8.550411 [DDD]
Janácek, L.:Taras Bulba *(rec Jan. 1990)* Naxos ▲ 8.550411 [DDD]

Petronsky (cnd)

Mageau, M.J.:Triple Con, w. A. Lorenz (vn), G. Williams (vc), W. Lorenz (pno) Vienna Modern Masters ▲ VMM 3001 [DDD]

C. Pollack (cnd)

Strauss (II), Joh.:Music of, w. Marilyn Hill Smith (sop)—Csárdás [from Fledermaus]; Goddess of Reason (quadrille); On the Banks of the Danube; First Love (romance); Clever Little Gretel (waltz); Take a Chance (gallop); Where the Lemon-Trees Blossom (waltz); New Csárdás [from Fledermaus]; If You Have a Sweet Beloved; Voices of Spring (waltz); The Slumbering Gables; First Thought; Odeon Waltz; A Verse for Dancing; Sweet Tears; Posthumous Waltz No. 4 *(rec Slovak Radio Concert Hall, Bratislava, May & Dec 1994)* Marco Polo ▲ 8.223276 [DDD]
Strauss (II), Joh.:Orchestral Music—Piccolo [march]; Auroraball, Op. 219 [polka]; Hirtenspiele, Op. 89 [waltz]; Sängerslust, Op. 328 [polka]; Sentenzen, Op. 233 [waltz]; Gruss aus Österreich, Op. 359 [polka mazurka]; Hommage au Public Russe [potpourri]; An der Moldau, Op. 366 [polka]; Gartenlaube, Op. 461 [waltz]; Soldatenspiel, Op. 430 [polka] *(rec House of Arts, Košice, Nov. 13–17, 1992)* Marco Polo ▲ 8.223242 [DDD]

Rowell (cnd)

Bestor, C.:Music of, Massachusetts Wind Ensemble—Ov. to a Romantic Comedy; Vars. for Orch; In Memoriam Bill Evans; Chaconne for Chamber Winds; 3 Portraits for Wind Octet *(rec Moyzes Hall, Bratislava, Slovakia)* Centaur ▲ CRC 2216 [DDD]

R. Stankovsky (cnd)

Bullen, G.:Elegy Eroica [composed to commemorate the 25th anniversary of the assassination of R.F. Kennedy] MMC ▲ MMC 2023
Burwasser, D.:A Well Traveled Road *(rec Slovak Radio & TV Studios, Slovak National Republic)* MMC ▲ MMC 2016 [DDD]
Colson, D.:Searching Schubert *(rec Slovak Radio & TV Studios, Slovak National Republic, June & Sept 1993)* MMC ▲ MMC 2015 [DDD]
Ernst, D.:Crossover *(rec Slovak Radio & TV Studios, Slovak National Republic, June & Sept 1993)* MMC ▲ MMC 2015 [DDD]
Fugarino Jr., J.:Riding on a Cloud MMC ▲ MMC 2017 [DDD]
Giusto, A.:Peace Cow (it's not a habit, I'm used to it) MMC ▲ MMC 2017 [DDD]
Hawthorne, D.:Night:Near the Wind's Eye, w. Kelvin Hawthorne (va) MMC ▲ MMC 2023
Hoiby, L.:Con 2 Pno, w. Stanley Babin (pno) Master Muscicians Collective ▲ MMC 2038 [DDD]
Kidde, G.:Quest *(rec Slovak Radio & TV Studios, Slovak National Republic, June & Sept 1993)* MMC ▲ MMC 2015 [DDD]
Levy, F.E.:Sym 4, "Structures of the Mind", w. Slovak Radio Chorus *(rec Slovak Radio & TV Studios)* Master Musicians Collective ▲ MMC 2021 [DDD]
McKinley, W.T.:Andante & Scherzo, w. Frances Burnett (pno) *(rec Slovak Radio & TV Studios)* MMC ▲ MMC 2009 [DDD]
McKinley, W.T.:Fant Variazioni, w. Elaine Comparone (hpd) *(rec Slovak Radio & TV Studios, Slovak National Republic)* MMC ▲ MMC 2016 [DDD]
Mascari, E.P.:Mount Washington MMC ▲ MMC 2023
Mosonyi, M.:Sym 1 Marco Polo ▲ 8.223539 [DDD]
Muncy, T.:Paean *(rec Slovak Radio & TV Studios, Slovak National Republic, June & Sept 1993)* MMC ▲ MMC 2015 [DDD]
Nelson, M.B.:Medead *(rec Slovak Radio & TV Studios, Slovak National Republic)* MMC ▲ MMC 2016 [DDD]
Packales, J.:I Was on the Sea, w. Slovak Radio Chorus *(rec Slovak Radio & TV Studios)* Master Muscicians Collective ▲ MMC 2021 [DDD]
Polay, B.:Cathedral Images MMC ▲ MMC 2023
Rendelman Jr., R.:Chorale & Toccata *(rec Slovak Radio & TV Studios)* MMC ▲ MMC 2009 [DDD]
Rubinstein, A.:Con 5 Pno, w. J. Banowetz (pno) *(rec Dec. 13–18, 1993)* Marco Polo ▲ 8.223489 [DDD]
Rubinstein, A.:Russian Capriccio, w. J. Banowetz (pno) *(rec Dec. 13–18, 1993)* Marco Polo ▲ 8.223489 [DDD]
Tepper, A.:Con Ob MMC ("Chamber Music" series) ▲ MMC 2010

J. E. Suben (cnd)

Anderson, B.:Minnesota Swale Opus One ▲ CD 156
Angeli, F. di A.:Pieces (2) Orch—Intermezzo; Pantokrator Opus One ▲ CD 170 [DDD]
Dellaira, M.:Three Rivers Opus One ▲ CD 170 [DDD]
Kenessey, S. de:Wintersong Opus One ▲ CD 170 [DDD]
Retzel, F.:Chansonnier Opus One ▲ CD 156
Scarmolin, A.L.:Sym 1 *(rec Bratislava, Jan 26–28, 1995)* New World ▲ 80502-2
Scarmolin, A.L.:Sym 2, w. Stanislav Bičák (bn), Peter Sivanič (hn), Miroslav Herák (vc) *(rec Bratislava, Jan 23–25, 1995)* New World ▲ 80502-2
Schubel, M.:Creatures of Mist Opus One ▲ CD 171 [DDD]
Schubel, M.:11 Come Once Opus One ▲ CD 171 [DDD]
Schubel, M.:Syngnet Opus One ▲ CD 171 [DDD]
Sichel, J.:3 Places Opus One ▲ CD 170 [DDD]
Strandberg, N.:The Legend of Emmeline Labiche Opus One ▲ CD 170 [DDD]

▲ = CD ♦ = Enhanced CD Δ = MD ■ = Cassette Tape □ = DCC

Slovak RSO Bratislava (cont.)
A. Tamayo (cnd)
Weber, C.M. von:Concertino Cl, w. D. Kloecker (cl) Novalis ▲ 150093
Weber, C.M. von:Con 1 Cl, w. D. Kloecker (cl) Novalis ▲ 150093
Weber, C.M. von:Con 2 Cl, w. D. Kloecker (cl) Novalis ▲ 150093
Weber, C.M. von:Music of, w. D. Klöcker (cl), Consortium Classicum Soloists—Concertino in C for Oboe & Winds; Romanza Siciliana for Flute & Orch.; Romanze Appassionata for Bassoon & Orch.; Divert. for Clarinet & Orch.; Andante & Rondo Ungarese for Bassoon & Orch., Op. 35; Concertino, Op. 45 Novalis ▲ 150100
E. Tomlinson (cnd)
Binge, R.:Con A Sax, w. K. Edge (a sax) *(rec Oct. 1992)* Marco Polo ("British Light Music" series) ▲ 8.223515 [DDD]
Binge, R.:Elizabethan Serenade *(rec Oct. 1992)* Marco Polo ("British Light Music" series) ▲ 8.223515 [DDD]
Binge, R.:Orch Music—Scottish Rhap.; Miss Melanie; Las Castañuelas; Madrugado; The Red Sombrero; Trade Winds; Faire Frou-Frou; String Song; Scherzo:Allegro molto; The Dance of the Snowflakes; High Stepper; Venetian Carnival; Sailing By *(rec Oct. 1992)* Marco Polo ("British Light Music" series) ▲ 8.223515 [DDD]
Tomlinson, E.:Dances from Aladdin *(rec Oct. 1992)* Marco Polo ("British Light Music" series) ▲ 8.223513 [DDD]
Tomlinson, E.:Light Music Suite *(rec Oct. 1992)* Marco Polo ("British Light Music" series) ▲ 8.223513 [DDD]
Tomlinson, E.:Music of, w. Czech-Slovak RSO Bratislava—Second Suite of English Folk Dances (1977); Silverthorn Suite; Cinderella Waltz; English Overture; Fairy Coach; Gaelic Lullaby; Hornpipe; Kielder Water; Little Serenade; Nautical Interlude; Nocturne; Sweet & Dainty Marco Polo (British Light Music) ▲ 8.223413 [DDD]
Tomlinson, E.:Orch Music—Comedy Ov.; Shenandoah; Cumberland Square; Passepied; Rigadoon; A Georgian Miniature *(rec Oct. 1992)* Marco Polo ("British Light Music" series) ▲ 8.223513 [DDD]
Tomlinson, E.:Rhapsody & Rondo, w. R. Watkins (hn) *(rec 1992)* Marco Polo ("British Light Music" series) ▲ 8.223513 [DDD]
Tomlinson, E.:Suite of English Folk Dances *(rec Oct. 1992)* Marco Polo ("British Light Music" series) ▲ 8.223513 [DDD]
P. Vronský (cnd)
Blak, K.:Con Cl, w. A. E. Klett (cl) *(rec Oct. 1993)* Tutl ▲ FKT 7
Rasmussen, S.:Grave, w. A. E. Klett (cl) *(rec Oct. 1993)* Tutl ▲ FKT 7
Rasmussen, S.:Landið, w. J. Johansen (sop) *(rec Oct. 1993)* Tutl ▲ FKT 7
Sandagerðl Paulli:Gerandisdagurl Havn, w. J. Johansen (sop) *(rec Oct. 1993)* Tutl ▲ FKT 7
J. Wildner (cnd)
Bizet, G.:Les Pêcheurs de perles (sels), w. Janez Lotrič (ten), Igor Morozov (bar)—Au fond du temple saint *(rec Slovak Radio Concert Hall, Bratislava, Feb. 15–24, 1994)* Naxos ▲ 8.553030 [DDD]
Donizetti, G.:Lucia di Lammermoor (sels), w. Janez Lotrič (ten), Igor Morozov (bar)—Orrida è questa notte *(rec Slovak Radio Concert Hall, Bratislava, Feb. 15–24, 1994)* Naxos ▲ 8.553030 [DDD]
Rossini, G.:Guillaume Tell (sels), w. J. Lortič (ten), I. Morozov (bar)—Arresta...Quali sguardi *(rec Bratislava, Feb. 15–24, 1994)* Naxos ▲ 8.553030 [DDD]
Spohr, L.:Con 2 Cl, w. Ernst Ottensamer (cl) *(rec Concert Hall of the Slovak Radio, Bratislava, Jan. 31–Feb. 4, 1994)* Naxos ▲ 8.550689 [DDD]
Spohr, L.:Con 4 Cl, w. Ernst Ottensamer (cl) *(rec Concert Hall of the Slovak Radio, Bratislava, Jan. 31–Feb. 4, 1994)* Naxos ▲ 8.550689 [DDD]
Spohr, L.:Fant & Vars on a Theme of Danzi, w. Ernst Ottensamer (cl) *(rec Concert Hall of the Slovak Radio, Bratislava, Feb. 20, 1994)* Naxos ▲ 8.550689 [DDD]
Spohr, L.:Potpourri, w. Ernst Ottensamer (cl) *(rec House of Arts, Košice)* Naxos ▲ 8.550688 [DDD]
Strauss (II), Joh.:Orchestral Music—Zivo!, Marsch, Op. 456; Architecten-Ball-Tänze, Walzer, Op. 36; Jäger-Polka française, Op. 229; Accelerationen, Walzer, Op. 234; Der Liebesbrunnen, Quadrille, Op. 10; Die Zietlose, Polka française; Königslieder, Walzer, Op. 334; Im Sturmschritt!, Polka schnell, Op. 348; Der Blitz Quadrille, Op. 59; Heut' ist heut', Walzer, Op. 471, Die Wahrsagerin, Polka mazurka, Op. 420 Marco Polo ▲ 8.223235
Strauss (II), Joh.:Orchestral Music, w. Bratislava City Chorus—Entrance March [from Der Zigeunerbaron]; Romance from Gounod's Faust [arr. Johann Strauss]; Kaiser-Alexander-Huldigungs-Marsch [arr. Kulling]; Ballet Music [from Indigo und die vierzig Räuber; arr. Schönherr]; Jubilee Waltz; Faust-Quadrille [from Gounod's Faust; arr. Kulling]; Kaiser Franz Joseph-Jubiläums-Marsch [unconfirmed]; Farewell to America Waltz; Sounds from Boston [both arr. Cohen]; Ballet Music [from Die Fledermaus]; Processional March [from Eine Nacht in Venedig] *(rec Bratislava Slovak Radio Concert Hall, Feb 1–4, 1994)* Marco Polo ▲ 8.223247 [DDD]
Verdi, G.:La forza del destino (sels), w. Janez Lotrič (ten), Igor Morozov (bar), Slovak Opera Chorus—Invano, Alvaro; Nè gustare m'è dato *(rec Slovak Radio Concert Hall, Bratislava, Feb. 15–24, 1994)* Naxos ▲ 8.553030 [DDD]
Verdi, G.:Otello (sels), w. Janez Lotrič (ten), Igor Morozov (bar)—Desdemona rea, si, per ciel *(rec Slovak Radio Concert Hall, Bratislava, Feb. 15–24, 1994)* Naxos ▲ 8.553030 [DDD]
Verdi, G.:I vespri siciliani (sels), w. Janez Lotrič (ten), Igor Morozov (bar)—Ebben? Non mi rispondi tu?; Quando al mio sen per te parlava *(rec Slovak Radio Concert Hall, Bratislava, Feb. 15–24, 1994)* Naxos ▲ 8.553030 [DDD]
Slovak State PO
The Dance Collection, w. Ondrej Lenard (cnd), Keith Clark (cnd), Stephen Gunzenhauser (cnd), Kenneth Jean (cnd), Barry Wordsworth (cnd), Adrian Leaper (cnd), Johannes Wildner (cnd), Czech RSO, Slovak RSO, Slovak PO, Royal PO, Slovak State PO, CRS SO, Thalia-Schrammeln Quartet *(rec Czechoslovak Radio Concert Hall, Bratislava, Feb 1–4, 1988)* Naxos 4-▲ 8.504015 [DDD]
Slovak State PO Košice
D. Amos (cnd)
Lopatnikoff, N.:Con for 2 Pnos, w. Dorothy Jonas (pno), Joshua Pierce (pno) Centaur ▲ CRC 2269
Malipiero, G.F.:Dialogo 7, w. Dorothy Jonas (pno), Joshua Pierce (pno) Centaur ▲ CRC 2269
Tansman, A.:Suite 2 Pnos, w. Dorothy Jonas (pno), Joshua Pierce (pno) Centaur ▲ CRC 2269
B. Kolman (cnd)
Antheil, G.:Archipelago *(rec House of Arts, Kosice, Slovakia, Oct 10–13 & Dec 4–5, 1995)* Centaur ▲ CRC 2293 [DDD]
Antheil, G.:Capital of the World *(rec House of Arts, Kosice, Slovakia, Oct 10–13 & Dec 4–5, 1995)* Centaur ▲ CRC 2293 [DDD]
Antheil, G.:Sym 5, "Joyous" *(rec House of Arts, Kosice, Slovakia, Oct 10–13 & Dec 4–5, 1995)* Centaur ▲ CRC 2293 [DDD]
Rubinstein, A.:Sym 3 *(rec Sept. 1993)* Centaur ▲ CRC 2185 [DDD]
Rubinstein, A.:Sym 5 *(rec Sept. 1993)* Centaur ▲ CRC 2185 [DDD]
C. Pollack (cnd)
Strauss (II), Joh.:Orchestral Music—Triumph-Marsch, Op. 69; Jugend-Träume, Op. 12; Das Comitat geht in die Höh! Op. 457; Die Königin von Leon, Op. 40; Neue steierische Tänze, Op. 61; Tanze mit dem Besenstiel! Op. 458; Spitzentuch-Quadrille, Op. 392; Schwungräder, Op. 223; Sonnenblume, Op. 459; Romanze No. 2 in g for Cello & Orchestra, Op. 255; Traumbild II; Symphonic Poem *(rec Feb. 9–12, 1992)* Marco Polo ▲ 8.223237 [DDD]
Strauss (II), Joh.:Orchestral Music—Ninetta-Marsch, Op. 447; Irenen-Walzer, Op. 32; Sylphen-Polka, Op. 309; Slaven-Ball Quadrille, Op. 88; Hell und voll, Op. 216; I Tipferl-Polka française, Op. 377; Klänge aus der Raimundzeit, Op. 479; Jabuka-Quadrille, Op. 460; Abschieds-Walzer in F; Unparteiische Kritiken, Op. 442 *(rec Feb. 9–12, 1992)* Marco Polo ▲ 8.223239 [DDD]
B. Rezucha (cnd)
Mendelssohn, F.:Cons 2 Pnos, w. Joshua Pierce (pno), Dorothy Jonas (pno) *(rec House of Art, Košice, Oct & Nov 1995)* Vox Classics ▲ VOX 7538 [DDD]
P. Robinson (cnd)
Lachner, F.P.:Sym 5 *(rec Oct. 16–18, 1992)* Marco Polo ▲ 8.223502 [DDD]
Lachner, F.P.:Sym 8 *(rec House of Arts, Košice, Oct. 18–20, 1992)* Marco Polo ▲ 8.223594 [DDD]
U. Schneider (cnd)
Raff, J.:Dame Kobald (ov) *(rec House of Arts, Košice, Jan. 14–17, 1994)* Marco Polo ▲ 8.223628 [DDD]

Slovak State PO Košice (cont.)
U. Schneider (cnd) (cont.)
Raff, J.:Ein feste Burg ist unser Gott *(rec Mar. 5, 1993)* Marco Polo ▲ 8.223455 [DDD]
Raff, J.:Festmarsch *(rec House of Arts, Košice, Jan. 14–17, 1994)* Marco Polo ▲ 8.223628 [DDD]
Raff, J.:Jubel-Ov *(rec House of Arts, Košice, Jan. 14–17, 1994)* Marco Polo ▲ 8.223628 [DDD]
Raff, J.:Konzert-Ov *(rec Apr. 27, 1993)* Marco Polo ▲ 8.223506 [DDD]
Raff, J.:Macbeth Ov *(rec House of Arts, Košice, Oct. 22–26, 1993)* Marco Polo ▲ 8.223630 [DDD]
Raff, J.:Romeo & Juliet Ov *(rec House of Arts, Košice, Oct. 22–26, 1993)* Marco Polo ▲ 8.223630 [DDD]
Raff, J.:Sym 2 *(rec House of Arts, Košice, Oct. 22–26, 1993)* Marco Polo ▲ 8.223630 [DDD]
Raff, J.:Sym 5 *(rec Apr. 13–15, 1992)* Marco Polo ▲ 8.223455 [DDD]
Raff, J.:Sym 6 *(rec House of Arts, Košice, Mar. 1–3, 1993)* Marco Polo ▲ 8.223628 [DDD]
Raff, J.:Sym 7 *(rec Mar. 4–6 1993)* Marco Polo ▲ 8.223506 [DDD]
R. Stankovsky (cnd)
Mendelssohn, F.:Capriccio brillante, w. B. Firth (pno) Naxos ▲ 8.550681 [DDD]
Mendelssohn, F.:Con 1 Pno, w. B. Firth (pno) Naxos ▲ 8.550681 [DDD]
Mendelssohn, F.:Con 2 Pno, w. B. Firth (pno) Naxos ▲ 8.550681 [DDD]
Mendelssohn, F.:Con 2 Pno, w. Benjamin Frith (pno) *(rec House of Arts, Košice, Apr 27–30, 1992)* Naxos ▲ 8.553267 [DDD]
Mendelssohn, F.:Rondo brilliant, w. B. Firth (pno) Naxos ▲ 8.550681 [DDD]
Mosonyi, M.:Con Pno, w. K. Körmendi (pno) Marco Polo ▲ 8.223539 [DDD]
Rubinstein, A.:Ivan the Terrible Marco Polo ▲ 8.223277
Rubinstein, A.:Sym 1 Marco Polo ▲ 8.223277
A. Walter (cnd)
Furtwängler, W.:Largo *(rec House of Arts, Košice, Feb. 12, 1993)* Marco Polo ▲ 8.223645 [DDD]
Furtwängler, W.:Ov *(rec House of Arts, Košice, June 30, 1993)* Marco Polo ▲ 8.223645 [DDD]
Furtwängler, W.:Sym in D—Allegro [1st movt.] *(rec House of Arts, Košice, Feb. 12, 1993)* Marco Polo ▲ 8.223645 [DDD]
Lachner, F.P.:Ball-Suite *(rec House of Arts, Košice, Sept. 3–4, 1993)* Marco Polo ▲ 8.223594 [DDD]
Spohr, L.:Sym 2 Marco Polo ▲ 8.223454
Spohr, L.:Sym 9 Marco Polo ▲ 8.223454
Strauss (II), Joh.:Orchestral Music—Wiener Garnison-Marsch, Op. 77; Damenspende, Op. 305; Faschings-Lieder, Op. 11; Serben-Quadrille, Op. 14; Nimm sie hin! Op. 358; Leitartikel, Op. 273; Eine Nacht in Venedig, Op. 416; Lagerlust, Op. 431; An der Elbe, Op. 477; Ninetta-Galopp, Op. 450; Zehner-Polka, Op. 121; Maskenzug-Polka française, Op. 240 *(rec Nov. 2–4, 1992)* Marco Polo ▲ 8.223238 [DDD]
Strauss (II), Joh.:Orchestral Music—Matador March, Op. 406 [orch. Gustav Fischer]; Kreuzfidel, Polka française, Op. 301; D' Woaldbuama, Walzer im Ländlerstil, Op. 66 [orch. Ludwig Babinski]; Process, Op. 294; Elfen Quadrille, Op. 16 [orch. A. Kulling]; Mephistos Höllenrufe Waltz, Op. 101; Bitte schön!, Op. 372; Die Extravaganten Waltz, Op. 205; Fledermaus Quadrille; Der Klügere gibt nach, Op. 401; Neu-Wien Waltz, Op. 342; Diplomaten Polka, Op. 448 Marco Polo ▲ 8.223236
Strauss (II), Joh.:Ovs—Der listige Krieg:Ov; Eine Nacht in Venedig:Ov & Prelude Act 3; Der Zigeunerbaron:Ov; Simplicius; Jabuka:Prelude Act 3; Waldmeister; Die Göttin der Vernuft:Ov; Aschenbrödel:Quadrille *(rec 1990 & 1993)* Marco Polo ▲ 8.223275 [DDD]
Strauss (II), Joh.:Ovs—Opéra comique [arr. C. Pollack]; Indigo und die vierzig Räuber; Intermezzo [from Tausend und eine Nacht]; Der Carneval in Rom; Die Fledermaus; Cagliostro in Wien; Prinz Methusalem; Blindekuh; Das Spitzentuch der Königin *(rec House of Arts, Košice)* Marco Polo ▲ 8.223249 [DDD]
Strauss, Josef:Music of—Avantgarde-Marsch, Op. 14; Mai-Rosen, Op. 34 (waltz); Caprice-Quadrille, Op. 65; Die Naive, Op. 77 (polka française); Die Lachtaube, Op. 117 (polka mazur); Assoziationen, Op. 143 (waltz); Sport-Polka, Op. 170 (schnell); Flick-Flock-Quadrille, Op. 187; Gnomen, Op. 217 (polka française); Ernst und Humor, Op. 254 (waltz); Ohne Sorgen, Op. 271 (polka schnell) *(rec House of Arts, Košice, Apr 25–28, 1994)* Marco Polo ▲ 8.223563 [DDD]
Strauss, Josef:Music of—Schottischer Tanz, Op. 20; 5 Kleeblad'ln, Op. 44 (waltz); Sympathie, Op. 73 (polka mazur); Diana-Polka, Op. 95; Amazonen-Quadrille, Op. 118; Sturmlauf, Op. 136 (polka schnell); Träumerei [trans of Schumann]; Petitionen, Op. 153 (waltz); Arabella, Op. 167 (polka française); Stiefmütterchen, Op. 183 (polka mazur); Genien-Polka, Op. 205; Tanz-Prioritäten, Op. 280 (waltz) *(rec House of Arts, Košice, Apr 25–28, 1994)* Marco Polo ▲ 8.223562 [DDD]
Suppé, F. von:Ovs—Die schöne Galatea [The Beautiful Galatea]; Isabella; Das Modell [The Model]; Tantalusqualen; Der Krämer und sein Kommis; Paragraph 3; Boccaccio; Fatinitza March; Donna Juanita [w. Karol Petroczi (vn)] *(rec House of Arts, Košice)* Marco Polo ▲ 8.223648 [DDD]
Suppé, F. von:Ovs—Dichter und Bauer [Poet & Peasant]; Irrfahrt um's Glück [Fortune's Labyrinth]; Juanita March [from Donna Juanita]; Carnaval; Menuet & Tarantella [from Boccaccio]; Die Frau Meisterin [The Mistress]; Banitenstreiche [Jolly Robbers]; Des Wanderers Ziel [The Goal of the Wanderer]; Die Kartenschlägerin [Pique-Dame or Queen of Spades] *(rec House of Arts, Košice, Aug. 26–31, 1993)* Marco Polo ▲ 8.223689 [DDD]
Suppé, F. von:Ovs—The Beautiful Galatea; Light Cavalry; Fantinitza; Boccaccio March; Fortune's Labyrinth; Morning, Noon & Night in Vienna; Jolly Robbers; Queen of Spades; Gay Blades; Poet & Peasant *(rec House of Arts, Košice, 1993–94)* Naxos ▲ 8.553935 [DDD]
Suppé, F. von:Ovs—Morning, Noon & Night in Vienna; Flotte Bursche; Über Berg, Über Tal, Marsch; Summer Night's Dream; Mozart; Zehn Mädchen und kein Mann; Kindereien; Journey through Africa [Afrikareise]; Solemn Ov *(rec House of Arts, Košice, June 13–25, 1994)* Marco Polo ▲ 8.223730 [DDD]
Waldteufel, E.:Waltzes, Polkas & Galops—Pomone, Op. 155 (waltz); Souveraine, Op. 255 (mazurka); Amour et Printemps (waltz); Sous la voûte étoilée, Op. 253 (waltz); Les folies, Op. 157 (polka); Mello, Op. 123 (waltz); Dolorès, Op. 170 (waltz); Mon rêve, Op. 151 (waltz); Grand vitesse, Op. 146 (galop) *(rec House of Arts, Košice, Dec 4–9, 1992)* Marco Polo ▲ 8.223451 [DDD]
J. Wildner (cnd)
Spohr, L.:Con 1 Cl, w. Ernst Ottensamer (cl) *(rec House of Arts, Košice)* Naxos ▲ 8.550688 [DDD]
Spohr, L.:Con 3 Cl, w. Ernst Ottensamer (cl) *(rec House of Arts, Košice)* Naxos ▲ 8.550688 [DDD]
Slovak SO
A. Nanut (cnd)
Smith, Hale:Innerflexions CRI ▲ CD 590 [DDD]
Slovenian PO
M. Hrvat (cnd)
Dvořák, A.:Sym 9, "From the New World" Stradivari Classics ▲ SCD 6030 [DDD] ■ SMC 6030 (D)
The Great Symphonies, w. Ljubljana SO [cnd:Anton Nanut], Slovak PO [cnd:Libor Pešek], Royal PO [cnd:Kurt Redel] Stradivari Classics ("Treasury of Great Classics" series) 5-▲ S5D 6082 [DDD] 5-■ S5C 6082 (D)
Slovenian Radio Jazz Quintet
V. Globokar (cnd)
Globokar, V.:Hallo, Do You Hear Me?, w. Slovenian RSO, Ljubljana Apz Tone Tomšič Chorus Harmonia Mundi France ▲ HMC 90933
Slovenian RSO
P. Freeman (cnd)
Bartók, B.:Con Va, w. M. Thompson (va) Centaur ▲ CRC 2150
Bloch, E.:Suite Va & Pno, w. M. Thompson (va) Centaur ▲ CRC 2150
Kabalevsky, D.:Con 3 Pno, w. J. Johnson (pno) Centaur ▲ CRC 2089 [DDD]
Muczynski, R.:Con 1 Pno, w. J. Johnson (pno) Centaur ▲ CRC 2089 [DDD]
V. Globokar (cnd)
Globokar, V.:Hallo, Do You Hear Me?, w. Slovenian Radio Jazz Quintet, Ljubljana Apz Tone Tomšič Chorus Harmonia Mundi France ▲ HMC 90933
Slovenian Radio-TV Orch
A. Nanut (cnd)
Casella, A.:Partita, w. J. Pierce (pno) *(rec Apr. 10–11, 1991)* Phoenix ▲ PHCD 124 [DDD]
Rachmaninoff, S.:Rhapsody on a Theme of Paganini, w. J. Pierce (pno) *(rec Apr. 10–11, 1991)* Phoenix ▲ PHCD 124 [DDD]
Respighi, O.:Toccata Pno, w. J. Pierce (pno) *(rec Apr. 10–11, 1991)* Phoenix ▲ PHCD 124 [DDD]
Slovenian SO
Arutiunian, A.:Con Tpt, w. Stanko Praprotnik (tpt) Audiophile Classics ▲ 101.040 [DDD]

ORCH. & ENS.

Slovenian SO (cont.)
Górecki, H.–M.:Sym 3, "Sym of Sorrowful Songs", w. Luisa Castellani (sop) Audiophile Classics ▲ 101.040 [DDD]
Smetana String Quartet
Dvořák, A.:Qt 12 Strs, "America" *(rec 1966)* Testament ▲ SBT 1074
Dvořák, A.:Qt 14 Strs *(rec 1967)* Testament ▲ SBT 1075
Dvořák, A.:Qnt Pno, Op. 5, w. J. Panenka (pno) Supraphon ▲ 10 4115-2 [DDD]
Dvořák, A.:Qnt Pno, Op. 81, w. J. Panenka (pno) Supraphon ▲ 10 4115-2 [DDD]
Dvořák, A.:Qnt Pno, Op. 81, w. Pavel Štěpán (pno) *(rec 1966)* Testament ▲ SBT 1074
Dvořák, A.:Qnt Strs, Op. 97, w. J. Suk (va) Supraphon ▲ SUP 111469 [DDD]
Dvořák, A.:Sextet, w. J. Suk (va), J. Schuchro (vc) Supraphon ▲ SUP 111469 [DDD]
Dvořák, A.:Terzetto *(rec 1966)* Testament ▲ SBT 1075
The 50th Anniversary of the Smetana Quartet Supraphon 6–▲ SUP 0076 [AAD/DDD]
Janáček, L.:Qt 1 Strs *(rec 1965)* Testament ▲ SBT 1074
Janáček, L.:Qt 2 Strs *(rec 1965)* Testament ▲ SBT 1075
Mendelssohn, F.:Octet Strs, w. Janáček String Quartet Supraphon Collection ▲ 11 0648-2 [ADD]
Mozart, W.A.:Qt 14 Strs Denon ▲ CO 1582 [DDD]
Mozart, W.A.:Qt 16 Strs Denon ▲ CO 1582 [DDD]
Schubert, Franz:Qt 10 Strs Denon/PCM Digital ▲ DEN 7546 [DDD]
Schubert, Franz:Qt 14 Strs Denon/PCM Digital ▲ DEN 7546 [DDD]
Smetana String Quartet Soloists
Brahms, J.:Sextet Strs, Op. 36, w. Kocian String Quartet Denon ▲ CO 2141 [DDD]
Smith String Quartet
Fitkin, G.:Frame, w. G. Fitkin (kbd), S. Sutherland (kbd) Argo ▲ 433690-2 [DDD]
Fitkin, G.:Huah, w. G. Fitkin (kbd), S. Sutherland (kbd) Argo ▲ 433690-2 [DDD]
Fitkin, G.:Slow, w. G. Fitkin (kbd), S. Sutherland (kbd) Argo ▲ 433690-2 [DDD]
Martland, S.:Patrol Catalyst ▲ 09026-62670-2 ■ 09026-62670-4
K. Jenkins (cnd)
Jenkins, K.:Music of, w. London PO—Diamond Music (Palladio); Adiemus Variations; Passacaglia (In memoriam Evelyn Mary Hopkins:1903–1995); Qt 2 Strs Sony Classical ▲ SK 62276 ■ ST 62276
Smith String Quartet [Ian Humphries (vn), Clive Hughes (vn), Nic Pendlebury (va), Deirdre Cooper (vc)]
Gough, O.:Late, w. Roger Heaton (cl), Melinda Maxwell (ob), Orlando Gough (kbd) *(rec London, 1995)* Catalyst ▲ 0902-668332-2 [DDD]
Smith String Quartet [Steve Smith (vn), Clive Hughes (vn), Nic Pendlebury (va), Sophie Harris (vc)]
Volans, K.:White Man Sleeps *(rec West German Radio, Cologne & Watershed Recording Studio, London)* United ▲ CAL 88034 [ADD]
Smithson String Quartet
Beethoven, L. van:Qts Strs (misc)—Op. 18, Nos. 1–6 [period instrs] Smithsonian Collection 6–▲ ND 0320
Mozart, W.A.:Kleine Nachtmusik, w. R. Myron (db) [period instrs] Smithsonian Collection ▲ ND 039
Mozart, W.A.:Kleine Nachtmusik, w. R. Myron (db) [period instrs] Smithsonian Collection 5–▲ ND 031
Mozart, W.A.:Musikalischer Spass [period instrs] Smithsonian Collection 5–▲ ND 031
Mozart, W.A.:Musikalischer Spass [period instrs] Smithsonian Collection ▲ ND 039
Mozart, W.A.:Qt 14 Strs Virgin Classics ▲ CDC 45029
Mozart, W.A.:Qt 15 Strs Virgin Classics ▲ CDC 45029
Mozart, W.A.:Qt 20 Strs [period instrs] Smithsonian Collection 5–▲ ND 031
Mozart, W.A.:Qnt Cl, K.581, w. L. McDonald (cl) [period instrs] Smithsonian Collection 5–▲ ND 031
Smithsonian CO
Mozart, W.A.:Serenade Vn, K.204, w. J. Schröder (vn) [period instrs] Smithsonian Collection 5–▲ ND 031
J. Schröder (cnd)
Beethoven, L. van:Sym 1 [period instrs] Smithsonian Collection 6–▲ ND 0320
Beethoven, L. van:Sym 2 [period instrs] Smithsonian Collection 6–▲ ND 0320
Beethoven, L. van:Sym 3, "Eroica" [period instrs] Smithsonian Collection 6–▲ ND 0320
Mozart, W.A.:Music of, w. Smithsonian String Quartet—Con. in A for Clarinet, K.622; Concertone in C for 2 Violins, K.166b; Ein musikalischer Spass, K.522; Qt. No. 1 for Flute & Strings, K.285; Qt. No. 20 in D for Strings; Qts. for Piano & Strings, K.478 & 493; Qnt. in A for Clarinet & Strings, K.581; Qnt. in E♭ for Horn & Strings, K.407; Serenade, K.204 in D, K.213a; Eine kleine Nachtmusik in G, K.525; Sinf. concertante, K.364; Trio in E♭ for Clarinet, Viola & Piano, K.498 Smithsonian Collection 5–■ NC 031
Mozart, W.A.:Sinf concertante Vn, K.364, w. J. Schroeder (vn), M. McDonald (va) [period instrs] Smithsonian Collection 5–▲ ND 031
Smithsonian Chamber Players
Boccherini, L.:Qnts Strs—3 Quintets—Op. 11, Nos. 4–6 Deutsche Harmonia Mundi ▲ 05472-77159-2
Brahms, J.:Sextet Strs, Op. 18, w. Anner Bylsma (vc), L'Archibudelli Sony Classical ("Vivarte" series) ▲ SK 68252
Brahms, J.:Sextet Strs, Op. 36, w. Anner Bylsma (vc), L'Archibudelli Sony Classical ("Vivarte" series) ▲ SK 68252
Couperin, F.:Concerts royaux (4) Deutsche Harmonia Mundi ▲ 05472-77327-2
Couperin, F.:Pièces de clavecin (sels) [performed on 2 harpsichords] Deutsche Harmonia Mundi ▲ 05472-77327-2
Gade, N.W.:Octet, w. L'Archibudelli Sony Classical ("Vivarte" series) ▲ SK 48307
Mendelssohn, F.:Octet Strs, w. L'Archibudelli Sony Classical ("Vivarte" series) ▲ SK 48307
Onslow, G.:Qnts (34) Strs, w. L'Archibudelli—in c, Op. 38 [The Bullet]; in E, Op. 39; in b, Op. 40 Sony Classical ("Vivarte" series) ▲ SK 64308
Spohr, L.:Double Qt 1, w. L'Archibudelli *(rec Jan. 21–24, 1993)* Sony Classical ▲ SK 53370 [DDD]
Spohr, L.:Qnts Strs, Op. 33, w. L'Archibudelli—in G *(rec Jan. 21–24, 1993)* Sony Classical ▲ SK 53370 [DDD]
Spohr, L.:Sxt Strs, w. L'Archibudelli *(rec Jan. 21–24, 1993)* Sony Classical ▲ SK 53370 [DDD]
Sweet Was The Song, w. Max Van Egmond (bass), [period instrs] Smithsonian Collection ▲ SMI ND 040
K. Slowik (cnd)
Bach, J.S.:St. John Passion, w. J. Baird (sop), J. Bryden (sop), J. Thomas (ten), D. Ripley (bar), J. Weaver (bass), Smithsonian Chamber Chorus [period instrs] [G] *(Slowik performs the original 1724 version, & includes the two choruses & three arias added to Bach's 1725 revision as appended tracks at the end of the discs, allowing the listener to either ignore the end tracks & hear the standard version or program the discs to play the 1725 sequence)* Smithsonian Collection 5–▲ ND 0380 [DDD]
Bach, J.S.:St. John Passion, w. J. Baird (sop), J. Bryden (sop), J. Thomas (ten), D. Ripley (bar), J. Weaver (bass), Smithsonian Chamber Chorus [period instrs] [G] Smithsonian Collection 2–▲ ND 0381 [DDD]
Barber, S.:Adagio Strs *(rec Purchase, NY, Oct. 18–20, 1994)* Deutsche Harmonia Mundi ▲ 05472-77343-2 [DDD]
Elgar, E.:Elegy Strs *(rec Purchase, NY, Oct. 18–20, 1994)* Deutsche Harmonia Mundi ▲ 05472-77343-2 [DDD]
Elgar, E.:Serenade Strs *(rec Purchase, NY, Oct. 18–20, 1994)* Deutsche Harmonia Mundi ▲ 05472-77343-2 [DDD]
Mahler, G.:Qt Strs *(rec Performing Arts Center, SUNY, Purchase, New York, Nov 28–Dec 1, 1995)* Deutsche Harmonia Mundi ▲ 05472-77374-2 [DDD]
Mahler, G.:Sym 5—Adagietto *(rec Performing Arts Center, SUNY, Purchase, New York, Nov 28–Dec 1, 1995)* Deutsche Harmonia Mundi ▲ 05472-77374-2 [DDD]
Schoenberg, A.:Verklärte Nacht *(rec Performing Arts Center, SUNY, Purchase, New York, Nov 28–Dec 1, 1995)* Deutsche Harmonia Mundi ▲ 05472-77374-2 [DDD]
Strauss, R.:Metamorphosen *(rec Purchase, NY, Oct. 18–20, 1994)* Deutsche Harmonia Mundi ▲ 05472-77343-2 [DDD]
Smithsonian Chamber Players [J. Schröder (vn), M. McDonald (vn), K. Slowik (vc), K. Junghänel (thb), J. Weaver (org)]
Corelli, A.:Trio Sons, Op. 3 [period instrs] Smithsonian Collection ▲ ND-035 [DDD]
Smithsonian Chamber Players [Kenneth Slowik (vl), Jaap Ter Linden (vl), Konrad Junghänel (thb)]
Marais, M.:Pièces for 2 Vls—Two Suites & Tombau Deutsche Harmonia Mundi ▲ 77146-2-RC [DDD]
Smithsonian Concerto Grosso
A. Dorati (cnd)
Handel, G.F.:Messiah, w. Edith Mathis (sop), James Bowman (alt), Claes Hakan Ahnsjö (ten), Richard Krause (ten), Univ of Maryland Choral Society [E] Pro Arte 2–▲ CDD 232 [DDD]; ■ PCD 232
Handel, G.F.:Music of, w. N. Simpson, Royal Promenade CO, Univ of Maryland Chorus—Royal Fireworks Music; Water Music Suite; Messiah (sels.); etc. Pro Arte ▲ CDM 810; ■ PCD 810
Smithsonian Quartet
J. Schröder (cnd)
Mozart, W.A.:Music of, w. Smithsonian CO—Con. in A for Clarinet, K.622; Concertone in C for 2 Violins, K.166b; Ein musikalischer Spass, K.522; Qt. No. 1 for Flute & Strings, K.285; Qt. No. 20 in D for Strings; Qts. for Piano & Strings, K.478 & 493; Qnt. in A for Clarinet & Strings, K.581; Qnt. in E♭ for Horn & Strings, K.407; Serenade, K.204 in D, K.213a; Eine kleine Nachtmusik in G, K.525; Sinf. concertante, K.364; Trio in E♭ for Clarinet, Viola & Piano, K.498 Smithsonian Collection 5–■ NC 031
Ethel Smyth Ensemble
J. Schmeller (cnd)
Smyth, E.:Songs (4) Mez, w. M. Petersen (mez) *(rec 1992)* Troubadisc ▲ TRO CD 01405 [DDD]
Société des Concerts du Conservatoire Orch—see Paris Conservatory Société des Concerts Orch
Society for New Music
Caltabiano, Godfrey, Murray (cnd)
Wagner, M.:Sextet Opus One ▲ CD 168
Murray (cnd)
Catabiano, R.:Torched Liberty Opus One ▲ CD 168
Society of Composers, Inc.
Potpurri Capstone ▲ CPS 8609
View from the Keyboard Capstone ▲ CPS 8606
Sofia Camerata Classica
I. Kozhouharov (cnd)
Albinoni, T.:Cons Obs, w. L. Oshavkova (fl)—in G Divertimento ▲ DIV 41001 [DDD]
Beethoven, L. van:Die Geschöpfe des Prometheus Divertimento ▲ DIV 41002 [DDD]
Benda, F.:Con in e Fl & Orch, w. L. Oshavkova (fl) Divertimento ▲ DIV 41001 [DDD]
Boccherini, L.:Con in D Fl [attrib], w. L. Oshavkova (fl) Divertimento ▲ DIV 41001 [DDD]
Mercadante, S.:Cons (6) Fl (1819), w. L. Oshavkova (fl)—in e Divertimento ▲ DIV 41001 [DDD]
Sofia CO
V. Kazandjiev (cnd)
Dvořák, A.:Serenade Strs Denon ▲ CO 8002 [DDD]
Tchaikovsky, P.:Serenade Strs Denon ▲ CO 8002 [DDD]
Sofia CO Soloists
Kralev, Kazandjiev (cnd)
Monteverdi, C.:Madrigals, w. Madrigal Chamber Ensemble, Bodra-Smyana Children's Choir—Ogni Amante e Guerrier; Si, Si Ch'io V'Amo; O Come Vaghi; O Viva Fiamma; Io Son Pur Vezzosetta Pastorella; Ardo e Scoprir; Chiomo d'Oro; Baci Soavi e Cari; Bel Pastor [Dialogo di Ninfa e Pastore] Forlane ▲ FRL 16546 [DDD/AAD]
Tabakov, Kralev (cnd)
Bach, J.S.:Christmas Oratorio, w. Ludmila Hadjieva (sop), Roumiana Tzatcheva (alt), Lubomir Diacovski (ten), Plamen Hidjov (bass), Madrigal Chamber Ensemble Pentagon 3–▲ 302 [DDD]
Sofia Festival Orch
J. Kovatchev (cnd)
Tchaikovsky, P.:Capriccio italien RS Prestige 6–▲ 6367-60/65
Tchaikovsky, P.:Con Vn, w. Vanya Milanova (vn) RS Prestige ▲ 951-0066 [DDD]
Tchaikovsky, P.:Francesca da Rimini RS Prestige 6–▲ 6367-60/65
Tchaikovsky, P.:Nutcracker Suite RS Prestige 6–▲ 6367-60/65
Tchaikovsky, P.:Ov 1812 RS Prestige 6–▲ 6367-60/65
Tchaikovsky, P.:Romeo & Juliet RS Prestige 6–▲ 6367-60/65
Tchaikovsky, P.:Sérénade mélancolique, w. Vanya Milanova (vn) RS Prestige ▲ 951-0066 [DDD]
Tchaikovsky, P.:Syms (comp) RS Prestige 6–▲ 6367-60/65
Tchaikovsky, P.:The Tempest RS Prestige 6–▲ 6367-60/65
E. Tchakarov (cnd)
Borodin, A.:Prince Igor, w. S. Evstatieva (sop), A. Milcheva (mez), B. Martinovich (b-bar), N. Ghiaurov (bass), N. Ghiuselev (bass), Sofia National Opera Chorus [R] Sony Classical 3–▲ S3K 44878 [DDD]
Glinka, M.:A Life for the Tsar, w. A. Pendachanska (sop), S. Toczyska (mez), C. Merritt (ten), B. Martinovich (bass), Sofia National Opera Chorus [R] Sony Classical 3–▲ S3K 46487 [DDD]
Mussorgsky, M.:Boris Godunov, w. S. Mineva (mez—Marina), M. Svetlev (ten—Gregory), N. Ghiaurov (bass—Boris), N. Ghiuselev (bass—Pimen), Sofia National Opera Chorus [R] Sony Classical ("Russian Opera" series) 3–▲ S3K 45763
Tchaikovsky, P.:Eugene Onegin, w. A. Tomowa-Sintow (sop), R. Troava-Mircheva (cta), N. Gedda (ten), Y. Mazurok (bar), N. Ghiuselev (bass), Sofia National Opera Chorus [R] Sony Classical 2–▲ S2K 45539 [DDD]
Tchaikovsky, P.:Queen of Spades, w. S. Evstatieva (sop), P. Dilova (mez), I. Konsulov (bar), Mazulok (bass), Bulgarian National Chorus [R] Sony Classical 3–▲ S3K 45720
Sofia Madrigal Ensemble
S. Kralev (cnd)
Monteverdi, C.:Madrigals, w. V. Kissyova (sop), N. Pankova (sop), A. Bovarian (alt), V. Vassilev (ten), K. Mirinski (bass)—Psalmus 121, "Laetatus sum"; Batto qui pianse; Chiome d'oro; Amor che deggio far?; O come sei gentile; Psalmus 147, "Lauda Jerusalem" Gega ▲ GD 174 [DDD]
Sofia National Opera Orch
Vol. 4, Classics Go to the Movies, w. Budapest SO, Budapest PO, Salzburg Mozarteum Orch, Christian Altenburger, Ernst Mayer-Schieming, German Bach Soloists LaserLight ▲ 15 644
D. Manolov (cnd)
Rimsky-Korsakov, N.:Golden Cockerel, w. Yavora Stoilova (sop—Golden Cockerel), Elena Stoyanova (sop—Queen), Evgenia Babacheva (mez—Amelfa), Lyubomir Bodourov (ten—Prince), Lyubomir Dyakovski (ten—Astrologer), Emil Ugrinov (bar—Afron), Nikolai Stoilov (bass—Tsar), Kosta Videv (bass—Polkan), Sofia National Opera Chorus *(rec Sofia, 1985)* Capriccio 2–▲ 10760/61 [DDD]
B. Spassov (cnd)
Minkus, L.:Ballets, w. Anna Takova-Baynova (vn), Valentina Raicheva (hp)—La bayadère (sels.) (1877); Paquita (complete) (1846) *(rec Studio I, Bulgarian National Radio, Sofia, Feb 1994)* Capriccio ▲ 10 544 [DDD]
E. Tchakarov (cnd)
Mussorgsky, M.:Khovanshchina, w. A. Miltcheva (mez), M. Popov (ten), K. Kaludov (ten), Z. Gadjev (bass), N. Ghiaurov (bass), N. Ghiuselev (bass), Sofia National Opera Chorus Sony Classical 3–▲ S3K 45831
P. Tiboris (cnd)
Verdi, G.:Requiem Mass, w. Maria Belcheva (sop), Stefka Mineva (mez), Roumen Doykov (ten), Dimiter Petkov (bass), Sofia National Opera Chorus *(rec Bulgarian National Radio Studio, Mar 14–17, 1994)* Elysium ▲ GRK 708 [DDD]
Sofia New Chamber Ensemble
I. Kozhouharov (cnd)
Mozart, W.A.:Con Fl Hp, w. L. Oshavkova (fl), C. Antonelli (hp) Divertimento ▲ DIV 31020 [DDD]
Sofia Orch Ensemble
B. Papazian (cnd)
Mozart, W.A.:Cons Hn, w. D. Bourgue (hn) Arion ▲ ARN 68198 [DDD]
Mozart, W.A.:Rondo Hn, K.371, w. D. Bourgue (hn) Arion ▲ ARN 68198 [DDD]

378 ▲ = CD ♦ = Enhanced CD Δ = MD ■ = Cassette Tape □ = DCC

Sofia Orch Ensemble (cont.)
B. Papazian (cnd) (cont.)
Mozart, W.A.:Rondo Hn, K.514 (compl'd Jeurissen), w. D. Bourgue (hn) Arion ▲ ARN 68198 [DDD]
Sofia Orthodox Ensemble
M. Popsavov (cnd)
Mystery of the East:Music from Russian Churches & Monasteries, w. Rybin Choir Moscow, Bulgarian National Choir [cnd:Georgi Robev] Capriccio ▲ 10 597 [DDD]
Sofia PO
Vol. 5, Classics Go to the Movies, w. Hannes Käster (org), Salzburg Mozarteum Orch, Bavarian RSO, Ludovic Spiess (ten), Virginia Zeani (sop), Rumanian Opera Orch, Rumanian Radio-TV Studio Orch, Budapest SO, Philharmonia Orch LaserLight ▲ 15 645
G. Bellini (cnd)
Puccini, G.:Madama Butterfly, w. Raina Kabaivanska (sop—Madama Butterfly), Alexandrina Milcheva (mez—Suzuki), Rossitza Troeva-Mircheva (cta—Kate Pinkerton), Nazzareno Antinori (ten—F.B. Pinkerton), Roumen Doikov (ten—Goro), Werther Vrachovski (ten—Il Principe Yamadori), Nelson Portella (bar—Sharpless), Kosta Dinkov (bass—Lo zio Bonzo), Svetoslav Obrenetov Bulgarian National Chorus *(rec Sophia, Bulgaria, Dec 1-13, 1982)* Arts Music 2-▲ 447161-2 [DDD]
Puccini, G.:Tosca, w. Raina Kabaivanska (sop—Floria Tosca), Nazzareno Antinori (ten—Mario Cavaradossi), Roumen Doikov (ten—Spoletta), Enzo Dara (bar—Casare Angelotti/Il sagrestano), Nelson Portella (bar—Il Barone Scarpia), Stoyan Balabanov (bass—Sciarrone/Un carceriere), Borislav Peev (sgr—Un Pastore), Bulgarian National Radio Children's Choir, Svetoslav Obrenetov Bulgarian National Chorus *(rec Sophia, Bulgaria, Nov 14-27, 1982)* Arts Music ▲ 47158-2 [DDD]
Y. Davov (cnd)
Haydn, J.:Con Hpd & Strs, H.XVIII/4, w. Nikolai Evrov (pno) Vivace ▲ E 569 [ADD]
Haydn, J.:Con Hpd, Obs, Hns & Strs, H.XVIII/11, w. Nikolai Evrov (pno) Vivace ▲ E 569 [ADD]
B. Fidetzis (cnd)
Kalomiris, M.:Sym 1, w. Bulgarian National Chorus Orata ▲ ORAML 62
Petridis, P.:Con grosso Ww, w. Bulgarian National Chorus Orata ▲ ORAML 62
R. Georgescu (cnd)
Waldrop, G.:Music of—Suite for Orch.:"From the Southwest" (1964); Pressures (1955); Prelude & Fugue (1963); "Songs of the Southwest" (1983) Gega ▲ GD 155 [DDD]
Waldrop, G.:Sym 1 Gega ▲ GD 155 [DDD]
V. Ghiaurov (cnd)
Tchaikovsky, P.:Sym 4 LaserLight ▲ 14 014 [DDD]
R. Raichev (cnd)
Verdi, G.:Arias, w. Anna Tomowa-Sintow (sop)—Air de Leonore [from Act 4 of La forza del destino]; Airs d'Aida [from Scenes 1 & 5 for Aida]; Willow Song; Ave Maria [both from Othello]; Air de Abigail [from Nabucco]; Récitatif et cavatine d'Elvire [from Hernani]; Scène et air de Violetta; Air de Violetta [both from La traviata] Forlane ▲ FRL 10506 [AAD]
G. Robev (cnd)
Mascagni, P.:Cavalleria rusticana (sels), w. Bulgarian National Chorus—Easterchorus Forlane ▲ FRL 16668 [ADD]
Orff, C.:Carmina burana, w. R. Bareva (sop), H. Kamenov (ten), Yanukov (bar), Bulgarian choirs [G, L] Forlane ▲ FOR 16556 [DDD]
Puccini, G.:Tosca (sels), w. Bulgarian National Chorus Forlane ▲ FRL 16668 [ADD]
Verdi, G.:Aida (sels), w. Bulgarian National Chorus—Triumphal March Forlane ▲ FRL 16668 [ADD]
Verdi, G.:Don Carlos (sels), w. Bulgarian National Chorus—Act 3 Finale Forlane ▲ FRL 16668 [ADD]
Verdi, G.:La forza del destino (sels), w. Bulgarian National Chorus Forlane ▲ FRL 16668 [ADD]
Verdi, G.:Nabucco (sels), w. Bulgarian National Chorus—Chorus of the Hebrew Slaves Forlane ▲ FRL 16668 [ADD]
Verdi, G.:La traviata (sels), w. Bulgarian National Chorus—Matadore Chorus; Gypsies Chorus Forlane ▲ FRL 16668 [ADD]
Verdi, G.:Il trovatore (sels), w. Bulgarian National Chorus—Bohemian Chorus Forlane ▲ FRL 16668 [ADD]
Wagner, R.:Lohengrin (sels), w. Bulgarian National Chorus—Bride-Chorus Forlane ▲ FRL 16668 [ADD]
Wagner, R.:Tannhäuser (sels), w. Bulgarian National Chorus—Entrance of the Knights Forlane ▲ FRL 16668 [ADD]
Weber, C.M. von:Der Freischütz (sels), w. Bulgarian National Chorus—The Hunters' Chorus Forlane ▲ FRL 16668 [ADD]
E. Tabakov (cnd)
Beethoven, L. van:Con 1 Pno, w. A. Dikov (pno) LaserLight ▲ 15 626 [DDD]
Beethoven, L. van:Con 2 Pno, w. A. Dikov (pno) LaserLight ▲ 15 626 [DDD]
Beethoven, L. van:Con 3 Pno, w. A. Dikov (pno) LaserLight ▲ 15 627 [DDD]
Beethoven, L. van:Con 4 Pno, w. A. Dikov (pno) LaserLight ▲ 15 627 [DDD]
Beethoven, L. van:Con 5 Pno, "Emperor", w. A. Dikov (pno) Capriccio ▲ 10 911 [DDD]
Beethoven, L. van:Con 5 Pno, "Emperor", w. A. Dikov (pno) Laserlight ▲ 15 523 [DDD]
Beethoven, L. van:Con 5 Pno, "Emperor", w. A. Dikov (pno) LaserLight ▲ 15 628 [DDD]
Beethoven, L. van:Fant Pno, Op. 80, "Choral Fant", w. A. Dikov (pno) Capriccio ▲ 10 911 [DDD]
Beethoven, L. van:Music of, w. London SO [cnd:Alfred Scholz] Laserlight ♦ 90020 [DDD]
Grieg, E.:Con Pno, Op. 16, w. S. Rodriguez (pno) Élan ▲ CD 2228 [DDD]
Liszt, F.:Con 1 Pno, w. S. Rodriguez (pno) Élan ▲ CD 2228 [DDD]
Mahler, G.:Sym 1 *(rec Bulgarian Concert Hall, Sofia, Mar 1989)* Capriccio 15-▲ 49043 [DDD]
Mahler, G.:Sym 2, w. Tiha Genova (sop), Vessela Zorova (alt), Bulgarian National Chorus *(rec Bulgarian Concert Hall, Sofia, Jan 1987)* Capriccio 15-▲ 49043 [DDD]
Mahler, G.:Sym 3, w. Brigitte Pretschner (alt), Bulgarian National Chorus, Bodra Smyana Children's Choir *(rec Bulgarian Concert Hall, Sofia, Apr 1990)* Capriccio 15-▲ 49043 [DDD]
Mahler, G.:Sym 4, w. Lyudmila Hadzhieva (sop) *(rec Bulgarian Concert Hall, Sofia, Jan 1990)* Capriccio 15-▲ 49043 [DDD]
Mahler, G.:Sym 5 *(rec Bulgarian Concert Hall, Sofia, Oct 1988)* Capriccio 15-▲ 49043 [DDD]
Mahler, G.:Sym 6 *(rec Bulgarian Concert Hall, Sofia, Oct 1993)* Capriccio 15-▲ 49043 [DDD]
Mahler, G.:Sym 7 *(rec Bulgarian Concert Hall, Sofia, Oct 1989)* Capriccio 15-▲ 49043 [DDD]
Mahler, G.:Sym 8, w. Lyudmila Hadzhieva (sop), Maria Temeshi (sop), Darina Takova (sop), Tamara Takac (alt), Boryana Tabakova (alt), Janos Bandi (ten), Pal Kovacs (bar), Tamash Syule (bass), Bulgarian National Chorus, Bulgarian National Radio Chorus, Bulgarian National Radio Children's Choir *(rec National Palace of Culture, Sofia, June 1991)* Capriccio 15-▲ 49043 [DDD]
Mahler, G.:Sym 9 *(rec Bulgarian Concert Hall, Sofia, Mar 1991)* Capriccio 15-▲ 49043 [DDD]
Mahler, G.:Sym 10 *(rec Bulgarian Concert Hall, Sofia, Apr 1987)* Capriccio 15-▲ 49043 [DDD]
Prokofiev, S.:Con 3 Pno, w. S. Rodriguez (pno) Élan ▲ CD 2220 [DDD]
Rachmaninoff, S.:Con 3 Pno, w. S. Rodriguez (pno) Élan ▲ CD 2220 [DDD]
Shostakovich, D.:Con 1 Vc, w. N. Rosen (vc) John Marks ▲ JMR 3
Stravinsky, I.:The Firebird Suite Gega ▲ GD 102 [DDD]
Tabakov, E.:Con Orch Gega ▲ GD 102 [DDD]
Tabakov, E.:Con for 15 Strs, w. Sofia Soloists CO Élan ▲ CD 2230 [DDD/ADD]
Tchaikovsky, P.:Con 1 Pno, w. S. Rodriguez (pno) Élan ▲ CD 2228 [DDD]
Tchaikovsky, P.:Pezzo capriccioso, w. N. Rosen (vc) John Marks ▲ JMR 3
Tchaikovsky, P.:Vars on a Rococo Theme, w. N. Rosen (vc) John Marks ▲ JMR 3
N. Uljanov (cnd)
Scriabin, A.:Con Pno, w. Evelyne Dubourg (pno) Tudor ▲ TUD 7025 [DDD]
Scriabin, A.:Sym 5 Tudor ▲ TUD 7025 [DDD]
V. Yampolsky (cnd)
Beethoven, L. van:Con Vn, Op. 61, w. N. Gotkovsky (vn) Pyramid ▲ PYR 13499 [DDD]
Berg, A.:Con Vn, w. N. Gotkovsky (vn) Pyramid ▲ PYR 13499 [DDD]
Sofia RSO
V. Kazandjiew (cnd)
Wagner, R:Music of, w. Budapest SO [cnd:György Lehel] Laserlight ♦ 90028 [DDD]
Sofia Solisti
P. Djurov (cnd)
From Yesterday to Penny Lane, w. Carlos Barbosa-Lima (gtr), Sofia Soloists Concord Concerto ▲ CCD 42041 [DDD]

Sofia Solisti (cont.)
E. Tabakov (cnd)
Stamitz, C.:Sinf Concertante, w. M. Minchev (vn), C. Paskalev (va) Vivace ▲ E 576 [ADD]
Sofia Solisti CO
Schütz, H.:Motets (misc), w. Madrigal Chamber Ensemble, Bodra-Smyana Children's Choir—Herr, Wenn ich Nur Dich Habe; Herr, Nun Lässest du Deiner in Frieden fahren Forlane ▲ FRL 16546 [DDD/AAD]
Schütz, H.:Musicalische Exequien, w. Madrigal Chamber Ensemble, Bodra-Smyana Children's Choir Forlane ▲ FRL 16546 [DDD/AAD]
G. Ben-Dor (cnd)
Bartók, B.:Divert Centaur ▲ 2239
Bartók, B.:For Children [trans. Rudolph Maros, Mihaly Horvath & Leo Weiner for str Orch] Centaur ▲ 2239
Bartók, B.:Romanian Folk Dances Pno [arr. Arthur Willner for str Orch] Centaur ▲ 2239
P. Djurov (cnd)
Bach, J.S.:Brandenberg Con 5, w. João Carlos Martins (pno), Lydia Oshavkova (fl), Liudmil Nenchev (vn) *(rec Salle Bulgaria, Sofia, Bulgaria, 1996)* Concord Concerto ▲ CCD 42042 [DDD]
Bach, J.S.:Con 2 Hpd, w. João Carlos Martins (pno) *(rec Salle Bulgaria, Sofia, Bulgaria, 1996)* Concord Concerto ▲ CCD 42042 [DDD]
Bach, J.S.:Con 4 Hpd, w. João Carlos Martins (pno) *(rec Salle Bulgaria, Sofia, Bulgaria, 1996)* Concord Concerto ▲ CCD 42042 [DDD]
V. Kazandjiev (cnd)
Schubert, Franz:Mass 2, w. E. Maksimova (sop), H. Kamenov (ten), I. Dobrev (bass), Rodina Chorus [L] Musique d'Abord ▲ HMA 190111 [AAD]
E. Tabakov (cnd)
Mozart, W.A.:Sinf concertante Vn, K.364, w. M. Minchev (vn), C. Paskalev (va) Vivace ▲ E 576 [ADD]
Mozart, W.A.:Sinf concertante Vn, K.364, w. M. Minchev (vn), C. Paskalev (va) Vivace 3-▲ E 316 [DDD]
Scriabin, A.:Sym 2 Élan ▲ CD 2230 [DDD/ADD]
Shostakovich, D.:Con 1 Vc, w. V. Spanoghe (vc) *(rec 1984)* Talent ▲ DOM 2910 11 [AAD]
Shostakovich, D.:Con 2 Vc, w. V. Spanoghe (vc) *(rec 1984)* Talent ▲ DOM 2910 11 [AAD]
Tabakov, E.:Con for 15 Strs, Sofia PO Élan ▲ CD 2230 [DDD/ADD]
Sofia State PO
C. Iliev (cnd)
Beethoven, L. van:Mass, Op. 86, w. Sofia State Chorus [L] Vivace ▲ E 567 [ADD]
Beethoven, L. van:Mass, Op. 86, w. E. Markova (sop), L. Parachikova (cta), C. Kamenev (ten), I. Petrov (bass), Sofia State Chorus [L] Musique d'Abord ▲ HMA 190109 [AAD]
I. Marinov (cnd)
Verdi, G.:Requiem Mass, w. Wiener-Chenisheva (sop), A. Milcheva-Nonova (mez), L. Bodourov (ten), N. Ghiuselev (bass), Sofia State Chorus [L] Vivace 3-▲ E 326 [ADD]
Sofia String Quartet
Borodin, A.:Qt 1 Strs *(rec Bulgaria Concert Hall Jan. 1992)* Gega ▲ GD 127 [DDD]
Borodin, A.:Qt 2 Strs Gega ▲ GD 127 [DDD]
Borodin, A.:Serenata alla spagnola Gega ▲ GD 127 [DDD]
Shostakovich, D.:Qt 8 Strs Gega ▲ GD 168 [DDD]
Shostakovich, D.:Qt 10 Strs Gega ▲ GD 168 [DDD]
Shostakovich, D.:Qt 11 Strs Gega ▲ GD 168 [DDD]
Sofia SO
Gounod, C.:Faust (sels), w. Alexandrina Pendachanska (sop—Margarethe), Giuseppe Sabbatini (ten—Faust), György Melis (bar—Valentin), Nicolai Ghiaurov (bass—Méphistophélès), Nikola Ghiuselev (bass—Méphistophélès), Berlin RSO, Vienna SO, Hungarian State Opera Orch, Bulgarian RSO, Bulgarian National Chorus, Bulgarian National Chorus Radio Choir—Intro; Vien ou bière; O sainte médaille...Avant de quitter ces lieux; Le veau d'or [all from Act 2]; Quel trouble inconnu me pénètre!...Salut! demeure chaste et pure; Je voudrais bien savoir...Il était un roi de Thule; Un bouquet!...O Dieu! que de bijoux [both from Act 3]; Gloire immortelle de nos aieux; Vous qui faites l'endormie [both from Act 4]; Intermezzo; Walpurgis Night [both from Act 5] Laserlight ▲ 14209 [DDD]
E. Lanev (cnd)
Bach, J.S.:Christmas Oratorio (sels), w. Sofia Sym Chorus RS Applausi ▲ 6367-220
Famous Opera Arias, w. Emil Ivanov (ten) Gega ▲ 190
I. Marinov (cnd)
Khachaturian, A.:Con Vn, w. Arusjak Baltanjan (vn) Audiophile Classics ▲ 101.049
Khachaturian, A.:Masquerade (ballet suite) Audiophile Classics ▲ 101.049
Khachaturian, A.:Spartacus (suites 1-3) Audiophile Classics ▲ 101.050 [DDD]
Nicola Ghiuselev, w. Nicola Ghiuselev (bass), Bulgarian National Phil Choir Gega ▲ GD 200 [DDD]
V. Stefanov (cnd)
Verdi, G.:Music of, w. Svetoslav Obretenov Bulgarian National Choir
Verdi, G.:Ovs & Preludes—La forza del destino; La traviata; Niabucco; Rigoletto; Un ballo in maschera; Otello; I vespri Siciliani; La battaglia di Legnano; Aida; Macbeth; Aroldo Laserlight ▲ 15 519
J. Vella (cnd)
Vella, J.:Con Pno, w. Natascha Chircop (pno) Gega ▲ GR 40
Vella, J.:Con Vn, w. Marcello Canci (vn) Gega ▲ GR 40
SoHo Quartet
Childs, M.E.:Four of One Another, w. Guy Klucevsek (acc) XI Compact Discs ▲ XI 114
Solati Trio
R. Black (cnd)
Skupinsky, G.:Wild n' Sexy, w. Slovak RSO Bratislava *(rec Slovak Radio & TV Studios, Slovak National Republic, June & Sept 1993)* MMC ▲ MMC 2015 [DDD]
Soldier String Quartet [Laura Seaton (vn), David Soldier (vn), Ron Lawrence (va), Mary Wooton (vc)]
Jenkins, L.:Off Duty Dryad *(rec live, Merkin Concert Hall, New York City, Apr. 9, 1992)* CRI ("eXchange" series) ▲ CD 663 [DDD]
Jenkins, L.:Themes & Improvisations on the Blues *(rec live, Merkin Concert Hall, New York City, Apr. 9, 1992)* CRI ("eXchange" series) ▲ CD 663 [DDD]
Soldier String Quartet [Regina Carter (vn), David Soldier (vn), Judith Insell (va), Dawn Buckholz (vc)]
Sharp, E.:Intifada, w. Elliot Sharp (cl) Tzadik ("Composer" series) ▲ TZA 7016 [DDD]
Sharp, E.:X-topia, w. Elliot Sharp (gtr) Tzadik ("Composer" series) ▲ TZA 7016 [DDD]
Solid Brass
Christmas with Solid Brass Dorian ▲ DOR 90114 [DDD]
Solid Brass at the Opera Dorian ▲ DOR 90108 [DDD]
Solist Band
P. Altrichter (cnd)
Milhaud, D.:Scaramouche Sax, w. Jiří Hlaváč (sax) *(rec ZK Motorlet Prague Studio, March 21, 1989)* Panton ▲ PAN 810884
S. Bogunia (cnd)
Bernstein, L.:Prelude, Fugue & Riffs, w. Jiří Hlaváč (cl) *(rec ZK Motorlet Prague Studio, Sept 4-6 & 14-15, 1986)* Panton ▲ PAN 810884
Stravinsky, I.:Ebony Con, w. Jiří Hlaváč (cl) *(rec ZK Motorlet Prague Studio, Sept 4-6 & 14-15, 1986)* Panton ▲ PAN 810884
I Solisti Aquilani
Albinoni, T.:Sinf (6) e con (6) à 5, Op. 2, w. M. Conti (fl)—Sinfs. in G & A Nuova Era ▲ 7066
Nardini, P.:Cons Fl, w. M. Conti (fl)—in D & G Nuova Era ▲ 7066
Tartini, G.:Con in F Fl, w. M. Conti (fl) Nuova Era ▲ 7066
V. Antonellini (cnd)
Bottesini, G.:Allegretto capriccio Db, w. M. Giorgi (db) Nuova Era ▲ 6810 [DDD]
Bottesini, G.:Elegy & Tarantella, w. M. Giorgi (db) Nuova Era ▲ 6810 [DDD]
Bottesini, G.:Gran Duo Cl, w. V. Mariozzi (cl), M. Giorgi (db) Nuova Era ▲ 6810 [DDD]
Bottesini, G.:Gran Duo Concertant, w. D. Conti (vn), M. Giorgi (db) Nuova Era ▲ 6810 [DDD]
Bottesini, G.:Introduction & Gavotte, w. M. Giorgi (db) Nuova Era ▲ 6810 [DDD]

I Solisti Aquilani (cont.)
V. Antonellini (cnd) (cont.)
Bottesini, G.:Passioni Amorose, w. D. Conti (vn), M. Giorgi (db) — Nuova Era ▲ 6810 [DDD]
Bottesini, G.:Vars on *La Sonnambula*, w. M. Giorgi (db) — Nuova Era ▲ 6810 [DDD]
Cherubini, L.:Sons (2) Hn, w. L. Giuliani (hn) — Nuova Era ▲ 6910 [DDD]
Mercadante, S.:Con in B♭ Cl, Op. 101, w. V. Mariozzi (cl) — Nuova Era ▲ 6910 [DDD]
Mercadante, S.:Con Hn, w. L. Giuliani (hn) — Nuova Era ▲ 6910 [DDD]
Rossini, G.:Intro, Theme & Vars Cl, w. V. Mariozzi (cl) — Nuova Era ▲ 6910 [DDD]
Tosti, P.F.:Songs, w. R. Bruson (bar) [string orch. trans. Giuseppe Piccinino]—Sogno; Malia; Ideale; Ridonami la calma; 'A Vucchella; La serenata; L'ultima canzone; Tristezza; La chanson de l'adieu; E morto Pulcinella; Vorrei morire; Non t'amo più [F,I] *(rec live, 9/19–21/86)* — Bongiovanni ▲ GB 2505 [DDD]

I Solisti Partenopei
I. Caiazza (cnd)
Durante, F.:Con Pno, w. Antonella Cristiano (pno) *(rec Mar 1996)* — Kicco Classics ▲ 396 [DDD]
Prati, A.:Con Pno, w. Antonella Cristiano (pno) *(rec Mar 1996)* — Kicco Classics ▲ 396 [DDD]
Ragazzi, A.:Con Grosso, w. Marco Rogliano (vn), Andrea Guerrini (vn), Eduardo Pitone (va), Aurelio Bertucci (vc), Antonella Cristiano (hpd) *(rec Mar 1996)* — Kicco Classics ▲ 396 [DDD]
Ragazzi, A.:Con Vn (1729), w. Marco Rogliano (vn) *(rec Mar 1996)* — Kicco Classics ▲ 396 [DDD]
Ragazzi, A.:Con Vn (1728), w. Marco Rogliano (vn) *(rec Mar 1996)* — Kicco Classics ▲ 396 [DDD]

Solna Brass
Live Brass, w. Massed Bands, Black Dyke Mills Band, James Shepherd Versatile Brass, Brighouse & Rastrick Band, Don Lusher Trombone Ensemble *(rec live at the National Brass Band Festiva, Gala Concerts 1977, 1978, 1979)* — Chandos ("Collect" series) ▲ CHAN 6561 [ADD]

Solomon Trio [Daniel Adni (pno), Rodney Friend (vn), Raphael Sommer (vc)]
Brahms, J.:Trio 1 Pno — IMP Classics 2-▲ IMP DMCD 94
Brahms, J.:Trio 2 Pno — IMP Classics ▲ IMP DMCD 94
Brahms, J.:Trio 3 Pno — IMP Classics ▲ IMP DMCD 94
Brahms, J.:Trio in A Pno (posth) — IMP Classics ▲ IMP DMCD 94

Sonare String Quartet [Jacek Klimkiewicz (vn), Laurentius Bonita (vn), Hideko Kobayashi (va), Emil Klein (vc)]
Boccherini, L.:Qts Strs, G.159–164 — CPO ▲ CPO 999123-2 [DDD]
Corrette, M.:Cons Org, Op. 26, w. H. Meyer (org), Noda (db)—concerto in A — Claves ▲ CD 8511 [DDD]
Durante, F.:Con Org, w. H. Meyer (org), Noda (db) — Claves ▲ CD 8511 [DDD]
Hindemith, P.:Qt Strs, Op. 2 — CPO ▲ CPO 999001-2 [DDD]
Hindemith, P.:Qt 5 Strs — CPO ▲ CPO 999001-2 [DDD]
Krenek, E.:Qts Strs (comp) — MD + G 4-▲ L 4280 [DDD]
Krenek, E.:Qt 1 Strs — MD + G ▲ L 3280 [DDD]
Krenek, E.:Qt 2 Strs — MD + G ▲ L 3280 [DDD]
Krenek, E.:Qt 3 Strs — MD + G ▲ L 3281 [DDD]
Krenek, E.:Qt 4 Strs — MD + G ▲ L 3283 [DDD]
Krenek, E.:Qt 5 Strs — MD + G ▲ L 3282 [DDD]
Krenek, E.:Qt 6 Strs — MD + G ▲ L 3283 [DDD]
Krenek, E.:Qt 7 Strs — MD + G ▲ L 3281 [DDD]
Krenek, E.:Qt 8 Strs — MD + G ▲ L 3282 [DDD]
Meyer, H.:Suite paysanne, w. H. Meyer (org), Noda (db) — Claves ▲ CD 8511 [DDD]
Paradies, P.D.:Con Org, w. I. Noda (db), H. Meyer (org) — Claves ▲ CD 8511 [DDD]
Rheinberger, J.:Qt 2 Strs — Thorofon 6-▲ BCTH 2161/6
Rheinberger, J.:Qt 2 Strs — Thorofon ▲ CTH 2061 [DDD]
Rheinberger, J.:Qnt Pno, w. H. Göbel (pno) — Thorofon ▲ CTH 2060 [DDD]
Rheinberger, J.:Qnt Pno, w. Horst Göbel (pno), Yumiko Noda (va) *(rec 1989)* — Thorofon 6-▲ BCTH 2161/6
Rheinberger, J.:Qnt Strings, w. Yumiko Noda (va) *(rec 1989)* — Thorofon 6-▲ BCTH 2161/6
Rheinberger, J.:Qnt Strings, w. Yumiko Noda (va) — Thorofon ▲ CTH 2060 [DDD]
Stanley, J.:Con in c Org, w. H. Meyer (org), Noda (db) — Claves ▲ CD 8511 [DDD]

Sonatori de la Gioiosa Marca
G. Carmignola (cnd)
Vivaldi, A.:Cons & Sinfs—in d, R.128 — RS Applausi ▲ 6367-25
Vivaldi, A.:Cons Vn, Op. 8/1–4, "The Four Seasons" — RS Applausi ▲ 6367-25
Vivaldi, A.:Con for 3 Vns — RS Applausi ▲ 6367-25
A. Curtis (cnd)
Monteverdi, C.:Ritorno d'Ulisse, w. Gloria Banditelli (cta), Villanueva (sgr), Tucker (sgr) [I] — Nuova Era ("Ancient Music" series) 3-▲ 7103/05 [DDD]

Sonatori Ensemble
Stamitz, C.:Trios Fl — Multisonic ▲ 31 0159-2 [DDD]

Sonatori Trio
Dussek, J.L.:Trio Son Pno, Op. 65 *(rec 4/90)* — FSM-Adagio ▲ FCD 97732 [DDD]
Gyrowetz, A.:Divertissement Pno *(rec 4/90)* — FSM-Adagio ▲ FCD 97732 [DDD]
Pleyel, I.:Grand Trio Pno *(rec 4/90)* — FSM-Adagio ▲ FCD 97732 [DDD]

Sones Contemporaneos Ensemble
J. Trigos (cnd)
Rasgado, V.:Music of—Rayo nocturnal; Axolote; Seis gestos sobre las cuartas; Rumores de la tierra — Spartacus ▲ 21092
Trigos, J.:Music of—Quartetto da do; Danza florida No. 1; Comentario I; Sax sin aliento — Spartacus ▲ 21092

Söngsveitin PO
P. Zukovsky (cnd)
Leifs, J.:Baldur, Sinfóíuhljómsveit Aeskunnar — CP2 Recordings 2-▲ CP2 106/7

Sonnerie Ensemble
Bach, J.S.:Cant 84, w. Nancy Argenta (sop) — Virgin Classics ▲ CDC 45059
Bach, J.S.:Cant 202, "Wedding Cant", w. Nancy Argenta (sop) — Virgin Classics ▲ CDC 45059
Bach, J.S.:Cant 209, w. Nancy Argenta (sop) — Virgin Classics ▲ CDC 45059
M. Huggett (cnd)
Bach, J.S.:Cant 51, w. N. Argenta (sop), M. Hugget (vn) — Virgin Classics ▲ CDC 45038
Bach, J.S.:Cant 82, w. N. Argenta (sop), M. Hugget (vn) — Virgin Classics ▲ CDC 45038
Bach, J.S.:Cant 199, w. N. Argenta (sop), M. Hugget (vn) — Virgin Classics ▲ CDC 45038

Sonnerie Ensemble [Monica Huggett (vn), Bruce Dickey (cnt), Sarah Cunningham (vc), Gary Cooper (hpd/org/vir)]
Cima, G.P.:Sons for 2–4 Instruments — Virgin Classics 2-▲ ZDCB 45199
Fontana, G.B.:Sons (18) Vns — Virgin Classics 2-▲ ZDCB 45199
Turini, F.:Sons Vns Bc — Virgin Classics 2-▲ ZDCB 45199

Sonnerie Trio
Corelli, A.:Sons Vn, Op. 5, w. N. North (archlt/thb/gtr)—comp. — Veritas 2-▲ VCD 7 90840-2 [DDD] 2-█ VC 7 90840-4 (D)
Corelli, A.:Sons Vn, Op. 5, w. N. North (archlt/gtr)—comp. — Virgin Classics 2-▲ ZDCB 59554
Gaudeamus Early Music Sampler, w. Great Consort, His Majesties Sagbutts & Cornetts, Rasumovsky String Quartet, Cappella Nova, Cardinall's Musick, Clerks' Group, Ex Cathedra, Gentlemen of the Chappell, Gonville & Caius College Choir Cambridge, et al. — ASV/Gaudeamus ▲ ASV 1002
Leclair, J.-M.:Sons Vn (Books 1–4)—Opp. 5/6 in c, 9/7 in G & 9/9 in E♭ — ASV ("Gaudeamus" series) ▲ CDGAU 106 [DDD]
Telemann, G.P.:Qts Vn, w. W. Hazelzet (fl)—Quartets 8 & 12, & the Concerto Primo in G & Sonata Primo in A from the first six quartets — Virgin Classics ▲ 59049 [DDD]

SONOR Ensemble of Univ of California San Diego
T. Nee (cnd)
Erickson, R.:Sierra, w. P. Larson (bar) *(rec 1987–91)* — CRI ▲ CD 616 [DDD]
B. Rands (cnd)
Rands, B.:Canti del Sole, w. C. Plantamura (sop), P. Sperry (ten) — CRI ▲ CD 591 [ADD]
R. Steiger (cnd)
Reynolds, R.:Personae, w. J. Négyesy (vn) — Neuma ▲ 450-78 [DDD]

SONOR Ensemble of Univ of California San Diego (cont.)
R. Steiger (cnd) (cont.)
Steiger, R.:Double Con, w. A. Karis (pno), S. Schick (perc) *(rec May 27–June 1, 1992)* — CRI ▲ CD 652 [DDD]
Xenakis, I.:Thalleïn — Neuma ▲ 450-86 [DDD]

SONOR Ensemble of Univ of California San Diego [E. Waterman (fl), R. Zelickman (cl), P. Michel (ob), S. Barrett (E hn), D. Savage (bn), W. Gref (hn)]
J. Fonville (cnd)
Ferneyhough, B.:Prometheus *(rec Feb. 23–24, 1992)* — CRI ▲ CD 652 [DDD]

SONOR Ensemble of Univ of California San Diego [J. Fonville (fl), R. Zelickman (cl), J. Négyesy (vn/va), P. Farrell (vc), A. Karis (pno)]
H. Sollberger (cnd)
Yuasa, J.:Mutterings, w. C. Plantamura (sop) *(rec Oct. 13–14, 1992)* — CRI ▲ CD 652 [DDD]

SONOR Ensemble of Univ of California San Diego [J. Fonville (fl/pic), R. Zelickman (cl), J. Négyesy (vn), P. Farrell (vc), A. Karis (pno)]
Reynolds, R.:Not only Night, w. C. Plantamura (sop) *(rec Dec. 1–2, 1992)* — CRI ▲ CD 652 [DDD]

Sonora Hungarica
Armando, G.:Con Ob, w. Pauline Oostenrijk (ob) *(rec Amsterdam, Feb 1993)* — Verdi Classics ▲ AU 32 251 [DDD]
Castelnuovo-Tedesco, M.:Con da Camera, w. Pauline Oostenrijk (ob) *(rec Amsterdam, Feb 1993)* — Verdi Classics ▲ AU 32 251 [DDD]
Cimarosa, D.:Con in C Ob, w. Pauline Oostenrijk (ob) *(rec Amsterdam, Feb 1993)* — Verdi Classics ▲ AU 32 251 [DDD]
Gibilaro, A.:Fant on British Airs, w. Pauline Oostenrijk (ob) *(rec Amsterdam, Feb 1993)* — Verdi Classics ▲ AU 32 251 [DDD]

Sonos Handbell Ensemble
J. Meredith (cnd)
Bach, J.S.:Chorale Preludes Org [arr for Handbell Ensemble]—O Mensch, bewein' dein' Sünde gross; Jesus bleibet meine Freude; Von Gott will ich nicht lassen — Well-Tempered Productions ▲ WTP 5182 [DDD]
Bach, J.S.:Toccata & Fugue Org, BWV 538, "Dorian" [arr for Handbell Ensemble] — Well-Tempered Productions ▲ WTP 5182 [DDD]
Christmas With Sonos Handbell Ensemble *(rec Scoring Stage, Skywalker Sound, Marin County, CA, June 1995)* — Well Tempered ▲ WTP 5176 [DDD]
Mozart, W.A.:Adagio Rondo, w. Carol Adee (fl), Noriko Kishi (vc), Kurt Rohde (va), Roger Wiesmeyer (ob) — Well-Tempered Productions ▲ WTP 5182 [DDD]
Mozart, W.A.:Son 11 Pno — Well-Tempered Productions ▲ WTP 5182 [DDD]
Sonos Handbell Ensemble — Well-Tempered Productions ▲ WTP 5170
Vivaldi, A.:Cons Vn, Op. 3/1–12, "L'estro armonico" [arr for Handbell Ensemble]—No. 8 — Well-Tempered Productions ▲ WTP 5182 [DDD]

Sonus [James Carrier (shms/rcr/hp/saz/oud/psaltery/gemshn/perc), Hazel Ketchum (voc/saz/lt/perc), John Holenko (chit/saz/psaltery/oud/rcr/perc)]
Songs & Dances of the Middle Ages — Dorian Discovery ▲ DIS 80109 [DDD]

Sophisticated Ladies
Sibelius, J.:Qt in a Strs — BIS ▲ CD 463 [DDD]
Sibelius, J.:Qt Strs, Op. 56 — BIS ▲ CD 463 [DDD]

Sorrel String Quartet [Gina McCormack (vn), Catherine Yates (vn), Vicci Wardman (va), Helen Thatcher (vc)]
Britten, B.:Alla Marcia — Chandos ▲ CHAN 9469
Britten, B.:Divertimenti (3) — Chandos ▲ CHAN 9469
Britten, B.:Qt 1 Strs — Chandos ▲ CHAN 9469
Britten, B.:Qt 3 Strs — Chandos ▲ CHAN 9469

Sound in Brass Handbells
Ringing Clear:The Art of Handbell Ringing, w. Launton Handbell Ringers, Four in Hand Grosmont Handbell Ringers, Change Ringing Handbell Group — Saydisc ▲ CDSDL 333 [AAD]

SoundStroke
R. C. Gipson (cnd)
Hennagin, M.:The Phantom Dances — Albany ▲ TROY 214 [DDD]
Maslanka, D.:Crown of Thorns — Albany ▲ TROY 214 [DDD]
Welcher, D.:Chameleon Music — Albany ▲ TROY 214 [DDD]
Wilkins, B.:Compendium — Albany ▲ TROY 214 [DDD]
Wilkins, B.:Twilight Offering Music — Albany ▲ TROY 214 [DDD]

Jean Sourisse Ensemble
J. Sourisse (cnd)
Chausson, E.:Duos, "La nuit" & "Le réveil", w. D. Collot (sop), B. Vinson (mez), J. Bouillat (ten), G. Wieclaw (bass), E. Strosser (pno), C. Desert (pno), Audite Nova Vocal Ensemble — FNAC Music ▲ 592224 [DDD]
Debussy, C.:Songs, w. D. Collot (sop), B. Vinson (mez), J. Bouillat (ten), G. Wieclaw (bass), C. Desert (pno), E. Strosser (pno), Audite Nova Vocal Ensemble—3 chansons de Chateau D'Orleans — FNAC Music ▲ 592224 [DDD]
Fauré, G.:Pavane Orch, w. D. Collot (sop), B. Vinson (mez), J. Bouillat (ten), G. Wieclaw (bass), C. Desert (pno), E. Strosser (pno), Audite Nova Vocal Ensemble — FNAC Music ▲ 592224 [DDD]
Fauré, G.:Songs, w. D. Collot (sop), B. Vinson (mez), J. Bouillat (ten), G. Wieclaw (bass), C. Desert (pno), E. Strosser (pno), Audite Nova Vocal Ensemble—Le Ruisseau, Op. 22; Puisqu'ici bas, Op. 10/1, Les Djinns, Op. 12 — FNAC Music ▲ 592224 [DDD]
Ravel, M.:Songs, w. D. Collot (sop), B. Vinson (mez), J. Bouillat (ten), G. Wieclaw (bass), E. Strosser (pno), C. Desert (pno), Audite Nova Vocal Ensemble—3 a capella songs — FNAC Music ▲ 592224 [DDD]
Saint-Saëns, C.:Choral Music, w. D. Collot (sop), B. Vinson (mez), J. Bouillat (ten), G. Wieclaw (bass), E. Strosser (pno), C. Desert (pno), Vocal Audite Nova Ensemble—Calme des nuits, Op. 68/1; Les fleurs et les arbres, Op. 68/2; Salterelle, Op. 74 — FNAC Music ▲ 592224 [DDD]

Sousa Band
Herbert L. Clarke, w. Clarke, Herbert L. (cnt), et al. *(rec 1900–01, 1904, 1908–09, 1911)* — Crystal ▲ CD 450
Trombone Solos, w. Pryor, Arthur (trbn), Pryor Band *(rec 1897–1911)* — Crystal █ C 451
J.P. Sousa (cnd)
Sousa, J.P.:Marches & Dances, w. Philadelphia Rapid Transit Company Band—Washington Post; Stars & Stripes Forever; 23 others — Pearl ▲ PEA 9249

South African Broadcasting Corp National SO
R. Cock (cnd)
Akpabot, S.:Nigerian Dances *(rec Radio Park, Johannesburg, Jan 1995)* — Marco Polo ▲ 8.223832 [DDD]
Bell, W.H.:A South African Sym *(rec Radio Park, Johannesburg, Jan 1994 & Jan 1995)* — Marco Polo ▲ 8.223833 [DDD]
Dijk, P.L. van:San Chronicle *(rec Radio Park, Johannesburg, Jan 1995)* — Marco Polo ▲ 8.223832 [DDD]
Dijk, P.L. van:San Gloria, w. South African Broadcating Corp National Chamber Choir *(rec Radio Park, Johannesburg, Jan 1995)* — Marco Polo ▲ 8.223832 [DDD]
Fagan, G.:Concert Ov *(rec Radio Park, Johannesburg, Jan 1994 & Jan 1995)* — Marco Polo ▲ 8.223833 [DDD]
Khumalo, M.:African Songs [arr P. L. Van Dijk for symphony] *(rec Radio Park, Johannesburg, Jan 1995)* — Marco Polo ▲ 8.223832 [DDD]
P. Marchbank (cnd)
Fagan, G.:Ilala *(rec Radio Park, Johannesburg, Jan 1994 & Jan 1995)* — Marco Polo ▲ 8.223833 [DDD]
Fagan, G.:Karoo Sym *(rec S.A.B.C. Radiopark, Auckland Park, Johannesburg, Jan. 1994)* — Marco Polo ▲ 8.223709 [DDD]
Glass, L.:Sym 5, "Svastica" *(rec Jan. 11–22, 1993)* — Marco Polo ▲ 8.223486
Glass, L.:Sym 6, "Birth of Scyldings" *(rec Jan. 11–22, 1993)* — Marco Polo ▲ 8.223486

South African Broadcasting Corp National SO (cont.)
P. Marchbank (cnd) (cont.)
Lissant-Collins, H.:Fuquoi in the Sugar Cane *(rec S.A.B.C. Radiopark, Auckland Park, Johannesburg, Jan. 1994)* Marco Polo ▲ 8.223709 [DDD]
Moerane, M.M.:My Country *(rec S.A.B.C. Radiopark, Auckland Park, Johannesburg, Jan. 1994)* Marco Polo ▲ 8.223709 [DDD]
Scott, C.:Aubade Marco Polo ▲ 8.223485
Scott, C.:Dances Marco Polo ▲ 8.223485
Scott, C.:Neapolitan Rhap Marco Polo ▲ 8.223485
Scott, C.:Passacaglias on Irish Themes Marco Polo ▲ 8.223485
Scott, C.:Suite fantastique Marco Polo ▲ 8.223485

South African National SO
O. Hadari (cnd)
Zaidel-Rudolph, J.:Fanfare Festival Ov Claremont ▲ GSE 1532
Zaidel-Rudolph, J.:Sefirot Sym Claremont ▲ GSE 1532
A. Stephenson (cnd)
Zaidel-Rudolph, J.:At the End of the Rainbow Claremont ▲ GSE 1532

South German CO
G. Wich (cnd)
Tchaikovsky, P.:Serenade Strs—Pezzo in forma di sonatina Interchord ▲ INT 892.934 [AAD]

South German Chamber Soloists
L. Lencsés (cnd)
Milhaud, D.:Les Rêves de Jacob *(rec Jan. 1986 & Jan. 1992)* CPO ▲ CPO 999114-2 [DDD]

South German PO
A. von Pitamic (cnd)
Mussorgsky, M.:Night Pro Arte ▲ 575

South German RSO
S. Celibidache (cnd)
Bruckner, A.:Sym 3, "Wagner" Exclusive ▲ EXL 59 [ADD]
Bruckner, A.:Sym 7 *(rec live 1971)* Andromeda ▲ ANR 2513 [ADD]
Haydn, J.:Sym 103, "Drum Roll" *(rec 1975)* Originals ▲ ORISH 808 [ADD]
Mozart, W.A.:Sym 38 *(rec 1975)* Originals ▲ ORISH 808 [ADD]
Ravel, M.:Boléro *(rec live, 1974)* Enterprise ("Documents" series) 2-▲ LV 946/47 (m/s) [ADD]
Ravel, M.:Ma mère l'oye Orch *(rec live, 1972)* Enterprise ("Documents" series) 2-▲ LV 946/47 (m/s) [ADD]
Ravel, M.:Le Tombeau de Couperin *(rec 1978–80)* Exclusive 2-▲ EXL 61 [ADD]
Ravel, M.:La Valse *(rec live, 1974)* Enterprise ("Documents" series) 2-▲ LV 946/47 (m/s) [ADD]
Stravinsky, I.:Le Baiser de la fée *(rec live, Stuttgart, 1970's)* As Disc ▲ ASD 2501
Stravinsky, I.:Le Baiser de la fée Originals ▲ ORISH 803 [ADD]
C. Eschenbach (cnd)
Gershwin, G.:Con Pno, w. S. Richter (pno) Originals ▲ ORISH 810 [DDD]
Saint-Saëns, C.:Con 1 Vn, w. S. Richter (vn) Originals ▲ ORISH 810 [DDD]
M. Inoue (cnd)
Chopin, F.:Con 2 Pno, w. M. Pollini (pno) Artists ▲ FED 56 [ADD]
M. Kagel (cnd)
Kagel, M.:Sankt-Bach-Passion, w. Anne Sofie von Otter (mez), Hans Peter Blochowitz (ten), Roland Hermann (bar), Peter Roggisch (narr), Gerd Zacher (org), Limburg Cathedral Boys' Chorus, Hamburg North German Choir Montaigne ▲ MO 782044
C. Kleiber (cnd)
Beethoven, L. van:Sym 7 Legend ▲ LGD 123 [ADD]
Strauss (II), Joh.:Die Fledermaus (sels)—Ov. Legend ▲ LGD 123 [ADD]
H. Müller-Kray (cnd)
Dvořák, A.:Con Vn, w. R. Ricci (vn) One-Eleven ▲ URS 93030 [ADD]
Goldmark, K.:Con 1 Vn, w. R. Ricci (vn) One-Eleven ▲ URS 93030 [ADD]
Verdi, G.:Requiem Mass, w. M. Stader (sop), M. Höffgen (cta), F. Wunderlich (ten), G. Frick (bass), South German Radio Sym Chorus *(rec live, Stuttgart, 11/2/60)* Myto 2-▲ 2 MCD 91648 [ADD]
H. Rosbaud (cnd)
Beethoven, L. van:Con Vn, Op. 61, w. Ginette Neveu (vn) *(rec Baden-Baden, Sept. 1949)* Music & Arts 2-▲ CD 837 [AAD]
C. Schuricht (cnd)
Brahms, J.:Sym 2 *(rec 1966)* Originals ▲ ORISH 816 [ADD]
Wagner, R.:Siegfried Idyll *(rec 1966)* Originals ▲ ORISH 816 [ADD]

South German SO
S. Celibidache (cnd)
Beethoven, L. van:Sym 3, "Eroica" *(rec 1971)* Artists ▲ FED 001
Bruckner, A.:Sym 4, "Romantic" *(rec live, Stuttgart 11/22/66)* Arkadia ▲ 751 [ADD]
Bruckner, A.:Sym 7 *(rec live, 1971)* As Disc ▲ ASD 2505
Rimsky-Korsakov, N.:Scheherazade *(rec live, Stuttgart, 1971)* Originals ▲ ORI SH 889
C. Schuricht (cnd)
Schubert, Franz:Sym 9 Theorema ▲ TH 121172

South Jutland SO
K. Andersen (cnd)
Saeverud, H.:Con Vn, w. T. Saeverud (vn) Simax ▲ PSC 1087 [DDD]
Saeverud, H.:Romanza Vn, w. T. Saeverud (vn) Simax ▲ PSC 1087 [DDD]
J. Frandsen (cnd)
Nielsen, C.:Amor (ov) *(rec "Musikhuset", DK-Sønderborg, 1982)* Paula ▲ PACD 18 [DAD]
Nielsen, C.:Cant for Centenary of Merchants, w. Sønderborg St. Marie Church Motet Choir—Danmark, i tusind år *(rec "Musikhuset", DK-Sønderborg, 1982)* Paula ▲ PACD 18 [DAD]
Nielsen, C.:Hagbarth og Signe—Ternernes dans; Min hjelm er mig for blank og tung [w. Ole Hedegaard (ten)] *(rec "Musikhuset", DK-Sønderborg, 1982)* Paula ▲ PACD 18 [DAD]
Nielsen, C.:Moderen—Tågen letter [w. Ib Nielsen (fl), Benedikte Johansen (hp)]; Min pige er så lys som rav; Dengang ørnen var flyveklar; Sa bittert var mit hjerte; Dengang døden var i vente [all w. Ole Hedegaard]; Forspil til 4. billede; March; Som en rejselysten flåde [w. The Sonder Jutland Kammerkor Chorus] *(rec "Musikhuset", DK-Sønderborg, 1982)* Paula ▲ PACD 18 [DAD]
Nielsen, C.:Springtime, w. Ole Hedegaard (ten)—Den milde dag er lys og lang *(rec "Musikhuset", DK-Sønderborg, 1982)* Paula ▲ PACD 18 [DAD]
Nielsen, C.:Tove, w. Ole Hedegaard (ten), Vi sletternes sønner *(rec "Musikhuset", DK-Sønderborg, 1982)* Paula ▲ PACD 18 [DAD]
Nielsen, C.:Willemoes—Havet omkring Danmark [w. Haderslev Vor Frue Cantori]; Forspil til 3. akt *(rec "Musikhuset", DK-Sønderborg, 1982)* Paula ▲ PACD 18 [DAD]
S. A. Johansen (cnd)
Blak, K.:Harpa Paetur og Elingorb Tutl ▲ FKT 2
F. Rasmussen (cnd)
Gade, N.W.:Comala, w. Canzone Choir Kontrapunkt ▲ KPT 32180 [DDD]
M. Schønwandt (cnd)
Schierbeck, P.:The Chinese Flute, w. Susanne Lange (sop) Point ▲ PCD 5085 [ADD]
Schierbeck, P.:Fête galante (ov) Point ▲ PCD 5085 [ADD]
Schierbeck, P.:The Night, w. Anne Øland (pno) Point ▲ PCD 5085 [ADD]
Schierbeck, P.:Sorceress, w. Susanne Lange (sop), Jens Kaas (org) Point ▲ PCD 5085 [ADD]
T. Vetö (cnd)
Sigurbjörnsson, T.:Columbine, w. Manuela Wiesler (fl) *(rec Denmark, Aug 1 & 4, 1995)* BIS ▲ CD 709 [DDD]
Sigurbjörnsson, T.:Eurydice, w. Manuela Wiesler (fl) *(rec Denmark, Aug 1 & 4, 1995)* BIS ▲ CD 709 [DDD]
Sigurbjörnsson, T.:Liongate, w. Manuela Wiesler (fl) *(rec Denmark, Aug 1 & 4, 1995)* BIS ▲ CD 709 [DDD]
J.-P. Wallez (cnd)
Pleyel, I.:Con in B♭ Cl, w. M. Lethiec (cl) *(rec Oct. 1992)* Talent ▲ DOM 2910 36 [DDD]
Pleyel, I.:Con in C for Fl, w. T. Jensen (fl) *(rec Oct. 1992)* Talent ▲ DOM 2910 36 [DDD]
Pleyel, I.:Con in G for Fl, w. T. Jensen (fl) *(rec Oct. 1992)* Talent ▲ DOM 2910 36 [DDD]

South Jutland SO members
Albinoni, T.:Con Tpt, Op. 7/2, w. P. Nielsen (tpt) Danica ▲ DCD 8095
Haydn, M.:Con Tpt, Hns & Strs, w. P. Nielsen (tpt) Danica ▲ DCD 8095
Mozart, L.:Con Tpt, w. P. Nielsen (tpt) Danica ▲ DCD 8095
Telemann, G.P.:Cons Tpt, w. P. Nielsen (tpt)—in D Danica ▲ DCD 8095
Tessarini, C.:Music of, w. P. Nielsen (tpt)—Son in D Danica ▲ DCD 8095
Torelli, G.:Sinf Tpt, w. P. Nielsen (tpt) Danica ▲ DCD 8095

South Westphalian PO
H. Ermert (cnd)
Cherubini, L.:Requiem Mass in c, w. South Westphalian Chorus [L] Koch Schwann ▲ 3-1346-2 [DDD]
F. Merz (cnd)
Schumann, R.:Con Vc, w. Julius Berger (vc) ebs ▲ ebs 6090
Schumann, R.:Con Vn, w. Hansheinz Schneeberger (vn) ebs ▲ ebs 6090
Schumann, R.:Ov, Scherzo & Finale Ebs ▲ 6091 [DDD]
Schumann, R.:Ov, Scherzo & Finale Capriccio 3-▲ CD 10997 [DDD]
Schumann, R.:Sym 4 Ebs ▲ 6091 [DDD]

Southern Bohemian Chamber PO Budweis
Mieg, P.:Double Con Pno, Vc, w. K-A Kolly (pno), D. Riniker (vc) Jecklin ▲ JS 297-2 [ADD]
D. Schmid (cnd)
Blum, R.:Seldwyla-Sinfonie *(rec June 1993)* Jecklin ▲ JS 297-2 [ADD]
Wehrli, W.:Sinfonietta Fl, w. G. Rumpel (fl), S. Andres (pno) *(rec 1993)* Jecklin ▲ JS 297-2

Southern PO
F. Stiedry (cnd)
Gluck, C.W.:Orfeo ed Euridice (sels), w. A. Ayars (sop), Z. Vlachopoulos (sop), K. Ferrier (cta), Glyndebourne Festival Chorus *(rec 1947)* Enterprise ("Palladio" series) ▲ ENTPD 4171 [ADD]

Southwest Chamber Music Society
Poulenc, F.:Élégie Hn Cambria ▲ CMB 1072 [DDD]
Poulenc, F.:Sxt Pno Cambria ▲ CMB 1072 [DDD]
Poulenc, F.:Trio Ob Cambria ▲ CMB 1072 [DDD]
Prokofiev, S.:Ov on Hebrew Themes Cambria ▲ CMB 1072 [DDD]
Prokofiev, S.:Qnt Ob Cambria ▲ CMB 1072 [DDD]

Southwest German CO
P. Angerer (cnd)
Divertimento for Trombone & Orchestra, w. Slokar, Branimir (trbn) Claves ▲ CD 906 [ADD]
V. Czarnedki (cnd)
The Trombone, w. Rosin, Armin (trbn), Michel Becquet (trbn), Berlin Trombone Quintet, Berlin RIAS Sinfonietta [cnd:Ernő Sebestyen], Lorraine PO [cnd:Jacques Houtmann] Koch Schwann ▲ SCH 313342 [DDD]

Southwest German CO Pforzheim
P. Angerer (cnd)
Albéniz, I.:Suite española (sels), w. K. Ragossnig (gtr)—No. 1, "Granada"; No. 3. "Sevilla" Allegretto ▲ ACD 8175 [ADD] ■ ACS 8175
Borodin, A.:Nocturne Str Orch Entrée ▲ 0051 [ADD]
Borodin, A.:Scherzo Str Qt [orch. P. Angerer] Entrée ▲ 0051 [ADD]
Corelli, A.:Concerti grossi, Op. 6, Nos. 1–12, comp. Vox Box 2-▲ CDX 5023 [ADD]
Falla, M. de:El sombrero de tres picos (sels), w. K. Ragossnig (gtr)—Miller's Dance Allegretto ▲ ACD 8175 [ADD] ■ ACS 8175
Fasch, J.F.:Con Gtr, w. K. Ragossnig (gtr) Allegretto ▲ ACD 8175 [ADD] ■ ACS 8175
Handel, G.F.:Concerti grossi, Op. 6 Vox Box 3-▲ CD3X 3005 [ADD]
Haydn, J.:Con Ob, w. Ingo Goritzki (ob) *(rec Pforzheim, 1975)* Claves ("Favor Collection" series) ▲ CLF 606 [ADD]
Liszt, F.:Malédiction, w. M. Ponti (pno) *(rec 1978)* Vox Box 2-▲ CDX 5067 [ADD]
Mercadante, S.:Con in B♭ Cl, Op. 101, w. Thomas Friedli (cl) Claves ▲ CD 813
Molter, J.M.:Con in D Cl, w. Thomas Friedli (cl) Claves ▲ CD 813
Mouravieff, L.:Nativité Entrée ▲ 0051 [ADD]
Mozart, W.A.:Con Ob, K.314, w. I. Goritzki (ob) *(rec Pforzheim, 1975)* Claves ("Favor Collection" series) ▲ CLF 606 [ADD]
Pleyel, I.:Con in C Cl, w. T. Friedli (cl) Claves ▲ CD 813
Rimsky-Korsakov, N.:Sostenuto & Allegro Entrée ▲ 0051 [ADD]
Stamitz, C.:Con 1 Vc, w. C. Starck (vc) *(rec Pforzheim, 1981)* Claves ("Favor Collection" series) ▲ CLF 8105 [ADD]
Stamitz, C.:Con 2 Vc, w. C. Starck (vc) *(rec Pforzheim, 1981)* Claves ("Favor Collection" series) ▲ CLF 8105 [ADD]
Stamitz, C.:Con 3 Vc, w. C. Starck (vc) *(rec Pforzheim, 1981)* Claves ("Favor Collection" series) ▲ CLF 8105 [ADD]
Tchaikovsky, P.:Elegy Entrée ▲ 0051 [ADD]
V. Czarnecki (cnd)
Albinoni, T.:Cons à 5 Obs, Op. 9, w. S. Dent (ob)—No. 2 in d Amati ▲ 9103 [DDD]
Bach, J.S.:Con Ob d'amore, w. S. Dent (ob d'amore) Amati ▲ 9103 [DDD]
Baldassare, P.:Son 1 Tpt, w. E. Schultz (tpt) ebs ▲ ebs 6053 [DDD]
Biscogli, F.:Con in D, w. E. Schultz (tpt), I. Franklin (ob), D. Haward (bn) ebs ▲ ebs 6054 [DDD]
Boccherini, L.:Cons Vc (comp), w. J. Berger (vc)—in C, G.481; in D, G.478; in D, G.483; in E♭, G.474 ebs ▲ ebs 6057 [DDD]
Boccherini, L.:Cons Vc (comp), w. Julius Berger (vc)—in C, G.573; in A, G.475; in E♭, G.deest; in G, G.480 ebs ▲ ebs 6055 [DDD]
Boccherini, L.:Cons Vc (comp), w. J. Berger (vc) ebs 3-▲ ebs 6058 [DDD]
Boccherini, L.:Cons Vc (comp), w. J. Berger (vc)—in B♭, G.482; in C, G.477; in D, G.476; in D, G.479 ebs ▲ ebs 6056 [DDD]
Cherubini, L.:Sons (2) Hn, w. I. James (hn) ebs ▲ ebs 6052 [DDD]
Cimarosa, D.:Con in C Ob, w. S. Dent (ob) Amati ▲ 9103 [DDD]
Corelli, A.:Son Tpt, w. E. Schultz (tpt) ebs ▲ ebs 6053 [DDD]
Crusell, B.H.:Divert Ob, w. S. Dent (cl) Amati ▲ 9103 [DDD]
Haydn, J.:Cons Hn, w. Ifor James (hn) ebs ▲ ebs 6052 [DDD]
Haydn, M.:Con 2 Tpt, w. Erik Schultz (tpt) ebs ▲ ebs 6053 [DDD]
Hertel, J.W.:Con à 6, w. E. Schultz (tpt), I. Franklin (ob) ebs ▲ ebs 6054 [DDD]
Honegger, A.:Con da camera, w. G. van Riet (fl), L. Lencsés (E hn) CPO ▲ CPO 999193-2 [ADD/DDD]
Ibert, J.:Symphonie concertante, w. L. Lencsés (ob) CPO ▲ CPO 999193-2 [ADD/DDD]
Molter, J.M.:Cons Cl, w. W. Meyer (tpt) Amati ▲ 9009 [DDD]
Molter, J.M.:Con 1 Tpt, w. E. Schultz (tpt) ebs ▲ ebs 6053 [DDD]
Mozart, L.:Con Tpt, w. E. Schultz (tpt) ebs ▲ ebs 6053 [DDD]
Mozart, W.A.:Con Ob, K.314, w. S. Dent (ob) Amati ▲ 9103 [DDD]
Neruda, J.B.G.:Con Hn, w. I. James (hn) ebs ▲ ebs 6052 [DDD]
Pezel, J.C.:Son Tpt, w. E. Schultz (tpt), D. Haward (bn) ebs ▲ ebs 6054 [DDD]
Telemann, G.P.:Con Hn, w. I. James (hn) ebs ▲ ebs 6092 [DDD]
Telemann, G.P.:Con for 2 Hns in E♭, w. I. James (hn), T. Schnirring (hn) ebs ▲ ebs 6092 [DDD]
Telemann, G.P.:Con for 3 Horns, w. I. James (hn), R. Teutsch (hn), T. Abramovici (hn) ebs ▲ ebs 6092 [DDD]
Telemann, G.P.:Suite for 4 Hns, w. I. James (hn), T. Abramovici (hn), A. Lewis (hn), R. Teutsch (hn) ebs ▲ ebs 6092 [DDD]
Wagenseil, G.C.:Cons Org, w. Stefan Johannes Bleicher (org) *(rec Peter & Paul Church, Mössingen, Oct 4–7, 1974)* ebs ▲ ebs 6089 [DDD]
J. E. Dähler (cnd)
Galuppi, B.:Magnificat, w. Ana-Maria Miranda (sop), Bern Chamber Choir *(rec Berner Münster, Dec 1977)* Claves ▲ CD 50801 [ADD]
Vivaldi, A.:Gloria, RV.589, w. Ana-Maria Miranda (sop), Ria Bollen (alt), Bern Chamber Choir *(rec Berner Münster, Dec 1977)* Claves ▲ CD 50801 [ADD]
H. Richter (cnd)
Françaix, J.:Con Gtr, w. E. Segre (gtr) Wergo ▲ WER 6198-2 [AAD]

ORCH. & ENS.

Southwest German CO Pforzheim (cont.)
F. Tilegant (cnd)
Telemann, G.P.:Suite in a Fl, w. F. Brüggen (rcr) Teldec ▲ 77620-2 [ADD]
Southwest German RSO
Con Eleganza, w. Renn Brass Quintet Bayer ▲ 100245 [DDD]
H. Müller-Kray (cnd)
Wieniawski, H.:Con 2 Vn, w. R. Ricci (vn) One-Eleven ▲ URS 93020 [ADD]
R. Reinhardt (cnd)
Aaron Rosand Plays Sibelius, Tchaikovsky, Berlioz, Chausson, Ravel, Saint-Saëns, Lalo, w. Rosand, Aaron (vn), Southwest German RSO Baden-Baden [cnd:Tibor Szöke] *(rec 1957-59)* Vox Box 2-▲ CDX 5116

Southwest German RSO Baden-Baden
K. Arp (cnd)
Bellini, V.:Norma (ov) Pierre Verany ▲ PVY 730050
Donizetti, G.:Ovs—Don Pasquale; Roberto Devereux Pierre Verany ▲ PVY 730050
Pierné, G.:Concertstück Hp, w. I. Moretti (hp) Koch Schwann ▲ SCH 313392 [ADD/DDD]
Rossini, G.:Ovs—Semiramide; Guillaume Tell Pierre Verany ▲ PVY 730050
Verdi, G.:Ovs & Preludes—La forza del destino; La traviata; Nabucco Pierre Verany ▲ PVY 730050
M. Bamert (cnd)
Delz, C.:Con Pno, w. C. Delz (pno) *(rec 9/26/88 & 8/29/86)* FSM ▲ FCD 97743 [ADD]
E. Bour (cnd)
Kelemen, M.:Changeant, w. Siegfried Palm (vc) *(rec Nov 1972)* BIS ▲ CD 742 [AAD]
Ligeti, G.:Lontano Wergo ▲ WER 60045-50
Ravel, M.:Boléro Intercord ▲ INT 892.923 [AAD]
Ruzicka, P.:Feedback, w. Zurich Sprechchor CPO ▲ CPO 999053 [DDD]
Wagemans, P.J.:Muziek II Donemus ▲ CV 28
Zinsstag, G.:Foris *(rec Oct. 15, 1988)* Grammont ▲ CTSP 36-2 [ADD]
S. Celibidache (cnd)
Respighi, O.:The Pines of Rome Originals ▲ ORI 860
Rimsky-Korsakov, N.:Scheherazade *(rec 1972)* Arlecchino ▲ ARL126
M. Gielen (cnd)
Busoni, F.:Con Pno, Op. 39, w. D. Lively (pno), Freiburg Vocal Ensemble Koch Schwann ▲ CD 311 160 [DDD]
Maderna, B.:Ausstrahlung Col Legno 2-▲ AU 31819
Nono, L.:A Carlo Scarpa Col Legno 2-▲ AU 31819
Schoenberg, A.:Chamber Sym 1 Philips ▲ 446683-2
Schoenberg, A.:Chamber Sym 2 Philips ▲ 446683-2
Schoenberg, A.:Con Pno, w. Alfred Brendel (pno) Philips ▲ 446683-2
Spahlinger, M.:Passage Col Legno 2-▲ AU 31819
Staude, C.:Morpheus Col Legno 2-▲ AU 31819
Wagner, R.:Tristan und Isolde (orch sels)—Liebestod Intercord ▲ INT 892.923 [AAD]
D. Hellmann (cnd)
Haydn, J.:Mass 14, "Harmoniemesse", w. Barbara Martig-Tüller (sop), Ria Bollen (alt), Adalbert Kraus (ten), Kurt Widmer (bass), Melitta Veits (org) Calig ▲ CAL 50490
G. Herbig (cnd)
Ruzicka, P.:Approach & Peace, w. Justus Frantz (pno) *(rec Nov 1984)* Thorofon ▲ CTH 2220
J. Horenstein (cnd)
Liszt, F.:A Faust Sym, w. F. Koch (ten), Southwest German Radio Chorus *(rec 1950s)* Vox Box ("Legends" series) 2-▲ CDX2 5504 [ADD]
Schoenberg, A.:Chamber Sym 1 *(rec Südwest Tonstudio, Stuttgart, 1956)* Vox Legends 2-▲ CDX2 5529
Schoenberg, A.:Verklärte Nacht *(rec Südwest Tonstudio, Stuttgart, 1956)* Vox Legends 2-▲ CDX2 5529
Wagner, R.:Eine Faust-Ov *(rec 1950s)* Vox Box ("Legends" series) 2-▲ CDX2 5504 [ADD]
K. Kord (cnd)
Delz, C.:In the Jungle *(rec 10/83)* FSM ▲ FCD 97742 [ADD]
Mussorgsky, M.:Pictures at an Exhibition *(rec 1983)* FSM ▲ FCD 97742 [ADD]
V. Neumann (cnd)
Dvořák, A.:Sym 9, "From the New World"—Largo Interchord ▲ INT 892.934 [AAD]
R. Reinhardt (cnd)
Bartók, B.:Rhap Pno, w. G. Sándor (pno) *(rec 1958-59)* Vox Box ("Legends" series) 2-▲ CDX2 5506 [ADD]
Bruch, M.:Con 1 Vn, w. Bronislaw Gimpel (vn) Vox Legends 2-▲ CDX 5523
Dvořák, A.:Con Vn, w. Bronislaw Gimpel (vn) Vox Legends 2-▲ CDX 5523
Goldmark, K.:Con 1 Vn, w. Bronislaw Gimpel (vn) Vox Legends 2-▲ CDX 5523
Sarasate, P. de:Carmen Fant, w. A. Rosand (vn) Allegretto ▲ ACD 8160 [ADD] ■ ACD 8160
Sarasate, P. de:Zigeunerweisen, w. A. Rosand (vn) Allegretto ▲ ACD 8160 [ADD] ■ ACS 8160
H. Rosbaud (cnd)
Beethoven, L. van:Con Vn, Op. 61, w. G. Neveu (vn) *(rec live, 1949)* Music & Arts ▲ CD 550 (m) [AAD]
Berg, A.:Pieces Orch, Op. 6 Adès ▲ ADE 202892 [AAD]
Bruckner, A.:Sym 7 *(rec 1958)* Vox Box 2-▲ CDX2 5518
Hindemith, P.:Con Vn, w. I. Gitlis (vn) *(rec live, 1962)* Music & Arts ▲ CD 627 (m) [AAD]
Mahler, G.:Das Lied von der Erde, w. Grace Hoffmann (alt), Helmut Melchert (ten) *(rec 1957)* Vox Box 2-▲ CDX2 5518
Mahler, G.:Sym 6 *(rec 1960)* Datum 2-▲ DAT 12303 [ADD]
Mahler, G.:Sym 7 *(rec Baden, Baden, Germany, Feb 20, 1957)* Agorá Music ("Phoenix" series) ▲ 702 [ADD]
Mozart, W.A.:Con Fl Hp, w. E. Bodensohn (fl), A.M. Schmeisser (hp) *(rec 1962)* Datum 2-▲ DAT 12303 [ADD]
Schoenberg, A.:Vars Orch, Op. 31 *(rec live, 1961)* Music & Arts ▲ CD 627 (m) [AAD]
Schubert, Franz:Sym 9 Wergo ▲ WER 6405-2
Stravinsky, I.:Agon Adès ▲ ADE 202892 [AAD]
Webern, A.:Pieces Orch, Op. 6 Adès ▲ ADE 202892 [AAD]
C. Schuricht (cnd)
Brahms, J.:Sym 3 Adès ▲ ADE 203062 [AAD]
Brahms, J.:Vars on a Theme by Haydn Adès ▲ ADE 203062 [AAD]
E. Smola (cnd)
Villa-Lobos, H.:Con Hmc, w. Tommy Reilly (hmc) Chandos ▲ CHAN 9248 [DDD]
L. Stokowski (cnd)
Prokofiev, S.:Romeo & Juliet (sels) *(rec 1951-70)* Music & Arts ▲ CD 831 [ADD]
T. Szöke (cnd)
Aaron Rosand Plays Sibelius, Tchaikovsky, Berlioz, Chausson, Ravel, Saint-Saëns, Lalo, w. Rosand, Aaron (vn), Southwest German RSO [cnd:Rolf Reinhardt] *(rec 1957-59)* Vox Box 2-▲ CDX 5116
Lalo, E.:Sym espagnole, w. A. Rosand (vn) Allegretto ▲ ACD 8058 [ADD]
Saint-Saëns, C.:Con 3 Vn, w. A. Rosand (vn) Allegretto ▲ ACD 8058 [ADD]
M. Viotti (cnd)
Poulenc, F.:Les Animaux modèles Claves ▲ CD 9111 [DDD]
Poulenc, F.:La Baigneuse de Trouville & Discours du général Claves ▲ CD 9111 [DDD]
Poulenc, F.:Les Biches Claves ▲ CD 9111 [DDD]
Poulenc, F.:2 marches et un intermède Claves ▲ CD 9111 [DDD]
L. Zagrosek (cnd)
Wildberger, J.:Die Stimme, die alte, schwächer werdende Stimme, w. K. Graf (sop), S. Palm (vc) [G] *(rec May 30, 1980)* Grammont ▲ CTSP 25-2 [ADD]
Southwest German SO
K. Donath (cnd)
Virtuoso Operatic Arias for Soprano & Obbligato Clarinet, w. Isolde Siebert, (sop), Dieter Klöcker (cl) Koch Schwann ▲ SCH 314018 [DDD]

Southwest German SO (cont.)
K. Kord (cnd)
Huber, N.A.:Nocturnes Col Legno ▲ AU 31821
Southwest RSO
E. Bour (cnd)
Hambreus, B.:Music of, w. H. Hellsten (org), W. Jacob (org)—Cendenza; Canvas with mirrors; Continuo MAP ▲ MAPCD 9131
Soviet Army Band
Soviet Army Chorus & Band, w. Soviet Army Chorus EMI Classics ▲ CDC 47833
Soviet Cinema Orch
Polianski (cnd)
Karetnikov, N.:Till Eulenspiegel, w. E. Mazo (sop), L. Mkrtchian (cta), A. Proujanski (ten), B. Koudriavtsev (bar), P. Glouboky (bass), A. Motchalov (bass), A. Martinov (sgr). Soviet Cinema Chorus *(rec Moscow, 1988)* Russian Season ("Russian Season" Series) 2-▲ LDC 288029/30 [DDD]
Soviet State RSO
N. Golovanov (cnd)
Glazunov, A.:Sym 7, "Pastoral" *(rec ca. 1950)* Pearl ▲ PEA 9404 (m) [AAD]
Spalato National Theater Orch
V. Sutej (cnd)
Mercadante, S.:La Vestale, w. G. Dimitrova (sop), D. Vejzovic (sop), G. Cecchele (ten), Romanò (sgr), Cepreaga (sgr), Kliskic (sgr), Sioli (sgr), Boldrini (sgr), Spalato National Theater Chorus [I] *(rec 4/9/87)* Bongiovanni 2-▲ GB 2065/66 [DDD]
Spanish National Orch
Classica de España, w. Madrid Concert Orch, Ernesto Bitetti (gtr), Alicia de Larrocha (pno) EMI Classics 2-▲ ZDMB 64241
A. Argenta (cnd)
Falla, M. de:El amor brujo, w. Manuel de Falla (kbd) Montilla ▲ MNT 3024
Falla, M. de:El sombrero de tres picos, w. Manuel De Falla (kbd) Montilla ▲ MNT 3024
J. Arámbarri (cnd)
Guridi, J.:Music of, w. P. Bayona (pno), Madrid Concert Orch—Amaya; 10 Melodias; Homenaje a Walt Disney *(rec 1959)* EMI Classics ▲ CDM 64558
R. F. de Burgos (cnd)
Falla, M. de:La vida breve, w. V. de los Angeles (sop), F. Cossutta (mez), I. Rivadeneyra (mez), Orféon Donostiarra [Sp] EMI Classics ▲ CDM 69590 [ADD]
Zarzuela Arias, w. Victoria de los Angeles (sop) EMI Classics ("Studio" series) ▲ CDM 69078
Spanish National Radio-TV SO
O. Alonso (cnd)
Guitarra Española:Rodrigo, Aranjuez, w. Yepes, Narciso (gtr), London SO [cnd:R. Frühbeck de Burgos] Deutsche Grammophon ▲ 435845-2
Rodrigo, J.:Concierto de Aranjuez, w. N. Yepes (gtr) Deutsche Grammophon ▲ 435845-2 [ADD]
I. Markevitch (cnd)
Falla, M. de:El amor brujo, w. I. Rivadeneyra (cta) *(rec 1966)* Philips ("Spanish" series) ▲ 432829-2 [ADD]
M. A. G. Martínez (cnd)
Falla, M. de:Noches en los jardines de España, w. L. Milà (pno) Regis Tro ▲ RTAC 002 [DDD]
Guridi, J.:Una Aventura de Don Quijote Regis Tro ▲ RTAC 002 [DDD]
Guridi, J.:Melodias vascas (10) Regis Tro ▲ RTAC 002 [DDD]
Milà, L.:Con 2 Pno, w. L. Milà (pno) Regis Tro ▲ RTAC 002 [DDD]
Turina, J.:Sinfonia sevillana Regis Tro ▲ RTAC 002 [DDD]
Spanish National Youth Orch
E. Colomer (cnd)
Falla, M. de:Atlántida, w. M. Bayo (sop), T. Berganza (mez), S. Estes (bass) Valois 2-▲ V 4685
Falla, M. de:Noches en los jardines de España, w. Rafael Orozco (pno)—4 Spanish Pieces; Nights in the Gardens of Spain; Fant. Baetica; Homage to Debussy; Homage to Paul Dukas Valois ▲ V 4724
Gerhard, R.:Epithalamion Auvidis Montaigne ▲ MO 782101
Gerhard, R.:La Peste, w. Michael Lonsdale (nar), BBC Sym Chorus Auvidis Montaigne ▲ MO 782101
Sparnaay/Kooistra/Abe Trio
Musiana 95:Electroacoustic Music from Denmark & Japan, w. Ensemble from the East, Hanne Andersen, Sofia Asunción Claro, Mari Kimura (hp/vn), Thomas Sandberg, Harry Sparnaay (b cl) Classico ▲ CLASSCD 139 [DDD]

Spectra Ensemble
F. Rathé (cnd)
Mendes, G.:Music of—Qualquer Música for Chamber Ensemble; Saudades do Parque Balneário Hotel for A Sax & Pno; Claro Clarone for Chamber Ensemble; Ulysses in Copacabana Surfing with James Joyce & Dorothy Lamour for Chamber Ensemble; Um Estudo? Eisler e Webern caminham nos mares do sul... for Pno; Longhorn Trio for Tpt, Trbn & Pno; Motetos à Feição de Lobo de Mesquita for Voice, Ob, Vc & Hpd; Sentimental Gentleman of Swing Revisited for Chamber Ensemble *(rec Steurbaut Sound Recording Centre, Ghent, Belgium, Jan 1996)* René Gailly ("Vox Temporis Productions" series) ▲ VTP CD 92030 [DDD]
Spectre de la Rose [M. Knight (baroque vn), A. Crum (vl), E. Liddle (vl), S. Pell (vl), D. Miller (thb/baroque gtr), T. Roberts (hpd)]
Marais, M.:Suites VI & Hpd—Suite in G *(rec Jan. 6-7, 1993)* Naxos ▲ 8.550750 [DDD]
Marais, M.:VI Music—Sonnerie de Sainte Geneviève du Mont de Paris; Le badinage; Le labyrinth; La rêveuse; L'arabesque; Prelude in G; Tombeau pour Monsieur de Sainte-Colombe *(rec Jan. 6-7, 1993)* Naxos ▲ 8.550750 [DDD]
Sainte-Colombe, M. de:VI Music—Le retour; Tombeau les Regrets *(rec Jan. 6-7, 1993)* Naxos ▲ 8.550750 [DDD]
Spectrum
G. Protheroe (cnd)
Harvey, J.:Bhakti NM Classics ▲ NMCD 001 [AAD]
Speculum Musicae
Crumb, G.:Federico's Little Songs, w. Susan Narucki (sop) Bridge ▲ 9069
Crumb, G.:Night Music I, w. Susan Narucki (sop) Bridge ▲ 9069
Crumb, G.:Quest, w. David Starobin (gtr) Bridge ▲ 9069
Crumb, G.:Songs, Drones & Refrains of Death, w. S. Sylvan (bar)—[Sp] *(rec 6/17/90)* Bridge ▲ BCD 9028 [DDD]
Kurtág, G.:Scenes from a Novel, w. Jan De Gaetani (mez) *(rec live, New York City, 1987)* Bridge ▲ BCD 9048 [ADD]
Moravec, P.:Kingdom CRI ▲ CD 641 [DDD]
Picker, T.:Sxt 3 Fl *(rec 1979)* CRI ▲ CD 589 [ADD]
Wen-Chung, C.:Music of, w. Boston Musica Viva, New Music Consort—Windswept Peaks; Suite for Hp & Ww Qnt; Echoes from the Gorge; Yü Ko Albany ▲ TROY 155
R. Black (cnd)
Carter, E.:In Sleep, In Thunder, w. J. Garrison (ten) [E] Bridge ▲ BCD 9014 [DDD]
J. Graham (cnd)
Kraft, William:Gallery '83 *(rec 1986)* CRI ▲ CD 639 [ADD/DDD]
D. Palma (cnd)
Anderson, A.:Charrette *(rec Feb 29, 1988)* CRI ▲ CD 617 [DDD]
Blaustein, S.:Commedia *(rec 10/23/87)* CRI ▲ CD 617 [DDD]
Carter, E.:A Mirror on Which to Dwell, w. C. Schadeberg (sop) [E] Bridge ▲ BCD 9014 [DDD]
Clement, S.:Chamber Con *(rec 3/18/86)* CRI ▲ CD 617 [DDD]
Hyla, L.:Pre-Pulse Suspended *(rec SUNY, Purchase, NY, Oct 24, 1995)* New World ▲ 80491-2
Rakowski, D.:Imaginary Dances *(rec 3/23/89)* CRI ▲ CD 617 [DDD]
Rasmussen, K.A.:Movts on a Moving Line *(rec American Academy of Arts & Letters, New York City, Apr. 19-21, 1994)* Bridge ▲ BCD 9054 [DDD]
Ruders, P.:Psalmodies, w. D. Starobin (gtr) Bridge ▲ BCD 9037 [DDD]
W. Purvis (cnd)
Abrahamsen, H.:Winternacht *(rec American Academy of Arts & Letters, New York City, Apr. 19-21, 1994)* Bridge ▲ BCD 9054 [DDD]

Speculum Musicae (cont.)
W. Purvis (cnd) (cont.)
Carter, E.:Syringa, w. K. Ciesinski (mez), J. Opalach (bass) — Bridge ▲ BCD 9014 [DDD]
Hyla, L.:Con 2 Pno, w. Aleck Karis (pno) *(rec SUNY, Purchase, NY, Oct 25, 1995)* — New World ▲ 80491-2
Jaffe, S.:Songs with Ensemble, w. D'Anna Fortunato (mez) *(rec Oct. 22 & 23, 1993)* — Bridge ▲ BCD 9047 [DDD]
Sanford, D.:Con 3 Cl, w. Allen Blustine (cl) *(rec Lefrak Hall, Queens College, New York, May 14, 1995)* — CRI ▲ CD 705 [DDD]
M. Rosenzweig (cnd)
Rosenzweig, M.:Delta, the Perfect King, w. William Purvis (hn) *(rec Recital Hall, SUNY, Purchase, New York, Oct 15, 1991)* — CRI ▲ CD 705 [DDD]
H. Sollberger (cnd)
Carter, E.:Syringa, w. J. DeGaetani (mez), T. Paul (bar), Group for Contemporary Music [E] *(rec 5/81)* — CRI ■ ACS 6003
Carter, E.:Syringa, w. J. DeGaetani (mez), T. Paul (bar), Group for Contemporary Music *(rec 5/81)* — CRI ▲ CD 610 [ADD]
D. Starobin (cnd)
Carter, E.:Poems (3) of Robert Frost, w. P. Mason (bar) [E] — Bridge ▲ BCD 9014 [DDD]
Ruders, P.:The Bells, w. Lucy Shelton (sop) *(rec American Academy of Arts & Letters, Apr 21, 1994)* — Bridge ▲ BCD 9057 [DDD]
Ruders, P.:The Bells, w. Lucy Shelton (sop) *(rec American Academy of Arts & Letters, New York City, Apr. 19–21, 1994)* — Bridge ▲ BCD 9054 [DDD]
Sørensen, B.:The Deserted Churchyards *(rec American Academy of Arts & Letters, New York City, Apr. 19–21, 1994)* — Bridge ▲ BCD 9054 [DDD]
Speculum Musicae [Elizabeth Brown (fl), Allen Blustine (cl), Ethan Silverman (bn), William Purvis (hn), Ray Mase (tpt), Hugh Eddy (trbn), Christopher Old father (pno), Jim Baker (perc), Eric Charlston (perc)]
D. Palma (cnd)
Chou Wen-Chung:Yün — Albany ▲ TROY 155 [DDD]
Speculum Musicae [Victoria Drake (hp), Elizabeth Brown (fl), Marcia Butler (ob), Allen Blustine (cl), Ethan Silverman (bn), William Purvis (hn)]
Chou Wen-Chung:Suite Hp — Albany ▲ TROY 155 [DDD]
Speculum Musicae members
Wuorinen, C.:Bearbeitungen über das Glogauer Liederbuch — Music & Arts ▲ CD 800 [ADD]
Wuorinen, C.:Trio Strs — Music & Arts ▲ CD 800 [ADD]
A. Brehm (cnd)
Bland, E.:Piece CO, Group for Contemporary Music — Cambria ▲ CD 1026
F. Sherry (cnd)
Wuorinen, C.:Speculum speculi — Music & Arts ▲ CD 800 [ADD]
Speculum Musicae String Quartet
Rhodes, P.:Autumn Setting, w. P. Bryn-Julson (sop) — CRI ■ C 301
Daniel Speer Trombone Consort
Bizet, G.:Carmen (sels), w. Carmen Oprisanu (mez), Rob Haertel (perc) [arr Gerard de Krom] — World Wind ▲ CD KK 9618 [DDD]
Boutry, R.:Pieces (5) a 4 — World Wind ▲ CD KK 9618 [DDD]
Carles, M.:Lamento — World Wind ▲ CD KK 9618 [DDD]
Gervaise, C.:French Dances of the 16th Century, w. Rob Haertel (perc) [arr Hans Mooren, 1961] — World Wind ▲ CD KK 9618 [DDD]
Lys, M.:Suite pour un poker d'as — World Wind ▲ CD KK 9618 [DDD]
Tomasi, H.:Etre ou ne pas être — World Wind ▲ CD KK 9618 [DDD]
Speranza Trio
Bruch, M.:Trios Cl, Va & Pno, Op. 83—Trio Nos. 2-8 — Partridge ▲ 1125-2 [DDD]
Mozart, W.A.:Trio Cl, K.498 — Partridge ▲ 1125-2 [DDD]
Schumann, R.:Nachtstücke — Partridge ▲ 1125-2 [DDD]
SPIT Orchestra
Wolfe, J.:Tell Me Everything — Point Music ▲ 454054-2
Spoleto Festival Orch
C. Badea (cnd)
Barber, S.:Antony & Cleopatra, w. E. Hinds (sop), J. Wells (bass), Westminster Choir [E] *(rec live at the Spoleto Festival in Spoleto, Italy, June 1983)* — New World 2-▲ 322/24-2 [AAD]
S. Mercurio (cnd)
Menotti, G.C.:Goya, w. Josie de Guzman (sgr), Daner (sgr), Hernandez (sgr), Wentzel (sgr), Westminster Choir [I] *(rec live 1991)* — Nuova Era 2-▲ 7060/61 [DDD]
La Stagione
M. Schneider (cnd)
Abel, C.F.:Cons Fl, K.46-50, w. K. Kaiser (fl)—Nos. 1 in C, 2 in e, 3 in D, 5 in G — CPO ▲ CPO 999208 [DDD]
Abel, C.F.:Syms, Op. 10 — CPO ▲ CPO 999207 [DDD]
Haydn, J.:L'Anima del filosofo, or Orfeo ed Euridice, w. Clara McFadden (sop), Marylin Schmiege (mez), Christoph Prégardien, Gotthold Schwarz (bass), La Stagione Choir — Deutsche Harmonia Mundi 2-▲ 05472-77229-2
Holzbauer, I.:Günther von Schwarzburg, w. Clara McFadden (sop), Christoph Prégardien (ten), Robert Wörle (ten), Michael Schopper (bass) — CPO 3-▲ CPO 999265
Scarlatti, A.:Passion Oratorio, w. M. Bach (sop), P. Geitner (sop), K. Wessel (alt), Frankfurt Vocal Ensemble — Capriccio 2-▲ CD 10 411/12
Stradella, A.:The Crucifixion & Death of our Lord Jesus Christ, w. Frankfurt Vocal Ensemble — Capriccio 2-▲ CD 10 411/12
Stradella, A.:Lamentation for Wednesday the Holy Week, w. Frankfurt Vocal Ensemble — Capriccio 2-▲ CD 10 411/12
Telemann, G.P.:Cants, w. *(soloists unknown)*—Herrn strafe mich nicht in Deinem Zorn; Funeral cant. for Siliem, "Schwanngesang" — CPO ▲ CPO 999212 [DDD]
Telemann, G.P.:Kapitänmusik—Danket dem Herrn (oratorio); Ihr rüstigen Wächter hamburgischer Zinnen (serenata) [both from 1755] *(rec live, Bremen, 1993)* — CPO 2-▲ CPO 999211 [DDD]
Stalder Wind Quintet
Gaudibert, E.:Astrance *(rec Sept. 7, 1980)* — Grammont ▲ CTSP 8-2 [ADD]
Onslow, G.:Grand Septuor Fl, w. R. Frei (db), W. Bärtschi (pno) *(rec 1979)* — Jecklin-Disco ▲ JD 554-2 [ADD]
Onslow, G.:Qnt Fl *(rec 1979)* — Jecklin-Disco ▲ JD 554-2 [ADD]
Widmer, E.:Qnt 2 Ww *(rec Jan. 7, 1979)* — Grammont ▲ CTSP 32-2 [ADD]
Stamic String Quartet
Brod, M.:Qnt Pno, w. Frantisek Kuda (pno) — Supraphon ▲ SUP 112188 [DDD]
Guastavino, C.:Jeromita Linares, w. Maria Isabel Siewers (gtr) — ASV ▲ ASV 933 [DDD]
Kozeluch, L.:Qts Strs, Op. 32 — Supraphon ▲ SUP 111529 [DDD]
Kozeluch, L.:Qts Strs, Op. 33 — Supraphon ▲ SUP 111528 [DDD]
Krommer, F.:Qnt Cl, w. Vlastimil Mares (cl) — Supraphon ▲ SUP 0017 [DDD]
Mozart, W.A.:Divert Hns Strs, K.247, w. Z. Tylšar (hn), B. Tylšar (hn) — Supraphon ▲ 111523-2 [DDD]
Mozart, W.A.:Divert Hns Strs, K.287, w. Z. Tylšar (hn), B. Tylšar (hn) — Supraphon ▲ 111524-2 [DDD]
Mozart, W.A.:Divert Hns Strs, K.334, w. Z. Tylšar (hn), B. Tylšar (hn) — Supraphon ▲ 11 1525-2 [DDD]
Mozart, W.A.:Qnt Cl, K.581, w. Vlastimil Mares (cl) — Supraphon ▲ SUP 0017 [DDD]
Reicha, A.:Qnt Cl, Op. 89, w. Vlastimil Mares (cl) — Supraphon ▲ SUP 0051
Reicha, A.:Qnt Ob, w. Vlastimil Mares (cl) — Supraphon ▲ SUP 0051
Vranicky, P.:Qts Strs—Op. 16/4 in F; 5 in C; 6 in d *(rec Panton Studio, Prague, Nov. 9–13, 1992)* — Panton ▲ PAN 811264
Vranicky, P.:Qts Strs—Nos. 1 in B♭, 2 in E♭ & 3 in D — Panton ▲ PAN 811046
Stamic String Quartet members
Guastavino, C.:Cantos Populares (3), w. Maria Isabel Siewers (gtr) — ASV ▲ ASV 933 [DDD]
Carl Stamitz Ensemble
Françaix, J.:Divert Bn, w. A. Wallez (bn) — Pierre Verany ▲ PVY 792102 [DDD]
Françaix, J.:Octet, w. J.-L. Sajot (cl), A. Wallez (bn) — Pierre Verany ▲ PVY 792102 [DDD]

Carl Stamitz Ensemble (cont.)
Françaix, J.:Qnt Cl, w. J.-L. Sajot (cl) — Pierre Verany ▲ PVY 792102 [DDD]
Reicha, A.:Octet Strs — Pierre Verany ▲ PV.789101 [DDD]
Reicha, A.:Qnt Cl, Op. 89 — Pierre Verany ▲ PV.789101 [DDD]
Schubert, Franz:Octet Ww, D.803 — Pierre Verany ▲ PV.790033 [DDD]
Weber, C.M. von:Intro, Theme & Vars Cl, w. J.-L. Sajot (cl) — Pierre Verany ▲ PV.792021 [DDD]
Weber, C.M. von:Qt Pno, w. P. Corre (pno) — Pierre Verany ▲ PV.792021 [DDD]
Weber, C.M. von:Qnt Cl, w. J.-L. Sajot (cl) — Pierre Verany ▲ PV.792021 [DDD]
Stamitz String Quartet
Dvořák, A.:Qts Strs (comp)—Nos. 1 & 9 — Bayer ▲ 100143 [DDD]
Dvořák, A.:Qts Strs (comp)—Nos. 5 & 6 — Bayer ▲ 100146 [DDD]
Dvořák, A.:Qts Strs (comp)—Nos. 10 & 14 — Bayer ▲ 100142 [DDD]
Dvořák, A.:Qts Strs (comp)—No. 11 — Bayer ▲ 100144 [DDD]
Dvořák, A.:Qts Strs (comp)—No. 1 — Bayer ▲ 100145 [DDD]
Dvořák, A.:Qts Strs (comp)—Nos. 12 & 13 — Bayer ▲ 100141 [DDD]
Dvořák, A.:Qnt Strs, Op. 77, w. J. Hudec (db) — Bayer ▲ 100184 [DDD]
Dvořák, A.:Qnt Strs, Op. 97, w. J. Talich (va) — Bayer ▲ 100184 [DDD]
Dvořák, A.:Waltzes Strs, B.105 — Bayer ▲ 100144 [DDD]
Janácek, L.:Qt 1 Strs — Bayer ▲ 100151 [DDD]
Janácek, L.:Qt 2 Strs — Bayer ▲ 100151 [DDD]
Krommer, F.:Qnts Fl, w. Bruno Meier (fl)—Opp. 49, 63 & 101 — Koch Schwann ▲ SCH 310972 [DDD]
Krommer, F.:Qnts Fl, w. B. Meier (fl)—Op. 55 in e;Op. 58 in C;Op. 109 in G — Koch Schwann ▲ 3-1049-2 [DDD]
Martinů, B.:Qts Strs — Bayer 3-▲ 100152/54 [DDD]
Mozart, W.A.:Adagio E hn, w. Lajos Lencsés (E hn) *(rec Bonnieux, July 1994)* — Capriccio ▲ 10525 [DDD]
Mozart, W.A.:Qt Ob, w. Lajos Lencsés (ob) *(rec Bonnieux, July 1994)* — Capriccio ▲ 10525 [DDD]
Mozart, W.A.:Qt 22 Strs *(rec Bonnieux, July 1994)* — Capriccio ▲ 10525 [DDD]
Mozart, W.A.:Qnt Ob, w. Lajos Lencsés (ob) *(rec Bonnieux, July 1994)* — Capriccio ▲ 10525 [DDD]
Stamitz String Quartet [Bohuslav Matousek (vn), Josef Kekula (vn), Jan Peruska (va), Vladimir Leixner (vc)]
Borodin, A.:Qt 1 Strs *(rec Temple de Dombresson, July 20–22, 1991)* — Alphée ▲ 9601006 [DDD]
Borodin, A.:Qt 2 Strs *(rec Temple de Dombresson, July 20–22, 1991)* — Alphée ▲ 9601006 [DDD]
Stamitz String Quartet members
Dvořák, A.:Terzetto — Bayer ▲ 100145 [DDD]
Martinů, B.:Madrigals Vn — Bayer 3-▲ 100152/54 [DDD]
Martinů, B.:Trio 2 Vn — Bayer 3-▲ 100152/54 [DDD]
Standard SO
A. Wallenstein (cnd)
Mozart, W.A.:Con 24 Pno, w. A. Schnabel (pno) *(rec live in Los Angeles, Dec. 1, 1946)* — Music & Arts ▲ CD 632 (m) [AAD]
Stanford String Quartet
Bolcom, W.:Qt 10 Strs — Laurel ▲ LR 847CD
Bridge, F.:Qt 1 Strs — Music & Arts ▲ CD 823 [DDD]
Fauré, G.:Qt Strs — Music & Arts ▲ CD 823 [DDD]
Johnston, B.:Qt 9 Strs — Laurel ▲ LR 847CD
Milhaud, D.:Qt 7 Strs — Music & Arts ▲ CD 823 [DDD]
Neikrug, M.:Qt Strs — Laurel ▲ LR 847CD
Stanislas Ensemble
Weill, K.:Songs—Moderato assai; Agitato; Shimmy Tempo; Andante con moto; Tango-Tempo; Allegretto; Foxtrot-Tempo *(rec Nov. 1991)* — Gallo ▲ CD 676 [DDD]
Stanislas Ensemble [J. Cohen (pno), A. Galpérine (vn), G. Lee (vn), P. Fenton (va), J. de Spengler (vc), J. Libouban (fl), P. Moinet (cl), N. Tacchi (bn), M. Shirotori (harm)]
Eisler, H.:Septet 1 *(rec Nov. 1991)* — Gallo ▲ CD 676 [DDD]
Eisler, H.:Septet 2, "Zirkus" *(rec Nov. 1991)* — Gallo ▲ CD 676 [DDD]
Schoenberg, A.:Songs—La Brigade de fer; Musique de Noël *(rec Nov. 1991)* — Gallo ▲ CD 676 [DDD]
Stanislas Ensemble [J. Libouban (fl), J. Guichard (ob), L. Causse (vn), G. Lee (vn), P. Fenton (va), J. de Spengler (vc)]
Rossini, G.:Serenade Fl — Gallo ▲ CD 721 [DDD]
Stanislas Ensemble [J. Libouban (fl), P. Moinet (cl), P. Riffault (hn), N. Tacchi (bn)]
Rossini, G.:Andante e Tema con variazioni — Gallo ▲ CD 721 [DDD]
Stanislas Ensemble [Jean-Louis Haguenauer (pno), Alexis Galpérine (vn), Gee Lee (vn), Paul Fenton (va), Jean de Spengler (vc), Sylvie Tournon (fl), Philippe Moinet (cl), Mari Shirotori (harm)]
Strauss (II), Joh.:Waltzes—Roses du Sud [trans Schoenberg]; Valse du "Baron Tzigane" [trans Webern]; Amier, Boire et Manger [trans Berg]; Valse de l'Empereur [trans Schoenberg] — Gallo ▲ CD 892 [ADD]
Stanislas Ensemble [L. Causse (vn), B. Huvenne (hp)]
Rossini, G.:Andante con variazioni Hp [arr. for violin & harp] — Gallo ▲ CD 721 [DDD]
Stanislas Ensemble [L. Causse (vn), P. Fenton (va), J. de Spengler (vc), E. Costa (db), J. Libouban (fl), P. Colombain (ob), P. Moinet (cl), P. Riffault (hn), N. Tacchi (bn)]
Spohr, L.:Nonet Strs — Gallo ▲ CD 721 [DDD]
Stanley String Quartet
Porter, Q.:Qt 8 Strs — CRI ■ C 118
Star of Indiana Drummers
Brass on Broadway, w. Canadian Brass, Luther Henderson (kbd), Edward Metz (perc) — Philips ▲ 442133-2
Starling CO
K. Sassmannshaus (cnd)
Samuel, G.:Transformations, w. Paul Yeager (vn) *(rec Corbett Auditorium, College-Conservatory of Music, Univ. of Cincinnati, OH, Sept 25, 1994)* — Centaur ▲ CRC 2238 [DDD]
State SO
G. A. Albrecht (cnd)
Koerppen, A.:Con a quattro — Ars Musici ▲ 1021
Koerppen, A.:Italian Madrigals, w. Hanover Theater School Chamber Choir — Ars Musici ▲ 1021
Koerppen, A.:Sym 2 — Ars Musici ▲ 1021
E. Chivzhel (cnd)
Martinů, B.:Rhap-Con Va, w. Mikhail Tolpygo (va) *(rec 1990)* — Consonance ▲ 81-0003 [DDD]
I. Golovshin (cnd)
Blumenfeld, F.:Sym, "To the Beloved Dead" — Russian Disc ▲ RUS 11052 [DDD]
Stauffer String Quartet [C. Feige (vn), A. Mastalini (vn), C. Pavolini (va), M. Decimo (vc)]
Sacchini, A.:Qts Strs — Arkadia-Akademia ▲ 141 [DDD]
Stavanger SO
A. Dmitriev (cnd)
Debussy, C.:Nocturnes, w. Stavanger Sym Women's Choir *(rec June 1993)* — Victoria ▲ VCD 19081
Ravel, M.:Ma mère l'oye Orch *(rec June 1993)* — Victoria ▲ VCD 19081
Ravel, M.:La Valse *(rec June 1993)* — Victoria ▲ VCD 19081
Saeverud, H.:Galdreslåtten *(rec Stavanger Konserthus, Stavanger, Norway, Nov 13–17, 1995)* — BIS ▲ CD 762 [DDD]
Saeverud, H.:Kjempeviseslåtten *(rec Stavanger Konserthus, Stavanger, Norway, Nov 13–17, 1995)* — BIS ▲ CD 762 [DDD]
Saeverud, H.:Peer Gynt Suites, w. Sveinung Sand (vn), Anna Dolezych (va), Kjersti Dahle (ob/E hn), Gyrid Erlandsen (cl), Bohumil Maliska (hn) *(rec Stavanger Konserthus, Stavanger, Norway, Nov 13–17, 1995)* — BIS ▲ CD 762 [DDD]
Saeverud, H.:Sinf dolorosa *(rec Stavanger Konserthus, Stavanger, Norway, Nov 13–17, 1995)* — BIS ▲ CD 762 [DDD]
Steintor Barock Bremen
W. Helbich (cnd)
Eybler, J.L.E. von:Requiem mit Libera, w. B. Schlick (sop), H. van der Kamp (bass), Alsfeld Vocal Ensemble — CPO ▲ CPO 999234 [DDD]

Stenzl Piano Duo [Hans-Peter Stenzl (pno), V. Stenzl (pno)]
Schubert, Franz:Fant Pno, D.940 Ars Musici ▲ 1087 [DDD]
Schubert, Franz:Son Pno 4-Hands, D.812 Ars Musici ▲ 1087 [DDD]
Sterling String Quartet [Megan Pound (vn), Rebecca Jones (vn), John Rayson (va), Brian Mullan (vc)]
Rubbra, E.:Qts Strs *(rec St. Martin's Church, Hampshire, England)*
Conifer Classics 2-▲ 75605-51260-2 [DDD]
Stoccarda RSO
J. Keilberth (cnd)
Beethoven, L. van:Con 5 Pno, "Emperor", w. Wilhelm Backhaus (pno) Stradivarius ▲ STV 10002 [ADD]
Stockholm Arts Trio [S. Bojsten (pno), D. Almgren (vn), T. Thedéen (vc)]
Wirén, D.:Music of—Trio No. 1, Op. 6; Sonatina for Violin & Piano, Op. 15; Ironiska smastycken for Piano, Op. 19; Sonatina for Cello & Piano, Op. 1; Trio No. 2, Op. 36 *(rec Aug. 28-30, 1992)*
BIS ▲ CD 582 [DDD]
Stockholm Chamber Brass
Bach, Jan:Laudes BIS ▲ CD 544 [DDD]
Bach, Jan:Rounds & Dances *(rec Danderyd Grammar School Gymnasium, June 26-30, 1994)*
BIS ▲ CD 699 [DDD]
Bernstein, L.:Dance Suite Brass *(rec Danderyd Grammar School Gymnasium, June 26-30, 1994)*
BIS ▲ CD 699 [DDD]
Danielsson, C.:Capriccio da camera Caprice ▲ CAP 21493
Ewald, V.:Qnt 1 Brass *(rec 1993)* BIS ▲ CD 613 [DDD]
Ewald, V.:Qnt 2 Brass *(rec 1993)* BIS ▲ CD 613 [DDD]
Ewald, V.:Qnt 3 Brass *(rec 1993)* BIS ▲ CD 613 [DDD]
Ewald, V.:Qnt 4 Brass *(rec 1993)* BIS ▲ CD 613 [DDD]
Heavy Metal BIS ▲ CD 544 [DDD]
Larsson, M.:Clockworks, w. Love Derwinger (pno), Rolan Pöntinen (pno), Johan Silvmark (perc) *(rec Studio 2, Swedish Radio, Nov. 13, 1994)* BIS ▲ CD 699 [DDD]
Previn, A.:4 Outings *(rec Danderyd Grammar School Gymnasium, June 26-30, 1994)*
BIS ▲ CD 699 [DDD]
Stravinsky, I.:L'Histoire du soldat (sels), w. Johan Silvmark (perc)—Tango; Waltz; Ragtime [all arr. Joakim Agnas for Brass] *(rec Danderyd Grammar School Gymnasium, June 26-30, 1994)*
BIS ▲ CD 699 [DDD]
Stravinsky, I.:Ragtime, w. Johan Silvmark (perc) [arr. Joakim Agnas for Brass Qnt] *(rec Danderyd Grammar School Gymnasium, June 26-30, 1994)* BIS ▲ CD 699 [DDD]
Stockholm Chamber Ensemble
Larsson, L.-E.:Concertinos, w. New Stockholm CO, Musica Sveciae, Musica Vitae, Umea Sinfonietta—G. von Bahr (fl) *(No. 1)*, H. Jahren (ob) *(No. 2)*, M. Lethiec (cl) *(No. 3)*, K. Sonstevold (bn) *(No. 4)*, S. Hermansson (hn) *(No. 5)*, U. Agnas (tpt) *(No. 6)*, C. Lindberg (trbn) *(No. 7)*, A. Kontra (vn) *(No. 8)*, B. Andersson (va) *(No. 9)*, F. Helmerson (vc) *(No. 10)*, H. Ehren (db) *(No. 11)*, H. Palsson (pno) *(No. 12)*
BIS 2-▲ CD 473/74 [AAD/DDD]
Larsson, L.-E.:Concertino Hn, w. Ib Lanzky-Otto (hn) Caprice ▲ CAP 21492
Sibelius, J.:Rakastava Strs Swedish Society ▲ SCD 1047
Sibelius, J.:Rondino Swedish Society ▲ SCD 1047
J.-O. Wedin (cnd)
Albinoni, T.:Adagio Org, w. G. von Bahr (fl) BIS ▲ CD 100
Molter, J.M.:Con Flauto d'amore, w. Gunilla von Bahr (fl) BIS ▲ CD 100
Mozart, W.A.:Rondo Fl, K.Anh.184, w. G. von Bahr (fl) BIS ▲ CD 175
Sun-Flute, w. Gunilla von Bahr (fl) BIS ▲ CD 100
Vivaldi, A.:Cons Pic, w. G. von Bahr (fl)—R.443 [w. K. Hindart (pno)]; R.444 & R.445 BIS ▲ CD 21
Werdin, E.:Concertino Fl, w. G. von Bahr (fl), D. Blanco (gtr) BIS ▲ CD 60 [AAD]
Stockholm CO
E. Ericson (cnd)
Sacred Songs, w. Barbara Hendricks (sop), Ericson's Chamber Choir EMI Classics ▲ CDC 54098 [DDD]
L. Markiz (cnd)
Schnittke, A.:Con grosso 3, w. P. Swedrup (vn), T. Olsson (vn) BIS ▲ CD 537 [DDD]
Schnittke, A.:Son Vn & CO, w. C. Bergqvist (vn) BIS ▲ CD 537 [DDD]
Schnittke, A.:Trio Son BIS ▲ CD 537 [DDD]
E.-P. Salonen (cnd)
Haydn, J.:Sym 22, "Der Philosoph" Sony Classical ▲ SK 45972
Haydn, J.:Sym 78 Sony Classical ▲ SK 45972
Haydn, J.:Sym 82, "The Bear" Sony Classical ▲ SK 45972
Haydn, J.:Sym 82, "The Bear"—Menuetto; Finale, Vivace assai
Sony Classical ▲ MLK 62369 [ADD/DDD]
Stravinsky, I.:Apollon musagète Sony Classical ▲ SK 46667
Stravinsky, I.:Con Str Sony Classical ▲ SK 46667
M. Tatlow (cnd)
Kraus, J.M.:Prosperin, w. Hillevi Martinpelto (sop), Susanne Rydén (sop), Anna Eklund-Tarantino (sgr), Peter Mattei (bar), Lars Arvidson (bass), Stephen Smith (sgr), Stockholm Chamber Choir
Musica Sveciae 2-▲ MSCD 422/23 [DDD]
Stockholm Chamber Soloists
Roman, J.H.:Con Vn, w. L. Berlin (vn), Philharmonic Chamber Ensemble Swedish Society ▲ SCD 1019
Stockholm Concert Band
G. Rozhdestvensky (cnd)
Khachaturian, A.:Soviet Police March Chandos ▲ CHAN 9444
Miaskovsky, N.:Sym 19 Chandos ▲ CHAN 9444
Prokofiev, S.:March, Op. 99 Chandos ▲ CHAN 9444
Rimsky-Korsakov, N.:Concertstück Cl, w. Alf Nilsson (cl) Chandos ▲ CHAN 9444
Rimsky-Korsakov, N.:Vars on a Theme of Glinka, w. Sölve Kingstedt (ob) Chandos ▲ CHAN 9444
Shostakovich, D.:March 1 Chandos ▲ CHAN 9444
Stravinsky, I.:Song of Volga Boatman (arr winds) Chandos ▲ CHAN 9444
Stockholm Concert Society Orch
W. Furtwängler (cnd)
Beethoven, L. van:Sym 9, "Choral Sym", w. H. Schymberg (sop), L. Tunell (cta), G. Bäckelin (ten), S. Björling (bar) *(rec Dec. 1, 1943)* Music & Arts ▲ CD 774 [AAD]
Wagner, R.:Tristan und Isolde (orch sels)—Isoldes Liebestod *(rec 1942)*
Grammofono 2000 ▲ GRM 78515 [AAD]
Stockholm Conservatory Soloists
Mozart, W.A.:Requiem, w. St. Jacob Choir Stockholm Prophone ▲ PCD 015
Stockholm Guitar Quartet
Bach, J.S.:Brandenburg Con 6 [arr for Gtr Qt] Opus 3 ▲ OP 7915
Bach, J.S.:Preludes (12) Hpd—Nos. 2 & 22 [arr for Gtr Qt] Opus 3 ▲ OP 7915
Cimarosa, D.:Music of—Larghetto in c [arr for Gtr Qt] Opus 3 ▲ OP 7915
Frescobaldi, G.:Aria detta "La Frescobalda" [arr for Gtr Qt] Opus 3 ▲ OP 7915
Telemann, G.P.:Cons Vn [arr for Gtr Qt] Opus 3 ▲ OP 7915
Stockholm New CO
J. Panula (cnd)
Glazunov, A.:Con Sax, w. P. Savijoki (sax) BIS ▲ CD 218 [DDD]
Larsson, L.-E.:Con Sax, w. Pekka Savijoki (a sax) BIS ▲ CD 218 [DDD]
Panula, J.:Adagio & Allegro, w. P. Savijoki (sax) BIS ▲ CD 218 [DDD]
Stockholm Philharmonic Brass Ensemble
Music for Brass Ensemble from the 16th-18th Centuries, w. Malmö Brass Ensemble
BIS ▲ CD 223 [ADD/DDD]
Music for Brass:Through Time & Space Caprice ▲ CAP 21258 [DDD]

Stockholm PO
Beethoven, L. van:Sym 9, "Choral Sym"—4th movt.; a stitched-together series of ten progressively earlier live performance selections conducted by, in order from bar one— Berglund [1988], Doráti [1976, 1967], Schmidt-Isserstedt [1960], Kletzki [1958], Fricsay [1957], E. Kleiber [1949], H. Abendroth [1943], Furtwängler [1943], V. Talich [1934] BIS 8-▲ CD 421/24 (m/s) [AAD]
Blomdahl, K.-B.:Sisyfos Swedish Society ▲ SCD 1037
75 Years (1914-1989), w. Yuri Ahronovitch (cnd), F. Busch (cnd), A. Dorati (cnd), W. Furtwängler (cnd), N. Grevillius (cnd), T. Mann (cnd), G. Rozhdestvensky (cnd), H. Schmidt-Isserstedt (cnd), V. Talich (cnd), Bruno Walter (cnd), et al. *(rec 1933-1988)* BIS 8-▲ CD 421/24 (m/s) [AAD]
Y. Ahronovitch (cnd)
Blomdahl, K.-B.:...the voyage this night, w. E. Söderström (sop) Caprice ▲ CAP 21365 [AAD]
Dvořák, A.:Sym 6 *(rec live, 1/26/84)* BIS 8-▲ CD 421/24 (m/s) [AAD]
Eklund, H.:Fant Vc Swedish Society ▲ SCD 1038
Eklund, H.:Music Orch Swedish Society ▲ SCD 1038
Eklund, H.:Small Talk Swedish Society ▲ SCD 1038
Eklund, H.:Sym 6 Swedish Society ▲ SCD 1038
Frumerie, G. de:Singoalla, w. Hägersten Motet Choir Caprice 2-▲ CAP 22023 [DDD]
Pettersson, G.A.:Sym 16—final movt. only *(rec live, 4/12/86)* BIS 8-▲ CD 421/24 (m/s) [AAD]
Pettersson, G.A.:Sym 16 Swedish Society ▲ SCD 1003
Rangström, T.:Sym 4, w. Erik Lundkvist (org) *(rec Stockholm Concert Hall, Jan. 16 & 18, 1985)*
Caprice ▲ CAP 21195 [DDD]
Shostakovich, D.:Sym 5 BIS ▲ CD 357 [DDD]
Tchaikovsky, P.:Suite 3—final movt. *(rec live, 9/15/84)* BIS 8-▲ CD 421/24 (m/s) [AAD]
J. Arnell (cnd)
Peterson-Berger, W.:Songs, w. Ingvar Wixell (bar)—Arnljots hälsningssang till Jämtland; Bland skogens höga furustammar; Böljeby-vals; När jag för mig själv i mörka skogen gar [Sw]
Musica Sveciae ▲ MSCD 617 [DDD]
Rangström, T.:Songs, w. I. Wixell (bar)—En visa om mig och narren Herkules; En visa om när jag var lustig; En visa till Karin när hon hade dansat; En visa till Karin ur fängelset; Kung Eriks sista visa [Sw]
Musica Sveciae ▲ MSCD 617 [DDD]
Söderman, A.:King Heimer & Aslog, w. I. Wixell (bar) [Sw] Musica Sveciae ▲ MSCD 617 [DDD]
Stenhammar, W.:Songs, w. I. Wixell (bar)—En positivvisa; Florez och Blanzeflor; I en skogskbacke; Kväll i Klara; Mellan broarna [Sw] *(rec 6/90)* Musica Sveciae ▲ MSCD 617 [DDD]
P. Berglund (cnd)
Strauss, R.:Burleske, w. S. Edelmann (pno) RCA Red Seal ▲ 60173-2-RC [DDD]
Strauss, R.:Don Juan RCA Red Seal ▲ 60173-2-RC [DDD]
Strauss, R.:Serenade Ww RCA Red Seal ▲ 60173-2-RC [DDD]
Strauss, R.:Till Eulenspiegels lustige Streiche RCA Red Seal ▲ 60173-2-RC [DDD]
H. Blomstedt (cnd)
Lidholm, I.:Poesis Swedish Society ▲ SCD 1027
F. Busch (cnd)
Berg, A.:Con Vn, w. L. Krasner (vn) *(rec live 4/20/38)* GM ▲ 2006 (m)
Larsson, L.-E.:Sym 2—3rd movt. *(rec live, 12/4/49)* BIS 8-▲ CD 421/24 (m/s) [AAD]
S. Comissiona (cnd)
Blomdahl, K.-B.:Forma ferritonans Caprice ▲ CAP 21365 [AAD]
Pettersson, G.A.:Sym 14 Phono Suecia ▲ PHN 12 [DDD]
Wirén, D.:Con Vn, w. Nils-Erik Sparf (vn) Caprice ▲ CAP 21326 [DDD/AAD]
A. Dorati (cnd)
Bartók, B.:The Miraculous Mandarin (suite) *(rec live, 2/4/70)* BIS 8-▲ CD 421/24 (m/s) [AAD]
Berwald, F.:Sym 2, "Sinfonie capricieuse" Swedish Society ▲ SCD 1046
Blomdahl, K.-B.:Sisyfos Caprice ▲ CAP 21365 [AAD]
Doráti, A.:Sym 1 *(rec 1972)* BIS ▲ CD 408 [ADD/DDD]
Doráti, A.:Sym 2, "Querela Pacis" *(rec 1988)* BIS ▲ CD 408 [ADD/DDD]
Kodály, Z.:Psalmus hungaricus, w. J. Simándy *(rec live, 12/16/67)* BIS 8-▲ CD 421/24 (m/s) [AAD]
Pettersson, G.A.:Sym 7 Swedish Society ▲ SCD 1003
Ravel, M.:Daphnis et Chloé (suite 2) *(rec live, 5/2/66)* BIS 8-▲ CD 421/24 (m/s) [AAD]
Sibelius, J.:Sym 2 Swedish Society ▲ SCD 1046
Stenhammar, W.:Serenade—abbreviated version *(rec live 2/4/70)* BIS 8-▲ CD 421/24 (m/s) [AAD]
S. Ehrling (cnd)
Atterberg, K.:Sym 3 Caprice ▲ CAP 21364 [AAD]
Blomdahl, K.-B.:Dance Suite 1 Caprice ▲ CAP 21424 [AAD]
Blomdahl, K.-B.:Dance Suite 2 Caprice ▲ CAP 21424 [AAD]
Blomdahl, K.-B.:In the Hall of Mirrors, w. *(soloists unknown)*, Swedish Radio Chorus
Caprice ▲ CAP 21424 [AAD]
Blomdahl, K.-B.:Sym 3, "Facetter" Swedish Society ▲ SCD 1037
Blomdahl, K.-B.:Sym 3, "Facetter" Caprice ▲ CAP 21365 [AAD]
Karkoff, M.:Sym 4 Swedish Society ▲ SCD 1023
P. Erös (cnd)
Nystroem, G.:Is havet Caprice ▲ CAP 21332 [ADD/DDD]
Nystroem, G.:Sinf breve Caprice ▲ CAP 21332 [ADD/DDD]
Nystroem, G.:Sinf seria Caprice ▲ CAP 21332 [ADD/DDD]
W. Furtwängler (cnd)
Beethoven, L. van:Leonore 2 *(rec Nov. 12, 1948)* Music & Arts ▲ CD 793 [AAD]
Beethoven, L. van:Sym 7 *(rec Nov. 13, 1948)* Music & Arts ▲ CD 793 [AAD]
Beethoven, L. van:Sym 8 *(rec Nov. 13, 1948)* Music & Arts ▲ CD 793 [AAD]
Beethoven, L. van:Sym 9, "Choral Sym", w. L. Tunell (alto), G. Bckelin (ten), S. Björling (bass) *(rec Dec. 1, 1943)* Music & Arts ▲ CD 2002 [AAD]
Brahms, J.:Ein Deutsches Requiem, w. K. Lindberg-Torlind (sop), B. Sonnerstedt (bar) *(rec 1948)*
Music & Arts 2-▲ CD 289 (m) [AAD]
Strauss, R.:Don Juan *(rec Nov. 25, 1942)* Music & Arts ▲ CD 814 [AAD]
Wagner, R.:Tristan und Isolde (prelude & liebestod) *(rec live, 11/25/42)*
BIS 8-▲ CD 421/24 (m/s) [AAD]
C. von Garaguly (cnd)
Pergament, M.:Rapsodie ebreica *(rec live, 3/30/49)* BIS 8-▲ CD 421/24 (m/s) [AAD]
Rosenberg, H.:Con 1 Orch *(rec 1950 for HMV)* BIS 8-▲ CD 421/24 (m/s) [AAD]
N. Grevillius (cnd)
Alfvén, H.:Swedish Rhap 1, "Midsommarvaka" *(rec Feb 24, 1939 for HMV)*
BIS 8-▲ CD 421/24 (m/s) [AAD]
Alfvén, H.:Sym 3 Swedish Society ▲ SCD 1008
J. Horenstein (cnd)
Mahler, G.:Sym 6 *(rec Apr. 15 & 17, 1966)* Music & Arts 4-▲ CD 785 [AAD]
A. Jansons (cnd)
Rosenberg, H.:Con 2 Vn, w. L. Spierer (vn) Caprice ▲ CAP 21367 [DDD]
Söderlundh, L.B.:Con Vn, w. L. Spierer (vn) Caprice ▲ CAP 21367 [DDD]
N. Järvi (cnd)
Alfvén, H.:Bergakungen—orchestral suite BIS ▲ CD 585 [DDD]
Alfvén, H.:Gustav II Adolph—Elegy BIS ▲ CD 585 [DDD]
Alfvén, H.:The Prodigal Son BIS ▲ CD 455 [DDD]
Alfvén, H.:Swedish Rhap 1, "Midsommarvaka" BIS ▲ CD 385 [DDD]
Alfvén, H.:Swedish Rhap 2, "Uppsala-rhapsodi" BIS ▲ CD 395
Alfvén, H.:Swedish Rhap 3, "Dalarhapsodien" BIS ▲ CD 455 [DDD]
Alfvén, H.:Sym 1 BIS ▲ CD 395
Alfvén, H.:Sym 2 BIS ▲ CD 385 [DDD]
Alfvén, H.:Sym 3 BIS ▲ CD 455 [DDD]
Alfvén, H.:Sym 4, "Fran havsbandet [From the Seaward Skerries]", w. C. Hogman (sop), C.-H. Ahnsjö (ten) BIS ▲ CD 505 [DDD]
Alfvén, H.:Sym 5 BIS ▲ CD 585 [DDD]
Alfvén, H.:A Tale from the Archipelago BIS ▲ CD 505 [DDD]

Stockholm PO (cont.)
O. Kamu (cnd)
Lindblad, A.F.:Sym 1 — Caprice ▲ CAP 21425 [DDD]
H. von Karajan (cnd)
Sibelius, J.:Sym 5—3rd movt. *(rec live, 11/7/49)* — BIS 8–▲ CD 421/24 (m/s) [AAD]
D. Kaye (cnd)
Tchaikovsky, P.:The Nutcracker (sels)—3 selections *(rec live, Unicef Gala, 11/17/73)* — BIS 8–▲ CD 421/24 (m/s) [AAD]
E. Klas (cnd)
Schnittke, A.:Sym 3 — BIS ▲ CD 477 [DDD]
R. Kubelik (cnd)
Stenhammar, W.:Serenade, w. E. Soderström (sop), N. Gedda (ten) — Swedish Society ▲ SCD 1016
C.R. Larsson (cnd)
Pettersson, G.A.:Sym 12, w. London Phil Choir, Univ of Uppsala Choir — Caprice ▲ CAP 21369 [AAD]
T. Mann (cnd)
Nystroem, G.:Sinf espressiva *(rec 1950 for HMV)* — BIS 8–▲ CD 421/24 (m/s) [AAD]
Stenhammar, W.:Sym 2 — Swedish Society ▲ SCD 1014
A. Öhrwall (cnd)
Olsson, O.:Requiem, w. M. A. Häggander (sop), E. Paaske (cta), A. Andersson (ten), L. Wedin (bar), Stockholm Phil Chorus — Caprice ▲ CAP 21368 [DDD]
J. Panula (cnd)
Nilsson, T.:Con 2 Pno, w. Hans Pålsson (pno) — Caprice ▲ CAP 21417 [DDD]
G. Rozhdestvensky (cnd)
Auber, D.–F.:Gustave III (ov) *(rec live, May 5, 1976)* — BIS 8–▲ CD 421/24 (m/s) [AAD]
Berwald, F.:Sym 3, "Sinfonie singulière" *(rec live Oct. 19, 1977)* — BIS 8–▲ CD 421/24 (m/s) [AAD]
Scriabin, A.:Sym 2 *(rec live 11/26/72)* — BIS 8–▲ CD 421/24 (m/s) [AAD]
H. Schmidt-Isserstedt (cnd)
Hindemith, P.:Con Orch *(rec live, 10/31/58)* — BIS 8–▲ CD 421/24 (m/s) [AAD]
Orff, C.:Carmina burana, w. E. Söderström (sop), G. Bäckelin (ten), S. Svanholm (ten), Stockholm Phil Chorus *(rec live, 11/26/54)* — BIS 8–▲ CD 421/24 (m/s) [AAD]
L. Segerstam (cnd)
Lidholm, I.:Kontakion — Caprice ▲ CAP 21366 [AAD]
Scriabin, A.:Con Pno, w. R. Pöntinen (pno) — BIS ▲ CD 475 [DDD]
Scriabin, A.:Sym 1, w. I. Blom (cta), L. Magnusson (ten), Stockholm Phil Chorus [R] — BIS ▲ CD 534 [DDD]
Scriabin, A.:Sym 3 — BIS ▲ CD 475 [DDD]
Scriabin, A.:Sym 5, w. Stockholm Phil Chorus — BIS ▲ CD 534 [DDD]
L. Stokowski (cnd)
Brahms, J.:Sym 1—2nd mvmt *(rec live, 5/25/39)* — BIS 8–▲ CD 421/24 (m/s) [AAD]
V. Talich (cnd)
Mahler, G.:Das Lied von der Erde, w. K. Thorborg (mez)—sels. *(rec live, 11/7/34)* — BIS 8–▲ CD 421/24 (m/s) [AAD]
A. Toscanini (cnd)
Brahms, J.:Sym 3—2nd mvmt. *(rec live, 12/3/33)* — BIS 8–▲ CD 421/24 (m/s) [AAD]
Rossini, G.:Ovs—Barber of Seville *(rec live 12/3/33)* — BIS 8–▲ CD 421/24 (m/s) [AAD]
N. Totsuka (cnd)
Boldemann, L.:Con Pno, w. D. Achatz (pno) — Swedish Society ▲ SKCD 1
O. Vänskä (cnd)
Rangström, T.:Vauxhall, w. Bengt Christiansson (fl), Lars Olof Loman (ob), Lars Almgren (cl), Sven Aarflot (bn), Rolf Bengtsson (hn), Rune Bodin (trbn), Rozalina Skytt (hp) *(rec Stockholm Concert Hall, Jan. 16 & 18, 1985)* — Caprice ▲ CAP 21195 [DDD]
B. Walter (cnd)
Mozart, W.A.:Sym 39 *(rec live, Sept. 8, 1950)* — BIS 8–▲ CD 421/24 (m/s) [AAD]
S. Westerberg (cnd)
Alfvén, H.:Bergakungen — Swedish Society ▲ SCD 1012
Alfvén, H.:Dalecarlian Rhap — Swedish Society ▲ SCD 1008
Alfvén, H.:Festspel — Swedish Society ▲ SCD 1012
Alfvén, H.:The Prodigal Son — Swedish Society ▲ SCD 1012
Alfvén, H.:Swedish Rhap 1, "Midsommarvaka" — Swedish Society ▲ SCD 1012
Frumerie, G. de:Con Hn, w. Ib Lanzky-Otto (hn) — Caprice ▲ CAP 21400 [AAD]
Frumerie, G. de:Vars & Fugue Pno, w. Laszlo Simon (pno) — Caprice ▲ CAP 21400 [AAD]
Koch, E. von:Impulsi Trilogy — Swedish Society ▲ SCD 1024
Koch, E. von:Lapland-Metamorphoses — Swedish Society ▲ SCD 1024
Koch, E. von:Oxberg Vars — Swedish Society ▲ SCD 1024
Larsson, L.–E.:Concertinos, w. L. Berlin (vn)—No. 8 for Violin (1956) — Swedish Society ▲ SCD 1004
Larsson, L.–E.:Con Vn, w. L. Berlin (vn) — Swedish Society ▲ SCD 1004
Larsson, L.–E.:En Vintersaga, w. L. Berlin (vn) — Swedish Society ▲ SCD 1004
Stenhammar, W.:Sym 2 — Caprice ▲ CAP 21151 [AAD]
A. Wiklund (cnd)
Wiklund, A.:Symphonic Prologue *(rec 6/5/39)* — BIS 8–▲ CD 421/24 (m/s) [AAD]

Stockholm PO Soloists
Blomdahl, K.–B.:Trio Bn, Cl & Ob — Swedish Society ▲ SCD 1037
Blomdahl, K.–B.:Trio Cl, Vc & Pno — Caprice ▲ CAP 21424 [AAD]
Eklund, H.:Qt 3 Strs — Swedish Society ▲ SCD 1038

Stockholm RSO
K. Husa (cnd)
Husa, K.:Mosaïques *(rec 1967)* — CRI ▲ CD 592 [ADD]
H. Müller-Kray (cnd)
Cherubini, L.:Les Deux journées, w. H. Hillebrecht (sop), F. Wunderlich (ten), M. Cordes (bar), R. Hoyem (sgr), Stockholm Radio Chorus *(rec live, Stockholm 1960)* — Melodram ▲ CDM 19507 [ADD]
C. Schuricht (cnd)
Haydn, J.:Sym 86 *(rec live, 1954)* — Melodram ▲ CDM 18047 [ADD]

Stockholm Royal Opera Orch
K. Bendix (cnd)
Mascagni, P.:Cavalleria rusticana, w. A. Nordmo-Lövberg (sop), A. Bjoerling (sop), M. Sehlmark (cta), J. Bjoerling (ten), G. Svedenbrandt (bass), Stockholm Royal Opera Chorus [I, Sw] *(rec live, Stockholm, 12/8/54)* — Legato Classics ▲ LCD 164-1 [ADD]
S. Ehrling (cnd)
Verdi, G.:Rigoletto, w. M. Hallin (sop), B. Nordin (sop), K. Meyer (mez), B. Ericson (mez), Kjellgren (mez), N. Gedda (ten), O. Sivall (ten), H. Hasslo (bar), I. Wixell (bar), B. Alstergård (bar), A. Tyrén (bass), Stockholm Royal Opera Chorus *(rec live Jan. 18, 1959)* — BIS ▲ CD 296 [AAD]
H. Sandberg (cnd)
Verdi, G.:La traviata, w. Hjördis Schymberg (sop), Jussi Björling (ten), Conny Molin (sgr), Stockholm Royal Opera Chorus — Grammofono 2000 2–▲ GRM 78640
Verdi, G.:La traviata, w. Hjördis Schymberg (sop), Jussi Björling (ten), Conni Molin (sgr), Stockholm Royal Theater Opera Chorus — Enterprise ("The 40's" series) 2–▲ ENT 331
C. Savina (cnd)
Verdi, G.:Un ballo in maschera (sels), w. Ragnar Ulfung (ten), Erik Saeden (bar), Lovberg (sgr)—Act III excerpts *(rec 1966)* — Arkadia 2–▲ 488

Stockholm Royal Orch
N. Grevillius (cnd)
Jussi Björling:The Golden Years, Vol. 1, w. Jussi Björling (ten) *(rec 1933–45)* — Iron Needle ▲ 1301 (m) [ADD]

Stockholm Sinfonietta
N. Järvi (cnd)
Gade, N.W.:Sym 1 — BIS ▲ CD 339
Gade, N.W.:Sym 2 — BIS ▲ CD 355
Gade, N.W.:Sym 3 — BIS ▲ CD 338
Gade, N.W.:Sym 4 — BIS ▲ CD 338

Stockholm Sinfonietta (cont.)
N. Järvi (cnd) (cont.)
Gade, N.W.:Sym 5 — BIS ▲ CD 356
Gade, N.W.:Sym 6 — BIS ▲ CD 356
Gade, N.W.:Sym 7 — BIS ▲ CD 355
Gade, N.W.:Sym 8 — BIS ▲ CD 339
Schubert, Franz:Ovs—Overture in C, "In the Italian Style" — BIS ▲ CD 387
Schubert, Franz:Ovs—Overture in D, "In the Italian Style," D.590 — BIS ▲ CD 453 [DDD]
Schubert, Franz:Sym 3 — BIS ▲ CD 453 [DDD]
Schubert, Franz:Sym 4 — BIS ▲ CD 453 [DDD]
Schubert, Franz:Sym 5 — BIS ▲ CD 387
Schubert, Franz:Sym 6 — BIS ▲ CD 387
Strauss, R.:Der Bürger als Edelmann (suite) — BIS ▲ CD 470 [DDD]
Strauss, R.:Con Ob, w. A. Nilsson (ob) — BIS ▲ CD 470 [DDD]
O. Kamu (cnd)
Schnittke, A.:Sym 4, w. S. Parkman (ten), M. Bellini (alt), Uppsala Academic Chamber Choir [L] — BIS ▲ CD 497 [DDD]
S. Parkman (cnd)
Schnittke, A.:Requiem, w. K. Salomonsson (sop), I. H. Sjöberg (sop), L. Lindholm (sop), A. F. Eker (cta), N. Högman (ten), Uppsala Academic Chamber Choir [L] — BIS ▲ CD 497 [DDD]
E.–P. Salonen (cnd)
Larsson, L.–E.:Little Serenade — BIS ▲ CD 285 [DDD]
Lidholm, I.:Musik — BIS ▲ CD 285 [DDD]
Söderlundh, L.B.:Concertino Ob, w. A. Nilsson (ob) — BIS ▲ CD 285 [DDD]
Wirén, D.:Serenade Strs — BIS ▲ CD 285 [DDD]
J.–O. Wedin (cnd)
Larsson, L.–E.:Divert 2 — Caprice ▲ CAP 21492
Mozart, W.A.:Con 21 Pno, w. Staffan Scheja (pno) — BIS ▲ CD 205
Mozart, W.A.:Sinf concertante Vn, K.364, w. B. Lysell (vn), N. Sparf (vn) — BIS ▲ CD 205
Wirén, D.:Triptyk — Caprice ▲ CAP 21326 [DDD/AAD]

Stockholm String Quartet
Larsson, L.–E.:Qt 3 Strs — Caprice ▲ CAP 21492
The String Quartet in Sweden:A Cavalcade of Its History, w. Barkel String Quartet, Garaguly String Quartet, Kyndel String Quartet, Ivan Ericson String Quartet, Grünfarb String Quartet, Skåne String Quartet, Hälsingborg String Quartet, Göteborg String Quartet, Galli Stri *(rec before 1951)* — Caprice 5–▲ CAP 21506 [AAD/ADD]

Stockholm Symphonic Wind Orch
Dahl, I.:Con A Sax — Caprice ▲ CAP 21414 [DDD]
Gregson, E.:Con Tuba — Caprice ▲ CAP 21414 [DDD]
Holst, G.:Hammersmith — Caprice ▲ CAP 21415 [DDD]
Keuris, T.:Catena:Refrains & Vars — Caprice ▲ CAP 21414 [DDD]
Khachaturian, A.:Music of—Uzbek March & Dancing Song; Armenian Folk Song & Dance — Caprice ▲ CAP 21415 [DDD]
Mellnäs, A.:Blow — Caprice ▲ CAP 21415 [DDD]
Morthenson, J.W.:Paraphonia — Caprice ▲ CAP 21414 [DDD]
Rimsky-Korsakov, N.:Concertstück Cl — Caprice ▲ CAP 21415 [DDD]
S. Ehrling (cnd)
Stravinsky, I.:Con Pno Ww, w. Nikolai Petrov (pno) *(rec Berwald Hall, Mar. 1991)* — Caprice ▲ CAP 21384 [DDD]
J. Hirokami (cnd)
Grondahl, L.:Con Trbn, w. Håkan Björkman (trbn) — Caprice ▲ CAP 21516
Maros, M.:Aurora — Caprice ▲ CAP 21516
Mayuzumi, T.:The Ritual Ov — Caprice ▲ CAP 21516
Mendelssohn, F.:Ov, Op. 24 — Caprice ▲ CAP 21516
Sallinen, A.:Chorali — Caprice ▲ CAP 21516
Schoenberg, A.:Theme & Vars Band — Caprice ▲ CAP 21516
P. Lyng (cnd)
Naumann, S.:Fanfarer *(rec Swedish Radio Studio 2, July 1989)* — Caprice ▲ CAP 21384 [DDD]
D. Porcelijn (cnd)
Schmitt, F.:Dionysiaques *(rec Swedish Radio Studio 2, Oct. 1990)* — Caprice ▲ CAP 21384 [DDD]
M. Turnovsky (cnd)
Dvořák, A.:Serenade Ww *(rec Swedish Radio Studio 2, Mar. 1991)* — Caprice ▲ CAP 21384 [DDD]

Stockholm SO
H. Schmidt-Isserstedt (cnd)
Lidholm, I.:Rites — Swedish Society ▲ SCD 1027
C. Schuricht (cnd)
Brahms, J.:Sym 2 *(rec live 1964)* — Melodram ▲ CDM 18046 [ADD]
Wagner, R.:Parsifal (prelude) *(rec live 1962)* — Melodram ▲ CDM 18046 [ADD]
G. Sjökvist (cnd)
Andrée, E.:Fritiof saga (suite) — Sterling ▲ 1016
Andrée, E.:Sym 2 — Sterling ▲ 1016

Stockholm Univ College of Music Orch
H. Kyhle (cnd)
Lindberg, O.:Requiem, w. I. Sörenson (sop), E. Thallang (alt), C. Solén (ten), E. Saedén (bass), O. Johansson (org), Englebrekt Church Oratory Choir *(rec Nov. 2, 1980)* — Sterling ▲ CDS 1013

Stockholm Wind Quintet
Eliasson, A.:La Fièvre — Caprice ▲ CAP 21402 [AAD]
Larsson, L.–E.:Quattro tempi — Caprice ▲ CAP 21492
Wirén, D.:Qnt Ww — Caprice ▲ CAP 21326 [DDD/AAD]

Leopold Stokowski SO
L. Stokowski (cnd)
Bach, J.S.:Jesu bleibet meine Freude—arr. Peter Schickele — Vanguard Classics ▲ OVC 8009 [ADD]
Bach, J.S.:Sheep May Safely Graze [arr. Stokowski] — Vanguard Classics ▲ OVC 8009 [ADD]
Bach Transcriptions — RCA Gold Seal ("Legendary Performers" series) ▲ 09026-60922-2
Beethoven, L. van:Son 14 Pno, "Moonlight Son"—Adagio [orchd. Stokowski] *(rec 1947)* — Music & Arts ▲ CD 846 [ADD]
Corelli, A.:Con grosso, Op. 6/8, "Christmas Con" — Vanguard Classics ▲ OVC 8009 [ADD]
Fantasia — Beuna Vista 2–▲ 60007
The Orchestra Landmarks of a Distinguished Career — EMI Classics ▲ CDM 65614
Solid Gold Baroque, w. English CO, [cnd:J. Somary] I Solisti Zagreb [cnd:Janigro], et al. — Vanguard Classics ▲ OVC 4021 [ADD]
The Stokowski Collection, Vol. 1 — Vanguard Classics ▲ OVC 8009 [ADD]
The Stokowski Collection, Vol. 3 — Vanguard Classics ▲ OVC 8013 [ADD]
Tchaikovsky, P.:Sleeping Beauty (sels) *(rec 1934)* — Iron Needle ▲ 1334
Tchaikovsky, P.:Sleeping Beauty (suite) — Enterprise ("Sirio" series) ▲ ENT SO 530010
Vivaldi, A.:Cons Vn, Op. 3/1-12, "L'estro armonico"—No. 11 in d — Vanguard Classics ▲ OVC 8009 [ADD]

Stour Music Festival CO
Purcell, H.:Love's Goddess Sure Was Blind, w. Deller Consort [E] — Musique d'Abord ▲ HMA 190222
Purcell, H.:Welcome to All the Pleasures, w. Deller Consort [E] — Musique d'Abord ▲ HMA 190222

Stow Festival Orch
B. Jones (cnd)
Beach, A.M.C.:Mass, "Grand Mass", w. Margot Law (sop), Martha Remington (mez), Ray Bauwens (ten), Joel Schneider (bar), Stow Festival Chorus *(rec Cathedral Church of St Paul, Tremont St, Boston, MA)* — Albany ▲ TROY 179 [DDD]

Strada
Nadal - Traditional Mediterranean Carols — Analekta Fleur de Lys ▲ FL 23059 [DDD]

Alessandro Stradella Consort
Stradella, A.:Crudo mar di fiamme orribili, w. Riccardo Ristori (bass) — Bongiovanni ▲ GB 2165 [DDD]

ORCH. & ENS.

Alessandro Stradella Consort (cont.)
Stradella, A.:Esule dalle sfere, w. Roberta Invernizzi (sop), Silvia Piccolo (sop), Marco Lazzara (alt), Mario Nuvoli (ten), Riccardo Ristori (bass), Carlo Lepore (bass) Bongiovanni ▲ GB 2165 [DDD]
Stradella, A.:Locutus est Dominus de nube ignis, w. Roberta Invernizzi (sop) Bongiovanni ▲ GB 2165 [DDD]
E. Velardi (cnd)
Glorias de España, 1492–1756, w. Josquino Salepico Chorus *(rec Oct. 8–10, 1992)* Bongiovanni ▲ GB 2161-2 [DDD]
Porpora, N.A.:Cant per la notte di Natale, w. Rosita Frisani (sop—Dorindo), Roberta Invernizzi (sop—Angelo), Marco Lazzara (cta—Montano) *(rec Genoa, Jan 29–30, 1995)* Bongiovanni 2-▲ GB 2181/2
Scarlatti, A.:Abramo, il tuo sembiante, w. S. Piccolo (sop), L. Bacchetta (sop), M. Lazzara (alt), M. Nuvoli (ten), G. Dagnino (bass) [period instrs] [l] Nuova Era ("Ancient Music" series) ▲ 7117 [DDD]
Steffani, A.:Vocal Music, w. S. Piccollo (sop), M. Mazzara (alt)—"Fileno Idolo Mio," Cantata for Soprano, 2 Violins & Continuo [attributed]; "Il Più Felice e Sfortunato Amante," Cantata for Alto, 2 Violins & Continuo [attributed]; "Porto L'Alma Incenerita," Chamber Duet for Soprano, Alto & Continuo [l] Bongiovanni ▲ GB 2123 [DDD]
Stradella, A.:Il moro per amore, w. R. Invernizzi (sop—Eurinda), S. Piccollo (sop—Lucinda), M. Grazia Liguori (sop—Fiorino), M. Lazzara (cta—Lindora), V. Matacchini (cta—Feraspe/Floridoro), M. Beasley (ten—Filandro), R. Ristori (bass—Rodrigo) [l] *(rec Oct. 31–Nov. 3, 1992)* Bongiovanni 3-▲ GB 2153/55
Stradella, A.:O di Cocito oscure deità, w. R. Invernizzi (sop—Proserpina), S. Piccollo (sop—Vendetta), M. Nuvoli (ten—Inganno), R. Ristori (bass—Plutone) *(rec Oct. 25, 1993)* Bongiovanni ▲ GB 2164 [DDD]
Stradella, A.:Lo schiavo liberto, w. R. Invernizzi (sop—Armida), M. Lazzara (cta—Rinaldo), M. Nuvoli (ten—Carlo), R. Ristori (bass—Ubaldo) *(rec Nov. 15, 1993)* Bongiovanni ▲ GB 2164 [DDD]
Stradella, A.:Vocal Music, w. E. Smith (hpd), G. Dagnino (bass), S. Piccollo (sop), M. Mazzara (alt), R. Balconi (ct)—Sinfonia in E from the Cantata "Crudo Mar"; Toccata in a for Harpsichord; Exultate in Deo Fideles, Motet for Bass Solo & Violins; Si Apra al Riso Ogni Labbro, Cantata for 3 Voices & Strings [l,L] Bongiovanni ▲ GB 2123 [DDD]

Stradivaria Ensemble
Leclair, J.-M.:Cons Vn, Op. 7, w. Daniel Cuiller (vn)—Nos. 1-3 & 5 Accord ▲ ACD 242552 [DDD]
P. Colléaux (cnd)
Charpentier, M.-A.:In honorem Sancti Xaverii canticum, w. E. Baudry (sop), C. Dune (sop), G. Ragon (ten), Nantes Vocal Ensemble [L] Arion ▲ ARN 68037 [DDD]
Charpentier, M.-A.:Judicum Salomonis, w. A. Zaepffel (ct), J. Benet (ten), Elwes (ten), G. Ragon (ten), J. Cabré (bar), G. Reinhart (bar), Nantes Vocal Ensemble [L] Arion ▲ ARN 68037 [DDD]
D. Cuiller (cnd)
Gluck, C.W.:Orfeo ed Euridice (sels), w. Alain Zaepffel (alt), Nantes Vocal Ensemble—Ballo; Che Puro Ciel Adda ▲ ADD 581050
Handel, G.F.:Samson (sels), w. Alain Zaepffel (alt), Paul Colleaux (cnd), Nantes Vocal Ensemble—The Body Comes; Return Oh God of Hosts Adda ▲ ADD 581050
Handel, G.F.:Theodora (sels), w. Alain Zaepffel (alt), Paul Colleaux (cnd), Nantes Vocal Ensemble—Sweet Rose & Lily; Unhappy, Happy Crew; Kind Heaven; Go Gen'rous Pious Youth Adda ▲ ADD 581050
Hasse, J.A.:Il trionfo di Clelia (sels), w. Alain Zaepffel (alt), Nantes Vocal Ensemble—Resta Cara Adda ▲ ADD 581050
Piccinni, N.:Tigrane (sels), w. Alain Zaepffel (alt), Paul Colleaux (cnd), Nantes Vocal Ensemble—Ah Cleopatra Adda ▲ ADD 581050
Traetta, T.:Ifigenia in Tauride (sels), w. Alain Zaepffel (alt), Nantes Vocal Ensemble—Scène avec Shoeurs Adda ▲ ADD 581050
Strängnäs Sinfonietta Ensemble
M. Maros (cnd)
Holewa, H.:Concertino 8, w. Magnus Andersson (gtr) Phono Suecia ▲ PHN 49 [ADD]
C. Merithz (cnd)
Holewa, H.:Concertino 9, w. Åse Enhamre (sop), Magnus Andersson (gtr) Phono Suecia ▲ PHN 49 [ADD]

Walther Straram Orch
E. Ansermet (cnd)
Stravinsky, I.:Capriccio, w. I. Stravinsky (pno) EMI Classics 2-▲ ZDCB 54607
Stravinsky, I.:Octet EMI Classics 2-▲ ZDCB 54607
W. Straram (cnd)
Poulenc, F.:Aubade Pno, w. F. Poulenc (pno) EMI Classics ▲ CDC 55036
Strasbourg Collegium Musicum Orch
R. Delage (cnd)
Chabrier, E.:Fisch-Ton-Kan, w. M. Delunsch (sop), B. Desnoues (sop), F. Dudziak (ten), C. Mehn (ten), J.-L. Georgel (bar) Arion ▲ ARN 68252 [DDD]
Chabrier, E.:Vaucochard & Son I, w. M. Delunsch (sop), B. Desnoues (sop), F. Dudziak (ten), C. Mehn (ten), J.-L. Georgel (bar) Arion ▲ ARN 68252 [DDD]
Chabrier, E.:A Wasted Education, w. M. Delunsch (sop), B. Desnoues (sop), F. Dudziak (ten), C. Mehn (ten), J.-L. Georgel (bar) Arion ▲ ARN 68252 [DDD]
Strasbourg Instrumental Percussion Group
P. Boulez (cnd)
Messiaen, O.:Couleurs de la cité céleste, w. Yvonne Loriod (pno), Domaine Musical Orch Sony Classical ("Pierre Boulez Edition" series) ▲ SMK 68332
Messiaen, O.:Et exspecto resurrectionem mortuorum, *(orch unknown)* Sony Classical ("Pierre Boulez Edition" series) ▲ SMK 68332

Strasbourg Opera Orch
F. Adam (cnd)
Wagner, R.:Der fliegende Holländer (sels), w. S. Jurinac (sop), N. Bailey (bar), A. Van Mill (bass), Strasbourg Opera Chorus—Senta's ballad (Jo-ho-hoe!...Traft ihr das Schiff) & Willst Du des Vaters Wahl [G] *(rec live, Strasbourg, 11/25/69)* Melodram 3-▲ CDM 37091 [ADD]
Strasbourg Percussion Ensemble
Ishii, M.:Concertante Mar & Perc, w. K. Abe (mar) Denon ▲ CO 73678 [DDD]
Xenakis, I.:Pleiades Denon ▲ CO 73678 [DDD]
Xenakis, I.:Pleiades Harmonia Mundi France ("Musique d'abord" series) ▲ HMA 1905185
G. van Gucht (cnd)
Denisov, E.:Con piccolo, w. C. Delangle (sax) *(rec Jan. 1990)* Pierre Verany ▲ PV.790112 [DDD]
Denisov, E.:Works (3) Perc *(rec Jan. 1990)* Pierre Verany ▲ PV.790112 [DDD]
R. Hayrabedian (cnd)
Ohana, M.:Cantigas, w. M. Quercia (sop), F. Atlan (mez), R. Conil (pno), Choeur Contemporain [Sp] Pierre Verany ▲ PV 787032 [DDD]
Stravinsky, I.:Les Noces, w. M. Quercia (sop), S. Cooper (mez), P. Capelle (ten), P. Marinov (bass), Vieuxtemps (pno), R. Conil (pno), Arzoumanian (pno), Raynaut (pno), Contemporary Choir Pierre Verany ▲ PV 787032 [DDD]

L. Vaillancourt (cnd)
Gougeon, D.:Un Train pour l'enfer, Nouvel Ensemble Moderne *(rec Strasbourg, Sept 29, 1993)* Ummus ▲ UMM 109

Strasbourg PO
L. Foster (cnd)
Romantic Interlude, w. The LIND Tapes, Monte Carlo PO, et al. Lind ■ LI 701
T. Guschlbauer (cnd)
Dvořák, A.:Con Pno, w. Claire Desert (pno) *(rec Strasbourg, July 10–12, 1995)* FNAC Music ▲ CD 592008 [DDD]
Grieg, E.:Con Pno, Op. 16, w. F.-R. Duchable (pno) Erato ▲ 92872-2 [DDD]
Indy, V. d':Saugefleurie Valois ▲ V 4686
Indy, V. d':Souvenirs Valois ▲ V 4686
Indy, V. d':Sym 3 Valois ▲ V 4686
Rachmaninoff, S.:Con 2 Pno, w. F.-R. Duchable (pno) Erato ▲ 92872-2 [DDD]

Strasbourg PO (cont.)
T. Guschlbauer (cnd) (cont.)
Scriabin, A.:Con Pno, w. Claire Desert (pno) *(rec Strasbourg, July 10–12, 1995)* FNAC Music ▲ CD 592008 [DDD]
Waldteufel, E.:Waltzes, Polkas & Galops FNAC Music ▲ 592311
F. Haider (cnd)
Donizetti, G.:Roberto Devereux, w. Edita Gruberová (sop), Delores Ziegler (mez), Don Bernardini (sgr), Ettore Kim (sgr), Rhine Opera Chorus Nightingale Classics 2-▲ NIG 70563
Raymond Leppard (cnd)
Music for Imaging, w. The LIND Tapes, London PO, et al. Lind ■ LI 201
A. Lombard (cnd)
Berlioz, H.:Ovs—Benevenuto Cellini; Carnaval romain Erato ("Bonsai" series) ▲ 2292-45925-2 ■ 2292-45925-4
Berlioz, H.:Sym fantastique Erato ("Bonsai" series) ▲ 2292-45925-2 ■ 2292-45925-4
Gounod, C.:Faust (sels), w. Montserrat Caballé (sop) Erato ("Recital" series) ▲ 98499-2
Mozart, W.A.:Così fan tutte, w. T. Stratas (sop), K. Te Kanawa (sop), F. von Stade (mez), Rhine Opera Chorus Erato 3-▲ 98494-2
Puccini, G.:Turandot, w. M. Caballé (sop—Turnadot), M. Freni (sop—Liu), J. Carreras (ten—Calaf), M. Sénéchal (ten—Emperor Altoum), V. Sardinero (bar—Ping), P. Plishka (bass—Timur), Maîtrise de la Cathédrale, Rhine Opera Chorus EMI Classics ▲ CDMB 65293
Puccini, G.:Turandot (sels), w. M. Caballé (sop), M. Freni (sop), J. Carreras (ten), M. Sénéchal (ten), Rhine Opera Chorus EMI Classics ("Studio" series) ▲ CDM 63410
Smetana, B.:The Moldau Erato ▲ 45928-2 [ADD]
Strauss, R.:4 Last Songs, w. Montserrat Caballé (sop) Erato ("Recital" series) ▲ 98499-2
Wagner, R.:Tannhäuser (sels), w. Montserrat Caballé (sop) Erato ("Recital" series) ▲ 98499-2
Wagner, R.:Tristan und Isolde (sels), w. Montserrat Caballé (sop) Erato ("Recital" series) ▲ 98499-2
Strasbourg SO
F.-R. Duchable (cnd)
Parish Alvars, E.:Con Hp, w. M. Nordmann (hp) *(rec June 22 & 30, 1992)* FNAC Music ▲ 592266 [DDD]

Strasbourg Theater Percussionists
Kabeláč, M.:Inventions *(rec 1971)* Praga ▲ PR 255 004
Kabeláč, M.:Sym 8, w. J. Jonasova (sop), V. Rabas (org) *(rec 1971)* Praga ▲ PR 255 004
Stratos [Cynthia Baehr (vn), Lorra Baylis (vn), Marie Flexer (vn), Michael Grossman (vn), Jennifer Kuan (vn), Stacy Lesartre (vn), Roy Lewis (vn), Kathryn Stenberg (vn), Cecily Ward (vn)]
Albinoni, T.:Adagio Org *(rec Skywalker Sound, Marin County, CA)* Warner Bros. ▲ 9-45995-2
Barber, S.:Adagio Strs *(rec Skywalker Sound, Marin County, CA)* Warner Bros. ▲ 9-45995-2
Corelli, A.:Con grosso, Op. 6/8, "Christmas Con" *(rec Skywalker Sound, Marin County, CA)* Warner Bros. ▲ 9-45995-2
Martin, F.:Etudes Str Orch *(rec Skywalker Sound, Marin County, CA)* Warner Bros. ▲ 9-45995-2
Shostakovich, D.:Chamber Sym, Op. 110a *(rec Skywalker Sound, Marin County, CA)* Warner Bros. ▲ 9-45995-2
Vivaldi, A.:Cons Vn, Op. 8/1–4, "The Four Seasons"—No. 2 [Summer] *(rec Skywalker Sound, Marin County, CA)* Warner Bros. ▲ 9-45995-2
Johann Strauss CO
J. Wildner (cnd)
Strauss (II), Joh.:Music of—Polka Mazurka, Op. 359; Polka schnell, Op. 326; Polka française, Op. 449; Polka Mazurka, Op. 322 Novalis ▲ 150122 [DDD]
Strauss (II), Joh.:Waltzes—Op. 234 & 418 Novalis ▲ 150122 [DDD]
Strauss, Josef:Music of—Polka schnell, Op. 133; Polka Mazurka, Op. 270; Polka schnell, Op. 76; Waltz, Op. 173; Waltz, Op. 184 Novalis ▲ 150122 [DDD]
Strauss Festival Orch
J. Francek (cnd)
Strauss (II), Joh.:Music of—Eljen a Magyar; Emperor Waltz; Morning Papers; Persian March; Seid umschlungen, Millionen; Roses From the South; Tritsch, Tratsch Polka; Wine, Women & Song LaserLight ▲ 15005 [DDD]
Strauss (II), Joh.:Waltzes—Emperor, Op. 437; Tritsch, Op. 214; Wine, Woman & Song, Op. 214; Eljen a Magyar, Op. 332; Morning Papers, OP. 279; Persian March, Op. 289; Seid umschlungen Millionen, Op. 443; Roses from the South, Op. 338 Laserlight ▲ 15 005
P. Guth (cnd)
Strauss, E.:Polkas & Waltzes—Auf und davon!, Op. 73 [fast polka] *(rec live, Salle Garniere, Monte Carlo, Monaco, May 8, 1994)* Discover International ▲ DICD 920240 [DDD]
Strauss (I), Joh.:Music of—Chinese Galop, Op. 20 *(rec live, Salle Garniere, Monte Carlo, Monaco, May 8, 1994)* Discover International ▲ DICD 920240 [DDD]
Strauss (II), Joh.:Music of—Ov. to Waldmeister; Vergnügungszug, Op. 281 [fast polka]; Roses from the South, Op. 388 [waltz from Das Spitzentuch der Königin]; Egyptian March, Op. 335; Champagne-Polka, Op. 211; Csárdás [from Ritter Pásmán]; Eljen a Magyar, Op. 332 [Hungarian fast polka]; Emperor-Waltz, Op. 437; On Hunting, Op. 373 [fast polka from Cagliostro in Wien] *(rec live, Salle Garniere, Monte Carlo, Monaco, May 8, 1994)* Discover International ▲ DICD 920240 [DDD]
Strauss, Josef:Music of—The Dragon-Fly, Op. 204 [polka mazur]; Dorfschwalben aus Österreich, Op. 164 [waltz] *(rec live, Salle Garniere, Monte Carlo, Monaco, May 8, 1994)* Discover International ▲ DICD 920240 [DDD]

Eduard Strauss Orch
E. Strauss (cnd)
Strauss (II), Joh.:Life & Music of—narration with selected excerpts from Blue Danube Waltz; Die Fledermaus; Pizzicato Polka; Singer's Joy Polka; Emperor Waltz; Vergnügungzug; Voices of Spring; Vienna Blood; Accelerations Waltz; Stadt und Land; Blue Danube Waltz; Roses from the South; Tales from the Vienna Woods; Gypsy Baron; A Thousand & One Nights, plus complete versions of Tales from the Vienna Woods, Blue Danube Waltz & Vienna Blood Waltz Vox Music Masters ("Music Masters" series) ▲ MMD 8514 [ADD] ■ MMC 8514
Johann Strauss Orch
W. Boskovsky (cnd)
Lehár, F.:Waltzes EMI Classics ▲ CDC 47020 [DDD]
Strauss (II), Joh.:Waltzes EMI Classics ▲ CDC 47052 [DDD]
Strauss (II), Joh.:Waltzes—Carnival in Vienna; Greetings from Austria; Music of Johann Strauss; Wine, Women & Song EMI Classics ▲ CDE 67788
J. Francek (cnd)
Schubert, Franz:Ovs—Einzugsmarsch & Ov. [from The Gypsy Baron]; Ov. [from Die Fledermaus]; Ov. [from Vienna Blood]; Ov. [from One Night in Venice]; Ov. [from Aschenbrödel]; Ov. [from Cagliostro in Vienna]; Radetzky March Laserlight ▲ 15 619
Strauss (II), Joh.:Ovs—Aschenbrödel, Cagliostro in Wien, Fledermaus, Gypsy Baron Overture & Einzugmarsch, One Night in Venice, Vienna Blood, Radetzky March LaserLight ▲ 15619 [DDD]
A. Rieu (cnd)
The Vienna I Love, w. André Rieu (vn) Philips ▲ 314-528786-2 ■ 314-528786-4
J. Rothstein (cnd)
Millöcker, C.:Der arme Jonathan (march) Chandos ▲ CHAN 8381 [DDD]
Millöcker, C.:Die sieben Schwaben (march) Chandos ▲ CHAN 8381 [DDD]
Strauss, E.:Music of—Knall und Fall (polka schnell), Op. 132; Leuchtkäferln Waltz, Op. 161; Hectograph (polka schnell), Op. 186 Chandos ▲ CHAN 8381 [DDD]
Strauss, E.:Music of—Blüthenkranz Johann Strauss'scher Walzer, Op. 292; Saat und Ernte (polka schnell), Op. 159; Weyprecht-Payer-Marsch, Op. 120; Mädchenlaune (polka-mazurka), Op. 99; Die Abonneten (waltz), Op. 116 Chandos ▲ CHAN 8527 [DDD]
Strauss (I), Joh.:Music of—Cachucha-Galopp, Op. 97 Chandos ▲ CHAN 8434 [DDD]
Strauss (II), Joh.:Music of—Morgenblätter (waltz), Op. 279; Tritsch-Tratsch-Polka, Op. 214; Kaiser Franz Josef-Marsch, Op. 67; Wiener Bonbons (waltz), Op. 307; Fata Morgana (polka-mazurka), Op. 330; Auf der Jagd (polka-schnell), Op. 373; Annen-Polka, Op. 117; An der schönen, blauen Donau, Op. 314 Chandos ▲ CHAN 8434 [DDD]

▲ = CD ♦ = Enhanced CD Δ = MD ■ = Cassette Tape □ = DCC

Johann Strauss Orch (cont.)
J. Rothstein (cnd) (cont.)
Strauss (II), Joh.:Music of—Concurrenzen Walzer, Op. 272; L'inconnue (polka française), Op. 182; Neuer csárdás (frm Die Fledermaus); Hoch Osterreich (march), Op. 371; Alexandrine-Polka, Op. 198 Chandos ▲ CHAN 8381 [DDD]
Strauss (II), Joh.:Music of—Pappacoda (polka-française), Op. 412; Quadrille on Themes from *Der lustige Krieg*, Op. 402; Klug Gretelein (waltz), Op. 462 Chandos ▲ CHAN 8527 [DDD]
Strauss (III), Joh.:Schlau-Schlau Chandos ▲ CHAN 8527 [DDD]
Strauss, Josef:Music of—For Ever (polka schnell), Op. 193; Defilir-Marsch, Op. 53; Farewell! (polka schnell), Op. 211 Chandos ▲ CHAN 8527 [DDD]
Strauss, Josef:Music of—Frohes leben walzer, Op. 272; Vorwärts! (schnell-polka), Op. 127; Nachtschatten (polka-mazurka), Op. 229; Elfen-Polka, Op. 74 Chandos ▲ CHAN 8381 [DDD]
Strauss, Josef:Music of—Ohne Sorgen! (polka schnell), Op. 271; Moulinet-Polka, Op. 57; Aquarellen (waltz), Op. 258 Chandos ▲ CHAN 8434 [DDD]

La Stravaganza
A. Manze (cnd)
Bach, J.S.:Cant 29, w. La Stravaganza—sinf. *(rec Emmanuel Church, Cologne-Rondorf, Oct. 24-29, 1994)* Denon 2-▲ DEN 78965 [DDD]
Bach, J.S.:Cant 146, w. La Stravaganza—sinf. *(rec Emmanuel Church, Cologne-Rondorf, Oct. 24-29, 1994)* Denon 2-▲ DEN 78965 [DDD]

La Stravaganza Cologne
Muffat, G.:Armonico tributo (5 sonatas for strings) (1682) *(rec July 20-22, 1992)* MD + G ▲ L 3459 [DDD]
Telemann, G.P.:Cons (misc), w. Masahiro Arita (trns fl/pic), Eric Hoeprich (chl), Hans Peter Westermann (ob), Dane Roberts (db), David Sinclair (db)—in E for Transverse Flute, Oboe d'amore, Viola d'amore, Strings & Continuo; in e for Transverse Flute, Violin, Strings & Continuo; in D for Transverse Flute, Strings & Continuo; in E♭ for Strings & Continuo; in G for Transverse Flute, Chalumeau, Oboe, 2 Double Basses, Strings & Continuo *(rec Cologne, May 30-June 3, 1994)* Denon ("Aliare" series) ▲ CO 78933 [DDD]
Telemann, G.P.:Ov Volker Denon ▲ CO 77398 [DDD]
Telemann, G.P.:Ov in f Denon ▲ CO 77398 [DDD]
Telemann, G.P.:Ov in g Denon ▲ CO 77398 [DDD]
Vivaldi, A.:Cons Vn, Op. 4, "La stravaganza", w. A. Manze (vn)—Nos. 1-4 Denon/PCM Digital ▲ DEN 75598 [DDD]
A. Manze (cnd)
Bach, J.S.:Ov Fl, BWV 1067, w. Masahiro Arita (trns fl) *(rec Sendesaal of German Radio, Cologne, June 2-3, 1994)* Denon 2-▲ DEN 78965 [DDD]
Bach, J.S.:Ov Obs, BWV 1066 *(rec Sendesaal of German Radio, Cologne, Oct. 24-29, 1994)* Denon 2-▲ DEN 78965 [DDD]
Bach, J.S.:Ov, BWV 1068 *(rec Sendesaal of German Radio, Cologne, Oct. 24-29, 1994)* Denon 2-▲ DEN 78965 [DDD]
Bach, J.S.:Ov, BWV 1069 *(rec Sendesaal of German Radio, Cologne, Oct. 24-29, 1994)* Denon 2-▲ DEN 78965 [DDD]

Streicher Trio [Charlene Brendler (pno), Katherine Kyme (vn), Sarah Freiberg (vc)]
Farrenc, J.-L.:Trio Vn Music & Arts ▲ CD 917
Schumann, C.:Trio Pno Music & Arts ▲ CD 917

Fred Stride Orch
F. Stride (cnd)
Kern, J.:Songs—Showboat Medley; The Last Time I Saw Paris; I Won't Dance; I'm Old Fashioned; Roberta; The Folks Who Live on the Hill; Who?; The Way You Look Tonight; I've Told Every Little Star; All the Things You Are; The Song is You *(rec The Orpheum, Vancouver)* CBC ▲ 1099 [DDD]

String Fever
M. Alsop (cnd)
Fever Pitch Koch International Classics ▲ KIC 7150 [DDD]

Strumenti Antichi
F. Colusso (cnd)
Carissimi, G.:Motets, w. Gruppo di Voci, Sulmona Phil Chorus—Vanitas Vanitatum I & II; Sponsa Canticorum; Tolle Sponsa [L] Bongiovanni ▲ GB 10003 [DDD]

Strung Out String Quartet
Stahmer, K.H.:Kristalgitter Pro Viva ▲ ISPV 167 [DDD]

Studio of Early Music
T. Binkley (cnd)
Carmina Burana:The Benediktbeuren Manuscript, ca. 1300 Teldec ("Das alte Werke" series) 2-▲ 95521-2

Stuttgart Bach Collegium
H. Rilling (cnd)
Bach, J.S.:Cants (misc), w. Württemberg CO, Gächinger Kantorei, Frankfurt Kantorei—Cantata Nos. 1, 36, 61, 63, 65, 91, 110, 121, 122, 132, 133, 153, 190 Hänssler Classic 4-▲ 98.836 [ADD]
Bach, J.S.:Cant 1, w. Gächinger Kantorei [G] Hänssler Classic ▲ 98.867 [AAD]
Bach, J.S.:Cant 2, w. H. Watts (cta), A. Baldin (ten), W. Heldwein (bass), Gächinger Kantorei Hänssler Classic ▲ 98.801 [AAD]
Bach, J.S.:Cant 3, w. Gächinger Kantorei [G] Hänssler Classic ▲ 98.873 [AAD]
Bach, J.S.:Cant 4, w. Gächinger Kantorei [G] Hänssler Classic ▲ 98.864 [AAD]
Bach, J.S.:Cant 5, w. A. Augér (sop), C. Watkinson (alt), A. Baldin (ten), W. Schöne (bass), Gächinger Kantorei [G] *(rec Feb & Oct 1979)* Hänssler Classic ▲ 98.816 [AAD]
Bach, J.S.:Cant 6, w. Gächinger Kantorei [G] Hänssler Classic ▲ 98.862 [AAD]
Bach, J.S.:Cant 7, w. H. Watts (cta), A. Kraus (ten), W. Schöne (bass), Gächinger Kantorei Hänssler Classic ▲ 98.802 [AAD]
Bach, J.S.:Cant 8, w. A. Augér (sop), H. Watts (cta), A. Kraus (ten), P. Huttenlocher (bar), Gächinger Kantorei [G] *(rec 1979)* Hänssler Classic ▲ 98.813 [AAD]
Bach, J.S.:Cant 9, w. Gächinger Kantorei [G] Hänssler Classic ▲ 98.859 [AAD]
Bach, J.S.:Cant 10, w. Gächinger Kantorei [G] Hänssler Classic ▲ 98.868 [AAD]
Bach, J.S.:Cant 11, "Ascension Oratorio", w. Gächinger Kantorei [G] Hänssler Classic ▲ 98.858 [AAD]
Bach, J.S.:Cant 13, w. Gächinger Kantorei [G] Hänssler Classic ▲ 98.874 [AAD]
Bach, J.S.:Cant 14, w. Gächinger Kantorei [G] Hänssler Classic ▲ 98.859 [AAD]
Bach, J.S.:Cant 16, w. G. Schreckenbach (cta), P. Schreier (ten), P. Huttenlocher (bar), Gächinger Kantorei [G] Hänssler Classic ▲ 98.871 [AAD]
Bach, J.S.:Cant 17, w. Gächinger Kantorei [G] Hänssler Classic ▲ 98.868 [AAD]
Bach, J.S.:Cant 20, w. V. Gohl (mez), M. Kessler (mez), T. Altmeyer (ten), A. Kraus (ten), W. Schöne (bass), Frankfurt Kantorei Hänssler Classic ▲ 98.801 [AAD]
Bach, J.S.:Cant 21, w. Gächinger Kantorei [G] Hänssler Classic ▲ 98.865 [AAD]
Bach, J.S.:Cant 23, w. A. Augér (sop), H. Watts (cta), A. Baldin (ten), N. Tütler (bass), Gächinger Kantorei [G] *(rec 1977)* Hänssler Classic ▲ 98.879 [AAD]
Bach, J.S.:Cant 24, w. A. Augér (sop), H. Watts (cta), K. Pugh (cta), A. Kraus (ten), W. Heldwein (bass), W. Schöne (bass), Gächinger Kantorei Hänssler Classic ▲ 98.803 [AAD]
Bach, J.S.:Cant 25, w. A. Augér (sop), A. Kraus (ten), P. Huttenlocher (bar), Gächinger Kantorei Hänssler Classic ▲ 98.810 [ADD]
Bach, J.S.:Cant 26, w. A. Augér (sop), D. Soffel (sop), A. Kraus (ten), P. Huttenlocher (bar), Gächinger Kantorei [G] *(rec 1979 & 1980)* Hänssler Classic ▲ 98.821 [AAD]
Bach, J.S.:Cant 28, w. A. Augér (sop), G. Schreckenbach (cta), A. Kraus (ten), W. Heldwein (bass), Gächinger Kantorei [G] *(rec Nov 1981 & Feb 1982)* Hänssler Classic ▲ 98.827 [AAD]
Bach, J.S.:Cant 29 [G] Hänssler Classic ▲ 98.857 [AAD]
Bach, J.S.:Cant 30, w. Gächinger Kantorei [G] Hänssler Classic ▲ 98.860 [AAD]
Bach, J.S.:Cant 32, w. Gächinger Kantorei [G] Hänssler Classic ▲ 98.873 [AAD]
Bach, J.S.:Cant 33, w. H. Watts (cta), F. Lang (ten), P. Huttenlocher (bar), Gächinger Kantorei Hänssler Classic ▲ 98.811 [AAD]
Bach, J.S.:Cant 34, w. H. Watts (cta), A. Kraus (ten), W. Schöne (bass), Gächinger Kantorei Hänssler Classic ▲ 98.887 [AAD]
Bach, J.S.:Cant 35, w. J. Hamari (cta) Hänssler Classic ▲ 98.811 [AAD]

Stuttgart Bach Collegium (cont.)
H. Rilling (cnd) (cont.)
Bach, J.S.:Cant 36, w. A. Augér (sop), G. Schreckenbach (cta), P. Schreier (ten), W. Heldwein (bass), Gächinger Kantorei [G] *(rec Oct 1980, Feb 1981 & Mar)* Hänssler Classic ▲ 98.823 [AAD]
Bach, J.S.:Cant 37, w. A. Augér (sop), C. Watkinson (mez), A. Kraus (ten), P. Huttenlocher (bar), Gächinger Kantorei [G] *(rec 1979)* Hänssler Classic ▲ 98.886 [AAD]
Bach, J.S.:Cant 38, w. A. Augér (sop), H. Watts (cta), L.-M. Harder (ten), P. Huttenlocher (bar), Gächinger Kantorei [G] *(rec Feb & Apr 1980)* Hänssler Classic ▲ 98.818 [AAD]
Bach, J.S.:Cant 39, w. A. Augér (sop), G. Schreckenbach (cta), F. Gerishen (bar), Gächinger Kantorei Hänssler Classic ▲ 98.802 [AAD]
Bach, J.S.:Cant 40, w. V. Gohl (mez), A. Kraus (ten), S. Nimsgern (b-bar), Stuttgart Gedächtnis Figural Choir [G] *(rec June-July 1970)* Hänssler Classic ▲ 98.824 [AAD]
Bach, J.S.:Cant 41, w. H. Donath (sop), M. Höffgen (mez), A. Kraus (ten), S. Nimsgern (b-bar), Gächinger Kantorei [G] Hänssler Classic ▲ 98.870 [AAD]
Bach, J.S.:Cant 43, w. A. Augér (sop), J. Hamari (cta), L.-M. Harder (ten), P. Huttenlocher (bar), Gächinger Kantorei [G] *(rec 1981-82)* Hänssler Classic ▲ 98.885 [AAD]
Bach, J.S.:Cant 44, w. A. Augér (sop), H. Watts (cta), A. Baldin (ten), W. Schöne (bass), Gächinger Kantorei [G] *(rec 1979)* Hänssler Classic ▲ 98.886 [AAD]
Bach, J.S.:Cant 46, w. H. Watts (cta), A. Kraus (ten), W. Schöne (bass), Gächinger Kantorei Hänssler Classic ▲ 98.808 [AAD]
Bach, J.S.:Cant 47, w. A. Augér (sop), P. Huttenlocher (bar), Gächinger Kantorei [G] *(rec 1982)* Hänssler Classic ▲ 98.815 [AAD]
Bach, J.S.:Cant 48, w. M. Hoffgen (mez), A. Baldin (ten), Gächinger Kantorei [G] *(rec 1973)* Hänssler Classic ▲ 98.813 [AAD]
Bach, J.S.:Cant 49, w. A. Augér (sop), P. Huttenlocher (bar) [G] *(rec Oct 1982)* Hänssler Classic ▲ 98.817 [AAD]
Bach, J.S.:Cant 50, w. Gächinger Kantorei [G] Hänssler Classic ▲ 98.857 [AAD]
Bach, J.S.:Cant 51, w. Gächinger Kantorei [G] Hänssler Classic ▲ 98.855 [AAD]
Bach, J.S.:Cant 51, w. A. Augér (sop), Gächinger Kantorei [G] Novalis ▲ 150029 [DDD]
Bach, J.S.:Cant 52, w. A. Augér (sop), Gächinger Kantorei [G] *(rec 1982 & 1983)* Hänssler Classic ▲ 98.821 [AAD]
Bach, J.S.:Cant 54, w. J. Hamari (cta) Hänssler Classic ▲ 98.805 [ADD]
Bach, J.S.:Cant 55, w. A. Kraus (ten), Gächinger Kantorei [G] *(rec 1982)* Hänssler Classic ▲ 98.819 [AAD]
Bach, J.S.:Cant 56, w. D. Fischer-Dieskau (bar), Gächinger Kantorei [G] Novalis ▲ 150029 [DDD]
Bach, J.S.:Cant 56, w. D. Fischer-Dieskau (bar), Gächinger Kantorei [G] *(rec ca 1986)* Hänssler Classic ▲ 98.903 [AAD]
Bach, J.S.:Cant 56, w. Gächinger Kantorei [G] Hänssler Classic ▲ 98.855 [AAD]
Bach, J.S.:Cant 57, w. A. Augér (sop), W. Heldwein (bass), Gächinger Kantorei [G] *(rec Nov 1981 & Feb 1982)* Hänssler Classic ▲ 98.825 [AAD]
Bach, J.S.:Cant 58, w. I. Reichelt (sop), W. Schöne (bass), Gächinger Kantorei [G] Hänssler Classic ▲ 98.871 [AAD]
Bach, J.S.:Cant 59, w. A. Augér (sop), N. Tüller (bass), Gächinger Kantorei [G] *(rec 1976-77)* Hänssler Classic ▲ 98.886 [AAD]
Bach, J.S.:Cant 60, w. H. Watts (cta), A. Kraus (ten), P. Huttenlocher (bar), Gächinger Kantorei [G] *(rec 1977 & 1978)* Hänssler Classic ▲ 98.821 [AAD]
Bach, J.S.:Cant 61, w. Gächinger Kantorei [G] Hänssler Classic ▲ 98.867 [AAD]
Bach, J.S.:Cant 62, w. I. Nielsen (sop), H. Watts (cta), A. Baldin (ten), P. Huttenlocher (bar), Gächinger Kantorei [G] *(rec Feb & Apr 1980)* Hänssler Classic ▲ 98.822 [AAD]
Bach, J.S.:Cant 63, w. A. Augér (sop), J. Hamari (mez), H. Laurich (cta), A. Kraus (ten), W. Heldwein (bass), W. Schöne (bass), Gächinger Kantorei [G] *(rec Feb 1971 & Feb 1981)* Hänssler Classic ▲ 98.823 [AAD]
Bach, J.S.:Cant 64, w. A. Augér (sop), A. Murray (mez), P. Huttenlocher (bar), Gächinger Kantorei [G] *(rec Jan 1978 & Mar 1981)* Hänssler Classic ▲ 98.825 [AAD]
Bach, J.S.:Cant 65, w. Gächinger Kantorei [G] Hänssler Classic ▲ 98.872 [AAD]
Bach, J.S.:Cant 66, w. G. Schreckenbach (cta), A. Kraus (ten), P. Huttenlocher (bar), W. Schöne (bass), Gächinger Kantorei [G] *(rec 1981)* Hänssler Classic ▲ 98.880 [AAD]
Bach, J.S.:Cant 68, w. A. Augèr (sop), P. Huttenlocher (bass), Gächinger Kantorei [G] *(rec 1980-81)* Hänssler Classic ▲ 98.890 [AAD]
Bach, J.S.:Cant 70, w. Gächinger Kantorei [G] Hänssler Classic ▲ 98.866 [AAD]
Bach, J.S.:Cant 71, w. Gächinger Kantorei [G] Hänssler Classic ▲ 98.863 [AAD]
Bach, J.S.:Cant 73, w. Gächinger Kantorei [G] Hänssler Classic ▲ 98.874 [AAD]
Bach, J.S.:Cant 74, w. H. Donath (sop), H. Laurich (cta), A. Kraus (ten), P. Huttenlocher (bar), Gächinger Kantorei Hänssler Classic ▲ 98.887 [AAD]
Bach, J.S.:Cant 75, w. I. Reichelt, V. Gohl (mez), J. Hamari (cta), A. Baldin (ten), A. Kraus (ten), H.-F. Kunz (bass), Frankfurt Kantorei [G] *(rec 1970)* Hänssler Classic ▲ 98.891 [AAD]
Bach, J.S.:Cant 76, w. Gächinger Kantorei [G] Hänssler Classic ▲ 98.869 [AAD]
Bach, J.S.:Cant 77, w. H. Donath (sop), J. Hamari (mez), A. Kraus (ten), W. Schöne (bar), Gächinger Kantorei Hänssler Classic ▲ 98.809 [AAD]
Bach, J.S.:Cant 78, w. Gächinger Kantorei [G] Hänssler Classic ▲ 98.861 [AAD]
Bach, J.S.:Cant 79, w. Gächinger Kantorei [G] Hänssler Classic ▲ 98.866 [AAD]
Bach, J.S.:Cant 82, w. D. Fischer-Dieskau (bar), Gächinger Kantorei [G] Novalis ▲ 150028 [DDD]
Bach, J.S.:Cant 82, w. Gächinger Kantorei [G] Hänssler Classic ▲ 98.855 [AAD]
Bach, J.S.:Cant 82, w. D. Fischer-Dieskau (bar), Gächinger Kantorei [G] *(rec ca 1986)* Hänssler Classic ▲ 98.903 [AAD]
Bach, J.S.:Cant 85, w. Gächinger Kantorei [G] Hänssler Classic ▲ 98.864 [AAD]
Bach, J.S.:Cant 86, w. A. Augér (mez), H. Watts (cta), A. Kraus (ten), W. Heldwein (bass), Gächinger Kantorei [G] *(rec 1979)* Hänssler Classic ▲ 98.885 [AAD]
Bach, J.S.:Cant 87, w. J. Hamari (cta), A. Baldin (ten), W. Heldwein (bass), Gächinger Kantorei [G] *(rec 1980-81)* Hänssler Classic ▲ 98.885 [AAD]
Bach, J.S.:Cant 88, w. I. Reichelt (sop), V. Gohl (mez), A. Kraus (ten), W. Schöne (bass), Remembrance Florid Church Chorus Hänssler Classic ▲ 98.804 [AAD]
Bach, J.S.:Cant 89, w. A. Augér (sop), H. Watts (cta), P. Huttenlocher (bar), Gächinger Kantorei [G] *(rec Sept & Dec 1977)* Hänssler Classic ▲ 98.818 [AAD]
Bach, J.S.:Cant 90, w. H. Watts (cta), A. Kraus (ten), Gächinger Kantorei [G] *(rec 1977 & 1978)* Hänssler Classic ▲ 98.821 [AAD]
Bach, J.S.:Cant 91, w. H. Donath (sop), H. Watts (cta), A. Kraus (ten), W. Schöne (bass), Württemberg CO, Gächinger Kantorei, Frankfurt Choir [G] *(rec Feb 1972)* Hänssler Classic ▲ 98.822 [AAD]
Bach, J.S.:Cant 93, w. Württemberg CO, Gächinger Kantorei [G] Hänssler Classic ▲ 98.865 [AAD]
Bach, J.S.:Cant 94, w. H. Donath (sop), E. Paaske (cta), A. Baldin (ten), H.-F. Kunz (bass), W. Schöne (bass), Württemberg CO, Gächinger Kantorei Hänssler Classic ▲ 98.808 [AAD]
Bach, J.S.:Cant 95, w. A. Augér (sop), A. Kraus (ten), W. Heldwein (bass), Württemberg CO, Gächinger Kantorei Hänssler Classic ▲ 98.812 [AAD]
Bach, J.S.:Cant 96, w. H. Donath (sop), M. Höffgen (mez), A. Kraus (ten), S. Nimsgern (b-bar), Württemberg CO, Gächinger Kantorei [G] *(rec 1973)* Hänssler Classic ▲ 98.814 [AAD]
Bach, J.S.:Cant 98, w. A. Augér (sop), J. Hamari (cta), L.-M. Harder (ten), W. Heldwein (bass), Gächinger Kantorei [G] *(rec Oct 1982 & July 1983)* Hänssler Classic ▲ 98.817 [AAD]
Bach, J.S.:Cant 99, w. A. Augér (sop), H. Watts (cta), L.-M. Harder (ten), J. Bröcheler (bar), Gächinger Kantorei [G] *(rec 1979)* Hänssler Classic ▲ 98.813 [AAD]
Bach, J.S.:Cant 100, w. Gächinger Kantorei [G] Hänssler Classic ▲ 98.858 [AAD]
Bach, J.S.:Cant 101, w. A. Augér (sop), H. Watts (cta), A. Baldin (ten), J. Bröcheler (bar), Gächinger Kantorei Hänssler Classic ▲ 98.809 [AAD]
Bach, J.S.:Cant 102, w. E. Randová (mez), K. Equiluz (ten), W. Schöne (bass), Gächinger Kantorei Hänssler Classic ▲ 98.809 [AAD]
Bach, J.S.:Cant 104, w. Gächinger Kantorei [G] Hänssler Classic ▲ 98.869 [AAD]
Bach, J.S.:Cant 107, w. A. Augér (sop), A. Baldin (ten), J. Bröcheler (bar), Gächinger Kantorei Hänssler Classic ▲ 98.805 [AAD]
Bach, J.S.:Cant 108, w. H. Donath (sop), M. Höffgen (mez), K. Equiluz (ten), H.-F. Kunz (bass), Gächinger Kantorei [G] *(rec 1980-81)* Hänssler Classic ▲ 98.884 [AAD]

Stuttgart Bach Collegium (cont.)
H. Rilling (cnd) (cont.)
Bach, J.S.:Cant 109, w. G. Schreckenbach (cta), K. Equiluz (ten), Gächinger Kantorei [G] *(rec Feb 1981)* Hänssler Classic ▲ 98.818 [AAD]
Bach, J.S.:Cant 110, w. K. Graf (sop), H. Gardow (sop), A. Baldin (ten), W. Schöne (bass), Gächinger Kantorei [G] *(rec Jan–Feb 1974)* Hänssler Classic ▲ 98.824 [AAD]
Bach, J.S.:Cant 111, w. Gächinger Kantorei [G] Hänssler Classic ▲ 98.874 [AAD]
Bach, J.S.:Cant 112, w. Gächinger Kantorei [G] Hänssler Classic ▲ 98.860 [AAD]
Bach, J.S.:Cant 113, w. A. Augér (sop), G. Schreckenbach (cta), A. Kraus (ten), N. Tüller (bass), Gächinger Kantorei Hänssler Classic ▲ 98.810 [ADD]
Bach, J.S.:Cant 114, w. G. Schnaut (mez), J. Hamari (cta), K. Equiluz (ten), W. Schöne (bass), Frankfurt Kantorei, Gächinger Kantorei [G] *(rec 1974)* Hänssler Classic ▲ 98.814 [AAD]
Bach, J.S.:Cant 115, w. A. Augér (sop), H. Watts (cta), L.-M. Harder (ten), W. Schöne (bass), Gächinger Kantorei [G] *(rec 1980)* Hänssler Classic ▲ 98.819 [AAD]
Bach, J.S.:Cant 116, w. A. Augér (sop), H. Watts (cta), L.-M. Harder (ten), P. Huttenlocher (bar), Gächinger Kantorei [G] *(rec 1980)* Hänssler Classic ▲ 98.820 [AAD]
Bach, J.S.:Cant 117, w. M. Georg (mez), A. Kraus (ten), A. Schmidt (bar), Gächinger Kantorei [G] Novalis ▲ 150028 [DDD]
Bach, J.S.:Cant 117, w. Gächinger Kantorei [G] Hänssler Classic ▲ 98.856 [AAD]
Bach, J.S.:Cant 121, w. A. Augér (sop), D. Soffel (cta), A. Kraus (ten), W. Schöne (bass), Gächinger Kantorei [G] *(rec Feb & Apr 1980)* Hänssler Classic ▲ 98.824 [AAD]
Bach, J.S.:Cant 122, w. A. Augér (sop), G. Schreckenbach (cta), A. Kraus (ten), N. Tüller (bass), Frankfurt Kantorei [G] *(rec Feb 1972)* Hänssler Classic ▲ 98.826 [AAD]
Bach, J.S.:Cant 123, w. Gächinger Kantorei [G] Hänssler Classic ▲ 98.872 [AAD]
Bach, J.S.:Cant 124, w. Gächinger Kantorei [G] Hänssler Classic ▲ 98.872 [AAD]
Bach, J.S.:Cant 126, w. H. Watts (cta), A. Kraus (ten), W. Schöne (bass), Gächinger Kantorei [G] *(rec 1980)* Hänssler Classic ▲ 98.878 [AAD]
Bach, J.S.:Cant 127, w. A. Augér (sop), L.-M. Harder (ten), W. Schöne (bass), Gächinger Kantorei [G] *(rec 1980)* Hänssler Classic ▲ 98.878 [AAD]
Bach, J.S.:Cant 128, w. G. Schreckenbach (cta), A. Baldin (ten), W. Schöne (bass), Gächinger Kantorei [G] *(rec 1980–81)* Hänssler Classic ▲ 98.886 [AAD]
Bach, J.S.:Cant 129 [G] Hänssler Classic ▲ 98.861 [AAD]
Bach, J.S.:Cant 131, w. Gächinger Kantorei [G] Hänssler Classic ▲ 98.866 [AAD]
Bach, J.S.:Cant 132, w. A. Augér (sop), H. Watts (cta), K. Equiluz (ten), W. Schöne (bass), Gächinger Kantorei [G] *(rec Sept 1976 & Jan & Apr 197)* Hänssler Classic ▲ 98.822 [AAD]
Bach, J.S.:Cant 133, w. A. Augér (sop), D. Soffel (cta), A. Baldin (ten), P. Huttenlocher (bar), Gächinger Kantorei [G] *(rec Feb–Mar 1980)* Hänssler Classic ▲ 98.826 [AAD]
Bach, J.S.:Cant 135, w. H. Watts (cta), A. Kraus (ten), P. Huttenlocher (bar), Gächinger Kantorei Hänssler Classic ▲ 98.802 [AAD]
Bach, J.S.:Cant 136, w. H. Watts (cta), K. Equiluz (ten), N. Tüller (bass), Gächinger Kantorei Hänssler Classic ▲ 98.806 [AAD]
Bach, J.S.:Cant 137, w. Gächinger Kantorei [G] Hänssler Classic ▲ 98.861 [AAD]
Bach, J.S.:Cant 138, w. A. Augér (sop), R. Bollen (cta), A. Baldin (ten), P. Huttenlocher (bar), Gächinger Kantorei Hänssler Classic ▲ 98.812 [AAD]
Bach, J.S.:Cant 139, w. I. Nelson (sop), H. Watts (cta), A. Kraus (ten), P. Huttenlocher (bar), Gächinger Kantorei [G] *(rec 1979 & 1980)* Hänssler Classic ▲ 98.820 [AAD]
Bach, J.S.:Cant 140, w. Gächinger Kantorei [G] Hänssler Classic ▲ 98.857 [AAD]
Bach, J.S.:Cant 140, w. A. Augér (sop), A. Baldin (ten), P. Huttenlocher (bar), Gächinger Kantorei [G] Novalis ▲ 150029 [DDD]
Bach, J.S.:Cant 143, w. E. Csapò (sop), A. Kraus (ten), W. Schöne (bass) [G] Hänssler Classic ▲ 98.870 [AAD]
Bach, J.S.:Cant 145, w. C. Cuccaro (sop), A. Kraus (ten), A. Schmidt (bass), Gächinger Kantorei [G] Novalis ▲ 150029 [DDD]
Bach, J.S.:Cant 145, w. Gächinger Kantorei [G] Hänssler Classic ▲ 98.856 [AAD]
Bach, J.S.:Cant 146, w. C. Watkinson (cta), P. Schreier (ten), P. Huttenlocher (bass), Gächinger Kantorei [G] *(rec 1973)* Hänssler Classic ▲ 98.884 [AAD]
Bach, J.S.:Cant 147, w. Gächinger Kantorei [G] Hänssler Classic ▲ 98.863 [AAD]
Bach, J.S.:Cant 148, w. H. Watts (cta), K. Equiluz (ten), Gächinger Kantorei [G] *(rec 1977)* Hänssler Classic ▲ 98.814 [AAD]
Bach, J.S.:Cant 149, w. A. Augér (sop), M. Georg (mez), A. Baldin (ten), P. Huttenlocher (bar), Gächinger Kantorei [G] *(rec 1984)* Hänssler Classic ▲ 98.815 [AAD]
Bach, J.S.:Cant 151, w. N. Gamo-Yamamoto (sop), H. Laurich (cta), A. Kraus (ten), H.-F. Kunz (bass), Frankfurt Kantorei [G] *(rec Feb 1971)* Hänssler Classic ▲ 98.825 [AAD]
Bach, J.S.:Cant 153, w. A. Murray (mez), A. Kraus (ten), W. Heldwein (bass), Gächinger Kantorei [G] Hänssler Classic ▲ 98.871 [AAD]
Bach, J.S.:Cant 154, w. Gächinger Kantorei [G] Hänssler Classic ▲ 98.872 [AAD]
Bach, J.S.:Cant 155, w. Gächinger Kantorei [G] Hänssler Classic ▲ 98.873 [AAD]
Bach, J.S.:Cant 159, w. J. Hamari (cta), A. Baldin (ten), P. Huttenlocher (bar), Gächinger Kantorei [G] *(rec 1983)* Hänssler Classic ▲ 98.879 [AAD]
Bach, J.S.:Cant 161, w. H. Laurich (cta), A. Kraus (ten), Gächinger Kantorei Hänssler Classic ▲ 98.812 [AAD]
Bach, J.S.:Cant 162, w. A. Augér (sop), A. Rogers (mez), K. Equiluz (ten), W. Schöne (bass), Frankfurt Kantorei [G] *(rec Dec 1975 & Mar 1976)* Hänssler Classic ▲ 98.816 [AAD]
Bach, J.S.:Cant 163, w. A. Augér (sop), H. Watts (cta), A. Kraus (ten), N. Tüller (bass), Gächinger Kantorei [G] *(rec 1976 & 1977)* Hänssler Classic ▲ 98.820 [AAD]
Bach, J.S.:Cant 164, w. E. Wiens (sop), J. Hamari (cta), L.-M. Harder (ten), W. Heldwein (bass), Gächinger Kantorei Hänssler Classic ▲ 98.811 [AAD]
Bach, J.S.:Cant 167, w. K. Graf (sop), H. Gardow (sop), A. Kraus (ten), N. Tüller (bass), Remembrance Florid Church Chorus Hänssler Classic ▲ 98.803 [AAD]
Bach, J.S.:Cant 170, w. Gächinger Kantorei Hänssler Classic ▲ 98.804 [AAD]
Bach, J.S.:Cant 172, w. Gächinger Kantorei [G] Hänssler Classic ▲ 98.864 [AAD]
Bach, J.S.:Cant 174, w. Gächinger Kantorei [G] Hänssler Classic ▲ 98.856 [AAD]
Bach, J.S.:Cant 176, w. I. Nielsen (sop), C. Watkinson (cta), W. Hedwein (bass), Gächinger Kantorei Hänssler Classic ▲ 98.801 [AAD]
Bach, J.S.:Cant 177, w. A. Augér (sop), J. Hamari (cta), P. Schreier (ten), Gächinger Kantorei Hänssler Classic ▲ 98.803 [AAD]
Bach, J.S.:Cant 178, w. G. Schreckenbach (cta), A. Baldin (ten), K. Equiluz (ten), W. Schöne (bass), Gächinger Kantorei Hänssler Classic ▲ 98.806 [AAD]
Bach, J.S.:Cant 179, w. A. Augér (sop), K. Equiluz (ten), W. Schöne (bass), Gächinger Kantorei Hänssler Classic ▲ 98.808 [AAD]
Bach, J.S.:Cant 180, w. A. Augér (sop), C. Watkinson (cta), A. Kraus (ten), W. Heldwein (sop), Gächinger Kantorei [G] *(rec Feb & Oct 1979)* Hänssler Classic ▲ 98.816 [AAD]
Bach, J.S.:Cant 181, w. A. Augér (sop), G. Schnaut (mez), G. Schreckenbach (cta), K. Equiluz (ten), N. Tütler (bass), Gächinger Kantorei [G] *(rec 1981)* Hänssler Classic ▲ 98.878 [AAD]
Bach, J.S.:Cant 182, w. D. Soffel (cta), A. Baldin (ten), P. Huttenlocher (bar), Gächinger Kantorei [G] *(rec 1975)* Hänssler Classic ▲ 98.880 [AAD]
Bach, J.S.:Cant 183, w. A. Augér (sop), J. Hamari (cta), P. Schreier (ten), W. Heldwein (bass), Gächinger Kantorei Hänssler Classic ▲ 98.801 [AAD]
Bach, J.S.:Cant 185, w. A. Augér (sop), H. Laurich (mez), A. Baldin (ten), P. Huttenlocher (bar), Frankfurt Kantorei Hänssler Classic ▲ 98.804 [AAD]
Bach, J.S.:Cant 186, w. A. Augér (sop), H. Watts (cta), K. Equiluz (ten), Gächinger Kantorei Hänssler Classic ▲ 98.805 [AAD]
Bach, J.S.:Cant 187, w. M. Friesenhausen (sop), H. Laurich (mez), W. Schöne (bass), Gächinger Kantorei Hänssler Classic ▲ 98.806 [AAD]
Bach, J.S.:Cant 190, w. H. Watts (cta), K. Equiluz (ten), N. Tüller (b-bar), Gächinger Kantorei [G] Hänssler Classic ▲ 98.870 [AAD]
Bach, J.S.:Cant 191, w. Gächinger Kantorei [G] Hänssler Classic ▲ 98.867 [AAD]
Bach, J.S.:Cant 192, w. Gächinger Kantorei [G] Hänssler Classic ▲ 98.863 [AAD]
Bach, J.S.:Cant 195, w. Gächinger Kantorei [G] Hänssler Classic ▲ 98.859 [AAD]

Stuttgart Bach Collegium (cont.)
H. Rilling (cnd) (cont.)
Bach, J.S.:Cant 198, w. J. Beckmann (sop), A. Kraus (ten), W. Heldwein (bass), Gächinger Kantorei [G] *(rec Sept 1976 & Jan 1977)* Hänssler Classic ▲ 98.827 [AAD]
Bach, J.S.:Cant 199, w. A. Augér (sop) Hänssler Classic ▲ 98.810 [ADD]
Bach, J.S.:Cant 200, w. Gächinger Kantorei [G] Hänssler Classic ▲ 98.858 [AAD]
Bach, J.S.:Cant 208, "Hunting Cant", w. Helen Donath (sop), Elisabeth Speiser (sop), Wilfrid Jochims (ten), Jakob Stämpfli (bass), Stuttgart Memorial Church Figuralchor *(rec Southwest Sound Studio, Stuttgart-Bottnang, May 1965)* Musicaphon ▲ 51351 [AAD]
Bach, J.S.:Cant 213, w. Sheila Armstrong (sop), Hertha Töpper (alt), Theo Altmeyer (ten), Jakob Stämpfli (bass) *(rec 1967)* Musicaphon ▲ 51356 [AAD]
Bach, J.S.:Cant 249a, w. Edith Mathis (sop), Hetty Plümacher (alt), Theo Altmeyer (ten), Jakob Stämpfli (bass), Stuttgart Memorial Church Figuralchor *(rec Gedächtniskirche Stuttgart, Mar 1967)* Musicaphon ▲ 51357 [AAD]
Bach, J.S.:Christmas Oratorio, w. A. Augér (sop), J. Hamari (cta), P. Schreier (ten), W. Schöne (bass), Gächinger Kantorei [G] *(rec 1984)* Hänssler Classic 5-▲ 98.976
Bach, J.S.:Christmas Oratorio, w. A. Augér (sop), J. Hamari (cta), P. Schreier (ten), W. Schöne (bass) Hänssler Classic 3-▲ 98.854 [DDD]
Bach, J.S.:Easter Oratorio, w. A. Augér (sop), J. Hamari (cta), A. Kraus (ten), P. Huttenlocher (bar), Gächinger Kantorei [G] *(rec 1980–81)* Hänssler Classic 5-▲ 98.976
Bach, J.S.:Easter Oratorio, w. Gächinger Kantorei [G] Hänssler Classic ▲ 98.862 [AAD]
Bach, J.S.:Magnificat, BWV 243, w. A. Augér (sop), A. Murray (mez), H. Watts (cta), A. Kraus (ten), P. Huttenlocher (bar), W. Schöne (bass), Gächinger Kantorei *(rec 1979)* Sony Classical ("Essential Classics" series) ▲ SBK 48280 [ADD] ■ SBT 48280
Bach, J.S.:Mass in b, BWV 232, w. *(soloists unknown)*, Gächinger Kantorei Odyssey 2-▲ MB2K 45615
Bach, J.S.:Motets (misc), w. Gächinger Kantorei [G]—O Jesu Christ, mein's Lebens Licht, BWV 118; Ich lasse dich nicht, du segnest mich denn, BWV Anh.159; Jauchzet dem Herrn, alle Welt, BWV Anh.160; Der Gerechte kommt um, BWV deest Hänssler Classic 2-▲ HR 98.965 [DDD]
Bach, J.S.:Motets, BWV 225–30, w. Gächinger Kantorei [G] Hänssler Classic 2-▲ HR 98.965 [DDD]
Bach, J.S.:St. Matthew Passion (sels), w. *(vocal soloists unknown)* Sony Classical (Essential Classics) ▲ SBK 46544 [ADD] ■ SBT 46544
Beethoven, L. van:Missa Solemnis, w. P. Coburn (sop), F. Quivar (cta), A. Baldin (ten), A. Schmidt (bar), Gächinger Kantorei [L] Hänssler Classic 2-▲ CD 98.956 [DDD] 2-■ MC 98.956 (D)
Brahms, J.:Ein Deutsches Requiem, w. D. Brown (sop), G. Cachemaille (bar), Gächinger Kantorei [G] Hänssler Classic ▲ 98.966 [DDD]
Handel, G.F.:Messiah, w. Donna Brown (sop), Cornelia Kallisch (cta), R. Sacca (ten), Alastair Miles (bass), Stuttgart Gächinger Kantorei Hänssler Classic 2-▲ HAN 98975 [DDD]
Handel, G.F.:Messiah (reorchd Mozart), w. Donna Brown (sop), Cornelia Kallisch (cta), R. Saccà (ten), Alastair Miles (bass), Gächinger Kantorei [G] Hänssler Classic 2-▲ 98.975 [DDD]
Haydn, J.:The Seven Last Words of Christ on the Cross, w. Pamela Coburn (sop), Ingeborg Danz (mez), Uwe Heilmann (ten), Andreas Schmidt (bar), Gächinger Kantorei [oratorio version] [G] Hänssler Classic ▲ 98.977 [DDD]
Haydn, M.:Requiem in B♭, w. Pamela Coburn (sop), Ingeborg Danz (mez), Andreas Schmidt (bar), Gächinger Kantorei [L] Hänssler Classic ▲ 98.977 [DDD]
Mozart, W.A.:Kyrie, K.341, w. Gächinger Kantorei [L] Hänssler Classic 2-▲ 98.979 [DDD]
Mozart, W.A.:Missa, K.427, w. C. Oelze (sop), I. Verebics (sop), S. Weir (ten), O. Widmer (bass), Gächinger Kantorei [L] Hänssler Classic 2-▲ 98.979 [DDD]
Mozart, W.A.:Requiem, w. C. Oelze (sop), I. Danz (mez), S. Weir (ten), A. Schmidt (bar), Gächinger Kantorei [L] Hänssler Classic 2-▲ 98.979 [DDD]

Stuttgart Bach Ensemble
Mozart, W.A.:Requiem, w. A. Augér (sop), C. Watkinson (cta), S. Jerusalem (ten), S. Nimsgern (b-bar), Gächinger Kantorei [L] Odyssey ▲ MBK 42614 ■ YT 42614

Stuttgart Baroque Orch
F. Bernius (cnd)
Bach, J.S.:Motets, BWV 225–30, w. Stuttgart Chamber Choir—BWV 225–229 Sony Classical ("Vivarte" series) ▲ SK 45859
Schütz, H.:Easter Oratorio, w. Musica Fiata, Stuttgart Chamber Choir Sony Classical ("Vivarte" series) ▲ SK 45943
Schütz, H.:Die Geburt unsers Herren Jesu Christi, w. Musica Fiata, Stuttgart Chamber Choir Sony Classical ("Vivarte" series) ▲ SK 45943

Stuttgart Brass Ensemble
Pärt, A.:Chamber Music, w. Gidon Kremer (vn), *(other artists unknown)*, Hilliard Ensemble—(works for brass, voice, strings & organ) Arbos; An den Wassern zu Babel; De Profundis; Es sang für langen Jahren; Summa ECM New Series ▲ 78118-21325-2 [DDD]; ■ 78118-21325-4 (D)

Stuttgart Chamber Music Players
Mozart, W.A.:Qts Fl Vivace 3-▲ E 319 [DDD]

Stuttgart CO
F. Bernius (cnd)
Jommelli, N.:Didone abbandonata, w. Dorothea Röschmann (sop), Mechthild Bach (mez), Martina Borst (mez), William Kendall (ct), Daniel Taylor (ct), Arno Raunig (ten)—Didone; Enea; Iarba; Selene; Araspe; Osmida Orfeo 3-▲ CD 381953 [DDD]
D. R. Davies (cnd)
Britten, B.:Lachrymae, w. K. Kashkashian (va) ECM New Series ▲ 78118-20002-2
Hindemith, P.:Trauermusik, w. K. Kashkashian (va) ECM New Series ▲ 78118-20002-2
Kancheli, G.:Abii ne viderem, w. Kim Kashkashian (va) *(rec Apr. 1994)* ECM New Series ▲ 78118-21510-2 [DDD]
Kancheli, G.:Evening Prayers, w. David James (ct), Rogers Covey-Crump (ten), John Potter (ten), Gordon Jones (bar) *(rec Apr. 1994)* ECM New Series ▲ 78118-21510-2 [DDD]
Kancheli, G.:Morning Prayers, w. Vasiko Tevdorashvili (sgr), Natalia Pschenitschnikova (alto flute) *(rec Apr. 1994)* ECM New Series ▲ 78118-21510-2 [DDD]
Mozart, W.A.:Con 21 Pno, w. Keith Jarrett (pno) *(rec Liederhalle, Stuttgart, Nov 1994 & Jan 1995)* ECM New Series 2-▲ 78118-21565-2 [DDD]
Mozart, W.A.:Con 23 Pno, w. Keith Jarrett (pno) *(rec Liederhalle, Stuttgart, Nov 1994 & Jan 1995)* ECM New Series 2-▲ 78118-21565-2 [DDD]
Mozart, W.A.:Con 27 Pno, w. Keith Jarrett (pno) *(rec Liederhalle, Stuttgart, Nov 1994 & Jan 1995)* ECM New Series 2-▲ 78118-21565-2 [DDD]
Mozart, W.A.:Mauerische Trauermusik *(rec Liederhalle, Stuttgart, Nov 1994 & Jan 1995)* ECM New Series 2-▲ 78118-21565-2 [DDD]
Mozart, W.A.:Sym 40 *(rec Liederhalle, Stuttgart, Nov 1994 & Jan 1995)* ECM New Series 2-▲ 78118-21565-2 [DDD]
Penderecki, K.:Con Va, w. K. Kashkashian (va) ECM New Series ▲ 78118-20002-2
K. Münchinger (cnd)
Albinoni, T.:Adagio Org London ▲ 411973-2 [DDD]
Albinoni, T.:Adagio Org London ▲ 430706-2 [DDD]
Bach, J.S.:Brandenburg Cons—Nos. 1-3 London ("Weekend Classics" series) ▲ 421027-2 [AAD]
Bach, J.S.:Brandenburg Cons—Nos. 4-6 London ("Weekend Classics" series) ▲ 421028-2 [AAD]
Bach, J.S.:Magnificat, BWV 243, w. E. Ameling (sop), H. van Bork (sop), H. Watts (cta), W. Krenn (ten), T. Krause (bass), Vienna Academy Chorus London ("Serenata" series) ▲ 433175-2 [ADD]
Bach, J.S.:Suite 2 Orch London ▲ 430706-2 [DDD]
Corelli, A.:Con grosso, Op. 6/8, "Christmas Con" London ("Weekend Classics" series) ▲ 417873-2 [AAD] ■ 417873-4
Handel, G.F.:Cons (16) Org, w. *(org unknown)*—No. 13 London ▲ 430706-2 [DDD]
Handel, G.F.:Cons (16) Org, w. F. Haselböck (org)—No. 13 London ▲ 411973-2 [DDD]
Handel, G.F.:Royal Fireworks Music London ▲ 417743-2 [DDD]
Handel, G.F.:Water Music (comp) London ▲ 417743-2 [DDD]
Mozart, W.A.:Divert Str Qt, K.136 IMP Collectors Series ▲ IMPX 9028 [AAD]
Mozart, W.A.:Kleine Nachtmusik—Andante Interchord ▲ INT 892.934 [AAD]
Mozart, W.A.:Kleine Nachtmusik IMP Collectors Series ▲ IMPX 9028 [AAD]
Mozart, W.A.:Musikalischer Spass IMP Collectors Series ▲ IMPX 9028 [AAD]
Pachelbel, J.:Canon London ▲ 411973-2 [DDD]

▲ = CD ♦ = Enhanced CD Δ = MD ■ = Cassette Tape ☐ = DCC

Stuttgart CO (cont.)
K. Münchinger (cnd) (cont.)
Pachelbel, J.:Canon — London ▲ 430706–2 [DDD]
Pergolesi, G.B.:Con Fl, w. J.–P. Rampal (fl) — London ("Weekend Classics" series) ▲ 417873–2 [AAD] ■ 417873–4
Stuttgart CO — London ▲ 411973–2 LH [DDD]
Vivaldi, A.:Cons Vn, Op. 8/1–4, "The Four Seasons" — London ■ 417051–4
Vivaldi, A.:Cons Vn, Op. 8/1–4, "The Four Seasons", w. W. Krotzinger (vn) — London ("Weekend Classics" series) ▲ 417873–2 [AAD] ■ 417873–4
M. Sieghart (cnd)
Françaix, J.:Divert Bn, w. M. Turkovic (bn) — Orfeo ▲ 223911 [DDD]
Gershwin, G.:Porgy & Bess (sels), w. M. Turkovic (bn) [suite arr. for bassoon & orchestra] — Orfeo ▲ 223911 [DDD]
Haydn, J.:Sym 47 — Orfeo ▲ 253931 [DDD]
Haydn, J.:Sym 62 — Orfeo ▲ 253931 [DDD]
Haydn, J.:Sym 75 — Orfeo ▲ 253931 [DDD]
Haydn, M.:Concertino Bn & Orch, w. Milan Turkovic (bn). — Orfeo ▲ 223911 [DDD]
Kraus, J.M.:Con Vn, w. E. Peinemann (vn) *(rec 3/91)* — Orfeo ▲ 254921 [DDD]
Kraus, J.M.:Symphony funèbre *(rec 3/91)* — Orfeo ▲ 254921 [DDD]
Kraus, J.M.:Sym in c *(rec 3/91)* — Orfeo ▲ 254921 [DDD]
Mozart, W.A.:Con Bn, w. M. Turkovic (bn) — Orfeo ▲ 223911 [DDD]
Mozart, W.A.:Diverts Str Qt, K.136–138 *(rec Ludwigsburg, Germany, Oct. 4–5, 1994)* — Discover International ▲ DI 920288 [DDD]
Mozart, W.A.:Sym 28 *(rec Ludwigsburg, Germany, Oct. 4–5, 1994)* — Discover International ▲ DI 920288 [DDD]
Villa-Lobos, H.:Ciranda das sete notas, w. M. Turkovič (bn) — Orfeo ▲ 223911 [DDD]

Stuttgart Ensemble
D. Kurz (cnd)
Wolf, H.:Choral Music, w. Alison Browner (sop), Württemburg Choir—Elfenlied; Der Feuerreiter; Dem Vaterland; Morgenhymnus; Frühlingschor *(rec live, Stuttgart, Feb 18, 1996)* — Claves ▲ CD 509622 [DDD]
Wolf, H.:Christnacht, w. Alison Browner (sop—Engel der Verkündigung), Katherin Koch (alt—Hirte), Christian Beller (ten), Württemburg Choir *(rec live, Stuttgart, Feb 18, 1996)* — Claves ▲ CD 509622 [DDD]

Stuttgart Hymnus Orch
E. Weyand (cnd)
Bach, J.S.:St. John Passion, w. C. Schäfer (sop), Y. Jänicke (mez), A. Kraus (ten), R. Hagen (bass), B. Possemeyer (bass), Stuttgart Hymnus Boys' Choir [G] *(rec 1990)* — Hänssler Classic 2–▲ 98.968

Stuttgart Philharmonia
H. Farberman (cnd)
Kupferman, M.:Divert Orch — Soundspells ▲ SP 112 [ADD]

Stuttgart Philharmonia Ensemble [W. Czelusta (trbn), K. Bäuerle (trbn), P. Redwig (trbn), F. Resch (trbn), M. Hug (org)]
H. Zanotelli (cnd)
Bruckner, A.:Motets, w. O. Pfaff (ten)—12 Motets *(rec Apr. 6–7, 1979)* — Calig ▲ CAL 50477 [ADD]

Stuttgart Phil Brass
Baroque Trombone & Brass, w. Armin Rosin (trbn), Franz Lehrendorfer (org) — Hännsler Classic ▲ 98.985 [AAD]

Stuttgart PO
R. Bader (cnd)
Mozart, W.A.:Requiem, w. U. Buckel (sop), M. Bence (cta), H.–U. Mielsch (ten), E. Wollitz (bass), Böblingen Bach Choir — Allegretto ▲ ACD 8060 [ADD] ■ ACS 8060
Weber, C.M. von:Missa sancta 2, w. Gertrude Stoklassa (sop), Emmy Lisken (cta), Manfred Raucamp (ten), Hans Kagel (bass), Stuttgart Phil Chorus — Koch Schwann ▲ SCH CD 316372
W. Boettcher (cnd)
Beethoven, L. van:Fant Pno, Op. 80, "Choral Fant", w. Alfred Brendel (pno), Stuttgart Teachers' Glee Club — Vox Box ("Legends" series) 3–▲ CDX3 3502 [ADD]
W.–D. Hauschild (cnd)
Coates, G.:Sym 4, "Chiaroscuro" *(rec Stuttgart, June 1990)* — CPO ▲ CPO 999392–2 [DDD]
M. Kuntzsch (cnd)
Grieg, E.:Con Pno, Op. 16, w. Eugene List (pno) *(rec Südwest Tonstudio, Stuttgart, 1976)* — Vox Legends 3–▲ CDX3 3504
Liszt, F.:Con 1 Pno, w. Eugene List (pno) *(rec Südwest Tonstudio, Stuttgart, 1976)* — Vox Legends 3–▲ CDX3 3504
Rachmaninoff, S.:Con 2 Pno, w. Eugene List (pno) — Vox Legends 3–▲ CDX3 3504
S. Köhler (cnd)
Tchaikovsky, P.:Vars on a Rococo Theme, w. L. Varga (vc) — Vox Box 3–▲ CD3X 3026 [ADD]
N. Pasquet (cnd)
Kalliwoda, J.W.:Vars et Rondo Bn, w. Albrecht Holder (bn) *(rec Stuttgart Phil Hall, June 1995)* — Naxos ▲ 8.553456 [DDD]
Kreutzer, C.:Fant Bn, w. Albrecht Holder (bn) *(rec Stuttgart Phil Hall, June 1995)* — Naxos ▲ 8.553456 [DDD]
Lindpaintner, P.J. von:Con Bn, w. Albrecht Holder (bn) *(rec Stuttgart Phil Hall, June 1995)* — Naxos ▲ 8.553456 [DDD]
Molter, J.M.:Con Bn, w. Albrecht Holder (bn) *(rec Stuttgart Phil Hall, June 1995)* — Naxos ▲ 8.553456 [DDD]
A. Paulmüller (cnd)
Hummel, J.N.:Con Pno, Op. 85, w. M. Galling (pno) — Preiser ▲ 90167 [ADD]
G. Schmöhe (cnd)
Coates, G.:Sym 7 *(rec Jan 1991)* — CPO ▲ CPO 999392–2 [DDD]

Stuttgart Piano Trio
Beethoven, L. van:Allegretto, Hess 48 *(rec 1992 & 1993)* — Naxos ▲ 8.550947 [DDD]
Beethoven, L. van:Trio 1 Pno *(rec 1992 & 1993)* — Naxos ▲ 8.550946 [DDD]
Beethoven, L. van:Trio 2 Pno *(rec 1992 & 1993)* — Naxos ▲ 8.550946 [DDD]
Beethoven, L. van:Trio 3 Pno *(rec 1992 & 1993)* — Naxos ▲ 8.550947 [DDD]
Beethoven, L. van:Trio 8 Pno *(rec 1992 & 1993)* — Naxos ▲ 8.550947 [DDD]
Beethoven, L. van:Vars on an Original Theme, Op. 44 *(rec 1992 & 1993)* — Naxos ▲ 8.550947 [DDD]
Mendelssohn, F.:Trio 1 Pno *(rec Sept. 20–22, 1992)* — Orfeo ▲ 308921 [DDD]
Mendelssohn, F.:Trio 2 Pno *(rec Sept. 20–22, 1992)* — Orfeo ▲ 308921 [DDD]
Schubert, Franz:Nocturne Pno *(rec 5/88)* — Naxos ▲ 8.550132 [DDD]
Schubert, Franz:Trio Pno, D.28 — Naxos ▲ 8.550131 [DDD]
Schubert, Franz:Trio 1 Pno — Naxos ▲ 8.550131 [DDD]
Schubert, Franz:Trio 2 Pno *(rec 5/88)* — Naxos ▲ 8.550132 [DDD]

Stuttgart Piano Trio [Monika Leonhard (pno), Rainer Kussmaul (vn), Helmar Stiehler (vc)]
Beethoven, L. van:Allegretto, WoO 39 *(rec 1992–93)* — Naxos ▲ 8.550949 [DDD]
Beethoven, L. van:Trio 6 Pno, "Archduke" *(rec 1992–93)* — Naxos ▲ 8.550949 [DDD]
Beethoven, L. van:Vars on "Ich bin der Schneider Kakadu" from Wenzel Müller's *Die Schwestern von Prag*, Op. 121a *(rec 1992–93)* — Naxos ▲ 8.550949 [DDD]

Stuttgart Pro Musica Orch
M. Couraud (cnd)
Vivaldi, A.:Gloria, RV.589, w. Friederike Sailer (sop), Margarethe Bence (alt) *(rec 1964)* — Tuxedo ▲ TUXCD 1032 [ADD]
Vivaldi, A.:Motets, w. Friederike Sailer (sop)—O qui coeli terraeque *(rec 1964)* — Tuxedo ▲ TUXCD 1032 [ADD]
Vivaldi, A.:Stabat Mater, w. Margarethe Bence (alt) *(rec 1964)* — Tuxedo ▲ TUXCD 1032 [ADD]
Vivaldi, A.:Stabat Mater, w. M. Bence (cta), Stuttgart Pro Musica Chorus *(rec 1957)* — Vox Box 2–▲ CDX 5081 [ADD]

Stuttgart Pro Musica Orch (cont.)
C. Cremer (cnd)
Kreisler, F.:Vn Pieces, w. Bronislaw Gimpel (vn)—Tartini:Fugue in A; La Gitana; Old Viennese Dance Melodies (3); Polichinelle – Serenade; Rimsky-Korsakov:Arab Song from Scheherazade; Perlude & Allegro (in the Style of Gaetano Pugnani); La Précieuse (in the Style of Louis Couperin); Caprice Viennois; Tambourin Chinois; Rachmaninoff:Marguerite; Falla:Danse Espagnole — Vox Legends ▲ CDX 5523

Stuttgart Radio Orch
Kelemen, M.:Grand Jeu Classic — Col legno ▲ AU 31803 [DDD]
C. Leonhardt (cnd)
Wagner, R.:Tannhäuser, w. T. Eipperle (sop), F. Krauss (bar), K. Schmitt-Walter (bar), S. Nilsson (bass), Stuttgart Radio Chorus [G] *(rec Oct. 24, 1937, mat. 39695)* — Preiser 3–▲ 90133 (m) [AAD]
Wagner, R.:Die Walküre (sels), w. M. Reining (sop), H. Jung (mez), F. Krauss (ten), R. Bockelmann (bar), J. von Manowarda (bass)—Act 2 (sels.); Act 3 (complete) *(rec Apr. 3, 1938)* — Preiser 2–▲ PRE 90207 [ADD]
Wagner, R.:Die Walküre (sels), w. M. Reining (sop), F. Krauss (ten)—4 solo arias from Act I Scene 3 *(Der Männer Sippe; Winterstürme wichen dem Wonnenmond; Du bist der Lenz; Siegmund heiss ich) [G] (rec April 3, 1938)* — Preiser 3–▲ 90133 (m) [AAD]
N. Marriner (cnd)
Haydn, J.:Die Schöpfung, w. Barbara Bonney (mez), Edith Wiens (sop), Hans–Peter Blochwitz (ten), Olaf Bär (bar), Jan–Herdrik Rootering (bass), Stuttgart Radio Chorus [G] — EMI Classics 2–▲ CDCB 54038 [DDD]

Stuttgart RSO
J. Barbirolli (cnd)
Mahler, G.:Sym 2, w. H. Donath (sop), B. Finnilä (cta), Stuttgart Radio Chorus [G] *(rec live 6/19/70)* — Arkadia 3–▲ 719 [ADD]
G. Bertini (cnd)
Debussy, C.:La Damoiselle élue, w. I. Cotrubas (sop), G. Maurice (mez), Stuttgart Radio Chorus [F] — Orfeo ▲ 012821 [DDD]
Debussy, C.:L'Enfant prodigue, w. J. Norman (sop), J. Carreras (ten), D. Fischer–Dieskau (bar), Stuttgart Radio Chorus [F] — Orfeo ▲ 012821
Ravel, M.:Con Pno (left hand), w. K. W. Paik (pno) — Orfeo ▲ 013821 [DDD]
Ravel, M.:Con in G Pno, w. K. W. Paik (pno) — Orfeo ▲ 013821 [DDD]
Stravinsky, I.:Abraham & Isaac, w. D. Fischer–Dieskau (bar) [E] — Orfeo ▲ 015821 [DDD]
Stravinsky, I.:Babel, w. D. Fischer–Dieskau (bar),[E] — Orfeo ▲ 015821 [DDD]
Stravinsky, I.:Songs, w. D. Fischer–Dieskau (bar),—2 Verlaine Songs, Op. 9 [F] — Orfeo ▲ 015821 [DDD]
Stravinsky, I.:Sym of Psalms, w. Stuttgart Radio Chorus [L] — Orfeo ▲ 015821 [DDD]
S. Celibidache (cnd)
Beethoven, L. van:Sym 3, "Eroica" *(rec 1974–82)* — Exclusive 2–▲ EXL 29 [AAD]
Beethoven, L. van:Sym 5 *(rec 1974–82)* — Exclusive 2–▲ EXL 29 [AAD]
Beethoven, L. van:Sym 6, "Pastorale" *(rec 1974–82)* — Exclusive 2–▲ EXL 29 [AAD]
Beethoven, L. van:Sym 7 *(rec 1974–82)* — Exclusive 2–▲ EXL 29 [AAD]
Bruckner, A.:Sym 5 *(rec Nov. 26, 1981)* — Exclusive 3–▲ EXL 44 [ADD]
Bruckner, A.:Sym 7 *(rec live, Stuttgart 6/8/71)* — Arkadia ▲ 763 [ADD]
Bruckner, A.:Sym 8 *(rec Nov. 13, 1977)* — Exclusive 3–▲ EXL 44 [ADD]
Dvořák, A.:Sym 9, "From the New World" *(rec 1970)* — Arlecchino ARL
Mozart, W.A.:Missa, K.427, w. Arleen Augér (sop), Heather Harper (sop), Horst Lubenthal (ten), Ulrik Cold (bass), Bavarian Radio Chorus, Southwest German Radio Chorus *(rec live, 1980's)* — Topazio ▲ TOP 26045
Schubert, Franz:Sym 5 *(rec live 1969)* — Memories ▲ HR 4190 (m)
Strauss, R.:Till Eulenspiegels lustige Streiche *(rec Stuttgart, 1962)* — Arkadia ▲ 487 [ADD]
Weber, C.M. von:Ovs—Oberon — Exclusive ▲ EXL 37 [ADD]
G. Chmura (cnd)
Schubert, Franz:Lazarus, or Die Feier der Auferstehung, w. E. Mathis (sop), C. Wulkopf (mez), H. Schwarz (mez), W. Hollweg (ten), H. Laubenthal (ten), H. Prey (bar), Stuttgart Radio Chorus [G] — Orfeo ▲ 011101 [DDD]
D. R. Davies (cnd)
Pärt, A.:Cantus in Memory of Benjamin Britten — ECM New Series ▲ 78118–21275–2 [DDD]; ■ 78118–21275–4
Trojahn, M.:Enrico, w. T. Schmidt (sop), L. Magnusson (ten), R. Salter (bar) — CPO 2–▲ CPO 999160 [DDD]
R. Frühbeck de Burgos (cnd)
Spohr, L.:Con 1 Cl, w. K. Leister (cl) — Orfeo ▲ 088101
Spohr, L.:Con 2 Cl, w. K. Leister (cl) — Orfeo ▲ 088201
Spohr, L.:Con 3 Cl, w. K. Leister (cl) — Orfeo ▲ 088201
Spohr, L.:Con 4 Cl, w. K. Leister (cl) — Orfeo ▲ 088101
G. Gelmetti (cnd)
Rossini, G.:Stabat Mater, w. Daniela Dessi (sop), Lucia Mazzaria (sop), Gloria Scalchi (mez), Pietro Ballo (ten), Chris Merritt (ten), Anatoli Kotscherga (bass), Roberto Scandiuzzi (bass), North German Radio Chorus, Southwest German Radio Chorus — Serenissima 2–▲ SER 360155 [DDD]
Verdi, G.:Requiem Mass, w. Lucia Mazzaria (sop), Daniela Dessi (sop), Gloria Scalchi (mez), Pietro Ballo (ten), Chris Merritt (ten), Anatoli Kotscherga (bass), Roberto Scandiuzzi (bass), North German Radio Chorus, Southwest German Radio Chorus — Serenissima 2–▲ SER 360155 [DDD]
M. Gielen (cnd)
Ruzicka, P.:Sinf for 25, w. South German Radio Chorus — CPO ▲ CPO 999053 [DDD]
B. Güller (cnd)
Lindpaintner, P.J. von:Sinfs concertante, Aulos Wind Quintet *(rec 1984)* — Koch Schwann ▲ CD 311 121 [ADD/DDD]
C. Kleiber (cnd)
Mozart, W.A.:Sym 40 — Exclusive ▲ EXL 28 [ADD]
C. Krauss (cnd)
Puccini, G.:La Bohème, w. H. Ranczak (sop), P. A. (ten), M. Ahlersmeyer (bar) *(rec 1938)* — Preiser 2–▲ PRE 90210 [ADD]
N. Marriner (cnd)
Barber, S.:Medea — Capriccio ▲ 10466 [DDD]
Beethoven, L. van:Coriolan Ov *(rec Stuttgart, Dec 7–8, 1994)* — Capriccio ▲ 10548 [DDD]
Beethoven, L. van:Egmont (ov) *(rec Stuttgart, Dec 14, 1991)* — Capriccio ▲ 10549 [DDD]
Beethoven, L. van:Fidelio (ov) *(rec Stuttgart, May 18, 1993)* — Capriccio ▲ 10549 [DDD]
Beethoven, L. van:Die Geschöpfe des Prometheus (sels)—Ov; Allegro vivace; Adagio; Pastorale; Andante; Finale. Allegretto *(rec Stuttgart)* — Capriccio ▲ 10548 [DDD]
Beethoven, L. van:König Stephen (ov) *(rec Stuttgart, Dec 7–8, 1993)* — Capriccio ▲ 10549 [DDD]
Beethoven, L. van:Leonore 1 *(rec Stuttgart, Nov 7, 1992)* — Capriccio ▲ 10549 [DDD]
Beethoven, L. van:Leonore 2 *(rec Stuttgart, May 17–18, 1993)* — Capriccio ▲ 10548 [DDD]
Beethoven, L. van:Leonore 3 *(rec Stuttgart, Nov 26, 1992)* — Capriccio ▲ 10548 [DDD]
Beethoven, L. van:Namensfeier Ov *(rec Stuttgart, Dec 7–8, 1993)* — Capriccio ▲ 10549 [DDD]
Beethoven, L. van:Die Ruinen von Athen (ov) *(rec Stuttgart, Dec 7–8, 1993)* — Capriccio ▲ 10549 [DDD]
Beethoven, L. van:Die Weihe des Hauses (ov) *(rec Stuttgart, Dec 7–8, 1993)* — Capriccio ▲ 10549 [DDD]
Bernstein, L.:Fancy Free (sels) — Capriccio ▲ 10466 [DDD]
Bernstein, L.:West Side Story (sels) — Capriccio ▲ 10466 [DDD]
Copland, A.:El salón México — Capriccio ▲ 10466 [DDD]
Gershwin, G.:Porgy & Bess (sels) — Capriccio ▲ 10466 [DDD]
Schumann, R.:Ov, Scherzo & Finale — Capriccio ▲ CDC 10063 [DDD]
Schumann, R.:Sym in g — Capriccio ▲ 10094 [DDD]
Schumann, R.:Syms (comp) — Capriccio 3–▲ CD 10097 [DDD]
Schumann, R.:Sym 2 — LaserLight ▲ 15 827 [DDD]
Schumann, R.:Sym 2 — Capriccio ▲ 10094 [DDD]

ORCH. & ENS.

Stuttgart RSO (cont.)
N. Marriner (cnd) (cont.)
Schumann, R.:Sym 3 Capriccio ▲ 10093 [DDD]
Schumann, R.:Sym 4 Capriccio ▲ 10093 [DDD]
Strauss, R.:Con Ob, w. L. Lencses (ob) Capriccio ▲ 10231 ■ 27231
Strauss, R.:Metamorphosen Capriccio ▲ 10231 ■ 27231
Tchaikovsky, P.:Suite 3 Capriccio ▲ 10200 [DDD]
Tchaikovsky, P.:Suite 4 Capriccio ▲ 10200 [DDD]
M. Minsky (cnd)
Joachim, J.:Con 3 Vn, w. T. Nishizaki (vn) Marco Polo ▲ 8.223373
Joachim, J.:Elegische Ov Marco Polo ▲ 8.223373
Joachim, J.:Hamlet Ov Marco Polo ▲ 8.223373
H. Müller-Kray (cnd)
Baur, J.:Romeo und Julia Thorofon ▲ CTH 2270
K. Münchinger (cnd)
Beethoven, L. van:Sym 6, "Pastorale" Intercord ▲ INT 820.547
Mozart, W.A.:Kleine Nachtmusik—Andante Intercord ▲ INT 892.934 [AAD]
Schubert, Franz:Sym 8—Andante con motto Intercord ▲ INT 892.934 [AAD]
N. Rescigno (cnd)
Bellini, V.:Il pirata (sels), w. Maria Callas (sop) *(rec Stuttgart, May 19, 1959)* Originals ▲ ORISH 850
Rossini, G.:Il barbiere di Siviglia (sels), w. Maria Callas (sop) *(rec Stuttgart, May 19, 1959)* Originals ▲ ORISH 850
Spontini, G.:La vestale (sels), w. Maria Callas (sop) *(rec Stuttgart, May 19, 1959)* Originals ▲ ORISH 850
Verdi, G.:Don Carlos (sels), w. Maria Callas (sop) *(rec Stuttgart, May 19, 1959)* Originals ▲ ORISH 850
Verdi, G.:Macbeth (sels), w. Maria Callas (sop) *(rec Stuttgart, May 19, 1959)* Originals ▲ ORISH 850
H. Rilling (cnd)
Bruckner, A.:Mass 3, w. *(soloists unknown)*, Gächinger Kantorei Hänssler Classic ▲ HAN 98983 [DDD]
Franck, C.:Les Béatitudes, w. D. Montague (mez), K. Lewis (ten), G. Cachemaille (bar), J. Cheek (bass), Gächinger Kantorei [F] Hänssler Classic 2-▲ 98.964 [DDD]
Verdi, G.:Messa per Rossini, w. G. Benačková-Cápova (sop), F. Quivar (mez), J. Wagner (ten), A. Agache (bar), A. Haugland (bass), Gächinger Kantorei, Prague Phil Chorus [L] Hänssler Classic 2-▲ CD 98.949 [DDD] 2-■ MC 96.949 (D)
C. Schuricht (cnd)
Beethoven, L. van:Coriolan Ov *(rec Stuttgart, Sept. 25, 1952)* Archiphon ▲ ARCH 2.8 (m) [ADD]
Beethoven, L. van:Sym 3, "Eroica" *(rec live, Stuttgart-Degerloch, Waldheim, Feb. 29, 1952)* Archiphon ▲ ARCH 2.8 (m) [ADD]
Brahms, J.:Ein Deutsches Requiem, w. M. Stader (sop), H. Prey (bar), Stuttgart Radio Chorus, Frankfurt Radio Chorus *(rec Nov. 7, 1959)* Archipon ▲ ARCH 2.2CD (m) [ADD]
Brahms, J.:Sym 2 *(rec 16 & 18 Mar. 1966)* Archipon ▲ ARCH 2.5CD [ADD]
Bruckner, A.:Sym 4, "Romantic" *(rec Apr. 5, 1955)* Archipon ▲ ARCH 2.4CD (m) [ADD]
Mahler, G.:Sym 3 *(rec Apr. 7, 1960)* Archipon 2-▲ ARCH 2.6/7 (m) [ADD]
Mozart, W.A.:Nozze di Figaro (ov) *(rec live, Stuttgart, Dec. 19, 1962)* Archiphon ▲ ARC 2.10 (m) [ADD]
Mozart, W.A.:Sinf concertante Ob, K.Anh.9 *(rec live, Stuttgart, Feb. 29, 1952)* Archiphon ▲ ARC 2.10 (m) [ADD]
Mozart, W.A.:Sym 40 *(rec live, Stuttgart, May 19, 1961)* Archiphon ▲ ARC 2.10 (m) [ADD]
Schumann, R.:Manfred, w. Stuttgart Radio Chorus *(rec Mar. 25, 1952)* Archipon ▲ ARCH 2.3CD (m) [ADD]
Strauss, R.:Eine Alpensinfonie *(rec Apr. 7, 1960)* Archipon 2-▲ ARCH 2.6/7 (m) [ADD]
Tchaikovsky, P.:Hamlet *(rec live, Stuttgart-Degerloch, Waldheim, Oct. 24, 1952)* Archiphon ▲ ARC 2.9 (m) [ADD]
Tchaikovsky, P.:Sym 4 *(rec live, Stuttgart-Degerloch, Waldheim, Nov. 26, 1954)* Archiphon ▲ ARC 2.9 (m) [ADD]
Wagner, R.:Parsifal (orch sels) *(rec 16 & 18 Mar. 1966)* Archipon ▲ ARCH 2.5CD [ADD]
U. Segal (cnd)
Françaix, J.:L'Horloge de Flore, w. L. Lencsés (ob) CPO ▲ CPO 999193-2 [ADD/DDD]
D. Shallon (cnd)
Mendelssohn, F.:Con in e Vn & Orch, Op. 64, w. András Adorján (fl) Orfeo ▲ 046831 [DDD]
Spohr, L.:Con 8 Vn, w. A. Adorján (fl) Orfeo ▲ 046831 [DDD]
S. Soltesz (cnd)
Famous Opera Arias, w. Bumbry, Grace (mez), Stuttgart Radio SO Orfeo ▲ C 081841 A [DDD] ■ M 081841 A (D)
J. Stárek (cnd)
Joachim, J.:Vars Vn, w. R. Odnoposoff (vn) *(rec June 7, 1974)* Doron ▲ DRC 4004 [ADD]
G. Varga (cnd)
Milhaud, D.:Aspen Serenade, w. L. Lencsès (ob) *(rec Jan. 1986 & Jan. 1992)* CPO ▲ CPO 999114-2 [DDD]
Milhaud, D.:Stanford Serenade, w. L. Lencsès (ob) *(rec Jan. 1986 & Jan. 1992)* CPO ▲ CPO 999114-2 [DDD]

Stuttgart Reich RSO
J. Keilberth (cnd)
Mozart, W.A.:Don Giovanni, w. Hedwig Jungkurth (sop—Elvira), Maria Reining (sop—Anna), Julius Patzak (ten—Ottavio), Karl Hammes (bar—Don Giovanni), Georg Hann (bass), Ludwig Weber (bass—Commandant), Stuttgart Radio Chorus *(rec Mar, 1936)* Preiser 2-▲ PRE 90263

Stuttgart Reichssenders Orch
C. Leonhardt (cnd)
Wagner, R.:Die Walküre (act 1), w. M. Reining (sop), F. Krauss (ten), J. von Manowarda (bass) *(rec April 28, 1940)* Preiser ▲ 90151 (m)

Stuttgart Sinfonia
W. Hofmann (cnd)
Hölszky, A.:Klangwerfer Koch Schwann ▲ 3-1062-2 [DDD]

Stuttgart Solisten
A. Grüber (cnd)
Hindemith, P.:Der Dämon—Con Suite *(rec 1971)* Allegretto ▲ ACD 8191

Stuttgart South Radio Orch
H. Müller-Kray (cnd)
Haydn, J.:Die Jahreszeiten, w. Agnes Giebel (sop—Hanne), Fritz Wünderlich (ten—Lukas), Kieth Engen (bass—Simon), Hesse Radio Chorus *(rec Schwetzingen, May 24, 1959)* Bella Voce 2-▲ 7204 [AAD]

Stuttgart State Opera Orch
D.R. Davies (cnd)
Glass, Philip:Akhnaten, w. Stuttgart State Opera Chorus CBS 2-▲ M2K 42457 [DDD]

Stuttgart String Sextet
Brahms, J.:Sextet Strs, Op. 18 *(rec 11/89)* Naxos ▲ 8.550436 [DDD]
Brahms, J.:Sextet Strs, Op. 36 *(rec 11/89)* Naxos ▲ 8.550436 [DDD]

Stuttgart Studio Ensemble
Kelemen, M.:Splintery Col legno ▲ AU 31803 [DDD]
Kelemen, M.:Varia Melodia Col legno ▲ AU 31803 [DDD]

Stuttgart SO
C. Kleiber (cnd)
Borodin, A.:Sym 2 *(rec live, Stuttgart 1972)* Memories ▲ HR 4410 [ADD]

Stuttgart Wind Quintet [Willy Freivogel (fl), Sigurd Michael (ob), Rainer Schumacher (cl), Friedheim Pütz (hn), Hermann Herder (bn)]
Curtis-Smith, C.:Sextet Pno, w. Dennis Russell Davies (pno) Albany ▲ TROY 148 [DDD]
Haas, P.:Qnt Wind [rev Lubomír Peduzzi] Orfeo ("Musica Rediviva" series) ▲ 386961 [DDD]

Stuyvesant String Quartet
B. Reibold (cnd)
Bach, J.S.:Cant 202, "Wedding Cant", w. E. Schumann (sop), M. Miller (mez), et al. *(rec RCA Victor Studio No. 2, New York, Oct 10 & Nov 22, 1939)* Pearl 2-▲ PEAS 9900 (m) [AAD]

ST-X Ensemble
C. Z. Bornstein (cnd)
Xenakis, I.:A la Mémoire de Witold Lutoslawski Mode ▲ MODE 56
Xenakis, I.:Akanthos *(rec live, Thread Waxing Space, New York, June 21, 1995)* Mode ▲ mode 53
Xenakis, I.:Akrata Mode ▲ MODE 56
Xenakis, I.:Échange, w. Michael Lowenstern (b cl) Mode ▲ MODE 56
Xenakis, I.:Eonta, w. Justin Rubin (pno) *(rec live, Thread Waxing Space, New York, June 21, 1995)* Mode ▲ mode 53
Xenakis, I.:N'shima, w. Catherine Aks (sop), April Lindevald (mez) *(rec live, Thread Waxing Space, New York, June 21, 1995)* Mode ▲ mode 53
Xenakis, I.:Plektó *(rec live, Thread Waxing Space, New York, June 21, 1995)* Mode ▲ mode 53
Xenakis, I.:Xas Mode ▲ MODE 56

Suisse Romande Orch—see Swiss Romande Orch

Suk CO
Lovely Time 1, w. Josef Suk (vn) Lotos ▲ LT 0002 [DDD]
Lovely Time 2, w. Josef Suk (vn) Lotos ▲ LT 0004 [DDD]
S. Bogunia (cnd)
Copland, A.:Con Cl, w. Jiří Hlaváč (cl), Hana Müllerová (hp), Ivan Klánský (pno) *(rec ZK Motorlet Prague Studio, Sept 4-6 & 14-15, 1986)* Panton ▲ PAN 810884
K. Donath (cnd)
Mozart, W.A.:Arias, w. Helen Donath (sop), Dieter Klöcker (cl), Josef Suk (vn), Karl-Otto Hartmann (bn)—Cor Sincerum; Jesus Amor Meus; Mens Sancta Deo [2 versions]; Jesu Dulcis Memoria; Salve Regina; Domine Deus Salutis Meae; Plasmator Deus; Die Hoffnung dient zum Stabe *(rec Cultural House, Prague, June 3-10, 1987)* Panton ▲ PAN 810860
P. Škvor (cnd)
Danzi, F.:Sinf concertante, w. D. Klöcker (cl), K.-O. Hartmann (bn) MD + G ▲ L 3365 [DDD]
Mozart, W.A.:Concertone Vns, w. D. Klöcker (cl), K.-O. Hartmann (bn) [arr. Anton Hoffmeister for clarinet & bassoon] MD + G ▲ L 3365 [DDD]
Schubert, J.F.:Con Cl, w. D. Klöcker (cl), K.-O. Hartmann (bn) MD + G ▲ L 3366 [DDD]
Winter, P. von:Concertino Cl, w. D. Klöcker (cl), K.-O. Hartmann (bn) MD + G ▲ L 3366 [DDD]
J. Suk (cnd)
Bach, J.S.:Brandenburg Cons, w. J. Suk (vn) *(rec 1989)* Vanguard Classics 2-▲ OVC 7002/03 [DDD]
Bach, J.S.:Suite 2 Orch, w. J. Válek (fl) Vanguard Classics 2-▲ OVC 7002/03 [DDD]
Besozzi, C.:Cons (3) Ob, w. J. Adamus (ob) Supraphon ▲ 11 1581-2 [DDD]
Dvořák, A.:Serenade Strs *(rec Oct. 6-16, 1985)* Supraphon ▲ 10 4136-2 [DDD]
Mozart, W.A.:Con 11 Pno, w. Susan Kagan (pno) *(rec Martinů Hall, Lichtenstein Palace, Prague, Jan 3-5, 1995)* Vox Classics ▲ VOX 7526 [DDD]
Mozart, W.A.:Con 12 Pno, w. Susan Kagan (pno) *(rec Martinů Hall, Lichtenstein Palace, Prague, Jan 3-5, 1995)* Vox Classics ▲ VOX 7526 [DDD]
Mozart, W.A.:Con 14 Pno, w. Susan Kagan (pno) *(rec Martinů Hall, Lichtenstein Palace, Prague, Jan 3-5, 1995)* Vox Classics ▲ VOX 7526 [DDD]
Mozart, W.A.:Con 2 Vn, w. J. Suk (vn) Vanguard Classics ▲ OVC 7001 [DDD]
Mozart, W.A.:Con 3 Vn, w. J. Suk (vn) Vanguard Classics ▲ OVC 7001 [DDD]
Mozart, W.A.:Sinf concertante Vn, K.364, w. J. Suk (vn), T. Kakuska (va) *(rec 1989)* Vanguard Classics ▲ OVC 7001 [DDD]
Suk, J.:Serenade Strs *(rec Oct. 6-16, 1985)* Supraphon ▲ 10 4136-2 [DDD]
F. Vajnar (cnd)
Zelenka, J.D.:Capriccios *(rec Studio Martínek, Prague)* Panton 2-▲ PAN 811235 [DDD]
Zelenka, J.D.:Con à 8, w. Jana Brozková (ob), Josef Suk (vn), Ludmila Vybíralová (vn), Ivo Laniar (vc), Jaroslav Kubita (bn) *(rec Studio Martínek, Prague)* Panton 2-▲ PAN 811235 [DDD]
Zelenka, J.D.:Hipocondrie à 7 *(rec Studio Martínek, Prague, Mar. 22-24 & 28, 1993)* Panton ("Protokol XX" series) ▲ PAN 811234
Zelenka, J.D.:Ov & Concertanti *(rec Studio Martínek, Prague, Mar. 22-24 & 28, 1993)* Panton ("Protokol XX" series) ▲ PAN 811234
Zelenka, J.D.:Sinfonia & Concertanti *(rec Studio Martínek, Prague, Mar. 22-24 & 28, 1993)* Panton ("Protokol XX" series) ▲ PAN 811234
J. Vlach (cnd)
Bach, J.S.:Con Vn & Ob, w. J. Suk (vn), J. Adamus (ob) Supraphon ▲ 10 4127 [DDD]
Bach, J.S.:Con Vn & Ob, w. J. Suk (vn), J. Adamus (ob) *(rec 1985)* Supraphon Collection ▲ 11 0642-2 [ADD]
Bach, J.S.:Con for 2 Vns, w. J. Suk (vn), M. Kosina (vn) *(rec 1982)* Supraphon ▲ 110281-2 [AAD]
Janáček, L.:Suite Str Orch Panton ▲ PAN 810954
Kalabis, V.:Diptych Panton ▲ PAN 810954
Kozeluch, L.:Sinf Francese MD + G ▲ L 3316 [DDD]
Kozeluch, L.:Sinf Francese Panton ▲ PAN 810953
Marcello, A.:Con Ob & Strs, w. J. Adamus (ob) Supraphon ▲ 10 4127 [DDD]
Martinů, B.:Partita (Suite 1) Panton ▲ PAN 810954
Martinů, B.:Serenade 2 Panton ▲ PAN 810954
Mysliveček, J.:Divert MD + G ▲ L 3316 [DDD]
Mysliveček, J.:Divert Panton ▲ PAN 810953
Mysliveček, J.:Sym in E Panton ▲ PAN 810953
Mysliveček, J.:Sym in E♭ MD + G ▲ L 3316 [DDD]
Telemann, G.P.:Cons Ob Orch, w. P. Verner (ob)—6 Concerti—in c, c, D, d, e & f *(rec 1987)* Supraphon ▲ 11 0122-2 [DDD]
Tuma, F.I.A.:Part Strs Panton ▲ PAN 810953
Vivaldi, A.:Cons Ob Vn, w. J. Adamus (ob), J. Suk (vn)—RV.576 Supraphon ▲ 10 4127 [DDD]
Vivaldi, A.:Cons Vn (misc), w. J. Suk (vn)—RV.230 Supraphon ▲ 10 4127 [DDD]
Vivaldi, A.:Cons Vn, Op. 3/1-12, "L'estro armonico", w. J. Suk (vn)—No. 9 in D *(rec June 16-19, 1985)* Supraphon ("Collection" series) ▲ 11 0685-2 [ADD]

Suk String Quartet
Dvořák, A.:Qnt Strs, Op. 97, w. Lubomir Maly (va) Praga ▲ PR 250078
Hába, A.:Qts Strs—Opp. 73/7, 76/8, 92/13, 95/15 & 98/16 *(rec 1978 & 1992)* Praga ▲ PR 255 005
Kopelent, M.:Qt 5 Strs Praga ▲ PR 255003

Suk String Quartet [A. Novák (vn), V. Jouza (vn), Karel Řehák (va), J. Štros (vc)]
Suk, J.:Qnt Pno, w. P. Štepán (pno) Supraphon (pn▲ SUP 111532 [DDD]

Suk String Quartet [Ivan Štraus (vn), Ludek Hašek (vn), Karel Řehák (va), František Host (vc)]
Fibich, Z.:Qt Pno, w. Radoslav Kvapil (pno) *(rec Bohuslav Martinů Hall in the Lichtenstejn Pallace, Prague, Apr 8-10, 1995)* Panton ▲ 811425-2 [DDD]
Fibich, Z.:Qnt Pno, w. Radoslav Kvapil (pno) [arr. for pno & str quartet] *(rec Bohuslav Martinů Hall in the Lichtenstejn Pallace, Prague, Apr 8-10, 1995)* Panton ▲ 811425-2 [DDD]

Suk String Quartet [Ivan Štraus (vn), Vojtech Jouza (vn), Karel Řehák (va), Jan Štros (vc)]
Suk, J.:Ballade Str Qt CRD ▲ CRD 3472 [DDD]
Suk, J.:Meditation on the Old Czech Hymn "St. Wenceslas" CRD ▲ CRD 3472 [DDD]
Suk, J.:Music for Strs—Barcarolle; Minuet CRD ▲ CRD 3472 [DDD]
Suk, J.:Qt Strs, Op. 11 CRD ▲ CRD 3472 [DDD]
Suk, J.:Qt Strs, Op. 31 CRD ▲ CRD 3472 [DDD]

Suk Trio [J. Panenka (pno), J. Suk (vn), J. Chuchra (vc)]
Mendelssohn, F.:Trio 1 Pno Supraphon Collection ▲ 11 0648-2 [ADD]
Suk, J.:Elegie Supraphon ▲ SUP 111532 [DDD]
Suk, J.:Trio Pno Supraphon ▲ SUP 111532 [DDD]
K. Masur (cnd)
Beethoven, L. van:Con Vn, Vc & Pno, "Triple Con", w. Czech PO *(rec 1973)* Supraphon ▲ 11 0707-2 [ADD]

▲ = CD ♦ = Enhanced CD ∆ = MD ■ = Cassette Tape □ = DCC

Brian Sullivan Orch
M. Abravanel (cnd)
Weill, K.:Street Scene, w. Anne Jeffreys (sgr), Polyna Stoska (sgr) *(rec 1949)* CBS ▲ MK 44668 (m) [ADD]
Summit Brass
American Tribute Summit ▲ DCD 127 [DDD]
Bach, J.S.:Music of—Toccata & Fugue in d, BWV 565; "Little" Fugue in g; Jesu, joy of man's desiring; Air from Orchestral Suite No. 3 Summit ▲ DCD 101 [DDD] ■ DC 101 (CrO2)
Bach, J.S.:Toccata & Fugue Org, BWV 565 Summit ▲ DCD 101 [DDD] ■ DC 101 (CrO2)
Cheetham, J.:Keystone Celebration Summit ▲ DCD 127 [DDD]
Delights Summit ▲ DCD 138 [DDD] ■ DCD 138
Erb, D.:Sonneries Summit ▲ DCD 127 [DDD]
Gabrieli, G.:Canzoni—3 sels. from Symphoniae Sacrae (1597) & 4 sels. from Canzoni e Sonate (1615); plus 3 Canzoni by contemporaries Orindio Bartolino, Girolamo Frescobaldi & Giosetto Guami Summit ▲ DCD 101 [DDD] ■ DC 101 (CrO2)
Hindemith, P.:Concert Music Pno, Brass & Hps, w. T. Lichtmann (pno), M. Walter (hp), P.L. Jenks (hp) Summit 2-▲ DCD 115 [DDD] 2-■ DCD 115
Hindemith, P.:Morgenmusik Summit 2-▲ DCD 115 [DDD] 2-■ DCD 115
Paving the Way *(rec Centre College, Danville, KT, June 20–21, 1994)* Summit ▲ DCD 171 [DDD]
Plog, A.:Music of, w. Thomas Bacon (nar), St. Louis Brass Quintet—Animal Ditties [poetry by Ogden Nash] for Narrator & Brass Ensemble (1989); Concerto for Trumpet, Brass Ensemble & Percussion (1989); Four Sketches for Brass Quintet (1989); Mini-Variations on Amazing Grace for Brass Ensemble (1987); Music for Brass Octet (1981) Summit ▲ DCD 116 [DDD]
Sampson, D.:Reflections on a Dance Summit ▲ DCD 127 [DDD]
Schuller, G.:Sym Brass Summit ▲ DCD 127 [DDD]
Stevens, J.:Moondance Summit ▲ DCD 127 [DDD]
Toccata & Fugue Summit ▲ DCD 101 [DDD] ■ DC 101 (CrO2)
Sundsvall CO
N. Willén (cnd)
Danzi, F.:Con Bn, w. Christian Davidsson (bn) *(rec Tonhallen, Sundsvall, Sweden, Dec. 5–10, 1994)* BIS ▲ CD 705 [DDD]
Hummel, J.N.:Con Bn, w. Christian Davidsson (bn) *(rec Tonhallen, Sundsvall, Sweden, Dec. 5–10, 1994)* BIS ▲ CD 705 [DDD]
Puteanus, E.:Quintetto Bn, w. Christian Davidsson (bn) *(rec Tonhallen, Sundsvall, Sweden, Dec. 5–10, 1994)* BIS ▲ CD 705 [DDD]
Weber, C.M. von:Andante & Rondo ungarese Bn, w. Christian Davidsson (bn) *(rec Tonhallen, Sundsvall, Sweden, Dec. 5–10, 1994)* BIS ▲ CD 705 [DDD]
Sundsvall Wind Quartet [Maria Garlöv (fl), Eva Lauenstein (ob), Inge Magnusson (cl), Maria Granberg (hn), Sixten Lindström (bn)]
Ibert, J.:Pièces brèves Caprice ▲ CAP 21497
Jacob, G.:Sextet Pno & Wind Qnt, w. Carl-Axel Dominique (pno) Caprice ▲ CAP 21497
Thuille, L.:Sxt Pno, w. Carl-Axel Dominique (pno) Caprice ▲ CAP 21497
Vinter, G.:Miniatures Caprice ▲ CAP 21497
Suske String Quartet
Beethoven, L. van:Minuet Str Qt Berlin Classics 2-▲ BER 9052 [DDD]
Beethoven, L. van:Qts Strs (comp)—Op. 18/1-6 Berlin Classics 2-▲ BER 9052 [DDD]
Beethoven, L. van:Qt 7 Strs Berlin Classics 2-▲ BER 9162
Beethoven, L. van:Qt 8 Strs Berlin Classics 2-▲ BER 9162
Beethoven, L. van:Qt 9 Strs Berlin Classics 2-▲ BER 9162
Beethoven, L. van:Qt 10 Strs, "Harp" Berlin Classics 2-▲ BER 9162
Beethoven, L. van:Qt 11 Strs, "Quartetto serioso" Berlin Classics 3-▲ BER 9163
Beethoven, L. van:Qt 12 Strs Berlin Classics 3-▲ BER 9163
Beethoven, L. van:Qt 13 Strs Berlin Classics 3-▲ BER 9163
Beethoven, L. van:Qt 14 Strs Berlin Classics 3-▲ BER 9163
Beethoven, L. van:Qt 15 Strs Berlin Classics 3-▲ BER 9163
Beethoven, L. van:Qt 16 Strs Berlin Classics 3-▲ BER 9163
Mozart, W.A.:Qts Strs (misc)—No. 14 in G, K.387; No. 15 in d, K.421; No. 16 in E♭, K.428; No. 17 in B♭, K.458; No. 18 in A, K.464; No. 19 in C, K.465; No. 20 in D, K.499; No. 21 in D, K.575; No. 22 in B♭, K.589; No. 23 in F, K.590 Berlin Classics 4-▲ BER 2116 [ADD]
Suske Trio
K. Masur (cnd)
Beethoven, L. van:Music of, w. Berlin State Orch, Berlin CO, Leipzig Gewandhaus Orch—Con for Piano in D, Op. 61; Son for Piano, Op. 14/1; Ländler; Minuets; Arias; plus others Berlin Classics 3-▲ BER 9131
Swedish Brass Quintet
Gaathaug, M.:Son Concertante, w. O. Baadsvik (tuba) Simax ▲ PSC 1101
Hindemith, P.:Son Bass Tuba, w. O. Baadsvik (tuba) Simax ▲ PSC 1101
Holmboe, V.:Qnt Brass DIS ▲ CD 78 [AAD/DDD]
Madsen, T.:Son Tuba, w. O. Baadsvik (tuba) Simax ▲ PSC 1101
Sivelov, N.:Son Tuba, w. O. Baadsvik (tuba) Simax ▲ PSC 1101
Swedish CO
S. Ehrling (cnd)
Wagner, R.:Siegfried Idyll Bluebell ▲ BLU 063 [DDD]
Wagner, R.:Sym in C Bluebell ▲ BLU 063 [DDD]
Wagner, R.:Wesendonck Songs, w. Helena Döse (sop) Bluebell ▲ BLU 063 [DDD]
P. Sakari (cnd)
Wirén, D.:Con Vc, w. Mats Rondin (vc) Caprice ▲ CAP 21513
Wirén, D.:Con Pno, w. Mats Widlund (pno) Caprice ▲ CAP 21513
Wirén, D.:Divert Caprice ▲ CAP 21513
Wirén, D.:Serenade Strs Caprice ▲ CAP 21513
Swedish Radio Orch
S. Ehrling (cnd)
Jussi Björling:In Song & Ballad, w. Jussi Björling (ten), Harry Ebert (pno), Bertil Bokstedt (pno), New York PO [cnd:Martti Similä] *(rec 1940, 1942 & 1957)* Bluebell ▲ BLU 050 [ADD]
Swedish RSO
Rossini, G.:Il barbiere di Siviglia (sels), w. Birgit Nilsson (sop), Set Svanholm (ten), Sigurd Björling (bar), Royal Stockholm PO—Largo al factotum Bluebell ▲ BLU 058 [ADD]
Verdi, G.:Otello (sels), w. Birgit Nilsson (sop), Set Svanholm (ten), Sigurd Björling (bar), Royal Stockholm PO—Desdemona rea!...Ora e per sempre adio...Si, pel ciel marmoreo giuro! Bluebell ▲ BLU 058 [ADD]
Wagner, R.:Arias & Scenes, w. Birgit Nilsson (sop), Set Svanholm (ten), Sigurd Björling (bar), Royal Stockholm PO—Morgenlich leuchtend [from Die Meistersinger von Nürnberg]; Ein Schwert verhiess mir der Vater [from Die Walküre]; Mime hiess ein mürrischer Zwerg...Brünnhilde, heilige Braut [from Götterdämmerung] Bluebell ▲ BLU 058 [ADD]
Weber, C.M. von:Der Freischütz (sels), w. Birgit Nilsson (sop), Set Svanholm (ten), Sigurd Björling (bar), Royal Stockholm PO—Durch die Wälder, durch die Auen Bluebell ▲ BLU 058 [ADD]
K. Atterberg (cnd)
Atterberg, K.:Aladdin (ov) Swedish Society ▲ SCD 1021
H. Blomstedt (cnd)
Eliasson, A.:Canto del Vagabondo, w. Swedish Radio Chorus, Eric Ericson Chamber Choir Caprice ▲ CAP 21402 [AAD]
Pettersson, G.A.:Con 2 Vn Orch, w. I. Haendel (vn) Caprice ▲ CAP 21359 [AAD]
Stenhammar, W.:Sången, w. Iwa Sörenson (sop), Anne Sofie von Otter (mez), Stefan Dahlberg (ten), Per-Arne Wahlgren (bar), Swedish Radio Chorus, Stockholm State Academy of Music Chamber Choir, Adolf Fredrik Music School Children's Choir Caprice ▲ CAP 21358
S. Celibidache (cnd)
Beethoven, L. van:Con 5 Pno, "Emperor", w. A. Benedetti Michelangeli (pno) *(rec live, Helsinki 5/20/69)* Arkadia ▲ 592 [ADD]

Swedish RSO (cont.)
S. Celibidache (cnd) (cont.)
Beethoven, L. van:Sym 2 *(rec live, 1967)* Artists ▲ FED 71 [ADD]
Beethoven, L. van:Sym 2 *(rec live, 1967)* As Disc ▲ ASD 2503
Beethoven, L. van:Sym 4 *(rec live, 1969)* As Disc ▲ ASD 2503
Beethoven, L. van:Sym 4 *(rec live, 1969)* Artists ▲ FED 71 [ADD]
Schumann, R.:Con Pno, w. A. Benedetti Michelangeli (pno) *(rec live, Stockholm, 11/19/67)* Arkadia ▲ 592 [ADD]
Sibelius, J.:En Saga Arkadia ▲ 616
S. Comissiona (cnd)
Mozart, W.A.:Con Bn, w. Knut Sönstevold (bn) Caprice ▲ CAP 21411 [DDD]
Pettersson, G.A.:Sym 7 Caprice ▲ CAP 21411 [DDD]
S. Ehrling (cnd)
Lundquist, I.T.:Sym 7, w. Anita Soldh (sop), Olle Persson (bar), Mikaeli Chamber Choir Caprice ▲ CAP 21419 [DDD]
Stravinsky, I.:Le Sacre du printemps Orch BIS ▲ CD 400
Stravinsky, I.:Sym of Psalms, w. Swedish Radio Chorus BIS ▲ CD 400
S. Frykberg (cnd)
Larsson, L.-E.:Con Vn, w. L. Kaufman (vn) *(rec Jan. 1955)* Music & Arts ▲ CD 667 (m) [AAD]
R. Goodman (cnd)
Berwald, F.:Music of—A Major Sym [frag]; 2 Ovs Hyperion 2-▲ CDA 67081/82
Berwald, F.:Syms (comp) Hyperion 2-▲ CDA 67081/82
F. Haider (cnd)
Donizetti, G.:Linda di Chamounix, w. Edita Gruberová (sop), Monica Groop (mez), Don Bernardini (sgr), Ettore Kim (sgr), Mikaeli Chamber Choir Nightingale Classics 3-▲ NIG 70561
E. Howarth (cnd)
Ligeti, G.:Double Con, w. *(soloists unknown)* BIS ▲ CD 53
Ligeti, G.:San Francisco Polyphony BIS ▲ CD 53
K. Ingebretsen (cnd)
Stenhammar, W.:Ithaka, w. Håkan Hagegård (bar) Caprice ▲ CAP 21358
N. Järvi (cnd)
Tubin, E.:Con Balalaika, w. E. Sheynkman (balalaika) BIS ▲ CD 351 [DDD]
Tubin, E.:Music for Strs BIS ▲ CD 351 [DDD]
Tubin, E.:Sym 1 BIS ▲ CD 351 [DDD]
Tubin, E.:Sym 2 BIS ▲ CD 304 [DDD]
Tubin, E.:Sym 3 BIS ▲ CD 342
Tubin, E.:Sym 6 BIS ▲ CD 304 [DDD]
Tubin, E.:Sym 8 BIS ▲ CD 342
G.L. Jochum (cnd)
Beethoven, L. van:Con 2 Pno, w. G. Gould (pno) BIS 2-▲ CD 323/24
Mozart, W.A.:Con 24 Pno, w. G. Gould (pno) BIS 2-▲ CD 323/24
O. Kamu (cnd)
Aulin, T.:Con 3 Vn, w. C. Bergqvist (vn) Musica Sveciae ▲ MSCD 622
Crusell, B.H.:Con 2 Cl, w. K.-I. Stevensson (cl), I. Olsen (hn), K. Sönstevold (bn) Musica Sveciae ▲ MSV 527 [DDD]
Crusell, B.H.:Intro, Theme & Vars on a Swedish Air, w. K.-I. Stevensson (cl), I. Olsen (hn), K. Sönstevold (bn) Musica Sveciae ▲ MSV 527 [DDD]
Crusell, B.H.:Sinf concertante, w. K.-I. Stevensson (cl), I. Olsen (hn), K. Sönstevold (bn) Musica Sveciae ▲ MSV 527 [DDD]
Strauss, E.:Polkas & Waltzes—Souvenir de Bade, Polka schnell, Op. 146 Myrthen-Sträusschen Walzer, Op. 87; Mit der Strömung Polka française, Op. 174 *(rec Oct. 4–6, 1993)* BIS ▲ CD 645 [DDD]
Strauss (I), Joh.:Music of—Concordia-Tänze Walzer, Op. 146; Versailler Galopp, Op. 107 *(rec Oct. 4–6, 1993)* BIS ▲ CD 645 [DDD]
Strauss (II), Joh.:Music of—Die Göttin der Vernunft:Ov. [w., U. Forsberg (violin)]; Simplicus, Act 2:Also, du bist ein Freiersmann? [w., E. Berg (soprano) & S. Dahlberg (tenor)]; Alexandrine-Polka française, Op. 198; Ritter Pasman, Act 3:Euch schlägt mein ganzes Herz entgegen [w. Berg, Dahlberg & Forsberg]; Carnevals-Spektakel-Quadrille, Op. 152; Cagliostro in Wien, Act. 2:Ha, welch' ein reizendes Gesicht! [w. Berg & Dahlberg] *(rec Oct. 4–6, 1993)* BIS ▲ CD 645 [DDD]
Strauss, Josef:Music of—Deutsche Grüsse Walzer, Op. 101 *(rec Oct. 4–6, 1993)* BIS ▲ CD 645 [DDD]
S. Köhler (cnd)
Peterson-Berger, W.:Romance Vn, w. M. Zetterqvist (vn) Musica Sveciae ▲ MSCD 630 [DDD]
Peterson-Berger, W.:Swedish Poetry, w. A. S. von Otter (mez)—Ask the East Wind, Ask the West Wind; Mumble Tumble Bumble Bee; Sift Sift Golden Grain; Did the East Wind See, Did the West Wind See; High Up on the Fern Thicket of the Slope [all from *Gullebarn's Lullabies*] [Sw] Musica Sveciae ▲ MSCD 630 [DDD]
Peterson-Berger, W.:Sym 3 Musica Sveciae ▲ MSCD 630 [DDD]
T. Mann (cnd)
Aulin, T.:Con 3 Vn, w. G. Kulonkampff (vn) Bluebell ▲ BLU 3003 [ADD]
Glazunov, A.:Con Vn, w. G. Kulenkampff (vn) Bluebell ▲ BLU 3003 [ADD]
E.-P. Salonen (cnd)
Berwald, F.:Sym 3, "Sinfonie singulière" *(rec Stockholm, Mar. 1990)* Musica Sveciae ▲ MSCD 531 [DDD]
Berwald, F.:Sym 4, "Sinfonie naïve" *(rec live, Edinburgh Aug. 29, 1987)* Musica Sveciae ▲ MSCD 531 [DDD]
Dallapiccola, L.:Il Prigioniero, w. Phyllis Bryn-Julson (sop), Sven-Erik Alexandersson (ten), Howard Haskin (ten), Jorma Hynninen (bar), Lage Wedin (bar), Eric Ericson Chamber Choir Sony Classical ▲ SK 68323
Lindberg, M.:Kraft Finlandia ▲ FIN 372 [DDD]
Nielsen, C.:Aladdin, w. Swedish Radio Chorus CBS ▲ MK 44934 [DDD]
Nielsen, C.:Choral Music, w. A. Båverstam (sop), L. Ekdahl (girl sop), A. Thors (boy sop), K. M. Sandve (ten), P. Hoyer (bar), Stockholm Boys' Choir, Swedish Radio Chorus—Springtime in Funen; The Blind Musician; The Old People; Dance Ballad *(rec Sept. 16–18, 1991)* Sony Classical ▲ SK 53276 [DDD]
Nielsen, C.:Con Cl, w. H. Rosengren (cl) *(rec Sept. 16–18, 1991)* Sony Classical ▲ SK 53276 [DDD]
Nielsen, C.:Con Fl, w. P. Flemström (fl) *(rec Sept. 16–18, 1991)* Sony Classical ▲ SK 53276 [DDD]
Nielsen, C.:Con Vn, w. C. L. Lin (vn) CBS ▲ MK 44548 [DDD]
Nielsen, C.:Helios CBS ▲ MK 42093
Nielsen, C.:Imaginary Trip *(rec Dec. 5–6, 1992)* Sony Classical ▲ SK 53276 [DDD]
Nielsen, C.:Maskarade—Overture; Act 2 Prelude; Dance of the Cockerels CBS ▲ MK 44547 [DDD]
Nielsen, C.:Pan & Syrinx CBS ▲ MK 44934 [DDD]
Nielsen, C.:Saul & David (sels)—Prelude to Act II *(rec Sept. 16–18, 1991)* Sony Classical ▲ SK 53276 [DDD]
Nielsen, C.:Sym 1 CBS ▲ MK 42321 [DDD]
Nielsen, C.:Sym 2 CBS ▲ MK 44934 [DDD]
Nielsen, C.:Sym 3 Sony Classical ▲ SK 46500
Nielsen, C.:Sym 4 CBS ▲ MK 42093
Nielsen, C.:Sym 5 CBS ▲ MK 44547 [DDD]
Nielsen, C.:Sym 6 Sony Classical ▲ SK 46500
A Nordic Festival Sony Classical ▲ SK 46668
Sibelius, J.:Con Vn, w. C.-L. Lin (vn) CBS ▲ MK 44548 [DDD]
Sibelius, J.:Finlandia Sony Classical ▲ SK 46668
Sibelius, J.:Valse triste Sony Classical ▲ SK 46668
Stenhammar, W.:Mid-Winter Musica Sveciae ▲ MSCD 626 [DDD]
Stravinsky, I.:Oedipus Rex, w. A. S. von Otter (mez/sop), V. Cole (ten), N. Gedda (ten), S. Estes (bass), H. Sotin (bass), P. Chéreau (nar), *(chorus unknown)* Sony Classical ▲ SK 48057
L. Segerstam (cnd)
Alfvén, H.:Sym 2 Swedish Society ▲ SCD 1005
Bloch, E.:Sym Trbn, w. C. Lindberg (trbn) BIS ▲ CD 538 [DDD]
Blomdahl, K.-B.:Sym 1 *(rec Feb. 24–25, 1993)* BIS ▲ CD 611 [DDD]

ORCH. & ENS.

Swedish RSO (cont.)
L. Segerstam (cnd) (cont.)
Blomdahl, K.-B.:Sym 2 *(rec Feb. 24-25, 1993)* BIS ▲ CD 611 [DDD]
Blomdahl, K.-B.:Sym 3, "Facetter" *(rec Oct. 23, 1991)* BIS ▲ CD 611 [DDD]
Holewa, H.:Con 1 Pno, w. José Ribera (pno) Phono Suecia ▲ PHN 49 [ADD]
Larsson, L.-E.:Con Sax, w. Christer Johnsson (a sax) Caprice ▲ CAP 21492
Lidholm, I.:Greetings from an Old World Caprice ▲ CAP 21366 [AAD]
Sandström, J.:Con Trbn, w. C. Lindberg (trbn) BIS ▲ CD 538 [DDD]
Sandström, S.-D.:The High Mass, w. Lena Hoel (sop), Sara Olsson (sop), Siri Torjesen (sop), Marianne Eklöf (mez), Annika Skoglund (mez), Peter Bengtson (org), Eric Ericson Chamber Choir *(rec live, Berwald Hall, Stockholm, Nov. 25 & 26, 1994)* Caprice 2-▲ CAP 22036
Sandström, S.-D.:Mute the Bereaved Memories Speak, w. Swedish Radio Chorus, Stockholm Chamber Choir, Stockholm Children's Choir Caprice 2-▲ CAP 22027 [AAD]
Serocki, K.:Con Trbn, w. C. Lindberg (trbn) BIS ▲ CD 538 [DDD]
Trombone Odyssey:20th Century Landmarks for Trombone & Orchestra, w. Christian Lindberg (trbn) BIS ▲ CD 538 [DDD]

E. Svetlanov (cnd)
Alfvén, H.:Bergakungen Musica Sveciae ▲ MSCD 614 [DDD]
Alfvén, H.:Sym 2 Musica Sveciae ▲ MSCD 627 [DDD]
Stenhammar, W.:Con 2 Pno, w. G. Erikson (pno) Musica Sveciae ▲ MSCD 622

T. Vetö (cnd)
Nørgård, P.:Gilgamesh, w. Swedish Radio Chorus, Swedish Radio Soloists *(rec Nov. 15, 1973)* Marco Polo ▲ DCCD 9001

S. Westerberg (cnd)
Alfvén, H.:Gustav II Adolph Swedish Society ▲ SCD 1013
Alfvén, H.:Sym 1 Swedish Society ▲ SCD 1001
Alfvén, H.:Sym 5 Swedish Society ▲ SCD 1013
Alfvén, H.:A Tale from the Archipelago Swedish Society ▲ SCD 1001
Atterberg, K.:Suite 3 Vn, w. M. Saulesco (vn), G. Roehr (va) Swedish Society ▲ SCD 1006
Atterberg, K.:Sym 1 *(rec Nov. 3-5, 1986)* Sterling ▲ CDS 1010
Atterberg, K.:Sym 2 Swedish Society ▲ SCD 1006
Eliasson, A.:Canti in Lontananza Caprice ▲ CAP 21402 [AAD]
Karkoff, M.:Chinese Impressions Swedish Society ▲ SCD 1023
Karkoff, M.:Pieces Orch Swedish Society ▲ SCD 1023
Karkoff, M.:Vision Swedish Society ▲ SCD 1023
Koch, E. von:Music of, w. Sigurd Rascher (a sax), Andreas Röhn (vn), Kerstin Hindart (pno), Munich PO—Nordiskt Capriccio; Skandinaviska Danser; Saxofonkonsert; Svensk Dansrapsodi; Karaktärer Föor Vn Och Pno Phono Suecia ▲ PHN 55 [ADD]
Lidholm, I.:Nausikaa Alone, w. E. Söderström (sop), Swedish Radio Chorus Caprice ▲ CAP 21366 [AAD]
Lindberg, O.:Florez & Blanzeflor *(rec Nov. 2, 1980)* Sterling ▲ CDS 1013
Lundquist, T.I.:Landscape, w. Michael Lind (tuba), Andraes Röhn (vn) Caprice ▲ CAP 21493
Nystroem, G.:Sinf concertante, w. E. B. Bengtsson (vc) Swedish Society ▲ SCD 1015
Nystroem, G.:Sym 3, w. E. Söderström (sop) Swedish Society ▲ SCD 1015
Pettersson, G.A.:Con 1 Str Orch Caprice ▲ CAP 21369 [AAD]
Pettersson, G.A.:Mesto Swedish Society ▲ SCD 1013
Pettersson, G.A.:Sym 2 Swedish Society ▲ SCD 1012
Pettersson, G.A.:Vox Humana, w. Marianne Mellnäs (sop), Margot Rödin (alt), Sven-Erik Alexandersson (ten), Erland Hagegård (bar), Swedish Radio Chorus *(rec Royal Swedish Academy of Music, Stockholm, Sweden, Mar. 22 & May 24, 1976)* BIS ▲ CD 55 [AAD]
Rosenberg, H.:Con 3 Orch Swedish Society ▲ SCD 1026
Rosenberg, H.:Suites Swedish Society ▲ SCD 1026
Sibelius, J.:King Christian II (suite) Swedish Society ▲ SCD 1047
Sibelius, J.:The Tempest (sels) Swedish Society ▲ SCD 1047
Stenhammar, W.:Florez och Blanzefor, w. I. Wixell (bar) EMI Classics ▲ CDM 65081
Stenhammar, W.:Sentimental Romances, w. Arve Tellefsen (vn) Caprice ▲ CAP 21358
Stenhammar, W.:Serenade EMI Classics ▲ CDM 65081
Swedish Highlights, w. Swedish Radio Choir Caprice ▲ CAP 21340 [DDD]
Wiklund, A.:Con 2 Pno, w. G. Erikson (pno) Caprice ▲ CAP 21363 [AAD]

Swedish RSO members
E.-P. Salonen (cnd)
Dallapiccola, L.:Canti di prigionia, w. Eric Ericson Chamber Choir, Swedish Radio Choir Sony Classical ▲ SK 68323

S. Westerberg (cnd)
Sonninen, A.:El amor pasa, w. Solveig Faringer (sop), Gunilla von Bahr (fl) *(rec Stockholm Concert Hall, Sweden, Sept. 17, 1974)* BIS ▲ CD 11 [AAD]

Swedish SO
Larsson, L.-E.:Concertinos—No. 11 for Double Bass (1957) Swedish Society ▲ SCD 1021
Larsson, L.-E.:God in Disguise, w. E. Söderström (sop), E. Sandaen (bar), L. Ekborg (nar) Swedish Society ▲ SCD 1020
Larsson, L.-E.:Orch Vars Swedish Society ▲ SCD 1020
Larsson, L.-E.:Pastoralsvit Swedish Society ▲ SCD 1020

Swiss CO
A. Duczmal (cnd)
Grieg, E.:Elegaic Melodies, Op. 34 ASV Quicksilva ▲ ASQ 6094 [ADD]
Grieg, E.:Holberg Suite ASV Quicksilva ▲ ASQ 6094 [ADD]

E. Mata (cnd)
Grieg, E.:Elegaic Melodies, Op. 34 ASV Quicksilva ▲ ASQ 6176
Grieg, E.:Holberg Suite ASV Quicksilva ▲ ASQ 6176

Swiss Clarinet Players
Mozart, W.A.:Adagio Cl, K.Anh.93 Claves ▲ CD 9212 [DDD]
Mozart, W.A.:Adagio Cls, K.411 Claves ▲ CD 9212 [DDD]
Pleyel, I.:Qts Cl Claves ▲ CD 9212 [DDD]
Salieri, A.:Qts Cl Claves ▲ CD 9212 [DDD]
Vanerovsky, F.:Qt Cl Claves ▲ CD 9212 [DDD]

Swiss Festival Orch
J. Fournet (cnd)
Fauré, G.:Requiem, w. E. Mathis (sop), K. Widmer (bass), Lucerne Festival Chorus *(rec 1984)* Koch Treasure ▲ 31619-2 [DDD]
Martin, F.:Maria-Triptychon, w. E. Mathis (sop), W. Schneiderhan (vn) *(rec 1984)* Koch Treasure ▲ 31619-2 [DDD]

Swiss Phil Workshop
M. Venzago (cnd)
Wildberger, J.:Und Füllet die Erde und machet sie euch untertan *(rec Oct. 2, 1989)* Grammont ▲ CTSP 25-2 [ADD]

Swiss Radio-TV Orch
C. Schuricht (cnd)
Brahms, J.:Con 2 Pno, w. Wilhelm Backhaus (pno) Stradivarius 2-▲ STV MSC 2001

Swiss Romande Orch
E. Ansermet (cnd)
Bach, J.S.:Cant 67, w. H. Watts (cta), W. Krenn (ten), T. Krause, Lausanne Pro Arte Choir London ("Serenata" series) ▲ 433175-2 [ADD]
Bach, J.S.:Cant 130, w. E. Ameling (sop), H. Watts (cta), W. Krenn (ten), T. Krause (bass), Lausanne Pro Arte Choir London ("Serenata" series) ▲ 433175-2 [ADD]
Borodin, A.:Prince Igor (ov) London ("Weekend Classics" series) ▲ 430219-2 [AAD]
Borodin, A.:Prince Igor (Polovtsian dances) London ("Weekend Classics" series) ▲ 430219-2 [AAD]
Borodin, A.:Sym 2 London ("Weekend Classics" series) ▲ 430219-2 [AAD]
Borodin, A.:Sym 3 London ("Weekend Classics" series) ▲ 430219-2 [AAD]
Chabrier, E.:España *(rec 1964)* London 2-▲ 443033-2 [ADD]
Chabrier, E.:Joyeuse Marche *(rec 1964)* London 2-▲ 443033-2 [ADD]

Swiss Romande Orch (cont.)
E. Ansermet (cnd) (cont.)
Debussy, C.:Petite suite *(rec 1961)* London ▲ 433711-2 [ADD]
Debussy, C.:Petite suite London ▲ 421171-2 [AAD] ■ 421171-4
Debussy, C.:Prélude à l'après-midi d'un faune London ▲ 421171-2 [AAD] ■ 421171-4
Debussy, C.:Prélude à l'après-midi d'un faune *(rec 1957)* London ▲ 433711-2 [ADD]
Debussy, C.:Première rapsodie, w. Robert (cl), Gugoltz (pno) *(rec 1964)* London ▲ 433711-2 [ADD]
España, w. London SO [cnd:Ataulfo Argenta] London ("Weekend Classics" series) ▲ 430217-2 LC [AAD]
Falla, M. de:El amor brujo London ("Weekend Classics" series) ▲ 417691-2 [AAD]
Falla, M. de:Atlántida, w. Montserrat Caballé (sop), Heinz Rehfuss (bar), Lausanne Youth Chorus, Swiss Romande Red Chorus, Villamont College Little Chorus Cascavelle ▲ CVL 2005 [ADD]
Falla, M. de:Homenajes (4) Orch Cascavelle ▲ CVL 2005 [ADD]
Fauré, G.:Masques et bergamasques (suite) London ("Weekend Classics" series) ▲ 421026-2 [AAD]
Fauré, G.:Pelléas et Mélisande (suite) London ("Weekend Classics" series) ▲ 421026-2 [AAD]
Fauré, G.:Requiem, w. S. Danco (sop), G. Souzay (bar), Tour de Peliz Union Chorus London ("Weekend Classics" series) ▲ 421026-2 [AAD]
First Performances of the Young Arturo Benedetti Michelangeli, w. Arturo Benedetti Michaelangeli (pno) Arkadia ▲ 624
Glazunov, A.:The Seasons London ("Enterprise" series) ▲ 430348-2 [ADD]
Glazunov, A.:Stenka Razin London ("Enterprise" series) ▲ 430348-2 [ADD]
Glazunov, A.:Valses de Concert, Opp. 47 & 51 London ("Enterprise" series) ▲ 430348-2 [ADD]
Martin, F.:Le Mystère de la Nativité, w. Elly Ameling (sop), Aafje Heynis (cta), Hugues Cuénod (ten), Louis Devos (ten), Eric Tappy (ten), Pierre Bollet (bar), Derrik Olsen (bar), Charles Clavensy (b-bar), André Vessières (bass), Jeunes de l'Eglise Chorus, Ceneva Motet Chorus Cascavelle 2-▲ CVL 2006 [ADD]
Martin, F.:Pilate, w. Ariette Chedel (cta), Eugenia Zareska (mez), Eric Tappy (ten), Derrik Olsen (bar), Jean-Christoph Benoit (bar), Lausanne Pro Arte Choir Cascavelle 2-▲ CVL 2006 [ADD]
Martinů, B.:Les Fresques de Piero della Francesca Cascavelle ▲ CVL 2007 [ADD]
Martinů, B.:Parables Cascavelle ▲ CVL 2007 [ADD]
Martinů, B.:Sym 4 Cascavelle ▲ CVL 2007 [ADD]
Prokofiev, S.:Romeo & Juliet (suites) *(rec 1961)* London 2-▲ 440630-2 [ADD]
Prokofiev, S.:Sym 5 *(rec ca. 1964)* IMP Collectors Series ▲ IMPX 9006 [ADD]
Ravel, M.:Boléro London ("Weekend Classics" series) ▲ 417691-2 [ADD]
Ravel, M.:Rapsodie espagnole London ("Weekend Classics" series) ▲ 417691-2 [ADD]
Ravel, M.:Shéhérazade Mez, w. R. Crespin (sop) [F] London ▲ 417813-2 [ADD]
Rieti, V.:Con Pnos, w. A. Gold (pno), R. Fizdale (pno) Premier ▲ PRCD 1033 [ADD]
Tchaikovsky, P.:The Nutcracker London 2-■ 417055-4
Tchaikovsky, P.:Nutcracker Suite 2 London ■ 417097-4
Tchaikovsky, P.:Swan Lake *(rec 1959)* London 2-▲ 440630-2 [ADD]

P. Ansermet (cnd)
Chabrier, E.:España London ("Weekend Classics" series) ▲ 417691-2 [AAD]
Debussy, C.:Clair de lune *(rec 1958)* London ▲ 433711-2
Debussy, C.:Clair de lune London ▲ 421171-2 [ADD]
Debussy, C.:Danse Pno, "Tarantelle styrienne" London ▲ 421171-2 [ADD] ■ 421171-4
Debussy, C.:Jeux *(rec 1958)* London ▲ 433711-2 [ADD]
Debussy, C.:La Mer London ▲ 421171-2 [ADD] ■ 421171-4
Debussy, C.:La Mer *(rec 1964)* London ▲ 433711-2 [ADD]
Debussy, C.:La Mer *(rec 1964)* London ▲ 433711-2 [ADD]
Debussy, C.:La Mer, London ▲ 421171-2 [ADD] ■ 421171-4
Rimsky-Korsakov, N.:Orchestral Music—Dubinushka, Op. 62; Sadko, Op. 5; May Night Ov.; Christmas Eve Suite; Snow Maiden Suite; The Flight of the Bumble Bee [from The Tale of Tsar Sultan] London ("Double Decker" series) 2-▲ 443464-2
Rimsky-Korsakov, N.:Scheherazade London ("Double Decker" series) 2-▲ 443464-2
Stravinsky, I.:The Firebird London ("Double Decker" series) 2-▲ 443467-2
Stravinsky, I.:Les Noces London ("Double Decker" series) 2-▲ 443467-2
Stravinsky, I.:Pétrouchka London ("Double Decker" series) 2-▲ 443467-2
Stravinsky, I.:Le Sacre du printemps Orch London ("Double Decker" series) 2-▲ 443467-2

E. Appia (cnd)
Wissmer, P.:Con 2 Vn, w. G. Devries (vn) *(rec 1959)* Quantum ▲ QM 6918

T. Beecham (cnd)
Mozart, W.A.:Sym 31 Cascavelle ▲ CVL 2002 [ADD]
Mozart, W.A.:Sym 35 Cascavelle ▲ CVL 2002 [ADD]
Mozart, W.A.:Sym 39 Cascavelle ▲ CVL 2002 [ADD]

R. Bonynge (cnd)
Delibes, L.:Coppélia, ou La fille aux yeux d'émail London ("Jubilee" series) 2-▲ 425472-2 [ADD/DDD]
Massenet, J.:Don Quichotte, w. R. Crespin (sop), M. Command (sop), G. Bacquier (bar), N. Ghiaurov (bass), Swiss Romande Chorus [F] London ("Grand Opera" series) 2-▲ 430636-2 [AAD]
Offenbach, J.:Les Contes d'Hoffmann, w. J. Sutherland (sop), H. Tourangeau (mez), P. Domingo (ten), H. Cuénod (ten), G. Bacquier (bar) London 2-▲ 417363-2 [ADD]
Offenbach, J.:Les Contes d'Hoffmann (sels)—Belle Nuit O Nuit D'Amour London ▲ 452485-2 ■ 452 485-4
Operetta Gala, w. Joan Sutherland (sop), New Philharmonia Orch, Ambrosian Light Opera Chorus London ("Opera Gala" series) ▲ 421880-2 LA [ADD]
Romantic French Arias, w.Joan Sutherland (sop), Geneva Grand Theater Chorus London ("Opera Gala" series) ▲ 421879-2 LA [ADD]

A. Erede (cnd)
The Early Recordings (1949-1952), w. Renata Tebaldi (sop), t. Cecilia Academy Orch London ("Historic" series) ▲ 425989-2 LM [ADD]

A. Jordan (cnd)
Debussy, C.:La Mer Erato ▲ 2292-45605-2 [DDD]
Debussy, C.:Nocturnes Erato ▲ 2292-45605-2 [DDD]
Debussy, C.:Prélude à l'après-midi d'un faune Erato ▲ 2292-45605-2 [DDD]
Martin, F.:Con for 7 Winds Erato ▲ 2292-45694-2 [DDD]
Martin, F.:Monologe (6) aus "Jedermann", w. G. Cachemaille (bar) Erato ▲ 2292-45694-2 [DDD]
Martin, F.:Petite sym concertante Erato ▲ 2292-45694-2 [DDD]
Rimsky-Korsakov, N.:Russian Easter Festival FNAC Music ▲ 592352
Rimsky-Korsakov, N.:Scheherazade FNAC Music ▲ 592352
Schumann, R.:Con Pno, w. M. Argerich (pno) *(rec live 1993)* Artists ▲ FED 69 [ADD]

N. Järvi (cnd)
Liszt, F.:Cons Pno, w. Geoffrey Tozer (pno) Chandos ▲ CHAN 9360 [DDD]
Liszt, F.:Symphonic Poems, w. Geoffrey Tozer (pno)—Nos. 3 & 6 Chandos ▲ CHAN 9360 [DDD]
Stravinsky, I.:Apollon musagète Chandos ▲ CHAN 9237 [DDD]
Stravinsky, I.:Canticum sacrum, w. Irene Friedli (alt), Frieder Lang (ten), Lausanne Pro Arte Choir Chandos ▲ CHAN 9408 [DDD]
Stravinsky, I.:Capriccio, w. G. Tozer (pno) Chandos ▲ CHAN 9238 [DDD]
Stravinsky, I.:Le Chant du rossignol Chandos ▲ CHAN 9238 [DDD]
Stravinsky, I.:Chorale Variations on the German Christmas Carol "Vom Himmel hoch da komm' ich her", w. Irene Friedli (alt), Frieder Lang (ten), Lausanne Pro Arte Choir Chandos ▲ CHAN 9408 [DDD]
Stravinsky, I.:Circus Polka Chandos ▲ CHAN 9237 [DDD]
Stravinsky, I.:Con Pno Ww, w. B. Berman (pno) Chandos ▲ CHAN 9239 [DDD]
Stravinsky, I.:Con Vn, w. L. Mordkovitch (vn) Chandos ▲ CHAN 9236 [DDD]
Stravinsky, I.:Music of, w. Romande Chamber Choir, Pro Arte Lausanne—Oedipus Rex; Sym. in Eb, Op. 1; Con. for Violin [w. L. Mordkovitch]; Petruchka (1911 version); Apollon Musagète; Circus Polka; Le chant du Rossignol; Sym. in 3 Movements; Capriccio for Piano & Orch. [w. G. Tozer]; Sym. in C; Sym. of Psalms; Con. for Piano & Winds [w. B. Berman] Chandos 5-▲ CHAN 9240 [DDD]
Stravinsky, I.:Pétrouchka [1911 version] Chandos ▲ CHAN 9237 [DDD]
Stravinsky, I.:Requiem Canticles, w. Irène Friedli (alt), Michel Brodard (bass), Lausanne Pro Arte Choir, Romande Chamber Choir Chandos ▲ CHAN 9408 [DDD]
Stravinsky, I.:Le Sacre du printemps Orch Chandos ▲ CHAN 9408 [DDD]

▲ = CD ♦ = Enhanced CD Δ = MD ■ = Cassette Tape □ = DCC

Swiss Romande Orch (cont.)
N. Järvi (cnd) (cont.)
Stravinsky, I.:Sym in C — Chandos ▲ CHAN 9239 [DDD]
Stravinsky, I.:Sym in 3 Movts — Chandos ▲ CHAN 9238 [DDD]
Stravinsky, I.:Sym of Psalms, w. Lausanne Pro Arte Choir, Romande Chamber Choir — Chandos ▲ CHAN 9239 [DDD]
P. Kletzki (cnd)
Hindemith, P.:Mathis der Maler (sym) — London ("Enterprise" series) ▲ 433081-2
H. Knappertsbusch (cnd)
Brahms, J.:Sym 2 *(rec 1947)* — Preiser ▲ PRE 90189 [AAD]
Wagner, R.:Die Meistersinger von Nürnberg (sels) *(rec 1947)* — Preiser ▲ PRE 90189 [AAD]
A. Lazarev (cnd)
The Ultimate Ballet Collection, w. Bolshoi SO — Erato ▲ 96969-2
J. Levine (cnd)
The Complete Solo Recordings, w. Jacques Thibaud (vn) Itit□(rec 1929–36) — APR 2-▲ APR 7028 [ADD]
H. Lewis (cnd)
Rossini, G.:Arias, w. M. Horne (mez). Royal PO, Ambrosian Opera Chorus [I] — London ▲ 421306-2 [ADD]
W. Sawallisch (cnd)
Vuataz, R.:Con Pno, w. S. Husson (pno) *(rec Feb. 13, 1974)* — Grammont ▲ CTSP 7-2 [ADD]
T. Schippers (cnd)
Bizet, G.:Carmen, w. Joan Sutherland (sop), Regina Resnik (mez), Mario del Monaco (ten) — London ("Double Decca" series) 2-▲ 443871-2
Bizet, G.:Carmen, w. R. Resnik (mez), J. Sutherland (sop), M. Del Monaco (ten), T. Krause (bar) — London 2-▲ 411630-2 [ADD]
C. Schuricht (cnd)
Beethoven, L. van:Sym 2 *(rec 1939–46)* — LYS ▲ LYS 129
Beethoven, L. van:Sym 6, "Pastorale" *(rec 1939–46)* — LYS ▲ LYS 129
Brahms, J.:Sym 1 *(rec Dec. 28, 1953)* — Archipon 2-▲ ARCH 2.1CD (m) [ADD]
L. Stokowski (cnd)
Mussorgsky, M.:Boris Godunov (sels) [symphonic synthesis by Stokowski] *(rec Opera House, Geneva, Switzerland, Sept 1968)* — London ("Phase 4 Stereo" series) ▲ 443896-2 [ADD]
H. Wallberg (cnd)
Mozart, W.A.:Nozze di Figaro (sels), w. R. Pütz (sop), T. Stich-Randall (mez), T. Berganza (mez), A.-R. Johnson (ten), G. Bacquier (bar), F. Corena (bass), Swiss Romande Chorus—Act IV — Melodram 2-▲ CDM 27094 [ADD]
P. Wissmer (cnd)
Wissmer, P.:Con 2 Pno, w. C. Perretti (pno) *(rec 1969)* — Quantum ▲ QM 6918
Swiss Romande Orch members
E. Ansermet (cnd)
Stravinsky, I.:L'Histoire du soldat, w. J. V. Gilles (nar), F. Simon (the Soldier), W. Jacques (the Devil) [F] *(rec 4/17/52)* — Claves ▲ CD 8918 (m) [ADD]
Stravinsky, I.:L'Histoire du soldat (sels), w. C.-F. Ramuz (nar) [F] *(rec 2/25/40)* — Claves ▲ CD 8918 (m) [ADD]
Stravinsky, I.:Japanese Lyrics, w. Y. Furusawa (sop) *(rec 11/3/50)* — Claves ▲ CD 8918 (m) [ADD]
Stravinsky, I.:Song of Volga Boatman (arr winds) *(rec 10/15/52)* — Claves ▲ CD 8918 (m) [ADD]
Swiss Romande RSO
R. Vuataz (cnd)
Vuataz, R.:Epopée antique *(rec June 1952)* — Grammont ▲ CTSP 7-2 [ADD]
Swiss Youth SO
A. Delfs (cnd)
Schoeck, O.:Concerto quasi una fantasia, w. B. Boller (vn) — Claves ▲ CD 9201 [DDD]
Schoeck, O.:Penthesilea (suite) — Claves ▲ CD 9201 [DDD]
Swiss-Italian Orch
M. Balderi (cnd)
Respighi, O.:Christus, w. C. Gaifa (ten), R. Hermann (bar), G. Sarti (bar), Swiss-Italian Chorus [L] — Claves ▲ CD 9203 [DDD]
M. de Bernart (cnd)
Rossini, G.:Torvaldo e Dorliska, w. A. Buda (sop), F. Pediconi (sop), M. Ciliento (mez), E. Palacio (ten), S. Antonucci (bar), A. Marani (b-bar), Cantemus, Swiss-Italian Radio-TV Chorus *(rec Jan. 11, 1992)* — Arkadia-Akademia 2-▲ 123 [DDD]
A. Jordan (cnd)
Regamey, C.:Alpha, w. E. Tappy (ten) [F] — Grammont ▲ CTSP 5-2 [ADD]
F. Martin (cnd)
Martin, F.:Maria-Triptychon, w. I. Seefried (sop), W. Schneiderhan (vn) [L] *(rec Sept. 3, 1970)* — Jecklin-Disco ▲ JD 645-2 [ADD]
Martin, F.:Petite sym concertante, w. E. Hunziker (hp), G. Vaucher-Clerc (hpd), D. Rosslaud (pno) *(rec Sept. 3, 1970)* — Jecklin-Disco ▲ JD 645-2 [ADD]
Martin, F.:Requiem, w. E. Speiser (sop), R. Bollen (cta), E. Tappy (ten), P. Lagger (bass), A. Luy (org), Union Chorale, Choir of Our Lady of Lausanne, Ars Laeta Vocal Group *(rec live, May 4, 1973)* — Jecklin-Disco ▲ JD 631-2 [ADD]
M. Rota (cnd)
Bellini, V.:I Capuleti e i Montecchi (sels), w. M. Devia (sop)—Oh quante volte *(rec June 4, 1992)* — Bongiovanni ▲ GB 2513 [DDD]
Bellini, V.:I Puritani (sels), w. M. Devia (sop)—Qui la voce...Vien diletto *(rec June 4, 1992)* — Bongiovanni ▲ GB 2513 [DDD]
Bellini, V.:La sonnambula (sels), w. M. Devia (sop)—Come per me sereno...Sovra il sen *(rec June 4, 1992)* — Bongiovanni ▲ GB 2513 [DDD]
Charpentier, G.:Louise (sels), w. M. Devia (sop) *(rec June 4, 1992)* — Bongiovanni ▲ GB 2513 [DDD]
Delibes, L.:Lakmé (sels), w. M. Devia (sop)—Aria delle campanelle *(rec June 4, 1992)* — Bongiovanni ▲ GB 2513 [DDD]
Donizetti, G.:Lucia di Lammermoor (sels), w. M. Devia (sop)—Ardon gli incensi *(rec June 4, 1992)* — Bongiovanni ▲ GB 2513 [DDD]
Gounod, C.:Roméo et Juliette (sels), w. M. Devia (sop)—Je veux vivre *(rec June 4, 1992)* — Bongiovanni ▲ GB 2513 [DDD]
N. Santi (cnd)
Leoncavallo, R.:Nuit de mai, w. Salvatore Fisichella (ten) — Accord ▲ ACD 201582 [DDD]
H. Stein (cnd)
Moret, N.:Tragiques *(rec Oct. 5, 1983)* — Grammont ▲ CTSP 23-2 [ADD]
Swiss-Italian RSO
M. Andreae (cnd)
Glass, Paul:Lamento dell'acqua *(rec Oct 5, 1990)* — Grammont ▲ CTSP 43 [AAD]
P. Argento (cnd)
Tchaikovsky, P.:Con 1 Pno, w. V. Cliburn (pno) *(rec 1962; 1968)* — Ermitage ▲ ERM 139
Tchaikovsky, P.:Romeo & Juliet, w. V. Cliburn (pno) *(rec 1962; 1968)* — Ermitage ▲ ERM 139
A. Cluytens (cnd)
Beethoven, L. van:Con 4 Pno, w. Friedrich Gulda (pno) *(rec Switzerland, 1965)* — Ermitage ▲ ERM 155
Franck, C.:Sym in d *(rec Switzerland, 1965)* — Ermitage ▲ ERM 155
T. Gotti (cnd)
Righini, V.:Alcide al Bivio, w. L. Serra (sop), S. Browne (cta), W. McKinney (ten), R. El Hage (bass), M. Barta (ob), P. Molinari (hpd), Swiss-Italian Radio Chorus *(rec 1979)* — Bongiovanni 2-▲ GB 2157/58 [ADD]
R. Kelterborn (cnd)
Lehmann, H.U.:Kammermusik II *(rec June 30, 1988)* — Grammont ▲ CTS P 4-2
H. Scherchen (cnd)
Beethoven, L. van:Sym 9, "Choral Sym", w. Magda Laszlo (sop), Lucienne Devallier (cta), Petre Monteanu (ten), Raffaele Arié (bass), Swiss-Italian Radio-TV Chorus — Accord ▲ ACD 201002 [AAD]
Mozart, W.A.:Con 15 Pno, w. A. Benedetti Michelangeli (pno) — Andromeda ▲ ANR 2503 [ADD]
Schumann, R.:Con Pno, w. A. Benedetti Michelangeli (pno) — Andromeda ▲ ANR 2503 [ADD]

Swiss-Italian RSO (cont.)
C. Schuricht (cnd)
Beethoven, L. van:Con 5 Pno, "Emperor", w. W. Backhaus (pno) *(rec Apr. 27, 1961)* — Ermitage ▲ ERM 144 [ADD]
Mendelssohn, F.:Die Hebriden *(rec Apr. 27, 1961)* — Ermitage ▲ ERM 144 [ADD]
Mozart, W.A.:Sym 40 *(rec Apr. 27, 1961)* — Ermitage ▲ ERM 144 [ADD]
I. Stravinsky (cnd)
Stravinsky, I.:Con CO *(rec 1954–55)* — Ermitage ▲ ERM 156
Stravinsky, I.:Con Str *(rec 1954–55)* — Ermitage ▲ ERM 156
Stravinsky, I.:Danses concertantes *(rec 1954–55)* — Ermitage ▲ ERM 156
Stravinsky, I.:Octet *(rec 1954–55)* — Ermitage ▲ ERM 156
Stravinsky, I.:Suites Orch *(rec 1954–55)* — Ermitage ▲ ERM 156
Swiss-Italian Radio-TV Orch
M. Andreae (cnd)
Donizetti, G.:Imelda de' Lambertazzi, w. D. D'Auria (sop), F. Sovilla (sop), F. Tenzi (ten), A. Martin (bar), G. Sarti (bar), Swiss-Italian Radio-TV Chorus [I] *(rec live)* — Nuova Era 2-▲ 6778/79 [DDD]
Pugnani, G.:Werther, w. M. Cei (sgr), A. Andreani (sgr), A. Flint (sgr), T. Yamashita (sgr) *(rec Dec. 14, 1989)* — Bongiovanni 2-▲ GB 5028/29 [DDD]
P. Antonini (cnd)
Vogel, W.:Pieces Perc—Verso-Inverso — Grammont ▲ CTSP 14-2 [ADD]
J. Balissat (cnd)
Balissat, J.:Bioméros — Grammont ▲ CTSP 17-2 [ADD]
Balissat, J.:Rückblick, w. B. Boller (vn) — Grammont ▲ CTSP 17-2 [ADD]
Perrin, J.:Sym 3 *(rec Sept 4–5, 1985)* — Grammont ▲ CTSP 45 [AAD]
J. Daetwyler (cnd)
Daetwyler, J.:Symphonie de la liberté, w. Barbara Martig Tüller (sop)—[F] — Grammont ▲ CTSP 15-2
E. Loehrer (cnd)
Mozart, W.A.:Litaniae de venerabili, w. Swiss-Italian Radio-TV Chorus — Accord ▲ ACD 201012 [AAD]
Mozart, W.A.:Litaniae Lauretanae, K.195, w. Swiss-Italian Radio-TV Chorus — Accord ▲ ACD 201012 [AAD]
Rossini, G.:Stabat Mater, w. Beatrice Haldas (sop), Lucia V. Terrani (mez), Antonio Savastano (ten), Raffaele Arié (bass), Swiss-Italian Radio-TV Chorus — Accord ▲ ACD 201752 [AAD]
H. Scherchen (cnd)
Bach, J.S.:The Art of the Fugue — Accord 2-▲ ACD 200412
Beethoven, L. van:Sym 6, "Pastorale" — Accord ▲ ACD 201762
M. Venzago (cnd)
Burkhard, W.:Con Va, w. C. Schiller (va) *(rec 1985 & 1989)* — Jecklin-Disco ▲ JD 647-2 [ADD]
Sydney Conservatorium for Music Orch
J. Hopkins (cnd)
Berlioz, H.:Requiem, "Grande Messe des Morts", w. D. Hamilton (ten), Sydney Conservatorium Choir, Willoughby Sym Chorus — Walsingham Classics ▲ WAL 8000 [DDD]
Sydney SO
The Pachelbel Canon & Other Favorites, w. Galway, James (fl) — RCA Victor ▲ 4063-2-RG [ADD] ■ AFK1-4063
W.A. Albert (cnd)
Hindemith, P.:Mathis der Maler (sym) *(rec Apr. & Aug. 1992)* — CPO ▲ CPO 999008 [DDD]
Hindemith, P.:Symphonia serena *(rec Apr. & Aug. 1992)* — CPO ▲ CPO 999008 [DDD]
Hindemith, P.:When Lilacs Last In The Dooryard Bloom'd—Prelude *(rec Apr. & Aug. 1992)* — CPO ▲ CPO 999008 [DDD]
S. Challender (cnd)
Banks, D.:Music of, w. D. Burrows, Judy Bailey Quintet—Nexus — Vox Australis ▲ VAST006-2 [DDD]
Humble, K.:Arcade V — Vox Australis ▲ VAST 006-2 [DDD]
C.L. Gee (cnd)
Ippolitov-Ivanov, M.:Caucasian Sketches, Opp. 10 & 42—Op. 10 & Op. 42 — Marco Polo ▲ 8.220369 [DDD]
H. Iwaki (cnd)
Kats-Chernin, E.:Music of—Stairs — Vox Australis ▲ VAST 006-2 [DDD]
R. Pikler (cnd)
Bach, J.S.:Music of—Toccata & Fugue in d, BWV 565; Passacaglia & Fugue in c, BWV 582; Adagio from the Toccata, Adagio & Fugue, BWV 564; Christ lag in Todesbanden (Chorale from the Cantata No. 4); Chorale Prelude, "Wir glauben all'an einen Gott," BWV 680; Fugue in g, BWV 578; Komm, süsser Tod, BWV 478 — Chandos ("Collect" series) ▲ CHAN 6532 [ADD]
Bach, J.S.:Passacaglia & Fugue Org — Chandos ("Collect" series) ▲ CHAN 6532 [ADD]
Bach, J.S.:Toccata & Fugue Org, BWV 565 — Chandos ("Collect" series) ▲ CHAN 6532 [ADD]
Berlioz, H.:L'Enfance du Christ (sels)—Prelude to Part 2, The Flight into Egypt — Chandos ("Collect" series) ▲ CHAN 6587 [ADD]
Berlioz, H.:Marche funèbre, w. Sydney Sym Chorus — Chandos ("Collect" series) ▲ CHAN 6587 [ADD]
Berlioz, H.:Ovs—Béatrice et Bénédict — Chandos ("Collect" series) ▲ CHAN 6587 [ADD]
Berlioz, H.:Roméo et Juliette (sels)—Scène d'amour — Chandos ("Collect" series) ▲ CHAN 6587 [ADD]
Berlioz, H.:Les Troyens (sels)—Royal Hunt & Storm — Chandos ("Collect" series) ▲ CHAN 6587 [ADD]
D. Porcelijn (cnd)
Mazurek, R.:Nocturnes — Vox Australis ▲ VAST 006-2 [DDD]
J. Serebrier (cnd)
Beethoven, L. van:Sym 3, "Eroica" — IMG/Pickwick ▲ PIC IMG 1615
Beethoven, L. van:Sym 8 — IMG/Pickwick ▲ PIC IMG 1615
Tchaikovsky, P.:Romeo & Juliet — ASV Quicksilva ▲ CD QS 6040 [DDD]
P. Thomas (cnd)
Smalley, R.:Sym — Vox Australis ▲ VAST 003-2
Sylvan Winds
Bernard, E.:Divert Winds — Koch International Classics ▲ KIC 7081-2 [DDD]
Indy, V. d':Chanson et Danses — Koch International Classics ▲ KIC 7081-2 [DDD]
Jongen, J.:Con Wind Qnt — Koch International Classics ▲ KIC 7081-2 [DDD]
Schmitt, F.:Lied et Scherzo — Koch International Classics ▲ KIC 7081-2 [DDD]
Symphonia Perusina
M. Ancillotti (cnd)
Boccherini, L.:Con in D Fl [attrib.], w. M. Ancillotti (fl) *(rec 1/91)* — Nuova Era ▲ 7026 [DDD]
Cambini, G.M.:Con Fl, w. M. Ancillotti (fl) *(rec 1/91)* — Nuova Era ▲ 7026 [DDD]
Martini, G.B.:Con Fl, w. M. Ancillotti (fl) *(rec 1/91)* — Nuova Era ▲ 7026 [DDD]
Piccinni, N.:Con Fl, w. M. Ancillotti (fl) — Nuova Era ▲ 7026 [DDD]
F. Ayo (cnd)
Tartini, G.:Cons Vn (misc), w. Felix Ayo (vn)—in D, D.15; in e, D.56; in b, D.125 *(rec St. Antonio Abate Church, Deruta, July 28–31, 1994)* — Dynamic ▲ CD 131 [DDD]
C. Casadei (cnd)
Bellafronte, R.:Orch Music—Forest; Aliàntes for Ob & Orch [w. Luciano Franca (ob)]; Sur le blanc for Fl & Orch [w. Massimo Mercelli (fl)] *(rec Chiesa S. Antonio Abate, Deruta, Feb 1995)* — Bongiovanni ▲ GB 5049-2 [DDD]
Symphonic Rock Orch
S. Gale (cnd)
Classical Highlights — PMG ("Vienna Masters" series) ▲ CD 160102 [DDD]
Symphonica of London
W. Morris (cnd)
Beethoven, L. van:Grosse Fuge Str Qt — IMP Classics 2-▲ IMP DPCD 1025
Bruckner, A.:Helgoland, w. Ambrosian Male Voice Chorus — IMP Classics ▲ IMP 1042 [DDD]
Chausson, E.:Poème de l'amour et de la mer, w. M. Caballé (sop) [F] — IMP Classics ▲ IMP PCD 1037 [DDD]
Mahler, G.:Sym 5 — IMP Classics ▲ IMP PCD 1033 [DDD]
Mahler, G.:Sym 8, w. Ambrosian Singers, New Philharmonia Chorus — IMP Classics 2-▲ IMP DPCD 1019 [DDD]
Mahler, G.:Sym 9 — IMP Classics 2-▲ IMP DPCD 1025

ORCH. & ENS.

Symphonica of London (cont.)
W. Morris (cnd) (cont.)
Wagner, R.:Das Liebesmahl der Apostel, w. Ambrosian Male Voice Chorus [G] IMP Classics ▲ IMP 1042 [DDD]

Symphony of the Air
A. Copland (cnd)
Copland, A.:Con Pno, w. Earl Wild (pno) *(rec 1961)* Vanguard Classics ▲ SVC 3 [AAD]
V. Golschmann (cnd)
Barber, S.:Essay 2 *(rec ca. 1960)* Vanguard Classics ▲ OVC 4016 [ADD]
Barber, S.:A Hand of Bridge, w. P. Neway (sop), E. Alberts (mez), W. Lewis (ten), P. Maero (bass) [E] *(rec ca. 1960)* Vanguard Classics ▲ OVC 4016 [ADD]
Barber, S.:Music for a Scene from Shelley *(rec ca. 1960)* Vanguard Classics ▲ OVC 4016 [ADD]
Barber, S.:Serenade *(rec ca. 1960)* Vanguard Classics ▲ OVC 4016 [ADD]
Barber, S.:A Stopwatch & an Ordnance Map, w. Robert DeCormier Chorale [E] *(rec ca. 1960)* Vanguard Classics ▲ OVC 4016 [ADD]
K. Kondrashin (cnd)
Rachmaninoff, S.:Con 3 Pno, w. Van Cliburn (pno) RCA Red Seal ▲ 6209-2-RC [ADD]
J. Krips (cnd)
Beethoven, L. van:Cons Pno (comp), w. A. Rubinstein (pno) RCA Gold Seal 3-▲ 09026-61260-2
J. Mester (cnd)
Menotti, G.C.:Con Pno, w. Earl Wild (pno) *(rec 1961)* Vanguard Classics ▲ SVC 3 [AAD]
L. Stokowski (cnd)
Bloch, E.:America, w. American Concert Choir *(rec 4/60)* Vanguard Classics ▲ OVC 8014 [ADD]
Enescu, G.:Romanian Rhap 1, RCA Victor SO RCA Living Stereo ▲ 09026-61503-2
Leopold Stokowski:The United Artists Recordings, 1958-59 EMI Classics ▲ ZDMB 65427
Liszt, F.:Hungarian Rhaps (orchestral versions), RCA Victor SO RCA Living Stereo ▲ 09026-61503-2
Schoenberg, A.:Verklärte Nacht *(rec Nov. 1960)* Library of Congress ▲ LOC 2 [ADD]
Smetana, B.:The Bartered Bride (ov), RCA Victor SO RCA Living Stereo ▲ 09026-61503-2
Smetana, B.:The Moldau, RCA Victor SO RCA Living Stereo ▲ 09026-61503-2
Stravinsky, I.:L'Histoire du soldat Suite Ensemble Vanguard Classics ▲ OVC 8013 [ADD]
Thomson, V.:The River (suite) Vanguard Classics ▲ SVC 1 [AAD]
Thomson, V.:The River (suite) Vanguard Classics ▲ OVC 8013 [ADD]
Vaughan Williams, R.:Fant on a Theme by Thomas Tallis *(rec Nov. 17, 1960)* Library of Congress ▲ LOC 2 [ADD]
Wagner, R.:Siegfried Idyll *(rec Nov. 1960)* Library of Congress ▲ LOC 2 [ADD]
Wagner, R.:Tannhäuser (orch sels), RCA Victor SO RCA Living Stereo ▲ 09026-61503-2
A. Wallenstein (cnd)
Chopin, F.:Con 2 Pno, w. A. Rubinstein (pno) RCA Red Seal ▲ 5612-2-RC [ADD]
Franck, C.:Symphonic Vars, w. A. Rubinstein (pno) *(rec 1956 & 1958)* RCA Gold Seal ▲ 09026-61496-2; ■ 09026-61496-4
Saint-Saëns, C.:Con 2 Pno, w. A. Rubinstein (pno) *(rec 1956 & 1958)* RCA Gold Seal ▲ 09026-61496-2 ■ 09026-61496-4
B. Walter (cnd)
Beethoven, L. van:Sym 4 *(rec Feb. 3, 1957)* Music & Arts ▲ CD 1010 [ADD]

SO of America
M. H. Phillips (cnd)
Chadwick, G.W.:Melpomene Albany ▲ TROY 103 [DDD]
Humiston, W.H.:A Southern Fant Albany ▲ TROY 103 [DDD]
Johnson, F.:Concert Band Marches & Dance Music—The Philadelphia Gray's Quickstep; The Princeton Grand March; Johnson's March Albany ▲ TROY 103 [DDD]
Kelley, E.S.:Aladdin Albany ▲ TROY 103 [DDD]
Shelley, H.R.:Santa Claus Ov Albany ▲ TROY 103 [DDD]

Synergy Percussion Quartet
Askill, M.:Lemurian Dances Vox Australis ▲ VAST 001
Cage, J.:Third Construction Vox Australis ▲ VAST 001
Edwards, R.:Prelude & Dragonfly Dance *(rec Studio 200 ABC Ultimo Centre, Apr 1994)* Tall Poppies ▲ TP 51 [DDD]
Kos, B.:Quasar Vox Australis ▲ VAST 001
Wesley-Smith, M.:For Mar & Tape Vox Australis ▲ VAST 001
Westlake, N.:Fabian Theory Vox Australis ▲ VAST 001
Westlake, N.:Moving Air Vox Australis ▲ VAST 001

Syracuse SO
C. Keene (cnd)
Heinrich, A.P.:The Ornithological Combat of Kings New World ▲ 80208-2

Syrinx Quintet
Françaix, J.:Qnt Fl MD + G ▲ L 3291 [DDD]
Hindemith, P.:Kleine Kammermusik MD + G ▲ L 3291 [DDD]
Ibert, J.:Pièces brèves MD + G ▲ L 3291 [DDD]
Taffanel, P.:Qnt Ww MD + G ▲ L 3291 [DDD]

Szeged PO
E. Acél (cnd)
Kabalevsky, D.:Sym 1 Olympia ▲ OLY 268 [DDD]
Kabalevsky, D.:Sym 2 Olympia ▲ OLY 268 [DDD]

Szeged SO
T. Pál (cnd)
Liszt, F.:Hungarian Rhaps—Nos. 2, 9 & 12 Hungaroton ▲ HCD 12721

Karol Szymanowski State PO
J. Kaspszyk (cnd)
Górecki, H.-M.:Sym 3, "Sym of Sorrowful Songs", w. Zofia Kilanowicz (sop) *(rec live, Breslau, Poland, Sept. 5, 1993)* EMI Classics ▲ CDC 55368 [DDD]
K. Penderecki (cnd)
Orff, C.:Carmina burana, w. Venceslava Hruba-Freiberger (sop), Rolf Havenstein (sgr), Piotr Kusiewicz (sgr), Karol Szymanowski State Phil Choir *(rec Cracow, Poland, Jan 27-28, 1989)* Arts Music ▲ 47177-2 [DDD]

Tafelmusik
Bach, J.S.:Brandenburg Cons, w. Jeanne Lamon (vn) Sony Classical ("Vivarte" series) 2-▲ S2K 66289
Bach, J.S.:Cons Vn (comp), w. Jeanne Lamon (vn) Sony Classical ("Vivarte" series) ▲ SK 66265
Bach, J.S.:Con for 2 Vns, w. Jeanne Lamon (vn) Sony Classical ("Vivarte" series) ▲ SK 66265
Boccherini, L.:Con Vc, G.476, w. A. Bylsma (vc) *(rec Sept. 15-17, 1992)* Sony Classical ▲ SK 53121 [DDD]
Boccherini, L.:Con Vc, G.573, w. A. Bylsma (vc) *(rec Sept. 15-17, 1992)* Sony Classical ▲ SK 53121 [DDD]
Boccherini, L.:Octet, w. A. Bylsma (vc) *(rec Sept. 15-17, 1992)* Sony Classical ▲ SK 53121 [DDD]
Boccherini, L.:Syms—D.519 & 521 *(rec Sept. 15-17, 1992)* Sony Classical ▲ SK 53121 [DDD]
It's Good to Be the King:Musical Delights for Kings, Queens, Princes & Royalty, w. Claudio Abbado (cnd), Eugene Ormandy (cnd), Esa-Pekka Salonen (cnd), Michael Tilson Thomas (cnd), Canadian Brass, Chicago SO, Philadelphia Orch, Royal PO, Tafelmusik Sony Classical ▲ SFK 57483 ■ SFT 57483
Music for Trumpet and Orchestra, w. Steele-Perkins, Crispian (tpt), Tafelmusik [cnd:J. Lanon] *(rec Mar. 30-Apr. 1, 1993)* Sony Classical ("Vivarte" series) ▲ SK 53365 [DDD]
Pachelbel, J.:Canon Reference ▲ RR 13CD
A. Curtis (cnd)
Handel, G.F.:Floridante (sels), w. Nancy Argenta (sop—Rossane), Ingrid Attrot (sop—Timante), Linda Maguire (mez—Elmira), Catherine Robbin (mez—Floridante), Mel Braun (bar—Coralbo/Orontes) [I] CBC ("SM 5000" series) ▲ SMCD 5110 [DDD]
J. Lamon (cnd)
Avison, C.:Concerti grossi (12)—Nos. 2,4,6 & 12 CBC ("SM 5000" series) ▲ SMCD 5061 [DDD]
Boccherini, L.:Con Vc, G.480, w. A. Bylsma (vc) Deutsche Harmonia Mundi ▲ 7867-2-RC [DDD]
Boccherini, L.:Con Vc, G.483, w. A. Bylsma (vc) Deutsche Harmonia Mundi ▲ 7867-2-RC [DDD]
Boccherini, L.:Syms—in B♭, G.497 & in d, G.506 Deutsche Harmonia Mundi ▲ 7867-2-RC [DDD]

Tafelmusik (cont.)
J. Lamon (cnd) (cont.)
Corelli, A.:Concerti grossi, Op. 6—Nos. 1,3,7,8,9 & 11 [period instrs] Deutsche Harmonia Mundi ▲ 7908-2-RC [DDD]
Geminiani, F.:Concerti grossi (misc)—Op. 2, Nos. 5 & 6; Op. 3, No. 3; Op. 7, Nos. 2,5 & 6 Sony Classical ("Vivarte" series) ▲ SK 48043
Gluck, C.W.:Orfeo ed Euridice, w. N. Argenta (sop), M. Chance (ct), F. Bernius (cnd), Stuttgart Chamber Choir Sony Classical ("Vivarte" series) 2-▲ SX2K 48040
Gluck, C.W.:Orfeo ed Euridice (dance of the blessed spirits), w. Claire Guimond (trns fl), Barthold Kuijken (trns fl) Sony Classical ▲ MLK 62369 [ADD/DDD]
Gluck, C.W.:Orfeo ed Euridice (dance of the blessed spirits), w. B. Kuijken (trns fl) Sony Classical ("Vivarte" series) ▲ SK 48045
Handel, G.F.:Concerti grossi, Op. 3 Sony Classical ▲ SK 52553 [DDD]
Handel, G.F.:Suite from 'Il pastor fido', HWV 8c Sony Classical ▲ SK 68257 [DDD]
Handel, G.F.:Water Music [period instrs] Sony Classical ▲ SK 68257 [DDD]
Haydn, J.:Con 1 Vc, w. Anner Bylsma (vc) Deutsche Harmonia Mundi ▲ 7757-2-RC [DDD] ■ 7757-4-RC (CrO2)
Haydn, J.:Con 2 Vc, w. Anner Bylsma (vc) Deutsche Harmonia Mundi ▲ 7757-2-RC [DDD] ■ 7757-4-RC (CrO2)
Haydn, J.:Con Fl, H.VIIf/D1, w. Barthold Kuijken (tran fl) Sony Classical ("Vivarte" series) ▲ SK 48045
Italian Concerti Grossi CBC Records ("SM 5000" series) ▲ SMCD 5099 [DDD] ■ SMC 5099 (D)
Kraft, A.:Con Vc, Op 4, w. A. Bylsma (vc) Deutsche Harmonia Mundi ▲ 7757-2-RC [DDD] ■ 7757-4-RC (CrO2)
Popular Masterworks of the Baroque Reference ▲ RR 13CD [ADD]
Purcell, H.:Abdelazer, or The Moor's Revenge—4 Dances *(rec Glenn Gould Studio, CBC Toronto, Apr 26-29, 1995)* CBC ▲ SM5 5147 [DDD]
Purcell, H.:Chacony *(rec Glenn Gould Studio, CBC Toronto, Apr 26-29, 1995)* CBC ▲ SM5 5147 [DDD]
Purcell, H.:Dido & Aeneas, w. Meredith Hall (sop—2nd Witch/Spirit), Ann Monoyios (sop—Belinda), Shari Saunders (sop—2nd Woman/1st Woman), Jennifer Lane (mez—Dido/Sorceress), Benjamin Butterfield (ten—Sailor), Russell Braun (bar—Aeneas), Tafelmusik Chamber Choir *(rec Glenn Gould Studio, CBC Toronto, Apr 26-29, 1995)* CBC ▲ SM5 5147 [DDD]
Purcell, H.:The Fairy Queen (sels)—2 Ovs.; Hornpipe; 5 Airs; Preludio; If love's a sweet passion; Jigg; Dance for Furies; Dance for the followers of Night; Sing while we trip it; Thus happy & free; Chacone *(rec Glenn Gould Studio, Toronto, Canada, Apr. 8-10, 1994)* Sony Classical ▲ SK 66169 [DDD]
Purcell, H.:The Indian Queen (sels)—Ov.; 2 Tpt. Tunes; 3 Airs; 2 Hornpipes; We the spirits of the air; Rondo *(rec Glenn Gould Studio, Toronto, Canada, Apr. 8-10, 1994)* Sony Classical ▲ SK 66169 [DDD]
Purcell, H.:King Arthur (sels)—Ov.; 4 Airs; Fairest isle; Hornpipe; How blest are shepherds; Round thy coast; Come, if you dare; 2 Tpt Tunes *(rec Glenn Gould Studio, Toronto, Canada, Apr. 8-10, 1994)* Sony Classical ▲ SK 66169 [DDD]
Purcell, H.:King Arthur (sels)—Ov; Aire Sony Classical ▲ MLK 62369 [ADD/DDD]
Purcell, H.:Ov Strs, Z.772 *(rec Glenn Gould Studio, CBC Toronto, Apr 26-29, 1995)* CBC ▲ SM5 5147 [DDD]
Purcell, H.:The Prophetess (sels)—Ov.; Preludio; Let the soldiers rejoice; Tpt Tune; Country Dance; Aire; Hornpipe; Aire; Canaries *(rec Glenn Gould Studio, Toronto, Canada, Apr. 8-10, 1994)* Sony Classical ▲ SK 66169 [DDD]
Richter, F.X.:Con in e Fl, w. B. Kuijken (trns fl) Sony Classical ("Vivarte" series) ▲ SK 48045
Schmelzer, J.H.:Ballet Suites—Ballet Fancesi for M.A. Cresti's "Nettunno e flora festeggianti" *(rec Apr. 5-7, 1993)* Sony Classical ▲ SK 53963 [DDD]
Schmelzer, J.H.:Duodena selectarum sonatarum—No. 10 *(rec Apr. 5-7, 1993)* Sony Classical ▲ SK 53963 [DDD]
Schmelzer, J.H.:Sons Instrs—Son. a 8 per chiesa e camera; Ciaccona a 3 chori; Son. ad tabulum a 4; Lamento sopra la morte Ferdinandi III; Son. a 5 per camera, "Al giorno della Correggie"; Son. terza from Sonatae unarum fidium; Son. a 5; Son. con ariae a 9, "Zu der Kayserlichen Serenade" *(rec Apr. 5-7, 1993)* Sony Classical ▲ SK 53963 [DDD]
Stamitz, C.:Con Fl, Op. 29, w. B. Kuijken (transverse fl) Sony Classical ("Vivarte" series) ▲ SK 48045
Vivaldi, A.:Cants, w. E. Kirkby (sop), Tafelmusik Chamber Choir [period instrs]—Lungi dal vago volto, RV.680 [L] Hyperion ▲ CDA 66247 [DDD]
Vivaldi, A.:Cons & Sinfs—Concerti RV.117, 134, 143 & 159 Sony Classical ("Vivarte" series) ▲ SK 48044
Vivaldi, A.:Cons Vc, w. A. Bylsma (vc)—RV.413 & 418 Sony Classical ("Vivarte" series) ▲ SK 48044
Vivaldi, A.:Cons Orch [period instrs]—RV.129 in d, "Concerto madrigalesco"; RV.151 in g, "Concerto alla Rustica"; RV.157 in g Hyperion ▲ CDA 66247 [DDD]
Vivaldi, A.:Cons Vn, Op. 8/1-4, "The Four Seasons", w. J. Lamon (vn) Sony Classical ("Vivarte" series) ▲ SK 48251 [DDD]
Vivaldi, A.:Con Vn Vc, RV.547 Sony Classical ("Vivarte" series) ▲ SK 48044
Vivaldi, A.:Con for 2 Vns Vcs Sony Classical ("Vivarte" series) ▲ SK 48044
Vivaldi, A.:Cons for 4 Vns—RV.549 Sony Classical ("Vivarte" series) ▲ SK 48044
Vivaldi, A.:Magnificat, RV.610, w. S. LeBlanc (sop), D. Forget (sop), R. Cunningham (alt), H. Ingram (ten), Tafelmusik Chamber Choir [L] Hyperion ▲ CDA 66247 [DDD]
Vivaldi, A.:Motets, w. E. Kirkby (sop), Tafelmusik Chamber Choir—"In turbata mare irato," RV.627 [L] Hyperion ▲ CDA 66247 [DDD]
Vivaldi, A.:Sinf, RV.169 Sony Classical ("Vivarte" series) ▲ SK 48251 [DDD]
B. Weil (cnd)
Beethoven, L. van:Con 1 Pno, w. Jos van Immerseel (pno) Sony Classical ("Vivarte" series) ▲ SK 68250
Beethoven, L. van:Con 2 Pno, w. Jos van Immerseel (pno) Sony Classical ("Vivarte" series) ▲ SK 68250
Gazzaniga, G.:Don Giovanni, w. L. Serra (sop), E. Szmytka (sop), E. Schmid-Lienbacher (sop), D. Johnson (sgr), F. Furlanetto (bass) Sony Classical ("Vivarte" series) ▲ SK 46693
Haydn, J.:Mass 7, "Kleine Orgelmesse", w. Geoffery Lancaster (org), Tölz Boys' Choir *(rec Germany, Sept. 5, 1993)* Sony Classical ("Vivarte" series) ▲ SK 53368 [DDD]
Haydn, J.:Mass 10, "Kriegsmesse", "Paukenmesse", w. Ann Monoyios (sop), Monica Groop (mez), Jörg Hering (ten), Harry van der Kamp (bass), Tölz Boys' Choir Sony Classical ("Vivarte" series) ▲ SK 68255
Haydn, J.:Salve regina, H.XXIIIb/1, w. Ann Monoyios (sop), Tölz Boys' Choir *(rec Bad Tolz, Germany, Sept. 5, 1993)* Sony Classical ▲ SK 53368 [DDD]
Haydn, J.:Die Schöpfung, w. Ann Monoyios (sop—Gabriel/Eva), Jörg Hering (ten—Uriel), Harry van der Kamp (bass—Raphael/Adam), Tölz Boys' Choir *(rec Bad Tolz, Germany, Aug. 31-Sept. 4, 1993)* Sony Classical ("Vivarte" series) 2-▲ SX2K 57965 [DDD]
Haydn, J.:Sym 41 Sony Classical ("Vivarte" series) ▲ SK 48370 [DDD]
Haydn, J.:Sym 42 Sony Classical ("Vivarte" series) ▲ SK 48370 [DDD]
Haydn, J.:Sym 43, "Mercury" Sony Classical ("Vivarte" series) ▲ SK 48370 [DDD]
Haydn, J.:Sym 44, "Trauer" Sony Classical ("Vivarte" series) ▲ SK 48371 [DDD]
Haydn, J.:Sym 45, "Farewell" *(rec Apr. 27-May 3, 1993)* Sony Classical ("Vivarte" series) ▲ SK 53986 [DDD]
Haydn, J.:Sym 46 *(rec Apr. 27-May 3, 1993)* Sony Classical ("Vivarte" series) ▲ SK 53986 [DDD]
Haydn, J.:Sym 47 *(rec Apr. 27-May 3, 1993)* Sony Classical ▲ SK 53986 [DDD]
Haydn, J.:Sym 50 *(rec Apr. 27-May 3, 1993)* Sony Classical ("Vivarte" series) ▲ SK 53985 [DDD]
Haydn, J.:Sym 51 Sony Classical ("Vivarte" series) ▲ SK 48371 [DDD]
Haydn, J.:Sym 52 Sony Classical ("Vivarte" series) ▲ SK 48371 [DDD]
Haydn, J.:Sym 60, "Il Distratto" *(rec Apr. 27-May 3, 1993)* Sony Classical ("Vivarte" series) ▲ SK 53985 [DDD]
Haydn, J.:Sym 65 *(rec Apr. 27-May 3, 1993)* Sony Classical ("Vivarte" series) ▲ SK 53985 [DDD]
Haydn, J.:Sym 82, "The Bear" *(rec Toronto, Feb. 15-19, 1994)* Sony Classical ("Vivarte" series) ▲ SK 66295 [DDD]
Haydn, J.:Sym 83, "The Hen" *(rec Toronto, Feb. 15-19, 1994)* Sony Classical ("Vivarte" series) ▲ SK 66295 [DDD]

▲ = CD ♦ = Enhanced CD Δ = MD ■ = Cassette Tape □ = DCC

Tafelmusik (cont.)
B. Weil (cnd) (cont.)
Haydn, J.:Sym 84, "In Nomine Domini" *(rec Toronto, Feb. 15-19, 1994)* Sony Classical ("Vivarte" series) ▲ SK 66295 [DDD]
Haydn, J.:Sym 85, "La Reine de France" *(rec Toronto, Feb. 15-19, 1994)* Sony Classical ("Vivarte" series) ▲ SK 66296 [DDD]
Haydn, J.:Sym 86 *(rec Toronto, Feb. 15-19, 1994)* Sony Classical ("Vivarte" series) ▲ SK 66296 [DDD]
Haydn, J.:Sym 87 *(rec Toronto, Feb. 15-19, 1994)* Sony Classical ("Vivarte" series) ▲ SK 66296 [DDD]
Haydn, J.:Sym 88 Sony Classical ("Vivarte" series) ▲ SK 66253
Haydn, J.:Sym 89 Sony Classical ("Vivarte" series) ▲ SK 66253
Haydn, J.:Sym 90 Sony Classical ("Vivarte" series) ▲ SK 66253
Mozart, W.A.:Ch'io mi scordi di te Sony Classical ("Vivarte" series) ▲ SK 47260
Mozart, W.A.:Cons Hn, w. A. Koster (hn) *(rec Sept. 11-13, 1992 & May 2)* Sony Classical ▲ SK 53369 [DDD]
Mozart, W.A.:German Dances—K.509, 536/537, 571, 586 Sony Classical ("Vivarte" series) ▲ SK 46696
Mozart, W.A.:Kleine Nachtmusik Sony Classical ("Vivarte" series) ▲ SK 46695
Mozart, W.A.:Ovs—Clemenza di Tito, Così fan tutte, Don Giovanni, Die Entführung aus dem Serail, Idomeneo, Le nozze di Figaro, Die Zauberflöte Sony Classical ("Vivarte" series) ▲ SK 46695
Mozart, W.A.:Rondo Hn, K.371, w. A. Koster (nat hn) *(rec Sept. 11-13, 1992 & May 2)* Sony Classical ▲ SK 53369 [DDD]
Mozart, W.A.:Serenade Vn, K.185 Sony Classical ("Vivarte" series) ▲ SK 47260
Mozart, W.A.:Serenade Vn, K.203 Sony Classical ("Vivarte" series) ▲ SK 47260
Mozart, W.A.:Serenade Vn, K.204 Sony Classical ("Vivarte" series) ▲ SK 47260
Mozart, W.A.:Serenade Vn, K.250 Sony Classical ("Vivarte" series) ▲ SK 47260
Mozart, W.A.:Serenade Ww, K.320 Sony Classical ("Vivarte" series) ▲ SK 47260

Taffanel Wind Quintet
Danzi, F.:Qnt Fl Denon ▲ CO 8004 [DDD]
Françaix, J.:Qnt Fl Denon ▲ CO 8004 [DDD]
Hindemith, P.:Kleine Kammermusik Denon ▲ CO 8004 [DDD]
Reicha, A.:Qnts Ww, Op. 88/2 Denon ▲ CO 8004 [DDD]
Rossini, G.:Andante e Tema con variazioni Denon ▲ CO 8004 [DDD]
Works for Wind Ensemble Denon ▲ CO 8004 [DDD]

Taipei Municipal Chinese Classical Orch
D. T. H. Chen (cnd)
Shui Man Pan:The Countryside Path Sunrise ▲ 8507
Shui Man Pan:Red Chamber Dream Sunrise ▲ 8507
Shui Man Pan:Romance Capriccio Sunrise ▲ 8507

Takács String Quartet [Edward Dusinberre (vn), Károly Schranz (vn), Roger Tapping (va), Andrs Fejer (vc)]
Bartók, B.:Qt Strs (comp) Hungaroton 3-▲ HCD 12502/04 [DDD]
Borodin, A.:Qt 2 Strs *(rec Enangelische Kirche, Honrath, Germany, Nov 28–Dec 1, 1995)* London ▲ 452239-2 [DDD]
Brahms, J.:Qt 1 Strs London ▲ 425526-2 [DDD]
Brahms, J.:Qt 2 Strs London ▲ 425526-2 [DDD]
Chausson, E.:Con Vn, Pno & Str Qt, w. J. Bell (vn), J.-Y. Thibaudet (pno) London ▲ 425860-2 [DDD]
Dvořák, A.:Bagatelles, Op. 47 London ▲ 430077-2 [DDD]
Dvořák, A.:Qt 12 Strs, "America" London ▲ 430077-2 [DDD]
Dvořák, A.:Qt 14 Strs London ▲ 430077-2 [DDD]
Haydn, J.:Qts Strs, Op. 76, "Erdödy Qts"—Nos. 4-6 London ▲ 425467-2 [DDD]
Haydn, J.:Qts Strs, Op. 76, "Erdödy Qts"—Nos. 1-3 London ▲ 421360-2 [DDD]
Haydn, J.:Qts Strs, Op. 77, "Lobkowitz Qts" London ▲ 430199-2 [DDD]
Haydn, J.:Qt Strs, Op. 103 London ▲ 430199-2 [DDD]
Mozart, W.A.:Adagio & Fugue Strs London ▲ 430772-2 [DDD]
Mozart, W.A.:Qnt Strs, K.515, w. G. Pauk (va) London ▲ 430772-2 [DDD]
Mozart, W.A.:Qnt Strs, K.593, w. D. Koromzay (va) Hungaroton ▲ HCD 12881 [DDD]
Mozart, W.A.:Qnt Strs, K.614, w. D. Koromzay (va) Hungaroton ▲ HCD 12881 [DDD]
Schubert, Franz:Qnt Pno, D.667, w. Z. Kocsis (pno) Hungaroton 2-▲ HCD 12918/19
Schumann, R.:Qts Strs, Op. 41 Hungaroton 2-▲ HCD 12918/19
Smetana, B.:Qt 1 Strs *(rec Enangelische Kirche, Honrath, Germany, Nov 28–Dec 1, 1995)* London ▲ 452239-2 [DDD]

Tal & Groethuysen Duo [Yaara Tal (pno), Andreas Groethuysen (pno)]
Brahms, J.:Hungarian Dances Pno 4-Hands *(rec Nov. 15-17, 1992)* Sony Classical ▲ SK 53285 [DDD]
Brahms, J.:Waltzes Pno, Op. 39 *(rec Nov. 15-17, 1992)* Sony Classical ▲ SK 53285 [DDD]
Dvořák, A.:From the Bohemian Forest Sony Classical ▲ SK 47199
Mendelssohn, Fanny:Pieces (3) Pno 4-Hands Sony Classical ▲ SK 48494 [DDD]
Mendelssohn, F.:Allegro brillant Sony Classical ▲ SK 48494 [DDD]
Mendelssohn, F.:Trio 2 Pno [arr. for piano 4-hands] Sony Classical ▲ SK 48494 [DDD]
Mendelssohn, F.:Vars Pno 4-Hands Sony Classical ▲ SK 48494 [DDD]
Rachmaninoff, S.:Duets Pno 4-Hands Sony Classical ▲ SK 47199
Reger, M.:Burlesques Sony Classical ▲ SK 47671
Reger, M.:Intro, Passacaglia & Fugue Pnos Sony Classical ▲ SK 47671
Reger, M.:Vars & Fugue on a Theme by Mozart Sony Classical ▲ SK 47671
Reger, M.:Waltzes-Caprices Sony Classical ▲ SK 47671
Rubinstein, A.:Characteristic Pictures Sony Classical ▲ SK 47199
Schubert, Franz:Allegro Pno 4-Hands, D.947 Sony Classical 2-▲ S2K 66256
Schubert, Franz:Divertissement sur des motifs originaux français, D.823 Sony Classical 2-▲ S2K 66256
Schubert, Franz:Grandes marches Pno Sony Classical 2-▲ S2K 66256
Schubert, Franz:Pno Music (4-hands) Sony Classical ▲ S2K 68240
Schubert, Franz:Pno Music (4-hands)—Fant in G, D.1; Fant in g, D.9; Fant in c, D.48; Ov in g, D.668; Deutscher with 2 trios & 2 Ländler, D.618; 4 Ländler, D.814; March in G, D.928; Allegro Moderato & Andante, D.968; Fugue in e, D.952 Sony Classical ▲ SK 68243
Schubert, Franz:Pno Music (4-hands) Sony Classical ▲ SK 68243
Schubert, Franz:Pno Music (4-hands)—Ov. in F, D.675; 8 Vars. on a Theme from Hérold's *Marie*; 3 marches heroiques, D.602; Fant. in f, D.940; 4 Vars. on an Orginal Theme, D.603 [Intro.]; Divertissement à l'hongroise Sony Classical 2-▲ S2K 58955 [DDD]
Schubert, Franz:Polonaises Pno, D.599 Sony Classical 2-▲ S2K 66256
Schubert, Franz:Rondo Pno, D.951 Sony Classical 2-▲ S2K 66256
Schubert, Franz:Vars on a French Song Pno 4-Hands, D.624 Sony Classical 2-▲ S2K 66256

Talan String Quartet [Vladimir Talanov (vn), Alexander Talanov (vn), Olga Bulakova (va), Alexei Steblov (vc)]
Taneyev, A.:Qt 1 Strs Olympia ▲ OLY 543 [DDD]
Taneyev, A.:Qt 2 Strs Olympia ▲ OLY 543 [DDD]
Taneyev, A.:Qt 3 Strs Olympia ▲ OLY 543 [DDD]

Tale String Quartet [T. Olsson (vn), P. Swedrup (vn), I. Kierkegaard (va), H. Nilsson (vc)]
Eliasson, A.:Disegno Trbn *(rec Jan. 31–Feb. 1, 1992)* BIS ▲ CD 603 [DDD]
Eliasson, A.:Qt Strs *(rec Jan. 31–Feb. 1, 1992)* BIS ▲ CD 603 [DDD]
Eliasson, A.:Qnt Hpd, w. L. Derwinger (pno) *(rec Sept. 26-27, 1992)* BIS ▲ CD 603 [DDD]
Penderecki, K.:Qt 1 Strs *(rec Feb. 18-20, 1994)* BIS ▲ CD 652 [DDD]
Penderecki, K.:Qt 2 Strs *(rec Feb. 18-20, 1994)* BIS ▲ CD 652 [DDD]
Penderecki, K.:Unterbrochene Gedanke *(rec Feb. 18-20, 1994)* BIS ▲ CD 652 [DDD]
Rosenberg, H.:Qt 11 Strs Caprice ▲ CAP 21380 [DDD]
Schnittke, A.:Canon in memoriam Igor Stravinsky BIS ▲ CD 547 [DDD]
Schnittke, A.:Qt 1 Strs BIS ▲ CD 467 [DDD]
Schnittke, A.:Qt 2 Strs BIS ▲ CD 467 [DDD]
Schnittke, A.:Qt 3 Strs BIS ▲ CD 467 [DDD]

Tale String Quartet (cont.)
Schnittke, A.:Qnt Pno, w. R. Pöntinen (pno) BIS ▲ CD 547 [DDD]

Tale String Quartet members
Schnittke, A.:Qt Pno, w. R. Pöntinen (pno) BIS ▲ CD 547 [DDD]
Schnittke, A.:Trio Strs BIS ▲ CD 547 [DDD]

Les Talens Lyriques
Couperin, F.:Motets, w. Sandrine Piau (sop), C. Pelon (sop), J.-P. Fouchécourt (ten), J. Corréas (bass)—Quatre versets d'un motet composé de l'ordre du Roy (1703); Verset du motet de l'année dernièr; Sept versets d'un motet composé de l'ordre du Roy (1704); Motet à Sainte Suzanne; Sept versets d'un motet composé de l'ordre du Roy (1705); Laudate Pueri Dominum, rec May 25–28, 1993 FNAC Music ▲ 592244 [DDD]

C. Rousset (cnd)
Broschi, R.:Arias, w. Ewa Mallas-Godlewska (sop), Derek Lee Ragin (ct)—Son qual nave ch'agitata; Se al labbro mio non credi; Ombra fedele anch'io Astrée ▲ E 8552 [DDD]
Broschi, R.:Arias, w. Ewa Mallas-Godlewska (sop), Derek Lee Ragin (ct)—Son qual nave ch'agitata; Se al labbro mio non credi; Ombra fedele anch'io *(rec Metz, France, July 1993)* Travelling ▲ K 1005 ▲ K 81005; ■ K 51005
Danielis, D.:Motets—Motets for 1 or 2 voices Koch Schwann ▲ SCH 310202
Handel, G.F.:Arias, w. E. Mallas-Godlewska (sop), D. L. Ragin (ct)—Handel Lascia ch'io pianga; Cara sposa *(rec Metz, France, July 1993)* Travelling ▲ K 1005 ▲ K 81005; ■ K 51005
Handel, G.F.:Riccardo Primo, w. Claire Brua (sop—Pulcheria), Sandrine Piau (sop—Costanza), Sara Mingardo (cta—Riccardo), Pascal Bertin (alt—Oronte), Roberto Scaltriti (bar—Isacio), Olivier Lallouette (bass—Berardo) L'oiseau Lyre ▲ 452 201-2
Handel, G.F.:Rinaldo (ov) *(rec Metz, France, July 1993)* Travelling ▲ K 1005 ▲ K 81005; ■ K 51005
Handel, G.F.:Scipione, w. Doris Lamprecht (sop), Sandrine Piau (sop), Vandaa Tabery (mez), Guy Flechter (ten), Oliver Lalouette (bass) [I] FNAC Music 3-▲ 592245 [DDD]
Hasse, J.A.:Arias, w. Ewa Mallas-Godlewska (sop), Derek Lee Ragin (ct)—Generoso risvegliati o core *(rec Metz, France, July 1993)* Travelling ▲ K 1005 ▲ K 81005; ■ K 51005
Hasse, J.A.:Artaserse (ov) *(rec Metz, France, July 1993)* Travelling ▲ K 1005 ▲ K 81005; ■ K 51005
Pergolesi, G.B.:Salve regina in a, w. Ewa Mallas-Godlewska (sop), Derek Lee Ragin (ct) *(rec Metz, France, July 1993)* Travelling ▲ K 1005; ▲ K 81005; ■ K 51005;
Porpora, N.A.:Arias, w. Ewa Mallas-Godlewska (sop), Derek Lee Ragin (ct) *(rec Metz, France, July 1993)* Travelling ▲ K 1005; ▲ K 81005; ■ K 51005;

Talich CO
Garnier, F.-J.:Con Ob, w. C. Villevielle (ob) Koch Schwann ▲ SCH 314752 [DDD]
Garnier, F.-J.:Sym Concertante 1, w. C. Villevielle (ob), J. Kolar (ob) Koch Schwann ▲ SCH 314752 [DDD]
Garnier, F.-J.:Sym Concertante 2, w. C. Villevielle (ob) Koch Schwann ▲ SCH 314752 [DDD]
Kreutzer, R.:Con Ob, w. C. Villevielle (ob) Koch Schwann ▲ SCH 314752 [DDD]

K. Redel (cnd)
Mozart, W.A.:Sinf concertante Vn, K.364, w. Jan Talich Sr. (vn), Jan Talich Jr. (va) Calliope ▲ CAL 9230

Talich String Quartet
Bartók, B.:Qt 2 Strs Collins Classics ▲ 11882 [DDD]
Bartók, B.:Qt 6 Strs Collins Classics ▲ 11882 [DDD]
Beethoven, L. van:Grosse Fuge Str Qt Calliope ▲ CAL 9635
Beethoven, L. van:Qts Strs (comp) Calliope 7-▲ CAL 9633/39
Beethoven, L. van:Qt 1 Strs Calliope 2-▲ CAL 9633/34
Beethoven, L. van:Qt 2 Strs Calliope 2-▲ CAL 9633/34
Beethoven, L. van:Qt 3 Strs Calliope 2-▲ CAL 9633/34
Beethoven, L. van:Qt 4 Strs Calliope 2-▲ CAL 9633/34
Beethoven, L. van:Qt 5 Strs Calliope 2-▲ CAL 9633/34
Beethoven, L. van:Qt 6 Strs Calliope 2-▲ CAL 9633/34
Beethoven, L. van:Qt 7 Strs Calliope ▲ CAL 9636
Beethoven, L. van:Qt 7 Strs Calliope ▲ CAL 9635
Beethoven, L. van:Qt 8 Strs Calliope ▲ CAL 9638
Beethoven, L. van:Qt 9 Strs Calliope ▲ CAL 9636
Beethoven, L. van:Qt 9 Strs Calliope ▲ CAL 9635
Beethoven, L. van:Qt 10 Strs, "Harp" Calliope ▲ CAL 9636
Beethoven, L. van:Qt 11 Strs, "Quartetto serioso" Calliope ▲ CAL 9635
Beethoven, L. van:Qt 12 Strs Calliope ▲ CAL 9635
Beethoven, L. van:Qt 13 Strs Calliope ▲ CAL 9637
Beethoven, L. van:Qt 14 Strs Calliope ▲ CAL 9638
Beethoven, L. van:Qt 15 Strs Calliope ▲ CAL 9639
Beethoven, L. van:Qt 16 Strs Calliope ▲ CAL 9639
Boccherini, L.:Qts Strs, G.242-247—No. 2 in E♭ Calliope ▲ CAL 9698 [ADD]
Borodin, A.:Qt 2 Strs Calliope ▲ CAL 9202
Brahms, J.:Qt 3 Strs Pyramid ▲ PYR 13489
Brahms, J.:Qnt Cl, w. P. Moragues (cl) Pyramid ▲ PYR 13489
Debussy, C.:Qt Strs Calliope ▲ CAL 9893 [ADD]
Dvořák, A.:Qt 11 Strs Calliope ▲ CAL 9617
Dvořák, A.:Qt 12 Strs, "America" Calliope ▲ CAL 9617
Dvořák, A.:Sextet, w. J. Najnar (va), V. Bernasek (vc) Calliope ▲ CAL 9217 [DDD]
Haydn, J.:Qts Strs, Op. 74—No. 3 Calliope ▲ CAL 9698 [ADD]
Janácek, L.:Qt 1 Strs Supraphon ▲ 11 1354-2 [DDD]
Janácek, L.:Qt 1 Strs Calliope ▲ CAL 9699
Janácek, L.:Qt 2 Strs Calliope ▲ CAL 9699
Janácek, L.:Qt 2 Strs Supraphon ▲ 11 1354-2 [DDD]
Mendelssohn, F.:Qt 2 Strs Calliope ▲ CAL 9698 [ADD]
Mica, J.A.F.:Qt 6 Strs Calliope ▲ CAL 9698 [ADD]
Mozart, W.A.:Adagio & Fugue Strs Calliope ▲ CAL 9245 [DDD]
Mozart, W.A.:Diverts Str Qt, K.136-138 *(rec 1993)* Calliope ▲ CAL 9248 [DDD]
Mozart, W.A.:Kleine Nachtmusik *(rec 1993)* Calliope ▲ CAL 9248 [DDD]
Mozart, W.A.:Qts Strs (misc)—Nos. 8-12 Calliope ▲ CAL 9247 [DDD]
Mozart, W.A.:Qt 1 Strs *(rec 1993)* Calliope ▲ CAL 9248 [DDD]
Mozart, W.A.:Qt 3 Strs Calliope ▲ CAL 9628
Mozart, W.A.:Qt 13 Strs *(rec 1993)* Calliope ▲ CAL 9248 [DDD]
Mozart, W.A.:Qt 20 Strs Calliope ▲ CAL 9244 [DDD]
Mozart, W.A.:Qt 21 Strs Calliope ▲ CAL 9244 [DDD]
Mozart, W.A.:Qt 22 Strs Calliope ▲ CAL 9245 [DDD]
Mozart, W.A.:Qt 23 Strs Calliope ▲ CAL 9245 [DDD]
Mozart, W.A.:Qnt Cl, K.581, w. Bohuslav Zahradnik (cl) Calliope ▲ CAL 9628
Mozart, W.A.:Qnt Cl, K.581, w. Bohuslav Zahardnik (cl), Karel Rehak (va) Calliope 3-▲ CAL 9231.3 [DDD]
Mozart, W.A.:Qnt Pno, K.452, w. K. Řehák (va) Calliope ▲ CAL 9232 [DDD]
Mozart, W.A.:Qnts Strs, w. Karel Rehak (va) Calliope 3-▲ CAL 9231.3 [DDD]
Mozart, W.A.:Qnt Strs, K.406, w. K. Řehák (va) Calliope ▲ CAL 9232 [DDD]
Mozart, W.A.:Qnt Strs, K.515 Calliope ▲ CAL 9231 [DDD]
Ravel, M.:Qt Strs Calliope ▲ CAL 9893 [ADD]
Schubert, Franz:Qt 10 Strs *(rec live, 1978)* Praga ▲ PR 250055
Shostakovich, D.:Qt 1 Strs *(rec 1976 & 1981)* Praga ▲ PR 254 042
Shostakovich, D.:Qnt Pno, w. M. Langer (pno) *(rec 1976 & 1981)* Praga ▲ PR 254 042
Smetana, B.:Qt 1 Strs Collins Classics ▲ COL 1323 [DDD]
Smetana, B.:Qt 1 Strs Calliope ▲ CAL 9690 [DDD]
Smetana, B.:Qt 2 Strs Collins Classics ▲ COL 1323 [DDD]
Smetana, B.:Qt 2 Strs Calliope ▲ CAL 9690 [DDD]
Suk, J.:Meditation on the Old Czech Hymn "St. Wenceslas" Collins Classics ▲ COL 1323 [DDD]
Tchaikovsky, P.:Qt 1 Strs Calliope ▲ CAL 9202

Talich String Quartet (cont.)
Z. Košler (cnd)
Schulhoff, E.:Con Str Qt, Czech PO Panton ▲ PAN 811225
Talich String Quartet [Petr Messiereur (vn), Jan Kvapil (vn), Jan Talich (va), Evzen Rattay (vc)]
Borodin, A.:Qt 2 Strs *(rec June 1986)* Approche ▲ CAL 6202 [DDD]
Mozart, W.A.:Qts Strs (misc)—Nos. 2-7, K.155-160, "The Milan Quartets" *(rec 1993)* Calliope ▲ CAL 9246 [DDD]
Mozart, W.A.:Qnt Cl, K.581, w. Bohuslav Zahradnik (cl) *(rec 1980–85)* Calliope ▲ CAL 6628 [ADD]
Tchaikovsky, P.:Qt 1 Strs *(rec June 1986)* Approche ▲ CAL 6202 [DDD]
Talich String Quartet [Petr Messiereur (vn), Vladimir Bukac (vn), Jan Talich (va), Evzen Rattay (vc)]
Dvořák, A.:Qnt Pno, Op. 81, w. K. Mimura (pno) *(rec 1993)* Calliope ▲ CAL 9229 [DDD]
Dvořák, A.:Qnt Strs, Op. 97, w. T. Adamopoulous (va) *(rec 1993)* Calliope ▲ CAL 9229 [DDD]
Haydn, J.:The Seven Last Words of Christ on the Cross *(rec 1995)* Calliope ▲ CAL 6202 [DDD]
Mozart, W.A.:Qnt Cl, K.581, w. Bohuslav Zahradnik (cl) Calliope ▲ CAL 9232 [DDD]
Mozart, W.A.:Qnt Strs, K.593, w. Karel Rehak (va) *(rec 1995)* Calliope ▲ CAL 9233 [DDD]
Mozart, W.A.:Qnt Strs, K.614, w. Karel Rehak (va) *(rec 1995)* Calliope ▲ CAL 9233 [DDD]
Schubert, Franz:Qt 10 Strs *(rec May 1994)* Calliope ▲ CAL 9234 [DDD]
Schubert, Franz:Qt 14 Strs *(rec May 1994)* Calliope ▲ CAL 9234 [DDD]
Schulhoff, E.:Qt 1 Strs *(rec 1973–1992)* Praga ▲ PR 255006
Tall Poppies Orch
D. Stanhope (cnd)
Vine, C.:The Battlers—"The Battlers" Suite; "The Battlers" theme; Dancy as Stranger; Dancy's Theme Revealed; "Moving On"; Dancy's First Yarn; Snow Goes Home; Snow Confronts His Family; Dancy Rescues Snow; Snow's Troubles; Dancy Teases Snow; The Storm; The Apostle Arrives; Snow in Hospital; Snow Says Goodbye; Charlie the Traindriver; Dancy & Jimmy Together; Dancy & Jimmy Get Closer; Looking for Dancy; On the Road; Jimmy Visits Prison; The Wedding & Prison; Paradise; Molly on the Warpath; "Love me Sweet"; Time Passes; "The Battlers" epilogue Tall Poppies ▲ TP 024 [DDD]
Tallinn CO
T. Kaljuste (cnd)
Pärt, A.:Berliner Messe, w. Estonian Phil Chamber Choir ECM New Series ▲ 78118-20003-2
Pärt, A.:Litany, w. David James (ct), Rogers Covey-Crump (ten), John Potter (ten), Gordon Jones (bass), Estonian Phil Chamber Choir *(rec Niguliste Church, Tallinn, Sept 1995)* ECM New Series ▲ 78118-21592-2 [DDD] ■ 78118-21592-4
Pärt, A.:Silouans Song, w. Estonian Phil Chamber Choir ECM New Series ▲ 78118-20003-2
Pärt, A.:Te Deum, w. Estonian Phil Chamber Choir ECM New Series ▲ 78118-20003-2
Tüür, E.-S.:Architectonics VI *(rec Estonia Concert Hall, Tallinn, 1994–95)* ECM ("ECM New" series) ▲ ECM 1590 [DDD]
Tüür, E.-S.:Crystallisatio *(rec Estonia Concert Hall, Tallinn, 1994–95)* ECM ("ECM New" series) ▲ ECM 1590 [DDD]
Tüür, E.-S.:Illusion Strs *(rec Estonia Concert Hall, Tallinn, 1994–95)* ECM ("ECM New" series) ▲ ECM 1590 [DDD]
Tüür, E.-S.:Music of, w. Estonian Phil Chamber Choir—Architectonics VI; Passion; Illusion; Chrystallisatio; Requiem ECM New Series ▲ 78118-21590-2
Tüür, E.-S.:Passion *(rec Estonia Concert Hall, Tallinn, 1994–95)* ECM ("ECM New" series) ▲ ECM 1590 [DDD]
Tüür, E.-S.:Requiem in memoriam Peeter Lilje, w. Kaia Urb (sop), Tiit Kogermann (ten), Estonian Phil Chamber Choir *(rec Estonia Concert Hall, Tallinn, 1994–95)* ECM ("ECM New" series) ▲ ECM 1590 [DDD]
Tallinn Linnamussikud Instrumental Ensemble
M. Bornus-Szczycinski (cnd)
Zielenski, M.:Communiones totius anni, w. Kira Borescko (sop), Marcin Borus-Szczycinski (alt), Ryszard Minkiewicz (ten), Robert Hugo (org), Bornus Consort, Tallin Linnamussikud Vocal Ensemble Urtext ▲ ACD 202662 [DDD]
Zielenski, M.:Offertoria totius anni, w. Kira Borescko (sop), Marcin Borus-Szczycinski (alt), Ryszard Minkiewicz (ten), Robert Hugo (org), Bornus Consort, Tallin Linnamussikud Vocal Ensemble Urtext ▲ ACD 202662 [DDD]
Tallinn String Quartet [Urmas Vulp (vn), Toomas Nestor (vn), Viljar Kuusk (va), Teet Järvi (vc)]
Pärt, A.:Fratres I, w. L. Derwinger (pno) BIS ▲ CD 574 [DDD]
Tobias, R.:Qt 1 Strs *(rec St Peter Paul Church, Tallinn, Estonia, Dec 17–20, 1994)* BIS ▲ CD 704 [DDD]
Tobias, R.:Qt 2 Strs *(rec St Peter Paul Church, Tallinn, Estonia, Dec 17–20, 1994)* BIS ▲ CD 704 [DDD]
Tubin, E.:Music of, w. L. Derwinger (pno)—String Qt.; Elegy; Piano Quartet BIS ▲ CD 574 [DDD]
Tüür, E.-S.:Qt Strs BIS ▲ CD 574 [DDD]
Talujon Percussion Quartet
Dun, T.:Elegy:Snow in June, w. A. Karttunen (vc) *(rec June 4, 1992)* CRI ▲ CD 655 [DDD]
Tambuco Camerata [Ricardo Gallardo (perc), Alfredo Bringas (perc), Ivan Manzanilla (perc), Raúl Tudón (perc)]
Chávez, C.:Tambuco, w. Rodrigo Alvarado (perc), Israel Moreno (perc) *(rec Sala Nezahualcóyotl, Mexican National Independent Univ., Oct. 1994)* Dorian ▲ DOR 90215 [DDD]
Chávez, C.:Toccata for 6 Perc, w. Rodrigo Alvarado (perc), Israel Moreno (perc) *(rec Sala Nezahualcóyotl, Mexican National Independent Univ., Oct. 1994)* Dorian ▲ DOR 90215 [DDD]
E. Mata (cnd)
Chávez, C.:Xochipilli, w. Rodrigo Alvarado (perc), Israel Moreno (perc) *(rec Sala Nezahualcóyotl, Mexican National Independent Univ., Oct. 1994)* Dorian ▲ DOR 90215 [DDD]
Támmittam Percussion Ensemble
G. Facchin (cnd)
Donatoni, F.:Cloches III, w. R. Maioli (pno), A. Orvieto (pno) Dynamic ▲ CD 97 [DDD]
Maderna, B.:Music of, w. R. Maioli (pno), A. Orvieto (pno)—Concerto for Two Pianos & Instruments (1948); Serenata per un satellite (1969) Dynamic ▲ CD 97 [DDD]
Tailleferre, G.:Music of, w. A. Orvieto (pno), R. Maioli (pno)—Hommage a Rameau (1964); Suite burlesque for Piano 4-Hands; Première prouesses for Piano 4-Hands Dynamic ▲ CD 97 [DDD]
Tampere PO
L. Grin (cnd)
Melartin, E.:Sym 1 Ondine ▲ ODE 841 [DDD]
Melartin, E.:Sym 2 Ondine ▲ ODE 822 [DDD]
Melartin, E.:Sym 3 Ondine ▲ ODE 841 [DDD]
Melartin, E.:Sym 4 Ondine ▲ ODE 822 [DDD]
Melartin, E.:Sym 5 Ondine ▲ ODE 799 [DDD]
Melartin, E.:Sym 6 Ondine ▲ ODE 799 [DDD]
Moszkowski, M.:Con Pno, w. M. Raekallio (pno) Ondine ▲ ODE 818 [DDD]
Prokofiev, S.:Autumn Ondine ▲ ODE 762-2 [DDD]
Prokofiev, S.:Pushkin Waltzes Ondine ▲ ODE 769-2 [DDD]
Prokofiev, S.:Summer Day Ondine ▲ ODE 769-2 [DDD]
Prokofiev, S.:Summer Night Ondine ▲ ODE 769-2 [DDD]
Prokofiev, S.:Sym 2 Ondine ▲ ODE 762-2 [DDD]
Prokofiev, S.:Waltz Suite Ondine ▲ ODE 762-2 [DDD]
Rubinstein, A.:Con 4 Pno, w. M. Raekallio (pno) Ondine ▲ ODE 818 [DDD]
Tchaikovsky, P.:Les Saisons [orch. arr. Alexander Gauk] Ondine ▲ ODE 782-2 [DDD]
T. Ollila (cnd)
Klami, U.:King Lear (ov) Ondine ▲ ODE 854
Klami, U.:Symphonie enfantine Ondine ▲ ODE 858
Klami, U.:Sym 1 Ondine ▲ ODE 854
Klami, U.:Sym 2 Ondine ▲ ODE 858
Sibelius, J.:Finlandia Ondine ▲ ODE 871
Sibelius, J.:Karelia Suite Ondine ▲ ODE 871
Sibelius, J.:Pohjola's Daughter Ondine ▲ ODE 871

Tampere PO (cont.)
T. Ollila (cnd) (cont.)
Sibelius, J.:En Saga Ondine ▲ ODE 871
Sibelius, J.:Valse triste Ondine ▲ ODE 871
A. Rasilainen (cnd)
Englund, S.E.:Sym 3 Ondine ▲ ODE 833 [DDD]
Englund, S.E.:Sym 7 Ondine ▲ ODE 833 [DDD]
L. Segerstam (cnd)
Schumann, R.:Con Vc, w. John Storgårds (vn) [arr composer for vn & orch] Ondine ▲ ODE CD 879
Schumann, R.:Con Vn, w. John Storgårds (vn) Ondine ▲ ODE CD 879
Segerstam, L.:Impressions of Nordic Nature *(rec 1992–93)* Kontrapunkt ▲ KPT 32165 [DDD]
Segerstam, L.:Nocturnal Thoughts *(rec 1992–93)* Kontrapunkt ▲ KPT 32165 [DDD]
Sibelius, J.:Songs, w. J. Hynninen (bar) Ondine ▲ ODE 823 [DDD]
Tchikashi Tanaka Ensemble
K. Toyoda (cnd)
Haydn, J.:Con 1 Vc, w. W. Boettcher (vc) Camerata ▲ 30CM 376
Haydn, J.:Con Org, Vn & Strs, H.XVIII/6, w. E. Hashimoto (hpd), H. Schneeberger (vn) Camerata ▲ 30CM 376
Taneyev String Quartet [Vladimir Ovcharek (vn), Girgory Luzkiy (vn), Vissarion Solovyov (va), Josef Levinson (vc)]
Miaskovsky, N.:Qt 1 Strs Russian Disc ▲ RUS 11013 [DDD]
Miaskovsky, N.:Qt 2 Strs *(rec 1982)* Russian Compact Disc ▲ RDCD 11031 [AAD]
Miaskovsky, N.:Qt 3 Strs *(rec 1982)* Russian Compact Disc ▲ RDCD 11032 [AAD]
Miaskovsky, N.:Qt 4 Strs Russian Disc ▲ RUS 11013 [DDD]
Miaskovsky, N.:Qt 5 Strs *(rec 1982)* Russian Compact Disc ▲ RDCD 11032 [AAD]
Miaskovsky, N.:Qt 6 Strs *(rec 1983)* Russian Compact Disc ▲ RDCD 11031 [AAD]
Miaskovsky, N.:Qt 7 Strs *(rec 1984)* Russian Compact Disc ▲ RDCD 11033 [AAD]
Miaskovsky, N.:Qt 8 Strs *(rec 1982)* Russian Compact Disc ▲ RDCD 11033 [AAD]
Miaskovsky, N.:Qt 9 Strs *(rec 1983)* Russian Compact Disc ▲ RDCD 11034 [AAD]
Miaskovsky, N.:Qt 10 Strs *(rec 1984)* Russian Compact Disc ▲ RDCD 11031 [AAD]
Miaskovsky, N.:Qt 11 Strs *(rec 1981)* Russian Compact Disc ▲ RDCD 11034 [AAD]
Miaskovsky, N.:Qt 12 Strs *(rec 1982)* Russian Compact Disc ▲ RD CD 11305 [AAD]
Miaskovsky, N.:Qt 13 Strs *(rec 1981)* Russian Compact Disc ▲ RD CD 11305 [AAD]
Salmanov, V.:Qt 1 Strs *(rec 1980)* Russian Disc ▲ RDCD 10048 [AAD]
Salmanov, V.:Qt 3 Strs *(rec 1966)* Russian Disc ▲ RDCD 10048 [AAD]
Salmanov, V.:Qt 4 Strs *(rec 1966)* Russian Disc ▲ RDCD 10048 [AAD]
Shostakovich, D.:Qt 4 Strs Praga ▲ PR 254054
Shostakovich, D.:Qt 5 Strs *(rec 1977)* Praga ▲ PR 250077
Shostakovich, D.:Qt 7 Strs *(rec 1976)* Praga ▲ PR 250077
Tanglewood Music Center Fellows
B. Lubman (cnd)
Zuidam, R.:Fishbone Donemus ▲ CV 27
Tanglewood Music Center Orch
O. Knussen (cnd)
del Tredici, D.:An Alice Sym, w. Phyllis Bryn-Julson (sop) *(rec Theatre-Concert Hall, Tanglewood, Lenox, MA, Aug. 7, 1991)* CRI ▲ CD 688 [DDD]
Tanglewood Percussion Quartet
Kraft, William:Qt Perc Crystal ▲ CD 124
Tango 7 [Daniel Binelli (band), Daniel Zisman (vn), Osvaldo Ciancio (vn), Eduardo Vassallo (vc), Gerardo Vila (pno/fl), Hugo Romero (gtr), Silvio Acosta (db)]
Música de Buenos Aires 2:Tango 7 *(rec Switzerland, Nov 1992)* Vox Classics ▲ VOX 7528
Tapestry
Angeli, Music of Angels, w. PAN Ensemble, William Hite (ten), Harlan B. Hokin (ten), Paul Cummings (bar) *(rec Studio A, National Music Center, Lenox, MA, Sept 11–14, 1995)* Telarc ▲ CD 80448 [DDD]
Tapiola Sinfonietta
Kortekangas, O.:A for Instruments & Choir, w. Tapiola Choir Ondine ▲ ODE 786-2 [DDD]
Rautavaara, E.:Children's Mass, w. Tapiola Choir Ondine ▲ ODE 786-2 [DDD]
P. Järvi (cnd)
Ibert, J.:Divert Orch *(rec June 4 & 9, 1993)* BIS ▲ CD 630 [DDD]
Jolivet, A.:Con Fl, w. M. Wiesler (fl) *(rec June 4 & 9, 1993)* BIS ▲ CD 630 [DDD]
Jolivet, A.:Fl Music (comp), w. Manuela Wiesler (fl), Erica Goodman (hp), Patrik Swedrup (vn), Håkan Olsson (va), Helena Nilsson (vc), Christian Davidsson (bn), Roland Pöntinen (pno), Kroumata Percussion Ensemble—Alla rustica for Fl & Hp; Chant de Linos for Fl, Hp & Str Trio; Pastorales de Noël for Fl, Bn & Hp; Con for Fl & Strs; Suite en concert for Fl & 4 Perc Players; Fant-Caprice for Fl & Pno; Cabrioles for Fl & Pno *(rec Danderyd Grammar School, Sweden, Tapiola Hall, Tapiola, Finland, Gothenburg Concert Hall, Sweden & Studio 2, Radiohuset, Stockholm, Sweden, June 21–22, 1995)* BIS ▲ CD 739 [DDD]
Roussel, A.:Sinfonietta Strs *(rec June 4 & 9, 1993)* BIS ▲ CD 630 [DDD]
J.-J. Kantorow (cnd)
Bartók, B.:Divert *(rec Tapiola Concert Hall, Finland, Mar 27–30, 1995)* BIS ▲ CD 740 [DDD]
Bartók, B.:Music for Strs, Perc & Cel *(rec Tapiola Concert Hall, Finland, Mar 27–30, 1995)* BIS ▲ CD 740 [DDD]
Bartók, B.:Romanian Folk Dances Pno *(rec Tapiola Concert Hall, Finland, Mar 27–30, 1995)* BIS ▲ CD 740 [DDD]
Schoenberg, A.:Chamber Sym 1 BIS ▲ CD 703 [DDD]
Schoenberg, A.:Qt 2 Strs, w. Christina Högman (sop) BIS ▲ CD 703 [DDD]
Schoenberg, A.:Verklärte Nacht BIS ▲ CD 703 [DDD]
J. Swensen (cnd)
Shostakovich, D.:Adagio & Allegretto Ondine ▲ ODE 845
Shostakovich, D.:Sym 14, w. Margareta Haverinen (sop), Petteri Salomaa (bass) Ondine ▲ ODE 845
O. Vänskä (cnd)
Britten, B.:Nocturne, w. C. Prégardien (ten) [E] *(rec 10–11/91)* BIS ▲ CD 540 [DDD]
Britten, B.:Now Sleeps the Crimson Petal, w. C. Prégardien, Ib Lanzky-Otto [E] *(rec 10–11/91)* BIS ▲ CD 540 [DDD]
Britten, B.:Serenade, Op. 31, w. C. Prégardien (ten), I. Lanzky-Otto (hn) [E] *(rec 10–11/91)* BIS ▲ CD 540 [DDD]
Britten, B.:Sinfonietta *(rec 10–11/91)* BIS ▲ CD 540 [DDD]
Crusell, B.H.:Concertino Bn, w. L. Hara (bn) BIS ▲ CD 495 [DDD]
Crusell, B.H.:Intro, Theme & Vars on a Swedish Air, w. A.-M. Korsimaa-Hursti (cl) BIS ▲ CD 495 [DDD]
Crusell, B.H.:Sinf concertante BIS ▲ CD 495 [DDD]
Dreams, w. [cnd:Erkki Pohjola], Tapiola Children's Choir Ondine ▲ ODE 786 [DDD]
Finland in Song, w. [cnd:Erkki Pohjola], Tapiola Children's Choir Ondine ▲ ODE 785 [DDD]
Rabe, F.:Con Trbn, w. C. Lindberg (trbn) BIS ▲ CD 568 [DDD]
Rimsky-Korsakov, N.:Con Trbn, w. C. Lindberg (trbn) BIS ▲ CD 568 [DDD]
Rota, N.:Con Trbn, w. C. Lindberg (trbn) BIS ▲ CD 568 [DDD]
Sallinen, A.:Con Vn, w. E. Koskinen (vn) BIS ▲ CD 560 [DDD]
Sallinen, A.:The Nocturnal Dances of Don Juanquixote, w. T. Thedéen (vc) BIS ▲ CD 560 [DDD]
Sallinen, A.:Some Aspects of Peltoniemi Hintrik's Funeral March BIS ▲ CD 560 [DDD]
Sallinen, A.:Vars BIS ▲ CD 560 [DDD]
Schnittke, A.:Dialogue Vc, w. C. Lindberg (vc) BIS ▲ CD 568 [DDD]
Tomasi, H.:Con Trbn, w. C. Lindberg (trbn) BIS ▲ CD 568 [DDD]
Tapiola Trio [I. Ranta (pno), J. Ilves (vn), R. Poutanen (vc)]
Sibelius, J.:Tone Poems—The Bard, Op. 64; The Dryad, Op. 45/1; En Saga, Op. 9; Finlandia, Op. 26; Luonnotar, Op. 70; Night-Ride and Sunrise, Op. 55; The Oceanides, Op. 73; Pohjola's Daughter, Op. 49; Spring Song, Op. 16; Tapiola, Op. 112) *(rec Oct. 1988)* Finlandia ▲ 4509-95858-2 [DDD]
Targu-Mures PO
F. Lamprecht (cnd)
Gounod, C.:Sym 1 Electrecord ▲ ELC 173 [DDD]
Gounod, C.:Sym 2 Electrecord ▲ ELC 173 [DDD]

▲ = CD ♦ = Enhanced CD Δ = MD ■ = Cassette Tape □ = DCC

Edward Tarr Brass Ensemble
Gabrieli, G.:Canzoni—7 Canzoni *(rec at St. Mark's Basilica, Venice, 1967)* CBS ▲ MK 42645 [ADD]
Gabrieli, G.:Sacred Music, w. E. P. Biggs (org), La Fenice Ensemble, Gregg Smith Singers, Texas Boys' Choir—Deus, in nomine tuo; Beata es, virgo Maria; Juilemus singuli; Deus, Deus meus, ad te de luce vigilo; O quam suavis est; Kyrie; Sanctus; Benedictus; Cantate Domino; Domine, exuadi orationem meam; Hodie completi sunt; Magnificat; Surrexit Christus; Nunc dimittis; Jubilate Deo; Intonatio *(rec San Marco, Venice, Sept 14–22, 1967)*
Sony Classical ("Essential Classics" series) ▲ SBK 62426 [ADD] ■ SBT 62426

Edward Tarr Trumpet Ensemble
The Silver Trumpets of Lisbon & Lusitanian Organ Music, w. Edward H. Tarr (tpt), Irmtraud Krüger (org) MD + G ▲ L 3348 [DDD]

Tasmanian Sym Chamber Players
18th Century Virtuoso String Music, w. B. J. Gilby (vn), Geoffrey Lancaster (pno) ABC Classics ▲ 432530–2 [DDD]
Ford, A.:Pastoral *(rec ABC's Odeon Theater, Hobart, Nov 1991)* Tall Poppies ▲ TP 053 [DDD]

Tasmanian SO
R. Mills (cnd)
Glanville-Hicks, P.:Sinf da Pacifica Vox Australis ▲ VAST 013
Kay, D.:Legend of Moinee Vox Australis ▲ VAST 013
Kay, D.:Tasmania Sym, w. Christian Wojtowicz (vc) Vox Australis ▲ VAST 013

Tátrai String Quartet
Dohnányi, E. von:Qnt 2 Pno, w. E. Szegedi (pno) Hungaroton ▲ HCD 11624 [ADD]
Haydn, J.:Qts Strs, Op. 1 Hungaroton 3–▲ HCD 31089/91 [DDD]
Haydn, J.:Qts Strs, Op. 2—Nos. 1,2,4 & 6 Hungaroton 3–▲ HCD 31089/91 [DDD]
Haydn, J.:Qts Strs, Op. 9 Hungaroton 2–▲ HCD 31296/97 [DDD]
Haydn, J.:Qts Strs, Op. 17 Hungaroton 2–▲ HCD 11382/83
Haydn, J.:Qts Strs, Op. 20, "Sun Qts" Hungaroton 2–▲ HCD 11332/33
Haydn, J.:Qts Strs, Op. 33, "Russian Qts" Hungaroton 2–▲ HCD 11887/88
Haydn, J.:Qt Strs, Op. 42 Hungaroton 3–▲ HCD 31089/91 [DDD]
Haydn, J.:Qts Strs, Op. 50, "Prussian Qts" Hungaroton 2–▲ HCD 11934/35
Haydn, J.:Qts Strs, Op. 54 Hungaroton 2–▲ HCD 12506/07
Haydn, J.:Qts Strs, Op. 55 Hungaroton 2–▲ HCD 12506/07
Haydn, J.:Qts Strs, Op. 64, "Tost Qts" Hungaroton 2–▲ HCD 11838/39
Haydn, J.:Qts Strs, Op. 71 Hungaroton 2–▲ HCD 12246/47
Haydn, J.:Qts Strs, Op. 74 Hungaroton 2–▲ HCD 12246/47
Haydn, J.:Qts Strs, Op. 76, "Erdödy Qts" Hungaroton 2–▲ HCD 12812/13
Haydn, J.:Qts Strs, Op. 77, "Lobkowitz Qts" Hungaroton ▲ HCD 11776
Haydn, J.:Qt Strs, Op. 103 Hungaroton 3–▲ HCD 31089/91 [DDD]
Haydn, J.:The Seven Last Words of Christ on the Cross [string quartet version] Hungaroton ▲ HCD 12036 [ADD]
Lajtha, L.:Qt 10 Strs [L,F] Hungaroton ▲ HCD 31453 [ADD]
Schubert, Franz:Qnt Strs, D.956, w. L. Szilvasy (vc) White Label ▲ HRC 056
M. Szabó (cnd)
Lajtha, L.:Hymns for the Holy Virgin, w. Liszt Academy of Music Chamber Choir, Győr Girls' Choir [L,F] Hungaroton ▲ HCD 31453 [ADD]
Lajtha, L.:Madrigals, w. Liszt Academy of Music Chamber Choir, Győr Girls' Choir [L,F] Hungaroton ▲ HCD 31453 [ADD]
Lajtha, L.:Magnificat, w. Liszt Academy of Music Chamber Choir, Győr Girls' Choir [L,F] Hungaroton ▲ HCD 31453 [ADD]

Tátrai String Quartet members
Dohnányi, E. von:Sextet, w. E. Szegedi (pno), B. Kovács (cl), F. Tarjáni (hn) Hungaroton ▲ HCD 11624 [ADD]

Taverner Players
DDD Christmas, w. Kathleen Battle (sop), Florence Quivar (mez), Taverner Consort, Taverner Choir, New York Choral Artists, Toronto Mendelssohn Choir, King's Singers, Empire Brass Angel ▲ CDM 63666
A. Parrott (cnd)
Bach, J.S.:Brandenburg Cons EMI Classics 2–▲ ZDCB 49806–2 [DDD]
Bach, J.S.:Jesu Bleibet Meine Freude, w. Taverner Consort Virgin Classics ▲ CDM 61304
Bach, J.S.:Magnificat, BWV 243, w. Taverner Consort, Taverner Consort EMI Classics ▲ CDC 54926
Bach, J.S.:Mass in b, BWV 232, w. E. Kirkby (sop), E. Van Evera (sop), R. Covey-Crump (ct), D. Thomas (bass), Taverner Consort, Tölz Boys' Choir [L] EMI Classics 2–▲ ZDCB 47292–2 [DDD]
Bach, J.S.:Sinfs—from Cantata 194 EMI Classics 2–▲ ZDCB 49806–2 [DDD]
Bach, J.S.:Sinfs—Sinf from Cants 29, 31, 106, 156 & 174 Virgin Classics ▲ CDM 61304
Bach, J.S.:Sons Vl, BWV 1027–1029 [trans. Duncan Druce]—BWV 1029 EMI Classics 2–▲ ZDCB 49806–2 [DDD]
The Carol Album:7 Centuries of Christmas Music, w. Taverner Consort, Taverner Choir EMI Classics ▲ CDC 49809
The Carol Album 2, w. Taverner Consort, Taverner Choir EMI Classics ▲ CDC 54902
Christmas Album, w. Taverner Consort, Taverner Choir EMI Classics ▲ CDC 54529
Gabrieli, G.:Music of, w. Taverner Consort [period instrs]—canzoni, sonatas & motets EMI Classics ▲ CDC 54265
Handel, G.F.:Carmelite Vespers, "Saeviat tellus inter vigores", w. Taverner Choir [L] EMI Classics 2–▲ CDCB 49749 [DDD]
Handel, G.F.:Con Hp Virgin Classics ▲ CDM 61304
Handel, G.F.:Dixit Dominus, w. Taverner Consort, Taverner Consort EMI Classics ▲ CDC 54926
Handel, G.F.:Israel in Egypt, w. Nancy Argenta (sop), Emily Van Evera (sop), Jan Wilson (mez), Anthony Rolfe Johnson (ten), Thomas (sgr), White (sgr), Taverner Choir [E] EMI Classics 2–▲ CDCB 54018 [DDD]
Handel, G.F.:Messiah, w. Emily van Evera (sop), Emma Kirkby (sop), Margaret Cable (alt), James Bowman (ct), Taverner Choir Virgin Classics 2–▲ ZDMB 61330
Handel, G.F.:Solomon (arrival of the queen of Sheba) Virgin Classics ▲ CDM 61304
Monteverdi, C.:Madrigals, Taverner Consort—Book Eight, 1638 EMI Classics ▲ CDC 54333
Pachelbel, J.:Canon Virgin Classics ▲ CDM 61304
Purcell, H.:Dido & Aeneas, w. E. Kirkby (sop), J. Nelson (mez), D. Thomas (bass), Taverner Choir [E] Chandos ("Chaconne" series) ▲ CHAN 0521 [DDD]
Purcell, H.:Fant 3 Fls Vn Virgin Classics ▲ CDM 61304
Purcell, H.:Music for the Theater, w. Taverner Consort Virgin Classics ▲ CDM 61304
Purcell, H.:Music of, w. Taverner Consort Virgin Classics ▲ CDC 45116
Purcell, H.:Rondeau EMI Classics ▲ CDD 64300 [DDD]
Purcell, H.:Te Deum & Jubilate, w. Taverner Choir Virgin Classics ▲ CDC 45061
Schütz, H.:Die Geburt unsers Herren Jesu Christi, w. Taverner Choir EMI Classics ▲ CDC 47633
Vivaldi, A.:Cons Vn, Op. 8/1–4, "The Four Seasons", w. J. Holloway (vn) Denon ▲ 7283 [DDD]
Vivaldi, A.:Gloria, RV.589, w. Taverner Choir [period instrs] Virgin Classics ▲ CDC 59326

Taylor Recorder Consort
The Wraggle Taggle Gypsies, w. Alfred Deller (ct), Desmond Dupré (lt/gtr) *(rec Walthamstow Town Hall, London, Feb 1956)* Vanguard Classics ("Alfred Deller Edition" series) ▲ OVC 8105 [ADD]

Tbilisi SO
D. Kakhidze (cnd)
Kancheli, G.:Sym 6 *(rec Tbilisi, Georgia, May, 1994)* Sony Classical ("St. Petersburg Classics" series) ▲ SMK 66590 [DDD]
Kancheli, G.:Sym 7 *(rec Tbilisi, Georgia, May, 1994)* Sony Classical ("St. Petersburg Classics" series) ▲ SMK 66590 [DDD]

Tchaikovsky CO
L. Gosman (cnd)
Boccherini, L.:Minuetto Sony Classical ▲ MLK 62369 [ADD/DDD]
Haydn, J.:Qts Strs, Op. 3—Serenade from Qt No. 5 for Strs Sony Classical ▲ MLK 62369 [ADD/DDD]

Tchaikovsky Piano Trio [Konstantin Bogino (pno), Alexandre Brussilovsky (vn), Anatole Liebermann (vc)]
Dvořák, A.:Trio 4 Pno, "Dumky" *(rec Rome, 1995)* Musicaimmagine ▲ MR 10017 [DDD]
Smetana, B.:Trio Pno *(rec Rome, 1995)* Musicaimmagine ▲ MR 10017 [DDD]
Tchaikovsky, P.:Serenade for Nikolai Rubinstein's Name-Day [arr. Alexander Gedike] Musicaimmagine ▲ MR 10009/10 [DDD]
Tchaikovsky, P.:Trio Pno Musicaimmagine ▲ MR 10009/10 [DDD]

Teatre Lliure CO
J. Pons (cnd)
Piazzolla, A.:Con Band, w. Pablo Mainetti (band) Harmonia Mundi France ▲ HMC 901595
Piazzolla, A.:Movimientos Tanguisticos Porteños Harmonia Mundi France ▲ HMC 901595
Piazzolla, A.:Music of—Decarísimo; Invierno Porteño; Adiós Nonino; Milonga del Ángel; La Muerte del Ángel Harmonia Mundi France ▲ HMC 901595

Teatro Armonico Instrumental Ensemble
Pasquini, B.:Cain & Abel, w. Il Teatro Armonico Vocal Ensemble Symphonia ▲ SYM 90S01 [DDD]

Teatro La Gran Guardia Orch
O. de Fabritiis (cnd)
Mascagni, P.:Il piccolo Marat, w. Virginia Zeani (sop), Clara Betner (mez), Umberto Borso (ten), Nicola Rossi-Lemeni (bass), Teatro La Gran Guardia Chorus [I] *(rec live, 10/26/61)* Fonè 2–▲ 88 F 17–37 [ADD]
G. Mucci (cnd)
Mascagni, P.:Lodoletta, w. L. Saldari (ten), Beltrami (sgr), Teatro La Gran Guardia Chorus [I] *(rec live, 10/2/60)* Fonè 2–▲ 88 F 16–36 [ADD]

Tedesco Duo [Barbara Hölzer (gtr), Eugène Hölzer (gtr)]
Benguerel, X.:Stella Splendens Koch Schwann ▲ CD 310 116 [DDD]
Brouwer, L.:Micro Piezas Koch Schwann ▲ CD 310 116 [DDD]
Castelnuovo-Tedesco, M.:Les Guitares bien tempérées Koch Schwann 2–▲ SCH 312242
Castelnuovo-Tedesco, M.:Preludes & Fugues (24) Koch Schwann 2–▲ SCH 312242
Petit, P.:Tarantelle & Toccata Gtrs Koch Schwann ▲ CD 310 116 [DDD]
Piazzolla, A.:Tango Suite Koch Schwann ▲ CD 310 116 [DDD]
Satie, E.:Gymnopédies [arr. for 2 guitars]—Nos. 1–3 Koch Schwann ▲ CD 310 116 [DDD]
Guitar Music from the Age of Viennese Classicism Koch Schwann ▲ SCH 310402 [DDD]

Telemann CO
L. Rémy (cnd)
Telemann, G.P.:Cants, w. Constanze Backes (sop), Mechthild Georg (mez), Klaus Mertens (bar), Andreas Post (sgr), Helko Siede (cnd), Michaelstein Chamber Choir—Christmas cantatas, "Siehe, ich verkündige Euch" (1761) & "Der Herr hat offenbaret" (1762) *(rec Apr 28–May 2, 1996)* CPO ▲ CPO 999419–2 [DDD]
Telemann, G.P.:Hirten an der Krippe zu Bethlehem, w. Constanze Backes (sop), Mechthild Georg (mez), Klaus Mertens (bar), Andreas Post (sgr), Helko Siede (cnd), Michaelstein Chamber Choir *(rec Apr 28–May 2, 1996)* CPO ▲ CPO 999419–2 [DDD]

Temianka CO
Schubert, Franz:Rondo Vn, D.438, w. H. Temianka (vn) *(rec 1937)* Biddulph 2–▲ LAB 059/60 [ADD]
H. Temianka (cnd)
Sibelius, J.:Humoresques, w. H. Temianka (vn)—Op. 89/4 *(rec 1937)* Biddulph 2–▲ LAB 059/60 [ADD]

Tempesta di Mare [Jim Bolyard (bn), Ann Marie Morgan (vc), Richard Stone (thb/lt), Web Wiggins (hpd/org)]
Veracini, F.M.:Sons Rcr, w. Gwyn Roberts (rcr)—Sons I–VI PGM ▲ PGM 107

Tenebrae
Semaine Sainte Studio SM ▲ 12 17.50

Tenerife SO
A. R. Marbà (cnd)
Vives, A.:Bohemios, w. M. Bayo (sop), L. Lima (ten), C. Alvarez (bass) Valois ▲ V 4711
Vives, A.:Doña Francisquita, w. R. Pierotti (sgr), S. S. Jerico (sgr) Valois 2–▲ V 4710
V. P. Pérez (cnd)
de Pablo, L.:Las Orilas Col Legno ▲ AU 31818
Dvořák, A.:Sym 8 Col Legno ▲ AU 31818
Gerhard, R.:Orch Music—Albada, Interludi I Dansa (1937); Don Quixote (1947); Pedrelliana (1941) Valois ▲ V 4660 [DDD]
Gerhard, R.:Sym 1 Valois ▲ V 4728
Gerhard, R.:Sym 3, "Collages" Valois ▲ V 4728
Halffter, E.:Dominus pastor meus, w. Susan Chilcott (sop), Claire Powell (mez), Joan Cabero (ten), José Antonio Carril (bass), La Laguna Univ Choir Discobi ▲ DIS 2009 [DDD]
Halffter, E.:Elegia en memoria de S.A.S. Príncipe Pierre de Polignac, w. La Laguna Univ Choir Discobi ▲ DIS 2009 [DDD]
Halffter, E.:Sinfonietta Discobi ▲ DIS 2009 [DDD]
Marco, Tomas:Pulsar Discobi ▲ DIS 2010 [DDD]
Marco, Tomas:Sym 4 Col Legno ▲ AU 31812
Turina, J.L.:Con Vn, w. Victor Martin (vn) Discobi ▲ DIS 2010 [DDD]

Terni CO
F. Maestri (cnd)
Pergolesi, G.B.:San Guglielmo Duca d'Aquitania, w. K. Gamberucci (sop), Caldini (sgr), B. Lucarini (sop), R. Girolami (bass), G. Gatti (bar), Herron (sgr) [I] *(rec live, 12/18/86)* Bongiovanni 2–▲ GB 2060/61 [DDD]

Terpsichore Ensemble
Renaissance Vocal & Instrumental Music Gallo ▲ CD 567 [ADD]

Tesoro String Quartet
Anthony, K.J.:Traces of My Self TCC ▲ 1030

Tetra Ensemble
Bayer, F.:Music of, w. Donatienne Michel-Dansac (sop), Alain Meunier (vc), Jean-Louis Haguenauer (pno), Renaud Francois, Francesca Paderni Pierre Verany ▲ PVY 796093

Texas Festival Orch
H. Ohyama (cnd)
Chopin, F.:Con 1 Pno, w. James Dick (pno) Round Top ▲ RTR 002
P. Verrot (cnd)
Prokofiev, S.:Con 3 Pno, w. James Dick (pno) Round Top ▲ RTR 002
Saint-Saëns, C.:Con 2 Pno, w. J. Dick (pno) *(rec Festival Concert Hall, Round Top, TX)* Round Top ▲ RTR 003 [DDD]
Welcher, D.:Con 1 Pno, w. James Dick (pno) *(rec Festival Concert Hall, Round Top, TX)* Round Top ▲ RTR 003 [DDD]

Texas Little Sym
A World of Folksong, w. [cnd:Gregg Smith], Gregg Smith Singers, Texas Boys' Choir, Dorthy Shaw Bell Choir *(rec Nov. 1981)* Premier ▲ PRCD 1031 [ADD]

Texas Tech Univ Symphonic Band
J. Sudduth (cnd)
Glazer, S.:Con Fl, w. M. Stoune (fl) Opus One ▲ 147
Van Appledorn, M.J.:Cycles of Moons & Tides Opus One ▲ CD 170 [DDD]

Texas Tech Univ Trombone Ensemble
R. Deahl (cnd)
Van Appledorn, M.J.:Atmospheres *(rec Texas Tech Univ., Hemmle Recital Hall, Lubbock Texas, Feb. 16, 1994)* Opus One ▲ CD 169

Texas Tech Univ Wind Ensemble
Soliloquy, w. Dale Underwood (sax), Texas Tech Univ Wind Ensemble [cnd:James Sudduth] Open Loop ▲ OL 013

Thalia–Schrammeln Quartet
The Dance Collection, w. Ondrej Lenard (cnd), Keith Clark (cnd), Stephen Gunzenhauser (cnd), Kenneth Jean (cnd), Barry Wordsworth (cnd), Adrian Leaper (cnd), Johannes Wildner (cnd), Czech RSO, Slovak RSO, Slovak PO, Royal PO, Slovak State PO, CRS SO, Thalia–Schrammeln Quartet *(rec Czechoslovak Radio Concert Hall, Bratislava, Feb 1–4, 1988)* Naxos 4–▲ 8.504015 [DDD]

Thames CO
D. Willcocks (cnd)
Bach, J.S.:St. Matthew Passion, w. F. Lott (sop), A. Hodgson (cta), R. Tear (ten), J. Shirley–Quirk (bar), S. Roberts (bar), Bach Choir [E] ASV Quicksilva 3–▲ ASQ 324 [ADD]

Thamyris [C. Boyd Waddell (sop), P. Brittan (fl), T. Gurch (cl/b cl), L. Gordy (pno), P. Benkeser (perc)]
Boelter, K.:Music of, w. C. Rex (vc)—To Know the Dark; One, Two, Three...Out; Peterborough Son.; No Longer of That World ACA Digital Recording ▲ CM 20007 [DDD]

Theater of Eternal Music Brass Ensemble
Young, L.:The Second Dream of the High–Tension Line Stepdown Transformer Gramavision ▲ R21S 79467

Théâtre Bouffes–Parisiens Orch & Ensemble
G. Calvi (cnd)
Offenbach, J.:Le Belle Hélène, w. Nicky Nancel (sgr) Accord 2–▲ ACD 290002 [AAD]

13 Étoiles Brass Band
Trombone Festival, w. Dany Bonvin (trbn) Gallo ▲ CD 474 [ADD]
G.–P. Moren (cnd)
Daetwyler, J.:Con Trbn, w. D. Bovin (trbn) Gallo ▲ CD 474 [ADD]
Langford, G.:Son, Serenade & Scherzo, w. D. Bovin (trtb) Gallo ▲ CD 474 [ADD]
Newsome, R.:Olympic Concertino, w. D. Bovin (trbn) Gallo ▲ CD 474 [ADD]
Voegelin, F.:Nordlicht–Variationen, w. Dany Bovin (trbn) Gallo ▲ CD 474 [ADD]

Thirteen Strings of Ottawa
B. Law (cnd)
Glick, S.I.:Divert Strs CBC ("Musica Viva" series) ▲ MVCD 1046 [DDD]

Bernard Thomas CO
J.–J. Kantorow (cnd)
Paganini, N.:Con 2 Vn, w. J.–J. Kanotorow (vn) Vox Box 3–▲ CD3X 3020 [ADD]
J. Pillement (cnd)
Boieldieu, F.–A.:La Fille mal gardée Thésis ▲ THC 82015 [DDD]
B. Thomas (cnd)
Boieldieu, F.–A.:Le Calife de Bagdad, w. N. Monestier (sop), Ouaki (sgr), S. Elloir (sgr), Plantak (sgr), Fokenoy (sgr), Patrick Marco Vocal Ensemble [F] Thésis ▲ THC 82015 [DDD]
Fauré, G.:Messe basse, w. Michel Piquemal (cnd), Patrick Marco (cnd), Michel Piquemal Vocal Ensemble, Petits Chanteurs de Paris, Argenteuil Vittoria Choir Forlane ▲ FRL 16536 [DDD]
Fauré, G.:Requiem, w. Michel Piquemal (cnd), Patrick Marco (cnd), Michel Piquemal Vocal Ensemble, Petits Chanteurs de Paris, Argenteuil Vittoria Choir Forlane ▲ FRL 16536 [DDD]

Michael Thompson Wind Quintet [Jonathan Snowden (fl), Derek Wickens (ob), Robert Hill (cl), Michael Thompson (hn), John Price (bn)]
Danzi, F.:Qnts Ww, Op. 56 *(rec St. Paul's Church, Rusthall, Kent, England, June 1994)* Naxos ▲ 8.553076 [DDD]
Reicha, A.:Qnts Ww, Op. 88—No. 2 *(rec St. Paul's Church, Rusthall, Kent, England, June 6–9, 1994)* Naxos ▲ 8.550432 [DDD]
Reicha, A.:Qnts Ww, Op. 100—No. 5 *(rec St. Paul's Church, Rusthall, Kent, England, June 6–9, 1994)* Naxos ▲ 8.550432 [DDD]

Thouvenel String Quartet [Eugene Purdue (vn), Edmund Stein (vn), Sally Chisholm (va), Jeffrey Levenson (vc)]
Krenek, E.:Qt 5 Strs *(rec Burbank, CA, July 1983)* CRI ▲ CD 678 [DDD]
Krenek, E.:Qt 8 Strs *(rec Burbank, CA, July 1983)* CRI ▲ CD 678 [DDD]

Three Rivers SO
G. Bellemare (cnd)
Leclerc, F.:Songs, w. J. Rouleau (bass) *(rec 1990)* Analekta ▲ AN2–8601 [DDD] ■ AN4–8601

Thüringen PO
O. Koch (cnd)
Sommerlatte, U.:Music of—Old Western Suite; Dream Ballet; The Rose of Shiraz; Traumulus; Romanesca; Doina; Venetian Suite; Metropolis; Night Express; Farewell (Adieu, Mona Lisa) Koch Schwann ▲ SCH 313192 [DDD]
Suder, J.:Symphonic Music II Calig ▲ CAL 50945 [DDD]
Koch, Ukigaya (cnd)
Erdmann, D.:Music of, w. Detlef Bensmann (sax), Pomorska PO—Con for Sax & Orch (1989); Saxophonata (1985); Fant Colorata for Ten Sax; Con for Alt Sax & Orch; Resonanze for Sax Qt; plus others Thorofon ▲ CTH 2269

Thüringian Saalfeld–Rudolstadt SO
K. Bach (cnd)
Wagner, S.:Schwarzschwanenreich, w. Beth Johanning (sop—Linda), Kerstin Quandt (cta—Ursula), Walter Raffeiner (ten—Ludwig), Lucian Chioreanu (ten—A Boy), André Wenhold (bar—Oswald), Roland Hartmann (sgr—Tempter/Priest), Jutta Maria Schmitz (sgr—Ash–Woman), Ksenija Lukie (sgr—A Girl), Thüringian Landestheater Rudolstadt Chorus *(rec Thüringer Landestheater, Rudolstadt, June 1994)* Marco Polo 2–▲ 8.223777–8 [DDD]

Thüringian SO
Wagner, S.:Der Bärenhäuter, w. B. Johanning (sop—Luise), K. Likic (sop—Lene), T. Koon (sop—Gunda), V. Horn (ten—Hans Kraft), A. Feilhaber (ten—Nikolaus Spitz), R. Hartmann (bar—Kaspar Wild), A. Wenhold (bar—Stranger), A. Waller (bass—Devil), H. Kiichli (bass—Melchior Fröhlich), Thüringian State Theater Chorus *(rec Rudolstadt, July 25–31, 1993)* Marco Polo ("Opera Classics" series) 2–▲ 8.223713/4 [DDD]
V. Gailis (cnd)
Wagner, S.:Banadietrich, w. Beth Johanning (sop), Vivian Hanner (sgr), Volker Horn (ten), André Wenhold (bar), Andreas Schmidt (bar), Adalbert Walker (bass), Rudolstadt Festival Chorus *(rec Rudolstädt, June 1995)* Marco Polo 2–▲ 8.223895–6 [DDD]

Thurston Clarinet Quartet
Clarinet Carnaval ASV ▲ ASV 2095 [DDD]
Clarinet Masquerade ASV ▲ ASV 2076 [DDD]

Tibetan Singing Bowl Ensemble
Mostel, R.:Jacob's Ladder Digital Fossils ▲ 10008–2 [DDD] ■ 10008–4
Mostel, R.:Nightsong Digital Fossils ▲ 10008–2 [DDD] ■ 10008–4
Mostel, R.:River Perc Digital Fossils ▲ 10009–2 [DDD] ■ 10009–4
Mostel, R.:River Tibetan Singing Bowls, w. Geoffrey Gordon (perc) *(rec live, WNYC Studios, Sept 18, 1987)* Digital Fossils ▲ 10009–2 [DDD]
Mostel, R.:Swiftly, w. Dan Erkkila (shakuhachi/ram's horn/Tibetan thighbone trumpets), John Charles Thomas (tube tpt/ram's horn), Geoffrey Gordon (perc) *(rec live, WNYC Studios, Sept 18, 1987)* Digital Fossils ▲ 10009–2 [DDD]

Tickmayer Formatio [Laura Levay (fl), Nikola Srdic (cl), Stéphane Gautier (bn), Sasa Dragovic (tpt), Branislav Askin (trbn), Milan Vrsajkov (vc), Steven Kovaks Tickmayer (pno/harm/perc)]
Tickmayer, S.K.:Wilhelm Dances—The Barber & the Death; Saving; Nervous Rehearsal; The Ladders of Heaven; Sticks; Fireman's Competiton; Pechan & Willy; Candles; Dance Competition I & II; Nervous Rehearsal II; The Barber, the Bear & the Man Without Legs; The Endgame ReR ▲ TFCD [DDD]

Timisoara Banatul PO
Timisoara Memorial, w. Timisoara Banatul Phil Chorus, Timisoara Romanian Opera Orch, various cnds & soloists Electrecord ▲ ELC 109 [AAD]
J.–F. Antonioli (cnd)
Weber, C.M. von:Con 1 Cl, w. Frederic Rapin (cl) Timpani ▲ 1031
Weber, C.M. von:Con 2 Cl, w. Frederic Rapin (cl) Timpani ▲ 1031

Timisoara Banatul PO (cont.)
N. Boboc (cnd)
Dragoiu, S.:Rustic Divert Electrecord ▲ ELCD 109 [AAD]
R. Georgescu (cnd)
Constantinescu, P.:Outlaw Ballad, w. A. Gutu (vc) *(rec 1983)* Olympia ▲ OCD 415 [AAD]
Enescu, G.:Suite châtelaine Marco Polo ▲ 8.223145
Enescu, G.:Voix de la nature Marco Polo ▲ 8.223145
Niculescu, S.:Sym 2 Olympia ▲ OCD 416 [AAD]

Timisoara PO
J.–F. Antonioli (cnd)
Honegger, A.:Amphion, w. Olivier Lallouette (bar—Apollon), Laurent Manzoni (bar—Amphion), Iona Bentoiu (sgr—muse), Theodora Ciucur (sgr—muse), Lucia Kriska (sgr—muse), Adriana Mestes (sgr—muse), Timisoara Banatul Phil Chorus, Timisoara Children's Chorus *(rec Salle Ion Vidu, Timisoara, Romania, Oct 28 & Nov 1, 1995)* Timpani ▲ 1035 [DDD]
Honegger, A.:L'Impératrice aux rochers *(rec Salle Ion Vidu, Timisoara, Romania, Oct 28 & Nov 1, 1995)* Timpani ▲ 1035 [DDD]
R. Georgescu (cnd)
Landowski, M.:Adagio Cantabile, w. Steliana Calos (sop), Pompei Harasteanu (bass), Dominique de Williencourt (vc), Jacques Taddei (org), Timisoara Chorus *(rec Mar. 16–18, 1993)* Chamade ▲ 5611 [DDD]
Landowski, M.:Leçons de Ténèbres, w. Steliana Calos (sop), Pompei Harasteanu (bass), Dominique de Williencourt (vc), Jacques Taddei (org), Timisoara Chorus *(rec Mar. 16–18, 1993)* Chamade ▲ 5611 [DDD]
Vieru, A.:Narration II, w. D. Kientzy (sax) Olympia ("Explorer" series) ▲ OCD 410 [AAD]

Timisoara Romanian Opera Orch
Timisoara Memorial, w. Timisoara Banatul PO, Timisoara Banatul Phil Chorus, various cnds & soloists Electrecord ▲ ELC 109 [AAD]

Timporg Trio [Markus Kühnis (org), Wolfgang Sieber (org), Christoph Kobelt (perc)]
Transcriptions for Organ 4–Hands & Percussion Koch Schwann ▲ SCH 315019 [DDD]

Tinturin Duo [Peter Tinturin (gtr), Noëlle Compinsky Tinturin (pno)]
Romancero Gitano:The Tinturin Duo Cambria ▲ CD 1099 [DAD]

Tîrgu Mures Philharmonic CO
Boldizsár, C.:Songs of Bravery *(rec 1976)* Electrecord ▲ ELCD 102 [AAD]
G. Dudea (cnd)
Terényi, E.:Baroque Rhap, w. P. Szeles (vc) Electrecord ▲ ELCD 124 [AAD]

Tivoli SO
M. Schønwandt (cnd)
Gade, N.W.:Elverskud, w. Susanne Elmark (sop–Elf–King's Daughter), Kirsten Dolberg (cta–Mother), Guido Paëvatalu (bar–Oluf), Tivoli Concert Choir *(rec Tivoli Concert Hall, Apr 29–30, May 4, 1996)* Marco Polo/Dacapo ▲ 8.224051 [DDD]
Gade, N.W.:Frühlings Fant, w. Anne Margrethe Dahl (sop), Kirsten Dolberg (cta), Gert Hennig–Jensen (ten), Sten Byriel (bass), Elisabeth Westenholz (pno) *(rec Tivoli Concert Hall, Apr 29–30, May 4, 1996)* Marco Polo/Dacapo ▲ 8.224051 [DDD]
R. Strauss (cnd)
Strauss, R.:Der Rosenkavalier (suite) *(rec 1926)* Koch Legacy ▲ 3–7132–2 H1

Toimii Ensemble
Lindberg, M.:Action–situation–signification Finlandia ▲ FIN 372 [AAD]

Tokyo Concert Orch
Shigenobu Yamaoka (cnd)
Plays His Favorite Encores, w. Jean–Pierre Rampal (fl) CBS ▲ MK 34559

Tokyo Flute Ensemble
M. Inoue (cnd)
Yoshimatsu, T.:Music of, w. New Japan PO—Threnody to Toki; Chikap; The Age of Birds; Digital Bird Suite; 4 Pieces in Bird Shape; Random Bird Vars; Sym No. 2 Camerata 2–▲ 30CM 178/9

Tokyo Imperial PO
W. Strickland (cnd)
Fine, V.:Alcestis CRI ▲ CD 692 [ADD]

Tokyo Metropolitan SO
Fascinating Orchestral Pieces Denon ▲ CO 8009 [DDD]
J. Fournet (cnd)
Berlioz, H.:Sym fantastique Denon/PCM Digital ▲ DEN 8097 [DDD]
Saint–Saëns, C.:Danse macabre Denon/PCM Digital ▲ DEN 8097 [DDD]
Y. Horigome (cnd)
Takemitsu, T.:Music of, w. K. Tsuruta (biwa), K. Yokoyama (shakuhachi)—Far Calls, Coming, Far! (1980); Requiem for Strings (1957); Nov. Steps (1967); Visions (1989) Denon/PCM Digital ▲ DEN 79441 [DDD]
M. Ishii (cnd)
Ishii, M.:Afro–Con Denon/PCM Digital ▲ DEN 76812 [DDD]
Ishii, M.:Fushi Denon/PCM Digital ▲ DEN 76812 [DDD]
Ishii, M.:Lost Sounds III Denon/PCM Digital ▲ DEN 76812 [DDD]
Ishii, M.:Polaritäten Denon/PCM Digital ▲ DEN 76812 [DDD]
H. Ishimaru (cnd)
Tchaikovsky, P.:Marche slave Denon/PCM Digital ▲ DEN 8085 [DDD]
H. Iwaki (cnd)
Matsumura, T.:Con 2 Pno, w. Minoru Nojima (pno) *(rec Jan 30, 1992)* Camerata ▲ 30 CM 261 [DDD]
Matsumura, T.:Prelude *(rec Jan 30, 1992)* Camerata ▲ 30 CM 261 [DDD]
Matsumura, T.:Sym *(rec Jan 30, 1992)* Camerata ▲ 30 CM 261 [DDD]
Mayuzumi, T.:Nirvana Sym, w. Tokyo Phil Chorus Denon ▲ DEN 78839
Masur (cnd)
Miki, M.:Music of, w. K. Mitsuhashi (shakuhachi), N. Yoshimura (koto), Y. Tanaka (shamisen), Tokyo PO, Leipzig Gewandhaus Orch—Jo No Kyoju; Prelude for Shakuhachi, Koto & Strings; Ha No Kyoku; Con. for Koto & Orch.; Kyu no Kyoku; Sym. for Two Worlds Camerata 2–▲ 30CM 223/24
Numajiri, Wakasugi (cnd)
Takemitsu, T.:Gémeaux, w. Masashi Honma (ob), Christian Lindberg (trbn) *(rec Tokyo Metropolitan Art Space, July 25–29, 1994)* Denon ▲ CO 78944 [DDD]
T. Otaka (cnd)
Hachimura, Y.:The Logic of Distraction, w. Yasuo Watanabe (pno) *(rec live, Tokyo Bunka–Kaikan, Large Hall, May 24, 1980)* Camerata ▲ 32CM–292 [AAD]
Mori, K.:Groom *(rec live, Tokyo Bunka–Kaikan, Large Hall, May 24, 1980)* Camerata ▲ 32CM–292 [AAD]
Noda, T.:Mutation, w. Katsuya Yokoyama (shak), Toshi Fujita (koto), Mikiko Haga (koto), Chieko Mori (koto) *(rec live, Tokyo Bunka–Kaikan, Large Hall, May 24, 1980)* Camerata ▲ 32CM–292 [AAD]
K. Sato (cnd)
Ikebe, S.–I.:Dimorphism, w. Naomi Matsui (org) Camerata ▲ 30CM 374 [DDD]
Ikebe, S.–I.:Sym 3 Camerata ▲ 30CM 374 [DDD]
H. Wakasugi (cnd)
Strauss, R.:Divert Denon ▲ CO 76330 [DDD]
Strauss, R.:Josephs–Legende Denon ▲ CO 2050 [DDD]
Strauss, R.:Romanze Vc, w. M. Fujiwara (vc) Denon/PCM Digital ▲ DEN 75860 [DDD]
Strauss, R.:Schlagobers Denon ▲ CO 73414 [DDD]
Strauss, R.:Sym in f Denon/PCM Digital ▲ DEN 75860 [DDD]
Strauss, R.:Tanzsuite Denon ▲ CO 76330 [DDD]
Takemitsu, T.:Dream/Window *(rec Tokyo Metropolitan Art Space, July 25–29, 1994)* Denon ▲ CO 78944 [DDD]
Takemitsu, T.:Spirit Garden *(rec Tokyo Metropolitan Art Space, July 25–29, 1994)* Denon ▲ CO 78944 [DDD]
Wagner, R.:Sym in C *(rec July 13–15, 1992)* Denon ▲ CO 75259 [DDD]
Wagner, R.:Sym in E *(rec July 13–15, 1992)* Denon ▲ CO 75259 [DDD]

▲ = CD ♦ = Enhanced CD Δ = MD ■ = Cassette Tape ☐ = DCC

Tokyo Metropolitan SO (cont.)
K. Yamada (cnd)
Fauré, G.:Requiem, w. K. Ito (sop), Ohga, Tokyo Metropolitan Sym Chorus [L] *(rec 1973)* CBS ▲ MK 44738 [ADD]

Tokyo PO
F. Haider (cnd)
The Anniversary Concert, w. Gruberova, Edita (sop) Nightingale Classics ▲ NIG CD 90560
Strauss, R.:Ein Heldenleben Nightingale Classics ▲ NIG 161864
Masur (cnd)
Miki, M.:Music of, w. K. Mitsuhashi (shakuhachi), N. Yoshimura (koto), Y. Tanaka (shamisen), Tokyo Metropolitan SO, Leipzig Gewandhaus Orch—Jo No Kyoju; Prelude for Shakuhachi, Koto & Strings; Ha No Kyoku; Con. for Koto & Orch.; Kyu no Kyoku; Sym. for Two Worlds Camerata 2-▲ 30CM 223/24
T. Otaka (cnd)
Fukushi, N.:Chromosphere, w. J. Arase (perc), M. Okada (perc), S. Sato (perc), H. Yamazaki (perc), S. Yoshihara (perc) *(rec live Tokyo Bunka-Kaikan, Large Hall, May 30, 1981)* Camerata ▲ 32CM 293 [AAD]
Hayashi, H.:The Second Sym, "Canciones", w. Yuji Takahashi (pno) Camerata ▲ 32CM 297
Ichiyanagi, T.:Con Vn, w. Paul Zukofsky (vn) Camerata ▲ 32CM 295
Irino, Y.:Symphonia Camerata ▲ 32CM 291
Kawanami, T.:Ondine, w. Kiyomi Toyoda (sop) Camerata ▲ 32CM 295
Kondo, J.:In the Woods *(rec Tokyo, June 2, 1990)* Camerata ▲ 32CM 190
Mahler, G.:Sym 5—Adagietto movt Camerata ("After Hours Classics" series) ▲ 20 CM 423 [DDD]
Otaka, A.:Image *(rec live Tokyo Bunka-Kaikan, Large Hall, May 30, 1981)* Camerata ▲ 32CM 293 [AAD]
Sato, S.:Sinf III Camerata ▲ 32CM 291
Suzuki, T.:Hymnos, w. Tokyo Phil Chorus *(rec Tokyo, June 2, 1990)* Camerata ▲ 32CM 190
Tada, E.:Sym 2 Pno, (The Min-On Contemporary Music Festival '85"), w. Y. Takahashi (pno) Camerata ▲ 32CM 297
Yoshimatsu, T.:Kamui-Chikap Sym *(rec Tokyo, June 2, 1990)* Camerata ▲ 32CM 190
Yuasa, J.:Scenes from Basho *(rec live Tokyo Bunka-Kaikan, Large Hall, May 30, 1981)* Camerata ▲ 32CM 293 [AAD]
R. Paternostro (cnd)
Verdi, G.:La traviata, w. L. Aliberti (sop), M. Dvorsky (ten), R. Bruson (bar), Tokyo Phil Chorus [I] *(rec live, Suntory Hall, Tokyo)* Capriccio 2-▲ 10274/75 [DDD]
W. Strickland (cnd)
Ives, C.:Holidays, w. Iceland SO, Finnish RSO, Göteborg SO, Iceland Sym Chorus [E] CRI ■ ACS 6014
Ives, C.:Washington's Birthday CRI ■ C 163
Tokyo String Quartet
Barber, S.:Qt Strs RCA Red Seal ▲ 09026-61387-2
Beethoven, L. van:Qts Strs (comp)—Op. 18, Nos. 1-6 RCA Red Seal 3-▲ 09026-61284-2
Beethoven, L. van:Qts Strs (comp) RCA Red Seal 9-▲ 09026-61621-2
Beethoven, L. van:Qts Strs (comp)—Nos. 7-11, Opp. 59/1-3, 74 & 95 RCA Red Seal 3-▲ 60462-2-RC [DDD]
Beethoven, L. van:Qts Strs (comp)—Nos. 12-16, Opp. 127, 130-132 & 135 RCA Red Seal 3-▲ 09026-60975-2 [DDD]
Beethoven, L. van:Qnt Strs, Op. 29, w. P. Zukerman (pno) RCA Red Seal 3-▲ 09026-61284-2
Beethoven, L. van:Son 9 Pno [arr in F for Strings] RCA Red Seal 3-▲ 09026-61284-2
Boccherini, L.:Qnts Gtr & Strs, w. K. Yamashita (gtr)—in D, G.448 & in G, G.450 RCA Red Seal ▲ 60421-2-RC [DDD]
Brahms, J.:Qnt Cl, w. Richard Stoltzman (cl) RCA Red Seal ▲ 09026-68049-2
Castelnuovo-Tedesco, M.:Qnt Gtr & Str, w. K. Yamashita (gtr) RCA Red Seal ▲ 60421-2-RC [DDD]
Debussy, C.:Qt Strs RCA Red Seal ▲ 09026-62552-2
Dvořák, A.:Qt 12 Strs, "America" CBS ▲ MK 44920 [DDD]
Dvořák, A.:Qnt Pno, Op. 81, w. H. Nakamura (pno) CBS ▲ MK 44920 [DDD]
Mozart, W.A.:Qts Fl RCA Red Seal ▲ 09026-60442-2 ■ 09026-60442-4
Mozart, W.A.:Qnt Strs, K.515, w. P. Zukerman (vn) RCA Red Seal ▲ 09026-60940-2
Ravel, M.:Intro & Allegro, w. Hedi Lehwalder (hp), Richard Stoltzman (cl), James Galway (fl) RCA Red Seal ▲ 09026-62552-2
Ravel, M.:Intro & Allegro, w. B. Allen (hp), Wilson (fl), D. Shifrin (cl) EMI Classics ▲ CDC 47520
Schubert, Franz:Qt 4 Strs RCA Red Seal ▲ 7990-2-RC [DDD]
Schubert, Franz:Qt 9 Strs RCA Red Seal ▲ 7750-2-RC [DDD]
Schubert, Franz:Qt 13 Strs RCA Red Seal ▲ 7750-2-RC [DDD]
Schubert, Franz:Qt 14 Strs RCA Red Seal ▲ 7990-2-RC [DDD]
Schubert, Franz:Qt 15 Strs RCA Red Seal ▲ 60199-2-RC [DDD]
Schumann, R.:Qnt Pno, w. A. de Larrocha (pno) RCA Red Seal ▲ 09026-61279-2
Weber, C.M. von:Qnt Cl, w. Richard Stoltzman (cl) RCA Red Seal ▲ 09026-68049-2
Tokyo String Quartet [Koichiro Harada (vn), Kikuei Ikeda (vn), Kazuhide Isomura (va), Sadao Harada (vc)]
Debussy, C.:Qt Strs *(rec New York City, Aug 2-4, 1977)* Sony Classical ("Essential Classics" series) ▲ SBK 62413 [ADD] ■ SBT 62413
Ravel, M.:Qt Strs *(rec New York City, Aug 2-4, 1977)* Sony Classical ("Essential Classics" series) ▲ SBK 62413 [ADD] ■ SBT 62413
Tokyo String Quartet [Peter Oundjian (vn), Kikuei Ikeda (vn), Kazuhide Isomura (va), Sadao Harada (vc)]
Bartók, B.:Qt Strs (comp) *(rec Richardson Auditorium, Princeton University, May 10-14 & 16-19, 1993)* RCA Red Seal 3-▲ 09026-68286-2 [DDD]
Brahms, J.:Qt 1 Strs Allegretto ▲ ACD 8200
Brahms, J.:Qt 3 Strs Allegretto ▲ ACD 8200
Britten, B.:Qt 2 Strs RCA Red Seal ▲ 09026-61387-2
Janácek, L.:Qt 1 Strs *(rec Richardson Auditorium, Princeton University, Sept 16 & 18, 1994)* RCA Red Seal 3-▲ 09026-68286-2 [DDD]
Janácek, L.:Qt 2 Strs *(rec Richardson Auditorium, Princeton University, Nov 21 & 22, 1994)* RCA Red Seal 3-▲ 09026-68286-2 [DDD]
Takemitsu, T.:Qt 1 Strs RCA Red Seal ▲ 09026-61387-2
Tokyo String Quartet members
Mozart, W.A.:Qts Fl, w. P. Robison (cl) Vanguard Classics ▲ OVC 4001 [ADD]
Mozart, W.A.:Qt Ob, K.370, w. J. Galway (fl) RCA Red Seal ▲ 09026-60442-2 ■ 09026-60442-4
Tokyo String Quintet
Mozart, W.A.:Qnt Cl, K.581, w. R. Stoltzman (cl) RCA Red Seal ▲ 60723-2 [DDD] ■ 60723-4 (CrO2)
Tokyo SO
K. Akiyama (cnd)
Mamiya, M.:Con III Pno, w. I. Tateno (pno) *(rec live Tokyo Metropolitan Theater, Large Hall, June 23, 1993)* Camerata ▲ 32CM 319 [DDD]
Matsunaga, M.:Constellations, w. Kayako Matsunaga (pno) Vienna Modern Masters ▲ VMM 3034 [DDD]
Nishimura, A.:Mantra of the Light, w. Tokyo Phil Chorus *(rec live Tokyo Metropolitan Theater, Large Hall, June 23, 1993)* Camerata ▲ 32CM 319 [DDD]
Tanaka, K.:Initium *(rec live, Tokyo Metropolitan Theater, Large Hall, June 23, 1993)* Camerata ▲ 32CM 319 [DDD]
R. Paternostro (cnd)
Strauss, R.:4 Last Songs, w. G. Jones (sop) [G] *(rec live, Suntory Hall, Tokyo, 5/29/91)* Koch Schwann ▲ CD 314081 [DDD]
Strauss, R.:Songs, w. G. Jones (sop)—Opp. 10/1, 27/1, 27/2, 27/4, 41/1, 48/1, 56/5, 56/6 [G] *(rec live, Suntory Hall, Tokyo, 5/29/91)* Koch Schwann ▲ CD 314081 [DDD]
Verdi, G.:Simon Boccanegra, w. M. Nicolesco (sop), G. Sabbatini (ten), R. Bruson (bar), S. Rinaldi-Miliani (bar), R. Scandiuzzi (bass), N. de Angelis (bass), Nikikai Chorus *(rec live 2/90)* Capriccio 2-▲ 60018-2 [DDD]

Tölz SO
E. Jochum (cnd)
Bach, J.S.:Christmas Oratorio, w. E. Ameling (sop), B. Fassbaender (mez), H. Laubenthal (ten), H. Prey (bar), Bavarian Radio Boys' Chorus—highlights Philips ("Silver Line" series) ▲ 422252-2 [ADD]
Tone Road Ramblers [John Fonville (fl), Eric Mandat (cl), Ray Sasaki (tpt), Morgan Powell (trbn), Jim Staley (trbn), Steven Butters (perc)]
Powell, Morgan:Outlaws *(rec Urbana, IL, Oct 5, 1995)* New World ▲ 80499-2
Powell, Morgan:THO *(rec live 1992)* Opus One ▲ CD 164
Tonhalle Orch
A. Mounk (cnd)
Duggan, M.:Babel Grammont ▲ CTSP 49-2
Tonkünstler Orch
T.C. David (cnd)
David, T.C.:Triple Con, w. Verdehr Trio Crystal ▲ CD 745
Top Brass
Angels Singing, Nowells Ringing, w. [cnd:Dennis Shrock], Canterbury Choral Society, Troubadour Ringers *(rec Watchorn Hall, 1st Presbyterian Church, Oklahoma City, OK, Sept. 24-25)* Integra Classic ▲ IMCD 944 [DDD]
Toronto CO
A. Davis (cnd)
The Baroque Album, w. J. Baxtresser (fl), O. Harnoy (vc), J. Cowell (tpt) Mastersound ▲ MST 19 [DDD]
P. Robinson (cnd)
Haydn, J.:Con 1 Vc, w. Ofra Harnoy (vc) *(rec Massey Hall, Toronto, Canada, 1983)* RCA Gold Seal ▲ 09026-60722-2 [DDD]
Haydn, J.:Con 2 Vc, w. Ofra Harnoy (vc) *(rec Massey Hall, Toronto, Canada, 1983)* RCA Gold Seal ▲ 09026-60722-2 [DDD]
Vivaldi, A.:Cons Vc, w. O. Harnoy (vc)—5 concerti—RV.399, 410, 405, 423, 538 RCA Red Seal ▲ 7774-2-RC [DDD] ■ 7774-4-RC (CrO2)
Vivaldi, A.:Cons Vc, w. O. Harnoy (vc)—in D, RV.404; in d, RV.407; in F, RV.411; in g, RV.417; in a, RV.420 RCA Red Seal ▲ 09026-61578-2; ■ 09026-61578-4
Vivaldi, A.:Cons Vc, w. O. Harnoy (vc)—7 concerti—RV.402, 403, 406, 412, 414, 422, 424 RCA Red Seal ▲ 60155-2-RC [DDD] ■ 60155-4-RC (CrO2) □ 09026-60155-5
Vivaldi, A.:Con Vc, RV.409, w. O. Harnoy (vc), J. McKay (bn) RCA Red Seal ▲ 7774-2-RC [DDD] ■ 7774-4-RC (CrO2)
Vivaldi, A.:Con Vn Vc, RV.544, w. O. Harnoy (vc) RCA Red Seal ▲ 09026-61578-2; ■ 09026-61578-4
Vivaldi, A.:Con Vn Vc, RV.547, w. Igor Oistrakh (vn), Ofra Harnoy (vc), *(Toronto, Feb 1992)* RCA Victor Red Seal ▲ 09026-68228-2 [DDD]
R. Stamp (cnd)
Vivaldi, A.:Cons Vc, w. Ofra Harnoy (vc)—Cons RV.408, 413, 416, 418 & 419, *(Toronto, Feb 1994)* RCA Victor Red Seal ▲ 09026-68228-2 [DDD]
Toronto Chamber Winds
C. Wealt (cnd)
Mozart, W.A.:Serenade Ww, K.375 CBC ("SM 5000" series) ▲ SMCD 5053 [DDD]
Mozart, W.A.:Serenade Ww, K.388 CBC ("SM 5000" series) ▲ SMCD 5053 [DDD]
Webber (cnd)
Mozart, W.A.:Serenade Ww, K.361 Crystal ■ C 646
Toronto Festival Pops Orch
B. Brott (cnd)
Addinsell, R.:Warsaw Con, w. V. Tyron (pno) Pro Arte ▲ CDD 422 [DDD]
Hooray for Hollywood, w. V. Tyron (pno) Pro Arte ▲ CDD 422 [DDD]
Toronto Percussion Ensemble
Chan Ka Nin:Everlasting Voices, w. R. Landry (sop) Centrediscs ▲ CD 3288
Toronto Ragtime Ensemble
Gershwin, G.:Music of—The Real American Folk Song [Is a Rag]; Prelude No. 2; Someone to Watch Over Me; Liza; Looking for a Boy; Embraceable You; 3 Quarter Blues; Jazzbo Brown; Impromptu in 2 Keys/Promenade; Lullaby; Swanee; Rialto Ripples; Somebody Loves Me; Our Love Is Here to Stay; My Man's Gone Now; Fascinating Rhythm IMP ("Classics" series) ▲ IMP 6700632
Toronto Sinfonietta
C. St. Clair (cnd)
Bolcom, W.:A Spring Concertino, w. H. Sargous (ob) Crystal ▲ CD326 [DDD]
Singer, L.:Sensazione II, w. H. Sargous (ob) Crystal ▲ CD326 [DDD]
Toronto SO
Trumpet Concertos, w. John Cowell (tpt) IMP ("Classics" series) ▲ IMP 6700602
K. Ančerl (cnd)
Beethoven, L. van:Con 5 Pno, "Emperor", w. Glenn Gould (pno) Sony Classical ("Glen Gould Edition" series) ▲ SMK 52687
M. Bernardi (cnd)
Dohnányi, E. von:Vars on a Nursery Song, w. A. Ozolins (pno) CBC ("SM 5000" series) ▲ SMCD 5052 [DDD]
Litolff, H.C.:Con Symphonique 3, w. Arthur Ozolins (pno)—Scherzo CBC ("SM 5000" series) ▲ SMCD 5052 [DDD]
Rachmaninoff, S.:Con 1 Pno, w. Arthur Ozolins (pno) CBC ("SM 5000" series) ▲ SMCD 5052 [DDD]
Rachmaninoff, S.:Con 2 Pno, w. A. Ozolins (pno) CBC ("SM 5000" series) ▲ SMCD 5108 [DDD] ■ SMC 5108 (D)
Rachmaninoff, S.:Vocalise CBC ("SM 5000" series) ▲ SMCD 5108 [DDD] ■ SMC 5108 (D)
Strauss, R.:Burleske, w. A. Ozolins (pno) CBC ("SM 5000" series) ▲ SMCD 5128 [DDD]
Willan, H.:Con Pno, w. A. Ozolins (pno) CBC ("SM 5000" series) ▲ SMCD 5108 [DDD] ■ SMC 5108 (D)
A. David (cnd)
Holst, G.:The Planets EMI Classics ▲ CDD 64300 [DDD]
A. Davis (cnd)
Beethoven, L. van:Con 5 Pno, "Emperor", w. Anton Kuerti (pno) *(rec Massey Hall, Toronto, 1986)* CBC ("SM 5000" series) ▲ SMCD 5155 [DDD]
Beethoven, L. van:Fant Pno, Op. 80, "Choral Fant", w. Anton Kuerti (pno), Toronto Mendelssohn Choir *(rec Massey Hall, Toronto, 1986)* CBC ("SM 5000" series) ▲ SMCD 5155 [DDD]
Beethoven, L. van:König Stephen (ov) *(rec Massey Hall, Toronto, 1986)* CBC ("SM 5000" series) ▲ SMCD 5155 [DDD]
Bizet, G.:L'Arlésienne (suites)—Suites 1 & 2 CBS ▲ MK 45649 [DDD]
Bizet, G.:L'Arlésienne (suites)—Suite No. 1 & Farandole from Suite No. 2 *(rec 1980)* Odyssey ▲ MBK 46275 [AAD] ■ YT 46275
Bloch, E.:Suite hébraïque, w. R. Golani (va) CBC ("SM 5000" series) ▲ SMCD 5087 [DDD] ■ 4-5087 (D)
Borodin, A.:Prince Igor (sels)—Ov; Polovtsian Dances *(rec Toronto, Nov 25, 1975)* Sony Classical ("Essential Classics" series) 2-▲ SB2K 62406 [ADD]
Borodin, A.:Prince Igor (Polovtsian dances) *(rec 1977)* Odyssey ▲ MBK 46275 [AAD] ■ YT 46275
Borodin, A.:Syms (comp) *(rec Toronto, Nov 25, 1975)* Sony Classical ("Essential Classics" series) 2-▲ SB2K 62406 [ADD]
Britten, B.:Lachrymae, w. R. Golani (va) CBC ("SM 5000" series) ▲ SMCD 5087 [DDD] ■ 4-5087 (D)
Colgrass, M.:Chaconne Va, w. R. Golani (va) CBC ("SM 5000" series) ▲ SMCD 5087 [DDD] ■ 4-5087 (D)
Handel, G.F.:Messiah, w. Kathleen Battle (sop), Florence Quivar (mez), John Aler (ten), Samuel Ramey (bass), Mendelssohn Club Chorus Philadelphia [E] EMI Classics ▲ CDC 49407 [DDD]; ■ 4DS 49407 (D)
Handel, G.F.:Messiah, w. Kathleen Battle (sop), Florence Quivar (mez), John Aler (ten), Samuel Ramey (bass), Mendelssohn Club Chorus Philadelphia [E] EMI Classics 2-▲ CDCB 49027 [DDD]; ■ 4D2S 49027 (D)

Toronto SO (cont.)
A. Davis (cnd) (cont.)
Hindemith, P.:Trauermusik, w. R. Golani (va)
CBC ("SM 5000" series) ▲ SMCD 5087 [DDD] ■ 4-5087 (D)
Janácek, L.:Taras Bulba *(rec Toronto, Nov 11, 1977)*
Sony Classical ("Essential Classics" series) ▲ SBK 62404 ■ SBT 62404
Schafer, R.M.:Con Hp, w. J. Loman (hp) CBC ("SM 5000" series) ▲ SMCD 5114 [DDD]
Strauss, R.:4 Last Songs, w. E. Martón (sop) [G] CBS ▲ MDK 44910 [DDD]
Strauss, R.:Ein Heldenleben CBC ("SM 5000" series) ▲ SMCD 5036 [DDD] ■ SMC 5036 (D)
Strauss, R.:Salome (final scene), w. E. Martón (sop) [G] CBS ▲ MDK 45650 [DDD]
Strauss, R.:Songs, w. Ben Heppner (ten)—Ewig einsam; Wenn du einst die Gauen [both from Guntram]; Love Scene [from Feuersnot]; Act II scene change; Falke, Falke, du wiedergefundener [both from Die Frau ohne Schatten]; No. 10b, Träumerei am Kamin; No. 10d, Fröhlicher Beschluss [both from Intermezzo]; Orch intro. to Act III; In Syriens Glut... [both from Die Liebe der Danae]; Was erblicke ich? [from Daphne]; Potpourri [from Die schweigsame Frau]; Di rigori armato il seno [from Der Rosenkavalier] *(rec Roy Thomson Hall, Toronto, Nov. 16, 18 & 20, 1994)*
CBC ▲ MVV 5142 [DDD]
Symphonic Spectaculars CBC Records ("SM 5000" series) ▲ SMCD 5068 [DDD] ■ SMC 5068 (D)
Tchaikovsky, P.:The Nutcracker (sels)—Suites 1 & 2 Odyssey ■ YT 44509
Tchaikovsky, P.:Nutcracker Suite *(rec 1978)* Odyssey ▲ MBK 46275 [AAD] ■ YT 46275
F.–P. Decker (cnd)
Beethoven, L. van:Con 5 Pno, "Emperor", w. W. Kempff (pno) *(rec Nov. 13, 1966)*
Music & Arts ▲ CD 768 [AAD]
V. Feldbrill (cnd)
Ridout, G.:Orch Music, w. Steven Dann (va)—Ballade No. 1 for Violin & String Orchestra; Cantiones Mysticae No. 1; Music for a Young Prince; No Mean City—Scenes from Childhood; La Prima Ballerina Suite No. 1 CBC ▲ CMCCD 3890 [DDD]
V. Golschmann (cnd)
Strauss, R.:Burleske, w. Glenn Gould (pno) Sony Classical ("Glenn Gould Edition" series) ▲ SMK 52687
G. Herbig (cnd)
Beethoven, L. van:Romances Vn, w. J. Israelievitch (vn) *(rec Sept. 21 & 22, 1990)*
Analekta ▲ AN 28201
Beethoven, L. van:Sym 3, "Eroica", w. J. Israelievitch (vn) *(rec Sept. 21 & 22, 1990)*
Analekta ▲ AN 28201
Schafer, R.M.:The Darkly Splendid Earth, w. J. Israelievitch (vn)
CBC ("SM 5000" series) ▲ SMCD 5114 [DDD]
E. MacMillan (cnd)
Bach, J.S.:Con 1 Hpd, w. G. Gould (pno) CBC ("Perspective" series) ▲ PSCD 2005 (m) [ADD]
Holst, G.:The Planets *(rec 1942)* Analekta ▲ AN 2 7804
Macmillan, E.:England *(rec Jan. 21, 1941)* Analekta ▲ AN 2 7804
Rachmaninoff, S.:Con 3 Pno, w. W. Kapell (pno) *(rec live, Apr. 13, 1948)*
VAI Audio ▲ VAIA/IPA 1027 [ADD]
S. Ozawa (cnd)
Berlioz, H.:Sym fantastique Odyssey ■ YT 31923
Toronto SO members
Adeste Fideles, w. Louis Quilico (bar), Gino Quilico (bar), Judy Loman (hp), Toronto SO members [cnd:Jean Ashworth Bartle], Toronto Children's Chorus
CBC Records ("SM 5000" series) ▲ SMCD 5119 [DDD]
Torres Quartet
Guitar Quartet *(rec 8/90)* Gallo ▲ CD 668 [AAD]
Spanish Guitar Music Vox ■ CT 4494
Toscana Accademia Strumentale
H. Handt (cnd)
Menichetti, D.:L'Epifania del Signore, w. K. Gamberucci (sop), F. Facini (bass), A. Palombi (sgr), A. Della Santa (sgr), F. Esposito (sgr), Polifonica Lucchese Bongiovanni ▲ GB 5033 [DDD]
Toscana Regional Orch
P. Bellugi (cnd)
Mozart, W.A.:Con 5 Vn, w. R. Ricci (vn) One-Eleven ▲ URS 93020 [ADD]
D. Renzetti (cnd)
Cherubini, L.:Ovs—Medea; Ifigenia in Aulide; Le crescendo *(rec Firenze, Italy, May 14–18, 1987)*
Arts Music ▲ 47102-2 [DDD]
Cherubini, L.:Sinf in D *(rec Firenze, Italy, May 14–18, 1987)* Arts Music ▲ 47102-2 [DDD]
Toscanini SO
E. Romagna (cnd)
Lattuada, F.:Le Preziose ridicole, w. S. Valayre (sop—Madelon), A. Catarci (sop—Marotte), A. Cicogna (mez—Cathos), S. Tedesco (ten—La Grange), E. Di Cesare (ten—Mascarille), A. Veccia (bar—Croissy), R. Servile (bar—Jodelet), E. Fissore (bass—Gorgibus), G. Masini (cnd), Rossini Teatro Comunale Chorus [I] *(rec live, 1991)* Ermitage ▲ ERM 404 [DDD]
Toulon Musica Antiqua
C. Mendoze (cnd)
Demantius, C.:Dances—Intradas, Nos. 1, 4, 6, 11 & 12; Galliardas, Nos. 1, 6, 9 & 10; Dances, Nos. 1, 3, 5, 6, 8, 9 & 10; Polish Dances, Nos. 1, 3, 9 & 12; Nachtanz, Polnischer Tanz, No. 1 *(rec Oct 16–17, 1992)* Pierre Verany ▲ PV 793032 [DDD]
Toulouse Capitole Orch
M. Plasson (cnd)
Bizet, G.:Orchestral Music—L'Arlesienne:Suite No. 1; Carmen:Suite No. 1; Jeux d'enfants; Les quatre coins; Marche funèbre; Ov. in A EMI Classics ▲ CDC 54765
Bizet, G.:Les Pêcheurs de perles, w. B. Hendricks (sop), J. Aler (ten), G. Quilico (bar), Toulouse Capitole Chorus [F] EMI Classics 2-▲ CDCB 49837 [DDD]
Chausson, E.:Soir de fête EMI Classics ▲ CDM 64686
Chausson, E.:Sym in B♭ EMI Classics ▲ CDM 64686
Chausson, E.:Viviane EMI Classics ▲ CDM 64686
Dukas, P.:L'Apprenti sorcier EMI Classics ▲ CDC 55385
Duparc, H.:Aux étoiles EMI Classics ▲ CDC 55385
Duparc, H.:Lénore EMI Classics ▲ CDC 55385
Franck, C.:Le Chasseur maudit EMI Classics ▲ CDC 55385
Franck, C.:Symphonic Vars, w. J. Collard (pno)
EMI Classics ("Studio DDD" series) ▲ CDD 63889 [DDD]
Gounod, C.:Faust, w. C. Studer (sop), R. Leech (ten), T. Hampson (bar), J. Van Dam (b-bar), Toulouse Capitole Chorus, *(highlights from the above)* EMI Classics ▲ CDC 54358 [DDD]
Gounod, C.:Faust, w. C. Studer (sop), R. Leech (ten), T. Hampson (bar), J. Van Dam (b-bar), Toulouse Capitole Chorus EMI Classics 3-▲ CDCC 54228 [DDD]
Gounod, C.:Mors et vita, w. B. Hendricks (sop), N. Denize (mez), J. Aler (ten), J. Van Dam (b-bar), Orféon Donostiarra [F] *(rec 1/92)* EMI Classics 2-▲ CDCB 54459
Gounod, C.:Roméo et Juliette, w. C. Malfitano (sop), A. Kraus (ten), L. Quilico (bar), J. Van Dam (b-bar), G. Bacquier (bar), Toulouse Capitole Chorus [F] EMI Classics 3-▲ CDCC 47365
Honegger, A.:Horace Victorieux Deutsche Grammophon ▲ 435438-2
Honegger, A.:Mermoz Deutsche Grammophon ▲ 435438-2
Honegger, A.:Pacific 231 Deutsche Grammophon ▲ 435438-2
Honegger, A.:Pacific 231 EMI Classics ▲ CDM 64275
Honegger, A.:Pastorale d'été Deutsche Grammophon ▲ 435438-2
Honegger, A.:Rugby Deutsche Grammophon ▲ 435438-2
Honegger, A.:Syms (comp)—Syms. 4 & 5 EMI Classics ▲ CDM 64275
Honegger, A.:Syms (comp)—Syms. 1–3 EMI Classics ▲ CDM 64274
Honegger, A.:La Tempête (prelude) Deutsche Grammophon ▲ 435438-2
Jaubert, M.:Film Music, w. M. Stewart (vn)—Le quai des brumes; Le jour se lève *(rec July 2–5, 1992)*
EMI Classics ▲ CDC 54764-2 [DDD]
Kosma, J.:Film Music, w. M. Stewart (vn)—Les portes de la nuit; Les enfants du paradis:Baptiste *(rec July 2–5, 1992)* EMI Classics ▲ CDC 54764-2 [DDD]
Lazzari, S.:Effet de nuit EMI Classics ▲ CDC 55385

Toulouse Capitole Orch (cont.)
M. Plasson (cnd) (cont.)
Massenet, J.:Don Quichotte, w. T. Berganza (mez—La Belle Dulcinée), A. Fondary (bar—Sancho Pana), J. Van Dam (b-bar—Don Quichotte), Toulouse Capitole Chorus EMI Classics ▲ CDCB 54767
Massenet, J.:Hérodiade, w. Cheryl Studer (sop—Salomé), Nadine Denize (mez—Hérodiade), Ben Heppner (ten—Jean), José Van Dam (b-bar—Phanuel), Thomas Hampson (bass—Hérode), Toulouse Capitole Chorus EMI Classics 3-▲ CDCC 55378
Milhaud, D.:Suite provençale Deutsche Grammophon ▲ 435437-2 [DDD]
Milhaud, D.:Sym 1 Deutsche Grammophon ▲ 435437-2 [DDD]
Milhaud, D.:Sym 2 Deutsche Grammophon ▲ 435437-2 [DDD]
Orff, C.:Carmina burana, w. Natalie Dessay (sop), Gérard Lesne (ct), Thomas Hampson (bar), Orféon Donostiarra, Midi-Pyrénées Children's Choir *(rec Halle-aux-Grains, Toulouse, Dec. 2, 4 & 6, 1994)*
EMI Classics ▲ CDC 55392 [DDD]
Prokofiev, S.:Peter & the Wolf, w. L. Wilson (nar) EMI Classics 2-▲ CDC 54465
Ropartz, G.:Sym 3, w. F. Pollet (sop), N. Stutzmann (cta), T. Dran (ten), F. Vassar (b-bar), Orféon Donostiarra EMI Classics ▲ CDM 64689-2
Saint-Saëns, C.:Carnival of the Animals, w. T. Barto (pno), M. Rudy (pno) EMI Classics 2-▲ CDC 54465
Saint-Saëns, C.:Cons Pno (comp), w. P. Entremont (pno) Odyssey 2-▲ MB2K 45624
Saint-Saëns, C.:Danse macabre EMI Classics ▲ CDC 55385
Toulouse CO
Musical Moments in the Garden, w. Academy of St. Martin in the Fields, Bournemouth SO, English CO, Hollywood Bowl SO, Toulouse Orch, Philharmonia Orch, L. Auriacombe (cnd), T. Beecham (cnd), C. Davis (cnd), R. Hickox (cnd), N. Marriner (cnd), M. Plasson (cnd), M. Sargent (cnd
Angel ▲ CDM 65203 ■ EG 65203
G. Armand (cnd)
Albinoni, T.:Cons à 5 Strs, Op. 5—No. 5 in a *(rec Chapelle des Italiens, Toulouse, Apr 1976)*
EMI Classics ▲ CDK 65337 [ADD]
Corelli, A.:Concerti grossi, Op. 6, w. Georges Armand (vn), Jean-Patrice Brosse (hpd)—Nos. 1 in D & 8 in g, "Christmas Concerto" EMI Classics ("Baroque" series) ▲ CDK 65731
Handel, G.F.:Concerti grossi, Op. 6—No. 1 in G; No. 6 in g *(rec Chapelle des Italiens, Toulouse, Oct. 1978)* EMI Classics ▲ CDK 65335 [ADD]
Handel, G.F.:Cons (16) Org, w. Lionel Rogg (org)—No. 11 [Op. 7/5] *(rec Eglise Abbatiale de Saint Michel de Gaillac, May 1974)* EMI Classics ▲ CDK 65335 [ADD]
L. Auriacombe (cnd)
Albinoni, T.:Adagio Org, w. Xavier Darasse (org) *(rec Chapelle des Italiens, Toulouse, Jan 1968)*
EMI Classics ▲ CDK 65337 [ADD]
Handel, G.F.:Con Hp, w. L. Laskine (hp) *(rec Chapelle des Italiens, Toulouse, July 1963)*
EMI Classics ▲ CDK 65335 [ADD]
Handel, G.F.:Cons (3) Ob, w. Pierre Pierlot (ob)—in g *(rec Chapelle des Italiens, Toulouse, July 1963)*
EMI Classics ▲ CDK 65335 [ADD]
Telemann, G.P.:Con Tpt Strs in D, w. Albert Calvayrac (tpt) *(rec Chapelle des Italiens, Toulouse, June 1965)* EMI Classics ▲ CDK 65340 [ADD]
Vivaldi, A.:Cons Diverse Instrs—(5) for 4 Violins in b; for Mandolin in C; for 2 Mandolins in G; for 2 Trumpets in C; for Flautino in C *(rec 1967 & 1969)* EMI Classics 2-▲ CDZB 769143-2 [ADD]
Vivaldi, A.:Cons Fl, Op. 10, w. M. Sanvoisin (fl) *(rec ca. 1967–69)*
EMI Classics 2-▲ CDZB 769143-2 [ADD]
Vivaldi, A.:Cons Fl, Op. 10 EMI Classics 2-▲ CDZB 69143
Vivaldi, A.:Con for 2 Fls EMI Classics 2-▲ CDZB 69143
Vivaldi, A.:Con Mand, RV.425 EMI Classics 2-▲ CDZB 69143
Vivaldi, A.:Con for 2 Mands EMI Classics 2-▲ CDZB 69143
Vivaldi, A.:Con for 2 Tpts EMI Classics 2-▲ CDZB 69143
Vivaldi, A.:Cons Vn, Op. 8/1–4, "The Four Seasons" *(rec ca. 1967–69)*
EMI Classics 2-▲ CDZB 69143-2 [ADD]
A. Moglia (cnd)
Haydn, J.:Cons Hn, w. Andre Cazalet (hn) *(rec Sept 1994)* Pierre Verany ▲ PVY 730029
Haydn, J.:Con Tpt, w. Thierry Caens (tpt) *(rec Sept 1994)* Pierre Verany ▲ PVY 730029
Haydn, M.:Concertino Hn, Trbn & Va, w. Andre Cazalet (hn) *(rec Sept 1994)*
Pierre Verany ▲ PVY 730029
Toulouse Mandolin Ensemble
A Tour of Europe with 40 Mandolins ARB ▲ 1422
Toulouse National CO
A. Moglia (cnd)
Corelli, A.:Concerti grossi, Op. 6 Pierre Verany ▲ PVY 730049
Debussy, C.:Danses sacrée et profane, w. Susanna Mildonian (hp) *(rec Apr 1995)*
Pavane ▲ ADW 7337 [DDD]
Françaix, J.:Con 2 Hps, w. Catherine Michel (hp), Susanna Mildonian (hp) *(rec Apr 1995)*
Pavane ▲ ADW 7337 [DDD]
Glazunov, A.:Suite Strs, w. Alain Moglia (vn) Pierre Verany ▲ PVY 730069
Gossec, F.-J.:Symphonie concertante for 2 Hps, w. Catherine Michel (hp), Susanna Mildonian (hp) *(rec Apr 1995)* Pavane ▲ ADW 7337 [DDD]
Malecki, M.:Concertino dans un style ancien, w. Catherine Michel (hp), Susanna Mildonian (hp) *(rec Apr 1995)* Pavane ▲ ADW 7337 [DDD]
Mozart, L.:Con Hn, w. Thierry Caens (tpt), Alain Moglia (vn), Les Cuivres Francais
Pierre Verany ▲ PVY 730070
Mozart, L.:Serenade Tpt, w. Thierry Caens (tpt), Alain Moglia (vn), Les Cuivres Francais
Pierre Verany ▲ PVY 730070
Mozart, L.:Toy Sym Pierre Verany ▲ PVY 730057 [DDD]
Mozart, W.A.:German Dances—in B♭ for 2 Vns & bass inst Pierre Verany ▲ PVY 730057 [DDD]
Mozart, W.A.:Minuet Vns, K.65a Pierre Verany ▲ PVY 730057 [DDD]
Mozart, W.A.:Musikalischer Spass Pierre Verany ▲ PVY 730057 [DDD]
Ravel, M.:Intro & Allegro, w. Susanna Mildonian (hp) *(rec Apr 1995)* Pavane ▲ ADW 7337 [DDD]
Tchaikovsky, P.:Serenade Strs, w. Alain Moglia (vn) Pierre Verany ▲ PVY 730069
Vivaldi, A.:Con Gtr, RV.93, w. Hugues Navez (gtr) Pierre Verany ▲ PVY 730038
Vivaldi, A.:Con Mand, RV.425, w. Hugues Navez (gtr) Pierre Verany ▲ PVY 730038
Vivaldi, A.:Cons Vn, Op. 8/1–4, "The Four Seasons", w. Alain Moglia (vn)
Pierre Verany ▲ PVY 730038
E. Plasson (cnd)
Lemeland, A.:Con funèbre, w. M.-A. Nicolas (vn) Skarbo ▲ SKR 3922 [DDD]
Lemeland, A.:Con Vn, w. M.-A. Nicolas (vn) Skarbo ▲ SKR 3922 [DDD]
Lemeland, A.:Con 2 Vn, w. M.-A. Nicolas (vn) Skarbo ▲ SKR 3922 [DDD]
Toulouse Orch
Musical Moments in the Garden, w. Academy of St. Martin in the Fields, Bournemouth SO, English CO, Hollywood Bowl SO, Philharmonia Orch, Toulouse CO, L. Auriacombe (cnd), T. Beecham (cnd), C. Davis (cnd), R. Hickox (cnd), N. Marriner (cnd), M. Plasson (cnd), M. Sargent (cnd)
Angel ▲ CDM 65203 ■ EG 65203
Toulouse Saqueboutiers
Gabrieli, G.:Sacrae symphoniae, w. Yasuko Uyama-Bouvard (org), A Sei Voci Adda ▲ ADD 242292
Schütz, H.:Magnificat anima mea, w. Clément Janequin Ensemble [L]
Harmonia Mundi France ▲ HMC 901255
Schütz, H.:Music of, w. Clément Janequin Ensemble—Die mit Tränen säen (motet), SWV.42; Anima mea & Adjuro vos (from Symphonia sacrae, Op. 6), SWV.263 & 264; Quemadmodum desiderat & Meine Seele erhebet den Herren (from Kleine geistliche Konzerte, Op. 9 & Op. 10), SWV.336 & 344; Erbarm dich mein, o Herre Gott, SWV.447; Ach Herr, du Schöpfer aller Ding (madrigal), SWV.450 [G,L] Harmonia Mundi France ▲ HMC 901255
Schütz, H.:The 7 Words of Jesus Christ on the Cross, w. Clément Janequin Ensemble [G]
Harmonia Mundi France ▲ HMC 901255
B. Fabre-Garrus (cnd)
Helfer, C. d':Missa pro defunctis, w. A Sei Voci, Psallette de Lorraine Astrée ▲ E 8521

▲ = CD ♦ = Enhanced CD Δ = MD ■ = Cassette Tape □ = DCC

Toulouse Saqueboutiers (cont.)
P. Herreweghe (cnd)
Monteverdi, C.:Vespro della Beata Vergine, w. A. Mellon (sop), G. Laurens (mez), H. Crook (ten), D. Thomas (bass), Chapelle Royale Choir, Collegium Vocale [L] Harmonia Mundi France 2-▲ HMC 901247/48 [DDD]
Le Tourdion
Guide des Instruments de la Renaissance, w. La Fenice, Ricercar Consort Ricercar 3-▲ 95001
Guy Touvron Brass Ensemble
Bach, J.S.:Music of—12 works trans. for brass quintet *(rec Classic Studio Berlin 1987)* Classic Studio Berlin ▲ CS 11308 [DDD]
Music for Brass Quintet Classic Studio Berlin ▲ CS 12108 [DDD]
J.-P. Lore (cnd)
Berlioz, H.:Requiem, "Grande Messe des Morts", w. French Oratorio Orch, French Oratorio Choir *(rec Dec. 7-13, 1987)* Esoldun 2-▲ MOS 1001 [DDD]
Berlioz, H.:Resurrexit, w. French Oratorio Orch, French Oratorio Choir *(rec June 10, 1987)* Esoldun 2-▲ MOS 1001 [DDD]
V. Tchernushenko (cnd)
Le Sueur, J.-F.:Sacred Music, w. *(soloists unknown)*, St. Petersburg Cappella Orch, St. Petersburg Capella Chorus—March; Unxerunt Salomonem; Tu es Petrus *(rec La Chaise-Dieu Abbey, Aug 22 & 23, 1995)* Koch Schwann ▲ SCH 312082
Paisiello, G.:Sacred Music, w. *(soloists unknown)*, St. Petersburg Cappella Orch, St. Petersburg Cappella—Mass; Te Deum *(rec La Chaise-Dieu Abbey, Aug 22 & 23, 1995)* Koch Schwann ▲ SCH 312082
Towson State Univ Sym Band
D. Rothlisberger (cnd)
Myers, T.:Cadenza & Lament, w. Edward Palanker (cl) Vienna Modern Masters ▲ VMM 3034 [DDD]
La Traditora
D. Vellard (cnd)
Agricola, A.:Motets, w. Cantus Figuratus Ensemble—Da pacem Domine; O quam glorifica K617 ▲ 7056
Compère, L.:Motet-Chansons, Cantus Figuratus Ensemble—O vos Omnes K617 ▲ 7056
Compère, L.:Motets, Cantus Figuratus Ensemble—Crux triumphans K617 ▲ 7056
Josquin Desprez:Motets, Cantus Figuratus Ensemble—In pace in idipsum K617 ▲ 7056
Lasson, M.:Motets, Cantus Figuratus Ensemble—Congratulamini mihi; Virtute magna; Anthoni pater inclyte K617 ▲ 7056
Obrecht, J.:Motets, Cantus Figuratus Ensemble—Si sumpsero K617 ▲ 7056
Therache, P. de:Missa 'O vos omnes', Cantus Figuratus Ensemble K617 ▲ 7056
Therache, P. de:Motets, Cantus Figuratus Ensemble—Verbum bonum et suave K617 ▲ 7056
Tragicomedia
La Dolce Vita, w. King's Singers EMI Classics ▲ CDC 54191
Early Music of the Netherlands, Vol. 1 (1400-1600), w. Gesualdo Consort, Concerto Palatino members *(rec Dec. 1988)* Emergo ▲ EC 3987 [DDD]
A Musicall Dreame, w. Michael Chance (ct), David Cordier (ct) Hyperion ▲ CDA 66335 [DDD]
Tragicomedia [S. Stubbs (lt), E. Headley (vl), A. Lawrence-King (hp)]
Bach, J.S.:Anna Magdalena Bach Notebook, w. S. Stubbs Teldec ("Das alte Werke" series) ▲ 91183
Biber, H. von:Mystery (or Rosary) Sons, w. J. Holloway (vn), D. Moroney (chamber org/hpd) Virgin Classics ("Veritas" series) 2-▲ 59551 [DDD]
Jones, Robert:Duets for 2 Cts, w. M. Chance (ct), D. Cordier (ct)—eleven duets by Jones, coupled with two duets by John Coprario & Angelo Notari, a solo song by John Dowland, & eight instrumental pieces by Dowland, Giles Farnaby & Tobias Hume Hyperion ▲ CDA 66335 [DDD]
Monteverdi, C.:Madrigals Teldec ▲ 91971-2
S. Stubbs (cnd)
Purcell, H.:Music of Teldec ("Das alte Werk" series) ▲ 95068-2
Purcell, H.:Songs—Welcome, viceregent of the mighty king, Z.340; O dive custos Auriacae domus, Z.504; Raise, raise the voice, Z.334; O let me ever, ever weep [from The Fairy Queen, Z.629]; Incassum, Lesbia, rogas [The Queen's Epicedium], Z.383; Young Thirsis' fate, Z.473; Why, why are all the Muses mute?, Z.343 *(rec St. Bartholomew's Church, Orford, Mar. 1994)* Teldec ("Das Alte Werk" series) ▲ 95068-2 [DDD]
Transylvanian PO Cluj
B. Hary (cnd)
Bretan, N.:The Evening Star, w. Adriana Croitoru (sop—King's Daughter), Elena Casian (mez—Lady-in-Waiting), Marius Budoiu (ten—Mariner), Ioan Pojar (ten—Page), Ionel Voineag (ten—Evening Star), Bálint Szabó (bass—Michael the Archangel) *(rec Cluj, Sept 1994)* Nimbus ▲ NI 5463 [DDD]
Transylvanian State PO Romania
J.-L. Petit (cnd)
Gounod, C.:Sym 2 Arion ▲ ARN 68239 [AAD]
Travelling Opera Orch
R. Dunk (cnd)
Bizet, G.:Carmen (sels)—Ov; Habañera; Sequidilla; Chanson bohème; Qnt; Flower Song & Response; Trio; Michael's Aria; Toreador's Song; Duet & Finale IMP ("Classics" series) ▲ IMP 6700892
Tre Musici [Elisabeth Zeuthen Schneider (vn), Ulrikke Høst-Madsen (vc)]
Henriques, F.:Børnetrio *(rec Copenhagen, Oct 1992)* Marco Polo ("dacapo" series) ▲ DC 9310 [DDD]
Tre Musici [John Damgaard (pno), Elisabeth Zeuthen Schneider (vn), Ulrikke Høst-Madsen (vc)]
Gade, N.W.:Trio Movt *(rec Copenhagen, Oct 1992)* Marco Polo/Dacapo ▲ DC 9310 [DDD]
Hartmann, J.P.E.:Andantino & 8 Vars *(rec Copenhagen, Oct 1992)* Marco Polo ("dacapo" series) ▲ DC 9310 [DDD]
Lange-Müller, P.E.:Trio Pno *(rec Copenhagen, Oct 1992)* Marco Polo ("dacapo" series) ▲ DC 9310 [DDD]
Tre Musici members [Elisabeth Zeuthen Schneider (vn), John Damgaard (pno)]
Langgaard, R.:Mountain Flowers *(rec Copenhagen, Oct 1992)* Marco Polo ("dacapo" series) ▲ DC 9310 [DDD]
Tremont String Quartet
Morrill, D.:Just a Shape, w. P. Jordan (sop) *(rec June 1991 & June 1992)* Centaur ▲ CRC 2143 [DDD]
Morrill, D.:Roxbury Preludes, w. Glenda Dove-Pellito (fl), Ernest Lascell (cl) *(rec June 1991 & June 1992)* Centaur ▲ CRC 2143 [DDD]
Trenkner-Speidel Piano Duo [Evelinde Trenkner (pno), Sontraud Speidel (pno)]
Bach, J.S.:Brandenburg Cons [trans M. Reger for pno 4-hands] MD + G 2-▲ MDG CD 3300635
Les Trésord d'Orphée
Purcell, D.:Music of—Shepherds Tune Your Pipes [ayre for solo sop]; Trio Son. in d for rcr, German fl & bc; Apollo & Daphne [cantata for sop & bc]; Son. in C for German fl & bc; She Whom Above Myself I Prize [cant. for sop & bc]; Son. in F for rcr & bc; Within A Verdant Grove [cant. for sop & bc]; Trio Son. in F for 2 rcrs & bc; Septimius & Acme [cant. for sop & bc]; Trio Son. in g for rcr, German fl & bc; My God, My God, Look Upon Me [anthem for sop, solo org & bc] Stradivarius ▲ STV 33360 [DDD]
Trieste PO
H. Hollreiser (cnd)
Tchaikovsky, P.:Sym 6 Allegretto ▲ ACD 8009 [ADD] ■ ACS 8009
T. Schippers (cnd)
Donizetti, G.:Il Duca d'Alba, w. Renato Cioni (ten), Wladimiro Ganzarolli (bar), Franco Ventriglia (bass) Melodram ▲ CDM 27036
Donizetti, G.:Il Duca d'Alba, w. Wladimiro Ganzarolli (bar), Louis Quilico (bar), Enzo Tei (sgr), Ivana Tosini (sgr) *(rec live at the Spoleto Festival, June 11, 1959)* Memories 2-▲ MEM 4579 [ADD]
Trieste Teatro Comunale Giuseppe Verdi Orch
F. Capuana (cnd)
Zandonai, R.:Francesca da Rimini, w. L. Gencer (sop—Francesca), R. Cioni (ten—Paolo), M. Ferrara (ten—Malatesino), Trieste Teatro Comunale G. Verdi Chorus *(rec Mar. 19. 1961)* Arkadia 2-▲ 597 [ADD]

Trieste Teatro Comunale Giuseppe Verdi Orch (cont.)
C.F. Cillario (cnd)
Massenet, J.:Werther, w. L. Gencer (sop), F. Tagliavini (ten). *(rec 1959)* Memories 2-▲ MEM 4554 [ADD]
O. de Fabritiis (cnd)
Donizetti, G.:Lucia di Lammermoor (sels), w. L. Gencer (sop), G. Prandelli (ten), N. Carta (bar), R. Botteghelli (bass), Hussu (sgr), Sabatucci (sgr), Trieste Teatro Comunale G. Verdi Chorus *(rec live 12/13/57 & 2/10/58)* Melodram ▲ MEL 15003 (m) [AAD]
G. Gavazzeni (cnd)
Smareglia, A.:La falena, w. Leyla Gencer (sop—La Falena), Rita Lantieri (sop—Albina, sua figlia), Ruggero Bondino (ten—Re Stellio), Dario Zerial (ten—Il ladro), Mario D'Anna (bar—Il vecchio Uberto), Aurio Tomicich (bass—Morio), Giuseppe Botta (sgr—Un marinaio), Trieste Teatro Comunale G. Verdi Chorus *(rec Trieste, Mar 18, 1876)* Bongiovanni 2-▲ GB 1131/32
L. Jia (cnd)
Mendelssohn, F.:Syms (comp), w. Gemma Bertagnolli (sop), Milena Rudiferia (mez), Wonjun Lee (ten), Ine Meisters (cnd), Trieste Teatro Comunale G. Verdi Chorus RS Prestige 3-▲ 953-0090 [DDD]
Mendelssohn, F.:Sym 2, w. Gemma Bertagnoli (sop), Milena Rudifera (sop), Wonjun Lee (ten), Trieste Teatro Comunale G. Verdi Chorus RS Applausi ▲ 6367-91
J. Kovatchev (cnd)
Dvořák, A.:Sym 1, "The Bells of Zlonice" RS Prestige 3-▲ 953-0131 [DDD]
Dvořák, A.:Sym 2 RS Prestige 3-▲ 953-0131 [DDD]
Dvořák, A.:Sym 3 RS Prestige 3-▲ 953-0131 [DDD]
Schumann, R.:Syms (comp) RS Prestige 2-▲ 6367 72/73
F. Molinari-Pradelli (cnd)
Verdi, G.:La battaglia di Legnano (sels), w. L. Gencer (sop), J. Gibin (ten), U. Savarese (bar), Trieste Teatro Comunale G. Verdi Chorus—extensive selections from Acts 1,3 & 4 [I] *(rec live 3/8/63)* Myto 2-▲ 2 MCD 89010 (m) [ADD]
Verdi, G.:Rigoletto, w. Gianna D'Angelo (sop), Aldo Protti (bar), Vito Susca (bass), Giorgio Tadeo (bass), Trieste Teatro Comunale G. Verdi Chorus Melodram 2-▲ CDM 27006
L. Toffolo (cnd)
Still, W.G.:Tristan und Isolde, w. C. Ligendza (sop), S. Anderson (cta), C. Heater (ten), A. Švorc (bass), M. Smith (bass), Trieste Teatro Comunale G. Verdi Chorus [G] *(rec live, Trieste, 12/13/69)* Melodram 3-▲ MEL 37072 (m) [AAD]
A. Votto (cnd)
Bellini, V.:Norma, w. M. Callas (sop), E. Nicolai (mez), F. Corelli (ten), B. Christoff (bass), Trieste Teatro Comunale G. Verdi Chorus *(rec live 11/19/53)* Melodram 2-▲ CDM 26031 [ADD]
Bellini, V.:Norma (sels), w. M. Callas (sop), E. Nicolai (mez), F. Corelli (ten), B. Christoff (bass), Trieste Teatro Comunale G. Verdi Chorus—13 arias [I] *(rec live 11/19/53)* Myto 2-▲ 2 MCD 91340 [ADD]
M. Wolf-Ferrari (cnd)
Smareglia, A.:Nozze istrane, w. Maria Chiara (sop—Marussa), Eleonora Iancovich (cta—Luze), Ruggero Bondino (ten—Lorenzo), Alessandro Cassis (bar—Nicola), Alessandro Maddalena (bar—Biagio), Carlo Zardo (bass—Bara Menico), Trieste Teatro Comunale G. Verdi Chorus *(rec Trieste, Feb 17, 1973)* Bongiovanni ("Il Mito dell'Opera" series) 2-▲ 1133/34-2 [ADD]
Trieste Trio
Beethoven, L. van:Trio 2 Pno Ermitage ▲ ERM 141
Brahms, J.:Trio Cl Deutsche Grammophon 2-▲ 437131-2 [ADD]
Brahms, J.:Trio Hn Deutsche Grammophon 2-▲ 437131-2 [ADD]
Brahms, J.:Trios (3) Pno Deutsche Grammophon 2-▲ 437131-2 [ADD]
Brahms, J.:Trio 2 Pno Ermitage ▲ ERM 141
Schubert, Franz:Nocturne Pno Nuova Era ▲ 7011 [DDD]
Schubert, Franz:Trio 1 Pno Nuova Era ▲ 7011 [DDD]
Trinity Baroque Orch
E. Milnes (cnd)
Bach, J.S.:St. John Passion, w. Tamara Matthews (sop), Jennifer Lane (alt), Mark Bleeke (ten—Evangelist), David Vanderwal (ten), Kevin Walsh (bar—Pilate), Nathaniel Watson (bass—Jesus), Trinity Cathedral Choir *(rec Trinity Cathedral, Portland, OR, Mar 31, 1996)* PGM 2-▲ PGM 111
Trio Basso
Brandmüller, T.:Cis-Cantus II Koch Schwann ▲ CD 310 041 [DDD]
Goldmann, F.:Trio Va, Vc & Db Koch Schwann ▲ CD 310 041 [DDD]
Huber, N.A.:Trio mit Stabpandeira Koch Schwann ▲ CD 310 040 [DDD]
Kagel, M.:Aus dem Nachlass Koch Schwann ▲ CD 310 040 [DDD]
Kalitzke, J.:Trio Infernal Koch Schwann ▲ CD 310 040 [DDD]
Kröll, G.:Capriccia sopra mi Koch Schwann ▲ CD 310 041 [DDD]
Niehaus, M.:Piège de Méduse Koch Schwann ▲ CD 310 041 [DDD]
Riehm, R.:Ich denk viel/Mr. President/pizz./13 Koch Schwann ▲ CD 310 041 [DDD]
Rihm, W.:Verzeichnung-Studie Koch Schwann ▲ CD 310 040 [DDD]
Trio Con Brio [Sergej Azizjan (vn), Hege Waldeland (vc), Poul Rosenbaum (pno)]
Babadjanyan, A.:Trio Pno Classico ▲ CLASSCD 137
Schoenberg, A.:Verklärte Nacht [arr E. Steuermann for pno trio] Classico ▲ CLASSCD 137
Trio di Bassetto [Jean-Claude Veilhan (cl/bas hn), Eric Lorho (bas hn), Jean-Louis Gauce (bas hn)]
Mozart, W.A.:Adagio Bas Hns, K.484d, w. Catherine Delaunay (cl), Jean Jeltsch (bas hn) *(rec Chapelle Notre-Dame de l'Hor, Moselle, June 29 - July 1, 1995)* K617 ▲ 7060 [DDD]
Mozart, W.A.:Adagio Cl, K.Anh.93, w. Catherine Delaunay (cl), Jean Jeltsch (bas hn) *(rec Chapelle Notre-Dame de l'Hor, Moselle, June 29 - July 1, 1995)* K617 ▲ 7060 [DDD]
Mozart, W.A.:Adagio Cl, K.Anh.94, w. Catherine Delaunay (cl), Jean Jeltsch (bas hn) *(rec Chapelle Notre-Dame de l'Hor, Moselle, June 29 - July 1, 1995)* K617 ▲ 7060 [DDD]
Mozart, W.A.:Adagio Cls, K.411, w. Catherine Delaunay (cl), Jean Jeltsch (bas hn) *(rec Chapelle Notre-Dame de l'Hor, Moselle, June 29 - July 1, 1995)* K617 ▲ 7060 [DDD]
Mozart, W.A.:Nozze di Figaro (winds), w. Catherine Delaunay (cl), Jean Jeltsch (bas hn) *(rec Chapelle Notre-Dame de l'Hor, Moselle, June 29 - July 1, 1995)* K617 ▲ 7060 [DDD]
Stadler, A.:Trios Bas Hns, w. Catherine Delaunay (cl), Jean Jeltsch (bas hn) *(rec Chapelle Notre-Dame de l'Hor, Moselle, June 29 - July 1, 1995)* K617 ▲ 7060 [DDD]
Trio di Clarone [Sabine Meyer (cl), Wolfgang Meyer (cl), Reiner Wehle (cl)], Peter Handsworth (cl), Eddie Daniels (cl)
Blues for Sabine:Sabine Meyer & Eddie Daniels EMI Classics ▲ CDC 55253
Trio Italiano [Giovanni Battista Rigon (pno), Sonick Tchakerian (vn), Teodora Campagnaro (vc)]
Beethoven, L. van:Trio 1 Pno *(rec Palazzo Giusti, Padova, Italy, May 1994)* Arts ▲ 47250-2 [DDD]
Beethoven, L. van:Trio 2 Pno *(rec Palazzo Giusti, Padova, Italy, May 1994)* Arts ▲ 47250-2 [DDD]
Beethoven, L. van:Trio 3 Pno *(rec Palazzo Giusti, Padova, Italy, May 1994)* Arts Music ▲ 47249-2 [DDD]
Beethoven, L. van:Trio 4 Pno, "Ghost" *(rec Padova, Italy, May 1994)* Arts ▲ 472512 [DDD]
Beethoven, L. van:Trio 5 Pno *(rec Padova, Italy, May 1994)* Arts ▲ 472512 [DDD]
Beethoven, L. van:Trio 6 Pno, "Archduke" *(rec Palazzo Giusti, Padova, Italy, May 1994)* Arts Music ▲ 47249-2 [DDD]
Beethoven, L. van:Vars on an Original Theme, Op. 44 *(rec Palazzo Giusti, Padova, Italy, May 1994)* Arts ▲ 47250-2 [DDD]
Beethoven, L. van:Vars on "Ich bin der Schneider Kakadu" from Wenzel Müller's *Die Schwestern von Prag*, Op. 121a *(rec Padova, Italy, May 1994)* Arts ▲ 472512 [DDD]
Debussy, C.:Trio Pno *(rec Vincenza, Italy, July 1992 & Mar 1993)* Arts ▲ 47238-2 [DDD]
Ravel, M.:Trio Pno *(rec Vincenza, Italy, July 1992 & Mar 1993)* Arts ▲ 47238-2 [DDD]
Schumann, R.:Fantasiestücke Vn *(rec 1/91)* Giulia 2-▲ GS 201002 [DDD]
Schumann, R.:Trios Pno (comp) *(rec Jan. 1991)* Giulia 2-▲ GS 201002 [DDD]
Trio 1790
Bach, Joh. Christian:Sons Hpd, T.313/1 CPO ▲ CPO 999254 [DDD]
Bach, Joh. Christian:Sons Hpd, T.323/5 CPO ▲ CPO 999254 [DDD]
Just, J.A.:Sons Hpd CPO ▲ CPO 999335

Trio Sonata [Anton Kuskin (fl), Donald Bender (ob), Gary Kessler (gtr)]
Clear out of Touch with Time — Boston Skyline ▲ BSD 120 [ADD/DDD]
Encore! More Music for Flute, Oboe & Guitar — Boston Skyline ▲ BSD 114 [ADD/DDD] ▮ BSC 114
Music for Flute, Oboe & Guitar — Boston Skyline ▲ BSD 110 [ADD/DDD] ▮ BSC 110

Trioalanterie [J. Schneiderman, J. von Einem, M. Chatfield (cello)]
Baron, E.G.:Con Lute *(rec Apr. 1-3, 1991)* — Audioquest ▲ AQCD 1005

Tripla Concordia
Castello, D.:Sonate concertate in stil moderno—3 sonatas from Book 2 for flute(s), cello & harpsichord — Nuova Era ("Ancient Music" series) ▲ 7041 [DDD]
Fontana, G.B.:Sons (18) Vns—Sonata Nos. 2,3 & 4; flute, cello & harpsichord — Nuova Era ("Ancient Music" series) ▲ 7041 [DDD]
Frescobaldi, G.:Canzonas II & IV — Nuova Era ("Ancient Music" series) ▲ 7041 [DDD]
Frescobaldi, G.:Canzoni da sonare (40)—Vol II — Nuova Era ("Ancient Music" series) 2-▲ NOU CD 7250
Frescobaldi, G.:Toccata XII — Nuova Era ("Ancient Music" series) ▲ 7041 [DDD]
Selma y Salaverde, B. de:Canzoni, fantasie et corrente (sels)—Canzon "Affetti"; Fantasia; "Vestiva i colli" — Nuova Era ("Ancient Music" series) ▲ 7041 [DDD]

Triton Trombone Quartet [Olaf Ott (trbn), Ulrich Dieckmann (trbn), Ulrich Behrends (trbn), Hermann Bäumer (trbn)]
Braun, P.M.:Chôrale (3) *(rec Furuby Church, Sweden, July 6-10, 1994)* — BIS ▲ CD 694 [DDD]
French Music for Trombones *(rec July 1992)* — BIS ▲ CD 604 [DDD]
German Music for Trombones *(rec July 3-5 & Aug. 6-7, 1993)* — BIS ▲ CD 644 [DDD]
Jansson, G.:Missa for 4 Trbns *(rec Furuby Church, Sweden, July 6-10, 1994)* — BIS ▲ CD 694 [DDD]
Kretz, J.:...alles Ding währt seine Zeit *(rec Furuby Church, Sweden, July 6-10, 1994)* — BIS ▲ CD 694 [DDD]
Maklakiewicz, T.:Chrysea Phorminx *(rec Furuby Church, Sweden, July 6-10, 1994)* — BIS ▲ CD 694 [DDD]
Peeters, F.:Suite 4 Trbns *(rec Furuby Church, Sweden, July 6-10, 1994)* — BIS ▲ CD 694 [DDD]
Serocki, K.:Suite for 4 Trbns *(rec Furuby Church, Sweden, July 6-10, 1994)* — BIS ▲ CD 694 [DDD]

Trombonissimo
Trombonissimo 2 *(rec Sept. 14-15, 1992)* — Bayer ▲ 100234 [DDD]

Trondheim SO
O.K. Ruud (cnd)
Groven, E.:Con Pno, w. W. Plagge (pno) — Simax ▲ PSC 3111
Groven, E.:Sym 2, w. W. Plagge (pno) — Simax ▲ PSC 3111
Halvorsen, J.:Norwegian Rhaps (2) — Simax ▲ PSC 1085 [DDD]
Halvorsen, J.:Scenes from Norwegian Tales — Simax ▲ PSC 1062 [DDD]
Halvorsen, J.:Sym 2, "Fate" — Simax ▲ PSC 1062 [DDD]
Halvorsen, J.:Sym 3 — Simax ▲ PSC 1062 [DDD]
Jensen, L.I.:The Return, w. A. Bolstad (sop), R. Sterne (alt), H. Bjørkey (ten), I. Gilhuus (ten), P. Vollestad (bar), C. Stabell (bass), Trondheim Sym Chorus, Nidarso Cathedral Choir — Simax 2-▲ PSC 3109
Madsen, T.:Con Hn, w. F. R. Werke (hn) — Simax ▲ PSC 1100
Nystedt, K.:Con Hn, w. F. R. Werke (hn) — Simax ▲ PSC 1100
Plagge, W.:Con Hn, w. F. R. Werke (hn) — Simax ▲ PSC 1100
Svendsen, J.:Andante Funèbre — Virgin Classics ▲ CDC 45128
Svendsen, J.:Carnival in Paris — Virgin Classics ▲ CDC 45128
Svendsen, J.:Festival Polonaise — Virgin Classics ▲ CDC 45128
Svendsen, J.:Norwegian Artists' Carnival — Virgin Classics ▲ CDC 45128
Svendsen, J.:Norwegian Rhaps — Simax ▲ PSC 1085 [DDD]
Svendsen, J.:Zorahayda — Virgin Classics ▲ CDC 45128

Trondheim Soloists
Grieg, E.:Music of, w. A. Kvalbein (vc), R. Askeland (pno), Oslo Piano Trio—Intermezzo for Cello & Piano; Andante con moto in c for Violin, Cello & Piano; Sonata in a for Cello & Piano, Op. 36; Holdberg Suite (sels.); Preludium; Sarabande; Gavotte; Air; Rigaudon *(rec May 1991)* — Victoria ▲ VCD 19071
B. Fiskum (cnd)
Grieg, E.:Lyric Pieces, w. B. Hoff (bass), G. Solum (hn)—Op. 68/4 & 5 [arr Grieg for orch] — Victoria ▲ VCD 19072
Grieg, E.:Melodies, Op. 53 — Victoria ▲ VCD 19072
Grieg, E.:Music of [arr. for string orch.]—Ase's Death, Op. 46/2; In Folk Style, Op. 63/1; String Quartet No. 1 in g; Two Elegiac Melodies *(rec June 1992)* — Victoria ▲ VCD 19066 [DDD]
Grieg, E.:Nordic Melodies, Op. 63 — Victoria ▲ VCD 19072
Sammartini, G.:Cons Rcr, w. P. Brochmann (rcr)—in F *(rec July 1993)* — Victoria ▲ VCD 19078
Telemann, G.P.:Con in C Rcr, w. P. Brochmann (rcr) *(rec July 1993)* — Victoria ▲ VCD 19078
Vivaldi, A.:Cons Rcr, w. P. Brochmann (rcr) *(rec July 1993)* — Victoria ▲ VCD 19078

Trondheim Wind Quintet
Alterhaug, B.:Sporadic Concentration on 5 Pictures of Ove Stokstad *(rec Trondheim Olavshalle, June 17-20, 1994)* — Vienna Modern Masters ▲ VMM 2007 [DDD]
Böttcher, E.:Movts (2) Ww *(rec Trondheim Olavshalle, June 17-20, 1994)* — Vienna Modern Masters ▲ VMM 2007 [DDD]
Ebenhöh, H.:Divertipentephonien *(rec Trondheim Olavshalle, June 17-20, 1994)* — Vienna Modern Masters ▲ VMM 2007 [DDD]
Hueber, K.A.:Qnt Winds *(rec Trondheim Olavshalle, June 17-20, 1994)* — Vienna Modern Masters ▲ VMM 2007 [DDD]
Johansen, B.P.:Höstscener *(rec Trondheim Olavshalle, June 17-20, 1994)* — Vienna Modern Masters ▲ VMM 2007 [DDD]

Troubadour Ringers
Angels Singing, Nowells Ringing, w. [cnd:Dennis Shrock], Canterbury Choral Society, Top Brass *(rec Watchorn Hall, 1st Presbyterian Church, Oklahoma City, OK)* — Integra Classic ▲ IMCD 944 [DDD]

TRT String Orch
G. Aykal (cnd)
Sinangil, A.D.:Suite Strs — Gallo ▲ CD 836 [ADD]

Tuba Ensemble
W. Brooks (cnd)
Tipei, S.:Cuniculi — Centaur ▲ CRC 2045 [DDD]

Tübingen Cantata Orch
B. Ader (cnd)
Rheinberger, J.:Con 1 Org, w. W. Rehfeldt (org) — Bayer ▲ 100074 [DDD]
Rheinberger, J.:Con 2 Org, w. W. Rehfeldt (org) — Bayer ▲ 100074 [DDD]

Tübingen Sinfonietta
R. Bohn (cnd)
Bartók, B.:Con 2 Vn, w. N. Chastain (vn) — Ars Produktion ▲ ARS 368319 [DDD]
Hindemith, P.:The Four Temperaments, w. F. Rieger (pno) — Ars Produktion ▲ ARS 368319 [DDD]

La Turbulente
Corelli, A.:Sons 2 Vns, Opp. 1-4 (sels)—Opp. 2/12; 3/5-8 & 11; 5/4 & 7 — Ligia Digital ▲ 0301027

Turicum Ensemble
L. A. da Brooks (cnd)
Pinto, L.A.:Te Deum Laudamus, w. Katharina Ott (sop), Luiz Alves da Silva (ct), Beat Mattmüller (ct), Andreas Schmidt (ct), Markus Schikora (ten), William Lombardi (ten), Peter Mächler (bass), Michael Leibundgut (bass) *(rec Studio DRS, Zurich, Sept 26-29, 1994)* — Claves ▲ CD 9521 [DDD]
L. A. da Silva (cnd)
Coelho Neto, M.:Maria mater gratiae, w. Luiz Alves da Silva (ct), Beat Mattmüller (ct), Markus Schikora (ten), Peter Mächler (b) *(rec Studio DRS, Zurich, Sept 26-29, 1994)* — Claves ▲ CD 9521 [DDD]
Garcia, J.M.N.:Motets, w. Katharina Ott (sop), Luiz Alves da Silva (ct), Beat Mattmüller (ct), Andreas Schmidt (ct), Markus Schikora (ten), William Lombardi (ten), Peter Mächler (bass), Michael Leibundgut (bass) *(rec Studio DRS, Zurich, Sept 26-29, 1994)* — Claves ▲ CD 9521 [DDD]

Turicum Ensemble (cont.)
L. A. da Silva (cnd) (cont.)
Mesquita, J.J.E.L. de:Antiphona de Nossa Senhora, w. Luiz Alves da Silva (ct), Beat Mattmüller (ct), Markus Schikora (ten), Peter Mächler (bass) *(rec Studio DRS, Zurich, Sept 26-29, 1994)* — Claves ▲ CD 9521 [DDD]
Mesquita, J.J.E.L. de:Tercio, w. Luiz Alves da Silva (ct), Beat Mattmüller (ct), Markus Schikora (ten), Michael Leibundgut (bass) *(rec Studio DRS, Zurich, Sept 26-29, 1994)* — Claves ▲ CD 9521 [DDD]
Mesquita, J.J.E.L. de:Tractus (4) para o Sábado Santo, w. Luiz Alves da Silva (ct), Beat Mattmüller (ct), Markus Schikora (ten), Michael Leibundgut (bass) *(rec Studio DRS, Zurich, Sept 26-29, 1994)* — Claves ▲ CD 9521 [DDD]

Turin EIAR SO
Opera Arias, w. Ebe Stignani (mez) *(rec 1937-1941)* — Preiser ("Lebendige Vergangenheit" series) ▲ PRE 89014 (m) [AAD]
V. Gui (cnd)
Bellini, V.:Norma, w. G. Cigna (sop), E. Stignani (mez), G. Breviario (ten), T. Pasero (bass), Turin EIAR Chorus *(rec 1937)* — Memories 2-▲ MEM 4552 [ADD]
Bellini, V.:Norma, w. Gina Signa (sop), Ebe Stignani (mez), Giovanni Breviario (ten), Tancredi Pasero (bass), Turin EIAR Chorus *(rec 1937)* — Grammofono 2000 2-▲ GRM 78583
H. von Karajan (cnd)
Mozart, W.A.:Sym 35 — Grammofon 2000 ▲ GRM 78663
Mozart, W.A.:Sym 41 — Grammofono 2000 ▲ GRM 78653

Turin Lyric Orch
Bellini, V.:La sonnambula (sels), w. Renata Scotto (sop)—arias:sels. unknown — Cetra Classic ("Classics Collection" series) ▲ 111 [ADD]
Bizet, G.:Les Pêcheurs de perles (sels), w. Renata Scotto (sop)—arias:sels. unknown — Cetra Classic ("Classics Collection" series) ▲ 111 [ADD]
Donizetti, G.:Don Pasquale (sels), w. Renata Scotto (sop)—arias:sels. unknown — Cetra Classic ("Classics Collection" series) ▲ 111 [ADD]
Mascagni, P.:Arias, w. Renata Scotto (sop), Giulietta Simionato (mez)—arias from Lodoletta & Cavalleria Rusticana — Cetra Classic ("Classics Collection" series) ▲ 111 [ADD]
Verdi, G.:Arias, w. Renata Scotto (sop), Giulietta Simionato (mez)—arias from La Traviata & Aida — Cetra Classic ("Classics Collection" series) ▲ 111 [ADD]

Turin PO
J. Kovatchev (cnd)
Chopin, F.:Con 1 Pno, w. Anna Malikova (pno) — RS Prestige ▲ 951-0019 [DDD]
Chopin, F.:Con 2 Pno, w. Anna Malikova (pno) — RS Prestige ▲ 951-0019 [DDD]
T. Sanderling (cnd)
Strauss, R.:Don Juan — RS Prestige ▲ 951-0170 [DDD]
Strauss, R.:Macbeth — RS Prestige ▲ 951-0170 [DDD]
Strauss, R.:Tod und Verklärung — RS Prestige ▲ 951-0170 [DDD]
M. Viotti (cnd)
Martin, F.:Ballade Pno, w. Jean-François Antonioli (pno) — Claves ▲ CD 8509 [DDD]
Martin, F.:Con 1 Pno, w. Jean-François Antonioli (pno) — Claves ▲ CD 8509 [DDD]
Martin, F.:Con 2 Pno, w. Jean-François Antonioli (pno) — Claves ▲ CD 8509 [DDD]
Rossini, G.:Il Signor Bruschino, w. Patrizia Orciani (sop), Katia Lytting (mez), Luca Canonici (ten), Fulvio Massa (ten), Bruno Praticò (bar), Pietro Spagnoli (bar), Natale de Carolis (b-bar) — Claves 2-▲ 50-8904/5
Rossini, G.:Il Signor Bruschino, w. P. Orciani (sop), K. Lytting (mez), L. Canonici (ten), F. Massa (ten), B. Praticò (bar), P. Spagnoli (bar), N. de Carolis (b-bar) [I] — Claves 8-▲ CD 9200 [DDD]

Turin Piano Trio [Giacomo Fuga (pno), Sergio Lamberto (vn), Dario Destefano (vc)]
Brahms, J.:Trio 2 Pno — RS Prestige ▲ 951-0175 [DDD]
Dvořák, A.:Trio 4 Pno, "Dumky" — RS Prestige ▲ 951-0175 [DDD]

Turin Radio Orch
J. Barbirolli (cnd)
Elgar, E.:Enigma Vars *(rec live, Turin 11/15/57)* — Arkadia 2-▲ 584 [ADD]
Mozart, W.A.:Sym 34 *(rec live, Turin, Nov. 25, 1957)* — Arkadia 2-▲ 584 [ADD]
P. Bellugi (cnd)
Rossini, G.:La donna del lago, w. M. Caballé (sop), J. Hamari (mez), F. Bonisolli (ten), R. Bottazzo (ten), Turin RAI Chorus [I] *(rec live 5/19/70)* — Standing Room Only 2-▲ SRO 803-2 (m) [ADD]
S. Celibidache (cnd)
Bartók, B.:Romanian Dances — Arkadia ▲ 526 [AAD]
Borodin, A.:Prince Igor (Polovtsian dances) — Arkadia ▲ 526 [AAD]
Dvořák, A.:Sym 9, "From the New World" *(rec 1962)* — Arkadia ▲ 526 [AAD]
M. Rossi (cnd)
Verdi, G.:I vespri siciliani, w. A. Cerquetti (sop), Ortica (sgr), C. Tagliabue (bar), B. Christoff (bass), Turin Radio Chorus [I] *(rec live, Turin, 11/16/55)* — Claque 2-▲ CLQ 2017 (m)
H. Scherchen (cnd)
Bach, J.S.:Cant 106, "Actus tragicus", w. M. László (sop), H. Handt (ten), J. Loomis (bass), Turin Radio Chorus [G] *(rec live, Jan 14, 1958)* — Memories ▲ HR 4160 (m) [ADD]
F. Vernizzi (cnd)
Virginia Zeani, Soprano Arias, w. Zeani, Virginia (sop), Nicola Rossi-Lemeni (bass) — Melodram 2-▲ CDM 27013 (m) [AAD]

Turin Radio-TV SO
A. Basile (cnd)
Cilea, F.:Adriana Lecouvreur (sels), w. Gabriella Tucci (sop), Guiseppe Taddei (bar)—Ecco il monologo... *(rec Concerto Martini & Rossi, Turin, Feb 15, 1960)* — Incontri Memorabili ▲ 5029 [ADD]
Donizetti, G.:Arias, w. Gabriella Tucci (sop), Guiseppe Taddei (bar)—Vien Leonora [from La Favorita]; Ah! tardi, troppo [from Linda di Chamounix] *(rec Concerto Martini & Rossi, Turin, Feb 15, 1960)* — Incontri Memorabili ▲ 5029 [ADD]
Massenet, J.:Hérodiade (sels), w. Gabriella Tucci (sop), Guiseppe Taddei (bar)—Divine volupté *(rec Concerto Martini & Rossi, Turin, Feb 15, 1960)* — Incontri Memorabili ▲ 5029 [ADD]
Mozart, W.A.:Don Giovanni (sels), w. Gabriella Tucci (sop), Guiseppe Taddei (bar)—Madamina il catalogo è questo *(rec Concerto Martini & Rossi, Turin, Feb 15, 1960)* — Incontri Memorabili ▲ 5029 [ADD]
Puccini, G.:Suor angelica (sels), w. Gabriella Tucci (sop), Guiseppe Taddei (bar)—Senza mamma *(rec Concerto Martini & Rossi, Turin, Feb 15, 1960)* — Incontri Memorabili ▲ 5029 [ADD]
Verdi, G.:Arias, w. Gabriella Tucci (sop), Guiseppe Taddei (bar)—Tacea la notte placida [from Il Trovatore]; Ave Maria! [from Otello] *(rec Concerto Martini & Rossi, Turin, Feb 15, 1960)* — Incontri Memorabili ▲ 5029 [ADD]
A. Simonetto (cnd)
Cilea, F.:Adriana Lecouvreur (sels), w. Elisabetta Barbato (sop)—Io Son l'Umile Ancella — Fonit Cetra ("Martini & Rossi" series) ▲ FCT CDMR 5009
Glinka, M.:A Life for the Tsar (sels), w. Boris Christoff (bass)—Monologo di Ivan — Fonit Cetra ("Martini & Rossi" series) ▲ FCT CDMR 5009
Meyerbeer, G.:Le Prophète (sels), w. Boris Christoff (bass) — Fonit Cetra ("Martini & Rossi" series) ▲ FCT CDMR 5009
Mozart, W.A.:Don Giovanni (sels), w. Boris Christoff (bass)—Madamina il Catalogo è Questo — Fonit Cetra ("Martini & Rossi" series) ▲ FCT CDMR 5009
Puccini, G.:Edgar (sels)—Preludio Atto Terzo — Fonit Cetra ("Martini & Rossi" series) ▲ FCT CDMR 5009
Puccini, G.:Tosca (sels), w. Elisabetta Barbato (sop)—Vissi d'Arte — Fonit Cetra ("Martini & Rossi" series) ▲ FCT CDMR 5009
Rossini, G.:La scala di seta (sels)—Sinf — Fonit Cetra ("Martini & Rossi" series) ▲ FCT CDMR 5009
Verdi, G.:Aida (sels), w. Elisabetta Barbato (sop) — Fonit Cetra ("Martini & Rossi" series) ▲ FCT CDMR 5009
Verdi, G.:La forza del destino (sels), w. Elisabetta Barbato (sop)—Pace, Mio Dio — Fonit Cetra ("Martini & Rossi" series) ▲ FCT CDMR 5009

Turin RAI Orch
The Best of the Original "Martini & Rossi" Concerts, w. Milan RAI Orch *(rec 1953-1960)* — Memories 2-▲ MEM 4419 (m) [ADD]
Rossini, G.:Music of — Cetra Classic ▲ CDON 42

402
▲ = CD ◆ = Enhanced CD Δ = MD ▮ = Cassette Tape ▯ = DCC

Turin RAI Orch (cont.)
A. Basile (cnd)
Bizet, G.:Carmen (sels), w. Margherita Benetti (sop—Micaela), Pia Tassinari (sop—Carmen), Franco Corelli (ten—Don José), Giangiacomo Guelfi (bar—Escamillo)—[Act. 1] È l'amore uno strano augello; Josè!...Micaela!...Ah! mi parla di lei; Mia madre io vedo ancor, sì, sì; Presso il bastion di Siviglia; Tacer, dì, non vuoi tu?; [Act 2] Con voi ber; Alto là! Chi va là?; Il fior che avevi a me tu dato; [Act 3] Andiam, nostra sorte sappiam!; [Act 4] Largo! Largo! L'Alcade; Sei tu?...Son io; Più non m'ama il tuo cor? *(rec Torino Dec. 15, 1961)* Myto ▲ MCD 953132
Verdi, G.:La forza del destino (sels), w. Franco Corelli (ten—Don Alvaro), Giangiacomo Guelfi (bar—Don Carlo)—[Act 3] La vita è inferno all'infelice...; O tu che in seno agli angeli; Al tradimento...; Amici in vita e in morte; Piano...qui posi...; Solenne in quest'ora; Morir!...tremenda cosa!...; Urna fatale del mio destino; E s'altra prova rinvenir potessi?...; E' salvo! oh gioia immensa; [Act 4] Giunge qualcuno...aprite...; Invano Alvaro ti celasti al mondo; Fratello...; Le minacce, i fieri accenti; Ah, la macchia del tuo stemma *(rec Torino Feb. 6, 1957)* Myto ▲ MCD 953132
P. Bellugi (cnd)
Rossini, G.:La donna del lago, w. M. Caballé (sop), J. Hamari (mez), F. Bonisolli (ten), R. Bottazzo (ten), Turin RAI Chorus [I] *(rec live 5/19/70)* Melodram 2–▲ MEL 27074 (m) [AAD]
E. Boncompagni (cnd)
Alfano, F.:Risurrezione, w. M. Olivero (Katiusha), A. Di Stasio (Matrena), Gismondo (Prince Dmitri), A. Boyer (Simonson) [I] *(rec live, Oct 22, 1971)* Standing Room Only 2–▲ SRO 839–2 [ADD]
S. Celibidache (cnd)
Beethoven, L. van:Egmont (ov) *(rec 1968)* Artists ▲ FED 001
Dvořák, A.:Slavonic Dances (sels)—8 sels from Op. 46 *(rec live, Turin, 1970)* Arkadia ▲ 615
Shostakovich, D.:Sym 5 *(rec live, Turin Feb. 21, 1955)* Arkadia ▲ 765 [ADD]
Sibelius, J.:Sym 5 Arkadia ▲ 616
O. de Fabritiis (cnd)
Magda Olivero & Flaviano Labò in Concert, w. Magda Olivero (sop), Flaviano Labò (ten), Jacques Bazire (cnd), Marsiglia Opera Orch, Raina Kabaivanska (sop), Gianpiero Matromei (bar), Carlo Meliciani (bar), La Scala Orch *(rec between 1969 & 1973)* Bongiovanni ▲ GB 1105 [ADD]
The Martini & Rossi Concerts, Vol. 3, w. Carosio, Margherita (sop), Giuseppe Di Stefano (ten) Fonit Cetra ("Martini & Rossi" series) ▲ FCT CDMR 5003
G. Ferro (cnd)
Chausson, E.:Poème de l'amour et de la mer, w. Shirley Verrett (mez) Fonit Cetra ("Italia" series) ▲ FCT CDC 90
Massenet, J.:Hérodiade (sels), w. Shirley Verrett (mez)—Je Ne l'Ai Pas Trouvée...Il Est Doux, Il Est Bon Fonit Cetra ("Italia" series) ▲ FCT CDC 90
Massenet, J.:Manon (sels), w. Shirley Verrett (mez)—Allons! Il le Faut!...Adieu Notre Petite Table; Je Marche sur Tous les Chemins...Obéissons Quand Leur Voix Appelle Fonit Cetra ("Italia" series) ▲ FCT CDC 90
Massenet, J.:Werther (sels), w. Shirley Verrett (mez)—Werther! Werther!...Je Vous Écris de Ma Petite Chambre Fonit Cetra ("Italia" series) ▲ FCT CDC 90
G. Gavazzeni (cnd)
Verdi, G.:Jérusalem, w. K. Ricciarelli (sop), J. Carreras (ten), S. Nimsgern (b-bar), Turin RAI Chorus [F] *(rec live 12/20/75)* Standing Room Only 2–▲ SRO 828–2 [ADD]
E. Gracis (cnd)
Donizetti, G.:La favorita, w. F. Cossotto (mez), J. Aragall (ten), A. Colzani (bar), Turin RAI Chorus *(rec live)* Melodram 2–▲ MEL 27020
R. Majone (cnd)
Mercadante, S.:Arias, w. M. Olivero (sop), Turin RAI Chorus—single arias from Virginia & Pelagio; Aria (La sette parole di nostro signore); Sinfonia from Rossini's Stabat Mater *(rec live, Turin, 11/23/70)* Melodram 2–▲ MEL 27099 [ADD]
F. Mannino (cnd)
Bellini, V.:Beatrice di Tenda, w. A. Gulin (sop), E. Zilio (mez), J. Carreras (ten), R. Bruson (bar), Turin RAI Chorus [I] *(rec live Oct. 9, 1973)* Golden Age of Opera 2–▲ GAO 158/59 [ADD]
F. Molinari-Pradelli (cnd)
Donizetti, G.:Lucia di Lammermoor, w. R. Scotto (sop—Lucia), L. Pavarotti (ten—Edgardo), P. Cappuccilli (bar—Enrico), Turin RAI Chorus [I] *(rec live, Turin 10/10/67)* Verona 2–▲ 27083/84
Flotow, F. von:Martha, w. E. Rizzieri (sop—Lady Enrichetta), P. Tassinari (sop—Nancy), F. Tagliavini (ten—Lionello), C. Tagliabue (bar—Plumkett), B. Carmassi (bass—Sir Tristano), Turin RAI Chorus *(rec 1953; Italian libretto)* Cetra Classic 2–▲ CDO 7 [AAD]
L. Pfaff (cnd)
Bartók, B.:Rhap Pno, w. Noël Lee (pno) Arion ▲ ARN 68250 [DDD]
Bartók, B.:Rhaps (2) Vn & Orch, w. Gérad Poulet (vn) Arion ▲ ARN 68250 [DDD]
Bartók, B.:The Wooden Prince Arion ▲ ARN 68250 [DDD]
F. Previtali (cnd)
Cilea, F.:Gloria, w. M. Roberti (sop), A. M. Rota (cta), F. Labò (ten), A. Albertini (bar), L. Testi (bar), E. Campi (bass), F. Mazzoli (bass), Turin RAI Chorus [I] *(rec live, Turin July 8, 1969)* Memories ▲ HR 4472 [ADD]
A. Questa (cnd)
Puccini, G.:Madama Butterfly, w. C. Petrella (sop—Madama Butterfly), M. Masini (mez—Suzuki), M. C. Foscale (sgr—Kate Pinkerton), F. Tagliavini (ten—Pinkerton), M. Caruso (ten—Goro), G. Taddei (bar—Sharpless), A. Albertini (bar—Yamadori), A. Biancardo (bass—Bonze), Cetra Chorus *(rec 1953)* Cetra Classic 2–▲ CDO 10 [AAD]
M. Rossi (cnd)
Rossini, G.:La Cenerentola, w. Ornella Rovero (sop), Miti Truccato Pace (mez), Giulietta Simionato (mez), Cesare Valletti (ten), Saturno Meletti (bar), Vito Susca (bass), Cristiano Dalamangas (sgr), Bruno Erminero (cnd), Turin RAI Chorus Fonit Cetra ("Classic Collection" series) ▲ FCT CDON 34
G. Santini (cnd)
Verdi, G.:La traviata (sels), w. Maria Callas (sop)—selected arias *(rec Milan, 1956)* Andromeda ▲ ANR 2541 [ADD]
N. Sanzogno (cnd)
Alda Noni, Sesto Bruscantini, w. Alda Noni (sop), Sesto Bruscantini (bass) *(rec Dec. 3, 1951)* Incontri Memorabili ("Martini & Rossi Concerts" series) ▲ 5016
G. Santini (cnd)
Verdi, G.:La traviata (sels), w. Maria Callas (sop)—selected arias *(rec Milan, 1956)* Andromeda ▲ ANR 2541 [ADD]
A. Simonetto (cnd)
Verdi, G.:Oberto, Conte di San Bonifacio, w. Elena Nicolai (mez), Giuseppe Modesti (bass), Gino Bonelli (sgr), Lydia Roan (sgr), Maria Vitale (sgr), Turin RAI Chorus Great Opera Performances 2–▲ GOP 774
F. Vernizzi (cnd)
Puccini, G.:Tosca, w. Magda Olivero (sop), Alvinio Misciano (ten), Turin RAI Chorus Melodram 2–▲ CDM 27025
Puccini, G.:Tosca, w. M. Olivero (sop), A. Misciano (ten), Fioravanti (sgr), Turin RAI Chorus *(rec live 1960)* Melodram 2–▲ MEL 27026
Puccini, G.:Tosca (sels), w. M. Olivero (sop), A. Misciano (ten)—3 duets [I] *(rec live, Turin, 3/7/60)* Myto 2–▲ 2 MCD 91136 [ADD]
A. Votto (cnd)
Ponchielli, A.:La Gioconda, w. M. Callas (sop—Gioconda), F. Barbieri (mez—Laura), M. Amadini (sgr—La Cieca), G. Poggi (ten—Enzo), P. Silveri (bar—Barnaba), G. Neri (bass—Alvise), Turin RAI Chorus *(rec 1952)* Cetra Classic 3–▲ CDO 8
Turin RAI Radio-TV SO
L. von Matačić (cnd)
Wagner, R.:Die Meistersinger von Nürnberg, w. Bruna Rizzoli (sop), Fernanda Cadoni (mez), Luigi Infantino (ten), Vito Tatone (ten), Renato Capecchi (bar), Giuseppe Taddei (bar), Boris Christoff (bass), Giovanni Ciavola (bass), James Loomis (bass), Silvo Maionica (bass), Vito Susca (bass), Raimondo Botteghelli (sgr), Walter Brunelli (sgr), Carlo Franzini (sgr), Ezio de Giorgi (sgr), Renzo Gonzales (sgr), Turin RAI Chorus Stradivarius 4–▲ STV 12310

Turin RAI Radio-TV SO (cont.)
G. Petrassi (cnd)
Petrassi, G.:Inni sacri, w. Aldo Bertocci (ten), Renato Cesari (bar) Stradivarius ▲ STV DTM 90001 [ADD]
Turin RAI SO
Arias, w. Maria Callas (sop), Rome RAI SO, Milan RAI SO, Royal Opera House Orch Covent Garden *(rec 1949–1962)* Verona 2–▲ 27058/59 (m) [AAD]
Boito, A.:Mefistofele (sels), w. Marcella Pobbe (sop), San Remo SO *(rec Turin & San Remo, 1954–58)* Cetra Classic ▲ CDON 110
Catalani, A.:La Wally (sels), w. Lejla Gencer (sop)—Aria Cetra Classic ("Classics Collection" series) ▲ 112 [ADD]
Cesare Siepi, w. Cesare Siepi (b-bar), Arturo Basile (cnd), Alfredo Simonetto (cnd), Franco Capuano (cnd), Gabriele Santini (cnd) *(rec Torino, 1955)* Cetra Classics ("Classic Collections" series) ▲ CDON 107
Donizetti, G.:Arias, w. Lejla Gencer (sop)—arias from Catarina Cornaro; Roberto Devereux; Maria Stuarda & Lucrezia Borgia Cetra Classic ("Classics Collection" series) ▲ 112 [ADD]
Gatta, Moffo, Rizzieri, Christoff & Mazzolli, w. Dora Gatta (sop), Anna Moffo (sop), Elena Rizzieri (sop), Boris Christoff (bass), Ferruccio Mazzoli (bass), Rome RAI SO *(rec Martini & Rossi Concert)* Incontri Memorabili ▲ CDMR 5033
Mascagni, P.:Isabeau (sels), w. Marcella Pobbe (sop), San Remo SO *(rec Torino & San Remo, 1954–58)* Cetra Classic ▲ CDON 110
Tebaldi, Barbieri & Valletti, w. Renata Tebaldi (sop), Fedora Barbieri (mez), Cesare Valletti (ten), Fighera, Nino Sanzogno (cnd), Milan RAI SO *(rec Martini & Rossi Concert, 1951 & 1953)* Incontri Memorabili ▲ CDMR 5012
Verdi, G.:Arias, w. Lejla Gencer (sop)—arias from Il Trovatore; La Forza del Destino; Aida; La Traviata Cetra Classic ("Classics Collection" series) ▲ 112 [ADD]
Verdi, G.:Music of Cetra Classic ▲ CDON 42
P. Argento (cnd)
Puccini, G.:Manon Lescaut (sels), w. Magda Olivero (sop—Manon), Giuseppe Venditelli (ten—Chevalier)—Oh, sarò la più bella! [Act 2] *(rec Turin, July 2, 1975)* Bella Voce 2–▲ BLV 107.221 [AAD]
A. Basile (cnd)
Giordano, U.:Andrea Chénier, w. R. Tebaldi (sop), U. Savarese (bar) Cetra Classic 2–▲ CDO 24
Giordano, U.:Andrea Chénier, w. Renata Tebaldi (sop), José Soler (ten), Ugo Savarese (bar) Fonit Cetra ("Classic Collection" series) 2–▲ FCT CDO 24
Basile, Cattini, Questa, Serafin (cnd)
Puccini, G.:Arias, w. Marcella Pobbe (sop), San Remo SO—from Suor Angelica, La Rondine, Tosca, Turandot, Manon Lescaut, La Bohème & Gianni Schicchi *(rec Torino & San Remo, 1954–58)* Cetra Classic ▲ CDON 110
F. Capuana (cnd)
Bellini, V.:La sonnambula, w. Anna Maria Anelli (sop), Lina Pagliughi (sop), Ferruccio Tagliavini (ten), Cesare Siepi (b-bar) Fonit Cetra ("Classic Collection" series) 2–▲ FCT CDO 16
S. Celibidache (cnd)
Brahms, J.:Sym 2 *(rec 1960)* Legend ▲ LGD 109 [ADD]
Strauss, R.:Tod und Verklärung *(rec Turin, Apr. 30, 1970)* Arkadia ▲ 487 [ADD]
A. Cluytens (cnd)
Brahms, J.:Con 2 Pno, w. Artur Rubinstein (pno) *(rec Torino, May 1962)* Emozioni ▲ ARCD 2027
O. De Fabritiis (cnd)
Maria Callas & Nicola Filacuridi, w. Maria Callas (sop), Nicola Filacuridi (ten) *(rec Milan, Feb. 18, 1952)* Incontri memorabili ("Martini & Rossi Concert" series) ▲ CDMR 5001 [ADD]
Franci, Lewis, Schippers (cnd)
Rossini, G.:Arias, w. Marylin Horne (mez), La Scala Orch—sels from Semiramide, Otello, La donna del Lago, Tancredi, La Cenerentola, L'Italiana in Algeri & L'Assedio di Dorinto *(rec live, 1968–71)* Enterprise ("Documents" series) ▲ ENT LV 979 (m)
G. Gavazzeni (cnd)
Boito, A.:Nerone, w. I. Ligabue (sop), R. Baldani (mez), B. Prevedi (bar), A. Ferrin (bass), Turin RAI Chorus *(rec live 1975)* Italian Opera Rarities 2–▲ IOR 7704 [ADD]
G. Gelmetti (cnd)
Rossini, G.:La gazza ladra, w. K. Ricciarelli (sop), W. Matteuzzi (ten), S. Ramey (bass) *(rec live, Rossini Opera Festival in Pesaro, Italy, Aug. 1989)* Sony Classical 3–▲ S3K 45850 [DDD]
F. Ghione (cnd)
Puccini, G.:Turandot, w. Gina Cigna (sop), Magda Olivero (sop), Francesco Merli (ten) *(rec 1938)* Phonographe 2–▲ PHG 5053
R. Leppard (cnd)
Purcell, H.:Dido & Aeneas, w. Helen Donath (sop—Belinda), Shirley Verrett (sop—Dido), Oralia Dominguez (mez—Sorceress), Carmen Lavani (alt—A Spirit), Margaret Lensky (cta—2nd Witch), Carlo Gaifa (ten—A Sailor), Dan Jordacescu (bar—Aeneas), Rosina Cavicchioli (sgr—A Woman), Lilia Teresita Reyes (sgr—1st Witch), Ambrosian Chorus *(rec Torino, May 20, 1971)* Arkadia ▲ 619 [ADD]
H. Lewis (cnd)
Meyerbeer, G.:Le Prophète, w. M. Rinaldi (sop), M. Horne (mez), N. Gedda (ten), R. El Hage (bass), Turin Radio Chorus [F] *(rec live 7/11/70)* Foyer 3–▲ FOY 2035 [ADD]
P. Maag (cnd)
Verdi, G.:Luisa Miller (sels), w. Luciano Pavarotti (ten)—Oh! fede negar potessi agl'occhi miei!; Quando le sere al placido *(rec Torino, 1969)* Goldies ▲ GLD 63202 [ADD]
P. Mascagni (cnd)
Mascagni, P.:L'amico Fritz, w. P. Tassinari (sop—Suzel), A. Pini (mez—Beppe), F. Tagliavini (ten—Fritz), A. Giannotti (ten—Frederico), S. Meletti (bar—David), P. L. Latinucci (bass—Hanezò), Turin Radio Chorus *(rec 1941)* Cetra Classic 2–▲ CDO 18
F. Molinari-Pradelli (cnd)
Donizetti, G.:Lucia di Lammermoor (sels), w. Renato Scotto (sop), Anna Di Stazio (mez), Luciano Pavarotti (ten)—Egli s'avanza; Sulla tomba che rinserra *(rec Torino, Oct 10, 1967)* Goldies ▲ GLD 63202 [ADD]
Massenet, J.:Werther, w. F. Tagliavini (ten), M. Cortis (bar), P.L. Latinucci (bass) *(rec 1953)* Cetra Classic 2–▲ CDO 15 [AAD]
F. M. Pradelli (cnd)
Rosanna Carteri, Carlo Bergonzi, w. Rosanna Carteri (sop), Carlo Bergonzi (ten), Turin RAI SO *(rec Jan. 30, 1960)* Incontri Memorabili ("Martini & Rossi Concerts" series) ▲ 5026
A. Questa (cnd)
Boito, A.:Mefistofele, w. Marcella Pobbe (sop), Ebe Ticozzi (mez), Ferruccio Tagliavini (ten), Giulio Neri (bass), Turin Teatro Regio Chorus Fonit Cetra ("Classic Collection" series) 2–▲ FCT CDO 19
Boito, A.:Mefistofele, w. M. Pobbe (sop—Margherita), D. De Cecco (sop—Elena), E. Ticozzi (mez—Marta), F. Tagliavini (ten—Faust), G. Neri (bass—Mefistofele), Turin Teatro Regio Chorus *(rec 1954)* Cetra Classic ▲ CDO 19
Verdi, G.:Un ballo in maschera, w. M. Curtis Verna (sop—Amelia), M. Erato (sop—Oscar), P. Tassinari (cta—Ulrica), F. Tagliavini (ten—Riccardo), G. Valdengo (bar—Renato), A. Albertini (bar—Silvano), M. Stefanoni (bass—Samuel), V. Susca (bass—Tom), Turin RAI Chorus *(rec 1954)* Cetra Classic 2–▲ CDO 13 [AAD]
A. Rodzinski (cnd)
Sibelius, J.:Sym 2 *(rec 1955)* Stradivarius ▲ DAT 12306 [ADD]
Stravinsky, I.:The Firebird Suite *(rec 1955)* Stradivarius 2–▲ DAT 12306 [ADD]
Szymanowski, K.:Stabat Mater, w. A. Martino (sop), A. M. Rota (alt), R. Capecchi (bar), Turin RAI Chorus *(rec 1955)* Stradivarius 2–▲ DAT 12306 [ADD]
M. Rossi (cnd)
Cimarosa, D.:Les Astuzie femminili (sels), w. Teresa Stich Randall (sop), Sesto Bruscantini (bass)—Le figliole che so' de vent'anni *(rec Concerto Martini & Rossi, Torino, Nov 9, 1959)* Incontri Memorabili ▲ 5027 [ADD]
Donizetti, G.:Don Pasquale, w. A. Noni (sop—Norina), C. Valletti (ten—Ernesto), M. Borriello (bar—Dr. Malatesta), S. Bruscantini (bass-bar—Pasquale), Turin RAI Chorus *(rec 1952)* Cetra Classic 2–▲ CDO 14 [AAD]

Turin RAI SO (cont.)
M. Rossi (cnd) (cont.)
Giordano, U.:Fedora, w. Maria Caniglia (sop), Aldo Bertocci (ten), Giacinto Prandelli (ten), Scipio Colombo (bar), Andrea Piccinni (bass), Capozzi (sgr), Turin RAI Chorus *(rec 1950)* Cetra Classic 2-▲ Don 35
Massenet, J.:Werther, w. M. Olivero (sop), A. Lazzari (ten), S. Meletti (bar), Turin Radio Chorus *(rec live, 6/12/63)* Melodram 2-▲ MEL 27065 (m) [AAD]
Mozart, W.A.:Arias, w. Teresa Stich Randall (sop), Sesto Bruscantini (bass)—Martern aller Arten [from Entführung aus dem Serail]; Tutto è disposto; E Susanna non vien! [both from Le nozze di Figaro]; Ei parte... Per pietà, ben mio perdona [from Così fan tutte]; Crudele?... Non mi dir, bell'idol mio [from Don Giovanni] *(rec Concerto Martini & Rossi, Torino, Nov 9, 1959)* Incontri Memorabili ▲ 5027 [ADD]
Rossini, G.:Il barbiere di Siviglia (sels), w. Teresa Stich Randall (sop), Sesto Bruscantini (bass)—Largo al factotum *(rec Concerto Martini & Rossi, Torino, Nov 9, 1959)* Incontri Memorabili ▲ 5027 [ADD]
Verdi, G.:Ernani (sels), w. Teresa Stich Randall (sop), Sesto Bruscantini (bass)—Gran Dio!... Ohe de' verd'anni miei *(rec Concerto Martini & Rossi, Torino, Nov 9, 1959)* Incontri Memorabili ▲ 5027 [ADD]
N. Sanzogno (cnd)
Ravel, M.:Con in G Pno, w. A. B. Michelangeli (pno) *(rec 2/1/52)* Arkadia ▲ 904 [ADD]
A. Silipigni (cnd)
Leoncavallo, R.:Zazà, w. C. Petrella (sop), E. Parker (mez), G. Campora (ten) *(rec 1969)* Memories 2-▲ MEM 4519 [AAD]
A. Simonetto (cnd)
Leoncavallo, R.:Pagliacci, w. C. Gavazzi (sop—Nedda), C. Bergonzi (ten—Canio), S. Di Tommaso (ten—Beppe), C. Tagliabue (bar—Tonio), M. Rossi (bar—Silvio), Turin RAI Chorus *(rec Turin, 1951)* Cetra Classic 2-▲ CDO 27 [ADD]
Puccini, G.:Gianni Schicchi, w. G. Rapisardi (sop), A. Dubbini (mez), G. Savio (ten), G. Taddei (bar) [I] *(rec 10/5/49)* Preiser ▲ 90074 (m) [AAD]
F. Vernizzi (cnd)
Pobbe, Sciutti & Siepi, w. Marcella Pobbe (sop), Graziella Sciutti (sop), Cesare Siepi (bass), Milan RAI SO [cnd:L. Toffolo] *(rec Martini & Rossi Concert, 1959)* Incontri Memorabili ▲ CDMR 5032
Puccini, G.:Arias, w. M. Olivero (sop), *(other soloists unknown)*—3 scenes from Tosca *(rec live, 3/7/60)* Melodram 2-▲ MEL 27065 (m) [AAD]
A. Votto (cnd)
Ponchielli, A.:La Gioconda, w. M. Callas (sop), F. Barbieri (mez), G. Poggi (ten), P. Silveri (bar), G. Neri (bass), Turin RAI Chorus *(rec 1952)* Andromeda 3-▲ ANR 2528 [ADD]
Ponchielli, A.:La Gioconda, w. M. Callas (sop), F. Barbieri (mez), G. Poggi (ten), P. Silveri (bar), G. Neri (bass), Turin RAI Chorus *(rec 1952)* Enterprise ("Palladio" series) ▲ ENT PD 4152 [DDD]
A. Zedda (cnd)
Pergolesi, G.B.:Stabat mater (sels), w. Lucia Valentini Terrani (sop) Kicco Classic ▲ 195
Rossini, G.:Arias, w. Lucia Valentini Terrani (sop)—from Otello; Cenerentola; Barbiere di Siviglia; Maometto II; Italiana in Algeri; Donna del Lago Kicco Classic ▲ 195
Rossini, G.:Arias, w. M. Horne (mez)—arias from Il barbiere di Siviglia, La gazza ladra, Maometto II, Tancredi [F,I,S] CBS ▲ MK 44820 [DDD]
Turin Strings
A. Molino (cnd)
Dall'Abaco, E.F.:Con Ob, w. Luca Avanzi (ob) Stradivarius ▲ STV 33346 [DDD]
Hasse, J.A.:Con Ob, w. Luca Avanzi (ob) Stradivarius ▲ STV 33346 [DDD]
Platti, G.B.:Cons Ob, w. Luca Avanzi (ob)—in g & G Stradivarius ▲ STV 33346 [DDD]
Sammartini, G.:Con Ob, Strs & Bc, w. Luca Avanzi (ob) Stradivarius ▲ STV 33346 [DDD]
Turin SO
F. Molinari-Pradelli (cnd)
Donizetti, G.:Lucia di Lammermoor (sels), w. Luciano Pavarotti (ten), Turin Sym Chorus—Tombe degl'avi miei *(rec live, June 30, 1967)* RCA Gold Seal ▲ 09026-68014-2 [ADD]
M. Rossi (cnd)
Verdi, G.:Rigoletto (sels), w. Luciano Pavarotti (ten)—Questa o quella; ella mi fu rapita...Parmi veder le lagrime; La donna è mobile *(rec live, Dec. 26, 1967)* RCA Gold Seal ▲ 09026-68014-2 [ADD]
Turin Teatro Regio Orch
B. Campanella (cnd)
Donizetti, G.:Don Pasquale, w. L. Serra (sop), E. Dara (bar), A. Corbelli (bar), Bartolo (sgr), Turin Teatro Regio Chorus [I] *(rec live)* Nuova Era 2-▲ 6715/16 [DDD]
Donizetti, G.:Don Pasquale, w. L. Serra (sop), E. Dara (bar), A. Corbelli (bar), Bartolo (sgr), Turin Teatro Regio Chorus [I] *(rec live)* Nuova Era ▲ 6766 [DDD]
F. Previtali (cnd)
Verdi, G.:Luisa Miller, w. K. Ricciarelli (sop—Luisa), M. G. Piolatto (mez—Laura), S. Silva (cta—Federica), J. Carreras (ten—Rodolfo), E. Pranod (ten—A Peasant), R. Bruson (bar—Miller), G. Casarini (bar—Wurm) M. Rinaudo (bass—Count Walter), Turin Teatro Regio Chorus *(rec May 9, 1976)* Legato Classics 2-▲ LCD 180 [ADD]
N. Santi (cnd)
Verdi, G.:Attila, w. Maria Chiara (sop), Silvano Carroli (bar), Nicolai Ghiuselev (bass), Turin Teatro Regio Chorus *(rec live, 1980)* Serenissima 2-▲ SER 360138
Turku PO
J. Mercier (cnd)
Heiniö, M.:Vuelo de Alambre, w. Karita Mattila (sop) Finlandia ▲ FIN 99403 [DDD]
Palmgren, S.:Cons Pno (comp), w. E. Heinonen (pno—No. 1), J. Lagerspetz (pno—Nos. 2 & 4), M. Raekallio (pno—No. 3), R. Kerppo (pno—No. 5) Finlandia 2-▲ 4509-95852-2 [DDD]
Palmgren, S.:Pictures from Finland Finlandia 2-▲ 4509-95852-2 [DDD]
Turtle Island String Quartet
Bimstein, P.K.:Dark Winds Rising, w. P. K. Bimstein (elec) Starkland ▲ ST 205 [DDD]
Turtle Island String Quartet [Darol Anger (vn), Tracy Silverman (vn), Danny Seidenberg (va), Mark Summer (vc)]
A Night in Tunisia, A Week in Detroit, w. Detroit SO [cnd:Neeme Järvi] Chandos ("New Direction" series) ▲ CHAN 9331 [DDD]
Turtle Mountain Naval Base Tactical Wind Ensemble
P. Schickele (cnd)
Schickele, P.:Music of—Grand Serenade for an Awful Lot of Winds & Percussion; "Dutch" Suite; Six Contrary Dances; Lip My Reeds; Door Prize Scene/Fanfare for Fred; March of the Cute Little Wood Sprites; Last Tango in Bayreuth *("Lip My Reeds" & "Last Tango..." are performed by the Tennessee Bassoon Quartet)* Telarc ▲ CD 80307 [DDD] ▮ CS 30307 (D)
Tuscan Orch
G. Gelmetti (cnd)
Rossini, G.:Il barbiere di Siviglia, w. A. Felle (sop), S. Mentzer (mez), J. Hadley (ten), T. Hampson (bass), S. Ramey (bass) EMI ▲ 54863-2
Tuscany Radio-TV Orch
D. Renzetti (cnd)
Schubert, Franz:Ovs—Ovs im italienischen Stil D.590 & 591; Ov Der Teufek als Hydraulicus; Ov Die Freunde von Salamanka; Ov D.470; Ov Die Zwillingsbrüder; Ov Alfonso und Estrella; Ov Fierrabras Arts ▲ 47168-2 [DDD]
Tutti Camarata Orch
Bernstein, L.:On the Town, w. M. Martin (sgr), N. Walker (sgr), B. Comden (sgr), A. Green (sgr), Leonard Joy Orch, Lynn Murray Orch, Lynn Murray Chorus MCA Classics ▲ MCAD 10280 (m) [AAD]
Tutti e solo [Malgorzata Mincak-Spychala (vn), Mariusz Derewecki (vn), Leszek Ziółko (vc), Barbara Mucha (hpd)]
Jarzebski, A.:Music of, w. Marcin Murawski (va)—Berlinesa; Cantate Domino; Tamburetta; Con Primo *(rec Grand Ballroom, Rydzyna Castle, Poland, Sept 1994)* Dorian Discovery ▲ DIS 80136 [DDD]
Mielczewski, M.:Canzona prima a 2 *(rec Grand Ballroom, Rydzyna Castle, Poland, Sept 1994)* Dorian Discovery ▲ DIS 80136 [DDD]
Milwid, A.:Semper mi Iesu, w. Benigna Jaskulska (sop) *(rec Grand Ballroom, Rydzyna Castle, Poland, Sept 1994)* Dorian Discovery ▲ DIS 80136 [DDD]
Rohaczewski, A.:Canzon a 4 *(rec Grand Ballroom, Rydzyna Castle, Poland, Sept 1994)* Dorian Discovery ▲ DIS 80136 [DDD]

Tutti e solo (cont.)
Sieprawski, P.:Justus germinavit, w. Benigna Jaskulska (sop) *(rec Grand Ballroom, Rydzyna Castle, Poland, Sept 1994)* Dorian Discovery ▲ DIS 80136 [DDD]
Stachowicz, D.:Veni Consolator, w. Benigna Jaskulska (sop), Roman Gryn (tpt) *(rec Grand Ballroom, Rydzyna Castle, Poland, Sept 1994)* Dorian Discovery ▲ DIS 80136 [DDD]
Szarzynski, S.S.:Son Vns *(rec Grand Ballroom, Rydzyna Castle, Poland, Sept 1994)* Dorian Discovery ▲ DIS 80136 [DDD]
Szarzynski, S.S.:Veni Sancte Spiritus, w. Benigna Jaskulska (sop) *(rec Grand Ballroom, Rydzyna Castle, Poland, Sept 1994)* Dorian Discovery ▲ DIS 80136 [DDD]
12 Cellos of the Berlin PO
A. Jordan, E. Inbal (cnds)
Sensual Classics II, w. A. Sultanov (pno), C. Katsaris (pno), Brodsky Quartet, London SO [cnd:M. Shostakovich], New York PO [cnd:Z. Mehta], BBC SO [cnd:A. Davis], Leipzig Gewandhaus Orch [cnd:K. Masur], et al. Teldec ▲ 92014-2 ▮ 92014-4
20th Century Classics Ensemble
Schoenberg, A.:Serenade Cl, w. Stephen Varcoe (bar) Koch International Classics ▲ KIC 7263-2 [DDD]
20th Century Consort
C. Kendall (cnd)
Albert, S.:To Wake the Dead, w. L. Shelton (sop) [E] Delos ▲ DCD 1016 [DDD]
Lazarof, H.:Concertante II Delos ▲ DE 3124 [DDD]
Lazarof, H.:Suite Perc Delos ▲ DE 3124 [DDD]
2E2M Ensemble
Rebotier, J.:Plages, w. Michaël Lonsdale (nar) Adès ▲ ADE 204472 [DDD/AAD]
P. Méfano (cnd)
Yun, I.:Con Fl, w. Pierre-Yves Artaud (fl) Adda ▲ ADD 243422 [DDD]
Yun, I.:Octet Cl Adda ▲ ADD 243422 [DDD]
Tzigane Piano Trio
Chaminade, C.:Pno Music (misc)—Pastorale enfantine; Ritournelle [both arr Elizabeth Marcus for pno trio]; Sérénade, Op. 29; Sérénade espagnole ASV ▲ ASV 965
Chaminade, C.:Trios Pno, Opp. 11 & 39 ASV ▲ ASV 965
Udine CO
W. Themel (cnd)
Backofen, J.G.:Con for 2 Cls, w. Nicola Bulfone (cl), Daniel Pacitti (cl) *(rec Oct 14-15, 1995)* Agora Musica ▲ 039 [DDD]
Devienne, F.:Sinf concertante Cls, w. Nicola Bulfone (cl), Daniel Pacitti (cl) *(rec Oct 14-15, 1995)* Agora Musica ▲ 039 [DDD]
Hoffmeister, F.A.:Con for 2 Cls, w. Nicola Bulfone (cl), Daniel Pacitti (cl) *(rec Auditorium di Remanzacco, Oct 12-13, 1995)* Agora Musica ▲ AG 033.1 [DDD]
Krommer, F.:Cons for 2 Cls, w. Nicola Bulfone (cl), Daniel Pacitti (cl) *(rec Auditorium di Remanzacco, Oct 12-13, 1995)* Agora Musica ▲ AG 023.1 [DDD]
Mendelssohn, F.:Concert Pieces, w. Nicola Bulfone (cl), Daniel Pacitti (cl) *(rec Auditorium di Remanzacco, Oct 12-13, 1995)* Agora Musica ▲ AG 023.1 [DDD]
Stamitz, C.:Con for 2 Cls, w. Nicola Bulfone (cl), Daniel Pacitti (cl) *(rec Oct 14-15, 1995)* Agora Musica ▲ 039 [DDD]
Tausch, F.W.:Concertante 2, w. Nicola Bulfone (cl), Daniel Pacitti (cl) *(rec Auditorium di Remanzacco, Oct 12-13, 1995)* Agora Musica ▲ AG 033.1 [DDD]
Telemann, G.P.:Con 2 Chl, w. Nicola Bulfone (cl), Daniel Pacitti (cl) *(rec Auditorium di Remanzacco, Oct 12-13, 1995)* Agora Musica ▲ AG 033.1 [DDD]
Ukrainian CO
F. Glushchenko (cnd)
Stankovich, E.:Chamber Sym 2 *(rec 1982)* Consonance ▲ 81-0006 [AAD]
A. Mogrelia (cnd)
Novák, V.:Serenade in F *(rec Concert Hall of the Ukrainian Radio, Kiev, Sept. 14-17, 1994)* Marco Polo ▲ 8.223649 [DDD]
Novák, V.:Serenade in D *(rec Concert Hall of the Ukrainian Radio, Kiev, Sept. 14-17, 1994)* Marco Polo ▲ 8.223649 [DDD]
Ukrainian National SO
O. Barvinskij (cnd)
Glass, Paul:Sinf 3 *(rec Kiev, 1991)* Grammont ▲ CTSP 43 [AAD]
T. Kuchar (cnd)
Kallinikov, V.:Sym 1 *(rec Concert Hall of the Ukrainian Radio, Kiev, Nov 2-6, 1994)* Naxos ▲ 8.553417 [DDD]
Kallinikov, V.:Sym 2 *(rec Concert Hall of the Ukrainian Radio, Kiev, Nov 2-6, 1994)* Naxos ▲ 8.553417 [DDD]
Prokofiev, S.:Autumm *(rec Ukranian Radio Concert Hall, Dec 1995)* Naxos ▲ 8.553053 [DDD]
Prokofiev, S.:Dreams *(rec Ukranian Radio Concert Hall, Dec 1995)* Naxos ▲ 8.553053 [DDD]
Prokofiev, S.:Sym 1 *(rec Ukranian Radio Concert Hall, Dec 1995)* Naxos ▲ 8.553053 [DDD]
Prokofiev, S.:Sym 2 *(rec Ukranian Radio Concert Hall, Dec 1995)* Naxos ▲ 8.553053 [DDD]
Prokofiev, S.:Sym 3 *(rec Concert Hall of the Ukrainian Radio, Kiev, Oct. 14-15, 1994)* Naxos ▲ 8.553054 [DDD]
Prokofiev, S.:Sym 5 *(rec Ukranian Radio Concert Hall, Kiev, Feb 3-7, 1995)* Naxos ▲ 8.553056 [DDD]
Prokofiev, S.:Sym 7 *(rec Concert Hall of the Ukrainian Radio, Kiev, Nov. 13-14, 1994)* Naxos ▲ 8.553054 [DDD]
Prokofiev, S.:The Year 1941 *(rec Ukranian Radio Concert Hall, Kiev, Feb 3-7, 1995)* Naxos ▲ 8.553056 [DDD]
Shostakovich, D.:5 Days-5 Nights *(rec Ukranian Radio Concert Hall, Kiev, Feb 1995)* Naxos ▲ 8.553299 [DDD]
Shostakovich, D.:The Gadfly *(rec Ukranian Radio Concert Hall, Kiev, Feb 1995)* Naxos ▲ 8.553299 [DDD]
Stankovich, E.:Sym 1 *(rec Ukrainian Radio Concert Hall, Jan 27-31, 1995)* Marco Polo ▲ 8.223792 [DDD]
Stankovich, E.:Sym 2 *(rec Ukrainian Radio Concert Hall, Jan 27-31, 1995)* Marco Polo ▲ 8.223792 [DDD]
A. Penny (cnd)
Brian, H.:Fant Vars on an Old Rhyme *(rec Concert Hall of the Ukraine Radio, Oct 28-30, 1994)* Marco Polo ▲ 8.223731 [DDD]
Brian, H.:Sym 20 *(rec Concert Hall of the Ukraine Radio, Oct 28-30, 1994)* Marco Polo ▲ 8.223731 [DDD]
Brian, H.:Sym 25 *(rec Concert Hall of the Ukraine Radio, Oct 28-30, 1994)* Marco Polo ▲ 8.223731 [DDD]
Holbrooke, J.:The Birds of Rhiannon *(rec Concert Hall of Ukrainian Radio, Kiev, Oct. 28-30, 1994)* Marco Polo ▲ 8.223721 [DDD]
Holbrooke, J.:The Children of Don (ov) *(rec Concert Hall of Ukrainian Radio, Kiev, Oct. 28-30, 1994)* Marco Polo ▲ 8.223721 [DDD]
Holbrooke, J.:Dylan (sels)—prelude *(rec Concert Hall of Ukrainian Radio, Kiev, Oct. 28-30, 1994)* Marco Polo ▲ 8.223721 [DDD]
Ukrainian Radio-TV SO
Liatoshinsky, B.:Lyric Poem Russian Disc ▲ RUS 11062 [DDD]
Liatoshinsky, B.:On the Banks of the Vistula Russian Disc ▲ RUS 11062 [DDD]
Liatoshinsky, B.:Sym 4 Russian Disc ▲ RUS 11062 [DDD]
A. Gharabekian (cnd)
Prokofiev, S.:Romeo & Juliet (suites)—Suite 1:VII; Suite 2:I-VII *(rec Ukranian Radio-TV Studio, Kiev, Nov 5-8, 1994)* Russian Disc ▲ RD CD 10090 [DDD]
Tchaikovsky, P.:Romeo & Juliet *(rec Ukranian Radio-TV Studio, Kiev, Nov 5-8, 1994)* Russian Disc ▲ RD CD 10090 [DDD]
V. Gnedash (cnd)
Liatoshinsky, B.:Romeo & Juliet (suite) Russian Disc ▲ RUS 11060 [DDD]
Liatoshinsky, B.:Sym 2 Russian Disc ▲ RUS 11 059

Ukrainian State SO

F. Glushchenko (cnd)

Liatoshinsky, B.:Slavonic Con, w. E. Rzhanov (pno) Russian Disc ▲ RUS 11 059
Stankovich, E.:The Night Before Christmas *(rec 1983)* Consonance ▲ 81-0006 [AAD]
Stankovich, E.:Sym of Pastorals *(rec 1982)* Consonance ▲ 81-0006 [AAD]

V. Gnedash (cnd)

Liatoshinsky, B.:Ov on 4 Ukrainian Themes Russian Disc ▲ RUS 11 055 [DDD]
Liatoshinsky, B.:Poem of Reunification Russian Disc ▲ RUS 11 055 [DDD]
Liatoshinsky, B.:Sym 1 Russian Disc ▲ RUS 11 055 [DDD]

T. Kuchar (cnd)

Liatoshinsky, B.:Grazhyna *(rec State Broadcasting Company of Ukraine Studio, Kiev, May 8, 13 & 15, 1994)* Marco Polo ▲ 8.223542 [DDD]
Liatoshinsky, B.:Sym 1 *(rec State Broadcasting Company of Ukraine Studio, Kiev, May 8, 13 & 15, 1994)* Marco Polo ▲ 8.223542 [DDD]
Liatoshinsky, B.:Sym 2 *(rec Kiev, June 4–9, 1993)* Marco Polo ▲ 8.223540 [DDD]
Liatoshinsky, B.:Sym 3 *(rec Kiev, June 4–9 1993)* Marco Polo ▲ 8.223540 [DDD]
Shchedrin, R.:Carmen *(rec Ukrainian State Broadcasting Co. Studio, Kiev, Apr. 28–30, 1994)* Naxos ▲ 8.553038 [DDD]
Shchedrin, R.:Con 1 Orch, "Naughty Limericks" *(rec Ukrainian State Broadcasting Co. Studio, Kiev, Apr. 28–30, 1994)* Naxos ▲ 8.553038 [DDD]
Stankovich, E.:Sym 4 *(rec Ukrainian Radio Concert Hall, Jan 27–31, 1995)* Marco Polo ▲ 8.223792 [DDD]

S. Turchak (cnd)

Liatoshinsky, B.:Sym 3 Russian Disc ▲ RUS 11060 [DDD]

Ulmer Brass Ensemble

Christmas Concert, w. Dach, Simon, Collegium Tubicense Ulm, Holzbläser Ensemble, Holzbläser CO Christophorus ▲ CD 74585

Ulsamer Collegium

Dance Music of the Renaissance, w. Konrad Ragossnig (lt/gtr) Archiv ▲ 415294-2 AH [ADD]
Praetorius, M.:Terpsichore, w. S. Behrend (gtr), S. Fink (perc), Collegium Terpsichore—36 sels IMP Collectors Series ▲ IMPX 9026 [AAD]

Ulster Orch

V. Handley (cnd)

Bax, A.:On the Sea Shore Chandos ▲ CHAN 8473 [DDD]
Beethoven, L. van:Egmont (ov) Chandos ▲ CHAN 8746 [DDD]
Bliss, A.:Checkmate (5 dances) Chandos ▲ CHAN 8503 [DDD]
Bliss, A.:A Colour Sym Chandos ▲ CHAN 8503 [DDD]
Bliss, A.:Con Vc, w. R. Wallfisch (vc) Chandos ▲ CHAN 8818 [DDD]
Bliss, A.:The Enchantress, w. L. Finnie (cta) [E] Chandos ▲ CHAN 8818 [DDD]
Bliss, A.:Hymn To Apollo [E] Chandos ▲ CHAN 8818 [DDD]
Britten, B.:Peter Grimes (sea interludes & passacaglia) Chandos ▲ CHAN 8473 [DDD]
Brahms, J.:Serenade 1 Orch Chandos ▲ CHAN 8612 [DDD]
Brahms, J.:Vars on a Theme by Haydn Chandos ▲ CHAN 8767 [DDD]
Brahms, J.:Vars on a Theme by Haydn Chandos ▲ CHAN 8612 [DDD]
Bridge, F.:The Sea—excerpt Chandos ("Collect" series) ▲ CHAN 6538 [ADD/DDD]
Bridge, F.:The Sea Chandos ▲ CHAN 8473 [DDD]
Delius, F.:Florida Chandos ▲ CHAN 8413 [DDD]
Delius, F.:North Country Sketches Chandos ▲ CHAN 8413 [DDD]
Dvořák, A.:Carnival Chandos ▲ CHAN 8453 [DDD]
Dvořák, A.:Carnival Chandos ▲ CHAN 8767 [DDD]
Dvořák, A.:In Nature's Realm Chandos ▲ CHAN 8453 [DDD]
Dvořák, A.:Othello Chandos ▲ CHAN 8453 [DDD]
Dvořák, A.:Scherzo Capriccioso Chandos ▲ CHAN 8453 [DDD]
Grieg, E.:Con Pno, Op. 16, w. M. Fingerhut (pno) Chandos ▲ CHAN 8723 [DDD]
Grieg, E.:Con Pno, Op. 16, w. Margaret Fingerhut (pno) Chandos ▲ CHAN 7040
Grieg, E.:Elegaic Melodies, Op. 34 Chandos ▲ CHAN 8524 [DDD]
Grieg, E.:Lyric Suite, Op. 54 Chandos ▲ CHAN 8723 [DDD]
Grieg, E.:Lyric Suite, Op. 54 Chandos ▲ CHAN 7040
Grieg, E.:Peer Gynt Suites, Opp. 46 & 55 Chandos ▲ CHAN 7040
Grieg, E.:Peer Gynt Suite 1 Chandos ▲ CHAN 8524 [DDD]
Grieg, E.:Peer Gynt Suite 1 Chandos ▲ CHAN 8767 [DDD]
Grieg, E.:Peer Gynt Suite 2 Chandos ▲ CHAN 8723 [DDD]
Grieg, E.:Sigurd Jorsalfar (suite) Chandos ▲ CHAN 8524 [DDD]
Grieg, E.:Symphonic Dances Chandos ▲ CHAN 8524 [DDD]
Moeran, E.J.:Con Vn, w. L. Mordkovitch (vn) Chandos ▲ CHAN 8807 [DDD]
Moeran, E.J.:In the Mountain Country Chandos ▲ CHAN 8639 [DDD]
Moeran, E.J.:Lonely Waters Chandos ▲ CHAN 8807 [DDD]
Moeran, E.J.:Nocturne, w. H. Mackey (bar), Renaissance Singers [E] Chandos ▲ CHAN 8808 [DDD]
Moeran, E.J.:Ov to a Masque Chandos ▲ CHAN 8577 [DDD]
Moeran, E.J.:Rhap 1 Chandos ▲ CHAN 8639 [DDD]
Moeran, E.J.:Rhap 2 [1941 version] Chandos ▲ CHAN 8639 [DDD]
Moeran, E.J.:Rhap Pno, w. M. Fingerhut (pno) Chandos ▲ CHAN 8639 [DDD]
Moeran, E.J.:Serenade—premiere rec'g of the complete work, incl. two sections dropped from the orig. published version Chandos ▲ CHAN 8808 [DDD]
Moeran, E.J.:Sym Chandos ▲ CHAN 8577 [DDD]
Moeran, E.J.:Whythorne's Shadow Chandos ▲ CHAN 8807 [DDD]
Mozart, W.A.:Sym 40 Chandos ▲ CHAN 8746 [DDD]
Schubert, Franz:Sym 8 Chandos ▲ CHAN 8746 [DDD]
Seascapes, w. Royal Scottish National Orch [cnd:A. Gibson], Bournemouth Sinfonietta [cnd:G. Hurst], London PO [cnd:B. Thomson] Chandos ("Collect" series) ▲ CHAN 6538 [ADD/DDD]
Stanford, C.V.:Concert Piece Org, w. G. Weir (org) Chandos ▲ CHAN 8861 [DDD]
Stanford, C.V.:Concert Vars upon an English Theme, w. M. Fingerhut (pno) Chandos ▲ CHAN 8736 [DDD]
Stanford, C.V.:Con Cl, w. J. Hilton (cl) Chandos ▲ CHAN 8991 [DDD]
Stanford, C.V.:Con 2 Pno, w. M. Fingerhut (pno) Chandos ▲ CHAN 8736 [DDD]
Stanford, C.V.:Irish Rhaps, w. R. Wallfisch (vc), L. Mordkovitch (vn) Chandos 2-▲ CHAN 7002/03 [DDD]
Stanford, C.V.:Irish Rhap 1 Chandos ▲ CHAN 8627 [DDD]
Stanford, C.V.:Irish Rhap 2 Chandos ▲ CHAN 9049 [DDD]
Stanford, C.V.:Irish Rhap 3, w. R. Wallfisch (vc) Chandos ▲ CHAN 8861 [DDD]
Stanford, C.V.:Irish Rhap 4 Chandos ▲ CHAN 8581 [DDD]
Stanford, C.V.:Irish Rhap 5 Chandos ▲ CHAN 8545 [DDD]
Stanford, C.V.:Irish Rhap 6, w. L. Mordkovitch (vn) Chandos ▲ CHAN 8884 [DDD]
Stanford, C.V.:Oedipus tyrannus (prelude) Chandos 2-▲ CHAN 7002/03 [DDD]
Stanford, C.V.:Oedipus tyrannus (prelude) Chandos ▲ CHAN 8884 [DDD]
Stanford, C.V.:Syms (comp) Chandos 4-▲ CHAN 9279 [DDD]
Stanford, C.V.:Sym 1 Chandos ▲ CHAN 9049 [DDD]
Stanford, C.V.:Sym 2 Chandos ▲ CHAN 8991 [DDD]
Stanford, C.V.:Sym 3 Chandos ▲ CHAN 8545 [DDD]
Stanford, C.V.:Sym 4 Chandos ▲ CHAN 8884 [DDD]
Stanford, C.V.:Sym 5 Chandos ▲ CHAN 8581 [DDD]
Stanford, C.V.:Sym 6 Chandos ▲ CHAN 8627 [DDD]
Tchaikovsky, P.:Romeo & Juliet Chandos ▲ CHAN 8767 [DDD]
Warlock, P.:Capriol Suite Chandos ▲ CHAN 8808 [DDD]
Warlock, P.:Serenade Chandos ▲ CHAN 8808 [DDD]

B. Thomson (cnd)

Bax, A.:The Garden of Fand Chandos ▲ CHAN 8307 [DDD]
Bax, A.:The Happy Forest Chandos ▲ CHAN 8307 [DDD]

Ulster Orch (cont.)

B. Thomson (cnd) (cont.)

Bax, A.:In The Faery Hills Chandos ▲ CHAN 8367 [DDD]
Bax, A.:Into the Twilight Chandos ▲ CHAN 8367 [DDD]
Bax, A.:November Woods Chandos ▲ CHAN 8307 [DDD]
Bax, A.:Roscatha Chandos ▲ CHAN 8367 [DDD]
Bax, A.:Summer Music Chandos ▲ CHAN 8307 [DDD]
Bax, A.:Sym 4 Chandos ▲ CHAN 8312 [DDD]
Bax, A.:The Tale the Pine-trees Knew Chandos ▲ CHAN 8367 [DDD]
Bax, A.:Tintagel Chandos ("Collect" series) ▲ CHAN 6538 [ADD/DDD]
Bax, A.:Tintagel Chandos ▲ CHAN 8312 [DDD]
Britten, B.:Peter Grimes (4 sea interludes)—Interludes Nos. 2 & 4 Chandos ("Collect" series) ▲ CHAN 6538 [ADD/DDD]
Elgar, E.:Nursery Suite Chandos ▲ CHAN 8318 [DDD]
Elgar, E.:The Wand of Youth Suites Chandos ▲ CHAN 8318 [DDD]
Handel, G.F.:Water Music (suites) [arr. Sir Hamilton Harty] Chandos ("Collect" series) ▲ CHAN 6583 [ADD]
Harty, H.:The Children of Lir Orch Chandos 3-▲ CHAN 7035
Harty, H.:The Children of Lir Sop & Orch, w. Heather Harper (sop) Chandos ▲ CHAN 7033
Harty, H.:A Comedy Ov Chandos ▲ CHAN 7034
Harty, H.:A Comedy Ov Chandos ▲ CHAN 8314 [DDD]
Harty, H.:Con Pno Chandos 3-▲ CHAN 7035
Harty, H.:Con Pno, w. Malcolm Binns (pno) Chandos ▲ CHAN 8321 [DDD]
Harty, H.:Con Pno, w. Malcolm Binns (pno) Chandos ▲ CHAN 7032
Harty, H.:Con Vn, w. Ralph Holmes (vn) Chandos ▲ CHAN 7032
Harty, H.:Con Vn Chandos 3-▲ CHAN 7035
Harty, H.:Con Vn, w. Ralph Holmes (vn) Chandos ▲ CHAN 8386
Harty, H.:In Ireland Chandos ▲ CHAN 7034
Harty, H.:In Ireland, w. Denise Kelley (hp), C. Fleming (fl) Chandos ("Collect" series) ▲ CHAN 6583 [ADD]
Harty, H.:In Ireland, w. Denise Kelley (hp), C. Fleming (fl) Chandos ▲ CHAN 8321 [DDD]
Harty, H.:Irish Sym Chandos 3-▲ CHAN 7035
Harty, H.:Irish Sym Chandos ▲ CHAN 7034
Harty, H.:Irish Sym Chandos ▲ CHAN 8314 [DDD]
Harty, H.:A John Field Suite Chandos ("Collect" series) ▲ CHAN 6583 [ADD]
Harty, H.:The Londonderry Air [arr for orch] Chandos ▲ CHAN 7033
Harty, H.:Ode to a Nightingale, w. Heather Harper (sop) Chandos ▲ CHAN 7033
Harty, H.:Vars on a Dublin Air, w. Ralph Holmes (vn) Chandos ▲ CHAN 8386
Harty, H.:Vars on a Dublin Air Chandos ▲ CHAN 7033
Harty, H.:With the Wild Geese Chandos ▲ CHAN 7034
Harty, H.:With the Wild Geese Chandos ▲ CHAN 8321 [DDD]

Y.P. Tortelier (cnd)

Berlioz, H.:Les Nuits d'été, w. B. Greevy (mez) [F] Chandos ▲ CHAN 8735 [DDD]
Bizet, G.:L'Arlésienne (suites) Chandos ("Collect" series) ▲ CHAN 6600 [DDD]
Bizet, G.:Carmen (suites) Chandos ("Collect" series) ▲ CHAN 6600 [DDD]
Chabrier, E.:España Chandos ▲ CHAN 8852 [DDD]
Chabrier, E.:Suite pastorale Chandos ▲ CHAN 8852 [DDD]
Chausson, E.:Poème de l'amour et de la mer, w. L. Finnie (mez) [F] Chandos ▲ CHAN 8952 [DDD]
Chausson, E.:Poème Vn, w. Y. P. Tortelier (vn) Chandos ▲ CHAN 8952 [DDD]
Debussy, C.:La Boîte à joujoux Chandos ▲ CHAN 7017
Debussy, C.:La Boîte à joujoux—orchestral version Chandos ▲ CHAN 8711 [DDD]
Debussy, C.:Children's Corner Chandos ▲ CHAN 7017
Debussy, C.:Clair de lune [orchd. André Caplet] *(rec May 29, 1991)* Chandos ▲ CHAN 9129 [DDD]
Debussy, C.:Danse Pno, "Tarantelle styrienne" Chandos ▲ CHAN 7017
Debussy, C.:Danse Pno, "Tarantelle styrienne" *(rec June 3–4, 1992)* Chandos ▲ CHAN 9129 [DDD]
Debussy, C.:Danses sacrée et profane, w. R. Masters (hp) Chandos ▲ CHAN 8972 [DDD]
Debussy, C.:Danses sacrée et profane Chandos ▲ CHAN 7018
Debussy, C.:Fant Pno Chandos ▲ CHAN 7018
Debussy, C.:Fant Pno, w. A. Queffélec (pno) Chandos ▲ CHAN 8972 [DDD]
Debussy, C.:Images Orch Chandos ▲ CHAN 8850 [DDD]
Debussy, C.:Images Orch Chandos ▲ CHAN 7016
Debussy, C.:L'Isle joyeuse [orchd. Molinari] *(rec Feb. 19–20, 1991)* Chandos ▲ CHAN 9129 [DDD]
Debussy, C.:Jeux Chandos ▲ CHAN 8903 [DDD]
Debussy, C.:Jeux Chandos ▲ CHAN 7016
Debussy, C.:Khamma Chandos ▲ CHAN 8903 [DDD]
Debussy, C.:Khamma Chandos ▲ CHAN 7016
Debussy, C.:Marche écossaise sur un thème populaire *(rec June 3–4, 1992)* Chandos ▲ CHAN 9129 [DDD]
Debussy, C.:Marche écossaise sur un thème populaire Chandos ▲ CHAN 7017
Debussy, C.:La Mer Chandos ▲ CHAN 9114 [DDD]
Debussy, C.:La Mer Chandos ("7000" series) ▲ CHAN 7015
Debussy, C.:Nocturnes, w. Renaissance Singers, Grosvenor High School Choir Chandos ▲ CHAN 8914 [DDD]
Debussy, C.:Nocturnes Chandos ("7000" series) ▲ CHAN 7015
Debussy, C.:Orchestral Music—La mer; Nocturnes; Printemps; Prélude à l'après-midi d'un faune; Images; Jeux; Khamma; La boîte à joujoux; Children's Corner; Petite suite; Marche écossaise sur un thème populaire; Danse; Fant for Pno & Orch; Première rapsodie; Danses; Rapsodie for A Sax & Orch; Sarabande; L'isle joyeuse; La plus que lente; Clair de lune Chandos 4-▲ CHAN 7019 [DDD]
Debussy, C.:Petite suite Chandos ▲ CHAN 7017
Debussy, C.:La Plus que lente *(rec Feb. 19–20, 1991)* Chandos ▲ CHAN 9129 [DDD]
Debussy, C.:Prélude à l'après-midi d'un faune Chandos ▲ CHAN 8893 [DDD]
Debussy, C.:Prélude à l'après-midi d'un faune Chandos ("7000" series) ▲ CHAN 7015
Debussy, C.:Première rapsodie, w. C. King (cl) Chandos ▲ CHAN 8972 [DDD]
Debussy, C.:Première rapsodie Chandos ▲ CHAN 7018
Debussy, C.:Printemps (suite) Chandos ▲ CHAN 9114 [DDD]
Debussy, C.:Printemps (suite) Chandos ("7000" series) ▲ CHAN 7015
Debussy, C.:Rapsodie, w. G. McChrystal (sax) *(rec June 3–4, 1992)* Chandos ▲ CHAN 9129 [DDD]
Debussy, C.:Sarabande *(rec Oct. 29–30, 1990)* Chandos ▲ CHAN 9129 [DDD]
Dukas, P.:L'Apprenti sorcier Chandos ▲ CHAN 8852 [DDD]
Dukas, P.:La péri Chandos ▲ CHAN 8852 [DDD]
Duparc, H.:Songs, w. B. Greevy (mez)—Chanson triste; Le Manoir de Rosemonde; L'invitation au voyage; Soupir; Phidylé; La vie antérieure; Sérénade florentine [F] Chandos ▲ CHAN 8735 [DDD]
Fauré, G.:Pavane Orch, w. Renaissance Singers Chandos ▲ CHAN 8952 [DDD]
Fauré, G.:Pelléas et Mélisande (suite) Chandos ▲ CHAN 8952 [DDD]
Ibert, J.:Divert Orch *(rec 5/91)* Chandos ▲ CHAN 9023 [DDD]
Milhaud, D.:Le Boeuf sur le toit *(rec 5/91)* Chandos ▲ CHAN 9023 [DDD]
Milhaud, D.:La Création du monde *(rec 5/91)* Chandos ▲ CHAN 9023 [DDD]
Poulenc, F.:Les Biches Chandos ▲ CHAN 9023 [DDD]
Ravel, M.:Alborada del gracioso Chandos ▲ CHAN 8850 [DDD]
Ravel, M.:Boléro Chandos ▲ CHAN 8903 [DDD]
Ravel, M.:Daphnis et Chloé, w. Belfast Philharmonic Society Chorus, Renaissance Singers Chandos ▲ CHAN 8893 [DDD]
Ravel, M.:Don Quichotte à Dulcinée, w. S. Roberts (bar) Chandos ▲ CHAN 8972 [DDD]
Ravel, M.:Intro & Allegro, w. R. Masters (hp) Chandos ▲ CHAN 8972 [DDD]
Ravel, M.:Ma mère l'oye Orch Chandos ▲ CHAN 8711 [DDD]
Ravel, M.:Orchestral Music—Une Barque sur l'Océan; Menuet antique; L'Eventail de Jéanne (Fanfare); Pavane pour une infante défunte Chandos ▲ CHAN 9129 [DDD]
Ravel, M.:Rapsodie espagnole Chandos ▲ CHAN 8850 [DDD]
Ravel, M.:Shéhérazade Mez, w. L. Finnie (mez) Chandos ▲ CHAN 8914 [DDD]
Ravel, M.:Shéhérazade Pno Chandos ▲ CHAN 8914 [DDD]

Ulster Orch (cont.)
Y.P. Tortelier (cnd) (cont.)
Ravel, M.:Trio Pno [orchd. version by Yan Pascal Tortelier] Chandos ▲ CHAN 9114 [DDD]
Ravel, M.:Tzigane, w. Y. P. Tortelier (vn) Chandos ▲ CHAN 8972 [DDD]
Ravel, M.:La Valse Chandos ▲ CHAN 8903 [DDD]
Saint-Saëns, C.:Sym 2 Chandos ▲ CHAN 8822 [DDD]
Saint-Saëns, C.:Sym 3, w. G. Weir (org) Chandos ▲ CHAN 8822 [DDD]
Umeå Sinfonietta
Larsson, L-E.:Concertinos, w. New Stockholm CO, Stockholm Chamber Ensemble, Musica Sveciae, Musica Vitae—G. von Bahr (fl) *(No. 1)*, H. Jahren (ob) *(No. 2)*, M. Lethiec (cl) *(No. 3)*, K. Sonstevold (bn) *(No. 4)*, S. Hermansson (hn) *(No. 5)*, U. Agnas (tpt) *(No. 6)*, C. Lindberg (trbn) *(No. 7)*, A. Kontra (vn) *(No. 8)*, B. Andersson (va) *(No. 9)*, F. Helmerson (vc) *(No. 10)*, H. Ehren (db) *(No. 11)*, H. Palsson (pno) *(No. 12)* [these twelve neo-classical, at times Hindemithesque, three-movement concertinos were composed to suit the performing abilities of the amateur orchestra] BIS 2-▲ CD 473/74 [AAD/DDD]
E. Chivzhel (cnd)
Atterberg, K.:Con Hn, w. Hermansson (hn) BIS ▲ CD 376 [DDD]
Jacob, G.:Con Hn, w. S. Hermansson (hn) BIS ▲ CD 376 [DDD]
Larsson, L-E.:Concertino Hn, w. Sören Hermansson (hn) BIS ▲ CD 376 [DDD]
Reger, M.:Scherzino, w. S. Hermansson (hn) BIS ▲ CD 376 [DDD]
Seiber, M.:Notturno Hn, w. S. Hermansson (hn) BIS ▲ CD 376 [DDD]
J.-P. Saraste (cnd)
Vanhal, J.B.:Con Bns, w. Annika Wallin (bn), Arne Nilsson (bn) BIS ▲ CD 288 [DDD]
Vanhal, J.B.:Sym in a BIS ▲ CD 288 [DDD]
Vanhal, J.B.:Sym in F BIS ▲ CD 288 [DDD]
Umeå SO
T. Svedlund (cnd)
Bach, C.P.E.:Cons Fl, w. Áshildur Haraldsdóttir (fl)—in G Intim Musik ▲ INT 38
Benda, F.:Con in e Fl & Orch, w. Áshildur Haraldsdóttir (fl) Intim Musik ▲ INT 38
Haydn, J.:Con Fl, H.VIIf/D1, w. Áshildur Haraldsdóttir (fl) Intim Musik ▲ INT 38
Unicorn Ensemble
Alfonso El Sabio:Cantigas de Santa Maria *(rec Tonstudio W-A-R, Nov. 24-27, 1994)* Naxos ▲ 8.553133 [DDD]
M. Posch (cnd)
Dufay, G.:Songs, w. Bernhard Landauer (ct)—J'ay mis mon cuer; Par droit je puis bien complaindre; Quel fronte signorille La dolce vista; Puisque vous estez campieur; Belle, que vous ay je mesfait; Vergene bella; Se la face ay pale; Donnes l'assault à la fortresse; Par le regard de vos beaux yeux; Resvelons nous; Ce jour de l'an; Mon chier amy; Pour l'amour de ma doulce amye; Helas mon dueil; Bon jour, bon mois; Resvelliés vous et faites chiere lye; Adieu ces bons vins de Lannoys *(rec Evangelische Kirche A.B., Vienna, Apr 15-18, 1995)* Naxos ▲ 8.553458 [DDD]
United States Air Force Academy Band members
R. Harris (cnd)
Harris, R.:Con Amplified Pno, w. Johana Harris (pno), International String Congress Orch *(rec Colorado Springs, CO, 1971)* Citadel ▲ CTD 88114
United States Air Force Band
An American Tribute, w. Mormon Tabernacle Choir, Singing Sergeants CBS ▲ MK 42133 [DDD] ■ MT 42133 (D)
H. Hanson (cnd)
Hanson, H.:Song of Democracy, w. Mormon Tabernacle Choir [E] CBS ▲ MK 42133 [DDD]
Universal Ensemble [Andreas Friedrich (vn), Cornel Anderes (va), Madleine Burkhalter (va), David Riniker (vc), Gallus Burkard (db)]
Mendelssohn, F.:Sextet, w. Karl-Andreas Kolly (pno) Pan ▲ 510 070 [DDD]
Univ Circle Wind Ensemble
G. Ciepluch (cnd)
Erb, D.:Cenotaph New World ▲ 80457-2
Erb, D.:Sym Ww New World ▲ 80457-2
Univ of Arizona Wind Orch
G.I. Hanson (cnd)
Maslanka, D.:Mass, w. Lydia Catherine Easley (sop), Charles Roe (bar), Jane Smith (org), Univ of Arizona Sym Choir, Arizona Chamber Choir, Tuscon Boys' Chorus *(rec St. Thomas the Apostle Church, Tuscon, Arizona, Apr 29-30, 1996)* Albany 2-▲ TROY 221-22 [DDD]
Univ of Calgary Wind Ensemble
G. Price (cnd)
Badings, H.:Con Fl, w. Tanya Dusevic (fl) *(rec Calgary Center for the Performing Arts)* Unical ▲ UC 9401 [DDD]
Ballenger, W.:Fant on "O Canada" *(rec Calgary Center for the Performing Arts)* Unical ▲ UC 9401 [DDD]
Coakley, D.:Lyric Essay *(rec Calgary Center for the Performing Arts)* Unical ▲ UC 9401 [DDD]
Irvine, J.S.:Epitaphium *(rec Calgary Center for the Performing Arts)* Unical ▲ UC 9401 [DDD]
Lukas, Z.:Musica Boema *(rec Calgary Center for the Performing Arts)* Unical ▲ UC 9401 [DDD]
Nelson, R.:Medieval Suite *(rec Calgary Center for the Performing Arts)* Unical ▲ UC 9401 [DDD]
Univ of California Los Angeles Wind Ensemble
J. Westbrook (cnd)
Grainger, P.:Lincolnshire Posy *(rec Jan. 1980)* Phoenix ▲ PHCD 119 [DDD]
Univ of California Santa Barbara Ensemble for Contemporary Music
Kraft, William:Qt for the Love of Time *(rec 1992)* CRI ▲ CD 639 [ADD/DDD]
Univ of Chicago Contemporary Chamber Players
C. Colnot (cnd)
Ran, S.:Con da Camera II, w. E. Gilmore (cl) *(rec 1979-91)* CRI ▲ CD 609 [ADD/DDD]
R. Shapey (cnd)
Shapey, R.:Concertante 1 Tpt, w. M. Anderson (trbn) New World ▲ NW 355-2 [DDD]
Shapey, R.:The Covenant, w. Elsa Charlston (sop) CRI ▲ CD 690 [ADD]
Shapey, R.:Incantations, w. Bethany Beardslee (sop) CRI ▲ CD 690 [ADD]
Thorne, F.:7 Set Pieces CRI ▲ CD 586 [ADD]
Univ of Chicago Contemporary Chamber Players String Quartet
Shapey, R.:Qt 7 Strs CRI ■ C 391
Univ of Florida Wind Ensemble
D. Waybright (cnd)
White, J.:But God's Own Descent, w. Univ of Florida Choir Opus One ▲ CD 167 [DDD]
Univ of Illinois Contemporary Chamber Players
Powell, Morgan:Qnt 2 Brass *(rec live 1985)* Opus One ▲ CD 164
E. London (cnd)
Powell, Morgan:Transitions, w. Daniel Perantoni (tuba) *(rec Univ of Illinois, 1976)* New World ▲ 80499-2
Univ of Illinois Contemporary Chamber Players [Ron Dewar (t sax), Charles Braugham (perc), Jon Dutton (perc), William Parsons (perc), Michael Ranta (perc), Thomas Fredrickson (db), Peter Farrell (vc)]
D. Gilbert (cnd)
Martirano, S.:Underworld *(rec 1966)* Centaur ▲ CRC 2266 [DDD]
Univ of Illinois New Music Ensemble
Powell, Morgan:Darkness I *(rec live 1988)* Opus One ▲ CD 164
J. Garvey (cnd)
Partch, H.:The Bewitched (final scene), w. Univ of Illinois Chorus CRI ■ ACS 6001
Partch, H.:The Bewitched (final scene), w. Univ of Illinois Chorus *(rec 1957, mono)* CRI ▲ CD 7000 (m/s) [AAD]
Univ of Illinois New Music Ensemble members
Partch, H.:The Bewitched, w. F. Schell (voc) CRI ▲ CD 7001 [ADD]
Univ of Iowa Center for New Music
25th Anniversary, 1966-1991 Music & Arts ▲ MUA 830 [DDD]
Univ of Iowa SO
J. Dixon (cnd)
Gaburo, K.:Antiphony IX, w. Iowa City Boys' Choir, Iowa City Girls' Choir Music & Arts ▲ CD 832 [DDD]
Wuorinen, C.:Con Amplified Vn, w. Paul Zukofsky (vn) Music & Arts ▲ CD 801 [ADD]
Univ of Maryland Flute Choir
R. Gibson (cnd)
Gibson, R.:Mirage Capstone ▲ CPS 8621
Univ of Massachusetts/Amherst Wind Ensemble
M. W. Rowell (cnd)
Copland, A.:Down a Country Lane Albany ▲ TROY 206 [DDD]
Grainger, P.:Early One Morning Albany ▲ TROY 206 [DDD]
Grainger, P.:Lincolnshire Posy Albany ▲ TROY 206 [DDD]
Grainger, P.:Molly on the Shore Albany ▲ TROY 206 [DDD]
Grainger, P.:Youthful Suite—English Waltz movt Albany ▲ TROY 206 [DDD]
Ives, C.:Country Band March Albany ▲ TROY 206 [DDD]
Khachaturian, A.:Armenian Dances Albany ▲ TROY 206 [DDD]
Maslanka, D.:Tears Albany ▲ TROY 206 [DDD]
Ticheli, F.:Postcard Albany ▲ TROY 206 [DDD]
Wilson, D.:Dance of the New World Albany ▲ TROY 206 [DDD]
Univ of Miami SO
T.M. Sleeper (cnd)
Brahms, J.:Ein Deutsches Requiem, w. Marvis Martin (sop), Kieth Spencer (bar), Univ of Miami Chorale Cane ▲ CR 1003
Ludwig, T.:Con Vn, w. Mark Peskanov (vn) *(rec Maurice Gusman Concert Hall, Miami, Oct 23, 1994)* Albany ▲ TROY 195 [DDD]
Surinach, C.:Double Con Fl, w. Christine Nield-Capote (fl), Lucas Drew (db) *(rec Maurice Gusman Concert Hall, The University of Miami, Florida, Oct 1993 & Nov 1994)* Centaur ▲ CRC 2256 [DDD]
Surinach, C.:Sinf chica, w. Christine Nield-Capote (fl), Lucas Drew (db) *(rec Maurice Gusman Concert Hall, The University of Miami, Florida, Oct 1993 & Nov 1994)* Centaur ▲ CRC 2256 [DDD]
Surinach, C.:Symphonic Melismas, w. Christine Nield-Capote (fl), Lucas Drew (db) *(rec Maurice Gusman Concert Hall, The University of Miami, Florida, Oct 1993 & Nov 1994)* Centaur ▲ CRC 2256 [DDD]
Univ of Miami Wind Ensemble
G. Green (cnd)
Colgrass, M.:Urban Requiem, w. David Fernandez (sax), Tom McCormick (sax), Stephen Welsh (sax), George Weremchuk (sax) *(rec Miami Beach, Feb 1996)* Albany ▲ TROY 212 [DDD]
Dahl, I.:Hymn Orch [arr J. Boyd for winds] *(rec Miami Beach, Feb 1996)* Albany ▲ TROY 212 [DDD]
Daugherty, M.:Motown Metal *(rec Miami Beach, Feb 1996)* Albany ▲ TROY 212 [DDD]
Univ of Michigan CO
Portrait of an Artist, Vol. 4, w. Ruggiero Ricci (vn), Helmut Barth, Rebecca Penneys (pno) One-Eleven ▲ URS 93040 [ADD]
Univ of Michigan Percussion Ensemble
C. Owen (cnd)
Suderburg, R.:Ritual Series Delfon ▲ DRS 2127 [DDD]
Univ of Michigan SO members
T. Hilbish (cnd)
Shifrin, S.:Odes of Shang, w. Univ of Michigan Chamber Choir *(rec Hill Auditorium, Univ of Michigan, Ann Arbor)* New World ▲ 80219-2
Thompson, R.:Americana, w. Univ of Michigan Chamber Choir *(rec Hill Auditorium, Univ of Michigan, Ann Arbor)* New World ▲ 80219-2
Univ of Minnesota Brass Band
A. Dorati (cnd)
Tchaikovsky, P.:Ov 1812, w. Minneapolis SO [Bronze cannon courtesy of U.S. Military Academy, West Point] Mercury Living Presence ▲ 434 360-2
Univ of Montreal Gamelan Ensemble
Seweca, I.W.:Sasih Kapan Ummus ▲ UMM 104
Valin, R.:Tat Ivam Asi Ummus ▲ UMM 104
Univ of New Mexico Contemporary Chamber Ensemble
Delio, T.:contrecoup... Neuma ▲ 450-81
Univ of New Mexico Percussion Ensemble
Garland, P.:Perc Music—The Three Strange Angels; Three Songs of Mad Coyote; Obstacles of Sleep; Apple Blossom ¿What Next? ▲ WN 0008 [DDD]
Univ of Northern Iowa Percussion Ensemble
Van De Vate, N.:Teufelstanz *(rec School of Music, Univ of Northern Iowa, Cedar Falls, Iowa, May 1993)* Vienna Modern Masters ▲ VMM 2015 [DDD]
Univ of Pennsylvania Chamber Players
R. Wernick (cnd)
Crumb, G.:Madrigals (4 books), w. J. DeGaetani (mez)—[Sp] New World ▲ NW 357-2
Univ of Redlands Chamber Ensemble
B. Childs (cnd)
Krumm, P.:Con B Cl, w. Scott Vance (b cl) Opus One ▲ CD 170 [DDD]
Univ of Southern California SO
D. Lewis (cnd)
Vazzana, A.:Odissea Vienna Modern Masters ▲ VMM 3031 [DDD]
Univ of Wisconsin-Milwaukee Orch
Downey, J.:What If?, w. Univ of Wisconsin-Milwaukee Chorus Gasparo ▲ GS 276 ■ GS 276C
Univ of Wisconsin-Milwaukee Wind Ensemble
Downey, J.:Octet Gasparo ▲ GS 276 ■ GS 276C
Upper Valley Duo [Tim Schwarz (vn), Dan Weiser (pno)]
Copland, A.:Rodeo (sels)—Hoe-Down Marquis ▲ MAR 179
Corigliano, J.:Son Vn & Pno Marquis ▲ MAR 179
Guarnieri, C.M.:Cantiga de Ninar Marquis ▲ MAR 179
Ives, C.:Son 2 Vn Marquis ▲ MAR 179
Uppsala Chamber Soloists
Linde, B.:Divert Fl, Vc & Pno MAP ▲ MAPCD 9025
Linde, B.:Son a tre Pno, Vn & Vc MAP ▲ MAPCD 9025
Linde, B.:Sonatina Pno MAP ▲ MAPCD 9025
Linde, B.:Trio Strs MAP ▲ MAPCD 9025
Mozart, W.A.:Duo Vn, K.423 Bluebell ▲ BLU 054 [DDD]
Mozart, W.A.:Grande Sestetto Concertante Bluebell ▲ BLU 054 [DDD]
Mozart, W.A.:Qnt Strs, K.406 Bluebell ▲ BLU 054 [DDD]
Uriarte-Mrongovius Duo [Begoña Uriarte (pno), Karl-Hermann Mrongovius (pno)]
Brahms, J.:Son for 2 Pnos Calig ▲ CAL 50893 [DDD]
Reger, M.:Vars & Fugue on a Theme by Mozart Calig ▲ CAL 50893 [DDD]
Soler, P.A.:Cons Kbds—Nos. 4 & 6 *(rec Sept. 6-8, 1991)* Calig ▲ CAL 50911 [DDD]
Soler, P.A.:Fandango *(rec Sept. 6-8, 1991)* Calig ▲ CAL 50911 [DDD]
Soler, P.A.:Sons Hpd—Nos. 21, 23, 24, 84, 90 & 100 *(rec Sept. 6-8, 1991)* Calig ▲ CAL 50911 [DDD]
USSR Large SO
G. Rozhdestvensky (cnd)
Glazunov, A.:Con Vn, w. S. Snitkovsky (vn) Vox Box 2-▲ CDX 5118 [ADD]
USSR Ministry of Culture SO
E. Khachaturian (cnd)
Prokofiev, S.:Hamlet, w. Elena Def-donskaya (sop), Sergei Balkov (bar) *(rec 1989)* Consonance ▲ 81-5005 [AAD]
G. Rozhdestvensky (cnd)
Miaskovsky, N.:Sym 1 Russian Disc ▲ RUS 11008 [AAD]

USSR Ministry of Culture SO (cont.)
G. Rozhdestvensky (cnd) (cont.)
Prokofiev, S.:Dreams *(rec 1985)* Consonance ▲ 81-5007 [AAD]
Shostakovich, D.:The Golden Mountains, Moscow PO Soloists Russian Disc ▲ RUS 11064 [AAD]
Shostakovich, D.:New Babylon, Moscow PO Soloists Russian Disc ▲ RUS 11064 [AAD]
Tchaikovsky, P.:Romeo & Juliet Erato ▲ 2292-45620-2 [DDD]
Tchaikovsky, P.:Sym 4 Erato ▲ 2292-45620-2 [DDD]
USSR Ministry of Defense Orch
A. Maltsev (cnd)
Glière, R.:Con Coloratura Sop, w. Timofei Dokschitzer (tpt) *(rec 1981)* RCA Gold Seal ▲ 74321-32045-2 [ADD]
USSR National Orch winds
Shostakovich, D.:Pieces by D. Scarlatti—Scarlatti's Sonatas, L.413 & 375 Praga ▲ PR 250090
USSR RSO
Mozart, W.A.:Con 20 Pno, w. Maria Yudina (pno) *(rec 1948)* Arlecchino ▲ ARL120
E. Chivzhel (cnd)
Gretchaninoff, A.:Sym 2, "Pastoral" Olympia ▲ OLY 586 [ADD]
Popov, G.N.:Sym 6 Olympia ▲ OLY 588 [ADD]
M. Ermler (cnd)
Shebalin, V.Y.:Sym 1 Olympia ▲ OLY 577 [ADD]
V. Fedoseyev (cnd)
Karamanov, A.:Sym 20 Olympia ▲ OLY 486 [ADD]
Karamanov, A.:Sym 23 Olympia ▲ OLY 486 [ADD]
V. Gergiev (cnd)
Shebalin, V.Y.:Sym 3 Olympia ▲ OLY 577 [ADD]
N. Golovanov (cnd)
Mussorgsky, M.:Boris Godounov (sels)—Polonaise *(rec 1947)* Arlecchino ▲ ARL101
Mussorgsky, M.:Night *(rec 1947)* Arlecchino ▲ ARL101
Mussorgsky, M.:Pictures *(rec 1947)* Arlecchino ▲ ARL101
A. Zhuraitis (cnd)
Gretchaninoff, A.:Sym 4 Olympia ▲ OLY 586 [ADD]
USSR Radio-TV Large Concert Orch
Mechem, K.:Sym 1, w. C. Brown *(rec live, Hall of Columns, Moscow, Mar, 30, 1991)* Russian Disc ▲ RCCD 10005 [DDD]
Mechem, K.:Sym 2, w. C. Brown *(rec live, Hall of Columns, Moscow, Mar, 30, 1991)* Russian Disc ▲ RCCD 10005 [DDD]
C. Brown (cnd)
Mechem, K.:The Jayhawk *(rec live, Hall of Columns, Moscow, 3/30/91)* Russian Disc ▲ RCCD 10 005 [DDD]
USSR Radio-TV Large SO
Berlioz, H.:Harold in Italy, w. Yuri Bashmet (vn) Audiophile Classics ▲ APL 101.514 [ADD]
Chausson, E.:Poème Vn, w. Igor Oistrakh (vn) Audiophile Classics ▲ APL 101.514 [ADD]
V. Fedoseyev (cnd)
Borodin, A.:In the Steppes of Central Asia Allegretto ▲ ACD 8182 [ADD] ■ ACS 8182
Borodin, A.:Prince Igor (Polovtsian dances) Allegretto ▲ ACD 8182 [ADD] ■ ACS 8182
Eshpay, A.:Sym 4 Russian Disc ▲ RUS 11051 [DDD]
Glazunov, A.:Sym 1 Vox Box 2-▲ CDX 5118 [ADD]
Glazunov, A.:Sym 2 Vox Box 2-▲ CDX 5118 [ADD]
Glazunov, A.:Sym 4 Vox Box 2-▲ CDX 5118 [ADD]
Ippolitov-Ivanov, M.:Caucasian Sketches, Op. 10 Allegretto ▲ ACD 8182 [ADD] ■ ACS 8182
Mussorgsky, M.:Night Allegretto ▲ ACD 8182 [ADD] ■ ACS 8182
Prokofiev, S.:Romeo & Juliet (suites)—No. 1 Audiophile Classics ("Legacy Collection" series) ▲ 101.506
Rachmaninoff, S.:Sym 2 Audiophile Classics ▲ APL 101518
Scriabin, A.:Rêverie Audiophile Classics ▲ APL 101517
Scriabin, A.:Sym 4 Audiophile Classics ▲ APL 101517
Stravinsky, I.:Pétrouchka Audiophile Classics ▲ APL 101.520 [ADD]
Taneyev, S.:Sym 2 Russian Disc ▲ RUS 11008 [AAD]
V. Gergiev (cnd)
Prokofiev, S.:Sym 2 Audiophile Classics ▲ APL 101517
D. Kakhidze (cnd)
Khachaturian, A.:Gayane Vox Box 2-▲ CDX 5119 [ADD]
Khachaturian, A.:Gayane Russian Disc 2-▲ RUS 11 029 [DDD]
A. Khachaturian (cnd)
Khachaturian, A.:Con-Rhap Vc, w. Mitsoslav Rostropovich (vc) Russian Disc ▲ RUS 11 014 [AAD]
Khachaturian, A.:Con-Rhap Pno, w. N. Petrov (pno) Russian Disc ▲ RUS 11 014 [AAD]
Khachaturian, A.:Ode to Joy, w. E. Obraztsova (mez), USSR Radio-TV Large Sym Chorus Russian Disc ▲ RUS 11 014 [AAD]
Khachaturian, A.:Spartacus (sels) Russian Disc ▲ RUS 11 014 [AAD]
B. Khaikin (cnd)
Glière, R.:Con Hp, w. Olga Erdeli (hp) *(rec 1968)* Consonance ▲ 81-3001 [AAD]
D. Kitayenko (cnd)
Prokofiev, S.:Sym 5 Audiophile Classics ("Legacy" series) ▲ 101.505 [ADD]
K. Kondrashin (cnd)
Mahler, G.:Sym 5 Audiophile Classics ("Legacy" series) ▲ 101.501 [ADD]
Miaskovsky, N.:Sym 15 Audiophile Classics ("Legacy" series) ▲ 101.503 [ADD]
A. Lazarev (cnd)
Strauss, R.:Con Vn, w. Valentin Zhuk (vn) Audiophile Classics ▲ APL 101519
F. Mansorov (cnd)
Prokofiev, S.:Pushkin Waltzes *(rec 1973)* Consonance ▲ 815008 [AAD]
L. Nikolayev (cnd)
Prokofiev, S.:Ode to the End of the War *(rec 1985)* Consonance ▲ 815008 [AAD]
V. Ovchinnikov (cnd)
Tchaikovsky, P.:Francesca da Rimini Allegretto ▲ ACD 8181 [ADD] ■ ACS 8181
Tchaikovsky, P.:Romeo & Juliet Allegretto ▲ ACD 8181 [ADD] ■ ACS 8181
G. Provatorov (cnd)
Banshchikov, G.:Duodecimet Russian Disc ▲ RUS 11052 [DDD]
Shebalin, V.Y.:Con Vn Russian Disc ▲ RUS 11052 [DDD]
G. Rozhdestvensky (cnd)
Chopin, F.:Con 1 Pno, w. Viktoria Postnikova (pno) Audiophile Classics ("Legacy Collection" series) ▲ 101.502
Dvořák, A.:Sym 2 Audiophile Classics ("Legacy" series) ▲ 101.509 [ADD]
Prokofiev, S.:Autumn *(rec 1962)* Consonance ▲ 81-5007 [AAD]
Prokofiev, S.:Chout *(rec 1962)* Consonance ▲ 815004 [AAD]
Prokofiev, S.:Cinderella Audiophile Classics ("Legacy Collection" series) 2-▲ 101.752
Prokofiev, S.:Cinderella *(rec 1966)* Consonance 2-▲ 81-5002 [AAD]
Prokofiev, S.:Con 5 Pno, w. Viktoria Postnikova (pno) Audiophile Classics ("Legacy Collection" series) ▲ 101.502
Prokofiev, S.:Con 1 Vn, w. Igor Oistrakh (vn) Audiophile Classics ("Legacy" series) ▲ 101.505 [ADD]
Prokofiev, S.:Con 1 Vn, w. Igor Oistrakh (vn) Allegretto ▲ ACD 8184 [ADD] ■ ACS 8184
Prokofiev, S.:The Steel Step (suite) *(rec 1966)* Consonance 2-▲ 81-5002 [AAD]
Prokofiev, S.:Sym 1 *(rec 1966)* Consonance ▲ 81-5007 [AAD]
Prokofiev, S.:Sym 1 Allegretto ▲ ACD 8184 [ADD] ■ ACS 8184
Prokofiev, S.:Sym 2 *(rec 1962)* Consonance ▲ 81-5006 [AAD]
Prokofiev, S.:Sym 3 Allegretto ▲ ACD 8184 [ADD] ■ ACS 8184
Prokofiev, S.:Sym 3 *(rec 1969)* Consonance ▲ 81-5006 [AAD]
Prokofiev, S.:Sym 5 *(rec 1965)* Consonance ▲ 815008 [AAD]
Prokofiev, S.:Sym 7 *(rec 1967)* Consonance ▲ 81-5007 [AAD]
Prokofiev, S.:Waltz Suite, w. Mikhail Chernykhovsky (vn) *(rec 1967)* Consonance ▲ 81-5005 [AAD]

USSR Radio-TV Large SO (cont.)
M. Shostakovich (cnd)
Svetlanov, E.:Con Pno, w. E. Svetlanov (pno) Russian Disc ▲ RUS 11 043 [ADD]
I. Shpiller (cnd)
Prokofiev, S.:Sym-Con Vc, w. Ivan Monighetti (vc) Audiophile Classics ("Legacy Collection" series) ▲ 101.506
E. Svetlanov (cnd)
Glazunov, A.:Stenka Razin Vox Box 2-▲ CDX 5118 [ADD]
USSR Radio-TV Orch
A. Khachaturian (cnd)
Khachaturian, A.:Con Pno, w. N. Petrov (pno) *(rec 1977)* Russian Disc ▲ RUS 11 012
Khachaturian, A.:Con Vn, w. D. Oistrakh (vn) *(rec 1965)* Russian Disc ▲ RUS 11 012
A. Zhuraitis (cnd)
Glazunov, A.:Con 1 Pno, w. A. Nasedkin (pno) Russian Disc ▲ RUS 11 024 [ADD]
Glazunov, A.:Mazurka-oberek, w. T. Gridenko (vn) Russian Disc ▲ RUS 11 024 [ADD]
USSR Radio-TV SO
V. Neumann (cnd)
Stravinsky, I.:Sym in C, Czech PO *(rec Prague, 1970)* Praga ▲ PR 250 063
G. Provatorov (cnd)
Popov, G.N.:Sym 2 Olympia ▲ OLY 576
G. Rozhdestvensky (cnd)
Stravinsky, I.:Sym in 3 Movts, Czech PO *(rec Prague, 1983)* Praga ▲ PR 250 063
Stravinsky, I.:Sym of Psalms, Czech PO *(rec Prague, 1977)* Praga ▲ PR 250 063
M. Shostakovich (cnd)
Vainberg, M.:Sym 12 Olympia ▲ OLY 472 [ADD]
USSR State Academy Orch
E. Svetlanov (cnd)
Khrennikov, T.:Con 1 Vn, w. Leonid Kogan (vn) Allegretto ▲ ACD 8179 [ADD] ■ ACS 8179
Khrennikov, T.:Sym 2 Allegretto ▲ ACD 8179 [ADD] ■ ACS 8179
USSR State Orch
K. Kondrashin (cnd)
Mozart, W.A.:Con 5 Vn, w. David Ostrakh (vn) *(rec 1958-59)* Tuxedo ▲ TUXCD 1052
USSR State SO
G. Rozhdestvensky (cnd)
Hindemith, P.:Con Vn, w. D. Oistrakh (vn) *(rec 1962)* Forlane ▲ FOR 16589 [AAD]
Hindemith, P.:Con Vn, w. David Oistrakh (vn) *(rec 1962)* Forlane ▲ FRL 16589 [AAD]
A. Shereshevsky (cnd)
Liszt, F.:Rhap espagnole, w. P. Serebryakov (pno) [arr. Busoni for orch.] *(rec 1951)* Multisonic ("Russian Treasures" series) ▲ 31 0190
Liszt, F.:Totentanz, w. P. Serebryakov (pno) *(rec 1958)* Multisonic ("Russian Treasures" series) ▲ 31 0190
Rubinstein, A.:Con 4 Pno, w. P. Serebryakov (pno) *(rec 1958)* Multisonic ("Russian Treasures" series) ▲ 31 0190
E. Svetlanov (cnd)
Prokofiev, S.:Sym 1 *(rec live, Royal Albert Hall, London 1968)* Intaglio ▲ INCD 7321 [ADD]
Rimsky-Korsakov, N.:The Legend of the Invisible City of Kitzeh (suite)—sels. *(rec 1968)* Intaglio ▲ ING 7481 [ADD]
Scriabin, A.:Sym 4 *(rec 1968)* Intaglio ▲ ING 7481 [ADD]
Shostakovich, D.:Con 2 Vn, w. D. Oistrakh (vn) *(rec live, Royal Albert Hall, London, August 1968)* Intaglio ▲ INCD 7241 [ADD]
Tchaikovsky, P.:Ov 1812 *(rec June 17, 1992)* Emergo ▲ EC 3968 [DDD]
Tchaikovsky, P.:Sym 5 *(rec June 13 & 14, 1993)* Emergo ▲ EC 3968 [DDD]
USSR SO
V. Fedoseyev (cnd)
Eshpay, A.:Sym 5 Russian Disc ▲ RUS 11051 [DDD]
Tchaikovsky, P.:Eugene Onegin, w. Lidiya Chernikh (sop), Tamara Sinyavskaya (mez), Alexander Vedernikov (bass), Alexander Fedin (sgr), Yuri Mazurok (sgr), Moscow SO, Fernseh SO Audiophile Classics ("Legacy Collection" series) 2-▲ 101.751
K. Ivanov (cnd)
Shostakovich, D.:The Sun Shines on Our Motherland, w. Moscow State Boys' Choir, Yurlov Russian Choir Russian Disc ▲ RUS 11 048 [AAD]
A. Katz (cnd)
Stravinsky, I.:Jeu de cartes Audiophile Classics ▲ APL 101.520 [ADD]
A. Khachaturian (cnd)
Khachaturian, A.:Gayane (sels)—9 sels. *(rec 1977)* Russian Disc ▲ RUS 11018 [AAD]
Khachaturian, A.:Sym 2 *(rec 1977)* Russian Disc ▲ RUS 11018 [AAD]
O. Koch (cnd)
Makarova, N.:Sym in d Russian Disc ▲ RUS 11 382 [DDD]
K. Kondrashin (cnd)
Miaskovsky, N.:Sym 6, w. Yurloff Russian Choir Russian Disc ▲ RUS 15 008 [ADD]
V. Kozhukar (cnd)
Bloch, E.:Sym Trbn, w. Grigory Khersonsky (trbn) *(rec 1988)* Consonance ▲ 81-0002 [DDD]
D. Oistrakh (cnd)
Shostakovich, D.:Sym 9 *(rec Aug. 6, 1969)* Russian Disc ▲ RUS 11192 [AAD]
G. Rozhdestvensky (cnd)
Knipper, L.K.:Con-Monologue, w. M. Rostropovich (vc) Russian Disc ▲ RUS 11 111 [AAD]
Levitin, Y.A.:Concertino Vc, w. M. Rostropovich (vc) Russian Disc ▲ RUS 11 111 [AAD]
Prokofiev, S.:The Prodigal Son *(rec 1979)* Consonance ▲ 815004 [AAD]
Vainberg, M.:Con Vc, w. M. Rostropovich (vc) Russian Disc ▲ RUS 11 111 [AAD]
S. Samosud, A. Orlov, A. Bron (cnds)
Recital, w. Kozlovsky, Ivan (ten), USSR SO Myto ▲ MCD 921.55 [ADD]
Recital, Vol. 2, w. Kozlovsky, Ivan (ten) Myto ▲ MCD 925.68 [ADD]
M. Shostakovich (cnd)
Shostakovich, D.:The Golden Age (suite) RCA Gold Seal ▲ 74321-32041-2 [ADD]
Shostakovich, D.:Michurin RCA Gold Seal ▲ 74321-32041-2 [ADD]
Shostakovich, D.:Sym 5 RCA Gold Seal ▲ 74321-32041-2 [ADD]
E. Svetlanov (cnd)
Arensky, A.:Sym 1 Allegretto ▲ ACD 8187 [ADD] ■ ACS 8187
Arensky, A.:Sym 2 Allegretto ▲ ACD 8187 [ADD] ■ ACS 8187
Boiko, R.:Peter's Chimes Russian Disc ▲ RUS 11 045 [AAD]
Boiko, R.:Sym 2 Russian Disc ▲ RUS 11 045 [AAD]
Boiko, R.:Vyata Songs Russian Disc ▲ RUS 11 045 [AAD]
Mendelssohn, F.:Sym 4 *(rec ca. 1983)* MCA Classics ▲ MLD 32130 [AAD]
Mendelssohn, F.:Sym 4 Allegretto ▲ ACD 8180 [ADD] ■ ACS 8180
Rachmaninoff, S.:Prince Rostislav Audiophile Classics ▲ APL 101518
Rossini, G.:Ovs—Guilaume Tell Allegretto ▲ ACD 8180 [ADD] ■ ACS 8180
Rossini, G.:Ovs—William Tell MCA Classics/Melodiya ▲ MLD 32130 [AAD]
Scriabin, A.:Rêverie *(rec live, Moscow, May 14, 1992)* Russian Disc ▲ RC CD 11 057 [DDD]
Scriabin, A.:Sym 1, w. N. Gaponova (sop), Andrei Salynikov (ten), USSR Radio Chorus *(rec live, Moscow, April 14, 1990)* Russian Disc ▲ RC CD 11 056 [ADD]
Scriabin, A.:Sym 2 *(rec live, Moscow May 14, 1992)* Russian Disc ▲ RC CD 11 057 [DDD]
Scriabin, A.:Sym 3 *(rec live, Moscow, April 14, 1990)* Russian Disc ▲ RC CD 11 058 [AAD]
Scriabin, A.:Sym 4 *(rec live, Moscow, April 14, 1990)* Russian Disc ▲ RC CD 11 056 [ADD]
Scriabin, A.:Sym 5, w. Sviatoslav Richter (pno) *(rec live April 12, 1988)* Russian Disc ▲ RC CD 11 058 [AAD]
Shchedrin, R.:Con 1 Pno, w. R. Shchedrin (pno) Russian Disc ▲ RUS 11129 [AAD]
Shchedrin, R.:Con 2 Pno, w. N. Petrov (pno) Russian Disc ▲ RUS 11129 [AAD]
Shchedrin, R.:Con 3 Pno, w. R. Shchedrin (pno) Russian Disc ▲ RUS 11129 [AAD]
Shostakovich, D.:Sym 1 *(rec Dec. 30, 1966)* Russian Disc ▲ RUS 11188 [AAD]

ORCH. & ENS.

USSR SO (cont.)
E. Svetlanov (cnd) (cont.)
Svetlanov, E.:Music of—Daybreak in the Field; 3 Russian Songs for Voice & Orchestra [w. R. Bobrineva (soprano)]; Pictures of Spain; Rhap. No. 2; Russian Vars. for Harp & Orchestra [w. N. Tostaya] Russian Disc ▲ RUS 11 044 [AAD]
Svetlanov, E.:Preludes:Symphonic Reflections Russian Disc ▲ RUS 11 043 [ADD]
Svetlanov, E.:The Red Gueler-Roser Russian Disc ▲ RUS 11 043 [ADD]
Taneyev, S.:At the Reading of a Psalm, w. Yuri Antonov (sgr), Yuri Belokrynkin (sgr), Ralsa Kotova (sgr), Adelina Kozlova (sgr), Yurloff State Choir Russian Disc ▲ RUS 10044 [AAD]
Tchaikovsky, P.:Capriccio italien *(rec Moscow, 1970)* Melodiya ▲ 74321-37879-2 [ADD]
Tchaikovsky, P.:Francesca da Rimini *(rec Moscow, 1970)* Melodiya ▲ 74321-37880-2 [ADD]
Tchaikovsky, P.:Manfred *(rec Moscow, 1967)* Melodiya ▲ 74321-37881-2 [ADD]
Tchaikovsky, P.:Romeo & Juliet *(rec Moscow, 1970)* Melodiya ▲ 74321-37881-2 [ADD]
Tchaikovsky, P.:Serenade Strs *(rec Moscow, 1970)* Melodiya ▲ 74321-37878-2 [ADD]
Tchaikovsky, P.:Suite 1 Melodiya ▲ 17099-2 [DDD]
Tchaikovsky, P.:Suite 2 Melodiya ▲ 17099-2 [DDD]
Tchaikovsky, P.:Suite 3 Melodiya ▲ 17100-2 [DDD]
Tchaikovsky, P.:Suite 4 Melodiya ▲ 17100-2 [DDD]
Tchaikovsky, P.:Sym 4 *(rec Moscow, 1967)* Melodiya ▲ 74321-37878-2 [ADD]
Tchaikovsky, P.:Sym 5 Vox Box 2-▲ CDX 5117 [ADD]
Tchaikovsky, P.:Sym 5 *(rec Moscow, 1967)* Melodiya ▲ 74321-37879-2 [ADD]
Tchaikovsky, P.:Sym 6 Vox Box 2-▲ CDX 5117 [ADD]
Tchaikovsky, P.:Sym 6 *(rec Moscow, 1967)* Melodiya ▲ 74321-37880-2 [ADD]

USSR SO String Group
V. Kozhukar (cnd)
Shostakovich, D.:Con 1 Pno, w. Mikhail Petukhov (pno) *(rec 1989)* Consonance ▲ 81-0009 [DDD]

Utah SO
Songs of Inspiration, w. Te Kanawa, Kiri (sop), Julius Rudel, Mormon Tabernacle Choir London ▲ 425431-2 LH [DDD]

M. Abravanel (cnd)
Anderson, L.:Music of—15 compositions Vanguard Classics ▲ OVC 6008 [ADD]
Beethoven, L. van:Egmont (incidental music), w. Netania Davrath (sop), Walther Reyer (nar) Vanguard Classics 2-▲ OVC 8084/85 [ADD]
Beethoven, L. van:Die Geschöpfe des Prometheus Vanguard Classics 2-▲ OVC 8084/85 [ADD]
Bloch, E.:Israel Sym *(rec 1967)* Vanguard Classics ▲ OVC 4047 [ADD]
Bloch, E.:Schelomo, w. Z. Nelsova (vc) *(rec 1967)* Vanguard Classics ▲ OVC 4047 [ADD]
Brahms, J.:Academic Festival Ov *(rec Mormon Tabernacle, Salt Lake City, May 17-24, 1976)* Vanguard Classics 3-▲ SVC 1719 [AAD]
Brahms, J.:Syms (comp) *(rec Mormon Tabernacle, Salt Lake City, May 17-24, 1976)* Vanguard Classics 3-▲ SVC 1719 [AAD]
Brahms, J.:Tragic Ov *(rec Mormon Tabernacle, Salt Lake City, May 17-24, 1976)* Vanguard Classics 3-▲ SVC 1719 [AAD]
Brahms, J.:Vars on a Theme by Haydn *(rec Mormon Tabernacle, Salt Lake City, May 17-24, 1976)* Vanguard Classics 3-▲ SVC 1719 [AAD]
Copland, A.:Appalachian Spring (suite) MCA Classics 2-▲ MCAD2-9800
Copland, A.:Billy the Kid (suite) MCA Classics 2-▲ MCAD2-9800
Copland, A.:Lincoln Portrait, w. C. Heston (nar) *(rec 12/61)* Vanguard Classics ▲ OVC 4037 [ADD]
Copland, A.:Our Town Orch *(rec 12/61)* Vanguard Classics ▲ OVC 4037 [ADD]
Copland, A.:An Outdoor Ov *(rec 12/61)* Vanguard Classics ▲ OVC 4037 [ADD]
Copland, A.:Quiet City *(rec 12/61)* Vanguard Classics ▲ OVC 4037 [ADD]
Copland, A.:Rodeo MCA Classics 2-▲ MCAD2-9800
Copland, A.:El salón México MCA Classics 2-▲ MCAD2-9800
Copland, A.:El salón México EMI Classics (American Composer Series) ▲ CDM 64307
Fiddle Faddle *(rec Salt Lake City, UT, 1967)* Vanguard Classics ▲ SVC 4 [AAD]
Gershwin, G.:Con Pno, w. R. Nibley (pno) MCA Classics 2-▲ MCAD2-9800
Glière, R.:The Red Poppy (suite), "Russian Sailors' Dance" *(rec Univ. of Utah Music Hall, Salt Lake City, 1967)* Vanguard Classics ▲ SVC 8 [AAD]
Glière, R.:The Red Poppy (suite), "Russian Sailors' Dance" *(rec 1967; originally released)* Vanguard Classics ("Everyman" series) ▲ OVC 5010 [ADD]
Goldmark, K.:Ländliche Hochzeit *(rec 1962)* Vanguard Classics ("Everyman" series) ▲ OVC 5002 [ADD]
Goldmark, K.:Ländliche Hochzeit *(rec Salt Lake City, UT)* Vanguard Classics ▲ SVC 10 [AAD]
Gottschalk, L.M.:Grande Tarantelle, w. Reid Nibley (pno) *(rec Univ. of Utah, Salt Lake City, Dec. 1962)* Vanguard Classics ▲ SVC 9 [AAD]
Gottschalk, L.M.:Grande Tarantelle, w. R. Nibley (pno) *(rec 1962)* Vanguard Classics ▲ OVC 4051 [ADD]
Gottschalk, L.M.:Sym 1, "La nuit des tropiques" *(rec 1962)* Vanguard Classics ▲ OVC 4051 [ADD]
Gottschalk, L.M.:Sym 1, "La nuit des tropiques" *(rec Univ. of Utah, Salt Lake City, Dec. 1962)* Vanguard Classics ▲ SVC 9 [AAD]
Gould, M.:Latin American Symphonette *(rec 12/62)* Vanguard Classics ▲ OVC 4037 [ADD]
Gould, M.:Latin American Symphonette *(rec Univ. of Utah, Salt Lake City, Dec. 1962)* Vanguard Classics ▲ SVC 9 [AAD]
Grieg, E.:Elegaic Melodies, Op. 34 *(rec 1975)* Vox Box 2-▲ CDX 5048 [ADD]
Grieg, E.:Holberg Suite *(rec 1975)* Vox Box 2-▲ CDX 5048 [ADD]
Grieg, E.:In Autumn *(rec 1975)* Vox Box 2-▲ CDX 5048 [ADD]
Grieg, E.:Lyric Pieces [orchd. Grieg]—Op. 65, No. 6, "Wedding Day at Troldhaugen," & Op. 68, Nos. 4 & 5, "Evening at the Mountains" & "Cradle Song" *(rec 1975)* Vox Box 2-▲ CDX 5048 [ADD]
Grieg, E.:Norwegian Dances, Op. 35 *(rec 1975)* Vox Box 2-▲ CDX 5048 [ADD]
Grieg, E.:Peer Gynt Suites, Opp. 46 & 55 *(rec 1975)* Vox Box 2-▲ CDX 5048 [ADD]
Grieg, E.:Pictures from Life in the Country [orch. by Johan Halvorsen]—No. 2, "The Bridal Procession Passes By" *(rec 1975)* Vox Box 2-▲ CDX 5048 [ADD]
Grieg, E.:Sigurd Jorsalfar (suite) *(rec 1975)* Vox Box 2-▲ CDX 5048 [ADD]
Grieg, E.:Symphonic Dances *(rec 1975)* Vox Box 2-▲ CDX 5048 [ADD]
Grofé, F.:Grand Canyon Suite Angel ("American Composer" series) ▲ CDM 64307
Handel, G.F.:Judas Maccabaeus, w. Martina Arroyo (sop), Grace Bumbry (mez), J. McCollum (ten), Marvin Sorensen (ten), D. Watts (bass), Utah Sym Chorus [E] *(rec ca. 1959)* MCA Classics 3-▲ MCAD3-10515 [ADD]
Honegger, A.:Judith, w. Netania Davrath (sop), Blanche Christensen (sop), Madeleine Milhaud (nar), Salt Lake City Symphonic Choir [F] *(rec Dec. 1964)* Vanguard Classics ▲ OVC 8088 [ADD]
Honegger, A.:Pacific 231 Vanguard Classics ▲ OVC 4031 [ADD]
Honegger, A.:Pacific 231 *(rec Salt Lake City, UT, 1968)* Vanguard Classics ▲ SVC 40 [AAD]
Honegger, A.:Le Roi David, w. Netania Davrath (sop), Jean Preston (mez), Marvin Sorenson (ten), M. Singher (nar), M. Milhaud (nar) [F] Vanguard Classics ▲ OVC 4038 [ADD]
Ippolitov-Ivanov, M.:Caucasian Sketches, Opp. 10 & 42—Suite No. 1, Op. 10 *(rec 1967; originally released)* Vanguard Classics ("Everyman" series) ▲ OVC 5010 [ADD]
Ippolitov-Ivanov, M.:Caucasian Sketches, Op. 10 *(rec Univ. of Utah Music Hall, Salt Lake City, 1967)* Vanguard Classics ▲ SVC 8 [AAD]
Mahler, G.:Syms Vanguard Classics 11-▲ SVC 2030
Mahler, G.:Sym 1 Vanguard Classics ▲ SVC 20 [AAD]
Mahler, G.:Sym 1 *(rec 1974)* Vanguard Classics ▲ OVC 4003 [ADD]
Mahler, G.:Sym 2, w. B. Sills (sop), F. Kopleff (cta) [G] *(rec 1967)* Vanguard Classics ▲ OVC 4004 [ADD]
Mahler, G.:Sym 2, w. B. Sills (sop), F. Kopleff (cta) *(rec Salt Lake City, 1967)* Vanguard Classics ▲ SVC 2 [AAD]
Mahler, G.:Sym 3, w. C. Krooskos (cta), Utah Sym Chorus [G] *(rec 1969)* Vanguard Classics 2-▲ OVC 4005/06 [ADD]
Mahler, G.:Sym 4, w. N. Davrath (sop) [G] *(rec 1974)* Vanguard Classics ▲ OVC 4007 [ADD]
Mahler, G.:Sym 5 Vanguard Classics ▲ SVC 25 [AAD]
Mahler, G.:Sym 6 Vanguard Classics ▲ SVC 26 [AAD]
Mahler, G.:Sym 7 Vanguard Classics ▲ SVC 27 [AAD]

Utah SO (cont.)
M. Abravanel (cnd) (cont.)
Mahler, G.:Sym 8 Vanguard Classics ▲ SVC 28 [AAD]
Mahler, G.:Sym 9 Vanguard Classics 2-▲ SVC 29/30 [AAD]
Mahler, G.:Sym 10 Vanguard Classics 2-▲ SVC 29/30 [AAD]
Milhaud, D.:La Création du monde *(rec Dec. 1961)* Vanguard Classics ▲ OVC 8088 [ADD]
Milhaud, D.:L'Homme et son désir, w. F. Kopleff (cta), L. Quilico (bar), Univ of Utah Chorus *(rec 1968)* Vanguard Classics ▲ OVC 8067 [ADD]
Milhaud, D.:Pacem in terris, w. F. Kopleff (cta), L. Quilico (bar), Univ of Utah Chorus *(rec 1965)* Vanguard Classics ▲ OVC 8067 [ADD]
Prokofiev, S.:Con 1 Pno, w. V. Ashkenazy (pno) *(rec live, Salt Lake Tabernacle, UT 11/3/73)* Intaglio ▲ INCD 7181 [ADD]
Rachmaninoff, S.:Songs, w. Netania Davrath (sop)—Chanson Georgienne Vanguard Classics ▲ SVC 8 [AAD]
Rachmaninoff, S.:Sym 3 Vanguard Classics ▲ SVC 8 [AAD]
Rimsky-Korsakov, N.:Antar *(rec Univ. of Utah Music Hall, Salt Lake City, 1967)* Vanguard Classics ▲ SVC 8 [AAD]
Satie, E.:Ballet Music—Parade; Mercure; Relâche; Jack in the Box (orchestrated by Milhaud); Gymnopédies 1 & 3 (orch. by Debussy); Trois morceaux en forme de poire (orch. by Desarmière); Cinq Grimaces pour "Le Songe d'une nuit d'été"; La belle excentrique/La grande ritournelle Vanguard Classics ▲ OVC 4030 [ADD]
Schubert, Franz:Rosamunde Vanguard Classics 2-▲ OVC 8084/85 [ADD]
Sibelius, J.:Syms (comp) *(rec Mormon Tabernacle, Salt Lake City, UT, May 1977)* Vanguard Classics 3-▲ SVC 3133 [AAD]
Tchaikovsky, P.:Francesca da Rimini Vox Box 2-▲ CDX 5005 [ADD]
Tchaikovsky, P.:Hamlet Vox Box 2-▲ CDX 5006 [ADD]
Tchaikovsky, P.:Marche slave Vox Box 2-▲ CDX 5005 [ADD]
Tchaikovsky, P.:The Nutcracker *(rec Salt Lake City, Sept 1961)* Vanguard Classics 2-▲ SVC 52/53 [AAD]
Tchaikovsky, P.:Nutcracker Suite *(rec 1961)* Vanguard Classics ("Everyman" series) ▲ OVC 5005 [ADD]
Tchaikovsky, P.:Orch Music Vox Box 2-▲ CDX 5005 [ADD]
Tchaikovsky, P.:Orch Music Vox Box 2-▲ CDX 5006 [ADD]
Tchaikovsky, P.:Orch Music Vox Box 2-▲ CDX 5004 [ADD]
Tchaikovsky, P.:Ov 1812 Vox Box 2-▲ CDX 5004 [ADD]
Tchaikovsky, P.:Romeo & Juliet Vox Box 2-▲ CDX 5006 [ADD]
Tchaikovsky, P.:Swan Lake *(rec April 1967)* Vanguard Classics ("Everyman" series) 2-▲ OVC 5008/09 [ADD]
Tchaikovsky, P.:Swan Lake (sels) MCA Classics 2-▲ MCAD2-9801
Tchaikovsky, P.:Swan Lake (suite) *(rec Salt Lake City, Sept 1961)* Vanguard Classics 2-▲ SVC 52/53 [AAD]
Tchaikovsky, P.:Sym 1 Vox Box 2-▲ CDX 5005 [ADD]
Tchaikovsky, P.:Sym 2 Vox Box 2-▲ CDX 5006 [ADD]
Tchaikovsky, P.:Sym 3 Vox Box 2-▲ CDX 5004 [ADD]
Tchaikovsky, P.:Sym 4 Vox Box 2-▲ CDX 5006 [ADD]
Tchaikovsky, P.:Sym 5 Vox Box 2-▲ CDX 5005 [ADD]
Tchaikovsky, P.:Sym 6 Vox Box 2-▲ CDX 5004 [ADD]
Tchaikovsky, P.:Sym 6—Adagio; Allegro non troppo Special Music Co. ("Classics of the Heart" series) ▲ SCD 5198
Tchaikovsky, P.:The Voyevoda, Op. 78 Vox Box 2-▲ CDX 5004 [ADD]
Varèse, E.:Amériques *(rec Salt Lake City, UT, 1968)* Vanguard Classics ▲ SVC 40 [AAD]
Varèse, E.:Amériques Vanguard Classics ▲ OVC 4031 [ADD]
Varèse, E.:Ecuatorial *(rec Salt Lake City, UT, 1968)* Vanguard Classics ▲ SVC 40 [AAD]
Varèse, E.:Ecuatorial Vanguard Classics ▲ OVC 4031 [ADD]
Varèse, E.:Nocturnal *(rec Salt Lake City, UT, 1968)* Vanguard Classics ▲ SVC 40 [AAD]
Varèse, E.:Nocturnal, w. A. Bybee (sop) Vanguard Classics ▲ OVC 4031 [ADD]
Vaughan Williams, R.:Dona nobis pacem, w. Blanche Christensen (sop), William Metcalf (bar) Vanguard Classics ▲ SVC 7 [ADD]
Vaughan Williams, R.:Fant on Greensleeves *(rec 1967)* Vanguard Classics ▲ OVC 4053 [ADD]
Vaughan Williams, R.:Fant on Greensleeves *(rec Salt Lake City, UT, 1966 & 1967)* Vanguard Classics ▲ SVC 43 [AAD]
Vaughan Williams, R.:Fant on a Theme by Thomas Tallis *(rec Salt Lake City, UT, 1966 & 1967)* Vanguard Classics ▲ SVC 43 [AAD]
Vaughan Williams, R.:Fant on a Theme by Thomas Tallis *(rec 1967)* Vanguard Classics ▲ OVC 4053 [ADD]
Vaughan Williams, R.:Flos Campi *(rec 1966)* Vanguard Classics ▲ OVC 4053 [ADD]
Vaughan Williams, R.:Flos Campi *(rec Salt Lake City, UT, 1966 & 1967)* Vanguard Classics ▲ SVC 43 [AAD]
Vaughan Williams, R.:Sym 6 Vanguard Classics ▲ SVC 7 [ADD]
Vaughan Williams, R.:Variants of "Dives & Lazarus" *(rec Salt Lake City, UT, 1966 & 1967)* Vanguard Classics ▲ SVC 43 [AAD]
Vaughan Williams, R.:Variants of "Dives & Lazarus" *(rec 1966)* Vanguard Classics ▲ OVC 4053 [ADD]
Walton, W.:Belshazzar's Feast, w. R. Peterson (bar), Univ of Utah Civic Chorale Allegretto ▲ ACD 8153 [ADD] ■ ACD 8153

S. Comissiona (cnd)
Mendelssohn, F.:Music of, w. J. Silverstein (vn), Houston SO—Violin Concerto in e, Op. 64; Midsummer Night's Dream (overture); etc. Pro Arte ▲ CDM 815 ■ PCD 815

A. Gerhardt (cnd)
Grieg, E.:Music of, w. J. Silverstein (vn), Russell Sherman (pno), London Royal Promenade Orch—Peer Gynt Suites 1 & 2; Holberg Suite; Piano Concerto (1st movt.) Pro Arte ▲ CDM 811 ■ PCD 811
World's Greatest Overtures, w. Royal Promenade Orch London Pro Arte ▲ CDM 813 ■ PCD 813

C. Ketchum (cnd)
Barber, S.:Con Vn, w. J. Silverstein (vn) Pro Arte ▲ CDD 241
Brahms, J.:Con Vn, w. J. Silverstein (vn) Pro Arte ▲ CDS 3431
Tiomkin, D.:Strangers on a Train (sels) Varése Sarabande ▲ VSD 47225
Waxman, F.:Suspicion (sels) Varése Sarabande ▲ VSD 47225
Webb, R.:Notorious (sels) Varése Sarabande ▲ VSD 47225
Williams, John:Family Plot (sels) Varése Sarabande ▲ VSD 47225

V. Kojian (cnd)
Berlioz, H.:Sym fantastique Reference ▲ RR 11CD
Brahms, J.:Tragic Ov Citadel ▲ CTD 88102 [DDD]
Korngold, E.W.:The Adventures of Robin Hood Varése Sarabande ▲ VSD 47202
Liszt, F.:Dante Sym, w. Utah Choral Citadel ▲ CTD 88102 [DDD]
Williams, John:Film Music—Star Wars; Empire Strikes Back & Return of the Jedi Varése Sarabande ▲ VSD 47201 ■ VSC 47201
Yardumian, R.:Armenian Suite Phoenix ▲ PHCD 112 [DDD]
Yardumian, R.:Sym 2 Phoenix ▲ PHCD 112 [DDD]

H. Lazarof (cnd)
Lazarof, H.:Spectrum, w. T. Stevens (tpt) CRI ▲ CD 588 [ADD]

J. Silverstein (cnd)
Barber, S.:Essay 2 Pro Arte ▲ CDD 241
Barber, S.:The School for Scandal Pro Arte ▲ CDD 241
Barber, S.:Vanessa (prelude & intermezzo) *(rec 6-86 & 8-86)* Pro Arte ▲ CDD 241
Beethoven, L. van:Con Vn, Op. 61, w. J. Silverstein (vn) Pro Arte ▲ CDD 228 [DDD]
Beethoven, L. van:Con Vn, Op. 61, w. J. Silverstein (vn) Pro Arte ▲ CDS 588 [DDD]
Beethoven, L. van:Die Weihe des Hauses (ov) Pro Arte ▲ CDD 228 [DDD]
Beethoven, L. van:Die Weihe des Hauses (ov), w. J. Silverstein (vn) Pro Arte ▲ CDS 588 [DDD]
Brahms, J.:Academic Festival Ov Pro Arte ▲ CDS 3431
Brahms, J.:Con Vn, w. J. Silverstein (vn) Pro Arte ▲ CDD 271
Dvořák, A.:Con Vn, w. J. Silverstein (vn) Pro Arte ▲ CDD 389

▲ = CD ♦ = Enhanced CD Δ = MD ■ = Cassette Tape □ = DCC

Utah SO (cont.)

J. Silverstein (cnd) (cont.)

Dvořák, A.:Serenade Strs — Pro Arte ▲ CDD 389
Mendelssohn, F.:Con in e Vn & Orch, Op. 64, w. Joseph Silverstein (vn) — Pro Arte ▲ CDD 187 [DDD]
Mendelssohn, F.:Ovs—Ruy Blas; Midsummer Night's Dream; Hebrides — Pro Arte ▲ CDD 187 [DDD]
Roman Carnival — Pro Arte ▲ CDS 543 [DDD]
Simple Gifts, w. Frederica von Stade (mez), Mormon Tabernacle Choir, John Longhurst (org) — London ▲ 436284-2 LH [DDD]

M. Tilson Thomas (cnd)

Copland, A.:Canticle of Freedom, w. Mormon Tabernacle Choir [E] — CBS ▲ MK 42140 [DDD] ■ MT 42140 (D)
Copland, A.:Old American Songs, w. Mormon Tabernacle Choir [E] — CBS ▲ MK 42140 [DDD] ■ MT 42140 (D)

C. Wilkins (cnd)

Kraft, William:Of Ceremonies, Pageants & Celebrations — Meet The Composer ▲ 79229-2 ■ 79229-4

Uttrecht SO

H. Vonk (cnd)

Beethoven, L. van:Con Vn, Op. 61, w. E. Verhey (vn) — Vivace 3-▲ E 324 [ADD/DDD]

Vagantes [Péter Kálmán (vl/vle/b lt/perc/voice), István Szabó (ct/bar/lt/thb/gtr/man), István Tóth (rcr/fl/goathorn/Turkish pipe/gtr/voice)]

Ekes Enekek:16th Century Hungarian Songs — Hungaroton ▲ HCD 31562 [DDD]
Esterházy, P.:Music of—On the Vanity of the World; On the Wisdom of God; On the Unsteadiness of Fortune; On the Blessed Virgin; Minden napunk; Más; Tota dulcis es, Maria; O gloriosa Domina—Salamon; On the Illness of a Friend; Son; On Warfare; Hatted Dances; On the Beasts of This Earth; On Garden Flowers; On the Pleasures of Hunting & Fowling; Bargamasco; On Spring; On Summer; Vlach Dances; On a Falcon; On a Swan; On a Little Hawk; Riders' Ballet; On a Beautiful Rose; Palas & Esther's Favourite Dance *(rec Hungaroton Classic Studios, 1995)* — Hungaroton ▲ HCD 31598 [DDD]
Hungarian Chronicle — Hungaroton ▲ HCD 31638 [DDD]

Valcour String Quartet [R. Williams (vn), L. Davis (vn), J. F. Hanna (va), D. Cassin (vc)]

Brody, W.K.:Qt Strs *(rec August 1991)* — Centaur ▲ CRC 2111 [DDD]

Valley String Quartet [William Hector (vn), Camille Ericson (vn), Mildred O'Donnell (va), Dorothy Muggeridge (vc)]

Levitch, L.:Qt 1 Strs — Cambria ▲ CD 1059 [ADD]

Vanberg Viennese Soloists

C. Vanberg (cnd)

Great Waltzes — Laserlight ▲ 15 512

Vanbrugh String Quartet [G. Ellis (vn), E. Charleson (vn), S. Sapell (va), C. Marwood (vc)]

Beckett, W.:Qt 1 Strs — Chandos ▲ CHAN 9295 [DDD]
Boydell, B.:Qt 2 Strs — Chandos ▲ CHAN 9295 [DDD]
Dohnányi, E. von:Qnt 1 Pno, w. Martin Roscoe (pno) — ASV ▲ ASV 915 [DDD]
Dohnányi, E. von:Qnt 2 Pno, w. Martin Roscoe (pno) — ASV ▲ ASV 915 [DDD]
Dvořák, A.:Qt 11 Strs — Collins Classics ▲ COL 1381 [DDD]
Fleischmann, A.:Qnt Pno, w. Hugh Tinney (pno) *(rec St. Georges, Bristol, Ireland, May 17-19, 1995)* — Marco Polo ("Irish Composer" series) ▲ 8.223888 [DDD]
Janácek, L.:Qt 1 Strs — Collins Classics ▲ COL 1381 [DDD]
Janácek, L.:Qt 2 Strs — Collins Classics ▲ COL 1381 [DDD]
Kinsella, J.:Qt 3 Strs — Chandos ▲ CHAN 9295 [DDD]
May, F.:Qt Strs *(rec St. Georges, Bristol, Ireland, May 17-19, 1995)* — Marco Polo ("Irish Composer" series) ▲ 8.223888 [DDD]
Simpson, R.:Qt 14 Strs — Hyperion ▲ CDA 66626
Simpson, R.:Qt 15 Strs — Hyperion ▲ CDA 66626
Simpson, R.:Qnt Cl, w. J. Farrall (cl), F. Cross (b cl) — Hyperion ▲ CDA 66626
Wilson, I.:Winter's Edge — Chandos ▲ CHAN 9295 [DDD]

Vancouver CO

K. Akiyama (cnd)

Baker, M.C.:Con Pno, w. R. Silverman (pno)—additional piano works by Baker — CBC ("SM 5000" series) ▲ SMCD 5107

Vancouver SO

Serenade to Music, w. [cnd:Bruce Pullan], Vancouver Bach Choir — CBC Records ("SM 5000" series) ▲ SMCD 5121 [DDD]

K. Akiyama (cnd)

Berlioz, H.:Ovs—Le roi Lear — CBC ("SM 5000" series) ▲ SMCD 5033 [DDD] ■ SMC 5033 (D)
Franck, C.:Sym in d — CBC ("SM 5000" series) ▲ SMCD 5033 [DDD] ■ SMC 5033 (D)
Glazunov, A.:The Seasons — CBC ("SM 5000" series) ▲ SMCD 5100 [DDD] ■ SMC 5100 (D)
Glazunov, A.:Valses de Concert, Opp. 47 & 51 — CBC ("SM 5000" series) ▲ SMCD 5100 [DDD] ■ SMC 5100 (D)
Schafer, R.M.:Con Fl, w. R. Aitken (fl) — CBC ("SM 5000" series) ▲ SMCD 5114 [DDD]

M. Bernardi (cnd)

French & Italian Opera Arias, w. Judith Forst (mez), Vancouver SO — CBC Records ("SM 5000" series) ▲ SMCD 5063 [DDD]

S. Comissiona (cnd)

Dvořák, A.:Slavonic Rhaps, Op. 45—No. 1 in D, No. 2 in g *(rec The Orpheum, Vancouver, B. C., June 13-14, 1994 & Mar 11, 1995)* — CBC ▲ 5166 [DDD]
Enescu, G.:Romanian Rhap 1 *(rec The Orpheum, Vancouver, B. C., June 13-14, 1994 & Mar 11, 1995)* — CBC ▲ 5166 [DDD]
Enescu, G.:Romanian Rhap 2 *(rec The Orpheum, Vancouver, B. C., June 13-14, 1994 & Mar 11, 1995)* — CBC ▲ 5166 [DDD]
Liszt, F.:Con Pno, Op. posth., w. J. Lowenthal (pno) — Music & Arts ▲ CD 803 [DDD]
Liszt, F.:Con 1 Pno, w. J. Lowenthal (pno) — Music & Arts ▲ CD 803 [DDD]
Liszt, F.:Hungarian Rhaps—No. 1 in f, No. 2 in d *(rec The Orpheum, Vancouver, B. C., June 13-14, 1994 & Mar 11, 1995)* — CBC ▲ 5166 [DDD]
Liszt, F.:Malédiction, w. J. Lowenthal (pno) [2 versions] — Music & Arts ▲ CD 803 [DDD]
Liszt, F.:Totentanz, w. J. Lowenthal (pno) — Music & Arts ▲ CD 803 [DDD]
Rachmaninoff, S.:Capriccio bohémien *(rec The Orpheum, Vancouver, June 1 & 4, 1993)* — CBC ▲ MVV 5143 [DDD]
Rachmaninoff, S.:Prelude Pno, Op. 3/2 [orchd. Lucien Cailliet] *(rec The Orpheum, Vancouver, June 1 & 4, 1993)* — CBC ▲ MVV 5143 [DDD]
Rachmaninoff, S.:Preludes Pno, Opp. 23 & 32—in g, Op. 23/5 [orchd. Lucien Cailliet] *(rec The Orpheum, Vancouver, June 1 & 4, 1993)* — CBC ▲ MVV 5143 [DDD]
Rachmaninoff, S.:Symphonic Dances *(rec The Orpheum, Vancouver, June 1 & 4, 1993)* — CBC ▲ MVV 5143 [DDD]

Varna PO

A. Andreev (cnd)

Shostakovich, D.:The Execution of Stepan Razin, w. A. Vassilev (bass), Varna Phil Chorus [R] — Koch International Classics ▲ KIC 7017-2 [DDD] ■ 3-7017-4 (D)
Sviridov, G.:Oratorio pathétique, w. A. Vassilev (bass), Varna Phil Chorus [R] — Koch International Classics ▲ KIC 7017-2 [DDD] ■ 3-7017-4 (D)

M. Mtakiev (cnd)

Stoyanov, L.:Liturgia Solemnis, w. A. Vassilev (bass), Slavonic Voices Male Chamber Choir [Slavonic] — Koch International Classics ▲ KIC 7033-2 [DDD] ■ 3-7033-4 (D)

Varsovia String Quartet

Bruzdowicz, J.:Qt 1 Strs, "La Vita" — Pavane ▲ ADW 7218 [DDD]
Bruzdowicz, J.:Qt 2 Strs, "Cantus Aeternus" — Pavane ▲ ADW 7218 [DDD]
Lutoslawski, W.:Petite Suite — Olympia ▲ OCD 328 [AAD]
Penderecki, K.:Qt 2 Strs — Olympia ▲ OCD 328 [AAD]
Szymanowski, K.:Qt 1 Strs — Olympia ▲ OCD 328 [AAD]
Szymanowski, K.:Qt 2 Strs — Olympia ▲ OCD 328 [AAD]
Zarebski, J.:Qnt Pno, w. W. Malicki (pno) — Pavane ▲ ADW 7218 [DDD]

Vedantic Arts Ensemble

J. Schienck (cnd)

Schlenck, J.:The Illumined Self *(rec San Francisco, 1986)* — Vedantic Arts ▲ VAR 001

Végh String Quartet

Beethoven, L. van:Grosse Fuge Str Qt — Valois ▲ V 4407 [AAD]
Beethoven, L. van:Grosse Fuge Str Qt — Valois 8-▲ V 4400 [AAD]
Beethoven, L. van:Qts Strs (comp)—Op. 18, Nos. 1 & 5 — Valois ▲ V 4401 [AAD]
Beethoven, L. van:Qts Strs (comp)—Op. 74 & Op. 127 — Valois ▲ V 4405 [AAD]
Beethoven, L. van:Qts Strs (comp)—Op. 95 & Op. 132 — Valois ▲ V 4406 [AAD]
Beethoven, L. van:Qts Strs (comp)—Op. 131 & Op. 135 — Valois ▲ V 4408 [AAD]
Beethoven, L. van:Qts Strs (comp)—Op. 59, Nos. 2 & 3 — Valois ▲ V 4404 [AAD]
Beethoven, L. van:Qts Strs (comp)—Op. 130 — Valois ▲ V 4407 [AAD]
Beethoven, L. van:Qts Strs (comp)—Op. 18/6 & Op. 59/1 — Valois ▲ V 4403 [AAD]
Beethoven, L. van:Qts Strs (comp)—Op. 18, Nos. 2,3 & 4 — Valois ▲ V 4402 [AAD]
Beethoven, L. van:Qts Strs (comp) — Valois 8-▲ V 4400 [AAD]
Beethoven, L. van:Qt 10 Strs, "Harp" — Auvidis Valois ▲ V 4405 [AAD]
Beethoven, L. van:Qt 11 Strs, "Quartetto serioso" — Auvidis Valois ▲ V 4406 [AAD]
Beethoven, L. van:Qt 12 Strs — Auvidis Valois ▲ V 4405 [AAD]
Beethoven, L. van:Qt 13 Strs — Auvidis Valois ▲ V 4407
Beethoven, L. van:Qt 14 Strs — Auvidis Valois ▲ V 4408 [AAD]
Beethoven, L. van:Qt 15 Strs — Auvidis Valois ▲ V 4406 [AAD]
Beethoven, L. van:Qt 16 Strs — Auvidis Valois ▲ V 4408 [AAD]

Venance Fortunat Ensemble

Angels, w. Concerto Soave, Ensemble Convivencia, Ensemble Lucidarum, La Fenice, Iberian Lyric Ensemble — L'Empreinte Digitale ▲ ED 13050

A.-M. Deschamps (cnd)

Daniel — L'Empreinte Digitale ▲ ED 13052
:Music Attributed to Fulbertus—Strips Jess (7 settings); Chorus novae; Benedicamus Domino (2 settings); O martyr; Iam super astra; Vir Dei Leobinus; Cumque gleba; Deus, Pater piissime; Aurea personet lyra; Alleluia dies sanctificatus; Solemn justitiae (4 settings); Ad nutum Domini [L,F] — Quantum ▲ QM 6899 [DDD]; ■ 1994
Sacred Lamentations in the Occidental Tradition *(rec 3/86)* — Solstice ▲ SOCD 48
Sacred Vocal Music from the Time of the Capetian Kings — Quantum ▲ QM 6892 [DDD] ■ QM 1987 (D)
Trouvères at the Court of Champagne — L'Empreinte Digitale ▲ ED 13045

La Venexiana

Marcello, B.:Cants & Duets, w. Rossana Bertini (sop), Claudio Cavina (alt)—Andromaca; Cassandra; La Lucrezia; La Stravaganza; plus others & duets — Opus 111 ▲ OPS 30-149

Venice Consort

Mainerio, G.:Il primo libro de balli *(rec Oct. 1-7, 1992)* — Tactus ▲ TC 531301 [DDD]

G. Toffano (cnd)

Cantar Alla Pavana, w. Accademia Strumentale Italiana *(rec Villa Beatrice, Monte Gemola, Baone, Padova, Oct 1995)* — Tactus ▲ TC 520002 [DDD]

Venice New Quintet [C. Montafia (fl), W. De Franceschi (ob), C. Lazari (vn), O. Trentin (bn), M. Liuzzi (clvd)]

Vivaldi, A.:Con Fl Ob, RV.88 — Tactus ▲ TC 672205 [DDD]
Vivaldi, A.:Con Fl Ob, RV.99 — Tactus ▲ TC 672205 [DDD]
Vivaldi, A.:Con Rcr Ob, RV.94 — Tactus ▲ TC 672205 [DDD]
Vivaldi, A.:Con Rcr Ob , RV.103 — Tactus ▲ TC 672205 [DDD]
Vivaldi, A.:Con Rcr Ob, RV.101 — Tactus ▲ TC 672205 [DDD]

Venice PO

P. Maag (cnd)

Malipiero, G.F.:Il finto Arlecchino (sels) *(rec March 1-8, 1991)* — Marco Polo ▲ 8.223397 [DDD]
Malipiero, G.F.:Invenzioni (4) *(rec March 1-8, 1991)* — Marco Polo ▲ 8.223397 [DDD]
Malipiero, G.F.:Invenzioni (7) *(rec March 1-8, 1991)* — Marco Polo ▲ 8.223397 [DDD]

Venice Solisti

The Ultimate Opera Collection, w. James Conlon (cnd), Armin Jordan (cnd), Raymond Leppard (cnd), Alain Lombard (cnd), Lorin Maazel (cnd), Claudio Scimone (cnd), London PO, Lyon Opera, et al. — Erato ▲ 2292-45797-2 ■ 2292-45797-4 AW

J.-C. Malgoire (cnd)

Vivaldi, A.:Cons Vn (misc), w. P. Toso (vn)—(2) RV.179 & RV.212a — Sony Classical ("Essential Classics" series) ▲ SBK 47662 ■ SBT 47662

C. Scimone (cnd)

Albinoni, T.:Cons à 5 Obs, Op. 7, w. M. Petri (rcr)—Nos. 3,6,9 & 12 — RCA Red Seal ▲ 60207-2 [DDD]
Albinoni, T.:Cons à 5 Obs, Op. 9, w. M. Petri (rcr)—Nos. 2,5,8 & 11 — RCA Red Seal ▲ 60207-2 [DDD]
Albinoni, T.:Il Nascimento de l'Aurora, w. June Anderson (sop), Susanne Klare (sop), Margarita Zimmermann (sop), Sandra Browne (alt), Yoshihisa Yamaj (ten) — Erato 2-▲ ERA SEL 96374 [DDD]
Baroque in Italy — Sony Classical ("Essential Classics" series) ▲ SBK 46547 [ADD] ■ SBT 46547
Bertoni, F.:Orfeo ed Euridice, w. Cecilia Gasdia (sop—Euridice), Delores Ziegler (mez—Orfeo), Bruce Ford (ten—Imeneo), John McCarthy (cnd), Ambrosian Opera Chorus *(rec Vicenza, Italy, Aug 3-7, 1990)* — Arts Music ▲ 47118-2 [DDD]
Boccherini, L.:Con Vc, G.482, w. O. Harnoy (vc) — RCA Red Seal ▲ 09026-61228-2 ■ 09026-61228-4
Boccherini, L.:Syms—in C, G.495; in d, G.506; in A, G.518 — Erato ▲ 2292-45486-2 [DDD]
Carnival in Venice, w. Guy Touvron (tpt) — RCA Red Seal ▲ 09026-61815-2
Cimarosa, D.:Con for 2 Fls, w. J.-P. Rampal (fl), Clémentine Scimone (fl) *(rec 1972)* — Erato ▲ 2292-45836-2 [ADD]
Devienne, F.:Sinf concertante for 2 Fls, w. J.-P. Rampal (fl), R. Wilson (fl) *(rec 1976)* — Erato ▲ 2292-45836-2 [ADD]
Galuppi, B.:Adamo, w. Susanna Rigacci (sop—Angelo di Misericordia), Mara Zampieri (sop—Eva), Marilyn Schmiege (mez—Angelo di Giustizia), Ernesto Palacio (ten—Adamo) — Erato 2-▲ ERA SEL 12984 [ADD]
Galuppi, B.:Concerti a quattro—1 sel — Erato 2-▲ ERA SEL 12984 [ADD]
Galuppi, B.:Con Fl, w. J. Galway (fl) — RCA Red Seal ▲ 09026-61164-2; ■ 09026-61164-4
Galuppi, B.:Cons Hpd, w. Edoardo Farina (hpd) — Erato 2-▲ ERA SEL 12984 [ADD]
Gianella, L.:Cons Fl (comp), w. J. Galway (fl)—Concerto lugubre — RCA Red Seal ▲ 09026-61164-2; ■ 09026-61164-4
Handel, G.F.:Messiah, w. Patricia Schuman (sop), Lucia Valentini Terrani (alt), Bruce Ford (ten), Gwynne Howell (bass), Bernard Soustrot (tpt), John McCarthy (cnd), Ambrosian Singers *(rec S. Francisco Church, Schio, Italy, June 23-30, 1989)* — Arts 2-▲ 471052 [DDD]
Italian Baroque Flute Concertos, w. Jean-Pierre Rampal (fl) — Sony Classical ▲ SK 47228
Mercadante, S.:Cons in D, e & E for Fl, w. J. Galway (fl) — RCA Red Seal ▲ 09026-61447-2
Mozart, W.A.:Cassation, K.100/62a *(rec Olimpic Theater, Vicenza, Italy, July 29-Aug 4, 1994)* — Arts Music ▲ 47277-2 [DDD]
Mozart, W.A.:Gallimathias musicum *(rec Olimpic Theater, Vicenza, Italy, June 10-14, 1994)* — Arts Music ▲ 47100-2 [DDD]
Mozart, W.A.:Sym, K.Anh.214 *(rec Olimpic Theater of Vicenza, Italy, July 29-Aug 4, 1994)* — Arts Music ▲ 47101-2 [DDD]
Mozart, W.A.:Sym, K.Anh.221 *(rec Olimpic Theater of Vicenza, Italy, July 29-Aug 4, 1994)* — Arts Music ▲ 47101-2 [DDD]
Mozart, W.A.:Sym, K.Anh.223 *(rec Olimpic Theater, Vicenza, Italy, June 10-14, 1994)* — Arts Music ▲ 47100-2 [DDD]
Mozart, W.A.:Sym 1 *(rec Olimpic Theater, Vicenza, Italy, June 10-14, 1994)* — Arts Music ▲ 47100-2 [DDD]
Mozart, W.A.:Sym 4 *(rec Olimpic Theater, Vicenza, Italy, June 10-14, 1994)* — Arts Music ▲ 47100-2 [DDD]
Mozart, W.A.:Sym 5 *(rec Olimpic Theater, Vicenza, Italy, June 10-14, 1994)* — Arts Music ▲ 47100-2 [DDD]

ORCH. & ENS.

Venice Solisti (cont.)
C. Scimone (cnd) (cont.)
Mozart, W.A.:Sym 6 *(rec Olimpic Theater, Vicenza, Italy, June 10–14, 1994)* Arts Music ▲ 47100-2 [DDD]
Mozart, W.A.:Sym 7 *(rec Olimpic Theater of Vicenza, Italy, July 29–Aug 4, 1994)* Arts Music ▲ 47101-2 [DDD]
Mozart, W.A.:Sym 8 *(rec Olimpic Theater of Vicenza, Italy, July 29–Aug 4, 1994)* Arts Music ▲ 47101-2 [DDD]
Mozart, W.A.:Sym 9 *(rec Olimpic Theater of Vicenza, Italy, July 29–Aug 4, 1994)* Arts Music ▲ 47101-2 [DDD]
Mozart, W.A.:Sym 10 *(rec Olimpic Theater, Vicenza, Italy, July 29–Aug 4, 1994)* Arts Music ▲ 47277-2 [DDD]
Mozart, W.A.:Sym 12 *(rec Olimpic Theater, Vicenza, Italy, July 29–Aug 4, 1994)* Arts Music ▲ 47277-2 [DDD]
Mozart, W.A.:Sym 13 *(rec Olimpic Theater, Vicenza, Italy, July 29–Aug 4, 1994)* Arts Music ▲ 47277-2 [DDD]
Mozart, W.A.:Sym 14 *(rec Olimpic Theater, Vicenza, Italy, July 29–Aug 4, 1994)* Arts Music ▲ 47277-2 [DDD]
Mysliveček, J.:Con Vc, w. O. Harnoy (vc) RCA Red Seal ▲ 09026-61228-2 ■ 09026-61228-4
Pergolesi, G.B.:Con Fl, w. J. Galway (fl) RCA Red Seal ▲ 09026-61164-2; ■ 09026-61164-4
Piacentino, R.A.:Con Fl, w. J. Galway (fl) RCA Red Seal ▲ 09026-61164-2; ■ 09026-61164-4
Rossini, G.:L'italiana in Algeri, w. K. Battle (sop), M. Horne (mez), E. Palacio (ten), S. Ramey (bass), N. Zaccaria (bass). Prague Phil Chorus [I] Erato ("Libretto" series) 2–▲ 2292-45404-2
Salieri, A.:Con Fl, w. Clementine Hoogendoorn (fl), Pietro Borgonovo (ob) Erato ▲ ERA SEL 12987 [DDD]
Salieri, A.:Cons Pno, w. Paul Badura-Skoda (pno)—in B♭ Erato ▲ ERA SEL 12987 [DDD]
Salieri, F.:Sinf la tempesta di mare Erato ▲ ERA SEL 12987 [DDD]
Tartini, G.:Con in G Fl, w. J. Galway (fl) RCA Red Seal ▲ 09026-61164-2 ■ 09026-61164-4
Trumpet Concertos, w. André Bernard (tpt), Helmut Hunger (tpt), et al., English CO [cnd:George Malcolm] Sony Classical ("Essential Classics" series) ▲ SBK 47663 ■ SBT 47663
Viotti, G.B.:Con Vc, w. O. Harnoy (vc) RCA Red Seal ▲ 09026-61228-2 ■ 09026-61228-4
Viotti, G.B.:Sym Concertante Fls, w. J.-P. Rampal (fl), R. Wilson (fl) *(rec 1976)* Erato ▲ 45836-2 [ADD]
Vivaldi, A.:Catone in Utica, w. Cecilia Gasdia (sop), Susanna Rigacci (sop), Marilyn Schmiege (sop), Lucretia Lendi (mez), Margarita Zimmerman (mez) Erato 2–▲ ERA SEL 11232 [DDD]
Vivaldi, A.:Cons Fl (misc), w. J. Galway (fl)—6 concerti—in a, RV.108; in D, RV.427; in D, RV.429; in G, RV.436; in G, RV.438; in a, RV.440 RCA Red Seal ▲ 7928-2-RC [DDD] ■ 7928-4-RC (CrO2)
Vivaldi, A.:Cons Fl (misc), w. J.-P. Rampal (fl)—RV.427 & 414 Erato ▲ 2292-45828-2 [ADD]
Vivaldi, A.:Cons Fl (misc), w. J.-P. Rampal (fl) Odyssey 2–▲ MB2K 45623
Vivaldi, A.:Cons Fl, Op. 10, w. J.-P. Rampal (fl) CBS ▲ MK 39062 [DDD]
Vivaldi, A.:Cons Fl, Op. 10, w. J.-P. Rampal (fl) Erato ▲ 2292-45828-2 [ADD]
Vivaldi, A.:Cons Rcr, w. M. Petri (rcr)—RV.108 & RV.441-445 RCA Red Seal ▲ 7885-2-RC [DDD]
Vivaldi, A.:Cons Vn, Op. 4, "La stravaganza" Erato ("CDouble" series) 2–▲ 2292-45450-2
Vivaldi, A.:Cons Vn, Op. 8/1-12, "Il cimento dell'armonia e dell'inventione", w. P. Toso (vn)—Nos. 1-6 & 8 Erato ("Bonsai" series) ▲ 2292-45945-2 ■ 2292-45945-4
Vivaldi, A.:Orlando Furioso, w. V. de los Angeles (sop), M. Horne (mez), L. Valentini-Terrani (mez), C. Gonzales (mez), Kosma (sgr), S. Bruscantini (bar), N. Zaccaria (bass) Erato 3–▲ 2292-45147-2 ZB

Venice String Quartet [Andrea Vio (vn), Alberto Battiston (vn), Luca Morassutti (va), Angelo Zanin (vc)]
Boccherini, L.:Qts Strs—Opp. 39/55; 41/56 & 57; 64/1 & 2 *(rec Dynamic Studios, Genoa, Oct. 19–21, 1994)* Dynamic ▲ CD 127 [DDD]
Boccherini, L.:Qts Strs, G.165-170 *(rec Dynamic's Studios, Genoa, Mar. 1–4, 1994)* Dynamic ▲ CDS 111 [DDD]
Boccherini, L.:Qts Strs G.232-235 *(rec Dynamic, Genoa, Italy, July 6–8, 1995)* Dynamic ▲ CD 154 [DDD]
Martucci, G.:Son Vn *(rec Oct. 23–25, 1992)* Ermitage ▲ ERM 410 [DDD]
Respighi, O.:Qnt Pno, w. P. Prati (vn) *(rec Oct. 23–25, 1992)* Ermitage ▲ ERM 410 [DDD]
Respighi, O.:Il Tramonto, w. C. Trakas (bar) [I] Koch International Classics ▲ KIC 7215 [DDD]

Venice Teatro La Fenice Orch
R. Abbado (cnd)
Verismo Arias, w. Freni, Mirella (sop) London ▲ 433316-2 LH [DDD]
B. Campanella (cnd)
Bellini, V.:I Capuleti e i Montecchi, w. K. Ricciarelli (sop), D. Montague (mez), D. Raffanti (ten), M. Lippi (bass), Venice Teatro La Fenice Chorus [I] *(rec 1991)* Nuova Era 2–▲ 7020/21 [DDD]
Bellini, V.:I Capuleti e i Montecchi (sels), w. Katia Ricciarelli (sop), Diana Montague (mez), Dano Raffanati (ten), Venice Teatro La Fenice Chorus Nuova Era ▲ NUO 7183 [DDD]
S. Celibidache (cnd)
Bäck, S.-E.:Intrada *(rec Oct. 31, 1965)* Originals ▲ ORISH 857
Cherubini, L.:Sinf in D *(rec Oct. 31, 1965)* Originals ▲ ORISH 857
Mussorgsky, M.:Pictures at an Exhibition *(rec Oct. 31, 1965)* Originals ▲ ORISH 857
J. Fisher (cnd)
Handel, G.F.:Rinaldo, w. Cecelia Gasdia (sop), Christine Weidinger (sop), Marylin Horne (mez), Ernesto Palacio (ten) *(rec live 1989)* Nuova Era 2–▲ 6813/14 [DDD]
C. Franci (cnd)
Rossini, G.:Armida, w. C. Deutekom (sop), P. Bottazzo (ten), O. Garaventa (ten), E. Gimenez (ten), B. Trotta (sgr), A. Maddalena (bass), G. Antonini (bass), Venice Teatro La Fenice Chorus *(rec live, Venice, 1970)* Foyer 2–▲ FOY 2030 [AAD]
Rossini, G.:Armida, w. C. Deutekom (sop), P. Bottazzo (ten), O. Garaventa (ten), E. Gimenez (ten), Venice Teatro La Fenice Chorus [I] *(rec live, 4/3/70)* Memories 2–▲ HR 4152/53 (m) [ADD]
G. Gavazzeni (cnd)
Donizetti, G.:Belisario, w. L. Gencer (sop), M. Pecile (cta), U. Grilli (ten), G. Taddei (bar), N. Zaccaria (bass), Venice Teatro La Fenice Chorus [I] *(rec live in Venice, 5/14/69)* Verona 2–▲ 27048/49 (m) [AAD]
Donizetti, G.:Belisario, w. L. Gencer (sop), M. Pecile (cta), U. Grilli (ten), G. Taddei (bar), N. Zaccaria (bass), Venice Teatro La Fenice Chorus [I] *(rec live, Venice 5/14/69)* Melodram 2–▲ MEL 27051 [AAD]
Donizetti, G.:Maria di Rohan, w. R. Scotto (sop—Maria), E. Zilio (mez—Armando di Gondi), U. Grilli (ten—Riccardo), R. Bruson (bar—Enrico), Venice Teatro La Fenice Chorus *(rec live Mar. 26, 1974)* Golden Age of Opera 2–▲ GAO 156/57 [ADD]
Verdi, G.:Jérusalem, w. Leyla Gencer (sop), Giacomo Aragall (ten), Giancarlo Guelfi (bar) [I] *(rec live 9/24/63)* Verona 2–▲ 27040/41 (m) [AAD]
Verdi, G.:Jérusalem, w. Leyla Gencer (sop), Giacomo Aragall (ten), Giancarlo Guelfi (bar), Venice Teatro La Fenice Chorus [I] *(rec live 9/24/63)* Melodram 2–▲ MEL 27004
Verdi, G.:Jérusalem, w. Leyla Gencer (sop), Giacomo Aragall (ten), Giancarlo Guelfi (bar), Venice Teatro La Fenice Chorus *(rec Venice, Sept 24, 1963)* Agorá Music ("Phoenix" series) 2–▲ 506
Verdi, G.:Macbeth (sels), w. L. Gencer (sop), G. Lamberti (ten), G. Guelfi (bar), Venice Teatro La Fenice Chorus [I] [highlights] *(rec live 4/9/68)* Melodram ▲ MEL 15002
G. Gelmetti (cnd)
Donizetti, G.:Les Martyrs, w. L. Gencer (sop), R. Bruson (bar), O. Garaventa (bar), F. Furlanetto (bass), Venice Teatro La Fenice Chorus *(rec 1978)* Italian Opera Rarities ▲ IOR 7716 [ADD]
V. Gui (cnd)
Bellini, V.:Beatrice di Tenda, w. L. Gencer (sop), J. Oncina (ten), M. Zanasi (bar), Venice Teatro La Fenice Chorus *(rec 1964)* Memories 2–▲ MEM 4543 [ADD]
J. Latham-König (cnd)
Leoncavallo, R.:La Bohème, w. L. Mazzaria (sop), M. Senn (mez), B. Praticò (sgr), M. Malagnini (sgr), J. Summers (bar), Venice Teatro La Fenice Chorus *(rec live, 1990)* Nuova Era 3–▲ 6917/19 [DDD]

Venice Teatro La Fenice Orch (cont.)
P. Maag (cnd)
Bizet, G.:Carmen, w. M. Chiara (sop—Micaela), A. Caminada (mez—Mercedes), F. Cossotto (mez—Carmen), F. Andreoli (ten—Il Remendado), P. M. Ferraro (ten—Don José), R. Bruson (bar—Escamillo), G. Zancanaro (bar—Morales), A. Carusi (bass—Il Dancairo), Venice Teatro La Fenice Chorus *(rec 1971)* Myto 2–▲ MCD 93487
I. Marin (cnd)
Rossini, G.:Arias, w. C. Bartoli (mez), Venice Teatro La Fenice Chorus—8 scenes from Donna del Lago, Elisabetta, Maometto II, Nozze di Teti e di Peleo, Semiramide, Zelmira [I] London ▲ 436075-2 [DDD] ■ 436075-4 □ 436075-5
Rossini, G.:Maometto II (sels), w. Cecilia Bartoli (mez). Venice Teatro La Fenice Chorus—Giusto ciel, in tal periglio *(rec 1991)* London ▲ 448300-2 [DDD]; ■ 448300-4
Rossini, G.:Semiramide (sels), w. Cecilia Bartoli (mez). Venice Teatro La Fenice Chorus—Bel raggio lusinghier *(rec 1991)* London ▲ 448300-2 [DDD]; ■ 448300-4
D. Mitropoulos (cnd)
Puccini, G.:La fanciulla del West, w. E. Steber (sop), M. del Monaco (ten), G. Guelfi (bar), Venice Teatro La Fenice Chorus *(rec live, 6/15/54)* Arkadia 2–▲ 565 (m)
R. Muti (cnd)
Beethoven, L. van:Christus am Ölberg, w. C. Deutekom (sop), L. Kozma (ten), F. Lindauer (sgr), Venice Teatro La Fenice Chorus [G] *(rec live, Venice 7/4/70)* Arkadia ▲ 743 [ADD]
D. Oren (cnd)
Primadonna:Bel Canto Italiano *(rec live, Piazza San Marco, Venice)* Musik Strasse ▲ MC 2104
N. Santi (cnd)
Bellini, V.:La sonnambula, w. R. Scotto (sop), A. Kraus (ten), I. Vinco (bass), Venice Teatro La Fenice Chorus [I] *(rec live, Venice 5/26/61)* Golden Age of Opera 2–▲ GAO 111/12 [ADD]
R. Weikert (cnd)
Mahler, G.:Songs, w. E. Lear (sop)—Es sungen drei Engel [from Sym. 3]; Urlicht [from Sym. 2] *(rec 1978)* VAI Audio ▲ VAIA 1061 (m) [ADD]

Vent d'Orient Ensemble
K. Komatsu (cnd)
Noda, T.:Poems I & II Camerata ▲ 32CM 58
Noda, T.:Serenade I Camerata ▲ 32CM 58

Veracini Trio [John Holloway (vn), David Watkins (vc), Lars Ulrik Mortensen (hpd)]
Corelli, A.:Sons Vn, Op. 5—complete, plus 2nd versions of Nos. 3 & 12 Novalis 2–▲ 150128 [DDD]

Verdehr Trio
The Making of a Medium, Vol. 1 Crystal ▲ CD 741
The Making Of A Medium, Vol. 2 Crystal ▲ CD 742

Verdehr Trio [Walter Verdehr (vn), Elsa Ludewig-Verdehr (cl), Gary Kirkpatrick (pno)]
Arutiunian, A.:Suite Vn Crystal ▲ CD 745
Averitt, W.:Tripartita Crystal ▲ CD 743 [DDD]
Bartók, B.:Contrasts Crystal ▲ CD 741
Bassett, L.:Trio Cl Leonarda ▲ LE 326
Bruch, M.:Trios Cl, Va & Pno, Op. 83—4 trios Leonarda ▲ LE 326
Currier, N.:Adagio & Vars Crystal ▲ CD 743 [DDD]
David, T.C.:Schubertiade Crystal ▲ CD 742
Dickinson, P.:Hymns, Rags & Blues Crystal ▲ CD 744
Frescobaldi, G.:Canzonas a due Canti [Canzoni seconda & quinta in violin-clarinet-piano arr. by the performers] Crystal ▲ CD 741
Freund, D.W.:Triomusic Crystal ▲ CD 744
Hoag, C.:Inventions on the Summer Solstice Leonarda ▲ LE 326
Hoover, K.:Images Leonarda ▲ LE 326
Hovhaness, A.:Lake Samish Crystal ▲ CD 741
Husa, K.:Son a tre Crystal ▲ CD 744
Liszt, F.:Hungarian Rhaps [arr. by M. Zearotti for violin, clarinet & piano]—Hungarian Rhapsody No. 13 Crystal ▲ CD 742
Mozart, W.A.:Son Pno 4-Hands, K.381 [arr. performers for violin, clarinet & piano] Crystal ▲ CD 741
Musgrave, T.:Pierrot Crystal ▲ CD 742
Pasatieri, T.:Theatrepieces Crystal ▲ CD 741
Rorem, N.:The End of Summer Crystal ▲ CD 742
Schickele, P.:Serenade for 3 Crystal ▲ CD 745
Schuller, G.:Trio Setting Vn Crystal ▲ CD 743 [DDD]
Sculthorpe, P.:Dream Tracks Crystal ▲ CD 745
Vanhal, J.B.:Trio Vn Crystal ▲ CD 742
T.C. David (cnd)
David, T.C.:Triple Con, w. Tonkünstler Orch Crystal ▲ CD 745

Verdi String Quartet
Berger, W.:Qnt Pno, w. Jost Michaels (pno) *(rec Leipzig, Jan.–Mar. 1964)* MD + G ("Gold" series) ▲ MDG 3080506 [DDD]
Bohnke, E.:Qt Strs MD + G 2–▲ MDG 3250531 [DDD]

Vermeer String Quartet [Shmuel Ashkenasi (vn), Mathias Tacke (vn), Richard Young (va), Marc Johnson (vc)]
Beethoven, L. van:Grosse Fuge Str Qt Teldec 3–▲ 4509-91496-2
Beethoven, L. van:Grosse Fuge Str Qt Teldec 9–▲ 9031-76457-2
Beethoven, L. van:Qts Strs (comp)—Nos. 1-6, Op. 18 Teldec 3–▲ 4509-91494-2
Beethoven, L. van:Qts Strs (comp) Teldec 9–▲ 9031-76457-2
Beethoven, L. van:Qts Strs (comp)—Nos. 12-16 Teldec 3–▲ 4509-91496-2
Beethoven, L. van:Qts Strs (comp)—Nos. 7-11, Opp. 59, 74 & 95 Teldec 3–▲ 4509-91495-2
Beethoven, L. van:Qt 12 Strs Teldec 9–▲ 9031-76457-2
Beethoven, L. van:Qt 12 Strs Teldec 3–▲ 4509-91496-2
Beethoven, L. van:Qt 13 Strs Teldec 9–▲ 9031-76457-2
Beethoven, L. van:Qt 13 Strs Teldec 3–▲ 4509-91496-2
Beethoven, L. van:Qt 14 Strs Teldec 9–▲ 9031-76457-2
Beethoven, L. van:Qt 14 Strs Teldec 3–▲ 4509-91496-2
Beethoven, L. van:Qt 15 Strs Teldec 9–▲ 9031-76457-2
Beethoven, L. van:Qt 15 Strs Teldec 3–▲ 4509-91496-2
Beethoven, L. van:Qt 16 Strs Teldec 9–▲ 9031-76457-2
Beethoven, L. van:Qt 16 Strs Teldec 3–▲ 4509-91496-2
Brahms, J.:Qnt Cl, w. K. Leister (cl) Orfeo ▲ 068831 [DDD]
Haydn, J.:The Seven Last Words of Christ on the Cross—w. introd. by Jason Robards, readings from the Gospels by Father Virgil P. Elizondo, Billy Graham, Rev. Kelly Clem, Dr. Martin E. Marty, Elder Dallin H. Oaks, Father Raymond E. Brown, Rev. Martin Luther King, Jr. & Pastor T.L. Barrett *(rec Northern Illinois Univ., May 1994)* Alden Productions 2–▲ AP 123046
Tchaikovsky, P.:Qt 2 Strs *(rec May & Oct. 1993)* Cedille ▲ CDR 90000 017 [DDD]
Tchaikovsky, P.:Souvenir de Florence, w. R. Solomonow (va), J. Sharp (vc) *(rec May–Oct., 1993)* Cedille ▲ CDR 90000 017 [DDD]

Vermont Festival Players
Hummel, J.N.:Septet Pno, w. Eugene List (pno) [variant arr. by Hummel for piano & string quartet] Monitor ■ 55002

Vermont SO members
R. Decormier (cnd)
Krása, H.:Brundibár, w. Constance Price (cnd), Essex Children's Choir, Vermont Sym Chorus members *(rec Ira Allen Chapel, Univ of Vermont, Burlington, VT, Jan 28, 1996)* Arabesque ▲ ARA 6680 [DDD]
Ullmann, V.:Kaiser von Atlantis, w. Vermont Sym Chorus members *(rec Ira Allen Chapel, Univ of Vermont, Burlington, VT, Jan 28, 1996)* Arabesque ▲ ARA 6681 [DDD]

Verna Trio
Mozart, W.A.:Trio Vn, K.563 REM ▲ 311119 XCD [DDD]

410 ▲ = CD ♦ = Enhanced CD Δ = MD ■ = Cassette Tape □ = DCC

Verona Istitutioni Harmoniche
M. Longhini (cnd)
Cavalieri, E. de:Rappresentatione di Anima et di Corpo, w. G. Bertagnolli (sop), C. Cavina (alt), B. Rossetti (sgr), G. Malatto (ten), R. Mattei (bar), A. Abete (sgr) Stradivarius ▲ STR 33339 [DDD]
Versailles CO
B. Wahl (cnd)
Mozart, W.A.:Divert Ob, K.251 Arion ▲ ARN 68140
Mozart, W.A.:Qt 4 Strs [arr. chamber orch.] Arion ▲ ARN 68140
Mozart, W.A.:Qt 7 Strs [arr. chamber orch.] Arion ▲ ARN 68140
Mozart, W.A.:Sym 13 Arion ▲ ARN 68140
Versailles Guitar Quartet [C. Chanel (gtr), N. Courtin (gtr), J. F. Fourichon (gtr), P. Rayer (gtr)]
Quatre Guitares à l'Abbaye de l'Epau Quantum ▲ QM 6926 [DDD]
Quatuor de guitares a l'abbaye de l'epau, Vol. 2 Quantum ▲ QM 6948
Versaille National Masters
J. Malgoire (cnd)
Les Chemins du Baroque [The Paths of the Baroque], Vol. 2:Mexico – Versailles:Vepres de l'Assomption, w. Compañia Musical de las Americas, La Grande Ecurie et la Chambre du Roy K617 ▲ 7026 [DDD]
Versailles Polyphonic Ensemble
S. Roger (cnd)
The Responsory of the Holy Week, w. [cnd:J.-P. Lore], St. Yves Choral Association *(rec May 24–26, 1980)* Esoldun ▲ MOS 1003 [ADD]
Vertavo String Quartet [Elise Batnes (vn), Berit Vaernes (vn), Henninge Batnes (va), Bjorg Vaernes (vc)]
Nielsen, C.:Qt 1 Strs *(rec Eldsvoll Church, Oct 20–21 & 24–25, 1995)* Simax ▲ PSC 1128 [DDD]
Nielsen, C.:Qt 2 Strs *(rec Eldsvoll Church, Oct 20–21 & 24–25, 1995)* Simax ▲ PSC 1128 [DDD]
Vestjysk Chamber Ensemble [F. Gislinge (ob), K. Brændstrup (cl), N. C. Øllgard (vn), J. Nielsen (va), F. Hansen (db)]
Prokofiev, S.:Qnt Ob *(rec Festival Hall, Esbjerg, Denmark, June 4–5, 1977)* BIS ▲ CD 155 [AAD]
Via Nova String Quartet
Fauré, G.:Qt Strs Erato ▲ ERA 96953 [ADD]
Fauré, G.:Qnts Pno & Strs, Opp. 89 & 115, w. Jean Hubeau (pno) Erato 3-▲ ERA 96953 [ADD]
Via Nova String Quartet members
Fauré, G.:Qts Pno, Opp. 15 & 45, w. Jean Hubeau (pno) Erato ▲ ERA 96953 [ADD]
Fauré, G.:Trio, w. Jean Hubeau (pno) Erato ▲ ERA 96953 [ADD]
Victoria SO
P. Freeman (cnd)
Saint-Saëns, C.:Con 1 Vc, w. O. Harnoy (vc) *(rec University of Victoria, British Columbia, 1983)* RCA Gold Seal ▲ 09026-68373-2 [DDD]
Tchaikovsky, P.:Vars on a Rococo Theme, w. Ofra Harnoy (vc) *(rec University of Victoria, British Columbia, 1983)* RCA Gold Seal ▲ 09026-68373-2 [DDD]
Victorian State Opera Orch
J. Hopkins (cnd)
Conyngham, B.:Fly, w. Victorian State Opera Chorus Move ▲ MD 3076 [DDD]
Videmus
Anderson, Thom Jefferson:Intermezzos Cl New World ▲ 80423-2
Baker, D.:Through This Vale of Tears [E] New World ▲ 80423-2
Fox, D.:Music of—Dialectics for Two Grand Pianos (1988); Duetto for Clarinet & Piano (1991); Four Chords from T.J.'s Intermezzi for Piano (1991); Jazz Sets & Tone Rows for Alto Saxophone & Piano (1991) New World ▲ 80423-2
Still, W.G.:Ennanga New World ▲ 80399-2 [DDD]
Still, W.G.:Instrumental Music—Summerland (1936); Out of the Silence (1940); Incantation and Dance (1942) New World ▲ 80399-2 [DDD]
Still, W.G.:Songs—Here's One (1941); Song for the Lonely (1953); Citadel (1956); Lift Every Voice & Sing [E] New World ▲ 80399-2 [DDD]
Still, W.G.:Songs of Separation [E] New World ▲ 80399-2 [DDD]
Wilson, O.:Sometimes New World ▲ 80423-2
Videmus members [L. Chang, V. Taylor]
Still, W.G.:Suite Vn New World ▲ 80399-2 [DDD]
Vienna Academy
Mozart:Missa Solemnis & Salieri:Te Deum (The Coronation Mass for Leopold II in Prague, September 1791), w. Ruth Ziesak (sop), E. von Magnus (mez), H. Wildahaber (ten), G. Hornik (bass), Hugo Distler Chorus, Vienna Hofburg Chapel Choir Novalis ▲ 150087 [DDD]
M. Haselböck (cnd)
Bach, J.S.:Brandenburg Cons [period instrs] Novalis 2-▲ 150035 [DDD]
Biber, H. von:Battalia *(rec Schloss Kammer & Vienna, May 1995)* Novalis ▲ 150124 [DDD]
Biber, H. von:Serenade Strs, "Nightwatchman's Call" *(rec Schloss Kammer & Vienna, May 1995)* Novalis ▲ 150124 [DDD]
Biber, H. von:Son a 5 Tpt *(rec Schloss Kammer & Vienna, May 1995)* Novalis ▲ 150124 [DDD]
Haydn, J.:Con Tpt, w. Reinhold Friedrich (tpt) *(rec Sofiensäle, Vienna, Oct 17–20, 1994)* Capriccio ▲ 10 598 [DDD]
Haydn, J.:Mass 5, "Missa Sancti Josephi", "Grosse Orgelmesse", w. Dorthea Röschmann (sop), Bernarda Fink (cta), Helmut Wildhaber (ten), Klaus Mertens (bar), Hugo Distler Choir Novalis ▲ 150095 [DDD]
Haydn, J.:Mass 7, "Kleine Orgelmesse", w. Dorthea Röschmann (sop), Bernarda Fink (cta), Helmut Wildhaber (ten), Klaus Mertens (bar), Hugo Distler Choir Novalis ▲ 150095 [DDD]
Haydn, J.:Salve regina, H.XXIIIb/2, w. Dorthea Röschmann (sop), Bernarda Fink (cta), Helmut Wildhaber (ten), Klaus Mertens (bar), Hugo Distler Choir Novalis ▲ 150095 [DDD]
Hummel, J.N.:Alma virgo, w. Amanda Halgrimson (sop), Susan McAdoo (mez), Helmut Wildhaber (ten), Petr Mikuláš (bass), Jan Engel (bass), Brünn Czech Phil Chorus Koch Schwann ▲ SCH CD 317792
Hummel, J.N.:Con in E♭ Tpt, S.49, w. Reinhold Friedrich (tpt) *(rec Sofiensäle, Vienna, Oct 17–20, 1994)* Capriccio ▲ 10 598 [DDD]
Hummel, J.N.:Mass in E♭, Op. 80, w. Amanda Halgrimson (sop), Susan McAdoo (mez), Helmut Wildhaber (ten), Petr Mikuláš (bass), Jan Engel (bass), Brünn Czech Phil Chorus Koch Schwann ▲ SCH CD 317792
Hummel, J.N.:Quod quod in orbe, w. Amanda Halgrimson (sop), Susan McAdoo (mez), Helmut Wildhaber (ten), Petr Mikuláš (bass), Jan Engel (bass), Brünn Czech Phil Chorus Koch Schwann ▲ SCH CD 317792
Mozart, W.A.:Con Fl, K.314, w. Christian Gurtner (fl) [period instrs] Novalis ▲ 150113 [DDD]
Mozart, W.A.:Marches Orch, K.335 *(rec Vienna, Feb. 1995)* Novalis ▲ 150109 [DDD]
Mozart, W.A.:Masonic Music, w. C. Prégardien (ten), H. Wildhaber (ten), G. Hornik (bass), P. Schneyder (bass), Chorus Viennensis—Masonic Cants., K.429, 471, 619, 623 & Songs, K.148, 468, 483, 484 [G] Novalis ▲ 150081 [DDD]
Mozart, W.A.:Maurerische Trauermusik Novalis ▲ 150081 [DDD]
Mozart, W.A.:Missa solemnis, K.337, w. R. Ziesak (sop), E. von Magnus (alt), H. Wildhaber (ten), G. Hornik (bar), H. Hüttler (cant), M. Jankowitsch (cant), P. Jelosits (cant), I. Rainer (org), Vienna Hofburg Chapel Choir [L] *(rec Apr. 1992)* Novalis ▲ 150087 [DDD]
Mozart, W.A.:Musikalischer Spass *(rec Vienna, Feb. 1995)* Novalis ▲ 150109 [DDD]
Mozart, W.A.:Serenade Ww, K.320 *(rec Vienna, Feb. 1995)* Novalis ▲ 150109 [DDD]
Mozart, W.A.:Sinf concertante Ob, K.Anh.9 [reconstructed by Robert D. Levin] Novalis ▲ 150113 [DDD]
Poglietti, A.:Music of—Canzon e capriccio sopra das Henner und Hannengeschray *(rec Schloss Kammer & Vienna, May 1995)* Novalis ▲ 150124 [DDD]
Puccini, M.:Concertone Fl, w. Christian Gurtner (fl), Lisa Klevit-Ziegler (cl), Reinhold Friedrich (tpt), Hector McDonald (nat hn) *(rec Sofiensäle, Vienna, Oct 17–20, 1994)* Capriccio ▲ 10 598 [DDD]
Telemann, G.P.:Cons (misc) [period instrs]—in D for 3 Tpts, 2 Obs, Strs, Timp & BC *(rec Vienna, Dec. 1994)* Novalis ▲ 150115 [DDD]

Vienna Academy (cont.)
M. Haselböck (cnd) (cont.)
Telemann, G.P.:Syms [period instrs]—Il grillo, TWV 50/1 *(rec Vienna, Dec. 1994)* Novalis ▲ 150115 [DDD]
Vejvanovsky, P.J.:Sons & Serenades—Son la posta; Son tribus quadrantibus; Son a 8 Sancti Petri et Pauli *(rec Schloss Kammer & Vienna, May 1995)* Novalis ▲ 150124 [DDD]
Vivaldi, A.:Con for 2 Vcs, w. M. Peters (vc), P. Sigl (vc) [period instrs] Novalis ▲ 150074 [DDD]
Vivaldi, A.:Cons Diverse Instrs [period instrs]—Concerti for 2 Trumpets, RV.537; Violin & Organ, RV.542; 2 Transverse Flutes, RV.533; 2 Cellos, RV.531; Oboe & Bassoon, RV.545; 2 Orchestras, RV.583 *(rec 11/90)* Novalis ▲ 150074 [DDD]
Vivaldi, A.:Con for 2 Fls, w. C. Gurtner (fl), L. Brunmayr (fl) [period instrs] Novalis ▲ 150074 [DDD]
Vivaldi, A.:Con Ob Bn, w. P. Frankenberg (ob), G. van der Wulp (bn) [period instrs] Novalis ▲ 150074 [DDD]
Vivaldi, A.:Con for 2 Orchs [period instrs] Novalis ▲ 150074 [DDD]
Vivaldi, A.:Con for 2 Tpts, w. S. Keavy (tpt), A. Lackner (tpt) [period instrs] Novalis ▲ 150074 [DDD]
Vivaldi, A.:Con Vn Org, RV.542, w. I. Kertész (vn), M. Haselböck (org) [period instrs] Novalis ▲ 150074 [DDD]
Weber, C.M. von:Concertino Hn, w. Hector McDonald (hn) Novalis ▲ 150113 [DDD]
Vienna Amadeus Ensemble
W. Kobera (cnd)
Mozart, W.A.:Arias, w. A. Raunig (ct), K. F. Schmid (cl), M. Dostal (org), Vienna Landstrasse Church Choir—Il padre adorato [from Idomneo]; Cara, lontano ancora [from Ascanio in Alba]; Parto, ma tu ben mio [from La clemenza di Tito] Divertimento ▲ DIV 31013 [DDD]
Mozart, W.A.:Exsultate, w. A. Raunig (ct), K. F. Schmid (cl), M. Dostal (org), Vienna Landstrasse Church Choir Divertimento ▲ DIV 31013 [DDD]
Salieri, A.:Arias, w. A. Raunig (ct), K. F. Schmid (cl), M. Dostal (org), Vienna Landstrasse Church Choir—Perdermi? [from Axur, Re d'ormus]; Lungi da te [from Armida]; A fulminas m'invita [from Anibale] Divertimento ▲ DIV 31013 [DDD]
Salieri, A.:Songs, w. A. Raunig (ct), K. F. Schmid (cl), M. Dostal (org), Vienna Landstrasse Church Choir—Fremat Thyrannus (motet) Divertimento ▲ DIV 31013 [DDD]
Vienna Bella Musica Ensemble
M. Dittrich (cnd)
Vienne Danses, 1850 Harmonia Mundi Plus ▲ HMP 3901013
Vienna Biedermeier Soloists
Fahrbach, P.:Im Kahlenbergerdörfel Camerata ▲ 32CM 210
Fahrbach, P.:Music of, w. Dieter Flury (fl), Peter Schmidl (cl)—Die Schwärmer, Op. 43; Talmi-Polka, Op. 304; Lerchenfelder-Polka, Op. 178; Vienna Polka, Op. 109; S'Schwarzblatl Aus'n Weanerwald, Op. 61; Wiener-Feuerwehr, Op. 280; Marien-Polka, Op. 164; Wiener Polka, Op. 109 *(rec Studio Baumgarten, Vienna, 1991–95)* Camerata ▲ 30CM 411 [DDD]
Fahrbach, P.:Music of—Im Kahlenbergerdörfel Camerata ▲ 32CM 129
Fahrbach (Jr.), P.:Music of, w. Dieter Flury (fl), Peter Schmidl (cl)—Der Klapperstorch, Op. 149; Wiener Lebensbilder, Op. 213; Reissausl, Op. 121; Pester Offiziers Casino Polka, Op. 83; Landsturm-Galopp, Op. 250; Erinnerung An Josef Strauss, Op. 53; Im Kahlenbergerdörfel, Op. 340 *(rec Studio Baumgarten, Vienna, 1991–95)* Camerata ▲ 30CM 411 [DDD]
Lanner, J.:Music of—Streyrische Tänze; Jägers Lust; Abensterne; Bruder Halt; Die Werber; Hans Jörgel-Polka Camerata ▲ 32CM 129
Strauss (II), Joh.:Music of—Jugendfeuer; Exeter Polka; Wiener Gemüths Walzer; Seufzer Galopp; Annen Polka; Hof Ball Tänze Camerata ▲ 32CM 210
Strauss (II), Joh.:Music of—Jugendfeuer; Exeter Polka; Wiener Gemüths Walzer; Seeufzer Galopp; Annen Polka; Hof Ball Tänze Camerata ▲ 32CM 129
Vienna Chamber Ensemble
Beethoven, L. van:Septet Strs Denon ▲ CO 75373
Beethoven, L. van:Sxt Hns, Op. 81b Denon ▲ CO 75373
Mozart, W.A.:Divert Hns Bn, K.205 Denon ▲ CO 77883 [DDD]
Mozart, W.A.:Divert Hns Strs, K.247 Denon ▲ CO 77883 [DDD]
Mozart, W.A.:Divert Ww, K.113 Denon ▲ CO 77882 [DDD]
Mozart, W.A.:March Hns, K.248 Denon ▲ CO 77883 [DDD]
Mozart, W.A.:March Hns, K.290 Denon ▲ CO 77883 [DDD]
Mozart, W.A.:March Hns, K.445 *(rec Apr.–May 1991)* Denon ▲ CO 77882 [DDD]
Vienna Chamber Ensemble members [Michael Werba (bn), Adalbert Skocic (vc)]
Mozart, W.A.:Son Bn *(rec Schottenstift, Vienna, Dec 15–19, 1991)* Canyon Classics ▲ 186
Vienna Chamber Ensemble members [Michael Werba (bn), Gerhart Hetzel (vn), Josef Hell (vn), Hatto Beyerle (va), Adalbert Skocic (vc)]
Devienne, F.:Qts Bn, Op. 73—No. 1 in C *(rec Schottenstift, Vienna, Dec 15–19, 1991)* Canyon Classics ▲ 186
Vienna Chamber Ensemble members [Norbert Taubl (cl), Gerhart Hetzel (vn), Josef Hell (vn), Hatto Beyerle (va), Adalbert Skocic (vc)]
Weber, C.M. von:Qnt Cl *(rec Schottenstift, Vienna, Dec 15–19, 1991)* Canyon Classics ▲ 186
Vienna Chamber Musicians
Schmidt, F.:Qnt Cl *(rec 1984)* Preiser ▲ 93357 [ADD]
Vienna CO
Mendelssohn, F.:Con in d Vn, Pno & Strs, w. O. Rudner (vn), P. Entremont (pno) Koch Schwann ▲ CD 311047 [DDD] ■ MC 211047 (D)
Viotti, G.B.:Con 3 Pno, w. P. Entremont (pno), O. Rudner (vn) Koch Schwann ▲ CD 311047 [DDD] ■ MC 211047 (D)
P. Entremont (cnd)
Haydn, J.:Con Ob, w. Pierre W. Feit (ob) Koch Schwann ▲ CD 311075
Haydn, J.:Sym 12 Musique d'Abord ▲ HMA 1901363
Haydn, J.:Sym 34 Musique d'Abord ▲ HMA 1901363
Haydn, J.:Sym 44, "Trauer" Musique d'Abord ▲ HMA 1901362
Haydn, J.:Sym 85, "La Reine de France" Musique d'Abord ▲ HMA 1901363
Haydn, J.:Sym 92, "Oxford" Musique d'Abord ▲ HMA 1901362
Mozart, W.A.:Con Ob, K.314, w. Pierre W. Feit (ob) Koch Schwann ▲ CD 311 075
Mozart, W.A.:Con 12 Pno, w. P. Entremont (pno) *(rec June 1985)* Koch Schwann ▲ 311157 G1 [DDD]
Mozart, W.A.:Con 14 Pno, w. P. Entremont (pno) *(rec June 1985)* Koch Schwann ▲ 311157 G1 [DDD]
Mozart, W.A.:Diverts Str Qt, K.136–138 Pro Arte ▲ CDS 579 [DDD]
Mozart, W.A.:Kleine Nachtmusik Pro Arte ▲ CDS 579 [DDD]
Mozart, W.A.:Sym 40 Pro Arte ▲ CDS 578
Mozart, W.A.:Sym 41 Pro Arte ▲ CDS 578
Tchaikovsky, P.:Serenade Strs *(rec Brussels, June 1990)* Naxos ▲ 8.553227 [DDD]
Tchaikovsky, P.:Serenade Strs *(rec 2/90)* Naxos ▲ 8.550404 [DDD]
Tchaikovsky, P.:Souvenir de Florence *(rec 2/90)* Naxos ▲ 8.550404 [DDD]
A. Fischer (cnd)
Mozart, W.A.:Arias, w. C. Bartoli (mez), A. Schiff (pno)—arias from Clemenza di Tito, Così fan tutte, Don Giovanni & Le nozze di Figaro; & three concert arias [I] London ▲ 430513-2 [DDD]
G. Fischer (cnd)
Mozart, W.A.:Arias, w. Cecilia Bartoli (mez)—Ch'io mi scordi di te? *(rec 1989)* London ▲ 448300-2 [DDD]; ■ 448300-4
Mozart, W.A.:Arias, w. C. Bartoli (mez)—Temerai...Come Scoglio; Ei Parte...per pieta; In nomini [all from Così fan tutte]; È Susanne non vien...Dove Sono [from Le nozze di Figaro]; Batti, batti; In quali eccessi...mi tradi [both from Don Giovanni] London ▲ 443452-2 ■ 443452-4 □ 443452-5
Mozart, W.A.:Arias, w. K. Te Kanawa (sop)—(7 concert arias) K.272, K.583, K.73d (79), K.582, K.490, K.528, K.383 [G,I] London ▲ 417756-2 [ADD]
Mozart, W.A.:Così fan tutte (sels), w. Cecilia Bartoli (mez)—Temerari!...Come scoglio; In uomini, in soldati *(rec 1993)* London ▲ 448300-2 [DDD]; ■ 448300-4
Mozart, W.A.:Davidde penitente, w. C. Bartoli (mez)—Lungi le cive ingrate London ▲ 443452-2 ■ 443452-4 □ 443452-5

Vienna CO (cont.)
G. Fischer (cnd) (cont.)
Mozart, W.A.:Don Giovanni (sels), w. Cecilia Bartoli (mez)—Batti, batti, o bel Masetto *(rec 1993)* London ▲ 448300-2 [DDD]; ■ 448300-4
Mozart, W.A.:Exsultate, w. C. Bartoli (mez) London ▲ 443452-2 ■ 443452-4 □ 443452-5
Mozart, W.A.:Nozze di Figaro (sels), w. Cecilia Bartoli (mez)—Voi che sapete; Giunse alfin il momento...Deh vieni *(rec 1989)* London ▲ 448300-2 [DDD]; ■ 448300-4
E. Märzendorfer (cnd)
Hummel, J.N.:Con Pno, Vn & Orch, Op. 17, w. Eugene List (pno), C. Glenn (vn) Monitor ■ 55002
B. Perrenoud (cnd)
Haydn, J.:Con 1 Vc, w. Tanja Tetzlaff (vc) *(rec Vienna, Feb 4–7, 1994)* Camerata ▲ 30CM 365 [DDD]
Haydn, J.:Con 2 Vc, w. Tanja Tetzlaff (vc) *(rec Vienna, Feb 4–7, 1994)* Camerata ▲ 30CM 365 [DDD]
Z. Topolski (cnd)
Mozart, W.A.:Con 20 Pno, w. Eugene List (pno) *(rec Baumgartner Casino, Vienna, 1966)* Vox Legends 3-▲ CDX3 3504
Mozart, W.A.:Con 26 Pno, w. Eugene List (pno) *(rec Baumgartner Casino, Vienna, 1966)* Vox Legends 3-▲ CDX3 3504
C. Traunfellner (cnd)
Mozart, W.A.:Arias, w. U. Fiedler (sop), C. Eisenberger (vn)—Exsultate, Jubilate; Voi avete un cor fedele; Misera, dove son!; Non temer, amato bene; Vedrai carino, se sei buonino; Bella mia fiamma, addio; Alma grande e nobil core; Chi sa, chi sa, qual sia Camerata ▲ 30CM-343
Vienna CO Soloists
Dvořák, A.:Qnt Pno, Op. 81, w. P. Entremont (pno) Pro Arte ▲ CDD 470 [DDD]
Mozart, W.A.:Qts Pno, w. P. Entremont (pno) Pro Arte ▲ CDD 469 [DDD]
Schubert, Franz:Qnt Pno, D.667, w. P. Entremont (pno) Pro Arte ▲ CDD 470 [DDD]
Vienna Chamber PO
C. Traunfellner (cnd)
Mozart, W.A.:Diverts Str Qt, K.136–138 *(rec Casino Zögarnitz, Vienna, June 1990)* Camerata ▲ 32CM 119 [DDD]
Mozart, W.A.:Kleine Nachtmusik *(rec Casino Zögarnitz, Vienna, June 1990)* Camerata ▲ 32CM 119 [DDD]
Mozart, W.A.:Serenata notturna *(rec Casino Zögarnitz, Vienna, June 1990)* Camerata ▲ 32CM 119 [DDD]
Vienna Classical Schrammel Quartet
Wien bleibt Wien Tudor ▲ 722 [ADD]
Vienna Concentus Musicus
Bach, J.S.:Cant 48, w. P. Esswood (ct), K. Equiluz (ten), Vienna Concentus Musicus Chorus [G] Teldec 2-▲ 2292-42560-2 ZL [AAD]
A. Deller (cnd)
Purcell, H.:The Prophetess, or The History of Dioclesian, w. H. Sheppard (sop), S. Le Sage (sop), A. Deller (ct), M. Worthley (ten), P. Todd (ten), M. Bevan (bar)—also includes incidental music from the play *(rec June 1965)* Vanguard Classics ("The Bach Guild" series) ▲ OVC 2517 [ADD]
Purcell, H.:The Prophetess (sels), w. Deller Consort—instrumental music Vanguard Classics ("The Bach Guild" series) ▲ OVC 2517 [ADD]
N. Harnoncourt (cnd)
Bach, J.S.:Brandenburg Cons—Nos. 1, 2, 4 Teldec ▲ 9031-75858-2 ■ 9031-75858-4
Bach, J.S.:Brandenburg Cons—Nos. 3, 5, 6 Teldec ▲ 9031-75859-2 ■ 9031-75859-4
Bach, J.S.:Brandenburg Cons Teldec 2-▲ 9031-77611-2
Bach, J.S.:Brandenburg Cons Teldec 2-▲ 95980-2
Bach, J.S.:Cant 1, w. P. Esswood (ct), K. Equiluz (ten), M. van Egmond (b-bar), Vienna Boys' Choir [G] Teldec 2-▲ 2292-42497-2 [AAD]
Bach, J.S.:Cant 2, w. P. Esswood (ct), K. Equiluz (ten), M. van Egmond (b-bar), Vienna Boys' Choir [G] Teldec 2-▲ 2292-42497-2 [AAD]
Bach, J.S.:Cant 3, w. P. Esswood (ct), K. Equiluz (ten), M. van Egmond (b-bar), Vienna Boys' Choir [G] Teldec 2-▲ 2292-42497-2 [AAD]
Bach, J.S.:Cant 4, w. P. Esswood (ct), K. Equiluz (ten), M. van Egmond (b-bar), Vienna Boys' Choir [G] Teldec 2-▲ 2292-42497-2 [AAD]
Bach, J.S.:Cant 5, w. P. Esswood (ct), K. Equiluz (ten), M. van Egmond (b-bar), Vienna Boys' Choir Teldec 2-▲ 2292-42498-2 [AAD]
Bach, J.S.:Cant 6, w. P. Esswood (ct), K. Equiluz (ten), M. van Egmond (b-bar), Vienna Boys' Choir Teldec 2-▲ 2292-42498-2 [AAD]
Bach, J.S.:Cant 11, "Ascension Oratorio", w. P. Esswood (ct), K. Equiluz (ten), M. van Egmond (b-bar), Vienna Concentus Musicus Chorus [G] Teldec 2-▲ 2292-42499-2 [AAD]
Bach, J.S.:Cant 17, w. P. Esswood (ct), K. Equiluz (ten), M. van Egmond (b-bar), Chorus Viennensis [G] Teldec 2-▲ 2292-42501-2 [AAD]
Bach, J.S.:Cant 18, w. P. Esswood (ct), K. Equiluz (ten), M. van Egmond (b-bar), Chorus Viennensis [G] Teldec 2-▲ 2292-42501-2 [AAD]
Bach, J.S.:Cant 19, w. P. Esswood (ct), K. Equiluz (ten), M. van Egmond (b-bar), Chorus Viennensis [G] Teldec 2-▲ 2292-42501-2 [AAD]
Bach, J.S.:Cant 20, w. P. Esswood (ct), K. Equiluz (ten), M. van Egmond (b-bar), Chorus Viennensis [G] Teldec 2-▲ 2292-42501-2 [AAD]
Bach, J.S.:Cant 21, w. P. Esswood (ct), K. Equiluz (ten), W. Wyatt (bass), Chorus Viennensis, Vienna Boys' Choir [G] Teldec 2-▲ 2292-42502-2 [AAD]
Bach, J.S.:Cant 24, w. P. Esswood (ct), K. Equiluz (ten), M. van Egmond (b-bar), Chorus Viennensis [G] Teldec 2-▲ 2292-42503-2 [AAD]
Bach, J.S.:Cant 25, w. K. Equiluz (ten), M. van Egmond (b-bar), Chorus Viennensis [G] Teldec 2-▲ 2292-42503-2 [AAD]
Bach, J.S.:Cant 26, w. P. Esswood (ct), K. Equiluz (ten), S. Nimsgern (b-bar), Chorus Viennensis [G] Teldec 2-▲ 2292-42503-2 [AAD]
Bach, J.S.:Cant 27, w. P. Esswood (ct), K. Equiluz (ten), S. Nimsgern (b-bar), Chorus Viennensis [G] Teldec 2-▲ 2292-42503-2 [AAD]
Bach, J.S.:Cant 28, w. P. Esswood (ct), K. Equiluz (ten), S. Nimsgern (b-bar), Chorus Viennensis [G] Teldec 2-▲ 2292-42504-2 [AAD]
Bach, J.S.:Cant 29, w. P. Esswood (ct), K. Equiluz (ten), M. van Egmond (b-bar), Chorus Viennensis [G] Teldec 2-▲ 2292-42504-2 [AAD]
Bach, J.S.:Cant 30, w. P. Esswood (ct), K. Equiluz (ten), M. van Egmond (b-bar), Chorus Viennensis [G] Teldec 2-▲ 2292-42504-2 [AAD]
Bach, J.S.:Cant 31, w. K. Equiluz (ten), S. Nimsgern (b-bar), Chorus Viennensis [G] Teldec 2-▲ 2292-42505-2 [AAD]
Bach, J.S.:Cant 34, w. P. Esswood (ct), K. Equiluz (ten), S. Nimsgern (b-bar) [G] Teldec 2-▲ 2292-42505-2 [AAD]
Bach, J.S.:Cant 35, w. P. Esswood (ct), Chorus Viennensis [G] Teldec 2-▲ 2292-42506-2 [AAD]
Bach, J.S.:Cant 36, w. P. Esswood (ct), K. Equiluz (ten), R. van der Meer (bass), Chorus Viennensis Teldec 2-▲ 2292-42506-2 [AAD]
Bach, J.S.:Cant 37, w. P. Esswood (ct), K. Equiluz (ten), R. van der Meer (bass), Chorus Viennensis [G] Teldec 2-▲ 2292-42506-2 [AAD]
Bach, J.S.:Cant 38, w. P. Esswood (ct), K. Equiluz (ten), R. van der Meer (bass), Chorus Viennensis [G] Teldec 2-▲ 2292-42506-2 [AAD]
Bach, J.S.:Cant 41, w. P. Esswood (ct), K. Equiluz (ten), R. van der Meer (bass), Vienna Concentus Musicus Chorus [G] Teldec 2-▲ 2292-42556-2 [AAD]
Bach, J.S.:Cant 42, w. P. Esswood (ct), K. Equiluz (ten), R. van der Meer (bass), Vienna Concentus Musicus Chorus [G] Teldec 2-▲ 2292-42556-2 [AAD]
Bach, J.S.:Cant 43, w. P. Esswood (ct), K. Equiluz (ten), R. van der Meer (bass), Vienna Concentus Musicus Chorus [G] Teldec 2-▲ 2292-42559-2 [AAD]
Bach, J.S.:Cant 44, w. P. Esswood (ct), K. Equiluz (ten), R. van der Meer (bass), Vienna Concentus Musicus Chorus [G] Teldec 2-▲ 2292-42559-2 [AAD]
Bach, J.S.:Cant 47, w. R. van der Meer (bass), Chorus Viennensis, Vienna Boys' Choir [G] Teldec 2-▲ 2292-42560-2 [AAD]

Vienna Concentus Musicus (cont.)
N. Harnoncourt (cnd) (cont.)
Bach, J.S.:Cant 49, w. R. van der Meer (bass), Chorus Viennensis, Vienna Boys' Choir [G] Teldec 2-▲ 2292-42560-2 [AAD]
Bach, J.S.:Cant 50, w. Chorus Viennensis, Vienna Boys' Choir [G] Teldec 2-▲ 2292-42560-2 [AAD]
Bach, J.S.:Cant 57, w. Vienna Boys' Choir [G] Teldec 2-▲ 2292-42423-2 [AAD]
Bach, J.S.:Cant 58, w. Vienna Boys' Choir [G] Teldec 2-▲ 2292-42423-2 [AAD]
Bach, J.S.:Cant 59, w. Vienna Boys' Choir [G] Teldec 2-▲ 2292-42423-2 [AAD]
Bach, J.S.:Cant 60, w. Vienna Boys' Choir Teldec 2-▲ 2292-42423-2 [AAD]
Bach, J.S.:Cant 61, w. S. Kronwitter (trb), K. Equiluz (ten), R. van der Meer (bass), Vienna Boys' Choir [G] Teldec 2-▲ 2292-42565-2 [AAD]
Bach, J.S.:Cant 62, w. P. Esswood (ct), P. Jelosits (ten), K. Equiluz (ten), R. van der Meer (bass), Vienna Concentus Musicus Chorus [G] Teldec 2-▲ 2292-42565-2 [AAD]
Bach, J.S.:Cant 63, w. P. Esswood (ct), P. Jelosits (ten), K. Equiluz (ten), R. van der Meer (bass), Vienna Concentus Musicus Chorus [G] Teldec 2-▲ 2292-42565-2 [AAD]
Bach, J.S.:Cant 64, w. P. Esswood (ct), P. Jelosits (ten), R. van der Meer (bass), Vienna Boys' Choir [G] Teldec 2-▲ 2292-42565-2 [AAD]
Bach, J.S.:Cant 65, w. Tölz Boys' Choir [G] Teldec 2-▲ 2292-42571-2 [AAD]
Bach, J.S.:Cant 68, w. Tölz Boys' Choir [G] Teldec 2-▲ 2292-42571-2 [AAD]
Bach, J.S.:Cant 69, w. W. Wiedl (trb), P. Esswood (ct), K. Equiluz (ten), R. van der Meer (bass), Concentus Musicus [G] Teldec 2-▲ 2292-42572-2 [ADD]
Bach, J.S.:Cant 70, w. W. Wiedl (trb), P. Esswood (ct), K. Equiluz (ten), L. Visser (bass), Tölz Boys' Choir [G] Teldec 2-▲ 2292-42572-2 [ADD]
Bach, J.S.:Cant 71, w. W. Wiedl (trb), P. Esswood (ct), K. Equiluz (ten), R. van der Meer (bass), Vienna Concentus Musicus Chorus [G] Teldec 2-▲ 2292-42572-2 [ADD]
Bach, J.S.:Cant 72, w. W. Wiedl (trb), P. Esswood (ct), R. van der Meer (bass), Tölz Boys' Choir [G] Teldec 2-▲ 2292-42572-2 [ADD]
Bach, J.S.:Cant 76, w. P. Esswood (ct), K. Equiluz (ten), R. van der Meer (bass), Vienna Concentus Musicus Chorus [G] Teldec 2-▲ 2292-42576-2 [ADD]
Bach, J.S.:Cant 78, w. P. Esswood (ct), K. Equiluz (ten), R. van der Meer (bass), Vienna Concentus Musicus Chorus [G] Teldec 2-▲ 2292-42576-2 [ADD]
Bach, J.S.:Cant 80, w. W. Wiedl (trb), P. Esswood (ct), K. Equiluz (ten), R. van der Meer (bass) [G] Teldec 2-▲ 2292-42577-2 [ADD]
Bach, J.S.:Cant 81, w. P. Esswood (ct), K. Equiluz (ten), R. van der Meer (bass) [G] Teldec 2-▲ 2292-42577-2 [ADD]
Bach, J.S.:Cant 82, w. P. Huttenlocher (bar) [G] Teldec 2-▲ 2292-42577-2 [ADD]
Bach, J.S.:Cant 83, w. K. Equiluz (ten), M. van Egmond (b-bar) [G] Teldec 2-▲ 2292-42577-2 [ADD]
Bach, J.S.:Cant 84, w. W. Wiedl (trb), Tölz Boys' Choir [G] Teldec 2-▲ 2292-42578-2 [ADD]
Bach, J.S.:Cant 85, w. W. Wiedl (trb), P. Esswood (ct), K. Equiluz (ten), Vienna Concentus Musicus Chorus [G] Teldec 2-▲ 2292-42578-2 [ADD]
Bach, J.S.:Cant 86, w. W. Wiedl (trb), P. Esswood (ct), K. Equiluz (ten), Vienna Concentus Musicus Chorus [G] Teldec 2-▲ 2292-42578-2 [ADD]
Bach, J.S.:Cant 87, w. P. Esswood (ct), K. Equiluz (ten), Vienna Concentus Musicus Chorus [G] Teldec 2-▲ 2292-42578-2 [ADD]
Bach, J.S.:Cant 91, w. Leonhardt Consort, G. Leonhardt (cnd) [G] Teldec 2-▲ 2292-42582-2 [ADD]
Bach, J.S.:Cant 92, w. Leonhardt Consort, G. Leonhardt (cnd) [G] Teldec 2-▲ 2292-42582-2 [ADD]
Bach, J.S.:Cant 93, w. Leonhardt Consort, G. Leonhardt (cnd) [G] Teldec 2-▲ 2292-42582-2 [ADD]
Bach, J.S.:Cant 94, w. Leonhardt Consort, G. Leonhardt (cnd) [G] Teldec 2-▲ 2292-42582-2 [ADD]
Bach, J.S.:Cant 95, w. W. Wiedl (trb), K. Equiluz (ten), P. Huttenlocher (bar) [G] Teldec ▲ 2292-42583-2 [ADD]
Bach, J.S.:Cant 96, w. W. Wiedl (trb), P. Esswood (ct), K. Equiluz (ten), P. Huttenlocher (bar) [G] Teldec ▲ 2292-42583-2 [ADD]
Bach, J.S.:Cant 97, w. W. Wiedl (trb), P. Esswood (ct), K. Equiluz (ten), P. Huttenlocher (bar) [G] Teldec ▲ 2292-42583-2 [ADD]
Bach, J.S.:Cant 99, w. W. Wiedl (trb), P. Esswood (ct), K. Equiluz (ten), P. Huttenlocher (bar) [G] Teldec ▲ 2292-42584-2
Bach, J.S.:Cant 101, w. W. Wiedl (trb), P. Esswood (ct), K. Equiluz (ten), P. Huttenlocher (bar) [G] Teldec ▲ 2292-42584-2
Bach, J.S.:Cant 102, w. W. Wiedl (trb), P. Esswood (ct), K. Equiluz (ten), P. Huttenlocher (bar) [G] Teldec ▲ 2292-42584-2
Bach, J.S.:Cant 104, w. K. Equiluz (ten), P. Huttenlocher (bar), Tölz Boys' Choir [G] Teldec ▲ 2292-42602-2
Bach, J.S.:Cant 105, w. W. Wiedl (trb), P. Esswood (ct), K. Equiluz (ten), M. van Egmond (b-bar), Tölz Boys' Choir [G] Teldec ▲ 2292-42602-2
Bach, J.S.:Cant 108, w. P. Esswood (ct), K. Equiluz (ten), M. van Egmond (b-bar) [G] Teldec 2-▲ 2292-42603-2
Bach, J.S.:Cant 109, w. P. Esswood (ct), K. Equiluz (ten), Tölz Boys' Choir [G] Teldec 2-▲ 2292-42603-2
Bach, J.S.:Cant 110, w. W. Wiedl (trb), S. Frangoulis (trb), P. Esswood (ct), Stumpf (sgr), K. Equiluz (ten), M. van Egmond (b-bar), S. Lorenz (b-bar), Tölz Boys' Choir [G] Teldec 2-▲ 2292-42603-2
Bach, J.S.:Cant 111, w. P. Esswood (ct), K. Equiluz (ten), K. Huber (ten), M. van Egmond (b-bar) [G] Teldec 2-▲ 2292-42606-2
Bach, J.S.:Cant 112, w. P. Esswood (ct), K. Equiluz (ten), K. Huber (ten), M. van Egmond (b-bar) [G] Teldec 2-▲ 2292-42606-2
Bach, J.S.:Cant 115 [G] Teldec 2-▲ 2292-42608-2
Bach, J.S.:Cant 116 [G] Teldec 2-▲ 2292-42608-2
Bach, J.S.:Cant 117 [G] Teldec 2-▲ 2292-42608-2
Bach, J.S.:Cant 119 [G] Teldec 2-▲ 2292-42608-2
Bach, J.S.:Cant 120 [G] Teldec 2-▲ 2292-42609-2
Bach, J.S.:Cant 121 [G] Teldec 2-▲ 2292-42609-2
Bach, J.S.:Cant 122 [G] Teldec 2-▲ 2292-42609-2
Bach, J.S.:Cant 123 [G] Teldec 2-▲ 2292-42609-2
Bach, J.S.:Cant 124 [G] Teldec ▲ 2292-42615-2
Bach, J.S.:Cant 125 [G] Teldec ▲ 2292-42615-2
Bach, J.S.:Cant 126 [G] Teldec ▲ 2292-42615-2
Bach, J.S.:Cant 127 [G] Teldec ▲ 2292-42615-2
Bach, J.S.:Cant 128 Teldec 2-▲ 2292-42617-2
Bach, J.S.:Cant 129 Teldec 2-▲ 2292-42617-2
Bach, J.S.:Cant 130, w. Gächinger Kantorei Teldec 2-▲ 2292-42617-2
Bach, J.S.:Cant 131 Teldec 2-▲ 2292-42617-2
Bach, J.S.:Cant 132 [G] Teldec 2-▲ 2292-42618-2
Bach, J.S.:Cant 133 [G] Teldec 2-▲ 2292-42618-2
Bach, J.S.:Cant 134 [G] Teldec 2-▲ 2292-42618-2
Bach, J.S.:Cant 135 [G] Teldec 2-▲ 2292-42618-2
Bach, J.S.:Cant 136 [G] Teldec ▲ 2292-42619-2
Bach, J.S.:Cant 137 [G] Teldec ▲ 2292-42619-2
Bach, J.S.:Cant 138 [G] Teldec ▲ 2292-42619-2
Bach, J.S.:Cant 139 [G] Teldec ▲ 2292-42619-2
Bach, J.S.:Cant 140 [G] Teldec 2-▲ 2292-42630-2 [DDD]
Bach, J.S.:Cant 143 [G] Teldec 2-▲ 2292-42630-2 [DDD]
Bach, J.S.:Cant 144 [G] Teldec 2-▲ 2292-42630-2 [DDD]
Bach, J.S.:Cant 145 [G] Teldec 2-▲ 2292-42630-2 [DDD]
Bach, J.S.:Cant 146 [G] Teldec 2-▲ 2292-42630-2 [DDD]
Bach, J.S.:Cant 147 [G] Teldec 2-▲ 2292-42631-2 [DDD]
Bach, J.S.:Cant 148 [G] Teldec 2-▲ 2292-42631-2 [DDD]
Bach, J.S.:Cant 152, w. C. Wegmann (trb), T. Hampson (b-bar) [G] Teldec 2-▲ 2292-42632-2 [DDD]
Bach, J.S.:Cant 153, w. S. Rampf (ct), K. Equiluz (ten), T. Hampson (b-bar), Tölz Boys' Choir [G] Teldec 2-▲ 2292-42632-2 [DDD]
Bach, J.S.:Cant 154, w. P. Esswood (ct), K. Equiluz (ten), T. Hampson (b-bar), Tölz Boys' Choir [G] Teldec 2-▲ 2292-42632-2 [DDD]

▲ = CD ♦ = Enhanced CD Δ = MD ■ = Cassette Tape □ = DCC

Vienna Concentus Musicus (cont.)
N. Harnoncourt (cnd) (cont.)
Bach, J.S.:Cant 155, w. A. Bergius (trb), P. Esswood (ct), K. Equiluz (ten), T. Hampson (b-bar), Tölz Boys' Choir [G] Teldec 2-▲ 2292-42632-2 [DDD]
Bach, J.S.:Cant 156, w. P. Esswood (ct), K. Equiluz (ten), T. Hampson (b-bar), Tölz Boys' Choir [G] Teldec 2-▲ 2292-42632-2 [DDD]
Bach, J.S.:Cant 161 [G] Teldec 2-▲ 2292-42633-2 [DDD]
Bach, J.S.:Cant 162 [G] Teldec 2-▲ 2292-42633-2 [DDD]
Bach, J.S.:Cant 163 [G] Teldec 2-▲ 2292-42633-2 [DDD]
Bach, J.S.:Cant 164, Leonhardt Consort [G] Teldec 2-▲ 2292-42634-2 [DDD]
Bach, J.S.:Cant 165, Leonhardt Consort [G] Teldec 2-▲ 2292-42634-2 [DDD]
Bach, J.S.:Cant 166, Leonhardt Consort [G] Teldec 2-▲ 2292-42634-2 [DDD]
Bach, J.S.:Cant 167, Leonhardt Consort [G] Teldec 2-▲ 2292-42634-2 [DDD]
Bach, J.S.:Cant 168, Leonhardt Consort [G] Teldec 2-▲ 2292-42634-2 [DDD]
Bach, J.S.:Cant 169, Leonhardt Consort [G] Teldec 2-▲ 2292-42634-2 [DDD]
Bach, J.S.:Cant 170, Leonhardt Consort [G] Teldec 2-▲ 2292-42635-2 [DDD]
Bach, J.S.:Cant 171, Leonhardt Consort [G] Teldec 2-▲ 2292-42635-2 [DDD]
Bach, J.S.:Cant 172, Leonhardt Consort [G] Teldec 2-▲ 2292-42635-2 [DDD]
Bach, J.S.:Cant 173, Leonhardt Consort [G] Teldec 2-▲ 2292-42635-2 [DDD]
Bach, J.S.:Cant 174, Leonhardt Consort [G] Teldec 2-▲ 2292-42635-2 [DDD]
Bach, J.S.:Cant 175, Leonhardt Consort [G] Teldec 2-▲ 2292-42428-2 [DDD]
Bach, J.S.:Cant 176, Leonhardt Consort [G] Teldec 2-▲ 2292-42428-2 [DDD]
Bach, J.S.:Cant 177, Leonhardt Consort [G] Teldec 2-▲ 2292-42428-2 [DDD]
Bach, J.S.:Cant 178, Leonhardt Consort [G] Teldec 2-▲ 2292-42428-2 [DDD]
Bach, J.S.:Cant 179, Leonhardt Consort [G] Teldec 2-▲ 2292-42428-2 [DDD]
Bach, J.S.:Cant 180, Leonhardt Consort [G] Teldec 2-▲ 2292-42738-2 [DDD]
Bach, J.S.:Cant 181, Leonhardt Consort [G] Teldec 2-▲ 2292-42738-2 [DDD]
Bach, J.S.:Cant 182, Leonhardt Consort [G] Teldec 2-▲ 2292-42738-2 [DDD]
Bach, J.S.:Cant 183, Leonhardt Consort [G] Teldec 2-▲ 2292-42738-2 [DDD]
Bach, J.S.:Cant 184, Leonhardt Consort [G] Teldec 2-▲ 2292-42738-2 [DDD]
Bach, J.S.:Cant 185, w. H. Wittek (trb), P. Esswood (ct), K. Equiluz (ten), T. Hampson (b-bar), Tölz Boys' Choir [G] Teldec 2-▲ 2292-44179-2 [DDD]
Bach, J.S.:Cant 186, w. R. Holl (bass), Tölz Boys' Choir [G] Teldec 2-▲ 2292-44179-2 [DDD]
Bach, J.S.:Cant 188, w. R. Holl (bass), Tölz Boys' Choir [G] Teldec 2-▲ 2292-44179-2 [DDD]
Bach, J.S.:Cant 192, Leonhardt Consort [G] Teldec ▲ 2292-44193-2
Bach, J.S.:Cant 194, Leonhardt Consort [G] Teldec ▲ 2292-44193-2
Bach, J.S.:Cant 195, Leonhardt Consort [G] Teldec ▲ 2292-44193-2
Bach, J.S.:Cant 196, Leonhardt Consort [G] Teldec 2-▲ 2292-44194-2
Bach, J.S.:Cant 197, Leonhardt Consort [G] Teldec 2-▲ 2292-44194-2
Bach, J.S.:Cant 198, Leonhardt Consort [G] Teldec 2-▲ 2292-44194-2
Bach, J.S.:Cant 199, Leonhardt Consort [G] Teldec 2-▲ 2292-44194-2
Bach, J.S.:Cant 208, "Hunting Cant", w. A. M. Blasi (sop), J. P. Kenny (alt), K. Equiluz (ten), R. Holl (bass), Arnold Schoenberg Choir [G] Teldec ▲ 2292-46151-2 [DDD]
Bach, J.S.:Cant 212, "Peasant Cant", w. A. M. Blasi (sop), R. Holl (bass), Arnold Schoenberg Choir [G] Teldec ▲ 2292-46151-2 [DDD]
Bach, J.S.:Christmas Oratorio, w. P. Esswood (ct), K. Equiluz (ten), S. Nimsgern (b-bar), Vienna Boys' Choir [G] Teldec ▲ 9031-74893-2
Bach, J.S.:Christmas Oratorio, w. P. Esswood (ct), K. Equiluz (ten), S. Nimsgern (b-bar) Teldec 2-▲ 9031-77610-2
Bach, J.S.:Magnificat, BWV 243, w. F. Palmer (sop), M. Lipovšek (mez), P. Langridge (ten), Arnold Schoenberg Choir [L] Teldec ▲ 2292-42984-2
Bach, J.S.:Mass in b, BWV 232, w. A. M. Blasi (sop), D. Ziegler (mez), J. Rappé (cta), K. Equiluz (ten), R. Holl (bass), Arnold Schoenberg Choir [L] Teldec 2-▲ 2292-42676-2 [DDD]
Bach, J.S.:Motets, BWV 225-30, w. Stockholm Bach Choir [G] Teldec ▲ 2292-42881-2
Bach, J.S.:Music of, Leonhardt Consort—arias and choruses from various cants. Teldec ▲ 93705-2
Bach, J.S.:St. John Passion, w. K. Equiluz (ten), M. Van Egmond (b-bar), J. Villisech (bass), Vienna Boys' Choir soloists Teldec ▲ 2292-42492-2
Bach, J.S.:St. Matthew Passion, w. J. Bowman (ct), P. Esswood (ct), T. Sutcliffe (ct), K. Equiluz (ten), M. van Egmond (b-bar) [G] Teldec 3-▲ 2292-42509-2 [AAD]
Bach, J.S.:Suites Orch, BWV 1066-1069 Teldec ▲ 92174-2
Fux, J.J.:Rondeau à 7 Teldec ("Das Alte Werk" series) 2-▲ 95989-2 [ADD]
Fux, J.J.:Serenada à 8 Teldec ("Das Alte Werk" series) 2-▲ 95989-2 [ADD]
Fux, J.J.:Son à Quattro Teldec ("Das Alte Werk" series) 2-▲ 95989-2 [ADD]
Handel, G.F.:Apollo e Dafne, w. R. Alexander (sop), T. Hampson (bass) Teldec ("Das alte Werk" series) ▲ 98645-2
Handel, G.F.:Choruses, w. Stockholm Bach Choir, Stockholm Chamber Choir, Arnold Schoenberg Choir Teldec ▲ 95498-2
Handel, G.F.:Concerti grossi, Op. 3 Teldec 4-▲ 95500-2
Handel, G.F.:Concerti grossi, Op. 6 Teldec 4-▲ 95500-2
Handel, G.F.:Cons (16) Org, w. H. Tachezi (org) Teldec ▲ 4509-91188-2
Handel, G.F.:Giulio Cesare in Egitto (sels), w. Roberta Alexander (sop), Thomas Hampson (bass) Teldec ("Das alte Werk" series) ▲ 98645-2
Handel, G.F.:Messiah, w. Elizabeth Gale (sop), Marjana Lipovšek (mez), Werner Hollweg (ten), Roderick Kennedy (bass) Teldec 2-▲ 9031-77615-2
Handel, G.F.:Messiah (sels), w. Elizabeth Gale (sop), Marjana Lipovsek (mez), Werner Hollweg (ten), Roderick Kennedy (bass), Stockholm Chamber Choir [E] Teldec ▲ 2292-42409-2
Handel, G.F.:Samson, w. Roberta Alexander (sop), Maria Venuti (sop), Jochen Kowalski (ct), Anthony Rolfe Johnson (ten), Aalstair Miles (bass), Anton Scharinger (bass), Arnold Schoenberg Choir Teldec ▲ 74871-2
Handel, G.F.:Theodora, w. Roberta Alexander (sop), Jard van Nes (cta), Jochen Kowalski (ct), Hans-Peter Blochwitz (ten), Anton Scharinger (bass), Arnold Schoenberg Choir [E] Teldec 2-▲ 2292-46447-2 [DDD]
Handel, G.F.:Utrecht Te Deum & Jubilate, w. Felicity Palmer (sop), Marjana Lipovšek (mez), Philip Langridge (ten), Arnold Schoenberg Choir [L] Teldec ▲ 2292-42984-2
Haydn, J.:Con Org & Strs, H.XVIII/2, w. Herbert Tachezi (pno) Teldec ▲ 2292-44196-2
Haydn, J.:Il Mondo della Luna (ov), w. Herbert Tachezi (pno) Teldec ▲ 2292-44196-2
Haydn, J.:The Seven Last Words of Christ on the Cross, w. Inge Nielsen (sop), Margaretha Hintermeier (cta), Anthony Rolfe Johnson (ten), Robert Holl (bass), Arnold Schoenberg Choir [oratorio version] Teldec ▲ 2292-46458-2 ZK
Haydn, J.:Sinf concertante Teldec ▲ 2292-44196-2
Haydn, J.:Sym 30, "Alleluja" Teldec ▲ 9031-76460-2
Haydn, J.:Sym 31, "Hornsignal" *(rec Vienna, Oct-Nov. 1993)* Teldec ▲ 90843-2 [DDD]
Haydn, J.:Sym 53, "L'Impériale" Teldec ▲ 9031-76460-2
Haydn, J.:Sym 59, "Fire" *(rec Vienna, Oct-Nov. 1993)* Teldec ▲ 90843-2 [DDD]
Haydn, J.:Sym 69, "Laudon" Teldec ▲ 9031-76460-2
Haydn, J.:Sym 73, "La Chasse" *(rec Vienna, Dec. 1992)* Teldec ▲ 90843-2 [DDD]
Leclair, J.-M.:Cons Vn, Opp. 7 & 10, w. J. Schröder (vn)—Op. 7/3 & 5; Op. 10/6 Teldec ▲ 92180
Monteverdi, C.:Combattimento, w. Joseph Schmidt (ten), Kurt Equiluz (ten), Werner Hollweg (ten) [I] Teldec ▲ 2292-43036-2
Monteverdi, C.:Combattimento Teldec ▲ 92181-2
Monteverdi, C.:Incoronazione, w. H. Donath (sop), E. Söderström (sop), C. Berberian (sop), P. Esswood (ct) [I] Teldec 4-▲ 2292-42547-2
Monteverdi, C.:Lamento della ninfa, w. Schmidt (ten), K. Equiluz (ten), W. Hollweg (ten) [I] Teldec ▲ 2292-43036-2
Monteverdi, C.:Lamento della ninfa Teldec ▲ 92181-2
Monteverdi, C.:Madrigals, (2) [I] Teldec ▲ 2292-43036-2
Monteverdi, C.:Ogni amante è guerrier Teldec ▲ 92181-2
Monteverdi, C.:Orfeo, w. R. Hansmann (sop), C. Berberian (sop), L. Kozma (ten), K. Equiluz (bar), M. Van Egmond (bass), Capella Antiqua München Teldec 2-▲ 42494-2

Vienna Concentus Musicus (cont.)
N. Harnoncourt (cnd) (cont.)
Monteverdi, C.:Ritorno d'Ulisse, w. P. Esswood (ct), K. Equiluz (ten), M. Dickie (ten), N. Rogers (ten), M. Van Egmond (bass) Teldec ▲ 42496-2
Monteverdi, C.:Vespro della Beata Vergine, w. M. Marshall (sop), F. Palmer (sop), P. Langridge (ten), K. Equiluz (ten), T. Hampson (bar), A. Korn (bass), Hamburg Monteverdi Chorus, Vienna Boys' Chorus Teldec 2-▲ 92629-2
Monteverdi, C.:Vespro della Beata Vergine, w. L. Marshall (sop), F. Palmer (sop), P. Langridge (ten), K. Equiluz (ten), T. Hampson (bar), A. Korn (bass), Hamburg Monteverdi Chorus, Vienna Boys' Chorus [L] Teldec 2-▲ 2292-42671-2
Mozart, W.A.:Ave verum corpus, w. Barbara Bonney (sop), Charlotte Margiono (sop), Sylvia McNair (sop), Elisabeth von Magnus (cta), Christoph Pregardien (ten), Thomas Hampson (bass), Arnold Schoenberg Choir Teldec ▲ 98928 2
Mozart, W.A.:Benedictus, w. Barbara Bonney (sop), Arnold Schoenberg Choir *(rec Casino Zögernitz, Vienna, Dec. 1990)* Teldec ("Das alte Werke" series) ▲ 96147-2 [DDD]
Mozart, W.A.:Cons Hn, w. Hermann Baumann (hn) Teldec ▲ 2292-42757-2
Mozart, W.A.:Divert Ob, K.251 [period instrs] Teldec ▲ 2292-44809-2 [DDD]
Mozart, W.A.:Dixit Dominus et Magnificat, w. E. Mei (sop), E. von Magnus (cta), K. Azesberger (ten), G. Cachemaille (bass), Arnold Schoenberg Choir Teldec ("Das alte Werke" series) ▲ 93025
Mozart, W.A.:Exsultate, w. B. Bonney (sop) [L] Teldec ▲ 2292-44180-2 [DDD]
Mozart, W.A.:Finta giardiniera, w. E. Gruberova (sop), C. Margiono (sop), M. Bacelli (sop), D. Upshaw (sop), U. Heilmann (ten), A. Scharinger (bass) Teldec 3-▲ 72309-2
Mozart, W.A.:Grabmusik, w. Barbara Bonney (sop), Charlotte Margiono (sop), Sylvia McNair (sop), Elisabeth von Magnus (cta), Christoph Pregardien (ten), Thomas Hampson (bass), Arnold Schoenberg Choir Teldec ("Das alte Werk" series) ▲ 98928-2
Mozart, W.A.:Kleine Nachtmusik Teldec ▲ 2292-44809-2 [DDD]
Mozart, W.A.:Kyrie, K.341, w. Arnold Schoenberg Choir Teldec ("Das alte Werke" series) ▲ 93025
Mozart, W.A.:Litaniae de venerabili, w. E. von Magnus (alt), A. Miles (bass), Arnold Schoenberg Choir Teldec ▲ 72304-2
Mozart, W.A.:Litaniae Lauretanae, K.109, w. Eva Mei (sop), Elisabeth von Magnus (alt), Kurt Azesberger (ten), Gilles Cachemaille (bass), Arnold Schoenberg Choir *(rec Casino Zögernitz, Vienna, Dec. 1992)* Teldec ("Das alte Werke" series) ▲ 96147-2 [DDD]
Mozart, W.A.:Litaniae Lauretanae, K.195, w. B. Bonney (sop), E. von Magnus (cta), U. Heilmann (tenor), G. Cachemaille (bass), Arnold Schoenberg Choir Teldec ("Das alte Werke" series) ▲ 93025
Mozart, W.A.:March Orch, K.215 Teldec ▲ 9031-72289-2
Mozart, W.A.:Missa, K.257, w. E. von Magnus (alt), A. Miles (bass), Arnold Schoenberg Choir Teldec ▲ 72304-2
Mozart, W.A.:Missa, K.317, w. J. Rodgers (sop), E. von Magnus (alt), J. Protschka (ten), L. Polgár (bass), Arnold Schoenberg Choir [L] Teldec ▲ 2292-43354-2
Mozart, W.A.:Missa, K.427, w. K. Láki (sop), Z. Dénes (sop), K. Equiluz (ten), R. Holl (bass), Vienna State Opera Chorus [L] Teldec ▲ 2292-43070-2
Mozart, W.A.:Missa solemnis, K.139, w. B. Bonney (sop), J. Rappé (ten), J. Protschka (ten), H. Hagegard (bar), Arnold Schoenberg Choir [L] Teldec ▲ 2292-44180-2 [DDD]
Mozart, W.A.:Missa brevis, K.275, w. E. Mei (sop), E. von Magnus (cta), K. Azesberger (ten), G. Cachemaille (bass), Arnold Schoenberg Choir Teldec ("Das alte Werke" series) ▲ 93025
Mozart, W.A.:Musikalischer Spass Teldec ▲ 2292-44809-2 [DDD]
Mozart, W.A.:Regina coeli, K.108, w. Charlotte Margiono (sop), Arnold Schoenberg Choir *(rec Casino Zögernitz, Vienna, Dec. 1991)* Teldec ("Das alte Werke" series) ▲ 96147-2 [DDD]
Mozart, W.A.:Regina coeli, K.127, w. Barbara Bonney (sop), Charlotte Margiono (sop), Sylvia McNair (sop), Elisabeth von Magnus (cta), Christoph Pregardien (ten), Thomas Hampson (bass), Arnold Schoenberg Choir Teldec ("Das alte Werk" series) ▲ 98928 2
Mozart, W.A.:Requiem, w. Rachel Yakar (sop), Ortrun Wenkel (cta), Kurt Equiluz (ten), Robert Holl (bass), Vienna State Opera Chorus [L] Teldec ▲ 2292-42911-2
Mozart, W.A.:Sacred Music, w. Arnold Schoenberg Choir—Venite populi, K.260 [rec Dec. 1991]; Inter natos mulierum, K.72 [rec Feb. 1992]; Ergo interest, an quie—Quaere superna, K.143 [rec Dec. 1990; w. Barbara Bonney (soprano)]; Te Deum laudamus, K.141 [rec Dec. 1990]; Alma Dei creatoris, K.277 [rec Dec. 1991; w. Charlotte Margiono (soprano), Elisabeth von Magnus (alto), Christoph Prégardien (tenor)]; Tantum ergo, K.197 [rec Dec. 1990]; Sub tuum praesidium, K.198 [rec Dec. 1990; w. Barbara Bonney (soprano), Elisabeth von Magnus (alto), Uwe Heilmann (tenor)]; Sancta Maria, mater Dei, K.273 [rec Feb. 1992] Teldec ("Das alte Werke" series) ▲ 96147-2 [DDD]
Mozart, W.A.:Sacred Music—K.125, 276 & 337 [L] Teldec ▲ 46339-2
Mozart, W.A.:Serenade Vn, K.204 Teldec ▲ 2292-72289-2
Mozart, W.A.:Sym 12 Teldec ▲ 74728-2
Mozart, W.A.:Sym 19 Teldec ▲ 74728-2
Mozart, W.A.:Sym 24 Teldec ▲ 74728-2
Mozart, W.A.:Sym 27 Teldec ▲ 9031-72289-2
Mozart, W.A.:Sym 39 Teldec 2-▲ 9031-74858-2
Mozart, W.A.:Sym 40 Teldec 2-▲ 9031-74858-2
Mozart, W.A.:Sym 41 Teldec 2-▲ 9031-74858-2
Mozart, W.A.:Vesperae solennes, w. J. Rodgers (sop), E. von Magnus (alt), J. Protschka (ten), L. Polgár (bass), Arnold Schoenberg Choir [L] Teldec ▲ 2292-43354-2
Music at the Court of Mannheim Teldec ▲ 44697-2
Purcell, H.:Dido & Aeneas, w. R. Yakar (sop), A. Murray (mez), A. Scharinger (bass), Arnold Schoenberg Choir Teldec ("Das alte Werke" series) ▲ 93686
Purcell, H.:Dido & Aeneas, w. R. Yakar (sop), A. Murray (mez), A. Scharinger (bass) [E] Teldec ▲ 2292-42959-2
Purcell, H.:Fants Vls, Z.732-734 *(rec Vienna, 1965)* Vanguard Classics ▲ OVC 8091 [ADD]
Purcell, H.:Fant Vls, Z.745 *(rec Vienna, 1965)* Vanguard Classics ▲ OVC 8091 [ADD]
Purcell, H.:In Nomine, Z.746 *(rec Vienna, 1965)* Vanguard Classics ▲ OVC 8091 [ADD]
Purcell, H.:In Nomine, Z.747 *(rec Vienna, 1965)* Vanguard Classics ▲ OVC 8091 [ADD]
Rameau, J.P.:Castor et Pollux, w. M. Schéle (sop), J. Scovotti (sop), R. Leanderson (bar), G. Souzay (bar), J. Villisech (bass) Teldec ▲ 42510-2
Schmelzer, J.H.:Sons Instrs—Son Natalitia a 3 Chori; Son II a 8, due cori; Son 4 [La Carolietta]; Son I a 8; Son a 3; Son IV a 6; Son a 5; Son a 3; Son a 3 Vns *(rec Casino Zögernitz, Vienna, 1969)* Teldec ("Das Alte Werk" series) 2-▲ 95989-2 [ADD]
Telemann, G.P.:Der Tag des Gerichts, w. R. Alexander (sop), K. Equiliz (ten), M. Van Egmond (bass), Monteverdi Choir Hamburg Teldec 2-▲ 77621-2
Telemann, G.P.:Ino, w. R. Alexander (sop), K. Equiliz (ten), M. Van Egmond (bar), Monteverdi Choir London Teldec 2-▲ 9031-77621-2
Vivaldi, A.:Cons Vn, Op. 8/1-12, "Il cimento dell'armonia e dell'inventione", w. A. Harnoncourt (vn)—Nos. 1-6 Teldec ▲ 91851-2

Harononcourt, Leonhardt (cnd)
Bach, J.S.:Cants (misc), w. *(various soloists & guest choirs)*, Leonhardt Consort—[Vol. 1] Nos. 1-14, 16-19; [Vol. 2] Nos. 20-36; [Vol. 3] 37-52, 54-60; [Vol. 4] Nos. 61-78; [Vol. 5] Nos. 79-99; [Vol. 6] Nos. 100-117; [Vol. 7] Nos. 119-137; [Vol. 8] Nos. 138-140, 143-159, 161-162; [Vol. 9] Nos. 163-182; [Vol. 10] Nos. 183-188, 192, 194-199 Teldec ("Das Alte Werk" series) 60-▲ 91765-2

H. Rilling (cnd)
Bach, J.S.:Cant 19, w. Gächinger Kantorei [G] Hänssler Classic ▲ 98.869 [AAD]

Vienna Concert House Orch
F. Grossmann (cnd)
Mozart, W.A.:Requiem, w. Vienna Concert House Chorus [L] Vivace 3-▲ E 326 [ADD]

Vienna Concert House String Quartet
Haydn, J.:Qts Strs (comp)—Op. 1/6; Op. 2/3, 5 & 6; Op. 3/1; Op. 9/1, 3, 4 & 5; Op. 17/3; Op. 20/3 & 4; Op. 76/3; Op. 77/3 Preiser 4-▲ PRE 90901 [ADD]
Haydn, J.:Qts Strs (comp)—Op. 1/5; Op. 33/3; Op. 50/5; Op. 51/1-7; Op. 55/3; Op. 64/1, 3 & 4; Op. 74/1; Op. 76/4, 5 & 6 Preiser 4-▲ PRE 90909 [ADD]
Haydn, J.:Qts Strs (comp)—Op. 2/4; Op. 3/5 & 6; Op. 9/6; Op. 17/1, 2 & 5; Op. 20/1, 2, 5 & 6; Op. 5/1 & 3; Op. 64/2; Op. 74/3; Op. 76/1 Preiser 4-▲ PRE 90905 [ADD]
Schmidt, F.:Qt Strs in G Preiser ▲ 93063 [ADD]

Vienna Concert Society Orch
Haydn, J.:Notturni (8) — Orfeo 2-▲ 246922 [DDD]
M. Sieghart (cnd)
Schoenberg, A.:Chamber Sym 1 — Orfeo ▲ 215901 [DDD]
Schoenberg, A.:Suite Ww — Orfeo ▲ 215901 [DDD]
Schoenberg, A.:Trans Chamber Ensemble—"Kaiserwalzer," after Joh. Strauss II (1925) — Orfeo ▲ 215901 [DDD]
Vienna Concilium Musicum
P. Angerer (cnd)
Attwood, T.:Trio Pno — Christophorus ▲ 77136 [DDD]
Austrian Church Music — Koch Schwann ▲ SCH 312522 [DDD]
Christmas with Ramón Vargas, w. Ramón Vargas (ten), Lucerne Boy's Choir *(rec live, Jesuitenkirche in Lucerne, Dec 21, 1995)* — Claves ▲ CD 509612 [DDD]
Freystadtler, F.J.:Con facile — Christophorus ▲ 77136 [DDD]
Haydn, J.:Applausus:Jubilaeum virtutis Palatium, w. Florian Erdl (sgr), Gert Füssi (sgr), Christian Graf (sgr), Helmut Wildhaber (ten), Georg Tichy (bass) [period instrs] — Koch Schwann ▲ SCH 314092
Old Viennese Dances — Koch Schwann ▲ SCH 312352 [DDD]
Schroeter, J.S.:Cons Pno, Op. 3, w. Paul Angerer (pno)—Nos. 1, 3, 4 & 6 — Koch Schwann ▲ SCH 312422 [DDD]
Storace, S.:Sextet Fl — Christophorus ▲ 77136 [DDD]
Vienna Concilium Musicum members
Sssmayr, F.X.:Divert I — Christophorus ▲ 77136 [DDD]
Vienna Ensemble
Lanner, J.:Die Mozartisten — Sony Classical ▲ SK 47672
Lanner, J.:Music of—Vermählungswalzer, Op. 15; Elisens und Katinkens Vereinigung [galopp], Op. 56; Jubelwalzer, Op. 100; Die Werber [waltz], Op. 103; Abendsterne [waltz], Op. 180; Hans-Jörgel Polka, Op. 194 — Sony Classical ▲ SK 52485 [DDD]
Mozart, W.A.:Diverts Str Qt, K.136–138 — Sony Classical ▲ SK 47672
Mozart, W.A.:German Dances, K.600 — Sony Classical ▲ SK 47672
Mozart, W.A.:German Dances, K.605—Nos. 1 & 3 — Sony Classical ▲ MLK 62369 [ADD/DDD]
Poulenc, F.:Music of, w. J. Levine (pno)—Elegie; Sextet; 2 Sonatas; Trio — Deutsche Grammophon ▲ 427639-2 [DDD]
Schubert, Franz:Con Vn, w. P. Guggenberger (vn) — Sony Classical ▲ SK 48386 [DDD]
Schubert, Franz:German Dances Pno, D.790 [arr. for string ensemble] — Sony Classical ▲ SK 48386 [DDD]
Schubert, Franz:Ländler Pno [arr. for string ensemble]—8 Wiener Damen-Ländler (D.784, Nos. 1,2,7,8,10,12,15 & 16) — Sony Classical ▲ SK 48386 [DDD]
Schubert, Franz:Ov Str Qt, D.8a — Sony Classical ▲ SK 48386 [DDD]
Schubert, Franz:Rondo Vn, D.438, w. P. Guggenberger (vn) — Sony Classical ▲ SK 48386 [DDD]
Strauss (I), Joh.:Music of—Kettenbrücke Walzer, Op. 4; Tivoli-Rutsch-Walzer, Op. 39; Cachucha Galopp, Op. 97; Gitana-Galopp, Op. 108; Eisele- und Beisele- Sprunge [polka], Op. 202 — Sony Classical ▲ SK 52485 [DDD]
Strauss, Josef:Music of—Die guten, alten Zeiten [waltz], Op. 26 — Sony Classical ▲ SK 52485 [DDD]
A Vienna Souvenir — Sony Classical ▲ SK 47187
P. Guggenberger (cnd)
Schubert, Franz:Polonaise Vn — Sony Classical ▲ SK 48386 [DDD]
Vienna Festival CO
W. Boettcher (cnd)
Torelli, G.:Music of, w. Karl Scheit (gtr)—Con in A for Gtr, Vn & Orch — Special Music Co. ("Classics of the Heart" series) ▲ SCD 5198
Vienna Festival Orch
V. Desarzens (cnd)
Mendelssohn, F.:Con in e Vn & Orch, Op. 64, w. Peter Rybar (vn) — Doron ▲ DRC 4005
Tchaikovsky, P.:Con Vn, w. Peter Rybar (vn) — Doron ▲ DRC 4005
J. Krips (cnd)
Strauss (II), Joh.:Music of—Le Beau Danube Blue [waltz]; Tipferl Polka; Chauve-souris Ov; Valse de l'Empereur; Baron Tzigane [march]; Waldmeister Ov — Accord ▲ ACD 200362 [AAD]
W. van Otterloo (cnd)
Rimsky-Korsakov, N.:Scheherazade, w. Lorand Fenyves (vn) — FNAC Music ("Via Classics" series) ▲ 642330
F. Prohaska (cnd)
Mahler, G.:Des Knaben Wunderhorn, w. M. Forrester (cta), H. Rehfuss (b-bar) *(rec 5 & 6/63)* — Vanguard Classics ▲ OVC 4045 [ADD]
Vienna Festival SO
W. Hall (cnd)
Britten, B.:War Requiem, w. *(vocalists unknown)*, Ladd Thomas (org), William Hall Chorale — Klavier ■ KC 544
Vienna Flautists [B. Gisler-Haase (fl), A. Kirchner (fl), A. Bauerle (fl), E. May (fl), G. Ahumada (a fl), G. Kugi (a fl), W. Tomasi (b fl), F. Rahbari (db fl)]
Mozart, W.A.:Adagio & Allegro Mechanical Org — Orfeo ▲ 239911 [DDD]
Mozart, W.A.:Andante & Vars Pno 4-Hands [arr. performers for flute ensemble] — Orfeo ▲ 239911 [DDD]
Mozart, W.A.:Andante Mechanical Org, K.616 — Orfeo ▲ 239911 [DDD]
Mozart, W.A.:Divert Str Qt, K.137 [arr. Mozart for flute ensemble] — Orfeo ▲ 239911 [DDD]
Mozart, W.A.:Fant Mechanical Org [arr. performers for flute ensemble] — Orfeo ▲ 239911 [DDD]
Prinz, A.:Zauberflötiana — Orfeo ▲ 239911 [DDD]
Rossini, G.:Sons Str Qt [arr. for flute ensemble]—Nos. 1,2,3 & 6 — Orfeo ▲ 280921 [DDD]
Vivaldi, A.:Cons Fl (misc)—No. 1 in A, RV.159; No. 13 in e, RV.134; No. 34 in F, RV.551; No. 35 in f, RV.143; No. 37 in C, RV.117; No. 44 in C, RV.114; in D, RV.549 (Op. 3/1); in e, RV.550 (Op. 3/4); in G, RV.151 (Op. 51/4); Sinfonietta No. 7 in b, RV.169 *(rec Slovak Radio Concert Hall, Bratislava, June 2–3, 1994)* — Discover International ▲ DICD 920230 [DDD]
Vivaldi, A.:Cons Vn, Op. 8/1–4, "The Four Seasons" [arr. for flute ensemble] — Orfeo ▲ 311931 [DDD]
Vienna Haydn Sinfonietta
M. Huss (cnd)
Haydn, J.:Diverts (misc)—H.1; H.II/9; H.II/D22 — Koch Schwann ▲ SCH 312862 [DDD]
Haydn, J.:Divert for 2 Cls, Hns & Strs, H.II/17 — Koch Schwann ▲ SCH 314812
Haydn, J.:Divert Strs, H.II/2 — Koch Schwann ▲ SCH 314812
Haydn, J.:Minuet with vars — Koch Schwann ▲ SCH 314812
Haydn, J.:Ovs—Acis e Galatea; Le Speziale; Le Pescatrici; L'Infedeltà delusa; Philemon und Baucis; Der Götterrath; Il Ritorno di Tobia; Die Feuersbrunst; L'Incontro improvviso; Il Mondo della Luna — Koch Schwann ▲ SCH 317232
Haydn, J.:Scherzandos — Koch Schwann ▲ SCH 314432 [DDD]
Vienna Haydn Trio
Mendelssohn, F.:Trio 2 Pno — Arabesque ▲ ARA 6651 [DDD]
Smetana, B.:Trio Pno — Arabesque ▲ ARA 6651 [DDD]
Vienna Kohonaden Orch
H. Hagen (cnd)
The Romantic Violin, w. Zsigmondy, Denes (vn), Anneliese Nissen (pno) — Klavier ▲ KCD 11037 [ADD]
Vienna Lanner Ensemble [Wolfgang Breinschmid (fl), Gerhard Breyer (vn), Wolfgang Breyer (ctbn), Manfred Kuhn (vn), Gregory Rogers (va), Jörg Wachsenegger (cl)]
Lanner, J.:Music of—Die Werber, Op. 103; Malapou-Galoppe, Op. 148; Dornbacher Länler, Op. 9; Cerrito Polka, Op. 189; Hofballtänze, Op. 161; Ungarischer Galoppe, Op. 97/3; Ber Herbst; Aufforderung zum Tanze, Op. 7; Marien Waltz, Op. 143; Die Schönbrunner, Op. 200 *(rec Vienna, July 5–8, 1994)* — Camerata ▲ 30CM 396 [DDD]
Vienna Mozart Academy
J. Wildner (cnd)
Mozart, W.A.:Con Bn, w. S. Turnovsky (bn) — Naxos ▲ 8.550345 [DDD]
Mozart, W.A.:Con Cl, w. E. Ottensamer (cl) *(rec Oct. 1989)* — Naxos ▲ 8.550345 [DDD]
Vienna Mozart Academy (cont.)
J. Wildner (cnd) (cont.)
Mozart, W.A.:Con Fl, K.314, w. M. Gabriel (ob) *(rec Oct. 1989)* — Naxos ▲ 8.550345 [DDD]
Vienna Mozart Ensemble
W. Boskovsky (cnd)
Mozart, W.A.:Cassation, K.100/62a *(rec Sofiensaal, Vienna)* — London 2-▲ 443458-2 [ADD]
Mozart, W.A.:Kleine Nachtmusik *(rec Sofiensaal, Vienna)* — London 2-▲ 443458-2 [ADD]
Mozart, W.A.:Serenade Vn, K.250 *(rec Sofiensaal, Vienna)* — London 2-▲ 443458-2 [ADD]
Mozart, W.A.:Serenade Ww, K.320 — London ■ 411846-4
Mozart, W.A.:Serenade Ww, K.320 *(rec Sofiensaal, Vienna)* — London 2-▲ 443458-2 [ADD]
Mozart, W.A.:Serenata notturna *(rec Sofiensaal, Vienna)* — London 2-▲ 443458-2 [ADD]
H. Kraus (cnd)
Mozart, W.A.:Con Bn, w. K. Hellmann (bn) — LaserLight ▲ 15 875 [DDD]
Mozart, W.A.:Cons Fl, w. K. Berger (fl) — LaserLight ▲ 15 624 [DDD]
Mozart, W.A.:Con Fl Hp, w. H. Friedrich (fl), A. Berger (hp) — LaserLight ▲ 15 873 [DDD]
Mozart, W.A.:Con Hn, K.412, w. B. Heiser (hn) — LaserLight ▲ 15 624 [DDD]
Mozart, W.A.:Con Hn, K.447, w. B. Heiser (hn) — LaserLight ▲ 15 624 [DDD]
Mozart, W.A.:Con 9 Pno, w. D. Gerard (pno) — LaserLight ▲ 15 632 [DDD]
Mozart, W.A.:Con 17 Pno, w. V. Fischer (pno) — LaserLight ▲ 15 618 [DDD]
Mozart, W.A.:Con 21 Pno, w. V. Fischer (pno) — Laserlight ▲ 15 618 [DDD]
Mozart, W.A.:Con 23 Pno, w. D. Gerard (pno) — LaserLight ▲ 15 632 [DDD]
Mozart, W.A.:Con 23 Pno, w. D. Gerard (pno) — LaserLight ▲ 15 649 [DDD]
Mozart, W.A.:Eine kleine Nachtmusik — LaserLight ▲ 15 861 [DDD]
Mozart, W.A.:Eine kleine Nachtmusik in G for Strings & Continuo, K.525 (1787) — Laserlight ♦ 90018 [DDD]
Mozart, W.A.:Music of Mozart, w. Franz Liszt CO [cnd:Janos Rolla], Camerata Academica Salzburg [cnd:Sándor Vegh] — Laserlight ♦ 90024 [DDD]
Vienna Mozart Orch
K. Leitner (cnd)
Mozart, W.A.:Music of, w. D. Robin (sop), A. Martin (bar), G. Grünbacher (cl), K. Leitner (pno)—features selections from Le nozze di Figaro, K.492; Con. No. 23 in A for Piano & Orch., K.488; Sym. No. 40 in g, K.550; Die Zauberflöte, K.620; Posthorn Serenade, K.320; Con. in A for Clarinet & Orch., K.622; Sym. No. 35 in in D, K.385 "Haffner" *(rec Feb. 9–13, 1990)* — Naxos ▲ 8.550867 [DDD]
Mozart, W.A.:Music of, w. D. Robin (sop), A. Martin (bar), G. Grünbacher (cl), K. Leitner (pno)—features selections from Die Entführung aus dem Serail, K.384; Don Giovanni, K.527; Serenade No. 13, K.525, "Eine kleine Nachtmusik"; Con. No. 21 in C for Piano & Orch., K.467; Symphony No. 41 in C, K.551, "Jupiter"; Con. No. 5 in A for Violin & Orch., K.219; Die Zauberflöte, K.620; Alla turca [arr. for orch.] *(rec Feb. 9–13, 1990)* — Naxos ▲ 8.550866 [DDD]
D. Robin (cnd)
Mozart, W.A.:Arias, w. A. Martin (bar), Capella Istropolitana—arias & duets from Entführung aus dem Serail, Così fan tutte, Don Giovanni, Die Zauberflöte, Le nozze di Figaro [G,I] — Naxos ▲ 8.550435 [DDD]
Vienna Mozart Winds
N. Harnoncourt (cnd)
Mozart, W.A.:Serenade Ww, K.361 — Teldec ▲ 2292-43003-2
Mozart, W.A.:Serenade Ww, K.375 — Teldec ▲ 2292-43056-2
Mozart, W.A.:Serenade Ww, K.388 — Teldec ▲ 2292-43056-2
Vienna Musica Antiqua [Eduard Melkus (vl), Alice Hoffner (vl), Gustav Leonhardt (b-vl), Nicholas Harnoncourt (b-vl)]
R. Clemencic (cnd)
A Celebration of Christmas:Carols through the Ages, w. Deller Consort — Vanguard Classics 4-▲ OVC 8050/53 [ADD]
Vienna Musikgesellschaft Orch
M. Gielen (cnd)
Rachmaninoff, S.:Con 2 Pno, w. F. Blumental (pno) — Allegretto ▲ ACD 8020 [ADD] ■ ACS 8020
Tchaikovsky, P.:Con 1 Pno, w. F. Blumental (pno) — Allegretto ▲ ACD 8020 [ADD] ■ ACS 8020
E. van Remoortel (cnd)
Mendelssohn, F.:Sym 4—Allegro — Special Music Co. ▲ SCD 5200
Mendelssohn, F.:Sym 4 — Allegretto ▲ ACD 8017 [ADD] ■ ACS 8017
Tchaikovsky, P.:Capriccio italien — Allegretto ▲ ACD 8017 [ADD] ■ ACS 8017
Vienna Musikverein Orch
M. Turnovsky (cnd)
Beethoven, L. van:Con 4 Pno, w. I. Moravec (pno) *(rec Oct. 6–7, 1963)* — VAI Audio ▲ VAIA 1021 [ADD]
Vienna Musikverein String Quartet
Beethoven, L. van:Qt 2 Strs — Platz ▲ PLZ 588 [DDD]
Beethoven, L. van:Qt 12 Strs — Platz ▲ PLZ 588 [DDD]
Haydn, J.:Qts Strs, Op. 76, "Erdödy Qts"—Nos. 3–5 — Platz ▲ PLZ 616 [DDD]
Vienna Octet members
Schubert, Franz:Qnt Pno, D.667, w. C. Curzon (pno) — London ▲ 417459-2 [ADD]
Vienna Opera Ball Orch
U. Thiemer (cnd)
Strauss (II), Joh.:Music of—orchestral highlights from Die Fledermaus, Die Zigeunerbaron & Indigo — Denon/PCM Digital ▲ DEN 77949 [DDD]
Vienna Opera Great SO
E. Graf (cnd)
Berlioz, H.:Sym fantastique — PWK Classics ▲ PWK 1129 [AAD]
Vienna Opera Orch
J.-M. Auberson (cnd)
Bach, J.S.:Cant 57, w. Maria Stader (sop), Heinz Rehfuss (bass) — FNAC Music ("Via Classics" series) ▲ 642329
P. Falk (cnd)
Strauss (II), Joh.:Music of—Gipsy Baron:Ov; Blue Danube; Emperor Waltz; Pizzicato Polka; Vienna Bonbons; Wine, Women & Song; Annen Polka; Roses from the South; Perpetuum Mobile, Op. 257 — Unison ▲ V 81245 ■ V 81474
Strauss (II), Joh.:Waltzes — Stradivari Classics ▲ SCD 6000 [DDD] ■ SMC 6000 (D)
Vienna Operetta Orch
Miklos Gafni Sings, w. Miklos Gafni (ten), Philharmonica Hungarica Orch — Aurora ▲ AUR 5051 [ADD]
E.-G. Scherzer (cnd)
Lehár, F.:Der Zarewitsch (sels), w. D. Koller (sop), G. di Stefano (ten), H. Holecek (bar), Original Volga Cossacks — Koch Schwann ▲ SCH 312732 [ADD]
Vienna Orch
C. F. Adler (cnd)
Bauer, M.:Prelude & Fugue — CRI ("American Masters" series) ▲ CD 714 [ADD]
Bauer, M.:Suite Strs — CRI ("American Masters" series) ▲ CD 714 [ADD]
Beethoven, L. van:Con 6 Pno, w. H. Schnabel (pno) *(rec early 1950s)* — Somerset ▲ SCD 10001 (m)
Luening, O.:Kentucky Rondo — CRI ■ ACS 6011
Luening, O.:Symphonic Fantasia — CRI ■ ACS 6011
Wigglesworth, F.:Sym 1 — CRI ▲ C 733 [ADD]
Wigglesworth, F.:Sym 1 — CRI ■ C 110
H. Gillesberger (cnd)
Mozart, W.A.:Ave verum corpus, w. Vienna Boys' Choir [L] — RCA Gold Seal ("Papillon Collection" series) ▲ 6535-2-RG [ADD] ■ 6535-4-RG
Mozart, W.A.:Requiem, w. Vienna Boys' Choir [L] — RCA Red Seal ("Papillon Collection" series) ▲ 6535-2 [ADD] ■ 6535-4
Vienna ORF SO
P. Steinberg (cnd)
Wagner, R.:Der fliegende Holländer, w. I. Haubold (sop—Senta), M. Schiml (mez—Nurse), P. Seiffert (ten—Erik), J. Hering (ten—Helsman), A. Muff (bar—The Dutchman), E. Knodt (bass—Sea Capt.), Budapest Radio Chorus [G] *(rec Sept. 1992)* — Naxos 2-▲ 8.660025/26 [DDD]

▲ = CD ♦ = Enhanced CD Δ = MD ■ = Cassette Tape ▯ = DCC

Vienna PO
Beethoven, L. van:Con Vn, Op. 61, w. B. Huberman (vn) *(rec 1934)* EMI Classics ("Great Recordings of the Century" series) ▲ CDH 63194 (m) [ADD]
Jurassic Classics, w. Berlin PO, Kirov Orch, Vienna PO, London PO, Boston SO, V. Gergiev (cnd), A. Previn (cnd), C. Davis (cnd), N. Marriner (cnd) Philips ▲ 442599-2 ■ 442599-4
Mad About Angels, w. Cheryl Studer (sop), Christa Ludwig (mez), Anne Sofie von Otter (mez), José Carreras (ten), New York PO [cnd:Leonard Bernstein], English Baroque Soloists [cnd:John Eliot Gardiner], Philharmonia Orch, Philharmonia Chorus [cnd:Carlo Maria Giulini], et.al. Deutsche Grammophon ▲ 449113-2 ■ 449113-4
Mozart, W.A.:Con 12 Pno, w. M. Pollini (pno) Exclusive ▲ EXL 35 [AAD]
Strauss (II), Joh.:Music of, w. *(cnd unknown)* *(rec 1929–40)* Preiser ▲ 90139 (m) [AAD]
Vienna Philharmonic:150th Anniversary Edition EMI Classics 5-▲ CDHE 64294 [ADD]
Viennese Waltzes & Polkas, w. various cnds Preiser ▲ PRE 90139 (m) [AAD]

C. Abbado (cnd)
Beethoven, L. van:Con 5 Pno, "Emperor", w. M. Pollini (pno) Exclusive ▲ EXL 64 [ADD]
Beethoven, L. van:Coriolan Ov Deutsche Grammophon ▲ 419597-2 [DDD] □ 419597-5
Beethoven, L. van:Coriolan Ov Deutsche Grammophon 6-▲ 427306-2 [DDD]
Beethoven, L. van:Egmont (ov) Deutsche Grammophon 6-▲ 427306-2 [DDD]
Beethoven, L. van:Fant Pno, Op. 80, "Choral Fant", w. M. Pollini (pno), Vienna State Opera Chorus [G] Deutsche Grammophon ▲ 419779-2 [DDD]
Beethoven, L. van:Leonore 2 Deutsche Grammophon 6-▲ 427306-2 [DDD]
Beethoven, L. van:Meeresstille und glückliche Fahrt, w. Vienna State Opera Chorus [G] Deutsche Grammophon 6-▲ 427306-2 [DDD]
Beethoven, L. van:Ovs—Die Weihe des Hauses, Coriolan, Die Geschöpfe des Prometheus, Egmont, Fidelio, König Stephen, Leonore 1–3, Namensfeier, Die Ruinen von Athen Deutsche Grammophon 2-▲ 429762-2 [DDD]
Beethoven, L. van:Syms (comp), w. Vienna State Opera Chorus Deutsche Grammophon 6-▲ 427306-2 [DDD]
Beethoven, L. van:Sym 3, "Eroica" Deutsche Grammophon ▲ 419597-2 [DDD] □ 419597-5
Beethoven, L. van:Sym 6, "Pastorale" Deutsche Grammophon ▲ 419779-2 [DDD]
Beethoven, L. van:Sym 6, "Pastorale" Deutsche Grammophon ("Masters" series) ▲ 445542-2
Beethoven, L. van:Sym 7 Deutsche Grammophon ▲ 423364-2 [DDD]
Beethoven, L. van:Sym 8 Deutsche Grammophon ▲ 423364-2 [DDD]
Beethoven, L. van:Sym 8 Deutsche Grammophon ("Masters" series) ▲ 445542-2
Beethoven, L. van:Sym 9, "Choral Sym", w. Vienna State Opera Chorus [G] Deutsche Grammophon ▲ 419598-2 [DDD] □ 419598-5
Berg, A.:Wozzeck, w. H. Behrens (sop), P. Langridge (ten), H. Zednik (ten), F. Grundheber (bar), A. Haugland (bass), Vienna State Opera Chorus, Vienna Boys' Choir [G] *(rec live, 6/88)* Deutsche Grammophon 2-▲ 423587-2 [DDD]
Brahms, J.:Hungarian Dances Orch Deutsche Grammophon ▲ 431594-2
Brahms, J.:Hungarian Dances Orch Deutsche Grammophon ▲ 410615-2 [DDD] □ 410615-5
Bruckner, A.:Sym 4, "Romantic" Deutsche Grammophon ▲ 431719-2 [DDD]
Bruckner, A.:Sym 7 Deutsche Grammophon ▲ 437518-2
Debussy, C.:Pelléas et Mélisande, w. M. Ewing (sop), C. Ludwig (mez), F. Le Roux (bar), J. Van Dam (bass–bar), J.–P. Courtis (bass), Vienna State Opera Chorus Deutsche Grammophon 2-▲ 435344-2 [DDD]
Ligeti, G.:Atmosphères Deutsche Grammophon ▲ 429260-2 [DDD]
Ligeti, G.:Lontano Deutsche Grammophon ▲ 429260-2 [DDD]
Mahler, G.:Sym 2, w. C. Studer (sop), W. Meier (mez), Arnold Schoenberg Choir Deutsche Grammophon ▲ 439953-2
Mahler, G.:Sym 3, w. J. Norman (sop), Vienna State Opera Chorus, Vienna Boys' Choir [G] Deutsche Grammophon 2-▲ 410715-2 [DDD]
Mozart, W.A.:Con 14 Pno, w. M. João Pires (pno) Deutsche Grammophon ▲ 437529-2
Mozart, W.A.:Con 26 Pno, w. M. João Pires (pno) Deutsche Grammophon ▲ 437529-2
Mozart, W.A.:Nozze di Figaro, w. Cecilia Bartoli (sop—Cherubino), Sylvia McNair (sop—Susanna), Cheryl Studer (sop—Countess Almaviva), Lucio Gallo (bar—Figaro), Boje Skovhus (bar—Count Almaviva), Vienna State Opera Chorus Deutsche Grammophon 3-▲ 445903-2
Nono, L.:Liebeslied, w. Vienna Boys' Choir Deutsche Grammophon ▲ 429260-2 [DDD]
Rossini, G.:L'italiana in Algeri, w. A. Baltsa (mez), F. Lopardo (ten), E. Dara (bar), R. Raimondi (bass), Vienna State Opera Chorus [I] Deutsche Grammophon 2-▲ 427331-2 [DDD]
Schoenberg, A.:A Survivor from Warsaw, w. G. Hornik (nar), Vienna State Opera Chorus Deutsche Grammophon ▲ 431774-2 [DDD]
Tchaikovsky, P.:Sym 4 Deutsche Grammophon ("Resonance" series) ▲ 429527-2 [ADD]
Tchaikovsky, P.:Sym 5 *(rec 1972–76)* Deutsche Grammophon ("Double" series) 2-▲ 437401-2
Verdi, G.:Un ballo in maschera, w. Gabriele Lechner (sop), Luciano Pavarotti (ten), Piero Cappuccilli (bar), Vienna State Opera Chorus *(rec live, 1986)* Serenissima 2-▲ SER 360118
Verdi, G.:Requiem Mass, w. C. Studer (sop), M. Lopivšek (cta), J. Carreras (ten), R. Riamondi (bass), Vienna State Opera Chorus Deutsche Grammophon 2-▲ 435884-2
Verdi, G.:quattro pezzi sacri, w. C. Studer (sop), M. Lopivšek (cta), J. Carreras (ten), R. Riamondi (bass), Vienna State Opera Chorus Deutsche Grammophon 2-▲ 435884-2
Wagner, R.:Lohengrin, w. Cheryl Studer (sop), Waltraud Meier (mez), Siegfried Jerusalem (ten), Andreas Schmidt (bar), Harmut Welker (bar), Kurt Moll (bass) Deutsche Grammophon 3-▲ 437808-2
Webern, A.:Bach Transcription, w. Vienna State Opera Chorus Deutsche Grammophon ▲ 431774-2 [DDD]
Webern, A.:Passacaglia, w. Vienna State Opera Chorus Deutsche Grammophon ▲ 431774-2 [DDD]
Webern, A.:Pieces Orch, Op. 6, w. Vienna State Opera Chorus Deutsche Grammophon ▲ 431774-2 [DDD]
Webern, A.:Pieces Orch, Op. 10, w. Vienna State Opera Chorus Deutsche Grammophon ▲ 431774-2 [DDD]
Webern, A.:Vars Orch, w. Vienna State Opera Chorus Deutsche Grammophon ▲ 431774-2 [DDD]

K. Alwin (cnd)
Mozart, W.A.:Entführung (sels), w. Margherita Perras (sop)—Welcher Kummer—Ach ich liebte Orfeo d'or ("Festspiel Dokumente" series) ▲ 394101

L. Bernstein (cnd)
Beethoven, L. van:Coriolan Ov Deutsche Grammophon ("Masters" series) ▲ 445505-2 [DDD]
Beethoven, L. van:Coriolan Ov Deutsche Grammophon ▲ 431025-2 [ADD]
Beethoven, L. van:Egmont (ov) Deutsche Grammophon ("Masters" series) ▲ 445505-2 [DDD]
Beethoven, L. van:Fidelio, w. G. Janowitz (sop), L. Popp (sop), R. Kollo (ten), H. Sotin (bass), D. Fischer–Dieskau (bar), Vienna State Opera Chorus [G] Deutsche Grammophon 2-▲ 419436-2 [ADD]
Beethoven, L. van:Fidelio (ov) Deutsche Grammophon ▲ 431024-2 [ADD]
Beethoven, L. van:König Stephen (ov) Deutsche Grammophon ▲ 431025-2 [ADD]
Beethoven, L. van:Leonore 3 Deutsche Grammophon ▲ 431049-2 [ADD]
Beethoven, L. van:Ovs—Coriolan, Die Geschöpfe des Prometheus, Egmont, Fidelio, König Stephen, Leonore 3 Deutsche Grammophon 6-▲ 423481-2 [ADD]
Beethoven, L. van:Qt 14 Strs [arr. for string orch.] *(rec live 1977)* Deutsche Grammophon ▲ 435779-2 [ADD]
Beethoven, L. van:Qt 16 Strs [arr. for string orch.] *(rec live 1989)* Deutsche Grammophon ▲ 435779-2 [ADD]
Beethoven, L. van:Syms (comp) Deutsche Grammophon 6-▲ 423481-2 [ADD]
Beethoven, L. van:Sym 3, "Eroica" Deutsche Grammophon ▲ 431024-2 [ADD]
Beethoven, L. van:Sym 5 Deutsche Grammophon ▲ 431049-2 [ADD]
Beethoven, L. van:Sym 5 Deutsche Grammophon ▲ 419435-2 [ADD]
Beethoven, L. van:Sym 6, "Pastorale" Deutsche Grammophon ▲ 431025-2 [ADD]
Beethoven, L. van:Sym 8 Deutsche Grammophon ▲ 419435-2 [ADD]
Beethoven, L. van:Sym 9, "Choral Sym" [G] Deutsche Grammophon ▲ 410859-2 [ADD]
Brahms, J.:Academic Festival Ov Deutsche Grammophon 4-▲ 415570-2 [DDD]
Brahms, J.:Academic Festival Ov Deutsche Grammophon ▲ 431029-2 [DDD]

Vienna PO (cont.)
L. Bernstein (cnd) (cont.)
Brahms, J.:Con 1 Pno, w. K. Zimerman (pno) Deutsche Grammophon ▲ 413472-2 [DDD]
Brahms, J.:Con 2 Pno, w. K. Zimerman (pno) Deutsche Grammophon ▲ 415359-2 [DDD]
Brahms, J.:Con Vn, w. G. Kremer (vn) Deutsche Grammophon ▲ 431031-2 [DDD]
Brahms, J.:Con Vn & Vc, "Double Con", w. G. Kremer (vn), M. Maisky (vc) Deutsche Grammophon ▲ 431031-2 [DDD]
Brahms, J.:Syms (comp) Deutsche Grammophon 4-▲ 415570-2 [DDD]
Brahms, J.:Sym 1 Deutsche Grammophon ("Masters" series) ▲ 445505-2 [DDD]
Brahms, J.:Sym 1 Deutsche Grammophon ▲ 431029-2 [DDD]
Brahms, J.:Sym 2 Deutsche Grammophon ("Masters" series) ▲ 445506-2 [DDD]
Brahms, J.:Sym 3 Deutsche Grammophon ("Masters" series) ▲ 445507-2
Brahms, J.:Sym 4 Deutsche Grammophon ▲ 410084-2 [DDD]
Brahms, J.:Sym 4 Deutsche Grammophon ("Masters" series) ▲ 445508-2
Brahms, J.:Tragic Ov Deutsche Grammophon 4-▲ 415570-2 [DDD]
Brahms, J.:Tragic Ov Deutsche Grammophon ▲ 410084-2 [DDD]
Brahms, J.:Tragic Ov Deutsche Grammophon ("Masters" series) ▲ 445508-2
Brahms, J.:Vars on a Theme by Haydn Deutsche Grammophon ("Masters" series) ▲ 445507-2
Brahms, J.:Vars on a Theme by Haydn Deutsche Grammophon 4-▲ 415570-2 [DDD]
Bruckner, A.:Sym 9 *(rec live)* Deutsche Grammophon ▲ 435350-2 [DDD]
Haydn, J.:Sym 92, "Oxford" Deutsche Grammophon ▲ 431034-2 [DDD]
Haydn, J.:Sym 94, "Surprise Sym" Deutsche Grammophon ▲ 431034-2 [DDD]
The Joy of Bernstein, w. New York PO, Los Angeles PO, Israel PO Deutsche Grammophon ▲ 445486-2
Mahler, G.:Kindertotenlieder, w. T. Hampson (bar) [G] Deutsche Grammophon 2-▲ 427697-2 [DDD]
Mahler, G.:Kindertotenlieder, w. T. Hampson (bar) Deutsche Grammophon ▲ 431682-2 [DDD]
Mahler, G.:Das Lied von der Erde, w. M. King (mez), D. Fischer–Dieskau (bar) [G] London ▲ 417783-2 [ADD]
Mahler, G.:Songs from Rückert, w. T. Hampson (bar) *(rec live, 2/90)* Deutsche Grammophon ▲ 431682-2 [DDD]
Mahler, G.:Syms, w. J. Blegen (sop), B. Hendricks (sop), M. Price (sop), G. Zeumer (sop), H. Wittek (trb), A. Baltsa (mez), C. Ludwig (mez), K. Riegel (ten), H. Prey (bar), A. Schmidt (bar), J. Van Dam (b–bar), New York PO, Royal Concertgebouw Orch, Westminster Choir, New York Choral Artists, Brooklyn Boys' Choir, Vienna Boys' Choir, Vienna State Opera Chorus, Vienna Singverein Deutsche Grammophon 13-▲ 435162-2 [DDD]
Mahler, G.:Sym 5 Deutsche Grammophon ▲ 423608-2 [DDD]
Mahler, G.:Sym 6 Deutsche Grammophon 2-▲ 427697-2 [DDD]
Mahler, G.:Sym 8, w. J. Blegen (sop), M. Price (sop), G. Zeumer (sop), A. Baltsa (mez), K. Riegel (ten), H. Prey (bar), A. Schmidt (bar), J. Van Dam (b–bar), Vienna State Opera Chorus, Vienna Boys' Choir *(rec Salzburg Festival, 1975)* Deutsche Grammophon 2-▲ 435102-2 [ADD]
Mahler, G.:Sym 10—Adagio only Deutsche Grammophon 2-▲ 435102-2 [ADD]
Mozart, W.A.:Con Cl, w. P. Schmidl (cl) Deutsche Grammophon ▲ 429221-2 [DDD]
Mozart, W.A.:Con 15 Pno, w. Leonard Bernstein (pno) London ("The Classic Sound" series) ▲ 448570-2
Mozart, W.A.:Sym 25 Deutsche Grammophon ▲ 429221-2 [DDD]
Mozart, W.A.:Sym 29 Deutsche Grammophon ▲ 429221-2 [DDD]
Mozart, W.A.:Sym 36 London ("The Classic Sound" series) ▲ 448570-2
Mozart, W.A.:Sym 39 Deutsche Grammophon ▲ 413776-2 [DDD] □
Mozart, W.A.:Sym 40 Deutsche Grammophon ("Masters" series) ▲ 445548-2
Mozart, W.A.:Sym 40 Deutsche Grammophon ▲ 413776-2 [DDD] □ 413776-5
Mozart, W.A.:Sym 40 Deutsche Grammophon ▲ 431040-2 [DDD]
Mozart, W.A.:Sym 41 Deutsche Grammophon ("Masters" series) ▲ 445548-2
Mozart, W.A.:Sym 41 Deutsche Grammophon ▲ 431040-2 [DDD]
Schumann, R.:Syms (comp) Deutsche Grammophon ("2CD" series) 2-▲ 453 049-2
Schumann, R.:Sym 1 Deutsche Grammophon ▲ 415274-2 [DDD]
Schumann, R.:Sym 4 Deutsche Grammophon ▲ 415274-2 [DDD]
Shostakovich, D.:Sym 6 Deutsche Grammophon ▲ 419771-2 [DDD]
Shostakovich, D.:Sym 9 Deutsche Grammophon ▲ 419771-2 [DDD]
Sibelius, J.:Sym 1 *(rec 1990)* Deutsche Grammophon ▲ 435351-2 [DDD]
Sibelius, J.:Sym 2 Deutsche Grammophon ▲ 419772-2 [DDD]
Sibelius, J.:Sym 5 Deutsche Grammophon ▲ 427647-2 [DDD]
Sibelius, J.:Sym 7 Deutsche Grammophon ▲ 427647-2 [DDD]
Strauss, R.:Der Rosenkavalier, w. G. Jones (sop), L. Popp (sop), C. Ludwig (mez), P. Domingo (ten), W. Berry (b–bar) [G] CBS 3-▲ M3K 42564 [ADD]

K. Böhm (cnd)
Bach, J.S.:Air on the G String *(rec Vienna, 1940–1944)* Preiser 2-▲ PRE 90922 [AAD]
Beethoven, L. van:Con 4 Pno, w. M. Pollini (pno) Deutsche Grammophon 10-▲ 435091-2
Beethoven, L. van:Con 5 Pno, "Emperor", w. E. Ney (pno) Datum 2-▲ DAT 12305 [ADD]
Beethoven, L. van:Coriolan Ov Deutsche Grammophon ("Double" series) 2-▲ 437368-2
Beethoven, L. van:Egmont (ov) Deutsche Grammophon ("Double" series) 2-▲ 437368-2
Beethoven, L. van:Die Geschöpfe des Prometheus (sels)—Ov. Deutsche Grammophon ("Double" series) 2-▲ 437368-2
Beethoven, L. van:Missa Solemnis, w. Margaret Price (sop), Christa Ludwig (mez), Wieslaw Ochman (ten), Martti Talvela (bass), Vienna State Opera Chorus *(rec 1957)* Deutsche Grammophon ("Double" series) 2-▲ 437386-2 [ADD]
Beethoven, L. van:Sym 1 Deutsche Grammophon ("Double" series) 2-▲ 439681-2
Beethoven, L. van:Sym 2 Deutsche Grammophon ("Double" series) 2-▲ 439681-2
Beethoven, L. van:Sym 3, "Eroica" Deutsche Grammophon ("Double" series) 2-▲ 437368-2
Beethoven, L. van:Sym 4 Deutsche Grammophon ("Double" series) 2-▲ 439681-2
Beethoven, L. van:Sym 5 Deutsche Grammophon ("Double" series) 2-▲ 439681-2
Beethoven, L. van:Sym 6, "Pastorale" Deutsche Grammophon ("Double" series) 2-▲ 437928-2
Beethoven, L. van:Sym 6, "Pastorale" *(rec Vienna, May 1971)* Deutsche Grammophon ▲ 447433-2 [ADD]
Beethoven, L. van:Sym 7 Deutsche Grammophon ("Double" series) 2-▲ 437928-2
Beethoven, L. van:Sym 8 Deutsche Grammophon ("Double" series) 2-▲ 437928-2
Beethoven, L. van:Sym 9, "Choral Sym", w. Gwyneth Jones (sop), Tatiana Troyanos (mez), Jess Thomas (ten), Karl Ridderbusch (bass), Vienna State Opera Chorus Deutsche Grammophon ("Double" series) 2-▲ 437368-2
Beethoven, L. van:Sym 9, "Choral Sym", w. Jessye Norman (sop), Brigitte Fassbaender (mez), Plácido Domingo (ten), Walter Berry (bass), Vienna State Opera Chorus Deutsche Grammophon ("Masters" series) ▲ 445503-2 [DDD]
Beethoven, L. van:Sym 9, "Choral Sym", w. Vienna State Opera Chorus [G] Deutsche Grammophon ("3D Classics" series) ▲ 427802-2 [DDD]
Beethoven, L. van:Sym 9, "Choral Sym", w. Vienna State Opera Chorus [G] Deutsche Grammophon ("Resonance" series) ■ 427196-4
Brahms, J.:Con Vn & Vc, "Double Con", w. W. Schneiderhan (vn), E. Mainardi (vc) Datum 2-▲ DAT 12305 [ADD]
Brahms, J.:Sym 1 *(rec Vienna, 1940–1944)* Preiser 2-▲ PRE 90922 [AAD]
Brahms, J.:Sym 2 *(rec Vienna, 1940–1944)* Preiser 2-▲ PRE 90922 [AAD]
Bruckner, A.:Sym 7 *(rec 1943)* Preiser ▲ PRE 90192 [AAD]
Dvořák, A.:Sym 9, "From the New World" *(rec live 1978)* Artists ▲ FED 33 [ADD]
Einem, G. von:Der Prozess, w. Lisa Della Casa (sop—Frl. Bürstner/Die Frau des Gerichtsdieners/Leni), Peter Klein (ten—Der Direktorstellvertreter/Der Student), Max Lorenz (ten—Josef K.), Erich Majkut (ten—Ein Bursche), László Szemere (ten—Titorelli), Alois Pernerstorfer (b-bar—Willem/Der Gerichtsdiener), Alfred Poell (b-bar—Der Advokat), Walter Berry (bass—Franz/Kanzleidirektor), Oskar Czerwenka (bass—Der Untersuchungsrichter/Der Prügler), Ludwig Hofmann (bass—Der Aufseher/Ein Passant/Der Geistliche/Der Fabrikant), Polly Batic (sgr—Frau Grubach), Endreh Koreh (sgr—Albert K.), Luise Leitner (sgr—Ein buckliges Mädchen), Vienna State Opera Chorus *(rec Aug 17, 1953)* Orfeo d'or ("Festspiel Dokumente" series) 2-▲ 392952 (m)

Vienna PO (cont.)

K. Böhm (cnd) (cont.)

Gluck, C.W.:Iphigénie en Aulide, w. Inge Borkh (sop—Klytämnestra), Christa Ludwig (mez—Iphigenie), Elisabeth Steiner (mez—Artemis), James King (ten—Achilles), Otto Edelmann (b-bar), Alois Pernerstorfer (b-bar), Walter Berry (bass), Salzburg Festival Chamber Choir, Vienna State Opera Chorus *(rec Salzburg, Aug 3, 1962)* Orfeo d'or ("Festspiel Dikumente" series) 2-▲ C 428962 (m) [ADD]
Haydn, J.:Sym 88 Deutsche Grammophon ("Resonance" series) ▲ 429523-2 [ADD]
Haydn, J.:Sym 89 Deutsche Grammophon ("Resonance" series) ▲ 429523-2 [ADD]
Haydn, J.:Sym 92, "Oxford" Deutsche Grammophon ("Resonance" series) ▲ 429523-2 [ADD]
Mozart, W.A.:Con Bn, w. D. Zeman (bn) Deutsche Grammophon ▲ 429816-2 [ADD] ■ 429816-4
Mozart, W.A.:Con Cl, w. A. Prinz (cl) Deutsche Grammophon ▲ 413552-2 [ADD]
Mozart, W.A.:Con Cl, w. A. Prinz (cl) Deutsche Grammophon ▲ 429816-2 [ADD] ■ 429816-4
Mozart, W.A.:Con Fl Hp, w. W. Schulz (fl), N. Zabaleta (hp) Deutsche Grammophon ▲ 413552-2 [ADD]
Mozart, W.A.:Con Fl Hp, w. W. Schulz (fl), N. Zabaleta (hp) Deutsche Grammophon ▲ 429815-2 [ADD]
Mozart, W.A.:Con Ob, K.314, w. G. Turetschek (ob) Deutsche Grammophon ▲ 429816-2 [ADD] ■ 429816-4
Mozart, W.A.:Con 18 Pno, w. M. Pollini (pno) Deutsche Grammophon ▲ 429812-2 [ADD]
Mozart, W.A.:Con 19 Pno, w. M. Pollini (pno) Deutsche Grammophon ▲ 429812-2 [ADD]
Mozart, W.A.:Con 23 Pno, w. M. Pollini (pno) Deutsche Grammophon ▲ 429812-2 [ADD]
Mozart, W.A.:Con 27 Pno, w. Emil Gilels (pno) Deutsche Grammophon ▲ 429810-2 [ADD]
Mozart, W.A.:Così fan tutte, w. E. Schwarzkopf (sop—Fiordiligi), C. Ludwig (sop—Dorabella), G. Sciutti (sop—Despina), W. Kmentt (ten—Ferrando), H. Prey (bar—Guglielmo), K. Dönch (bar—D. Alfonso), Vienna State Opera Chorus [I] *(rec live, Salzburg, Aug. 8, 1962)* Arkadia 2-▲ 455 [ADD]
Mozart, W.A.:Così fan tutte (sels), w. Elisabeth Schwarzkopf (sop), Irmgard Seefried (sop), Christa Ludwig (mez), Anton Dermota (ten), Erich Kunz (bar), Paul Schoeffler (b-bar)—Sento, o Dio; Sorella, cosa dici?—Prenderò quel brunettino Orfeo d'or ("Festspiel Dokumente" series) ▲ 394201
Mozart, W.A.:Così fan tutte (sels), w. G. Janowitz (sop), R. Grist (sop), B. Fassbaender (mez), P. Schreier (ten), H. Prey (bar), R. Panerai (bar), Vienna State Opera Chorus—scenes & arias Deutsche Grammophon ▲ 429824-2 [ADD]
Mozart, W.A.:Don Giovanni (sels), w. A. Tomowa-Sintow (sop), T. Zylis-Gara (sop), E. Mathis (sop), S. Milnes (bar), W. Berry (bass), Vienna State Opera Chorus—Scenes & Arias Deutsche Grammophon ▲ 429823-2 [ADD]
Mozart, W.A.:Kleine Nachtmusik *(rec 1943)* Orfeo ▲ 376941 (m)
Mozart, W.A.:Requiem, w. E. Mathis (sop), J. Hamari (mez), W. Ochman (ten), K. Ridderbusch (bass), Vienna State Opera Chorus [L] Deutsche Grammophon ▲ 413553-2 [ADD]
Mozart, W.A.:Sym 35 *(rec Vienna, 1940-1944)* Preiser 2-▲ PRE 90922 [AAD]
Mozart, W.A.:Sym 40 Deutsche Grammophon ▲ 413547-2 [ADD]
Mozart, W.A.:Sym 41 *(rec 1943)* Orfeo ▲ 376941 (m)
Mozart, W.A.:Sym 41 Deutsche Grammophon ▲ 413547-2 [ADD]
Mozart, W.A.:Zauberflöte, w. H. Gueden (sop), W. Lipp (sop), L. Simoneau (ten), W. Berry (bass), K. Bohme (bass), Vienna State Opera Chorus London ("Grand Opera" series) 2-▲ 414362-2 [ADD]
Schubert, Franz:Sym 5 *(rec Vienna, Dec 1979)* Deutsche Grammophon ▲ 447433-2 [ADD]
Schubert, Franz:Sym 8 *(rec Vienna, 1940-1944)* Preiser 2-▲ PRE 90922 [AAD]
Schumann, R.:Con Pno, w. W. Backhaus (pno) Datum 2-▲ DAT 12305 [ADD]
Strauss, R.:Arabella, w. M. Reining (sop), L. Della Casa (sop), H. Taubmann (ten), H. Hotter (b-bar) *(rec Salzburg Festival, 1947)* Deutsche Grammophon 3-▲ 445342-2 (m) [ADD]
Strauss, R.:Arabella, w. L. Della Casa (sop), M. Reining (sop), R. Anday (cta), H. Hotter (b-bar), G. Hann (bass), J. Patzak (ten), Vienna State Opera Chorus *(rec live, Salzburg Festival, 8/12/47)* Melodram 3-▲ MEL 37077
Strauss, R.:Ariadne auf Naxos, w. L. Della Casa (sop), H. Güden (sop), I. Seefried (sop), R. Schock (ten), P. Schöffler (bass) *(rec Salzburg Festival, 1954)* Deutsche Grammophon 2-▲ 445332-2 (m) [ADD]
Strauss, R.:Con 2 Hn, w. Gottfried von Freiberg (hn) *(rec 1943)* Orfeo ▲ 376941 (m)
Strauss, R.:Der Rosenkavalier, w. E. Mathis (sop), C. Ludwig (mez), T. Troyanos (mez), O. Wiener (bar), T. Adam (b-bar) *(rec Salzburg Festival, 1969)* Deutsche Grammophon 3-▲ 445338-2 [ADD]
Strauss, R.:Die Schweigsame Frau, w. H. Güden (sop), F. Wunderlich (ten), H. Prey (bar), H. Hotter (b-bar) *(rec Salzburg Festival, 1959)* Deutsche Grammophon 2-▲ 445335-2 (m) [ADD]
Strauss, R.:Die Schweigsame Frau, w. G. von Milinkovic (mez), F. Wunderlich (ten), H. Hotter (b-bar), H. Prey (bar), Vienna State Opera Chorus *(rec live, Salzburg Festival, 8/8/59)* Melodram 2-▲ MEL 27071 (m) [AAD]
Wagner, R.:Die Meistersinger von Nürnberg, w. Irmgard Seefried (sop—Eva), Else Schürhoff (mez—Magdelene), Peter Klein (ten—David), August Seider (ten—Walther), Erich Kunz (bar—Beckmesser), Paul Schoeffler (b-bar—Hans Sachs), Herbert Alsen (bass—Pogner), Vienna State Opera Chorus *(rec Vienna, Nov. & Dec. 1944)* Preiser 4-▲ PRE 90234 [ADD]
Weber, C.M. von:Ovs—Der Freischütz *(rec live 1978)* Artists ▲ FED 33 [ADD]

K. Böhm, Moralt (cnds)

Mozart, W.A.:Don Giovanni (sels), w. Hilde Konetzni (sop), Emmy Loose (sop), Irmgard Seefried (sop), Anton Dermota (ten), Erich Kunz (bar), Paul Schöffler (b-bar), Herbert Alsen (bass) *(rec 1944)* Preiser ▲ PRE 90249 [ADD]
Mozart, W.A.:Entführung (sels), w. Hilde Konetzni (sop), Emmy Loose (sop), Irmgard Seefried (sop), Anton Dermota (ten), Erich Kunz (bar), Paul Schöffler (b-bar), Herbert Alsen (bass) *(rec 1944)* Preiser ▲ PRE 90249 [ADD]
Mozart, W.A.:Zauberflöte (sels), w. Hilde Konetzni (sop), Emmy Loose (sop), Irmgard Seefried (sop), Anton Dermota (ten), Erich Kunz (bar), Paul Schöffler (b-bar), Herbert Alsen (bass) *(rec 1944)* Preiser ▲ PRE 90249 [ADD]

W. Boskovsky (cnd)

Strauss (II), Joh.:Music of—An der schönen blauen Donau, Op. 314; Fruhlingstimmen, Op. 410; Wein, Weiber und Gesang, Op. 333; Tausend und eine Nacht, Op. 346; Kaiserwaltzer, Op. 437 London ("Double Decker" series) 2-▲ 443473-2
Strauss (II), Joh.:Waltzes London ("Weekend Classics" series) ▲ 417885-2 [AAD] ■ 417885-4
Wiener Tanzgala I London ▲ 436781-2

P. Boulez (cnd)

Mahler, G.:Sym 5 Deutsche Grammophon ▲ 453 416-2
Mahler, G.:Sym 6 Deutsche Grammophon ("4D Audio" series) ▲ 445835-2

M.-W. Chung (cnd)

Rossini, G.:Stabat Mater, w. Luba Orgonasova (sop), Cecilia Bartoli (mez), Raul Gimenez (ten), Roberto Scandiuzzi (bass), Vienna State Opera Chorus Deutsche Grammophon ▲ 449 178-2

A. Cluytens (cnd)

Humperdinck, E.:Hänsel und Gretel, w. Lislotte Maikl (sop—Sandman/Dew Fairy), Anneliese Rothenberger (sop—Gretel), Irmgard Seefried (sop—Hänsel), Grace Hoffman (mez—Gertrude), Elisabeth Höngen (cta—Witch), Walter Berry (bass—Peter), Vienna Boys' Choir EMI Classics 2-▲ CDMB 65661

C. Davis (cnd)

Berlioz, H.:Roméo et Juliette, w. Olga Borodina (mez), Thomas Moser (ten), Alastair Miles (bass), Bavarian Radio Chorus Philips ▲ 442134-2
Berlioz, H.:Sym fantastique Philips ▲ 432151-2 [DDD] □ 432151-5

I. Dobrowen (cnd)

Bach, J.S.:Cons Vn (comp), w. B. Huberman (vn) *(rec 1934)* Pearl ▲ PEA 9341 (m)
Mozart, W.A.:Con 3 Vn, w. B. Huberman (vn) *(rec 1934)* Pearl ▲ PEA 9341 (m) [AAD]

C. von Dohnányi (cnd)

Berg, A.:Lulu, w. A. Silja (sop), B. Fassbaender (mez), W. Berry (b-bar), K. Moll (bass), H. Hotter (b-bar), A. Szramek (sgr) London 2-▲ 430415-2 [ADD]
Berg, A.:Wozzeck, w. A. Silja (sop), G. Jahn (mez), H. Laubenthal (ten), H. Zednik (ten), E. Waechter (bar) London 2-▲ 417348-2 [DDD]
Glass, Philip:Con Vn, w. G. Kremer (vn) Deutsche Grammophon ▲ 437091-2
Mendelssohn, F.:Sym 4 London ▲ 430722-2 [DDD]
Schnittke, A.:Con grosso 5, w. G. Kremer (vn) Deutsche Grammophon ▲ 437091-2
Schoenberg, A.:Erwartung, w. A. Silja (sop) [G] London 2-▲ 417348-2 [DDD]
Strauss, R.:Don Juan London ▲ 430508-2 [DDD] □ 430508-5

Vienna PO (cont.)

C. von Dohnányi (cnd) (cont.)

Strauss, R.:Metamorphosen London ▲ 430508-2 [DDD] □ 430508-5
Strauss, R.:Salome, w. Catherine Malfitano (sop), Hanna Schwarz (mez), Kenneth Riegel (ten), Bryn Terfel (b-bar) London 2-▲ 444178-2
Strauss, R.:Tod und Verklärung London ▲ 430508-2 [DDD]
Tchaikovsky, P.:Ov 1812 London ▲ 425792-2 [DDD]
Tchaikovsky, P.:Sym 4 London ▲ 425792-2 [DDD]
Wagner, R.:Der fliegende Holländer, w. H. Beherns (sop—Senta), I. Vermillion (mez—Mary), U. Heilmann (ten—Helmsman), J. Protschka (ten—Erik), R. Hale (bar—The Dutchman), K. Rydl (bass—Daland), Vienna State Opera Chorus London 2-▲ 436418-2 [DDD]

F. Fricsay (cnd)

Einem, G. von:Dantons Tod, w. M. Cebotari (sop—Lucille Desmoulins), R. Anday (cta—Frau des Simon), P. Klein (ten—de Séchelles), J. Patzak (ten—Camille Desmoulins), J. Witt (ten—Robspierre), P. Schöffler (bar—Danton), L. Weber (bass—Saint Just), Vienna State Opera Chorus *(rec Aug. 6, 1947)* Stradivarius 2-▲ STR 10067 [ADD]

W. Furtwängler (cnd)

Albert, E. d':Tiefland (ov) *(rec live, 1944)* As Disc ▲ ASD 2506
Beethoven, L. van:Egmont (ov) *(rec live, Vienna Sept.24, 1948)* Melodram 2-▲ CDM 25009 [ADD]
Beethoven, L. van:Egmont (ov) *(rec Sept. 4, 1953)* Music & Arts ▲ CD 792 [AAD]
Beethoven, L. van:Fidelio, w. K. Flagstad (sop), J. Patzak (ten), P. Schöffler (b-bar), J. Greindl (bass), Vienna State Opera Chorus [G] *(rec live 1950)* Arkadia 2-▲ 354
Beethoven, L. van:Fidelio, w. S. Jurinac (sop), M. Mödl (sop), W. Windgassen (ten), A. Poell (bar), O. Edelmann (bass), G. Frick (bass) *(rec Oct. 1953)* EMI Classics 2-▲ CDHB 64496
Beethoven, L. van:Fidelio, w. K. Flagstad (sop), J. Patzak (ten), J. Griendl (bass), Vienna State Opera Chorus EMI Classics 2-▲ CDC 64901
Beethoven, L. van:Fidelio, w. K. Flagstad (sop), J. Patzak (ten), P. Schöffler (b-bar), J. Greindl (bass), Vienna State Opera Chorus [G] *(rec live, Salzburg 8/5/50)* Verona 2-▲ 27044/45 (m) [AAD]
Beethoven, L. van:Fidelio (sels), w. W. Windgassen—3 selections from Act 2—aria "Gott, welch' Dunkel hier...In des lebens Frühlingstagen," trio "Euch werde Lohn!" [w. Martha Mödl & Gottlob Frick] & duet "O namenlose Freude" [w. Martha Mödl] [G] *(rec 1953)* Memories 2-▲ HR 4424/25 [ADD]
Beethoven, L. van:Grosse Fuge Str Qt *(rec live, Salzburg 8/30/54)* Music & Arts ▲ CD 520 [AAD]
Beethoven, L. van:Grosse Fuge Str Qt *(rec live, Salzburg 8/30/54)* Arkadia ▲ 363 [ADD]
Beethoven, L. van:Leonore 3 *(rec live, June 2, 1944)* AS Disc ▲ ASD 2900
Beethoven, L. van:Syms (comp), w. E. Schwarzkopf (sop), E. Höngen (mez), H. Hopf (ten), O. Edelmann (bass), Bayreuth Festival Orch, Bayreuth Festival Chorus *(rec 1948-54)* EMI Classics 5-▲ CDHE 63606
Beethoven, L. van:Sym 1 *(rec 1952)* Arkadia ▲ 504 (m) [AAD]
Beethoven, L. van:Sym 1 *(rec live 11/30/52)* Music & Arts ▲ CD 711-1 [AAD]
Beethoven, L. van:Sym 1 *(rec Sept. 4, 1953)* Music & Arts ▲ CD 792 [AAD]
Beethoven, L. van:Sym 3, "Eroica" *(rec Dec 16, 1944)* Iron Needle 3-▲ IN 1348/50 [ADD]
Beethoven, L. van:Sym 3, "Eroica" *(rec Dec. 1944)* Music & Arts ▲ CD 814 [AAD]
Beethoven, L. van:Sym 4 *(rec Sept. 4, 1953)* Music & Arts ▲ CD 792 [AAD]
Beethoven, L. van:Sym 5 *(rec live, Copenhagen, 10/1/50)* Danacord ▲ DACOCD 301 (m)
Beethoven, L. van:Sym 5 *(rec 1952)* EMI Classics ("Great Recordings of the Century" series) ▲ CDH 69803 (m) [ADD]
Beethoven, L. van:Sym 6, "Pastorale" *(rec Dec. 1943)* Preiser ▲ PRE 90199 [ADD]
Beethoven, L. van:Sym 7 *(rec 1950)* EMI Classics ("Great Recordings of the Century" series) ▲ CDH 69803 (m) [ADD]
Brahms, J.:Vars on a Theme by Haydn *(rec Dec. 18, 1943)* Music & Arts 4-▲ CD 804 [ADD]
Brahms, J.:Vars on a Theme by Haydn EMI Classics 2-▲ ZDHC 65513
Brahms, J.:Vars on a Theme by Haydn *(rec Dec. 1943)* Preiser ▲ PRE 90199 [ADD]
Bruckner, A.:Sym 4, "Romantic" *(rec Oct. 29, 1951)* Music & Arts ▲ CD 796 [AAD]
Bruckner, A.:Sym 5 *(rec live, Salzburg Festival, 1951)* EMI Classics ▲ CDM 65750
Bruckner, A.:Sym 5 *(rec live, Salzburg 8/19/51)* Arkadia ▲ 360 [ADD]
Bruckner, A.:Sym 8 *(rec Oct. 17, 1944)* Music & Arts ▲ CD 764 [AAD]
Early Studio Recordings 1929-43, w. Berlin PO Music & Arts 4-▲ MUA CD 954
Franck, C.:Sym in d [2 recordings] Arlecchino ARL
Furtwängler, W.:Sym 2 *(rec live, Feb. 22, 1953)* Orfeo ▲ 375941 (m)
Glazunov, A.:Stenka Razin *(rec live, 1944)* As Disc ▲ ASD 2506
Hindemith, P.:Die Harmonie der Welt *(rec live Salzburg, Aug. 30, 1952)* EMI Classics ▲ ZDMB 65353
Liszt, F.:Les Préludes Historical Performers ▲ HPS 14
Mahler, G.:Lieder eines fahrenden Gesellen, w. D. Fischer-Dieskau (bar) [G] *(rec Salzburg, 8/19/51)* Verona 2-▲ 27062/63 (m) [AAD]
Mozart, W.A.:Con 10 Pno, w. Paul Badura-Skoda (pno), Dagmar Bella (pno) Music & Arts ▲ CD 895
Mozart, W.A.:Don Giovanni, w. E. Schwarzkopf (sop), E. Grümmer (sop), E. Berger (sop), A. Dermota (ten), C. Siepi (b-bar), O. Edelmann (b-bar), W. Berry (bass), Vienna State Opera Chorus *(rec Salzburg, Aug. 3, 1953)* EMI Classics ("Great Recordings of the Century" series) 2-▲ CDHB 63860
Mozart, W.A.:Don Giovanni, w. E. Schwarzkopf (sop), E. Grümmer (sop), E. Berger (sop), A. Dermota (ten), C. Siepi (b-bar), O. Edelmann (b-bar), W. Berry (bass), Vienna State Opera Chorus *(rec 1953)* Arkadia 3-▲ 509 (m) [AAD]
Mozart, W.A.:Nozze di Figaro, w. Elisabeth Schwarzkopf (sop—Countess), Irmgard Seefried (sop—Susanna), Hilde Güden (mez—Cherubino), Paul Schöffler (bar—Almaviva), Erich Kunz (bass—Figaro), Vienna State Opera Chorus *(rec Salzburg Festival, Aug 8, 1953)* EMI Classics 3-▲ CDHC 66080
Mozart, W.A.:Zauberflöte, w. Wilma Lipp (sop), Irmgard Seefried (sop), Peter Klein (ten), Walther Ludwig (ten), Karl Schmitt-Walter (bar), Josef Greindl (bass), Paul Schöffler (sgr), Vienna State Opera Chorus *(rec 1949)* Music & Arts 3-▲ CD 882 [AAD]
Mozart, W.A.:Zauberflöte, w. I. Seefried (sop-Pamina), W. Lipp (sop—Queen of the Night), A. Dermota (ten—Tamino), E. Kunz (bar—Papageno), J. Greindl (bass—Sarastro), Vienna State Opera Chorus [G] *(rec live, Salzburg, Aug. 6, 1951)* Arkadia 3-▲ 361 [ADD]
Mozart, W.A.:Zauberflöte, w. I. Seefried (sop-Pamina), W. Lipp (sop—Queen of the Night), A. Dermota (ten—Tamino), E. Kunz (bar—Papageno), J. Greindl (bass—Sarastro), Vienna State Opera Chorus *(rec live 1951)* EMI Classics 3-▲ CDMC 65356
Mozart, W.A.:Zauberflöte (sels), w. I. Seefried (sop), W. Lipp (sop), W. Ludwig (ten), K. Schmitt-Walter (bar), J. Greindl (bass), Vienna State Opera Chorus—Ov. & 11 arias *(rec live, Salzburg, July, 27, 1949)* Arkadia 3-▲ 361 [ADD]
Schubert, Franz:Sym 9 *(rec live, Salzburg, Aug. 30, 1952)* EMI Classics ▲ ZDMB 65353
Sibelius, J.:En Saga, Berlin PO [2 versions] *(rec Feb. 7-8, 1943 & Sept. 25)* Music & Arts ▲ CD 799 [AAD]
Smetana, B.:The Moldau *(rec Vienna, 1951)* Historical Performers ▲ HPS 14
Strauss, R.:Don Juan EMI Classics ▲ ZDMB 65353
Verdi, G.:Otello, w. Carla Martinis (sop—Desdemona), Sieglinde Wagner (mez—Emilia), Anton Dermota (ten—Cassio), Paul Schöffler (ten—Iago), Ramon Vinay (ten—Otello), Josef Greindl (bass—Lodovico), Vienna State Opera Chorus *(rec live, Salzburg Festival, Aug 7, 1951)* EMI Classics ▲ CDMB 65751

J.E. Gardiner (cnd)

Chabrier, E.:España *(rec Vienna, Mar 1995)* Deutsche Grammophon ▲ 447 751-2 [DDD]
Chabrier, E.:Gwendoline (ov) *(rec Vienna, Mar 1995)* Deutsche Grammophon ▲ 447 751-2 [DDD]
Chabrier, E.:Habanera *(rec Vienna, Mar 1995)* Deutsche Grammophon ▲ 447 751-2 [DDD]
Chabrier, E.:Joyeuse Marche *(rec Vienna, Mar 1995)* Deutsche Grammophon ▲ 447 751-2 [DDD]
Chabrier, E.:Larghetto, w. Ronald Janezic (hn) *(rec Vienna, Mar 1995)* Deutsche Grammophon ▲ 447 751-2 [DDD]
Chabrier, E.:Prélude pastoral *(rec Vienna, Mar 1995)* Deutsche Grammophon ▲ 447 751-2 [DDD]
Chabrier, E.:Le Roi malgré lui (fête polonaise) *(rec Vienna, Mar 1995)* Deutsche Grammophon ▲ 447 751-2 [DDD]
Chabrier, E.:Suite pastorale *(rec Vienna, Mar 1995)* Deutsche Grammophon ▲ 447 751-2 [DDD]
Lehár, F.:Die lustige Witwe, w. Cheryl Studer (sop), Barbara Bonney (sop), Boje Skovhus (bar), Bryn Terfel (b-bar), Monteverdi Choir London Deutsche Grammophon ▲ 439911-2

▲ = CD ♦ = Enhanced CD Δ = MD ■ = Cassette Tape □ = DCC

Vienna PO (cont.)

J. E. Gardiner, J. Levine (cnds)

Mad About Love, w. Cheryl Studer (sop), Kiri Te Kanawa (sop), José Carreras (ten), Jerry Hadley (ten), Philharmonia Orch [cnd:Giuseppe Sinopoli], Bastille Opera Orch [cnd:Myung-Whun Chung], Boston SO [cnd:Seiji Ozawa] Deutsche Grammophon ▲ 449112-2 ■ 449112-4

C.M. Giulini (cnd)

Brahms, J.:Sym 1 Deutsche Grammophon ▲ 435347-2 [DDD]

Brahms, J.:Sym 4 Deutsche Grammophon ▲ 429403-2 [DDD]

Brahms, J.:Tragic Ov Deutsche Grammophon ▲ 429403-2 [DDD]

Bruckner, A.:Sym 8 Deutsche Grammophon ("Digital Midprice" series) 2-▲ 445529-2 [DDD]

Bruckner, A.:Sym 9 Deutsche Grammophon ▲ 427345-2 [DDD]

Franck, C.:Symphonic Vars, w. Paul Crossley (pno) *(rec Musikverein, Grosser Saal, Vienna, Austria, June 12 & 13, 1993)* Sony Classical ▲ S2K 58958 [DDD]

Franck, C.:Sym in d *(rec Musikverein, Grosser Saal, Vienna, Austria, June 12 & 13, 1993)* Sony Classical ▲ S2K 58958 [DDD]

Grieg, E.:Pno Music (sels), w. E. Kissin (pno) Sony Classical ▲ SK 52567

Grieg, E.:Pictures from Life in the Country, w. E. Kissin (pno)—No. 3, "Carnival Scene" Sony Classical ▲ SK 52567

Liszt, F.:Soirées de Vienne, w. Y. Kissin (pno)—Valse-caprice No. 6-First Version Sony Classical ▲ SK 52567

Schubert, Franz:Qnt Pno, D.667, w. Y. Kissin (pno) Sony Classical ▲ SK 52567

Schubert, Franz:Songs (misc), w. Y. Kissin (pno)—Erlkönig, D.328 Sony Classical ▲ SK 52567

B. Haitink (cnd)

Brahms, J.:Con 2 Pno, w. V. Ashkenazy (pno) London ▲ 410199-2

Bruckner, A.:Sym 3, "Wagner" Philips ▲ 422411-2 [DDD]

Bruckner, A.:Sym 5 Philips □ 434724-5

N. Harnoncourt (cnd)

Mozart, W.A.:Cons Vn Orch, w. Gidon Kremer (vn)—Nos. 1-5 Deutsche Grammophon ("2CD" series) 2-▲ 453 043-2

Mozart, W.A.:Sinf Concertante Vn Va Orch, w. Gidon Kremer (vn), Kim Kashkashian (va) Deutsche Grammophon ("2CD" series) 2-▲ 453 043-2

R. Heger (cnd)

Strauss, R.:Der Rosenkavalier, w. L. Lehmann (sop), E. Schumann (sop) EMI Classics 2-▲ CDHB 64487

Strauss, R.:Der Rosenkavalier, w. L. Lehmann (sop), E. Schumann (sop), M. Olczewska (mez), R. Mayr (bass), Vienna State Opera Chorus—abridged performance [G] *(rec 1933 for HMV)* Pearl 2-▲ GEMMCDS 9365 (m) [AAD]

F. Huybrechts (cnd)

Janácek, L.:Lachian Dances London 2-▲ 430372-2 [ADD]

H. von Karajan (cnd)

Beethoven, L. van:Fidelio, w. C. Goltz (sop), S. Jurinac (sop), G. Zampieri (ten), P. Schöffler (b-bar), O. Edelmann (bass), Vienna State Opera Chorus [G] *(rec live, Salzburg Festival 7/27/57)* Claque 2-▲ CLQ 2007 (m)

Bizet, G.:Carmen, w. G. Bumbry (sop), M. Freni (sop), J. Vickers (ten), J. Diaz (bass), Vienna State Opera Chorus [F] *(rec live, Salzburg 1967)* Arkadia 3-▲ 221 [ADD]

Bizet, G.:Carmen, w. L. Price (sop), M. Freni (sop), F. Corelli (ten), R. Merrill (bar), Vienna State Opera Chorus [F] RCA Gold Seal ▲ 60190-2-RG [ADD] ■ 60190-4-RG

Bizet, G.:Carmen, w. L. Price (sop), M. Freni (sop), F. Corelli (ten), R. Merrill (bar), Vienna State Opera Chorus [F] RCA Gold Seal 3-▲ 6199-2-RG [ADD] 2-■ 6199-4-RG

Bizet, G.:Carmen (sels), w. Mirella Freni (sop), Leontyne Price (sop), Franco Corelli (ten), Vienna State Opera Chorus RCA Victor ▲ 09026-68021-2; ■ 09026-68021-4

Bizet, G.:Carmen (sels), w. Mirella Freni (sop), Grace Bumbry (mez), Jon Vickers (ten) *(rec Salzburg, 1967)* Arkadia 3-▲ 498

Brahms, J.:Ein Deutsches Requiem, w. B. Hendricks (sop), J. Van Dam (bar), Vienna Singverein [G] *(rec 1986)* Deutsche Grammophon ▲ 431651-2 [DDD]

Brahms, J.:Ein Deutsches Requiem, w. E. Schwarzkopf (sop), H. Hotter (bar), Vienna Singverein [G] *(rec 10/47)* EMI Classics ("Great Recordings of the Century" series) ▲ CDH 61010 (m) [ADD]

Bruckner, A.:Sym 7 Deutsche Grammophon ▲ 429226-2 [DDD]

Bruckner, A.:Sym 7 *(rec Great Hall, Musikverein, Vienna, Apr 1989)* Deutsche Grammophon ("Karajan Gold" series) ▲ 439037-2 [DDD]

Bruckner, A.:Sym 8 [1890 version, ed. Haas] Deutsche Grammophon 2-▲ 427611-2 [DDD]

A Christmas Offering, w. Price, Leontyne (sop) London ■ 411614-4

Gluck, C.W.:Orfeo ed Euridice, w. S. Jurinac (sop), G. Sciutti (sop), G. Simionato (mez), Vienna State Opera Chorus *(rec live 1959)* Memories 2-▲ HR 4382/83 (m)

Granada:The Greatest Hits of Plácido Domingo, w. Domingo, Plácido (ten), London SO [cnd:C. Abbado], Los Angeles PO [cnd:C. M. Giulini], Royal Opera House Orch, Covent Garden [cnd:Z. Mehta], Philharmonia Orch [cnd:Giuseppe Sinopoli] Deutsche Grammophon ▲ 445777-2 ■ 445777-4

Haydn, J.:Die Schöpfung, w. Gundula Janowitz (sop—Gabriel), Fritz Wünderlich (ten—Uriel), Kim Borg (bass—Raphael), Vienna Singverein *(rec Salzburg, Aug 29, 1965)* Bella Voce 2-▲ 7204 [AAD]

Mozart, W.A.:Con 23 Pno, w. M. Pollini (pno) *(rec 1974)* Enterprise ("Document" series) ▲ ENT LV 938 [ADD]

Mozart, W.A.:Don Giovanni, w. L. Price (sop), H. Gueden (sop), G. Sciurri (sop), F. Wunderlich (ten), E. Wächter (bar), W. Berry (bass), Vienna State Opera Chorus [I] *(rec live, 1963)* Verona 3-▲ 27065/67 (m) [AAD]

Mozart, W.A.:Don Giovanni, w. G. Janowitz (sop), T. Zylis-Gara (sop), M. Freni (sop), A. Kraus (ten), R. Panerai (bar), V. von Halem (bass), N. Ghiaurov (bass), Vienna State Opera Chorus [I] *(rec live, Salzburg, Aug. 1, 1969)* Memories 3-▲ HR 4362/64 (m) [ADD]

Mozart, W.A.:Nozze di Figaro, w. E. Schwarzkopf (sop), I. Seefried (sop), S. Jurinac (sop), E. Höngen (cta), G. London (bar), E. Kunz (bar), Vienna State Opera Chorus—omitting recitatives [I] *(rec 1950)* EMI Classics ("Studio" series) 2-▲ CDMB 69639 (m) [ADD]

Mozart, W.A.:Nozze di Figaro (sels), w. Anna Tomowa-Sintow (sop), José van Dam (b-bar), Controbas (sgr) London ▲ 421317-2 [ADD]

Mozart, W.A.:Requiem, w. A. Tomowa-Sintow (sop), H. Müller Molinari (cta), V. Cole (ten), P. Burchuladze (bass), Vienna Singverein [L] Deutsche Grammophon ("Karajan Gold" series) ▲ 439023-2 [DDD]

Mozart, W.A.:Requiem, w. L. Price (sop), H. Rössl-Majdan (mez), F. Wunderlich (ten), W. Berry (bass), Vienna Singverein [L] *(rec live, Salzburg Festival, Aug. 24, 1960)* Melodram ▲ MEL 18003

Mozart, W.A.:Zauberflöte, w. Reri Grist (sop), Edita Gruberová (sop), Edith Mathis (sop), Rene Kollo (ten), Gerhard Unger (ten), Hermann Prey (bar), José Van Dam (b-bar), Peter Meven (bass), Vienna State Opera Chorus *(rec live, Salzburg, July 26, 1974)* Arkadia 2-▲ 233

Mozart, W.A.:Zauberflöte, w. I. Seefried (sop-Pamina), W. Lipp (sop—Queen of the Night), A. Dermota (ten—Tamino), E. Kunz (bar—Papageno), J. Greindl (bass—Sarastro), Musikfreunde Chorus [without dialogue; G] *(rec 1950)* EMI Classics ("Studio" series) 2-▲ CDHB 69631 (m)

Mozart, W.A.:Zauberflöte (sels), w. Vienna Singverein Classics for Pleasure ("Eminence" series) ▲ CDEMX 2220 [ADD]

Mussorgsky, M.:Boris Godunov, w. N. Dobrianova (sop), S. Jurinac (sop), D. Usunow (ten), N. Ghiaurov (bass), N. Ghiuselev (bass), A. Diakov (bass), Vienna State Opera Chorus [R] *(rec live in Salzburg, 7/26/64)* Arkadia 2-▲ 210 (m) [ADD]

The Opera Lover's Broadway:Great Voices Sing Broadway's Greatest Hits, w. New Philharmonia Orch [cnd:Richard Bonynge], Roland Shaw Orch, London SO [cnd:John Mauceri], Nelson Riddle & His Orch, London Festival Orch [cnd:Robert Sharples] London ▲ 448282-2 ■ 448282-4

Opera Arias, w. Cebotari, Maria (sop), Vienna PO [cnd:Prohaska], Philharmonia Orch [cnd:Krips], et al. *(rec ca. 1934-1949)* Preiser ▲ PRE 90034 (m) [AAD]

Puccini, G.:Madama Butterfly, w. M. Freni (sop), C. Ludwig (mez), L. Pavarotti (ten), R. Kerns (bar) [I] London 3-▲ 417577-2 [ADD]

Puccini, G.:Madama Butterfly (sels), w. M. Freni (sop), C. Ludwig (mez), L. Pavarotti (ten), R. Kerns (bar) [I] London ▲ 421247-2 [ADD] ■ 421247-4

Puccini, G.:Tosca, w. L. Price (sop), G. di Stefano (ten), G. Taddei (bar), Vienna State Opera Chorus [I] London 2-▲ 421670-2 [ADD]

Vienna PO (cont.)

H. von Karajan (cnd) (cont.)

Puccini, G.:Turandot, w. K. Ricciarelli (sop), B. Hendricks (sop), P. Domingo (ten), R. Raimondi (bass), Vienna State Opera Chorus [I] Deutsche Grammophon 2-▲ 423855-2 [DDD]

Puccini, G.:Turandot (sels), w. K. Ricciarelli (sop), B. Hendricks (sop), P. Domingo (ten), R. Raimondi (bass), Vienna State Opera Chorus [I] Deutsche Grammophon ▲ 435409-2 [DDD]

Schumann, R.:Con Pno, w. M. Pollini (pno) *(rec 1974)* Enterprise ("Document" series) ▲ ENT LV 938 [ADD]

Schumann, R.:Con Pno, w. *(soloist unknown)* Exclusive ▲ EXL 17 [ADD]

Strauss (II), Joh.:Die Fledermaus, w. H. Gueden (sop), E. Köth (sop), R. Resnik (mez), W. Kmentt (ten), G. Zampieri (ten), E. Wächter (bar), W. Berry (bass), E. Kunz (bar), Vienna State Opera Chorus, with Gala Sequence [G] London 2-▲ 421046-2 [ADD]

Strauss (II), Joh.:Music of, w. H. Gueden (sop), Vienna Men's Choral Association—5 waltzes & polkas—Blue Danube; Annen-Polka; Pizzicato Polka; Voices of Spring; Imperial Waltz [G] Arkadia 3-▲ 215 (m) [ADD]

Strauss, R.:Also sprach Zarathustra London ("The Classic Sound" series) ▲ 448582-2

Strauss, R.:Don Juan London ("The Classic Sound" series) ▲ 448582-2

Strauss, R.:Elektra, w. A. Varnay (sop/mez), M. Mödl (sop/mez), H. Hillebrecht (sop), J. King (ten), E. Wächter (bar), Vienna State Opera Chorus [G] *(rec 1964)* Melodram 2-▲ MEL 27044 [AAD]

Strauss, R.:Elektra (sels), w. A. Varnay (sop/mez), H. Hillebrecht (sop), J. King (ten), Vienna State Opera Chorus [G] *(rec live in Salzburg, 8/11/64)* Arkadia 3-▲ 213 (m) [ADD]

Strauss, R.:Der Rosenkavalier, w. E. Schwarzkopf (sop—Feldmarschallin), A. Rothenberger (sop—Sophie), S. Jurinac (sop—Octavian), O. Edelmann (bass—Baron Ochs) *(rec live, Salzburg, 8/1/64)* Arkadia 3-▲ 227 [ADD]

Strauss, R.:Der Rosenkavalier, w. L. Della Casa (sop), H. Gueden (sop), S. Jurinac (sop), E. Kunz (bar), O. Edelmann (b-bar). Vienna State Opera Chorus [G] *(rec live in Salzburg, 7/26/60)* Arkadia 3-▲ 213 [ADD]

Strauss, R.:Der Rosenkavalier, w. A. Tomowa-Sintow (sop), J. Perry (sop), A. Baltsa (mez), K. Moll (bass), Vienna State Opera Chorus [G] Deutsche Grammophon 3-▲ 423850-2 [DDD]

Strauss, R.:Der Rosenkavalier (sels), w. L. Della Casa (sop—Feldmarschallin), S. Jurinac (sop—Octavian) *(rec live, Salzburg, 7/26/60)* Arkadia 3-▲ 227 [ADD]

Strauss, R.:Salome, w. H. Behrens (sop), A. Baltsa (mez), H. Angervo (alt), K.W. Böhm (ten), W. Ochman (ten), J. van Dam (bar) EMI Classics 2-▲ CDCB 49358

Strauss, R.:Salome (dance) London ("The Classic Sound" series) ▲ 448582-2

Strauss, R.:Till Eulenspiegels lustige Streiche London ("The Classic Sound" series) ▲ 448582-2

Tchaikovsky, P.:Con Vn, w. Anne-Sophie Mutter (vn) *(rec live, Salzburg 1988)* Deutsche Grammophon ▲ 419241-2 [DDD]

Tchaikovsky, P.:Sym 4 Deutsche Grammophon ▲ 439018-2

Verdi, G.:Aida, w. R. Tebaldi, (sop) G. Simionato (mez), C. Bergonzi (ten), C. MacNeil (bar), A. van Mill (bass), Vienna State Opera Chorus [I] London 3-▲ 414087-2 [ADD]

Verdi, G.:Aida, w. R. Tebaldi (sop), G. Simionato (mez), C. Bergonzi (ten), C. MacNeil (bar), A. van Mill (bass), Vienna State Opera Chorus [I] London ("Jubilee" series) ▲ 417763-2 [ADD]

Verdi, G.:Aida, w. L. Freni (sop), K. Ricciarelli (sop), A. Baltsa (mez), J. Carreras (ten), P. Cappuccilli (bar), G. Raimondi (ten), J. Van Dam (b-bar), Vienna State Opera Chorus [I] EMI Classics (Studio) 3-▲ CDMC 69300 [ADD]

Verdi, G.:Un ballo in maschera, w. J. Barstow (sop), S. Jo (sop), F. Quivar (mez), P. Domingo (ten), L. Nucci (bar), Vienna State Opera Chorus [I] Deutsche Grammophon 2-▲ 427635-2 [DDD]

Verdi, G.:Don Carlos, w. S. Jurinac (sop), G. Simionato (mez), E. Fernandi (ten), E. Bastianini (bar), C. Siepi (b-bar), Vienna State Opera Chorus [I] *(rec live, Salzburg 7/26/58)* Arkadia 2-▲ 220 [ADD]

Verdi, G.:Otello, w. R. Tebaldi (sop), M. Del Monaco (ten), A. Protti (bar) [I] London 2-▲ 411618-2 [ADD]

Verdi, G.:Otello, w. M. Freni (sop), J. Vickers (ten), P. Glossop (bar) *(rec 1971)* Memories 2-▲ MEM 4533 [ADD]

Verdi, G.:Requiem Mass, w. Hilde Zadek (sop), Margarete Klose (cta), Helge Roswaenge (ten), Boris Christoff (bass), Vienna Singverein Stradivarius 2-▲ STV DTM 12323 [ADD]

Verdi, G.:Requiem Mass, w. Anna Tomowa-Sintow (sop), Agnes Baltsa (mez), José Carreras (ten), José Van Dam (bass-bar), Vienna State Opera Chorus, Sofia National Opera Chorus *(rec Great Hall, Musikverein, Vienna, June 1984)* Deutsche Grammophon 2-▲ 439033-2 [DDD]

Vivaldi, A.:Cons Vn, Op. 8/1-4, "The Four Seasons", w. A. S. Mutter (vn) EMI Classics ▲ CDC 47043

Wagner, R.:Siegfried Idyll Deutsche Grammophon ▲ 423613-2 [DDD]

Wagner, R.:Tannhäuser (ov) Deutsche Grammophon ▲ 423613-2 [DDD]

Karajan, Kubelik, Böhm, Jochum (cnd)

Wagner, R.:Ovs, Preludes & Orch Sels, Berlin PO, Bayreuth Festival Orch, Bavarian RSO, Berlin Opera Orch—sels. from Rienzi, Die fliegende Holländer, Tannhäuser, Lohengrin, Parsifal, Die Meistersinger von Nürnberg, Die Walküre, Siegfried, Götterdämmerung *(rec 1958 & 1981)* Deutsche Grammophon ("Double" series) 2-▲ 439687-2 [ADD]

R. Kempe (cnd)

Pfitzner, H.:Palestrina (sels), w. M. Lorenz (ten), P. Schöffler (b-bar)—solo tenor aria & one duet from Act I *(rec live, Salzburg, 8/1/55)* Myto 3-▲ 3 MCD 92259 [ADD]

Wagner, R.:Lohengrin, w. E. Grümmer (sop), C. Ludwig (mez), J. Thomas (ten), D. Fischer-Dieskau (bar), G. Frick (bass), Vienna State Opera Chorus [G] EMI Classics 3-▲ CDCC 49017 [ADD]

I. Kertész (cnd)

Brahms, J.:Serenade 1 Orch London 2-▲ 448200-2

Brahms, J.:Serenade 2 Orch London 2-▲ 448197-2

Brahms, J.:Sym 1 London 2-▲ 448197-2

Brahms, J.:Sym 2 London 2-▲ 448197-2

Brahms, J.:Sym 3 London 2-▲ 448200-2

Brahms, J.:Sym 4 London 2-▲ 448200-2

Brahms, J.:Vars on a Theme by Haydn London 2-▲ 448197-2

Dvořák, A.:Sym 9, "From the New World" London ("Weekend Classics" series) ▲ 417678-2 [AAD]

Mozart, W.A.:Entführung (sels), w. Fritz Wunderlich (ten)—Konstanze, dich wiederzusehen Orfeo d'or ("Festspiel Dokumente" series) ▲ 394301

Mozart, W.A.:Requiem, w. E. Ameling (sop), M. Horne (mez), U. Benelli (bar), T. Franc (bass), Vienna State Opera Chorus London ("Weekend Classics" series) ▲ 417681-2 [ADD] ■ 417681-4

Smetana, B.:The Moldau London ("Weekend Classics" series) ▲ 417678-2 [AAD]

A. Khachaturian (cnd)

Khachaturian, A.:Gayane (sels) London ▲ 425619-2 [ADD]

Khachaturian, A.:Sym 2 London ▲ 425619-2 [ADD]

C. Kleiber (cnd)

Beethoven, L. van:Sym 5 Deutsche Grammophon ▲ 415861-2 [ADD]

Beethoven, L. van:Sym 5 Deutsche Grammophon ("The Originals" series) ▲ 447400-2

Beethoven, L. van:Sym 7 *(rec 1982)* Exclusive ▲ EXL 25 [ADD]

Beethoven, L. van:Sym 7 Deutsche Grammophon ("The Originals" series) ▲ 447400-2

Beethoven, L. van:Sym 7 Deutsche Grammophon ▲ 415862-2 [ADD]

Berg, A.:Wozzeck (sels), w. D. Vejzovic (sop), Vienna Boys' Choir *(rec Feb. 28, 1982)* Exclusive ▲ EXL 47 [ADD]

Brahms, J.:Sym 2 Exclusive ▲ EXL 10 [ADD]

Brahms, J.:Sym 4 Exclusive ▲ EXL 28 [ADD]

Brahms, J.:Sym 4 Deutsche Grammophon ▲ 400037-2 [DDD]

Haydn, J.:Sym 94, "Surprise Sym" *(rec 1982-88)* Exclusive ▲ EXL 13 [ADD]

Kleiber Conducts Strauss Sony Classical ▲ SK 45938 [DDD]

Mozart, W.A.:Sym 33 *(rec Dec. 16, 1979)* Exclusive ▲ EXL 47 [ADD]

Mozart, W.A.:Sym 36 *(rec 1982-88)* Exclusive ▲ EXL 13 [ADD]

New Year's Concert, 1989 CBS 2-▲ MK2 45564 [DDD] ■ MT 45564 (D)

New Year's Concert, 1992 Sony Classical ▲ SK 48376

Still, W.G.:Tristan und Isolde, w. Catarina Ligendza (sop), Ruša Baldani (mez), Hans Hopf (ten), Hans Sotin (bass), Vienna State Opera Chorus *(rec Vienna, Oct. 7, 1973)* Pantheon 3-▲ PHE 6601 (m)

Weber, C.M. von:Der Freischütz (sels) *(rec 1979)* Exclusive ▲ EXL 25 [ADD]

Weber, C.M. von:Ovs—Die Frieschütz Exclusive ▲ EXL 10 [ADD]

Vienna PO (cont.)
E. Kleiber (cnd)
Beethoven, L. van:Sym 3, "Eroica" *(rec 1955)* Theorema 2-▲ TH 121211/212
Mozart, W.A.:Sym 38 Grammofono 2000 ▲ GRM 78609 (m)
Mozart, W.A.:Sym 38 *(rec 1929)* Preiser ▲ 90115 (m) [AAD]
Strauss (II), Joh.:Music of—2 waltzes—Du und Du, Op. 367; Künstlerleben, Op. 316; G. Szell (cnd)—Pizzicato Polka; Tritsch-tratsch Polka, Op. 214; Frühlingsstiummen walzer, Op. 410; An der schönen blauen Donau, Op. 314 *(rec 1929 & 1934)* Preiser ▲ 90115 (m) [AAD]
Strauss, Josef:Music of—Dorfschwalben aus Österreich (waltz), Op. 164 *(rec 1929, issued as HMV C 168)* Preiser ▲ 90115 (m) [AAD]
Strauss, R.:Der Rosenkavalier, w. M. Reining (sop), H. Gueden (sop), S. Jurinac (sop), L. Weber (bass), Vienna State Opera Chorus [G] London ("Historic" series) ▲ 425950-2 (m) [ADD]
O. Klemperer (cnd)
Bruckner, A.:Sym 5 *(rec June 2, 1968)* Music & Arts ▲ CD 836 (s) [ADD]
Bruckner, A.:Sym 5 Topazio ▲ TOP 260411
Mahler, G.:Sym 2, w. Galina Vishnevskaya (sop), Hilde Rössl-Majdan (alt), Vienna Phil Chorus Music & Arts ▲ CD 881 [ADD]
Mahler, G.:Sym 9 *(rec live in Vienna, 6/9/68)* Arkadia 2-▲ 578 (m) [ADD]
Mozart, W.A.:Maurerische Trauermusik [performed in memory of Sen. Robert Kennedy, assassinated June 6, 1968] *(rec live in Vienna, June 9, 1968)* Arkadia 2-▲ 578 (m) [ADD]
Schubert, Franz:Sym 8 *(rec live, 1968)* Enterprise ("Palladio" series) ▲ ENTPD 4208 [ADD]
Wagner, R.:Ovs, Preludes & Orch Sels—Meistersinger—Overture; Tristan—Act 1 Prelude *(rec live, Vienna, 6/16/68)* Arkadia 2-▲ 578 (m) [ADD]
P. Kletzki (cnd)
Mahler, G.:Sym 1 Royal Classics ▲ ROY 6446
H. Knappertsbusch (cnd)
Beethoven, L. van:Con 4 Pno, w. Wilhelm Backhaus (pno) Stradivarius ▲ STV 10002 [ADD]
Bruckner, A.:Sym 3, "Wagner" *(rec 1954)* Andromeda ▲ ANR 2511 [ADD]
Bruckner, A.:Sym 4, "Romantic" *(rec ca. 1950s)* Enterprise ▲ ENT PD 4105
Bruckner, A.:Sym 4, "Romantic" *(rec 1955)* Andromeda ▲ ANR 2502 [ADD]
Bruckner, A.:Sym 5 *(rec 1954)* Andromeda ▲ ANR 2517 [ADD]
Bruckner, A.:Sym 7 *(rec Vienna, Aug. 30, 1949)* Music & Arts ▲ CD 209 [ADD]
Mozart, W.A.:Sym 40 *(rec 1941)* Preiser ▲ PRE 90951 [AAD]
Mozart, W.A.:Sym 41 *(rec 1941)* Preiser ▲ PRE 90951 [AAD]
Schubert, Franz:Sym 9 *(rec live, May 1962)* Music & Arts ▲ MUA CD 936
Strauss (II), Joh.:Music of—Leichtes Blut Polka; Pizzicato Polka *(rec 1940)* Preiser ▲ 90116 (m) [AAD]
Verdi, G.:Aida (sels) Grammofono 2000 ▲ GRM 78522
Verdi, G.:Aida (sels) *(rec 1940)* Preiser ▲ 90116 (m) [AAD]
Wagner, R.:Götterdämmerung (rhine journey & funeral)—Siegfried's Journey; Funeral Music Grammofono 2000 ▲ GRM 78522
Wagner, R.:Ovs, Preludes & Orch Sels—Rienzi Overture *(rec 1940)* Preiser ▲ 90116 (m) [AAD]
Wagner, R.:Rienzi, der Letzte der Tribunen (ov) Grammofono 2000 ▲ GRM 78522
Weber, C.M. von:Euryanthe (ov) *(rec live, May 1962)* Music & Arts ▲ MUA CD 936
K. Kondrashin (cnd)
Beethoven, L. van:Con Vn, Op. 61, w. K.-W. Chung (vn) London ("Jubilee" series) ▲ 425035-2 [ADD]
Beethoven, L. van:Con Vn, Op. 61, w. K.-W. Chung (vn) London ("Ovation" series) ▲ 430752-2 [DDD]
Dvořák, A.:Sym 9, "From the New World" London ("Jubilee" series) ▲ 430702-2 [DDD]
C. Krauss (cnd)
Beethoven, L. van:Sym 2 *(rec 1929-30)* Preiser ▲ PRE 90258
Brahms, J.:Hungarian Dances Orch—Nos. 1 & 3 *(rec 1929-30)* Preiser ▲ PRE 90258
Brahms, J.:Sym 3 *(rec 1930)* Koch Legacy ▲ 3-7129-2 H1
Brahms, J.:Sym 3 *(rec 1929-30)* Preiser ▲ PRE 90258
Bruckner, A.:Sym 4, "Romantic" *(rec 1929-30)* Preiser ▲ PRE 90258
Haydn, J.:Die Jahreszeiten, w. Trude Eipperle (sop), Julius Patzak (ten), Georg Hann (bass), Vienna State Opera Chorus [G] *(rec live, June 1942)* Preiser 2-▲ PRE 93053 [AAD]
Haydn, J.:Die Schöpfung, w. Trude Eipperle (sop), Julius Patzak (ten), Georg Hann (bass), Vienna State Opera Chorus *(rec early 1940's)* Preiser 2-▲ PRE 90104 [AAD]
Haydn, J.:Sym 88 *(rec June 1929)* Koch Legacy ▲ 3-7011-2 (m) [DDD] ■ 3-7011-4 (m)
Haydn, J.:Sym 88 *(rec 6-7/29)* Preiser ▲ 90112 (m) [AAD]
Mozart, W.A.:Nozze di Figaro, w. Irma Beilke (sop), Helena Braun (sop), Gerda Sommerschuh (sop), Josef Witt (ten), Hans Hotter (bar), Erich Kunz (bar), Gustav Neidlinger (b-bar), Vienna State Opera Chorus *(rec live, Salzburg Festival, Aug. 1942)* Preiser 3-▲ PRE 90203 [ADD]
Pfitzner, H.:Von deutscher Seele, w. Trude Eipperle (sop), Luise Willer (mez), Julius Patzak (ten), Ludwig Weber (bass), Vienna State Opera Chorus *(rec Jan 1945)* Preiser 2-▲ PRE 90255 [ADD]
Strauss (II), Joh.:Die Fledermaus, w. H. Gueden (sop), J. Patzak (ten), A. Dermota (ten), A. Jaresch (ten), A. Poell (b-bar), W. Lipp (sop), S. Wagner (mez), K. Preger (ten) *(rec early 1950s)* London ("Historic" series) 2-▲ 425990-2 [AAD]
Strauss (II), Joh.:Music of—Perpetuum Mobile; Annen Polka; Morning Papers Waltz; 1001 Nights Waltz; Liebeslieder Waltz *(rec 1929-31, from HMV 78s)*; Blue Danube Waltz; Egyptian March; Roses from the South *(rec 1940, from Telefunken 78s)*; Voices of Spring *(rec 1940, unissued)* Biddulph ▲ WHL 001 [ADD]
Strauss (II), Joh.:Music of—Im Krapfenwald, Pizzicato Polka, etc. *(rec early 1950s)* London ("Historic" series) 2-▲ 425990-2 [AAD]
Strauss (II), Joh.:Music of—Annen Polka; Die Fledermaus Overture; Leichtes Blut Polka; Liebeslieder Waltz; Morgenblätter Waltz; Perpetuum mobile; Tausend und eine Nacht Waltz; Die Zigeunerbaron (entrance march) *(rec 1929-31 for HMV)* Preiser ▲ 90112 (m) [AAD]
Strauss (II), Joh.:Music of—Frühlingsstimmen, Op. 410; Rosen aus dem Süden, Op. 388; An der schönen blauen Donau, Op. 314; Morgenblätter, Op. 279; Annen Polka, Op. 117; Perpetuum mobile, Op. 257; Ägyptischer Marsch, Op. 335; Tausendundeine Nacht Walzer, Op. 346; Liebeslieder Walzer, Op. 114 *(rec 1929-40)* Iron Needle ▲ 1318 (m) [ADD]
Strauss (II), Joh.:Music of—Morgenblätter; Ägyptischer Marsch; Tausendundeine Nacht; Frühlingsstimmen; Spährenklänge; Feuerfest; Rosen aus dem Süden; An der schönen blauen Donau; others Enterprise ("The Radio Years" series) ▲ ENT RY 57
Strauss (II), Joh.:Der Zigeunerbaron, w. Emmy Loose (sop), Hilde Zadek (sop), Rosette Anday (cta), Julius Patzak (ten), Karl Dönch (bar), Alfred Poell (bar), Steffi Leverenz (sgr), Vienna State Opera Chorus Phonographe 2-▲ PHG 5020 [AAD]
Strauss, Josef:Music of—Sphärenklänge, Op. 235; Feuerfest, Op. 269 *(rec 1929-40)* Iron Needle ▲ 1318 (m) [ADD]
Strauss, Josef:Music of—Sphärenklänge Waltz *(rec 1931 for HMV)* Preiser ▲ 90112 (m) [AAD]
Strauss, Josef:Music of—Music of the Spheres; Feuerfest Polka *(rec 1931 & 1940)* Biddulph ▲ WHL 001 [ADD]
Strauss, R.:Der Bürger als Edelmann (suite) *(rec 1929)* Koch Legacy ▲ 3-7129-2 H1
Strauss, R.:Die Liebe der Danae, w. A. Kupper (sop), J. Traxel (ten), L. Szemere (ten), P. Schöffler (b-bar), Vienna State Opera Chorus [G] *(rec live, Salzburg, 8/14/52)* Melodram 3-▲ MEL 37061 (m) [AAD]
Strauss, R.:Salome (dance) *(rec 1941)* Koch Legacy ▲ 3-7129-2 H1
Ziehrer, C.M.:Weaner Mad'ln Waltz *(rec Jan. 17, 1931 for HMV)* Biddulph ▲ WHL 001 [ADD]
Ziehrer, C.M.:Weaner Mad'ln Waltz *(rec 1/17/31 for HMV)* Preiser ▲ 90112 (m) [AAD]
J. Krips (cnd)
Haydn, J.:Sym 94, "Surprise Sym" *(rec ca. 1957/58)* PWK Classics ▲ PWK 1155
Mozart, W.A.:Don Giovanni, w. S. Danco (sop), L. della Casa (sop), A. Dermota (ten), C. Siepi (b-bar), F. Corena (bass), Vienna State Opera Chorus London 3-▲ 411626-2 [ADD]
R. Kubelik (cnd)
Brahms, J.:Syms (comp) Theorema 3-▲ TH 121147/149
Mozart, W.A.:Kleine Nachtmusik Royal Classics ▲ ROY 6410
Mozart, W.A.:Sym 35 Royal Classics ▲ ROY 6410
Mozart, W.A.:Sym 36 Royal Classics ▲ ROY 6410
Mozart, W.A.:Sym 38 EMI Classics ▲ CDE 67776

Vienna PO (cont.)
R. Kubelik (cnd) (cont.)
Mozart, W.A.:Sym 41 EMI Classics ▲ CDE 67780
Mozart, W.A.:Sym 41 EMI Classics ▲ CDE 67776
Smetana, B.:Má Vlast London ("Weekend Classics" series) ▲ 421167-2 [AAD]
F. Lehár (cnd)
Lehár, F.:Music of, w. E. Réthy (sop), M. Reining (sop), J. Novotna (sop), R. Tauber (ten), Vienna SO—6 orchestral sels. *(Musikalische Memorien I-IV; Die lustige Witwe—Overture; Eva—Prelude)*; 4 Arias from Giuditta *(Du bist meine Sonne—Tauber; Freunde, das Leben ist lebenswert—Tauber; Schön wie die blaue Sommernacht—Novotna & Tauber; Schönste der Frauen—Tauber)*; 1 Song & 5 Arias sung by Esther Réthy *(Wien, du bist das Herz der Welt; Giuditta—Meine Lippen, sie küssenso heiss; Paganini—Liebe, du Himmel auf Erden; Schön ist die Welt—Ich bin verliebt; Der Zarewitsch—Einer wird kommen; Zigeunerliebe—Hör ich Cymbalklänge)*; 2 Arias sung by Maria Reining *(Eva—Im heimlichen Dämmer der silbernen Ampel; Friederike—Warum hast du mich wachgeküsst?) (rec 1934-1942 Odeon & HMV rec)* Preiser ▲ 90150 (m) [AAD]
E. Leinsdorf (cnd)
Mozart, W.A.:Don Giovanni, w. Birgit Nilsson (sop—Donna Anna), Leontyne Price (sop—Donna Elvira), Eugenia Ratti (sop—Zerlina), Cesare Valletti (ten—Don Ottavio), Heinz Blankenburg (bar—Masetto), Fernando Corena (b-bar—Leporello), Arnold van Mill (b-bar—Il Commendatore), Cesare Siepi (b-bar—Don Giovanni), Vienna State Opera Chorus [I] London 3-▲ 444594-2 [ADD]
J. Levine (cnd)
Beethoven, L. van:Missa Solemnis, w. C. Studer (sop), J. Norman (sop), P. Domingo (ten), K. Moll (bass), Leipzig Radio Chorus, Eric Ericson Chamber Chorus Deutsche Grammophon 2-▲ 435770-2 [DDD]
Brahms, J.:Alto Rhap, w. Anne Sofie von Otter (mez), Arnold Schoenberg Choir Deutsche Grammophon ("4D Audio" series) ▲ 439887-2
Brahms, J.:Sym 3 Deutsche Grammophon ("4D Audio" series) ▲ 439887-2
Brahms, J.:Tragic Ov Deutsche Grammophon ("4D Audio" series) ▲ 439887-2
Carmen Fantasy, w. Mutter, Anne-Sophie (vn) Deutsche Grammophon ▲ 437544-2 ■ 437544-4
Mozart, W.A.:Adagio Vn, K.261, w. Itzhak Perlman (vn) Deutsche Grammophon ("Digital Midprice" series) 2-▲ 445535-2 [DDD]
Mozart, W.A.:Cons Vn, w. Itzhak Perlman (vn)—Nos. 1-5 Deutsche Grammophon ("Digital Midprice" series) 2-▲ 445535-2 [DDD]
Mozart, W.A.:Con 1 Vn, w. I. Perlman (vn) Deutsche Grammophon ▲ 415958-2 [DDD]
Mozart, W.A.:Con 2 Vn, w. I. Perlman (vn) Deutsche Grammophon ▲ 415975-2 [DDD]
Mozart, W.A.:Con 3 Vn, w. I. Perlman (vn) Deutsche Grammophon ▲ 410020-2 [DDD]
Mozart, W.A.:Con 3 Vn, w. I. Perlman (vn) Deutsche Grammophon ("3D Classics" series) ▲ 431282-2 [DDD]
Mozart, W.A.:Con 4 Vn, w. I. Perlman (vn) Deutsche Grammophon ▲ 415975-2 [DDD]
Mozart, W.A.:Con 4 Vn, w. I. Perlman (vn) Deutsche Grammophon ("3D Classics" series) ▲ 431282-2 [DDD]
Mozart, W.A.:Con 5 Vn, w. I. Perlman (vn) Deutsche Grammophon ▲ 410020-2 [DDD]
Mozart, W.A.:Così fan tutte, w. Kiri Te Kanawa (sop), Marie McLaughlin (sop), Ann Murray (mez), Hans-Peter Blochwitz (ten), Thomas Hampson (bar), G. Furlanetto (bar), Vienna State Opera Chorus [I] Deutsche Grammophon 3-▲ 423897-2 [DDD]
Mozart, W.A.:Kleine Nachtmusik Deutsche Grammophon ▲ 445555-2
Mozart, W.A.:Missa, K.427, w. K. Battle (sop), L. Cuberli (sop), P. Seiffert (ten), K. Moll (bass), Vienna State Opera Chorus Deutsche Grammophon ▲ 423664-2 [DDD]
Mozart, W.A.:Rondo Vn, K.269, w. I. Perlman (vn) Deutsche Grammophon ("3D Classics" series) ▲ 431282-2 [DDD]
Mozart, W.A.:Rondo Vn, K.269, w. I. Perlman (vn) Deutsche Grammophon ▲ 415958-2 [DDD]
Mozart, W.A.:Rondo Vn, K.373, w. Itzhak Perlman (vn) Deutsche Grammophon ("Digital Midprice" series) 2-▲ 445535-2 [DDD]
Mozart, W.A.:Rondo Vn, K.373, w. I. Perlman (vn) Deutsche Grammophon ▲ 415958-2 [DDD]
Mozart, W.A.:Serenade Ww, K.320 Deutsche Grammophon ▲ 445555-2
Mozart, W.A.:Syms (comp) Deutsche Grammophon 11-▲ 435360-2 [DDD]
Mozart, W.A.:Sym 32 Deutsche Grammophon ▲ 445555-2
Mozart, W.A.:Sym 40 Deutsche Grammophon ▲ 429731-2 [DDD]
Mozart, W.A.:Sym 41 Deutsche Grammophon ▲ 429731-2 [DDD]
Smetana, B.:The Bartered Bride (ov) Deutsche Grammophon ▲ 427340-2 [DDD]
Smetana, B.:The Bartered Bride (dances) Deutsche Grammophon ▲ 427340-2 [DDD]
Smetana, B.:From Bohemian Fields & Groves Deutsche Grammophon ▲ 427340-2 [DDD]
Smetana, B.:Vyšehrad Deutsche Grammophon ▲ 427340-2 [DDD]
Strauss, R.:Ariadne auf Naxos, w. A. Tomowa-Sintow (sop), K. Battle (sop), A. Baltsa (mez), G. Lakes (ten), H. Prey (bar) Deutsche Grammophon 2-▲ 419225-2 [DDD]
Tchaikovsky, P.:Nutcracker Suite Deutsche Grammophon ▲ 437806-2
Tchaikovsky, P.:Sleeping Beauty (suite) Deutsche Grammophon ▲ 437806-2
Tchaikovsky, P.:Swan Lake (suite) Deutsche Grammophon ▲ 437806-2
L. Maazel (cnd)
Beethoven, L. van:Fidelio, w. Birgit Nilsson (sop—Leonore), Graziella Sciutti (sop—Marzelline), Kurt Equiluz (ten—Erster Gefangener), Donald Grobe (ten—Jacquino), James McCracken (ten—Florestan), Tom Krause (bar—Don Pizarro), Hermann Prey (bar—Don Fernando), Kurt Böhme (bass—Rocco), Günther Adam (sgr—Zweiter Gefangener), Vienna State Opera Concert Association Chorus *(rec Sofiensaal, Vienna, Mar 1964)* London 2-▲ 448104-2 [ADD]
Beethoven, L. van:Sym 5 CBS ▲ MDK 44783 [DDD]
Beethoven, L. van:Wellington's Victory, "Battle Sym" CBS ▲ MDK 44901 [DDD]
Beethoven, L. van:Wellington's Victory, "Battle Sym" CBS ▲ MK 37252 [DDD]
Dvořák, A.:Sym 8 Deutsche Grammophon ("Masters" series) ▲ 445510-2 [DDD]
Dvořák, A.:Sym 9, "From the New World" Deutsche Grammophon ("Masters" series) ▲ 445510-2 [DDD]
Lanner, J.:Music of—Die Schönbrunner, Op. 200 *(rec Jan. 1, 1994)* Sony Classical ▲ SK 46694 [DDD]
Mahler, G.:Kindertotenlieder, w. A. Baltsa (mez) [G] CBS 2-▲ M2K 42403 [DDD]
Mahler, G.:Syms Sony Classical 14-▲ SX14K 48198 [DDD]
Mahler, G.:Sym 1 CBS ▲ MDK 44907 [DDD] ■ MDT 44907 (D)
Mahler, G.:Sym 2, w. E. Marton (sop), J. Norman (sop), Vienna State Opera Chorus [G] CBS 2-▲ M2K 38667 [DDD]
Mahler, G.:Sym 3, w. A. Baltsa (mez), Vienna Phil Chorus [G] CBS 2-▲ M2K 42403 [DDD]
Mahler, G.:Sym 4, w. K. Battle (sop) CBS ▲ MDK 44908 [DDD] ■ MDT 44908 (D)
Mahler, G.:Sym 5 CBS ▲ MDK 44782 [DDD] ■ MDT 44782 (D)
Mahler, G.:Sym 5—Adagietto CBS ▲ MDK 44907 [DDD] ■ MDT 44907 (D)
Mahler, G.:Sym 6 CBS 3-▲ M3K 42495 [DDD]
Mahler, G.:Sym 7 CBS 3-▲ M3K 42495 [DDD]
Mahler, G.:Sym 8, w. *(chorus unknown) [G,L]* Sony Classical 2-▲ S2K 45754 [DDD]
Schubert, Franz:Sym 8 CBS ▲ MDK 44783 [DDD]
Strauss, E.:Polkas & Waltzes—Mit Vergnügen [With Pleasure] (polka rapide), Op. 228 *(rec live, Vienna, Jan 1, 1996)* RCA Red Seal 2-▲ 09026-68421-2
Strauss, E.:Polkas & Waltzes—Mit Chic, Op. 221 *(rec Jan. 1, 1994)* Sony Classical ▲ SK 46694 [DDD]
Strauss (I), Joh.:Radetzky March *(rec live, Vienna, Jan 1, 1996)* RCA Red Seal 2-▲ 09026-68421-2
Strauss (I), Joh.:Radetzky March *(rec Jan. 1, 1994)* Sony Classical ▲ SK 46694 [DDD]
Strauss (II), Joh.:Die Fledermaus (sels) [arr. H. Swarowsky] *(rec Jan. 1, 1994)* Sony Classical ▲ SK 46694 [DDD]
Strauss (II), Joh.:Music of—Festival March; Floral Festive Polka; Waldmeister (ov); The Goddess of Reason (ov); Seconds Polka, Op. 258; Furioso-Polka, Op. 278 *(rec live, Vienna, Jan 1, 1996)* RCA Red Seal 2-▲ 09026-68421-2
Strauss (II), Joh.:Music of—Carrousel March, Op. 133; Accelerationen, Op. 234; Lieder Quadrille, Op. 275; L'Enfantillage, Op. 202; Ein Herz, ein Sinn, Op. 323Csárdás; G'schichten aus dem Wienerwald, Op. 325 [w. Maazel & Werner Hink (violins)] Sony Classical ▲ SK 46694 [DDD]
Strauss (II), Joh.:Waltzes—Lagoon Waltz; The Wings of the Phoenix; Emperor Waltz, Op. 437; The Blue Danube, Op. 314 *(rec live, Vienna, Jan 1, 1996)* RCA Red Seal 2-▲ 09026-68421-2

▲ = CD ♦ = Enhanced CD Δ = MD ■ = Cassette Tape □ = DCC

Vienna PO (cont.)

L. Maazel (cnd) (cont.)

Strauss, Josef:Music of—Feuerfest, Op. 269; Aus der Ferne, Op. 270; Ohne Sorgen, Op. 271 *(rec Jan. 1, 1994)* Sony Classical ▲ SK 46694 [DDD]

Strauss, Josef:Music of, w. Lorin Maazel (vn), Lorin Maazel (glock)—The Girl from Nasswald, Op. 267; The Dancing Muse, Op. 266; Jockey Polka, Op. 278 *(rec live, Vienna, Jan 1, 1996)* RCA Red Seal 2-▲ 09026-68421-2

Tchaikovsky, P.:Marche slave CBS ▲ MK 37252 [DDD]

Tchaikovsky, P.:Ov 1812, w. Vienna State Opera Chorus CBS ▲ MDK 44786 [DDD]

Ziehrer, C.M.:Waltzes & Other Dances—Viennese Citizens, Op. 419 *(rec live, Vienna, Jan 1, 1996)* RCA Red Seal 2-▲ 09026-68421-2

C. Mackerras (cnd)

Janácek, L.:The Cunning Little Vixen, w. L. Popp (sop), E. Randová (mez), D. Jedlička (bass) [Cz] London 2-▲ 417129-2 [DDD]

Janácek, L.:The Cunning Little Vixen (suite) [arr Václav Talich; rev Václav Smetáček] London 2-▲ 417129-2

Janácek, L.:From the House of the Dead, w. I. Zítek (sgr), V. Zítek (ten), D. Jedlička (bass), Vienna Opera Chorus London 2-▲ 430375-2 [DDD]

Janácek, L.:Jenůfa, w. L. Popp (sop), E. Söderström (sop), E. Randová (mez), M. Dvorsky (ten), W. Ochman (ten) [Cz] London 2-▲ 414483-2 [DDD]

Janácek, L.:Kát'a Kabanová, w. E. Söderström (sop), N. Kniplová (mez), P. Dvorsky (ten), V. Krejčík (ten), Z. Svehla (ten), D. Jedlica (bass) London 2-▲ 421852-2 [ADD]

Janácek, L.:The Makropulos Affair, w. E. Söderström (sop), V. Krejčík (ten), Z. Švehla (ten), V. Zítek (ten), D. Jedlička (bass), Vienna Opera Chorus London 2-▲ 430372-2 [ADD]

Janácek, L.:Nursery Rhymes London 2-▲ 430375-2 [DDD]

Janácek, L.:Sinfonietta London ▲ 410138-2 [DDD]

Janácek, L.:Taras Bulba London ▲ 410138-2 [DDD]

Janácek, L.:Taras Bulba London ▲ 430727-2 [DDD]

Janácek, L.:Youth London 2-▲ 430375-2 [DDD]

E. Märzendorfer (cnd)

Ginastera, A.:Con Pno, w. Hilde Somer (pno) Phoenix ▲ PHCD 110 [AAD]

Z. Mehta (cnd)

Beethoven, L. van:Con 4 Pno, w. V. Ashkenazy (pno) London ("Jubilee" series) ▲ 430704-2 [ADD]

Beethoven, L. van:Con 5 Pno, "Emperor", w. V. Ashkenazy (pno) London ("Jubilee" series) ▲ 430704-2 [ADD]

Mahler, G.:Sym 2, w. Ileana Cotrubas (sop), Christa Ludwig (cta), Vienna State Opera Chorus *(rec 1975)* London ("Double Decker" series) 2-▲ 440615-2 [ADD]

Mozart, W.A.:Entführung, w. Reri Grist (sop—Blondchen), Anneliese Rothenberger (sop—Konstanze), Gerhard Unger (ten—Pedrillo), Fritz Wunderlich (ten—Belmonte), Fernando Corena (bass—Osmin), Michael Heltau (nar—Selim), Vienna State Opera Chorus *(rec July 28, 1965)* Orfeo d'or ("Festspiel Dokumente" series) 2-▲ 392952 (m)

New Year's Concert 1990 *(rec live, Vienna's Grosser Musikvereinssaal, 1/1/90)* Sony Classical ▲ SK 45808 [DDD]

Schmidt, F.:Sym 4 *(rec 1971)* London ("Double Decker" series) 2-▲ 440615-2 [ADD]

Strauss, E.:Polkas & Waltzes—Electric Polka Sony Classical ▲ SK 66860

Strauss (I), Joh.:Music of—Alice-Polka, Op. 238; Radetzky March Sony Classical ▲ SK 66860

Strauss (I), Joh.:Music of—Indianer (galopp), Op. 111 *(rec live in Vienna, 1/1/90)* Sony Classical ▲ SK 45808 [DDD]

Strauss (I), Joh.:Radetzky March *(rec live in Vienna, 1/1/90)* Sony Classical ▲ SK 45808 [DDD]

Strauss (II), Joh.:Music of—Riding March, Op. 428; Morning Papers Waltz, Op. 279; Trial-Polka, Op. 294; Mephistos Calls from Hell, Op. 101; Perpetuum mobile, Op. 257; Russian March Fant.; The Blue Danube Sony Classical ▲ SK 66860

Strauss (II), Joh.:Music of—polkas—Die Emancipierte, Op. 73; Im Sturmschritt, Op. 348; Tritsch-Tratsch-Polka, Op. 214; Explosions-Polka, Op. 43, waltzes—Donauweibchen; Wiener Blut, Op. 354; Geschichten aus dem Wienerwald, Op. 325; An der schönen, blauen Donau, Op. 314, march—Einzugsmarsch, from Die Zigeunerbaron *(rec live in Vienna, 1/1/90)* Sony Classical ▲ SK 45808 [DDD]

Strauss, Josef:Music of, "New Year's Concert 1990"—three polkas:Eingesendet, Op. 240; Sport-Polka, Op. 170; Sympathie, Op. 73 *(rec live in Vienna, 1/1/90)* Sony Classical ▲ SK 45808 [DDD]

Strauss, Josef:Music of—Arm in Arm [from Polka Mazur, Op. 215]; Favorite Polka, Op. 201; Thalia-Polka Mazur, Op. 195; My Way through Life Is Love & Pleasure; On Vacation Sony Classical ▲ SK 66860

Suppé, F. von:Ovs—The Beautiful Galatea; The Fortune Teller; The Jolly Robbers; Light Cavalry; Morning, Noon & Night in Vienna; Poet & Peasant; The Quen of Spades; Tantalus's Torment; Vienna Jubilation CBS ▲ MK 44932 [DDD]

D. Mitropoulos (cnd)

Brahms, J.:Con Vn, w. Z. Francescatti (vn) *(rec live, Salzburg 8/24/58)* Intaglio ▲ IND 706-1 [ADD]

Mahler, G.:Sym 8, w. *(soloists unknown),* Vienna Phil Chorus Enterprise 2-▲ ENT LV 1000

Mozart, W.A.:Don Giovanni, w. E. Grümmer (sop—D. Anna), R. Streich (sop—Zerlina), L. Della Casa (sop—D. Elvira), L. Simoneau (ten—Don Ottavio), C. Siepi (bass-baritone—Don Giovanni), W. Borry (bass—Masetto), G. Frick (bass—Il Commendatore), F. Corena (bass—Leporello), Vienna State Opera Chorus *(rec Salzburg, July 24, 1956)* Sony Classical 3-▲ SM3K 64263 [ADD]

Mozart, W.A.:Don Giovanni, w. E. Grümmer (sop), L. Della Casa (sop), R. Streich (sop), L. Simoneau (ten), C. Siepi (b-bar), G. Frick (bass), W. Berry (bass), F. Corena (bass), Vienna State Opera Chorus [I] *(rec live, Salzburg, July 24, 1956)* Arkadia 3-▲ 552 (m) [ADD]

Schmidt, F.:Das Buch mit sieben Siegeln, w. Hilde Gueden (sop), Ira Malaniuk (cta), Anton Dermota (ten), Fritz Wunderlich (ten), Walter Berry (bass), Vienna Singverein Sony Classical ("Festspiel Dokumente:Salzburger Festspiele" series) 2-▲ SM2K 68442

Schmidt, F.:Das Buch mit sieben Siegeln, w. H. Gueden (sop), I. Malaniuk (cta), A. Dermota (ten), F. Wunderlich (ten), W. Berry (bass), Vienna Singverein *(rec live, Salzburg Festival 1959)* Melodram 2-▲ MEL 27078

P. Monteux (cnd)

Beethoven, L. van:Sym 1 London ("Double Decker" series) 2-▲ 440627-2

Beethoven, L. van:Sym 3, "Eroica" London ("Double Decker" series) 2-▲ 440627-2

Beethoven, L. van:Sym 6, "Pastorale" London ("Double Decker" series) 2-▲ 440627-2

Beethoven, L. van:Sym 8 London ("Double Decker" series) 2-▲ 440627-2

R. Muti (cnd)

Donizetti, G.:Don Pasquale, w. E. Ravaglia (sop), P. Bottazzo (ten), A. Frati (ten), R. Panerai (bar), F. Corena (bass), Vienna State Opera Chorus [I] *(rec live, Salzburg, 8/11/71)* Melodram 2-▲ CDM 27094 [ADD]

Mozart, W.A.:Clemenza, w. Christine Barbaux (sop—Servilia), Carol Vaness (sop—Viellia), Martha Senn (mez—Annio), Delores Ziegler (mez—Sesto), Gösta Winbergh (ten—Tito), László Polgár (bass—Publio), Vienna State Opera Chorus *(rec live, Salzburg Festival, 1988)* EMI Classics 2-▲ CDCB 55489

Mozart, W.A.:Don Giovanni, w. S. Studer (sop), C. Vaness (sop), W. Shimell (bar), S. Ramey (bass) EMI Classics 3-▲ CDCC 54255

Mozart, W.A.:Don Giovanni (sels), w. C. Studer (sop), C. Vaness (sop) EMI Classics ▲ CDC 54323

Mozart, W.A.:Nozze di Figaro, w. M. Price (sop), K. Battle (sop), M. Nicolesco (sop), A. Murray (mez), J. Hynninen (bar), K. Rydl (bass), Vienna State Opera Chorus [I] EMI Classics 3-▲ CDCC 47978 [DDD]

Mozart, W.A.:Nozze di Figaro (sels), w. M. Price (sop), K. Battle (sop), M. Nicolesco (sop), A. Murray (mez), J. Hynninen (bar), K. Rydl (bass), Vienna State Opera Chorus [I] EMI Classics ▲ CDC 54321

Mozart, W.A.:Sym 36 Philips ▲ 434107-2

Mozart, W.A.:Sym 40 Philips ▲ 434107-2

New Year's Concert From Vienna 1993 Philips ▲ 438493-2 [DDD]

Schubert, Franz:Rosamunde—sels. EMI Classics ▲ CDC 54873

Schubert, Franz:Sym 2 EMI Classics ▲ CDC 54873

M. Olszewska (cnd)

Strauss, R.:Songs, w. L. Lehmann (sop), E. Schumann (sop), R. Mayr (bass) EMI Classics 2-▲ CDHB 64487

S. Ozawa (cnd)

Dvořák, A.:The Noon Witch Philips ▲ 434990-2

Vienna PO (cont.)

S. Ozawa (cnd) (cont.)

Dvořák, A.:Sym 8 Philips ▲ 434990-2

Dvořák, A.:Sym 9, "From the New World" Philips ▲ 432996-2 [DDD]

Rimsky-Korsakov, N.:Russian Easter Festival Philips ▲ 438941-2

Rimsky-Korsakov, N.:Scheherazade Philips ▲ 438941-2

M. Pollini (cnd)

Mozart, W.A.:Con 14 Pno, w. M. Pollini (pno) Exclusive ▲ EXL 35 [AAD]

Mozart, W.A.:Con 20 Pno, w. M. Pollini (pno) Exclusive ▲ EXL 35 [AAD]

A. Previn (cnd)

Dvořák, A.:Con Vc, w. H. Schiff (vc) Philips ▲ 434914-2

Dvořák, A.:Rondo, w. H. Schiff (vc) Philips ▲ 434914-2

Dvořák, A.:Silent Woods, w. H. Schiff (vc) Philips ▲ 434914-2

Orff, C.:Carmina burana, w. B. Bonney (sop), F. Lopardo (ten), A. Michaels-Moore (bar), Arnold Schoenberg Choir, Vienna Boys' Choir Deutsche Grammophon ▲ 439950-2

Strauss (II), Joh.:Die Fledermaus, w. K. Te Kanawa (sop), E. Gruberová (sop), B. Fassbaender (mez), W. Brendel (bar), R. Leech (ten), O. Bär (bar), T. Krause (bar), Vienna State Opera Chorus [G] Philips 2-▲ 432157-2 [DDD]

Strauss (II), Joh.:Die Fledermaus (sels), w. K. Te Kanawa (sop), E. Gruberova (sop), B. Fassbaender (mez), R. Leech (ten), W. Brendel (bar), O. Bär (bar) Philips ▲ 438503-2

Strauss, R.:Eine Alpensinfonie Telarc ▲ CD 80211 [DDD]

Strauss, R.:Also sprach Zarathustra Telarc ▲ CD 80167 [DDD]

Strauss, R.:Capriccio (sels) Deutsche Grammophon ▲ 437790-2 [DDD]

Strauss, R.:Don Juan Telarc ▲ CD 80262 [DDD]

Strauss, R.:Don Quixote, w. F. Bartolomey (vc) Telarc ▲ CD 80262 [DDD]

Strauss, R.:4 Last Songs, w. A. Augér (sop) [G] Telarc ▲ CD 80180 [DDD]

Strauss, R.:Ein Heldenleben [G] Telarc ▲ CD 80180 [DDD]

Strauss, R.:Der Rosenkavalier (suite) Deutsche Grammophon ▲ 437790-2 [DDD]

Strauss, R.:Salome (dance) Deutsche Grammophon ▲ 437790-2 [DDD]

Strauss, R.:Symphonic Interludes Deutsche Grammophon ▲ 437790-2 [DDD]

Strauss, R.:Till Eulenspiegels lustige Streiche EMI Classics ("DDD Midline" series) ▲ CDD 64106 [DDD]

Strauss, R.:Tod und Verklärung Telarc ▲ CD 80167 [DDD]

J. Pritchard (cnd)

Mozart, W.A.:Idomeneo, w. L. Popp (sop), E. Gruberova (sop), A. Baltsa (mez), L. Pavarotti (ten), L. Nucci (bar), Vienna State Opera Chorus [I] London 3-▲ 411805-2 [DDD]

F. Reiner (cnd)

Verdi, G.:Requiem Mass, w. Leontyne Price (sop), Rosalind Elias (mez), Jussi Björling (ten), Giorgio Tozzi (bass), French Musical Society Vocal Group *(rec 1959)* London ("Double Decker" series) 2-▲ 444833-2 [ADD]

Verdi, G.:Requiem Mass, w. L. Price (sop), R. Elias (mez), J. Björling (ten), G. Tozzi (bass), Vienna Singverein [L] London 2-▲ 421608-2 [ADD]

Wagner, R.:Die Meistersinger von Nürnberg, w. I. Seefried (sop), H. Beirer (ten), P. Schoeffler (b-bar), Vienna State Opera Chorus *(rec live, Vienna, 1955)* Melodram 4-▲ MEL 47083

M. Sargent (cnd)

Sibelius, J.:Finlandia, BBC SO EMI Classics ▲ CDE 67787

Sibelius, J.:En Saga, BBC SO EMI Classics ▲ CDE 67787

F. Schalk (cnd)

Beethoven, L. van:Sym 6, "Pastorale" *(rec April 1928)* Preiser ▲ 90111 (m) [AAD]

Beethoven, L. van:Sym 6, "Pastorale" *(rec 1928)* EMI Classics 5-▲ CDHE 64294 [ADD]

Beethoven, L. van:Sym 8 *(rec April 1928)* Preiser ▲ 90111 (m) [AAD]

U. Schirmer (cnd)

Strauss, R.:Capriccio, w. Kiri Te Kanawa (sop—Gräfin), Brigitte Fassbaender (mez—Clairon), Uwe Heilmann (ten—Flamand), Werner Hollweg (ten—Taupe), Olaf Bär (bar—Olivier), Håkan Hagegård (bar—Graf), Victor von Halem (b-bar—La Roche) [G] *(rec Vienna, Dec 1993)* London 2-▲ 444405-2 [DDD]

C. Schuricht (cnd)

Beethoven, L. van:Egmont (ov) *(rec General Assembly, United Nations, New York, Dec. 10, 1956)* Archiphon ▲ ARCH 4.0 (m) [ADD]

Beethoven, L. van:Sym 7 *(rec General Assembly, United Nations, New York, Dec. 10, 1956)* Archiphon ▲ ARCH 4.0 (m) [ADD]

Bruckner, A.:Sym 5 *(rec Vienna, Feb. 24, 1963)* Memories ▲ MEM 4582 [ADD]

Bruckner, A.:Sym 5 Stradivarius 2-▲ STV MSC 2001

Mendelssohn, F.:A Midsummer Night's Dream (sels)—Scherzo *(rec General Assembly, United Nations, New York, Dec. 10, 1956)* Archiphon ▲ ARCH 4.0 (m) [ADD]

Mozart, W.A.:Sym 35 *(rec General Assembly, United Nations, New York, Dec. 10, 1956)* Archiphon ▲ ARCH 4.0 (m) [ADD]

G. Solti (cnd)

Beethoven, L. van:Sym 5 London ▲ 430505-2 [DDD]

Brahms, J.:Con 1 Pno, w. A. Schiff (pno) London ▲ 425110-2 [DDD]

Humperdinck, E.:Hänsel und Gretel, w. L. Popp (sop), B. Fassbaender (mez), J. Hamari (mez), A. Schlemm (mez), W. Berry (bass) London 2-▲ 421111-2 [ADD]

Mendelssohn, F.:Sym 4 London ▲ 440476-2 [DDD]

Mozart, W.A.:Entführung, w. E. Gruberova (sop), K. Battle (sop), G. Winbergh (ten), H. Zednik (ten), M. Talvela (bass), Will Quadflieg (nar) [G] London 2-▲ 417402-2 [DDD]

Mozart, W.A.:Requiem, w. A. Augér (sop), C. Bartoli (mez), V. Cole (ten), R. Pape (bass), Vienna Phil Chorus [L] *(rec live 12/5/91)* London ▲ 433688-2 [DDD] □ 433688-5

Mozart, W.A.:Zauberflöte, w. P. Lorengar (sop), C. Deutekom (sop), S. Burrows (ten), H. Prey (bar), D. Fischer-Dieskau (bar), M. Talvela (bass) [G] London 3-▲ 414568-2

Mozart, W.A.:Zauberflöte, w. S. Jo (sop), R. Ziesak (sop), U. Heilmann (ten), A. Kraus (ten), K. Moll (bass), Vienna State Opera Chorus London 2-▲ 433210-2 [DDD]

Mozart, W.A.:Zauberflöte (sels), w. Pilar Lorengar (sop), Cristina Deutekom (sop), Stuart Burrows (ten), Hermann Prey (bar), Martti Talvela (bass) London ▲ 421302-2 [ADD]

Mozart, W.A.:Zauberflöte (sels), w. S. Jo (sop), R. Ziesak (sop), U. Heilmann (ten), A. Kraus (ten), K. Moll (bass), Vienna State Opera Chorus London ▲ 433667-2 [DDD]

Schubert, Franz:Sym 9 London ▲ 400082-2 [DDD]

Shostakovich, D.:Sym 5 London ▲ 440476-2 [DDD]

Shostakovich, D.:Sym 9 London ▲ 430505-2 [DDD]

The Solti Edition, w. Chicago SO, London PO, London SO, New Philharmonia Orch, Royal Opera House Orch, CO of Europe London 25-▲ 436600-2

Strauss, R.:Arabella, w. L. Della Casa (sop), H. Gueden (sop), I. Malaniuk (cta), A. Dermota (ten), W. Kmentt (ten), G. London (bar), O. Edelmann (bass) [G] London ("Grand Opera" series) 2-▲ 430387-2 [ADD]

Strauss, R.:Elektra, w. B. Nilsson (sop), M. Collier (sop), R. Resnik (mez), G. Stolze (ten), T. Krause (bar) [G] London 2-▲ 417345-2 [ADD]

Strauss, R.:4 Last Songs, w. K. Te Kanawa (sop) [G] London ▲ 430511-2 [DDD]

Strauss, R.:Die Frau ohne Schatten, w. J. Varady (sop), H. Behrens (sop), P. Domingo (ten), J. Van Dam (b-bar), Vienna State Opera Chorus [G] London 3-▲ 436243-2

Strauss, R.:Der Rosenkavalier, w. R. Crespin (sop), H. Donath (sop), Y. Minton (mez), M. Jungwirth (bass) [G] London 3-▲ 417493-2 [ADD]

Strauss, R.:Salome, w. B. Nilsson (sop), G. Hoffman (mez), G. Stolze (ten), W. Kmentt (ten), E. Wächter (bar) [G] London 2-▲ 414414-2 [ADD]

Verdi, G.:Requiem Mass, w. J. Sutherland (sop), M. Horne (mez), L. Pavarotti (ten), M. Talvela (bass), Vienna State Opera Chorus [L] London 2-▲ 411944-2 [ADD]

Wagner, R.:Götterdämmerung, w. B. Nilsson (sop), J. Watson (sop), C. Ludwig (mez), W. Windgassen (ten), D. Fischer-Dieskau (bar), G. Frick (bass) [G] London 4-▲ 414115-2 [ADD]

Wagner, R.:Lohengrin, w. J. Norman (sop), E. Randová (mez), P. Domingo (ten), D. Fischer-Dieskau (bar), S. Nimsgern (b-bar), H. Sotin (bass), Vienna State Opera Chorus [G] London 4-▲ 421053-2 [DDD]

Vienna PO (cont.)
G. Solti (cnd) (cont.)
Wagner, R.:Lohengrin, w. J. Norman (sop), E. Randová (mez), P. Domingo (ten), D. Fischer-Dieskau (bar), S. Nimsgern (b-bar), H. Sotin (bass), Vienna State Opera Chorus [G] London ▲ 425530-2 [DDD]
Wagner, R.:Die Meistersinger von Nürnberg, w. H. Bode (sop), J. Hamari (mez), A. Kollo (ten), N. Bailey (bar), B. Weikl (bar), K. Moll (bass), Vienna State Opera Chorus [G] London 4-▲ 417497-2 [ADD]
Wagner, R.:Ovs, Preludes & Orch Sels—Tristan und Isolde Prelude; Tannhäuser Ov.; Lohengrin Prelude; Die Meistersinger von Nürnberg Prelude & Hymn; Parsifal Prelude London ("Double Decker" series) 2-▲ 440606-2
Wagner, R.:Ovs, Preludes & Orch Sels—Der fliegende Holländer *(Overture)*, Götterdämmerung *(Siegfried's Funeral March)*, Lohengrin *(Prelude to Act 3; Bridal Chorus)*, Tannhäuser *(Overture; Venusberg Music)*, Tristan *(Act 1 Prelude)* London ▲ 440107-2 [ADD/DDD]
Wagner, R.:Parsifal, w. C. Ludwig (mez), A. Kollo (ten), D. Fischer-Dieskau (bar), Z. Kelemen (bar), G. Frick (bass), Vienna State Opera Chorus, Vienna Boys' Choir [G] London 4-▲ 417143-2 [ADD]
Wagner, R.:Das Rheingold, w. K. Flagstad (sop), J. Madeira (mez), S. Svanholm (ten), G. London (bar), G. Neidlinger (b-bar), K. Böhme (bass) [G] London 3-▲ 414101-2 [ADD]
Wagner, R.:Der Ring des Nibelungen, w. B. Nilsson (sop), K. Flagstad (sop), R. Crespin (sop), C. Watson (sop), C. Ludwig (mez), J. Madeira (mez), S. Svanholm (ten), J. King (ten), G. Stolze (ten), W. Windgassen (ten), G. London (bar), D. Fischer-Dieskau (bar), H. Hotter (b-bar), G. Neidlinger (b-bar), G. Frick (bass) [G] London 15-▲ 414100-2 [ADD]
Wagner, R.:Der Ring des Nibelungen (sels), w. Deryck Cooke (nar)—narrated guide to the Ring Cycle w. 193 musical examples London 2-▲ 443581-2
Wagner, R.:Der Ring des Nibelungen (sels), w. B. Nilsson (sop), W. Windgassen (ten), H. Hotter (b-bar) London ▲ 421313-2 [ADD]
Wagner, R.:Der Ring des Nibelungen (orch sels) London ▲ 410137-2 [DDD] □ 410137-5
Wagner, R.:Siegfried, w. B. Nilsson (sop), W. Windgassen (ten), G. Stolze (ten), H. Hotter (b-bar), G. Neidlinger (b-bar) [G] London 4-▲ 414110-2 [ADD]
Wagner, R.:Tannhäuser, w. H. Dernesch (sop), C. Ludwig (mez), A. Kollo (ten), H. Braun (bar), H. Sotin (bass) [Paris version] [G] London 3-▲ 414581-2 [ADD]
Wagner, R.:Tristan und Isolde, w. B. Nilsson (sop), R. Resnik (mez), H.-M. Uhle (ten), R. Krause (ten), A. van Mill (bass) [G] London ("Grand Opera" series) 4-▲ 430234-2 [ADD]
Wagner, R.:Die Walküre, w. B. Nilsson (sop), R. Crespin (sop), C. Ludwig (mez), J. King (ten), H. Hotter (b-bar), G. Frick (bass) [G] London 4-▲ 414105-2 [ADD]
Wagner, R.:Die Walküre (magic fire) London ▲ 440107-2 [ADD/DDD]
Wagner, R.:Die Walküre (ride of the valkyries) London ▲ 440107-2 [ADD/DDD]

H. Stein (cnd)
Beethoven, L. van:Con 5 Pno, "Emperor", w. F. Gulda (pno) *(rec ca. 1971)* PWK Classics ▲ PWK 1146 [AAD]
Verdi, G.:Don Carlos, w. Gundula Janowitz (sop), Shirley Verrett (mez), Franco Corelli (ten), Eberhard Waechter (bar), Nicolai Ghiaurov (bass), Martti Talvela (bass), Vienna State Opera Chorus *(rec Vienna, Oct. 25, 1970)* Pantheon 2-▲ PHE 6614

R. Strauss (cnd)
Strauss, R.:Orchestral Music (comp)—Don Juan, Op. 20; Till Eulenspiegels lustige Streiche, Op. 28; Also sprach Zarathustra, Op. 30; Ein Heldenleben, Op. 40; Der Bürger als Edelmann, Op. 60; Tod und Verklärung, Op. 24; Sinf. Domestica, Op. 53 *(rec Feb. & June 1944)* Preiser 3-▲ PRE 90216 [ADD]

G. Szell (cnd)
Beethoven, L. van:Con Vn, Op. 61, w. B. Huberman (vn)—Allegro ma non troppo; Larghetto; Rondo *(rec 1934)* Preiser ▲ 90118 (m)
Beethoven, L. van:Con Vn, Op. 61, w. Branislaw Huberman (vn) *(rec June 18-20, 1934)* APR ("Signature" series) ▲ APR 5506 [ADD]
Lalo, E.:Sym espagnole, w. Branislaw Huberman (vn) *(rec 1934 for Columbia Records)* The Classical Collector ▲ FDC 2003 (m) [AAD]
Lalo, E.:Sym espagnole, w. Branislaw Huberman (vn) *(rec June 20 & 22, 1934)* APR ("Signature" series) ▲ APR 5506 [ADD]
Lalo, E.:Sym espagnole, w. Branislaw Huberman (vn)—Allegro non troppo; Scherzando; Andante; Rondo *(rec 1934)* Preiser ▲ 90118 (m)
Liebermann, R.:Die Schule der Frauen, w. Anneliese Rothenberger (sop—Agnes), Christa Ludwig (mez—Georgette), Nicolai Gedda (ten—Horace), Alois Pernerstorfer (b-bar—Gronte), Walter Berry (bass—Poquelin), Kurt Böhme (bass—Arnolphe) *(rec Salzburg, Aug 17, 1957)* Orfeo d'or ("Festspiel Dikumente" series) 2-▲ C 429962 (m) [ADD]
Mozart, W.A.:Entführung (sels), w. Erika Köth (sop), Rudolf Schock (ten)—Welch' ein Geschick Orfeo d'or ("Festspiel Dokumente" series) ▲ 394201
Mozart, W.A.:Zauberflöte, w. L. Della Casa (sop), E. Köth (sop), G. Sciurri (sop), L. Simoneau (ten), W. Berry (bass), K. Böhme (bass), Vienna State Opera Chorus [G] *(rec live at the Salzburg Festival, July 27, 1959)* Melodram ("Connaisseur" series) 2-▲ MEL 27505 (m) [AAD]
Strauss (II), Joh.:Waltzes—An der schönen blauen Donau, Walzer Op. 314; Frühlingsstimmen, Walzer Op. 410 *(rec 1934)* Preiser ▲ 90118 (m)

A. Toscanini (cnd)
Mozart, W.A.:Zauberflöte, w. Jarmila Novotna (sop), Helge Roswaenge (ten), Alexander Kipnis (bass), Julie Osvath (sgr), Vienna State Opera Chorus Enterprise ("The 40's" series) 2-▲ ENT 321
Mozart, W.A.:Zauberflöte, w. D. Komarek (sop), J. Novotna (sop), J. Osvath (sop), H. Roswaenge (ten), W. Domgraf-Fassbaender (bar), A. Kipnis (bass), Vienna Phil Chorus [G] *(rec live, Salzburg, July 30, 1937)* Melodram 3-▲ MEL 37040 (m) [AAD]
Mozart, W.A.:Zauberflöte (sels), w. Helge Roswaenge (ten), Helge Roswaenge (ten) *(Dies Bildnis ist bezaubernd schön)*, Jarmila Novotna (sop), Willy Domgraf-Fassbaender (bar) *(Bei Männern, welche Liebe fühlen)*, Alexander Kipnis (bass) *(In diesen heil'gen Hallen)* Orfeo d'or ("Festspiel Dokumente" series) ▲ 394101
Verdi, G.:Falstaff, w. Dino Borgioli (ten), Ismildo Tedeschi (ten), Mariano Stabile (bar), Vienna State Opera Chorus *(rec live, Salzburg Festival, 1936)* Arkadia 2-▲ 625
Verdi, G.:Falstaff, w. Augusta Ottrabella (sop—Nannetta), Franca Somigli (sop—Alice), Angelica Cravcenko (mez—Mrs. Quickly), Mita Vasari (mez—Meg), Dino Borgioli (ten—Fenton), Giuseppe Nessi (ten—Bardolfo), Alfredo Tedeschi (ten—Dr. Cajus), Piero Biasini (bar—Ford), Mariano Stabile (bar—Falstaff), Virgilio Lazzari (bass—Pistola), Vienna State Opera Chorus *(rec Salzburg, Aug 23, 1937)* Minerva 2-▲ MN A36/37 (m) [ADD]
Wagner, R.:Die Meistersinger von Nürnberg, w. M. Reining (sop), H. Noort (ten), A. Dermota (ten), H. H. Nissen (bar), H. Alsen (bass) *(rec live, Salzburg, 1937)* Melodram 4-▲ MEL 47041

B. Walter (cnd)
Beethoven, L. van:Con 5 Pno, "Emperor", w. W. Giesking (pno) *(rec 1939)* Grammofono 2000 ▲ GRM 78506 [ADD]
Beethoven, L. van:Con 5 Pno, "Emperor", w. Walter Gieseking (pno) *(rec Vienna, Sept. 10 & 11, 1934)* APR ▲ APR 5512 [ADD]
Beethoven, L. van:Con 5 Pno, "Emperor", w. Walter Gieseking (pno) Enterprise ("The Radio Years" series) ▲ ENT RY 61
Beethoven, L. van:Leonore 3 *(rec Vienna, 1936)* Grammofono 2000 ▲ GRM 78517 [ADD]
Beethoven, L. van:Leonore 3 *(rec May 21, 1936)* Koch Legacy ▲ 370112 (m) [DDD] ■ 370114 (m)
Beethoven, L. van:Leonore 3 Enterprise ("Sirio" series) ▲ ENT SO 53005
Beethoven, L. van:Leonore 3 *(rec between 1935-36)* Preiser ▲ PRE 90157 [AAD]
Beethoven, L. van:Ovs—Leonore No. 3 *(rec 5/21/36)* Koch Legacy ▲ 3-7011-2 (m) [DDD] ■ 3-7011-4 (m)
Beethoven, L. van:Sym 6, "Pastorale" *(rec between 1935-36)* Preiser ▲ PRE 90157 [AAD]
Brahms, J.:Sym 1 Enterprise ("Sirio" series) ▲ ENT SO 53005
Brahms, J.:Sym 1 *(rec 5/37)* Preiser ▲ 90114 (m) [AAD]
Brahms, J.:Sym 1 *(rec Vienna, 1937)* Grammofono 2000 ▲ GRM 78517 [ADD]
Brahms, J.:Sym 3 *(rec 1936 for HMV)* Koch Legacy ▲ 3-7120-2 H1
Bruckner, A.:Te Deum, w. Hilde Güden (sop), Hilde Zadeck (cta), Erich Majkut (ten), Gottlob Frick (bass), Vienna State Opera Chorus *(rec live, 1955)* Enterprise ("Palladio" series) ▲ ENTPD 4209 [ADD]
Haydn, J.:Sym 96, "Miracle" *(rec 5/37)* Preiser ▲ 90114 (m) [AAD]

Vienna PO (cont.)
B. Walter (cnd) (cont.)
Haydn, J.:Sym 96, "Miracle" *(rec 1937)* Pearl ▲ PEA 9945 (m) [AAD]
Haydn, J.:Sym 100, "Military" Grammofono 2000 ▲ GRM 78629
Haydn, J.:Sym 100, "Military" *(rec Jan. 10, 1938; from HMV D)* Preiser ▲ 90141 (m) [AAD]
Mahler, G.:Kindertotenlieder, w. K. Ferrier (cta) [G] EMI Classics ("Great Recordings of the Century" series) ▲ CDH 61003 (m)
Mahler, G.:Das Lied von der Erde, w. Kerstin Thorborg (mez), Charles Kullmann (ten) *(rec Vienna, May 1936)* Grammofono 2000 ▲ GRM 78553
Mahler, G.:Das Lied von der Erde, w. K. Thorberg (mez), C. Kullman (ten) Enterprise ("Palladio" series) ▲ ENTPD 4172 [ADD]
Mahler, G.:Songs, w. E. Schwarzkopf (sop)—Ich atmet' einen Linden Duft; Ich bin der Welt abhanden gekommen; Wo die schönen Trumpeten blasen [G] *(rec live, May 29, 1960)* Music & Arts 2-▲ CD 705-2 [AAD]
Mahler, G.:Songs, w. K. Thorborg (mez)—Ich bin der Welt abhanden gekommen [G] *(rec live, Vienna, 5/24/36)* Music & Arts ▲ CD 749-1 (m) [AAD]
Mahler, G.:Songs, w. E. Schwarzkopf (sop) *(rec May, 1960)* Arkadia ▲ 767 [ADD]
Mahler, G.:Songs from Rückert, w. K. Thorborg (mez)—Ich bin der Welt abhanden gekommen [G] *(rec live in the Musikvereinsaal, Vienna, 5/24/36)* Pearl ▲ PEA 9413 (m) [AAD]
Mahler, G.:Sym 4, w. E. Schwarzkopf (sop) *(rec live, May 29, 1960)* Music & Arts 2-▲ CD 705-2 [AAD]
Mahler, G.:Sym 4, w. E. Schwarzkopf (sop) *(rec May 1960)* Arkadia ▲ 767 [ADD]
Mahler, G.:Sym 5—Adagietto *(rec 1/38)* Preiser ▲ 90114 (m) [AAD]
Mahler, G.:Sym 5—Adagietto *(rec live in the Musikvereinsaal, Vienna, 1/15/38)* Pearl ▲ PEA 9413 (m) [AAD]
Mahler, G.:Sym 5—Adagietto *(rec Jan. 15, 1938)* Music & Arts ▲ CD 749-1 (m) [AAD]
Mahler, G.:Sym 9 *(rec 1938)* EMI Classics ("Great Recordings of the Century" series) ▲ CDH 63029 (m) [ADD]
Mahler, G.:Sym 9 Enterprise ("Palladio" series) ▲ ENTPD 4172 [ADD]
Mozart, W.A.:Con 20 Pno, w. B. Walter (pno) *(rec 1937, from Victor M 420)* Pearl ▲ PEA 9940 (m) [AAD]
Mozart, W.A.:Con 20 Pno, w. B. Walter (pno) *(rec May 7, 1937; from HMV DB)* Preiser ▲ 90141 (m) [AAD]
Mozart, W.A.:Con 20 Pno, w. B. Walter (pno) EMI Classics ("Great Recordings of the Century" series) 3-▲ CDHC 63912
Mozart, W.A.:Don Giovanni, w. L. Helletsgruber (sop), E. Rethberg (sop), M. Bokor (mez), D. Borgioli (ten), K. Ettl (bass), E. Pinza (bass), Vienna State Opera Chorus *(rec Salzburg, Aug. 2, 1937)* Melodram 3-▲ MLO 37506 [ADD]
Mozart, W.A.:German Dances, K.605 *(rec 1937, from HMV DA 1570)* Pearl ▲ PEA 9940 (m) [AAD]
Mozart, W.A.:German Dances, K.605 EMI Classics ("Great Recordings of the Century" series) 3-▲ CDHC 63912
Mozart, W.A.:Kleine Nachtmusik *(rec 1937, from HMV DB 3075/6)* Pearl ▲ PEA 9940 (m) [AAD]
Mozart, W.A.:Kleine Nachtmusik EMI Classics ("Great Recordings of the Century" series) 3-▲ CDHC 63912
Mozart, W.A.:Nozze di Figaro, w. Jarmila Novotna (sop), Aulikki Rautawaara (sop), Esther Réthy (sop), Agostino Lazzari (ten), Mariano Stabile (bar), Ezio Pinza (bass), Vienna State Opera Chorus *(rec live, 1937)* Melodram ▲ CDI 205003
Mozart, W.A.:Ovs— Le nozze di Figaro EMI Classics ("Great Recordings of the Century" series) 3-▲ CDHC 63912
Mozart, W.A.:Requiem, w. Lisa della Casa (sop), Ira Malaniuk (cta), Anton Dermota (ten), Cesare Siepi (b-bar), Vienna State Opera Chorus *(rec Salzburg, July 26, 1956)* Orfeo d'or ("Festspiel Dikumente" series) ▲ C 430961 (m) [ADD]
Mozart, W.A.:Requiem, w. E. Schumann (sop), K. Thorborg (mez), A. Dermota (ten), A. Kipnis (bass), Vienna State Opera Chorus EMI Classics ("Great Recordings of the Century" series) 3-▲ CDHC 63912
Mozart, W.A.:Sym 25 *(rec Salzburg, July 26, 1956)* Orfeo d'or ("Festspiel Dikumente" series) ▲ C 430961 (m) [ADD]
Mozart, W.A.:Sym 38 *(rec 1937)* Pearl ▲ PEA 9940 (m) [AAD]
Mozart, W.A.:Sym 38 EMI Classics ("Great Recordings of the Century" series) 3-▲ CDHC 63912
Mozart, W.A.:Sym 41 EMI Classics ("Great Recordings of the Century" series) 3-▲ CDHC 63912
Mozart, W.A.:Sym 41 *(rec Jan. 11, 1938; from HMV D)* Preiser ▲ 90141 (m) [AAD]
Mozart, W.A.:Sym 41 Enterprise ("Palladio" series) ▲ ENTPD 4169 [ADD]
Schubert, Franz:Sym 8 *(rec Vienna, May 29, 1960)* Music & Arts 2-▲ CD 705-2 [ADD]
Schubert, Franz:Sym 8 Enterprise ("Palladio" series) ▲ ENTPD 4169 [ADD]
Schubert, Franz:Sym 8 *(rec 1937)* Pearl ▲ PEA 9945 (m) [AAD]
Wagner, R.:Siegfried Idyll Enterprise ("Palladio" series) ▲ ENTPD 4169 [ADD]
Wagner, R.:Siegfried Idyll *(rec between 1935-36)* Preiser ▲ PRE 90157 [AAD]
Wagner, R.:Die Walküre (act 1), w. L. Lehmann (sop), E. List (bass) [G] *(rec 6/20-22/35)* Danacord 2-▲ DACOCD 317/18 (m)
Wagner, R.:Die Walküre (act 1), w. L. Lehmann (sop), L. Melchior (ten), E. List (bass) *(rec 1935)* EMI Classics ("Great Recordings of the Century" series) ▲ CDH 61020 (m) [ADD]

F. von Weingartner (cnd)
Beethoven, L. van:Con Vn, Vc & Pno, "Triple Con", w. R. Odnoposoff (vn), S. Auber (vc), A. Morales (pno) *(rec 10/20-21/37)* Pearl ▲ PEA 9358 (m) [AAD]
Beethoven, L. van:Sym 3, "Eroica" *(rec May 1936)* Preiser ▲ 90113 (m) [AAD]
Beethoven, L. van:Sym 8 *(rec February 1936)* Preiser ▲ 90113 (m) [AAD]
Beethoven, L. van:Sym 9, "Choral Sym" [soloists L. Helletsgrüber, R. Anday, G. Maikl, R. Mayr] *(rec 1935 for Columbia Records)* Music Memoria ▲ 30378
Beethoven, L. van:Sym 9, "Choral Sym", w. Vienna State Opera Chorus [G] *(rec 1935)* Pearl ▲ PEA 9407 (m) [AAD]
Beethoven, L. van:Sym 9, "Choral Sym", w. Luise Helletsgruber (sop), Rosette Anday (cta), Georg Maikl (ten), Richard Mayr (bass), Vienna State Opera Chorus *(rec Feb. 2-5, 1935)* Preiser ▲ PRE 90193 [ADD]

Zimerman, Bernstein (cnd)
Beethoven, L. van:Cons Pno (comp), w. K. Zimerman (pno) *(rec 1989)* Deutsche Grammophon 3-▲ 435467-2 [DDD]

Vienna PO String Quartet
Schubert, Franz:Qt 14 Strs London ▲ 417459-2 [ADD]

Vienna Philharmonic Trio [Peter Wächter (vn), Martin Lemberg (va), Robert Nagy (vc)]
Mozart, W.A.:Trio Vn Va *(rec Studio Baumgarten, Vienna, Sept 1995)* Camerata ▲ 30 CM 417 [DDD]
Schubert, Franz:Trio 2 Strs *(rec Studio Baumgarten, Vienna, Sept 1995)* Camerata ▲ 30 CM 417 [DDD]

Vienna Piano Trio [Stefan Mendl (pno), Wolfgang Redik (vn), Marcus Trefny (vc)]
Brahms, J.:Trio 1 Pno *(rec Mar. 1993)* Naxos ▲ 8.550746 [DDD]
Brahms, J.:Trio 2 Pno *(rec Mar. 1993)* Naxos ▲ 8.550746 [DDD]
Brahms, J.:Trio 3 Pno *(rec Sept. 30-Oct. 3, 1993)* Naxos ▲ 8.550747 [DDD]
Brahms, J.:Trio in A Pno (posth) *(rec Sept. 30-Oct. 3, 1993)* Naxos ▲ 8.550747 [DDD]
Dvořák, A.:Trio 1 Pno *(rec Concert Hall of the Nimbus Foundation, Wyastone Leys, Monmouth, May 24-27, 1995)* Nimbus ▲ NI 5472 [DDD]
Dvořák, A.:Trio 4 Pno, "Dumky" *(rec Concert Hall of the Nimbus Foundation, Wyastone Leys, Monmouth, May 24-27, 1995)* Nimbus ▲ NI 5472 [DDD]

Vienna Pro Musica Orch
M. Gielen (cnd)
Bartók, B.:Con 2 Pno, w. György Sándor (pno) *(rec 1959)* Tuxedo ▲ TUXCD 1014
Bartók, B.:Con 3 Pno, w. György Sándor (pno) *(rec 1959)* Tuxedo ▲ TUXCD 1014
V. Hladky (cnd)
Hummel, J.N.:Con Mand & Strs, w. Edith Bauer-Slais (mand) *(rec 1973)* Tuxedo ▲ TUXCD 1026
H. Hollreiser (cnd)
Honegger, A.:Concertino Pno & Orch, w. W. Klien (pno) Allegretto ▲ ACD 8157 [ADD] ■ ACS 8157

▲ = CD ♦ = Enhanced CD Δ = MD ■ = Cassette Tape □ = DCC

Vienna Pro Musica Orch (cont.)
M. Lange (cnd)
Mendelssohn, F.:Con in a Pno, Op. posth., w. Rena Kyriakou (pno)—Allegro; Adagio; Finale Allegro ma non tropo Tuxedo ▲ TUXCD 1011
H. Swarowsky (cnd)
Mendelssohn, F.:Capriccio brillante, w. Rena Kyriakou (pno)—Andante Allegro con fuoco Tuxedo ▲ TUXCD 1011
Mendelssohn, F.:Rondo brilliant, w. Rena Kyriakou (pno)—Presto Tuxedo ▲ TUXCD 1011
Mendelssohn, F.:Serenade & Allegro giocoso, w. Rena Kyriakou (pno)—Andante; Allegro giocoso Tuxedo ▲ TUXCD 1011
Vienna Quintet [Hansgeorg Schmeiser (fl), Harald Hörth (ob), Helmut Hödl (cl), Martin Bramböck (hn), Maximilian Feyertag (bn)]
Danzi, F.:Qnts Ww, Op. 56—No. 2 Nimbus ▲ NI 5479 [DDD]
Farkas, F.:Antique Hungarian Dances Nimbus ▲ NI 5479 [DDD]
Haydn, J.:Divert for 2 Obs, Hns, Bns & Serpent, H.II/46 Nimbus ▲ NI 5479 [DDD]
Mozart, W.A.:Divert Obs, K.213 Nimbus ▲ NI 5479 [DDD]
Mozart, W.A.:Zauberflöte Winds [duets for fl & cl] Nimbus ▲ NI 5479 [DDD]
Takács, J.:Serenade nach Alt-Grazer Kontratänzen Nimbus ▲ NI 5479 [DDD]
Vienna RSO
M. Caridis (cnd)
Kalomiris, M.:Sym 1, w. Vienna Singverein *(rec live, 10/31/86)* Koch Schwann ▲ CD 311110 [ADD]
F. Lehár (cnd)
Lehár, F.:Giuditta (sels), w. Vienna Opera Chorus Bel Age 2-▲ BLA 103.352
Lehár, F.:Paganini (sels), w. Vienna Radio Chorus Bel Age 2-▲ BLA 103.351
Lehár, F.:Schön ist die Welt (sels) Bel Age 2-▲ BLA 103.352
Lehár, F.:Wo die Lerche singt (sels), w. Vienna Radio Chorus Bel Age 2-▲ BLA 103.352
K. Tenner (cnd)
Marschner, H.A.:Der Vampyr, w. L. Synek (sop), L. Heppe (ten), G. Oeggl (bar), Rathauscher (sgr), Skladal (sgr), Sperlbauer (sgr), Weise (sgr), Vienna Radio Chorus [G] *(rec live, Vienna, 4/9/51)* Memories 2-▲ HR 4466/67 [ADD]
Vienna Radio Winds
M. Turkovic (cnd)
Dvořák, A.:Serenade Ww *(rec live, Vienna, Aug 26-27, 1994)* Camerata ▲ 30CM 406 [DDD]
Eder, H.:Suite with Intermezzi *(rec live, Vienna, May 12, 1994)* Camerata ▲ 30CM 406 [DDD]
Strauss, R.:Serenade Ww *(rec Studio Baumgarten, Vienna, Apr 17, 1994)* Camerata ▲ 30CM 406 [DDD]
Vienna Recorder Ensemble
Musik der Renaissance Tudor ▲ 719
Vienna Ring Ensemble
Lehár, F.:Die lustige Witwe (sels)—Da geh' ich zu Maxim; Vilja Lied; Lippen schweigen; Ja, das Studium der Weiber *(rec Ishihara Hall, Osaka, Oct. 1993)* Platz ▲ PLZ 618
Mozart, W.A.:German Dances, K.602 *(rec Vienna, Sept. 1984)* Platz ▲ PLCC 558
Nicolai, O.:Lustigen Weiber (ov) *(rec Ishihara Hall, Osaka, Oct. 1993)* Platz ▲ PLZ 618
Strauss (II), Joh.:Die Fledermaus (sels)—Ov.; Quadrille; Czárdás; Tick, Tack [Duet] *(rec Ishihara Hall, Osaka, Oct. 1993)* Platz ▲ PLZ 618
Strauss (II), Joh.:Der Zigeunerbaron (sels)—Ov.; Wer uns getraut; Ja, das alles auf Ehr'; Ja, das Schreiben und das Lesen *(rec Ishihara Hall, Osaka, Oct. 1993)* Platz ▲ PLZ 618
Vienna Ring Ensemble [Paul Guggenberger (vn), Peter Götzel (vn), Alois Posch (db)]
Beethoven, L. van:German Dances, WoO 8—Nos. 1-8 & 12 *(rec Vienna, Sept. 1984)* Platz ▲ PLCC 558
Haydn, J.:German Dances, H.IX/12, "Tedeschi di ballo" *(rec Vienna, Sept. 1984)* Platz ▲ PLCC 558
Mozart, W.A.:German Dances, K.600 *(rec Vienna, Sept. 1984)* Platz ▲ PLCC 558
Mozart, W.A.:German Dances, K.605—Nos. 1 & 3 *(rec Vienna, Sept. 1984)* Platz ▲ PLCC 558
Vienna Sinfonietta
K. Rapf (cnd)
Dittersdorf, K.D. von:Syms (Metamorphoses) Calig 2-▲ CAL 50885/86 [DDD]
Vienna State Opera CO
V. Golschmann (cnd)
Bach, J.S.:Cons Vn (comp), w. M. Elman (vn)—No. 2 *(rec June 1960)* Vanguard Classics ▲ OVC 8033 [ADD]
Nardini, P.:Con Vn, w. M. Elman (vn) *(rec June 1960)* Vanguard Classics ▲ OVC 8033 [ADD]
Vivaldi, A.:Cons Vn (misc), w. M. Elman (vn) *(rec June 1960)* Vanguard Classics ▲ OVC 8033 [ADD]
Vienna State Opera Orch
Arias & Duets (1974-1986), w. Giuseppe Taddei (bar), P. Domingo (ten), L. Pavarotti (ten), et al., Vienna State Opera Orch [var. cnd] Acanta ▲ 49402
German University Songs, w. [cnd:Franz Litschauer], Vienna State Opera Men's Chorus, Erich Kunz (bar) Vanguard Classics ▲ OVC 6009 [ADD]
German University Songs, Vol. 2, w. Erich Kunz (bar), Vienna State Opera Male Chorus [cnd:Anton Paulik] *(rec Brahmssaal, Musikverein, Vienna, June 1956)* Vanguard Classics ▲ OVC 6010 [ADD]
Recital, w. Anton Dermota (ten), Vienna State Opera Orch [cnd:K. Böhm, J. Krips, R. Moralt, et al.] *(rec live, 1942-1970)* Melodram 2-▲ CDM 26522 [AAD]
Vienna State Opera:Historic Live Recordings, 1933-1944 *(rec 1933-1944)* Koch Schwann ▲ SCH 314502 [DDD]
Vienna State Opera Live, Vol. 1:1933-36 Koch Schwann 2-▲ SCH 314512 [ADD]
Vienna State Opera Live, Vol. 4, 1933-1942 *(rec 1933-1942)* Koch Schwann 2-▲ SCH 314542 [ADD]
C. Abbado (cnd)
Mussorgsky, M.:Khovanshchina, w. M. Lipovsek (mez), V. Atlantov (ten), P. Burchuladze (bass), A. Haugland (bass), Slovak Phil Chorus [Shostakovich version] [R] Deutsche Grammophon 3-▲ 429758-2 [DDD]
Adler, Buketoff (cnd)
Gottschalk, L.M.:Music of, w. Trinidad Paniagua (sop), José Alberto Esteves (ten), Pablo Garcia (bar), Eugene List (pno), Cary Lewis (pno), Brady Millican (pno), Berlin SO—Grande Tarantelle for Piano & Orchestra, Op. 67; Symphony No. 1, "La nuit des tropiques"; Symphony No. 2, "A Montevideo"; The Union (concert paraphrase on American national airs) for Piano & Orchestra, Op. 48; Variations on the Portuguese National Hymn for Piano & Orchestra, Op. 91; Grande fantaisie triomphale sur l'hymne national brésilien for Piano & Orchestra, Op. 69; Marche solennelle for Orchestra; Marcha triunfal y final de opera for Orchestra; Escenas campestres (opera in one act); Five Pieces for Piano Duet [Radieuse, Op. 72; Ses yeux, Op. 66; La Gallina, Op. 53; Ojos criollos, Op. 37; Pasquinade, Op. 59] Vox Box 2-▲ CDX 5009 [ADD]
K. Alwin (cnd)
Mascagni, P.:Cavalleria rusticana (sels), w. Alfred Piccaver (ten—Turiddu), Emil Schipper (bar—Alfio) *(rec May 10, 1937)* Koch Schwann 2-▲ SCH 314632 [ADD]
Mozart, W.A.:Entführung (sels), w. Maria Ivogün (sop), Leo Slezak (ten), Richard Tauber (ten)—Hier soll ich dich; Konstanzel... wie ängstlich; Martern aller Arten *(rec 1905 - 1944)* Minerva ▲ MN A14 [ADD]
Rosette Anday, w. Rosette Anday (cta), Berlin State Opera Orch [cnd:Julius Prüwer], London SO [cnd:Robert Heger] Preiser ("Lebendige Vergangenheit" series) ▲ PRE 89046 (m) [AAD]
Verdi, G.:Aida (sels), w. Maria Nemeth (sop—Aida), Rosette Anday (cta—Amneris), Benjamino Gigli (ten—Radames), Alexander Kipnis (bass—Ramfis) *(rec May 23, 1937)* Koch Schwann 2-▲ SCH 314632 [ADD]
G. Barati (cnd)
Haydn, J.:Mass 6, "Nikolai-messe", "6/4-Takt-Messe", w. Elisabeth Thoman (sop), Rose Bahl (cta), Kurt Equiluz (ten), Vienna Academy Chamber Choir *(rec 1964)* Tuxedo ▲ TUXCD 1055 [ADD]
Haydn, J.:Mass 14, "Harmoniemesse", w. Christiane Sorell (sop), Elisabeth Thoman (sop), Rose Bahl (cta), Maura Moreira (cta), Kurt Equiluz (ten), Gerhard Eder (bass), P. Wimburger (bass), Vienna Academy Chamber Choir *(rec 1964)* Tuxedo ▲ TUXCD 1055 [ADD]

Vienna State Opera Orch (cont.)
G. Barati (cnd) (cont.)
Schubert, Franz:Mass 1, w. Laurence Dutoit (sop), Rose Bahl (alt), Kurt Equiluz (ten), Kunikazu Ohashi (bass), Xaver Mayer (org), Vienna Academy Chamber Choir *(rec 1960)* Tuxedo ▲ TUXCD 1040 [ADD]
Schubert, Franz:Mass 4, w. Laurence Dutoit (sop), Rose Bahl (alt), Kurt Equiluz (ten), Kunikazu Ohashi (bass), Xaver Mayer (org), Vienna Academy Chamber Choir *(rec 1960)* Tuxedo ▲ TUXCD 1040 [ADD]
L. Blech (cnd)
Wagner, R.:Die Walküre (sels), w. F. Leider (sop), G. Ljungberg (sop), E. Leisner (cta), F. Schorr (b-bar)—nine selections from Acts 2 & 3 [G] *(rec 1927)* Pearl ▲ PEA 9357 (m) [AAD]
K. Böhm (cnd)
Beethoven, L. van:Fidelio, w. H. Konetzni (sop), I. Seefried (sop), P. Klein (ten), T. Ralf (ten), P. Schöffler (b-bar), H. Alsen (bass), Vienna State Opera Chorus *(rec Feb. 1944)* Preiser 2-▲ PRE 90195 [AAD]
Mozart, W.A.:Nozze di Figaro (sels), w. M. Reining (sop—Countess), M. Cebotari (sop—Susanna), M. Ahlersmeyer (bar—Count Almaviva) *(rec Nov. 7, 1941)* Koch Schwann 2-▲ SCH 314602
Rossini, G.:Il barbiere di Siviglia, w. R. Grist (sop), F. Wunderlich (ten), E. Wächter (bar), O. Czerwenka (bass), Kunz (sgr), Vienna State Opera Chorus *(rec live, Vienna 4/28/66)* Myto 2-▲ 2 MCD 91752 [ADD]
Strauss, R.:Ariadne auf Naxos, w. L. Rysanek (sop), J. Scovotti (sop), T. Troyanos (mez), J. King (ten), P. Schöffler (b-bar), Vienna State Opera Chorus *(rec 1967)* Melodram 2-▲ MLO 270105 [ADD]
Strauss, R.:Ariadne auf Naxos, w. M. Reining (sop), I. Seefried (sop), A. Noni (sop), M. Lorenz (ten), J. Witt (ten), E. Kunz (bar), P. Schöffler (bass) *(rec Strauss' 80th Birthday Festival, June 11, 1944)* Preiser 2-▲ PRE 90217 [ADD]
Strauss, R.:Ariadne auf Naxos (sels), w. Alda Noni (sop—Zerbinetta), Maria Reining (sop—Ariadne), Irmgard Seefried (sop—Composer), Max Lorenz (ten—Bacchus), Paul Schöffler (b-bar—Musiklehrer) *(rec Vienna, June 11, 1944)* Koch Schwann 2-▲ SCH 314732 [ADD]
Strauss, R.:Die Frau ohne Schatten (sels), w. H. Konetzni (sop—Die Kaiserin), E. Schulz (sop—Die Färberin), T. RA. (ten—Der Kaiser), J. Herrmann (bar—Barak), Vienna State Opera Chorus *(rec Nov. 23, 1943)* Koch Schwann 2-▲ SCH 314552 [ADD]
Verdi, G.:Macbeth, w. C. Ludwig (mez), C. Cossutta (ten), K. Ridderbusch (bass), S. Milnes (bass), Vienna State Opera Chorus *(rec live 1970)* Legato Classics 2-▲ LCD 143-2 [ADD]
Verdi, G.:Macbeth, w. E. Höngen (cta), J. Witt (ten), M. Ahlersmeyer (bar), H. Alsen (bass), Vienna State Opera Chorus *(rec 1943)* Preiser 2-▲ PRE 90175 [AAD]
Verdi, G.:Otello, w. Hilde Konetzni (sop), Elena Nikolaidi (cta), Torsten Ralf (ten), Paul Schöffler (b-bar), Vienna State Opera Chorus *(rec live, Aug. 1944)* Preiser 2-▲ PRE 90230 [ADD]
Wagner, R.:Die Meistersinger von Nürnberg (sels), w. Maria Reining (sop—Eva), Peter Klein (ten—David), Max Lorenz (ten—Walther), Josef Hermann (bar—Hans Sachs), Erich Kunz (bar—Beckmesser) *(rec Vienna, Jan. 19, 1943)* Koch Schwann 2-▲ SCH 314732 [ADD]
Wagner, R.:Die Meistersinger von Nürnberg (sels), w. Maria Reining (sop—Eva), Torsten Ralf (ten—Walther), Josef Herrman (bar—Hans Sachs), Erich Kunz (bar—Beckmesser), Kurt Böhme (bass—Pogner) *(rec Vienna, 1944)* Koch Schwann 2-▲ SCH 314682 [ADD]
A. Boult (cnd)
Holst, G.:The Planets MCA Classics 2-▲ MCAD2-9813 [AAD]
Vaughan Williams, R.:English Folk Song Suite MCA Classics 2-▲ MCAD2-9813 [AAD]
Vaughan Williams, R.:Fant on Greensleeves MCA Classics 2-▲ MCAD2-9813 [AAD]
Vaughan Williams, R.:Fant on a Theme by Thomas Tallis MCA Classics 2-▲ MCAD2-9813 [AAD]
M. Caridis (cnd)
Bach, J.S.:Con 1 Hpd, w. Anton Heiller (hpd) *(rec Brahmsall, Vienna, May 1958)* Vanguard Classics ("The Bach Guild" series) 2-▲ OVC 2523/24 [ADD]
Bach, J.S.:Con 4 Hpd, w. Anton Heiller (hpd) *(rec Brahmsall, Vienna, May 1958)* Vanguard Classics ("The Bach Guild" series) 2-▲ OVC 2523/24 [ADD]
Bach, J.S.:Con 5 Hpd, w. Anton Heiller (hpd) *(rec Brahmsall, Vienna, May 1958)* Vanguard Classics ("The Bach Guild" series) 2-▲ OVC 2523/24 [ADD]
A. Fistoulari (cnd)
Liszt, F.:Hungarian Rhaps—Nos. 2, 5, 6, 9, 12 & 14 *(rec 1958)* Vanguard Classics ("Everyman" series) ▲ OVC 5007 [ADD]
W. Furtwängler (cnd)
Beethoven, L. van:Fidelio (sels), w. E. Schlüte (sop), L. della Casa (sop), J. Patzak (ten), R. Schock (ten), F. Frantz (b-bar), H. Alsen (bass), Vienna State Opera Chorus—Overture, 16 arias & choruses *(rec live, Salzburg Festspielhaus Aug. 3, 1948)* Melodram 2-▲ CDM 25009 [ADD]
Wagner, R.:Die Meistersinger von Nürnberg (sels), w. Maria Reining (sop—Eva), Max Lorenz (ten—Walther), Erich Zimmermann (ten—David), Karl Kamann (bar—Hans Sachs) *(rec Vienna, Nov. 25, 1937)* Koch Schwann 2-▲ SCH 314702 [ADD]
Wagner, R.:Die Meistersinger von Nürnberg (sels), w. T. Lemnitz (sop), E. Laholm (ten), R. Bockelmann (bar), E. Fuchs (bar), Vienna State Opera Chorus *(rec Sept. 5, 1938)* Koch Schwann 2-▲ SCH 314522 [ADD]
Wagner, R.:Tannhäuser (sels), w. Maria Müller (sop), Anna Báthy (sop), Max Lorenz (ten) Koch Schwann 2-▲ SCH 314702 [ADD]
Wagner, R.:Tristan und Isolde (sels), w. Anny Konetzni (sop—Isolde), Margarete Klose (cta—Brangäne), Max Lorenz (ten—Tristan), Paul Schöffler (b-bar—Kurwenal), Herbert Alsen (bass—King Marke), Vienna State Opera Chorus—extended excerpts from Acts 1 & 2; Act 3 (comp.) *(rec Vienna, Jan. 2, 1943)* Koch Schwann 2-▲ SCH 314612 [ADD]
Wagner, R.:Tristan und Isolde (sels), w. A. Konetzni (sop—Isolde), M. Klose (cta—Brangäne), M. Lorenz (ten—Tristan), Vienna State Opera Chorus *(rec Dec. 25, 1941)* Koch Schwann 2-▲ SCH 314562 [ADD]
Wagner, R.:Die Walküre (sels), w. Anny Konetzni (sop—Brunnhilde), Maria Müller (sop—Sieglinde), Franz Völker (ten—Siegmund), Walter Grossmann (bass—Wotan) *(rec Vienna, Feb. 13-17, 1936)* Koch Schwann 2-▲ SCH 314702 [ADD]
L. Gardelli (cnd)
Verdi, G.:Nabucco, w. E. Suliotis (sop), B. Prevedi (ten), T. Gobbi (ten), C. Cava (bass), Vienna State Opera Chorus [I] London 2-▲ 417407-2 [ADD]
H. Gillesberger (cnd)
Haydn, J.:Mass 7, "Kleine Orgelmesse", w. Eiko Katonosaka (sop), Elfriede Jahn (alt), Kurt Equiluz (ten), Leo Heppe (bass), Vienna Chamber Choir *(rec 1965)* Tuxedo ▲ TUXCD 1025
Haydn, J.:Mass 10, "Kriegsmesse", "Paukenmesse", w. Elisabeth Thomann (sop), Elfriede Jahn (alt), Stafford Wing (ten), Eishi Kawamura (bass), Vienna Chamber Choir *(rec 1965)* Tuxedo ▲ TUXCD 1025
V. Golschmann (cnd)
Bartók, B.:Rhaps (2) Vn & Orch, w. R. Totenberg (vn)—No. 1 *(rec 1961)* Vanguard Classics ▲ OVC 4046 [ADD]
Bloch, E.:Con symphonique, w. M. Mitchell (pno) *(rec 1961)* Vanguard Classics ▲ OVC 4052 [ADD]
Bloch, E.:Con Vn, w. R. Totenberg (vn) *(rec 1961)* Vanguard Classics ▲ OVC 4046 [ADD]
Enescu, G.:Romanian Rhap 1 *(rec 1960)* Vanguard Classics ("Everyman" series) ▲ OVC 5002 [ADD]
Enescu, G.:Romanian Rhap 1 *(rec Musikverein, Vienna)* Vanguard Classics ▲ SVC 10 [AAD]
Enescu, G.:Romanian Rhap 2 *(rec 1960)* Vanguard Classics ("Everyman" series) ▲ OVC 5002 [ADD]
Enescu, G.:Romanian Rhap 2 *(rec Musikverein, Vienna)* Vanguard Classics ▲ SVC 10 [AAD]
Kabalevsky, D.:The Comedians *(rec 1958)* Vanguard Classics ("Everyman" series) ▲ OVC 5010 [ADD]
Khachaturian, A.:Con Vn, w. M. Elman (vn) *(rec 1959)* Vanguard Classics ▲ OVC 8035 [ADD]
Khachaturian, A.:Gayane (suites)—Suite No. 1 *(rec 1958)* Vanguard Classics ("Everyman" series) ▲ OVC 5010 [ADD]
Lalo, E.:Sym espagnole, w. Mischa Elman (vn) *(rec 1959)* Vanguard Classics ▲ OVC 8034 [ADD]
Litolff, H.C.:Con Symphonique 4, w. M. Mitchell (pno)—Scherzo *(rec 1961)* Vanguard Classics ▲ OVC 4052 [ADD]
Mendelssohn, F.:Con in e Vn & Orch, Op. 64, w. M. Elman (vn) *(rec 1959)* Vanguard Classics ▲ OVC 8034 [ADD]
Saint-Saëns, C.:Introduction & Rondo capriccioso, w. Elman (vn) *(rec 1959)* Vanguard Classics ▲ OVC 8035 [ADD]

Vienna State Opera Orch (cont.)
E. Goossens (cnd)
Prokofiev, S.:Peter & the Wolf, w. J. Ferrer (nar)—two separate performances, in English & Spanish *(rec ca. 1960)* MCA Classics 2-▲ MCAD2-9820 [AAD]
R. Heger (cnd)
Pfitzner, H.:Palestrina, w. S. Jurinac (sop), C. Ludwig (mez), F. Wunderlich (ten), G. Stolze (ten), O. Wiener (bar), G. Frick (bass), W. Berry (bass), Vienna State Opera Chorus *(rec live, Vienna 12/16/64)* Myto 3-▲ 3 MCD 92259 [ADD]
Wagner, R.:Götterdämmerung (sels), w. G. Kappel (sop—Brünhilde), J. Kalenberg (ten—Siegfried), J. von Manowarda (bass—Mime), Vienna State Opera Chorus *(rec June 15, 1933)* Koch Schwann 2-▲ SCH 314592
Wagner, R.:Siegfried (sels), w. G. Kappel (sop—Brünhilde), R. Schubert (ten—Siegfried), E. Zimmermann (ten—Mime), Vienna State Opera Chorus *(rec June 13, 1933)* Koch Schwann 2-▲ SCH 314592
Wagner, R.:Tannhäuser (sels), w. Lotte Lehmann (sop—Elisabeth), Josef Kalenberg (ten—Tannhäuser), Richard Mayr (bass—Landgraf), Friedrich Schorr (bass—Wolfram) *(rec Vienna, Sept. 25, 1933)* Koch Schwann 2-▲ SCH 314622 [ADD]
H. Hollreiser (cnd)
Krenek, E.:Jonny spielt auf, w. E. Lear (sop—Anita), L. Popp (sop—Yvonne), W. Blankenship (ten—Max), K. Equiluz (ten—Station Announcer), L. Heppe (ten—Manager), T. Stewart (bar—Daniello), G. Feldhoff (bass—Jonny) [G] Vanguard Classics ▲ OVC 8048 [ADD]
J. Horenstein (cnd)
Strauss (II), Joh.:Music of—Die Fledermaus Overture; Perpetuum Mobile; Emperor Waltz; Tritsch-Tratsch-Polka; Tales from the Vienna Woods; Artist's Life; Der Zigeunerbaron Overture; Annen-Polka; Wine, Women and Song *(rec 1962)* Chesky ▲ CD70 [ADD]
Strauss (II), Joh.:Waltzes—Tausend und eine Nächter; Rosen aus dem Suden; Über Donner- und Blitz-Schnellpolka; Wo die Zitronen bluh'n; Lagunen Walzer; Morgenblatter; Frühlingsstimmen; Weiner Blut; An der schönen, blauen Donau *(rec Dec. 1962 & Sept. 1969)* Chesky ▲ CD 95 [ADD]
H. von Karajan (cnd)
Puccini, G.:La Bohème, w. M. Freni (sop), H. Gueden (sop), G. Raimondi (ten), G. Taddei (bar), Vienna State Opera Chorus [I] *(rec live 11/30/63)* Melodram 2-▲ MELCD 27007
Puccini, G.:La Bohème (sels), w. M. Freni (sop), H. Gueden (sop), G. Raimondi (ten), R. Panerai (bar)—7 arias & scenes [I] *(rec live 11/9/63)* Verona 2-▲ 27079/80
Strauss (II), Joh.:Die Fledermaus, w. H. Gueden (sop), R. Streich (sop), G. Di Stefano (ten), G. Stolze (ten), G. Zampieri (ten), E. Wächter (bar), W. Berry (bass), E. Kunz (bar), Vienna State Opera Chorus [G] Arkadia 3-▲ 215 (m) [ADD]
Strauss, R.:Die Frau ohne Schatten, w. L. Rysanek (sop), Hoffman (sgr), Thomas (sgr), Vienna State Opera Chorus [G] *(rec live, Vienna, 6/11/64)* Arkadia 3-▲ 207 (m) [ADD]
Wagner, R.:Parsifal, w. C. Ludwig (mez), E. Höngen (cta), H.-M. Uhle (ten), H. Hotter (b-bar), T. Franc (bass), W. Berry (bass), Vienna State Opera Chorus [G] *(rec live 4/1/61)* Arkadia 3-▲ 219 (m) [ADD]
I. Kertész (cnd)
Mozart, W.A.:Clemenza, w. M. Casula (sop), L. Popp (sop), T. Berganza (mez), B. Fassbaender (mez), T. Franc (bass), F. Krenn (bass), Vienna State Opera Chorus London ("Grand Opera" series) 2-▲ 430105-2 [ADD]
C. Kleiber (cnd)
Bizet, G.:Carmen, w. E. Obraztsova (mez), P. Domingo (ten), J. Mazurok (bar), Vienna State Opera Chorus Exclusive 2-▲ EXL 11 [ADD]
Still, W.G.:Tristan und Isolde, w. C. Ligendza (sop), R. Baldani (mez), H. Hopf (ten), A. Dermota (ten), H. Sotin (bass), G. Neidlinger (bass), Vienna State Opera Chorus *(rec Oct. 7, 1973)* Exclusive 3-▲ EXL 18 [ADD]
Wagner, R.:Tristan und Isolde (sels), w. Catarina Ligendza (sop), Ruŝa Baldani (mez), Hans Hopf (ten) *(rec live, 1973)* AS Disc ▲ ASD 2510
B. Klobucar (cnd)
Verdi, G.:La traviata, w. A. Moffo (sop), G. Janowitz (sop), G. Zampieri (ten), E. Bastianini (bar), Vienna State Opera Chorus [I] *(rec live, Vienna, 1964)* Melodram (Connaisseur) 2-▲ CDM 27510 [ADD]
H. Knappertsbusch (cnd)
Mozart, W.A.:Zauberflöte (sels), w. Erna Berger (sop—Queen of the Night), Maria Reining (sop—Pamina), Josef von Manowarda (bass—Sarastro) *(rec Vienna, Dec. 4, 1941)* Koch Schwann 2-▲ SCH 314672 [ADD]
Strauss, R.:Elektra (sels), w. Hilde Konetzni (sop—Chrysothemis), Gertrude Rünger (cta/sop—Elektra) *(rec Vienna, Nov. 21, 1941)* Koch Schwann 2-▲ SCH 314662 [ADD]
Strauss, R.:Der Rosenkavalier (sels), w. Lotte Lehmann (sop—Feldmarschallin), Elisabeth Schumann (sop—Sophie), Eva Hadrabavá (sop—Octavian) *(rec Vienna, Apr. 22, 1936)* Koch Schwann 2-▲ SCH 314622 [ADD]
Strauss, R.:Der Rosenkavalier (sels), w. Margit Bokor (sop—Octavian), Hilde Konetzni (sop—Marschallin), Elisabeth Schumann (sop—Sophie) *(rec Salzburg, June 13, 1937)* Koch Schwann 2-▲ SCH 314672 [ADD]
Wagner, R.:Götterdämmerung (sels), w. Gertrude Rünger (sop—Brünnhilde), Julius Pölzer (ten—Siegfried) *(rec Vienna, Sept. 25, 1938)* Koch Schwann 2-▲ SCH 314662 [ADD]
Wagner, R.:Parsifal (sels), w. Fred Destal (bar—Amfortas), Herbert Alsen (bass—Gurnemanz), Nikolaus Zec (bass-Titurel) *(rec Nov. 1, 1937)* Koch Schwann 2-▲ SCH 314632 [ADD]
Wagner, R.:Parsifal (sels), w. A. Konetzni (sop), H. Grahl (ten), H. Weidemann (bar), H. Alsen (bass), Vienna State Opera Chorus *(rec Apr. 6, 1939)* Koch Schwann 2-▲ SCH 314522 [ADD]
Wagner, R.:Der Ring des Nibelungen (sels), w. Adele Kern (sop), Anny Konetzni (sop), Hilde Konetzni (sop), Elisabeth Schumann (sop), Enid Szantho (cta), Josef Kalenberg (ten), Max Lorenz (ten), Set Svanholm (ten), Erich Zimmermann (ten), Hans Hotter (bar), Jaro Prohaska (bar), Emil Schipper (bar), Paul Schöffler (b-bar), Ludwig Hoffmann (bass) *(rec Vienna, 1937–1943)* Koch Schwann 2-▲ SCH 314742 [ADD]
Wagner, R.:Siegfried (sels), w. E. Szantho (cta—Erda), M. Lorenz (ten—Siegfried), W. Wernigk (ten—Mime), L. Hoffmann (bass—Wanderer), Vienna State Opera Chorus *(rec June 16, 1937)* Koch Schwann 2-▲ SCH 314602
Wagner, R.:Siegfried (sels), w. A. Konetzni (sop—Brünhilde), J. Kalenberg (ten—Siegfried), Vienna State Opera Chorus *(rec Apr. 18, 1936)* Koch Schwann 2-▲ SCH 314562 [ADD]
Wagner, R.:Tannhäuser (sels), w. Maria Reining (sop—Elisabeth), Max Lorenz (ten—Tannhäuser), Arno Schellenberg (bar—Wolfram) *(rec Vienna, Nov. 20, 1937)* Koch Schwann 2-▲ SCH 314672 [ADD]
Wagner, R.:Die Walküre (sels), w. A. Konetzni (sop—Brünhilde), L. Hofmann (bass—Wotan), Vienna State Opera Chorus *(rec Oct. 28, 1942)* Koch Schwann 2-▲ SCH 314562 [ADD]
Weber, C.M. von:Der Freischütz (sels), w. Tiana Lemnitz (sop—Agathe), Michael Bohnen (b-bar—Kaspar) *(rec Salzburg, Aug. 3, 1939)* Koch Schwann 2-▲ SCH 314672 [ADD]
C. Krauss (cnd)
Strauss, R.:Die ägyptische Helena (sels), w. V. Ursuleac (sop—Helena), F. Völker (ten—Menelas), H. Roswaenge (ten—Da-Ud), E. Kunz (bar—Arbace), Vienna State Opera Chorus *(rec Sept. 20, 1933)* Koch Schwann 2-▲ SCH 314552 [ADD]
Strauss, R.:Arabella (sels), w. Margit Bokor (sop—Zdenka), Viorica Ursuleac (sop—Arabella), Alfred Jerger (bar—Mandryka), Richard Mayr (bass—Waldner) *(rec Vienna, Oct. 29, 1933)* Koch Schwann 2-▲ SCH 314625 [ADD]
Strauss, R.:Ariadne auf Naxos, w. Erna Berger (sop), Miliza Korjus (sop), Viorica Ursuleac (sop), Helge Rosvaenge (ten), *(other soloists unknown)*, Vienna State Opera Chorus *(rec 1935)* Arlecchino 3-▲ ARL 14/16
Strauss, R.:Die Frau ohne Schatten (sels), w. Viorica Ursuleac (sop—Die Kaiserin), Gertrude Rünger (cta/sop—Elisabetta), Franz Völker (ten—Der Kaiser) *(rec Vienna, June 1, 1933)* Koch Schwann 2-▲ SCH 314662 [ADD]
Strauss, R.:Friedenstag, w. Viorica Ursuleac (sop—Maria), Anton Dermota (ten—Ein Piemonteser), Hans Hotter (b-bar—Kommandant), Herbert Alsen (bass—Wachtmeister) *(rec Vienna, Oct. 16, 1941)* Koch Schwann 2-▲ SCH 314625 [ADD]
Strauss, R.:Salome, w. Maria Cebotari (sop—Salome), Elisabeth Höngen (mez—Herodias), Karl Friedrich (ten—Narraboth), Julius Patzak (ten—Herod), Marko Rothmüller (bar—Jokanaan), Vienna State Opera Chorus *(rec Covent Garden, London, Sept 30, 1947)* Legato 2-▲ LCD 211-2 [ADD]

Vienna State Opera Orch (cont.)
C. Krauss (cnd) (cont.)
Verdi, G.:Don Carlos (sels), w. Viorica Ursuleac (sop—Elisabetta), Franz Völker (ten—Don Carlo), Josef von Manowarda (bass—Filippo) *(rec Vienna, Feb. 25, 1933)* Koch Schwann 2-▲ SCH 314662 [ADD]
Verdi, G.:Otello (sels), w. Viorica Ursuleac (sop—Desemona), Franz Völker (ten—Otello), Josef von Manowarda (bass—Iago) *(rec Vienna, Dec. 15, 1933)*. Koch Schwann 2-▲ SCH 314662 [ADD]
Wagner, R.:Götterdämmerung (sels), w. Henny Trundt (sop—Brünnhilde), Josef Kalenberg (ten—Siegfried), Emil Schipper (bar—Gunther), Josef von Manowarda (bass—Hagen) *(rec Mar. 7, 1933)* Koch Schwann 2-▲ SCH 314642 [ADD]
Wagner, R.:Die Meistersinger von Nürnberg (sels), w. V. Ursuleac (sop—Eva), F. Völker (ten—Walther), A. Jerger (b-bar—Hans Sachs), Vienna State Opera Chorus *(rec Apr. 13, 1934)* Koch Schwann 2-▲ SCH 314602
Wagner, R.:Die Meistersinger von Nürnberg (sels), w. Viorica Ursuleac (sop—Eva), Rudolf Bockelmann (ten—Hans Sachs), Josef Kalenberg (ten—Walther), Hermann Wiedemann (bar—Beckmesser), Vienna State Opera Chorus *(rec Jan. 20, 1933)* Koch Schwann 2-▲ SCH 314642 [ADD]
Wagner, R.:Die Meistersinger von Nürnberg (sels), w. V. Ursuleac (sop—Eva), M. Lorenz (ten—Walther), E. Zimmermann (ten—David), A. Jerger (b-bar—Hans Sachs), Vienna State Opera Chorus *(rec Feb. 26, 1933)* Koch Schwann 2-▲ SCH 314562 [ADD]
Wagner, R.:Parsifal (sels), w. Gertrude Fünger (cta—Kundry), Gunnar Graarud (ten—Parsifal), Emil Schipper (bar—Amfortas), Josef von Manowarda (bass—Gurnemanz) *(rec Apr. 13, 1933)* Koch Schwann 2-▲ SCH 314642 [ADD]
Wagner, R.:Das Rheingold (sels), w. Erich Zimmermann (ten—Mime), Herrmann Wiedemann (bar—Alberich), Josef von Manowarda (bass—Wotan) *(rec Feb. 28, 1933)* Koch Schwann 2-▲ SCH 314642 [ADD]
Wagner, R.:Die Walküre (sels), w. Maria Jeritza (sop—Brünnhilde), Felice Hüni-Mišek (sop—Sieglinde), Franz Völker (ten—Siegmund), Friedrich Schorr (b-bar—Wotan) *(rec June 11, 1933)* Koch Schwann 2-▲ SCH 314642 [ADD]
Wagner, R.:Die Walküre (sels), w. Lotte Lehmann (sop—Sieglinde), Maria Jeritza (sop—Brünnhilde), Franz Völker (ten—Siegmund), Friedrich Schorr (bass—Wotan) *(rec Vienna, Sept. 14, 1933)* Koch Schwann ▲ SCH 314622 [ADD]
Krauss, Knappertsbusch (cnd)
Wagner, R.:Die Walküre (sels), w. Viorica Ursuleac (sop—Sieglinde), Hilde Konetzni (sop—Sieglinde), Gertrude Rünger (sop—Brünnhilde), Franz Völker (ten—Siegmund), Richard Mayr (bass—Hunding) Koch Schwann 2-▲ SCH 314662 [ADD]
J. Krips (cnd)
Gounod, C.:Faust (sels), w. Luise Helletsgruber (sop—Marguerite), Helge Roswaenge (ten—Faust), Joel Berglund (ten—Mephistopheles) *(rec Vienna, Nov. 10, 1936)* Koch Schwann 2-▲ SCH 314622 [ADD]
Smetana, B.:Dalibor, w. L. Rysanek (sop), L. Spiess (ten), E. Wächter (bar), Vienna State Opera Chorus *(rec live, Vienna, 10/19/69)* Myto 2-▲ 2 MCD 92465 [ADD]
Wagner, R.:Das Rheingold (sels), w. A. Konetzni (sop—Fricka), J. Prohaska (bar—Wotan), N. Zec (b-bar—Fasolt), H. Alsen (bass—Fafner), Vienna State Opera Chorus *(rec Jan. 18, 1937)* Koch Schwann 2-▲ SCH 314592
Wagner, R.:Rienzi, der Letzte der Tribunen (sels), w. Rosette Andsy (cta—Adriano), Hermann Gallos (ten—Baroncelli), Franz Völker (tenor-Rienzi), Karl Ettl (bass—Cecco) *(rec Vienna, May 15, 1933)* Koch Schwann 2-▲ SCH 314662 [ADD]
R. Leibowitz (cnd)
Mozart, W.A.:Ave verum corpus, w. Vienna State Opera Chorus [L] *(rec 1958)* MCA Classics 2-▲ MCAD2-9816 [AAD]
Mozart, W.A.:Regina coeli, K.108, w. Vienna State Opera Chorus [L] *(rec 1958)* MCA Classics 2-▲ MCAD2 9816 [AAD]
Mozart, W.A.:Requiem, w. S. Jurinac (sop), L. West (alt), H. Loeffler (ten), F. Gutherie (bass), Vienna State Opera Chorus [L] *(rec 1958)* MCA Classics 2-▲ MCAD2 9816 [AAD]
Mozart, W.A.:Sancta Maria, w. Vienna State Opera Chorus [L] *(rec 1958)* MCA Classics 2-▲ MCAD2 9816 [AAD]
Mozart, W.A.:Te Deum, w. Vienna State Opera Chorus [L] *(rec 1958)* MCA Classics 2-▲ MCAD2-9816 [AAD]
W. Loibner (cnd)
Mozart, W.A.:Nozze di Figaro (sels), w. Maria Reining (sop—Countess), Margherita Perras (sop—Susanna), Alfred Jerger (b-bar—Count), Paul Schöffler (b-bar—Figaro) *(rec May 24, 1938)* Koch Schwann 2-▲ SCH 314632 [ADD]
L. Ludwig (cnd)
Verdi, G.:Aida (sels), w. D. Illitsch (sop—Aida), E. Nikolaidi (cta), M. Lorenz (ten), Vienna State Opera Chorus *(rec Sept. 22, 1942)* Koch Schwann 2-▲ SCH 314562 [ADD]
L. Maazel (cnd)
Puccini, G.:Turandot (sels), w. E. Martón (sop), K. Ricciarelli (sop), J. Carreras (ten), Vienna State Opera Chorus [I] CBS ▲ MK 42168 [DDD] ■ MT 42168 (D)
C. Mackerras (cnd)
Gluck, C.W.:Orfeo ed Euridice, w. H. Steffek (sop—Amore), T. Stich-Randall (mez—Euridice), M. Forrester (cta—Orfeo), Vienna State Opera Chorus [Italian version w. additions composed for the French production] *(rec 6/66)* Vanguard Classics 2-▲ OVC 4039/40 [ADD]
F. Molinari-Pradelli (cnd)
Puccini, G.:Turandot, w. B. Nilsson (sop), L. Price (sop), G. di Stefano (ten), T. Gobbi (bar), Vienna State Opera Chorus [I] *(rec live, 6/22/61)* Legato Classics 2-▲ LCD 153-2 (m) [ADD]
R. Moralt (cnd)
Strauss, R.:Ariadne auf Naxos (sels), w. Adele Kern (sop—Zerbinetta), Anny Konetzni (sop—Ariadne), Set Svanholm (ten—Bacchus), Else Schulz (sgr—Composer) *(rec Vienna, Oct. 16, 1941)* Koch Schwann 2-▲ SCH 314625 [ADD]
Strauss, R.:Daphne (sels), w. M. Reining (sop—Daphne), A. Dermota (ten—Leukippos), Vienna State Opera Chorus *(rec May 8, 1942)* Koch Schwann 2-▲ SCH 314552 [ADD]
Weber, C.M. von:Der Freischütz (sels), w. Maria Reining (sop—Agathe), Elisabeth Rutgers (mez—Ännchen), Julius Pölzer (ten—Max), Herbert Alsen (bass—Kaspar) *(rec Jan. 1, 1939)* Koch Schwann 2-▲ SCH 314632 [ADD]
A. Paulik (cnd)
Strauss, E.:Polkas & Waltzes—Bahn frei, Op. 45; Mit Extrapost, Op. 259; Jugendfeuer, Op. 210 Vanguard Classics 3-▲ OVC 8078/80 [ADD]
Strauss (I), Joh.:Music of—Sperl, Op. 133; Loreley-Rheinklänge, Op. 154; Donaulieder, Op. 127 Vanguard Classics 3-▲ OVC 8078/80 [ADD]
Strauss (I), Joh.:Radetzky March Vanguard Classics 3-▲ OVC 8078/80 [ADD]
Strauss (II), Joh.:Music of—10 popular polkas & waltzes—Pizzicatto Polka; Aus der Ferne; Annen-Polka; Tritsch-Tratsch Polka; Voices of Spring; On the Beautiful Blue Danube; Tales from the Vienna Woods; Artist's Life; Wine, Women & Song; Emperor Waltz Vanguard Classics ▲ OVC 4028 [ADD]
Strauss (II), Joh.:Music of—On the Beautiful Blue Danube, Op. 314; Wiener Blut, Op. 354; Frisch ins Feld, Op. 398; Auf der Jagd, Op. 373; Bandit's Galop, Op. 378; Artists' Life, Op. 316; Pizzacato Polka [composed w. Josef Strauss]; Tritsch-Tratsch, Op. 214; Eiljen a Magyar, Op. 332; Emperor Waltz, Op. 437; Czárdás [from Ritter Pasman]; Vienna Bonbons, Op. 307; Wine, Women & Song, Op. 333; Entrance March [from The Gypsy Baron]; Voice of Spring, Op. 410; Perpetuum mobile, Op. 257; Thunder & Lightening, Op. 324; Acceleration Waltz, Op. 234; The Dot on the "I", Op. 377; Roses from the South, Op. 388 Vanguard Classics 3-▲ OVC 8078/80 [ADD]
Strauss (II), Joh.:Der Zigeunerbaron, w. Emmy Loose (sop—Arsena), Gerda Scheyrer (sop—Saffi), Elisabeth Fez (cta—Mirabella), Hilde Rössl-Majdan (cta—Czipra), Waldemar Kmentt (ten—Barinkay), Paul Spani (ten—Ottokar), Erich Kunz (bar—Homonay), Kurt Pregar (bar—Zsupan), Eberhard Wächter (bass—Carnero), Vienna State Opera Chorus *(rec Brahmssaal, Vienna, Austria, June 1956)* Vanguard Classics 2-▲ OVC 8082/83 [ADD]
Strauss, Josef:Music of—Music of the Spheres, Op. 235; Pizzicato Polka [composed w. J. Strauss II]; My Life Is Love & Joyl, Op. 263; Aquarellen, Op. 258; Jockey, Op. 278; Village Swallows, Op. 164; Delirien, Op. 212 Vanguard Classics 3-▲ OVC 8078/80 [ADD]

▲ = CD ♦ = Enhanced CD Δ = MD ■ = Cassette Tape □ = DCC

Vienna State Opera Orch (cont.)
F. Prohaska (cnd)
Bach, J.S.:Cant 4, w. L. Dutoit (trb), K. Equiluz (ten), H. Braun (bar), Vienna Chamber Choir [G] *(rec 1959)* Vanguard Classics ("The Bach Guild" series) ▲ OVC 2001 [ADD]
Bach, J.S.:Cant 50, w. Vienna State Opera Chorus [G] *(rec June 1957)* Vanguard Classics ("The Bach Guild" series) ▲ OVC 2010 [ADD]
Bach, J.S.:Cant 70, w. A. Felbermayer (sop), E. Wiens (sop), H. M. Welfing (ten), N. Foster (bass), Vienna State Opera Chorus [G] *(rec June 1957)* Vanguard Classics ("The Bach Guild" series) ▲ OVC 2010 [ADD]
Bach, J.S.:Cant 140, w. L. Dutoit (trb), K. Equiluz (ten), H. Braun (bar), Vienna State Opera Chorus [G] *(rec 1959)* Vanguard Classics ("The Bach Guild" series) ▲ OVC 2001 [ADD]
Bach, J.S.:Magnificat, BWV 243, w. M. Coertse (sop), M. Sjöstedt (sop), H. Rössl-Majdan (mez), A. Dermota (ten), F. Guthrie (bass), Vienna State Opera Chorus [L] *(rec June 1957)* Vanguard Classics ("The Bach Guild" series) ▲ OVC 2010 [ADD]
Debussy, C.:Première rapsodie, w. Jack Brymer (cl) *(rec Vienna, June 1966)* Vanguard Classics ▲ OVC 8090 [ADD]
Gluck, C.W.:Orfeo ed Euridice (dance of the blessed spirits), w. Julius Baker (fl) *(rec Vienna, 1966)* Vanguard Classics ▲ SVC 55 [AAD]
Krommer, F.:Con Cl, w. Jack Brymer (cl) *(rec Vienna, June 1966)* Vanguard Classics ▲ OVC 8090 [ADD]
Meyerbeer, G.:L'Africaine (sels), w. Paul Schoeffler (bass)—Figlia de Rè *(rec Musikverein, Vienna, Austria, May 1995)* Vanguard Classics ▲ OVC 8054 [ADD]
Mozart, W.A.:Con 2 Fl, w. Julius Baker (fl) *(rec Vienna, 1966)* Vanguard Classics ▲ SVC 55 [AAD]
Verdi, G.:Arias, w. Paul Schoeffler (bass)—M'ardon le tempia! [from Simon Boccanegra]; O tu Palermo [from I Vespri Siciliani] *(rec Musikverein, Vienna, Austria, May 1995)* Vanguard Classics ▲ OVC 8054 [ADD]
Vivaldi, A.:Cons Pic, w. Julius Baker (fl)—Cons in C & a, R.444 & 445 *(rec Vienna, 1966)* Vanguard Classics ▲ SVC 55 [AAD]
Wagner, R.:Adagio Cl, w. Jack Brymer (cl) *(rec Vienna, June 1966)* Vanguard Classics ▲ OVC 8090 [ADD]
Wagner, R.:Arias & Scenes, w. Paul Schoeffler (bass)—Wotan's Farewell & Magic Fire Music [from Die Walküre]; Hans Sachs' Fliedermonolog [from die Meistersinger]; Amfortas's Monologue [from Parsifal] *(rec Musikverein, Vienna, Austria, May 1995)* Vanguard Classics ▲ OVC 8054 [ADD]
Weber, C.M. von:Concertino Cl, w. Jack Brymer (cl) *(rec Vienna, June 1966)* Vanguard Classics ▲ OVC 8090 [ADD]

H. Reichenberger (cnd)
Mascagni, P.:Cavalleria rusticana (sels), w. Maria Jeritza (sop—Santuzza), Helge Roswaenge (ten—Turiddu) *(rec Vienna, Sept. 26, 1933)* Koch Schwann 2-▲ SCH 314622 [ADD]

L. Reichwein (cnd)
Wagner, R.:Der fliegende Holländer (sels), w. Wilhelm Rode (bar—Holländer), Josef von Manowarda (bass—Daland) *(rec Jan. 6, 1939)* Koch Schwann 2-▲ SCH 314632 [ADD]
Wagner, R.:Götterdämmerung (sels), w. M. Lorenz (ten—Siegfried), P. Schöffler (b-bar—Gunther), J. von Manowarda (bass—Hagen), Vienna State Opera Chorus *(rec Sept. 10, 1942)* Koch Schwann 2-▲ SCH 314562 [ADD]

Reichwein, Knappertsbusch (cnd)
Wagner, R.:Parsifal (sels), w. H. Braun (sop—Kundry), M. Lorenz (ten—Parsifal), P. Schöffler (b-bar—Amfortas), Vienna State Opera Chorus *(rec Apr. 4, 1942)* Koch Schwann 2-▲ SCH 314562 [ADD]

M. Rossi (cnd)
A Demonstration of the Instruments of the Orchestra, w. David Randolph (nar) *(rec Vienna, 1957)* Vanguard Classics 2-▲ OVC 8096/97 [ADD]
Prokofiev, S.:Peter & the Wolf, w. B. Karloff (nar) *(rec 1957)* Vanguard Classics ("Everyman" series) ▲ OVC 5005 [ADD]

F. Rühlmann (cnd)
Wagner, R.:Lohengrin (sels), w. Franz Völker (ten—Lohengrin), Josef von Manowarda (bass—King Henry), Zdenka Zika (sgr—Titurel) *(rec Vienna, June 3, 1933)* Koch Schwann 2-▲ SCH 314662 [ADD]

H. Scherchen (cnd)
Bach, J.S.:Brandenburg Cons *(rec 1960)* MCA Classics (Double Decker) 2-▲ MCAD2-9831 [AAD]
Bach, J.S.:Mass in b, BWV 232, w. P. Alarie (sop), N. Merriman (cta), L. Simoneau (ten), G. Neidlinger (bass), Vienna Academy Chorus [L] MCA Classics 2-▲ MCAD2-9821 [AAD]
Bach, J.S.:St. John Passion, w. P. Curtin (sop), E. Thomann (sop), E. Alberts (cta), W. Kmentt, J. Van Kesteren (ten), R. Springer (bar), O. Wiener (bar), D. Smith (b-bar), F. Guthrie (bass), F. Lukasowsky (bass), Vienna Academy Chorus [G] *(rec ca 1960)* MCA Classics 2-▲ MCAD2-9804
Bach, J.S.:St. John Passion, w. P. Curtin (sop), E. Alberts (cta), W. Kmentt (ten), O. Weiner (ten), Vienna Academy Chorus *(rec 1962)* Enterprise ("Documents" series) ▲ ENT LV 925
Beethoven, L. van:Syms (comp), London Philharmonic SO—Syms. 3, 4, 6 & 7 Enterprise ("Palladio" series) ▲ ENT PD 4144 [ADD]
Beethoven, L. van:Sym 1 MCA Classics 2-▲ MCAD2-9802
Beethoven, L. van:Sym 3, "Eroica" MCA Classics 2-▲ MCAD2-9802
Beethoven, L. van:Sym 6, "Pastorale" *(rec 1958)* Andromeda ▲ ANR 2520 [ADD]
Beethoven, L. van:Sym 6, "Pastorale" MCA Classics 2-▲ MCAD2-9802
Beethoven, L. van:Sym 7 *(rec 1952)* Andromeda ▲ ANR 2520 [ADD]
Beethoven, L. van:Sym 9, "Choral Sym", w. M. László (sop), P.-L. Munteanu (ten), Vienna Singakademie *(rec 1954)* Andromeda ▲ ANR 2533 [ADD]
Haydn, J.:The Seven Last Words of Christ on the Cross, w. Albert (sop), John Van Kesteren (ten), Otto Wiener (bar), Anatoli Babikian (bass), Vienna State Opera Chorus [oratorio version] [G] *(rec 1962)* MCA Classics 2-▲ MCAD2-9816 [AAD]
Liszt, F.:Music of—Mephisto Waltz; Les Préludes; Battle of the Huns; Mazeppa; Hungarian Rhaps. 1, 2, 3, 4, 5 & 6 *(rec 1957)* Enterprise ("Palladio" series) ▲ ENT PD 4160 [ADD]
Mahler, G.:Lieder eines fahrenden Gesellen, w. Lucretia West (alt), Vienna Academy Chorus Theorema ▲ TH 121203/04
Mahler, G.:Sym 2, w. M. Coertse (sop), L. West (alt), Vienna State Opera Chorus *(rec 1958)* Enterprise ("Palladio" series) ▲ ENTPD 4180 [ADD]
Mahler, G.:Sym 2, w. Mimi Coertse (sop), Lucretia West (alt) Theorema 2-▲ TH 121203/04
Mahler, G.:Sym 5 *(rec 1952)* Andromeda ▲ ANR 2516 [ADD]
Mozart, W.A.:Requiem, w. S. Jurinac (sop), L. West (alt), H. Loeffler (ten), F. Gutherie (bass), Vienna State Opera Chorus *(rec 1958)* Andromeda ▲ ANR 2525 [ADD]
Rimsky-Korsakov, N.:Scheherazade Enterprise ("Palladio" series) ▲ ENT PD 4159 [DDD]
Saint-Saëns, C.:Danse macabre Enterprise ("Palladio" series) ▲ ENT PD 4159 [DDD]
Tchaikovsky, P.:Ov 1812 *(rec 1958)* Theorema ▲ TH 121153
Tchaikovsky, P.:Romeo & Juliet MCA Classics 2-▲ MCAD2-9805

T. Scherman (cnd)
Handel, G.F.:Judas Maccabaeus, w. Martina Arroyo (sop), Mary Davenport (mez), Lawrence Avery (ten), Jan Peerce (ten), David Smith (bar), Vienna Academy Chorus Vox Box 2-▲ CDX 5125 [ADD]

H. Stein (cnd)
Cherubini, L.:Médée, w. L. Popp (sop), L. Rysanek (sop), M. Lilowa (mez), B. Prevedi (ten), N. Ghiuselev (bass), Vienna State Opera Chorus *(rec live, Vienna 1/31/72)* Melodram 2-▲ CDM 27087 [ADD]

R. Strauss (cnd)
Mozart, W.A.:Idomeneo (sels), w. E. Réthy (sop—Idamante), A. Konetzni (sop—Ismene), J. Sabel (ten—Idomeneo), E. Kunz (bar—Arbace), Vienna State Opera Chorus *(rec Dec. 3, 1941)* Koch Schwann 2-▲ SCH 314532 [ADD]
Strauss, R.:Salome (sels), w. E. Schulz (sop—Salome), A. Dermota (ten—Narraboth), J. Witt (ten—Herodes), H. Hotter (bar—Jochanaan), P. Schöffler (b-bar—Jochanaan), Vienna State Opera Chorus *(rec Feb. 15 & May 6, 1942)* Koch Schwann 2-▲ SCH 314532 [ADD]

H. Swarowsky (cnd)
Chopin, F.:Con 1 Pno, w. Mieczyslaw Horszowsky (pno) Relief 4-▲ CR 911020-23
Humperdinck, E.:Königskinder (sels)—Hellafest; Kinderreigen; Intro to Act III *(rec 1958)* Tuxedo ▲ TUXCD 1054 [ADD]

Vienna State Opera Orch (cont.)
H. Swarowsky (cnd) (cont.)
Humperdinck, E.:Orchestral Suites—Tone Pictures from Sleeping Beauty; Fant on theme from Hänsel und Gretel *(rec 1958)* Tuxedo ▲ TUXCD 1054 [ADD]

H. Tietjen (cnd)
Wagner, R.:Lohengrin (sels), w. Maria Müller (sop—Elsa), Margarete Klose (mez—Ortrud), Franz Völker (ten—Lohengrin), Jaro Prohaska (bar—Telramund), Josef von Manowarda (bass—King Heinrich) *(rec Vienna, 1938)* Koch Schwann 2-▲ SCH 314682 [ADD]

S. Varviso (cnd)
Verdi, G.:Don Carlos, w. S. Jurinac (sop—Elisabetta), L. Rysanek (sop—Celestial Voice), F. Cossotto (mez—Princess Eboli), L. Dutoit (boy sop—Tebaldo), P. Domingo (ten—Don Carlo), E. Majkut (ten—Count of Lerma), M. Sereni (bar—Rodrigo), C. Siepi (bass—Philip II), I. Vinco (bass—Grand Inquisitor), T. Franc (bass—Friar), Vienna State Opera Chorus Standing Room Only 2-▲ SRO 850 [ADD]

B. Walter (cnd)
Verdi, G.:Don Carlos (sels), w. H. Konetzni (sop—Elisabetta), F. Völker (ten—Don Carlos), A. Kipnis (bass—Filippo), Vienna State Opera Chorus *(rec Dec. 16, 1936)* Koch Schwann 2-▲ SCH 314602
Wagner, R.:Die Walküre (sels), w. H. Konetzni (sop—Sieglinde), R. Merker (sop—Brünhilde), F. Völker (ten—Sigmund), L. Hofmann (bass—Wotan), Vienna State Opera Chorus *(rec Oct. 19, 1936)* Koch Schwann 2-▲ SCH 314592

F. von Weingartner (cnd)
Nicolai, O.:Lustigen Weiber (sels), w. A. Jerger (b-bar—Herr Fluth), L. Hofmann (bass—Falstaff) *(rec Oct. 28, 1935)* Koch Schwann 2-▲ SCH 314602
Wagner, R.:Die Meistersinger von Nürnberg (sels), w. Lotte Lehmann (sop—Eva), Eyvind Laholm (ten—Walther), Ludwig Hofmann (bass—Hans Sachs), Vienna State Opera Chorus *(rec Vienna, Sept. 20, 1935)* Koch Schwann 2-▲ SCH 314622 [ADD]

M. Wöldike (cnd)
Haydn, J.:Mass 10, "Kriegsmesse", "Paukenmesse", w. Netania Davrath (sop), Hilde Rössl-Majdan (alt), Anton Dermota (ten), W. Bery (bass), Anton Heiller (org), R. Harand (vc), Vienna State Opera Chorus *(rec May 14-16, 1960)* Vanguard Classics ("The Bach Guild" series) ▲ OVC 2518 [ADD]
Haydn, J.:Die Schöpfung, w. Anny Felbermayer (sop—Eve), Teresa Stich-Randall (sop—Gabriel), Anton Dermota (ten—Uriel), Paul Schöffler (b-bar—Adam), Frederick Guthrie (bass—Raphael), Franz Holletschek (cembalo), Vienna State Opera Chorus *(rec Musikverein, Vienna, Austria, May 1955)* Vanguard Classics 2-▲ SVC 34/35 [AAD]
Haydn, J.:Sym 99 *(rec Brahmssaal, Musikverein, Vienna, June 1956)* Vanguard Classics 3-▲ SVC 14/16 [AAD]
Haydn, J.:Sym 100, "Military" *(rec Brahmssaal, Musikverein, Vienna, June 1956)* Vanguard Classics 3-▲ SVC 14/16 [AAD]
Haydn, J.:Sym 101, "Clock" *(rec Brahmssaal, Musikverein, Vienna, June 1956)* Vanguard Classics 3-▲ SVC 14/16 [AAD]
Haydn, J.:Sym 102 *(rec Brahmssaal, Musikverein, Vienna, June 1956)* Vanguard Classics 3-▲ SVC 14/16 [AAD]
Haydn, J.:Sym 103, "Drum Roll" *(rec Brahmssaal, Musikverein, Vienna, June 1956)* Vanguard Classics 3-▲ SVC 14/16 [AAD]
Haydn, J.:Sym 104, "London" *(rec Brahmssaal, Musikverein, Vienna, June 1956)* Vanguard Classics 3-▲ SVC 14/16 [AAD]
Mozart, W.A.:March Orch, K.249 *(rec Brahmssaal, Vienna, June 1957)* Vanguard Classics ("Historical Anthology:The Bach Guild" series) ▲ OVC 2516 [ADD]
Mozart, W.A.:Serenade Vn, K.250 *(rec Brahmssaal, Vienna, June 1957)* Vanguard Classics ("Historical Anthology:The Bach Guild" series) ▲ OVC 2516 [ADD]

Vienna State Opera Orch Soloists
H. Scherchen (cnd)
Bach, J.S.:Brandenburg Cons Theorema 2-▲ TH 121136/137

Vienna Strauss Festival Orch
W. Buchler (cnd)
Strauss (II), Joh.:Music of—Uwertura do operetki; Wiener Blut, Op. 354; Leichtes Blut, Op. 319; Banditen Galopp, Op. 378; Einzugsmarsch; Frühlingsstimmen, Op. 410; Tritsch-Trasch, Op. 214; Kaiserwalzer, Op. 437; Neue Pizzicato-Polka, Op. 449; Auf der Jagd, Op. 373; An der schönen, blauen Donau, Op. 314 Polskie Nagrania ▲ PNCD 159 [DDD]

O. Lenárd (cnd)
Strauss (II), Joh.:Waltzes—Artist's Life; Blue Danube; Emperor Waltz; Roses from the South; Tales from the Vienna Woods; Treasure Waltz from "Gypsy Baron"; Voices of Spring; Wiener Blut; Wine, Women & Song Naxos ▲ 8.550152 [DDD]

Vienna Strauss Orch
Classics Go to the Movies, Vol. 1, w. Hungarian State Opera Orch, Jenő Jandó (pno), Plovdiv PO, Dresden PO, New Leipzig Bach Collegium Musicum, Budapest SO LaserLight ▲ 15 641

J. Francek (cnd)
Music of Johann Strauss (II), w. Luxembourg Radio Sym [cnd:Kurt Redel] Laserlight ♦ 90027 [DDD]

Vienna String Quartet [Werner Hink (vn), Hubert Kroisamer (vn), Klaus Peisteiner (va), Fritz Dolezal (vc)]
Bärmann, H.J.:Adagio Cl Str Qt, w. Karl Leister (cl) Camerata ("After Hours Classics" series) ▲ 20 CM 424 [DDD]
Berg, A.:Qt Strs Camerata ▲ 32CM 99
Brahms, J.:Qnt Cl, w. Karl Leister (cl)—Adagio movt Camerata ("After Hours Classics" series) ▲ 20 CM 424 [DDD]
Crusell, B.H.:Qnt Cl, w. Karl Leister (cl)—Romanze cantabile movt Camerata ("After Hours Classics" series) ▲ 20 CM 424 [DDD]
Dvořák, A.:Cypresses *(rec Vienna, June 1994)* Camerata ▲ 30 CM 350 [DDD]
Dvořák, A.:Music of—When Thy Sweet Glances Fall; The Old Letter in My Book; Thou Only Dear One, But For Thee; Qt 12 Strs [Adagio cantabile]; Qt 13 Strs [Adagio ma non troppo] Camerata ("After Hours Classics" series) ▲ 20 CM 422 [DDD]
Dvořák, A.:Qt 9 Strs *(rec Studio Baumgarten, Vienna, Nov 30 & Dec 1, 1995)* Camerata ▲ 30 CM 400 [DDD]
Dvořák, A.:Qt 10 Strs Camerata ▲ 32CM 250
Dvořák, A.:Qt 12 Strs, "America" Camerata ▲ 32CM 250
Dvořák, A.:Qt 13 Strs *(rec Studio Baumgarten, Vienna, Feb 20, 22, 23, 1995)* Camerata ▲ 30 CM 400 [DDD]
Dvořák, A.:Qt 14 Strs *(rec Vienna, June 1994)* Camerata ▲ 30 CM 350 [DDD]
Haydn, J.:Qts Strs (misc)—Qt Strs Op.76/3 [Poco adagio cantabile]; Qt Strs, Op. 76/2 [Andante O più tosto allegretto]; Qt Strs, Op. 64/5 [Adagio cantabile]; Qt Strs, Op. 76/4 [Adagio]; Qt Strs, Op. 3/5 [Andante (Serenade)] Camerata ("After Hours Classics" series) ▲ 20 CM 422 [DDD]
Haydn, J.:Qts Strs, Op. 76, "Erdödy Qts"—Nos. 3 & 4 *(rec Studio Baumgarten, Vienna, Apr 3-16, 1988)* Camerata ▲ 25CM90 [DDD]
Mozart, W.A.:Music of—Qt 19 Strs [Andante cantabile]; Qt 23 Strs [Andante]; Qt 15 Strs [Andante]; Qt 14 Strs [Andante cantabile]; Qt 20 Strs [Adagio]; Qt 18 Strs [Andante]; Qt 21 Strs [Andante]; Qt 17 Strs [Adagio]; Qt 16 Strs [Andante con moto] Camerata ("After Hours Classics" series) ▲ 20 CM 421 [DDD]
Mozart, W.A.:Qts Strs (misc)—Nos. 14-23 Camerata 5-▲ 25CM 151/5
Mozart, W.A.:Qt 21 Strs *(rec Studio Baumgarten, Vienna, Mar. 1990)* Camerata ▲ 25CM 349 [DDD]
Mozart, W.A.:Qt 22 Strs *(rec Studio Baumgarten, Vienna, Mar. 1990)* Camerata ▲ 25CM 349 [DDD]
Mozart, W.A.:Qt 23 Strs *(rec Studio Baumgarten, Vienna, May 1990)* Camerata ▲ 25CM 349 [DDD]
Mozart, W.A.:Qnt Cl, K.581, w. Karl Leister (cl)—Larghetto movt Camerata ("After Hours Classics" series) ▲ 20 CM 424 [DDD]
Reger, M.:Qnt Cl, w. Karl Leister (cl)—Largo movt Camerata ("After Hours Classics" series) ▲ 20 CM 424 [DDD]
Schubert, Franz:Music of—Qt 14 Strs [Andante]; Qt 1 Strs [Andante]; Qt 10 Strs [Adagio]; Qt 9 Strs [Andantino]; Qt 4 Strs [Andante con moto]; Qt 13 Strs [Andante]; Qt 11 Strs [Andante]; Qt 2 Strs [Andante]; Qt 6 Strs [Andante]; Qt 15 Strs [Andante un poco moto] Camerata ("After Hours Classics" series) ▲ 20 CM 420 [DDD]

ORCH. & ENS.

Vienna String Quartet (cont.)
Weber, C.M. von:Qnt Cl, w. Karl Leister (cl) *(rec Casino Zögarnitz, TELDEC Studio, Vienna, Dec. 1982)* Camerata ▲ 25CM 331 [DDD]
Weber, C.M. von:Qnt Cl, w. Karl Leister (cl) Camerata 2-▲ 25CM71-2 [DDD]
Weber, C.M. von:Qnt Cl, w. Karl Leister (cl)—Fantasia, Adagio ma non troppo movt Camerata ("After Hours Classics" series) ▲ 20 CM 424 [DDD]
Webern, A.:Movts Str Qt Camerata ▲ 32CM 99
Zemlinsky, A. von:Qt 1 Strs Camerata ▲ 32CM 99

Vienna String Quintet [Thomas Christian (vn), Peter Wächter (vn), Hans Peter Ochsenhofer (va), Michael Hell (vc), Wolfgand Gürtler (db)]
Dvořák, A.:Qnt Strs, Op. 77 *(rec Fuchu-no-Mori Art Theater, Wien Hall, Jan 7-8, 1992)* Camerata ▲ 32CM242 [DDD]
Dvořák, A.:Waltzes Strs, B.105 *(rec Fuchu-no-Mori Art Theater, Wien Hall, Jan 7-8, 1992)* Camerata ▲ 32CM242 [DDD]
Hindemith, P.:Stücke (8) Str Qnt *(rec Fuchu-no-Mori Art Theater, Wien Hall, Jan 12, 1992)* Camerata ▲ 32CM242 [DDD]

Vienna String Quintet [Thomas Christian (vn), Peter Wächter (vn), Tobias Lea (va), Hans Peter Ochsenhofer (va), Michael Hell (vc)]
Bruckner, A.:Intermezzo Str Qnt *(rec Toso Bunka-Kaikan, Sept 23-25, 1994)* Camerata ▲ 30CM399 [DDD]
Bruckner, A.:Qnt Strs *(rec Toso Bunka-Kaikan, Sept 23-25, 1994)* Camerata ▲ 30CM399 [DDD]

Vienna String Trio [J. Pospichal (vn), W. Klos (va), W. Rehm (vc)]
Bach, J.S.:Music of—Adagio & Fugue in d; Adagio & Fugue in g; Adagio & Fugue in F; Adagio & Fugue in d; Largo & Fugue in E♭ & c; Adagio & Fugue in f [all arr Mozart] Calig ▲ CAL 50920
Beethoven, L. van:Serenade Strs, Op. 8 Calig ▲ CD 50835
Beethoven, L. van:Trios Strs, Op. 9—No. 3 in c Calig ▲ CD 50835
Busch, A.:String Trio, Op. 24 Calig ▲ CAL 50896 [DDD]
Dittersdorf, K.D. von:Divert Vn Calig ▲ CAL 50876 [DDD]
Dohnányi, E. von:Serenade Calig ▲ CAL 50896 [DDD]
Einem, G. von:Trio Strs Calig ▲ CAL 50896 [DDD]
Haydn, J.:Trio Vn, Va & Vc *(rec June 10-11, 1985)* Calig ▲ CAL 50847 [DDD]
Hummel, J.N.:Pno Piece Calig ▲ CAL 50876 [DDD]
Krenek, E.:Trio Strs Calig ▲ CAL 50861 [DDD]
Mozart, W.A.:Trio Vn, K.563 Calig ▲ CD 50497
Pleyel, I.:Trio 3 Strs Calig ▲ CAL 50876 [DDD]
Pössinger, F.A.:Trio Strs Calig ▲ CAL 50876 [DDD]
Reger, M.:Trios Vn Va Calig ▲ CAL 50906 [DDD]
Schoenberg, A.:Trio Strs Calig ▲ CAL 50861 [DDD]
Schubert, Franz:Trio Strs, D.471—fragment *(rec June 10-11, 1985)* Calig ▲ CAL 50847 [DDD]
Schubert, Franz:Trio Strs, D.581 *(rec June 10-11, 1985)* Calig ▲ CAL 50847 [DDD]
Webern, A.:Piece Str Trio Calig ▲ CAL 50861 [DDD]
Webern, A.:Trio Strs Calig ▲ CAL 50861 [DDD]

Vienna SO
Akademie Chamber Choir & Vienna SO, w. [cnd:Ferdinand Grossmann], Akademie Chamber Choir, Elisabeth Roon (sop), Laurence Dutoit (sop), Daagmar Herrmann-Braun (cta), Erich Majkut (ten), W. Berry (bass) Vox 90s ■ V9-9903
The Best of Christmas in Vienna, w. Plácido Domingo (ten), Charles Aznavour (sgr), José Carreras (ten), Sissel Kyrkjebø (sgr), Dionne Warwick (sgr) *(rec Vienna)* Sony Classical ▲ SK 62696 ■ ST 62696
Gounod, C.:Faust (sels), w. Alexandrina Pendachanska (sop—Margarethe), Giuseppe Sabbatini (ten—Faust), György Melis (bar—Valentin), Nicolai Ghiaurov (bass—Méphistophélès), Nikola Ghiuselev (bass—Méphistophélès), Berlin RSO, Hungarian State Opera Orch, Bulgarian RSO, Sofia SO, Bulgarian National Chorus, Bulgarian National Chorus Radio Choir—Intro; Vien ou bière; O sainte médaille...Avant de quitter ces lieux; Le veau d'or [all from Act 2]; Quel trouble inconnu me pénètrel...Salut! demeure chaste et pure; Je voudrais bien savoir...Il était un roi de Thule; Un bouquet!...O Dieu! que de bijoux [both from Act 3]; Gloire immortelle de nos aieux; Vous qui faites l'endormie [both from Act 4]; Intermezzo; Walpurgis Night [both from Act 5] Laserlight ▲ 14209 [DDD]
Of Gods & Demons, w. George London (b-bar), Columbia SO, Metropolitan Opera Orch, Rudolf Moralt (cnd), Jean-Paul Moral (cnd), Kurt Adler (cnd) Sony Classical ("Masterworks Heritage" series) ▲ MHK 62758

Y. Ahronovitch (cnd)
Grieg, E.:Peer Gynt Suite 2 LaserLight ▲ 15 617 [DDD]
Liszt, F.:Music of Pro Arte ▲ CDM 804 ■ PCD 804
Liszt, F.:Les Préludes Laserlight ▲ 15 503 [DDD]
Smetana, B.:The Moldau Laserlight ▲ 15 503 [DDD]
Tchaikovsky, P.:Music of Pro Arte ▲ CDM 804 ■ PCD 804
Tchaikovsky, P.:Music of, w. Bavarian RSO [cnd:Hans Vonk], Budapest SO [cnd:András Ligeti] Laserlight ♦ 90029 [DDD]
Wagner, R.:Wagner Concert Pro Arte ▲ CDM 804 ■ PCD 804

Ahronovitch, Lehel (cnd)
Wagner, R.:Ovs, Preludes & Orch Sels, Budapest SO Laserlight ▲ 15 521 [DDD]

G. Anda (cnd)
Mozart, W.A.:Con 20 Pno, w. G. Anda (pno) RCA Silver Seal ▲ 60484-2 [ADD] ■ 60484-4 (CrO2)
Mozart, W.A.:Con 21 Pno, w. G. Anda (pno) RCA Silver Seal ▲ 60484-2 [ADD] ■ 60484-4 (CrO2)
Mozart, W.A.:Con 21 Pno, w. Géza Anda (pno) RCA Gold Seal ▲ 09026-68113-2 [ADD]

G. Bertini (cnd)
Brahms, J.:Serenade 1 Orch Orfeo ▲ 008101 [ADD]
Brahms, J.:Serenade 2 Orch Orfeo ▲ 008101 [ADD]

K. Böhm (cnd)
Strauss, R.:Daphne, w. H. Gueden (sop), F. Wunderlich (ten), J. King (ten), P. Schöffler (bass), Vienna State Opera Chorus *(rec live 1963)* Deutsche Grammophon 2-▲ 445322-2
Strauss, R.:Die Frau ohne Schatten, w. B. Nilsson (sop), L. Rysanek (sop), R. Hesse (mez), J. King (ten), W. Berry (bass) Deutsche Grammophon 3-▲ 445325-2

O. Caetani (cnd)
Donizetti, G.:Poliuto, w. K. Ricciarelli (sop), J. Carreras (ten), J. Pons (bar), Vienna Chorus CBS 2-▲ M2K 44821

S. Celibidache (cnd)
Ravel, M.:Con Pno (left hand), w. R. Casadesus (pno) *(rec live, 1952)* Enterprise ("Documents" series) 2-▲ LV 946/47 (m/s) [ADD]

H. Esser (cnd)
Paganini, N.:Con 1 Vn, w. S. Ashkenasi (vn) Deutsche Grammophon ("Resonance" series) ▲ 429524-2 [ADD]
Paganini, N.:Con 2 Vn, w. S. Ashkenasi (vn) Deutsche Grammophon ("Resonance" series) ▲ 429524-2 [ADD]

F. Fricsay (cnd)
Mozart, W.A.:Sym 29 *(rec 1960-61)* Deutsche Grammophon ("Double" series) 2-▲ 437386-2 [ADD]
Mozart, W.A.:Sym 39 *(rec 1960-61)* Deutsche Grammophon ("Double" series) 2-▲ 437386-2 [ADD]
Mozart, W.A.:Sym 40 *(rec 1960-61)* Deutsche Grammophon ("Double" series) 2-▲ 437386-2 [ADD]
Mozart, W.A.:Sym 41 *(rec 1960-61)* Deutsche Grammophon ("Double" series) 2-▲ 437386-2 [ADD]

H. Froschauer (cnd)
Ave Maria, w. Plácido Domingo (ten), Vienna Boys Choir RCA Gold Seal ▲ 07863-53835-2
Plácido Domingo, w. Plácido Domingo (ten), Vienna Boys Choir RCA Gold Seal ▲ 07863-53835 ■ ARK1-3835

H. Gillesberger (cnd)
Schubert, Franz:Deutsche Messe, w. Elisabeth Thomann (sop), Gertrude Jahn (alt), Stafford Wing (ten), Kunikazu Ohashi (bass), Vienna Chamber Choir Tuxedo ▲ TUXCD 1074 [ADD]

Vienna SO (cont.)

H. Gillesberger (cnd) (cont.)
Schubert, Franz:Mass 3, w. Elisabeth Thomann (sop), Gertrude Jahn (alt), Stafford Wing (ten), Kunikazu Ohashi (bass), Vienna Chamber Choir Tuxedo ▲ TUXCD 1074 [ADD]

F. Grossmann (cnd)
Bach, J.S.:Christmas Oratorio, w. E. Roon (sop), D.H. Braun (mez), E. Majkut (ten), W. Berry (bass), L. Dutoit (echo), B. Seidlhofer (hpd), J. Nebois (org), Akademie Chamber Choir Vox Box 2-▲ CDX 5096 [ADD]
Schubert, Franz:Die Verschworenen, w. Ilona Steingruber (sop—Countess), Elizabeth Roon (mez—Helene), Laurence Dutoit (trb—Isella), Walter Anton (ten—Udolin), Walter Berry (bar—Count), Rudolf Kreutzberger (sgr—Astolf), Vienna Academy Chamber Choir Theorema ▲ TH 121178

T. Guschlbauer (cnd)
Mozart, W.A.:Andante Fl, K.315/285a, w. J.-P. Rampal (fl) *(rec 1966)* Erato ▲ 45832-2 [ADD] ■ 45832-4
Mozart, W.A.:Con Fl, K.313, w. J.-P. Rampal (fl) *(rec 1966)* Erato ▲ 45832-2 [ADD] ■ 45832-4

N. Harnoncourt (cnd)
Haydn, J.:Die Jahreszeiten, w. Angela Maria Blasi (sop), Josef Protschka (ten), Robert Holl (bass), Arnold Schoenberg Choir [G] Teldec 2-▲ 2292-42699-2
Haydn, J.:Die Schöpfung, w. Edita Gruberova (sop), Josef Protschka (ten), Robert Holl (bass), Arnold Schoenberg Choir [G] Teldec 2-▲ 2292-42682-2
Schubert, Franz:Rosamunde (sels)—Overture, etc. Teldec ("Digital Experience" series) ▲ 9031-74785-2 AW [DDD] ■ 9031-74785-4
Schubert, Franz:Sym 8 Teldec ("Digital Experience" series) ▲ 9031-74785-2 AW [DDD] ■ 9031-74785-4
Strauss (II), Joh.:Der Zigeunerbaron, w. Pamela Coburn (sop), Christiane Oelze (sop), Julia Hamari (mez), Elisabeth von Magnus (alt), Herbert Lippert (ten), Rudolf Schasching (ten), Wolfgang Holzmair (bar), Jurgen Flimm (sgr), Robert Florianschutz (sgr), Hans-Jurgen Lazar (sgr), Arnold Schoenberg Choir *(rec Vienna, 1994)* Teldec 2-▲ 94555-2

Helles (cnd)
Mozart, W.A.:Con 19 Pno, w. I. Haebler (pno) Allegretto ▲ ACD 8011 [ADD] ■ ACS 8011

P. Hindemith (cnd)
Hindemith, P.:When Lilacs Last In The Dooryard Bloom'd, w. Elisabeth Höngen (mez), Hans Braun (bar), Vienna State Opera Chorus *(rec 1956)* Tuxedo ▲ TUXCD 1061

Hollreiser, Gielen (cnd)
Bartók, B.:Cons Pno (comp), w. G. Sándor (pno), Bamberg SO *(rec 1958-59)* Vox Box ("Legends" series) 2-▲ CDX2 5506 [ADD]

J. Horenstein (cnd)
Bach, J.S.:Brandenburg Cons *(rec 1954)* Vox Box 2-▲ CDX2 5519
Bartók, B.:Con 2 Vn, w. I. Gitlis (vn) *(rec 1954-57)* Vox Box ("Legends" series) 2-▲ CDX2 5505 [ADD]
Bruch, M.:Con 1 Vn, w. I. Gitlis (vn) *(rec 1954-57)* Vox Box ("Legends" series) 2-▲ CDX2 5505 [ADD]
Bruckner, A.:Sym 9 Vox Box ("Legends" series) 2-▲ CDX2 5508
Mahler, G.:Sym 1 Vox Box ("Legends" series) 2-▲ CDX2 5508
Mahler, G.:Sym 9 *(rec 1954)* Vox Box ("Legends" series) 2-▲ CDX2 5509 [ADD]
Mozart, W.A.:Missa, K.317, w. Wilma Lipp (sop), Christa Ludwig (alt), Murray Dickie (ten), Walter Berry (bass) Vox Legends 2-▲ CDX 5524
Mozart, W.A.:Sym 38 Vox Legends 2-▲ CDX 5524
Mozart, W.A.:Sym 39 Vox Legends 2-▲ CDX 5524
Mozart, W.A.:Sym 41 Vox Legends 2-▲ CDX 5524
Mozart, W.A.:Vesperae solennes, w. Wilma Lipp (sop), Christa Ludwig (alt), Murray Dickie (ten), Walter Berry (bass) Vox Legends 2-▲ CDX 5524
Sibelius, J.:Con Vn, w. I. Gitlis (vn) *(rec ca. 1954-57)* Vox Box ("Legends" series) 2-▲ CDX2 5505 [ADD]
Tchaikovsky, P.:Con Vn, w. I. Gitlis (vn) *(rec ca. 1954-57)* Vox Box ("Legends" series) 2-▲ CDX2 5505 [ADD]

E. Inbal (cnd)
Beethoven, L. van:Sym 9, "Choral Sym", w. Vienna Singakademie, Chorus Viennensis [G] *(rec live, Konzerthaus, 12/30/89 & 1/1/90)* Denon ▲ CO 76646 [DDD]
Mahler, G.:Kindertotenlieder, w. D. Soffel (mez) *(rec Konzerthaus, Vienna, June 9-10, 1992)* Denon/PCM Digital ▲ DEN 75969 [DDD]
Mahler, G.:Lieder eines fahrenden Gesellen, w. D. Soffel (mez) *(rec Konzerthaus, Vienna, July 4-5, 1992)* Denon/PCM Digital ▲ DEN 75969 [DDD]
Mahler, G.:Songs from Rückert, w. D. Soffel (mez) *(rec Konzerthaus, Vienna, July 4-5, 1992)* Denon/PCM Digital ▲ DEN 75969 [DDD]
Schumann, R.:Con Pno, w. M. Dalberto (pno) Denon/PCM Digital ▲ DEN 75859 [DDD]
Schumann, R.:Intro & Allegro appassionato, Op. 92, w. M. Dalberto (pno) Denon/PCM Digital ▲ DEN 75859 [DDD]
Schumann, R.:Intro & Allegro, Op. 134, w. M. Dalberto (pno) Denon/PCM Digital ▲ DEN 75859 [DDD]
Shostakovich, D.:Sym 1 *(rec Konzerthaus, Vienna, Oct. 12-15, 1992)* Denon ▲ DEN 78948 [DDD]
Shostakovich, D.:Sym 2, w. Vienna Singverein Women's Chorus *(rec Oct. 16-18, 1992)* Denon/PCM Digital ▲ DEN 75719 [DDD]
Shostakovich, D.:Sym 3, w. Vienna Boys' Choir Denon/PCM Digital ▲ CO 75444 [DDD]
Shostakovich, D.:Sym 4 *(rec Jan. 20-24, 1992)* Denon ▲ CO 75330 [DDD]
Shostakovich, D.:Sym 5, w. Chorus Viennensis *(rec Nov. 26-29, 1990)* Denon/PCM Digital ▲ DEN 75719 [DDD]
Shostakovich, D.:Sym 6 *(rec Konzerthaus, Vienna, Jan 22-25, 1991)* Denon ▲ DEN 78968 [DDD]
Shostakovich, D.:Sym 7 Denon/PCM Digital ▲ CO 79942 [DDD]
Shostakovich, D.:Sym 8 Denon ▲ CO 78910 [DDD]
Shostakovich, D.:Sym 9 Denon/PCM Digital ▲ CO 75444 [DDD]
Shostakovich, D.:Sym 10 Denon/PCM Digital ▲ CO 79474 [DDD]
Shostakovich, D.:Sym 11 *(rec Konzerthaus, Vienna, May 23-27, 1992)* Denon ▲ CO 78920 [DDD]
Shostakovich, D.:Sym 12 *(rec Konzerthaus, Vienna, Apr 27-30, 1994)* Denon ▲ DEN 78968 [DDD]
Shostakovich, D.:Sym 13, w. R. Holl (bass), Chorus Viennensis *(rec May 13-17, 1993)* Denon/PCM Digital ▲ CO 75887 [DDD]
Shostakovich, D.:Sym 14, w. Elena Prokina (sop), Sergei Aleksashkin (bass), Wilfried Rehm (vc) *(rec Konzerthaus, Vienna, Apr 26-29, 1993)* Denon ▲ CO 78821 [DDD]
Shostakovich, D.:Sym 15 *(rec Konzerthaus, Vienna, Oct. 16-19, 1992)* Denon ▲ DEN 78948 [DDD]

A. Janigro (cnd)
Respighi, O.:La Boutique fantastique *(rec Vienna, 1965)* Vanguard Classics ▲ SVC 41 [AAD]
Respighi, O.:Rossiniana *(rec Vienna, 1965)* Vanguard Classics ▲ SVC 41 [AAD]

O. Kabasta (cnd)
Schubert, Franz:Sym 3 *(rec 1940-43)* Preiser ▲ PRE CD 90303
Schubert, Franz:Sym 5 *(rec 1940-43)* Preiser ▲ PRE CD 90303

C. Kalmar (cnd)
Alcalay, L.:fluchtpunktzeile, w. C. Ascher (mez), M. Hemm (b-bar) Vienna Modern Masters ▲ VMM 3020 [AAD]

H. von Karajan (cnd)
Bach, J.S.:Mass in b, BWV 232, w. E. Schwarzkopf (sop), C. Ludwig (mez), K. Ferrier (cta), A. Poell (b-bar), Schöffler (bass) [L] *(rec live at Vienna's International Bach Festival, June 15, 1950)* Verona 2-▲ 27073/74 (m) [AAD]
Bach, J.S.:Mass in b, BWV 232, w. E. Schwarzkopf (sop), C. Ludwig (mez), K. Ferrier (cta), A. Poell (b-bar), Schöffler (bass), Vienna Singverein—6 arias excerpted from the above rec'g Verona ▲ 27076 (m) [AAD]
Bach, J.S.:St. Matthew Passion, w. I. Seefried (sop), C. Ludwig (mez), K. Ferrier (cta), O. Edelmann (b-bar), P. Schoeffler (bass), Vienna Singverein [G] *(rec live June 9, 1950)* Verona 3-▲ 27070/72 (m) [AAD]
Bach, J.S.:St. Matthew Passion (sels), w. I. Seefried (sop), C. Ludwig (mez), K. Ferrier (cta), O. Edelmann (b-bar), P. Schöffler (bass), Vienna Singverein Verona ▲ 27076 (m) [AAD]

Vienna SO (cont.)
H. von Karajan (cnd) (cont.)
Bizet, G.:Carmen, w. H. Gueden (sop), G. Simionato (mez), N. Gedda (ten), Vienna Singverein *(rec live, Vienna Oct. 1954)* Melodram 2-▲ MEL 27012
C. Kleiber (cnd)
Mahler, G.:Das Lied von der Erde, w. C. Ludwig (mez), W. Kmentt (ten) Exclusive ▲ EXL 53 [ADD]
Mozart, W.A.:Sym 33 *(rec live, Vienna 1967)* Memories ▲ HR 4410 [ADD]
E. Kleiber (cnd)
Verdi, G.:Requiem Mass, w. O. Rovero (sop), J. Madeira (mez), J. Lambert (sgr), G. Neri (bass), Vienna Singverein *(rec live, Vienna 11/23/55)* Melodram 2-▲ CDM 28044 [ADD]
O. Klemperer (cnd)
Beethoven, L. van:Con 4 Pno, w. G. Novaes (pno) Vox Box ("Legends" series) 2-▲ CDX2 5501 [ADD]
Beethoven, L. van:Leonore 3 Allegretto ▲ ACD 8039 [ADD] ■ ACS 8039
Beethoven, L. van:Missa Solemnis, w. Ilona Steingruber (sop), Else Schuerhoff (alt), Ernst Majkut (ten), Otto Wiener (bass), Akademie Chamber Choir *(rec Vienna, 1950)* Vox Legends 2-▲ CDX2 5527
Beethoven, L. van:Sym 5 Allegretto ▲ ACD 8039 [ADD] ■ ACS 8039
Beethoven, L. van:Sym 5 *(rec Vienna, 1950)* Vox Legends 2-▲ CDX2 5527
Beethoven, L. van:Sym 6, "Pastorale" *(rec Vienna, 1950)* Vox Legends 2-▲ CDX2 5527
Beethoven, L. van:Sym 6, "Pastorale" Allegretto ▲ ACD 8000 [ADD] ■ ACS 8000
Beethoven, L. van:Sym 6, "Pastorale"—Allegretto Special Music Co. ▲ SCD 5200
Bruckner, A.:Sym 4, "Romantic" *(rec 1951)* Vox Box 2-▲ CDX2 5520
Bruckner, A.:Sym 4, "Romantic" Enterprise ("Documents" series) ▲ ENT LV 939 [ADD]
Chopin, F.:Con 2 Pno, w. G. Novaes (pno) Vox Box ("Legends" series) 2-▲ CDX2 5501 [ADD]
Guiomar Novaes, w. Guiomar Novaes (pno) *(rec 1950s & early 1960s)* Vox Box 2-▲ CDX2 5501 [ADD]
Mahler, G.:Lied von der Erde, w. Elsa Cavelti (alt), Anton Dermota (ten) *(rec 1957)* Tuxedo ▲ TUXCD 1036 [ADD]
Schumann, R.:Con Pno, w. G. Novaes (pno) Vox Box ("Legends" series) 2-▲ CDX2 5501 [ADD]
C. Krauss (cnd)
Beethoven, L. van:Cant on the Death of the Emperor Joseph II, w. Ilona Steingruber (sop), Alfred Poell (b-bar), Vienna Academy Chamber Choir *(rec live, 1953)* Originals ▲ ORISH 825 [ADD]
Lehel, Ahronovitch (cnd)
Wagner, R.:Ovs, Preludes & Orch Sels, Budapest SO—Fliegende Holländer, Lohengrin, Meistersinger, Parsifal, Tannhäuser, Tristan und Isolde LaserLight ▲ 15521 [DDD]
F. Lehár (cnd)
Lehár, F.:Music of, w. E. Réthy (sop), M. Reining (sop), J. Novotna (sop), R. Tauber (ten), Vienna PO—6 orchestral sels. *(Musikalische Memorien I-IV; Die lustige Witwe—Overture; Eva—Prelude)*; 4 Arias from Giuditta *(Du bist meine Sonne—Tauber; Freunde, das Leben ist lebenswert—Tauber; Schön wie die blaue Sommernacht—Novotna & Tauber; Schönste der Frauen—Tauber)*; 1 Song & 5 Arias sung by Esther Rethy *(Wien, du bist das Herz der Welt; Giuditta—Meine Lippen, sie küssenso heiss; Paganini—Liebe, du Himmel auf Erden; Schön ist die Welt—Ich bin verliebt; Der Zarewitsch—Einer wird kommen; Zigeunerliebe—Hör ich Cymbalklänge)*; 2 Arias sung by Maria Reining *(Eva—Im heimlichen Dämmer der silbernen Ampel; Friederike—Warum hast du mich wachgeküsst?) (rec 1934-1942 Odeon & HMV rec)* Preiser ▲ 90150 (m) [AAD]
F. Leitner (cnd)
Beethoven, L. van:Leonore (opera), w. H. Zadek (sop), A. Dermota (ten), P. Schöffler (b-bar), O. von Rohr (bass), Vienna State Opera Chorus [G] *(rec live, Bregenz 1960)* Melodram 2-▲ CDM 27085 [AAD]
I. Marin (cnd)
Mozart, W.A.:Arias, w. F. Furlanetto (b-bar)—(15 arias) from Così fan tutte *(Donne mie; Rivolgete a lui lo sguardo)*, Don Giovanni *(Deh, vienni alla finestra; Finch'han dal vino; Ho, capito, Signor, si; Madamina! il catologo è questo; Metà di voi qua vadano)*, Le nozze di Figaro *(Hai già vinta la causa; Non più andrai; La vendetta; Se vuol ballare; Tutte è disposto)*, Die Zauberflöte *(In diesen heiligen Hallen; Ein Mädchen oder Weibchen; Der Vogelfänger bin ich ja)* [G,I] Sony Classical ▲ SK 47192
Rossini, G.:Arias, w. A. Baltsa (mez), Vienna State Opera Chorus—arias from Barbiere di Siviglia, Cenerentola, Donna del lago, Italiana in Algeri, Maometto II, Semiramide, Tancredi [I] Sony Classical ▲ SK 45964
G.-F. Masini (cnd)
Verdi, G.:Giovanna d'Arco, w. Edita Gruberova (sop), Salvatore Fisichella (ten), Giorgio Zancanaro (bar) *(rec live, 1985)* Serenissima 2-▲ SER 360133
K. Melles (cnd)
Mozart, W.A.:Con 18 Pno, w. Ingrid Haebler (pno) Allegretto ▲ ACD 8011 [ADD] ■ ACS 8011
Mozart, W.A.:Con 20 Pno, w. I. Haebler (pno) Allegretto ▲ ACD 8011 [ADD] ■ ACS 8011
R. Moralt (cnd)
Albert, E. d':Tiefland, w. G. Brouwenstijn, H. Hopf, W. Kmentt, E. Wächter, P. Schöffler, O. Czerwenka *(rec 1957)* Philips 2-▲ 434781-2
Mozart, W.A.:Con 11 Pno, w. L. Kraus (pno) Vox Box ("Legends" series) 2-▲ CDX2 5510 [ADD]
Mozart, W.A.:Con 19 Pno, w. L. Kraus (pno) Vox Box ("Legends" series) 2-▲ CDX2 5510 [ADD]
Wagner, R.:Parsifal, w. Anny Konetzni (sop—Kundry), Günther Treptow (ten—Parsifal), Paul Schöffler (bar—Amfortas), Hans Braun (bass—Titurel), Adolf Vogel (bass—Klingsor), Ludwig Weber (bass—Gurnemanz), Vienna State Opera Chorus *(rec Vienna)* Myto 4-▲ 4 MCD 954.136
Wagner, R.:Die Walküre (sels), w. Hilde Konetzni (sop—Sieglinde), Günther Treptow (ten—Siegmund), Herbert Alsen (bass—Hunding)—Act 1 Myto 4-▲ 4 MCD 954.136
D. Oistrach (cnd)
Bach, J.S.:Cons Vn (comp), w. David Oistrach (vn) Deutsche Grammophon ("The Originals" series) 2-▲ 447427-2
A. Paulik (cnd)
Strauss (II), Joh.:Eine Nacht in Venedig, w. E. Réthy (sop), M. Schober (sop), R. Boesch (bar), K. Friedrich (ten), A. Jerger (b-bar), K. Preger (ten), Bregenz Festival Choir [G] *(rec 1951)* Koch Schwann ▲ 3-1272-2 [ADD]
J. Perlea (cnd)
Ballet Music from Grand Opera, w. Württemberg State Orch Allegretto ▲ ACD 8122 [ADD] ■ ACS 8122
Mozart, W.A.:Con 21 Pno, w. M. Tipo (pno) Vox Box ("Legends" series) 2-▲ CDX2 5515 [ADD]
Mozart, W.A.:Con 25 Pno, w. M. Tipo (pno) Vox Box ("Legends" series) 2-▲ CDX2 5515 [ADD]
W. Perry (cnd)
Perry, W.:Film Music, w. Richard Hayman (hmc), Rome PO, Slovak PO, Slovak Phil Chorus, Vienna Boys' Choir [scores for 6 Mark Twain films originally produced for PBS in the 1980s]—Adventures of Huckleberry Finn; The Innocents Abroad; Life on the Mississippi; The Mysterious Stranger; The Private History of a Campaign That Failed; Pudd'head Wilson Premier ▲ PRCD 1015 [DDD]
G. Prêtre (cnd)
Saint-Saëns, C.:La Jeunesse d'Hercule Erato ▲ 2292-45696-2 [DDD]
Saint-Saëns, C.:Sym 1 Erato ▲ 2292-45695-2 ZK
Saint-Saëns, C.:Sym 2 Erato ▲ 2292-45695-2 ZK
Saint-Saëns, C.:Sym 3, w. M.-C. Alain (org) Erato ▲ 2292-45696-2 [DDD]
E. van Remoortel (cnd)
Chabrier, E.:España Allegretto ▲ ACD 8025 [ADD] ■ ACS 8025
Debussy, C.:Prélude à l'après-midi d'un faune Allegretto ▲ ACD 8041 [ADD] ■ ACS 8041
Debussy, C.:Prélude à l'après-midi d'un faune Allegretto ▲ ACD 8025 [ADD] ■ ACS 8025
Dukas, P.:L'Apprenti sorcier Allegretto ▲ ACD 8025 [ADD] ■ ACS 8025
Grieg, E.:Elegaic Melodies, Op. 34 Allegretto ▲ ACD 8066 [ADD] ■ ACS 8066
Grieg, E.:Symphonic Dances Allegretto ▲ ACD 8066 [ADD] ■ ACS 8066
Ravel, M.:Boléro Allegretto ▲ ACD 8025 [ADD] ■ ACS 8025
Tchaikovsky, P.:Sleeping Beauty (sels) Allegretto ▲ ACD 8024 [ADD] ■ ACS 8024
Tchaikovsky, P.:Swan Lake (sels) Allegretto ▲ ACD 8024 [ADD] ■ ACS 8024
G. Rozhdestvensky (cnd)
Tchaikovsky, P.:Con 1 Pno, w. V. Postnikova (pno) London ▲ 430725-2 [DDD]

Vienna SO (cont.)
W. Sawallisch (cnd)
Brahms, J.:Choral Music, w. Wilma Lipp (sop), Aafje Heynis (cta), Franz Crass (bar), Vienna Singverein—Ein deutsches Requiem, Op. 45; Academic Festival Ov., Op. 80; Tragic Ov., Op. 81; Schicksalslied, Op. 54; Alto Rhap., Op. 53; Var. on a Theme of Haydn, Op. 56a Philips ▲ 438760-2
Brahms, J.:Syms (comp) Philips ("Duo" series) 2-▲ 438757-2
Haydn, J.:Sym 100, "Military" Philips ▲ 422973-2 [ADD]
Haydn, J.:Sym 101, "Clock" Philips ▲ 422973-2 [ADD]
Hindemith, P.:When Lilacs Last In The Dooryard Bloom'd, w. B. Fassbaender (mez), D.Fischer-Dieskau (bar), Vienna State Opera Chorus [E] *(rec live, 11/1/83)* Orfeo ▲ 112851 [DDD]
Strauss (II), Joh.:Music of Philips ("Miniature" series) ▲ 422277-2 [ADD]
H. Scherchen (cnd)
Mahler, G.:Sym 7 *(rec 1960)* Legend ▲ LGD 131 [ADD]
Mahler, G.:Sym 9 *(rec live, Vienna, 5/19/50)* Melodram ▲ MEL 18038 [ADD]
S. Soltesz (cnd)
Tchaikovsky, P.:Swan Lake (sels) Denon/PCM Digital ▲ DEN 8078 [DDD]
H. Stein (cnd)
Schmidt, F.:Das Buch mit sieben Siegeln, w. Gabriele Fontana (sop), Margareta Hintermeier (alt), Kurt Azesberger (ten), Eberhard Büchner (ten—Johannes), Robert Holl (bass—Voice of the Lord), Robert Holzer (bass), Martin Haselböck (org), Vienna Sym Chorus *(rec live, Vienna Music Hall, May 1996)* Calig 2-▲ CAL 50978/9 [DDD]
R. Stolz (cnd)
The Best of Johann Strauss, Jr., w. Berlin SO Victrola ("Victrola Best of" series) ▲ 60774-2-RV [ADD] ■ 60774-4-RV
Komzák, K.:Badener Madeln *(rec 1969)* Tuxedo ▲ TUXCD 1023
Lehár, F.:Waltzes—Gold und Silber *(rec 1969)* Tuxedo ▲ TUXCD 1023
Stolz, R.:Music of—Gruss aus Wien (marsch); Melodien; Uno-Marsch; Wiener Café; Frühjahrsparade (marschlied) *(rec 1969)* Tuxedo ▲ TUXCD 1023
Strauss (II), Joh.:Die Fledermaus (ov) *(rec 1969)* Tuxedo ▲ TUXCD 1023
Strauss (II), Joh.:Polkas—Annen-Polka, Op. 117 (1852) *(rec 1969)* Tuxedo ▲ TUXCD 1023
Strauss (II), Joh.:Wiener Blut (sels), w. M. Schramm (sop), H. Gueden (sop), R. Schock (ten), B. Kusche (bar) [G] Eurodisc ▲ 25-8370 [ADD]
Strauss (II), Joh.:Der Zigeunerbaron (ov) *(rec 1969)* Tuxedo ▲ TUXCD 1023
W. Strickland (cnd)
Cowell, H.:Sym 7 CRI ■ ACS 6005
Ward, R.:Jubilation Ov CRI ■ C 159
V. Šutej (cnd)
Plácido Domingo:The Best of Christmas in Vienna, w. Plácido Domingo (ten), José Carreras (ten), Dionne Warwick (sgr), Charles Aznavour, Sissel Kyrkjebø Sony Classical ▲ SK 62696 ■ ST 62696
H. Swarowsky (cnd)
Chopin, F.:Con 1 Pno, w. M. Horszowski (pno) Vox Box ("Legends" series) 2-▲ CDX2 5511 [ADD]
Falla, M. de:Noches en los jardines de España, w. G. Novaes (pno) *(rec 1950s)* Vox Box ("Legends" series) 2-▲ CDX2 5513 [ADD]
Grieg, E.:Con Pno, Op. 16, w. G. Novaes (pno) *(rec 1950s)* Vox Box ("Legends" series) 2-▲ CDX2 5513 [ADD]
Mendelssohn, F.:Con in e Vn & Orch, Op. 64, w. I. Gitlis (vn) *(rec ca. 1954-57)* Vox Box ("Legends" series) 2-▲ CDX2 5505 [ADD]
Mozart, W.A.:Con 9 Pno, w. G. Novaes (pno) *(rec 1950s)* Vox Box ("Legends" series) 2-▲ CDX2 5512 [ADD]
Mozart, W.A.:Con 20 Pno, w. G. Novaes (pno) *(rec 1950s)* Vox Box ("Legends" series) 2-▲ CDX2 5512 [ADD]
Mozart, W.A.:Don Giovanni, w. G. Grob-Prandl (sop), H. Konetzni (sop), M. Stabile (bar), A. Pernerstorfer (b-bar), O. Czerwenka (bass), Vienna State Opera Chorus *(rec 1950)* Preiser 2-▲ PRE 90166 [AAD]
H. Swoboda (cnd)
Goldmark, K.:Con 1 Vn, w. P. Rybar (vn) *(rec 1950)* Doron ▲ DRC 4003 [ADD]
B. Weil (cnd)
Mozart, W.A.:Entführung, w. C. Studer (sop), E. Szmytka (sop), K. Streit (ten), R. Gambill (ten), G. Missenhardt (bar), M. Heltau (nar), Vienna State Opera Chorus Sony Classical 2-▲ S2K 48053
Mozart, W.A.:Entführung (sels), w. C. Studer (sop), E. Szmytka (sop), K. Streit (ten), R. Gambill (ten), Gunter Missenhardt (bar), Vienna State Opera Chorus *(rec Vienna, Apr. 2-10, 1991)* Sony Classical ("Opera Highlights" series) ▲ SMK 53500 [DDD]
Offenbach, J.:Ovs—La fille du tambour major; Orpheus in the Underworld; La belle Hélène; Barbe-Bleue; La Grande-Duchesse de Gerolstein; Monsieur et Madame Denis; La vie pariesienne; Vert-Vert *(rec Dec. 11-14, 1992)* Sony Classical ▲ SK 53288 [DDD]
Vienna SO Johann Strauss Ensemble
J. Wildner (cnd)
Strauss, E.:Polkas & Waltzes—Auf und davon! (polka schnell) *(rec 1992)* Orfeo ▲ 291931 [DDD]
Strauss (I), Joh.:Music of—Fortuna-Galopp, Op. 69 *(rec 1992)* Orfeo ▲ 291931 [DDD]
Strauss (II), Joh.:Music of—Cagliostro in Wien (overture); Tritsch-Tratsch-Polka, Op. 214; Morgenblätter (waltz), Op. 279; Persischer Marsch, Op. 289; Accelerationen (waltz), Op. 234; Wiener Blut (waltz), Op. 354 *(rec 1992)* Orfeo ▲ 291931 [DDD]
Strauss, Josef:Music of—Die Emancipirte (polka mazur), Op. 282; Lock (polka française), Op. 233; Sphären-Klänge (waltz), Op. 235 *(rec 1992)* Orfeo ▲ 291931 [DDD]
Vienna Tonkunstler Orch
Z. Topolski (cnd)
Liszt, F.:Fant on Hungarian Folk Tunes, w. Eugene List (pno) *(rec Südwest Tonstudio, Stuttgart, 1976)* Vox Legends 3-▲ CDX3 3504
Tchaikovsky, P.:Con 1 Pno, w. Eugene List (pno) *(rec Südwest Tonstudio, Stuttgart, 1976)* Vox Legends 3-▲ CDX3 3504
Vienna Unterhaltung Orch
H. Hagen (cnd)
Anton Karas, w. Karas, Anton (zither) Tuxedo ▲ 5003
Karas, A.:Third Man Theme, w. Anton Karas (zither) Tuxedo ▲ 5003
Vienna Virtuosi
Beethoven, L. van:Dances, WoO 17 *(rec Zögernitz Casino, Vienna, Dec 20-21, 1994 & Mar 20-)* Canyon Classics ▲ 301
Beethoven, L. van:Septet Strs *(rec Zögernitz Casino, Vienna, Dec 20-21, 1994 & Mar 20-)* Canyon Classics ▲ 301
Vienna Volksoper Orch
F. Bauer-Theussl (cnd)
Benatzky, R.:Im weissen Rössl (sels), w. F. Loor (sop), H. Brauner (cta), K. Equiluz (ten), K. Terkal (ten), Vienna Volksoper Chorus [G] Koch Präsent ▲ CD 399225 [AAD]
Golden Operetta, Vol. 1, w. Vienna Volksoper Chorus, various soloists Koch Präsent ▲ 399 223 [AAD]
Golden Operetta, Vol. 2:Operetta Melodies, w. Vienna Volksoper Chorus, Renate Holm (sop), Lotte Rysanek (sop), Dagmar Hermann (mez), Kurt Equiluz (ten), Horst Winter (ten), et al. Koch Präsent ▲ 399 224 [AAD]
Golden Operetta, Vol. 3, w. Vienna Volksoper Chorus Koch Präsent ▲ 399 225 [AAD]
Golden Operetta, Vol. 4, w. Vienna Volksoper Chorus Koch Präsent ▲ 399 226 [AAD]
Kálmán, I.:Die Csárdásfürstin (sels), w. E. Liebesberg (sop), L. Rysanek (sop), R. Christ (ten), H. Prikopa (bar), Vienna Volksoper Chorus [G] Koch Präsent ▲ CD 399223 [AAD]
Lehár, F.:Der Graf von Luxemburg (sels), w. Renate Holm (sop), Else Liebesberg (sop), Hilde Brauner (cta), Dagmar Hermann (mez), Rudolf Christ (ten), Herbert Prikopa (bar), Vienna Volksoper Chorus [G] Koch Präsent ▲ CD 399223 [AAD]
Lehár, F.:Paganini (sels), w. E. Liebesberg (sop), E. Mechera (sop), Rudolf Christ (ten), K. Equiluz (ten), Vienna Volksoper Chorus [G] Koch Präsent ▲ CD 399226 [AAD]

Vienna Volksoper Orch (cont.)
F. Bauer-Theussl (cnd) (cont.)
Straus, O.:Ein Walzertraum (sels), w. H. Brauner (cta), R. Holm (sop), E. Liebesberg (sop), D. Hermann (mez), R. Christ (ten), H. Prikopa (bar), Vienna Volksoper Chorus [G] — Koch Präsent ▲ CD 399223 [AAD]
Strauss (II), Joh.:Waltzes — Philips ▲ 411119-2
R. Bibl (cnd)
Strauss (II), Joh.:Wiener Blut, w. H. Papouschek (sop), S. Martikke (sop), E. Kales (sop), A. Dallapozza (ten), K. Ruzicka (ten), E. Kuchar (ten), W. Kandutsch (bar), K. Dönch (bar), O. Kolmann (bass), Vienna Volksoper Chorus — Denon 2-▲ CO 8105 [DDD]
P. Falk (cnd)
Strauss (I), Joh.:Radetzky March — PMG ("Vienna Master" series) 3-▲ CD 160303-5 [DDD]
Strauss, R.:Music of—Roses from the South Waltz — Special Music Co. ("Classics of the Heart" series) ▲ SCD 5198
E. Gold (cnd)
Castelnuovo-Tedesco, M.:Coplas, w. M. Nixon (sop) [Sp] *(rec Sept. 28–29, 1974)* — Crystal ▲ CD501
Gold, E.:Songs of Love & Parting, w. M. Nixon (sop) [E] *(rec Sept. 28–29, 1974)* — Crystal ▲ CD 501
H. Lambrecht (cnd)
Lehár, F.:Das Land des Lächelns, w. Dagmar Koller (sop), Valorie Goodall (sop), Guiseppe di Stefano (ten), Heinz Holecek (bass) [G] *(rec 1967)* — Preiser ▲ 93144 [ADD]
P. Maag (cnd)
Mozart, W.A.:Masonic Music, w. K. Equiluz (ten), K. Rapf (pno/org), Vienna Volksoper Chorus—Adagios, K.410 & 411; Adagio & Fugue, K.546; Adagio & Rondo, K.617; Anhang zum Schluss der Freimaurerloge, K.623a; Cants, K.429, 471, 619 & 623; Graduale, K.273; Lieder, K.148, 468, 483 & 484; Maurerische; Motet, K.618; Psalm 129, K.93 *(rec 1966)* — Vox Box 2-▲ CDX 5055 [ADD]
C. Michalski (cnd)
Strauss (II), Joh.:Music of—17 favorite waltzes, polkas & marches — Vivace 2-▲ G 214 [DDD]
G. Patanè (cnd)
Rossini, G.:Arias, w. C. Bartoli (mez)—arias from L'italiana in Algeri, La donna del lago, Tancredi, Otello, Stabat Mater, La pietra del paragone, Cenerentola — London ▲ 425430-2 [DDD]
A. Paulik (cnd)
Millöcker, C.:Bettelstudent, w. Wilma Lipp (sop—Laura), Esther Rethy (sop—Bronislava), Rosette Anday (cta—Palmatica), Rudolf Christ (ten—Symon), Kurt Preger (ten—Ollendorf), Eberhard Waechter (bar—Jan), Vienna Volksoper Chorus *(rec Brahmssaal, Vienna, June 1995)* — Omega 2-▲ OCD 1018/19 [ADD]
L. Schifrin (cnd)
Vienna, w. Migenes, Julia (sop) — Erato ▲ 4509-92875-2
A. Scholz, P. Falk, C. Michalski (cnds)
Strauss (II), Joh.:Music of—25 waltzes, polkas, marches — PMG ("Vienna Master" series) 3-▲ CD 160303-5 [DDD]
E. Strauss (cnd)
Strauss (II), Joh.:Waltzes—An der schönen, blauen Donau, Op. 314; Frühlingsstimmen, Op. 410; G'schichten aus dem Wiener Wald, Op. 325; Kaiserwalzer, Op. 437; Wiener Blut, Op. 354; Rosen aus dem Süden, Op. 388; Kunstlerleben, Op. 316 — Preiser ▲ 90013 [AAD]

Vienna Wind Soloists
Beethoven, L. van:Qnt Pno, Ob, Cl, Hn & Bn, w. A. Previn (pno) — Telarc ▲ CD 80114 [DDD]
Mozart, W.A.:Qnt Pno, K.452, w. A. Previn (pno) — Telarc ▲ CD 80114 [DDD]

Vienna Youth Orch
H. Boeck (cnd)
Schmidt, F.:Chaconne, w. Karl-Andreas Kolly (pno) — Pan Classics ▲ 510081 [DDD]
Schmidt, F.:Con Pno Left Hand, w. Karl-Andreas Kolly (pno) — Pan Classics ▲ 510081 [DDD]

Vienna–Berlin Ensemble
Barber, S.:Summer Music — Sony Classical ▲ SK 48052 [DDD]
Berio, L.:Opus Number Zoo — Sony Classical ▲ SK 48052 [DDD]
Debussy, C.:Chansons de Bilitis (recitation), w. C. Deneuve (nar) [F] — Deutsche Grammophon ▲ 429738-2 [DDD]
Debussy, C.:Son Fl — Deutsche Grammophon ▲ 429738-2 [DDD]
Debussy, C.:Syrinx — Deutsche Grammophon ▲ 429738-2 [DDD]
Eder, H.:Qnt 3 Ww, "Begegnung" — Sony Classical ▲ SK 48052 [DDD]
Françaix, J.:Qnt Fl — Sony Classical ▲ SK 48052 [DDD]
Lachner, F.P.:Nonet — Sony Classical ▲ SK 58971
Ligeti, G.:Bagatelles — Sony Classical ▲ SK 48052 [DDD]
Ravel, M.:Intro & Allegro — Deutsche Grammophon ▲ 429738-2 [DDD]
Ravel, M.:Pavane pour une infante défunte — Deutsche Grammophon ▲ 429738-2 [DDD]
Ravel, M.:Son Vn Vc — Deutsche Grammophon ▲ 429738-2 [DDD]
Rheinberger, J.:Nonet Fl — Sony Classical ▲ SK 58971

Vienna–Szasz CO
J. Dobra (cnd)
Bengraf, J.:Sacred Music, w. Ingrid Kertesi (sop), Katalin Gémes (mez), Gábor Kállay (ten), Ákos Ambrus (bar), István Ella (org), Zsolt Kovács (vc), Balázs Arnóth (bn), Vilmos Buza (db), Tomkins Vocal Ensemble—Te Deum; O sacrum convivium; Libera me; Gloria [from Missa solemnis in D] — Hungaroton ▲ HCD 31609 [DDD]
Druschetzky, G.:Missa solemnis, w. Ingrid Kertesi (sop), Katalin Gémes (mez), Gábor Kállay (ten), Ákos Ambrus (bar), István Ella (org), Zsolt Kovács (vc), Balázs Arnóth (bn), Vilmos Buza (db), Tomkins Vocal Ensemble — Hungaroton ▲ HCD 31609 [DDD]
J. Mezei (cnd)
Werner, G.J.:Laetaniae de Venerabili Sacramento, w. St. Cecilia Vocal Ensemble *(rec St. Columba's Presbyterian Church, Budapest, June 12–15, 1995)* — Hungaroton ▲ HCD 31646 [DDD]
Werner, G.J.:Vesperae de Apostolis, w. Agnes Dobszay (sop), Péter Patay (cta), Tamás Bubnó (ten), Péter Cser (bass), Budapest Schola Cantorum *(rec St. Columba's Presbyterian Church, Budapest, June 12–15, 1995)* — Hungaroton ▲ HCD 31646 [DDD]
Werner, G.J.:Vesperae de Confessoris, w. Éva Bodrogi (sop), Regina Fülöp (cta), Kornél Pechan (ten), Péter Cser (bass), János Mezei (org), Budapest Schola Cantorum *(rec St. Columba's Presbyterian Church, Budapest, June 12–15, 1995)* — Hungaroton ▲ HCD 31646 [DDD]

Viennese Ladies' Opera Ball Orch
Viennese Ladies' Opera Ball Orch. — Koch Schwann ▲ SCH 311170 [DDD]

Viento Ensemble
Hidas, F.:Qnt 3 Winds *(rec Scottish Rite Temple, Portland, OR, Mar. 1992)* — Centaur ▲ CRC 2211 [DDD]
Janácek, L.:Moravian Dances Orch *(rec Scottish Rite Temple, Portland, OR, Mar. 1992)* — Centaur ▲ CRC 2211 [DDD]
Sabaneyev, L.L.:Suite Ww *(rec Scottish Rite Temple, Portland, OR, Mar. 1992)* — Centaur ▲ CRC 2211 [DDD]
Svoboda, T.:Trio Fl *(rec Scottish Rite Temple, Portland, OR, Mar. 1992)* — Centaur ▲ CRC 2211 [DDD]
Zeiger, J.:Estonian Suite *(rec Scottish Rite Temple, Portland, OR, Mar. 1992)* — Centaur ▲ CRC 2211 [DDD]

VIF Flute Quartet [Hildegard Schattenberg (fl), Stefan Boots (fl), Christiane Oxenfort (fl), Andreas Dahmen (fl)]
Beckmann, H.:Levada — New Classic Colours ▲ ♦ NCC 8001 [DDD]
Beckmann, H.:Uptime — New Classic Colours ▲ ♦ NCC 8001 [DDD]
Bozza, E.:Jour d'été à la montagne — New Classic Colours ♦ NCC 8001 [DDD]
Gluck, C.W.:Orfeo ed Euridice (sels) [arr Oliver Peters for 4 fls] — New Classic Colours ♦ NCC 8001 [DDD]
Gulda, F.:Fuge Pno [arr Oliver Peters for 4 fl] — New Classic Colours ♦ NCC 8001 [DDD]
Lins, I.:Setembro [arr Oliver Peters for 4 fl] — New Classic Colours ♦ NCC 8001 [DDD]
Peters, O.:Feu VIF, w. Kölner Saxophone Mafia — New Classic Colours ♦ NCC 8001 [DDD]

Viklarbo Chamber Ensemble
Newman, Alfred:Robe, w. Amelite Consortium — Raptoria Caam ▲ RCD 1004
Newman, M.:Chamber Music, Amelite Consortium—Solus for Violin & Cello; Ornitholites for Cl Qnt; Dances for Deliverence for solo Violin — Raptoria Caam ▲ RCD 1004

Viklarbo Chamber Ensemble (cont.)
Newman, M.:Music of, w. Randy Newman (nar)—On a Pincushion; A Guide to Chamber Music; The Happy Prince for Vn & Nar — Raptoria Caam ▲ RCD 1002

Viklarbo Chamber Ensemble [M. Newman (vn), Jeff Elmassian (cl), S. Toettcher (vc), W. Prober (pno)]
Schickele, P.:Qt Vn *(rec Alfred Newman's home, 1990)* — Raptoria Caam ▲ RCD 1005

Viklarbo Chamber Ensemble [M. Newman (vn), Jeff Elmassian (cl), W. Prober (pno)]
Freund, D.W.:Triomusic *(rec Skip Saylor Studios, 1990)* — Raptoria Caam ▲ RCD 1005

Viklarbo Chamber Ensemble [M. Newman (vn), S. Toettcher (vc), J. Elmassian (cl)]
Dahl, I.:Concerto à tre *(rec Deep Sleep Studios, 1990)* — Raptoria Caam ▲ RCD 1005

Villa Marigola Festival Orch
Malipiero, G.F.:Dialogo 1, w. G. Garbarino — Nuova Era ▲ 6998 [DDD]
Malipiero, G.F.:Grottesco, w. G. Garbarino — Nuova Era ▲ 6998 [DDD]
G. Garbarino (cnd)
Casella, A.:L'Adieu à la vie, w. L. Zürcher (mez) [F] — Nuova Era 2-▲ 7143/44 [DDD]
Casella, A.:Con Vc, w. S. Palm (vc) — Nuova Era 2-▲ 7143/44 [DDD]
Casella, A.:Con Strs, Pno, Timp & Perc — Nuova Era 2-▲ 7143/44 [DDD]
Casella, A.:Serenata — Nuova Era 2-▲ 7143/44 [DDD]
Malipiero, G.F.:Con Vc, w. S. Palm (vc) — Nuova Era ▲ 6998 [DDD]
Malipiero, G.F.:Ricercari — Nuova Era ▲ 6998 [DDD]

Villa Musica Ensemble
Fauré, G.:Qt 1 Pno — MD + G ▲ MDG 3040536 [DDD]
Fauré, G.:Qt 2 Pno — MD + G ▲ MDG 3040536 [DDD]
Fuchs, R.:Qnt Cl — Marco Polo ▲ 8.223282 [DDD]
Hindemith, P.:Die junge Magd, w. Cornelia Kollisch (mez) — MD + G ▲ MDG 3040535 [DDD]
Hindemith, P.:Melancholie, w. Cornelia Kollisch (mez) — MD + G ▲ MDG 3040535 [DDD]
Hindemith, P.:Octet Winds & Strs — MD + G ▲ L 3447 [DDD]
Hindemith, P.:Qt Cl, Vn, Vc & Pno — MD + G ▲ MDG 3040537 [DDD]
Hindemith, P.:Qnt Cl — MD + G ▲ L 3447 [DDD]
Hindemith, P.:Septet Winds & Tpt — MD + G ▲ L 3447 [DDD]
Hindemith, P.:Die Serenaden, w. Christiane Oelze (sop) — MD + G ▲ MDG 3040535 [DDD]
Hindemith, P.:Son for 4 Hns — MD + G ▲ MDG 3040537 [DDD]
Hindemith, P.:Des Todes Tod, w. Christiane Oelze (sop) or Cornelia Kollisch (mez) — MD + G ▲ MDG 3040535 [DDD]
Hindemith, P.:Trio Pno — MD + G ▲ MDG 3040537 [DDD]
Hindemith, P.:Wie es wär', wenn's anders wär, w. Christiane Oelze (sop) or Cornelia Kallisch (mez) — MD + G ▲ MDG 3040535 [DDD]
Janácek, L.:Concertino Pno — MD + G ▲ L 3439 [DDD]
Janácek, L.:Fairy Tale — MD + G ▲ L 3439 [DDD]
Janácek, L.:Presto — MD + G ▲ L 3439 [DDD]
Janácek, L.:Son Vn — MD + G ▲ L 3439 [DDD]
Klein, G.:Divert Ob — MD + G ▲ MDG 3040618
Klein, G.:Duo Vn & Vc — MD + G ▲ MDG 3040618
Klein, G.:Movements Str Qt — MD + G ▲ MDG 3040618
Klein, G.:Son Pno — MD + G ▲ MDG 3040618
Klein, G.:Trio Vn — MD + G ▲ MDG 3040618
Lachner, F.P.:Septet Winds & Strs — Marco Polo ▲ 8.223282 [DDD]
MD & G Portraits:Ensemble Villa Musica — MD + G ▲ MDG 3492 [DDD]
Milhaud, D.:Chamber Syms — MD + G ▲ L 3449 [DDD]
Milhaud, D.:Les Rêves de Jacob — MD + G ▲ L 3449 [DDD]
Milhaud, D.:Suite d'après Corrette — MD + G ▲ L 3449 [DDD]
Mozart, W.A.:Qts Fl, w. J. C. Gérard (fl) *(rec Aug. 29–30, 1990)* — Naxos ▲ 8.550438 [DDD]
Reinecke, C.:Octet Ww — MD + G ▲ MDG 3040478 [DDD]
Reinecke, C.:Qnt Pno — MD + G ▲ MDG 3040478 [DDD]
Reinecke, C.:Sxt Ww — MD + G ▲ MDG 3040478 [DDD]
Schubert, Franz:Qnt Strs, D.956 — Naxos ▲ 8.550388 [DDD]
Schubert, Franz:Trio 2 Pno — Naxos ▲ 8.550388 [DDD]
Schulhoff, E.:The Cloud Pump — MD + G ▲ MDG 3040617
Schulhoff, E.:Concertino Fl — MD + G ▲ MDG 3040617
Schulhoff, E.:Divertissement Ob — MD + G ▲ MDG 3040617
Schulhoff, E.:Duo Vn — MD + G ▲ MDG 3040617
Schulhoff, E.:Son Fl — MD + G ▲ MDG 3040617
Spohr, L.:Qnt Fl — MD + G ▲ L 3448 [DDD]
Spohr, L.:Qnt Pno — MD + G ("Gold" series) ▲ MDG 3040534 [DDD]
Spohr, L.:Spt Fl — MD + G ("Gold" series) ▲ MDG 3040534 [DDD]
Spohr, L.:Sxt Strs — MD + G ▲ L 3448 [DDD]

Villanella Ensemble
S. Berger (cnd)
Tugend und Untugend:German Secular Songs & Instrumental Music from the Time of Luther, w. Convivium Musicum *(rec School of Music & Musicology, Gothenburg)* — Naxos ▲ 8.553352 [DDD]

Vilnius String Quartet
Balakauskas, O.:Qt 2 Strs — Academy ▲ ACA 8503
Juzeliunas, J.:Kantata — Academy ▲ ACA 8503-2
Kutavičus, B.:Anno cum tettigonia — Academy ▲ ACA 8503
Mozart, W.A.:Qnt Cl, K.581, w. Eddy Vanoosthuyse (cl) *(rec Vilnius Recording Studio, Vilnius, Lithuania, Mar 1995)* — Infinity Digital ▲ QK 69270 [DDD]
Narbutaite, O.:Qt 2 Strs — Academy ▲ ACA 8503-2
Weber, C.M. von:Qnt Cl, w. Eddy Vanoosthuyse (cl) *(rec Vilnius Recording Studio, Vilnius, Lithuania, Mar 1995)* — Infinity Digital ▲ QK 69270 [DDD]

Vincenzo Bellini Theater Orch
A. Quadri (cnd)
Bellini, V.:I Puritani (sels), w. Gabriella Tucci (sop—Elvira), Vittorina Magnaghi (mez—Enrichetta di Francia), Luciano Pavarotti (ten—Lord Arturo Talbo), Aldo Protti (bar—Sir Riccardo Forth), Ruggero Raimondi (bass—Sir Giorgio), Catania Teatro Massimo Bellini Chorus — Budget ("The Greatest Voice in Opera" series) ▲ SYP 106

Les Violons du Roy
C. Jackson (cnd)
Desmarets, H.:Motets, w. Sarah Leonard (sop), Jean-Paul Fouchécourt (ten), Norman Richard (b-bar), Montreal Ancient Music Ensemble—Domine ne in furore; Usquequo Domine Confitebor Tibi Domine; Lauda Jerusalem; Marche Lorraine — K617 2-▲ 7053
B. Labadie (cnd)
Bach, C.P.E.:Sinfs, H.654–656—Sinf in E♭, H.654 *(rec Church of Saint-Isidore, Quebec, Feb 1996)* — Dorian ▲ DOR 90239 [DDD]
Bach, Joh. Christian:Sinfs Orch, Op. 6—Sinf in g, Op.6/6 *(rec Church of Saint-Isidore, Quebec, Feb 1996)* — Dorian ▲ DOR 90239 [DDD]
Bach, J.C.F:Sinf, HW.I/3 *(rec Church of Saint-Isidore, Quebec, Feb 1996)* — Dorian ▲ DOR 90239 [DDD]
Bach, J.S.:Cant 173a, w. D. Röschmann (sop), H. Saint-Gelais (ten), K. McMillan (bar) *(rec Quebec City, Jan 1994)* — Dorian ▲ DOR 90199 [DDD]
Bach, J.S.:Cant 204, w. Dorothea Röschmann (sop) *(rec Saint-Isidore Church, Québec, May 1994)* — Dorian ▲ DOR 90207 [DDD]
Bach, J.S.:Cant 210, w. Dorothea Röschmann (sop) *(rec Saint-Isidore Church, Québec, May 1994)* — Dorian ▲ DOR 90207 [DDD]
Bach, J.S.:Cant 211, "Coffee Cant", w. D. Röschmann (sop), H. Saint-Gelais (ten), K. McMillan (bar) *(rec Quebec City, Jan 1994)* — Dorian ▲ DOR 90199 [DDD]
Bach, J.S.:Cant 212, "Peasant Cant", w. D. Röschmann (sop), H. Saint-Gelais (ten), K. McMillan (bar) *(rec Quebec City, Jan 1994)* — Dorian ▲ DOR 90199 [DDD]
Bach, W.F.:Ov *(rec Church of Saint-Isidore, Quebec, Feb 1996)* — Dorian ▲ DOR 90239 [DDD]
Bach, W.F.:Sinf in d *(rec Church of Saint-Isidore, Quebec, Feb 1996)* — Dorian ▲ DOR 90239 [DDD]

426 ▲ = CD ♦ = Enhanced CD Δ = MD ■ = Cassette Tape □ = DCC

Les Violons du Roy (cont.)
B. Labadie (cnd) (cont.)
Pergolesi, G.B.:Stabat mater, w. D. Röschmann (sop), C. Robbin (mez) Dorian ▲ DOR 90196 [DDD]
Simphonies des Noëls:A Treasury of Baroque Christmas Concerti Dorian ▲ DOR 90180 [DDD]
Vivaldi, A.:Motets, w. D. Röschmann (sop), C. Robbin (mez) Dorian ▲ DOR 90196 [DDD]
Vivaldi, A.:Stabat Mater Cta, w. C. Robbin (mez) Dorian ▲ DOR 90196 [DDD]
Viotta Ensemble
Coenan, J.M.:Qnt Winds NM Classics ▲ NM 92035
Röntgen, J.:Serenade NM Classics ▲ NM 92035
Van Bree, J.B.:Allegro NM Classics ▲ NM 92035
Viotti CO
L. Borin (cnd)
Viotti, G.B.:Cons Vn, w. F. Mezzena (vn)—No. 1 in C, No. 2 in E, & No. 19 in g Dynamic ▲ CD 86 [DDD]
Viotti, G.B.:Cons Vn, w. F. Mezzena (vn)—No. 8 in D, No. 11 in A, & No. 12 in B♭ Dynamic ▲ CD 63 [DDD]
Viotti String Quartet
Pierné, G.:Qnt Pno, w. J. Hubeau (pno) Erato ("Musifrance" series) ▲ 2292-45525-2 [AAD/DDD]
Virgin Consort
K. Brown (cnd)
Charpentier, M.-A.:Messe de minuit pour Noël *(rec Church of St. Mary the Virgin, NYC)* Gothic ▲ G 49077 [DDD]
Virtual Orch
Winstin, R.I.:Con 1 Pno, w. R. I. Winstin (pno) E.R.M. ▲ CCC 6660 [DDD]
Winstin, R.I.:Music of, w. R. I. Winstin (pno)—In Memoria:J.S. Bach; Nursery Rhymes E.R.M. ▲ CCC 6660 [DDD]
Winstin, R.I.:Sym 4, w. R. I. Winstin (pno) E.R.M. ▲ CCC 6660 [DDD]
I Virtuosi Dell'Accademia
Bonporti, F.A.:Concerti (10) à Quattro, Op. 11—Nos. 4-6, 8 & 9 *(rec 12/90)* Nuova Era ▲ 7000 [DDD]
Virtuosi Quintet
Baksa, R.:Qnt (No. 1) Ww Capstone ▲ CPS 8608 [DDD]
Virtuosi Quintet members
Baksa, R.:Qt Pno & Winds, w. A. Kim (pno) Capstone ▲ CPS 8608 [DDD]
Virtuosi Saxoniae
Concertos for Trumpet & Corno da caccia, w. Ludwig Güttler (tpt) Berlin Classics ▲ BER 1102 [DDD]
The Golden Trumpet, w. Ludwig Güttler (tpt/hunting hn) Berlin Classics 2-▲ BER 9053
Ludwig Güttler:Trompete, Corno da Caccia, Posthorn, w. Ludwig Güttler (tpt), F. Kircheis (hpd), J. Bischof (vc), W. Zeibig (db) *(rec 1988-92)* Berlin Classics ▲ BER 1053 [DDD]
L. Güttler (cnd)
Ariosti, A.:Sacred Music, w. P. Schreier (ten)—O quam suavis est Berlin Classics ▲ BER 1077 [DDD]
Bach, J.S.:Brandenburg Cons Berlin Classics 3-▲ BER 1033 [DDD]
Fux, J.J.:Plaudite, sonat tuba, w. P. Schreier (ten) Berlin Classics ▲ BER 1077 [DDD]
Hasse, J.A.:Mass for Dresden, "Terza messa", w. Thüringian Academic Sing Circle Berlin Classics ▲ BER 1006 [DDD]
Heinichen, J.D.:Sacred Music, w. P. Schreier (ten)—Lamentatio I Berlin Classics ▲ BER 1077 [DDD]
Pisendel, J.G.:Con grossi—in E♭ & D Berlin Classics ▲ BER 1079 [DDD]
Pisendel, J.G.:Sinf in B♭ Berlin Classics ▲ BER 1079 [DDD]
Quantz, J.J.:Cons for 2 Fls—in g *(rec Feb. 1988)* Berlin Classics ▲ BER 1002 [DDD]
Scarlatti, A.:Su le sponde del Tebro, w. P. Schreier (ten) Berlin Classics ▲ BER 1077 [DDD]
Telemann, G.P.:Cons (misc)—in F Berlin Classics ▲ BER 1079 [DDD]
Telemann, G.P.:Cons Vn—in D *(rec 1988)* Berlin Classics ▲ BER 1002 [DDD]
Vivaldi, A.:Con Ob, RV.456 Berlin Classics ▲ BER 1082 [DDD]
Vivaldi, A.:Con Va d'amore Lt Berlin Classics ▲ BER 1082 [DDD]
Vivaldi, A.:Con Vn Obs, RV.576 Berlin Classics ▲ BER 1082 [DDD]
Vivaldi, A.:Cons for 2 Vns—in D, RV.564a *(rec Feb. 1988)* Berlin Classics ▲ BER 1002 [DDD]
Vivaldi, A.:Con for 2 Vns Rcrs Berlin Classics ▲ BER 1082 [DDD]
Vivaldi, A.:Cons for 4 Vns Berlin Classics ▲ BER 1082 [DDD]
Vivaldi, A.:Gloria, RV.589, w. Hallenser Madrigal Singers Berlin Classics ▲ BER 1003 [DDD]
Vivaldi, A.:Magnificat, RV.611, w. Hallenser Madrigal Singers Berlin Classics ▲ BER 1003 [DDD]
Vivaldi, A.:Motets, w. Hallenser Madrigal Singers—in D, RV.642, "Ostro picta" Berlin Classics ▲ BER 1003 [DDD]
Zelenka, J.D.:Capriccios Berlin Classics 4-▲ BER 1150 [DDD]
Zelenka, J.D.:Capriccios—in A for 2 Oboes, Bassoon, 2 Corni da caccia, Strings & Continuo *(rec Feb. 1988)* Berlin Classics ▲ BER 1002 [DDD]
Zelenka, J.D.:Confitebor, w. Burkhard Glaetzner (ob), Thüringian Academic Sing Circle Berlin Classics 4-▲ BER 1150 [DDD]
Zelenka, J.D.:Laudate pueri, w. Thüringian Academic Sing Circle Berlin Classics 4-▲ BER 1150 [DDD]
Zelenka, J.D.:Missa Dei Patris, w. Thüringian Academic Sing Circle Berlin Classics ▲ BER 1078
Zelenka, J.D.:Missa Dei Patris, w. Thüringian Academic Sing Circle Berlin Classics 4-▲ BER 1150 [DDD]
Zelenka, J.D.:Music of, w. P. Schreier (ten)—Laudate pieri Berlin Classics ▲ BER 1077 [DDD]
Virtuoso Strings
C. Kendell (cnd)
Stewart, R.:Idyll Strs MMC ("Chamber Music" series) ▲ MMC 2010
Vivaldi Consort
Vivaldi, A.:Cons Diverse Instrs—in D for Vn & Fl; in g for Fl, Ob & Bn; in D for Vn, Fl & Bn; in g for Fl, Vn & Bn; in F for Fl, Vn & Bn; in d for Vn, Fl & Bn Rivoalto ▲ RIV 9010 [DDD]
Vivaldi, A.:Sons Ob, w. P. Pollastri (ob)—in c, RV.53; in g, RV.81; in B♭, RV.34; in g, RV.51; in C, RV.48; in C (unpubl.); in g, RV.28 Tactus ▲ TC 672203
Le Vivaldiane CO
Corelli, A.:Concerti grossi, Op. 6 *(rec Italy, Apr 1-3, 1995 & Jul 10-12)* Agorá 2-▲ 011/012 [DDD]
Vivant Trio
Jalousie Pro Arte ▲ CDD 586 [DDD]
Joyful Tidings Intersound ▲ CHD 1525 [DDD]
Palm Court Encores *(rec 1/91)* Pro Arte ▲ CDD 565 [DDD]
Palm Court Pleasures Pro Arte ▲ CDD 369 [DDD]
Vivenza
Encore Skylark ▲ 9101 [DDD]
In Palm Court Style Skylark ▲ 9001 [DDD]
Vivo Duo [L. Hunter (sax), B. Connelly (pno)]
Bolcom, W.:Lilith Crystal ▲ CD 651 [DDD] ■ C 651 (D)
Gottschalk, A.:Jeu de chat Crystal ▲ CD 651 [DDD] ■ C 651 (D)
Rogers, R.:The Nature of This Whirling Wheel Crystal ▲ CD 651 [DDD] ■ C 651 (D)
Vivo Duo [L. Hunter (sax), B. Connelly (syn)]
Galante, S.:Shu Gath Manna Crystal ▲ CD 651 [DDD] ■ C 651 (D)
Vlach String Quartet [Jana Vlachová (vn), Karel Stadtherr (vn), Petr Verner (va), Mikael Ericsson (vc)]
Beethoven, L. van:Qts Strs (comp) *(rec 1960-67)* Praga 7-▲ PR 254 009/15
Brahms, J.:Qt 2 Strs Praga ▲ PR 250074
Brahms, J.:Qt 3 Strs Praga ▲ PR 250074
Dvořák, A.:Bagatelles, Op. 47 *(rec by Czech Radio 1957-67)* Praga 3-▲ PR 250004/06
Dvořák, A.:Qt 8 Strs *(rec Martinek Hall, Prague, Oct 12, 1995)* Naxos ▲ 8.553372 [DDD]
Dvořák, A.:Qt 9 Strs *(rec by Czech Radio 1957-67)* Praga 3-▲ PR 250004/06
Dvořák, A.:Qt 9 Strs *(rec Martinek Studio, Prague, 1995)* Naxos ▲ 8.553373 [DDD]
Dvořák, A.:Qt 11 Strs *(rec Martinek Hall, Prague, Oct 12, 1995)* Naxos ▲ 8.553372 [DDD]
Dvořák, A.:Qt 11 Strs *(rec by Czech Radio 1957-67)* Praga 3-▲ PR 250004/06
Dvořák, A.:Qt 12 Strs, "America" *(rec by Czech Radio 1957-67)* Praga 3-▲ PR 250004/06
Dvořák, A.:Qt 13 Strs *(rec by Czech Radio 1957-67)* Praga 3-▲ PR 250004/06
Dvořák, A.:Qt 14 Strs *(rec by Czech Radio 1957-67)* Praga 3-▲ PR 250004/06

Vlach String Quartet (cont.)
Haydn, J.:Qts Strs, Op. 74—No. 3 *(rec live, Czech Radio broadcasts, 1965)* Praga ▲ PR 250098 (m)
Janácek, L.:Qt 1 Strs Panton ▲ PAN 811203
Janácek, L.:Qt 2 Strs Panton ▲ PAN 811203
Mozart, W.A.:Qt 17 Strs *(rec live, Czech Radio broadcasts, 1965)* Praga ▲ PR 250098 (m)
Mozart, W.A.:Qt 19 Strs *(rec live, Czech Radio broadcasts, 1963)* Praga ▲ PR 250098 (m)
Vlach String Quartet members
Dvořák, A.:Terzetto *(rec by Czech Radio 1957-67)* Praga 3-▲ PR 250004/06
Voces Intimae String Quartet [Jorma Rahkonen (vn), Ari Angervo (vn), Mauri Pietikäinen (va), Veikko Höylä (vc)]
Arriaga, J.C.:Qts (3) Strs MD + G ▲ L 3236 [DDD]
Enescu, G.:Qts Strs, Op. 22 *(rec 1980)* Olympia ▲ OCD 413 [AAD]
Ligeti, G.:Qt 1 Strs BIS ▲ CD 53
Rautavaara, E.:Qt 4 Strs *(rec June 27, 1976)* BIS ▲ CD 66 [AAD]
Sallinen, A.:Qt 3 Strs BIS ▲ CD 41 [AAD]
Schumann, R.:Qts Strs, Op. 41—No. 3 BIS ▲ CD 10
Shostakovich, D.:Qt 8 Strs BIS ▲ CD 26 [AAD]
Sibelius, J.:Qt Strs, Op. 56 BIS ▲ CD 10
Voces Intimae String Quartet members
Enescu, G.:Qt 1 Pno, w. Y. Piedemonte (pno) *(rec 1981)* Olympia ▲ OCD 412 [AAD]
Enescu, G.:Qt 2 Pno, w. Y. Piedemonte (pno) *(rec 1981)* Olympia ▲ OCD 412 [AAD]
Voces String Quartet
Enescu, G.:Oct Strs, w. Euterpe String Quartet Marco Polo ▲ 8.223147
Vogler String Quartet
Bartók, B.:Qt 2 Strs RCA Red Seal ▲ 09026-61185-2
Beethoven, L. van:Qt 7 Strs RCA Red Seal ▲ 09026-61185-2
Berg, A.:Lyric Suite RCA Red Seal ▲ 09026-60855-2
Brahms, J.:Qt 2 Strs RCA Red Seal ▲ 09026-61866-2
Brahms, J.:Qt 3 Strs RCA Red Seal ▲ 09026-61438-2
Debussy, C.:Qt Strs RCA Red Seal ▲ 09026-61816-2
Janácek, L.:Qt 1 Strs RCA Red Seal ▲ 09026-61816-2
Schumann, R.:Qts Strs, Op. 41—No. 1 RCA Red Seal ▲ 09026-61438-2
Schumann, R.:Qt Strs, Op. 41/1 RCA Red Seal ▲ 09026-61866-2
Shostakovich, D.:Qt 11 Strs RCA Red Seal ▲ 09026-61816-2
Verdi, G.:Qt Strs RCA Red Seal ▲ 09026-60855-2
Vogtland PO Greiz/Reichenbach
H.-R. Förster (cnd)
Stavenhagen, B.:Con 2 Pno, w. V. Lehmann (pno) ebs ▲ ebs 6079 [DDD]
Stavenhagen, B.:Songs, w. H. Spatzek (sop), T. Pfeiffer (bar) ebs ▲ ebs 6079 [DDD]
Voices of Ascension Orch
Duruflé, M.:Mass, "Cum jubilo", w. François le Roux (bar), D. Keene (cnd), Voices of Ascension Chorus *(rec Church of the Ascension, New York City, May 13, 17 & 18, 1995)* Delos ▲ DE 3169 [DDD]
Duruflé, M.:Requiem, w. Patricia Spence (mez), François le Roux (bar), D. Keene (cnd), Voices of Ascension Chorus *(rec Church of the Ascension, New York City, June 5-6, 1994)* Delos ▲ DE 3169 [DDD]
Volharding Orch
Dias, A.V.:Pranto Attacca ▲ 8953-6 [DDD]
Manen, W. van:Mikroskoop Attacca ▲ 8953-6 [DDD]
Martland, S.:Shoulder to Shoulder Attacca ▲ 8953-6 [DDD]
Norden, M. van:Cookie Girl Attacca ▲ 8953-6 [DDD]
Padding, M. van:Remote Places Attacca ▲ 8953-6 [DDD]
Wolfe, J.:Arsenal of Democracy Point Music ▲ 454054-2
Wallace Collection
Gabrieli, G.:Canzoni Nimbus ▲ NI 5236-2 [DDD]
J. Wallace (cnd)
Berlioz, H.:Grande Symphonie funèbre et triomphale, w. Leeds Festival Chorus Nimbus ▲ NI 5175 [DDD]
Sousa, J.P.:Marches & Dances—marches & incidental music Nimbus ▲ NI 5129 [DDD]
Warren-Green, Wallace (cnd)
Weber, C.M. von:Marcia Vivace, Philharmonia Orch members Nimbus ▲ NI 5065 [DDD]
S. Wright (cnd)
Hindemith, P.:Concert Music Pno, Brass & Hps, w. J. Wallace (tpt), R. Kapil (pno), Philharmonia Orch Nimbus ▲ NI 5103 [DDD]
Vačkář, D.C.:Jazz Con, w. John Wallace (tpt), Radoslav Kapil (pno), Philharmonia Orch members Nimbus ▲ NI 5103 [DDD]
Wallfisch Duo [Ernst Wallfisch (va), Lory Wallfisch (pno)]
Brahms, J.:Son 1 Cl Bayer ▲ CD 200050 (m) [AAD]
Mendelssohn, F.:Son Va Bayer ▲ CD 200050 (m) [AAD]
Schumann, R.:Märchenbilder Bayer ▲ CD 200050 (m) [AAD]
Wallonie Opera Royal Orch
R. Rossel (cnd)
Verdi, G.:Arias, w. Marcel Vanaud (bar)—Nabucco; Stiffelio; Rigoletto; Il Trovatore; La Traviata; Un Ballo in Maschera; La Forza del destino; Don Carlo Ligia Digital ▲ 0203035
Verdi, G.:La forza del destino (ov) Ligia Digital ▲ 0203035
Verdi, G.:Nabucco (ov) Ligia Digital ▲ 0203035
Wallonie Royal CO
G. Octors (cnd)
Dvořák, A.:Serenade Strs Cypres ▲ 2615 [DDD]
Elgar, E.:Serenade Strs Cypres ▲ 2615 [DDD]
Tchaikovsky, P.:Serenade Strs Cypres ▲ 2615 [DDD]
Uy, P.:Choral pour la Paix, w. Dinah Bryant (sop), Zeger Vandersteene (ten), Philippe Huttenlocher (bar), Alain Carré (nar), Dominique Cornil (pno), Denis Menier (cnd), Namur Chamber Choir *(rec Aulne, Belgium, 1995)* Cypres ▲ 2611 [DDD]
Walloon & French Community of Belgium CO
Mozart, W.A.:Con 7 Pnos, w. O. Ouziel (pno), D. Ouziel (pno), G. Octors (pno) [arr. for 2 Pianos by Mozart] *(rec Jan. 1991)* Pavane ▲ ADW 7257 [DDD]
Mozart, W.A.:Con 10 Pnos, w. O. Ouziel (pno), D. Ouziel (pno) *(rec Jan. 1991)* Pavane ▲ ADW 7257 [DDD]
Walloon CO
Marc Grauwels & Friends, w. Marc Grauwels (fl), Marie-Noelle de Callataÿ (sop), Hiroko Masaki (sop), Dennis James (glass hmc), Ingrid Procureur (hp), Yves Storms (gtr), Yvietta Matison (va), Mark Drobinsky (vc), Alain De Rijckere (bn), Daniel Blumenthal (pno), Frank Michiels (perc), Belgian RSO Syrinx 2-▲ 96101 [DDD]
B. Labadie (cnd)
Bréval, J.B.:Sym concertante, w. M. Grauwels (fl), A. De Rijckere (bn) Syrinx ▲ 92101 [DDD]
Devienne, F.:Con 2 Fl, w. M. Grauwels (fl) Syrinx ▲ 92101 [DDD]
Devienne, F.:Con 7 Fl, w. M. Grauwels (fl) Syrinx ▲ 92101 [DDD]
Wanderer Trio
Chausson, E.:Trio Vn *(rec Feb. 2-6, 1993)* K617 ▲ 7031 [DDD]
Warmia National Orch
B. Amaducci (cnd)
Opera Arias, w. Giuseppe Morino (ten) Nuova Era ▲ NUO 6851 [DDD]
S. Frontalini (cnd)
Bellini, V.:Ariette da camera (6), w. J. Omilian (sop) [I] Bongiovanni ▲ GB 2098 [DDD]
Bellini, V.:Sinfs (3) Bongiovanni ▲ GB 2098 [DDD]
Cimarosa, D.:Requiem pro defunctis, w. K. Rymarczyk (sop), B. Krahel (mez), I. Jakubowski (ten), A. Niemierowicz (bar), Olsztyn Academy Chorus [L] Bongiovanni ▲ GB 2088 [DDD]
Mancinelli, L.:Ov romantica Bongiovanni ▲ GB 5505 [DDD]

ORCH. & ENS.

Warmia National Orch (cont.)
S. Frontalini (cnd) (cont.)
Mercadante, S.:Orchestral Music—Fantasia funèbre; Il Lamento del Bardo; Il Montanaro (sinfonia); Overture in D; Sinfonia fantastica; Lo Zampognato Napoletano Bongiovanni ▲ GB 2099 [DDD]
Warner Brothers Orch
E.W. Korngold (cnd)
Korngold, E.W.:Film Music—selections from Captain Blood; The Green Pastures; Anthony Adverse; The Prince & the Pauper; The Adventures of Robin Hood; Juarez; The Private Lives of Elizabeth & Essex; The Sea Hawk; The Sea Wolf; Kings Row; The Constant Nymph; Devotion; Between Two Worlds; Of Human Bondage; Escape Me Never; Deception *(rec 1935–1946)* Rhino Movie Music 2–▲ R2 72243

Warsaw Chamber Opera Orch
M. Nowakowski (cnd)
Dankowski, A.:Sym in E♭ Elysium ▲ GRK 704 [DDD]
Wanski, J.:Sym in D Elysium ▲ GRK 704 [DDD]
Warsaw CO
Polish Stars Sing the Carols, w. Teresa Zylis-Gara (sop), Wieslaw Ochman (ten), Polish Radio-TV SO [cnd:Stefan Stuligrosz], Poznan State PO Men's & Boys' Choir Polskie Nagrania Edition ▲ ECD 025
J. Dobrzanski (cnd)
Zebrowski, M.J.:Magnificat, Musica Antiquae Collegium Varsoviense [L] *(rec 1968)* Olympia ▲ OCD 317 [AAD]
E. Kajdasz (cnd)
Moniuszko, S.:Mass in E♭, w. H. Slonicka (sop), A. Malewicz (mez), W. Pilewski (bass), Polish Radio Chorus Olympia ▲ OLY 395 [ADD]
Moniuszko, S.:Sacred Music, w. H. Slonicka (sop), A. Malewicz (mez), W. Pilewski (bass), Polish Radio Chorus—Ne memineris; Vide humilitatem meam; Litanie Ostrobramskie, No. 1 Olympia ▲ OLY 395 [ADD]
W. Lutoslawski (cnd)
Lutoslawski, W.:Preludes & Fugue *(rec Warsaw, 1974)* Polskie Nagrania ▲ PNCD 043 [AAD]
M. Sewen (cnd)
Dankowski, A.:Sym in E♭ *(rec 1992)* Olympia ▲ OCD 380 [DDD]
Engel, J.:Sym in E♭ *(rec 1992)* Olympia ▲ OCD 380 [DDD]
Engel, J.:Sym in F *(rec 1992)* Olympia ▲ OCD 380 [DDD]
Mozart, W.A.:Con 20 Pno, w. Y. Okada (pno) Emergo ("Corneille" series) ▲ EC 3971
Mozart, W.A.:Con 27 Pno, w. Y. Okada (pno) Emergo ("Corneille" series) ▲ EC 3971
Namieyski:Sym in D Olympia ▲ OCD 380 [DDD]
Orlowski, M.:Sym in F Olympia ▲ OCD 380 [DDD]
Pawlowski, J.:Allegro Olympia ▲ OCD 380 [DDD]
K. Teutsch (cnd)
Handel, G.F.:Cons (16) Org, w. J. Bucher (org)—Nos. 7-10 Vivace ▲ 591 [ADD]
Warsaw Military District Band
Marsz, Marsz Polonia, w. Krakow Garrison Military Band, Polish Air Force Band, Polish Army Band, Polish Navy Band, Pomeranian Military District Band, Silesian Military District Band Polskie Nagrania Edition ▲ ECD 064 [DDD]
Warsaw National PO
R. Black (cnd)
MMC Warsaw Series, Vol. 2, w. Warsaw National Chorus, Victoria Griswold Master Musicians Collective ▲ MMC 2004 [DDD]
Warsaw National Philharmonic SO
K. Kord (cnd)
Elsner, J.:Passio Domini Nostri Jesu Christi, w. B. Harasimowicz (sop), K. Szmyt (ten), C. Galka (bar), P. Nowacki (bass), Warsaw National Philharmonic Sym Chorus *(rec 1990)* Muza ▲ PNCD 078 [DDD]
Warsaw Opera Orch
Latoszewski, Rezler (cnd)
Puccini, G.:Arias, w. Maria Foltyn (sop), Franciszek Arno (ten), Polish National RSO Katowice—Mi chiamano Mimi [from Cyganeria]; Ah! que gli ochi; Vissi d'arte [both from Tosca] Polskie Nagrania ▲ PNCD 275
Rezler, Latoszewski (cnd)
Moniuszko, S.:Halka (sels), w. Maria Foltyn (sop), Franciszek Arno (ten), Polish National RSO Katowice—Gdyby rannym slonkiem; O mój malenki Polskie Nagrania ▲ PNCD 275
Verdi, G.:Arias, w. Maria Foltyn (sop), Franciszek Arno (ten), Polish National RSO Katowice—O Patria mia [from Aida]; Ma dall'arido stelo [from Bal Maskowy]; Pace, pace, mio Dio [from Moc Przeznaczenia] Polskie Nagrania ▲ PNCD 275
Wagner, R.:Lohengrin (sels), w. Maria Foltyn (sop), Franciszek Arno (ten), Polish National RSO Katowice—Einsam in truben Tagen Polskie Nagrania ▲ PNCD 275
R. Satanowski (cnd)
Debussy, C.:Petite suite Olympia ▲ OCD 318 [DDD]
Honegger, A.:Sym 3 Olympia ▲ OCD 318 [DDD]
Massenet, J.:Thaïs (sels)—Méditation (intermezzo) Olympia ▲ OCD 318 [DDD]
Ravel, M.:Daphnis et Chloé (suite 2) Olympia ▲ OCD 318 [DDD]
Szymanowski, K.:Harnasie, w. J. Stepien (ten), Warsaw National Opera Chorus Koch Schwann ▲ CD 311064 [DDD]
Szymanowski, K.:Mandragora, w. P. Raptis (ten), Warsaw National Opera Chorus Koch Schwann ▲ CD 311064 [DDD]
Warsaw Orch
S. Frontalini (cnd)
Caggiano, N.:Adelchi Bongiovanni ▲ GB 5032 [DDD]
Warsaw Philharmonic CO
K. Teutsch (cnd)
Bach, J.S.:Air on the G String Polskie Nagrania ▲ PNCD 151 [ADD]
Bach, J.S.:Brandenburg Con 5—Allegro Polskie Nagrania ▲ PNCD 151 [ADD]
Bach, J.S.:Con 2 Vn—Allegro Polskie Nagrania ▲ PNCD 151 [ADD]
Bach, J.S.:Sons Fl, BWV 1030–35—Siciliana [from Son, BWV 1031] Polskie Nagrania ▲ PNCD 151 [ADD]
Handel, G.F.:Cons (16) Org, w. J. Bucher (org)—Op. 7/1–3 *(rec 1973)* Polskie Nagrania ▲ PNCD 170 [ADD]
Vivaldi, A.:Cons Vn, Op. 8/1–4, "The Four Seasons", w. Konstanty Andrzej Kulka (vn) *(rec Warsaw, 1970)* Polskie Nagrania ▲ PNCD 136 [ADD]
Warsaw PO
R. Black (cnd)
Carbon, J.:Inner Voices Master Musicians Collective ▲ MMC 2003 [DDD]
Kelly, P.:Sym 1 *(rec Mar. 4–6, 1991)* Vienna Modern Masters ▲ VMM 3005 [DDD]
Lennon, J.A.:Con A Sax, w. *(soloist unknown)* Master Musicians Collective ▲ MMC 2003 [DDD]
Lennon, J.A.:Sym Rhap Master Musicians Collective ▲ MMC 2003 [DDD]
McKinley, W.T.:New York Ov *(rec Mar. 4–6, 1991)* Vienna Modern Masters ▲ VMM 3005 [DDD]
McKinley, W.T.:Sym 3 Master Musicians Collective ▲ MMC 2003 [DDD]
McKinley, W.T.:Sym 5, "Irish" *(rec Mar. 4–6, 1991)* Vienna Modern Masters ▲ VMM 3005 [DDD]
Z. Gorzynski (cnd)
Chopin, F.:Con 2 Pno, w. Vladimir Ashkenazy (pno) Testament ▲ TESSBT 1045 (m) [ADD]
J. Katlewicz (cnd)
Mozart, W.A.:Don Giovanni (ov) *(rec Warsaw, 1969)* Polskie Nagrania ▲ PNCD 137 [ADD]
Mozart, W.A.:Nozze di Figaro (ov) *(rec Warsaw, 1969)* Polskie Nagrania ▲ PNCD 137 [ADD]
Mozart, W.A.:Zauberflöte (ov) *(rec Warsaw, 1969)* Polskie Nagrania ▲ PNCD 137 [ADD]
K. Kord (cnd)
Chopin, F.:Andante Spianato & Grande Polonaise, w. Halina Czerny-Stefanska (pno) *(rec Warsaw Philharmonic Hall, June 27–30, 1994)* Canyon Classics ▲ CD 248
Chopin, F.:Con 1 Pno, w. P. Paleczny (pno) *(rec Apr. 22-26, 1991)* Canyon Classics ▲ 3650 [DDD]
Chopin, F.:Con 2 Pno, w. A. Harasiewicz (pno) LaserLight ▲ 14 003 [DDD]
Chopin, F.:Con 2 Pno, w. Chopin, Frédéric, Adam Harasiewicz (pno) Laserlight ♦ 90017 [DDD]
Chopin, F.:Con 2 Pno, w. P. Paleczny (pno) *(rec Apr. 22-26, 1991)* Canyon Classics ▲ 3650 [DDD]

Warsaw PO (cont.)
K. Kord (cnd) (cont.)
Chopin, F.:Grand Fant on Polish Airs, w. Janusz Olejniczak (pno) *(rec Warsaw Philharmonic Hall, June 27–30, 1994)* Canyon Classics ▲ CD 248
Chopin, F.:Krakowiak, w. Piotr Paleczny (pno) *(rec Warsaw Philharmonic Hall, June 27–30, 1994)* Canyon Classics ▲ CD 248
Chopin, F.:Vars on Mozart's *La ci darem la mano*, w. Elzbieta Karas-Krasztel (pno) *(rec Warsaw Philharmonic Hall, June 27–30, 1994)* Canyon Classics ▲ CD 248
Elsner, J.:Passio Domini Nostri Jesu Christi, w. Bozena Harasimowicz (sop), Krzysztof Szmyt (ten), Czeslaw Galka (bar), Bogdan Sliwa (bar), Piotr Nowacki (bass), Henryk Wojnarowski (cnd), Ewa Marchwicka (cnd), Warsaw National Phil Chorus, E. Mlynarski State School of Music Children's Choir *(rec National Philharmonic, Warsaw, 1990)* Polskie Nagrania ▲ PNCD 078 [DDD]
Górecki, H.-M.:Sym 3, "Sym of Sorrowful Songs", w. J. Koslowska (sop) Philips ("Solo" series) ▲ 442411-2
Lutoslawski, W.:Chain 2, w. Krzysztof Jakowicz (vn) Polskie Nagrania ▲ PNCD 044 [AAD]
Mlynarski, E.:Con 2 Vn, w. Konstanty Andrzej Kulka (vn) *(rec Concert Hall of the National Philharmonic, Warsaw, June 21–27, 1990)* Polskie Nagrania ▲ PNCD 074 [DDD]
Mlynarski, E.:Sym in F *(rec Concert Hall of the National Philharmonic, Warsaw, June 21–27, 1990)* Polskie Nagrania ▲ PNCD 074 [DDD]
Mozart, W.A.:Requiem, w. Barbara Nieman (sop), Krystyna Szostek-Radkowa (mez), Wieslaw Ochman (ten), Leonard Mróz (bass), Henryk Wojnarowski (cnd), Warsaw National Phil Chorus *(rec Warsaw, 1979)* Polskie Nagrania ▲ PNCD 135 [ADD]
J. Krenz (cnd)
Chopin, F.:Con 2 Pno, w. Fabio Bidini (pno) *(rec National Philharmonic Concert Hall, Warsaw, June 1, 1991)* Polskie Nagrania ▲ PNCD 126 [DDD]
Lutoslawski, W.:Livre *(rec Warsaw, 1969)* Polskie Nagrania ▲ PNCD 042 [AAD]
W. Lutoslawski (cnd)
Lutoslawski, W.:Paroles tissées, w. Louis Devos (ten) *(rec Warsaw, 1968)* Polskie Nagrania ▲ PNCD 042 [AAD]
Lutoslawski, W.:Sym 2 *(rec Warsaw, 1968)* Polskie Nagrania ▲ PNCD 041 [AAD]
A. Markowski (cnd)
Bacewicz, G.:Con 7 Vn, w. P. Janowski (vn) Olympia ▲ OLY 392 [ADD]
Penderecki, K.:Dimensions, w. Warsaw National Phil Chorus Polskie Nagrania 2–▲ PNCD 017 A/B
Penderecki, K.:Psalms, w. Warsaw National Phil Chorus Polskie Nagrania 2–▲ PNCD 017 A/B
Penderecki, K.:Utrenia, w. Delfina Ambroziak (sop), Stefania Woytowicz (sop), Krystyna Szczepanska (mez), Kazimierz Pustelak (ten), Boris Carmeli (bass), Wlodzimierz Denysenko (bass), Józef Bok (cnd), Stanislaw Skoraczewski (cnd), Warsaw National Phil Chorus, Pioneer Choir *(rec Warsaw, 1973)* Polskie Nagrania ▲ PNCD 018
H. Rotman (cnd)
Tchaikovsky, P.:Iolanta, w. Michaela Gurevich (sop—Iolanta), Jaqueline Miura (sop—Brigitta), Tatjana Tabachuk (mez—Martha), Annette Kuhn (mez—Laura), Ian Denolfo (ten—Godefroy), Keith Alexander Bolves (ten—Alméric), Alexander Ben (bar—Robert), Georg Lehner (bar—Ibn-Hakia), Arutiun Kotchinian (bass—René), Kurt Geysen (bass—Bertrand), ECOV Ensemble Members *(rec Vooruit Center of the Arts, Ghent, Belgium, Aug 28–29, 1993)* CPO 2–▲ CPO 999456-2 [DDD]
W. Rowicki (cnd)
Chopin, F.:Andante Spianato & Grande Polonaise, w. Halina Czerny-Stefanska (pno) *(rec Warsaw, 1959–60)* Polskie Nagrania ▲ PNCD 308
Chopin, F.:Andante Spianato & Grande Polonaise, w. Halina Czerny-Stefanska (pno) *(rec Warsaw, 1959)* Polskie Nagrania ▲ PNCD 306 B
Chopin, F.:Grand Fant on Polish Airs, w. Wladyslaw Kedra (pno) *(rec Warsaw, 1959–60)* Polskie Nagrania ▲ PNCD 308
Chopin, F.:Krakowiak, w. Wladyslaw Kedra (pno) *(rec Warsaw, 1959–60)* Polskie Nagrania ▲ PNCD 308
Chopin, F.:Vars on Mozart's *La ci darem la mano*, w. Wladyslaw Kedra (pno) *(rec Warsaw, 1959–60)* Polskie Nagrania ▲ PNCD 308
Lutoslawski, W.:Venetian Games *(rec Warsaw, 1962)* Polskie Nagrania ▲ PNCD 041 [AAD]
Mendelssohn, F.:A Midsummer Night's Dream (comp) *(rec Warsaw, 1960)* Polskie Nagrania ▲ PNCD 141 [ADD]
Mussorgsky, M.:Pictures, w. Piotr Paleczny (pno) [both versions] Polskie Nagrania Edition ▲ ECD 026
Penderecki, K.:Threnody for the Victims of Hiroshima Polskie Nagrania 2–▲ PNCD 017 A/B
Prokofiev, S.:Con 5 Pno, w. S. Richter (pno) Deutsche Grammophon ▲ 415119-2 [ADD]
Ravel, M.:Boléro *(rec Warsaw, 1960)* Polskie Nagrania ▲ PNCD 141 [ADD]
Rimsky-Korsakov, N.:Scheherazade Polskie Nagrania ▲ PNCD 253
Schumann, R.:Con Pno, w. A. Benedetti Michelangeli (pno) *(rec live, Warsaw, 1955)* Melodram 2–▲ CD 28019 (m)
Schumann, R.:Con Pno, w. Sviatoslav Richter (pno) *(rec National Philharmonic, Warsaw, Oct 1958)* Deutsche Grammophon ("The Originals" series) ▲ 447440-2 [ADD]
Stravinsky, I.:Pétrouchka Polskie Nagrania ▲ PNCD 260
Szymanowski, K.:Concert Ov Polskie Nagrania ▲ PLN 62 [ADD]
Szymanowski, K.:Con 1 Vn, w. Wanda Wikomirska (vn) Polskie Nagrania ▲ PLN 64 [ADD]
Szymanowski, K.:Con 2 Vn, w. Wanda Wikomirska (vn) Polskie Nagrania ▲ PLN 64 [ADD]
Szymanowski, K.:Harnasie, w. Kazimierz Pustelak (ten), Antoni Szalinski (cnd), Warsaw National Phil Chorus Polskie Nagrania ▲ PNCD 242 [AAD]
Szymanowski, K.:Litany to the Virgin Mary, w. Stefania Woytowicz (sop), Warsaw National Phil Chorus—12-note Zither; Like a Dwarf Bush *(rec Concert Hall at the National PO, Warsaw, 1961)* Polskie Nagrania ▲ PLN 063 [ADD]
Szymanowski, K.:Stabat Mater, w. Stefania Woytowicz (sop), Krystyna Szczepanska (alt), Andrzej Hiolski (bar), Warsaw National Phil Chorus *(rec Concert Hall at the National PO, Warsaw, 1961)* Polskie Nagrania ▲ PLN 063 [ADD]
Szymanowski, K.:Sym 2 Polskie Nagrania ▲ PLN 62 [ADD]
Szymanowski, K.:Sym 3, w. Stefania Woytowicz (sop), Warsaw National Phil Chorus *(rec Concert Hall at the National PO, Warsaw, 1961)* Polskie Nagrania ▲ PLN 063 [ADD]
Szymanowski, K.:Sym 4, w. Tadeusz Zmudzinski (pno) Polskie Nagrania ▲ PLN 62 [ADD]
Tchaikovsky, P.:Sleeping Beauty (suite) Deutsche Grammophon ("Resonance" series) ▲ 427219-2 [AAD] ■ 427219-4
Tchaikovsky, P.:Swan Lake (suite) Deutsche Grammophon ("Resonance" series) ▲ 427219-2 [AAD] ■ 427219-4
J. Semkow (cnd)
Bizet, G.:Carmen (sels), w. Krystyna Szczepanska (alt—Carmen), Bogdan Paprocki (ten—Don José), Andrzej Hiolski (bar—Escamillo), Alina Bolechowska (sgr—Micaela), Warsaw National Phil Chorus Polskie Nagrania ▲ PNCD 213 [AAD]
Rimsky-Korsakov, N.:Capriccio espagnol Polskie Nagrania ▲ PNCD 253
T. Strugala (cnd)
Chopin, F.:Con 1 Pno, w. S. Bunin (pno) *(rec 11th International Chopin Piano Competition, Warsaw 1985)* Capriccio ▲ 10217
Maciejewski, R.:Missa pro defunctis, w. Zdzislawa Donat (sop), Jadwiga Rappé (alt), Jerzy Knetig (ten), Janusz Niziolek (bass), Henryk Wojnarowski (cnd), Warsaw National Phil Chorus *(rec National Philharmonic, Warsaw, May 2–15, 1989)* Polskie Nagrania 2–▲ PNCD 039 A/B
Melcer, H.:Con 1 Pno, w. M. Ponti (pno) Olympia ▲ OLY 398 [DDD]
J. Swoboda (cnd)
Black, R.:Capriccio Orch, "Blown Apart" Bridge ▲ BCD 9061 [DDD]
Bokhour, R.:Angel Butcher, w. Ray Bokhour (nar) MMC ▲ MMC 2027 [DDD]
Goodman, J.:Sym 2 MMC ▲ MMC 2027 [DDD]
P. Tiboris (cnd)
Beethoven, L. van:Die Weihe des Hauses (ov) Albany ▲ TROY 089 [DDD]
Mahler, G.:Beethoven's Sym 5 Albany ▲ TROY 110
Mahler, G.:Beethoven's Sym 7 Albany ▲ TROY 110
Schubert, Franz:Sym 5 Albany ▲ TROY 089 [DDD]
S. Wislocki (cnd)
Beethoven, L. van:Coriolan Ov *(rec Warsaw, 1970)* Polskie Nagrania ▲ PNCD 137 [ADD]

428 ▲ = CD ♦ = Enhanced CD Δ = MD ■ = Cassette Tape □ = DCC

Warsaw PO (cont.)
S. Wislocki (cnd) (cont.)
Beethoven, L. van:Egmont (ov) *(rec Warsaw, 1970)* — Polskie Nagrania ▲ PNCD 137 [ADD]
Beethoven, L. van:Leonore 2 *(rec Warsaw, 1970)* — Polskie Nagrania ▲ PNCD 137 [ADD]
Rachmaninoff, S.:Con 2 Pno, w. S. Richter (pno) — Deutsche Grammophon ▲ 415119-2 [ADD]
Schumann, R.:Intro & Allegro, Op. 134, w. Sviatoslav Richter (pno) *(rec National Philharmonic, Warsaw, Apr 1959)* — Deutsche Grammophon ("The Originals" series) ▲ 447440-2 [ADD]

Warsaw Philharmonic SO
A. Markowski (cnd)
Turski, Z.:Sym 2 *(rec 1968)* — Olympia ▲ OCD 327 [AAD]
W. Rowicki (cnd)
Karlowicz, M.:Con Vn, w. Wanda Wilkomirska (vn) *(rec National Philharmonic Concert Hall, Warsaw, 1963)* — Polskie Nagrania ▲ PNCD 142 [DDD]
Szymanowski, K.:Con 1 Vn, w. Wanda Wilkomirska (vn) *(rec National Philharmonic Concert Hall, Warsaw, 1961)* — Polskie Nagrania ▲ PNCD 142 [DDD]
S. Wislocki (cnd)
Turski, Z.:Con 1 Vn, w. T. Wronski (vn) *(rec 1962)* — Olympia ▲ OCD 327 [AAD]

Warsaw Piano Quintet
Bacewicz, G.:Qnt 2 Pno — Olympia ▲ OLY 387 [ADD]

Warsaw RSO
S. Heinrich (cnd)
Liszt, F.:Legend of Saint Elizabeth, w. Maria Szechowska (sop), Doreen Millmann (mez), Klaus Lapins (bar), István Bercewy (bass), Warsaw Radio Chorus [G] *(rec 1983)* — Koch Schwann 2-▲ 3-1291-2 [ADD]
S. Rachon (cnd)
Rimsky-Korsakov, N.:The Tale of Tsar Saltan Orch, Op. 57 — Polskie Nagrania ▲ PNCD 253

Warsaw Radio-TV Orch
W. Kamirski (cnd)
Tchaikovsky, P.:Sleeping Beauty (suite) *(rec Warsaw, 1980)* — Polskie Nagrania ▲ PNCD 153 [ADD]
Tchaikovsky, P.:Swan Lake (suite) *(rec Warsaw, 1980)* — Polskie Nagrania ▲ PNCD 153 [ADD]

Warsaw Sinfonia
T. Bugaj (cnd)
Gluck, C.W.:La Corona, w. A. Slowakiewicz (sop), H. Gorzynska (sop), L. Juranek (sop), B. Nowicka (mez) [I] — Orfeo 2-▲ 135872 [DDD]
Gluck, C.W.:La Danza, w. E. Ignatowicz (sop), K. Myrlak (ten) [I] — Orfeo 2-▲ 135872 [DDD]
E. Krivine (cnd)
Mozart, W.A.:Sym 26 — Denon ▲ CO 77202 [DDD]
Mozart, W.A.:Sym 29 — Denon ▲ CO 77202 [DDD]
Mozart, W.A.:Sym 39 — Denon ▲ CO 77202 [DDD]

Warsaw Soloists
A. Mysinski (cnd)
Pergolesi, G.B.:Stabat mater, w. Brigitte Fournier (sop), Artur Stefanowicz (ct) *(rec Warsaw Philharmonic Concert Hall, Warsaw, 1992)* — Elysium ▲ GRK 705 [DDD]
Vivaldi, A.:Stabat Mater, w. Brigitte Fournier (sop), Artur Stefanowicz (ct) *(rec Warsaw Philharmonic Concert Hall, Warsaw, 1992)* — Elysium ▲ GRK 705 [DDD]

Warsaw State Opera House Orch
Z. Gorzynski (cnd)
Moniuszko, S.:Halka, w. Barbara Nieman (sop), Halina Sloniowska (sop), Jan Góralski (ten), Bogdan Paprocki (ten), Leslaw Pawluk (ten), Kazimierz Pustelak (ten), Andrzej Hiolski (bar), Edmund Kossowski (bass), Edward Pawlak (bass), Warsaw National Opera Chorus *(rec Warsaw, 1965)* — Polskie Nagrania ▲ PNCD 092 [AAD]
Rozycki, L.:Pan Twardowski (sels) — Olympia ▲ OCD 306 [AAD]
W. Rowicki (cnd)
Moniuszko, S.:Haunted Manor, w. Halina Slonicka (sop), Bozena Brun-Baranska (mez), Barbara Lawcewicz (mez), Krystyna Szczepanska (mez), Zdzislaw Nikodem (ten), Bogdan Paprocki (ten), Andrzej Hiolski (bar), Edmund Kossowski (bass), Bernard Ladysz (bass), Warsaw National Opera Chorus *(rec Warsaw, 1965)* — Polskie Nagrania ▲ PNCD 093 [AAD]

Warsaw Strings
M. Sewen (cnd)
Lipinski, K.J.:Caprice 20 Strs *(rec 1977)* — Olympia ▲ OCD 389 [AAD]

Warsaw SO
J. Bok (cnd)
Bach, J.S.:St. Mark Passion, w. K. Myrlak (ten), B. Jaszkowski (bar), et al., Warsaw Chamber Opera Chorus [G] — Bongiovanni 2-▲ GB 2024/25 [ADD]
J. Przybylski (cnd)
Castelnuovo-Tedesco, M.:Sérénade, w. D. Hopf (gtr), M. Tröster (gtr) *(rec Aug. 1992)* — Thorofon ▲ CTH 2171 [DDD]

Warsaw Teatr Wielki Orch
Z. Gorzynski (cnd)
Gounod, C.:Faust (sels)—Seena z 1 aktu; Aria Walentyna; Piesn o zlotym cielcu; Wale; Aria Siebla; Cavatina Fausta; Aria Malgorzaty; Duet Malgorzaty i Fausta; Chór Zolnierzy; Serenada Metista; Final — Polskie Nagrania ▲ PNCD 222 [AAD]
Verdi, G.:Il trovatore (sels), w. Warsaw Teatr Wielki Chorus—Introdukcja I Cavatina Ferranda; Cavatina Leonory; Tercet Leonory, Manrica I Di Luny; Chór Cyganów; Canzona Azuceny; Duet Manrica I Azuceny; Aria Di Luny; Introdukcja I Chór Zolierzy; Scena I Aria Manrica; Scena I Aria Leonory-Miserere; Duet Leonory I Di Luny; Tercet Manrica, Leonory I Azuceny — Polskie Nagrania ▲ PNCD 228 [AAD]
R. Satanowski (cnd)
Moniuszko, S.:Halka, w. B. Zagòrzanka (sop), R. Racewicz (mez), W. Ochman (ten), A. Hiolski (bar), J. Ostapuik (bass), Warsaw Teatr Wielki Chorus *(rec live, 10/14/86)* — CPO 2-▲ CPO 999032-2 [DDD]
Szymanowski, K.:King Roger, w. B. Zagórzanka (sop—Roger), S. Kowalski (ten—Shepherd), Z. Nikodem (ten—Edrisi), F. Skulski (bar—Roger II), Warsaw Teatr Wielki Chorus [Polish] — Koch Schwann 2-▲ CD 314 014 [DDD]
Wicherek (cnd)
Moniuszko, S.:Songs & Arias, w. Hanna Rumowska-Machnikowska (sop), Anna Pawluk (pno), Polish Radio-TV SO, Polish RSO—Do Faona; Przasniczka; Mogila; Nad Rzeka; Powiedzcie Mi; Czy Powroci; Gdyby Kto Mnie Kochal Szczerze; Przepioreczka; Nawrócona; Hola Ptaszki; O, Sama Nie Wiem; Oj, Polece Ja Daleko; Jako Od Wichru Krzew Polamany; Oi Jakzebym Kleczec Juz Chciala Gdyby Rannym Slonkiem; Hal Dzieciatko Nam Umiera O Mój Malenki — Polskie Nagrania ("Polskie Radio" series) ▲ PNCD 322

Warsaw Wind Quintet
Poulenc, F.:Sxt Pno, w. M. Otaki (pno) — Koch Schwann ▲ SCH 313942 [DDD]
Tansman, A.:Danse de la sorcière, w. M. Otaki (pno) — Koch Schwann ▲ SCH 313942 [DDD]
Thuille, L.:Sxt Pno, w. M. Otaki (pno) — Koch Schwann ▲ SCH 313942 [DDD]

Warschauer SO
J. Przybylski (cnd)
Moreno Torroba, F.:Concierto de Castilla, w. M. Tröster (gtr) *(rec Aug. 1992)* — Thorofon ▲ CTH 2171 [DDD]
Rodrigo, J.:Concierto de Aranjuez, w. M. Tröster (gtr) *(rec Aug. 1992)* — Thorofon ▲ CTH 2171 [DDD]

Washington Camerata Ensemble
Faith, R.:Fant Trio *(rec Livingston, MD, July 1994)* — Vernissage ▲ VR 1019 [DDD]
Khachaturian, A.:Trio Cl *(rec Livingston, MD, July 1994)* — Vernissage ▲ VR 1019 [DDD]
Milhaud, D.:Suite Vn *(rec Livingston, MD, July 1994)* — Vernissage ▲ VR 1019 [DDD]
Mozart, W.A.:Trio Cl, K.498 *(rec Livingston, MD, July 1994)* — Vernissage ▲ VR 1019 [DDD]

Washington Chamber Soloists
E. Carroll (cnd)
Handel, G.F.:Water Music (comp) — Infinity Digital ▲ QK 62384 [DDD]
Handel, G.F.:Water Music (sels)—Air; Bourrée; Hornpipe — Sony Classical ▲ MLK 62369 [ADD/DDD]

Washington Music Ensemble
Lazar (cnd)
Siegmeister, E.:Langston Hughes Songs, w. C. Williams (bar) [E] — CRI ■ C 532

Washington Winds
K. Brion (cnd)
Sousa, J.P.:Marches & Dances—Semper fidelis; Fugue on Yankee Doodle; Liberty Bell; Free Lance; Willow Blossoms; Untitled March; Hands across the Sea; El Capitan; Pirates of Penzance (sels); Sabre & Spurs; Manhattan Beach March; I've Made My Plans for the Summer; Washington Post; Thunderer; Black Horse Troop; Songs of Grace & Songs of Glory; Invincible Eagle; Stars & Stripes Forever *(rec Omega Studios, Rockville, MD)* — Walking Frog ▲ WFR 137 [DDD]
E. Peterson (cnd)
Barker, W.:By the River's Bend *(rec Omega Studios, Rockville, MD)* — Walking Frog ▲ WFR 105 [DDD]
Barker, W.:Danny Boy [trad; arr Barker] *(rec Omega Studios, Rockville, MD)* — Walking Frog ▲ WFR 105 [DDD]
Barker, W.:Deir in De *(rec Omega Studios, Rockville, MD)* — Walking Frog ▲ WFR 105 [DDD]
Barker, W.:Ov a la Russe *(rec Omega Studios, Rockville, MD)* — Walking Frog ▲ WFR 105 [DDD]
Barnhouse, C.L.:Marches—Harmony Heaven; Messenger March *(rec Omega Studios, Rockville, MD)* — Walking Frog ▲ WFR 101 [DDD]
Classics! *(rec Omega Studios, Rockville, MD)* — Walking Frog ▲ WFR 129 [DDD]
Hilliard, Q.:Vars on an African Hymnsong *(rec Omega Studios, Rockville, MD)* — Walking Frog ▲ WFR 105 [DDD]
Huckeby, E.:Music of—Explorations; Declaration, Ballade & Finale; Fanfare & Toccata; Prelude & Primal Dance; Of a Distant Star; On Wings of Eagles; Concertante for Winds; Pine River Trilogy; Overtura; Blue Lake Reflections; Jubiloso; Intrada & Festival; Acclamations *(rec Omega Studios, Rockville, MD)* — Walking Frog ▲ WFR 103 [DDD]
Jewell, F.:E Pluribus Unum March *(rec Omega Studios, Rockville, MD)* — Walking Frog ▲ WFR 101 [DDD]
Jutras, A.:A Barrie North Celebration *(rec Omega Studios, Rockville, MD)* — Walking Frog ▲ WFR 105 [DDD]
King, K.L.:Marches—Barnum & Bailey's Favorite [arr Bainum]; Allied Honor; Alamo March; Valley Forge March; United Nations March; Bonds of Unity; Coast Guards March [all arr Swearingen]; Trombone King; Hosts of Freedom; Broadway One-Step; Purple Pageant [all arr Paynter]; Walking Frog [arr Foster] *(rec Omega Studios, Rockville, MD)* — Walking Frog ▲ WFR 101 [DDD]
Kopetz, B.:Knightsbridge Chronicles *(rec Omega Studios, Rockville, MD)* — Walking Frog ▲ WFR 105 [DDD]
Niehaus, L.:Morro Bay *(rec Omega Studios, Rockville, MD)* — Walking Frog ▲ WFR 105 [DDD]
Richards, J.J.:Emblem of Unity March *(rec Omega Studios, Rockville, MD)* — Walking Frog ▲ WFR 101 [DDD]
Shaffer, D.:Regatta *(rec Omega Studios, Rockville, MD)* — Walking Frog ▲ WFR 105 [DDD]
Shaffer, D.:Suncoast Carnival *(rec Omega Studios, Rockville, MD)* — Walking Frog ▲ WFR 105 [DDD]
Sheldon, R.:Music of—Danse Celestiale; West Highlands Sojurn; Symphonic Narrative; Images; Fanfare & Intermezzo; Lindbergh Vars; Ocean Ridge Rhap; Corsair's Landing; Lost Colony *(rec Omega Studios, Rockville, MD)* — Walking Frog ▲ WFR 104 [DDD]
Swearingen, J.:Music of—Centuria; Child's Lullaby; Exaltation; Legacy; Novena; Silvercrest; Exordium; All Glory Told; Invicta; Covington Square; Romanesque; Chesford Portrait; Majestia *(rec Omega Studios, Rockville, MD)* — Walking Frog ▲ WFR 138 [DDD]
Swearingen, J.:Music of—Dawn of a New Day; Let the Spirit Soar; In All Its Glory; Blue Ridge Saga; Celebration & Dance; Proud Spirit; Light Eternal; Where the River Flows; Fant on an American Classic; Seagate Ov *(rec Omega Studios, Rockville, MD)* — Walking Frog ▲ WFR 102 [DDD]

Waterloo CO
U. Waterlot (cnd)
Le Rossignol de l'Opera:Musique Française de la Belle Epoque, w. Marc Grauwels (fl) — Syrinx ▲ 93102 [DDD]

Waverly Consort
A Waverly Consort Christmas:Christmas from East Anglia to Appalachia — Virgin Classics ▲ CDC 55193 ■ 4DS 55193
M. Jaffee (cnd)
Alfonso El Sabio:Cantigas de Santa Maria, w. J. DeGaetani (sop), C. Cassolas (ten), N. Kepros (troubadour) [Port] *(rec 1972)* — Vanguard Classics ("The Bach Guild" series) ▲ OVC 2013 [ADD]
1492:Music from the Age of Discovery — Angel ▲ CDC 54506
Renaissance Favorites — CBS ■ IMT 37845 (D)

Wawelskie Trio [Kaja Danczowska (vn), Jerzy Klocek (vc), Jerzy Lukowicz (pno)]
Meyer, K.:Trio Vn *(rec Munich, 1995)* — Pro Viva ▲ ISPV 176 CD [DDD]

Wayal Duo [Hayet Ayad (voc/perc), Nanette van Zanten (fid/hp cithara)]
Voices of the Medieval Mediterranean — Solstice ▲ SOL 103

Helga Weber Instrumentalkreis
Brassart, J.:Ave Maria, w. A. Teichert-Hailperin (sop), K. Smith (ct), W. Jochesn (ten), M. Nitz (ten) — Entrée ▲ 0041 [ADD]
Dufay, G.:Magnificat, w. A. Teichert-Hailperin (sop), K. Smith (ct), W. Jochesn (ten)—Octavi toni for 3 voices — Entrée ▲ 0041 [ADD]
Dunstable, J.:Sacred Music, w. A. Teichert-Hailperin (sop), K. Smith (ct), W. Jochens (ten), M. Nitz (ten), H. Deutsch (bar)—Sancta Maria; Beata dei genetrix; Beata mater et innupta virgo; Speciosa facta es; Alma redemptoris mater — Entrée ▲ 0041 [ADD]
Hildegard Of Bingen:Sacred Songs, w. A. Teichert-Hailperin (sop), K. Smith (ct), W. Jochens (ten), M. Nitz (ten), H. Deutsch (bar)—Caritas abundat in omnia; O virtus sapientiae; O quam mirabilis; Hodie aperuit nobis clausa porta; Alleluia. O virga, mediatrix; O clarissima mater; O frodens virga — Entrée ▲ 0041 [ADD]
Love Songs from the 14th & 15th Centuries, w. Almut Teichert-Hailperin (sop), Kevin Smith (ct), Wilfried Jochens (ten), Martin Nitz (ten) — Entrée ▲ CHE 0042-2 [ADD]

Wegelius CO
J. Storgårds (cnd)
Nordgren, P.H.:Con 4 Vn, w. John Storgards (vn) — Ondine ▲ ODE CD 873
Nordgren, P.H.:Cronaca — Ondine ▲ ODE CD 873

Weilerstein Duo [Donald Weilerstein (vn), Vivian Hornik Weilerstein (pno)]
Bloch, E.:Abodah, "God's Worship" — Arabesque ▲ Z 6605
Bloch, E.:Baal Shem, "3 Pictures of Chassidic Life" — Arabesque ▲ Z 6606
Bloch, E.:Music for Vn & Pno — Arabesque ▲ Z 6605/06
Bloch, E.:Nuit exotique — Arabesque ▲ Z 6606
Bloch, E.:Son 1 Vn — Arabesque ▲ Z 6605
Bloch, E.:Son 2 Vn, "Poème mystique" — Arabesque ▲ Z 6606
Bloch, E.:Suite hébraïque — Arabesque ▲ Z 6605

Weisberg Ensemble
Mayer, William:Two News Items, w. C. Rowe (sop) — CRI ■ C 291

Weiss Duo [Sidney Weiss (vn), Jeanne Weiss (pno)]
Grieg, E.:Sons Vn, Opp. 8, 13 & 45—No. 2 — Summit ▲ DCD 107 [DDD]
Grieg, E.:Son 2 Vn — Summit ▲ SMT 107
Mozart, W.A.:Sons Vn Pno (misc) — Summit ▲ SMT 107
Weiss Duo
Weiss Duo in Recital — Summit ▲ DCD 107 [DDD]

Welsh Guards Band
Music from the 1994 Royal Tournament, w. Coldstream Guards Band, Grenadier Guards Band, Irish Guards Band, Life Guards Band, et al. — Bandleader ▲ BND 5094 [DDD]
M. Reed (cnd)
Classical Spectacular, w. Royal PO, London Choral Society, Scots Guards Band — RPO Records 2-▲ CDRPD 9001 [DDD]
Classical Spectacular 1, w. Royal PO, Scots Guards Band, Musketeers of the Sealed Knot, London Choral Society — RPO Records ▲ RPO 5009 [DDD]

Welsh Guards Band (cont.)
M. Reed (cnd) (cont.)
Classical Spectacular 2, w. Royal PO, Gunnar Gudbjornsson (ten), J. Howard (bar), Scots Guards Band, London Choral Society RPO Records ▲ CDRPO 5010 [DDD]
P. Hannam (cnd)
Music from the Changing of the Guard Bandleader ▲ BND 5045 [DDD]
Welsh Guards Fanfare Trumpeters
Celebration:Christmas Fanfares & Carols, w. [cnd:John Hugh Thomas], BBC Welsh Chorus, Huw Tregelles Williams (org), Aled Jones (nar) Nimbus ▲ NI 5310 [DDD]
The Spirit of Christmas Present, w. Kansas City Chorale [cnd:Charles Bruffy], BBC Welsh Chorus [cnd:John Hugh Thomas], Huw Tregelles Williams (org), Christ Church Cathedral Choir [cnd:Stephen Darlington], Gulbenkian Orch [cnd:Michel Swierczewski], et.al. Nimbus ▲ NI 7034 [DDD]
Welsh National Opera Orch
R. Armstrong (cnd)
Britten, B.:Serenade, Op. 31, w. R. Tear (ten), A. Civil (hn) EMI Classics ▲ CDM 69522
R. Bonynge (cnd)
Bellini, V.:Norma, w. J. Sutherland (sop), M. Caballé (sop), L. Pavarotti (sop), S. Ramey (bass), Welsh National Opera Chorus [I] London 3-▲ 414476-2 [DDD]
Cilea, F.:Adriana Lecouvreur, w. J. Sutherland (sop), C. Bergonzi (ten), L. Nucci (bar), Welsh National Opera Chorus London 2-▲ 425815-2 [DDD]
Donizetti, G.:Anna Bolena, w. J. Sutherland (sop), S. Mentzer (mez), B. Manca di Nissa (cta), J. Hadley (ten), S. Ramey (bass) [I] London 3-▲ 421096-2 [DDD]
Thomas, A.:Hamlet, w. J. Sutherland (sop), S. Milnes (bar), Welsh National Opera Chorus London ("Grand Opera" series) 3-▲ 433857-2 [DDD]
Verdi, G.:I masnadieri, w. J. Sutherland (sop), F. Bonisolli (ten), M. Manugerra (bar), S. Ramey (bass), Welsh National Opera Chorus London ("Grand Opera" series) 2-▲ 433854-2 [DDD]
R. Goodall (cnd)
Wagner, R.:Parsifal, w. Waltraud Meier (mez—Kundry), Warren Ellsworth (ten—Parsifal), Nicholas Folwell (bar—Klingsor), Philip Joll (b-bar—Amfortas), Donald McIntyre (b-bar—Gurnemanz), Welsh National Opera Chorus EMI Classics 2-▲ CDMD 65665
G. Lloyd (cnd)
Lloyd, G.:The Vigil of Venus, w. Carolyn James (sop), Thomas Booth (ten), Welsh National Opera Chorus Albany ▲ TROY 170 [DDD]
C. Mackerras (cnd)
The Artistry of Fernando de la Mora, w. Fernando de la Mora (ten) *(rec Brangwyn Hall, Swansea, Wales & Music Hall, Cincinnati, OH, Nov. 10–11, 1994 & Feb. 1)* Telarc ▲ CD 80411 [DDD]
Britten, B.:Gloriana, w. J. Barstow (sop—Queen Elizabeth I), D. Jones (mez—Lady Essex), P. Langridge (ten—Earl of Essex), J. M. Ainsley (ten—Spirit of the Masque), J. Summers (bar—Lord Mountjoy), J. Shirley-Quirk (bar—Recorder of Norwich), B. Terfel (b-bar—Henry Cuffe), Welsh National Opera Chorus Argo 2-▲ 440213-2 [DDD]
Delius, F.:Aquarelles (2) Argo ▲ 433704-2 [DDD]
Delius, F.:Brigg Fair:An English Rhapsody Argo ▲ 430202-2 [DDD]
Delius, F.:Con Vn, w. T. Little (vn) Argo ▲ 433704-2 [DDD]
Delius, F.:Dance Rhap 1 Argo ▲ 433704-2 [DDD]
Delius, F.:Dance Rhap 2 Argo ▲ 433704-2 [DDD]
Delius, F.:Fennimore & Gerda (intermezzo) Argo ▲ 433704-2 [DDD]
Delius, F.:Florida Argo ▲ 430206-2 [DDD]
Delius, F.:In a Summer Garden Argo ▲ 430202-2 [DDD]
Delius, F.:Irmelin (prelude) Argo ▲ 433704-2 [DDD]
Delius, F.:North Country Sketches Argo ▲ 430202-2 [DDD]
Delius, F.:On Hearing the 1st Cuckoo Argo ▲ 433704-2 [DDD]
Delius, F.:Sea Drift, w. T. Hampson (bar), Welsh National Opera Chorus Argo ▲ 430206-2 [DDD]
Delius, F.:Songs Argo ▲ 433704-2 [DDD]
Gilbert, W.S.:Trial by Jury, w. Rebecca Evans (sop—Plaintiff), Barry Banks (ten—Defendant), Gareth Rhys-Davies (bar—Foreman of the Jury), Peter Savidge (bar—Counsel for the Plaintiff), Donald Adams (bass—Usher), Richard Suart (bass—The Learned Judge), Welsh National Opera Chorus *(rec Brangwyn Hall, Swasea, Wales, Apr 18–30 & May 1, 1995)* Telarc 2-▲ CD 80404 [DDD]
Gilbert, W.S.:The Yeomen of the Guard, w. Felicity Palmer (sop—Dame Carruthers), Pamela Helen Stephens (mez—Phoebe Meryll), Alwyn Mellor (sgr—Elsie Maynard), Clare O'Neill (sgr—Kate), Neill Archer (ten—Col Fairfax), Peter Hoare (ten—Leonard Meryll), Ralph Mason (ten—1st Yeoman), Donald Maxwell (bar—Wilfred Shadbolt), Peter Savidge (bar—Lieutenant Sir Richard Cholmondely), Donald Adams (bass—Sergeant Meryll), Richard Suart (bass—Jack Point), Peter Lloyd Evans (sgr—2nd Yeoman), Welsh National Opera Chorus *(rec Brangwyn Hall, Swasea, Wales, Apr 18–30 & May 1, 1995)* Telarc 2-▲ CD 80404 [DDD]
Sullivan, A.:HMS Pinafore, w. F. Palmer (sop—Little Buttercup), R. Evans (mez—Josephine), M. Schade (ten—Ralph Rackstraw), T. Allen (bar—Capt. Corcoran), R. Suart (bass—Rt. Hon. Sir Joseph Porter, K.C.B.), D. Adams (bass—Dick Deadeye), R. Van A. (bass—Bill Bobstay), Welsh National Opera Chorus *(rec Swansea, Wales, June 5–8, 1994)* Telarc ▲ CD 80374 [DDD]
Sullivan, A.:The Mikado, w. M. McLaughlin (sop), A. Howells (mez), J. Watson (sop), F. Palmer (sop/mez), D. Adams (bass), A. Rolfe Johnson (ten), R. Stuart (bar), R. Van Allan (bass), N. Folwell (bar), Welsh National Opera Chorus—Ov & dialogue omitted [E] Telarc ▲ CD 80284 [DDD]; ■ CS 30284 (D)
Sullivan, A.:The Pirates of Penzance, w. R. Evans (sop—Mabel), G. Knight (mez—Ruth), J. Gossage (mez—Edith), J. M. Ainsley (ten—Frederic), R. Suart (bar—Maj.-Gen. Stanley), N. Folwell (bar—Samuel), D. Adams (b-bar—Pirate King), R. Van Allan (bass—Sergeant of Police), Welsh National Opera Chorus *(rec May 4–6, 1993)* Telarc ▲ CD 80353 [DDD]; ■ CS 30353
Sullivan, A.:Trial by Jury, w. Rebecca Evans (sop—Plaintiff), Barry Banks (ten—Defendant), Gareth Rhys-Davies (bar—Foreman of the Jury), Peter Savidge (bar—Counsel for the Plaintiff), Donald Adams (bass—Usher), Richard Suart (bass—The Learned Judge), Welsh National Opera Chorus *(rec Brangwyn Hall, Swasea, Wales, Apr 18–30 & May 1, 1995)* Telarc 2-▲ CD 80404 [DDD]
Sullivan, A.:The Yeomen of the Guard, w. Felicity Palmer (sop—Dame Carruthers), Pamela Helen Stephens (mez—Phoebe Meryll), Neill Archer (ten—Col Fairfax), Peter Hoare (ten—Leonard Meryll), Ralph Mason (ten—1st Yeoman), Donald Maxwell (bar—Wilfred Shadbolt), Peter Savidge (bar—Lieutenant Sir Richard Cholmondely), Donald Adams (bass—Sergeant Meryll), Richard Suart (bass—Jack Point), Peter Lloyd Evans (sgr—2nd Yeoman), Alwyn Mellor (sgr—Elsie Maynard), Clare O'Neill (sgr—Kate), Welsh National Opera Chorus *(rec Brangwyn Hall, Swasea, Wales, Apr 18–30 & May 1, 1995)* Telarc 2-▲ CD 80404 [DDD]
Tchaikovsky, P.:Eugene Onegin, w. K. Te Kanawa (sop—Tatiana), P. Bardon (mez—Olga), N. Rosenshein (ten—Lensky), T. Hampson (b-bar—Eugene Onegin), J. Connell (bass—Prince Gremin), Welsh National Opera Chorus [E] EMI Classics ▲ CDCB 55004
C. Rizzi (cnd)
Gounod, C.:Faust, w. C. Gasdia (sop), B. Fassbaender (mez), S. Mentzer (mez), J. Hadley (ten), A. Agache (bar), P. Fourcade (bass), Welsh National Opera Chorus Teldec 3-▲ 90872
Hadley & Hampson, w. Jerry Hadley (ten), Thomas Hampson (bass) Teldec ▲ 73283-2
The Incomparable Alfredo Kraus, w. Alfredo Kraus (ten), Welsh National Opera Chorus Philips ▲ 442785-2
Verdi, G.:Rigoletto, w. L. Vaduva (sop), J. Larmore (mez), R. Leech (ten), A. Agache (bar), S. Ramey (bass) Teldec ▲ 90851-2
August Wenzinger Ensemble
Handel, G.F.:Cants, w. L. M. Åkerlund (sop)—Qual ti riveggio; No se Emenderá Jamás; Clori, mia bella Clori Accord ▲ ACD 201102 [DDD]
August Wenzinger Ensemble [Gottfried Bach (hpd), Yasunori Iamamura (lt), Hannelore Müller (vl), August Wenzinger (vl)]
Telemann, G.P.:Chamber Music—Sons in e, A, a & A; Fant in D; Son (Trio) in G Accord ▲ ACD 220282 [DDD]
Weser-Renaissance Ensemble
The Spirit of the Renaissance CPO ▲ CPO 999294 [DDD]
Stoltzer, T.:Missa duplex per totum annum, w. Manfred Cordes (cnd), Weser-Renaissance CPO ▲ CPO 999295
Stoltzer, T.:Psalm Motets, w. Manfred Cordes (cnd), Weser-Renaissance—3 sels CPO ▲ CPO 999295
Weser-Renaissance Ensemble [Mona Spagele (sop), Detlef Bratschke (alt), Andre Cats (ten), Martin Post (ten), Rein de Vries (bass), William Dongois (cnt), Olek Anderson (trbn), Cas Gevers (trbn), Henning Plumeyer (trbn), Manfred Cordes (trbn/org), Thomas Ihlenfeldt (lt)]
M. Cordes (cnd)
Lechner, L.:Sacred & Secular Songs—17 German Songs CPO ▲ CPO 999370
Wesleyan Univ New World Consort
Lucier, A.:Septet Lovely Music ▲ LCD 1018 [ADD]
West Australian SO
D. Masson (cnd)
Smalley, R.:Con Pno, w. R. Smalley (pno) Vox Australis ▲ VAST 003-2
H. Schönzeler (cnd)
Bliss, A.:Checkmate (5 dances) Chandos ("Collect" series) ▲ CHAN 6576 [ADD/DDD]
West Austrian SO
H. Moltkau (cnd)
Beethoven, L. van:Con Vn, Op. 61, w. P. Rybar (vn) Doron ▲ DRC 4001 [ADD]
Brahms, J.:Con Vn, w. P. Rybar (vn) Doron ▲ DRC 4001 [ADD]
West German Orch
R. Kraus (cnd)
Verdi, G.:Macbeth, w. Astrid Varnay (sop—Lady Macbeth), Trude Roesler (mez—Lady-in-waiting), Hasso Eschert (ten—Malcolm), Walter Geisler (ten—Macduff), Joseph Metternich (bar—Macbeth), Ludwig Weber (bass—Banquo), West German Chorus *(rec Cologne, 1954)* Myto 2-▲ 952128
West German Radio Orch
D. Mitropoulos (cnd)
Schoenberg, A.:Con Vn, w. L. Krasner (vn) *(rec live 7/16/54)* GM ▲ 2006
G. Solti (cnd)
Verdi, G.:Requiem Mass, w. Gré Brouwenstijn (sop), Oralia Dominguez (mez), Giuseppe Zampieri (ten), Nicola Zaccaria (bass), West German Radio Chorus Globe 2-▲ GLO 5141 [ADD]
West German RSO
C. Kleiber (cnd)
Berg, A.:Wozzeck (sels) [I] *(rec 1972)* Artists 2-▲ FED 45 [ADD]
West German Sinfonia
D. Joeres (cnd)
Brahms, J.:Serenade 1 Orch *(rec Broadcasting Hall, German Radio, Cologne, June 1992)* IMP ▲ IMP 2046
Brahms, J.:Serenade 2 Orch IMP ▲ IMP 2046
Haydn, J.:Con Org & Strs, H.XVIII/2, w. D. Joeres (pno) *(rec 3–3/91)* IMP Classics ▲ PCD 969 [DDD]
Mozart, W.A.:Con 12 Pno, w. D. Joeres (pno) IMP Classics ▲ PCD 969 [DDD]
Mozart, W.A.:Rondo Pno Orch, K.386, w. D. Joeres (pno) IMP Classics ▲ PCD 969 [DDD]
Schubert, Franz:Sym 2 IMP Classics ▲ IMP PCD 1052 [DDD]
Schubert, Franz:Sym 5 IMP Classics ▲ IMPPCD 1046 [DDD]
Voříšek, J.V.:Sym, Op. 24 IMP Classics ▲ IMP PCD 1052 [DDD]
West Jutland Chamber Ensemble
Britten, B.:Sinfonietta BIS ▲ CD 31 [AAD]
West Point Military Band
MacDonally (cnd)
Sousa & American Marches Tuxedo ▲ 5032
Sousa, J.P.:Marches & Dances—Gladiators; U. S. Field Artillery; Bride Elect; King Cotton Tuxedo ▲ 5032
Sousa, J.P.:Stars & Stripes Forever Tuxedo ▲ 5032
Westchester PO
P.L. Dunkel (cnd)
Sessions, R.:Con Pno, w. R. Taub (pno) *(rec Jan. 17, 1994)* New World ▲ 80443-2
Thorne, F.:Con 3 Pno, w. U. Oppens (pno) *(rec Jan. 18, 1993)* New World ▲ 80443-2
Westchester SO
S. Landau (cnd)
Glière, R.:The Red Poppy (sels)—Heroic Dance of the Coolies; Scene; Phoenix; Dance of the Russian Sailors Allegretto ▲ ACD 8161 [ADD] ■ ACS 8161
Ippolitov-Ivanov, M.:Caucasian Sketches, Op. 10 Allegretto ▲ ACD 8161 [ADD] ■ ACS 8161
Kurka, R.:The Good Soldier Schweik (suite) *(rec 1974)* Allegretto ▲ ACD 8191
Still, W.G.:Darker America *(rec 1973)* Vox Box ("The American Composers" series) 2-▲ CDX 5157
Still, W.G.:From the Black Belt *(rec 1973)* Vox Box ("The American Composers" series) 2-▲ CDX 5157
Weill, K.:Kleine Dreigroschenmusik *(rec 1974)* Vox Box 2-▲ CDX 5043 [ADD]
Western Brass Quintet
Husa, K.:Landscapes *(rec 1977)* CRI ▲ CD 592 [ADD]
Western Wind
Christmas in the New World, w. Albert de Ruiter (bass), Louise Schulman (vn), Wendy Gillespie (vl), Joseph Karpienia (gtr), Elaine Comparone (hpd) MusicMasters ▲ 01612-67176-2
Morrow, C.:Birth [E] Laurel ▲ LR 840CD [DDD]
An Old-Fashioned Christmas:Caroling with the Western Wind Elektra/Nonesuch ▲ 79053-2 ■ 79053-4
Westminster Abbey Consort
Adeste Fideles! Christmas Down the Ages, w. Emma Kirkby (sop), English CO [cnd:Martin Neary], Westminster Abbey Ensemble, Westminster Abbey Choir Sony Classical ▲ SK 62688 ■ ST 62688
Westminster Abbey Ensemble
Adeste Fideles! Christmas Down the Ages, w. Emma Kirkby (sop), English CO [cnd:Martin Neary], Westminster Abbey Consort, Westminster Abbey Choir Sony Classical ▲ SK 62688 ■ ST 62688
Westminster Abbey Orch
S. Preston (cnd)
Handel, G.F.:Dixit Dominus, w. Arleen Augér (sop), Lynne Dawson (sop), Diana Montague (mez), Leigh Nixon (ten), Simon Birchall (bass), Westminster Abbey Choir [L] Archiv ▲ 423594-2 [DDD]
Handel, G.F.:Nisi Dominus, w. Diana Montague (mez), John Mark Ainsley (ten), Simon Birchall (bass), Westminster Abbey Choir [L] Archiv ▲ 423594-2 [DDD]
Westminster CO
W. Ehmann (cnd)
Bach, J.S.:Motets, BWV 225–30, w. Daniel Beckwith (org), Westminster Choir [G]—final chorales of BWV 226 & 229 are omitted Gothic ▲ G 49052
Westminster Concert Bell Choir
D. E. Alfred (cnd)
Westminster Bell Choir Gothic ▲ GOT 49042
Westminster PO
K. Alwyn (cnd)
Steiner, M.:Film Music—Casablanca;The Caine Mutiny; Treasure of the Sierra Madre; A Summer Place; Helen of Troy; A Distant Trumpet; Adventures of Mark Twain; Gone with the Wind Silva America ▲ SILCD 1035
Waxman, F.:Film Music—The Bride of Frankenstein; The Invisible Ray Silva America ▲ SIL 1028 [DDD]
Westphalia CO
W. Gundlach (cnd)
Weill, K.:Down in the Valley, w. I. Davidson (sop), M. Acito (ten), D. Collup (bar), J. Mabry (sgr), D. P. Lang (sgr), Westphalia Kantorei Capriccio ▲ 60 020-1 [DDD]
Weill, K.:Der Jasager, w. H. Helling (cta), T. Schmeisser (treb), T. Bräutigam (ten), T. Fischer (ten), U. Schütte (bar), M. Knöppel (bass), Westphalia Kantorei Capriccio ▲ 60 020-1 [DDD]
Westphalia PO
F. Obstfeld (cnd)
Haas, P.:Study EDA ▲ 0092 [DDD]
Krása, H.:Ov Small Orch EDA ▲ 0092 [DDD]
Martinů, B.:Sextet Strs [arr composer for str orch] EDA ▲ 0092 [DDD]

 ▲ = CD ♦ = Enhanced CD Δ = MD ■ = Cassette Tape □ = DCC

Westphalia PO (cont.)
F. Obstfeld (cnd) (cont.)
Schreker, F.:Intermezzo Strs EDA ▲ 0092 [DDD]
Schreker, F.:Scherzo Strs EDA ▲ 0092 [DDD]
Westphalia PO Chamber Ensemble [Barbara Doll (vn), Pal Banda (vc), Heiner Rekeszus (cl), Alan Leighton (hn), Michael Allan (pno)]
Schreker, F.:Der Wind EDA ▲ 0092 [DDD]
Westphalia SO
R. Kapp (cnd)
Thalberg, S.:Con Pno, w. M. Ponti (pno) *(rec 1973)* Vox Box 2–▲ CDX 5066 [ADD]
S. Landau (cnd)
Korngold, E.W.:Much Ado About Nothing *(rec 1974)* Allegretto ▲ ACD 8191
Liapunov, S.:Rhap on Ukranian Themes, w. M. Ponti (pno) *(rec 1975)* Vox Box 2–▲ CDX 5068 [ADD]
Liszt, F.:Hexaméron, w. Eugene List (pno) *(rec Tonstudio Englesmann, Germany, 1973)* Vox Legends 3–▲ CDX3 3504
Liszt, F.:Odes funèbres—No. 3 Le triomphe funèbre du Tasse [epilogue to Tasso, S.95] Allegretto ▲ ACD 8158 [ADD] ■ ACS 8158
Liszt, F.:Les Préludes Allegretto ▲ ACD 8158 [ADD] ■ ACS 8158
Liszt, F.:Tasso—Lamento e Trionfo Allegretto ▲ ACD 8158 [ADD] ■ ACS 8158
Liszt, F.:Von der Wiege bis zum Grabe Allegretto ▲ ACD 8158 [ADD] ■ ACS 8158
Macdowell, E.:Con 2 Pno, w. E. List (pno) *(rec 1972)* Vox Box 2–▲ CDX 5069 [ADD]
Saint-Saëns, C.:Con 2 Vc, w. L. Varga (vc) Vox Box 2–▲ CDX 5084 [ADD]
Schumann, R.:Con Vc, w. L. Varga (vc) Vox Box 2–▲ CDX 5027 [ADD]
H. Reichert (cnd)
Beethoven, L. van:Con Vn, Op. 61, w. S. Lautenbacher (vn) Allegretto ▲ ACD 8014 [ADD] ■ ACS 8014
Goldmark, K.:Ländliche Hochzeit *(rec 1970)* Allegretto ▲ ACD 8173 [ADD] ■ ACS 8173
Mozart, W.A.:Con Cl, w. J. Michaels (cl) Allegretto ▲ ACD 8013 [ADD] ■ ACS 8013
Mozart, W.A.:Con Cl, w. Jost Michaels (cl)—Allegro Special Music Co. ("Classics of the Heart" series) ▲ SCD 5196
Mozart, W.A.:Con Cl, w. Jost Michaels (cl)—Allegro Special Music Co. ▲ SCD 5200
Saint-Saëns, C.:Wedding Cake, w. R. Kyriakou (pno) Vivace 3–▲ E 321 [DDD]
Westphalia SO Recklinghausen
P. Freeman (cnd)
Kay, U.:Dances *(rec 1973)* Vox Box ("The American Composers" series) 2–▲ CDX 5157
R. Kapp (cnd)
Bronsart von Schellendorf, H.:Con Pno, w. M. Ponti (pno) *(rec 1972)* Vox Box 2–▲ CDX 5067 [ADD]
S. Landau (cnd)
Balakirev, M.:Con 2 Pno, w. M. Ponti (pno) *(rec 1975)* Vox Box 2–▲ CDX 5068 [ADD]
Beach, A.M.C.:Con Pno, w. M.-L. Boehm (pno) *(rec 1976)* Vox Box 2–▲ CDX 5069 [ADD]
Coolidge, P.S.:Blue Planet *(rec 1975)* Vox Box ("The American Composers" series) 2–▲ CDX 5157
Coolidge, P.S.:New England Autumn *(rec 1975)* Vox Box ("The American Composers" series) 2–▲ CDX 5157
Coolidge, P.S.:Pioneer Dances *(rec 1975)* Vox Box ("The American Composers" series) 2–▲ CDX 5157
Coolidge, P.S.:Rhap Hp, w. Aristid von Wurtzler (hp) *(rec 1975)* Vox Box ("The American Composers" series) 2–▲ CDX 5157
Coolidge, P.S.:Spirituals in Sunshine & Shadow *(rec 1975)* Vox Box ("The American Composers" series) 2–▲ CDX 5157
Mason, D.G.:Prelude & Fugue *(rec 1976)* Vox Box ("The American Composers" series) 2–▲ CDX 5157
Schillings, M. von:Mona Lisa (suite) *(rec ca. 1973)* Vox Box 2–▲ CDX 5043 [ADD]
Weill, K.:Quodlibet *(rec ca. 1973)* Vox Box 2–▲ CDX 5043 [ADD]
Westphalia Trombone Quartet
Bozza, E.:Pièces (3) for 4 Trbns MD + G ▲ L 3094
Bruckner, A.:Motets—2 motets MD + G ▲ L 3094
Serocki, K.:Suite for 4 Trbns MD + G ▲ L 3094
Staden, J.:Partita Trbn MD + G ▲ L 3094
Sweelinck, J.P.:Fant chromatica MD + G ▲ L 3094
Trombone Quartets MD + G ▲ L 3094 [DDD]
Trombone Quartets 2 MD + G ▲ L 3295 [DDD]
Westwood String Quartet
Glinka, M.:Qt 2 Strs Protone ■ CSPR 164
Mendelssohn, F.:Qt in E♭ Strs Protone ■ CSPR 164
Toch, E.:Qt Strs, Op. 18 Protone ■ CSPR 165
Westwood String Trio
Toch, E.:Serenade Protone ■ CSPR 165
Westwood Wind Quintet
Barber, S.:Summer Music Crystal ▲ CD 750 ■ C 750
Bergsma, W.:Con Ww Qnt *(rec May 1992 & Jan 1993)* Crystal ▲ CD 752
Berio, L.:Children's Play Crystal ■ C 250
Biggs, J.:Scherzo Ww Qnt *(rec May 1992 & Jan 1993)* Crystal ▲ CD 752
Carlson, M.:Nightwings Crystal ▲ CD 750
Carlson, M.:Nightwings Crystal ■ C 750
Carter, E.:Qnt Ww *(rec May 1992 & Jan 1993)* Crystal ▲ CD 752
Dahl, I.:Allegro & Arioso Crystal ▲ CD 751
Husa, K.:Serenade, w. L. Bergman (pno) Crystal ▲ CD 751 [DDD]
Klughardt, A.:Qnt Winds Crystal ■ C 250
Ligeti, G.:Bagatelles Crystal ▲ CD 750
Ligeti, G.:Bagatelles Crystal ■ C 750
Mathias, W.:Qnt Ww Crystal ■ C 250
Mathias, W.:Qnt Ww Crystal ▲ CD 750
Moyse, L.:Qnt Ww Crystal ▲ CD 751
Pleyel, I.:Miniatures Va, w. J. Dunham (va) Crystal ■ C 647
Plog, A.:Animal Ditties *(rec May 1992 & Jan 1993)* Crystal ▲ CD 752
Rochberg, G.:To the Dark Wood *(rec May 1992 & Jan 1993)* Crystal ▲ CD 752
Sapieyevski, J.:Arioso, w. J. Dunham (va), Boatman (perc) Crystal ■ C 647
Sapieyevski, J.:Arioso, w. R. Pressley (tpt) Crystal ▲ CD 751
Schuller, G.:Suite Ww Qnt *(rec May 1992 & Jan 1993)* Crystal ▲ CD 752
Schuman, W.:Dances Ww Qnt *(rec May 1992 & Jan 1993)* Crystal ▲ CD 752
Westwood Wind Quintet members
Revueltas, S.:Little Serious Pieces, w. T. Stevens (tpt) Crystal ▲ CD 667
Wettinger CO
Schoeck, O.:Der Postillon, w. K. Grenacher (pno), E. Haefliger (ten), Wettinger Chamber Chorus, Seminarchor Wettingen [G] *(rec 1967)* Jecklin-Disco ▲ JD 504–2 [ADD]
Schoeck, O.:Songs (misc), w. K. Grenacher (pno), E. Haefliger (ten), Wettinger Chamber Chorus, Seminarchor Wettingen [G] *(rec 1967)* Jecklin-Disco ▲ JD 504–2 [ADD]
Paul Whiteman Orch
Gershwin, G.:Rhap in Blue, w. George Gershwin (pno) Claremont ▲ CDGSE 785065
W. Dailey (cnd)
Gershwin, G.:Con Pno, w. R. Bargy (pno) [Ferde Grofé's 1928 "jazz band" orchestration] *(rec 1928)* Preamble ▲ PRCD 1785 [AAD]
P. Whiteman (cnd)
Gershwin, G.:Rhap in Blue, w. G. Gershwin (pno) RCA ■ ALK1–7114 (m)
Gershwin, G.:Rhap in Blue, w. G. Gershwin (pno) Pro Arte ▲ CDD 433 (m)
Gershwin, G.:Rhap in Blue, w. G. Gershwin (pno) *(rec 4/21/27 for Victor)* Pearl 2–▲ PEAS 9483 (m) [AAD]
Grofé, F.:Grand Canyon Suite *(rec 1932)* Preamble ▲ PRCD 1785 [AAD]
Rodgers, R.:Slaughter on 10th Avenue Claremont ▲ CDGSE 785065

Whiteman Orch
Whiteman, Sinatra (cnd)
Rodgers, R.:Music of, w. B. Crosby (sgr), R. Vallee (sgr), J. Macdonald (sgr), A. Jolson (sgr), et al., Sinatra Orch, Paramount Studio Orch—On Your Toes; Jumbo; Present Arms; One Damn Thing After Another; The Boys from Syracuse; Heads Up; Lido Lady; Peggy Ann; Love Me Tonight; Higher & Higher; Spring is Here; The Girl Friend; Simple Simon; Hallelujah; I'm a Bum Pearl ("Flapper" series) ▲ PAST CD 9794 [AAD]
John Whitney Trio [John Whitney (pno), John Beal (db), Ronnie Zito (dr)]
In a Classical Groove, w. Dave Samuels (vib) *(rec Clinton Recording Studio, New York City, Sept 18–20, 1995)* Golden String ▲ GSCD 028A
The Whole Noyse
W. Stewart (cnd)
Cavalieri, E. de:Rappresentatione di Anima et di Corpo, w. Judith Nelson (mez), Paul Hillier (bass) Koch International Classics ▲ KIC 7363
The Whole Noyse [Stephen Escher (cnt/fl/rcr), Brian Howard (cnt/fl/rcr), Richard Van Hessel (fl/rcr/gittern), D. Sanford Stadtfeld (rcr), Herbert Myers (curtal fl/rcr/va/shm)]
Lo Splendore D'Italia Helicon Classics ▲ HE 1011
Wichita State Univ Faculty Ensemble
W. Mays (cnd)
Mays, W.:Con A Sax, w. John Sampen (a sax) CRI ■ C 361
Clara Wieck Trio
Schumann, C.:Trio Pno Bayer ▲ BR 100094 [DDD]
Wilanów String Quartet
Bacewicz, G.:Qt 3 Strs Olympia ▲ OLY 387 [ADD]
Bacewicz, G.:Qt 5 Strs Olympia ▲ OLY 387 [ADD]
Bargielski, Z.:ArnolD SCHöNBErG in Memoriam Pro Viva ▲ ISPV 173
Bloch, A.:Music for Cl & Str Qt, w. E. Brunner (cl) *(rec Jan. 21 & 23, 1986)* Pro Viva ▲ ISPV 147 CD [DDD]
Grieg, E.:Qt Strs (unfinished) Accord ▲ ACD 201552 [DDD]
Grieg, E.:Qt Strs, Op. 27 Accord ▲ ACD 201552 [DDD]
Meyer, K.:Qts Strs—Nos. 4–6, Opp. 33, 42, 51 *(rec June 1982)* Pro Viva ▲ ISPV 162 CD [ADD]
Meyer, K.:Qts Strs—Nos. 1, 7–8, Opp. 8a, 65, 67 *(rec Mar. 17, 1986)* Pro Viva ▲ ISPV 151 CD [DDD]
Meyer, K.:Qt 9 Strs *(rec SFB Studio Kleiner Sendesaal, Berlin, June 1992)* Pro Viva ▲ ISPV 171 [DDD]
Meyer, K.:Qnt Cl, w. E. Brunner (cl) *(rec Nov. 10–11, 1986)* Pro Viva ▲ ISPV 147 CD [DDD]
Meyer, K.:Qnt Pno, w. Krzysztof Meyer (pno) *(rec SFB Studio Kleiner Sendesaal, Berlin, June 1992)* Pro Viva ▲ ISPV 171 [DDD]
Reger, M.:Qnt Cl, w. E. Brunner (cl) Tudor ▲ 724 [DDD]
Szymanowski, K.:Qt 1 Strs Koch Schwann ▲ 311552 [DDD]
Szymanowski, K.:Qt 2 Strs Koch Schwann ▲ 311552 [DDD]
Yun, I.:Qnt Cl, w. Eduard Brunner (cl) Col Legno ▲ AU 31808
Wilanów String Quartet [Tadeusz Gadzina (vn), Pawel Losakiewicz (vn), Artur Paciorkiewicz (va), Wojciech Walasek (vc)]
Lutoslawski, W.:Qt Strs Polskie Nagrania Edition ▲ ECD 035
Meyer, K.:Qt 3 Strs Polskie Nagrania Edition ▲ ECD 035
Penderecki, K.:Qt 1 Strs Polskie Nagrania Edition ▲ ECD 035
Penderecki, K.:Qt 2 Strs Polskie Nagrania Edition ▲ ECD 035
Stachowski, M.:Qt 2 Strs *(rec Polish Radio Studio S2, Warsaw, Oct. 1976)* Polskie Nagrania ▲ PLN 076 [ADD]
Szymanowski, K.:Qt 1 Strs Polskie Nagrania Edition ▲ ECD 035
Szymanowski, K.:Qt 2 Strs *(rec Concert Hall at the National PO, Warsaw, 1975)* Polskie Nagrania ▲ PLN 065 [ADD]
Wilanów String Quartet [Tadeusz Gadzina (vn), Pawel Losakiewicz (vn), Ryszard Duz (va), Marian Wasiólka (vc)]
Beethoven, L. van:Grosse Fuge Str Qt *(rec Concert Hall of the National Philharmonic, Warsaw, Apr 5–6, 1982)* Polskie Nagrania ▲ PNCD 072 [ADD]
Beethoven, L. van:Qt 12 Strs *(rec Concert Hall of the National Philharmonic, Warsaw, Jan 7–10, 1985)* Polskie Nagrania ▲ PNCD 070 [ADD]
Beethoven, L. van:Qt 13 Strs *(rec Concert Hall of the National Philharmonic, Warsaw, Feb 10–16, 1982)* Polskie Nagrania ▲ PNCD 070 [ADD]
Beethoven, L. van:Qt 14 Strs *(rec Concert Hall of the National Philharmonic, Warsaw, Aug 17–22, 1981)* Polskie Nagrania ▲ PNCD 071 [ADD]
Beethoven, L. van:Qt 15 Strs *(rec Concert Hall of the National Philharmonic, Warsaw, Nov 14–18, 1983)* Polskie Nagrania ▲ PNCD 072 [ADD]
Beethoven, L. van:Qt 16 Strs *(rec Concert Hall of the National Philharmonic, Warsaw, Aug 17–22, 1981)* Polskie Nagrania ▲ PNCD 071 [ADD]
Lutoslawski, W.:Qt Strs Accord ▲ ACD 201142 [DDD]
Wilbraham Brass Soloists
Gabrieli, G.:Choral Music, w. David Willcocks (cnd), Bach Choir, King's College Choir Cambridge EMI Classics ("Doublefforte" series) 2–▲ CDFB 68631
Scheidt, S.:Choral Music, w. David Willcocks (cnd), Bach Choir, King's College Choir Cambridge EMI Classics ("Doublefforte" series) 2–▲ CDFB 68631
Schütz, H.:Choral Music, w. David Willcocks (cnd), Bach Choir, King's College Choir Cambridge EMI Classics ("Doublefforte" series) 2–▲ CDFB 68631
D. Willcocks (cnd)
Schütz, H.:Lobet den Herrn in seinem Heiligtum, w. Cambridge Univ Musical Society Chorus, King's College Choir Cambridge EMI Classics ("Baroque" series) ▲ CDK 65736
Wilhan String Quartet [Leos Cepicky (vn), Jan Schulmeister (vn), Jirí Zigmund (va), Ales Kasprík (vc)]
Janácek, L.:Qt 1 Strs Studio Matous ▲ MAT 32 [DDD]
Janácek, L.:Qt 2 Strs Studio Matous ▲ MAT 32 [DDD]
Williams Fairey Band
J.G. Hurdley (cnd)
Bone Idyll, w. Brett Baker (trbn) Chandos ("Brass" series) ▲ CHAN 4543
P. Parkes (cnd)
Sousa, J.P.:Marches & Dances—Semper Fidelis; The Crusader; El Capitan; The Invincible Eagle; King Cotton; Hands across the Sea; Manhattan Beach; Our Flirtations; The Picadore; The Gladiator; The Free Lance; The Washington Post; The Beau Ideal; High School Cadets; Fairest of the Fair; The Thunderer; The Occidental; The Liberty Bell; The Corcoran Cadets; National Fencibles; The Black Horse Troop; The Gridiron Club; The Directorate; The Belle of Chicago Chandos ("Brass" series) ▲ CHAN 4535 [DDD]
Wind Quintette of the 1900s
Ghedini, G.F.:Qnt Ww *(rec 3/89)* Fonè ▲ 90F01
Malipiero, G.F.:Dialogo 4 *(rec 3/89)* Fonè ▲ 90F01
Malipiero, R.:Musica da camera—Canto crepuscolare; Canto Notturno; Il canto della lontananza; Il canto nell'infinito *(rec 3/89)* Fonè ▲ 90F01
Respighi, O.:Qnt Ww *(rec 3/89)* Fonè ▲ 90F01
Windham String Quartet [Ivan Chan (vn), Naomi Katz (vn), Hsin-Yun Hyuang (va), Wilhelmina Smith (vc)]
Lazarof, H.:Divert 3 Vn, w. Ani Kavafian (vn) *(rec SUNY, Purchase, Nov 1993)* Laurel LR 856 [DDD]
Wingra Woodwind Quintet
Mitchell, R.:Cutouts Lovely Music ▲ LCD 2021 [AAD]
Winnipeg SO
K. Koizumi (cnd)
Debussy, C.:Danse Pno, "Tarantelle styrienne" CBC ("SM 5000" series) ▲ SMCD 5080 [DDD] ■ SMC 5080 (D)
Dvořák, A.:Legends, Op. 59—No. 4, orch. ver. CBC ("SM 5000" series) ▲ SMCD 5039 [DDD]

Winnipeg SO (cont.)
K. Koizumi (cnd) (cont.)
Eckhardt-Gramatté, S.-C.:Capriccio-Concertante
CBC ("SM 5000" series) ▲ SMCD 5089 [DDD] ▮ SMC 5089 (D)
Glinka, M.:Kamarinskaya CBC ("SM 5000" series) ▲ SMCD 5089 [DDD] ▮ SMC 5089 (D)
Kodály, Z.:Galanta Dances CBC ("SM 5000" series) ▲ SMCD 5039 [DDD]
Louie, A.:Songs of Paradise CBC ("SM 5000" series) ▲ SMCD 5080 [DDD] ▮ SMC 5080 (D)
Mendelssohn, F.:Meeresstille CBC ("SM 5000" series) ▲ SMCD 5080 [DDD] ▮ SMC 5080 (D)
Morawetz, O.:Carnival Ov CBC ("SM 5000" series) ▲ SMCD 5039 [DDD]
Respighi, O.:Trittico botticelliano CBC ("SM 5000" series) ▲ SMCD 5080 [DDD] ▮ SMC 5080 (D)
Rodrigo, J.:Concierto de Aranjuez, w. N. Kraft (gtr)
CBC ("SM 5000" series) ▲ SMCD 5066 [DDD] ▮ SMC 5066 (D)
Takemitsu, T.:Requiem CBC ("SM 5000" series) ▲ SMCD 5080 [DDD] ▮ SMC 5080 (D)
Tchaikovsky, P.:Suite 1 CBC ("SM 5000" series) ▲ SMCD 5089 [DDD] ▮ SMC 5089 (D)
Tchaikovsky, P.:Suite 4 CBC ("SM 5000" series) ▲ SMCD 5039 [DDD]
Villa-Lobos, H.:Con Gtr, w. N. Kraft (gtr)
CBC ("SM 5000" series) ▲ SMCD 5066 [DDD] ▮ SMC 5066 (D)

E. Kunzel (cnd)
Kunzel's Best! Mastersound ▲ DFCDI 213 [DDD]
Winnipeg SO

B. Tovey (cnd)
Buhr, G.:Con Pno, w. Christina Petrowska (pno) *(rec Winnipeg, Manitoba, Mar. 16 & 18, 1993)*
CBC ("SM 5000" series) ▲ SMCD 5141 [DDD]
Luedeke, R.:The Transparency of Time, w. André Laplant (pno) *(rec Winnipeg, Manitoba, Mar. 19-20, 1990)* CBC ("SM 5000" series) ▲ SMCD 5141 [DDD]
Nishimura, A.:Heterophony, w. Shirley Sawatzky (pno), Judith Kehler Siebert (pno) *(rec Winnipeg, Manitoba, Mar. 16 & 18, 1993)* CBC ("SM 5000" series) ▲ SMCD 5141 [DDD]

Winston-Salem Piedmont Triad SO
P. Perret (cnd)
Shaffer, S.:Con Orch Vienna Modern Masters ▲ VMM 3013 [DDD]
Ward, R.:Con Vn, w. S. Johnson (vn) Albany ▲ TROY 126 [DDD]
Ward, R.:Scarlet Letter (suite) Albany ▲ TROY 126 [DDD]

Winterthur Baroque Quintet
Holzbauer, I.:Nocturni Fl, w. R. Weber (va), R. Frei (db) *(rec 1969)*
Jecklin-Disco ▲ JD 4406-2 [ADD]
Holzbauer, I.:Qnt Fl, w. R. Weber (va) *(rec 1969)* Jecklin-Disco ▲ JD 4406-2 [ADD]

Winterthur Musicum Collegium
W.A. Albert (cnd)
Schoeck, O.:Con Hn, w. Bruno Schneider (hn) CPO ▲ CPO 999337
Schoeck, O.:Don Ranudo de Colibrados (sels), w. Bruno Schneider (hn)—Serenade for Ob, Eng Hn & Strs CPO ▲ CPO 999337
Schoeck, O.:Praeludium CPO ▲ CPO 999337
Schoeck, O.:Suite Strs CPO ▲ CPO 999337

Winterthur State Orch members
V. Desarzens (cnd)
Martin, F.:Le Vin herbé, w. B. Retchitzka (sop), H. Morath (cta), O. de Nyzankowskyi (ten), H. Rehfuss (bar), D. Olsen (bass), F. Martin (pno) Jecklin-Disco 2-▲ JD 581/2-2 [ADD]

Winterthur String Orch
C. Dahinden (cnd)
Vaughan Williams, R.:Con accademico, w. L. Kaufman (vn) *(rec 1951)*
Music & Arts ▲ CD 667 (m) [AAD]

Winterthur String Quartet [Willi Zimmermann (vn), Pär Näsbom (vn), Jürg Dähler (va), Cäcilia Chmel (vc)]
Goetz, H.:Qt Strs *(rec May 1995)* Jecklin ▲ JEC 703 [DDD]
Rauchenecker, G.W.:Qt 1 Strs *(rec May 1995)* Jecklin ▲ JEC 703 [DDD]

Winterthur SO
F. Busch (cnd)
Mendelssohn, F.:Sym 4 *(rec 1950)*
Arlecchino ARL
Schubert, Franz:Sym 5 *(rec 1950)*
Arlecchino ARL

W. Goehr (cnd)
Tartini, G.:Cons Vn (misc), w. M. Rostal (vn)—in g Symposium ▲ 1079

H. Swoboda (cnd)
Beethoven, L. van:Con 3 Pno, w. C. Haskil (pno) *(rec 1950)*
Enterprise ("Palladio" series) ▲ ENTPD 4179 [ADD]
Mozart, W.A.:Con 20 Pno, w. C. Haskil (pno) *(rec 1950)*
Enterprise ("Palladio" series) ▲ ENTPD 4179 [ADD]

Wisconsin Brass Quintet [J. Aley (tpt), D. Cooper (tpt), N. Smith (hn), W. Richardson (trbn), J. Stevens (tuba)]
Stevens, J.:Fabrics Summit ▲ DCD 164 [DDD]
Stevens, J.:Seasons Summit ▲ DCD 164 [DDD]

Wisconsin Brass Quintet [J. Aley (tpt), D. Cooper (tpt), S. Hermansson (hn), W. Richardson (trbn), J. Stevens (tuba)]
Reynolds, V.:Qnt Brass Summit ▲ DCD 164 [DDD]

Wizards! [Mark Weiger (ob/ob d'amore), Andrea Gullickson (ob/ob d'amore), S. Blake Duncan (E hn), Greg Morton (bn)]
A Double Reed Consort, w. Iowa Double Reed Consort [Lissa Stolz (ob), Debra Hawk-Burt (ob/e hn), Ronald Tyree (bn), Ronald Snitker (bn/ctbn), Trevor Johnson (hpd)] *(rec Clapp Recital Hall, Univ. of Iowa, Iowa City, Jan. 1993 & May 1994)* CRS Master ▲ CRS 9460

Women's Philharmonic
Armer, E.:Music of, w. Ursula Le Guin (nar), Elinor Armer (nar), Women's Philharmonic, Elizabeth Appling (cnd), JoAnn Falletta (cnd), San Francisco Girls' Chorus, San Francisco Boys' Chorus, San Francisco Chamber Singers—The Great Instrument of the Geggerets; Anithaca; The Seasons of Oling; Eating with the Hoi; Open & Shut; Sailing Among the Pheromones; On the Antiorietal Shores; Island Earth Koch International Classics 2-▲ KIC 7331 [DDD]

J. Falletta (cnd)
Boulanger, L.:D'un matin de printemps Orch Koch International Classics ▲ KIC 7169-2 [DDD]
Boulanger, L.:D'un soir triste Koch International Classics ▲ KIC 7169-2 [DDD]
Chen, Y.:Music of, w. Liu Wei-shan (guzheng), Zhao Yang-qin (yangqin), Chen Jie-bing (erhu), Min Xiao-fen (pipa), Chanticleer—Duo Ye No. 2; Sym 2; Ge Xu; Chinese Myths Cant; Pan Gu Creates Heaven & Earth; Nu Wa Creates Human Beings; Weaving Maid & Cowherd; Song of Weaving Maid & Cowherd *(rec Skywalker Sound, San Rafael, CA, June 1996)* New Albion ▲ NA 090
Mendelssohn, Fanny:Ov Orch Koch International Classics ▲ KIC 7169-2 [DDD]
Schumann, C.:Con Pno, w. A. Cheng (pno) Koch International Classics ▲ KIC 7169-2 [DDD]
Tailleferre, G.:Concertino Hp, w. G. Benet (hp) Koch International Classics ▲ KIC 7169-2 [DDD]

Woodwind Arts Quintet
Downey, J.:Agort Gasparo ▲ GS 276 ▮ GS 276C

World Casio Quartet [B. Charles, E. Sandrof, D. First, K. Sparke]
First, D.:Strange over *(rec July 1988)* O.O. Discs ▲ OO 5 [DDD]

World Orch for Peace
G. Solti (cnd)
Bartók, B.:Con Orch *(rec Victoria Hall, Geneva, July 5, 1995)* London ▲ 448901-2 [DDD]
Beethoven, L. van:Fidelio (sels), w. Evelyn Herlitzius (sop—Leonore), Ruth Ziesak (sop—Marzelline), Stig Andersen (ten—Florestan), Herbert Lippert (ten—Jaquino), Albert Dohmen (bar—Don Pizarro), Andreas Kohn (bass—Don Fernando), Hans Tschammer (bass—Rocco), London Voices—Finale Act II *(rec Victoria Hall, Geneva, July 5, 1995)* London ▲ 448901-2 [DDD]
Rossini, G.:Guillaume Tell (ov) *(rec Victoria Hall, Geneva, July 5, 1995)* London ▲ 448901-2 [DDD]

World SO
M. Atzmon (cnd)
Haydn, J.:Die Schöpfung, w. Edith Mathis (sop), Christoph Prégardien (ten), Harald Stamm (bass), Pécs Chamber Choir, Berlin Academy of Arts Chamber Choir, Shin-Yuh Kai Choir [G] *(rec Basilica San Francesco in Assisi, as part of the IPPNW "Hiroshima Concert 1990")* BIS 2-▲ CD 493/94 [DDD]

World Youth SO Interlochen
H. Hanson (cnd)
Hanson, H.:Extended Theme *(rec live, Kresge Auditorium, Interlochen, Michigan, Aug 7, 1977)*
Citadel ▲ CTD 88116 [ADD]
Hanson, H.:Pan & the Priest *(rec live, Kresge Auditorium, Interlochen, Michigan, Aug 7, 1977)*
Citadel ▲ CTD 88116 [ADD]
Hanson, H.:Rhythmic Vars on 2 Ancient Hymns *(rec live, Kresge Auditorium, Interlochen, Michigan, Aug 7, 1977)* Citadel ▲ CTD 88116 [ADD]
Hanson, H.:Sym 7, "A Sea Sym", w. National Music Camp High School Choir *(rec live, Kresge Auditorium, Interlochen, Michigan, Aug 7, 1977)* Citadel ▲ CTD 88116 [ADD]

Wren Baroque Soloists
Peerson, M.:Music of Collins Classics ▲ COL 1437 [DDD]

Wroclaw Orch
Gorczycki, G.G.:Sacred Choral Music, w. R. Stacewicz (sop), I. Tkaczyk (alt), A. Pagowska (alt), E. Sasiadek (ten), W. Brychcy (bass), S. Galonski (cnd), Edmund Kajdasz (cnd), Capella Bydgostiensis Pro Musica Antiqua, Madrigalists Choir, Polish Radio Chorus—Completorium; In virtute tua; Iudica me deus; Laetatus sum; Missa paschalis [L] *(rec 1966)* Olympia ▲ OCD 320 [AAD]

Wuppertal SO
P. Gülke (cnd)
Reicha, A.:Ov in D MD + G ▲ MDG 3350661
Reicha, A.:Sinf concertante, w. Ida Bieler (vn), Jena-Claude Gerard (fl) MD + G ▲ MDG 3350661
Reicha, A.:Sym in E♭ MD + G ▲ MDG 3350661

Württemberg CO
The Pachelbel Canon & Other Baroque Favorites, w. Mainz CO, various soloists
Allegretto ▲ ACD 8098 [ADD] ▮ ACS 8098

F. Bernius (cnd)
Haydn, J.:Stabat Mater, w. Krisztina Láki (sop), Júlia Hamari (mez), Claes Hakan Ahnsjö (ten), Richard Anlauf (bass), Stuttgart Chamber Choir *(rec 1978)* Vox Box 2-▲ CDX 5081 [ADD]

R. Ewerhart (cnd)
Bach, J.S.:Cant 202, "Wedding Cant", w. Ursula Buckel (sop), Willy Schnell (ob), Werner Keltsch (vn), Peter Buck (vc), Martin Galling (hpd) *(rec 1965)* Vox Box 3-▲ CD3X 3039
Bach, J.S.:Cant 204, w. Elisabeth Speiser (sop), Helmuth Steinkraus (fl), Willi Schnell (ob), Dietmar Keller (ob), Susanne Lautenbacher (vn) *(rec 1966)* Vox Box 3-▲ CD3X 3039
Bach, J.S.:Cant 209, w. Elisabeth Speiser (sop), Helmuth Steinkraus (fl), Martin Galling (hpd) *(rec 1966)* Vox Box 3-▲ CD3X 3039
Bach, J.S.:Cant 211, "Coffee Cant", w. Wilfrid Jochims (nar), Elisabeth Speiser (sop—Lieschen), Claus Ocker (bass—Schlendrian) *(rec 1966)* Vox Box 3-▲ CD3X 3039
Bach, J.S.:Cant 212, "Peasant Cant", w. Ursula Buckel (sop), Claus Ocker (bass), Gabriele Zimmerman (fl), Peter Buck (vc), Martin Galling (hpd) *(rec 1965)* Vox Box 3-▲ CD3X 3039

G. K. Faerber (cnd)
The Virtuoso French Horn, w. Mainz CO, various soloists Allegretto ▲ ACD 8144 [ADD] ▮ ACS 8144

J. Faerber (cnd)
Albinoni, T.:Adagio Org, w. D. Haas (org) Allegretto ▲ ACD 8098 [ADD] ▮ ACS 8098
Albinoni, T.:Cons à 5 Obs, Op. 9, w. Maurice André (tpt), Guy Touvron (tpt)—No. 9 in C [played on tpts] *(rec Eglise Evangélique, Heilbronn, May 1979)* EMI Classics ▲ CDK 65337 [ADD]
Albinoni, T.:Con Tpt, "San Marco", w. Maurice André (tpt) *(rec Salle Wagram, Paris, June 1978)*
EMI Classics ▲ CDK 65337 [ADD]
Bach, C.P.E.:Cons Fl, w. J. Galway (fl)—in F, H.426, in A, H.438 (W.168) & in G, H.445 (W.169)
RCA Red Seal ▲ 60244-2-RC [DDD] ▮ 60244-4-RC (CrO2)
Bach, J.S.:Con Fl, Vn & Hpd, w. G. Höller (fl), G. Egger (vn) *(rec 1978)*
Vox Box 3-▲ CD3X 3018 [ADD]
Bach, J.S.:Con Fl, Vn & Hpd, w. J. Galway (fl), R. Wolters (vn), U. Deutschler (hpd)
RCA Red Seal ▲ 09026-60900-2 ▮ 09026-60900-4 ◻ 09026-60900-5
Bach, J.S.:Cons Hpd, BWV 1052-1058, w. C. Jaccottet (hpd), C. Sartoretti (hpd), N. Hostettler (hpd), L. Klinckerfus (hpd) *(rec 1978)* Vox Box 3-▲ CD3X 3018 [ADD]
Bach, J.S.:Cons for 2 Hpds (comp), w. C. Jaccottet (hpd), C. Sartoretti (hpd), N. Hostettler (hpd), L. Klinckerfus (hpd) *(rec 1978)* Vox Box 3-▲ CD3X 3018 [ADD]
Bach, J.S.:Cons for 3 Hpds (comp), w. C. Jaccottet (hpd), C. Sartoretti (hpd), N. Hostettler (hpd), L. Klinckerfus (hpd) *(rec 1978)* Vox Box 3-▲ CD3X 3018 [ADD]
Bach, J.S.:Suite 2 Orch, w. J. Galway (fl)
RCA Red Seal ▲ 09026-60900-2 ▮ 09026-60900-4 ◻ 09026-60900-5
Danzi, F.:Concertante Fl, w. A. Nicolet (fl), E. Brunner (cl) Tudor ▲ 702 [ADD]
Danzi, F.:Concertante Fl, w. D. Becker (fl), W. Meyer (cl) *(rec 1/91)* MD + G ▲ L 3396 [DDD]
Danzi, F.:Concertante Fl, w. J. Galway (fl), S. Meyer (cl)
RCA Red Seal ▲ 09026-61976-2; ▮ 09026-61976-4
Danzi, F.:Con 2 Fl, w. J. Galway (fl) RCA Red Seal ▲ 09026-61976-2; ▮ 09026-61976-4
Danzi, F.:Phantasie on "La ci darem la mano" from Mozart's *Don Giovanni*, w. S. Meyer (cl)
RCA Red Seal ▲ 09026-61976-2; ▮ 09026-61976-4
Hartmann, K.A.:Con funèbre, w. Susanne Lautenbacher (vn) Vox Box 2-▲ CDX 5134 [ADD]
Krommer, F.:Con Cl, w. D. Glazer (cl) Preiser ▲ 90167 [ADD]
Molter, J.M.:Cons Tpt, w. G. Touvron (tpt), G. Messler (tpt) RCA Red Seal ▲ 09026-61200-2
Molter, J.M.:Con 2 Tpt, w. G. Touvron (tpt) RCA Victor ▲ 09026-61857-2; ▮ 09026-61857-4
Molter, J.M.:Con 3 Tpt, w. G. Touvron (tpt) RCA Victor ▲ 09026-61857-2; ▮ 09026-61857-4
Mouravieff, L.:Nativité Vox Box 3-▲ CD3X 3021 [ADD]
Mozart, W.A.:Adagio Vn, w. Frank Peter Zimmermann (vn) EMI Classics 2-▲ CDFB 69355
Mozart, W.A.:Andante Fl, K.315/285a, w. R. Siebert (fl) Vox Box 3-▲ CD3X 3003 [ADD]
Mozart, W.A.:Cons Fl, w. R. Siebert (fl) Vox Box 3-▲ CD3X 3003 [ADD]
Mozart, W.A.:Con Fl Hp, w. R. Siebert (fl), C. Michel (hp) Vox Box 3-▲ CD3X 3003 [ADD]
Mozart, W.A.:Cons Vn, w. Frank Peter Zimmermann (vn)—Nos. 1-5 EMI Classics 2-▲ CDFB 69355
Mozart, W.A.:Con 4 Vn, w. G. Pauk (vn) Allegretto ▲ ACD 8141 [ADD] ▮ ACS 8141
Mozart, W.A.:Con 5 Vn, w. G. Pauk (vn) Allegretto ▲ ACD 8141 [ADD] ▮ ACS 8141
Mozart, W.A.:Rondo Fl, K.Anh.184, w. R. Siebert (fl) Vox Box 3-▲ CD3X 3003 [ADD]
Mozart, W.A.:Rondo in B♭ Vn, w. Frank Peter Zimmermann (vn) EMI Classics 2-▲ CDFB 69355
Mozart, W.A.:Rondo Vn, K.373, w. Frank Peter Zimmermann (vn) EMI Classics 2-▲ CDFB 69355
An Old World Christmas, w. [cnd:Paul Holstein], Southwest German Radio Children's Choir
Vox 90s ▮ V9-9901
Pleyel, I.:Sinf concertante 5, w. D. Becker (fl), P. Meyer (cl), Schottstädt (bn), Schneider (hn)
MD + G ▲ L 3396 [DDD]
Quantz, J.J.:Cons Fl & Orch, w. J. Galway (fl)
RCA Red Seal ▲ 60247-2-RC [DDD] ▮ 60247-4-RC (CrO2)
Rossini, G.:Intro, Theme & Vars Cl, w. E. Brunner (cl) Tudor ▲ 702 [ADD]
Salieri, A.:Con Fl, w. D. Becker (fl), L. Lenczés (ob) MD + G ▲ L 3396 [DDD]
Schaeuble, H.:Concertino Ob, w. S. Fuchs (ob), S. Lautenbacher (vn), G. Egger (vn)
Gallo ▲ CD 577 [DAD]
Schaeuble, H.:Music for 2 Vns, w. S. Lautenbacher (vn), G. Egger (vn) Gallo ▲ CD 577 [DAD]
Schaeuble, H.:Sym for Strs, "In Memoriam", w. S. Lautenbacher (vn), G. Egger (vn)
Gallo ▲ CD 577 [DAD]
Stamitz, A.:Con Fls, w. A. Nicolet (fl), C. Nicolet (fl) Tudor ▲ 702 [ADD]
Trumpet Concertos, w. Maurice André (tpt), Franz Liszt CO [cnd:Jesus Lopez-Cobos], Academy of St. Martin in the Fields [cnd:Neville Marriner], London PO [cnd:Jesus Lopez-Cobos], Philharmonia Orch [cnd:Riccardo Muti] EMI Classics 2-▲ CDZB 69152 [ADD]
Vanhal, J.B.:Con Va, w. E. Wallfisch (va) Bayer ▲ BR 200028 [ADD]

▲ = CD ♦ = Enhanced CD Δ = MD ▮ = Cassette Tape ◻ = DCC

Württemberg CO (cont.)
J. Faerber (cnd) (cont.)
Vivaldi, A.:Cons Diverse Instrs, w. Anton Stingl (lt)—in D for Lt & Strs
Special Music Co. ("Classics of the Heart" series) ▲ SCD 5198
Vivaldi, A.:Cons Vn, Op. 8/1–4, "The Four Seasons", w. Susanne Lautenbacher (vn)—Winter
Special Music Co. ▲ SCD 5200
Vivaldi, A.:Cons Vn, Op. 8/1–4, "The Four Seasons"–Autumn
Special Music Co. ("Classics of the Heart" series) ▲ SCD 5196
Vivaldi, A.:Cons Vn, Op. 8/1–4, "The Four Seasons", w. S. Lautenbacher (vn)
Allegretto ▲ ACD 8002 [ADD] ■ ACS 8002
Vivaldi, A.:Life & Music of, w. S. Lautenbacher (vn)—narration & selected excerpts from Con. for Bassoon; Con. No. 1 for Violin, Op. 4; Con. in B♭ for Flute; Con. No. 11, Op. 8; Gloria in D; The Nymph and the Shepherd; Con. No. 12, Op. 4; Con. No. 10, Op. 3; Four Seasons, Op. 8; Bach:Con. for 4 Harpsichords, BWV 1065; Con. 2, Op. 9
Vox Music Masters ("Music Masters" series) ▲ MMD 8510 [ADD] ■ MMC 8510
Weber, C.M. von:Con Bn, w. George Zukerman (bn) *(rec 1965)* Allegretto ▲ ACD 8189
Weber, C.M. von:Con 1 Cl, w. David Glazer (cl) *(rec 1967)* Allegretto ▲ ACD 8189
D. Kurz (cnd)
Mozart, W.A.:Davidde penitente, w. E. Csapo (sop), G. Koban (sop), A. Baldin (ten), Württemburg Choir *(rec 1978)* Allegretto ▲ ACD 8164 [ADD] ■ ACS 8164
H. Rilling (cnd)
Bach, J.S.:Cants (misc), w. Stuttgart Bach Collegium, Gächinger Kantorei, Frankfurt Kantorei—Cantata Nos. 1, 36, 61, 63, 65, 91, 110, 121, 122, 132, 133, 153, 190
Hänssler Classic 4–▲ 98.836 [ADD]
Bach, J.S.:Cant 11, "Ascension Oratorio", w. C. Cuccaro (sop), M. Georg (alt), A. Kraus (ten), A. Schmidt (bass), Gächinger Kantorei [G] Novalis ▲ 150028 [DDD]
Bach, J.S.:Cant 11, "Ascension Oratorio", w. C. Cuccaro (sop), M. Georg (alt), A. Kraus (ten), A. Schmidt (bass), Gächinger Kantorei [G] *(rec 1984)* Hänssler Classic 5–▲ 98.976
Bach, J.S.:Cant 80, w. Antonia Fahberg (sop), Bargarete Bence (cta), Theophil Maier (ten), Ulrich Schaible (bass), Stuttgart Memorial Church Figuralchor *(rec 1964)* Vox Box 3–▲ CD3X 3039
Bach, J.S.:Cant 80, w. A. Augér (sop), G. Schreckenbach (cta), L.–M. Harder (ten), P. Huttenlocher (bar), Gächinger Kantorei [G] *(rec 1976 & 1983)* Hänssler Classic ▲ 98.819 [AAD]
Bach, J.S.:Cant 91, w. H. Donath (sop), H. Watts (cta), A. Kraus (ten), W. Schöne (bass), Stuttgart Bach Collegium, Gächinger Kantorei, Frankfurt Choir [G] *(rec Feb 1972)*
Hänssler Classic ▲ 98.822 [AAD]
Bach, J.S.:Cant 93, w. Stuttgart Bach Collegium, Gächinger Kantorei [G]
Hänssler Classic ▲ 98.865 [AAD]
Bach, J.S.:Cant 94, w. H. Donath (sop), E. Paaske (cta), A. Baldin (ten), H.–F. Kunz (bass), W. Schöne (bass), Stuttgart Bach Collegium, Gächinger Kantorei Hänssler Classic ▲ 98.808 [AAD]
Bach, J.S.:Cant 95, w. A. Augér (sop), A. Kraus (ten), W. Heldwein (bass), Stuttgart Bach Collegium, Gächinger Kantorei Hänssler Classic ▲ 98.812 [AAD]
Bach, J.S.:Cant 96, w. H. Donath (sop), M. Höffgen (mez), A. Kraus (ten), S. Nimsgern (b–bar), Stuttgart Bach Collegium, Gächinger Kantorei [G] *(rec 1973)* Hänssler Classic ▲ 98.814 [AAD]
Bach, J.S.:Cant 100, w. A. Augér (sop), J. Hamari (cta), A. Kraus (ten), P. Huttenlocher (bar), Gächinger Kantorei [G] *(rec 1983–84)* Hänssler Classic 5–▲ 98.976
Bach, J.S.:Cant 169, w. C. Watkinson (cta), Gächinger Kantorei [G] *(rec 1983)*
Hänssler Classic ▲ 98.815 [AAD]
Bach, J.S.:Cant 171, w. A. Augér (sop), J. Hamari (cta), A. Badin (ten), W. Heldwein (bass), Gächinger Kantorei [G] Hänssler Classic ▲ 98.871 [AAD]
Bach, J.S.:Cant 188, w. A. Augér (sop), J. Hamari (cta), A. Baldin (ten), W. Heldwein (bass), Gächinger Kantorei [G] *(rec June & Sept 1983)* Hänssler Classic ▲ 98.817 [AAD]
Württemberg Clarinet Quartet
Contemporary Clarinet Quartets Koch Schwann ▲ SCH 310067 [DDD]
Jelinek, H.:Divert for 2 Cls Koch Schwann ▲ CD 310067 [DDD]
Jettel, R.:Qt for 3 Cls Koch Schwann ▲ CD 310067 [DDD]
Stark, R.:Serenade Koch Schwann ▲ CD 310067 [DDD]
Uhl, A.:Serenade Koch Schwann ▲ CD 310067 [DDD]
Württemberg PO
D. Agrafiotis (cnd)
Komma, K.M.:Con 1 Pno, w. Karl Michael Komma (pno) Bayer ▲ 800880
Komma, K.M.:Signals Bayer ▲ 800880
J.–M. Burfin (cnd)
Indy, V. d':Fant sur des thèmes populaires français, w. P. Cousu (ob) *(rec Baden–Baden, 1992–93)*
Marco Polo ▲ 8.223659 [DDD]
S. Friedmann (cnd)
Komma, K.M.:Con 2 Pno, w. Karl Michael Komma (pno) Bayer ▲ 800880
G. Nopre (cnd)
Indy, V. d':L'Etranger—Prelude to Act II *(rec Baden–Baden, 1992–93)*
Marco Polo ▲ 8.223659 [DDD]
Indy, V. d':Fervaal (sels)—Prelude to Act I *(rec Baden–Baden, 1992–93)*
Marco Polo ▲ 8.223659 [DDD]
Indy, V. d':Karadec Marco Polo ▲ 8.223654 [DDD]
Indy, V. d':Médée Marco Polo ▲ 8.223654 [DDD]
Indy, V. d':Saugefleurie *(rec Baden–Baden, 1992–93)* Marco Polo ▲ 8.223659 [DDD]
Indy, V. d':Souvenirs Marco Polo ▲ 8.223654 [DDD]
Indy, V. d':Tableaux de voyage *(rec Baden–Baden, 1992–93)* Marco Polo ▲ 8.223659 [DDD]
J. Rotter (cnd)
Clementi, M.:Pno Music (comp), w. Aldo Antognazzi (pno), Christian Badian (pno), Jose Maria Brusco (pno), Daniela Lanzillo (pno), Federico Wiman (pno)—Con in C for Pno; Sons (6) for Pno, Op. 1, Nos. 1–3; "Son inedita" in A♭ Aura Classics ▲ AU 32070
Württemberg State Orch
J. Ferencsik (cnd)
Ballet Music from Operas, w. Hungarian State Orch [cnd:I. Fischer], Hungarian State Opera Orch
White Label ▲ HRC 058
J. Perlea (cnd)
Ballet Music from Grand Opera, w. Vienna SO Allegretto ▲ ACD 8122 [ADD] ■ ACS 8122
Würzburg Guitar Trio
Granados, E.:Valses poeticos (7) CPO ▲ CPO 999059–2 [DDD]
Wytko Saxophone Quartet
Karlins, M.W.:Qt 1 Saxs ACA Digital Recording ▲ CM 20012
Karlins, M.W.:Qt 2 Saxs ACA Digital Recording ▲ CM 20012
Myers, R.:Qt Sax ACA Digital Recording ▲ CM 20012
Xalapa SO
Gershwin, G.:Music of, w. J. Brook (pno)—Strike up the Band; The Man I Love; Foggy Day; Embraceable You; Love Walked in; My Man's Gone Now; But Not for Me; Love Is Sweeping the Country; Of Thee I Sing IMP Classics ▲ IMPPCD 1057 [DDD]
H. de la Fuente (cnd)
Falla, M. de:Noches en los jardines de España, w. J. F. Osorio (pno)
IMP Classics ▲ IMPPCD 1074 [DDD]
Revueltas, S.:Noche de los Mayas Catalyst ▲ 09026–62672–2
Shostakovich, D.:Con 1 Vc, w. C. Prieto (vc) IMP Classics ▲ IMPPCD 1084 [DDD]
Spanish Fiesta, w. London SO, Rafael Frühbeck de Burgos (cnd), M. Conn (gtr)
Pickwick ("The Orchid" series) ▲ PICORCD 11014
Tchaikovsky, P.:Con 1 Pno, w. J. F. Osorio (pno) IMP Classics ▲ IMPPCD 1074 [DDD]
Tchaikovsky, P.:Sym 4 IMP ("Classics" series) ▲ IMP 6700052
Josh Levine (cnd)
Gershwin, G.:"I Got Rhythm" Vars, w. *(pianist unknown)* IMP Classics ▲ IMPPCD 1057 [DDD]
Xenakis Ensemble
H. Kerstens (cnd)
Wagemans, P.J.:Viderunt omnes Donemus ▲ CV 28

XLNT Sinfonietta
Cohn, J.:Con Cl, w. J. Manasse (cl) *(rec Oct. 1993)* XLNT ▲ CD 18009 [DDD]
Cohn, J.:Mount Gretna Suite *(rec Sept. 1992)* XLNT ▲ CD 18007 [DDD]
Gershwin, G.:Preludes (3) Pno, w. J. Manasse (cl) [arr. for clarinet & strings James Cohn] *(rec Oct. 1993)*
XLNT ▲ CD 18009 [DDD]
XTET
A. Stern (cnd)
Kubik, G.:Gerald McBoing Boing, w. W. Klemperer (speaker) Delos ▲ DE 6001 [DDD] ■ CS 6001 (D)
Rogers, B.:The Musicians of Bremen, w. Carl Reiner (nar) Delos ▲ DE 6001 [DDD] ■ CS 6001 (D)
Stern, A.:The Fairy's Gift, w. A. Grebner (speaker) Delos ▲ DE 6001 [DDD] ■ CS 6001 (D)
Yale Cellos
M. Bresnick (cnd)
Bresnick, M.:B.'s Garlands, w. Yale Cellos *(rec Sprague Hall, Yale Univ., Jan. 16, 1994)*
CRI ▲ CD 682 [DDD]
Parisot (cnd)
Bach, J.S.:Music of Delos ▲ DCD 3041
Villa–Lobos, H.:Bachiana brasileira 1 Delos ▲ DCD 3041
Villa–Lobos, H.:Bachiana brasileira 5, w. A. Augér (sop) Delos ▲ DCD 3041
Yale String Quartet
Beethoven, L. van:Qt 12 Strs *(rec 1968)* Vanguard Classics ("Everyman" series) ▲ OVC 5012 [ADD]
Beethoven, L. van:Qt 14 Strs *(rec 1970)* Vanguard Classics ("Everyman" series) ▲ OVC 5012 [ADD]
Beethoven, L. van:Qt 15 Strs *(rec 1967)* Vanguard Classics ("Everyman" series) ▲ OVC 5003 [ADD]
Beethoven, L. van:Qt 16 Strs *(rec 1971)* Vanguard Classics ("Everyman" series) ▲ OVC 5003 [ADD]
Yerevan RSO
R. Mangasarian (cnd)
Operatic Arias & Neapolitan Songs, w. David Varjabed (bar), Yerevan String Orch [cnd:Kevork Adjemian] Doremi ▲ 71121 [AAD]
Yerevan String Orch
K. Adjemian (cnd)
Operatic Arias & Neapolitan Songs, w. David Varjabed (bar), Yerevan RSO [cnd:Rafael Mangasarian]
Doremi ▲ 71121 [AAD]
Ymir Ensemble
Eirlksdottlr, Karolina:Renku Music from Iceland ▲ ITM 803
Ingólfsson, A.:Musubl Music from Iceland ▲ ITM 803
Másson, A.:Snow Music from Iceland ▲ ITM 803
Pórdarson, H.:3 Places in Japan Music from Iceland ▲ ITM 803
Tómasson, J.:Sonata XXI Music from Iceland ▲ ITM 803
Yoan Kukuzel–Angeloglasniyat Chamber Ensemble
D. Dimitrov (cnd)
Church Music Gega ▲ GD 101 [DDD]
Yomiuri Nippon SO
C.–S. Chen (cnd)
Wut, M.–C.:Ambush on All Sides, w. Ku Hui–Man (P'i P'a) Sunrise ▲ 8515
H. Sung–jen (cnd)
Shui–Lung, M.:Con Bamboo Fl, w. Chen Chung–sen (bamboo fl) Sunrise ▲ 8501
Shui–Lung, M.:The Peacock Flies Southeast, w. Kifu Mitsuhashi (hsiao) Sunrise ▲ 8501
Yordanov Ensemble
Nikolov, L.:Metamorphoses 4 Gega ▲ GD 149 [DDD]
York Piano Trio
Dvořák, A.:Trio 3 Pno Meridian ▲ CDE 84187
Dvořák, A.:Trio 4 Pno, "Dumky" Meridian ▲ CDE 84187
Mendelssohn, F.:Trio 1 Pno Meridian ▲ MER 84200 [DDD]
Mendelssohn, F.:Trio 2 Pno Meridian ▲ MER 84200 [DDD]
Schumann, R.:Fantasiestücke Vn Meridian ▲ MER 84200 [DDD]
York Waits
The City Musicke:Wind Bands of Renaissance Europe, 1550–1600 *(rec St. Botolph's Church, Bossall, 1993)* Brewhouse Music ▲ BHCD 9409 [DDD]
Old Christmas Return'd Saydisc ▲ CDSDL 398 [DDD]
Young PO
P. Hirsch (cnd)
Brahms, J.:Qt 1 Pno *(rec Sept. 15, 1993)* Pavane ▲ ADW 7303 [DDD]
Janácek, L.:Lachian Dances *(rec Sept. 15, 1993)* Pavane ▲ ADW 7303 [DDD]
Strauss (II), Joh.:Waltzes—Eljan a Magyar, Op. 332 *(rec Sept. 15, 1993)*
Pavane ▲ ADW 7303 [DDD]
Young Russia State SO Moscow
M. Gorenstein (cnd)
Shchedrin, R.:Carmen *(rec Moscow Conservatory Great Hall, May & Sept 1994)*
PopeMusic ▲ PM 10022 [DDD]
Shostakovich, D.:Ballet Suite 5 *(rec Moscow Conservatory Great Hall, May & Sept 1994)*
PopeMusic ▲ PM 10022 [DDD]
Ysaÿe String Quartet
Boucourechliev, A.:Les Archipels, w. Brigitte Sylvestre (hp), Elisabeth Chojnacka (hpd), Françoise Rieunier (org), Roland Auzet, Jean–Pierre Drouet (perc), Hakon Austbö (pno), Françoise–Frédéric Guy (pno), Claude Helffer (pno), Georges Pludermacher (pno), Les Pléiades Ensemble
Musique Francaise d'Aujourd'hui ("Collection MFA–Radio France" series) ▲ MFA 216001
Ysaÿe String Quartet [C. Giovaninetta (vn), L.–M. Aguera (vn), M. da Silva (va), M. Poulet (vc)]
Debussy, C.:Qt Strs London ▲ 430434–2 [DDD]
Mendelssohn, F.:Qts Strs (comp) London ▲ 436325–2 [DDD]
Mendelssohn, F.:Qt 2 Strs London ▲ 436325–2 [DDD]
Mendelssohn, F.:Qt 3 Strs London ▲ 440369–2 [DDD]
Mendelssohn, F.:Qt 4 Strs *(rec Jan. 17–20, 1993)* London ▲ 440369–2 [DDD]
Mendelssohn, F.:Qt 6 Strs London ▲ 436325–2 [DDD]
Ravel, M.:Qt Strs London ▲ 430434–2 [DDD]
Eugene Ysaÿe String Trio
Devienne, F.:Qts Bn, Op. 73, w. F. Pollet (bn)—No. 3 in g Syrinx ▲ 93103 [DDD]
Mozart, W.A.:Duo Bn Vc, w. F. Pollet (bn) Syrinx ▲ 93103 [DDD]
Stamitz, C.:Qt Bn, w. F. Pollet (bn) Syrinx ▲ 93103 [DDD]
Vogel, J.C.:Qts Bn, w. F. Pollet (bn)—No. 1 in F Syrinx ▲ 93103 [DDD]
Yugoslavia RSO
P. Freeman (cnd)
Liszt, F.:Totentanz, w. A. Bromeley McCune (pno) Pro Arte ▲ 575
Rachmaninoff, S.:The Isle of the Dead Pro Arte ▲ 575
Yuval Trio
Arensky, A.:Trio 1 Pno Relief ▲ CR 900012
Dvořák, A.:Trio 2 Pno Relief ▲ CR 900012
Saint–Saëns, C.:Trio 1 Pno *(rec live)* Relief ▲ CR 891009 [ADD]
Saint–Saëns, C.:Trio 2 Pno *(rec live)* Relief ▲ CR 891009 [ADD]
Shostakovich, D.:Trio 2 Pno Relief ▲ CR 891 008 [DDD]
Tchaikovsky, P.:Trio Pno Relief ▲ CR 891 008 [DDD]
Zaanstad Opera Orch
J. Schaap (cnd)
Donizetti, G.:Il borgomastro di Saardam, w. Philipp Langridge (ten), Renato Capecchi (bar), Let Kiel (sgr), Zaanstad Opera Chorus *(rec 1973)* Pantheon 2–▲ PHE 6630 (m)
Zagreb Festival Orch
M. Halász (cnd)
Rossini, G.:Ovs—Il Barbiere di Siviglia; La scala di seta; Semiramide; Signor Bruschino; Guilaume Tell; L'italiana in Algeri; La Cenerentola; La gazza ladra *(rec Lisinski Concert Hall, Zagreb, Jan 9–11, 1989)*
Naxos 4–▲ 8.504013 [DDD]

ORCH. & ENS.

Zagreb Festival Orch (cont.)
M. Halász (cnd) (cont.)
Rossini, G.:Ovs—Barber of Seville; Cenerentola; Gazza ladra; Italiana in Algeri; Scala di seta; Semiramide; Signor Bruschino; William Tell — Naxos ▲ 8.550236 [DDD]

Zagreb Musici
Albinoni, T.:Music of—Con à cinque in g — Special Music Co. ("Classics of the Heart" series) ▲ SCD 5197
J. Rolla (cnd)
Concerto Barock, w. Liszt CO — Vivace 2-▲ G 216 [DDD]

Zagreb Opera Orch
S. Hubada (cnd)
Puccini, G.:La Bohème (sels), w. M. Olivero (sop), J. Oncina (ten)—one solo soprano aria (Si, mi chiamano Mimi) & one duet (O soave fanciulla) [I] *(rec live 5/3/64)* — Myto 2-▲ 2 MCD 91136 [ADD]

Zagreb PO
R. Edlinger (cnd)
Beethoven, L. van:Sym 2 *(rec 9/88)* — Naxos ▲ 8.550177 [DDD]
Beethoven, L. van:Sym 4 *(rec 9/88)* — Naxos ▲ 8.550180 [DDD]
Beethoven, L. van:Sym 5 *(rec 9/88)* — Naxos ▲ 8.550289 [DDD]
Beethoven, L. van:Sym 5 *(rec 9/88)* — Naxos ▲ 8.550177 [DDD]
Beethoven, L. van:Sym 7 *(rec 9/88)* — Naxos ▲ 8.550180 [DDD]
Beethoven, L. van:Sym 8 *(rec Zagreb, Sept 1988)* — Naxos 4-▲ 8.504012 [DDD]
Beethoven, L. van:Sym 9, "Choral Sym" *(rec 9/88)* — Naxos ▲ 8.550181 [DDD]
L. von Matačić (cnd)
Monteverdi, C.:Vespro della Beata Vergine, w. Croatian Radio-TV Choir *(rec live, 1974)* — Memories 2-▲ MEM 4598

Zagreb RSO
A. Janigro (cnd)
Haydn, J.:Sym 44, "Trauer" — Vanguard Classics ("Historical Anthology:The Bach Guild" series) 2-▲ SVC 5/6 [ADD]
Haydn, J.:Sym 45, "Farewell" — Vanguard Classics ("Historical Anthology:The Bach Guild" series) ▲ SVC 5/6 [ADD]
Haydn, J.:Sym 46 — Vanguard Classics ("Historical Anthology:The Bach Guild" series) ▲ SVC 5/6 [ADD]
Haydn, J.:Sym 47 — Vanguard Classics ("Historical Anthology:The Bach Guild" series) ▲ SVC 5/6 [ADD]
Haydn, J.:Sym 48, "Maria Theresia" — Vanguard Classics ("Historical Anthology:The Bach Guild" series) ▲ SVC 5/6 [ADD]
Haydn, J.:Sym 49, "La Passione" — Vanguard Classics ("Historical Anthology:The Bach Guild" series) ▲ SVC 5/6 [ADD]

Zagreb Solisti
Bach, J.S.:Con in e Fl, w. J. Galway (fl) — RCA Red Seal ("Papillon Collection" series) ▲ 6517-2-RG [ADD] ■ 6517-4-RG
Bach, J.S.:Con 8 Hpd, w. J. Galway (fl) [arr for fl & orch in a] — RCA Gold Seal ("Papillon Collection" series) ▲ 6517-2-RG [ADD] ■ 6517-4-RG
Bach, J.S.:Suite 2 Orch, w. J. Galway (fl) — RCA Gold Seal ("Papillon Collection" series) ▲ 6517-2-RG [ADD] ■ 6517-4-RG
Baroque Treasures — PMG ("Vienna Masters" series) ▲ CD 160105 [DDD]
Haydn, J.:Con 1 Vc, w. Mario Brunello (vc) — RS Applausi ▲ 6367-04
Haydn, J.:Con 2 Vc, w. Mario Brunello (vc) — RS Applausi ▲ 6367-04
Vivaldi, A.:Music of — PMG ("Vienna Master" series) ▲ CD 160229 [DDD]
J. Galway (cnd)
Vivaldi, A.:Cons Vn, Op. 8/1-4, "The Four Seasons", w. J. Galway (fl) — RCA Gold Seal ▲ 60748-2 [ADD] ■ 60748-4 (CrO2)
A. Janigro (cnd)
Barber, S.:Adagio Strs *(rec ca. 1963)* — Vanguard Classics ▲ OVC 4016 [ADD]
Boyce, W.:Syms, Op. 2, w. Herbert Tachezi (hpd/org) *(rec Grossesaal, Musikverein, Vienna, 1965)* — Vanguard Classics ▲ SVC 46 [ADD]
Castelnuovo-Tedesco, M.:Con 1 Gtr, w. Alirio Diaz (gtr) *(rec Grossesaal, Musikverein, Vienna, June 1965)* — Vanguard Classics ▲ OVC 8069 [ADD]
Kohaut, K.:Cons Lt & Strs, w. Alirio Diaz (gtr)—in F *(rec Grossesaal, Musikverein, Vienna, June 1965)* — Vanguard Classics ▲ OVC 8069 [ADD]
Mozart, L.:Toy Sym *(rec 1958)* — Vanguard Classics ("Everyman" series) ▲ OVC 5005 [ADD]
Mozart, W.A.:Andante Fl, w. Julius Baker (fl) *(rec Vienna, 1965)* — Vanguard Classics ▲ SVC 54 [AAD]
Mozart, W.A.:Con 1 Fl, w. Julius Baker (fl) *(rec Vienna, 1965)* — Vanguard Classics ▲ SVC 54 [AAD]
Mozart, W.A.:Con Fl Hp, w. J. Baker (fl), H. Jelinek (hp) *(rec 1962)* — Vanguard Classics ("Everyman" series) ▲ OVC 5011 [ADD]
Mozart, W.A.:Con Fl Hp, w. Julius Baker (fl), Hubert Jelinek (hp) *(rec Baumgarten Hall, Vienna, May 5-7, 1962)* — Vanguard Classics ▲ SVC 42 [AAD]
Mozart, W.A.:Con 9 Pno, w. A. Brendel (pno) — Vanguard Classics ▲ OVC 4015 [ADD]
Mozart, W.A.:Con 14 Pno, w. A. Brendel (pno) — Vanguard Classics ▲ OVC 4015 [ADD]
Solid Gold Baroque, w. English CO — Vanguard Classics ▲ OVC 4021 [ADD]
Telemann, G.P.:Suite in a Fl, w. Julius Baker (fl) *(rec Baumgarten Hall, Vienna, May 5-7, 1962)* — Vanguard Classics ▲ SVC 42 [AAD]
Telemann, G.P.:Suite in a Fl, w. J. Baker (fl) *(rec 1962)* — Vanguard Classics ("Everyman" series) ▲ OVC 5011 [ADD]
Vaughan Williams, R.:Fant on Greensleeves, w. Julius Baker (fl) *(rec Vienna, 1965)* — Vanguard Classics ▲ SVC 54 [AAD]
Vivaldi, A.:Cons Bn, w. R. Klepač (bn)—RV.501 in g *(rec 1964)* — Vanguard Classics ("The Bach Guild" series) ▲ OVC 2006 [ADD]
The Virtuoso Trumpet, w. Helmut Wobisch (tpt) *(rec 1961)* — Vanguard Classics ("The Bach Guild" series) ▲ OVC 2008 [ADD]
Vivaldi, A.:Cons Fl (misc), w. J. Baker (fl)—RV.439 in B♭, "La Notte" *(rec 1964)* — Vanguard Classics ("The Bach Guild" series) ▲ OVC 2006 [ADD]
Vivaldi, A.:Cons Fl (misc), w. Julius Baker (fl)—in D, R.428, "Il cardellino" *(rec Vienna, 1965)* — Vanguard Classics ▲ SVC 54 [AAD]
Vivaldi, A.:Con Fl Bn, w. Julius Baker (fl), Karl Hoffmann (bn) *(rec Baumgarten Hall, Vienna, May 5-7, 1962)* — Vanguard Classics ▲ SVC 42 [AAD]
Vivaldi, A.:Con for 2 Mands, w. A. Ganoci (mand), F. Pavlinek (mand) *(rec 1964)* — Vanguard Classics ("The Bach Guild" series) ▲ OVC 2006 [ADD]
Vivaldi, A.:Cons Orch—RV.158 in A, "Concerto Ripieno" *(rec 1964)* — Vanguard Classics ("The Bach Guild" series) ▲ OVC 2006 [ADD]
Vivaldi, A.:Cons Pic, w. Julius Baker (fl)—Con in C, RV.443 *(rec Vienna, 1965)* — Vanguard Classics ▲ SVC 54 [AAD]
Vivaldi, A.:Cons Vn (misc), w. J. Stanic (vn)—RV.179 in C *(rec 1964)* — Vanguard Classics ("The Bach Guild" series) ▲ OVC 2006 [ADD]
T. Ninič (cnd)
Bartók, B.:Divert *(rec 6/91)* — IMP Classics ▲ PCD 1000 [DDD]
Bartók, B.:Romanian Folk Dances Pno *(rec 6/91)* — IMP Classics ▲ PCD 1000 [DDD]
Shostakovich, D.:Chamber Sym, Op. 110a — IMP Classics ▲ PCD 1000 [DDD]
Shostakovich, D.:Scherzo Orch — IMP Classics ▲ PCD 1000 [DDD]
Vivaldi, A.:Cons Bn, w. D. Smith (bn)—Concerti RV.473, 478, 483, 485, 497, 498, 502 — ASV ▲ ASV 752 [DDD]
Vivaldi, A.:Cons Bn, w. D. Smith (bn)—Concerti RV.480, 484, 489, 493, 503, 504 — ASV ▲ ASV 751 [DDD]
Vivaldi, A.:Cons Bn, w. D. Smith (bn)—Concerti RV.471, 475, 490, 492, 495, 496 — ASV ▲ ASV 734 [DDD]

Zagreb String Quartet
Boccherini, L.:Qnt Pno, G.413-418, w. R. Caramella (pno)—in A, B♭ & e, G.413-415 — Nuova Era ▲ NUO 7160 [DDD]

Zagreb Youth Orch
I. Davidovac (cnd)
Kreisler, F.:Cadenzas for Beethoven's Con Vn, w. R. Ricci (vn)—Beethoven:Con., Op. 61 — One-Eleven ▲ URS 91050 [ADD]
Mozart, W.A.:Con 4 Vn, w. R. Ricci (vn) — One-Eleven ▲ URS 91050 [ADD]

Zagros Ensemble
J. Storgårds (cnd)
Nevanlinna, T.:Spin — Finlandia ▲ FIN 12179 [DDD]
Suilamo, H.:KOTVA — Finlandia ▲ FIN 12179 [DDD]
Suilamo, H.:NAALA — Finlandia ▲ FIN 12179 [DDD]
Vuori, H.:Les Mouvements interrompus — Finlandia ▲ FIN 12179 [DDD]

Zapolski String Quartet
Shostakovich, D.:Qt 2 Strs — Classico ▲ 135
Shostakovich, D.:Qt 8 Strs — Classico ▲ 135

Zaslav Duo [Bernard Zaslav (va), Naomi Zaslav (pno)]
Bloch, E.:In the Night — Music & Arts ▲ CD 902 [DDD]
Bloch, E.:Meditation & Processional — Music & Arts ▲ CD 902 [DDD]
Bloch, E.:Sketches (5) in Sepia — Music & Arts ▲ CD 902 [DDD]
Bloch, E.:Suite hébraïque — Music & Arts ▲ CD 902 [DDD]
Bloch, E.:Suite Va — Music & Arts ▲ CD 902 [DDD]
Bloch, E.:Suite Va & Pno — Music & Arts ▲ CD 902 [DDD]

Zefiro Ensemble
Mozart, W.A.:Divert Obs, K.213 — Astrée ▲ E 8529
Mozart, W.A.:Divert Obs, K.240 — Astrée ▲ E 8529
Mozart, W.A.:Divert Obs, K.252 — Astrée ▲ E 8529
Mozart, W.A.:Divert Obs, K.253 — Astrée ▲ E 8529
Mozart, W.A.:Divert Obs, K.270 — Astrée ▲ E 8529
Mozart, W.A.:Divert Ww, K.186 [period instrs] — Astrée ▲ E 8573
Mozart, W.A.:Serenade Winds, K.388 [period instrs] — Astrée ▲ E 8573
Mozart, W.A.:Serenade Winds, K.375 [period instrs] — Astrée ▲ E 8573
Zelenka, J.D.:Sons Obs—Sons 1, 3 & 4 — Astrée ▲ E 8563
Zelenka, J.D.:Trio Sons Obs—Nos. 2, 5 & 6 — Astrée ▲ E 8511

Zeitgeist [Bob Samarotto (ww), Tom Linker (pno/syn), Jay Johnson (mar/perc), Heather Barringer (vib/perc)]
Budd, H.:In Delius' Sleep, w. Harold Budd (voc/pno) *(rec Westminster Church, Minneapolis, MN, Nov. 20, 1993)* — New Albion ▲ NA066
Budd, H.:She Is a Phantom, w. Harold Budd (voc/pno) *(rec Westminster Church, Minneapolis, MN, Nov. 20, 1993)* — New Albion ▲ NA066
Riley, T.:Music of—Intuitive Leaps; Salome's excellent extension; The room of rememberance — Work Music ▲ WRK 00-3
Rzewski, F.:Crusoe *(rec Studio M, St. Paul, MN, Mar. 1994)* — O.O. Discs ▲ OO 15
Rzewski, F.:The Lost Melody, w. Joseph Holmquist (perc) *(rec Studio M, St. Paul, MN, Mar. 1994)* — O.O. Discs ▲ OO 15
Rzewski, F.:Spots, w. Joseph Holmquist (perc) *(rec Studio M, St. Paul, MN, Mar. 1994)* — O.O. Discs ▲ OO 15
Rzewski, F.:Wails, w. Joseph Holmquist (perc) *(rec Studio M, St. Paul, MN, Mar. 1994)* — O.O. Discs ▲ OO 14

Zemlinsky Trio [Thomas Friedli (cl), Annick Gautier (vc), Patricia Thomas (pno)]
Maggini, E.:Chamber Music—Torso III "Cinque Visioni"; Torso VIII; Torso IX; Torso X; Canto XI; Atem; Canto I-III "Tre canti sacri" *(rec 1993)* — Jecklin ▲ JS 295-2 [ADD]

Zephyrus [Courtney Westcott (fl), Ingrid Matthews (vn), Shelley Taylor (vc), Byron Schenkman (hpd/pno)]
Holzbauer, I.:Qnt Fl, w. Dana Maiben (va) *(rec Faith Lutheran Church, Bloomington, July 5-7, 1994)* — Focus ▲ FOCUS 945 [DDD]
Toeschi, C.J.:Quartetto *(rec Faith Lutheran Church, Bloomington, July 5-7, 1994)* — Focus ▲ FOCUS 945 [DDD]

Zephyrus [Courtney Westcott (fl), Ingrid Matthews (vn), Shelley Taylor (vc)]
Mozart, W.A.:Qt Fl, K.Anh.171 *(rec Faith Lutheran Church, Bloomington, July 5-7, 1994)* — Focus ▲ FOCUS 945 [DDD]

Zephyrus members [Courtney Westcott (fl), Shelley Taylor (vc)]
Danzi, F.:Petits Duos (3)—No. 2 in D *(rec Faith Lutheran Church, Bloomington, July 5-7, 1994)* — Focus ▲ FOCUS 945 [DDD]

Zephyrus members [Ingrid Matthews (vn), Byron Schenkman (pno)]
Lebrun, F.:Son Vn *(rec Faith Lutheran Church, Bloomington, July 5-7, 1994)* — Focus ▲ FOCUS 945 [DDD]

Zetterqvist String Quartet
Brahms, J.:Qnt Cl, w. K. Fagéus (b cl) — Opus 3 ▲ OP 19301
Mozart, W.A.:Qnt Cl, K.581, w. K. Fagéus (b cl) — Opus 3 ▲ OP 19301

Zingara Trio
E. Heath (cnd)
Beethoven, L. van:Con Vn, Vc & Pno, "Triple Con", w. English CO — IMP ("Classics" series) ▲ IMP 6700912

Zurich Baroque Strings
V. Kazandjiev (cnd)
Barber, S.:Adagio Strs — Denon ▲ CO 8002 [DDD]

Zurich Beromünster Orch
P. Burkhard (cnd)
Sibelius, J.:Con Vn, w. Peter Rybar (vn) *(rec live, Zurich, 1952)* — Doron ("Legendary Artists" series) ▲ DRC 4009 [ADD]

Zurich Camerata
R. Tschupp (cnd)
Bach, J.C.:Sinfs, Op. 6, w. G. Rumpel (fl), A. Raoult (ob) *(rec 1969, 1981)* — Jecklin ▲ J 4408 [ADD]
Cimarosa, D.:Con for 2 Fls, w. P.-L. Graf (fl), G. Guéneux (fl) *(rec 1968)* — Jecklin-Disco ▲ JD 506-2 [ADD]
Gluck, C.W.:Con Fl, w. P.-L. Graf (fl) *(rec 1968)* — Jecklin-Disco ▲ JD 506-2 [ADD]
Haller, H.:Per la Camerata — Grammont ▲ CTSP 10-2 [ADD]
Krommer, F.:Concertino Fl, Op. 65, w. G. Rumpel (fl), A. Raoult (ob) *(rec 1969, 1981)* — Jecklin ▲ J 4408 [ADD]
Mäder, U.:Vergänglich *(rec 1996)* — Jecklin ▲ JS 3072 [DDD]
Marek, C.:Rural Scenes, w. Jeannette Fischer (sop) *(rec Dec 1993-Dec 1994)* — Jecklin ▲ JEC 306
Müller-Zurich, P.:Sonate Str — Grammont ▲ CTSP 20-2
Vanhal, J.B.:Sym in g, w. G. Rumpel (fl), A. Raoult (ob) *(rec 1969, 1981)* — Jecklin ▲ J 4408 [ADD]
Vogel, W.:Hörformen Pno, w. Werner Bärtschi (pno) *(rec Dec 1993-Dec 1994)* — Jecklin ▲ JEC 306

Zurich Chamber Ensemble
C. Keller (cnd)
Eisler, H.:Chamber Music (comp) — Accord 4-▲ ACD 201712 [DDD]
R. Tschupp (cnd)
Boccherini, L.:Con in D Fl [attrib.], w. P.-L. Graf (fl) *(rec 1968)* — Jecklin-Disco ▲ JD 506-2 [ADD]

Zurich CO
Caplet, A.:Conte fantastique, w. Ursula Holliger (hp) — Claves ▲ CD 50280 [ADD]
Czerny, C.:Gott erhalte Franz den Kaiser, w. M. Jones (pno) — Jecklin-Disco ▲ JD 608-2 [ADD]
Ravel, M.:Intro & Allegro, w. Ursula Holliger (hp), Perter-Lukas Graf (fl), Hans Rudolf Stalder (cl) — Claves ▲ CD 50280 [ADD]
M. Jones (cnd)
Hänsel, P.:Qt Strs — Jecklin-Disco ▲ JD 608-2 [ADD]
E. de Stoutz (cnd)
Bach, J.S.:Suite 2 Orch, w. Syrinx (fl) *(rec 1986)* — Analekta ▲ AN2-8501 [DDD] ■ AN4-8501
Bartók, B.:Divert *(rec Zurich, July 17, 1960)* — Vanguard Classics ▲ OVC 8055 [ADD]

▲ = CD ♦ = Enhanced CD Δ = MD ■ = Cassette Tape □ = DCC

Zurich CO (cont.)
E. de Stoutz (cnd) (cont.)
Beethoven, L. van:Romances Vn, w. S. Ashkenasi (vn) — Tudor ▲ 723 [ADD]
Bellini, V.:Con in E♭ Ob, w. M. André (tpt) [arr. André] — EMI Classics ▲ CDC 54086 [DDD]
Boccherini, L.:Con in D Fl, w. Syrinx (fl) *(rec 1986)* — Analekta ▲ AN2–8501 [DDD] ■ AN4–8501
Haydn, J.:Con Tpt, w. Maurice André (tpt) — EMI Classics ▲ CDC 54086 [DDD]
Hummel, J.N.:Vars Ob, w. M. André (tpt) [arr. André] — EMI Classics ▲ CDC 54086 [DDD]
Martin, F.:Pavane couleur du temps — Gallo ▲ CD 713 [ADD]
Martin, F.:Petite sym concertante, w. C. Mathieu (hp), C. Rütti (hpd), V. Graf (pno) — Gallo ▲ CD 713 [ADD]
Martin, F.:Polyptyque (6 images de la Passion du Christ), w. Z. Czapzynski (vn) — Gallo ▲ CD 713 [ADD]
Mozart, W.A.:Con Bn, w. Klaus Thunemann (bn) *(rec Kirche Altstetten/ZH, June 1982)* — Claves ▲ CD 508205 [DDD]
Mozart, W.A.:Con Cl, w. Thomas Friedli (cl) *(rec Kirche Altstetten/ZH, June 1982)* — Claves ▲ CD 508205 [DDD]
Mozart, W.A.:Con Ob, K.314, w. M. André (tpt) [trans Maurice André for Tpt] — EMI Classics ▲ CDC 54086 [DDD]
Mozart, W.A.:Con 2 Vn, w. Z. Francescatti (vn) *(rec 1968; from CBS Masterwork)* — Sony Masterworks ("Portrait" series) ▲ MPK 52526 [ADD]
Mozart, W.A.:Con 5 Vn, w. S. Ashkenasi (vn) — Tudor ▲ 723 [ADD]
Mozart, W.A.:Con 5 Vn, w. Z. Francescatti (vn) *(rec 1968; from CBS Masterwork)* — Sony Masterworks ("Portrait" series) ▲ MPK 52526 [ADD]
Stravinsky, I.:Con CO, Zurich Tonhalle Orch Winds *(rec Zurich, July 17, 1960)* — Vanguard Classics ▲ OVC 8055 [ADD]
Stravinsky, I.:Con Str *(rec Zurich, July 17, 1960)* — Vanguard Classics ▲ OVC 8055 [ADD]
Tartini, G.:Cons Vn (misc), w. A. Gertler (vn)—(5) in D, D.24; in D, D.30; in F, D.68; in G, D.83; in A, D.95 *(rec 1962-63)* — Hungaroton ▲ HCD 31529 [ADD]

Zurich Chamber Players
Martin, F.:Pavane couleur du temps *(rec 1989/90)* — Jecklin–Disco ▲ JD 646–2 [ADD]
Martin, F.:Qnt Pno, w. H. Schmid–Wyss (pno) *(rec 1989/90)* — Jecklin–Disco ▲ JD 646–2 [ADD]
Martin, F.:Trio sur les mélodies populaires irlandaises, w. H. Schmid–Wyss (pno) *(rec 1989/90)* — Jecklin–Disco ▲ JD 646–2 [ADD]
Martin, F.:Trio Vn *(rec 1989/90)* — Jecklin–Disco ▲ JD 646–2 [ADD]
Raff, J.:Octet Strs, w. B. Langbein (vn), M. Lehmann (va), R. Reichel *(rec 1978)* — Jecklin–Disco ▲ JD 547–2 [ADD]
Reger, M.:Sextet Vns *(rec 1977)* — Jecklin–Disco ▲ JD 543–2 [ADD]
Weber, C.M. von:Intro, Theme & Vars Cl, w. H. R. Stalder (cl) *(rec 1972, 1975 & 1982)* — Jecklin–Disco ▲ JD 536–2 [ADD]

Zurich Chamber Players [Jürg Dähler (vn), Andreas Pfenninger (vn), Cornel Anderes (va), Valérie Dähler-Mulet (va), Raffaele Altwegg (vc), Luciano Pezzani (vc)]
Schoenberg, A.:Verklärte Nacht *(rec 1995)* — Jecklin ▲ JEC 702
Schulhoff, E.:Sxt Strs *(rec 1995)* — Jecklin ▲ JEC 702
Spohr, L.:Double Qt 1, w. B. Langbein (vn), M. Lehmann (va), R. Reichel *(rec 1978)* — Jecklin–Disco ▲ JD 547–2 [ADD]
Spohr, L.:Fant & Vars on a Theme of Danzi, w. H. R. Stalder (cl) *(rec 1972, 1975 & 1982)* — Jecklin–Disco ▲ JD 536–2 [ADD]

Zurich Chamber Soloists
Rosauro, N.:Con Mar, w. S. Balzer (mar) — Gallo ▲ CD 599 [AAD]

A.-H. Lilienthal (cnd)
Cornell, K.:Widerschein — Gallo ▲ CD–569 [ADD]
Felder, A.:Metamorphose — Gallo ▲ CD 569 [ADD]
Felder, A.:...pasar por la calle... — Gallo ▲ CD 569 [ADD]

Zurich Clarinet Trio
Lehmann, H.U.:Triplum *(rec July 2, 1984)* — Grammont ▲ CTS P 4–2

Zurich Collegium Musicum Orch
P. Sacher (cnd)
Maurice André Trumpet Masterpieces, w. Maurice André (tpt), Munich CO [cnd:Hans Stadlmair], English CO [cnd:Charles Mackerras], Munich Bach Orch [cnd:Karl Richter] — Deutsche Grammophon ("Double" series) 2–▲ 413853–2
Moret, N.:Con Vc, w. Mstislav Rostropovitch (vc) — Musiques Suisses ▲ CD 6103 [DDD]
Moret, N.:Double Con, w. R. Pezzani (vn), L. Pezzani (vc) *(rec live Nov. 18, 1992)* — Grammont ▲ CTSP 23–2 [ADD]
Mozart, W.A.:Cassation, K.63 *(rec 1969)* — Jecklin ▲ J 44042 [ADD]
Mozart, W.A.:Cassation, K.99/63a *(rec 1969)* — Jecklin ▲ J 44042 [ADD]
Paul Sacher & New Music, w. Basel CO, Basel Percussion Ensemble — Ars Musici 3–▲ 1155

P. Siegwart (cnd)
Mäder, U.:Mit Nacht beladen, w. Verena–Barbara Gohl (alt), Michael Gohl (cl) *(rec 1996)* — Jecklin ▲ JS 3072 [DDD]

Zurich Mozart Opera Orch
N. Harnoncourt (cnd)
Mozart, W.A.:Entführung, w. Yvonne Kenny (sop), Carolyn Watson (cta), Peter Schreier (ten), Wilfried Gamlich (ten), Matti Salminen (bass), Wolfgang Reichmann (nar), Zurich Mozart Opera Chorus [G] — Teldec 2–▲ 2292–42643–2

Zurich New Music Ensemble [Hans Peter Frehner (fl), Hansruedi Bissegger (cl), Mattias Eser (perc), Viktor Müller (hpd), Urs Bumbacher (vn), D. Riniker (vc), Xenia Schindler (hp), Cornel Anderes (va)]
J. Henneberger (cnd)
Berio, L.:Folk Songs Mez, w. H. Fassbender (mez)—[arr. by Berio] Black is the color (USA); I wonder as I wander (USA); The moon has risen (Armenian); Little nightingale (France); May the Lord send fine weather... (Italy); The ideal woman (Italy); Dance (Italy); Songs of sadness (Sardinia); Wretched is he (France); The Spinner (France); Azerbaijan love song (Azerbaijan) *(rec 1993)* — Jecklin–Disco ▲ JD 684–2 [DDD]
Denisov, E.:La Vie en Rouge, w. H. Fassbender (mez)—I'd like; A real joke; The atom-bomb waltz; The yellow waltz; The Prisoner; What I live for; The last waltz *(rec 1993)* — Jecklin–Disco ▲ JD 684–2 [DDD]

Zurich New Music Ensemble [Hans Peter Frehner (fl), Hansruedi Bissegger (cl), Mattias Eser (perc), Viktor Müller (pno), Urs Bumbacher (vn), Samuel Brunner (vc)]
Crumb, G.:Eleven Echoes of Autumn *(rec Radio Studio Zurich, Jan 1996)* — Jecklin ▲ JD 7052 [DDD]

Zurich New Music Ensemble [Hans Peter Frehner (fl), Samuel Brunner (vc), Viktor Müller (pno)]
Crumb, G.:Vox balaenae *(rec Radio Studio Zurich, Jan 1996)* — Jecklin ▲ JD 7052 [DDD]

Zurich New Music Ensemble [Urs Bumbacher (vn), Hansruedi Bissegger (cl), Xenia Schindler (hp), D. Riniker (hpd)]
Berio, L.:Chamber Music, w. H. Fassbender (mez)—Strings in the Earth; All day; Winds of May *(rec 1993)* — Jecklin–Disco ▲ JD 684–2 [DDD]

Zurich New Music Ensemble [Urs Bumbacher (vn), Jürg Henneberger (pno)]
Crumb, G.:Nocturnes (4) (Night Music II) *(rec Radio Studio Zurich, Jan 1996)* — Jecklin ▲ JD 7052 [DDD]

Zurich New Music Ensemble [Urs Bumbacher (vn), Samuel Brunner (vc), Viktor Müller (pno), Matthias Eser (perc)]
J. Henneberger (cnd)
Crumb, G.:Dream Sequence (Images II) *(rec Radio Studio Zurich, Jan 1996)* — Jecklin ▲ JD 7052 [DDD]

Zurich Opera Orch
N. Harnoncourt (cnd)
Mozart, W.A.:Clemenza, w. L. Popp (sop), R. Ziesack (sop), A. Murray (mez), D. Ziegler (mez), P. Langridge (ten), L. Polgar (bass), T. Grabowski (hpd), C. Hermann (vc), Zurich Opera House Chorus — Teldec 2–▲ 90857–2

Zurich Opera Orch (cont.)
N. Harnoncourt (cnd) (cont.)
Mozart, W.A.:Zauberflöte, w. E. Gruberova (sop), B. Bonney (sop), G. Schmid (sop), H.-P. Blochwitz (ten), T. Hampson (bar), M. Salminen (bass), A. Scharinger (bass), Zurich Opera House Chorus [G] — Teldec 2–▲ 2292–42716–2

R. Weikert (cnd)
Marti, H.:Wachsende Bedrohung — Grammont ▲ CTS P 22–2 [DDD]
Zemlinsky, A. von:Kleider machen Leute, w. E. Mathis (sop), H. Winkler (ten), V. Vogel (ten), C. Otelli (bar), H. Franzen (bass), R. Scholze (bass), W. Slabbert (sgr), Zurich Opera House Chorus [G] *(rec live, Zurich Opera House, 6/29/90)* — Koch Schwann 2–▲ CD 314 069 [DDD]

F. Welser-Möst (cnd)
Opera Themes & Variations for Clarinet & Orchestra, w. Sabine Meyer (cl) — EMI Classics ▲ CDC 56137

Zurich Pro Arte Wind Quintet
Milhaud, D.:Le Cheminée du Roi René — Nimbus ▲ NI 5327 [ADD]

Zurich RSO
F. Lehár (cnd)
Lehár, F.:Music of, w. Richard Tauber (ten)—Music from Das Land des Lächelns; Giuditta; Der Graf von Luxemburg; Das Füstenkind; others *(rec June 5, 1946)* — Koch Schwann ▲ SCH 310982 [AAD]

J. Sternberg (cnd)
Bassett, L.:Vars Orch — CRI ▲ CD 677 [ADD]

Zurich SO
D. Schweizer (cnd)
Dupré, M.:Sym, Op. 25, w. U. Meldau (pno) — Motette ▲ CD 40111 [DDD]
Keller, A.:Ossia — Grammont ▲ CTSP 19–2 [ADD]
Müller–Zurich, P.:Consenso *(rec Sept. 1991)* — Jecklin–Disco ▲ JD 663–2 [DDD]
Müller–Zurich, P.:Sinfonietta I *(rec Sept. 1991)* — Jecklin–Disco ▲ JD 663–2 [DDD]
Müller–Zurich, P.:Sinfonietta II *(rec Sept. 1991)* — Jecklin–Disco ▲ JD 663–2 [DDD]

Zurich Tonhalle Orch
O. Ackermann (cnd)
Beethoven, L. van:Sym 5 — Stradivarius 2–▲ STV DTM 12324 [ADD]
Beethoven, L. van:Sym 7 — Stradivarius 2–▲ STV DTM 12324 [ADD]
Chopin, F.:Con 1 Pno, w. D. Lipatti (pno) *(rec live, 1950)* — EMI Classics ▲ CDH 63497 (m) [ADD]
Chopin, F.:Con 1 Pno, w. D. Lipatti (pno) *(rec live Feb. 7, 1950)* — Jecklin–Disco ▲ JD 541–2 [ADD]
Dvořák, A:Con Vc — Stradivarius 2–▲ STV DTM 12324 [ADD]
Dvořák, A:Sym 9, "From the New World" — Stradivarius 2–▲ STV DTM 12324 [ADD]

J. Krips (cnd)
Brahms, J.:Academic Festival Ov — Accord ▲ ADE 132742 [AAD]
Brahms, J.:Sym 2 — Accord ▲ ADE 132742 [AAD]
Mozart, W.A.:Ovs—La nozze di Figaro; Don Juan; Le directeur de theatre; Die Entführung aus dem Serail; La clemence de Tito; Così fan tutte; La fainta giardiniera; Idomeneo — Adès ▲ ADE 203072 [DDD]

M. Stern (cnd)
Derungs, M.:Music of, w. Mary Woodside (vn)—Con for Vn; Giarsun; Con for Rcr, Db, Hpd & Strs; Scene teatrali for Ww Oct — Grammont ▲ CTSP 51–2
Prokofiev, S.:Cons Vn (comp), w. B. Belkin (vn) — Denon/PCM Digital ▲ CO 75891 [DDD]
Stravinsky, I.:Agon *(rec Tonhalle, Zurich, Feb. & Sept. 1993)* — Denon ▲ CO 78972 [DDD]
Stravinsky, I.:The Firebird Suite *(rec Tonhalle, Zurich, Feb. & Sept. 1993)* — Denon ▲ CO 78972 [DDD]
Stravinsky, I.:Jeu de cartes *(rec Tonhalle, Zurich, Feb. & Sept. 1993)* — Denon ▲ CO 78972 [DDD]

F. Travis (cnd)
Moeschinger, A.:On ne traverse pas la nuit — Grammont ▲ CTSP 1–2 [ADD]

H. Wakasugi (cnd)
Ringger, R.U.:Nachhall *(rec live Sept. 3, 1986)* — Grammont ▲ CTSP 29–2 [ADD]

Zurich Tonhalle Orch Soloists
Haydn, J.:Diverts for 2 Obs, Cls, Hns, Bns & Ctbn, H.II/41-46 *(rec 1973)* — Jecklin ▲ J 4407–2 [ADD]

Zurich Tonhalle Orch Winds
E. de Stoutz (cnd)
Stravinsky, I.:Con CO, w. Zurich CO *(rec Zurich, July 17, 1960)* — Vanguard Classics ▲ OVC 8055 [ADD]

Zurich Wind Octet
Krommer, F.:Octet-Partitas — Tudor ▲ TUD 7001 [DDD]
Salieri, A.:Armonia per un tempio della notte — Tudor ▲ 779 [DDD]
Triebensee, J.:Suite — Tudor ▲ 779 [DDD]

INSTRUMENTALISTS

Aaberg, Philip (instr)
Mozart, W.A.:Music of, w. Todd Boekelheide, Chris Botti, Henry Adam Curtis, Steve Erquiaga, Béla Fleck, Eugene Friesen, Paul McCandless, Tim Story, Richard Schönherz, Tracy Scott Silverman, Thea Suits-Silverman, ValGardena, Modern Mandolin Quartet Imaginary Road ▲ 314534065-2 ■ 314534065-4

Aabo, Lars (cl)
Brahms, J.:Son 1 Cl, w. Semion Balshem (pno) *(rec Aarhus, Denmark, July 1995)* Rondo Grammofon ▲ RCD 8348 [DDD]
Reger, M.:Son Cl, Op. 107, w. Semion Balshem (pno) *(rec Aarhus, Denmark, July 1995)* Rondo Grammofon ▲ RCD 8348 [DDD]
Winding, A.:Fants Cl, w. Semion Balshem (pno) *(rec Aarhus, Denmark, July 1995)* Rondo Grammofon ▲ RCD 8348 [DDD]

Aadne, T. (hn)—see ORCHESTRAS & ENSEMBLES Danish Wind Octet

Aarflot, Sven (bn)
Rangström, T.:Vauxhall, w. Bengt Christiansson (fl), Lars Olof Loman (ob), Lars Almgren (cl), Rolf Bengtsson (hn), Rune Bodin (trbn), Rozalina Skytt (hp), O. Vänskä (cnd), Stockholm PO *(rec Stockholm Concert Hall, Jan. 16 & 18, 1985)* Caprice ▲ CAP 21195 [DDD]

Aaron, Richard (vc)
Heiden, B.:Serenade, w. David DeBolt (bn), Stephanie Sant'Ambrogio (vn), Katherine DeBolt (va) Crystal ▲ CD 347

Aasen, H. P. (bn)—see ORCHESTRAS & ENSEMBLES Oslo Wind Ensemble

Abbenes, Arie (car)
Kagel, M.:Nah und Fern, w. Andreas Adam (tpt), Marco Blaauw (tpt), Achim Gorsch (tpt), Markus Stockhausen (tpt), M. Kagel (cnd) Montaigne ▲ MO 782062

Abberger, John (ob)—see ORCHESTRAS & ENSEMBLES L'Archibudelli

Abbott, Leo (org)
The E. & G. G. Hook Organ, Op. 801 (1875) AFKA ▲ SK 519 ■ SK 329

Abe, Keiko (mar/vib)
Ishii, M.:Concertante Mar & Perc, w. Strasbourg Percussion Ensemble Denon ▲ CO 73678 [DDD]
Matsushita, I.:Airscope II BIS ▲ CD 462 [DDD]
Miki, M.:Mar Spiritual, w. Kroumata Percussion Ensemble BIS ▲ CD 462 [DDD]
Miyoshi, A.:Rin-sai, w. Kroumata Percussion Ensemble BIS ▲ CD 462 [DDD]
Nishimura, A.:Kala, w. Kroumata Percussion Ensemble BIS ▲ CD 462 [DDD]
Play Works for Marimba & Percussion, w. Kroumata Percussion Ensemble BIS ▲ CD 462 [DDD]
Ptaszynska, M.:Con Mar, w. S. Kawalla (cnd), Polish National RSO Cracow *(rec Cracow Philharmonic, May 8-10, 1986)* Polskie Nagrania ▲ PLN 075 [ADD]
Takemitsu, T.:Music of, w. Y. Nagano Tashi (mez), H. Ibe (gtr), M. Nagasako (hpY. Takahashi (pno), R. Noguchi (fl), M. Hamada (lt), T. Koizumi (picc), S. Ueki (vn), Y. Hattori (vc), R. Stoltzman (cl), P. Serkin (pno), Ozawa, Wakasugi (cnd), Boston SO—Quatrain; Stanza I; Sacrifice; Ring; Valeria; A Flock Descends into the Pentagonal Garden
Deutsche Grammophon ("20th Century Classics" series) ▲ 423253-2 [ADD]

Abe, Yoko (pno)
Holt, S. ten:Horizon, w. Polo de Haas (pno), Margaret Krill (pno), Fred Oldenburg (pno) Donemus 2-▲ CV 5/6

Abel, David (vn)
Cage, J.:Nocturne, w. J. Steinberg (pno) New Albion ▲ NA 036 [DDD]
Curran, A.:VSTG, w. S. Wood (vn), M. Tichener (va), D. Weinschelbaum (vc) CRI ▲ CD 668 [DDD]
Dresher, P.:Double Ikat, w. J. Steinberg (pno), W. Winant (perc) *(rec 1992)* New Albion ▲ NA 053
Feldman, Morton:Rothko Chapel, w. D. Dietrich (sop), K. Rosenak (pno), W. Winant (perc), Philip Brett (cnd), Univ of California at Berkeley Chamber Chorus *(rec 10/90)* New Albion ▲ NA 039 [DDD]
Harrison, L.:Suite Vn & American Gamelan, w. J. Bergamo (gamelan cnd) New Albion ▲ NA 015 [ADD];
Zorn, J.:Elegy, w. Mike Patton (sgr), Barbara Chaffe (fl), Scummy (gtr), David Shea (turntables), David Slusser (sound effects), William Winant (perc) Tzadik ▲ TZA 7302 [ADD]

Abel, David (vn/hi-hat/dog whistle)
Curran, A.:Schtyx, w. J. Steinberg (pno/prepared pno/hmc/bass dr/vn/dog whistle), W. Winant (perc/vn/dog whistle) CRI ▲ CD 668 [DDD]

Abel, Jenny (vn)
Schumann, R.:Adagio & Allegro Hn, w. Roberto Szidon (pno) Ars Musici 2-▲ 1038
Schumann, R.:Fantasiestücke Cl, w. Roberto Szidon (pno) Ars Musici 2-▲ 1038
Schumann, R.:Märchenbilder, w. Roberto Szidon (pno) Ars Musici 2-▲ 1038
Schumann, R.:Romances Ob, w. Roberto Szidon (pno) Ars Musici 2-▲ 1038
Schumann, R.:Son 1 Vn, w. Roberto Szidon (pno) Ars Musici 2-▲ 1038
Schumann, R.:Son 2 Vn, w. Roberto Szidon (pno) Ars Musici 2-▲ 1038
Schumann, R.:Son 3 Vn, w. Roberto Szidon (pno) Ars Musici 2-▲ 1038
Schumann, R.:Stücke im Volkston, w. Roberto Szidon (pno) Ars Musici 2-▲ 1038
Villa-Lobos, H.:Son 1 Vn, w. Roberto Szidon (pno) Bayer ▲ BR 100119 [DDD]
Villa-Lobos, H.:Son 2 Vn, w. Roberto Szidon (pno) Bayer ▲ BR 100119 [DDD]
Villa-Lobos, H.:Son 3 Vn, w. Roberto Szidon (pno) Bayer ▲ BR 100119 [DDD]

Aberg, Kerstin (pno)
Franck, C.:Les Djinns, w. O. Kamu (cnd), Gothenburg SO *(rec May 31, 1979)* BIS ▲ CD 137 [AAD]
Franck, C.:Prélude, choral et fugue *(rec Oct. 15, 1979)* BIS ▲ CD 137 [AAD]
Franck, C.:Symphonic Vars, w. O. Kamu (cnd), Gothenburg SO *(rec May 31, 1979)* BIS ▲ CD 137 [AAD]
Kodály, Z.:Adagio Vn, w. E. Lavotha (vc) BIS ▲ CD 172 [AAD]
Kodály, Z.:Son Vc & Pno, Op. 4, w. E. Lavotha (vc) BIS ▲ CD 172 [AAD]
Kodály, Z.:Sonatina Vc & Pno, w. E. Lavotha (vc), K. Aberg (pno) BIS ▲ CD 172 [AAD]
Lidholm, I.:Pieces Vc & Pno, w. E. Lavotha (vc) BIS ▲ CD 72 [AAD]
Martinů, B.:Son 1 Vc, w. E. Lavotha (vc) BIS ▲ CD 72 [AAD]
Popular & Serious Music for Cello & Piano, w. E. Lavotha (vc) BIS ▲ CD 72 [AAD]
Strauss, E.:Son Vc, w. E. Lavotha (vc) *(rec Feb. 24-25, 1978)* BIS ▲ CD 49 [AAD]

Aberg, Mats (org)
Mats Aberg, w. Pär Sjöberg (ob) *(rec Jan. 28, 1983)* BIS ▲ CD 229 [DDD]

Åberg, Sven (chit)
Carissimi, G.:Ferma lascia ch'io parli, w. Lena Nordin (sop), Maria Wieslander (org), Chrichan Larsson (vc), Nanette Nowels-Stenholm (pno), M. Guidarini (cnd), *(orch unknown)* Swedish Society ▲ SCD 1076
Donizetti, G.:Maria Stuarda (sels), w. Lena Nordin (sop), Carina Morling (mez), Ingus Petterssons (ten), Anders Bergström (bar), Tord Wallström (bar), Maria Wieslander (org), Chrichan Larsson (vc), Nanette Nowels-Stenholm (pno), M. Guidarini (cnd), *(orch unknown)* Swedish Society ▲ SCD 1076

Åberg, Sven (lt)
The Royal Court of the Vasa Kings, 1523-1611, w. M. Bellini (ct), Lennart Löwgren (ct), Carl Unander-Scharin (ten), Lars Arvidson (bass), Sven-Anders Benktsson (bass), Hortus Musicus, Tallinn [cnd:Andres Mustonen] Musica Sveciae ▲ MSV 202 [DDD]

Åberg, Sven (thb/lt/gtr)
Roman, J.H.:Songs, w. S. Rydén (sop), N. E. Sparf (vn), K. Ottesen (vc), B. Gäfvert (org/hpd)—Thet är en kostelig ting; 4 Songs from *Vûrbetraktelser* [text by Jacob Freese]:Mit hierta rörs af frögd/I foglar, vilde djur/Min andagt/Gud, alla härars Gud; Ihr Augen worzu nutzt ihr mir [w. E. Nordenfelt (harpsichord)]; Sein eigen Hertze fressen [w. Nordenfelt]; Kom tysta enslighet; La Ragion gli affetti ascolta; The Happy Man; For the Few Hours; Herren lofver af Himlen hög [Ps. 148]; 5 Songs by Olof von Dalin:Åta litet, dricka vatten/At ju mûngen har idag/Födas, grûta dij och lindas/Är det hela tidsfördrifvet/Den är lycklig född til Verlden; Herre när jag tig hafver; Jag förtröstar pû Herran; Gud, jag will sjunga om din makt *(rec May 9-11 & July 10, 1994)* Swedish Society ▲ SCD 1066

Ablitzer, Jean-Charles (org)
Bach, J.S.:Das Orgelbüchlein [at the org of Sainte-Croix d'Aubusson] Harmonic ▲ HAR 8508 [DDD]
Buxtehude, D.:Org Music (comp) Harmonic ▲ HAR 8718 [DDD]
Buxtehude, D.:Org Music (comp) Harmonic ▲ HAR 8826 [DDD]
Buxtehude, D.:Org Music (comp) [the historic organ at the Evangelical Reformed Church, Weener] Harmonic ▲ HAR 8830 [DDD]

Abraham, C. (fl)
Wallach, J.:Mourning Madrigals, w. K. Birnbaum (sop), F. Urrey (ten), A. Tarantiles (hp) [E] Capstone ▲ CPS 8613

Abram, B. (pno)
Kupferman, M.:Triple Play, w. N. Drucker (cl), S. Drucker (cl) Soundspells ▲ SP 102

Abramenkov, A. (vn)—see ORCHESTRAS & ENSEMBLES Borodin String Quartet

Abramenkov, Andrei (vn)
Telemann, G.P.:Cons Ob, w. Pierre Pierlot (ob), Evgeni Nepalov (ob), Piotr Dubrov (ob), Rudolf Barshai (vn), Leonid Poleess (vn), R. Barshaï (cnd), Moscow CO—in B♭ for 3 Obs, 3 Vns & Bc *(rec Salle Wagram, Paris, June 1964)* EMI Classics ▲ CDK 65340 [ADD]

Abramovic, Charles (pno)
Black, R.:Pieces (3) Vn, w. Gregory Fulkerson (vn) Bridge ▲ BCD 9061 [DDD]
Davidson, T.:Blue Dawn (The Promised Fruit), w. Carol Brown (fl), Lloyd Shorter (E hn), Charles Holdeman (bn) CRI ▲ CD 681 [DDD]
Davidson, T.:Fire on the Mountain, w. Anthony Orlando (mar), Don Liuzzi (vib) CRI ▲ CD 681 [DDD]
Davidson, T.:I Hear the Mermaids Singing, w. Kathleen Carol (va), Lori Barnet (vc) CRI ▲ CD 681 [DDD]
Davidson, T.:Lullaby, w. Marshall Taylor (sax), Carol Brown (fl), Lloyd Shorter (E hn), Charles Holdeman (bn) CRI ▲ CD 681 [DDD]
Levinson, G.:Bronze Music, w. J. Freeman (pno) CRI ▲ CD 642 [DDD]
Levinson, G.:Morning Star, w. J. Freeman (pno) CRI ▲ CD 642 [DDD]
Schwantner, J.:Distant Runes & Incantations, w. J. Freeman (cnd), Orch 2001 *(rec Lang Concert Hall, Swarthmore College)* CRI ▲ CD 723 [DDD]

Abramovich, Michael (pno)
Debussy, C.:Son Vn, w. Ittai Shapira (vn) Meridian ▲ MER 84284 [DDD]
Janácek, L.:Son Vn, w. Ittai Shapira (vn) Meridian ▲ MER 84284 [DDD]
Strauss, R.:Son Vn, w. Ittai Shapira (vn) Meridian ▲ MER 84284 [DDD]

Abramovici, T. (hn)
Telemann, G.P.:Con for 3 Horns, w. I. James (hn), R. Teutsch (hn), V. Czarnecki (cnd), Southwest German CO Pforzheim ebs ▲ ebs 6092 [DDD]
Telemann, G.P.:Suite for 4 Hns, w. I. James (hn), A. Lewis (hn), R. Teutsch (hn), V. Czarnecki (cnd), Southwest German CO Pforzheim ebs ▲ ebs 6092 [DDD]

Abramovitz, David (pno)
Sauguet, H.:Mélodies sur les poèmes symbolistes, w. C. Antonicelli (sop) Sonpact ▲ SPT 93008 [DDD]
Sauguet, H.:Neiges, w. M. Masquelin (sop) Sonpact ▲ SPT 93008 [DDD]
Sauguet, H.:Les Pénitents en maillot roses, w. C. Mortagne (ten) Sonpact ▲ SPT 93008 [DDD]
Sauguet, H.:Visions infernales, w. P. Brechbüller (bar) Sonpact ▲ SPT 93008 [DDD]
Saylor, B.:Songs from Water St, w. C. Beavon (mez), M. Hoffman (va) [E] CRI ▲ CD 578 [DDD]

Abramowicz, Sylvia (b vl)
Sainte-Colombe, M. de:Vl Music, w. Jonathan Dunford (b vl)—Suite in d; Concert [Le meslé]; Suite in B; Concert [Les roulades]; Concert [Le Varié]; Suite in G; Concert [Tombeau, les regret]; Vielle in D Adès ▲ ADE 204912

Abramson, A. (cl)
Iannaccone, A.:Trio Fl, w. R. Hill (fl), E. Jacobson (pno) Opus One ▲ CD 154

Abramyan, V. (vn)
Glinka, M.:Trio pathétique, w. A. Bourikov (vc), G. Dzubenko (pno) *(rec Firma Melodiya, Big Studio, 1995)* Russian Compact Disc ▲ RCD 10401 [DDD]
Rachmaninoff, S.:Trio élégiaque 1, w. G. Dzubenko (pno), A. Bourikov (vc) *(rec Firma Melodiya, Big Studio, 1995)* Russian Compact Disc ▲ RCD 10401 [DDD]
Shostakovich, D.:Trio 2 Pno, w. G. Dzubenko (pno), A. Bourikov (vc) *(rec Firma Melodiya, Big Studio, 1995)* Russian Compact Disc ▲ RCD 10401 [DDD]

Abreu, Joaquim (perc)—see ORCHESTRAS & ENSEMBLES Duo Dialogos

Abt, Walter (gtr)
Boccherini, L.:Qnts Gtr & Strs, w. Hugo Wolf String Quartet—Nos. 1, 4 & 9 *(rec Munich, Apr.-June 1994)* Calig ▲ CAL 50936 [DDD]
Brouwer, L.:Estudios Sencillos Koch Schwann ▲ SCH 317132 [DDD]
Brouwer, L.:Paisaje cubano con campanas Koch Schwann ▲ SCH 317132 [DDD]
Dyens, R.:Fuoco Koch Schwann ▲ SCH 317132 [DDD]
Gismonti, E.:Gtr Music—Agua y Vinho; Central Gtr; Vars on Frevo; Memoria e Fado Koch Schwann ▲ SCH 317132 [DDD]
Pereira, M.S.:Circulo das Cuerdas Koch Schwann ▲ SCH 317132 [DDD]

Abt, Walter (vih)
Dreams of a Lost Era Koch Schwann ▲ SCH 314262

Abt-Greenfield, Meryl (E♭ cl)
Brings, A.:Concert Piece for 4 Cls, w. P. Gallo (a cl), E. Gilmore (cl), B. Hysong (b cl) *(rec 1989-90)* Centaur ▲ CRC 2079 [ADD]

Abt-Greenfield, Meryl (cl)
Brings, A.:Inventions (3) for 2 Cls, w. E. Gilmore (cl) *(rec 1989-90)* Centaur ▲ CRC 2079 [ADD]

Accardo, Salvatore (vn)
Bach, J.S.:Con 1 Vn, w. S. Accardo (cnd), English CO EMI Classics 3-▲ CDMC 69878
Bach, J.S.:Con for 2 Vns, w. A.-S. Mutter (vn), S. Accardo (cnd), English CO EMI Classics ▲ CDC 47005-2 [DDD]
Bach, J.S.:Con for 2 Vns, w. A.-S. Mutter (vn), S. Ozawa (cnd), French National Orch EMI Classics 3-▲ CDMC 69878
Bartók, B.:Son in e Vn & Pno, w. N. Lee (pno) *(rec live 1968)* Dynamic ▲ CDS 110 [ADD]
Beethoven, L. van:Con Vn, Op. 61, w. C.M. Giulini (cnd), La Scala Orch *(rec Milan Teatro Abanella, Italy, Dec. 10-13, 1992)* Sony Classical ▲ SK 53287 [DDD]
Beethoven, L. van:Qnt Strs, Op. 29, w. M. Batjer (vn), T. Hoffman (va), S. Gazeau (va), G. Hoffman (vc) Nuova Era ▲ 6870 [DDD]
Beethoven, L. van:Romances Vn, w. C.M. Giulini (cnd), La Scala Orch *(rec Milan Teatro Abanella, Italy, Dec. 10-13, 1992)* Sony Classical ▲ SK 53287 [DDD]
Chausson, E.:Con Vn, Pno & Str Qt, w. B. Canino (pno), Naples String Quartet Dynamic ▲ CD 44
Elgar, E.:Con Vn, w. R. Hickox (cnd), London SO Collins Classics ▲ COL 1338 [DDD]
Ginastera, A.:Con Vn, w. M. di Bonaventura (cnd), Hopkins Center Orch *(rec live 1968)* Dynamic ▲ CDS 110 [ADD]
Haydn, J.:Con Org, Vn & Strs, H.XVIII/6, w. Bruno Canino (hpd), S. Accardo (cnd), English CO Philips 2-▲ 438797-2
Haydn, J.:Con 1 Vn, w. S. Accardo (cnd), English CO Philips 2-▲ 438797-2
Haydn, J.:Con 3 Vn, w. S. Accardo (cnd), English CO Philips 2-▲ 438797-2
Haydn, J.:Con 4 Vn, w. S. Accardo (cnd), English CO Philips 2-▲ 438797-2
Mendelssohn, F.:Qnt 2 Strs, w. M. Batjer (vn), T. Hoffman (va), S. Gazeau (vc), G. Hoffman (db) Nuova Era ▲ 6870 [DDD]
Mozart, W.A.:Concertone Vns, w. M. Batjer (vn), S. Accardo (cnd), Prague CO Nuova Era ▲ 6949 [DDD]
Mozart, W.A.:Qts Fl, w. J-P. Rampal (fl), I. Stern (vn), M. Rostropovich (vc) CBS ▲ MK 42320 [DDD]
Mozart, W.A.:Sinf concertante Vn, K.364, w. T. Hoffman (va), S. Accardo (cnd), Prague CO Nuova Era ▲ 6949 [DDD]
Paganini, N.:Caprices Vn Deutsche Grammophon ("Galleria" series) ▲ 429714-2 [ADD]

436 ▲ = CD ♦ = Enhanced CD Δ = MD ■ = Cassette Tape □ = DCC

Accardo, Salvatore (vn) (cont.)
Paganini, N.:Con 1 Vn, w. C. Dutoit (cnd), London PO — Deutsche Grammophon ▲ 415378-2 [ADD]
Paganini, N.:Con 2 Vn, w. C. Dutoit (cnd), London PO — Deutsche Grammophon ▲ 415378-2 [ADD]
Paganini, N.:Con 3 Vn, w. C. Dutoit (cnd), London PO — Deutsche Grammophon ▲ 423370-2 [ADD]
Paganini, N.:Con 4 Vn, w. C. Dutoit (cnd), London PO — Deutsche Grammophon ▲ 423370-2 [ADD]
Paganini, N.:Con 5 Vn, w. C. Dutoit (cnd), London PO — Deutsche Grammophon ▲ 423578-2 [DDD]
Paganini, N.:Maestoso son sentimentale, w. C. Dutoit (cnd), London PO — Deutsche Grammophon ▲ 423578-2 [ADD]
Paganini, N.:Son Vn "La Primavera", w. C. Dutoit (cnd), London PO — Deutsche Grammophon ▲ 423578-2 [ADD]
Paganini's Violin:Salvatore Accardo Plays Paganini's Guarneri del Gesù 1742, wLaura Manzini (pno) *(rec Dynamic's, Genova, Mar 13–14, 1995)* — Dynamic ▲ CDS 175 [DDD]
Penderecki, K.:Con Vn, w. K. Penderecki (cnd), Orch Giovanile Italiana *(rec live 1987)* — Nuova Era ▲ 6705 [DDD]
Sibelius, J.:Con Vn, w. C. Davis (cnd), Boston SO — Philips ("Duo" series) 2-▲ 446160-2
Tchaikovsky, P.:Qt 1 Strs, w. *(other artists unknown)* — Nuova Era ▲ 6866 [DDD]
Tchaikovsky, P.:Souvenir de Florence, w. *(other artists unknown)* — Nuova Era ▲ 6866 [DDD]
Vivaldi, A.:Cons Vn (misc), Italian Camerata Orch — RCA Silver Seal ▲ 60542-2 [ADD/DDD] ■ 60542-4
Vivaldi, A.:Cons Vn, Op. 8/1–4, "The Four Seasons", Italian Camerata Orch — RCA Silver Seal ▲ 60542-2 [ADD/DDD] ■ 60542-4
Vivaldi, A.:Cons Vn, Op. 8/1–4, "The Four Seasons", Italian Camerata Orch — RCA Victrola ▲ 7732-2 RV [DDD] ■ 7732-4 RV (CrO2)
Vivaldi, A.:Music of, w. Frederico Agostini (vn), Heinz Holliger (ob), Ida Levin (vn), Aurele Nicolet (fl), Massimo Paris (va d'amore), Angel Romero (gtr), Celedonio Romero (gtr), Celine Romero (gtr), Henryk Szeryng (vn), Pinchas Zukerman (vn), Academy of St. Martin in the Fields, English CO, I Musici, Naples Weekly International Soloists, St. Paul CO, Dresden Staatskapelle—The Four Seasons [Winter]; Con in D for Gtr [Largo]; Con in D for Fl, "Il gardellino" [Cantabile]; Con in C for Diverse Insts [Andante molto]; Con in g for Strs [Andante molto]; Con in D for 2 Vns & 2 Vcs [Largo]; Con in g for Ob, Vn, Ww & Strs [Larghetto]; Con in a for Gtr, "L'estro armonico" [Largo]; Con in F for 3 Vns [Andante]; Con in F for Fl [Largo]; Con in d for Va D'Amore [Largo]; Con in E for Vn & Strs, "Il riposo" [Allegro]; Con in G for Ob, Bn & Strs [Largo]; Con in B♭ for Vn & Strs [Largo]; Con in A for Gtr & Strs [Larghetto]; Con in E for Vn & Strs, "L'amoroso" [Allegro]; Con in G for Fl [Largo]; Con in A for Vn [Larghetto]; Con in c for Vn & Strs, "Il sospetto" [Andante]; Con in a for 2 Obs & Strs [Largo]; Con in g for Orch [Largo non molto]; Con in a for Vn [Largo]; Con in C for Ob [Adagio]; Con in g for Fl, "La notte" [Largo] — Philips ▲ 454051-2 ■ 454 051-4
Walton, W.:Con Va, w. R. Hickox (cnd), London SO — Collins Classics ▲ COL 1338 [DDD]

Accurso, Fabio (medieval fl/perc)—see ORCHESTRAS & ENSEMBLES Vox

Achatz, Dag (pno)
Beckman, B.:Pno Music—String Play — Musica Sveciae ▲ MSV 628 [DDD]
Bernstein, L.:Fancy Free — BIS ▲ CD 352
Bernstein, L.:Touches — BIS ▲ CD 352
Bernstein, L.:West Side Story (ballet music) — BIS ▲ CD 352
Boldemann, L.:Con Pno, w. N. Totsuka (cnd), Stockholm PO — Swedish Society ▲ SKCD 1
Boldemann, L.:Kleine Liebeslieder — Swedish Society ▲ SKCD 1
Boldemann, L.:Morgenstern Sänger — Swedish Society ▲ SKCD 1
Debussy, C.:Children's Corner *(rec Nacka Aula, Nacka, Sweden, May 1, 1980)* — BIS ▲ CD 28 [AAD]
Debussy, C.:Lindaraja, w. Y. Nagai (pno) — BIS ▲ CD 526 [DDD]
Debussy, C.:La Mer, w. Y. Nagai (pno) [2-piano arr. André Caplet] — BIS ▲ CD 526 [DDD]
Debussy, C.:Nocturnes, w. Y. Nagai (pno) [2-piano trans. Maurice Ravel] — BIS ▲ CD 526 [DDD]
Debussy, C.:Petite suite, w. Y. Nagai (pno) — BIS ▲ CD 526 [DDD]
Eriksson, J.:Kleine Klavierstücke (6) — Musica Sveciae ▲ MSV 628 [DDD]
Fauré, G.:Fant Fl, w. G. von Bahr (fl) — BIS ▲ CD 160 [AAD]
For Children *(rec Apr. 30–May 1, 1980 & May)* — BIS ▲ CD 158 [AAD/DDD]
Fryklöf, H.:Little Pieces (8) — Musica Sveciae ▲ MSV 628 [DDD]
Gershwin, G.:Pno Music—complete works composed or arranged by Gershwin for solo piano:The George Gershwin Song Book; Rhapsody in Blue; Three Preludes; Impromptu in two keys; Rialto Ripples; Merry Andrew; Three-Quarter Blues; Promenade — BIS ▲ CD 404 [DDD]
Liszt, F.:Pno Music (misc) [Liszt's own American Chickering grand piano in the Liszt Academy, Budapest]—Ballade No. 2 in b; Am Grabe Richard Wagners; Consolation No. 3; En rêve; Hungarian Rhasody No. 3; Les jeux d'eau à la villa d'Este; Liebesträum No. 3; La lugubre gondola No. 2; Nuages gris — BIS ▲ CD 244 [DDD]
Liszt, F.:Son Pno *(rec Nacka Aula, Nacka, Sweden, June 12–13, 1979)* — BIS ▲ CD 144 [AAD]
Lundberg, L.:Pno Music—Legend, Op 55/1; Barcarolle, Op. 7/1; Epilogue — Musica Sveciae ▲ MSV 628 [DDD]
Messiaen, O.:La Merle noir, w. G. von Bahr (fl) — BIS ▲ CD 160 [AAD]
Pierné, G.:Con Pno, w. J. Houtmann (cnd), Lorraine PO — BIS ("BIS Twins" series) 2-▲ CD 375/381
Pierné, G.:Con Pno, w. J. Houtmann (cnd), Lorraine PO — BIS ▲ CD 381 [DDD]
Poulenc, F.:Son Fl, w. G. von Bahr (fl) — BIS ▲ CD 160 [AAD]
Rachmaninoff, S.:Pno Transcriptions, w. Yukie Nagai (pno)—Glazunov:Sym No. 6 *(rec Växjö Concert Hall, Sweden, Aug 6–8, 1995)* — BIS ▲ CD 746 [DDD]
Rachmaninoff, S.:The Rock, w. Yukie Nagai (pno) [trans Rachmaninoff for Pno Duo] *(rec Växjö Concert Hall, Sweden, Aug 6–8, 1995)* — BIS ▲ CD 746 [DDD]
Ravel, M.:Boléro, w. Y. Nagai (pno) [piano duet version] — BIS ▲ CD 489 [DDD]
Ravel, M.:Con Pno (left hand), w. L. Ferré (cnd), Milan SO — EPM ▲ EPM 982372 [AAD]
Ravel, M.:Daphnis et Chloé (suite 2), w. Y. Nagai (pno) [2-piano trans. by Lucien Garbon & Dag Achatz] — BIS ▲ CD 489 [DDD]
Ravel, M.:Ma mère l'oye Pno, w. Y. Nagai (pno) — BIS ▲ CD 489 [DDD]
Ravel, M.:Rapsodie espagnole, w. Y. Nagai (pno) [Ravel's two-piano arr.] — BIS ▲ CD 489 [DDD]
Rhené-Baton:Passacaille, w. G. von Bahr (fl) — BIS ▲ CD 160 [AAD]
Romantic & Picturesque Music for Flute with Piano or Organ, w. Hans Fagius (org) — BIS ▲ CD 160 [AAD]
Roussel, A.:Joueurs de flûte, w. G. von Bahr (fl) — BIS ▲ CD 160 [AAD]
Schumann, R.:Fant Pno *(rec Nacka Aula, Nacka, Sweden, June 12–13, 1979)* — BIS ▲ CD 144 [AAD]
Schumann, R.:Kinderszenen *(rec Nacka Aula, Nacka, Sweden, Apr. 30, 1980)* — BIS ▲ CD 144 [AAD]
Scriabin, A.:Pno Music (misc), w. Roland Pöntinen (pno)—Études, Opp. 2/1, 8/12 & 42/3; Mazurka, Op. 3/3; Préludes, Opp. 16/4, 27/2 & 48/4; Feuillet d'album, Op. 45/1; Danse languide, Op. 51/4; Nuances, Op. 56/3; Désir, Op. 57/1; Caresse dansée, Op. 57/2; Poèmes, Op. 69/1 & 2; Vers la flamme, Op. 72; Sons Nos. 5, 7, 9 & 10 *(rec Nacka Aula, Nacka, Sweden & Danderyd Grammer School, Sweden)* — BIS ▲ CD 119 [AAD/DDD]
Scriabin, A.:Sym 4, w. Yukie Nagai (pno) [trans Leon Conus for Pno Duo] *(rec Växjö Concert Hall, Sweden, Aug 6–8, 1995)* — BIS ▲ CD 746 [DDD]
Stravinsky, I.:The Firebird Suite [solo piano arr.] — BIS ▲ CD 188 [DDD]
Stravinsky, I.:Le Sacre du printemps Orch [solo pno arr.] — BIS ▲ CD 188 [DDD]
Tchaikovsky, P.:Sleeping Beauty (sels), w. Y. Nagai (pno) [arr. Rachmaninoff for 2 pianos] *(rec Oct. 9–12, 1993)* — BIS ▲ CD 627 [DDD]
Tchaikovsky, P.:Swan Lake (sels), w. Y. Nagai (pno) [arr. for 2 pianos Debussy] *(rec Oct. 9–12, 1993)* — BIS ▲ CD 627 [DDD]
Tchaikovsky, P.:Sym 5, w. Y. Nagai (pno) [arr. Taneyev for 2 pianos] *(rec Oct. 9–12, 1993)* — BIS ▲ CD 627 [DDD]

Acheva, Kremena (fl)
Bond, V.:Shenblu — Gega ▲ GD 197 [DDD]

Achim, Erzsébet (org)
Handel, G.F.:Cons (16) Org, w. Budapest Strings [organ of the Franciscan church at Vác, Hungary]—Op. 4 — Capriccio ▲ 10 533 [DDD]

Achucarro, Joaquin (pno)
Schubert, Franz:Son Pno, D.575 — Masters of Art ▲ AAOC 9385
Schumann, R.:Sym Etudes — Masters of Art ▲ AAOC 9385

Ackerman, Mary (gtr)
Schubert, Franz:Choral Music, w. N. MacKenzie (pno), R. Shaw (cnd), Robert Shaw Chamber Singers—Die Nacht; Der Nachtigall [w. K. Dent (tenor)]; Wehmuth; Der Gondelfahrer; Mondenschein [w. Dent]; Nachthelle [w. Dent]; Das Dörfchen [w. Dent]; Die Einsiedelei; Sehnsucht; Grab und Mond; Frühlingsgesang [w. Dent & R. Clement (tenor)]; Liebe; Widerspruch; An den Frühling; La pastorella; Ständchen [w. M. Hart (mezzo-soprano)]; Der Entfernten *(rec Oct. 17–18, 1992)* — Telarc ▲ CD 80340 [DDD]

Acosta, Silvio (db)—see ORCHESTRAS & ENSEMBLES Tango 7

Adam, Andreas (tpt)
Kagel, M.:Nah und Fern, w. Marco Blaauw (tpt), Achim Gorsch (tpt), Markus Stockhausen (tpt), Arie Abbenes (car), M. Kagel (cnd) — Montaigne ▲ MO 782062

Adam, Doris (pno)
Beethoven, L. van:Son 5 Vn, "Spring", w. Karin Adam (vn) *(rec Studio Baumgarten, Vienna, Apr 10–11, 1992)* — Camerata ▲ 32CM 266 [DDD]
Beethoven, L. van:Son 9 Vn, "Kreutzer", w. Karin Adam (vn) *(rec Studio Baumgarten, Vienna, Jan 2–4, 1988)* — Camerata ▲ 32CM 266 [DDD]
Schmidt, F.:Concertante Variations on a Theme of Beethoven, w. A. Eschwé (cnd), Austrian RSO — Preiser ▲ 93395 [ADD]

Adam, Karin (vn)
Beethoven, L. van:Son 5 Vn, "Spring", w. Doris Adam (pno) *(rec Studio Baumgarten, Vienna, Apr 10–11, 1992)* — Camerata ▲ 32CM 266 [DDD]
Beethoven, L. van:Son 9 Vn, "Kreutzer", w. Doris Adam (pno) *(rec Studio Baumgarten, Vienna, Jan 2–4, 1988)* — Camerata ▲ 32CM 266 [DDD]
Brahms, J.:Con Vn, w. A. Wit (cnd), Polish National RSO Katowice *(rec Katowice, May 21–23, 1991)* — Camerata ▲ 32CM 219
Sibelius, J.:Con Vn, w. A. Wit (cnd), Polish National RSO Katowice *(rec Katowice, May 21–23, 1991)* — Camerata ▲ 32CM 219

Adamczewski, Marc (org)
Orgue historique de chantilly — Musidisc ▲ MUS 291392 [DDD]

Adamopoulos, Tasso (va)
Dvořák, A.:Qnt Strs, Op. 97, w. Talich String Quartet *(rec 1993)* — Calliope ▲ CAL 9229 [DDD]

Adamopoulos, Tasso (vn)—see also ORCHESTRAS & ENSEMBLES Monnaie Piano Trio
Lekeu, G.:Qt Pno, Vn, Va & Vc, w. D. Blumenthal (pno), C. Desjardins (va), G. Zanlonghi (vc) — Koch Schwann ▲ CD 310185 [DDD]

Adamovitch, Michaïl (pno)
Rabinovitch, A.:Music for Pnos, w. A. Rabinovitch (pno), M. Argerich (pno), A. Ieriomine (pno), A. Batagov (pno)—Musique Populaire for 2 Pianos; La Belle Musique for 4 Pianos; Liebliches Lied for Piano 4-hands; Musique triste, parfois tragique *(rec 1990 & 1992)* — Valois ▲ V 4694 [DDD]

Adams, Clinton (pno)
Zaimont, J.L.:Hidden Heritage, w. Karen Moratz (fl), David Krakauer (cl/b cl/t sax), David Finkel (vc), Barry Dove (perc), D. Kosloff (cnd) *(rec SUNY Purchase, Theatre C, Jan 8–10 & Feb 20, 1995)* — Arabesque ▲ ARA 6667 [DDD]

Adams, John Luthers (perc)
Adams, J.L.:Earth & the Great Weather, w. R. Lorentz (vn/perc), R. Lawrence (va), M. Finckel (vc), R. Black (db/perc), A. Knoles (perc), J. Nageak (Iñupiat Eskimo performer), D. Simmonds (Iñupiat Eskimo performer), L. Tritt (Gwich'in Indian performer), A. P. Raboff (Gwich'in Indian performer), D. Hunsaker (Latin voice), J.L. Adams (cnd) *(rec Fairbanks, Mar. 8–11, 1993)* — New World ▲ 80459-2

Adams, Julia (va)—see ORCHESTRAS & ENSEMBLES Portland String Quartet

Adams, Monty (fl)
Opera by Request, w. Phyllis Adams (hp) — Adams Disques ▲ ADA 1 [DDD]
Universal Peace, w. Phyllis Adams (hp) — Adams Disques ▲ AD 9602 [DDD]

Adams, Peter (vc)—see ORCHESTRAS & ENSEMBLES Rogeri Trio

Adams, Phyllis (hp)
Opera by Request — Adams Disques ▲ ADA 1 [DDD]
Universal Peace — Adams Disques ▲ AD 9602 [DDD]

Adams, Piers (rcr)
The English Nightingale, w. P. Adams (rcrs), Howard Beach (hpd/pno), D. Watkin (vc) — Albany ▲ TROY 088-2 [DDD]
Vivaldi, A.:Cons Rcr, w. Ray Goodman (vn), Miles Golding (vn), Jane Compton (va), Jane Coe (vc), Mandy MacNamara (db), David Miller (archlt), Robert King (hpd/org)—in F for Treble Rcr, Op. 10/1; in a for Sopranino Rcr, RV.440; in c for Treble Rcr, RV.441; in D for Sopranino Rcr, Op. 10/3; in g for Treble Rcr, Op. 10/2; in C for Sopranino Rcr, RV.443 *(rec Radley College, Abingdon, Oxon)* — United ▲ CAL 88015 [DDD]

Adams, Steve (instr)
Riley, T.:In C, w. Bruce Ackley, Don R. Baker, Chris Brown, George Brooks, Steve Coughlin, Blake Derby, Bill Douglass, Mihr'un'Nisa Douglass, Hank Dutt, David Harrington, Don Howe, Joan Jeanrenaud, Alden Jenks, Warner Jepson, Henry Kaiser, Jaron Lanier, Bill Maginnis, George Marsh, Shabda Owens, Jon Raskin, Gyan Riley, Terry Riley, Gino Robair, John Sackett, Ramón Sender, John Sherba, Toyji Tomita, Danny Tunick, William Winant, Evan Ziporyn *(rec Jan. 14, 1990)* — New Albion ▲ NA 071

Adámska, A. (vn)—see ORCHESTRAS & ENSEMBLES Erato String Quartet

Adamus, Jan (ob)
Bach, J.S.:Con Vn & Ob, w. J. Suk (vn), J. Vlach (cnd), Suk CO — Supraphon ▲ 10 4127 [DDD]
Bach, J.S.:Con Vn & Ob, w. J. Suk (vn), J. Vlach (cnd), Suk CO *(rec 1985)* — Supraphon Collection ▲ 11 0642-2 [ADD]
Besozzi, C.:Cons (3) Ob, w. J. Suk (cnd), Suk CO — Supraphon ▲ 11 1581-2 [DDD]
Druschetzky, G.:Con Ob, w. P. Altrichter (cnd), Pardubice Chamber PO — Panton ▲ PAN 810940
Gyrowetz, A.:Sinf concertante, w. P. Altrichter (cnd), Pardubice Chamber PO — Panton ▲ PAN 810940
Marcello, A.:Con Ob & Strs, w. J. Vlach (cnd), Suk CO — Supraphon ▲ 10 4127 [DDD]
Mozart, W.A.:Sinf concertante Ob, K.Anh.9, w. Frantisek Bláha (cl), Svatopluk Čech (bn), Zdenek Divoky (hn), J. Belohlávek (cnd), Dvořák CO — Panton ▲ PAN 811206
Reicha, J.:Con Ob, w. P. Altrichter (cnd), Pardubice Chamber PO — Panton ▲ PAN 810940
Vivaldi, A.:Cons Ob Vn, w. J. Suk (vn), J. Vlach (cnd), Suk CO—R.576 — Supraphon ▲ 10 4127 [DDD]

Adee, Carol (fl)
Bach, J.S.:Suites Vc, BWV 1007–1012—Nos. 2, 3 & 5, BWV 1008, 1009 & 1011 — Well-Tempered Productions ▲ WPT 5171 [DDD]
Mozart, W.A.:Adagio Rondo, w. Noriko Kishi (vc), Kurt Rohde (va), Roger Wiesmeyer (ob), J. Meredith (cnd), Sonos Handbell Ensemble — Well-Tempered Productions ▲ WTP 5182 [DDD]

Adeney, Richard (fl)
Mozart, W.A.:Qts Fl, w. Melos Ensemble — ASV Quicksilva ▲ ASQ 6099 [DDD]
Song Recital, w. V. Masterson (sop), Roger Vignoles (pno) — Pearl ▲ PEA 9590 [DDD]

Ader, Alice (pno)
Brahms, J.:Ballades, Op. 10 — Accord ▲ ACD 204922 [DDD]
Brahms, J.:Intermezzos Pno, Op. 117 — Accord ▲ ACD 204922 [DDD]
Brahms, J.:Pieces Pno, Op. 76 — Accord ▲ ACD 204922 [DDD]
Koechlin, C.:Little Pieces, w. Hervé Joulain (hn), Jean-Jacques Kantorow (vn)—2 sels — Arion ▲ ARN 68311 [DDD]
Messiaen, O.:Regards sur l'Enfant Jésus — Adda 2-▲ ADD 581061 [DDD]
Nunes, E.:Litanies — Adda ▲ ADD 581095 [DDD]
Schubert, Franz:Ländler Pno — Harmonia Mundi France ("Musique d'abord" series) ▲ HMA 1905233
Schubert, Franz:Waltzes Pno—Valses nobles; Valses sentimentales — Harmonia Mundi France ("Musique d'abord" series) ▲ HMA 1905233
Strauss, F.:Nocturne, w. Hervé Joulain (hn) — Arion ▲ ARN 68311 [DDD]

Ader, B. (org)
Rheinberger, J.:Sons Org—Nos. 1, 3, 4 & 8 — Bayer ▲ CD 100254 [DDD]

Adjemova, Yelena (vn)
Artyomov, V.:Gurian Hymn, w. Y. Smirnov (vn), T. Gridenko (vn), D. Kitayenko (cnd), Moscow PO — Olympia ▲ OLY 515 [DDD]

INSTRUMENT.

Adkins, Christopher (vc)
Sargon, S.:Music of, w. Lila Deis (sop), Stephen Dubov (ten), Stephen Girko (cl), Vesselin Demirev (vn), Deborah Baron (fl), Simon Sargon (pno)—Shemà [Hear] for Sop, Fl, Cl, Vc & Pno; Before the Ark for Vn & Pno; Wedding Dance for Vn & Pno; Klezmuzik for Cl & Pno; At Gradmother's Knee [5 Yiddish Folk Songs] for Ten & Pno; Meditation for Vc & Pno; At Grandfather's Knee [5 Judeo–Spanish Folk Songs] for Sop & Pno *(rec Caruth Auditorium, SMU, Dallas, TX, Jan 1996)* Gasparo ▲ GAS 318

Adler, Jonathan (pno)
Beethoven, L. van:Trio 7 Pno, w. S. Shinohe (cl), D. Schwalke (vc) Classic Studio Berlin ▲ CS 10 308 [DDD]
Brahms, J.:Trio Cl, w. S. Shinohe (cl), D. Schwalke (vc) Classic Studio Berlin ▲ CS 10 308 [DDD]
Debussy, C.:Son Vc, w. D. Schwalke (vc) *(rec 1984)* Classic Studio Berlin ▲ CS 10708 [DDD]
Fauré, G.:Son 1 Vn, w. C. Bolze (vn) *(rec 1984)* Classic Studio Berlin ▲ CS 10808 [DDD]
Popper, D.:Elfentanz Vc, w. D. Schwalke (vc) *(rec 1984)* Classic Studio Berlin ▲ CS 10708 [DDD]
Ravel, M.:Berceuse sur le nom de Gabriel Fauré, w. C. Bolze (vn) *(rec 1984)* Classic Studio Berlin ▲ CS 10808 [DDD]
Ravel, M.:Son Vn Pno, w. C. Bolze (vn) *(rec 1984)* Classic Studio Berlin ▲ CS 10808 [DDD]
Ravel, M.:Sonate posthume, w. C. Bolze (vn) *(rec 1984)* Classic Studio Berlin ▲ CS 10808 [DDD]
Reger, M.:Sons Cl, Op. 49, w. S. Shinohe (cl)—No. 2 *(rec 1986)* Classic Studio Berlin ▲ CS 10908 [DDD]
Reger, M.:Son Cl, Op. 107, w. S. Shinohe (cl) *(rec 1986)* Classic Studio Berlin ▲ CS 10908 [DDD]
Schubert, Franz:Winterreise, w. B. McDaniel (bar) [G] Classic Studio Berlin ▲ CS 30208 [DDD]
Schumann, R.:Fantasiestücke Cl, w. D. Schwalke (vc) *(rec 1984)* Classic Studio Berlin ▲ CS 10708 [DDD]
Strauss, R.:Son Vc, w. D. Schwalke (vc) *(rec 1984)* Classic Studio Berlin ▲ CS 10708 [DDD]

Adler, Kurt–Theo (cl)—see also ORCHESTRAS & ENSEMBLES Sabine Meyer Wind Ensemble
Stravinsky, I.:Elegy for J.F.K., w. D. Fischer–Dieskau (bar), H. Gruber (cl), K. Berger (cl) [E] Orfeo ▲ 015821 [DDD]

Adni, Daniel (pno)—see also ORCHESTRAS & ENSEMBLES Solomon Trio
Debussy, C.:Pno Music (misc)—Golliwogg's Cake–Walk [Children's Corner No. 6]; Suite bergamasque; Ballade; Mouvement [Images, Book 1/3]; Arabesques No. 1 in E & No. 2 in G; L'isle joyeuse; Poissons d'or [Images, Book 2/3]; La fille auz cheveux de lin [Preludes, Book 1/8]; Feux d'artifice [Preludes, Book 2/12] Classics for Pleasure ("Eminence" series) ▲ CFP–2055 [ADD]
Favorite Piano, w. A. Brownridge (pno), J. Février (pno), M. Lympany (pno), J. Ogdon (pno), G. Tacchino (pno) Classics for Pleasure ▲ CDCFP 4622 [ADD/DDD]
Martinů, B.:Qt 1 Pno, w. Isabelle van Keulen (vn), Rainer Moog (va), Young–Chang Cho (vc) *(rec Australian Festival of Chamber Music, July 1994)* Naxos ▲ 8.553916 [DDD]
Martinů, B.:Son 1 Va, w. Rainer Moog (va) *(rec Australian Festival of Chamber Music, July 1994)* Naxos ▲ 8.553916 [DDD]
Mendelssohn, F.:Lieder ohne Worte Pno EMI Classics 2–▲ CDFB 69352

Adorján, András (fl)
Benda, F.:Cons (3) Fl & Orch, w. M. Munclinger (cnd), Ars Rediviva Orfeo ▲ 151101 [DDD] ■ 151101 (D)
Boehm, T.:Compositions Fl, w. W. Bennett (fl), U. Burkhard (fl), M. Debost (fl), I. Grafenauer (fl), A. Nicolet (fl), B. Weber (pno)—works for Flute & Piano *(Andante pastorale, from Souvenir des Alpes; Elegie in A♭, Op. 47; Fantaisie sur un air allemand, Op. 22; Fantaisie in A♭ on a Theme by Schubert; Grande Polonaise in D, Op. 16; Variations on Nel cor più non mi sento)*; works for Flute Ensemble *(Duettino in D, Pièce facile in C & Romanza in F [Nos. 66–68]; plus a six–flute ensemble performance of the 2nd movt. from Boismortier's Flute Concerto No. 1 in G)* *(rec live, Cuvilliés Theater, Munich 11/27/81)* Orfeo ▲ 018821 [DDD]
Danzi, F.:Cons (4) Fl, w. H. Stadlmair (cnd), Munich CO Orfeo 2–▲ 003812 [DDD]
Debussy, C.:Chansons de Bilitis (recitation), w. A. Lochner (nar), M. Larrieu (fl), S. Mildonian (hp), Y. Nagae (hp), E. Sun (cel) [F] Quantum ▲ QM 6912 [DDD]
Devienne, F.:Cons Fl (comp), w. H. Stadlmair (cnd), Munich CO—Concerto No. 9 in e; Concerto No. 12 in A; Concerto in G, Op. Posth. Tudor ▲ TUD 782 [DDD]
Devienne, F.:Cons Fl (comp), w. H. Stadlmair (cnd), Munich CO—Nos. 4 in G, 5 in G, 6 in D & 7 in e Tudor ▲ TUD 765 [DDD]
Doppler, A.F.:Con Fls, w. J.–P. Rampal (fl), C. Scimone (cnd), Monte Carlo Opera Orch *(rec 1977)* Erato ▲ 2292–45836–2 [ADD]
Hummel, J.N.:Adagio, Vars & Rondo on "Schöne Minka", w. P. Gililov (pno), B. Pergamenschikow (vc) *(rec Apr. 23–25, 1991)* Orfeo ▲ 252931 [DDD]
Lieberson, P.:King Gesar, w. Yo–Yo Ma (vc), Emanuel Ax (pno), Peter Serkin (pno), Omar Ebrahim (nar), Deborah Marshall (cl), William Purvis (hn), David Taylor (trbn), Stefan Huge (perc) Sony Classical ▲ SK 57971
Lobanow, W.:Son Fl, w. W. Lobanow (pno) Tudor ▲ 727 [DDD]
Lyrical Melodies of Japan, w. Ayako Shinozaki (hp) Denon ("Repertoire" series) ▲ CO 8114 [DDD]
Mendelssohn, F.:Con in e Vn & Orch, Op. 64, w. D. Shallon (cnd), Stuttgart RSO Orfeo ▲ 046831 [DDD]
Mercadante, S.:Duetto Concertante, w. Aurèle Nicolet (fl) Tudor ▲ TUD 763 [DDD]
Mercadante, S.:Fant Fl Tudor ▲ TUD 763 [DDD]
Mercadante, S.:Qts Fl, w. Munich String Trio Tudor ▲ 730 [DDD]
Mercadante, S.:La Serenata, w. Han–An Liu (hp), Dieter Savelwski (Eng hn), Julius Berger (vc) Tudor ▲ TUD 763 [DDD]
Mercadante, S.:Serenate for 3 Fls, w. Aurèle Nicolet (fl), Marianne Hendel (fl) Tudor ▲ TUD 763 [DDD]
Mercadante, S.:Trio for 2 Fls, w. Aurèle Nicolet (fl) Tudor ▲ TUD 763 [DDD]
Mozart, W.A.:Andante Fl, K.315/285a, w. H. Stadlmair (cnd), Munich CO Denon ▲ 7803 [DDD]
Mozart, W.A.:Cons Fl, w. H. Stadlmair (cnd), Munich CO Denon ▲ 7803 [DDD]
Mozart, W.A.:Con Fl Hp, w. Susanna Mildonian (hp), H. Stadlmair (cnd), Munich CO Denon ▲ 7804 [DDD]
Mozart, W.A.:Concertone Vns, w. J.J. Kantorow (violin), H. Stadlmair (cnd), Munich CO [arr. flute & violin] Denon ▲ 7804 [DDD]
Mozart, W.A.:Rondo Fl, K.Anh.184, w. H. Stadlmair (cnd), Munich CO Denon ▲ 7804 [DDD]
Reger, M.:Allegretto grazioso, w. A. Kontarsky (pno) Tudor ▲ TUD 755 [DDD]
Reger, M.:Serenades Fl, Opp. 77a & 141a, w. A. Chumachenco (vn), O. Lysy (va) Tudor ▲ TUD 755 [DDD]
Reinecke, C.:Music for Fl & Pno, w. Christian Ivaldi (pno)—Son for Fl & Pno, Op. 167 [Undine]; Suite for Fl & Pno, Op. 202 [Von der Wiege bis zum Grabe]; Ballade; Sonatines Nos. 1 in F, 2 in G & 3 in B♭ Tudor ▲ TUD 792 [DDD]
Reinecke, C.:Son Fl, w. C. Ivaldi (pno) Tudor ▲ TUD 798 [DDD]
Shostakovich, D.:Waltzes Fl, w. E. Brunner (cl), R. Levin (pno) Tudor ▲ 727 [DDD]
Spohr, L.:Con 8 Vn, w. D. Shallon (cnd), Stuttgart RSO Orfeo ▲ 046831 [DDD]
Weber, C.M. von:Trio Fl, w. B. Pergamenschikow (vc), G. Oppitz (pno) Orfeo ▲ 187891

Adorján, András (pic)
Janácek, L.:Pno Music, w. Gilead Mishory (pno), Saschko Gawriloff (vn), Wen–Sinn Yang (vc)—Son. for Vn & Pno; Allegro for Vn & Pno; Romance for Vn & Pno; Dumka for Vn & Pno; Tema Con Vars. for Pno; Fairy Tale for Vc & Pno; Presto for Vc & Pno; March of the Bluebreasts for Pic & Pno; Music for Excercises w. Clubs for Pno; In Memoriam for Pno; Reminiscence for Pno Tudor ▲ TUD 7003 [DDD]

Adriaans, Frank (fl)
Fauré, G.:Fant Fl, w. G. Oskamp (cnd), Limburg SO *(rec Nov. 1992 & May 1993)* Erasmus ▲ WVH 099 [DDD]

Adrien, Brandon (instr)
Brooke, N.:Obomobile, w. Jennifer Baker, Karen Birch, Daniel Cate, Judy Christy, Richard Cochran, Jessica Cooper, Leslie Dominguez, Erin Hannigan, Dorothy Knight, Jason Lichtenwalter, Jay Moore, Hwa–Ling Russell, Toyin Spellman, Sarah Weiner, Jay Weinland Opus One ▲ CD 160

Adzenyah, A. (African drums/conga)
Kabat, J.:Poems by H. D., w. J. Kabat (voice/glass hmc/saw/African drums/kalimba), B. Hudson (vn), M. Crispell (pno) [E] Leonarda ■ LE 319 (D)

Aebersold, Claire (pno)
Brahms, J.:Con 1 Pno, w. Ralph Neiweem (pno) [arr. Brahms for Piano 4–Hands] *(rec WFMT Radio, Chicago, IL)* Summit ▲ SMT 184 [DDD]
Brahms, J.:Waltzes Pno, Op. 39, w. Ralph Neiweem (pno) *(rec WFMT Radio, Chicago, IL)* Summit ▲ SMT 184 [DDD]

Aerts, M. (vle)—see ORCHESTRAS & ENSEMBLES Kuijken Consort

Aeschbacher, Adrian (pno)
Beethoven, L. van:Con 1 Pno, w. W. Furtwängler (cnd), Lucerne Festival Orch *(rec Aug. 1947)* Music & Arts ▲ CD 839 [ADD]

Afanassiev, Valery (pno)
Afanassiev, V.:Pno Music—The River Doesn't Welcome the Same Man [Homage to Heraclitus]; Forgiveness; The Ineffable Name; The Immortality of the Human Race; From Here to Eternity; others Denon ▲ DEN 78979
Bach, J.S.:Das wohltemperierte Klavier—Book 1 *(rec Musica Théâtre, La Chaux–de–Fonds, Apr 10–14, 1995)* Denon 2–▲ CO 78834–35 [DDD]
Beethoven, L. van:Bagatelles (24)—Opp. 119 & 126 Denon ▲ CO 72433 [DDD]
Beethoven, L. van:Son 31 Pno Denon ▲ DEN 78979
Brahms, J.:Ballades, Op. 10 Denon ▲ CO 78906 [DDD]
Brahms, J.:Fants Pno, Op. 116 Denon ▲ CO 78906 [DDD]
Brahms, J.:Rhaps Pno, Op. 79 Denon ▲ CO 78906 [DDD]
Brahms, J.:Son for 2 Pnos, w. Vadim Suchanov (pno) *(rec Musica–Théâtre, La Chaux–de–Fonds, Oct. 31–Nov. 2, 1994)* Denon ▲ DEN 78976 [DDD]
Brahms, J.:Souvenir de la Russie, w. Vadim Suchanov (pno) *(rec Musica–Théâtre, La Chaux–de–Fonds, Oct. 31–Nov. 2, 1994)* Denon ▲ DEN 78976 [DDD]
Mozart, W.A.:Adagio Pno, K.540 *(rec Musica Théâtre, La Chaux–de–Fonds, Apr. 6–7, 1993)* Denon ▲ CO 78945 [DDD]
Mozart, W.A.:Fant Pno, K.396 *(rec Musica Théâtre, La Chaux–de–Fonds, Apr. 6–7, 1993)* Denon ▲ CO 78945 [DDD]
Mozart, W.A.:Fant Pno, K.397 *(rec Musica Théâtre, La Chaux–de–Fonds, Apr. 6–7, 1993)* Denon ▲ CO 78945 [DDD]
Mozart, W.A.:Fant Pno, K.475 *(rec Musica Théâtre, La Chaux–de–Fonds, Apr. 6–7, 1993)* Denon ▲ CO 78945 [DDD]
Mozart, W.A.:Son 14 Pno *(rec Musica Théâtre, La Chaux–de–Fonds, Apr. 6–7, 1993)* Denon ▲ CO 78945 [DDD]
Schubert, Franz:Schwanengesang, w. J. Van Dam (b–bar) [G] Forlane ▲ FOR 16647 [DDD]
Schumann, R.:Kreisleriana Denon/PCM Digital ▲ DEN 75714

Afriat, N. (pno)
Scriabin, A.:Etudes Pno, Op. 8 Forlane ▲ FOR 16623 [DDD]
Scriabin, A.:Etudes Pno, Op. 42 Forlane ▲ FOR 16623 [DDD]

Afshar, Lily (gtr)
Castelnuovo–Tedesco, M.:Caprichos (24) de Goya—Nos. 3, 13 & 18 Summit ▲ DCD 167 [DDD]

Agelao, Massimiliano (vc)
Respighi, O.:Adagio con variazioni Vc Orch, w. R. Tigani (cnd), Sassari SO *(rec Rome, Oct 11–14, 1994)* Bongiovanni ▲ GB 2166 [DDD]

Aggesea, Niels Erik (org)
Lady Plays the Bass, w. M. Hanskoy (db), T. Lønskov (pno) *(rec Apr. 1991)* Danacord ▲ DACOCD 378 [DDD]

Agopian, Edmond (vn)
A Little Romance, w. Charles Foreman (pno) *(rec Calgary Center for the Performing Arts)* Unical ▲ UC 9502 [DDD]

Agosti, Guido (pno)
Beethoven, L. van:Son 3 Vn, w. F. von Vecsey (vn) *(rec early 1930s)* Pearl ▲ PEA 9498 (m) [AAD]

Agosti, Riccardo (vc)—see also ORCHESTRAS & ENSEMBLES Paganini String Quartet
Paganini, N.:Divertimenti carnevaleschi, w. Stefan Milenkovich (vn), Pier Domenico Sommati (vn) *(rec Dynamic's, Genova, Feb 22–24, 1995)* Dynamic ▲ CD 105 [DDD]
Paganini, N.:Duetti Vn, w. Stefan Milenkovich (vn) *(rec Dynamic's, Genova, Feb 22–24, 1995)* Dynamic ▲ CD 105 [DDD]
Paganini, N.:In cuor più non mi sento, w. Stefan Milenkovich (vn), Pier Domenico Sommati (vn) *(rec Dynamic's, Genova, Feb 22–24, 1995)* Dynamic ▲ CD 105 [DDD]
Sivori, C.:Music for Pno Trio, w. B. Pignata (vn), F. Giacosa (pno)—Mira la bianca luna on Rossini's Soirées musicales; La Pesca e La Promessa on Rossini's Soirées musicales; Il coro delle sirene on Weber's Oberon *(rec Jan. 12–14, 1994)* Dynamic ▲ CDS 115 [DDD]

Agostini (hp)
Hovhaness, A.:Firdausi, w. Lawrence Sobol (cl), Boyar (perc) Grenadilla ■ GSC 1008

Agostini, Federico (vn)
Vivaldi, A.:Music of, w. Salvatore Accardo (vn), Heinz Holliger (ob), Ida Levin (vn), Aurele Nicolet (fl), Massimo Paris (va d'amore), Angel Romero (gtr), Celedonio Romero (gtr), Celine Romero (gtr), Henryk Szeryng (vn), Pinchas Zukerman (vn), Academy of St. Martin in the Fields, English CO, I Musici, Naples Weekly International Soloists, St. Paul CO, Dresden Staatskapelle—The Four Seasons [Winter]; Con in D for Gtr [Largo]; Con in D for Fl, "Il gardellino" [Cantabile]; Con in C for Diverse Insts [Andante molto]; Con in g for Strs [Andante molto]; Con in D for 2 Vns & 2 Vcs [Largo]; Con in g for Ob, Vn, Ww & Strs [Larghetto]; Con in a for Gtr, "L'estro armonico" [Largo]; Con in F for 3 Vns [Andante]; Con in F for Fl [Largo]; Con in d for Va D'Amore [Largo]; Con in E for Vn & Strs, "Il riposo" [Allegro]; Con in G for Ob, Bn & Strs [Largo]; Con in B♭ for Vn & Strs [Largo]; Con in A for Gtr & Strs [Larghetto]; Con in E for Vn & Strs, "L'amoroso" [Allegro]; Con in G for Fl [Largo]; Con in A for Vn [Larghetto]; Con in c for Vn & Strs, "Il sospetto" [Andante]; Con in a for 2 Obs & Strs [Largo]; Con in g for Orch [Largo non molto]; Con in a for Vn [Largo]; Con in C for Ob [Adagio]; Con in g for Fl, "La notte" [Largo] Philips ▲ 454051–2 ■ 454 051–4

Agostino, Gregory d' (org)
Bach, J.S.:Org Music (misc)—Liebster Jesu, wir sind hier, BWV 731; Nun freut euch, lieben Christen g'mein, BWV 734; Passacaglia in c, BWV 582 *(rec National City Christian Church, Washington, D.C., Sept 20–24, 1994)* Centaur ▲ CRC 2246 [DDD]
Karg–Elert, S.:Pastels—Soul of the Lake [No. 1]; The Sun's Evensong [No. 5]; Hymn to the Stars [No. 7] *(rec National City Christian Church, Washington, D.C., Sept 20–24, 1994)* Centaur ▲ CRC 2246 [DDD]
Liszt, F.:Am Grabe Richard Wagners *(rec National City Christian Church, Washington, D.C., Sept 20–24, 1994)* Centaur ▲ CRC 2246 [DDD]
Liszt, F.:Consolations—in E & D♭ *(rec National City Christian Church, Washington, D.C., Sept 20–24, 1994)* Centaur ▲ CRC 2246 [DDD]
Liszt, F.:Prelude & Fugue on the name B–A–C–H *(rec National City Christian Church, Washington, D.C., Sept 20–24, 1994)* Centaur ▲ CRC 2246 [DDD]
Wagner, R.:Die Meistersinger von Nürnberg (ov) *(rec National City Christian Church, Washington, D.C., Sept 20–24, 1994)* Centaur ▲ CRC 2246 [DDD]

Aguera, L.–M. (vn)—see ORCHESTRAS & ENSEMBLES Ysaÿe String Quartet

Aguessy, Fréderic (pno)
Bloch, E.:Son 1 Vn, w. Alexis Galperine (vn) Accord ▲ ACD 240132 [DDD]
Bloch, E.:Son 2 Vn, "Poème mystique", w. Alexis Galperine (vn) Accord ▲ ACD 240132 [DDD]

Aguilar, David (fl)—see ORCHESTRAS & ENSEMBLES Aguilar–Delgado Duo

Agus, Ayke (pno)
An American Collage Vol. II, w. Constance Keene (pno), Anita Swearingen (pno), Michael Lang (pno), Diane Lang Bryan (cl), James Smith (gtr), Sherry Kloss (vn), Laila Padorr (fl), Victor Morosco (a sax) Protone ▲ PRCD 1114 [DDD]
Musical Momentos of Jascha Heifetz Protone ▲ PRCD 1108 [DDD]
Plays Forgotten Gems from the Heifetz Legacy, w. S. Kloss (vn) Protone ▲ PRCD 1104 [A/DDD] ■ CSPR 170

Aharonian, Ruben (vn)
Glazunov, A.:Con Vn, w. M. Gorenstein (cnd), Russian SO Russian Disc ▲ RUS 10039 [DDD]

▲ = CD ♦ = Enhanced CD Δ = MD ■ = Cassette Tape □ = DCC

Ahlert, B. (gtr)
Sor, F.:Divert militaire, w. M. Dossow (gtr) Ambitus ▲ 97860 [ADD]
Sor, F.:Fant Gtrs Ambitus ▲ 97860 [ADD]
Ahlgrimm, Isolde (hpd)
Bach, J.S.:Sons Vl, BWV 1027–1029, w. S. Pank (vl) Capriccio ▲ CDC 10043 [DDD]
Vivaldi, A.:Sons Vc, w. C. Starck (vc), M. Frey (vc)—Op. 14/1-5; Son in a, RV.44; Sons in B♭, E♭ & g Tudor 2-▲ 709 [ADD]
Ahlstrom, Albert (org)
Parker, H.:Org Music [1895 Miller & Abel Org, St Joseph's Catholic Church, New York City]—Recital Pieces [21 compositions] Organ Historical Society ▲ OAR 340 [DDD]
Ahmas, Harri (bn)
Gubaidulina, S.:Con Bn, w. O. Vänskä (cnd), Lahti Chamber Ensemble *(rec Aug. 16–19, 1993)* BIS ▲ CD 636 [DDD]
Ahn, Mee-Hyun (pno)
Chopin, F.:Con 2 Pno, w. M. Avetisyan (cnd), Moscow Orch Russian Compact Disc ▲ RCD 30005 [DDD]
Scriabin, A.:Con Pno, w. M. Avetisyan (cnd), Moscow Orch Russian Compact Disc ▲ RCD 30005 [DDD]
Ahrens, Sieglinde (org)
Eben, Petr:Choral Phantasies (2) Multisonic ▲ 31 0097 [DDD]
Eben, Petr:Landscapes of Patmos, w. M. Lenniger (perc) Multisonic ▲ 31 0097 [DDD]
Eben, Petr:Laudes Multisonic ▲ 31 0097 [DDD]
Ahumada, G. (a fl)—see ORCHESTRAS & ENSEMBLES Vienna Flautists
Aïche, P. (vn)—see ORCHESTRAS & ENSEMBLES Kandinsky Quartet
Aide, William (pno)
The Art of Ofra Harnoy, Vol. 1, w. O. Harnoy (vc), Helena Bowkun (pno) Mastersound ▲ DFCD1-012
Brahms, J.:Son 1 Vc, w. Ofra Harnoy (vc) RCA Gold Seal ▲ 09026-68371-2
Brahms, J.:Son 2 Vc, w. Ofra Harnoy (vc) RCA Gold Seal ▲ 09026-68371-2
Chopin, F.:Études (24) CBC ("Musica Viva" series) ▲ MVCD 1017 [DDD]
Franck, C.:Son Vn, w. O. Harnoy (vc) [cello-piano arr.] Mastersound ▲ DFCD1-012
Harman, C.P.:Poem, w. Lawrence Cherney (b ob) *(rec St Martin-in-the-Fields Church, Toronto, July 1995)* Centrediscs ▲ CMC 5395 [DDD]
Ofra Harnoy Collection, Vol. 4, w. O. Harnoy (vc) *(rec Timothy Eaton Memorial Church, Toronto, Canada, 1982)* RCA Gold Seal ▲ 09026-68369-2 [ADD]
Somers, H.:Miniatures, w. Lawrence Cherney (ob) *(rec St Martin-in-the-Fields Church, Toronto, July 1995)* Centrediscs ▲ CMC 5395 [DDD]
Aigmüller, Andreas (dr)
Caprioli, A.:Serenata per Francesca, w. V. Fuchsberger (sgr), G. Schneider (vn), S. Winiarczyk (ob), R. Crow (instr), R. Huber (instr), K. Ager (cnd), Austrian Ensemble for New Music *(rec 1987)* Pro Viva ▲ ISPV 148 CD [ADD]
Aigner, Albert (gtr)—see ORCHESTRAS & ENSEMBLES Duett Konzertant
Aike, Jeri-Lou (vn)
In Sweet Rejoicing Music for Christmas:Ars Antique Choralis, Vol 3, w. [cnd:Richard Proulx], Cathedral Singers, Mary Hickey (fl), Elizabeth Anderson (vc), Samuel Soria Jr. (org) *(rec Oct. 17–19 & 24–26, 1993)* GIA ▲ CD 323 ■ CS 323
Aimard, Pierre-Laurent (pno)
Amy, G.:Trio Cl, w. Alain Damiens (cl), Maryvonne Le Dizes (vn) Adda ▲ ADD 581142 [DDD]
Bartók, B.:Contrasts, w. Alain Damiens (cl), Maryvonne Le Dizes (vn) Adda ▲ ADD 581142 [DDD]
Berg, A.:Adagio, w. Alain Damiens (cl), Maryvonne Le Dizes (vn) Adda ▲ ADD 581142 [DDD]
Boulez, P.:Notations Pno, w. P. Boulez (cnd), Ensemble InterContemporain Deutsche Grammophon ▲ 445833-2
Boulez, P.:Son 1 Pno Erato ▲ 2292-45648-2 [DDD]
Boulez, P.:Sonatine Fl & Pno, w. S. Cherrier (fl) Erato ▲ 2292-45648-2 [DDD]
Boulez, P.:Structures, w. P. Boulez (cnd), Ensemble InterContemporain—Book II Deutsche Grammophon ▲ 445833-2
Janácek, L.:Fairy Tale, w. Anne Gastinel (vc) Valois ▲ V 4748
Kodály, Z.:Son Vc & Pno, Op. 4, w. Anne Gastinel (vc) Valois ▲ V 4748
Lachenmann, H.:Allegro sostenuto, w. Alain Damiens (cl), Pierre Strauch (vc) Accord ▲ ACD 202082 [DDD]
Lachenmann, H.:Wiegenmusik Accord ▲ ACD 202082 [DDD]
Ligeti, G.:Con Pno, w. P. Boulez (cnd), Ensemble InterContemporain Deutsche Grammophon ▲ 439808-2
Ligeti, G.:The Ligeti Edition, w. Phyllis Bryn-Julson (sop), Rosemary Hardy (sop), Christiane Oelze (sop), Rose Taylor (mez), Sibylle Ehlert (sgr), Omar Ebrahim (bar), E.-P. Salonen (cnd), Philharmonia Orch, King's Singers—Vocal Works; Madrigals; Mysteries; Adventures; Songs; Nonsense Madrigals Sony Classical ▲ SK 62311
Ligeti, G.:The Ligeti Edition—Piano Solos Sony Classical ▲ SK 62308
Liszt, F.:Elegie 1, w. Anne Gastinel (vc) Valois ▲ V 4748
Liszt, F.:Elegie 2, w. Anne Gastinel (vc) Valois ▲ V 4748
Liszt, F.:La Lugubre gondola Vn & Pno, w. Anne Gastinel (vc) Valois ▲ V 4748
Strauss, R.:Son Vc, w. A. Gastinel (vc) Valois ▲ V 4692
Stravinsky, I.:L'Histoire du soldat Suite Vn, w. Maryvonne Le Dizes (vn), Alain Damiens (cl) Adda ▲ ADD 581142 [DDD]
Aitken, Dianne (fl)
Evangelista, J.:O Bali, w. R. Aitken (fl), New Music Concerts CBC ("Musica Viva" series) ▲ MVCD 1057 [DDD]
Aitken, Robert (fl)
Aitken, R.:Berceuse (For Those Who Sleep Before Us), w. A. Pauk (cnd), Esprit Orch *(rec Studioasis, Toronto, Apr 10–11, 1995)* CBC ("SM 5000" series) ▲ SM5 5154 [DDD]
Böhm, T.:Grande polonaise, w. Elisabeth Westenholz (pno) BIS ▲ CD 166
Bozza, E.:Image *(rec Nacka Aula, Nacka, Sweden, Sept. 14–16, 1980)* BIS ▲ CD 183 [AAD]
Damase, J.-M.:Son Fl & Hp, w. Erica Goodman (hp) *(rec Elora, Ontario, Canada, Sept–Oct, 1993)* BIS ▲ CD 650 [DDD]
Donizetti, G.:Son Fl & Hp, w. Erica Goodman (hp) *(rec Castle Wik, Sweden, June 2–4, 1979)* BIS ▲ CD 143 [AAD]
Doppler, A.F.:Fant pastorale hongroise, w. Per Oien (fl), Geir Henning Braaten (pno), Elisabeth Westenholz (pno) BIS ▲ CD 166
Doppler, A.F.:Music Fl & Pno, w. P. Oien (fl), Gier Hanning Braaten (pno) BIS 2-▲ CD 145/46
Evangelista, J.:O Bali, w. New Music Concerts CBC ("Musica Viva" series) ▲ MVCD 1057 [DDD]
Flute & Harp, w. Erica Goodman (hp) BIS ▲ CD 320
French Flute Music, w. Robin McCabe (pno) BIS ▲ CD 184 [AAD]
Hovhaness, A.:The Garden of Adonis, w. Erica Goodman (hp) *(rec Castle Wik, Sweden, June 2–4, 1979)* BIS ▲ CD 143 [AAD]
Inghelbrecht, D.-E.:Sonatina en trois parties, w. Erica Goodman (hp) *(rec Elora, Ontario, Canada, Sept–Oct, 1993)* BIS ▲ CD 650 [DDD]
Jeux à Deux, w. Aitken, Robert (fl), Erica Goodman (hp) Marquis Classics ▲ ERAD 101 [DDD]
Krumpholtz, J.-B.:Son Fl & Hp, w. Erica Goodman (hp) *(rec Castle Wik, Sweden, June 2–4, 1979)* BIS ▲ CD 143 [AAD]
Lauber, J.:Medieval Dances, w. Erica Goodman (hp) *(rec Elora, Ontario, Canada, Sept–Oct, 1993)* BIS ▲ CD 650 [DDD]
McPhee, C.:Kambing Slem, w. M. Widner (pno) CBC ("Musica Viva" series) ▲ MVCD 1057 [DDD]
McPhee, C.:Lagoe Sesoeloelingan Ardja, w. M. Widner (pno) CBC ("Musica Viva" series) ▲ MVCD 1057 [DDD]
Marais, M.:Vars on *Folies d'Espagne* *(rec Nacka Aula, Nacka, Sweden, Sept. 14–16, 1980)* BIS ▲ CD 183 [AAD]
Meyer, K.:Trio Fl, w. Eckart Schloifer (va), Reinbert Evers (gtr) *(rec Munich, 1995)* Pro Viva ▲ ISPV 176 CD [DDD]
Mozart, F.X.W.:Rondo Fl, w. Robin McCabe (pno) *(rec Nacka Aula, Nacka, Sweden, Sept. 14–16, 1980)* BIS ▲ CD 183 [AAD]

Aitken, Robert (fl) (cont.)
Mozart, W.A.:Andante Fl, K.315/285a, w. F. Mannino (cnd), National Arts Center Canada Orch CBC ("SM 5000" series) ▲ SMCD 5076 [DDD] ■ SMC 5076 (D)
Mozart, W.A.:Cons Fl, w. F. Mannino (cnd), National Arts Center Canada Orch CBC ("SM 5000" series) ▲ SMCD 5076 [DDD] ■ SMC 5076 (D)
Mozart, W.A.:Rondo Fl, K.Anh.184, w. F. Mannino (cnd), National Arts Center Canada Orch CBC ("SM 5000" series) ▲ SMCD 5076 [DDD] ■ SMC 5076 (D)
Petra-Basacopol, C.:Son Fl Hp, w. Erica Goodman (hp) *(rec Elora, Ontario, Canada, Sept–Oct, 1993)* BIS ▲ CD 650 [DDD]
Reinecke, C.:Son Fl, w. Robin McCabe (pno) *(rec. Studio BIS, Djursholm, Sweden, May 31 & June 2, 1981)* BIS ▲ CD 183 [AAD]
Schafer, R.M.:Con Fl, w. K. Akiyama (cnd), Vancouver SO CBC ("SM 5000" series) ▲ SMCD 5114 [DDD]
Schubert, Franz:Intro & Vars Fl on "Tröckne Blumen", w. Robin McCabe (pno) *(rec Studio BIS, Djursholm, Sweden, May 31 & June 2, 1981)* BIS ▲ CD 183 [AAD]
Spohr, L.:Son 3 Vn, w. Erica Goodman (hp) [trans. fl & hp] *(rec Castle Wik, Sweden, June 2–4, 1979)* BIS ▲ CD 143 [AAD]
Spohr, L.:Son 4 Vn, w. Erica Goodman (hp) [trans. fl & hp] *(rec Castle Wik, Sweden, June 2–4, 1979)* BIS ▲ CD 143 [AAD]
Spohr, L.:Son 5 Vn, w. Erica Goodman (hp) [trans. fl & hp] *(rec Castle Wik, Sweden, June 2–4, 1979)* BIS ▲ CD 143 [AAD]
Sveinsson, A.H.:Con Fl, w. P.P. Pálsson (cnd), Iceland SO ITM ▲ ITM 706
Taffanel, P.:Fant on Freischütz, w. Elisabeth Westenholz (pno), or Per Oien (fl), Geir Henning Braaten (pno) BIS ▲ CD 166
Takemitsu, T.:Toward the Sea III, w. Erica Goodman (hp) *(rec Elora, Ontario, Canada, Sept–Oct, 1993)* BIS ▲ CD 650 [DDD]
Aivazian, Rouben (org)
Ave Maria, w. E. Chakoyan (sop) Leonarda ▲ LE 341 [DDD]
Ajemian, Anahid (vn)
Feldman, Morton:The Va in My Life, w. K. Phillips (va), M. Feldman (cnd) *(rec 12/7/70)* CRI ▲ CD 620 [ADD]
Rieti, V.:Partita Hpd, w. S. Marlowe (hpd), S. Baron (fl), R. Roseman (ob), C. Libove (vn), H. Zaratzian (va), C. McCraken (vc) CRI ▲ CD 601 [ADD]
Weill, K.:Con Vn, w. I. Solomon (cnd), MGM Wind Orch—& Lady In the Dark:"Dance of the Tumblers"; Lost In the Stars:"Gold" Polydor ▲ 839727-2 (m) ■ 839727-4 (m)
Ajemian, Maro (pno)
Cage, J.:A Book of Music, w. Joshua Pierce (pno) *(rec 1976–89)* Wergo ▲ WER 6158-2 [ADD]
Ajemian, Maro (prepared pno)
Cage, J.:Sons & Interludes *(rec Carnegie Hall, New York City, 1950)* CRI ▲ CD 700 [ADD]
Akahoshi, Akira (db)
Stephan, R.:Music for 7 Stringed Instrs, w. B. Hartog (vn), I. Schliephake (vn), S. Passaggio (va), G. Donderer (vc), C. Tainton (pno), M. Schmidt (hp) *(rec 1983)* Koch Schwann ▲ CD 311 122 [ADD]
Akamatsu, Nami (db)
Cohn, J.:Music of, w. M. Piccinini (fl), M. Dine (ob), J. Manasse (cl), M. Finn (bn), J. Tarpley (hn), S. Alderking (pno)—Wind Quintet, Op. 36b (1981); Goldfinch Variations for Wind Trio, Op. 61 (1984); Little Overture for Wind Quartet, Op. 59 (1982); Suite Champêtre for Wind Quintet (after Rameau), Op. 47 (1968) XLNT ■ C 2
Cohn, J.:Music of, w. M. Piccinini (fl), M. Dine (ob), J. Manasse (cl), M. Finn (bn), J. Tarpley (hn), S. Alderking (pno)—Wind Quintet, Op. 36b (1981); Little Overture for Wind Quintet, Op. 59 (1982); Sonatina for Clarinet & Piano, Op. 56 (1981); Sonata Romantica for Double Bass & Piano, Op. 18 (1952); Sonata Robusta for Bassoon & Piano, Op. 55 (1980); Sonata for Flute & Piano, Op. 52 (1974); Goldfinch Variations for Three Treble Instruments, Op. 61 (1984) *(rec 1985)* XLNT ▲ CD 18006 [ADD]
Akao, M. (fue)
Shinohara, M.:Cooperation, w. A. Nishigata (shamisen), K. Mitsuhashi (shakuhachi), S. Yaotani (hichiriki), K. Ishikawa (sho), C. Fukunaga (koto), J. Ueda (biwa), M. Yoshizawa (kokyu), I. Tsuji (oboe), T. Takahashi (cl), G. Kitamura (tpt), A. Murata (trbn), S. Eiso (perc), S. Ueki (vn), S. Katsuta (vc), Y. Shibuya (pno), K. Komatsu (cnd) *(rec live Casals Hall, Tokyo, Mar. 5, 1994)* Camerata ▲ 30CM 375 [DDD]
Akatsu, Makoto (vn)—see ORCHESTRAS & ENSEMBLES Affetti Musicali members
Åkerlund, L. (rcr)
Pergament, M.:Little Suite, w. E. Hagberg (rcr) *(rec Dec. 17–18, 1976)* BIS ▲ CD 37 [AAD]
Akl, Walid (pno)
Bach, J.S.:Chaconne—transcriptions of the Chaconne for piano by Brahms, Busoni, & Raff Pavane ▲ ADW 7255 [DDD]
Busoni, F.:Chaconne Pno Pavane ▲ ADW 7255 [DDD]
Handel, G.F.:Chaconne Hpd Pavane ▲ ADW 7255 [DDD]
Liszt, F.:Transcriptions & Paraphrases—Tannhäuser Ov. [Wagner] Pavane ▲ 7322
Liszt, F.:Transcriptions & Paraphrases Pavane ▲ ADW 7255 [DDD]
Nietzsche, F.:Pno Music—complete pno works Pavane ▲ 7322
Raff, J.:Chaconne Pno Pavane ▲ ADW 7255 [DDD]
Scriabin, A.:Etudes Pno, Op. 42—No. 5 Pavane ▲ 7322
Scriabin, A.:Son 1 Pno Pavane ▲ 7322
Aklexeev, Dimitri (pno)
Sings Spirituals, w. B. Hendricks (sop) EMI Classics ▲ CDC 47026 [DDD]
Akopov, S. (db)
Vivaldi, A.:Sons Vc, w. A. Dmitriev (vc)—(6) R.40, 41, 43, 45–47 Arkadia-Akademia ▲ 119 [DDD]
Alain, Marie-Claire (org)
Alain, A.:Org Music (misc)—Scherzo; Andante in B; Carillon sur Laufa Sion; Andantino; Carillon de Bougival *(rec Sept. 1991)* Gallo ▲ CD 683 [DDD]
Alain, J.:Deuxième fantaisie—Litanies; Organ Music (misc.); Variations sur un thème de Clément Jannequin *(rec Sept. 1991)* Gallo ▲ CD 683 [DDD]
Alain, J.:Litanies—Deuxième fantaisie; Organ Music (misc.); Variations sur un thème de Clément Jannequin *(rec Sept. 1991)* Gallo ▲ CD 683 [DDD]
Alain, J.:Org Music (misc)—Le jardin suspendu;Choral dorien; Choral phrygien; Premieère fantaisie; Aria; Variations sur un thème de Clément Jannequin for Organ; Litanies; Deuxième fantaisie *(rec Sept. 1991)* Gallo ▲ CD 683 [DDD]
Alain, J.:Vars sur un thème de Jannequin—Deuxième fantaisie; Litanies; Organ Music (misc.) *(rec Sept. 1991)* Gallo ▲ CD 683 [DDD]
Bach, J.S.:Chorale Preludes (Schübler) Erato (Bonsai) ▲ 2292-45922-2 ■ 2292-45922-4
Bach, J.S.:Fugue Org, BWV 578 Erato ("Bonsai" series) ▲ 2292-45922-2 ■ 2292-45922-4
Bach, J.S.:Org Music (comp)—Preludes & Fugues, BWV 534 & 546; Partita BWV 768; Fant. BWV 570; Chorales BWV 633–644 Erato ▲ 91702-2
Bach, J.S.:Org Music (misc)—Orgelbüchlein, BWV 618–632; Prelude & Fugue BWV 535; Toccatas & Fugues, BWV 538 & 566 Erato ▲ 2292-45701-2 ZK
Bach, J.S.:Org Music (misc)—Chorales BWV 694, 710 & 733; Partita BWV 767; Preludes & Fugues BWV 539, 545 & 551; etc. Erato ▲ 2292-45702-2 ZK
Bach, J.S.:Passacaglia & Fugue Org Erato ("Bonsai" series) ▲ 2292-45922-2 2292-45922-4
Bach, J.S.:Toccata, Adagio & Fugue Org, BWV 564—Chorale Preludes (Schübler Chorales), BWV 645-650; Fugue in g, BWV 578; Passacaglia & Fugue in c; Toccata & Fugue in d, BWV 565; Toccata & Fugue in E, BWV 566 Erato ("Bonsai" series) ▲ 2292-45922-2 ■ 2292-45922-4
Bach, J.S.:Toccata & Fugue Org, BWV 565 Erato ("Bonsai" series) ▲ 2292-45922-2 ■ 2292-45922-4
Bach, J.S.:Toccata & Fugue Org, BWV 566 Erato ("Bonsai" series) ▲ 2292-45922-2 ■ 2292-45922-4

INSTRUMENT.

Alain, Marie–Claire (org) (cont.)
Buxtehude, D.:Org Music (misc)—Praeludium in g; Wie Schön Leuchtet der Morgenstern; Praeludium in f#; In Dulci Jubilo; Praeludium in D; Nun Komm, der Heiden Heiland; Praeludium in C; Durch Adams Fall ist Ganz Verderbt; Praeludium in d; Komm, Heiliger Geist, Herre Gott; Praeludium in e; Ach Herr, Mich Armen Sünder; Praeludium in F; Praeludium in a; Fuga in C; Passacaglia in d; Ciacona in e; ciacona in c; Canzonetta in G; Magnificat Primi Toni; Der Tag, Der ist so Freudenreich; Toccata in d; Te Deum Laudamus; Toccata in F; Nimm von Uns, Herr Erato 2–▲ ERA SEL 12979 [DDD]
Charpentier, M.–A.:Magnificat, w. Martha Angelici (sop), Jocelyn Chamonin (sop), André Mallabrera (ct), Rémy Corazza (ten), Georges Abdoun (bar), Jacques Mars (bass), Maurice André (tpt), L. Martini (cnd), Jean–François Paillard CO, French Jeunesses Musicales Chorale *(rec Paris, Mar 15, 1963)* Vanguard Classics ▲ OVC 8075 [ADD]
Charpentier, M.–A.:Te Deum, H. 146, w. Martha Angelici (sop), Jocelyn Chamonin (sop), André Mallabrera (ct), Rémy Corazza (ten), Georges Abdoun (bar), Jacques Mars (bass), Maurice André (tpt), L. Martini (cnd), Jean–François Paillard CO, French Jeunesses Musicales Chorale *(rec Paris, Mar 15, 1963)* Vanguard Classics ▲ OVC 8075 [ADD]
Famous Music for Organ Erato ▲ 45976–2 [ADD/DDD] ■ 45976–4
Great Toccatas Erato ▲ 94812
Handel, G.F.:Cons (16) Org, Jean–François Paillard CO [Haerpfer–Ermann positive organ, Eglise des Maronites, Paris]—Nos. 1 in g, 2 in B♭, 3 in g, 4 in F, 5 in F & 6 in B♭ Boston Skyline ▲ BSD 133 [ADD]
Mendelssohn, F.:Andante & Vars Org Erato ▲ ERA 96957 [ADD]
Mendelssohn, F.:Preludes & Fugues Org, Op. 37 Erato ▲ ERA 96957 [ADD]
Mendelssohn, F.:Sons Org—Nos. 1, 3 & 6 Erato ▲ ERA 96957 [ADD]
Organ Encores Erato ▲ 92888–2
Saint–Saëns, C.:Sym 3, w. G. Prêtre (cnd), Vienna SO Erato ▲ 2292–45696–2 [DDD]
Trompette et Orgue, w. M. André (tpt) Erato ▲ 4509–92124–2

Alanko, Petri (a fl)
Saariaho, K.:...à la fumée, w. A. Karttunen (vc), E.–P. Salonen (cnd), Los Angeles PO Ondine ▲ Ode 804 [DDD]
Sallinen, A.:Chamber Music II, w. O. Vänskä (cnd), Lahti SO *(rec Church of the Cross, Lahti, Finland, Aug 8–11, 1995)* BIS ▲ CD 687 [DDD]

Alanko, Petri (fl)
Bach, J.S.:Partita Fl, BWV 1013, w. Anssi Mattila (hpd) *(rec Järvenpää, Dec 1995)* Naxos ▲ 8.553754 [DDD]
Bach, J.S.:Partita Fl, BWV 1013 *(rec Järvenpää Hall, Dec 1995)* Naxos ▲ 8.553754 [DDD]
Bach, J.S.:Sons Fl, BWV 1030–35, w. Anssi Mattila (hpd)—BWV 1031, 1032 & 1034 [w. Jukka Rautasalo (vc)] *(rec Järvenpää Hall, Dec 1995)* Naxos ▲ 8.553754 [DDD]
Bach, J.S.:Sons Fl, BWV 1030–35, w. Anssi Mattila (hpd)—BWV 1031, 1032 & 1034 [w. Jukka Rautasalo (vc)] *(rec Järvenpää, Dec 1995)* Naxos ▲ 8.553754 [DDD]
Ibert, J.:Con Fl, w. J.–P. Saraste (cnd), Finnish RSO Ondine ▲ ODE 802 [DDD]
Jolivet, A.:Con Fl, w. T. Pulakka (cnd), Avanti! CO Ondine ▲ ODE 802 [DDD]
Nielsen, C.:Con Fl, w. J.–P. Saraste (cnd), Finnish RSO Ondine ▲ ODE 802 [DDD]

Alanko, Petri (fl/a fl)
Marttinen, T.:Con espagnole, w. O. Vänskä (cnd), Lahti SO *(rec Church of the Cross, Lahti, Finland, Aug 8–11, 1995)* BIS ▲ CD 687 [DDD]

Alanko, Petri (pic/fl/a fl/b fl)
Bashmakov, L.:Impressioni marine, w. O. Vänskä (cnd), Lahti SO *(rec Church of the Cross, Lahti, Finland, Aug 8–11, 1995)* BIS ▲ CD 687 [DDD]
Rautavaara, E.:Dances with the Winds, w. O. Vänskä (cnd), Lahti SO *(rec Church of the Cross, Lahti, Finland, Aug 8–11, 1995)* BIS ▲ CD 687 [DDD]

Alanne, Kari (hn)—see ORCHESTRAS & ENSEMBLES Helsinki Wind Quintet

Alba, Alessio (tamboura)
Battiato, F.:Ricerca sul Terzo, w. Franco Battiato (voc), Antonio Ballista (pno), Marco Boni (vc), Debendra Kanti Chakraborty (tabla), Guido Corti (cnt), Filippo Destrieri (kbd/computer), John Giblin (bass), Buddhadeu Das Gupta (sarod), Gavin Harrison (dr/perc), Jakko Jakszyk (gtr), Roberto Mazza (ob), Fabrizio Merlini (va), Angelo Privitera (kbd/computer), Mino Bordignon (cnd), Milan Chamber Music Choir Hemisphere ▲ 837234–2

Albach, Carl (tpt)
Sowerby, L.:Festival Musick, w. Susan Radcliff (tpt), Jeffrey Caswell (trbn), Tom Hutchinson (trbn), Dan Haskins (timp), David Mulbury (org), J. Welsh (cnd), Fairfield Orch *(rec St. Bartholomew's Church, New York City, May 5, 1994)* Marco Polo ▲ 8.223725 [DDD]

Albani, Adele (pno)
Italy's Love Songs, w. A. B. Rawn III (bass) *(rec Alhambra, Sept 8, 1996)* Classic Digital ▲ B1996 [DDD]

Albee, Jeananne (pno)
Austin, E.:Circling, w. Mary Lou Rylands (vc) Capstone ▲ CPS 8625
Austin, E.:Music of, w. Jerome Reed (pno), Mary Lou Rylands (vc), Ursula Trede–Boettcher (hpd), Markus Lücke (cl), Sibylle Dotzauer (pno), Constitution Brass, Gerald Kegelmann (cnd), Heidelberg State Music School Chamber Choir—To Begin for Brass Qnt; Klavier Double for Pno & Tape; Circling for Vc & Pno; Lighthouse I for solo Hpd; Gathering Threads for solo Cl; Zodiac Suite for Pno; An Die Nachgeborenen [To Those Born Later] Capstone ▲ CPS 8625

Alberman, David (vn)—see also ORCHESTRAS & ENSEMBLES Arditti String Quartet
Nono, L.:Hay que caminar, w. Irvine Arditti (vn) Montaigne ▲ MO 789005

Albers, Walter (vn)
Reichardt, J.F.:Rondeau, w. B. Hoffmann (glass hmc), H. Anrath (vn), E. Nippes (va), H. Plumacher (vc), G. Nose (db) Allegretto ▲ ACD 8174 [ADD] ■ ACS 8174
Röllig, K.L.:Qnt Glass Hmc, w. B. Hoffmann (glass hmc), H. Anrath (vn), E. Nippes (va), H. Plumacher (vc) Allegretto ▲ ACD 8174 [ADD] ■ ACS 8174

Albert, Eugene d (pno)
D'Albert Symposium ▲ SYM 1046

Albertson, Julie (hp)
Rutter, J.:Requiem, w. Karyn List (sop), Kathy Farmer (fl), Barbara Cook (ob), Mary Alice Swope (vc), Tom Alderman (org), Jennifer Mautz (timp), Mike Del Campo (perc), Michael O'Neal (cnd), Michael O'Neal Singers *(rec Roswell United Methodist Church, Atlanta, GA, Mar 27, 1995)* ACA Digital Recording ▲ CM 20048 [DDD]

Albertsson, Ólafur Vignir (pno)
Leifs, J.:Music of, w. Sigrídur Ella Magnúsdóttir (mez), Ólafur Vignir Albertsson (pno), Sólveig Anna Jónsdóttir (pno), Hjálmar Ragnarsson (pno), Edda Erlendsdóttir (pno), Marteinn Hunger Fridriksson (org), Hildigunnur Halldórsdóttir (vn), Gréta Gudnadóttir (vn), Gudmundur Kristmundsson (va), Sigurdur Halldórsson (vc), Richard Korn (db), Iceland SO, Icelandic Opera Chorus, Langholts Church Graduale Choir, Hamrahlíd Choir—Icelandic Cant, Op. 13/4; Valse Lento, Op. 2/1; Icelandic Dance, Op. 11/2 [Tempo Giusto]; Requiem; Lullaby [After the Riots]; Fairy–Tale in the Wood [from Baldr, Op. 34]; Funeral March; Separation [from Elegy, Op. 53]; Galdra Loftur Ov, Op. 10; Funeral March, Op. 6; Reverie; Reunion [from Elegy, Op. 53]; Fine I, Op. 55; Andante [The Last Supper]; Preludia Organo, Op. 16/3 [In the Church]; The Tear of Stone [from Elegy, Op. 53] Music From Iceland ▲ ITM 605 [DDD]
Ragnarsson, H.:Music of, w. S. E. Magnúsdóttir (mez), H. Halldórsdóttir (vn), G. Gudnadóttir (vn), G. Kristmundsson (va), S. Halldórsson (vc), R. Korn (db), Ó. V. Albertsson (pno), S. A. Jónsdóttir (pno), H. Ragnarsson (pno), E. Erlendsdóttir (pno), M. H. Fridriksson (org), Sakari, Wilkinson (cnd), Iceland SO, G. Cortes (cnd), J. Stefánsson (cnd), T. Ingólfsdóttir (cnd), Hamrahlíd Choir, Icelandic Opera Chorus, Langholts Church Graduale Choir—Meine kleine Freundin [In the Ballroom]; Lovers Duet; After the concert; Meine kleine Freundin [Annie listens to the Radio]; Lif's Theme [On the Beach]; Lif's Theme II [Night Prayer]; Composing Ov [Vars I, II & III] Music From Iceland ▲ ITM 605 [DDD]

Albrecht, Kenneth (hn)
Schickele, P.:Pentangle, w. J. Mester (cnd), Louisville Orch Albany ▲ TROY 024–2 [ADD]

Albrecht, Timothy (org)
Messiaen, O.:Messe de la Pentecôte—Offertoire ACA Digital Recording ▲ CM 20024

Albrecht, Timothy (org) (cont.)
Tomorrow Shall Be My Dancing Day:Christmas at Emory University, w. [cnd:Alfred Calabrese], Emory Univ Concert Choir, Jane Flynn (org), Nella Rigell (hp) *(rec Cathedral of St. Philip, Atlanta, GA, Apr. 30 & May 1, 1994)* ACA Digital ▲ CM 20035

Albright, William (pno)
Johnson, J.P.:Stride Pieces—Mule–Walk Stomp; Eccentricity–Syncopated Waltz; Modernistic (You've Got to Be); Snowy Morning Blues; Carolina Shout MusicMasters ▲ 01612–67135–2 [ADD]
Joplin, S.:Pno Music—The Crush Collision March; Harmony Club Waltz; Combination March; Swipesy Cake Walk; Augustan Club Waltz; Sunflower Slow Drag; Cleopha; March Majestic; Something Doing; Bethena; Rosebud; Binks' Waltz; Antoinette; Heliotrope Bouquet; Lily Queen; Pleasant Moments; Felicity Rag; Kismet Rag MusicMasters ▲ 01612–67102–2 [DDD]
Joplin, S.:Pno Music—A Breeze from Alabama; The Cascades; The Chrysanthemum; Country club; The Easy winners; Elite syncopations; The Entertainer; Eugenia; Euphonic sounds; The Favorite; Fig leaf rag; Gladiolus rag; Leola; Magnetic rag; Maple leaf rag; Nonpareil; Original rag; Palm leaf rag; Paragon rag; Peacherine rag; Pine apple rag; The Ragtime dance; Reflection rag; Rose leaf rag; Scott Joplin's new rag; Searchlight rag; Silver swan rag; Solace; Stoptime rag; The Strenuous life; Sugar cane; The Sycamore; Wall Street rag; Weeping willow MusicMasters 2–▲ 7061–2–C

Albulescu, Eugene (pno)
Liszt, F.:Pno Music (misc)—Legend No. 2; Son. in b; Grand Etude de Paganini No. 3; Nuages Gris; Romance oubliée; La Lugubre Gondola 2; En Rêve; Valse de l'Opera Faust Manu ▲ MAN 1446

Alchourroun, Dominique (pno/rainsticks)
Cage, J.:Four^3, w. Ami Flammer (vn/rainsticks), Martine Joste (pno/rainsticks), Jean Michaut (rainsticks) *(rec Radio France, Paris, Jan. 18–4, 1994)* Mode ▲ mode 44

Aldao, Federico (pno)
Clementi, M.:Pno Music (comp), w. Aldo Antognazzi (pno), Ana Chavez (pno), Lorena Di Florio (pno), Marcela Paludi (pno), Ricardo Zanon (pno)—Sons (6) for Pno, Op. 1, Nos. 4–6; Sons (6) for Pno, Op. 2, Nos. 2, 4 & 6 Aura Classics ▲ AU 32072

Alder, Jonathan (pno)
Brahms, J.:Sons Vc (comp), w. D. Schwalke (vc) Classic Studio Berlin ▲ CS 10108 [DDD]
Brahms, J.:Son 2 Vn, w. R. Alleson (vn) *(rec 1989)* Classic Studio Berlin ▲ CS 11908 [DDD]
Courts, E.:Son 2 Vn & Pno, w. R. Alleson (vn) *(rec 1989)* Classic Studio Berlin ▲ CS 11908 [DDD]
Milhaud, D.:Le Bal martiniquais, w. P. Moll (pno) Classic Studio Berlin ▲ CS 11108 [DDD]
Milhaud, D.:Scaramouche for 2 Pnos, w. P. Moll (pno) Classic Studio Berlin ▲ CS 11108 [DDD]
Musik für Violine und Klavier, w. Alleson, Robin (vn) Classic Studio Berlin ▲ CS 11908 [DDD]
Poulenc, F.:Capriccio Pnos, w. P. Moll (pno) *(rec 1985)* Classic Studio Berlin ▲ CS 11108 [DDD]
Poulenc, F.:Elégie Pnos, w. P. Moll (pno) Classic Studio Berlin ▲ CS 11108 [DDD]
Poulenc, F.:L'Embarquement pour Cythère, w. P. Moll (pno) Classic Studio Berlin ▲ CS 11108 [DDD]
Poulenc, F.:Son for 2 Pnos, w. P. Moll (pno) *(rec 1985)* Classic Studio Berlin ▲ CS 11108 [DDD]
Schubert, Franz:Son Arpeggione, w. D. Schwalke (vc) Classic Studio Berlin ▲ CS 10108 [DDD]

Alderking, Sean (pno)
Cohn, J.:Music of, w. M. Piccinini (fl), M. Dine (ob), J. Manasse (cl), M. Finn (bn), J. Tarpley (hn), N. Akamatsu (db)—Wind Quintet, Op. 36b (1981); Little Overture for Wind Quintet, Op. 59 (1982); Sonatina for Clarinet & Piano, Op. 56 (1981); Sonata Romantica for Double Bass & Piano, Op. 18 (1952); Sonata Robusta for Bassoon & Piano, Op. 55 (1980); Sonata for Flute & Piano, Op. 52 (1974); Goldfinch Variations for Three Treble Instruments, Op. 61 (1984) *(rec 1985)* XLNT ▲ CD 18006 [ADD]
Cohn, J.:Music of, w. M. Piccinini (fl), M. Dine (ob), J. Manasse (cl), M. Finn (bn), J. Tarpley (hn), N. Akamatsu (db)—Wind Quintet, Op. 36b (1981); Goldfinch Variations for Wind Trio, Op. 61 (1984); Little Overture for Wind Quartet, Op. 59 (1982); Suite Champêtre for Wind Quintet (after Rameau), Op. 47 (1968) XLNT ■ C 2

Alderman, Tom (org)
Rutter, J.:Requiem, w. Karyn List (sop), Kathy Farmer (fl), Barbara Cook (ob), Julie Albertson (hp), Mary Alice Swope (vc), Jennifer Mautz (timp), Mike Del Campo (perc), Michael O'Neal (cnd), Michael O'Neal Singers *(rec Roswell United Methodist Church, Atlanta, GA, Mar 27, 1995)* ACA Digital Recording ▲ CM 20048 [DDD]

Aldrich, Ronnie (pno)
Adagio:21 Great Melodies from the Classics, w. *(orch unknown)* London ("Phase 4 Stereo") ▲ 444 787–2 [ADD]

Aldwell, Edward (pno)
Bach, J.S.:Goldberg Vars Biddulph ▲ FLW 001
Bach, J.S.:Das wohltemperierte Klavier—Book 2 Elektra/Nonesuch 2–▲ 79200–2–R 2–■ 79200–4–R
Bach, J.S.:Das wohltemperierte Klavier—Book 1 Elektra/Nonesuch 2–▲ 79272–2
Fauré, G.:Nocturnes (13) Pno—No. 4 in E♭, Op. 36; No. 7 in c#, Op. 74; No. 13 in b, Op. 119 *(rec Academy of Arts & Letters, NY, July 15 & 16, 1995)* Pro Piano ▲ PPR224508
Hindemith, P.:Ludus Tonalis *(rec Academy of Arts & Letters, New York, July 15–16, 1995)* Pro Piano ▲ PPR 224508

Aldwinckle, Robert (hpd)
Bach, J.S.:Capriccio Departure MCA Classics ▲ MCAD 25924 [DDD]
Bach, J.S.:Chromatic Fant & Fugue MCA Classics ▲ MCAD 25924 [DDD]
Bach, J.S.:French Suites—BWV 816 IMP Classics ▲ PCD 817 [DDD]
Bach, J.S.:Italian Con IMP Classics ▲ PCD 817 [DDD]
Bach, J.S.:Toccatas Hpd, BWV 910–16—BWV 913 in d IMP Classics ▲ PCD 817 [DDD]
English Madrigals, w. C. Brett (cnd), Amaryllis Consort Allegro ▲ ALG PCD 873
Harpsichord Masterpieces IMP Classics ("Masters" series) ▲ PCD 850 [DDD]

Aldwinckle, Robert (org)
Melgaz, D.D.:Motets, w. C. Harper (hp), M. Brown (cnd), Pro Cantione Antiqua Hyperion ▲ CDA 66715
Morago, E.L.:Motets, w. C. Harper (hp), M. Brown (cnd), Pro Cantione Antiqua Hyperion ▲ CDA 66715

Alessandrini, Raymond (bc)
Bach, C.P.E.:Sons Vl, w. P. Pandolfo (vl)—in g (w. obbligato keyboard), H.510 (W.88); in C & D, H.558–559 (W.136–137) Tactus ▲ TC 710201 [DDD]

Alessandrini, Raymond (hpd)
Frescobaldi, G.:Fiori musicali [newly restored 16th–cent. Antegnati organ, St. Maurizio, Milan]—3 organ masses Astrée 2–▲ E 8714/15

Alessandrini, Raymond (org)
Leclair, J.–M.:Premier livres de sonates, w. F. Biondi (vn), M. Naddeo (vc), P. Montelheit (thb)—Sons. III, VII, VIII, XI Arcana ▲ ACA 39 [DDD]
Vivaldi, A.:Cons Vn Org, w. F. Biondi (vn), F. Biondi (cnd), Europa Galante—RV.541 *(rec Apr. 1993)* Opus 111 ▲ OPS 3086 [DDD]

Alessandrini, Raymond (pno)
Rossini, G.:Petite messe solennelle, w. Françoise Pollet (sop), Jacqueline Mayeur (mez), Jean–Luc Viala (ten), Michel Piquemal (bar), Emmanuel Mandrin (harm), Michel Piquemal (cnd), Michel Piquemal Vocal Ensemble Accord 2–▲ ACD 203562 [DDD]

Alessandrini, Rinaldo (hpd)—see also ORCHESTRAS & ENSEMBLES Europa Galante
Bach, J.S.:Sons Vl, BWV 1027–1029, w. Paolo Pandolfo (vl) Harmonia Mundi France ("Documenta" series) ▲ HMC 905218
Bach, J.S.:Sons Vn, w. Fabio Biondi (vn)—BWV 1014–1019 Opus 111 2–▲ OPS 30–127/128
Festa Italiana, w. Barbara Schlick (sop), Fabio Biondi (vn), Pascal Monteilhet (va), Maurizio Naddeo (vc), Concerto Italiano, Europa Galante Opus 111 5–▲ 2001
Frescobaldi, G.:Toccate d'intavolatura (12) Arcana 2–▲ ACA 904
150 Years of Italian Music, 1550–1799:From Valente to Scarlatti, Vol. 1 Opus 111 ▲ OPS 30–118
Scarlatti, A.:Toccatas Hpd Arcana ▲ ACA 3 [DDD]
Tartini, G.:Sons Vn & Continuo, w. F. Biondi (vn), M. Naddeo (vc), P. Montheillet (thb)—5 Sonatas—in g (B g11); in B♭ (B b3); in g (B g10); in A (B A15); in G (B G17) Opus 111 ▲ OPS 59–9205 [DDD]
Veracini, F.M.:Sonate accademiche, w. Fabio Biondi (vn), Maurizio Naddeo (vc), Pascal Monteilhet (tiorba)—Nos. 7 in d, 8 in e, 9 in A, 12 in d; Capriccio in g Opus 111 ▲ OPS 30–138
Vivaldi, A.:Sons Vn, w. F. Biondi (vn), M. Naddeo (vc), P. Pandolfo (db), R. Lislevand (thb/lt)—Manchester Sons. 1, 2, 3, 6, 8 & 10 Arcana ▲ ACA 4 [DDD]
Vivaldi, A.:Sons Vn, w. F. Biondi (vn), M. Naddeo (vc), P. Pandolfo (db), R. Lislevand (thb/lt)—Manchester Sons. 4, 5, 7, 9, 11 & 12 Arcana ▲ ACA 5 [DDD]

Alessandrini, Rinaldo (hpd/org)
150 Years of Italian Music, Vol. 3 — Opus 111 ▲ OPS 30-125

Alessandrini, Roberta (hp)
Dussek, J.L.:Con Hp, w. V. Parisi (cnd), Mantova Orch *(rec Jan 1995)* — Naxos ▲ 8.553622 [DDD]
Dussek, J.L.:Sons Hp, Op. 34, w. V. Parisi (cnd), Mantova Orch members *(rec Jan 1995)* — Naxos ▲ 8.553622 [DDD]
Krumpholtz, J.-B.:Con 6 Hp, w. V. Parisi (cnd), Mantova Orch *(rec Jan 1995)* — Naxos ▲ 8.553622 [DDD]
Wagenseil, G.C.:Con in G Hp, w. V. Parisi (cnd), Mantova Orch members *(rec Jan 1995)* — Naxos ▲ 8.553622 [DDD]

Alessandro, Maurizio d' (cl)—see also ORCHESTRAS & ENSEMBLES Rara Ensemble
Setaccioli, G.:Son Cl, w. Maurizio Aschelter (pno) *(rec Audiovisivi S. Paolo–Albano Laziale, 1995)* — Bongiovanni ▲ 5560 [DDD]

Alessi, Joseph (trbn)
Bernstein, L.:Elegy for Mippy II — Cala Records ("New York Legends" series) ▲ CAL CACD 508 [DDD]
Ewazen, E.:Son Hn, w. John McNeely (pno) — Cala Records ("New York Legends" series) ▲ CAL CACD 508 [DDD]
Massenet, J.:Méditation, w. Barbara Allen (hp) [trans Hartmann for trbn & hp] — Cala Records ("New York Legends" series) ▲ CAL CACD 508 [DDD]
Peaslee, R.:Arrows of Time, w. John McNeely (pno) — Cala Records ("New York Legends" series) ▲ CAL CACD 508 [DDD]
Ropartz, J.G.:Concert Piece, w. John McNeely (pno) — Cala Records ("New York Legends" series) ▲ CAL CACD 508 [DDD]
Rouse, C.:Con Trbn, w. M. Alsop (cnd), Colorado SO, *(Denver, Feb 1995)* — RCA Victor Red Seal ▲ 09026-68410-2 [DDD]
Rush, S.:Rebellion, w. John McNeely (pno), Christopher Lamb (perc) — Cala Records ("New York Legends" series) ▲ CAL CACD 508 [DDD]

Alessi, Oscar (pno)
Oyf'n Prip'chok:Jewish Melodies of the 20th Century, w. A. Jona (bar) — Nuova Era ▲ NUO 7261

Aleven, Douceline (hp)
Andriessen, L.:Anachrony 1, w. Nico de Rooij (pno), Sepp Grotenhuis (cel), Arthur Cune (vib), Nicolette Heerema (org), H. Williams (cnd), Netherlands Ballet Orch *(rec Amsterdam Music Theater, Oct 3–6, 1994)* — Donemus ▲ CV 54 [DDD]

Alexander, Alonzo (pno)
Samuel, G.:Nocturne on an Impossible Dream, w. Yehonatan Berick (vn), Helen Russell (cl), G. Samuel (cnd), CCM Contemporary Music Ensemble *(rec Corbett Auditorium, Cincinnati Conservatory, OH)* — Acoma ▲ GXD 5733 [DDD]

Alexander, Catherine Edward (perc)
The Ancient Music of Christmas, w. E. James (h-g/perc/harm/dlc/saz/port org/gtr) *(rec Reptile's Cloister, Hollywood, CA)* — Hannibal ▲ HNCD 1398

Alexander, Juraj (vc)
Romberg, A.:Qnts Fl, w. V. Brunner (fl), V. Simcisko (vn), M. Telecky (va), J. Cút (va) — Trevak ▲ TRE 40007 [DDD]
Sperger, J.:Trios, w. M. Jukovic (fl), V. Dufka (ob), V. Simcisko (vn), M. Telecky (va), sels. unknown — Trevak ▲ TRE 40002 [DDD]
Zimmermann, A.:Cassations, w. V. Brunner (fl), J. Brunner (fl), J. Vondra (hn), P. Sivanic (hn), V. Simcisko (vn), M. Tedla (vn), M. Telecky (va)—in G, D & D — Trevak ▲ TRE 40008 [DDD]

Alexander, Meyrick (bn)
Vivaldi, A.:Cons Bn, w. C. Warren-Green (cnd), London CO—RV.502 in B♭ — Virgin Classics ▲ 59609 [DDD]

Alexander, Millette (pno)—see ORCHESTRAS & ENSEMBLES Alexander & Daykin Piano Duo

Alexander, Peter (cl)
Kupferman, M.:Con Cl, w. L. Botstein (cnd), Boston Pro Arte CO — CRI ▲ CD 575 [DDD]
Kupferman, M.:Qnt Cl, w. Bronx Arts Ensemble — Soundspells ▲ CD 108 [DDD]

Alexandru, Nicolae (fl)
Enescu, G.:Dectet Ww, w. M. Teodorescu (fl), C. Silvestri (cnd) — Electrecord ▲ ELCD 122 [AAD]
Enescu, G.:Oct Strs, w. M. Teodorescu (fl), C. Silvestri (cnd) — Electrecord ▲ ELCD 122 [AAD]

Alexeev, Dmitri (pno)
Chopin, F.:Preludes, Op. 28 — EMI Classics (Classics for Pleasure) ▲ CDM 64117
Grieg, E.:Con Pno, Op. 16, w. Y. Temirkanov (cnd), Royal PO — Classics for Pleasure ▲ CDEMX 2195 [DDD]
Medtner, N.:Con 1 Pno, w. A. Lazarev (cnd), BBC SO — Hyperion ▲ CDA 66744
Medtner, N.:Knight Errant, w. N. Demidenko (pno) — Hyperion ▲ CDA 66654 [DDD]
Medtner, N.:Qnt Pno, w. New Budapest String Quartet — Hyperion ▲ CDA 66744
Medtner, N.:Russian Round Dance (A Tale), w. N. Demidenko (pno) — Hyperion ▲ CDA 66654 [DDD]
Rachmaninoff, S.:Russian Rhap, w. N. Demidenko (pno) — Hyperion ▲ CDA 66654 [DDD]
Rachmaninoff, S.:Suite 2 for 2 Pnos, w. N. Demidenko (pno) — Hyperion ▲ CDA 66654 [DDD]
Rachmaninoff, S.:Symphonic Dances, w. N. Demidenko (pno) — Hyperion ▲ CDA 66654 [DDD]
Schumann, R.:Con Pno, w. Y. Temirkanov (cnd), Royal PO — Classics for Pleasure ▲ CDEMX 2195 [DDD]

Aley, J. (tpt)—see also ORCHESTRAS & ENSEMBLES Wisconsin Brass Quintet
Balada, L.:Son Winds, w. D. Wakefield (hn), R. Borror (tenor trbn), R. Biddlecome (bass trbn), American Brass Quintet — New World ▲ 80442-2

Alfonso, Ilse (gtr)
Two Centuries of Spanish Guitar Music, w. N. Alfonso (gtr) — René Gailly ▲ CD 86005 [ADD]

Alfonso, Nicolas (gtr)
Two Centuries of Spanish Guitar Music, w. Ilse Alfonso (gtr) — René Gailly ▲ CD 86005 [ADD]

Alieva, Adilia (pno)
Adilia Alieva Plays Piano, w. A. Alieva (pno) — Gallo ▲ CD 707 [ADD]
Balakirev, M.:Paraphrase Pno — Gallo ▲ CD 832 [DDD]
Beethoven, L. van:Con 4 Pno, w. W. Proost (cnd), San Remo SO — Gallo ▲ CD 891 [DDD]
Cornissimo, w. Cass, Gregory (hn) *(rec June 28–30, 1992)* — Gallo ▲ CD 741
Ibrahimova, S.:Transcriptions de chants populaires azerbaïdjans — Gallo ▲ CD 832 [DDD]
Liszt, F.:Song Transcriptions—Le Rossignol — Gallo ▲ CD 832 [DDD]
Mustafa-Zade, W.:Con Pno, w. A. Scharoev (cnd), Kiev National Phil CO — Gallo ▲ CD 832 [DDD]
Prokofiev, S.:Con 2 Pno, w. W. Proost (cnd), San Remo SO — Gallo ▲ CD 849 [DAD]
Rachmaninoff, S.:Pno Music (misc)—Prélude (1891); 4 Pièces pour Pno, Op. 1; Marguerites, Op. 38/3 — Gallo ▲ CD 832 [DDD]
Rachmaninoff, S.:Rhapsody on a Theme of Paganini, w. W. Proost (cnd), San Remo SO — Gallo ▲ CD 849 [DAD]
Radjabov, O.:Tableaux (6) de la vie hébraïque — Gallo ▲ CD 832 [DDD]

Alin, Andreas (fl)
Delage, M.:Poèmes hindous, w. Anne Sofie von Otter (mez), Peter Rydström (fl/pic), Ulf Bjurenhed (ob/E hn), Lars Paulsson (cl), Per Billman (cl/b cl), Nils-Erik Sparf (vn), Ulf Forsberg (vn), Matti Hirvikangas (va), Mats Lindström (vc), Lisa Viguier (hp) *(rec Stockholm, Nov 1994)* — Deutsche Grammophon ▲ 447 752-2 [DDD]
Martin, F.:Chants de Noël, w. Anne Sofie von Otter (mez), Bengt Forsberg (pno) *(rec Stockholm, Nov 1994)* — Deutsche Grammophon ▲ 447 752-2 [DDD]
Poulenc, F.:Rapsodie nègre, w. Anne Sofie von Otter (mez), Lars Paulsson (cl), Nils-Erik Sparf (vn), Ulf Forsberg (vn), Matti Hirvikangas (va), Mats Lindström (vc), Bengt Forsberg (pno) *(rec Stockhom, Nov 1994)* — Deutsche Grammophon ▲ 447 752-2 [DDD]
Ravel, M.:Trois poèmes de Stéphane Mallarmé, w. Anne Sofie von Otter (mez), Peter Rydström (fl/pic), Andreas Alin (fl), Lars Paulsson (cl), Per Billman (cl/b cl), Nils-Erik Sparf (vn), Ulf Forsberg (vn), Matti Hirvikangas (va), Mats Lindström (vc), Bengt Forsberg (pno) *(rec Stockholm, Nov 1994)* — Deutsche Grammophon ▲ 447 752-2 [DDD]
Saint-Saëns, C.:Une Flûte invisible, w. Anne Sofie von Otter (mez), Bengt Forsberg (pno) *(rec Stockhom, Nov 1994)* — Deutsche Grammophon ▲ 447 752-2 [DDD]

Alin, Folke (pno)
Alfvén, H.:Choral Music, w. C.-H. Ahnsjö (ten), R. Sund (cnd), Orphei Drängar—Hör I Orphei Drängar; Dawn at Sea; Papillon; Gustaf Frödings Funeral; Berceuse; Spring in Roslagen; Sweden's Flag; My Sweetheart; Serenade; Night; Evening; Lullaby; So Take My Heart; Quiet Hours; Scents of Summer; You Are Peaceful Calm; I Long for You; The Forest Sleeps; The Trial; Flowers of Joy; Värmlandsvisan; Oxberg March; Swedish Dance; Fatheads; Herdboy's Song; Andrew Was a Lively Lad; And the Maiden Joins the Ring; In Our Meadow; Mood [Sw] *(rec Feb 6–7 & Sept 4–5, 1993)* — BIS ▲ CD 633 [DDD]
Söderman, A.:Choral Music, w. C.-H. Ahnsjö (ten), Orphei Drängar [arr. Alfvén]—In the Gleam of the Moon — BIS ▲ CD 633 [DDD]
A Swedish Bouquet, w. Mats Nilsson (pno), Uppsala Univ Choir [cnd:Cecilia Rydinger-Alin] — BIS ▲ CD 591 [DDD]

Allan, Michael (pno)—see also ORCHESTRAS & ENSEMBLES Westphalia PO Chamber Ensemble
Ullmann, V.:Die Weise von Liebe und Tod, w. Gert Westphal (nar) *(rec Siemensvilla, Berlin-Lankwitz, Aug. 1994)* — EDA ▲ EDA 008-2 [DDD]

Allan, Susie (pno)
Parry, H.:A Garland of (6) Old-Fashioned Songs, w. Henry Wickham (bar) — Meridian ▲ MER 84279 [DDD]
Somervell, A.:Maud, w. Henry Wickham (bar) — Meridian ▲ MER 84279 [DDD]
Woodforde-Finden, A.:Indian Love Lyrics, w. Henry Wickham (bar) — Meridian ▲ MER 84279 [DDD]

Allard, Maurice (bn)
Poulenc, F.:Trio Ob, w. Pierre Pierlot (ob), Francis Poulenc (pno) — Adès ▲ ADE 202522 [AAD]
Telemann, G.P.:Son Bn, w. Richard Siegel (hpd) *(rec Lutheran Church of la Villette, Sept 13 & 17, 1983)* — Studio SM ▲ 2527
Telemann, G.P.:Sons Ob, w. Reynald Parrot (ob)—Son in a *(rec Lutheran Church of la Villette, Sept 13 & 17, 1983)* — Studio SM ▲ 2527
Telemann, G.P.:Suite Ob, w. Reynald Parrot (ob), Richard Siegel (hpd) *(rec Lutheran Church of la Villette, Sept 13 & 17, 1983)* — Studio SM ▲ 2527

Allard, Régis (org)
Scheidemann, H.:Org Music—Magnificats in the 1st, 5th, 7th & 8th tones; Praeambulums in D, & in F — Arion ▲ ARN 68207 [AAD]

Allcoat, Nigel (org)
L'Orgue Baroque — Herald ▲ HAVPCD 171

Allen (hp)
Debussy, C.:Arabesques (2)—& Rèverie] — EMI Classics ▲ CDC 47520 [DDD]
Rochberg, G.:Slow Fires of Autumn, w. C. Wincenc (fl) — CRI ■ ACS 6013

Allen, Barbara (hp)—see also ORCHESTRAS & ENSEMBLES Auréole, Musicians' Accord members
Debussy, C.:Danses sacrée et profane, w. G. Schwarz (cnd), Los Angeles CO — EMI Classics ▲ CDC 47520 [DDD]
Debussy, C.:Épigraphes antiques, w. L. Gilbert (fl) [trans. V. Drake for flute & harp] — Koch International Classics ▲ KIC 7055-2 [DDD]
Debussy, C.:Suite bergamasque — EMI Classics ▲ CDC 47520 [DDD]
Imbrie, A.W.:Three Piece Suite, w. Edmund Niemann (pno) *(rec Mar. 14, 1994)* — New World ▲ 80441-2
Massenet, J.:Méditation, w. Joseph Alessi (trbn) [trans Hartmann for trbn & hp] — Cala Records ("New York Legends" series) ▲ CAL CACD 508 [DDD]
Ravel, M.:Intro & Allegro, w. Wilson (fl), D. Shifrin (cl), Tokyo String Quartet — EMI Classics ▲ CDC 47520
Ravel, M.:Ma mère l'oye Pno—2 selections — EMI Classics ▲ CDC 47520 [DDD]
Riley, D.:Apparitions, w. M. Kaufman (fl), M. Gallagher (va) — CRI ▲ CD 595 [DDD]

Allen, Bryan (tpt)—see ORCHESTRAS & ENSEMBLES Fine Arts Brass Ensemble

Allen, Gregory (pno)
Debussy, C.:Rêverie [solo harp trans.] — EMI Classics ▲ CDC 47520 [DDD]
Rodrigo, J.:Pno Music (comp), w. A. Nel (pno)—Suite for Piano (1923); Berceuse d'automne (1923); Cinco piezas infantiles (1924); Preludio al Gallo mañanero, Zarabanda lejana, Pastorale & Bagatela (1926); Berceuse de printemps (1928); Air de Ballet (1930); Serenata española (1931); Sonada de Adios (1935); Cuatra Piezas (1936–38); Tres Danzas de España & Gran Marcha de los Subsecretarios (1941); A l'ombre de Torre Bermeja (1945); Cuatra Estampas Andaluzas (1946–52); El Album de Cecilia (1948); Cinco Sonatas de Castilla (1950–51); Danza de la Amapola (1972); Artadecer (1975); Sonatina para dos Muñecas (1977); Tres Evocaciones (1980–81); Preludio de Añoranza (1987) — Bridge 2-▲ BCD 9027 [DAD]

Allen, J. (vn)
Pfiffner, E.:Monologue on Peace & War, w. F. Reinmann (bar), A. Rosenfeld (vn), C. Anderes (va), G. Pawlica (vc) *(rec May 1992)* — Pro Viva ▲ ISPV 170 [DDD]

Allen, Jamie (wood fl)
Allen, J.:Midnight Sun, w. Carol Redman (fl) *(rec Santuario de Guadalupe, Sante Fe, NM, Sept 29–30, 1995)* — Wild Iris ▲ WI 001

Allen, Jonathan (vn)—see ORCHESTRAS & ENSEMBLES Kammermusik Ensemble Chamäleon

Allen, M. (vib)—see ORCHESTRAS & ENSEMBLES Gavin Bryars Ensemble

Allen, Nancy (hp)
A Celebration for Harp — EMI Classics ("Studio" series) ▲ CDM 69070 [DDD]
Joy to the World, w. Empire Brass — Angel ▲ CDC 49097
Mozart, W.A.:Con Fl Hp, w. S. Palma (fl), Orpheus CO — Deutsche Grammophon ▲ 427677-2 [DDD]
Mozart, W.A.:Con Fl Hp, w. S. Palma (fl), Orpheus CO — Deutsche Grammophon 3-▲ 431665-2 [DDD]
Romance, w. R. Stoltzman (cl), Irma Vallecillo (pno) — RCA Red Seal ▲ 60198-2-RC [DDD]
Villanelle:French Masterworks for Horn, w. D. Jolley (hn), Joyce Guyer (sop), Samuel Sanders (pno) *(rec SUNY, Purchase Recital Hall, May 24–26, 1995)* — Arabesque ▲ Z 6678 [DDD]
Wilson, R.:The Ballad of Longwood Glen, w. P. Sperry (ten) — CRI ▲ CD 602 [ADD]

Allen, Susan (hp)—see ORCHESTRAS & ENSEMBLES Just Strings Ensemble

Aller, Eleanor (vc)—see ORCHESTRAS & ENSEMBLES Hollywood String Quartet members, Hollywood String Quartet

Aller, Victor (pno)
Brahms, J.:Qts Pno (comp), w. Hollywood String Quartet members *(rec Studio A, Capitol Tower, Hollywood & Melrose Studio, Hollywood, Jan–June 1956)* — Testament 3-▲ SBT 3063 (m) [ADD]
Brahms, J.:Qnt Pno, w. Hollywood String Quartet members *(rec Hollywood, Mar 30–31, 1954)* — Testament 3-▲ SBT 3063 (m) [ADD]
Franck, C.:Qnt Pno, w. Hollywood String Quartet *(rec 1953)* — Testament ▲ SBT 1077
Schumann, R.:Qnt Pno, w. Hollywood String Quartet *(rec 1955)* — Testament 3-▲ SBT 3063
Schumann, R.:Qnt Pno, w. Hollywood String Quartet *(rec Melrose Studio, Hollywood, May 13–16, 1955)* — Testament 3-▲ SBT 3063 (m) [ADD]
Shostakovich, D.:Qnt Pno, w. Hollywood String Quartet *(rec 1952)* — Testament ▲ SBT 1077

Alleson, Robin (vn)
Brahms, J.:Scherzo Vn, w. J. Lenehan (pno) *(rec 1987)* — Classic Studio Berlin ▲ CS 11408 [DDD]
Brahms, J.:Sons Vn (comp), w. J. Lenehan (pno) *(rec 1987)* — Classic Studio Berlin ▲ CS 11408 [DDD]
Brahms, J.:Son 2 Vn, w. J. Alder (pno) *(rec 1989)* — Classic Studio Berlin ▲ CS 11908 [DDD]
Courts, E.:Son Vn & Pno, w. J. Lenehan (pno) *(rec 1987)* — Classic Studio Berlin ▲ CS 11408 [DDD]
Courts, E.:Son 2 Vn & Pno, w. J. Alder (pno) *(rec 1989)* — Classic Studio Berlin ▲ CS 11908 [DDD]
Musik für Violine und Klavier, w. Jonathan Alder (pno) — Classic Studio Berlin ▲ CS 11908 [DDD]

Allessi, Joseph (trbn)
Four of a Kind:Music for Trombone Quartet, w. Blair Bollinger (trbn), Scott A. Hartman (trbn), Mark H. Lawrence (trbn) — Summit ▲ DCD 123 [DDD] ■ DCD 123

Alley, J. (org)
Holst, G.:Psalms 86 & 148, w. R. Hickox (cnd), City of London Sinfonia, Britten Singers [E] — Chandos ▲ CHAN 8997 [DDD]

Alley, John (pno)
Britten, H.:Suite Vn, w. Alexander Barantschik (vn) — EMI Classics ("Anglo-American Chamber Music" series) ▲ CDC 55398

Allocco, Gian Luca (vn)—see ORCHESTRAS & ENSEMBLES Paganini String Quartet

Almarza, Alberto (fl)
Vali, R.:Folk Songs Set 9, w. Alvaro Bitrán (vc) *(rec Rodef Shalom, Pittsburgh, Apr. 13, 1994)* New Albion ▲ NAO 77
Vali, R.:Music of, w. Alvaro Bitran (vc), J.P. Izquierdo (cnd), Carnegie Mellon PO, Latin American String Quartet New Albion ▲ NA 077
Almasi, Z. (vn)
Rheinberger, J.:Qt Pno, w. H. Göbel (pno), D. Cofré (vc) *(rec 1989)* Thorofon 6–▲ BCTH 2161/6
Alme, Waldemar (pno)
Beethoven, L. van:Songs, w. K. Flagstad (sop), An die Hoffnung, Op. 94 [G] Acanta ▲ 43189
Sinding, C.:Songs, w. K. Flagstad (sop)—Eg vil deg'kje elske; Eg tykkjer det er reint langsmt; Eg tarv ikkje ljose aa kveikje Acanta ▲ 43189
Strauss, R.:Songs, w. K. Flagstad (sop)—Im Abendrot, Op. 4 [G] Acanta ▲ 43189
Almeida, Laurindo (gtr)
Almeida, L.:Con 1 Gtr, w. L. Almeida (cnd), Los Angeles CO Concord Concerto ■ CC 2001
Almeida, L.:Lobiana, w. L. Almeida (cnd), Los Angeles CO Concord Concerto ■ CC 2001
The Art of Laurindo Almeida, w. Deltra Eamon (sop) *(rec Hollywood, CA, 1970)* Orion ▲ 7816-2 [AAD]
3 Guitars 3, w. S. Isbin (gtr), Larry Coryell (gtr) Pro Arte ▲ CDD 235 ■ PCD 235
Almgren, D. (vn)—see ORCHESTRAS & ENSEMBLES Stockholm Arts Trio
Almgren, Lars (cl)
Rangström, T.:Vauxhall, w. Bengt Christiansson (fl), Lars Olof Loman (ob), Sven Aarflot (bn), Rolf Bengtsson (hn), Rune Bodin (trbn), Rozalina Skytt (hp), O. Vänskä (cnd), Stockholm PO *(rec Stockholm Concert Hall, Jan. 16 & 18, 1985)* Caprice ▲ CAP 21195 [DDD]
Almond, Frank (vn)
Cage, J.:Nocturne, w. J. Pierce (pno) Wergo ▲ WER 60157-50
Satoh, S.:Music of, w. Leng Tan (pno), Messier (sop), Pugliese (perc)—Birds in Warped Time II for Violin & Piano (1980); The Heavenly Spheres are Illuminated by Lights for Soprano, Piano & Percussion (1979); Incarnation II for solo Piano with tape delay (1970); Litania for 2 Pianos with tape delay (1973); A Gate into the Stars for solo Piano (1962) New Albion ▲ NA 008 [ADD]
Aloni, Pamela Highbaugh (vc)—see ORCHESTRAS & ENSEMBLES Lafayette String Quartet
Aloni, Y. (va)—see ORCHESTRAS & ENSEMBLES Aviv String Quartet
Alpenheim, Ilse von (hpd)
Haydn, J.:Con Org & Strs, H.XVIII/2, w. A. Dorati (cnd), Bamberg SO Vox Box 2–▲ CDX 5017 [ADD]
Alpenheim, Ilse von (pno)—see also ORCHESTRAS & ENSEMBLES Arion Trio
Haydn, J.:Con Hpd & Strs, H.XVIII/3, w. A. Dorati (cnd), Bamberg SO Vox Box 2–▲ CDX 5017 [ADD]
Haydn, J.:Con Hpd & Strs, H.XVIII/4, w. A. Dorati (cnd), Bamberg SO Vox Box 2–▲ CDX 5017 [ADD]
Haydn, J.:Con Hpd, Vns & Bass Instrument, H.XVIII/9, w. A. Dorati (cnd), Bamberg SO Vox Box 2–▲ CDX 5017 [ADD]
Haydn, J.:Con Hpd, Obs, Hns & Strs, H.XVIII/11, w. A. Dorati (cnd), Bamberg SO Vox Box 2–▲ CDX 5017 [ADD]
Haydn, J.:Divert Hpd, Vns & Strs, H.XIV/4, w. A. Dorati (cnd), Bamberg SO Vox Box 2–▲ CDX 5017 [ADD]
Haydn, J.:Sons Pno—Sonatas in E♭, H.XIV/52 & in C, H.XVI/50 Vox Box 2–▲ CDX 5017 [ADD]
Mendelssohn, F.:Lieder ohne Worte Pno Philips ("Duo" series) 2–▲ 438709-2
Mozart, W.A.:Trio Cl, K.498, w. A. Morf (cl), C. Veress (va) BIS 2–▲ CD 513/14 [DDD]
Schubert, Franz:Fant Vn, D.934, w. I. Ozim (vn) BIS 4–▲ CD 521/24 [DDD]
Schubert, Franz:Rondo Vn, D.895, w. I. Ozim (vn) BIS 4–▲ CD 521/24 [DDD]
Schubert, Franz:Son Arpeggione, w. W. Grimmer (vc) BIS 4–▲ CD 521/24 [DDD]
Schubert, Franz:Son Vn, D.574, w. I. Ozim (vn) BIS 4–▲ CD 521/24 [DDD]
Schubert, Franz:Sonatinas Vn, w. I. Ozim (vn) BIS 4–▲ CD 521/24 [DDD]
Alperin, Yoram (vc)
Caplet, A.:Conte fantastique, w. A. Giles (hp), R. Kaminkovsky (vn), R. Mozes (vn), Y. Kaminkovsky (va) PWK Classics ▲ PWK 1141 [DDD]
Ravel, M.:Intro & Allegro, w. A. Giles (hp), E. Talmi (fl), A. Arnheim (cl), R. Kaminkovsky (vn), R. Mozes (vn), Y. Kaminkovsky (va) PWK Classics ▲ PWK 1141 [DDD]
Alpermann, Raphael (hpd)
Jochen Kowalski:Aria from Berlin's Operatic History, w. J. Kowalski (ct), C. Schornsheim (hpd), H. Friedrich (vc), Markus Stauch (db), Berlin CO [cnd:M. Pommer] Berlin Classics ▲ BER 1050 [DDD]
Alpermann, Raphael (org)
Pergolesi, G.B.:Salve regina in c, w. J. Kowalski (alt), H. Haenchen (cnd), C.P.E. Bach CO *(rec Apr. 1994)* Berlin Classics ▲ BER 1047-2 [DDD]
Pergolesi, G.B.:Stabat mater, w. D. Naseband (trb), J. Kowalski (alt), H. Haenchen (cnd), C.P.E. Bach CO *(rec Apr. 1992)* Berlin Classics ▲ BER 1047-2 [DDD]
Alpert, Pauline (pno)
Keyboard Wizards of the Gershwin Era, Vol. 1:Pauline Alpert *(rec 1927–44)* Pearl ▲ PEA 9201 [ADD]
Altena, J. E. van Regteren (vn)
Berio, L.:Tempi Concertati, w. L. Pameijer (fl), D. Porcelijn (cnd), Asko Ensemble *(rec live, Amsterdam 3/6/90)* Attacca ▲ Babel 9057-4 [DDD]
Altena, Quirijn van Regteren (db)
Andriessen, L.:Elegie, w. Peter Beijersbergen van Henegouwen (pno) Olympia ▲ OLY 467 [DDD]
Desenclos, A.:Aria & Rondo, w. Peter Beijersbergen van Henegouwen (pno) Olympia ▲ OLY 467 [DDD]
Ginastera, A.:Pampeana 2, w. Peter Beijersbergen van Henegouwen (pno) Olympia ▲ OLY 467 [DDD]
Hindemith, P.:Son Db, w. Peter Beijersbergen van Henegouwen (pno) Olympia ▲ OLY 467 [DDD]
Thilman, J.P.:Charaktere, w. Peter Beijersbergen van Henegouwen (pno) Olympia ▲ OLY 467 [DDD]
Wilder, A.:Small Suite, w. Peter Beijersbergen van Henegouwen (pno) Olympia ▲ OLY 467 [DDD]
Altenbach, Richard (vn)
Egilsson:Contemplation, w. Endeé Granat (vn), Janet Lakatos (va), Douglas Davis (vc), Árni Egilsson (db) Cambria ▲ CD 1033
Egilsson:Get Down!, w. Endeé Granat (vn), Janet Lakatos (va), Douglas Davis (vc), Árni Egilsson (db) Cambria ▲ CD 1033
Egilsson:Is It?, w. Endeé Granat (vn), Janet Lakatos (va), Douglas Davis (vc), Árni Egilsson (db) Cambria ▲ CD 1033
Egilsson:What If?, w. Endeé Granat (vn), Janet Lakatos (va), Douglas Davis (vc), Árni Egilsson (db) Cambria ▲ CD 1033
Egilsson:Why?, w. Endeé Granat (vn), Janet Lakatos (va), Douglas Davis (vc), Árni Egilsson (db) Cambria ▲ CD 1033
Altenburger, Christian (va)
Mozart, W.A.:Sinf concertante Vn, K.364, w. W. Christ (va), H. Winschermann (cnd), German Bach Soloists LaserLight ▲ 15 650 [DDD]
Mozart, W.A.:Sinf concertante Vn, K.364, w. W. Christ (va), H. Winschermann (cnd), German Bach Soloists LaserLight ▲ 15 880 [DDD]
Altenburger, Christian (vn)
Bottesini, G.:Gran Duo Concertant, w. W. Harrer (db), G. Meditz (cnd), New Vienna Soloists Koch Schwann ▲ CD 311112 [DDD] ■ MC 211112 (D)
Classics Go to the Movies, Vol. 4, w. Budapest SO, Budapest PO, Salzburg Mozarteum Orch, Ernst Mayer-Schieming, German Bach Soloists, Sofia National Opera Orch LaserLight ▲ 15 644
Killmayer, W.:Brahms-Bildnis, w. S. Mauser (pno), J. Berger (vc) CPO ▲ CPO 999020-2 [DDD]
Killmayer, W.:Qt Pno, w. S. Mauser (pno), B. Westphal (va), J. Berger (vc) CPO ▲ CPO 999020-2 [DDD]
Killmayer, W.:Qt Strs, w. G. Weinmeister (vn), B. Westphal (va), J. Berger (vc) CPO ▲ CPO 999020-2 [DDD]
Killmayer, W.:Romances, w. S. Mauser (pno) CPO ▲ CPO 999020-2 [DDD]
Killmayer, W.:Trio for 2 Vns & Vc, w. G. Weinmeister (vn), J. Berger (vc) CPO ▲ CPO 999020-2 [DDD]
Mozart, W.A.:Cons Vn, w. H. Winschermann (cnd), German Bach Soloists—sels. from Cons. 3 & 5 for Violin LaserLight ▲ 15 650 [DDD]
Altenburger, Christian (vn) (cont.)
Mozart, W.A.:Con 3 Vn, w. H. Winschermann (cnd), German Bach Soloists LaserLight ▲ 15 525 [DDD]
Mozart, W.A.:Con 3 Vn, w. H. Winschermann (cnd), German Bach Soloists LaserLight ▲ 15 879 [DDD]
Mozart, W.A.:Con 4 Vn, w. H. Winschermann (cnd), German Bach Soloists LaserLight ▲ 15 879 [DDD]
Mozart, W.A.:Con 4 Vn, w. H. Winschermann (cnd), German Bach Soloists Laserlight ▲ 15 525 [DDD]
Mozart, W.A.:Con 4 Vn, w. H. Winschermann (cnd), German Bach Soloists LaserLight ▲ 15 650 [DDD]
Mozart, W.A.:Con 5 Vn, w. H. Winschermann (cnd), German Bach Soloists LaserLight ▲ 15 880 [DDD]
Mozart, W.A.:Con 5 Vn, w. H. Winschermann (cnd), German Bach Soloists Laserlight ▲ 15 525 [DDD]
Altenburger, Sylvie (va)—see ORCHESTRAS & ENSEMBLES Rubin String Quartet
Altenstadt, Tinta S. von (vn)—see ORCHESTRAS & ENSEMBLES Rubin String Quartet
Altisent, Feliu Gasuli i (gtr)
Orrego-Salas, J.:Glosas, w. Ginette Decuyper (vn) *(rec Musical Arts Ctr, Bloomington, IN, Dec 2, 1988)* Indiana Univ School of Music ▲ IUSM 02
Altman, Yevgeni (vc)
Schnittke, A.:Qt 2 Strs, w. A. Krysa (vn), N. Zabavnikov (vn), F. Dnizhinin (va) Vox Box 2–▲ CDX 5121 [ADD]
Altmann, Hans (pno)
Schubert, Franz:Songs (misc), w. H. Hotter (bar)—10 songs—D.291, 530, 553, 583, 649, 674, 776, 778, 870, 933 [G] *(rec 1952 & 1959)* Preiser ▲ 93145 (m) [AAD]
Schumann, R.:Dichterliebe, w. H. Hotter (b-bar) [G] *(rec 1954)* Preiser ▲ 93145 (m) [AAD]
Alton, Ann (pno)
Blanchard, P.:Music of, w. J. Brown (gtr), J. Vinci (fl)—Lament; Frolic Albany ▲ TROY 086 [DDD]
Fine, V.:Canzones y Dances, w. J. Brown (gtr), J. Vinci (fl) Albany ▲ TROY 086
Holland, A.:Poems Without Words, w. J. Brown (gtr), J. Vinci (fl) Albany ▲ TROY 086
York, A.:Transilience, w. J. Brown (gtr), J. Vinci (fl) Albany ▲ TROY 086
Altwegg, Raffaele (vc)—see also ORCHESTRAS & ENSEMBLES Zurich Chamber Players
Bach, J.S.:Arias, w. Kathrin Graf (sop), Peter-Lukas Graf (fl), Michio Kobayashi (hpd/pno)—Meine Seele sie vergnügt [from Cantata No. 204, Von der Vergnügsamkeit] *(rec Protestant Chuch Seon, 1976)* Claves ("Favor Collection" series) ▲ CD 604 [ADD]
Handel, G.F.:Arias, w. K. Graf (sop), P. Graf (fl), M. Kobayashi (hpd/pno)—Meine Seele hört im Sehen [from 9 German Arias] *(rec Protestant Chuch Seon, 1976)* Claves ("Favor Collection" series) ▲ CD 604 [ADD]
Müller-Zurich, P.:Trio Strs, w. B. Langbein (vn), D. Corti (va) Grammont ▲ CTSP 20-2
Ravel, M.:Chansons madécasses, w. Kathrin Graf (sop), Peter-Lukas Graf (fl), Michio Kobayashi (hpd/pno) *(rec Protestant Chuch Seon, 1976)* Claves ("Favor Collection" series) ▲ CD 604 [ADD]
Scarlatti, A.:Solitudini amene, apriche collinette, w. Kathrin Graf (sop), Peter-Lukas Graf (fl), Michio Kobayashi (hpd/pno) *(rec Protestant Chuch Seon, 1976)* Claves ("Favor Collection" series) ▲ CD 604 [ADD]
Alvanis, L. D. (pno)
Brahms, J.:Hungarian Dances Pno Meridian ▲ MER 84268 [DDD]
Brahms, J.:Rhaps Pno, Op. 79 Meridian ▲ MER 84268 [DDD]
Brahms, J.:Studies (5) Piano Meridian ▲ MER 84268 [DDD]
Alvarado, Rodrigo (perc)
Chávez, C.:Tambuco, w. Israel Moreno (perc), Tambuco Camerata *(rec Sala Nezahualcóyotl, Mexican National Independent Univ., Oct. 1994)* Dorian ▲ DOR 90215 [DDD]
Chávez, C.:Toccata for 6 Perc, w. Israel Moreno (perc), Tambuco Camerata *(rec Sala Nezahualcóyotl, Mexican National Independent Univ., Oct. 1994)* Dorian ▲ DOR 90215 [DDD]
Chávez, C.:Xochipilli, w. Israel Moreno (perc), E. Mata (cnd), Tambuco Camerata *(rec Sala Nezahualcóyotl, Mexican National Independent Univ., Oct. 1994)* Dorian ▲ DOR 90215 [DDD]
Alvarez-Parejo, Juan Antonio (pno)
Canciones Españolas, w. M. Bayo (sop) Claves ▲ CD 9205 [DDD]
Falla, M. de:Canciones populares españolas (7), w. Teresa Berganza (mez) Claves ▲ 50-8405
Granados, E.:Songs, w. Teresa Berganza (mez) (6) Claves ▲ 50-8704
Guridi, J.:Canciones Castellanas (6), w. Teresa Berganza (mez) Claves ▲ 50-8704
Toldrá, E.:Songs, w. Teresa Berganza (mez)—6 sels Claves ▲ 50-8704
Turina, J.:Poema en forma de canciones, w. Teresa Berganza (mez) Claves ▲ 50-8704
Alvarosi, A. (ob)
Vivaldi, A.:Cons for 2 Obs, w. A. Caroldi (ob), P. Santi (cnd), Milan Virtuosi—RV.535 Allegretto ▲ ACD 8036 [ADD] ■ ACS 8036
Vivaldi, A.:Cons Obs Cls, w. A. Caroldi (ob), E. Schiani (cl), A. Gerbi (cl), P. Santi (cnd), Milan Virtuosi Allegretto ▲ ACD 8036 [ADD] ■ ACS 8036
Alvini, Laura (hpd)
Bach, J.S.:Italian Con Tactus ▲ TC 680201
Bach, J.S.:Sons Vl, BWV 1027-1029, w. R. Gini (vl) Tactus ▲ TC 680201
Boccherini, L.:Trio Sons Hpd, G.143-148, w. E. Gatti (vn), R. Gini (vc) *(rec June 27-30, 1991)* Tactus ▲ TC 740202
Cherubini, L.:Sons (6) Hpd—Nos. 1-6 Nuova Era ("Ancient Music" series) ▲ 6867 [DDD]
Durante, F.:Sons (12) Divided into Etudes & Divertimentos Tactus ▲ TC 680402 [DDD]
Scarlatti, A.:Toccatas Hpd—(2) in g & a Tactus ▲ TC 680402 [DDD]
Scarlatti, A.:Variations on *La Follia* Tactus ▲ TC 680402 [DDD]
Alvini, Laura (pno)—see also ORCHESTRAS & ENSEMBLES Concerto Ensemble
Boccherini, L.:Qnt Pno, G.407-412, w. E. Gatti (vn), O. Edouard (vn), E. Moreno (va), R. Gini (vc)—Nos. 1, 5 & 6 Tactus ▲ TC 740203
Mendelssohn, F.:Lied ohne Worte Vc, w. S. Righini (vc) Giulia ▲ 201012 [DDD]
Mendelssohn, F.:Son 1 Vc, w. S. Righini (vc) Giulia ▲ 201012 [DDD]
Mendelssohn, F.:Son 2 Vc, w. S. Righini (vc) Giulia ▲ 201012 [DDD]
Mendelssohn, F.:Vars concertantes, w. S. Righini (vc) Giulia ▲ 201012 [DDD]
Mozart, W.A.:Pno Music (misc)—Themes & Vars. Symphonia ▲ SYM 91T03 [DDD]
Rossini, G.:Péchés de vieillesse (sels)—Preludes Symphonia ▲ SYM 92S14 [DDD]
Amade, Jacques (org)
Albinoni, T.:Cons Tpt, w. F. Presle (tpt) [at the Grand Organ of St. Martin's Church, Masevaux]—in D, a, F, B♭, f, B♭ & D *(rec Oct 4-6, 1993)* Chamade ▲ 5617 [DDD]
Franck, C.:Fant Org [Great Cavaillé-Coll Org of the Abbey of St. Ouen, Rouen, France] Chamade ▲ 5627
Franck, C.:Final [Great Cavaillé-Coll Org of the Abbey of St. Ouen, Rouen, France] Chamade ▲ 5627
Franck, C.:Grande pièce symphonique [Great Cavaillé-Coll Org of the Abbey of St. Ouen, Rouen, France] Chamade ▲ 5627
Franck, C.:Pastorale [Great Cavaillé-Coll Org of the Abbey of St. Ouen, Rouen, France] Chamade ▲ 5627
Franck, C.:Prière [Great Cavaillé-Coll Org of the Abbey of St. Ouen, Rouen, France] Chamade ▲ 5627
Recital for Trumpet & Organ, w. F. Presle (tpt) Chamade ▲ 5629
Telemann, G.P.:Cons Tpt & Org, w. F. Presle (tpt) [the Grand Organ of St. Martin's Church, Masevaux]—in D, E♭, g, A & B♭; Son. de concert *(rec Oct. 5-7, 1992)* Chamade ▲ 5605 [DDD]
Vierne, L.:Pièces en style libre [Cavaillé-Coll Organ of St. Joseph's Church, Marseille] *(rec Oct. 21-23, 1992)* Chamade 2–▲ 5651/52 [DDD]
Amado, Carol Stein (vn)
Davison, J.:Son 1 Vn, w. Albert Lotto (pno) Albany ▲ TROY 199 [DDD]
Amario, Bruno Battisti d (gtr)
Donizetti, G.:Qnts Gtr, w. Rome Solisti—Nos. 2, 3 & 5 *(rec Rome, 1996)* musicaimmagine ▲ MR 10031
Amati, Nicolò (vc)—see ORCHESTRAS & ENSEMBLES Paraíba Quintet
Amato, Albert Carlo (pno)
New York Farewell Recital, w. T. Schipa (ten) *(rec Nov 1962)* Standing Room Only ▲ SRO 817-1 [ADD]
Amato, Donna (pno)
Balakirev, M.:Son Pno Olympia ▲ OCD 354 [DDD]
Debussy, C.:Pno Music (misc)—Arabesque No. 1; La Cathédral engloutie; Clair de lune; La Fille aux cheveux de lin; La plus que lente *(rec Norway 4/90)* Olympia ▲ OCD 352 [DDD]
Dutilleux, H.:Son Pno Olympia ▲ OCD 354 [DDD]

▲ = CD ♦ = Enhanced CD Δ = MD ■ = Cassette Tape □ = DCC

Amato, Donna (pno) (cont.)
Gershwin, G.:Preludes (3) Pno *(rec Norway, 4/90)* Olympia ▲ OCD 352 [DDD]
Gershwin, G.:Rhap in Blue *(rec Norway 4/90)* Olympia ▲ OCD 352 [DDD]
Gershwin, G.:Songs—trans. of I Got Rhythm; I'll Build a Stairway to Paradise; The Man I Love; Oh Lady Be Good; Swanee; 'S wonderful *(rec Norway 4/90)* Olympia ▲ OCD 352 [DDD]
Hinton, A.:Vars & Fugue on a Theme of Grieg Altarus ▲ CD 9021
Liszt, F.:Pno Music (misc)—Consolation No. 3; Hungarian Rhapsody No. 2; Liebesträum No. 3 Olympia ▲ OCD 352 [DDD]
Macdowell, E.:Con 1 Pno, w. P. Freeman (cnd), London PO Olympia ▲ OLY 353 [DDD]
Macdowell, E.:Con 2 Pno, w. P. Freeman (cnd), London PO Olympia ▲ OLY 353 [DDD]
Nevin, A.:Pno Music—From Edgeworth Hills; Toccatella Altarus ▲ CD 9024
Nevin, E.:Pno Music—Napoli; Water Scenes, Op. 13; Un Giorno in Venezia, Op. 25; Maggio in Toscana, Op. 21; O'er Hill & Dale; The Rosary; Mighty Lak' a Rose; Etudes, Op. 18/1 & 2 Altarus ▲ CD 9024
Ravel, M.:Pavane pour une infante défunte Olympia ▲ OCD 352 [DDD]
Scriabin, A.:Pno Music (misc)—Sonatas, Opp. 66, 68, 70; Two Préludes, Op. 67; Two Poems, Op. 69; Two Poems, Op. 71; Two Danses, Op.73; Five Préludes, Op.74 Altarus ▲ CD 9020
Sorabji, K.S.:Fant Espagnole Altarus ▲ CD 9022
Sorabji, K.S.:Pno Music—Quære reliqua hujus materiei inter secretiora (1940); St. Bertrand de Comminges:"He was laughing in the tower" (1941); Toccatinetta sopra C.G.F. (1929); Sutra sul nome dell'amico Alexis (1981); Sutra "Per il caro amico quasi Nipote – Alexis" (?1984); Passeggiata arlecchinesca sopra un frammento di Busoni *(rec 1981–82)* Altarus ▲ AIR CD 9025
Sorabji, K.S.:Variazione maliziosa e perversa on Grieg's "La morte d'Ase" Altarus ▲ CD 9021
Stevenson, R.:Pno Music—Den Bergtekne [Taken into the Mountains] (ballad after Grieg); Norse Elegy for Ella Nygaard; Beltane Bonfire Altarus ▲ CD 9021

Ambache, Diana (pno)
Donizetti, G.:Instrumental Music, w. J. Polmear (ob/hn)—Concertino in G for English Horn & Orchestra; Sonata in F for Oboe & Piano; Waltz in C for Piano; Il barcaiolo Meridian ▲ CDE 84147
Liszt, F.:Réminiscences de Lucia di Lammermoor Meridian ▲ CDE 84147
Mozart, W.A.:Con 8 Pno, w. D. Ambache (cnd), Ambache CO IMP Classics ▲ PCD 931 [DDD]
Mozart, W.A.:Con 9 Pno, w. D. Ambache (cnd), Ambache CO IMP Classics ▲ PCD 931 [DDD]
Mozart, W.A.:Con 21 Pno, w. D. Ambache (cnd), Ambache CO Virgin Classics ▲ CDZ 59647
Mozart, W.A.:Con 25 Pno, w. D. Ambache (cnd), Ambache CO Virgin Classics ▲ CDZ 59647
Mozart, W.A.:Qts Pno, w. Ambache Chamber Ensemble—K.493 Meridian ▲ CDE 84142
Mozart, W.A.:Qt Pno, K.493, w. Ambache Chamber Ensemble Meridian ▲ MER 84329 [AAD]
Mozart, W.A.:Rondo Pno Orch, K.386, w. D. Ambache (cnd), Ambache CO IMP Classics ▲ PCD 931 [DDD]
Mozart, W.A.:Sons Vn Pno (misc), w. Adrian Levine (vn)—in G, K.301 Meridian ▲ MER 84329 [AAD]
Mozart, W.A.:Trio Pno, K.542, w. Ambache Chamber Ensemble Meridian ▲ CDE 84142
Mozart, W.A.:Trio Pno, K.542, w. Ambache Chamber Ensemble members Meridian ▲ MER 84329 [AAD]
Pasculli, A.:Concerto on Themes from Donizetti's *La Favorita,* w. J. Polmear (ob) Meridian ▲ CDE 84147
Pasculli, A.:Fantaisie on Themes from Donizetti's *Poliuto,* w. J. Polmear (ob) Meridian ▲ CDE 84147

Ambartsumian, Levon (vn)
Eshpai, A.Y.:Son 1 Vn, w. Anatoly Sheludyakov (pno) *(rec Large Hall, Moscow Conservatory, July 10 & 12, 1989)* Russian Compact Disc ▲ RDCD 10001 [DDD]
Khachaturian, K.:Son Vn, w. Anatoly Sheludyakov (pno) *(rec Large Hall, Moscow Conservatory, July 10 & 12, 1989)* Russian Compact Disc ▲ RDCD 10001 [DDD]
Prokofiev, S.:Son Vn, Op. 94bis, w. Anatoly Sheludyakov (pno) *(rec Large Hall, Moscow Conservatory, July 10 & 12, 1989)* Russian Compact Disc ▲ RDCD 10001 [DDD]
Schnittke, A.:Son 2 Vn, w. Anatoly Sheludyakov (pno) *(rec Large Hall, Moscow Conservatory, July 10 & 12, 1989)* Russian Compact Disc ▲ RDCD 10001 [DDD]

Ambrose, Melissa (org)
It's a Grand Old Flag *(rec 1/91)* Pro Arte ▲ CDS 560 [DDD]

Ambrosini, Marco (va d'amore)
Vivaldi, A.:Sons Vn, w. Riccardo Delfino (va da rota), Thomas Wimmer (va da gamba)—RV.23, 53 & 58 Preiser ▲ PRE 90276
Vivaldi, A.:Sons for 2 Vns, Op. 1, w. Riccardo Delfino (va da rota), Thomas Wimmer (va da gamba)—No. 12 [La Follia] Preiser ▲ PRE 90276

Ambrus, Károly (hn)
Janácek, L.:Concertino Pno, w. Thomas Hlawatsch (pno), Béla Nagy (vn), Vilmos Oláh (vn), Csaba Babácsi (va), Géza Bánhegyi (cl), István Hartenstein (bn) *(rec Budapest, May 1995)* Naxos ▲ 8.553587 [DDD]

Amelotti, Ferruccio (pno)
Donizetti, G.:Sons Pno 4–Hands, w. P. Dirani (pno)—7 Sonatas—in F ("La solita Suonata"), in B♭ ("Per Dolci e Donizetti"), in E♭ ("L'inaspettata"), in F ("Sonata a quattro sanfe"), in D, in C, & in F *(rec 7/90)* Fonè ▲ 91F21 [DDD]

Amfitheatrof, M. (vc)
Strauss, R.:Don Quixote, w. S. Celibidache (cnd), Milan RAI SO *(rec 4/11/68)* Arkadia ▲ 570 [ADD]

Amico, Anthony d' (db)
Cage, J.:Ryoanji for 4 Soloists, w. Fenwick Smith (fl), Michael Miller (ob), Petur Eiriksson (b trbn), S. Drury (cnd), New England Conservatory Avant–Garde Ensemble *(rec New England Conservatory of Music, Boston, MA, Mar. 4 & 6, 1991)* Mode ▲ MODE 41

Amis, Kenneth (tuba)—see ORCHESTRAS & ENSEMBLES Empire Brass Quintet

Amlin, Martin (pno)
Hollingsworth, S.:Son Ob, w. Wayne Rapier (ob) Boston Records ▲ BR 1013
Koechlin, C.:Morceau de lecture, w. F. Smith (fl) Hyperion ▲ CDA 66414 [DDD]
Koechlin, C.:Pieces Fl & Pno, Op. 149, w. F. Smith (fl) [F] Hyperion ▲ CDA 66414 [DDD]
Koechlin, C.:Pieces Fl, Op. 157, w. F. Smith (fl) Hyperion ▲ CDA 66414 [DDD]
Koechlin, C.:Premier album de Lilian, w. J. West (sop), F. Smith (fl) [F] Hyperion ▲ CDA 66414 [DDD]
Koechlin, C.:Son Fl & Pno, w. F. Smith (fl) Hyperion ▲ CDA 66414 [DDD]
Piston, W.:Suite Ob, w. Wayne Rapier (ob) Boston Records ▲ BR 1013
Saint–Saëns, C.:Son Ob, w. W. Rapier (ob) Boston Records ▲ BR 1013

Amoretti, Alessandro (pno)
Berlioz, H.:Les Nuits d'été, w. M. Lazzara (alt) Bongiovanni ▲ GB 5540 [DDD]
Verdi, G.:Romances Voice, w. M. Lazzara (alt) Bongiovanni ▲ GB 5540 [DDD]
Verdi, G.:Romance without Words Bongiovanni ▲ GB 5540 [DDD]

Amory, Misha (va)
Barker, T.E.:Trikhyálo, w. F. Sherry (vc), R. Schulte (vn) *(rec Nov. 1992)* CRI ▲ CD 661 [DDD]

Amoyal, Pierre (vn)
Janácek, L.:Son Vn, w. Charles Mackerras (pno) EMI Classics ▲ CDC 55585
Spohr, L.:Double Qt 1, w. J. Heifetz (vn), I. Baker (vn), P. Rosenthal (vn), M. Thomas (va), A. Harshman (va), G. Piatigorsky (vc), L. Lesser (vc) RCA Gold Seal ▲ 7870–2–RG (m/s) [ADD]
Tchaikovsky, P.:Con Vn, w. C. Dutoit (cnd), Philharmonia Orch Erato ▲ 45971–2
Tchaikovsky, P.:Con Vn, w. C. Dutoit (cnd), Philharmonia Orch Erato ▲ 92865–2
Tchaikovsky, P.:Sérénade mélancolique, w. C. Dutoit (cnd), Philharmonia Orch Erato ▲ 45971–2
Tchaikovsky, P.:Trio Pno, w. P. Rogè (pno), F. Lodeon (vc) Erato ▲ 45972–2
Tchaikovsky, P.:Valse–Scherzo Vn, w. C. Dutoit (cnd), Philharmonia Orch Erato ▲ 45971–2

Ampleyev, Sergei (perc)—see ORCHESTRAS & ENSEMBLES Moscow Contemporary Music Ensemble

Amrein, Marianne (fl douce/perc)
The Lausanne Vocal Ensemble Euterpe in Concert, w. [cnd:Christophe Gesseney], Euterpe, Christine Sortoretti (hpd), Yves Rechsteiner (org), C. Delafontaine (pic) Gallo ▲ CD 766 [DDD]

Anagnoson, James (pno)
Arensky, A.:Suites (4) for 2 Pnos, w. L. Kinton (pno) CBC ("Musica Viva" series) ▲ MVCD 1036 [DDD]
Dvořák, A.:Slavonic Dances (comp), w. Leslie Kinton (pno) *(rec Glenn Gould Studio, CBC Toronto, June 28–29, 1993)* CBC ("Musica Viva" series) ▲ MVCD 1088 [DDD]
Matton, R.:Con for 2 Pnos, w. L. Kinton (pno), R. Armenian (cnd), Kitchener–Waterloo SO CBC ("SM 5000" series) ▲ SMCD 5120 [DDD]

Anagnoson, James (pno) (cont.)
Milhaud, D.:Scaramouche for 2 Pnos, w. L. Kinton (pno) CBC ("SM 5000" series) ▲ SMCD 5120 [DDD]
Poulenc, F.:Con for 2 Pnos, w. L. Kinton (pno), R. Armenian (cnd), Kitchener–Waterloo SO CBC ("SM 5000" series) ▲ SMCD 5120 [DDD]
Saint–Saëns, C.:Carnival of the Animals, w. L. Kinton (pno), J. Campbell (cnd), Festival of the Sound Ensemble *(rec Glenn Gould Studio, CBC Toronto, Mar. 26–27, 1994)* CBC ("Musica Viva" series) ▲ MVV 1089 [DDD]
Stravinsky, I.:Con CO, w. L. Kinton (pno) CBC ("SM 5000" series) ▲ SMCD 5120 [DDD]

Anatoly, A. (hn)
Rubinstein, A.:Qnt Pno, w. A. Nasedkin (pno), V. Zverov (fl), V. Sokolov (cl), S. Krasavin (bn) Russian Disc ("The A. Rubinstein Edition" series) ▲ RUS 11 061 [ADD]

Ancillotti, Mario (fl)
Boccherini, L.:Con in D Fl [attrib.], w. M. Ancillotti (cnd), Symphonia Perusina *(rec 1/91)* Nuova Era ▲ 7026 [DDD]
Cambini, G.M.:Con Fl, w. M. Ancillotti (cnd), Symphonia Perusina *(rec 1/91)* Nuova Era ▲ 7026 [DDD]
Martini, G.B.:Con Fl, w. M. Ancillotti (cnd), Symphonia Perusina *(rec 1/91)* Nuova Era ▲ 7026 [DDD]
Mercadante, S.:Qts Fl, w. Quartetto Academica members—Quartet in a Nuova Era ▲ 6901 [DDD]
Molique, W.B.:Intro, Andante & Polonaise, w. P. Masi (pno) Dynamic ▲ CD 104
Petrassi, G.:Ala, w. Luciano Tristano (fl), Leonardo Bartelloni (pno) Koch Schwann ▲ SCH 315242
Petrassi, G.:Con Fl, w. H. Soudant (cnd), Sicilian SO Koch Schwann ▲ SCH 315242
Petrassi, G.:Dialogo angelico, w. Luciano Tristano (fl) Koch Schwann ▲ SCH 315242
Piccinni, N.:Con Fl, w. M. Ancillotti (cnd), Symphonia Perusina Nuova Era ▲ 7026 [DDD]
Reinecke, C.:Son Fl, w. P. Masi (pno) Dynamic ▲ CD 104
Rietz, J.:Son Fl, w. P. N. Masi (pno) Dynamic ▲ CD 104
Rolla, A.:Qt 3 Fl, w. Quartetto Academica members Nuova Era ▲ 6901 [DDD]
Viotti, G.B.:Qts Fl, Op. 22, w. Quartetto Academica members—Nos 1 & 2 Nuova Era ▲ 6901 [DDD]

Anda, Géza (pno)
Bartók, B.:Cons Pno (comp), w. F. Fricsay (cnd), Berlin RSO Deutsche Grammophon ("The Originals" series) ▲ 447399–2
Bartók, B.:Con 3 Pno, w. H. von Karajan (cnd), Dresden Staatskapelle *(rec live, 1972)* AS Disc ▲ ASD 2508
Bartók, B.:For Children *(rec 1954–55)* Testament ▲ SBT 1065
Bartók, B.:Sonatina Pno *(rec London, 1954)* Testament ▲ SBT 1067
Beethoven, L. van:Son 7 Pno *(rec 1958)* Testament ▲ SBT 1070
Beethoven, L. van:Son 14 Pno, "Moonlight Son" *(rec 1955)* Testament ▲ SBT 1070
Beethoven, L. van:Son 28 Pno *(rec 1958)* Testament ▲ SBT 1070
The Best of Chopin, w. John Browning (pno), Emanuel Ax (pno), Peter Serkin (pno), et al. Victrola ("Victrola Best of" series) ▲ 60770–2–RV [ADD] ■ 60770–4–RV
Brahms, J.:Intermezzos Pno, Op. 117 *(rec London, 1953 & 1957)* Testament ▲ SBT 1068
Brahms, J.:Son 3 Pno *(rec London, 1953 & 1957)* Testament ▲ SBT 1068
Brahms, J.:Vars on a Theme by Paganini *(rec London, 1953 & 1957)* Testament ▲ SBT 1068
Chopin, F.:Ballade Pno, Op. 23 *(rec London 1956)* Testament ▲ SBT 1066
Chopin, F.:Con 1 Pno, w. A. Galliera (cnd), Philharmonia Orch *(rec London 1956)* Testament ▲ SBT 1066
Chopin, F.:Études (24)—12 études; sels unknown *(rec London 1956)* Testament ▲ SBT 1066
Chopin, F.:Waltzes RCA Victrola ▲ 7744–2–RV [ADD] ■ 7744–4–RV (CrO2)
Delibes, L.:Coppélia (sels)—Valse lente [arr Ernö Dohnanyi for pno] *(rec London, 1954)* Testament ▲ SBT 1067
Liszt, F.:Con 1 Pno, w. O. Ackermann (cnd), Philharmonia Orch *(rec May 1955)* Testament ▲ SBT 1071
Liszt, F.:Études de concert (3) Pno—Un sospiro *(rec London, 1954)* Testament ▲ SBT 1067
Liszt, F.:Études d'exécution transcendante d'après Paganini, S.140—La Campanella [arr Ferruccio Busoni for pno] *(rec London, 1954)* Testament ▲ SBT 1067
Liszt, F.:Fant on Hungarian Folk Tunes, w. O. Ackermann (cnd), Philharmonia Orch *(rec May 1955)* Testament ▲ SBT 1071
Liszt, F.:Mephisto Waltz 1 Pno *(rec London, 1954)* Testament ▲ SBT 1067
Liszt, F.:Son Pno *(rec London, 1954)* Testament ▲ SBT 1067
Mozart, W.A.:Cons Pno, w. G. Anda (cnd), Salzburg Mozarteum Camerata Academica—Nos. 1–6, 8, 9 & 11–27 Deutsche Grammophon 10–▲ 429001–2 [ADD]
Mozart, W.A.:Con 6 Pno, w. G. Anda (cnd), Salzburg Mozarteum Camerata Academica *(rec Neues Festspielhaus, Salzburg, Apr 1962)* Deutsche Grammophon ▲ 447436–2 [ADD]
Mozart, W.A.:Con 17 Pno, w. G. Anda (cnd), Salzburg Mozarteum Camerata Academica *(rec Neues Festspielhaus, Salzburg, May 1961)* Deutsche Grammophon ▲ 447436–2 [ADD]
Mozart, W.A.:Con 20 Pno, w. G. Anda (cnd), Vienna SO RCA Silver Seal ▲ 60484–2 [ADD] ■ 60484–4 (CrO2)
Mozart, W.A.:Con 21 Pno, w. G. Anda (cnd), Salzburg Mozarteum Camerata Academica *(rec Neues Festspielhaus, Salzburg, May 1961)* Deutsche Grammophon ▲ 447436–2 [ADD]
Mozart, W.A.:Con 21 Pno, w. G. Anda (cnd), Vienna SO RCA Gold Seal ▲ 09026–68113–2 [ADD]
Mozart, W.A.:Con 21 Pno, w. G. Anda (cnd), Vienna SO RCA Silver Seal ▲ 60484–2 [ADD] ■ 60484–4 (CrO2)
Rachmaninoff, S.:Con 2 Pno, w. A. Galliera (cnd), Philharmonia Orch Testament ▲ SBT 1064
Rachmaninoff, S.:Preludes Pno, Opp 23 & 32, w. A. Galliera (cnd), Philharmonia Orch—2 Preludes Testament ▲ SBT 1064
Saint–Saëns, C.:Carnival of the Animals, w. Béla Siki (pno), I. Markevitch (cnd), Philharmonia Orch *(rec Jan 1954)* Testament ▲ SBT 1071
Schumann, R.:Carnaval Pno *(rec London, 1953 & 1955)* Testament ▲ SBT 1069
Schumann, R.:Kreisleriana *(rec London, 1953 & 1955)* Testament ▲ SBT 1069
Schumann, R.:Sym Etudes *(rec London, 1953 & 1955)* Testament ▲ SBT 1069
Tchaikovsky, P.:Con 1 Pno, w. A. Galliera (cnd), Philharmonia Orch Testament ▲ SBT 1064

Anderer, J. (hn)—see ORCHESTRAS & ENSEMBLES Boehme Quintet

Anderes, Cornel (va)—see also ORCHESTRAS & ENSEMBLES Universal Ensemble, Zurich Chamber Players, Zurich New Music Ensemble
Pfiffner, E.:Monologue on Peace & War, w. F. Reinmann (bar), J. Allen (vn), A. Rosenfeld (vn), G. Pawlica (vc) *(rec May 1992)* Pro Viva ▲ ISPV 170 [DDD]

Anders, U. (perc)
Gulda, F.:Gegenwart, w. F. Gulda (clav/recs) *(rec Jan. 1976)* Celestial Harmonies ▲ 19003–2

Andersen, Diane (pno)
Biarent, A.:Music of, w. M. Drobinsky (vc)—Poco lento; Presto furioso; Lamento; Un peu lent *(rec 1980; 1993)* Talent ▲ DOM 2910 14 [DDD]
Chausson, E.:Pièce Vc & Pno, w. M. Drobinsky (vc) *(rec 1980/1993)* Talent ▲ DOM 2910 14 [DDD]
Kozeluch, L.:Sons Pno—Op. 30/1–3; in D [sans opus] Talent ▲ DOM 291032 [DDD]
Pâque, D.:Sons Pno (comp) Koch Schwann ▲ SCH 317192 [DDD]

Andersen, Georg Svendsen (va)
Kuhlau, F.:Qnts Fl, w. Eyvind Rafn (fl), Kim Sjøgren (vn), Bjarne Boye Rasmussen (va), Lars Holm Johansen (vc) *(rec Torpen Kapel, Humlebaek, Nordsjaelland, Denmark, Aug 1985)* Naxos ▲ 8.553303 [DDD]

Andersen, Peter (bn)—see also ORCHESTRAS & ENSEMBLES Scandinavian Wind Quintet
Maegaard, J.:Musica Riservata II, w. Klas Sjöblom (ob/E hn), Jesper Helmuth Madsen (cl), Jørgen Bove (sax) *(rec Copenhagen, 1995–96)* Marco Polo/Dacapo ▲ 8.224050 [DDD]

Anderson, A. (pno)
Ravel, M.:Gaspard de la nuit Klavier ▲ KCD 11016 [DDD]
Ravel, M.:Jeux d'eau Klavier ▲ KCD 11016 [DDD]
Ravel, M.:Pno Music—Valses nobles et sentimentales; Jeux d'eau; Gaspard de la Nuit; Sonatine; Pièce en forme de Habanera Klavier ▲ KCD 11016 ■ KC 7038
Ravel, M.:Pièce en forme de Habanera Klavier ▲ KCD 11016 [DDD]
Ravel, M.:Sonatine Pno Klavier ▲ KCD 11016 [DDD]
Ravel, M.:Valses nobles et sentimentales Klavier ▲ KCD 11016 [DDD]

Anderson, Amy (ob)
Shewan, S.:The Widow's Lament in Springtime, w. Jill Richardson (sop), Rebecca Patterson (vc), Stephen Shewan (pno) Albany ▲ TROY 149 [DDD]
Anderson, Dean (perc)
Kraft, William:Con Perc, w. Renee Krimsier (fl), Diane Heffner (cl), Nancy Cirillo (vn/va), Ronald Lowry (vc), Hugh Hinton (pno) Albany ▲ TROY 218 [DDD]
Kraft, William:Settings from Pierrot Lunaire, w. Jane Manning (sop), Renee Krimsier (fl), Diane Heffner (cl), Nancy Cirillo (vn/va), Ronald Lowry (vc), Hugh Hinton (pno) Albany ▲ TROY 218 [DDD]
Anderson, Elizabeth (hpd)
Recital Move ▲ MD 3078
Anderson, Elizabeth (vc)
Giuliani, M.:Serenade Vn, w. J. Swensen (vn), K. Yamashita (gtr) RCA Red Seal ▲ 09026-60237-2
Hanson, H.:Con da Camera, w. B. Preston (vn), I. Swenson (vn), C. Wiersma (vn), M. Lambros (va) Albany ▲ TROY 129 [DDD]
In Sweet Rejoicing Music for Christmas:Ars Antique Choralis, Vol 3, w. [cnd:Richard Proulx], Cathedral Singers, Mary Hickey (fl), Jeri-Lou Aike (vn), Samuel Soria Jr. (org) *(rec Oct. 17-19 & 24-26, 1993)* GIA ▲ CD 323 ■ CS 323
Anderson, John (ob)
Albinoni, T.:Cons à 5 Obs, Op. 7, w. S. Wright (cnd), Philharmonia Orch—Nos. 3 & 6 *(rec St. Jude-on-the-Hill, Hampstead, Jan. 5-6, 1989)* Nimbus ▲ NI 7027 [DDD]
Benjamin, A.:Con Ob Strs, w. S. Wright (cnd), Philharmonia Orch *(rec St. Jude-on-the-Hill, Hampstead, Jan. 5-6, 1989)* Nimbus ▲ NI 7027 [DDD]
Capriccio:Classics for Oboe, w. Gordon Back (pno) ASV ▲ ASV 2100
Françaix, J.:L'Horloge de Flore, w. S. Wright (cnd), Philharmonia Orch Nimbus ▲ NI 5330 [DDD]
Haydn, J.:Sym 96, "Miracle", w. Hugh Bean (vn), Nicholas Whiting (vn), L. Slatkin (cnd), Philharmonia Orch *(rec Abbey Road Studio No. 1, London, Aug 1993)* RCA Red Seal ▲ 09026-68424-2 [DDD]
Italian Oboe Concertos, w. Philharmonia Orch [cnd:Simon Wright] Nimbus ▲ NI 5188 [DDD]
Marcello, A.:Cons Ob, w. S. Wright (cnd), Philharmonia Orch—in d *(rec St. Jude-on-the-Hill, Hampstead, Jan. 5-6, 1989)* Nimbus ▲ NI 7027 [DDD]
Martinů, B.:Con Ob, w. S. Wright (cnd), Philharmonia Orch Nimbus ▲ NI 5330 [DDD]
Strauss, R.:Con Ob, w. S. Wright (cnd), Philharmonia Orch Nimbus ▲ NI 5330 [DDD]
Strauss, R.:Con Ob, w. N. del Mar (cnd), BBC SO IMP ("BBC Radio Classics" series) ▲ IMP 9138
Summertime:Music for Oboe & Guitar, w. Simon Wynberg (gtr) Chandos ("Collect" series) ▲ CHAN 6581 [DDD]
Vivaldi, A.:Cons Ob, w. S. Wright (cnd), Philharmonia Orch—in F, R.461; in D, R.453; in F, R.455 *(rec St. Jude-on-the-Hill, Hampstead, Jan. 5-6, 1989)* Nimbus ▲ NI 7027 [DDD]
Anderson, L. (vn)
Foss, L.:Paradigm, w. J. Williams (perc), J. Grassel (electric gtr), S. Basson (bn), R. Dagon (cl) *(rec 1989-90)* Koss Classics ▲ KC 1006 [DDD]
Anderson, M. (perc)
Kinney, M.:You Are So Stingingly Demure, w. T. Cora (vc), M. Kinney (vc), S. Mensah (perc) Innova ▲ MN 107
Anderson, Mark (pno)
Brahms, J.:Son 3 Pno *(rec Nimbus Foundation Concert Hall, Nov. 17-19, 1993)* Nimbus ▲ NI 5422 [DDD]
Liszt, F.:Années de pèlerinage 2—No. 7, "Dante Son." *(rec Nimbus Foundation Concert Hall, Nov. 17-19, 1993)* Nimbus ▲ NI 5422 [DDD]
Liszt, F.:Années de pèlerinage 2—Sonetto 104 del Petrarca Nimbus ▲ NI 5484 [DDD]
Liszt, F.:Années de pèlerinage 3—Les jeux d'eau à la Villa d'Este Nimbus ▲ NI 5484 [DDD]
Liszt, F.:Études de concert (2) Pno Nimbus ▲ NI 5484 [DDD]
Liszt, F.:Légendes Nimbus ▲ NI 5484 [DDD]
Liszt, F.:Mephisto Waltz 3 Pno Nimbus ▲ NI 5484 [DDD]
Liszt, F.:Pno Music (misc)—4 kleine Klavierstücke Nimbus ▲ NI 5484 [DDD]
Liszt, F.:Rhap espagnole Nimbus ▲ NI 5484 [DDD]
Schumann, R.:Toccata Pno Nimbus ▲ NI 5422 [DDD]
Anderson, Miles (trbn)
Baley, V.:Partita 1 Trbns, w. Virko Baley (pno) *(rec Univ. of Nevada, Las Vegas)* Cambria ▲ CMB 1077 [DDD]
Shapey, R.:Concertante 1 Tpt, w. R. Shapey (cnd), Univ of Chicago Contemporary Chamber Players New World ▲ NW 355-2 [DDD]
Anderson, Neil (gtr)—see ORCHESTRAS & ENSEMBLES Folios Guitar Duo
Anderson, Olek (trbn)—see ORCHESTRAS & ENSEMBLES Weser-Renaissance Ensemble
Anderson, Ronald (tpt)
Fine, V.:Qt Brass, w. Allan Dean (tpt), David Jolley (hn), Lawrence Benz (b trbn) CRI ▲ CD 692 [ADD]
Anderson, William (gtr)
Kupferman, M.:Dark Orpheus, w. L. Varga (pno) Soundspells ▲ CD 105
Kupferman, M.:Night Voices, w. L. Varga (vc), K. Rosenak (pno) Soundspells ▲ CD 105
Mertz, K.J.:Gtr Music—Pieces (6) from Bardenklange, Op. 13; 6 Schubert Lieder; Ländler (6), Op. 9; Le Gondolier; Mazurkas & Polonaises, Op. 3 *(rec Sarah Lawrence College, July & Aug 1993)* Titanic ▲ Ti 218 [DDD]
Andersson, E. (cl)
Beethoven, L. van:Qnt Pno, Ob, Cl, Hn & Bn, w. E. Knardahl (pno), A. Linder (hn), E. Schleiffer (bn) BIS ▲ CD 44 [AAD]
Berwald, F.:Qt Pno, Cl, Hn & Bn, w. E. Knardahl (pno), A. Linder (hn), E. Schleiffer (bn) BIS ▲ CD 44 [AAD]
Rimsky-Korsakov, N.:Qnt Fl, w. E. Schleiffer (bn), A. Linder (hn), E. Knardahl (pno) BIS ▲ CD 44 [AAD]
Andersson, Gert-Inge (va)
Brask, P.:Son Va, w. E. Skjoldan (pno) *(rec Dec. 1992)* Classico ▲ CLASSCD 107
Vesth, T.:Music of, w. Jan Sommer (gtr), Nils Sylvest Jeppesen (vc), Per Friman (vn), Berit Spaelling (hp), Bent Larsen (fl), Bjorn Nielsen (ob), Svend Rasmussen (cl), Henrik Simonsen (db)—Cuddling Rain; Waltz the Blue Sea; Kaspers Lullaby; Autumn Sunshine; Red Fox Hunting Tea Party; Off White Eternity; Tartan Fl Danica ▲ DCD 8142
Andersson, K. (cl)—see ORCHESTRAS & ENSEMBLES Frösunda Wind Quintet
Andersson, Magnus (gtr)
Ferneyhough, B.:Kurze Schatten II Montaigne ▲ MO 782029
Holewa, H.:Concertino 8, w. M. Maros (cnd), Strängnäs Sinfonietta Ensemble Phono Suecia ▲ PHN 49 [ADD]
Holewa, H.:Concertino 9, w. Åse Enhamre (sop), C. Merithz (cnd), Strängnäs Sinfonietta Ensemble Phono Suecia ▲ PHN 49 [ADD]
Holewa, H.:Duettino 1, w. Emil Dekov (vn) Phono Suecia ▲ PHN 49 [ADD]
Holewa, H.:Duettino 2, w. Stig Bengtson (fl) Phono Suecia ▲ PHN 49 [ADD]
Anderszewski, Piotr (pno)
Debussy, C.:Son Vn, w. Viktoria Mullova (vn) Philips ▲ 446091-2
Janácek, L.:Son Vn, w. Viktoria Mullova (vn) Philips ▲ 446091-2
Prokofiev, S.:Son 1 Vn, w. Viktoria Mullova (vn) Philips ▲ 446091-2
Andolfi, Godfroy (pno)
Falla, M. de:Canciones populares españolas (7), w. Ninon Vallin (sop)—Seguidilla murciana; Nana; Jota *(rec 1930)* VAI Audio ▲ VAIA 1127 [ADD]
Schumann, R.:Frauenliebe und -leben, w. Ninon Vallin (sop) [Fr. trans. Jules Barbier] *(rec 1920)* VAI Audio ▲ VAIA 1127 [ADD]
Schumann, R.:Liederkreis, Op. 39, w. Ninon Vallin (sop)—Au loin *(rec 1931)* VAI Audio ▲ VAIA 1127 [ADD]
Strauss, R.:Songs, w. Ninon Vallin (sop)—Sérénade; Rêve crépusculaire *(rec 1931)* VAI Audio ▲ VAIA 1127 [ADD]
Andorjan, A. (fl)
Schoenberg, A.:Chamber Sym 1, w. E. Brunner (cl), D. Sitkovetzky (vn), D. Geringas (vc), G. Oppitz (pno) [Webern's 1923 arr. for Flute, Clarinet, Violin, Cello & Piano] Tudor ▲ 717 [DDD]

Andrade, Cisneiro de (hn)—see ORCHESTRAS & ENSEMBLES Brasil Brass Quintet
Andrade, L. (va)—see ORCHESTRAS & ENSEMBLES Arditti String Quartet
Andranian, Chantal (pno)
Sauguet, H.:Con 3 Pno, w. Gisèle Andranian (pno) [arr Sauguet] Arcobaleno ▲ AAOC 93732 [DDD]
Sauguet, H.:Les Jeux de l'amour et du hasard, w. Gisèle Andranian (pno) Arcobaleno ▲ AAOC 93732 [DDD]
Sauguet, H.:Valse brève, w. Gisèle Andranian (pno) Arcobaleno ▲ AAOC 93732 [DDD]
Sauguet, H.:Vines aux mains de fée, w. Gisèle Andranian (pno) Arcobaleno ▲ AAOC 93732 [DDD]
Andranian, Gisèle (pno)
Sauguet, H.:Con 3 Pno, w. Chantal Andranian (pno) [arr Sauguet] Arcobaleno ▲ AAOC 93732 [DDD]
Sauguet, H.:Les Jeux de l'amour et du hasard, w. Chantal Andranian (pno) Arcobaleno ▲ AAOC 93732 [DDD]
Sauguet, H.:Valse brève, w. Chantal Andranian (pno) Arcobaleno ▲ AAOC 93732 [DDD]
Sauguet, H.:Vines aux mains de fée, w. Chantal Andranian (pno) Arcobaleno ▲ AAOC 93732 [DDD]
André, Maurice (tpt)
L'Adagio d'Albinoni EPM ("RYM Musique" series) ▲ EPM RYM 191619
Albinoni, T.:Cons à 5 Obs, Op. 9, w. Guy Touvron (tpt), J. Faerber (cnd), Württemberg CO—No. 9 in C [played on tpts] *(rec Eglise Evangélique, Heilbronn, May 1979)* EMI Classics ▲ CDK 65337 [ADD]
Albinoni, T.:Con Tpt, "San Marco", w. J. Faerber (cnd), Württemberg CO *(rec Salle Wagram, Paris, June 1978)* EMI Classics ▲ CDK 65337 [ADD]
The Art of Maurice André EMI Classics 4-▲ DMD 64100
La Belle Époque Erato ▲ 4509-92126-2
Bellini, V.:Con in E♭ Ob, w. E. de Stoutz (cnd), Zurich CO [arr. André] EMI Classics ▲ CDC 54086 [DDD]
Bolling, C.:Toot Suite, w. C. Bolling (pno) CBS ▲ MK 36731
Charpentier, M.-A.:Magnificat, w. Martha Angelici (sop), Jocelyn Chamonin (sop), André Mallabrera (ct), Rémy Corazza (ten), Georges Abdoun (bar), Jacques Mars (bass), Marie-Claire Alain (org), L. Martini (cnd), Jean-François Paillard CO, French Jeunesses Musicales Chorale *(rec Paris, Mar 15, 1963)* Vanguard Classics ▲ OVC 8075 [ADD]
Charpentier, M.-A.:Te Deum, H. 146, w. Martha Angelici (sop), Jocelyn Chamonin (sop), André Mallabrera (ct), Rémy Corazza (ten), Georges Abdoun (bar), Jacques Mars (bass), Marie-Claire Alain (org), L. Martini (cnd), Jean-François Paillard CO, French Jeunesses Musicales Chorale *(rec Paris, Mar 15, 1963)* Vanguard Classics ▲ OVC 8075 [ADD]
Children's Songs, w. St. Laurent Children's Choir [cnd:François Rauber], St. Laurent Instrumental Ensemble, Jean-Pierre Rampal (fl) CBS ▲ MK 39669
Fasch, J.F.:Con Tpt & 2 Obs, w. Jacques Chambon (ob), Pierre Pierlot (ob), J.-F. Paillard (cnd), Jean-François Paillard CO *(rec 1968)* Erato ▲ 98475-2 [ADD]
Haydn, J.:Con Tpt, w. E. de Stoutz (cnd), Zurich CO EMI Classics ▲ CDC 54086 [DDD]
Haydn, J.:Con Tpt, w. J. López-Cobos (cnd), London PO EMI Classics 2-▲ CDZB 69152 [DDD]
Hummel, J.N.:Vars Ob, w. E. de Stoutz (cnd), Zurich CO [arr. André] EMI Classics ▲ CDC 54086 [DDD]
Italian Baroque Concertos, w. various orch Erato ▲ 4509-92124-2
Maurice André Trumpet Masterpieces, w. Munich CO [cnd:Hans Stadlmair], English CO [cnd:Charles Mackerras], Zurich Collegium Musicum Orch [cnd:Paul Sacher], Munich Bach Orch [cnd:Karl Richter] Deutsche Grammophon ("Double" series) 2-▲ 413853-2
Mozart, W.A.:Con Ob, K.314, w. E. de Stoutz (cnd), Zurich CO [trans Maurice André for Tpt] EMI Classics ▲ CDC 54086 [DDD]
Scarlatti, A.:Su le sponde del Tebro, w. Helen Donath (sop), N. Marriner (cnd), Academy of St. Martin in the Fields EMI Classics ("Baroque" series) ▲ CDK 65735
Telemann, G.P.:Con Tpt Strs in D, w. C. Mackerras (cnd), English CO Deutsche Grammophon ("Musikfest" series) ▲ 413256-4 [AAD] ■ 413256-4
Trompette et Orgue, w. Marie-Clair Alain (org) Erato ▲ 4509-92124-2
Trompette Hors-Série EPM ("RYM Musique" series) ▲ EPM RYM 191634
Trumpet & Organ Recital, w. Hedwig Bilgram (org) EMI Classics ▲ CDC 54330
Trumpet Concertos, w. Franz Liszt CO [cnd:Jesus Lopez-Cobos], Württemberg CO [cnd:Jörg Faerber], Academy of St. Martin in the Fields [cnd:Neville Marriner], London PO [cnd:Jesus Lopez-Cobos], Philharmonia Orch [cnd:Riccardo Muti] EMI Classics 2-▲ CDZB 69152 [ADD]
Trumpet Voluntary, w. various orch Erato ▲ 4509-92123-2
Vivaldi, A.:Cons Tpt, w. Iona Brown (vn), N. Marriner (cnd), Academy of St. Martin in the Fields—in B♭ for Tpt & Vn Classics for Pleasure ("Eminence" series) ▲ CFP 2235
Vivaldi, A.:Con for 2 Tpts, w. Bernard Soustrot (tpt), N. Marriner (cnd), Academy of St. Martin in the Fields Classics for Pleasure ("Eminence" series) ▲ CFP 2235
Andreasen, Henrik Wenzel (fl)
Frøhlich, J.F.:Son Fl *(rec College of Music, Malmö, Sweden, Aug 8-9, 1994)* Naxos ▲ 8.553333 [DDD]
Hartmann, J.P.E.:Prelude Fl *(rec College of Music, Malmö, Sweden, Aug 8-9, 1994)* Naxos ▲ 8.553333 [DDD]
Hartmann, J.P.E.:Son Fl *(rec College of Music, Malmö, Sweden, Aug. 8-9, 1994)* Naxos ▲ 8.553333 [DDD]
Kuhlau, F.:Duos brillants, w. Anna Øland (pno)—No. 1 *(rec College of Music, Malmö, Sweden, Aug 8-9, 1994)* Naxos ▲ 8.553333 [DDD]
Weyse, C.E.F.:Rondeau Fl, w. Anna Øland (pno) *(rec College of Music, Malmö, Sweden, Aug. 8-9, 1994)* Naxos ▲ 8.553333 [DDD]
Andreasen, J. (pno)
Rasmussen, S.:Music of, w. W. Gaffron (vn), A. Turner (vc), E. Dalsgarò (fl), A. Klett (cl), P. Sólstein (hn), S.A. Johansen (cnd), *(orch unknown)*—"Warnings I"—The Naked Destruction Tutl ▲ FKT 4
Andreassen, T. O. (fl)—see ORCHESTRAS & ENSEMBLES Oslo Wind Ensemble
Andreasson, G. (vn)—see ORCHESTRAS & ENSEMBLES Busch String Quartet
André-Combes, Marie-Noëlle (pno)
Ives, C.:Songs, w. Nicholas Isherwood (bass), Eric Watson (pno)—Tom Sails Away; Ann Street; Thoreau; Maple Leaves; The Cage; 1, 2, 3; Evening; Serenity; A Unison Chant; The New River; The White Gulls; Slugging a Vampire; West London [A Sonnet]; From the Incantation; Charlie Rutlage; Slow March; The Indians; Walt Whitman [from 20th Stanza]; Afterglow; His Exaltation; At the River; In the Mornin'; The Camp Meeting; The Circus Band; From Paracelsus; Premonitions; On the Counter; A Sea Dirge; Like a Sick Eagle; Soliloquy [or A Study in 7th & Other Things]; Memories; The One Way; Remembrance; A Farewell to Land Accord ▲ ACD 201812 [DDD]
Andreotti, Maria-Tecla (trns fl)—see ORCHESTRAS & ENSEMBLES Limoges Baroque Ensemble Soloists
Andres, S. (vn)
Wyttenbach, J.:Vn Songs *(rec May 19-20, 1990)* Grammont ▲ CTSP 37-2 [ADD]
Andres, Stefi (pno)
Bassi, L.:Divert, w. Bernhard Röthlisberger (cl) Gallo ▲ CD 916 [DDD]
Cavallini, E.:Adagio sentimentale, "Una lagrima sulla tomba dell'immortale Rossini", w. Bernhard Röthlisberger (cl) Gallo ▲ CD 916 [DDD]
Cavallini, E.:Fant on Motifs from Bellini's *I somnambula* , w. Bernhard Röthlisberger (cl) Gallo ▲ CD 916 [DDD]
Czerny, C.:Duo concertant, w. G. Rumpel (fl) *(rec 1977)* Jecklin ▲ J 44102 [ADD]
Donizetti, G.:Son Fl & Pno, w. G. Rumpel (fl) *(rec 1977)* Jecklin ▲ J 44102 [ADD]
Kreutzer, C.:Son Concertante, w. G. Rumpel (fl) *(rec 1977)* Jecklin ▲ J 44102 [ADD]
Labanchi, G.:Fant on Verdi's *Aida*, w. Bernhard Röthlisberger (cl) Gallo ▲ CD 916 [DDD]
Lovreglio, D.:Fant da concerto on Motifs of Verdi's *La traviata*, w. Bernhard Röthlisberger (cl) Gallo ▲ CD 916 [DDD]
Panizza, G.:Ballabile, w. Bernhard Röthlisberger (cl) Gallo ▲ CD 916 [DDD]
Rossini, G.:Andante & Allegro Fl, w. G. Rumpel (fl) *(rec 1977)* Jecklin ▲ J 44102 [ADD]
Rossini, G.:Fant Cl, w. G. Rumpel (fl) [arr flute] *(rec 1977)* Jecklin ▲ J 44102 [ADD]
Spadina, A.:Duetto Concertante on Motifs from Bellini's *Norma*, w. Bernhard Röthlisberger (cl) Gallo ▲ CD 916 [DDD]
Wehrli, W.:Sinfonietta Fl, w. G. Rumpel (fl), D. Schmid (cnd), Southern Bohemian Chamber PO Budweis *(rec 1993)* Jecklin ▲ JS 297-2

444 ▲ = CD ♦ = Enhanced CD Δ = MD ■ = Cassette Tape □ = DCC

Andresen, Mogens (b trbn)
Biber, H. von:Son à 3 for 2 Vns, B Trbn, w. Troels Svendsen (vn), Wim ten Have (vn), Karen Englund (hpd) *(rec Strandmarks Church, Copenhagen, Denmark, Sept 1994)* Rondo Gramophon ▲ RCD 8343 [DDD]
Marini, B.:Sons, Syms & Retornelli, w. Mogens Rasmussen (vl), Karen Englund (hpd)—Son *(rec Strandmarks Church, Copenhagen, Denmark, Sept 1994)* Rondo Gramophon ▲ RCD 8343 [DDD]
Andresen, Mogens (eup)—see ORCHESTRAS & ENSEMBLES Royal Danish Brass
Andrews, Julie (bn)
Strauss, R.:Duet-Concertino, w. Joy Farrall (cl), N. Cleobury (cnd), Britten Sinfonia Classics for Pleasure ("Eminence" series) ▲ CFP 2238
Andrews, Mitchell (pno)
Baker, D.:Jazz Suite Vn, w. R. Ricci (vn) Grenadilla ■ 1056
Kay, U.:Portraits, w. R. Ricci (vn) Grenadilla ■ 1056
Andreyev, Elena (vc)
Aperghis, G.:L'origine des espèces, w. Françoise Degeorges (sop), Donatienne Michel-Dansac (sop), Emmanuelle Zoll (sop), Valérie Joly (mez), Frédérique Wolf-Michaux (cta) Musique Française d'Aujourd'hui ▲ MFA 216004
Andreza, Glauco (perc)
Manuel Do Espírito Santo, A.:Music of, w. Brasil Brass Quintet—220 [arr. Adail Fernandes] *(rec Cultural Foundation Theatre, João Pessoa, Paraíba, Brazil, Mar 22-26, 1995)* Nimbus ▲ NI 5462 [DDD]
Segundo Sedícias, D.:Music of, w. Brasil Brass Quintet—Trilogia matuta *(rec Cultural Foundation Theatre, João Pessoa, Paraíba, Brazil, Mar 22-26, 1995)* Nimbus ▲ NI 5462 [DDD]
Ursicino da Silva, J.:Music of, w. Brasil Brass Quintet—Suite Recife; Gonzagueando; Concertino para Trompete; Brass Music No. 1; Marquinhos no frevo; Andrezza; Coletânea '93; Serenata no Capibaribe; Nairam; Tema para um trompetista *(rec Cultural Foundation Theatre, João Pessoa, Paraíba, Brazil, Mar 22-26, 1995)* Nimbus ▲ NI 5462 [DDD]
Villa-Lobos, H.:Cirandas Pno, w. Brasil Brass Quintet [3 Cirandas arr. José Alberto Kaplan] *(rec Cultural Foundation Theatre, João Pessoa, Paraíba, Brazil, Mar 22-26, 1995)* Nimbus ▲ NI 5462 [DDD]
Andriaccio, Michael (gtr)—see ORCHESTRAS & ENSEMBLES Castellani-Andriaccio Duo
Andrie, Karen (vc)
Tailleferre, G.:Chansons populaires françaises, w. Patrice Maginnis (sop), John Fairweather (vn), David Ryther (vn), Jill Cohen (va), Elizabeth Bodine (ob), Andy Connell (cl), Gordon Mumma (hn), June Orzel (bn), N. Paiement (cnd) *(rec UC, Santa Cruz, May 1992)* Helicon Classics ▲ HE 1008
Tailleferre, G.:Image, w. John Fairweather (vn), David Ryther (vn), Jill Cohen (va), Elizabeth Bodine (ob), Andy Connell (cl), Gordon Mumma (hn), June Orzel (bn), N. Paiement (cnd) *(rec UC, Santa Cruz, May 1992)* Helicon Classics ▲ HE 1008
Andriessen, Louis (pno)
Andriessen, L.:Melody Fl, w. F. Brüggen (fl) Attacca ▲ Babel 9267-6 [DDD]
Andriessen, Rik (b fl)—see ORCHESTRAS & ENSEMBLES Ives Ensemble members
Andriessen, Rik (fl)—see ORCHESTRAS & ENSEMBLES Ives Ensemble members
Andriessen, Willem (pno)
Falla, M. de:Noches en los jardines de España, w. O. Klemperer (cnd), Royal Concertgebouw Orch *(rec live March 29, 1951)* Music & Arts ▲ CD 752-1 (m) [AAD]
Andriesson, L. (pno)—see ORCHESTRAS & ENSEMBLES Icebreaker
Andrus, Brice (hn)
Kodály, Z.:Galanta Dances, w. Laura Ardan (cl), Y. Levi (cnd), Atlanta SO *(rec Atlanta, 1995-96)* Telarc ▲ CD 80413 [DDD]
Andsnes, Leif Ove (pno)
Brahms, J.:Sons Cl (comp), w. L. A. Tomter (va) Broadway Angel ▲ CDC 59154
Chopin, F.:Études (24)—Op. 10/6; Op. 25/3, 4, 10 & 11 Virgin Classics 2-▲ ZDMB 61317
Chopin, F.:Mazurkas—4 Mazurkas, Op. 17 Virgin Classics 2-▲ ZDMB 61317
Chopin, F.:Pno Music (misc)—5 Etudes:Op. 10, No. 6 & Op. 25, Nos. 3,4,10 & 11; 4 Mazurkas:Op. 17 Virgin Classics 2-▲ 59072 [DDD]
Chopin, F.:Sons Pno (comp) Virgin Classics 2-▲ ZDMB 61317
Chopin, F.:Son Pno, Op. 4 Virgin Classics 2-▲ 59072 [DDD]
Chopin, F.:Son Pno, Op. 35 Virgin Classics 2-▲ 59072 [DDD]
Chopin, F.:Son Pno, Op. 58 Virgin Classics 2-▲ 59072 [DDD]
Concerto Sampler, w. various artists, Bergen PO [cnd:D. Kitayenko] Virgin Classics 2-▲ CDC 59083
Grieg, E.:Con Pno, Op. 16, w. D. Kitayenko (cnd), Bergen PO Virgin Classics ▲ 59613 [DDD]
Grieg, E.:Lyric Pieces—Op. 65, Nos. 1-6 Virgin Classics ▲ 59613 [DDD]
Grieg, E.:Lyric Pieces Virgin Classics ▲ CDC 59300
Grieg, E.:Son Pno Virgin Classics ▲ CDC 59300
Janácek, L.:In the Mists Virgin Classics ▲ CDC 59639
Janácek, L.:On an Overgrown Path Virgin Classics ▲ CDC 59639
Janácek, L.:Son October 1, 1905 Pno Virgin Classics ▲ CDC 59639
Liszt, F.:Con 2 Pno, w. D. Kitayenko (cnd), Bergen PO Virgin Classics ▲ 59613 [DDD]
Nielsen, C.:Chaconne Virgin Classics ▲ CDC 45129
Nielsen, C.:Humoreske-Bagateller Virgin Classics ▲ CDC 45129
Nielsen, C.:Pieces Pno, Op. 3 Virgin Classics ▲ CDC 45129
Nielsen, C.:Pieces Pno, Op. 59 Virgin Classics ▲ CDC 45129
Nielsen, C.:Suite Pno Virgin Classics ▲ CDC 45129
Prokofiev, S.:Con 3 Pno, w. O.K. Ruud (cnd), Bergen PO Simax ▲ PSC 1060 [DDD]
Rachmaninoff, S.:Con 3 Pno, w. P. Berglund (cnd), Oslo PO Virgin Classics ▲ CDC 45173
Schumann, R.:Märchenbilder, w. L. A. Tomter (va) Broadway Angel ▲ CDC 59154
Anedda, R. (vn)
Milesi, P.:Modi 2, w. L. M. Pickova (sop), Françoise Goddard (alt), M. Ferradini (ten), B. Andersen (bass), D. Cassamagnaghi (fl), S. Scanziani (ob), A. Bianchi (cl/b cl), E. Crisafulli (bn), C. Gazzola (hn), F. Gualandris (tuba), A. Girardi (celtic hp), E. Groppo (vn), M. Pagani (vn), M. Ravasio (va), S. Righini (vc), P. Rizzi (db), J. Scully (perc), P. Milesi (cnd) Cuneiform ▲ RUNE 63
Angarola, Anisa (gtr)
Giuliani, M.:Grand Son Fl, w. V. King (fl) Discovery ▲ DSCD 203 [DDD]
Giuliani, M.:Serenade Fl, w. V. King (fl) Discovery ▲ DSCD 203 [DDD]
Giuliani, M.:Vars on "I bin a Kohlbauern Bub" Discovery ▲ DSCD 203 [DDD]
Angel, David (vn)—see ORCHESTRAS & ENSEMBLES Maggini String Quartet
Angel, Rita (pno)—see ORCHESTRAS & ENSEMBLES Santa Fe Trio
Angelich, Nicholas (pno)
Brahms, J.:Son 1 Cl, w. Laurent Verney (va) Harmonia Mundi France ("Les Nouveaux Interprètes" series) ▲ HMN 911565
Brahms, J.:Son 2 Cl, w. Laurent Verney (va) Harmonia Mundi France ("Les Nouveaux Interprètes" series) ▲ HMN 911565
Rachmaninoff, S.:Études-tableaux, Opp. 33 & 39 Harmonia Mundi France ("Les Nouveaux Interprètes" series) ▲ HMN 911547
Rachmaninoff, S.:Preludes Pno, Opp 23 & 32 Harmonia Mundi France ("Les Nouveaux Interprètes" series) ▲ HMN 911547
Angelini, J. (fl)
Mozart, W.A.:Cons Fl, w. A. Lizzio (cnd), Mozart Festival Orch Vivace 3-▲ E 315 [DDD]
Angelis, Antonella De (fl)—see ORCHESTRAS & ENSEMBLES Bilitis Ensemble
Angelloz, Guy (fl)
Flute & Organ at Notre Dame, Paris, w. Arnold Batselaere (org) *(rec 4/85)* Pierre Verany ▲ 785094 [DDD]
Anger, Darol (vn)—see ORCHESTRAS & ENSEMBLES Turtle Island String Quartet
Angerer, Ixi (hp)
Bortnyansky, D.:Sinf concertante, w. H. Kann (pno), *(bn unknown)*, H. Bondarenko (vn), W. Knieps (va), A. Schober (vc) Entrée ▲ 0051 [ADD]
Angerer, Paul (pno)
Schroeter, J.S.:Cons Pno, Op. 3, w. P. Angerer (cnd), Vienna Concilium Musicum—Nos. 1, 3, 4 & 6 Koch Schwann ▲ SCH 312422 [DDD]
Angervo, Ari (vn)—see ORCHESTRAS & ENSEMBLES Voces Intimae String Quartet

Angervo, Ilari (va)
Gothoni, R.:The Bull & His Herdsman:A Zen Story from Ancient China, w. Soile Isokoski (sop), Jorma Hynninen (bar), Jan Söderblom (vn), Jan-Erik Kustafsson (vc), Heini Kärkkäinen (pno), R. Gothoni (cnd) Ondine ▲ ODE 832 [DDD]
Anghelescu, Christina (vn)
Enescu, G.:Mélodies, Op. 4, w. H. Andreescu (cnd), Romanian National RSO, Romanian National Radio Chorus—No. 1 [arr for Vn & Orch] Olympia ▲ OLY 496
Anievas, Augustin (pno)
Chopin, F.:Impromptus—(3) EMI Classics ▲ CDE 67769
Chopin, F.:Waltzes EMI Classics ▲ CDE 67769
Rachmaninoff, S.:Cons Pno (comp), w. M Atzmon (cnd), New Philharmonia Orch EMI Classics ("Doublefforte" series) 2-▲ CDFB 68619
Rachmaninoff, S.:Con 2 Pno, w. M. Atzmon (cnd), New Philharmonia Orch EMI Classics ▲ CDE 67783
Rachmaninoff, S.:Preludes Pno, Opp 23 & 32, w. M. Atzmon (cnd), New Philharmonia Orch EMI Classics ▲ CDE 67783
Rachmaninoff, S.:Rhapsody on a Theme of Paganini, w. R. Frühbeck de Burgos (cnd), New Philharmonia Orch EMI Classics ("Doublefforte" series) 2-▲ CDFB 68619
Anjos, Antonietta (va)
Danzi, F.:Qts Bn, Op. 40, w. M. Monguzzi (bn), G. Maestri (vn), A. Riccardi (vc) Bongiovanni ▲ GB 5520 [DDD]
Krommer, F.:Qt Bn, Op. 46/1, w. M. Monguzzi (cl), G. Maestri (vn), A. Riccardi (vc) Bongiovanni ▲ GB 5520 [DDD]
Annetteruel, M. von (lt)
Adriaenssen, E.:Music of, w. Lautentrio Ricardo Correa—Qts. Villanella & "Als ick u vinde"; Trio "Madonna mia pieta" Christophorus ▲ CHR 74527 [ADD]
Annis, Robert (cl)—see also ORCHESTRAS & ENSEMBLES Collage New Music Ensemble
Bazelon, I.:Legends & Love Letters, w. J. Heller (sop), F. Epstein (perc), C. Oldfather (pno), J. Scolnik (fl), J. Moerchel (vc), C. Fussell (cnd), Collage New Music Ensemble Albany ▲ TROY 054 [DDD]
Annunziati, Marco (gtr)
Gragnani, F.:Gtr Music, w. R. Bini (gtr), C. Mascilli Migliorini (gtr), M. Fornaciari (vn)—3 Sonatas for Violin & Guitar; 3 Duets for 2 Guitars Foné ▲ FON 93F 18 [DDD]
Anrath, Herbert (vn)
Reichardt, J.F.:Rondeau, w. B. Hoffmann (glass hmc), W. Albers (vn), E. Nippes (va), H. Plumacher (vc), G. Nose (db) Allegretto ▲ ACD 8174 [ADD] ■ ACS 8174
Röllig, K.L.:Qnt Glass Hmc, w. B. Hoffmann (glass hmc), W. Albers (vn), E. Nippes (va), H. Plumacher (vc) Allegretto ▲ ACD 8174 [ADD] ■ ACS 8174
Ansel, S. (va)
Schoenberg, A.:Verklärte Nacht, w. S. Chase (vn), L. Chang (vn), M. Thompson (va), R. Thomas (vc), M. Djokic (vc) *(rec Methuen, MA, Dec. 1990)* Northeastern ▲ NOR 249 [DDD]
Tchaikovsky, P.:Souvenir de Florence, w. A. Delmoni (vn), L. Chang (vn), M. Thompson (va), R. Thomas (vc), M. Reynolds (vc) *(rec Weston, MA, Jan. 1993)* Northeastern ▲ NOR 249 [DDD]
Ansell, Steven (va)—see ORCHESTRAS & ENSEMBLES Muir String Quartet
Antál, Mátyás (pno)
Mozart, W.A.:Con 7 Pnos, w. J. Jandó (pno), D. Várjon (pno), Concentus Hungaricus [arr. Mozart for 2 pianos & orch.] *(rec Jan. 7-10, 1991)* Naxos ▲ 8.550210 [DDD]
Mozart, W.A.:Con 10 Pnos, w. J. Jandó (pno), Concentus Hungaricus Naxos ▲ 8.550206 [DDD]
Antalffy, Gabor (hpd/pno)
Bach, C.P.E.:Kbd Music—H.244, 245, 186, 243 & 187 (W.55/1-6); H.260, 246, 261, 269, 262 & 270 (W.56/1-6); H.265, 247, 271, 208, 266 & 173 (W.57/1-6); H.276, 273, 274, 188, 267, 277 & 278(W.58/1-7); H.281, 268, 282, 283, 279 & 284 (W.59/1-6); H.209 (W.60) *(rec Apr, May & July, 1991)* CPO 4-▲ CPO 999100-2 [DDD]
Antognazzi, Aldo (pno)
Clementi, M.:Pno Music (comp), w. Federico Aldao (pno), Ana Chavez (pno), Lorena Di Florio (pno), Marcela Paludi (pno), Ricardo Zanon (pno)—Sons (6) for Pno, Op. 1, Nos. 4-6; Sons (6) for Pno, Op. 2, Nos. 2, 4 & 6 Aura Classics ▲ AU 32072
Clementi, M.:Pno Music (comp), w. Christian Badian (pno), Jose Maria Brusco (pno), Daniela Lanzillo (pno), Federico Wiman (pno), J. Rotter (cnd), Württemberg PO—Con in C for Pno; Sons (6) for Pno, Op. 1, Nos. 1-3; "Son inedita" in A♭ Aura Classics ▲ AU 32070
Clementi, M.:Pno Music (comp), w. Christian Badian (pno), Eduardo Cazaban (pno), Cristina Da Souza (pno), Dao Di Renzo (pno), Pablo Lavandera (pno), Yi Fang Huang (vn), Silvina Cardenas (fl), Nestor Herzbaum (fl)—Sons (6) for Pno, Op. 2, Nos. 1, 3 & 5 (w. flutes); Duets (3) for Piano 4-Hands, Op. 3, Nos. 2 & 3; Sons (3) for Pno & Vn, Op. 3, No. 4 Aura Classics ▲ AU 32287
Clementi, M.:Pno Music (comp), w. Augusto Miravalle (pno), Yi Fang Huang (vn)—Sons (3) for Pno & Vn, Op. 3, Nos. 5 & 6; Sons (6) for Pno & Vn, Op. 4 Aura Classics ▲ AU 32288
Antognini, Ivo (pno)
Bolling, C.:Con Gtr, w. Franco Trentin (gtr), Rino Rossi (db), Matteo Mazza (dr) Gallo ▲ CD 820 [DDD]
Antonelli, Claudia (hp)
Bach, C.P.E.:Son Hp *(rec Rome, Italy, 1987)* Arts ▲ 47202-2 [DDD]
Boieldieu, F.-A.:Con Harp, w. H.L. Hirsch (cnd), Innsbruck CO *(rec ORF Landesstudio Tirol, Innsbruck, June 1983)* Arts ▲ 47285-2 [DDD]
Britten, H.:Suite Hp *(rec Rome, Italy, 1987)* Arts ▲ 47202-2 [DDD]
Dittersdorf, K.D. von:Con Harp, w. H.L. Hirsch (cnd), Innsbruck CO *(rec ORF Landesstudio Tirol, Innsbruck, June 1983)* Arts ▲ 47285-2 [DDD]
Fauré, G.:Impromptu Hp *(rec Rome, Italy, 1987)* Arts ▲ 47202-2 [DDD]
Handel, G.F.:Con Hp, w. H.L. Hirsch (cnd), Innsbruck CO *(rec ORF Landesstudio Tirol, Innsbruck, June 1983)* Arts ▲ 47285-2 [DDD]
Mozart, W.A.:Con Fl Hp, w. L. Oshavkova (fl), I. Kozhouharov (cnd), Sofia New Chamber Ensemble Divertimento ▲ DIV 31020 [DDD]
Saint-Saëns, C.:Fant Hp *(rec Rome, Italy, 1987)* Arts ▲ 47202-2 [DDD]
Spohr, L.:Fant Hp in c *(rec Rome, Italy, 1987)* Arts ▲ 47202-2 [DDD]
Viotti, G.B.:Son Hp *(rec Rome, Italy, 1987)* Arts ▲ 47202-2 [DDD]
Antonini, Claire (lt)
Boësset, A.:Music of, w. Marcel Bozonnet (nar), Véronique Dietschy (sop), Alain Zaepffel (ct), Christophe Le Paludier (ten), Jacques Bone (bass), Marianne Muller (vl)—Madame de la fayette; Airs de cour; La princesse de cleves (sels) Adès ▲ ADE 204722
Antonioli, Jean-François (pno)
Busoni, F.:Konzertstück Pno, w. L. Foster (cnd), Lausanne CO Claves ▲ CD 8806 [DDD]
Martin, F.:Ballade Pno, w. M. Viotti (cnd), Turin PO Claves ▲ CD 8509 [DDD]
Martin, F.:Con 1 Pno, w. M. Viotti (cnd), Turin PO Claves ▲ CD 8509 [DDD]
Martin, F.:Con 2 Pno, w. M. Viotti (cnd), Turin PO Claves ▲ CD 8509 [DDD]
Raff, J.:Con Pno, w. L. Foster (cnd), Lausanne CO Claves ▲ CD 8806 [DDD]
Raff, J.:Ode au printemps, w. L. Foster (cnd), Lausanne CO Claves ▲ CD 8806 [DDD]
Antonioni, Beatrice (vn)
Tartini, G.:Cons Vn (misc), w. S. Frontalini (cnd), Kaunas CO—in C, D.12; in D, D.15; in G, D.78 *(rec Kaunas, Lithuania, 1993)* Bongiovanni ▲ GB 2177 [DDD]
Antoniotti, Luca (org)
Queens of the Night, w. Yovanka Marville (hpd), Raoul Esmerode (perc) Gallo ▲ CD 658 [ADD]
Antonova, Natalya (pno)
Adler, S.:Duo Son, w. Barry Snyder (pno) Gasparo ▲ GS 298 [DDD/DAD]
Antonsen, Ole Edvard (tpt)
Haydn, J.:Con Tpt, w. J. Tate (cnd), English CO EMI Classics ▲ CDC 54897
Hummel, J.N.:Con in E♭ Tpt, S.49, w. J. Tate (cnd), English CO EMI Classics ▲ CDC 54897
Neruda, J.B.G.:Con Tpt, w. J. Tate (cnd), English CO EMI Classics ▲ CDC 54897
Shostakovich, D.:Con 1 Pno, w. Mikhail Rudy (pno), M. Jansons (cnd), Berlin PO EMI Classics ▲ CDC 55361
Tartini, G.:Con Tpt, w. J. Tate (cnd), English CO EMI Classics ▲ CDC 54897
Telemann, G.P.:Con Tpt Strs in D, w. J. Tate (cnd), English CO EMI Classics ▲ CDC 54897

Antonsen, Ole Edvard (tpt) (cont.)
20th Century Works for Solo Trumpet or Trumpet & Piano, w. Einar Henning Smebye (pno) Simax ▲ PSC 1041 [DDD]

Anugama (syn)
Classic Fantasy II Nightingale ▲ NGH 350 [ADD]

Anyz, Ivo (a vl)—see ORCHESTRAS & ENSEMBLES Pro Arte Antiqua Prague

Anyz, Ivo (va)
Biber, H. von:Son Tpt, 2 Vns, Vc, w. Richard Steuart (tpt), Oldrich Vlcek (vn), Sylvie Hessova (vn), Vaclav Jirovec (vc) *(rec Prague, Nov. 1994)* Discover International ▲ DI 920244 [DDD]

Anzellotti, Teodoro (acc)
Holliger, H.:Beiseit, w. David James (ct), Elmar Schmid (cl), Johannes Nied (db), H. Holliger (cnd) ECM New Series ▲ 78118-21540-2 [ADD]
Keller, M.:Aushalten und bewegen *(rec June 1994–Apr 1995)* Jecklin ▲ JEC 310 [DDD]

Anzelmo, F. (va)
Rendano, A.:Qnt Pno, w. R. Caporali (pno), R. Bonucci (vn), M. Fiorini (vn), A. Bonucci (vc) *(rec Mar. 29-31, 1989)* Ermitage ▲ ERM 409 [ADD]

Apap, Gilles (vn)
Gilles Apap & the Transylvanian Mountain Boys, w. Jean-Marc Apap (va), Chris Judge (gtr), Brendan Statom (db) Sony Classical ▲ SK 62374

Apap, Jean-Marc (va)
Gilles Apap & the Transylvanian Mountain Boys, w. G. Apap (vn), Chris Judge (gtr), Brendan Statom (db) Sony Classical ▲ SK 62374

Apel, W. (pno)
Mauersberger, R.:Trio Pno, w. R. Straumer (vn), A. Priebst (vc) *(rec June 1991)* Thorofon ▲ CTH 2112 [DDD]

Appel, Andrew (hpd)—see also ORCHESTRAS & ENSEMBLES Four Nations Ensemble
Bach, J.S.:Capriccio Departure Bridge ▲ BCD 9005
Bach, J.S.:Chromatic Fant & Fugue Bridge ▲ BCD 9005
Bach, J.S.:Fants Hpd—Fantasia & Fugue in a, BWV 904; Fantasia in c, BWV 906 Bridge ▲ BCD 9005
Bach, J.S.:Italian Con Bridge ▲ BCD 9005
Bach, J.S.:Toccatas Hpd, BWV 910-16—BWV 912 Bridge ▲ BCD 9005

Appel, Toby (va)
Seasons Remembered 2, w. J. L. Stillman (pno), John Deak (db), Eliot Porter (db), Diaz Trio, Lutz Rath (vc), Fenwick Smith (fl), Ruth Waterman (vn) North Star ▲ 9837-40052-2 ■ 9837-40052-4

Appenheimer, Yoma (hpd)
Il Flauto Dolce, w. B. Bonitz (rcr), Irene Gudel (vc) Arcadia ▲ ARC 1993-2 [DDD]

Appleman, Gerald (vc)
Corigliano, J.:Soliloquy, w. Stanley Drucker (cl), Kerry McDermott (vn), Lisa Kim (vn), Rebecca Young (va) Cala Records ("New York Legends" series) ▲ CAL CACD 509 [DDD]
Schumann, R.:Andante & Vars Hn, w. Thomas Hecht (pno), Sandra Shapiro (pno), Alan Stepansky (vc), L. William Kuyper (Fr hn) *(rec Performing Arts Ctr/Purchase College-State Univ of NY Recital Hall, May 8, 1995)* Elysium ▲ GRK 709 [DDD]

Appleton, Jon (synclavier)
Appleton, J.:Brush Canyon Centaur ▲ CRC 2052 [DDD]
Appleton, J.:Degitaru Ongaku Centaur ▲ CRC 2052 [DDD]

Apro, A. (va)—see ORCHESTRAS & ENSEMBLES Danubius Quartet

Apter, David (pno)
Bridge, F.:Scherzetto Vc, w. Rebecca Rust (vc) *(rec Munich, Feb. 21-25, 1994)* Marco Polo ▲ 8.223637 [DDD]
Bridge, F.:Son Vc, w. Rebecca Rust (vc) *(rec Munich, Feb. 21-25, 1994)* Marco Polo ▲ 8.223637 [DDD]
Enescu, G.:Son Vc, w. R. Rust (vc) Marco Polo ▲ 8.223298
Tovey, D.F.:Elegiac Vars, w. Rebecca Rust (vc) *(rec Munich, Feb. 21-25, 1994)* Marco Polo ▲ 8.223637 [DDD]
Tovey, D.F.:Son Vc, w. Rebecca Rust (vc) *(rec Munich, Feb. 21-25, 1994)* Marco Polo ▲ 8.223637 [DDD]
Villa-Lobos, H.:Vc Pno Music, w. R. Rust (vc)—O canto do capodócio & O canto da nossa terra [prelude & aria from the Bachianas brasilieras]; Divigaçao (1946); Sonhar, Op. 14 (1915); O canto do Cisne Negro; Berceuse, Op. 50 (1915) Marco Polo ▲ 8.223298

Aqua, Karen (perc)
Field, K.:Music of, w. Ken Field (sax/perc/syn/fl), Ken Winokur (perc), Mike Rivard (elec bass), John Fleagle (voice), Karen Gruber (perc)—A Space in a Place; Om on the Range; Takuskanskan; 5 Saxophones in Search of Meaning; Sanity; Perpetual Motion; Thoughts Unspoken; Berrendo; Sympathetic Magic; The Missing Soul; When I Fall in Love *(rec The Henge, Roswell, NM, Wellspring Sound, Concord, MA, The Chicken Loft, Cambridge, MA & The Basement, Cambridge, MA, 1988–1995)* O.O. Discs ▲ OO 25

Ara, León (vn)
Rodrigo, J.:Canciones Valencianas, w. E. de Cranck (pno) CPO ▲ CPO 999186 [DDD]
Rodrigo, J.:Capriccio CPO ▲ CPO 999186 [DDD]
Rodrigo, J.:2 Esbozos, w. E. de Cranck (pno) CPO ▲ CPO 999186 [DDD]
Rodrigo, J.:Rumaniana, w. E. de Cranck (pno) CPO ▲ CPO 999186 [DDD]
Rodrigo, J.:Son pimpante, w. E. de Cranck (pno) CPO ▲ CPO 999186 [DDD]

Arai, Yoshiko (vn)
Sibelius, J.:Music for Vn Pno, w. E. Heinonen (pno)—2 Pieces, Op. 2; 2 Pieces, Op. 77; 4 Pieces, Op. 78; 6 Pieces, Op. 79 Ondine ▲ ODE 720-2 [DDD]
Sibelius, J.:Music for Vn Pno, w. E. Heinonen (pno) Ondine ▲ ODE 756-2 [DDD]
Sibelius, J.:Novelette, w. E. Heinonen (pno) Ondine ▲ ODE 756-2 [DDD]
Sibelius, J.:Pieces Vn Pno, Op. 81, w. E. Heinonen (pno) Ondine ▲ ODE 756-2 [DDD]
Sibelius, J.:Pieces Vn Pno, Op. 115, w. E. Heinonen (pno) Ondine ▲ ODE 756-2 [DDD]
Sibelius, J.:Pieces Vn Pno, Op. 116, w. E. Heinonen (pno) Ondine ▲ ODE 756-2 [DDD]
Sibelius, J.:Sonatina Vn, w. I. Tateno (pno) *(rec Apr. 1980)* Finlandia ▲ 4509-95853-2 [AAD]

Aranovskaya, Alla (vn)—see also ORCHESTRAS & ENSEMBLES St. Petersburg String Quartet
Saint-Saëns, C.:Con 3 Vn, w. A. Tchernushenko (cnd), St. Petersburg State Academic Cappella SO Audiophile Classics ▲ 101.042

Arase, J. (perc)
Fukushi, N.:Chromosphere, w. M. Okada (perc), S. Sato (perc), H. Yamazaki (perc), S. Yoshihara (perc), T. Otaka (cnd), Tokyo PO *(rec live Tokyo Bunka-Kaikan, Large Hall, May 30, 1981)* Camerata ▲ 32CM 293 [AAD]

Arbuszov, Alexei (tuba)
Ustvolskaya, G.:Composition 1, w. Michail Tokarev (pic), Oleg Malov (pno) *(rec St. Petersburg Radio House, Jan. 1994)* Megadisc ▲ 7867

Archer, Carol (pno)
Hermit Songs, w. T. Palmer (cl) Koch International Classics ▲ KIC 7148 [DDD]

Archibald, P. (tpt)
Saint-Saëns, C.:Spt Tpt, w. I. Brown (pno), Nash Ensemble Virgin Classics ▲ 59514 [DDD]

Arciuli, Emanuele (pno)
Kogoj, M.:Music of, w. Crtomir Siskovic (vn)—Andante in E; Prelude; Portrait; 7 Pieces; Piano [complete collection] Stradivarius ▲ STV 33342

Arco, Annie d' (pno)
Boëllmann, L.:Son Vc, w. A. Navarra (vc) Calliope ▲ CAL 9854 [ADD]
Chopin, F.:Son Vc, w. A. Navarra (vc) Calliope ▲ CAL 9854 [ADD]
Eight Japanese Melodies, w. A. Navarra (vc) Calliope ▲ CAL 9818 [ADD]
Fauré, G.:Après un rêve, w. A. Navarra (vc) [cello-piano arr.] Calliope ▲ CAL 9854 [ADD]
Fauré, G.:Elégie, w. A. Navarra (vc) Calliope ▲ CAL 9854 [ADD]
Fauré, G.:Papillon, w. A. Navarra (vc) Calliope ▲ CAL 9854 [ADD]
Fauré, G.:Romance Vc, w. A. Navarra (vc) Calliope ▲ CAL 9854 [ADD]
Fauré, G.:Sérénade, w. A. Navarra (vc) Calliope ▲ CAL 9854 [ADD]
Saint-Saëns, C.:Allegro appassionato, w. A. Navarra (vc) Calliope ▲ CAL 9854 [ADD]
Saint-Saëns, C.:Son 1 Vc, w. A. Navarra (vc) Calliope ▲ CAL 9818 [ADD]

Arco, Annie d' (pno) (cont.)
Saint-Saëns, C.:Son 2 Vc, w. A. Navarra (vc) Calliope ▲ CAL 9818 [ADD]

Arcu, V. (vc)
Enescu, G.:Symphonie concertante, w. I. Conta (cnd), Romanian Radio-TV Orch Marco Polo ▲ 8.223141

Ardan, Laura (cl)—see also ORCHESTRAS & ENSEMBLES Atlanta Chamber Players
Kodály, Z.:Galanta Dances, w. Brice Andrus (hn), Y. Levi (cnd), Atlanta SO *(rec Atlanta, 1995-96)* Telarc ▲ CD 80413 [DDD]

Ardašev, Igor (pno)
Beethoven, L. van:Son 29 Pno, "Hammerklavier" Supraphon ▲ SUP 112194 [DDD]
Dvořák, A.:Slavonic Dances (comp), w. Renata Ardasev (pno) Supraphon ▲ SUP 0001 [DDD]
Liszt, F.:Pno Music (misc)—Études de concert (Waldesrauschen; Gnomenreigen; La Leggierezza); Sonetto 123 del Petrarca; Valse oubliée No. 1 in F# Supraphon ▲ 11 1519-2 [DDD]
Liszt, F.:Rhap espagnole Supraphon ▲ 11 1519-2 [DDD]
Liszt, F.:Son Pno Supraphon ▲ 11 1519-2 [DDD]
Mussorgsky, M.:Pictures at an Exhibition Supraphon ▲ SUP 112194 [DDD]
Novák, V.:My May Supraphon ▲ SUP 3183
Smetana, B.:Rêves Supraphon ▲ SUP 3183
Suk, J.:Pieces Pno, Op. 7—Idylls (1891); Love Song (1893) Supraphon ▲ SUP 3183
Suk, J.:Spring Supraphon ▲ SUP 3183
Tchaikovsky, P.:Con 1 Pno, w. J. Belohlávek (cnd), Czech PO *(rec 3/89)* Supraphon ▲ 110952-2 [DDD]
Tchaikovsky, P.:Pno Music—Capriccio, Op. 19/5; Nocturne, Op. 10/1; Piano Pieces, Op. 9/2 & Op. 14/72 Supraphon ▲ 110952-2 [DDD]
Ullmann, V.:Con Pno, w. G. Albrecht (cnd), Czech PO *(rec live, 1994-95)* Orfeo ("Musica Rediviva" series) ▲ 366951 [DDD]

Ardasev, Renata (pno)
Dvořák, A.:Slavonic Dances (comp), w. Igor Ardasev (pno) Supraphon ▲ SUP 0001 [DDD]

Ardeleanu, Mircea (perc)
Henze, H.-W.:El Cimarrón, w. P. Yoder (bar), M. Faust (fl), R. Evers (gtr) Koch Schwann 2-▲ 314 030 [DDD]

Arden, David (pno)
Berio, L.:Pno Music—5 Vars; Wasserklavier; Sequenza IV; Rounds; Erdenklavier; Luftklavier; Feuerklavier; Brin; Leaf; Petite Suite *(rec Ozawa Hall, Tanglewood, MA, Aug 16-18, 1996)* New Albion ▲ NA 089
Brown, E.:Music of—Folio; 4 Systems; 25 Pages; Corroboree; Perspectives; 3 Pieces; Forgotten Piece; Summer Suite, '95 New Albion ▲ NA 082
Górecki, H.-M.:Preludes (4) Pno Koch International Classics ▲ KIC 7301 [DDD]
Górecki, H.-M.:Son 1 Pno Koch International Classics ▲ KIC 7301 [DDD]
Pärt, A.:Für Alina Koch International Classics ▲ KIC 7301 [DDD]
Pärt, A.:Variationen zur Gesundung von Arinuschka Koch International Classics ▲ KIC 7301 [DDD]
Ustvolskaya, G.:Preludes Pno Koch International Classics ▲ KIC 7301 [DDD]
Ustvolskaya, G.:Son 6 Pno Koch International Classics ▲ KIC 7301 [DDD]

Arditti, Irvine (vn)—see also ORCHESTRAS & ENSEMBLES Arditti String Quartet
Berio, L.:Corale, w. J. Nott (cnd), Moscow PO *(rec Great Hall, Tchaikovsky Conservatory, Moscow, Mar 11-14, 1995)* BIS ▲ CD 772 [DDD]
Cage, J.:Freeman Études Vn—Books 3 & 4 *(rec Sept. 13 & 14, 1993)* Mode ▲ mode 37
Cage, J.:Freeman Études Vn Mode ▲ mode 32
Carter, E.:Riconoscenza (per Goffredo Petrassi) Montaigne ▲ MO 789003
Dillon, J.:Music of—Del cuarto elemento for Violin Montaigne ▲ MO 789003
Donatoni, F.:Argot Montaigne ▲ MO 789003
Estrada, J.:Canto oculto Montaigne ▲ MO 789003
Ferneyhough, B.:Intermedio alla ciaccona (1977) Montaigne ▲ MO 789003
Ferneyhough, B.:Terrain, w. Asko Ensemble Montaigne ▲ MO 782029
Hosokawa, T.:Vertical Time Study III, w. Icharo Nodaira (pno) Montaigne ▲ MO 782078
Mira Fornés, R.:Desde Tan Tien, w. J. Nott (cnd), Moscow PO *(rec Great Hall, Tchaikovsky Conservatory, Moscow, Mar 11-14, 1995)* BIS ▲ CD 772 [DDD]
Nono, L.:Hay que caminar, w. David Alberman (vn) Montaigne ▲ MO 789005
Nono, L.:Lontananza, w. A. Richard (tapes/sound effects) Montaigne ▲ MO 782004 [DDD]
Nono, L.:Madrigale per piu "caminantes", w. A. Richard (tapes/sound effects) Montaigne ▲ MO 782004 [DDD]
Pablo, L. de:Il Violino spagnolo Montaigne ▲ MO 789003
Xenakis, I.:DOX-ORKH, w. J. Nott (cnd), Moscow PO *(rec Great Hall, Tchaikovsky Conservatory, Moscow, Mar 11-14, 1995)* BIS ▲ CD 772 [DDD]

Arel, Gaston (org)
Chaconnes et Passacailles REM ▲ 311154 [DDD]

Arends, André (a sax)—see ORCHESTRAS & ENSEMBLES Aurelia Saxophone Quartet

Arens, Rolf-Dieter (pno)
Mozart, W.A.:Rondo Pno, K.485 LaserLight ▲ 15 877 [DDD]
Mozart, W.A.:Son 11 Pno LaserLight ▲ 15 877 [DDD]
Mozart, W.A.:Vars Pno, K.265 LaserLight ▲ 15 877 [DDD]
Webern, A.:Songs, w. Roswitha Trexler (sop), C.P. Flor (cnd), Berlin SO Berlin Classics ▲ BER 9049 [DDD]

Argerich, Martha (pno)
Bach, J.S.:Sons VI, BWV 1027-1029, w. M. Maisky (vc) Deutsche Grammophon ▲ 415471-2 [DDD]
Bartók, B.:Son Pno Exclusive ▲ EXL 48 [AAD]
Bartók, B.:Son 1 Vn & Pno, w. G. Kremer (vn) Deutsche Grammophon ▲ 427351-2 [DDD]
Beethoven, L. van:Con 1 Pno, w. S. Ozawa (cnd), Bavarian RSO *(rec live 1983)* Artists ▲ FED 69 [ADD]
Beethoven, L. van:Con 1 Pno, w. G. Sinopoli (cnd), Philharmonia Orch Deutsche Grammophon ("Masters" series) ▲ 445504-2
Beethoven, L. van:Con 2 Pno, w. G. Sinopoli (cnd), Philharmonia Orch Deutsche Grammophon ("Masters" series) ▲ 445504-2
Beethoven, L. van:Die Geschöpfe des Prometheus (sels), w. C. Abbado (cnd), Berlin PO, Berlin Singakademie *(rec May 23-25, 1993)* Sony Classical ▲ SK 53978 [DDD]
Beethoven, L. van:Son 1 Vc, w. M. Maisky (vc) Deutsche Grammophon ▲ 431801-2 [DDD]
Beethoven, L. van:Son 2 Vc, w. M. Maisky (vc) Deutsche Grammophon ▲ 431801-2 [DDD]
Beethoven, L. van:Son 3 Vc, w. M. Maisky (vc) Deutsche Grammophon ▲ 437514-2 [DDD]
Beethoven, L. van:Son 4 Vc, w. M. Maisky (vc) Deutsche Grammophon ▲ 437514-2 [DDD]
Beethoven, L. van:Son 5 Vc, w. M. Maisky (vc) Deutsche Grammophon ▲ 437514-2 [DDD]
Beethoven, L. van:Son 1 Vn, w. G. Kremer (vn) Deutsche Grammophon ▲ 415138-2 [DDD]
Beethoven, L. van:Son 2 Vn, w. G. Kremer (vn) Deutsche Grammophon ▲ 415138-2 [DDD]
Beethoven, L. van:Son 3 Vn, w. G. Kremer (vn) Deutsche Grammophon ▲ 415138-2 [DDD]
Beethoven, L. van:Son 4 Vn, w. G. Kremer (vn) Deutsche Grammophon ▲ 419787-2 [DDD]
Beethoven, L. van:Son 5 Vn, "Spring", w. G. Kremer (vn) Deutsche Grammophon ▲ 419787-2 [DDD]
Beethoven, L. van:Son 6 Vn, w. Gidon Kremer (vn) Deutsche Grammophon ▲ 445652-2
Beethoven, L. van:Son 7 Vn, w. Gidon Kremer (vn) Deutsche Grammophon ▲ 445652-2
Beethoven, L. van:Son 8 Vn, w. Gidon Kremer (vn) Deutsche Grammophon ▲ 445652-2
Beethoven, L. van:Son 9 Vn, "Kreutzer", w. Gidon Kremer (vn) *(rec Auditorium Stravinski, Montreux, Mar 1994)* Deutsche Grammophon ▲ 447054-2 [DDD]
Beethoven, L. van:Son 10 Vn, w. Gidon Kremer (vn) *(rec Auditorium Stravinski, Montreux, Mar 1994)* Deutsche Grammophon ▲ 447054-2 [DDD]
Beethoven, L. van:Vars on "Ein Mädchen oder Weibchen" from Mozart's *Die Zauberflöte*, w. M Maisky (vc) Deutsche Grammophon ▲ 431801-2 [DDD]
Beethoven, L. van:Vars on "See, the Conquering Hero Comes" from Handel's *Judas Maccabaeus*, w. M. Maisky (vc) Deutsche Grammophon ▲ 437514-2
Beethoven, L. van:Vars on "Bei Männern" from Mozart's *Die Zauberflöte*, w. M. Maisky (vc) Deutsche Grammophon ▲ 431801-2 [DDD]

▲ = CD ♦ = Enhanced CD Δ = MD ■ = Cassette Tape □ = DCC

Argerich, Martha (pno) (cont.)
Brahms, J.:Rhaps Pno, Op. 79 *(rec 1960 & 1971)* Deutsche Grammophon ("The Originals" series) ▲ 447430-2
Brahms, J.:Son for 2 Pnos, w. A. Rabinovitch (pno) *(rec Berlin, Apr. 1993)* Teldec ▲ 92257-2 [DDD]
Brahms, J.:Vars on a Theme by Haydn, w. A. Rabinovitch (pno) *(rec Berlin, Apr. 1993)* Teldec ▲ 92257-2 [DDD]
Brahms, J.:Waltzes Pno, Op. 39, w. A. Rabinovitch (pno) *(rec Berlin, Apr. 1993)* Teldec ▲ 92257-2 [DDD]
Chopin, F.:Barcarolle Pno *(rec 1960 & 1971)* Deutsche Grammophon ("The Originals" series) ▲ 447430-2
Chopin, F.:Con 1 Pno, w. J. Levine (cnd), London SO Exclusive ▲ EXL 48 [AAD]
Chopin, F.:Con 1 Pno, w. A. Orizio (cnd), Gasparo da Salò Orch *(rec live, Brescia 6/6/67)* Arkadia ▲ 574 [ADD]
Chopin, F.:Con 1 Pno, w. C. Abbado (cnd), London SO *(rec Walthamstow Town Hall, London, Feb 1968)* Deutsche Grammophon ("The Originals" series) ▲ 449719-2 [ADD]
Chopin, F.:Con 1 Pno, w. A. Orizio (cnd), Gasparo da Salò Orch *(rec live 6/67)* Fonè ▲ 91F03 [ADD]
Chopin, F.:Music of—Preludes (24), Op. 28; Preludes Nos. 25 & 26; Mazurkas, Op. 59, Nos. 1–3; Scherzo No. 3, Op. 39 Deutsche Grammophon ▲ 431584-2
Chopin, F.:Pno Music (misc)—Barcarolle, Op. 60; Etude in c# Op. 10/4; 3 Mazurkas (Op. 24/2, & 59/1 & 2); 2 Nocturnes, Opp. 15/1 & 55/2; Scherzo in c#, Op. 39 Arkadia ▲ 574 [ADD]
Chopin, F.:Pno Music (misc)—Barcarolle, Op. 60; Etude, Op. 10/4; Mazurkas, Opp. 24/2, 59/1 & 2; Nocturnes, Opp. 15/1, 55/2; Scherzo, Op. 39/3 *(rec live 6/67)* Fonè ▲ 91F03 [ADD]
Chopin, F.:Pno Music (misc), w. Vladimir Ashkenazy (pno), Stanislav Bunin (pno), Halina Czerny-Stefanska (pno), Jan Ekier (pno), Yuval Fichman (pno), Kemal Gekic (pno), Adam Harasiewicz (pno), Krzysztof Jablonski (pno), Louis Kentner (pno), Jean-Marc Luisada (pno), Garrick Ohlsson (pno), Ivo Pogorelich (pno), Maurizio Pollini (pno), Dang Thai Son (pno)—includes Ballade (Nos. 1 & 2); Barcarolle, Op. 60; Concerto Nos. 1 & 2; Etudes (Op. 10, Nos. 1, 5, 8, 10 & 12 & Op. 25, No. 10, 18 & 25); Grand valse brillante; Impromptus (Nos. 3 & 4); Mazurkas (Op. 24, Nos. 1–4; Op. 30, Nos. 1–4; Op. 50, No. 32; Op. 59, Nos. 1–3); Nocturnes (Op. 9, No. 3; Op. 37, No. 12; Op. 48, No. 13; Op. 55, No. 16)Polonaise (Op. 40, Nos. 3 & 4; Op. 44, No. 5; Op. 53, No. 6; Op. 61, No. 7); Preludes (Op. 28 Nos. 13–18, 21–24 & Op. 45, No. 25); Scherzos (Nos. 1–3); Sonatas (Nos. 2 & 3); Waltzes (No. 1 & 6) LaserLight 5–▲ 15 961 [ADD/DDD]
Chopin, F.:Preludes, Op. 28 Deutsche Grammophon ▲ 431584-2 [ADD]
Chopin, F.:Scherzos—Op. 39/3 *(rec 1960 & 1971)* Deutsche Grammophon ("The Originals" series) ▲ 447430-2
Debussy, C.:Estampes Exclusive ▲ EXL 65 [ADD]
Debussy, C.:Estampes Enterprise ("Documents") ▲ ENT LV 960 [ADD]
Janácek, L.:Son Vn, w. G. Kremer (vn) Deutsche Grammophon ▲ 427351-2 [DDD]
Liszt, F.:Con 1 Pno, w. C. Abbado (cnd), London SO *(rec Walthamstow Town Hall, London, Feb 1968)* Deutsche Grammophon ("The Originals" series) ▲ 449719-2 [ADD]
Liszt, F.:Études de concert (3) Pno— No. 2, "La leggierezza" Arkadia ▲ 574 [ADD]
Liszt, F.:Hungarian Rhaps—No. 6 *(rec 1960 & 1971)* Deutsche Grammophon ("The Originals" series) ▲ 447430-2
Liszt, F.:Prometheus, w. C. Abbado (cnd), Berlin PO, Berlin Singakademie *(rec May 23–25, 1993)* Sony Classical ▲ SK 53978 [DDD]
Liszt, F.:Son Pno *(rec 1960 & 1971)* Deutsche Grammophon ("The Originals" series) ▲ 447430-2
The Lockenhaus Collection:Encore! Musical Jokes with Gidon Kremer and Friends, w. Borodin String Quartet, et al. Philips ▲ 432252-2 PH [DDD]
Mendelssohn, F.:Con in d Vn, Pno & Strs, w. G. Kremer (vn), Orpheus CO Deutsche Grammophon ▲ 427338-2 [DDD]
Messiaen, O.:Thème et vars, w. G. Kremer (vn) Deutsche Grammophon ▲ 427351-2 [DDD]
Mozart, W.A.:Andante & Vars Pno 4-Hands, w. A. Rabinovitch (pno) *(rec Berlin, Nov. 1992 & Dec. 1993)* Teldec ▲ 91378-2 [DDD]
Mozart, W.A.:Son Pno 4-Hands, K.381, w. A. Rabinovitch (pno) *(rec Berlin, Nov. 1992 & Dec. 1993)* Teldec ▲ 91378-2 [DDD]
Mozart, W.A.:Son Pno 4-Hands, K.521, w. A. Rabinovitch (pno) *(rec Berlin, Nov. 1992 & Dec. 1993)* Teldec ▲ 91378-2 [DDD]
Mozart, W.A.:Son Pnos, K.448, w. A. Rabinovitch (pno) *(rec Berlin, Nov. 1992 & Dec. 1993)* Teldec ▲ 91378-2 [DDD]
Prokofiev, S.:Con 3 Pno, w. C. Abbado (cnd), Berlin PO Deutsche Grammophon 3–▲ 435151-2 [ADD]
Prokofiev, S.:Con 3 Pno, w. C. Abbado (cnd), Berlin PO Deutsche Grammophon ▲ 415062-2 [AAD]
Prokofiev, S.:Con 3 Pno, w. C. Abbado (cnd), Berlin PO *(rec Jesus-Christus-Kirche, Berlin, May–June 1967)* Deutsche Grammophon ▲ 447438-2 [ADD]
Prokofiev, S.:Mélodies, w. G. Kremer (vn) Deutsche Grammophon ▲ 431803-2 [DDD]
Prokofiev, S.:Son 7 Pno—3rd movt. Arkadia ▲ 574 [ADD]
Prokofiev, S.:Son 7 Pno Exclusive ▲ EXL 65 [ADD]
Prokofiev, S.:Son Vn, Op. 94bis, w. G. Kremer (vn) Deutsche Grammophon ▲ 431803-2 [DDD]
Prokofiev, S.:Son 1 Vn, w. G. Kremer (vn) Deutsche Grammophon ▲ 431803-2 [DDD]
Prokofiev, S.:Toccata Pno *(rec 1960 & 1971)* Deutsche Grammophon ("The Originals" series) ▲ 447430-2
Rabinovitch, A.:Music for Pnos, w. A. Rabinovitch (pno), M. Adamovitch (pno), A. Ieriomine (pno), A. Batagov (pno)—Musique Populaire for 2 Pianos; La Belle Musique for 4 Pianos; Liebliches Lied for Piano 4-hands; Musique triste, parfois tragique *(rec 1990 & 1992)* Valois ▲ V 4694 [DDD]
Rachmaninoff, S.:Con 3 Pno, w. R. Chailly (cnd), Berlin RSO *(rec live, Berlin)* Philips ▲ 446673-2
Rachmaninoff, S.:Suite 1 for 2 Pnos, w. A. Rabinovich (pno) Teldec ▲ 9031-74717-2 ZK
Rachmaninoff, S.:Suite 2 for 2 Pnos, w. A. Rabinovich (pno) Teldec ▲ 9031-74717-2 ZK
Rachmaninoff, S.:Symphonic Dances, w. A. Rabinovich (pno) Teldec ▲ 9031-74717-2 ZK
Ravel, M.:Con in G Pno, w. C. Abbado (cnd), Rome RAI SO Enterprise ("Documents" series) ▲ ENT LV 960 [ADD]
Ravel, M.:Con in G Pno, w. C. Abbado (cnd), London SO Deutsche Grammophon ▲ 423665-2 [DDD]
Ravel, M.:Con in G Pno, w. C. Abbado (cnd), Rome RAI SO Exclusive ▲ EXL 65 [ADD]
Ravel, M.:Con in G Pno, w. C. Abbado (cnd), Rome RAI SO Originals ▲ ORISH 851
Ravel, M.:Con in G Pno, w. C. Abbado (cnd), Berlin PO *(rec Jesus-Christus-Kirche, Berlin, May–June 1967)* Deutsche Grammophon ▲ 447438-2 [ADD]
Ravel, M.:Gaspard de la nuit *(rec Studio Lankwitz, Berlin, Nov 1974)* Deutsche Grammophon ▲ 447438-2 [ADD]
Ravel, M.:Jeux d'eau *(rec 1960 & 1971)* Deutsche Grammophon ("The Originals" series) ▲ 447430-2
Saint-Saëns, C.:Carnival of the Animals, w. N. Freire (pno), G. Kremer (vn), I. van Keulen (vn), T. Zimmermann (va), M. Maisky (vc), et al. Philips ("Digital Classics" series) ▲ 416841-2 [DDD]
Schubert, Franz:Son Arpeggione, w. M. Maisky (vc) Philips ▲ 412230-2 [DDD]
Schumann, R.:Con Pno, w. N. Harnoncourt (cnd), CO of Europe *(rec Graz, Germany, July 1992)* Teldec ▲ 90696-2 [DDD]
Schumann, R.:Con Pno, w. A. Jordan (cnd), Swiss Romande Orch *(rec live 1993)* Artists ▲ FED 69 [ADD]
Schumann, R.:Fant Pno EMI Classics ("Studio" series) ▲ CDM 63576 [ADD]
Schumann, R.:Fant Pno Enterprise ("Documents" series) ▲ ENT LV 960 [ADD]
Schumann, R.:Fant Pno Exclusive ▲ EXL 48 [AAD]
Schumann, R.:Fantasiestücke Cl, w. M. Maisky (vc) Philips ▲ 412230-2 [DDD]
Schumann, R.:Fantasiestücke Pno, Op. 12 EMI Classics ("Studio" series) ▲ CDM 63576 [ADD]
Schumann, R.:Kinderszenen Deutsche Grammophon ▲ 410653-2 [DDD]
Schumann, R.:Kreisleriana Deutsche Grammophon ▲ 410653-2 [DDD]
Schumann, R.:Son 1 Vn, w. M. Kremer (ten) Deutsche Grammophon ▲ 419235-2 [DDD]
Schumann, R.:Son 2 Vn, w. M. Kremer (ten) Deutsche Grammophon ▲ 419235-2 [DDD]
Schumann, R.:Stücke im Volkston, w. M. Maisky (vc) Philips ▲ 412230-2 [DDD]
Scriabin, A.:Sym 5, w. C. Abbado (cnd), Berlin PO, Berlin Singakademie *(rec May 23–25, 1993)* Sony Classical ▲ SK 53978 [DDD]
Strauss, R.:Burleske, w. C. Abbado (cnd), Berlin PO *(rec Dec. 31, 1992)* Sony Classical ▲ SK 52565

Argerich, Martha (pno) (cont.)
Stravinsky, I.:Les Noces, w. A. Mory (sop), P. Parker (mez), J. Mitchinson (ten), P. Hudson (bass), H. Francesch (pno), K. Zimerman (pno), C. Katsaris (pno), L. Bernstein (cnd), English Bach Festival Orch, English Bach Festival Chorus [R] Deutsche Grammophon ("20th Century Classics" series) ▲ 423251-2 [ADD]
Tchaikovsky, P.:Con 1 Pno, w. C. Dutoit (cnd), Royal PO Deutsche Grammophon ▲ 415062-2 [ADD]
Tchaikovsky, P.:Con 1 Pno, w. C. Abbado (cnd), Berlin PO *(rec Berlin, Dec 1994)* Deutsche Grammophon ▲ 449816-2 [DDD]
Tchaikovsky, P.:Con 1 Pno, w. C. Dutoit (cnd), Royal PO Deutsche Grammophon ▲ 431609-2
Tchaikovsky, P.:Con 1 Pno, w. K. Kondrashin (cnd), Bavarian RSO *(rec 1980)* Philips ▲ 446673-2
Tchaikovsky, P.:Nutcracker Suite, w. Nicolas Economou (pno) [arr N. Economou for 2 pnos] *(rec Munich, Mar 1983)* Deutsche Grammophon ▲ 449816-2 [DDD]

Arico, Fortunato (vc)
Brahms, J.:Sextet Strs, Op. 36, w. P. Carmirelli (vn), J. Toth (vn), P. Naegele (va), C. Levine (va), D. Reichenberger (vc) Sony Classical ▲ SMK 46249 [ADD] ■ SMT 46249

Arimany, Claude (fl)
Abel, C.F.:Son Fl, Vc & Hpd, w. A. Schmöller (vc), M. Grüber (hpd) Motette ▲ MOT CD 30141 [DDD]
Bach, C.P.E.:Trio Son Fl, H.586, w. A. Schmöller (vc), M. Grüber (hpd) Motette ▲ MOT CD 30141 [DDD]
Devienne, F.:Cons Fl (comp), w. V. Esipov (cnd), Russian CO—Nos. 6, 11 & 12 Aura Classics ▲ AU 32172
Devienne, F.:Cons Fl (comp), w. D. Mihailovic (cnd), Russian CO—Nos. 3, 8 & 10 Aura Classics ▲ AU 32162
Devienne, F.:Cons Fl (comp), w. J. Przybylski (cnd), Gdansk SO—Nos. 2, 4, 5 & 7 Aura Classics ▲ AU 32002
Kirnberger, J.P.:Son Fl, w. A. Schöller (vc), M. Grüber (hpd) Motette ▲ MOT CD 30141 [DDD]
Mozart, W.A.:Andante Fl, w. J.-P. Rampal (cnd), Hungarian Virtuosi CO PROdigital ▲ PRO 2419 [DDD]
Mozart, W.A.:Con 1 Fl, w. J.-P. Rampal (cnd), Hungarian Virtuosi CO PROdigital ▲ PRO 2419 [DDD]
Mozart, W.A.:Rondo Fl, w. J.-P. Rampal (cnd), Hungarian Virtuosi CO PROdigital ▲ PRO 2419 [DDD]
Müthel, J.G.:Son Fl, w. A. Schöller (vc), M. Grüber (hpd) Motette ▲ MOT CD 30141 [DDD]

Arita, Chiyoko (hpd)
18th Century "New Generation" German Flute Music, w. M. Arita, Tetsuya Nakano (vl) *(rec Nov. 11–12, 1991 & Feb. 2)* Denon ▲ CO 75025 [DDD]
Rameau, J.P.:Pièces de clavecin en concert, w. N. Wakamatsu (vn), W. Kuijken (vl), M. Arita (trns fl/pic) Denon ▲ CO 79045 [DDD]

Arita, Masahiro (fl)
Bach, J.S.:Ov Fl, BWV 1067, w. A. Manze (cnd), La Stravaganza Cologne *(rec Sendesaal of German Radio, Cologne, June 2–3, 1994)* Denon 2–▲ DEN 78965 [DDD]
18th Century "New Generation" German Flute Music, w. Chiyoko Arita (hpd), Tetsuya Nakano (vl) *(rec Nov. 11–12, 1991 & Feb. 2)* Denon ▲ CO 75025 [DDD]
Telemann, G.P.:Fants Fl Denon ▲ CO 76685 [DDD]
Telemann, G.P.:Qts, Book 4, w. Ryo Terakado (baroque vn), Kaori Uemura (vl), Cristophe Rousset (hpd) Denon ▲ DEN 78844 [DDD]
Vivaldi, A.:Cons Fl (misc), w. Bach-Mozart Ensemble Tokyo—RV.438 & 440 *(rec June 22–26, 1992)* Denon ▲ CO 75198 [DDD]
Vivaldi, A.:Cons Fl, Op. 10, w. Bach-Mozart Ensemble Tokyo Denon ▲ CO 77288 [DDD]
Vivaldi, A.:Con Fl Ob, RV.107, w. M. Homma (ob), N. Wakamatsu (vn), K. Dosaka (bn), Bach-Mozart Ensemble Tokyo *(rec June 22–26, 1992)* Denon ▲ CO 75198 [DDD]

Arita, Masahiro (fl/pic)
Rameau, J.P.:Pièces de clavecin en concert, w. C. Arita (hpd), N. Wakamatsu (vn), W. Kuijken (vl) Denon ▲ CO 79045 [DDD]
Telemann, G.P.:Cons (misc), w. Eric Hoeprich (chl), Hans Peter Westermann (ob), Dane Roberts (db), David Sinclair (db), La Stravaganza Cologne—in E for Transverse Flute, Oboe d'amore, Viola d'amore, Strings & Continuo; in e for Transverse Flute, Violin, Strings & Continuo; in D for Transverse Flute, Strings & Continuo; in E♭ for Strings & Continuo; in G for Transverse Flute, Chalumeau, Oboe, 2 Double Basses, Strings & Continuo *(rec Cologne, May 30–June 3, 1994)* Denon ("Aliare" series) ▲ CO 78933 [DDD]

Arkadiev, Mikhail (pno)
Borodin, A.:Songs, w. Dmitri Hvorostovsky (bar)—For the shores of your distant homeland Philips ▲ 442536-2
Rachmaninoff, S.:Songs, w. Dmitri Hvorostovsky (bar)—'Tis Pleasant Here; Everything Passes; Answer Was Given; Song for My Cornfield; Heed Me Not, Dear; I Wait for You; Night; Night Is Sad; I Am Alone Again Philips ▲ 446666-2
Rachmaninoff, S.:Songs, w. Dmitri Hvorostovsky (bar)—Morning; Child, you are beautiful like a flower; How I languish; Spring waters Philips ▲ 442536-2
Rimsky-Korsakov, N.:Songs, w. Dmitri Hvorostovsky (bar)—The clouds begin to scatter; The octave; The wave breaks into spray Philips ▲ 442536-2
Sviridov, G.:Russia Cast Adrift, w. Dmitri Hvorostovsky (bar)—Autumn; I Left My Home Behind; Open before Me, O My Guardian Angel; Silver Path; Russia Cast Adrift; Simon, Peter... Where Are You? Come to Me; Where Are You, O My Father's House; Beyond the Hills of the Milky Way; It Sounds, It Sounds, the Fateful Trumpet; An Owl Cries in Autumn; Oh I Believe, I Believe in Happiness!; O My Homeland, O Happy & Eternal Hour Philips ▲ 446666-2
Tchaikovsky, P.:Songs, w. Dmitri Hvorostovsky (bar)—Ah, if only you could for 1 moment; Amid the din of the ball; I should like in a single word; My protector, my angel, my friend; It happened in the early spring; I bless you, forests; Not a word, beloved; The love of a dead man; On the golden cornfields; Whether the day reigns; We sat together Philips ▲ 442536-2

Arm, Theodore (vn)
Herrmann, B.:Souvenirs de Voyage, w. D. Schifrin (cl), P. Frank (vn), W. Trampler (va), W. Lash (vc) *(rec 6 & 7/90)* Delos ▲ 3088 [DDD]
Porter, Q.:Qnt Cl, w. D. Schifrin (cl), E. Sato (vn), P. Neubauer (va), W. Lash (vc) *(rec 6 & 7/90)* Delos ▲ 3088 [DDD]
Vienna Nocturne:The Mair-Davis Duo & Friends Play Waltzes & Sonatas of the Golden Age, w. Mair-Davis Duo, Mary Lou Rylands (vc), Susan Thomas (fl) North Star ▲ NS0034 [DDD]

Armand, Georges (vn)
Corelli, A.:Concerti grossi, Op. 6, w. Jean-Patrice Brosse (hpd), G. Armand (cnd), Toulouse CO—Nos. 1 in D & 8 in g, "Christmas Concerto" EMI Classics ("Baroque" series) ▲ CDK 65731

Armbruster, Frank (gtr)—see ORCHESTRAS & ENSEMBLES Duo Favori

Armengaud, Jean-Pierre (pno)
Poulenc, F.:Chamber Music, w. France Radio PO Soloists—Son for Vn & Pno; Son for Ob & Pno; Elegy for Hn & Pno; Son for 2 Cls; Son for Vc & Pno; Sxt for Pno, Fl, Ob, Cl, Bn & Hn; Son for Fl & Pno; Trio for Pno, Ob & Bn; Son for Cl & Pno; Villanelle for Pic & Pno; Son for Cl & Bn; Son for Hn, Tpt & Trbn Accord 2–▲ ACD 202022 [DDD]
Russian Avant-Garde Music Nuova Era ▲ NUO CD 7263
Satie, E.:Aperçus désagréables, w. Dominique Merlet (pno) Mandala ▲ MAN 4882
Satie, E.:La belle excentrique, w. Dominique Merlet (pno) Mandala ▲ MAN 4882
Satie, E.:En habit de cheval, w. Dominique Merlet (pno) Mandala ▲ MAN 4882
Satie, E.:Morceaux en forme de poire, w. Dominique Merlet (pno) Mandala ▲ MAN 4882
Satie, E.:Parade, w. Dominique Merlet (pno) [arr for pno 4-hands] Mandala ▲ MAN 4882
Satie, E.:Petites pièces montées, w. Dominique Merlet (pno) Mandala ▲ MAN 4882

Armin, Adele (vn)—see also ORCHESTRAS & ENSEMBLES Catherine Wilson Trio
Duets:Ofra Harnoy & Friends, w. O. Harnoy (vc), Michael Dussek (pno), Orford String Quartet, Maureen Forrester (cta), Andrew Davis (pno), Jeanne Baxtresser (fl), Catherine Wilson (pno), Paul Brodie (sax), Shauna Rolston (vc), Armin Strings, Canadian Piano Trio, Adele Armin (vn) Mastersound ▲ MST 30 [DDD]

Armon, William (vn)
Bach, Joh. Christian:Sinf concertante Fl, w. J. Galway (fl), D. Wickens (ob), N. Jones (vc), L. Jones (cnd), London Little Orch Elektra/Nonesuch ■ 71165-4

Armstrong, D. (elec bass)—see ORCHESTRAS & ENSEMBLES Present Music

INSTRUMENT.

INSTRUMENTALISTS 447

Armstrong, D. C. (perc)
Crawford, R.:Songs (3), w. P. Berlin (mez), J. Ostryniec (ob), P. Hoffman (pno) CRI ▲ CD 658 [ADD]
Armstrong, E. Duncan (fl)—see ORCHESTRAS & ENSEMBLES Pennsylvania Wind Quintet
Armstrong-Ouellette, Susan (org)
Bonnet, J.:Vars de Concert AFKA ▲ SK 518
Buck, D.:Home, Sweet Home [1892 Johnson & Son Opus 778 Org, Sacred Heart Church, Waterbury, CT] AFKA ▲ SK 520
Guilmant, A.:Son 8 Org AFKA ▲ SK 518
Hannahs, R.:Tpt Tune AFKA ▲ SK 518
A Methuen Mosaic AFKA ▲ AFK 531
Musique de la Basilique *(rec Basilica of Our Lady of Perpetual Help Mission Church, Boston)* AFKA ▲ SK 538
Parker, H.:Son Org [1892 Johnson & Son Opus 778 Organ, Sacred Heart Church, Waterbury, CT] AFKA ▲ SK 520
Rheinberger, J.:Sons Org [1892 Johnson & Son Opus 778 Org, Sacred Heart Church, Waterbury, CT] AFKA ▲ SK 520
Rheinberger, J.:Sons Org—No. 17 in B, Op. 181 AFKA ▲ SK 518
Widor, C.M.:Bach's Memento [1892 Johnson & Son Org, Op. 778] *(rec Sacred Heart Church, Waterbury, CT)* Afka ▲ SK 520
Widor, C.M.:Transcriptions [1892 Johnson & Son Opus 778 Organ, Sacred Heart Church, Waterbury, CT]—Bach's Memento (Pastorale; Miserere Mei; Aria; Marche du Veilleur de Nuit; Sicilienne; Mattheus-Finale AFKA ▲ SK 520
Armytage, Christopher Green (pno)
Simpson, R.:Qt Hn, w. R. Watkins (hn), P. Lowbury (vn), C. Dearnley (vc) Hyperion ▲ CDA 66695
Simpson, R.:Son Vn, w. Pauline Lowbury (vn) Hyperion ▲ CDA 66737
Simpson, R.:Trio Hn, w. R. Watkins (hn), P. Lowbury (vn) Hyperion ▲ CDA 66695
Arnaltes, Edemiro (pno)
The Art of Alfredo Kraus, w. A. Kraus (ten), Canaria Grand PO [cnd:Gian Paolo Sanzogno] RNE/Spanish Radio 3-▲ 65015/16/17
Arnaud, Jean-Pierre (ob)
Klein, G.:Divert Ob, w. Jean-Marc Liet (ob), Rémi Lerner (cl), Christian Rocca (cl), Michel Tavernier (bn), Amaury Wallez (bn), Éric Karcher (hn), Philippe Queyraud (hn) Arion ▲ ARN 68272 [DDD]
Arner, Leonard (ob)
Bach, J.S.:Cant 131, w. Loren Driscoll (ten), Robert Oliver (bass), R. Craft (cnd), Columbia SO Sony Classical ("Essential Classics" series) 2-▲ SB2K 62656
Arnheim, Avigail (cl)
Ravel, M.:Intro & Allegro, w. A. Giles (hp), E. Talmi (fl), R. Kaminkovsky (vn), R. Mozes (vn), Y. Kaminkovsky (va), Y. Alperin (vc) PWK Classics ▲ PWK 1141 [DDD]
Arnheim, Yossi (fl)
Dvořák, A.:Sonatina Vn, w. Daniel Gortler (pno) Meridian ▲ MER 84320 [DDD]
Martinů, B.:Madrigal Son, w. Irit Rub-Levi (pno), Elyakum Saltzman (vn) Kontrapunkt ▲ KPT 32205
Martinů, B.:Promenades, w. Elyakum Saltzman (vn), Irit Rub-Levi (pno) Kontrapunkt ▲ KPT 32205
Martinů, B.:Son Fl & Pno, w. Irit Rub-Levi (pno) Kontrapunkt ▲ KPT 32205
Martinů, B.:Son Fl, Vn & Pno, w. Elyakum Saltman (vn), Irit Rub-Levi (pno) Kontrapunkt ▲ KPT 32205
Martinů, B.:Trio Fl, w. Marcel Bergman (vc), Irit Rub-Levi (pno) Kontrapunkt ▲ KPT 32205
Reinecke, C.:Son Fl, w. Daniel Gortler (pno) Meridian ▲ MER 84320 [DDD]
Schubert, Franz:Intro & Vars Fl on "Tröckne Blumen", w. Daniel Gortler (pno) Meridian ▲ MER 84320 [DDD]
Arnold, Bruce (processed gtr)—see ORCHESTRAS & ENSEMBLES Act of Finding
Arnold, Peter (hn)
Dauprat, L.-F.:Qnt Hn & Strs, w. A. Grötzinger (vn), A. Henschke (vn/va), H.-B. Henscke (va), P. Gerschwitz (vc) Bayer ▲ BR 100236 [DDD]
Mozart, W.A.:Qnt Hn, K.407, w. A. Grötzinger (vn), A. Henschke (vn/va), H.-B. Henscke (va), P. Gerschwitz (vc) Bayer ▲ BR 100236 [DDD]
Stamitz, A.:Qnt Hn, w. A. Grötzinger (vn), A. Henschke (vn/va), H.-B. Henscke (va), P. Gerschwitz (vc) Bayer ▲ BR 100236 [DDD]
Arnold, S. (pno)
Liszt, F.:Études d'exécution transcendante d'après Paganini, S.140 Ambitus ▲ 97878 [DDD]
Liszt, F.:Harmonies poétiques et religieuses—Funerailles Ambitus ▲ 97878 [DDD]
Liszt, F.:Son Pno Ambitus ▲ 97878 [DDD]
Arnold, Stanko (tpt)
Eben, Petr:Windows, w. Irena Chribková (org) Multisonic ▲ MUL 310347 [DDD]
Arnóth, Balázs (bn)
Bengraf, J.:Sacred Music, w. Ingrid Kertesi (sop), Katalin Gémes (mez), Gábor Kállay (ten), Ákos Ambrus (bar), István Ella (org), Zsolt Kovács (vc), Vilmos Buza (db), J. Dobra (cnd), Vienna-Szász CO, Tomkins Vocal Ensemble—Te Deum; O sacrum convivium; Libera me; Gloria [from Missa solemnis in D] Hungaroton ▲ HCD 31609 [DDD]
Druschetzky, G.:Missa solemnis, w. Ingrid Kertesi (sop), Katalin Gémes (mez), Gábor Kállay (ten), Ákos Ambrus (bar), István Ella (org), Zsolt Kovács (vc), Vilmos Buza (db), J. Dobra (cnd), Vienna-Szász CO, Tomkins Vocal Ensemble Hungaroton ▲ HCD 31609 [DDD]
Arnowitz, Cecil (va)
Purcell, H.:Chamber Music, w. Alberto Lysy (vn), Robert Masters (vn), Yehudi Menuhin (vn), Walter Gerhard (va), Derek Simpson (vc), Ambrose Gauntlett (vl), Roy Jesson (hpd/org)—Trio Sons Nos. 2 in C, 6 in G & 8 in G; Fants Nos. 4 in g, 7 in c, 8 in d & 13 in F, "Upon One Note" EMI Classics ("Baroque" series) ▲ CDK 65734
Arntorp, Stig (perc)
Bäck, S.-E.:Favola, w. Thore Janson (cl), Bengt Arsenius (perc), Roland Johansson (perc), Björn Liljequist (perc) Caprice ▲ CAP 21490
Aronov, Ben (pno)
The Other Portrait, w. K. Peplowski (cl), Ken Peplowski (t sax), Ken Peplowski Jazz Quartet, Bulgarian National SO [cnd:Ljubomir Denev] Concord Concerto ▲ CCD 42043 [DDD]
Aronowitz, Cecil (va)
Brahms, J.:Qnt 1 Strs, w. Amadeus String Quartet Deutsche Grammophon 3-▲ 419875-2 [ADD]
Brahms, J.:Qnt 2 Strs, w. Amadeus String Quartet Deutsche Grammophon 3-▲ 419875-2 [ADD]
Brahms, J.:Sextet Strs, Op. 18, w. A. Pleeth (vc), Amadeus String Quartet Deutsche Grammophon 3-▲ 419875-2 [ADD]
Brahms, J.:Sextet Strs, Op. 36, w. A. Pleeth (vc), Amadeus String Quartet Deutsche Grammophon 3-▲ 419875-2 [ADD]
Brahms, J.:Songs, Op. 91, w. Janet Baker (mez), André Previn (pno) EMI Classics ("Doublefforte" series) 2-▲ CDFB 68667
Purcell, H.:Fants, w. Alberto Lysy (vn), Robert Masters (vn), Yehudi Menuhin (vn), Walter Gerhard (va), Derek Simpson (vc), Ambrose Gauntlett (vl), Roy Jesson (hpd/org)—Nos. 4 in g, 7 in c, 8 in d, 13 in F EMI Classics ▲ CDK 65734
Purcell, H.:Sons (22) Vns, w. Alberto Lysy (vn), Robert Masters (vn), Yehudi Menuhin (vn), Walter Gerhard (va), Derek Simpson (vc), Ambrose Gauntlett (vl), Roy Jesson (hpd/org)—Nos. 2, 6, & 8 EMI Classics ▲ CDK 65734
Aronsky, Peter (pno)
Raff, J.:Ode au printemps, w. J. Meier (cnd), Basel RSO Tudor ▲ TUD 784 [ADD]
Aronson, Henry (elec)—see ORCHESTRAS & ENSEMBLES Postcards
Arpin, Christopher (pno)—see also ORCHESTRAS & ENSEMBLES Meininger Trio
Boulanger, L.:D'un matin de printemps Fl & Pno, w. Christiane Meininger (fl) Bayer ▲ BR 100 266 [DDD]
Boulanger, L.:Nocturne, w. Christiane Meininger (fl) Bayer ▲ BR 100 266 [DDD]
Gubaidulina, S.:Allegro rustico, w. Christiane Meininger (fl) Bayer ▲ BR 100 266 [DDD]
Arpin, John (pno)
French Connection, w. L. Nashman (fl) Pro Arte ▲ CDD 585 [DDD]
Arpin, John (pno) (cont.)
Gottschalk, L.M.:Pno Music—Bamboula; Le bananier; The Banjo; Berceuse; Creole Eyes; Dying Poet; La Gallina; Grand scherzo; Minuit à Séville; Pasquinade; Souvenirs D'Andalousie; Souvenir de Porto Rico; Tournament Galop *(rec 9/89)* Pro Arte/Fanfare ▲ CDD 515 [DDD]
Joplin, S.:Pno Music—Bethena Waltz; Cleopha; Easy Winners; Elite Syncopations; The Entertainer; Heliotrope Bouquet; Magnetic Rag; Maple Leaf Rag; Pineapple Rag; Ragtime Dance; Solace; Stoptime Rag; Wall St. Rag; Weeping Willow *(rec 2/3/88)* Pro Arte/Fanfare ▲ CDD 397 [DDD]
Joplin, S.:Pno Music—Antoinette; Augustine Club Waltzes; Cascades; Chrysanthemum; Country Club; Eugenia; Euphonic Sounds; Gladiolus; Leola; Pleasant Moments; Rose Leaf Rag; Scott Joplin's New Rag; Searchlight Rag; Something Doing; Sugar Cane Rag; Sunflower Slow Drag; Swipsy Cake Walk *(rec 6-7/91)* Pro Arte/Fanfare ▲ CDD 562 [DDD]
Lamb, J.:Pno Music—American Beauty Rag; Bohemia; Champagne Rag; Cleopatra Rag; Contentment Rag; Ethiopia; Excelsior Rag; Patricia Rag; Ragtime Nightingale; Reindeer Ragtime Two-Step; Sensation—A Rag; Topliner Rag Pro Arte/Fanfare ▲ CDD 497 [DDD]
Lullabies, w. Forrester, Maureen (cta) *(rec 5/88)* Pro Arte ▲ CDD 411 [DDD]
Arpino, André (perc)
Loussier, J.:Lumières, w. Déborah Rees (sop), James Bowman (ct), J.-P. Wallez (cnd), Harmonia Nova Orch, Patrick Marco Vocal Ensemble *(rec Studio de Miraval, 1957)* Media 7 ▲ CD 707 [DDD]
Arrau, Claudio (pno)
Arrau Edition, Vol. 1 Philips 11-▲ 432301-2 [ADD]
Arrau Edition, Vol. 2:Debussy Philips ▲ 434626-2 PH [DDD]
Arrau Edition, Vol. 4 Philips 2-▲ 432304-2 [ADD]
Arrau Edition, Vol. 5 Philips 5-▲ 432305-2 [ADD]
Arrau Edition, Vol. 6 Philips 7-▲ 432306-2 [ADD]
Bach, J.S.:Partitas Hpd, BWV 825-830—Nos. 1, 2, 3 & 5 Philips ▲ 434904-2
Beethoven, L. van:Cons Pno (comp), w. C. Davis (cnd), Dresden Staatskapelle Philips 3-▲ 422149-2 [DDD]
Beethoven, L. van:Con 3 Pno, w. C. Schuricht (cnd), Paris National Orch *(rec live, Paris 3/24/59)* Melodram ("Connaisseur" series) 2-▲ CD 27504 (m) [AAD]
Beethoven, L. van:Con 5 Pno, "Emperor", w. C. Davis (cnd), Dresden Staatskapelle Philips ▲ 416215-2 [DDD] ◻ 416215-5
Beethoven, L. van:Con 5 Pno, "Emperor", w. E. Inbal (cnd), New Philharmonia Orch Philips ("Duo" series) 2-▲ 442580-2
Beethoven, L. van:Sons Pno (comp) *(rec 1960s)* Philips 11-▲ 432301-2 [ADD]
Beethoven, L. van:Son 3 Pno Philips ▲ 420153-2 [DDD]
Beethoven, L. van:Son 8 Pno, "Pathétique" Philips ▲ 420153-2 [DDD]
Beethoven, L. van:Son 8 Pno, "Pathétique" Philips ▲ 422970-2 [ADD]
Beethoven, L. van:Son 9 Pno Philips ▲ 426314-2 [DDD]
Beethoven, L. van:Son 10 Pno Philips ▲ 426314-2 [DDD]
Beethoven, L. van:Son 12 Pno, "Funeral March" Philips ▲ 426256-2 [DDD]
Beethoven, L. van:Son 14 Pno, "Moonlight Son" Philips ▲ 422970-2 [ADD]
Beethoven, L. van:Son 15 Pno, "Pastoral" Philips ▲ 426256-2 [DDD]
Beethoven, L. van:Son 19 Pno Philips ▲ 426256-2 [DDD]
Beethoven, L. van:Son 20 Pno Philips ▲ 426256-2 [DDD]
Beethoven, L. van:Son 21 Pno, "Waldstein" Philips ▲ 426068-2 [ADD]
Beethoven, L. van:Son 23 Pno, "Appassionata" Philips ▲ 422970-2 [ADD]
Beethoven, L. van:Son 26 Pno, "Les Adieux" Philips ▲ 426068-2 [ADD]
Beethoven, L. van:Son 27 Pno, w. C. Arrau Philips ▲ 426314-2 [DDD]
Beethoven, L. van:Son 28 Pno Philips ▲ 426314-2 [DDD]
Beethoven, L. van:Sons Vn (comp), w. J. Szigeti (vn) Vanguard Classics 4-▲ OVC 8060/63 (m) [ADD]
Beethoven, L. van:Son 2 Vn, w. Arthur Grumiaux (vn) Philips ("Solo" series) ▲ 442651-2
Beethoven, L. van:Son 4 Vn, w. Arthur Grumiaux (vn) Philips ("Solo" series) ▲ 442651-2
Beethoven, L. van:Son 5 Vn, "Spring", w. Arthur Grumiaux (vn) Philips ("Solo" series) ▲ 442651-2
Beethoven, L. van:Son 5 Vn, "Spring", w. Joseph Szigeti (vn) Enterprise ("Sirio" series) ▲ ENT SO 530012
Beethoven, L. van:Son 8 Vn, w. Arthur Grumiaux (vn) Philips ("Solo" series) ▲ 442651-2
Beethoven, L. van:Son 9 Vn, "Kreutzer", w. Joseph Szigeti (vn) Enterprise ("Sirio" series) ▲ ENT SO 530012
Beethoven, L. van:Vars on an Original Theme, Op. 34 Philips 11-▲ 432301-2 [ADD]
Beethoven, L. van:Vars & Fugue Pno, Op. 35, "Eroica" Philips 11-▲ 432301-2 [ADD]
Beethoven, L. van:Vars Pno, WoO 80 Philips 11-▲ 432301-2 [ADD]
Brahms, J.:Con 1 Pno, w. B. Haitink (cnd), Royal Concertgebouw Orch Philips 2-▲ 438320-2
Brahms, J.:Con 2 Pno, w. B. Haitink (cnd), Royal Concertgebouw Orch Philips 2-▲ 438320-2
Brahms, J.:Vars & Fugue on a Theme by Handel *(rec live, Lugano 5/20/63)* Ermitage ▲ ERM 104 [ADD]
Busoni, F.:Sonatina 6 Pno *(rec ca. 1929 for HMV)* Pearl ▲ PEA 9928 (m) [AAD]
Chopin, F.:Allegro de concert *(rec 1929-50)* Arlecchino ARL
Chopin, F.:Ballades Pno (comp) *(rec 1929-50)* Arlecchino ARL
Chopin, F.:Ballades Pno (comp) Arlecchino ▲ ARL100
Chopin, F.:Ballades Pno (comp)—Op. 47 Philips ▲ 420655-2 [ADD] ■ 420655-4
Chopin, F.:Barcarolle Pno Philips ▲ 420655-2 [ADD] ■ 420655-4
Chopin, F.:Barcarolle Pno Arlecchino ▲ ARL100
Chopin, F.:Con 1 Pno, w. E. Inbal (cnd), London SO Philips ("Insignia" series) ▲ 434145-2 [ADD]
Chopin, F.:Con 2 Pno, w. E. Inbal (cnd), London SO Philips ("Insignia" series) ▲ 434145-2 [ADD]
Chopin, F.:Études (24) EMI Classics (Great Recordings of the Century) ▲ CDH 61016 (m)
Chopin, F.:Études (24) *(rec 1929-50)* Arlecchino ARL
Chopin, F.:Fant Philips ▲ 420655-2 [ADD] ■ 420655-4
Chopin, F.:Impromptus Arlecchino ▲ ARL100
Chopin, F.:Impromptus—No. 4 Philips ▲ 420655-2 [ADD] ■ 420655-4
Chopin, F.:Music of, w. E. Inbal (cnd), London SO Philips 2-▲ 438338-2
Chopin, F.:Music of, w. Nikita Magaloff (pno), Rotterdam PO [cnd:David Zinman], E. Inbal (cnd), London PO—Con. No. 2 in f for Pno, Op. 21 [Larghetto]; Berceuse in D♭, Op. 57; Nocturnes No. 1 in b♭, Op. 9/1; No. 2 in E♭, Op. 9/2; No. 5 in F#, Op. 15/2; No. 8 in D♭, Op. 27/2; No. 20 in c#, Op. posth.; No. 21 in c, Op. posth.; Prelude No. 7 in A, Op. 28; Andante spianato; Prelude No. 4 in e, Op. 28; Waltz No. 9 in A♭, Op. 69/1; Con. No. 1 in e for Pno, Op. 11 [Romance] Philips ▲ 446629-2 ■ 446629-4
Chopin, F.:Nocturnes Philips 2-▲ 416440-2 [ADD]
Chopin, F.:Nouvelles études EMI Classics (Great Recordings of the Century) ▲ CDH 61016 (m)
Chopin, F.:Pno Music (misc)—Ballade No. 3 in A♭, Op. 47 & Scherzo in c#, Op. 39 [rec. 1939]; 4 Etudes:Op. 10, Nos. 3,4,8 & 9; Waltz in F, Op. 34/3 [rec. 1929] Pearl ▲ PEA 9928 (m) [AAD]
Chopin, F.:Pno Music (misc)—Ballade No. 3; Barcarolle; Fantaisie in f; Impromptu No. 4; 2 Nocturnes; 1 Prelude; 2 Waltzes Philips ▲ 420655-2 [ADD] ■ 420655-4
Chopin, F.:Pno Music (misc), w. E. Inbal (cnd), London SO Philips 2-▲ 438338-2
Chopin, F.:Polonaises Philips ("Solo" series) ▲ 442407-2
Chopin, F.:Preludes, Op. 28 *(rec 1929-50)* Arlecchino ARL
Chopin, F.:Preludes, Op. 28 Odyssey ■ YT 35934 (m)
Chopin, F.:Scherzos Arlecchino ARL
Chopin, F.:Scherzos Philips ("Solo" series) ▲ 442407-2
Chopin, F.:Son Pno, Op. 58 Arlecchino ARL
Chopin, F.:Tarantelle *(rec 1929-50)* Arlecchino ARL
Chopin, F.:Waltzes Philips ▲ 400025-2 [ADD]
Debussy, C.:Estampes Philips ▲ 420393-2 [ADD]

▲ = CD ♦ = Enhanced CD Δ = MD ■ = Cassette Tape ◻ = DCC

Arrau, Claudio (pno) (cont.)
Debussy, C.:Images (6) Pno—Set 1 Philips ▲ 420393-2 [ADD]
Debussy, C.:Images (6) Pno Philips 2-▲ 432304-2 [ADD]
Debussy, C.:Pno Music (misc)—Jardins sous la pluie (from Estampes) & Danse, "Tarantele styrienne" *(rec 1939 Parlophone recording)* Pearl ▲ PEA 9928 (m) [AAD]
Debussy, C.:La Plus que lente Philips ▲ 434626-2 [DDD]
Debussy, C.:Preludes Pno Philips 2-▲ 432304-2 [ADD]
Debussy, C.:Preludes Pno—Book 1 Philips ▲ 420393-2 [ADD]
Debussy, C.:Sarabande Philips ▲ 434626-2 [DDD]
Debussy, C.:Suite bergamasque Philips ▲ 434626-2 [DDD]
Debussy, C.:Valse romantique Philips ▲ 434626-2 [DDD]
Liszt, F.:Années de pèlerinage 2—No. 7, "Dante Sonata" Philips ▲ 411055-2 [DDD]
Liszt, F.:Années de pèlerinage 3—No. 4, "Les Jeux d'eaux à la Villa d'Este" *(rec 1928 Parlophone recording)* Pearl ▲ PEA 9928 (m) [AAD]
Liszt, F.:Cons Pno, w. C. Davis (cnd), London SO Philips ▲ 416461-2 [ADD]
Liszt, F.:Con 1 Pno, w. E. Ormandy (cnd), Philadelphia Orch *(rec Feb 1952)* Sony Classical ("Masterworks Heritage" series) ▲ MHK 62338 [ADD]
Liszt, F.:Études d'exécution transcendante, S.139 Philips 5-▲ 432305-2 [ADD]
Liszt, F.:Études d'exécution transcendante, S.139 Philips ▲ 416458-2 [ADD]
Liszt, F.:Fant on Hungarian Folk Tunes, w. E. Ormandy (cnd), Philadelphia Orch *(rec Feb 1952)* Sony Classical ("Masterworks Heritage" series) ▲ MHK 62338 [ADD]
Liszt, F.:Harmonies poétiques et religieuses—Funérailles Philips ▲ 411055-2 [DDD]
Liszt, F.:Hungarian Rhaps—Nos. 8, 9, 10, 11 & 13 *(rec 1951–52)* Sony Classical ("Masterworks Heritage" series) ▲ MHK 62338 [ADD]
Liszt, F.:Liebesträume—No. 3 Philips ▲ 422060-2 [DDD]
Liszt, F.:Mephisto Waltz 3 Pno Philips ▲ 422060-2 [DDD]
Liszt, F.:Pno Music (misc)—Etude de concert, "Gnomenreigen"; Mephisto Waltz; Chopin song transcription, "Mes joies" *(rec live, Lugano, 5/20/63)* Ermitage ▲ ERM 104 [ADD]
Liszt, F.:Pno Music (misc)—Après une lecture du Dante; 6 Chants polonais de Frédéric Chopin; Funérailles; Verdi Opera Paraphrases; Bénédiction de Dieu dans la solitude; Il lamento; La leggierezza; Un sospiro; Sonetto 104 del Petrarca; Sonetto 123 del Petrarca; Ballade No. 2; Vallée d'Obermann; Valse Oubliée No. 1; Les jeux d'eaux à la Villa d'Este; Waldesrauschen; Gnomenreigen Philips 5-▲ 432305-2 [ADD]
Liszt, F.:Son Pno Philips ▲ 422060-2
Liszt, F.:Son Pno Philips 5-▲ 432305-2 [ADD]
Liszt, F.:Song Transcriptions—Chopin:6, from Op. 74 Philips ▲ 411055-2 [DDD]
Mozart, W.A.:Adagio Pno, K.540 Philips 7-▲ 432306-2 [ADD]
Mozart, W.A.:Fant Pno, K.397 Philips 7-▲ 432306-2 [ADD]
Mozart, W.A.:Fant Pno, K.475 Philips 7-▲ 432306-2 [ADD]
Mozart, W.A.:Rondo Pno, K.485 Philips 7-▲ 432306-2 [ADD]
Mozart, W.A.:Rondo Pno, K.511 Philips 7-▲ 432306-2 [ADD]
Mozart, W.A.:Sons Pno Philips 7-▲ 432306-2 [ADD]
Mozart, W.A.:Son 9 Pno Naxos ▲ 8.550446 [DDD]
Ravel, M.:Gaspard de la nuit *(rec live, Lugano, 5/20/63)* Ermitage ▲ ERM 104 [ADD]
Schubert, Franz:Impromptus Pno, D.935 Philips ▲ 434101-2
Schubert, Franz:Pieces Pno, D.946 Philips ▲ 434101-2
Schumann, R.:Carnaval Pno *(rec 1939)* Pearl ▲ PEA 9928 (m) [AAD]
Schumann, R.:Carnaval Pno Philips ("Silver Line" series) ▲ 420871-2 [ADD]
Schumann, R.:Kinderszenen Philips ("Silver Line" series) ▲ 420871-2 [ADD]

Arriaga, Gerado (gtr)
Murcia, S. de:Gtr Music—Obra por 8 Tono Natural; Folias Italianas; Folias Gallegas; Marizapalos; Tarantelas; Cancion; La Babet; La Bretaigne O Paspied; La Guastala; Pasacalles for Radio La E; 6 Menuets; 8 Pasacalles *(rec Madrid, Dec 14–18, 1987)* RNE/Spanish National Radio ▲ AME 001 [DDD]

Arrignon, Daniel (ob)
Albinoni, T.:Cons à 5 Obs, Op. 9, w. N. Marriner (cnd), Academy of St. Martin in the Fields—No. 3 in F Classics for Pleasure ("Eminence" series) ▲ CFP 2235
Bach, J.S.:Con 1 for 2 Hpds, w. Bernard Mathern (vn), J.–P. Berlingen (cnd), Normandy Orchestral Ensemble [reconstructed for ob & vn in d] *(rec Kusatsu Concert Hall, Nov 2–3, 1991)* Camerata ▲ 32CM284 [DDD]
Bach, J.S.:Con Vn & Ob, w. Philip Bride (vn), French Instrumental Ensemble *(rec Nov 5 & 6, 1988)* Pierre Verany ▲ PVY 730020 [DDD]

Arrignon, Michel (cl)
Burgan, P.:Music of, w. Liliane Mazeron (sop), Clara Novakova (fl), Alain Jacquon (pno), Henry Trio—Jeux de femmes [6 Erotic Poems of Verlaine]; Rondes Nocturnes; Bavardage; Berceuse Maguelone ▲ 350.529
Honegger, A.:Chamber Music (comp), w. D.–S. Kang (vn), P.–H. Xuereb (va), R. Wallfisch (vc), M. Arrignon (cl), A. Haraldsdottir (fl), C. Moreaux (ob), T. Caens (tpt), M. Becquet (trbn), P. Zanlonghi (hp), P. Devoyon (pno), F. Kondo (mez), Ludwig String Quartet—Sonatine for Clarinet & Piano (1921–22); Rapsodie for 2 Flutes, Clarinet & Piano (1917); Danse de la Chèvre for Solo Flute (1921); Romance for Flute & Piano (1953); Petite Suite for 2 Flutes & Piano (1934); Trois Contrepoints for Piccolo, Oboe, Violin & Cello (1922); Intrada for Trumpet & Piano (1947); Hommage du trombone exprimant la tristesse de l'auteur absent for Trombone & Piano (1925); J'avais un fidèle amant for String Quartet (1929); Chanson de Ronsard & 3 Chansons de la petite Sirène for Mezzo, Flute & String Quartet (1924); Introduction et Danse for Flute, Harp & String Trio [undated]; Colloque for Flute, Celesta, Violin & Viola [undated] Timpani ▲ IC1010 [DDD]
Honegger, A.:Sonatina Cl, w. P. Devoyon (pno) Timpani ▲ IC1010 [DDD]
Stravinsky, I.:Ebony Con, w. P. Boulez (cnd), Ensemble InterContemporain Deutsche Grammophon ("The Originals" series) ▲ 447405-2

Arron, Edward (vc)
Brubeck, C.:Songs, w. Frederica von Stade (sop), Jenny Elkus (sgr), Bill Crofut (sgr/banjo), Chris Brubeck (sgr/trbn/pno/db), Mark Vinci (fl), Frank Brown (cl), Dan Brubeck (dr/perc)—The Distance between Us; La Paloma azul; Strange Meadowlark; Across Your Dreams; Summer Song; Polly; Blue Rondo–A Tribute to Dave; Autumn in Our Town; Thinking of You Thinking of Me; It's a Raggy Waltz; Heart of Winter; In the Grace of Your Room; Lonely on Both Ends of the Road *(rec Sandisfield, MA; Fantasy Studios, Berkeley, CA)* Telarc ▲ CD 80467 [DDD]

Arroyo, Rafael (pno)
Albéniz, I.:Cantos de España—Cordoba [No. 4] Adès ▲ ADE 132072 [AAD]
Albéniz, I.:España—No. 2 [Tango] Adès ▲ ADE 132072 [AAD]
Albéniz, I.:Suite española (sels)—Sevilla Adès ▲ ADE 132072 [AAD]
Falla, M. de:El amor brujo (ritual fire dance) Adès ▲ ADE 132072 [AAD]
Falla, M. de:Pièces espagnoles (4)—Andaluza Adès ▲ ADE 132072 [AAD]
Granados, E.:Allegro di Concierto Adès ▲ ADE 132072 [AAD]
Granados, E.:Goyescas—No. 4 [Quejas o la Maja y el Ruisenor] Adès ▲ ADE 132072 [AAD]
Turina, J.:Danzas fantásticas Adès ▲ ADE 132072 [AAD]

Arsenius, Bengt (perc)
Bäck, S.–E.:Favola, w. Thore Janson (cl), Stig Arntorp (perc), Roland Johansson (perc), Björn Liljequist (perc) Caprice ▲ CAP 21490

Artaud, Pierre-Yves (fl)
Cage, J.:Ryoanji Fl & Octobass, w. J.–C. François (perc) Neuma ▲ 450-77 [DDD]
Chaynes, C.:Oginoha, "Lights from Japanese Poetry", w. Y. Nara (sop), D. Megévand (celtic hp), C. Giot (perc) REM ▲ REM 311194 [DDD]
Contemporary Flute Music, w. Jean–Charles François (perc) Neuma ▲ 450-77 [DDD]
Ferneyhough, B.:Casandra's Dream Song Neuma ▲ 450-72 [DDD]
Hosokawa, T.:Fragmente II, w. Arditti String Quartet Montaigne ▲ MO 782078
Korde, S.:Goldbach's Conjecture Neuma ▲ 450-77 [DDD]
Mabry, D.:5.4.88 Neuma ▲ 450-77 [DDD]
Mefano, P.:Traits Suspendus Neuma ▲ 450-77 [DDD]
Radulescu, H.:Music of, w. H. Radulescu (cnd), French Flute Orch—Dizzy Divinity I; Byzantine Prayer; Frenetico il Longing di Amare; Capricorn's Nostalgic Crickets II Adda ▲ ADD 581298 [DDD]

Artaud, Pierre-Yves (fl) (cont.)
Radulescu, H.:Sensual Sky, w. N. Andreassian (cnd), Polychromie Ensemble Adès ▲ ADE 204482 [DDD]
Tanguy, É.:Con Fl, w. C. Bardon (cnd), Caen Orch *(rec Feb. 25–27, 1994)* Chamade ▲ 5606 [DDD]
Varèse, E.:Density 21.5 Neuma ▲ 450-77 [DDD]
Yun, I.:Con Fl, w. P. Méfano (cnd), 2E2M Ensemble Adda ▲ ADD 581166 [DDD]
Yun, I.:Con Fl, w. P. Méfano (cnd), 2E2M Ensemble Adda ▲ ADD 243422 [DDD]
Yun, I.:Etudes Fl Adda ▲ ADD 243422 [DDD]
Yun, I.:Etudes Fl Adda ▲ ADD 581166 [DDD]
Yun, I.:Garak, w. Jacqueline Mefano (pno) Adda ▲ ADD 243422 [DDD]
Yun, I.:Garak, w. Jacqueline Mefano (pno) Adda ▲ ADD 581166 [DDD]

Arthur, Howard (gtr)—see ORCHESTRAS & ENSEMBLES Rhythm & Bluefield Band

Artman, Gilbert (dr)—see ORCHESTRAS & ENSEMBLES Heldon

Artymiw, Lydia (pno)
Brahms, J.:Chorale Preludes, Op. 122—Nos. 4,5 & 8–11 [pno trans by Busoni] Chandos ▲ CHAN 8410 [DDD]
Brahms, J.:Qnt Pno, w. American String Quartet *(rec Tuscon Winter Chamber Festival; Mar 10, 1995)* Arizona Friends of Chamber Music ▲ AFCD 19952
Brahms, J.:Sarabande Piano Chandos ▲ CHAN 8410 [DDD]
Brahms, J.:Suite Pno Chandos ▲ CHAN 8410 [DDD]
Brahms, J.:Vars & Fugue on a Theme by Handel Chandos ▲ CHAN 8410 [DDD]
Debussy, C.:Ariettes oubliées, w. Benita Valente (sop) *(rec Rutgers Church, New York City, Jan 23–26, 1989)* Centaur ▲ CRC 2220 [DDD]
Debussy, C.:Chansons de jeunesse (4), w. Benita Valente (sop) *(rec Rutgers Church, New York City, Jan 23–26, 1989)* Centaur ▲ CRC 2220 [DDD]
Debussy, C.:Fêtes galantes 1, w. Benita Valente (sop) *(rec Rutgers Church, New York City, Jan 23–26, 1989)* Centaur ▲ CRC 2220 [DDD]
Fauré, G.:Mélodies 'de Venise', Op. 58, w. Benita Valente (sop)—Mandoline; En Sourdine; Green; A Clymene; C'est l'extase; Au bord de l'eau; Fleur jetée [all texts Verlaine] *(rec Rutgers Church, New York City, Jan 23–26, 1989)* Centaur ▲ CRC 2220 [DDD]
Rorem, N.:The Santa Fe Songs, w. Kurt Ollman (bar), Sheryl Staples (vn), Heiichiro Ohyama (va), Peter Rejto (vc) *(rec live, Tucson Chamber Music Festival, Mar 12, 1995)* Arizona Friends of Chamber Music ▲ 1995 [DDD]
Tchaikovsky, P.:Les Saisons Chandos ▲ CHAN 8349 [DDD]

Artzt, Alice (gtr)—see ORCHESTRAS & ENSEMBLES Alice Artzt Guitar Trio

Arutiunyan, A. (pno)
Babadjanyan, A.:Music of, w. Arno Babadjanyan (pno), B. Chekmenyov (gtr), A. Tarasov (gtr), A. Nikolayev (perc), Silantiev, Mavisakhalyan (cnd), All–Union Radio–TV Sym Variety Orch, Armenian Radio–TV Orch—Nocturne; Prelude & Vagarshapat Dance; Capriccio; Polyphonic Son; Exprompt; Armenian Rhap; Elegy in Commemoration of A. Khachaturyan; 6 Pictures; Melody & Humoresque; Fant on Give Me My Music Back; Fant on Dum spiro spero; Fant on Winer Love; Fant on Call Me; Piece for the Pno & Orch [Dreams] *(rec 1953–83)* Russian Compact Disc ("Talents of Russia" series) ▲ RCD 16251 [ADD]

Arzoumanian (pno)
Stravinsky, I.:Les Noces, w. M. Quercia (sop), S. Cooper (mez), P. Capelle (ten), P. Marinov (bass), Vieuxtemps (pno), R. Conil (pno), Raynaut (pno), R. Hayrabedian (cnd), Strasbourg Percussion Ensemble, Contemporary Choir Pierre Verany ▲ PV 787032 [DDD]

Arzruni, Sahan (pno)
Babadjanyan, A.:Son Vn, w. A. Kavafian (vn) Positively Armenian PA 105C
Hovhaness, A.:Armenian Folk Songs Positively Armenian ■ PA 106C
Hovhaness, A.:Flute Player of the Armenian Mountains, w. A. Berberian (bass) [Armenian] *(rec 1985)* Positively Armenian ■ PA 104C
Hovhaness, A.:Pno Music—Pastoral No. 1, Op. 111/1; Hymn to a Celestial Musician, Op. 111/2; Achtamar, Op. 64/1; 2 Ghazals, Op. 36a–b; Child in the Garden, Op. 168 (piano duet, with the composer) Positively Armenian ■ PA 106C
Hovhaness, A.:Songs, w. A. Berberian (bass)—4 songs [Armenian] *(rec 1985)* Positively Armenian ■ PA 104C
Hovhaness, A.:Suite Pno Positively Armenian ■ PA 106C
Hovhaness, A.:Visionary Landscapes Positively Armenian ■ PA 106C
Hovhaness, A.:Visions of St. Mesrob, w. A. Kavafian (vn) Positively Armenian ■ PA 105C
Khachaturian, A.:Dance Vn & Pno, w. A. Kavafian (vn) Positively Armenian ■ PA 105C
Khachaturian, A.:Nocturne, w. A. Kavafian (vn) Positively Armenian ■ PA 105C
Khachaturian, A.:Song–Poem, w. A. Kavafian (vn) Positively Armenian ■ PA 105C

Asai, Michiko (pno)
Miyoshi, A.:Collection of Songs, w. Y. Tanaka (pno), F. Kuyiyama (cnd), Chorale OMP Camerata ▲ 32CM-28
Miyoshi, A.:Symphonic Choral Poem, w. A. Miyoshi (nar), Y. Tanaka (pno), F. Kuyiyama (cnd), Chorale OMP Camerata ▲ 32CM-28

Asawa, Kazue Frances (fl)
Hirai, K.:Son Koto & Fl, w. K. Kudo (koto) Crystal ▲ CD 316 [DDD]
Japanese Music for Koto & Flute, w.K. Kudo (koto) Crystal ▲ CD 316 [DDD]
Miyagi, M.:Haru no Umi, w. K. Kudo Crystal ▲ CD 316 [DDD]
Sawai, T.:Flower, w. K. Kudo (koto) Crystal ▲ CD 316 [DDD]
Yamamoto, H.:Ichikotsu, w. K. Kudo (koto) Crystal ▲ CD 316 [DDD]

Asawa, Kazue Frances (shak)
Miyagi, M.:Izumi, w. K. Kudo (koto) Crystal ▲ CD 316 [DDD]

Aschelter, Maurizio (pno)—see also ORCHESTRAS & ENSEMBLES Rara Ensemble
Setaccioli, G.:Dall'Album *(rec Audiovisivi S. Paolo–Albano Laziale, 1995)* Bongiovanni ▲ 5560 [DDD]
Setaccioli, G.:Romances Vn, w. Massimiliano Destro (vn) *(rec Audiovisivi S. Paolo–Albano Laziale, 1995)* Bongiovanni ▲ 5560 [DDD]
Setaccioli, G.:Son Cl, w. Maurizio D'Alessandro (cl) *(rec Audiovisivi S. Paolo–Albano Laziale, 1995)* Bongiovanni ▲ 5560 [DDD]

Ascher, Christina (perc)
Brandmüller, T.:Despedida, w. Christina Ascher (mez), Volker Höh (gtr) *(rec Altensteig, July 18–20, 1996)* Signum ▲ X 74-00 [DDD]
Heyn, V.:I(–na), w. Christina Ascher (mez), Volker Höh (gtr) *(rec Altensteig, July 18–20, 1996)* Signum ▲ X 74-00 [DDD]
Spassov, B.:Calliope, w. Christina Ascher (mez), Volker Höh (gtr) *(rec Altensteig, July 18–20, 1996)* Signum ▲ X 74-00 [DDD]

Asheim, Nils Henrik (pno)
Engleskyts:Angels' Arrows, w. Berntsen, Anne–Lise (sop) Norway Music ▲ FXCD 136

Ashkenasi, Shmuel (vn)—see ORCHESTRAS & ENSEMBLES Amici Quartet, Vermeer String Quartet

Ashkenasi, Shnuel (vn)
Beethoven, L. van:Romances Vn, w. E. de Stoutz (cnd), Zurich CO Tudor ▲ 723 [ADD]
Mozart, W.A.:Con 5 Vn, w. E. de Stoutz (cnd), Zurich CO Tudor ▲ 723 [ADD]
Paganini, N.:Con 1 Vn, w. H. Esser (cnd), Vienna SO Deutsche Grammophon ("Resonance" series) ▲ 429524-2 [ADD]
Paganini, N.:Con 2 Vn, w. H. Esser (cnd), Vienna SO Deutsche Grammophon ("Resonance" series) ▲ 429524-2 [ADD]

Ashkenazy, Dmitri (cl)
Françaix, J.:Con Cl, w. C. Mueller (cnd), Cincinnati PO Pan Classics ▲ 510082 [DDD]
Gerber, R.:Chamber Music, w. Fränzi Badertscher–Jaquiéry (fl), Gunhard Mattes (ob), Claude Delley (cl), Pierre–Yves Dubois (cl), Anne de Dadelsen (pno)—Pièce lente; Habanera; Berceuse [all for Cl & Pno]; Trio for Fl, Ob & Pno; Son for Fl & Pno; Ballet for Fl & Pno; Sonatine for 3 Cl; Pavane for Fl & Pno; Suite for Fl & Pno; Prélude et fugue sur le nom de Bach for Cl Gallo ▲ CD 788 [DAD]
Mendelssohn, F.:Concert Pieces, w. Peter Furniss (bas hn), Karl–Andreas Kolly (pno) Pan ▲ 510 070 [DDD]
Mendelssohn, F.:Lieder ohne Worte Pno, w. Karl–Andreas Kolly (pno)—Opp. 19/1 & 4, 38/1 & 53/2 [arr. for cl & pno] Pan ▲ 510 070 [DDD]

INSTRUMENT.

Ashkenazy, Dmitri (cl) (cont.)

- Mendelssohn, F.:Son Cl, w. Karl–Andreas Kolly (pno) — Pan ▲ 510 070 [DDD]
- Moser, R.:Con Cl, w. C. Mueller (cnd), Cincinnati PO — Pan Classics ▲ 510082 [DDD]
- Rimsky–Korsakov, N.:Concertstück Cl, w. C. Mueller (cnd), Cincinnati PO — Pan Classics ▲ 510082 [DDD]
- Strauss, R.:Duet–Concertino, w. K. Walker (bn), V. Ashkenazy (cnd), Berlin RSO — London ▲ 436415–2 [DDD]
- Stravinsky, I.:Ebony Con, w. V. Ashkenazy (cnd), Berlin German SO *(rec Aug.–Sept. 1992)* — London ▲ 440229–2 [DDD]
- Taneyev, S.:Canzona Cl, w. C. Mueller (cnd), Cincinnati PO — Pan Classics ▲ 510082 [DDD]

Ashkenazy, Vladimir (pno)

- Arensky, A.:Trio 1 Pno, w. R. Stamper (vn), C. Jackson (vc) *(rec Nov 1990)* — Naxos ▲ 8.550467 [DDD]
- Beethoven, L. van:Bagatelles (24) — London 3–▲ 425582–2 [ADD]
- Beethoven, L. van:Bagatelle, WoO 59, "Für Elise" — London 3–▲ 425582–2 [ADD]
- Beethoven, L. van:Bagatelle, WoO 59, "Für Elise" — London 2–▲ 436380–2 [ADD/DDD]
- Beethoven, L. van:Cons Pno (comp), w. V. Ashkenazy (cnd), Cleveland Orch — London 3–▲ 421718–2 [DDD]
- Beethoven, L. van:Cons Pno (comp), w. G. Solti (cnd), Cleveland Orch — London 3–▲ 425582–2 [ADD]
- Beethoven, L. van:Con 2 Pno, w. G. Solti (cnd), Chicago SO — London ▲ 417703–2 [ADD]
- Beethoven, L. van:Con 3 Pno, w. V. Ashkenazy (cnd), Cleveland Orch — London □ 433321–5
- Beethoven, L. van:Con 3 Pno, w. V. Ashkenazy (cnd), Royal PO *(rec live 11/89)* — RPO ▲ CDRPO 7014 [DDD]
- Beethoven, L. van:Con 3 Pno, w. G. Solti (cnd), Chicago SO — London ▲ 417740–2 [ADD]
- Beethoven, L. van:Con 4 Pno, w. V. Ashkenazy (cnd), Cleveland Orch — London □ 433321–5
- Beethoven, L. van:Con 4 Pno, w. G. Solti (cnd), Chicago SO — London 2–▲ 436380–2 [ADD]
- Beethoven, L. van:Con 4 Pno, w. G. Solti (cnd), Chicago SO — London ▲ 417740–2 [ADD]
- Beethoven, L. van:Con 4 Pno, w. Z. Mehta (cnd), Vienna PO — London ("Jubilee" series) ▲ 430704–2 [ADD]
- Beethoven, L. van:Con 5 Pno, "Emperor", w. G. Solti (cnd), Chicago SO — London 2–▲ 436380–2 [ADD]
- Beethoven, L. van:Con 5 Pno, "Emperor", w. G. Solti (cnd), Chicago SO — London ▲ 417703–2 [ADD]
- Beethoven, L. van:Con 5 Pno, "Emperor", w. Z. Mehta (cnd), Vienna PO — London ("Jubilee" series) ▲ 430704–2 [ADD]
- Beethoven, L. van:Fant Pno, Op. 80, "Choral Fant", w. V. Ashkenazy (cnd), Cleveland Orch — London 3–▲ 421718–2 [DDD]
- Beethoven, L. van:Sons Vc (comp), w. L. Harrell (vc) — London 2–▲ 417628–2 [DDD]
- Beethoven, L. van:Sons Pno (comp) — London 10–▲ 425590–2 [ADD]
- Beethoven, L. van:Son 8 Pno, "Pathétique" — London ▲ 410260–2 [ADD]
- Beethoven, L. van:Son 8 Pno, "Pathétique" — London 2–▲ 436380–2 [ADD/DDD]
- Beethoven, L. van:Son 14 Pno, "Moonlight Son" — London ▲ 410260–2 [ADD]
- Beethoven, L. van:Son 14 Pno, "Moonlight Son" — London ▲ 425838–2 [DDD] □ 425838–5
- Beethoven, L. van:Son 14 Pno, "Moonlight Son" — London 2–▲ 436380–2 [ADD/DDD]
- Beethoven, L. van:Son 18 Pno — Russian Disc ▲ RUS 11208 [AAD]
- Beethoven, L. van:Son 21 Pno, "Waldstein" — London ▲ 425838–2 [DDD] □ 425838–5
- Beethoven, L. van:Son 21 Pno, "Waldstein" — Berlin Classics ("Dokumente" series) ▲ BER 2133 [ADD]
- Beethoven, L. van:Son 23 Pno, "Appassionata" — London ▲ 410260–2 [ADD]
- Beethoven, L. van:Son 23 Pno, "Appassionata" — London ▲ 425838–2 [DDD] □ 425838–5
- Beethoven, L. van:Son 28 Pno — London ▲ 436735–2 [DDD]
- Beethoven, L. van:Son 28 Pno — London ("Two–Fers" series) 2–▲ 452176–2
- Beethoven, L. van:Son 29 Pno, "Hammerklavier" — London ▲ 436735–2 [DDD]
- Beethoven, L. van:Son 29 Pno, "Hammerklavier" — London ("Two–Fers" series) 2–▲ 452176–2
- Beethoven, L. van:Son 30 Pno — London ("Two–Fers" series) 2–▲ 452176–2
- Beethoven, L. van:Son 30 Pno — London ▲ 436076–2 [DDD]
- Beethoven, L. van:Son 31 Pno — London ▲ 436076–2 [DDD]
- Beethoven, L. van:Son 31 Pno — London ("Two–Fers" series) 2–▲ 452176–2
- Beethoven, L. van:Son 32 Pno — Berlin Classics ("Dokumente" series) ▲ BER 2133 [ADD]
- Beethoven, L. van:Son 32 Pno — London ▲ 436076–2 [DDD]
- Beethoven, L. van:Son 32 Pno — London ("Two–Fers" series) 2–▲ 452176–2
- Beethoven, L. van:Sons Vn (comp), w. I. Perlman (vn) — London ("Jubilee" series) 4–▲ 421453–2 [ADD]
- Beethoven, L. van:Son 5 Vn, "Spring", w. I. Perlman (vn) — London ▲ 410554–2 [ADD]
- Beethoven, L. van:Son 7 Vn, w. I. Perlman (vn) — London ▲ 411948–2 [ADD]
- Beethoven, L. van:Son 9 Vn, "Kreutzer", w. I. Perlman (vn) — London ▲ 410554–2 [ADD]
- Beethoven, L. van:Son 10 Vn, w. I. Perlman (vn) — London ▲ 411948–2
- Beethoven, L. van:Trio 6 Pno, "Archduke", w. I. Perlman (vn), L. Harrell (vc) — EMI Classics ▲ CDC 47010 [DDD]
- Beethoven, L. van:Trio 10 Pno, w. Ashkenazy, Perlman, Harrell — EMI Classics ▲ CDC 47010 [DDD]
- Brahms, J.:Con 1 Pno, w. B. Haitink (cnd), Royal Concertgebouw Orch — London ▲ 410009–2 [DDD]
- Brahms, J.:Con 2 Pno, w. B. Haitink (cnd), Vienna PO — London ▲ 410199–2
- Brahms, J.:Qnt Pno, w. Cleveland Orch String Quartet — London ▲ 425839–2 [DDD]
- Brahms, J.:Sons Cl (comp), w. F. Cohen (cl) — London ▲ 430149–2 [DDD]
- Brahms, J.:Sons Vn (comp), w. I. Perlman (vn) — EMI Classics ▲ CDC 47403 [DDD]
- Brahms, J.:Trio Cl, w. F. Cohen (cl), et al. — London ▲ 425839–2 [DDD]
- Brahms, J.:Trio Hn, w. B. Tuckwell (hn), I. Perlman (vn) — London ▲ 414128–2 [ADD]
- Brahms, J.:Trios (3) Pno, w. I. Perlman (vn), L. Harrell (vc) — EMI Classics ▲ CDCB 54725
- Brahms, J.:Trio in A Pno (posth), w. I. Perlman (vn), L. Harrell (vc) — EMI Classics ▲ CDCB 54725
- Chopin, F.:Ballades Pno (comp) — London ▲ 417474–2 [DDD/ADD]
- Chopin, F.:Ballades Pno (comp) — Russian Disc ▲ RUS 11208 [AAD]
- Chopin, F.:Ballades Pno (comp)—Op. 38 — Testament ▲ TESSBT 1046 (m) [ADD]
- Chopin, F.:Barcarolle Pno — Testament ▲ TESSBT 1045 (m) [ADD]
- Chopin, F.:Con 2 Pno, w. Z. Gorzynski (cnd), Warsaw PO — Testament ▲ TESSBT 1045 (m) [ADD]
- Chopin, F.:Con 2 Pno, w. D. Zinman (cnd), London SO — London ▲ 417750–2 [ADD]
- Chopin, F.:Études (24)—Nos. 1 (Op. 10/1) & 15 (Op. 25/3) — Testament ▲ TESSBT 1045 (m) [ADD]
- Chopin, F.:Études (24) — London ▲ 414127–2 [ADD]
- Chopin, F.:Fant — London ▲ 417475–2 [ADD]
- Chopin, F.:Impromptus — London ▲ 417476–2 [DDD/ADD]
- Chopin, F.:Mazurkas — London 2–▲ 417584–2 [DDD/ADD]
- Chopin, F.:Mazurkas—in f, Op. 68/4 *(rec June 24–25, 1992)* — London ▲ 436821–2 [DDD]
- Chopin, F.:Mazurkas — London 2–▲ 448086–2
- Chopin, F.:Mazurkas—Nos. 21, 29, 35 & 36 — Testament ▲ TESSBT 1046 (m) [ADD]
- Chopin, F.:Nocturnes — London ▲ 414564–2 [ADD/DDD]
- Chopin, F.:Nocturnes—Opp. 9/2, 15/2, 27/1 & 2, 32/1 & 2, 37/2 — London ("Ovation" series) ▲ 430751–2 [DDD]
- Chopin, F.:Pno Music (misc), w. Martha Argerich (pno), Stanislav Bunin (pno), Halina Czerny–Stefanska (pno), Jan Ekier (pno), Yuval Fichman (pno), Kemal Gekic (pno), Adam Harasiewicz (pno), Krzysztof Jablonski (pno), Louis Kentner (pno), Jean–Marc Luisada (pno), Garrick Ohlsson (pno), Ivo Pogorelich (pno), Maurizio Pollini (pno), Dang Thai Son (pno)—includes Ballade (Nos. 1 & 2); Barcarolle, Op. 60; Concerto Nos. 1 & 2; Études (Op. 10, Nos. 1, 5, 8, 10 & 12 & Op. 25, No. 10, 18 & 25); Grand valse brillante; Impromptus (Nos. 3 & 4); Mazurkas (Op. 24, Nos. 1–4; Op. 30, Nos. 1–4; Op. 50, No. 32; Op. 59, Nos. 1–3); Nocturnes (Op. 9, No. 3; Op. 37, No. 12; Op. 48, No. 13; Op. 55, No. 16)Polonaise (Op. 40, Nos. 3 & 4; Op. 44, No. 5; Op. 53, No. 6; Op. 61, No. 7); Preludes (Op. 28 Nos. 13–18, 21–24 & Op. 45, No. 25); Scherzos (Nos. 1–3); Sonatas (Nos. 2 & 3); Waltzes (No. 1 & 6) — LaserLight 5–▲ 15 961 [ADD/DDD]
- Chopin, F.:Pno Music (misc)—4 etudes, 2 preludes, 2 waltzes, etc. — London ▲ 410180–2 [ADD]
- Chopin, F.:Pno Music (misc)— Fantasie impromptu; Grand valse brillante; Mazurkas; etc. — London ("Jubilee" series) ▲ 417798–2 [DDD]
- Chopin, F.:Pno Music (misc)—Piano Sonata No. 2; Berceuse , Op. 57; selected Nocturnes, Polonaises, Preludes, Waltzes, etc. — London 2–▲ 436389–2 [ADD/DDD]

Ashkenazy, Vladimir (pno) (cont.)

- Chopin, F.:Pno Music (misc)—Grande Valse, Op. 18; Fant.–impromptu, Op. 66; Nocturnes, Opp. 9/2, 15/2, 32/1 & 55/1; Waltzes, Opp. 34/2, 69/1, 69/2, 70/1, 64/1 & 64/2; Mazurkas, Opp. 33/2 & 7/1; Scherzos, Opp. 31& 39; Ballades, Opp. 23 & 47; Polonaises, Opp. 53 & 40/1; Preludes, Opp. 45 & 28/15; Etudes, Opp. 10/12, 10/5, 25/11 & 10/3; Barcarolle in F#, Op. 60 *(rec 1972, 1976, 1978, 1979, 1)* — London 2–▲ 444830–2 [DDD/ADD]
- Chopin, F.:Preludes, Op. 28 — London ▲ 417476–2 [DDD/ADD]
- Chopin, F.:Preludes, Op. 28 *(rec June 24–25, 1992)* — London ▲ 436821–2 [DDD]
- Chopin, F.:Scherzos — London ▲ 417474–2 [DDD/ADD]
- Chopin, F.:Scherzos—No. 4, Op. 54 — Testament ▲ TESSBT 1045 (m) [ADD]
- Chopin, F.:Son Pno, Op. 35 — London ▲ 417475–2 [ADD]
- Chopin, F.:Son Pno, Op. 35 — London 2–▲ 436389–2 [ADD/DDD]
- Chopin, F.:Son Pno, Op. 58 — Testament ▲ TESSBT 1045 (m) [ADD]
- Chopin, F.:Son Pno, Op. 58 *(rec June 24–25, 1992)* — London ▲ 436821–2 [DDD]
- Chopin, F.:Son Pno, Op. 58 — London ▲ 417475–2 [ADD]
- Chopin, F.:Waltzes — London ▲ 414600–2 [ADD/DDD]
- Chopin, F.:Waltzes—Opp. 18 ("Grande valse brillante"), 34/2 & 3, 69/1 & 2, 70/1–3, & Waltz in e, Op. posth. — London ("Ovation" series) ▲ 430751–2 [DDD]
- Chopin, F.:Waltzes—Nos. 2 & 6 — Testament ▲ TESSBT 1046 (m) [ADD]
- Debussy, C.:Clair de lune — Russian Disc ▲ RUS 11208 [AAD]
- Debussy, C.:Pno Music (misc) — Russian Disc ▲ RUS 11208 [AAD]
- Debussy, C.:Son Vc, w. Lynn Harrell (vc) *(rec Henry Wood Hall, London, May 1994)* — London ▲ 444318–2 [DDD]
- Debussy, C.:Son Vn, w. Itzhak Perlman (vn) *(rec Henry Wood Hall, London, May 1994)* — London ▲ 444318–2 [DDD]
- Franck, C.:Son Vn, w. I. Perlman (vn) — London ▲ 414128–2 [ADD]
- Largo I, w. Alfred Brendel (pno), Alicia de Larrocha (pno), Julius Katchen (pno), András Schiff (pno), Iliana Vered (pno), et al. — Celestial Harmonies ▲ 35509–2 2–■ 35509–4
- Largo II, w. Alfred Brendel (pno), Alicia de Larrocha (pno), Julius Katchen (pno), András Schiff (pno), Iliana Vered (pno), et al. — Celestial Harmonies ▲ 19504–2 ■ 19504–4
- Liszt, F.:Études d'exécution transcendante, S.139—No. 5 — Testament ▲ TESSBT 1046 (m) [ADD]
- Liszt, F.:Mephisto Waltz 1 Pno—pno transcription, S.514 (1859–60) — Testament ▲ TESSBT 1046 (m) [ADD]
- Mozart, W.A.:Cons Pno, w. V. Ashkenazy (cnd), Philharmonia Orch—Nos. 1–6, 8, 9 & 11–27 — London 12–▲ 425557–2 [ADD]
- Mozart, W.A.:Cons 1–4 Pno, w. D. Barenboim (cnd), Philharmonia Orch — London 2–▲ 421577–2 [ADD]
- Mozart, W.A.:Con 5 Pno, w. D. Barenboim (cnd), Philharmonia Orch — London 2–▲ 421577–2 [ADD]
- Mozart, W.A.:Con 6 Pno, w. D. Barenboim (cnd), Philharmonia Orch — London 2–▲ 421577–2 [ADD]
- Mozart, W.A.:Con 7 Pnos, w. D. Barenboim (pno), Fou Ts'ong (pno), Philharmonia Orch — London 2–▲ 421577–2 [ADD]
- Mozart, W.A.:Con 10 Pnos, w. D. Barenboim (pno), V. Ashkenazy (cnd), English CO — London ▲ 421036–2 [ADD]
- Mozart, W.A.:Con 17 Pno, w. V. Ashkenazy (cnd), Philharmonia Orch — London ▲ 411947–2 [ADD]
- Mozart, W.A.:Con 20 Pno, w. V. Ashkenazy (cnd), Philharmonia Orch — London 2–▲ 436383–2 [ADD]
- Mozart, W.A.:Con 21 Pno, w. V. Ashkenazy (cnd), Philharmonia Orch — London 2–▲ 436383–2 [ADD/DDD]
- Mozart, W.A.:Con 21 Pno, w. V. Ashkenazy (cnd), Philharmonia Orch — London ▲ 411947–2 [ADD]
- Mozart, W.A.:Con 22 Pno, w. V. Ashkenazy (cnd), Philharmonia Orch — London ▲ 421036–2 [ADD]
- Mozart, W.A.:Con 23 Pno, w. V. Ashkenazy (cnd), Philharmonia Orch — London 2–▲ 436383–2 [ADD/DDD]
- Mozart, W.A.:Con 25 Pno, w. V. Ashkenazy (cnd), Philharmonia Orch — London ▲ 411810–2 [DDD]
- Mozart, W.A.:Con 26 Pno, w. V. Ashkenazy (cnd), Philharmonia Orch — London ▲ 411810–2 [DDD]
- Mozart, W.A.:Con 27 Pno, w. V. Ashkenazy (cnd), Philharmonia Orch — London 2–▲ 436383–2 [ADD/DDD]
- Mozart, W.A.:Rondo Pno, K.511 — London 2–▲ 436383–2 [ADD/DDD]
- Mozart, W.A.:Son 17 Pno — London 2–▲ 436383–2 [ADD/DDD]
- Mussorgsky, M.:Pictures at an Exhibition — London ▲ 414386–2
- Prokofiev, S.:Cons Pno (comp), w. A. Previn (cnd), London SO — London 2–▲ 425570–2 [ADD]
- Prokofiev, S.:Con 1 Pno, w. M. Abravanel (cnd), Utah SO *(rec live, Salt Lake Tabernacle, UT 11/3/73)* — Intaglio ▲ INCD 7181 [ADD]
- Prokofiev, S.:Con 2 Pno, w. K. Kondrashin (cnd), Moscow PO *(rec live, Royal Festival Hall, London, 9/15/63)* — Intaglio ▲ INCD 7181 [ADD]
- Prokofiev, S.:Con 3 Pno, w. W. Steinberg (cnd), Pittsburgh SO *(rec live 11/7/69)* — Intaglio ▲ INCD 7181 [ADD]
- Prokofiev, S.:Son 7 Pno — Testament ▲ TESSBT 1046 (m) [ADD]
- Prokofiev, S.:Son Vn, Op. 94bis, w. I. Perlman (vn) — RCA Gold Seal ▲ 09026–61454–2
- Prokofiev, S.:Son 1 Vn, w. I. Perlman (vn) — RCA Gold Seal ▲ 09026–61454–2
- Rachmaninoff, S.:Cons Pno (comp), w. A. Previn (cnd), London SO — London 2–▲ 425576–2 [ADD]
- Rachmaninoff, S.:Cons Pno (comp), w. A. Previn (cnd), London SO *(rec Kingsway Hall, London, Apr 1970 to Nov 1971)* — London 2–▲ 444839–2 [ADD]
- Rachmaninoff, S.:Cons Pno (comp), w. B. Haitink (cnd), Royal Concertgebouw Orch — London 2–▲ 421590–2 [DDD]
- Rachmaninoff, S.:Con 1 Pno, w. A. Previn (cnd), London SO — London ("Jubilee" series) ▲ 425004–2 [ADD]
- Rachmaninoff, S.:Con 2 Pno, w. B. Haitink (cnd), Royal Concertgebouw Orch — London ▲ 414475–2 [DDD] ■ 414475–4 □ 414475–5
- Rachmaninoff, S.:Con 2 Pno, w. A. Previn (cnd), London SO — London ▲ 417702–2 [ADD]
- Rachmaninoff, S.:Con 2 Pno, w. A. Previn (cnd), London SO — London 2–▲ 436386–2 [ADD]
- Rachmaninoff, S.:Con 3 Pno, w. B. Haitink (cnd), Royal Concertgebouw Orch — London ▲ 417239–2 [DDD]
- Rachmaninoff, S.:Con 3 Pno, w. A. Previn (cnd), London SO — London ▲ 417764–2 [ADD]
- Rachmaninoff, S.:Con 3 Pno, w. A. Previn (cnd), London SO — London 2–▲ 436386–2 [ADD]
- Rachmaninoff, S.:Con 4 Pno, w. B. Haitink (cnd), Royal Concertgebouw Orch — London ▲ 414475–2 [DDD] ■ 414475–4 □ 414475–5
- Rachmaninoff, S.:Con 4 Pno, w. A. Previn (cnd), London SO — London ("Jubilee" series) ▲ 425004–2 [ADD]
- Rachmaninoff, S.:Études–tableaux, Opp. 33 & 39—Op. 39, Nos. 1,2 & 5 — London 2–▲ 436386–2 [ADD]
- Rachmaninoff, S.:Études–tableaux, Opp. 33 & 39 *(rec All Sants' Church, Petersham & St George the Martyr, 1977 & 1981)* — London ("Double Decker" series) 2–▲ 444845–2 [ADD]
- Rachmaninoff, S.:Prelude Pno, Op. 3/2 — London 2–▲ 436386–2 [ADD]
- Rachmaninoff, S.:Prelude Pno, Op. 3/2 — London ("Double Decca" series) 2–▲ 443841–2
- Rachmaninoff, S.:Preludes Pno, Opp 23 & 32 — London 2–▲ 414417–2
- Rachmaninoff, S.:Preludes Pno, Opp 23 & 32—Op. 23/2 & 5; Op. 32/10 & 13 — London ▲ 417764–2 [ADD]
- Rachmaninoff, S.:Preludes Pno, Opp 23 & 32—4 Preludes:Op. 23, Nos. 2 & 5; Op. 32, Nos. 10 & 13 — London 2–▲ 436386–2 [ADD]
- Rachmaninoff, S.:Preludes Pno, Opp 23 & 32 — London ("Double Decca" series) 2–▲ 443841–2
- Rachmaninoff, S.:Rhapsody on a Theme of Paganini, w. A. Previn (cnd), London SO — London ▲ 417702–2 [ADD]
- Rachmaninoff, S.:Rhapsody on a Theme of Paganini, w. A. Previn (cnd), London SO — London 2–▲ 436386–2 [ADD]
- Rachmaninoff, S.:Russian Rhap, w. André Previn (pno) *(rec Kingsway Hall, London, 1979)* — London ("Double Decker" series) 2–▲ 444845–2 [ADD]
- Rachmaninoff, S.:Son 2 Pno — London 2–▲ 414417–2 [ADD]
- Rachmaninoff, S.:Son 2 Pno — London ("Double Decca" series) 2–▲ 443841–2
- Rachmaninoff, S.:Suite 1 for 2 Pnos, w. André Previn (pno) *(rec All Sants' Church, Petersham, 1974)* — London ("Double Decker" series) 2–▲ 444845–2 [ADD]

450 ▲ = CD ♦ = Enhanced CD Δ = MD ■ = Cassette Tape □ = DCC

Ashkenazy, Vladimir (pno) (cont.)
Rachmaninoff, S.:Suite 2 for 2 Pnos, w. André Previn (pno) *(rec All Saints' Church, Petersham, 1974)* London ("Double Decker" series) 2-▲ 444845-2 [ADD]
Rachmaninoff, S.:Symphonic Dances, w. André Previn (pno) *(rec Kingsway Hall, London, 1979)* London ("Double Decker" series) 2-▲ 444845-2 [ADD]
Rachmaninoff, S.:Variations on a Theme by Corelli *(rec Kingsway Hall, London, 1972)* London ("Double Decker" series) 2-▲ 444845-2 [ADD]
Rachmaninoff, S.:Variations on a Theme by Corelli Testament ▲ TESSBT 1046 (m) [ADD]
Rachmaninoff, S.:Vocalise, w. Mats Lidström (vc) *(rec Gothenburg Concert Hall, Sweden, 1995)* BIS ▲ CD 719 [DDD]
Ravel, M.:Trio Pno, w. Itzhak Perlman (vn), Lynn Harrell (vc) *(rec Henry Wood Hall, London, May 1994)* London ▲ 444318-2 [DDD]
Schumann, R.:Blumenstück London ▲ 425109-2 [DDD]
Schumann, R.:Davidsbündlertänze London ▲ 425109-2 [DDD]
Schumann, R.:Fantasiestücke Cl, w. F. Cohen (cl) London ▲ 430149-2 [DDD]
Schumann, R.:Fantasiestücke Pno, Op. 12 London ▲ 425109-2 [DDD]
Schumann, R.:Kinderszenen London ▲ 421290-2 [DDD]
Schumann, R.:Son 1 Pno London ▲ 421290-2 [DDD]
Schumann, R.:Waldscenen London ▲ 421290-2 [DDD]
Scriabin, A.:Con Pno, w. L. Maazel (cnd), London PO London ▲ 417252-2 [ADD]
Scriabin, A.:Con Pno, w. B. Haitink (cnd), London PO *(rec 1972)* Intaglio ▲ ING 7481 [ADD]
Scriabin, A.:Sons Pno (comp)—Nos. 1-10 London 2-▲ 425579-2 [DDD/ADD]
Strauss, R.:Das Alphorn, w. M. McLaughlin (sop), B. Tuckwell (hn) London ▲ 430370-2 [DDD]
Strauss, R.:Andante Hn, w. B. Tuckwell (hn) London ▲ 430370-2 [DDD]
Strauss, R.:Intro, Theme & Vars, w. B. Tuckwell (hn) London ▲ 430370-2 [DDD]
Stravinsky, I.:Con Pnos, w. A. Gavrilov (pno) London ▲ 433829-2 [DDD]
Stravinsky, I.:Le Sacre du printemps Orch, w. A. Gavrilov (pno) [2-pno trans.] London ▲ 433829-2 [DDD]
Stravinsky, I.:Scherzo à la russe, w. A. Gavrilov (pno) [2-pno trans.] London ▲ 433829-2 [DDD]
Stravinsky, I.:Son Pnos, w. A. Gavrilov (pno) London ▲ 433829-2 [DDD]
Tchaikovsky, P.:Con 1 Pno, w. L. Maazel (cnd), London SO London ▲ 417750-2 [ADD]
Tchaikovsky, P.:Trio Pno, w. R. Stamper (vn), C. Jackson (vc) *(rec Nov. 1990)* Naxos ▲ 8.550467 [DDD]
Tchaikovsky, P.:Trio Pno, w. I. Perlman (vn), L. Harrell (vc) EMI Classics ▲ CDC 47988 [ADD]

Ashley, Robert (syn)
Ashley, R.:Superior 7, w. Tom Hamilton (cmpt/syn), Barbara Held (cmpt) *(rec 10 Beach St, NYC)* New World ▲ 80460-2

Ashton, Graham (tpt)
Bach, J.S.:Brandenburg Con 2, w. J. Rees (cnd), Scottish Ensemble Virgin Classics ▲ CDZ 59688-2
Clarke, J.:Suite Tpt, w. L. Pearson (org) IMP Classics ▲ PCD 986 [DDD]
Music for Trumpet & Organ, w. Leslie Pearson (org), John Orford (bn), Gordon Hunt (ob), Denis Vigay (vc) IMP Classics ▲ PCD 986 [DDD]
Shostakovich, D.:Con 1 Pno, w. M. Jones (pno), W. Boughton (cnd), English SO *(rec 11/90)* Nimbus ▲ NI 5308 [DDD]
Trumpet & Organ:Sonatas & Suites, w. Leslie Pearson (org), Gordon Hunt (ob), John Orford (bn), Denis Vigay (vc) IMP ("Classics" series) ▲ IMP 6700922
Vivaldi, A.:Con for 2 Tpts, w. G. Ruddock (tpt), C. Warren-Green (cnd), London CO Virgin Classics ▲ 59609 [DDD]

Ashton, Graham (tpt/flgl)
Contemporary Trumpet Music, w. T. Fry (perc), I. Watson (pno) Virgin Classics ▲ CDC 45003

Ashwander, Donald (pno)
Ashwander, D.:Pno Music—Request; Saratoga Rag; Sunday Night, Manhattan; October; Old Streets; Summer Garden; The Garden at Night; We Danced Premier ▲ PRCD 1038 [ADD/DDD]
Ashwander, D.:Traditional Patterns Premier ▲ PRCD 1038 [ADD/DDD]

Ashworth, T. (trbn)
Solo Pro:Contest Music for Trombone, w. T. Lichtmann (cnd) Summit ■ DCD 105

Asiedu, Nana Yaw (perc)
Childs, B.:The Distant Land, w. Carmen Lundy (mez), Billy Childs (pno), Thomas Kelley (perc) *(rec Masonic Auditorium, Cleveland, OH, Feb 27, 1995)* Telarc ▲ CD 80409 [DDD]

Asikainen, Seppo (perc)
Crumb, G.:Madrigals (4 books), w. A.-M. Mühle (sop), A.-M. Bergström (fl), S. Lüannerholm (hp), S. Röjder (db)—[Sp] *(rec digital)* BIS ▲ CD 261
Crumb, G.:Music For A Summer EveningMusic for a Summer Evening (Makrokosmos III), w. B. Dahlman (pno), I. Lindgren (pno), R. Kuisma (perc) *(rec analog)* BIS ▲ CD 261

Askeland, Reidun (pno)
Grieg, E.:Music of, w. A. Kvalbein (vc), Oslo Piano Trio, Trondheim Soloists—Intermezzo for Cello & Piano; Andante con moto in c for Violin, Cello & Piano; Sonata in a for Cello & Piano, Op. 36; Holdberg Suite (sels.); Preludium; Sarabande; Gavotte; Air; Rigaudon *(rec May 1991, Jan. & Mar. 199)* Victoria ▲ VCD 19071

Áskelsson, Hördur (org)
Sigurbjörnsson, T.:Auf meinen lieben Gott Music from Iceland ▲ ITM 702 [ADD]

Askenase, Stefan (pno)
Mozart, W.A.:Con 21 Pno, w. K. Böhm (cnd), Berlin PO Datum 2-▲ DAT 12305 [ADD]

Askew, K. (va)
Rorem, N.:Hearing, w. R. Rees (sop), K. Wheeler (mez), M. Galloway (ten), R. Hilley (bar), R. Wagner (cl), J. Hamlin (tpt), D. Starobin (mand), D. Davidson (vn), J. Babich (db), P. Suits (pno), D. Druckman (perc), G. Smith (cnd) Premier ▲ PRCD 1035 [ADD]

Askill, Michael (mar)
Edwards, R.:Marimba Dances *(rec Digital Audio Studios)* Tall Poppies ▲ TP 51 [DDD]

Askill, Michael (perc)
Wesley-Smith, M.:Nonsense, Truth & Lewis Carroll, w. David Miller (kbd), John Grundy (cnd), Sydney Philharmonia Motet Choir Vox Australis 2-▲ VAST 010-2
Wesley-Smith, M.:VENCEREMOS, w. Robert Constable (prepared pno), Martin Wesley-Smith (elec) *(rec Electronic Music Studio, Sydney Conservatorium of Music)* Tall Poppies ▲ TP 072 [DDD]

Askin, Branislav (trbn)—see ORCHESTRAS & ENSEMBLES Tickmayer Formatio

Åslund, Viktor (pno)
Strauss, R.:4 Last Songs, w. Britt Marie Aruhn (sop), S. Köhler (cnd), Royal Stockholm Orch Bluebell ▲ BLU 062 [DDD]
Strauss, R.:Songs, w. Britt Marie Aruhn (sop), S. Köhler (cnd), Royal Stockholm Orch—Begegnung, AV.72; Die Nacht, Op. 10; Allerseelen, Op. 10; Wie sollten wir geheim sie halten, Op. 19; Du meines herzens Krönelein, Op. 21; Cäcilie, Op. 27; Morgen, Op. 27; Befreit, Op. 39; Wiegenlied, Op. 41; Freundliche Vision, Op. 48; Sie wissen's nicht, Op. 49; Frühlingsfeier, Op. 56; Ich wolt' ein Sträusslein binden, Op. 68; Säusle, liebe Myrthe, Op. 68; Malven, AV.304 Bluebell ▲ BLU 062 [DDD]

Asma, F. (org)
Mendelssohn, F.:Sons Org—Nos. 1-4 Festivo ▲ FECD 092 [ADD]

Asper, Frank (org)
The Great Thanksgiving:Hymns & Songs of Thanks & Brotherhood, w. Mormon Tabernacle Choir, Alexander Schreiner (org) *(rec Salt Lake City, Utah)* Sony Classical ▲ SMK 61983 ■ SMT 61983

Assad, Odair (gtr)
Alma Brasileira Elektra/Nonesuch ▲ 79179-2 ■ 79179-4
Bach, J.S.:Das wohltemperierte Klavier, w. S. Assad (gtr)—Book 1 Elektra/Nonesuch ▲ 79292-2 ■ 79292-4
Castelnuovo-Tedesco, M.:Con for 2 Gtrs, w. S. Assad (gtr), J. Neschling (cnd), St. Gallen SO GHA ▲ 126.018
Gnattali, R.:Brasiliana 8, w. S. Assad (gtr) *(rec 1984)* GHA ▲ 126.021 [AAD]
Gnattali, R.:Corta jaca & Valsa, w. S. Assad (gtr) *(rec 1984)* GHA ▲ 126.021 [AAD]
Guitar Music of Brouwer, Pascoal, Piazzolla, et al., w. S. Assad (gtr) Elektra/Nonesuch ▲ 79116-2 ■ 79116-4
Piazzolla, A.:Escolaso, w. S. Assad (gtr) GHA ▲ 126.021 [AAD]

Assad, Odair (gtr) (cont.)
Piazzolla, A.:Lo que vendra, w. S. Assad (gtr) GHA ▲ 126.021 [AAD]
Rodrigo, J.:Concierto madrigal, w. S. Assad (gtr), J. Neschling (cnd), St. Gallen SO GHA ▲ 126.018
Rodrigo, J.:Tonadilla, w. S. Assad (gtr) GHA ▲ 126.021 [AAD]
Rodrigo, J.:Tonadilla, w. Sergio Assad (gtr) GHA ▲ 126.034
Sergio & Odair Assad, w. S. Assad (gtr) Elektra/Nonesuch ▲ 79292-2 ■ 79292-4

Assad, Sérgio (gtr)
Alma Brasileira, w. Odair Assad (gtr) Elektra/Nonesuch ▲ 79179-2 ■ 79179-4
Bach, J.S.:Das wohltemperierte Klavier, w. O. Assad (gtr)—Book 1 Elektra/Nonesuch ▲ 79292-2 ■ 79292-4
Castelnuovo-Tedesco, M.:Con for 2 Gtrs, w. O.Assad (gtr), J. Neschling (cnd), St. Gallen SO GHA ▲ 126.018
Gnattali, R.:Brasiliana 8, w. O. Assad (gtr) *(rec 1984)* GHA ▲ 126.021 [AAD]
Gnattali, R.:Corta jaca & Valsa, w. O. Assad (gtr) *(rec 1984)* GHA ▲ 126.021 [AAD]
Guitar Music of Brouwer, Pascoal, Piazzolla, et al., w. Odair Assad (gtr) Elektra/Nonesuch ▲ 79116-2 ■ 79116-4
Piazzolla, A.:Escolaso, w. O. Assad (gtr) GHA ▲ 126.021 [AAD]
Piazzolla, A.:Lo que vendra, w. O. Assad (gtr) GHA ▲ 126.021 [AAD]
Rodrigo, J.:Concierto madrigal, w. O. Assad (gtr), J. Neschling (cnd), St. Gallen SO GHA ▲ 126.018
Rodrigo, J.:Tonadilla, w. O. Assad (gtr) GHA ▲ 126.021 [AAD]
Rodrigo, J.:Tonadilla, w. Odair Assad (gtr) GHA ▲ 126.034
Sergio & Odair Assad, w. Odair Assad (gtr) Elektra/Nonesuch ▲ 79292-2 ■ 79292-4

Assael, D. (vc)
Polishook, M.:The Tribute, w. P. Van Dewater (vn), M. Gibson (vn), M. Ewing (va) Vienna Modern Masters ▲ VMM 2008 [DDD]

Assat, Georganne (hp)
Veeneman, C.:The Wiry Concord, w. Susan Werner (banjo), Forrest Covington (hammered dlc/cimbalom), Georganne Assat (hpd), Donald Martin Jenni (hpd), Mark Johnson (hpd), Barbara Phillips Farley (pno), James Austin (pno), Marta Soderberg (va), James Knutson (perc), Patrick Doyle (perc), Steven Butters (perc), James Popejoy (perc), M. Geary (cnd) Capstone ▲ SCI 6

Assayag, I. (hpd)
Rossé, F.:Music of, w. Y. Haym (ob), P. Ruby (gtr), M. Michalakakos (va), C. Roy (vc)—Zembrocordal; Digitales; Lance du Souvenant; Impromptu 0990; For a Little Hot Quaint Time Quantum ▲ QM 6949

Asti, Eugene (pno)
Coates, E.:First Meeting, w. Michael Ponder (va) *(rec St. Silas, London, Jan 25-27, 1994)* Marco Polo ▲ 8.223806 [DDD]
Coates, E.:Songs, w. Richard Edgar-Wilson (ten)—4 Old English Songs; The Mill o' Dreams; Rise up & Reach the Stars; At Vesper Bell; The Young Lover; The Grenadier; Because I Miss You So; Sigh No More, Ladies; Tell Me Where Is Fancy Bred; The Fairy Tales of Ireland; Music of the Night; Betty & Johnny; When I Am Dead; the Little Green Balcony; Ship of Dream; The Outlaw's Song; Your Name; Beautiful Lady Moon; Princess of the Dawn *(rec St. Silas, London, Jan 25-27, 1994)* Marco Polo ▲ 8.223806 [DDD]

Åstrand, Christina (vn)—see ORCHESTRAS & ENSEMBLES LINensemble

Atamian, Dickran (pno)
Beethoven, L. van:Son 8 Pno, "Pathétique" *(rec May 5 & 7, 1993)* Lyra House ▲ LHL 1004 [DDD]
Beethoven, L. van:Son 23 Pno, "Appassionata" *(rec May 5 & 7, 1993)* Lyra House ▲ LHL 1004 [DDD]
Beethoven, L. van:Son 28 Pno *(rec May 5 & 7, 1993)* Lyra House ▲ LHL 1004 [DDD]
Chopin, F.:Ballades Pno (comp)—Op. 47 Lyra House ▲ LHL 1001 [DDD]
Chopin, F.:Mazurkas—Nos. 1-4 Lyra House ▲ LHL 1001 [DDD]
Chopin, F.:Preludes, Op. 28—Nos. 4, 7, 10 & 22 Lyra House ▲ LHL 1001 [DDD]
Chopin, F.:Scherzos—Op. 39/3 Lyra House ▲ LHL 1001 [DDD]
Khachaturian, A.:Con Pno, w. G. Schwarz (cnd), Seattle SO *(rec Nov. 22-23, 1993)* Delos ▲ DE 3155 [DDD]
Mussorgsky, M.:Pictures at an Exhibition Lyra House ▲ LHL 1003 [DDD]
Prokofiev, S.:Con 3 Pno, w. G. Schwarz (cnd), Seattle SO *(rec Nov. 22-23, 1993)* Delos ▲ DE 3155 [DDD]
Prokofiev, S.:Son 6 Pno Lyra House ▲ LHL 1003 [DDD]

Atanasov, Atanas (org)
Mozart, W.A.:Adagio & Rondo Glass Armonica, w. L. Oshavkova (fl), C. T. Kasmetski (ob), Ognian Stantchev (va), N. Bespalov (vc) Divertimento ▲ DIV 31020 [DDD]

Atanasov, Atanas (harm)
Britten, H.:Missa brevis, w. T. Atanassov (sop), M. Alexandrova (sop), A. Blagoeva (cnd), Sofia Boys' Choir [arr. A. Blagoeva for sopranos, organ & boy's chorus] Gega ▲ GD 153 [DDD]

Athanasiadès, Georges (org)
The Largest Church Organ in the World Tudor ▲ 726 [DDD]
Mozart, W.A.:Andante Mechanical Org, K.616 *(rec Dec. 1989)* Tudor ▲ 754 [DDD]
Roland Schnorhk, w. R. Schnorhk (trbn) Studio SM ("Resonance Collection" series) ▲ 2544 [ADD]

Athanassova, Roumiana (pno)
Chopin, F.:Ballades Pno (comp)—in f, Op. 52 *(rec Dec. 15-17, 1993)* Ligia Digital ▲ 0103012 [DDD]
Chopin, F.:Études (24)—in E, G♭ & F, Op. 10/3, 5 & 8; in A♭, c# & a, Op. 25/1, 7 & 11 *(rec Dec. 15-17, 1993)* Ligia Digital ▲ 0103012 [DDD]
Chopin, F.:Nocturnes—in F#, Op. 15/2; in c#, Op. 27/1 *(rec Dec. 15-17, 1993)* Ligia Digital ▲ 0103012
Chopin, F.:Son Pno, Op. 35 *(rec Dec. 15-17, 1993)* Ligia Digital ▲ 0103012 [DDD]

Atherholt, Robert (ob)
Picker, T.:Romances & Interludes, w. C. Eschenbach (cnd), Houston SO Virgin Classics ▲ 59007 [DDD]
Ung, C.:Tall Wind, w. Joan Heller (sop), Keith Underwood (fl), David Starobin (gtr), Chris Finckel (vc), A. Weisberg (cnd) *(rec Vanguard Recording Studio, New York, 1982)* CRI ▲ CRI 710 [DDD/ADD]

Atherton, Joan (vn)
Matthews, C.:Suns Dance, w. Sebastian Bell (pic), Gareth Hulse (ob), Michael Collins (b cl), John Orford (ctbn), Michael Thompson (hn), Nona Liddell (vn), Joan Atherton (vn), Paul Silverthorne (va), Christopher van Kampen (vc), Robin McGee (db) *(rec All Saint's Church, Petersham, Oct 1992)* Deutsche Grammophon ▲ 447067-2 [DDD]

Atherton, Sonia Wieder (vc)
Grieg, E.:Son Vc, w. David Oei (pno) Adda ▲ ADD 581128 [DDD]
Schumann, R.:Adagio & Allegro Hn, w. David Oei (pno) Adda ▲ ADD 581128 [DDD]
Schumann, R.:Fantasiestücke Cl, w. David Oei (pno) Adda ▲ ADD 581128 [DDD]
Schumann, R.:Stücke im Volkston, w. David Oei (pno) Adda ▲ ADD 581128 [DDD]

Athparia, C. (pno)
Lee, H.:entends, etends le passé qui marche... New Concert Discs ▲ NCD 0294 [DDD]

Atkins (cl)
Thompson, R.:Suite Ob, w. P. Christ (ob), De Veritch (va) Crystal ▲ CD 321

Atkins, Jane (vl)
Damase, J.-M.:Qnt Fl, Hp & Strs, w. Anna Noakes (fl), Gillian Tingay (hp), Richard Friedman (vn), Ferenc Szucs (vc) ASV ▲ ASV 898 [DDD]

Atkins, John (pno)
Hoiby, L.:Con Pno & Orch, w. J. Krenz (cnd), Polish National RSO Katowice *(rec 1966)* Citadel ▲ CTD 88118 [ADD]

Atmacayan, Garbis (vc)
Scharwenka, X.:Qt Pno, w. Seta Tanyel (pno), Levon Chilingirian (vn), Ivo-Jan Van Der Werff (va) Collins Classics ▲ COL 1419 [DDD]
Scharwenka, X.:Trio 2 Pno, w. Seta Tanyel (pno), Levon Chilingirian (vn) Collins Classics ▲ COL 1419 [DDD]

Atri, Gloria d' (pno)
Haydn, J.:Con Org & Strs, H.XVIII/2, w. E. Aadland (cnd), European Community CO *(rec 8/90)* IMP Classics ▲ PCD 964 [DDD]

Atticciati, C. (hpd)
Frescobaldi, G.:Hpd Music [Primo Libro di Toccate...(1615)]—Toccatas Nos. 1 & 8; 14 Partitas on l'Aria di Romanesca; 6 Partitas on l'Aria di Follia; [Secondo Libro di Toccate...(1627)]—Canzonas Nos. 3 & 4; Toccata No. 9; Aria detta balletto; Ancidetemi Pur d'Arcadelt passaggiato; [Primo Libro di Capricci...(1624)—Capriccio sesto sopra la spagnoletta *(rec Jan. 21 & 22, 1992)* Bongiovanni ▲ GB 5527 [DDD]

Auber, Stefan (vc)
Beethoven, L. van:Con Vn, Vc & Pno, "Triple Con", w. R. Odnoposoff (vn), A. Morales (pno), F. von Weingartner (cnd), Vienna PO *(rec 10/20–21/37)* Pearl ▲ PEA 9358 (m) [AAD]

Aubert, Lucien (cl)
Donizetti, G.:Concertino Cl, w. O. Vlček (cnd), Prague Virtuosi ICN ▲ 008 [DDD]
Mercadante, S.:Con in E♭ Cl, w. O. Vlček (cnd), Prague Virtuosi ICN ▲ 008 [DDD]
Mercadante, S.:Con in B♭ Cl, Op. 101, w. O. Vlček (cnd), Prague Virtuosi ICN ▲ 008 [DDD]
Poulenc, F.:Son Cl Bn, w. Alexandre Ouzounoff (bn) Accord ▲ ACD 205192 [DDD]
Poulenc, F.:Son for 2 Cls, w. Jacques di Donato (cl) Accord ▲ ACD 205192 [DDD]
Rossini, G.:Vars Cl, w. O. Vlček (cnd), Prague Virtuosi ICN ▲ 008 [DDD]

Aubert-Tackett, Catherine (pno)
Flury, R.:Romantic Pieces (50) Gallo ▲ CD 908 [DAD]
Gerber, R.:Pno Music—Fantaisie sur un air de Bach; Douze divertissements; Variations sur LA-DO-RÉ; Petite suite; Cahier I–IV; 8 marches françaises Gallo ▲ CD 677 [DAD]
Gerber, R.:Sonatine (6) du Terroir Parisien Gallo ▲ CD 685 [AAD]

Aubier, Eric (tpt)
Bach, J.S.:Mass in b, BWV 232, w. Hélène Obadia (sop), Madeleine Jalbert (alt), Adrian Brand (ten), Paul Gay (bass), P. Kuentz (cnd), Paul Kuentz Orch, Paul Kuentz Choir Pierre Verany ▲ PVY 730060 [DDD]
French Trumpet in Japan, w. Hiroshi Hagao (pno) *(rec Hiroshima, Oct. 1990)* Maguelone ▲ 351.006 [DDD]
Jolivet, A.:Arioso barocco, w. *(other artists unknown)* Pierre Verany ▲ PVY 796092
Jolivet, A.:Concertino Tpt, w. *(other artists unknown)* Pierre Verany ▲ PVY 796092
Jolivet, A.:Con 2 Tpt, w. *(other artists unknown)* Pierre Verany ▲ PVY 796092
Jolivet, A.:Heptade, w. *(other artists unknown)* Pierre Verany ▲ PVY 796092

Aubut, Alain (vc)
Vivaldi, A.:Con for 2 Vcs, w. Y. Turovsky (vc), Y. Turovsky (cnd), Montreal Musici Chandos ▲ CHAN 8408 [DDD]
Vivaldi, A.:Con for 2 Vns Vc, R.565, w. E. Turovsky (vn), E. Skerjanc (vn), Y. Turovsky (cnd), Montreal Musici—RV.542 in F Chandos ▲ CHAN 8651 [DDD]
Vivaldi, A.:Con for 2 Vns Vcs, w. C. Prevost (vn), L. Hall (vn), B. Hurtubise (vc), Y. Turovsky (cnd), Montreal Musici—RV.542 in F Chandos ▲ CHAN 8651 [DDD]

Audin, Gilbert (bn)
Haydn, J.:Trios Fls & Vc, "London Trios", w. Jean-Pierre Rampal (fl), W. Schulz (fl) [trans. for 2 flutes & bassoon] Sony Classical ▲ SK 48061 [DDD]
Landowski, M.:Music of, w. Nadine Sautereau (sop), Jean-Christophe Benoit (bar), Xavier Depraz (bass), Michel Bouquet (spkr), Evelyne Aïello, Didier Bouture, Ludovic Chevalier, Laurent Decker, Françoise Deslogères, Landowski, Tzipine (cnd), Colonne Association des Concerts Orch, Boulogne-Billancourt Orch Conservatory, Paris Conservatory Société des Concerts Orch, L'Itinéraire Ensemble, Harmonia Nova Orch Ensemble—Con Bn; Con pour ondes Martenot; Femme sans passé; Hauts de Hurlevent; Horologe; Mouvement; Notes de Nuit; Souvenir d'un jardin d'enfance; Ventriloque Chamade 3-▲ 5639/40/41 [AAD/DDD]

Audoli, Jean-Philippe (vn)
Honegger, A.:Chamber Music (comp), w. D.-S. Kang (vn), P.-H. Xuereb (va), R. Wallfisch (vc), J. Rossi (db), P. Devoyon (pno)—Sonatine for 2 Violins (1920); Sonatine for Violin & Cello (1932); Sonata for Cello & Piano (1920); Sonata for Viola & Piano (1920); Trio in f for Violin, Cello & Piano (1914); Paduana for Solo Cello (1945); Prelude for Double Bass & Piano (1932) Timpani ▲ IC1009 [DDD]

Auer, Christian (hn)
Mozart, W.A.:Don Giovanni, w. Gernot Schmalfub (ob), Christian Hartmann (ob), Dieter Klöcker (cl), Waldemar Wandel (cl), Sara Willis (hn), Karl-Otto Hartmann (bn), Eberhard Buschmann (bn), Jürgen Normann (db), Consortium Classicum Bayer ▲ BR 100 135 [DDD]

Auer, Edward (pno)
Chopin, F.:Pno Music (misc)—Ballade No. 1 in g, Op. 23; Waltz No. 17 in E♭, Op. posth.; Ballade No. 3 in A♭, Op. 47; Rondeau in E♭, Op. 16; Prélude in A♭, Op. posth.; Ballade No. 2 in F, Op. 38; Souvenir de Paganini; Prélude in c♯, Op. 45; Contredanse in G♭; Ballade No. 4 in f, Op. 52 Camerata ▲ 32CM 263
Schubert, Franz:Sonatinas Vn, w. A. Delmoni (vn)—1 Sonatina *(rec Dec. 1993)* Clarity ▲ CCP 1007
Schubert, Franz:Trio 2 Pno, w. A. Delmoni (vn), N. Rosen (vc) *(rec Dec. 1993)* Clarity ▲ CCD 1007

Auger, François (perc)
Chronolyse, w. R. Pinhas (syns/gtr), Didier Batard (bass) Cuneiform ▲ Rune 30
East/West, w. R. Pinhas (syns/gtr), Norman Spinrad (voc), Dominique E. (voc), Patrick Gauthier (syn), G. Grunblatt (syn), Steve Shehan (perc), Didier Batard (bass gtr) Cuneiform ▲ Rune 31
L'Ethique, w. R. Pinhas (syns/gtr), Gilles Deleuze (voc), J. P. Goude (syn/perc), G. Grunblatt (syn), Patrick Gauthier (syn/bass), Bernard Paganotti (bass), Clément Bailly (drums) Cuneiform ▲ Rune 36X
Iceland, w. R. Pinhas (syns/gtr), Jean-Philippe Goude (syn) Cuneiform ▲ Rune 44X
Rhizosphere/Live, Paris 1982, w. R. Pinhas (syns/gtr), Patrick Gauthier (syns), Bernard Paganotti (bass), Clement Bailly (perc) Cuneiform ▲ Rune 61

Augst, Gert (org)
Brandmüller, T.:Wie Du unsern Vätern geschworen hast, w. U. Mayer-Reinach (mez), Mayence Brass Quartet [G] Gallo ▲ CD 604 [AAD]
Eben, Petr:Vitraux, w. D. Tasa (tpt) Gallo ▲ CD 604 [AAD]
Gilboa, J.:Chagall sur la Bible, w. U. Mayer-Reinach (mez), Mayence Brass Quartet Gallo ▲ CD 604 [AAD]

Auric, Georgis (pno)
Satie, E.:En habit de cheval, w. Jacques Fevrier (pno) Adès ▲ ADE 203842 [AAD]
Satie, E.:Morceaux en forme de poire, w. Jacques Fevrier (pno) Adès ▲ ADE 203842 [AAD]
Satie, E.:Petites pièces montées, w. Jacques Fevrier (pno) Adès ▲ ADE 203842 [AAD]

Auriol, Adele (vn)
Schwartz, E.:Memorial in 2 Parts, w. Bernard Fauchet (pno) Capstone ▲ CPS 863300

Aussel, Roberto (gtr)
Buxtehude, D.:Gtr Music—Suite in e *(rec Apr. 1993)* GHA ▲ 126.024
Ginastera, A.:Son Gtr GHA ▲ 126.007
Kleynjans, F.:A l'aube du dernier jour GHA ▲ 126.007
Ponce, M.:Sonatina meridional Gtr GHA ▲ 126.007
Rodrigo, J.:Gtr Music—En los trigales; Fandango GHA ▲ 126.007
Scarlatti, D.:Sons Kbd—K.14, 32 & 391 GHA ▲ 126.034
Scarlatti, D.:Sons Kbd—K.11, 14, 32, 391 & 533 *(rec Apr. 1993)* GHA ▲ 126.024
Tansman, A.:Cavatina GHA ▲ 126.007
Weiss, S.L.:Lt Music—Suite No. 25, "L'infidèle" *(rec Apr. 1993)* GHA ▲ 126.024

Austbø, Håkon (harm)
Schoenberg, A.:Trans Chamber Ensemble, w. Michel Béroff (perc), Isabelle Berteletti (perc), Louise Bessette (pno), Marc Marder (db), Paul Meyer (cl), Michel Moraguès (fl), Arditti String Quartet—Busoni:Berceuse élégiaque (1920); Mahler:Songs of a Wayfarer (1920) [w. Jean-Luc Chaignaud (baritone)]; Joh. Strauss:Kaiserwalzer (1925); Roses from the South (1921) Montaigne ▲ MO 789011 [DDD]
Schoenberg, A.:Weihnachtsmusik, w. Louise Bessette (pno), Arditti String Quartet members Montaigne ▲ MO 789011 [DDD]

Austbø, Håkon (pno)
Boucourechliev, A.:Les Archipels, w. Brigitte Sylvestre (hp), Elisabeth Chojnacka (hpd), Françoise Rieunier (org), Roland Auzet, Jean-Pierre Drouet (perc), Françoise-Frédéric Guy (pno), Claude Helffer (pno), Georges Pludermacher (pno), Ysaÿe String Quartet, Les Pléiades Ensemble Musique Francaise d'Aujourd'hui ("Collection MFA-Radio France" series) ▲ MFA 216001

Austbø, Håkon (pno) (cont.)
Debussy, C.:En blanc et noir, w. C. Helffer (pno) Musique d'Abord ▲ HMA 190957
Debussy, C.:Epigraphes antiques, w. C. Helffer (pno) Musique d'Abord ▲ HMA 190957
Debussy, C.:Lindaraja, w. C. Helffer (pno) Musique d'Abord ▲ HMA 190957
Debussy, C.:Marche écossaise sur un thème populaire, w. C. Helffer (pno) Musique d'Abord ▲ HMA 190957
Debussy, C.:Petite suite, w. C. Helffer (pno) Musique d'Abord ▲ HMA 190957
Messiaen, O.:Regards sur l'Enfant Jésus *(rec St. Martin's Church, East Woodhay, England, Aug. 11–13 & 16–18, 1993)* Naxos 2-▲ 8.550829/30 [DDD]

Austin, James (pno)
Veeneman, C.:The Wiry Concord, w. Susan Werner (banjo), Forrest Covington (hammered dlc/cimbalom), Georganne Assat (hp), Donald Martin Jenni (hpd), Mark Johnson (hpd), Barbara Phillips Farley (pno), James Austin (pno), Marta Soderberg (va), James Knutson (perc), Patrick Doyle (perc), Steven Butters (perc), James Popejoy (perc), M. Geary (cnd) Capstone ▲ SCI 6

Austin, Linda (gtr)
Exquisite Corpses from P.S. 122, w. D. Watson (shears/stick vn/gtr/tpt), Judy Dunaway (gtr/balloons), Anthony Coleman (sampler), Raissa St. Pierre (drums), Guy Yarden (vn/pno), Leslie Ross (bn), Bruce Kaplan (gtr), Doug Henderson (peckhorn/bass/toy pno), Sue Ann Harkey (gtr), Cinnie Cole (sampler), Mike Sap ¿What Next? ▲ WN 0002 [ADD]

Austin, Michael (org)
Organ Classics Chandos ("Collect" series) ▲ CHAN 6518 [ADD]
Pipes of Splendor:Organ Favorites, w. F. Jackson (org) Chandos ▲ CHAN 6602 [DDD]

Austin-Allen, Toni (pno)
Allen, J.:Vars on Desire *(rec Santuario de Guadalupe, Sante Fe, NM, Sept 29–30, 1995)* Wild Iris ▲ WI 001

Austin-Allen, Toni (pno/claves)
Allen, J.:Di Me, Lluvia, w. Carol Redman (fl/whistle), Sam Lunt (bongos), Tom Maguire (perc) *(rec Santuario de Guadalupe, Sante Fe, NM, Sept 29–30, 1995)* Wild Iris ▲ WI 001

Auviol, Adèle (vn)
Kurtz, E.:From Time to Time, w. B. Fauchet (pno) *(rec Nov. 1992)* CRI ▲ CD 661 [DDD]

Avanzi, Luca (ob)
Dall'Abaco, E.F.:Con Ob, w. A. Molino (cnd), Turin Strings Stradivarius ▲ STV 33346 [DDD]
Hasse, J.A.:Con Ob, w. A. Molino (cnd), Turin Strings Stradivarius ▲ STV 33346 [DDD]
Platti, G.B.:Cons Ob, w. A. Molino (cnd), Turin Strings—in g & G Stradivarius ▲ STV 33346 [DDD]
Sammartini, G.:Con Ob, Strs & Bc, w. A. Molino (cnd), Turin Strings Stradivarius ▲ STV 33346 [DDD]

Avat, Danielle Torchon d' (pno)
Moscheles, I.:Grande Son Pno 4-Hands, w. Sylvie Midena (pno) *(rec Festetich Castle, Budapest, June 1994)* Pyramid ▲ 13513 [DDD]
Moscheles, I.:Grande sonate symphonique 2, w. Sylvie Midena (pno) *(rec Festetich Castle, Budapest, June 1994)* Pyramid ▲ 13513 [DDD]
Moscheles, I.:Hommage à Händel, w. Sylvie Midena (pno) *(rec Festetich Castle, Budapest, June 1994)* Pyramid ▲ 13513 [DDD]

Avehaus, Silke (pno)
Szymanowski, K.:Caprices, w. Thomas Zehetmair (vn) EMI Classics ▲ CDC 55607
Szymanowski, K.:Romance, w. Thomas Zehetmair (vn) EMI Classics ▲ CDC 55607

Avery, James (pno)
Bartók, B.:Son for 2 Pnos, w. J. Simms (pno), T. L. Davis (perc), S. Schick (perc) Music & Arts ▲ CD 648 [AAD/ADD]
Lewis, P.T.:Music of, w. J. Ferrell (vn), S. Schick (perc), Peter Tod Lewis (elec), Center for New Music Ensemble, Columbia String Quartet—Bricolage (1979); Gestes (1973); Manestar (1970); ...of bells...and time (1967); Signs & Circuits—String Quartet No. 2 (1969) *(rec 1978–82)* CRI ▲ CD 619 [ADD]

Avery, James (pno/perc)
Stockhausen, K.:Kontakte, w. S. Schick (perc), J. Spek (elec) Music & Arts ▲ CD 648 [AAD/ADD]

Avila, Zoraida (hp)
Debussy, C.:Son Fl, w. Conchi Vacas (fl), Alison Montoya (va) *(rec Madrid, Oct 1–3 1990)* RNE/Spanish National Radio ▲ M3/06 [DDD]
Falla, M. de:Psyché, w. Elena Montaña (sop), Conchi Vacas (fl), Wen-Yu Ku (vn), Alison Montoya (va), Gloria Cuerda (vc) *(rec Madrid, Oct 1–3 1990)* RNE/Spanish National Radio ▲ M3/06 [DDD]
Ginastera, A.:Cantos del Tucumán, w. Elena Montaña (sop), Conchi Vacas (fl), Wen-Yu Ku (vn), Conchi Sangregorio (perc) *(rec Madrid, Oct 1–3 1990)* RNE/Spanish National Radio ▲ M3/06 [DDD]
Guibert, A.:The Bath Tub, w. Elena Montaña (sop), Conchi Vacas (fl), Wen-Yu Ku (vn), Alison Montoya (va), Gloria Cuerda (vc) *(rec Madrid, Oct 1–3 1990)* RNE/Spanish National Radio ▲ M3/06 [DDD]
Roussel, A.:Sérénade, w. Conchi Vacas (fl), Wen-Yu Ku (vn), Alison Montoya (va), Gloria Cuerda (vc) *(rec Madrid, Oct 1–3 1990)* RNE/Spanish National Radio ▲ M3/06 [DDD]
Tournier, M.:Nocturno, w. Gloria Guerda (vc) *(rec Madrid, Oct 1–3 1990)* RNE/Spanish National Radio ▲ M3/06 [DDD]

Avramenko, Alexander (vn)
Scriabin, A.:Sym 2, w. I. Golovshin (cnd), Moscow SO *(rec Mosfilm Studio, Oct 1995)* Naxos ▲ 8.553581 [DDD]

Avshalian, Charles (vn)
Bolcom, W.:Qt Pno, w. Joseph Gurt (pno), David Ireland (va), Jerome Jelinek (vc) *(rec Univ of Michigan, May 1979)* CRI ▲ CD 711 [ADD]
Finney, R.L.:Trio 2 Pno, w. Joseph Gurt (pno), Jerome Jelinek (vc) *(rec Univ of Michigan, Oct 1980)* CRI ▲ CD 711 [ADD]

Avshalomov, Daniel (va)—see also ORCHESTRAS & ENSEMBLES American String Quartet
Avshalomov, A.:Songs, w. Robert McDonald (pno)—Nocturne/Kwei Fei's Lamnet; Lantern Dance [arr J. Avshalomov] Albany ▲ TROY 216 [DDD]
Avshalomov, D.:Torn Curtain, w. Robert McDonald (pno) Albany ▲ TROY 216 [DDD]
Avshalomov, J.:Evocations, w. Robert McDonald (pno) Albany ▲ TROY 216 [DDD]
Avshalomov, J.:Sonatine, w. Robert McDonald (pno) Albany ▲ TROY 216 [DDD]

Ax, Emanuel (hpd)
Haydn, J.:Con Hpd & Strs, H.XVIII/3, w. Franz Liszt CO Sony Classical ▲ SK 48383 [DDD]
Haydn, J.:Con Hpd & Strs, H.XVIII/4, w. Franz Liszt CO Sony Classical ▲ SK 48383 [DDD]

Ax, Emanuel (pno)
Basic 100, Vol. 54, w. Eugene Ormandy (cnd) RCA Victor ▲ 09026-68023-2 ■ 09026-68023-4
Beethoven, L. van:Con 3 Pno, w. A. Previn (cnd), Royal PO RCA Silver Seal ▲ 60476-2-RV [DDD] ■ 60476-4-RV
Beethoven, L. van:Con 4 Pno, w. A. Previn (cnd), Royal PO RCA Silver Seal ▲ 60476-2-RV [DDD] ■ 60476-4-RV
Beethoven, L. van:Con 5 Pno, "Emperor", w. A. Previn (cnd), Royal PO RCA Silver Seal ▲ 09026-61213-2 ■ 09026-61213-4
Beethoven, L. van:Con 5 Pno, "Emperor", w. A. Previn (cnd), Royal PO RCA Victor ▲ 09026-61714-2; ■ 09026-61714-4
Beethoven, L. van:Fant Pno, Op. 80, "Choral Fant", w. Z. Mehta (cnd), New York PO, New York Choral Artists RCA Silver Seal ▲ 09026-61213-2 ■ 09026-61213-4
Beethoven, L. van:Polonaise Pno RCA Silver Seal ▲ 09026-61213-2 ■ 09026-61213-4
Beethoven, L. van:Qt Pno, Op. 16, w. I. Stern (vn), J. Laredo (va), Y. Ma (vc) *(rec Mar. 9–12, 1992)* Sony Classical ▲ SK 53339 [DDD]
Beethoven, L. van:Sons Vc (comp), w. Yo Yo Ma (vc) CBS 2-▲ M2K 42446 [DDD]
Beethoven, L. van:Son 1 Vc, w. Yo Yo Ma (vc) CBS ▲ MK 37251 [DDD] ■ IMT 37251 (D)
Beethoven, L. van:Son 2 Vc, w. Yo Yo Ma (vc) CBS ▲ MK 37251 [DDD] ■ IMT 37251 (D)
Beethoven, L. van:Son 3 Vc, w. Yo Yo Ma (vc) CBS ▲ MK 39024 [DDD] ■ IMT 39024 (D)
Beethoven, L. van:Son 4 Vc, w. Yo Yo Ma (vc) CBS ▲ MK 42121 [DDD]
Beethoven, L. van:Son 5 Vc, w. Yo Yo Ma (vc) CBS ▲ MK 39024 [DDD] ■ IMT 39024 (D)
Beethoven, L. van:Vars on "Ein Mädchen oder Weibchen" from Mozart's *Die Zauberflöte*, w. Yo Yo Ma (vc) CBS 2-▲ M2K 42446 [DDD]
Beethoven, L. van:Vars on "Ein Mädchen oder Weibchen" from Mozart's *Die Zauberflöte*, w. Yo Yo Ma (vc) CBS ▲ MK 42121 [DDD]

Ax, Emanuel (pno) (cont.)
- Beethoven, L. van:Vars on "See, the Conquering Hero Comes" from Handel's *Judas Maccabaeus*, w. Yo Yo Ma (vc) CBS ▲ MK 42121 [DDD]
- Beethoven, L. van:Vars on "Bei Männern" from Mozart's *Die Zauberflöte*, w. Yo Yo Ma (vc) CBS 2-▲ M2K 42446 [DDD]
- Beethoven, L. van:Vars on "Bei Männern" from Mozart's *Die Zauberflöte*, w. Yo Yo Ma (vc) CBS ▲ MK 42121 [DDD]
- The Best of Chopin, w. Géza Anda (pno), John Browning (pno), Peter Serkin (pno), et al. Victrola ("Victrola Best of" series) ▲ 60770-2-RV [ADD] ■ 60770-4-RV
- Bolcom, W.:Sons (2) for 2 Pnos, Bass & Perc, w. C. Bolling (pno), C. Sorin (db), C. Cordelette (perc) CBS ▲ MK 45646 [DDD]
- Brahms, J.:Fants Pno, Op. 116 Sony Classical ▲ SK 69284
- Brahms, J.:Intermezzos Pno, Op. 117 Sony Classical ▲ SK 69284
- Brahms, J.:Pieces Pno, Op. 118 Sony Classical ▲ SK 48046
- Brahms, J.:Qts Pno (comp), w. Isaac Stern (vn), Jalme Laredo (va), Yo-Yo Ma (vc) Sony Classical ("Isaac Stern:A Life in Music" series) 3-▲ SM3K 64520
- Brahms, J.:Qts Pno (comp), w. I. Stern (vn), J. Laredo (va), Yo-Yo Ma (vc) Sony Classical 2-▲ S2K 45846 [DDD] 2-■ S2T 45846 (D)
- Brahms, J.:Qt 3 Pno, w. I. Stern (vn), J. Laredo (va), Yo-Yo Ma (vc) CBS ▲ MK 42387 [DDD]
- Brahms, J.:Rhaps Pno, Op. 79 Sony Classical ▲ SK 48046
- Brahms, J.:Sons Vc (comp), w. Yo-Yo Ma (vc) RCA Gold Seal ▲ 09026-61355-2 ■ 09026-61355-4
- Brahms, J.:Sons Vc (comp), w. Yo-Yo Ma (vc) Sony Classical Δ SM 48191 [DDD]
- Brahms, J.:Sons Vc (comp), w. Yo-Yo Ma (vc) Sony Classical ▲ SK 48191 [DDD]
- Brahms, J.:Son 2 Pno Sony Classical ▲ SK 69284
- Brahms, J.:Son 3 Vn, w. Yo-Yo Ma (vc) [trans. for cello & piano] Sony Classical ▲ SK 48191 [DDD]
- Brahms, J.:Theme & Vars Pno Sony Classical 2-▲ S2K 45820
- Brahms, J.:Vars & Fugue on a Theme by Handel Sony Classical ▲ SK 48046
- Britten, H.:Son Vc, w. Yo-Yo Ma (vc) CBS ▲ MK 44980 [DDD]
- Chopin, F.:Ballades Pno (comp) RCA Silver Seal ▲ 60480-2-RV [DDD] ■ 60480-4-RV (CrO2)
- Chopin, F.:Con 1 Pno, w. E. Ormandy (cnd), Philadelphia Orch RCA Silver Seal ▲ 60789-2-RV [ADD/DDD] ■ 60789-4-RV
- Chopin, F.:Con 1 Pno, w. E. Ormandy (cnd), Philadelphia Orch RCA Victor ▲ 09026-68023-2; ■ 09026-68023-4
- Chopin, F.:Con 2 Pno, w. E. Ormandy (cnd), Philadelphia Orch *(rec analog)* RCA Silver Seal ▲ 60789-2-RV [ADD/DDD] ■ 60789-4-RV
- Chopin, F.:Con 2 Pno, w. E. Ormandy (cnd), Philadelphia Orch RCA Victor ▲ 09026-68023-2; ■ 09026-68023-4
- Chopin, F.:Mazurkas—Opp. 6/2, 24/2, 56/3 & 59/1-3 CBS ▲ MK 44544 [DDD]
- Chopin, F.:Scherzos CBS ▲ MK 44544 [DDD]
- Chopin, F.:Son Vc, w. Yo-Yo Ma (vc) *(rec Jordan Hall, New England Conservatory, Boston, MA, June 8-10, 1992)* Sony Classical ▲ SK 53112 [DDD]
- Chopin, F.:Son Pno, Op. 35 RCA Silver Seal ▲ 60480-2-RV [DDD] ■ 60480-4-RV (CrO2)
- Chopin, F.:Trio Pno, w. Pamela Frank (vn), Yo-Yo Ma (vc) *(rec Jordan Hall, New England Conservatory, Boston, MA, June 8-10, 1992)* Sony Classical ▲ SK 53112 [DDD]
- Dvořák, A.:Trio 3 Pno, w. Y. U. Kim (vn), Yo Yo Ma (vc) CBS ▲ MK 44527 [DDD]
- Dvořák, A.:Trio 4 Pno, "Dumky", w. Y. U. Kim (vn), Yo Yo Ma (vc) CBS ▲ MK 44527 [DDD]
- Fauré, G.:Qt 1 Pno, w. J. Laredo (vn), I. Stern (vn), Y.-Y. Ma (vc) Sony Classical ▲ SK 48066 [DDD]
- Fauré, G.:Qt 2 Pno, w. J. Laredo (vn), I. Stern (vn), Y.-Y. Ma (vc) Sony Classical ▲ SK 48066 [DDD]
- Haydn, J.:Con Hpd, Obs, Hns & Strs, H.XVIII/11, Franz Liszt CO Sony Classical ▲ SK 48383 [DDD]
- Haydn, J.:Sons Pno—Nos. 33, 38, 58, 60 CBS ▲ MK 44918 [DDD]
- Haydn, J.:Sons Pno—No. 47 in b, H.XVI/32; No. 53 in e, H.XVI/34; No. 32 in g, H.XVI/44; No. 59 in D♭, H.XVI/49 *(rec Oct. 13-14, 1993)* Sony Classical ▲ SK 53635 [DDD]
- Lieberson, P.:King Gesar, w. Yo-Yo Ma (vc), Peter Serkin (pno), Omar Ebrahim (nar), Andras Adorjan (fl), Deborah Marshall (cl), William Purvis (hn), David Taylor (trbn), Stefan Huge (perc) Sony Classical ▲ SK 57971
- Liszt, F.:Album d'un voyageur—Book I, No. 4 [Vallée d'Obermann] Sony Classical ▲ SK 48484 [DDD]
- Liszt, F.:Con 1 Pno, w. E.-P. Salonen (cnd), Philharmonia Orch *(rec Dec. 20-21, 1992)* Sony Classical ▲ SK 53289 [DDD]
- Liszt, F.:Con 2 Pno, w. E.-P. Salonen (cnd), Philharmonia Orch *(rec Dec. 20-21, 1992)* Sony Classical ▲ SK 53289 [DDD]
- Liszt, F.:Operatic Paraphrases & Transcriptions—Aida & Rigoletto Sony Classical ▲ SK 48484 [DDD]
- Liszt, F.:Son Pno Sony Classical ▲ SK 48484 [DDD]
- Mozart, W.A.:Con 17 Pno, w. P. Zukerman (cnd), St. Paul CO RCA Victrola ▲ 60136-2 [DDD] ■ 60136-4 (D)
- Mozart, W.A.:Con 18 Pno, w. P. Zukerman (cnd), St. Paul CO RCA Victrola ▲ 60136-2 [DDD] ■ 60136-4 (D)
- Piazzolla, A.:Music of, w. Pablo Ziegler (pno)—Revirado; Fuga y misterio; Milonga del ángel; Decarissimo; Soledad; La muerte del ángel; Adiós Nonino; Libertango; Verano porteño; Michelangelo; Buenos Aires hora cero; Tangata [arr 2 pnos Pablo Ziegler] *(rec Am Acad of Arts & Letters, NY, June 19-20, 1996)* Sony Classical ▲ SK 62728 [DDD]
- Prokofiev, S.:Son Vc, w. Yo-Yo Ma (vc) Sony Classical ▲ SK 46486 ■ ST 46486
- Rachmaninoff, S.:Son Vc, w. Yo-Yo Ma (vc) Sony Classical ▲ SK 46486 ■ ST 46486
- Schoenberg, A.:Con Pno, w. E.-P. Salonen (cnd), Philharmonia Orch *(rec Dec. 20-21, 1992)* Sony Classical ▲ SK 53289 [DDD]
- Schubert, Franz:Die Schöne Müllerin, w. H. Hagegård (bar) RCA Red Seal ▲ 09026-61705-2
- Schumann, R.:Adagio & Allegro Hn, w. Yo-Yo Ma (vc) CBS ▲ MK 42663 [DDD]
- Schumann, R.:Fantasiestücke Cl, w. Yo Yo Ma (vc) CBS ▲ MK 42663 [DDD]
- Schumann, R.:Qt Pno, Op. 47, w. Cleveland Quartet RCA Red Seal ▲ 6498-2-RC [DDD]
- Schumann, R.:Qt Pno, Op. 47, w. I. Stern (vn), J. Laredo (va), Y. Ma (vc) *(rec Mar. 9-12, 1992)* Sony Classical ▲ SK 53339 [DDD]
- Schumann, R.:Qnt Pno, w. Cleveland Quartet RCA Red Seal ▲ 6498-2-RC [DDD]
- Schumann, R.:Stücke im Volkston, w. Yo Yo Ma (vc) CBS ▲ MK 42663 [DDD]
- Shostakovich, D.:Son Vc, w. Yo Yo Ma (vc) CBS ▲ MK 44664 [DDD]
- Shostakovich, D.:Trio 2 Pno, w. I. Stern (vn), Yo Yo Ma (vc) CBS ▲ MK 44664 [DDD]
- Strauss, R.:Son Vc, w. Yo Yo Ma (vc) CBS ▲ MK 44980 [DDD]

Ayad, Hayet (voc/perc)—see ORCHESTRAS & ENSEMBLES Wayal Duo

Ayats, R. Cortes (pno)
- Mompou, F.:Pno Music (misc)—Suburbis; Scènes d'enfants; Cançons i Dansas; Préludes Pavane ▲ ADW 7192 [DDD]

Ayerst, Jonathan (pno)
- Liszt, F.:Music of, w. Chris Nicholls (vn)—Grand Duo con.; Duo [Son.]; Epithalam; Valse Caprice after Schubert [arr. Oistrakh]; Consolation No. 3 [arr. Milstein]; Hungarian Rhap. No. 12 [arr. Joachim]; Mephisto Waltz No. 1 [arr. Milstein]; Valse oubliée [arr. Hubay] Hyperion ▲ CDA 66743

Aymes, Jean-Marc (hpd)—see also ORCHESTRAS & ENSEMBLES Concerto Soave, La Fenice Ensemble
- Late 16th Century Venetian Harpsichord, w. Maria Cristina Kiehr (sop) L'Empreinte Digitale ▲ ED 13042

Ayo, Felix (vn)
- Alfredo Kraus in Concerto, w. A. Kraus (ten), Italian Music Academy Orch [cnd:Franco Mannino] *(rec live Apr. 3, 1989)* Fonit Cetra ▲ CDC 42 [DDD]
- Mendelssohn, F.:Con in d Vn & Strs, w. M.B. Darman (cnd), Castilla y León SO *(rec Estudios Cinearte, Madrid, July 14, 1992)* Dynamic ▲ CD 153 [DDD]
- Mendelssohn, F.:Con in d Vn, Pno & Strs, w. Emma Jimenez (pno), M.B. Darman (cnd), Castilla y León SO *(rec Estudios Cinearte, Madrid, Apr 12, 1992)* Dynamic ▲ CD 153 [DDD]
- Tartini, G.:Cons Vn (misc), w. F. Ayo (cnd), I Giovani Musici Italiani—in C, D.12; in F, D.67; in G, D.78; *(rec Rome, Italy, Apr 1-3, 1996)* Dynamic ▲ CDS 163 [DDD]
- Tartini, G.:Cons Vn (misc), w. F. Ayo (cnd), Pesaro Rossini Orch—Cons. in A, D.96; in d, D.45; in E *(rec Mar. 5-7, 1993)* Dynamic ▲ CDS 92 [DDD]
- Tartini, G.:Cons Vn (misc), w. F. Ayo (cnd), Symphonia Perusina—in D, D.15; in e, D.56; in b, D.125 *(rec St. Antonio Abate Church, Deruta, July 28-31, 1994)* Dynamic ▲ CD 131 [DDD]

Ayo, Felix (vn) (cont.)
- Vivaldi, A.:Cons Vn (misc), I Musici—RV.271 Philips ▲ 416611-2 [ADD]
- Vivaldi, A.:Cons Vn, Op. 8/1-4, "The Four Seasons", I Musici Philips ▲ 416611-2 [ADD]

Ayres, Paul (org)
- Essentially Christmas, w. East London Chorus, A. Doyle (sop), S. Liley (ten), J. Lister (hp), M. Kibbelwhite (cnd), Locke Brass Consort Koch International Classics ▲ KIC 7202 [DDD]

Ayrton, P. (hpd)—see ORCHESTRAS & ENSEMBLES La Dada

Azizjan, Sergej (vn)—see ORCHESTRAS & ENSEMBLES Trio Con Brio

Azkoul, Jad (gtr)
- Barrios, A.:Gtr Music—Chôro do Saudade; Confesion; Danza Paraguaya Forlane ▲ FOR 16666 [DDD]
- Carlevaro, A.:American Preludes Forlane ▲ FOR 16666 [DDD]
- Silvestre, L.:Gtr Music—Illustrations vulgaires; Micro-Chôros Nos. 1 & 2 Forlane ▲ FOR 16666 [DDD]
- Villa-Lobos, H.:Preludes Gtr Forlane ▲ FOR 16666 [DDD]

Azuma, Cristina (gtr)
- Contatos, w. C. Azuma (gtr) *(rec Samurai Sound, Petaluma, CA)* GSP ▲ GSP 1009

Azzaro, Teresa (pno)
- Bartók, B.:Bagatelles, Op. 6 Giulia ▲ GIU 201036 [DDD]
- Bartók, B.:Rondos (3) on Folk Tunes Giulia ▲ GIU 201036 [DDD]

Azzolini, Sergio (bn)—see also ORCHESTRAS & ENSEMBLES Sabine Meyer Wind Ensemble
- Beethoven, L. van:Duo 1 Fl & Bn, w. S. Milan (fl) Chandos ▲ CHAN 9108 [DDD]
- Beethoven, L. van:Trio Fl, WoO 37, w. S. Milan (fl), I. Brown (pno) Chandos ▲ CHAN 9108 [DDD]
- Mozart, W.A.:Con Bn, w. E. Aadland (cnd), European Community CO IMP Classics ▲ IMPCD 1054 [DDD]

Baader, Adelheid (va)
- Stamitz, C.:Qts Cl, w. E. Brunner (cl), G. Schneider (vn), H. Veihelmann (vc) Koch Schwann ▲ CD 310003 [DDD]

Baadsvik, Oystein (tuba)
- Gaathaug, M.:Son Concertante, w. Swedish Brass Quintet Simax ▲ PSC 1101
- Hindemith, P.:Son Bass Tuba, w. Swedish Brass Quintet Simax ▲ PSC 1101
- Kraft, William:Encounters II Simax ▲ PSC 1101
- Madsen, T.:Son Tuba, w. Swedish Brass Quintet Simax ▲ PSC 1101
- Sivelov, N.:Son Tuba, w. Swedish Brass Quintet Simax ▲ PSC 1101

Babácsi, Csaba (va)
- Janácek, L.:Concertino Pno, w. Thomas Hlawatsch (pno), Béla Nagy (vn), Vilmos Oláh (vn), Géza Bánhegyi (cl), Károly Ambrus (hn), István Hartenstein (bn) *(rec Budapest, May 1995)* Naxos ▲ 8.553587 [DDD]

Babadjanyan, Arno (pno)
- Babadjanyan, A.:Music of, w. A. Arutiunyan (pno), B. Chekmenyov (gtr), A. Tarasov (gtr), A. Nikolayev (perc), Silantiev, Mavisakhalyan (cnd), All-Union Radio-TV Sym Variety Orch, Armenian Radio-TV Orch—Nocturne; Prelude & Vagarshapat Dance; Capriccio; Polyphonic Son; Exprompt; Armenian Rhap; Elegy in Commemoration of A. Khachaturyan; 6 Pictures; Melody & Humoresque; Fant on Give Me My Music Back; Fant on Dum spiro spero; Fant on Winer Love; Fant on Call Me; Piece for the Pno & Orch [Dreams] *(rec 1953-83)* Russian Compact Disc ("Talents of Russia" series) ▲ RCD 16251 [ADD]

Babayan, Sergei (pno)
- Liszt, F.:Ballade 2 Pno *(rec Nov. 1992)* Connoisseur Society ▲ CD 4195
- Prokofiev, S.:Sarcasms *(rec Nov. 1992)* Connoisseur Society ▲ CD 4195
- Ravel, M.:Gaspard de la nuit *(rec Nov. 1992)* Connoisseur Society ▲ CD 4195
- Scarlatti, D.:Sons Kbd—K.8, 17, 45, 54, 79, 118, 141, 198, 239, 247, 365, 425, 427, 445, 454, 487, 491, 502 & 547 *(rec Academy of Arts & Letters, NY, July 11-12, 1995)* Pro Piano ▲ PPR 224506

Babcock, Martha (vc)
- Clarke, R.:Pieces (2) Va, w. P. McCarty (va) Northeastern ("Classical Arts" series) ▲ NR 212-CD

Babich, J. (db)
- Rorem, N.:Hearing, w. R. Rees (sop), K. Wheeler (mez), M. Galloway (ten), R. Hilley (bar), R. Wagner (cl), J. Hamlin (tpt), D. Starobin (mand), D. Davidson (vn), K. Askew (va), J. Babich (db), P. Suits (pno), D. Druckman (perc), G. Smith (cnd) Premier ▲ PRCD 1035 [ADD]

Babin, Stanley (pno)
- Hoiby, L.:Con 2 Pno, w. R. Stankovsky (cnd), Slovak RSO Bratislava Master Muscicians Collective ▲ MMC 2038 [DDD]

Babini, Italo (vc)
- Bréval, J.B.:Son Vc, w. M. Meirelles (pno) Centaur ▲ CRC 2058 [DDD]
- Kabalevsky, D.:Son Vc, w. M. Meirelles (pno) Centaur ▲ CRC 2058 [DDD]
- Schumann, R.:Fantasiestücke Cl, w. M. Meirelles (pno) [cello & piano trans.] Centaur ▲ CRC 2058 [DDD]
- Tchaikovsky, P.:Nocturne Vc, w. M. Meirelles (pno) Centaur ▲ CRC 2058 [DDD]
- Tchaikovsky, P.:Vars on a Rococo Theme, w. P. Freeman (cnd), London SO Centaur ▲ CRC 2058 [DDD]
- Walker, G.:Son Vc, w. George Walker (pno) Albany ▲ TROY 154 [DDD]
- Weber, C.M. von:Rondo Vc, w. M. Meirelles (pno) Centaur ▲ CRC 2058 [DDD]

Babinsky, Margarete (pno)
- Mozart, W.A.:Son 11 Pno—Andante grazioso LaserLight ▲ 14 224

Bacalov, Luis (pno)
- Rota, N.:Music of [trans. Bacalov]—Preludes for Piano; O Venezia, Venaga, Venusia; L'Uccello Magico; L'Intermezzo della Mantide Religiosa; The Great Mouna; Il Duca di Wurttenberg; Poupee Automate CAM ▲ CVS 015

Baccaro, Karen (tpt)
- Tailleferre, G.:Galliarde, w. Michael McGuishin (pno) *(rec UC, Santa Cruz, May 1992)* Helicon Classics ▲ HE 1008

Bacchus, P. J. (fl)
- Newman, Anthony:Chamber Music, w. M. Mills (pno), Y. Waldman (vn), D. Wan, Flute Force, Laurentian String Quartet—Qnt for Piano & Strings, "Easter"; Qt for 4 Flutes; Introduction & Toccata for Flute & Piano; Vars & Toccata for Violin Newport Classic ▲ NCD 60032 [DDD]

Baccini, Alessandro (ob)
- Mozart, W.A.:Con Ob, K.314, w. E. Aadland (cnd), European Community CO IMP ▲ IMP 2047
- Mozart, W.A.:Con Ob, K.314, w. E. Aadland (cnd), European Community CO IMP Classics ▲ IMPCD 1054 [DDD]

Bacelar, Alejandro (vc)
- Hazzan Rishon, Legendary Cantorial Recitativi, Opuses 1 & 2, w. Montefiore, David (cant), C. Vineburg (pno), V. Zeltser (vn), G. Lochner (vc), C. Morrison (va) Behar/Berg 2-▲ 001494

Bach, Erik (pno)
Stolarczyk, W.:Earth Air Fire Water, w. Amalie Malling (pno), John Damgaard (pno), Anne Øland (pno), Teddy Teirup (pno), Friedrich Gürtler (pno), Rosalind Bevan (pno), Poul Rosenbaum (pno), Rodolfo Llambias (pno), Bella Horn-Ribera (pno), Anders Riber (pno), Elisabeth Sigurdsson (pno), Thomas Tronheim (pno), Elsebeth Broderson (pno), Erik Kaltoft (pno), Jørgen Hald Nielsen (pno), Aino Gilemann (pno), Birgit Kjær (pno), Jørgen Thomsen (pno), Gunhild Donslund (pno), Henrik Bo Hansen (pno), Lone Karlsson (pno), Erik Fessel (pno), Lasse Nilsson (pno), Janos Ferenczi (pno), Axel Momme (pno), Arne de Cros Dich (pno), Sven Micha Slot (pno), Hanne Bramsen Buhl (pno), Lili Olesen (pno), Susannah Carlsson (pno), Ulla Erml (pno), Vagn Sørensen (pno), Leif Greibe (pno), Bodil Krogh (pno), Kirsten Ottosen (pno), Inger Bergenholz (pno), Karsten Gylendorf (pno), Bjønr Elkjær (pno), Jacob Bjørn Jensen (pno), Jørgen Kaad (pno), Anne Marie Hjelm (pno), Carl Ulrik Munk Andersen (pno), Poul Lumbye (pno), Oluf Hildebrandt Nielsen (pno), Joachim Olsson (pno), Peter Pade Ramsøe Jacobsen (pno), Astrid Pollmann (pno), Jette Borsch (pno), Kirsten Karlshøj (pno), Maria Teresa Assing (pno), Allan Dahl Hansen (pno), Johan Hugossen (pno), Tine Fenger Pederson (pno), Arne Jørgen Fæø (pno), Anja Høgsted (pno), Anne Sophie Parbo (pno), Inga Lindmark (pno), Teresa Drabik Stathakis (pno), Anne Ruth Ferenczi (pno), Irene Hasager (pno), Yuka Ichikawa (pno), Birgitte Baur (pno), Malene Thastum (pno), Jens E. Rasmussen (pno), Birgitte Zielke (pno), Claus Zielke (pno), Stefan Kasch (pno), Bin Qiao (pno), Inger Johanne Teirup (pno), Lindy Rosborg (pno), Liisa Heininen (pno), David Højer (pno), Ellen Refstrup (pno), Thomas K. Søorensen (pno), Erik Kure (pno), Michael Rauff (pno), Jan beck Eriksson (pno), Tanja Zapolski (pno), Vibeke Skagbo (pno), Pål Eide Lindtner (pno), Ha-Young Sul (pno), Benedicte Palko (pno), Inke Kesseler (pno), Anne Marie Meineche (pno), Sverre Larsen (pno), Kasper Peter Bach (pno), Elisabetta Eliseo (pno), Olga Magieres (pno), Carl Erik Kühl (pno), Thorkild Borup Nielsen (pno), Valeria Zanini (pno), Lars Stenhoft (perc), Dennis Boel (perc), Winnie Dahlgren (perc), Susanne Vind (perc), Claus Byrith (elec), Anne Marie Storm (elec), J. Ribera (cnd) *(rec live, Koldinghaus Castle, Denmark, May 2, 1996)* — Danica ▲ DCD 1996

Bach, Franz (perc)
Hummel, B.:Music of, w. S. Gagelmann (perc), E. Guggeis (perc), Peter Sadlo (perc)—Tempo di valse, Op. 76c; 5 Szenen für 2 Schlagzeuger, Op. 58; Marimbana, Op. 95d; 5 Aspekte für Schlagzeuger, Op. 88d; Quattro pezzi für Schlagzeuger, Op. 92; Freken 70 für vier Schlagzeuger, Op. 38 *(rec Gasteig Munich, Dec. 1993)* — Thorofon ▲ CTH 2233 [DDD]

Bach, Gottfried (hpd)—see ORCHESTRAS & ENSEMBLES August Wenzinger Ensemble, Freiburg Baroque Soloists

Bach, Michael (vc)
Bach, J.S.:Suites Vc, BWV 1007-1012 *(rec Germany, Apr 21-22, 1994)* — Mode ▲ mode 52 [DDD]
Lachenmann, H.:Allegro sostenuto, w. B. Wambach (pno), D. Smeyers (cl) — CPO ▲ CPO 999102-2 [DDD]
Lachenmann, H.:Pression — CPO ▲ CPO 999102-2 [DDD]
Schnebel, D.:Inventionen Vc *(rec Germany, Apr 21-22, 1994)* — Mode ▲ mode 52 [DDD]
Schnebel, D.:Mit diesen Händen, w. Metchild Seitz (mez) *(rec Germany, Apr 21-22, 1994)* — Mode ▲ mode 52 [DDD]
Zimmermann, B.A.:Intercommunicazione, w. B. Waumbach (pno) — CPO ▲ CPO 999198 [DDD]
Zimmermann, B.A.:Short Studies Vc — CPO ▲ CPO 999198 [DDD]
Zimmermann, B.A.:Son Vc — CPO ▲ CPO 999198 [DDD]

Bacha, Abdel Rahman El (pno)
Bach, J.S.:Con 1 Hpd, w. K. Redel (cnd), Grenoble Instrumental Ensemble — Forlane ▲ FRL 16537 [DDD]
Bach, J.S.:Con 4 Hpd, w. K. Redel (cnd), Grenoble Instrumental Ensemble — Forlane ▲ FRL 16537 [DDD]
Bach, J.S.:Con 5 Hpd, w. K. Redel (cnd), Grenoble Instrumental Ensemble — Forlane ▲ FRL 16537 [DDD]
Beethoven, L. van:Son 8 Pno, "Pathétique" — Forlane ▲ FRL 16612 [DDD]
Beethoven, L. van:Son 9 Pno — Forlane ▲ FRL 16612 [DDD]
Beethoven, L. van:Son 10 Pno — Forlane ▲ FRL 16612 [DDD]
Beethoven, L. van:Son 11 Pno — Forlane ▲ FRL 16612 [DDD]
Ravel, M.:Gaspard de la nuit — Forlane ▲ FRL 16737 [DDD]
Ravel, M.:Miroirs — Forlane ▲ FRL 16737 [DDD]
Ravel, M.:Le Tombeau de Couperin — Forlane ▲ FRL 16737 [DDD]
Schubert, Franz:Pieces Pno, D.946 — Forlane ▲ FRL 16756 [DDD]
Schubert, Franz:Son Pno, D.784 — Forlane ▲ FRL 16756 [DDD]
Schubert, Franz:Son Pno, D.894 — Forlane ▲ FRL 16756 [DDD]

Bachauer, Gina (pno)
Beethoven, L. van:Con 4 Pno, w. A. Dorati (cnd), London SO — Mercury Living Presence ▲ 432018-2 [ADD]
Beethoven, L. van:Con 5 Pno, "Emperor", w. S. Skrowaczewski (cnd), London SO — Mercury Living Presence ▲ 432018-2 [ADD]
Beethoven, L. van:Son 9 Pno *(rec London, July 9, 1963)* — Mercury Living Presence ▲ 434340-2
Brahms, J.:Con 2 Pno, w. S. Skrowaczewski (cnd), London SO *(rec London, July 6 & 7, 1962)* — Mercury Living Presence ▲ 434340-2
Brahms, J.:Vars on a Theme by Paganini *(rec New York, Feb. 20 & 26, 1963)* — Mercury Living Presence ▲ 434340-2
Chopin, F.:Con 1 Pno, w. A. Dorati (cnd), London SO — Mercury Living Presence ▲ 434374-2
Chopin, F.:Con 2 Pno, w. A. Dorati (cnd), London SO — Mercury Living Presence ▲ 434374-2
Debussy, C.:Pour le piano — Mercury Living Presence ▲ 434359-2
Debussy, C.:Preludes Pno (sels)—Cathédrale engloutie; Danseuses de Delphe [both from Book 1]; Bruyères [from Book 2] — Mercury Living Presence ▲ 434359-2
Liszt, F.:Hungarian Rhaps—No. 12 *(rec New York, Feb. 20 & 26, 1963)* — Mercury Living Presence ▲ 434340-2
Ravel, M.:Gaspard de la nuit, w. John Gielgud (nar)—includes readings of poems by Bertrand [Ondine, Le Gibet & Scarbo] — Mercury Living Presence ▲ 434359-2
Stravinsky, I.:Scenes Pno — Mercury Living Presence ▲ 434359-2

Bächer, Mihály (pno)
Beethoven, L. van:Son 5 Vn, "Spring", w. D. Kovács (vn) — White Label ▲ HRC 105 [ADD]
Beethoven, L. van:Son 9 Vn, "Kreutzer", w. D. Kovács (vn) — White Label ▲ HRC 105 [ADD]

Bächli, Tomas (pno)
Tenney, J.:Flocking, w. Gertrud Schneider (pno) — Hat Hut ("Now" series) ▲ ART CD 6193 [DDD]

Bachlin, Kerstin (vn)
Johansson, O.:Poem for Kerstin Bachlin *(rec Oct 1979)* — Point ▲ PCD 5118

Bachman Vas, Meg (pno)
Cory, E.:Pas de Quatre, w. Jayn Rosenfeld (fl), Diane Bruce Sinclair (vn), Charles Forbes (vc), New York Camerata — Soundspells ▲ CD 116 [DDD]
Fauré, G.:Après un rêve, w. Arturo Delmoni (vn) — John Marks ▲ JMR 8
Fauré, G.:Après un rêve, w. A. Delmoni (vn) [violin-piano arr.] — Mobile Fidelity ▲ MFCD 781 [AAD]
Fauré, G.:Son 1 Vn, w. Arturo Delmoni (vn) — John Marks ▲ JMR 8
Fauré, G.:Son 1 Vn, w. A. Delmoni (vn) — Mobile Fidelity ▲ MFCD 781 [AAD]
Franck, C.:Son Vn, w. Arturo Delmoni (vn) — John Marks ▲ JMR 8
Franck, C.:Son Vn, w. A. Delmoni (vn) — Mobile Fidelity ▲ MFCD 781 [AAD]
Songs My Mother Taught Me, w. A. Delmoni (vn) *(rec 1982)* — John Marks Records ▲ JMR 1
Songs My Mother Taught Me, w. A. Delmoni (vn) — North Star ■ DS 0004

Bachmann, Maria (va)
Glinsky, A.:Toccata-Scherzo, w. J. Klibonoff (pno) — Catalyst ▲ 09026-61824-2

Bachmann, Maria (vn)
Beethoven, L. van:Son 9 Vn, "Kreutzer", w. J. Klibonoff (pno) — Connoisseur Society ▲ CD 4178 [DDD]
Bolcom, W.:Son 2 Vn, w. Jon Kilbonoff (pno) — Catalyst ▲ 09026-62668-2
Copland, A.:Nocturne, w. Jon Kilbonoff (pno) — Catalyst ▲ 09026-62668-2
Corigliano, J.:Son Vn & Pno, w. J. Klibonoff (pno) — Catalyst ▲ 09026-61824-2
Dresher, P.:Double Ikat 2, w. Jon Kilbonoff (pno) — Catalyst ▲ 09026-62668-2
Macmillan, J.:Kiss on Wood, w. Jon Kilbonoff (pno) — Catalyst ▲ 09026-62668-2

Bachmann, Maria (vn) (cont.)
Messiaen, O.:Quatuor pour la fin du temps, w. J. Klibonoff (pno)—Praise to the Immortality of Jesus Christ [8th movt.] — Catalyst ▲ 09026-61824-2
Moravec, P.:Son Vn, w. J. Klibonoff (pno) — Catalyst ▲ 09026-61824-2
Pärt, A.:Fratres II, w. J. Klibonoff (pno) [arr vn & pno] — Catalyst ▲ 09026-61824-2
Rochberg, G.:Son Vn, w. J. Klibonoff (pno) — Connoisseur Society ▲ CD 4178 [DDD]
Schnittke, A.:Son 1 Vn, w. Jon Kilbonoff (pno) — Catalyst ▲ 09026-62668-2

Back, Gordon (pno)
Capriccio:Classics for Oboe, w. J. Anderson (ob) — ASV ▲ ASV 2100
Jeux d'Enfants, w. Christopher Hyde-Smith (fl/pic), Emma Johnson (cl), George MacDonald (cl), Academy of St. Martin in the Fields [cnd:Neville Marriner], Mexico City PO, Mexico State SO, Royal PO [cnd:Enrique Bátiz], Northern Sinfonia of England [cnd — ASV Quicksilva ▲ ASQ 6182

Backer, I. (bn)
Vogel, W.:Sonances, w. H. Peter-Indermühle (fl), H. Elhorst (ob), K. Weber (cl), K. Hanke (hn), U. Lehmann (vn), L. Dober (vn), H. Forster (va), M. Liechti (vc), R. Tschupp (cnd) — Grammont ▲ CTSP 14-2 [ADD]

Backhaus, Wilhelm (pno)
Beethoven, L. van:Con 4 Pno, w. G. Cantelli (cnd), New York PO *(rec live, 1956)* — Legend ▲ LGD 121
Beethoven, L. van:Con 4 Pno, w. H. Knappertsbusch (cnd), Vienna PO — Stradivarius ▲ STV 10002 [ADD]
Beethoven, L. van:Con 5 Pno, "Emperor", w. J. Keilberth (cnd), Stoccarda RSO — Stradivarius ▲ STV 10002 [ADD]
Beethoven, L. van:Con 5 Pno, "Emperor", w. C. Schuricht (cnd), Swiss-Italian RSO *(rec Apr. 27, 1961)* — Ermitage ▲ ERM 144 [ADD]
Beethoven, L. van:Son 4 Pno *(rec Salzburg Festival, 1967)* — Enterprise ("Documents" series) ▲ ENTLV 964 [ADD]
Beethoven, L. van:Son 6 Pno — Fortissimo ▲ CDE 3020
Beethoven, L. van:Son 21 Pno, "Waldstein" — Fortissimo ▲ CDE 3020
Beethoven, L. van:Son 25 Pno — Fortissimo ▲ CDE 3020
Beethoven, L. van:Son 28 Pno *(rec Salzburg Festival, 1967)* — Enterprise ("Documents" series) ▲ ENTLV 964 [ADD]
Beethoven, L. van:Son 30 Pno *(rec Salzburg Festival, 1967)* — Enterprise ("Documents" series) ▲ ENTLV 964 [ADD]
Beethoven, L. van:Son 32 Pno — Fortissimo ▲ CDE 3020
Brahms, J.:Ballades, Op. 10—Nos. 1 & 2 *(rec , London 1933 from HMV 78s)* — Memories 2-▲ HR 4442/43 [ADD]
Brahms, J.:Ballades, Op. 10 *(rec between 1933 & 1939)* — Grammofono 2000 ▲ GRM 78507 [ADD]
Brahms, J.:Ballades, Op. 10—Nos. 1 & 2 *(rec , London 1933 from HMV 78s)* — Pearl ▲ PEA 9385 (m) [AAD]
Brahms, J.:Con 2 Pno, w. K. Böhm (cnd), Saxon State Orch *(rec Dresden 1939 from HMV 78s)* — Memories 2-▲ HR 4442/43 [ADD]
Brahms, J.:Con 2 Pno, w. K. Böhm (cnd), Saxon State Orch — Enterprise ("Piano Library" series) ▲ ENT PL 213
Brahms, J.:Con 2 Pno, w. C. Schuricht (cnd), Swiss Radio-TV Orch — Stradivarius 2-▲ STV MSC 2001
Brahms, J.:Con 2 Pno, *(cnd & orch unknown)* — Memories 2-▲ MEM CD 3009
Brahms, J.:Hungarian Dances Pno—Nos. 6 & 7 *(rec , Berlin 1934 from HMV 78s)* — Memories 2-▲ HR 4442/43 [ADD]
Brahms, J.:Hungarian Dances Pno—Nos. 6 & 7 *(rec , Berlin 1934 from HMV 78s)* — Pearl ▲ PEA 9385 (m) [AAD]
Brahms, J.:Pno Music (misc)—Pieces, Op. 76/7 & 8; Intermezzos, Op. 117/1 & 2; Pieces, Op. 118; Ballades; Hungarian Rhapsodies; Rhaps., Op. 79; Scherzo in e♭; Vars. on an Original Theme, Op. 21/1; Waltzes, Op. 39/1, 2, 12, 13, 14, 15 & 16 *(rec London & Berlin, 1933 & 1935 from HMV 78s)* — Memories 2-▲ HR 4442/43 [ADD]
Brahms, J.:Pno Music (misc)—Intermezzos, Op. 17/1 & 2; Klavierstücke, Op. 76/7 & 8 & Op. 118/1-6; Ballades; Hungarian Dances Piano; Rhaps.; Vars., Op. 21/1 *(rec between 1933 & 1939)* — Grammofono 2000 ▲ GRM 78507 [ADD]
Brahms, J.:Pno Music (misc)—Pieces, Op. 76/7 & 8; Intermezzos. Op. 117/1 & 2; Pieces, Op. 118; Ballades, Nos. 1 & 2; Hungarian Dances; Rhaps., Op. 79; Scherzo in e♭; Vars. on an Original Theme, Op. 21/1; Waltzes, Op. 39/1, 2 & 15 *(rec London & Berlin, 1933 & 1935 from HMV 78s)* — Pearl ▲ PEA 9385 (m) [AAD]
Brahms, J.:Pno Music (misc)—Ballads, Op. 10/1 & 2; Waltzes, Op. 39/1, 2 & 12-16; Pieces for Pno, Op. 76/7-8 & Op. 118/1-6; 2 Rhaps, Op. 70/1 & 2; Hungarian Dances, Nos. 6 & 7; Intermezzi, Op. 117/1 & 2; Vars on an Orig Theme, Op. 21/1 — Enterprise ("The Piano Library" series) ▲ ENT 192
Brahms, J.:Rhaps Pno, Op. 79 *(rec London 1933 from HMV 78s)* — Memories 2-▲ HR 4442/43 [ADD]
Brahms, J.:Rhaps Pno, Op. 79 *(rec between 1933 & 1939)* — Grammofono 2000 ▲ GRM 78507 [ADD]
Brahms, J.:Rhaps Pno, Op. 79 *(rec London, 1933 from HMV 78s)* — Pearl ▲ PEA 9385 (m) [AAD]
Brahms, J.:Scherzo Pno, Op. 4 *(rec London 1933 from HMV 78s)* — Memories 2-▲ HR 4442/43 [ADD]
Brahms, J.:Scherzo Pno, Op. 4 *(rec London 1933 from HMV 78s)* — Pearl ▲ PEA 9385 (m) [AAD]
Brahms, J.:Vars on an Original Theme *(rec between 1933 & 1939)* — Grammofono 2000 ▲ GRM 78507 [ADD]
Brahms, J.:Vars on an Original Theme *(rec Berlin, 1935 from HMV 78s)* — Memories 2-▲ HR 4442/43 [ADD]
Brahms, J.:Vars on an Original Theme *(rec Berlin, 1935 from HMV 78s)* — Pearl ▲ PEA 9385 (m) [AAD]
Brahms, J.:Vars on a Theme by Paganini — Enterprise ("Piano Library" series) ▲ ENT PL 213
Brahms, J.:Waltzes Pno, Op. 39—Nos. 1, 2 & 15 *(rec London for HMV 78s, 1933)* — Pearl ▲ PEA 9385 (m) [AAD]
Brahms, J.:Waltzes Pno, Op. 39—Nos. 1, 2, 12, 13, 14, 15 & 16 *(rec London for HMV '78s, 1933)* — Memories 2-▲ HR 4442/43 [ADD]
Chopin, F.:Études (24) *(rec 1927 for HMV)* — Pearl ▲ PEA 9902 (m) [AAD]
Chopin, F.:Pno Music (misc)—Berceuse, Op. 57; Fantaisie-Impromptu, Op. 66; Grande Valse Brillante, Op. 18; Waltz in D♭, Op. 64/1 *(rec 1925-33 for HMV)* — Pearl ▲ PEA 9902 (m) [AAD]
Great Pianists of the Golden Era:Wihelm Backhaus, w. Backhaus, Wilhelm (pno) — Fonè ▲ FON 90F11 [DDD]
Liszt, F.:Études de concert (2) Pno *(rec 1925 for HMV)* — Pearl ▲ PEA 9902 (m) [AAD]
Schumann, R.:Con Pno, w. K. Böhm (cnd), Vienna PO — Datum 2-▲ DAT 12305 [ADD]

Backhouse, Peter (org)
Famous Hymns of Praise, w. [cnd:Dennis Townhill], St. Mary's Episcopal Cathedral Choir Edinburgh — Priory ▲ PRCD 376 [DDD]

Bacon, Ernst (pno)
Bacon, E.:Songs from Dickenson, w. Helen Boatwright (sop), John Kirkpatrick (pno)—It's All I Have to Bring; Eden; I'm Nobody; As Well as Jesus ; A Word; Weeping and Sighing; O Friend; She Went; A Threadless Way; The Imperial Hear; Summer's Lapse; Is There Such a Thing as Day?; To Make a Prairie; A Spider; The Grass So Little Has to Do; The Snake; So Bashful; Alabaster Wool; Eternity; Sunset; The Simple Days; On this Wondrous Sea *(rec 1954 & 1964)* — CRI ▲ CD 675 [ADD]
Ives, C.:Songs, w. Helen Boatwright (sop), John Kirkpatrick (pno)—Abide with Me; Walking; Where the Eagle; Disclosure; The White Gulls; Two Little Flowers; The Greatest Man; The Children's Hour; Berceuse; Ann Street; General William Booth Enters into Heaven; Autumn; Swimmers; Evening; Harpalus; Tarrant Moss; Serenity; At the River; The See'r; Maple Leaves; "1, 2, 3"; Tom Sails away; He Is There!; In Flanders Fields *(rec 1954 & 1964)* — CRI ▲ CD 675 [ADD]

Bacon, Thomas (hn)
Fantasie, w. Bacon, Thomas (hn), Phillip Moll (pno) — Crystal ■ C 379
Gottschalk, A.:Section for 4 Hns, w. J. Wilson (hn), N. Goodearl (hn), J. Graber (hn), R. Brown (timp) — Summit ▲ DCD 135 [DDD]
Hindemith, P.:Son for 4 Hns, w. A. D. Krehbiel (hn), L. Strieby (hn), G. Williams (hn) — Summit 2-▲ DCD 115 [DDD] 2-■ DCD 115

▲ = CD ♦ = Enhanced CD Δ = MD ■ = Cassette Tape □ = DCC

Bacon, Thomas (hn) (cont.)
Leclaire, D.:Qt Hns, w. G. Hustis (hn), W. Caballero (hn), Erik Ralske (hn) Summit ▲ DCD 135 [DDD]
Pinkston, R.:Qt for 4 Hns, w. J. Landsman (hn), N. Goodearl (hn), J. Horrocks (hn) Summit ▲ DCD 135 [DDD]
Schultz, Arthur:Dragons in the Sky, w. R. Brown (perc/elec) Summit ▲ DCD 135 [DDD]
Schultz, Arthur:T-Rex, w. B. Connelly (pno) Summit ▲ DCD 135 [DDD]
Wilder, A.:Easy Pieces Hn, w. Phillip Moll (pno) *(rec Arizona State Univ., May 16–18, 1994)* Summit ▲ DCD 170 [DDD]
Wilder, A.:Son 1 Hn, w. Phillip Moll (pno) *(rec Arizona State Univ., May 16–18, 1994)* Summit ▲ DCD 170 [DDD]
Wilder, A.:Son 2 Hn, w. Phillip Moll (pno) *(rec Arizona State Univ., May 16–18, 1994)* Summit ▲ DCD 170 [DDD]
Wilder, A.:Son 3 Hn, w. Phillip Moll (pno) *(rec Arizona State Univ., May 16–18, 1994)* Summit ▲ DCD 170 [DDD]
Wilder, A.:Suite Hn, w. Phillip Moll (pno) *(rec Arizona State Univ., May 16–18, 1994)* Summit ▲ DCD 170 [DDD]

Badaloni, Francesco (cl)
Curran, A.:Crystal Psalms, An Homage to Kristallnacht, w. D. Keberlee (cl), M. Riesler (cl), A. Santoloci (cl), M. Capone (acc), L. Dublanchet (tuba), D. Rueff (tuba), A. Caggiano (perc), w. Ensemble Vocale Sesquialtera [cnd:E. Razzicchia], Radio France Chamber Choir [cnd:D. LaBorde]—[F] New Albion ▲ NA 067

Badertscher-Jaquiéry, Fränzi (fl)
Gerber, R.:Chamber Music, w. Gunhard Mattes (ob), Dimitri Ashkenazy (cl), Claude Delley (cl), Pierre-Yves Dubois (cl), Anne de Dadelsen (pno)—Pièce lente; Habanera; Berceuse [all for Cl & Pno]; Trio for Fl, Ob & Pno; Son for Fl & Pno; Ballet for Fl & Pno; Sonatine for 3 Cl; Pavane for Fl & Pno; Suite for Fl & Pno; Prélude et fugue sur le nom de Bach for Cl Gallo ▲ CD 788 [DAD]

Badev, G. (vn)
Mozart, W.A.:Con 1 Vn, w. C. Iliev (cnd), Philharmonia Bulgarica Vivace ▲ 516
Mozart, W.A.:Con 1 Vn, w. C. Iliev (cnd), Philharmonia Bulgarica Vivace 2-▲ G 217 [ADD]
Mozart, W.A.:Con 2 Vn, w. C. Iliev (cnd), Philharmonia Bulgarica Vivace ▲ 516
Mozart, W.A.:Con 2 Vn, w. C. Iliev (cnd), Philharmonia Bulgarica Vivace 2-▲ G 217 [ADD]

Badgley, Barbara (vc)
Kosins, M.S.:Love Letters:A Dialogue, w. B. Shank (fl), P. Terry (hp) *(rec 1980)* Centaur ▲ CRC 2105 [ADD]

Badian, Christian (pno)
Clementi, M.:Pno Music (comp), w. Aldo Antognazzi (pno), Jose Maria Brusco (pno), Daniela Lanzillo (pno), Federico Wiman (pno), J. Rotter (cnd), Württemberg PO—Con in C for Pno; Sons (6) for Pno, Op. 1, Nos. 1–3; "Son inedita" in A♭ Aura Classics ▲ AU 32070
Clementi, M.:Pno Music (comp), w. Aldo Antognazzi (pno), Eduardo Cazaban (pno), Cristina Da Souza (pno), Dao Di Renzo (pno), Pablo Lavandera (pno), Yi Fang Huang (vn), Silvina Cardenas (fl), Nestor Herzbaum (fl)—Sons (6) for Pno, Op. 2, Nos. 1, 3 & 5 (w. flutes); Duets (3) for Piano 4-Hands, Op. 3, Nos. 2 & 3; Sons (3) for Pno & Vn, Op. 3, No. 4 Aura Classics ▲ AU 32287

Badings, Vera (hp)
Debussy, C.:Orchestral Music, w. George Pieterson (cl), Beinum (cnd), Royal Concertgebouw Orch—Berceuse héroique; Danses for Harp & Orch.; Images; Jeux; Marche écossaise; La mer; Nocturnes; Prélude à l'après-midi d'un faune; Première rapsodie for Clarinet & Orch. Philips 2-▲ 438742-2

Badura-Skoda, Paul (pno)
Bach, J.S.:Partitas Hpd, BWV 825–830 MCA Classics 2-▲ MCAD2-9840 (m) [ADD]
Beethoven, L. van:Con 4 Pno, Collegium Aureum Editio Classica ▲ 77063-2-RG [ADD]
Beethoven, L. van:Con Vn, Vc & Pno, "Triple Con", w. F. Maier (vn), A. Bylsma (vc), Collegium Aureum Editio Classica ▲ 77063-2-RG [ADD]
Brahms, J.:Intermezzos Pno, Op. 117 Auvidis ▲ AV 6115 [AAD]
Brahms, J.:Pieces Pno, Op. 118 Auvidis ▲ AV 6115 [AAD]
Brahms, J.:Pieces Pno, Op. 119 Auvidis ▲ AV 6115 [AAD]
Haydn, J.:Sons Pno—6 Lost Pno Sons Koch Schwann ▲ SCH 315722 [DDD]
Martin, F.:Con 2 Pno, w. F. Martin (cnd), Luxembourg RSO *(rec 1971)* Jecklin-Disco ▲ JD 632-2 [ADD]
Mozart, W.A.:Adagio Pno, K.540 Astrée ▲ E 7710 [AAD]
Mozart, W.A.:Complete Mozart Edition, w. Ingrid Haebler (pno), Ludwig Hoffmann (pno), Jörg Demus (pno) Philips 2-▲ 422516-2 [ADD]
Mozart, W.A.:Con 10 Pno, w. Dagmar Bella (pno), W. Furtwängler (cnd), Vienna PO Music & Arts ▲ CD 895
Mozart, W.A.:Con 20 Pno, w. P. Badura-Skoda (cnd), Prague CO Valois ▲ V 4664
Mozart, W.A.:Con 21 Pno, w. P. Badura-Skoda (cnd), Prague CO *(rec 1971)* Supraphon Collection ▲ 11 0610-2 [ADD]
Mozart, W.A.:Con 21 Pno, w. P. Badura-Skoda (cnd), Prague CO Valois ▲ V 4664
Mozart, W.A.:Con 23 Pno, w. P. Badura-Skoda (cnd), Prague CO Valois ▲ V 4687
Mozart, W.A.:Con 24 Pno, w. P. Badura-Skoda (cnd), Prague CO *(rec 1970)* Supraphon Collection ▲ 11 0610-2 [ADD]
Mozart, W.A.:Con 25 Pno, w. P. Badura-Skoda (cnd), Prague CO Valois ▲ V 4687
Mozart, W.A.:Fant Pno, K.397 Astrée ▲ E 7710 [AAD]
Mozart, W.A.:Pno Music (misc)—Marche funèbre, K.453a; Minuet in D, K.355; Gigue in G, K.574 Astrée ▲ E 7710 [AAD]
Mozart, W.A.:Prelude & Fugue Pno Astrée ▲ E 7710 [AAD]
Mozart, W.A.:Qts Pno, w. Festetics String Quartet Arcana ▲ ACA 7 [DDD]
Mozart, W.A.:Qts Pno, w. Festetics String Quartet Arcana 3-▲ ACA 903 [DDD]
Mozart, W.A.:Rondo Pno, K.511 Astrée ▲ E 7710 [AAD]
Mozart, W.A.:Vars Pno, K.265 Astrée ▲ E 7710 [AAD]
Music at the Time of Beaumarchais, w. Montserrat Figueras (sop), Lawrence Monteyro (sop), Raphel Oleg (vn), Miguel da Silva (va), Christophe Coin (vc), Marc Coppey (vc), José Miguel Moreno (gtr), Philippe Cassard (pno), Éric Le Sage (pno), et al. Valois ▲ V 4767
Salieri, A.:Cons Pno, w. C. Scimone (cnd), Venice Solisti—in B♭ Erato ▲ ERA SEL 12987 [DDD]
Schubert, Franz:Fant Pno, D.760, "Wandererfantasie" *(rec 1987)* Music & Arts ▲ CD 267 [DDD]
Schubert, Franz:Ländler Pno—Lerchenwalzer [from D.145] *(rec 1987)* Music & Arts ▲ CD 267 [DDD]
Schubert, Franz:Moments musicaux *(rec 1987)* Music & Arts ▲ CD 267 [DDD]
Schubert, Franz:Pno Music (4-hands), w. Andrea Bonatta (pno)—Fant.; Rondo; Vars.; Grandes Marches; Trio 5 & 6; 3 Marches Militaires Valois ▲ V 4720
Schubert, Franz:Scherzos Pno, D.593—No. 1 *(rec 1987)* Music & Arts ▲ CD 267 [DDD]
Schubert, Franz:Sons Pno (comp)—Son. 8, D.571; Son. 16, D.850 Arcana ▲ ACA 15 [DDD]
Schubert, Franz:Sons Pno (comp)—Son. 11, D.625; Son. 18, D.958 Arcana ▲ ACA 17 [DDD]
Schubert, Franz:Son Pno, D.459 Arcana ▲ ACA 14 [DDD]
Schubert, Franz:Son Pno, D.537 Arcana ▲ ACA 16 [DDD]
Schubert, Franz:Son Pno, D.784 Arcana ▲ ACN 942018 [DDD]
Schubert, Franz:Son Pno, D.845 Arcana ▲ ACA 14 [DDD]
Schubert, Franz:Son Pno, D.894 Arcana ▲ ACA 16 [DDD]
Schubert, Franz:Son Pno, D.959 Arcana ▲ ACN 942018 [DDD]
Schubert, Franz:Songs (misc), w. E. Söderström (sop) [ca. 1824 Conrad Graf piano]—13 songs—D.118, 162, 216, 257, 328, 367, 544, 717, 720, 764, 877/2-4 [G] Astrée ▲ E 7783 [DDD]
Schubert, Franz:Waltzes Pno—14 waltzes *(rec 1987)* Music & Arts ▲ CD 267 [DDD]
Schumann, R.:Carnaval Pno Valois ▲ V 4699 [DDD]
Schumann, R.:Etudes in the Form of Free Variations on a Theme by Beethoven Koch Treasure ▲ 31627-2 [ADD]
Schumann, R.:Kinderszenen Valois ▲ V 4699 [DDD]
Schumann, R.:Waldscenen Valois ▲ V 4699 [DDD]

Bae, Ik-Hwan (vn)—see also ORCHESTRAS & ENSEMBLES Bargemusic
Bartók, B.:Contrasts, w. D. Shifrin (cl), W. Doppmann (pno) Delos ▲ CD 3043 [DDD]
Messiaen, O.:Quatuor pour la fin du temps, w. D. Shifrin (cl), W. Lash (vc), W. Doppmann (pno) Delos ▲ CD 3043 [DDD]

Baeckelandt, G. (instr)—see ORCHESTRAS & ENSEMBLES Quintessens
Baehr, Cynthia (vn)—see ORCHESTRAS & ENSEMBLES Stratos

Baerg, Irmgard (pno)
Davies, V.:Con 1 Pno, "Mennonite Pno Con", w. B. Brott (cnd), London SO Campion ▲ 1304 [DDD]

Baert, Edmont (vc)
Brahms, J.:Son in D Vc, w. Serge Bémant (pno) Pavane 2-▲ ADW 7124/25
Chopin, F.:Intro & Polonaise, "Polonaise brilliante", w. Serge Bémant (pno) Pavane 2-▲ ADW 7124/25
Franck, C.:Son Vn, w. Serge Bémant (pno) Pavane 2-▲ ADW 7124/25
Servais, A.-F.:Fant Polonaise Vc, w. Serge Bémant (pno) Pavane 2-▲ ADW 7124/25
Servais, A.-F.:Souvenir de Spa, w. Serge Bémant (pno) Pavane 2—▲ ADW 7124/25

Baert, Lieven (vc)
Rossini, G.:Tancredi, w. Sumi Jo (sop—Amenaide), Lucretia Lendi (mez—Roggiero), Anna Maria di Micco (mez—Isaura), Ewa Podles (cta—Tancredi), Stanford Olsen (ten—Argirio), Pietro Spagnoli (bar—Orbazzano), Ewald Demeyere (hpd), Franck Coryn (db), A. Zedda (cnd), Collegium Instrumentale Brugense, Capella Brugensis *(rec Poissy Theatre & Centre Musical-Lyrique-Phonographique, Ile de France, Jan. 26–31, 1994)* Naxos ("Opera Classics" series) 2-▲ 8.660037/38 [DDD]

Baeyens, Edmond (vc)
Boeck, A. de:Cantilena, w. Robert Wasmuth (pno) *(rec Belgian Radio-TV Concerthall, Feb 8, 1982)* Phaedra ▲ 492 002 [ADD]
Dvořák, A.:Con Vc, w. F. Terby (cnd), BRTN PO Brussels *(rec Belgian Radio-TV Concerthall, Jan 1978)* Phaedra ▲ 492 002 [ADD]
Schumann, R.:Con Vc, w. F. Terby (cnd), BRTN PO Brussels *(rec Belgian Radio-TV Concerthall, May 1978)* Phaedra ▲ 492 002 [ADD]

Bagg, Jonathan (va)—see also ORCHESTRAS & ENSEMBLES Ciompi String Quartet, Arman Ensemble
Fuchs, R.:Fantstücke Va, w. Jane Hawkins (pno) *(rec Baldwin Audit., Durham, NC, Dec 16–18, 1994)* Centaur ▲ CRC 2278 [DDD]
Fuchs, R.:Son Va, w. Jane Hawkins (pno) *(rec Baldwin Audit., Durham, NC, Dec 16–18, 1994)* Centaur ▲ CRC 2278 [DDD]
Fuchs, R.:Trio Vn, Va & Pno, w. Fritz Gearhart (vn), Jane Hawkins (pno) *(rec Baldwin Audit., Durham, NC, Dec 16–18, 1994)* Centaur ▲ CRC 2278 [DDD]
Hoiby, L.:Bermudas, w. Terry Rhodes (sop), Ellen Williams (mez), Hsiao-mei Ku (vn), Fred Raimi (vc), Thomas Warburton (pno) Albany ▲ TROY 172 [DDD]
Ward, R.:Serenade for Mallarmé, w. Anna Wilson (fl), Fred Raimi (vc), Jane Hawkins (pno) Albany ▲ TROY 204 [DDD]

Bagger, Louis (hpd)
Bach, J.S.:The Art of the Fugue Titanic ▲ Ti 151 [DDD]
Byrd, W.:Consort Music, w. New York Consort of Viols—Prelude & Voluntary; Fant. a 3 in C; Fant. a 3 in C; Ut re mi fa sol la; Fant. a 4 in G; Fant. a 4 in D; Prelude [from Pavana, Gagliarda Ph. Tregian]; The Maiden's Songe *(rec Leverett, MA, May 24–26 & June 23, 1993)* Lyrichord ▲ LEMS 8015 [DDD]
Byrd, W.:Songs, w. Tamara Crout (sop), Lawrence Lipnik (ct), New York Consort of Viols—Rejoice unto the Lord; Delight is dead; Farewell, false love; Who made thee, Hob, forsake the plough?; My mistress had a little dog; Browning (The leaves bee greene); Ye Sacred Muses *(rec Leverett, MA, May 24–26 & June 23, 1993)* Lyrichord ▲ LEMS 8015 [DDD]

Bagliano, Stefano (rcr)—see also ORCHESTRAS & ENSEMBLES Collegium Pro Musica
Bach, J.S.:Sons Fl, BWV 1030–35, w. O. Dantone (hpd)—in c, BWV 1030 [trans. Dantone & Bagliano]; in C, BWV 1032 [trans. Reinhald Gerlach & Dantone] *(rec June 1993)* Dynamic ▲ CDS 77 [DDD]
Bach, J.S.:Trio Sons Org, BWV 525–530, w. O. Dantone (hpd)—in d, BWV 527 & in F, BWV 527 [trans. Dantone & Bagliano] *(rec June 1993)* Dynamic ▲ CDS 77 [DDD]
Scarlatti, A.:Cants, w. S. Picollo (sop), R. Balconi (ten), Collegium Pro Musica—includes Clori mia, Clori bella; Filli che esprime la sua fede a Fileno; Ardo e ver per te d'amore; Tu sei quella che al nime sembri giusta, plus others Nuova Era ("Ancient Music" series) ▲ NUO 7162 [DDD]

Bagratuni, Suren (vc)
Crumb, G.:Son Vc *(rec New Hope Methodist Church, Methuen, MA, May 22–23, 1995)* Ongaku ▲ 024-104 [DDD]
Hindemith, P.:Son Vc, Op. 25/3 *(rec New Hope Methodist Church, Methuen, MA, May 22–23, 1995)* Ongaku ▲ 024-104 [DDD]
Khudoyan, A.:Nostalgia, w. Natalia Knoma (vc) *(rec New Hope Methodist Church, Methuen, MA, May 22–23, 1995)* Ongaku ▲ 024-104 [DDD]
Khudoyan, A.:Son 1 Vc *(rec New Hope Methodist Church, Methuen, MA, May 22–23, 1995)* Ongaku ▲ 024-104 [DDD]
Khudoyan, A.:Son 2 Vc *(rec New Hope Methodist Church, Methuen, MA, May 22–23, 1995)* Ongaku ▲ 024-104 [DDD]
Khudoyan, A.:Son 3 Vc *(rec New Hope Methodist Church, Methuen, MA, May 22–23, 1995)* Ongaku ▲ 024-104 [DDD]
Khudoyan, A.:Son for 2 Vcs, w. Natalia Knoma (vc) *(rec New Hope Methodist Church, Methuen, MA, May 22–23, 1995)* Ongaku ▲ 024-104 [DDD]

Bagwell, Thomas (pno)
Dvořák, A.:Music of, w. Scott St. John (vn)—2 Slavonic Dances; Humoresque; Mazurek; Capriccio; Romantic Pieces; Son. for Violin & Piano Marquis Classics ▲ MAR 159 [DDD]

Bahng, Grace Mihi (vc)—see ORCHESTRAS & ENSEMBLES Blair String Quartet

Bahr, Gunilla von (fl)
Albinoni, T.:Adagio Org, w. J.-O. Wedin (cnd), Stockholm Chamber Ensemble BIS ▲ CD 100
Bach, C.P.E.:Son Fl, H.562 BIS ▲ CD 21
Bach, J.S.:Partita Fl, BWV 1013 BIS ▲ CD 21
Bach, J.S.:Suite 2 Orch, w. C. Génetay (cnd), National Museum CO BIS ▲ CD 21
Badings, H.:Dialogues Fl Org, w. H. Fagius (org) BIS ▲ CD 160 [AAD]
Bashmakov, L.:Quattro bagatelle, w. Rainer Kuisma (perc) *(rec Castle Wik, Sweden, Oct. 22, 1974)* BIS ▲ CD 11 [AAD]
Castelnuovo-Tedesco, M.:Sonatina Fl & Gtr, w. D. Blanco (gtr) BIS ▲ CD 60 [AAD]
Debussy, C.:Syrinx BIS ▲ CD 100
Debussy, C.:Syrinx *(rec Castle Wik, Sweden, Sept. 6, 1975)* BIS ▲ CD 28 [AAD]
Dorothy Dorow, w. D. Dorow (sop), L. Negro (pno) *(rec Aug. 31, 1975 & Jan. 24–2)* BIS ▲ CD 45 [AAD]
Fauré, G.:Fant Fl, w. D. Achatz (pno) BIS ▲ CD 160 [AAD]
Ibert, J.:Entracte, w. D. Blanco (gtr) BIS ▲ CD 60 [AAD]
Martin, F.:Son da chiesa, w. Hans Fagius (org) *(rec Härnösand Cathedral, Sweden, Feb 29, 1980)* BIS ▲ CD 71 [AAD]
Martinů, B.:Son Fl & Pno, w. K. Hindart (pno) *(rec 4/73)* BIS ▲ CD 234 [AAD]
Messiaen, O.:La Merle noir, w. D. Achatz (pno) BIS ▲ CD 160 [AAD]
Molter, J.M.:Con Flauto d'amore, w. J.-O. Wedin (cnd), Stockholm Chamber Ensemble BIS ▲ CD 100
Mozart, W.A.:Rondo Fl, K.Anh.184, w. J.-O. Wedin (cnd), Stockholm Chamber Ensemble BIS ▲ CD 175
Music for Flute & Guitar, w. Diego Blanco (gtr) BIS ▲ CD 60 [AAD]
Nordic Solo Flute Music BIS ▲ CD 150 [AAD]
Olsson, O.:Romance Fl, w. H. Fagius (org) BIS ▲ CD 160 [AAD]
Pergament, M.:Pezzo, w. P. Pohjola (vn), Z. Zirchev (vn), Z. Tchavdarov (va), U. Vrethammar (vc) *(rec Jan. 25, 1973)* BIS ▲ CD 37 [AAD]
Pergament, M.:Son Fl Pno, w. K. Hindart (pno) *(rec Apr. 15, 1973)* BIS ▲ CD 37 [AAD]
Pergament, M.:Sonatina Fl Strs, w. S. Westerberg (cnd), Musica Sveciae *(rec Feb. 20, 1976)* BIS ▲ CD 37 [AAD]
Poulenc, F.:Son Fl, w. D. Achatz (pno) BIS ▲ CD 160 [AAD]
Rachmaninoff, S.:Vocalise, w. H. Fagius (org) BIS ▲ CD 175 [AAD]
Rautavaara, E.:Son Fl, w. D. Blanco (gtr) BIS ▲ CD 60 [AAD]
Rautavaara, E.:Son Fl, w. D. Blanco (gtr) *(rec June 25, 1975)* BIS ▲ CD 66 [AAD]
Rhené-Baton:Passacaille, w. D. Achatz (pno) BIS ▲ CD 160 [AAD]

Bahr, Gunilla von (fl) (cont.)
Romantic & Picturesque Music for Flute with Piano or Organ, w. Dag Achatz (pno), Hans Fagius (org) BIS ▲ CD 160 [AAD]
Rosenblüth, L.:Jewish Liturgical Music, w. L. Rosenblüth (cant), A. Vitolius (org), M. Thyresson (org), E. Ericson (cnd), Stockholm Royal Conservatory Chamber Choir—Psalms 93 & 155, plus 5 settings for High Holidays, Rosh Hashanah, Sabbath & Yom Kippur BIS ▲ CD 1 [AAD]
Roussel, A.:Joueurs de flûte, w. D. Achatz (pno) BIS ▲ CD 160 [AAD]
Sonninen, A.:El amor pasa, w. Solveig Faringer (sop), S. Westerberg (cnd), Swedish RSO members *(rec Stockholm Concert Hall, Sweden, Sept. 17, 1974)* BIS ▲ CD 11 [AAD]
Sun-Flute, w. Stockholm Chamber Ensemble [cnd:Jan-Olav Wedin] BIS ▲ CD 100
Sun-Flute 2/3 BIS ▲ CD 175 [AAD]
Sun-Flute 4, w. Karin Langebo (hp), Musica Vitae [cnd:Jan-Olav Wedin] BIS ▲ CD 350 [DDD]
Telemann, G.P.:Cants, w. Rolf Leanderson (bar), Hans Fagius (org)—Kleine Kantate von Wald und Au; Ew'ge Quelle, milder Strom *(rec Johannes Church, Stockholm, Sweden, May 16 & 17, Oct 20, 1978)* BIS ▲ CD 127 [AAD]
Vivaldi, A.:Cons Pic, w. J.-O. Wedin (cnd), Stockholm Chamber Ensemble—R.443 [w. K. Hindart (pno)]; R.444 & R.445 BIS ▲ CD 21
Werdin, E.:Concertino Fl, w. D. Blanco (gtr), J.-O. Wedin (cnd), Stockholm Chamber Ensemble BIS ▲ CD 60 [AAD]
Works for Flute & Guitar, w. Diego Blanco (gtr) BIS ▲ CD 90 [AAD]

Bahr, Gunilla von (pic/fl)
Bashmakov, L.:Con da camera, w. Paavo Pohjola (vn), Mona Nordin (vn), Zahari Tchavdarov (va), Elemér Lavotha (vc) *(rec Grünewald Hall, Stockholm, Sweden, May 11, 1974)* BIS ▲ CD 11 [AAD]

Baiano, Enrico (org/hpd)
Sui Palchi Delle Stelle:Sacred Music in the Neapolitan Conservatories at the Time of Francesco Provenzale, w. [cnd:Antonio Florio], Cappella Pietà de Turchini, Antonella Ippolito (sop), Jane Haughton (sop), Daniela del Monaco (alt), Sebastiano Cassarà (vn), Rosario Di Meglio (vn), Antonella Bologna (va), Paolo Dionisio (vl), Antonio Florio (vc), Pierluigi Ciappareli (thb) Symphonia ▲ SY 93S20 [DDD]

Bailes, Anthony (lt)
Vivaldi, A.:Music of, w. Wim Ten Have (va), Raymond Leppard (hpd), Hans-Martin Linde (fl/rcr), Leppard, Linde (cnd), English CO, Prague CO, Danske Strings members—Concertino in D, RV.121; Cons. in f, RV.156; in G, RV.435 [Op. 10/4]; in D, RV.429; in F, RV.434 [Op. 10/5]; in D, RV.93; in d, RV.540; Son. in E♭, RV.130 [Al Santo Sepolcro] Classics for Pleasure ▲ CDCFP 4656 [ADD]

Bailey, John (fl)—see also ORCHESTRAS & ENSEMBLES Moran Woodwind Quintet
Snyder, R.:Qnt 3 Fl, w. William McMullen (ob), Eric Ginsberg (cl), Allen French (hn), Gary Echols (bn) Coronet ▲ COR 400-9

Bailey, Michael (org)
Byrd, W.:Org Music Duo ▲ 89027 [DDD]

Bailey, Owain (fl)
Gregson, E.:Metamorphoses, w. Karen Fotherby (cl), E. Gregson (cnd), Royal Northern College of Music Wind Orch Doyen ▲ CD 043 [DDD]

Bailey, R. (vc)—see ORCHESTRAS & ENSEMBLES Delmé String Quartet

Baillie, Alexander (vc)
Holst, G.:Orchestral Works, w. L. MacAslan (vn), D. Atherton (cnd), London PO, London SO—A Winter Idyll; Elegy in Memoriam William Morris; Indra, Symphonic Poem for Orchestra, Op. 13; A Song of the Night, Op. 19/1; Sita:Interlude from Act III, Op. 23; Invocation, Op. 19/2; The Lure; Dances from the Morning of the Year, Op. 45/2 Lyrita ▲ SRCD 209
Respighi, O.:Adagio con variazioni Vc Orch, w. G. Simon (cnd), Philharmonia Orch *(rec Goldsmith's College, London, Dec 19-22, 1990)* Cala ▲ CACD 1007 [DDD]
Stevens, B.:Con Vc, w. E. Downes (cnd), BBC PO Meridian ▲ CDE 84124
Tippett, M.:Con Vn Va, w. E. Kovacic (vn), G. Caussé (va), M. Tippett (cnd), BBC PO Nimbus ▲ NI 5301 [DDD]

Bailly, Clément (drums)
L'Ethique, w. Pinhas, Richard (syns/gtr), Gilles Deleuze (voc), J. P. Goude (syn/perc), G. Grunblatt (syn), Patrick Gauthier (syn/bass), Bernard Paganotti (bass), François Auger (drums) Cuneiform ▲ Rune 36X

Bailly, Clément (perc)
Rhizosphere/Live, Paris 1982, w. R. Pinhas (syns/gtr), Patrick Gauthier (syns), Bernard Paganotti (bass), François Auger (perc) Cuneiform ▲ Rune 61

Baines, Anthony (db)—see ORCHESTRAS & ENSEMBLES London Chamber Players

Baines, Francis (b vl)—see ORCHESTRAS & ENSEMBLES In Nomine Players

Baitz, Rick (synclavier)
Baitz, R.:Kaleidocycles Centaur ▲ CRC 2039 [DDD]

Baker, Brett (trbn)
Bone Idyll, w. J.G. Hurdley (cnd), Williams Fairey Band Chandos ("Brass" series) ▲ CHAN 4543

Baker, Charles (pno)
Encores, w. P. Casals (vc), Eugene Istomin (pno) *(rec 1915-1954)* Sony Classical ("Casals Edition" series) ▲ SMK 66573 [ADD]

Baker, Dian (pno)
Duo, w. R. Drinkall (vc) Klavier ▲ KCD 11043 [DDD]
Gubaidulina, S.:Pno Music (comp)—Chaconne; Invention; Toccata-Troncata; Son; Musical Toys [A Collection of Piano Pieces of Children] Stradivarius ▲ STV 33393 [DDD]
Hindemith, P.:Son Vc & Pno, Op. 11/3, w. Roger Drinkall (vc) Pyramid ▲ PYR 13505
Kodály, Z.:Son Vc & Pno, Op. 4, w. Roger Drinkall (vc) Pyramid ▲ PYR 13505
Martinů, B.:Son 3 Vc, w. Roger Drinkall (vc) Pyramid ▲ PYR 13505
Weill, K.:Son Vc, w. Roger Drinkall (vc) Pyramid ▲ PYR 13505

Baker, Don R. (instr)
Riley, T.:In C, w. Bruce Ackley, Steve Adams, Chris Brown, George Brooks, Steve Coughlin, Blake Derby, Bill Douglass, Mihr'un'Nisa Douglass, Hank Dutt, David Harrington, Don Howe, Joan Jeanrenaud, Alden Jenks, Warner Jepson, Henry Kaiser, Jaron Lanier, Bill Maginnis, George Marsh, Shabda Owens, Jon Raskin, Gyan Riley, Terry Riley, Gino Robair, John Sackett, Ramón Sender, John Sherba, Toyji Tomita, Danny Tunick, William Winant, Evan Ziporyn *(rec Jan. 14, 1990)* New Albion ▲ NA 071

Baker, Israel (vn)
Brahms, J.:Sextet Strs, Op. 36, w. J. Heifetz (vn), W. Primrose (va), V. Majewski (va), G. Piatigorsky (vc), G. Rejto (vc) RCA Gold Seal ▲ 7965-2-RG [ADD]
Mozart, W.A.:Qnt Strs, K.516, w. J. Heifetz (vn), W. Primrose (va), V. Majewski (va), G. Piatigorsky (vc) RCA Gold Seal ▲ 7869-2 (m/s) [ADD] ■ 7869-4 (m/s)
Schubert, Franz:Qnt Strs, D.956, w. J. Heifetz (vn), W. Primrose (va), G. Piatigorsky (vc), G. Rejto (vc) RCA Gold Seal ▲ 7964-2-RG [ADD] ■ 7964-4-RG (CrO2)
Spohr, L.:Double Qt 1, w. J. Heifetz (vn), P. Amoyal (vn), P. Rosenthal (vn), M. Thomas (va), A. Harshman (va), G. Piatigorsky (vc), L. Lesser (vc) RCA Gold Seal ▲ 7870-2-RG (m/s) [ADD]

Baker, Jennifer (instr)
Brooke, N.:Obomobile, w. Brandon Adrien, Karen Birch, Daniel Cate, Judy Christy, Richard Cochran, Jessica Cooper, Leslie Dominguez, Erin Hannigan, Dorothy Knight, Jason Lichtenwalter, Jay Moore, Hwa-Ling Russell, Toyin Spellman, Sarah Weiner, Jay Weinland Opus One ▲ CD 160

Baker, Jim (perc)—see ORCHESTRAS & ENSEMBLES Speculum Musicae

Baker, Julius (fl)
Amram, D.:Theme & Vars on "Red River Valley", w. R.A. Clark (cnd), Manhattan CO Newport Classic ▲ NPD 85546 [DDD]
Debussy, C.:Prélude à l'après-midi d'un faune, w. L. Emenheiser Logan (pno) [flute & piano trans. J. Jaubert] *(rec live, 1982)* VAI Audio ▲ VAIA 1022 [ADD]
Franck, C.:Son Vn, w. L. E. Logan (pno) *(rec live 1982)* VAI Audio ▲ VAIA 1022 [ADD]
Gluck, C.W.:Orfeo ed Euridice (dance of the blessed spirits), w. F. Prohaska (cnd), Vienna State Opera Orch *(rec Vienna, 1966)* Vanguard Classics ▲ SVC 55 [AAD]
Handel, G.F.:Semele, w. Flute Force—Where'er you walk [arr Cooper] *(rec Queens College, NY, Sept 1993)* VAI Audio ▲ VAIA 1133 [DDD]
In Recital, Vol. 2, w. Harriet Wingreen (pno) *(rec live 1983)* VAI Audio ▲ VAIA 1033

Baker, Julius (fl) (cont.)
Mozart, W.A.:Andante Fl, w. A. Janigro (cnd), Zagreb Solisti *(rec Vienna, 1965)* Vanguard Classics ▲ SVC 54 [AAD]
Mozart, W.A.:Con 1 Fl, w. A. Janigro (cnd), Zagreb Solisti *(rec Vienna, 1965)* Vanguard Classics ▲ SVC 54 [AAD]
Mozart, W.A.:Con 2 Fl, w. F. Prohaska (cnd), Vienna State Opera Orch *(rec Vienna, 1966)* Vanguard Classics ▲ SVC 55 [AAD]
Mozart, W.A.:Con Fl Hp, w. H. Jelinek (hp), A. Janigro (cnd), Zagreb Solisti *(rec 1962)* Vanguard Classics ("Everyman" series) ▲ OVC 5011 [ADD]
Mozart, W.A.:Con Fl Hp, w. Hubert Jelinek (hp), A. Janigro (cnd), Zagreb Solisti *(rec Baumgarten Hall, Vienna, May 5-7, 1962)* Vanguard Classics ▲ SVC 42 [AAD]
Muczynski, R.:Son Fl, w. L. Emenheiser Logan (pno) *(rec live 1982)* VAI Audio ▲ VAIA 1022 [ADD]
Music from Cranberry Isles, w. S. S. Frank (sop), Sara Lambert Bloom (ob), et al. Centaur ▲ CRC 2084
Nielsen, C.:Con Fl, w. L. Bernstein (cnd), New York PO *(rec 1966)* Sony Classical 4-▲ S4K 45989 [ADD]
Nielsen, C.:Con Fl, w. L. Bernstein (cnd), New York PO Sony Classical ▲ SMK 47599
Poulenc, F.:Son Fl, w. L. Emenheiser Logan (pno) *(rec live 1982)* VAI Audio ▲ VAIA 1022 [ADD]
Ravel, M.:Daphnis et Chloé (suite 2), w. Flute Force [arr Rie Schmidt] *(rec Queens College, NY, Sept 1993)* VAI Audio ▲ VAIA 1133 [DDD]
Telemann, G.P.:Suite in a Fl, w. A. Janigro (cnd), Zagreb Solisti *(rec 1962)* Vanguard Classics ("Everyman" series) ▲ OVC 5011 [ADD]
Telemann, G.P.:Suite in a Fl, w. A. Janigro (cnd), Zagreb Solisti *(rec Baumgarten Hall, Vienna, May 5-7, 1962)* Vanguard Classics ▲ SVC 42 [AAD]
Vaughan Williams, R.:Fant on Greensleeves, w. A. Janigro (cnd), Zagreb Solisti *(rec Vienna, 1965)* Vanguard Classics ▲ SVC 54 [AAD]
Vivaldi, A.:Cons Fl (misc), w. A. Janigro (cnd), Zagreb Solisti—RV.439 in B♭, "La Notte" *(rec 1964)* Vanguard Classics ("The Bach Guild" series) ▲ OVC 2006 [ADD]
Vivaldi, A.:Cons Fl (misc), w. A. Janigro (cnd), Zagreb Solisti—in D, R.428, "Il cardellino" *(rec Vienna, 1965)* Vanguard Classics ▲ SVC 54 [AAD]
Vivaldi, A.:Con Fl Bn, w. Karl Hoffmann (bn), A. Janigro (cnd), Zagreb Solisti *(rec Baumgarten Hall, Vienna, May 5-7, 1962)* Vanguard Classics ▲ SVC 42 [AAD]
Vivaldi, A.:Cons Pic, w. A. Janigro (cnd), Zagreb Solisti—Con in C, R.443 *(rec Vienna, 1965)* Vanguard Classics ▲ SVC 54 [AAD]
Vivaldi, A.:Cons Pic, w. F. Prohaska (cnd), Vienna State Opera Orch—Cons in C & a, R.444 & 445 *(rec Vienna, 1966)* Vanguard Classics ▲ SVC 55 [AAD]

Baker, Martin (org)
Tavener, J.:Akathist of Thanksgiving, w. J. Bowman (ct), T. Wilson (ten), M. Neary (cnd), BBC SO, Westminster Abbey Choir, BBC Singers *(rec Jan. 21, 1994)* Sony Classical ▲ SK 64446 [DDD]
Tavener, J.:Innocence, w. Patricia Rozario (sop), Leigh Nixon (ten), Graham Titus (bass), Alice Neary (vc), Charles Fullbrook (bells), Martin Neary (cnd), Westminster Abbey Choir *(rec Westminster Abbey, May 1-5, 1995)* Sony Classical ▲ SK 66613 [DDD]

Baker, Melissa (va)
Dvořák, A.:Qnt Pno, Op. 81, w. J. Lateiner (pno), J. Heifetz (vn), J. de Pasquale (va), G. Piatigorsky (vc) RCA Gold Seal ▲ 7965-2-RG [ADD]

Bakhchiev, Alexander (pno)
Levina, Z.:Sons Vn & Pno, w. G. Kalacheva (vn)—1 Son., "Poem" Russian Disc ▲ RUS 11 382 [DDD]
Liapunov, S.:Con 2 Pno, w. B. Khaikin (cnd), Moscow RSO Russian Disc ▲ RUS 11 024 [ADD]
Rubinstein, A.:Pno Music—selected short works Russian Disc ("The A. Rubinstein Edition" series) ▲ RUS 11 337 [ADD]
Rubinstein, A.:Pno Music—selected short works Russian Disc ▲ RUS 11049 [ADD]

Bakker, Harm (vl)
Einhorn, R.:Voices of Light, w. Susan Narucki (sop), Corrie Pronk (alt), Frank Hameleers (ten), Henk van Heijnsbergen (b-bar), Ronald Hoogeveen (vn), Michael Feves (vl), Naomi Hirschfeld (vl), S. Mercurio (cnd), Netherlands Radio PO, Martin Wright (cnd), Anonymous 4, Netherlands Radio Chorus *(rec Music Center of the Netherlands Radio & TV, Aug 23-25, 1995)* Sony Classical ▲ SK 62006 [DDD]

Bakowski, Krysztof (vn)
Krauze, Z.:Quatour pour la naissance, w. Miroslaw Pokrzywinski (cl), Andrzej Bauer (vc), Zygmunt Krauze (pno) *(rec National Philharmonic, Warsaw, Mar. 1991)* Polskie Nagrania ▲ PLN 113 [DDD]
Lutoslawski, W.:Chain 2, w. A. Wit (cnd), Polish National RSO Katowice *(rec Polish Radio Concert Hall, Katowice, Dec 19-22, 1994)* Naxos ▲ 8.553202 [DDD]
Lutoslawski, W.:Partita Vn, Orch & Obbligato Pno, w. A. Wit (cnd), Polish National RSO Katowice *(rec Polish Radio Concert Hall, Katowice, Dec 19-22, 1994)* Naxos ▲ 8.553202 [DDD]

Bakulin, V. (va)—see ORCHESTRAS & ENSEMBLES Northern Crown Soloists Ensemble

Bal, János (rcr/fl)—see ORCHESTRAS & ENSEMBLES Affetti Musicali

Bala, Gabriel (va)
5 Centuries of German Music in Transylvania, w. H. Andreescu (cnd), Bucharest Virtuosi, Georgeta Stoleriu (sop), Adrian Petrescu (ob), René Cristian Popescu (vn), Stefan Thomasz (db), Nicolae Licaret (hpd) Electrecord ▲ ELC EDC 168 [DDD]

Balanescu, Alexander (vn)—see also ORCHESTRAS & ENSEMBLES Gavin Bryars Ensemble, Balanescu String Quartet, Arditti String Quartet
Bryars, G.:After the Requiem, w. A. Balanescu, G. Bryars, B. Frisell, R. Heaton, et al. ECM New Series ▲ 78118-21424-2 [DDD]
Bryars, G.:Alaric I or II, w. A. Balanescu, G. Bryars, B. Frisell, R. Heaton, et al. ECM New Series ▲ 78118-21424-2 [DDD]
Bryars, G.:Allegrasco, w. A. Balanescu, G. Bryars, B. Frisell, R. Heaton, et al. ECM New Series ▲ 78118-21424-2 [DDD]
Bryars, G.:The Last Days, w. Clare Connors (vn) Argo ▲ 448175-2 [DDD]
Bryars, G.:The Old Tower of Löbenicht, w. R. Heaton (cl), B. Frisell (elec gtr), G. Bryars (db), et al. ECM New Series ▲ 78118-21424-2 [DDD]
Hopkins, B.:Music of, w. A. Wells (sop), R. Bernas (cnd), Music Projects London—En attendant for Flute, Oboe, Cello & Harpsichord; 2 Pomes for Soprano, Bass Cittern; Trumpet, Harp & Viola; Penandt for Violin; Sensation for Soprano, Saxophone, Trumpet, Harp & Viola NM Classics ▲ NMCD 014 [DDD]
Nyman, M.:Zoo Caprices TER Limited ▲ CDTER 1123 [DDD] ■ CSTER 1123 (D)
Vivaldi, A.:Con for 3 Vns, w. C. Warren-Green (vn), E. Layton (vn), C. Warren-Green (cnd), London CO—RV.551 in F Virgin Classics ▲ 59609 [DDD]

Balazs, Tatjana (pno)
Chopin, F.:Etudes (24) *(rec Aug. 15-17, 1993)* Posh Boy ▲ 8161-2

Balbi, Jesús Castro (gtr)
Barrios, A.:Gtr Music—Aconquija; Aire de zamba; Alms for the Love of God; The Bees; Caazapá; La catedral; Chôro da saudade; Danza paraguaya; Dream in the Forest; Estudio de concierto; Julia Florida; Mazurka appasionata; Oración; Prelude in c; Prelude in g; Romance in Imitation of the Cello; Waltz in d; Waltz in G *(rec Feb. 1992)* Opus 111 ▲ OPS 49-9209 [DDD]
Clásicos de las Américas, w. Margot Pares-Reyna (sop), Marcel Quillevéré (ten), Noël Lee (pno), Georges Rabol (pno), Erwartung Ensemble [cnd:Bernard Desgraupes], Jazzogène Orch [cnd:Jean-Luc Fillon] Opus 111 6-▲ 2000

Balcytis, Marius (lure)
Habbestad, K.:The Articles of Norwegian Christian Law, w. Ståle Bjørnhaug (nar), Adomas Kontautas (lure), Zigmas Kazlauskas (lure), Rimantas Valanctus (lure) Norway Music ▲ 2912

Baldi, Livia (va)—see ORCHESTRAS & ENSEMBLES Ricordanze String Quartet

Baldin, Dileno (hn)—see ORCHESTRAS & ENSEMBLES L'Astrée Ensemble

Balding, Caroline (vn)—see also ORCHESTRAS & ENSEMBLES Scaramouche
Telemann, G.P.:Suite for 2 Vns, w. Andrew Manze (vn) Harmonia Mundi France ▲ HMU 907137

Baldwin, Dalton (pno)
Amazing Grace, w. J. Norman (sop), Geoffrey Parsons (pno), Christopher Bowers-Broadbent (org), Alexander Gibson (cnd), Willis Patterson (cnd), Royal PO, Ambrosian Singers Philips ▲ 432546-2 PH [DDD] ■ 432546-4 PH
Brahms, J.:Gypsy Songs (8), w. S.-C. Süssmann (mez) [G] Arcobaleno ▲ SBCD 1506
Debussy, C.:Songs, w. F. von Stade (sop)—complete edition of Debussy's songs EMI Classics 3-▲ CDMC 64095

▲ = CD ♦ = Enhanced CD Δ = MD ■ = Cassette Tape ◻ = DCC

Baldwin, Dalton (pno) (cont.)
Duparc, H.:Songs, w. G. Souzay (bar)—L'invitation au voyage; Extase; Phidylé; Le manoir de Rosemonde; Lamento; Soupir [F] Denon ▲ CO 2252 [DDD]
Fauré, G.:La bonne chanson, w. G. Souzay (bar) [F] Denon ▲ CO 2252 [DDD]
Fauré, G.:La Chanson d'Eve, w. S.-C. Süssmann (mez) [F] Arcobaleno ▲ SBCD 1506 SBCD 1506
Fauré, G.:Songs, w. Ameling (sop), G. Souzay (bar) [complete edition of Fauré's songs] EMI Classics 4-▲ CDMD 64079
Ives, C.:Songs, w. William Parker (bar)—At the River; His Exaltation; Watchman!; The Camp Meeting; Sunrise [w. Ani Kavafian (vn)]; Chanson de Florian; Rosamunde; Qu'il m'irait bien; Élégie *(rec Columbia Recording Studios, New York City)* New World ▲ 80463-2
Korngold, E.W.:Songs, w. S. Kimbrough (bar)—Six Songs, Op. 9, Nos. 1-6; Four Songs, Op. 14; Three Songs, Op. 18; Two Songs, Op. 41/3 & 4 [G] Acanta ▲ 43539 [DDD]
Korngold, E.W.:Songs, w. S. Kimbrough (bar) Koch Schwann ▲ SCH 310942 [DDD]
Love Songs Delos ▲ DCD 3029 [DDD]
Mozart, W.A.:Complete Mozart Edition, w. Elly Ameling (sop), Netherlands Wind Ensemble Philips 2-▲ 422524-2 [ADD]
Poulenc, F.:Songs, w. E. Ameling (sop), G. Souzay (bar)—complete EMI Classics 4-▲ CDMD 64087
Ravel, M.:Don Quichotte à Dulcinée, w. Gérard Souzay (bar) [F] Denon ▲ CO 2252 [DDD]
Rossini, G.:Arias, w. A. Aug(acu)er (sop), J. Larmore (mez), M. Kimbrough (bar)—La Pesca (duet); Il Trovatore Arabesque ▲ Z 6623 [ADD]
Rossini, G.:Péchés de vieillesse (sels), w. A. Auger (sop), J. Larmore (mez), J. Aler (ten), S. Kimbrough (bar)—Les Amants de Séville; Chanson de Zora; L'Esule; La Fioraia Fiorentina; La Lontananza; Musique Anodine; L'Orpheline du Tyrol; La Passegiata Quartettino; L'Ultimo Ricordo; Un Sou Complainte [I,F] Arabesque ▲ Z 6623 [ADD]
Schoenberg, A.:Songs, w. S. Kimbrough (bar) Koch Schwann ▲ SCH 310942 [DDD]
Schreker, F.:Songs, w. S. Kimbrough (bar) Koch Schwann ▲ SCH 310942 [DDD]
Schubert, Franz:Songs (misc), w. E. Ameling (sop)—13 songs [G] Philips ("Silver Line" series) ▲ 420870-2 [ADD]
Schubert, Franz:Winterreise, w. J. Van Dam (bar) [G] Forlane ▲ FOR 16622 [DDD]
Schumann, R.:Dichterliebe, w. J. Van Dam (b-bar) [G] Forlane ▲ FOR 16595 [DDD]
Schumann, R.:Frauenliebe und -leben, w. S.-C. Süssmann (mez) [G] Arcobaleno ▲ SBCD 1506
Schumann, R.:Songs, w. J. van Dam (bar)—12 Kerner-Lieder, Op. 35; Die beiden Grenadiere, Op. 49 [G] Forlane ▲ FOR 16595 [DDD]
Weigl, K.:Songs, w. S. Kimbrough (bar)—7 Songs, Op. 1 Koch Schwann ▲ SCH 310942 [DDD]
Weill, K.:Songs, w. S. Kimbrough (bar) [E,G] Arabesque ▲ Z 6579

Balestracci, Guido (vl)—see also ORCHESTRAS & ENSEMBLES Labyrinto, Les Cyclopes
Forqueray, A.:Suites (5) Va da Gamba, w. Paolo Pandolfo (vl), Eduardo Eguez (thb/baroque gtr), Rolf Lislevand (thb/baroque gtr), Guido Morini (clvd) Glossa 2-▲ 920401

Balestracci, Serbio (rcr)—see ORCHESTRAS & ENSEMBLES Il Desiderio

Balet, Jean-Jacques (pno)
Orff, C.:Carmina burana, w. Brigitte Fournier (sop), Peter Sigrist (ten), Michel Brodard (bar), Mayumi Kameda (pno), Geneva Percussion Ensemble [version for 2 pnos & perc] Cascavelle ▲ CVL 1009 [DDD]
Rogg, L.:Music of, w. M. Larrieu (fl), T. Friedli (cl), J.-P. Goy (ob), M. Kameda (pno), L. Rogg (syn), M. Kameda (piano) *(8 Etudes [1990]; Jazzic J.-J. Balet (piano) (Cinq petites pièces lyriques [1952]; Trois pièces [1952]; Valse [1952]; Cinq petites géométries [1958]),* Kameda, Balet *(Face à face for 2 Pianos [1987]),* J.-P. Goy, L. Rogg *(Pièce for Oboe & Synthesizer [1991]),* T. Friedli *(Pièce for solo Clarinet [1986]); M. Larrieu (Suite for solo Flute [1991])* BIS ▲ CD 546 [DDD]

Baley, Virko (pno)
Baley, V.:Duo Concertante, w. Natalia Khoma (vc) *(rec Longy School of Music, Cambridge, Massachusetts, June 15, 1995)* Cambria ▲ CD 1087
Baley, V.:Partita 1 Trbns, w. Miles Anderson (trbn) *(rec Univ. of Nevada, Las Vegas)* Cambria ▲ CMB 1077 [DDD]
Baley, V.:Sculptured Birds, w. William Powell (cl) *(rec California Institute of the Arts)* Cambria ▲ CMB 1077 [DDD]

Bálint, János (fl)
Bach, Joh. Christian:Sinf concertante, T.289/4, w. Lajos Lencsés (ob), Béla Bánfalvi (vn), Károly Botvay (vc), Budapest Strings Capriccio ▲ 10509 [DDD]
Mendelssohn, F.:Con in d Vn & Strs, w. P.G. Morandi (cnd), Budapest SO Hungaroton ▲ HCD 31481 [DDD]
Mendelssohn, F.:Con in e Vn & Orch, Op. 64, w. P.G. Morandi (cnd), Budapest SO Hungaroton ▲ HCD 31481 [DDD]
Paganini, N.:Con 2 Vn, w. P.G. Morandi (cnd), Budapest SO—3rd movt. Hungaroton ▲ HCD 31481 [DDD]
The Romance Collection, w. Nóra Mercz (hp) *(rec Rottenbiller Street Studio, Budapest, Dec 14-18, 1992)* Naxos 4-▲ 8.504005 [DDD]
Romantic Music for Flute & Harp, w. Nóra Mercz (hp) *(rec Dec. 1992)* Naxos ▲ 8.550741 [DDD]

Ball, Andrew (pno)
Boulanger, L.:Choral Music, w. M. Hill (ten), J. Wood (cnd), New London Chamber Choir—Les Sireènes; Soir sur la Plaine; Hymne au Soleil; Pour les funérailles d'un soldat Hyperion ▲ CDA 66726
Boulanger, L.:Clairiès dans le ciel, w. M. Hill (ten) Hyperion ▲ CDA 66726
Boulanger, L.:Renouveau, w. M. Hill (ten), J. Wood (cnd), New London Chamber Choir Hyperion ▲ CDA 66726
Brahms, J.:Sons Cl (comp), w. D. Campbell (cl) Collins Quest ▲ COL 3010 [DDD]
Delius, F.:Songs, w. S. Douse (ten), Elysian Singers London Continuum ▲ CON 1054
Gerhard, R.:Alegrías, Divertissement Flamenco, w. J. Jacobson (pno) Largo ▲ 5119 [DDD]
Gerhard, R.:Dos Apunts Largo ▲ 5119 [DDD]
Gerhard, R.:Pandora, w. J. Jacobson (pno), R. Benjafield (perc) Largo ▲ 5119 [DDD]
Gerhard, R.:Soirées de Barcelona Largo ▲ 5119 [DDD]
Mayerl, W.J.:Music of, w. G. Carpenter (cnd), Slovak RSO Bratislava—Marigold; A L. Pond; 4 Aces Suite; From a Spanish Lattice; Minuet by Candlelight; Aquarium Suite; Autumn Crocus; Bats in the Belfry; Pastoral Sketches; Fireside Fusiliers; Parade of the Sandwich-Board Men; Waltz for a Lonely Heart; Busybody *(rec Oct. 1992)* Marco Polo ("British Light Music" series) ▲ 8.223514 [DDD]
Mendelssohn, F.:Son Cl, w. D. Campbell (cl) Collins Quest ▲ COL 3010 [DDD]
Tippett, M.:Purcell Realizations, w. Martyn Hill (ten)—If music be the food of love; An Epithalamium; The Fatal hour comes on apace [w. Graig Ogden (gtr)]; Mad Bess; Sweeter than roses Hyperion ▲ CDA 66700
Tippett, M.:Songs, w. Martyn Hill (ten)—Music; Songs for Ariel [Come unto these Yello sands/Full fathom five/Where the bee sucks]; Songs for Achilles [In the Tent/ Across the Plain/ By the Sea; w. Graig Ogden (gtr)]; Boyhood's End; The Heart's Assurance [Song/Compassion/The Dance/Remember Your Lovers] Hyperion ▲ CDA 66700

Ballard, Jeremy (vn)
Britten, H.:Young Apollo, w. P. Donohoe (pno), F. Kok (vn), P. Cole (va), M. Kaznowski (vc), S. Rattle (cnd), City of Birmingham SO *(rec 4/82)* EMI Classics 2-▲ CDCB 54270 [DDD]

Baller, Adolph (pno)
Bloch, E.:Suite Va & Pno, w. Gabor Rejto (vc) [arr. for vc & pno Baller & Rejto] *(rec Los Angeles & Columbus, 1969 & 1979)* Orion ▲ 7813-2 [AAD]

Ballista, Antonio (pno)
Battiato, F.:Haiku, w. Franco Battiato (voc), Pouran Ghaffarpour (voc), Marco Boni (vc), Guido Corti (cnt), Filippo Destrieri (kbd/computer), John Giblin (bass), Gavin Harrison (dr/perc), Jakko Jakszyk (gtr), Roberto Mazza (ob), Fabrizio Merlini (va), Angelo Privitera (kbd/computer), Mino Bordignon (cnd), Milan Chamber Music Choir Hemisphere ▲ 837234-2
Battiato, F.:L'Ombra della Luce, w. Franco Battiato (voc), Roger Chase (va), Filippo Destrieri (kbd/computer), Anthony Pleeth (vc), Gavin Wright (vn), G. Pio (cnd), London Astarte Orch Hemisphere ▲ 837234-2
Battiato, F.:Povera Patria, w. Franco Battiato (voc), Roger Chase (va), Filippo Destrieri (kbd/computer), Anthony Pleeth (vc), Gavin Wright (vn), G. Pio (cnd), London Astarte Orch Hemisphere ▲ 837234-2

Ballista, Antonio (pno) (cont.)
Battiato, F.:Ricerca sul Terzo, w. Franco Battiato (voc), Alessio Alba (tamboura), Marco Boni (vc), Debendra Kanti Chakraborty (tabla), Guido Corti (cnt), Filippo Destrieri (kbd/computer), John Giblin (bass), Buddhadeu Das Gupta (sarod), Gavin Harrison (dr/perc), Jakko Jakszyk (gtr), Roberto Mazza (ob), Fabrizio Merlini (va), Angelo Privitera (kbd/computer), Mino Bordignon (cnd), Milan Chamber Music Choir Hemisphere ▲ 837234-2
Battiato, F.:Le Sacre Sinfonie del Tiempo, w. Franco Battiato (voc), Roger Chase (va), Filippo Destrieri (kbd/computer), Anthony Pleeth (vc), Gavin Wright (vn), G. Pio (cnd), London Astarte Orch Hemisphere ▲ 837234-2
Ligeti, G.:Pieces for 2 Pnos, w. Bruno Canino (pno) Wergo ▲ WER 60100-50 [DDD]
Petrassi, G.:Coro di morti, w. Bruno Canino (pno), G. Petrassi (cnd), Milan Angelicum Instrumentalists, Milan Polyphonic Choir Stradivarius ▲ STV DTM 90001 [ADD]

Balmain, Ian (tpt)
Haydn, J.:Con Tpt, w. S. Kovacevich (cnd), Liverpool PO Classics for Pleasure ▲ CDCFP 4589 [DDD]

Balmer, Christopher (va)
Vaughan Williams, R.:Flos Campi, w. V. Handley (cnd), Royal Liverpool PO, Royal Liverpool Phil Choir Classics for Pleasure ("Eminence" series) ▲ CDEMX 9512 [DDD]

Balogh, Ferenc (vn)—see also ORCHESTRAS & ENSEMBLES New Budapest String Quartet
Bartók, B.:Duos (44), w. A. Kiss (vn) Hyperion ▲ CDA 66453
Hubay, J.:Hejre Kati, w. M. Antál (cnd), Hungarian State Orch *(rec 4/88)* Naxos ▲ 8.550142 [DDD]

Balogh, József (bas hn)
Mozart, W.A.:Qnt Cl Bas Hn, K.580b, w. B. Kovács (cl), Danubius Quartet members [completed Franz Beyer] *(rec Sept. 23-25, 1991)* Naxos ▲ 8.550390 [DDD]

Balogh, József (cl)—see also ORCHESTRAS & ENSEMBLES Danubius Quartet
Beethoven, L. van:Septet Strs, w. Ildikó Hegyi (vn), Győző Máthé (va), Péter Szabó (vc), István Tóth (db), Jenő Keveházi (hn), József Vajda (bn) *(rec Scottish Church, Budapest, Apr. 21-23 & May 29-31, 1)* Naxos ▲ 8.553090 [DDD]
Brahms, J.:Qnt Cl, w. C. Onczay (vc), Danubius Quartet *(rec Oct. 16-18, 1991)* Naxos ▲ 8.550391 [DDD]
Brahms, J.:Trio Cl, w. C. Onczay (vc), J. Jandó (pno) *(rec Oct. 16-18, 1991)* Naxos ▲ 8.550391 [DDD]
Mozart, W.A.:Qts Cl, w. Danubius Quartet—No. 2 in E♭ from K.380 *(rec Sept. 25, 1991)* Naxos ▲ 8.550390 [DDD]
Mozart, W.A.:Qnt Cl, K.581, w. Danubius Quartet *(rec Sept. 23-25, 1991)* Naxos ▲ 8.550390 [DDD]

Balogh, Sándor (pno)
Cornologia, w. Budapest Festival Horn Quartet, Zoltán Varga (timp/perc), Dimitris Politis (gtr), Ferenc Gayer (db/bass gtr), János Weszely (dr) *(rec Hungaroton Classic Studio, Feb 15-16, 1996)* Hungaroton ▲ HCD 31652 [ADD/DDD]

Baloghova, Dagmar (pno)
Tchaikovsky, P.:Con 1 Pno, w. K. Ančerl (cnd), Czech PO Supraphon ▲ SUP 111944 [AAD]

Balsa, E. (vc)—see ORCHESTRAS & ENSEMBLES Concerto Rococo

Balsam, Artur (pno)
Beethoven, L. van:Son 5 Vn, "Spring", w. Nathan Milstein (vn) Bridge ▲ BRI 9066
Beethoven, L. van:Son 8 Vn, w. N. Milstein (vn) *(rec 1939)* Biddulph ▲ LAB 063 [ADD]
Brahms, J.:Liebeslieder Waltzes SATB, w. J. Kahn (pno), W. Preston (cnd), *(chorus unknown)* [G] RCA Gold Seal ▲ 60260-2-RG [ADD] ▇ 60260-4-RG (CrO2)
Brahms, J.:Liebeslieder Waltzes SATB, w. J. Kahn (pno), *(chorus unknown)* [G] *(rec Studio 8-H broadcast, Nov 27, 1948)* RCA Gold Seal 4-▲ 60325-2-RG (m) [ADD] 4-▇ 60325-4-RG (CrO2)
Brahms, J.:Son 3 Vn, w. Nathan Milstein (vn) *(rec Library of Congress, Mar 13, 1953)* Bridge ▲ 9066
Dvořák, A.:Slavonic Dances (comp), w. G. Raps (pno) Arabesque ▲ Z 6559
Guarnieri, C.M.:Son 2 Vn, w. Louis Kaufman (vn) Cambria ("Historical" series) ▲ CD 1078 [ADD]
Mozart, W.A.:Andante & Vars Pno 4-Hands, w. Gena Raps (pno) *(rec SUNY, Purchase Theatre C, June 15-18, 1992)* Arabesque ▲ ARA 6652 [DDD]
Mozart, W.A.:Fant Mechanical Org, w. Gena Raps (pno) [arr. for pno 4-hands] *(rec SUNY, Purchase Theatre C, June 15-18, 1992)* Arabesque ▲ ARA 6652 [DDD]
Mozart, W.A.:Pno Music 4-Hands, w. G. Raps (pno)—Son. in F, K.497; Fant. No. 1 in f, K.594; Son. in B♭, K.358 Arabesque ▲ ARA 6635 [DDD]
Mozart, W.A.:Son Pno 4-Hands, K.381, w. Gena Raps (pno) *(rec SUNY, Purchase Theatre C, June 15-18, 1992)* Arabesque ▲ ARA 6652 [DDD]
Mozart, W.A.:Son Pno 4-Hands, K.521, w. Gena Raps (pno) *(rec SUNY, Purchase Theatre C, June 15-18, 1992)* Arabesque ▲ ARA 6652 [DDD]
Mozart, W.A.:Sons Vn Pno (misc), w. N. Milstein (vn)—K.296 *(rec 1939)* Biddulph ▲ LAB 063 [ADD]
Rachmaninoff, S.:Trio élégiaque 2, w. Joseph Roisman (vn), Mischa Schneider (vc) *(rec Coolidge Auditorium, Library of Congress, Apr 4, 1952)* Bridge ▲ BRIDGE 9063
Stamitz, C.:Con Vn, w. N. Milstein (vn) [arr. for violin & piano]—Adagio & Rondo movts. *(rec 1940)* Biddulph ▲ LAB 063 [ADD]
Suk, J.:Burleska, w. N. Milstein (vn) *(rec 1940)* Biddulph ▲ LAB 063 [ADD]
Tartini, G.:Son Vn "Devil's Trill", w. Y. Menuhin (vn) *(rec 1932)* Biddulph ▲ LAB 046 [ADD]
A Tribute to Nathan Milstein, w. N. Milstein (vn) One-Eleven ▲ URS 50020 [ADD]
The Young Yehudi Menuhin:The 1932 HMV Recordings, w. Y. Menuhin (vn) Biddulph ▲ LAB 046 [ADD]

Balser, Uwe (pno)
Medtner, N.:Forgotten Melodies 3 Koch Schwann ▲ SCH 317872
Medtner, N.:Morceaux, Op. 31—Improvisation, Op. 31/1 Koch Schwann ▲ SCH 317872
Medtner, N.:Son romantica Koch Schwann ▲ SCH 317872

Balshem, Semion (pno)
Brahms, J.:Son 1 Cl, w. Lars Aabo (cl) *(rec Aarhus, Denmark, July 1995)* Rondo Grammofon ▲ RCD 8348 [DDD]
Reger, M.:Son Cl, Op. 107, w. Lars Aabo (cl) *(rec Aarhus, Denmark, July 1995)* Rondo Grammofon ▲ RCD 8348 [DDD]
Winding, A.:Fants Cl, w. Lars Aabo (cl) *(rec Aarhus, Denmark, July 1995)* Rondo Grammofon ▲ RCD 8348 [DDD]

Balssa, V. (fl)
Telemann, G.P.:Con Fl, Hpd, w. A. Frigé (org) Nuova Era ("Ancient Music" series) ▲ NUO 7135 [DDD]

Baltanjan, Arusjak (vn)
Khachaturian, A.:Con Vn, w. I. Marinov (cnd), Sofia SO Audiophile Classics ▲ 101.049

Baltayan, Seta (vc)—see ORCHESTRAS & ENSEMBLES Academic Chamber Ensemble

Baltensperger, Susanne (hpd)
Fritz, G.:Sons Vn, Op. 2, w. A.-K. Graf (vn) *(rec 1993)* Jecklin-Disco ▲ JD 668-2 [DDD]

Balter, Alan (cl)
Baker, D.:Jazz Suite Cl, "3 Ethnic Dances", w. A. Balter (cnd), Akron SO *(rec Masonic Auditorium, Cleveland, OH, Feb 22, 1993)* Telarc ▲ CD 80409 [DDD]

Balzaretti, Carlo (pno)
Copland, A.:Con Cl, w. Daniel Pacitti (cl), D. Pacitti (cnd), Moldavian Radio-TV SO Agorá ▲ 026 [DDD]
Guastavino, C.:Son Cl, w. Daniel Pacitti (cl) Agorá ▲ 026 [DDD]

Balzer, Severin (mar)
Bach, J.S.:Suites Vc, BWV 1007-1012—Suite No. 3 [trans for solo mar] Gallo ▲ CD 599 [AAD]
Fink, S.:Batu Ferringhi Gallo ▲ CD 599 [AAD]
Rosauro, N.:Con Mar, w. Zurich Chamber Soloists Gallo ▲ CD 599 [AAD]
Stout, G.:Mexican Dances Gallo ▲ CD 599 [AAD]

Banaszak, Greg (sax)
Bach, J.S.:Sons Fl, BWV 1030-35, w. Christopher Casey (pno)—Siciliano/Waltz [from Son in E♭; arr Ricker for Sax & Pno] *(rec Bailey Hall, Cornell Univ, Ithaca, NY, Dec 19-23, 1993)* Open Loop ▲ OL 018 [DDD]
Dobbins, B.:Son Sax, w. Christopher Casey (pno) *(rec Bailey Hall, Cornell Univ, Ithaca, NY, Dec 19-23, 1993)* Open Loop ▲ OL 018 [DDD]
Koch, F.:Latin Moods, w. Christopher Casey (pno) *(rec Bailey Hall, Cornell Univ, Ithaca, NY, Dec 19-23, 1993)* Open Loop ▲ OL 018 [DDD]

INSTRUMENT.

Banaszak, Greg (sax) (cont.)
Ricker, R.:Solar Chariots, w. Christopher Casey (pno) *(rec Bailey Hall, Cornell Univ, Ithaca, NY, Dec 19–23, 1993)* Open Loop ▲ OL 018 [DDD]
Wilder, A.:Suite 1 Sax, w. Christopher Casey (pno) *(rec Bailey Hall, Cornell Univ, Ithaca, NY, Dec 19–23, 1993)* Open Loop ▲ OL 018 [DDD]
Yasinitsky, G.:Double Edge, w. Christopher Casey (pno) *(rec Bailey Hall, Cornell Univ, Ithaca, NY, Dec 19–23, 1993)* Open Loop ▲ OL 018 [DDD]
Young, C.R.:Double Vision, w. Christopher Casey (pno) *(rec Bailey Hall, Cornell Univ, Ithaca, NY, Dec 19–23, 1993)* Open Loop ▲ OL 018 [DDD]

Banat, Gabriel (vn)
Penderecki, K.:Miniatures Vn Pno, w. Ilana Vered (pno) *(rec Feb 1972)* Vox Box 2-▲ CDX 5142

Banchini, Chiara (vn)—see ORCHESTRAS & ENSEMBLES Ensemble 415

Banda, E. (vc)
Brahms, J.:Sextet Strs, Op. 36, w. G. Konrád (va), Bartók String Quartet *(rec 1971–74)* Hungaroton 3-▲ HCD 11591/93 [ADD]
Liszt, F.:Music of, w. A. Kiss (n), Z. Tóth (va), M. Perényi (vc), H. Lubik (hp), I. Lantos (pno/org), S. Margittay (harm)—Angelus; La lugubre gondola; Epithalam; Am Grabe Richard Wagners; Romance oubliée; Elégies 1 & 2; Offertorium; Benedictus Hungaroton ▲ HCD 11798 [DDD]
Schubert, Franz:Qt Fl, w. Z. Jeney (fl), P. Lukács (va), Szendrey-Karper (gtr) White Label ▲ HRC 146 [ADD]

Banda, Pal (vc)—see ORCHESTRAS & ENSEMBLES Westphalia PO Chamber Ensemble

Bandera, J. (gtr)
Albéniz, I.:Iberia Suite, w. P. de Lucia (gtr), J. Cañizares (gtr) [trans Paco de Lucia for 3 gtrs] Verve ▲ 314-510301-2

Bandt, Ros (rcr/fl/psalter/perc)
Codax, M.:Cantigas d'amigo (7), w. H. Newnham (ct/perc), R. Wilkinson (vielle/rcr), J. Griffiths (lt/gtr morisca) Vox Australis ▲ VAST 005-2
Codax, M.:Music of, w. H. Newnham (ct/perc), R. Wilkinson (vielle/rcr), J. Griffiths (lt/gtr morisca)—L'Autrier Jost' una Sebissa; Istanpitta Gaetta; Bel m'es Quant Son Li Fruit Madur; Slatarello Vox Australis ▲ VAST 005-2

Banegas, Cristina Garcia (org)
Zipoli, D.:Choral Music, w. G. Garrido (cnd), Buenos Aires Affetti Ensemble, Ensemble Elyma, Cordoba Children's Chorus—Misa brevis; O gloriosa virgunum; Sacris solemnis; Tantum ergo; Letania I in c; Letania II in f; Ave maris stella; Zoipaqui; Deus in adjutorium; Dixit Dominus K617 ▲ 7036
Zipoli, D.:Org Music—Retirada del Emperador; Primavera; Del principe K617 ▲ 7036

Bánfalvi, Béla (vn)
Bach, Joh. Christian:Sinf concertante, T.289/4, w. János Bálint (fl), Lajos Lencsés (ob), Károly Botvay (vc), Budapest Strings Capriccio ▲ 10509 [DDD]
Bach, Joh. Christian:Sinf concertante, T.284/6, w. Zsuzsanna Németh (vn), Lajos Lencsés (ob), Budapest Strings Capriccio ▲ 10509 [DDD]
Bach, Joh. Christian:Sinf concertante, T.284/4, w. Károly Botvay (vc), Budapest Strings Capriccio ▲ 10509 [DDD]
Bach, J.S.:Con Vn & Ob, w. Emilia Csánky (ob), Budapest Strings *(rec Unitarian Church, Budapest, Nov 1991)* Naxos ▲ 8.553028 [DDD]
Bach, J.S.:Easter Oratorio, w. Emilia Csánky (ob), Budapest Strings—Adagio *(rec Unitarian Church, Budapest, Nov 1991)* Naxos ▲ 8.553028 [DDD]
Beethoven, L. van:German Dances, WoO 42, w. S. Falvai (pno) Hungaroton ▲ HCD 12303
Beethoven, L. van:Vars Fl, Op. 105, w. S. Falvai (pno) Hungaroton ▲ HCD 12303
Boëllmann, L.:Qt Pno & Strs, w. I. Prunyi (pno), J. Fejévári (va), K. Botvay (vc) Marco Polo ▲ 8.223524
Boëllmann, L.:Trio Pno, w. I. Prunyi (pno), J. Fejévári (va), K. Botvay (vc) Marco Polo ▲ 8.223524
Pierné, G.:Trio Pno, w. N. Szelecsenyi (pno), K. Vass (vc) Marco Polo ▲ 8.223189
Rózsavölgyi, M.:Csárdás, w. Budapest Strings Capriccio ▲ 10 528 [DDD]
Vivaldi, A.:Cons Vn, Op. 8/1–4, "The Four Seasons", w. K. Botvay (cnd), Budapest Strings Laserlight ▲ 15 518 [DDD]
Vivaldi, A.:Cons for 2 Vns, w. Zsuzsa Németh (vn), Budapest Strings—in G, RV.516 *(rec Unitarian Church, Budapest, Nov. 1991)* Naxos ▲ 8.553028 [DDD]

Banfield, Volker (pno)
Goetz, H.:Con 1 Pno, w. W.A. Albert (cnd), Hanover North German Radio PO CPO ▲ CPO 999098 [DDD]
Goetz, H.:Con 2 Pno, w. W.A. Albert (cnd), Hanover North German Radio PO CPO ▲ CPO 999098 [DDD]
Pettersson, G.A.:Lamento CPO ▲ CPO 999169 [DDD]
Pfitzner, H.:Con Pno, w. W.A. Albert (cnd), Munich PO CPO ▲ CPO 999045-2 [AAD]
Schumann, R.:Sons Pno (comp) CPO ▲ CPO 999217 [DDD]

Bánhegyi, Géza (cl)
Janácek, L.:Concertino Pno, w. Thomas Hlawatsch (pno), Béla Nagy (vn), Vilmos Oláh (vn), Csaba Babácsi (va), Károly Ambrus (hn), István Hartenstein (bn) *(rec Budapest, May 1995)* Naxos ▲ 8.553587 [DDD]

Bania, Maria (fl)
Agrell, J.:Con Fl, w. A. Manze (cnd), Concerto Copenhagen *(rec Aug 1992)* Chandos ("Chaconne" series) ▲ CHAN 0535 [DDD]
Scheibe, J.A.:Con Fl in A, w. A. Manze (cnd), Concerto Copenhagen *(rec Aug. 8–10, 1992)* Chandos ("Chaconne" series) ▲ CHAN 0535 [DDD]

Banic, Joze (bn)
The Mozart Collection, w. Pietro Cavaliere (cl), Ruda Kosi (hp), Joze Falout (hn), Dubrovka Tomsic (pno), Ljubljana SO [cnd:Anton Nanut, Marko Munih, Alexander Pitamic, Mihail Glinka] Stradivari Classics ("Treasury of Great Classics" series) 5-▲ S5D 61000 [DDD] 5-■ S5C 61000 (D)

Bank, Chris (sax)—see also ORCHESTRAS & ENSEMBLES Rhythm & Bluefield Band
Clazzual Sax, w. D. Bluefield (sax) D'Blue ▲ DB 10001

Banks, Jon (hp/sackbut/org/vl/perc)—see ORCHESTRAS & ENSEMBLES Sirinu

Banovetz, Bill (ob)
Debussy, C.:Songs, w. B. Lister-Sink (pno)—Apparition; Claire de lune; Pantomime; Pierrot [trans. for oboe & piano] Well-Tempered Productions ▲ WPT 5163 [DDD]
Dvořák, A.:Love Songs, Op. 83, w. B. Lister-Sink (pno)—Never Will Love Lead Us to That Glad Goal; Nature Lies Peaceful in Slumber and Dreaming; In Deepest Forest Glade I Stand; I Know That on My Love to Thee; When Thy Sweet Glances on Me Fall; Thou Only Dear One, but for Thee [trans. for oboe & piano] Well-Tempered Productions ▲ WPT 5163 [DDD]
Falla, M. de:Canciones populares españolas (7), w. B. Lister-Sink (pno)—Apparition; Claire de lune; Pantomime; Pierrot [trans. for oboe & piano] Well-Tempered Productions ▲ WPT 5163 [DDD]
Fauré, G.:Songs, w. B. Lister-Sink (pno)—Nell; Ici-basl; Après un rêve; Le papillon et la fluer; Prison; Fleur jetée [trans. for oboe & piano] Well-Tempered Productions ▲ WPT 5163 [DDD]
Strauss, R.:Songs, w. B. Lister-Sink (pno) [trans. for oboe & piano]—Allerseelen; Ich schwebe; Nacht; Ständchen; Freundliche Vision; Kling! Well-Tempered Productions ▲ WPT 5163 [DDD]

Banowetz, Joseph (pno)
Balakirev, M.:Mazurkas (comp) Marco Polo ▲ 8.220447 [DDD]
Balakirev, M.:Scherzi (comp) Marco Polo ▲ 8.220447 [DDD]
Bottesini, G.:Fants & Vars, w. Ronald Stevenson (pno) *(rec Genoa, May 2–5, 1994)* Dynamic ▲ CDS 122 [DDD]
Busoni, F.:Fant contrappuntistica Pno 4-Hands, w. Ronald Stevenson (pno) Altarus ▲ CD 9044
Busoni, F.:Finnländische Volksweisen, w. Ronald Stevenson (pno) Altarus ▲ CD 9044
Busoni, F.:Fugue on the folksong *O du lieber Augustin*, w. Ronald Stevenson (pno) Altarus ▲ CD 9044
Huang, A.:Con Pno, w. K. Schermerhorn (cnd), Hong Kong PO—Allegro only *(rec Lyric Theatre of the Hong Kong Academy for Performing Arts, June 28, 1986)* Marco Polo ("Chinese Contemporary" series) ▲ 8.223915 [DDD]
Liszt, F.:Cons Pno, w. O. Dohnányi (cnd), Czech-Slovak RSO Bratislava *(rec 11/88)* Naxos ▲ 8.550187 [DDD]
Liszt, F.:Con 1 Pno, w. O. Dohnányi (cnd), Czech-Slovak Republic SO *(rec Concert Hall, Czechoslovak Radio, Bratislava, Nov, 1988)* Naxos ▲ 8.553267 [DDD]

Banowetz, Joseph (pno) (cont.)
Liszt, F.:Totentanz, w. O. Dohnányi (cnd), Czech-Slovak RSO Bratislava *(rec 11/88)* Naxos ▲ 8.550187 [DDD]
Mozart, W.A.:Fant Mechanical Org, w. Ronald Stevenson (pno) [arr Busoni for pno 4-hands] Altarus ▲ CD 9044
Rubinstein, A.:Con 1 Pno, w. A. Walter (cnd), Czech-Slovak State PO *(rec March 3–7, 1992)* Marco Polo ▲ 8.223456 [DDD]
Rubinstein, A.:Con 2 Pno, w. A. Walter (cnd), Czech-Slovak State PO *(rec March 3–7, 1992)* Marco Polo ▲ 8.223456 [DDD]
Rubinstein, A.:Con 3 Pno, w. R. Stankovsky (cnd), Czech-Slovak State PO Marco Polo ▲ 8.223382 [DDD]
Rubinstein, A.:Con 4 Pno, w. R. Stankovsky (cnd), Czech-Slovak State PO Marco Polo ▲ 8.223382 [DDD]
Rubinstein, A.:Con 5 Pno, w. R. Stankovsky (cnd), Slovak RSO Bratislava *(rec Dec. 13–18, 1993)* Marco Polo ▲ 8.223489 [DDD]
Rubinstein, A.:Concertstück, w. O. Dohnányi (cnd), Czech-Slovak RSO Bratislava Marco Polo ▲ 8.223190
Rubinstein, A.:Fant Pno, w. O. Dohnányi (cnd), Czech-Slovak RSO Bratislava Marco Polo ▲ 8.223190
Rubinstein, A.:Pno Music—Soirées musicales, Op. 109 Marco Polo ▲ 8.223177
Rubinstein, A.:Pno Music—Album de Peterhof, Op. 75, Nos. 1-12 Marco Polo ▲ 8.223176
Rubinstein, A.:Russian Capriccio, w. R. Stankovsky (cnd), Slovak RSO Bratislava *(rec Dec. 13–18, 1993)* Marco Polo ▲ 8.223489 [DDD]
Stevenson, R.:Pno Music—Fugue on a fragment of Chopin; 20th Century Music Diary; Symphonic Elegy for Liszt; A Scottish Triptych; Motus perpetuus temporibus fatalibus Altarus ▲ CD 9089
Tchaikovsky, P.:Con 1 Pno, w. O. Lenárd (cnd), Czech RSO *(rec Czechoslovak Radio Concert Hall, Bratislava, May 29–June 1, 1988)* Naxos 4-▲ 8.504011 [DDD]
Tchaikovsky, P.:Con 1 Pno, w. O. Lenárd (cnd), Czech-Slovak RSO Bratislava *(rec 1988)* Naxos ▲ 8.550137 [DDD]
Tchaikovsky, P.:Eugene Onegin (sels), w. O. Lenárd (cnd), Czech RSO—Polonaise; Waltz *(rec Czechoslovak Radio Concert Hall, Bratislava, May 29–June 1, 1988)* Naxos 4-▲ 8.504011 [DDD]
Tchaikovsky, P.:The Tempest, w. O. Lenárd (cnd), Czech RSO *(rec Czechoslovak Radio Concert Hall, Bratislava, May 29–June 1, 1988)* Naxos 4-▲ 8.504011 [DDD]

Banz, Bertram (va)
Reger, M.:Cantatas, w. V. Schweizer (sop), A. Hellmann (alt), R. Julius Koch (ob), R. Hellmann, U. Soldan (vn), C. Hellmann (vc), C. Fink (db), H. Bilgram (org), D. Hellmann (cnd), Mainz Bach Choir Entrée ▲ 0049 [ADD]

Banzo, Eduardo López (hpd)—see ORCHESTRAS & ENSEMBLES Al Ayre Español

Baptista, Cyro (perc)
So Many Stars, w. K. Battle (sop), Antonio Hart (sax), Grover Washington Jr (sax), Tom Harrell (flgl), James Carter (b cl), Cyrus Chestnut (pno), Jon Herrington (gtr), Romero Lubambo (gtr), Ira Coleman (elec bass), Christian McBride (elec bass), Steven Berrios (perc) *(rec Hit Factory, Clinton Recording Studios, R.P.M. Sound Studios, Unique Recording Studios, Power Station)* Sony Classical ▲ SK 68473 [DDD]

Bär, Alwin (pno)
Romantic Piano Favorites Vivace 3-▲ E 330 [ADD/DDD]

Barab, Seymour (vc)
Feldman, Morton:False Relationships & the Extended Ending, w. M. Raimondi (vn), P. Jacobs (pno), Y. Takahashi (pno), M. Feldman (cnd) *(rec 6/8/70)* CRI ▲ CD 620 [ADD]

Barab, Seymour (vl)
Music of the Middle Ages, Vol. 4:English Polyphony of the 13th & Early 14th Centuries, w. R. Oberlin (ct), C. Bressler (ten), D. Perry (ten), M. Blackman (vl) Lyrichord ▲ LYR 8004 [ADD]
Music of the Middle Ages, Vol. 5:English Medieval Songs of the 12th & 13th Centuries, w. R. Oberlin (ct) Lyrichord ▲ LYR 8005 [ADD]
Notre Dame Organa Leonius & Perotinus Magister, w. R. Oberlin (ct), C. Bressler (ten), D. Perry (ten) Lyrichord ▲ LYR 8002 [ADD]
Troubadour & Trouvere Songs, w. R. Oberlin (ct) Lyrichord ▲ LYR 8001 [ADD]

Baraglioli, Jean-Pierre (sax)
Escaich, T.:Intermezzi (3), w. Yves Queyroux (fl), Sylvain Frydman (cl) *(rec Apr 16–17, Nov 4 & 26, 19)* Chamade ▲ CHCD 5638 [DDD]

Barakhovsky, Anton (vn)
Tchaikovsky, P.:Con Vn, w. V. Tchernushenko (cnd), St. Petersburg State Academic Cappella SO Audiophile Classics ▲ 101.042

Baraldi, Roberto (vn)—see also ORCHESTRAS & ENSEMBLES Milan Quartet
Haydn, J.:Sons Vn & Pno, w. Massimo Palumbo (pno)—Nos. 1, 3, 4 & 6 Nuova Era ▲ NUO 7229

Baran, Peter (vc)—see ORCHESTRAS & ENSEMBLES Bratislava String Trio

Barantschik, Alexander (vn)
Britten, H.:Suite Vn, w. John Alley (pno) EMI Classics ("Anglo-American Chamber Music" series) ▲ CDC 55398
Delius, F.:Son 3 Vn & Pno, w. Israela Margalit (pno) EMI Classics ("Anglo-American Chamber Music" series) ▲ CDC 55399
Elgar, E.:Qnt Pno Strs, w. Israela Margalit (pno), Janice Graham (vn), Paul Silverthorne (va), Moray Welsh (vc) EMI Classics ("Anglo-American Chamber Music" series) ▲ CDC 55403

Baranyay, László (bn)
Dohnányi, E. von:Con 1 Pno, w. G. Györványi-Ráth (cnd), Budapest SO Hungaroton ▲ HCD 31555 [DDD]
Dohnányi, E. von:Con 2 Pno, w. G. Györványi-Ráth (cnd), Budapest SO Hungaroton ▲ HCD 31555 [DDD]

Barbagallo, James (pno)
Harrison, L.:Con in slendro, w. Daniel Kobialka (vn), Machiko Kobialka (pno), Patricia Jennerjohn (cel), Don Marconi (perc), J. Neff (perc), R. Hughes (cnd) *(rec 1972)* CRI ▲ CD 613 [ADD]
Macdowell, E.:Amourette *(rec Fisher Hall, Santa Rosa, CA, May 2–5, 1994)* Marco Polo ▲ 8.223632 [DDD]
Macdowell, E.:Erste moderne Suite *(rec Fisher Hall, Santa Rosa, CA, May 2–5, 1994)* Marco Polo ▲ 8.223632 [DDD]
Macdowell, E.:Forgotten Fairytales *(rec Fisher Hall, Santa Rosa, CA, Aug. 2–4, 1994)* Marco Polo ▲ 8.223633 [DDD]
Macdowell, E.:Idyllen *(rec Fisher Hall, Santa Rosa, CA, May 2–5, 1994)* Marco Polo ▲ 8.223632 [DDD]
Macdowell, E.:In Lilting Rhythm *(rec Fisher Hall, Santa Rosa, CA, May 2–5, 1994)* Marco Polo ▲ 8.223632 [DDD]
Macdowell, E.:Pno Music—Woodland Scketches, Op. 51; Sea Pieces, Op. 55; Fireside Tales, Op. 61; New England Idyls, Op. 62 Marco Polo ▲ 8.223631
Macdowell, E.:Poems after Heine *(rec Fisher Hall, Santa Rosa, CA, Aug. 2–4, 1994)* Marco Polo ▲ 8.223633 [DDD]
Macdowell, E.:Son 3 Pno *(rec Fisher Hall, Santa Rosa, CA, May 2–5, 1994)* Marco Polo ▲ 8.223632 [DDD]
Macdowell, E.:Son 4 Pno *(rec Fisher Hall, Santa Rosa, CA, Aug. 2–4, 1994)* Marco Polo ▲ 8.223633 [DDD]
Macdowell, E.:Virtuoso Etudes *(rec Fisher Hall, Santa Rosa, CA, Aug. 2–4, 1994)* Marco Polo ▲ 8.223633 [DDD]

Barbagelata, Cinzia (vn)—see ORCHESTRAS & ENSEMBLES Aglàia Ensemble

Barbareschi, Piero (hpd)—see ORCHESTRAS & ENSEMBLES Collegium Pro Musica

Barbareschi, Piero (pno)
Casella, A.:Pupazzetti, w. S. Ragni (pno) Nuova Era 2-▲ 7143/44 [DDD]

Barbé, Henriette (hpd)
Bach, J.S.:Partita Fl, BWV 1013, w. P. Graf (fl), J. Koch (vl) [trans. for additional instrs.] Jecklin-Disco 2-▲ JEC CD 4400 [ADD]
Bach, J.S.:Sons Fl, BWV 1030–35, w. P. Graf (fl), J. Koch (vl) [trans. for additional instr.] Jecklin-Disco 2-▲ JEC CD 4400 [ADD]

458 ▲ = CD ♦ = Enhanced CD Δ = MD ■ = Cassette Tape □ = DCC

Barbé, Henriette (hpd) (cont.)
Telemann, G.P.:Der Getreue Music-Meister (sels), w. M. Zürcher (rcr)—2 Sonatas *(rec 1970)* Jecklin-Disco ▲ JEC CD 4403 [ADD]
Telemann, G.P.:Kleine Kammermusik, w. M. Zürcher (rcr) *(rec 1970)* Jecklin-Disco ▲ JEC CD 4403 [ADD]

Barber, Amy Lynn (perc)—see ORCHESTRAS & ENSEMBLES Prague Percussion Project

Barber, Gail (hp)
Barber, G.:Songs of Destiny, w. Cynthia Vonn Preid (mez) Opus One ▲ CD 169
Van Appledorn, M.J.:Rhap, w. Willie Strieder (tpt) *(rec Texas Tech Univ., Hemmle Recital Hall, Lubbock Texas, Feb. 16, 1994)* Opus One ▲ CD 169
Van Appledorn, M.J.:Sonic Mutation *(rec Texas Tech Univ., Hemmle Recital Hall, Lubbock Texas, Feb. 17, 1994)* Opus One ▲ CD 169

Barber, Graham (org)
Böhm, G.:Org Music [the organ at the Church of St. Peter Mancroft, Norwich]—Prelude in C; Chorales; Prelude in d; Chorale Variations; Capriccio in D; Prelude in a ASV ("Gaudeamus" series) ▲ GAU 128 [DDD]
Buxtehude, D.:Org Music (misc)—Praeludiums, BuxWV 139, 145, 146, 149 & 137; Chorales, BuxWV 193, 76/1, 223 & 178; Fugue, BuxWV 174; Klag-Lied, BuxWV 76/2; Ciacona, BuxWV 159 [Church of St. Peter Org] *(rec Church of St. Peter, Mancroft, Norwich)* ASV/Gaudeamus ▲ ASV 130
European Organ Tour, w. Marc Rochester (org), Kimberly Marshall (org), John Scott Whiteley (org) *(rec 1983-88)* Priory ▲ PRCD 903
Great European Organs, Vol. 20, w. S. Cleobury (org) Priory ▲ PRCD 297 [DDD]
Great European Organs, Vol. 25, w. S. Cleobury (org) Priory ▲ PRCD 373 [DDD]
Great European Organs, Vol. 27, w. S. Cleobury (org) Priory ▲ PRCD 391 [DDD]
Jackson, F.:Son 3 Org Priory ▲ PRCD 373 [DDD]
Karg-Elert, S.:Sym Org, w. G. Barber (org) Priory ▲ PRCD 373 [DDD]
Sowerby, L.:Pageant of Autumn Priory ▲ PRCD 373 [DDD]

Barber, Ian (org)
Peace I Leave With You:A Sequence of Music for the Holy Eucharist, w. Belfast Cathedral Choir [cnd:David Drinkell] *(rec Belfast Cathedral, Northern Ireland)* Guild ▲ GMCD 7126 [DDD]

Barber, Samuel (pno)
Barber, S.:Hermit Songs, w. L. Price (sop) *(rec 1953)* RCA Gold Seal ▲ 09026-61983-2
Barber, S.:Hermit Songs, w. L. Price (sop) [E] *(rec 1954)* Sony Masterworks ("Portrait" series) ▲ MPK 46727 [ADD]

Barbero, Ero Maria (clvd)—see ORCHESTRAS & ENSEMBLES Conserto Vago

Barbier, Jean-Joël (pno)
Albéniz, I.:Pno Music—Torre Bermeja [Serenata]; Tango Espagnol in a; Granada [Serenata]; Mallorca [Barcarolle]; Rumores de la Caleta [Malaguena]; Tango in D; Chants d'Espagne [Prélude; Orientale; Sous le Palmier]; Espagne Souvenirs [Prélude]; Asturias Accord ▲ ACD 200332 [AAD]
Chabrier, E.:Bourée fantasque Accord ▲ ACD 200312 [AAD]
Chabrier, E.:Habanera Accord ▲ ACD 200312 [AAD]
Chabrier, E.:Pièces pittoresques Accord ▲ ACD 200312 [AAD]
Chabrier, E.:Pièces posthumes—Feuillet d'album Accord ▲ ACD 200312 [AAD]
Satie, E.:Pno Music (comp)—4 Ogives; 3 Gymnopédies; 6 Gnossiennes; Pièces froides [Airs à faire fuir; Danses de travers]; Je te veux; Le Picadilly; 3 Sarabandes Accord ▲ ACD 200072 [AAD]
Satie, E.:Pno Music (comp)—Véritables préludes flasques [Pour un chien]; Descriptions automatiques; Embryons desséchés; Croquis et agaceries d'un gros bonhomme en bois; Chapitres tournés en tous sens; Vieux sequins et vielles cuirasses; Menus propos enfantins; Enfantillages pittoresques; Peccadilles importunes; Sports et divertissements; Les trois valses distinguées du précieux dégoûté; Avant-dernières Pensées; Sonatine bureaucratique Accord ▲ ACC 221362 [AAD]
Satie, E.:Pno Music (comp), w. Jean Wiener (pno)—Prélude de la porte heroïque du ciel; Poudre d'or; Aperçus désagréables [quatre mains]; En habit de cheval [quatre mains]; Heures séculaires et instanées; Cinq nocturnes; Premier menuet; Fête donnée par les chevaliers normands en l'honneur d'une jeune demoiselle; Passacaille; Songe creux; Prélude en tapisserie; Nouvelles pièces froides; Deux rêveries nocturnes; Préludes falsques [Pour un chien] Accord ▲ ACD 200902 [AAD]

Barbizet, Pierre (pno)
Beethoven, L. van:Son 4 Vn, w. C. Ferras (vn) *(rec 1971)* FNAC Music ▲ 642327
Beethoven, L. van:Son 6 Vn, w. C. Ferras (vn) *(rec 1971)* FNAC Music ▲ 642327
Beethoven, L. van:Son 7 Vn, w. C. Ferras (vn) *(rec 1971)* FNAC Music ▲ 642327
Chausson, E.:Con Vn, Pno & Str Qt, w. C. Ferras (vn), Lamoureux Concerts Orch members EMI Classics ▲ CDM 64365

Barbolini, Giorgio (hpd)
Bach, J.S.:Sons Fl, BWV 1030-35, w. C. Mendoze (rcr), B. Re (vl)—BWV 1035 Pierre Verany ▲ PV 787023 [DDD]
Corelli, A.:Sons Vn, Op. 5, w. C. Mendoze (rcr), B. Re (vl)—No. 9 Pierre Verany ▲ PV 787023 [DDD]
Handel, G.F.:Sons Fl, w. Christian Mendoze (rcr), Bruno Re (vl)—Op. 1, Nos. 4 & 7 Pierre Verany ▲ PV 787023 [DDD]
Telemann, G.P.:Son Rcr in F, w. C. Mendoze (rcr), B. Re (vl) Pierre Verany ▲ PV 787023 [DDD]
Vivaldi, A.:Il pastor fido, w. C. Mendoze (rcr), B. Re (viol)—No. 6 Pierre Verany ▲ PV 787023 [DDD]

Barbosa, Antonio (pno)
Debussy, C.:Preludes Pno (sels)—Book 2 Connoisseur Society ▲ CD 4190
Liszt, F.:Années de pèlerinage 2—Après une lecture du Dante *(rec Tarrytown Music Hall, 1993)* Connoisseur Society ▲ CD 4192
Liszt, F.:Consolations—No. 3 in D♭ *(rec Tarrytown Music Hall, 1993)* Connoisseur Society ▲ CD 4192
Liszt, F.:Transcriptions & Paraphrases—Schubert Transcriptions:Die Forelle; Erlkönig; Auf dem Wasser zu singen; Du bist die Ruh; Hark, hark, the Lark; Wohin?; Frühlingsglaube; Gretchen am Spinnrade; Ave Maria *(rec Tarrytown Music Hall, 1993)* Connoisseur Society ▲ CD 4192
Milhaud, D.:Saudades do Brasil Connoisseur Society ▲ CD 4190

Barbosa-Lima, Carlos (gtr)
Brazil with Love, w. S. Isbin (gtr) Concord Picante ▲ CCD 4320 ■ CJP 320-C
From Yesterday to Penny Lane, w. Sofia Soloists [cnd:Plamen Djurov] Concord Concerto ▲ CCD 42041 [DDD]
Impressions Concord Concerto ■ CC 2009 (D)
Rhapsody in Blue/West Side Story, w. S. Isbin (gtr) Concord Concerto ▲ CCD 42012 ■ CC 2012-C

Barboteu, Georges (hn)
Bochsa, N.C.:Andante sostenuto, w. Lily Laskine (hp) Erato ▲ 94801-2
Corrette, M.:Cons Comiques, w. Michel Berges (hn), Gilbert Coursier (hn), Daniel Dubar (hn), J.-F. Paillard (cnd), Jean-François Paillard CO—No. 14 for Hns & Orch [La Choisy] Erato ▲ 94801-2
Mozart, W.A.:Rondo Hn, K.371, w. T. Guschlbauer (cnd), Bamberg SO Erato ▲ 94801-2
Telemann, G.P.:Con Hn, w. J.-F. Paillard (cnd), Jean-François Paillard CO—Allegro; Andante; Allegro Erato ▲ 94801-2

Barbuceanu, Valeriu (cl)
Enescu, G.:Dectet Ww, w. Virgil Francu (fl), Nicolae Maxin (fl), Valeriu Barbuceanu (cl), Leontin Boanta (cl), Adrian Petrescu (ob), Viorica Feher (bn), Goedri Orban (bn), Florin Ionoaia (Eng hn), Dan Cinca (hn), Simon Jebeleanu (hn), H. Andreescu (cnd) Olympia ▲ OLY 445 [DDD]

Barcellona (fl)
Holst, G.:Terzetto Fl, w. P. Christ (ob), J. Dunham (va) Crystal ■ C 647

Bard, Christine (perc)
Gisberg:Music of, w. Christina Sun (erhu), Jeff O'Malley (nar), Jacqueline Leclair (ob), Quentin Chiappetta (sampler/pno/cpsr), Reuben Radding (bass instrument), Gisburg (voice/fl/cpsr)—Opening; No Stranger Not At All; Imaginary Movielandscape 1; Portrait; "Jowohl"; Mein Herz hat nicht vergessen [tango]; Ritual; Dying Takes Its Time; Fruits; Mic' N Drums Tzadik ("The Composers" series) ▲ TZA 7007 [DDD]
Gisberg:Music of, w. Gisburg (sgr/fl), Jeff O'Malley (nar), Midori Seiler (vn), Ron Lawrence (va), Guy Tyler (db), Anthony Coleman (pno)—Low-End; Since You Have Left; The Woman Is Perfected; Sharks; Night & Wind; Saturnspacemonsters Walking on a Sandy Surface; Old Moon in Winter; Never Saw the Stars So Bright; Habe Die Liebe Verschlafen; W.A.L.S.H. Tzadik ▲ TZA CD 7019 [DDD]

Bard, Matthew (gtr)
First, D.:Lens Pt 2, w. D. First (gtr), C. Henderson (gtr), E. Sandrof (syn) *(rec Oct. 1987)* O.O. Discs ▲ OO 5 [DDD]

Bardèche, Jean-Marie (pno)
de Clerck, P.:Già, w. Marc Danel (vn) *(rec Ravenstein Hall, May & June 1994)* Megadisc ▲ 7866
de Clerck, P.:Pianokwintet, w. Danel String Quartet *(rec Ravenstein Hall, May & June 1994)* Megadisc ▲ 7866

Bardo, Lucy (b vl)—see ORCHESTRAS & ENSEMBLES New York Consort of Viols
Bardo, Lucy (vl)—see ORCHESTRAS & ENSEMBLES Calliope

Bardon, Pierre (org)
Bach, J.S.:Cons solo Hpd, BWV 972-987, w. K. Redel (cnd), Munich Pro Arte Orch—BWV 972 & 975 *(rec 1980)* Pierre Verany ▲ PV.79801 [ADD]
Bach, J.S.:Cons Org, BWV 592-597, w. K. Redel (cnd), Munich Pro Arte Orch—BWV 593 & 594 *(rec 1980)* Pierre Verany ▲ PV.79801 [ADD]
Bach, J.S.:Org Music (misc)—Fantasy & Fugue, BWV 542; Passacaglia, BWV 582; Toccata & Fugue, BWV 540 & 565 *(rec 1981)* Pierre Verany ▲ PV.710811 [ADD]
Clérambault, L.N.:Premier livre d'orgue contents deux suites—Suite du premier ton; Suite du deuxième ton Pierre Verany ▲ PV.784011 [ADD]
Dandrieu, J.F.:Offertoire sur les Grands Jeux pour la Fête de Paques Pierre Verany ▲ PV.784011 [ADD]
Daquin, L.-C.:Noëls pour l'orgue ou le clavecin—Nos. 1-12 *(rec 1983)* Pierre Verany ▲ PV.783122 [ADD]
Grigny, N. de:Mass Org *(rec 10/85)* Pierre Verany ▲ PV.790031
Grigny, N. de:Premier livre d'orgue *(rec 10/91)* Pierre Verany ▲ PV.792041 [DDD]
Jewels of Early Music, w. Loïnhdana Ensemble, Musica Antiqua, John Elwes (ten), André Isoir (org) *(rec 1982-86)* Pierre Verany ▲ 791051 [DDD]
Marchand, L.:Pieces Org—Grand Jeu in C, from Book 2 Pierre Verany ▲ PV.784011 [ADD]
Raison, A.:Le Vive-le-Roy des Parisiens Pierre Verany ▲ PV.784011 [ADD]

Barella, Washington (ob)
Bach, C.P.E.:Son Ob, H.549, w. V. de Hoog (vc), C. Farr (kbd) Channel Classics ▲ CCS 2091 [DDD]
Bach, J.S.:Partita Fl, BWV 1013 Channel Classics ▲ CCS 2091 [DDD]
Bach, J.S.:Sons Fl, BWV 1030-35, w. C. Farr (hpd)—BWV 1030 Channel Classics ▲ CCS 2091 [DDD]
Bach, J.S.:Sons Vn, w. C. Farr (hpd)—BWV 1020 [doubtful; trans. for oboe & continuo] Channel Classics ▲ CCS 2091 [DDD]
Bach, W.F.:Fugues, w. C. Farr (harpsichord)—3 fugues Channel Classics ▲ CCS 2091 [DDD]

Barenboim, Daniel (pno)
Bach, J.S.:Goldberg Vars *(rec live, 1988)* Erato 2-▲ 2292-45468-2-ZK
Bartók, B.:Con 1 Pno, w. P. Boulez (cnd), Philharmonia Orch *(rec 1967)* EMI Classics ▲ CDC 54770-2
Bartók, B.:Con 3 Pno, w. P. Boulez (cnd), Philharmonia Orch *(rec 1967)* EMI Classics ▲ CDC 54770-2
Beethoven, L. van:Cons Pno (comp), w. O. Klemperer (cnd), New Philharmonia Orch EMI Classics ("Studio" series) 3-▲ CDMC 63360
Beethoven, L. van:Con 1 Pno, w. D. Barenboim (cnd), Berlin PO Sony Classical ▲ SK 45830 [DDD]
Beethoven, L. van:Con Vn, Vc & Pno, "Triple Con", w. Itzhak Perlman (vn), Yo-Yo Ma (vc), Berlin PO EMI Classics ▲ CDC 55516
Beethoven, L. van:Fant Pno, Op. 80, "Choral Fant", w. O. Klemperer (cnd), New Philharmonia Orch, John Alldis Choir [G] EMI Classics ("Studio" series) 3-▲ CDMC 63360 [ADD]
Beethoven, L. van:Fant Pno, Op. 80, "Choral Fant", Berlin PO EMI Classics ▲ CDC 55516
Beethoven, L. van:Fant Pno, Op. 80, "Choral Fant", w. O. Klemperer (cnd), New Philharmonia Orch, John Alldis Choir [G] EMI Classics ("Studio" series) 2-▲ CDMB 69538 [ADD]
Beethoven, L. van:Grosse Fuge for 2 Pnos, w. A. Brendel (pno) *(rec live, Brighton Festival 1970)* Arkadia 2-▲ 589 [ADD]
Beethoven, L. van:Qnt Pno, Ob, Cl, Hn & Bn, w. H. Schellenberger (ob), L. Combs (cl), D. Damiano (bn), D. Clevenger (hn) Erato ▲ 96359-2
Beethoven, L. van:Sons Vc (comp), w. J. Du Pré (vc) EMI Classics 2-▲ ZDMB 63015
Beethoven, L. van:Son 3 Vc, w. J. Du Pré (vc) EMI Classics 2-▲ ZDMB 69707
Beethoven, L. van:Sons Pno (comp)—Nos. 1-15 Deutsche Grammophon 6-▲ 413759-2 [DDD]
Beethoven, L. van:Sons Pno (comp)—Nos. 16-32 Deutsche Grammophon 6-▲ 413766-2 [DDD]
Beethoven, L. van:Sons Pno (comp) EMI Classics 10-▲ CDZJ 62863
Beethoven, L. van:Son 8 Pno, "Pathétique" Deutsche Grammophon ▲ 419602-2 [DDD]
Beethoven, L. van:Son 8 Pno, "Pathétique" MCA Classics 2-▲ MCAD2-9803
Beethoven, L. van:Son 14 Pno, "Moonlight Son" Deutsche Grammophon ▲ 419602-2 [DDD]
Beethoven, L. van:Son 14 Pno, "Moonlight Son" MCA Classics 2-▲ MCAD2-9803
Beethoven, L. van:Son 23 Pno, "Appassionata" MCA Classics 2-▲ MCAD2-9803
Beethoven, L. van:Son 23 Pno, "Appassionata" Deutsche Grammophon ▲ 419602-2 [DDD]
Beethoven, L. van:Son 2 Vn, w. P. Zukerman (vn) *(rec Sept. 9, 1971)* Ermitage ▲ ERM 125 [ADD]
Beethoven, L. van:Son 3 Vn, w. P. Zukerman (vn) *(rec Sept. 9, 1971)* Ermitage ▲ ERM 125 [ADD]
Beethoven, L. van:Son 5 Vn, "Spring", w. P. Zuckerman (vn) EMI Classics ▲ CDM 64631
Beethoven, L. van:Son 8 Vn, w. P. Zuckerman (vn) EMI Classics ▲ CDM 64631
Beethoven, L. van:Son 8 Vn, w. P. Zukerman (vn) *(rec Sept. 9, 1971)* Ermitage ▲ ERM 125 [ADD]
Beethoven, L. van:Son 9 Vn, "Kreutzer", w. P. Zuckerman (vn) EMI Classics ▲ CDM 64631
Beethoven, L. van:Trios Pno (comp), w. P. Zukerman (vn), J. Du Pré (vc) EMI Classics ("Studio" series) 3-▲ ZDMC 63124 [ADD]
Beethoven, L. van:Trio 3 Pno, w. P. Zukerman (vn), J. Du Pré (vc) *(rec live, Brighton Festival 1970)* Arkadia 2-▲ 589 [ADD]
Beethoven, L. van:Trio 5 Pno, w. P. Zukerman (vn), J. Du Pré (vc) *(rec live, Brighton Festival 1970)* Arkadia 2-▲ 589 [ADD]
Beethoven, L. van:Trio 5 Pno, w. P. Zukerman (vn), J. Du Pré (vc) EMI Classics 2-▲ ZDMB 69707
Beethoven, L. van:Trio 6 Pno, "Archduke", w. P. Zukerman (vn), J. Du Pré (vc) *(rec live, Brighton Festival 1970)* Arkadia 2-▲ 589 [ADD]
Beethoven, L. van:Trio 7 Pno, w. G. De Peyer (cl), J. Du Pré (vc) *(rec live, Brighton Festival 1970)* Arkadia 2-▲ 589 [ADD]
Beethoven, L. van:Vars on "See, the Conquering Hero Comes" from Handel's *Judas Maccabaeus*, w. J. Du Pré (vc) EMI Classics 2-▲ ZDMB 63015
Beethoven, L. van:Vars on "Bei Männern" from Mozart's *Die Zauberflöte*, w. J. Du Pré (vc) EMI Classics 2-▲ ZDMB 63015
Beethoven, L. van:Vars on a waltz by Diabelli, Op. 120 Erato ▲ 94810
Beethoven, L. van:Vars on a waltz by Diabelli, Op. 120 MCA Classics 2-▲ MCAD2-9803
Berg, A.:Chamber Con, w. Saschko Gawriloff (vn), P. Boulez (cnd), London SO Sony Classical ("Pierre Boulez Edition" series) ▲ SMK 68331
Berg, A.:Chamber Con, w. Pinchas Zukerman (vn), P. Boulez (cnd), Ensemble InterContemporain Deutsche Grammophon ("The Originals" series) ▲ 447405-2
Brahms, J.:Con 1 Pno, w. Z. Mehta (cnd), New York PO Odyssey 3-▲ MB3K 45828
Brahms, J.:Con 2 Pno, w. Z. Mehta (cnd), New York PO Odyssey 3-▲ MB3K 45828
Brahms, J.:Con 2 Pno, w. Z. Mehta (cnd), New York PO Odyssey ▲ MBK 42608 [ADD] ■ YT 42608
Brahms, J.:Duets, Op. 28, w. Janet Baker (mez), Dietrich Fischer-Dieskau (bar) EMI Classics ("Doublefforte" series) 2-▲ CDFB 68667
Brahms, J.:Scherzo Vn, w. P. Zukerman (vn) Deutsche Grammophon ▲ 437248-2 [ADD]
Brahms, J.:Sons Vc (comp), w. J. Du Pré (vc) EMI Classics ("Studio" series) ▲ CDM 63298 [ADD]
Brahms, J.:Sons Cl (comp), w. P. Zukerman (va) Deutsche Grammophon ▲ 437248-2 [ADD]
Brahms, J.:Sons Vn (comp), w. I. Perlman (vn) Sony Classical ▲ SK 45819 [DDD]
Chopin, F.:Music of—selected Nocturnes Deutsche Grammophon ▲ 431586-2
Chopin, F.:Nocturnes—Opp. 9/2, 15/1-3, 27/1, 32/1, 37/1-2, 48/1-2, 55/1, 62/2, 72/1 Deutsche Grammophon 2-▲ 415117-2 [DDD]
Chopin, F.:Nocturnes Deutsche Grammophon ("Galleria" series) 2-▲ 423916-2 [DDD]
Chopin, F.:Nocturnes *(rec 1982)* Deutsche Grammophon ("Double" series) 2-▲ 437464-2 [DDD]
Chopin, F.:Son Vc, w. J. Du Pré (vc) EMI Classics ▲ CDM 63184

INSTRUMENT.

Barenboim, Daniel (pno) (cont.)
Franck, C.:Son Vn, w. J. Du Pré (vc) EMI Classics ▲ CDM 63184
Liszt, F.:Années de pèlerinage 2—No. 7 Après une lecture du Dante Teldec ▲ 77340
Mahler, G.:Songs from Rückert, w. D. Fischer-Dieskau (bar) [G] EMI Classics ▲ CDC 47657 [ADD]
Mendelssohn, F.:Lieder ohne Worte Pno
Deutsche Grammophon ("Galleria" series) 2-▲ 423931-2 [ADD]
Messiaen, O.:Quatuor pour la fin du temps, w. C. Desurmont (cl), L. Yordanoff (vn), A. Tetard (vc)
Deutsche Grammophon ("20th Century Classics" series) ▲ 423247-2 [ADD]
Mozart, W.A.:Cons Pno, w. D. Barenboim (cnd), English CO EMI Classics 10-▲ CDZJ 62825
Mozart, W.A.:Con 7 Pnos, w. V. Ashkenazy (pno), Fou Ts'ong (pno), Philharmonia Orch
London 2-▲ 421577-2 [ADD]
Mozart, W.A.:Con 7 Pnos, w. A. Schiff (pno), G. Solti (pno), G. Solti (cnd), English CO
London ▲ 430232-2 [DDD]
Mozart, W.A.:Con 9 Pno, w. D. Barenboim (cnd), Berlin PO Teldec ▲ 9031-73128-2 ZK [DDD]
Mozart, W.A.:Con 10 Pnos, w. V. Ashkenazy (pno), V. Ashkenazy (cnd), English CO
London ▲ 421036-2 [ADD]
Mozart, W.A.:Con 14 Pno, w. D. Barenboim (cnd), English CO
EMI Classics ("Studio" series) ▲ CDM 69124 [ADD]
Mozart, W.A.:Con 15 Pno, w. D. Barenboim (cnd), English CO
EMI Classics ("Studio" series) ▲ CDM 69124 [ADD]
Mozart, W.A.:Con 16 Pno, w. D. Barenboim (cnd), English CO
EMI Classics ("Studio" series) ▲ CDM 69124 [ADD]
Mozart, W.A.:Con 17 Pno, w. D. Barenboim (cnd), Berlin PO Teldec ▲ 9031-73128-2 ZK [DDD]
Mozart, W.A.:Con 18 Pno, w. D. Barenboim (cnd), Berlin PO *(rec live, Philharmonie Hall, Berlin, Apr. 1993)* Teldec ▲ 90674-2 [DDD]
Mozart, W.A.:Con 19 Pno, w. D. Barenboim (cnd), Berlin PO *(rec live, Philharmonie Hall, Berlin, Apr. 1994)* Teldec ▲ 90674-2 [DDD]
Mozart, W.A.:Con 20 Pno, w. D. Barenboim (cnd), Berlin PO Teldec 4-▲ 9031-72024-2 [DDD]
Mozart, W.A.:Con 20 Pno, w. D. Barenboim (cnd), Berlin PO Teldec ▲ 9031-75710-2 [DDD]
Mozart, W.A.:Con 21 Pno, w. D. Barenboim (cnd), Berlin PO Teldec 4-▲ 9031-72024-2 [DDD]
Mozart, W.A.:Con 21 Pno, w. D. Barenboim (cnd), Berlin PO Teldec ▲ 9031-75710-2 [DDD]
Mozart, W.A.:Con 22 Pno, w. D. Barenboim (cnd), Berlin PO Teldec ▲ 9031-75711-2 [DDD]
Mozart, W.A.:Con 22 Pno, w. D. Barenboim (cnd), Berlin PO Teldec 4-▲ 9031-72024-2 [DDD]
Mozart, W.A.:Con 23 Pno, w. D. Barenboim (cnd), Berlin PO Teldec ▲ 9031-75711-2 [DDD]
Mozart, W.A.:Con 23 Pno, w. D. Barenboim (cnd), Berlin PO Teldec 4-▲ 9031-72024-2 [DDD]
Mozart, W.A.:Con 24 Pno, w. D. Barenboim (cnd), Berlin PO Teldec 4-▲ 9031-72024-2 [DDD]
Mozart, W.A.:Con 24 Pno, w. D. Barenboim (cnd), Berlin PO Teldec ▲ 9031-75715-2 [DDD]
Mozart, W.A.:Con 25 Pno, w. D. Barenboim (cnd), Berlin PO Teldec 4-▲ 9031-72024-2 [DDD]
Mozart, W.A.:Con 25 Pno, w. D. Barenboim (cnd), Berlin PO Teldec ▲ 9031-75715-2 [DDD]
Mozart, W.A.:Con 26 Pno, w. D. Barenboim (cnd), Berlin PO Teldec 4-▲ 9031-72024-2 [DDD]
Mozart, W.A.:Con 26 Pno, w. D. Barenboim (cnd), Berlin PO Teldec ▲ 9031-75716-2 [DDD]
Mozart, W.A.:Con 27 Pno, w. D. Barenboim (cnd), Berlin PO Teldec 4-▲ 9031-72024-2 [DDD]
Mozart, W.A.:Con 27 Pno, w. D. Barenboim (cnd), Berlin PO Teldec ▲ 9031-75716-2 [DDD]
Mozart, W.A.:Qnt Pno, K.452, w. H. Schellenberger (ob), L. Combs (cl), D. Damiano (bn), D. Clevenger (hn) Erato ▲ 96359-2
Mozart, W.A.:Rondo Pno Orch, K.382, w. D. Barenboim (cnd), Berlin PO *(rec live, Philharmonie Hall, Berlin, Apr. 1994)* Teldec ▲ 90674-2 [DDD]
Mozart, W.A.:Sons Vn Pno (misc), w. I. Perlman (vn)—K.454 & 481
Deutsche Grammophon ▲ 431673-2 [DDD]
Mozart, W.A.:Sons Vn Pno (misc), w. I. Perlman (vn)—K.526 & 547
Deutsche Grammophon ▲ 431687-2 [DDD]
Mozart, W.A.:Sons Vn Pno (misc), w. I. Perlman (vn)—K.378, 379 & 380
Deutsche Grammophon ▲ 423229-2 [DDD]
Mozart, W.A.:Sons Vn Pno (misc), w. I. Perlman (vn)—(16) K.296, 301-306, 376-380, 454, 481, 526 & 547 Deutsche Grammophon 4-▲ 431784-2 [DDD]
Mozart, W.A.:Vars Pno (complete)—(15) K.24, K.25, K.180/173c, K.179/189a, K.354/299a, K.265/300e, K.353/300f, K.264/315d, K.352/374c, K.398/416e, K.455, K.500, K.54 (Anh.138a/547b), K.573, K.613 *(rec 1991)* EMI Classics 3-▲ CDCC 54362 [DDD]
Schoenberg, A.:Pierrot lunaire, w. Y. Minton (speaker), P. Zukerman (vn/va), L. Harrell (vc), M. Debost (fl/pic), A. Pay (cl/b cl), P. Boulez (cnd) *(rec June 20-21, 1977)*
Sony Classical ▲ SMK 48466 [ADD]
Schubert, Franz:Fant Vn, D.934, w. Isaac Stern (vn) Sony Classical 2-▲ SM2K 64528 [ADD/DDD]
Schubert, Franz:Impromptus Pno, D.935 Erato ▲ 91700-2
Schubert, Franz:Rondo Vn, D.895, w. Isaac Stern (vn) Sony Classical 2-▲ SM2K 64528 [ADD/DDD]
Schubert, Franz:Son Pno, D.960 Erato ▲ 91700-2
Schubert, Franz:Son Vn, D.574, w. Isaac Stern (vn) Sony Classical 2-▲ SM2K 64528 [ADD/DDD]
Schubert, Franz:Sonatinas Vn, w. P. Zukerman (vn)—Nos. 2 & 3 *(rec Sept. 9, 1971)*
Ermitage ▲ ERM 125 [ADD]
Schubert, Franz:Sonatinas Vn, w. Isaac Stern (vn) Sony Classical 2-▲ SM2K 64528 [ADD/DDD]
Schumann, R.:Con Pno, w. D. Fischer-Dieskau (cnd), London PO EMI Classics ▲ CDM 64626
Schumann, R.:Frauenliebe und -leben, w. Janet Baker (mez)
EMI Classics ("Doublefforte" series) 2-▲ CDFB 68667
Schumann, R.:Intro & Allegro, Op. 134, w. D. Fischer-Dieskau (cnd), London PO
EMI Classics ▲ CDM 64626

Barere, Simon (pno)
Liszt, F.:Con 1 Pno, w. D. Brockman (cnd), *(orch unknown)* *(rec May 17, 1946)*
APR 2-▲ APR 7007 [AAD]
Liszt, F.:Études de concert (2) Pno—Gnomenreigen [2 versions] *(rec Nov 18, 1946 & Feb 7, 194)*
APR 2-▲ APR 7007 [AAD]
Liszt, F.:Harmonies poétiques et religieuses—Funérailles, S.173/7 *(rec Mar 9, 1947)*
APR 2-▲ APR 7007 [AAD]
Liszt, F.:Hungarian Rhaps—No. 12 in c#, S.244 *(rec Mar 9, 1947)* APR 2-▲ APR 7007 [AAD]
Liszt, F.:Rhap espagnole *(rec Mar 9, 1947)* APR 2-▲ APR 7007 [AAD]
Liszt, F.:Son Pno *(rec Nov 11, 1947)* APR 2-▲ APR 7007 [AAD]
Liszt, F.:Transcriptions & Paraphrases—Gounod:Valse de l'opéra Faust, S.407 *(rec Nov 11, 1946 & Feb 7, 194)* APR 2-▲ APR 7007 [AAD]
Simon Barere at the Carnegie Hall, Vol. 1 APR ▲ APR 7008 [AAD]
Simon Barere at the Carnegie Hall, Vol. 2 APR ▲ APR 7009 [AAD]
Simon Barere:The Complete HMV Recordings (1936-36) APR ▲ APR 7001 [AAD]

Bares, Alessandro (baroque vn)—see ORCHESTRAS & ENSEMBLES Ensemble Barocco Padua Sans Souci

Bares, Peter (org)
Bares, P.:Org Improvs on the Measured Studies of the West Facade of St. Peter in Sinzig
Pro Viva ▲ ISPV 166

Bargy, Roy (pno)
Gershwin, G.:Con Pno, w. W. Dailey (cnd), Paul Whiteman Orch [Ferde Grofé's 1928 "jazz band" orchestration] *(rec 1928)* Preamble ▲ PRCD 1785 [AAD]

Barham, P. (sax)
Waschka (II), R.:Last Night, w. Y. Mayama-Livesay (pno) Centaur ▲ CRC 2133 [DDD]

Barik, R. (s sax)—see ORCHESTRAS & ENSEMBLES Prism Saxophone Quartet

Barile, Claudio (fl)
Ginastera, A.:Impresiones de la Puna, Camerata Bariloche CO Argentina *(rec Troy Savings Bank Music Hall, Troy, NY, Feb. 1994)* Dorian ▲ DOR 90202 [DDD]

Bar-Illan, David (pno)
Beethoven, L. van:Son 3 Pno Audiofon ▲ CD 72009
Beethoven, L. van:Son 14 Pno, "Moonlight Son" Audiofon ▲ CD 72009
Beethoven, L. van:Son 21 Pno, "Waldstein" Audiofon ▲ CD 72009
Beethoven, L. van:Vars & Fugue Pno, Op. 35, "Eroica" Audiofon ▲ CD 72009
Chopin, F.:Ballades Pno (comp)—Op. 52 Audiofon ▲ CD 72031

Bar-Illan, David (pno) (cont.)
Chopin, F.:Études (24)—7 sels. InSync ■ C 4160
Debussy, C.:Pno Music (misc)—Feux d'artifice; Toccata (from Pour le piano) InSync ■ C 4161
Franck, C.:Symphonic Vars, w. J.-J. DuBois (cnd), French Concerts Orch Audiofon ▲ CD 72006
Franck, C.:Symphonic Vars, w. J.-J. DuBois (cnd), French Concerts Orch InSync ■ C 4161
Liszt, F.:Années de pèlerinage 2—No. 7, "Dante Sonata" Audiofon ▲ CD 72031
Liszt, F.:Con 1 Pno, w. J.-J. DuBois (cnd), French Concerts Orch Audiofon ▲ 72030
Liszt, F.:En rêve Audiofon ▲ CD 72031
Moszkowski, M.:Con Pno, w. A. Antonini (cnd), Bavarian RSO—& Etude in A♭, Op. 72/11
InSync ■ C 4160
Moszkowski, M.:Con Pno, w. A. Antonini (cnd), Bavarian RSO Audiofon ▲ CD 72006
Moszkowski, M.:Con Pno, w. A. Antonini (cnd), Bavarian RSO Audiofon ▲ CD 72065
Moszkowski, M.:Études de virtuosité Audiofon ▲ CD 72065
Mussorgsky, M.:Pictures at an Exhibition Audiofon ▲ CD 72031
Recital Audiofon ▲ CD 72030
Saint-Saëns, C.:Con 2 Pno, w. D, J.-J. DuBois (cnd), French Concerts Orch InSync ■ C 4161
Saint-Saëns, C.:Con 2 Pno, w. J.-J. DuBois (cnd), French Concerts Orch Audiofon ▲ CD 72006
Tchaikovsky, P.:Con 2 Pno, w. D. Bar-Illan, J.-J. DuBois (cnd), French Concerts Orch
Audiofon ▲ CD 72030
Tchaikovsky, P.:Con 2 Pno, w. J.-J. DuBois (cnd), French Concerts Orch Audiofon ▲ CD 72065
Weber, C.M. von:Sons Pno—No. 2 Audiofon ▲ CD 72031

Barinova, G. (vn)
Sibelius, J.:Con Vn, w. A. Orlov (cnd), Moscow RSO *(rec 1947)*
Multisonic ("Russian Treasures" series) ▲ 31 0238

Barker, Edwin (db)
Ives, C.:Largo cantabile, w. Lydian String Quartet Centaur ▲ CRC 2069 [DDD]
Schulhoff, E.:Concertino Fl, w. F. Smith (fl), M. Ludwig (va)—Andante con moto moderato; Furiant; Andante; Rondino *(rec May 1992)* Northeastern ▲ NR 248-CD

Barker, Thurman (dr)
Jenkins, L.:Monkey on the Dragon, w. Leroy Jenkins (vn), Henry Threadgill (fl), Don Byron (cl), Marth Ehrlich (b cl), Janet Frice (bn), Vincent Chancey (hn), Frank Gordon (tpt), Jeff Hoyer (trbn), David Soldier (vn), Jane Henry (vn) Ron Lawrence (va), Mary Wooton (vc), Lindsey Horner (db), Myra Melford (pno), T. Léon (cnd) *(rec live, Merkin Concert Hall, New York City, Apr. 9, 1992)*
CRI ("eXchange" series) ▲ CD 663 [DDD]
Lebaron, A.:The E. & O. Line (sels), w. Louise Cloutier (mez—Eurydice/Vendors), Hugh Panero (ten—Hermes), Lawrence Hamilton (bar—Orpheus/Men), Frank London (tpt), Marcus Rojas (tuba), Myra Melford (pno/kbd), Davey Williams (gtr), Fred Hopkins (elec bass), A. LeBaron (cnd)—Juke Joint Jam Session; Eurydice Meets Hermes; Eurydice's Death [Funeral Band]; Eurydice's River Journey; Orpheus Laments [Looked Away] *(rec Coolidge Auditorium, Library of Congress, 1987)* Mode ▲ Mode 42

Barlett, Eric (vc)
Fine, V.:Missa Brevis, w. Jan DeGaetani (mez), David Finckel (vc), Michael Finckel (vc), Maxine Neuman (vc) CRI ▲ CD 692 [ADD]

Barlow, Jeremy (rcrs/perc)—see ORCHESTRAS & ENSEMBLES Broadside Band

Barlow, Robert (hp)
Suesse, D.:Music of, w. Cy Coleman (pno), Dana Suesse (pno), F. Fennell (cnd), American SO, All City Concert Choir—Con Romantico for Pno & Orch; A Little Light Music; Young Man with Harp for Hp & Orch; The Blues [from Con in 3 Rhythms]; Coronach for Hp & Orch; Jazz Con for Combo & Orch; The Night Is Young & You're So Beautiful for Orch & Chorus *(rec Carnegie Hall, Dec 1974)*
Premier ▲ PRCD 1055

Barna, Thomas D. (pno)
Kosins, M.S.:Songs of the Seeker, w. J. Carradine (nar), A. Kavafian (vn), R. Williams (bn) *(rec 1980)*
Centaur ▲ CRC 2105 [ADD]

Barnes, Darrell (va)
Beethoven, L. van:Serenade Fl, Op. 25, w. J. Berg (fl), M. Rabinovitsj (vn) *(rec 1975-79)*
Vox Box 3-▲ CD3X 3014 [ADD]
Brahms, J.:Qnt Cl, w. G. Siflies (cl), J. Korman (vn), J. Beiler (vn), J. Sant'Ambrogio (vc) *(rec 1975-79)*
Vox Box 3-▲ CD3X 3014 [ADD]

Barnes, James (cimbalom)
Kodály, Z.:Háry János (suite), w. Ted Gurch (sax), Reid Harris (va), Y. Levi (cnd), Atlanta SO *(rec Atlanta, 1995-96)* Telarc ▲ CD 80413 [DDD]

Barnes, James Earl (perc)
Persichetti, V.:Cant 2 Fl, w. E. A. Schultz (fl), T. Brooks (cnd), Mendelssohn Club Chorus Philadelphia
New World ▲ 80316-2

Barnes, Linn (gtr/lt)
Yule, w. L. Barnes (gtr/lt), Allison Hampton (hp) *(rec Inner Ear Studios, Arlington, VA)*
Oak Leaf ▲ OL 2110

Barnes, Paul (pno)
Pinkham, D.:Songs, w. Margaret Kennedy (sop), William McMullen (ob)—Carols & Cries; Music, Thou Soul of Heaven; Slow, Slow, Fresh Fount; The Hour Glass; Heaven-Haven/World Welter; The Moon Was But a Chin of Gold; To Make a Prairie; A Partridge in a Pear Tree; 3 Canticles from Luke; For Echo is the Soul of the Voice; When Love Was Gone; 3 Alleluias Arkay ▲ ARK 6153 [DDD]

Barnes, Robert (va)
Mozart, W.A.:Qts Fl, w. P. Fried (fl), V. Romanul (vn), R. Feldman (vc) Golden Tone ▲ GT 003

Barneschi, Stefano (vn)—see ORCHESTRAS & ENSEMBLES Ricordanze String Quartet

Barnet, Lori (vc)—see ORCHESTRAS & ENSEMBLES Penn Contemporary Players

Barnett, Lori (vc)
Davidson, T.:I Hear the Mermaids Singing, w. Kathleen Carol (va), Charles Abramovic (pno)
CRI ▲ CD 681 [DDD]
Musgrave, T.:Orfeo III, w. Pamela Guidetti (fl), Mei Chen Liao Cope (vn), Igor Szwec (vn), Michael Strauss (va), Miles B. Davis (db), J. Freeman (cnd) *(rec Lang Concert Hall, Swarthmore College)*
CRI ▲ CD 723 [DDD]

Barnhart, S. (perc)
Schwartz, E.:Sinf Juxta, w. E. Schwartz (pno), S. Jones (tpt), B. Theurer (tpt)
Capstone ▲ CPS 8612 CD [DDD]

Baron, Art (conch shell/trbn/didjerido)
Lockwood, A.:Thousand Year Dreaming, w. Liby Van Cleve (ob/E hn), Jon Gibson (didjeridu), J.D. Parran (cl), Michael Publiese (perc), Scott Robinson (conch shell/perc), John Snyder (didjeridu/waterphone), Charles Wood (tam-tam, stones), Peter Zummo (trbn/didjeridu)
¿What Next? ▲ WN 0010

Baron, Deborah (fl)—see also ORCHESTRAS & ENSEMBLES Dallas Tryptych Players
Mamlok, U.:Vars Fl CRI ■ C 212
Perle, G.:Monody CRI ■ ACS 6015
Piston, W.:Con Fl, w. U. Barnea (cnd), Billings SO CRS ▲ CD 8840
Sargon, S.:Music of, w. Lila Deis (sop), Stephen Dubov (ten), Stephen Girko (cl), Christopher Adkins (vc), Vesselin Demirev (vn), Simon Sargon (pno)—Shemà [Hear] for Sop, Fl, Cl, Vc & Pno; Before the Ark for Vn & Pno; Wedding Dance for Vn & Pno; Klezmuzik for Cl & Pno; At Gradmother's Knee [5 Yiddish Folk Songs] for Ten & Pno; Meditation for Vc & Pno; At Grandfather's Knee [5 Judeo-Spanish Folk Songs] for Sop & Pno *(rec Caruth Auditorium, SMU, Dallas, TX, Jan 1996)* Gasparo ▲ GAS 318
Telemann, G.P.:Sons Fl & Hpd, w. E. Brewer (hpd)—in c Elektra/Nonesuch ■ 71352-4
Ward-Steinman, D.:Fragments from Sappho, w. P. Curtin (sop), D. Glazer (cl), D. Ward-Steinman (pno) [E] CRI ■ C 238

Baron, Joey (perc)
Sato, M.:Improvs, w. Michihiro Sato (tsugaru shamisen), Bill Frisell (elec gtr), Fred Frith (elec gtr), Tenko (sgr), Mark Miller (elec bass), Nicolas Collins (elec), Christian Marclay (turntables), Steve Colemann (sax), Tom Cora (vc), Mark Dresser (elec bass), Gerry Hemingway (perc), Toh Ban Djan, Semantics—23 improvisations with various accompaniment combinations *(rec Baby Monster Studio, NY, Apr. 11-16, 1988)* Hat Hut ▲ hat ART CD 6015 [ADD]

460 ▲ = CD ♦ = Enhanced CD Δ = MD ■ = Cassette Tape □ = DCC

Baron, Samuel (fl)—see also ORCHESTRAS & ENSEMBLES New York Woodwind Quintet members, New York Woodwind Quintet
Bach, J.S.:Sons Fl, BWV 1030–35, w. G. Ranck (hpd), T. Eddy (vc)—Sons. BWV 1030-1032, 1034 & 1035 Soundspells ▲ CD 106 [DDD]
Kupferman, M.:Line Fant from Infinities I CRI ■ C 212
Martin, F.:Ballade Fl, w. U. Barnea (cnd), Billings SO [orchestral version] CRS ▲ CD 8840
Martino, D.:Quodlibets CRI ▲ CD 693 [ADD]
Martino, D.:Quodlibets CRI ■ C 212
Mozart, W.A.:Qts Fl, w. Fine Arts String Quartet members Boston Skyline ▲ BSD 142 [AAD]
Rieti, V.:Con Hpd, w. S. Marlowe (hpd), chamber orch CRI ▲ CD 601 [ADD]
Rieti, V.:Partita Hpd, w. S. Marlowe (hpd), R. Roseman (ob), C. Libove (vn), A. Ajemian (vn), H. Zaratzian (va), C. McCraken (vc) CRI ▲ CD 601 [ADD]
Telemann, G.P.:Qt Bn, w. A. Weisberg (bn), R. Roseman (ob), E. Brewer (hpd)—in d Elektra/Nonesuch ■ 71352-4
Walton, W.:Façade, w. J. Bookspan (nar), C. Russon (cl), H. Estrin (sax), M. Broiles (tpt), K. Moore (vc), H. Harris (perc), D. Epstein (cnd) Allegretto ▲ ACD 8153 [ADD] ■ ACD 8153
Wigglesworth, F.:Lake Music CRI ■ C 212
Wigglesworth, F.:Lake Music CRI ▲ C 733 [ADD]

Baroncini, S. (hn)
Rossini, G.:Prelude, Theme & Vars Hn, w. V. Terekiev (pno) Nuova Era 2-▲ 7100/01 [DDD]

Barontini, I. (pno)
Beethoven, L. van:Notturno, w. M. Fornaciari (va) Fonè ▲ FON 93F 20 [DDD]
Beethoven, L. van:Son 9 Vn, "Kreutzer", w. M. Fornaciari (vn) Fonè ▲ FON 93F 20 [DDD]

Barova, Snezhana (pno)—see ORCHESTRAS & ENSEMBLES Academic Chamber Ensemble

Barr, E. (ob)—see ORCHESTRAS & ENSEMBLES Dallas Chamber Players

Barr, Nick (va)—see ORCHESTRAS & ENSEMBLES Lyric String Quartet

Barr, R. (ob)
Hertel, J.W.:Con à 6, w. R. Giangiulio (tpt), R. Neal (cnd), Dallas CO Crystal ▲ CD 512

Barratt-Due, Stephan (vn)
Hvoslef, K.:Duodu, w. S.-M. Chung (va) *(rec 1993)* Victoria ▲ VCD 19067
Mozart, W.A.:Duos Vn, w. S.-M. Chung (va) *(rec 1993)* Victoria ▲ VCD 19067
Nordheim, A.:Duplex, w. S. M. Chung (va) *(rec 1993)* Victoria ▲ VCD 19067

Barrell, S. (clvd)
Bach, W.F.:Polonaises, F.12, w. S. Barrell Globe ▲ GLO 5035 [DDD]

Barrett, Michael (pno)—see also ORCHESTRAS & ENSEMBLES New York Festival of Song
Bernstein, L.:Arias & Barcarolles, w. Judy Kaye (mez), William Sharp (bar), Steven Blier (pno) [E] Koch International Classics ▲ KIC 7000-2 [DDD] ■ 3-7000-4 (D)
Bernstein, L.:Songs & Duets, w. Judy Kaye (sop), William Sharp (bar), S. Blier (pno), S. Sant'Ambrogio (vc)—sels. from On The Town, 1944 *(Some other time; Lonely town; Carried away; I can cook)*; Peter Pan, 1949 *(Dream with me)*; Wonderful Town, 1952 *(A little bit in love)*; Songfest, 1977 *(Storyette, H.M.; To what you said)* [E] Koch International Classics ▲ KIC 7000-2 [DDD] ■ 3-7000-4 (D)
Blitzstein, M.:Con Pno, w. L. Foss (cnd), Brooklyn PO CRI ▲ CD 554 [DDD]

Barrett, Nerine (pno)
Gottschalk, L.M.:Pno Music, w. A. Marks (pno)—Réponds moi (danse cubaine), Op. 50; Printemps d'amour, Op. 40; Marche de Nuit, Op. 17; Ses Yeux, Op. 66; La Jota Argonesa, Op. 14; Le Bananier, Op. 5; Ojos Criollos, Op. 37; Orfa (grande polka), Op. 71; La Scintilla, Op. 21; Marche funèbre, Op. 64; La Gallina, Op. 53; Radieuse, Op. 72; Grande Tarantelle, Op. 67 Nimbus ▲ NI 5324 [DDD]

Barrett, S. (E hn)—see ORCHESTRAS & ENSEMBLES SONOR Ensemble of Univ of California San Diego members

Barringer, Heather (vib/perc)—see ORCHESTRAS & ENSEMBLES Zeitgeist

Barrio, Isidro (pno)
Beethoven, L. van:Vars on a waltz by Diabelli, Op. 120 Koch Schwann ▲ SCH 314422
Soler, P.A.:Sons Kbd—Sons 1-8 Pno Koch Schwann ▲ SCH 317302
Soler, P.A.:Sons Kbd, Sons 9-18 Pno Koch Schwann ▲ SCH 317312

Barritt, Jonathan (va)
Jolivet, A.:Petite suite, w. Anna Noakes (fl), Gillian Tingay (hp) ASV ("French Chamber Music" series) ▲ ASV 948

Barritt, Paul (vn)
Ireland, J.:Chamber Music, w. Catherine Edwards (pno)—Bagatelle; Berceuse; Catavina; The Holy Boy Hyperion ▲ CDA 66853
Ireland, J.:Son 1 Vn, w. Catherine Edwards (pno) Hyperion ▲ CDA 66853
Ireland, J.:Son 2 Vn, w. Catherine Edwards (pno) Hyperion ▲ CDA 66853
Mozart, W.A.:Qts Fl, w. J. Hall (fl), G. Clarkson (va), J. Horder (vc) Collins Quest ▲ 3044 [DDD]
Rheinberger, J.:Suite Vn, Op. 150, w. Christopher Herrick (org) Hyperion ▲ CDA 66883
Rheinberger, J.:Suite Vn Vc, w. Richard Lester (vc), Christopher Herrick (org) Hyperion ▲ CDA 66883
Rimsky-Korsakov, N.:Golden Cockerel (sels), w. O. Dohnányi (cnd), English CO—Hymn to the Sun *(rec St. Silas Church, London, Dec 1994)* Novalis ▲ 150119 [DDD]
Rózsa, M.:North Hungarian Peasant Songs & Dances, w. Julian Jacobson (pno) Silva Classics ▲ SIL 6006 [DDD]
Rózsa, M.:Son Vn Silva Classics ▲ SIL 6006 [DDD]

Barro, Jean-Claude (hn)
Schumann, R.:Konzertstück Hns, w. Alain Courtois (hn), Jean-Paul Gantiez (hn), Jean-Jacques Justafre (hn), *(orch unknown)*—Lebhaft; Romanze Erato ▲ 94801-2

Barron, Ronald (trbn)
All American Trombone, w. Fredrik Wanger (pno), Harvard Univ Wind Ensemble, Atlantic Brass Quintet *(rec Sanders Theater, Harvard Univ; Symphony Hall, Boston; Morse Auditorium, Boston Univ, Nov 7, Dec 8-9, 1995; Jan)* Boston Brass ▲ BB 1003
Hindemith on Trombone Boston Brass ▲ BB 1002CD ■ BB 1002CT
Hindemith, P.:Chansons [w his trbn ensemble] [arr. for trombone ensemble] Boston Brass ▲ BB 1002CD ■ BB 1002CT
Hindemith, P.:Leichte Stücke, w. F. Wanger (pno) [tran for trbn & pno] Boston Brass ▲ BB 1002CD ■ BB 1002CT
Hindemith, P.:Morgenmusik [w trbn qt] Boston Brass ▲ BB 1002CD ■ BB 1002CT
Hindemith, P.:Son Alto Hn, w. F. Wanger (pno) Boston Brass ▲ BB 1002CD ■ BB 1002CT
Hindemith, P.:Son Trbn, w. F. Wanger (pno) Boston Brass ▲ BB 1002CD ■ BB 1002CT
Hindemith, P.:Stücke (4) Bn & Vc, w. D. Yeo (trbn) [arr. for tenor & bass trombones] Boston Brass ▲ BB 1002CD ■ BB 1002CT
Hindemith, P.:Trauermusik, w. *(ensemble unknown)* Boston Brass ▲ BB 1002CD ■ BB 1002CT
In The Family, w. Marianne Gedigian (fl), Ann Hobson Pilot (hp), Douglas Yeo (trbn), Edwin Barker (bass), Thomas Gauger (perc) *(rec Morse Auditorium, Boston Univ, Dec 1995)* Boston Brass ▲ BB 1004
Le Trombone français *(rec Jan. 1976)* Boston Brass ■ BB 1001

Barrows, John (hn)—see ORCHESTRAS & ENSEMBLES New York Woodwind Quintet

Barrueco, Manuel (gtr)
Falla, M. de:Canciones populares españolas (7), w. A. Monoyios (sop) EMI Classics ▲ CDC 54456
Granados, E.:Danzas españolas (10), w. T. Müller-Pering (gtr) EMI Classics ▲ CDC 54456
Manuel Barrueco Plays Lennon & McCartney, w. David Tanenbaum (gtr), London SO [cnd:Jeremy Lubbock] Angel ▲ CDC 55228
Plays Albéniz & Turina EMI Classics ▲ CDC 54382
Pure Barrueco, w. David Tanenbaum (gtr), London SO [cnd:Jeremy Lubbock] EMI Classics ▲ CDC 55315
300 Years of Guitar Masterpieces Vox Box 3-▲ CD3X 3007 [ADD]

Barsalkin, Valeri (db)
Schnittke, A.:Hymns Vc, w. A. Ivashkin (vc), Y. Rudometkin (bn), I. Pashinskaya (hp), V. Chasovennaya (hpd), V. Grishin, N. Grishin (perc/bells)—No. 1 for Cello, Harp & Timpani [Quasi andante]; No. 2 for Cello & Double *(rec National Radio House, Moscow, 1987)* Vox Box 2-▲ CDX 5121 [ADD]

Barshaï, Rudolf (vn)
Telemann, G.P.:Cons Ob, w. Pierre Pierlot (ob), Evgeni Nepalov (ob), Piotr Dubrov (ob), Andrei Abramenkov (vn), Leonid Poleess (vn), R. Barshaï (cnd), Moscow CO—in B♭ for 3 Obs, 3 Vns & Bc *(rec Salle Wagram, Paris, June 1964)* EMI Classics ▲ CDK 65340 [ADD]

Barshay, Nina (vn)
Bortnyansky, D.:Qnt Vn, Vl, w. Boris Dobrokhotov (vl), Vladimir Berlinsky (vc), Olga Erdeli (hp), Sergey Dizhur (pno) *(rec 1950)* Multisonic ("Russian Treasures" series) ▲ 31 0253
Bortnyansky, D.:Sinf concertante, w. Boris Dobrokhotov (vl), Vladimir Berlinsky (vc), Olga Erdeli (hp), Sergey Dizhur (pno), Moscow CO *(rec 1984)* Multisonic ("Russian Treasures" series) ▲ 31 0253

Barshay, Rudolf (va)
Hindemith, P.:Son Va, Op. 25/1 Multisonic ▲ MUL 310355
Mozart, W.A.:Duos Vn & Va, w. Igor Oistrakh (vn)—K.424 Multisonic ▲ MUL 310355
Schumann, R.:Märchenbilder, w. Vladimir Shraybman (pno) Multisonic ▲ MUL 310355

Bársony, László (va)—see also ORCHESTRAS & ENSEMBLES New Budapest String Quartet
Mozart, W.A.:Qts Fl, w. J. Szebenyi (fl), A. Kiss (vn), K. Botvay (vc) White Label ▲ HRC 128 [ADD]
Truscott, H.:Trio Fl, w. Imre Kovács (fl), Béla Nagy (vn) *(rec Alpha-Line Studio, Festetich Castle, Budapest, 1994)* Marco Polo ▲ 8.223727 [DDD]
Vivaldi, A.:Cons Va d'amore, w. J. Rolla (cnd), Franz Liszt CO—5 concerti, RV.392-396 Hungaroton ▲ HCD 12162
Vivaldi, A.:Con Va d'amore Lt, w. D. Benkő (lt), J. Rolla (cnd), Franz Liszt CO Hungaroton ▲ HCD 11978

Barstow, Margaret (vc)
Telemann, G.P.:Canonic Son 2 Bn, w. Christopher Weait (bn) D'Note Classics ▲ DND 1008 [DDD]

Bárta, Aleš (hps/postivie org)—see ORCHESTRAS & ENSEMBLES Pro Arte Antiqua Prague

Bárta, Aleš (org)
Bach, J.S.:Org Music (misc)—Chorale Preludes BWV 659 & 734; Concerto in G, BWV 592; Pastorale in F, BWV 590; Prelude & Fugue in G, BWV 541; Toccata, Adagio & Fugue in C, BWV 564; Toccata & Fugue in d, BWV 565 Supraphon ▲ 11 1289-2 [DDD]
Jewels of Baroque Music, w. J. Suk (vn) Lotos ▲ LT 0009 [DDD]
Liszt, F.:Org Music—Variations on a Theme by Bach, S.180; Pontifical Anthem; Prelude & Fugue, S.260; Fantasy & Fugue on the Chorale "Ad Nos, Ad Salutarem Undam" *(rec 1991-92)* Praga ▲ 250037

Barta, Jiří (vc)
Pärt, A.:Fratres I, w. Marian Lapsansky (pno) [arr vc & pno] Supraphon ▲ SUP 112156 [DDD]
Rachmaninoff, S.:Son Vc, w. Marian Lapsansky (pno) Supraphon ▲ SUP 112156 [DDD]
Schnittke, A.:Son Vc, w. Marian Lapsansky (pno) Supraphon ▲ SUP 112156 [DDD]
Schulhoff, E.:Son Vc, w. Jan Cech (pno) Supraphon ▲ SUP 112169 [DDD]

Barta, M. (ob)
Righini, V.:Alcide al Bivio, w. L. Serra (sop), S. Browne (cta), W. McKinney (ten), R. El Hage (bass), P. Molinari (hpd), T. Gotti (cnd), Swiss-Italian RSO, Swiss-Italian Radio Chorus *(rec 1979)* Bongiovanni 2-▲ GB 2157/58 [ADD]

Bartelloni, Leonardo (pno)
Petrassi, G.:Ala, w. Mario Ancillotti (fl), Luciano Tristano (fl) Koch Schwann ▲ SCH 315242

Bartlett, Dale (pno)
Coulthard, J.:Son Rhap, w. Robert Verebes (va) *(rec Boucherville, Quebec)* SNE ▲ 550
Hindemith, P.:Son in C Va & Pno, w. Robert Verebes (va) SNE 2-▲ 546/7
Hindemith, P.:Son Va & Pno, Op. 11/4, w. Robert Verebes (va) SNE 2-▲ 546/7
Hindemith, P.:Son Va & Pno, Op. 25/4, w. Robert Verebes (va) SNE 2-▲ 546/7
Martinů, B.:Son 1 Va, w. Robert Verebes (va) *(rec Boucherville, Quebec)* SNE ▲ 550
Mendelssohn, F.:Son Va, w. Robert Verebes (va) *(rec Boucherville, Quebec)* SNE ▲ 550

Bartlett, Eric (vc)
Moravec, P.:Open Secret, w. R. Schulte (vn), E. Garth (pno) CRI ▲ CD 641 [DDD]

Barto, Tzimon (pno)
Chopin, F.:Con 1 Pno, w. A. Fischer (cnd), Royal PO *(rec Dec. 9, 1991)* EMI Classics ▲ CDC 54648-2 [DDD]
Chopin, F.:Pno Music (misc)—Cantabile; Contredanse; 3 Nocturnes EMI Classics ▲ CDC 54367
Chopin, F.:Preludes, Op. 28 EMI Classics ▲ CDC 54367
Liszt, F.:Con 2 Pno, w. A. Fischer (cnd), Royal PO *(rec Dec. 9, 1991)* EMI Classics ▲ CDC 54648-2 [DDD]
Popular Encores, w. T. Barto (pno) EMI Classics ▲ CDC 54900
Saint-Saëns, C.:Carnival of the Animals, w. M. Rudy (pno), M. Plasson (cnd), Toulouse Capitole Orch EMI Classics 2-▲ CDC 54465

Bartók, Béla (pno)
Bartók at the Piano Hungaroton 6-▲ HCD 12326/31 (m) [ADD]
Bartók, B.:Allegro barbaro EMI Classics ▲ CDC 55031
Bartók, B.:Contrasts, w. B. Goodman (cl), Szigeti (vn) CBS ▲ MK 42227 ■ MYT 42227
Bartók, B.:Contrasts, w. B. Goodman (cl), Szigeti (vn) *(rec 1940)* Hungaroton 6-▲ HCD 12326/31 (m) [ADD]
Bartók, B.:Contrasts, w. B. Goodman (cl), Szigeti (vn) *(rec 1940)* Sony Masterworks ("Portrait" series) ▲ MPK 47676 [ADD]
Bartók, B.:Mikrokosmos—31 sels. *(rec 1940)* Sony Masterworks ("Portrait" series) ▲ MPK 47676 [ADD]
Bartók, B.:Pno Music, w. V. Medgyaszay (sop), M. Basilides (cta), F. Székelyhidy (ten), J. Szigeti (vn), B. Goodman (cl), D. Bartók Pásztory (pno), H. J. Baker, E. J. Rubsam (perc)—studio, broadcast & piano roll recordings of music by Bartók, Kodály, Beethoven, Debussy, Liszt & Scarlatti, chronologically arranged from ca. 1920 through 1945—Sonatina; 6 Romanian Folk Dances; Evening in Transylvania; 8 sels. from 15 Hungarian Peasant Songs; Suite, Op. 14 (both the issued & test recordings); Allegro barbaro; 5 sels. from 2 Romanian Dances, 3 Burlesques, 10 Easy Pieces & 14 Bagatelles; & 4 Sons. by D. Scarlatti (test recordings); 8 sels. from 15 Hungarian Peasant Songs; 4 sels. from 9 Little Piano Pieces, Petite Suite & 3 Rondos on Folk Melodies; & "Sursum corda" from Liszt's Années de pèlerinage; 20 Hungarian Folk Songs; 5 Hungarian Folk Tunes; 8 Hungarian Folksongs; Hungarian Folk Tunes; 6 Romanian Folk Dances; Rhap. 1 Violin & Piano; Contrasts for Clarinet, Violin & Piano; 2 sels. from Mikrokosmos; 32 sels. from Mikrokosmos; Rhap. 1; Son. No. 2; Beethoven's "Kreutzer" Son.; Debussy's Son. 3; Son. 2 Pianos & Percussion; Petite Suite; 3 Hungarian Folk Tunes; 11 sels. from Improvs. on Hungarian Peasant Songs; Mikrokosmos; 3 Rondos on Folk Melodies; 9 Little Piano Pieces; 14 Bagatelles; 15 sels. from For Children & 2 sels. from 10 Easy Pieces Hungaroton 6-▲ HCD 12326/31 (m) [ADD]
Bartók, B.:Rhaps Vn & Pno, Sz.86 & 89, w. J. Szigeti (vn) *(rec 1940)* Vanguard Classics ▲ OVC 8008 [AAD]
Bartók, B.:Rhaps Vn & Pno, Sz.86 & 89, w. J. Szigeti (vn) [two performances of No. 1] *(rec 1940)* Hungaroton 6-▲ HCD 12326/31 (m) [ADD]
Bartók, B.:Son 2 Vn & Pno, w. J. Szigeti (vn) *(rec 1940)* Vanguard Classics ▲ OVC 8008 [AAD]
Bartók, B.:Son 2 Vn & Pno, w. J. Szigeti (vn) *(rec 1940)* Hungaroton 6-▲ HCD 12326/31 (m) [ADD]
Bartók, B.:Songs, w. *(vocalists unknown)*, J. Szigeti (vn) EMI Classics ▲ CDC 55031
Bartók, B.:Suite Pno EMI Classics ▲ CDC 55031
Bartók, B.:Suite Pno Hungaroton 6-▲ HCD 12326/31 (m) [ADD]
Beethoven, L. van:Son 9 Vn, "Kreutzer", w. J. Szigeti (vn) *(rec live, Library of Congress, Washington D.C. 4/13/40)* Hungaroton 6-▲ HCD 12326/31 (m) [ADD]
Beethoven, L. van:Son 9 Vn, "Kreutzer", w. J. Szigeti (vn) *(rec 1940)* Vanguard Classics ▲ OVC 8008 [AAD]
Debussy, C.:Son Vn, w. J. Szigeti (vn) *(rec 1940)* Vanguard Classics ▲ OVC 8008 [AAD]
Debussy, C.:Son Vn, w. J. Szigeti (vn) *(rec live, Library of Congress, Washington D.C. 4/13/40)* Hungaroton 6-▲ HCD 12326/31 (m) [ADD]
Kodály, Z.:Hungarian Folk Music, w. V. Medgyaszay (sop), M. Basilides (mez), F. Székelyhidy (ten) [arr. by Kodály for solo voice & piano]—20 Hungarian folk songs *(rec Budapest, 1928)* Hungaroton 6-▲ HCD 12326/31 (m) [ADD]
Liszt, F.:Années de pèlerinage 3 *(rec Budapest, ca.1936)* Hungaroton 6-▲ HCD 12326/31 (m) [ADD]

Bartók, Béla (pno) (cont.)
The Recordings with Béla Bartók & Andor Foldes, w. J. Szigeti (vn), Benny Goodman (cl) *(rec 1940–41)* Biddulph ▲ BID LAB 070 [ADD]
Bartoletti, Angelo (va)—see ORCHESTRAS & ENSEMBLES Italian Piano Quartet
Bartoli, René (gtr)
Guitar Recital Harmonia Mundi Plus ▲ HMP 390928
Bartoli, Riccardo (pno)
Castelnuovo-Tedesco, M.:Son Cl & Pno, w. Sergio Bosi (cl) *(rec Potenza Picena Teatro "B. Mugellini", June 3–6, 1994)* Bongiovanni ▲ GB 5563 [DDD]
Reinecke, C.:Fantasiestücke Cl, w. S. Bossi (cl) *(rec June 19–22, 1993)* Bongiovanni ▲ GB 5537 [DDD]
Reinecke, C.:Fantasiestücke Pno *(rec June 19–22, 1993)* Bongiovanni ▲ GB 5537 [DDD]
Reinecke, C.:Fantasiestücke Va, w. R. Molinelli (va) *(rec June 19–22, 1993)* Bongiovanni ▲ GB 5537 [DDD]
Rota, N.:Son Cl Pno, w. Sergio Bosi (cl) *(rec Potenza Picena Teatro "B. Mugellini", June 3–6, 1994)* Bongiovanni ▲ GB 5563 [DDD]
Setaccioli, G.:Son Cl, w. Sergio Bosi (cl) *(rec Potenza Picena Teatro "B. Mugellini", June 3–6, 1994)* Bongiovanni ▲ GB 5563 [DDD]
Bartolomey, Franz (vc)—see also ORCHESTRAS & ENSEMBLES Vienna Ring Ensemble
Strauss, R.:Don Quixote, w. A. Previn (cnd), Vienna PO Telarc ▲ CD 80262 [DDD]
Barton, Ena Bronstein (pno)
Rahbee, D.G.:Mosaic, w. P. A. Lehrer (pno) *(rec The Music Room)* Seda ▲ 333 [DDD]
Barton, Hanus (pno)
Dussek, J.L.:Qt Pno, w. Apollo String Quartet members Studio Matous ▲ MAT 20 [DDD]
Dussek, J.L.:Qnt Pno, w. Apollo String Quartet Studio Matous ▲ MAT 20 [DDD]
Dussek, J.L.:Son Pno, Op. 77, "L'invocation" Studio Matous ▲ MAT 20 [DDD]
Janácek, L.:Vocal Music, w. Eva Struplová (sop), Stanislav Predota (ten), Adam Skoumal (pno), L. Cerny (cnd), *(ensemble unknown)*, Milan Uherek (cnd), Severácek Children's Choir—Little Queens; Folk Poetry from Hukvaldy; Folk Nocturnes; Nursery Rhymes Studio Matous ▲ MAT 16 [DDD]
Barton, Rachel (vn)
Sarasate, P. de:Carmen Fant, w. S. Sanders (pno) [arr. violin & piano] Dorian ▲ DOR 90183 [DDD]
Sarasate, P. de:Intro & Tarantella, w. S. Sanders (pno) [arr. violin & piano] Dorian ▲ DOR 90183 [DDD]
Sarasate, P. de:Spanish Dances, w. S. Sanders (pno) Dorian ▲ DOR 90183 [DDD]
Sarasate, P. de:Vn & Pno Music, w. S. Sanders (pno)—Muiñera; Miramar; Adios, montaños mias Dorian ▲ DOR 90183 [DDD]
Barton, V. (vc)
Pellegrini, E.:Divert a tre Bn, w. D. N. Joseph (bn), M. Schmidt (vc) CRS ▲ CD 8949
Bartos, Samuel (pno)
Bach, J.S.:Chromatic Fant & Fugue Connoisseur Society ▲ CD 4176 [DDD]
Bach, J.S.:Goldberg Vars Connoisseur Society ▲ CD 4176 [DDD]
Bärtschi, Werner (pno)
Bach, C.P.E.:Con Hpd & Strs, H.427, w. A. Marasch (cnd), Hallé Collegium Instrumentale *(rec Waldenburg, Switzerland, Apr–May, 1995)* Jecklin ▲ JD 701-2 [DDD]
Bach, C.P.E.:Con Hpd & Strs, H.430, w. A. Marasch (cnd), Hallé Collegium Instrumentale *(rec Waldenburg, Switzerland, Apr–May, 1995)* Jecklin ▲ JD 701-2 [DDD]
Bach, C.P.E.:Con Hpd & Strs, H.443, w. A. Marasch (cnd), Hallé Collegium Instrumentale *(rec Waldenburg, Switzerland, Apr–May, 1995)* Jecklin ▲ JD 701-2 [DDD]
Bach, C.P.E.:Kbd Music—Sons, H.47, 75, 247 & 280; Rondo, H.283; Fant, H.284 *(rec 1992)* Jecklin ▲ JD 683-2 [DDD]
Bartschi, W.:Frühmorgens am Daubensee ECM New Series ▲ 78118-21377-2 [DDD]
Busoni, F.:Toccata Pno ECM New Series ▲ 78118-21377-2 [DDD]
Hindemith, P.:Pno Music—In einer Nacht, Op. 15; Reihe kleiner Stück *(rec 1982)* Jecklin ▲ JD 686-2
Hindemith, P.:Pno Music—In Einer Nacht, Op. 15; Reihe Kleiner Stücke, Op. 37/11 Jecklin ▲ JD 691
Marek, C.:Toccata Pno *(rec Dec 1993–Dec 1994)* Jecklin ▲ JEC 306
Marti, H.:Echos de Détresse, w. R. Fritz (harm) Grammont ▲ CTS P 22-2 [ADD]
Mozart, W.A.:Fant Pno, K.475 ECM New Series ▲ 78118-21377-2
Mozart, W.A.:Son 13 Pno ECM New Series ▲ 78118-21377-2 [DDD]
Onslow, G.:Grand Septuor Fl, w. R. Frei (db), Stalder Wind Quintet *(rec 1979)* Jecklin-Disco ▲ JD 554-2 [ADD]
Pärt, A.:Für Alina ECM New Series ▲ 78118-21377-2 [DDD]
Satie, E.:Gymnopédies Accord ▲ ACD 220522 [DDD]
Satie, E.:Pno Music (misc)—Heurs séulaires et instantanées; Lent for Pno; Rêverie du pauvre Accord ▲ ACD 220522 [DDD]
Satie, E.:Socrate, w. Kathrin Graf (sop) Accord ▲ ACD 220522 [DDD]
Scelsi, G.:Illustrazioni Pno ECM New Series ▲ 78118-21377-2 [DDD]
Schmitt, F.:Qnt Pno, w. Bern String Quartet Accord ▲ ACD 220982
Schoeck, O.:Pieces Pno *(rec Dec 1993–Dec 1994)* Jecklin ▲ JEC 306
Vogel, W.:Epitaffio per Alban Berg Grammont ▲ CTSP 14-2 [ADD]
Vogel, W.:Hörformen Pno, w. R. Tschupp (cnd), Zurich Camerata *(rec Dec 1993–Dec 1994)* Jecklin ▲ JEC 306
Vogel, W.:Intervalle *(rec Dec 1993–Dec 1994)* Jecklin ▲ JEC 306
Vogel, W.:Mondträume [G] Grammont ▲ CTSP 14-2 [ADD]
Vogel, W.:Sprechlieder, w. K. Widmer (bass) [G] Grammont ▲ CTSP 14-2 [ADD]
Vogel, W.:Vars Pno Grammont ▲ CTSP 14-2 [ADD]
Vogel, W.:Variétude *(rec Dec 1993–Dec 1994)* Jecklin ▲ JEC 306
Werner Bärtschi-Live *(rec Oct. 19–23, 1988)* Jecklin ▲ JEC 629-2 [ADD]
Zinsstag, G.:Wenn Zum Beispiel..., w. A. Brunner, M. Burg, D. Dyk, R. Ericksson, B. Köhler, M. Maassen, E. Nowak, H. Suter, W. A. Wohlgemuth [G] *(rec Aug. 27, 1976)* Grammont ▲ CTSP 36-2 [ADD]
Barwahser, Hubert (fl)
Mozart, W.A.:Con Fl Hp, w. Berghout (hp), E. van Beinum (cnd), Royal Concertgebouw Orch Philips ■ 411174-4
Bary, Philippe (vc)
Cras, J.:La Flûte de Pan, w. D. Henry (bar), T. Prevost (fl), M.-C. Milliere (vn), J.-F. Benatar (va)—[F] Quantum ▲ QM 6897 [DDD] ■ QM 1992 (D)
Cras, J.:Qnt, w. C. Michel (hp), T. Prevost (fl), M.-C. Milliere (vn), J.-F. Benatar (va) Quantum ▲ QM 6897 [DDD] ■ QM 1992 (D)
Cras, J.:Trio, w. M.-C. Milliere (vn), J.-F. Benatar (va) Quantum ▲ QM 6897 [DDD] ■ QM 1992 (D)
Martinů, B.:Duo Vn & Vc, w. M. Milliere (vn) Quantum ▲ QM 6910 [DDD] ■ QM 2004 (D)
Saint-Saëns, C.:Trio 1 Pno, w. Angéline Pondepeyre (pno), Jeanne-Marie Conquer (vn) REM ▲ REM 311273 [DDD]
Saint-Saëns, C.:Trio 2 Pno, w. Angéline Pondepeyre (pno), Jeanne-Marie Conquer (vn) REM ▲ REM 311273 [DDD]
Basch, Wolfgang (tpt)
Chamber Music for Trumpet & Winds, w. Bob Van Asperen (org/hpd/cnd) Deutsche Harmonia Mundi ▲ 7976-2-RC [DDD]
Gros, J.A.:Con Tpt, Orpheus CO Koch Schwann ▲ CD 311 071 [DDD]
Haydn, J.:Con Tpt, w. M. Andreae (cnd), Bamberg SO Koch Schwann ▲ CD 311005 [DDD]
Hertel, J.W.:Con Tpt, Orpheus CO Koch Schwann ▲ CD 311071 [DDD]
Hummel, J.N.:Con in E♭ Tpt, S.49, Orpheus CO Koch Schwann ▲ CD 311071 [DDD]
Mozart, L.:Con Tpt, w. M. Andreae (cnd), Bamberg SO Koch Schwann ▲ CD 311005 [DDD]
Reutter, J.G. von:Con 2 Tpt, w. M. Andreae (cnd), Bamberg SO Koch Schwann ▲ CD 311005 [DDD]
Telemann, G.P.:Con Tpt Strs in D, w. M. Andreae (cnd), Bamberg SO Koch Schwann ▲ CD 311005 [DDD]
Baschiera, Alfonso (gtr)
Carulli, F.:Gtr Music—Introduction, Theme & Variations, Op. 142; Andanti (4) from Op. 320; Les Adieux, Op. 229; Sonatas (3) from Op. 229; Waltzes (3) from Op. 101 *(rec 6/91)* Nuova Era ▲ 7102

Baschiera, Alfonso (gtr) (cont.)
The Easy Guitar Rivo Alto ▲ RIV 9402 [DDD]
Baselga, Miguel (pno)
Falla, M. de:Pno Music—Nocturno; Mazurka; Serenata andaluza; Canción; Vals-Capricho; Cortejo de gnomos; Serenata; Allegro de concierto; Piezas españolas; Fantasía Bética; Homenaje 'Le tombeau de Claude Debussy'; Canto de los remeros del Volga; Pour le Tombeau de Paul Dukas *(rec Danderyd Grammar School, Sweden, Aug 5–7, 1996)* BIS ▲ CD 773 [DDD]
Bashkirova, Elena (pno)
Mozart, W.A.:Songs, w. J. Varady (sop)—(10 songs) Ridente la calma, K.152; Oiseaux, si tous les ans, K.307; Dans un bois solitaire, K.308; An die Einsamkeit, K.391; Der Zauberer, K.472; Das Veilchen, K.476; Die Alte, K.517; Als Luise die Briefe..., K.520; Abendempfindung, K.523; Un moto di gioia, K.579 [F,G,I] Orfeo ▲ 248921 [DDD]
Schumann, R.:Dichterliebe, w. S. Jerusalem (ten) Erato ▲ 2292-45740-2 ZK
Schumann, R.:Liederkreis, Op. 39, w. S. Jerusalem (ten) Erato ▲ 2292-45740-2 ZK
Strauss, R.:Songs, w. J. Varady (sop)—Schlagende Herzen, Op. 29/2; Meinem Kinde, Op. 37/3; Befreit, Op. 39/4; Waldseligkeit, Op. 49/1; Frühlingsfeier, Op. 56/5; Ich wollt' ein Sträusslein binden, Op. 68/2; Säusle, liebe Myrte, Op. 68/3; Schlechtes Wetter, Op. 69/5 [G] Orfeo ▲ 248921 [DDD]
Bashkirova, Elena (pno/nar)
Meschwitz, F.:Tier Gebete, w. G. Kremer (nar) Philips ("Digital Classics" series) ▲ 416841-2 [DDD]
Bashmet, Yuri (va)
Beethoven, L. van:Serenade Strs, Op. 8, w. Oleg Kagan (vn), Natalia Gutman (vc) *(rec Hohenems Schubertiade, June 22, 1988)* Live Classics ("Kagan Edition" series) ▲ 142
Beethoven, L. van:Trios Strs, Op. 9, w. Oleg Kagan (vn), Natalia Gutman (vc)—Nos. 1 & 3 *(rec Hohenems Schubertiade & Kuhmo Chamber Festival)* Live Classics ("Kagan Edition" series) ▲ 141
Berlioz, H.:Harold in Italy, w. E. Inbal (cnd), Frankfurt RSO Denon ▲ CO 73207 [DDD]
Berlioz, H.:Harold in Italy, w. USSR Radio-TV Large SO Audiophile Classics ▲ APL 101.514 [ADD]
Britten, H.:Lachrymae, w. S. Richter (pno) MK ▲ MKA 418015 [DDD]
Britten, H.:Lachrymae, w. Moscow Soloists RCA Red Seal ▲ 60464-2-RC [DDD]
Bruch, M.:Kol Nidrei, w. M. Muntian (pno) [arr. viola-piano] RCA Red Seal ▲ 60112-2-RC [DDD]
Enescu, G.:Concertpiece Va, w. M. Muntian (pno) RCA Red Seal ▲ 60112-2-RC [DDD]
Glinka, M.:Son Va, w. M. Muntian (pno) RCA Red Seal ▲ 09026-61273-2
Hindemith, P.:Sons Va & Pno, w. Sviatoslav Richter (pno)—Op. 11/4 (1919); Op. 25/4 (1922); Sonata (1939) MK ▲ MKA 418015 [DDD]
Hindemith, P.:Trauermusik, w. Moscow Soloists RCA Red Seal ▲ 60464-2-RC [DDD]
Reger, M.:Suites Va—Suite No. 1 in g RCA Red Seal ▲ 60464-2-RC [DDD]
Roslavets, N.:Son Va, w. M. Muntian (pno)—not advised of which sonata is played here RCA Red Seal ▲ 09026-61273-2
Schnittke, A.:Con Va, w. M. Rostropovich (cnd), London SO RCA Red Seal ▲ 60446-2-RC [DDD]
Schnittke, A.:Con for 3, w. Gidon Kremer (vn), Mstislav Rostropovich (vc), Y. Bashmet (cnd), Moscow Soloists EMI Classics ▲ CDC 55627
Schnittke, A.:Menuet Vn, w. Gidon Kremer (vn), Mstislav Rostropovich (vc) EMI Classics ▲ CDC 55627
Schnittke, A.:Monologue Va RCA Red Seal ▲ 60464-2-RC [DDD]
Schnittke, A.:Trio Strs, w. Gidon Kremer (vn), Mstislav Rostropovich (vc) EMI Classics ▲ CDC 55627
Schubert, Franz:Son Arpeggione, w. Y. Bashmet, M. Muntian [viola-piano arr.] RCA Red Seal ▲ 60112-2-RC [DDD]
Schubert, Franz:Trio Strs, D.471, w. Oleg Kagan (vn), Natalia Gutman (vc) *(rec Hohenems Schubertiade, June 22, 1988)* Live Classics ("Kagan Edition" series) ▲ 142
Schubert, Franz:Trio Strs, D.581, w. Oleg Kagan (vn), Natalia Gutman (vc) *(rec Hohenems Schubertiade, June 22, 1988)* Live Classics ("Kagan Edition" series) ▲ 142
Schumann, R.:Adagio & Allegro Hn, w. M. Muntian (pno) RCA Red Seal ▲ 60112-2-RC [DDD]
Schumann, R.:Märchenbilder, w. M. Muntian (pno) RCA Red Seal ▲ 60112-2-RC [DDD]
Shostakovich, D.:Son Va, w. M. Muntian (pno) RCA Red Seal ▲ 09026-61273-2
Shostakovich, D.:Son Va, w. S. Richter (pno) MK ▲ MKA 418015 [DDD]
Baskin, Theodore (ob)
Vivaldi, A.:Cons Ob, w. Y. Turovsky (cnd), Montreal Musici—RV.447 Chandos ▲ CHAN 8651 [DDD]
Vivaldi, A.:Cons Ob, w. Y. Turovsky (cnd), Montreal Musici—in C, RV.449 & in d, RV.454 Chandos ▲ CHAN 8444 [DDD]
Vivaldi, A.:Cons Ob Vn, w. E. Turovsky (vn), Y. Turovsky (cnd), Montreal Musici—RV.548 Chandos ▲ CHAN 8651 [DDD]
Baslawskaya, Mila (pno)
Miaskovsky, N.:Son 2 Vc, w. D. Perschtman (vc) Globe ▲ GLO 5041 [DDD]
Schnittke, A.:Son Vc, w. D. Perschtman (vc) Globe ▲ GLO 5041 [DDD]
Shostakovich, D.:Son Vc, w. D. Perschtman (vc) Globe ▲ GLO 5041 [DDD]
Basquin, Peter (pno)
Harris, R.:Con Cl, w. Lawrence Sobol (cl), Long Island Chamber Ensemble Grenadilla ■ GSC 1007
Levinson, G.:Dreamlight, w. A. Emelianoff (vc), P. Hostetter (perc), B. Ramirez (perc) CRI ▲ CD 642 [DDD]
Macdowell, E.:Pieces Cl, w. L. Sobol (cl) Grenadilla ■ GSC 1008
McPhee, C.:Tabuh-Tabuhan, w. Christopher Oldfather (pno), D. R. Davies (cnd), American Composers Orch *(rec Manhattan Center, New York, May 1994)* Argo ▲ 444560-2 [DDD]
Bäss, Hajo (vn)—see ORCHESTRAS & ENSEMBLES Capella Clementina
Bass, Howard (lt/gtr)—see ORCHESTRAS & ENSEMBLES La Rondinella
Bass, Walden (vc)
Liptak, D.:Rhaps, w. L. Greene (fl), J. Friedrichs (cl), D. Gerikh (vn), S. Heyman (pno) Opus One ▲ CD 168 [DDD]
Bassi, A. (pno)
Respighi, O.:Ancient Airs & Dances, w. M. Palumbo (pno) Bongiovanni ▲ GB 5528 [DDD]
Respighi, O.:Gösdemlan, w. M. Palumbo (pno) Bongiovanni ▲ GB 5528 [DDD]
Respighi, O.:Little Pieces Pno, w. M. Palumbo (pno) Bongiovanni ▲ GB 5528 [DDD]
Respighi, O.:Waltz Pno, w. M. Palumbo (pno) Bongiovanni ▲ GB 5528 [DDD]
Bässler, Klaus (pno)
Brahms, J.:Liebeslieder Waltzes SATB, w. Barbara Hoene (sop), Gisela Pohl (alt), Armin Ude (ten), Siegfried Lorenz (bar), Dieter Zechlin (pno), W.-D. Hauschild (cnd), Berlin RSO Berlin Classics ▲ BER 9269
Brahms, J.:Neue Liebeslieder Waltzes, w. Barbara Hoene (sop), Gisela Pohl (alt), Armin Ude (ten), Siegfried Lorenz (bar), Dieter Zechlin (pno), W.-D. Hauschild (cnd), Berlin RSO Berlin Classics ▲ BER 9269
Basson, S. (bn)
Foss, L.:Paradigm, w. J. Williams (perc), J. Grassel (electric gtr), R. Dagon (cl), L. Anderson (vn) *(rec 1989–90)* Koss Classics ▲ KC 1006 [DDD]
Bassoon, Claude (ob)
Poulenc, F.:Trio Ob, w. Alexandre Ouzounoff (bn), Kun Woo Paik (pno) Accord ▲ ACD 205192 [DDD]
Bastian, Dorothy (gtr)
Barney, N.:Strs of Light, w. A. Haas (hpd) Neuma ▲ 450-72 [DDD]
Bastock, Chris (perc)
A Secret Place, w. S. Rebello (perc), Andrew Scott (a sax), Liz Gilliver (mar), Kalengo Percussion Ensemble, Eryl Roberts (perc), John Melbourne (perc), Richard Dyson (perc) *(rec Zion Institute, Manchester, 1995)* Doyen ▲ CD 040 [DDD]
Batagov, Anton (pno)
Rabinovitch, A.:Music for Pnos, w. A. Rabinovitch (pno), M. Argerich (pno), M. Adamovitch (pno), A. Ieriomine (pno)—Musique Populaire for 2 Pianos; La Belle Musique for 4 Pianos; Liebliches Lied for Piano 4-hands; Musique triste, parfois tragique *(rec 1990 & 1992)* Valois ▲ V 4694 [DDD]
Ravel, M.:Gaspard de la nuit *(rec 1987)* Arbiter ▲ CD 102 [ADD]
Ravel, M.:Le Tombeau de Couperin *(rec 1987)* Arbiter ▲ CD 102 [ADD]
Ravel, M.:Valses nobles et sentimentales *(rec 1987)* Arbiter ▲ CD 102 [ADD]
Batard, Didier (bass gtr)
Chronolyse, w. R. Pinhas (syns/gtr), François Auger (perc) Cuneiform ▲ Rune 30
East/West, w. R. Pinhas (syns/gtr), Norman Spinrad (voc), Dominique E. (voc), Patrick Gauthier (syn), G. Grunblatt (syn), François Auger (perc), Steve Shehan (perc) Cuneiform ▲ Rune 31

462 ▲ = CD ♦ = Enhanced CD Δ = MD ■ = Cassette Tape ☐ = DCC

Bate, Jennifer (org)
Dickinson, P.:Con Org, w. D. Atherton (cnd), BBC SO — EMI ▲ CDC7 47584 [DDD]
Liszt, F.:Fant & Fugue on "Ad nos, ad salutarem undam" Org — ASV Quicksilva ▲ ASQ 6127 [ADD]
Liszt, F.:Prelude & Fugue on the name B-A-C-H — ASV Quicksilva ▲ ASQ 6127 [ADD]
Messiaen, O.:L'Ascension Org — Unicorn-Kanchana 2-▲ DKP CD 9024/25 [DDD]
Messiaen, O.:Le Banquet céleste — Unicorn-Kanchana ▲ DKP CD 9005 [DDD]
Messiaen, O.:Les Corps glorieux — Unicorn-Kanchana ▲ DKP CD 9004 [DDD]
Messiaen, O.:Diptyque — Unicorn-Kanchana ▲ DKP CD 9004 [DDD]
Messiaen, O.:Méditations sur le mystère la Sainte Trinité — Unicorn-Kanchana 2-▲ DKP CD 9024/25 [DDD]
Messiaen, O.:Messe de la Pentecôte — Unicorn-Kanchana 2-▲ DKP CD 9024/25 [DDD]
Messiaen, O.:La Nativité du Seigneur — Unicorn-Kanchana ▲ DKP CD 9005 [DDD]
Program 3, w. D. Dolmetsch (vir), François (trb rcr), Jeanne Dolmetsch (trb rcr), Marguerite Dolmetsch (vl), Nigel Foster (hpd), Kathleen Livingstone (sop), John Hancorn (bass), et al. — IMP Allegro ▲ PCD 995 [DDD]
Schumann, R.:Sketches Pedal Pno — ASV Quicksilva ▲ ASQ 6127 [ADD]

Bate, Jennifer (pno)
Liszt, F.:Vars on "Weinen, Klagen, Sorgen, Zagen", S.179 — ASV Quicksilva ▲ ASQ 6127 [ADD]

Bates, Leon (pno)
Corea, C.:Children's Songs — Naxos ▲ 8.550341 [DDD]
Gershwin, G.:Preludes (3) Pno *(rec 12/89)* — Naxos ▲ 8.550341 [DDD]
Gershwin, G.:Songs—Fascinatin' Rhythm; I've Got Rhythm; Lisa; Man I Love; Somebody Loves Me; Strike Up the Band *(rec 12/89)* — Naxos ▲ 8.550341 [DDD]

Bates, Susan (va)
Harrison, L.:Pieces (3) Gamelan, w. Scott L. Hartman (hn), L. Harrison (suling) — CRI ■ ACS 6006

Bates, Susan (vn)
Harrison, L.:Pieces (3) Gamelan, w. Sekar Kembar (gamelan), Scott L. Hartman (hn—Main), S. Bates (vn—Threnody), L. Harrison (suling—Serenade) *(rec 1979)* — CRI ▲ CD 613 [ADD]

Batiashvili, Tamaz (vn)—see ORCHESTRAS & ENSEMBLES Georgian State String Quartet

Batik, Roland (pno)
Batik, R.:Con 1 Pno, w. R. Batik (cnd), Das Klein Orchester — Camerata ▲ 30CM 347
Batik, R.:New Impressions, w. R. Batik (cnd), Das Klein Orchester — Camerata ▲ 30CM 347
Corea, C.:Sea Journey, w. R. Batik (cnd), London Little Orch — Camerata ▲ 30CM 347
Schabata, W.:St. Marx, w. R. Batik (cnd), Das Klein Orchester — Camerata ▲ 30CM 347

Batjer, Margaret (vn)
Beethoven, L. van:Qnt Strs, Op. 29, w. S. Accardo (vn), T. Hoffman (va), S. Gazeau (va), G. Hoffman (vc) — Nuova Era ▲ 6870 [DDD]
Mendelssohn, F.:Qnt 2 Strs, w. S. Accardo (vn), T. Hoffman (va), S. Gazeau (vc), G. Hoffman (db) — Nuova Era ▲ 6870 [DDD]
Mozart, W.A.:Concertone Vns, w. S. Accardo (vn), S. Accardo (cnd), Prague CO — Nuova Era ▲ 6949 [DDD]

Batnes, Elise (vn)—see ORCHESTRAS & ENSEMBLES Vertavo String Quartet
Batnes, Henninge (va)—see ORCHESTRAS & ENSEMBLES Vertavo String Quartet

Batselaere, Arnold (org)
Flute & Organ at Notre Dame, Paris, w. G. Angelloz (fl) *(rec 4/85)* — Pierre Verany ▲ 785094 [DDD]

Battaglia, Lucien (gtr)
Sor, F.:Gtr Music—Studies Nos. 1-20 *(rec 1981)* — Pierre Verany ▲ PVY 730026

Battersby, Edmund (pno)
Granados, E.:Goyescas—Nos. 1-6 — Koch International Classics ▲ KIC 7062-2 [DDD]
Nin-Culmell, J.:Tonadas—ten sels., from all volumes — Koch International Classics ▲ KIC 7062-2 [DDD]
Rachmaninoff, S.:Études-tableaux, Opp. 33 & 39—Op. 39, Nos. 1, 2, 6 & 8 *(rec Feb. & Mar. 1991)* — Koch International Classics ▲ KIC 7098 [DDD]
Rachmaninoff, S.:Preludes Pno, Opp 23 & 32—Op.23, Nos. 4-7; Op. 32, Nos. 7-11 *(rec Feb. & Mar. 1991)* — Koch International Classics ▲ KIC 7098 [DDD]

Battey, David (hn)
Beethoven, L. van:Sxt Hns, Op. 81b, w. G. Hustis (hn), R. Neal (cnd), Dallas CO — Crystal ▲ CD 512
Linek, J.:Intradas, w. G. Hustis (hn), D. Howard (timp), Dallas SO Trumpet Section — Crystal ▲ CD234

Battista, Michele Francesco (pno)
Ginastera, A.:Son 1 Pno — Kicco Classic ▲ 294
Rota, N.:Preludes Pno — Kicco Classic ▲ 294
Rota, N.:Variations & Fugue on the Name B-A-C-H — Kicco Classic ▲ 294

Battistelli, P. (s fl)—see ORCHESTRAS & ENSEMBLES Il Cortegiano
Battiston, Alberto (vn)—see ORCHESTRAS & ENSEMBLES Venice String Quartet

Bauer, Andrzej (vc)
Brahms, J.:Son 1 Vc, w. E. Kupiec (pno) [arr Friedrich Grützmacher] *(rec 1990)* — Koch Schwann ▲ 3-1187-2 [DDD]
Krauze, Z.:Quatour pour la naissance, w. Miroslaw Pokrzywinski (cl), Krysztof Bakowski (vn), Zygmunt Krauze (pno) *(rec National Philharmonic, Warsaw, Mar. 1991)* — Polskie Nagrania ▲ PLN 113 [DDD]
Mendelssohn, F.:Lied ohne Worte Vc, w. E. Kupiec (pno) *(rec 1990)* — Koch Schwann ▲ 3-1187-2 [DDD]
Prokofiev, S.:Son Vc, w. Ewa Kupiec (pno) — Koch Schwann ▲ SCH 314362
Schubert, Franz:Son Arpeggione, w. E. Kupiec (pno) *(rec 1990)* — Koch Schwann ▲ 3-1187-2 [DDD]
Schumann, R.:Adagio & Allegro Hn, w. E. Kupiec (pno) *(rec 1990)* — Koch Schwann ▲ 3-1187-2 [DDD]
Shostakovich, D.:Son Vc, w. Ewa Kupiec (pno) — Koch Schwann ▲ SCH 314362
Stravinsky, I.:Suite italienne Vc, w. Ewa Kupiec (pno) — Koch Schwann ▲ SCH 314362
Weber, C.M. von:Adagio & Rondo Harm, w. E. Kupiec (pno) [arr. for cello & piano by Gregor Piatigorsky] *(rec 1990)* — Koch Schwann ▲ 3-1187-2 [DDD]

Bauer, Frida (pno)
Bartók, B.:Sons (2) Vn & Pno, w. D. Oistrakh (vn), G. Kremer(vn), O. Maisenberg (pno) *(rec 1969, 1972 & 1978)* — Praga ▲ PR 250 038
Beethoven, L. van:Son 5 Vn, "Spring", w. David Oistrakh (vn) *(rec live Smetana Hall, Prague, May 19, 1969)* — Praga ▲ PR 250 058
Brahms, J.:Son 1 Vn, w. David Oistrakh (vn) *(rec live Smetana Hall, Prague, July 17, 1994)* — Praga ▲ PR 250 058
Brahms, J.:Son 3 Vn, w. D. Oistrakh (vn) *(rec live Prague Spring Festival, 1966)* — Multisonic (Prague Spring Collection) ▲ 31 0109-2 [ADD]
Brahms, J.:Son 3 Vn, w. David Oistrakh (vn) *(rec live in Prague, Smetana Hall, May 18, 1966)* — Praga ▲ PR 250 058
Prokofiev, S.:Mélodies, w. D. Oistrakh (vn) *(rec live, Czechoslovak Radio Prague, 1966)* — Multisonic ("Prague Spring Collection" series) ▲ 31 0109-2 [ADD]
Prokofiev, S.:Mélodies, w. D. Oistrakh (vn) *(rec 1966, 1969 & 1970)* — Praga ▲ PR 250 041
Prokofiev, S.:Son 1 Vn, w. D. Oistrakh (vn) *(rec 1966, 1969 & 1970)* — Praga ▲ PR 250 041
Ravel, M.:Son Vn Pno, w. D. Oistrakh (vn) *(rec live, Czechoslovak Radio Prague, 1966)* — Multisonic ("Prague Spring Collection" series) ▲ 31 0109-2 [ADD]
Schubert, Franz:Son Vn, D.574, w. D. Oistrakh (vn) *(rec live, Czechoslovak Radio Prague, 1966)* — Multisonic ("Prague Spring Collection" series) ▲ 31 0109-2 [ADD]

Bauer, Harold (pno)
Bach, J.S.:Chromatic Fant & Fugue [trans. von Bülow] — Nimbus ("Grand Piano" series) ▲ NI 8808
Bach, J.S.:Inventions (30) Hpd—2-Part, Nos. 1, 6, 8 — Nimbus ("Grand Piano" series) ▲ NI 8808
Bach, J.S.:Jesu bleibet meine Freude [trans. Bauer] — Nimbus ("Grand Piano" series) ▲ NI 8808
Bach, J.S.:Music of, w. Ignaz Friedman (pno), Percy Grainger (pno), Myra Hess (pno), Harold Samuel (pno)—Toccata No. 3 in G; Toccata & Fugue in d for Org [trans Tausig]; Well-Tempered Clavier Book 1, Nos. 5 & 21; Chorale [from Cant 147; trans Bauer]; Chromatic Fant & Fugue [trans von Bülow]; 2-Part Inventions Nos. 1, 6 & 8; Fant & Fugue in g for Org [trans Liszt]; Toccata & Fugue in g; French Suite No. 6; Gigue [from Partita in B♭, Book 1, No. 1] [all pno rolls] — Nimbus ("Grand Piano" series) ▲ NI 8808 [DDD]
Bach, J.S.:Das wohltemperierte Klavier—Book 1, No. 5 in D — Nimbus ("Grand Piano" series) ▲ NI 8808

Bauer, Harold (pno) (cont.)
Beethoven, L. van:Son 14 Pno, "Moonlight Son" *(rec 1926 Victor)* — Biddulph ▲ LHW 007 [ADD]
Beethoven, L. van:Son 23 Pno, "Appassionata" *(rec 1927 Victor)* — Biddulph ▲ LHW 007 [ADD]
Brahms, J.:Qnt Pno, w. Flonzaley String Quartet *(rec Dec. 21 & 23, 1925)* — Biddulph 2-▲ LAB 072/73 [ADD]
Grieg, E.:Albumblade, Op. 28—Nos. 1 & 3 — Biddulph ▲ LHW 011
Grieg, E.:Lyric Pieces—Op. 38, No. 1; Op. 43, Nos. 1 & 6; Op. 47, No. 1; Op. 54, No. 4 — Biddulph ▲ LHW 011
Grieg, E.:Pno Music (sels)—Humoresque, Op. 6, No. 3 — Biddulph ▲ LHW 011
Grieg, E.:Pictures from Life in the Country—No. 2, "The Bridal Procession" — Biddulph ▲ LHW 011
Liszt, F.:Études de concert (2) Pno—Waldesrauschen — Biddulph ▲ LHW 011
Liszt, F.:Études de concert (3) Pno—Un sospiro — Biddulph ▲ LHW 011
The 1924-1928 Victor Recordings, w. Bauer, Harold (pno) — Biddulph ▲ LHW 007 [ADD]
The 1929 Victor & 1939 Schirmer Recordings, w. Bauer, Harold (pno) — Biddulph ▲ LHW 009 [ADD]
Schumann, R.:Fantasiestücke Pno, Op. 12 — Biddulph ▲ LHW 011
Schumann, R.:Pno Music (misc)—In der Nacht [from Op. 12]; Novellette [from Op. 21, No. 2] — Biddulph ▲ LHW 011
Schumann, R.:Son 1 Pno — Nimbus ("Grand Piano" series) ▲ NI 8804
Schumann, R.:Toccata Pno — Nimbus ("Grand Piano" series) ▲ NI 8804

Bauer, Ivo (va)—see ORCHESTRAS & ENSEMBLES Avantgarde Ensemble, Leipzig String Quartet

Bauer, S. (hpd)
Bach, J.S.:Goldberg Vars — Ars Musici ▲ 1103 [DDD]

Bauer, Sabine (rcr)
Handel, G.F.:Sons Rcr, w. Michael Schneider (rcr), Cologne Camerata—8 Sonatas—Op. 1, Nos. 2, 4, 7 & 11; Sonatas in B♭, d & G; Sonata in F for 2 Recorders — Editio Classica ▲ 77104-2-RG [DDD]

Bauer, Tony (va)
Lindblad, A.F.:Qnt Strs, w. Peter Olofsson (vn), Patrik Swedrup (vn), Jonal Lindgård (va), Lars Frykholm (vc) — Musica Sveciae ▲ MSV 522 [DDD]
Randel, A.:Qt Strs, w. Peter Olofsson (vn), Patrik Swedrup (vn), Jonal Lindgård (va), Lars Frykholm (vc) — Musica Sveciae ▲ MSV 522 [DDD]

Bauerle, A. (fl)—see ORCHESTRAS & ENSEMBLES Vienna Flautists
Bäuerle, K. (trbn)—see ORCHESTRAS & ENSEMBLES Stuttgart Philharmonia Ensemble

Bauer-Slais, Edith (mand)
Hummel, J.N.:Con Mand & Strs, w. V. Hladky (cnd), Vienna Pro Musica Orch *(rec 1973)* — Tuxedo ▲ TUXCD 1026
Music for Lute, Guitar & Mandolin, w. K. Ragossnig (gtr), Anton Stingl (lt), Michael Schäffer (lt), Karl Scheit (gtr), Leo Witoszinskyj (gtr), William Matthews (gtr), Paul Grund (mand), Artur Rumetsch (mand), Elfriede Kunschak (mand) — Vox Box 3-▲ CD3X 3022

Baum, Carol (hp)
La Montaine, J.:Lessons of Christmas, w. Polly Jo Baker (sop), David Griffith (ten), Scott Shepherd (perc), J. Montaine (cnd), Fredonia Singers — Fredonia Discs ▲ FDCD 14
Pinkham, D.:Advent Cant, w. Ariel Wind Quintet, Boston Cecilia *(rec Dec. 1992)* — Koch International Classics ▲ KIC 7180 [DDD]

Baumann, Anett (vn)
Helmschrott, R.:Cross & Freedom, w. Helmut Schatz, Nancy Gibson (sop), Frieder Aurich (ten), Matthias Weichert (bass), Manfred Ball (nar), Frank Philliptsch, Linda Robbins, Gerhard Wolf, Martin Homann (perc), Robert M. Helmschrott (org), H.-C. Rademann (cnd), Munich Trombone Quartet, Dresden Chamber Choir — Vienna Modern Masters ▲ VMM 3027 [DDD]

Baumann, Hermann (hn)
Beethoven, L. van:Qnt Pno, Ob, Cl, Hn & Bn, w. A. Brendel (pno), H. Holliger (ob), E. Brunner (cl), K. Thunemann (bn) — Philips ▲ 420182-2 [DDD]
Beethoven, L. van:Sxt Hns, Op. 81b, w. Gewandhaus String Quartet — Philips ▲ 426440-2
Chabrier, E.:Larghetto, w. K. Masur (cnd), Leipzig Gewandhaus Orch — Philips ▲ 416380-2 [DDD]
Danzi, F.:Con Hn, w. J. Schröder (cnd), Concerto Amsterdam *(rec 1969)* — Teldec ▲ TEL SEL 12324 [ADD]
Dukas, P.:Villanelle, w. K. Masur (cnd), Leipzig Gewandhaus Orch — Philips ▲ 416380-2 [DDD]
Glière, R.:Con Hn, w. K. Masur (cnd), Leipzig Gewandhaus Orch — Philips ▲ 416380-2 [DDD]
Haydn, J.:Con 1 Hn, w. J. Schröder (cnd), Concerto Amsterdam *(rec 1969)* — Teldec ▲ TEL SEL 12324 [ADD]
Haydn, M.:Romance, w. Gewandhaus String Quartet — Philips ▲ 426440-2
Ligeti, G.:Trio Hn, Vn & Pno, w. S. Gawriloff (vn), E. Besch (pno) — Wergo ▲ WER 60100-50 [DDD]
Mozart, L.:Con 2 Hns, w. M. Cakar (hn), J. Schröder (cnd), Concerto Amsterdam — Acanta ▲ 43278
Mozart, L.:Sym in G, "Sinf da caccia", w. J. Schröder (cnd), Concerto Amsterdam — Acanta ▲ 43278
Mozart, W.A.:Cons Hn, w. P. Zukerman (cnd), St. Paul CO — Philips ▲ 412737-2 [DDD]
Mozart, W.A.:Cons Hn, w. N. Harnoncourt (cnd), Vienna Concentus Musicus — Teldec ▲ 2292-42757-2
Mozart, W.A.:Divert Ob, K.251, w. H. Holliger (ob), Orlando String Quartet — Philips ▲ 412618-2 [DDD]
Mozart, W.A.:Qnt Hn, K.407, w. Gewandhaus String Quartet — Philips ▲ 426440-2
Mozart, W.A.:Qnt Pno, K.452, w. A. Brendel (pno), H. Holliger (ob), E. Brunner (cl), K. Thunemann (bn) — Philips ▲ 420182-2 [DDD]
Pokorny, F.X.:Con Hns, w. C. Kohler (hn), J. Schröder (cnd), Concerto Amsterdam — Acanta ▲ 43278
Reicha, A.:Qnt Hn, w. Gewandhaus String Quartet — Philips ▲ 426440-2
Rosetti, F.A.:Cons Hn, w. J. Schröder (cnd), Concerto Amsterdam—Con. in F — Acanta ▲ 43278
Rosetti, F.A.:Cons Hn, w. J. Schröder (cnd), Concerto Amsterdam—in d *(rec 1969)* — Teldec ▲ TEL SEL 12324 [ADD]
St. Hubert Mass, w. horn ensemble — Philips ▲ 426301-2 PH
Saint-Saëns, C.:Morceau de concert Hn, w. K. Masur (cnd), Leipzig Gewandhaus Orch — Philips ▲ 416380-2 [DDD]
Strauss, R.:Con 1 Hn, w. K. Masur (cnd), Leipzig Gewandhaus Orch — Philips ▲ 412237-2 [DDD]
Strauss, R.:Con 2 Hn, w. K. Masur (cnd), Leipzig Gewandhaus Orch — Philips ▲ 412237-2 [DDD]
Telemann, G.P.:Cons for 2 Hns, w. T. Brown (hn), I. Brown (cnd), Academy of St. Martin in the Fields — Philips ▲ 412226-2 [DDD]
Telemann, G.P.:Cons Hns, w. T. Brown (hn), N. Hill (hn), I. Brown (cnd), Academy of St. Martin in the Fields — Philips ▲ 412226-2 [DDD]
Weber, C.M. von:Concertino Hn, w. K. Masur (cnd), Leipzig Gewandhaus Orch — Philips ▲ 412237-2 [DDD]
Witt, F.:Con Hns, w. M. Cakar (hn), J. Schröder (cnd), Concerto Amsterdam—in F — Acanta ▲ 43278

Baumann, Jörg (vc)
Bach, J.S.:Suites Vc, BWV 1007-1012—No. 6 in D — Camerata ▲ 25CM 373
Barrière, F.:Son Vc & Db, w. Klauss Stoll (db) — Camerata ▲ 32CM 5
Boismortier, J.B. de:Sons, Op. 40, w. K. Stoll (db)—No. 2 — Koch Schwann ▲ SCH 313382 [ADD/DDD]
Couperin, F.:Con Vc, w. Klauss Stoll (db) — Camerata ▲ 32CM 5
Holewa, H.:Trio Vn, Va & Vc, w. Leon Spierer (vn), Ulrich Fritze (va) — Phono Suecia ▲ PHN 49 [ADD]
Mozart, W.A.:Duo Bn Vc, w. Klauss Stoll (db) — Camerata ▲ 32CM 5
Mozart, W.A.:Son Bn Vc, w. K. Stoll (db) — Camerata ▲ 25CM 373
Reger, M.:Suites Vc—No. 3 in a — Camerata ▲ 25CM 373
Rossini, G.:Duet Vc, w. Klauss Stoll (db) — Camerata ▲ 32CM 5

Baumann, Michael (pno)
Hindemith, P.:Motets, w. C. Baumann (sop)—Exiit edictum; Pastores loquebantur; Dicebat Jesus scribis et pharisaeis; Dixit Jesus Petro; Angelus Domini apparuit; Erat Joseph et Maria; Defuncto Herode; Cum natus esset; Cum factus esset Jesus; Vidit Joannes Jesum; Nuptiae factae sunt; Cum descendisset Jesus; Ascendente Jesu in naviculam — Christophorus ▲ CD 74546 [DDD]

Baumel, Michèl (org)
Exsultate Deo:The Liturgy of St. Wandrille, w. St. Wandrille Abbey Monks' Choir — Studio SM ▲ 12 20.77
Trumpet & Organ in St. Wandrille Abbey, w. P. Dambreville (tpt) — Studio SM ▲ 12 18 58 [DDD]

Bäumer, Hermann (trbn)—see ORCHESTRAS & ENSEMBLES Triton Trombone Quartet

Baumgartner, R. (pno)
Janácek, L.:In Memoriam — Gallo ▲ CD 659 [AAD]
Janácek, L.:In the Mists — Gallo ▲ CD 659 [AAD]

Baumgartner, R. (pno) (cont.)
Janácek, L.:On an Overgrown Path Gallo ▲ CD 659 [AAD]
Janácek, L.:Reminiscence Gallo ▲ CD 659 [AAD]
Janácek, L.:Son October 1, 1905 Pno Gallo ▲ CD 659 [AAD]
Janácek, L.:Thema con variazioni Gallo ▲ CD 659 [AAD]

Baumgratz, Wolfgang (org)
Telemann, G.P.:Organ Music (misc)—Concerto in g (after Bach's solo Harpsichord concerto, BWV 985); Passacaglia in b; 4 Chorale Preludes (Allein Gott in der Höh sei Ehr; Vater unser im Himmelreich; Herr Jesu Christ, dich zu uns wend; Komm heiliger Geist, Herre Gott); Fantasia in D; Sonata for 2 manuals & pedal in D; 2 Chorale Variations on "Nun freut euch lieben Christen gemein"; Concerto per la chiesa in G (after J.G. Walther) MD + G ▲ L 3078 [DDD]

Baumont, Olivier (hpd)
Anglebert, J.-H. d':Pièces de clavecin—6 pieces in g; Prelude & 5 pieces in C REM ▲ 310990 XCD [DDD]
Balbastre, C.-B.:Hpd Music REM ▲ 310990 XCD [DDD]
Caix D'Hervelois, L. de:Pieces (4) Hpd REM ▲ 310990 XCD [DDD]
Couperin, F.:Pièces de clavecin (sels)—Les fastes de la grande et ancienne ménestrandise; Les baricades mistérieuses; Le tic-toc-choc ou les maillotins; others Erato ▲ ERA 11471 [DDD]
Couperin, F.:Pièces de clavecin (sels)—Book 1 Erato 3-▲ ERA 10694 [DDD]
Couperin, F.:Pièces de clavecin (sels), w. Davitt Moroney (hpd)—13th-19th books Erato 2-▲ ERA 92859 [DDD]
Couperin, F.:Pièces de clavecin (sels)—Book Four Erato 2-▲ 2292-45824-2 ZA
Dandrieu, J.F.:Pièces de clavecin (3 books) Accord ▲ ACD 242072 [DDD]
Mozart, W.A.:Sons Fl Hpd (misc), w. Jean-Christophe Frisch (fl), Antoine Ladrette (vc)—No. 1 in B♭, K.10; No. 2 in G, K.11; No. 3 in A, K.12; No. 4 in F, K.13; No. 5 in C, K.14; No. 6 in B♭, K.15 Adda ▲ ADD 581229 [DDD]
Purcell, H.:Suites Hpd Erato ▲ ERA 10695 [DDD]
Rameau, J.P.:Hpd Music (comp solo)—Premier Livre; Les petits marteaux; Menuet en rondeau; Pieces de clavecin; Nouvelles suites de pieces de clavecin; 5 Pieces; Les indes galantes; La dauphine Adda 3-▲ ADD 581901

Baumont, Olivier (pno)
Dandrieu, J.F.:Pno Music—Premier livre; Deuxième livre; Troisième livre Adda ▲ ADD 581073 [DDD]
Rameau, J.P.:La Dauphine Adda ▲ ADD 581150 [DDD]
Rameau, J.P.:Les Indes Galantes (airs) Adda ▲ ADD 581150 [DDD]

Baun, Nancy (vc)—see ORCHESTRAS & ENSEMBLES Eaken Piano Trio

Bauni, Axel (pno)
Hindemith, P.:Songs, w. Julianne Banse (sop)—34 sels including Lieder mit Klavier, Op. 18; Gesang; Vier Lieder nach Texten des Angelus Silesius; Abendständchen; Singet leise; Wer wusste je das Leben; Der Einsiedler; Du bist mein; Zum Abscheid meiner Tochter; Ich will Trauern lassen stehn; Abendwolke Orfeo ▲ 413961 [DDD]
Krenek, E.:Songs, w. Christine Schäfer (sop)—O lacrymosa, Op. 48; Monolog der Stella, Op. 57; Die nachtigall, Op. 68; 5 Lieder, Op. 82; 4 Songs, Op. 112; The Flea, Op. 175; Wechselrahmen, Op. 189 *(rec Studio 3, Bavarian Radio, Aug. 16, 17, 22 & 23, 199)* Orfeo ▲ 373951 [DDD]
Reimann, A.:Nightpiece, w. Christine Schäfer (sop) *(rec Studio II, Radio Free Berlin, May 1995)* Orfeo ▲ C 412 961 [DDD]
Reimann, A.:Wie, die wie der Strandhafer wahren, w. Ursula Hesse (mez) *(rec Studio II, Radio Free Berlin, June 1995)* Orfeo ▲ C 412 961 [DDD]
Ullmann, V.:Songs, w. Christine Schäfer (sop), Liat Himmelheber (mez), Yaron Windmüller (bar)—5 Liebeslieder, Op. 18; 6 Lieder, Op. 17; 3 Sonette, Op. 29; 6 Sonnets, Op. 34; Geistliche Lieder, Op. 20; Liederbuch das Hafis, op. 30; Der Mensch und sein Tag, Op. 47; Immer inmitten; Chinesische Lieder; 3 Lieder *(rec Oct. 25-27 & Dec. 7-8, 19)* Orfeo 2-▲ 380952 [DDD]

Bavaj, Lorenzo (hpd)
Bach, Joh. Christian:Trio for 2 Fls, Op. 2, w. M. Larrieu (fl), M. Mercelli (fl)—in G Bongiovanni ▲ GB 5529 [DDD]
Bach, W.F.:Trios Fls, F.47-49, w. M. Larrieu, M. Mercelli—Nos. 1-3 Bongiovanni ▲ GB 5529 [DDD]

Bavaj, Lorenzo (pno)
Donizetti, G.:Arias, w. Taro Ichihara (ten)—Una lacrima *(rec 1995)* Bongiovanni ▲ GB 2519 [DDD]
Donizetti, G.:Music for Pno 4-Hands, w. G. Valentini (pno)—La solita suonata; Una delle più matte; Sons. in D, C, G & A; Polacca in G Bongiovanni ▲ GB 5515 [DDD]
Gasparini, F.:Arias, w. Taro Ichihara (ten)—Lasciar d'amarti *(rec 1995)* Bongiovanni ▲ GB 2519 [DDD]
Giordani, G.:Arias, w. Taro Ichihara (ten)—Caro mio ben *(rec 1995)* Bongiovanni ▲ GB 2519 [DDD]
José Carreras in Recital, w. J. Carreras (ten) *(rec Seattle, 5/4/89)* Legato Classics ▲ LCD 156-1 [AAD]
Martini, J.P.A.:Arias, w. Taro Ichihara (ten)—Piacer d'amor *(rec 1995)* Bongiovanni ▲ GB 2519 [DDD]
Rossini, G.:Arias, w. Taro Ichihara (ten)—L'orgia; La promessa; La partenza; L'esule; La gita in gondola *(rec 1995)* Bongiovanni ▲ GB 2519 [DDD]
Scarlatti, A.:Cants, w. Taro Ichihara (ten)—Già il sole dal gange *(rec 1995)* Bongiovanni ▲ GB 2519 [DDD]
Tosti, P.F.:Songs, w. Taro Ichihara (ten)—La Serenata; Ideale; 'A vucchella; Marechiare; L'Ultima canzone *(rec 1995)* Bongiovanni ▲ GB 2519 [DDD]

Bavouzet, Jean-Efflam (cel)
Stockhausen, K.:Refrain, w. Gérard Frémy (pno), Florent Jodelet (perc) Accord ▲ ACD 202742 [DDD]

Bavouzet, Jean-Efflam (pno)
Haydn, J.:Fant Pno Harmonic ▲ CD 9141 [DDD]
Haydn, J.:Sons Pno—H.XVI/24, 46, 48 & 49 Harmonic ▲ CD 9141 [DDD]

Bax, Arnold (pno)
Bax, A.:Son Va & Pno, w. L. Tertis (va) *(rec 1929)* Pearl ▲ PEA 9918 (m) [AAD]
Delius, F.:Son 1 Vn & Pno, w. May Harrison (vn) *(rec 1929)* Symposium ▲ SYM 1140
Delius, F.:Son 3 Vn & Pno, w. May Harrison (vn) *(rec private recording, ca. 1937)* Symposium ▲ 1075

Baxa, Jiri (vn)
Schubert, Franz:Qnt Strs, D.956, w. Josef Suk (vn), Ladislav Černý (va), Saša Večtomov (vc), Josef Simandl (vc) *(rec live, 1971)* Praga ▲ PR 250055

Baxtresser, Jeanne (fl)
Barber, S.:Canzone Fl & Pno, w. Israela Margalit (pno) EMI Classics ("Anglo-American Chamber Music" series) ▲ CDC 55400
Barber, S.:Summer Music, w. Joseph Robinson (ob), Stanley Drucker (cl), Judith LeClair (bn), Philip Myers (hn) EMI Classics ("Anglo-American Chamber Music" series) ▲ CDC 55400
The Baroque Album, w. A. Davis (cnd), Toronto CO, O. Harnoy (vc), J. Cowell (tpt) Mastersound ▲ MST 19 [DDD]
Bolling, C.:Suite 1 Fl, w. Eric Robertson Trio IMP ("Classics" series) ▲ IMP 6700962
Copland, A.:Duo Fl, w. Israela Margalit (pno) EMI Classics ("Anglo-American Chamber Music" series) ▲ CDC 55405
Duets:Ofra Harnoy & Friends, w. O. Harnoy (vc), Michael Dussek (pno), Orford String Quartet, Maureen Forrester (cta), Andrew Davis (pno), Catherine Wilson (pno), Paul Brodie (sax), Shauna Rolston (vc), Armin Strings, Canadian Piano Trio, Adele Armin (vn) Mastersound ▲ MST 30 [DDD]
Ofra Harnoy & Friends, w. Harnoy, Ofra (vc), Orford String Quartet, M. Forrester (cta), P. Brodie (sax), M. Dussek (pno), et al. Pro Arte ▲ CDD 552 [DDD]

Bay, Emanuel (pno)
Bach, J.S.:Sinfs, w. J. Heifetz (vn)—Nos. 3 in D, 4 in d & 9 in f RCA Gold Seal ▲ 7964-2-RG [ADD] ■ 7964-4-RG (CrO2)
Beethoven, L. van:Sons Vn (comp), w. J. Heifetz—Nos. 1-4 RCA Gold Seal ▲ 7704-2 RC (m) [ADD] ■ 7704-4 RC (m)
Beethoven, L. van:Sons Vn (comp), w. J. Heifetz (vn)—Nos. 5-7 RCA Gold Seal ▲ 7705-2 RC (m) [ADD] ■ 7705-4 RC (m)
Beethoven, L. van:Sons Vn (comp), w. J. Heifetz (vn)—Nos. 8-10 RCA Gold Seal ▲ 7706-2 RC (m) [ADD] ■ 7706-4 RC (m)

Bay, Emanuel (pno) (cont.)
Brahms, J.:Son 2 Vn, w. Jascha Heifetz (vn) *(rec RCA Studio 3, New York, Jan 31, 1936)* RCA Gold Seal 2-▲ 09026-61735-2 [ADD]
Brahms, J.:Son 2 Vn, w. J. Heifetz (vn) *(rec 1936)* Biddulph ▲ LAB 011 [ADD]
Debussy, C.:Preludes Pno (sels), w. J. Heifetz (vn) [arr. for violin & piano]—Book 1, No. 8, "La fille aux cheveux de lin" RCA Gold Seal ▲ 7871-2-RG (m) [ADD]
Debussy, C.:Son Vn, w. J. Heifetz (vn) RCA Gold Seal ▲ 7871-2-RG (m/s) [ADD]
The Decca Masters, Vol. 1, w. J. Heifetz (vn), Milton Kaye (pno) *(rec 1944-46)* MCA Classics ▲ MCAD 42211 (m) [ADD]
The Decca Masters, Vol. 2 (1944-1946), w. J. Heifetz (vn), Milton Kaye (pno), Bing Crosby (sgr) *(rec 1944-46)* MCA Classics ▲ MCAD 42212 (m) [ADD]
Fauré, G.:Son 1 Vn, w. Jascha Heifetz (vn) *(rec RCA Studio 3, New York, Feb 10, 1936)* RCA Gold Seal 2-▲ 09026-61735-2 [ADD]
Fauré, G.:Son 1 Vn, w. J. Heifetz (vn) *(rec 1936)* Biddulph ▲ LAB 065 [ADD]
Grieg, E.:Sons Vn, Opp. 8, 13 & 45, w. J. Heifetz (vn)—Sonata No. 2, Op. 13 *(rec 1936)* Biddulph ▲ LAB 065 [ADD]
Handel, G.F.:Sons Vn & Kbd, w. Jascha Heifetz (vn)—No. 15 in E *(rec Radio Recorders, Hollywood, Nov 30, 1953)* RCA Gold Seal 2-▲ 09026-61740-2 (m) [ADD]
Mozart, W.A.:Sons Vn Pno (misc), w. J. Heifetz (vn)—K.378 & 454 *(rec 1936 for HMV)* Biddulph ▲ LAB 012 [AAD]
Mozart, W.A.:Sons Vn Pno (misc), w. Jascha Heifetz (vn)—in B♭, K.378; in B♭, K.454 *(rec RCA Studio 3, New York City, Feb 10, 1936)* RCA Gold Seal 2-▲ 09026-61740-2 (m) [ADD]
Respighi, O.:Son Vn, w. J. Heifetz (vn) RCA Gold Seal ▲ 7871-2-RG (m/s) [ADD]
Schubert, Franz:Ave Maria! Jungfrau mild!, w. J. Heifetz (vn) RCA Gold Seal ▲ 7964-2-RG [ADD] ■ 7964-4-RG (CrO2)

Bayer, A. (vn)
Vivaldi, A.:Sons Ob, w. B. Glaetzner (ob), I. Goritzki (ob), K. Suske (vn), T. Reinhardt (bn), S. Pank (vl), C. Schornsheim (org/hpd)—RV.28, 34, 53, 81 & 779 Capriccio ▲ CD 10143 [DDD] ■ CAS 27153 (CrO2)

Bayer St. Mary, Maura (fl)
del Aguila, M.:Herbsttag, w. J. Farmer (bn), G. Mossyrsch (hp), H. Earle (cnd), American Music Ensemble Vienna Albany ▲ TROY 066 [DDD]

Baylac, Pascal (hpd)
Le Roux, G.:Kbd Music, w. I. Pappas (hpd)—Suites 1-7 Arkadia-Akademia ▲ 127 [DDD]

Bayless, John (pno)
Bach Meets the Beatles Pro Arte ▲ CDD 211 ■ PCD 211
Puccini, G.:Arias—improvisations on melodies from La Bohème, Madama Butterfly, Tosca, Turnadot, La Rondine & Gianni Schicchi EMI Classics ▲ CDC 54801-2 ■ CDC 54801-4
West Side Story Variations Angel ▲ CDC 54507 ■ 4DS 54507

Baylis, Lorra (vn)—see ORCHESTRAS & ENSEMBLES Stratos

Bayona, P. (pno)
Guridi, J.:Music of, w. J. Arámbarri (cnd), Madrid Concert Orch, Spanish National Orch—Amaya; 10 Melodias; Homenaje a Walt Disney *(rec 1959)* EMI Classics ▲ CDM 64558

Bazelaire, P. (vc)
Saint-Saëns, C.:Son 1 Vc, w. I. Philipp (pno) Pearl ▲ PEA 9174 [ADD]
Saint-Saëns, C.:Son 2 Vc, w. I. Philipp (pno) Pearl ▲ PEA 9174 [ADD]

Bazsinka, József (tuba)
Bogár, I.:Con Tuba, w. Gusztáv H *(rec Jul 3-7, 1995)* Hungaroton ▲ HCD 31612 [DDD]
Dubrovay, L.:Buzzing - Polka, w. Gusztáv H *(rec Jul 3-7, 1995)* Hungaroton ▲ HCD 31612 [DDD]
Hidas, F.:Folksongs of Békés County, w. Gusztáv H *(rec Jul 3-7, 1995)* Hungaroton ▲ HCD 31612 [DDD]
Hidas, F.:Folksongs of the Balaton, w. Gusztáv H *(rec Jul 3-7, 1995)* Hungaroton ▲ HCD 31612 [DDD]
Lendvay, K.:The Last Message from Maestro Tchaikovsky, w. Gusztáv H *(rec Jul 3-7, 1995)* Hungaroton ▲ HCD 31612 [DDD]
Ránki, G.:The Magic Potion, w. Gusztáv Hóna (harsona/bn), L. Marosi (cnd), Budapest Symphonic Band *(rec Jul 3-7, 1995)* Hungaroton ▲ HCD 31612 [DDD]
Ránki, G.:The Tales of Father Goose, w. Gusztáv Hóna (harsona/bn), L. Marosi (cnd), Budapest Symphonic Band *(rec Jul 3-7, 1995)* Hungaroton ▲ HCD 31612 [DDD]
Waves, w. Bazsinka, József (tuba) Hungaroton ▲ HCD 31642 [DDD]

Beach, Howard (hpd/org)
The English Nightingale, w. P. Adams (rcrs), D. Watkin (vc) Albany ▲ TROY 088-2 [DDD]

Beal, John (db)—see ORCHESTRAS & ENSEMBLES John Whitney Trio

Bean, Hugh (vn)
Bach, J.S.:Cons Vn (comp), w. A. Davidson (cnd), England Virtuosi Classics for Pleasure ("Silver Doubles" series) 2-▲ CFP CDCFP 4769 [ADD]
Bach, J.S.:Con for 2 Vns, w. Kenneth Sillito (vn), A. Davidson (cnd), England Virtuosi Classics for Pleasure ("Silver Doubles" series) 2-▲ CFP CDCFP 4769 [ADD]
Elgar, E.:Con Vn, w. C. Groves (cnd), Liverpool PO Classics for Pleasure ▲ CDCFP 4632 [ADD]
Elgar, E.:Son Vn, w. D. Parkhouse (pno) Classics for Pleasure ▲ CDCFP 4632 [ADD]
Haydn, J.:Sym 96, "Miracle", w. Nicholas Whiting (vn), John Anderson (ob), L. Slatkin (cnd), Philharmonia Orch *(rec Abbey Road Studio No. 1, London, Aug 1993)* RCA Red Seal ▲ 09026-68424-2 [DDD]
Vaughan Williams, R.:The Lark Ascending, w. A. Boult (cnd), New Philharmonia Orch EMI Classics (British Composers) ▲ CDM 64022
Vaughan Williams, R.:Son Vn, w. Music Group of London EMI Classics ▲ CDM 65100
Vivaldi, A.:Cons Vn, Op. 8/1-4, "The Four Seasons", w. L. Stokowski (cnd), New Philharmonia Orch London ("Weekend Classics" series) ▲ 433680-2 [ADD]

Bean, Nancy (vn)
Vaughan Williams, R.:Songs, w. R. Golden (sop), T. Woodman (bar), L. Rothfuss (pno)—From the House of Life; 4 Last Songs; Linden Lea; The Sky Above the Roof; Dreamland; Claribel; If I Were a Queen; 4 Poems by Fredegond Shove; Adieu; Think of Me; Along the Field *(rec Apr. 1992)* Koch International Classics ▲ KIC 7168 [DDD]

Beaser, Robert (pno)
Beaser, R.:The Old Men Admiring Themselves In The Water, w. P. Robison (fl) New World ▲ 80403-2 [DDD]

Beaufort, Raphaël (pno)
Ibert, J.:Impromptu Tpt & Pno, w. Roger Delmotte (tpt) Adès ▲ ADE 203462 [AAD]

Beaufreton, B. (sax)
Moser, R.:Wal, w. I. Roth (sax), M. Weiss (sax), J.-G. Koerper (sax), P. Egholm (sax), M. Venzago (cnd), Basel SO Grammont ▲ CTSP 12-2 [ADD]

Beaulieu, M. (vn)
Kirchner, L.:Qt 1 Strs, w. C. Hoener (vn), S. Woolweaver (va), A. Mark (vc) Albany ▲ TROY 137 [DDD]
Kirchner, L.:Qt 2 Strs, w. C. Hoener (vn), S. Woolweaver (va), A. Mark (vc) Albany ▲ TROY 137 [DDD]
Kirchner, L.:Qt 3 Strs, w. C. Hoener (vn), S. Woolweaver (va), A. Mark (vc) Albany ▲ TROY 137 [DDD]

Beaumadier, Jean-Louis (fl)
Busoni, F.:Divert Fl, w. Jacques Raynaut (pno) Calliope ▲ CAL 9227 [DDD]
Doppler, A.F.:Music of, w. A. Marion (fl), E. Exerjean (pno)—Souvenir, Op. 24; Sommnambula, Op. 42; Chanson d'amour, Op. 20; L'oiseau des bois; Casilda fant. [w. F. Pierre (harp)]; Duettino americain, Op. 37; Duettino hongrois, Op. 36 *(rec 1993)* Calliope ▲ CAL 9224 [DDD]
Fouad, H.:Thâksim, w. Jacques Raynaut (pno) Calliope ▲ CAL 9227 [DDD]
Henze, H.-W.:Sonatine Fl & Pno, w. Jacques Raynaut (pno) Calliope ▲ CAL 9227 [DDD]
Lenot, J.:Dans la rue du Jeune Anacharsis, w. Jacques Raynaut (pno) Calliope ▲ CAL 9227 [DDD]
Petronio, A.:Structures mobiles, w. Jacques Raynaut (pno) Calliope ▲ CAL 9227 [DDD]
Schubert, Franz:Intro & Vars Fl on "Tröckne Blumen", w. Noel Lee (pno) Approche ▲ 6209
Schubert, Franz:Son Arpeggione, w. Noel Lee (pno) [arr for fl & pno] Approche ▲ 6209
Schubert, Franz:Sonatina Vn, D.385, w. Noel Lee (pno) [arr for fl & pno] Approche ▲ 6209
Vivaldi, A.:Cons Pic, w. J.-P. Rampal (fl), French National Orch—RV.443, 444, 445 Calliope ▲ CAL 9630

▲ = CD ♦ = Enhanced CD Δ = MD ■ = Cassette Tape ☐ = DCC

Beaumadier, Jean-Louis (pic)
Damaré, E.:Music of, w. Christophe Poiget (vn), Marc Giradot (ophicleide/tuba), Circe Wind Quintet, La Follia Instrumental Ensemble—La Capricieuse, Op. 270; Feux follets, Op. 378; Les Échos des bois, Op. 220; Le Merle blanc, Op. 161; Tarentelle, Op. 391; L'Oiseau et les roses, Op. 153; Le Tourbillon, Op. 212; L'Alouette, Op. 172; Pizzicato, Op. 426; La Danse des grillons, Op. 380 *(rec 1996)* Calliope ▲ CAL 9869 [DDD]
Vivaldi, A.:Cons Rcr, w. J.-P. Rampal (cnd), French National Orch—RV.108 Calliope ▲ CAL 9630

Beauséjour, Luc (hpd)
Boismortier, J.B. de:Sons Fl & Continuo, w. Claire Guimond (baroque fl)—Nos. 1–6 Analekta ▲ ATM 29730
Boismortier, J.B. de:Sons Fl, Op. 91, w. C. Guimond (fl)—in D, g, G, e, A, c *(rec Aug. 22–24, 1994)* Analekta Fleur de Lys ▲ FL 2 3008 [DDD]
Little Notebook for Anna Magdalena Bach, w. K. Gauvin (sop), Sergeï Istomin (vc) Analekta Fleur de Lys ▲ FL 23064 [DDD]
Scarlatti, D.:Sons Kbd—18 sels Analekta ▲ ATM 29720

Beauséjour, Luc (org)
Böhm, G.:Org Music—Vater unser im Himmelreich *(rec Knox College, Toronto, May 1995)* Analekta Fleur de Lys ▲ FL 23063 [DDD]
Bruhns, N.:Preludes & Fugues (4) Org—in e *(rec Knox College, Toronto, May 1995)* Analekta Fleur de Lys ▲ FL 23063 [DDD]
Buxtehude, D.:Org Music (misc)—Prelude in C; Ach Herr, mich armen Sünder; Nun lob, mein Seel, den Herren; Fugue in C; Nun komm, der Heiden Heiland; Puer natus in Bethlehem; Toccata in G; Prelude in e *(rec Knox College, Toronto, May 1995)* Analekta Fleur de Lys ▲ FL 23063 [DDD]
Hanff, J.N.:Org Music—Ach Gott, vom Himmel sieh darein *(rec Knox College, Toronto, May 1995)* Analekta Fleur de Lys ▲ FL 23063 [DDD]
Scheidemann, H.:Org Music—Praeambulum in G *(rec Knox College, Toronto, May 1995)* Analekta Fleur de Lys ▲ FL 23063 [DDD]
Weckmann, M.:Org Music (misc)—Magnificat II & Toni; Ach wir armen Sünder *(rec Knox College, Toronto, May 1995)* Analekta Fleur de Lys ▲ FL 23063 [DDD]

Beauséjour, Luc (org/hpd)
Kuhnau, J.:Musicalische Vorstellung einiger biblischer Historien *(rec Presbyterian College Chapel, McGill Univ, Montréal, Québec, Mar 1994)* CBC ("Musica Viva" series) ▲ MVCD 1086 [DDD]

Beauvais, William (gtr)
Berg, O.:Memory Palace Centaur ▲ CRC 2167 [DDD]
Berg, O.:Odd Trio, w. K. Smith (vn), T. Tureski (mar) Centaur ▲ CRC 2167 [DDD]
Dances & Romances for Violin, w. M. Hammer (vn), Valerie Tryon (pno) Musica Viva ▲ MVCD 1071 [DDD]

Beaver, Martin (vn)
Fossa, F. de:Trios, Op. 18, w. S. Wynberg (gtr), B. Epperson (vc) *(rec St. John's Church, Elora, Ontario, Mar. 23–25, 1993)* Naxos ▲ 8.550760 [DDD]
Strauss, R.:Till Eulenspiegels lustige Streiche, w. James Campbell (cl), James McKay (bn), James Sommerville (hn), Joel Quarrington (db)—[arr. Franz Hasenöhrl as Einmal Anders! (frolic for 5 instruments; 1954)] *(rec Glenn Gould Studio, CBC Toronto, Mar. 26–27, 1994)* CBC ("Musica Viva" series) ▲ MVV 1089 [DDD]
Weinzweig, J.:Son Vn, w. Mary Kenedi (pno) *(rec live, Walter Hall, Univ. of Toronto, Mar. 11, 1993)* Centrediscs ▲ CMC 5295 [DDD]

Beck, J. (perc/elec)
Schindler, A.:At the Edge *(rec Sept. 1992)* Centaur ▲ CRC 2170 [DDD]

Beck, Janice (org)
Mendelssohn, F.:Sons Org Arkay ▲ AR 6103 [DDD]

Becker, Bob (perc)—see ORCHESTRAS & ENSEMBLES Nexus

Becker, Bob (pno/kbd perc)
Becker, B.:Mudra *(rec Holman Sound, Houston, TX, Aug. 8–12, 1994)* Nexus ▲ 10328 [DDD]
Becker, B.:Noodrem *(rec Holman Sound, Houston, TX, Aug. 8–12, 1994)* Nexus ▲ 10328 [DDD]
Becker, B.:Prisoners of the Image Factory *(rec Holman Sound, Houston, TX, Aug. 8–12, 1994)* Nexus ▲ 10328 [DDD]
Becker, B.:There is a Time *(rec Holman Sound, Houston, TX, Aug. 8–12, 1994)* Nexus ▲ 10328 [DDD]
Becker, B.:Turning Point *(rec Holman Sound, Houston, TX, Aug. 8–12, 1994)* Nexus ▲ 10328 [DDD]

Becker, Bob (xyl/perc)
Cahn, W.:In Ancient Temple Gardens, w. Joseph Werner (pno) Nexus ▲ 10339 [DDD]

Becker, Dagmar (fl)
Danzi, F.:Concertante Fl, w. W. Meyer (cl), J. Faerber (cnd), Württemberg CO *(rec 1/91)* MD + G ▲ L 3396 [DDD]
Pleyel, I.:Sinf concertante 5, w. P. Meyer (cl), Schottstädt (bn), Schneider (hn), J. Faerber (cnd), Württemberg CO MD + G ▲ L 3396 [DDD]
Salieri, A.:Con Fl, w. L. Lenczés (ob), J. Faerber (cnd), Württemberg CO MD + G ▲ L 3396 [DDD]

Becker, I. (syns/pno)—see ORCHESTRAS & ENSEMBLES Antifonale Chamber Ensemble

Becker, Jörg (hpd)
Chambonnières, J.C. de:Hpd Music—Suites Berlin Classics ▲ BER 9183
Couperin, L.:Suites Hpd Berlin Classics ▲ BER 9183
Soler, P.A.:Fandango Berlin Classics ▲ BER 9183
Soler, P.A.:Sons Hpd Berlin Classics ▲ BER 9183

Becker, Jörg (pno)
Sonate Facile Capriccio ▲ 10415 [DDD]

Becker, Kristi (pno)
Kagel, M.:Rrrrrrr... Cl, Vn & Pno, w. M. Riessler (cl), G. Wharton (vn) Montaigne ▲ MO 782003 [DDD]

Beckett, Edward (fl)
Yoshioka, T.:Rhap Mar, w. Evelyn Glennie (mar), Roy Howitt (cl), Chris Laurence (db), Ralph Salmins (dr) *(rec Whitfield Street Studios, London, Sept. 22–29, 1994)* Catalyst ▲ 09026-68193-2 [DDD]

Beckett, Harry (tpt)—see ORCHESTRAS & ENSEMBLES austraLYSIS members

Beckett, Rachel (fl)
Handel, G.F.:Sons Solo Instrs, w. Lisa Beznosiuk (rcr), Paul Goodwin (ob), Locatelli Trio Hyperion 3-▲ CDA 66921/23

Beckwith, Daniel (org)
Bach, J.S.:Motets, BWV 225–30, w. W. Ehmann (cnd), Westminster CO, Westminster Choir [G]—final chorales of BWV 226 & 229 are omitted Gothic ▲ G 49052

Becquet, Michel (trbn)
Constant, M.:Con Trbn, w. J. Kaltenbach (cnd), Nancy SO *(rec Salle Poirel, Nancy, Apr. 4, 1990)* Erato ▲ 94815-2 [DDD]
Honegger, A.:Chamber Music (comp), w. D.-S. Kang (vn), P.-H. Xuereb (va), R. Wallfisch (vc), M. Arrignon (cl), A. Marion (fl), A. Haraldsdottir (fl), C. Moreaux (ob), T. Caens (tpt), P. Zanlonghi (hp), P. Devoyon (pno), F. Kondo (mez), Ludwig String Quartet—Sonatine for Clarinet & Piano (1921–22); Rapsodie for 2 Flutes, Clarinet & Piano (1917); Danse de la Chêvre for Solo Flute (1921); Romance for Flute & Piano (1953); Petite Suite for 2 Flutes & Piano (1934); Trois Contrepoints for Piccolo, Oboe, Violin & Cello (1922); Intrada for Trumpet & Piano (1947); Hommage du trombone exprimant la tristesse de l'auteur absent for Trombone & Piano (1925); J'avais un fidèle amant for String Quartet (1929); Chanson de Ronsard & 3 Chansons de la petite Sirène for Mezzo, Flute & String Quartet (1924); Introduction et Danse for Flute, Harp & String Trio [undated]; Colloque for Flute, Celesta, Violin & Viola [undated] Timpani ▲ IC1010 [DDD]
Landowski, M.:Music of, w. J. Loriod (ondes Martenot), A. Marion (fl), F. Clidat (pno), J. Houtmann (cnd), Lorraine PO—Concerto for Ondes Martenot & Orchestra; Concerto for Flute & Strings; Concerto for Piano & Orchestra; Concertino for Trombone & Strings Koch Schwann ▲ CD 311175 [DDD]
Rimsky-Korsakov, N.:Con Trbn, w. N. Nozy (cnd), Belgian Guides Symphonic Band René Gailly ▲ CD 87075 [DDD]
The Trombone, w. A. Rosin (trbn), Berlin Trombone Quintet, Berlin RIAS Sinfonietta [cnd:Ernő Sebestyen], Lorraine PO [cnd:Jacques Houtmann], Southwest German CO [cnd:Vladislav Czernedki] Koch Schwann ▲ SCH 313342 [DDD]

Bédard, D. (org)
Handel, G.F.:Cons (16) Org, w. Carl Philipp Ensemble Analekta Fleur de Lys ▲ FL 2 3027

Bedford, Steuart (pno)
Britten, H.:The Holy Sonnets of John Donne, w. Philip Langridge (ten) Collins Classics ▲ COL 1468
Britten, H.:Sonnets of Michelangelo, w. Philip Langridge (ten) Collins Classics ▲ COL 1468
Britten, H.:Winter Words, w. Philip Langridge (ten) Collins Classics ▲ COL 1468
Schubert, Franz:Schwanengesang, w. John Shirley-Quirk (bar) ASV Quicksilva ▲ ASQ 6171

Beecham, Thomas (pno)
Delius, F.:Songs, w. D. Labbette (sop)—Cradle Song; The Nightingale; Twilight Fancies *(rec June 24 & July 10, 1929)* Dutton Laboratories ▲ CDLX 7011 [ADD]
Schumann, R.:Con Pno, w. T. Beecham (cnd), Royal PO EMI Classics ▲ CDH 69792

Beegle, Raymond (pno)—see CHORAL GROUP New York Vocal Arts Ensemble

Beenhouwer, Josef de (pno)
Schumann, C.:Pno Music—Sonata (newly discovered, first recording); cherzo; Romances; etc. Partridge ▲ 1129-2 [DDD]
Schumann, C.:Pno Music—Caprices (9) en forme de Valse, Op. 2; Romance variée, Op. 3; Valses romantique, Op. 4; Souvenir de Vienne (impromptu), Op. 9; Trois Romances, Op. 11; Preludes & Fugues (3), Op. 16; Variations on a Theme of Robert Schumann, Op. 20 Partridge ▲ 1130-2 [DDD]
Schumann, C.:Pno Music—Concert Variations on a Cavatine from Bellini's "Il pirata," Op. 8 (1837); Fugues (3) on Themes by J.S. Bach (1845); Pièces caractéristiques (4), Op. 5 (1835); Pièces fugitives (4), Op. 15 (ca. 1840/44); Polonaises (4), Op. 1 (1828–30); Romances (3), Op. 21 (1853) Partridge ▲ 1131-2 [DDD]

Beer, Robert (gtr)
Brouwer, L.:Gtr Music, w. John Draper (gtr), Carl Ljungstrom (gtr), Steven Patterson (gtr)—Musica Incidental Campesina; Vier Mikropiezas; Cuban Landscape with Rain; Preludios Epigrammaticos; El Decameron Negro; other works Koch Schwann ▲ SCH 311742 [DDD]

Beerman, Burton (cl)
Electric Clarinet:Contemporary Works for Clarinet & Various Electronic Processes, w. Errante, F. Gerard (cl) Capstone ▲ CPS 8607 [DDD]

Beetem, Anne (pno)
Voices That Are Gone:Songs from Victorian America, w. R. Turner (ten) Corvus ▲ RT 1196

Béghin, Alain (perc)
Arma, P.:Music of, w. Josette Morata (nar), Fabrice Moretti (sax), Régis Poulain (bn), Jean-Marie Cottet (pno), Francis Petit (perc), J.-L. Petit (cnd), Avray Atelier Musique—Phases contre phases for S Sax & Pno; Celui qui dort et dort for Nar, Bn, Xyl & Perc [after poems by Max Jacob]; 5 esquisses for Pno [from a Hungarian Theme]; Divertissement 1600 for Fls [w. Jean-Noël Catrice (fl), Béatrice Delpierre (fl), Pascale Haarscher (fl), Marie-Aude Menou (fl)]; 3 Regards for solo Ob [w. Jacques Vandeville (ob)]; Divert No. 6 for Cl & Pno [w. Dominique Vidal (cl)]; Parlando for solo Fl [w. Patrice Bocquillon (fl)] REM ▲ REM 311266 [DDD]

Beghin, Tom (pno)
Haydn, J.:Arianna a Naxos, w. Andrea Folan (sop) *(rec Sage Chapel, Cornell Univ., Itahca, NY, Mar 21–23, 1995)* Bridge ▲ BCD 9059 [DDD]
Haydn, J.:Songs (52) solo Voice & Kbd, w. Andrea Folan (sop)—Das strickende Mädchen; Cupido; Der erste Kuss; Eine sehr gewöhnliche Geschichte; Die Verlassene; Der Gleichsinn; An Iris; An Thyrsis; Trost unglücklicher Liebe; Die Landlust; Liebeslied; Die zu späte Ankunft der Mutter [H.XXVIa/1–12] *(rec Sage Chapel, Cornell Univ., Itahca, NY, Mar 21–23, 1995)* Bridge ▲ BCD 9059 [DDD]

Begnis, E. (vn)—see ORCHESTRAS & ENSEMBLES Quartetto Modì

Behrend, Roger (eup)
Elegance, w. Richard A. Donn (pno/hpd) Coronet ▲ COR 400-0

Behrend, Siegfried (gtr)
Carulli, F.:Con Gtr, I Musici Deutsche Grammophon (Musikfest) ■ 413664-4
Castelnuovo-Tedesco, M.:Con 1 Gtr, w. R. Peters (cnd), Berlin PO Deutsche Grammophon ("Resonance" series) ▲ 427214-2 [AAD]
Giuliani, M.:Con 1 Gtr, I Musici Deutsche Grammophon ("Musikfest" series) ■ 413664-4
Praetorius, M.:Terpsichore, w. S. Fink (perc), Collegium Terpsichore, Ulsamer Collegium—36 sels IMP Collectors Series ▲ IMPX 9026 [AAD]
Rodrigo, J.:Concierto de Aranjuez, w. R. Peters (cnd), Berlin PO Deutsche Grammophon ("Resonance" series) ▲ 427214-2 [AAD]
Siegfried Behrend in Memoriam Thorofon 2-▲ CTH 2201/2 [AAD]

Behrends, A. (org)
Bach, J.S.:Partite diverse sopra *O Gott, du frommer Gott* *(rec Apr 90)* Ambitus ▲ 97854 [DDD]
Tunder, F.:Org Music—Preludium in g *(rec 4/90)* Ambitus ▲ 97854 [DDD]
Weckmann, M.:O lux beata trinitas Ambitus ▲ 97854 [DDD]

Behrends, Ulrich (trbn)—see ORCHESTRAS & ENSEMBLES Triton Trombone Quartet

Behringer, Michael (org)
Jenkins, J.:Consort Music, w. J. Savall (cnd), Hespèrion XX (pavans & fantasies) Astrée ▲ E 8724

Beier, Michael (fl)—see ORCHESTRAS & ENSEMBLES Collegium Musicum Soloists

Beier, Mikael (fl)
Popular Music for Flute & Harp, w. Marie Eriksson (hp) Danacord ▲ DACOCD 306 [DDD]

Beier, Paul (archlt)
Piccinini, A.:Intavolature Nuova Era ("Ancient Music" series) ▲ 7114 [DDD]

Beier, Paul (lt)
Galilei, M.:Lt Music 1—Six Sonatas & Passamezzo e Saltarello Nuova Era ("Ancient Music" series) ▲ 6869 [DDD]
Molinaro, S.:Lt Music—Book One (1599) Nuova Era ("Ancient Music" series) ▲ 6923 [DDD]

Beijer, Erik (fid/vl)—see ORCHESTRAS & ENSEMBLES Camerata Trajectina

Beiler, Jonathan (vn)
Brahms, J.:Qnt Cl, w. G. Siflies (cl), J. Korman (vn), D. Barnes (va), J. Sant'Ambrogio (vc) *(rec 1975–79)* Vox Box 3-▲ CD3X 3014 [ADD]

Beinvenu, Lily (pno)
Ravel, M.:Songs, w. Irma Kolassi (mez)—Sainte; Manteau de fleur; Les grands vents venus d'outremer; Trois poèmes de Stéphane Mallarmé *(rec 1961)* Mémoire Vive ▲ 262014 (m)

Beiser, Maya (vc)—see also ORCHESTRAS & ENSEMBLES Bang on a Can members, Bang on a Can
Gordon, M.:Industry *(rec Air Recording Studios, Lyndhurst Hall, Hampstead, London, June 29–July 3, 1994)* Sony Classical ▲ SK 66483
Gubaidulina, S.:In Croce, w. Dorothy Papadakos (org) Koch International Classics ▲ KIC 7258 [DDD]
Gubaidulina, S.:Preludes (10) Vc Koch International Classics ▲ KIC 7258 [DDD]
Radzynski, J.:Music of, w. A Erez (pno), Aviv String Quartet, *(Qt. for Strings Y. Aloni (viola), A. Erez (Canto for Piano [rec. 1991]),* M. Beiser, Z. Plesser *(5 Duets for 2 Cellos [rec. 1992])* CRI ▲ CD 649 [DDD]
Ustvolskaya, G.:Grand Duet Vc, w. Christopher Oldfather (pno) Koch International Classics ▲ KIC 7258 [DDD]
Wolfe, J.:Lick, w. Evan Ziporyn (s sax), Mark Stewart (elec gtr), Steven Schick (perc), Lisa Moore (pno), Robert Black (db) *(rec Air Recording Studios, Lyndhurst Hall, Hampstead, London, June 29–July 3, 1994)* Sony Classical ▲ SK 66483 [DDD]

Bekova, Alfia (vc)—see also ORCHESTRAS & ENSEMBLES Bekova Sisters
Brahms, J.:Sons Vc (comp), w. Eleonora Bekova (pno) Chandos ▲ CHAN 9479
Gubaidulina, S.:Meditation on a Bach Chorale, w. Elisabeth Chojnacka (hpd), Hanna Weinmeister (vn), Elvira Bekova (vn), Marius Stravinsky (va), Alois Posch (db) *(rec Lockenhaus Festival, Austria, 1995)* BIS ▲ CD 810 [DDD]

Bekova, Eleonora (pno)—see also ORCHESTRAS & ENSEMBLES Bekova Sisters
Brahms, J.:Sons Vc (comp), w. Alfia Bekova (vc) Chandos ▲ CHAN 9479

Bekova, Elvira (vn)—see also ORCHESTRAS & ENSEMBLES Bekova Sisters
Gubaidulina, S.:Meditation on a Bach Chorale, w. Elisabeth Chojnacka (hpd), Hanna Weinmeister (vn), Marius Stravinsky (va), Alfia Bekova (vc), Alois Posch (db) *(rec Lockenhaus Festival, Austria, 1995)* BIS ▲ CD 810 [DDD]

Bélanger, Marc (vn)
Vivier, C.:Kopernikus, "A Ritual Opera of Death", w. Y. Parent (sop), P. Vaillancourt (sop), M.-D. Parent (sop), J. Fleury (cta), D. Doane (ten), M. Ducharme (bar), Y. Saint-Amant (bass), F. Martel (cl), L. Bouchard (tpt), L. Vaillancourt (cnd), *(orch unknown) (rec Feb. 1991)* CBC ("Musica Viva" series) ▲ MVCD 1047 [DDD]

Belcher, David (pno)—see ORCHESTRAS & ENSEMBLES Hawthorne Trio

Belcher, Diane Meredith (org)
Duruflé, M.:Suite Org Direct-to-Tape Recording ▲ DTR 8403CD ■ DTR 8403
Jongen, J.:Symphonie Concertante, w. J. Primavera (cnd), Philadelphia Youth Orch Direct-to-Tape Recording ▲ DTR 8804CD ■ DTR 8804
Reger, M.:Son 2 Org—Invocation Direct-to-Tape Recording ▲ DTR 8403CD ■ DTR 8403
Rheinberger, J.:Sons Org—No. 8 in e, Op. 132 [Introduction & Fugue] Direct-to-Tape Recording ▲ DTR 8403CD ■ DTR 8403
Shout the Glad Tidings, w. Memphis Chamber Choir, Memphis Boychoir *(rec 1992)* Pro Organo ▲ POCD 7037 [DDD]
What Sweeter Music:Carols for the Year Round, w. Memphis Chamber Choir, Memphis Boychoir *(rec 1991)* Pro Organo ▲ POCD 7031 [DDD]
Widor, C.M.:Sym 6 Org, w. D. M. Belcher—Intermezzo Direct-to-Tape Recording ▲ DTR 8403CD ■ DTR 8403

Belden, David (vn)—see ORCHESTRAS & ENSEMBLES Ad Hoc String Quartet

Belder, Pieter-Jan (rcr)
17th & 18th Century Chamber Music, w. René Schiffer (baroque vc), H. Stinders (hpd) *(rec Nov. 1991)* Erasmus ▲ WVH 058 [DDD]

Beldi, Christian (pno)
Mendelssohn, F.:Lied ohne Worte Vc, w. E. Klein (vc) *(rec 1988)* Ambitus ▲ 97832 [DDD]
Mendelssohn, F.:Son 1 Vc, w. E. Klein (vc) *(rec 1988)* Ambitus ▲ 97832 [DDD]
Mendelssohn, F.:Son 2 Vc, w. E. Klein (vc) *(rec 1988)* Ambitus ▲ 97832 [DDD]
Mendelssohn, F.:Vars concertantes, w. E. Klein (vc) *(rec 1988)* Ambitus ▲ 97832 [DDD]

Belkin, Boris (vn)
Brahms, J.:Sons Vn (comp), w. Michel Dalberto (pno) *(rec Musica Théâtre, La Chaux-de-Fonds, Switzerland, May 24-29, 1994)* Denon ▲ DEN 78962 [DDD]
Bruch, M.:Con 1 Vn, w. J. Hirokami (cnd), Royal PO *(rec All Saints Church, Tooting, London, May 3-5, 1994)* Denon ▲ CO 78951 [DDD]
Mozart, W.A.:Con 5 Vn, w. Salzburg Chamber Soloists *(rec Mozarteum Grosse Saal, Salzburg, Feb. 21-23, 1994)* Denon ▲ CO 78918 [DDD]
Mozart, W.A.:Sinf concertante Vn, K.364, w. Lavard Skou Larsen (va), Salzburg Chamber Soloists *(rec Mozarteum Grosse Saal, Salzburg, Feb. 21-23, 1994)* Denon ▲ CO 78918 [DDD]
Prokofiev, S.:Cons Vn (comp), w. M. Stern (cnd), Zurich Tonhalle Orch Denon/PCM Digital ▲ CO 75891 [DDD]
Shostakovich, D.:Con 1 Vn, w. V. Ashkenazy (cnd), Royal PO London ▲ 425793-2 [DDD]
Sibelius, J.:Con Vn, w. J. Hirokami (cnd), Royal PO *(rec All Saints Church, Tooting, London, May 3-5, 1994)* Denon ▲ CO 78951 [DDD]
Strauss, R.:Con Vn, w. V. Ashkenazy (cnd), Berlin RSO London ▲ 436415-2 [DDD]

Bell, David (org)
Mozart, W.A.:Requiem, w. Felicity Lott (sop), Cella Jones (mez), Keith Lewis (ten), Willard White (bass), F. Welser-Möst (cnd), London PO, London Phil Choir Classics for Pleasure ("Eminence" series) ▲ CDEMX 2150 [DDD]

Bell, Joshua (vn)
Brahms, J.:Con Vn, w. C. von Dohnányi (cnd), Cleveland Orch London ▲ 444811-2
Bruch, M.:Con 1 Vn, w. N. Marriner (cnd), Academy of St. Martin in the Fields London ▲ 421145-2 [DDD] ■ 421145-4
Chausson, E.:Con Vn, Pno & Str Qt, w. J.-Y. Thibaudet (pno), Takács String Quartet London ▲ 425860-2 [DDD]
Debussy, C.:Son Vn, w. J.-Y. Thibaudet (pno) London ▲ 421817-2 [DDD]
Fauré, G.:Son 1 Vn, w. J.-Y. Thibaudet (pno) London ▲ 421817-2 [DDD]
Franck, C.:Son Vn, w. J.-Y. Thibaudet (pno) London ▲ 421817-2 [DDD]
Joshua Bell, w. Samuel Sanders (pno) London ▲ 417891-2 LH [DDD]
Kreisler, F.:Music of, w. Paul Coker (pno)—Praeludium & Allegro; Schon Rosmarin; Tambourin Chinois; Caprice Viennois; La Precieuse; Liebesfreud; Liebeslied; La Gitana; Bercuse Romantique; Polinchinelle; Rondino; Tempo Di Minuetto; Toy Soldier's March; Allegretto; Marche miniature viennoise; Aucassin & Nicolette; Menuett; Sicilienne & Riguadon; Syncopation London ▲ 444409-2
Lalo, E.:Sym espagnole, w. C. Dutoit (cnd), Montreal SO London ▲ 425501-2 [DDD]
Mendelssohn, F.:Con in e Vn & Orch, Op. 64, w. N. Marriner (cnd), Academy of St. Martin in the Fields London ▲ 421145-2 [DDD] ■ 421145-4
Mozart, W.A.:Adagio Vn, K.261, w. P. Maag (cnd), English CO London ▲ 436376-2 [DDD]
Mozart, W.A.:Con 3 Vn, w. P. Maag (cnd), English CO London ▲ 436376-2 [DDD]
Mozart, W.A.:Con 5 Vn, w. P. Maag (cnd), English CO London ▲ 436376-2 [DDD]
Mozart, W.A.:Rondo Vn, K.373, w. P. Maag (cnd), English CO London ▲ 436376-2 [DDD]
Poème, w. Royal PO [cnd:Andrew Litton] London ("Digital" series) ▲ 433519-2 LH [DDD] □ 433519-5
Prokofiev, S.:Cons Vn (comp), w. C. Dutoit (cnd), Montreal SO London ▲ 440331-2
Prokofiev, S.:The Love for 3 Oranges (suite), w. C. Dutoit (cnd), Montreal SO London ▲ 440331-2
Prokofiev, S.:Mélodies, w. Olli Mustonen (pno) London ▲ 440926-2 [DDD]
Prokofiev, S.:Son Vn, Op. 94bis, w. Olli Mustonen (pno) London ▲ 440926-2 [DDD]
Prokofiev, S.:Son 1 Vn, w. Olli Mustonen (pno) London ▲ 440926-2 [DDD]
Saint-Saëns, C.:Con 3 Vn, w. C. Dutoit (cnd), Montreal SO London ▲ 425501-2 [DDD]
Schumann, R.:Con Vn, w. C. von Dohnányi (cnd), Cleveland Orch London ▲ 444811-2
Tchaikovsky, P.:Con Vn, w. V. Ashkenazy (cnd), Cleveland Orch London ▲ 421716-2 [DDD]
Wieniawski, H.:Con 2 Vn, w. V. Ashkenazy (cnd), Cleveland Orch London ▲ 421716-2 [DDD]

Bell, Larry (pno)
Bell, L.:Son Pno *(rec Recital Hall of the Univ at Albany, May 25-26, 1995)* North/South ▲ N/S R 1007 [DDD]

Bell, Majken (acc)
Werner, S.E.:Tango Studies, w. Heidi Hansen (acc), Carsten Holbek (acc), Hans Jorgen Holbek (acc), Lelo Nika (acc), Morten Rossen (acc), Anders Vesterdahl (acc) *(rec Danish Accordian Academy, Oct. 1994)* Marco Polo ("dacapo" series) ▲ 8.224006 [DDD]

Bell, Sebastian (fl)
Takemitsu, T.:Music of, w. J. Williams (gtr), G. Hulse (ob), E.-P. Salonen (cnd), London Sinfonietta—To the Edge of Dream (for Guitar & Orchestra); Vers, L'arc-en-ciel, Palma (for Guitar & Oboe); Toward the Sea (for Alto Flute & Guitar); Folios (for solo Guitar); 12 Songs for Guitar (selections) Sony Classical ▲ SK 46720
Takemitsu, T.:Rain Coming, w. O. Knussen (cnd), London Sinfonietta Virgin Classics ▲ CDC 59020

Bell, Sebastian (pic)
Matthews, C.:Suns Dance, w. Gareth Hulse (ob), Michael Collins (b cl), John Orford (ctbn), Michael Thompson (hn), Nona Liddell (vn), Joan Atherton (vn), Paul Silverthorne (va), Christopher van Kampen (vc), Robin McGee (db) *(rec All Saint's Church, Petersham, Oct 1992)* Deutsche Grammophon ▲ 447067-2 [DDD]

Bell, Sian (vc)—see ORCHESTRAS & ENSEMBLES Balanescu String Quartet

Bell, Stephen (hn)
Mozart, W.A.:Qnt Hn, w. Lindsay String Quartet ASV ▲ ASV CD 968

Bella, Dagmar (pno)
Mozart, W.A.:Con 10 Pno, w. Paul Badura-Skoda (pno), W. Furtwängler (cnd), Vienna PO Music & Arts ▲ CD 895

Bellaich, Alain (synthesized gtr)
D.W.W., w. R. Pinhas (syns/gtr), J. Philippe Goude (syn programming/drums/gtr), Patrick Gauthier (syns/pno/drums), Bernard Paganotti (bass gtr) Cuneiform ▲ Rune 40

Bellato, Andrea (vc)
Gragnani, F.:Gtr Music, w. Marco Riboni (gtr), Leopoldo Saracino (gtr), Andrea Pecola (vn), Emilio Vapi (fl), Anna Maria Giaquinta (cl)—Qt in A for Vn, Cl & 2 Gtrs, Op. 8; Duet No. 1 in A for Vn & Gtr; Trio in D for Fl, Vn & Gtr, Op. 13; Duet No. 2 in A for Vn & Gtr; Sxt in A for Fl, Cl, Vn, 2 Gtrs & Vc, Op. 9 Stradivarius ▲ STV 33385 [DDD]

Belli, Massimo (vn)
Donizetti, G.:Larghetto, Theme & Vars, w. V. Terekiev (pno) Nuova Era 2-▲ 7100/01 [DDD]

Bellik, Daniele (pno)
Furtwängler, W.:Qnt Pno, w. Elyséen String Quartet Bayer ▲ 100269 [ADD]

Bellinati, Paulo (gtr)
Guitares du Brésil, w. Bellinati, Paulo (gtr) GHA ▲ 126.015
Sardinha, A.A.:Gtr Music—(24 selections) Duas Contas; Inspiração; Lamentos do Morro; Um Rosto de Mulher; Sinal dos Tempos; Debussyana; A Caminho dos Estados Unidos; Mazurka 3; Carioquinha; Voltarei; Desvairada; Improviso; Meditação; Naqueles Velhos Tempos; Gracioso; Vivo Sonhando; Enigma; Esperança; Nosso Chôro; Chôro Triste 1 & 2; Doce Lembrança; Jorge do Fusa; Gente Humilde GSP Recordings ▲ GSP 1002CD ■ GSP 1002C

Bellio, E. (pno)
Dvořák, A.:From the Bohemian Forest, w. M. Somenzi (pno) *(rec 5/91)* Giulia 2-▲ GS 201004 [DDD]
Dvořák, A.:Legends, Op. 59, w. M. Somenzi (pno) *(rec 5/91)* Giulia 2-▲ GS 201004 [DDD]
Dvořák, A.:Slavonic Dances (comp), w. M. Somenzi (pno) [piano 4-hands] *(rec 5/91)* Giulia 2-▲ GS 201004 [DDD]

Bellocchio, M. G. (pno)
Duffy String Quartet with M. G. Bellocchio & the Ensemble Nuove Sincronie, w. Duffy String Quartet, Ensemble Nuove Sincronie Stradavarius ▲ SIP 1011

Bellocq, Eric (thb)
Clérambault, L.N.:Cants, w. Noémi Rime (sop), Jean-Paul Fouchécourt (ten), Nicolas Rivenq (bass), Hiro Kurosaki (vn), Ryo Terakado (vn), Marc Hantaï (fl), Elisabeth Matiffa (b vl), Bruno Croscet (basse de vn), W. Christie (cnd), Les Arts Florissants—Pyrame et Tisbé, La Muse de l'opéra ou les Caractères Lyriques, La Mort d'Hercule, Orphée Musique d'Abord ▲ HMA 1901329
Rebel, J.-F.:Sons 2 or 3 Parts, w. Frédéric Martin (vn), Odile Edouard (vn), Christine Plumbeau (vl), Noëlle Spieth (hpd)—Nos. 1-7 [L'immortelle; L'apollon; Tombeau de monsieur de Lully; La venus; La flore; La pallas; La junon] Adda ▲ ADD 581265 [DDD]

Bellotti, Eduardo (org)
Bach, J.S.:Cons solo Hpd, BWV 972-987—BWV 972, 973, 974, 975, 976, 978 & 981 Fonè ▲ FON 93F 22 [DDD]

Bellows, Beverly (hp)
Harrison, L.:Pieces (4) Hp Phoenix ▲ PHCD 118 [AAD]

Bellson, Louis (dr)
Farberman, H.:Con Jazz Drummer, w. H. Farberman (cnd), Bournemouth SO BIS ("BIS Twins" series) 2-▲ CD 232/382 [DDD]
Farberman, H.:Con Jazz Drummer, w. H. Farberman (cnd), Bournemouth SO BIS ▲ CD 382 [DDD]

Belnick, Arnold (vn)
Bacewicz, G.:Partita Vn, w. Sergei Silvansky (pno) *(rec Univ of Southern California, July 1995)* Cambria ▲ CD 1052 [DDD]
Bacewicz, G.:Son 3 Vn & Pno, w. Sergei Silvansky (pno) *(rec Univ of Southern California, July 1995)* Cambria ▲ CD 1052 [DDD]
Bacewicz, G.:Son 4 Vn & Pno, w. Sergei Silvansky (pno) *(rec Univ of Southern California, July 1995)* Cambria ▲ CD 1052 [DDD]
Bacewicz, G.:Son 5 Vn & Pno, w. Sergei Silvansky (pno) *(rec Univ of Southern California, July 1995)* Cambria ▲ CD 1052 [DDD]
Grieg, E.:Sons Vn, Opp. 8, 13 & 45, w. Adrian Ruiz (pno) *(rec May 1993)* Cambria ▲ CD 1076 [DDD]
Prokofiev, S.:Mélodies, w. A. Dominguez (pno) Cambria ▲ CMB 1096 [DDD]
Prokofiev, S.:Son Vn, Op. 94bis, w. A. Dominguez (pno) Cambria ▲ CMB 1096 [DDD]
Prokofiev, S.:Son 1 Vn, w. A. Dominguez (pno) Cambria ▲ CMB 1096 [DDD]

Belskaya, Irina (vn)
Mozart, W.A.:Serenata Notturna, w. Alexander Mayorov (vn), Ilya Shpiegelman (va), Sergey Kirichenko (db), A. Rudin (cnd), Musica Viva CO *(rec Moscow Conservatory Great Hall, 1996)* Russian Compact Disc ▲ RCD 30201 [DDD]

Belton, Ian (vn)—see ORCHESTRAS & ENSEMBLES Brodsky String Quartet

Béluse, Pierre (perc)
Tremblay, G.:Aubes—or Initial, w. Robert Cram (fl), René Gosselin (db) Centrediscs ▲ CMC 5094 [DDD]
Tremblay, G.:le sifflement des vents porteurs de l'amour, w. Robert Cram (fl) Centrediscs ▲ CMC 5094 [DDD]

Bémant, Serge (pno)
Brahms, J.:Son in D Vc, w. Edmont Baert (vc) Pavane 2-▲ ADW 7124/25
Chopin, F.:Intro & Polonaise, "Polonaise brilliante", w. Edmont Baert (vc) Pavane 2-▲ ADW 7124/25
Franck, C.:Son Vn, w. Edmont Baert (vc) Pavane 2-▲ ADW 7124/25
Servais, A.-F.:Fant Polonaise Vc, w. Edmont Baert (vc) Pavane 2-▲ ADW 7124/25
Servais, A.-F.:Souvenir de Spa, w. Edmont Baert (vc) Pavane 2-▲ ADW 7124/25

Bénatar, Jean-François (va)
Cras, J.:La Flûte de Pan, w. D. Henry (bar), T. Prevost (fl), M.-C. Milliere (vn), P. Bary (vc)—[F] Quantum ▲ QM 6897 [DDD] ■ QM 1992 (D)
Cras, J.:Qnt, w. C. Michel (hp), T. Prevost (fl), M.-C. Milliere (vn), P. Bary (vc) Quantum ▲ QM 6897 [DDD] ■ QM 1992 (D)
Cras, J.:Trio, w. M.-C. Milliere (vn), P. Bary (vc) Quantum ▲ QM 6897 [DDD] ■ QM 1992 (D)
Juon, P.:Chamber Music, w. Claire Vergnory-Mion (cl), Pierre Lenert (va), Philippe Nadal (vc), Hélène Calef (pno)—Trio Miniatures for Cl, Vc & Pno; Son in D for Va & Pno, Op. 15; Divert for Cl & 2 Vas, Op. 34; Trio for Cl, Vc & Pno, Op. 17 REM ▲ REM 311267 [DDD]
Martinů, B.:Madrigals Vn, w. M. Milliere (vn) Quantum ▲ QM 6910 [DDD] ■ QM 2004 (D)

Benck, Ayrton (tpt/flgl)—see ORCHESTRAS & ENSEMBLES Brasil Brass Quintet

Benedetti Michelangeli, Arturo (pno)—see Michelangeli, Arturo Benedetti

Benda, Christian (vc)
Benda, J.G.:Con Vn, w. C. Benda (cnd), Prague CO [trans for vc & strs] *(rec Prague, Nov 1994)* Naxos ▲ 8.553346 [DDD]
Stamitz, C.:Con 1 Vc, w. C. Benda (cnd), Prague CO *(rec Jan. 1993)* Naxos ▲ 8.550865 [DDD]
Stamitz, C.:Con 2 Vc, w. C. Benda (cnd), Prague CO *(rec Jan. 1993)* Naxos ▲ 8.550865 [DDD]
Stamitz, C.:Con 3 Vc, w. C. Benda (cnd), Prague CO *(rec Jan. 1993)* Naxos ▲ 8.550865 [DDD]

Benda, Sebastian (pno)
Martin, F.:Ballade Pno, w. F. Martin (cnd), Lausanne CO *(rec 1971)* Jecklin-Disco ▲ JD 529-2 [ADD]

Bender, Donald (ob)—see ORCHESTRAS & ENSEMBLES Trio Sonata

Bendixen, Kirsten (hn)—see ORCHESTRAS & ENSEMBLES Brass Ring

Benedetti, Fred (gtr)
Gold, E.:Music of, w. H. Dilworth (sop), G. Nestor (gtr), R. Gianattosio (pno), Holmby String Quartet—Sonata for Piano (1980); Songs of Love & Parting (1963); Quartet No. 1 for Strings (1948) *(rec 1983 & 1990)* Cambria ▲ CD 1062 [DDD/ADD]

Benedetto, Sirio (sax)
Albanese, G.:Songs, w. Luana Gentile (sop), Antonella Trovarelli (sop), Marina Gentile (mez), Stefano Consolini (ten), Paolo Speca (bar), Andrea De Mele (vn), Roberto Rupo (pno)—Aria di Natale; Duettino e coro muto (w. Carlo Moreno) [both w. Giorgina Dell'Immagine, Tito Petralia (cnd), EIAR Orch & Chorus]; Passione (M. Gentile); Serenata (Speca); Alzati, o bella... (Trovarelli); Mattinata (Speca); Il sogno d'una suora (Trovarelli); Ninna Nanna (M. Gentile); Barcarola (Rupo); Madrigale (L. Gentile); Ninna nanna...900 (L. Gentile); Variazioni (L. Gentile); Non so qual io mi voglia... (L. Gentile); Io sono un augellin... (L. Gentile); Bravo, bene, bis...(va bene) (Consolini & Di Benedetto); Che caviale (Consolini); Ma non sapete chi sono io? (Consolini & L. & M. Gentile); Grappoli di stelle (Consolini); Notte di Capri (Consolini & Di Mele); Una rosa di ferro battuto (Consolini, Speca & L. & M. Gentile) *(rec Ortona, Teatro Zambra, Feb 21, 22, 23 & Mar 1 &)* Bongiovanni ▲ GB 5054-2 [DDD]

▲ = CD ♦ = Enhanced CD Δ = MD ■ = Cassette Tape □ = DCC

Beneš, J. (instr)
Janácek, L.:The Danube Sop & Orch, w. K. Dvořákové (sop), F. Jílek (cnd), Brno State PO *(rec Jan. 22–25, 1992)* Supraphon ▲ 111522–2 [DDD]
Janácek, L.:Schluck und Jau, w. M. Gajdošová (vn), F. Jílek (cnd), Brno State PO *(rec Jan. 22–25, 1992)* Supraphon ▲ 111522–2 [DDD]

Benet, G. (pno)—see also ORCHESTRAS & ENSEMBLES Atlantic Sinfonietta members
Dun, T.:In Distance, w. K.–L. Wilson (pic), T. Dun (dr) *(rec June 4, 1992)* CRI ▲ CD 655 [DDD]

Benet, Gillian Vivia (hp)
Ginastera, A.:Con Hp, w. J. Yannatos (cnd), Harvard–Radcliffe Orch AFKA ▲ SK 509
Tailleferre, G.:Concertino Hp, w. J. Falletta (cnd), Women's PO Koch International Classics ▲ KIC 7169–2 [DDD]

Bengen, J. (perc/santouri)—see ORCHESTRAS & ENSEMBLES Estampie

Bengtson, Peter (org)
Sandström, S.–D.:The High Mass, w. Lena Hoel (sop), Sara Olsson (sop), Siri Torjesen (sop), Marianne Eklöf (mez), Annika Skoglund (mez), L. Segerstam (cnd), Swedish RSO, Eric Ericson Chamber Choir *(rec live, Berwald Hall, Stockholm, Nov. 25 & 26, 1994)* Caprice 2–▲ CAP 22036

Bengtson, Stig (fl)
Holewa, H.:Duettino 2, w. Magnus Andersson (gtr) Phono Suecia ▲ PHN 49 [ADD]

Bengtsson, Erling Bløndal (vc)
Bach, J.S.:Suites Vc, BWV 1007–1012 *(rec Mar–May 1984)* Danacord 2–▲ DACOCD 331/32 [ADD]
Boccherini, L.:Con Vc, G.482, w. I. Stupel (cnd), Artur Rubinstein PO *(rec Apr. 1993)* Danacord ▲ DACOCD 416 [DDD]
Dvořák, A.:Con Vc, w. I. Stupel (cnd), Artur Rubinstein PO Danacord ▲ DACOCD 413 [DDD]
Erling Blöndal Bengtsson, w. Ingolf Olsen (gtr) *(rec Sept. 22–25, 1986)* Danacord ▲ DACOCD 335
Haydn, J.:Con 1 Vc, w. I. Stupel (cnd), Artur Rubinstein PO *(rec Apr. 1993)* Danacord ▲ DACOCD 416 [DDD]
Haydn, J.:Con 2 Vc, w. I. Stupel (cnd), Artur Rubinstein PO *(rec Apr. 1993)* Danacord ▲ DACOCD 416 [DDD]
Holmboe, V.:Con Vc, w. J. Ferencsik (cnd), Danish National RSO BIS ▲ CD 78 [AAD/DDD]
Koppel, H.D.:Con Vc, w. O. Schmidt (cnd), Danish National RSO BIS ▲ CD 80 [AAD]
Nordal, J.:Con Vc, w. P. Sakari (cnd), Iceland SO Music from Iceland ▲ ITM 602 [DDD]
Nørholm, I.:Con Vc, w. T. Vetö (cnd), Aalborg SO Kontrapunkt ▲ 32099 [DDD]
Nystroem, G.:Sinf concertante, w. S. Westerberg (cnd), Swedish RSO Swedish Society ▲ SCD 1015
Rachmaninoff, S.:Son Vc, w. N. Kavtaradze (pno) Kontrapunkt ▲ 32018 [DDD]
Reger, M.:Suites Vc *(rec July 1992)* Danacord ▲ CACOCD 372 [DDD]
Schumann, R.:Con Vc, w. I. Stupel (cnd), Artur Rubinstein PO Danacord ▲ DACOCD 413 [DDD]
Shostakovich, D.:Son Vc, w. N. Kavtaradze (pno) Kontrapunkt ▲ 32018 [DDD]
Ysaÿe, E.:Son Vc *(rec July 1992)* Danacord ▲ CACOCD 372 [DDD]

Bengtsson, Rolf (hn)
Rangström, T.:Vauxhall, w. Bengt Christiansson (fl), Lars Olof Loman (ob), Lars Almgren (cl), Sven Aarflot (bn), Rune Bodin (trbn), Rozalina Skytt (hp), O. Vänskä (cnd), Stockholm PO *(rec Stockholm Concert Hall, Jan. 16 & 18, 1985)* Caprice ▲ CAP 21195 [DDD]

Ben–Haim, Paul (pno)
Ben–Haim, P.:A Star Fell Down, w. U. Mayer–Reinach (mez) [He] Gallo ▲ CD 530 [AAD]

Benítez, B. (gtr)
Piazzolla, A.:Music of—Acentuado and Romantico; Campadre; Campero; Contrabajeando; Milonga del angel; La muerte del angel; Primavera porteña; Tristón; Verano porteño Canal Grande ▲ CCS 9322 [DDD]

Benjafield, Richard (perc)—see also ORCHESTRAS & ENSEMBLES Ensemble Bash
Gerhard, R.:Pandora, w. A. Ball (pno), J. Jacobson (pno) Largo ▲ 5119 [DDD]

Benjamin, George (pno)
Benjamin, G.:Son Pno *(rec 1982)* Nimbus ▲ NI 1415 [ADD]

Benjamin, Jeanne (vn)—see ORCHESTRAS & ENSEMBLES Contemporary Chamber Players

Benjamin, Keith (tpt)—see also ORCHESTRAS & ENSEMBLES Missouri Brass Quintet
Albright, W.:Jericho, w. M. Turnquist (org) Gothic ▲ G 49067 [DDD]
Eben, Petr:Windows, w. M. Turnquist (org) Gothic ▲ G 49067 [DDD]
Hamelin, P.:Sonata ben melodico, w. M. Turnquist (org) Gothic ▲ G 49067 [DDD]
Nelhybel, V.:Metamorphosis, w. M. Turnquist (org) Gothic ▲ G 49067 [DDD]
Starer, R.:Preludes Tpt, w. M. Turnquist (org) Gothic ▲ G 49067 [DDD]

Benkeser, P. (perc)—see ORCHESTRAS & ENSEMBLES Thamyris

Benkö, Dániel (gtr)
Paganini, N.:Centone di sonate, w. M. Szenthelyi (vn)—Nos. 1–4 Hungaroton ▲ HCD 31478 [DDD]
Paganini, N.:Duetto amoroso Vn, w. M. Szenthelyi (vn) Hungaroton ▲ HCD 31478 [DDD]
Paganini, N.:Sons Vn & Gtr, w. M. Szenthelyi (vn)—Son. concertata in A, Son. per novene (No. 2) in E & Son. in A, Op. 3/1 Hungaroton ▲ HCD 31478 [DDD]

Benkö, Dániel (lt)
Vivaldi, A.:Con Lt, w. J. Rolla (cnd), Franz Liszt CO Hungaroton ▲ HCD 11978
Vivaldi, A.:Con Va d'amore Lt, w. L. Bársony (va), J. Rolla (cnd), Franz Liszt CO Hungaroton ▲ HCD 11978
Vivaldi, A.:Trio Sons Vn Lt, w. J. Rolla (va), Z. Pertis (hpd) Hungaroton ▲ HCD 11978

Bennett, Elinor (hp)
Images & Impressions:Music for Flute & Harp, w. J. Hall (fl) Nimbus ▲ NI 5247 [DDD]
Mathias:Sante Fe Suite & Other 20th Century Harp Classics *(rec Concert Hall of the Nimbus Foundation, Wyastone Leys, Monmouth, Dec 6–8, 1993)* Nimbus ▲ NI 5441 [DDD]
Sea of Glass Lorelt ▲ LNT 105

Bennett, George (vn)—see ORCHESTRAS & ENSEMBLES Lyric Art String Quartet

Bennett, Hye Yun Chung (hp)
Musical Colors, w. W. Hendrick (fl) Klavier ▲ KCD 11063 [DDD]

Bennett, Karen (fl)
Telemann, G.P.:Con Rcr, Fl, w. M. Petri (rcr), I. Brown (cnd), Academy of St. Martin in the Fields Philips ▲ 410041–2 [DDD]
Thofanidis, C.:Suite Fl, w. Chris Theofanidis (pno) Albany ▲ TROY 158 [DDD]

Bennett, Mark (tpt)
Biber, H. von:Sonatae tam aris quam aulis servientes, w. Michael Laird (tpt), Katherine McGillvray (va), Jane Rogers (va), Tim Cronin (va), Purcell Quartet Chandos ▲ CHAN 0591
Haydn, J.:Con Tpt, w. T. Pinnock (cnd), English Concert Archiv ▲ 431678–2 [DDD]
Telemann, G.P.:Cons Tpts, w. Michael Harrison (tpt), Nicholas Thompson (tpt), Paul Goodwin (ob), Lorraine Wood (ob), T. Pinnock (cnd), English Concert—in D *(rec Henry Wood Hall, London, Mar 1993)* Archiv Produktion ▲ 439893–2 [DDD]
Vivaldi, A.:Con for 2 Tpts, w. A. Crowley (tpt), L. Friedman (cnd), St. Andrew Camerata Omega ▲ OCD 1012 [DDD]

Bennett, Richard Rodney (pno)
Arlen, H.:Ballet Music [arr. Bennett for 2 pianos]—Civil War Ballet; Hero Ballet DRG ▲ DRG 6102 [DDD]
Bennett, Richard Rodney:Suite for Skip & Sadie, w. C. Rosenberger (pno) Delos ▲ DE 6002 [DDD] ■ CS 6002 (D)
Gershwin, G.:Pno Music—Gershwin Songbook; Preludes Nos. 1–3; Promenade; Merry Andrew; Jasbo Brown Blues; Impromptu in 2 Keys; 2 Waltzes in C; 3–Quarter Blues; Rialto Ripples; Little Jazz Bird; Bess, Oh Where's My Bess; Someone to Watch Over Me IMP ("Classics" series) ▲ IMP 6700372
Holst, G.:The Planets, w. R. Bradshaw (pno) [2–piano version] Facet ▲ FCD 8002 [AAD]
Porter, C.:Within the Quota [arr. Bennett for 2 pianos] DRG ▲ DRG 6102 [DDD]
Rodgers, R.:Ballet Music [arr. Bennett for 2 pianos]—Ghost Town DRG ▲ DRG 6102 [DDD]
Walton, W.:Duets for Children, w. C. Rosenberger (pno) Delos ▲ DE 6002 [DDD] ■ CS 6002 (D)

Bennett, Richard Rodney (pno/nar)
Bennett, Richard Rodney:Partridge Pie Delos ▲ DE 6002 [DDD] ■ CS 6002 (D)
Bennett, Richard Rodney:7 Days a Week Delos ▲ DE 6002 [DDD] ■ CS 6002 (D)
Bennett, Richard Rodney:A Week of Birthdays Delos ▲ DE 6002 [DDD] ■ CS 6002 (D)

Bennett, Samm (perc)
Sato, M.:Improvs, w. Michihiro Sato (tsugaru shamisen), Bill Frisell (elec gtr), Fred Frith (elec gtr), Tenko (sgr), Mark Miller (elec bass), Nicolas Collins (elec), Christian Marclay (turntables), Steve Colemann (sax), Tom Cora (vc), Joey Baron (perc), Mark Dresser (elec bass), Gerry Hemingway (perc), Toh Ban Djan—23 improvisations with various accompaniment combinations *(rec Baby Monster Studio, NY, Apr. 11–16, 1988)* Hat Hut ▲ hat ART CD 6015 [ADD]

Bennett, Steve (hp gtr)
The Classical Banjo, w. J. Bullard (banjo), John Patykula (gtr), William Comita (vc), Greg Giannascoli (vib) *(rec Big Audio, Richmond, VA, May–July 1992, Oct. 1994)* Dargason Music ▲ DM 115 [DDD]; ■ DM 115

Bennett, William (fl)
Bach, J.S.:Sons Fl, BWV 1030–35, w. G. Malcolm (hpd) ASV Quicksilva ▲ 6108 [DDD]
Bizet, G.:L'Arlésienne (sels), w. Clifford Benson (pno)—Minuet *(rec Japan, Sept 2 & 3, 1991)* Camerata ▲ 30CM 390 [DDD]
Bizet, G.:Carmen (sels), w. Clifford Benson (pno)—Intermezzo *(rec Japan, Sept 2 & 3, 1991)* Camerata ▲ 30CM 390 [DDD]
Boehm, T.:Compositions Fl, w. A. Adorján (fl), U. Burkhard (fl), M. Debost (fl), I. Grafenauer (fl), A. Nicolet (fl), B. Weber (pno)—works for Flute & Piano *(Andante pastorale, from Souvenir des Alpes; Elegie in A♭, Op. 47; Fantaisie sur un air allemand, Op. 22; Fantaisie in A♭ on a Theme by Schubert; Grande Polonaise in D, Op. 16; Variations on Nel cor più non mi sento)*; works for Flute Ensemble *(Duettino in D, Pièce facile in C & Romanza in F [Nos. 66–68]; plus a six–flute ensemble performance of the 2nd movt. from Boismortier's Flute Concerto No. 1 in G)* *(rec live, Cuvilliés Theater, Munich 11/27/81)* Orfeo ▲ 018821 [DDD]
Chopin, F.:Vars on Rossini's *Non più mesta,* w. Clifford Benson (pno) *(rec Japan, Sept 2 & 3, 1991)* Camerata ▲ 30CM 390 [DDD]
Corelli, A.:Concerti grossi, Op. 6, w. M. Eade (vn), J.L. Garcia (vn), N. Black (ob), I. Watson (hpd/org), English CO—No. 2 in F Virgin Classics ▲ CDZ 59656
Debussy, C.:Chamber Music, w. David Campbell (cl), James Campbell (cl), Nicholas Daniel (ob), Robert Makell (hn), Richard Watkins (hn), Robin Kennard (bn), Rachel Gough (bn), Simon Haram (sax), Ieuan Jones (hp), Clifford Benson (pno), Julius Drake (pno), John York (pno), Roger Tapping (va)—Rapsodie for Eng hn; Syrinx; Première rapsodie; Son for Fl, Va & Hp; Le petit nègre; Petite pièce; Rapsodie for Sax *(rec All Saints' Church, East Finchley, London, Jan 12–20, 1994)* Cala 2–▲ CACD 1017 [DDD]
Debussy, C.:Son Fl, w. S. Shingles (va), S. Kanga (hp) Chandos ▲ CHAN 8621 [DDD]
Franck, C.:Son Vn, w. Clifford Benson (pno) *(rec Oct 14, 1987)* Camerata ▲ 32CM 204 [DDD]
Handel, G.F.:Duets for 2 Fls, Op. 2, w. G. L. Petrucci (fl) Bongiovanni ▲ GB 5516 [DDD]
Hommages, w. M. Fingerhut (pno), Margaret Cable (mez), Kenneth Sillito (vn), Clifford Benson (pno) Chandos ▲ CHAN 8578 [DDD]
Mozart, W.A.:Con Fl, Hp, w. Osian Ellis (hp), R. Leppard (cnd), English CO ASV ▲ ASV 532
Mozart, W.A.:Così fan tutte (sels), w. Clifford Benson (pno)—Adagio & Rondo *(rec Japan, Oct 21, 1987)* Camerata ▲ 30CM 390 [DDD]
Pergolesi, G.B.:Con Fl, w. English CO Virgin Classics ▲ CDZ 59656
Poulenc, F.:Chamber Music, w. Peter Sidhom (bar), David Campbell (cl), James Campbell (cl), Nicholas Daniel (ob), Richard Watkins (hn), Rachel Gough (bn), Peter Carter (vn), Chris West (db), Ieuan Jones (hp), Clifford Benson (pno), Julius Drake (pno), John York (pno)—Son for Ob; L'invitation au château; Villanelle; Son 2 Cls; Trio; Sxt; Son for Cl & Bn; Rapsodie nègre; Son for Cl; Mouvements perpétuels; Son for Fl *(rec All Saints' Church, East Finchley, London, Jan 12–20, 1994)* Cala ▲ CACD 1018 [DDD]
Poulenc, F.:Son Fl, w. Clifford Benson (pno) *(rec Japan, Sept 2 & 3, 1991)* Camerata ▲ 30CM 390 [DDD]
Ravel, M.:Intro & Allegro, w. S. Kanga (hp), A. Marriner (cl), Academy of St. Martin in the Fields Chamber Ensemble Chandos ▲ CHAN 8621 [DDD]
Ravel, M.:Intro & Allegro, w. Ieuan Jones (hp), James Campbell (cl), Allegri String Quartet *(rec All Saints' Church, East Finchley, London, Jan 12–20, 1994)* Cala 2–▲ CACD 1018 [DDD]
Ravel, M.:Vocalise–étude en forme de habanera, w. Clifford Benson (pno) *(rec Japan, Sept 2 & 3, 1991)* Camerata ▲ 30CM 390 [DDD]
Ries, F.:Qnt Fl, w. M. Kosi (va), Novsak Trio *(rec 1990)* Jecklin–Disco ▲ JD 633–2 [DDD]
Romberg, A.:Qnts Fl, w. M. Kosi (va), Novsak Trio—Op. 21/4–5 *(rec 1990)* Jecklin–Disco ▲ JD 633–2 [DDD]
Saint–Saëns, C.:Chamber Music, w. D. Campbell (cl), J. Campbell (cl), N. Daniel (ob), R. Makell (hn), R. Watkins (hn), R. Kennard (bn), R. Gough (bn), S. Haram (sax), I. Jones (hp), C. Benson (pno), J. Drake (pno), J. York (pno), R. Tapping (va)—Odelette, Op. 162; Son for Cl, Op. 167; Feuillet d'album, Op. 81; Son for Bn, Op. 168; Caprice on Danish & Russian Airs, Op. 79; Son for Ob, Op. 166; Romance in D♭, Op. 37; Tarantelle, Op. 6 *(rec All Saints' Church, East Finchley, London, Jan 12–20, 1994)* Cala 2–▲ CACD 1017 [DDD]
Saint–Saëns, C.:Odelette Fl, w. C. Benson (pno) *(rec Japan, Oct 21, 1987)* Camerata ▲ 30CM 390 [DDD]
Schubert, Franz:Intro & Vars Fl on "Tröckne Blumen", w. Clifford Benson (pno) *(rec Oct 14, 1987)* Camerata ▲ 32CM 204 [DDD]
Schubert, Franz:Son Arpeggione, w. Clifford Benson (pno) (tran fl & pno) Camerata ▲ 25CM 14 [DDD]
Schubert, Franz:Son Vn, D.574, w. Clifford Benson (pno) [tran fl & pno] Camerata ▲ 25CM 14 [DDD]
Schubert, Franz:Songs (misc), w. Clifford Benson (pno)—Gute Nacht; Der Lindenbaum; Das Fischermadchen; Standchen; Am Meer; Die Taubenpost [trans fl & pno] Camerata ▲ 25CM 14 [DDD]
Stalder, J.F.X.D.:Con Fl, w. H. Griffiths (cnd), English CO Novalis ▲ 150031 [DDD]
Taffanel, P.:Mignon Fant, w. Clifford Benson (pno) *(rec Oct 14, 1987)* Camerata ▲ 32CM 204 [DDD]
Vivaldi, A.:Con for 2 Fls, w. F. Smith (fl), N. Marriner (cnd), Academy of St. Martin in the Fields Philips ▲ 412892–2 [DDD]
Widor, C.M.:Suite Fl, w. Clifford Benson (pno) *(rec Japan, Oct 21, 1987)* Camerata ▲ 30CM 390 [DDD]

Bennett, William (ob)
Harbison, J.:Con Ob, w. H. Blomstedt (cnd), San Francisco SO *(rec Oct. 8, 1993)* London ▲ 443376–2 [DDD]

Bennion, Karl (vc)
Blavet, M.:Sons Trns Fl, w. Robert Stallman (fl), Edwin Swanborn (hpd)—Op. 2/2, 4 & 6; Op. 3/2, 4 & 6 VAI Audio ▲ VAIA 1101
Handel, G.F.:Sons Fl, w. Robert Stallman (fl), Edwin Swanborn (hpd), Op. 1, Nos. 1, 2, 4, 5, 7, 9 & 11 VAI Audio ▲ VAIA 1091
Leclair, J.–M.:Sons Vn (Books 1–4), w. R. Stallman (fl), E. Swanborn (hpd)—Opp. 2/1, 3 & 11; 9/2 & 7 *(rec Mar. 21–24, 1993)* VAI Audio ▲ VAIA 1068 [DDD]

Benoit, Prisca (pno)
Scarlatti, D.:Sons Kbd—K.1, 2, 27, 125, 162, 193, 247, 322, 380, 415, 441, 466, 476, 481, 531 Pavane ▲ 7326

Benoit, Regis (pno)
Pfitzner, H.:Songs, w. L. Maxwell (mez)—12 songs—Op. 2, Nos. 2,4 & 6; Op. 9, Nos. 2,3 & 5; Opp. 11/4, 24/4 & 26/2 & 3 & 29/2; Folk song, "Untreu und Trost" [G] Centaur ▲ CRC 2070 [DDD]
Strauss, R.:Songs, w. L. Maxwell (mez)—9 songs—Opp. 10/8, 21/1, 41b/2, 48/3–5, 49/5 & 69/5; Weinachtsgefühl (1899) [G] Centaur ▲ CRC 2070 [DDD]

Ben Omar, Maurizio (gtr/perc)
Scelsi, G.:Music of, w. Michiko Hirayama (sop), Federico Mondelci (sax), A. Brizzi (cnd), Gruppo Musica Insieme, Nuovo Ensemble Italiano—Pranam I for Voice, 12 Instrs & Band; Ko–Tha [3 danses de Shiva] for Gtr; I presagi for 11 Instruments; Riti [I funerali di Alessandro Magno]; Trio for 3 Percussionists; Manto per quattro for Voice, Fl, Trbn & Vc; Kya for Sax & 7 Instruments; Entretiens avec Giacento Scelsi Memoire Vive ▲ CD 262009 [ADD/DDD]

Ben Omar, Maurizio (perc)
Scelsi, G.:Khoom, w. Michiko Hirayama (sop), Frank Lloyd (hn), A. Brizzi (cnd), Arditti String Quartet Salabert ▲ SCD 8904–5

Ben-Or, Nelly (pno)
Beethoven, L. van:Qt Pno, Op. 16, w. Jerusalem String Trio — Meridian ▲ CDE 84154
Chopin, F.:Pno Music (misc)—Bolero, Op. 19; Mazurkas, Op. 17, No. 4, Op. 24, No. 2, Op. 30, No. 3, Op. 33, No. 2, Op. 50, No. 3, Op. 68, Nos. 1 & 4; Polonaises, Op. 26, No. 1, Op. 40, No. 1, Op. 44; Waltzes, Op. 42, Op. 64, Nos. 1 & 2 — Meridian ▲ CDE 84186
Dvořák, A.:Qts Pno Strs, Opp. 23 & 87, w. Jerusalem String Trio—Op. 87 — Meridian ▲ CDE 84179
Fibich, Z.:Qt Pno, w. Jerusalem String Trio — Meridian ▲ CDE 84179

Bensel, Paul (rec/crumhorn/perc)—see ORCHESTRAS & ENSEMBLES La Rondinella

Bensmann, Detlef (sax)—see also ORCHESTRAS & ENSEMBLES Berlin Saxophone Quartet
Borck, E. von:Con Sax, w. R. Wolf (cnd), Leipzig RSO — MD + G ▲ L 3451 [DDD]
Erdmann, D.:Music of, w. Koch, Ukigaya (cnd), Thüringen PO, Pomorska PO—Con for Sax & Orch (1989); Saxophonata (1985); Fant Colorata for Ten Sax; Con for Alt Sax & Orch; Resonanze for Sax Qt; plus others — Thorofon ▲ CTH 2269
Glazunov, A.:Con Sax, w. D. Shallon (cnd), Berlin RSO — Koch Schwann ▲ SCH 313352 [DDD]
Saxophone & Piano, w. Michael Rische (pno) — Koch Schwann ▲ SCH 310071 [ADD]
Schulhoff, E.:Hot Son Sax, w. M. Rische (pno) — Koch Schwann ▲ SCH 313352 [DDD]

Benson, Clifford (pno)
Arnold, Bernstein, Debussy, Martinů, Poulenc, Saint-Saëns, w. G. Gray (cl) *(rec June 1992)* — Centaur ▲ CRC 2165 [DDD]
Bizet, G.:L'Arlésienne (sels), w. William Bennett (fl)—Minuet *(rec Japan, Sept 2 & 3, 1991)* — Camerata ▲ 30CM 390 [DDD]
Bizet, G.:Carmen (sels), w. William Bennett (fl)—Intermezzo *(rec Japan, Sept 2 & 3, 1991)* — Camerata ▲ 30CM 390 [DDD]
Brahms, J.:Trio Cl, w. T. King (cl), K. Georgian (vc) — Hyperion ▲ CDA 66107
Chopin, F.:Vars on Rossini's *Non più mesta*, w. William Bennett (fl) *(rec Japan, Sept 2 & 3, 1991)* — Camerata ▲ 30CM 390 [DDD]
Debussy, C.:Chamber Music, w. William Bennett (fl), David Campbell (cl), James Campbell (cl), Nicholas Daniel (ob), Robert Makell (hn), Richard Watkins (hn), Robin Kennard (bn), Rachel Gough (bn), Simon Haram (sax), Ieuan Jones (hp), Julius Drake (pno), John York (pno), Roger Tapping (va)—Rapsodie for Eng hn; Syrinx; Première rapsodie; Son for Fl, Va & Hp; Le petit nègre; Petite pièce; Rapsodie for Sax *(rec All Saints' Church, East Finchley, London, Jan 12-20, 1994)* — Cala 2-▲ CACD 1017 [DDD]
Fauré, G.:Elégie, w. T. Igloi (vc) — CRD ▲ 3316
Fauré, G.:Sicilienne, w. T. Igloi (vc) — CRD ▲ 3316
Fauré, G.:Son 1 Vc, w. T. Igloi (vc) — CRD ▲ 3316
Fauré, G.:Son 2 Vc, w. T. Igloi (vc) — CRD ▲ 3316
Ferguson, H.:Discovery, w. Lydia Mordkovitch (vn) — Chandos ▲ CHAN 9316 [DDD]
Ferguson, H.:Irish Folksongs, Op. 17, w. Lydia Mordkovitch (vn) — Chandos ▲ CHAN 9316 [DDD]
Ferguson, H.:Mediaeval Carols (3), w. Lydia Mordkovitch (vn) — Chandos ▲ CHAN 9316 [DDD]
Ferguson, H.:Short Pieces Cl, Op. 6, w. Jane Hilton (cl) — Chandos ▲ CHAN 9316 [DDD]
Ferguson, H.:Sketches, Op. 14, w. David Butt (fl) — Chandos ▲ CHAN 9316 [DDD]
Ferguson, H.:Son 1 Vn, w. Lydia Mordkovitch (vn) — Chandos ▲ CHAN 9316 [DDD]
Ferguson, H.:Son 2 Vn, w. Lydia Mordkovitch (vn) — Chandos ▲ CHAN 9316 [DDD]
Finzi, G.:Song Cycles Bar, w. S. Varcoe (bar)—Earth & Air & Rain, Op. 15; Before & After Summer, Op. 16; I Said to Love, Op. 19b [E] — Hyperion 2-▲ CDA 66161/62
Finzi, G.:Song Cycles Ten, w. M. Hill (ten)—A Young Man's Exhortation, Op. 14; Till Earth Outwears, Op. 19a [E] — Hyperion 2-▲ CDA 66161/62
Franck, C.:Son Vn, w. William Bennett (fl) *(rec Oct 14, 1987)* — Camerata ▲ 32CM 204 [DDD]
Hommages, w. M. Fingerhut (pno), Margaret Cable (mez), William Bennett (fl), Kenneth Sillito (vn) — Chandos ▲ CHAN 8578 [DDD]
Mozart, W.A.:Così fan tutte (sels), w. William Bennett (fl)—Adagio & Rondo *(rec Japan, Oct 21, 1987)* — Camerata ▲ 30CM 390 [DDD]
Nielsen, C.:Son 1 Vn, w. L. Mordkovitch (vn) — Chandos ▲ CHAN 8598 [DDD]
Nielsen, C.:Son 2 Vn, w. L. Mordkovitch (vn) — Chandos ▲ CHAN 8598 [DDD]
Poulenc, F.:Chamber Music, w. Peter Sidhom (bar), William Bennett (fl), David Campbell (cl), James Campbell (cl), Nicholas Daniel (ob), Richard Watkins (hn), Rachel Gough (bn), Peter Carter (vn), Chris West (db), Ieuan Jones (hp), Julius Drake (pno), John York (pno)—Son for Ob; L'invitation au château; Villanelle; Son 2 Cls; Trio; Sxt; Son for Cl & Bn; Rapsodie nègre; Son for Cl; Mouvements perpétuels; Son for Fl *(rec All Saints' Church, East Finchley, London, Jan 12-20, 1994)* — Cala ▲ CACD 1018 [DDD]
Poulenc, F.:Son Fl, w. William Bennett (fl) *(rec Japan, Sept 2 & 3, 1991)* — Camerata ▲ 30CM 390 [DDD]
Ravel, M.:Pièce en forme de Habanera, w. Peter Carter (vn) *(rec All Saints' Church, East Finchley, London, Jan 12-20, 1994)* — Cala ▲ CACD 1018 [DDD]
Ravel, M.:Son Vn Pno, w. Lydia Mordkovitch (vn) — Chandos ▲ CHAN 9351 [DDD]
Ravel, M.:Sonate posthume, w. Lydia Mordkovitch (vn) — Chandos ▲ CHAN 9351 [DDD]
Ravel, M.:Vocalise-étude en forme de habanera, w. William Bennett (fl) *(rec Japan, Sept 2 & 3, 1991)* — Camerata ▲ 30CM 390 [DDD]
Respighi, O.:Son Vn, w. Lydia Mordkovitch (vn) — Chandos ▲ CHAN 9351 [DDD]
Saint-Saëns, C.:Chamber Music, w. W. Bennett (fl), D. Campbell (cl), J. Campbell (cl), N. Daniel (ob), R. Makell (hn), R. Watkins (hn), R. Kennard (bn), R. Gough (bn), S. Haram (sax), I. Jones (hp), C. Benson (pno), J. Drake (pno), J. York (pno), R. Tapping (va)—Odelette, Op. 162; Son for Cl, Op. 167; Feuillet d'album, Op. 81; Son for Bn, Op. 168; Caprice on Danish & Russian Airs, Op. 79; Son for Ob, Op. 166; Romance in D♭, Op. 37; Tarantelle, Op. 6 *(rec All Saints' Church, East Finchley, London, Jan 12-20, 1994)* — Cala 2-▲ CACD 1017 [DDD]
Saint-Saëns, C.:Odelette Fl, w. W. Bennett (fl) *(rec Japan, Oct 21, 1987)* — Camerata ▲ 30CM 390 [DDD]
Schubert, Franz:Intro & Vars Fl on "Tröckne Blumen", w. William Bennett (fl) *(rec Oct 14, 1987)* — Camerata ▲ 32CM 204 [DDD]
Schubert, Franz:Son Arpeggione, w. William Bennett (fl) (tran fl & pno) — Camerata ▲ 25CM 14 [DDD]
Schubert, Franz:Son Vn, D.574, w. William Bennett (fl) [tran fl & pno] — Camerata ▲ 25CM 14 [DDD]
Schubert, Franz:Songs (misc), w. William Bennett (fl)—Gute Nacht; Der Lindenbaum; Das Fischermadchen; Standchen; Am Meer; Die Taubenpost [trans fl & pno] — Camerata ▲ 25CM 14 [DDD]
Shostakovich, D.:Son Vn, w. L. Mordkovitch (vn) — Chandos ▲ CHAN 8988 [DDD]
Taffanel, P.:Mignon Fant, w. William Bennett (fl) *(rec Oct 14, 1987)* — Camerata ▲ 32CM 204 [DDD]
Widor, C.M.:Suite Fl, w. William Bennett (fl) *(rec Japan, Oct 21, 1987)* — Camerata ▲ 30CM 390 [DDD]

Benson, Joan (clvd)
Bach, C.P.E.:Kbd Music—Fant. in c; Rondo in B♭; Rondo, "Abschied von Silbermannschen Clavier" — Focus ▲ 931 [AAD]
Kuhlau, F.:Biblical Sons—No. 2 — Focus ▲ 931 [AAD]

Bentley, Judith (fl)
Bresgen, C.:Son Fl, w. R. Spano (pno) — Capstone ▲ CPS 8605
Genzmer, H.:Son Fl, w. R. Spano (pno) — Capstone ▲ CPS 8605
Hindemith, P.:Pieces (8) Fl & Pno, w. R. Spano (pno) — Capstone ▲ CPS 8605
Hindemith, P.:Son Cl, w. R. Spano (pno) — Capstone ▲ CPS 8605
Raphael, G.:Son Fl, w. R. Spano (pno) — Capstone ▲ CPS 8605

Bentzon, Niels Viggo (pno)
Bentzon, N.V.:Copenhagen Suites — Classico ▲ CLASSCD 108
Bentzon, N.V.:Son 19 Pno — Classico ▲ CD 152
Bentzon, N.V.:Son 20 Pno — Classico ▲ CD 152
Bentzon, N.V.:Son 29 Pno, "Taiwanese" — Classico ▲ CD 152
Bentzon, N.V.:Son for 2 Pnos, w. Nikolaj Bentzon (pno) — Classico ▲ CD 152
Bentzon, N.V.:Sons Sax, Opp. 320, 471, 478 & 498, w. P. Egholm (sax) *(rec 9/86)* — Kontrapunkt ▲ 32017

Bentzon, Nikolaj (pno)
Bentzon, N.V.:Son for 2 Pnos, w. Niels Viggo Bentzon (pno) — Classico ▲ CD 152

Benvenutti, Joseph (pno)
"Le Patron" of the Saxophone, w. M. Mule (sax), Guy Chauvet (ten), G. Charon (sgr), F. l'Homme (sgr), P. Romby (sgr), Eugène Bozza (cnd), Francis Çebron (cnd), Phillipe Gaubert (cnd), *(orchs unknown)*, Marcel Gaveau (pno), Marthe Pellas-Lenom (pno), François Combelle (sax) *(rec 1930-1940)* — Clarinet Classics ▲ CC 0013 [AAD]

Benyacs, Zoltan (va)
Escher, R.:Chamber Music, w. Jacques Zoon (fl), Herman De Boer (cl), Bart Schneemann (ob), Dmitri Ferschtman (vc), Glen Wilson (hpd)—includes Le Tombeau de Ravel; Trio for Strings; Trio for Cl, Va & Pno — NM Classics ▲ NM 92026

Benyamini, Daniel (va)
Berlioz, H.:Harold in Italy, w. Z. Mehta (cnd), Israel PO *(rec early/mid 1970s)* — PWK Classics ▲ PWK 1152 [ADD]

Benyus, S. (db)
Monteverdi, C.:Music of, w. M. Spányi (org), B. Máté (vc), I. Szabó (thb), Monteverdi Chamber Choir—Laudate pueri, Lauda Ierusalem, Nisi Dominus — Hungaroton ▲ HCD 31273 [DDD]

Benz, Lawrence (b trbn)
Fine, V.:Qt Brass, w. Ronald Anderson (tpt), Allan Dean (tpt), David Jolley (hn) — CRI ▲ CD 692 [ADD]

Benz, Lawrence (trbn)—see ORCHESTRAS & ENSEMBLES Calliope

Beran, J. (pno/perc/elec instrs)
Beran, J.:Music of—Landscape Mohenjo-daro; Cirri 1 & 2; Still life with metal bridge; Sundarban; Still life with glass, pearls & water; Khajurabo; Cotton Club *(rec June 16, 1990)* — Centaur ▲ CRC 2100 [DDD]

Beránek, Rudolf (hn)
Beethoven, L. van:Qnt Ob, 3 Hns & Bn, w. J. Mihule (ob), Z. Tylšar (hn), B. Tylšar (hn), F. Herman (bn) — Supraphon ▲ 11 1445-2 [DDD]

Béranger, Vinciane (va)—see ORCHESTRAS & ENSEMBLES Cecilia Piano Quartet

Berard, M. (ob)
Mozart, W.A.:Adagio & Rondo Glass Armonica, w. J. Petric (acc), M. Hammer (fl), D. Perry (va), D. Hetherington (vc) [trans. for accordion & string quartet] *(rec June 12-13, 1991)* — CBC ("Musica Viva" series) ▲ MVCD 1056 [DDD]

Berchot, Erik (pno)
Legrand, H.:Andante, w. M. Stilz (vc) — Arcobaleno ▲ SBCD 7300
Legrand, H.:Attila — Arcobaleno ▲ SBCD 7300
Legrand, H.:Concertino Vn, w. R. Muller (vn), J.-J. Werner (cnd), Youth Orch — Arcobaleno ▲ SBCD 7300
Saint-Saëns, C.:Allegro appassionato, w. Emmanauel Gaugué (vc) [arr for vc & pno] — Chamade ▲ 5628
Saint-Saëns, C.:Le Cygne, w. Emmanauel Gaugué (vc) — Chamade ▲ 5628
Saint-Saëns, C.:Romance Vc, w. Emmanauel Gaugué (vc) — Chamade ▲ 5628
Saint-Saëns, C.:Son 1 Vc, w. Emmanauel Gaugué (vc) — Chamade ▲ 5628
Saint-Saëns, C.:Son 2 Vc, w. Emmanauel Gaugué (vc) — Chamade ▲ 5628

Bereau, Marie (vn)—see ORCHESTRAS & ENSEMBLES Manfred String Quartet

Berekovsky, Boris (pno)
Chopin, F.:Études (24) — Teldec ▲ 9031-73129-2 [DDD]
Chopin, F.:Nouvelles études — Teldec ▲ 9031-73129-2 [DDD]

Berends, David (pno)
Berends, D.:15 Exceptions — Albany ▲ TROY 097 [ADD]

Berényi, Bea (fl)
Doppler, A.F.:Music Fl & Pno, w. Ákos Dratsay (fl), László Révész (pno)—for 2 fls & pno composed by A. Doppler:Andante et Rondeau, Op. 25; Fantasie sur des motifs hongrois, Op. 35; Duettino sur des motifs hongrois, Op. 36; Duettino sur motifs Americains, Op. 37; La Sonnambula, Op. 42; for 2 fls & pno composed by A. Doppler & K. Doppler:Souvenir de Prague, Op. 24; Valse di Bravura, Op. 33; Rigoletto-fantasie, Op. 38 *(rec Jan 22-24, 1996)* — Hungaroton ▲ HCD 31648 [DDD]

Berezovsky, Boris (pno)
Rachmaninoff, S.:Con 3 Pno, w. E. Inbal (cnd), Philharmonia Orch — Teldec ▲ 9031-73797-2 ZK
Rachmaninoff, S.:Preludes Pno, Opp 23 & 32—5 Preludes — Teldec ▲ 9031-73797-2 ZK
Rachmaninoff, S.:Son 1 Pno — Teldec ▲ 90890
Rachmaninoff, S.:Variations on a Theme by Chopin — Teldec ▲ 90890
Ravel, M.:Gaspard de la nuit *(rec Berlin, Jan. 1994)* — Teldec ▲ 94539-2 [DDD]
Ravel, M.:Sonatine Pno *(rec Berlin, Jan. 1994)* — Teldec ▲ 94539-2 [DDD]
Ravel, M.:La Valse [trans. for piano] *(rec Berlin, Jan. 1994)* — Teldec ▲ 94539-2 [DDD]
Ravel, M.:Valses nobles et sentimentales *(rec Berlin, Jan. 1994)* — Teldec ▲ 94539-2 [DDD]
Schumann, R.:Davidsbündlertänze — Teldec ▲ 77476-2
Schumann, R.:Son 2 Pno — Teldec ▲ 77476-2
Tchaikovsky, P.:Con 1 Pno, w. D. Kitayenko (cnd), Moscow PO — Teldec ▲ 2292-46010-2 [DDD]

Berg, Bruce (vn)—see ORCHESTRAS & ENSEMBLES Ciompi String Quartet

Berg, Jacob (fl)
Barber, S.:Capricorn Con, w. Peter Bowman (ob), Susan Slaughter (tpt), L. Slatkin (cnd), St. Louis SO *(rec Powell Symphony Hall, St. Louis, MO, May 7, 1995)* — RCA Red Seal ▲ 09026-68283-2 [DDD]
Beethoven, L. van:Serenade Fl, Op. 25, w. M. Rabinovitsj (vn), D. Barnes (va) *(rec 1975-79)* — Vox Box 3-▲ CD3X 3014 [ADD]

Berg, L. P. (ob)—see ORCHESTRAS & ENSEMBLES Oslo Wind Ensemble

Berg, Stefan (va)—see also ORCHESTRAS & ENSEMBLES Fanny Mendelssohn String Quartet
Milhaud, D.:Catalogue de fleurs, w. Ulrike Sonntag (sop), Irmela Nolte (fl), Deborah Marshall (cl), Michael Weigel (bn), Renate Eggebrecht (vn), Friedemann Kupsa (vc), Arpat György (db) *(rec Ludwigsburg, Germany, Jan. 1995)* — Troubadisc ▲ TROCD 01410 [DDD]
Milhaud, D.:Machines agricoles, w. Ulrike Sonntag (sop), Irmela Nolte (fl), Deborah Marshall (cl), Michael Weigel (bn), Renate Eggebrecht (vn), Friedemann Kupsa (vc), Arpat György (db) *(rec Ludwigsburg, Germany, Jan. 1995)* — Troubadisc ▲ TROCD 01410 [DDD]

Bergaglio, Jorge (pno)
Deux Pianos:Mozart, Ravel, Milhaud, Bartók, Guastavino, Piazzolla, w. L. Sainz (pno) — Gallo ▲ CD 800 [ADD]

Bergé, Luc (hn)
Amon, J.A.:Qt Hn, Op. 20/1, w. Arriaga String Quartet — Eufoda ▲ 1207 [DDD]
Hoffmeister, F.A.:Qnt Hn, w. Arriaga String Quartet — Eufoda ▲ 1207 [DDD]
Mozart, W.A.:Qnt Hn, K.407, w. Arriaga String Quartet — Eufoda ▲ 1207 [DDD]
Stich, J.V.:Qt Hn, w. Arriaga String Quartet — Eufoda ▲ 1207 [DDD]

Bergemann, Karl (pno)
Breville, P. de:Sonatine Ob, w. Lajos Lencsés (ob) — Bayer ▲ BR 100227 [DDD]
Dutilleux, H.:Son Ob, w. Lajos Lencsés (ob) — Bayer ▲ BR 100227 [DDD]
Poulenc, F.:Son Ob, w. Lajos Lencsés (ob) — Bayer ▲ BR 100227 [DDD]
Saint-Saëns, C.:Son Ob, w. L. Lencsés (ob) — Bayer ▲ BR 100227 [DDD]

Bergen, Peter van (sax)
Andriessen, L.:Ittrospezione 3, w. Gerard Bouwhuis (pno), Sepp Grotenhuis (pno), Marjan Damsté (db), H. Williams (cnd), Netherlands Ballet Orch *(rec Amsterdam Music Theater, Oct 3-6, 1994)* — Donemus ▲ CV 54 [DDD]

Bergenholz, Inger (pno)
Stolarczyk, W.:Earth Air Fire Water, w. Amalie Malling (pno), John Damgaard (pno), Anne Øland (pno), Teddy Teirup (pno), Friedrich Gürtler (pno), Rosalind Bevan (pno), Poul Rosenbaum (pno), Rodolfo Llambias (pno), Bella Horn–Ribera (pno), Anders Riber (pno), Elisabeth Sigurdsson (pno), Thomas Tronheim (pno), Elsebeth Broderson (pno), Erik Kaltoft (pno), Jørgen Hald Nielsen (pno), Aino Gilemann (pno), Birgit Kjær (pno), Jørgen Thomsen (pno), Gunhild Donslund (pno), Henrik Bo Hansen (pno), Lone Karlsson (pno), Erik Fessel (pno), Lasse Nilsson (pno), Janos Ferenczi (pno), Erik Bach (pno), Axel Momme (pno), Arne de Cros Dich (pno), Sven Micha Slot (pno), Hanne Bramsen Buhl (pno), Lili Olesen (pno), Susannah Carlsson (pno), Ulla Erml (pno), Vagn Sørensen (pno), Leif Greibe (pno), Bodil Krogh (pno), Kirsten Ottosen (pno), Karsten Gylendorf (pno), Bjønr Elkjær (pno), Jacob Bjørn Jensen (pno), Jørgen Kaad (pno), Anne Marie Hjelm (pno), Carl Ulrik Munk Andersen (pno), Poul Lumbye (pno), Oluf Hildebrandt Nielsen (pno), Joachim Olsson (pno), Peter Pade Ramsøe Jacobsen (pno), Astrid Pollmann (pno), Jette Borsch (pno), Kirsten Karlshøj (pno), Maria Teresa Assing (pno), Allan Dahl Hansen (pno), Johan Hugossen (pno), Tine Fenger Pederson (pno), Arne Jørgen Fæø (pno), Anja Høgsted (pno), Anne Sophie Parbo (pno), Inga Lindmark (pno), Teresa Drabik Stathakis (pno), Anne Ruth Ferenczi (pno), Irene Hasager (pno), Yuka Ichikawa (pno), Birgitte Baur (pno), Malene Thastum (pno), Jens E. Rasmussen (pno), Birgitte Zielke (pno), Claus Zielke (pno), Stefan Kasch (pno), Bin Qiao (pno), Inger Johanne Teirup (pno), Lindy Rosborg (pno), Liisa Heininen (pno), David Højer (pno), Ellen Refstrup (pno), Thomas K. Søorensen (pno), Erik Kure (pno), Michael Rauff (pno), Jan beck Eriksson (pno), Tanja Zapolski (pno), Vibeke Skagbo (pno), Pål Eide Lindtner (pno), Ha–Young Sul (pno), Benedicte Palko (pno), Inke Kesseler (pno), Anne Marie Meineche (pno), Sverre Larsen (pno), Kasper Peter Bach (pno), Elisabetta Eliseo (pno), Olga Magieres (pno), Carl Erik Kühl (pno), Thorkild Borup Nielsen (pno), Valeria Zanini (pno), Lars Stenhoft (perc), Dennis Boel (perc), Winnie Dahlgren (perc), Susanne Vind (perc), Claus Byrith (elec), Anne Marie Storm (elec), J. Ribera (cnd) *(rec live, Koldinghaus Castle, Denmark, May 2, 1996)* Danica ▲ DCD 1996

Berger, Angelica (hp)
Mozart, W.A.:Con Fl Hp, w. H. Friedrich (fl), H. Kraus (cnd), Vienna Mozart Ensemble LaserLight ▲ 15 873 [DDD]

Berger, Julius (vc)
Bach, C.P.E.:Con Vc, H.432, w. J. M. Händler (cnd), Dall'Arco CO ebs ▲ ebs 6069 [DDD]
Bach, C.P.E.:Con Vc, H.436, w. J. M. Händler (cnd), Dall'Arco CO ebs ▲ ebs 6069 [DDD]
Bach, C.P.E.:Con Vc, H.439, w. J. M. Händler (cnd), Dall'Arco CO ebs ▲ ebs 6069 [DDD]
Bach, J.S.:Suites Vc, BWV 1007–1012 [1700 5–stringed vc] Orfeo 2–▲ 146852 [DDD]
Bloch, E.:From Jewish Life, w. A. Wit (cnd), Polish National RSO Katowice—Prayer [arr. A. Antonini for cello & orch.] ebs ▲ ebs 6070 [DDD]
Bloch, E.:Schelomo, w. A. Wit (cnd), Polish National RSO Katowice ebs ▲ ebs 6070 [DDD]
Bloch, E.:Voice in the Wilderness, w. A. Wit (cnd), Polish National RSO Katowice ebs ▲ ebs 6070 [DDD]
Boccherini, L.:Cons Vc (comp), w. V. Czarnecki (cnd), Southwest German CO Pforzheim—in B♭, G.482; in C, G.477; in D, G.476; in D, G.479 ebs ▲ ebs 6056 [DDD]
Boccherini, L.:Cons Vc (comp), w. V. Czarnecki (cnd), Southwest German CO Pforzheim—in C, G.481; in D, G.478; in D, G.483; in E♭, G.474 ebs ▲ ebs 6057 [DDD]
Boccherini, L.:Cons Vc (comp), w. V. Czarnecki (cnd), Southwest German CO Pforzheim—in C, G.573; in A, G.475; in E♭, G.deest; in G, G.480 ebs ▲ ebs 6055 [DDD]
Boccherini, L.:Cons Vc (comp), w. V. Czarnecki (cnd), Southwest German CO Pforzheim ebs 3–▲ ebs 6058 [DDD]
Boccherini, L.:Fugues, G.73, w. H.–J. Sung (vc), M. Galling (pno) ebs ▲ EBS 6032 [DDD]
Boccherini, L.:Sons (34) Vc, w. M. Galling (hpd)—Sonatas in A, F & c; Sonata in E♭ for 2 Cellos (w. Hyun–Jung Sung) ebs ▲ ebs 6031 [DDD]
Boccherini, L.:Sons (34) Vc, w. H.–J. Sung (vc), M. Galling (pno)—G.6, 565, 571 & 572 ebs ▲ EBS 6032 [DDD]
Boccherini, L.:Sons (5) Vc & Db, w. A. Posch (vc), J. Bleicher (org), A. Spiri (hpd/pno) ebs ▲ ebs 6011 [DDD]
Bruch, M.:Adagio on a Celtic Theme, w. A. Wit (cnd), Polish National RSO Katowice ebs ▲ ebs 6060 [DDD]
Bruch, M.:Ave Maria Vc, w. A. Wit (cnd), Polish National RSO Katowice ebs ▲ ebs 6060 [DDD]
Bruch, M.:Canzone Vc, w. A. Wit (cnd), Polish National RSO Katowice ebs ▲ ebs 6060 [DDD]
Bruch, M.:Kol Nidrei, w. A. Wit (cnd), Polish National RSO Katowice ebs ▲ ebs 6060 [DDD]
Cage, J.:One[8] Wergo ▲ WER 6288–2
Dittersdorf, K.D. von:Qnts Strs, w. Franz Schubert String Quartet—Nos. 3 & 6 CPO ▲ CPO 999122–2 [DDD]
Enescu, G.:Son Vc, w. Lory Wallfisch (pno) Ebs ▲ 6043 [DDD]
Gubaidulina, S.:In Croce, w. Stefan Hussong (acc) Wergo ▲ WER 6263–2
Gubaidulina, S.:Preludes (10) Vc Wergo ▲ WER 6288–2
Gubaidulina, S.:The Seven Last Words, w. Stefan Hussong (acc), F. Rosensteiner (cnd), CO Diagonal Wergo ▲ WER 6263–2
Killmayer, W.:Brahms–Bildnis, w. S. Mauser (pno), C. Altenburger (vn) CPO ▲ CPO 999020–2 [DDD]
Killmayer, W.:Qt Pno, w. S. Mauser (pno), C. Altenburger (vn), B. Westphal (va) CPO ▲ CPO 999020–2 [DDD]
Killmayer, W.:Qt Strs, w. C. Altenburger (vn), G. Weinmeister (vn), B. Westphal (va) CPO ▲ CPO 999020–2 [DDD]
Killmayer, W.:Trio for 2 Vns & Vc, w. C. Altenburger (vn), G. Weinmeister (vn) CPO ▲ CPO 999020–2 [DDD]
Korngold, E.W.:Con Vc, w. W. A. Albert (cnd), Northwest German PO CPO ▲ CPO 999077–2 [DDD]
Korngold, E.W.:Symphonic Serenade, w. W. A. Albert (cnd), Northwest German PO CPO ▲ CPO 999077–2 [DDD]
Mercadante, S.:La Serenata, w. Andras Adorjan (fl) or Aurèle Nicolet (fl), Han–An Liu (hp), Dieter Savelwski (Eng hn) Tudor ▲ TUD 763 [DDD]
Pfitzner, H.:Duo Vn, w. S. Gawriloff (vn), W.A. Albert (cnd), Bamberg SO CPO ▲ CPO 999079–2 [DDD]
Saint–Saëns, C.:Elévation, ou Communion Vivace 3–▲ E 321 [DDD]
Schulhoff, E.:Sxt Strs, w. G. Kremer (vn), P. Hirschhorn (vn), N. Imai (va), K. Kashkasian (va), D. Geringas (vc) *(rec Lockenhaus Festival, 1986)* ECM New Series 2–▲ 78118–21347–2 [DDD]
Schumann, R.:Con Vc, w. F. Merz (cnd), South Westphalian PO ebs ▲ ebs 6090
Vivaldi, A.:Sons Vc, w. S. J. Bleicher (org)—(10) RV.39–47 & Sonata in A Orfeo 2–▲ 251912 [DDD]

Berger, Kurt (b cl)
Janácek, L.:Youth, w. Aulos Wind Quintet Koch Schwann ▲ CD 310 051 [DDD]

Berger, Kurt (cl)
Stravinsky, I.:Elegy for J.F.K., w. D. Fischer–Dieskau (bar), H. Gruber (cl), K. T. Adler (cl) [E] Orfeo ▲ 015821 [DDD]

Berger, Kurt (fl)
Mozart, W.A.:Cons Fl, w. H. Kraus (cnd), Vienna Mozart Ensemble LaserLight ▲ 15 624 [DDD]

Berger, Melvin (va)
Starer, R.:Con Va, w. J. Snashall (cnd), English CO *(rec 1965)* Vox Box ("The American Composers" series) 2–▲ CDX 5158

Bergeron, Sylvain (instr)—see ORCHESTRAS & ENSEMBLES Da Sonar Ensemble

Bergeron, Sylvain (oud/psaltery/bells)—see ORCHESTRAS & ENSEMBLES La Nef

Berges, Michel (hn)
Corrette, M.:Cons Comiques, w. Georges Barboteu (hn), Gilbert Coursier (hn), Daniel Dubar (hn), J.–F. Paillard (cnd), Jean–François Paillard CO—No. 14 for Hns & Orch [La Choisy] Erato ▲ 94801–2

Bergfelt, Ingemar (pno)
Schubert, Franz:Songs (misc), w. Märta Schéle (sop), Albert Linder (hn)—Auf dem Strome, Op. 119 *(rec Gothenburg Concert Hall, Sweden, May 8, 1976)* BIS ▲ CD 34 [AAD]

Bergh, Arthur (pno)
Opera Arias & Songs, w. A. Kipnis (bass), Frank Bibb (pno), Robert Hood Bowers (cnd) Sony Classical ("Masterworks Heritage" series) ▲ MHK 62354
Schumann, R.:Songs, w. A. Kipnis (bass)—Wanderlied, Op. 35/3; Mondnacht, Op. 39/5 *(rec New York City, 10/24/29)* Music & Arts 2–▲ CD 661 (m) [AAD]

Bergh, Arthur (pno) (cont.)
Strauss, R.:Songs, w. A. Kipnis (bass)—Zueignung, Op. 10/1; Traum durch die Dämmerung, Op. 29/1 *(rec New York City, 10/23/29)* Music & Arts 2–▲ CD 661 (m) [AAD]

Berghout (hp)
Mozart, W.A.:Con Fl Hp, w. H. Barwahser (fl), E. van Beinum (cnd), Royal Concertgebouw Orch Philips ■ 411174–4

Bergman, Borah (pno)
Cage, J.:Pno Music, w. Joshua Pierce (pno), Dorothy Jones (pno), Joseph Kubera (pno), Myra Meldorf (pno), Fumiko Miyanoo (pno)—Music Walk; Jazz Study; Experiences I & II; plus others Wergo ▲ WER 61592

Bergman, L. (pno)
Husa, K.:Serenade, w. Westwood Wind Quintet Crystal ▲ CD 751 [DDD]

Bergman, Marcel (vc)
Beethoven, L. van:Trio 7 Pno, w. O. Volkov (pno), E. Eban (cl) Meridian ▲ CDE 84122
Brahms, J.:Trio Cl, w. E. Eban (cl), A. Volkov (pno) Meridian ▲ CDE 84122
Martinů, B.:Trio Fl, w. Yossi Arnheim (fl), Irit Rub–Levi (pno) Kontrapunkt ▲ KPT 32205

Bergmann, Maria (pno)
Bartók, B.:Son for 2 Pnos, w. H. Rosbaud (pno), W. Grabinger (perc), E. Seiler (perc) *(rec live, 1953)* Music & Arts ▲ CD 627 (m) [AAD]
Faisst, C.:Adagio consolante, w. T. Blees (vc) FSM ▲ FCD 97 728 [DDD]
Farrenc, J.–L.:Son Vc, w. T. Blees (vc) FSM ▲ FCD 97 728 [DDD]
Lebeau, L.A.:Romanze, w. T. Blees (vc) FSM ▲ FCD 97728 [DDD]
Mayer, E.:Son Vc, w. T. Blees (vc) FSM ▲ FCD 97728 [DDD]
Music for Cello & Piano by Female Composers of the 19th Century, w. T. Blees FSM ▲ 97728 [DDD]

Bergmann, Walter (hpd)
Purcell, H.:Music of, w. April Cantelo (sop), Alfred Deller (ct), Maurice Bevan (bar), Neville Marriner (vn), Peter Gibbs (vn), Granville Jones (vn), Desmond Dupré (vl), George Malcolm (hpd)—15 Songs & Airs; Fantasia upon a Ground in d for 3 Violins & Continuo, Z.731; Fantasia upon One Note in F for 5 Viols, Z.745; Hornpipe in e (from The Old Bachelor); Music Lessons 1–12 from Musick's Hand–Maid, Part II; A New Irish Tune, "Lilliburlero," Z.646; Pavan in g for 3 Violins & Bass Viol, Z.752; Sonata in g for Violin & Continuo, Z.780; Sonata No. 9 in F, "Golden Sonata," Z.810 (from Ten Sonatas in Four Parts); Suite in D for Harpsichord, Z.667 Vanguard Classics ("The Bach Guild" series) 2–▲ OVC 2002/03 [ADD]

Bergqvist, Christian (vn)
Aulin, T.:Con 3 Vn, w. O. Kamu (cnd), Swedish RSO Musica Sveciae ▲ MSCD 622
Schnittke, A.:Son 1 Vn, w. R. Pöntinen (pno) BIS ▲ CD 364 [DDD]
Schnittke, A.:Son Vn & CO, w. L. Markiz (cnd), Stockholm CO BIS ▲ CD 537 [DDD]
Shostakovich, D.:Son Vn, w. R. Pöntinen (pno) BIS ▲ CD 364 [DDD]
Stravinsky, I.:Duo Concertant, w. R. Pöntinen (pno)—"Dithyramb" section BIS ▲ CD 364 [DDD]

Bergström, Anne–Maria (fl)
Crumb, G.:Madrigals (4 books), w. A.–M. Mühle (sop), S. Lüannerholm (hp), S. Röjder (db), S. Asikainen (perc)—[Sp] *(rec digital)* BIS ▲ CD 261

Bergström, Lars–Olof (vc)—see ORCHESTRAS & ENSEMBLES Crafoord String Quartet

Berick, Yehonatan (vn)
Samuel, G.:Nocturne on an Impossible Dream, w. Helen Russell (cl), Alonzo Alexander (pno), G. Samuel (cnd), CCM Contemporary Music Ensemble *(rec Corbett Auditorium, Cincinnati Conservatory, OH)* Acoma ▲ GXD 5733 [DDD]

Berix, I. (cl)
Krása, H.:Chamber Music, w. K. Slowioczek (bar), La Roche String Quartet—String Quartet (1923); Tanz for String Trio (1943); Theme & Variations for String Quartet; Three Songs for Baritone, Clarinet, Viola & Cello (1943) Channel Classics ▲ CCS 3792 [DDD]

Berkes, Kálamán (cl)
Krommer, F.:Con Cl, w. K. Berkes (cnd), Nicolaus Esterházy Sinfonia *(rec Scottish Church, Budapest, July 14–17, 1994)* Naxos ▲ 8.553178 [DDD]
Krommer, F.:Cons for 2 Cls, w. K. Berkes (cnd), Nicolaus Esterházy Sinfonia—Op. 35 [w. Kaori Tsutsui (cl)]; Op. 91 [w. Tomoko Takashima (cl)] *(rec Scottish Church, Budapest, July 14–17, 1994)* Naxos ▲ 8.553178 [DDD]
Weber, C.M. von:Grand duo concertant Cl, w. Jenõ Jandó (pno) *(rec Scottish Church, Budapest, Aug. 23–27, 1994)* Naxos ▲ 8.553122 [DDD]
Weber, C.M. von:Intro, Theme & Vars Cl, w. Auer String Quartet *(rec Scottish Church, Budapest, Aug. 23–27, 1994)* Naxos ▲ 8.553122 [DDD]
Weber, C.M. von:Qnt Cl, w. Auer String Quartet *(rec Scottish Church, Budapest, Aug. 23–27, 1994)* Naxos ▲ 8.553122 [DDD]
Weber, C.M. von:Vars on a Theme from *Silvana* Cl, w. Jenõ Jandó (pno) *(rec Scottish Church, Budapest, Aug. 23–27, 1994)* Naxos ▲ 8.553122 [DDD]

Berkey, Jackson (pno)
Beethoven, L. van:Son 30 Pno American Gramaphone ▲ AGCD 381 [DDD]
Berkey, J.:The Mountains & the Sea, w. Soli Deo Gloria Cantorum SDG ▲ SDGCD 92
Debussy, C.:Clair de lune American Gramaphone ▲ AGCD 381 [DDD]
Debussy, C.:Preludes Pno (sels)—four sels. from Book 1:No. 1, "Danseuses de Delphes"; No. 6, "Des pas sur la neige"; No. 8, "La fille aux cheveux de lin"; No. 12, "Minstrels" American Gramaphone ▲ AGCD 381 [DDD]
Plays Beethoven, Debussy & Scriabin American Gramaphone ▲ AGCD 381 [DDD]
Scriabin, A.:Pno Music (misc)—Etude in c#, Op. 2/1; Prelude for the Left Hand Alone (1894); Prelude in e, Op. 11/4 American Gramaphone ▲ AGCD 381 [DDD]

Berki, Sándor (hn)
Beethoven, L. van:Qnt Ob, 3 Hns & Bn, w. Ottó Rácz (ob), Jenõ Keveházi (hn), János Keveházi (hn), József Vajda (bn) Naxos ▲ 8.553090 [DDD]

Berkofsky, Martin (pno)
Bruch, M.:Con for 2 Pnos, w. D. Hogan (pno), L. Herbig (cnd), Berlin SO *(rec 1977)* Allegretto ▲ ACD 8169 [ADD] ■ ACS 8169
Bruch, M.:Fant for 2 Pnos, w. D. Hogan (pno) Allegretto ▲ ACD 8169 [ADD] ■ ACS 8169
Bruch, M.:Swedish Dances, w. D. Hogan (pno) Allegretto ▲ ACD 8169 [ADD] ■ ACS 8169

Berkovsky, Martin (pno)
Hovhaness, A.:Saturn, w. Kate Hurney (sop), Lawrence Sobol (cl) Crystal ▲ CD 808

Berkowitz, Paul (pno)
Schubert, Franz:Fant Pno, D.760, "Wandererfantasie" Meridian ▲ MER 84285 [DDD]
Schubert, Franz:Son Pno, D.537 Meridian ▲ MER 84265 [DDD]
Schubert, Franz:Son Pno, D.568 Meridian ▲ MER 84265 [DDD]
Schubert, Franz:Son Pno, D.575 Meridian ▲ MER 84285 [DDD]
Schubert, Franz:Son Pno, D.664 Meridian ▲ MER 84265 [DDD]
Schubert, Franz:Son Pno, D.784 Meridian ▲ MER 84201 [DDD]
Schubert, Franz:Son Pno, D.840 Meridian ▲ MER 84285 [DDD]
Schubert, Franz:Son Pno, D.845 Meridian ▲ MER 84202 [DDD]
Schubert, Franz:Son Pno, D.850 Meridian ▲ MER 84202 [DDD]
Schubert, Franz:Son Pno, D.894 Meridian ▲ MER 84201 [DDD]
Schumann, R.:Davidsbündlertänze [Schumann's 1st version] Meridian ▲ CDE 84156
Schumann, R.:Kreisleriana [Schumann's 1st version] Meridian ▲ CDE 84156

Berkowitz, Ralph (pno)
Stravinsky, I.:Vn Pno Music, w. E. Shapiro (vn)—Suite d'apres des themes fragments et morceaux de Pergolesi; Variation d'Apollon; Berceuse & Scherzo from "Firebird"; Chanson Russe from "Mavra"; Ballade from "Fairy's Kiss"; Danse Russe from "Pétrouchka" Crystal ▲ CD302
Toch, E.:Son Vn, w. E. Shapiro (vn) Crystal ▲ CD302

Berkowitz, Sheldon (cl)—see also ORCHESTRAS & ENSEMBLES Musicians' Accord members
Kassel, R.:Res Facta, w. W. A. Trigg (percussion) Mode ▲ 23

Berl, P. (pno)
Victoria de los Angeles Live in Concert, w. V. de los Angeles (sop), Pablo Casals (pno) *(rec 1952–60)* VAI Audio 2–▲ VAIA 1025 (m) [ADD]

Berlin, Leo (vn)
Larsson, L.-E.:Concertinos, w. S. Westerberg (cnd), Stockholm PO—No. 8 for Violin (1956) Swedish Society ▲ SCD 1004
Larsson, L.-E.:Con Vn, w. S. Westerberg (cnd), Stockholm PO Swedish Society ▲ SCD 1004
Larsson, L.-E.:En Vintersaga, w. S. Westerberg (cnd), Stockholm PO Swedish Society ▲ SCD 1004
Roman, J.H.:Con Vn, w. Philharmonic Chamber Ensemble, Stockholm Chamber Soloists Swedish Society ▲ SCD 1019
Sjögren, E.:Son 1 Vn, w. G. Erikson (pno) Swedish Society ▲ SCD 1028
Sjögren, E.:Son 2 Vn, w. G. Erikson (pno) Swedish Society ▲ SCD 1028

Berlinski, Herman (org)
Berlinski, H.:Das Gebet Bonhoeffers, w. Nancy Gibson (sop), Matthias Weichert (bass), Olaf Georgi (fl), Bernhard Hentrich (vc), Holger Miersch (cel), Martin Homann (perc), Hans-Christoph Rademann (cnd), Dresden Chamber Choir Vienna Modern Masters ▲ VMM 3027 [DDD]

Berlinsky, Ludmilla (pno)
Mahler, G.:Qt Pno [1 movt], w. Borodin String Quartet Virgin Classics ▲ CDC 59040
Schnittke, A.:Qnt Pno, w. Borodin String Quartet Virgin Classics ▲ CDC 59040

Berlinsky, Vladimir (vc)—see also ORCHESTRAS & ENSEMBLES Borodin String Quartet
Bortnyansky, D.:Qnt Vn, Vl, w. Nina Barshay (vn), Boris Dobrokhotov (vl), Olga Erdeli (hp), Sergey Dizhur (pno) *(rec 1950)* Multisonic ("Russian Treasures" series) ▲ 31 0253
Bortnyansky, D.:Sinf concertante, w. Nina Barshay (vn), Boris Dobrokhotov (vl), Olga Erdeli (hp), Sergey Dizhur (pno), Moscow CO *(rec 1984)* Multisonic ("Russian Treasures" series) ▲ 31 0253

Berman (pno)
Rachmaninoff, S.:Con 3 Pno, w. C. Abbado (cnd), London SO CBS ▲ MYK 37809 [AAD] ■ MYT 37809

Berman, Bart (pno)—see also ORCHESTRAS & ENSEMBLES Duo Beersheva
Martin, F.:Ballade Trbn (or T Sax), w. Stewart Taylor (trbn) Gallo ▲ CD 633 [DDD]

Berman, Boris (pno)
Buxtehude, D.:Prelude & Fugue in d Org [trans Prokofiev for solo piano] Chandos ▲ CHAN 9017 [DDD]
Debussy, C.:Elégie Chandos ▲ CHAN 9294 [DDD]
Debussy, C.:Epigraphes antiques Chandos ▲ CHAN 9294 [DDD]
Debussy, C.:Pno Music (misc)—Pour le piano; Images I & II; Berceuse héroïque; Elégie; Epigraphes antiques (6) Chandos ▲ CHAN 9294 [DDD]
Debussy, C.:Pour le piano Chandos ▲ CHAN 9294 [DDD]
Franck, C.:Son Vn, w. A. Nicolet (fl) [flute-piano arr.] Tudor ▲ 721 [ADD]
Franck, C.:Son Vn, w. A. Nicolet (fl) Titanic ▲ Ti 164 [DDD]
Janácek, L.:Capriccio, w. T. Fischer (cnd), Netherlands Wind Ensemble Chandos ▲ CHAN 9399 [DDD]
Janácek, L.:Concertino Pno, w. T. Fischer (cnd), Netherlands Wind Ensemble Chandos ▲ CHAN 9399 [DDD]
Janácek, L.:March of the Blue Boys, w. *(piccolo player unknown)* Chandos ▲ CHAN 9399 [DDD]
Pärt, A.:Collage on the Theme B-A-C-H, w. *(soloists unknown)*, N. Järvi (cnd), Philharmonia Orch Chandos ▲ CHAN 9134 [DDD]
Pärt, A.:Credo, w. N. Järvi (cnd), Philharmonia Orch, Philharmonia Chorus Chandos ▲ CHAN 9134 [DDD]
Pärt, A.:Wenn Bach Bienen gezüchtet hätte, w. N. Järvi (cnd), Philharmonia Orch Chandos ▲ CHAN 9134 [DDD]
Prokofiev, S.:Cinderella Pno, Op. 95 Chandos ▲ CHAN 9069 [DDD]
Prokofiev, S.:Cinderella Pno, Op. 97 Chandos ▲ CHAN 8976 [DDD]
Prokofiev, S.:Cinderella Pno, Op. 102 Chandos ▲ CHAN 9017 [DDD]
Prokofiev, S.:Cons Pno (comp), w. H. Gutiérrez (pno), N. Järvi (cnd), Royal Concertgebouw Orch Chandos 2-▲ CHAN 8938 [DDD]
Prokofiev, S.:Con 1 Pno, w. N. Järvi (cnd), Royal Concertgebouw Orch Chandos ▲ CHAN 8791 [DDD]
Prokofiev, S.:Con 4 Pno, w. N. Järvi (cnd), Royal Concertgebouw Orch Chandos ▲ CHAN 8791 [DDD]
Prokofiev, S.:Con 5 Pno, w. N. Järvi (cnd), Royal Concertgebouw Orch Chandos ▲ CHAN 8791 [DDD]
Prokofiev, S.:Dumka Pno Chandos ▲ CHAN 9017 [DDD]
Prokofiev, S.:Gavotte Pno, Op. 77bis Chandos ▲ CHAN 9017 [DDD]
Prokofiev, S.:Gavotte Pno [from Sym 1] Chandos ▲ CHAN 9361 [DDD]
Prokofiev, S.:March & Scherzo Pno Chandos ▲ CHAN 8851 [DDD]
Prokofiev, S.:Mélodies, w. M. Lubotsky (vn) Ottavo ▲ OTT 79136 [DDD]
Prokofiev, S.:Mïsli Chandos ▲ CHAN 9069 [DDD]
Prokofiev, S.:Music for Children Chandos ▲ CHAN 8926 [DDD]
Prokofiev, S.:Pno Music (comp) Chandos ▲ CHAN 9119 [DDD]
Prokofiev, S.:Pno Music (misc)—March; Allegretto; Minuet; Waltz; Scherzo; Etude-Scherzo [Juvenilia] Chandos ▲ CHAN 9361 [DDD]
Prokofiev, S.:Pieces Pno, Op. 4 Chandos ▲ CHAN 8851 [DDD]
Prokofiev, S.:Pieces Pno, Op. 4 Chandos ▲ CHAN 8976 [DDD]
Prokofiev, S.:Pieces Pno, Op. 4 Chandos ▲ CHAN 9017 [DDD]
Prokofiev, S.:Pieces Pno, Op. 12 Chandos ▲ CHAN 9069 [DDD]
Prokofiev, S.:Pieces Pno, Op. 52 Chandos ▲ CHAN 8926 [DDD]
Prokofiev, S.:Pieces Pno, Op. 59 Chandos ▲ CHAN 9017 [DDD]
Prokofiev, S.:Pieces Pno, Op. 96 Chandos ▲ CHAN 9017 [DDD]
Prokofiev, S.:Romeo & Juliet Pno Chandos ▲ CHAN 8851 [DDD]
Prokofiev, S.:Sarcasms Chandos ▲ CHAN 8881 [DDD]
Prokofiev, S.:Son 2 Pno Chandos ▲ CHAN 9017 [DDD]
Prokofiev, S.:Son 3 Pno Chandos ▲ CHAN 9069 [DDD]
Prokofiev, S.:Son 4 Pno Chandos ▲ CHAN 8926 [DDD]
Prokofiev, S.:Son 5 Pno Chandos ▲ CHAN 8851 [DDD]
Prokofiev, S.:Son 5 Pno Chandos ▲ CHAN 9361 [DDD]
Prokofiev, S.:Son 6 Pno Chandos ▲ CHAN 9361 [DDD]
Prokofiev, S.:Son 7 Pno Chandos ▲ CHAN 8881 [DDD]
Prokofiev, S.:Son 8 Pno Chandos ▲ CHAN 8976 [DDD]
Prokofiev, S.:Son 10 Pno Chandos ▲ CHAN 9361 [DDD]
Prokofiev, S.:Son Vn, Op. 94bis, w. M. Lubotsky (vn) Ottavo ▲ OTT 79136 [DDD]
Prokofiev, S.:Son 1 Vn, w. M. Lubotsky (vn) Ottavo ▲ OTT 79136 [DDD]
Prokofiev, S.:Sonatinas Pno Chandos ▲ CHAN 9017 [DDD]
Prokofiev, S.:Tales of an Old Grandmother Chandos ▲ CHAN 8881 [DDD]
Prokofiev, S.:Toccata Pno Chandos ▲ CHAN 9361 [DDD]
Prokofiev, S.:Visions fugitives Chandos ▲ CHAN 8881 [DDD]
Prokofiev, S.:Waltzes (suite) Chandos ▲ CHAN 9017 [DDD]
Schnittke, A.:Son 1 Pno Chandos ▲ CHAN 8962 [DDD]
Scriabin, A.:Sons Pno (comp)—Nos. 1-5 Music & Arts ▲ CD 605 [DDD]
Scriabin, A.:Sons Pno (comp)—Nos. 6-10 Music & Arts ▲ CD 621 [DDD]
Scriabin, A.:Sons Pno (comp) Music & Arts 2-▲ CD 865 [DDD]
Stravinsky, I.:Con Pno Ww, w. N. Järvi (cnd), Swiss Romande Orch Chandos ▲ CHAN 9239 [DDD]
Stravinsky, I.:Pno-Rag-Music Chandos ▲ CHAN 8962 [DDD]
Stravinsky, I.:Serenade Pno Chandos ▲ CHAN 8962 [DDD]
Stravinsky, I.:Son Pno Chandos ▲ CHAN 8962 [DDD]
Weber, C.M. von:Sons Pno, w. A. Nicolet (fl) [19th cent. flute-piano arr.]—Son. No. 2 Tudor ▲ 721 [ADD]

Berman, G. (va)—see ORCHESTRAS & ENSEMBLES Kegelstaat Trio Amsterdam

Berman, Lazar (pno)
Beethoven, L. van:Son 8 Vn, w. P. Berman (vn) *(rec live Dec. 16, 1990)* Audiofon ▲ CD 72040
Beethoven, L. van:Son 9 Vn, "Kreutzer", w. P. Berman (vn) Discover International ▲ DICD 920142 [DDD]
Beethoven, L. van:Turkish March Audiofon ▲ CD 72041
Bloch, E.:Nigun, w. P. Berman (vn) *(rec live 12/16/90)* Audiofon ▲ CD 72040
Brahms, J.:Con 1 Pno, w. P. Altrichter (cnd), Prague SO *(rec 1992)* Supraphon ▲ SUP 111832 [DDD]

Berman, Lazar (pno) (cont.)
Brahms, J.:Son 3 Vn, w. P. Berman (vn) *(rec live Dec. 16, 1990)* Audiofon ▲ CD 72040
Liszt, F.:Années de pèlerinage (comp) Deutsche Grammophon 3-▲ 437206-2
Liszt, F.:Harmonies poétiques et religieuses—Funérailles Audiofon ▲ CD 72041
Liszt, F.:Mephisto Waltz 3 Pno Audiofon ▲ CD 72041
Liszt, F.:Pno Music (misc)—Mephisto Waltz; Transcendental Etudes Nos. 8,11 & 12; Dante Son.; Nuages gris; Trauergondel [2nd version]; 3 Schubert Song Transcriptions [Ave Maria, Erlkönig, Gretchen am Spinnrade]; Transcription of the March from Beethoven's Ruins of Athens *(rec live, Bergamo, May 21, 1971)* Arkadia ▲ 922 [ADD]
Liszt, F.:Sonetti del Petrarca Pno—Sonetto 104 Audiofon ▲ CD 72041
Liszt, F.:Transcriptions & Paraphrases—Schubert:Ave Maria; Gretchen am Spinnrade; Erlkönig; Die junge Nonne; Der Leiermann; Tauschung; Wagner—Isoldens Liebestod Audiofon ▲ CD 72041
Mozart, W.A.:Sons Vn Pno (misc), w. P. Berman (vn)—in e, K.304 Discover International ▲ DICD 920142 [DDD]
Mozart, W.A.:Sons Vn Pno (misc), w. P. Berman (vn)—K.304 *(rec live 12/16/90)* Audiofon ▲ CD 72040
Prokofiev, S.:Son Vn, Op. 94bis, w. P. Berman (vn) *(rec live Dec. 16, 1990)* Audiofon ▲ CD 72040
Prokofiev, S.:Son Vn, Op. 94bis, w. P. Berman (vn) Discover International ▲ DICD 920142 [DDD]
Rachmaninoff, S.:Moments musicaux—No. 4 only Audiofon ▲ CD 72041
Tchaikovsky, P.:Con 1 Pno, w. H. von Karajan (cnd), Berlin PO Deutsche Grammophon ("Resonance" series) ▲ 429166-2 [ADD]
Tchaikovsky, P.:Con 1 Pno, w. Y. Temirkanov (cnd), Berlin RSO [original version] Koch Schwann ▲ CD 311 037 [DDD]

Berman, Pavel (vn)
Beethoven, L. van:Son 8 Vn, w. L. Berman (pno) *(rec live Dec. 16, 1990)* Audiofon ▲ CD 72040
Beethoven, L. van:Son 9 Vn, "Kreutzer", w. L. Berman (pno) Discover International ▲ DICD 920142 [DDD]
Bloch, E.:Abodah, "God's Worship", w. A. Epperson (pno) Koch International Classics ▲ KIC 7116 [DDD]
Bloch, E.:Baal Shem, "3 Pictures of Chassidic Life", w. A. Epperson (pno) Koch International Classics ▲ KIC 7116 [DDD]
Bloch, E.:Nigun, w. L. Berman (pno) *(rec live 12/16/90)* Audiofon ▲ CD 72040
Brahms, J.:Con Vn, w. P. Altrichter (cnd), Prague SO *(rec 1992)* Supraphon ▲ SUP 111832 [DDD]
Brahms, J.:Son 3 Vn, w. L. Berman (pno) *(rec live Dec. 16, 1990)* Audiofon ▲ CD 72040
Mozart, W.A.:Sons Vn Pno (misc), w. L. Berman (pno)—K.304 *(rec live 12/16/90)* Audiofon ▲ CD 72040
Mozart, W.A.:Sons Vn Pno (misc), w. L. Berman (pno)—in e, K.304 Discover International ▲ DICD 920142 [DDD]
Prokofiev, S.:Son Vn, Op. 94bis, w. L. Berman (pno) *(rec live Dec. 16, 1990)* Audiofon ▲ CD 72040
Prokofiev, S.:Son Vn, Op. 94bis, w. L. Berman (pno) Discover International ▲ DICD 920142 [DDD]

Berman, R. (vc)
Feldman, Morton:Untitled Composition, w. K. Wieringa (pno) *(rec 1990)* Attacca ▲ Babel 9160-3 [DDD]

Bernabò, Giorgio (fl)
Veracini, F.M.:Sons Fl, w. Alan Curtis (hpd)—Nos. 1-5 & 11-12 *(rec Villa Trissino-Marzotto, Vicenza, Italy, Jan. 15-17, 1994)* Dynamic ▲ CDS 114 [DDD]

Bernar, Miguel (perc)—see ORCHESTRAS & ENSEMBLES Contemporain Duo

Bernard, André (tpt)
Musiques Nuptiales, w. Jean-Louis Gil (org) *(various orchs & cnds)* Forlane ▲ FRL 16754 [DDD]

Bernašek, Václav (vc)—see also ORCHESTRAS & ENSEMBLES Kocian String Quartet
Dvořák, A.:Sextet, w. J. Najnar (va), Talich String Quartet Calliope ▲ CAL 9217 [DDD]
Schulhoff, E.:Duo Vn, w. *(vn soloist unknown)* *(rec 1973-1992)* Praga ▲ PR 255006

Bernathova, Eva (pno)
Bartók, B.:Con 3 Pno, w. K. Ančerl (cnd), Czech PO *(rec 1961-63)* Supraphon ▲ SUP 11 1957 [AAD]

Berne, Tim (br sax)
Hyla, L.:We Speak Etruscan, w. Tim Smith (b cl) *(rec Dec. 18, 1994)* New World ▲ 80491-2

Bernfeld, Jay (vl)—see also ORCHESTRAS & ENSEMBLES Pariser Quartet
Couperin, F.:Pièces de violes avec la bass chifrée, w. S. Sempé (cnd), Capriccio Stravagante *(rec New York, 1993)* Deutsche Harmonia Mundi ▲ 05472-77315-2 [DDD]
Couperin, F.:La Sultane, w. S. Sempé (cnd), Capriccio Stravagante *(rec New York, 1993)* Deutsche Harmonia Mundi ▲ 05472-77315-2 [DDD]
Couperin, F.:La Superbe, w. S. Sempé (cnd), Capriccio Stravagante *(rec New York, 1993)* Deutsche Harmonia Mundi ▲ 05472-77315-2 [DDD]
Couperin, F.:Vl Music, w. S. Sempé (cnd), Capriccio Stravagante—Le Dodo ou l'amour au berceau *(rec New York, 1993)* Deutsche Harmonia Mundi ▲ 05472-77315-2 [DDD]
Italian Arias & Cantatas, w. J. Bowman (ct), Skip Sempé (org) *(rec 10/87)* Arion ▲ ARN 68046 [DDD]

Bernhardt, Lynn (timp/military dr)—see ORCHESTRAS & ENSEMBLES New York Trumpet Ensemble

Berni, Monica (fl)
Bottesini, P.:Andante e Tema con variazioni, w. Ciro Scarponi (cl), Rome Solisti *(rec Rome, 1996)* musicaimmagine ▲ MR 10031
Mercadante, S.:Qts Fl, w. Rome Solisti—in a *(rec Rome, 1996)* musicaimmagine ▲ MR 10031
Petrassi, G.:Serenata Fls, w. A. Vismara (va), F. Fraioli (db), V. de Vita (pno), M. Vinci (perc) Bongiovanni ▲ GB 5534 [DDD]

Bernier, Sylvia (pno)
Musiques De Salon, w. Guy Penson (pno) Ricercar ▲ RIC 147135 [ADD]

Bernold, Philippe (fl)
Schubert, Franz:Intro & Vars Fl on "Tröckne Blumen", w. Laurent Cabasso (pno) Harmonia Mundi France ▲ HMN 911535
Weber, C.M. von:Sons Vn, w. Laurent Cabasso (pno)—1 Son. for fl & pno on Schubert theme Harmonia Mundi France ▲ HMN 911535
Weber, C.M. von:Trio Fl, w. Jean-Guihen Queyras (vc), Laurent Cabasso (pno) Harmonia Mundi France ("Les Nouveaux Interprètes" series) ▲ HMN 911535

Bernstein, Leonard (pno)
Beethoven, L. van:Con 1 Pno, w. L. Bernstein (cnd), New York PO Sony Classical ▲ SMK 47519 [ADD]
Bernstein, L.:Anniversaries (7) Pno *(rec 1947)* RCA Gold Seal ▲ 09026-60915-2 ■ 09026-60915-4
Copland, A.:Son Pno *(rec before 1955)* RCA Gold Seal ▲ 09026-60915-2 ■ 09026-60915-4 (CrO2)
Gershwin, G.:An American in Paris, w. L. Bernstein (cnd), New York PO Polskie Nagrania ▲ PNCD 150 [ADD]
Gershwin, G.:Rhap in Blue, w. L. Bernstein (cnd), Columbia SO CBS ▲ MYK 37242 [ADD] ■ MYT 37242
Gershwin, G.:Rhap in Blue, w. L. Bernstein (cnd), Columbia SO CBS ▲ MLK 39454 ■ PMT 39454
Gershwin, G.:Rhap in Blue, w. L. Bernstein (cnd), Columbia SO *(rec Brooklyn, June 23, 1959)* Sony Classical ("Bernstein:The Royal Edition" series) ▲ SMK 47529 [ADD] Δ SM 47529 [ADD]
Gershwin, G.:Rhap in Blue, w. L. Bernstein (cnd), Los Angeles PO Deutsche Grammophon ("3D Classics" series) ▲ 427806-2 [DDD]
Gershwin, G.:Rhap in Blue, w. L. Bernstein (cnd), Los Angeles PO Deutsche Grammophon ▲ 431048-2 [DDD]
Gershwin, G.:Rhap in Blue, w. L. Bernstein (cnd), Columbia SO CBS ▲ MK 42264 [ADD]
Gershwin, G.:Rhap in Blue, w. L. Bernstein (cnd), Columbia SO Polskie Nagrania ▲ PNCD 150 [ADD]
Mahler, G.:Lieder eines fahrenden Gesellen, w. D. Fischer-Dieskau (bar) [G] *(rec live at Lincoln Center, New York, 11/8/68)* Myto ▲ 1 MCD 89008 (m) [ADD]
Mahler, G.:Songs from Rückert, w. D. Fischer-Dieskau (bar)—4 songs:Blicke mir nicht in die Lieder; Ich atmet' einen Linden Duft; Ich bin der Welt abhanden; Um Mitternacht [G] *(rec live at Lincoln Center, New York, 11/8/68)* Myto ▲ 1 MCD 89008 (m) [ADD]

▲ = CD ♦ = Enhanced CD Δ = MD ■ = Cassette Tape □ = DCC

Bernstein, Leonard (pno) (cont.)
Mozart, W.A.:Con 15 Pno, w. L. Bernstein (cnd), Vienna PO
London ("The Classic Sound" series) ▲ 448570-2
Mozart, W.A.:Con 25 Pno, w. L. Bernstein (cnd), Israel PO Sony Classical ▲ SMK 47519 [ADD]
Ravel, M.:Con in G Pno, w. L. Bernstein (cnd), Columbia SO *(rec 1958)*
Sony Classical ("Bernstein:The Royal Edition" series) ▲ SMK 47571 [ADD]
Shostakovich, D.:Con 2 Pno, w. L. Bernstein (cnd), New York PO *(rec Jan. 6, 1958)*
Sony Classical ▲ SMK 47618 [ADD]
Strauss (I), Joh.:Radetzky March, w. L. Bernstein, New York PO *(rec Oct. 20, 1970)*
Sony Classical ▲ SMK 47626 [ADD]

Bernstein, Walter-Heinz (hpd)
Bach, J.S.:Anna Magdalena Bach Notebook, w. Burkhardt, Schreier, H. Grüss (cnd), Capella Fidicinia Leipzig Capriccio ▲ CDC 10031 [DDD]
Zelenka, J.D.:Trio Sons Obs, w. B. Glaetzner (ob), I. Goritzki (ob), K. Sønstevold (bn), A. Beyer (vn), S. Pank (vl) Berlin Classics 2-▲ BER 1070 [DDD]
Zelenka, J.D.:Trio Sons Obs, w. Burkhard Glaetzer (ob), Ingo Goritzki (ob), Knut Sønstevold (bn), Achim Beyer (vn), Siegfried Pank (va) Berlin Classics 4-▲ BER 1150 [DDD]

Béroff, Michel (perc)
Schoenberg, A.:Trans Chamber Ensemble, w. Hakon Ausbö (harm), Isabelle Berteletti (perc), Louise Bessette (pno), Marc Marder (db), Paul Meyer (cl), Michel Moraguès (fl), Arditti String Quartet—Busoni:Berceuse élégiaque (1920); Mahler:Songs of a Wayfarer (1920) [w. Jean-Luc Chaignaud (baritone)]; Joh. Strauss:Kaiserwalzer (1925); Roses from the South (1921)
Montaigne ▲ MO 789011 [DDD]

Béroff, Michel (pno)
Bizet, G.:Jeux d'enfants, w. Jean-Philippe Collard (pno) EMI Classics ▲ CDC 55347
Debussy, C.:Pno Music (complete solo)—Préludes [premier livre]; D'un cahier d'esquisses ["From a Sketchbook"]; Morceau de concouours; Hommage à Haydn; Le petit nègre; Children's Corner
Denon ▲ DEN 78847 [DDD]
Debussy, C.:Pno Music (complete solo)—Préludes [deuxième livre]; La plus que lente ["As Slow as Possible"]; Berceuse héroïque; 6 épigraphes antiques Denon ▲ DEN 78848 [DDD]
Debussy, C.:Prélude à l'après-midi d'un faune, w. Jean-Philippe Collard (pno) [arr 2 pianos]
EMI Classics ▲ CDC 55347
Dukas, P.:L'Apprenti sorcier, w. Jean-Philippe Collard (pno) [arr 2 pianos] EMI Classics ▲ CDC 55347
Prokofiev, S.:Cons Pno (comp), w. K. Masur (cnd), Leipzig Gewandhaus Orch
EMI Classics 2-▲ CDZB 62542
Prokofiev, S.:Visions fugitives EMI Classics 2-▲ CDZB 62542
Ravel, M.:Con Pno (left hand), w. C. Abbado (cnd), London SO
Deutsche Grammophon ▲ 423665-2 [DDD]
Ravel, M.:Rapsodie espagnole, w. Jean-Philippe Collard (pno) [arr 2 pianos]
EMI Classics ▲ CDC 55347
Stravinsky, I.:Pno Music, w. S. Ozawa (cnd), Orch de Paris EMI Classics 2-▲ CDZB 67276
Szymanowski, K.:Caprices, w. Ulf Hoelscher (vn) *(rec West German Radio Studio 2, Cologne, May 18–20, 1982)* EMI Classics ▲ CDC 55169 [DDD]
Szymanowski, K.:Myths, w. Ulf Hoelscher (vn) *(rec West German Radio Studio 2, Cologne, May 18–20, 1982)* EMI Classics ▲ CDC 55169 [DDD]
Szymanowski, K.:Notturno e Tarantella, w. Ulf Hoelscher (vn) *(rec West German Radio Studio 2, Cologne, May 18–20, 1982)* EMI Classics ▲ CDC 55169 [DDD]
Szymanowski, K.:Romance, w. Ulf Hoelscher (vn) *(rec West German Radio Studio 2, Cologne, May 18–20, 1982)* EMI Classics ▲ CDC 55169 [DDD]

Berofsky, Aaron (vn)—see also ORCHESTRAS & ENSEMBLES Chester String Quartet
Kernis, A.J.:Mozart en Route, w. David Harding (va), Tom Rosenberg (vc) *(rec Manhattan Center Studios, New York, May 31–June 3, 1995)* New Albion ♦ NA 083CD

Berrette, Jean-Michel (vn)—see ORCHESTRAS & ENSEMBLES Paris String Quartet

Berrios, Steven (perc)
So Many Stars, w. K. Battle (sop), Antonio Hart (sax), Grover Washington Jr (sax), Tom Harrell (flgl), James Carter (b cl), Cyrus Chestnut (pno), Jon Herrington (gtr), Romero Lubambo (gtr), Ira Coleman (elec bass), Christian McBride (elec bass), Cyro Baptista (perc), *(rec Hit Factory, Clinton Recording Studios, R.P.M. Sound Studios, Unique Recording Studios, Power Station)*
Sony Classical ▲ SK 68473 [DDD]

Berry, George (bn)
Beethoven, L. van:Qnt Ob, 3 Hns & Bn, w. A. Simon (ob), R. Woodhams (hn), G. Stilfies (hn), R. Pandolfi (bn) *(rec 1975–79)* Vox Box 3-▲ CD3X 3014 [ADD]
Mozart, W.A.:Qnt Pno, K.452, w. W. Klien (pno), P. Bowman (ob), G. Silfies (cl), R. Pandolfi (hn) *(rec 1975–79)* Vox Box 3-▲ CD3X 3014 [ADD]

Berry, Richard (hn)
Danzi, F.:Sextet Ob, w. Michael Thompson (hn), John Bradburg (cl), Robert Hill (cl), John Price (bn), Philip Tarlton (bn)—version for Harmonie ensemble *(rec St. Paul's Church, Rusthall, Kent, England, June 1994)* Naxos ▲ 8.553076 [DDD]

Berteletti, Isabella (perc)
Schoenberg, A.:Trans Chamber Ensemble, w. Hakon Ausbö (harm), Michel Béroff (perc), Louise Bessette (pno), Marc Marder (db), Paul Meyer (cl), Michel Moraguès (fl), Arditti String Quartet—Busoni:Berceuse élégiaque (1920); Mahler:Songs of a Wayfarer (1920) [w. Jean-Luc Chaignaud (baritone)]; Joh. Strauss:Kaiserwalzer (1925); Roses from the South (1921)
Montaigne ▲ MO 789011 [DDD]

Berteletti, Isabella (prepared pno)
Cage, J.:Amores, w. Hêlios Percussion Quartet Wergo ▲ WER 6203-2 [DDD]
Cage, J.:First Construction, w. P. Chaignon (additional perc), Hêlios Percussion Quartet
Wergo ▲ WER 6203-2 [DDD]
Cage, J.:She Is Asleep, w. M. Viard (voice), Hêlios Percussion Quartet Wergo ▲ WER 6203-2 [DDD]

Berthiaume, Gerald (cel)
Read, G.:Chamber Music, w. Janet Packer (vn), Leslie Stratton Norris (hp), Barbara Harbach (hpd), Joseph Holt (pno), Howard Karp (pno), Boston Composers String Quartet—5 Aphorisms, Op. 150; Son. da Chiesa, Op. 61; Sonoric Fant. No. 1, Op. 102; Qt. 1 Strings, Op. 100
Northeastern ▲ NOR 253 [DDD]
Read, G.:Sonoric Fantasia 1, w. Leslie Stratton Norris (hp), Barbara Harbach (hpd) *(rec KWSU-TV Studios, Pullman, WA, Nov. 1993)* Northeastern ("Classical Arts, Contemporary" series) ▲ NR 253

Berthiaume, Gerald (pno)
Jolivet, A.:Chant de Linos, w. Ann Marie Yasinitsky (fl) Vienna Modern Masters ▲ VMM 2013 [DDD]
Starer, R.:At Home Alone Albany ▲ TROY 205 [DDD]
Starer, R.:Caprices Albany ▲ TROY 205 [DDD]
Starer, R.:Electric Church Albany ▲ TROY 205 [DDD]
Starer, R.:Excursions for a Pianist Albany ▲ TROY 205 [DDD]
Starer, R.:Israeli Sketches Albany ▲ TROY 205 [DDD]
Starer, R.:Sketches in Color Albany ▲ TROY 205 [DDD]
Starer, R.:Son 1 Pno Albany ▲ TROY 205 [DDD]

Berthier, Jacques (org)
Flute & Organ, w. Brother Hubert (fl) Studio SM ▲ 12 17 48

Berthold, Beate (pno)
Banter, H.:Rhap Intermezzo, w. M. Jurowski (cnd), Northwest German PO *(rec Cologne Phil Hall, Mar 1995)* Marco Polo ▲ 8.223860 [DDD]

Berths, Vera (vn)
Keulen, G. van:Con Vn, w. G. van Keulen (cnd), Omroep Orch Donemus ▲ CV 33

Bertoldi, Francesco (pno)
Franck, C.:Fants Pno—Fantasies (2) on arias from Dalayrac's opera "Gulistan," Op. 11 & Op. 12; Fantasy in D, Op. 14; Fantasy on two Air Polonais, Op. 15; Great Fantasy, Op. 19
Dynamic ▲ CD 95 [DDD]
Glinka, M.:Pno Music (comp) Nuova Era ▲ NUO 7232 [DDD]
Weber, C.M. von:Sons Vn, w. Lorenzo Bertoldi (vn)
Enterprise ("Tiziano" series) ▲ ENT TZ 96006 [DDD]

Bertoldi, Francesco (pno) (cont.)
Weber, C.M. von:Vars on the Air de ballet from Vogler's *Castor et Pollux* Pno, J.40
Enterprise ("Tiziano" series) ▲ ENT TZ 96006 [DDD]
Weber, C.M. von:Vars on a Norwegian Air Vn Enterprise ("Tiziano" series) ▲ ENT TZ 96006 [DDD]

Bertoldi, Lorenzo (vn)
Weber, C.M. von:Sons Vn, w. Francesco Bertoldi (pno)
Enterprise ("Tiziano" series) ▲ ENT TZ 96006 [DDD]

Bertram, Simon (org)
French Romantic Organ Music, w. Bertram, Simon (org)
Unicorn-Kanchana ("Souvenir" series) ▲ UKCD 2070

Bertucci, Aurelio (vc)
Ragazzi, A.:Con Grosso, w. Marco Rogliano (vn), Andrea Guerrini (vn), Eduardo Pitone (va), Antonella Cristiano (hpd), I. Caiazza (cnd), I Solisti Partenopei *(rec Mar 1996)* Kicco Classics ▲ 396 [DDD]

Besch, Eckart (pno)
Ligeti, G.:Trio Hn, Vn & Pno, w. H. Baumann (hn), S. Gawriloff (vn) Wergo ▲ WER 60100-50 [DDD]

Beschi, Emanuele (va)—see ORCHESTRAS & ENSEMBLES Flautarte Quartet

Bespalov, Nikolai (vc)
Mozart, W.A.:Adagio & Rondo Glass Armonica, w. A. Atanasov (org), L. Oshavkova (fl), C. T. Kasmetski (ob), Ognian Stantchev (va) Divertimento ▲ DIV 31020 [DDD]

Bessette, Louise (pno)
Foley, D.:Oiseaux excentriques CBC ("Musica Viva" series) ▲ MVCD 1064 [DDD]
Hétu, J.:Petite Suite CBC ("Musica Viva" series) ▲ MVCD 1064 [DDD]
Ives, C.:Son 2 Pno *(rec live, 12/87)* CBC ("Musica Viva" series) ▲ MVCD 1041 [DDD]
Louie, A.:Music (set of 4 pieces) Pno CBC ("Musica Viva" series) ▲ MVCD 1064 [DDD]
Messiaen, O.:Regards sur l'Enfant Jésus—Nos. 11, 14 & 20 *(rec live 12/87)*
CBC ("Musica Viva" series) ▲ MVCD 1041 [DDD]
Schoenberg, A.:Trans Chamber Ensemble, w. Hakon Ausbö (harm), Michel Béroff (perc), Isabelle Berteletti (perc), Marc Marder (db), Paul Meyer (cl), Michel Moraguès (fl), Arditti String Quartet—Busoni:Berceuse élégiaque (1920); Mahler:Songs of a Wayfarer (1920) [w. Jean-Luc Chaignaud (baritone)]; Joh. Strauss:Kaiserwalzer (1925); Roses from the South (1921)
Montaigne ▲ MO 789011 [DDD]
Schoenberg, A.:Weihnachtsmusik, w. Hakon Ausbö (harm), Arditti String Quartet members
Montaigne ▲ MO 789011 [DDD]
Smith, L.C.:Zart CBC ("Musica Viva" series) ▲ MVCD 1064 [DDD]
Southam, A.:Rivers—Set 2, "The Bells" Nos. 1, 3 & 4; Set 3, "Rivers" No. 5
CBC ("Musica Viva" series) ▲ MVCD 1064 [DDD]

Bessler, B. (vn)
Beethoven, L. van:Vars on Grétry's romance "Un fièvre brûlante", WoO 72, w. M. Grauwels (fl), C. Springuel (va), G. H. (hp), Y. Stormes (gtr) Syrinx ▲ 94101 [DDD]
Spohr, L.:Son 4 Vn, w. M. Grauwels (fl), C. Springuel (va), G. H. (hp), Y. Stormes (gtr)
Syrinx ▲ 94101 [DDD]

Bessonnet, Georges (org)
Saint-Saëns, C.:Fants Org [Grande Org, Cavaillé-Coll, Cathédrale d'Orléans]—Op. 157
Accord ▲ ACD 243062 [DDD]
Saint-Saëns, C.:Fant Org, Op. 101 [Grandes Org, Cathédrale d'Orléans] Adda ▲ ADD 581279 [DDD]
Saint-Saëns, C.:Improvisations [Grande Org, Cavaillé-Coll, Cathédrale d'Orléans]
Accord ▲ ACD 243062 [DDD]
Saint-Saëns, C.:Improvisations Org [Grandes Org, Cathédrale d'Orléans] Adda ▲ ADD 581279 [DDD]
Saint-Saëns, C.:Preludes & Fugues, Op. 99 [Grande Org, Cavaillé-Coll, Cathédrale d'Orléans]
Accord ▲ ACD 243062 [DDD]
Saint-Saëns, C.:Preludes & Fugues, Op. 99 [Grandes Org, Cathédrale d'Orléans]
Adda ▲ ADD 581279 [DDD]

Best, Roger (va)
Britten, H.:Lachrymae, w. W. Boughton (cnd), English String Orch Nimbus ▲ NI 5025
Debussy, C.:Son Fl, w. McNicol (fl), Kelly (hp) Chandos ▲ CHAN 8385 [ADD]
Vaughan Williams, R.:Flos Campi, w. S. Darlington (cnd), English String Orch, Christ Church Cathedral Choir Oxford Nimbus ▲ NI 5166 [DDD]

Beths, Gijs (vn)
Beethoven, L. van:Ländler Dances, WoO 15, w. V. Beths (vn), A. Bijlsma (vc) *(rec 6/90)*
Channel Classics ▲ CCS 1491 [DDD]

Beths, Vera (vn)—see also ORCHESTRAS & ENSEMBLES L'Archibudelli
Antheil, G.:Son 1 Vn, w. Reinbert de Leeuw (pno) Montaigne ▲ MO 782022 [DDD]
Antheil, G.:Son 2 Vn, w. Reinbert de Leeuw (pno) Montaigne ▲ MO 782022 [DDD]
Antheil, G.:Son 4 Vn, w. Reinbert de Leeuw (pno) Montaigne ▲ MO 782022 [DDD]
Beethoven, L. van:Folksong Arrs, w. M. Kweksilber (sop), S. Hoogland (pno), A. Bijlsma (vc)—Irish Songs, WoO 152, Nos. 1,5,8 & 11; Scottish Songs, Op. 108, Nos. 2,3,5,7,8,17,20 & 24 [E] *(rec 6/90)* Channel Classics ▲ CCS 1491 [DDD]
Beethoven, L. van:Ländler Dances, WoO 15, w. G. Beths (vn), A. Bijlsma (vc) *(rec 6/90)*
Channel Classics ▲ CCS 1491 [DDD]
Beethoven, L. van:Trio 10 Pno, w. S. Hoogland, A. Bijlsma *(rec June 1990)*
Channel Classics ▲ CCS 1491 [DDD]
Dotzauer, F.:Canon for 2 Vns, w. Lisa Rautenberg (vn) *(rec New York City, Jan. 19–22, 1994)*
Sony Classical ("Vivarte" series) ▲ SK 64307 [DDD]
Dotzauer, F.:Qt Strs, w. Jody Gatwood (vn), Lisa Rautenberg (va), Anner Bylsma (vc) *(rec New York City, Jan. 19–22, 1994)* Sony Classical ▲ SK 66259 [DDD]
Dotzauer, F.:Qnt Strs, w. Jody Gatwood (vn), Lisa Rautenberg (va), Anner Bylsma (vc), Kenneth Slowik (vc) *(rec New York City, Jan. 19–22, 1994)* Sony Classical ("Vivarte" series) ▲ SK 64307 [DDD]
Escher, R.:Son Vn, w. Stanley Hoogland (pno) *(rec Sept 4, 1984)* Donemus ▲ CV 47 [ADD]
Haydn, J.:Trios Pno, Vn & Vc, w. Robert Levin (pno), Anner Bylsma (vc)—No. 25 in C, H.XV:27; No. 26 in E, H.XV:28; No. 30 in E♭, H.XV:30 *(rec Sept. 2–5, 1992)* Sony Classical ▲ SK 53120 [DDD]
Mozart, W.A.:Concertone Vns, w. R. Kussmaul (vn), Amsterdam Mozart Players *(rec Mar. 1991)*
Channel Classics ▲ CCS 3992 [DDD]
Mozart, W.A.:Qts Cl, w. C. Neidich (cl), J. Kussmaul (va), A. Bylsma (vc)—in B♭ after K.378
Sony Classical ("Vivarte" series) ▲ SK 53366 [DDD]
Mozart, W.A.:Qnt Cl, K.581, w. C. Neidich (cl), J. Kussmaul (va), A. Bylsma (vc)
Sony Classical ("Vivarte" series) ▲ SK 53366 [DDD]
Mozart, W.A.:Sinf concertante Vn, K.Anh.104, w. J. Kussmaul (va), A. Bulsma (vc) *(rec Mar. 1991)*
Channel Classics ▲ CCS 3992 [DDD]
Mozart, W.A.:Trio Cl, K.498, w. C. Neidich (vn), J. Kussmaul (va), A. Bylsma (vc)
Sony Classical ("Vivarte" series) ▲ SK 53366 [DDD]
Schubert, Franz:Rondo Vn, D.438, w. et al. Sony Classical ("Vivarte" series) ▲ SK 46669
Schubert, Franz:Trio 1 Pno, w. Jos van Immerseel (pno), Anner Blysma (vc)
Sony Classical ("Vivarte" series) ▲ SK 62695
Schubert, Franz:Trio 2 Pno, w. Jos van Immerseel (pno), Anner Blysma (vc)
Sony Classical ("Vivarte" series) ▲ SK 62695
Tchaikovsky, P.:Souvenir d'un lieu cher, w. A. Lascae (cnd), Arion Ensemble [trans. for solo vn & strings A. Lascae] Partridge ▲ 1126-2 [DDD]
Ustvolskaya, G.:Duet Vn, w. Reinbert de Leeuw (pno) *(rec De Vereeniging, Nijmegen, Oct. 5 & 6, 1991)*
Hat Hut ("NOW." series) ▲ hat ART CD 6115 [DDD]
Ustvolskaya, G.:Trio Cl, w. Harmen de Boer (cl), Reinbert de Leeuw (pno) *(rec De Vereeniging, Nijmegen, Oct. 5 & 6, 1991)* Hat Hut ("NOW." series) ▲ hat ART CD 6115 [DDD]

Bettelheim, Dorf (vn)
Schumann, R.:Qnt Pno, w. S. Rhodes (va), Beaux Arts Trio Philips ▲ 420791-2 [ADD]

Betteridge, Stephen (pno)
An Album of Victorian Song, Vol. 1, w. P. Allanson (bar) Symposium ▲ SYM 1074
Harrison, M.:The May Song, w. Peter Allanson (bar) *(rec 1989)* Symposium ▲ 1075
Horder, M.:Songs (40), w. Winifred Soutter (sop), Peter Allanson (bar), Carl Murray (bar), Gordon Kirkwood (pno) Symposium ▲ 1039

Bettez, M. (bn)—see ORCHESTRAS & ENSEMBLES Pentaèdre Ensemble

INSTRUMENT.

Bettridge, J. (bgp)
Mozart, L.:Bauernhochzeit, w. P. Freeman (cnd), Chicago Sinfonietta Centaur ▲ CRC 2062 [DDD]
Betz, Karl (pno)
Janácek, L.:In the Mists Koch Schwann ▲ 310038 [DDD]
Schubert, Franz:German Dances Pno, D.790 Koch Schwann ▲ CD 310066 [ADD]
Schubert, Franz:Ländler Pno—16 selections from 17 Ländler D.145 & Wiener Damen-ändler D.734 Koch Schwann ▲ CD 310066 [ADD]
Schubert, Franz:Waltzes Pno—34 sels. from 12 Waltzes D.145, 34 Valses sentimentales D.779 & 12 Valses nobles D.969; plus Waltz ina, D.366, No. 3 Koch Schwann ▲ CD 310066 [ADD]
Beuckels, Patrick (fl)
Telemann, G.P.:Con in F Rcr Fl, w. F. de Roos (rcr), Ricercar Consort Ricercar ▲ RIC 44021 [DDD]
Beukels, Patrick (trns fl)
Bach, W.F.:Duets Fls, F.54-59, w. Daniele Etienne (trns fl) *(rec 1992)* Ricercar 2-▲ 089125/26
Bach, W.F.:Trios Fls, F.47-49, w. Daniele Etienne (trns fl), Guy Penson (hpd) *(rec 1992)* Ricercar 2-▲ 089125/26
Bevan, Paul (slide tpt/rcr/pipe & tabor/perc)—see ORCHESTRAS & ENSEMBLES Dufay Collective
Bevan, Rosalind (pno)—see also ORCHESTRAS & ENSEMBLES Danish Trio
Nielsen, C.:Songs, w. Jøorgen Klint (bass)—Sang bag Ploven; I Aften; Balladen om Bjøornen; Den blinde Spillemand [w. Jens Schou (cl)]; Solnedgang; I Seraillets Have; Til Asali; Irmelin Rose; Har Dagen sanket al sin Sorg; Jeronimus Sang; Jeg baerer med Smil min Byrde; Jens Vejmand; Se dig ud en Sommerdag; Det bødes der for; Det villeste; Nu lyser løov i Lunde; Min lille Fugl; Vi Sletternes Sønner; Jeg ved en Laerkerede; Den Danske Sang; Danmark i Tusind År; Forunderligt at sige *(rec Nov 1987)* Paula ▲ PACD 56
Olsen, P.R.:Concertino Cl, w. Jens Schou (cl), Peder Elbaek (vn), Verner Skovlund (va), Svend Winsløv (vc) *(rec PAULA's Recording Hall, 1984)* Paula ▲ PACD 36 [AAD]
Olsen, P.R.:Images Paula ▲ PACD 76 [DAD]
Olsen, P.R.:Medardus Paula ▲ PACD 76 [DAD]
Olsen, P.R.:Nocturnes Paula ▲ PACD 76 [DAD]
Olsen, P.R.:Preludes Paula ▲ PACD 76 [DAD]
Olsen, P.R.:Serenade Vn, w. Peder Elbaek (vn) *(rec PAULA's Recording Hall, 1984)* Paula ▲ PACD 36 [AAD]
Olsen, P.R.:Trio II Pno, w. Peder Elbaek (vn), Svend Winsløv (vc) *(rec PAULA's Recording Hall, 1984)* Paula ▲ PACD 36 [AAD]
Stolarczyk, W.:Earth Air Fire Water, w. Amalie Malling (pno), John Damgaard (pno), Anne Øland (pno), Teddy Teirup (pno), Friedrich Gürtler (pno), Poul Rosenbaum (pno), Rodolfo Llambias (pno), Bella Horn-Ribera (pno), Anders Riber (pno), Elisabeth Sigurdsson (pno), Thomas Tronheim (pno), Elsebeth Broderson (pno), Erik Kaltoft (pno), Jørgen Hald Nielsen (pno), Aino Gilemann (pno), Birgit Kjær (pno), Jørgen Thomsen (pno), Gunhild Donslund (pno), Henrik Bo Hansen (pno), Lone Karlsson (pno), Erik Fessel (pno), Lasse Nilsson (pno), Janos Ferenczi (pno), Erik Bach (pno), Axel Momme (pno), Arne de Cros Dich (pno), Sven Micha Slot (pno), Hanne Bramsen Buhl (pno), Lili Olesen (pno), Susannah Carlsson (pno), Ulla Erml (pno), Vagn Sørensen (pno), Leif Greibe (pno), Bodil Krogh (pno), Kirsten Ottosen (pno), Inger Bergenholz (pno), Karsten Gylendorf (pno), Bjønr Elkjær (pno), Jacob Bjørn Jensen (pno), Jørgen Kaad (pno), Anne Marie Hjelm (pno), Carl Ulrik Munk Andersen (pno), Poul Lumbye (pno), Oluf Hildebrandt Nielsen (pno), Joachim Olsson (pno), Peter Pade Ramsøe Jacobsen (pno), Astrid Pollmann (pno), Jette Borsch (pno), Kirsten Karlshøj (pno), Maria Teresa Assing (pno), Allan Dahl Hansen (pno), Johan Hugossen (pno), Tine Fenger Pederson (pno), Arne Jørgen Fæø (pno), Anja Høgsted (pno), Anne Sophie Parbo (pno), Inga Lindmark (pno), Teresa Drabik Stathakis (pno), Anne Ruth Ferenczi (pno), Irene Hasager (pno), Yuka Ichikawa (pno), Birgitte Baur (pno), Malene Thastum (pno), Jens E. Rasmussen (pno), Birgitte Zielke (pno), Claus Zielke (pno), Stefan Kasch (pno), Bin Qiao (pno), Inger Johanne Teirup (pno), Lindy Rosborg (pno), Liisa Heininen (pno), David Højer (pno), Ellen Refstrup (pno), Thomas K. Søorensen (pno), Erik Kure (pno), Michael Rauff (pno), Jan beck Eriksson (pno), Tanja Zapolski (pno), Vibeke Skagbo (pno), Pål Eide Lindtner (pno), Ha-Young Sul (pno), Benedicte Palko (pno), Inke Kesseler (pno), Anne Marie Meineche (pno), Sverre Larsen (pno), Kasper Peter Bach (pno), Elisabetta Eliseo (pno), Olga Magieres (pno), Carl Erik Kühl (pno), Thorkild Borup Nielsen (pno), Valeria Zanini (pno), Lars Stenhoft (perc), Dennis Boel (perc), Winnie Dahlgren (perc), Susanne Vind (perc), Claus Byrith (elec), Anne Marie Storm (elec), J. Ribera (cnd) *(rec live, Koldinghaus Castle, Denmark, May 2, 1996)* Danica ▲ DCD 1996
Bex, Robert (vc)
Bach, C.P.E.:Con Vc, H.439, w. P. Boulez (cnd), *(orch unknown)* Harmonia Mundi Plus ▲ HMP 390545
Bach, C.P.E.:Cons Fl, w. P. Boulez (cnd), *(orch unknown)*—in d Harmonia Mundi Plus ▲ HMP 390545
Beyer, Achim (vl)
Fasch, J.F.:Trio Sons, w. B. Glaetzner (ob), I. Goritzki (ob), T. Reinhardt (bn), S. Pank (vl), C. Schornsheim (hpd) Berlin Classics ▲ BER 1069 [DDD]
Beyer, Achim (vn)
Zelenka, J.D.:Trio Sons Obs, w. Burkhard Glaetzer (ob), Ingo Goritzki (ob), Knut Sønstevold (bn), Siegfried Pank (va), Walter-Heinz Bernstein (hpd) Berlin Classics 4-▲ BER 1150 [DDD]
Zelenka, J.D.:Trio Sons Obs, w. B. Glaetzner (ob), I. Goritzki (ob), K. Sønstevold (bn), S. Pank (vl), W. H. Bernstein (hpd) Berlin Classics 2-▲ BER 1070 [DDD]
Beyer, Christoph Otto (vc)
Duruflé, M.:Requiem, w. C. Guber (mezzo-soprano), P. Sefcik (baritone), T. Götting (organ), Kammerorchester, H. Hennig (cnd), Hanover Youth Choir Ars Musici ▲ AM 1098-2 [DDD]
Beyer, Franz (va)
Dittersdorf, K.D. von:Son Va, w. P. Breuer (db) FSM-Adagio ▲ FCD 91 009 [ADD]
Beyer, Willi (db)
Berg, A.:Adagio, w. Hans-Udo Heinzmann (fl), Malte Lammers (ob), Walter Hermann (cl), Heinrich Horlein (vn), Jaap Zeijl (va), Seven Forsberg (vc), Jurgen Lamke (pno), Werner Hagen (pno), Volker Kneip (perc) [arr chamber ensemble] Koch Schwann ▲ SCH CD 311912
Busoni, F.:Berceuse élégiaque, w. Hans-Udo Heinzmann (fl), Malte Lammers (ob), Walter Hermann (cl), Heinrich Horlein (vn), Jaap Zeijl (va), Seven Forsberg (vc), Jurgen Lamke (pno), Werner Hagen (pno), Volker Kneip (perc) [arr Stein for chamber ensemble] Koch Schwann ▲ SCH CD 311912
Debussy, C.:Prélude à l'après-midi d'un faune, w. Hans-Udo Heinzmann (fl), Malte Lammers (ob), Walter Hermann (cl), Heinrich Horlein (vn), Jaap Zeijl (va), Seven Forsberg (vc), Jurgen Lamke (pno), Werner Hagen (pno), Volker Kneip (perc) [arr Sachs for chamber ensemble] Koch Schwann ▲ SCH CD 311912
Schoenberg, A.:Chamber Sym 1, w. Hans-Udo Heinzmann (fl), Malte Lammers (ob), Walter Hermann (cl), Heinrich Horlein (vn), Jaap Zeijl (va), Seven Forsberg (vc), Jurgen Lamke (pno), Werner Hagen (pno), Volker Kneip (perc) [arr Webern for chamber ensemble] Koch Schwann ▲ SCH CD 311912
Beyerle, Hatto (va)—see also ORCHESTRAS & ENSEMBLES Vienna Chamber Ensemble members
Spohr, L.:Con Str Qt, w. E. Sebestyen (vn), H. Ganz (vn), M. Ostertag (vc), G. Albrecht (cnd), Berlin RSO Koch Schwann ▲ CD 311088 [DDD] ■ MC 211088 (D)
Spohr, L.:Var, Op. 6, w. E. Sebestyen (vn), H. Ganz (vn), M. Ostertag (vc) Koch Schwann ▲ CD 311088 [DDD] ■ MC 211088 (D)
Beznosiuk, Lisa (fl)
Bach, J.S.:Con Fl, Vn & Hpd, w. S. Standage (vn), T. Pinnock (hpd), T. Pinnock (cnd), English Concert Archiv ▲ 413731-2 [DDD]
Bach, J.S.:Con Fl, Vn & Hpd, w. Elizabeth Wallfisch (vn), Paul Nicholson (hpd), E. Wallfisch (cnd), Orch of the Age of Enlightenment Virgin Classics ▲ CD 45190
Concord of Sweet Sounds, w. Nigel North (lt/gtr) Amon Ra ▲ CDSAR 33 [DDD]
Mozart, W.A.:Con Fl, K.313, w. C. Hogwood (cnd), Academy of Ancient Music L'Oiseau-Lyre ▲ 417622-2 [DDD] ▯ 417622-5
Mozart, W.A.:Con Fl Hp, w. F. Kelly (hp), C. Hogwood (cnd), Academy of Ancient Music—No. 1 L'Oiseau-Lyre ▲ 417622-2 [DDD] ▯ 417622-5
Beznosiuk, Lisa (rcr)
Handel, G.F.:Sons Solo Instrs, w. Rachel Beckett (fl), Paul Goodwin (ob), Locatelli Trio Hyperion 3-▲ CDA 66921/23

Beznosiuk, Pavlo (vn)—see also ORCHESTRAS & ENSEMBLES Hausmusik
Purcell, H.:Sons (12) Vns, Z.790-801, w. Rachel Podger (vn), Christophe Coin (b vl), Christopher Hogwood (org) *(rec Emmanuel College, Cambridge, Feb-Aug 1994)* L'Oiseau-Lyre ▲ 444449-2 [DDD]
The Spirits of England & France, Vol. 1, w. Gothic Voices [cnd:Christopher Page] Hyperion ▲ CDA 66739
The Spirits of England & France, Vol. 2, w. E. Kirkby (sop), Robert White (bgp), Nick Bicat (perc), Gothic Voices [cnd:Christopher Page] Hyperion ▲ CDA 66773
Bezrodny, Sergei (hpd)
Bach, J.S.:Con Fl, Vn & Hpd, w. E. Duran (fl), V. Spivakov (vn), V. Spivakov (cnd), Moscow Virtuosi RCA Red Seal ▲ 7991-2-RC [DDD]
Bezrodny, Sergei (pno)
It Ain't Necessarily So & Other Violin Miniatures, w. V. Spivakov (vn) RCA Red Seal ▲ 09026-60861-2
It's Peaceful Here, w. V. Spivakov (vn) RCA Red Seal ▲ 09026-62524-2
Bezzina, Gilbert (vn)
Locatelli, P.:Cons for 4 Vns, w. G. Bezzina (cnd), Nice Baroque Ensemble Adda ▲ ADD 581118 [DDD]
Vivaldi, A.:Cons Vn, Op. 4, "La stravaganza", w. G. Bezzina (cnd), Nice Baroque Ensemble—Nos. 2, 3, 6, 7, 9 & 12 *(rec Sept 1992)* Pierre Verany ▲ PVY 730028
Vivaldi, A.:Cons Vn, Op. 4, "La stravaganza", w. G. Bezzina (cnd), Nice Baroque Ensemble Pierre Verany 2-▲ PVY 793022 [DDD]
Biancalana, Jeffrey (tpt)—see ORCHESTRAS & ENSEMBLES New World Brass
Bianchi, A. (cl)
Milesi, P.:Modi 1, w. D. Cassamagnaghi (fl), F. Pomarico (ob), L. Dosso (bn), G. Govi (vn), D. Tellini (vn), M. Ravasio (va), S. Righini (vc), P. Rizzi (db), C. Vignani (hpd), J. Scully (perc), P. Milesi (cnd) Cuneiform ▲ RUNE 63
Bianchi, A. (cl/b cl)
Milesi, P.:Modi 2, w. L. M. Pickova (sop), Françoise Goddard (alt), M. Ferradini (ten), B. Andersen (bass), D. Cassamagnaghi (fl), S. Scanziani (ob), E. Crisafulli (bn), C. Gazzola (hn), F. Gualandris (tuba), A. Girardi (celtic hp), R. Anedda (vn), E. Groppo (vn), M. Pagani (vn), M. Ravasio (va), S. Righini (vc), P. Rizzi (db), J. Scully (perc), P. Milesi (cnd) Cuneiform ▲ RUNE 63
Bianchi, Luigi Alberto (vn)
Kreisler, F.:Vn Pieces, w. P. Masi (pno)—Tambourin Chinois; Schön Rosmarin; Liebesleid; Liebesfreud; Caprice Viennoise; Gypsy Caprice; La Gitana; Syncopation; Londonderry Air; Dancing Doll; Polichinelle Serenade; Rondino; Toy Soldiers March; Old Refrain; Marche Miniature Viennoise; Viennese Rapsodic Fantasietta; Recitativo und Scherzo *(rec 6/91)* Dynamic ▲ CD 88 [DDD]
Paganini, N.:Cantabile, w. Maurizio Preda (gtr) *(rec Dynamic's, Genova, June 22-23, 1995)* Dynamic ▲ CD 148 [DDD]
Paganini, N.:Cantibile, w. Maurizio Preda (gtr) *(rec Dynamic Studio, Genoa, Italy, June 22-23, 1995)* Dynamic 3-▲ 1571 [DDD]
Paganini, N.:Caprices Vn *(rec Dynamic Studio, Genoa, Italy, June 22-23, 1995)* Dynamic 3-▲ 1571 [DDD]
Paganini, N.:Caprices Vn—No. 24 *(rec Dynamic's, Genova, June 22-23, 1995)* Dynamic ▲ CD 148 [DDD]
Paganini, N.:Centone di sonate, w. M. Preda (gtr)—Nos. 7-12 Dynamic ▲ CD 84 [DDD]
Paganini, N.:Centone di sonate, w. M. Preda (gtr)—Nos. 13-18 Dynamic ▲ CD 34 [DDD]
Paganini, N.:Centone di sonate, w. Maurizio Preda (gtr) *(rec Dynamic Studio, Genoa, Italy, Jan 1991; Oct 1991; June)* Dynamic 3-▲ 1571 [DDD]
Paganini, N.:Centone di sonate, w. Maurizio Preda (gtr)—Nos. 1-6 *(rec Dynamic's, Genova, June 22-23, 1995)* Dynamic ▲ CD 148 [DDD]
Paganini, N.:Sons Vn & Gtr, w. M. Preda (gtr)—30 Sons Dynamic 2-▲ CD 43/1-2
Weber, C.M. von:Sons Vn, w. Caroline Haffner (pno) *(rec Dynamic's, Genova, May 23-25, 1995)* Dynamic ▲ CDS 149 [DDD]
Weber, C.M. von:Vars on a Norwegian Air Vn, w. Caroline Haffner (pno) *(rec Dynamic's, Genova, May 23-25, 1995)* Dynamic ▲ CDS 149 [DDD]
Bianchi, V. (bn)
Vivaldi, A.:Cons Bn, w. P. Santi (cnd), Milan Virtuosi—RV.501 Allegretto ▲ ACD 8036 [ADD] ■ ACS 8036
Bianconi, P. (pno)
Schubert, Franz:Die Schöne Müllerin, w. H. Prey (bar) [G] Denon ▲ CO 1072 [DDD]
Bibb, Frank (pno)
Opera Arias & Songs, w. A. Kipnis (bass), Arthur Bergh (pno), Robert Hood Bowers (cnd) Sony Classical ("Masterworks Heritage" series) ▲ MHK 62354
Biberauer, Bernhard (vn)—see ORCHESTRAS & ENSEMBLES Biedermeier Ensemble
Bibl, Rudolf (pno)
Liederabend, w. G. di Stefano (ten) *(rec Vienna, June 22, 1968)* Koch Schwann ▲ SCH 318332
Bicák, Stanislav (bn)
Scarmolin, A.L.:Sym 2, w. Peter Sivanič (hn), Miroslav Herák (vc), J. E. Suben (cnd), Slovak RSO Bratislava *(rec Bratislava, Jan 23-25, 1995)* New World ▲ 80502-2
Bicat, Nick (perc)
The Spirits of England & France, Vol. 2, w. E. Kirkby (sop), Robert White (bgp), Pavlo Beznosiuk (fid), Gothic Voices [cnd:Christopher Page] Hyperion ▲ CDA 66773
Bicket, Harry (org)
Carols from Christ Church, w. Christ Church Cathedral Choir Oxford [cnd:Francis Grier], Frances Kelley (hp) ASV ▲ ASV CD 2097
Finzi, G.:Choral Music, w. P. Spicer (cnd), Finzi Singers—works for mixed chorus, a cappella & with organ, composed 1926-1954)—Three Short Elegies, Op. 5; Seven Partsongs, Op. 17; Lo, the full, final sacrifice, Op. 26; My lovely one, God is gone up & Welcome sweet & sacred feast (Op. 27, Nos. 1-3); Thou didst delight my eyes, Op. 32; All this night, Op. 33; Let us now praise famous men, Op. 35; Magnificat, Op. 36; White-flowering days, Op. 37 [E] Chandos ▲ CHAN 8936 [DDD]
Howells, H.:Choral Music, w. Paul Spicer (cnd), Finzi Singers—A Sequence for St. Michael (1961); House of the Mind (motet—1949) [E] Chandos ▲ CHAN 9019 [DDD]
Howells, H.:Requiem, w. Paul Spicer (cnd), Finzi Singers Chandos ▲ CHAN 9019 [DDD]
Vaughan Williams, R.:Choral Music, w. Paul Spicer (cnd), Finzi Singers—A Vision of Aeroplanes (1955); Lord, Thou hast been our Refuge (motet); Prayer to the Father of Heaven (motet) Chandos ▲ CHAN 9019 [DDD]
Biddlecome, R. (bass trbn)
Balada, L.:Son Winds, w. J. Aley (tpt), D. Wakefield (hn), R. Borror (tenor trbn), American Brass Quintet New World ▲ 80442-2
Bidini, Fabio (pno)—see also ORCHESTRAS & ENSEMBLES Clementi Quartet
Beethoven, L. van:Son 23 Pno, "Appassionata" *(rec Resurrection Lutheran Church, Plano, TX, Oct 29-30, 1995)* Encore ▲ EPR 9510 [DDD]
Bellini, V.:Ariette da camera (6), w. Eva Mei (sop) *(rec Bavarian Radio, Munich, June 7-10, 1994)* RCA Red Seal ▲ 09026-68025-2 [DDD]
Busoni, F.:Bach Transcriptions—Chaconne in d *(rec Resurrection Lutheran Church, Plano, TX, Oct 29-30, 1995)* Encore ▲ EPR 9510 [DDD]
Chopin, F.:Con 2 Pno, w. J. Krenz (cnd), Warsaw PO *(rec National Philharmonic Concert Hall, Warsaw, June 1, 1991)* Polskie Nagrania ▲ PNCD 126 [DDD]
Chopin, F.:Impromptus—in F#, Op. 36 *(rec National Philharmonic Concert Hall, Warsaw, June 1, 1991)* Polskie Nagrania ▲ PNCD 126 [DDD]
Chopin, F.:Nocturnes—in c#, Op. posth.; in F#, Op. 15/2 *(rec National Philharmonic Concert Hall, Warsaw, June 1, 1991)* Polskie Nagrania ▲ PNCD 126 [DDD]
Chopin, F.:Scherzos—in B♭, Op. 31 *(rec National Philharmonic Concert Hall, Warsaw, June 1, 1991)* Polskie Nagrania ▲ PNCD 126 [DDD]
Clementi, M.:Sons Pno—in b, Op. 40/2 *(rec Resurrection Lutheran Church, Plano, TX, Oct 29-30, 1995)* Encore ▲ EPR 9510 [DDD]
Donizetti, G.:Composizioni da camera, w. Eva Mei (sop) *(rec Bavarian Radio, Munich, June 7-10, 1994)* RCA Red Seal ▲ 09026-68025-2 [DDD]

472 ▲ = CD ♦ = Enhanced CD Δ = MD ■ = Cassette Tape ▯ = DCC

Bidini, Fabio (pno) (cont.)
Grieg, E.:Sons Vn, Opp. 8, 13 & 45, w. Alessandro Perpich (vn) *(rec Mesquite Performing Arts Center, TX, Apr 1996)* EPR ▲ EPR 9613 [DDD]
Rossini, G.:Les Soirées musicales, w. Eva Mei (sop)—La Promessa; Il Rimprovero; la Partenza; L'Orgia; L'Invito; La Pastorella delle alpi; La Gita in Gondola; La Danza *(rec Bavarian Radio, Munich, June 7–10, 1994)* RCA Red Seal ▲ 09026-68025-2 [DDD]
Schubert, Franz:Pieces Pno, D.946—No. 2 *(rec Resurrection Lutheran Church, Plano, TX, Oct 29–30, 1995)* Encore ▲ EPR 9510 [DDD]

Bidlo, Karel (bn)
Mozart, W.A.:Con Bn, w. K. Ančerl (cnd), Czech PO *(rec 1952–1966)* Supraphon ▲ CD 111935 [AAD]

Bidoli, Paolo (pno)
Dussek, J.L.:Trio Son Pno, Op. 65, w. Francesca Pagnini (fl), Mauro Valli (vc) Enterprise ("Tiziano" series) ▲ ENT TZ 96002 [DDD]
Kalkbrenner, F.:Son Fl, w. Francesca Pagnini (fl), Mauro Valli (vc) Enterprise ("Tiziano" series) ▲ ENT TZ 96002 [DDD]
Kreutzer, C.:Son Fl, Vc & Pno, w. Francesca Pagnini (fl), Mauro Valli (vc) Enterprise ("Tiziano" series) ▲ ENT TZ 96002 [DDD]

Biegel, Jeffrey (pno)
Cui, C.:Preludes Pno, Op. 64 Marco Polo ▲ 8.223496

Bielby, Jonathan (org)
Great European Organs, Vol. 21, w. S. Cleobury (org) Priory ▲ PRCD 298 [DDD]
Romantic Music of Yesteryear, w. J. Bielby (org) *(rec 1982–84)* Priory ▲ PRCD 904 [AAD/DDD]

Bieler, Ida (vn)—see also ORCHESTRAS & ENSEMBLES Melos String Quartet
Bartók, B.:Sons (2) Vn & Pno, w. Nina Tichman (pno) MD + G ("Ensemble Villa Musica" series) ▲ MDG 3040666
Reicha, A.:Sinf concertante, w. Jena-Claude Gerard (fl), P. Gülke (cnd), Wuppertal SO MD + G ▲ MDG 3350661

Biely, Peter (vn)—see also ORCHESTRAS & ENSEMBLES Albrecht String Quartet
Godár, V.:Déploration sur la mort de Witold Lutoslawski, w. Eleonóra Škutová-Slaničková (pno), Ivana Pristašová (vn), Peter Šesták (va), Jozef Lupták (vc) *(rec Residence of Slovak Composers, Apr 1996)* Slovart ▲ SR 0018-2-131 [DDD]

Biery, James (org)
Dupré, M.:Sym-Passion, "The World Awaiting the Saviour" [at the org of the Cathedral of St. Joseph, Hartford] *(rec Hartford, CT, May 17–18, 1994)* Afka ▲ SK 537
Dupré, M.:Les vêpres de la Vierge [at the org of the Cathedral of St. Joseph, Hartford] *(rec Hartford, CT, May 17–18, 1994)* Afka ▲ SK 537

Biessen, Emile (fl)
Honegger, A.:Con da camera, w. Miriam Hannecart-Jakes (E hn), J. Fournet (cnd), Netherlands Radio PO *(rec Hilversum Music Center, Netherlands, May & Dec, 1993)* Denon ▲ CO 78831 [DDD]

Bigley, Roger (va)
Simpson, R.:Qnt Strs, w. Coull String Quartet Hyperion ▲ CDA 66503

Bigo, Bernard (gtr)
Christmas Cithare, w. Murray, Martial (zither) Studio SM ▲ 1222.49 [AAD]

Bihari, Endre (vc)—see ORCHESTRAS & ENSEMBLES Innsbruck Salon Quintet

Bijlsma, Anner (vc)
Beethoven, L. van:Folksong Arrs, w. M. Kweksilber (sop), S. Hoogland (pno), V. Beths (vn)—Irish Songs, WoO 152, Nos. 1,5,8 & 11; Scottish Songs, Op. 108, Nos. 2,3,5,7,8,17,20 & 24 [E] *(rec 6/90)* Channel Classics ▲ CCS 1491 [DDD]
Beethoven, L. van:Ländler Dances, WoO 15, w. G. Beths (vn), V. Beths (vn) *(rec 6/90)* Channel Classics ▲ CCS 1491 [DDD]
Beethoven, L. van:Trio 10 Pno, w. S. Hoogland, V. Beths, A. Bijlsma *(rec June 1990)* Channel Classics ▲ CCS 1491 [DDD]
Boccherini, L.:Qnts Strs, w. Boccherini String Quartet—Quintet in F, Op. 39/2 (G.338); Quintettino in E♭, Op. 27/4 (G.304) Channel Classics ▲ CCS 3692 [DDD]

Bik, Annette (vn)
Shostakovich, D.:Movts Str Qt, w. G. Kremer (vn), V. Hagen (va), T. Demenga (vc) *(rec Lockenhaus Festival, 1986)* ECM New Series 2-▲ 78118-21347-2 [DDD]

Bilek, Frantisek (cl)—see ORCHESTRAS & ENSEMBLES Prague Chamber Ensemble

Bilger, David (tpt)—see also ORCHESTRAS & ENSEMBLES New York Trumpet Ensemble
Baroque Trumpetissimo, w. Stephen Burns (tpt), Edward Carroll (tpt), Alex Holton (tpt), Raymond Mase (tpt), Timothy Morrison (tpt), Lee Soper (tpt), Atsuko Sato (bn), Ben Harms (timp), Edward Brewer (org/hpd), Philharmonia Virtuosi [cnd:Richard Kapp] ESS.A.Y ▲ ESS 1035 [DDD]

Bilgram, Hedwig (hpd)
Bach, J.S.:Cons for 3 Hpds (comp), w. M. Galling (hpd), F. Lehrndorfer (hpd), G. Kehr (cnd), Mainz CO Vox Box 2-▲ CDX 5040
Bach, J.S.:Con for 4 Hpds, w. M. Galling (hpd), F. Lehrndorfer (hpd), K.-H. Stolze (hpd), G. Kehr (cnd), Mainz CO Vox Box 2-▲ CDX 5040
Bach, J.S.:Lt Music, w. Paul Meisen (fl)—Partita in c, BWV 997 [arr for Fl & Hpd] *(rec Augustinian Monastery Mens' Choir, Polling, West Germany, Sept 21–24, 1977)* Camerata ▲ 32CM 281 [AAD]
Bach, J.S.:Sons Fl, BWV 1030–35, w. Paul Meisen (fl)—in b, BWV 1030; in A, BWV 1032 *(rec Augustinian Monastery Mens' Choir, Polling, West Germany, Sept 21–24, 1977)* Camerata ▲ 32CM 281 [AAD]
Bach, J.S.:Sons Vn, w. Paul Meisen (fl)—in g, BWV 1020 [arr for Fl & Hpd] *(rec Augustinian Monastery Mens' Choir, Polling, West Germany, Sept 21–24, 1977)* Camerata ▲ 32CM 281 [AAD]
Trumpet & Organ Recital, w. M. André (tpt) EMI Classics ▲ CDC 54330
Works for Oboe & Organ, w. H. Schellenberger (ob) *(rec July 29–Aug. 1, 1991)* Denon ▲ CO 75081 [DDD]

Bilgram, Hedwig (org)
Organ Music from the Church Year (org) *(rec 1993)* Calig ▲ CAL 50928 [DDD]
Reger, M.:Cantatas, w. V. Schweizer (sop), A. Hellmann (alt), R. Julius Koch (ob), R. Hellmann, U. Soldan (vn), B. Banz (va), C. Hellmann (vc), C. Fink (db), D. Hellmann (cnd), Mainz Bach Choir Entrée ▲ 0049 [ADD]
Reger, M.:Easy Chorale Preludes—No. 52, "O wie selig seid ihr doch" Entrée ▲ 0049 [ADD]
Reger, M.:Intro & Passacaglia Entrée ▲ 0049 [ADD]
Reger, M.:Little Chorale Preludes—Von Himmel hoch, da komm ich her; O Haupt voll Blut und Wunden; Meinum Jesum lass ich nicht Entrée ▲ 0049 [ADD]

Billaut, Hervé (pno)
Castérède, J.:Hommage à Thelonious Monk REM ▲ 311092 [DDD]
Castérède, J.:Son Pno REM ▲ 311092 [DDD]

Billeter, Bernhard (pno)
Fröhlich, F.T.:Choral Music, w. E. Speiser (sop), P. Steiner (ten), J. Krattiger (bass), C. Spring (pno), Winterthur Vocal Ensemble [G] *(rec 1988)* Jecklin-Disco ▲ JD 627-2 [ADD]
Hindemith, P.:Pno Music—previously unpublished piano works *(rec 1989)* Jecklin-Disco ▲ JD 644-2 [DDD]

Billing, Klaus (pno)
Schubert, Franz:Schwanengesang, w. D. Fischer-Dieskau (bar) [G] *(rec live, Berlin, 1/19–25/48)* Melodram ▲ MEL 18017
Schubert, Franz:Songs (misc), w. D. Fischer-Dieskau (bar)—7 songs—D.138; D.771; D.911 [Winterreise], Nos. 1,11,13 & 24; D.932 [G] *(rec live, Berlin, 1/19–25/48)* Melodram ▲ MEL 18017

Billman, Per (cl/b cl)
Delage, M.:Poèmes hindous, w. Anne Sofie von Otter (mez), Andreas Alin (fl), Peter Rydström (fl/pic), Ulf Bjurenhed (ob/E hn), Lars Paulsson (cl), Nils-Erik Sparf (vn), Ulf Forsberg (vn), Matti Hirvikangas (va), Mats Lindström (vc), Lisa Viguier (hp) *(rec Stockholm, Nov 1994)* Deutsche Grammophon ▲ 447 752-2 [DDD]

Billman, Per (cl/b cl) (cont.)
Ravel, M.:Trois poèmes de Stéphane Mallarmé, w. Anne Sofie von Otter (mez), Peter Rydström (fl/pic), Andreas Alin (fl), Lars Paulsson (cl), Nils-Erik Sparf (vn), Ulf Forsberg (vn), Matti Hirvikangas (va), Mats Lindström (vc), Bengt Forsberg (pno) *(rec Stockholm, Nov 1994)* Deutsche Grammophon ▲ 447 752-2 [DDD]

Billmeyer, Dean (org)
Albright, W.:A Song to David, w. Melissa Semmes (nar), Charles Russell (nar), Deborah Carbaugh (sop), Susan Sacquitne-Druck (mez), Rick Penning (ten), James Bohn (bass), Howard Don Small (cnd), St. Mark's Cathedral Choir Minneapolis *(rec live, St. Mark's Cathedral, Minneapolis, MN, Apr. 28, 1991)* Gothic ▲ G 49066 [DDD]

Bilson, Malcolm (pno)
Beethoven, L. van:Son 1 Vc, w. A. Bylsma (baroque vc) Elektra/Nonesuch ▲ 79152-2 [DDD] ■ 79152-4 (D)
Beethoven, L. van:Son 2 Vc, w. A. Bylsma (vc) Elektra/Nonesuch ▲ 79152-2 [DDD] ■ 79152-4 (D)
Haydn, J.:Sons Pno (Nos. 49, 52) Elektra/Nonesuch ▲ 78018-2
Mozart, W.A.:Allegro & Andante & Rondo Hungaroton 2-▲ HCD 31013/14 [DDD]
Mozart, W.A.:Cons Pno, w. J. E. Gardiner (cnd), English Baroque Soloists—Nos. 1–6, 8, 9 & 11–27; No. 7 [w. R. Levin & M. Tan]; No. 10 [w. R. Levin] Deutsche Grammophon 9-▲ 431211-2 [DDD]
Mozart, W.A.:Cons 1–4 Pno, w. T. Crawford (cnd), Old Fairfield Academy Orch [period instrs] MusicMasters ▲ 01612-67095-2
Mozart, W.A.:Con 9 Pno, w. J. E. Gardiner (cnd), English Baroque Soloists Archiv ▲ 447291-2
Mozart, W.A.:Con 17 Pno, w. J. E. Gardiner (cnd), English Baroque Soloists Archiv ▲ 447291-2
Mozart, W.A.:Con 20 Pno, w. J. E. Gardiner (cnd), English Baroque Soloists Archiv ▲ 419609-2 [DDD]
Mozart, W.A.:Con 21 Pno, w. J. E. Gardiner (cnd), English Baroque Soloists Archiv ▲ 419609-2 [DDD]
Mozart, W.A.:Con 22 Pno, w. J. E. Gardiner (cnd), English Baroque Soloists Deutsche Grammophon ▲ 447283-2
Mozart, W.A.:Con 26 Pno, w. J. E. Gardiner (cnd), English Baroque Soloists Deutsche Grammophon ▲ 447283-2
Mozart, W.A.:Fant Pno, K.475 Hungaroton 2-▲ HCD 31013/14 [DDD]
Mozart, W.A.:Pno Music 4-Hands, w. Robert Levin (pno)—Fugue in c, K.426; Larghetto & Allegro in E♭ [compl. Levin] Elektra/Nonesuch ■ 78023-4
Mozart, W.A.:Rondo Pno Orch, K.382, w. J. E. Gardiner (cnd), English Baroque Soloists Archiv ▲ 447291-2
Mozart, W.A.:Sons Pno—No. 2, K.280; No. 3, K.281; No. 5, K.283; No. 9, K.311; No. 10, K.330; No. 11, K.331 Hungaroton 2-▲ HCD 31009/10 [DDD]
Mozart, W.A.:Sons Pno—Sonatas No. 6, K.284; No. 8, K.310; No. 12, K.332; No. 13, K.333; No. 16, K.570; No. 17, K.576 Hungaroton 2-▲ HCD 31011/12 [DDD]
Mozart, W.A.:Sons Pno [1989 fortepiano built by P. McNulty, Amsterdam, after an instrument by A. Walter, Vienna, ca. 1790]—No. 1 in C, K.279; No. 4 in E♭, K.282; No. 7 in C, K.309; No. 14 in c, K.457; No. 15 in C, K.545 Hungaroton 2-▲ HCD 31013/14 [DDD]
Mozart, W.A.:Son Pnos, K.448, w. R. Levin (pno) Elektra/Nonesuch ■ 78023-4
Mozart, W.A.:Sons Vn Pno (misc), w. S. Luca (vn)—K.454, 481, 526 & 547 Elektra/Nonesuch 2-▲ 79112-2 [DDD]
Schubert, Franz:Son Pno, D.537 *(rec Utrecht, The Netherlands, May, 1995)* Hungaroton ▲ HCD 31587 [DDD]
Schubert, Franz:Son Pno, D.568 *(rec Oude Katholiek Kerk, Utrecht, The Netherlands, Dec 8 & 9, 1994)* Hungaroton ▲ HCD 31586 [DDD]
Schubert, Franz:Son Pno, D.850 *(rec Oude Katholiek Kerk, Utrecht, The Netherlands, Dec 8 & 9, 1994)* Hungaroton ▲ HCD 31586 [DDD]
Schubert, Franz:Son Pno, D.959 *(rec Utrecht, The Netherlands, May, 1995)* Hungaroton ▲ HCD 31587 [DDD]

Biltcliffe, Edwin (pno)
Love's Secrets & Other Songs By American Composers, w. Steber, Eleanor (sop), Milldred Miller (mez), John McCollum (ten), Donald Gramm (bass-bar), Richard Cumming (pno) Vox Box ("The American Composers" series) 2-▲ CDX 5129

Bilyeu, Landon (pno)
Bartók, B.:Contrasts, w. Charles West (cl), Laura Roelofs (vn) Klavier ▲ KCD 11072 [DDD]
Glinka, M.:Trio pathétique, w. Charles West (cl), Bruce Hammel (bn) Klavier ▲ KCD 11072 [DDD]
Mozart, W.A.:Qnt Pno, K.452, w. Philip Teachey (ob), Charles West (cl), Bruce Hammel (bn), Alan Paterson (hn) Klavier ▲ KCD 11072 [DDD]

Binelli, Daniel (band)—see ORCHESTRAS & ENSEMBLES Tango 7, New Tango Sex-tet

Bingham, John (pno)
Beethoven, L. van:Con 4 Pno, w. C. Hoey (cnd), Singapore SO Meridian ▲ CDE 84172
Beethoven, L. van:Con 5 Pno, "Emperor", w. C. Hoey (cnd), Singapore SO Meridian ▲ CDE 84172
Elgar, E.:Music of, w. Barbara Leigh-Hunt (nar), Richard Pasco (nar), Medici String Quartet—includes excerpts from Start of the Play; Qnt. for Pno; Qt. for Strs [slow movt.]; In the South; The Wand of Youth [suite]; Chanson de Matin; Salut d'Amour; Starlight Express; Son. for Vn; Son. for Vc; Adieu; others *(rec Gateway Studios, London)* Medici Quartet ▲ MQT 7001 [DDD]
Elgar, E.:Qnt Pno Strs, w. Medici String Quartet Medici Quartet ▲ MQT 8001 [DDD]
Elgar, E.:Qnt Pno Strs, w. Medici String Quartet Meridian ▲ ECD 84082
Elgar, E.:Son Vn, w. Paul Robertson (vn) Medici Quartet ▲ MQT 7001 [DDD]
Franck, C.:Qnt Pno, w. Medici String Quartet Nimbus ▲ NI 5114 [DDD]
Liszt, F.:Song Transcriptions—10 Schubert songs Meridian ▲ CDE 84019
Liszt, F.:Transcriptions & Paraphrases—Die Taubenpost; Der Müller und der Bach; Rastlose Liebe; Des Mädchens Klage; Der Lindenbaum; Erlkönig; Die Forelle (1st version); Der Doppelgänger; Morgenständchen; Das Sterbeglöcklein Meridian ▲ CDE 84019
Schlegel, L.:Qt Pno, w. Orpheus String Quartet NM Classics ▲ NM 92046
Shostakovich, D.:Qnt Pno, w. Medici String Quartet Nimbus ▲ NI 5156 [DDD]

Bingham, Kaoru (pno)
Liszt, F.:Transcriptions & Paraphrases Meridian ▲ MER 84249 [DDD]

Bini, Ricardo (gtr)
Gragnani, F.:Gtr Music, w. M. Annunziati (gtr), C. Mascilli Migliorini (gtr), M. Fornaciari (vn)—3 Sonatas for Violin & Guitar; 3 Duets for 2 Guitars Fonè ▲ FON 93F 18 [DDD]

Binkley, George (vn)—see ORCHESTRAS & ENSEMBLES L'Atelier String Trio

Binkley, Paul (mandola/gtr)—see ORCHESTRAS & ENSEMBLES Modern Mandolin Quartet

Binko, P. (org)
Myers, T.:Festival Fant CRS ▲ CD 9153

Binns, Malcolm (pno)
Balakirev, M.:Con 1 Pno, w. D. Lloyd-Korsakov (cnd), English Northern Philharmonia Hyperion ▲ CDA 66640
Balakirev, M.:Con 2 Pno, w. D. Lloyd-Korsakov (cnd), English Northern Philharmonia Hyperion ▲ CDA 66640
Bennett, W.S.:Adagio, w. N. Braithwaite (cnd), London PO Lyrita ▲ SRCD 205 [DDD]
Bennett, W.S.:Caprice, w. N. Braithwaite (cnd), London PO Lyrita ▲ SRCD 204 [DDD]
Bennett, W.S.:Con 1 Pno, w. N. Braithwaite (cnd), London PO Lyrita ▲ SRCD 204 [DDD]
Bennett, W.S.:Con 2 Pno, w. N. Braithwaite (cnd), London PO Lyrita ▲ SRCD 205 [DDD]
Bennett, W.S.:Con 3 Pno, w. N. Braithwaite (cnd), London PO Lyrita ▲ SRCD 204 [DDD]
Bennett, W.S.:Con 5 Pno, w. N. Braithwaite (cnd), London PO Lyrita ▲ SRCD 205 [DDD]
Chopin, F.:Études (24) Pearl ▲ PEA 9641
Chopin, F.:Nouvelles études Pearl ▲ PEA 9641
Fauré, G.:Ballade Pno, w. R. Leppard (cnd), BBC Northern SO IMP ("BBC Radio Classics" series) ▲ IMP 9136
Harty, H.:Con Pno, w. B. Thomson (cnd), Ulster Orch Chandos ▲ CHAN 7032
Harty, H.:Con Pno, w. B. Thomson (cnd), Ulster Orch Chandos ▲ CHAN 8321 [DDD]
Rimsky-Korsakov, N.:Con Pno, w. D. Lloyd-Jones (cnd), English Northern Philharmonia Hyperion ▲ CDA 66640

Biondi, Fabio (vn)—see also ORCHESTRAS & ENSEMBLES Europa Galante
Bach, J.S.:Sons Vn, w. Rinaldo Alessandrini (hpd)—BWV 1014–1019 Opus 111 2–▲ OPS 30–127/128
Casella, A.:Scarlattiana, w. L. di Ilio (pno)—Minuet [arr. for violin & piano] *(rec July 1991)* Opus 111 ▲ OPS 44–9202 [DDD]
Festa Italiana, w. Barbara Schlick (sop), Pascal Monteilhet (va), Maurizio Naddeo (vc), Rinaldo Alessandrini (hpd), Concerto Italiano, Europa Galante Opus 111 5–▲ 2001
Leclair, J.–M.:Premier livres de sonates, w. M. Naddeo (vc), P. Montelheit (thb), R. Alessandrini (org)—Sons. III, VII, VIII, XI Arcana ▲ ACA 39 [DDD]
Malipiero, G.F.:Vn & Pno Music, w. L. di Ilio (pno) *(rec July 1991)* Opus 111 ▲ OPS 44–9202 [DDD]
Pizzetti, I.:Canti Vn, w. L. Di Ilio (pno) *(rec July 1991)* Opus 111 ▲ OPS 44–9202 [DDD]
The Poet–Violinist Opus 111 ▲ OPS 30–95
Respighi, O.:Vn Pno Music, w. L. Di Ilio (pno)—Aubade; Berceuse; Humoresque; Madrigale; Melodia; Romanza *(rec July 1991)* Opus 111 ▲ OPS 44–9202 [DDD]
Schubert, Franz:Son Vn, D.574, w. Olga Tverskaya (pno) Opus 111 ▲ OPS 30–126
Schubert, Franz:Sonatinas Vn, w. Olga Tverskaya (pno) Opus 111 ▲ OPS 30–126
Schumann, C.:Romances Vn, w. L. Di Ilio (pno) [period instrs] Opus 111 ▲ OPS 30–77
Schumann, R.:Son 1 Vn, w. L. Di Ilio (pno) [period instrs] Opus 111 ▲ OPS 30–77
Schumann, R.:Son 2 Vn, w. L. Di Ilio (pno) [period instrs] Opus 111 ▲ OPS 30–77
Tartini, G.:Sons Vn & Continuo, w. M. Naddeo (vc), R. Alessandrini (hpd), P. Montheillet (thb)—5 Sonatas—in g (B g11); in B♭ (B b3); in g (B g10); in A (B A15); in G (B G17) Opus 111 ▲ OPS 59–9205 [DDD]
Veracini, F.M.:Sonate accademiche, w. Maurizio Naddeo (vc), Rinaldo Alessandrini (hpd), Pascal Monteilhet (tiorba)—Nos. 7 in d, 8 in e, 9 in A, 12 in d; Capriccio in g Opus 111 ▲ OPS 30–138
Vivaldi, A.:Cons Vn (misc), w. F. Biondi (cnd), Europa Galante—RV.281 & 286 *(rec Apr. 1993)* Opus 111 ▲ OPS 3086 [DDD]
Vivaldi, A.:Cons Vn, Op. 8/1–4, "The Four Seasons", Europa Galante Opus 111 ▲ OPS 56–9120
Vivaldi, A.:Cons Vn Org, w. R. Alessandrini (org), F. Biondi (cnd), Europa Galante—RV.541 *(rec Apr. 1993)* Opus 111 ▲ OPS 3086 [DDD]
Vivaldi, A.:Cons for 2 Vns, w. F. Cipriani (vn), F. Biondi (cnd), Europa Galante—RV.511 *(rec Apr. 1993)* Opus 111 ▲ OPS 3086 [DDD]
Vivaldi, A.:Sons Vn—in d, RV.14 Adda ▲ ADD 581053 [ADD]
Vivaldi, A.:Sons Vn, w. R. Alessandrini (hpd), M. Naddeo (vc), P. Pandolfo (db), R. Lislevand (thb/lt)—Manchester Sons. 1, 2, 3, 6, 8 & 10 Arcana ▲ ACA 4 [DDD]
Vivaldi, A.:Sons Vn, w. R. Alessandrini (hpd), M. Naddeo (vc), P. Pandolfo (db), R. Lislevand (thb/lt)—Manchester Sons. 4, 5, 7, 9, 11 & 12 Arcana ▲ ACA 5 [DDD]
Vivaldi, A.:Sons Vn, Op. 2, w. Il Seminario Musicale—No. 3 Adda ▲ ADD 241872 [ADD]

Birch, John (db)
Haydn, J.:Salve regina, H.XXIIIb/2, w. Arleen Auger (sop), Alfreda Hodgson (cta), Anthony Rolfe Johnson (ten), Gwynne Howell (bass), L. Heltay (cnd), Argo CO, London Chamber Choir *(rec St. Jude's, London, Feb 1979)* London 2–▲ 443027–2 [ADD]

Birchmeier, Oskar (org)
Schoeck, O.:Songs (comp), w. Nathan Berg (bar), Julius Drake (pno)—3 geistliche Gesänge, Op. 11; 3 Lieder, Op. 7; 2 Gesänge, Op. 9; 5 Lieder, Op. 31; 12 Eichendorff–Lieder, Op. 30 *(rec Sept 1995)* Jecklin ▲ JD 672
Zachow, F.W.:Kbd Music, w. Egon Schwarb (org)—Vars on "Jesu, meine Freude" *(rec Pere Casulleras, CH–Waldenburg 1992)* Jecklin ▲ JS 309–2 [DDD]

Bird, Alberto (org)
Freeman, J.:Suite Org, w. J. Somary (cnd), Bronx Arts Ensemble Premier ▲ PRCD 1042 [DDD]

Biret, Idil (pno)
Bach, J.S.:Kbd Music (misc)—Es ist gewisslich an der Zeit, BWV 307/Nun freut euch, liebe Christeng'mein, BWV 734; Herzlich tut mich verlangen, BWV 727; In dulci jubilo, BWV 751; Jesu bleibet meine Freude, from BWV 727; Nun komm der Heiden Heiland, BWV 659a; Siciliano, from BWV 1031; Sinfonia, from BWV 29; Wachet auf! ruft uns die Stimme, BWV 645 *(rec Nov–Dec 1991)* Marco Polo ▲ 8.223452 [DDD]
Brahms, J.:Etudes (5) Pno *(rec 1993)* Naxos ▲ 8.550509 [DDD]
Brahms, J.:Exercises Pno, WoO 6 *(rec Clara Wieck Auditorium, Sandhausen, 1995)* Naxos ▲ 8.553425 [DDD]
Brahms, J.:Hungarian Dances Pno *(rec 1992)* Naxos ▲ 8.550355 [DDD]
Brahms, J.:Pno Music (misc)—Theme & Vars. in d [from Sextet No. 1 for Strings, Op. 18]; Gavotte in A by Gluck; Sarabande & 2 Gavottes; Gigue in a; Sarabande in b; Gigue in b; Kleines Klavierstück; Canon; Canon (Inverted); Rakoczy March; Sarabande in A; Impromptu Naxos ▲ 8.550958 [DDD]
Brahms, J.:Son 1 Pno *(rec 11/89)* Naxos ▲ 8.550351 [DDD]
Brahms, J.:Son 2 Pno *(rec 11/89)* Naxos ▲ 8.550351 [DDD]
Brahms, J.:Vars & Fugue on a Theme by Handel *(rec Nov. 1989)* Naxos ▲ 8.550350 [DDD]
Brahms, J.:Vars on a Hungarian Song *(rec 1993)* Naxos ▲ 8.550509 [DDD]
Brahms, J.:Vars on an Original Theme *(rec 1993)* Naxos ▲ 8.550509 [DDD]
Brahms, J.:Vars on a Theme by Paganini *(rec Nov. 1989)* Naxos ▲ 8.550350 [DDD]
Brahms, J.:Vars on a Theme of Robert Schumann, Op. 9 *(rec Nov. 1989)* Naxos ▲ 8.550350 [DDD]
Brahms, J.:Waltzes Pno, Op. 39 *(rec 1992)* Naxos ▲ 8.550355 [DDD]
Chopin, F.:Andante Spianato & Grande Polonaise *(rec Apr. 1991)* Naxos ▲ 8.550361 [DDD]
Chopin, F.:Andante Spianato & Grande Polonaise, w. R. Stankovsky (cnd), Czech–Slovak State PO Naxos ▲ 8.550368 [DDD]
Chopin, F.:Con 1 Pno, w. R. Stankovsky (cnd), Czech–Slovak State PO Naxos ▲ 8.550368 [DDD]
Chopin, F.:Con 2 Pno, w. R. Stankovsky (cnd), Czech–Slovak State PO *(rec 11/90 & 6/91)* Naxos ▲ 8.550369 [DDD]
Chopin, F.:Études (24) *(rec 3/90)* Naxos ▲ 8.550364 [DDD]
Chopin, F.:Krakowiak, w. R. Stankovsky (cnd), Czech–Slovak State PO *(rec 11/90 & 6/91)* Naxos ▲ 8.550369 [DDD]
Chopin, F.:Mazurkas—Opp. 6, 7, 17, 24, 30, 33, 41/1 *(rec 3/90)* Naxos ▲ 8.550358 [DDD]
Chopin, F.:Nocturnes—Op. 9/1–3, 15/1–3, 27/1–2, 32/1–2; Nos. 20 & 21 *(rec July & Sept. 1991)* Naxos ▲ 8.550356 [DDD]
Chopin, F.:Pno Music (misc)—Barcarolle; Bolero; Bourrée I & II; Wiosna; Feuille d'Album; Fugue *(rec March & Sept. 1991, Feb.)* Naxos ▲ 8.550366 [DDD]
Chopin, F.:Pno Music (misc)—Contredanse in G♭; Three Ecossaises *(rec March & Sept. 1991)* Naxos ▲ 8.550365 [DDD]
Chopin, F.:Pno Music (misc)—Rondo in c, Op. 1; Rondo in F, Op.5; Rondo in E♭, Op. 16; Rondo in C, Op. 73; 6 Mazurkas; Variations *(rec March, Apr, & Sept. 1991)* Naxos ▲ 8.550367 [DDD]
Chopin, F.:Pno Music (misc)—Ballades; Berceuse; Études; Fantasie, Op. 49; Gallop Marquis; Largo; Funeral March; Cantabile *(rec March, April, Sept. 1991)* Naxos ▲ 8.550508 [DDD]
Chopin, F.:Pno Music (misc)—Impromptu No. 4 in c#, Op. 66; Nocturnes, No. 2 in E♭, Op. 9/2; No. 8 in D♭, Op. 27/2; Waltzes, No. 1 in E♭, Op. 18; No. 6 in D♭, Op. 64/1; No. 7 in c#, Op. 64/2; Son. No. 2, Op. 35; Mazurka No. 5 in B♭, Op. 7/1; Polonaises, No. 3 in A, Op. 40/1; No. 6 in A♭, Op. 53; Prelude No. 15 in D♭, Op. 28/15; Études, No. 3 in E, Op. 10/3; No. 5 in G♭, Op. 10/5; No. 12 in c, Op. 10/12; Ballade No. 1 in g, Op. 23 Naxos ▲ 8.553170 [DDD]
Chopin, F.:Polonaises Naxos ▲ 8.550360 [DDD]
Chopin, F.:Polonaises—9 polonaises *(rec Apr. 1991)* Naxos ▲ 8.550361 [DDD]
Chopin, F.:Prelude in A♭ *(rec March & Sept. 1991, Feb.)* Naxos ▲ 8.550366 [DDD]
Chopin, F.:Preludes, Op. 28 *(rec March & Sept. 1991, Feb.)* Naxos ▲ 8.550366 [DDD]
Chopin, F.:Prelude, Op. 45 *(rec March & Sept. 1991, Feb.)* Naxos ▲ 8.550366 [DDD]
Chopin, F.:Son Pno, Op. 4 *(rec Tonstudio von Geest, Heidelberg, Germany, Sept 3–5, 1990)* Naxos ▲ 8.553237 [DDD]
Chopin, F.:Son Pno, Op. 35 *(rec Tonstudio von Geest, Heidelberg, Germany, Sept 3–5, 1990)* Naxos ▲ 8.553237 [DDD]
Chopin, F.:Tarantelle *(rec March & Sept. 1991)* Naxos ▲ 8.550365 [DDD]
Chopin, F.:Vars on Mozart's *La ci darem la mano,* w. R. Stankovsky (cnd), Czech–Slovak State PO *(rec 11/90 & 6/91)* Naxos ▲ 8.550369 [DDD]
Chopin, F.:Waltzes *(rec March & Sept. 1991)* Naxos ▲ 8.550365 [DDD]

Biret, Idil (pno) (cont.)
Famous Piano Music Naxos 4–▲ 8.504010 [DDD]
Gluck, C.W.:Orfeo ed Euridice (ballet music & reigen der seliger geister) *(rec 11–12/91)* Marco Polo ▲ 8.223452 [DDD]
Handel, G.F.:Menuet Pno *(rec 11–12/91)* Marco Polo ▲ 8.223452 [DDD]
Kempff, W.:Pno Music—Italian Suite, Op. 68 (1953); Sonata in g, Op. 47 (1947) *(rec 11–12/91)* Marco Polo ▲ 8.223452 [DDD]
Liszt, F.:Transcriptions & Paraphrases—Berlioz:Symphonie Fantastique *(rec June 1992)* Naxos ▲ 8.550725 [DDD]
Mozart, W.A.:Pastorale variée Marco Polo ▲ 8.223452 [DDD]
Rachmaninoff, S.:Études–tableaux, Opp. 33 & 39 Naxos ▲ 8.550347 [DDD]
Rachmaninoff, S.:Moments musicaux *(rec Oct. 1989)* Naxos ▲ 8.550349 [DDD]
Rachmaninoff, S.:Morceaux de fant *(rec Oct. 1989 & Oct. 1990)* Naxos ▲ 8.550348 [DDD]
Rachmaninoff, S.:Pno Transcriptions—Liebesfreud; Liebeslied [F. Kreisler] Naxos ▲ 8.550466 [DDD]
Rachmaninoff, S.:Preludes Pno, Opp 23 & 32—Op. 23 *(rec Oct. 1989 & Oct. 1990)* Naxos ▲ 8.550348 [DDD]
Rachmaninoff, S.:Preludes Pno, Opp 23 & 32—Op. 32 Naxos ▲ 8.550466 [DDD]
Rachmaninoff, S.:Son 2 Pno *(rec Oct. 1989)* Naxos ▲ 8.550349 [DDD]
Rachmaninoff, S.:Variations on a Theme by Corelli *(rec Oct. 1989)* Naxos ▲ 8.550349 [DDD]
Saint–Saëns, C.:Con 2 Pno, w. J. Loughran (cnd), Philharmonia Orch Naxos ▲ 8.550334 [DDD]
Saint–Saëns, C.:Con 4 Pno, w. J. Loughran (cnd), Philharmonia Orch Naxos ▲ 8.550334 [DDD]

Birgisson, Snorri Sigfús (pno)
Cello, w. Bryndís Halla Gylfadóttir (vc), Marta Guthrún Halldórsdóttir (sop) Music from Iceland ▲ ITM 804

Birkeland, Øystein (vc)
Grieg, E.:Intermezzo, w. H. Gimse (pno) *(rec May & Aug. 1993)* Naxos ▲ 8.550878 [DDD]
Grieg, E.:Son Vc, w. H. Gimse (pno) *(rec May & Aug. 1993)* Naxos ▲ 8.550878 [DDD]
Halvorsen, J.:Passacaglia & Sarabande con variazioni, w. Atle Sponberg (vn) [arr for Vn & Vc] Simax ▲ PSC 1104
Kodály, Z.:Duo Vn & Vc, w. Atle Sponberg (vn) Simax ▲ PSC 1104
Ravel, M.:Son Vn Vc, w. Atle Sponberg (vn) Simax ▲ PSC 1104

Birkeland, Roger (sax)—see ORCHESTRAS & ENSEMBLES Chicago Saxophone Quartet

Birkelund, Poul (fl)
Ibert, J.:Con Fl, w. M. Caridis (cnd), Danish National RSO Canzone ▲ CAN 33008 [ADD]
Jolivet, A.:Con Fl, w. E. Tuxen (cnd), Danish National RSO Canzone ▲ CAN 33008 [ADD]
Nielsen, C.:Con Fl, w. E. Tuxen (cnd), Danish National RSO Canzone ▲ CAN 33008 [ADD]

Birnie, T. (pno)
Holland, Dulcie:Pno Music, w. D. Holland (pno)—A Scattering of Leaves; Nocturne; Asterisk; A Night for Ghosts; Son.; Mini–Toccata; Asterisk; other solo pieces Southern Cross ▲ SCCD 1028 [DDD]

Birnstigl, R. (db)
Balissat, J.:Vars (7), w. P. Genet, F. Gottraux (vn), N. Pache (va), M. Jaermann (vc), F. Rapin (cl), F. Schmocker (bn), M. Veillon (hn), J. Balissat (cnd) Grammont ▲ CTSP 17–2 [ADD]

Birnstingl, Roger (bn)
Berio, L.:Opus Number Zoo, w. B. Demottaz (ob), B. Schenkel (fl), R. Meyer (cl), G. Cass (hn) *(rec June 1987)* Gallo ▲ CD 527
Bizet, G.:Jeux d'enfants, w. B. Demottaz (fl), B. Schenkel (ob), R. Meyer (cl), G. Cass (hn) *(rec June 1987)* Gallo ▲ CD 527
Ibert, J.:Pièces brèves, w. G. Cass (hn), B. Demottaz, R. Meyer, B. Schenkel *(rec June 1987)* Gallo ▲ CD 527
Saint–Saëns, C.:Carnival of the Animals, w. B. Demottaz (ob), B. Schenkel (inst), R. Meyer (cl), G. Cass (horn) *(rec June 1987)* Gallo ▲ CD 527

Biron, Avner (fl)
Handel, G.F.:Cants, w. M. Zakai (cta), A. Shavel (hpd)—"Mal palpita il cor" [I] Koch International Classics ▲ KIC 7021–2 [DDD] ■ 3–7021–4 (D)
Ravel, M.:Chansons madécasses, w. M. Zakai (cta), M. Haran (vc), Y. Zak (pno) [F] Koch International Classics ▲ KIC 7021–2 [DDD] ■ 3–7021–4 (D)

Biros, Philippe (pno)
Fauré, G.:Songs, w. Vincent Le Texier (bar)—Les Roses d'Ispahan; Hymne; Chanson du pêcheur; Les matelots; Chant d'automne; L'absent; Fleur jetée; Le Voyageur; Chanson d'amour; Automne; Le Secret; Les Larmes; Au Cimetière; Les Berceaux; Tristesse; Chant d'automne; Nocturne; Nell; Poème d'un jour; L'absent; L'Horizon chimérique Valois ▲ V 4747
Ropartz, G.:Songs, w. V. Le Téxier (bar)—Veilles de départ; Il pleut; En mai; Tout le long de la nuit; Chanson de bord; Le Temps des Saintes; Chant d'automne; Si j'étais roi; Quatre poèmes Valois ▲ V 4701 [DDD]

Bisaro, Xavier (org)
Lefébure–Wély, L.J.A.:Music of, w. Sylvie de May (sop), Catherine Ravenne (alt), Vincent Genvrin (org), La Lyre Seraphique, L'Accent Grave Vocal Ensemble—Adoremus et procidamus; Marche en mib majeur; Adoro te [alterné]; Tantum ergo; Sacris solemnis; Elévation en la mineur; Marche en ut majeur; Noël varié, offertoire pour le jour de Noël; Sanctus; O Salutaris; Pastorale en sol majeur; Agnus Dei; Communion en fa majeur; Domine salvum; Missum redemptorem; Sortie en sib majeur et Cloches Media 7 ▲ 005 [DDD]

Bischof, Andrea (vn)—see ORCHESTRAS & ENSEMBLES Mosaïques String Quartet

Bischof, J. (vc)
Ludwig Güttler:Trompete, Corno da Caccia, Posthorn, w. L. Güttler (tpt), Virtuosi Saxoniae, F. Kircheis (hpd), W. Zeibig (db) *(rec 1988–92)* Berlin Classics ▲ BER 1053 [DDD]

Bischoff–Oswald, Tamara (hp)
Gawthrop, D.:This Child, This King, w. Rebecca Parkinson (org), Dennis Griffin (timp), Will Kesling (cnd), Utah State Univ Chamber Singers *(rec Kent Concert Hall, USU Chase Fine Arts Center, Logan, UT, Feb. 4–5, 1995)* Integra Classic ▲ IMCD 951 [DDD]

Bisengaliev, Marat (vn)
Brian, H.:Con Vn, w. L. Friend (cnd), BBC Scottish SO *(rec Jan. 12–15, 1993)* Marco Polo ▲ 8.223479 [DDD]
Lalo, E.:Sym espagnole, w. J. Wildner (cnd), Polish National RSO Katowice *(rec Jan. 31–Feb. 3, 1992)* Naxos ▲ 8.550494 [DDD]
Ravel, M.:Tzigane, w. J. Wildner (cnd), Polish National RSO Katowice *(rec Jan. 31–Feb. 3, 1992)* Naxos ▲ 8.550494 [DDD]
Saint–Saëns, C.:Havanaise Vn, w. J. Wildner (cnd), Polish National RSO Katowice *(rec Jan. 31–Feb. 3, 1992)* Naxos ▲ 8.550494 [DDD]
Sarasate, P. de:Zigeunerweisen, w. J. Wildner (cnd), Polish National RSO Katowice *(rec Jan. 31–Feb. 3, 1992)* Naxos ▲ 8.550494 [DDD]
Wieniawski, H.:Con 1 Vn, w. A. Wit (cnd), Polish National RSO Katowice *(rec Katowice, Poland, Aug 1995)* Naxos ▲ 8.553517 [DDD]
Wieniawski, H.:Con 2 Vn, w. A. Wit (cnd), Polish National RSO Katowice *(rec Katowice, Poland, Aug 1995)* Naxos ▲ 8.553517 [DDD]
Wieniawski, H.:Fant brilliante on Themes from Gounod's *Faust,* w. A. Wit (cnd), Polish National RSO Katowice *(rec Katowice, Poland, Aug 1995)* Naxos ▲ 8.553517 [DDD]
Wieniawski, H.:Vn & Pno Music, w. J. Lenehan (pno)—Souvenir de Moscou, Op. 6; Capriccio–valse in E, Op. 7; Vars. on an Original Theme, Op. 15; Polonaise brillante, Op. 4; Le carnaval russe, Op. 11; Gigue in e, Op. 23; Saltarello [arr. Lenehan]; Mazurkas, Opp. 12/2 & 19/1 Naxos ▲ 8.550744 [DDD]

Bish, Diane (org)
Bish, D.:A Sym of Hymns, w. Sung Sook Lee (sop), D. James Kennedy (nar), R. McMurrin (cnd), Coral Ridge Orch, Coral Ridge Chorus [E] VQR Digital ▲ QR 2041 [DDD]
Bish, D.:A Sym of Hymns, w. Sung Sook Lee (sop), D. James Kennedy (nar), R. McMurrin (cnd), Coral Ridge Orch, Coral Ridge Chorus [E] VQR Digital ▲ QR 2041 [DDD]

Bissegger, Hansruedi (cl)—see also ORCHESTRAS & ENSEMBLES Zurich New Music Ensemble
Wyttenbach, J.:Lamentoroso, w. L. Akerlund (sop), N. Calame (cl), M. Maurer (cl), E. Molinari (cl), M. Weber (cl), H. Zwahlen (cl) *(rec May 19–20, 1990)* Grammont ▲ CTSP 37–2 [ADD]

Bissenger, Hansruedi (cl)—see ORCHESTRAS & ENSEMBLES Zurich New Music Ensemble

Bissiri, Gary (gtr)
The Gypsy Influence, w. S. Novacek (gtr) — Ambassador ▲ ARC 1005 [ADD] ■ ARC 1005
Rodrigo, J.:Tonadilla, w. S. Novacek (gtr) — Ambassador ▲ ARC 1005 [ADD] ■ ARC 1005

Bitetti, Ernesto (gtr)
Classica de España, w. Madrid Concert Orch, National Orch of Spain, Alicia de Larrocha (pno) — EMI Classics 2–▲ ZDMB 64241
Rodrigo, J.:Concierto de Aranjuez, w. A. Ros–Marbá (cnd), Philharmonia Orch — Classics for Pleasure ▲ CDCFP 4614 [DDD]
Rodrigo, J.:Fant para un gentilhombre, w. A. Ros–Marbá (cnd), Philharmonia Orch — Classics for Pleasure ▲ CDCFP 4614 [DDD]
Rodrigo, J.:Gtr Music, w. A. Ros–Marbá (cnd), Philharmonia Orch—En Los Trigales; Sonata a la Española — Classics for Pleasure ▲ CDCFP 4614 [DDD]

Bitrán, Alvaro (vc)—see also ORCHESTRAS & ENSEMBLES Latin American String Quartet
Vali, R.:Folk Songs Set 9, w. Alberto Almarza (fl) *(rec Rodef Shalom, Pittsburgh, Apr. 13, 1994)* — New Albion ▲ NAO 77
Vali, R.:Music of, w. Alberto Almarza (fl), J.P. Izqueirdo (cnd), Carnegie Mellon PO, Latin American String Quartet — New Albion ▲ NA 077

Bitrán, Arón (vn)—see ORCHESTRAS & ENSEMBLES Latin American String Quartet

Bitrán, Saúl (vn)—see ORCHESTRAS & ENSEMBLES Latin American String Quartet

Bitterman, Craig (perc)
Cage, J.:But What About The Noise...?, w. Eberhard Blum, Patti Cudd, Thomas Furminger, Erik Oña, Christopher Swist *(rec Slee Concert Hall, Univ. at Buffalo, NY, May 28 – June 1, 1995)* — Hat Art ("Hat Now" series) ▲ 6179 [DDD]

Bitzinger, Christoph (va)
Weichlein, R.:Encaenia musices, w. Gunar Letzbor (vn), Daniel Sepec (vn), Herbert Lindsberger (va), Michael Oman (vl), Gaetano Nasillo (vc), Roberto Sensi (vn), Andreas Lackner (nat tpt), Herbert Walser (nat tpt), Norbert Kirchner (hpd/org), G. Letzbor (cnd), Ars Antiqua Austria—Sons. Nos. I in C, II in g, III in a, IV in E, V in C & VI in F — Symphonia ▲ SY 93S23

Bjerken, X. (vc)—see ORCHESTRAS & ENSEMBLES Mobius

Björklund, Staffan (org)
Björklund, S.:Org Music—Organ Symphony (1975–6); Melody for Organ (1982); Choral Fantasy for organ on Swedish Psalm 43, "Bereden väg för Herran" (1979) — BIS ▲ CD 417 [DDD]
Björklund, S.:Org Music — Proprius ▲ PRCD 9051

Björkman, Håkan (trbn)
Grondahl, L.:Con Trbn, w. J. Hirokami (cnd), Stockholm Symphonic Wind Orch — Caprice ▲ CAP 21516

Bjørkøe, C. (pno)
Barber, S.:Prayers of Kierkegaard, w. S. Skov (pno), J. Koch (pno), Safri Duo, La Camerata — Danica ▲ DCD 8154
Britten, H.:Flower Songs, w. S. Skov (sop), J. Koch (pno), Safri Duo, La Camerata — Danica ▲ DCD 8154
Grainger, P.:Songs, w. S. Skov (sop), J. Koch (pno), M. Bojesen (cnd), Camerata, Safri Duo—No Nighean Dhu; O Mistress Mine; 6 Dukes Went a–Fishing; Mary Thompson; Old Irish Tune — Danica ▲ DCD 8154
Holmboe, V.:Songs, w. S. Skov (sop), J. Koch (pno), Safri Duo—Americana — Danica ▲ DCD 8154
Nørholm, I.:Songs, w. S. Skov (sop), J. Koch (pno), Camerata, Safri Duo—Song at Sunset — Danica ▲ DCD 8154

Björlin, Ulf (ob)
Roman, J.H.:Con grosso, Cappella Coloniensis — Capriccio ▲ 10 624 [DDD]

Bjørn–Larsen, Jens (tuba)—see ORCHESTRAS & ENSEMBLES Royal Danish Brass

Björnsson, Oddur (trbn)
Sveinsson, A.H.:Jubilus II, w. P.P. Pálsson (cnd), Iceland SO — ITM ▲ ITM 706

Bjørslev, Jørgen (gtr)
Albéniz, I.:Gtr Music—Asturias; Granada — Danica ▲ DCD 8146
Falla, M. de:Homenaje 'Le tombeau de Debussy' — Danica ▲ DCD 8146
Moreno Torroba, F.:Gtr Music—Torija; Turegano — Danica ▲ DCD 8146
Murcia, S. de:Gtr Music—Partita in d [from Passacailles y Obras] — Danica ▲ DCD 8146
Narváez, L. de:Seys libros—Con que la lavare la tex de la mia cara; Cancion del Emperador; Fant del primero tono; Differencias sobre Guarda me las vacas — Danica ▲ DCD 8146
Sor, F.:Gtr Music—Intro & Vars sur "Malbroug", Op. 28 — Danica ▲ DCD 8146
Turina, J.:Gtr Music—Sevillana — Danica ▲ DCD 8146

Bjurenhed, Ulf (ob/E hn)
Delage, M.:Poèmes hindous, w. Anne Sofie von Otter (mez), Andreas Alin (fl), Peter Rydström (fl/pic), Lars Paulsson (cl), Per Billman (cl/b cl), Nils–Erik Sparf (vn), Ulf Forsberg (vn), Matti Hirvikangas (va), Mats Lindström (vc), Lisa Viguier (hp) *(rec Stockholm, Nov 1994)* — Deutsche Grammophon ▲ 447 752–2 [DDD]

Blaas, Mikuláš (va)—see ORCHESTRAS & ENSEMBLES Bratislava String Trio

Blaauw, Marco (tpt)
Kagel, M.:Nah und Fern, w. Andreas Adam (tpt), Achim Gorsch (tpt), Markus Stockhausen (tpt), Arie Abbonos (oar), M. Kagol (cnd) — Montaigne ▲ MO 782062

Blacher, Kolja (vn)
Beethoven, L. van:Missa Solemnis, w. Julia Varady (sop), Iris Vermillion (mez), Vinson Cole (ten), Rene Pape (bass), G. Solti (cnd), Berlin PO, Berlin Radio Chorus — London ▲ 444337–2 [DDD]
Blacher, B.:Con Vn, w. N. Athinäos (cnd), Frankfurt on the Oder SO — Signum ▲ X 40–00 [DDD]
Dehmel Lieder, w. D. Fischer–Dieskau (bar), Aribert Reimann (pno) — Orfeo d'or ▲ 390951
Hindemith, P.:Kammermusik 4, w. C. Abbado (cnd), Berlin PO — EMI Classics ▲ CDC 56160

Black (pno)
Pollock, R.:Violament, w. J. Graham (va) — CRI ■ ACS 6016 (CrO2)

Black, B. (tpt)
Haydn, J.:Con Tpt, w. C. Scimone (cnd), Philharmonia Orch — EMI Classics ▲ CDC 54620
Hummel, J.N.:Con in E♭ Tpt, S.49, w. C. Scimone (cnd), Philharmonia Orch — EMI Classics ▲ CDC 54620
Vivaldi, A.:Con for 2 Tpts, w. C. Scimone (cnd), Philharmonia Orch — EMI Classics ▲ CDC 54620

Black, Gavin (hpd)
Böhm, G.:Hpd Music—Praeludium in g *(rec American Academy of Arts & Letters, New York City, June 6, 1994)* — PGM ▲ PGM 101 [DDD]
Buxtehude, D.:La Capricciosa *(rec St. Peter's Church, Great Valley, Malvern, PA)* — PGM ▲ PGM 105
Buxtehude, D.:More Palatino *(rec St. Peter's Church, Great Valley, Malvern, PA)* — PGM ▲ PGM 105
Buxtehude, D.:Suite Kbd, BuxWV 230 *(rec St. Peter's Church, Great Valley, Malvern, PA)* — PGM ▲ PGM 105
Buxtehude, D.:Suite Kbd, BuxWV 233 *(rec St. Peter's Church, Great Valley, Malvern, PA)* — PGM ▲ PGM 105
Buxtehude, D.:Suite Kbd, BuxWV 235 *(rec St. Peter's Church, Great Valley, Malvern, PA)* — PGM ▲ PGM 105
Froberger, J.J.:Hpd Music—Ricercars Nos. 4 & 6; Suites Nos. 1 & 6; Toccata No. 6 *(rec American Academy of Arts & Letters, New York City, June 6, 1994)* — PGM ▲ PGM 101 [DDD]
Kuhnau, J.:Biblical Sons—Death & Burial of Jacob *(rec American Academy of Arts & Letters, New York City, June 6, 1994)* — PGM ▲ PGM 101 [DDD]
Kuhnau, J.:Musicalische Vorstellung einiger biblischer Historien—Death & Burial of Jacob *(rec American Academy of Arts & Letters, New York City, June 6, 1994)* — PGM ▲ PGM 101 [DDD]

Black, Neil (ob d'amore)
Bach, J.S.:Con 4 Hpd, w. Christopher Hogwood (bc), Nicholas Kraemer (bc), N. Marriner (cnd), Academy of St. Martin in the Fields [trans for ob d'amore] *(rec St. John's, Smith Square, London, Aug 1974 & Feb 1975)* — Boston Skyline ▲ BSD 127 [ADD]

Black, Neil (ob)
Albinoni, T.:Cons Obs, w. J. L. Garcia (vn), M. Eade (vn), English CO—in d — Virgin Classics ▲ CDZ 59656
Bach, J.S.:Con 2 Hpd, w. Christopher Hogwood (bc), Nicholas Kraemer (bc), N. Marriner (cnd), Academy of St. Martin in the Fields [trans for ob] *(rec St. John's, Smith Square, London, Aug 1974 & Feb 1975)* — Boston Skyline ▲ BSD 127 [ADD]

Black, Neil (ob) (cont.)
Corelli, A.:Concerti grossi, Op. 6, w. M. Eade (vn), J.L. Garcia (vn), W. Bennett (fl), I. Watson (hpd/org), English CO—No. 2 in F — Virgin Classics ▲ CDZ 59656
Falla, M. de:Con Hpd, w. R. Puyana (hpd), D. Sandeman (fl), T. King (cl), R. Cohen (vn), T. Weill (vc), C. Mackerras (cnd) *(rec 1969)* — Philips ("Spanish" series) ▲ 432829–2 [ADD]
Mozart, W.A.:Con Ob, K.314, w. N. Marriner (cnd), Academy of St. Martin in the Fields — Philips ▲ 416483–2 [DDD]
Strauss, R.:Con Ob, w. D. Barenboim (cnd), English CO — Sony Classical ("Essential Classics" series) ▲ SBK 62652 ■ SBT 62652

Black, Robert (bass gtr)
Andriessen, L.:Hoketus, w. Katherine Pendry (panpipes), James Poke (panpipes), Evan Ziporyn (a sax), Richard Craig (a sax), Steven Schick (congas), Amy Knoles (congas), Lisa Moore (Fender Rhodes), Damian LeGassick (Fender Rhodes), Cees van Zeeland (pno), Gerard Bouwhuis (pno), Mark Stewart (bass gtr) *(rec Air Recording Studios, Lyndhurst Hall, Hampstead, London, June 29–July 3, 1994)* — Sony Classical ▲ SK 66483 [DDD]

Black, Robert (db)—see also ORCHESTRAS & ENSEMBLES Bang on a Can
Bolle, J.:Duo Vn & Db, w. Veronica Macchia–Kadlubkiewicz (vn) — Gasparo ▲ GSCD 317 [DDD]
Cage, J.:Ryoanji, w. John Patrick Thomas (voc), Gudrun Reschke (ob), Eberhard Blum (fl), Iven Hausmann (trbn), Jan Williams (perc) *(rec Akademie der Künste, Berlin, June 22, 1995)* — Hat Hut ("Now" series) ▲ hat ART CD 6183 [DDD]
Kernis, A.J.:America(n) (Day) Dreams, w. Kim Barber (mez), Mary Rowell (vn), Leslie Tomkins (va), Tonya Tomkins (vc), Kathleen Nester (fl), Larry Guy (cl/b cl), John Dent (tpt), Anthony Cecere (hn), Leslie Stifelman (pno), Susan Jolles (hp), Jeffrey Milarsky (perc), M. Barrett (cnd)—A Navajo Blanket; Wednesday at the Waldorf; The Pregnant Dream; The Blue Bottle; "So Long" to the Moon from the Men of Apollo; Epilogue:The Pure Suit of Happiness *(rec Manhattan Center Studios, New York, May 31–June 3, 1995)* — New Albion ♦ NA 083CD
Wolfe, J.:Lick, w. Evan Ziporyn (s sax), Mark Stewart (elec gtr), Steven Schick (perc), Lisa Moore (pno), Maya Beiser (vc) *(rec Air Recording Studios, Lyndhurst Hall, Hampstead, London, June 29–July 3, 1994)* — Sony Classical ▲ SK 66483 [DDD]

Black, Robert (db/midi bass/elec bass/processed bass)
State of Bass — O. O. Discs ▲ OO 14

Black, Robert (db/perc)
Adams, J.L.:Earth & the Great Weather, w. R. Lorentz (vn/perc), R. Lawrence (va), M. Finckel (vc), A. Knoles (perc), J. L. Adams (perc), J. Nageak (Iñupiat Eskimo performer), D. Simmonds (Iñupiat Eskimo performer), L. Tritt (Gwich'in Indian performer), A. P. Raboff (Gwich'in Indian performer), D. Hunsaker (Latin voice), J.L. Adams (cnd) *(rec Fairbanks, Mar. 8–11, 1993)* — New World ▲ 80459–2

Black, Robert (elec bass/elec)
Dresher, P.:Mirrors — Starkland ▲ ST 204

Black, Robert (pno)
Babbitt, M.:Composition Va, w. J. Graham (va) — CRI ■ ACS 6016 (CrO2)
Ghent, E.:Entelechy, w. J. Graham (va) — CRI ■ ACS 6016 (CrO2)

Black, Stanley (pno)
Gershwin, G.:Rhap in Blue, w. S. Black (cnd), London Festival Orch *(rec Kingsway Hall, London, Dec 1965)* — London ("Phase 4 Stereo" series) ▲ 444785–2 [ADD]

Black, Virginia (harm)
Dvořák, A.:Bagatelles, Op. 47, w. Alberni String Quartet members *(rec 10–11/1988)* — CRD ▲ 3457 [DDD]

Black, Virginia (hpd)
The Essential Harpsichord — Collins Classics ▲ COL 5024 [DDD]
Program 4, w. A. Dolmetsch (vir), Carl Dolmetsch (rcr), François Dolmetsch (rcr), Marguerite Dolmetsch (rcr), et al. — IMP Allegro ▲ PCD 1010 [DDD]
Scarlatti, D.:Sons Kbd—K.24, 113, 119, 120, 146, 213, 318, 319, 380, 381, 466, 501, 502 — CRD ▲ CD 3442

Black, William (pno)
Diamond, D.:Preludes & Fugues (52)—in C; in e; in c# [from Vol 1] *(rec RCA Studio A, New York City)* — New World ▲ 80508–2
Diamond, D.:Preludes & Fugues (52)—3 from Vol. 1—in C, c# & e — Grenadilla ■ GSC 1064
Diamond, D.:Sons (2) Vn, w. Robert McDuffie (vn) *(rec RCA Studio A, New York City)* — New World ▲ 80508–2
Diamond, D.:Sons (2) Vn, w. Robert McDuffie (vn) — Grenadilla ■ GSC 1064
Gershwin, G.:Rhap in Blue, w. E. Corporon (cnd), Cincinnati College Conservatory of Music Wind Sym [scored Grofé] — Klavier ▲ KCD 11047 [DDD]
Johnson, H.:Son Pno — Albany ▲ TROY 061 [DDD]
Rachmaninoff, S.:Con 4 Pno, w. I. Buketoff (cnd), Iceland SO [original 1927 version] — Chandos ▲ CHAN 8987 [DDD]

Blackman, Martha (vl)
Music of the Middle Ages, Vol. 4:English Polyphony of the 13th & Early 14th Centuries, w. Oberlin, Russell (ct), C. Bressler (ten), D. Perry (ten), S. Barab (vl) — Lyrichord ▲ LYR 8004 [ADD]
Music of the Middle Ages, Vol. 6:English Polyphony of the 14th & Early 15th Centuries, w. Oberlin, Russell (ct), C. Bressler (ten), R. Price (ten), G. Meyers (bar) — Lyrichord ▲ LYR 8006 [ADD]
Music of the Middle Ages, Vol. 7, w. French Ars Antiqua, Russell Oberlin (ct), Charles Bressler (ten), R. Price (ten), G. Meyers (bar), P. Wolfe (org) — Lyrichord ▲ LYR 8007 [ADD]

Blackwood, Easley (pno)
Blackwood, E.:Son Vc, w. K. Scholes (vc) — Cedille ▲ CDR 90000 008 [DDD]
Bridge, F.:Son Vc, w. K. Scholes (vc) — Cedille ▲ CDR 90000 008 [DDD]
Casella, A.:Pezzi, Op. 24 — Cedille ▲ CDR 90000 003 [DDD]
Casella, A.:Sonatina Pno — Cedille ▲ CDR 90000 003 [DDD]
Copland, A.:Son Pno — Cedille ▲ CDR 90000 005 [DDD]
Ives, C.:Son 2 Pno, w. R. Graef (fl) — Cedille ▲ CDR 90000 005 [DDD]
Radical Piano:Modernist Masterpieces from the 1st Half of the 20th Century, w. Blackwood, Easley (pno) *(rec WFMT, Chicago, 1994–96)* — Cedille ▲ CDR 90000 027 [DDD]
Reger, M.:Son Cl, Op. 107, w. John Bruce Yeh (cl) *(rec WFMT Chicago, Feb. 19–21, 1995)* — Cedille ▲ CDR 90000 022 [DDD]
Wuorinen, C.:Variations Pno *(rec live)* — Music & Arts ▲ CD 800 [ADD]

Blackwood, Easley (polyfusion syn)
Blackwood, E.:Fanfare in 19–note Equal Tuning *(rec 1979–81)* — Cedille ▲ CDR 90000 018
Blackwood, E.:Microtonal Etudes (12) *(rec 1979–81)* — Cedille ▲ CDR 90000 018

Blaha, Bernadene (pno)
Chopin, F.:Ballades Pno (comp)—Op. 23 — Round Top ▲ RTR 8615
Chopin, F.:Nocturnes—in B & c# — Round Top ▲ RTR 8615
Chopin, F.:Polonaise–fant — Round Top ▲ RTR 8615
Chopin, F.:Son Pno, Op. 58 — Round Top ▲ RTR 8615
Chopin, F.:Waltzes—Grand Valse in A♭ — Round Top ▲ RTR 8615

Bláha, František (cl)
Mozart, W.A.:Sinf concertante Ob, K.Anh.9, w. Jan Adamus (ob), Svatopluk Cech (bn), Zdenek Divoky (hn), J. Belohlávek (cnd), Dvořák CO — Panton ▲ PAN 811206

Blak, Kristian (pno)
Blak, K.:Addeq, w. L. Kullgren (gtr), P. Janson (db), M. Cissokho (perc) — Tutl ▲ HJF 22
Blak, K.:Music of, w. S. Rasmussen (perc)—8 (sels.) *(rec Dec. 1990)* — Tutl ▲ HJF 24

Blak, Kristian (pno/perc/sgr)
Blak, K.:Con Grotto, w. John Tchicai (t sax/sgr/perc), Lennart Kullgren (gtr/fl/sgr/perc), Anders Hagberg (fl/perc/sgr), Anders Jormin (bass instr/perc/sgr), Karin Korpelainen (perc/sgr), Sharon Weiss (perc/kaval) *(rec Lidargjógv, Sandoy, Aug. 1984)* — Tutl ▲ HJF 33

Blak, Kristian (pno/sgr)
Blak, K.:Drangar, w. Anders Hagberg (fl/s sax/perc), Tore Brunborg (s sax/t sax/perc), Lennart Kullgren (gtr/sgr), Anda Kuitse (sgr/perc), Anders Jormin (bass instr/perc), Karin Korpelainen (dr/perc) *(rec Nordic House, Tórshavn, Jan. 1995)* — Tutl ▲ HJF 33

Blake, Susan (vc)
Broadstock, B.:Eheu Fugaces, w. Marilyn Richardson (sop), Christine Draeger (fl), Roslyn Dunlop (cl), Fiona Ziegler (vn), David Miller (pno), Daryl Pratt (perc) Vox Australis ▲ VAST018–2 [DDD]
Sculthorpe, P.:The Stars Turn, w. Marilyn Richardson (sop), David Miller (pno) Vox Australis ▲ VAST018–2 [DDD]
Sitsky, L.:Deep in My Hidden Country, w. Marilyn Richardson (sop), Christine Draeger (fl), David Miller (pno), Daryl Pratt (perc) Vox Australis ▲ VAST018–2 [DDD]

Blakely, John (pno)
Beethoven, L. van:Son 5 Vn, "Spring", w. L. McAslan (vn) IMP ▲ PCD 833 [DDD]
Beethoven, L. van:Son 9 Vn, "Kreutzer", w. L. McAslan (vn) IMP ▲ PCD 833 [DDD]
Britten, H.:Reveille Vn, w. L. McAslan (vn) Continuum ▲ CCD 1022 [DDD]
Britten, H.:Suite Vn, w. L. McAslan (vn) Continuum ▲ CCD 1022 [DDD]
Bridge, F.:Cradle Song Vn, w. L. McAslan (vn) Continuum ▲ CCD 1022 [DDD]
Bridge, F.:Heart's Ease, w. L. McAslan (vn) Continuum ▲ CCD 1022 [DDD]
Bridge, F.:Norse Legend, w. L. McAslan (vn) Continuum ▲ CCD 1022 [DDD]
Bridge, F.:Serenade Vn, w. L. McAslan (vn) Continuum ▲ CCD 1022 [DDD]
Bridge, F.:Son Vn, w. L. McAslan (vn) Continuum ▲ CCD 1022 [DDD]
Bridge, F.:Vn & Pno Music, w. L. McAslan (vn)—Romanze Continuum ▲ CCD 1022 [DDD]
Elgar, E.:Son Vn, w. Lorraine McAslan (vn) ASV/Quicksilva ▲ ASQ CD 6191
Fauré, G.:Berceuse Vn, w. K. Smietana (vn) Meridian ▲ MER 84259 [DDD]
Fauré, G.:Sicilienne, w. K. Smietana (vn) Meridian ▲ MER 84259 [DDD]
Fauré, G.:Son 1 Vn, w. K. Smietana (vn) Meridian ▲ MER 84259 [DDD]
Fauré, G.:Son 2 Vn, w. K. Smietana (vn) Meridian ▲ MER 84259 [DDD]
Walton, W.:Son Vn & Pno, w. Lorraine McAslan (vn) ASV/Quicksilva ▲ ASQ CD 6191

Blanchard, Pierre (vn)
Blanchard, P.:Music of, w. V. Pagliarin (vn), C. Mouton (bass), C. Terranova (kbd), L. Robin (dr), M. Garay (perc)—Isidora; Koid'9; Perdoname; Folklores; Train de sables; Lithops; Marquesas Keys; Bodas de sangue *(rec Nov. 1992)* OMD ▲ CD 1538 [DDD]

Blanchard, Terence (hn)
Howard, J.N.:Primal Fear, w. Barbara Northcutt (E hn), A. Kane (cnd), *(orch unknown)* *(rec Paramount Pictures, Scoring Stage M, Los Angeles)* Milan ▲ 73138–35716–2 [DDD]

Blanco, Diego (gtr)
Castelnuovo–Tedesco, M.:Sonatina Fl & Gtr, w. G. von Bahr (fl) BIS ▲ CD 60 [AAD]
Favorite Guitar Music BIS ▲ CD 233 [DDD]
Ibert, J.:Entracte, w. G. von Bahr (fl) BIS ▲ CD 60 [AAD]
Music for Flute & Guitar, w. G. von Bahr (fl) BIS ▲ CD 60 [AAD]
Popular Guitar Music *(rec 1975 & 1979)* BIS ▲ CD 133 [AAD]
Rautavaara, E.:Son Fl, w. G. von Bahr (fl) BIS ▲ CD 60 [AAD]
Rautavaara, E.:Son Fl, w. G. von Bahr (fl) *(rec June 25, 1975)* BIS ▲ CD 66 [AAD]
Tárrega, F.:Recuerdos de la Alhambra BIS ▲ CD 233 [DDD]
Villa–Lobos, H.:Suite populaire brésilienne BIS ▲ CD 233 [DDD]
Werdin, E.:Concertino Fl, w. G. von Bahr (fl), J.–O. Wedin (cnd), Stockholm Chamber Ensemble BIS ▲ CD 60 [AAD]
Works for Flute & Guitar, w. G. von Bahr (fl) BIS ▲ CD 90 [AAD]

Blank, J. (ob)—see ORCHESTRAS & ENSEMBLES Roseau Wind Quintet
Blank, W. (perc)—see ORCHESTRAS & ENSEMBLES Linea Ensemble

Blankestijn, Marieke (vn)
Bach, J.S.:Con Vn & Ob, w. D. Boyd (ob), A. Schneider (cnd), CO of Europe ASV ("CO of Europe" series) ▲ CDCOE 803 [DDD]

Blasdale, Justin (pno)—see also ORCHESTRAS & ENSEMBLES Dunsmuir Piano Quartet
Kingman, D.:Dances & Ghost Dances, w. Betty Woo (pno) Innova ▲ INNOVA 504

Blasejewicz, Gerd (gtr)—see ORCHESTRAS & ENSEMBLES Rotenbeck Trio

Blashenov, Sergei (bn)
Vivaldi, A.:Con Ob Bn, w. Sergei Bliznetzov (ob), L. Korkhin (cnd), Collegium dell'Arte Infinity Digital ▲ QK 66724 [DDD]

Blasio, Chris de (pno)
de Blasio, C.:All the Way through Evening, w. Michael Dash (bar) CRI ▲ CD 729 [DDD]

Blas–Net (pno)
Bow & Baton:Complete 1929–30 HMV Singles & 1928 London Symphony Recordings, w. Casals, Pablo (vc), Otto Schulhof (pno) Pearl ▲ PEA 9128 [ADD]

Blatchly, Mark (org)
Coates, E.:Music of—Calling All Workers; London Bridge; Knightsbridge; Oxford Street; Tarantella [Covent Garden]; Dance in the Twilight; By the Sleepy Lagoon; The Dam Busters Priory ▲ PRI 521 [DDD]
Elgar, E.:Pomp & Circumstance Marches Priory ▲ PRI 521 [DDD]

Blatt, Josef (pno)
Bach, J.S.:Sons & Partitas Vn, BWV 1001–1006, w. Nathan Milstein (vn)—Son in g, BWV 1001 *(rec Coolidge Auditorium, Library of Congress, Oct 7, 1946)* Bridge ▲ BCD 9064
Chopin, F.:Nocturnes, w. Nathan Milstein (vn)—No. 20 in c# [arr Milstein for vn & pno] *(rec Coolidge Auditorium, Library of Congress, Oct 7, 1946)* Bridge ▲ BCD 9064
Mendelssohn, F.:Con in e Vn & Orch, Op. 64, w. Nathan Milstein (vn) *(rec Coolidge Auditorium, Library of Congress, Oct 7, 1946)* Bridge ▲ BCD 9064
Milstein, N.:Paganiniana, w. Nathan Milstein (vn) *(rec Coolidge Auditorium, Library of Congress, Oct 7, 1946)* Bridge ▲ BCD 9064
Vitali, T.A.:Chaconne Vn Pno, w. Nathan Milstein (vn) *(rec Coolidge Auditorium, Library of Congress, Oct 7, 1946)* Bridge ▲ BCD 9064
Wieniawski, H.:Vn & Pno Music, w. Nathan Milstein (vn)—Scherzo–Tarantelle *(rec Coolidge Auditorium, Library of Congress, Oct 7, 1946)* Bridge ▲ BCD 9064

Blau, Andreas (fl)
Mozart, W.A.:Con Fl, K.313, w. J. Galway (fl), F. Helmis (hp), H. von Karajan (cnd), Berlin PO EMI Classics ▲ CDM 69187
Mozart, W.A.:Con Fl Hp, w. J. Galway (fl), F. Helmis (hp), H. von Karajan (cnd), Berlin PO EMI Classics ▲ CDM 69187
Mozart, W.A.:Qts Fl, w. Amadeus String Quartet Deutsche Grammophon ▲ 429819–2 [ADD]
Mozart, W.A.:Qts Fl, w. Amadeus String Quartet members Deutsche Grammophon 2–▲ 437137–2 [ADD]

Blaumane, Kristine (vc)
Vasks, P.:Book *(rec Riga Recording Studio, Latvia, Dec 1995)* Conifer Classics ▲ 51272 [DDD]

Blees, Thomas (vc)
Faisst, C.:Adagio consolante, w. M. Bergmann (pno) FSM ▲ FCD 97 728 [DDD]
Farrenc, J.–L.:Son Vc, w. M. Bergmann (pno) FSM ▲ FCD 97 728 [DDD]
Lebeau, L.A.:Romanze, w. M. Bergmann (pno) FSM ▲ FCD 97728 [DDD]
Mayer, E.:Son Vc, w. M. Bergmann (pno) FSM ▲ FCD 97728 [DDD]
Music for Cello & Piano by Female Composers of the 19th Century, w. Maria Bergmann (pno) FSM ▲ 97728 [DDD]
Penderecki, K.:Son Vc, w. A. Springer (cnd), Luxembourg RSO *(rec Feb 1972)* Vox Box 2–▲ CDX 5142

Bleicher, Stefan Johannes (org)
Basilika Birnau:Duette für Orgel, w. M. Hospach–Martini (org) *(rec June 7–8, 1993)* Orfeo ▲ 341941 [DDD]
Boccherini, L.:Sons (5) Vc & Db, w. J. Berger (vc), A. Posch (vc), A. Spiri (hpd/pno) ebs ▲ ebs 6011 [DDD]
Meditations, w. James, Ifor (hn) ebs ▲ ebs 6040 [DDD]
Vivaldi, A.:Sons Vc, w. J. Berger (vc)—(10) RV.39–47 & Sonata in A Orfeo 2–▲ 251912 [DDD]
Wagenseil, G.C.:Cons Org, w. V. Czarnecki (cnd), Southwest German CO Pforzheim *(rec Peter & Paul Church, Mössingen, Oct 4–7, 1974)* ebs ▲ ebs 6089 [DDD]

Blet, Stéphane (pno)
Blet, S.:Prélude Pno Forlane ▲ FRL 16752 [DDD]

Blet, Stéphane (pno) (cont.)
Chopin, F.:Preludes, Op. 28—No. 16 Forlane ▲ FRL 16752 [DDD]
Liszt, F.:Album d'un voyageur—Les cloches de Genève [Book 1, No. 3] Forlane ▲ FRL 16752 [DDD]
Liszt, F.:Consolations—Nos. 1–3 & 6 Forlane ▲ FRL 16752 [DDD]
Liszt, F.:En rêve Forlane ▲ FRL 16752 [DDD]
Liszt, F.:Valse impromptu Forlane ▲ FRL 16752 [DDD]
Satie, E.:Le Piccadilly Forlane ▲ FRL 16752 [DDD]
Scarlatti, D.:Sons Kbd—in E, L.21 Forlane ▲ FRL 16752 [DDD]
Schumann, R.:Kreisleriana—Intermezzo Forlane ▲ FRL 16752 [DDD]
Stravinsky, I.:Studies Pno—No. 4 Forlane ▲ FRL 16752 [DDD]

Blewett, Brenda (pno)—see ORCHESTRAS & ENSEMBLES Musica Domestica

Blidar, Radu (vn)
Constant, M.:Chamber Music, w. Bruno Pasquier (va), Francis Pierre (hp), Elizabeth Chojnacka (hpd) Salabert ▲ SCD 9401

Blier, Steven (pno)—see also ORCHESTRAS & ENSEMBLES New York Festival Of Song
Bernstein, L.:Arias & Barcarolles, w. Judy Kaye (mez), William Sharp (bar), Michael Barrett (pno) [E] Koch International Classics ▲ KIC 7000–2 [DDD] ■ 3–7000–4 (D)
Bernstein, L.:Songs & Duets, w. Judy Kaye (sop), William Sharp (bar), M. Barrett (pno), S. Sant'Ambrogio (vc)—sels. from On The Town, 1944 *(Some other time; Lonely town; Carried away; I can cook)*; Peter Pan, 1949 *(Dream with me)*; Wonderful Town, 1952 *(A little bit in love)*; Songfest, 1977 *(Storyette, H.M.; To what you said)* [E] Koch International Classics ▲ KIC 7000–2 [DDD] ■ 3–7000–4 (D)
Blitzstein, M.:Songs, w. K. Holvik (sop), W. Sharp (bar)—Monday morning blues; Croon–spoon; The new suit ("Zipperfly"); In the clear; Then; I wish it so; In twos; Penny candy; Emily (Ballad of the bombardier); Displaced; Four e e cummings Songs (o by the by; until and i heard; open your heart; jimmy's got a goil); What will it be for me; Rose song; Blues; Nickel under the foot; The cradle will rock; Bird upon the tree; Stay in my arms [E] Koch International Classics ▲ KIC 7050–2 [DDD]
Bowles, P.:Songs Bar, w. W. Sharp (bar)—Four Blue Mountain Ballads; Sleeping song; April fool baby; A little closer, please; Three; Letter to Freddy; Secret words; My sister's hand in mine [E] New World ▲ NW 369–2 [DDD]
Gershwin, G.:Songs, w. J. Kaye (sop), W. Sharp (bar)—20 solo songs & duets Koch International Classics ▲ KIC 7028–2 [DDD] ■ 3–7028–4 (D)
Musto, J.:Recuerdo, w. W. Sharp (bar) [E] New World ▲ NW 369–2 [DDD]
Thomson, V.:Songs Bar, w. W. Sharp (bar)—Prayer to St. Catherine (1959); If thou a reason dost desire to know (1955); Two by Marianne Moore (1963); John Peel (1955); At the spring (1955) [E] New World ▲ NW 369–2 [DDD]

Blinderman, S. (pno)
Van Appledorn, M.J.:Con Brevis, w. J. Russo (cnd), National Festival Orch CRS ▲ CD 9052

Bliznetzov, Sergei (ob)
Vivaldi, A.:Con Ob Bn, w. Sergei Blashenov (bn), L. Korkhin (cnd), Collegium dell'Arte Infinity Digital ▲ QK 66724 [DDD]

Bloch, Boris (pno)
Liszt, F.:Operatic Paraphrases & Transcriptions—Reminiscences de Norma [Bellini]; Reminiscences de Lucia di Lammermoor [Donizetti]; Miserere d'Il Trovatore; Rigoletto Paraphrase; Danza Sacra e Duetto Finale d'Aida [all Verdi] Accord ▲ ACD 201722 [DDD]
Mussorgsky, M.:Pno Music—complete [17 pieces] Accord 2–▲ ACD 202152 [DDD]

Bloch, David (pno)
Avni, T.:Beside the Depths of a River, w. E. Berendsen (sgr) Symposium ▲ 1110

Bloch, J. (pno)
Crawford, R.:Preludes (9) CRI ▲ CD 658 [ADD]
Crawford, R.:Study in Mixed Accents CRI ▲ CD 658 [ADD]

Block, Michel (pno)
Albéniz, I.:España IMP ("Classics" series) ▲ IMP 6700042
Brahms, J.:Intermezzos Pno, Op. 117 *(rec New York, June 22 & 23, 1994)* Pro Piano ▲ PPR 224504 [DDD]
Brahms, J.:Pieces Pno, Op. 76—Intermezzos Nos. 3 in A♭, 4 in B♭ & 7 in a *(rec American Academy of Arts & Letters, New York, June 22 & 23, 1994)* ProPiano ▲ PPR 224504 [DDD]
Cerf, M.:Ma plus belle histoire d'amour *(rec live, Bloomington, IN, 1980)* Pro Piano ▲ PPR 224514
Chopin, F.:Mazurkas—in a, Op. 67/4 (Op. posth.) *(rec New York, June 22 & 23, 1994)* Pro Piano ▲ PPR 224504 [DDD]
Chopin, F.:Mazurkas—Op. 7/2 & 3; Op. 17/4; Op. 24/1 & 4; Op. 30/4; Op. 41/1 & 2; Op. 50/1–3; Op. 56/1–3; Op. 59/1 & 2; Op. 63/2 & 3; Op. 67/3; Op. 68/3 & 4; Notre Temps No. 2 in a *(rec Academy of Arts & Letters, New York, July 13–14, 1995)* Pro Piano ▲ PPR 224507
Chopin, F.:Polonaise–fant *(rec American Academy of Arts & Letters, New York, June 22 & 23, 1994)* ProPiano ▲ PPR 224504 [DDD]
Debussy, C.:Children's Corner—Serenade for the Doll *(rec Musical Arts Center, Bloomington, IN, Sept 15, 1980)* Pro Piano ▲ PPR 224514 [ADD]
Debussy, C.:Images (3) Pno—Quelques aspects de "Nour n'irons plus au bois," parce qu'il fait un temps *(rec Musical Arts Center, Bloomington, IN, Sept 15, 1980)* Pro Piano ▲ PPR 224514 [ADD]
Debussy, C.:Pno Music (misc)—Serenade for the Doll [from Children's Corner]; Quelques aspects de "Nous n'irons plus au bois", parce qu'il fait un temps insupportable [from Images (oubliées)] *(rec live, Bloomington, IN, 1980)* Pro Piano ▲ PPR 224514
Falla, M. de:Pièces espagnoles (4) IMP ("Classics" series) ▲ IMP 6700042
Fauré, G.:Nocturnes (13) Pno—No. 6 in D♭, Op. 63 *(rec New York, June 22 & 23, 1994)* Pro Piano ▲ PPR 224504 [DDD]
Godowsky, L.:Transcriptions & Paraphrases—Andante in C, trans. from J.S. Bach's Son. No. 2 in A for solo Violin, BWV 1003 *(rec New York, June 22 & 23, 1994)* Pro Piano ▲ PPR 224504 [DDD]
Granados, E.:Danzas españolas (10) IMP ("Classics" series) ▲ IMP 6700042
Granados, E.:Escenas poeticas IMP ("Classics" series) ▲ IMP 6700042
Schumann, R.:Novelettes *(rec Musical Arts Center, Bloomington, IN, Sept 15, 1980)* Pro Piano ▲ PPR 224514 [ADD]
Scriabin, A.:Son 2 Pno *(rec New York, June 22 & 23, 1994)* Pro Piano ▲ PPR 224504 [DDD]

Bloemendal, Coenraad (vc)—see also ORCHESTRAS & ENSEMBLES Rembrandt Trio
The Cantorial Voice of the Cello, w. Valerie Tryon (pno), Andrés Díaz (vc), Andrew Mark (vc) *(rec Troy Savings Bank Music Hall, Troy, NY, May 1994)* Dorian ▲ DOR 90208 [DDD]

Blok, Leonid (pno)
Violin Suites, w. I. Kaler (vn) Art & Electronics ▲ AED 10527 [DDD]

Blondin, Suzanne (pno)
Bloch, E.:Meditation & Processional, w. Robert Verebes (va) SNE ▲ 612
Bloch, E.:Suite hébraïque, w. Robert Verebes (va) SNE ▲ 612
Bruch, M.:Romanze Va, w. Robert Verebes (va) SNE ▲ 612
Enescu, G.:Concertpiece Va, w. Robert Verebes (va) SNE ▲ 612
Kodály, Z.:Adagio, w. Robert Verebes (va) SNE ▲ 612
Schubert, Franz:Son Arpeggione, w. Robert Verebes (va) *(rec Montreal)* SNE ▲ 580
Schumann, R.:Märchenbilder, w. Robert Verebes (va) *(rec Montreal)* SNE ▲ 580
Vaughan Williams, R.:Romance Va, w. Robert Verebes (va) SNE ▲ 612
Vieuxtemps, H.:Elégie, w. Robert Verebes (va) SNE ▲ 612
Vieuxtemps, H.:Son Va, w. Robert Verebes (va) *(rec Montreal)* SNE ▲ 580
Wieniawski, H.:Rêverie, w. Robert Verebes (va) SNE ▲ 612

Blonk, Stefan (hn)—see ORCHESTRAS & ENSEMBLES L'Archibudelli

Bloom, Arthur (cl)—see also ORCHESTRAS & ENSEMBLES Contemporary Chamber Players
Cordero, R.:Qnt Fl, w. John Wion (fl), Kees Kooper (vn), Fred Sherry (vc), Mary Louise Boehm (pno) Albany ▲ TROY 153 [DDD]
Martino, D.:Trio Cl, w. Paul Zukofsky (vn), Gilbert Kalish (pno) CRI ▲ CD 693 [ADD]
Palmer, R.:Qnt Cl, w. K. Kooper (vn), P. Doktor (va), Fred Sherry (vc), Mary Louise Boehm (pno) Albany ▲ TROY 153

Bloom, Claudia (vn)—see ORCHESTRAS & ENSEMBLES Ciompi String Quartet
Bloom, Jane Ira (s sax)—see ORCHESTRAS & ENSEMBLES Jazzantiqua

▲ = CD ♦ = Enhanced CD Δ = MD ■ = Cassette Tape ▯ = DCC

Bloom, Myron (hn)
Brahms, J.:Trio Hn, w. M. Tree (vn), R. Serkin (pno) Sony Classical ▲ SMK 46249 [ADD] ■ SMT 46249

Bloom, Sara Lambert (ob)
Handel, D.:Trio Ob, w. Benjamin Jew (E hn), Frank Weinstock (pno) Vienna Modern Masters ▲ VMM 2019 [DDD]
Handel, D.:The Tyger, w. Mary Henderson (sop), Gabrielle Robinson (vn), Jina Lee (vn), Rebecca Boughton (va), Deborah Netanel (vc), Mark Butler (pno), C. Zimmerman (cnd) Vienna Modern Masters ▲ VMM 2019 [DDD]
Music from Cranberry Isles, w. S. S. Frank (sop), Julius Baker (fl), et al. Centaur ▲ CRC 2084
Premiere Chamber Works, w. Amernet String Quartet, various soloists Centaur ▲ CRC 2217 [DDD]

Bloomquist, William (pno)
Brahms, J.:Sons Cl (comp), w. Charles Stier (cl) Halcyon 2-▲ HP 30101 [DDD]
Brahms, J.:Son 1 Cl, w. C. Stier (cl) Élan ▲ CD 2224 [DDD]
Brahms, J.:Son 2 Cl, w. C. Stier (cl) Élan ▲ CD 2238 [DDD]
Gade, N.W.:Fantasistykker, w. Charles Stier (cl) Halcyon 2-▲ HP 30101 [DDD]
Gade, N.W.:Fantasistykker, w. C. Stier (cl) Élan ▲ CD 2238 [DDD]
Reger, M.:Albumblatt & Romanze, w. C. Stier (cl)—Romanze Élan ▲ CD 2238
Reger, M.:Albumblatt & Tarantella, w. Charles Stier (cl) Halcyon 2-▲ HP 30101 [DDD]
Reger, M.:Albumblatt & Tarantella, w. C. Stier (cl) Élan ▲ CD 2238 [DDD]
Reger, M.:Son Cl, Op. 107, w. C. Stier (cl) Élan ▲ CD 2224 [DDD]
Schumann, R.:Fantasiestücke Cl, w. Charles Stier (cl) Halcyon 2-▲ HP 30101 [DDD]
Schumann, R.:Fantasiestücke Cl, w. C. Stier (cl) Élan ▲ CD 2238 [DDD]
Weber, C.M. von:Grand duo concertant Cl, w. Charles Stier (cl) Halcyon 2-▲ HP 30101 [DDD]
Weber, C.M. von:Grand duo concertant Cl, w. C. Stier (cl) Élan ▲ CD 2238 [DDD]

Bloss, Michael (org)
Bach, J.S.:Cant 156, w. Ofra Harnoy (vc)—Arioso [arr for vc & org] *(rec Church of the Blessed Sacrament, Toronto, 1981)* RCA Gold Seal ▲ 09026-68368-2 [ADD]
Bach, J.S.:Con 2 Vn, w. Ofra Harnoy (vc)—Adagio [arr for vc & org] *(rec Church of the Blessed Sacrament, Toronto, 1981)* RCA Gold Seal ▲ 09026-68368-2 [ADD]
Bach, J.S.:Toccata, Adagio & Fugue Org, BWV 564, w. Ofra Harnoy (vc)—Adagio [arr for vc & org] *(rec Church of the Blessed Sacrament, Toronto, 1981)* RCA Gold Seal ▲ 09026-68368-2 [ADD]
Bruch, M.:Kol Nidrei, w. Ofra Harnoy (vc) [arr for vc & org] *(rec Church of the Blessed Sacrament, Toronto, 1981)* RCA Gold Seal ▲ 09026-68368-2 [ADD]
Casals, P.:El Cant dels ocells, w. Ofra Harnoy (vc) [arr for vc & org] *(rec Church of the Blessed Sacrament, Toronto, 1981)* RCA Gold Seal ▲ 09026-68368-2 [ADD]
Corelli, A.:Sons Vn, Op. 5, w. Ofra Harnoy (vc)—No. 8 [arr for vc & org] *(rec Church of the Blessed Sacrament, Toronto, 1981)* RCA Gold Seal ▲ 09026-68368-2 [ADD]
Mozart, W.A.:Ave verum corpus, w. Ofra Harnoy (vc) [arr for vc & org] *(rec Church of the Blessed Sacrament, Toronto, 1981)* RCA Gold Seal ▲ 09026-68368-2 [ADD]
Vitali, T.A.:Chaconne Vn, w. Ofra Harnoy (vc) [arr for vc] *(rec Church of the Blessed Sacrament, Toronto, 1981)* RCA Gold Seal ▲ 09026-68368-2 [ADD]

Blount, William (cl)
Copland, A.:Con Cl, w. D. R. Davies (cnd), Orch of St. Luke MusicMasters ▲ 7005-2-C [DDD]
Liebman, D.:Remembrance, w. David Taylor (b trbn), Stephen Taylor (ob), Alan Cox (fl), Dennis Godburn (bn) New World ▲ 80494-2
Rzewski, F.:Moonrise with Memories, w. David Taylor (b trbn), David Carp (kazoo), Allan Dean (tpt), Louise Schulman (vn), Robert Wolinsky (gtr), Bill Moersch (mar/dlc) *(rec RCA Studios, NYC, June 4, 1981)* New World ▲ 80494-2

Bluefield, David (pno)—see ORCHESTRAS & ENSEMBLES Rhythm & Bluefield Band

Bluefield, David (sax)
Clazzual Sax, w. Chris Bank (sax) D'Blue ▲ DB 10001

Bluestone, Joel (dr/cym/hand perc)
Jones, D.E.:Still Life Dancing, w. J. Ferrari (vib/perc), D. Kennedy (mar/perc) Centaur ▲ CRC 2052 [DDD]

Blum, Eberhard (fl)
Brown, E.:Music of, w. Jan Williams (perc)—1991 [versions 1 & 2]; For Ann [versions 1 & 2]; 1980 [versions 1 & 2] [all from Folio II] *(rec Slee Concert Hall, Buffalo, New York, June 1–2, 1995)* Hat Hut ("Now" series) ▲ CD 6176 [DDD]
Cage, J.:Ryoanji, w. John Patrick Thomas (voc), Gudrun Reschke (ob), Iven Hausmann (trbn), Robert Black (db), Jan Williams (perc) *(rec Akademie der Künste, Berlin, June 22, 1995)* Hat Hut ("Now" series) ▲ hat ART CD 6183 [DDD]
Cage, J.:Vars I–IV, w. Jan Williams (perc)—Vars III [version 1 for perc; version 2 for fl & sound objects] *(rec Slee Concert Hall, Buffalo, New York, June 1–2, 1995)* Hat Hut ("Now" series) ▲ CD 6176 [DDD]
Feldman, Morton:For Christian Wolff, w. Nils Vigeland (pno/cel) *(rec Sender Freies Berlin, June 16 & 17, 1992)* Hat Hut ("NOW." series) 3-▲ hat ART CD 3-61201/02 [DDD]
Feldman, Morton:Why Patterns, w. M. Feldman (vn), J. Williams (perc) *(rec 12/17/78)* CRI ▲ CD 620 [ADD]
Fukushima, K.:A Hymn of Spring *(rec Sender Freies Berlin, Mar. 23–24, 1992)* Hat Hut ("NOW." series) ▲ hat ART CD 6114 [DDD]
Fukushima, K.:Kadha Karuna, w. Steffen Schleiermacher (pno) *(rec Sender Freies Berlin, Mar. 23–24, 1992)* Hat Hut ("NOW." series) ▲ hat ART CD 6114 [DDD]
Fukushima, K.:Mei *(rec Sender Freies Berlin, Mar. 23–24, 1992)* Hat Hut ("NOW." series) ▲ hat ART CD 6114 [DDD]
Fukushima, K.:Pieces (3) from Chu–u, w. Steffen Schleiermacher (pno) *(rec Sender Freies Berlin, Mar. 23–24, 1992)* Hat Hut ("NOW." series) ▲ hat ART CD 6114 [DDD]
Fukushima, K.:Requiem *(rec Sender Freies Berlin, Mar. 23–24, 1992)* Hat Hut ("NOW." series) ▲ hat ART CD 6114 [DDD]
Haubenstock–Ramati, R.:Interpolation *(rec Hessen Radio, Frankfurt, Aug 14–15, 1995)* Hat Hut ("Now" series) ▲ CD 6180 [DDD]
Pablo, L. de:Condicionado *(rec Hessen Radio, Frankfurt, Aug 14–15, 1995)* Hat Hut ("Now" series) ▲ CD 6180 [DDD]
Scherchen–Hsiao, T.:In Fl *(rec Hessen Radio, Frankfurt, Aug 14–15, 1995)* Hat Hut ("Now" series) ▲ CD 6180 [DDD]
Wolff, C.:Edges, w. Jan Williams (perc)—Realization for Fl & Perc [Versions 1 & 2] *(rec Slee Concert Hall, Buffalo, New York, June 1–2, 1995)* Hat Hut ("Now" series) ▲ CD 6176 [DDD]
Wolff, C.:Exercises, w. Roland Dahinden (trbn), Steffen Schleiermacher (pno), Jan Williams (perc) *(rec Hessischer Radio, Frankfurt, Aug 6–7, 1994)* Hat Hut ("Now" series) ▲ CD 6167 [DDD]
Wolff, C.:Pairs, w. Steffen Schleiermarcher (pno)—Versions 1 & 2 *(rec Hessen Radio, Frankfurt, Dec. 16–17, 1993)* Hat Hut ("NOW." series) ▲ hat ART CD 6146 [DDD]
Zimmermann, B.A.:Tempus loquendi *(rec Hessen Radio, Frankfurt, Aug 14–15, 1995)* Hat Hut ("Now" series) ▲ CD 6180 [DDD]

Blum, Eberhard (fl/sound objects)
Brown, E.:Music of, w. Steffen Schleiermacher (pno/cel), Jan Williams (perc)—4 Systems; Hodograph 1, Versions 1 & 2; Octet 1 *(rec Hessen Radio, Frankfurt, Dec. 16–17, 1993)* Hat Hut ("NOW." series) ▲ hat ART CD 6146 [DDD]
Cage, J.:Vars I–IV, w. Jan Williams (perc)—Var II *(rec Hessen Radio, Frankfurt, Dec. 16–17, 1993)* Hat Hut ("NOW." series) ▲ hat ART CD 6146 [DDD]

Blum, Eberhard (pic/fl/alt fl)
Cage, J.:Atlas Eclipticalis—flute parts *(rec Hessen Radio, Frankfurt, Feb. 10–11, 1992* Hat Hut ("NOW." series) ▲ hat ART CD 6111 [DDD]
Cage, J.:But What About The Noise...?, w. Craig Bitterman, Patti Cudd, Thomas Furminger, Erik Oña, Christopher Swist *(rec Slee Concert Hall, Univ. at Buffalo, NY, May 28 – June 1, 1995)* Hat Art ("Hat Now" series) ▲ 6179 [DDD]

Blum, Eberhard (pic/fl/alt fl) (cont.)
Cage, J.:Winter Music, w. Mats Persson (pno), Steffen Schleiermacher (pno), Kristine Scholz (pno), Nils Vigeland (pno)—for 4 pianos; for 4 pianos with flute parts from Atlas Eclipticalis *(rec Sender Freies Berlin & Hessen Radio, Frankfurt, Feb. 10–11, 1992 & June 6)* Hat Hut ("NOW." series) ▲ hat ART CD 6141 [DDD]
Feldman, Morton:For Philip Guston, w. Jan Williams (chimes/glock/mar/vib), Nils Vigeland (pno/cel) *(rec Buffalo, NY, Aug. 19–21, 1991)* Hat Hut ("NOW." series) 4-▲ hat ART CD 4-61041/44 [DDD]
Fukushima, K.:Ekagura, w. Steffen Schleiermacher (pno) *(rec Sender Freies Berlin, Mar. 23–24, 1992)* Hat Hut ("NOW." series) ▲ hat ART CD 6114 [DDD]
Stiebler, E.:3 in 1 *(rec Sender Freies Berlin, Sept 22, 1995)* Hat Hut ("Now" series) ▲ CD 6169 [DDD]

Blume, Norbert (va d'amore)
Hindemith, P.:Kammermusik (comp), w. R. Brautigam (pno), L. Harrell (vc), K. Kulka (vn), K. Kashkashian (va), L. van Doeselaar (org), R. Chailly (cnd), Royal Concertgebouw Orch—No. 1 for Small Orchestra, Op. 24/1 (1922); No. 2 (Piano Concerto) for Piano & 12 Instruments, Op. 36/1 (1924); No. 3 (Cello Concerto), foe Cello & 10 Instruments, Op. 36/2 (1925); No. 4 (Violin Concerto) for Violin & Large Orchestra, Op. 36/3 (1925); No. 5 (Viola Concerto) for Viola & Large Chamber Orchestra, Op. 36/4 (1927); No. 6 (Viola d'amore Concerto) for Viola d'amore & Chamber Orchestra, Op. 46/1 (1927); No. 7 (Organ Concerto) for Organ & chamber Orchestra, Op. 46/2 (1927) London 2-▲ 433816-2 [DDD]

Blumenstock, Elizabeth (baroque vn)—see ORCHESTRAS & ENSEMBLES American Baroque, Musica Pacifica

Blumenthal, Daniel (pno)—see also ORCHESTRAS & ENSEMBLES Monnaie Piano Trio, Algae Trio
Arensky, A.:Children's Suite, w. R. Groslot (pno) [arr. for 2 pnos] *(rec Heidelberg, Aug 1992)* Marco Polo ▲ 8.223497 [DDD]
Arensky, A.:Suite 1 for 2 Pnos, w. R. Groslot (pno) *(rec Heidelberg, Aug 1992)* Marco Polo ▲ 8.223497 [DDD]
Arensky, A.:Suite 2 for 2 Pnos, "Silhouettes", w. R. Groslot (pno) *(rec Heidelberg, Aug 1992)* Marco Polo ▲ 8.223497 [DDD]
Arensky, A.:Suite 3 for 2 Pnos, "Vars", w. R. Groslot (pno) *(rec Heidelberg, Aug 1992)* Marco Polo ▲ 8.223497 [DDD]
Arensky, A.:Suite 4 for 2 Pnos, w. R. Groslot (pno) *(rec Heidelberg, Aug 1992)* Marco Polo ▲ 8.223497 [DDD]
Beethoven, L. van:Son Hn, w. L. Van Marcke (hn) *(rec Apr. 1993)* Pavane ▲ ADW 7295 [DDD]
Bülow, H. von:Piano Transcriptions—Gluck:Tanzwisen; Rêveri fantastique, Op. 7; Tarantella, Op. 19; Valse de L'ingénu, No. 1 from trois valses caractéristique; Verdi:Arabesques sur un thème de l'opéra Rigoletto, Op. 2; Wagner:Paraphrase of the quintet from Act III of Die Meistersinger von Nürnberg *(rec Sept. 1991)* Marco Polo ▲ 8.223421 [DDD]
Busoni, F.:Etudes Pno, op. 16 Pavane ▲ ADW 7316 [DDD]
Busoni, F.:Etude en forme de variations Pno Pavane ▲ ADW 7316 [DDD]
Busoni, F.:Vars & Fugue in free form on Chopin's Prelude No. 20 Pavane ▲ ADW 7316 [DDD]
Czerny, C.:Fant on a Romantic Var Etcetera ▲ KTC 2023
Czerny, C.:Son 1 Pno Etcetera ▲ KTC 2023
Czerny, C.:Son 2 Pno Etcetera ▲ KTC 2023
Czerny, C.:Son 3 Pno Etcetera ▲ KTC 2023
Czerny, C.:Son 4 Pno Etcetera ▲ KTC 2023
Czerny, C.:Vars on "Vienna Waltz" Etcetera ▲ KTC 2023
David, Felicien:Mélodies orientales Marco Polo ▲ 8.223376 [DDD]
Debussy, C.:Arrs for 2 Pnos, w. R. Groslot (pno)—Saint-Saëns:Introduction & Rondo Capriccioso; Etienne Marcel; Tchaikovsky:Swan Lake; Gluck/Saint-Saëns:Caprice; Schumann:6 Etudes, Op. 56; Wagner:The Flying Dutchman:Overture *(rec Mar. 18–20, 1991)* Marco Polo ▲ 8.223378 [DDD]
Devreese, F.:Con 2 Pno, w. F. Devreese (cnd), Brussels Belgian Radio–TV PO *(rec Jan. 26, 1991)* Marco Polo ▲ 8.223505 [DDD]
Devreese, F.:Con 3 Pno, w. F. Devreese (cnd), Brussels Belgian Radio–TV PO *(rec Nov. 19–22, 1991)* Marco Polo ▲ 8.223505 [DDD]
Devreese, F.:Con 4 Pno, w. F. Devreese (cnd), Brussels Belgian Radio–TV PO *(rec Nov. 19–22, 1991)* Marco Polo ▲ 8.223505 [DDD]
Feld, J.:Son Fl, w. Carlo Jans (fl) Pavane ▲ ADW 7358 [DDD]
Franck, C.:Duo 1 sur le God Save the King, w. J. Bogart (pno) *(rec Sept. 1991)* Koch Schwann ▲ SCH 313772 [DDD]
Franck, C.:Duo 2 sur le quatuor de Lucile de Grétry, w. J. Bogart (pno) *(rec Sept. 1991)* Koch Schwann ▲ SCH 313772 [DDD]
Franck, C.:Hulda (sels), w. J. Bogart (pno) *(rec Sept. 1991)* Koch Schwann ▲ SCH 313772 [DDD]
Fuchs, R.:Fantasiestücke Vc, Op. 78, w. M. Drobinsky (vc) Marco Polo ▲ 8.223423 [DDD]
Fuchs, R.:Jugendklänge Marco Polo ▲ 8.223474
Fuchs, R.:Son 1 Pno Marco Polo ▲ 8.223377 [DDD]
Fuchs, R.:Son 1 Pno Marco Polo ▲ 8.223423 [DDD]
Fuchs, R.:Son 2 Pno Marco Polo ▲ 8.223423 [DDD]
Fuchs, R.:Son 2 Pno Marco Polo ▲ 8.223377 [DDD]
Fuchs, R.:Son 3 Pno Marco Polo ▲ 8.223474
Fuchs, R.:Waltzes Pno, Op. 110 Marco Polo ▲ 8.223474
Gistelinck, E.:Music of, w. Jenny Spanoghe (vn)—Music for René for Vn & Pno, Op. 35; Clowns for Pno, Op. 45; 3 Songs for Children for Vn & Pno, Op. 49; Kleine Treurmuziek voor Che for Pno, Op. 22/a; Horizon 250 for Vn & Pno, Op. 46; 5 Preludes for a Little Boy for Pno, Op. 29; Prelude 6 for Pno, Op. 34; Lullaby for Nathaly for Vn & Pno, Op. 31 *(rec BRTN, Studio 4, Brussels)* René Gailly ▲ CD 87113 [DDD]
Hindemith, P.:Echo Fl & Pno, w. Marc Grauwels (fl) Syrinx ▲ 95101
Hindemith, P.:Son Fl, w. Marc Grauwels (fl) Syrinx ▲ 95101
Joplin, S.:Pno Music—Maple Leaf Rag; The Easy Winners; The Entertainer; The Cascades; The Strenuous Life; Bethena; Binks' Waltz; Heliotrope Bouquet; Gladiolus Rag; Pine Apple Rag; Wall Street Rag; Solace; Euphonic Sounds; Paragon Rag; Felicity Rag; Scott Joplin's New Rag; Magnetic Rag Pavane ▲ 7317
Koechlin, C.:Morceau de lecture, w. Barry Tuckwell (hn) [arr hn & pno] ASV ▲ ASVCD 716
Koechlin, C.:Pieces Hn & Pno, w. Barry Tuckwell (hn) ASV ▲ ASVCD 716
Koechlin, C.:Son Hn, w. Barry Tuckwell (hn) ASV ▲ ASVCD 716
Legley, V.:Burlesque, w. Jenny Spanoghe (vn) *(rec BRTN, Studio 4, Brussels)* René Gailly ▲ CD 87114 [DDD]
Legley, V.:Drie Meisjes, w. Jenny Spanoghe (vn) *(rec BRTN, Studio 4, Brussels)* René Gailly ▲ CD 87114 [DDD]
Legley, V.:Romance, w. Jenny Spanoghe (vn) *(rec BRTN, Studio 4, Brussels)* René Gailly ▲ CD 87114 [DDD]
Legley, V.:Son Vn & Pno, w. Jenny Spanoghe (vn) *(rec BRTN, Studio 4, Brussels)* René Gailly ▲ CD 87114 [DDD]
Lekeu, G.:Qt Pno, Vn, Va & Vc, w. T. Adamopoulos (vn), C. Desjardins (va), G. Zanlonghi (vc) Koch Schwann ▲ CD 310185 [DDD]
Lekeu, G.:Son Vc, w. G. Zanlonghi (vc) Koch Schwann ▲ CD 310185 [DDD]
Marc Grauwels & Friends, w. M. Grauwels (fl), Marie–Noelle de Callataÿ (sop), Hiroko Masaki (sop), Dennis James (glass hmc), Ingrid Procureur (hp), Yves Storms (gtr), Yvietta Matison (va), Mark Drobinsky (vc), Alain De Rijckere (bn), Frank Michiels (perc), Belgian RSO, W Syrinx 2-▲ 96101 [DDD]
Martinů, B.:Son 1 Fl, w. Carlo Jans (fl) Pavane ▲ ADW 7358 [DDD]
Prokofiev, S.:Son Fl, w. Carlo Jans (fl) Pavane ▲ ADW 7358 [DDD]
Schubert, Franz:Intro & Vars Fl on "Tröckne Blumen", w. M. Grauwels (fl) Syrinx ▲ 93105 [DDD]
Schulhoff, E.:Son Fl, w. Carlo Jans (fl) Pavane ▲ ADW 7358 [DDD]
Schumann, R.:Album für die Jugend *(rec 1988)* Approche ▲ CAL 6208 [DDD]
Schumann, R.:Album für die Jugend Calliope ▲ CAL 9208 [DDD]
Schumann, R.:Etudes after Paganini's Caprices, Op. 3 *(rec 1995)* Calliope ▲ CAL 9271 [DDD]
Schumann, R.:Intermezzos *(rec 1995)* Calliope ▲ CAL 9271 [DDD]
Schumann, R.:Kinderszenen *(rec 1995)* Calliope ▲ CAL 9271 [DDD]

Blumenthal, Daniel (pno) (cont.)
Schumann, R.:Papillons *(rec 1995)* Calliope ▲ CAL 9271 [DDD]
Schumann, R.:Vars on A-B-E-G-G *(rec 1995)* Calliope ▲ CAL 9271 [DDD]
Wolf, H.:Mörike-Lieder (sels), w. Dinah Bryant (sop)—Auf einer Wanderung; Eine Stündlein wohl vor Tag; Erstes Liebeslied eine Mädchens; Das Verlassene Mägdlein; Nixe Binsefuss; Gesang Weylas; Fussreise; Schlafendes Jesuskind; Lied vom Winde; Im Frühling; Verborgenheit; Elfenlied; Zitronenfalter im April; Heimweh; Er ist's; Abschied Pavane ▲ ADW 7323 [DDD]
Blumenthal, Felicja (pno)
Rachmaninoff, S.:Con 2 Pno, w. M. Gielen (cnd), Vienna Musikgesellschaft Orch Allegretto ▲ ACD 8020 [ADD] ■ ACS 8020
Szymanowski, K.:Mazurkas—2 Mazurkas EMI Classics ▲ CDM 65307
Szymanowski, K.:Pno Music (comp)—Theme & Vars, Op. 3 EMI Classics ▲ CDM 65307
Tchaikovsky, P.:Con 1 Pno, w. M. Gielen (cnd), Vienna Musikgesellschaft Orch Allegretto ▲ ACD 8020 [ADD] ■ ACS 8020
Blustine, Allen (b cl)—see ORCHESTRAS & ENSEMBLES New Music Consort
Blustine, Allen (cl)—see also ORCHESTRAS & ENSEMBLES Speculum Musicae
Cory, E.:Profiles, w. C. Finckel (vc), A. Karis (pno) *(rec 1981 & 1986; originally r)* CRI ▲ CD 621 [ADD]
Rosenzweig, M.:Diptych, w. S. Palma (fl), B. Hudson (vn), C. Finckel (vc), E. Garth (pno), M. Rosenzweig Centaur ▲ CRC 2103 [DDD]
Sanford, D.:Con 3 Cl, w. W. Purvis (cnd), Speculum Musicae *(rec Lefrak Hall, Queens College, New York, May 14, 1995)* CRI ▲ CD 705 [DDD]
Blyme, Anker (pno)
Gade, N.W.:Pno Music (comp)—3 Piano Pieces; Scherzo in f#/F#; Little Piano Story; Dithyrambe; Impromptu in f#; Allegretto grazioso; 30 Scandanavian Folksongs; Saltarella in D; 10 Watercolor Sketches, Op. 19; 3 Album Leaves *(rec 5-11/90)* Marco Polo/Dacapo ▲ DCCD 9115 [DDD]
Gade, N.W.:Pno Music (comp)—Calendar; Scherzino & Barcarolle; Arabesque, Op. 27; Sonata in e, Op. 28; 4 Fantasy Pieces, Op. 31; Folk Dance & Romance; 8 Piano Pieces (from the Sketch-Book); 4 Idylls, Op. 34 *(rec 5-11/90)* Marco Polo/Dacapo ▲ DCCD 9116 [DDD]
Blysma, Anner (vc)
Schubert, Franz:Trio 1 Pno, w. Jos van Immerseel (pno), Vera Beths (vn) Sony Classical ("Vivarte" series) ▲ SK 62695
Schubert, Franz:Trio 2 Pno, w. Jos van Immerseel (pno), Vera Beths (vn) Sony Classical ("Vivarte" series) ▲ SK 62695
Boanta, Leontin (cl)
Enescu, G.:Dectet Ww, w. Virgil Francu (fl), Nicolae Maxin (fl), Valeriu Barbuceanu (cl), Adrian Petrescu (ob), Viorica Feher (bn), Goedri Orban (bn), Florin Ionoaia (Eng hn), Dan Cinca (hn), Simon Jebeleanu (hn), H. Andreescu (cnd) Olympia ▲ OLY 445 [DDD]
Boardman, Reginald (pno)
The Art of Roland Hayes, w. R. Hayes (sgr) Smithsonian Collection ▲ SMI RD 041 (m)
Boatman (perc)
Sapieyevski, J.:Arioso, w. J. Dunham (va), Westwood Wind Quintet Crystal ■ C 647
Boatman, James (a sax)—see ORCHESTRAS & ENSEMBLES New Century Saxophone Quartet
Bobesco, Lola (vn)—see also ORCHESTRAS & ENSEMBLES Arte del Suono String Quartet
Beethoven, L van:Con Vn, Op. 61, w. E. Doneux (cnd), RTBF New SO Talent ▲ 2910501
Fauré, G.:Andante Vn, w. J. Genty (pno) *(rec 1980)* Pavane 2-▲ ADW 7292/93
Fauré, G.:Berceuse Vn, w. J. Genty (pno) *(rec 1980)* Pavane 2-▲ ADW 7292/93
Fauré, G.:Son 1 Vn, w. J. Genty (pno) *(rec 1980)* Pavane 2-▲ ADW 7292/93
Fauré, G.:Son 2 Vn, w. J. Genty (pno) *(rec 1980)* Pavane 2-▲ ADW 7292/93
Franck, C.:Son Vn, w. Jacques Genty (pno) *(rec 1980)* Pavane 2-▲ ADW 7292/93
Lekeu, G.:Son Vn, w. J. Genty (pno) *(rec 1980)* Pavane 2-▲ ADW 7292/93
Mendelssohn, F.:Con in e Vn & Orch, Op. 64, w. E. Doneux (cnd), RTBF New SO Talent ▲ 2910501
Pleyel, I.:Duets Vns, w. J. Rubinstein (vn) Talent ▲ DOM 291016 [ADD]
Villette, P.:Qts Strs, w. J.-M. Defalque (vn), D. Huybrechts (va), S. Mariage (vc)—Nos. 1-6 in A, C, F, B♭, E♭ & E Talent ▲ DOM 2910 46 [DDD]
Viotti, G.B.:Con 22 Vn, w. K. Redel (cnd), Rhineland-Palatinate State PO Talent ▲ DOM 291013 [ADD]
Viotti, G.B.:Con 23 Vn, w. K. Redel (cnd), Rhineland-Palatinate State PO Talent ▲ DOM 291013 [ADD]
Bobo, Roger (tuba)
Bobissimo!, w. R. Bobo (tuba), Ralph Grierson (pno) Crystal ▲ CD 125
Galliard, J.E.:Son 5 Tuba, w. R. Grierson (pno) *(rec 1969)* Crystal ▲ CD 125
Hindemith, P.:Son Bass Tuba, w. R. Grierson (pno) *(rec 1969)* Crystal ▲ CD 125
Reynolds, V.:Signals, w. T. Stevens (tpt), Los Angeles Brass Society Crystal ▲ CD 667
Wilder, A.:Children's Suite:Effie the Elephant, w. R. Grierson (pno) *(rec 1969)* Crystal ▲ CD 125
Bobo, Roger (tuba/b hn)—see ORCHESTRAS & ENSEMBLES Prunes
Bobritskaya, Rimma (pno)
Prokofiev, S.:Music for Children Russian Season ("Russian Season" series) ▲ LDC 288034 [DDD]
Shostakovich, D.:Pno Music—Berceuse; Contredanse; Danse; Danse espagnole; Nocturne; Seven Children's Pieces Russian Season ("Russian Season" series) ▲ LDC 288034 [DDD]
Tchaikovsky, P.:Album pour enfants Russian Season ▲ LDC 288034 [DDD]
Bobylev, Leonid (pno)
The Spirit of Russia, w. G. Kremer (vn), Vladimir Malinin (vn), Mark Pekarsky (cymbals), Alexander Melnikov (vn) Vox Box 2-▲ CDX 5115 [ADD]
Bocchino, Alberto (gtr)—see ORCHESTRAS & ENSEMBLES Duo Chitarristico
Boch, Richard (vc)
Rózsa, M.:Sinf concertante, w. Igor Gruppman (vn), J. Sedares (cnd), New Zealand SO Koch International Classics ▲ KIC 7304 [DDD]
Bochet, H. (bn)
Suter, R.:Musikalisches Tagesbuch 1, w. B. Geiser-Payer (alt), H. Haldemann (pic/fl), H. Holliger (ob), J. Joubert (vn), J. Semper (va), W. Eugster (vc), M. Dellanoy (db) *(rec 1962)* Grammont ▲ CSTP 6-2 [AAD]
Bochkovskaya, Julia (pno)
Roslavets, N.:Dances, w. Mark Lubotsky (vn) Olympia ▲ OLY 559 [DDD]
Roslavets, N.:Nocturne, w. Mark Lubotsky (vn) Olympia ▲ OLY 559 [DDD]
Roslavets, N.:Poema, w. Mark Lubotsky (vn) Olympia ▲ OLY 559 [DDD]
Roslavets, N.:Preludes in All the Keys, w. Mark Lubotsky (vn) Olympia ▲ OLY 559 [DDD]
Roslavets, N.:Son 1 Vn, w. Mark Lubotsky (vn) Olympia ▲ OLY 558 [DDD]
Roslavets, N.:Son 2 Vn, w. Mark Lubotsky (vn) Olympia ▲ OLY 558 [DDD]
Roslavets, N.:Son 4 Vn, w. Mark Lubotsky (vn) Olympia ▲ OLY 558 [DDD]
Roslavets, N.:Son 6 Vn, w. Mark Lubotsky (vn) Olympia ▲ OLY 558 [DDD]
Böcker, Martin (org)
Baroque Organ Music Ambitus ▲ AMB 97829 [DDD]
Bockman, Sigurd (cl)
Kodály, Z.:Galanta Dances, w. F. Reiner (cnd), Pittsburgh SO *(rec Mar 1945)* Sony Classical ("Masterworks Heritage" series) ▲ MHK 062343 [ADD]
Bocquillon, Patrice (fl)
Gossec, F.-J.:Qts Fl, Op. 14, w. Millière String Trio Koch Schwann ▲ CD 310 081 [DDD]
Bodanza, Giuseppe (tpt)
Puccini, M.:Concertone Fl, w. Mencarelli (fl), di Girolamo (cl), Caproni (hn), G. Cosmi (cnd), Lucca Teatro Comunale del Giglio Orch Bongiovanni ▲ GB 2048 [DDD]
Rota, N.:Film Music, w. Stefano Pagliani (vn), R. Muti (cnd), La Scala Orch—Ballet Suite [from La Strada]; Dances [from Il Gattopardo] *(rec Abanella Theatre, Milan, Italy, Apr. 9-14, 1994)* Sony Classical ▲ SK 66279 [DDD]
Bode, Cornelia (vc)—see ORCHESTRAS & ENSEMBLES Manchester Chamber Players
Bode, Ulrich (vc)
Fuchs, R.:Qt Pno, w. K. Schilde (pno), K. Heymann (vn), J. Rieber (va) MD + G ▲ L 3165
Mahler, G.:Qt Pno [1 movt], w. K. Schilde (pno), K. Heymann (vn), J. Rieber (va) MD + G ▲ L 3165

Bodensohn, E. (fl)
Mozart, W.A.:Con Fl Hp, w. A.M. Schmeisser (hp), H. Rosbaud (cnd), Southwest German RSO Baden-Baden *(rec 1962)* Datum 2-▲ DAT 12303 [ADD]
Bodin, Rune (trbn)
Rangström, T.:Vauxhall, w. Bengt Christiansson (fl), Lars Olof Loman (ob), Lars Almgren (cl), Sven Aarflot (bn), Rolf Bengtsson (hn), Rozalina Skytt (hp), O. Vänskä (cnd), Stockholm PO *(rec Stockholm Concert Hall, Jan. 16 & 18, 1985)* Caprice ▲ CAP 21195 [DDD]
Bodine, Elizabeth (ob)
Tailleferre, G.:Chansons populaires françaises, w. Patrice Maginnis (sop), John Fairweather (vn), David Ryther (vn), Jill Cohen (va), Karen Andrie (vc), Andy Connell (cl), Gordon Mumma (hn), June Orzel (bn), N. Paiement (cnd) *(rec UC, Santa Cruz, May 1992)* Helicon Classics ▲ HE 1008
Tailleferre, G.:Image, w. John Fairweather (vn), David Ryther (vn), Jill Cohen (va), Karen Andrie (vc), Andy Connell (cl), Gordon Mumma (hn), June Orzel (bn), N. Paiement (cnd) *(rec UC, Santa Cruz, May 1992)* Helicon Classics ▲ HE 1008
Bodini, Maria Rosa (pno)
Falla, M. de:Serenata andaluza Nuova Era ▲ 6809 [DDD]
Falla, M. de:Serenata Pno Nuova Era ▲ 6809 [DDD]
Bodle, Douglas (org)
To God Sing Praise, w. G. Evans (ten) Pro Arte ▲ CDD 3403 [DDD]
Bodolai, C. (va)—see ORCHESTRAS & ENSEMBLES Danubius Quartet
Boecke, Kees (vls)—see ORCHESTRAS & ENSEMBLES Little Consort
Boeckman, Vicki (rcr)
Castello, D.:Sons (3) Rcr, w. F. Hansen (vl), L. U. Mortensen (hpd) *(rec 9/90)* Kontrapunkt ▲ 32059 [DDD]
Cima, G.P.:Sons 1 & 2 Rcr, w. F. Hansen (db), L. U. Mortensen (hpd) *(rec 9/90)* Kontrapunkt ▲ 32059 [DDD]
Fontana, G.B.:Sons 2, 3 & 4 Rcr, w. F. Hansen (vl), L. U. Mortensen (hpd) *(rec 9/90)* Kontrapunkt ▲ 32059 [DDD]
Frescobaldi, G.:Canzona detta la Bernadinia, w. F. Hansen (db), L. U. Mortensen (hpd) *(rec 9/90)* Kontrapunkt ▲ 32059 [DDD]
Frescobaldi, G.:Canzona quatra, w. F. Hansen (db), L. U. Mortensen (hpd) *(rec 9/90)* Kontrapunkt ▲ 32059 [DDD]
Merula, T.:Music for Rcr, w. F. Hansen (vl), L. U. Mortensen (hpd)—La Merula; L'Arisia; La Dada; & La Pighetta *(rec 9/90)* Kontrapunkt ▲ 32059 [DDD]
Telemann, G.P.:Sons (6) Rcr, w. F. Hansen (vl), L.U. Mortensen (hpd) *(rec 9/88)* Kontrapunkt ▲ 32014 [DDD]
Boegner, Michèle (pno)
Bach, J.S.:Con 1 Hpd, w. J.-C. Hartemann (cnd), French Soloists Calliope ▲ CAL 6629 [ADD]
Bach, J.S.:Con 5 Hpd, w. J.-C. Hartemann (cnd), French Soloists Calliope ▲ CAL 6629 [ADD]
Mon ami piano:42 Pieces from Bach to Stravinsky Adès 2-▲ ADE 203742 [AAD]
Boehm, Mary Louise (pno)
Beach, A.M.C.:Con Pno, w. S. Landau (cnd), Westphalia SO Recklinghausen *(rec 1976)* Vox Box 2-▲ CDX 5069 [ADD]
Cordero, R.:Qnt Fl, w. John Wion (fl), Arthur Bloom (cl), Kees Kooper (vn), Fred Sherry (vc) Albany ▲ TROY 153 [DDD]
Palmer, R.:Qnt Cl, w. A. Bloom (cl), K. Kooper (vn), P. Doktor (va), Fred Sherry (vc) Albany ▲ TROY 153
Rochberg, G.:Trio Pno, w. Kees Kooper (vn), Fred Sherry (vc) Albany ▲ TROY 153
Schelling, E.:Pno Music—Theme & Vars; Fatalisme; Romance; Valse Gracieuse; Ragusa [Nocturne]; Improvisation; Un Petit Rien; Au Chateau de Wiligrad; Ritmicissimo *(rec Oct 9-12, 1995)* Albany ▲ TROY 193 [DDD]
Boeke, Kees (rcr)
Boeke, K.:Lacrime, w. Amsterdam Loeki Stardust Quartet *(rec 1/91)* Channel Classics ▲ CCS 2891 [DDD]
Boeke, Kees (vl)
Frescobaldi, G.:Canzonas, Caprici & Ricercari, w. L. Cavasanti (rcr), G. Capocaccia (rcr), C. Boersma (vc), S. Ciomei (hpd/org)—Canzoni Trigesima, detta ia Cittadellia; Vigesimasesta, detta la Moricona; Vigesimaottiva, detta le Lanberta; Prima a tre; Trigesimaseconda detta l'Altogradina; Vigesimaquarta, detta la Nobile; Vigesimesttima, detta la Lanciona; Quintedecima, detta la Lievoratta; Terza a quattro; Vigesimaquinta, detta la Garzoncina; Prima a tre; Decmasesta, detta la Samminiata; Trigesimaprima, detta l'Arnolfinia; Quarta a tre; Quinta a tre; Decimasettima, detta la Diodata; Seconda a quattro; Seconda a tre; Vigesimanona, detta la Bocellina; Terza a tre Trigesimaquarta, detta la Sandoninia Nuova Era ("Ancient Music" series) ▲ 7131
Holborne, A.:Instrumental Consort Music, w. Amsterdam Loeki Stardust Quartet—Amoretta; Bona Speranza; Ecce quam bonum; The Funerals; Galliard; Image of Melancolly; Infernum; Muy Linda; Nec invideo; Paradizo; Pavana Ploravit; Sic semper soleo; The Sighes; Teares of the Muses *(rec 1/91)* Channel Classics ▲ CCS 2891 [DDD]
Boekelheide, Todd (instr)
Mozart, W.A.:Music of, w. Philip Aaberg, Chris Botti, Henry Adam Curtis, Steve Erquiaga, Béla Fleck, Eugene Friesen, Paul McCandless, Tim Story, Richard Schönherz, Tracy Scott Silverman, Thea Suits-Silverman, ValGardena, Modern Mandolin Quartet Imaginary Road ▲ 314534065-2 ■ 314534065-4
Boer, Harmen de (cl)
Bernstein, L.:Prelude, Fugue & Riffs Cl, w. R. Dufallo (cnd), Netherlands Wind Ensemble Chandos ("New Direction" series) ▲ CHAN 9210 [DDD]
Ustvolskaya, G.:Trio Cl, w. Vera Beths (vn), Reinbert de Leeuw (pno) *(rec De Vereeniging, Nijmegen, Oct. 5 & 6, 1991)* Hat Hut ("NOW." series) ▲ hat ART CD 6115 [DDD]
Boer, Herman de (cl)
Escher, R.:Chamber Music, w. Jacques Zoon (fl), Bart Schneemann (ob), Zoltan Benyacs (va), Dmitri Ferschtman (vc), Glen Wilson (hpd)—includes Le Tombeau de Ravel; Trio for Strings; Trio for Cl, Va & Pno NM Classics ▲ NM 92026
Boer, Johannes (vl)—see ORCHESTRAS & ENSEMBLES Royal Consort
Boersma, Caroline (vc)
Frescobaldi, G.:Canzonas, Caprici & Ricercari, w. K. Boeke (vl), L. Cavasanti (rcr), G. Capocaccia (rcr), S. Ciomei (hpd/org)—Canzoni Trigesima, detta ia Cittadellia; Vigesimasesta, detta la Moricona; Vigesimaottiva, detta le Lanberta; Prima a tre; Trigesimaseconda detta l'Altogradina; Vigesimaquarta, detta la Nobile; Vigesimesttima, detta la Lanciona; Quintedecima, detta la Lievoratta; Terza a quattro; Vigesimaquinta, detta la Garzoncina; Prima a tre; Decmasesta, detta la Samminiata; Trigesimaprima, detta l'Arnolfinia; Quarta a tre; Quinta a tre; Decimasettima, detta la Diodata; Seconda a quattro; Seconda a tre; Vigesimanona, detta la Bocellina; Terza a tre Trigesimaquarta, detta la Sandoninia Nuova Era ("Ancient Music" series) ▲ 7131
Mancini, F.:Sons Rcr, w. L. Cavasanti (rcr), S. Ciomei (hpd) Nuova Era ("Ancient Music" series) ▲ NUO 7138 [DDD]
Sacchini, A.:La contandina in corte, w. S. Rigacci (sop—Tancia), E. Palacio (ten—Ruggiero), G. Gatti (bar—Berto), M. Clavenna (db), M. T. Conti (hpd), G. Catalucci (cnd), Sassari SO *(rec Dec. 17-18, 1991)* Bongiovanni 2-▲ GB 2145/46 [DDD]
Telemann, G.P.:Con in a for Rcr, Ob, w. L. Cavasanti (rcr), P. Faldi (ob), D. Moore (vn), S. Ciomei (hpd) *(rec July 23-26, 1991)* Nuova Era ("Ancient Music" series) ▲ NUO 7067 [DDD]
Boettcher, Marianne (vn)
Alotin, Y.:Sonatina Vn, w. Ursula Trede-Boettcher (pno) Bayer ▲ 100169 [DDD]
Beau, L.A. le:Son Vn, w. Ursula Trede-Boettcher (pno) Bayer ▲ 100169 [DDD]
Boulanger, L.:D'un matin de printemps Fl & Pno, w. Ursula Trede-Boettcher (pno) Bayer ▲ 100169 [DDD]
Danzi, M.:Son 1 Vn, w. Ursula Trede-Boettcher (pno) Bayer ▲ 100169 [DDD]
Mendelssohn, Fanny:Adagio, w. Ursula Trede-Boettcher (pno) Bayer ▲ 100169 [DDD]
Zieritz, G. von:Triptychion Bayer ▲ 100169 [DDD]
Boettcher, Wolfgang (vc)—see also ORCHESTRAS & ENSEMBLES Brandis String Quartet
Bloch, A.:Duet Vn & Vc, w. Ulf Hoelscher (vn) Pro Viva ▲ ISPV 172
Bloch, A.:Suplicazioni Vc, w. Ursula Trede-Boettcher (pno) Pro Viva ▲ ISPV 172

Boettcher, Wolfgang (vc) (cont.)
Boccherini, L.:Con Vc, G.480, w. J. Velazco (cnd), Berlin RIAS Sinfonietta
Koch Schwann ▲ CD 311101 [ADD]
Danzi, F.:Con Vc, w. J. Velazco (cnd), Berlin RIAS Sinfonietta Koch Schwann ▲ CD 311101 [ADD]
Gomezanda, A.:Logos, w. Alan Marks (pno), J. Velazco (cnd), Berlin SO Koch Schwann ▲ SCH 310232
Haydn, J.:Con 1 Vc, w. K. Toyoda (cnd), Tchikashi Tanaka Ensemble Camerata ▲ 30CM 376
Haydn, J.:Trios Pno, Fl & Vc, w. Josef Pálaníček (pno), N. Nishida (fl)—in D Camerata ▲ 30CM 376
Hindemith, P.:Duet Va & Vc, w. Wilfried Strehle (va) Nimbus ▲ NI 5473 [DDD]
Schubert, Franz:Qnt Strs, D.956, w. Melos String Quartet Harmonia Mundi France ▲ HMC 901494

Boeykens, Anne (cl)
Hoffmeister, F.A.:Con for 2 Cls, w. Walter Boeykens (cl), J. Caeyers (cnd), Belgium New CO
Musique d'abord ▲ HMA 1901433
Krommer, F.:Cons for 2 Cls, w. Walter Boeykens (cl), J. Caeyers (cnd), Belgium New CO
Musique d'abord ▲ HMA 1901433

Boeykens, Walter (cl)—see also ORCHESTRAS & ENSEMBLES Walter Boeykens Ensemble
Brahms, J.:Qnt Cl, w. J.-J. Kantarow (vn), A. Czifra (vn), V. Mendelssohn (va), H.-J. Stegenga (vc)
Erasmus ▲ WVH 017 [DDD]
Bruch, M.:Pieces Cl, Op. 83/1–8, w. Thérèse-Marie Gilissen (va), Roel Dieltiens (vc), Robert Groslot (pno) *(rec 1991)* Musique D'Abord ▲ HMA 1901371
Hoffmeister, F.A.:Con for 2 Cls, w. Anne Boeykens (cl), J. Caeyers (cnd), Belgium New CO
Musique d'abord ▲ HMA 1901433
Krommer, F.:Cons for 2 Cls, w. Anne Boeykens (cl), J. Caeyers (cnd), Belgium New CO
Musique d'abord ▲ HMA 1901433
Rimsky-Korsakov, N.:Concertstück Cl, w. N. Nozy (cnd), Belgian Guides Symphonic Band
René Gailly ▲ CD 87075 [DDD]
Wagemans, P.J.:Sym 6, w. A. van Beek (cnd), Rotterdam Conservatory Symphonic Band
Donemus ▲ CV 56 [DDD]
Weber, C.M. von:Concertino Cl, w. J. Conlon (cnd), Rotterdam PO Erato ▲ 2292-45459-2-ZK
Weber, C.M. von:Con 1 Cl, w. J. Conlon (cnd), Rotterdam PO Erato ▲ 2292-45459-2-ZK
Weber, C.M. von:Con 1 Cl, w. J. Conlon (cnd), Rotterdam PO—Rondo-allegretto *(rec Doelen, Rotterdam, Jan. 1989)* Erato ▲ 94679-2
Weber, C.M. von:Con 2 Cl, w. J. Conlon (cnd), Rotterdam PO—Alla Polacca *(rec Doelen, Rotterdam, Jan. 1989)* Erato ▲ 94679-2
Weber, C.M. von:Con 2 Cl, w. J. Conlon (cnd), Rotterdam PO Erato ▲ 2292-45459-2-ZK
Weber, C.M. von:Grand duo concertant Cl, w. Walter Boeykens Ensemble
Harmonia Mundi France ▲ HMC 901481
Weber, C.M. von:Qnt Cl, w. Walter Boeykens Ensemble Harmonia Mundi France ▲ HMC 901481
Weber, C.M. von:Vars on a Theme from *Silvana* Cl, w. Walter Boeykens Ensemble
Harmonia Mundi France ▲ HMC 901481
Zemlinsky, A. von:Trio Cl, w. Thérèse-Marie Gilissen (va), Roel Dieltiens (vc), Robert Groslot (pno) *(rec 1991)* Musique d'Abord ▲ HMA 1901371

Bogaart, Jacob (pno)
Crumb, G.:Celestial Mechanics (Makrokosmos IV), w. R. Nasveld (pno) Attacca ▲ CD 8740
Schäfer, D.:Qnt Pno, w. Orpheus String Quartet NM Classics ▲ NM 92046

Bogacz, Pavel (vn)—see ORCHESTRAS & ENSEMBLES Bratislava String Trio

Bogart, John (pno)
Franck, C.:Duo 1 sur le God Save the King, w. D. Blumenthal (pno) *(rec Sept. 1991)*
Koch Schwann ▲ SCH 313772 [DDD]
Franck, C.:Duo 2 sur le quatuor de Lucile de Grétry, w. D. Blumenthal (pno) *(rec Sept. 1991)*
Koch Schwann ▲ SCH 313772 [DDD]
Franck, C.:Hulda (sels), w. D. Blumenthal (pno) *(rec Sept. 1991)*
Koch Schwann ▲ SCH 313772 [DDD]

Bogas, R. (pno)
Imbrie, A.W.:Son Vc, w. R. Sayre (vc) *(rec Dec. 18, 1971; originally)* CRI ▲ CD 632 [ADD]

Bogatin, Barbara (vc)
Bach, J.S.:Sons Fl, BWV 1030–35, w. J. Solum (fl), I. Kipnis (hpd)—BWV 1030–1035 [period instrs]
Arabesque ▲ Z 6589

Bogdanas, Constantin (vn)—see ORCHESTRAS & ENSEMBLES Enesco String Quartet

Bogdanović, Dusan (gtr)—see also ORCHESTRAS & ENSEMBLES Falla Trio
Bach, J.S.:Inventions (30) Hpd, w. E. Comparone (hpd) *(rec Aug 2–4, 1993)*
ESS.A.Y ▲ CD 1039 [DDD]
Bach, J.S.:Trio Sons Org, BWV 525–530, w. E. Comparone (hpd) [trans performers for gtr & hpd]
ESS.A.Y ▲ CD 1023 [DDD]
Bogdanovic, D.:Gtr Music—Mysterious Habitats; Jass Sonatina; 7 Little Secrets; Omar's Fancy; 4 Polymetric Studies; Intro, Passacaglia & Fugue [For the Golden Flower]; Son No. 2; A Fairytale with Vars *(rec Samurai Sound, Petaluma, CA)* GSP ▲ GSP 1014

Bogino, Konstantin (pno)—see also ORCHESTRAS & ENSEMBLES Tchaikovsky Piano Trio
Tchaikovsky, P.:Songs, w. M. Vitas (sop)—Do Not Believe My Friend; Not a Word, My Friend [both from 6 Songs, Op. 6]; Lullaby [from 6 Songs, Op. 16]; Say, What Does the Nightingale Sing [from 6 Songs, Op. 57]; Mid a Turbulent Ball [from 6 Songs, Op. 38]; Had I Known; In the Field [both from 7 Songs, Op. 47]; Lullaby in the Storm [from 16 Children's Songs, Op. 54]; O Senseless Night; I Shall Not Tell You Anything; O Nightingale [all from 12 Songs, Op. 60]; Zemphir's Song [!]
Musicaimmagine ▲ MR 10011 [DDD]

Bognár, Ferenc (pno)
Debussy, C.:Première rapsodie, w. Karl Leister (cl) *(rec Vienna, June & Dec 1995)*
Camerata ▲ 30 CM 415 [DDD]
Elgar, E.:Romance Bn, w. Milan Turkovic (bn) *(rec Studio Baumgarten, Vienna, June 30–July 1, 1994)*
Camerata ▲ 30CM 370 [DDD]
Françaix, J.:Theme & Vars Cl, w. Karl Leister (cl) *(rec Vienna, June & Dec 1995)*
Camerata ▲ 30 CM 415 [DDD]
Gade, N.W.:Fantasistykker, w. Karl Leister (cl) Camerata ▲ 30CM 370
Glinka, M.:Trio pathétique, w. Karl Leister (cl), Milan Turkovic (bn) *(rec Studio Baumgarten, Vienna, June 30–July 1, 1994)* Camerata ▲ 30CM 370 [DDD]
Hindemith, P.:Son Bn, w. Milan Turkovic (bn) Sony Classical ▲ SK 64400
Hindemith, P.:Son Cl, w. Karl Leister (cl) Camerata ▲ 30CM 358 [DDD]
Hindemith, P.:Son E Hn, w. Hansjörg Schellenberger (E hn) Sony Classical ▲ SK 64400
Hindemith, P.:Son Fl, w. Wolfgang Schulz (fl) Sony Classical ▲ SK 64400
Hindemith, P.:Son Hn, w. Günter Högner (hn) Sony Classical ▲ SK 64400
Milhaud, D.:Son Cl, w. Karl Leister (cl) *(rec Vienna, June & Dec 1995)*
Camerata ▲ 30 CM 415 [DDD]
Poulenc, F.:Son Cl Pno, w. Karl Leister (cl) *(rec Vienna, June & Dec 1995)*
Camerata ▲ 30 CM 415 [DDD]
Saint-Saëns, C.:Son Cl, w. Karl Leister (cl) *(rec Vienna, June & Dec 1995)*
Camerata ▲ 30 CM 415 [DDD]
Widor, C.M.:Intro & Rondo Cl, w. Karl Leister (cl) *(rec Vienna, June & Dec 1995)*
Camerata ▲ 30 CM 415 [DDD]

Bogorad, Julia (fl)
Daugherty, M.:Mxyzptlk, w. S. Y. Lee (fl), M. Singher (cnd), Oberlin CO Opus One ▲ 138
Holst, G.:A Fugal Con, w. K. Greenbank (vn), R. Tecco (vn), L. Shank (vn), J. Koestenbaum (vc), C. Hogwood (cnd), St. Paul CO *(rec May 1992)* London ▲ 440376-2
Love Songs & Lullabies, w. Isbin, Sharon (gtr), Benita Valente (sop), Thomas Allen (bar), Guadencio Thiago de Mello (perc) Virgin Classics ▲ 59226
Macy, C.:Solstice & Equinox, w. Adam Keunzel (fl), John Jensen (pno) *(rec Macalester College, Mar 11–12, 1994)* Innova ▲ 503
Scelsi, G.:Anahit, w. Paul Zukofsky (vn), Peggy Russell (fl), Courtney Westcott (fl), Lawrence McDonald (cl), Joan Waryha (cl), Jean Hansen (b cl), Bill Suite (e hn), Nita VanPelt (sax), Bob Zobal (tpt), John Carter (trbn), Martin Lydecker (trbn), Stan Cortman (hn), Robert Ward (hn), William Curry (va), Jody Rowitsch (va), Irene Wade (va), Anne Fagerburg (vc), John Gockel (vc), Sue Manz (bass), Steven Stearman (bass) *(rec Oberlin Conservatory of Music, Oct 8, 1973)* CP² ▲ CP2 108 [AAD]

Boquet, Jean (pno)
Debussy, C.:Pno Music (complete solo) *(rec 1970)* Tudor 4–▲ 731/34 [ADD]

Boguk, Alina (mand)
Vivaldi, A.:Con for 2 Mands, w. T. Kostyanaia (mand), L. Korkhin (cnd), Renaissance CO
Infinity Digital ▲ QK 57244 [DDD]

Bogunia, Stanislav (pno)
Beethoven, L. van:Sons Vn (comp), w. Petr Messiereur (vn) Calliope 3–▲ CAL 9251.3 [DDD]
Beethoven, L. van:Son 5 Vn, "Spring", w. Petr Messiereur (vn) Calliope ▲ CAL 9252
Beethoven, L. van:Son 6 Vn, w. Petr Messiereur (vn) Calliope ▲ CAL 9252
Beethoven, L. van:Son 7 Vn, w. Petr Messiereur (vn) Calliope ▲ CAL 9252
Dvořák, A.:Moravian Duets, Opp. 20, 32 & 38, w. P. Kühn (cnd), Kühn Chorus
Supraphon ▲ 10 4093-2 [DDD]
Martinů, B.:Primrose, w. P. Messiereur (vn), P. Kühn (cnd), Kühn Women's Chorus
Supraphon 2–▲ 11 0752-2 [DDD]
Martinů, B.:The Prophecy of Isaiah, w. N. Romanová (sop), D. Drobková (alto), R. Novák (bass), V. Kozderka (tpt), J. Peruška (va), I. Kiezlich (timp), P. Kühn (cnd), Prague Radio Men's Chorus, Kühn Chorus [Cz] *(rec 2–3/88)* Supraphon ▲ 11 0751-2 [DDD]
Mozart, W.A.:Sons Vn Pno (misc), w. Petr Messiereur (vn)—K.376, K.481 *(rec 1980–85)*
Calliope ▲ CAL 6628 [ADD]
Mozart, W.A.:Sons Vn Pno (misc), w. P. Messiereur (vn)—K.296 Calliope ▲ CAL 9244

Boguslavsky, Igor (va)
Schnittke, A.:Suite in the Old Style, w. Alla Litvinenko (hpd), Viktor Grishin (vib), Viktor Gabinsky (mar), Vadim Vasilykov (bells) [arr. unknown] *(rec 1989)* Consonance ▲ 81-0009 [DDD]

Bogyo, Kristine (vc)
Beethoven, L. van:Sons Vc (comp), w. A. Kuerti (pno) Analekta ▲ CM 2902
Chopin, F.:Intro & Polonaise, "Polonaise brilliante", w. A. Kuerti (pno) Analekta ▲ CM 2902
Falla, M. de:Suite populaire espagnole, w. A. Kuerti (pno) [trans for vc & pno by Maurice Maréchal]
Analekta ▲ CM 2902
Fauré, G.:Elégie, w. A. Kuerti (pno) Analekta ▲ CM 2902
Schumann, R.:Fantasiestücke Cl, w. A. Kuerti (pno) [trans. cello & piano] Analekta ▲ CM 2902

Böhm, Bernhard (fl)
Montéclair, M.P. de:Concerts Suites, w. Hedos Ensemble—Nos. 1–4 CPO ▲ CPO 999213 [DDD]

Böhm, Bernhard (rcr/trns fl/bgp/Rauschpfeife)—see ORCHESTRAS & ENSEMBLES Hedos Ensemble

Böhm, Bernhard (trns fl)
Platti, G.B.:Sons Fl, w. R. Zipperling (vc), G. Wilson (hpd) CPO ▲ CPO 999021-2 [DDD]

Böhm, Bernhard (trns fl/rcr)
Boismortier, J.B. de:Suites Fl, Op. 35, w. J. Hübscher (lt/baroque gtr), A. Weigel (gamba)
CPO ▲ CPO 999048-2 [DDD]

Böhme, Ullrich (org)
Mendelssohn, F.:Sons Org [Sauer Organ, St. Thomas' Church, Leipzig]
Capriccio ("Famous European Organs" series) ▲ CD 10702 [DDD]

Böhn, Ole (vn)
Carter, E.:Con Vn, w. O. Knussen (cnd), London Sinfonietta Virgin Classics ▲ CDC 59271
Kleven, A.:Son Vn, w. G. H. Braaten (pno) Simax ("Norway in Music" series) ▲ PSC 3106 [DDD]

Böhner, Georg (hn)
Schumann, R.:Konzertstück Hns, w. P. Damm (hn), H. Märker (hn), W. Pilz (hn), F. Konwitschny (cnd), Leipzig Gewandhaus Orch *(rec 1960–61)* Berlin Classics ("Eterna" series) 3–▲ BER 2016 [ADD]

Bohrig, Matthias (db)
Zimmermann, H.W.:Neujahrslied Db, w. Robert M. Helmschrott (org), Hans-Christoph Rademann (cnd), Dresden Chamber Choir Vienna Modern Masters ▲ VMM 3027 [DDD]

Boico, Efim (vn)—see ORCHESTRAS & ENSEMBLES Fine Arts String Quartet

Boissenin, Anne-Sophie (vc)—see ORCHESTRAS & ENSEMBLES Cecilia Piano Quartet

Bojsten, Stefan (pno)—see also ORCHESTRAS & ENSEMBLES Stockholm Arts Trio
Marianne Eklöf & Stefan Bojsten, w. Eklöf, Marianne (mez) MAP ▲ MAPCD 8922
Schulhoff, E.:Son Vc, w. Torleif Thedéen (vc) *(rec Danderyd Grammar School, Sweden, May 11, 1996)*
BIS ▲ CD 679 [DDD]

Bok, Henri (reeds)—see ORCHESTRAS & ENSEMBLES Duo Novair, Contemporain Duo

Bokstedt, Bertil (pno)
Jussi Björling:In Song & Ballad, w. J. Björling (ten), Harry Ebert (pno), Swedish Radio Orch [cnd:Sixten Ehrling], New York PO [cnd:Martti Similä] *(rec 1940, 1942 & 1957)* Bluebell ▲ BLU 050 [ADD]

Boland, Jan (fl)
Owen, J.:Intimate Dances, w. Cynthia Egger (gtr) *(rec Aug 10, 1991)* Centaur ▲ CRC 2233 [DDD]
Rossini, Mozart et al.:Serenades from the 19th Century Salon on Period Instruments, w. John Dowdall (gtr) Titanic ▲ Ti 182 [DDD]

Bolcolm, William (pno)
After the Ball, w. J. Morris (mez) Elektra/Nonesuch ▲ 79148-2
Blue Skies:Songs by Irving Berlin, w. J. Morris (mez) Elektra/Nonesuch ▲ 79120-2 ▮ 79120-4
Bolcom, W.:Aubade, "For the Continuation of Life", w. H. Sargous (ob) Crystal ▲ CD326 [DDD]
Bolcom, W.:Con Pno, w. S. Hodkinson (cnd), Rochester PO *(rec 1983)* Vox Classics ▲ VOX 7509
Cornet Favorites, w. G. Schwarz (tpt) Elektra/Nonesuch ▲ 79157-2
Gershwin, G.:The George Gershwin Songbook Elektra/Nonesuch ▲ 79151-2 [AAD]
Gershwin, G.:Pno Music—Rialto Ripples; Three Preludes; Impromptu in Two Keys; Three-Quarter Blues; Merry Andrew; Piano Playin' Jazzbo Brown; Promenade Elektra/Nonesuch ▲ 79151-2 [AAD]
Gershwin, G.:Preludes (3) Pno Elektra/Nonesuch ▲ 79151-2 [AAD]
Gershwin, G.:Songs, w. J. Morris (bass) Elektra/Nonesuch ▲ 79151-2 [AAD]
Joplin, S.:Music of—Collaborative Rags:Swipesy Cake Walk; Lily Queen; Sunflower Slow Drag; Something Doing; Felicity Rag MusicMasters ▲ 01612-67135-2 [ADD]
Joplin, S.:Pno Music Omega ▲ OCD 3001 [DDD]
Kern, J.:Songs, w. J. Morris (bass) Arabesque ▲ Z 6515 [DDD]
Let's Do It:Bolcolm & Morris at Aspen, w. J. Morris (mez) *(rec live in concert at the Aspen Music Festival, 7/22/89)* Omega Classics ▲ OCD 3004 [DDD]
Matthews & Scott:Pastimes & Piano Rags, w. W. Bolcolm (pno) Elektra/Nonesuch ▮ 71299-4
Night & Day:The Cole Porter Album, w. J. Morris (mez) Omega Classics ▲ OCD 3002 [DDD]
Silver Linings:Songs by Jerome Kern, w. J. Morris (mez) Arabesque ▲ Z 6515

Bolet, Jorge (pno)
Busoni, F.:Chaconne Pno RCA Gold Seal ▲ 7710-2-RG [ADD]
Chausson, E.:Con Vn, Pno & Str Qt, w. I. Perlman (vn), Juilliard String Quartet
CBS ▲ MK 37814 [DDD]
Chopin, F.:Con 1 Pno, w. C. Dutoit (cnd), Montreal SO London ▲ 425859-2 [DDD]
Chopin, F.:Con 2 Pno, w. C. Dutoit (cnd), Montreal SO London ▲ 425859-2 [DDD]
Chopin, F.:Études (24)—in E, Op. 10/3; in G♭, Op. 10/5 [Black Key]; in c, Op. 10/12 [Revolutionary] *(rec Belock Recording Studio, Bayside, Queens, NY)* Everest ▲ EVC 9028 [AAD]
Chopin, F.:Impromptus—No. 4 [Fant-Impromptu] *(rec Belock Recording Studio, Bayside, Queens, NY)*
Everest ▲ EVC 9028 [AAD]
Chopin, F.:Nocturnes—Opp. 27/1–2, 55/1, 62/2 London ▲ 421363-2 [DDD]
Chopin, F.:Nocturnes—in E♭, Op. 9/2 *(rec Belock Recording Studio, Bayside, Queens, NY)*
Everest ▲ EVC 9028 [AAD]
Chopin, F.:Polonaises—in A, Op. 40/1 [Military]; in A♭, Op. 53 *(rec Belock Recording Studio, Bayside, Queens, NY)* Everest ▲ EVC 9028 [AAD]
Chopin, F.:Preludes, Op. 28—No. 15 in D♭ *(rec Belock Recording Studio, Bayside, Queens, NY)*
Everest ▲ EVC 9028 [AAD]
Chopin, F.:Preludes, Op. 28 London ▲ 421363-2 [DDD]
Chopin, F.:Preludes, Op. 28 RCA Gold Seal ▲ 7710-2 RG [ADD]
Chopin, F.:Waltzes—in D♭, Op. 64/1 [Minute]; in c♯, Op. 64/2 *(rec Belock Recording Studio, Bayside, Queens, NY)* Everest ▲ EVC 9028 [AAD]
Grieg, E.:Con Pno, Op. 16, w. R. Chailly (cnd), Berlin RSO London ▲ 430719-2 [DDD]
Liszt, F.:Études de concert (2) Pno *(rec July 19, 1972)* Lyra House ▲ LHL 1002 [AAD]
Liszt, F.:Études d'exécution transcendante, S.139 London ▲ 414601-2 [DDD]

INSTRUMENT.

Bolet, Jorge (pno) (cont.)
Liszt, F.:Pno Music (misc)—Liebestraum No. 3; Au bord d'une source; Sonetto 104 del Petrarca; Les jeux d'eau à la Villa d'Este; Die Forelle; Auf dem Wasser zu singen; Wanderer Fantasy (all Schubert/Liszt); Gnomenreigen; Un sospiro; Tarantella (Venezia e Napoli) London ▲ 425689-2 [DDD]
Liszt, F.:Pno Music (misc)—Liebestraum No. 3 in A♭; Mephisto Waltz No. 1; Funérailles [from Harmonies poétiques et religieuses]; Réminiscences de Don Juan; La campanella [from Grandes études de Paganini]; Die Forelle; Erlkönig [both trans from Schubert]; Hungarian Rhap No. 12 in c#; Consolation No. 3; Sonetto 104 del Petrarca; Les Jeux d'eau à la Villa d'Este; Au bord d'une source; Gnomenreigen [from 2 Études de concert]; Un sospiro [from 3 Études de concert]; Rigoletto [concert paraphrase from Verdi]; Son in b *(rec 1978–85)* London ("Double Decker" series) 2-▲ 444851-2
Liszt, F.:Pno Music (misc)—Spanish Rhapsody *(rec July 19, 1972)* Lyra House ▲ LHL 1002 [AAD]
Liszt, F.:Totentanz, w. I. Fischer (cnd), London SO London ("Jubilee" series) ▲ 430736-2 [DDD]
Prokofiev, S.:Con 2 Pno, w. A. Cox (cnd), Nuremberg SO Genesis ▲ GCD 104 [ADD]
Prokofiev, S.:Con 3 Pno, w. A. Cox (cnd), Nuremberg SO Genesis ▲ GCD 104 [ADD]
Rachmaninoff, S.:Con 3 Pno, *(orch unknown)* *(rec June 30, 1969)* Lyra House ▲ LHL 1002 [AAD]
Schumann, R.:Con Pno, w. R. Chailly (cnd), Berlin RSO London ▲ 430719-2 [DDD]
Wagner, R.:Ovs, Preludes & Orch Sels [arr. for piano by Liszt]—Tannhäuser overture RCA Gold Seal ▲ 7710-2-RG [ADD]

Bolkvadze, Elisso (pno)
Liszt, F.:Fant on Hungarian Folk Tunes, w. J. Mardjani (cnd), Georgian Festival Orch Infinity Digital ▲ QK 57260 [DDD]

Bolla, Michele (pno)
Beethoven, L. van:Son 21 Pno, "Waldstein" Walsingham Classics ("The Sydney International Piano Competition" series) ▲ WAL 8019 [DDD]

Bollard, David (cl)
Evocations:The Poet Tall Poppies ▲ TP 10 [DDD]

Bollard, David (pno)—see also ORCHESTRAS & ENSEMBLES Australia Ensemble
Brahms, J.:songs, w. David Pereira (vc)—Feldeinsamkeit; Wie Melodien zieht es mir; Sappische Ode; Wiegenlied; Liebstreu; Minnelied [all arr Norbert Salter for vc & pno] Tall Poppies ▲ TP 078 [DDD]
Edwards, R.:The Tower of Remoteness, w. Nigel Westlake (cl) *(rec Sir John Clancy Auditorium, Univ of NSW, July 1990)* Tall Poppies ▲ TP 51 [DDD]
Falla, M. de:Suite populaire espagnole vc, w. David Pereira (vc) Tall Poppies ▲ TP 078 [DDD]
Ginastera, A.:Pampeana 2, w. David Pereira (vc) Tall Poppies ▲ TP 078 [DDD]
Nin, J.:songs, w. David Pereira (vc)—Montañesa; Tonada murciana; Saeta; Granadina [all arr Kochanski for vn & pno & tran for vc] Tall Poppies ▲ TP 078 [DDD]
Schubert, Franz:Der Hirt auf dem Felsen, w. J. Bates (sop), N. Westlake (cl), Australia Ensemble [G] *(rec July 1991)* Tall Poppies ▲ TP 011 [DDD]
Schumann, R.:Stücke im Volkston, w. David Pereira (vc) Tall Poppies ▲ TP 078 [DDD]
Shostakovich, D.:Ballet Suite 2, w. David Pereira (vc) [arr vc & pno] Tall Poppies ▲ TP 078 [DDD]
Songs of Sea & Sky, w. Bollard, David (pno), Nigel Westlake (cl) Tall Poppies ▲ TP 4 [DDD]
Souvenir, w. Graham Wood (vn) *(rec Sir John Clancy Auditorium, Univ of NSW, Sydney, June 1993)* Tall Poppies ▲ TP 56 [DDD]

Boller, Bettina (vn)
Balissat, J.:Rückblick, w. J. Balissat (cnd), Swiss-Italian Radio-TV Orch Grammont ▲ CTSP 17-2 [ADD]
Schoeck, O.:Concerto quasi una fantasia, w. A. Delfs (cnd), Swiss Youth SO Claves ▲ CD 9201 [DDD]

Bolleter, Ross (acc)
Bolleter, R.:Euridice in Hades Tall Poppies ▲ TP 45 [DDD]
Bolleter, R.:Nethermost Parts of the Dark Tall Poppies ▲ TP 45 [DDD]

Bolleter, Ross (acc/nar)
Bolleter, R.:The Complete History of a Minute Tall Poppies ▲ TP 45 [DDD]

Bolleter, Ross (acc/ruined pno/nar)
Bolleter, R.:Labyrinth, w. L. Brodalka (nar), F. Brodalka (nar) Tall Poppies ▲ TP 45 [DDD]

Bolleter, Ross (ruined pno)
Bolleter, R.:Myo Sei/Dark Sky Tall Poppies ▲ TP 45 [DDD]

Bolling, Claude (pno)
Bolcom, W.:Sons (2) for 2 Pnos, Bass & Perc, w. E. Ax (pno), C. Sorin (db), C. Cordelette (perc) CBS ▲ MK 45646 [DDD]
Bolling, C.:California Suite, w. H. Laws (fl), C. Damonico (db), S. Manne (perc) CBS ▲ MK 36691
Bolling, C.:Music of, w. J.-P. Rampal (fl), A. Lagoya (gtr), et al.—California Suite, Concerto for Classic Guitar & Jazz Piano, Flute & Jazz Piano Suites Nos. 1 & 2, Violin & Jazz Piano Suite, Picnic Suite, & Toot Suite CBS ▲ MK 44608 ■ FMT 44608
Bolling, C.:Suite 2 Fl, w. J.-P. Rampal (fl), C. Sorin (db), C. Cordelette (perc) CBS ▲ MK 42318 [DDD] ■ FMT 42318 (D)
Bolling, C.:Suite Jazz Pno, w. J.-P. Rampal (cnd), English CO CBS ▲ MK 37798
Bolling, C.:Toot Suite, w. M. André (tpt) CBS ▲ MK 36731

Bollinger, Blair (trbn)
Four of a Kind:Music for Trombone Quartet, w. J. Allessi (trbn), Scott A. Hartman (trbn), Mark H. Lawrence (trbn) Summit ▲ DCD 123 [DDD] ■ DCD 123

Bologna, Antonella (va)
Sui Palchi Delle Stelle:Sacred Music in the Neapolitan Conservatories at the Time of Francesco Provenzale, w. [cnd:Antonio Florio], Cappella Pietà de Turchini, Antonella Ippolito (sop), Jane Haughton (sop), Daniela del Monaco (alt), Sebastiano Cassarà (vn), Rosario Di Meglio (vn), Antonella Bologna (va), Paolo Dionisio (vl), Antonio Florio (vc), Pierluigi Ciapparelli (thb), Enrico Baiano (org/hpd) Symphonia ▲ SY 93S20 [DDD]

Bolognese, Vincenzo (vn)
Heifetz, J.:Transcriptions Vn, w. Luisa Prayer (pno)—trans. of works by Rameau, Chopin, Saint-Saëns, Dvořák, Prokofiev, Mozart, Schumann, Debussy, Rachmaninoff, Gershwin, others Musikstrasse ▲ 2107
Respighi, O.:Con Vn, w. R. Tigani (cnd), Sassari SO *(rec Rome, Oct 11–14, 1994)* Bongiovanni ▲ GB 2166 [DDD]

Bolsi, Corrado (vn)—see ORCHESTRAS & ENSEMBLES Italian Piano Quartet

Bolton, Ivor (hpd)
Bach, J.S.:Cons Hpd, BWV 1052–1058, w. I. Bolton (cnd), St. James' Baroque Players—Nos. 1 & 4–6 IMP Classics ▲ PCD 864 [DDD]
Bach, J.S.:Con 1 Hpd, w. I. Bolton (cnd), St. James' Baroque Players IMP ("Classics" series) ▲ IMP 6700692
Bach, J.S.:Con 2 Hpd, w. I. Bolton (cnd), St. James' Baroque Players IMP Classics ▲ PCD 901 [DDD]
Bach, J.S.:Con 3 Hpd, w. I. Bolton (cnd), St. James' Baroque Players IMP Classics ▲ PCD 901 [DDD]
Bach, J.S.:Con 4 Hpd, w. I. Bolton (cnd), St. James' Baroque Players IMP ("Classics" series) ▲ IMP 6700692
Bach, J.S.:Con 5 Hpd, w. I. Bolton (cnd), St. James' Baroque Players IMP ("Classics" series) ▲ IMP 6700692
Bach, J.S.:Con 6 Hpd, w. I. Bolton (cnd), St. James' Baroque Players IMP ("Classics" series) ▲ IMP 6700692
Bach, J.S.:Con 7 Hpd, w. I. Bolton (cnd), St. James' Baroque Players IMP Classics ▲ PCD 901 [DDD]

Bolyard, Jim (bn)—see ORCHESTRAS & ENSEMBLES Tempesta di Mare

Bolze, C. (vn)
Fauré, G.:Son 1 Vn, w. J. Adler (pno) *(rec 1984)* Classic Studio Berlin ▲ CS 10808 [DDD]
Ravel, M.:Berceuse sur le nom de Gabriel Fauré, w. J. Adler (pno) *(rec 1984)* Classic Studio Berlin ▲ CS 10808 [DDD]
Ravel, M.:Son Vn Pno, w. J. Adler (pno) *(rec 1984)* Classic Studio Berlin ▲ CS 10808 [DDD]
Ravel, M.:Sonate posthume, w. J. Adler (pno) *(rec 1984)* Classic Studio Berlin ▲ CS 10808 [DDD]

Bomont, Yves (bn)—see ORCHESTRAS & ENSEMBLES Belgian Wind Quintet

Bon, Maarten (pno)
Hindemith, P.:Son Hn, w. H. Dullaert (hn) *(rec Oct. & Dec. 1992)* CPO ▲ CPO 999229 [DDD]
Hindemith, P.:Son Alto Hn, w. H. Dullaert (hn) *(rec Oct. & Dec. 1992)* CPO ▲ CPO 999229 [DDD]
Messiaen, O.:Visions de l'Amen, w. Reinbert de Leeuw (pno) Montaigne ▲ MO 782050

Bonafosse, Pierre-Marie (sax)
Constant, M.:Choruses & Interludes, w. Jean-Jacques Justafre (hn), François Moutin (b gtr), Pierre Guignon (dr), Andy Emler (pno), J. Kaltenbach (cnd), Nancy SO *(rec Salle Poirel, Nancy, Apr. 4, 1990)* Erato ▲ 94815-2 [DDD]

Bonaldi, Clara (vn)
Ravel, M.:Berceuse sur le nom de Gabriel Fauré, w. Noël Lee (pno) Adda ▲ ADD 581065 [DDD]
Ravel, M.:Son Vn Vc, w. Yvan Chiffoleau (vc) Adda ▲ ADD 581065 [DDD]
Ravel, M.:Sonate posthume, w. Noël Lee (pno) Adda ▲ ADD 581065 [DDD]
Ravel, M.:Trio Pno, w. Noël Lee (pno), Yvan Chiffoleau (vc) Adda ▲ ADD 581065 [DDD]

Bonatta, Andrea (pno)
Brahms, J.:Ballades, Op. 10 Astrée ▲ E 8753
Brahms, J.:Sons Vn (comp), w. M.-A. Nicolas (vn) Valois ▲ V 4709 [DDD]
Brahms, J.:Vars & Fugue on a Theme by Handel Astrée ▲ E 8753
Brahms, J.:Vars on an Original Theme Astrée ▲ E 8753
Schubert, Franz:Pno Music (4-hands), w. Paul Badura-Skoda (pno)—Fant.; Rondo; Vars.; Grandes Marches; Trio 5 & 6; 3 Marches Militaires Valois ▲ V 4720

Bonaventura, Anthony di (pno)
Balada, L.:Transparencies of Chopin's 1st Ballade New World ▲ 80442-2
Chopin, F.:Barcarolle Pno Titanic ▲ Ti 208 [DDD]
Chopin, F.:Polonaise-fant Titanic ▲ Ti 208 [DDD]
Chopin, F.:Scherzos—Op. 54 Titanic ▲ Ti 208 [DDD]
Chopin, F.:Son Pno, Op. 58 Titanic ▲ Ti 208 [DDD]
Rachmaninoff, S.:Preludes Pno, Opp 23 & 32—Op. 32 Titanic ▲ Ti 195 [DDD]
Scarlatti, D.:Sons Kbd—K.11 in c; K.29 in D; K.32 in d; K.44 in F; K.113 in A; K.132 in C; K.146 in G; K.162 in E; K.201 in G; K.209 in A; K.366 in F; K.380 in E; K.435 in D; K.513 in C Titanic ▲ Ti 194 [DDD]

Bond, Danny (bn)
Boismortier, J.B. de:Sons, Op. 40, w. R. van der Meer (vc)—No. 1 Accent ▲ 58331 [DDD]
Boismortier, J.B. de:Sons, Op. 26, w. R. van der Meer (vc), R. Kohnen (hpd)—Nos. 1, 2 & 3 Accent ▲ 58331 [DDD]
Corrette, M.:Sons, w. R. van der Meer (vc), R. Kohnen (hpd)—Sons. 1, 3 & 5 Accent ▲ 58331 [DDD]
Devienne, F.:Sons Bn, Op. 24, w. R. van der Meer (vc), R. Kohnen (hpd) *(rec Dec. 1992)* Accent ▲ 9290
Mozart, W.A.:Con Bn, w. C. Hogwood (cnd), Academy of Ancient Music L'Oiseau-Lyre ▲ 417622-2 [DDD] □ 417622-5
Zelenka, J.D.:Trio Sons Obs, w. P. Dombrecht (ob), et al. Accent 2-▲ 8848

Bond, Timothy (org)
Messiaen, O.:L'Ascension Org IMP ("BBC Radio Classics" series) ▲ IMP 5691602

Bondarenko, Alexander (vn)
Stetsenko, K.:The Divine Liturgy of St. J. Chrysostom, w. A. Bondarenko (cnd), Frescoes of Kiev Erasmus ▲ WVH 120 [DDD]

Bondarenko, Helena (vn)
Bortnyansky, D.:Sinf concertante, w. H. Kann (pno), *(bn unknown)*, I. Angerer (hp), W. Knieps (va), A. Schober (vc) Entrée ▲ 0051 [ADD]

Bone, Elizabeth (vc)—see ORCHESTRAS & ENSEMBLES Canterbury Cellists

Bône, N. (va)—see ORCHESTRAS & ENSEMBLES Kandinsky Quartet

Bonell, Carlos (gtr)
Bach, J.S.:Partita Lt, BWV 997 Elektra/Nonesuch ■ H4-71403
Bach, J.S.:Suite Lt, BWV 996 RCA Red Seal ▲ RCD1-5841
John Williams & Friends, w. J. Williams (gtr), Brian Gascoigne (mar/vib), Morris Pert (mar/vib), Keith Marjoram (db) CBS ▲ MK 35108 [AAD]
Music of Spain Elektra/Nonesuch ■ N5-71390
Purcell, H.:The Fairy Queen (sels) [arr for solo gtr] Elektra/Nonesuch ■ H4-71403
Rodrigo, J.:Concierto de Aranjuez, w. C. Dutoit (cnd), Montreal SO London ▲ 430703-2 [DDD]
Visée, R. de:Gtr Pieces (sels)—Suite in G Elektra/Nonesuch ■ H4-71403
Weiss, S.L.:Lt Music—Tombeau sur la mort de M. Comte de Logy Elektra/Nonesuch ■ H4-71403

Bonelli, Ilde (hp)
19th Century Music for Flute & Harp, w. G. Mugnolo (fl) Bongiovanni ▲ GB 5039 [DDD]

Bonet-Manrique, Javier (hn)—see ORCHESTRAS & ENSEMBLES L'Archibudelli

Bonfanti, Sergio (vc)—see ORCHESTRAS & ENSEMBLES Fauré Trio

Bongiovanni, Ettore (hn)—see ORCHESTRAS & ENSEMBLES Arnold Quintet, Italiano Octet

Boni, Marco (vc)
Battiato, F.:Haiku, w. Franco Battiato (voc), Pouran Ghaffarpour (voc), Antonio Ballista (pno), Guido Corti (cnt), Filippo Destrieri (kbd/computer), John Giblin (bass), Gavin Harrison (dr/perc), Jakko Jakszyk (gtr), Roberto Mazza (ob), Fabrizio Merlini (va), Angelo Privitera (kbd/computer), Mino Bordignon (cnd), Milan Chamber Music Choir Hemisphere ▲ 837234-2
Battiato, F.:Ricerca sul Terzo, w. Franco Battiato (voc), Alessio Alba (tamboura), Antonio Ballista (pno), Debendra Kanti Chakraborty (tabla), Guido Corti (cnt), Filippo Destrieri (kbd/computer), John Giblin (bass), Buddhadeu Das Gupta (sarod), Gavin Harrison (dr/perc), Jakko Jakszyk (gtr), Roberto Mazza (ob), Fabrizio Merlini (va), Angelo Privitera (kbd/computer), Mino Bordignon (cnd), Milan Chamber Music Choir Hemisphere ▲ 837234-2
Brahms, J.:Trio Cl, w. Gaspare Tirincanti (cl), Maurizio Deoriti (pno) Stradivarius ▲ STV SIP 27 [DDD]
Brahms, J.:Trio Cl, w. G. Trinicanti (cl), M. Deoriti (pno) *(rec June 1993)* Sipario Dischi ▲ CS 27 C

Bönig, Winfried (org)
Buxtehude, D.:Org Music (misc)—Canzonetta, BuxWV.171; Chaconne in c, BuxWV.159; Chorale Preludes, BuxWV.182, 183, 207, 214, 223; Preludes in D, BuxWV.139, in f#, BuxWV.146 & in a, BuxWV.153; Fugue in C, BuxWV.174; Passacaglia in d, BuxWV.161; Toccata in F, BuxWV.157 *(rec 8/88)* Ambitus ▲ 97835 [DDD]
La Toccata Française Ambitus ▲ AMB 97823 [DDD]

Bonita, Laurentius (vn)—see ORCHESTRAS & ENSEMBLES Sonare String Quartet

Bonitz, Benedikta (rcr)
Il Flauto Dolce, w. Bonitz, Benedikta (rcr), Irene Gudel (vc), Yoma Appenheimer (hpd) Arcadia ▲ ARC 1993-2 [DDD]

Bonn, James (pno)
Hartke, S.:Son-Vars, w. Ronald Copes (vc) *(rec Hancock Auditorium, USC, Los Angeles, CA, Nov. 25–27, 1994)* New World ▲ 80461-2
Shostakovich, D.:Trio 2 Pno, w. Ani Kavafian (vn), Colin Carr (vc) *(rec Tuscon Winter Chamber Festival; Mar 13, 1994)* Arizona Friends of Chamber Music ▲ AFCD 19941
Shostakovich, D.:Trio 2 Pno, w. Ani Kavafian (vn), Colin Carr (vc) *(rec live, Tucson Chamber Music Festival, Mar 13, 1994)* Arizona Friends of Chamber Music ▲ 1994 [DDD]

Bonneau, Jacqueline (pno)
Mozart, W.A.:Songs, w. Terese Stich-Randall (mez)—La violette; Sentiment du soir; L'image du rêve; Viens, chère cithare; Nostalgie du printemps; A chloé; Chant de séparation Accord ▲ ACD 201452 [AAD]
Schubert, Franz:Songs (misc), w. Terese Stich-Randall (sop)—A la musique; Petite rose des bruyères; Tu es le repos; Rire et pleurer; La truite; Foi printanière; Ave maria; Amour sans repos; Nuit et rêves Accord ▲ ACD 201452 [AAD]

Bonnell, Robin (vc)—see ORCHESTRAS & ENSEMBLES Earplay, Earplay members

Bønnerup, Inge (org)
Buxtehude, D.:Org Music (comp) *(rec May 1991)* Danacord ▲ DACOCD 384 [DDD]
Buxtehude, D.:Org Music (comp) *(rec Oct. 1991)* Danacord ▲ DACOCD 385 [DDD]
Buxtehude, D.:Org Music (comp) *(rec Jun. 1991)* Danacord ▲ DACOCD 383 [DDD]
Buxtehude, D.:Org Music (comp) *(rec Apr. 1991)* Danacord ▲ DACOCD 381 [DDD]
Buxtehude, D.:Org Music (comp) *(rec Nov. 1991)* Danacord ▲ DACOCD 386 [DDD]
Buxtehude, D.:Org Music (comp) *(rec Feb. 1991)* Danacord ▲ DACOCD 382 [DDD]
Thybo, L.:Con 2 Org *(rec Vangede Church, Mar. 13, Apr. 11, 12 & 25)* Marco Polo/Dacapo ▲ 8.224009 [DDD]

▲ = CD ♦ = Enhanced CD Δ = MD ■ = Cassette Tape □ = DCC

Bonnevie, Robert (hn)
Schumann, R.:Konzertstück Hns, w. R. Bonnevie (hn), et al., G. Schwarz (cnd), Seattle SO
Delos ▲ DE 3084 [DDD]
Bonnier, Pascale (pno)
Couperin, G.-F.:Music of, w. Lucette Touzet (pno), Blandine Virard (pno)—Vars on Ah! Ça Ira
Adda ▲ ADD 581114
Jadin, L.E.:Sons Pno 4-Hands, Op. 2, w. Lucette Touzet (pno), Blandine Virard (pno)—No. 1
Adda ▲ ADD 581114
Méhul, E.-N.:Sons Hpd, Op. 1, w. Lucette Touzet (pno), Blandine Virard (pno)—No. 3
Adda ▲ ADD 581114
Rigel, H.-J.:Kbd Music, w. Lucette Touzet (pno), Blandine Virard (pno)—Son No. 3, Op. 3
Adda ▲ ADD 581114
Tapray, J.F.:Sons Hpd, Op. 24, w. Lucette Touzet (pno), Blandine Virard (pno)—No. 3
Adda ▲ ADD 581114
Bontrager, L. J. (hn)—see ORCHESTRAS & ENSEMBLES Pennsylvania Wind Quintet
Bontrager, Laura (vc)—see ORCHESTRAS & ENSEMBLES CELLO
Bonucci, Arturo (vc)—see also ORCHESTRAS & ENSEMBLES Mezzena-Bonucci Trio
Rendano, A.:Qnt Pno, w. R. Caporali (pno), R. Bonucci (vn), M. Fiorini (vn), F. Anzelmo (va) *(rec Mar. 29–31, 1989)*
Ermitage ▲ ERM 409 [ADD]
Bonucci, Rodolfo (vn)
Fauré, G.:Berceuse Vn, w. E. Bátiz (cnd), Mexico City PO — ASV ▲ ASV 686
Fauré, G.:Con Vn, w. E. Bátiz (cnd), Mexico City PO — ASV ▲ ASV 686
Rendano, A.:Qnt Pno, w. R. Caporali (pno), M. Fiorini (vn), F. Anzelmo (va), A. Bonucci (vc) *(rec Mar. 29–31, 1989)*
Ermitage ▲ ERM 409 [ADD]
Bonvin, Dany (trbn)
Trombone Festival, w. 13 Etoiles Brass Band — Gallo ▲ CD 474 [ADD]
Boomkamp, Carel van Leeuwen (vc)—see ORCHESTRAS & ENSEMBLES Alma Musica Ensemble
Booth, Colin (hpd)
Bach, J.S.:Chaconne—BWV 964 [arr. Bach] — Olympia ▲ OLY 437 [DDD]
Bach, J.S.:Chromatic Fant & Fugue—BWV 964 [arr. Bach] — Olympia ▲ OLY 437 [DDD]
Bach, J.S.:Cons solo Hpd, BWV 972–987—BWV 976 — Olympia ▲ OLY 437 [DDD]
Bach, J.S.:Sons (5) Kbd—BWV 964 [arr. Bach] — Olympia ▲ OLY 437 [DDD]
Booth, Colin (org)
Bach, C.P.E.:Sons Hpd—W.62/5, 6 & 7; W.65/13 & 20 — Olympia ▲ OLY 433 [DDD]
Booth, J. (vn)
Lentz, G.:Caeli enarrant...IV, w. Georges Lentz (vn), D. Wicks (va), P. Morrison (vc)
Tall Poppies ▲ TP 35
Boothby, Richard (vl)—see ORCHESTRAS & ENSEMBLES Purcell Quartet
Boots, Stefan (fl)—see ORCHESTRAS & ENSEMBLES VIF Flute Quartet
Boquet, Pascale (archlt)
Vivaldi, A.:Sons Fl, w. Jean-Christophe Frisch (trns fl), Christine Plubeau (vl), Claude Wassmer (bn), Alessandro de Marchi (hpd)—in F, d, e, g, c, D & g — Adda ▲ ADD 241882
Borbei, Evelina (pno)
Levinas, M.:Anaglyphe — REM ▲ REM 311270 [DDD]
Liszt, F.:Son Pno — REM ▲ REM 311270 [DDD]
Schumann, R.:Fant Pno — REM ▲ REM 311270 [DDD]
Borciani, Mario (pno)
Martucci, G.:Qnt Pno, w. Giovane Quartetto Italiano — Claves ▲ CD 9210 [DDD]
Martucci, G.:Trio 1 Pno, w. Giovane Quartetto Italiano members — Claves ▲ CD 9210 [DDD]
Borciani, Paolo (vn)—see ORCHESTRAS & ENSEMBLES Quartetto Italiano
Borczon, Ron (gtr)—see ORCHESTRAS & ENSEMBLES B & B Duo
Borden, D. (kbd/syns)—see also ORCHESTRAS & ENSEMBLES Mother Mallard
Borden, D.:Music of—Esty Point, Summer 1978 [w. H. Roberts (cello), J. Hyman (violin), G. Borden (guitar)]; Enfield in Winter; Enfield in Summer; Ah Eden, a Rib; Droneland; Her Inner Lock; Unjust Malaise; for Rose Mary Harbison [w. J. Hyman (violin)]; for Bob Haskins; for Laurie Spiegel
Cuneiform ▲ RUNE 58
Borden, G. (gtr)—see ORCHESTRAS & ENSEMBLES Mother Mallard
Bordner, Gary (tpt)
Copland, A.:Quiet City, w. T. Tempel (E hn), H. Wolff (cnd), St. Paul CO
Teldec ▲ 2292-46314-2 [DDD]
Borel, S. (perc)
Gaudibert, E.:Feuillages, w. M. Favrod (perc), J. Hostettler (perc) — Gallo ▲ CD 630 [AAD]
Borge, Victor (pno)
Victor Borge Live(!) — Sony Masterworks ▲ MDK 48482 (m) [ADD] ■ MGT 48482
Borgonovo, Pietro (ob)
Salieri, A.:Con Fl, w. Clementine Hoogendoorn (fl), C. Scimone (cnd), Venice Solisti
Erato ▲ ERA SEL 12987 [DDD]
Villa-Lobos, H.:Duo Ob, w. Rino Vernizzi (bn) *(rec Chiesa della Misericordia, Torino, Italy, Feb 1987)*
Arts Music ▲ 447200-2 [DDD]
Villa-Lobos, H.:Qt Fl, w. Andrea Griminelli (fl), Michele Carulli (cl), Rino Vernizzi (bn) *(rec Chiesa della Misericordia, Torino, Italy, Feb 1987)* — Arts Music ▲ 447200-2 [DDD]
Villa-Lobos, H.:Qnten forme de chôros, w. Andrea Griminelli (fl), Michele Carulli (cl), Francesco Pomarico (E hn), Rino Vernizzi (bn) *(rec Chiesa della Misericordia, Torino, Italy, Feb 1987)*
Arts Music ▲ 447200-2 [DDD]
Villa-Lobos, H.:Trio Ob, w. Michele Carulli (cl), Rino Vernizzi (bn) *(rec Chiesa della Misericordia, Torino, Italy, Feb 1987)* — Arts Music ▲ 447200-2 [DDD]
Borioli, Orazio (sax)
Music for Saxophone, w. Cesarini (pno) — Gallo ▲ CD 516
Boriskin, Michael (pno)
Bernstein, L.:Anniversaries (13) Pno *(rec April 1992)* — New World ▲ 80426-2
Brahms, J.:Theme & Vars Pno — Music & Arts ▲ CD 7261
Brahms, J.:Vars & Fugue on a Theme by Handel — Music & Arts ▲ CD 726-1
Brahms, J.:Vars on a Hungarian Song — Music & Arts ▲ CD 726-1
Brahms, J.:Vars on an Original Theme — Music & Arts ▲ CD 726-1
Danielpour, R.:Son Pno *(rec April 1992)* — New World ▲ 80426-2
del Tredici, D.:Soliloquy — New World ▲ NW 380-2 [DDD]
del Tredici, D.:Virtuoso Alice — New World ▲ NW 380-2 [DDD]
Fine, I.:Music for Pno — New World ▲ 80402-2 [DDD]
Liebermann, L.:Gargoyles *(rec April 1992)* — New World ▲ 80426-2
Menotti, G.C.:Ricercare & Toccata on a Theme from *The Old Maid & the Thief*
New World ▲ 80402-2 [DDD]
Perle, G.:Fant-Vars Pno — New World ▲ NW 342-2 [DDD]
Perle, G.:Lyric Intermezzo — New World ▲ NW 380-2 [DDD]
Perle, G.:New Etudes — New World ▲ NW 342-2 [DDD]
Perle, G.:Pantomime, Interlude & Fugue — New World ▲ NW 342-2 [DDD]
Perle, G.:Short Son Pno — New World ▲ NW 342-2 [DDD]
Perle, G.:Sonatina Pno — New World ▲ NW 380-2 [DDD]
Perle, G.:Suite Pno — New World ▲ NW 342-2 [DDD]
Ruggles, C.:Evocations — New World ▲ 80402-2 [DDD]
Shapero, H.:Sons Pno — New World ▲ 80402-2 [DDD]
Slonimsky, S.:Transformational Etudes *(rec April 1992)* — New World ▲ 80426-2
Thorne, N.:Love Songs — New World ▲ NW 380-2 [DDD]
Thorne, N.:Son Pno — New World ▲ NW 380-2 [DDD]

Borisova, Roza (vc)
Vivaldi, A.:Cons Vn, Op. 8/1–4, "The Four Seasons", w. Jerome Franke (vn), Karine Garibova (vn), Pasquale Laurino (vn), Olga Miliaeva (va), Mika Hennessy (db), Melanie Panush (ham dlc), Stanislav Venglevski (bayan), Mike Kashou (arabic tabla), Daryl Stuermer (gtr), Ed Palouсek (celtic fid), Gary Bottoni (highland pipe), Dubuffet String Quartet *(rec July-Sept 1995)*
EarthBeat! ▲ 35270-2 [DDD]
Borisovsky, Vadim (va)—see ORCHESTRAS & ENSEMBLES Beethoven String Quartet
Börlin, Heinz (pno)
Les Plus belles transcriptions pour contrebass et piano, w. Y. Goïlav (db) — Gallo ▲ CD 675 [DDD]
Bornkamp, Arno (sax)
Charpentier, J.:Gavambodi 2, w. I. Janssen (pno) — Globe ▲ GLO 5032 [DDD]
Denisov, E.:Son A Sax, w. I. Janssen (pno) — Globe ▲ GLO 5032 [DDD]
Desenclos, A.:Prélude, cadence et finale, w. I. Janssen (pno) — Globe ▲ GLO 5032 [DDD]
Schmitt, F.:Légende, w. I. Janssen (pno) — Globe ▲ GLO 5032 [DDD]
Works for Saxophone & Piano, w. A. Bornkamp (sax) — Globe ▲ GLO 5032 [DDD]
Bornkamp, Arno (t sax)—see ORCHESTRAS & ENSEMBLES Aurelia Saxophone Quartet
Borowsky, Alexander (pno)
Bach, J.S.:Fant & Fugue Org, BWV 542 [trans Liszt for pno] — Pearl 2-▲ PEA CD 9235
Busoni, F.:Bach Transcriptions—Con in d; Con in f — Pearl 2-▲ PEA CD 9235
Liszt, F.:Album d'un voyageur—Au Bord d'un source — Pearl 2-▲ PEA CD 9235
Liszt, F.:Hungarian Rhaps—Nos. 1–15 — Pearl 2-▲ PEA CD 9235
Borràs, Xavier (pno)
Debussy, C.:Son Vn, w. Francisca Mendoza (vn) *(rec Barcelona, July 8, 9, 22 & 23, 1994)*
Edicions Albert Moraleda ▲ 1294-18 [DDD]
Prokofiev, S.:Son Vn, Op. 94bis, w. Francisca Mendoza (vn) *(rec Barcelona, July 8, 9, 22 & 23, 1994)*
Edicions Albert Moraleda ▲ 1294-18 [DDD]
Borrett, Joanna (vc)—see ORCHESTRAS & ENSEMBLES Double Image members
Borries, Siegfried (vn)
Lehár, F.:Paganini (sels), w. Melitta Muszely (sop), Rudolf Schock (ten), W. Schmidt-Boelcke (cnd), FFB Orch, Gunther Arndt Chorus — Emperor Operetta ▲ KO 86343
Borror, Ron (trbn)—see ORCHESTRAS & ENSEMBLES New Music Consort
Borror, Ronald (tenor trbn)
Balada, L.:Son Winds, w. J. Aley (tpt), D. Wakefield (hn), R. Biddlecome (bass trbn), American Brass Quintet — New World ▲ 80442-2
Borror, Ronald (trbn)
Roussakis, N.:Trigono, w. Steven Paysen (vib), Gregory Charnon (perc) — CRI ▲ CD 709 [DDD]
Stravinsky, I.:Octet, w. M. Parloff (fl), D. Schiffrin (cl), F. Morelli (bn), S. Heinneman (bn), R. Mase (tpt), C. Gekker (tpt), D. Taylor (trbn), G. Schuller (cnd) *(rec Sep. 1991)* — GM ▲ GM 2030
Wuorinen, C.:Trio Trbn, w. D. Druckman (mar), A. Feinberg (pno) *(rec Sept. 11–13, 1991)*
Koch International Classics ▲ KIC 7123-2 [DDD]
Borsódy, László (tpt)—see ORCHESTRAS & ENSEMBLES Affetti Musicali
Borst, Katherine (fl)
Telemann, G.P.:Qt Bn Fls, w. Christopher Weait (bn), Craig J. Kirchhoff (fl), Nelson Harper (hpd)
D'Note Classics ▲ DND 1008 [DDD]
Borth, Dorothea (vc)—see ORCHESTRAS & ENSEMBLES Chalumeau Trio
Borys, Roman (vc)—see ORCHESTRAS & ENSEMBLES Gryphon Piano Trio
Bos, Coenraad V. (pno)
Wolf, H.:Michelangelo-Lieder, w. A. Kipnis (bass) *(rec 1933, "Hugo Wolf Society")*
Music & Arts 2-▲ CD 661 (m) [AAD]
Wolf, H.:Michelangelo-Lieder, w. A. Kipnis (bass) *(rec 1933, "Hugo Wolf Society")*
Preiser 2-▲ 89204 (m) [AAD]
Wolf, H.:Songs (misc), w. A. Kipnis (bass), Gerald Moore (pno), Ernst Victor Wolff (pno)—Grenzen der Menschheit; Um Mitternacht; Sterb' ich, so hüllt in Blumen meine Glieder; Michelangelo-Lieder I-III *[w. Bos, rec. 1933–4]*; Cophtisches Lied I; Der Musikant; Der Soldat I; Der Schreckenberger *[w. Moore, rec. 1935]*; Wie glänzt der helle Mond; Nun lasst uns Frieden schliessen; Wir haben beide lange Zeit geschwiegen; Geselle, woll'n wir uns in Kutten hüllen; Heb' auf dein blondes Haupt; Wie viele Zeit verlor ich; Was für ein Lied soll dir gesungen werden *[w. Wolff, rec. 1934] (rec "Hugo Wolf Society," 1933–35)* — Music & Arts 2-▲ CD 661 (m) [AAD]
Wolf, H.:Songs (misc), w. A. Kipnis (bass), Gerald Moore (pno), Ernst Victor Wolff (pno)—Grenzen der Menschheit; Um Mitternacht; Sterb' ich, so hüllt in Blumen meine Glieder; Michelangelo-Lieder I-III *[w. Bos, rec. 1933–4]*; Cophtisches Lied I; Der Musikant; Der Soldat I; Der Schreckenberger *[w. Moore, rec. 1935]*; Wie glänzt der helle Mond; Nun lasst uns Frieden schliessen; Wir haben beide lange Zeit geschwiegen; Geselle, woll'n wir uns in Kutten hüllen; Heb' auf dein blondes Haupt; Wie viele Zeit verlor ich; Was für ein Lied soll dir gesungen werden *[w. Wolff, rec. 1934] (rec 1933–35)*
Preiser 2-▲ 89204 (m) [AAD]
Bosbach, Philipp (vc)—see also ORCHESTRAS & ENSEMBLES Capella Clementina
Schobert, J.:Music of, w. L. Sgrizzi (pno), C. Ganchini (vn), V. Méjean (vn)—Qts. in f, Op. 7/2 & in E♭, Op. 14/1; Sons. in d & A, Op. 14/4 & 5; Trios in D & B♭, Op. 16/1 & 4
Musique d'Abord ▲ HMA 1901294
Boschetti, Victor (pno)
Mozart, W.A.:Rè pastore (sels), w. Maria Gerhart (sop), Gustav Liebich (vn) *(rec 1905 - 1944)*
Minerva ▲ MN A14 [ADD]
Boschi, Hélène (pno)
Schubert, Franz:Son Pno, D.664 — REM ▲ REM 311269 [AAD]
Schubert, Franz:Son Pno, D.960 — REM ▲ REM 311269 [AAD]
Schubert, Franz:Valses sentimentales — REM ▲ REM 311269 [AAD]
Boschiero, R. (hp)
Haik-Vantoura, S.:The Song of Songs, w. S. Haik-Vantoura (mez), M.-L. Banzet (bar), S. Chefson (fl), E. Dutrieux (cnd), *(chorus unknown)* [He] *(rec 1986)* — Alienor ▲ AL 1045 [DDD]
Boscole, Christopher (pno)
O Christmas Tree — Centaur ▲ CRC 2137
Boselli, Guido (vc)
Zimmermann, B.A.:Short Studies Vc — Stradivarius ▲ STR 33340
Zimmermann, B.A.:Son Vc — Stradivarius ▲ STR 33340
Boshniakovich, Oleg (pno)
Tchaikovsky, P.:Songs, w. D. Hvorostovsky (bar)—9 songs—A tear trembles; None but the lonely heart; Reconciliation; The fearful minute; Don Juan's serenade; The nightingale; Exploit; I opened the window; Again, as before, alone — Philips ▲ 432119-2 [DDD] ◻ 432119-5
Bosi, Sergio (cl)
Castelnuovo-Tedesco, M.:Son Cl & Pno, w. Riccardo Bartoli (pno) *(rec Potenza Picena Teatro "B. Mugellini", June 3–6, 1994)* — Bongiovanni ▲ GB 5563 [DDD]
Rota, N.:Son Cl Pno, w. Riccardo Bartoli (pno) *(rec Potenza Picena Teatro "B. Mugellini", June 3–6, 1994)* — Bongiovanni ▲ GB 5563 [DDD]
Setaccioli, G.:Son Cl, w. Riccardo Bartoli (pno) *(rec Potenza Picena Teatro "B. Mugellini", June 3–6, 1994)* — Bongiovanni ▲ GB 5563 [DDD]
Boskovsky, Willi (vn)
Mozart, W.A.:Sons Vn Pno (comp), w. L. Kraus (pno)
EMI Classics ("Great Recordings of the Century" series) 6-▲ CDHF 63873
Bosna, Pietro (hpd)
Campogalliani, E.:Music of, w. Luca Bertazzi, Umberto Bertetti, Dino Miglioli, Emanuela Moreschi, Rinaldo Rossi — Bongiovanni ▲ GB 5050
Geminiani, F.:Sons Vc & Continuo, Op. 5, w. V. Paternoster (vc), A. Coen (vc)—No. 3
Bongiovanni ▲ GB 10015 [DDD]
Marcello, B.:Son Vc, Op. 2/4, w. A. Coen (vc), V. Paternoster (vc) — Bongiovanni ▲ GB 10015 [DDD]
Martino, F.:Son Vc, w. V. Paternoster (vc), A. Coen (vc) — Bongiovanni ▲ GB 10015 [DDD]
Pergolesi, G.B.:Sinf Vc, w. V. Paternoster (vc), A. Coen (vc) — Bongiovanni ▲ GB 10015 [DDD]
Scipriani, F.P.:Sinf Vc, w. V. Paternoster (vc), A. Coen (cv) — Bongiovanni ▲ GB 10015 [DDD]
Bosna, Pietro (vc)—see ORCHESTRAS & ENSEMBLES L'Arte dell'Arco

Bossard, Suzy (pno)
Debussy, C.:Son Vc, w. A. Gastinel (vc) *(rec 7/90)* Ottavo ▲ OTR C79032 [DDD]
Debut Recital, w. A. Gastinel (vc) Ottavo ▲ 79032 [DDD]
Fauré, G.:Elégie, w. A. Gastinel (vc) *(rec 7/90)* Ottavo ▲ OTR C79032 [DDD]
Fauré, G.:Son 2 Vc, w. A. Gastinel (vc) *(rec 7/90)* Ottavo ▲ OTR C79032 [DDD]
Gastinel, G.:Marutz, w. A. Gastinel (vc) *(rec 7/90)* Ottavo ▲ OTRC 79032 [DDD]
Marais, M.:La Folia, w. A. Gastinel (vc) *(rec 7/90)* Ottavo ▲ OTR C79032 [DDD]
Merlet, M.:Une Soirée à Nohant, w. A. Gastinel (vc) *(rec 7/90)* Ottavo ▲ OTR C79032 [DDD]

Bosse, Gerhard (vn)
Beethoven, L. van:Missa Solemnis, w. Anna Tomowa-Sintow (sop), Annelies Burmeister (alt), Peter Schreier (ten), Hermann Christian Polster (bass), Hannes Kastner (org), K. Masur (cnd), Leipzig Gewandhaus Orch, Leipzig Radio Chorus Berlin Classics ("Masur Edition" series) ▲ BER 9160

Bossers, Johan (pno)
Brewaeys, L.:Trajet, w. Champ d'Action *(rec Blauwe Zaal, deSingel, Oct. 1994)* Megadisc ▲ 7869

Bosshart, Verena (fl)
Daetwyler, J.:Divert Fl, Vn & Vc, w. Hans-Walter Hirzel (vn), Nicolas Hartmann (vc) Grammont ▲ CTSP 15-2
Karg-Elert, S.:Sinfonische Kanzone, w. Stefan Fahrni (pno) *(rec Radio Studio Bern, 1993)* Jecklin ▲ JS 302-2 [DDD]
Karg-Elert, S.:Son Fl, Op. 68, w. Stefan Fahrni (pno) *(rec Radio Studio Bern, 1993)* Jecklin ▲ JD 686-2 [DDD]
Karg-Elert, S.:Suite pointillistique, w. Verena Bosshart (fl), Stefan Fahrni (pno) *(rec Radio Studio Bern, 1993)* Jecklin ▲ JD 686-2 [DDD]

Bossi, Serfio (cl)
Reinecke, C.:Fantasiestücke Cl, w. R. Bartoli (pno) *(rec June 19-22, 1993)* Bongiovanni ▲ GB 5537 [DDD]

Bosso, Ezio (db)
Bottesini, G.:Music for Db, w. Luca Brancaleon (pno)—Gran Duo; Rêverie; Duo concertant sure thèmes des Les Puritaines de Bellini; Melodie; Passioni amorose; Grande allegro; Gran duo concertant Stradivarius ▲ STV 33397 [DDD]

Bostrom, Erik (org)
Messiaen, O.:Org Music (comp) Proprius 7-▲ PRCD 9009/15
The Oscar Church Organ Proprius ▲ PRCD 9002

Botapek, Kathryn (vn)—see ORCHESTRAS & ENSEMBLES Chester String Quartet

Botár, Ecaterina (hpd)
Haydn, M.:Con Org, w. Alexandru Iosif Thurzo (va), E. Acél (cnd), Oradea PO Olympia ("Explorer" series) ▲ OCD 406 [AAD]
Terényi, E.:Vivaldiana, w. G. Costea, C. Mandeal, Cluj-Napoca CO *(Vivaldiana)*, Costea, et al. *(Gallant Dances)*, P. Szeles, G. Dudea, Tîrgu Mures Phil. CO *(Baroque Rhap.)*, "G. Dima" Conservatory Percussion Ensemble of Cluj-Napoca *(Swing Suite)* Electrecord ▲ ELCD 124 [AAD]

Botnen, Geir (pno)
Grieg, E.:Holberg Suite *(rec Eidsvoll Church, Jan 15-16, 1996)* Simax ▲ PSC 1133 [DDD]
Grieg, E.:Improvisations on 2 Norwegian Folksongs *(rec Eidsvoll Church, Jan 15-16, 1996)* Simax ▲ PSC 1133 [DDD]
Grieg, E.:Norwegian Dances, Op. 35, w. Jens Harald Bratlie (pno) *(rec Eidsvoll Church, Jan 15-16, 1996)* Simax ▲ PSC 1133 [DDD]
Grieg, E.:Norwegian Folk Songs, Op. 66 *(rec Eidsvoll Church, Jan 15-16, 1996)* Simax ▲ PSC 1133 [DDD]
Grieg, E.:Norwegian Folk Songs, Op. 66, w. K. Hamre (sgr), H. Fiddle (sgr), R. Horvei (sgr) Simax ▲ PSC 1102
Grieg, E.:Norwegian Peasant Dances, Op. 72, w. K. Hamre (sgr), H. Fiddle (sgr), R. Horvei (sgr) Simax ▲ PSC 1102
Tveitt, G.:Danse Pno Simax ▲ 1121 [DDD]
Tveitt, G.:Son 29 Pno Simax ▲ 1121 [DDD]
Tveitt, G.:2 Part Inventions Simax ▲ 1121 [DDD]

Botti, Chris (instr)
Mozart, W.A.:Music of, w. Philip Aaberg, Todd Boekelheide, Henry Adam Curtis, Steve Erquiaga, Béla Fleck, Eugene Friesen, Paul McCandless, Tim Story, Richard Schönherz, Tracy Scott Silverman, Thea Suits-Silverman, ValGardena, Modern Mandolin Quartet Imaginary Road ▲ 314534065-2 ▮ 314534065-4

Bottoni, Gary (highland pipe)
Vivaldi, A.:Cons Vn, Op. 8/1-4, "The Four Seasons", w. Jerome Franke (vn), Karine Garibova (vn), Pasquale Laurino (vn), Olga Miliaeva (va), Roza Borisova (vc), Mika Hennessy (db), Melanie Panush (ham dlc), Stanislav Venglevski (bayan), Mike Kashou (arabic tabla), Daryl Stuermer (gtr), Ed Palouçek (celtic fid), Dubuffet String Quartet *(rec July-Sept 1995)* EarthBeat! ▲ 35270-2 [DDD]

Botvay, Károly (vc)—see also ORCHESTRAS & ENSEMBLES New Budapest String Quartet
Bach, Joh. Christian:Sinf concertante, T.289/4, w. János Bálint (fl), Lajos Lencsés (ob), Béla Bánfalvi (vn), Budapest Strings Capriccio ▲ 10509 [DDD]
Bach, Joh. Christian:Sinf concertante, T.287/2, w. Lajos Lencsés (ob), Emilia Csánky (ob), B. Bánfalvi (cnd), Budapest Strings Capriccio ▲ 10509 [DDD]
Bach, Joh. Christian:Sinf concertante, T.284/4, w. Béla Bánfalvi (vn), Budapest Strings Capriccio ▲ 10509 [DDD]
Boëllmann, L.:Qt Pno & Strs, w. I. Prunyi (pno), B. Bánfalvi (vn), J. Fejévári (va) Marco Polo ▲ 8.223524
Boëllmann, L.:Trio Pno, w. I. Prunyi (pno), B. Bánfalvi (vn), J. Fejévári (va) Marco Polo ▲ 8.223524
Brahms, J.:Qt 1 Pno, w. C. Szabó (pno), P. Kolmós (vn), G. Németh (va) *(rec 1972-74)* Hungaroton 2-▲ HCD 11597/98 [ADD]
Brahms, J.:Qt 2 Pno, w. I. Lantos (pno), P. Kolmós (vn), G. Németh (va) *(rec 1972-74)* Hungaroton 2-▲ HCD 11597/98 [ADD]
Brahms, J.:Qt 3 Pno, w. S. Falvai (pno), P. Kolmós (vn), G. Németh (va) *(rec 1972-74)* Hungaroton 2-▲ HCD 11597/98 [ADD]
Mozart, W.A.:Qts Fl, w. J. Szebenyi (fl), A. Kiss (vn), L. Bársony (va) White Label ▲ HRC 128 [ADD]

Bouchard, Antoine (org)
Bach, J.S.:Preludes & Fugues, BWV 531-552—BWV 544 & 548 Rem 2-▲ 311130 [DDD]
L'Orgue Français Classique en Nouvelle France, w. Bouchard, Antoine (org) REM ▲ 311201 [DDD]

Bouchard, Lise (tpt)
Lebaron, A.:Lamentation/Invocation, w. A. Shearer (sgr), R. Yamins (sgr), M. Shapiro (vc), N. Kellman (perc), New Music Consort [E] Mode ▲ 30
Vivier, C.:Kopernikus, "A Ritual Opera of Death", w. Y. Parent (sop), P. Vaillancourt (sop), M.-D. Parent (sop), J. Fleury (cta), D. Doane (ten), M. Ducharme (bar), Y. Saint-Amant (bass), F. Martel (cl), M. Bélanger (vn), L. Vaillancourt (cnd), *(orch unknown)* *(rec Feb. 1991)* CBC ("Musica Viva" series) ▲ MVCD 1047 [DDD]

Boucher, Jacques (org)
Bonnet, J.:Org Music—Six versets en forme de variations, Op. 10/7; Prelude au Salve Regina, Op. 7/1; Trois versets sur l'hymne "Ave Maris Stella," Op. 5/5; Variations de concert, Op. 1 REM ▲ 311162 [DDD]
Widor, C.M.:Sym 9 Org REM ▲ 311162 [DDD]

Boucher, Rémi (gtr)
Abril, A.G.:Music of, w. R. Dessaints (cnd), Amati Ensemble—Concierto Mudéjar Analekta ▲ AN 29502
Asencio, V.:Collectici Intim Analekta ▲ AN 28775
Castelnuovo-Tedesco, M.:Capriccio diabolico, "Homage to Paganini" Analekta Fleur de Lys ▲ FL 2 3057
Duarte, J.:Vars sur un thème Catalan Analekta Fleur de Lys ▲ FL 2 3057
Granados, E.:Valses poeticos (7) Analekta Fleur de Lys ▲ FL 2 3057
Regondi, G.:Intro et caprice Analekta Fleur de Lys ▲ FL 2 3057
Rodrigo, J.:Son giocosa Analekta Fleur de Lys ▲ FL 2 3057

Boudler, John (perc)
Thomson, V.:Portraits, w. Y. Mikhashoff (pno), M. Herr (sop), D. Kuehn (tpt)—30 sels composed from 1926-1982 New Albion ▲ NA 034 [ADD]

Boughton, Rebecca (va)
Handel, D.:The Tyger, w. Mary Henderson (sop), Sara Lambert Bloom (ob), Gabrielle Robinson (vn), Jina Lee (vn), Deborah Netanel (vc), Mark Butler (pno), C. Zimmerman (cnd) Vienna Modern Masters ▲ VMM 2019 [DDD]

Boukoff, Y. (pno)
Wissmer, P.:Con 3 Pno, w. L. de Froment (cnd), Luxembourg RSO Quantum ▲ QM 6908

Boulay, Laurence (hpd)
Boismortier, J.B. de:Hpd Music—La Caverneuse; La Marguillère; La Transalpine; La Alétudinaire; La Décharnée Erato ▲ ERA SEL 12983 [ADD]
Couperin, F.:Pièces de clavecin (sels), w. Françoise Lengellé (hpd)—Concerts royaux pour 2 Hpds [Nos. 1-4]; Allemande à 2 Hpds [from Neuvième ordre]; Muséte de choisi & muséte de taverni à 2 Hpds [from Quinzième ordre] Erato ▲ ERA SEL 12982 [ADD]

Boulay, Laurence (hpd/org)
Couperin, F.:Leçons de ténèbres (for Good Friday), w. M. Van Der Sluis (sop), G. Laurens (mez), P. Monteilhet (lt), M. Muller (vl)—[L] Erato (Musifrance) ▲ 2292-45012-2 [DDD]
Couperin, F.:Magnificat, w. M. Van Der Sluis (sop), G. Laurens (mez), P. Monteilhet (lt), M. Muller (vl)—[L] Erato (Musifrance) ▲ 2292-45012-2 [DDD]

Boulier, Christophe (vn)
10 Pièces pour violin et piano, w. Miklos Schön (pno) REM ▲ 311256

Boulware, H. (pno)
Joplin, S.:Pno Music, w. S. Joplin (pno)—14 piano rolls of Joplin compositions:3 hand-played by Joplin himself, the others from rolls produced by Hal Boulware in the 1960s:Maple leaf rag; Something doing; Weeping willow rag *(preceding three are original Joplin rolls)*; The entertainer; The easy winners; Pine apple rag; Solace; Gladiolus rag; The ragtime dance; Sugar cane; The crush collision march; Bethena (a concert waltz); Combination march; A breeze from Alabama Biograph ▲ BCD 101 [DDD]
Joplin, S.:Pno Music, w. S. Joplin (pno)—16 piano rolls, including 15 Joplin compositions and one by W.C. Handy; 3 selections hand-played by Joplin himself, the others from rolls produced by Hal Boulware in the 1960s:Maple leaf rag; Ole Miss rag [W.C. Handy]; Magnetic rag *(preceding three are original Joplin rolls)*; Elite syncopations; Country club; Paragon rag; Eugenia; Cleopha; A real slow drag; Scott Joplin's new rag; Leola (two-step); Lily Queen; The chrysanthemum; Heliotrope bouquet; Reflection rag; Silver swan rag (ragtime two-step) Biograph ▲ BCD 102 [DDD]

Bouman, Henk (hpd)
Campra, A.:Motets, w. Haydn-Héritage Ensemble—O Jesu amantissime; Immensus es Domine; Quis ego Domine [L] REM ▲ 311110 XCD [DDD]

Bourachoff, Israel (fl)
Downey, J.:A Dolphin, w. D. Nelson (ten), B. Zaslav (va), B. Burda (perc), J. Downey (pno) Gasparo ▲ GS 276 ▮ GS 276C

Bourdin, Roger (fl)
Debussy, C.:Son Fl, w. C. Lequien (va), A. Challan (hp) Philips ▲ 422839-2 [ADD]

Bourgue, Daniel (hn)
Mozart, W.A.:Cons Hn, w. B. Papazian (cnd), Sofia Orch Ensemble Arion ▲ ARN 68198 [DDD]
Mozart, W.A.:Rondo Hn, K.371, w. B. Papazian (cnd), Sofia Orch Ensemble Arion ▲ ARN 68198 [DDD]
Mozart, W.A.:Rondo Hn, K.514 (compl'd Jeurissen), w. B. Papazian (cnd), Sofia Orch Ensemble Arion ▲ ARN 68198 [DDD]

Bourgue, Maurice (ob)
Albinoni, T.:Cons à 5 Obs, Op. 7, w. H. Holliger (ob), I Musici Philips ▲ 432115-2 [DDD]
French Chamber Music for Piano & Wind, w. P. Rogé (pno), Catherine Cantin (fl), et al. London ▲ 425861-2 [DDD]
Poulenc, F.:Sxt Pno, w. P. Rogé (pno), P. Gallois (fl), M. Portal (cl), A. Wallez (bn), A. Cazalet (hn) London ▲ 421581-2 [DDD]
Poulenc, F.:Son Ob, w. P. Rogé (pno) London ▲ 421581-2 [DDD]
Poulenc, F.:Trio Ob, w. A. Wallez (bn), P. Rogé (pno) London ▲ 421581-2 [DDD]
Vaughan Williams, R.:Con Ob, w. W. Boughton (cnd), English String Orch Nimbus ▲ NI 5019
Vaughan Williams, R.:Con Ob, w. W. Boughton (cnd), English String Orch Nimbus 4-▲ NI 5210/13 [DDD]

Bourikov, A. (vc)
Glinka, M.:Trio pathétique, w. V. Abramyan (vn), G. Dzubenko (pno) *(rec Firma Melodiya, Big Studio, 1995)* Russian Compact Disc ▲ RCD 10401 [DDD]
Rachmaninoff, S.:Trio élégiaque 1, w. G. Dzubenko (pno), V. Abramyan (vn) *(rec Firma Melodiya, Big Studio, 1995)* Russian Compact Disc ▲ RCD 10401 [DDD]
Shostakovich, D.:Trio 2 Pno, w. G. Dzubenko (pno), V. Abramyan (vn) *(rec Firma Melodiya, Big Studio, 1995)* Russian Compact Disc ▲ RCD 10401 [DDD]

Bourin, Odile (vc)
Bouknik, M.:Fant Vc, w. Bernard Cazauran (db) Gallo ▲ CD 795 [ADD]
Franchomme, A.:Caprices, Op. 7, w. Bernard Cazauran (db)—No. 11 [arr performers for vc & db] Gallo ▲ CD 795 [ADD]
Genzmer, H.:Bagatelles (6), w. Bernard Cazauran (db) Gallo ▲ CD 795 [ADD]
Lindner, A.:Diverts for Young Cellists, w. Bernard Cazauran (db) [arr performers for vc & db] Gallo ▲ CD 795 [ADD]
Rossini, G.:Duet Vc, w. Bernard Cazauran (db) Gallo ▲ CD 795 [ADD]

Bournet, Pascal (gtr)
Carreño, I.:Fant, w. Inocente Carreno (vn) *(rec Studio Damiens, Boulogne, 1994)* Iris ▲ 269 [DDD]
Gonzalez, F.:Music of, w. Inocente Carreno (vn)—Danza de Los Amantes Efimeros; Brisas Del Pamplomita; El Diablo Suelto; Intro et Pasillo *(rec Studio Damiens, Boulogne, 1994)* Iris ▲ 269 [DDD]
Machado, C.:Music of, w. Inocente Carreno (vn)—Pacoga choro; Pé de Moleque *(rec Studio Damiens, Boulogne, 1994)* Iris ▲ 269 [DDD]
Piazzolla, A.:Music of, w. Inocente Carreno (vn)—Café 1930; Nightclub 1960 *(rec Studio Damiens, Boulogne, 1994)* Iris ▲ 269 [DDD]
Villa-Lobos, H.:Music of, w. Inocente Carreno (vn)—Modinha; Distribução de Flores *(rec Studio Damiens, Boulogne, 1994)* Iris ▲ 269 [DDD]

Bousfield, Ian (trbn)
Martin, F.:Ballade Trbn (or T Sax), w. M. Bamert (cnd), London PO Chandos ▲ CHAN 9380 [DDD]

Bousseau, Pierre (org)
Liszt, F.:Org Music—Intro a La légende de Sainte Élizabeth; Ora Pro Nobis Litanie; Ave Maria D'Arcadelt; Ave Maris Stella; Salve Regina; Via Crucis; Missa Pro Organo Adda ▲ ADD 581030
Liszt, F.:Org Music [at the St. Salomon Church Org, St. Grégoire de Pithiviers, France]—Resignazione; Angélus, prière aux anges gardiens; Rosario; Requiem; Ungarn's gott; Am grabe Richard Wagner's; Il sposalizio; O sacrum convivium; Ave maria; Introitus Adda ▲ ADD 581089

Bouton, William (vn)
Elgar, E.:Music of, w. L. Hall (pno)—includes Chanson de nuit, Chanson de matin, Salute d'amour, Sospiri, La Capricieuse, Sonata in e for Violin & Piano, & others IMP Classics 2-▲ IMP 1039 [DDD]
Harrison, L.:Music for Vn, w. Richard Dee (cheng), William Colvig (sheng/fang-hsiang), Lou Harrison (piri), Helen Rifas (hp) Phoenix ▲ PHCD 118 [AAD]

Boutry, Roger (pno)
La Clarinette de la Belle Epoque, w. S. Hue (cl) REM ▲ 311209 [DDD]
Fauré, G.:Songs, w. Suzanne Danco (sop)—Prison Memoire Vive ▲ CD 262024
Suzanne Danco in Concert, w. S. Danco (sop) *(rec between Mar. 1949 & Aug.)* Memoire Vive ▲ 262002 (m) [ADD]

Bouvard, Michel (org)
Couperin, F.:Org Music—Fants Nos 12, 26, 58 & 59 *(rec St. Martin's Church, Le Mesnil-Amelot)* Chamade ▲ 5621

Bouvard, Michel (org) (cont.)
du Caurroy, E.:Fant on Une Jeune Filette *(rec St. Martin's Church, Le Mesnil-Amelot)* Chamade ▲ 5621
du Mont, H.:Org Music—Preludes Nos 3, 7, 10 & 14 *(rec St. Martin's Church, Le Mesnil-Amelot)* Chamade ▲ 5621
Racquet, C.:Fant Org *(rec St. Martin's Church, Le Mesnil-Amelot)* Chamade ▲ 5621
Titelouze, J.:Ave maris stella *(rec St. Martin's Church, Le Mesnil-Amelot)* Chamade ▲ 5621

Bouwhuis, Gerard (pno)
Andriessen, L.:Contra tempus, w. Sepp Grotenhuis (pno), Tomoko Mukaiyama (elec pno), Nico de Rooij (elec pno) *(rec Amsterdam Music Theater, Oct 3–6, 1994)* Donemus ▲ CV 54 [DDD]
Andriessen, L.:Hoketus, w. Katherine Pendry (panpipes), James Poke (panpipes), Evan Ziporyn (a sax), Richard Craig (a sax), Steven Schick (congas), Amy Knoles (congas), Lisa Moore (Fender Rhodes), Damian LeGassick (Fender Rhodes), Cees van Zeeland (pno), Robert Black (bass gtr), Mark Stewart (bass gtr) *(rec Air Recording Studios, Lyndhurst Hall, Hampstead, London, June 29–July 3, 1994)* Sony Classical ▲ SK 66483 [DDD]
Andriessen, L.:Ittrospezione 3, w. Sepp Grotenhuis (pno), Peter van Bergen (sax), Marjan Damsté (db), H. Williams (cnd), Netherlands Ballet Orch *(rec Amsterdam Music Theater, Oct 3–6, 1994)* Donemus ▲ CV 54 [DDD]
Andriessen, L.:De Staat, w. C. van Zeeland (pno) Attacca ▲ BABEL 8949–2 [DDD]
Holt, S. ten:Canto ostinato, w. Gene Carl (pno), A. Vernède (pno), C. van Zeeland (pno) *(rec live, Jan 10, 1988)* Donemus 3–▲ CV 2/3/4
Ives, C.:Three Quarter-Tone Pieces, w. C. van Zeeland (pno) *(rec Jan. 1992)* Channel Classics ▲ CCS 4592 [DDD]
Martland, S.:Drill, w. Cees van Zeeland (pno) *(rec Maltings, Snape, Suffolk, Mar 26, 1989)* Catalyst ▲ 09026–68397–2 [DDD]
Messiaen, O.:Visions de l'Amen, w. C. van Zeeland (pno) *(rec Jan. 1992)* Channel Classics ▲ CCS 4592 [DDD]
Schat, P.:Anathema Donemus ▲ CV 19
Schat, P.:Canto general, w. Lucia Meeuwsen (sop), Frank de Groot (vn) Donemus ▲ CV 19
Stravinsky, I.:Agon, w. C. van Zeeland (pno) [Stravinsky's 2-piano arr.] Attacca ▲ BABEL 8949–2 [DDD]
Wagenaar, D.:Music of, w. Cees van Zeeland (pno), Netherlands Wind Ensemble, The Hague Percussion Group—La Volta; Stadium; Solenne; Liederen; Metrum Donemus ▲ CV 29
Zeeland, C. van:Initials, w. C. van Zeeland (pno) *(rec Jan. 1992)* Channel Classics ▲ CCS 4592 [DDD]

Bouwhuis, Gerard (prepared pno)
Cage, J.:Dances (3) for 2 Prepared Pnos, w. C. van Zeeland (prepared pno) Attacca ▲ BABEL 8949–2 [DDD]

Bova, Lucia (hp)
Dashow, J.:Reconstructions *(rec Wonderland Studio, Rome)* Neuma ▲ 45090 [DDD]
Dashow, J.:Reconstructions, w. James Dashow (cmpt) *(rec Studio Wonderland, Rome, June 1993)* Pro Viva ▲ ISPV 177 CD [DDD]

Bove, Jørgen (sax)
Maegaard, J.:Musica Riservata II, w. Klas Sjöblom (ob/E hn), Jesper Helmuth Madsen (cl), Peter Andersen (bn) *(rec Copenhagen, 1995–96)* Marco Polo/Dacapo ▲ 8.224050 [DDD]

Bovet, Guy (org)
À l'orgue de la Basilique de Valère (1390), Vol. 1 Gallo ▲ CD 088 [AAD]
Alain, J.:Org Music (misc)—Litanies; De Jules Lemaître; Monodie; Petite pièce; Vars sur un thème de Clément Janequin; 2 Préludes Profanes; Aria; Prélude & Fugue; Berceuse sur 2 notes qui cornent; Ballade en mode phrygien; Grave; 2 chorals; 3 danses *(rec Maison de la Dîme, Romainmôtier, Switzerland, Apr 19–21, 1995)* Gallo ▲ CD 851 [ADD]
All'Organo di Carasso Gallo ▲ CD 536 [AAD]
Bach, J.S.:Chorale Preludes Org—BWV 717 Gallo ▲ CD 453
Bach, J.S.:Chorale Preludes (Schübler)—BWV 645, 648 Gallo ▲ CD 453
Bach, J.S.:Chorale Settings, BWV 651–668—BWV 659 Gallo ▲ CD 453
Bach, J.S.:Fant & Fugue Org, BWV 542 Gallo ▲ CD 453
Bach, J.S.:Fant Org, BWV 573 Gallo ▲ CD 453
Bach, J.S.:Prelude & Fugue Org, BWV 568 & 577 Gallo ▲ CD 453
Bach, J.S.:Toccata & Fugue Org, BWV 565 Gallo ▲ CD 453
Bovet, G.:Org Music—Improvisation Gallo ▲ CD 536
Gershwin, G.:Rhap in Blue [Wurlitzer Cinema Org] [solo arr.] Gallo ▲ CD 583 [AAD]
Organs of Mexico, Vol. 3 Gallo ▲ CD 560 [AAD]
Orgues de la Cathédrale de Mexico Gallo ▲ CD 439
Plays the 1390 Gothic Organ of the Valère Cathedral at Sion Gallo ▲ CD 281 [AAD]
Plays the 1390 Gothic Organ of the Valère Cathedral at Sion, Vol. 2 Gallo ▲ CD 440
Racquet, C.:Fant Org Gallo ▲ CD 536
Raison, A.:Org Music—extraits de la Messe du Deuxieme Ton Gallo ▲ CD 536
Rameau, J.P.:Music of—Air de Jupiter; Air en Rondeau; Air de chasse Gallo ▲ CD 536
Saint-Saëns, C.:Danse macabre [Wurlitzer Cinema Organ] Gallo ▲ CD 583 [AAD]

Bovet, Jeanne (pno)
Bach, J.S.:Partitas Hpd, BWV 825–830—No. 1 in b, BWV 825 Gallo ▲ CD 772 [ADD]
Bach, J.S.:Preludes & Fugues Hpd—in C, BWV 846 Gallo ▲ CD 746 [AAD]
Debussy, C.:Children's Corner Gallo ▲ CD 746 [AAD]
Handel, G.F.:Chaconne Hpd [arr. for piano] Gallo ▲ CD 772 [ADD]
Scarlatti, D.:Sons Kbd Gallo ▲ CD 772 [ADD]
Schumann, R.:Kinderszenen Gallo ▲ CD 746 [AAD]
Schumann, R.:Waldscenen Gallo ▲ CD 746 [AAD]

Bovin, Dany (trbn)
Daetwyler, J.:Con Trbn, w. G.–P. Moren (cnd), 13 Étoiles Brass Band Gallo ▲ CD 474 [ADD]
Langford, G.:Son, Serenade & Scherzo, w. G.–P. Moren (cnd), 13 Étoiles Brass Band Gallo ▲ CD 474 [ADD]
Newsome, R.:Olympic Concertino, w. G.–P. Moren (cnd), 13 Étoiles Brass Band Gallo ▲ CD 474 [ADD]
Voegelin, F.:Nordlicht-Variationen, w. G.–P. Moren (cnd), 13 Étoiles Brass Band Gallo ▲ CD 474 [ADD]

Bowen, Frank (fl)—see ORCHESTRAS & ENSEMBLES Santa Fe Trio

Bower, K. (pno)
Ave Maria, w. Miriam Hayward (sop) Segal, M. Keough (hp) Symposium ▲ SYM 1175 [DDD]

Bowers-Broadbent, Christopher (org)
Amazing Grace, w. J. Norman (sop), Dalton Baldwin (pno), Geoffrey Parsons (pno), Alexander Gibson (cnd), Willis Patterson (cnd), Royal PO, Ambrosian Singers Philips ▲ 432546–2 PH [DDD] ■ 432546–4 PH
Bryars, G.:The Black River, w. S. Leonard (sop) ECM New Series ▲ 78118–21495–2
Byrd, W.:Mass in 4 Parts, w. Theater of Voices *(rec Feb. 1992)* ECM New Series ▲ 78118–21512–2 [DDD]
Davies, P.M.:Voluntaries (2) ECM New Series ▲ 78118–21431–2 [DDD]
Glass, Philip:Org Music—Satyagraha; Danca IV ECM New Series ("New" series) ▲ 78118–21431–2
Górecki, H.–M.:O Domina Nostra, w. S. Leonard (sop) ECM New Series ("New" series) ▲ 78118–21495–2
Macmillan, J.:Cantos Sagrados, w. James MacMillan (cnd), Polyphony *(rec St. John-at-Hackney, London, Sept. 28–30, 1994)* Catalyst ▲ 09026–68125–2 [DDD]; ■ 09026–68125–4
Messiaen, O.:Méditations sur le mystère la Sainte Trinité *(rec Hofkirche, Lucerne, June 1992)* ECM New Series ▲ 78118–21494–2 [DDD]
Milhaud, D.:Preludes Org, Nos. 1 & 2 ECM New Series ▲ 78118–21495–2
Pärt, A.:Annum per annum ECM New Series ▲ 78118–21431–2 [DDD]
Pärt, A.:Mein Weg hat Gipfel und Wellentäler ECM New Series ▲ 78118–21431–2 [DDD]
Pärt, A.:Org Music—Trivium; Mein Weg hat Gipfel und Wellentaler; Annum per annum ECM New Series ▲ 78118–21431–2 [DDD]
Pärt, A.:Pari intervallo ECM New Series ▲ 78118–21431–2 [DDD]
Pärt, A.:Trivium ECM New Series ▲ 78118–21431–2 [DDD]
Satie, E.:Messe des pauvres, w. S. Leonard (sop) ECM New Series ▲ 78118–21495–2

Bowers-Broadbent, Christopher (org) (cont.)
Tavener, J.:Choral Music, w. Simon Joly (cnd), BBC Singers—Thunder Entered Her; The Lamb; The Tiger; Hymn to the Mother of God; Hymn for the Dormition of the Mother of God; Responorium in memoriam Annon Lee Silver; Song for Athene; Eonia; God is With Us *(rec live, St Giles, Cripplegate, Jan 22, 1994)* United ▲ CAL 88023 [DDD]
Taverner, J.:In nomine *(rec Feb. 1992)* ECM New Series ▲ 78118–21512–2 [DDD]

Bowes, Thomas (vn)
Vivaldi, A.:Cons for 4 Vns, w. C. Warren-Green (vn), R. Furniss (vn), B. Davison (vn), C. Warren-Green (cnd), London CO—RV.580 in b Virgin Classics ▲ 59609 [DDD]

Bowkun, Helena (pno)
The Art of Ofra Harnoy, Vol. 1, w. O. Harnoy (vc), William Aide (pno) Mastersound ▲ DFCD1–012
Salut d'Amour, w. O. Harnoy (vc), Michael Dussek (pno), Catherine Wilson (pno) RCA Red Seal ▲ 60697–2–RC [AAD/DDD]
Tchaikovsky, P.:Nocturne Vc, w. Ofra Harnoy (vc) *(rec Walter Hall, University of Toronto & Timothy Eaton Memorial Church, Toronto, 1980)* RCA Gold Seal ▲ 09026–68373–2 [DDD]

Bowles, David (baroque vc)
Bach, J.S.:Anna Magdalena Bach Notebook, w. N. McGegan (hpd/clvd), L. Hunt (sop)—French Suite No. 1, BWV 812; French Suite No. 2, BWV 813—first 3 sections; various minuets & other short pieces; 5 solo clavichord sels.; 4 Polonaises, in d,F,G & g; Prelude No. 1 from the Well-tempered Clavier Book 1; 5 Arias & Recitatives for Soprano & Continuo instruments *(Arias—Bist du bei mir, BWV 508; Willst du mein Herz mir schenken, BWV 518; Gedenke doch, mein Geist; Schlummert, ein; Recitative—Ich habe genug)* Harmonia Mundi USA ▲ HMU 907042

Bowman, Brian (eup)
Adler, S.:Dialogs (9) Eup, w. G. Stout (mar) Crystal ■ C393
Boda, J.:Sonatina Crystal ■ C393
Brian Bowman, w. B. Bowman (eup), Gordon Stout (mar), Marjorie Lee (pno) Crystal ■ C393
Ross, W.:Partita Eup, w. Lee (pno) Crystal ■ C393

Bowman, Peter (ob)
Bach, J.S.:Brandenburg Con 2, w. D. Hickman, T. Rolston (cnd), Banff Festival Strings *(rec Aug 6–8, 1990)* Summit ▲ DCD 118 [DDD] ■ DCD 118
Barber, S.:Capricorn Con, w. Jacob Berg (fl), Susan Slaughter (tpt), L. Slatkin (cnd), St. Louis SO *(rec Powell Symphony Hall, St. Louis, MO, May 7, 1995)* RCA Red Seal ▲ 09026–68283–2 [DDD]
Hertel, J.W.:Con à 6, w. D. Hickman (tpt), T. Rolston (cnd), Banff Festival Strings *(rec Aug. 6–8, 1990)* Summit ▲ DCD 118 [DDD] ■ DCD 118
Mozart, W.A.:Qnt Pno, K.452, w. W. Klien (pno), G. Silfies (cl), G. Berry (bn), R. Pandolfi (hn) *(rec 1975–79)* Vox Box 3–▲ CD3X 3014 [ADD]
Tower, J.:Island Prelude, w. L. Slatkin (cnd), St. Louis SO Elektra/Nonesuch ▲ 79245–2–ZK ■ 79245–4–AW

Bowman, Randolph (fl)—see ORCHESTRAS & ENSEMBLES Collage New Music Ensemble

Bowman, Robin (pno)
Ives, C.:Songs, w. H. Herford (bar)—General William Booth enters into Heaven; There is a certain garden; In Flanders Fields; etc. Unicorn-Kanchana ▲ DKP CD 9111 [DDD]
Ives, C.:Songs, w. H. Herford (bar)—In summer fields; In the alley; Religion; Luck & work; The Cage; Grantchester; Premonitions; Nov. 2, 1920; Duty; from "Lincoln, the Great Commoner"; Thoreau; Walt Whitman; The greatest man; So may it be! (The rainbow); Walking; August; September; December; Autumn; Afterglow; from the "Incantation"; Spring song; At sea; Tarrant moss; Waltz; Romanzo di Central Park; Canon; Mirage; Maple leaves; Charlie Rutlage; The camp-meeting Unicorn-Kanchana ▲ DKP CD 9112 [DDD]

Bowyer, Kevin (org)
Alkan, C.–V.:Org Music Nimbus ▲ NI 5089 [DDD]
Bach, J.S.:Org Music (comp) [at the modern classical Marcussen organ of Sct. Hans Kirke, Odense, Denmark]—Aus tiefer Not schrei ich zu dir, BWV 1099; Concerto in G, BWV 592; Erbarm dich mein, o Herre Gott, BWV 721; Fantasia & Fugue in g, BWV 542; Pastorale in F, BWV 590; Toccata & Fugue in d, BWV 565; Trio Sonata No. 1 in E♭, BWV 525 Nimbus ▲ NI 5280
Bach, J.S.:Org Music (comp) [at the modern classical Marcussen organ of Sct. Hans Kirke, Odense, Denmark]—6 Chorale Preludes (BWV 697, 720, 722, 729, 738, 751); Fugue in g, BWV 577; Preludes & Fugues (BWV 532, 536, 541); Trio Sonata No. 5, BWV 529 Nimbus ▲ NI 5289
Bach, J.S.:Org Music (comp)—Toccata in g, BWV 915; Fugue in b on a theme by Albinoni, BWV 951; Fugue in c, BWV 575; 8 Short Preludes & Fugues; Fantasia in b, BWV 563; Fugue in A on a theme by Albinoni, BWV 950; Toccata in G, BWV 916 Nimbus ▲ NI 5377
Bach, J.S.:Org Music (comp) [at the Marcussen Organ of Sct. Hans Kirke, Odense, Denmark] Nimbus ▲ NI 5400
Bach, J.S.:Org Music (misc)—Prelude & Fugue in f; Trio Sonata in c; Partita "Sei gegrüsset, Jesu gütig"; Concerto in d (after Vivaldi); Prelude & Fugue in a Nimbus ▲ NI 5290 [DDD]
Bach, J.S.:Org Music (misc)—6 Chorale Preludes; Fugue in G; Grand Fantasy & Fugue in g; Grand Fugue in E♭; Grand Prelude & Fugue in D; Toccata & Fugue in d Priory ▲ PRCD 267 [DDD]
Bach, J.S.:Das Orgelbüchlein, w. Alice Joensen (cnd), Fynske Chamber Choir [at the Marcussen Org] *(rec St. Hans Church, Odense, Denmark, May 14–17, 1995)* Nimbus 2–▲ NI 5457/58 [DDD]
Bach, J.S.:Preludes & Fugues, BWV 531–552—in e, BWV 533; in g, BWV 535 *(rec St. John Church, Odense, Denmark, Mar 23–24, 1993)* Nimbus ▲ NI 5423 [DDD]
Bach, J.S.:Preludes & Fugues, BWV 531–552—in e, BWV 533; in g, BWV 535 *(rec St. John Church, Odense, Denmark, Mar. 23–24, 1993)* Nimbus ▲ NI 5423 [DDD]
Bach, J.S.:Toccata, Adagio & Fugue Org, BWV 564 *(rec St. John Church, Odense, Denmark, Mar. 23–24, 1993)* Nimbus ▲ NI 5423 [DDD]
Bach, J.S.:Toccata & Fugue Org, BWV 566 *(rec St. John Church, Odense, Denmark, Mar 23–24, 1993)* Nimbus ▲ NI 5423 [DDD]
Bach, J.S.:Trio Sons Org, BWV 525–530 *(rec St. John Church, Odense, Denmark, Mar. 23–24, 1993)* Nimbus ▲ NI 5423 [DDD]
Bach, J.S.:Trio Son Org, BWV 584 *(rec St. John Church, Odense, Denmark, Mar 23–24, 1993)* Nimbus ▲ NI 5423 [DDD]
Brahms, J.:Chorale Preludes, Op. 122 Nimbus ▲ NI 5262 [DDD]
Brahms, J.:Org Musc (comp) [the organ of Odense Cathedral, Denmark] Nimbus ▲ NI 5262 [DDD]
Christmas Organ Music Nimbus ▲ NI 7711 [DDD]
Hinton, A.:Pansophiae for John Ogdon [organ of St. Mary Redcliffe, Bristol] Altarus 2–▲ AIR-CD 9063
Langlais, J.:Org Music [Carthy Organ, Calgary]—Sym. No. 1; Nazard; Arabesque sur les flûtes [from Suite Française]; Suite Brève; Sym. No. 2, "Alla Webern"; Poem of Happiness *(rec Sept. 6–8, 1992)* Nimbus ▲ NI 5408 [DDD]
Sorabji, K.S.:Sym 1 Org Continuum 2–▲ CCD 1001/2
Stevenson, R.:Prelude & Fugue on a Theme by Liszt [organ of St. Mary Redcliffe, Bristol] Altarus 2–▲ AIR-CD 9063

Bowyer, Kevin (pno)
Busoni, F.:Fant contrappuntistica Pno [the organ of St. Mary Redcliffe, Bristol] [trans. Wilhelm Middelschulte] Altarus 2–▲ AIR-CD 9063

Boyar (perc)
Hovhaness, A.:Firdausi, w. Lawrence Sobol (cl), Agostini (hp) Grenadilla ■ GSC 1008

Boyd, Bonita (fl)
Adler, S.:Con Fl, w. D. Effron (cnd), Rochester PO *(rec 1983)* Vox Classics ▲ VOX 7509
Adler, S.:Son Fl *(rec 1995)* Vox Classics ▲ VOX 7509
Benson, W.:5 Lyrics of Louise Bogan, w. Jan DeGaetani (mez) [E] Gasparo ▲ GS 261
Brandt, H.:Angels & Devils, w. D. Hunsberger (cnd), Eastman Wind Ensemble Centaur ▲ CRC 2014 [AAD]
Martinů, B.:Promenades, w. C. Castleman (vn), B. Harbach (hpd) Albany ▲ TROY 041–2
Rubbra, E.:Cant Pastorale, w. B. Harbach (hpd), et al. Albany ▲ TROY 041–2
Rubbra, E.:Fant on a Theme of Machaut, w. B. Harbach (hpd), et al. Albany ▲ TROY 041–2

Boyd, Douglas (ob)—see also ORCHESTRAS & ENSEMBLES CO of Europe Soloists
Bach, J.S.:Con 8 Hpd, Orpheus CO Deutsche Grammophon ▲ 429225–2 [DDD]
Bach, J.S.:Con Ob, BWV 1053, Orpheus CO Deutsche Grammophon ▲ 429225–2 [DDD]
Bach, J.S.:Con Ob d'amore, Orpheus CO Deutsche Grammophon ▲ 429225–2 [DDD]

Boyd, Douglas (ob) (cont.)
Bach, J.S.:Con Vn & Ob, w. M. Blankestijn (vn), A. Schneider (cnd), CO of Europe ASV ("CO of Europe" series) ▲ CDCOE 803 [DDD]
Mozart, W.A.:Qt Ob, K.370, w. Gabrieli String Quartet IMP Classics ▲ PCD 810 [DDD]

Boyd, Liona (gtr)
The Best of Liona Boyd CBS ▲ MK 37788 [ADD] ■ FMT 37788
Christmas Dreams, w. Toronto Children's Choir A&M ▲ CD 9513 ■ CS 9513
Encore! A&M ▲ CD 9509 ■ CS 9509
Persona CBS ▲ MK 42120
The Romantic Guitar of Liona Boyd CBS ▲ MK 42016 [ADD] ■ FMT 42016

Boyd, Mary (pno)
Ashford, R.:Pieces (4) Pno—Children's Dance; Father Rondo; Summer's End; Where Are the Hereos & Heroines Nigel Classics ▲ NC 10101
Ashford, R.:Rise & Fall & Peaceful Rest, w. Mayumi Plumohira (vn), Gregory Wood (vc) Nigel Classics ▲ NC 10101

Boyd, Michael (pno)
Popper, D.:Vc & Pno Music, w. Marc Moskovitz (vc)—Romanze, Op. 5; Im Walde, Op. 50; Nocturne, Op. 42; Polonaise de Concert, Op. 14; Suite for 2 Vc, Op. 16 [w. Steven Shumway (vc)]; Requiem for 3 Vc & Pno [w. Steven Shumway (vc), Freya Samuels (vc)] *(rec Collingwood Arts Center Theater, Toledo, OH, Apr. 25–26 & May 11, 1994)* VAI Audio ▲ VAIA 1109

Boyer, Jean (org)
Clérambault, L.N.:Premier livre d'orgue contents deux suites [the historic Organ of the Abbey of St. Michel, Thiérache] *(rec June 20–24, 1993)* FNAC Music 2–▲ 592316 [DDD]
Salve Regina:Musiques festives mariales du grégorien au 17ème siècle, w. A Sei Voci Accord ▲ ACD 205072 [DDD]

Boyle, D. (pno)
Beethoven, L. van:Vars on a waltz by Diabelli, Op. 120 Centaur ▲ CRC 2040 [DDD]

Boysen, Bjørn (org)
Vierne, L.:Sym 4 Org [Organ of St. Catherine Church, Stockholm] Simax ▲ PSC 1050

Bozek–Musialska, Urszula (pno)
The Polish Violin, w. Lasocki, Roman (vn), Polish National Radio Orch [cnd:Karol Stryja] *(rec 1986 & 1988)* Olympia ▲ OCD 323 [AAD]
Twardowski, R.:Spanish Fant, w. R. Lasocki (vn) Olympia ▲ OCD 323 [AAD]

Bozeman, George (org)
Historic Organs of New Orleans, w. James S. Darling (org), Jesse E. Eschbach (org), Gerald D. Frank (org), John Gearhart (org), James Hammann (org), Frederick Hohman (org), Lenora McCroskey (org), Mary Gifford Matthys (org), Lorenz Maycher (org), Donald Messer (org) *(rec June 1989)* Organ Historical Society 2–▲ OHS 89

Bozok, Tayfun (vn)
Brahms, J.:Son 1 Vn, w. A. Golovin (pno) Gallo ▲ CD 609 [AAD]
Strauss, R.:Son Vn, w. A. Golovin (pno) Gallo ▲ CD 609 [AAD]

Braaten, Geir Henning (pno)
Alfvén, H.:Notturno elegiaco, w. Ingegärd Øien (hn) *(rec Sweden, 1980 & 1982)* BIS ▲ CD 171 [AAD]
Bozza, E.:Divertissement Sax, w. Steinar Hannevold (E hn) [arr for E hn & pno] Norway Music ▲ 0096–0038 [DDD]
Bozza, E.:Fant pastoral, w. Steinar Hannevold (ob) Norway Music ▲ 0096–0038 [DDD]
Bozza, E.:Recit, Sicilienne et Rondo, w. Per Hannevold (bn) Norway Music ▲ 0096–0038 [DDD]
Doppler, A.F.:Fant pastorale hongroise, w. Robert Aikten (fl), Per Oien (fl), Elisabeth Westenholz (pno) BIS ▲ CD 166
Doppler, A.F.:Music Fl & Pno, w. R. Aitken (fl), P. Oien (fl) BIS 2–▲ CD 145/46
Grieg, E.:Pno Music (comp)—Waltz–Caprices, Op. 37; Lyrical Pieces, Op. 38; Holberg Suite, Op. 40; 6 Song Arrangements, Op. 41 *(rec 1992)* Victoria ▲ VCD 19028
Grieg, E.:Pno Music (comp)—Lyric Pieces, Op. 71; Norwegian Peasant Dances, Op. 72 Victoria ▲ VCD 19033
Grieg, E.:Pno Music (comp)—Opp. 65 & 68; 2 Norwegian Folk Songs, Op. 66 Victoria ▲ VCD 19032
Grieg, E.:Pno Music (comp)—Opp. 57 & 62; 2 Nordic Melodies Victoria ▲ VCD 19031
Grieg, E.:Pno Music (comp)—2 Melodies for String Orchestra, Op. 53; Lyric Pieces, Op. 54; Peer Gynt Suite No. 2, Op. 55; 3 Orchestral Pieces from Sigurd Jorsalfar, Op. 56 *(rec Dec. 1992 & Jan. 1993)* Victoria ▲ VCD 19030
Grieg, E.:Pno Music (comp)—Lyric Pieces Opp. 43 & 47; Peer Gynt Suite No. 1; Olav Trygvason (scenes); Transcriptions of Original Songs, Op. 52 *(rec Autumn 1992)* Victoria ▲ VCD 19029
Grieg, E.:Pno Music (comp)—Moods, Op. 73; Larvik Polka; 23 Short Pieces Victoria ▲ VCD 19034
Grieg, E.:Pno Music (comp)—Ballade, Op. 24; Four Album Leaves, Op. 28; Improvisations on Two Norwegian Folk Songs, Op. 29; Two Elegiac Melodies, Op. 34; Four Norwegian Dances, Op. 35 Victoria ▲ VCD 19027
Grieg, E.:Pno Music (comp)—25 Norwegian Folk Songs & Dances, Op. 25; Pictures from Folk Life (Humoresques), Op. 19; Sigurd Jorsalfar, Op. 22; Peer Gynt (5 scenes), Op. 23 Victoria ▲ VCD 19026
Grieg, E.:Pno Music (comp)—Four Piano Pieces, Op. 1; Poetical Tone Pictures, Op. 3; Humoresques, Op. 6; Sonata in e, Op. 7; Lyric Pieces Vol. 1, Op. 12 *(rec 6/90)* Victoria ▲ VCD 19025 [DDD]
Grieg, E.:Pno Music (comp)—3 Pieces; Nordraak's Funeral March in a; At the Halfdan Kjerulf Statue; Albumblade; 6 Norwegian Mountain Tunes; Dance of the Mountain King's Daughter, Op. 23/9; 3 Pieces; Bergliot, Op. 42 Victoria ▲ VCD 19035–A
Grieg, E.:Pno Music (comp)—Norway's Melodies; 6 Norwegian Mountain Melodies; 3 Piano Pieces; Album Leaf; Entry of the Boyars; Dance of the Mountain King's Daughter *(rec 1993)* Victoria ▲ VCD 19035B
Jeppesen, K.:Little Trio Fl, Hn & Pno, w. Per Øien (fl), Ingegärd Øien (hn) *(rec Sweden, 1980 & 1982)* BIS ▲ CD 171 [AAD]
Kleven, A.:Son Vn, w. O. Bohn (vn) Simax ("Norway in Music" series) ▲ PSC 3106 [DDD]
Kvandal, J.:Intro & Allegro, w. Ingegärd Øien (hn) *(rec Sweden, 1980 & 1982)* BIS ▲ CD 171 [AAD]
Nielsen, C.:Canto serioso, w. Ingegärd Øien (hn) *(rec Sweden, 1980 & 1982)* BIS ▲ CD 171 [AAD]
The Norwegian Flute, w. P. Øien (fl), Norwegian CO *(rec 1978 & 1980)* BIS ▲ CD 103 [AAD]
Poulenc, F.:Trio Ob, w. Steinar Hannevold (ob), Per Hannevold (bn) Norway Music ▲ 0096–0038 [DDD]
Saint–Saëns, C.:Son Bn, w. Per Hannevold (bn) Norway Music ▲ 0096–0038 [DDD]
Saint–Saëns, C.:Son Ob, w. Steinar Hannevold (ob) Norway Music ▲ 0096–0038 [DDD]
Taffanel, P.:Fant on Freischütz, w. Robert Aikten (fl), Elisabeth Westenholz (pno), or Per Oien (fl) BIS ▲ CD 166
Valen, F.:Con Pno, w. C. Eggen (cnd), Norwegian Broadcasting Orch Simax ▲ PSC 3116

Brabec, Ludomír (gtr)
Music From the Heart of Europe, w. Josef Suk (vn), Rudolf Firkušný (pno), Vaclav Neumann (cnd), Jiří Belohlávek (cnd), Panocha Quartet, Czech PO, Prague CO, Prague Musica Antiqua, et al. Supraphon ▲ SUP 0063 [DDD]
Rodrigo, J.:Concierto de Aranjuez, Prague CO Supraphon ▲ 11 1563–2 [DDD]
Rodrigo, J.:Fant para un gentilhombre, Prague CO Supraphon ▲ 11 1563–2 [DDD]
Sor, F.:Gtr Music—Mozart Vars; Intro & Vars, Op. 28; Allegretto; Grand Solo, Op. 14; Andante Largo; Étude No. 11; Fant No. 2, Op. 7 Supraphon ▲ SUP 0004 [DDD]
Trojan, V.:Bagaja, w. Pavel Dreser (acc), Václav Hudeček (vn) Supraphon ▲ SUP 112203 [DDD]
Trojan, V.:The Emperor's Nightengale, w. Pavel Dreser (acc), Václav Hudeček (vn) Supraphon ▲ SUP 112203 [DDD]
Vivaldi, A.:Cons Diverse Instrs, w. Václav Hudeček (cl), Jiří Stivín (va), G. Delogu (cnd), Janáček CO, Prague CO—in C for 2 Rcrs, 2 Bns, 2 Vns, 2 Gtrs, Vc, Strings & Cont, RV.558; in d for Vn, Gtr, Strs & Cont, RV.540; in F for Vn, Gtr, Strs & Cont, RV.542; in a for Rcr, Strs & Cont, RV.108; in C for 2 Vns, 2 Gtrs, 2 Fls, 2 Rcrs, 2 Strs & 2 Conts, RV.565 Supraphon ▲ SUP 3023
Vivaldi, A.:Con Lt, w. O. Vlček (cnd), Prague CO Supraphon ▲ 10 4126–2 [DDD]
Vivaldi, A.:Con Mand, RV.425, w. O. Vlček (cnd), Prague CO Supraphon ▲ 10 4126–2 [DDD]
Vivaldi, A.:Con for 2 Mands, w. M. Mysliviček (gtr), O. Vlček (cnd), Prague CO Supraphon ▲ 10 4126–2 [DDD]

Brabec, Ludomír (gtr) (cont.)
Vivaldi, A.:Con Va d'amore Lt, w. L. Malý (va), O. Vlček (cnd), Prague CO Supraphon ▲ 10 4126–2 [DDD]

Brackman, Bernd (pno)
Escher, R.:Son Fl, w. Jacques Zoon (fl) *(rec Singelkerk, Amsterdam, Aug 14–15, 1995)* NM Classics ▲ 92059 [DDD]
Geraedts, J.:Sonatine Fl, w. Jacques Zoon (fl) *(rec Singelkerk, Amsterdam, Aug 14–15, 1995)* NM Classics ▲ 92059 [DDD]
Keuris, T.:Aria Fl & Pno, w. Jacques Zoon (fl) *(rec Singelkerk, Amsterdam, Aug 14–15, 1995)* NM Classics ▲ 92059 [DDD]
Loevendie, T.:Music Fl & Pno, w. Jacques Zoon (fl) *(rec Singelkerk, Amsterdam, Aug 14–15, 1995)* NM Classics ▲ 92059 [DDD]
Pijper, W.:Son Fl, w. Jacques Zoon (fl) *(rec Singelkerk, Amsterdam, Aug 14–15, 1995)* NM Classics ▲ 92059 [DDD]

Bradburg, John (cl)
Danzi, F.:Sextet Ob, w. Richard Berry (hn), Michael Thompson (hn), Robert Hill (cl), John Price (bn), Philip Tarlton (bn)—version for Harmonie ensemble *(rec St. Paul's Church, Rusthall, Kent, England, June 1994)* Naxos ▲ 8.553076 [DDD]

Bradbury, Colin (cl)
The Art of the Clarinettist:Fantaisies & Paraphrases for Clarinet & Piano, w. Oliver Davies (pno) Clarinet Classics 2–▲ CC 0008
The Bel Canto Clarinettist, w. Oliver Davies (pno) *(rec St. George's Brandon Hill, Bristol)* Clarinet Classics ▲ CC 0014 [DDD]

Bradbury, John (cl)
Dodgson, S.:Last of the Leaves, w. Michael George (b–bar), R. Zollman (cnd), Northern Sinfonia of England *(rec St Nicholas Hospital, Newcastle–upon–Tyne, Oct 23–24, 1992)* Biddulph ▲ LAW 013 [DDD]

Braden, Martha (pno)
Finney, R.L.:Fant Pno CRI ▲ CD 560 [DDD]
Finney, R.L.:Narrative in Retrospect CRI ▲ CD 560 [DDD]
Finney, R.L.:Son 3 Pno CRI ▲ CD 560 [DDD]
Finney, R.L.:Son quasi una fant CRI ▲ CD 560 [DDD]

Bradetich, Jeff (db)
Classics for All to Hear, w. Judi Rockey Bradetich (pno) Music for All to Hear ▲ 9101 ■ 9101

Bradetich, Judi Rockey (pno)
Classics for All to Hear, w. J. Bradetich (db) Music for All to Hear ▲ 9101 ■ 9101

Bradshaw, David (pno)—see also ORCHESTRAS & ENSEMBLES Bradshaw & Buono Piano Duo
Liszt, F.:Pno Music (misc), w. Cosmo Buono (pno)—Hungarian Rhapsody No. 2 (piano duet arr., 1874); Fest–Polonaise for Piano Four–Hands (1874); Four Operatic Transcriptions (Benediction & Sermon from Berlioz's Benvenuto Cellini; March & Cavatina from Donizetti's Lucia di Lammermoor; Fantasy & Fugue on the Chorale "Ad nos, ad salutarem undam" from Meyerbeer's Le Prophète; The Entrance of the Guests from Wagner's Tannhäuser) Albany ▲ TROY 039–2 [DDD]
Schubert, Franz:Divertissement à l'hongroise, D.818, w. F. Buono (pno) Albany ▲ TROY 069 [DDD]

Bradshaw, R. (pno)
Holst, G.:The Planets, w. R. Bennett (pno) [2–piano version] Facet ▲ FCD 8002 [AAD]

Bradshaw, Susan (pno)
Mayer, J.:Dance Suite, w. Georgina Dobrée (cl) Clarinet Classics ▲ CC 0012 [AAD]
Schubert, Franz:Fant Pno, D.940, w. F. Buono (pno) Albany ▲ TROY 069 [DDD]
Schubert, Franz:Ländler Pno, w. F. Buono (pno) [arr. J. Brahms]—11 of 17 Ländler, D. 366 Albany ▲ TROY 069 [DDD]
Schubert, Franz:Marche militaire, D.733/1, w. F. Buono (pno) Albany ▲ TROY 069 [DDD]
Wellesz, E.:Pieces Cl, w. Georgina Dobrée (cl) Clarinet Classics ▲ CC 0012 [AAD]

Brady, Mary (vc)
Martinů, B.:Son 1 Vc, w. C. Hedinger (pno) Koch Schwann ▲ 310 107 [DDD]
Martinů, B.:Trio Fl, w. F. Renggli (fl), C. Hedinger (pno) Koch Schwann ▲ 310 107 [DDD]

Brændstrup, K. (cl)—see ORCHESTRAS & ENSEMBLES Vestjysk Chamber Ensemble

Bragato, José (vc)—see ORCHESTRAS & ENSEMBLES New Tango Sex–tet

Brahms, Johannes (pno)
Brahms, J.:Hungarian Dances Pno—the 1889 Edison cylinder rec'g of Brahms speaking, & playing his Hungarian Dance No. 1 Pearl 6–▲ PEA 99049 (m) [AAD]

Braillard, Bertrand (vc)
Kodály, Z.:Duo Vn & Vc, w. Jean–Luc Pouchet (vn) Analekta ▲ ATM 29721

Brailowsky, Alexander (pno)
Alexander Brailowsky:The Leschetizky Tradition *(rec 1928–34)* Pearl ▲ PEA 9132 [ADD]
Bach, J.S.:Cons Org, BWV 592–597—in d, BWV 596 *(rec 1938)* APR ▲ APR 5501 [AAD]
Beethoven, L. van:Rondo a capriccio, "Rage Over a Lost Penny" *(rec London, 1938 HMV recordings)* APR ▲ APR 5501 [AAD]
The Berlin Polydor Recordings, 1928–1934, Vol. 1 Danacord 2–▲ DACOCD 336/337 (m) [ADD]
The Berlin Polydor Recordings, 1928–1934, Vol. 2 Danacord 2–▲ DACOCD 338/339 (m) [ADD]
Chopin, F.:Berceuse *(rec London 1938 HMV recordings)* APR ▲ APR 5501 [AAD]
Chopin, F.:Con 1 Pno, w. J. Prüwer (cnd), Berlin PO *(rec 1928)* Danacord 2–▲ DACOCD 336/37 (m) [ADD]
Chopin, F.:Con 1 Pno, w. W. Steinberg (cnd), RCA Victor SO RCA Gold Seal ▲ 09026–61656–2 [AAD]
Chopin, F.:Con 2 Pno, w. C. Munch (cnd), Boston SO RCA Gold Seal ▲ 09026–61656–2 [AAD]
Chopin, F.:Ecossaises (3) *(rec 1938)* APR ▲ APR 5501 [AAD]
Chopin, F.:Nocturnes—No. 2, Op. 27 RCA Gold Seal ▲ 09026–61656–2 [AAD]
Chopin, F.:Pno Music (misc)—Sonata No. 3, Op. 58; Berceuse, Op. 57; 3 nouvelles études; Nocturnes; Waltzes; FantaisiE Impromptu, Op. 66; Ecossaises, Op. 72/3; Etudes; Sonata No. 2, Op. 35; Impromptu, Op. 29 RCA Gold Seal 2–▲ 09026–68164–2
Chopin, F.:Pno Music (misc)—Ballade No. 1 in g, Op. 23; Barcarolle in F#, Op. 60; Etudes, Op. 10, Nos. 3–5 & Op. 25, Nos. 1–3,9,11 & 12; Impromptus in A♭, Op. 29 & in c#, Op. 66; Mazurka in B♭, Op. 7/1; Nocturne in E♭, Op. 9/2; Polonaise in A♭, Op. 53; Preludes, Op. 28, Nos. 3,6 & 15; Waltzes, Opp. 34/1, 64/2, 69/1 & Op. posth.; *(rec 1928–34)* Danacord 2–▲ DACOCD 336/37 (m) [ADD]
Chopin, F.:Son Pno, Op. 35 *(rec 1932)* Danacord 2–▲ DACOCD 336/37 (m) [ADD]
Chopin, F.:Son Pno, Op. 58 *(rec 1938)* APR ▲ APR 5501 [AAD]
Chopin, F.:Son Pno, Op. 58 Sony Classical (Essential Classics) ▲ SBK 46346 [ADD] ■ SBT 46346
Chopin, F.:Waltzes—in E♭, Op. 18 *(rec 1938)* APR ▲ APR 5501 [AAD]
Chopin, F.:Waltzes—1 waltz in E RCA Gold Seal ▲ 09026–61656–2 [AAD]
Chopin, F.:Waltzes—14 waltzes Sony Classical (Essential Classics) ▲ SBK 46346 [ADD] ■ SBT 46346
Liszt, F.:Con 1 Pno, w. J. Prüwer (cnd), Berlin PO *(rec 1928)* Danacord 2–▲ DACOCD 338/339 (m) [ADD]
Liszt, F.:Pno Music (misc)—Hungarian Rhapsodies 2,6 & 12; Gnomenreigen; Liebestraum No. 3 in A♭; Valse impromptu; Transcriptions of Wagner's Tannhäuser overture & Spinnerlied from Fliegende Holländer, & Schubert's Morgenständchen *(rec 1928–34)* Danacord 2–▲ DACOCD 338/339 (m) [ADD]
Liszt, F.:Totentanz, w. E. Ormandy (cnd), Philadelphia Orch Sony Classical ("Essential Classics" series) ▲ SBK 48167 ■ SBT 48167
Rachmaninoff, S.:Music of, w. Anna Moffo (sop), Alexis Weissenberg (pno), Leonard Pennario (pno) (cnd) (cnd), *(orch unknown)* RCA ■ 5697–4–RV
Tausig, C.:Trans & Arr—3 Scarlatti sons *(rec London, 1938 HMV recordings)* APR ▲ APR 5501 [AAD]

Brain, Aubrey (hn)—see also ORCHESTRAS & ENSEMBLES Adolf Busch Chamber Players
Brahms, J.:Trio Hn, w. Adolf Brusch (vn), Rudolf Serkin (pno) *(rec 1933)* Enterprise ("Strings" series) ▲ ENT QT 99302
Brahms, J.:Trio Hn, w. Adolf Busch (vn), Rudolf Serkin (pno) *(rec 1933)* Iron Needle 2–▲ IN 1342/43 (m) [ADD]
Brahms, J.:Trio Hn, w. A. Busch (vn), R. Serkin (pno) EMI Classics ▲ CDH 64495

484 ▲ = CD ♦ = Enhanced CD Δ = MD ■ = Cassette Tape □ = DCC

Brain, Aubrey (hn) (cont.)
Mozart, W.A.:Con Hn, K.447, w. A. Boult (cnd), BBC SO EMI Classics ▲ CDM 64198
Mozart, W.A.:Divert Hns Strs, K.334, w. D. Brain (hn), Léner String Quartet EMI Classics ▲ CDM 64198

Brain, Dennis (hn)
Britten, H.:Serenade, Op. 31, w. Peter Pears (ten), B. Britten (cnd), Boyd Neel String Orch Pearl ▲ PEA 9177 [ADD]
Hindemith, P.:Con Hn, w. P. Hindemith (cnd), Philharmonia Orch EMI Classics 2-▲ ZDCB 55032
Mozart, W.A.:Cons Hn, w. H. von Karajan (cnd), Philharmonia Orch EMI Classics ("Great Recordings of the Century" series) ▲ CDH 61013 (m)
Mozart, W.A.:Con Hn, K.417, w. W. Susskind (cnd), Philharmonia Orch EMI Classics ▲ CDM 64198
Mozart, W.A.:Divert Hns Strs, K.334, w. A. Brain (hn), Léner String Quartet EMI Classics ▲ CDM 64198
Strauss, R.:Con 1 Hn, w. W. Sawallisch (cnd), Philharmonia Orch EMI Classics ▲ CDC 47834 (m)
Strauss, R.:Con 2 Hn, w. W. Sawallisch (cnd), Philharmonia Orch EMI Classics 2-▲ CDC 47834 (m)

Brain, Leonard (E hn)
Stravinsky, I.:Pastorale, w. Neville Taweel (vn), Derek Wickens (ob), Thomas Kelly (cl), John Price (bn), L. Stokowski (cnd), Royal PO *(rec Kingsway Hall, London, England, June 16–17, 1969)* London ("Phase 4 Stereo" series) ▲ 443898-2 [ADD]

Brainin, Norbert (vn)
Mozart, W.A.:Concertone Vns, w. Peter Schidlof (va), A. Gibson (cnd), English CO Chandos ▲ CHAN 8315 [DDD]
Mozart, W.A.:Sinf concertante Vn, K.364, w. P. Schidlof (va), A. Gibson (cnd), English CO Chandos ▲ CHAN 8315 [DDD]

Braitberg, David (vn)
Mozart, W.A.:Adagio E Hn, w. Patrick McFarland (E hn), Beth Newdome (vn), Paul Murphy (va), Dona Klein (vc) [trans Renate Rosenbaltt] Arundax ▲ 21339
Rachmaninoff, S.:Vocalise, w. Patrick McFarland (E hn), Beth Newdome (vn), Paul Murphy (va), Dona Klein (vc), Larry LeMaster (vc), Gloria Jones (db) [trans John Wildermuth] Arundax ▲ 21339

Braito, Eva (hpd)
Farkas, F.:Concertino Hpd, w. P. Kantschieder (cnd), *(orch unknown)* Koch Schwann ▲ SCH 314222
Françaix, J.:Con Hpd, w. P. Kantschieder (cnd), *(orch unknown)* Koch Schwann ▲ SCH 314222
Jelinek, H.:2 Blue O's, w. P. Kantschieder (cnd), *(orch unknown)* Koch Schwann ▲ SCH 314222
Martinů, B.:Con Hpd, w. P. Kantschieder (cnd), *(orch unknown)* Koch Schwann ▲ SCH 314222

Brake, K. (pno)
Barber, S.:Son Vc, w. S. Honigberg (vc) Albany ▲ TROY 082 [DDD]
Bernstein, L.:Mass (sels), w. S. Honigberg (vc)—Three Meditations Albany ▲ TROY 082 [DDD]
Diamond, D.:Kaddish, w. S. Honigberg (vc) Albany ▲ TROY 082 [DDD]
Foss, L.:Capriccio, w. S. Honigberg (vc) Albany ▲ TROY 082 [DDD]

Braley, Frank (pno)
Bach, J.S.:Cons for 3 Hpds (comp), w. S. Prutsman (pno), B. Ganz (pno), P. Peire (cnd), Collegium Instrumentale Brugense René Gailly ▲ CD 87065 [DDD]
Mozart, W.A.:Con 7 Pnos, w. S. Prutsman (pno), B. Ganz (pno), P. Peire (cnd), Collegium Instrumentale Brugense René Gailly ▲ CD 87065 [DDD]
Rachmaninoff, S.:Pno Music (pno 6–hands), w. Brian Ganz (pno), Stephen Prutsman (pno)—Romance; Valse René Gailly ▲ CD 87065 [DDD]
Schubert, Franz:Pieces Pno, D.946 Harmonia Mundi France ("Les Nouveaux Interprètes" series) ▲ HMN 911546
Schubert, Franz:Son Pno, D.959 Harmonia Mundi France ("Les Nouveaux Interprètes" series) ▲ HMN 911546

Bramböck, Martin (hn)—see ORCHESTRAS & ENSEMBLES Vienna Quintet

Brancaleon, Luca (pno)
Bottesini, G.:Music for Db, w. Ezio Bosso (db)—Gran Duo; Rêverie; Duo concertant sure thèmes des Les Puritaines de Bellini; Melodie; Passioni amorose; Grande allegro; Gran duo concertant Stradivarius ▲ STV 33397 [DDD]

Brancart, E. (pno)
Carter, E.:Son Vc, w. A. Ross (vc) Boston Records ▲ BR 1006
Rachmaninoff, S.:Son Vc, w. A. Ross (vc) Boston Records ▲ BR 1006

Brand, Natan (pno)
Chopin, F.:Ballades Pno (comp)—Op. 52 APR 2-▲ APR 7022
Chopin, F.:Scherzos—No. 1 in b APR 2-▲ APR 7022
Haydn, J.:Fant Pno APR 2-▲ APR 7022
Haydn, J.:Pno Music—Vars in f APR 2-▲ APR 7022
Mussorgsky, M.:Pictures at an Exhibition APR 2-▲ APR 7022
Schubert, Franz:Impromptus Pno, D.899—No. 4 in A♭ APR 2-▲ APR 7022
Schubert, Franz:Moments musicaux—No. 2 in A♭ APR 2-▲ APR 7022
Schumann, R.:Blumenstück APR 2-▲ APR 7022
Schumann, R.:Kreisleriana APR 2-▲ APR 7022
Schumann, R.:Sym Etudes APR 2-▲ APR 7022

Brandenburg, C. (cl)—see ORCHESTRAS & ENSEMBLES Kegelstaat Trio Amsterdam

Brandenburg, Mark (cl)
Bowles, P.:Son Ob & Cl, w. Roger Weismeyer (ob) Koch International Classics ▲ KIC 7343 [DDD]

Brandenmüller, Theo (org)
Brandmüller, T.:Con Org, w. M. Pommer (cnd), Leipzig RSO MD + G ▲ MDG 6250551 [DDD]
Brandmüller, T.:Enigma, w. Christiane Edinger (vn) MD + G ▲ MDG 6250551 [DDD]

Brandis, Thomas (vn)—see also ORCHESTRAS & ENSEMBLES Brandis String Quartet
Mozart, W.A.:Kleine Nachtmusik, w. G. Cappone (va), K. Böhm (cnd), Berlin PO Deutsche Grammophon ("Resonance" series) ▲ 427208-2 [ADD]
Mozart, W.A.:Serenata notturna, w. G. Cappone (va), K. Böhm (cnd), Berlin PO Deutsche Grammophon ("Resonance" series) ▲ 427208-2 [ADD]
Mozart, W.A.:Sinf concertante Vn, K.364, w. G. Cappone (va), K. Böhm (cnd), Berlin PO Deutsche Grammophon ("Resonance" series) ▲ 427208-2 [ADD]
Vivaldi, A.:Cons Vn (misc), w. H. von Karajan (cnd), Berlin PO—RV.271 Deutsche Grammophon ("Galleria" series) ▲ 419046-2 [ADD]

Brandon, David (gtr)
Virtuoso Duets, w. C. Parkening (gtr) EMI Classics ▲ CDC 49406

Brandwynne, L. (pno)
Imbrie, A.W.:Serenade Fl, w. L. DiTullio (fl), W. Trampler (va) *(rec Aug. 17, 1971; originally)* CRI ▲ CD 632 [ADD]

Brannick, Chris (perc)—see ORCHESTRAS & ENSEMBLES Ensemble Bash

Brandt, Henry (org)
Brandt, H.:Kingdom Come, w. Samuel (cnd), Oakland SO, Oakland Youth Orch Phoenix ▲ PHCD 127

Brandt, Henry (pno)
Ives, C.:Songs, w. M. Ingham (sgr)—Ann Street; His exaltation; The see'r; The last reader; General William Booth enters into heaven; The things our fathers loved; Walking; Luck and work; An election; Tom sails away; from "Paracelsus"; Walt Whitman; The camp meeting; 1,2,3; Grantchester; The new river; The cage; The Housatonic at Stockbridge; Charlie Rutledge; Requiem; Slugging a vampire; A sea dirge; Soliloquy; September; December; Majority; The swimmers; On the Antipodes *(rec Aug. 1991)* AmCam ▲ ACR 10306CD [DDD]

Bratchkova, D. (vn)
Dietrich, A.:Trio 1 Pno, w. Aldo Orvieto (pno), Michel Dispa (vc) *(rec Dynamic's, Genova, May 17–19, 1994)* Dynamic ▲ CD 121 [DDD]
Dietrich, A.:Trio 2 Pno, w. Aldo Orvieto (pno), Michel Dispa (vc) *(rec Dynamic's, Genova, May 17–19, 1994)* Dynamic ▲ CD 121 [DDD]
Paganini, N.:Serenata Vns, w. G. Hartmann (vn), A. Sebastiani (gtr) Dynamic ▲ CD 76 [DDD]
Paganini, N.:Terzetto Vn, w. A. Noferini (vc), A. Sebastiani (gtr) Dynamic ▲ CD 76 [DDD]
Paganini, N.:Terzetto Vns, w. G. Hartmann (vn), A. Sebastiani (gtr) Dynamic ▲ CD 76 [DDD]

Bratke, Marcelo (pno)
Berg, A.:Son Pno Olympia ▲ OLY 392 [ADD]

Bratke, Marcelo (pno) (cont.)
Krenek, E.:Sons Pno—No. 2, Op. 59 (1928); No. 3, Op. 92/4 (1943) Olympia ▲ OLY 392 [ADD]
Villa-Lobos, H.:Pno Music—The Little Broken Musical Box; The Baby's Family No. 1; Little Children's Rounds; Children's Carnival Olympia ▲ OLY 455 [DDD]
Webern, A.:Vars Pno Olympia ▲ OLY 392 [ADD]

Bratlie, Jens Harald (pno)—see also ORCHESTRAS & ENSEMBLES Oslo Piano Trio
Grieg, E.:Norwegian Dances, Op. 35, w. Geir Botnen (pno) *(rec Eidsvoll Church, Jan 15–16, 1996)* Simax ▲ PSC 1133 [DDD]
Johansen, D.M.:Portraits from the Middle Ages Simax ▲ PSC 3119
Johansen, D.M.:Suite 2 Pno Simax ▲ PSC 3119
Johansen, D.M.:Suite 3 Pno Simax ▲ PSC 3119
Madsen, T.:Hommage à Ravel Norway Music ▲ CD 2913
Madsen, T.:Preludes Pno Norway Music ▲ CD 2913
Madsen, T.:Prelude & Fugue on the Name of Bach Norway Music ▲ CD 2913
Madsen, T.:Son Hn, w. Frøydis Ree Wekre (hn) Crystal ▲ CD 678
Madsen, T.:Variations & Fugue over a Theme by Beethoven Norway Music ▲ CD 2913

Bratlie, Jorunn Marie (pno)
Olsen, O.:Petite suite, w. C. Eggen (cnd), Norwegian RSO NKF ▲ NKFCD 50024
Piano Works by 7 Women Composers NKF ▲ NKFCD 50024-2

Braucher, Ernest (va)—see ORCHESTRAS & ENSEMBLES Aira String Quartet, Paganini String Quartet
Braucher, Ernest (vn)—see ORCHESTRAS & ENSEMBLES Conserto Vago

Brauchli, Bernard (hpd/clvd)
18th Century Music for 2 Keyboard Instruments, w. Esteban Elizondo (org/clvd) Titanic ▲ Ti 185 [DDD]

Brauchli, Bernard (org)
The Iberian Organ, Vol. 2 Titanic ▲ Ti 157 [DDD]
Seixas, C. de:Sons Kbd—3 sonatas:Nos. 1,8 & 22 Titanic ▲ Ti 157 [DDD]
Soler, P.A.:Cons Kbds, w. E. Elizondo (org)—Nos. 1 & 2—2 clavichords; Nos. 3 & 6—harpsichord & organ; Nos. 4 & 5—2 organs Titanic ▲ Ti 152 [DDD]

Brauchner, Ernest (vn)—see ORCHESTRAS & ENSEMBLES Conserto Vago
Braugham, Charles (perc)—see ORCHESTRAS & ENSEMBLES Univ of Illinois Contemporary Chamber Players

Braumann, Susanne (vl)—see also ORCHESTRAS & ENSEMBLES Royal Consort
Marais, M.:Suites VI & Hpd, w. Fred Jacobs (thb)—in e; in a; in D; in e *(rec Utrecht, Oct. 1994)* Globe ▲ GLO 5122 [DDD]

Braun, Richard (pno)
Mendelssohn, Fanny:Songs, w. Michaela Krämer (sop), Gerhild Romberger (alt), Alastair Thompson (ten), Gerrit Miehlke (bass), Willi Gundlach (cnd), Dortmund Univ Chamber Choir—Morgendämmerung; Im Herbste; Unter des Laubdachs Hut; Ich stand gelehnet an den Mast; Mitternacht; Abschied; Lockung; Abend; Aus meinen Tränen; Wenn ich in deine Augen seh'; Im wunderschönen Monat Mai; Schöne Fremde; Schweigend sinkt die Nacht hernieder; Nacht liegt auf den fremden Wegen; Hochzeitsbitter; Wandl' ich in dem Wald; Frühzeitiger Frühling; Blumengruss; O Herbst; Schilflied; Feldlied; März; Lichter Mai; Waldruhe; Nachtreigen *(rec Musikhochschule Detmold, Dortmund, Oct 1995)* Thorofon ▲ CTH 2299 [DDD]

Braunholz, Bernhard (vc)
Fauré, G.:Qt 1 Pno, w. J. Eymar (pno), G. Kehr (vn), E. Sichermann (va) *(rec 1966)* Vox Box 2-▲ CDX 5073 [ADD]
Fauré, G.:Qt 2 Pno, w. J. Eymar (pno), G. Kehr (vn), E. Sichermann (va) *(rec 1966)* Vox Box 2-▲ CDX 5073 [ADD]
Fauré, G.:Qnts Pno & Strs, Opp. 89 & 115, w. J. Eymar (pno), G. Kehr (vn), W. Neuhaus (vn), E. Sichermann (va) *(rec 1970)* Vox Box 2-▲ CDX 5073 [ADD]

Braunstein, Mark (va)
Elgar, E.:Con Vc, w. R. Stamp (cnd), Academy of London Orch Virgin Classics ▲ CDZ 59643

Brautigam, Ronald (pno)
Beethoven, L. van:Son 1 Pno *(rec July 1993)* Globe ▲ GLO 5100 [DDD]
Beethoven, L. van:Son 2 Pno *(rec July 1993)* Globe ▲ GLO 5100 [DDD]
Beethoven, L. van:Son 3 Pno *(rec July 1993)* Globe ▲ GLO 5100 [DDD]
Beethoven, L. van:Son 19 Pno *(rec July 1993)* Globe ▲ GLO 5100 [DDD]
Beethoven, L. van:Son 20 Pno *(rec July 1993)* Globe ▲ GLO 5100 [DDD]
Beethoven, L. van:Vars on Ditterdorf's arietta "Es war einmal ein alter Mann", WoO 66 *(rec Dec. 1992)* Globe ▲ GLO 5095 [DDD]
Beethoven, L. van:Vars on Haibel's "Menuet à la Viganò", WoO 68 *(rec Dec. 1992)* Globe ▲ GLO 5095 [DDD]
Beethoven, L. van:Vars on Paisiello's aria "Quant' è più bello", WoO 69 *(rec Dec. 1992)* Globe ▲ GLO 5095 [DDD]
Beethoven, L. van:Vars on Paisiello's duet "Nel cor più non mi sento", WoO 70 *(rec Dec. 1992)* Globe ▲ GLO 5095 [DDD]
Beethoven, L. van:Vars on a Russian Dance from P. Wranitzky's ballet "Das Waldmachen", WoO 71 *(rec Dec. 1992)* Globe ▲ GLO 5095 [DDD]
Beethoven, L. van:Vars on Grétry's romance "Un fièvre brûlante", WoO 72 *(rec Dec. 1992)* Globe ▲ GLO 5095 [DDD]
Beethoven, L. van:Vars on Salieri's duet "La stessa, le stessissima", WoO 73 *(rec Dec. 1992)* Globe ▲ GLO 5095 [DDD]
Beethoven, L. van:Vars on Winter's "Kind, willst du ruhig schlafen", WoO 75 *(rec Dec. 1992)* Globe ▲ GLO 5095 [DDD]
Bosmans, H.:Concertino Pno, w. E. Spanjaard (cnd), Netherlands Radio CO *(rec Geertekerk, Utrecht, May 14, 1994)* NM Special ▲ 92095 [DDD]
Bosmans, H.:Concertino Pno, w. E. Spanjaard (cnd), Netherlands Radio CO NM Classics ▲ NM 92044
Debussy, C.:Son Vn, w. Isabelle van Keulen (vn) Koch Schwann ▲ SCH 315272 [DDD]
Escher, R.:Sonate concertante, w. Harro Ruysenaars (vc) *(rec Mar 7, 1984)* Donemus ▲ CV 47 [ADD]
Fauré, G.:Son 1 Vn, w. Isabelle von Keulen (vn) Koch Schwann ▲ SCH 315272 [DDD]
Hindemith, P.:Kammermusik (comp), w. L. Harrell (vc), K. Kulka (vn), K. Kashkashian (va), N. Blume (va d'amore), L. van Doeselaar (org), R. Chailly (cnd), Royal Concertgebouw Orch—No. 1 for Small Orchestra, Op. 24/1 (1922); No. 2 (Piano Concerto) for Piano & 12 Instruments, Op. 36/1 (1924); No. 3 (Cello Concerto), foe Cello & 10 Instruments, Op. 36/2 (1925); No. 4 (Violin Concerto) for Violin & Large Orchestra, Op. 36/3 (1925); No. 5 (Viola Concerto) for Viola & Large Chamber Orchestra, Op. 36/4 (1927); No. 6 (Viola d'amore Concerto) for Viola d'amore & Chamber Orchestra, Op. 46/1 (1927); No. 7 (Organ Concerto) for Organ & chamber Orchestra, Op. 46/2 (1927) London 2-▲ 433816-2 [DDD]
Mendelssohn, F.:Capriccio brillante, w. L. Markiz (cnd), Amsterdam New Sinfonietta *(rec Concertgebouw, Haarlem, Holland, May 18–20, 1995)* BIS ▲ CD 713 [DDD]
Mendelssohn, F.:Con in a Pno, Op. posth., w. L. Markiz (cnd), Amsterdam New Sinfonietta *(rec Concertgebouw, Haarlem, Holland, May 20–21, 1995)* BIS ▲ CD 718 [DDD]
Mendelssohn, F.:Con 1 Pno, w. L. Markiz (cnd), Amsterdam New Sinfonietta *(rec Concertgebouw, Haarlem, Holland, Aug 4, 1994)* BIS ▲ CD 718 [DDD]
Mendelssohn, F.:Con 2 Pno, w. L. Markiz (cnd), Amsterdam New Sinfonietta *(rec Concertgebouw, Haarlem, Holland, Aug 5, 1994)* BIS ▲ CD 718 [DDD]
Mendelssohn, F.:Con in d Vn, Pno & Strs, w. Isabelle Van Keulen (vn), L. Markiz (cnd), Amsterdam New Sinfonietta *(rec Concertgebouw, Haarlem, Holland, July 4–5, 1995)* BIS ▲ CD 713 [DDD]
Mendelssohn, F.:Rondo brilliant, w. L. Markiz (cnd), Amsterdam New Sinfonietta *(rec Concertgebouw, Haarlem, Holland, May 18–20, 1995)* BIS ▲ CD 713 [DDD]
Mendelssohn, F.:Serenade & Allegro giocoso, w. L. Markiz (cnd), Amsterdam New Sinfonietta *(rec Concertgebouw, Haarlem, Holland, May 18–20, 1995)* BIS ▲ CD 713 [DDD]
Pijper, W.:Con Pno, w. R. van Driesten (cnd), Residentie Orch The Hague Olympia ▲ OCD 504 [AAD]
Poulenc, F.:Son Vn, w. Isabelle von Keulen (vn) Koch Schwann ▲ SCH 315272 [DDD]
Schumann, R.:Allegro Pno Olympia ▲ OLY 436 [DDD]
Schumann, R.:Fantasiestücke Pno, Op. 111 Olympia ▲ OLY 436 [DDD]
Schumann, R.:Gesänge der Frühe Olympia ▲ OLY 436 [DDD]
Schumann, R.:Novelettes Olympia ▲ OLY 436 [DDD]

INSTRUMENT.

Brautigam, Ronald (pno) (cont.)
Shostakovich, D.:Con 1 Pno, w. P. Masseurs (tpt), R. Chailly (cnd), Royal Concertgebouw Orch London ▲ 433702-2 [DDD]
Smit, L.:Con Pno, w. E. Spanjaard (cnd), Netherlands Radio CO NM Classics ▲ NM 92044

Braxton, Anthony (fl/s sax/a sax)
Braxton, A.:Composition 144, w. Seppo Baron Paakkunainen (fl/t sax/br sax), Pentti Lahti (fl/s sax/a sax), Pepa Päivinen (fl/t sax/sop sax/b cl), Mircea Stan (trbn), Mikko-Ville Luolajan-Mikkola (vn), Teppo Hauta-aho (db/vc), Jukka Wasama (dr) *(rec Järvenpää House, Järvenpää, Finland, Nov 7, 1988)* Leo ▲ LR 233
Braxton, A.:Composition 145, w. Seppo Baron Paakkunainen (fl/t sax/br sax), Pentti Lahti (fl/s sax/a sax), Pepa Päivinen (fl/t sax/sop sax/b cl), Mircea Stan (trbn), Mikko-Ville Luolajan-Mikkola (vn), Teppo Hauta-aho (db/vc), Jukka Wasama (dr) *(rec Järvenpää House, Järvenpää, Finland, Nov 7, 1988)* Leo ▲ LR 233

Braxton, Anthony (sax)
Braxton, A.:Composition 107 (sels), w. D. Rosenboom (pno), W. Winant (perc) Centaur ▲ CRC 2110 [DDD]
Rosenboom, D.:A Precipice in Time, w. D. Rosenboom (elec), W. Winant (perc), et al. Centaur ▲ CRC 2110 [DDD]

Braxton, Anthony (sax/cl/fl)
Teitelbaum, R.:Con Grosso, w. George Lewis (trbn), Richard Teitelbaum (kbd/elec) *(rec Klaviere & Computer Festival, Cologne, May 3, 1985)* Hat Hut ▲ hat ART CD 6004 [AAD]

Braynard, David (tuba)
Wuorinen, C.:Trio Bass Trbn, w. D. Taylor (trbn), D. Palma (db) *(rec Sept. 11-13, 1991)* Koch International Classics ▲ KIC 7123-2 [DDD]

Brázada, Joseph (hn)
Haydn, J.:Con 1 Hn, w. L. Sagrestano (cnd), Prague Musici Accord ▲ ACD 220462 [DDD]

Brazzel, Russel (gtr)
Ardévol, J.:Gtr Music—Son. Centaur ▲ CRC 2155
Brouwer, L.:Gtr Music—Zapateo; Ojos Brujos; Guajìra criolla; Canciòn de Cuna; Danza caracteristica; Elogio de la Danze; Canticum Centaur ▲ CRC 2155
Galàn, N.:Gtr Music—Sonata Breve; Sonata Fàcile; Suite Cubana Centaur ▲ CRC 2155

Bream, Julian (gtr)
Albéniz, I.:Gtr Music—Mallorca; Suite Española; Cordoba RCA ▲ RCD1-4378 [DDD]
Albéniz, I.:Gtr Music RCA Gold Seal 2-▲ 09026-61608-2 [AAD]; ■ 09026-61608-4
Arnold, M.:Con Gtr, w. S. Rattle (cnd), City of Birmingham SO EMI Classics ▲ CDC 54661-2
Bach, J.S.:Chaconne EMI Classics ▲ CDC 55123
Bach, J.S.:Suite Lt, BWV 995 RCA Gold Seal ▲ 09026-61603-2 ■ 09026-61603-4
Bach, J.S.:Trio Sons (misc)—2 sons RCA Gold Seal ▲ 09026-61603-2 ■ 09026-2D61603-2D4
Bach, J.S.:Trio Sons Org—BWV 525 & 529 RCA Red Seal ▲ RCD1-5841
The Baroque Guitar Victrola ▲ 60494-2-RV [ADD] ■ 60494-4-RV
Berkeley, L.:Con Gtr, *(orch unknown)* RCA Gold Seal 2-▲ 09026-61605-2 [AAD]
Berkeley, L.:Con Gtr, w. J.E. Gardiner (cnd), Monteverdi Orch RCA ■ ALK1-9535
Britten, H.:Music of, w. Peter Pears (ten) RCA Gold Seal ▲ 09026-61601-2
Britten, H.:Nocturnal Gtr EMI Classics ▲ CDC 54901
Brouwer, L.:Con 3 Gtr, "Con Elegíaco", w. J. E. Gardiner (cnd), *(orch unknown)* RCA Gold Seal 2-▲ 09026-61605-2 [AAD]
Brouwer, L.:Con 3 Gtr, "Con Elegíaco", w. L. Brouwer (cnd), RCA Victor CO RCA Red Seal ▲ 7718-2-RC [DDD]
Brouwer, L.:Gtr Music—Son. in 3 movements EMI Classics ▲ CDC 54901
Carulli, F.:Serenade for 2 Gtrs, w. J. Williams (gtr) RCA ■ ARK1-0456
A Celebration of Andrés Segovia RCA Gold Seal ▲ 09026-61353-2 ■ 09026-61353-4
Giuliani, M.:Variazioni Concertanti, w. J. Williams (gtr) RCA ■ ARK1-0456
Granados, E.:Gtr Music RCA Gold Seal 2-▲ 09026-61608-2; ■ 09026-61608-4
Guitar Greatest Hits RCA Victor ▲ 09026-62663-2 ■ 09026-62663-4
La Guitarra Romantica RCA Red Seal ▲ 60429-2-RC [DDD] ■ 60429-4-RC
Highlights from the Julian Bream Edition, w. George Malcolm (hpd), John Eliot Gardiner (cnd), Monteverdi Orch, Julian Bream Consort RCA Gold Seal ▲ 09026-61848-2
Julian & John Together, w. John Williams (gtr) RCA Gold Seal ▲ 09026-61450-2 ■ 09026-61450-4
Julian & John Together Again, w. John Williams (gtr) RCA Gold Seal ▲ 09026-61452-2 ■ 09026-61452-4
Julian Bream Edition:The Ultimate Guitar Collection RCA Gold Seal 28-▲ 09026-61583-2
Lutoslawski, W.:Melodie ludowe EMI Classics ▲ CDC 54901
Martin, F.:Pièces brèves EMI Classics ▲ CDC 54901
Milán, L. de:Music of RCA Gold Seal ▲ 09026-61606-2
Narváez, L. de:Seys libros RCA Gold Seal ▲ 09026-61606-2
Popular Classics for Spanish Guitar RCA Gold Seal ▲ 09026-61591-2 ■ 09026-61591-4
Rodrigo, J.:Concierto de Aranjuez, w. J.E. Gardiner (cnd), Monteverdi Orch RCA Victor ▲ 09026-61724-2; ■ 09026-61724-4 (CrO2)
Rodrigo, J.:Concierto de Aranjuez, w. S. Rattle (cnd), City of Birmingham SO EMI Classics ▲ CDC 54661
Rodrigo, J.:Concierto de Aranjuez, w. J.E. Gardiner (cnd), Monteverdi Orch RCA ■ ALK1-9535
Rodrigo, J.:Concierto de Aranjuez, w. *(orch unknown)* RCA Gold Seal 2-▲ 09026-61605-2
Rodrigo, J.:Concierto de Aranjuez, w. J.E. Gardiner (cnd), Monteverdi Orch RCA Gold Seal ▲ 6525-2-RG [ADD] ■ 6525-4-RG (CrO2)
Rodrigo, J.:Fant para un gentilhombre, w. L. Brouwer (cnd), RCA Victor CO RCA Red Seal ▲ 7718-2-RC [DDD]
Rodrigo, J.:Fant para un gentilhombre, w. L. Brouwer (cnd), RCA Victor CO RCA Victor ▲ 09026-61724-2; ■ 09026-61724-4 (CrO2)
The Romantic Guitar RCA Gold Seal ▲ 6798-2-RG [ADD] ■ 6798-4-RG
Seiber, M.:Music of, w. Peter Pears (ten) RCA Gold Seal ▲ 09026-61601-2
Takemitsu, T.:All in Twilight EMI Classics ▲ CDC 54901
Takemitsu, T.:To the Edge of Dream, w. S. Rattle (cnd), City of Birmingham SO EMI Classics ▲ CDC 54661
Tárrega, F.:Gtr Music RCA Red Seal ▲ 60429-2-RC [DDD] ■ 60429-4-RC (CrO2)
Villa-Lobos, H.:Con Gtr, w. A. Previn (cnd), London SO RCA Gold Seal ▲ 6525-2-RG [ADD] ■ 6525-4-RG (CrO2)
Villa-Lobos, H.:Preludes Gtr RCA Victor ▲ 09026-61724-2 ■ 09026-61724-4 (CrO2)
Walton, W.:Music of, w. Peter Pears (ten) RCA Gold Seal ▲ 09026-61601-2

Bream, Julian (lt)
Bach, J.S.:Suite Lt, BWV 996 EMI Classics ▲ CDC 55123
Monteverdi, C.:Ballo delle ingrate, w. April Cantelo (sop—Una dell' Ingrate), Eileen McLoughlin (sop—Amore), Alfred Deller (alt—Venere), David Ward (bass—Plutone), Desmond Dupre (vl), A. Deller (cnd), London Chamber Players *(rec Walthamstow Hall, London)* Vanguard Classics ▲ OVC 8100 [ADD]

Brecker, Michael (sax)
Grana, E.D.:Stones, Time & Elements:A Humanist Requiem, w. R.A. Clark (cnd), Manhattan CO, Magic Circle Opera Ensemble Newport Classic ▲ NPT 85573

Breika, H. (trbn)
Bruckner, A.:Motets, w. H. P. Blochwitz (ten), H. Skarba (trbn), H. Weimer (trbn), S. Rommelspacher (org), Freiburg Vocal Ensemble—Os justi; Afferentur regi; Christus factus est; Tota pulchra es Maria; Vexilla regis prodeunt; Ecce sacerdos magnus; Pange lingua; Locus iste; Ave Maria; Virga Jesse floruit Entrée ▲ 0039 [ADD]

Breiner, P. (pno)
Granados, E.:Pno Music (misc), w. G. Garcia (gtr), Czech State PO [arranged by cond. for guitar & orch.]—Spanish Dances Nos. 2,6,8 & 11; Zapateado Naxos ▲ 8.550220 [DDD]

Breiner, Peter (pno)
Mozart, W.A.:Con 20 Pno, w. O. Trhlík (cnd), Philharmonia Cassovia *(rec House of Arts, Kosice, Jan. 31, 1990)* Lydian ▲ 18102 [DDD]

Breinschmid, Wolfgang (fl)—see ORCHESTRAS & ENSEMBLES Vienna Lanner Ensemble

Breitman, David (pno)
Barber, S.:Hermit Songs, w. S. Sylvan (bar) Elektra/Nonesuch ▲ 79259-2
Chanler, T.:Epitaphs (8), w. S. Sylvan (bar) Elektra/Nonesuch ▲ 79259-2
Chopin, F.:Études (24), w. K. Scholes (vc)—No. 9 [trans. K. Scholes for cello & piano] *(rec June 1990)* Titanic ▲ TI 197 [DDD]
Chopin, F.:Intro & Polonaise, "Polonaise brilliante", w. K. Scholes (vc) *(rec June 1990)* Titanic ▲ TI 197 [DDD]
Chopin, F.:Son Vc, w. K. Scholes (vc) *(rec June 1990)* Titanic ▲ TI 197 [DDD]
Chopin, F.:Waltzes, w. K. Scholes (vc)—Op. 34/2 *(rec June 1990)* Titanic ▲ TI 197 [DDD]
Copland, A.:Poems (8) of Emily Dickinson, w. S. Sylvan (bar) Elektra/Nonesuch ▲ 79259-2
Schubert, Franz:Die Schöne Müllerin, w. S. Sylvan (bar) Elektra/Nonesuch ▲ 79293-2

Brem, Peter (vn)—see ORCHESTRAS & ENSEMBLES Brandis String Quartet

Brembeck, Christian (org)
Famous European Organs Capriccio ▲ CD 10 351 [DDD]
Orgel-Impressionen:Book of Hours *(rec St. Willibald, Munich, Aug-Sept 1995)* Calig ▲ CAL 50965 [DDD]
Orgel-Impressionen:Seasons *(rec St. Willibald, Munich, Aug-Sept 1995)* Calig ▲ CAL 50966 [DDD]
Virtuoso Organ Music of the North German Baroque Classic Studio Berlin ▲ CS 11508 [DDD]

Brembeck, Christian (org/hpd)
Kuhnau, J.:Musicalische Vorstellung einiger biblischer Historien Capriccio ▲ CD 10 350 [DDD]

Bremsteller, Ulrich (org)
Trumpet & Organ, w. Lange, Arno (tpt), Joachim Pliquett (tpt), Arvid Gast (org) Classic Studio Berlin ▲ CS 12 208 [DDD]

Brendel, Alfred (pno)
The Alfred Brendel Collection Vanguard Classics 6-▲ OVC 4015 and OVC 4023-4027 [ADD]
Bach, J.S.:Chromatic Fant & Fugue Philips ▲ 412252-2 [ADD]
Bach, J.S.:Italian Con Philips ▲ 412252-2 [ADD]
Beethoven, L. van:Andante, WoO 57, "Andante favori" Philips ▲ 438472-2
Beethoven, L. van:Andante, WoO 57, "Andante favori" *(rec 1964)* VoxBox 2-▲ CDX 5112
Beethoven, L. van:Bagatelles (24)—Op. 126 Philips ▲ 412227-2 [DDD]
Beethoven, L. van:Bagatelles (24) *(rec 1964)* Vox Box 2-▲ CDX 5112
Beethoven, L. van:Bagatelle, WoO 59, "Für Elise" Philips ▲ 412227-2
Beethoven, L. van:Bagatelle, WoO 60 *(rec 1964)* Vox Box 2-▲ CDX 5112
Beethoven, L. van:Cons Pno (comp), w. J. Levine (cnd), Chicago SO *(rec live)* Philips 3-▲ 411189-2 [DDD]
Beethoven, L. van:Cons Pno (comp)—No. 1 [w. Wilfried Boettcher (cnd), Stuttgart PO]; No. 2 [w. Heinz Walberg (cnd), Vienna Volksoper Orch.]; Nos. 3 & 4 [both w. Heinz Walberg (cnd), Vienna SO]; No. 5 [w. Zubin Mehta (cnd), Vienna SO] Vox Box ("Legends" series) 3-▲ CDX3 3502 [ADD]
Beethoven, L. van:Con 1 Pno, w. J. Levine (cnd), Chicago SO Philips ▲ 412787-2 [DDD]
Beethoven, L. van:Con 2 Pno, w. J. Levine (cnd), Chicago SO Philips ▲ 412787-2 [DDD]
Beethoven, L. van:Con 3 Pno, w. J. Levine (cnd), Chicago SO Philips ▲ 412788-2 [DDD]
Beethoven, L. van:Con 4 Pno, w. R. Kubelik (cnd), Bavarian RSO *(rec 1970)* Arkadia ▲ 494
Beethoven, L. van:Con 4 Pno, w. R. Kubelik (cnd), Bavarian RSO Artists ▲ FED 47 [ADD]
Beethoven, L. van:Con 4 Pno, w. J. Levine (cnd), Chicago SO Philips ▲ 412788-2 [DDD]
Beethoven, L. van:Con 5 Pno, "Emperor", w. B. Haitink (cnd), London PO Philips ("Insignia" series) ▲ 434148-2 [ADD]
Beethoven, L. van:Con 5 Pno, "Emperor", w. J. Levine (cnd), Chicago SO Philips ▲ 412789-2 [DDD]
Beethoven, L. van:Fant Pno, Op. 80, "Choral Fant", w. W. Boettcher (cnd), Stuttgart PO, Stuttgart Teachers' Glee Club Vox Box ("Legends" series) 3-▲ CDX3 3502 [ADD]
Beethoven, L. van:Fant Pno, Op. 80, "Choral Fant", w. B. Haitink (cnd), London PO Philips 2-▲ 454038-2
Beethoven, L. van:Fant Pno, Op. 80, "Choral Fant", w. B. Haitink (cnd), London PO, London Phil Chorus Philips ("Insignia" series) ▲ 434148-2 [DDD]
Beethoven, L. van:Grosse Fuge for 2 Pnos, w. D. Barenboim (pno) *(rec live, Brighton Festival 1970)* Arkadia 2-▲ 589 [ADD]
Beethoven, L. van:Pno Music (misc)—Allegretto, WoO 53; Ecossaises (6), WoO 83; Für Elise, WoO 59; Polonaise, Op. 89; Rondo, Op. 51/2 *(rec 1961-63)* Vox Box 3-▲ CD3X 3017 [ADD]
Beethoven, L. van:Pno Music (misc), w. J. Levine (cnd), Chicago SO—Andante for Pno, WoO 57; Bagatelles for Pno, Op. 126 & WoO 59; Cons for Pno Nos. 4 & 5; Ecossaises; Sons Op. 2/3, 22, 31/3, 57, 78, 106, 109; Vars for Pno:Op. 34, 35, 120 & WoO 70 & 79 Philips 25-▲ 446920-2
Beethoven, L. van:Qnt Pno, Ob, Cl, Hn & Bn, w. Hungarian Quintet members Allegretto ▲ ACD 8150 [ADD] ■ ACS 8150
Beethoven, L. van:Qnt Pno, Ob, Cl, Hn & Bn, w. H. Holliger (ob), E. Brunner (cl), K. Thunemann (bn), H. Baumann (hn) Philips ▲ 420182-2 [DDD]
Beethoven, L. van:Rondos Pno, Op. 51 *(rec 1964)* Vox Box 2-▲ CDX 5112
Beethoven, L. van:Rondo a capriccio, "Rage Over a Lost Penny" *(rec 1964)* Vox Box 2-▲ CDX 5112
Beethoven, L. van:Sons Pno (comp) Philips 11-▲ 412575-2
Beethoven, L. van:Sons Pno (comp) Philips 10-▲ 446 909-2
Beethoven, L. van:Sons Pno (comp)—Sonata Nos. 27-32 Vox Box 2-▲ CDX 5028 [ADD]
Beethoven, L. van:Sons Pno (comp)—Nos. 16-19, 21-23, & 26 *(rec 1962-64)* Vox Box 2-▲ CDX 5042 [ADD]
Beethoven, L. van:Sons Pno (comp)—Nos. 1, 5, 6, 9, 10, 13-15, 25 *(rec 1962-64)* Vox Box 2-▲ CDX 5056 [ADD]
Beethoven, L. van:Sons Pno (comp)—Nos. 2, 3, 7, 8, 11, 12 & 24 *(rec 1962-64)* Vox Box 2-▲ CDX 5060 [ADD]
Beethoven, L. van:Son 1 Pno Philips ▲ 442124-2
Beethoven, L. van:Son 2 Pno Philips ▲ 442124-2
Beethoven, L. van:Son 3 Pno Philips ▲ 442124-2
Beethoven, L. van:Son 4 Pno *(rec 1961-63)* Vox Box 3-▲ CD3X 3017 [ADD]
Beethoven, L. van:Son 4 Pno Philips ▲ 446 624-2
Beethoven, L. van:Son 5 Pno Philips ▲ 446664-2
Beethoven, L. van:Son 6 Pno Philips ▲ 446664-2
Beethoven, L. van:Son 7 Pno Philips ▲ 446664-2
Beethoven, L. van:Son 8 Pno, "Pathétique" Philips ▲ 411470-2 [ADD]
Beethoven, L. van:Son 8 Pno, "Pathétique" Philips 2-▲ 438730-2
Beethoven, L. van:Son 8 Pno, "Pathétique" Philips ▲ 442774-2
Beethoven, L. van:Son 9 Pno Philips ▲ 442774-2
Beethoven, L. van:Son 10 Pno Philips ▲ 442774-2
Beethoven, L. van:Son 11 Pno Philips ▲ 442774-2
Beethoven, L. van:Son 12 Pno, "Funeral March" Originals ▲ ORI 801 [DDD]
Beethoven, L. van:Son 12 Pno, "Funeral March" *(rec Neumarkt, Germany, Apr. 2-8, 1993)* Philips ▲ 438863-2
Beethoven, L. van:Son 13 Pno *(rec Neumarkt, Germany, Apr. 2-8, 1993)* Philips ▲ 438863-2
Beethoven, L. van:Son 14 Pno, "Moonlight Son" Originals ▲ ORI 801 [DDD]
Beethoven, L. van:Son 14 Pno, "Moonlight Son" Philips ▲ 411470-2 [ADD]
Beethoven, L. van:Son 14 Pno, "Moonlight Son" Philips 2-▲ 438730-2
Beethoven, L. van:Son 14 Pno, "Moonlight Son" *(rec Neumarkt, Germany, Apr. 2-8, 1993)* Philips ▲ 438863-2
Beethoven, L. van:Son 15 Pno, "Pastoral" Philips ▲ 446 624-2
Beethoven, L. van:Son 16 Pno Philips ▲ 438134-2
Beethoven, L. van:Son 17 Pno, "Tempest" Philips ▲ 438134-2
Beethoven, L. van:Son 17 Pno, "Tempest" Philips 2-▲ 438730-2
Beethoven, L. van:Son 18 Pno Philips ▲ 438134-2
Beethoven, L. van:Son 19 Pno *(rec Neumarkt, Germany, Apr. 2-8, 1993)* Philips ▲ 438863-2
Beethoven, L. van:Son 20 Pno Philips ▲ 446 624-2
Beethoven, L. van:Son 20 Pno *(rec 1961-63)* Vox Box 3-▲ CD3X 3017 [ADD]
Beethoven, L. van:Son 21 Pno, "Waldstein" Philips ▲ 438472-2

▲ = CD ♦ = Enhanced CD ∆ = MD ■ = Cassette Tape ▯ = DCC

Brendel, Alfred (pno) (cont.)
Beethoven, L. van:Son 21 Pno, "Waldstein" Philips 2–▲ 438730–2
Beethoven, L. van:Son 21 Pno, "Waldstein" Originals ▲ ORI 801 [DDD]
Beethoven, L. van:Son 22 Pno Philips ▲ 438472–2
Beethoven, L. van:Son 23 Pno, "Appassionata" Philips ▲ 411470–2 [ADD]
Beethoven, L. van:Son 23 Pno, "Appassionata" Philips 2–▲ 438730–2
Beethoven, L. van:Son 23 Pno, "Appassionata" Philips ▲ 442787–2
Beethoven, L. van:Son 24 Pno Philips ▲ 442787–2
Beethoven, L. van:Son 25 Pno Philips ▲ 442787–2
Beethoven, L. van:Son 26 Pno, "Les Adieux" Philips 2–▲ 438730–2
Beethoven, L. van:Son 26 Pno, "Les Adieux" Philips ▲ 446093–2
Beethoven, L. van:Son 27 Pno Philips 2–▲ 438323–2
Beethoven, L. van:Son 27 Pno Philips 2–▲ 438374–2
Beethoven, L. van:Son 27 Pno Philips ▲ 442787–2
Beethoven, L. van:Sons 28–32 Pno, "The Late Sons" Philips 2–▲ 438374–2
Beethoven, L. van:Son 28 Pno Philips ▲ 438472–2
Beethoven, L. van:Son 29 Pno, "Hammerklavier" Philips ▲ 446093–2
Beethoven, L. van:Son 30 Pno Philips ▲ 446701–2
Beethoven, L. van:Son 31 Pno Philips ▲ 412789–2
Beethoven, L. van:Son 31 Pno Philips ▲ 446701–2
Beethoven, L. van:Son 32 Pno Philips ▲ 446701–2
Beethoven, L. van:Vars Pno—Vars, Opp. 34 & 76; Vars, WoO 64, 65, 66, 69, 70, 71, 72, 73, 75, 76, 77, 78, 79 & 80; Vars & Fugue in E♭ for Pno, Op. 35 Vox Box 3–▲ CD3X 3017 [ADD]
Beethoven, L. van:Vars & Fugue Pno, Op. 35, "Eroica" Philips ▲ 412227–2 [DDD]
Beethoven, L. van:Vars on a waltz by Diabelli, Op. 120 *(rec 1964)* Vox Box 2–▲ CDX 5112
Brahms, J.:Con 1 Pno, w. C. Abbado (cnd), Berlin PO Philips ▲ 420071–2 [DDD]
Brahms, J.:Pno Music (misc), w. Abbado, Holliger (cnd), Berlin PO, London SO—Ballades, Op. 10; Cons for Pno Nos. 1 & 2; Sxt–Vars Philips 25–▲ 446920–2
Brahms, J.:Theme & Vars Pno Philips ("Digital Classics" series) ▲ 426272–2 [DDD]
Chopin, F.:Andante Spianato & Grande Polonaise Vanguard Classics ▲ OVC 4023 [ADD]
Chopin, F.:Polonaises—in c, Op. 40/2; in f#, Op. 44; in A♭, Op. 53 Vanguard Classics ▲ OVC 4023 [ADD]
Chopin, F.:Polonaise–fant Vanguard Classics ▲ OVC 4023 [ADD]
Haydn, J.:Adagio in F Pno, H.XVII/9 Philips ▲ 412228–2 [DDD]
Haydn, J.:Adagio in F Pno, H.XVII/9 Philips 4–▲ 416643–2 [DDD]
Haydn, J.:Fant Pno Philips 4–▲ 416643–2 [DDD]
Haydn, J.:Fant Pno Philips ▲ 412228–2 [DDD]
Haydn, J.:Pno Music, w. Imogen Cooper (pno), N. Marriner (cnd), Academy of St. Martin in the Fields—Andante w. Vars (H.XVII/6); Sons Nos. 49, 50 & 52 Philips 25–▲ 446920–2
Haydn, J.:Sons Pno—H.XVI/32, 34, 42 Philips ▲ 412228–2 [DDD]
Haydn, J.:Sons Pno—H.XVI/48, 50, 51 Philips ▲ 411045–2 [DDD]
Haydn, J.:Sons Pno—H.XVI/20, 32, 34, 37, 40, 42, 48, 49, 50, 51, 52 Philips 4–▲ 416643–2 [DDD/ADD]
Haydn, J.:Sons Pno—H.XVI/37, 40, 52 Philips ▲ 416365–2 [DDD]
Haydn, J.:Son Pno, H.XVII/6, "Andante with Vars" Philips 4–▲ 416643–2 [DDD]
Haydn, J.:Son Pno, H.XVII/6, "Andante with Vars" Philips ▲ 416365–2 [DDD]
Largo I, w. Vladimir Ashkenazy (pno), Alicia de Larrocha (pno), Julius Katchen (pno), András Schiff (pno), Iliana Vered (pno), et al. Celestial Harmonies ▲ 35509–2 2–■ 35509–4
Largo II, w. Vladimir Ashkenazy (pno), Alicia de Larrocha (pno), Julius Katchen (pno), András Schiff (pno), Iliana Vered (pno), et al. Celestial Harmonies ▲ 19504–2 ■ 19504–4
Liszt, F.:Années de pèlerinage 1 Philips ▲ 420202–2 [DDD]
Liszt, F.:Années de pèlerinage 2 Philips ▲ 420169–2 [DDD]
Liszt, F.:Harmonies poétiques et religieuses—Funérailles Philips ▲ 434078–2 [DDD]
Liszt, F.:Hungarian Rhaps—Nos. 2, 3, 8, 13, 15 & 17; plus Csárdás obstiné Vanguard Classics ▲ OVC 4024 [ADD]
Liszt, F.:Operatic Paraphrases & Transcriptions—Wagner:Isolde's Liebestod Philips ▲ 420202–2 [DDD]
Liszt, F.:Pno Music (misc)—Nuages gris; En rêve; Klavierstück, S.192/3 Philips ▲ 434078–2 [DDD]
Liszt, F.:Pno Music (misc)—Vexilla regis prodeunt; Années de pèlerinage III—Sursum corda; Weihnachtsbaum—Abendglocken; Harmonies poétiques et religieuses—Invocation Philips ▲ 420156–2 [DDD]
Liszt, F.:Pno Music (misc), w. B. Haitink (cnd), London PO—Années de pèlerinage I, II, III, Nos. 2–5; Bénédiction de Dieu; Berceuse; Cons for Pno Nos. 1 & 2; Csardas Macabre; Danse Macabre; En Rêve; Evening Bells; Fantasy & Fugue on BACH; Funerailles; Invocation; Klavierstück in F; Lugubrious Gondola Nos. 1 & 2; Mosonyis Grabgeleit; Nuages Gris; Pensée des morts; Richard Wagner Venezia; St. Francis Preaching & Walking; Schlaflos; Son in b; Unstern - Sinestre; Valse Oubliée; Vexilla Regis Prodeunt; Wagner–Liszt:Isolde's Death; Weinen, Klagen, Sorgen, Zagen Philips 25–▲ 446920–2
Liszt, F.:Son Pno Philips ▲ 434078–2 [DDD]
Mendelssohn, F.:Vars sérieuses Philips ("Digital Classics" series) ▲ 426272–2 [DDD]
Mozart, W.A.:Arias, w. E. Schwarzkopf (sop), G. Szell (cnd), London SO—4 Concert arias EMI Classics ▲ CDH 63702
Mozart, W.A.:Complete Mozart Edition, w. Stephen Bishop Kovacevich (pno), Bruno Hoffmann (glass armonica), Beaux Arts Trio Philips 5–▲ 422514–2 [ADD]
Mozart, W.A.:Con 5 Pno, w. N. Marriner (cnd), Academy of St. Martin in the Fields Philips ▲ 416366–2 [DDD]
Mozart, W.A.:Con 6 Pno, w. N. Marriner (cnd), Academy of St. Martin in the Fields Philips ▲ 416366–2 [DDD]
Mozart, W.A.:Con 8 Pno, w. N. Marriner (cnd), Academy of St. Martin in the Fields Philips ▲ 411468–2 [DDD]
Mozart, W.A.:Con 9 Pno, w. N. Marriner (cnd), Academy of St. Martin in the Fields Philips ("Duo" series) 2–▲ 442571–2
Mozart, W.A.:Con 9 Pno, w. A. Janigro (cnd), Zagreb Solisti Vanguard Classics ▲ OVC 4015 [ADD]
Mozart, W.A.:Con 14 Pno, w. A. Janigro (cnd), Zagreb Solisti Vanguard Classics ▲ OVC 4015 [ADD]
Mozart, W.A.:Con 15 Pno, w. N. Marriner (cnd), Academy of St. Martin in the Fields Philips ▲ 400018–2 [DDD]
Mozart, W.A.:Con 15 Pno, w. N. Marriner (cnd), Academy of St. Martin in the Fields Philips ("Duo" series) 2–▲ 442571–2
Mozart, W.A.:Con 20 Pno, w. N. Marriner (cnd), Academy of St. Martin in the Fields Philips ♦ 0062635488
Mozart, W.A.:Con 20 Pno, w. N. Marriner (cnd), Academy of St. Martin in the Fields Philips ("Concert Classics" series) ▲ 420867–2
Mozart, W.A.:Con 21 Pno, w. N. Marriner (cnd), Academy of St. Martin in the Fields Philips ♦ 0062635488
Mozart, W.A.:Con 21 Pno, w. N. Marriner (cnd), Academy of St. Martin in the Fields Philips ▲ 400018–2 [DDD]
Mozart, W.A.:Con 22 Pno, w. N. Marriner (cnd), Academy of St. Martin in the Fields Philips ("Duo" series) 2–▲ 442571–2
Mozart, W.A.:Con 23 Pno, w. N. Marriner (cnd), Academy of St. Martin in the Fields Philips ▲ 420487–2 [ADD]
Mozart, W.A.:Con 24 Pno, w. N. Marriner (cnd), Academy of St. Martin in the Fields Philips ("Concert Classics" series) ▲ 420867–2 [ADD]
Mozart, W.A.:Con 25 Pno, w. O. Klemperer (cnd), New Philharmonia Orch *(rec live, Royal Festival Hall 1970)* Foyer ▲ FOY 2037 [AAD]
Mozart, W.A.:Con 25 Pno, w. N. Marriner (cnd), Academy of St. Martin in the Fields Philips ("Duo" series) 2–▲ 442571–2
Mozart, W.A.:Con 26 Pno, w. N. Marriner (cnd), Academy of St. Martin in the Fields Philips ▲ 411468–2 [DDD]
Mozart, W.A.:Con 27 Pno, w. N. Marriner (cnd), Academy of St. Martin in the Fields Philips ▲ 420487–2 [ADD]

Brendel, Alfred (pno) (cont.)
Mozart, W.A.:Con 27 Pno, w. N. Marriner (cnd), Academy of St. Martin in the Fields Philips ("Duo" series) 2–▲ 442571–2
Mozart, W.A.:Fant Pno, K.396 Vanguard Classics ▲ OVC 4025 [ADD]
Mozart, W.A.:Pno Music (misc), w. Imogen Cooper (pno), N. Marriner (cnd), Academy of St. Martin in the Fields—Adagio K.540; Cons for Pno Nos. 10, 14, 15, 19, 21, 26, 27; Fant K.475; Rondo K.511; Sons Nos. 8, 11, 13, 14 Philips 25–▲ 446920–2
Mozart, W.A.:Pno Music (misc)—Son in a, K.310; Fant in c, K.475; Son in c, K.457; Son in B♭, K.333; Son in A, K.331; Adagio in b, K.540; 9 Vars on a Minuet by Duport, K.573; Rondo in a, K.511 Philips ("Duo" series) 2–▲ 454 244–2
Mozart, W.A.:Qt Pno, K.478, w. Thomas Zehetmair (vn), Tabea Zimmermann (va), Richard Duven (vc), Peter Riegelbauer (db) Philips ▲ 446001–2
Mozart, W.A.:Qnt Pno, K.452, w. H. Holliger (ob), E. Brunner (cl), K. Thunemann (bn), H. Baumann (hn) Philips ▲ 420182–2 [DDD]
Mozart, W.A.:Qnt Pno, K.452, w. Hungarian Quintet members Allegretto ▲ ACD 8150 [ADD] ■ ACS 8150
Mozart, W.A.:Rondo Pno, K.511 Vanguard Classics ▲ OVC 4025 [ADD]
Mozart, W.A.:Rondo Pno Orch, K.382, w. N. Marriner (cnd), Academy of St. Martin in the Fields Philips ("Concert Classics" series) ▲ 420867–2 [ADD]
Mozart, W.A.:Son 8 Pno Vanguard Classics ▲ OVC 4025 [ADD]
Mozart, W.A.:Vars Pno, K.573 Philips ("Digital Classics" series) ▲ 426272–2 [DDD]
Mozart, W.A.:Vars Pno, K.573 Vanguard Classics ▲ OVC 4025 [ADD]
Mussorgsky, M.:Pictures at an Exhibition Philips ▲ 420156–2 [DDD]
Schoenberg, A.:Con Pno, w. M. Gielen (cnd), Southwest German RSO Baden–Baden Philips ▲ 446683–2
Schoenberg, A.:Con Pno, w. R. Kubelik (cnd), Bavarian RSO Deutsche Grammophon ("20th Century Classics" series) ▲ 431740–2 [ADD]
Schubert, Franz:Allegretto Pno, D.915 Philips ▲ 422229–2 [DDD]
Schubert, Franz:Fant Pno, D.760, "Wandererfantasie" Philips ("Silver Line" series) ▲ 420644–2 [ADD]
Schubert, Franz:German Dances Pno (misc)—10, from D.783 Philips ▲ 422229–2 [DDD]
Schubert, Franz:German Dances Pno (misc)—10, from D.783 Vanguard Classics ▲ OVC 4026 [ADD]
Schubert, Franz:Impromptus Pno (comp) Philips ▲ 422237–2 [DDD] □ 422237–5
Schubert, Franz:Moments musicaux Philips ▲ 422076–2 [DDD]
Schubert, Franz:Pno Music (misc) Philips 6–▲ 426128–2 [DDD]
Schubert, Franz:Pno Music (misc)—Allegretto D.915; 11 Ecossaises D.781; German Dances D.790; 16 German Dances; Hungarian Melody D.817; 6 Moments Musicaux D.780; Sons D.537, D.664, D.784, D.840, D.845, D.850, D.894, D.958, D.959, D.960; Wanderer Fant Philips 25–▲ 446920–2
Schubert, Franz:Pieces Pno, D.946 Philips ("Duo" series) 2–▲ 438703–2
Schubert, Franz:Pieces Pno, D.946 Philips ▲ 422075–2 [DDD]
Schubert, Franz:Qnt Pno, D.667, w. Cleveland String Quartet Philips ▲ 400078–2 [ADD]
Schubert, Franz:Qnt Pno, D.667, w. Thomas Zehetmair (vn), Tabea Zimmermann (va), Richard Duven (vc), Peter Riegelbauer (db) Philips ▲ 446001–2
Schubert, Franz:Schwanengesang, w. D. Fischer–Dieskau (bar) [G] Philips ▲ 411051–2 [DDD]
Schubert, Franz:Son Pno, D.537 Philips ("Digital Classics" series) ▲ 410605–2 [DDD]
Schubert, Franz:Son Pno, D.664 Philips ("Digital Classics" series) ▲ 410605–2 [DDD]
Schubert, Franz:Son Pno, D.840 Philips ▲ 422340–2 [DDD]
Schubert, Franz:Son Pno, D.840 Vanguard Classics ▲ OVC 4026 [ADD]
Schubert, Franz:Son Pno, D.845 Philips ▲ 422075–2 [DDD]
Schubert, Franz:Son Pno, D.894 Philips ▲ 422340–2 [DDD]
Schubert, Franz:Son Pno, D.958 Philips ▲ 422076–2 [DDD]
Schubert, Franz:Son Pno, D.958 Philips ("Duo" series) 2–▲ 438703–2
Schubert, Franz:Son Pno, D.958 Vanguard Classics ▲ OVC 4026 [ADD]
Schubert, Franz:Son Pno, D.959 Philips ▲ 422229–2 [DDD]
Schubert, Franz:Son Pno, D.959 Philips ("Duo" series) 2–▲ 438703–2
Schubert, Franz:Son Pno, D.960 Philips ("Silver Line" series) ▲ 420644–2 [ADD]
Schubert, Franz:Son Pno, D.960 Philips ▲ 422062–2 [DDD]
Schubert, Franz:Son Pno, D.960 Philips ("Duo" series) 2–▲ 438703–2
Schubert, Franz:Winterreise, w. D. Fischer–Dieskau (bar) Philips ▲ 411463–2 [DDD]
Schumann, R.:Con Pno, w. C. Abbado (cnd), London SO Philips ▲ 412251–2 [ADD]
Schumann, R.:Dichterliebe, w. D. Fischer–Dieskau (bar), A [G] Philips ▲ 416352–2 [DDD]
Schumann, R.:Fant Pno Vanguard Classics ▲ OVC 4027 [ADD]
Schumann, R.:Fant Pno Philips ▲ 411049–2 [DDD]
Schumann, R.:Fantasiestücke Pno, Op. 12 Philips ▲ 411049–2 [DDD]
Schumann, R.:Fantasiestücke Pno, Op. 12 Philips ▲ 434732–2
Schumann, R.:Kinderszenen Philips ▲ 434732–2
Schumann, R.:Kreisleriana Philips ▲ 434732–2
Schumann, R.:Liederkreis, Op. 39, w. D. Fischer–Dieskau (bar) [G] Philips ▲ 416352–2 [DDD]
Schumann, R.:Pno Music (misc), w. L. Maazel (cnd), Berlin PO, London SO—Abendleid; Adagio & Allegro; Con in a; Fant in C; Fantasiestücke; Kinderszenen; Kreisleriana; 3 Stücke in Volkston; 3 Romances; Symphonic Studies Philips 25–▲ 446920–2
Schumann, R.:Sym Etudes Vanguard Classics ▲ OVC 4027 [ADD]

Brendler, Charlene (pno)—see ORCHESTRAS & ENSEMBLES Streicher Trio

Brendstrup, Henrik (vc)
Bartók, B.:Rhap 1 Vc, w. Katrine Gislinge (pno) Kontrapunkt ▲ KPT 32217
Chopin, F.:Intro & Polonaise, "Polonaise brilliante", w. C. Edwards (pno) Kontrapunkt ▲ 32026 [DDD]
Chopin, F.:Son Vc, w. C. Edwards (pno) Kontrapunkt ▲ 32026 [DDD]
Gubaidulina, S.:Detto 2 Vc, w. F. Widekind (cnd), Athela Ensemble Kontrapunkt ▲ KPT 32176 [DDD]
Gubaidulina, S.:In Croce, w. J. Christiansen (org) Kontrapunkt ▲ KPT 32176 [DDD]
Gubaidulina, S.:Preludes (10) Vc Kontrapunkt ▲ KPT 32176 [DDD]
Janácek, L.:Fairy Tale, w. Katrine Gislinge (pno) Kontrapunkt ▲ KPT 32217
Janácek, L.:Presto, w. Katrine Gislinge (pno) Kontrapunkt ▲ KPT 32217
Kodály, Z.:Adagio Vn, w. Katrine Gislinge (pno) Kontrapunkt ▲ KPT 32217
Kodály, Z.:Son Vc & Pno, Op. 4, w. Katrine Gislinge (pno) Kontrapunkt ▲ KPT 32217
Kodály, Z.:Sonatina Vc & Pno, w. Katrine Gislinge (pno) Kontrapunkt ▲ KPT 32217
Liszt, F.:Vc & Pno Music, w. C. Edwards (pno)—Elegies Nos. 1 & 2, S.130 & S.131; Romance oubliée, S.132; La lugubre gondola, S.134 Kontrapunkt ▲ 32026 [DDD]
Maegaard, J.:Elegy, w. Anette Simonsen (mez), Eva Feldbæk (org) *(rec Copenhagen, 1995–96)* Marco Polo/Dacapo ▲ 8.224050 [DDD]
Mendelssohn, F.:Lied ohne Worte Vc, w. C. Edwards (pno) Kontrapunkt ▲ 32007 [DDD]
Mendelssohn, F.:Son 1 Vc, w. C. Edwards (pno) Kontrapunkt ▲ 32007 [DDD]
Mendelssohn, F.:Son 2 Vc, w. C. Edwards (pno) Kontrapunkt ▲ 32007 [DDD]
Mendelssohn, F.:Vars concertantes, w. C. Edwards (pno) Kontrapunkt ▲ 32007 [DDD]

Brennan, Jack (perc)
Handel, D.:The Poems of Our Climate, w. Sheryl Woods (sop), Pamela Watson (fl), Brian Delay (gtr), Val Griffen (vc), Anton Nel (pno), James Culley (perc), Allen Otte (perc), G. Samuel (cnd) Vienna Modern Masters ▲ VMM 2019 [DDD]

Brenner, E. (b ob)
Vivaldi, A.:Cons Diverse Instrs, w. G. Vicari (mand), C. de Filippis (mand), J. Wummer (fl), R. Morris (fl), W. Vacchiano (tpt), N. Prager (tpt), C. Stavrache (hp), A. Wurtzler (hp), J. Gorigliano (vn), L. Varga (vc), L. Bernstein (cnd), New York PO—in C, RV.558 *(rec Dec. 15, 1958)* Sony Classical ("Leonard Bernstein:The Royal Edition" series) ▲ SMK 47642 [ADD]

Brero, Vittorio (vn)
Brahms, J.:Qt 1 Pno, w. E. Fischer (pno), R. Nel (va), T. Schürgers (vc) *(rec Berlin, ca. 1939/41, Electrola DB)* Koch Historic ▲ 7701–2 [AAD]

INSTRUMENTALISTS 487

Bresciani, Vittorio (pno)
Liszt, F.:Operatic Paraphrases & Transcriptions—Reminiscences de Don Juan; Lacrimosa [based on Mozart's Requiem]; La serenata e l'orgia, grande fantaisie on Rossini's Soirées musicale; La gita in gondola, Soirée musicale No. 4; La pastorella dell'Alpi e Li marinari, 2nd fant. on Rossini's Soirées musicales; Fant. on 2 Motifs from Mozart's Figaro *(rec Dec. 1992)* Dynamic ▲ CDS 108 [DDD]
Liszt, F.:Song Transcriptions—18 Schubert transcriptions—12 Lieder (1838)—Auf dem Wasser zu singen; Ave Maria; Du bist die Ruh; Erlkönig; Frühlingsglaube; Gretchen am Spinnrade; Die junge Nonne; Meerestille; Rastlose Liebe; Sei mir gegrüsst; Ständchen (Horch, horch, die Lerch); Der Wanderer; 6 Müllerlieder (1847)—Der Jager; Der Müller und der Bach; Ungeduld; Das Wandern; Wohin? Dynamic ▲ CD 73 [DDD]

Bress, Hyman (vn)
Bloch, E.:Con Vn, w. J. Rohan (cnd), Prague SO *(rec Apr. 25–29, 1966)* Supraphon ("Collection" series) ▲ 11 0674-2 [ADD]
Bloch, E.:Suite hébraïque, w. J. Rohan (cnd), Prague SO *(rec Apr. 25–29, 1966)* Supraphon ("Collection" series) ▲ 11 0674-2 [ADD]

Breteau, Claire (vc)—see ORCHESTRAS & ENSEMBLES Denis Clavier String Quartet

Breuer, Cordula (rcr)
Vivaldi, A.:Cons Rcr, Concerto Cologne LaserLight ▲ 15634 [DDD]
Vivaldi, A.:Cons Rcr, w. Martin Sandhoff (rcr), Concerto Cologne LaserLight ▲ 14036 [DDD]

Breuer, Paul (db)
Dittersdorf, K.D. von:Son Va, w. F. Beyer (va) FSM-Adagio ▲ FCD 91 009 [ADD]

Brevig, Per-Christian (trbn)
Starer, R.:Con a 3, w. J. Rabbai (cl), G. Schwarz (tpt), A. Kaplan (cnd), Camerata String Orch *(rec 1972)* CRI ▲ CD 612 [ADD]

Brewer, Aline (hp)
Farnon, R.:Music of, w. R. Cohen (vn), Farnon, Gamley (cnd), Royal PO—Capt. Horatio Hornblower Suite; A la claire fontaine; Intermezzo for Harp & Strings; Lake of the Woods; A Promise of Spring; Rhapsody for Violin & Orchestra; State Occasion *(rec 1991)* Reference ▲ RR 47CD [DDD]
Mozart, W.A.:Con Fl Hp, w. J. Stinton (fl), T. Vásáry (cnd), Philharmonia Orch Collins Classics 2-▲ 70052 [DDD]
Romantic Works for Flute & Harp, w. J. Stinton (fl) Collins Classics ▲ COL 1008 [DDD]
The Flute Album, w. K. Jones (fl), Jane Pendlebury (vc), Catherine Edwards (pno) Conifer Classics 2-▲ 75605-51905-2 [DDD]

Brewer, Edward (hpd)
Albinoni, T.:Con in C Tpt, w. Gerard Schwarz (tpt), Ronald Roseman (ob), Susan Weiner (ob), Virginia Brewer (ob), Ronald MacCourt (bn), William Scribner (bn) Vox Box 2-▲ CDX 5124 [ADD]
Battistin, J.B.:Héraclitie et Démocrite, w. D. Fortunato (mez), J. Ostendorf (b-bar), R. Palmer (cnd), Brewer CO [period instrs] *(rec 1985)* Erasmus ▲ WVH 071 [DDD]
Handel, G.F.:Faramondo, w. Julianne Baird (sop—Clotilde), Mary Ellen Callahan (sop—Adolfo), D'Anna Fortunado (mez—Faramondo), Jennifer Lane (mez—Rosimonda), Drew Minter (alt—Gernando), Peter Castaldi (bar—Gustavo), Mark Singer (bar—Tebaldo), R. Palmer (cnd), Brewer CO [period instrs] Vox Classics 3-▲ VOX3 7536 [DDD]
Handel, G.F.:Imeneo, w. Julianne Baird (sop—Rosmene), Beverly Hoch (sop—Clomiri), D'Anna Fortunato (cta—Tirinto), Jan Opalach (bass—Argenio), John Ostendorf (bass—Imeneo), R. Palmer (cnd), Brewer CO Vox Box 2-▲ CDX 5135 [DDD]
Handel, G.F.:Sosarme, Rè di Media, w. Julinne Baird (sop—Elmira), D'Anna Fortunato (mez—Sosarme), Jennifer Lane (mez—Erenice), Drew Minter (ct—Melo), Rarmond Pellerin (ct—Argone), John Aler (ten—King Haliate), Nathaniel Watson (bass—Varo) Newport Classic 2-▲ NPT 85575 [DDD]
Hertel, J.W.:Con à cinque, w. Gerard Schwarz (tpt), Ronald Roseman (ob), Susan Weiner (ob), Virginia Brewer (ob), Ronald MacCourt (bn), William Scribner (bn) Vox Box 2-▲ CDX 5124 [ADD]
Telemann, G.P.:Cons Tpt, w. Gerard Schwarz (tpt), Ronald Roseman (ob), Susan Weiner (ob), Virginia Brewer (ob), Ronald MacCourt (bn), William Scribner (bn) Vox Box 2-▲ CDX 5124 [ADD]
Telemann, G.P.:Qt Bn, w. A. Weisberg (bn), S. Baron (fl), R. Roseman (ob)—in d Elektra/Nonesuch ■ 71352-4
Telemann, G.P.:Sons Fl & Hpd, w. D. Baron (fl)—in c Elektra/Nonesuch ■ 71352-4
Vivaldi, A.:Con Lt, w. P. Press (gtr), P. Peabody (vn), E. Lim (vn), J. Haffner (va), T. Mook (vc) ESS.A.Y ▲ CD 1004 [DDD] ■ C 1004 (D)
Vivaldi, A.:Trio Sons Gtr Vn, w. P. Press (gtr), P. Peabody (vn), R. Shell (vc)—(2) in C, RV.82 & in g, RV.85 ESS.A.Y ▲ CD 1004 [DDD] ■ C 1004 (D)
Vivaldi, A.:Trio Sons Vn Lt, w. Paul Peabody (vn), Peter Press (gtr), Roger Shell (vc) ESS.A.Y ▲ ESS 1004 [DDD]

Brewer, Edward (hpd/positiv org)
Telemann, G.P.:Con Tpt Strs in D, w. Edward Carroll (tpt/pic tpt), Diane Bruce (vn), Elizabeth Field (vn), Annabelle Hoffman (vc), Dongsok Shin (positiv org) *(rec Rye Presbyterian Church)* Helicon Classics ▲ HE 1009
Telemann, G.P.:Musique héroïque, w. Edward Carroll (tpt/pic tpt), Diane Bruce (vn), Elizabeth Field (vn), Annabelle Hoffman (vc), Dongsok Shin (positiv org) *(rec Rye Presbyterian Church)* Helicon Classics ▲ HE 1009
Telemann, G.P.:Sons Tpt, w. Edward Carroll (tpt/pic tpt), Diane Bruce (vn), Elizabeth Field (vn), Annabelle Hoffman (vc), Dongsok Shin (positiv org) *(rec Rye Presbyterian Church)* Helicon Classics ▲ HE 1009
Telemann, G.P.:Trio Sons, w. Edward Carroll (tpt/pic tpt), Diane Bruce (vn), Elizabeth Field (vn), Annabelle Hoffman (vc), Dongsok Shin (positiv org) *(rec Rye Presbyterian Church)* Helicon Classics ▲ HE 1009

Brewer, Edward (org)
Clérambault, L.N.:Cants, w. D. Fortunato (mez), J. Ostendorf (bass-bar), R. Palmer (cnd), Brewer CO—Le Soleil vainqueur (1721); Léandre et Héro [from Livre II (1713)] *(rec 1985)* Erasmus ▲ WVH 071 [DDD]

Brewer, Edward (org/hpd)
Baroque Trumpetissimo, w. D. Bilger (tpt), Stephen Burns (tpt), Edward Carroll (tpt), Alex Holton (tpt), Raymond Mase (tpt), Timothy Morrison (tpt), Lee Soper (tpt), Atsuko Sato (bn), Ben Harms (timp), Edward Brewer (org/hpd), Philharmonia Virtuosi [cnd:Richard Kapp] ESS.A.Y ▲ ESS 1035 [DDD]

Brewer, Virginia (ob)
Albinoni, T.:Con in C Tpt, w. Gerard Schwarz (tpt), Ronald Roseman (ob), Susan Weiner (ob), Ronald MacCourt (bn), William Scribner (bn), Edward Brewer (hpd) Vox Box 2-▲ CDX 5124 [ADD]
Bach, J.S.:Con Vn & Ob, w. Y. Waldman (vn), J. Somary (cnd), Amor Artis Orch Omega ▲ OCD 1013 [DDD]
Hertel, J.W.:Con à cinque, w. Gerard Schwarz (tpt), Ronald Roseman (ob), Susan Weiner (ob), Ronald MacCourt (bn), William Scribner (bn), Edward Brewer (hpd) Vox Box 2-▲ CDX 5124 [ADD]
Telemann, G.P.:Cons Tpt, w. Gerard Schwarz (tpt), Ronald Roseman (ob), Susan Weiner (ob), Ronald MacCourt (bn), William Scribner (bn), Edward Brewer (hpd) Vox Box 2-▲ CDX 5124 [ADD]

Brey, Carter (vc)
Farrenc, J.-L.:Trio Vn, w. K. Hoover (fl), B. Weintraub (pno) Leonarda ■ LE 304
Kernis, A.J.:Still Movement with Hymn, w. Pamela Frank (vn), Paul Neubauer (va), Christopher O'Riley (pno) *(rec Florence Gould Auditorium, Seiji Ozawa Hall, Tanglewood, June 19 & 20, 1995)* Argo ▲ 448174-2 [DDD]
Lipkis, L.:Scaramouche Vc & Orch, w. D. Spieth (cnd), Lehigh Valley CO Koch International Classics ▲ KIC 7166 [DDD]
Milhaud, D.:La Création du monde (suite), w. André Previn (pno), Ani Kavafian (vn), Julie Rosenfeld (vn), Toby Hoffman (va) *(rec Manhattan Center Studios, New York City, May 25-26, 1993)* RCA Red Seal ▲ 09026-68181-2 [DDD]
O'Connor, M.:Qt Vn, w. Mark O'Connor (vn), Daniel Phillips (va), Edgar Meyer (db) *(rec Blair Recital Hall, Vanderbilt Univ., Nashville, TN, Dec. 1990)* Warner Bros. ▲ 45846-2
Saint-Saëns, C.:Spt Tpt, w. André Previn (pno), Thomas Stevens (tpt), Julie Rosenfeld (vn), Ani Kavafian (vn), Toby Hoffman (va), Jack Kulowitsch (db) *(rec Manhattan Center Studios, New York City, May 25-26, 1993)* RCA Red Seal ▲ 09026-68181-2 [DDD]
Ulehla, L.:Elegy, w. K. Hoover (fl), B. Weintraub (pno) Leonarda ■ LE 304

Breyer, Gerhard (vn)—see ORCHESTRAS & ENSEMBLES Vienna Lanner Ensemble

Breyer, Wolfgang (ctbn)—see ORCHESTRAS & ENSEMBLES Vienna Lanner Ensemble

Brezina, Josef (vn)
Bach, J.S.:Cons Vn (comp), w. E. Duvier (cnd), Camerata Romana PMG ("Vienna Master" series) ▲ CD 160101 [DDD]
Bach, J.S.:Con for 2 Vns, w. F. Elias (vn), E. Duvier (cnd), Camerata Romana PMG ("Vienna Master" series) ▲ CD 160101 [DDD]
Bruch, M.:Con 1 Vn, w. A. Scholz (cnd), London Festival Orch PMG ("Vienna Master" series) ▲ CD 160112 [DDD]

Bria, Giovanni (pno)
Paganini, N.:Caprices Vn, w. Ingolf Turban (vn) [arr. R. Schumann for violin & piano] *(rec Nov. 1993, May, June & Ju)* Claves ▲ CD 9416 [DDD]

Briasco, Giuseppe (gtr)—see ORCHESTRAS & ENSEMBLES Paganini String Quartet

Briasco, Pino (vn)—see also ORCHESTRAS & ENSEMBLES Paganini String Quartet
Paganini, N.:Duetto amoroso Vn, w. Bruno Pignata (vn) *(rec Dynamic's Genoa, Dec 10–13, 1995)* Dynamic ▲ CD 152 [DDD]

Bride, Kathleen (hp)
Bach, J.S.:Con 1 for 2 Hpds, w. Jon Gillock (org)—Adagio [arr for org & hp] *(rec Church of the Ascension, New York, Nov 1995)* Milan ▲ 73138-35764-2 [DDD]
Grandjany, M.:Aria in Classic Style, w. Jon Gillock (org) *(rec Church of the Ascension, New York, Nov 1995)* Milan ▲ 73138-35764-2 [DDD]
Grandjany, M.:Rhap Hp *(rec Church of the Ascension, New York, Nov 1995)* Milan ▲ 73138-35764-2 [DDD]
Handel, G.F.:Con Hp [arr for hp] *(rec Church of the Ascension, New York, Nov 1995)* Milan ▲ 73138-35764-2 [DDD]
Mysteries Beyond:Songs & Chants in Praise of Mary, w. [cnd:Dennis Keene], Voices of Ascension, V. Cole (ten), Patrick Stephens (pno), M. Kruczek (org) *(rec Apr. 17, 28–30, 1993)* Delos ▲ DE 3138 [DDD]
White, L.:Suite Hp, w. Jon Gillock (org)—Aria; Fugue *(rec Church of the Ascension, New York, Nov 1995)* Milan ▲ 73138-35764-2 [DDD]

Bride, Philip (vn)
Bach, J.S.:Con 1 Vn, w. French Instrumental Ensemble *(rec Nov 5 & 6, 1988)* Pierre Verany ▲ PVY 730020 [DDD]
Bach, J.S.:Con 2 Vn, w. French Instrumental Ensemble *(rec Nov 5 & 6, 1988)* Pierre Verany ▲ PVY 730020 [DDD]
Bach, J.S.:Con Vn & Ob, w. Daniel Arrignon (ob), French Instrumental Ensemble *(rec Nov 5 & 6, 1988)* Pierre Verany ▲ PVY 730020 [DDD]
Bach, J.S.:Con for 2 Vns, w. Christian Crenne (vn), French Instrumental Ensemble *(rec Nov 5 & 6, 1988)* Pierre Verany ▲ PVY 730020 [DDD]
Mozart, W.A.:Concertone Vns, w. Christian Crenne (vn), K. Redel (cnd), French Instrumental Ensemble *(rec Apr. 9 & 10, 1990)* Pierre Verany ▲ PVY 730024 [DDD]
Mozart, W.A.:Sinf concertante Vn, K.364, w. Serge Soufflard (va), K. Redel (cnd), French Instrumental Ensemble *(rec Apr. 9 & 10, 1990)* Pierre Verany ▲ PVY 730024 [DDD]

Bridger, Ellen (vc)
Beside Thy Cradle, w. [cnd:Ralph B. Woodward], Salt Lake Children's Choir, Tamara B. Oswald (hp), Janet Peterson (hp), Kelly Parkinson (vn), Victoria Ferris (vn), Hadley Ferris (va) *(rec Maurice Abravanel Hall, Salt Lake City)* Cherbourne ▲ CH 121

Bridges, S. (cl)
Goosen, F.:Son Cl, w. P. Hood (pno) CRI ▲ CD 665 [ADD]

Bridgewater, Adrienne (hp)
A Baby's Prayer, w. C. Mellis (fl) PHD ▲ PHD 570016

Brient, Patrice (h-g/rebeck/voc)
Tensons e partimens de Trobairitz, Vol. 3, w. G. Zuchetto (sgr), Katia Caré (sgr), Gisela Bellsolà (sgr), Guy Robert (medieval lt/oud/hp) Gallo ▲ CD 769 [DDD]
Troubador Songs of the 12th & 13th Centuries, w. G. Zuchetto (sgr), Jacques Khoudir (perc) Gallo ▲ CD 529

Brigandi, Loredana (pno)
Moscheles, I.:Studien Nuova Era ▲ NUO 7226

Briggs, Claire (hn)
Mozart, W.A.:Cons Hn, w. S. Kovacevich (cnd), Royal Liverpool PO Classics for Pleasure ▲ CDCFP 4589 [DDD]

Briggs, David (org)
Alain, J.:Le Jardin suspendu Priory ▲ PRI 568 [DDD]
Bach, J.S.:Preludes & Fugues, BWV 531–552—in G, BWV 541; in E♭, BWV 552 Priory ▲ PRI 568 [DDD]
Cochereau, P.:Boléro on a Theme of Charles Racquet Priory ▲ PRI 568 [DDD]
Dukas, P.:L'Apprenti sorcier—Scherzo Priory ▲ PRI 568 [DDD]
Franck, C.:Pièce héroïque Priory ▲ PRI 568 [DDD]
Great European Organs, Vol. 16, w. S. Cleobury (org) Priory ▲ PRCD 284 [DDD]
Haydn, J.:Flute-Clock Pieces—3 sels Priory ▲ PRI 568 [DDD]
Improvisation:The Illusionist's Art Priory ▲ PRI 428 [DDD]
Tchaikovsky, P.:Nutcracker Suite—Miniature-Ov; Waltz of the Flowers Priory ▲ PRI 568 [DDD]

Brind, Alan (vn)
Chausson, E.:Poème Vn, w. V. Handley (cnd), Royal PO Chandos ("Collect" series) ▲ CHAN 6514 [DDD]
Sibelius, J.:Con Vn, w. V. Handley (cnd), Royal PO Chandos ("Collect" series) ▲ CHAN 6514 [DDD]

Bringas, Alfredo (perc)—see ORCHESTRAS & ENSEMBLES Tambuco Camerata

Brings, Allen (pno)
Brings, A.:Son Cl, w. E. Gilmore (cl) Centaur ▲ CRC 2156
Clementi, M.:Sons Pno 4-Hands, w. G. Chinn (pno)—Sons., Opp. 3/2; 6/1; 14/1 & 3 Centaur ▲ CRC 2046 [AAD]

Brink, Frank van den (cl)
Bavicchi, J.:Short Son, w. Pinkham (hpd) CRI ■ C 138
Cowell, H.:Prelude, w. Pinkham (hpd) CRI ■ C 109
Hovhaness, A.:Duet Vn & Hpd, w. Pinkham (hpd) CRI ■ C 109
Pinkham, D.:Cantilena & Capriccio, w. D. Pinkham (hpd) CRI ■ C 109
Rossini, G.:Vars Cl, w. J. Reynolds (cnd), European CO Per Musica *(rec Aug. 1986)* Globe ▲ GLO 6014 [DDD]
Rossini, G.:Vars Obbligato Instruments, w. J. Reynolds (cnd), European CO Per Musica *(rec Aug. 1986)* Globe ▲ GLO 6014 [DDD]
Roussel, A.:Chamber Music, w. Paul Verhey (fl/pic), Hans Roerade (ob), Jos de Lange (bn), Herre-Jan Stegenga (vc), Jet Röling (pno), Schoenberg String Quartet—Trio for Fl, Va & Vc, Op. 40; Qt for Strs, Op. 45; Andante & Scherzo for Fl & Pno, Op. 51; Pipe for Pic & Pno; Trio for Strs, Op. 58; Music from Elpenor for Fl & Str Qt, Op. 59; Andante from an unfinished Ww Trio for Ob, Cl & Bn Olympia ▲ OLY 460 [DDD]
Schubert, Franz:Der Hirt auf dem Felsen, w. D. Aalbers (sop), S. Hoogland (pno) [G] Partridge ▲ 1132-2 [DDD]

Brissot, Irène (hp)
Ropartz, G.:Choral Music, w. Christian Papis (nar), Didier Henry (bar), Vincent Le Texier (b-bar), Christine Lajarrige (pno), Eric Lebrun (org), M. Piquemal (cnd), Nancy SO, French Radio Chorus Soloists, Vittoria Regional French Choir—Psaume 136; Dimanche; Nocturne; Les Vêpres sonnent; Le Miracle de Saint Nicolas *(rec Salle Poirel, Nancy, Apr. 22–24, 1994)* Marco Polo ▲ 8.223774 [DDD]

Brito, Rodolfo (pno)
Lecuona, E.:Pno Music—Ante el Escorial; Danzas Afro-Cubanas; A la Antigua; Crisantemo Vals; Vals Azul; Danzas Cubanas; Córdoba; Malagueña [from Andalucia Suite] *(rec Univ of Maryland, Baltimore, Apr 1996)* Elan ("La Musica de Cuba" series) ▲ CD 82272 [DDD]
Touzet, R.:Dedicación al Maestro Elan ("La Musica de Cuba" series) ▲ 82272 [DDD]
Touzet, R.:Pno Music—Siboney/Noche Azul (paraphrase); Dedicacion al Maestro *(rec Univ of Maryland, Baltimore, Apr 1996)* Elan ("La Musica de Cuba" series) ▲ CD 82272 [DDD]

488 ▲ = CD ♦ = Enhanced CD Δ = MD ■ = Cassette Tape □ = DCC

Brittan, P. (fl)—see ORCHESTRAS & ENSEMBLES Thamyris

Britten, Benjamin (pno)
- Britten, H.:Folksong Arrs, w. J. Cross (sop), P. Pears (ten) — EMI Classics ▲ CDMB 64727
- Britten, H.:Hölderlin-Fragmente, w. P. Pears (ten) — London 2-▲ 433200-2
- Britten, H.:The Holy Sonnets of John Donne, w. P. Pears (ten) [E] — London 3-▲ 417428-2 [ADD]
- Britten, H.:The Holy Sonnets of John Donne, w. P. Pears (ten) — EMI Classics ▲ CDC 54605
- Britten, H.:Introduction & Rondo alla burlesca & Mazurka elegiaca, w. Clifford Curzon (pno) *(rec 1941–44)* — Pearl ▲ PEA 9177 [ADD]
- Britten, H.:Introduction & Rondo alla burlesca & Mazurka elegiaca, w. S. Richter (pno)—No. 1 *(rec live, Aldeburgh 1967)* — Music & Arts ▲ CD 709-1 [AAD]
- Britten, H.:Sonnets of Michelangelo, w. Peter Pears (ten) *(rec 1941–44)* — Pearl ▲ PEA 9177 [ADD]
- Britten, H.:Sonnets of Michelangelo, w. P. Pears (ten) — EMI Classics ▲ CDC 54605
- Bridge, F.:Son Vc, w. Mstislav Rostropovich (vc) — London ("The Classic Sound" series) ▲ 443575-2
- Debussy, C.:En blanc et noir, w. S. Richter (pno) *(rec live, Aldeburgh 1967)* — Music & Arts ▲ CD 709-1 [AAD]
- Kathleen Ferrier Edition, Vol. 4, w. K. Ferrier (cta) *(rec 1948)* — London ▲ 433471-2 LM [ADD]
- McPhee, C.:Balinese Ceremonial Music, w. Colin McPhee (pno) — Pearl ▲ PEA 9177 [ADD]
- Mozart, W.A.:Son Pno 4-Hands, K.521, w. S. Richter (pno) *(rec live, Aldeburgh, 1967)* — Memories 2-▲ HR 4366/67 (m) [ADD]
- Mozart, W.A.:Son Pno 4-Hands, K.521, w. S. Richter (pno) *(rec live 1966)* — Music & Arts ▲ CD 721-1 [AAD]
- Mozart, W.A.:Son Pnos, K.448, w. S. Richter (pno) *(rec live, Aldeburgh, 1967)* — Music & Arts ▲ CD 709-1 [AAD]
- Schubert, Franz:Divertissement sur des motifs originaux français, D.823, w. S. Richter (pno)—Andantino varié [movt No. 2] *(rec live 1965)* — Music & Arts ▲ CD 722-1
- Schubert, Franz:Fant Pno, D.940, w. S. Richter (pno) *(rec live 1965)* — Music & Arts ▲ CD 722-1
- Schubert, Franz:Son Arpeggione, w. Mstislav Rostropovich (vc) — London ("The Classic Sound" series) ▲ 443575-2
- Schubert, Franz:Son Pno 4-Hands, D.812, w. S. Richter (pno) *(rec live 1965)* — Music & Arts ▲ CD 721-1 [AAD]
- Schubert, Franz:Vars on an Original Theme Pno 4-Hands, w. S. Richter (pno) *(rec live 1964)* — Music & Arts ▲ CD 722-1
- Schumann, R.:Bilder aus Osten, w. S. Richter (pno) *(rec live 1966, Aldeburgh)* — Music & Arts ▲ CD 709-1 [AAD]

Brittin, Anthony (hn)
- Van Appledorn, M.J.:Patterns, w. J. Whitaker (hn), M. Walzel (hn), L. Dawson (hn), H. Landers (hn) — Opus One ▲ CD 162

Britton, David (org)
- Bach, Buxtehude, & Friends — Delos ▲ DE 1020 [ADD]
- Gargoyles & Chimeras:Exotic Works for Organ — Delos ▲ DCD 3077 [DDD]
- Organo Deco:Sophisticated American Organ Music, ca. 1915–1950 — Delos ▲ DE 3111 [DDD]

Britton, Harold (org)
- Franck, C.:Panis angelicus [arr for org; Walsall Town Hall Org] — ASV Quicksilva ▲ ASQ 6175
- Organ Extravaganza — ASV ("White Line" series) ▲ ASV 2064 [DDD]
- Pachelbel, J.:Canon — ASV ("White Line" series) ▲ WHL 2064 [DDD]
- Widor, C.M.:Sym 5 Org [organ of the Royal Albert Hall, London] — ASV Quicksilva ▲ QS 6051 [ADD/DDD]

Bro, Paul (s sax)—see also ORCHESTRAS & ENSEMBLES Chicago Saxophone Quartet
- Linn, R.:Con S Sax, w. J. Boyd (cnd), Indiana State Univ Symphonic Wind Ensemble *(rec 1994)* — Truemedia ▲ D 94127

Broadbent, Alan (pno)
- Vivaldi, A.:Cons Vn, Op. 8/1–4, "The Four Seasons", w. Eddie Daniels (cl), Peter Erskine (dr), Dave Carpenter (db) *(rec California State University, Long Beach, CA, Mar 15, 1996)* — Shanachie ▲ SHA 5017 ■ SHA 5017

Broadway, Kenneth (pno)
- Mélange:French Music for Bassoon, w. C. Millard (bn), Camille Churchfield (fl) — Summit ▲ DCD 128 [DDD] ■ DCD 128
- Saint-Saëns, C.:Carnival of the Animals, w. P. Schickele (nar), R. Markham (pno), Y. Levi (cnd), Atlanta SO [poems by Schickele] *(rec Mar. 20 & June 16, 1993)* — Telarc ▲ CD 80350 [DDD] ■ CS 30350
- Vaughan Williams, R.:Con Pno, w. R. Markham (pno), Y. Menuhin (cnd), Royal PO — Virgo ▲ CDZ 61105
- Vaughan Williams, R.:Sym 5, w. R. Markham (pno), Y. Menuhin (cnd), Royal PO — Virgo ▲ CDZ 61105

Brochmann, Per (rcr)
- Sammartini, G.:Cons Rcr, w. B. Fiskum (cnd), Trondheim Soloists—in F *(rec July 1993)* — Victoria ▲ VCD 19078
- Telemann, G.P.:Con in C Rcr, w. B. Fiskum (cnd), Trondheim Soloists *(rec July 1993)* — Victoria ▲ VCD 19078
- Vivaldi, A.:Cons Rcr, w. B. Fiskum (cnd), Trondheim Soloists *(rec July 1993)* — Victoria ▲ VCD 19078

Brock, John (org)
- A Tonnoccoo Organ Tour:8 Pipe Organs, Historic & Recent, w. J. Brock (org) *(rec May, June & July, 1992)* — Raven ▲ OAR 270

Brockman, M. (sax)
- Karpen, R.:Saxonomy, w. R. Karpen (elec) — Centaur ▲ CRC 2144 [DDD]

Brodard, Thierry (vn)—see ORCHESTRAS & ENSEMBLES Paris String Quartet

Broderson, Elsebeth (pno)
- Stolarczyk, W.:Earth Air Fire Water, w. Amalie Malling (pno), John Damgaard (pno), Anne Øland (pno), Teddy Teirup (pno), Friedrich Gürtler (pno), Rosalind Bevan (pno), Poul Rosenbaum (pno), Rodolfo Llambias (pno), Bella Horn-Ribera (pno), Anders Riber (pno), Elisabeth Sigurdsson (pno), Thomas Tronheim (pno), Erik Kaltoft (pno), Jørgen Hald Nielsen (pno), Aino Gilemann (pno), Birgit Kjær (pno), Jørgen Thomsen (pno), Gunhild Donslund (pno), Henrik Bo Hansen (pno), Lone Karlsson (pno), Erik Fessel (pno), Lasse Nilsson (pno), Janos Ferenczi (pno), Erik Bach (pno), Axel Momme (pno), Arne de Cros Dich (pno), Sven Micha Slot (pno), Hanne Bramsen Buhl (pno), Lili Olesen (pno), Susannah Carlsson (pno), Ulla Erml (pno), Vagn Sørensen (pno), Leif Greibe (pno), Bodil Krogh (pno), Kirsten Ottosen (pno), Inger Bergenholz (pno), Karsten Gylendorf (pno), Bjønr Elkjær (pno), Jacob Bjørn Jensen (pno), Jørgen Kaad (pno), Anne Marie Hjelm (pno), Carl Ulrik Munk Andersen (pno), Poul Lumbye (pno), Oluf Hildebrandt Nielsen (pno), Joachim Olsson (pno), Peter Pade Ramsøe Jacobsen (pno), Astrid Pollmann (pno), Jette Borsch (pno), Kirsten Karlshøj (pno), Maria Teresa Assing (pno), Allan Dahl Hansen (pno), Johan Hugossen (pno), Tine Fenger Pederson (pno), Arne Jørgen Fæø (pno), Anja Høgsted (pno), Anne Sophie Parbo (pno), Inga Lindmark (pno), Teresa Drabik Stathakis (pno), Anne Ruth Ferenczi (pno), Irene Hasager (pno), Yuka Ichikawa (pno), Birgitte Baur (pno), Malene Thastum (pno), Jens E. Rasmussen (pno), Birgitte Zielke (pno), Claus Zielke (pno), Stefan Kasch (pno), Bin Qiao (pno), Inger Johanne Teirup (pno), Lindy Rosborg (pno), Liisa Heininen (pno), David Højer (pno), Ellen Refstrup (pno), Thomas K. Søorensen (pno), Erik Kure (pno), Michael Rauff (pno), Jan beck Eriksson (pno), Tanja Zapolski (pno), Vibeke Skagbo (pno), Pål Eide Lindtner (pno), Ha-Young Sul (pno), Benedicte Palko (pno), Inke Kesseler (pno), Anne Marie Meineche (pno), Sverre Larsen (pno), Kasper Peter Bach (pno), Elisabetta Eliseo (pno), Olga Magieres (pno), Carl Erik Kühl (pno), Thorkild Borup Nielsen (pno), Valeria Zanini (pno), Lars Stenhoft (perc), Dennis Boel (perc), Winnie Dahlgren (perc), Susanne Vind (perc), Claus Byrith (elec), Anne Marie Storm (elec), J. Ribera (cnd) *(rec live, Koldinghaus Castle, Denmark, May 2, 1996)* — Danica ▲ DCD 1996

Brodie, Gary (cl/bass chalumeaux)
- The Early Clarinet Family, w. K. Puddy (cl), P. Price (bass chalumeaux), Susan Dent (baroque hn), Alastair Mitchell (8-keyed bn), Malcolm Martineau (pno) — Clarinet Classics ▲ CC 0004

Brodie, Paul (sax)
- Duets:Ofra Harnoy & Friends, w. O. Harnoy (vc), Michael Dussek (pno), Orford String Quartet, Maureen Forrester (cta), Andrew Davis (pno), Jeanne Baxtresser (fl), Catherine Wilson (pno), Shauna Rolston (vc), Armin Strings, Canadian Piano Trio, Adele Armin (vn) — Mastersound ▲ MST 30 [DDD]
- The Golden Age of the Saxophone, w. Myriam Schechter (pno) — Musica Viva ▲ MVCD 1005 [ADD]
- Ofra Harnoy & Friends, w. O. Harnoy (vc), Orford String Quartet, J. Baxtresser (fl), M. Forrester (cta), M. Dussek (pno), et al. — Pro Arte ▲ CDD 552 [DDD]

Brodo, Amy (vc)
- Baroque Favorites, w. Kol, B. (rcr), D. Shemer (hpd) — PWK Classics ▲ PWK 1138 [DDD]

Brodsky, Vadim (vn)
- Sibelius, J.:Con Vn, w. J. Salwarowski (cnd), Polish National RSO Katowice — ASV Quicksilva ▲ QS 6016 [DDD]
- Tchaikovsky, P.:Con Vn, w. A. Wit (cnd), Polish National RSO Katowice — ASV Quicksilva ▲ QS 6016 [DDD]
- Tchaikovsky, P.:Con Vn, w. A. Straszynski (cnd), Polish National RSO Katowice *(rec Katowice, Poland, Aug 1988)* — Arts ▲ 447144-2 [DDD]
- Tchaikovsky, P.:Sérénade méloncolique, w. A. Straszynski (cnd), Polish National RSO Katowice *(rec Katowice, Poland, Aug 1988)* — Arts ▲ 447144-2 [DDD]
- Tchaikovsky, P.:Valse-Scherzo Vn, w. A. Straszynski (cnd), Polish National RSO Katowice *(rec Katowice, Poland, Aug 1988)* — Arts ▲ 447144-2 [DDD]

Brodzky, Thomas (vn)
- Bach, J.S.:Con for 2 Vns, w. A. Stadlmayer (vn), T. Karolski (cnd), Camerata Romana — Vivace ▲ E 506

Broek, W. van den (org)
- Mendelssohn, F.:Sons Org [organ of the Old Church, Delft] *(rec Sept. 17, 1992)* — Emergo ▲ EC 3999 [DDD]
- Reger, M.:Monologe *(rec June 4, 1992)* — Emergo ▲ EC 3998 [DDD]

Broiles, M. (tpt)
- Walton, W.:Façade, w. J. Bookspan (nar), S. Baron (fl), C. Russon (cl), H. Estrin (sax), K. Moore (vc), H. Harris (perc), D. Epstein (cnd) — Allegretto ▲ ACD 8153 [ADD] ■ ACD 8153

Brokowski, Marian (pno)
- Polish Piano Music, w. Teresa Rutkowska (pno), Maria Nosowska (pno), Baroara Halska (pno) — Olympia ▲ OLY 394 [AAD]

Bron, Zakhar (vn)
- Prokofiev, S.:Mélodies, w. I. Vinogradova (pno) — Giulia ▲ GS 201017 [DDD]
- Tchaikovsky, P.:Sérénade mélancolique, w. I. Vinogradova (pno) — Giulia ▲ GS 201017 [DDD]

Bronfman, Yefim (pno)
- Arensky, A.:Trio 1 Pno, w. C.-L. Lin (vn), G. Hoffman (vc) *(rec Aug 25–27, 1992)* — Sony Classical ▲ SK 53269 [DDD]
- Bartók, B.:Cons Pno (comp), w. E.-P. Salonen (cnd), Los Angeles PO — Sony Classical ▲ SK 66718
- Brahms, J.:Sons Vn (comp), w. I. Stern (vn) *(rec Dec. 18–19, 1991)* — Sony Classical ▲ SK 53107 [DDD]
- Mozart, W.A.:Sons Vn Pno (comp), w. I. Stern (vn)—in C, K.296; in B♭, K.454; in A, K.526 *(rec Mar. 13–16, 1993)* — Sony Classical ▲ SK 53972 [DDD]
- Mozart, W.A.:Sons Vn Pno (comp), w. Isaac Stern (vn)—K.304, 377, 481 & 547 — Sony Classical ▲ SK 61962
- Mozart, W.A.:Sons Vn Pno (misc), w. Isaac Stern (vn)—K. 302, 303, 305, 376, 380 — Sony Classical ▲ SK 64309
- Mussorgsky, M.:Pictures at an Exhibition — Sony Classical ▲ SK 46481
- Prokofiev, S.:Con 1 Pno, w. Z. Mehta (cnd), Israel PO *(rec Nov. 14–25, 1991)* — Sony Classical ▲ SK 52483 [DDD]
- Prokofiev, S.:Con 2 Pno, w. Z. Mehta (cnd), Israel PO *(rec July 8–17, 1993)* — Sony Classical ▲ SK 58966 [DDD]
- Prokofiev, S.:Con 3 Pno, w. Z. Mehta (cnd), Israel PO *(rec Nov. 14–25, 1991)* — Sony Classical ▲ SK 52483 [DDD]
- Prokofiev, S.:Con 4 Pno, w. Z. Mehta (cnd), Israel PO *(rec July 8–17, 1993)* — Sony Classical ▲ SK 58966 [DDD]
- Prokofiev, S.:Con 5 Pno, w. Z. Mehta (cnd), Israel PO *(rec Nov. 14–25, 1991)* — Sony Classical ▲ SK 52483 [DDD]
- Prokofiev, S.:Ov on Hebrew Themes, w. Giora Feidman (cl), Juilliard String Quartet *(rec Richardson Auditorium, Alexander Hall, Princeton Univ, Princeton, NJ, May 18, 1994)* — Sony Classical ("Greatest Hits" series) ▲ MLK 69249 [DDD] ■ LT 69
- Prokofiev, S.:Ov on Hebrew Themes, w. G. Feidman (cl), Juilliard String Quartet *(rec May 18, 1994)* — Sony Classical ▲ SK 58966 [DDD]
- Prokofiev, S.:Son 1 Pno *(rec Sept. 17–21, 1991)* — Sony Classical ▲ SK 52484 [DDD]
- Prokofiev, S.:Son 4 Pno *(rec Sept. 17–21, 1991)* — Sony Classical ▲ SK 52484 [DDD]
- Prokofiev, S.:Son 6 Pno *(rec Sept. 17–21, 1991)* — Sony Classical ▲ SK 52484 [DDD]
- Prokofiev, S.:Son 7 Pno — CBS ▲ MK 44680 [DDD]
- Prokofiev, S.:Son 8 Pno — CBS ▲ MK 44680 [DDD]
- Rachmaninoff, S.:Con 2 Pno, w. E.-P. Salonen (cnd), Philharmonia Orch — Sony Classical ▲ SK 47183
- Rachmaninoff, S.:Con 3 Pno, w. E.-P. Salonen (cnd), Philharmonia Orch — Sony Classical ▲ SK 47183
- Stravinsky, I.:Scenes Pno — Sony Classical ▲ SK 46481
- Tchaikovsky, P.:Pno Music—Dumka (Russian Rustic Scene), Op. 59 — Sony Classical ▲ SK 46481
- Tchaikovsky, P.:Trio Pno, w. C.-L. Lin (vn), G. Hoffman (vc) *(rec Aug. 25–27, 1992)* — Sony Classical ▲ SK 53269 [DDD]

Bronne, Ariana (vn)
- Vivaldi, A.:Cons Vn, Op. 8/1–4, "The Four Seasons", w. Monosoff (vn), Kwalwasser (va), G. Koutzen (vc), M. Goberman (cnd), New York Sinfonietta — Odyssey ■ YI 60132

Bronstein, F. (pno)—see ORCHESTRAS & ENSEMBLES Aequalis

Bronzi, Enrico (vc)—see ORCHESTRAS & ENSEMBLES Collegium Pro Musica

Brook, J. (pno)
- Gershwin, G.:Music of, w. Xalapa SO—Strike up the Band; The Man I Love; Foggy Day; Embraceable You; Love Walked in; My Man's Gone Now; But Not for Me; Love Is Sweeping the Country; Of Thee I Sing — IMP Classics ▲ IMPPCD 1057 [DDD]

Brook, Paige (fl)
- Falla, M. de:Con Hpd, w. I. Kipnis (hpd), H. Gomberg (ob), S. Drucker (cl), E. Chapo (vn), L. Munroe (vc), P. Boulez (cnd), New York PO *(rec Mar. 2, 1975)* — Sony Classical ▲ SBK 53264 ■ SBT 53264

Brooker, A. (vn)—see ORCHESTRAS & ENSEMBLES Florida String Quartet

Brooks, Davis (vn)
- Purcell, H.:Come Ye Sons of Art, w. Laura Goetz (ob), Sarah Weiner (ob), Lisa Brooks (vn), Jann Cosart (va), Mary Burke (vl), Vance Reese (db), Thomas Gerber (hpd), Henry H. Leck (cnd), Indianapolis Children's Choir [arr. Maurice Blower] *(rec The Lodge, May & June 1995)* — VAI Audio ▲ VAIA 1130 [DDD]
- Purcell, H.:Fly, Bold Rebellion (sels), w. Laura Goetz (ob), Sarah Weiner (ob), Lisa Brooks (vn), Jann Cosart (va), Mary Burke (vl), Vance Reese (db), Thomas Gerber (hpd), Henry H. Leck (cnd), Indianapolis Children's Choir—Be Welcome Then, Great Sir [arr. Steven Rickards] *(rec The Lodge, May & June 1995)* — VAI Audio ▲ VAIA 1130 [DDD]
- Purcell, H.:King Arthur (sels), w. Laura Goetz (ob), Sarah Weiner (ob), Lisa Brooks (vn), Jann Cosart (va), Mary Burke (vl), Vance Reese (db), Thomas Gerber (hpd), Henry H. Leck (cnd), Indianapolis Children's Choir—Fairest Isle [arr. Steven Rickards] *(rec The Lodge, May & June 1995)* — VAI Audio ▲ VAIA 1130 [DDD]

Brooks, George (instr)
- Riley, T.:In C, w. Bruce Ackley, Steve Adams, Don R. Baker, Chris Brown, Steve Coughlin, Blake Derby, Bill Douglass, Mihr'un'Nisa Douglass, Hank Dutt, David Harrington, Don Howe, Joan Jeanrenaud, Alden Jenks, Warner Jepson, Henry Kaiser, Jaron Lanier, Bill Maginnis, George Marsh, Shabda Owens, Jon Raskin, Gyan Riley, Terry Riley, Gino Robair, John Sackett, Ramón Sender, John Sherba, Toyji Tomita, Danny Tunick, William Winant, Evan Ziporyn *(rec Jan. 14, 1990)* — New Albion ▲ NA 071

Brooks, Lisa (vn)
- Purcell, H.:Come Ye Sons of Art, w. Laura Goetz (ob), Sarah Weiner (ob), Davis Brooks (vn), Jann Cosart (va), Mary Burke (vl), Vance Reese (db), Thomas Gerber (hpd), Henry H. Leck (cnd), Indianapolis Children's Choir [arr. Maurice Blower] *(rec The Lodge, May & June 1995)* — VAI Audio ▲ VAIA 1130 [DDD]
- Purcell, H.:Fly, Bold Rebellion (sels), w. Laura Goetz (ob), Sarah Weiner (ob), Davis Brooks (vn), Jann Cosart (va), Mary Burke (vl), Vance Reese (db), Thomas Gerber (hpd), Henry H. Leck (cnd), Indianapolis Children's Choir—Be Welcome Then, Great Sir [arr. Steven Rickards] *(rec The Lodge, May & June 1995)* — VAI Audio ▲ VAIA 1130 [DDD]

Brooks, Lisa (vn) (cont.)
Purcell, H.:King Arthur (sels), w. Laura Goetz (ob), Sarah Weiner (ob), Davis Brooks (vn), Jann Cosart (va), Mary Burke (vl), Vance Reese (db), Thomas Gerber (hpd), Henry H. Leck (cnd), Indianapolis Children's Choir—Fairest Isle [arr. Steven Rickards] *(rec The Lodge, May & June 1995)* VAI Audio ▲ VAIA 1130 [DDD]

Brookshire, Bradley (hpd)
Bach, J.S.:The Art of the Fugue, w. Robert Hill (hpd) Music & Arts ▲ CD 279
Handel, G.F.:Tolomeo, Rè di Egitto, w. Brenda Harris (sop—Seleuce), Andrea Matthews (sop—Elisa), Mary Ann Hart (mez—Alessandro), Jennifer Lane (mez—Tolomeo), Peter Castaldi (bar—King Araspe), R.A. Clark (cnd), Manhattan CO *(rec St. Jean Baptiste Church, NY, Mar 1995)* Vox Classics 3-▲ VOX 7530

Brosse, Jean-Patrice (hpd)—see also ORCHESTRAS & ENSEMBLES Concerto Rococo
Balbastre, C.-B.:Hpd Music—La Malesherbe; La D'Esclignac; La Marche des Marseillais et L'air Ça ira Pierre Verany ▲ PV 789094 [DDD]
Corelli, A.:Concerti grossi, Op. 6, w. Georges Armand (vn), G. Armand (cnd), Toulouse CO—Nos. 1 in D & 8 in g, "Christmas Concerto" EMI Classics ("Baroque" series) ▲ CDK 65731
Dussek, J.L.:Hpd Music—La mort de Marie-Antoinette; Variations sur "God Save the King" Pierre Verany ▲ PV 789094 [DDD]
The Golden Age of the Harpsichord *(rec 2/88)* Pierre Verany ▲ 789093 [DDD]
The Harpsichord at the End of the Old Regime *(rec 2/89)* Pierre Verany ▲ 789094 [DDD]
The Harpsichord at the Time of Louis XIV Pierre Verany ▲ 789092
Purcell, H.:Hpd Music (misc)—Ov, Air & Jig [from The Virtuous Wife]; Jig, Air [from Abdelazar]; Chaconne [from Timon of Athens]; Canary [from The Indian Queen]; various jigs [Kroll Hpd, 1774] EMI Classics ("Baroque" series) ▲ CDK 65734

Brosse, Jean-Patrice (org)
Bach, J.S.:Cons solo Hpd, BWV 972-987—BWV 972 Pierre Verany ▲ PV 787091 [DDD]
Bach, J.S.:Cons Org, BWV 592-597—omitting BWV 597 Pierre Verany ▲ PV 787091 [DDD]
Bach, J.S.:Org Music (misc)—Chorales BWV 615, 639, 645, 659, 680, 721, 734; Fantasy, BWV 572; Passacaglia & Fugue, BWV 582; Pastorale, BWV 590; Toccata & Fugue, BWV 565 Pierre Verany ▲ PV.789104
Dandrieu, J.F.:Mass & Vespers for Easter Sunday Pierre Verany ▲ PVY 794034 [DDD]
Purcell, H.:Org Music—Tpt Tune in C [from The Indian Queen]; The Queens' Dolour; Tpt Tune in D EMI Classics ▲ CDK 65734

Brosse, Jean-Patrice (org/hpd)
Bach, J.S.:Org Music (misc)—Clavierübung Part 3:Prelude & Fugue in E♭, BWV 552a/b; 21 Chorale Preludes, BWV 669-689; Four Duets, BWV 802-805 Pierre Verany 2-▲ PV.790052/53 [DDD]

Brotbek, Conradin (vc)—see ORCHESTRAS & ENSEMBLES Aria String Quartet

Brott, Denis (vc)—see also ORCHESTRAS & ENSEMBLES Orford String Quartet
Brahms, J.:Sons Vc (comp), w. Glen Montgomery (pno) *(rec St Augustin de Mirabel Church, Québec, Nov 1994)* Analekta Fleur de Lys ▲ FL 2 3009 [DDD]
Brahms, J.:Son in D Vc, w. Glen Montgomery (pno) *(rec St Augustin de Mirabel Church, Québec, Nov 1994)* Analekta ▲ AN 29901 [DDD]
Brott, A.:Arabesque Vc, w. B. Brott (cnd), McGill CO Analekta ▲ ANC 9801

Brovan, A. (pno)
Foss, L.:Thirteen Ways of Looking at a Blackbird, w. E. LaBruce (mez), C. Meves (fl), M. Shadd (perc) [E] *(rec 1989-90)* Koss Classics ▲ KC 1006 [DDD]

Browder, Risa (vn/va)
Purcell, H.:Music for 2 or 3 Vns, w. Purcell Quartet—Chacony in g, Z.730; Fantasia upon a Ground in D, Z.731; Pavan in A, Z.748; Pavan in g, Z.751 Chandos ▲ CHAN 8663 [DDD]

Brown, A. (bn)
Telemann, G.P.:Kleine Kammermusik, w. H. Lucarelli (ob), G. Ranck (hpd) Well-Tempered Productions ▲ WPT 5169 [ADD]

Brown, Ashley (perc)—see ORCHESTRAS & ENSEMBLES austraLYSIS members

Brown, Ashley (vc)—see ORCHESTRAS & ENSEMBLES Canterbury Cellists

Brown, Carol (fl)
Davidson, T.:Blue Dawn (The Promised Fruit), w. Lloyd Shorter (E hn), Charles Holdeman (bn), Charles Abramovic (pno) CRI ▲ CD 681 [DDD]
Davidson, T.:Lullaby, w. Marshall Taylor (sax), Lloyd Shorter (E hn), Charles Holdeman (bn), Charles Abramovic (pno) CRI ▲ CD 681 [DDD]

Brown, Elizabeth (fl)—see also ORCHESTRAS & ENSEMBLES Speculum Musicae
Wigglesworth, F.:Psalm 148, w. Kathy Fink (fl), Jeanne Wilson (fl), Kevin James (trbn), David Taylor (trbn), D. Schuler (cnd), Church of St. Luke in the Fields Choir CRI ▲ C 733 [DDD]

Brown, Frank (cl)
Brubeck, C.:Songs, w. Frederica von Stade (sop), Jenny Elkus (sgr), Bill Crofut (sgr/banjo), Chris Brubeck (sgr/trbn/pno/db), Mark Vinci (fl), Edward Arron (vc), Dan Brubeck (dr/perc)—The Distance between Us; La Paloma azul; Strange Meadowlark; Across Your Dreams; Summer Song; Polly; Blue Rondo-A Tribute to Dave; Autumn in Our Town; Thinking of You Thinking of Me; It's a Raggy Waltz; Heart of Winter; In the Grace of Your Room; Lonely on Both Ends of the Road *(rec Sandisfield, MA; Fantasy Studios, Berkeley, CA)* Telarc ▲ CD 80467 [DDD]

Brown, Ian (pno)—see also ORCHESTRAS & ENSEMBLES Nash Ensemble
Beethoven, L. van:Trio Fl, WoO 37, w. S. Milan (fl), S. Azzolini (bn) Chandos ▲ CHAN 9108 [DDD]
Debussy, C.:Petite pièce, w. R. Fallows (cl) Chandos ▲ CHAN 8385 [ADD]
Debussy, C.:Première rapsodie, w. R. Fallows (cl) Chandos ▲ CHAN 8385 [ADD]
Debussy, C.:Son Vc, w. S. Orton (vc) Chandos ▲ CHAN 8385 [ADD]
Debussy, C.:Son Vc, w. C. Van Kampen (vc) Virgin Classics ▲ 59604 [DDD]
Debussy, C.:Son Vn, w. M. Crayford (vn) Virgin Classics ▲ 59604 [DDD]
Debussy, C.:Son Vn, w. Maguire (vn) Chandos ▲ CHAN 8385 [ADD]
Delius, F.:Music of, w. A. Shulman (pno)—works for cello & piano—Creole Dance (from *Koanga*); 3 Pieces (from *Hassan*); Romance; Summer Night on the Water *(rec 9/87)* Continuum ▲ CCD 1025
Delius, F.:Son Vc & Pno, w. A. Shulman (vc) *(rec 9/87)* Continuum ▲ CCD 1025
Dyson, G.:Music of, w. A. Shulman (vc)—Prelude, Fantasy & Chaconne; 2 Pieces *(rec 9/87)* Continuum ▲ CCD 1025
Flute Fantaisie:Virtuoso French Flute Repertoire, w. Milan, Susan (fl) Chandos ▲ CHAN 8609 [DDD]
Gaubert, P.:Fl & Pno Music, w. S. Milan (fl)—Romance (1905); Nocturne et Allegro scherzando (1906); Berceuse (1907); Madrigal (1908); Sur l'eau (1910); Fantaisie (1912); Deux esquisses (1914); Sicilienne (1914); Sonata No. 1 (1917); Suite (1921); Sonata No. 2 (1924); Ballade (1927); Sonata No. 3 (1933); Sonatina (1937) Chandos 2-▲ CHAN 8981/82 [DDD]
Handel, G.F.:Ovs, w. N. Marriner (cnd), Academy of St. Martin in the Fields—Ov in D; Ov in B♭ Philips ▲ 420397-2 [ADD]
Ireland, J.:The Holy Boy, w. Karine Georgian (vc) Chandos ▲ CHAN 9377/8 [DDD]
Ireland, J.:Phantasie Trio, w. Lydia Mordkovitch (vn), Karine Georgian (vc) Chandos ▲ CHAN 9377/8 [DDD]
Ireland, J.:Son Vc, w. Karine Georgian (vc) Chandos ▲ CHAN 9377/8 [DDD]
Ireland, J.:Son 1 Vn, w. Lydia Mordkovitch (vn) Chandos ▲ CHAN 9377/8 [DDD]
Ireland, J.:Son 2 Vn, w. Lydia Mordkovitch (vn) Chandos ▲ CHAN 9377/8 [DDD]
Ireland, J.:Trio 2 Pno, w. Lydia Mordkovitch (vn), Karine Georgian (vc) Chandos ▲ CHAN 9377/8 [DDD]
Ireland, J.:Trio 3 Pno, w. Lydia Mordkovitch (vn), Karine Georgian (vc) Chandos ▲ CHAN 9377/8 [DDD]
Lambert, C.:Con Pno, w. L. Friend (cnd), Nash Ensemble Hyperion ▲ CDA 66754
Lambert, C.:Mr. Bear Squash-you-all-flat, w. L. Friend (cnd), Nash Ensemble Hyperion ▲ CDA 66754
Lambert, C.:Poems by Li-Po, w. Philip Langridge (ten), Nigel Hawthorne (nar), L. Friend (cnd), Nash Ensemble Hyperion ▲ CDA 66754
Lambert, C.:Son Pno Hyperion ▲ CDA 66754
Martinů, B.:Son Fl & Pno, w. S. Milan (fl) Chandos ▲ CHAN 8823 [DDD]
Poulenc, F.:Capriccio Pnos, w. S. Tanyel (pno) Chandos ▲ CHAN 8519 [DDD]
Poulenc, F.:Elégie Pnos, w. S. Tanyel (pno) Chandos ▲ CHAN 8519 [DDD]
Poulenc, F.:L'Embarquement pour Cythère, w. S. Tanyel (pno) Chandos ▲ CHAN 8519 [DDD]
Poulenc, F.:Son Pno 4-Hands, w. S. Tanyel (pno) Chandos ▲ CHAN 8519 [DDD]

Brown, Ian (pno) (cont.)
Poulenc, F.:Son for 2 Pnos, w. S. Tanyel (pno) Chandos ▲ CHAN 8519 [DDD]
Reinecke, C.:Son Fl, w. S. Milan (fl) Chandos ▲ CHAN 8823 [DDD]
Saint-Saëns, C.:Carnival of the Animals, w. S. Tomes (pno), Nash Ensemble Virgin Classics ▲ 59514 [DDD]
Saint-Saëns, C.:Carnival of the Animals, w. A. Goldstone (pno), O.A. Hughes (cnd), Royal PO ASV Quicksilva ▲ CD QS 6017 [ADD]
Saint-Saëns, C.:Spt Tpt, w. P. Archibald (tpt), Nash Ensemble Virgin Classics ▲ 59514 [DDD]
Saint-Saëns, C.:Trio 1 Pno, w. M. Crayford (vn), C. Van Kampen (vc) Virgin Classics ▲ 59514 [DDD]
Schubert, Franz:Der Hirt auf dem Felsen, w. F. Lott (sop), M. Collins (cl) [G] IMP Classics ▲ PCD 868 [DDD]
Schubert, Franz:Intro & Vars Fl on "Tröckne Blumen", w. S. Milan (fl) Chandos ▲ CHAN 8823 [DDD]
Virtuoso Violin, w. M. Hasson (vn), St. John's Smith Square Orch [cnd:John Lubbock] ASV ("Quicksilva" series) ▲ ASV 6034 [ADD]

Brown, Iona (vn)
Vaughan Williams, R.:The Lark Ascending, w. N. Marriner (cnd), Academy of St. Martin in the Fields Argo ▲ 414595-2 [ADD] ■ 421227-4
Vivaldi, A.:Cons Tpt, w. Maurice André (tpt) or Bernard Soustrot (tpt), N. Marriner (cnd), Academy of St. Martin in the Fields—in B♭ for Tpt & Vn Classics for Pleasure ("Eminence" series) ▲ CFP 2235
Vivaldi, A.:Cons Vn (misc), w. I. Brown (cnd), Academy of St. Martin in the Fields—RV.356 Philips ▲ 412624-2 [DDD]
Vivaldi, A.:Cons Vn, Op. 8/1-4, "The Four Seasons", w. I. Brown (cnd), Academy of St. Martin in the Fields *(rec London, Sept 1995)* Hänssler Classic ▲ CD 98.017 [DDD]
Vivaldi, A.:Cons Vn, Op. 8/1-4, "The Four Seasons", w. N. Marriner (cnd), Academy of St. Martin in the Fields Philips ▲ 420482-2 [ADD]
Vivaldi, A.:Con Vn Obs, RV.563, w. M. Laird (tpt), W. Houghton (tpt), N. Marriner (cnd), Academy of St. Martin in the Fields Philips ▲ 412892-2 [DDD]
Vivaldi, A.:Cons for 2 Vns, w. Johnathan Rees (vn), Briony Shaw (vn), Ralph de Souza (vn), I. Brown (cnd), Academy of St. Martin in the Fields—Nos. 3 & 10 *(rec London, Sept 1995)* Hänssler Classic ▲ CD 98.017 [DDD]
Walton, W.:Con Vn, w. E. Downes (cnd), London SO IMP ("BBC Radio Classics" series) ▲ IMP 5691732

Brown, Jeremy (pno)
Arutiunian, A.:Armenian Rhap, w. S. Tanyel (pno) Chandos ▲ CHAN 8466 [DDD]
Bax, A.:Pno Music for 2 Pnos, w. S. Tanyel (pno)—Moy Mell (1917); Hardanger (1927); The Poisoned Fountain (1928); The Devil that Tempted St. Anthony (1929); Red Autumn (1931) Chandos ▲ CHAN 8603 [DDD]
Bax, A.:Son for 2 Pnos, w. S. Tanyel (pno) Chandos ▲ CHAN 8603 [DDD]
Khachaturian, A.:Suite 2 Pnos, w. Seta Tanyel (pno) Chandos ▲ CHAN 8466 [DDD]
Shostakovich, D.:Concertino for 2 Pnos, w. Seta Tanyel (pno) Chandos ▲ CHAN 8466 [DDD]
Shostakovich, D.:Suite for 2 Pnos, w. Seta Tanyel (pno) Chandos ▲ CHAN 8466 [DDD]

Brown, Joel (gtr)
Blanchard, P.:Music of, w. J. Vinci (fl), A. Alton (pno)—Lament; Frolic Albany ▲ TROY 086 [DDD]
Chobanian, L.:Images Albany ▲ TROY 086
Chords & Thyme:English Folksongs for Guitar *(rec Troy, NY, Apr. 1994)* Dorian ▲ DOR 90204 [DDD]
Fine, V.:Canzones y Dances, w. J. Vinci (fl), A. Alton (pno) Albany ▲ TROY 086
Holland, A.:Poems Without Words, w. J. Vinci (fl), A. Alton (pno) Albany ▲ TROY 086
York, A.:Transilience, w. J. Vinci (fl), A. Alton (pno) Albany ▲ TROY 086

Brown, Kirwan (elec bass)—see ORCHESTRAS & ENSEMBLES Rhythm & Bluefield Band

Brown, Kyler (org)
Masterpieces from the Church of St. Mary the Virgin Gothic ▲ G 49085

Brown, Niall (vc)
Hindemith, P.:A Frog He Went a-Courting, w. Isabelle Trüb (pno) *(rec Théâtre de Poche, Vevey Mar 11-12, 1995)* Doron ▲ DRC 3024 [DDD]
Hindemith, P.:Kleine Son Vc, w. Isabelle Trüb (pno) *(rec Théâtre de Poche, Vevey Mar 11-12, 1995)* Doron ▲ DRC 3024 [DDD]
Hindemith, P.:Leichte Stücke, w. Isabelle Trüb (pno) *(rec Théâtre de Poche, Vevey Mar 11-12, 1995)* Doron ▲ DRC 3024 [DDD]
Hindemith, P.:Pieces (3) Vc & Pno, w. Isabelle Trüb (pno) *(rec Théâtre de Poche, Vevey Mar 11-12, 1995)* Doron ▲ DRC 3024 [DDD]

Brown, R. (vn)
Vivaldi, A.:Cons for 2 Vns, w. J. Schröder (vn), S. Ritchie (vn), N. TeBrake (vn), J. Griffin (va), M. Lutszke (vc), M. Willems (db), A. Fuller (hpd) *(rec June 6-8, 1986)* Reference ▲ RR 23 CD [DDD]

Brown, Rachel (fl)—see also ORCHESTRAS & ENSEMBLES Les Éléments
Bach, Joh. Christian:Con 2 Fl, w. A. Halstead (cnd), Hanover Band *(rec Rosslyn Hill Chapel, London, Mar-Apr 1995)* CPO ▲ CPO 999347-2 [DDD]
Boehm, T.:Compositions Fl, w. Simon Nicholls (pno)—Grande Polonaise, Op. 16; First Potpourri of Waltzes on Franz Schubert's & other Favourite Melodies, Op. 18; Fant. on a Schubert Air, Op. 21 Chandos ("Chaconne" series) ▲ CHAN 0565 [DDD]
Martin, F.:Ballade Fl, w. R. Kapp (cnd), Philharmonia Virtuosi [orchestral version] ESS.A.Y ▲ CD 1014 [DDD]
Schubert, Franz:Intro & Vars Fl on "Tröckne Blumen", w. Simon Nicholls (pno) Chandos ("Chaconne" series) ▲ CHAN 0565 [DDD]
Schubert, Franz:Schwanengesang, w. Simon Nicholls (pno)—Am Meer [arr. Theobald Boehm for fl & pno] Chandos ("Chaconne" series) ▲ CHAN 0565 [DDD]
Schubert, Franz:Winterreise, w. Simon Nicholls (pno)—Gute Nacht; Der Lindenbaum [both arr. Leopold Jansa for fl & pno] Chandos ("Chaconne" series) ▲ CHAN 0565 [DDD]
Telemann, G.P.:Con Fl Vn in e, w. S. Standage (vn), S. Standage (cnd), Collegium Musicum 90 Chandos ("Chaconne" series) ▲ CHAN 0519 [DDD]
Telemann, G.P.:Cons for 2 Fls, w. S. Peasgood (fl), S. Standage (vn), J. Coe (vc), S. Standage (cnd), Collegium Musicum 90—(1) in D Chandos ("Chaconne" series) ▲ CHAN 0512 [DDD]

Brown, Ray (db)
Jazz Meets the Symphony:Works of Lalo Schifrin, w. London PO, Grady Tate (dr) Atlantic ▲ 82506-2 P ■ 82506-4 P
Kiri Sidetracks, w. K. Te Kanawa (sop), André Previn (pno), Mundell Lowe (gtr) Philips ▲ 434092-2 PH [DDD] ■ 434092-4 PH (D)

Brown, Richard (perc/elec)
Schultz, Arthur:Dragons in the Sky, w. T. Bacon (hn) Summit ▲ DCD 135 [DDD]

Brown, Richard (timp)
Gottschalk, A.:Section for 4 Hns, w. T. Bacon (hn), J. Wilson (hn), N. Goodearl (hn), J. Graber (hn) Summit ▲ DCD 135 [DDD]

Brown, Ryan (vn)—see ORCHESTRAS & ENSEMBLES Four Nations Ensemble

Brown, Stephanie (pno)
Schubert, Franz:Fant Vn, D.934, w. J. Laredo (vn) Dorian 2-▲ DOR 90137 [DDD]
Schubert, Franz:Rondo Vn, D.895, w. J. Laredo (vn) Dorian 2-▲ DOR 90137 [DDD]
Schubert, Franz:Son Vn, D.574, w. J. Laredo (vn) Dorian 2-▲ DOR 90137 [DDD]
Schubert, Franz:Sonatinas Vn, w. J. Laredo (vn) Dorian 2-▲ DOR 90137 [DDD]

Brown, Stephen (pno)
Constantinides, D.:Vocal Music, w. Cynthia Dewey (nar), Angela DeVerger (sop), Evelyn Petros (sop), Susan Faust Straley (sop), Eugenia Epperson (fl), Richard Jernigan (cl), Kelly Smith Toney (vn), Hye-Yun Chung (hp), John Raush (perc), D. Constantinides (cnd), Louisiana State Univ New Music Ensemble—Reflections IV for Sop, Fl, Hp & Pno; Intimations [1 Act Opera]; 4 Songs on Poems by Sappho; Mutability for Sop & Str Qt.; 4 Greek Songs Vestige ▲ 04

Brown, Thomas (org)
Alain, J.:Org Music (misc) [at the St. Michael's Parish Quimby Organ, Litchfield, CT]—Litanies; Choral dorien RBW ▲ RBWCD 003
Duruflé, M.:Suite Org [at the St. Michael's Parish Quimby Organ, Litchfield, CT] RBW ▲ RBWCD 003
Franck, C.:Chorals Org, M.38-40 [at the St. Michael's Parish Quimby Organ, Litchfield, CT]—No. 2 RBW ▲ RBWCD 003

490

▲ = CD ♦ = Enhanced CD Δ = MD ■ = Cassette Tape □ = DCC

Brown, Thomas (org) (cont.)
Vierne, L.:Pièces de fant—Carillon de Westminster [org the St. Michael's Parish Quimby Organ, Litchfield, CT] RBW ▲ RBWCD 003
Vierne, L.:Pièces en style libre—Berceuse [org the St. Michael's Parish Quimby Organ, Litchfield, CT] RBW ▲ RBWCD 003
Widor, C.M.:Sym 9 Org—Andante sostenuto [at the St. Michael's Parish Quimby Organ, Litchfield, CT] RBW ▲ RBWCD 003

Brown, Timothy (hn)
Haydn, J.:Con 1 Hn, w. C. Hogwood (cnd), Academy of Ancient Music L'Oiseau-Lyre ▲ 417610-2 [DDD]
Telemann, G.P.:Cons for 2 Hns, w. H. Baumann (hn), I. Brown (cnd), Academy of St. Martin in the Fields Philips ▲ 412226-2 [DDD]
Telemann, G.P.:Cons Hns, w. H. Baumann (hn), N. Hill (hn), I. Brown (cnd), Academy of St. Martin in the Fields Philips ▲ 412226-2 [DDD]
Vivaldi, A.:Cons for 2 Hns, w. D. Hill (hn), N. Marriner (cnd), Academy of St. Martin in the Fields—RV.539 Philips ▲ 412892-2 [DDD]

Browne, Geoffrey (E hn)
Alwyn, W.:Autumn Legend, w. W. Alwyn (cnd), London PO Lyrita ▲ SRCD 230 [ADD]
Honegger, A.:Con da camera, w. J. Stinton (fl), S. Bedford (cnd), Scottish CO Collins Classics ▲ 12102 [DDD]
Honegger, A.:Con da camera, w. J. Stinton (fl), S. Bedford (cnd), Scottish CO Collins Classics 2-▲ 70052 [DDD]
Ibert, J.:Con Fl, w. J. Stinton (fl), S. Bedford (cnd), Scottish CO Collins Classics 2-▲ 70052 [DDD]

Browning, John (pno)
Barber, S.:Ballade MusicMasters ▲ 01612-67122-2 [DDD]
Barber, S.:Con Pno, w. L. Slatkin (cnd), St. Louis SO RCA Red Seal ▲ 60732-2-RC [DDD] ■ 60732-4-RC (CrO2)
Barber, S.:Excursions MusicMasters ▲ 01612-67122-2 [DDD]
Barber, S.:Interlude 1, "Adagio for Jeanne" MusicMasters ▲ 01612-67122-2 [DDD]
Barber, S.:Nocturne, "Homage to John Field" MusicMasters ▲ 01612-67122-2 [DDD]
Barber, S.:Son Pno Phoenix ▲ PHCD 105 [AAD]
Barber, S.:Son Pno MusicMasters ▲ 01612-67122-2 [DDD]
Barber, S.:Songs, w. C. Studer (sop), T. Hampson (b-bar), Emerson String Quartet Deutsche Grammophon 2-▲ 435867-2 [DDD]
The Best of Chopin, w. Géza Anda (pno), Emanuel Ax (pno), Peter Serkin (pno), et al. Victrola ("Victrola Best of" series) ▲ 60770-2-RV [ADD] ■ 60770-4-RV
The Best of Tchaikovsky, w. Philadelphia Orch [cnd:E. Ormandy], Chicago SO [cnd:F. Reiner], London SO [cnd:S. Ozawa], et al. Victrola ("Victrola Best of" series) ▲ 60775-2-RV [ADD] ■ 60775-4-RV
Chopin, F.:Études (24) RCA Victrola ▲ 60131-2-RV [ADD] ■ 60131-4-RV
Cumming, R.:Preludes (24) Pno Phoenix ▲ PHCD 105 [AAD]
Liszt, F.:Années de pèlerinage 2—No. 7, "Dante Sonata" Delos ▲ DCD 3022 [DDD]
Liszt, F.:Son Pno Delos ▲ DCD 3022 [DDD]
Liszt, F.:Sonetti del Petrarca Pno Delos ▲ DCD 3022 [DDD]
Mussorgsky, M.:Pno Music—Hopak [orig. version & Rachmaninoff's arr.]; Impromptu passionné; Sonata Delos ▲ DCD 1008 [AAD]
Mussorgsky, M.:Pictures at an Exhibition Delos ▲ DCD 1008 [AAD]
Rachmaninoff, S.:Études-tableaux, Opp. 33 & 39—Op. 33/2, 3; Op. 39/5 Delos ▲ DCD 3044 [DDD]
Rachmaninoff, S.:Moments musicaux—No. 5 Delos ▲ DCD 3044 [DDD]
Rachmaninoff, S.:Pno Music (misc)—Daisies, Op. 38/3; Études-tableaux; Moments; Preludes; Son. 2 Delos ▲ DCD 3044 [DDD]
Rachmaninoff, S.:Preludes Pno, Opp 23 & 32—Op. 23, Nos. 4,5 & 6; Op. 32, Nos. 5,12 & 13 Delos ▲ DCD 3044 [DDD]
Rachmaninoff, S.:Son 2 Pno Delos ▲ DCD 3044 [DDD]
Scarlatti, D.:Sons Kbd—K.14, 6, 106, 161, 490, 3, 32, 53, 105, 391, 45, 175, 145, 206, 327, 184, 407, 109, 496, 132, 402, 427, 466, 193, 215, 532, 443, 283, 380, 487 *(rec Apr. 25-27, 1994)* MusicMasters ▲ 01612-67146-2 [DDD]
Tchaikovsky, P.:Con 1 Pno, w. S. Ozawa (cnd), London SO RCA Silver Seal ▲ 60491-2-RV [ADD] ■ 60491-4-RV (CrO2)

Brownridge, Angela (pno)
Favorite Piano, w. Daniel Adni (pno), J. Février (pno), M. Lympany (pno), J. Ogdon (pno), G. Tacchino (pno) Classics for Pleasure ▲ CDCFP 4622 [ADD/DDD]
Tchaikovsky, P.:Les Saisons United ▲ UNI 88008 [DDD]
Tchaikovsky, P.:Son Pno, Op. 37 United ▲ UNI 88008 [DDD]

Brozková, Jana (ob)
Zelenka, J.D.:Con à 8, w. Josef Suk (vn), Ludmila Vybíralová (vn), Ivo Laniar (vc), Jaroslav Kubita (bn), F. Vajnar (cnd), Suk CO *(rec Studio Martínek, Prague, May 15-17 & Nov. 8-13, 19)* Panton 2-▲ PAN 811235 [DDD]
Zelenka, J.D.:Trio Sons Obs, w. Vojtech Jouza (ob), Jan Jouza (vn), Jaroslav Kubita (bn), Václav Hoskovec (db), Frantisek Xaver Thuri (hpd)—Nos. 1-3 Studio Matous ▲ MAT 8 [DDD]
Zelenka, J.D.:Trio Sons Obs, w. Vojtech Jouza (ob), Jaroslav Kubita (bn), Václav Hoskovec (db), Frantisek Xaver Thuri (hpd)—Nos. 4-6, ZWV 181 Studio Matous ▲ MAT 9 [DDD]

Brubaker, Bruce (pno)
Brahms, J.:Fants Pno, Op. 116 Vital Music ▲ VC 003
Steuermann, E.:Son Pno Vital Music ▲ VC 003
Wagner, R.:Pno Music—Album Leaf for Frau Betty Schott; Ankunft bei den schwarzen Schwänen [Arrival at the Black Swans'] Vital Music ▲ VC 003

Brubaker, Catherine (va)
Beethoven, L. van:Serenade Strs, Op. 8, w. D. Pettys (vn), D. Hopman (vc) [violin-viola-guitar arr.] Gajo ▲ GR 1002 [DAD]

Brubaker, Scott (hn)
Brahms, J.:Son 1 Vc, w. R. Levy (pno) [trans S. Brubaker for hn & pno] Koch International Classics ▲ KIC 7034-2 [DDD]
Brahms, J.:Son 2 Cl, w. R. Levy (pno) [trans S. Brubaker for hn & pno] Koch International Classics ▲ KIC 7034-2 [DDD]
Ewazen, E.:Son Hn, w. Eric Ewazen (pno) *(rec Recital Hall, SUNY Purchase, 1993)* Well-Tempered Productions ▲ WTP 5172 [DDD]
Krommer, F.:Con for 2 Hns, w. C. Kavalovski (hn), S. Richman (cnd), Harmonie Ensemble/New York Music & Arts ▲ CD 691-1 [DDD]

Brubeck, Chris (trbn/pno/db/sgr)
Brubeck, C.:Songs, w. Frederica von Stade (sop), Jenny Elkus (sgr), Bill Crofut (sgr/banjo), Mark Vinci (fl), Frank Brown (cl), Edward Arron (vc), Dan Brubeck (dr/perc)—The Distance between Us; La Paloma azul; Strange Meadowlark; Across Your Dreams; Summer Song; Polly; Blue Rondo-A Tribute to Dave; Autumn in Our Town; Thinking of You Thinking of Me; It's a Raggy Waltz; Heart of Winter; In the Grace of Your Room; Lonely on Both Ends of the Road *(rec Sandisfield, MA; Fantasy Studios, Berkeley, CA)* Telarc ▲ CD 80467 [DDD]

Brubeck, Dan (dr/perc)
Brubeck, C.:Songs, w. Frederica von Stade (sop), Jenny Elkus (sgr), Bill Crofut (sgr/banjo), Chris Brubeck (sgr/trbn/pno/db), Mark Vinci (fl), Frank Brown (cl), Edward Arron (vc)—The Distance between Us; La Paloma azul; Strange Meadowlark; Across Your Dreams; Summer Song; Polly; Blue Rondo-A Tribute to Dave; Autumn in Our Town; Thinking of You Thinking of Me; It's a Raggy Waltz; Heart of Winter; In the Grace of Your Room; Lonely on Both Ends of the Road *(rec Sandisfield, MA; Fantasy Studios, Berkeley, CA)* Telarc ▲ CD 80467 [DDD]

Brubeck, Dave (pno)—see ORCHESTRAS & ENSEMBLES Dave Brubeck Quartet

Bruce, Diane (vn)
Telemann, G.P.:Con Tpt Strs in D, w. Edward Carroll (tpt/pic tpt), Elizabeth Field (vn), Annabelle Hoffman (vc), Dongsok Shin (positiv org), Edward Brewer (hpd/positiv org) *(rec Rye Presbyterian Church)* Helicon Classics ▲ HE 1009

Bruce, Diane (vn) (cont.)
Telemann, G.P.:Musique héroïque, w. Edward Carroll (tpt/pic tpt), Elizabeth Field (vn), Annabelle Hoffman (vc), Dongsok Shin (positiv org), Edward Brewer (hpd/positiv org) *(rec Rye Presbyterian Church)* Helicon Classics ▲ HE 1009
Telemann, G.P.:Sons Tpt, w. Edward Carroll (tpt/pic tpt), Elizabeth Field (vn), Annabelle Hoffman (vc), Dongsok Shin (positiv org), Edward Brewer (hpd/positiv org) *(rec Rye Presbyterian Church)* Helicon Classics ▲ HE 1009
Telemann, G.P.:Trio Sons, w. Edward Carroll (tpt/pic tpt), Elizabeth Field (vn), Annabelle Hoffman (vc), Dongsok Shin (positiv org), Edward Brewer (hpd/positiv org) *(rec Rye Presbyterian Church)* Helicon Classics ▲ HE 1009

Bruce, Neely (pno)
Duckworth, W.E.:The Time Curve Preludes I-XXIV Lovely Music ▲ LCD 2031 [ADD]

Bruck, Wilhelm (gtr)
Lachenmann, H.:Salut für Caldwell, w. T. Ross (gtr) Col Legno ▲ AU 31804 [DDD]

Brugge, H. Ter (vc)—see ORCHESTRAS & ENSEMBLES Ensemble 415

Brüggen, Daniel (rcr)—see ORCHESTRAS & ENSEMBLES Amsterdam Loeki Stardust Quartet

Brüggen, Frans (fl)—see also ORCHESTRAS & ENSEMBLES Amsterdam Quartet, Paris Quartet
Andriessen, L.:Melody Fl, w. L. Andriessen (pno) Attacca ▲ Babel 9267-6 [DDD]
Little Consort with Frans Brüggen, w. Little Consort Channel Classics ▲ CCS 0390 [DDD]
Rameau, J.P.:Pièces de clavecin en concert, w. S. Kuijken (vn), W. Kuijken (vn), G. Leonhardt (vn) Teldec ▲ 77618-2

Brüggen, Frans (rcr)
Naudot, J.-C.:Con Rcr, w. J. Schröder (vn), N. Harnoncourt (cnd), Concentus Musicus Soloists—No. 5 in G Teldec ▲ 92180
Telemann, G.P.:Con Rcr, Fl, w. F. Vester (fl), A. Rieu (cnd), Amsterdam CO Teldec ▲ 77620-2 [ADD]
Telemann, G.P.:Fantasias Rcr—in d, g, a, C, B♭ & F [TWV 40:4, 9, 11, 2, 12 & 8] Teldec ("Das Alte Werk" series) ▲ 93688-2 [ADD]
Telemann, G.P.:Sons Rcr, w. Anner Bylsma (vc), Gustav Leonhardt (hpd)—in F, B♭, C, f, d & C [TWV 41:F2, B3, C5, f1, d4 & C2] Teldec ("Das Alte Werk" series) ▲ 93688-2 [ADD]
Telemann, G.P.:Suite in a Fl, w. F. Tilegant (cnd), Southwest German CO Pforzheim Teldec ▲ 77620-2 [ADD]
Vivaldi, A.:Music of, w. S. Kuijken (vn), St. Mary's Chamber Players, La Petite Bande—The 4 Seasons; Bn Con in E♭; Ob Con in F; etc. Pro Arte ▲ CDM 816 ■ PCD 816

Bruine, Frank de (ob)—see also ORCHESTRAS & ENSEMBLES Biedermeier Quintet, Schönbrunn Ensemble Amsterdam
Vivaldi, A.:Cons Ob, w. C. Hogwood (cnd), Academy of Ancient Music—in C, RV.447; in F, RV.457; in a RV.461; in a RV.463 London ▲ 433674-2
Vivaldi, A.:Cons Ob Vn, w. S. Ritchie (vn), C. Hogwood (cnd), Academy of Ancient Music—in g, RV.460 L'Oiseau-Lyre ▲ 436172-2 [DDD]
Vivaldi, A.:Cons for 2 Obs, w. S. Hammer (ob), C. Hogwood (cnd), Academy of Ancient Music—RV.535 London ▲ 433674-2
Vivaldi, A.:Cons Obs Cls, w. S. Hammer (ob), E. Hoeprich (cl), A. Pay (cl), C. Hogwood (cnd), Academy of Ancient Music—RV.559 London ▲ 433674-2

Bruins, Theo (pno)
Beethoven, L. van:Vars on a waltz by Diabelli, Op. 120 *(rec Aug. 1989)* Canal Grande ▲ CG 9324
Beethoven, L. van:Vars on a waltz by Diabelli, Op. 120 Channel Classics ▲ CCS 9324 [DDD]
Beethoven, L. van:Vars on Salieri's duet "La stessa, le stessissima", WoO 73 *(rec Aug. 1989)* Canal Grande ▲ CG 9324
Beethoven, L. van:Vars on "Rule Britannia", WoO 79 *(rec Aug. 1989)* Canal Grande ▲ CG 9324
Escher, R.:Arcana *(rec live, Royal Conservatory, The Hague, June 5, 1980)* Donemus ▲ CV 47 [ADD]
Pijper, W.:Con Pno, w. R. van Driesten (cnd), Rotterdam PO Donemus ▲ CV 1

Bruna, Francesco La (vn)—see ORCHESTRAS & ENSEMBLES Il Ruggiero

Brunborg, Tore (s sax/t sax/perc)
Blak, K.:Drangar, w. Anders Hagberg (fl/s sax/perc), Lennart Kullgren (gtr/sgr), Kristian Blak (pno/sgr), Anda Kuitse (sgr/perc), Anders Jormin (bass instr/perc), Karin Korpelainen (dr/perc) *(rec Nordic House, Tórshavn, Jan. 1995)* Tutl ▲ HJF 33

Bruncel, Carlos (fl)
Rossini, G.:Qts Fl, w. Het Trio—Sons 1 in G, 2 in A, 4 in B & 6 in Đ; Divert Eufoda ▲ EUF 1139

Brundage, K. (perc)
Erb, D.:Drawing down the Moon, w. J. Gippo (pic) New World ▲ 80457-2

Brunelle, Philip (org)
Serenade for Christmas Night, w. P. Brunelle (cnd) Virgin Classics ▲ CDC 59198

Brunello, Mario (vc)
Haydn, J.:Con 1 Vc, w. Zagreb Solisti RS Applausi ▲ 6367-04
Haydn, J.:Con 2 Vc, w. Zagreb Solisti RS Applausi ▲ 6367-04

Bruni, Paola (pno)
Mozart, W.A.:Con 8 Pno, w. E. Aadland (cnd), European Community CO IMP Classics ▲ PCD 964 [DDD]

Brunmayr, L. (fl)
Vivaldi, A.:Con for 2 Fls, w. C. Gurtner (fl), M. Haselböck (cnd), Vienna Academy [period instrs] Novalis ▲ 150074 [DDD]

Brunner, A. (instr)
Zinsstag, G.:Wenn Zum Beispiel..., w. W. Bärtschi, M. Burg, D. Dyk, R. Ericksson, B. Köhler, M. Maassen, E. Nowak, H. Suter, W. A. Wohlgemuth [G] *(rec Aug. 27, 1976)* Grammont ▲ CTSP 36-2 [ADD]

Brunner, Christoph (perc)
Keller, M.:Neungestalt *(rec June 1994-Apr 1995)* Jecklin ▲ JEC 310 [DDD]

Brunner, Eduard (cl)
Beethoven, L. van:Qnt Pno, Ob, Cl, Hn & Bn, w. A. Brendel (pno), H. Holliger (ob), K. Thunemann (bn), H. Baumann (hn) Philips ▲ 420182-2 [DDD]
Beethoven, L. van:Trio 7 Pno, w. Elisso Wirssaladze (pno), Natalia Gutman (vc) *(rec Wildbad Kreuth, July 3, 1992)* Live Classics ▲ LCL 622 [DDD]
Benjamin, A.:Con Ob Strs, w. H. Stadlmair (cnd), Munich CO [arr for cl & strs] Tudor ▲ 728 [DDD]
Bloch, A.:Clarinetto Divertente *(rec Aug. 21 & 23, 1986)* Pro Viva ▲ ISPV 147 CD [DDD]
Bloch, A.:Music for Cl & Str Qt, w. Wilanów String Quartet *(rec Jan. 21 & 23, 1986)* Pro Viva ▲ ISPV 147 CD [DDD]
Bruch, M.:Con Cl & Va, w. L. Zagrosek (cnd), Bamberg SO Koch Schwann ▲ CD 311065 [DDD]
Carnevale de Venezia Tudor ▲ 728 [DDD]
Cimarosa, D.:Con Cl, w. H. Stadlmair (cnd), Munich CO Tudor ▲ 728 [DDD]
Compositions for Clarinet & Piano, w. Margarita Höhenrieder (pno) Calig ▲ CAL 50907 [DDD]
Copland, A.:Con Cl, w. U. Schneider (cnd), Bavarian RSO Koch Schwann ▲ 3-1035-2 [DDD]
Danzi, F.:Concertante Fl, w. A. Nicolet (fl), J. Faerber (cnd), Württemberg CO Tudor ▲ 702 [ADD]
Danzi, F.:Concertino Cl, w. K. Thunemann (bn), H. Stadlmair (cnd), Munich CO Tudor ▲ 718 [DDD]
Danzi, F.:Phantasie on "La ci darem la mano" from Mozart's *Don Giovanni*, w. H. Stadlmair (cnd), Munich CO Tudor ▲ 718 [DDD]
Devienne, F.:Son 1 Cl, w. Mariko Hayashi (pno) *(rec Maebashi Shimin Bunka Kaikan, Aug 31-Sept 2, 1984)* Camerata ▲ 25CM 356 [DDD]
Devienne, F.:Son 2 Cl, w. Mariko Hayashi (pno) *(rec Maebashi Shimin Bunka Kaikan, Aug 31-Sept 2, 1984)* Camerata ▲ 25CM 356 [DDD]
Donizetti, G.:Concertino Cl, w. H. Stadlmair (cnd), Munich CO Tudor ▲ 728 [DDD]
Eybler, J.L.E. von:Con Cl, Bamberg SO Tudor ▲ TUD 782 [DDD]
Françaix, J.:Theme & Vars Cl, w. R. Werthen (cnd), I Fiamminghi CO Koch Schwann ▲ SCH 310262
Giampieri, A.:Il Carnevale di Venezia, w. H. Stadlmair (cnd), Munich CO Tudor ▲ 728 [DDD]
Haydn, J.:Trios Cl, Vn & Vc, H.IV/Es1, Es2 & B1, w. Hiroaki Ozeki (vn), Mineo Hayachi (vc) *(rec Maebashi Shimin Bunka Kaikan, Aug 31-Sept 2, 1984)* Camerata ▲ 25CM 356 [DDD]
Hindemith, P.:Con Cl, w. U. Schneider (cnd), Bavarian RSO Koch Schwann ▲ 3-1035-2 [DDD]
Hoffmeister, F.A.:Con 2 Cl, w. H. Stadlmair (cnd), Munich CO Tudor ▲ TUD 7008 [DDD]
Krommer, F.:Con Cl, w. H. Stadlmair (cnd), Bamberg SO Tudor ▲ TUD 782 [DDD]

Brunner, Eduard (cl) (cont.)
Kurtág, G.:Hommage à R. Schumann, w. Kim Kashkashian (va), Robert Levin (pno) *(rec Beethovenhaus, Bonn, Aug. 1992 & May & Sept. 1)* ECM New Series ▲ 78118-21508-2 [DDD]
Lobanow, W.:Son Cl, w. W. Lobanow (pno) Tudor ▲ 727 [DDD]
Mercadante, S.:Con in B♭ Cl, Op. 101, w. H. Stadlmair (cnd), Munich CO Tudor ▲ 728 [DDD]
Merikanto, A.:Con Vn Cl, Horn & Strs, w. O. Kagan (vn), D. Jolley (hn), et al., U. Söderblom (cnd) Ondine ▲ ODE 703-2
Messiaen, O.:Quatuor pour la fin du temps, w. Fontenay Trio Teldec ▲ 9031-73239-2 ZK [DDD]
Meyer, K.:Qnt Cl, w. Wilanów String Quartet *(rec Nov. 10-11, 1986)* Pro Viva ▲ ISPV 147 CD [DDD]
Mihalovici, M.:Nocturne, w. R. Werthen (cnd), I Fiamminghi CO Koch Schwann ▲ SCH 310262
Milhaud, D.:Con Cl, w. U. Schneider (cnd), Bavarian RSO Koch Schwann ▲ 3-1035-2 [DDD]
Milhaud, D.:Scaramouche Cl, w. U. Schneider (cnd), Bavarian RSO Koch Schwann ▲ 3-1035-2 [DDD]
Milhaud, D.:Son Cl, w. O. Maisenberg (pno) Orfeo ▲ 060831
Milhaud, D.:Son Fl, Cl, Ob & Pno, w. O. Maisenberg (pno), A. Nicolet (fl), H. Holliger (ob) Orfeo ▲ 060831
Mozart, W.A.:Qnt Pno, K.452, w. A. Brendel (pno), H. Holliger (ob), K. Thunemann (bn), H. Baumann (hn) Philips ▲ 420182-2 [DDD]
Pokorny, F.X.:Cons (2) Cl, w. H. Stadlmair (cnd), Munich CO Tudor ▲ TUD 7008 [DDD]
Prokofiev, S.:Son Fl, w. R. Levin (pno) [clarinet-piano trans. by Brunner] Tudor ▲ 727 [DDD]
Reger, M.:Albumblatt & Tarantella, w. G. Oppitz (pno) Tudor ▲ 724 [DDD]
Reger, M.:Qnt Cl, w. Wilanów String Quartet Tudor ▲ 724 [DDD]
Reger, M.:Son Cl, Op. 107, w. G. Oppitz (pno) Tudor ▲ 724 [DDD]
Rivier, J.:Con Cl, w. R. Werthen (cnd), I Fiamminghi CO Koch Schwann ▲ SCH 310262
Rossini, G.:Intro, Theme & Vars Cl, w. J. Faerber (cnd), Württemberg CO Tudor ▲ 702 [ADD]
Rossini, G.:Vars Cl, w. H. Stadlmair (cnd), Munich CO Tudor ▲ 728 [DDD]
Schoenberg, A.:Chamber Sym 1, w. A. Andorjan (fl), D. Sitkovetzky (vn), D. Geringas (vc), G. Oppitz (pno) [Webern's 1923 arr. for Flute, Clarinet, Violin, Cello & Piano] Tudor ▲ 717 [DDD]
Schumann, R.:Fantasiestücke Cl, w. Robert Levin (pno) *(rec Beethovenhaus, Bonn, Aug. 1992 & May & Sept. 1)* ECM New Series ▲ 78118-21508-2 [DDD]
Schumann, R.:Märchenerzählungen, w. Kim Kashkashian (va), Robert Levin (pno) *(rec Beethovenhaus, Bonn, Aug. 1992 & May & Sept. 1)* ECM New Series ▲ 78118-21508-2 [DDD]
Shostakovich, D.:Waltzes Fl, w. A. Adorján (fl), R. Levin (pno) Tudor ▲ 727 [DDD]
Stamitz, C.:Con Cl Bn, w. K. Thunemann (bn), H. Stadlmair (cnd), Munich CO Tudor ▲ 718 [DDD]
Stamitz, C.:Cons Cl, w. H. Stadlmair (cnd), Munich CO—in B♭ for Vn & Cl; in B♭ for Cl & Bn; No. 6 in B♭; No. 10 in B♭ Tudor ▲ TUD 7004 [DDD]
Stamitz, C.:Con Cl, w. H. Stadlmair (cnd), Munich CO Tudor ▲ 718 [DDD]
Stamitz, C.:Qts Cl, w. G. Schneider (vn), A. Baader (va), H. Veihelmann (vc) Koch Schwann ▲ CD 310003 [DDD]
Stamitz, J.W.A.:Con Cl, w. H. Stadlmair (cnd), Munich CO Tudor ▲ TUD 7008 [DDD]
Strauss, R.:Duet-Concertino, w. M. Turkovic (bn), M. Graf (hp), L. Zagrosek (cnd), Bamberg SO Koch Schwann ▲ CD 311065 [DDD]
Suder, J.:Arietta & Burlesque, w. M. Höhenrieder (pno) Calig ▲ CAL 50888 [DDD]
Tomasi, H.:Con Cl, w. R. Werthen (cnd) Koch Schwann ▲ SCH 310262
Weber, C.M. von:Concertino Cl, w. O. Caetani (cnd), Bamberg SO Orfeo ▲ 067831 [DDD]
Weber, C.M. von:Con 1 Cl, w. O. Caetani (cnd), Bamberg SO Orfeo ▲ 067831 [DDD]
Weber, C.M. von:Con 2 Cl, w. O. Caetani (cnd), Bamberg SO Orfeo ▲ 067831 [DDD]
Weber, C.M. von:Grand duo concertant Cl, w. G. Oppitz (pno) Orfeo ▲ 187891
Weber, C.M. von:Vars on a Theme from *Silvana* Cl, w. G. Oppitz (pno) Orfeo ▲ 187891
Yun, I.:Con Cl, w. P. Thomas (cnd), Bavarian RSO Camerata ▲ 30CM 46
Yun, I.:Piri Cl Col Legno ▲ AU 31808
Yun, I.:Piri Cl & Orch, w. P. Thomas (cnd), Bavarian RSO Camerata ▲ 30CM 46
Yun, I.:Piri Ob *(rec Studio 3, Bavarian Radio, Nov 25, 1982)* Camerata ▲ 25CM 356 [DDD]
Yun, I.:Qnt Cl, w. Akiko Tatsumi String Quartet *(rec Maebashi Shimin Bunka Kaikan, Aug 31-Sept 2, 1984)* Camerata ▲ 25CM 356 [DDD]
Yun, I.:Qnt Cl, w. Akiko Tatsumi String Quartet *(rec Maebashi City Auditorium, Aug 31, 1984)* Camerata ▲ 30CM 70 [AAD]
Yun, I.:Qnt Cl, w. Wilanów String Quartet Col Legno ▲ AU 31808
Yun, I.:Recontre, w. Marion Hofmann (hp), Walter Grimmer (vc) Col Legno ▲ AU 31808
Yun, I.:Riul, w. A. Kontarsky (pno) Camerata ▲ 30CM 46
Zemlinsky, A. von:Trio Cl, w. D. Geringas (vc), G. Oppitz (pno) Tudor ▲ 717 [DDD]

Brunner, Eduard (ob)
Lutoslawski, W.:Con Ob, w. M. Graf (hp), L. Zagrosek (cnd), Bamberg SO Koch Schwann ▲ CD 311065 [DDD]

Brunner, J. (fl)
Zimmermann, A.:Cassations, w. V. Brunner (fl), J. Vondra (hn), P. Sivanic (hn), V. Simcisko (vn), M. Tedla (vn), M. Telecky (va), J. Alexander (vc)—in G, D & D Trevak ▲ TRE 40008 [DDD]

Brunner, Samuel (vc)—see ORCHESTRAS & ENSEMBLES Zurich New Music Ensemble

Brunner, Vladislav (fl)
Romberg, A.:Qnts Fl, w. V. Simcisko (vn), M. Telecky (va), J. Cút (va), J. Alexander (vc) Trevak ▲ TRE 40007 [DDD]
Zimmermann, A.:Cassations, w. J. Brunner (fl), J. Vondra (hn), P. Sivanic (hn), V. Simcisko (vn), M. Tedla (vn), M. Telecky (va), J. Alexander (vc)—in G, D & D Trevak ▲ TRE 40008 [DDD]

Brunner, Wolfgang (pno)
Mozart, W.A.:Pno Music (misc)—Fant in d, KV 397; Son mouvement in g, KV 312; Rondo in F, KV 494 [1st version]; Fant in c, KV 475; Son in E♭, KV 282; Vars (8) on Schack, KV 613; Son in C, KV 330 [Andante cantabile] *(rec Ljubljana, Aug 8, 1993)* CPO ▲ CPO 999430-2 [DDD]
Orff, C.:Songs & Hymns, w. Mechthild Bach (sop), Gerd Rürk (ten), Michael Schopper (bar) Wergo ▲ WER 6279-2

Bruns, Barbara (pno)
Pinkham, D.:Wedding Cant, w. C. Swistro (sop), T. W. Bridge (ten), Boston Cecilia *(rec Dec. 1992)* Koch International Classics ▲ KIC 7180 [DDD]

Bruns, Peter (vc)
Brahms, J.:Son 1 Vc, w. Olga Tverskaya (pno) Opus 111 ▲ OPS 30-144
Brahms, J.:Son 2 Vc, w. Olga Tverskaya (pno) Opus 111 ▲ OPS 30-144

Brunsvik, Anders (pno)
Bibalo, A.:Balkan Dances *(rec Eidsvoll Church, Apr 10-11 & 20-21, 1995)* Simax ▲ PSC 1103 [DDD]
Bibalo, A.:Hommages (3) *(rec Eidsvoll Church, Apr 10-11 & 20-21, 1995)* Simax ▲ PSC 1103 [DDD]
Bibalo, A.:Miniatures (12)—Study for the left hand; Lonely Doll *(rec Eidsvoll Church, Apr 10-11 & 20-21, 1995)* Simax ▲ PSC 1103 [DDD]
Bibalo, A.:Pno Solo in Evening *(rec Eidsvoll Church, Apr 10-11 & 20-21, 1995)* Simax ▲ PSC 1103 [DDD]
Bibalo, A.:Son 1 Pno, "In due movimenti" *(rec Eidsvoll Church, Apr 10-11 & 20-21, 1995)* Simax ▲ PSC 1103 [DDD]
Bibalo, A.:Son 2 Pno, "La Notte" Norway Music ▲ SOL 10913 [DDD]
Bibalo, A.:Son 2 Pno, "La Notte" *(rec Eidsvoll Church, Apr 10-11 & 20-21, 1995)* Simax ▲ PSC 1103 [DDD]
Bibalo, A.:Toccata *(rec Eidsvoll Church, Apr 10-11 & 20-21, 1995)* Simax ▲ PSC 1103 [DDD]
Meyers, R.:Elegiac Memories, w. E. Zeppezauer (db) Norway Music ▲ SOL 10913 [DDD]
Meyers, R.:Meditation 5 Norway Music ▲ SOL 10913 [DDD]

Brunt, Peter (vn)
Jeths, W.:Glenz, w. L. Markiz (cnd), Amsterdam New Sinfonietta NM Classics ▲ NM 92041
Tchaikovsky, P.:Nocturne Vc, w. L. Markiz (cnd), Amsterdam New Sinfonietta *(rec Oct. & Dec. 1990)* Globe ▲ GLO 6021 [DDD]

Brusch, Adolf (vn)
Brahms, J.:Trio Hn, w. Aubrey Brain (hn), Rudolf Serkin (pno) *(rec 1933)* Enterprise ("Strings" series) ▲ ENT QT 99302

Brusco, Jose Maria (pno)
Clementi, M.:Pno Music (comp), w. Aldo Antognazzi (pno), Christian Badian (pno), Daniela Lanzillo (pno), Federico Wiman (pno), J. Rotter (cnd), Württemberg PO—Con in C for Pno; Sons (6) for Pno, Op. 1, Nos. 1-3; "Son inedita" in A♭ Aura Classics ▲ AU 32070

Brusilow, Anshel (vn)
Bach, J.S.:Brandenburg Con 5, w. Fernando Valenti (hpd), William Kincaid (fl), L. Stokowski (cnd), Philadelphia Orch *(rec Feb 25, 1960)* Sony Classical ("Masterworks Heritage" series) 2-▲ MH2K 62345 [ADD]

Brussilovsky, Alexandre (vn)—see ORCHESTRAS & ENSEMBLES Tchaikovsky Piano Trio

Brustaux, Y. (perc)—see also ORCHESTRAS & ENSEMBLES Linea Ensemble
Vuataz, R.:Destin, w. P. Collet (sax), E. Guibentif (hp)—3rd movt. *(rec Nov. 1980)* Grammont ▲ CTSP 7-2 [ADD]

Bruton, Laura (va)—see ORCHESTRAS & ENSEMBLES Clementi Quartet

Bruun, Mogens (va)—see ORCHESTRAS & ENSEMBLES Copenhagen String Quartet

Bruylants, Betty (hpd)
Bartók, B.:Mikrokosmos—sels. from Vols. 2, 3, 4, 5 & 6 René Gailly ▲ CD 87089 [DDD]

Bryan, Diane Lang (cl)
An American Collage Vol. II, w. Constance Keene (pno), Ayke Agus (pno), Anita Swearingen (pno), Michael Lang (pno), James Smith (gtr), Sherry Kloss (vn), Laila Padorr (fl), Victor Morosco (a sax) Protone ▲ PRCD 1114 [DDD]

Bryan, John (hpd)
Tomkins, T.:Instr & Voc Music, w. Timothy Roberts (hpd/org), Rose Consort of Viols, Red Byrd—Pavan in F; Almain in F; In Nomine; Above the stars; Fant. XIV; Fant. I; A Fancy, for 2 to play; Ut re mi; O Lord, let me know mine end; Fant. XII; In Nomine II; Pavan & galliard, Earl Strafford; Fant. for 6 Vls; Miserere; Voluntary; Pavan in a; Galliard; Thou art my King, O God *(rec Forde Abbey, Dorset, Apr. 27-28, May 12, 25-27)* Naxos ("Early Music" series) ▲ 8.550602 [DDD]

Bryan, Keith (fl)
Gould, M.:Con Fl, w. Z. Chen (cnd), Slovak RSO Bratislava *(rec Concert Hall of Slovak Radio, Bratislava, June 20-24, 1994)* Premier ▲ PR 1045 [DDD]
Griffes, C.T.:Poem Fl, w. Z. Chen (cnd), Czech RSO Premier ▲ PRCD 1026 [DDD]
Hindemith, P.:Son Fl, w. Karen Keys (pno) *(rec OPUS Studio 1, Bratislava, Slovak Republic, July 1989)* Premier ▲ PRCD 1053 [DDD]
Ibert, J.:Con Fl, w. Z. Chen (cnd), Czech RSO Premier ▲ PRCD 1026 [DDD]
La Montaine, J.:Con Fl, w. Z. Chen (cnd), Slovak RSO Bratislava *(rec Concert Hall of Slovak Radio, Bratislava, June 20-24, 1994)* Premier ▲ PR 1045 [DDD]
Martinů, B.:Son Fl & Pno, w. Karen Keys (pno) *(rec OPUS Studio 1, Bratislava, Slovak Republic, July 1989)* Premier ▲ PRCD 1053 [DDD]
Nielsen, C.:Con Fl, w. Z. Chen (cnd), Czech RSO Premier ▲ PRCD 1026 [DDD]
Perry, W.:Summer Nocturne, w. Z. Chen (cnd), Czech RSO Premier ▲ PRCD 1026 [DDD]
Poulenc, F.:Son Fl, w. Karen Keys (pno) *(rec OPUS Studio 1, Bratislava, Slovak Republic, July 1989)* Premier ▲ PRCD 1053 [DDD]
Prokofiev, S.:Son Fl, w. Karen Keys (pno) *(rec OPUS Studio 1, Bratislava, Slovak Republic, July 1989)* Premier ▲ PRCD 1053 [DDD]

Bryant, Allan (gtr)
Bryant, A.:Gtr Music—Whirling Take-Off; A Bouncing People Planet; Space Guitars; A Rocket Is a Drum; Space Train; Insect Takeover; Space Storm CRI ▲ CD 699

Bryant, Jeffrey (hn)
Britten, H.:Serenade, Op. 31, w. M. Hill (ten), V. Ashkenazy (cnd), Royal PO *(rec live, Moscow, 11/89)* RPO ▲ CDRPO 7015 [DDD]
Mozart, W.A.:Cons Hn, w. T. Dausgaard (cnd), Royal PO Tring ▲ TRP 47 [DDD]
Mozart, W.A.:Rondo Hn, K.371, w. T. Dausgaard (cnd), Royal PO Tring ▲ TRP 47 [DDD]

Bryars, Gavin (db)—see also ORCHESTRAS & ENSEMBLES Icebreaker, Gavin Bryars Ensemble
Bryars, G.:After the Requiem, w. A. Balanescu, B. Frisell, R. Heaton, et al. ECM New Series ▲ 78118-21424-2 [DDD]
Bryars, G.:Alaric I or II, w. A. Balanescu, B. Frisell, R. Heaton, et al. ECM New Series ▲ 78118-21424-2 [DDD]
Bryars, G.:Allegrasco, w. A. Balanescu, B. Frisell, R. Heaton, et al. ECM New Series ▲ 78118-21424-2 [DDD]
Bryars, G.:The Old Tower of Löbenicht, w. A. Balanescu (vn), R. Heaton (cl), B. Frisell (elec gtr), et al. ECM New Series ▲ 78118-21424-2 [DDD]

Brydon, Russell (org)
Russian Showpieces, w. E. Diazmunoz (cnd), Mexico State SO Pickwick ("The Orchid" series) ▲ PICORCD 11004

Bryla, Bartosz (vn)—see ORCHESTRAS & ENSEMBLES Chopin Trio

Brymer, Jack (cl)—see also ORCHESTRAS & ENSEMBLES Beaux Arts Trio
Brahms, J.:Qnt Cl, w. Medici String Quartet Medici Quartet ▲ MQT 8001 [DDD]
Debussy, C.:Première rapsodie, w. F. Prohaska (cnd), Vienna State Opera Orch *(rec Vienna, June 1966)* Vanguard Classics ▲ OVC 8090 [ADD]
Krommer, F.:Con Cl, w. F. Prohaska (cnd), Vienna State Opera Orch *(rec Vienna, June 1966)* Vanguard Classics ▲ OVC 8090 [ADD]
Liszt, F.:Songs, w. Margaret Price (sop), James Lockhart (pno)—O lieb', so lang du lieben kannst!; Die Lorelei; Die stille Wasserrose; Es muss ein Wunderbares sein; Kling leise, mein Lied Classics for Pleasure ▲ CFP 4669
Mozart, W.A.:Con Cl, w. N. Marriner (cnd), Academy of St. Martin in the Fields Philips ▲ 416483-2 [ADD]
Schubert, Franz:Songs (misc), w. Margaret Price (sop), James Lockhart (pno)—Auf der Riesenkoppe, D.611; Der Hirt auf dem Felsen [The Shepherd on the Rock], D.965 Classics for Pleasure ▲ CFP 4669
Siegmeister, E.:Con Cl, w. E. Siegmeister (pno), London SO *(rec 1973)* Premier ("Composer" series) ▲ PRCD 1010 [ADD]
Tchaikovsky, P.:Songs, w. Margaret Price (sop), James Lockhart (pno)—None but the Weary Heart, Op. 6/6; Do Not Believe, My Friend, Op. 6/1; At the Ball, Op. 38/3 Classics for Pleasure ▲ CFP 4669
Wagner, R.:Adagio Cl, w. F. Prohaska (cnd), Vienna State Opera Orch *(rec Vienna, June 1966)* Vanguard Classics ▲ OVC 8090 [ADD]
Weber, C.M. von:Concertino Cl, w. F. Prohaska (cnd), Vienna State Opera Orch *(rec Vienna, June 1966)* Vanguard Classics ▲ OVC 8090 [ADD]

Buble, Jan (vn)
Reicha, A.:Qts Fl, w. Jiri Válek (fl), Jan Marek (va), Ladislav Pospfsil (vc) Panton ▲ PAN 811003

Buccheri, Elizabeth (pno)
Argento, D.:Songs About Spring, w. Patrice Michaels Bedi (sop) *(rec Mandel Hall, Univ of Chicago, June 17-21, 1996)* Cedille ▲ CDR 90000029 [DDD]
Argento, D.:To Be Sung Upon The Water, w. Patrice Michaels Bedi (sop), Larry Combs (cl) *(rec Mandel Hall, Univ of Chicago, June 17-21, 1996)* Cedille ▲ CDR 90000029 [DDD]

Buchbinder, Rudolf (pno)
Beethoven, L. van:Son 30 Pno Teldec ("Digital Experience" series) ▲ 9031-75855-2 AW [DDD] ■ 9031-75855-4
Beethoven, L. van:Son 31 Pno Teldec ("Digital Experience" series) ▲ 9031-75855-2 AW [DDD] ■ 9031-75855-4
Beethoven, L. van:Son 32 Pno Teldec ("Digital Experience" series) ▲ 9031-75855-2 AW [DDD] ■ 9031-75855-4
Brahms, J.:Son 1 Vc, w. J. Starker (vc) RCA Red Seal ▲ 09026-61562-2
Schumann, R.:Adagio & Allegro Hn, w. J. Starker (vc)—No. 1 in e RCA Red Seal ▲ 09026-61562-2

Bucher, Anne-Catherine (org)
The Organ in Lorraine:Works by Composers of the Region from 1537 to the Present, w. Michel Chapuis (org), Francois Menissier (org), Norbert Petry (org) K617 2-▲ 7055

Bucher, Josef (org)
Handel, G.F.:Cons (16) Org, w. K. Teutsch (cnd), Warsaw CO—Nos. 7-10 Vivace ▲ 591 [ADD]

▲ = CD ♦ = Enhanced CD Δ = MD ■ = Cassette Tape □ = DCC

Bucher, Josef (org) (cont.)

Handel, G.F.:Cons (16) Org, w. K. Teutsch (cnd), Warsaw Philharmonic CO—Op. 7/1–3 *(rec 1973)* Polskie Nagrania ▲ PNCD 170 [ADD]

Buchholz, Matthias (va)—see ORCHESTRAS & ENSEMBLES Bartholdy Piano Quartet

Buchman, Noam (fl)

Ibert, J.:Con Fl, w. E. Acél (cnd), Oradea PO *(rec 4/91)* Olympia ▲ OCD 420 [DDD]

Nielsen, C.:Con Fl, w. E. Acél (cnd), Oradea PO *(rec 4/91)* Olympia ▲ OCD 420 [DDD]

Partos, O.:Visions, w. E. Acél (cnd), Oradea PO *(rec 4/91)* Olympia ▲ OCD 420 [DDD]

Buchy, Chantal de (pno)—see ORCHESTRAS & ENSEMBLES Ravel Trio

Buck, Fred (vc)

Rosenmüller, J.:Lamentationes Jeremiae, w. Fritz Wünderlich (ten), Lisedor Praetorius (hpd) *(rec Stuttgart, Mar 24, 1957)* Bella Voce ▲ 7003 [AAD]

Buck, Peter (vc)—see also ORCHESTRAS & ENSEMBLES Melos String Quartet

Bach, J.S.:Cant 202, "Wedding Cant", w. Ursula Buckel (sop), Willy Schnell (ob), Werner Keltsch (vn), Martin Galling (hpd), R. Ewerhart (cnd), Württemberg CO *(rec 1965)* Vox Box 3–▲ CD3X 3039

Bach, J.S.:Cant 212, "Peasant Cant", w. Ursula Buckel (sop), Claus Ocker (bass), Gabriele Zimmerman (fl), Martin Galling (hpd), R. Ewerhart (cnd), Württemberg CO *(rec 1965)* Vox Box 3–▲ CD3X 3039

Buckholz, Dawn (vc)—see also ORCHESTRAS & ENSEMBLES Soldier String Quartet

Rosenhaus, S.:Kol Nidre Prelude, w. Tina Pelikan (va) *(rec Tom Tom Studios, NYC)* Capstone ▲ CPS 8616 [ADD]

Buckland, David (ctbn)

Denisov, E.:Peinture, w. T. Otaka (cnd), BBC Welsh National SO *(rec Brangwyn Hall, Swansea, Wales, Jan 31, 1994 & Feb 1, 199)* BIS ▲ CD 665 [DDD]

Schnittke, A.:Sym 7, w. Nigel Seaman (tuba), Michael Wright (db), T. Otaka (cnd), BBC Welsh National SO *(rec Brangwyn Hall, Swansea, Wales, July 26–27, 1995)* BIS ▲ CD 747 [DDD]

Buckley, Diedre (va)—see also ORCHESTRAS & ENSEMBLES Ad Hoc String Quartet

Rosner, A.:Duet Va, w. Mark Ottesen (va) Albany ▲ TROY 210 [DDD]

Bucknall, Nicholas (cl)

Tausch, F.W.:Concertante 2, w. T. King (cl), L. Heger (cnd), English CO Hyperion ▲ CDA 66504

Tausch, F.W.:Con 1 for 2 Cls, w. T. King (cl), L. Hager (cnd), English CO Hyperion ▲ CDA 66504

Buckoke, Peter (db)

Dvořák, A.:Qnt Strs, Op. 77, w. Coull String Quartet Hyperion ▲ CDA 66679

Budgey, Andrea (hp/rcr/darabukka)—see ORCHESTRAS & ENSEMBLES Sine Nomine Ensemble

Budway, D. (pno)

Green, P.:The Man from Galilee (interpretations) Alanna ▲ ALA 5554 [DDD]

Green, P.:Mass of St. Francis of Assisi, "Let Me Bring Love", w. Bernadette Greevy (mez), Sydney MacEwan (bar), Cork Children's Choir Alanna ▲ ALA 5553

Buechner, David (pno)

The American Flute, w. R. Stallman (fl) ASV ▲ ASV 869 [DDD]

Brahms, J.:Rhaps Pno, Op. 79 Connoisseur Society ▲ CD 4179 [DDD]

Brahms, J.:Vars on a Hungarian Song Connoisseur Society ▲ CD 4179 [DDD]

Busoni, F.:Pno Music—Toccata (1920); Introduction & Capriccio [Paganinesco] (1909) Connoisseur Society ▲ CD 4174 [DDD]

Busoni, F.:Vars & Fugue in free form on Chopin's Prelude No. 20 Connoisseur Society ▲ CD 4174 [DDD]

The Cinema Classics Collection, Vol. 1, w. Angeles String Quartet, London SO, New Zealand SO, Phoenix SO Koch International Classics ▲ KIC 7604

Dvořák, A.:Pieces Pno, Op. 52—Impromptu, Intermezzo, Gigue, Eclogue Connoisseur Society ▲ CD 4179 [DDD]

Dvořák, A.:Theme with Vars Connoisseur Society ▲ CD 4179 [DDD]

Gershwin, G.:Pno Music—Clap Yo' Hands; Impromptu in 2 Keys; Looking for a Boy; Maybe; Sleepless Night; So Am I; Someone to Watch Over Me; Sweet and Low-Down; That Certain Feeling *(rec Pequot Auditorium, Southport, CT, Nov 29 & 30, 1991)* Connoisseur Society ▲ CD 4191

Gershwin, G.:Preludes (3) Pno *(rec Pequot Auditorium, Southport, CT, Nov 29 & 30, 1991)* Connoisseur Society ▲ CD 4191

Gershwin, G.:Rhap in Blue [trans. by Gershwin for solo pno] *(rec Pequot Auditorium, Southport, CT, Nov 29 & 30, 1991)* Connoisseur Society ▲ CD 4191

Gershwin, G.:Second Rhap [trans. by David Buechner for solo pno] *(rec Pequot Auditorium, Southport, CT, Nov 29 & 30, 1991)* Connoisseur Society ▲ CD 4191

Herrmann, B.:Con Macabre, w. J. Sedares (cnd), New Zealand SO Koch International Classics ▲ KIC 7225 [DDD]

Herrmann, B.:Prelude Pno Koch International Classics ▲ KIC 7225 [DDD]

Mozart, W.A.:Adagio Pno, K.540 *(rec Music Hall, Tarrytown, NY, Feb 19–21, 1994)* Connoiseur Society ▲ CD 4202

Mozart, W.A.:Allegro & Andante & Rondo *(rec Music Hall, Tarrytown, NY, Feb 19–21, 1994)* Connoisseur Society ▲ CD 4202

Mozart, W.A.:Allegro in Son form *(rec Music Hall, Tarrytown, NY, Feb 19–21, 1994)* Connoiseur Society ▲ CD 4202

Mozart, W.A.:Allegro Pno, K.400 *(rec Music Hall, Tarrytown, NY, Feb 19–21, 1994)* Connoiseur Society ▲ CD 4202

Mozart, W.A.:Gigue Pno, K.574 *(rec Music Hall, Tarrytown, NY, Feb 19–21, 1994)* Connoiseur Society ▲ CD 4202

Mozart, W.A.:Minuet Pno, K.355 *(rec Music Hall, Tarrytown, NY, Feb 19–21, 1994)* Connoiseur Society ▲ CD 4202

Mozart, W.A.:Sons Pno—K.310, 312, 400 *(rec Music Hall, Tarrytown, NY, Feb 19–21, 1994)* Connoiseur Society ▲ CD 4202

Mozart, W.A.:Son 8 Pno *(rec Music Hall, Tarrytown, NY, Feb 19–21, 1994)* Connoiseur Society ▲ CD 4202

North, A.:Rhap Pno, w. J. Sedares (cnd), New Zealand SO [w. Tpt Obbligato] Koch International Classics ▲ KIC 7225 [DDD]

Stravinsky, I.:Scenes Pno Connoisseur Society ▲ CD 4174 [DDD]

Turina, J.:Bailete Pno Connoisseur Society ▲ CD 4186 [DDD]

Turina, J.:Danzas andaluzas Connoisseur Society ▲ CD 4186 [DDD]

Turina, J.:Mujeres de Sevilla Connoisseur Society ▲ CD 4186 [DDD]

Turina, J.:Mujeres Españolas Connoisseur Society ▲ CD 4186 [DDD]

Waxman, F.:Rhap Pno, w. J. Sedares (cnd), New Zealand SO Koch International Classics ▲ KIC 7225 [DDD]

York, W.:Music for Strs [written for piano] *(rec May 1987)* New World ▲ 80439-2

York, W.:My Heart Is Different, w. S. Botti (sop) *(rec Feb. 1989)* New World ▲ 80439-2

Buffa, Mario (vn)—see also ORCHESTRAS & ENSEMBLES Rome Solisti

Dashow, J.:Some Dream Songs, w. J. Logue (sop), G. Simonacci (pno)—[E] CRI ▲ CD 578 [DDD]

Buhl, Hanne Bramsen (pno)

Stolarczyk, W.:Earth Air Fire Water, w. Amalie Malling (pno), John Damgaard (pno), Anne Øland (pno), Teddy Teirup (pno), Friedrich Gürtler (pno), Rosalind Bevan (pno), Poul Rosenbaum (pno), Rodolfo Llambias (pno), Bella Horn-Ribera (pno), Anders Riber (pno), Elisabeth Sigurdsson (pno), Thomas Tronheim (pno), Elsebeth Broderson (pno), Erik Kaltoft (pno), Jørgen Hald Nielsen (pno), Aino Gilemann (pno), Birgit Kjær (pno), Jørgen Thomsen (pno), Gunhild Donslund (pno), Henrik Bo Hansen (pno), Lone Karlsson (pno), Erik Fessel (pno), Lasse Nilsson (pno), Janos Ferenczi (pno), Erik Bach (pno), Axel Momme (pno), Arne de Cros Dich (pno), Sven Micha Slot (pno), Lili Olesen (pno), Susannah Carlsson (pno), Ulla Erml (pno), Vagn Sørensen (pno), Leif Greibe (pno), Bodil Krogh (pno), Kirsten Ottosen (pno), Inger Bergenholz (pno), Karsten Gylendorf (pno), Bjønr Elkjær (pno), Jacob Bjørn Jensen (pno), Jørgen Kaad (pno), Anne Marie Hjelm (pno), Carl Ulrik Munk Andersen (pno), Poul Lumbye (pno), Oluf Hildebrandt Nielsen (pno), Joachim Olsson (pno), Peter Pade Ramsøe Jacobsen (pno), Astrid Pollmann (pno), Jette Borsch (pno), Kirsten Karlshøj (pno), Maria Teresa Assing (pno), Allan Dahl Hansen (pno), Johan Hugossen (pno), Tine Fenger Pederson (pno), Arne Jørgen Fæø (pno), Anja Høgsted (pno), Anne Sophie Parbo (pno), Inga Lindmark (pno), Teresa Drabik Stathakis (pno), Anne Ruth Ferenczi (pno), Irene Hasager (pno), Yuka Ichikawa (pno), Birgitte Baur (pno), Malene Thastum (pno), Jens E. Rasmussen (pno), Birgitte Zielke (pno), Claus Zielke (pno), Stefan Kasch (pno), Bin Qiao (pno), Inger Johanne Teirup (pno), Lindy Rosborg (pno), Liisa Heininen (pno), David Højer (pno), Ellen Refstrup (pno), Thomas K. Søorensen (pno), Erik Kure (pno), Michael Rauff (pno), Jan beck Eriksson (pno), Tanja Zapolski (pno), Vibeke Skagbo (pno), Pål Eide Lindtner (pno), Ha-Young Sul (pno), Benedicte Palko (pno), Inke Kesseler (pno), Anne Marie Meineche (pno), Sverre Larsen (pno), Kasper Peter Bach (pno), Elisabetta Eliseo (pno), Olga Magieres (pno), Carl Erik Kühl (pno), Thorkild Borup Nielsen (pno), Valeria Zanini (pno), Lars Stenhoft (perc), Dennis Boel (perc), Winnie Dahlgren (perc), Susanne Vind (perc), Claus Byrith (elec), Anne Marie Storm (elec), J. Ribera (cnd) *(rec live, Koldinghaus Castle, Denmark, May 2, 1996)* Danica ▲ DCD 1996

Bukac, Vladimir (vn)—see ORCHESTRAS & ENSEMBLES Talich String Quartet

Bulakova, Olga (va)—see ORCHESTRAS & ENSEMBLES Talan String Quartet

Bulen, Jay (trbn)

Dempster, S.:Music of, w. Stuart Dempster (trbn/didjeridu/conch), Jeff Domoto (trbn), Moc Escobedo (trbn/didjeridu/conch), Scott Higbee (trbn), Gretchen Hopper (trbn), Nathaniel Irby-Oxford (trbn), Chad Kirby (trbn/conch), Dave Marriott (trbn), Greg Powers (trbn), Debra Sykes (cym)—Conch Calling; Morning Light; Didjerilayover; Secret Currents; Melodic Communion; Shell Shock; Cloud Landings *(rec Fort Worden, Port Townsend, WA, June 18, 1994)* New Albion ▲ NA 076

Bulfone, Nicola (cl)

Backofen, J.G.:Con for 2 Cls, w. Daniel Pacitti (cl), W. Themel (cnd), Udine CO *(rec Oct 14–15, 1995)* Agora Musica ▲ 039 [DDD]

Devienne, F.:Sinf concertante Cls, w. Daniel Pacitti (cl), W. Themel (cnd), Udine CO *(rec Oct 14–15, 1995)* Agora Musica ▲ 039 [DDD]

Hoffmeister, F.A.:Con for 2 Cls, w. Daniel Pacitti (cl), W. Themel (cnd), Udine CO *(rec Auditorium di Remanzacco, Oct 12–13, 1995)* Agora Musica ▲ AG 033.1 [DDD]

Krommer, F.:Cons for 2 Cls, w. Daniel Pacitti (cl), W. Themel (cnd), Udine CO *(rec Auditorium di Remanzacco, Oct 12–13, 1995)* Agora Musica ▲ AG 023.1 [DDD]

Mendelssohn, F.:Concert Pieces, w. Daniel Pacitti (cl), W. Themel (cnd), Udine CO *(rec Auditorium di Remanzacco, Oct 12–13, 1995)* Agora Musica ▲ AG 023.1 [DDD]

Stamitz, C.:Con for 2 Cls, w. Daniel Pacitti (cl), W. Themel (cnd), Udine CO *(rec Oct 14–15, 1995)* Agora Musica ▲ 039 [DDD]

Tausch, F.W.:Concertante 2, w. Daniel Pacitti (cl), W. Themel (cnd), Udine CO *(rec Auditorium di Remanzacco, Oct 12–13, 1995)* Agora Musica ▲ AG 033.1 [DDD]

Telemann, G.P.:Con 2 Chl, w. Daniel Pacitti (cl), W. Themel (cnd), Udine CO *(rec Auditorium di Remanzacco, Oct 12–13, 1995)* Agora Musica ▲ AG 033.1 [DDD]

Bulkely, E. (instr)

For Citizens & Peasants:Popular Tunes from Old Norwegian Music Books, w. N. Almquist (sgr), J. Arnold, T. Chancey, E. Bulkely Folger Consort ▲ BDCD1 9003 [DDD]

Bullard, John (banjo)

The Classical Banjo, w. John Patykula (gtr), Steve Bennett (hp gtr), William Comita (vc), Greg Giannascoli (vib) *(rec Big Audio, Richmond, VA, May-July 1992, Oct. 1994)* Dargason Music ▲ DM 115 [DDD]; ■ DM 115

Bullock, Robin (6- /12-string citterns)

Green Fields:Celtic Music for Cittern & Guitar Dorian Discovery ▲ DIS 80112 [DDD]

Bullock, Robin (gtr/cittern/fid)

Man with the Wooden Flute, w. C. Norman (fl), Ann Marie Morgan (vl), Pete Sutherland (fid) Dorian ▲ DOR 90166 [DDD]

Bulow, Harry (cl)

Bulow, H.:Contours Capstone ▲ CPS 8631

Bulsma, A. (vc)

Mozart, W.A.:Sinf concertante Vn, K.Anh.104, w. V. Beths (vn), J. Kussmaul (va) *(rec Mar. 1991)* Channel Classics ▲ CCS 3992 [DDD]

Bulva, Josef (pno)

Liszt, F.:Hungarian Rhaps—No. 2 Critics Choice 2–▲ CCD 943 [DDD]

Bumanis, Nora (hp)

Dances for 2 Harps, w. Julia Shaw (hp) CBC Records ("Musica Viva" series) ▲ MVCD 1062 [DDD]

Bumbacher, Urs (vn)—see ORCHESTRAS & ENSEMBLES Zurich New Music Ensemble

Buncke, J. (cl)

Baksa, R.:Ov Cl Capstone ▲ CPS 8610

Bungarten, Frank (gtr)

Bach, J.S.:Sons & Partitas Vn, BWV 1001–1006 [trans. Bungarten]—BWV 1001, 1003, 1005 MD + G ▲ L 3306 [DDD]

Sor, F.:Etudes—24 Etudes, selected from Opp. 6, 29, 31, 35 & 60 MD + G ▲ L 3390 [DDD]

Bunin, Stanislav (pno)

Bach, J.S.:English Suites—No. 3 EMI Classics 2–▲ CDFB 69479

Bach, J.S.:Italian Con EMI Classics 2–▲ CDFB 69479

Chopin, F.:Con 1 Pno, w. T. Strugala (cnd), Warsaw PO *(rec 11th International Chopin Piano Competition, Warsaw 1985)* Capriccio ▲ 10217

Chopin, F.:Con 1 Pno, w. Y. Toyama (cnd), NHK SO *(rec live 8/86)* MK ▲ 418026

Chopin, F.:Pno Music (misc), w. Martha Argerich (pno), Vladimir Ashkenazy (pno), Halina Czerny-Stefanska (pno), Jan Ekier (pno), Yuval Fichman (pno), Kemal Gekic (pno), Adam Harasiewicz (pno), Krzysztof Jablonski (pno), Louis Kentner (pno), Jean-Marc Luisada (pno), Garrick Ohlsson (pno), Ivo Pogorelich (pno), Maurizio Pollini (pno), Dang Thai Son (pno)—includes Ballade (Nos. 1 & 2); Barcarolle, Op. 60; Concerto Nos. 1 & 2; Études (Op. 10, Nos. 1, 5, 8, 10 & 12 & Op. 25, No. 10, 18 & 25); Grand valse brillante; Impromptus (Nos. 3 & 4); Mazurkas (Op. 24, Nos. 1–4; Op. 30, Nos. 1–4; Op. 50, No. 32; Op. 59, Nos. 1–3); Nocturnes (Op. 9, No. 3; Op. 37, No. 12; Op. 48, No. 13; Op. 55, No. 16)Polonaise (Op. 40, Nos. 3 & 4; Op. 44, No. 5; Op. 53, No. 6; Op. 61, No. 7); Preludes (Op. 28 Nos. 13–18, 21–24 & Op. 45, No. 25); Scherzos (Nos. 1–3); Sonatas (Nos. 2 & 3); Waltzes (No. 1 & 6) LaserLight 5–▲ 15 961 [ADD/DDD]

Chopin, F.:Preludes, Op. 28—Nos. 13–18 *(rec live, 11th International Chopin Piano Competition, Warsaw 1985)* Capriccio ▲ 10217

Chopin, F.:Son Pno, Op. 58 *(rec 8/86)* MK ▲ 418027 [DDD]

Haydn, J.:Sons Pno—H.XVI/23 *(rec 8/86)* MK ▲ 418027 [DDD]

Mozart, W.A.:Con 23 Pno, w. Y. Toyama (cnd), NHK SO *(rec live Aug. 1986)* MK ▲ 418026

Mozart, W.A.:Son 11 Pno *(rec Aug. 1986)* MK ▲ 418027 [DDD]

Bunin, Vladimir (pno)

Feinberg, S.:Con 3 Pno, w. G. Cherkasov (cnd), Ostankino Radio-TV Large SO *(rec 1990)* Consonance ▲ 81-0002 [DDD]

Liszt, F.:Transcriptions & Paraphrases—trans. of works by Schubert, Schumann, Rossini Calig ▲ CAL 50933

Büning, Till (vn)—see ORCHESTRAS & ENSEMBLES Avantgarde Ensemble, Leipzig String Quartet

Bunke, J. (cl)

Schwartz, E.:Extended Cl, w. E. Schwartz (tape) CRI ▲ CD 598 [ADD]

Bunke, J. (cl) (cont.)
Schwartz, E.:Souvenir, w. L. Raver (org) CRI ▲ CD 598 [ADD]
Buono, Cosmo (pno)—see also ORCHESTRAS & ENSEMBLES Bradshaw & Buono Piano Duo
Liszt, F.:Pno Music (misc), w. David Bradshaw (pno)—Hungarian Rhapsody No. 2 (piano duet arr., 1874); Fest-Polonaise for Piano Four-Hands (1874); Four Operatic Transcriptions (Benediction & Sermon from Berlioz's Benvenuto Cellini; March & Cavatina from Donizetti's Lucia di Lammermoor; Fantasy & Fugue on the Chorale "Ad nos, ad salutarem undam" from Meyerbeer's Le Prophète; The Entrance of the Guests from Wagner's Tannhäuser) Albany ▲ TROY 039-2 [DDD]
Buono, F. (pno)
Schubert, Franz:Divertissement à l'hongroise, D.818, w. D. Bradshaw (pno) Albany ▲ TROY 069 [DDD]
Schubert, Franz:Fant Pno, D.940, w. S. Bradshaw (pno) Albany ▲ TROY 069 [DDD]
Schubert, Franz:Ländler Pno, w. S. Bradshaw (pno) [arr. J. Brahms]—11 of 17 Ländler, D. 366 Albany ▲ TROY 069 [DDD]
Schubert, Franz:Marche militaire, D.733/1, w. S. Bradshaw (pno) Albany ▲ TROY 069 [DDD]
Buonocore, William (gtr)—see also ORCHESTRAS & ENSEMBLES Folios Guitar Duo
Electro Accoustic Music III, w. Camilla Hoitenga (fl), Maria Tegzes (sop), Jacques Linder (pno), Robert McCormick (perc) Neuma ▲ 450-87 [DDD]
Buonocore, William (mand)
Pinkham, D.:Intro, Nocturne & Rondo, w. J. Curtis (gtr) *(rec Dec. 1992)* Koch International Classics ▲ KIC 7180 [DDD]
Buraglia, Maurice (thb)
Marais, M.:Tombeau pour Monsieur de Ste Colombe, w. Nima Ben David (vl) Astrée ▲ E 8592
Buranovsky, Daniel (pno)
Suk, J.:Songs, Op. 15, w. Marian Lapšanský (pno), Josef Pancík (cnd), Prague Chamber Choir Chandos ▲ CHAN 9257 [DDD]
Buranskas, Karen (vc)—see also ORCHESTRAS & ENSEMBLES Notre Dame String Trio
Haimo, E.:Contrasts, w. William Cerny (pno) *(rec Annenberg Audit., Snite Museum of Art, Univ. of Notre Dame, May & June 1994 & Jan 199)* Centaur ▲ CRC 2253 [DDD]
Burba, M. (tpt/pno/didgeridoo/tools/eup/alphn)
Les Vertige des Profondeurs, w. M. Liebermann (sop) *(rec 1985, 1986, 1990, 1992 &)* Thorofon ▲ CTH 2198 [AAD/DDD]
Burchell, David (hpd/org)
Insalata, w. I Fagiolini, E. Kenny (theorbo), Riona D.(baroque vn), T. Cronin (baroque vn), D. Clasen (bar) Metronome ▲ METCD 1004
Burchell, David (org)
Tomkins, T.:3rd or Great Service, w. E. Higginbottom (cnd), New College Choir Oxford *(rec July 16–18, 1990)* CRD ▲ CRD 3467 [DDD]
Burda, Bernard (perc)
Downey, J.:A Dolphin, w. D. Nelson (ten), Bourachoff (fl), B. Zaslav (va), J. Downey (pno) Gasparo ▲ GS 276 ■ GS 276C
Burdick, Daniel (tuba)—see ORCHESTRAS & ENSEMBLES Missouri Brass Quintet
Burg, M. (instr)
Zinsstag, G.:Wenn Zum Beispiel..., w. W. Bärtschi, A. Brunner, D. Dyk, R. Ericksson, B. Köhler, M. Maassen, E. Nowak, H. Suter, W. A. Wohlgemuth [G] *(rec Aug. 27, 1976)* Grammont ▲ CTSP 36-2 [ADD]
Burge, Russell (perc)
Handel, D.:Barge Music, w. Bradley Garner (a fl), Rodney Studky (gtr), Jon Pascolini (db), Allen Otte (perc) Vienna Modern Masters ▲ VMM 2019 [DDD]
Burger, Klaus (tuba/pic tpt)
Nono, L.:guai ai gelidi mostri, w. Susanne Otto (cta), Helena Rasker (alt), Stefano Scodanibbio (db), A. Richard (cnd), Rechêrche Ensemble Montaigne ▲ MO 782047
Burger, Richard (pno)
Cage, J.:Four Walls, w. J. Clayton (voice) Tomato ▲ R2-70696
Burgess, D. (gtr)
Music for Violin & Guitar, w. A. Delmoni (vn) Athena ▲ ACSC 10006 [ADD]
Burgess, J. (tpt)
Gregson, E.:Celebration, w. M. Kane (tpt), D. Papp (tpt), E. Corporon (cnd), Cincinnati College Conservatory of Music Wind Sym Klavier ▲ KCD 11047 [DDD]
Burgueras, Manuel (pno)
Divas in Song:Marylin Horne, a 60th Birthday Celebration, w. Montserrat Caballé (sop), H. Donath (sop), R. A. Swenson (sop), F. von Stade (mez), R. Fleming (mez), S. Ramey (bass), J. Levine (cnd), M. Katz (pno), W. Jones (pno), K. Donath (pno) RCA Red Seal ▲ 09026-62547-2
Burkard, Gallus (db)—see ORCHESTRAS & ENSEMBLES Universal Ensemble
Burke, Mary (vl)
Purcell, H.:Come Ye Sons of Art, w. Laura Goetz (ob), Sarah Weiner (ob), Davis Brooks (vn), Lisa Brooks (vn), Jann Cosart (va), Vance Reese (db), Thomas Gerber (hpd), Henry H. Leck (cnd), Indianapolis Children's Choir [arr. Maurice Blower] *(rec The Lodge, May & June 1995)* VAI Audio ▲ VAIA 1130 [DDD]
Purcell, H.:Fly, Bold Rebellion (sels), w. Laura Goetz (ob), Sarah Weiner (ob), Davis Brooks (vn), Lisa Brooks (vn), Jann Cosart (va), Vance Reese (db), Thomas Gerber (hpd), Henry H. Leck (cnd), Indianapolis Children's Choir—Be Welcome Then, Great Sir [arr. Steven Rickards] *(rec The Lodge, May & June 1995)* VAI Audio ▲ VAIA 1130 [DDD]
Purcell, H.:King Arthur (sels), w. Laura Goetz (ob), Sarah Weiner (ob), Davis Brooks (vn), Lisa Brooks (vn), Jann Cosart (va), Vance Reese (db), Thomas Gerber (hpd), Henry H. Leck (cnd), Indianapolis Children's Choir—Fairest Isle [arr. Steven Rickards] *(rec The Lodge, May & June 1995)* VAI Audio ▲ VAIA 1130 [DDD]
Burke, Mary Louise (pno)
A Colorado Kind of Christmas, w. [cnd:Duain Wolfe], Colorado Children's Chorale, Mike Fitzmaurice (db), Rod Garnet (fl), William Hill (perc), Deborah Schmit-Lobis (pno), Brett Walace (vc), Laurie Kahler (pno), Helen Hope (hp) *(rec Denver Center Media)* Colorado Children's Chorale ▲ XMAS
Burkert, Julie (fl)—see ORCHESTRAS & ENSEMBLES B & B Duo
Burkhalter, Laurence (va)—see also ORCHESTRAS & ENSEMBLES Ames Piano Quartet
Strauss, R.:Qt Pno, w. W. David (pno), M. Darlington (vn), G. Work (vc) *(rec Oct. 1991)* Dorian ▲ DOR 90167 [DDD]
Widor, C.M.:Qt Pno, w. W. David (pno), M. Darlington (vn), G. Work (vc) *(rec Oct. 1991)* Dorian ▲ DOR 90167 [DDD]
Burkhalter, Madleine (va)—see ORCHESTRAS & ENSEMBLES Universal Ensemble
Burkhard, S. (pno)
Pfiffner, E.:Don Quijote, w. F. Reinmann (bar) *(rec May 1992)* Pro Viva ▲ ISPV 170 [DDD]
Burkhard, Ursula (fl)
Boehm, T.:Compositions Fl, w. A. Adorján (fl), W. Bennett (fl), M. Debost (fl), I. Grafenauer (fl), A. Nicolet (fl), B. Weber (pno)—works for Flute & Piano *(Andante pastorale, from Souvenir des Alpes; Elegie in A♭, Op. 47; Fantaisie sur un air allemand, Op. 22; Fantaisie in A♭ on a Theme by Schubert; Grande Polonaise in D, Op. 16; Variations on Nel cor più non mi sento)*; works for Flute Ensemble *(Duettino in D, Pièce facile in C & Romanza in F [Nos. 66–68]; plus a six-flute ensemble performance of the 2nd movt. from Boismortier's Flute Concerto No. 1 in G)* *(rec live, Cuvilliés Theater, Munich 11/27/81)* Orfeo ▲ 018821 [DDD]
Lehmann, H.U.:Tractus, w. P. Fuchs (ob), H. R. Stalder (cl) *(rec Jan. 13, 1978)* Grammont ▲ CTS P 4-2
Burkhardt, Rick (gtr)—see ORCHESTRAS & ENSEMBLES Illinois Performers' Workshop Ensemble
Burleson, Geoffrey (pno)
Abdel-Gawad, R.:Funeral Ceremony at the Pyramid of Mankara *(rec Paine Hall, Harvard Univ., Apr 14, 1991)* Vienna Modern Masters ▲ VMM 2015 [DDD]
Eisler, H.:Klavierstücke, Op. 32—Nos. 2 & 5 Neuma ▲ 45083 [DDD]
Eisler, H.:Son 2 Pno Neuma ▲ 45083 [DDD]
Eisler, H.:Songs, w. M. Tegzes (sop)—Die Maske des Bösens; Lied eines Freudenmädchens; Hollywood Elegy; Wie der Wind weht; Lied der Kupplerin; Andere die Welt, sie braucht es Neuma ▲ 45083 [DDD]
Burleson, Geoffrey (pno) (cont.)
Harsh, E.:Songs, w. Maria Tegzes (sop)—be not the slave of words/i fear loquacios odes Neuma ▲ 45083 [DDD]
Looten, C.:...Incoronata Poeta *(rec Tsai Performance Center, Boston Univ., Sept 14, 1991)* Vienna Modern Masters ▲ VMM 2015 [DDD]
Schoenberg, A.:The Cabaret Songs, w. M. Tegzes (sop) Neuma ▲ 45083 [DDD]
Burley, Elizabeth (pno)
Chabrier, E.:Pno Music (misc), w. Kathryn Stott (pno)—10 Pièces pittoresques; Impromptu; 5 morceaux pour pno; 3 valses romantiques Unicorn-Kanchana ▲ DKP CD 9158
Burley, Raymond (gtr)—see ORCHESTRAS & ENSEMBLES Alice Artzt Guitar Trio
Burman-Hall, Linda (hpd)
Bach, C.P.E.:Sons Fl, w. L. Miller (baroque fl), R. Hutchinson (vl)—in G, H.548 (W.134); in G, H.550 (W.123); in e, H.551 (W.124); in B♭, H.552 (W.125); in D, H.553 (W.126); in G, H.554 (W.127) Centaur ▲ CRC 2087 [DDD]
Burnett (pno)
Hummel, J.N.:Son Va, w. Holmes (violin) Amon Ra ▲ CD-SAR 12
Burnett, Dana (pno)
Zaimont, J.L.:Doubles, w. Lisa Kozenko (ob) *(rec SUNY Purchase, Theatre C, Jan 8–10 & Feb 20, 1995)* Arabesque ▲ ARA 6667 [DDD]
Burnett, Frances (pno)
Barber, S.:Son Vc, w. Gordon Epperson (vc) *(rec Bryan Hall, Moore College of Musical Arts, Bowling Green State Univ, Bowling Green, OH, Aug 2–3, 1994)* Centaur ▲ CRC 2275 [DDD]
Bartók, B.:Rhap 1 Vc, w. Gordon Epperson (vc) *(rec Bryan Hall, Moore College of Musical Arts, Bowling Green State Univ, Bowling Green, OH, Aug 2–3, 1994)* Centaur ▲ CRC 2275 [DDD]
Bavicchi, J.:Son 2 Vc, w. Gordon Epperson (vc) *(rec Bryan Hall, Moore College of Musical Arts, Bowling Green State Univ, Bowling Green, OH, Aug 2–3, 1994)* Centaur ▲ CRC 2275 [DDD]
McKinley, W.T.:Andante & Scherzo, w. R. Stankovsky (cnd), Slovak RSO Bratislava *(rec Slovak Radio & Television Studios)* MMC ▲ MMC 2009 [DDD]
Martinů, B.:Son 2 Vc, w. Gordon Epperson (vc) *(rec Bryan Hall, Moore College of Musical Arts, Bowling Green State Univ, Bowling Green, OH, Aug 2–3, 1994)* Centaur ▲ CRC 2275 [DDD]
Melloni, R.C.:Sym Pno, w. S. Black (cnd), Slovak RSO Bratislava Master Musicians Collective ▲ MMC 2020
Burnett, Richard (chamber org/spinet/hpd/pno)
Clarinet Collection, w. A. Hacker (cl) Amon Ra ▲ CDSAR 10
Burnett, Richard (pno)
Beethoven, L. van:Son 5 Vn, "Spring", w. R. Holmes (vn) Amon Ra ▲ CD-SAR 9
Beethoven, L. van:Son 7 Vn, w. R. Holmes (vn) Amon Ra ▲ CD-SAR 9
Beethoven, L. van:Son 8 Vn, w. R. Holmes (vn) [1820 Graf fortepiano] Amon Ra ▲ CD-SAR 16 [DDD]
Beethoven, L. van:Son 9 Vn, "Kreutzer", w. R. Holmes (vn) [1820 Graf fortepiano] Amon Ra ▲ CD-SAR 16 [DDD]
Brahms, J.:Sons Cl (comp), w. A. Hacker (cl) [period instrs] Amon Ra ▲ CD-SAR 37 [DDD]
Brahms, J.:Trio Cl, w. A. Hacker (cl), J. Ward Clarke (vc) [period instrs] Amon Ra ▲ CD-SAR 37 [DDD]
Clementi, M.:Monferrinas [1822 grand fortepiano] Amon Ra ▲ CD-SAR 8 [AAD]
Clementi, M.:Son Pno, Op. 50/3, "Didone abbandonata" [1822 grand fortepiano] Amon Ra ▲ CD-SAR 8 [AAD]
Czerny, C.:Vars on "La Ricordanza" Amon Ra ▲ CD-SAR 7
Field, J.:Pno Music [historic pianos—several early 19th cent. Viennese fortepianos & a ca. 1825 cabinet piano by Clementi & Co., London] [Solos]—Nocturnes (Nos. 1–6, 11, 12 & 14); Grand Pastorale in E; Variations in B♭ on a Russian Air (Kamarinskaya); Variations in d on a Russian Song; [Duets]—Andante in c; The Bear Dance; Variations in a on a Russian Air, w. L. Fulford (2nd piano) Amon Ra ▲ CD-SAR 48 [DDD]
Field, J.:Son Pno, Op. 1/1 [1822 grand pianoforte by Clementi & Co., London] Amon Ra ▲ CD-SAR 48 [DDD]
Gottschalk, L.M.:Pno Music—Ballade No. 6; Le bananier (chanson nègre); Berceuse; Chanson du Gitano; The Dying Poet (méditation); La gallina (danse cubaine); Le mancenillier (sérénade); Manchega (étude de concert); Mazurk; Minuit à Seville (caprice); Polka in A♭; Polka in B♭; Romance; La savane (ballade creole); Souvenir de Porto Rico (marche des gibaros); Souvenirs d'Andalousie (caprice concert); Suis moi (caprice) [historic pnos] Amon Ra ▲ CD-SAR 32 [DDD]
Haydn, J.:Sons Pno—Nos. 35, 41, 60, 61 Amon Ra ▲ CD-SAR 5
Hummel, J.N.:Nocturne, w. Ralph Holmes (vn) Amon Ra ▲ CD-SAR 12
Hummel, J.N.:Son Vn & Pno, Op. 50, w. Ralph Holmes (vn) Amon Ra ▲ CD-SAR 12
Hummel, J.N.:Vars on a theme from Gluck's *Armide* Amon Ra ▲ CD-SAR 7
Kalliwoda, J.W.:Morceau de Salon, w. R. Canter (ob) Amon Ra ▲ CD-SAR 22 [DDD]
Keyboard Collection Amon Ra ▲ CDSAR 6 [AAD]
Mendelssohn, F.:Concert Pieces, w. A. Hacker (cl), L. Schatzberger (bas hn) [period instrs] Amon Ra ▲ CD-SAR 38 [DDD]
Mendelssohn, F.:Lieder ohne Worte Pno—(6) Opp. 53/4 in F, 62/6 in A, 67/2 in f#, 67/4 in C, "Venetian Gondola Song" in a, Op. 62/5 & "Venetian Gondola Song" in A (1842) Amon Ra ▲ CD-SAR 38 [DDD]
Mendelssohn, F.:Rondo capriccioso [1823 Broadwood piano] Amon Ra ▲ CD-SAR 38 [DDD]
Mendelssohn, F.:Son Cl, w. A. Hacker (cl) [period instrs] Amon Ra ▲ CD-SAR 38 [DDD]
Mendelssohn, F.:Vars sérieuses Amon Ra ▲ CD-SAR 38 [DDD]
Mozart, W.A.:Qts Pno, w. Salomon String Quartet [period instrs] Amon Ra ▲ CD-SAR 31 [DDD]
Music for Mandolin, w. A. Stephens (mand), Sue Mossop (mand), Poppy Holden (sop) Amon Ra ▲ CDSAR 53 [DDD]
Schubert, Franz:Pno Music (misc)—Ländler, D.145/2–5; Ecossaises, D.145/1–3 & D.421/1,2; Letzte Walzer, D.146/1,20 Amon Ra ▲ CD-SAR 7
Schumann, R.:Kinderszenen Amon Ra ▲ CD-SAR 7
Schumann, R.:Qt Pno, Op. 47, w. Fitzwilliam String Quartet members [period instrs] Amon Ra ▲ CD-SAR 54 [DDD]
Schumann, R.:Qnt Pno, w. Fitzwilliam String Quartet [period instrs] Amon Ra ▲ CD-SAR 54 [DDD]
Schumann, R.:Son 1 Vn, w. L. Russell (vn) Amon Ra ▲ CD-SAR 54 [DDD]
Walmisley, T.A.:Sonatina 2 Ob, w. R. Canter (ob) Amon Ra ▲ CD-SAR 22 [DDD]
Weber, C.M. von:Sons Vn & Pno, w. Preston (fl)—Nos. 1, 3, 4, 6 Amon Ra ▲ CD-SAR 21 [DDD]
Weber, C.M. von:Trio Fl, w. Preston (fl), J. .W. Clarke (vc) Amon Ra ▲ CD-SAR 21 [DDD]
Burnett, Richard (square pno)
Music in Miniature Amon Ra ■ CSAR 20
Burns, Jeffrey (pno)
Humel, G.:Universe Academy ▲ ACA 8501
Ligeti, G.:Bagatelles—Désordre; Fanfares; Cordes Vides; Touches bloquée; Arc-en-ciel; Automne à Varsovie Academy ▲ ACA 8505 [ADD]
Reimann, A.:Spektren Academy ▲ ACA 8505 [ADD]
Yun, I.:Interludium A Academy ▲ ACA 8505 [ADD]
Burns, Stephen (tpt)
Baroque Trumpetissimo, w. D. Bilger (tpt), Edward Carroll (tpt), Alex Holton (tpt), Raymond Mase (tpt), Timothy Morrison (tpt), Lee Soper (tpt), Atsuko Sato (bn), Ben Harms (timp), Edward Brewer (org/hpd), Philharmonia Virtuosi [cnd:Richard Kapp] ESS.A.Y ▲ ESS 1035 [DDD]
Shostakovich, D.:Con 1 Pno, w. C. Rosenberger (pno), G. Schwarz (cnd), Los Angeles CO Delos ▲ DCD 3021 [DDD]
Stock, D.:Tekiah, w. D. Stock (cnd), Pittsburgh New Music Ensemble *(rec Levy Hall, Rodef Shalom Temple, Pittsburgh, Feb. 11, 1990)* Northeastern ("Contemporary" series) ▲ NR 255 [DDD]
Telemann, G.P.:Air de Trompette, w. S. Burns (cnd), American Concerto Orch *(rec Academy of Arts & Letters, New York City, Apr. 29–May 1, 1994)* Dorian Discovery ▲ DIS 80132 [DDD]
Telemann, G.P.:Cons Tpt, w. S. Burns (cnd), American Concerto Orch—in D for Tpt, Strs & Bc; in D for Tpt, 2 Obs, Bn & Hpd; in D for Tpt, Obs, Bn, Strs & Bc *(rec Academy of Arts & Letters, New York City, Apr. 29–May 1, 1994)* Dorian Discovery ▲ DIS 80132 [DDD]
Telemann, G.P.:Sons Tpt, w. S. Burns (cnd), American Concerto Orch—in D for Tpt, Strs & Bc *(rec Academy of Arts & Letters, New York City, Apr. 29–May 1, 1994)* Dorian Discovery ▲ DIS 80132 [DDD]

494 ▲ = CD ♦ = Enhanced CD ∆ = MD ■ = Cassette Tape □ = DCC

Burns, Stephen (tpt) (cont.)
Telemann, G.P.:Suites Tpt, w. S. Burns (cnd), American Concerto Orch—in D for Tpt, Strs & Bc *(rec Academy of Arts & Letters, New York City, Apr. 29–May 1, 1994)* Dorian Discovery ▲ DIS 80132 [DDD]
Trumpet Voluntary, w. Crispian Steele-Perkins (tpt), Gerald Gifford (org) ASV ("Quicksilva" series) ▲ ASV 6081 [ADD/DDD]

Burr, Tony (cl)
O'Rourke, J.:Terminal Pharmacy, w. Jeff Cortazzo (b trbn), John McEntire (dr), Rob Prosser (acc), Isha Suftin (acc), Mike Dockter (vc), Hattie Franck (vc), Robert Keck (vc), Mary LaBreque (vc), Dan Loch (vc), Stan Saderk (vc), Lisa Hemmer (fl), Sue Oberg (fl), Wendi Lev (fl), Jim Vanden (fl), Jim O'Rourke (gtr), Steve Braack (elec) Tzadik ▲ TZA 7011 [DDD]

Burrell, Charles (db)
Encore, w.Colorado Children's Chorale [cnd:Duain Wolfe], Rick Chinski (gtr), Robert Davine (acc), Laurie Kahler (pno), Samuel Lancaster (pno), Barry Oliver (pno), Marylin Preston (fl), Karen Yonovitz (fl), Peter Cooper (ob), Andy Stevens (cl), Lionel Young (vn), Basil Vendreys (va), Wayne Templeman (vc), et al. *(rec Denver Center Media)* Colorado Children's Chorale ▲ 001

Burrows, D. (instr)
Banks, D.:Music of, w. S. Challender (cnd), Sydney SO, Judy Bailey Quintet—Nexus Vox Australis ▲ VAST006-2 [DDD]

Burton, G. (cl)
Gershwin, G.:Music of, w. D. Grusin, L. Ritenour, E. Daniels (cl), J. Pattitucci— instrumental jazz improvisations on 14 Gershwin tunes:That certain feeling; Soon; Fascinating rhythm; Prelude II; How long has this been going on?; There's a boat dat's leavin' soon for New York; My man's gone now; Maybe; Our love is here to stay; 'S Wonderful; I've got plenty o' nuthin; Nice work if you can get it; Medley (Bess, you is my woman now/I loves you, Porgy) GRP ▲ GRD 2005 [ADD]

Burton, Gary (vib)
Brasil, w. R. Stoltzman (cl), Eddie Gomez (db), Danny Gottlieb (perc) RCA Victor ▲ 60708-2-RC [DDD] ■ 60708-4-RC (CrO2)

Burton, Margot (va)—see ORCHESTRAS & ENSEMBLES Rome Solisti

Burton, W. (bar sax)
Kallman, D.:Forecasts, w. E. Finney (sop sax), S. Hyslop (alt sax), K. Claussen (ten sax) Innova ▲ MN 109
Macy, C.:4 Saxes, w. E. Finney (sop sax), S. Hyslop (a sax), K. Claussen (ten sax) Innova ▲ MN 109

Burward-Hoy, Kenneth (va)
Levitch, L.:Fant Ob, w. Greg Donovetsky (ob), Alexander Treger (vn), Janice Foy (vc) Cambria ▲ CD 1059 [ADD]

Busch, A. (vn)—see ORCHESTRAS & ENSEMBLES Busch String Quartet

Busch, Alfred (vn)
Bach, J.S.:Brandenburg Cons, w. A. Busch (cnd), Adolf Busch Chamber Players *(rec mid 1930s)* EMI Classics (Great Recordings of the Century) 3-▲ ZDHC 64047-2
Bach, J.S.:Sons & Partitas Vn, BWV 1001-1006—in g, BWV 1001 Music & Arts 3-▲ CD 877 [ADD]
Bach, J.S.:Sons & Partitas Vn, BWV 1001-1006—Partita No. 2 in d, BWV 1004 *(rec for HMV, 1929)* Pearl ▲ PEA 9942 (m) [AAD]
Bach, J.S.:Sons Vn, w. Rudolf Serkin (pno)—in g, BWV 1001; in E, BWV 1016 Music & Arts 3-▲ CD 877 [ADD]
Bach, J.S.:Sons Vn, w. R. Serkin (pno)—BWV 1021 & 1929 Pearl ▲ PEA 9942 (m) [AAD]
Bach, J.S.:Suites Orch, BWV 1066-1069, w. A. Busch (cnd), Adolf Busch Chamber Players *(rec mid 1930s)* EMI Classics ("Great Recordings of the Century" series) 3-▲ CDHC 64047-2
Beethoven, L. van:Con Vn, Op. 61, w. F. Busch (cnd), New York PO *(rec live, New York 1942)* Melodram ▲ CDM 18040 [ADD]
Beethoven, L. van:Romances Vn, w. H. Münch (cnd), Basel SO *(rec Dec. 18, 1951)* Music & Arts ▲ CD 861 [AAD]
Beethoven, L. van:Son 3 Vn, w. Rudolf Serkin (pno) Enterprise ("The Piano Library" series) ▲ ENT 189
Beethoven, L. van:Son 3 Vn, w. R. Serkin (pno) *(rec 1930 for HMV)* Pearl ▲ PEA 9942 (m) [AAD]
Beethoven, L. van:Son 3 Vn, w. Rudolf Serkin (pno) *(rec May 5, 1931)* APR ▲ APR 5541 [ADD]
Beethoven, L. van:Son 5 Vn, "Spring", w. Rudolf Serkin (pno) *(rec May 17, 1933)* APR ▲ APR 5541 [ADD]
Beethoven, L. van:Son 7 Vn, w. Rudolf Serkin (pno) *(rec Sept 23, 1932 & May 16, 1)* APR ▲ APR 5541 [ADD]
Beethoven, L. van:Son 8 Vn, w. Rudolf Serkin (pno) Music & Arts 3-▲ CD 877 [ADD]
Beethoven, L. van:Son 9 Vn, "Kreutzer", w. Rudolf Serkin (pno), B. Walter (cnd), New York Philharmonic SO Biddulph ▲ LHW 026
Brahms, J.:Con Vn, w. H. Münch (cnd), Basel Orch *(rec Dec. 18, 1951)* Music & Arts ▲ CD 861 [AAD]
Brahms, J.:Con Vn & Vc, "Double Con", w. H. Busch (vc), P. Kletzki (cnd), French National RSO *(rec live, Strasbourg Festival 1949)* Melodram ▲ CDM 18040 [ADD]
Brahms, J.:Qt 2 Pno, w. R. Serkin (pno), Busch String Quartet *(rec 1938)* EMI Classics ▲ CDH 64702
Brahms, J.:Qnt Pno, w. R. Serkin (pno), Busch String Quartet *(rec 1938)* EMI Classics ▲ CDH 64702
Brahms, J.:Son 1 Vn, w. R. Serkin (pno) EMI Classics ▲ CDH 64495
Brahms, J.:Son 2 Vn, w. R. Serkin (pno) EMI Classics ▲ CDH 64495
Brahms, J.:Son 2 Vn, w. R. Serkin (pno) *(rec 1932 HMV recording)* Pearl ▲ PEA 9942 (m) [AAD]
Brahms, J.:Son 3 Vn, w. Rudolf Serkin (pno) Music & Arts 3-▲ CD 877 [ADD]
Brahms, J.:Trio Hn, w. Aubrey Brain (hn), Rudolf Serkin (pno) *(rec 1933)* Iron Needle 2-▲ IN 1342/43 (m) [ADD]
Brahms, J.:Trio Hn, w. A. Brain (hn), R. Serkin (pno) EMI Classics ▲ CDH 64495
Busch, A.:Son Vn, w. Rudolf Serkin (pno) Music & Arts 3-▲ CD 877 [ADD]
Busoni, F.:Con Vn, w. B. Walter (cnd), Royal Concertgebouw Orch *(rec Mar. 12, 1936)* Music & Arts ▲ CD 861 [AAD]
Mozart, W.A.:Sons Vn Pno (misc), w. Rudolf Serkin (pno)—in E♭, K.380; in E♭, K.481 Music & Arts 3-▲ CD 877 [ADD]
Schubert, Franz:Rondo Vn, D.895, w. Rudolf Serkin (pno) Music & Arts 3-▲ CD 877 [ADD]
Schumann, R.:Son 1 Vn, w. Rudolf Serkin (pno) Music & Arts 3-▲ CD 877 [ADD]
Schumann, R.:Son 1 Vn, w. Rudolf Serkin (pno) Enterprise ("The Piano Library" series) ▲ ENT 189
Schumann, R.:Son 2 Vn, w. Rudolf Serkin (pno) Music & Arts 3-▲ CD 877 [ADD]

Busch, Christine (vn)
Turina, J.:Escena andaluza, w. P. Coletti (va), F. Rieger (pno), N. Chastain (vn), A. B. Deutschler (va), F. Goutou (vc) *(rec May 25–28, 1993)* Claves ▲ CD 9403 [DDD]
Turina, J.:Qnt Pno, w. Menuhin Festival Piano Quartet *(rec May 25–28, 1993)* Claves ▲ CD 9403 [DDD]

Busch, H. (vc)—see ORCHESTRAS & ENSEMBLES Busch String Quartet

Busch, Hermann (vc)
Brahms, J.:Con Vn & Vc, "Double Con", w. A. Busch (vn), P. Kletzki (cnd), French National RSO *(rec live, Strasbourg Festival 1949)* Melodram ▲ CDM 18040 [ADD]

Busch, U. (gtr)
Moreno Torroba, F.:Sonatina 1 Gtr Ambitus ▲ 97881
Palacios y Sojo, P.:Son Gtr Ambitus ▲ 97881
Rodrigo, J.:Piezas españolas Ambitus ▲ 97881

Buschmann, Eberhard (bn)
Mozart, W.A.:Don Giovanni, w. Gernot Schmalfub (ob), Christian Hartmann (ob), Dieter Klöcker (cl), Waldemar Wandel (cl), Sara Willis (hn), Christian Auer (hn), Karl-Otto Hartmann (bn), Jürgen Normann (db), Consortium Classicum Bayer ▲ BR 100 135 [DDD]

Buschnakowski, Werner (org)
Kol Nidre:Sacred Music of the Synagogue, w. G. Seipelt (alt), Leo Roth (ten), Rudolf Wiebel (bar), Harry Foss (org), Leipzig RSO members, Jewish Congregation Choir Berlin, Leipzig Synagogue Choir EMI Classics ▲ CDM 65457

Bush, Catherine (vn)
Ashford, R.:Because, w. Mayumi Plumohira (vn), Bruce Plumohira (va), Gregory Wood (vc) Nigel Classics ▲ NC 10101

Bush, Catherine (vn) (cont.)
Ashford, R.:Summer's End, w. Mayumi Plumohira (vn), Bruce Plumohira (va), Gregory Wood (vc) Nigel Classics ▲ NC 10101

Bush, Geoffrey (pno)
Bush, G.:Air & Round-O, "Hommage to Matthew Locke", w. English CO Wind Ensemble Chandos ▲ CHAN 8819 [DDD]
Bush, G.:Dialogue Ob, w. English CO Wind Ensemble Chandos ▲ CHAN 8819 [DDD]
Bush, G.:Qnt Ww, w. English CO Wind Ensemble Chandos ▲ CHAN 8819 [DDD]
Bush, G.:Trio Ob, Bn & Pno, w. English CO Wind Ensemble Chandos ▲ CHAN 8819 [DDD]

Bush, Philip (pno)
Bouchard, L.:Black Burned Wood, w. D. Ohrenstein (sop), M. Rowell (vn/va), J. Cirker (dr/perc), B. Ruyle (mar/xyl/perc) *(rec Feb. & Apr. 1993)* CRI ▲ CD 654 [DDD]
Bruch, M.:Romanze Va, w. P. Coletti (va) Ars Produktion ▲ FCD 368316 [DDD]
Childs, M.E.:Night, w. Dora Ohrenstein (sop) XI Compact Discs ▲ XI 114
Davis, A.:Lost Moon Sisters, w. D. Ohrenstein (sop), M. Rowell (vn), J. Cirker (mar/vib) *(rec Feb. & Apr. 1993)* CRI ▲ CD 654 [DDD]
Johnston, B.:Calamity Jane to Her Daughter, w. D. Ohrenstein (sop), M. Rowell (vn), B. Ruyle (perc) *(rec Feb. & Apr. 1993)* CRI ("Emergency Music" series) ▲ CD 654 [DDD]
Schubert, Franz:Son Arpeggione, w. P. Coletti (va) Ars Produktion ▲ FCD 368316 [DDD]
Shostakovich, D.:Son Va, w. P. Coletti (va) Ars Produktion ▲ FCD 368316 [DDD]

Bush, Philip (pno/syn)
Johnson, S.:Confetti on Flesh, w. D. Ohrenstein (sop), M. Rowell (vn), J. Cirker (mar/dr set) *(rec Feb. & Apr. 1993)* CRI ("Emergency Music" series) ▲ CD 654 [DDD]
Lebaron, A.:Dish, w. D. Ohrenstein (sop), M. Rowell (vn), J. Thompson (elec bass), J. Cirker (dr), B. Ruyle (perc) *(rec Feb. & Apr. 1993)* CRI ("Emergency Music" series) ▲ CD 654 [DDD]

Bushkov, Yevgheny (vn)
Romance & Dances for Violin, w. Y. Bushkov (vn), Marcelle Dedieu-Vidal (pno) Valois ▲ V 4727

Buskirk, John van (pno)
Foster, S.C.:Songs, w. J. Baird (sop), L. Russell (alt/mountain dulcimer), F. Urrey (ten), R. Enslow (fid)—The Glendy Burke; Nelly Was a Lady; Melinda May; The Soirée Polka; The Moustache Song; O Willie, Is It You, Dear?; Mr. & Mr Albany ▲ TROY 119
Rorem, N.:3 Sisters Who Are Not Sisters, w. Andrea Matthews (sop—Jenny), Carol Flamm (sop—Helen), Madeline Tsingopoulos (sgr—Ellen), Frederick Urrey (ten—Samuel), Mark Singer (sgr—Sylvester) Newport Classic ▲ NPT 85594 [DDD]

Buskirk, Tessa van (vn)
Sowerby, L.:Songs, w. D'Anna Fortunato (mez), Veronica Macchia-Kadlubkiewicz (vn), Virginia Christensen (va), Michael Curry (vc)—Premonition; Kisses; Midnight; Reassurance; Adventure [all text L. E. Thomas] Gasparo ▲ GSCD 315 [DDD]

Busoni, Ferruccio (pno)
Bach, J.S.:Chorale Preludes Org—Nun freut euch, BWV 734 [arr Busoni] Symposium ▲ SYM 1145
Bach, J.S.:Preludes & Fugues Hpd—No. 1 in C, BWV 846 Symposium ▲ SYM 1145
Beethoven, L. van:Ecossaises, WoO 83 [arr Busoni] Symposium ▲ SYM 1145
Chopin, F.:Études (24)—in G♭, Op. 10/5; in e, Op. 25/5 Symposium ▲ SYM 1145
Chopin, F.:Nocturnes—in f♯, Op. 15/2 Symposium ▲ SYM 1145
Chopin, F.:Preludes, Op. 28, in A, Op. 28/7 Symposium ▲ SYM 1145
The Complete Recordings (1919–1922) Pearl ▲ PEA 9347 (m) [AAD]
Great Composers at the Keyboard: Ferruccio Busoni Foné ▲ FON 90F13 [DDD]
Liszt, F.:Hungarian Rhaps—No. 13 Symposium ▲ SYM 1145
Liszt, F.:Pno Music (misc)—La Campanella; Feux Follets *(rec 1900–10)* Adès ▲ ADE 203932 [AAD]

Bussotti, Carlo (pno)
Bloch, E.:Son 1 Vn, w. J. Szigeti (vn) Music & Arts 4-▲ CD 720-4 [AAD]
Hindemith, P.:Son in E Vn & Pno, w. J. Szigeti (vn) Sony Masterworks ("Portrait" series) ▲ MPK 52569 (m) [ADD]
Ravel, M.:Son Vn Pno, w. J. Szigeti (vn) *(rec 1953)* Sony Masterworks ("Portrait" series) ▲ MPK 52569 (m) [ADD]
Schubert, Franz:Rondo Vn, D.895, w. J. Szigeti (vn) *(rec 1952; from Columbia LP ML)* Sony Masterworks ("Portrait" series) ▲ MPK 52538 (m) [ADD]

Bustabo, Guila (vn)
Paganini, N.:Con 1 Vn, w. F. Zaun (cnd), Berlin City Orch—1st movt., Allegro, w. cadenza by Wilhelmj *(rec 1940, orig. issued as Col)* Biddulph ▲ LAB 051 [ADD]

Buswell IV, James Oliver (vn)
Vaughan Williams, R.:Con accademico, w. A. Previn (cnd), London SO RCA Gold Seal ▲ 60581-2-RG [ADD]

Butler, M. (vn)—see ORCHESTRAS & ENSEMBLES Chilingirian String Quartet

Butler, Marcia (ob)—see ORCHESTRAS & ENSEMBLES Speculum Musicae, Continuum Chamber Ensemble

Butler, Mark (pno)
Handel, D.:The Tyger, w. Mary Henderson (sop), Sara Lambert Bloom (ob), Gabrielle Robinson (vn), Jina Lee (vn), Rebecca Boughton (va), Deborah Netanel (vc), C. Zimmerman (cnd) Vienna Modern Masters ▲ VMM 2019 [DDD]

Butler Shannon, Nanette (pno)
Moss, L.:Songs to Poems, w. Pamela Jordan (sop) Capstone ▲ CPS 8619

Butt, David (fl)
Ferguson, H.:Sketches, Op. 14, w. Clifford Benson (pno) Chandos ▲ CHAN 9316 [DDD]

Butt, John (hpd)
Bach, J.S.:Con for 4 Hpds, w. Phebe Craig (hpd), Johathan Dimmock (hpd), Jeffrey Thomas (hpd), J. Thomas (cnd), American Bach Soloists Koch International Classics ▲ KIC 7237 [DDD]
Kuhnau, J.:Frische Clavier Früchte *(rec Oct. 1991)* Harmonia Mundi USA ▲ HMU 907097

Butt, John (hpd/clvd/org)
Kuhnau, J.:Musicalische Vorstellung einiger biblischer Historien *(rec Sept 22-24, 1994)* Harmonia Mundi France ▲ HMU 907133

Butt, John (org)
Bach, J.S.:Trio Sons Org, BWV 525-530 Harmonia Mundi USA ▲ HMU 907055
Blow, J.:Org Music—Voluntaries (6) Harmonia Mundi USA ▲ HMU 907103 [DDD]
Cabanilles, J.B.J.:Obras de Organo *(rec 8/91)* Harmonia Mundi USA ▲ HMU 907047
Fauré, G.:Messe basse (in 3 movts), w. Arleen Augér (sop), King's College Choir Cambridge Classics for Pleasure ("Eminence" series) ▲ CDEMX 2166 [DDD]
Fauré, G.:Requiem, w. Arleen Augér (sop), Benjamin Luxon (bar), English CO, King's College Choir Cambridge Classics for Pleasure ("Eminence" series) ▲ CDEMX 2166 [DDD]
Frescobaldi, G.:Capricci Kbd Harmonia Mundi ▲ 907178
Locke, M.:Org Music—Voluntaries (7) Harmonia Mundi USA ▲ HMU 907103 [DDD]
Pachelbel, J.:Hexachordum Apollinis Harmonia Mundi USA ▲ HMU 907029
Pachelbel, J.:Org Music—Chaconne in D; Chaconne in f Harmonia Mundi USA ▲ HMU 907029

Butterfield, Adrian (vn)—see ORCHESTRAS & ENSEMBLES Revolutionary Drawing Room String Quartet

Butterfield, Don (instr)
Cage, J.:Music of, w. John Cage, Xenia Cage, Michael Colgrass, Merce Cunningham, et al.—6 Short Inventions for 7 Instruments; First Construction in Metal; Imaginary Landscape No. 1; The Wonderful Widow of 18 Springs; She Is Asleep; Son. & Interludes; Music for Carillon; Williams Mix; Con. for Piano & Orch. Wergo 3-▲ WER 6247-2

Butterly, Nigel (pno)
Cage, J.:Music for Marcel Duchamp Tall Poppies ▲ TP 025
Cage, J.:Sons & Interludes Tall Poppies ▲ TP 025
Cage, J.:The Wonderful Widow of Eighteen Springs, w. G. English (ten) Tall Poppies ▲ TP 025

Butters, Steve (perc)—see also ORCHESTRAS & ENSEMBLES Tone Road Ramblers
Lund, E.:Due Process *(rec live 1992)* Opus One ▲ CD 164
Veeneman, C.:The Wiry Concord, w. Susan Werner (banjo), Forrest Covington (hammered dlc/cimbalom), Georganne Assat (hp), Donald Martin Jenni (hpd), Mark Johnson (hpd), Barbara Phillips Farley (pno), James Austin (pno), Marta Soderberg (va), James Knutson (perc), Patrick Doyle (perc), James Popejoy (perc), M. Geary (cnd) Capstone ▲ SCI 6

INSTRUMENT.

Buttrick, John (pno)
Busoni, F.:Bach Transcriptions—Nun komm, der Heiden Heiland; Wachet auf, ruft uns die Stimme *(rec 1988)* Jecklin-Disco ▲ JD 623-2
Busoni, F.:Fant nach J. S. Bach Pno *(rec 1988)* Jecklin-Disco ▲ JD 623-2
Busoni, F.:Vars & Fugue in free form on Chopin's Prelude No. 20 *(rec 1988)* Jecklin-Disco ▲ JD 623-2
Haydn, J.:Arianna a Naxos, w. Elisabeth Speiser (sop) [I] *(rec 1987)* Jecklin-Disco ▲ JD 621-2 [ADD]
Haydn, J.:Canzonettas, w. Elisabeth Speiser (sop)—Nos. 32, 34, 41, 42, 50 [E] *(rec 1987)* Jecklin-Disco ▲ JD 621-2 [ADD]
Haydn, J.:Sons Pno—No. 50 *(rec 1987)* Jecklin-Disco ▲ JD 621-2 [ADD]
Haydn, J.:Son Pno, H.XVII/6, "Andante with Vars" *(rec 1987)* Jecklin-Disco ▲ JD 621-2 [ADD]
Reger, M.:Intermezzi *(rec 1985)* Jecklin-Disco ▲ JD 601-2 [ADD]
Reger, M.:Träume am Kamin *(rec 1985)* Jecklin-Disco ▲ JD 601-2 [ADD]
Reger, M.:Trio Vn Vc, w. C. Ragaz (vn), R. Häusler (vc) *(rec 1985)* Jecklin-Disco ▲ JD 604-2 [ADD]
Schubert, Franz:Songs (misc), w. E. Speiser (sop)—20 songs [G] *(rec 1988)* Jecklin-Disco ▲ JD 630-2 [ADD]
Strauss, R.:Enoch Arden, w. G. Westphal (nar) *(rec 1984)* Jecklin-Disco ▲ JD 592-2 [ADD]

Buxtorf, Brigette (fl)
Haydn, J.:Con Fl & Orch, w. B. Dupaquier (cnd), Jura CO Gallo ▲ CD 623 [DDD]

Buyse, Leone (fl)
Contrasts:American Music for Flute & Harp, w. Ann Hobson Pilot (hp) *(rec Seiji Ozawa Hall, Tanglewood, Lenox, MA, July 18-19, 1994)* Boston Records ▲ BR 1011
Koechlin, C.:Son for 2 Fls, w. F. Smith (fl) Hyperion ▲ CDA 66414 [DDD]

Buza, Vilmos (db)
Bengraf, J.:Sacred Music, w. Ingrid Kertesi (sop), Katalin Gémes (mez), Gábor Kállay (ten), Ákos Ambrus (bar), István Ella (org), Zsolt Kovács (vc), Balázs Arnóth (bn), J. Dobra (cnd), Vienna-Szász CO, Tomkins Vocal Ensemble—Te Deum; O sacrum convivium; Libera me; Gloria [from Missa solemnis in D] Hungaroton ▲ HCD 31609 [DDD]
Druschetzky, G.:Missa solemnis, w. Ingrid Kertesi (sop), Katalin Gémes (mez), Gábor Kállay (ten), Ákos Ambrus (bar), István Ella (org), Zsolt Kovács (vc), Balázs Arnóth (bn), J. Dobra (cnd), Vienna-Szász CO, Tomkins Vocal Ensemble Hungaroton ▲ HCD 31609 [DDD]

Bychkov, Semyon (pno)
Mozart, W.A.:Con 7 Pnos, w. K. Labèque (pno), M. Labèque (pno), S. Bychkov (cnd), Berlin PO Philips ("Digital Classics" series) ▲ 426241-2

Bylsma, Anner (vc)—see also ORCHESTRAS & ENSEMBLES Amsterdam Quartet, L'Archibudelli, Paris Quartet
Bach, C.P.E.:Cons Vc, H.432, 436 & 439, w. G. Leonhardt (cnd), Orch of the Age of Enlightenment Virgin Classics ▲ CDC 59541-2 [DDD]
Bach, J.C.F:Son Vc, w. B. van Asperen (org) Sony Classical ("Vivarte" series) ▲ SK 45945
Bach, J.S.:Partita Fl, BWV 1013 Deutsche Harmonia Mundi ▲ 7998-2-RC [DDD]
Bach, J.S.:Sons & Partitas Vn, BWV 1001-1006—BWV 1003 & 1006 only Deutsche Harmonia Mundi ▲ 7998-2-RC [DDD]
Bach, J.S.:Sons Vl, BWV 1027-1029, w. B. van Asperen (org) Sony Classical ("Vivarte" series) ▲ SK 45945
Bach, J.S.:Suites Vc, BWV 1007-1012 [Violoncello Stradivarius "Servais," from the collection of the Smithsonian Institution] Sony Classical ("Vivarte" series) 2-▲ S2K 48047 [DDD]
Beethoven, L. van:Con Vn, Vc & Pno, "Triple Con", w. F. Maier (vn), P. Badura-Skoda (pno), Collegium Aureum Editio Classica ▲ 77063-2-RG [ADD]
Beethoven, L. van:Son 1 Vc, w. M. Bilson (pno) Elektra/Nonesuch ▲ 79152-2 [DDD] ■ 79152-4 (D)
Beethoven, L. van:Son 2 Vc, w. M. Bilson (pno) Elektra/Nonesuch ▲ 79152-2 [DDD] ■ 79152-4 (D)
Boccherini, L.:Con Vc, G.476, Tafelmusik *(rec Sept. 15-17, 1992)* Sony Classical ▲ SK 53121 [DDD]
Boccherini, L.:Con Vc, G.480, w. J. Lamon (cnd), Tafelmusik Deutsche Harmonia Mundi ▲ 7867-2-RC [DDD]
Boccherini, L.:Con Vc, G.483, w. J. Lamon (cnd), Tafelmusik Deutsche Harmonia Mundi ▲ 7867-2-RC [DDD]
Boccherini, L.:Con Vc, G.573, Tafelmusik *(rec Sept. 15-17, 1992)* Sony Classical ▲ SK 53121 [DDD]
Boccherini, L.:Fugues, G.73, w. K. Slowik (vc)—in c, G.2; in B♭, G.8; in F, G.9 *(rec Sept. 6-7, 1992)* Sony Classical ▲ SK 53362 [DDD]
Boccherini, L.:Octet, Tafelmusik *(rec Sept. 15-17, 1992)* Sony Classical ▲ SK 53121 [DDD]
Boccherini, L.:Sons (34) Vc, w. K. Slowik (vc), B. Van Asperen (hpd)—in c, G.2; in B♭, G.8; in F, G.9 *(rec Sept. 6-7, 1992)* Sony Classical ▲ SK 53362 [DDD]
Brahms, J.:Sextet Strs, Op. 18, w. L'Archibudelli, Smithsonian Chamber Players Sony Classical ("Vivarte" series) ▲ SK 68252
Brahms, J.:Sextet Strs, Op. 36, w. L'Archibudelli, Smithsonian Chamber Players Sony Classical ("Vivarte" series) ▲ SK 68252
Brahms, J.:Sons Vc (comp), w. Lambert Orkis (pno) Sony Classical ("Vivarte" series) ▲ SK 68249
Dotzauer, F.:Etudes (3) Vc *(rec New York City, Jan. 19-22, 1994)* Sony Classical ("Vivarte" series) ▲ SK 64307 [DDD]
Dotzauer, F.:Pieces Vc, Op. 104, w. Steven Doane (vc), Kenneth Slowik (vc) *(rec New York City, Jan. 19-22, 1994)* Sony Classical ("Vivarte" series) ▲ SK 64307 [DDD]
Dotzauer, F.:Qt Strs, w. Vera Beths (vn), Jody Gatwood (vn), Lisa Rautenberg (va) *(rec New York City, Jan. 19-22, 1994)* Sony Classical ▲ SK 66259 [DDD]
Dotzauer, F.:Qnt Strs, w. Vera Beths (vn), Jody Gatwood (vn), Lisa Rautenberg (va), Kenneth Slowik (vc) *(rec New York City, Jan. 19-22, 1994)* Sony Classical ("Vivarte" series) ▲ SK 64307 [DDD]
Frescobaldi, G.:Music Vc, w. B. Van Asperen (org), L. Schifes—Canzone VIII, XV, XVI; Ricercari I-VII; Canon Deutsche Harmonia Mundi ▲ 7978-2-RC [DDD]
Haydn, J.:Con 1 Vc, w. J. Lamon (cnd), Tafelmusik Deutsche Harmonia Mundi ▲ 7757-2-RC [DDD] ■ 7757-4-RC (CrO2)
Haydn, J.:Con 2 Vc, w. J. Lamon (cnd), Tafelmusik Deutsche Harmonia Mundi ▲ 7757-2-RC [DDD] ■ 7757-4-RC (CrO2)
Haydn, J.:Mass 4, Missa 'Sunt bona mixta malis', w. Anthony Woodrow (db), Bob Van Asperen (org), B. Weil (cnd), Tölz Boys' Choir *(rec Bad Tolz, Germany, June 6, 1992)* Sony Classical ("Vivarte" series) ▲ SK 53368 [DDD]
Haydn, J.:Non nobis, Domine, w. Anthony Woodrow (db), Bob Van Asperen (org), B. Weil (cnd), Tölz Boys' Choir *(rec Bad Tolz, Germany, June 4, 1992)* Sony Classical ("Vivarte" series) ▲ SK 53368 [DDD]
Haydn, J.:Trios Pno, Vn & Vc, w. Robert Levin (pno), Vera Beths (vn)—No. 25 in C, H.XV:27; No. 26 in E, H.XV:28; No. 30 in E♭, H.XV:30 *(rec Sept. 2-5, 1992)* Sony Classical ▲ SK 53120 [DDD]
Jacchini, G.M.:Sons Vc, w. L. Schifes (continuo instr), B. Van Asperen (org)—Op. 1/7 & 8; Op. 3/9 & 10 Deutsche Harmonia Mundi ▲ 7978-2-RC [DDD]
Kox, H.:Con Vc, w. S. Goldberg (cnd), Netherlands CO *(rec 1970)* Attacca ▲ Babel 9262-1 [ADD/DDD]
Kraft, A.:Con Vc, Op 4, w. J. Lamon (cnd), Tafelmusik Deutsche Harmonia Mundi ▲ 7757-2-RC [DDD] ■ 7757-4-RC (CrO2)
Mozart, W.A.:Qts Cl, w. C. Neidich (cl), V. Beths (vn), J. Kussmaul (va)—in B♭ after K.378 Sony Classical ("Vivarte" series) ▲ SK 53366 [DDD]
Mozart, W.A.:Qnt Cl, K.581, w. C. Neidich (cl), V. Beths (vn), J. Kussmaul (va) Sony Classical ("Vivarte" series) ▲ SK 53366 [DDD]
Mozart, W.A.:Trio Cl, K.498, w. C. Neidich (vn), V. Beths (vn), J. Kussmaul (va) Sony Classical ("Vivarte" series) ▲ SK 53366 [DDD]
Schubert, Franz:Qnt Strs, D.956, w. L. Rautenberg (vn), J. Gatwood (vn), S. Dann (va), K. Slowick (vc) Sony Classical ("Vivarte" series) ▲ SK 46669
Schumann, R.:Stücke im Volkston, w. Lambert Orkis (pno) Sony Classical ("Vivarte" series) ▲ SK 68249
Telemann, G.P.:Sons Rcr, w. Frans Brüggen (rcr), Gustav Leonhardt (hpd)—in F, B♭, C, f, d & C [TWV 41:F2, B3, C5, f1, d4 & C2] Teldec ("Das Alte Werk" series) ▲ 93688-2 [ADD]

Bylsma, Anner (vc) (cont.)
Vivaldi, A.:Cons Vc, w. J. Lamon (cnd), Tafelmusik—RV.413 & 418 Sony Classical ("Vivarte" series) ▲ SK 48044

Byram-Wigfield, Timothy (org)
The Organ of St. Mary's Cathedral, Edinburgh Herald ▲ HAVPCD 169
Scarlatti, D.:Salve regina, w. C. Harris (trb), N. Clapton (alt) Hyperion ▲ CDA 66182 [DDD]
Vaughan Williams, R.:O Taste & See, w. D. Hill (cnd), Winchester Cathedral Choir Argo ▲ 436120-2 [DDD]
Walton, W.:Coronation Te Deum, w. D. Hill (cnd), Bournemouth SO, Winchester Cathedral Choir Argo ▲ 436120-2 [DDD]
Walton, W.:Jubilate Deo, w. D. Hill (cnd), Winchester Cathedral Choir, Waynflete Singers Argo ▲ 436120-2 [DDD]
Weelkes, T.:Cathedral Music, w. David Hill (cnd), Winchester Cathedral Choir—All Laud and Praise; Alleluia, I Heard a Voice; Give Ear, O Lord; Give the King Thy Judgements; Gloria in excelsis Deo; Hosanna to the Son of David; If King Manasses; Laboravi in gemitu meo; Magnificat; Nunc dimittis; O How Amiable; O Jonathan; O Lord Arise; When David Heard [E,L] Hyperion ▲ CDA 66477

Byron, Don (cl)
Jenkins, L.:Monkey on the Dragon, w. Leroy Jenkins (vn), Henry Threadgill (fl), Marth Ehrlich (b cl), Janet Frice (bn), Vincent Chancey (hn), Frank Gordon (tpt), Jeff Hoyer (trbn), David Soldier (vn), Jane Henry (vn) Ron Lawrence (va), Mary Wooton (vc), Lindsey Horner (db), Thurman Barker (traps), Myra Melford (pno), T. Léon (cnd) *(rec live, Merkin Concert Hall, New York City, Apr. 9, 1992)* CRI ("eXchange" series) ▲ CD 663 [DDD]
Jenkins, L.:Panorama 1, w. Leroy Jenkins (vn), Henry Threadgill (fl), Marty Ehrlich (b cl), Vincent Chancey (hn) *(rec live, Merkin Concert Hall, New York City, Apr. 9, 1992)* CRI ("eXchange" series) ▲ CD 663 [DDD]

Byzantine, Julian (gtr)
Albéniz, I.:Recuerdos de Viaje Classics for Pleasure ▲ CDCFP 4631 [DDD]
Albéniz, I.:Suite española [arr. Byzantine] Classics for Pleasure ▲ CDCFP 4631 [DDD]
Bach, J.S.:Lt Music Classics for Pleasure ▲ CDCFP 9014 [DDD]
Scarlatti, D.:Sons Kbd—Sonata in A, K.322; Sonata in E, K.380 Classics for Pleasure ▲ CDCFP 9014 [DDD]
Weiss, S.L.:Lt Music—Tombeau sur la mort de M. Comte de Logy; Fantasie; Passacaille form Suite XIV Classics for Pleasure ▲ CDCFP 9014 [DDD]

Caballero, William (hn)
Leclaire, D.:Qt Hns, w. T. Bacon (hn), G. Hustis (hn), Erik Ralske (hn) Summit ▲ DCD 135 [DDD]
Lees, B.:Con Hn, w. L. Maazel (cnd), Pittsburgh SO *(rec Pittsburgh, May 10-12, 1996)* New World ▲ 805032 [DDD]

Cabasso, Laurent (pno)
Schubert, Franz:Intro & Vars Fl on "Tröckne Blumen", w. Philippe Bernold (fl) Harmonia Mundi France ▲ HMN 911535
Schumann, R.:Andante & Vars Hn, w. Marie-Josèphe Jude (pno), Roland Pidoux (vc), Michel François (vc), Hervé Joulain (hn) Harmonia Mundi France ("Les Nouveaux Interprètes" series) ▲ HMN 911559
Schumann, R.:Songs, w. Marie-Josèphe Jude (pno), Roland Pidoux (vc), Michel François (vc), Hervé Joulain (hn)—Abendlied, Op. 107/6 Harmonia Mundi France ("Les Nouveaux Interprètes" series) ▲ HMN 911559
Weber, C.M. von:Sons Vn, w. Philippe Bernold (fl)—1 Son. for fl & pno on Schubert theme Harmonia Mundi France ▲ HMN 911535
Weber, C.M. von:Trio Fl, w. Philippe Bernold (fl), Jean-Guihen Queyras (vc) Harmonia Mundi France ("Les Nouveaux Interprètes" series) ▲ HMN 911535

Cabaud-Chiaparin, Myriam (fl)
Benedict, J.:La Gitane et l'oiseau, w. Caryn Hartglass (sop) *(rec Châteaugay Church, France, June 1995)* Ligia Digital ▲ 0201033 [DDD]
Bernstein, L.:Mass (sels), w. Caryn Hartglass (sop), Bernard Leroy (pno)—A Simple Song; I Go On *(rec Châteaugay Church, France, June 1995)* Ligia Digital ▲ 0201033 [DDD]
Longas, F.:Le Rossignol et l'Empereur, w. Caryn Hartglass (sop) *(rec Châteaugay Church, France, June 1995)* Ligia Digital ▲ 0201033 [DDD]

Cabestany, Rose-Marie (pno)
Kodály, Z.:Son Vc & Pno, Op. 4, w. Lluís Claret (vc) Harmonia Mundi France ("Musique d'abord" series) ▲ HMA 1901325

Cabral, Pedro (gtr)
Guitarra Portuguesa GHA ▲ 126.014

Cacioppo, Curt (pno)
Cacioppo, C.:Wolf, w. Janice Fiore (sop), David Geber (vc) Capstone ▲ CPS 8632

Cadiz, Monserrat (fl)
Kam, D.:Fant Vars, w. Dennis Kam (pno) *(rec Studio Center, Miami)* Capstone ▲ CPS 8631

Cadranel, B. (hpd)
Bach, J.S.:Preludium & Fugue Hpd, BWV 894 Klavier ■ KC 7028
Scarlatti, D.:Sons Kbd—Sons., K.54, K.215, K.216, K.49, K.518, K.519 Klavier ■ KC 7028

Caens, Thierry (tpt)
The Art of the Cornet, w. Lyon Wind Quintet Arion ▲ ARN 60267
Haydn, J.:Con Tpt, w. A. Moglia (cnd), Toulouse CO *(rec Sept 1994)* Pierre Verany ▲ PVY 730029
Honegger, A.:Chamber Music (comp), w. D.-S. Kang (vn), P.-H. Xuereb (va), R. Wallfisch (vc), M. Arrignon (cl), A. Marion (fl), A. Haraldsdottir (fl), C. Moreaux (ob), M. Becquet (trbn), P. Zanlonghi (hp), P. Devoyon (pno), F. Kondo (mez), Ludwig String Quartet—Sonatine for Clarinet & Piano (1921-22); Rapsodie for 2 Flutes, Clarinet & Piano (1917); Danse de la Chèvre for Solo Flute (1921); Romance for Flute & Piano (1953); Petite Suite for 2 Flutes & Piano (1934); Trois Contrepoints for Piccolo, Oboe, Violin & Cello (1922); Intrada for Trumpet & Piano (1947); Hommage du trombone exprimant la tristesse de l'auteur absent for Trombone & Piano (1925); J'avais un fidèle amant for String Quartet (1929); Chanson de Ronsard & 3 Chansons de la petite Sirène for Mezzo, Flute & String Quartet (1924); Introduction et Danse for Flute, Harp & String Trio [undated]; Colloque for Flute, Celesta, Violin & Viola [undated] Timpani ▲ 1C1010 [DDD]
Mozart, L.:Con Hn, w. Alain Moglia (vn), A. Moglia (cnd), Toulouse National CO, Les Cuivres Francais Pierre Verany ▲ PVY 730070
Mozart, L.:Serenade Tpt, w. Alain Moglia (vn), A. Moglia (cnd), Toulouse National CO, Les Cuivres Francais Pierre Verany ▲ PVY 730070

Caffagni, Livia (rcr/h-g/sgr)—see ORCHESTRAS & ENSEMBLES La Reverdie

Cage, John (instrs)
Cage, J.:Music of, w. Xenia Cage, Don Butterfield, Michael Colgrass, Merce Cunningham, et al.—6 Short Inventions for 7 Instruments; First Construction in Metal; Imaginary Landscape No. 1; The Wonderful Widow of 18 Springs; She Is Asleep; Son. & Interludes; Music for Carillon; Williams Mix; Con. for Piano & Orch. Wergo 3-▲ WER 6247-2

Cage, John (pno)
Wolff, C.:Duo for Pianists I, w. David Tudor (pno)—2 versions *(rec Oct 1, 1960)* Hat Hut ("Now" series) ▲ CD 6181 [ADD]

Cage, Xenia (instr)
Cage, J.:Music of, w. John Cage, Don Butterfield, Michael Colgrass, Merce Cunningham, et al.—6 Short Inventions for 7 Instruments; First Construction in Metal; Imaginary Landscape No. 1; The Wonderful Widow of 18 Springs; She Is Asleep; Son. & Interludes; Music for Carillon; Williams Mix; Con. for Piano & Orch. Wergo 3-▲ WER 6247-2

Caggiano, Antonio (perc)
Curran, A.:Crystal Psalms, An Homage to Kristallnacht, w. F. Badaloni (cl), D. Keberlee (cl), M. Riesler (cl), A. Santoloci (cl), M. Capone (acc), L. Dublanchet (tuba), D. Rueff (tuba), w. Ensemble Vocale Sesquialtera [cnd:E. Razzicchia], Radio France Chamber Choir [cnd:D. LaBorde]—[F] New Albion ▲ NA 067

Cagnon, François (hn)
Original Works & Transcriptions for Horn & Harp, w. Marie-Pierre Cochereau (hp) Solstice ▲ SOCD 53

Cahn, B. (perc)—see ORCHESTRAS & ENSEMBLES Nexus

Cahn, Ruth (timp)
Cahn, W.:Raga 1 Nexus ▲ 10339 [DDD]

Cahuzac, Louis (cl)
Hindemith, P.:Con Cl, w. P. Hindemith (cnd), Philharmonia Orch EMI Classics 2-▲ ZDCB 55032
Nielsen, C.:Con Cl, w. J. Frandsen (cnd), Copenhagen Opera Orch *(rec Nov. 3 & 4, 1947)* Clarinet Classics ▲ CC 0002

Caillat, Gui-Michel (pno)
Gerber, R.:Con Pno & Winds, w. C. Delley (cnd), Provence Camerata Genève Gallo ▲ CD 861 [ADD]

Cain, Sim (perc)
Shea, D.:Hsi-Yu Chi, w. Hideki Kato (bass instrument), Wu Man (pipa), Zeena Parkins (hp/pno/acc), Jim Pugliese (perc), Mark Ribot (gtr/banjo), David Shea (sampler/pno/turntables), Alex Tobias (celtic dr/misc.), Rebecca Wilson (screaming), John Zorn (a sax) Tzadik ("The Composers" series) ▲ TZA 7005 [DDD]

Caird, George (ob)
Leighton, K.:Veris gratia, w. Raphael Wallfisch (vc), V. Handley (cnd), Royal Liverpool PO Chandos ▲ CHAN 8471 [DDD]

Caister, Tim (hn)
Vivaldi, A.:Cons Diverse Instrs, w. Joanna Graham (bn), Ruth McDowall (cl), David Rix (ct), Deborah Davis (fl), Duke Dobing (fl), Stephen Stirling (hn), Christopher Hooker (ob), Helen McQueen (ob), Michael Meekes (tpt), Crispian Steele-Perkins (tpt), Nicholas Kraemer (hpd), N. Kraemer (cnd), London Sinfonietta—Cons. in F, RV.539; in C, RV.533; in D, RV.122; in C, RV.537; in C, RV.560; in F, RV.538; in G, RV.545 *(rec All Saints Church, East Finchley, Oct. 1994 & Jan. 1995)* Naxos ("Vivaldi Collection" series) ▲ 8.553204 [DDD]

Cakar, M. (hn)
Mozart, L.:Con 2 Hns, w. H. Baumann (hn), J. Schröder (cnd), Concerto Amsterdam Acanta ▲ 43278
Witt, F.:Con Hns, w. H. Baumann (hn), J. Schröder (cnd), Concerto Amsterdam—in F Acanta ▲ 43278

Calame, G. (pno)
Guyonnet, J.:La Cantate interrompue, w. F. Rochaix (nar), S. Stenhammar (sop), S. Seban (pno), G. Calame (pno), E. Séjourne (perc), P. Geiss, E. Tarr (tpt), B. Nilsson (tpt), H. Ries (trbn), H. Rückert (trbn), J.-M. Collet, J. Guyonnet (cnd), Geneva Collegium Academicum [F] *(rec Nov. 15, 1986)* Grammont ▲ CTSP 30-2

Calame, N. (cl)
Wyttenbach, J.:Lamentoroso, w. L. Akerlund (sop), H. Bissegger (cl), M. Maurer (cl), E. Molinari (cl), M. Weber (cl), H. Zwahlen (cl) *(rec May 19-20, 1990)* Grammont ▲ CTSP 37-2 [ADD]

Calderón, Javier (gtr)
Spanish & Latin Music *(rec Jan. 1993)* Centaur ▲ CRC 2179

Caldwell, Phyllis (vc)
Weber, C.M. von:Qnt Cl, w. L. Fuchs (cl), M. Solms (vn), O. Sipahi (vn), D. Morice (va) Gallo ▲ CD 570 [DDD]

Calef, Hélène (pno)
Juon, P.:Chamber Music, w. Claire Vergnory-Mion (cl), Jean-François Benatar (va), Pierre Lenert (va), Philippe Nadal (vc)—Trio Miniatures for Cl, Vc & Pno; Son in D for Va & Pno, Op. 15; Divert for Cl & 2 Vas, Op. 34; Trio for Cl, Vc & Pno, Op. 17 REM ▲ REM 311267 [DDD]

Calef, Iosef (vc)—see ORCHESTRAS & ENSEMBLES Crawford Trio

Calhoun, David (vc)—see ORCHESTRAS & ENSEMBLES Hudson River String Trio

Call, P. (fl)
Zappa, E.A.:Hydra Son, w. M. Graber (pno) CRS ▲ CD 9257

Callahan, Charles (org)
Guilmant, A.:Org Music—Grand Triumphant Chorus, Op. 47/2; Melody in D (Song without Words), Op. 45; Paraphrase (on a chorus from *Judas Maccabaeus*), Op. 90/16; The Manger (Pastoral & Adoration), Op. 50/3; Fuga "alla Handel," Op. 49/6; Melody in G (Song without Words), Op. 46/4; March upon a Theme of Handel, Op. 15/2; Cantilene Pastorale (Souvenir), Op. 15; Prayer in F, Op. 16/2; Caprice, Op. 20; Offertory upon "O Filii," Op. 49/2 Pro Organo ▲ CD 7006
Stanford, C.V.:Sons Org (misc)—No. 2 in G, Op. 151, "Eroica" (1917); No. 3 in D, Op. 152, "Britannica" (1917); No. 4 in C, Op. 153, "Celtica" (1918) Pro Organo ■ 7010

Callahan, J. (org)
Oberdoerffer, F.:Fant & Fugue Org Centaur ▲ CRC 2081 [DAD]
Reger, M.:Org Music (misc)—Introduction & Passacaglia in d; Canon in E & Pastorale in F (from Op. 59) Centaur ▲ CRC 2081 [DAD]
Rheinberger, J.:Sons Org—No. 7 in f, Op. 127 Centaur ▲ CRC 2081 [DAD]
Schmidt, F.:Chorale Preludes Centaur ▲ CRC 2081 [DAD]

Callandrelli, Jorge (pno)
Symphonic Boleros, w. V. Lewis (cnd), Royal PO, Ettore Stratta (cnd), Ernie Watts (sax), Sal Marquez (tpt), Clare Fischer (pno), Brian Monroney (gtr) Teldec ▲ 91180-2 ■ 91180-4

Callaway, Paul (org)
La Montaine, J.:Wilderness Journal, w. Donald Gramm (b-bar), A. Dorati (cnd), National SO Washington D.C. *(rec live, Kennedy Center, Oct 10, 1972)* Fredonia Discs ■ FDC 11
La Montaine, J.:Wilderness Journal, w. Donald Gramm (b-bar), A. Dorati (cnd), National SO Washington D.C. *(rec live, Kennedy Center, Oct 10, 1972)* Fredonia Discs ▲ FDCD 12

Calligaris, Sergio (pno)
Calligaris, S.:Con Pno, w. M. de Bernart (cnd), Albanian Radio-TV Orch Agora Musica ▲ AG 042.1 [DDD]
Calligaris, S.:Son-Fant Agora Musica ▲ AG 042.1 [DDD]

Callinicos, Constantine (pno)
Three Tenors of the Golden Age, w. J. Björling (ten), Mario Lanza (ten), Jan Peerce (ten), John Corigliano (vn), Frederick Schauwecker (pno), RCA Victor Orch [cnd:Renato Cellini, Constantine Callinicos, Erich Leinsdorf, Sylvan Levin, Maximilian Pilzer, Frieder Weissmann], Rome Opera Orch, Rome Opera Chorus [cnd:Eri RCA Gold Seal ▲ 09026-68531-2 [ADD] ■ 09026-68531-4

Calnan, Patricia (vn)—see ORCHESTRAS & ENSEMBLES Lyric String Quartet

Calogero, Antonio (gtr)
Saariaho, K.:Gtr Music—Oltre la Porta, al Di del Muro; Il Ritorno; Il Piano; Il Primo Inverno; 1580 Hayes Street; La Rosa del Deserto; Flusso Creativo; Pre America/Post America; San Francisco; Cosi Chiaro...Nel Buio; La Port D'Oro *(rec Osnabruck, Germany, Dec. 1995)* Acoustic Music ▲ 319-1092-2 [DDD]

Calvayrac, Albert (tpt)
Telemann, G.P.:Con Tpt Strs in D, w. L. Auriacombe (cnd), Toulouse CO *(rec Chapelle des Italiens, Toulouse, June 1965)* EMI Classics ▲ CDK 65340 [ADD]

Calvetti (db)
Peck, R.:Automobile, w. Ragains (sop), Middleton (fl), Johnson (perc) CRI ■ C 367

Cambreling, Frédérique (hp)
Milhaud, D.:Con Hp, w. K. Nagano (cnd), Lyon Opera Orch Erato ("Musifrance" series) ▲ 2292-45820-2-ZK

Camden, Anthony (ob)
Albinoni, T.:Cons à 5 Obs, Op. 9, w. J. Georgiadis (cnd), London Virtuosi—Nos. 2, 5, 8 & 11; Nos. 3 & 9, w. Julia Girdwood *(rec Oct 11-12, 1992)* Naxos ▲ 8.550739 [DDD]
Barbirolli, J.:Con on Themes of Peroglisi, w. N. Ward (cnd), City of London Sinfonia *(rec East Finchley, England, Apr 1995)* Naxos ▲ 8.553433 [DDD]
Bellini, V.:Con in E♭ Ob, w. N. Ward (cnd), City of London Sinfonia *(rec East Finchley, England, Apr 1995)* Naxos ▲ 8.553433 [DDD]
Cimarosa, D.:Con in C Ob, w. N. Ward (cnd), City of London Sinfonia *(rec East Finchley, England, Apr 1995)* Naxos ▲ 8.553433 [DDD]
Corelli, A.:Con Ob, w. N. Ward (cnd), City of London Sinfonia *(rec East Finchley, England, Apr 1995)* Naxos ▲ 8.553433 [DDD]
Fiorillo, F.:Sinf concertante, w. Julia Girdwood (ob), N. Ward (cnd), City of London Sinfonia—in F *(rec East Finchley, England, Apr 1995)* Naxos ▲ 8.553433 [DDD]
Handel, G.F.:Cons (3) Ob, w. N. Ward (cnd), City of London Sinfonia *(rec All Saints Church, East Finchley, Apr 24 & 27, 1995)* Naxos ▲ 8.553430 [DDD]

Camden, Anthony (ob) (cont.)
Handel, G.F.:Hpd Music, w. N. Ward (cnd), City of London Sinfonia—Air in g & Rondo in G [orchd A. Camden] *(rec All Saints Church, East Finchley, Apr 24 & 27, 1995)* Naxos ▲ 8.553430 [DDD]
Handel, G.F.:Ottone, Rè di Germania (ov), w. Julia Girdwood (ob), N. Ward (cnd), City of London Sinfonia *(rec All Saints Church, East Finchley, Apr 24 & 27, 1995)* Naxos ▲ 8.553430 [DDD]
Handel, G.F.:Suites Hpd, w. Julia Girdwood (ob), N. Ward (cnd), City of London Sinfonia—in g [trans by A. Camden] *(rec All Saints Church, East Finchley, Apr 24 & 27, 1995)* Naxos ▲ 8.553430 [DDD]
Righini, V.:Con Ob, w. N. Ward (cnd), City of London Sinfonia *(rec East Finchley, England, Apr 1995)* Naxos ▲ 8.553433 [DDD]
Williams, G.:Music of, w. Snell, Groves (cnd), London SO, Royal PO, English CO—Fant on Welsh Nursery Tunes; Sea Sketches; Penillion; Carillions Ob; Con for Tpt Lyrita ▲ SRCD 323

Cameron, M. (db)—see ORCHESTRAS & ENSEMBLES Ciosoni Trio

Cameron, Michael (db)
Bach, J.S.:Suites Vc, BWV 1007-1012 [trans for db] Zuma Records ▲ ZMA 304
Baker, C.:Omaggi e Fant Db, w. D. Liptak (pno) Gasparo ▲ GS 286
Hindemith, P.:Son Db, w. Ian Hobson (pno) Zuma Records ▲ ZMA 304
Johnston, B.:Progression, w. Ian Hobson (pno) Zuma Records ▲ ZMA 304
Segall, A.J.:Fant Db, w. Ian Hobson (pno) Zuma Records ▲ ZMA 304
Shostakovich, D.:Night, w. Ian Hobson (pno) Zuma Records ▲ ZMA 304

Camilleri, Marie-Laurence (vn)—see ORCHESTRAS & ENSEMBLES Cecilia Piano Quartet

Camino, Bruno (pno)
Beethoven, L. van:Son 3 Vc, w. Jan Vogler (vc) Berlin Classics ▲ BER 1167
Beethoven, L. van:Vars on "Ein Mädchen oder Weibchen" from Mozart's *Die Zauberflöte*, w. Jan Vogler (vc) Berlin Classics ▲ BER 1167
Beethoven, L. van:Vars on "See, the Conquering Hero Comes" from Handel's *Judas Maccabaeus*, w. Jan Vogler (vc) Berlin Classics ▲ BER 1167
Beethoven, L. van:Vars on "Bei Männern" from Mozart's *Die Zauberflöte*, w. Jan Vogler (vc) Berlin Classics ▲ BER 1167
Schumann, R.:Fantasiestücke Cl, w. Jan Vogler (vc) Berlin Classics ▲ BER 1167

Camosi, Jean (perc)
Martinů, B.:Double Con Pno & Timp, w. J.-F. Heisser (pno), A. Planès (pno), J. Conlon (cnd), French National Orch Erato ▲ 2292-45499-2 ZK

Camp, Manel (pno)
Camp, M.:Pno Music—Coratge; Primavera perduda; Anhels; Imatges suggestives; Nocturn *(rec Albert Moraleda Studios, July 24-26, 1995)* Edicions Albert Moraleda ▲ 95327 [DDD]

Campagnaro, Teodora (vc)—see also ORCHESTRAS & ENSEMBLES Trio Italiano
Dragonetti, D.:Duo Vc & Db, w. Ubaldo Fioravanti (db) *(rec Sala San Bovo, Padova, Italy, Jan 17-19, 1995)* Dynamic ▲ CD 133 [DDD]
Dragonetti, D.:Qt 4 Strs, w. Stefano Furini (vn), Pietro Juvarra (vn), Giancarlo di Vacri (va) *(rec Sala San Bovo, Padova, Italy, Jan 17-19, 1995)* Dynamic ▲ CD 133 [DDD]

Campagne, Augusta (hpd)
Vivaldi, A.:Cons Hpd—RV.230 Preiser ▲ PRE 90276

Campanella, Michele (pno)
Liszt, F.:Hungarian Rhaps Philips 2-▲ 438371-2

Campbell, Crispin (vc)
Hurley, S.:Wind River Songs, w. Nicole Philibosian (sop), Michael Coonrod (pno) *(rec Interlochen Center for the Arts)* Capstone ▲ CPS 8618

Campbell, David (cl)
Brahms, J.:Sons Cl (comp), w. A. Ball (pno) Collins Quest ▲ COL 3010 [DDD]
Debussy, C.:Chamber Music, w. William Bennett (fl), James Campbell (cl), Nicholas Daniel (ob), Robert Makell (hn), Richard Watkins (hn), Robin Kennard (bn), Rachel Gough (bn), Simon Haram (sax), Ieuan Jones (hp), Clifford Benson (pno), Julius Drake (pno), John York (pno), Roger Tapping (va)—Rapsodie for Eng hn; Syrinx; Première rapsodie; Son for Fl, Va & Hp; Le petit nègre; Petite pièce; Rapsodie for Sax *(rec All Saints' Church, East Finchley, London, Jan 12-20, 1994)* Cala 2-▲ CACD 1017 [DDD]
Krauze, Z.:Quatuor pour la naissance, w. M. Mitchell (vn), C. van Kampen (vc), J. MacGregor (pno) Collins Classics ▲ COL 1393 [DDD]
Mendelssohn, F.:Son Cl, w. A. Ball (pno) Collins Quest ▲ COL 3010 [DDD]
Messiaen, O.:Quatuor pour la fin du temps, w. M. Mitchell (vn), C. van Campen (vc), J. MacGregor (pno) Collins Classics ▲ COL 1393 [DDD]
Mozart, W.A.:Con Cl, w. R. Hickox (cnd), City of London Sinfonia IMP ▲ IMP 2011
Poulenc, F.:Chamber Music, w. Peter Sidhom (bar), William Bennett (fl), James Campbell (cl), Nicholas Daniel (ob), Richard Watkins (hn), Rachel Gough (bn), Peter Carter (vn), Chris West (db), Ieuan Jones (hp), Clifford Benson (pno), Julius Drake (pno), John York (pno)—Son for Ob; L'invitation au château; Villanelle; Son 2 Cls; Trio; Sxt; Son for Cl & Bn; Rapsodie nègre; Son for Cl; Mouvements perpétuels; Son for Fl *(rec All Saints' Church, East Finchley, London, Jan 12-20, 1994)* Cala ▲ CACD 1018 [DDD]
Ravel, M.:Intro & Allegro, w. V. McKeand (hp), C. Wincenc (fl), Allegri String Quartet Virgin Classics ▲ CDZ 59695
Ravel, M.:Le Tombeau de Couperin, w. V. McKeand (hp), C. Wincenc (fl), Allegri String Quartet Virgin Classics ▲ CDZ 59695
Saint-Saëns, C.:Chamber Music, w. W. Bennett (fl), J. Campbell (cl), N. Daniel (ob), R. Makell (hn), R. Watkins (hn), R. Kennard (bn), R. Gough (bn), S. Haram (sax), I. Jones (hp), C. Benson (pno), J. Drake (pno), J. York (pno), R. Tapping (va)—Odelette, Op. 162; Son for Cl, Op. 167; Feuillet d'album, Op. 81; Son for Bn, Op. 168; Caprice on Danish & Russian Airs, Op. 79; Son for Ob, Op. 166; Romance in D♭, Op. 37; Tarantelle, Op. 6 *(rec All Saints' Church, East Finchley, London, Jan 12-20, 1994)* Cala 2-▲ CACD 1017 [DDD]
Schubert, Franz:Songs (misc), w. Lynda Russell (sop), Peter Hill (pno)—Ganymed, D.544; Liebhaber in allen Gestalten, D.558; Nacht und Träume, D.827; Geheimes, D.719; Abendstern, D.806; Der Hirt auf dem Felsen, D.965; Suleika, D.720; Seligkeit, D.433; Wiegenlied, D.498; Gretchen am Spinnrade, D.118; An die Entfernte, D.765; Im Frühling, D.882; Suleikas zweiter Gesang, D.717; Du bist die Ruh, D.776; Lied der Mignon, D.877/4; Nachtviolen, D.752; Der Musensohn, D.764; Die Forelle, D.550 *(rec St. Martin's Church, East Woodhay, Hampshire, England, Nov 7-9, 1994)* Naxos ▲ 8.553113 [DDD]
Weber, C.M. von:Vars on a Theme from *Silvana* Cl, w. Christine Croshaw (pno) Meridian ▲ MER 84260 [DDD]

Campbell, G. (sax)
Swack, I.:Elegy for Moss Land, w. Valcour String Quartet *(rec Aug. 1991)* Centaur ▲ CRC 2111 [DDD]

Campbell, James (cl)—see also ORCHESTRAS & ENSEMBLES Indiana Trio
Beethoven, L. van:Trio 7 Pno, w. L. Edlina (pno), Y. Turovsky (vc) Chandos ▲ CHAN 8655 [DDD]
Berg, A.:Pieces (4) Cl, w. J. York (pno) Crystal ■ C331
Brahms, J.:Son 1 Cl, w. G. Simon (cnd), London SO [orchd. Berio] *(rec St Jude-on-the-Hill, Hampstead Garden Suburb, London, Oct 1-4, 1990)* Cala ▲ CACD 1006 [DDD]
Brahms, J.:Trio Cl, w. Y. Turovsky (vc), L. Edlina (pno) Chandos ▲ CHAN 8606 [DDD]
Copland, A.:Con Cl, w. F.-P. Decker (cnd), National Arts Center Canada Orch CBC ("SM 5000" series) ▲ SMCD 5096 [DDD] ■ SMC 5096 (D)
Debussy, C.:Chamber Music, w. William Bennett (fl), David Campbell (cl), Nicholas Daniel (ob), Robert Makell (hn), Richard Watkins (hn), Robin Kennard (bn), Rachel Gough (bn), Simon Haram (sax), Ieuan Jones (hp), Clifford Benson (pno), Julius Drake (pno), John York (pno), Roger Tapping (va)—Rapsodie for Eng hn; Syrinx; Première rapsodie; Son for Fl, Va & Hp; Le petit nègre; Petite pièce; Rapsodie for Sax *(rec All Saints' Church, East Finchley, London, Jan 12-20, 1994)* Cala 2-▲ CACD 1017 [DDD]
Debussy, C.:Première rapsodie, w. Glenn Gould (pno) Sony Classical ("Glen Gould Edition" series) ▲ SMK 52661
Debussy, C.:Première rapsodie, w. G. Simon (cnd), Philharmonia Orch *(rec St. Jude-on-the-Hill, Hampstead, London, Jan 2-6, 1990)* Cala ▲ CACD 1001 [DDD]

INSTRUMENT.

Campbell, James (cl) (cont.)
Françaix, J.:Heure du berger Orch, w. Suzanne Shulman (fl), James Mason (ob), James Sommerville (hn), James McKay (bn), André Laplante (pno) *(rec Glenn Gould Studio, CBC Toronto, Mar. 26–27, 1994)* CBC ("Musica Viva" series) ▲ MVV 1089 [DDD]
Glick, S.I.:Suite Hébraïque 1, w. V. Tyron (pno) CBC ("Musica Viva" series) ▲ MVCD 1046 [DDD]
Glick, S.I.:Suite Hébraïque 5, w. S. Shulman (fl), A. Dawes (vn), D. Domb (vc) CBC ("Musica Viva" series) ▲ MVCD 1046 [DDD]
James Campbell, w. John York (pno) Crystal ■ C331
Louie, A.:Cadenzas, w. B. Johnston (perc) Centrediscs ▲ CMCCD 2786
Martinů, B.:La Revue de Cuisine, w. James McKay (bn), Guy Few (tpt), Moshe Hammer (vn), Tsuyoshi Tsutsumi (vc), André Laplante (pno) *(rec Glenn Gould Studio, CBC Toronto, Mar. 26–27, 1994)* CBC ("Musica Viva" series) ▲ MVV 1089 [DDD]
Milhaud, D.:Suite Vn, w. Moshe Hammer (vn), André Laplante (pno) *(rec Glenn Gould Studio, CBC Toronto, Mar. 26–27, 1994)* CBC ("Musica Viva" series) ▲ MVV 1089 [DDD]
Mozart, W.A.:Con Cl, w. F.–P. Decker (cnd), National Arts Center Canada Orch CBC ("SM 5000" series) ▲ SMCD 5096 [DDD] ■ SMC 5096 (D)
Mozart, W.A.:Qnt Cl, K.581, w. Orford String Quartet CBC ("Musica Viva" series) ▲ MVCD 1032 [DDD]
Mozart, W.A.:Trio Cl, K.498, w. R. Dubinsky (va), L. Edlina (pno) Chandos ▲ CHAN 8655 [DDD]
Nielsen, C.:Serenata in vano, w. James McKay (bn), James Sommerville (hn), Tsuyoshi Tsutsumi (vc), Joel Quarrington (db) *(rec Glenn Gould Studio, CBC Toronto, Mar. 26–27, 1994)* CBC ("Musica Viva" series) ▲ MVV 1089 [DDD]
Piché, J.:Steal the Thunder, w. B. Johnston (perc) Centrediscs ▲ CMC CD 2786
Poulenc, F.:Chamber Music, w. Peter Sidhom (bar), William Bennett (fl), David Campbell (cl), Nicholas Daniel (ob), Richard Watkins (hn), Rachel Gough (bn), Peter Carter (vn), Chris West (db), Ieuan Jones (hp), Clifford Benson (pno), Julius Drake (pno), John York (pno)—Son for Ob; L'invitation au château; Villanelle; Son 2 Cls; Trio; Sxt; Son for Cl & Bn; Rapsodie nègre; Son for Cl; Mouvements perpétuels; Son for Fl *(rec All Saints' Church, East Finchley, London, Jan 12–20, 1994)* Cala ▲ CACD 1018 [DDD]
Poulenc, F.:Son Cl Pno, w. J. York (pno) Crystal ■ C331
Prokofiev, S.:Ov on Hebrew Themes, w. E. Turovsky (vn), R. Golani (va), Borodin Trio [orig. chamber version] Chandos ▲ CHAN 8924 [DDD]
Ravel, M.:Intro & Allegro, w. Ieuan Jones (hp), William Bennett (fl), Allegri String Quartet *(rec All Saints' Church, East Finchley, London, Jan 12–20, 1994)* Cala 2–▲ CACD 1018 [DDD]
Saint-Saëns, C.:Chamber Music, w. W. Bennett (fl), D. Campbell (cl), N. Daniel (ob), R. Makell (hn), R. Watkins (hn), R. Kennard (bn), R. Gough (bn), S. Haram (sax), I. Jones (hp), C. Benson (pno), J. Drake (pno), J. York (pno), R. Tapping (va)—Odelette, Op. 162; Son for Cl, Op. 167; Feuillet d'album, Op. 81; Son for Bn, Op. 168; Caprice on Danish & Russian Airs, Op. 79; Son for Ob, Op. 166; Romance in D♭, Op. 37; Tarantelle, Op. 6 *(rec All Saints' Church, East Finchley, London, Jan 12–20, 1994)* Cala 2–▲ CACD 1017 [DDD]
Schumann, R.:Fantasiestücke Cl, w. J. York (pno) Crystal ■ C331
Stolen Gems, w. Allegri String Quartet *(rec 8/85)* Marquis Classics ▲ ERAD 119 [DDD]
Strauss, R.:Till Eulenspiegels lustige Streiche, w. James McKay (bn), James Sommerville (hn), Martin Beaver (vn), Joel Quarrington (db)—[arr. Franz Hasenöhrl as Einmal Anders! (frolic for 5 instruments; 1954)] *(rec Glenn Gould Studio, CBC Toronto, Mar. 26–27, 1994)* CBC ("Musica Viva" series) ▲ MVV 1089 [DDD]
Weber, C.M. von:Concertino Cl, w. F.–P. Decker (cnd), National Arts Center Canada Orch CBC ("SM 5000" series) ▲ SMCD 5096 [DDD] ■ SMC 5096 (D)
Weber, C.M. von:Qnt Cl, w. Orford String Quartet CBC ("Musica Viva" series) ▲ MVCD 1032 [DDD]

Campbell, James (fl)
After Hours, w. Gene DiNovi Trio, S. Lemelin (pno) Marquis Classics ▲ MAR 153 [DDD]

Campbell, Laura (fl)
Fairlie–Kennedy, M.:Windrider/Final Ascent, w. Christopher Morgan Loy (pno) *(rec MasterView SoundCrafts Recording Studios)* Capstone ▲ CPS 8631

Campbell, Nancy (sax)
Exquisite Corpses from P.S. 122, w. D. Watson (shears/stick vn/gtr/tpt), Judy Dunaway (gtr/balloons), Anthony Coleman (sampler), Raissa St. Pierre (drums), Guy Yarden (vn/pno), Leslie Ross (bn), Linda Austin (gtr), Bruce Kaplan (gtr), Doug Henderson (peckhorn/bass/toy pno), Sue Ann Harkey (gtr), Cinnie Cole (sampler), et al. ¿What Next? ▲ WN 0002 [ADD]

Campen, C. van (vc)
Messiaen, O.:Quatuor pour la fin du temps, w. D. Campbell (cl), M. Mitchell (vn), J. MacGregor (pno) Collins Classics ▲ COL 1393 [DDD]

Campion, David (timp/perc)
Bach, J.S.:Music of, w. Wendy Humphreys (sop), Daniel Lichti (b–bar), Stuart Laughton (tpt/nat tpt/Renaissance cnt), William O'Meara (org)—Prelude & Fugue in G; Grosser Herr [from Christmas Oratorio]; Mein gläubiges Herz [from Cant 68]; 3 Chorale Preludes; Prelude & Fugue in A Doremi ▲ DHR 9303 [DDD]
Baroque Banquet, w. W. Humphreys (sop), Daniel Lichti (b–bar), Stuart Laughton (tpt/nat tpt/cnt), William O'Meara (org) Doremi ▲ 9303
Franceschini, P.:Son à 7, w. Stuart Laughton (tpt), William O'Meara (org) Doremi ▲ DHR 9303 [DDD]
Handel, G.F.:Samson (sels), w. Wendy Humphreys (sop), Daniel Lichti (b–bar), Stuart Laughton (tpt/nat tpt/Renaissance cnt), William O'Meara (org)—Let the Bright Seraphim Doremi ▲ DHR 9303 [DDD]
Scarlatti, A.:Endimione e Cintia, w. Wendy Humphreys (sop), Daniel Lichti (b–bar), Stuart Laughton (tpt/nat tpt/Renaissance cnt), William O'Meara (org)—Vaga Cintia Doremi ▲ DHR 9303 [DDD]
Susato, T.:Music of, w. Stuart Laughton (tpt), William O'Meara (org)—Renaissance Dance Suite Doremi ▲ DHR 9303 [DDD]
Telemann, G.P.:Musique héroïque, w. Stuart Laughton (tpt), William O'Meara (org) Doremi ▲ DHR 9303 [DDD]

Campion, Guy (pno)—see ORCHESTRAS & ENSEMBLES Duo Campion–Vachon

Campo, Mike del (perc)
Rutter, J.:Requiem, w. Karyn List (sop), Kathy Farmer (fl), Barbara Cook (ob), Julie Albertson (hp), Mary Alice Swope (vc), Tom Alderman (org), Jennifer Mautz (timp), Michael O'Neal (cnd), Michael O'Neal Singers *(rec Roswell United Methodist Church, Atlanta, GA, Mar 27, 1995)* ACA Digital Recording ▲ CM 20048 [DDD]

Campoli, Alfredo (vn)
Bliss, A.:Con Vn, w. A. Bliss (cnd), London PO Beulah ▲ 3PD10 (m) [ADD]
Bliss, A.:Theme & Cadenza, w. A. Bliss (cnd), London PO Beulah ▲ 3PD10 (m) [ADD]
Bruch, M.:Scottish Fant Vn, w. A. Boult (cnd), London PO IMP Collectors Series ▲ IMPX 9031 [ADD]
Campoli's Choice Flapper ▲ PAST CD 9744 (m) [AAD]
Elgar, E.:Con Vn, w. A. Boult (cnd), London PO Beulah ▲ 1PD10
Mendelssohn, F.:Con in e Vn & Orch, Op. 64, w. A. Boult (cnd), London PO Beulah ▲ 1PD10
Mendelssohn, F.:Con in e Vn & Orch, Op. 64, w. A. Boult (cnd), London PO IMP Collectors Series ▲ IMPX 9031 [ADD]
Tchaikovsky, P.:Con Vn, w. A. Argenta (cnd), London SO PWK Classics ▲ PWK 1145 [AAD]
Tchaikovsky, P.:Con Vn, w. A. Argenta (cnd), London SO Beulah ▲ 3PD10 [ADD]

Canales, Marisa (fl)
Schifrin, L.:Tangos, w. Lidia Tamayo (hp) Urtext ▲ URT 1 [DDD]
Zyman, S.:Con Fl, w. B. J. Echenique (cnd), Mexico City CO Urtext ▲ URT 1 [DDD]
Zyman, S.:Son Fl, w. Ana Maria Tradatti (pno) Urtext ▲ URT 1 [DDD]

Canci, Marcello (vn)
Vella, J.:Con Vn, w. J. Vella (cnd), Sofia SO Gega ▲ GR 40

Candamio, Clarece (org)
Christmas in Dallas, w. C. Harmon (org), Jeffery Curnow (tpt), Adam Gordon (tpt), Gregory Hustis (hn) *(rec Lover's Lane United Methodist Church, Dallas)* Hester Park ▲ 7706 [DDD]

Candela, Jean–Yves (pno)
Chevalier, C.:Music of, w. Teca Calazans (sgr), Ze–Luis (sgr), Regina Machado (sgr), Nigel Scragg (fl/a sax), Rosihna de Valenca (gtr), Wilson das Neves (perc), Regina Machado (perc), Silvano Michelino (perc)—Comme d'habitude; Couleur café; Une histoire d'amour; Les feuilles mortes; Les moulins de mon coeur; Syracuse; Je t'aimerai; Ces petits rien; La valse des lilas; L'absent; Que reste–il de nos amours; Un homme et une femme *(rec Studio Bastille)* Iris ▲ 010 [DDD]

Cani, R. (vn)
Bruckner, A.:Son 2 Vn, w. J. Swann (pno) *(rec Milan, Dec. 16–18, 1993)* Arkadia–Akademia ▲ 143 [DDD]
Respighi, O.:Son Vn, w. J. Swann (pno) *(rec Milan, Dec. 16–18, 1993)* Arkadia–Akademia ▲ 143 [DDD]

Canihac, Jean–Pierre (cnt)
Merula, T.:Arias & Capriccios, w. M. Figueras (sop), T. Koopman (hpd), J. Savall (vl), R. Lislevand (thb), A. Laurence–King (hp), L. Duftschmid (vn) Astrée ▲ E 8503

Canin, Serena (vn)—see also ORCHESTRAS & ENSEMBLES Continuum Chamber Ensemble
Martin, F.:Con Vn, w. K. Nagano (cnd), Berkeley SO *(rec Los Medanos College, Pittsburgh, CA, Feb 25–26, 1995)* New Albion ▲ NA 086
Martin, F.:Maria–Triptychon, w. Sara Ganz (sop), K. Nagano (cnd), Berkeley SO *(rec Los Medanos College, Pittsburgh, CA, Feb 25–26, 1995)* New Albion ▲ NA 086

Canino, Bruno (hpd)
Haydn, J.:Con Org, Vn & Strs, H.XVIII/6, w. Salvatore Accardo (vn), S. Accardo (cnd), English CO Philips 2–▲ 438797–2
Locatelli, P.:Sons Vn & Hpd, w. Cristiano Rossi (vn) *(rec Dynamic's Studio, Genova, Italy, Mar. 2–3 & 7–8, 1994)* Dynamic ▲ CDS 105 [DDD]

Canino, Bruno (pno)
Bach, J.S.:Goldberg Vars Ermitage ▲ ERM 412
Bach, J.S.:Sons Vn, w. V. Mullova (vn)—1014, 1015 & 1019; BWV 1024 [spurious] Philips ▲ 434084–2
Bartók, B.:Rhaps Vn & Pno, Sz.86 & 89, w. M. Kaplan (vn) Arabesque ▲ ARA 6649 [DDD]
Bartók, B.:Romanian Folk Dances Vn, w. M. Kaplan (vn) Arabesque ▲ ARA 6649 [DDD]
Beethoven, L. van:Sons Vc (comp), w. Jan Vogler (vc)—Nos. 4 & 5, Op. 102 Berlin Classics ▲ BER 1100 [DDD]
Beethoven, L. van:Son 1 Vc, w. Jan Vogler (vc) Berlin Classics ▲ BER 1122
Beethoven, L. van:Son 2 Vc, w. Jan Vogler (vc) Berlin Classics ▲ BER 1122
Brahms, J.:Son 2 Vc, w. Jan Vogler (vc) Berlin Classics ▲ BER 1029 [DDD]
Bussotti, S.:O, w. C. Berberian (sop) Wergo ▲ WER 60054–50
Cage, J.:Songs, w. C. Berberian (mez)—A Flower; The Wonderful Widow of Eighteen Springs Wergo ▲ WER 60054–50
Casella, A.:A notte alta Stradivarius ▲ STV 33350 [DDD]
Casella, A.:Pavane Stradivarius ▲ STV 33350 [DDD]
Casella, A.:Pezzi, Op. 24 Stradivarius ▲ STV 33350 [DDD]
Casella, A.:Sonatina Pno Stradivarius ▲ STV 33350 [DDD]
Casella, A.:Vars sur une Chaconne Stradivarius ▲ STV 33350 [DDD]
Chausson, E.:Con Vn, Pno & Str Qt, w. S. Accardo (vn), Naples String Quartet Dynamic ▲ CD 44
Debussy, C.:Son Vc, w. Jan Vogler (vc) Berlin Classics ▲ BER 1029 [DDD]
Hindemith, P.:The Four Temperaments, w. C. Mackerras (cnd), Basel SO *(rec Stadtcasino Basel, Musiksaal & Ref. Kirche Arlesheim, Mar 1995)* Novalis ▲ 150118 [DDD]
Kagel, M.:An Tasten, w. Saschko Gawriloff (vn), Siegfried Palm (vc) Montaigne ▲ MO 782043
Kagel, M.:Klangwölfe, w. Saschko Gawriloff (vn), Siegfried Palm (vc) Montaigne ▲ MO 782043
Kagel, M.:Trio Pno, w. Saschko Gawriloff (vn), Siegfried Palm (vc) Montaigne ▲ MO 782043
Kagel, M.:Unguis incarnatus est, w. Saschko Gawriloff (vn), Siegfried Palm (vc) Montaigne ▲ MO 782043
Kreisler, F.:Transcriptions, w. D. Sitkovetzky (vn) Orfeo ▲ 048831 [DDD]
Ligeti, G.:Pieces for 2 Pnos, w. Antonio Ballista (pno) Wergo ▲ WER 60100–50 [DDD]
Mendelssohn, F.:Lied ohne Worte Vc, w. L. Harrell (vc) London ▲ 430198–2 [DDD]
Mendelssohn, F.:Lieder ohne Worte Pno, w. L. Harrell (vc)—Op. 19/1 [trans for vc & pno] London ▲ 430198–2 [DDD]
Mendelssohn, F.:Son 1 Vc, w. L. Harrell (vc) London ▲ 430198–2 [DDD]
Mendelssohn, F.:Son 2 Vc, w. L. Harrell (vc) London ▲ 430198–2 [DDD]
Mendelssohn, F.:Vars concertantes, w. L. Harrell (vc) London ▲ 430198–2 [DDD]
Noda, T.:Developpements Camerata ▲ 32CM 58
Petrassi, G.:Coro di morti, w. Antonia Ballista (pno), G. Petrassi (cnd), Milan Angelicum Instrumentalists, Milan Polyphonic Choir Stradivarius ▲ STV DTM 90001 [ADD]
Rachmaninoff, S.:Vocalise, w. Jan Vogler (vc) Berlin Classics ▲ BER 1029 [DDD]
Sarasate, P. de:Vn & Pno Music, w. M. Kaplan (vn)—Navarra for 2 Violins & Piano, Op. 33 *(M. Kaplan plays both violins)*; Malagueña, Op. 21/1; Habanera, Op. 21/2; Romanza Andaluza, Op. 22/2; Jota Navarra, Op. 22/4; Playera, Op. 23/1; Zapateado, Op. 23/2; Caprice Basque, Op. 24; Spanish Dance (untitled), Op. 26/1; Spanish Dance (untitled), Op. 26/2; Bolero, Op. 30; Zortzico D'Iparaguirre, Op. 39; Miramar (Zortzico), Op. 42; Introductions & Tarantelle, Op. 43 Arabesque ▲ Z 6614
Savinio, A.:Les Chants de la mi–mort Stradivarius ▲ STR 33309 [DDD]
Schnittke, A.:Son Vc, w. Jan Vogler (vc) Berlin Classics ▲ BER 1029 [DDD]
Schumann, R.:Adagio & Allegro Hn, w. Jan Vogler (vc) Berlin Classics ▲ BER 1122
Schumann, R.:Stücke im Volkston, w. Jan Vogler (vc) Berlin Classics ▲ BER 1100 [DDD]
Weber, C.M. von:Sons Vn, w. A. Nicolet (fl) Novalis ▲ 150065 [DDD]
Weber, C.M. von:Trio Fl, w. A. Nicolet (fl), R. Filippini (vc) Novalis ▲ 150065 [DDD]
Wolf–Ferrari, E.:Italian Songbook, w. Yvi Janicke (mez) CPO ▲ CPO 999270
Wolf–Ferrari, E.:Pno Music—Rispetti, Op. 11 & 12; 3 Impromptus, Op. 13; 3 Piano Pieces, Op. 14 CPO ▲ CPO 999270

Canino, Bruno (pno/cel)
Savinio, A.:Album 1914, w. L. Castellani (sop), A. Jona (sgr), D. Zaffaroni (bn) Stradivarius ▲ STR 33309 [DDD]

Canino, Bruno (pno/hpd)
"MagnifiCathy":The Many Voices of Cathy Berberian Wergo ▲ WER 60054–50

Cañizares, Juan (gtr)
Albéniz, I.:Iberia Suite, w. P. de Lucia (gtr), J. Bandera (gtr) [trans Paco de Lucia for 3 gtrs] Verve ▲ 314–510301–2

Cann, Antoinette (pno)
Claire & Antoinette Cann, w. C. Cann (pno) Pianissimo ▲ PP 21192 [DDD]

Cann, Claire (pno)
Claire & Antoinette Cann, w. Antoinette Cann (pno) Pianissimo ▲ PP 21192 [DDD]

Canter, Robin (ob)
Bach, J.S.:Sons Fl, BWV 1030–35, w. P. Nicholson (hpd)—BWV 1030 & 1031 *(rec May 1992)* Amon Ra ▲ CD–SAR 60 [DDD]
Bach, J.S.:Sons Vl, BWV 1027–1029, w. P. Nicholson (hpd)—BWV 1027 *(rec May 1992)* Amon Ra ▲ CD–SAR 60 [DDD]
Bach, J.S.:Sons Vn, w. P. Nicholson (hpd)—BWV 1020 *(rec May 1992)* Amon Ra ▲ CD–SAR 60 [DDD]
Kalliwoda, J.W.:Morceau de Salon, w. R. Burnett (pno) Amon Ra ▲ CD–SAR 22 [DDD]
Marais, M.:Vars on *Folies d'Espagne* Amon Ra ▲ CD–SAR 22 [DDD]
Mozart, W.A.:Divert Ob, K.251, w. London Baroque [period instrs] Amon Ra ▲ CD–SAR 34 [DDD]
Mozart, W.A.:Qt Ob, K.370, w. London Baroque [period instrs] Amon Ra ▲ CD–SAR 34 [DDD]
Mozart, W.A.:Qnt Ob, K.516b, w. London Baroque [period instrs] Amon Ra ▲ CD–SAR 34 [DDD]
Oboe Collection, w. Anthony Pleeth (vc), Melvyn Tan (hpd), Richard Burnett (pnos), James Wood (perc) Amon Ra ▲ CDSAR 22 [DDD]
Routh, F.:Tragic Interludes *(rec BBC Studio 2, June 1987)* Redcliffe ▲ RR 006
Strauss, R.:Con Ob, w. J. Judd (cnd), London SO IMP ("Masters" series) ▲ IMP 6600212
Strauss, R.:Con Ob, w. J. Judd (cnd), London SO IMP Masters ▲ IMPMCD 58 [DDD]
Vaughan Williams, R.:Con Ob, w. J. Judd (cnd), London SO IMP ("Masters" series) ▲ IMP 6600212
Vaughan Williams, R.:Con Ob, w. J. Judd (cnd), London SO IMP Masters ▲ IMPMCD 58 [DDD]
Vaughan Williams, R.:Studies in English Folk–Song, w. J. Judd (cnd), London SO [arr Canter] IMP ("Masters" series) ▲ IMP 6600212
Vaughan Williams, R.:Studies in English Folk–Song, w. J. Judd (cnd), London SO [arr. for oboe] IMP Masters ▲ IMPMCD 58 [DDD]
Walmisley, T.A.:Sonatina 2 Ob, w. R. Burnett (pno) Amon Ra ▲ CD–SAR 22 [DDD]

Cantin, Catherine (fl)
French Chamber Music for Piano & Wind, w. P. Rogé (pno), M Bourgue (ob), et al. London ▲ 425861–2 [DDD]
Messiaen, O.:Concert à Quatre, w. Heinz Holliger (ob), Yvonne Loriod (pno), Mstislav Rostropovich (vc), M.–W. Chung (cnd), Bastille Opera Orch Deutsche Grammophon ("4D Audio" series) ▲ 445947–2
Cantor, Emile (va)—see ORCHESTRAS & ENSEMBLES Orpheus String Quartet
Cantos, M. L. (pno)
Nin–Culmell, J.:Tonadas *(rec Jan. 1993)* Marco Polo ▲ 8.223534 [DDD]
Canuti, Stefano (bn)
Caix D'Hervelois, L. de:La Gracieuse, w. Jennifer Paull (ob), Christine Sartoretti (hpd) *(rec English Church, Villars, Switzerland, Apr 21–22, 1995)* Doron ▲ DRC 5006 [DDD]
Caix D'Hervelois, L. de:Les Vendangeuses, w. Jennifer Paull (ob), Christine Sartoretti (hpd) *(rec English Church, Villars, Switzerland, Apr 21–22, 1995)* Doron ▲ DRC 5006 [DDD]
Marais, M.:Vars on *Folies d'Espagne,* w. Jennifer Paull (ob), Christine Sartoretti (hpd) *(rec English Church, Villars, Switzerland, Apr 21–22, 1995)* Doron ▲ DRC 5006 [DDD]
Čap, Jan (pno)—see ORCHESTRAS & ENSEMBLES Crawford Trio
Čap, Ludek (vn)—see ORCHESTRAS & ENSEMBLES Kubín String Quartet
Čáp, Petr (b cl)
Janácek, L.:Youth, w. Prague Wind Quintet Supraphon ▲ 11 1354–2 [DDD]
Capalletti, A. (vn)
Respighi, O.:Con gregoriano, w. M. Bamert (cnd), Philharmonia Orch Koch Schwann ▲ SCH 311242 [DDD]
Capelli, Norberto (pno)
Brahms, J.:Academic Festival Ov, w. Hector Moreno (pno) [arr pno 4–hands] *(rec Accademia Bartolomeo Cristofori, Florence, Italy, Aug 1993)* Arts ▲ 4471362 [DDD]
Brahms, J.:Hungarian Dances Pno 4–Hands, w. Hector Moreno (pno) *(rec Accademia Bartolomeo Cristofori, Florence, Italy, Aug 1993)* Arts ▲ 4471362 [DDD]
Caplan, Stephen (ob)—see also ORCHESTRAS & ENSEMBLES Sierra Winds
Baley, V.:Orpheus Singing, w. Continuum Chamber Ensemble *(rec Juilliard School, NYC, Apr 22, June 21, July 12)* Cambria ▲ CD 1087
Diamond, D.:Partita Ob, Bn & Pno, w. K. Wolfe (bn), L. Spitzer (pno) Cambria ▲ 1091 [DDD]
Caplurcenko, Rita (vn)—see ORCHESTRAS & ENSEMBLES Prague Chamber Ensemble
Capocaccia, G. (rcr)
Frescobaldi, G.:Canzonas, Caprici & Ricercari, w. K. Boeke (vl), L. Cavasanti (rcr), C. Boersma (vc), S. Ciomei (hpd/org)—Canzoni Trigesima, detta la Cittadellia; Vigesimasesta, detta la Moricona; Vigesimaottiva, detta le Lanberta; Prima a tre; Trigesimaseconda detta l'Altogradina; Vigesimaquarta, detta la Nobile; Vigesimesttima, detta la Lanciona; Quintedecima, detta la Lievoratta; Terza a quattro; Vigesimaquinta, detta la Garzoncina; Prima a tre; Decmasesta, detta la Samminiata; Trigesimaprima, detta l'Arnolfinia; Quarta a tre; Quinta a tre; Decimasettima, detta la Diodata; Seconda a quattro; Seconda a tre; Vigesimanona, detta la Bocellina; Terza a tre Trigesimaquarta, detta la Sandoninia Nuova Era ("Ancient Music" series) ▲ 7131
Capone, Morris (acc)
Curran, A.:Crystal Psalms, An Homage to Kristallnacht, w. F. Badaloni (cl), D. Keberlee (cl), M. Riesler (cl), A. Santoloci (cl), L. Dublanchet (tuba), D. Rueff (tuba), A. Caggiano (perc), w. Ensemble Vocale Sesquialtera [cnd:E. Razzicchia], Radio France Chamber Choir [cnd:D. LaBorde]—[F] New Albion ▲ NA 067
Caporali, R. (pno)
Rendano, A.:Pieces Pno *(rec Mar. 29–31, 1989)* Ermitage ▲ ERM 409 [ADD]
Rendano, A.:Qnt Pno, w. R. Bonucci (vn), M. Fiorini (vn), F. Anzelmo (va), A. Bonucci (vc) *(rec Mar. 29–31, 1989)* Ermitage ▲ ERM 409 [ADD]
Cápová, Silvia (pno)
Beethoven, L. van:Son 8 Pno, "Pathétique" Lydian ▲ LYD 18021 [DDD]
Beethoven, L. van:Son 14 Pno, "Moonlight Son" Lydian ▲ LYD 18021 [DDD]
Beethoven, L. van:Son 23 Pno, "Appassionata" Lydian ▲ LYD 18021 [DDD]
Binge, R.:Prelude:The Whispering Valley, w. E. Tomlinson (cnd), Slovak RSO *(rec Oct. 1992)* Marco Polo ("British Light Music" series) ▲ 8.223515 [DDD]
The Great Classics, w. Ljubljana SO [cnd:Marko Munih] Stradivari Classics ("Treasury of Great Classics" series) 5–▲ S5D 6083 [DDD] 5–■ S5C 6083 (D)
Liszt, F.:Cons Pno, Slovak PO Critics Choice 2–▲ CCD 943 [DDD]
Liszt, F.:Pno Music (misc)—Consolation in E; Liebesträume Critics Choice 2–▲ CCD 943 [DDD]
Piano Masterpieces, w. Capova, Sylvia (pno) Stradivari Classics ▲ SCD 6020 [DDD] ■ SMC 6020 (D)
Cappelletti, Andrea (vn)
Tartini, G.:Sons solo Vn—(8) Piccole sonate Koch Schwann ▲ SCH 311262 [DDD]
Cappelli, Giorgio (org)
Ricci, F.P.:Org Music Nuova Era ▲ NUO 7244
Cappone, Guisto (va)
Mozart, W.A.:Kleine Nachtmusik, w. T. Brandis (vn), K. Böhm (cnd), Berlin PO Deutsche Grammophon ("Resonance" series) ▲ 427208–2 [ADD]
Mozart, W.A.:Serenata notturna, w. T. Brandis (vn), K. Böhm (cnd), Berlin PO Deutsche Grammophon ("Resonance" series) ▲ 427208–2 [DDD]
Mozart, W.A.:Sinf concertante Vn, K.364, w. Thomas Brandis (vn), K. Böhm (cnd), Berlin PO Deutsche Grammophon ("Resonance" series) ▲ 427208–2 [ADD]
Caproni (hn)
Puccini, M.:Concertone Fl, w. Mencarelli (fl), di Girolamo (cl), G. Bodanza (tpt), G. Cosmi (cnd), Lucca Teatro Comunale del Giglio Orch Bongiovanni ▲ GB 2048 [DDD]
Carabetta, Samuel (org)
Anthems & Motets, w. [cnd:Samuel Carabetta], St. John's Episcopal Church Choir Lafayette Sq. Washington D.C. *(rec 1991)* Gothic ▲ GOT 49050
Caracilly, Yvon (vn)
Onslow, G.:Qt Strs, Op. 8/1, w. French String Trio *(rec 1978)* Koch Treasure ▲ 316232 [ADD]
Onslow, G.:Qnt Strs, Op. 78/1, w. B. Pasquier (va), French String Trio *(rec 1978)* Koch Treasure ▲ 316232 [ADD]
Caramella, Riccardo (pno)
Boccherini, L.:Qnt Pno, G.413–418, w. Zagreb String Quartet—in A, B♭ & e, G.413–415 Nuova Era ▲ NUO 7160 [DDD]
Milhaud, D.:Le Carnaval d'Aix, w. P. Bender (cnd), Cannes–Provençe Alpes–Côte d'Azur Regional Orch Nuova Era ▲ 7130 [DDD]
Milhaud, D.:Fant pastorale, w. P. Bender (cnd), Cannes–Provençe Alpes–Côte d'Azur Regional Orch Nuova Era ▲ 7130 [DDD]
Rossini, G.:Chamber Music, w. Sergio Lamberto (vn), Guido Corti (hn), Sergio del Mastro (cl) Nuova Era ▲ NUO 7245
Yin, C.–Z.:Yellow River Con, w. Y. Fang (cnd), Beijing RSO—also includes Yunan Scenes Nuova Era ▲ 6722
Caramiello, Francesco (pno)
Martucci, G.:Con 2 Pno, w. F. d' Avalos (cnd), Philharmonia Orch ASV ▲ ASV 691 [DDD]
Martucci, G.:Pno Music—3 pieces, Op. 64; Prelude, Toccata & Gigue, Op. 61; 3 Scherzos, Op. 53; Theme & Vars, Op. 58 ASV ▲ ASV 897 [DDD]
Caratelli (fl)
Bach, J.S.:Suite 2 Orch, w. F. Reiner (cnd), Pittsburgh SO *(rec 1945–46)* LYS ▲ LYS 126
Beethoven, L. van:Sym 2, w. F. Reiner (cnd), Pittsburgh SO *(rec 1945–46)* LYS ▲ LYS 126
Carbonare, Alessandro (cl)
Bassi, L.:Divert on Verdi's *Il Trovatore,* w. Andrea Dindo (pno) *(rec Jungle Studios, Milan, July 29–31, 1995)* Agora Musica ▲ AG 017.1 [DDD]
Bassi, L.:Fant di concerto on Verdi's *Rigoletto,* w. Andrea Dindo (pno) *(rec Jungle Studios, Milan, July 29–31, 1995)* Agora Musica ▲ AG 017.1 [DDD]
Carulli, B.:Fant on Verdi's *Macbeth,* w. Andrea Dindo (pno) *(rec Jungle Studios, Milan, July 29–31, 1995)* Agora Musica ▲ AG 017.1 [DDD]
Carbonare, Alessandro (cl) (cont.)
Leonesi, G.:Capriccio on Verdi's *Un ballo in maschera,* w. Andrea Dindo (pno) *(rec Jungle Studios, Milan, July 29–31, 1995)* Agora Musica ▲ AG 017.1 [DDD]
Lovreglio, D.:Fant da concerto on Motifs of Verdi's *La traviata,* w. Andrea Dindo (pno) *(rec Jungle Studios, Milan, July 29–31, 1995)* Agora Musica ▲ AG 017.1 [DDD]
Poulenc, F.:Sxt Pno, w. Andrea Dindo (pno), Gianpaolo Pretto (fl), Paolo Grazia (ob), Roberto Giaccaglia (bn), Stefano Pignatelli (hn) *(rec Sala Maffeiana dell'Accademia Filarmonica di Verona, May 7–9, 1995)* Agorá ▲ 021 [DDD]
Poulenc, F.:Son Cl Pno, w. Andrea Dindo (pno) *(rec Sala Maffeiana dell'Accademia Filarmonica di Verona, May 7–9, 1995)* Agorá ▲ 021 [DDD]
Serafini, M.:Fantasia on Verdi's *Aida,* w. Andrea Dindo (pno) *(rec Jungle Studios, Milan, July 29–31, 1995)* Agora Musica ▲ AG 017.1 [DDD]
Verdi, G.:Music of, w. Andrea Dindo (pno)—melodies from Ballo in Maschera; Aida; Macbeth; Il Trovatore; La Traviata; Rigoletto Agorá ▲ 017
Carbonel, Sylvie (pno)
Schumann, R.:Fantasiestücke Pno, Op. 12 Pavane ▲ ADW 7259 [DDD]
Schumann, R.:Humoreske Pno Pavane ▲ ADW 7259 [DDD]
Carbotta, Mario (fl)
Casella, A.:Barcarola et scherzo, w. R. Cognazzo (pno) Nuova Era ▲ NUO 7185 [DDD]
Casella, A.:Sicilienne et burlesque Fl & Pno, w. R. Cognazzo (pno) Nuova Era ▲ NUO 7185 [DDD]
Cortese, L.:Intro e Allegro, w. R. Cognazzo (pno) Nuova Era ▲ NUO 7185 [DDD]
Cortese, L.:Melodia, w. R. Cognazzo (pno) Nuova Era ▲ NUO 7185 [DDD]
Fioroni, G.A.:Son Fl, w. R. Cognazzo (pno) *(rec 3/91)* Nuova Era ▲ 7022 [DDD]
Krakamp, E.:Characteristic Pieces, w. Roberto Cognazzo (pno) Nuova Era ▲ NUO 7193 [DDD]
Pilati, M.:Son Fl, w. R. Cognazzo (pno) Nuova Era ▲ NUO 7185 [DDD]
Rota, N.:Pieces Fl, w. R. Cognazzo (pno)—5 Pieces Nuova Era ▲ NUO 7185 [DDD]
Sammartini, G.:Sons Fl, w. R. Cognazzo (hpd) *(rec 3/91)* Nuova Era ▲ 7022 [DDD]
Zuccari, C.:Son Fl, w. R. Cognazzo (hpd) *(rec 3/91)* Nuova Era ▲ 7022 [DDD]
Cardenas, Silvina (fl)
Clementi, M.:Pno Music (comp), w. Aldo Antognazzi (pno), Christian Badian (pno), Eduardo Cazaban (pno), Cristina Da Souza (pno), Dao Di Renzo (pno), Pablo Lavandera (pno), Yi Fang Huang (vn), Nestor Herzbaum (fl)—Sons (6) for Pno, Op. 2, Nos. 1, 3 & 5 (w. flutes); Duets (3) for Piano 4–Hands, Op. 3, Nos. 2 & 3; Sons (3) for Pno & Vn, Op. 3, No. 4 Aura Classics ▲ AU 32287
Cárdenes, Andrés (vn)
It's Peaceful Here:Little Gems for the Violin, w. Luz Manriquez (pno) Arabesque ▲ ARA 6655 [DDD]
Made in the U.S.A., w. Luz Manríquez (pno) *(rec Carnegie Library of Homestead, Munhall, PA, Oct 21–23, 1996)* Ocean ▲ OR 103
Cardenes, Andrew (vn)
Arensky, A.:Trio 1 Pno, w. M. Golabek (pno), J. Solow (vc) Delos ▲ DE 3056 [DDD]
Tchaikovsky, P.:Trio Pno, w. M. Golabek (pno), J. Solow (vc) Delos ▲ DE 3056 [DDD]
Cardi, S. (gtr)
Paganini, N.:Music of, w. R. Ricci (vn)—Cantabile in D; Taratella; Nel cor piu non mi sento; Cantabile & Waltz, Centone Son. No. 1; Son., Op. 2/1 & 4; Son., Op. 3/1–4 & 6; Moses Fant.; Variazioni di bravura; Son. in A, Op. posth. One–Eleven ▲ URS 93070 [DDD]
Paganini, N.:Qts (15) Vn, w. R. Ricci (vn), A. Vismara (va), L. Signorini (vc)—No. 7 Bongiovanni ▲ GB 5507 [DDD]
Paganini, N.:Son concertata, w. R. Ricci (vn) Bongiovanni ▲ GB 5507 [DDD]
Paganini, N.:Terzetto concertante Va, w. A. Vismara (va), L. Signorini (vc) Bongiovanni ▲ GB 5507 [DDD]
Paganini, N.:Terzetto Vn, w. R. Ricci (vn), L. Signorini (vc) Bongiovanni ▲ GB 5507 [DDD]
Cardin, Michel (baroque lt)
Weiss, S.L.:Lt Music—The Londres Manuscript Analekta ▲ CLCD 2017
Carey, Colm (org)
Fauré, G.:Messe basse (in 3 movts), w. Lisa Beckley (sop), J. Summerly (cnd), Oxford Camerata, Oxford Schola Cantorum *(rec Hertford College Chapel, Oxford, May 17 & 18, 1993)* Naxos ▲ 8.550765 [DDD]
Fauré, G.:Requiem, w. Lisa Beckley (sop), Nicholas Gedge (b–bar), J. Summerly (cnd), Oxford Camerata, Oxford Schola Cantorum *(rec Hertford College Chapel, Oxford, May 17 & 18, 1993)* Naxos ▲ 8.550765 [DDD]
Séverac, D. de:Tantum ergo, w. Jeremy Summerly (cnd), Oxford Schola Cantorum, Oxford Camerata *(rec Hertford College Chapel, Oxford, May 17 & 18, 1993)* Naxos ▲ 8.550765 [DDD]
Vierne, L.:Org Music—Andantino *(rec Hertford College Chapel, Oxford, May 17 & 18, 1993)* Naxos ▲ 8.550765 [DDD]
Carey, Colm (pno)
Brahms, J.:Sons Cl (comp), w. E. Vardi (va) Finnadar ■ 90519–4
Carfi, Martha (vn)—see also ORCHESTRAS & ENSEMBLES Munich Violin Duo
Viotti, G.B.:Con 2 Vn, w. L. Michal (vn), L. Michal (cnd), Bavarian CO Calig ▲ CAL 50917 [DDD]
Viotti, G.B.:Sym Concertante 1, w. L. Michal (vn), L. Michal (cnd), Bavarian CO Calig ▲ CAL 50917 [DDD]
Viotti, G.B.:Sym Concertante 2, w. L. Michal (vn), L. Michal (cnd), Bavarian CO Calig ▲ CAL 50917 [DDD]
Carhart, David (pno)—see also ORCHESTRAS & ENSEMBLES Double Image members
Schumann, C.:Variations on a Theme by Robert Schumann Meridian ▲ MER 84312 [DDD]
Carl, Gene (pno)
Holt, S. ten:Canto ostinato, w. Gerard Bouwhuis (pno), A. Vernède (pno), C. van Zeeland (pno) *(rec live, Jan 10, 1988)* Donemus 3–▲ CV 2/3/4
Carles, Nicolas (va)
Eccles, H.:Son Db, w. B. Cazauran (db), J. M. Denis (vn), A. Loger (vn), E. Petit (vc) *(rec Aug. 29–30, 1992)* Gallo ▲ CD 753 [ADD]
Carli, Maria Isabella de (cembalo)
Marcello, B.:Sons Vc, w. A. Pocaterra (vc), B. Ferrari (vn) Rivoalto ▲ CRA 9008 [ADD]
Vivaldi, A.:Sons Vn, Op. 5, w. F. Fantini (vn), M. Ferarris (vn), A. Ephrikaim (vn), A. Pocaterra (vc), G. Ghetti (vc), V. Luccini (cembalo) Rivoalto ▲ CRA 9005 [ADD]
Carli, Maria Isabella de (hpd)
Marcello, B.:Sons Vc, w. Antonio Pocaterra (vc), Benito Ferraris (vn) Rivoalto ▲ RIV 9008 [ADD]
Carlin, Seth (pno)
Beethoven, L. van:Bagatelles (24)—Op. 126 Titanic ▲ Ti 167 [DDD]
Beethoven, L. van:Bagatelles (24)—Op. 126 Titanic ▲ Ti 467 [DDD]
Beethoven, L. van:Son 15 Pno, "Pastoral" Titanic ▲ Ti 167 [DDD]
Beethoven, L. van:Son 21 Pno, "Waldstein" Titanic ▲ Ti 167 [DDD]
Schubert, Franz:Moments musicaux—Nos. I, II & V Titanic ▲ Ti 198 [DDD]
Schubert, Franz:Son Pno, D.537 Titanic ▲ Ti 198 [DDD]
Schubert, Franz:Son Pno, D.894 Titanic ▲ Ti 198 [DDD]
Carlsen, Douglas (tpt)
Vivaldi, A.:Con for 2 Tpts, w. D. Hickman (tpt), T. Rolston (cnd), Banff Festival Strings *(rec Aug. 6–8, 1990)* Summit ▲ DCD 118 [DDD] ■ DCD 118
Carlsen, M. (t sax)—see ORCHESTRAS & ENSEMBLES Antifonale Chamber Ensemble
Carlsen, Mary Jo (vn)—see ORCHESTRAS & ENSEMBLES Penumbra
Carlson, Andrew (vn)
Schoenberg, A.:Pierrot lunaire, w. Leslie Boucher (nar), Julie Stone (fl/pic), Tod Kerstetter (cl/b cl), Philip Singleton (va), Juanita Karpf (vc), F. Joseph Lozier (pno) *(rec Roswell United Methodist Church, Roswell, GA, July 20, Aug. 2 & Sept. 1)* ACA Digital ▲ CM 20027
Zwilich, E.T.:Passages, w. Leslie Boucher (sop), Julie Stone (fl/pic), Tod Kerstetter (cl/b cl), Philip Singleton (va), Juanita Karpf (vc), F. Joseph Lozier (pno), Joanna Parks (perc), Shannon O'Kelley (perc) *(rec Roswell United Methodist Church, Roswell, GA, July 20, Aug. 2 & Sept. 1)* ACA Digital ▲ CM 20027
Carlsson, Roger (perc)
Másson, A.:Con Mar, Gothenburg SO Intim Musik ▲ INT 19 [DDD]
Nørgård, P.:For a Change, Gothenburg SO Intim Musik ▲ INT 19 [DDD]

INSTRUMENT.

Carlsson, Roger (perc) (cont.)
Sallinen, A.:Sym 2, Gothenburg SO — Intim Musik ▲ INT 19 [DDD]

Carlsson, Susannah (pno)
Stolarczyk, W.:Earth Air Fire Water, w. Amalie Malling (pno), John Damgaard (pno), Anne Øland (pno), Teddy Teirup (pno), Friedrich Gürtler (pno), Rosalind Bevan (pno), Poul Rosenbaum (pno), Rodolfo Llambias (pno), Bella Horn-Ribera (pno), Anders Riber (pno), Elisabeth Sigurdsson (pno), Thomas Tronheim (pno), Elsebeth Broderson (pno), Erik Kaltoft (pno), Jørgen Hald Nielsen (pno), Aino Gilemann (pno), Birgit Kjær (pno), Jørgen Thomsen (pno), Gunhild Donslund (pno), Henrik Bo Hansen (pno), Lone Karlsson (pno), Erik Fessel (pno), Lasse Nilsson (pno), Janos Ferenczi (pno), Erik Bach (pno), Axel Momme (pno), Arne de Cros Dich (pno), Sven Micha Slot (pno), Hanne Bramsen Buhl (pno), Lili Olesen (pno), Ulla Erml (pno), Vagn Sørensen (pno), Leif Greibe (pno), Bodil Krogh (pno), Kirsten Ottosen (pno), Inger Bergenholz (pno), Karsten Gylendorf (pno), Bjørn Elkjær (pno), Jacob Bjørn Jensen (pno), Jørgen Kaad (pno), Anne Marie Hjelm (pno), Carl Ulrik Munk Andersen (pno), Poul Lumbye (pno), Oluf Hildebrandt Nielsen (pno), Joachim Olsson (pno), Peter Pade Ramsøe Jacobsen (pno), Astrid Pollmann (pno), Jette Borsch (pno), Kirsten Karlshøj (pno), Maria Teresa Assing (pno), Allan Dahl Hansen (pno), Johan Hugossen (pno), Tine Fenger Pederson (pno), Arne Jørgen Fæø (pno), Anja Høgsted (pno), Anne Sophie Parbo (pno), Inga Lindmark (pno), Teresa Drabik Stathakis (pno), Anne Ruth Ferenczi (pno), Irene Hasager (pno), Yuka Ichikawa (pno), Birgitte Baur (pno), Malene Thastum (pno), Jens E. Rasmussen (pno), Birgitte Zielke (pno), Claus Zielke (pno), Stefan Kasch (pno), Bin Qiao (pno), Inger Johanne Teirup (pno), Lindy Rosborg (pno), Liisa Heininen (pno), David Højer (pno), Ellen Refstrup (pno), Thomas K. Sørensen (pno), Erik Kure (pno), Michael Rauff (pno), Jan beck Eriksson (pno), Tanja Zapolski (pno), Vibeke Skagbo (pno), Pål Eide Lindtner (pno), Ha-Young Sul (pno), Benedicte Palko (pno), Inke Kesseler (pno), Anne Marie Meineche (pno), Sverre Larsen (pno), Kasper Peter Bach (pno), Elisabetta Eliseo (pno), Olga Magieres (pno), Carl Erik Kühl (pno), Thorkild Borup Nielsen (pno), Valeria Zanini (pno), Lars Stenhoft (perc), Dennis Boel (perc), Winnie Dahlgren (perc), Susanne Vind (perc), Claus Byrith (elec), Anne Marie Storm (elec), J. Ribera (cnd) *(rec live, Koldinghaus Castle, Denmark, May 2, 1996)* — Danica ▲ DCD 1996

Carlyss, Earl (vn)
Rorem, N.:Night Music, w. A. Schein (pno) — Phoenix ▲ PHCD 123

Carmagnola, Andrea (fl)—see ORCHESTRAS & ENSEMBLES Consort Fontegara

Carmelli, Zwi (va)
Roussel, A.:Chamber Music, w. Majken Bjerno (sop), Toke Lund Christiansen (fl), Bjørn Carl Nielsen (ob), Niels Thomsen (cl), Per Jacobsen (hn), Asger Svendsen (bn), Ketil Christensen (tpt), Anne Søe Hansen (vn), Piotr Zelazny (va), Niels Ullner (vc), Michael Dabelsteen (db), Tine Rehling (hp), Morten Mogensen (pno), Per Salo (pno), Per Jensen (perc)—Divertissement, Op. 6; Trio, Op. 40; Joueurs de Flute, Op. 27; Sérenade, Op. 30; Le marchand de sable qui passe, Op. 13; Andante et scherzo, Op. 13; 2 poèmes de ronsard, Op. 26; Aria; Elpenor, Op. 59; Pipe — Kontrapunkt 2-▲ KPT 32218 [DDD]

Carmignola, Giuliano (vn)
Vivaldi, A.:Cons Vn, Op. 8/1–4, "The Four Seasons", w. A. Orizio (cnd), Brescia & Bergamo Festival CO — Fonè ▲ 87 F04-16 [DDD]

Carmirelli, Pina (vn)
Brahms, J.:Sextet Strs, Op. 36, w. J. Toth (vn), P. Naegele (va), C. Levine (va), F. Arico (vc), D. Reichenberger (vc) — Sony Classical ▲ SMK 46249 [ADD] ■ SMT 46249
Vivaldi, A.:Cons Vn, Op. 8/1–4, "The Four Seasons", I Musici — Philips ▲ 410001-2 [DDD]

Carnelli, Maurizio (pno)
Haydn, J.:Arianna a Naxos, w. Lucia Valentini Terrani (mez) — Kicco Classic ▲ KC 196 [DDD]
Rossini, G.:Giovanna d'Arco, w. Lucia Valentini Terrani (mez) — Kicco Classic ▲ KC 196 [DDD]
Rossini, G.:Songs, w. Lucia Valentini Terrani (mez)—Addio di Rossini; Canzonetta spagnola; Ave Maria; La danza — Kicco Classic ▲ KC 196 [DDD]

Carney, Laurie (vn)—see ORCHESTRAS & ENSEMBLES American String Quartet

Carney, Ralph (sax/b cl/bar hn)
Waits, T.:The Black Rider:The Casting of Magic Bullets, w. Angelika Thomas (sgr—Anne), Annette Paulmann (sgr—Kätchen), Sona Cervena (sgr—Bird/Messenger/Spoonwoman), Monika Tahal (sgr—Witness/Bird/Shrink/Wilhelm's Double/Skeleton), Susi Eisenkolb (sgr—Bridesmaid/Pegleg's Double), Heinz Vossbrink (sgr—Kuno), Dominique Horwitz (sgr—Pegleg), Gerd Kunath (sgr—Bertram), Stefan Kurt (sgr—Wilhelm), Klaus Schreiber (sgr—Robert/Man on Stag/Georg Schmid), Jörg Holm (Old Uncle/Duke), Jan Moritz Steffen (sgr—Young Kuno/Bird/Shrink/Skeleton), Tom Waits (vocals/coliope/organ/chamberlain/mar/emax/guitar/train whistle), Bill Douglas (bass instr), Kenny Wollesen (perc) — Island ▲ 314518559-2

Carno, Zita (pno)
Beethoven, L. van:Son Hn, w. J. Cerminaro (hn) — Crystal ▲ CD 676
Bernstein, L.:Son Cl, w. D. Howard (cl) *(rec Aug. 6-7 & 9, 1991)* — Centaur ▲ CRC 2201 [DDD]
Bozza, E.:Badinage, w. T. Stevens (tpt) — Crystal ■ C 367
Bozza, E.:Caprice, w. T. Stevens (tpt) — Crystal ■ C 367
Bozza, E.:En forêt, w. J. Cerminaro (hn) — Crystal ▲ CD 676
Bozza, E.:Lied Tpt & Pno, w. T. Stevens (tpt) — Crystal ■ C 367
Frøydis Ree Wekre, Horn, w. Wekre, Frøydis Ree (hn), Sequoia String Quartet *(rec 1980 & 1983)* — Crystal ▲ CD 377
Heiden, B.:Son Hn, w. John Cerminaro (hn) — Crystal ▲ CD 676
Henderson, W.P.H.:Easy Pieces — Grenadilla ■ GSC 1069
Henderson, W.P.H.:Juxtaposition — Grenadilla ■ GSC 1069
Henderson, W.P.H.:Toujours Amoureux — Grenadilla ■ GSC 1069
Hindemith, P.:Son Cl, w. D. Howard (cl) *(rec Aug. 6-7 & 9, 1991)* — Centaur ▲ CRC 2201 [DDD]
Hindemith, P.:Son Hn, w. John Cerminaro (hn) — Crystal ▲ CD 676
Ibert, J.:Impromptu Tpt & Pno, w. T. Stevens (tpt) — Crystal ■ C 367
John Cerminaro:Horn, w. J. Cerminaro — Crystal ▲ CD676
Lutoslawski, W.:Dance Preludes Cl, Hp, Pno, Perc & Strs, w. D. Howard (cl), *(other soloists unknown) (rec Aug. 6-7 & 9, 1991)* — Centaur ▲ CRC 2201 [DDD]
Poulenc, F.:Son Cl Pno, w. D. Howard (cl) *(rec Aug. 6-7 & 9, 1991)* — Centaur ▲ CRC 2201 [DDD]
Powell, J.:Rhap nègre, w. C. Simmons (cnd), Los Angeles PO — New World ▲ 80228-2
Ralph Sauer, Trombone, w. R. Sauer (trbn) — Crystal ▲ CD 380
Ropartz, G.:Andante & Allegro, w. T. Stevens (tpt) — Crystal ■ C 367
Smith, Hale:The Valley Wind, w. Harris (sgr) — CRI ■ C 301
Strauss, F.:Nocturne, w. J. Cerminaro (hn) — Crystal ▲ CD 676
Thomas Stevens, w. T. Stevens (tpt) — Crystal ▲ CD 665
Tomasi, H.:Triptyque, w. T. Stevens (tpt) — Crystal ■ C 367

Carol, Henri (org)
Anthologie de Musique Italienne — REM ▲ 311117 [ADD]

Carol, Kathleen (va)
Davidson, T.:I Hear the Mermaids Singing, w. Lori Barnet (vc), Charles Abramovic (pno) — CRI ▲ CD 681 [DDD]

Carolan, Lucy (hpd)—see ORCHESTRAS & ENSEMBLES L'École d'Orphée

Carolan, Lucy (kbd)
Flute Collection, w. S. Preston (fl) — Amon Ra ▲ CDSAR 19 [DDD]

Caroldi, A. (ob)
Vivaldi, A.:Cons for 2 Obs, w. A. Alvarosi (ob), P. Santi (cnd), Milan Virtuosi—RV.535 — Allegretto ▲ ACD 8036 [ADD] ■ ACS 8036
Vivaldi, A.:Cons Obs Cls, w. A. Alvarosi (ob), E. Schiani (cl), A. Gerbi (cl), P. Santi (cnd), Milan Virtuosi — Allegretto ▲ ACD 8036 [ADD] ■ ACS 8036

Caroli, Enzo (fl)
The Flute from '700 to '900, w. E. Caroli (fl), Renato Maioli (pno), Daniela Colonna Romano (hp) — Stradavarius ▲ SIP 25

Carp, David (kazoo)
Rzewski, F.:Moonrise with Memories, w. David Taylor (b trbn), Bill Blount (cl), Allan Dean (tpt), Louise Schulman (vn), Robert Wolinsky (gtr), Bill Moersch (mar/dlc) *(rec RCA Studios, NYC, June 4, 1981)* — New World ▲ 80494-2

Carpenter, Dave (db)
Vivaldi, A.:Cons Vn, Op. 8/1–4, "The Four Seasons", w. Eddie Daniels (cl), Peter Erskine (dr), Alan Broadbent (pno) *(rec California State University, Long Beach, CA, Mar 15, 1996)* — Shanachie ▲ SHA 5017 ■ SHA 5017

Carpenter, Nicholas (cl)
Arnold, M.:Sonatina Cl, w. David McArthur (pno) — Herald ▲ HAVPCD 152
Dunhill, T.:Phantasy Suite, w. David McArthur (pno) — Herald ▲ HAVPCD 152
Finzi, G.:Bagatelles, Op. 23, w. David McArthur (pno) — Herald ▲ HAVPCD 152
Henry, M.:Jazz Song, w. David McArthur (pno) — Herald ▲ HAVPCD 152
Ireland, J.:Fant-Son Cl & Pno, w. David McArthur (pno) — Herald ▲ HAVPCD 152
McCabe, J.:Pieces Cl, w. David McArthur (pno) — Herald ▲ HAVPCD 152

Carr, Colin (vc)—see also ORCHESTRAS & ENSEMBLES Golub/Kaplan/Carr Trio
Brahms, J.:Sextet Strs, Op. 36, w. Benny Kim (vn), Ani Kavafian (vn), Cynthia Phelps (va), Randolph Kelly (va), Peter Rejto (vc) *(rec live, Tucson Chamber Music Festival, Mar 11, 1994)* — Arizona Friends of Chamber Music ▲ 1994 [DDD]
Brahms, J.:Trio Cl, w. D. Shifrin (cl), D. Golub (pno) — Arabesque ▲ Z 6608
Brahms, J.:Trio 1 Pno, w. D. Golub (pno), M. Kaplan (vn) — Arabesque ▲ Z 6607
Brahms, J.:Trio 2 Pno, w. D. Golub (pno), M. Kaplan (vn) — Arabesque ▲ Z 6608
Brahms, J.:Trio 3 Pno, w. D. Golub (pno), M. Kaplan (vn) — Arabesque ▲ Z 6608
Britten, H.:Suite 3 Vc *(rec Oct. 1990)* — GM ▲ GM2031 [DDD]
Crumb, G.:Son Vc *(rec Oct. 1990)* — GM ▲ GM2031 [DDD]
Kodály, Z.:Son Vc, Op. 8 *(rec Oct. 1990)* — GM ▲ GM2031 [DDD]
Mendelssohn, F.:Trio 1 Pno, w. D. Golub (pno), M. Kaplan (vn) — Arabesque ▲ Z 6599
Mendelssohn, F.:Trio 2 Pno, w. D. Golub (pno), M. Kaplan (vn) — Arabesque ▲ Z 6599
Mozart, W.A.:Qnt Strs, K.516, w. Ani Kavafian (vn), Benny Kim (vn), Randolph Kelly (va), Cynthia Phelps (va) *(rec Tuscon Winter Chamber Festival; Mar 11, 1994)* — Arizona Friends of Chamber Music ▲ AFCD 19951
Mozart, W.A.:Qnt Strs, K.516, w. Ani Kavafian (vn), Benny Kim (vn), Randolph Kelley (va), Cynthia Phelps (va) *(rec 1994–95)* — Arizona Friends of Chamber Music ▲ 1994/5 [DDD]
Scharwenka, X.:Son Vc, w. Seta Tanyel (pno) — Collins Classics ▲ COL 1448 [DDD]
Scharwenka, X.:Trio 1 Pno, w. Seta Tanyel (pno), Lydia Mordkovitch (vn) — Collins Classics ▲ COL 1448 [DDD]
Schubert, Franz:Nocturne Pno, w. D. Golub (pno), M. Kaplan (vn) — Arabesque 2-▲ Z 6580-2
Schubert, Franz:Trio Pno, D.28, w. M. Kaplan (vn), D. Golub (pno) — Arabesque 2-▲ Z 6580-2
Schubert, Franz:Trio 1 Pno, w. D. Golub (pno), M. Kaplan (vn) — Arabesque 2-▲ Z 6580-2
Schubert, Franz:Trio 2 Pno, w. D. Golub (pno), M. Kaplan (vn)—includes both the traditional finale as well as the first recording of the original finale, which contains 100 bars cut by Schubert prior to publication — Arabesque 2-▲ Z 6580-2
Schuller, G.:Fant Vc *(rec Oct. 1990)* — GM ▲ GM2031 [DDD]
Schumann, C.:Trio Pno, w. J. Silverstein (vn), V. Jochum (pno) — Tudor ▲ TUD 788 [DDD]
Shostakovich, D.:Trio 2 Pno, w. James Bonn (pno), Ani Kavafian (vn) *(rec Tuscon Winter Chamber Festival; Mar 13, 1994)* — Arizona Friends of Chamber Music ▲ AFCD 19941
Shostakovich, D.:Trio 2 Pno, w. Ani Kavafian (vn), James Bonn (pno) *(rec live, Tucson Chamber Music Festival, Mar 13, 1994)* — Arizona Friends of Chamber Music ▲ 1994 [DDD]

Carr, Ian (tpt/flgl)
Carr, I.:Music of, w. J. Taylor (org)—12 works inspired by Shakespeare *(rec May 30-31, 1992)* — Celestial Harmonies ▲ 13064-2

Carreno, Inocente (vn)
Carreño, I.:Fant, w. Pascal Bournet (gtr) *(rec Studio Damiens, Boulogne, 1994)* — Iris ▲ 269 [DDD]
Gonzalez, F.:Music of, w. Pascal Bournet (gtr)—Danza de Los Amantes Efimeros; Brisas Del Pamplomita; El Diablo Suelto; Intro et Pasillo *(rec Studio Damiens, Boulogne, 1994)* — Iris ▲ 269 [DDD]
Machado, C.:Music of, w. Pascal Bournet (gtr)—Pacoga choro; Pé de Moleque *(rec Studio Damiens, Boulogne, 1994)* — Iris ▲ 269 [DDD]
Piazzolla, A.:Music of, w. Pascal Bournet (gtr)—Café 1930; Nightclub 1960 *(rec Studio Damiens, Boulogne, 1994)* — Iris ▲ 269 [DDD]
Villa-Lobos, H.:Music of, w. Pascal Bournet (gtr)—Modinha; Distribução de Flores *(rec Studio Damiens, Boulogne, 1994)* — Iris ▲ 269 [DDD]

Carrier, James (shm/rcr/oud/hp/gemshn)—see also ORCHESTRAS & ENSEMBLES Sonus
Sonus Chanterai:Music of Medieval France, w. Hazel Ketchum (sgr/saz-lt/perc), J. Holenko (oud/chitarra/psaltery/saz-lt/perc), Will Mason (saz-lt/chitarra/vih/ham dlc/perc) *(rec St. John's Episcopal Church, Columbia, MD, Sept. 1993)* — Dorian Discovery ▲ DIS 80123 [DDD]

Carrington, John (hp)
Hovhaness, A.:Starry Night, w. Scott Goff (fl), Ronald Johnson (xyl) *(rec St Thomas Center Chapel, Bothell, WA, Jan 1995)* — Crystal ▲ CD 811 [DDD]

Carroll, Edward (tpt)—see also ORCHESTRAS & ENSEMBLES New York Trumpet Ensemble
Albinoni, T.:Con Tpt, Op. 7/3, w. H. Friesen (cnd), Concerto Rotterdam *(rec Apr 26-27, 1988)* — Erasmus ▲ WVH 005 [DDD]
Baldassare, P.:Son 1 Tpt, w. H. Friesen (cnd), Concerto Rotterdam *(rec Apr. 26-27, 1988)* — Erasmus ▲ WVH 005 [DDD]
Baroque Trumpetissimo, w. D. Bilger (tpt), Stephen Burns (tpt), Alex Holton (tpt), Raymond Mase (tpt), Timothy Morrison (tpt), Lee Soper (tpt), Atsuko Sato (bn), Ben Harms (timp), Edward Brewer (org/hpd), Philharmonia Virtuosi [cnd:Richard Kapp] — ESS.A.Y ▲ ESS 1035 [DDD]
Franceschini, P.:Son à 7, w. A. van Zon, H. Friesen (cnd), Concerto Rotterdam *(rec Apr. 26-27, 1988)* — Erasmus ▲ WVH 005 [DDD]
Handel, G.F.:Music of, w. Anthony Newman (org), New York Trumpet Ensemble—Ov; Bourrée; La Paix; La Rejouissance; Minuets I & II [all from Royal Fireworks Music]; Grand Fugues Nos. 2, 3 & 6 in G, B♭ & c [from Fugues faciles]; Martial Sym [from Belshazzar]; Tpt Ov [from Atalanta]; 2 Marches [from Floridante]; Grand March [from Rinaldo]; March in D [from Hercules]; Chorus & March [from Judas Maccabaeus]; Con in B♭ [from Select Harmony]; Suite in D [from Water Music] *(rec Rye Presbyterian Church, Rye, NY, Sept 1985)* — Allegretto ▲ ACD 8205
Purcell, H.:Trumpet Tune & Ayre, w. William Nell (org) — Sony Classical ▲ MLK 62369 [ADD/DDD]
Torelli, G.:Con Tpt, w. H. Friesen (cnd), Concerto Rotterdam *(rec Apr. 26-27, 1988)* — Erasmus ▲ WVH 005 [DDD]
Vivaldi, A.:Con Ob, RV.451, w. H. Friesen (cnd), Concerto Rotterdam [arr. for trumpet] *(rec Apr. 26-27, 1988)* — Erasmus ▲ WVH 005 [DDD]
Vivaldi, A.:Con for 2 Tpts, w. A. van Zon (tpt), H. Friesen (cnd), Concerto Rotterdam *(rec Apr. 26-27, 1988)* — Erasmus ▲ WVH 005 [DDD]

Carroll, Edward (tpt/pic tpt)
Telemann, G.P.:Con Tpt Strs in D, w. Diane Bruce (vn), Elizabeth Field (vn), Annabelle Hoffman (vc), Dongsok Shin (positiv org), Edward Brewer (hpd/positiv org) *(rec Rye Presbyterian Church)* — Helicon Classics ▲ HE 1009
Telemann, G.P.:Musique héroïque, w. Diane Bruce (vn), Elizabeth Field (vn), Annabelle Hoffman (vc), Dongsok Shin (positiv org), Edward Brewer (hpd/positiv org) *(rec Rye Presbyterian Church)* — Helicon Classics ▲ HE 1009
Telemann, G.P.:Sons Tpt, w. Diane Bruce (vn), Elizabeth Field (vn), Annabelle Hoffman (vc), Dongsok Shin (positiv org), Edward Brewer (hpd/positiv org) *(rec Rye Presbyterian Church)* — Helicon Classics ▲ HE 1009
Telemann, G.P.:Trio Sons, w. Diane Bruce (vn), Elizabeth Field (vn), Annabelle Hoffman (vc), Dongsok Shin (positiv org), Edward Brewer (hpd/positiv org) *(rec Rye Presbyterian Church)* — Helicon Classics ▲ HE 1009

Carroll, Paul (bn)—see ORCHESTRAS & ENSEMBLES Badinage

Carroll, Paul (fl)—see ORCHESTRAS & ENSEMBLES Badinage

Carroll, Paul (fl/rcr/bn/ob)—see ORCHESTRAS & ENSEMBLES Badinage

Carteng, Cammi (handbells)
Vees, J.:Stigmata non Grata, w. Dorian Ringers (handbells), Jan Dudiet (handbells), JoAnn Kerns (handbells), Monica McGowan (handbells), B. Mathis (cnd) — CRI ("Emergency Music" series) ▲ CD 730 [DDD]

▲ = CD ♦ = Enhanced CD Δ = MD ■ = Cassette Tape ◻ = DCC

Carter, James (b cl)

So Many Stars, w. K. Battle (sop), Antonio Hart (sax), Grover Washington Jr (sax), Tom Harrell (flgl), Cyrus Chestnut (pno), Jon Herrington (gtr), Romero Lubambo (gtr), Ira Coleman (elec bass), Christian McBride (elec bass), Cyro Baptista (perc), Steven Berrios (perc) *(rec Hit Factory, Clinton Recording Studios, R.P.M. Sound Studios, Unique Recording Studios, Power Station)* Sony Classical ▲ SK 68473 [DDD]

Carter, John (trbn)

Scelsi, G.:Anahit, w. Paul Zukofsky (vn), Julie Bogorad (fl), Peggy Russell (fl), Courtney Westcott (fl), Lawrence McDonald (cl), Joan Waryha (cl), Jean Hansen (b cl), Bill Suite (e hn), Nita VanPelt (sax), Bob Zobal (tpt), Martin Lydecker (trbn), Stan Cortman (hn), Robert Ward (hn), William Curry (va), Jody Rowitsch (va), Irene Wade (va), Anne Fagerburg (vc), John Gockel (vc), Sue Manz (bass), Steven Stearman (bass) *(rec Oberlin Conservatory of Music, Oct 8, 1973)* CP² ▲ CP2 108 [AAD]

Carter, Nora (vn)—see ORCHESTRAS & ENSEMBLES Meaux String Quartet

Carter, Peter (vn)—see also ORCHESTRAS & ENSEMBLES Allegri String Quartet

Poulenc, F.:Chamber Music, w. Peter Sidhom (bar), William Bennett (fl), David Campbell (cl), James Campbell (cl), Nicholas Daniel (ob), Richard Watkins (hn), Rachel Gough (bn), Chris West (db), Ieuan Jones (hp), Clifford Benson (pno), Julius Drake (pno), John York (pno)—Son for Ob; L'invitation au château; Villanelle; Son 2 Cls; Trio; Sxt; Son for Cl & Bn; Rapsodie nègre; Son for Cl; Mouvements perpétuels; Son for Fl *(rec All Saints' Church, East Finchley, London, Jan 12–20, 1994)* Cala ▲ CACD 1018 [DDD]

Ravel, M.:Pièce en forme de Habanera, w. Clifford Benson (pno) *(rec All Saints' Church, East Finchley, London, Jan 12–20, 1994)* Cala ▲ CACD 1018 [DDD]

Carter, Regina (vn)—see ORCHESTRAS & ENSEMBLES Soldier String Quartet

Carter, Roy (ob)

Bach, J.S.:Music of—Christ lag in Todesbanden; Wachet auf, ruft uns die stimme; Jesu, joy of man's desiring; Air on a G string; etc. Blue Note ▲ B21Z 80510

Britten, H.:Metamorphoses Ob EMI Classics ("Anglo–American Chamber Music" series) ▲ CDC 55398

Elgar, E.:Harmony Music I–V, w. Michael Cox (fl), Paul Edmund–Davies (fl), Nicholas Rodwell (cl), Martin Gatt (bn)—No. 4, "The Farmyard" EMI Classics ("Anglo–American Chamber Music" series) ▲ CDC 55403

Muldowney, D.:Con Ob, w. M. Tilson Thomas (cnd), London SO NM Classics ▲ NMCD 018

Carter, William (thb/gtr)—see ORCHESTRAS & ENSEMBLES Palladian Ensemble

Cartwright, George (sax/fl)

Exquisite Corpses from P.S. 122, w. D. Watson (shears/stick vn/gtr/tpt), Judy Dunaway (gtr/balloons), Anthony Coleman (sampler), Raissa St. Pierre (drums), Guy Yarden (vn/pno), Leslie Ross (bn), Linda Austin (gtr), Bruce Kaplan (gtr), Doug Henderson (peckhorn/bass/toy pno), Sue Ann Harkey (gtr), Cinnie Cole (sampler), et al. ¿What Next? ▲ WN 0002 [ADD]

Carulli, Michele (cl)

Mozart, W.A.:Con Cl, w. E. Aadland (cnd), European Community CO IMP Classics ▲ IMPCD 1054 [DDD]

Mozart, W.A.:Con Cl, w. E. Aadland (cnd), European Community CO IMP ▲ IMP 2047

Villa–Lobos, H.:Chôro 2, w. Andrea Griminelli (fl) *(rec Chiesa della Misericordia, Torino, Italy, Feb 1987)* Arts Music ▲ 447200–2 [DDD]

Villa–Lobos, H.:Qt Fl, w. Andrea Griminelli (fl), Pietro Borgonovo (ob), Rino Vernizzi (bn) *(rec Chiesa della Misericordia, Torino, Italy, Feb 1987)* Arts Music ▲ 447200–2 [DDD]

Villa–Lobos, H.:Qnten forme de chôros, w. Andrea Griminelli (fl), Pietro Borgonovo (ob), Francesco Pomarico (E hn), Rino Vernizzi (bn) *(rec Chiesa della Misericordia, Torino, Italy, Feb 1987)* Arts Music ▲ 447200–2 [DDD]

Villa–Lobos, H.:Trio Ob, w. Pietro Borgonovo (ob), Rino Vernizzi (bn) *(rec Chiesa della Misericordia, Torino, Italy, Feb 1987)* Arts Music ▲ 447200–2 [DDD]

Caruthers, Yvonne (vc)

Adler, S.:Close Encounters, w. W. Steck (vn) Gasparo ▲ GS 297

Adler, S.:Music of, w. W. Steck (vn), G. Peachey (pno), C. Lewis (pno)—Sons. 2–4; Etudes (4), "Meadowmountetudes"; Double Portrait; Little Suite; Close Encounters Gasparo ▲ GS 297 [DDD/ADD]

Caryevschi, Jorge (fl)

Ledesma, M.R.:Divert Marcial, w. Jacques Ogg (pno) *(rec Madrid, Feb 6–10, 1989)* RNE/Spanish National Radio ▲ AME 006 [DDD]

Ribas, J.M. del C.:Music for Fl Pno, w. Jacques Ogg (pno)—El Sereni; La Cachucha; Fant Octava *(rec Madrid, Feb 6–10, 1989)* RNE/Spanish National Radio ▲ AME 006 [DDD]

Casadei, C. (vc)

Haydn, J.:Trios Fls & Vc, "London Trios", w. Maxence Larrieu (fl), M. Mercelli (fl) Bongiovanni ▲ GB 5508 [DDD]

Haydn, J.:Trios Pno, Vn & Vc, w. L. Mercelli (pno), M. Mercelli (vn)—HXV No. 30 in F—piano–flute–cello Bongiovanni ▲ GB 5508 [DDD]

Casademunt, Sergi (vl)—see ORCHESTRAS & ENSEMBLES L'Academia d'Harmonia

Casadesus, Gaby (pno)

Beethoven, L. van:Son 5 Vn, "Spring", w. Z. Francescatti (vn) Sony Classical ("Essential Classics" series) ▲ SBK 46342 [ADD] ■ SBT 46342

Beethoven, L. van:Son 9 Vn, "Kreutzer", w. Z. Francescatti (vn) Odyssey ▲ MBK 42528

Casadesus, R.:Danses Mediterranéenes, Op. 36, w. R. Casadesus (pno) *(rec 1950)* Sony Masterworks (Portrait) ▲ MPK 52527 [AAD]

Debussy, C.:En blanc et noir, w. R. Casadesus (pno) *(rec 1963; from CBS Masterwork)* Sony Masterworks (Portrait) ▲ MPK 52527 [AAD]

Debussy, C.:Petite suite, w. R. Casadesus (pno) *(rec 1959; from CBS Masterwork)* Sony Masterworks (Portrait) ▲ MPK 52527 [AAD]

Fauré, G.:Ballade Pno, w. L. Bernstein (cnd), New York PO *(rec 1961)* Sony Classical ▲ SMK 47548 [ADD]

Fauré, G.:Dolly, w. R. Casadesus (pno) *(rec 1959)* Sony Masterworks (Portrait) ▲ MPK 52527 [AAD]

Franck, C.:Symphonic Vars, w. E. Ormandy (cnd), Philadelphia Orch Odyssey ■ YT 31274

Indy, V. d':Sym on a French Mountain Air, w. E. Ormandy (cnd), Philadelphia Orch Odyssey ■ YT 31274

Satie, E.:Morceaux en forme de poire, w. R. Casadesus (pno) *(rec 1959)* Sony Masterworks ("Portrait" series) ▲ MPK 52527 [AAD]

Casadesus, Jean–Claude (perc)

Berio, L.:Circles, w. C. Berberian (sop), F. Pierre (hp), J.–P. Drouet (perc) *(rec 1967)* Wergo ▲ WER 6021–2 [AAD]

Casadesus, Robert (pno)

Beethoven, L. van:Son 14 Pno, "Moonlight Son" Sony Classical ("Essential Classics" series) ▲ SBK 46345 [ADD] ■ SBT 46345

Beethoven, L. van:Son 23 Pno, "Appassionata" Sony Classical ("Essential Classics" series) ▲ SBK 46345 [ADD] ■ SBT 46345

Beethoven, L. van:Son 24 Pno Sony Classical ("Essential Classics" series) ▲ SBK 46345 [ADD] ■ SBT 46345

Beethoven, L. van:Son 26 Pno, "Les Adieux" Sony Classical ("Essential Classics" series) ▲ SBK 46345 [ADD] ■ SBT 46345

Beethoven, L. van:Son 4 Vn, w. Z. Francescatti (vn) *(rec 1961)* Sony Masterworks ("Portrait" series) ▲ MPK 52534 [ADD]

Beethoven, L. van:Son 5 Vn, "Spring", w. Z. Francescatti (vn) Odyssey ▲ MBK 42528

Beethoven, L. van:Son 6 Vn, w. Z. Francescatti (vn) *(rec 1961)* Sony Masterworks ("Portrait" series) ▲ MPK 52534 [ADD]

Beethoven, L. van:Son 7 Vn, w. Z. Francescatti (vn) *(rec 1961)* Sony Masterworks ("Portrait" series) ▲ MPK 52534 [ADD]

Beethoven, L. van:Son 8 Vn, w. Z. Francescatti (vn) *(rec 1961)* Sony Masterworks ("Portrait" series) ▲ MPK 52534 [ADD]

Beethoven, L. van:Son 9 Vn, "Kreutzer", w. Z. Francescatti (vn) Sony Classical ("Essential Classics" series) ▲ SBK 46342 [ADD] ■ SBT 46342

Casadesus, Robert (pno) (cont.)

Beethoven, L. van:Son 10 Vn, w. Z. Francescatti (vn) Sony Classical ("Essential Classics" series) ▲ SBK 46342 [ADD] ■ SBT 46342

Brahms, J.:Con 2 Pno, w. C. Schuricht (cnd), *(orch unknown)* Melodram ▲ CDM 18049

Brahms, J.:Sons Vn (comp), w. Z. Francescatti (vn) *(rec 1949 & 1952)* Library of Congress ▲ LOC 3 [ADD]

Casadesus, R.:Danses Mediterranéenes, Op. 36, w. G. Casadesus (pno) *(rec 1950)* Sony Masterworks (Portrait) ▲ MPK 52527 [AAD]

Debussy, C.:En blanc et noir, w. G. Casadesus (pno) *(rec 1963; from CBS Masterwork)* Sony Masterworks (Portrait) ▲ MPK 52527 [AAD]

Debussy, C.:Petite suite, w. G. Casadesus (pno) *(rec 1959; from CBS Masterwork)* Sony Masterworks (Portrait) ▲ MPK 52527 [AAD]

Debussy, C.:Son Vc, w. Maurice Marechal (vc) *(rec 1929 – 1943)* Iron Needle ▲ IN 1324 [ADD]

Debussy, C.:Son Vc, w. M. Marechal (vc) *(rec 1930 for French Columbia)* Pearl ▲ PEA 9348 (m) [AAD]

Fauré, G.:Dolly, w. G. Casadesus (pno) *(rec 1959)* Sony Masterworks (Portrait) ▲ MPK 52527 [AAD]

Mozart, W.A.:Con 21 Pno, w. G. Szell (cnd), Cleveland Orch CBS ▲ MYK 38523 [AAD] ■ MYT 38523

Mozart, W.A.:Con 21 Pno, w. R. Kubelik (cnd), Bavarian RSO *(rec 1971)* Arkadia ▲ 494

Mozart, W.A.:Con 21 Pno, w. G. Szell (cnd), Cleveland Orch Sony Classical 3–▲ SM3K 46519

Mozart, W.A.:Con 22 Pno, w. G. Szell (cnd), Columbia SO Sony Classical 3–▲ SM3K 46519

Mozart, W.A.:Con 23 Pno, w. G. Szell (cnd), Columbia SO Sony Classical 3–▲ SM3K 46519

Mozart, W.A.:Con 24 Pno, w. G. Szell (cnd), Cleveland Orch CBS ▲ MYK 38523 [AAD] ■ MYT 38523

Mozart, W.A.:Con 24 Pno, w. G. Szell (cnd), Cleveland Orch Sony Classical 3–▲ SM3K 46519

Mozart, W.A.:Con 26 Pno, w. G. Szell (cnd), Columbia SO Sony Classical 3–▲ SM3K 46519

Mozart, W.A.:Con 27 Pno, w. G. Szell (cnd), Columbia SO Sony Classical 3–▲ SM3K 46519

Ravel, M.:Con Pno (left hand), w. S. Celibidache (cnd), Vienna SO *(rec live, 1952)* Enterprise ("Documents" series) 2–▲ LV 946/47 (m/s) [ADD]

Saint–Saëns, C.:Con 4 Pno, w. L. Bernstein (cnd), New York PO Sony Classical ▲ SMK 47608

Satie, E.:Morceaux en forme de poire, w. G. Casadesus (pno) *(rec 1959)* Sony Masterworks ("Portrait" series) ▲ MPK 52527 [AAD]

Casalonga, Nicole (org/hpd)

Missa Coriscia in Monticellu, w. A Cumpagnia *(rec Mar. 18–23, 1994)* K617 ▲ 7043

Casals, Pablo (pno)

Victoria de los Angeles Live in Concert, w. V. de los Angeles (sop), P. Berl (pno) *(rec 1952–60)* VAI Audio 2–▲ VAIA 1025 (m) [ADD]

Casals, Pablo (vc)

Bach, J.S.:Music of, w. E. Ormandy, E. P. Biggs (org), Moog Synthesizer CBS ■ MGT 31261

Bach, J.S.:Sons VI, BWV 1027–1029, w. M. Horszowski (pno)—BWV 1027 *(rec live, July 8, 1956)* Music & Arts 4–▲ CD 689 (m) [AAD]

Bach, J.S.:Sons VI, BWV 1027–1029, w. Mieczyslaw Horszowsky (pno)—No. 1 in G; No. 2 in D Andromeda ▲ ANR 2524

Bach, J.S.:Suites Vc, BWV 1007–1012—No. 6 *(rec Paris, 1938)* Iron Needle ▲ IN 1308

Bach, J.S.:Suites Vc, BWV 1007–1012—No. 3 in C, BWV 1009 *(rec live 1950s)* Music & Arts 4–▲ CD 688 (m) [AAD]

Bach, J.S.:Suites Vc, BWV 1007–1012 *(rec 1936–39)* Grammofono 2000 2–▲ GRM 78627

Bach, J.S.:Suites Vc, BWV 1007–1012—Nos. 4–6 *(rec 1938 & 1939)* EMI Classics ("Great Recordings of the Century" series) ▲ CDH 61029–2 (m)

Bach, J.S.:Suites Vc, BWV 1007–1012—Nos. 1–3 *(rec 1936 & 1938)* EMI Classics ("Great Recordings of the Century" series) ▲ CDH 61028–2 (m)

Beethoven, L. van:Minuets Orch, WoO 7—No. 2 in D [cello–piano arr.] Pearl 4–▲ PEAS 9935 (m) [AAD]

Beethoven, L. van:Minuets Orch, WoO 7, w. O. Schulhof (pno)—No. 2 in D [cello–piano arr.] *(rec 1930 for HMV)* Pearl 2–▲ PEAS 9461 (m) [AAD]

Beethoven, L. van:Sons Vc (comp), w. R. Serkin (pno) *(rec Perpignan, France; Prades, France)* Sony Classical ("The Casals Edition" series) 2–▲ SM2K 58985 [ADD]

Beethoven, L. van:Son 3 Vc, w. R. Serkin (pno) *(rec 1953)* Sony Masterworks ("Portrait" series) ▲ MPK 45682 [ADD]

Beethoven, L. van:Son 4 Vc, w. R. Serkin (pno) Sony Masterworks ("Portrait" series) ▲ MPK 45682 [ADD]

Beethoven, L. van:Son 4 Vc, w. Mieczyslaw Horszowsky (pno) *(rec London, 1936)* Iron Needle ▲ IN 1308

Beethoven, L. van:Son 5 Vc, w. M. Horszowski (pno) *(rec live June 1953)* Music & Arts 4–▲ CD 688 (m) [AAD]

Beethoven, L. van:Son 5 Vc, w. Mieczyslaw Horzowsky (pno) *(rec 1953)* Historical Performers ▲ HPS 31

Beethoven, L. van:Son 5 Vc, w. R. Serkin (pno) Sony Masterworks ("Portrait" series) ▲ MPK 45682 [ADD]

Beethoven, L. van:Trio 1 Pno, w. E. Istomin (pno), J. Fuchs (vn) *(rec Prades, France, July 5, 1953)* Sony Classical ("The Casals Edition" series) ▲ SMK 58988 [ADD]

Beethoven, L. van:Trio 2 Pno, w. E. Istomin (pno), A. Schneider (vn) *(rec Perpignan, France, Aug. 1951)* Sony Classical ("The Casals Edition" series) ▲ SMK 58989 [ADD]

Beethoven, L. van:Trio 3 Pno, w. H. Menuhin (pno), Y. Menuhin (vn) *(rec live July 18, 1959)* Music & Arts 4–▲ CD 688 (m) [AAD]

Beethoven, L. van:Trio 4 Pno, "Ghost", w. E. Istomin (pno), J. Fuchs (vn) *(rec Prades, France, July 8–9, 1953)* Sony Classical ("The Casals Edition" series) ▲ SMK 58991 [ADD]

Beethoven, L. van:Trio 4 Pno, "Ghost", w. R. Serkin (pno), S. Goldberg (vn) *(rec live June 18, 1954)* Music & Arts 4–▲ CD 688 (m) [AAD]

Beethoven, L. van:Trio 5 Pno, w. E. Istomin (pno), A. Schneider (vn) *(rec Perpignan, France, Aug. 1951)* Sony Classical ("The Casals Edition" series) ▲ SMK 58991 [ADD]

Beethoven, L. van:Trio 5 Pno, w. R. Serkin (pno), S. Goldberg (vn) *(rec live, June 18, 1954)* Music & Arts 4–▲ CD 688 (m) [AAD]

Beethoven, L. van:Trio 6 Pno, "Archduke", w. Mieczyslaw Horzowsky (pno), Sandor Végh (vn) *(rec 1956)* Historical Performers ▲ HPS 31

Beethoven, L. van:Trio 6 Pno, "Archduke", w. E. Istomin (pno), A. Schneider (vn) *(rec Perpignan, France, Aug. 1951)* Sony Classical ("The Casals Edition" series) ▲ SMK 58990 [ADD]

Beethoven, L. van:Trio 7 Pno, w. A. Cortot (pno), J. Thibaud (vn) *(rec Nov.–Dec. 1928)* EMI Classics 3–▲ 64057–2 (m) [ADD]

Beethoven, L. van:Trio 7 Pno, w. E. Istomin (pno), A. Schneider (vn) *(rec Perpignan, France, Aug. 1951)* Sony Classical ("The Casals Edition" series) ▲ SMK 58990 [ADD]

Beethoven, L. van:Trio 9 Pno, "Kakadu", w. A. Cortot (pno), J. Thibaud (vn) *(rec July 6, 1926)* EMI Classics 3–▲ 64057 (m) [ADD]

Beethoven, L. van:Trio 9 Pno, "Kakadu", w. R. Serkin (pno), S. Goldberg (vn) Music & Arts 4–▲ CD 688 (m) [AAD]

Beethoven, L. van:Vars on "Ein Mädchen oder Weibchen" from Mozart's *Die Zauberflöte,* w. R. Serkin (pno) *(rec Perpignan, France, July 31, 1951)* Sony Classical ("The Casals Edition" series) 2–▲ SM2K 58985 [ADD]

Beethoven, L. van:Vars on "Ein Mädchen oder Weibchen" from Mozart's *Die Zauberflöte,* w. M. Horszowsky (pno) AS Disc (Notes) ▲ ASDPGP 11032 [ADD]

Beethoven, L. van:Vars on "See, the Conquering Hero Comes" from Handel's *Judas Maccabaeus,* w. R. Serkin (pno) *(rec Perpignan, France, Aug. 1951)* Sony Classical ("The Casals Edition" series) ▲ SMK 58991 [ADD]

Beethoven, L. van:Vars on "Bei Männern" from Mozart's *Die Zauberflöte,* w. A. Cortot (pno) *(rec June 21, 1927)* EMI Classics 3–▲ 64057–2 (m) [ADD]

Beethoven, L. van:Vars on "Bei Männern" from Mozart's *Die Zauberflöte,* w. A. Cortot (pno) *(rec 1927 for HMV)* Pearl 2–▲ PEAS 9461 (m) [AAD]

Beethoven, L. van:Vars on "Bei Männern" from Mozart's *Die Zauberflöte,* w. A. Cortot (pno) Pearl 4–▲ PEAS 9935 (m) [AAD]

Beethoven, L. van:Vars on "Bei Männern" from Mozart's *Die Zauberflöte,* w. R. Serkin (pno) *(rec Perpignan, & Prades, France)* Sony Classical ("The Casals Edition" series) 2–▲ SM2K 58985 [ADD]

Casals, Pablo (vc) (cont.)
Boccherini, L.:Con Vc, G.482, w. L. Ronald (cnd), London SO *(rec for HMV, 1936)* Pearl ▲ PEA 9349 (m) [AAD]
Boccherini, L.:Con Vc, G.482, w. L. Ronald (cnd), London SO Pearl 4–▲ PEAS 9935 (m) [AAD]
Bow & Baton:Complete 1929–30 HMV Singles & 1928 London Symphony Recordings, w. Casals, Pablo (vc), Blas-Net (pno), Otto Schulhof (pno) Pearl ▲ PEA 9128 [ADD]
Brahms, J.:Con Vn & Vc, "Double Con", w. J. Thibaud (vn), A. Cortot (cnd), Barcelona Pau Casals Orch *(rec May 1929)* EMI Classics 3–▲ 64057-2 (m) [ADD]
Brahms, J.:Con Vn & Vc, "Double Con", w. J. Thibaud (vn), A. Cortot (cnd), Barcelona Pau Casals Orch *(rec between May 11–12, 1929)* Koch Historic 2–▲ 7705-2 [ADD]
Brahms, J.:Con Vn & Vc, "Double Con", w. Jacques Thibaud (vn), A. Cortot (cnd), Barcelona Pau Casals Orch Dutton Laboratories ▲ DUT 5006 [ADD]
Brahms, J.:Con Vn & Vc, "Double Con", w. J. Thibaud (vn), A. Cortot (cnd), Barcelona Pau Casals Orch *(rec 1929 for HMV)* Pearl ▲ PEA 9363 (m) [AAD]
Brahms, J.:Con Vn & Vc, "Double Con", w. J. Thibaud (vn), A. Cortot (cnd), Barcelona Pau Casals Orch Pearl 4–▲ PEAS 9935 (m) [AAD]
Brahms, J.:Sextet Strs, Op. 18, w. I. Stern (vn), A. Schneider (vn), M. Katims (va), M. Thomas (va), M. Foley (vc) *(rec Prades, France, June 23–July 3, 1952)* Sony Classical ("The Casals Edition" series) ▲ SMK 58994 [ADD]
Brahms, J.:Sextet Strs, Op. 18, w. I. Stern (vn), A. Schneider (vn), M. Katims (va), M. Thomas (va), M. Foley (vc) *(rec 1952)* Sony Masterworks ("Portrait" series) ▲ MPK 44851 [ADD]
Brahms, J.:Sons Vc (comp), w. M. Horszowski (pno) Pearl 4–▲ PEAS 9935 (m) [AAD]
Brahms, J.:Son 2 Vc, w. M. Horszowski (pno) *(rec 1936 for HMV)* Pearl ▲ PEA 9363 (m) [AAD]
Brahms, J.:Son 2 Vc, w. Mieczyslaw Horszowsky (pno) *(rec 1936)* Iron Needle ▲ IN 1308
Brahms, J.:Trio Cl, w. D. Oppenheim (cl), E. Istomin (pno) *(rec live July 3, 1955)* Music & Arts 4–▲ CD 689 (m) [AAD]
Brahms, J.:Trio 1 Pno, w. M. Hess (pno), I. Stern (vn) *(rec Prades, France, June 23–July 3, 1952)* Sony Classical ("The Casals Edition" series) ▲ SMK 58994 [ADD]
Brahms, J.:Trio 1 Pno, w. Eugene Istomin (pno), Yehudi Menuhin (vn) Stradivarius ▲ STV 10020 [ADD]
Brahms, J.:Trio 1 Pno, w. E. Istomin (pno), Y. Menuhin (vn) *(rec live July 13, 1955)* Music & Arts 4–▲ CD 689 (m) [AAD]
Brahms, J.:Trio 2 Pno, w. Myra Hess (pno), Joseph Szigeti (vn) *(rec Prades, June 16, 1952)* Sony Classical ▲ SMK 66571 [ADD]
Brahms, J.:Trio 2 Pno, w. M. Hess (pno), J. Szigeti (vn) *(rec 1952)* Sony Masterworks ("Portrait" series) ▲ MPK 52535 (m) [ADD]
Brahms, J.:Trio 2 Pno, w. E. Istomin (pno), Y. Menuhin (vn) *(rec live July 13, 1955)* Music & Arts 4–▲ CD 689 (m) [AAD]
Brahms, J.:Trio 3 Pno, w. Eugene Istomin (pno), Yehudi Menuhin (vn) Stradivarius ▲ STV 10020 [ADD]
Brahms, J.:Trio 3 Pno, w. E. Istomin (pno), Y. Menuhin (vn) *(rec live July 13, 1955)* Music & Arts 4–▲ CD 688 (m) [AAD]
Bruch, M.:Kol Nidrei, w. L. Ronald (cnd), London SO *(rec 1936)* Pearl ▲ PEA 9349 (m) [AAD]
Bruch, M.:Kol Nidrei, w. L. Ronald (cnd), London SO Pearl 4–▲ PEAS 9935 (m) [AAD]
Bruch, M.:Kol Nidrei, w. L. Ronald (cnd), London SO *(rec 1936)* EMI Classics ("Great Recordings of the Century" series) ▲ CDH 63498 (m) [ADD]
Casals Pearl 4–▲ PEA 9935 (m) [AAD]
Dvořák, A.:Con Vc, w. G. Szell (cnd), Czech PO Dutton Laboratories ▲ DUT 5002
Dvořák, A.:Con Vc, w. G. Szell (cnd), Czech PO *(rec 1937)* EMI Classics (Great Recordings of the Century) ▲ CDH 63498 (m) [ADD]
Dvořák, A.:Con Vc, w. G. Szell (cnd), Czech PO *(rec 1937)* Pearl ▲ PEA 9349 (m) [AAD]
Dvořák, A.:Con Vc, w. G. Szell (cnd), Czech PO Pearl 4–▲ PEAS 9935 (m) [AAD]
Elgar, E.:Con Vc, w. A. Boult (cnd), BBC SO *(rec 1945)* EMI Classics (Great Recordings of the Century) ▲ CDH 63498 (m) [ADD]
Encores, w. Charles Baker (pno), Eugene Istomin (pno) *(rec 1915–1954)* Sony Classical ("Casals Edition" series) ▲ SMK 66573 [ADD]
Encores Pearl ▲ PEA 9363 [AAD]
Haydn, J.:Trios Pno, Vn & Vc, w. Alfred Cortot (pno), Jacques Thibaud (vn)—No. 25 only *(rec 6/20/27)* Biddulph ▲ LAB 028 [ADD]
Legendary Performers:Casals Early Recordings, 1925–28 *(rec between 1925 & 1928)* RCA Gold Seal ▲ 09026-61616-2
Mendelssohn, F.:Trio 1 Pno, w. Mieczyslaw Horszowski (pno), Alexander Schneider (vn) *(rec White House, Washington, D.C., Nov 13, 1961)* Sony Classical ▲ SMK 66571 [ADD]
Mendelssohn, F.:Trio 1 Pno, w. Alfred Cortot (pno), Jacques Thibaud (vn) *(rec June 1927)* Iron Needle 2–▲ IN 1342/43 (m) [ADD]
Mendelssohn, F.:Trio 1 Pno, w. A. Cortot (pno), J. Thibaud (vn) *(rec June 1927)* EMI Classics 3–▲ 64057-2 (m) [ADD]
Mendelssohn, F.:Trio 1 Pno, w. A. Cortot (pno), J. Thibaud (vn) *(rec 1927 for HMV)* Biddulph ▲ LHW 002 [ADD]
Mozart, W.A.:Qt Pno, K.493, w. M. Horszowski (pno), Y. Menuhin (vn), W. Wallfisch (va) *(rec live, Prades Festival, July 7, 1956)* Music & Arts 4–▲ CD 688 (m) [AAD]
Schubert, Franz:Qnt Strs, D.956, w. I. Stern (vn), A. Schneider (vn), M. Katims (va), P. Tortelier (vc) *(rec 1952)* CBS 4–▲ M4K 42003 (m/s) [ADD]
Schubert, Franz:Qnt Strs, D.956, w. I. Stern (vn), A. Schneider (vn), M. Katims (va), P. Tortelier (vc) *(rec Prades, France, July 1–2, 1952)* Sony Classical ("The Casals Edition" series) ▲ SMK 58992 [ADD]
Schubert, Franz:Trio 1 Pno, w. E. Istomin (pno), A. Schneider (vn) *(rec Perpignan, France, Aug. 1951)* Sony Classical ("Casals Edition" series) ▲ SMK 58989 [ADD]
Schubert, Franz:Trio 1 Pno, w. A. Cortot (pno), J. Thibaud (vn) *(rec 1926)* EMI Classics 3–▲ 64057-2 (m) [ADD]
Schubert, Franz:Trio 1 Pno, w. Alfred Cortot (pno), Jaques Thibaud (vn) Memories ▲ MEM CD 4605
Schubert, Franz:Trio 2 Pno, w. M. Horszowski (pno), A. Schneider (vn) *(rec Prades, France, July 5–6, 1952)* Sony Classical ("The Casals Edition" series) ▲ SMK 58988 [ADD]
Schumann, R.:Adagio & Allegro Hn, w. Clifford Curzon (pno) Andromeda ▲ ANR 2524
Schumann, R.:Con Vc, w. E. Ormandy (cnd), Prades Festival Orch Andromeda ▲ ANR 2524
Schumann, R.:Con Vc, w. E. Ormandy (cnd), Prades Festival Orch *(rec Prades, France, May 28–29, 1953)* Sony Classical ("The Casals Edition" series) ▲ SMK 58993 [ADD]
Schumann, R.:Stücke im Volkston, w. L. Mannes (pno) *(rec Prades, France, May 28–29, 1953)* Sony Classical ("The Casals Edition" series) ▲ SMK 58993 [ADD]
Schumann, R.:Trio 1 Pno, w. A. Cortot (pno), J. Thibaud (vn) *(rec 1928 for HMV)* Biddulph ▲ LHW 004 [ADD]
Schumann, R.:Trio 1 Pno, w. A. Cortot (pno), J. Thibaud (vn) *(rec 1928 for HMV)* EMI Classics 3–▲ 64057-2 (m) [ADD]
Schumann, R.:Trio 1 Pno, w. M. Horszowski (pno), A. Schneider (vn) *(rec Prades, France, July 4, 1952)* Sony Classical ("The Casals Edition" series) ▲ SMK 58993 [ADD]
Schumann, R.:Trio 2 Pno, w. Y. Menuhin (vn), M. Horszowski (pno) *(rec live 1950s)* Music & Arts 4–▲ CD 689 (m) [AAD]
Schumann, R.:Trio 3 Pno, w. S. Vegh (vn), R. Serkin (pno) *(rec live July 11, 1956)* Music & Arts 4–▲ CD 688 (m) [AAD]
Tovey, D.F.:Con Vc, w. A. Boult (cnd), BBC SO *(rec live Nov. 17, 1937)* Symposium ▲ 1115
The Victor Recordings (1926–1928), w. Nikolai Mednikoff (pno) Biddulph ▲ LAB 017 [ADD]

Casart, Chris (perc)
Snyder, R.:Enneagram Studies, w. Eric Ginsberg (cl), Stephen Krahn (pno), Rick Schaefer (perc), Kelly Scheef (perc), Jason Varga (perc), Scott Zimmerman (perc) Coronet ▲ COR 400-9

Casazza, Enrico (vn)
Vivaldi, A.:Cons Vn, Op. 8/1–12, "Il cimento dell'armonia e dell'inventione", San Rocco Accademia—Nos. 1–6 *(rec Silvelle, Treviso, Italy, Mar 1996)* Arts ▲ 473692 [DDD]

Case, Lynn (vn)—see ORCHESTRAS & ENSEMBLES Peter Garland Ensemble

Casella, Alfredo (pno)
Great Composers at the Keyboard, w. Sergei Prokofiev (pno), Georges Enescu (pno) Fonè ▲ FON 90F15 [DDD]

Casen, Petra (hpd)
Weir, J.:Chamber Music, w. William Howard (pno), Susan Tomes (pno), Domus Chamber Ensemble, Schubert Ensemble—Distance & Enchantment; The Bagpiper's Trio; I Broke Off a Golden Branch; El Rey de Francia; The Art of Touching the Keyboard; The King of France; Ardnamurchan Point Collins Classics ▲ COL 1453

Casey, Christopher (pno)
Bach, J.S.:Sons Fl, BWV 1030–35, w. Greg Banaszak (sax)—Siciliano/Waltz [from Son in E♭; arr Ricker for Sax & Pno] *(rec Bailey Hall, Cornell Univ, Ithaca, NY, Dec 19–23, 1993)* Open Loop ▲ OL 018 [DDD]
Dobbins, B.:Son Sax, w. Greg Banaszak (sax) *(rec Bailey Hall, Cornell Univ, Ithaca, NY, Dec 19–23, 1993)* Open Loop ▲ OL 018 [DDD]
Koch, F.:Latin Moods, w. Greg Banaszak (sax) *(rec Bailey Hall, Cornell Univ, Ithaca, NY, Dec 19–23, 1993)* Open Loop ▲ OL 018 [DDD]
Ricker, R.:Solar Chariots, w. Greg Banaszak (sax) *(rec Bailey Hall, Cornell Univ, Ithaca, NY, Dec 19–23, 1993)* Open Loop ▲ OL 018 [DDD]
Wilder, A.:Suite 1 Sax, w. Greg Banaszak (sax) *(rec Bailey Hall, Cornell Univ, Ithaca, NY, Dec 19–23, 1993)* Open Loop ▲ OL 018 [DDD]
Yasinitsky, G.:Double Edge, w. Greg Banaszak (sax) *(rec Bailey Hall, Cornell Univ, Ithaca, NY, Dec 19–23, 1993)* Open Loop ▲ OL 018 [DDD]
Young, C.R.:Double Vision, w. Greg Banaszak (sax) *(rec Bailey Hall, Cornell Univ, Ithaca, NY, Dec 19–23, 1993)* Open Loop ▲ OL 018 [DDD]

Casier, Robert (ob)
Lemeland, A.:Scansions Skarbo ▲ SKR 3901 [AAD]

Caskel, Christoph (perc)
Bartók, B.:Son for 2 Pnos, w. Alfons Kontarsky (pno), Aloys Kontarsky (pno), H. König (perc) Deutsche Grammophon ("20th Century Classics" series) ▲ 437027-2 [ADD]

Casola, Fabio di (cl)
Messiaen, O.:Quatuor pour la fin du temps, w. Emilie Haudenschild (vn), Emeric Kostyak (vc), Ricardo Castro (pno) Accord ▲ ACD 201772 [AAD]

Càsoli, Elena (gtr)
Giuliani, M.:Gtr Music—Etudes Rivoalto ▲ RIV 9401 [DDD]

Cass, Gregory (hn)
Berio, L.:Opus Number Zoo, w. B. Demottaz (ob), B. Schenkel (fl), R. Meyer (cl), R. Birnstingl (bn) *(rec June 1987)* Gallo ▲ CD 527
Bizet, G.:Jeux d'enfants, w. B. Demottaz (fl), B. Schenkel (ob), R. Meyer (cl), R. Birnstingl (bn) *(rec June 1987)* Gallo ▲ CD 527
Cornissimo, w. Adilia Alieva (pno) *(rec June 28–30, 1992)* Gallo ▲ CD 741
Ibert, J.:Pièces brèves, w. R. Birnstingl (bn), B. Demottaz, R. Meyer, B. Schenkel *(rec June 1987)* Gallo ▲ CD 527
Saint-Saëns, C.:Carnival of the Animals, w. B. Demottaz (ob), B. Schenkel (inst), R. Meyer (cl), R. Birnstingl (bn) *(rec June 1987)* Gallo ▲ CD 527

Cass, Jennifer (hp)
Tailleferre, G.:Son Hp *(rec UC, Santa Cruz, May 1992)* Helicon Classics ▲ HE 1008

Cassado, Gaspar (vc)
Dvořák, A.:Con Vc, w. J. Perlea (cnd), Pro Musica Orch *(rec 1950s)* Vox Box ("Legends" series) 2–▲ CDX2 5502 [ADD]
Fauré, G.:Elégie, w. J. Perlea (cnd), Bamberg SO Allegretto ▲ ACD 8143 [ADD] ■ ACS 8143
Gaspar Cassado Performs Cello Masterpieces, w. Bamberg SO, Pro Musica Orch [cnd:Jonel Perlea] *(rec mid–late 1950s)* Vox Box 2–▲ CDX2 5502 [ADD]
Lalo, E.:Con Vc, w. J. Perlea (cnd), Bamberg SO Allegretto ▲ ACD 8143 [ADD] ■ ACS 8143
Respighi, O.:Adagio con variazioni Vc Orch, w. J. Perlea (cnd), Pro Musica Orch *(rec 1950s)* Vox Box ("Legends" series) 2–▲ CDX2 5502 [ADD]
Saint-Saëns, C.:Con 1 Vc, w. J. Perlea (cnd), Bamberg SO Allegretto ▲ ACD 8143 [ADD] ■ ACS 8143
Schubert, Franz:Con Vc, w. J. Perlea (cnd), Bamberg SO *(rec 1950s)* Vox Box ("Legends" series) 2–▲ CDX2 5502 [ADD]
Schumann, R.:Con Vc, w. J. Perlea (cnd), Bamberg SO *(rec 1950s)* Vox Box ("Legends" series) 2–▲ CDX2 5502 [ADD]
Tchaikovsky, P.:Vars on a Rococo Theme, w. J. Perlea (cnd), Pro Musica Orch *(rec 1950s)* Vox Box ("Legends" series) 2–▲ CDX2 5502 [ADD]

Cassamagnaghi, D. (fl)
Milesi, P.:Modi 1, w. F. Pomarico (ob), A. Bianchi (cl), L. Dosso (bn), G. Govi (vn), D. Tellini (vn), M. Ravasio (va), S. Righini (vc), P. Rizzi (db), C. Vignani (hpd), J. Scully (perc), P. Milesi (cnd) Cuneiform ▲ RUNE 63
Milesi, P.:Modi 2, w. L. M. Pickova (sop), Françoise Goddard (alt), M. Ferradini (ten), B. Andersen (bass), S. Scanziani (ob), A. Bianchi (cl/b cl), E. Crisafulli (bn), C. Gazzola (hn), F. Gualandris (tuba), A. Girardi (celtic hp), R. Anedda (vn), E. Groppo (vn), M. Pagani (vn), M. Ravasio (va), S. Righini (vc), P. Rizzi (db), J. Scully (perc), P. Milesi (cnd) Cuneiform ▲ RUNE 63

Cassara, Frank (perc)—see also ORCHESTRAS & ENSEMBLES New Music Consort
Lebaron, A.:Rite of the Black Sun, w. W.A. Trigg (perc), P. Guerguerian (perc), M. Pugliese (perc), C. Heldrich (cnd), New Music Consort Mode ▲ 30
Monk, T.:Round Midnight, w. Ted Mook (vc), Dean Drummond (zmz), Dominic Donato (zmz) [arr. Drummond for cello & 3 zoomoozophones] *(rec The Magic Shop, New York City, Jan. 31, 1993)* Mode ▲ MODE 33

Cassará, Sebastiano (vn)—see also ORCHESTRAS & ENSEMBLES L'Astrée Ensemble
Sui Palchi Delle Stelle:Sacred Music in the Neapolitan Conservatories at the Time of Francesco Provenzale, w. [cnd:Antonio Florio], Cappella Pietà de Turchini, Antonella Ippolito (sop), Jane Haughton (sop), Daniela del Monaco (alt), Rosario Di Meglio (vn), Antonella Bologna (va), Paolo Dionisio (vl), Antonio Florio (vc), Pierluigi Ciappareli (thb), Enrico Baiano (org/hpd) Symphonia ▲ SY 93S20 [DDD]

Cassard, Philippe (pno)
Beethoven, L. van:Qts Pno, WoO 36, w. Raphael Oleg (vn), Miguel da Siva (va), Marc Copey (vc) Valois 2–▲ V 4715
Beethoven, L. van:Qt Pno, Op. 16, w. Raphael Oleg (vn), Miguel da Siva (va), Marc Copey (vc) Valois 2–▲ V 4715
Beethoven, L. van:Son 27 Pno Adda ▲ ADD 581108 [DDD]
Colonel Chabert, w. Pasquier, Régis (vn), Lluís Claret (vc), Pierre Hantaï (hpd) Travelling ▲ K 1013
Debussy, C.:Pno Music (complete solo)—Etudes; Arabesques; Rêverie; Berceuse; Ballade; Nocturne Astrée ▲ E 8549
Debussy, C.:Pno Music (misc)—Images [premier & deuxième livre]; Images Oubliées; Estampes; Trois Pièces de 1904 Accord ▲ ACD 242092 [DDD]
Debussy, C.:Preludes Pno (sels)—7 sels Adda ▲ ADD 581108 [DDD]
Debussy, C.:Songs, w. Véronique Dietschy (sop)—Ariettes oubliées; 5 poèmes de Baudelaire [La balcon; Harmonie du soir; Le jet d'eau; Recueillement; La mort des amants]; Jane; Caprice; Fêtes galantes [En sourdine; Fantoches; Clair de lune] Adès ▲ ADE 202682 [DDD]
Liszt, F.:Pno Music (misc)—Après une lecture du Dante [fant] Adda ▲ ADD 581108 [DDD]
Music at the Time of Beaumarchais, w. Montserrat Figueras (sop), Lawrence Monteyro (sop), Raphel Oleg (vn), Miguel da Silva (va), Christophe Coin (vc), Marc Coppey (vc), José Miguel Moreno (gtr), Paul Badura-Skoda (pno), Eric Le Sage (pno), Bob Van Asperen (hpd), et al. Valois ▲ V 4767
Ravel, M.:Valses nobles et sentimentales Adda ▲ ADD 581108 [DDD]
Schubert, Franz:Moments musicaux Adda ▲ ADD 241912
Schubert, Franz:Pieces Pno, D.946 Adda ▲ ADD 581287 [DDD]
Schubert, Franz:Son Pno, D.850 Adda ▲ ADD 581287 [DDD]

Cassidy, Paul (va)—see ORCHESTRAS & ENSEMBLES Brodsky String Quartet

Cassidy-Polera, Noreen (pno)
Cellist's Holliday, w. W. De Rosa (vc) Audiofon ▲ CD 72046

Cassin, Dan (vc)—see ORCHESTRAS & ENSEMBLES Busoni String Quartet, Valcour String Quartet

Cassin, Jennifer Harris (va)—see ORCHESTRAS & ENSEMBLES Busoni String Quartet

Cassone, Gabriele (nat tpt)

Cazzati, M.:Sons 5 Instr, Op. 35, w. Pian e Forte Ensemble—Nos. 10 & 11 *(rec Feb. 17–20, 1992)* Nuova Era ("Ancient Music" series) ▲ NUO 7128 [DDD]

Melani, A.:Cants, w. E. Gambarini (sop), Pian e Forte Ensemble—"All'armi, pensieri" & "Qual bellici, accenti" [I] Nuova Era ("Ancient Music" series) ▲ 7009 [DDD]

Milanese Instrumental Songs of the 17th Century, w. Cassone, Gabriel (nat tpt), Antonio Frigé (hpd), C. Frigerio (vc) Nuova Era ▲ NUO 7184 [DDD]

Cassone, Gabriele (tpt)

Gabrielli, D.:Son 2 Tpt, w. Pian e Forte Ensemble *(rec Feb. 17–20, 1992)* Nuova Era ("Ancient Music" series) ▲ NUO 7128 [DDD]

Gabrielli, D.:Son 5 Tpt, w. Pian e Forte Ensemble *(rec Feb. 17–20, 1992)* Nuova Era ("Ancient Music" series) ▲ NUO 7128 [DDD]

Grossi, A.:Sons, Op. 3, w. G. Cassone (cnd), Pian e Forte Ensemble—Nos. 10 & 11 *(rec Feb. 17–20, 1992)* Nuova Era ("Ancient Music" series) ▲ NUO 7128 [DDD]

Jacchini, G.M.:Sons Tpt, w. Pian e Forte Ensemble—Nos. 5 & 6 *(rec Feb. 17–20, 1992)* Nuova Era ("Ancient Music" series) ▲ NUO 7128 [DDD]

Scarlatti, A.:Su le sponde del Tebro, w. E. Gambarini (sop), Pian e Forte Ensemble [I] Nuova Era ("Ancient Music" series) ▲ 7009 [DDD]

Telemann, G.P.:Con Tpt 2 Obs, w. Pian e Forte Ensemble *(rec 4/91)* Giulia ▲ GS 201008 [DDD]

Telemann, G.P.:Con Tpt 2 Obs, w. Pian e Forte Ensemble *(rec Milan, Apr 1991)* Arts ▲ 47320–2 [DDD]

Telemann, G.P.:Con Tpt 2 Vns, w. Pian e Forte Ensemble *(rec Milan, Apr 1991)* Arts ▲ 47320–2 [DDD]

Telemann, G.P.:Con Tpt 2 Vns, w. Pian e Forte Ensemble *(rec 4/91)* Giulia ▲ GS 201008 [DDD]

Torelli, G.:Sinf Tp, w. Pian e Forte Ensemble *(rec Feb. 17–20, 1992)* Nuova Era ("Ancient Music" series) ▲ NUO 7128 [DDD]

Torelli, G.:Son Tpt, G.1, w. Pian e Forte Ensemble *(rec Feb. 17–20, 1992)* Nuova Era ("Ancient Music" series) ▲ NUO 7128 [DDD]

Torelli, G.:Tpt Music, w. P.–O. Lindeke (tpt), D. Staff (tpt), E. Tarr (tpt), S. Vartolo (cnd), San Petronio Cappella Musicale Orch—Sinfs., G.1, 2, 8, 10, 11, 26, 29, 30, 31, 33; Sons. G.3–6, 13, 15–25; Con. G.27 Bongiovanni 3–▲ GB 5523/25

Castagner, Jacques (fl)

Ibert, J.:Entr'Acte, w. Elisabeth Fontan–Binoche (hp) Adès ▲ ADE 203462 [AAD]

Jolivet, A.:Pastorale de Noël, w. Gerard Faisandier (bn), Lily Laskine (hp) Adès ▲ ADE 203492 [ADD]

Castellani, Joanne (gtr)—see ORCHESTRAS & ENSEMBLES Castellani–Andriaccio Duo

Castellanos, Ofelia (org)

Autour du livre d'orgue de Mexico, w. Gustavo Delgado Parra (org) K617 ▲ 7059

Castérède, Jacques (pno)

Castérède, J.:Feux Croisés, w. G. Ibanez (pno) REM ▲ 311092 [DDD]

Castilano, Edward (db)

Willey, J.:Society Music, w. L. Greene (fl), G. Coble (tpt), W. Harris (trbn), D. Resue (hn), S. Heyman (pno), E. Gustafson (via), G. Macero (vc), L. Luttinger (perc), E. Murray (cnd) Opus One ▲ CD 168 [DDD]

Castillo, Anabel Garcia del (vn)

Bartók, B.:Romanian Folk Dances Vn, w. Agustin Serrano (pno) *(rec Madrid, Oct 1–3, 1990)* RNE/Spanish National Radio ▲ M3/10 [DDD]

Debussy, C.:Son Vn, w. Agustin Serrano (pno) *(rec Madrid, Oct 1–3, 1990)* RNE/Spanish National Radio ▲ M3/10 [DDD]

Stravinsky, I.:Suite italienne Vc, w. Agustin Serrano (pno) *(rec Madrid, Oct 1–3, 1990)* RNE/Spanish National Radio ▲ M3/10 [DDD]

Turina, J.:Son 1 Vn, w. Agustin Serrano (pno) *(rec Madrid, Oct 1–3, 1990)* RNE/Spanish National Radio ▲ M3/10 [DDD]

Castillo, P. (hn)—see ORCHESTRAS & ENSEMBLES Danish Wind Octet

Castleman, Charles (vn)—see also ORCHESTRAS & ENSEMBLES Castleman/Hodgkinson Violin–Piano Duo

Adler, S.:Son 2 Vn, w. B. Harbach (hpd) Albany ▲ TROY 041

Amram, D.:Con Vn, w. R.A. Clark (cnd), Manhattan CO *(rec SUNY, Oct 1993)* Newport Classics ▲ NPD 85601 [DDD]

Dvořák, A.:Bagatelles, Op. 47 Albany ▲ TROY 041–2

Martinů, B.:Promenades, w. B. Boyd (fl), B. Harbach (hpd) Albany ▲ TROY 041–2

Milhaud, D.:Son Vn & Hpd, Op. 257, w. B. Harbach (hpd) Albany ▲ TROY 041–2

Piston, W.:Sonatina Vn, w. B. Harbach (hpd) Albany ▲ TROY 041–2

Sarasate, P. de:Vn & Pno Music, w. Charles Tauber (pno), Barbara Lister-Sink (pno)—Faust Fant.; Carmen; Zigeunerweisen; Les Adieux; Zapateado; Malaguena; Romance; others Music & Arts ▲ CD 855 [DDD]

Ysaÿe, E.:Sons Vn Music & Arts ▲ CD 854 [ADD]

Castro, Ricardo (pno)

Messiaen, O.:Quatuor pour la fin du temps, w. Fabio di Casola (cl), Emilie Haudenschild (vn), Emeric Kostyak (vc) Accord ▲ ACD 201772 [AAD]

Casu, Poalo (perc)—see ORCHESTRAS & ENSEMBLES L'Homme Armé

Casularo, Enrico (fl)—see also ORCHESTRAS & ENSEMBLES Meister Consort

Clementi, M.:Sons Pno, Fl & Vc, Op. 21, w. A. Coen (hpd), V. Paternoster (vc) Bongiovanni ▲ GB 10007 [DDD]

Clementi, M.:Sons Pno, Fl & Vc, Op. 22, w. A. Coen (hpd), V. Paternoster (vc) Bongiovanni ▲ GB 10007 [DDD]

Giuliani, M.:Music for Fl & Gtr (sels), w. J. Fresno (gtr)—Rondeau, Op. 68; Divertimento in G; Qual mesto gemito, 3 Pièces, Op. 74 *(rec 1989)* Jecklin–Disco ▲ JD 624–2 [ADD]

Caswell, Jeffrey (trbn)

Sowerby, L.:Festival Musick, w. Carl Albach (tpt), Susan Radcliff (tpt), Tom Hutchinson (trbn), Dan Haskins (timp), David Mulbury (org), J. Welsh (cnd), Fairfield Orch *(rec St. Bartholomew's Church, New York City, May 5, 1994)* Marco Polo ▲ 8.223725 [DDD]

Catalini, Franco (db)—see ORCHESTRAS & ENSEMBLES L'Arte dell'Arco

Catalucci, Gabriele (hpd)

Haydn, J.:Lo Speziale, w. Gil Manuel Beltran (ten—Sempronio), Daniela Broganelli (sgr—Volpino), Cinzia Forte (sgr—Grilletta), Paolo Pellegrini (sgr—Mengone), Maurizio Gambini (vc), Marco Tinarelli (db), F. Maestri (cnd), In Canto CO *(rec 1993)* Bongiovanni 2–▲ GB 2171/72 [DDD]

Sarro, D.N.:Son Fl, w. U. Giani (fl), E. Rohrmann (vc), M. Tinarelli (db) *(rec Dec. 8, 1992)* Bongiovanni ▲ GB 2147 [DDD]

Scarlatti, D.:Sons Vn, w. C. Cornoldi (vn) *(rec live, 1988)* Bongiovanni ▲ GB 2026 [DDD]

Cate, Daniel (instr)

Brooke, N.:Obomobile, w. Brandon Adrien, Jennifer Baker, Karen Birch, Judy Christy, Richard Cochran, Jessica Cooper, Leslie Dominguez, Erin Hannigan, Dorothy Knight, Jason Lichtenwalter, Jay Moore, Hwa-Ling Russell, Toyin Spellman, Sarah Weiner, Jay Weinland Opus One ▲ CD 160

Catemario, Edoardo (gtr)

Albéniz, I.:Gtr Music—Asturias; Sevilla; Cataluña *(rec Monteggiori, Italy, Sept 1993)* Arts Music ▲ 47145–2 [DDD]

Durante, F.:Sons (12) Divided into Etudes & Divertimentos—Diverts I & II; Study II [arr E. Catemario for gtr] *(rec Lucca, Italy, Sept 1994)* Arts ▲ 47356–2 [DDD]

Granados, E.:Gtr Music—La Maja de Goya; Danzas Nos. 4 & 5 *(rec Monteggiori, Italy, Sept 1993)* Arts Music ▲ 47145–2 [DDD]

Moreno Torroba, F.:Sonatina Gtr *(rec Monteggiori, Italy, Sept 1993)* Arts Music ▲ 47145–2 [DDD]

Pergolesi, G.B.:Sons—in F [arr E. Catemario for gtr] *(rec Lucca, Italy, Sept 1994)* Arts ▲ 47356–2 [DDD]

Scarlatti, D.:Sons Kbd, Sons, K.11, 32, 77, 178, 198, 208, 380 & 533 [arr E. Catemario for gtr] *(rec Lucca, Italy, Sept 1994)* Arts ▲ 47356–2 [DDD]

Catemario, Edoardo (gtr) (cont.)

Tárrega, F.:Gtr Music—Capricho Arabe; Mazurka en Sol; Recuerdos de la Alhambra *(rec Monteggiori, Italy, Sept 1993)* Arts Music ▲ 47145–2 [DDD]

Caudle, M. (vc)—see ORCHESTRAS & ENSEMBLES Invocation

Caudle, Mark (b vl)

Couperin, F.:Leçons de ténèbres (for Ash Wednesday), w. J. Bowman (ct), M. Chance (ct), R. King (trb) Hyperion ▲ CDA 66474

Purcell, H.:Songs, w. B. Bonney (sop), S. Gritton (sop), J. Bowman (ct), R. Covey-Crump (ten), C. Daniels (ten), M. George (bass), D. Miller (archlt/thb/baroque gtr), R. King (chamber org)—Draw near, you lovers; While Thyrsis, wrapt in downy sleep; Love, thou canst hear, I lov'd fair Celia; What hope for us remains now he is gone; Pastora's beauties, when unblown; A thousand sev'ral ways I tried; Urge me no more; Farewell all joys; If music be the food of love [1st setting]; Amidst the shades and cool refreshing streams; They say you're angry; Let each gallant heart; This poet sings the Trojan wars; Ah, how pleasant 'tis to love; My heart whenever you appear; On the brow of Richard Hill; Rashly I swore I would disown; Since the pox or the plague; Beneath a dark and melancholy grove; Musing on cares of human fate; Whilst Cynthia sung, all angry winds lay still Hyperion ▲ CDA 66710

Purcell, H.:Songs, w. B. Bonney (sop), S. Gritton (sop), J. Bowman (ct), R. Covey-Crump (ten), C. Daniels (ten), M. George (bass), D. Miller (archlt/thb/baroque gtr), R. King (org/hpd), King's Consort—Incassum Lesbia; Gentle Shepherds, you that know the charms; I love and I must; Through mournful shades and solitary groves; The Knotting Song Hyperion ▲ CDA 66720 [DDD]

Cauhape, Jean (va)

Albrechtsberger, J.G.:Concertino 5 Instrs, w. Armando Ghitalla (tpt), Robert Shermont (vn), Alfred Zighera (vc), James Weaver (pno) *(rec Dec 1963 & Jan 1964)* Crystal ▲ CD 760

Caussé, Gérard (va)

Bach, J.S.:Goldberg Vars, w. Sitkovetsky (vn), Maisky (vc) [string Trio version arr. Dmitri Sitkovetsky] Orfeo ▲ 138851 ■ 138851

Berlioz, H.:Harold in Italy, w. J. E. Gardiner (cnd), Orch Révolutionnaire et Romantique Philips ▲ 446676–2

Brahms, J.:Qnt 2 Strs, w. Melos String Quartet Harmonia Mundi France ▲ HMC 901349

Bruch, M.:Con Cl & Va, w. P. Meyer (cl), K. Nagano (cnd), Lyon Opera Orch Erato ▲ 2292–45483–2 ZK [DDD]

Bruch, M.:Pieces Cl, Op. 83/1–8, w. Paul Meyer (cl), François-René Duchable (pno)—No. 8 [Moderato in e♭] *(rec Studio 106, Radio France, Feb. 1989)* Erato ▲ 94679–2

Bruch, M.:Romanze Va, w. K. Nagano (cnd), Lyon Opera Orch Erato ▲ 2292–45483–2 ZK [DDD]

Bruch, M.:Trios Cl, Va & Pno, Op. 83, w. P. Meyer (cl), F.–R. Duchable (pno) Erato ▲ 2292–45483–2 ZK [DDD]

Dvořák, A.:Qnt Pno, Op. 81, w. Roberte Mamou (pno), Ami Flammer (vn), Silvia Marcovici (vn), Robert Cohen (vc) *(rec Mozart Festival, Lille, France, 1994)* Verdi Classics ▲ AU 32 250

Dvořák, A.:Terzetto, w. Ami Flammer (vn), Silvia Marcovici (vn) *(rec Mozart Festival, Lille, France, 1994)* Verdi Classics ▲ AU 32 250

Grisey, G.:Chamber Music, w. Claude Delangle (sax), Rophé, Foster (cnd), Itinéraire Ensemble—Talea for ensemble; Prologue for Va & Ww; Anubis for Sax; Jour Contre Jour Accord ▲ ACD 201952 [DDD]

Tippett, M.:Con Vn Va, w. E. Kovacic (vn), A. Baillie (vc), M. Tippett (cnd), BBC PO Nimbus ▲ NI 5301 [DDD]

Caussé, Gérard (vn)

Norman, L.:Qt Pno, Op. 10, w. Christian Ivaldi (pno), Sylvie Gazeau (vn), Alain Meunier (vc) Musica Sveciae ▲ MSV 518 [DDD]

Causse, L. (vn)—see ORCHESTRAS & ENSEMBLES Stanislas Ensemble

Cavalcante, Ronedilk (vn)—see ORCHESTRAS & ENSEMBLES Paraíba Quintet

Cavaliere, Pietro (cl)

The Mozart Collection, w. Joze Banic (bn), Ruda Kosi (hp), Joze Falout (hn), Dubrovka Tomsic (pno), Ljubljana SO [cnd:Anton Nanut, Marko Munih, Alexander Pitamic, Mihail Glinka] Stradivari Classics ("Treasury of Great Classics" series) 5–▲ S5D 61000 [DDD] 5–■ S5C 61000 (D)

Cavalieri, Claudio (vn)

Amendola, F.:Ricercari, w. D. Patumi (db), A. Frederico (elecs/pno), A. Flore (voc), G. Lanzini (cl), L. Ciolfi (vn), C. Sanzo (vc), O. Mangiavacchi (perc), Donizetti Ensemble Bongiovanni ▲ GB 5519 [DDD]

Cavallo, Enrica (pno)

Mendelssohn, F.:Con in d Vn, Pno & Strs, w. F. Gulli (vn), P. Urbini (cnd), Angelicum CO Koch Treasure ▲ 31622–2 [ADD]

Mendelssohn, F.:Con in d Vn, Pno & Strs, w. Franco Gulli (vn), P. Urbini (cnd), Milano Angelicum Orch Sarx ▲ SRX 2027 [ADD]

Mendelssohn, F.:Son Vn (1838), w. F. Gulli (vn) Koch Treasure ▲ 31622–2 [ADD]

Mendelssohn, F.:Son Vn (1838), w. Franco Gulli (vn) Sarx ▲ SRX 2027 [ADD]

Paganini, N.:Cantabile, w. F. Gulli (vn) [arr for vn & pno] *(rec 1963)* Dynamic ▲ CD 30U [AAD]

Paganini, N.:I palpiti, w. F. Gulli (vn) [arr vn & pno] *(rec 1963)* Dynamic ▲ CD 30U [AAD]

Paganini, N.:Sons Vn & Gtr, Op. 3, w. F. Gulli (vn)—No. 6 *(rec 1963)* Dynamic ▲ CD 30U [AAD]

Cavasanti, Lorenzo (rcr)

Frescobaldi, G.:Canzonas, Caprici & Ricercari, w. K. Boeke (vl), G. Capocaccia (rcr), C. Boersma (vc), S. Ciomei (hpd/org)—Canzoni Trigesima, detta ia Cittadellia; Vigesimasesta, detta la Moricona; Vigesimaottiva, detta le Lanberta; Prima a tre; Trigesimaseconda detta l'Altogradina; Vigesimaquarta, detta la Nobile; Vigesimesttima, detta la Lanciona; Quintedecima, detta la Lievoratta; Terza a quattro; Vigesimaquinta, detta la Garzoncina; Prima a tre; Decmasesta, detta la Samminiata; Trigesimaprima, detta l'Arnolfinia; Quarta a tre; Quinta a tre; Decimasettima, detta la Diodata; Seconda a quattro; Seconda a tre; Vigesimanona, detta la Bocellina; Terza a tre Trigesimaquarta, detta la Sandoninia Nuova Era ("Ancient Music" series) ▲ 7131

Mancini, F.:Sons Rcr, w. C. Boersma (vc), S. Ciomei (hpd) Nuova Era ("Ancient Music" series) ▲ NUO 7138 [DDD]

Telemann, G.P.:Con in a for Rcr, Ob, w. P. Faldi (ob), D. Moore (vn), C. Boersma (vc), S. Ciomei (hpd) *(rec July 23–26, 1991)* Nuova Era ("Ancient Music" series) ▲ NUO 7067 [DDD]

Telemann, G.P.:Quartet in G for Recorder, Oboe, Violin & Continuo, w. P. Faldi (ob), D. Moore (vn), S. Ciomei (hpd) *(rec July 23–26, 1991)* Nuova Era ("Ancient Music" series) ▲ NUO 7067 [DDD]

Cave, Michael (pno)

Cave, M.:Son Cl & Pno, w. G. De Peyer (cl) MCM ■ 0086.1

Debussy, C.:Preludes Pno (sels)—Book 1 MCM ■ 0080.1

Gervase De Peyer, w. G. De Peyer (cl) MCM ■ 0086.1

Schubert, Franz:Son Arpeggione, w. G. de Peyer (cl) MCM ■ 0086.1

Schumann, R.:Arabeske Pno MCM ■ 0084.3

Schumann, R.:Carnaval Pno MCM ■ 0084.1

Schumann, R.:Davidsbündlertänze MCM ■ 0084.1

Schumann, R.:Fant Pno MCM ■ 0080.1

Schumann, R.:Fantasiestücke Pno, Op. 12 MCM ■ 0084.2

Schumann, R.:Faschingsschwank aus Wien MCM ■ 0084.4

Schumann, R.:Gesänge der Frühe MCM ■ 0084.4

Schumann, R.:Kinderszenen MCM ■ 0084.2

Schumann, R.:Kreisleriana MCM ■ 0084.3

Schumann, R.:Nachtstücke—Nos. 3 & 4 only MCM ■ 0084.3

Schumann, R.:Papillons MCM ■ 0084.1

Schumann, R.:Pno Music (misc) MCM 4–■ 0084.1–4

Schumann, R.:Romances Ob, w. G. De Peyer (cl) MCM ■ 0086.1

Schumann, R.:Son 2 Pno MCM ■ 0084.4

Schumann, R.:Sym Etudes MCM ■ 0084.2

Schumann, R.:Toccata Pno MCM ■ 0084.2

Weber, C.M. von:Vars on a Theme from *Silvana* Cl, w. G. De Peyer (cl) MCM ■ 0086.1

Cazaban, Eduardo (pno)

Clementi, M.:Pno Music (comp), w. Aldo Antognazzi (pno), Christian Badian (pno), Cristina Da Souza (pno), Dao Di Renzo (pno), Pablo Lavandera (pno), Yi Fang Huang (vn), Silvina Cardenas (fl), Nestor Herzbaum (fl)—Sons (6) for Pno, Op. 2, Nos. 1, 3 & 5 (w. flutes); Duets (3) for Piano 4–Hands, Op. 3, Nos. 2 & 3; Sons (3) for Pno & Vn, Op. 3, No. 4 Aura Classics ▲ AU 32287

Cazal, Olivier (pno)
Schubert, Franz:Son Pno, D.960
Walsingham Classics ("The Sydney International Piano Competition" series) ▲ WAL 8019 [DDD]

Cazalet, André (hn)
Haydn, J.:Cons Hn, w. A. Moglia (cnd), Toulouse CO *(rec Sept 1994)* Pierre Verany ▲ PVY 730029
Haydn, M.:Concertino Hn, Trbn & Va, w. A. Moglia (cnd), Toulouse CO *(rec Sept 1994)* Pierre Verany ▲ PVY 730029
Ligeti, G.:Trio Hn, Vn & Pno, w. G. Commentale (vn), C. Huvé (pno) Montaigne ▲ MO 782006 [DDD]
Poulenc, F.:Sxt Pno, w. P. Rogé (pno), P. Gallois (fl), M. Bourgue (ob), M. Portal (cl), A. Wallez (bn) London ▲ 421581-2 [DDD]

Cazauran, Bernard (db)
Bouknik, M.:Fant Vc, w. Odile Bourin (vc) Gallo ▲ CD 795 [ADD]
Dittersdorf, K.D. von:Con Db *(rec Aug. 29–30, 1992)* Gallo ▲ CD 753 [ADD]
Eccles, H.:Son Db, w. J. M. Denis (vn), A. Loger (vn), N. Carles (va), E. Petit (vc) *(rec Aug. 29–30, 1992)* Gallo ▲ CD 753 [ADD]
Franchomme, A.:Caprices, Op. 7, w. Odile Bourin (vc)—No. 11 [arr performers for vc & db] Gallo ▲ CD 795 [ADD]
Genzmer, H.:Bagatelles (6), w. Odile Bourin (vc) Gallo ▲ CD 795 [ADD]
Lindner, A.:Diverts for Young Cellists, w. Odile Bourin (vc) [arr performers for vc & db] Gallo ▲ CD 795 [ADD]
Rossini, G.:Duet Vc, w. Odile Bourin (vc) Gallo ▲ CD 795 [ADD]
Salles, B.:Con Db, w. M. Maunas (cnd), Pau Orch *(rec Aug. 29–30, 1992)* Gallo ▲ CD 753 [ADD]
Zbinden, J.-F.:Hommage à J. S. Bach *(rec Aug. 29–30, 1992)* Gallo ▲ CD 753 [ADD]

Cazauran, Jacques (db)
Schubert, Franz:Qnt Pno, D.667, w. I. Haebler (pno), Grumiaux Trio Philips ▲ 422838-2 [ADD]

Cebro, Carlos (pno)
Ibert, J.:Songs, w. Marie-Jose Dolorian (sop)—Berceuse de Galiane; Chanson; Chanson du Rien; 2 Chansons de Melpomène; 4 Chants; Complainte de Florinde; Le Jardin du Ciel; La Verdure dorée; 3 sels from Livre d'Amour; 3 sels from Roi d'Yvetot Media 7 ▲ 007 [DDD]
Mompou, F.:Songs Sop, w. C. Bustamante (sop)—(22) Becquerianas (set of 6 songs); Cinq Mélodies [P. Valery]; Combat del Somni (set of 3 songs); etc. Arcobaleno ▲ SBCD 1502 [DDD]

Cebulski, M. (perc)
Adams, J.L.:Night Peace, w. C. Bray Lower (sop), N. Rigel (hp) *(rec Sept. 1992)* New Albion ▲ NA 061

Cecchetti, Riccardo (pno)—see ORCHESTRAS & ENSEMBLES Italian Piano Quartet

Cecere, Anthony (hn)
Kernis, A.J.:America(n) (Day) Dreams, w. Kim Barber (mez), Mary Rowell (vn), Leslie Tomkins (va), Tonya Tomkins (vc), Robert Black (db), Kathleen Nester (fl), Larry Guy (cl/b cl), John Dent (tpt), Leslie Stifelman (pno), Susan Jolles (hp), Jeffrey Milarsky (perc), M. Barrett (cnd)—A Navajo Blanket; Wednesday at the Waldorf; The Pregnant Dream; The Blue Bottle; "So Long" to the Moon from the Men of Apollo; Epilogue:The Pure Suit of Happiness *(rec Manhattan Center Studios, New York, May 31–June 3, 1995)* New Albion ♦ NA 083CD

Cecere, Giuseppe Paolo (Medieval strs/organistrum/slide tpt)—see ORCHESTRAS & ENSEMBLES Vox

Cech, Jan (pno)
Schulhoff, E.:Hot Son Sax, w. Stepan Koutnik (a sax) Supraphon ▲ SUP 112169 [DDD]
Schulhoff, E.:Son Vc, w. Jiří Barta (vc) Supraphon ▲ SUP 112169 [DDD]
Schulhoff, E.:Son Fl, w. Pavel Foltyn (fl) Supraphon ▲ SUP 112169 [DDD]

Čech, Svatopluk (bn)
Martinů, B.:Sxt Fl, Ob, Cl, 2 Bns & Pno, w. Jan Riedlbauch (fl), Jurij Likin (ob), Vlastimil Mareš (cl), Lumír Vanek (bn), Ivan Klánsky (pno) *(rec Studio Martínek, Prague, Mar 3, 1995)* Panton ("Protokol XX" series) ▲ 811348-2 [DDD]
Mozart, W.A.:Sinf concertante Ob, K.Anh.9, w. Jan Adamus (ob), Frantisek Bláha (cl), Zdenek Divoky (hn), J. Belohlávek (cnd), Dvořák CO Panton ▲ PAN 811206

Cedillo, Idelfonso (vc)
Ponce, M.:Music of, w. Joseph Olechovsky (pno)—Son for Vc & Pno; Preludes; Granada; Estrellita Spartacus ▲ SPR 21008 [DDD]

Celeghin, Angelica (fl)—see ORCHESTRAS & ENSEMBLES Rara Ensemble

Celeghin, Luigi (org)
Fantasia for Trumpet & Organ, w. G. Touvron (tpt) *(rec Church of Sts Felice & Fortunato di Noale, Venice, Oct 29 & 30, 1995)* Bongiovanni ▲ GB 5589 [DDD]
Grand Duett:Music for 2 Organs, w. István Ella (org), János Sebestyén (org) Hungaroton ▲ HCD 31464 [DDD]

Celli, Joseph (ob/E hn)
Celli, J.:Improvisations, w. Mukha Veena (Yamaha WX-7 midi breath controller with TX-802), J. H. Kim (komungo, changgo & electric komungo)—Types of Asia for Changgo & English Horn (without reeds); Dasreng for solo Komungo; Mukhan O.O. Discs ▲ OO 2 [DDD]
Celli, J.:Improvisations, w. J. H. Kim (komungo & electric komungo)—Triple AAA [w. A. Plack (didgeridoo)]; April One [w. Shelley Hirsh (voice)]; Baccalau Trio [w. A. Curran (synthesizer & computer samplers)]; My Friend [w. M. Thiam (African percussion) O.O. Discs ▲ OO 4 [DDD]
Celli, J.:Sky:S for J O.O. Discs ▲ OO 1 [AAD]
Goldstein, M.:A Summoning of Focus O.O. Discs ▲ OO 1 [AAD]
Kim, J.H.:Piri Qt, w. Chung Jae-Guk (piri), Park Jong-Sol (piri), Yang Myung-Sok (piri) O. O. Discs ▲ OO24
Schwartz, E.:Extended Ob O.O. Discs ▲ OO 1 [AAD]
Thorington, H.:Partial Perceptions, w. Shelley Hirsch (sgr), Helen Thorington (elec) ¿What Next? ▲ WN 0013

Celli, Joseph (syn)
First, D.:Matador *(rec Oct. 1987)* O.O. Discs ▲ OO 5 [DDD]

Cellier, Marcel (org)
Zamfir, G.:Music of, w. G. Zamfir (panpipes)—34 (sels.) Analekta 3-▲ AN 28401-3 [AAD]

Cenarill, Sigrid (vn)
Bach, J.S.:Con for 2 Vns, w. J.-J. Kantorow (vn), H. Stadlmair (cnd), Munich CO Denon ▲ CO 7096 [DDD]

Cepicky, Leos (vn)—see ORCHESTRAS & ENSEMBLES Wilhan String Quartet

Čermáková, Ludmila (pno)
Dvořák, A.:Moravian Duets, Opp. 20, 32 & 38, w. B. Kulínský (cnd), Bambini di Praga Multisonic ▲ 31 0111-2 [DDD]
Suk, J.:Songs, Op. 15, w. B. di Praga, J. Šaroun (pno), B. Kulínský (cnd)—Zal; Tuzba; Společný hrob; Pastýři na jaro; Diviná voda; Vily; Pastýř a pastyřka; Zpominky; Choutka po vdaní; Kéz byVedeli [Cz] Multisonic ▲ 31 0111-2 [DDD]

Cerminaro, John (hn)
Beethoven, L. van:Son Hn, w. Z. Carno (pno) Crystal ▲ CD 676
Bozza, E.:En forêt, w. Z. Carno (pno) Crystal ▲ CD 676
Brahms, J.:Trio Hn, w. N. Salerno-Sonnenberg (vn), C. Licad (pno) EMI Classics ▲ CDC 54800
Heiden, B.:Son Hn, w. Zita Carno (pno) Crystal ▲ CD 676
Hindemith, P.:Son Hn, w. Zita Carno (pno) Crystal ▲ CD 676
John Cerminaro:Horn, w. J. Cerminaro (hn), Zita Carno (pno) Crystal ▲ CD676
Poulenc, F.:Son Tpt, w. T. Stevens (tpt), R. Sauer (trbn) Crystal ■ C 367
Strauss, F.:Nocturne, w. Z. Carno (pno) Crystal ▲ CD 676

Cerne, Charles (pno)
Paganini, N.:Con 1 Vn, w. Vása Příhoda (vn) [arr for Vn & Pno] Biddulph ▲ LAB 135
Paganini, N.:I palpiti, w. Vása Příhoda (vn) Biddulph ▲ LAB 135
Paganini, N.:Son 12 Vn, w. Vása Příhoda (vn) Biddulph ▲ LAB 135
Paganini, N.:Le Streghe, w. Vása Příhoda (vn) [arr Vn & Pno] Biddulph ▲ LAB 135

Černy, Ladislav (va)
Schubert, Franz:Qnt Strs, D.956, w. Josef Suk (vn), Jirí Baxa (vn), Saša Večtomov (vc), Josef Šimandl (vc) *(rec live, 1971)* Praga ▲ PR 250055

Černý, Pavel (org)
Albinoni, T.:Con Tpt & Org, w. Jaroslav Halíř (tpt) *(rec Mirror Chapel of the Prague Klementinum, Mar 31, 1995)* Panton ▲ 811368-2 [DDD]
Purcell, H.:Son Tpt, w. Jaroslav Halíř (tpt), Marek Vajo (tpt), Radek Nemec (tpt), Jan Vobořil (hn), Jiří Nauš (trbn), Lubomír Maryška (tuba), Oldřich Satava (timp) [trans. F. Antonín Vaigl] *(rec Mirror Chapel of the Prague Klementinum, Mar 26, 1995)* Panton ▲ 811368-2 [DDD]

Cerny, William (pno)
Haimo, E.:Contrasts, w. Karen Buranskas (vc) *(rec Annenberg Audit., Snite Museum of Art, Univ. of Notre Dame, May & June 1994 & Jan 199)* Centaur ▲ CRC 2253 [DDD]

Cervera, Marçal (vl)
Bach, J.S.:Sons Vl, BWV 1027-1029, w. Rafael Puyana (hpd) Philips 2-▲ 438809-2

Cesaraccio, Alberto (ob)
Respighi, O.:Di Sera, w. Emanuela Saba (ob), R. Tigani (cnd), Sassari SO *(rec Rome, Oct 11-14, 1994)* Bongiovanni ▲ GB 2166 [DDD]
Respighi, O.:Gli uccelli, w. Stefano Mancini (fl), Antonio Puglia (cl), Paloma Tironi (hp), Stefano Melis (cel), R. Tigani (cnd), Sassari SO *(rec Rome, Oct 11-14, 1994)* Bongiovanni ▲ GB 2166 [DDD]

Cesarini (pno)
Music for Saxophone, w. O. Borioli (sax) Gallo ▲ CD 516

Chabot, Christian de (gtr)
Flûte et Guitare, w. K. Redel (fl) Arion ▲ ARN 68213 [DDD]

Chadwick, Eric (org)
Handel, G.F.:Messiah (sels), w. Elsie Morison (sop), Marjorie Thomas (cta), Richard Lewis (ten), James Milligan (bass), M. Sargent (cnd), Royal Liverpool PO, Huddersfield Choral Society Classics for Pleasure ▲ CDCFP 9007 [ADD]

Chaffe, Barbara (fl)
Zorn, J.:Elegy, w. Mike Patton (sgr), David Abel (vn), Scummy (gtr), David Shea (turntables), David Slusser (sound effects), William Winant (perc) Tzadik ▲ TZA 7302 [ADD]

Chaignon, P. (perc)
Cage, J.:First Construction, w. I. Berteletti (prepared pno), Hêlios Percussion Quartet Wergo ▲ WER 6203-2 [DDD]

Chai-Hsio, Tsai (pno)
Children's Suite:Chinese Piano Music, w. T. Chai-Hsio (pno) *(rec Dec 1988)* Thorofon ▲ CTH 2034 [ADD]

Chaisemartin, Suzanne (org)
Brahms, J.:Chorale Preludes, Op. 122—3 Preludes REM ▲ 311079 XCD [DDD]
Dupré, M.:Le Chemin de la croix [Cavaille Organ of the Abbey of St. Etienne de Caen] Esoldun ▲ MOS 1006
Liszt, F.:Prelude & Fugue on the name B-A-C-H *(rec 5/86)* REM ▲ 311079 XCD [DDD]
Mendelssohn, F.:Sons Org—No. 6 REM ▲ 311079 XCD [DDD]
Schumann, R.:Sketches Pedal Pno *(rec 5/86)* REM ▲ 311079 XCD [DDD]

Chakraborty, Debendra Kanti (tabla)
Battiato, F.:Ricerca sul Terzo, w. Franco Battiato (voc), Alessio Alba (tamboura), Antonio Ballista (pno), Marco Boni (vc), Debendra Kanti Chakraborty (tabla), Guido Corti (cnt), Filippo Destrieri (kbd/computer), John Giblin (bass), Buddhadeu Das Gupta (sarod), Gavin Harrison (dr/perc), Jakko Jakszyk (gtr), Roberto Mazza (ob), Fabrizio Merlini (va), Angelo Privitera (kbd/computer), Mino Bordignon (cnd), Milan Chamber Music Choir Hemisphere ▲ 837234-2

Chalifour, Martin (vn)
Debussy, C.:Danses sacrée et profane, w. Y. Kondonassis (hp), F. Cohen (cl), W.-F. Gu (va), S. Konopka (va), R. Weiss (vc), T. Sperl (db), J. Smith (instr) *(rec Nov. 23-25, 1992)* Telarc ▲ CD 80361 [DDD]
Ravel, M.:Intro & Allegro, w. Y. Kondonassis (hp), J. Smith (fl), F. Cohen (cl), W.-F. Gu (va), S. Konopka (va), R. Weiss (vc), T. Sperl (db) *(rec Nov. 23-25, 1992)* Telarc ▲ CD 80361 [DDD]
Ravel, M.:Pavane pour une infante défunte, w. Y. Kondonassis (hp), J. Smith (fl), F. Cohen (cl), W.-F. Gu (va), S. Konopka (va), R. Weiss (vc), T. Sperl (db) [arr. by Kondonassis] *(rec Nov. 23-25, 1992)* Telarc ▲ CD 80361 [DDD]

Challan, Annie (hp)
Debussy, C.:Son Fl, w. R. Bourdin (fl), C. Lequien (va) Philips ▲ 422839-2 [ADD]

Chalmers, David (org)
Music of the Americas, 1492-1992, w. [cnd:Elizabeth C. Patterson], Gloriae Dei Cantores, James E. Jordan Jr. (org) Paraclete 2-▲ PCL 10 [DDD] 2-■ PCL 10
Organ Music of America:20th Century "Romantics", w. James E. Jordan Jr. (org) *(rec Church of the Advent, Boston)* Paraclete ▲ PCL 9 [DDD] ■ PCL 9
Organ Music of America (1891-1991), w. James E. Jordan Jr. (org) Paraclete ▲ GDCD 009 ■ GDC 009
Organ Music of America II:The Boston Classicists, w. James E. Jordan Jr. (org) *(rec Mechanics Hall, Worcester, MA)* Paraclete ▲ PCL 11 [DDD] ■ PCL 11
Organ Music of America II (1868-1908), w. D. Jordan (org), J. E. Jordan, Jr. (org) Paraclete ▲ GDCD 011 ■ GDC 011
Rheinberger, J.:Mass, Op. 187, w. Elizabeth C. Patterson (cnd), Gloriae Dei Cantores Paraclete ▲ GDCD 018 [DDD]
Rheinberger, J.:Mass, Op. 190, w. Elizabeth C. Patterson (cnd), Gloriae Dei Cantores Paraclete ▲ GDCD 018 [DDD]
San Marco 1527-1740, w. [cnd:Elizabeth C. Patterson], Gloriae Dei Cantores, James E. Jordan Jr. (org) Paraclete 2-▲ GDCD 014 [DDD] 2-■ GDC 014 I & II
Sowerby, L.:Canon, Chacony & Fugue Paraclete 2-▲ GCCD 016
Sowerby, L.:Choral Music, w. J. E. Jordan Jr. (org), E.C. Patterson (cnd), Gloriae Dei Cantores—Great Is the Lord; Hear My Cry, O God; The Lord Is My Shepherd; How Long Wilt Thou Forget Me; Turn Thou to Thy God; Whoso Dwelleth; An Angel Stood by the Alter Of Paraclete 2-▲ GCCD 016
Sowerby, L.:Org Music [Organ of All Saints Church, Worcester, MA]—Carillon; Arioso; Prelude, "Were You There?"; Bright, Blithe & Brisk Paraclete 2-▲ GCCD 016

Chalmers, David (pno)
This Worldes Joie, w. [cnd:Elizabeth C. Patterson], Gloriae Dei Cantores, James E. Jordan Jr. (org) *(rec Mechanics Hall, Worcester, MA)* Paraclete ▲ GDCD 020

Chamberlain, Robert (pno)
Grieg, E.:Son 1 Vn, w. Marina Marsden (vn) *(rec Iwaki Auditorium, ABC, Melbourne, Sept 1994)* Tall Poppies ▲ TP 67 [DDD]
Heim, C.:Transformation, w. Marina Marsden (vn) *(rec Iwaki Auditorium, ABC, Melbourne, Sept 1994)* Tall Poppies ▲ TP 67 [DDD]
Nielsen, C.:Son 1 Vn, w. Marina Marsden (vn) *(rec Iwaki Auditorium, ABC, Melbourne, Sept 1994)* Tall Poppies ▲ TP 67 [DDD]

Chambon, Jacques (ob)
Fasch, J.F.:Con Tpt & 2 Obs, w. Maurice André (tpt), Pierre Pierlot (ob), J.-F. Paillard (cnd), Jean-François Paillard CO *(rec 1968)* Erato ▲ 98475-2 [ADD]
Japanese Melodies, w. J.-F. Paillard (cnd), Jean-François Paillard CO, Lily Laskine (hp) Denon ("Repertoire" series) ▲ CO 8116 [DDD]
Telemann, G.P.:Musique de Table, w. B. Gabel (tpt), J.-F. Paillard (cnd), Jean-François Paillard CO—sels. Erato ▲ 92868-2

Champney, Wendy (va)—see ORCHESTRAS & ENSEMBLES Carmina String Quartet

Chan, David (vn)
Gershwin, G.:Songs, w. Robert Koenig (pno)—Summertime; A Woman Is a Sometime Thing [arr vn & pno] *(rec Joan & Irving Harris Concert Hall, Aspen, CO, May 1995)* Ambassador ▲ ARC 1017 [DDD]
Paganini, N.:Con 2 Vn, w. Robert Koenig (pno)—3rd movt [arr for vn & pno] *(rec Joan & Irving Harris Concert Hall, Aspen, CO, May 1995)* Ambassador ▲ ARC 1017 [DDD]
Saint-Saëns, C.:Son 1 Vn, w. Robert Koenig (pno) *(rec Joan & Irving Harris Concert Hall, Aspen, CO, May 1995)* Ambassador ▲ ARC 1017 [DDD]
Tartini, G.:Son Vn "Devil's Trill", w. Robert Koenig (pno) *(rec Joan & Irving Harris Concert Hall, Aspen, CO, May 1995)* Ambassador ▲ ARC 1017 [DDD]

Chan, David (vn) (cont.)
Tchaikovsky, P.:Mélodie, w. Robert Koenig (pno) [tran for vn & pno] *(rec Joan & Irving Harris Concert Hall, Aspen, CO, May 1995)* Ambassador ▲ ARC 1017 [DDD]
Tchaikovsky, P.:Valse-Scherzo Vn, w. Robert Koenig (pno) *(rec Joan & Irving Harris Concert Hall, Aspen, CO, May 1995)* Ambassador ▲ ARC 1017 [DDD]
Ysaÿe, E.:Son 6 Vn *(rec Joan & Irving Harris Concert Hall, Aspen, CO, May 1995)* Ambassador ▲ ARC 1017 [DDD]

Chan, Ivan (vn)—see ORCHESTRAS & ENSEMBLES Windham String Quartet

Chan, L. (vn)
Pachelbel, J.:Canon, w. P. Cochand (vn), P. Cochand (cnd), Classico CO Ensemble *(rec Oct. 19–21, 1992)* Gallo ▲ CD 723 DAD
Richter, F.X.:Grandes simphonies, w. P. Cochand (vn), P. Cochand (cnd), Classico CO Ensemble—in G *(rec Oct. 19–21, 1992)* Gallo ▲ CD 723 DAD
Telemann, G.P.:Don Quichotte (suite), w. P. Cochand (vn), P. Cochand (cnd), Classico CO Ensemble *(rec Oct. 19–21, 1992)* Gallo ▲ CD 723 DAD
Vivaldi, A.:Cons Vn, Op. 3/1–12, "L'estro armonico", w. P. Cochand (vn), P. Cochand (cnd), Classico CO Ensemble *(rec Oct. 19–21, 1992)* Gallo ▲ CD 723 DAD

Chancey, Tina (trb vl/b vl/rebec/kamenj/lyra/rec/perc)—see ORCHESTRAS & ENSEMBLES La Rondinella

Chancey, Vincent (hn)
Jenkins, L.:Monkey on the Dragon, w. Leroy Jenkins (vn), Henry Threadgill (fl), Don Byron (cl), Marth Ehrlich (b cl), Janet Frice (bn), Frank Gordon (tpt), Jeff Hoyer (trbn), David Soldier (vn), Jane Henry (vn) Ron Lawrence (va), Mary Wooton (vc), Lindsey Horner (db), Thurman Barker (traps), Myra Melford (pno), T. Léon (cnd) *(rec live, Merkin Concert Hall, New York City, Apr. 9, 1992)* CRI ("eXchange" series) ▲ CD 663 [DDD]
Jenkins, L.:Panorama 1, w. Leroy Jenkins (vn), Henry Threadgill (fl), Don Byron (cl), Marty Ehrlich (b cl) *(rec live, Merkin Concert Hall, New York City, Apr. 9, 1992)* CRI ("eXchange" series) ▲ CD 663 [DDD]

Chandra, Arun (gtr)—see ORCHESTRAS & ENSEMBLES Illinois Performers' Workshop Ensemble

Chanel, C. (gtr)—see ORCHESTRAS & ENSEMBLES Versailles Guitar Quartet

Chanel, Philippe (clvd)
Philippe Chanel Gallo ▲ CD 545 [AAD]

Chaney, Harold (hpd)
Roussakis, N.:Son Hpd *(rec Studio 2037 Broadway, New York, May, 1970)* CRI ▲ CD 709 [DDD]

Chang, Choong-Jin (va)
Hush, D.:Qt 1 Strs, w. G.J. Schenk (vn), J. Ingolfsson (vn), M. Ingolfsson (vc) CRS ▲ CD 9257
Rorem, N.:Studies for 11, w. E. Ostling (fl), K. Lord (ob), G. Raden (cl), J. Sutte (tpt), S. Copes (vn), C.-J. Chang (va), J. Lastrapes (vc), K. Englichova (hp), R. Uchida (pno), A. LaFargue (perc), R. Laveille (perc), R. Milanov (cnd) New World ▲ 80445-2
Van Appledorn, M.J.:Ayre, w. G.J. Schenk (vn), J. Ingolfsson (vn), D. Foster (va), M. Ingolfsson (vc), S. Shao (vc) CRS ▲ CD 9257

Chang, Hae-won (pno)
Haydn, J.:Con Hpd & Strs, H.XVIII/4, w. R. Stankovsky (cnd), Camerata Cassovia *(rec Sept. 7–12, 1992)* Naxos ▲ 8.550713 [DDD]
Haydn, J.:Con Hpd, Vns & Bass Instrument, H.XVIII/9, w. R. Stankovsky (cnd), Camerata Cassovia *(rec Sept. 7–12, 1992)* Naxos ▲ 8.550713 [DDD]
Haydn, J.:Con Hpd, Obs, Hns & Strs, H.XVIII/11, w. R. Stankovsky (cnd), Camerata Cassovia *(rec Sept. 7–12, 1992)* Naxos ▲ 8.550713 [DDD]
Haydn, J.:Con Org, Vns & Bass Instrument, H.XVIII/7, w. R. Stankovsky (cnd), Camerata Cassovia *(rec Sept. 7–12, 1992)* Naxos ▲ 8.550713 [DDD]
Hummel, J.N.:Con Pno, Op. 85, w. T. Pál (cnd), Budapest CO *(rec Budapest, May 28–30, 1987)* Naxos ▲ 8.550837 [DDD]
Hummel, J.N.:Con Pno, Op. 89, w. T. Pál (cnd), Budapest CO *(rec Budapest, May 28–30, 1987)* Naxos ▲ 8.550837 [DDD]
Pierné, G.:Pno Music—Fifteen Pieces, Op. 3; Serenade to Columbine; Serenade to Izeyl; Concert Scherzando; Concert Study, Op. 13 Marco Polo ▲ 8.223115

Chang, Han-Na (vc)
Bruch, M.:Kol Nidrei, w. M. Rostropovich (cnd), London SO EMI Classics ▲ CDC 56126
Fauré, G.:Elégie, w. M. Rostropovich (cnd), London SO EMI Classics ▲ CDC 56126
Saint-Saëns, C.:Con 1 Vc, w. M. Rostropovich (cnd), London SO EMI Classics ▲ CDC 56126
Tchaikovsky, P.:Vars on a Rococo Theme, w. M. Rostropovich (cnd), London SO EMI Classics ▲ CDC 56126

Chang, Li-Kuo (va)
Dittersdorf, K.D. von:Son Va, w. J. Fuller (db) Musical Arts Society ▲ CD 41592 [DDD] ■ CS 41592 (D)
Romberg, B.:Trios Va, w. Gary Stucka (vc), Jerry Fuller (db)—No. 1 in e *(rec WTMT Studio 1, Jan 24, 1993)* Musical Arts Society ▲ MAS 41595 [DDD]
Vanhal, J.B.:Divert Strs, w. David Taylor (vn), Jerry Fuller (db) *(rec WTMT Studio 1, Jan 24, 1993)* Musical Arts Society ▲ MAS 41595 [DDD]

Chang, Lynn (vn)—see also ORCHESTRAS & ENSEMBLES Videmus members
Foote, A.:Nocturne, w. F. Smith (fl), V. Uritzky (vn), K. Murdock (va), B. Coppock (vc) Northeastern ("Classical Arts" series) ▲ NR 227-CD
Kirchner, L.:Triptych, w. Yo-Yo Ma (vc) *(rec May 7–8, 1991)* Sony Classical ▲ SK 53126 [DDD]
Schoenberg, A.:Verklärte Nacht, w. S. Chase (vn), M. Thompson (va), S. Ansel (va), R. Thomas (vc), M. Djokic (vc) *(rec Methuen, MA, Dec. 1990)* Northeastern ▲ NOR 249 [DDD]
Tchaikovsky, P.:Souvenir de Florence, w. A. Delmoni (vn), M. Thompson (va), S. Ansel (va), R. Thomas (vc), M. Reynolds (vc) *(rec Weston, MA, Jan. 1993)* Northeastern ▲ NOR 249 [DDD]

Chang, Sarah (vn)
Debut, w. Sandra Rivers (pno) EMI Classics ▲ CDC 54352 [DDD] ■ 4DS 54352
Lalo, E.:Sym espagnole, w. C. Dutoit (cnd), Royal Concertgebouw Orch *(rec Concertgebouw, Amsterdam, Jan. 4–8, 1995)* EMI Classics ▲ CDC 55292 [DDD]
Paganini, N.:Con 1 Vn, w. W. Sawallisch (cnd), Philadelphia Orch EMI Classics ▲ CDC 55026
Saint-Saëns, C.:Havanaise Vn, w. W. Sawallisch (cnd), Philadelphia Orch EMI Classics ▲ CDC 55026
Saint-Saëns, C.:Introduction & Rondo capriccioso, w. W. Sawallisch (cnd), Philadelphia Orch EMI Classics ▲ CDC 55026
Sarasate, P. de:Carmen Fant, w. S. Rivers (pno) EMI Classics ▲ CDC 54352 [DDD] ■ 4DS 54352
Tchaikovsky, P.:Con Vn, w. C. Davis (cnd), London SO EMI Classics ▲ CDC 54753 ■ 4DS 54753
Vieuxtemps, H.:Con 5 Vn, w. C. Dutoit (cnd), Philharmonia Orch *(rec Henry Wood Hall, London, Dec. 22–23, 1994)* EMI Classics ▲ CDC 55292 [DDD]

Chang, Yi-an (pno)
Chou Wen-Chung:The Willows Are New CRI ▲ CD 691 [ADD]

Chapelet, Francis (org)
Vol. 2 (org) *(rec Cholula, Mexico, Oct. 21–24, 1994)* K617 ▲ 7048 [DDD]

Chapelin-Dubar, Anne (hpd)
Rameau, J.P.:Hpd Music (comp solo)—Pièces de clavecin (1706); Pièces de clavecin (1724); Nouvelles suites de pièces de clavecin (1728); La d Dauphine (1747); Menuet & Rondeau Koch Schwann 2-▲ CD 310043 [DDD]

Chapin, Earl (hn)—see ORCHESTRAS & ENSEMBLES New York Woodwind Soloists

Chapiro, Fania (pno)
Chopin, F.:Nocturnes—Op. 62/1 Fidelio ▲ FID 8840 [DDD]

Chapman, Jane (hpd)
Couperin, L.:Hpd Music—Suites in a & d; Prelude in C; Pavanne in f# Collins Classics ▲ COL 1421 [DDD]
Frescobaldi, G.:Hpd Music—Capriccio in G; Fant in e Collins Classics ▲ COL 1421 [DDD]
Froberger, J.J.:Hpd Music—Suites in a & G; Toccata in a; Ricercar in C Collins Classics ▲ COL 1421 [DDD]

Chapo, Eliot (vn)
Falla, M. de:Con Hpd, w. I. Kipnis (hpd), P. Brook (fl), H. Gomberg (ob), S. Drucker (cl), L. Munroe (vc), P. Boulez (cnd), New York PO *(rec Mar. 2, 1975)* Sony Classical ▲ SBK 53264 ■ SBT 53264

Chappuis, Claude (gtr)
Balsons des Fleurs, w. E. Mattmann (sop) Gallo ▲ CD 751 [DDD]

Chapuis, Michel (org)
Couperin, F.:Leçons de ténèbres (for Good Friday), w. A. Deller (ct), P. Todd (ten), R. Perulli (va da gamba) [L] Musique d'Abord ▲ HMA 190210
Couperin, F.:Pièces d'orgue consistantes en deux Messes—No. 1 Musique d'Abord ▲ HMA 190714
The Organ in Lorraine:Works by Composers of the Region from 1537 to the Present—, w. Anne-Catherine Bucher (org), Francois Menissier (org), Norbert Petry (org) K617 2-▲ 7055

Charbonnier, Bernadette (vn)
Jacquet De La Guerre, E.:Pièces de clavecin qui peuvent se jouer sur le viollon, w. G. Guillard (hpd) Arion 2-▲ ARN 268012 [AAD]
Jacquet De La Guerre, E.:Trio Sons for 2 Vns, w. Catherine Giardelli (vn), Claire Giardelli (vc), G. Guillard (hpd)—No. 4 Arion 2-▲ ARN 268012 [AAD]

Charial, Pierre (barrel org)
Constant, M.:Con Barrel Org, w. J. Kaltenbach (cnd), Nancy SO *(rec Salle Poirel, Nancy, Apr. 4, 1990)* Erato ▲ 94815-2 [DDD]

Charles, B. (instr)—see ORCHESTRAS & ENSEMBLES World Casio Quartet

Charles, Brian (ob)
Hays, S.:Take a Back Country Road, w. Sorrel Hays (elec sax/elec), Marilyn Ries (elec) New World ▲ 805202 [DDD]

Charleson, E. (vn)—see ORCHESTRAS & ENSEMBLES Vanbrugh String Quartet

Charlier, Olivier (vn)
Beethoven, L. van:Son 7 Vn, w. Brigitte Engerer (pno) Harmonia Mundi France ▲ HMC 901580
Beethoven, L. van:Son 8 Vn, w. Brigitte Engerer (pno) Harmonia Mundi France ▲ HMC 901580
Beethoven, L. van:Son 9 Vn, "Kreutzer", w. Brigitte Engerer (pno) Harmonia Mundi France ▲ HMC 901580
Dutilleux, H.:L'Arbre de songes, w. Y. P. Tortelier (cnd), BBC PO Chandos ▲ CHAN 9504
Mendelssohn, F.:Con in d Vn & Strs, w. L. Foster (cnd), Monte Carlo PO Erato ▲ 92869-2
Mendelssohn, F.:Con in e Vn & Orch, Op. 64, w. L. Foster (cnd), Monte Carlo PO Erato ▲ 92869-2
Pierné, G.:Son Vn, w. J. Hubeau (pno) Erato ("Musifrance" series) ▲ 2292-45525-2 [AAD/DDD]
Saint-Saëns, C.:Son 1 Vn, w. J. Hubeau (pno) Erato ("Musifrance" series) ▲ 2292-45017-2-ZK
Saint-Saëns, C.:Son 2 Vn, w. J. Hubeau (pno) Erato ("Musifrance" series) ▲ 2292-45017-2-ZK
Schumann, R.:Romances Ob, w. B. Engerer (pno) [trans. for violin & piano] Harmonia Mundi France ▲ HMC 901405
Schumann, R.:Son 1 Vn, w. B. Engerer (pno) Harmonia Mundi France ▲ HMC 901405
Schumann, R.:Son 2 Vn, w. B. Engerer (pno) Harmonia Mundi France ▲ HMC 901405

Charlston, Eric (perc)—see also ORCHESTRAS & ENSEMBLES Speculum Musicae, Continuum Chamber Ensemble, New Generation
Kraft, L.:Episodes, w. E. Gilmore (cl) *(rec 1989–1990)* Centaur ▲ CRC 2079 [ADD]
Léon, T.:Batéy, w. D. Ponce (conga), J. Passaro (perc), T. Léon (cnd), Western Wind CRI ▲ CD 662 [DDD]

Charlston, Terence (hpd/org)
Il Flauto Dolce:Italian Music from 3 Centuries, w. A. Solomon (fl/rcr), Jan Spencer (vc) Meridian ▲ MER 84292 [DDD]

Charnon, Gregory (perc)
Roussakis, N.:Trigono, w. Ronald Borror (tbn), Steven Paysen (vib) CRI ▲ CD 709 [DDD]

Charnstrom, Christine (chromelodeon)
Partch, H.:Barstow, w. William Wendlant (voc), Harry Partch (adapted gtr/voc), Lee Hoiby (kitara) *(rec 1945)* Innova 4-▲ 401
Partch, H.:By the Rivers of Babylon, w. William Wendlandt (bar), Lee Hoiby (kithara), Harry Partch (adapted va) *(rec 1945)* Innova 4-▲ 401
Partch, H.:Dark Brother, w. William Wendlandt (bar), Lee Hoiby (kithara), Harry Partch (adapted va), Fralia Hancock (Indian dr) *(rec 1945)* Innova 4-▲ 401
Partch, H.:San Francisco, w. Harry Partch (adapted va/ voc), Lee Hoiby (kitara) *(rec 1945)* Innova 4-▲ 401
Partch, H.:US HIghball, w. William Wendlandt (bar), Harry Partch (adapted gtr/voc), Lee Hoiby (kitara), Fralia Hancock (db canon) *(rec 1946)* Innova 4-▲ 401

Charpentier, Marcel (vn)—see ORCHESTRAS & ENSEMBLES Parrenin String Quartet

Charrez, Jean-Claude (pno)
Marescotti, A.-F.:Insomnies, w. Michel Brodard (bass) [arr for Bass & Pno] Grammont ▲ CTSP 13-2

Charvát, Přemsyi (pno)
Berman, K.:Songs (4), "Poupata", w. K. Berman (bass) [Czech] *(rec 2-3/85)* Channel Classics ▲ CCS 3191 [ADD]
Berman, K.:Suite Pno *(rec 2-3/85)* Channel Classics ▲ CCS 3191 [ADD]

Chase, Roger (va)—see also ORCHESTRAS & ENSEMBLES Nash Ensemble, Hausmusik
Battiato, F.:L'Ombra della Luce, w. Franco Battiato (voc), Antonio Ballista (pno), Filippo Destrieri (kbd/computer), Anthony Pleeth (vc), Gavin Wright (vn), G. Pio (cnd), London Astarte Orch Hemisphere ▲ 837234-2
Battiato, F.:Povera Patria, w. Franco Battiato (voc), Antonio Ballista (pno), Filippo Destrieri (kbd/computer), Anthony Pleeth (vc), Gavin Wright (vn), G. Pio (cnd), London Astarte Orch Hemisphere ▲ 837234-2
Battiato, F.:Le Sacre Sinfonie del Tiempo, w. Franco Battiato (voc), Antonio Ballista (pno), Filippo Destrieri (kbd/computer), Anthony Pleeth (vc), Gavin Wright (vn), G. Pio (cnd), London Astarte Orch Hemisphere ▲ 837234-2
Britten, H.:Lachrymae, w. L. Friend (cnd), Nash Ensemble Hyperion ▲ CDA 66845
Debussy, C.:Son Fl, w. P. Davies (fl), Marisa Robles (hp) Virgin Classics ▲ 59604 [DDD]
Mozart, W.A.:Sinf concertante Vn, K.364, w. S. Chase (vn), R. Goodman (cnd), Hanover Band [period instrs] *(rec Blackheath Concert Halls, London, May 18–20, 1992)* Cala 2-▲ CACD 1014 [DDD]
Panufnik, A.:Sxt Strs, w. Stephen Orion (vc), Chilingirian String Quartet Conifer Classics ▲ 74321-16190-2

Chase, Stephanie (vn)
Beethoven, L. van:Con Vn, Op. 61, w. R. Goodman (cnd), Hanover Band [period instrs] *(rec Blackheath Concert Halls, London, Feb 27–29, 1992)* Cala ▲ CACD 1013 [DDD]
Beethoven, L. van:Romances Vn, w. R. Goodman (cnd), Hanover Band [period instrs] *(rec Blackheath Concert Halls, London, Feb 27–29, 1992)* Cala ▲ CACD 1013 [DDD]
Borodin, A.:Nocturne Vn & Orch, w. G. Simon (cnd), Philharmonia Orch *(rec All Hallows Church, Gospel Oak, London, Feb 21–24 & Apr 8–10, 199)* Cala ▲ CAL 1011 [DDD]
Brahms, J.:Trio Hn, w. L. Greer (nat hn), S. Lubin (pno) Harmonia Mundi USA ▲ HMU 907037
Copland, A.:Threnodies I & II, w. F. Smith (fl), K. Murdock (va), R. Thomas (vc) Northeastern ("Classical Arts" series) ▲ NR 227-CD
Mozart, W.A.:Con 3 Vn, w. R. Goodman (cnd), Hanover Band [period instrs] *(rec Blackheath Concert Halls, London, May 18–20, 1992)* Cala 2-▲ CACD 1014 [DDD]
Mozart, W.A.:Con 5 Vn, w. R. Goodman (cnd), Hanover Band [period instrs] *(rec Blackheath Concert Halls, London, May 18–20, 1992)* Cala 2-▲ CACD 1014 [DDD]
Mozart, W.A.:Sinf concertante Vn, K.364, w. R. Chase (va), R. Goodman (cnd), Hanover Band [period instrs] *(rec Blackheath Concert Halls, London, May 18–20, 1992)* Cala 2-▲ CACD 1014 [DDD]
Ravel, M.:Tzigane, w. G. Simon (cnd), Philharmonia Orch *(rec St. Jude-on-the-HIll, Hampstead, London, Feb 8–12, 1991)* Cala ▲ CACD 1004 [DDD]
Schoenberg, A.:Verklärte Nacht, w. L. Chang (vn), M. Thompson (va), S. Ansel (va), R. Thomas (vc), M. Djokic (vc) *(rec Methuen, MA, Dec. 1990)* Northeastern ▲ NOR 249 [DDD]
Shostakovich, D.:Trio 2 Pno, w. R. Hodgkinson (pno), R. Thomas (vc) *(rec Methuen, MA, Jan. 1990)* Northeastern ▲ NOR 245 [DDD]

Chasovennaya, Vera (hpd)
Schnittke, A.:Hymns Vc, w. A. Ivashkin (vc), Y. Rudometkin (bn), I. Pashinskaya (hp), V. Barsalkin (db), V. Grishin, N. Grishin (perc/bells)—No. 1 for Cello, Harp & Timpani [Quasi andante]; No. 2 for Cello & Double *(rec National Radio House, Moscow, 1987)* Vox Box 2-▲ CDX 5121 [ADD]

Chastain, Nora (vn)—see also ORCHESTRAS & ENSEMBLES Menuhin Festival Piano Quartet
Bartók, B.:Con 2 Vn, w. R. Bohn (cnd), Sinfonietta Tübingen Ars Produktion ▲ ARS 368319 [DDD]

Chastain, Nora (vn) (cont.)
Debussy, C.:Son Vn, w. F. Rieger (pno) Ars Produktion ▲ FCD 368311 [DDD]
Fauré, G.:Son 1 Vn, w. F. Rieger (pno) Ars Produktion ▲ FCD 368311 [DDD]
Honegger, A.:Sons Vn, w. F. Rieger (pno)—Sonata No. 1 for Violin & Piano (1916–18) Ars Produktion ▲ FCD 368311 [DDD]
International Menuhin Music Academy, w. International Menuhin Music Academy, Paul Coletti (vn), Hu-Kun (vn), Mi-Kyung Lee (vn), Alberto Lysy (vn) Arcobaleno ▲ SBCD 4700 [DDD]
Turina, J.:Escena andaluza, w. P. Coletti (va), F. Rieger (pno), C. Busch (vn), A. B. Deutschler (va), F. Goutou (vc) *(rec May 25–28, 1993)* Claves ▲ CD 9403 [DDD]

Chateauneuf, Paula (gtr)
Purcell, H.:Music of, w. Catherine Bott (sop), Emma Kirkby (sop), James Bowman (alt), Anthony Rooley (lt), Monica Huggett (vn), Catherine Mackintosh (vn), Christophe Coin (vc), Hill, Hogwood (cnd), Academy of Ancient Music, Brandenburg Consort, David Hill (cnd), Anthony Lewis (cnd), St. Anthony Singers, Taverner Choir, Winchester Cathedral Choir—The Double Dealer; Come Ye Sons of Art; The Old Bachelor; Birthday Song for Queen Mary; Oedipus; King Arthur; Bonduca; The Fairy Queen; Son. No. 9 in F; Dido & Aeneas; Abdelazer; Bess of Bedlam; The Married Beau; Hear My Prayer, O Lord; Rejoice in the Lord Always London ("Editions de l'oiseau-lyre" series) ▲ 444620-2

Chateauneuf, Paula (gtr/thb)
Blow, J.:Songs, w. J. M. Ainsley (ten), T. Roberts (spinet/hpd/chamber org)—No More, the Dear, Lovely Nymph's No More; Lovely Selina, Innocent & Free; O Turn Not Those Fine Eyes away; Fairest Work of Happy Nature; Flavia Grown Old; Oh! That Mine Eyes Would Melt into a Flood; O Might God, Who Sit'st on High; Sabina Has a Thousand Charms; Of All the Torments, All the Cares; No, Lesbia, You Ask in Vain *(rec Jan. 25–27, 1993)* Hyperion ▲ CDA 66646 [DDD]

Chatfield, M. (vc)—see ORCHESTRAS & ENSEMBLES Trioalanterie, Trio Galanterie

Chatham, R. (tpt)
Behrman, D.:Music of, w. T. Kosugi (vn), B. Neill (tpt), C. Mondshine (sound effects), jakino (keyboard improvisation)—Interspecies Small Talk (1984); Leapday Night (1983–86); A Traveller's Dream Journal (1988–90) Lovely Music ▲ LCD 1042 [ADD]

Chatton, M. (lt)—see ORCHESTRAS & ENSEMBLES Lautentrio Ricardo Correa

Chauveau, Mélisande (pno)
Liszt, F.:Chorales Pno—Vexilla regis prodeunt; Was Gott tut, das ist wohlgetan Arion ▲ ARN 68024 [DDD]
Liszt, F.:Études de concert (3) Pno—No. 2, "La leggierezza" Arion ▲ ARN 68024 [DDD]
Liszt, F.:Études d'exécution transcendante, S.139—No. 8 Arion ▲ ARN 68024 [DDD]
Liszt, F.:Harmonies poétiques et religieuses—Funérailles Arion ▲ ARN 68024 [DDD]
Liszt, F.:Transcriptions & Paraphrases—Allegri & Mozart—A la Chapelle Sixtine; Mozart—2 Pieces from the Requiem; Schumann—Widmung Arion ▲ ARN 68024 [DDD]
Messiaen, O.:Regards sur l'Enfant Jésus Forlane 2-▲ FRL 16709 [DDD]

Chavaukina, Lidiya (vn)
Taneyev, S.:Trio Strs, Op. 21, w. Sergei Ryabov (vn), Andrei Kevorkov (va) Allegretto ▲ ACD 8178 [DDD] ■ ACS 8178

Chavez, Ana (pno)
Clementi, M.:Pno Music (comp), w. Federico Aldao (pno), Aldo Antognazzi (pno), Lorena Di Florio (pno), Marcela Paludi (pno), Ricardo Zanon (pno)—Sons (6) for Pno, Op. 1, Nos. 4–6; Sons (6) for Pno, Op. 2, Nos. 2, 4 & 6 Aura Classics ▲ AU 32072

Chaynes-Decaux, Odette (pno)
Chaynes, C.:Au-delà de l'espérance, w. H. Jossoud (mez) REM ▲ REM 311194 [DDD]

Cheetham, Richard (trbn)
Bruckner, A.:motets, w. Adrian Lane (trbn), Steven Saunders (trbn), Simon Wills (trbn), Matthew Morley (org), Robert James (cnd), James St. Bride's Church Choir—Os justi; Locus iste; Libera me [in f, 1854]; Ave maria; Ecce sacerdos; Vexilla regis; Salvum fac populum tuum [1884]; Afferentur regi; Pange lingua; Tota pulchra es [Daniel Norman (tenor)]; Virga Jesse; Inveni David; Iam lucis orto sidere [Hymnus, 1868]; Tantum ergo [in D, 1988]; Christus factus est *(rec St. Bride's Church, Fleet Street, London, Jan. 27–29, 1994)* Naxos ▲ 8.550956 [DDD]

Chee-Yun (vn)
Debussy, C.:Son Vn, w. A. Eguchi (pno) *(rec May 1990)* Denon/PCM Digital ▲ CO 75625 [DDD]
Fauré, G.:Son 1 Vn, w. A. Eguchi (pno) *(rec May 1990)* Denon/PCM Digital ▲ CO 75625 [DDD]
Franck, C.:Son Vn, w. Akira Eguchi (pno) *(rec Chichibu-Muse Park, Music Hall, Saitama-prefecture, Japan, Oct. 17–20, 1994)* Denon ▲ CO 78954 [DDD]
Mendelssohn, F.:Con in e Vn & Orch, Op. 64, w. J. López-Cobos (cnd), London PO Denon ▲ CC 78913
Saint-Saëns, C.:Son 1 Vn, w. A. Eguchi (pno) *(rec May 1990)* Denon/PCM Digital ▲ CO 75625 [DDD]
Szymanowski, K.:Son Vn, w. Akira Eguchi (pno) *(rec Chichibu-Muse Park, Music Hall, Saitama-prefecture, Japan, Oct. 17–20, 1994)* Denon ▲ CO 78954 [DDD]
Vocalise, w. Akira Eguchi (pno) *(rec July 31–Aug. 1, 1992)* Denon ▲ CO 75118 [DDD]

Chefson, Sabine (hp)
Haik-Vantoura, S.:The Song of Songs, w. S. Haik-Vantoura (mez), M.-L. Banzet (bar), R. Boschiero (hp), E. Dutrieux (cnd), *(chorus unknown)* [He] *(rec 1986)* Alienor ▲ AL 1045 [DDD]
Lemeland, A.:L'Automne et sens envols d'etourneaux, w. J.-L. Homs (E hn), M. Tardue (cnd), Grenoble Instrumental Ensemble Skarbo ▲ SKR 3913 [DDD]
Lemeland, A.:Con Hp, w. M. Tardue (cnd), Grenoble Instrumental String Ensemble Skarbo ▲ SKR 2338 [DDD]

Cheifetz, Hamilton (vc)
Diamond, D.:Qnt Cl, w. D. Schifrin (cl), P. Neubauer (va), W. Trampler (va), W. Lash (vc) *(rec 6 & 7/90)* Delos ▲ 3088 [DDD]

Chekina, Tatiana (pno)
Bartók, B.:Sons (2) Vn & Pno, w. Oleh Krysa (vn) *(rec Moscow Conservatory, July 1995)* Triton ▲ 17007 [DDD]

Chekmenyov, B. (gtr)
Babadjanyan, A.:Music of, w. A. Arutiunyan (pno), Arno Babadjanyan (pno), A. Tarasov (gtr), A. Nikolayev (perc), Silantiev, Mavisakhalyan (cnd), All-Union Radio-TV Sym Variety Orch, Armenian Radio-TV Orch—Nocturne; Prelude & Vagarshapat Dance; Capriccio; Polyphonic Son; Exprompt; Armenian Rhap; Elegy in Commemoration of A. Khachaturyan; 6 Pictures; Melody & Humoresque; Fant on Give Me My Music Back; Fant on Dum spiro spero; Fant on Winer Love; Fant on Call Me; Piece for the Pno & Orch [Dreams] *(rec 1953–83)* Russian Compact Disc ("Talents of Russia" series) ▲ RCD 16251 [ADD]

Chen, Hung-Kuan (pno)
Chopin, F.:Nocturnes—Op. 61/1 & 2 MusicMasters ▲ 7063-2-C [DDD]
Chopin, F.:Preludes, Op. 28 MusicMasters ▲ 7063-2-C [DDD]

Chen, Jie-bing (erhu)
Chen, Y.:Music of, w. Liu Wei-shan (guzheng), Zhao Yang-qin (yangqin), Min Xiao-fen (pipa), J. Falletta (cnd), Women's PO, Chanticleer—Duo Ye No. 2; Sym 2; Ge Xu; Chinese Myths Cant; Pan Gu Creates Heaven & Earth; Nu Wa Creates Human Beings; Weaving Maid & Cowherd; Song of Weaving Maid & Cowherd *(rec Skywalker Sound, San Rafael, CA, June 1996)* New Albion ▲ NA 090

Chen, Melvin (pno)
Julette Kang, w. J. Kang (vn) *(rec Indianapolis, Nov. 1994)* Discover International ▲ DICD 920241 [DDD]

Chen, Robert (vn)
Tchaikovsky, P.:Con Vn, w. P. Kogan (cnd), Hanover North German Radio PO Berlin Classics ▲ BER 1169
Tchaikovsky, P.:Sérénade mélancolique, w. P. Kogan (cnd), Hanover North German Radio PO Berlin Classics ▲ BER 1169
Tchaikovsky, P.:Souvenir d'un lieu cher, w. P. Kogan (cnd), Hanover North German Radio PO Berlin Classics ▲ BER 1169

Chenault, Elizabeth (org)
Christmas at Spivey Hall, w. Raymond Chenault (org) Gothic ▲ GOT CD 49084
Vol. 2, 20th Century Organ Music for Two, w. Raymond Chenault (org) Gothic ▲ GOT 49073 [DDD]

Chenault, Raymond (org)
Christmas at Spivey Hall, w. E. Chenault (org) Gothic ▲ GOT CD 49084
Vol. 2, 20th Century Organ Music for Two, w. E. Chenault (org) Gothic ▲ GOT 49073 [DDD]

Cheng, Angela (pno)
Mozart, W.A.:Con 9 Pno, w. M. Bernardi (cnd), CBC Vancouver SO CBC ("SM 5000" series) ▲ SMCD 5104 [DDD] ■ SMC 5104 (D)
Mozart, W.A.:Con 17 Pno, w. M. Bernardi (cnd), CBC Vancouver SO CBC ("SM 5000" series) ▲ SMCD 5104 [DDD] ■ SMC 5104 (D)
Schumann, C.:Con Pno, w. J. Falletta (cnd), Women's PO Koch International Classics ▲ KIC 7169-2 [DDD]
Schumann, C.:Pièces fugitives *(rec Glenn Gould Studio, CBC Toronto, Jan 6–8, 1995)* CBC ("Musica Viva" series) ▲ MVCD 1087 [DDD]
Schumann, C.:Preludes & Fugues—No. 2 *(rec Glenn Gould Studio, CBC Toronto, Jan 6–8, 1995)* CBC ("Musica Viva" series) ▲ MVCD 1087 [DDD]
Schumann, C.:Scherzo Pno *(rec Glenn Gould Studio, CBC Toronto, Jan 6–8, 1995)* CBC ("Musica Viva" series) ▲ MVCD 1087 [DDD]
Schumann, C.:Variations on a Theme by Robert Schumann *(rec Glenn Gould Studio, CBC Toronto, Jan 6–8, 1995)* CBC ("Musica Viva" series) ▲ MVCD 1087 [DDD]
Schumann, R.:Arabeske Pno *(rec Glenn Gould Studio, CBC Toronto, Jan 6–8, 1995)* CBC ("Musica Viva" series) ▲ MVCD 1087 [DDD]
Schumann, R.:Faschingsschwank aus Wien *(rec Glenn Gould Studio, CBC Toronto, Jan 6–8, 1995)* CBC ("Musica Viva" series) ▲ MVCD 1087 [DDD]
Schumann, R.:Son Pno, Op. 14—Vars on a theme by Clara Wieck *(rec Glenn Gould Studio, CBC Toronto, Jan 6–8, 1995)* CBC ("Musica Viva" series) ▲ MVCD 1087 [DDD]

Cheng, Chiung-Ying (pno)
Boettcher, E.:Birthday Vars, w. Eun-Joo Kwak (pno) Northwestern Univ School of Music ▲

Cheng, Gloria (pno)
Carter, E.:Pastoral E hn, w. Carolyn Hove (E hn) *(rec Little Bridges Auditorium, Pomona College, Dec 1994 & Jan 1996)* Crystal ▲ CD 328 [DDD]
Hindemith, P.:Son E Hn, w. Carolyn Hove (E hn) *(rec Little Bridges Auditorium, Pomona College, Dec 1994 & Jan 1996)* Crystal ▲ CD 328 [DDD]
Marvin, J.:Pieces E hn & Pno, w. Carolyn Hove (E hn) *(rec Little Bridges Auditorium, Pomona College, Dec 1994 & Jan 1996)* Crystal ▲ CD 328 [DDD]
Messiaen, O.:Cantéyodjayâ Koch International Classics ▲ KIC 7267 [DDD]
Messiaen, O.:Études (4) de Rhythme Koch International Classics ▲ KIC 7267 [DDD]
Messiaen, O.:Petites esquisses d'oiseaux Koch International Classics ▲ KIC 7267 [DDD]
Messiaen, O.:Pièce pour le tombeau de Paul Dukas Koch International Classics ▲ KIC 7267 [DDD]
Salonen, E.-P.:Second Meeting, w. Carolyn Hove (ob) *(rec Little Bridges Auditorium, Pomona College, Dec 1994 & Jan 1996)* Crystal ▲ CD 328 [DDD]

Cherkassky, Shura (pno)
Bach, J.S.:Partitas Hpd, BWV 825–830—in e, BWV 830 *(rec Salzburg, Aug 3, 1968)* Orfeo d'or ("Festspiel Dikumente" series) 2-▲ C 431962 (m) [ADD]
Beethoven, L. van:Ecossaises, WoO 83 Biddulph ▲ LHW 034
Beethoven, L. van:Son 13 Pno Nimbus ▲ NI 5021 [DDD]
Bennett, Richard Rodney:Studies (5) Pno *(rec Salzburg, Aug 3, 1968)* Orfeo d'or ("Festspiel Dikumente" series) 2-▲ C 431962 (m) [ADD]
Berg, A.:Son Pno Nimbus ▲ NI 5021 [DDD]
Bernstein, L.:Touches Nimbus ▲ NI 5091 [DDD]
Brahms, J.:Son 3 Pno *(rec Salzburg, Aug 3, 1968)* Orfeo d'or ("Festspiel Dikumente" series) 2-▲ C 431962 (m) [ADD]
Brahms, J.:Vars on a Theme by Paganini Nimbus ▲ NI 5020 [DDD]
Busoni, F.:Chaconne Pno Nimbus ▲ NI 5021 [DDD]
Chasins, A.:Chinese Pieces (3)—Rush Hour in Hong Kong Nimbus ▲ NI 5020 [DDD]
Cherkassky, S.:Prélude pathétique Biddulph ▲ LHW 034
Chopin, F.:Andante Spianato & Grande Polonaise *(rec June 11 & Oct. 16–17, 198)* Nimbus ▲ NI 7701 [DDD]
Chopin, F.:Andante Spianato & Grande Polonaise Nimbus ▲ NI 5044 [DDD]
Chopin, F.:Andante Spianato & Grande Polonaise *(rec Nimbus Records, Wyastone Leys, Monmouth, 1984–85)* Nimbus ▲ NI 7708 [DDD]
Chopin, F.:Ballades Pno (comp)—Opp. 23 & 38 *(rec 1977)* Tudor ▲ 720 [ADD]
Chopin, F.:Barcarolle Pno Tudor ▲ 720 [ADD]
Chopin, F.:Fant Tudor ▲ 720 [ADD]
Chopin, F.:Mazurkas—in b, Op. 33/4; in c#, Op. 63/3 *(rec Nimbus Records, Wyastone Leys, Monmouth, 1984–85)* Nimbus ▲ NI 7708 [DDD]
Chopin, F.:Mazurkas—Op. 33/4 & Op. 63/3 Nimbus ▲ NI 5044 [DDD]
Chopin, F.:Nocturnes—Opp. 27/2, 62/2, 72 Nimbus ▲ NI 5044 [DDD]
Chopin, F.:Nocturnes—in Db, Op. 27/2; in E, Op. 62/2; in e, Op. 72 *(rec Nimbus Records, Wyastone Leys, Monmouth, 1984–85)* Nimbus ▲ NI 7708 [DDD]
Chopin, F.:Pno Music (misc)—"Revolutionary" Etude; "Heroic" Polonaise; Scherzo No. 4 in c# ASV ("Quicksilva" series) ▲ ASQ 6109 [DDD]
Chopin, F.:Polonaises Deutsche Grammophon ("Resonance" series) ▲ 429516-2 [ADD]
Chopin, F.:Polonaise-fant Deutsche Grammophon ("Resonance" series) ▲ 429516-2 [ADD]
Chopin, F.:Preludes, Op. 28 *(rec Salzburg, Aug 3, 1968)* Orfeo d'or ("Festspiel Dikumente" series) 2-▲ C 431962 (m) [ADD]
Chopin, F.:Preludes, Op. 28 ASV ("Quicksilva" series) ▲ ASQ 6109 [DDD]
Chopin, F.:Scherzos—No. 1 Nimbus ▲ NI 5043 [DDD]
Chopin, F.:Scherzos—in b, Op. 20 *(rec Nimbus Records, Wyastone Leys, Monmouth, 1984–85)* Nimbus ▲ NI 7708 [DDD]
Chopin, F.:Scherzos Tudor ▲ 720 [ADD]
Chopin, F.:Son Pno, Op. 58 Nimbus ▲ NI 5044 [DDD]
Chopin, F.:Son Pno, Op. 58 *(rec June 11 & Oct. 16–17, 198)* Nimbus ▲ NI 7701 [DDD]
Chopin, F.:Vars on Mozart's *La ci darem la mano* Nimbus ▲ NI 5091 [DDD]
Chopin, F.:Waltzes—waltz in e Biddulph ▲ LHW 034
80th Birthday Recital at Carnegie Hall, w. Cherkassky, Shura (pno) *(rec December 1991)* London ▲ 433654-2 LH [DDD]
Franck, C.:Prélude, choral et fugue Nimbus ▲ NI 5090 [DDD]
Franck, C.:Prélude, choral et fugue *(rec Apr. 14–16, 1987)* Nimbus ▲ NI 7705 [DDD]
Godowsky, L.:Transcriptions & Paraphrases—Paraphrase on Johann Strauss's "Wein, Weib und Gesang" for Piano Nimbus ▲ NI 5043 [DDD]
Gould, M.:Boogie Woogie Etude London ▲ 433654-2 [DDD]
Grieg, E.:Son Pno Nimbus ▲ NI 5090 [DDD]
Hofmann, J.:Kaleidoskop Nimbus ▲ NI 5020 [DDD]
Ives, C.:Three-Page Son London ▲ 433654-2 [DDD]
Last of the Great Piano Romantics, Vol. 1, w. Cherkassky, Shura (pno) ASV ("Quicksilva" series) ▲ ASQ 6096 [ADD]
Liszt, F.:Fant on Hungarian Folk Tunes, w. H. von Karajan (cnd), Berlin PO Deutsche Grammophon 2-▲ 415967-2 [ADD]
Liszt, F.:Fant on Hungarian Folk Tunes, w. H. von Karajan (cnd), Berlin PO Deutsche Grammophon ("Resonance" series) ▲ 429156-2 [ADD]
Liszt, F.:Fant on Hungarian Folk Tunes, w. H. von Karajan (cnd), Berlin PO Deutsche Grammophon ("Galleria" series) ▲ 419862-2 [ADD]
Liszt, F.:Harmonies poétiques et religieuses—No. 7 [Funérailles] *(rec Nimbus Records, Wyastone Leys, Monmouth, 1984–85)* Nimbus ▲ NI 7708 [DDD]
Liszt, F.:Harmonies poétiques et religieuses—Funérailles Nimbus ▲ NI 5021 [DDD]
Liszt, F.:Hungarian Rhaps—No. 2 Nimbus ▲ NI 5045 [DDD]
Liszt, F.:Hungarian Rhaps *(rec June 11 & Oct. 16–17, 198)* Nimbus ▲ NI 7701 [DDD]
Liszt, F.:Hungarian Rhaps—No. 2 *(rec Nimbus Records, Wyastone Leys, Monmouth, 1984–85)* Nimbus ▲ NI 7708 [DDD]

Cherkassky, Shura (pno) (cont.)
Liszt, F.:Hungarian Rhaps—No. 12 in c# *(rec 1982)* Vox Box 2-▲ CDX 5139 [ADD]
Liszt, F.:Hungarian Rhaps, w. H. von Karajan (cnd), Berlin PO—Nos. 2, 5, 6, 9, 12 & 14 Deutsche Grammophon ("Resonance" series) ▲ 429156-2 [ADD]
Liszt, F.:Liebesträume—No. 3 *(rec 1982)* Vox Box 2-▲ CDX 5139 [ADD]
Liszt, F.:Pno Music (misc)—Polonaise No. 2; Rigoletto Paraphrase ASV ("Quicksilva" series) ▲ ASQ 6109 [DDD]
Liszt, F.:Polonaises Pno—No. 2 in E *(rec Salzburg, Aug 3, 1968)* Orfeo d'or ("Festspiel Dikumente" series) 2-▲ C 431962 (m) [ADD]
Liszt, F.:Son Pno Nimbus ▲ NI 5045 [DDD]
Liszt, F.:Son Pno *(rec June 11 & Oct. 16-17, 198)* Nimbus ▲ NI 7701 [DDD]
Live from Queen Elizabeth Hall, w. Cherkassky, Shura (pno) London ▲ 433653-2 LH [ADD]
Mana-Zucca, G.:Prelude Pno Biddulph ▲ LHW 034
Mendelssohn, F.:Fant ou caprices—No. 2 Biddulph ▲ LHW 034
Mendelssohn, F.:Lieder ohne Worte Pno—Op. 19, No. 3 Biddulph ▲ LHW 034
Mendelssohn, F.:Preludes & Fugues Pno, Op. 35—No. 1 in e Biddulph ▲ LHW 034
Mendelssohn, F.:Rondo capriccioso *(rec 1982)* Vox Box 2-▲ CDX 5139 [ADD]
Messiaen, O.:Études (4) de Rhythme—Nos. 1 & 2 Nimbus ▲ NI 5090 [DDD]
Pabst, P.:Concert Paraphrase on Tchaikovsky's *Eugen Onegin* Nimbus ▲ NI 5091 [DDD]
Piano Recital, w. Cherkassky, Shura (pno) *(rec Dec. 5, 1963)* Ermitage ▲ ERM 133
Rachmaninoff, S.:Son Vc, w. Marcel Hubert (vc) Biddulph ▲ LHW 034
Rachmaninoff, S.:Variations on a Theme by Corelli Nimbus ▲ NI 5090 [DDD]
Rameau, J.P.:Pièces de clavecin avec une méthode sur la mécanique des doigts—Tambourin [arr. Godowsky] Biddulph ▲ LHW 034
Schubert, Franz:Impromptus Pno, D.899—in E♭ & G♭, Op. 90/2 & 3 Nimbus ▲ NI 5043 [DDD]
Schubert, Franz:Impromptus Pno, D.899—Nos. 2 in E♭ & 3 in G♭ *(rec Nimbus Records, Wyastone Leys, Monmouth, 1984-85)* Nimbus ▲ NI 7708 [DDD]
Schubert, Franz:Son Pno, D.664 London ▲ 433653-2 [ADD]
Schubert, Franz:Son Pno, D.664 Nimbus ▲ NI 5091 [DDD]
Schumann, R.:Kreisleriana Nimbus ▲ NI 5043 [DDD]
Schumann, R.:Kreisleriana *(rec May 13-14 & June 10, 1985)* Nimbus ▲ NI 7705 [DDD]
Schumann, R.:Sym Etudes *(rec 1984)* Nimbus ▲ NI 7705 [DDD]
Schumann, R.:Sym Etudes London ▲ 433654-2 [DDD]
Schumann, R.:Sym Etudes Nimbus ▲ NI 5020 [DDD]
Stravinsky, I.:Scenes Pno Nimbus ▲ NI 5045 [DDD]
Tchaikovsky, P.:Con 2 Pno, w. W. Susskind (cnd), Cincinnati SO *(rec 1981)* Vox Box 2-▲ CDX 5139 [ADD]

Cherney, Lawrence (E hn)
Weinzweig, J.:Divert 11 E Hn, w. V. Feldbrill (cnd), *(orch unknown)* *(rec live, Walter Hall, Univ. of Toronto, Mar. 11, 1993)* Centrediscs ▲ CMC 5295 [DDD]

Cherney, Lawrence (bass ob)
Harman, C.P.:Poem, w. William Aide (pno) *(rec St Martin-in-the-Fields Church, Toronto, July 1995)* Centrediscs ▲ CMC 5395 [DDD]

Cherney, Lawrence (ob)
Chan Ka Nin:The Charmer, w. G. Kulesha (cnd), chamber ensemble *(rec St Martin-in-the-Fields Church, Toronto, July 1995)* Centrediscs ▲ CMC 5395 [DDD]
Cherney, B.:River of Fire, w. Erica Goodman (hp) *(rec St Martin-in-the-Fields Church, Toronto, July 1995)* Centrediscs ▲ CMC 5395 [DDD]
Hui, M.:San Rocco, w. Russell Hartenberger (perc), Noel Edison (cnd), Elora Festival Singers *(rec St Martin-in-the-Fields Church, Toronto, July 1995)* Centrediscs ▲ CMC 5395 [DDD]
Lake, L.:Psalm Centrediscs ▲ CD 3288
Mather, B.:Vouvray, w. Erica Goodman (hp) *(rec St Martin-in-the-Fields Church, Toronto, July 1995)* Centrediscs ▲ CMC 5395 [DDD]
Somers, H.:Miniatures, w. William Aide (pno) *(rec St Martin-in-the-Fields Church, Toronto, July 1995)* Centrediscs ▲ CMC 5395 [DDD]

Cherney, Lawrence (ob/ob d'amore/E hn)
Tongues of Angels Centrediscs ▲ CMC 4793 [DDD]

Chernykhovsky, Mikhail (vn)
Prokofiev, S.:Waltz Suite, w. G. Rozhdestvensky (cnd), USSR Radio-TV Large SO *(rec 1967)* Consonance ▲ 81-5005 [AAD]

Chernyshov, Igor (pno)
Brahms, J.:Son 2 Vn, w. Marina Yashvili (vn) *(rec 1991)* Russian Compact Disc ("Talents of Russia" series) ▲ RCD 16252 [ADD]

Cherrier, Sophie (fl)
Boulez, P.:Mémoriale, w. P. Boulez (cnd), Ensemble InterContemporain Erato ▲ 2292-45648-2 [DDD]
Boulez, P.:Sonatine Fl & Pno, w. P.-L. Aimard (pno) Erato ▲ 2292-45648-2 [DDD]

Chertok, Michael (org)
Strauss, R.:Festliches Präludium, w. J. López-Cobos (cnd), Cincinnati SO *(rec Music Hall, Cincinnati, OH, Oct. 2-3, 1994)* Telarc ▲ CD 80371 [DDD]

Chertok, Michael (pno)
Cinematic Piano Telarc ▲ CD 80357

Chestnut, Cyrus (pno)
So Many Stars, w. K. Battle (sop), Antonio Hart (sax), Grover Washington Jr (sax), Tom Harrell (flgl), James Carter (b cl), Jon Herrington (gtr), Romero Lubambo (gtr), Ira Coleman (elec bass), Christian McBride (elec bass), Cyro Baptista (perc), Steven Berrios (perc) *(rec Hit Factory, Clinton Recording Studios, R.P.M. Sound Studios, Unique Recording Studios, Power Station)* Sony Classical ▲ SK 68473 [DDD]

Chevailler, Jean-Pierre (eup)
The Classic Euphonium, w. Chevailler, Jean-Pierre (eup) Albany ▲ TROY 201-2 [DDD] ■ TROY 201-4 (D)
Danzi, F.:Con Bn, w. G. Lloyd (cnd), City of London Sinfonia Albany ▲ TROY 201-2 [DDD] ■ TROY 201-4 (D)
Handel, G.F.:Con Eup, w. G. LLoyd (cnd), City of London Sinfonia Albany ▲ TROY 201-2 [DDD]; ■ TROY 201-4 (D)
Mozart, W.A.:Con Bn, w. G. Lloyd (cnd), City of London Sinfonia Albany ▲ TROY 201-2 [DDD] ■ TROY 201-4 (D)

Chiarappa, Carlo (vn)
Bach, J.S.:Con Fl, Vn & Hpd, w. C. Chiarappa (cnd), Accademia Bizantina *(rec Il Liceo Musicale A. Masini di Forli, 1991)* Denon 2-▲ CO 78970 [DDD]
Bach, J.S.:Con 1 Hpd, w. C. Chiarappa (cnd), Accademia Bizantina *(rec Il Liceo Musicale A. Masini di Forli, 1991)* Denon 2-▲ CO 78970 [DDD]
Bach, J.S.:Con 5 Hpd, w. C. Chiarappa (cnd), Accademia Bizantina *(rec Il Liceo Musicale A. Masini di Forli, 1991)* Denon 2-▲ CO 78970 [DDD]
Bach, J.S.:Con 1 for 2 Hpds, w. C. Chiarappa (cnd), Accademia Bizantina *(rec Il Liceo Musicale A. Masini di Forli, 1991)* Denon 2-▲ CO 78970 [DDD]
Bach, J.S.:Con 2 for 3 Hpds, w. C. Chiarappa (cnd), Accademia Bizantina *(rec Il Liceo Musicale A. Masini di Forli, 1991)* Denon 2-▲ CO 78970 [DDD]
Bach, J.S.:Cons Vn (comp), w. C. Chiarappa (cnd), Accademia Bizantina *(rec Il Liceo Musicale A. Masini di Forli, 1991)* Denon 2-▲ CO 78970 [DDD]
Bach, J.S.:Con for 2 Vns, w. C. Chiarappa (cnd), Accademia Bizantina *(rec Il Liceo Musicale A. Masini di Forli, 1991)* Denon 2-▲ CO 78970 [DDD]
Bach, J.S.:A Musical Offering, w. C. Chiarappa (cnd), Accademia Bizantina Denon/PCM Digital ▲ DEN 75861 [DDD]
Berio, L.:Pezzi (2) Vn, w. R. Valentini (pno) Denon/PCM Digital ▲ CO 75448
Berio, L.:Sequenza VIII Denon/PCM Digital ▲ CO 75448
Ghedini, G.F.:Con Vn, "Il Belprato", w. C. Chiarappa (cnd), Accademia Bizantina *(rec Rocca Sforzesca, Imola, Italy, July, 20-22, 1993)* Denon ▲ CO 78916 [DDD]
Respighi, O.:Ancient Airs & Dances, w. C. Chiarappa (cnd), Accademia Bizantina—Set No. 3 *(rec Rocca Sforzesca, Imola, Italy, July, 20-22, 1993)* Denon ▲ CO 78916 [DDD]

Chiarappa, Carlo (vn) (cont.)
Schubert, Franz:Con Vn, w. C. Chiarappa (cnd), Accademia Bizantina *(rec Ravenna, Italy, Oct 27-29, 1987)* Arts Music ▲ 447210-2 [DDD]
Schubert, Franz:Polonaise Vn, w. C. Chiarappa (cnd), Accademia Bizantina *(rec Ravenna, Italy, Oct 27-29, 1987)* Arts Music ▲ 447210-2 [DDD]
Schubert, Franz:Rondo Vn, D.438, w. C. Chiarappa (cnd), Accademia Bizantina *(rec Ravenna, Italy, Oct 27-29, 1987)* Arts Music ▲ 447210-2 [DDD]
Tartini, G.:Cons Vn (misc), w. C. Chiarappa (cnd), Accademia Bizantina—in e, D.56; in G, D.78; in A, D.96; in b, D.125 *(rec Presso Museo S. Vitale, Ravenna, Oct. 1-4, 1993)* Denon ▲ DEN 78969 [DDD]

Chiaro, Giovanni de (gtr)
Christmas on Guitar Centaur ▲ CRC 2101
Joplin, S.:Music of—The Heliotrope Bouquet; Eugenia; Bethena:A Concert Waltz; The Pine Apple Rag; The Weeping Willow; The Sunflower Slow Drag; Solace:A Mexican Serenade; Elite Syncopation; The Chrysanthemum; The Maple Leaf Rag *(rec May 30 & 31, 1989)* Centaur ▲ CRC 2163 [DDD]

Chiffoleau, Yvan (vc)
Alkan, C.-V.:Chamber Music, w. Dong-Suk Kang (vn), O. Gardon (pno)—Grand Duo concertant for Violin & Piano, Op. 21; Sonate de Concert for Cello & Piano, Op. 47; Trio for Piano, Violin & Cello, Op. 30 Timpani ▲ 1C 1013 [DDD]
Ladmirault, P.:Son Vc, w. Robert Plantard (pno) *(rec Radio-France, Paris, 1980)* Skarbo ▲ SK 4952 [ADD]
Ravel, M.:Son Vn Vc, w. Clara Bonaldi (vn) Adda ▲ ADD 581065 [DDD]
Ravel, M.:Trio Pno, w. Noël Lee (pno), Clara Bonaldi (vn) Adda ▲ ADD 581065 [DDD]

Childs, B. (pno)
Childs, B.:The Distant Land, w. Carmen Lundy (mez), Nana Yaw Asiedu (perc), Thomas Kelley (perc) *(rec Masonic Auditorium, Cleveland, OH, Feb 27, 1995)* Telarc ▲ CD 80409 [DDD]
Schwartz, E.:Reading Session, w. P. Rehfeldt, B. Childs Capstone ▲ CPS 8609 CD

Childs, Nicholas (eup)
Curnow, J.:Rhap Eup, w. H. Snell (cnd), Brittania Building Society Band Doyen ▲ CD 002 [DDD]
Howarth, E.:Cantabile for John Fletcher, w. Robert Childs (eup) Doyen ▲ CD 002 [DDD]
Phillips, John:Romance, w. Robert Childs (eup), H. Snell (cnd), Brittania Building Society Band Doyen ▲ CD 002 [DDD]
Sparke, P.:Fant Eup, w. H. Snell (cnd), Brittania Building Society Band Doyen ▲ CD 002 [DDD]
Stephens, D.:Rhap Eup, w. H. Snell (cnd), Brittania Building Society Band Doyen ▲ CD 002 [DDD]

Childs, Robert (eup)
Bowen, B.:Eup Music, w. H. Snell (cnd), Brittania Building Society Band Doyen ▲ CD 002 [DDD]
Golland, J.:Con 1 Eup, w. H. Snell (cnd), Brittania Building Society Band Doyen ▲ CD 002 [DDD]
Howarth, E.:Cantabile for John Fletcher, w. Nicholas Childs (eup) Doyen ▲ CD 002 [DDD]
Phillips, John:Romance, w. Nicholas Childs (eup), H. Snell (cnd), Brittania Building Society Band Doyen ▲ CD 002 [DDD]

Chiles, R. (pno)
Van Appledorn, M.J.:Liquid Gold, w. D. Underwood (sax) Opus One ▲ 147

Chilingirian, Levon (vn)—see also ORCHESTRAS & ENSEMBLES Chilingirian String Quartet
Beethoven, L. van:Serenade Fl, Op. 25, w. S. Milan (fl), L. Williams (va) Chandos ▲ CHAN 9108 [DDD]
Scharwenka, X.:Qt Pno, w. Seta Tanyel (pno), Ivo-Jan Van Der Werff (va), Garbis Atmacayan (vc) Collins Classics ▲ COL 1419 [DDD]
Scharwenka, X.:Trio 2 Pno, w. Seta Tanyel (pno), Garbis Atmacayan (vc) Collins Classics ▲ COL 1419 [DDD]
Tippett, M.:Triple Con, w. Simon Rowland-Jones (va), Philip de Groote (vc), R. Hickox (cnd), Bournemouth SO Chandos ▲ CHAN 9384 [DDD]

Chinn, Genevieve (pno)
Brings, A.:Son Pno Centaur ▲ CRC 2156
Brings, A.:Trio Cl, Vc & Pno, w. E. Gilmore (cl), A. Kouguell (vc) *(rec 1989-90)* Centaur ▲ CRC 2079 [ADD]
Clementi, M.:Sons Pno 4-Hands, w. A. Brings (pno)—Sons., Opp. 3/2; 6/1; 14/1 & 3 Centaur ▲ CRC 2046 [AAD]

Chinski, Rick (gtr)
Encore, w. Colorado Children's Chorale [cnd:Duain Wolfe], Robert Davine (acc), Laurie Kahler (pno), Samuel Lancaster (pno), Barry Oliver (pno), Marylin Preston (fl), Karen Yonovitz (fl), Peter Cooper (ob), Andy Stevens (cl), Lionel Young (vn), Basil Vendreys (va), Wayne Templeman (vc), Charle *(rec Denver Center Media)* Colorado Children's Chorale ▲ 001

Chircop, Natascha (pno)
Vella, J.:Con Pno, w. J. Vella (cnd), Sofia SO Gega ▲ GR 40

Chirivi, N. (vc)
Handel, G.F.:Con for 2 Vns & Vc, w. M. Domini (vn), A. Reale (vn), M. Peca (cnd), Rome Stradivari Ensemble Bongiovanni ▲ GB 2100 [DDD]

Chisholm, Sally (va)—see ORCHESTRAS & ENSEMBLES Thouvenel String Quartet

Chislett, Laura (fl)
The Flute Ascendant Vox Australis ▲ VAST 007-2

Chitta, A. (vc)
Füssl, K.H.:Duo Vc & Pno, w. S. Chitta (pno) *(rec Vienna, Jan. 1989)* Vienna Modern Masters ▲ VMM 2010 [DDD]
Hueber, K.A.:Capriccio Vc *(rec Vienna, Jan. 1989)* Vienna Modern Masters ▲ VMM 2010 [DDD]
Hueber, K.A.:Son 2 Vc *(rec Vienna, Jan. 1989)* Vienna Modern Masters ▲ VMM 2010 [DDD]
Hueber, K.A.:Son Vc & Pno, w. S. Chitta (pno) *(rec Vienna, Jan. 1989)* Vienna Modern Masters ▲ VMM 2010 [DDD]

Chitta, S. (pno)
Füssl, K.H.:Duo Vc & Pno, w. A. Chitta (vc) *(rec Vienna, Jan. 1989)* Vienna Modern Masters ▲ VMM 2010 [DDD]
Füssl, K.H.:Fünf Töne—Fünf Finger *(rec Vienna, Jan. 1989)* Vienna Modern Masters ▲ VMM 2010 [DDD]
Hueber, K.A.:Son Vc & Pno, w. A. Chitta (vc) *(rec Vienna, Jan. 1989)* Vienna Modern Masters ▲ VMM 2010 [DDD]
Hueber, K.A.:Son Pno *(rec Vienna, Jan. 1989)* Vienna Modern Masters ▲ VMM 2010 [DDD]

Chiu, Frederic (pno)
Busoni, F.:Bach Transcriptions—Three Chorale Preludes—Nun komm die heiden Heiland; Nun freut euch, liebe Christen; Wachet auf, ruft uns die Stimme Harmonia Mundi USA ▲ HMU 907054
Busoni, F.:Pno Music—Schoenberg's Klavierstück, Op. 11, No. 2 [trans.] Harmonia Mundi USA ▲ HMU 907054
Decaux, A.:Clairs de lune Harmonia Mundi France ▲ HMU 907166
Liszt, F.:Operatic Paraphrases & Transcriptions Harmonia Mundi USA ▲ HMU 907054
Liszt, F.:Song Transcriptions—Schubert:Horst, horst die Lerche; Der Lindenbaum; Schumann Harmonia Mundi USA ▲ HMU 907054
Liszt, F.:Transcriptions & Paraphrases—Rossini:William Tell Overture *(rec July 1992)* Harmonia Mundi USA ▲ HMU 907102
Mendelssohn, F.:Rondo capriccioso Harmonia Mundi USA ▲ HMU 907117
Mendelssohn, F.:Son Pno, Op. 6 Harmonia Mundi USA ▲ HMU 907117
Mendelssohn, F.:Son Pno, Op. 105 Harmonia Mundi USA ▲ HMU 907117
Mendelssohn, F.:Son Pno, Op. 106 Harmonia Mundi USA ▲ HMU 907117
Piano Transcriptions Harmonia Mundi ▲ HMU 907054
Prokofiev, S.:Cinderella Pno, Op. 95 Harmonia Mundi USA ▲ HMU 907150
Prokofiev, S.:Cinderella Pno, Op. 97 Harmonia Mundi USA ▲ HMU 907150
Prokofiev, S.:Lt Kijé Suite—Romance & The Marriage of Kijé [trans Chiu for pno] Harmonia Mundi USA 3-▲ HMU 907086/88
Prokofiev, S.:Pieces Pno, Op. 3 Harmonia Mundi France ▲ HMU 907169
Prokofiev, S.:Pieces Pno, Op. 4 Harmonia Mundi France ▲ HMU 907169
Prokofiev, S.:Pieces Pno, Op. 52 Harmonia Mundi ▲ HMU 907189
Prokofiev, S.:Pieces Pno, Op. 59 Harmonia Mundi ▲ HMU 907189
Prokofiev, S.:Pieces Pno, Op. 96 Harmonia Mundi USA ▲ HMU 907150

INSTRUMENT.

Chiu, Frederic (pno) (cont.)
Prokofiev, S.:Romeo & Juliet Pno Harmonia Mundi USA ▲ HMU 907150
Prokofiev, S.:Sarcasms Harmonia Mundi France ▲ HMU 907169
Prokofiev, S.:Sons Pno (comp)—Nos. 1-9 Harmonia Mundi USA 3-▲ HMU 907086/88
Prokofiev, S.:Son 1 Pno Harmonia Mundi ▲ HMU 907197
Prokofiev, S.:Son 2 Pno Harmonia Mundi ▲ HMU 907197
Prokofiev, S.:Son 3 Pno Harmonia Mundi ▲ HMU 907197
Prokofiev, S.:Son 4 Pno Harmonia Mundi ▲ HMU 907197
Prokofiev, S.:Son 5 Pno Harmonia Mundi ▲ 907198
Prokofiev, S.:Son 6 Pno Harmonia Mundi ▲ 907198
Prokofiev, S.:Son 7 Pno Harmonia Mundi ▲ 907198
Prokofiev, S.:Son 8 Pno Harmonia Mundi ("Production USA" series) ▲ HMU 907199
Prokofiev, S.:Son 9 Pno Harmonia Mundi ("Production USA" series) ▲ HMU 907199
Prokofiev, S.:Sonatinas Pno Harmonia Mundi ▲ HMU 907189
Prokofiev, S.:Toccata Pno Harmonia Mundi France ▲ HMU 907169
Prokofiev, S.:Visions fugitives Harmonia Mundi France ▲ HMU 907169
Prokofiev, S.:Waltzes (suite) Harmonia Mundi USA ▲ HMU 907054
Rachmaninoff, S.:Pno Transcriptions—Bach—Prelude, Gavotte & Gigue from the Violin Partita in E (1933); Schubert—Wohin? (1925) Harmonia Mundi USA ▲ HMU 907054 ■
Ravel, M.:Miroirs Harmonia Mundi France ▲ HMU 907166
Rossini, G.:Péchés de vieillesse (sels)—Awakening with a Start; A Deep Sleep; Enough of Souvenirs—Let's Dance; A Nightmare; Souvenirs of Man; Specimen of My Time; The Would-Be Dramatic Prelude *(rec July 1992)* Harmonia Mundi USA ▲ HMU 907102
Schoenberg, A.:Pieces Pno, Op. 11 Harmonia Mundi France ▲ HMU 907166
Schulz-Evler, A.:Arabesque on Themes from Johann Strauss' *The Beautiful Blue Danube* Harmonia Mundi USA ▲ HMU 907054

Chiu, Tom Teh (vn)
Baley, V.:Con 1 quasi una fant, w. J. Sachs (cnd), New Juilliard Ensemble *(rec Juilliard School, NYC, Apr 22, June 21, July 12)* Cambria ▲ CD 1087

Chivers, Dana (gtr)
Matiegka, W.T.:Grand Trio Vn, Va & Gtr, w. H. Williams (vn), R. Smissen (va) Erasmus ▲ WVH 086
Matiegka, W.T.:Serenade Fl, Va & Gtr, w. E. Frank (fl), R. Smissen (va) Erasmus ▲ WVH 086

Chiorzempa, D. (org)
Saint-Saëns, C.:Sym 3, w. P. Maag (cnd), Bern SO IMP ▲ IMP 2010

Chmel, Cäcilia (vc)—see ORCHESTRAS & ENSEMBLES Winterthur String Quartet

Chmielewski, Tadeusz (pno)
Szymanowski, K.:Roxana's Song, w. Wanda Wikomirska (vn) Polskie Nagrania ▲ PLN 64 [ADD]
Szymanowski, K.:Son Vn, w. Wanda Wikomirska (vn) Polskie Nagrania ▲ PLN 64 [ADD]

Cho, Young-Chang (vc)
Martinů, B.:Qt 1 Pno, w. Daniel Adni (pno), Isabelle van Keulen (vn), Rainer Moog (va) *(rec Australian Festival of Chamber Music, July 1994)* Naxos ▲ 8.553916 [DDD]
Martinů, B.:Qnt Strs, w. Charmian Gadd (vn), Solomia Soroka (vn), Rainer Moog (va), Theodore Kuchar (va) *(rec Australian Festival of Chamber Music, July 1994)* Naxos ▲ 8.553916 [DDD]

Choate, Carol Beth (org)
Messiaen, O.:Méditations sur le mystère la Sainte Trinité [Austin Cathedral Org, St. Joseph Cathedral, Hartford, CT] Afka ▲ SK 532

Chochlov, Vladimir (pno)
Rachmaninoff, S.:Songs, w. Inessa Galante (sop)—Sing Not to Me Beautiful Maiden [from Songs (6), Op. 4/4 (1890-93)]; They Answered; How Fair This Place [both from Songs (12), Op. 21/4 & 7 (1902)]; Before My Window [from Songs (15), Op.26/10 (1906)] Campion ▲ 1340 [AAD]

Chojnacka, Elisabeth (hpd)
Boucourechliev, A.:Les Archipels, w. Brigitte Sylvestre (hp), Françoise Rieunier (org), Roland Auzet, Jean-Pierre Drouet (perc), Hakon Austbö (pno), Françoise-Frédéric Guy (pno), Claude Helffer (pno), Georges Pludermacher (pno), Ysaÿe String Quartet, Les Pléiades Ensemble Musique Francaise d'Aujourd'hui ("Collection MFA-Radio France" series) ▲ MFA 216001
Constant, M.:Chamber Music, w. Radu Blidar (vn), Bruno Pasquier (va), Francis Pierre (hp) Salabert ▲ SCD 9401
Gubaidulina, S.:Meditation on a Bach Chorale, w. Hanna Weinmeister (vn), Elvira Bekova (vn), Marius Stravinsky (va), Alfia Bekova (vc), Alois Posch (db) *(rec Lockenhaus Festival, Austria, 1995)* BIS ▲ CD 810 [DDD]
Joplin, S.:Music of—Maple Leaf Rag; Magnetic Rag; Elite Syncopations; Peacherine Rag; Kismet Rag; Swipsey; Stoptime; Dethena; Original Rag; Pineapple Rag; Scott Joplin's New Rag; Sunflower Slow Drag; Something Doing Valois ▲ V 4704
Ligeti, G.:Continuum Wergo ▲ WER 60100-50 [DDD]
Ligeti, G.:Hungarian Rock Wergo ▲ WER 60100-50 [DDD]
Ligeti, G.:Passacaglia ungherese Wergo ▲ WER 60100-50 [DDD]

Cholakian, A. (vc)—see ORCHESTRAS & ENSEMBLES Cassatt String Quartet

Cholette, Daniel (pno)
Koechlin, C.:Premier album de Lilian, w. Kathrin Graf (sop), Philippe Racine (fl), Christine Simonin (ondes martinot) Accord ▲ ACD 201232 [DDD]
Koechlin, C.:Second album de Lilian, w. Philippe Racine (fl), Christine Simonin (ondes martinot) Accord ▲ ACD 201232 [DDD]

Chopin, S.-V. (org)
Boëllmann, L.:Suite gothique Studio SM ▲ 12 21.14
Grunenwald, J.-J.:Allégresse Studio SM ▲ 12 21.14
Grunenwald, J.-J.:Improv Org Studio SM ▲ 12 21.14
Grunenwald, J.-J.:La Mélodie Intérieure Studio SM ▲ 12 21.14
Mendelssohn, F.:Sons Org—No. 6 Studio SM ▲ 12 21.14
Reger, M.:Intro, Passacaglia & Fugue Org Studio SM ▲ 12 21.14

Chorberg, Israel (vn)
Surinach, C.:Con Str Orch, w. P. Zinger (cnd), Bronx Arts Ensemble *(rec 1992)* New World ▲ 80428-2
Surinach, C.:Flamenco cyclothymia, w. P. Zinger (pno) *(rec 1992)* New World ▲ 80428-2
Surinach, C.:Qt Pno, w. P. Zinger (pno), Bronx Arts Ensemble *(rec 1992)* New World ▲ 80428-2

Chorzempa, Daniel (org)
Bach, J.S.:Org Music (misc) Philips □ 410038-5
Bach, J.S.:Preludes & Fugues, BWV 531-552—BWV 535, 538, 545, 550 Philips ("Silver Line" series) ▲ 420860-2 [ADD]
Bach, J.S.:Toccata & Fugue Org, BWV 565 Philips ("Silver Line" series) ▲ 420860-2
Mozart, W.A.:Complete Mozart Edition, w. Helmut Winschermann (ob), German Bach Soloists Philips 2-▲ 422521-2 [ADD]
Widor, C.M.:Sym 5 Org Philips ▲ 410054-2 [DDD]
Widor, C.M.:Sym 10 Org Philips ▲ 410054-2 [DDD]

Chou, C. (pno)—see ORCHESTRAS & ENSEMBLES Parnassus Trio

Chribkova, Irena (org)
Eben, Petr:Windows, w. Stanko Arnold (tpt) Multisonic ▲ MUL 310347 [DDD]
Ropek, J.:Org Music—Vars on Victimae Paschali Laudes Multisonic ▲ MUL 310347 [DDD]
Seger, J.:Kbd Music—Toccata & Fugue in a; Pastoral & Fugue on a Czech Christmas Song Multisonic ▲ MUL 310347 [DDD]
Wiedermann, B.A.:Org Music—Toccata & Fugue in f Multisonic ▲ MUL 310347 [DDD]
Zach, J.:Org Music—Prelude & Fugue in c Multisonic ▲ MUL 310347 [DDD]

Christ, P. (ob)
Ginastera, A.:Duo Fl, w. G. Shanley (fl) Crystal ▲ CD 321
Holst, G.:Terzetto Fl, w. Barcellona (fl), J. Dunham (va) Crystal ■ C 647
Persichetti, V.:Parable 3 Crystal ■ C 321
Persichetti, V.:Parable 3 Crystal ▲ CD 321
Schmidt, W.:The Sparrow and The Amazing Mr. Avaunt, w. Vlazinskaya (nar) [E] Crystal ▲ CD 321
Schmidt, W.:The Sparrow and The Amazing Mr. Avaunt, w. Vlazinskaya (nar) Crystal ■ C 321
Still, W.G.:Miniatures, w. G. Shanley (fl), S. Davis (pno) Crystal ■ C 321

Christ, P. (ob) (cont.)
Still, W.G.:Miniatures, w. G. Shanley (fl), S. Davis (pno) Crystal ▲ CD 321
Thompson, R.:Suite Ob, w. Atkins (cl), De Veritch (va) Crystal ▲ CD 321
Thompson, R.:Suite Ob, w. Atkins (cl), De Veritch (va) Crystal ■ C 321

Christ, Wolfram (va)
Bartók, B.:Con Va, w. S. Ozawa (cnd), Berlin PO Deutsche Grammophon ▲ 437993-2 [DDD]
Hindemith, P.:Kammermusik 5, w. C. Abbado (cnd), Berlin PO EMI Classics ▲ CDC 56160
Mozart, W.A.:Sinf concertante Vn, K.364, w. C. Altenburger (va), H. Winschermann (cnd), German Bach Soloists LaserLight ▲ 15 650 [DDD]
Mozart, W.A.:Sinf Concertante, K.364, w. Rainer Kussmaul (vn), C. Abbado (cnd), Berlin PO Sony Classical ▲ SK 66859
Mozart, W.A.:Sinf concertante Vn, K.364, w. C. Altenburger (va), H. Winschermann (cnd), German Bach Soloists LaserLight ▲ 15 880 [DDD]
Schubert, Franz:Qt Fl, w. J. Levine (pno), G. Hetzel (vn), G. Faust (vc), A. Posch (db) Deutsche Grammophon ▲ 431783-2
Schubert, Franz:Qnt Pno, D.667, w. J. Levine (pno), G. Hetzel (vn), G. Faust (vc), A. Posch (db) Deutsche Grammophon ▲ 431783-2

Christensen, Cindy (cl)
Concertos for Clarinets & Military Band, w. D. Christensen (cl), Leipzig Radio Wind Orch [cnd:Motti Miron] Koch Schwann ▲ SCH 310672 [DDD]

Christensen, Don (cl)
Concertos for Clarinets & Military Band, w. Cindy Christensen (cl), Leipzig Radio Wind Orch [cnd:Motti Miron] Koch Schwann ▲ SCH 310672 [DDD]

Christensen, Jacob (gtr)
Cantos de España, w. Michaela Fukacová (vc) Kontrapunkt ▲ 32044 [DDD]
Nørholm, I.:Chamber Music, w. B. Rørbeck (vn), N. Ullner (vc), P. Salo (pno/hpd), G. Sørensen (perc), Kuhlau Flute Quartet—Before Silence, Op. 83; Contrast-Continuum, Op. 70; Guitar Sonata No. 2; The Orthodox Dream; So to Say, Op. 74; Turbulens-Laminar, Op. 93; Variants, Op. 19 *(rec 9/90)* Kontrapunkt ▲ 32065 [DDD]

Christensen, Jens E. (org)
Bach, J.S.:Chorale Preludes Org—Chorale Preludes, BWV 552a, 552b, 669-689 & 802-805 Kontrapunkt 2-▲ 32055/56 [DDD]
Brorson, H.A.:Hymns, w. Aage Haugland (bass)—Arise! All That God Hath Made; Here Come Your Little Poor Beings; The Loveliest Rose is Found; My Heart Always Abides; Oh, My Rose Withers Away; The One That God Hath Born & Bred; My Bridegroom, the Delicate, Handsome & Sweet; Peace is the Best Treasure of the Soul; others Kontrapunkt ▲ KPT 32214 [DDD]
Gubaidulina, S.:In Croce, w. H. Brendstrup (vc) Kontrapunkt ▲ KPT 32176 [DDD]
Iberian Organ Music (1500-1750) Kontrapunkt ▲ 32035 [DDD]
Nørgård, P.:Org Music—Canon; Partita Concertante; Trepartita *(rec 4/91)* Kontrapunkt ▲ 32081 [DDD]

Christensen, Ketil (tpt)
Danish Chirstmas Carols, w. St. Annae Girls' Choir, Flemming Dreisig (org), Erling Pedersen (org) Danica ▲ DCD 8103
Hansen, T.:Con Waltz, w. Jøorgen Andersen (pno) *(rec Anneberg Mansion, Denmark, 1982)* Rondo Grammofon ▲ RCD 8350
Hansen, T.:Qnt Brass, w. Bjarne Nielsen (tpt), Mogens Andresen (eup), Keld Jørgensen (trbn), Henning Hansen (Fr hn) *(rec Anneberg Mansion, Denmark, 1983)* Rondo Grammofon ▲ RCD 8350
Hansen, T.:Romance Tpt, w. Jøorgen Andersen (pno) *(rec Anneberg Mansion, Denmark, 1982)* Rondo Grammofon ▲ RCD 8350
Hansen, T.:Scherzo Tpt, w. Jøorgen Andersen (pno) *(rec Anneberg Mansion, Denmark, 1982)* Rondo Grammofon ▲ RCD 8350
Hansen, T.:Son Tpt, w. Jørgen Andersen (pno) *(rec Anneberg Mansion, Denmark, 1982)* Rondo Grammofon ▲ RCD 8350
Haydn, J.:Con Tpt, w. H. Farkač (cnd), Boemia CO Rondo Grammofon ▲ RCD 8337
Horovitz, J.:Concertino Classico, w. Ole Andersen (tpt), H. Farkač (cnd), Boemia CO Rondo Grammofon ▲ RCD 8337
Horovitz, J.:Concertino Classico, w. Ole Andersen (tpt), J.M. Jensen (cnd), Danish Concert Band Rondo Grammofon ▲ RCD 8340
Hummel, J.N.:Con in E♭ Tpt, S.49, w. H. Farkač (cnd), Boemia CO Rondo Grammofon ▲ RCD 8337
Jørgensen, A.:Caprice orientale, w. Jøorgen Andersen (pno) *(rec Anneberg Mansion, Denmark, 1982)* Rondo Grammofon ▲ RCD 8350
Jørgensen, A.:Qnt Brass, w. Bjarne Nielsen (tpt), Mogens Andresen (eup), Keld Jørgensen (trbn), Henning Hansen (Fr hn) *(rec Anneberg Mansion, Denmark, 1983)* Rondo Grammofon ▲ RCD 8350
Langgaard, R.:Ribe Early Morning, w. Bjarne Nielsen (tpt), Mogens Andresen (eup), Keld Jørgensen (trbn), Henning Hansen (Fr hn) *(rec Anneberg Mansion, Denmark, 1986)* Rondo Grammofon ▲ RCD 8350
Martinussen, L.:Dialogue, w. Ole Andersen (tpt), J.M. Jensen (cnd), Danish Concert Band Rondo Grammofon ▲ RCD 8340
Roussel, A.:Chamber Music, w. Majken Bjerno (sop), Toke Lund Christiansen (fl), Bjørn Carl Nielsen (ob), Niels Thomsen (cl), Per Jacobsen (hn), Asger Svendsen (bn), Ketil Christensen (tpt), Anne Søe Hansen (vn), Zwi Carmelli (va), Piotr Zelazny (va), Niels Ullner (vc), Michael Dabelsteen (db), Tine Rehling (hp), Morten Mogensen (pno), Per Salo (pno), Per Jensen (perc)—Divertissement, Op. 6; Trio, Op. 40; Joueurs de Flute, Op. 27; Serenade, Op. 30; Le marchand de sable qui passe, Op. 13; Andante et scherzo, Op. 13; 2 poèmes de ronsard, Op. 26; Aria; Elpenor, Op. 59; Pipe Kontrapunkt 2-▲ KPT 32218 [DDD]
Sehested, H.:Suite Cnt, w. Alice Nørregaard (pno) [arr. Christensen & Nørregaard] *(rec Anneberg Mansion, Denmark, 1995)* Rondo Grammofon ▲ RCD 8350
Tartini, G.:Con Tpt, w. H. Farkač (cnd), Boemia CO Rondo Grammofon ▲ RCD 8337
Trumpet Concertos, Vol. 2, w. Ole Andersen (tpt), Lars Ole Schmidt (tpt), Boemia CO [cnd:Hynec Farkac] Rondo Grammofon ▲ RCD 8339
Trumpet Concertos, Vol. 3, w. Ole Andersen (tpt), Lars Ole Schmidt (tpt), Moravian-Silesian CO [cnd:Preben Norgaard Christensen, Pavel Vitek] Rondo Grammofon ▲ RCD 8345
Vivaldi, A.:Con for 2 Tpts, w. Ole Andersen (tpt), H. Farkač (cnd), Boemia CO Rondo Grammofon ▲ RCD 8337

Christensen, Leif (gtr)
Llobet, M.:Gtr Music—Variaciones sobre un tema de Sor; Preludios in E & A; Romanza in c; Estudio in E; Estudio Capricho in D; Mazurka; Scherzo-Vals; Canciones Populares Catalanas *(rec Kollemorten, Denmark, May-June 1982)* Paula ▲ PACD 59 [AAD]
Tárrega, F.:Gtr Music—Preludes Nos. 2 & 5; Marieta; Adelita; transciptions by Albéniz [Pavana-capricho, Op. 12], Schumann [Au soir, Op. 12] & Thalberg [Tema y estudio de concierto] *(rec Fruering Kirke, Denmark, Oct 1987)* Paula ▲ PACD 59 [AAD]

Christensen, Roy (vc)—see also ORCHESTRAS & ENSEMBLES L'Atelier String Trio
Adler, S.:Trio 2 Pno, w. Elizabeth Wright (pno), Veronica Kadlubkiewicz (vn) Gasparo ▲ GS 298 [DDD/DAD]
Hindemith, P.:Son Vc, Op. 25/3 Gasparo ▲ 1009
Hindemith, P.:Stücke (4) Bn & Vc, w. Otto Eifert (bn) Gasparo ▲ 1009

Christensen, Virginia (va)—see also ORCHESTRAS & ENSEMBLES L'Atelier String Trio
Sowerby, L.:Songs, w. D'Anna Fortunato (mez), Veronica Macchia-Kadlubkiewicz (vn), Tessa van Buskirk (vn), Michael Curry (vc)—Premonition; Kisses; Midnight; Reassurance; Adventure [all text L. E. Thomas] Gasparo ▲ GSCD 315 [DDD]

Christian, Thomas (vn)—see ORCHESTRAS & ENSEMBLES Vienna String Quintet

Christiansen, Anne Lund (vc)
Haydn, J.:Trios Pno, Fl & Vc, w. Elisabeth Westenholz (pno), Toke Lund Christiansen (fl) Kontrapunkt ▲ 32071 [DDD]
Kuhlau, F.:Grand Trio, w. T. L. Christiansen (fl), E. Westenholz (pno) [arr fl, vc & pno] Kontrapunkt ▲ 32064 [DDD]
Martinů, B.:Trio Fl, w. T.L. Christiansen (fl), E. Westenholz (pno) Kontrapunkt ▲ 32064 [DDD]

Christiansen, Asger Lund (vc)—see ORCHESTRAS & ENSEMBLES Copenhagen String Quartet

508 ▲ = CD ♦ = Enhanced CD Δ = MD ■ = Cassette Tape □ = DCC

Christiansen, Clay (org)
Pipe Organ of the Mormon Tabernacle, Salt Lake City Klavier ▲ KCD 11044 [DDD] ■ KC 7044
Christiansen, J. B. (hpd)
Mattheson, J.:Sons Trns Fl, w. T. L. Christiansen (tran fl) Kontrapunkt 2-▲ 32060/61 [DDD]
Christiansen, Toke Lund (fl)—see also ORCHESTRAS & ENSEMBLES Collegium Musicum Soloists
Andersen, J.:Fl & Pno Music, w. P. Salo (pno)—Valse Caprice, Op. 44; Impromptu, Op. 7; Morceaux pour la flûte, Op. 57; Fant on Bellini's *Norma;* Leichte Stücke, Op. 56; 8 Vortragsstücke, Op. 55 *(rec Mar 1991)* Kontrapunkt ▲ 32079 [DDD]
Beethoven, L. van:Qnt Fl, Vn, 2 Vas & Vc, w. J. Søe Hansen (vn), H. Olsen (va), M. Dolgin (va), T.S. Hermansen (vc) Kontrapunkt 2-▲ 32160/61 [DDD]
Entr'acte, w. M. Debost (fl), Tine Rehling (hp) Kontrapunkt ▲ 32043 [DDD]
Haydn, J.:Qts Strs, Op. 77, "Lobkowitz Qts", w. Elisabeth Westenholz (pno) [arr. for flute & piano]—No. 1 Kontrapunkt ▲ 32071 [DDD]
Haydn, J.:Trios Pno, Fl & Vc, w. Elisabeth Westenholz (pno), Anne Lund Christiansen (vc) Kontrapunkt ▲ 32071 [DDD]
Ibert, J.:Pièce Fl Kontrapunkt ▲ KPT 32202
Ives, C.:Son 2 Pno, w. P. Salo (pno), J. Jorgensen (va) Kontrapunkt ▲ 32046 [DDD]
Kuhlau, F.:Grand Trio, w. A. L. Christiansen (vc), E. Westenholz (pno) [arr fl, vc & pno] Kontrapunkt ▲ 32064 [DDD]
Kuhlau, F.:Qnts Fl, w. J. Søe Hansen (vn), M. Dolgin (va), H. Olsen (va), T.S. Hermansen (vc) Kontrapunkt 2-▲ 32160/61 [DDD]
Kuhlau, F.:Sons Fl (comp), w. E. Westenholz (pno)—Sonatas Op. 64, Op. 69, Op. 71, Op. 83/1-3, Op. 85, Op. 110/1-3 Kontrapunkt 3-▲ 32114/16 [DDD]
Maegaard, J.:Canon, w. Henrik Svitzer (fl), Ulla Miilmann Jørgensen (fl) *(rec Copenhagen, 1995-96)* Marco Polo/Dacapo ▲ 8.224050 [DDD]
Martinů, B.:Trio Fl, w. A. L. Christiansen (vc), E. Westenholz (pno) Kontrapunkt ▲ 32064 [DDD]
Mattheson, J.:Sons Trns Fl, w. J. B. Christiansen (hpd) Kontrapunkt 2-▲ 32060/61 [DDD]
Nielsen, C.:Con Fl, w. M. Schønwandt (cnd), Danish National RSO Chandos ▲ CHAN 8894 [DDD]
Nørholm, I.:Chamber Music, w. B. Rørbech (vn), M. Vitek (vn), H. Olsen (va), I. Olsen (gtr), N. Ullner (vc), A. Øland (pno)—Essai Prismatique; Medusa's Shadow; Mosaic; Prelude to My Wintermorning; Sonata Quasi Variazioni *(rec 2/89)* Kontrapunkt ▲ 32019 [DDD]
Roussel, A.:Chamber Music, w. Majken Bjerno (sop), Bjørn Carl Nielsen (ob), Niels Thomsen (cl), Per Jacobsen (hn), Asger Svendsen (bn), Ketil Christensen (tpt), Anne Søe Hansen (vn), Zwi Carmelli (va), Piotr Zelazny (va), Niels Ullner (vc), Michael Dabelsteen (db), Tine Rehling (hp), Morten Mogensen (pno), Per Salo (pno), Per Jensen (perc)—Divertissement, Op. 6; Trio, Op. 40; Joueurs de Flute, Op. 27; Serenade, Op. 30; Le marchand de sable qui passe, Op. 13; Andante et scherzo, Op. 13; 2 poèmes de ronsard, Op. 26; Aria; Elpenor, Op. 59; Pipe Kontrapunkt 2-▲ KPT 32218 [DDD]
Schubert, Franz:Intro & Vars Fl on "Tröckne Blumen", w. et al. [octet arr. by Christiansen for flute, strings & winds] Kontrapunkt ▲ 32024 [DDD]
Schubert, Franz:Qt Fl, w. H. Olsen (va), I. Olsen (gtr), N. Ullner (vc) Kontrapunkt ▲ 32024 [DDD]
Schubert, Franz:Son Arpeggione, w. E. Westenholz (pno) [flute-piano version] Kontrapunkt ▲ 32024 [DDD]

Christiansson, Bengt (fl)
Rangström, T.:Vauxhall, w. Lars Olof Loman (ob), Lars Almgren (cl), Sven Aarflot (bn), Rolf Bengtsson (hn), Rune Bodin (trbn), Rozalina Skytt (hp), O. Vänskä (cnd), Stockholm PO *(rec Stockholm Concert Hall, Jan. 16 & 18, 1985)* Caprice ▲ CAP 21195 [DDD]
Christie, James David (org)
Pinkham, D.:Christmas Cant, w. Lenox Brass, Boston Cecilia *(rec Dec. 1992)* Koch International Classics ▲ KIC 7180 [DDD]
Pinkham, D.:Son 3 Vns, w. J. Sedares (cnd), London SO Koch International Classics ▲ KIC 7179 [DDD]
Sweelinck, J.P.:Org Music [the C.B. Fisk Organ at Houghton Chapel, Wellesley College]—Toccata in C; Ball del granduca; Ricercar; Malle Sijmen; Mein junges Leben hat ein End'; Echo Fantasia in a; Onder een linde groen; Toccata in a; Erbarm dich mein, o Herr Naxos ▲ 8.550904 [DDD]
Christie, William (hpd)
Couperin, F.:L'Apothéose de Lully, w. Christophe Rousset (hpd) Harmonia Mundi 12-▲ 2901442.52
Fischer, J.C. Ferdinand:Musicalischer Parnassus—Nos. 6, "Euterpe" & 9, "Urania" Musique d'Abord ▲ HMA 1901026
Fischer, J.C. Ferdinand:Praeludium 6 & 8 Musique d'Abord ▲ HMA 1901026
Purcell, H.:Dido & Aeneas, w. Véronique Gens (sop—Dido), Sophie Marin-Degor (sop—Belinda), Sophie Daneman (sop—2nd woman/1st witch), Gaëlle Mechaly (sop—2nd witch), Claire Brua (mez—Sorceress), Steve Dugardin (alt—Chorus), Jean-Paul Fouchécourt (ten—Spirit/Sailor), Nathan Berg (b-bar—Aeneas), Jonathan Arnold (bass—Chorus), W. Christie (cnd), Les Arts Florissants *(rec Massy Opera Theatre, Nov. 8-11, 1994)* Erato ▲ 98477-2 [DDD]
Purcell, H.:Songs, w. A. Deller (ct), R. Skeaping (vn), W. Kuijken (vl), J. Ryan (vl), R. Elliott (hpd)—An Evening Hymn; Fairest Isle; From Rosy Bow'rs; I Attempt From Love's Sickness; If Music Be the Food of Love; Not All My Torments; O Lead Me to Some Peaceful Gloom; O Solitude; The Plaint; Retired From My Dear Astrea's Sight; Sweeter Than Roses; Thrice Happy Lovers *(rec April 1979)* Harmonia Mundi ▲ HML 590249
Rameau, J.P.:Nouvelles suites Musique d'Abord 2-▲ HMA 1901120/21
Rameau, J.P.:Pièces de clavecin avec une méthode sur la mécanique des doigts Musique d'Abord 2-▲ HMA 1901120/21
Royer, J.-N.-P.:Pièces de clavecin Musique d'Abord ▲ HMA 1901037
Christie, William (org)
Campra, A.:Motets, w. J. Nicolas (sop), A.-M. Lasla (bass vl)—O Dulcis amor; Salve Regina; Quemadmodum desiderat cervus; Ubi es, deus meus; O Sacrum convivium; Jubilate deo Pierre Verany ▲ PV.784093 [DDD]
Couperin, F.:L'Apothéose de Lully, w. C. Rousset (hpd)—2-harpsichord version Harmonia Mundi France ▲ HMC 901269 [DDD]
Couperin, F.:Le Parnasse, L'apothéose de Corelli, w. C. Rousset (hpd)—2-harpsichord version Harmonia Mundi France ▲ HMC 901269 [DDD]
Couperin, F.:Pièces de clavecin (sels)—4 selections from Ordres 14-16 for solo harpsichord; Allemande for 2 harpsichords from Ordre 9 [w. C. Rousset] Harmonia Mundi France ▲ HMC 901269 [DDD]

Christof, Josef (pno)
Brown, E.:Tracking Pierrot, w. Andreas Seidel (vn) *(rec Sender Freies Berlin, Jan 16-17, 1995)* Hat Hut ("Now" series) ▲ CD 6177 [DDD]
Christopoulos, Vangelis (ob)
Karaindrou, E.:Film Music, w. Jan Garbarek (t sax), Anthis Sokratis (tpt), Nikos Guinos (cl), Tassos Diakoyiorgis (santouri), Vangelis Skouras (hn), Petros Protopapas (fl), Andreas Tsekouras (acc), Christos Sfetsas (vc), Eleni Karaindrou (pno/voc), L. Chalkiadakis (cnd), *(ensemble unknown)*—Farewell Theme; Scream; Improv. On Farewell & Waltz Theme; Farewell Theme II [all from The Beekeeper; w. Jan Garbarek (ten sax), Tassos Diakoyiorgis (satouri), Vassilis Dertilis (kbd), Eleni Karaindrou (pno), Lefteris Chalkiadakis (cnd)]; Elegy for Rosa; Rosa's Song (text:Christofis) [both from Rosa; w. Vangelis Skouras (Fr hn), Petros Protopapas (fl), Alekos Christidis (timp), Eleni Karaindrou (voc), Lefteris Chalkiadakis (cnd)]; Fairytale; Parade; Return; Song [all from Happy Homecoming, Comrade; w. Vangelis Skouras (Fr hn), Christos Sfetsas (vc), Aliki Krithari (hp), Andreas Tsekouras (acc), Eleni Karaindrou (pno), Nelli Semitekolo (pno), Anthis Sokratis (tpt), Lefteris Chalkiadakis (cnd)]; Wandering in Alexandria (2 vers) [both from Wandering; w. Tassos Diakoyiorgis (santouri), Nelli Semitekolo (prepared pno), Anthis Sokratis (tpt), Nikos Guinos (cl), Katerina Ktona (hpd), Christos Sfetsas (vc)]; The Journey [from Voyage to Cythera]; Adagio [from Landscape in the Mist] [both w. Vangelis Christopoulos (ob), str orch, Lefteris Chalkiadakis (cnd)] ECM ▲ 78118-21429-2 [AAD]
Karaindrou, E.:The Suspended Step of the Stork, w. Ada Rouva (hp), Christos Sfetsas (vc), Nikos Spinoulas (hn), Andreas Tsekouras (acc), Dimitris Vraskos (vn), L. Chalkiadakis (cnd), *(orch unknown) (rec Sound, Athens, Apr & Aug 1991)* ECM ▲ 78118-21456-2 [AAD]
Christy, Judy (instr)
Brooke, N.:Obomobile, w. Brandon Adrien, Jennifer Baker, Karen Birch, Daniel Cate, Richard Cochran, Jessica Cooper, Leslie Dominguez, Erin Hannigan, Dorothy Knight, Jason Lichtenwalter, Jay Moore, Hwa-Ling Russell, Toyin Spellman, Sarah Weiner, Jay Weinland Opus One ▲ CD 160

Chtchennikov, Viatcheslav (tpt)
Shostakovich, D.:Con 1 Pno, w. Valentina Lisitsa (pno), S. Caldwell (cnd), Ekaterinburg PO Audiofon ▲ CD 72060
Chubinishvili, Otar (vc)—see ORCHESTRAS & ENSEMBLES Georgian State String Quartet
Chuchra, Josef (vc)—see ORCHESTRAS & ENSEMBLES Suk Trio
Chuchro, Josef (vc)
Dvořák, A.:Con Vc, w. V. Neumann (cnd), Czech PO Supraphon ▲ SUP CD 3093
Dvořák, A.:Qts Pno Strs, Opp. 23 & 87, w. J. Hála (pno), Suk (vn), J. Kodousek (va)—Op. 23 & Op. 87 Supraphon ▲ 11 1464-2 [DDD]
Martinů, B.:Con 1 Vc, w. Z. Košler (cnd), Czech PO Supraphon ▲ SUP CD 3093
Martinů, B.:Sons Vc, w. J. Hála (pno) Supraphon ▲ SUP 110992 [DDD]
Chumachenco, Ana (vn)
Reger, M.:Romanze Vn, w. A. Kontarsky (pno) Tudor ▲ TUD 755 [DDD]
Reger, M.:Serenades Fl, Opp. 77a & 141a, w. A. Adorján (fl), O. Lysy (va) Tudor ▲ TUD 755 [DDD]
Reger, M.:Suite Vn Pno, w. A. Kontarsky (pno) Tudor ▲ TUD 755 [DDD]
Schubert, Franz:Son Vn, D.574, w. R. Gothoni (pno) Ondine ▲ ODE 746-2 [DDD]
Schubert, Franz:Sonatinas Vn, w. R. Gothoni (pno) Ondine ▲ ODE 746-2 [DDD]
Chumbley, Robert (pno)
Copland, A.:Qt Pno, w. Broyhill Chamber Ensemble *(rec Appalachian State Univ, July 1995)* MMC ▲ MMC 2041 [DDD]
Chung, Hye-Yun (hp)—see also ORCHESTRAS & ENSEMBLES Louisiana State Univ New Music Ensemble
Constantinides, D.:Vocal Music, w. Cynthia Dewey (nar), Angela DeVerger (sop), Evelyn Petros (sop), Susan Faust Straley (sop), Eugenia Epperson (fl), Richard Jernigan (cl), Kelly Smith Toney (vn), Stephen Brown (pno), John Raush (perc), D. Constantinides (cnd), Louisiana State Univ New Music Ensemble—Reflections IV for Sop, Fl, Hp & Pno; Intimations [1 Act Opera]; 4 Songs on Poems by Sappho; Mutability for Sop & Str Qt.; 4 Greek Songs Vestige ▲ 04
Debussy, C.:Son Vn, w. R. Lupu (pno) London ▲ 421154-2 [ADD]
Chung, Hye-Yun (vn)
Mendelssohn, F.:Con in e Vn & Orch, Op. 64, w. C. Dutoit (cnd), Montreal SO London ▲ 410011-2 [DDD]
Chung, Jae-Guk (piri)
Kim, J.H.:Piri Qt, w. Park Jong-Sol (piri), Yang Myung-Sok (piri), Joseph Celli (ob/E hn) O. O. Discs ▲ 0024
Chung, Kyung-Wha (vn)—see also ORCHESTRAS & ENSEMBLES Chung Trio
Bach, J.S.:A Musical Offering, w. J. Galway (fl), P. Moll (hpd)—Trio Sonata Section RCA Red Seal ("Papillon Collection" series) ▲ 6517-2-RG [ADD] ■ 6517-4-RG
Bach, J.S.:Son Fl, BWV 1079, w. J. Galway (fl), P. Moll (hpd), M. Welsh (vc) RCA Gold Seal ("Papillon Collection" series) ▲ 6517-2-RG [ADD] ■ 6517-4-RG
Bach, J.S.:Trio Son for 2 Fls, BWV 1039, w. J. Galway (fl), P. Moll (hpd), M. Welsh (vc) RCA Gold Seal ("Papillon Collection" series) ▲ 6517-2-RG [ADD] ■ 6517-4-RG
Bartók, B.:Con 1 Vn, w. G. Solti (cnd), Chicago SO London ▲ 425015-2 [DDD/ADD]
Bartók, B.:Con 2 Vn, w. S. Rattle (cnd), City of Birmingham SO EMI Classics ▲ CDC 54211
Bartók, B.:Con 2 Vn, w. G. Solti (cnd), London PO London ▲ 425015-2 [ADD/DDD]
Bartók, B.:Rhaps (2) Vn & Orch, w. S. Rattle (cnd), City of Birmingham SO EMI Classics ▲ CDC 54211
Beethoven, L. van:Con Vn, Op. 61, w. K. Tennstedt (cnd), London PO EMI Classics ▲ CDC 54072
Beethoven, L. van:Con Vn, Op. 61, w. K. Kondrashin (cnd), Vienna PO London ("Ovation" series) ▲ 430752-2 [DDD]
Beethoven, L. van:Con Vn, Op. 61, w. K. Kondrashin (cnd), Vienna PO London ("Jubilee" series) ▲ 425035-2 [ADD]
Beethoven, L. van:Trio 6 Pno, "Archduke", w. M.-W. Chung (pno), M.-W. Chung (vc) EMI Classics ▲ CDC 55187
Beethoven, L. van:Trio 7 Pno, w. M.-W. Chung (pno), M.-W. Chung (vc) EMI Classics ▲ CDC 55187
Bruch, M.:Con 1 Vn, w. K. Tennstedt (cnd), London PO EMI Classics ▲ CDC 54072
Bruch, M.:Scottish Fant Vn, w. R. Kempe (cnd), Royal PO London ("Jubilee" series) ▲ 425035-2 [ADD]
Dvořák, A.:Con Vn, w. R. Muti (cnd), Philadelphia Orch EMI Classics ▲ CDC 49858 [DDD]
Dvořák, A.:Romance Vn, w. R. Muti (cnd), Philadelphia Orch EMI Classics ▲ CDC 49858 [DDD]
Franck, C.:Son Vn, w. R. Lupu (pno) London ▲ 421154-2 [ADD]
Mendelssohn, F.:Con in e Vn & Orch, Op. 64, w. C. Dutoit (cnd), Montreal SO London ("Ovation" series) ▲ 430752-2 [DDD]
Prokofiev, S.:Cons Vn (comp), w. A. Previn (cnd), London SO London ("Jubilee" series) ▲ 425003-2 [ADD]
Respighi, O.:Son Vn, w. K. Zimerman (pno) Deutsche Grammophon ▲ 427617-2 [DDD]
Saint-Saëns, C.:Havanaise Vn, w. C. Dutoit (cnd), Royal PO London ("Jubilee" series) ▲ 425021-2 [ADD]
Saint-Saëns, C.:Introduction & Rondo capriccioso, w. C. Dutoit (cnd), Royal PO London ("Jubilee" series) ▲ 425021-2 [ADD]
Sibelius, J.:Con Vn, w. A. Previn (cnd), London SO London ("The Classic Sound" series) ▲ 425080-2
Strauss, R.:Son Vn, w. K. Zimerman (pno) Deutsche Grammophon ▲ 427617-2 [DDD]
Stravinsky, I.:Con Vn, w. A. Previn (cnd), London SO London ("Jubilee" series) ▲ 425003-2 [ADD]
Tchaikovsky, P.:Con Vn, w. C. Dutoit (cnd), Montreal SO London ▲ 410011-2 [DDD]
Tchaikovsky, P.:Con Vn, w. C. Dutoit (cnd), Montreal SO London ▲ 430725-2 [DDD]
Tchaikovsky, P.:Con Vn, w. A. Previn (cnd), London SO London ("The Classic Sound" series) ▲ 425080-2
Chung, Myung-Whun (pno)—see also ORCHESTRAS & ENSEMBLES Chung Trio
Beethoven, L. van:Trio 6 Pno, "Archduke", w. K.-W. Chung (vn), M.-W. Chung (vc) EMI Classics ▲ CDC 55187
Beethoven, L. van:Trio 7 Pno, w. K.-W. Chung (vn), M.-W. Chung (vc) EMI Classics ▲ CDC 55187
Berlioz, H.:Songs, w. Cecilia Bartoli (mez)—La Mort d'Ophelie; Zaide London ▲ 452667-2 ■ 452667-4
Bizet, G.:Songs, w. Cecilia Bartoli (mez)—Chant d'amour; Oeuvre ton coeur; Adieux de l'hotesse arabe; Tarantelle; La Coccinelle London ▲ 452667-2 ■ 452667-4
Delibes, L.:Les Filles de Cadix, w. Cecilia Bartoli (mez) London ▲ 452667-2 ■ 452667-4
Ravel, M.:Songs, w. Cecilia Bartoli (mez)—Chanson française; Chanson espagnole; Chanson italienne; Chanson hébraïque; Vocalise-Etude; Kaddisch; L'Enigme eternelle; Tripatos London ▲ 452667-2 ■ 452667-4
Viardot-Garcia, P.:Songs, w. Cecilia Bartoli (mez)—Hai luli; Havanaise; Les Filles de Cadix London ▲ 452667-2 ■ 452667-4
Chung, Myung-Whun (vc)—see also ORCHESTRAS & ENSEMBLES Chung Trio
Beethoven, L. van:Trio 6 Pno, "Archduke", w. M.-W. Chung (pno), K.-W. Chung (vn) EMI Classics ▲ CDC 55187
Beethoven, L. van:Trio 7 Pno, w. M.-W. Chung (pno), K.-W. Chung (vn) EMI Classics ▲ CDC 55187
Chung, Soon-Mi (va)
Hvoslef, K.:Duodu, w. S. Barratt-Due (vn) *(rec 1993)* Victoria ▲ VCD 19067
Mozart, W.A.:Duos Vn, w. S. Barratt-Due (vn) *(rec 1993)* Victoria ▲ VCD 19067
Nordheim, A.:Duplex, w. S. Barratt-Due (vn) *(rec 1993)* Victoria ▲ VCD 19067
Chung-sen, Chen (bamboo fl)
Shui-Lung, M.:Con Bamboo Fl, w. H. Sung-jen (cnd), Yomiuri Nippon SO Sunrise ▲ 8501
Chuprik, Ethella (pno)
Beethoven, L. van:Con 5 Pno, "Emperor", w. R. Seifried (cnd), Czech-Slovak State PO Lydian ▲ LYD 18122
Beethoven, L. van:Son 15 Pno, "Pastoral" Lydian ▲ LYD 18116 [DDD]
Beethoven, L. van:Son 17 Pno, "Tempest" Lydian ▲ LYD 18117 [DDD]
Beethoven, L. van:Son 21 Pno, "Waldstein" Lydian ▲ LYD 18116 [DDD]
Beethoven, L. van:Son 26 Pno, "Les Adieux" Lydian ▲ LYD 18117 [DDD]
Beethoven, L. van:Son 31 Pno Lydian ▲ LYD 18117 [DDD]
Liszt, F.:Mazeppa Pno *(rec Budapest, Mar. 1992)* Lydian ▲ 18121 [DDD]
Liszt, F.:Mephisto Waltz 1 Pno *(rec Budapest, Mar. 1992)* Lydian ▲ 18121 [DDD]

Chuprik, Ethella (pno) (cont.)
Liszt, F.:Nuages gris *(rec Budapest, Mar. 1992)* Lydian ▲ 18121 [DDD]
Liszt, F.:Rhap espagnole *(rec Budapest, Mar. 1992)* Lydian ▲ 18121 [DDD]
Liszt, F.:Son Pno *(rec Budapest, Mar. 1992)* Lydian ▲ 18121 [DDD]
Tchaikovsky, P.:Con 1 Pno, w. R. Seifried (cnd), Czech-Slovak State PO Lydian ▲ LYD 18122
Chuquisengo, Juan Jose (pno)
García, M.:Songs, w. Ernesto Palacio (ten), Juan Carlos Rivera (gtr)—Yo que soy contrabandista; Y otras canciones; I Who Am a Bandit; others Almaviva ▲ 0114
Churchfield, Camille (fl)
Mélange:French Music for Bassoon, w. C. Millard (bn), Kenneth Broadway (pno) Summit ▲ DCD 128 [DDD] ■ DCD 128
Churchill (tpt)
Vivaldi, A.:Con for 2 Tpts, w. P. Jones (tpt), N. Marriner (cnd), Academy of St. Martin in the Fields London ■ 417100-4
Cialini, Annalisa (cel)—see ORCHESTRAS & ENSEMBLES Bilitis Ensemble
Ciampa, Leonard (org)
No Room at the Inn, w. L. Ciampa (org) *(rec 1991-93)* AFKA ▲ SK 428
Ciampi, Maurizio (org)
Demessieux, J.:Etudes (6) *(rec Pontificio Santuario di Pompei, Napoli)* Stradivarius ▲ STV 33384 [DDD]
Demessieux, J.:Méditations sur le Saint Esprit (7) *(rec Pontificio Santuario di Pompei, Napoli)* Stradivarius ▲ STV 33384 [DDD]
Ciancio, Osvaldo (vn)—see ORCHESTRAS & ENSEMBLES Tango 7
Cianfoni, Filippo (fl)—see ORCHESTRAS & ENSEMBLES Rara Ensemble
Ciani, Dino (pno)
Asioli, B.:Capriccio Pno *(rec live, July 14, 1966)* Arkadia 3-▲ 901 [ADD]
Beethoven, L. van:Bagatelles (24)—6 sels, Op. 126 Fonit Cetra ("Italia" series) ▲ FCT CDC 37
Beethoven, L. van:Fant Pno, Op. 80, "Choral Fant", w. R. Muti (cnd), La Scala Orch, La Scala Chorus [G] *(rec live, Milan 11/5/70)* Arkadia ▲ 743 [ADD]
Hummel, J.N.:Rondo Pno *(rec live, Milan, 7/14/66)* Arkadia 3-▲ 901 [ADD]
Hummel, J.N.:Son 2 Pno *(rec live, Milan, 7/14/66)* Arkadia 3-▲ 901 [ADD]
Kozeluch, L.:Son Pno, Op. 35/1 *(rec live, Milan, 7/14/66)* Arkadia 3-▲ 901 [ADD]
Rossini, G.:Péchés de vieillesse—Vol. 7, "Album de chaumière" & Vol. 8, "Album de château" *(rec 1968)* Arkadia 3-▲ 901 [ADD]
Schumann, R.:Novelettes Fonit Cetra ("Italia" series) ▲ FCT CDC 37
Ciani, Suzanne (pno)
Ciani, S.:History of My Heart Private Music ▲ 2058-2-P ■ 2058-4-P
Ciani, S.:Hotel Luna Private Music ▲ 01005-82090-2 ■ 01005-82090-4
Ciani, S.:Neverland Private Music ▲ 2036-2-P ■ 2036-4-P
Ciani, S.:Pianissimo Private Music ▲ 2073-2-P ■ 2073-4-P
Ciani, S.:The Private Music of Suzanne Ciani Private Music ▲ 01005-82103-2 ■ 01005-82103-4
Ciani, S.:Seven Waves Private Music ▲ 2046-2-P ■ 2046-4-P (CrO2)
Ciani, S.:The Velocity of Love Private Music ▲ 01005-82085-2 ■ 01005-82085-4
Ciapparelli, Pierluigi (thb)
Sui Palchi Delle Stelle:Sacred Music in the Neapolitan Conservatories at the Time of Francesco Provenzale, w. [cnd:Antonio Florio], Cappella Pietà de Turchini, Antonella Ippolito (sop), Jane Haughton (sop), Daniela del Monaco (alt), Sebastiano Cassarà (vn), Rosario Di Meglio (vn), Antonella Bologna (va), Paolo Dionisio (vl), Antonio Florio (vc), Enrico Baiano (org/hpd) Symphonia ▲ SY 93S20 [DDD]
Ciaravolo, Sylvain (org)
Corrette, M.:Pièces pour l'orgue dans un genre nouveau [Grandes Org, Koenig de Saint-Avold] Adda ▲ ADD 581138
Grigny, N. de:Premier livre d'orgue [Historic Org of the St Pierre des Chartreux Church, Toulouse] Adda ▲ ADD 581251 [DDD]
Ciarla, Giusi (hp)—see ORCHESTRAS & ENSEMBLES Bilitis Ensemble
Ciccarelli, Enrica (pno)
Beethoven, L. van:Son 28 Pno *(rec Jungle Studios, Milan, Nov 25-27, 1995)* Agora Musica ▲ 029 [DDD]
Mussorgsky, M.:Pictures at an Exhibition Agora Music ▲ 006
Prokofiev, S.:Son 7 Pno Agora Music ▲ 006
Rachmaninoff, S.:Preludes Pno, Opp 23 & 32—Opp. 23/5 & 32/12 Agora Music ▲ 006
Schubert, Franz:Son Pno, D.537 *(rec Jungle Studios, Milan, Nov 25-27, 1995)* Agora Musica ▲ 029 [DDD]
Schumann, C.:Con Pno, w. F. Layer (cnd), Montpellier Languedoc-Roussillon PO—Romanze [w. Cyrille Tricoire (vc)] *(rec Opera Berlioz, Le Corum, Montpellier, June 14-16, 1995)* Agorá ▲ 014 [DDD]
Schumann, R.:Con Pno, w. F. Layer (cnd), Montpellier Languedoc-Roussillon PO *(rec Opera Berlioz, Le Corum, Montpellier, June 14-16, 1995)* Agorá ▲ 014 [DDD]
Weber, C.M. von:Son 2 Pno *(rec Jungle Studios, Milan, Nov 25-27, 1995)* Agora Musica ▲ 029 [DDD]
Ciccolini, A. (vn)—see ORCHESTRAS & ENSEMBLES Modo Antiquo
Ciccolini, Aldo (pno)
Albéniz, I.:Con 1 Pno, w. E. Bátiz (cnd), London SO IMG/Pickwick ▲ PICIMG 1607
Albéniz, I.:España—Cataluña IMG/Pickwick ▲ PICIMG 1607
Albéniz, I.:Iberia Suite, w. E. Bátiz (cnd), London SO IMG/Pickwick ▲ PICIMG 1607
Albéniz, I.:Navarra IMG/Pickwick ▲ PICIMG 1607
Beethoven, L. van:Son 1 Pno *(rec Euphonic Sound Studio, Montebelluna, Italy, Apr 10-11, 1995)* Bongiovanni ▲ GB 5580 [DDD]
Beethoven, L. van:Son 5 Pno *(rec Euphonic Sound Studio, Montebelluna, Italy, June 16-17, 1955)* Bongiovanni ▲ GB 5582 [DDD]
Beethoven, L. van:Son 9 Pno *(rec Euphonic Sound-Studio, Montebelluna, Italy, May 7-8, 1995)* Bongiovanni ▲ GB 5581 [DDD]
Beethoven, L. van:Son 10 Pno *(rec Euphonic Sound-Studio, Montebelluna, Italy, May 7-8, 1995)* Bongiovanni ▲ GB 5581 [DDD]
Beethoven, L. van:Son 11 Pno *(rec Euphonic Sound Studio, Montebelluna, Italy, Apr 10-11, 1995)* Bongiovanni ▲ GB 5580 [DDD]
Beethoven, L. van:Son 14 Pno, "Moonlight Son" *(rec Euphonic Sound Studio, Montebelluna, Italy, Apr 10-11, 1995)* Bongiovanni ▲ GB 5580 [DDD]
Beethoven, L. van:Son 17 Pno, "Tempest" *(rec Euphonic Sound Studio, Montebelluna, Italy, June 16-17, 1955)* Bongiovanni ▲ GB 5582 [DDD]
Beethoven, L. van:Son 20 Pno *(rec Euphonic Sound-Studio, Montebelluna, Italy, May 7-8, 1995)* Bongiovanni ▲ GB 5581 [DDD]
Beethoven, L. van:Son 30 Pno *(rec Euphonic Sound Studio, Montebelluna, Italy, June 16-17, 1955)* Bongiovanni ▲ GB 5582 [DDD]
Beethoven, L. van:Son 32 Pno *(rec Euphonic Sound-Studio, Montebelluna, Italy, May 7-8, 1995)* Bongiovanni ▲ GB 5581 [DDD]
Debussy, C.:La Boîte à joujoux EMI Classics ▲ CDC 54448
Debussy, C.:Pno Music (complete solo)—Etudes, Books 1 & 2; Children's Corner; Etude retrouvée EMI Classics ▲ CDC 54450
Debussy, C.:Pno Music (complete solo)—Preludes, Book 2; Danse bohémienne; (Six) Epigraphes antiques; Hommage à Haydn; Mazurka; Morceau de concours; Page d'album; Le petit nègre; La plus que lente EMI Classics ▲ CDC 54449
Debussy, C.:Pno Music (complete solo)—Deux Arabesques; Berceuse héroïque; D'un cahier d'esquisses; Elégie; L'Isle joyeuse; Masques; Nocturne; Pour le piano; Suite bergamasque; Tarantelle styrienne EMI Classics ▲ CDC 54451
Debussy, C.:Pno Music (complete solo)—Preludes, Book 1; La Boîte à joujoux EMI Classics ▲ CDC 54448
Debussy, C.:Pno Music (complete solo)—Ballade; Estampes; Images 1 & 2; Images oubliées; Rêverie; Valse romantique EMI Classics ▲ CDC 54447
Debussy, C.:Preludes Pno (sels)—Book 1 EMI Classics ▲ CDC 54448

Ciccolini, Aldo (pno) (cont.)
Massenet, J.:Con Pno, w. S. Cambreling (cnd), Monte Carlo PO EMI Classics ▲ CDM 64277
Massenet, J.:Pno Music—10 Pièces de genre, Op. 10 (1866); etc. EMI Classics ▲ CDM 64277
Mozart, W.A.:Allegro & Andante *(rec EMS Studios, Brussels, 1990)* Discover International ▲ DICD 920199 [DDD]
Mozart, W.A.:Fant Pno, K.475 Arcobaleno ▲ SBCD 1401
Mozart, W.A.:Son 1 Pno *(rec EMS Studios, Brussels, 1990)* Discover International ▲ DICD 920200 [DDD]
Mozart, W.A.:Son 2 Pno Arcobaleno ▲ SBCD 1401
Mozart, W.A.:Son 4 Pno Arcobaleno ▲ SBCD 1401
Mozart, W.A.:Son 5 Pno *(rec EMS Studios, Brussels, 1990)* Discover International ▲ DICD 920200 [DDD]
Mozart, W.A.:Son 6 Pno *(rec EMS Studios, Brussels, 1990)* Discover International ▲ DICD 920198 [DDD]
Mozart, W.A.:Son 8 Pno *(rec EMS Studios, Brussels, 1990)* Discover International ▲ DICD 920215 [DDD]
Mozart, W.A.:Son 9 Pno *(rec EMS Studios, Brussels, 1990)* Discover International ▲ DICD 920198 [DDD]
Mozart, W.A.:Son 11 Pno *(rec EMS Studios, Brussels, 1990)* Discover International ▲ DICD 920200 [DDD]
Mozart, W.A.:Son 11 Pno *(rec EMS Studios, Brussels, 1990)* Discover International ▲ DICD 920215 [DDD]
Mozart, W.A.:Son 14 Pno Arcobaleno ▲ SBCD 1401
Mozart, W.A.:Son 14 Pno *(rec EMS Studios, Brussels, 1990)* Discover International ▲ DICD 920215 [DDD]
Mozart, W.A.:Son 16 Pno *(rec EMS Studios, Brussels, 1990)* Discover International ▲ DICD 920199 [DDD]
Mozart, W.A.:Son 17 Pno *(rec EMS Studios, Brussels, 1990)* Discover International ▲ DICD 920198 [DDD]
Mozart, W.A.:Son Vn, K.547, w. *(vn unknown)* *(rec EMS Studios, Brussels, 1990)* Discover International ▲ DICD 920199 [DDD]
Recital, 29 June 1969, w. E. Schwarzkopf (sop) Arkadia ▲ 802 [ADD]
Saint-Saëns, C.:Cons Pno (comp), w. S. Baudo (cnd), Orch de Paris EMI Classics ("Studio" series) 2-▲ CDMB 69443 [ADD]
Satie, E.:Choses vues à droite et à gauche, w. Y. P. Tortelier (vn) Virgin Classics 2-▲ CDZB 62877
Satie, E.:Geneviève de Brabant, w. A. Guiot (sop), M. Mesplé (sop), D. Millet (sop), A. Esposito (sop), J.C. Benoit (bar), P. Dervaux (cnd), Orch de Paris, Paris Opera Chorus Virgin Classics 2-▲ CDZB 62877
Satie, E.:Les Pantins dansent Virgin Classics 2-▲ CDZB 62877
Satie, E.:Pno Music (comp) EMI Classics ▲ CDC 49702 [DDD]
Satie, E.:Pno Music (comp) EMI Classics ▲ CDC 49703 [DDD]
Satie, E.:Pno Music (comp) EMI Classics ▲ CDC 49713 [DDD]
Satie, E.:Pno Music (comp) EMI Classics ▲ CDC 49714 [DDD]
Satie, E.:Pno Music (comp) EMI Classics ▲ CDC 49760 [DDD]
Satie, E.:Pno Music (comp) EMI Classics 2-▲ CDZB 67282
Satie, E.:Le Piège de Méduse Virgin Classics 2-▲ CDZB 62877
Scarlatti, D.:Sons Kbd—K.406, 9, 492, 205, 87 & 268 EMI Classics ("Baroque" series) ▲ CDK 65735
Čičvački, Borislav (ob)
Tickmayer, S.K.:Music of Forgotten Times, Camerata Academica Novi Sad Emergo ▲ EC 3950 [DDD]
Ciechanski, Aleksander (vc)
Chopin, F.:Trio Pno, w. Wladyslaw Szpilman (pno), Tadeusz Wronski (vn) *(rec Warsaw, 1961)* Polskie Nagrania ▲ PNCD 309
Cinca, Dan (hn)
Enescu, G.:Dectet Ww, w. Virgil Francu (fl), Nicolae Maxin (fl), Valeriu Barbuceanu (cl), Leontin Boanta (cl), Adrian Petrescu (ob), Viorica Feher (bn), Goedri Orban (bn), Florin Ionoaia (Eng hn), Simon Jebeleanu (hn), H. Andreescu (cnd) Olympia ▲ OLY 445 [DDD]
Cincera, Andreas (db)
Schubert, Franz:Chamber Music Pno, w. C. Veress (va), Arion Trio BIS 4-▲ CD 521/24 [DDD]
Schubert, Franz:Qnt Pno, D.667, w. C. Veress (va), Arion Trio BIS 4-▲ CD 521/24 [DDD]
Ciolfi, Luciana (vn)
Amendola, F.:Ricercari, w. D. Patumi (db), A. Frederico (elecs/pno), A. Flore (voc), G. Lanzini (cl), C. Cavalieri (vn), C. Sanzo (vc), O. Mangiavacchi (perc), Donizetti Ensemble Bongiovanni ▲ GB 5519 [DDD]
Ciomei, Sergio (hpd)
Mancini, F.:Sons Rcr, w. L. Cavasanti (rcr), C. Boersma (vc) Nuova Era ("Ancient Music" series) ▲ NUO 7138 [DDD]
Telemann, G.P.:Con in a for Rcr, Ob, w. L. Cavasanti (rcr), P. Faldi (ob), D. Moore (vn), C. Boersma (vc) *(rec July 23-26, 1991)* Nuova Era ("Ancient Music" series) ▲ NUO 7067 [DDD]
Telemann, G.P.:Quartet in G for Recorder, Oboe, Violin & Continuo, w. L. Cavasanti (rcr), P. Faldi (ob), D. Moore (vn) *(rec July 23-26, 1991)* Nuova Era ("Ancient Music" series) ▲ NUO 7067 [DDD]
Ciomei, Sergio (hpd/org)
Frescobaldi, G.:Canzonas, Caprici & Ricercari, w. K. Boeke (vl), L. Cavasanti (rcr), G. Capocaccia (rcr), C. Boersma (vc)—Canzoni Trigesima, detta la Cittadellia; Vigesimasesta, detta la Moricona; Vigesimaottiva, detta le Lanberta; Prima a tre; Trigesimaseconda detta l'Altogradina; Vigesimaquarta, detta la Nobile; Vigesimesttima, detta la Lanciona; Quintedecima, detta la Lievoratta; Terza a quattro; Vigesimaquinta, detta la Garzoncina; Prima a tre; Decmasesta, detta la Samminiata; Trigesimaprima, detta l'Arnolfinia; Quarta a tre; Quinta a tre; Decimasettima, detta la Diodata; Seconda a quattro; Seconda a tre; Vigesimanona, detta la Bocellina; Terza a tre Trigesimaquarta, detta la Sandoninia Nuova Era ("Ancient Music" series) ▲ 7131
Cionco, Richard (pno)
Fauré, G.:Fant Fl, w. Laurel Zucker (fl) *(rec California State Univ Recital Hall, Sacramento)* Cantilena ▲ 66011-2 [DDD]
Kingman, D.:La Commedia Innova ▲ INNOVA 504
Kingman, D.:Fant-Mosaic Innova ▲ INNOVA 504
Kingman, D.:Scénario musical 1, w. James Een (va), Susan Lamb Cook (vc) Innova ▲ INNOVA 504
Cipriana, Guy-Joel (perc)
Bartók, B.:Son for 2 Pnos, w. J.-F. Heisser (pno), G. Pludermacher (pno), G. Perotin (perc) Erato ▲ 2292-45861-2
Cipriani, Fabrizio (vn)—see also ORCHESTRAS & ENSEMBLES Aira String Quartet, Collegium Pro Musica
Stanley, J.:Cons Org, Op. 10, w. A Frigé (hpd), R. Pietropaolo (vn), A. Fantinuoli (db), *(w. accompaniments for 2 vn & db)* Nuova Era ("Ancient Music" series) ▲ 7152
Torelli, G.:Concertino per camera, w. A. Fantinuoli (vc)—No. 2 *(rec Feb. 17-20, 1992)* Nuova Era ("Ancient Music" series) ▲ NUO 7128 [DDD]
Vivaldi, A.:Cons for 2 Vns, w. F. Biondi (vn), F. Biondi (cnd), Europa Galante—RV.511 *(rec Apr. 1993)* Opus 111 ▲ OPS 3086 [DDD]
Cipriani, P. (vn)—see ORCHESTRAS & ENSEMBLES Modo Antiquo
Cirillo, Nancy (vn)
Brings, A.:Son Vn Centaur ▲ CRC 2156
Kraft, William:Gallery 4-5, w. Diane Heffner (cl), Ronald Copes (va), Ronald Lowry (vc), Hugh Hinton (pno) Albany ▲ TROY 218 [DDD]
Cirillo, Nancy (vn/va)
Kraft, William:Con Perc, w. Dean Anderson (perc), Renee Krimsier (fl), Diane Heffner (cl), Ronald Lowry (vc), Hugh Hinton (pno) Albany ▲ TROY 218 [DDD]
Kraft, William:Settings from Pierrot Lunaire, w. Jane Manning (sop), Renee Krimsier (fl), Diane Heffner (cl), Ronald Lowry (vc), Dean Anderson (perc), Hugh Hinton (pno) Albany ▲ TROY 218 [DDD]
Cirker, J. (perc)
Bouchard, L.:Black Burned Wood, w. D. Ohrenstein (sop), M. Rowell (vn/va), Phillip Bush (pno), B. Ruyle (mar/xyl/perc) *(rec Feb. & Apr. 1993)* CRI ▲ CD 654 [DDD]

▲ = CD ♦ = Enhanced CD Δ = MD ■ = Cassette Tape □ = DCC

Cirker, J. (perc) (cont.)
Davis, A.:Lost Moon Sisters, w. D. Ohrenstein (sop), M. Rowell (vn), P. Bush (pno) *(rec Feb. & Apr. 1993)* CRI ▲ CD 654 [DDD]
Johnson, S.:Confetti on Flesh, w. D. Ohrenstein (sop), M. Rowell (vn), P. Bush (pno/syn) *(rec Feb. & Apr. 1993)* CRI ("Emergency Music" series) ▲ CD 654 [DDD]
Lebaron, A.:Dish, w. D. Ohrenstein (sop), M. Rowell (vn), P. Bush (pno/syn), J. Thompson (elec bass), B. Ruyle (perc) *(rec Feb. & Apr. 1993)* CRI ("Emergency Music" series) ▲ CD 654 [DDD]
Cislowski, Tamara-Anna (pno)
Rawsthorne, A.:Con Pnos, w. G. Tozer (pno), M. Bamert (cnd), London PO Chandos ▲ CHAN 9125 [DDD]
Cissokho, M. (perc)
Blak, K.:Addeq, w. L. Kullgren (gtr), K. Blak (pno), P. Janson (db) Tutl ▲ HJF 22
Civil, Alan (hn)
Britten, H.:Serenade, Op. 31, w. R. Tear (ten), R. Armstrong (cnd), Welsh National Opera Orch EMI Classics ▲ CDM 69522
Handel, G.F.:Royal Fireworks Music, w. Derek Wickens (ob), John Wilbraham (tpt), Harold Lester (hpd), J. Somary (cnd), English CO *(rec Conway Hall, London, 1973)* Vanguard Classics ▲ SVC 47 [AAD]
Handel, G.F.:Water Music (comp), w. Derek Wickens (ob), John Wilbraham (tpt), Harold Lester (hpd), J. Somary (cnd), English CO *(rec Conway Hall, London, 1973)* Vanguard Classics ▲ SVC 47 [AAD]
Mozart, W.A.:Con Hn, K.495, w. L. Foster (cnd), Royal PO IMP Collectors Series ▲ IMPX 9012
Civval, Sally (vc)—see ORCHESTRAS & ENSEMBLES Badinage
Claesson, Søren Kaas (vn)
Pape, A.:I've Never Seen A Butterfly Here, w. Lise-Lotte Nielsen (sop), Geir Draugsvoll (acc) *(rec Oct 1995–Jan 1996)* Marco Polo/Dacapo ▲ 8.224028 [DDD]
Clamor, Thomas (tpt)
Hindemith, P.:Septet Winds & Tpt, w. Manfred Preis (b cl), Berlin Philharmonic Wind Quintet *(rec Berlin-Spandau, Sept 11–14, 1995)* BIS ▲ CD 752 [DDD]
Clancy, Robert (baroque gtr)
Caccini, G.:Le nuove musiche, w. Montserrat Figueras (sop), J. Savall (vl), H. Smith (baroque gtr), X. Schindler (hp), Schola Cantorum Basiliensis Editio Classica ▲ 77164-2-RG [ADD]
Clapp, S. (vn)—see ORCHESTRAS & ENSEMBLES Oberlin Trio
Clapton, Eric (gtr)
Pavarotti & Friends for War Child, w. L. Pavarotti (ten), Eric Clapton (sgr), Sheryl Crow (sgr), Elton John (sgr), Liza Minelli (sgr), Joan Osborne (sgr), Jon Secada (sgr), John McLaughlin (gtr), Marco Armiliato, Edoardo Bennato, José Molina, Al DiMeola, Kelly Family, Ligabue, Litfiba, P *(rec Modena, Italy, 1996)* London ▲ 452900-2 ■ 452900-4
Claret, Gerard (vn)
Montsalvatge, X.:Concertino 1 + 13, w. G. Claret (cnd), Andorra National CO Nimbus ▲ NI 5482 [DDD]
Claret, Lluís (vc)
Bach, J.S.:Suites Vc, BWV 1007-1012 Valois 2-▲ V 4695
Chopin, F.:Son Vc, w. Alain Planès (pno) Musique d'Abord ▲ HMA 1901370
Colonel Chabert, w. R. Pasquier (vn), Philippe Cassard (pno), Pierre Hantaï (hpd) Travelling ▲ K 1013
In Memoriam Pablo Casals, w. Seon-Hee Myong (pno), Barcelona Cello Ensemble Valois ▲ V 4733
Kodály, Z.:Son Vc, Op. 8 Harmonia Mundi France ("Musique d'abord" series) ▲ HMA 1901325
Kodály, Z.:Son Vc & Pno, Op. 4, w. Rose-Marie Cabestany (pno) Harmonia Mundi France ("Musique d'abord" series) ▲ HMA 1901325
Strauss, R.:Son Vc, w. Alain Planès (pno) Musique d'Abord ▲ HMA 1901370
Clark, Harry (vc)—see also ORCHESTRAS & ENSEMBLES Fidelio
Starer, R.:Episodes Va, w. Lois Martin (va), Sanda Schuldmann (pno) Albany ▲ TROY 152 [DDD]
Starer, R.:Remembering Felix, w. Robert J. Lurtsema (nar), Sanda Schuldmann (pno) Albany ▲ TROY 151 [DDD]
Clark, James (vn)
Davies, P.M.:Strathclyde Con 5, w. C. Marwood (vc), P. M. Davies (cnd), Scottish CO Collins Classics ▲ COL 1303 [DDD]
Clark, Kate (trns fl)
Philidor, P.:Music of, w. W. Hazelet (trns fl), M. Fentross (lt/thb), T. Zwart (vl), J. Ogg (hpd)—Trios 1 & 2 in G & e for 2 Flutes & Continuo; Suite No. 3 in D for 2 Flutes; Suites Nos. 5, 6 & 12 in e, b & D for Flute & Continuo *(rec June 1993)* Globe ▲ GLO 5107 [DDD]
Clark, S. (va)
Lachner, F.P.:Qnt 2 Pno, w. H. Göbel (pno), O. Duliba (vn), T. Jahnel (vn), S. Dörfler (vc) *(rec June 10, 1991)* Thorofon ▲ CTH 2132 [DDD]
Clark, Stanley (trbn)
Contrasts, w. Avis Romm (pno) ebs ▲ ebs 6023 [DDD]
Clarke, Herbert L. (cnt)
Herbert L. Clarke, w. Sousa Band, et al. *(rec 1900–01, 1904, 1908–09, 1)* Crystal ▲ CD 450
Clarke, Herbert L. (tpt)
Cornet Soloist Crystal ■ C 450 (m)
Clarke, Jennifer Ward (vc)—see also ORCHESTRAS & ENSEMBLES Salomon String Quartet
Bassoon Collection, w. F. Eustace (bn), Andrew Watts (bn), Paul Nicholson (kbds) Amon Ra ▲ CDSAR 35 [DDD]
Brahms, J.:Trio Cl, w. A. Hacker (cl), R. Burnett (pno) [period instrs] Amon Ra ▲ CD-SAR 37 [DDD]
Weber, C.M. von:Trio Fl, w. Preston (fl), R. Burnett (pno) Amon Ra ▲ CD-SAR 21 [DDD]
Clarke, Kate (fl)
Bach, C.P.E.:Trio Son for 2 Fls, H.580, w. Wilbert Hazelzet (fl), Alda Stuurop (vn), Richte van der Meer (vc), Jacques Ogg (hpd) *(rec Utrecht, Sept 1993)* Globe ▲ GLO 5110 [DDD]
Clarke, Pip (vn)
Chausson, E.:Poème Vn, w. S. Holshouser (pno) [trans. for violin & piano] Classic Jewel ▲ CJL 0101-2
Kreisler, F.:Vn Pieces, w. S. Holshouser (pno)—Recitativo & Scherzo-caprice, Op. 6 Classic Jewel ▲ CJL 0101-2
Saint-Saëns, C.:Son 1 Vn, w. S. Holshouser (pno) Classic Jewel ▲ CJL 0101-2
Tchaikovsky, P.:Valse-Scherzo Vn, w. S. Holshouser (pno) Classic Jewel ▲ CJL 0101-2
Waxman, F.:Carmen Fant, w. S. Holshouser (pno) [trans. for violin & piano] Classic Jewel ▲ CJL 0101-2
Clarke, Raymond (pno)
Simpson, R.:Michael Tippett, His Mystery Hyperion ▲ CDA 66827
Simpson, R.:Son Pno Hyperion ▲ CDA 66827
Simpson, R.:Variations & Finale on a Theme by Beethoven Hyperion ▲ CDA 66827
Simpson, R.:Variations & Finale on a Theme by Haydn Hyperion ▲ CDA 66827
Stevenson, R.:Passacaglia on DSCH *(rec London, Feb. 20, 1993)* Marco Polo ▲ 8.223545 [DDD]
Clarkson, Gustav (va)
Mozart, W.A.:Qts Fl, w. J. Hall (fl), P. Barritt (vn), J. Horder (vc) Collins Quest ▲ 3044 [DDD]
Claro, Sofia Asunción (elec)
Musiana 95:Electroacoustic Music from Denmark & Japan, w. Ensemble from the East, Trio Sparnaay/Kooistra/Abe, Hanne Andersen, Sofia Asunción Claro, Mari Kimura (hp/vn), Thomas Sandberg, Harry Sparnaay (b cl) Classico ▲ CLASSCD 139 [DDD]
Clarvis, Paul (perc)
Gough, O.:Currulao, w. Beverly Davison (vn), Roger Heaton (cl), Bruce Nockles (tpt), John Pigneguy (hn), David Stewart (trbn), Tracey Goldsmith (acc), Orlando Gough (kbd) *(rec London, 1995)* Catalyst ▲ 0902-668332-2 [DDD]
Class, Kevin (pno)—see also ORCHESTRAS & ENSEMBLES Duo Nuova
Chopin, F.:Mazurkas—Op. 24/1-4 *(rec Solid Sound Studio, Ann Arbor; Oct 25 & 26, 1994)* Jackal ▲ JCD 0001
Chopin, F.:Nocturnes—Op. 27, No. 2 *(rec Solid Sound Studio, Ann Arbor; Oct 25 & 26, 1994)* Jackal ▲ JCD 0001
Chopin, F.:Polonaises—Op. 44 in f# *(rec Solid Sound Studio, Ann Arbor; Oct 25 & 26, 1994)* Jackal ▲ JCD 0001
Chopin, F.:Son Pno, Op. 35 *(rec Solid Sound Studio, Ann Arbor; Oct 25 & 26, 1994)* Jackal ▲ JCD 0001

Class, Kevin (pno) (cont.)
Chopin, F.:Waltzes—Op. 34/2 in a *(rec Solid Sound Studio, Ann Arbor; Oct 25 & 26, 1994)* Jackal ▲ JCD 0001
Clausen, Thomas (pno)
Clausen, T.:Songs (3), w. Mads Viding (db), Jesper Grove Jørgensen (cnd), Lille MUKO Point ▲ PCD 5125
Claussen, K. (t sax)
Kallman, D.:Forecasts, w. E. Finney (sop sax), S. Hyslop (alt sax), W. Burton (bar sax) Innova ▲ MN 109
Macy, C.:4 Saxes, w. E. Finney (sop sax), S. Hyslop (a sax), W. Burton (bar sax) Innova ▲ MN 109
Clavenna, M. (db)
Sacchini, A.:La contandina in corte, w. S. Rigacci (sop—Tancia), E. Palacio (ten—Ruggiero), G. Gatti (bar—Berto), C. Boersma (vc), M. T. Conti (hpd), G. Catalucci (cnd), Sassari SO *(rec Dec. 17–18, 1991)* Bongiovanni 2-▲ GB 2145/46 [DDD]
Clavier, Denis (vn)—see ORCHESTRAS & ENSEMBLES Denis Clavier String Quartet
Clavreul, Robin (vc)
Duparc, H.:Son Vc, w. B. Nedeltchev (pno) Gega ▲ GD 151 [DDD]
Poulenc, F.:Son Vc, w. B. Nedeltchev (pno) Gega ▲ GD 151 [DDD]
Clayton, Nigel (pno)
Rossini, G.:Petite messe solennelle, w. M. Musacchio (sop), C. Bandera (alt), G. Dominguez (ten), J. Mannov (bass), U. Koella (pno), F. Näf (cnd), *(chorus unknown)* Ars Musici ▲ AM 1091 [DDD]
20th Century Recital, w. L. McAslan (vn) Collins Classics ▲ COL 1173 [DDD]
Clearfield, Andrea (pno)
Clearfield, A.:Songs of the Wolf, w. Frøydis Ree Wekre (hn) Crystal ▲ CD 678
Cleeman, P. (va)
Carter, E.:Triple Duo, w. P. Racine (fl), E. Molinari (cl), H. Schneeberger (vn), T. Demenga (vc), G. Huber (perc) ECM New Series ▲ 78118-21391-2 [DDD]
Cleemann, Paul (pno)
Dünki, J.-J.:Tétraptéron O-IV, w. J.-J. Dünki (clvd), S. Reymond (hpd), P. Sublet (cel) *(rec Sept. 18, 1992)* Jecklin ▲ JS 289-2 [ADD]
Pepi, J.:Metamorfosis I *(rec May 28, 1992)* Jecklin ▲ JS 289-2 [ADD]
Clein, Natalie (vc)
Duruflé, M.:Mass, "Cum jubilo", w. Aaron Webber (trb), Simon Keenlyside (bar), Iain Simcock (org), James O'Donnell (cnd), Westminster Cathedral Choir Hyperion ▲ CDA 66757
Duruflé, M.:Motets on Gregorian Chants, Op. 10, w. Aaron Webber (trb), Simon Keenlyside (bar), Iain Simcock (org), J. O'Donnell (cnd), Westminster Cathedral Choir Hyperion ▲ CDA 66757
Duruflé, M.:Notre Père, w. Aaron Webber (trb), Simon Keenlyside (bar), Iain Simcock (org), J. O'Donnell (cnd), Westminster Cathedral Choir Hyperion ▲ CDA 66757
Duruflé, M.:Requiem, w. Aaron Webber (trb), Simon Keenlyside (bar), Iain Simcock (org), J. O'Donnell (cnd), Westminster Cathedral Choir Hyperion ▲ CDA 66757
Clemencic, René (fl)—see ORCHESTRAS & ENSEMBLES Clemencic Consort
Clemencic, René (rcr)
Flûte à bec, Luth et Giutare, w. Andras Kecskés (lt/gtr) Harmonia Mundi ▲ HMC 90427
Gabrieli, G.:Music of, w. A. Heiller (hpd), H. Tachezi (pno), E. Appia (cnd), Gabrieli Festival Orch, Gabrieli Festival Chorus—Processional & Ceremonial Music from Sacrae Symphoniae [1597, 1615] & Concerti [1587]; originally released as Bach Guild BGS 5004)—Sancta et immaculata virginitas; O magnum mysterium; Nunc dimittis; Angelus ad pastores; O Jesu mi dulcissime; Exaudi Deus; Hodie completi sunt; O Domine Jesu Christe; Canzona Quarti Toni a 15 (ricercar); Inclina Domine *(rec Vienna, Feb. 1958)* Vanguard Classics ("The Bach Guild" series) ▲ OVC 2007 [ADD]
Plays 21 Recorders Harmonia Mundi ▲ HMA 190384
Clement, Manfred (ob)
Strauss, R.:Con Ob, w. R. Kempe (cnd), Dresden Staatskapelle EMI Classics 3-▲ CDZC 64342
Clemente, A. (hpd)—see ORCHESTRAS & ENSEMBLES Modo Antiquo
Clemente, Anna (cembalo)
Geminiani, F.:The Art of Playing the Gtr or Citra, w. Carlo Mascilli Migliorini (gtr) Koch Schwann ▲ SCH 313592
Marella, G.:Compositions, w. Carlo Mascilli Migliorini (gtr) Koch Schwann ▲ SCH 313592
Clemmow, Caroline (pno)—see also ORCHESTRAS & ENSEMBLES Hartley Piano Trio
Bainton, E.:Miniature Suite, w. Anthony Goldstone (pno) *(rec 1996)* Albany ▲ TROY 198 [DDD]
Bury, F.:Prelude & Fugue, w. Anthony Goldstone (pno) *(rec 1996)* Albany ▲ TROY 198 [DDD]
Elgar, E.:Serenade Strs, w. Anthony Goldstone (pno) [arr Elgar for 2 Pnos] *(rec 1996)* Albany ▲ TROY 198 [DDD]
German, E.:Pno Music, w. Anthony Goldstone (pno)—Suite for Pno 4-Hands (1896) *(rec St. John the Baptist Church, Alkborough, South Humberside, Aug. 1994)* Amphion ▲ PHI 129 [DDD]
Holst, G.:The Planets, w. Anthony Goldstone (pno) [arr Holst for 2 Pnos] *(rec 1996)* Albany ▲ TROY 198 [DDD]
Holst, G.:Sym, "The Cotswolds", w. Anthony Goldstone (pno)—Elegy, In Memoriam William Morris [arr Holst for 2 Pnos] *(rec 1996)* Albany ▲ TROY 198 [DDD]
Massenet, J.:Pièces Pno 4-Hands, w. Anthony Goldstone (pno) *(rec St. John the Baptist Church, Alkborough, South Humberside, Aug. 1994)* Amphion ▲ PHI 129 [DDD]
Play Virtuoso Variations for Piano Duet, w. A. Goldstone (pno) Symposium ▲ SYM 1037
Rachmaninoff, S.:Duets Pno 4-Hands, w. Anthony Goldstone (pno) *(rec St. John the Baptist Church, Alkborough, South Humberside, Aug. 1994)* Amphion ▲ PHI 129 [DDD]
Sinding, C.:Suite Pno 4-Hands, w. Anthony Goldstone (pno) *(rec St. John the Baptist Church, Alkborough, South Humberside, Aug. 1994)* Amphion ▲ PHI 129 [DDD]
Cleobury, Stephen (org)
Alcock, W.:Intro & Passacaglia *(rec King's College, Cambridge)* Priory ▲ PRI 5 [DDD]
Britten, H.:Prelude & Fugue on a Theme of Vittoria *(rec King's College, Cambridge)* Priory ▲ PRI 5 [DDD]
Fauré, G.:Cantique de Jean Racine, w. G. Guest (cnd), St. John's College Choir Cambridge [F] London ("Jubilee" series) ▲ 430360-2 [ADD]
Great European Organs, Vol. 1 Priory ▲ PRCD 185 [DDD]
Great European Organs, Vol. 5, w. James Lancelot (org) Priory ▲ PRCD 228 [DDD]
Great European Organs, Vol. 6, w. Keith John (org) Priory ▲ PRCD 235 [DDD]
Great European Organs, Vol. 7, w. Jane Watts (org) Priory ▲ PRCD 237 [DDD]
Great European Organs, Vol. 10, w. Keith John (org) Priory ▲ PRCD 262 [DDD]
Great European Organs, Vol. 15, w. Colin Walsh (org) Priory ▲ PRCD 281 [DDD]
Great European Organs, Vol. 16, w. David Briggs (org) Priory ▲ PRCD 284 [DDD]
Great European Organs, Vol. 18, w. Jane Watts (org) Priory ▲ PRCD 286 [DDD]
Great European Organs, Vol. 19, w. Jane Watts (org) Priory ▲ PRCD 294 [DDD]
Great European Organs, Vol. 20, w. Graham Barber (org) Priory ▲ PRCD 297 [DDD]
Great European Organs, Vol. 21, w. Jonathan Bielby (org) Priory ▲ PRCD 298 [DDD]
Great European Organs, Vol. 22, w. Naji Hakim (org) Priory ▲ PRCD 327 [DDD]
Great European Organs, Vol. 25, w. Graham Barber (org) Priory ▲ PRCD 373 [DDD]
Great European Organs, Vol. 26, w. Keith John (org) Priory ▲ PRCD 370
Great European Organs, Vol. 27, w. Graham Barber (org) Priory ▲ PRCD 391 [DDD]
The King's Trumpeter:Music for Trumpet & Organ from King's College Cambridge, w. C. Steele-Perkins (tpt) Priory ▲ PRCD 189 [DDD]
Leighton, K.:Org Music—Paean *(rec King's College, Cambridge)* Priory ▲ PRI 5 [DDD]
Liszt, F.:Vars on "Weinen, Klagen, Sorgen, Zagen", S.179 Priory ▲ PRCD 185 [DDD]
Mathias, W.:Partita Org, Op. 19 *(rec King's College, Cambridge)* Priory ▲ PRI 5 [DDD]
Mendelssohn, F.:Sons Org—No. 3 Priory ▲ PRCD 185 [DDD]
Mozart, W.A.:Fant Mechanical Org Priory ▲ PRCD 185 [DDD]
Parry, H.:Fant & Fugue Org *(rec King's College, Cambridge)* Priory ▲ PRI 5 [DDD]
Reger, M.:Pieces Org, Op. 145—No. 2, "Dankpsalm" Priory ▲ PRCD 185 [DDD]
The Splendour of King's:Essential Organ Favorites Collins Classics ▲ COL 1401 [DDD]
Cleveland, D. (vn)—see ORCHESTRAS & ENSEMBLES Audubon String Quartet
Cleveland, Douglas (org)
Dupré, M.:Vars sur un vieux Noël [at the Princeton Univ. Chapel Grand Organ] RBW ▲ RBWCD 004
Howells, H.:Rhap 1 Organ [Princeton Univ Chapel Grand Organ] RBW ▲ RBWCD 004

INSTRUMENT.

Cleveland, Douglas (org) (cont.)
Tournemire, C.:Chorales Org—Improvisation sur le Victimae Paschali [at the Princeton Univ Chapel Grand Organ] RBW ▲ RBWCD 004
Vierne, L.:Sym 6 Org—Finale [Princeton Univ Chapel Grand Organ] RBW ▲ RBWCD 004
Whitlock, P.:Org Music—Plymouth Suite [at the Princeton Univ. Chapel Grand Organ] RBW ▲ RBWCD 004

Clevenger, Dale (hn)
Beethoven, L. van:Qnt Pno, Ob, Cl, Hn & Bn, w. D. Barenboim (pno), H. Schellenberger (ob), L. Combs (cl), D. Damiano (bn) Erato ▲ 96359–2
Mozart, W.A.:Cons Hn, Franz Liszt CO Sony Classical ("Essential Classics" series) ▲ SBK 62639 ■ SBT 62639
Mozart, W.A.:Cons Hn, Franz Liszt CO—No. 1 [natural horn]; Nos. 2–4 [valve horn] CBS ▲ MDK 44906 [DDD] ■ MDT 44906 (D)
Mozart, W.A.:Con Movt Hn, K.494a, Franz Liszt CO CBS ▲ MDK 44906 [DDD] ■ MDT 44906 (D)
Mozart, W.A.:Qnt Pno, K.452, w. D. Barenboim (pno), H. Schellenberger (ob), L. Combs (cl), D. Damiano (bn) Erato ▲ 96359–2
Mozart, W.A.:Rondo Hn, K.371, Franz Liszt CO Sony Classical ("Essential Classics" series) ▲ SBK 62639 ■ SBT 62639
Mozart, W.A.:Rondo Hn, K.371, Franz Liszt CO CBS ▲ MDK 44906 [DDD] ■ MDT 44906 (D)

Cliburn, Van (pno)
Barber, S.:Son Pno RCA Gold Seal ▲ 60415–2–RG [ADD] ■ 60415–4–RG (CrO2)
Beethoven, L. van:Con 3 Pno, w. E. Ormandy (cnd), Philadelphia Orch RCA Gold Seal ▲ 09026–60419–2 [ADD] ■ 09026–60419–4
Beethoven, L. van:Con 4 Pno, w. F. Reiner (cnd), Chicago SO RCA Gold Seal ▲ 7943–2–RG [ADD] ■ 7943–4–RG
Beethoven, L. van:Con 5 Pno, "Emperor", w. F. Reiner (cnd), Chicago SO RCA Gold Seal ▲ 7943–2–RG [ADD] ■ 7943–4–RG
Beethoven, L. van:Con 5 Pno, "Emperor", w. F. Reiner (cnd), Chicago SO RCA Living Stereo ▲ 09026–61961–2 [AAD]; ■ 09026–61961–4
Beethoven, L. van:Son 8 Pno, "Pathétique" RCA Gold Seal ▲ 60356–2–RG [ADD] ■ 60356–4–RG
Beethoven, L. van:Son 14 Pno, "Moonlight Son" RCA Gold Seal ▲ 60356–2–RG [ADD] ■ 60356–4–RG
Beethoven, L. van:Son 23 Pno, "Appassionata" RCA Gold Seal ▲ 60356–2–RG [ADD] ■ 60356–4–RG
Beethoven, L. van:Son 26 Pno, "Les Adieux" RCA Gold Seal ▲ 60356–2–RG [ADD] ■ 60356–4–RG
Brahms, J.:Con 1 Pno, w. E. Leinsdorf (cnd), Boston SO RCA Gold Seal ▲ 60357–2–RG [ADD] ■ 60357–4–RG (CrO2)
Brahms, J.:Con 2 Pno, w. F. Reiner (cnd), Chicago SO RCA Gold Seal ▲ 7942–2–RG [ADD] ■ 7942–4–RG (CrO2)
Brahms, J.:Con 2 Pno, w. F. Reiner (cnd), Chicago SO RCA Living Stereo ▲ 09026–68480–2 ■ 09026–68480–4
Brahms, J.:Con 2 Pno, w. K. Kondrashin (cnd), Moscow PO *(rec 1972)* RCA Red Seal ▲ 09026–62695–2 [ADD] ■ 09026–62695–4
Brahms, J.:Fants Pno, Op. 116—Nos. 3 & 6 RCA Gold Seal ▲ 09026–60419–2 [ADD] ■ 09026–60419–4
Brahms, J.:Intermezzos Pno, Op. 117—Nos. 1 & 2 RCA Gold Seal ▲ 7942–2–RG [ADD] ■ 7942–4–RG (CrO2)
Brahms, J.:Pieces Pno, Op. 118 RCA Gold Seal ▲ 09026–60419–2 [ADD] ■ 09026–60419–4
Brahms, J.:Pieces Pno, Op. 119—Nos. 1–3 RCA Gold Seal ▲ 7942–2–RG [ADD] ■ 7942–4–RG (CrO2)
Brahms, J.:Rhaps Pno, Op. 79 RCA Gold Seal ▲ 09026–60419–2 [ADD] ■ 09026–60419–4
Brahms, J.:Vars & Fugue on a Theme by Handel RCA Gold Seal ▲ 60357–2–RG [ADD] ■ 60357–4–RG (CrO2)
Chopin, F.:Con 1 Pno, w. E. Ormandy (cnd), Philadelphia Orch RCA Gold Seal ▲ 7945–2–RG [ADD] ■ 7945–4–RG (CrO2)
Chopin, F.:Pno Music (misc)—Ballade in A♭, Op. 47; Barcarolle, Op. 60; 2 Etudes, Op. 10/3 & Op. 25/11; Fantaisie in f, Op. 49; Nocturne in B, Op. 62/1; Polonaise in A♭, Op. 53; Scherzo No. 3, Op. 39; 2 Waltzes, Op. 64/1 ("Minute Waltz") & 2 RCA Gold Seal ▲ 60358–2–RG [ADD] ■ 60358–4–RG (CrO2)
Chopin, F.:Son Pno, Op. 35 RCA Gold Seal ▲ 09026–60417–2 [ADD] ■ 09026–60417–4 (CrO2)
Chopin, F.:Son Pno, Op. 58 RCA Gold Seal ▲ 09026–60417–2 [ADD] ■ 09026–60417–4 (CrO2)
Debussy, C.:Pno Music (misc)—Estampes—Nos. 2, "Soirée dans Grenade" & 3, "Jardins sous la pluie"; Etude No. 5 (Etude in Octaves); Images—Book 1, No. 1, "Reflets dans l'eau"; Preludes—Book 2, Nos. 7, "Terrasses des audiences au clair de lune" & 12, "Feux d'artifice" RCA Gold Seal ▲ 60415–2–RG [ADD] ■ 60415–4–RG (CrO2)
Grieg, E.:Con Pno, Op. 16, w. E. Ormandy (cnd), Philadelphia Orch RCA Gold Seal ▲ 7834–2–RG [ADD] ■ 7834–4–RG (CrO2)
Liszt, F.:Cons Pno, w. E. Ormandy (cnd), Philadelphia Orch RCA Gold Seal ▲ 7834–2–RG [ADD] ■ 7834–4–RG (CrO2)
Liszt, F.:Pno Music (misc)—Mephisto Waltz; Sonetto del Petrarca No. 123; Un sospiro RCA Gold Seal ▲ 09026–60417–2 [ADD] ■ 09026–60417–4 (CrO2)
Liszt, F.:Son Pno RCA Gold Seal ▲ 60414–2–RG [ADD] ■ 60414–4–RG (CrO2)
Macdowell, E.:Con 2 Pno, w. W. Hendl (cnd), Chicago SO RCA Gold Seal ▲ 60420–2–RG [ADD] ■ 60420–4–RG (CrO2)
Macdowell, E.:Con 2 Pno, w. W. Hendl (cnd), Chicago SO RCA Living Stereo ▲ 09026–68480–2 ■ 09026–68480–4
Macdowell, E.:To a Wild Rose RCA Gold Seal ▲ 60420–2–RG [ADD] ■ 60420–4–RG (CrO2)
Mozart, W.A.:Son 10 Pno RCA Gold Seal ▲ 60415–2 [ADD] ■ 60415–4 (CrO2)
My Favorite Encores RCA Gold Seal ▲ 60726–2–RG [ADD] ■ 60726–4–RG
Prokofiev, S.:Con 3 Pno, w. W. Hendl (cnd), Chicago SO *(rec 1960)* RCA Living Stereo ▲ 09026–62691–2 [ADD]; ■ 09026–62691–4
Prokofiev, S.:Con 3 Pno, w. W. Hendl (cnd), Chicago SO RCA Red Seal ▲ 6209–2–RC [ADD]
Prokofiev, S.:Son 6 Pno RCA Gold Seal ▲ 7941–2–RG [ADD] ■ 7941–4–RG (CrO2)
Rachmaninoff, S.:Con 2 Pno, w. F. Reiner (cnd), Chicago SO RCA Living Stereo ▲ 09026–61961–2 [AAD]; ■ 09026–61961–4 [DD
Rachmaninoff, S.:Con 2 Pno, w. F. Reiner (cnd), Chicago SO RCA Red Seal ▲ 07863–55912–2 [ADD] ■ 07863–55912–4
Rachmaninoff, S.:Con 3 Pno, w. K. Kondrashin (cnd), Symphony of the Air RCA Red Seal ▲ 6209–2–RC [ADD]
Rachmaninoff, S.:Études-tableaux, Opp. 33 & 39—Op. 39, No. 5 RCA Gold Seal ▲ 7941–2–RG [ADD] ■ 7941–4–RG (CrO2)
Rachmaninoff, S.:Preludes Pno, Opp 23 & 32—Op. 23, No. 4 RCA Gold Seal ▲ 7941–2–RG [ADD] ■ 7941–4–RG (CrO2)
Rachmaninoff, S.:Rhapsody on a Theme of Paganini, w. K. Kondrashin (cnd), Moscow PO *(rec 1972)* RCA Red Seal ▲ 09026–62695–2 [ADD] ■ 09026–62695–4
Rachmaninoff, S.:Rhapsody on a Theme of Paganini, w. E. Ormandy (cnd), Philadelphia Orch RCA Gold Seal ▲ 7945–2–RG [ADD] ■ 7945–4–RG (CrO2)
Rachmaninoff, S.:Son 2 Pno RCA Gold Seal ▲ 7941–2–RG [ADD] ■ 7941–4–RG (CrO2)
A Romantic Collection RCA Gold Seal ▲ 60414–2–RG [ADD] ■ 60414–4–RG
Schumann, R.:Con Pno, w. F. Reiner (cnd), Chicago SO *(rec 1960)* RCA Living Stereo ▲ 09026–62691–2 [ADD]; ■ 09026–62691–4
Schumann, R.:Con Pno, w. F. Reiner (cnd), Chicago SO RCA Gold Seal ▲ 60420–2–RG [ADD] ■ 60420–4–RG (CrO2)
Tchaikovsky, P.:Con 1 Pno, w. P. Argento (cnd), Swiss-Italian RSO *(rec 1962; 1968)* Ermitage ▲ ERM 139
Tchaikovsky, P.:Con 1 Pno, w. K. Kondrashin (cnd), RCA Victor SO RCA Red Seal ▲ 07863–55912–2 [ADD] ■ 07863–55912–4
Tchaikovsky, P.:Romeo & Juliet, w. P. Argento (cnd), Swiss-Italian RSO *(rec 1962; 1968)* Ermitage ▲ ERM 139

Clidat, France (pno)
Chopin, F.:Mazurkas—Opp. 6, 7, 17, 24, 30, 33, 41 & 48 Forlane ▲ FOR 16729 [DDD]
Chopin, F.:Polonaises—Op. 26, Nos. 1 & 2; Op. 40, Nos. 1 & 2; Op. 44; Op. 53; Op. 61; Op. 71, Nos. 1–3 Forlane ▲ FOR 16615 [DDD]
Franck, C.:Symphonic Vars, w. Z. Macal (cnd), Philharmonia Orch Forlane ▲ FRL 16673 [ADD]
Landowski, M.:Music of, w. J. Loriod (ondes Martenot), A. Marion (fl), M. Becquet (trbn), J. Houtmann (cnd), Lorraine PO—Concerto for Ondes Martenot & Orchestra; Concerto for Flute & Strings; Concerto for Piano & Orchestra; Concertino for Trombone & Strings Koch Schwann ▲ CD 311175 [DDD]
Rachmaninoff, S.:Con 3 Pno, w. Z. Macal (cnd), Royal PO Forlane ▲ FRL 13 [AAD]
Satie, E.:Pno Music (comp)—[Disc 1] Gymnopédies; Nocturnes Nos. 1–3; Gnossiennes Nos. 1–3; Avant-dernières pensées; Je te veux valse; Prélude de la porte héroïque du ciel; Les trois valses distinguées du précieux dégoûté; Poudre d'or; Sonneries de la rose croix; Descritions automatiques; Heures séculaires et instantanées; Pièces froides; [Disc 2] Nouvelles pièces froides; Gnossiennes Nos. 4–6; Embryons desséchés; Caresse; Préludes flasques; Véritables préludes flasques; Le fils des étoiles; Croques et agaceries d'un gros bonhomme en bois; Vieux sequins et vieelles cuirasses; Sarabandes; Chapitres tournés en tous sens; [Disc 3] Nocturnes No. 4 & 5; 2 Rêveries nocturnes; Rêverie l'enfance de pantagruel; Songe creux; 1st pensée rose croix; Douze petits chorals; Menus propos enfantins; Enfantillages pittoresques; Peccadilles importunes; Sports et divertissements; Valse-ballet, Op. 62; Fant-Valse; Sonatine bureaucratique; Premier menuet; Petit Ov; A Danser; Prélude en tapisserie; Les pantins dansent; Passacaille; Le piccadilly Forlane 3–▲ FRL 16592 [AAD]
Satie, E.:Pno Music (misc)—Trois Gymnopédies; Gnossiennes Nos. 1–4; Nocturnes Nos. 1–3; Avant-dernières pensées; Sports et divertissements; Embryons desséchés; Trois valses du précieux dégôuté; Je te veux; Poudre d'or; Prélude de la porte héroïque du ciel Forlane ▲ FOR 10514 [DDD]

Cload, Julia (pno)
Bach, J.S.:Goldberg Vars Meridian ▲ MER 84291 [DDD]
Haydn, J.:Sons Pno—Nos. 39, 41, 44, 48 & 49 Meridian ▲ MER 84210

Clothier-Angeroth, Kathleen (vn)
Hoffman, D.:Trio Cl, Vn & Pno, w. Rhonda Gowen (cl), Julie Schwartz (pno) Meyer ▲ MC 0108

Clottu, Dagmar (pno)
Gerber, R.:Sarabande, w. Tamas Weber (vc) Gallo ▲ CD 861 [ADD]
Gerber, R.:Son Vn, w. Freidmann Sarnau (vn) Gallo ▲ CD 861 [ADD]

Cobb, John (pno)
Fennelly, B.:Son seria *(rec 1980)* New World ▲ 80448–2

Coble, George (tpt)
Caltabiano, R.:Torched Liberty, w. N. Pilgrim (sop), V. Pritsker (vn), G. Macero (vc), L. Greene (pic/fl/alt fl), K. Schempf (E♭/A/B♭ cl), S. Heyman (pno), L. Luttinger (perc), R. Caltabiano (cnd) Opus One ▲ CD 168 [DDD]
Willey, J.:Society Music, w. L. Greene (fl), W. Harris (trbn), D. Resue (hn), S. Heyman (pno), E. Gustafson (via), G. Macero (vc), E. Castilano (db), L. Luttinger (perc), E. Murray (cnd) Opus One ▲ CD 168 [DDD]

Cobo, Ricardo (gtr)
Brouwer, L.:Con 3 Gtr, "Con Elegíaco", w. R. Kapp (cnd), Kiev Pro Musica *(rec Kiev, Ukraine, Nov. 1–3, 1994)* ESS.A.Y ▲ CD 1040 [DDD]
Brouwer, L.:Con 4 Gtr, "De Toronto", w. R. Kapp (cnd), Kiev Pro Musica *(rec Kiev, Ukraine, Nov. 1–3, 1994)* ESS.A.Y ▲ CD 1040 [DDD]
Brouwer, L.:El Decameron Negro ESS.A.Y ▲ CD 1034 [DDD]
Brouwer, L.:Two Suggestions ESS.A.Y ▲ CD 1034 [DDD]
Dyens, R.:Libra Sonatatina ESS.A.Y ▲ CD 1034 [DDD]
Koshkin, N.:Usher ESS.A.Y ▲ CD 1034 [DDD]
Piazzolla, A.:La muerte del angel ESS.A.Y ▲ CD 1034 [DDD]
Piazzolla, A.:Primavera portena ESS.A.Y ▲ CD 1034 [DDD]

Cochand, P. (vn)
Pachelbel, J.:Canon, w. L. Chan (vn), P. Cochand (cnd), Classico CO Ensemble *(rec Oct. 19–21, 1992)* Gallo ▲ CD 723 DAD
Richter, F.X.:Grandes simphonies, w. L. Chan (vn), P. Cochand (cnd), Classico CO Ensemble—in G *(rec Oct. 19–21, 1992)* Gallo ▲ CD 723 DAD
Telemann, G.P.:Don Quichotte (suite), w. L. Chan (vn), P. Cochand (cnd), Classico CO Ensemble *(rec Oct. 19–21, 1992)* Gallo ▲ CD 723 DAD
Vivaldi, A.:Cons Vn, Op. 3/1–12, "L'estro armonico", w. L. Chan (vn), P. Cochand (cnd), Classico CO Ensemble *(rec Oct. 19–21, 1992)* Gallo ▲ CD 723 DAD

Cochereau, Marie-Pierre (hp)
Original Works & Transcriptions for Horn & Harp, w. Cagnon, François (hn) Solstice ▲ SOCD 53

Cochereau, Pierre (org)
Organist of Notre Dame Cathedral 1955–84 Solstice 3–▲ SOC 94
Pierre Cochereau at the Great Organs of Notre-Dame de Paris *(rec 1966)* Fnac Music ("Via Classique" series) ▲ 642301
Saint-Saëns, C.:Sym 3, w. H. von Karajan (cnd), Berlin PO Deutsche Grammophon ("Karajan Gold" series) ▲ 439014–2

Cochran, Richard (ob)
Brooke, N.:Obomobile, w. Brandon Adrien, Jennifer Baker, Karen Birch, Daniel Cate, Judy Christy, Jessica Cooper, Leslie Dominguez, Erin Hannigan, Dorothy Knight, Jason Lichtenwalter, Jay Moore, Hwa-Ling Russell, Toyin Spellman, Sarah Weiner, Jay Weinland Opus One ▲ CD 160

Cochrane, Chris (gtr)
Exquisite Corpses from P.S. 122, w. D. Watson (shears/stick vn/gtr/tpt), Judy Dunaway (gtr/balloons), Anthony Coleman (sampler), Raissa St. Pierre (drums), Guy Yarden (vn/pno), Leslie Ross (bn), Linda Austin (gtr), Bruce Kaplan (gtr), Doug Henderson (peckhorn/bass/toy pno), Sue Ann Harkey (gtr), Cinnie Cole (sampler), et al. ¿What Next? ▲ WN 0002 [ADD]

Cock, Kaat de (va)
Berkeley, M.:For the Savage Messiah, w. Kristof van Gryspeere (pno), Dirk Lievens (vn), Stefaan Craeynest (vc), Jan Verheye (db) *(rec Steurbaut Sound Recording Ctr)* René Gailly ▲ CD87 118 [DDD]

Cocozza, Giancarlo (pno)
Catalani, A.:Songs, w. M. Rosa Bersanetti (sop)—La viola; Ad una stella; Fior di collina; O rea Gomorra, o Sodoma perversa; Sognal; Chanson groenlandaise; L'odalisque; In riva al mare; Il m'aimait tant; Le gondolier; Senza baci; La pescatrice Ducale ▲ DUC 17 [DDD]
Martucci, G.:Songs, w. M. Rosa Bersanetti (sop)—Alma gentile; Sogno di morte; Sogno d'amore; 6 liriche, Op. 68; Ballando; 3 liriche, Op. 84 *(rec July 7–9, 1993)* Ducale ▲ DUC 17 [DDD]

Cocset, Bruno (vc)—see ORCHESTRAS & ENSEMBLES Fitzwilliam Ensemble, Fitzwilliam Ensemble members

Coe, Jane (vc)
Arne, T.:Songs, w. John Mark Ainsley (ten), Miles Golding (vn), Roy Goodman (vn), Anthony Robson (sop rcr), Robert King (hpd/org)—Under the Greenwood Tree; Come Away Death; Where the Bee Sucks *(rec St Jude-on-the-Hill, London, Dec 20–21, 1968)* United ▲ CAL 88002 [DDD]
Humfrey, P.:Anthems, w. James Bowman (ct), Robert King (org), R. King (cnd), King's Consort—A Hymn to God the Father *(rec St Jude-on-the-Hill, London, Dec 20–21, 1968)* United ▲ CAL 88002 [DDD]
Telemann, G.P.:Cons for 2 Fls, w. R. Brown (fl), S. Peasgood (fl), S. Standage (vn), S. Standage (cnd), Collegium Musicum 90—(1) in D Chandos ("Chaconne" series) ▲ CHAN 0512 [DDD]
Vivaldi, A.:Con for 2 Vcs, w. D. Watkin (vc), S. Standage (cnd), Collegium Musicum 90 Chandos ("Chaconne" series) ▲ CHAN 0528 [DDD]
Vivaldi, A.:Cons Rcr, w. Piers Adams (rcr), Ray Goodman (vn), Miles Golding (vn), Jane Compton (va), Mandy MacNamara (db), David Miller (archlt), Robert King (hpd/org)—in F for Treble Rcr, Op. 10/1; in a for Sopranino Rcr, RV.440; in c for Treble Rcr, RV.441; in D for Sopranino Rcr, Op. 10/3; in g for Treble Rcr, Op. 10/2; in C for Sopranino Rcr, RV.443 *(rec Radley College, Abingdon, Oxon)* United ▲ CAL 88015 [DDD]

Coehand, P. (vn)
Mozart, W.A.:Sons Vn Pno (misc), w. M. Ganz (pno)—in C, K.296 & in G, K.301 Gallo ▲ CD 701

▲ = CD ♦ = Enhanced CD Δ = MD ■ = Cassette Tape ◻ = DCC

Coehand, P. (vn) (cont.)
Schubert, Franz:Sonatina Vn, D.408, w. M. Ganz (pno) Gallo ▲ CD 701

Coen, A. (vc)
Geminiani, F.:Sons Vc & Continuo, Op. 5, w. V. Paternoster (vc), P. Bosna (hpd)—No. 3 Bongiovanni ▲ GB 10015 [DDD]
Marcello, B.:Son Vc, Op. 2/4, w. V. Paternoster (vc), P. Bosna (hpd) Bongiovanni ▲ GB 10015 [DDD]
Martino, F.:Son Vc, w. V. Paternoster (vc), P. Bosna (hpd) Bongiovanni ▲ GB 10015 [DDD]
Pergolesi, G.B.:Sinf Vc, w. V. Paternoster (vc), P. Bosna (hpd) Bongiovanni ▲ GB 10015 [DDD]
Scipriani, F.P.:Sinf Vc, w. V. Paternoster (vc), P. Bosna (hpd) Bongiovanni ▲ GB 10015 [DDD]

Coen, Andrea (hpd)—see also ORCHESTRAS & ENSEMBLES L'Arte dell'Arco
Clementi, M.:Sons Pno, Fl & Vc, Op. 21, w. E. Casularo (fl), V. Paternoster (vc) Bongiovanni ▲ GB 10007 [DDD]
Clementi, M.:Sons Pno, Fl & Vc, Op. 22, w. E. Casularo (fl), V. Paternoster (vc) Bongiovanni ▲ GB 10007 [DDD]

Coen, Bart (fl)—see ORCHESTRAS & ENSEMBLES Romanesque

Coen, Massimo (vn)—see ORCHESTRAS & ENSEMBLES Rome Solisti

Coffey, Melinda (pno)
Brahms, J.:Pieces Pno, Op. 119 Meridian ▲ CDE 84164
Brahms, J.:Sons Cl (comp), w. E. Eban (cl) Meridian ▲ CDE 84164
Davies, V.:Trio 1 Pno, "Silhouettes", w. Arthur Polson (vn), Ian Hampton (vc) Campion ▲ RRCD 1339 [DDD]

Cofré, D. (vc)
Rheinberger, J.:Qt Pno, w. H. Göbel (pno), Z. Almasi (vn) *(rec 1989)* Thorofon 6–▲ BCTH 2161/6

Cogan, Dmitriy (pno)
Encores, w. A. Markov (vn) Erato ▲ 98481–2

Cognazzo, Roberto (hpd)
Sammartini, G.:Sons Fl, w. M. Carbotta (fl) *(rec 3/91)* Nuova Era ▲ 7022 [DDD]
Zuccari, C.:Son Fl, w. M. Carbotta (fl) *(rec 3/91)* Nuova Era ▲ 7022 [DDD]

Cognazzo, Roberto (pno)
Casella, A.:Barcarola et scherzo, w. M. Carbotta (fl) Nuova Era ▲ NUO 7185 [DDD]
Casella, A.:Sicilienne et burlesque Fl & Pno, w. M. Carbotta (fl) Nuova Era ▲ NUO 7185 [DDD]
Cortese, L.:Intro e Allegro, w. M. Carbotta (fl) Nuova Era ▲ NUO 7185 [DDD]
Cortese, L.:Melodia, w. M. Carbotta (fl) Nuova Era ▲ NUO 7185 [DDD]
Fioroni, G.A.:Son Fl, w. M. Carbotta (fl) *(rec 3/91)* Nuova Era ▲ 7022 [DDD]
Krakamp, E.:Characteristic Pieces, w. Mario Carbotta (fl) Nuova Era ▲ NUO 7193 [DDD]
Pilati, M.:Son Fl, w. M. Carbotta (fl) Nuova Era ▲ NUO 7185 [DDD]
Rota, N.:Pieces Fl, w. M. Carbotta (fl)—5 Pieces Nuova Era ▲ NUO 7185 [DDD]
Tosti, P.F.:Songs, w. R. Bruson (bar), 33 songs, w. lyrics by Gabriele D'Annunzio [I] *(rec Nov. 30 & Dec. 8, 1991)* Nuova Era 2–▲ 7090/91

Cohen, Arnaldo (pno)
Cohen, A.:Song of Myself, w. R. Lee (tpt) *(rec Brooklyn College, Apr. 1993 & May 1994)* Capstone ▲ CPS 8620 [DDD]
Cohen, A.:Wings of Desire, w. R. Lee (tpt) *(rec Brooklyn College, Apr. 1993 & May 1994)* Capstone ▲ CPS 8620 [DDD]
Haydn, J.:Trios Pno, Vn & Vc, w. Erich Höbarth (vn), Christophe Coin (vc)—H.XV/12–14 Harmonia Mundi France ▲ HMC 901277 [DDD]

Cohen, Franklin (cl)
Brahms, J.:Sons Cl (comp), w. V. Ashkenazy (pno) London ▲ 430149–2 [DDD]
Brahms, J.:Trio Cl, w. V. Ashkenazy (pno), et al. London ▲ 425839–2 [DDD]
Debussy, C.:Danses sacrée et profane, w. Y. Kondonassis (hp), M. Chalifour (vn), W.–F. Gu (va), S. Konopka (va), R. Weiss (vc), T. Sperl (db), J. Smith (instr) *(rec Nov. 23–25, 1992)* Telarc ▲ CD 80361 [DDD]
Ravel, M.:Intro & Allegro, w. Y. Kondonassis (hp), J. Smith (fl), M. Chalifour (vn), W.–F. Gu (va), S. Konopka (va), R. Weiss (vc), T. Sperl (db) *(rec Nov. 23–25, 1992)* Telarc ▲ CD 80361 [DDD]
Ravel, M.:Pavane pour une infante défunte, w. Y. Kondonassis (hp), J. Smith (fl), M. Chalifour (vn), W.–F. Gu (va), S. Konopka (va), R. Weiss (vc), T. Sperl (db) [arr. by Kondonassis] *(rec Nov. 23–25, 1992)* Telarc ▲ CD 80361 [DDD]
Schumann, R.:Fantasiestücke Cl, w. V. Ashkenazy (pno) London ▲ 430149–2 [DDD]]

Cohen, Fredric (ob)
Thomson, V.:Portraits, w. A. Tommasini (pno), S. Leventhal (vn), J. Miller (vc), R. Haroutunian (bn)—Selected Portraits (13) for Pno (1935–42); Five Ladies for Vn & Pno (1930; 1940; 1983); A Portrait of 2, for Ob, Bn & Pno (1984); 3 Portraits for Pno (1940; arr Samuel Dushkin in 1947 for Vn & Pno); Etude for Vc & Pno:A Portrait of Frederic James (1966); Lili Hastings for Vc & Pno (1983) Northeastern ▲ NR 240–CD

Cohen, Fredric (ob/E hn)
Macchia, S.:Chamber Con 3, w. J. Tanner (fl/alt fl), M. Sussman (cl), D. Fedora (bn), L. Klock (hn), V. Kadlubkiewicz (vn), J. Messina (db), P. Tanner (perc) *(rec July 1992)* Gasparo ▲ GS 226 [DDD]

Cohen, Greg (db)
The Other Portrait, w. K. Peplowski (cl/t sax), Bulgarian National SO [cnd:Ljubomir Denev] Concord Concerto ▲ CCD 42043 [DDD]

Cohen, Harriet (pno)
Bax, A.:Son Va & Pno, w. W. Primrose (va) *(rec 1937)* Pearl ▲ PEA 9453 (m) [AAD]
Brahms, J.:Son 2 Cl, w. L. Tertis (va) *(rec 1933)* Pearl ▲ PEA 9918 (m) [AAD]

Cohen, I. (vn)—see ORCHESTRAS & ENSEMBLES Beaux Arts Trio

Cohen, Jeffrey (pno)—see also ORCHESTRAS & ENSEMBLES Stanislas Ensemble
Fauré, G.:Songs, w. Natalie Dessay (sop), Béatrice Uria–Monzon (mez), Jean–Paul Fouchécourt (ten), François Le Roux (bar)—complete songs grouped by poets [Leconte de Lisle; Charles Baudelaire; Paul Verlaine; Jean de la Ville de Mirmont; Armand Silvestre; Victor Hugo; Théophile Gautier; 5 Melodies of Venice; Sully Prudhomme; Albert Samain; Louis Pommey; Paul de Chodens; Marc Monnier; Romain Bussine; Victor Wilder; Georgette Deblads; Villiers de l'Isle Adam; Charles Grandmougin; Henri de Régnier; Stéphan Bordèse; Charles Van Lerberghe; Baronne de Brimont; Maurice Maeterlinck; Edmond Haraucourt; Molière REM 4–▲ REM 311179 [DDD]
Folk Songs, w. M. Kobayashi (mez) REM ▲ 311253
Mélodies Françaises en duo, w. C. Alliot–Lugaz (sop), François Le Roux (bar) *(rec 9/88)* REM ▲ 311086 [DDD]
Weill, K.:Mahagonny, w. U. Lemper (sop), H. Jungwirth (sop), H. Wildhaber (ten), P. Haage (ten), T. Mohr (bar), S. Tremper (sgr), J. Mauceri (cnd), Berlin RIAS Chamber Ensemble [G] London ▲ 430168–2 [DDD]

Cohen, Jill (va)
Tailleferre, G.:Chansons populaires françaises, w. Patrice Maginnis (sop), John Fairweather (vn), David Ryther (vn), Karen Andrie (vc), Elizabeth Bodine (ob), Andy Connell (cl), Gordon Mumma (hn), June Orzel (bn), N. Paiement (cnd) *(rec UC, Santa Cruz, May 1992)* Helicon Classics ▲ HE 1008
Tailleferre, G.:Image, w. John Fairweather (vn), David Ryther (vn), Karen Andrie (vc), Elizabeth Bodine (ob), Andy Connell (cl), Gordon Mumma (hn), June Orzel (bn), N. Paiement (cnd) *(rec UC, Santa Cruz, May 1992)* Helicon Classics ▲ HE 1008

Cohen, Joël (lt)
Hugues Cuenod, w. H. Cuénod (ten), Rose Dobos (pno) Memoire Vive ▲ CD 262020 [ADD]

Cohen, Lynette Diers (bn)
Banfield, W.:4 Persons, w. Fred Ormand (cl), Harry Sargous (ob), Ellen Weckler (pno) Innova ▲ 510 [DDD]

Cohen, P. (vc)—see ORCHESTRAS & ENSEMBLES Apple Hill Chamber Players

Cohen, Pablo (gtr)
Guastavino, C.:Jeromita Linares, Camerata Bariloche CO Argentina *(rec Troy Savings Bank Music Hall, Troy, NY, Feb. 1994)* Dorian ▲ DOR 90202 [DDD]

Cohen, Patrick (pno)
Adalid Y Gurréa, M. del:El Lamento *(rec Auditorio de Cuenca, Apr 1995)* Glossa ▲ GCD 920501 [DDD]
Adalid Y Gurréa, M. del:Petits riens *(rec Auditorio de Cuenca, Apr 1995)* Glossa ▲ GCD 920501 [DDD]

Cohen, Patrick (pno) (cont.)
Adalid Y Gurréa, M. del:El Último adiós *(rec Auditorio de Cuenca, Apr 1995)* Glossa ▲ GCD 920501 [DDD]
Allú, M.S.:El peregrino *(rec Auditorio de Cuenca, Apr 1995)* Glossa ▲ GCD 920501 [DDD]
Beethoven, L. van:Son 1 Vc, w. Christophe Coin (vc) Musique d'Abord ▲ HMA 1901179
Beethoven, L. van:Son 2 Vc, w. Christophe Coin (vc) Musique d'Abord ▲ HMA 1901179
Beethoven, L. van:Trio 1 Pno, w. Erich Höbarth (vn), Christophe Coin (vc) Harmonia Mundi France ("Musique d'abord" series) ▲ HMA 1901361
Beethoven, L. van:Trio 2 Pno, w. Erich Höbarth (vn), Christophe Coin (vc) Harmonia Mundi France ("Musique d'abord" series) ▲ HMA 1901361
Beethoven, L. van:Trio 3 Pno, w. E. Höbarth (vn), C. Coin (vc) Harmonia Mundi France ▲ HMC 901475
Beethoven, L. van:Trio 7 Pno, w. W. Meyer (vn), C. Coin (vc) Harmonia Mundi France ▲ HMC 901475
Boccherini, L.:Qnt Pno, G.407–412, w. Mosaïques String Quartet—G.407, 408 & 411 Astrée ▲ E 8518 [DDD]
de Quesada, A.:Allegro de concierto *(rec Auditorio de Cuenca, Apr 1995)* Glossa ▲ GCD 920501 [DDD]
de Quesada, A.:Grandes estudios (6) *(rec Auditorio de Cuenca, Apr 1995)* Glossa ▲ GCD 920501 [DDD]
Fauré, G.:Trio, w. Pascal Moraguès (cl), Christophe Coin (vc) Adès ▲ ADE 203952 [DDD]
Haydn, J.:Sons Pno—H.XVI/21–26 Valois ▲ V 4668
Haydn, J.:Trios Pno, Fl & Vc, w. Konrad Hüntler (fl), Christophe Coin (vc) Harmonia Mundi France ▲ HMC 901521
Haydn, J.:Trios Pno, Vn & Vc, w. Erich Höbarth (vn), Christophe Coin (vc)—Nos. 32–34, H.XV/18–20 Harmonia Mundi France ▲ HMC 901314
Haydn, J.:Trios Pno, Vn & Vc, w. Erich Höbarth (vn), Christophe Coin (vc)—H.XV/35–37 Harmonia Mundi France ▲ HMC 901400
Haydn, J.:Trios Pno, Vn & Vc, w. Erich Höbarth (vn), Christophe Coin (vc) Harmonia Mundi France ▲ HMC 901572
Haydn, J.:Trios Pno, Vn & Vc, w. Erich Höbarth (vn), Christophe Coin (vc) Harmonia Mundi France ▲ HMC 901514
Indy, V. d':Trio Cl, w. Pascal Moraguès (cl), Christophe Coin (vc) Adès ▲ ADE 203952 [DDD]
Jadin, H.:Sons Pno, Op. 4 Valois ▲ V 4689
Jadin, H.:Sons Pno, Op. 5 Valois ▲ V 4689
Mozart, W.A.:Con 20 Pno, w. C. Coin (cnd), Limoges Baroque Ensemble Astrée ▲ E 8589
Mozart, W.A.:Con 21 Pno, w. C. Coin (cnd), Limoges Baroque Ensemble Astrée ▲ E 8589
Mozart, W.A.:Son 1 Pno [performed on fortepiano (Anton Walter, Vienna ca 1790)] *(rec Oberschützen, Austria, Feb 1996)* Glossa ▲ GCD 920503 [DDD]
Mozart, W.A.:Son 2 Pno [performed on fortepiano (Anton Walter, Vienna ca 1790)] *(rec Oberschützen, Austria, Feb 1996)* Glossa ▲ GCD 920503 [DDD]
Mozart, W.A.:Son 3 Pno [performed on fortepiano (Anton Walter, Vienna ca 1790)] *(rec Oberschützen, Austria, Feb 1996)* Glossa ▲ GCD 920503 [DDD]
Mozart, W.A.:Son 4 Pno [performed on fortepiano (Anton Walter, Vienna ca 1790)] *(rec Oberschützen, Austria, Feb 1996)* Glossa ▲ GCD 920503 [DDD]
Mozart, W.A.:Sons Vn Pno (misc), w. Erich Höbarth (vn)—K.301–305 Astrée ▲ E 8542
Mozart, W.A.:Sons Vn Pno (misc), w. Erich Höbarth (vn) [period instrs] Auvidis Astrée ▲ E 8581
Mozart, W.A.:Trio Cl, K.498, w. W. Meyer (cl), A. Mitterer (va) Astrée ▲ E 8736
Mozart, W.A.:Vars Vn, K.360/374b, w. Erich Höbarth (vn) [period instrs] Auvidis Astrée ▲ E 8581
Ocón, E.:Bolero *(rec Auditorio de Cuenca, Apr 1995)* Glossa ▲ GCD 920501 [DDD]
Power, T.:Barcarola Pno *(rec Auditorio de Cuenca, Apr 1995)* Glossa ▲ GCD 920501 [DDD]
Soler, P.A.:Sons Kbd Glossa ("Los Siglos de Oro" series) ▲ 920502

Cohen, Raymond (vn)—see also ORCHESTRAS & ENSEMBLES Cohen Piano Trio, Cohen Piano Trio members
Beethoven, L. van:Sons Vn (comp), w. A. Rael (pno) Duo 3–▲ 89019 [DDD]
Falla, M. de:Con Hpd, w. R. Puyana (hpd), D. Sandeman (fl), N. Black (ob), T. King (cl), T. Weill (vc), C. Mackerras (cnd) *(rec 1969)* Philips ("Spanish" series) ▲ 432829–2 [ADD]
Farnon, R.:Music of, w. A. Brewer (hp), Farnon, Gamley (cnd), Royal PO—Capt. Horatio Hornblower Suite; A la claire fontaine; Intermezzo for Harp & Strings; Lake of the Woods; A Promise of Spring; Rhapsody for Violin & Orchestra; State Occasion *(rec 1991)* Reference ▲ RR 47CD [DDD]

Cohen, Richard (hn)
Wagner, R.:Siegfried Idyll, w. T. Holowach (vn), M. Skazinetsky (vn), L. Toman (va), R. Laurie (vc), C. Elliott (db), S. Shulman (fl), T. Maloney (cl), J. Valdepenas (cl), J. Fetherston (cl), S. Mosher (bn), S. Wilson (hn), J. Cowell (tpt), G. Gould (cnd) *(rec July 27–29 & Sept. 8, 198)* Sony Classical ▲ SMK 52650 [ADD]

Cohen, Robert (vc)—see also ORCHESTRAS & ENSEMBLES Cohen Piano Trio
Beethoven, L. van:Con Vn, Vc & Pno, "Triple Con", w. Frank Peter Zimmermann (vn), Wolfgang Manz (pno), J.–P. Saraste (cnd), English CO Classics for Pleasure ("Silver Doubles" series) 2–▲ CFP CDCFP 4775 [ADD/DDD]
Dvořák, A.:Con Vc, w. Z. Macal (cnd), London PO Classics for Pleasure ("Silver Doubles" series) 2–▲ CFP CDCFP 4775 [ADD/DDD]
Dvořák, A.:Qnt Pno, Op. 81, w. Roberte Mamou (pno), Ami Flammer (vn), Silvia Marcovici (vn), Gerard Causse (va) *(rec Mozart Festival, Lille, France, 1994)* Verdi Classics ▲ AU 32 250
Dvořák, A.:Rondo, w. Roberte Mamou (pno) [arr for vc & pno] *(rec Mozart Festival, Lille, France, 1994)* Verdi Classics ▲ AU 32 250
Elgar, E.:Con Vc, w. N. del Mar (cnd), London PO Classics for Pleasure ▲ CDCFP 9003 [ADD]
Elgar, E.:Con Vc, w. N. del Mar (cnd), London PO Classics for Pleasure ("Silver Doubles" series) 2–▲ CFP CDCFP 4775 [ADD/DDD]
Elgar, E.:Con Vc, w. N. del Mar (cnd), London PO Classics for Pleasure 2–▲ CFP CFPSD 4775 [ADD/DDD]
Elgar, E.:Elegy Strs, w. N. del Mar (cnd), London PO Classics for Pleasure ▲ CDCFP 9003 [ADD]
Elgar, E.:In the South, w. N. del Mar (cnd), London PO Classics for Pleasure ▲ CDCFP 9003 [ADD]
Grieg, E.:Son Vc, w. R. Vignoles (pno) CRD ▲ 3391 [ADD]
Haydn, J.:Con 1 Vc, w. Y. Menuhin (cnd), English CO Start Classics ▲ SCD 13
Schubert, Franz:Qnt Strs, D.956, w. Amadeus String Quartet—Adagio *(rec Abbey Road Studios, London, Nov 10–11, 1994)* Argo ▲ 444873–2
Tchaikovsky, P.:Vars on a Rococo Theme, w. Z. Macal (cnd), London PO Classics for Pleasure ("Silver Doubles" series) 2–▲ CFP CDCFP 4775 [ADD/DDD]
Walton, W.:Con Vc, w. A. Litton (cnd), Bournemouth SO London ▲ 443450–2

Cohen, Steven (cl)
Dankner, S.:Trio Cl, w. Allen Nisbet (vc), Peter Collins (pno) Albany ▲ TROY 144 [DDD]

Cohl, Deborah (fl)
Serenade, w. Nancy Dygert (hp) PHD ▲ PHD 570004 [DDD]

Cohler, Jonathan (cl)
Bärmann, H.J.:Qnt 3 Cl, w. J. Gordon (pno) [arr. for Clarinet & Piano]—Adagio *(rec May 29–30, 1992)* Ongaku ▲ 024–101 [DDD]
Brahms, J.:Son 1 Cl, w. J. Gordon (pno) *(rec May 29–30, 1992)* Ongaku ▲ 024–101 [DDD]
Brahms, J.:Son 2 Cl, w. R. Hodgkinson (pno) *(rec Aug. 28–29, 1993)* Ongaku ▲ 024–102 [DDD]
Koch, E. von:Monolog 3 Cl *(rec New Hope Methodist Church, Methuen, MA, Aug 11–Sept 2, 1995)* Ongaku ▲ 024–105 [DDD]
Martino, D.:A Set *(rec New Hope Methodist Church, Methuen, MA, Aug 11–Sept 2, 1995)* Ongaku ▲ 024–105 [DDD]
Messiaen, O.:Quatuor pour la fin du temps—Abîme des oiseaux *(rec New Hope Methodist Church, Methuen, MA, Aug 11–Sept 2, 1995)* Ongaku ▲ 024–105 [DDD]
Milhaud, D.:Sonatina Cl, w. R. Hodgkinson (pno) *(rec Aug. 28–29, 1993)* Ongaku ▲ 024–102 [DDD]
Moonflowers, Baby!, w. J. Gordon (pno) *(rec Aug. 23–24, 1993)* Crystal ▲ CD 733 [DDD]
Osborne, W.:Rhap Bn *(rec New Hope Methodist Church, Methuen, MA, Aug 11–Sept 2, 1995)* Ongaku ▲ 024–105 [DDD]
Persichetti, V.:Parable 13 *(rec New Hope Methodist Church, Methuen, MA, Aug 11–Sept 2, 1995)* Ongaku ▲ 024–105 [DDD]

Cohler, Jonathan (cl) (cont.)
Poulenc, F.:Son Cl Pno, w. R. Hodgkinson (pno) *(rec Aug. 28–29, 1993)* Ongaku ▲ 024-102 [DDD]
Sargon, S.:Deep Ellum Nights, w. J. Gordon (pno) *(rec May 29–30, 1992)* Ongaku ▲ 024-101 [DDD]
Schumann, R.:Fantasiestücke Cl, w. R. Hodgkinson (pno) *(rec Aug. 28–29, 1993)* Ongaku ▲ 024-102 [DDD]
Smith, W.O.:Pieces Cl *(rec New Hope Methodist Church, Methuen, MA, Aug 11–Sept 2, 1995)* Ongaku ▲ 024-105 [DDD]
Stravinsky, I.:Pieces Cl, w. R. Hodgkinson (pno) *(rec Aug. 28–29, 1993)* Ongaku ▲ 024-102 [DDD]
Weber, C.M. von:Grand duo concertant Cl, w. J. Gordon (pno) *(rec May 29–30, 1992)* Ongaku ▲ 024-101 [DDD]
Wellesz, E.:Suite Cl *(rec New Hope Methodist Church, Methuen, MA, Aug 11–Sept 2, 1995)* Ongaku ▲ 024-105 [DDD]

Cohn, Al (t sax)
Wolpe, S.:Qt Tpt, w. Bob Nagel (tpt), Al Howard (perc), Jack Maxin (pno), S. Baron (cnd) *(rec Esoteric Studios, NY, 1954)* Hat Hut ▲ CD 6182 [AAD]

Coid, Marshall (vn)—see ORCHESTRAS & ENSEMBLES Musicians' Accord members

Coin, Christophe (b vl)
Purcell, H.:Sons (12) Vns, Z.790–801, w. Pavlo Beznosiuk (vn), Rachel Podger (vn), Christopher Hogwood (org) *(rec Emmanuel College, Cambridge, Feb–Aug 1994)* L'Oiseau-Lyre ▲ 444449-2 [DDD]
Purcell, H.:Sons (10) Vns, Z.802–811, w. C. Mackintosh (vn), M. Huggett (vn), C. Hogwood (chamber org/spinet) L'Oiseau-Lyre ▲ 433190-2 [ADD]

Coin, Christophe (pic vc/cnd)
Bach, J.S.:Cant 85, w. Barbara Schlick (sop), Andreas Scholl (alt), Christoph Prégardien (ten), Gotthold Schwarz (bass), Leipzig Vocal Concerto, Limoges Baroque Ensemble Astrée ▲ E 8544
Bach, J.S.:Cant 175, w. Barbara Schlick (sop), Andreas Scholl (alt), Christoph Prégardien (ten), Gotthold Schwarz (bass), Leipzig Vocal Concerto, Limoges Baroque Ensemble Astrée ▲ E 8544
Bach, J.S.:Cant 183, w. Barbara Schlick (sop), Andreas Scholl (alt), Christoph Prégardien (ten), Gotthold Schwarz (bass), Leipzig Vocal Concerto, Limoges Baroque Ensemble Astrée ▲ E 8544
Bach, J.S.:Cant 199, w. Barbara Schlick (sop), Andreas Scholl (alt), Christoph Prégardien (ten), Gotthold Schwarz (bass), Leipzig Vocal Concerto, Limoges Baroque Ensemble Astrée ▲ E 8544

Coin, Christophe (vc)—see also ORCHESTRAS & ENSEMBLES Mosaïques String Quartet
Beethoven, L. van:Son 1 Vc, w. Patrick Cohen (pno) Musique d'Abord ▲ HMA 1901179
Beethoven, L. van:Son 2 Vc, w. Patrick Cohen (pno) Musique d'Abord ▲ HMA 1901179
Beethoven, L. van:Trio 1 Pno, w. Patrick Cohen (pno), Erich Höbarth (vn) Harmonia Mundi France ("Musique d'abord" series) ▲ HMA 1901361
Beethoven, L. van:Trio 2 Pno, w. Patrick Cohen (pno), Erich Höbarth (vn) Harmonia Mundi France ("Musique d'abord" series) ▲ HMA 1901361
Beethoven, L. van:Trio 3 Pno, w. P. Cohen (pno), E. Höbarth (vn) Harmonia Mundi France ▲ HMC 901475
Beethoven, L. van:Trio 7 Pno, w. P. Cohen (pno), W. Meyer (vn) Harmonia Mundi France ▲ HMC 901475
Boccherini, L.:Con Vc, G.476, w. C. Coin (cnd), Baroque Instrumental Ensemble Astrée ▲ E 8517 [DDD]
Boccherini, L.:Con Vc, G.480, w. C. Coin (cnd), Baroque Instrumental Ensemble Astrée ▲ E 8517 [DDD]
Boccherini, L.:Con Vc, G.482, w. C. Coin (cnd), Baroque Instrumental Ensemble Astrée ▲ E 8517 [DDD]
Fauré, G.:Trio, w. Patrick Cohen (pno), Pascal Moraguès (cl) Adès ▲ ADE 203952 [DDD]
Haydn, J.:Trios Pno, Fl & Vc, w. Patrick Cohen (pno), Konrad Hüntler (fl) Harmonia Mundi France ▲ HMC 901521
Haydn, J.:Trios Pno, Vn & Vc, w. Arnaldo Cohen (pno), Erich Höbarth (vn)—H.XV/12–14 Harmonia Mundi France ▲ HMC 901277 [DDD]
Haydn, J.:Trios Pno, Vn & Vc, w. Partick Cohen (pno), Erich Höbarth (vn)—Nos. 32–34, H.XV/18–20 Harmonia Mundi France ▲ HMC 901314
Haydn, J.:Trios Pno, Vn & Vc, w. Partick Cohen (pno), Erich Höbarth (vn)—H.XV/35–37 Harmonia Mundi France ▲ HMC 901400
Haydn, J.:Trios Pno, Vn & Vc, w. Patrick Cohen (pno), Erich Höbarth (vn) Harmonia Mundi France ▲ HMC 901514
Haydn, J.:Trios Pno, Vn & Vc, w. Patrick Cohen (pno), Erich Höbarth (vn) Harmonia Mundi France ▲ HMC 901572
Indy, V. d':Trio Cl, w. Pascal Moraguès (cl), Patrick Cohen (pno) Adès ▲ ADE 203952 [DDD]
Music at the Time of Beaumarchais, w. Montserrat Figueras (sop), Lawrence Monteyro (sop), Raphel Oleg (vn), Miguel da Silva (va), Marc Coppey (vc), José Miguel Moreno (gtr), Paul Badura-Skoda (pno), Philippe Cassard (pno), Eric Le Sage (pno), Bob Van Asperen (hpd), et al. Valois ▲ V 4767
Purcell, H.:Music of, w. Catherine Bott (sop), Emma Kirkby (sop), James Bowman (alt), Anthony Rooley (lt), Paula Chateauneuf (gtr), Monica Huggett (vn), Catherine Mackintosh (vn), Hill, Hogwood (cnd), Academy of Ancient Music, Brandenburg Consort, David Hill (cnd), Anthony Lewis (cnd), St. Anthony Singers, Taverner Choir, Winchester Cathedral Choir—The Double Dealer; Come Ye Sons of Art; The Old Bachelor; Birthday Song for Queen Mary; Oedipus; King Arthur; Bonduca; The Fairy Queen; Son. No. 9 in F; Dido & Aeneas; Abdelazer; Bess of Bedlam; The Married Beau; Hear My Prayer, O Lord; Rejoice in the Lord Always London ("Editions de l'oiseau-lyre" series) ▲ 444620-2
Vivaldi, A.:Cons Vc, w. C. Hogwood (cnd), Academy of Ancient Music—3 Concerti—RV.402, 406, 414 L'Oiseau-Lyre ▲ 433052-2 [DDD]
Vivaldi, A.:Cons Vc, w. C. Hogwood (cnd), Academy of Ancient Music—5 concerti—RV. 401, 412, 413, 416, 418, 424 L'Oiseau-Lyre ▲ 421732-2 [DDD] □ 421732-5
Vivaldi, A.:Cons Diverse Instrs, w. Il Giardino Armonico Ensemble—in g, RV.531; in F, RV.544; in F, RV.551; in D, RV.564; in A, RV.552; in C, RV.561 Teldec ("Das alte Werk" series) ▲ 94552-2
Vivaldi, A.:Sons Vc, Op. 14, w. C. Hogwood (hpd) L'Oiseau-Lyre ▲ 421060-2 [DDD]

Coin, Christophe (vl)—see ORCHESTRAS & ENSEMBLES Limoges Baroque Ensemble Soloists

Coker, Paul (pno)
Beethoven, L. van:Sons Vc (comp), w. Patrick Demenga (vc) Accord 2-▲ ACD 204302 [DDD]
Beethoven, L. van:Vars on "Ein Mädchen oder Weibchen" from Mozart's *Die Zauberflöte*, w. Patrick Demenga (vc) Accord ▲ ACD 204302 [DDD]
Beethoven, L. van:Vars on "See, the Conquering Hero Comes" from Handel's *Judas Maccabaeus*, w. Patrick Demenga (vc) Accord ▲ ACD 204302 [DDD]
Kreisler, F.:Music of, w. Joshua Bell (vn)—Praeludium & Allegro; Schon Rosmarin; Tambourin Chinois; Caprice Viennois; La Precieuse; Liebesfreud; Liebeslied; La Gitana; Bercuse Romantique; Polinchinelle; Rondino; Tempo Di Minuetto; Toy Soldier's March; Allegretto; Marche miniature viennoise; Aucassin & Nicolette; Menuett; Sicilienne & Riguadon; Syncopation London ▲ 444409-2
Prokofiev, S.:Son Vc, w. K. B. Dinitzen (vc) Kontrapunkt ▲ KPT 32146 [DDD]
Reger, M.:Sons Cl, Op. 49, w. Steven Kanoff (cl) Accord ▲ ACD 204432 [DDD]

Cokkinias, P. (cl)—see ORCHESTRAS & ENSEMBLES Scarborough Chamber Players

Col, V. de (pno)
Clementi, M.:Sons Pno—in B, Op. 47/2; in g, Op. 34/2 Entrée ▲ 0038 [ADD]
Clementi, M.:Waltzes, Op. 38, w. K. Künstler (tambourine), M. Dietrich (triangle) Entrée ▲ 0038 [ADD]

Colan, Ruxandra (vn)
Martin, P.:Elegies, w. Philip Martin (pno) Altarus ▲ CD 9011
Martin, P.:Songs for the 4 Parts of the Night, w. Penelope Price Jones (sop) Altarus ▲ CD 9011

Colard, Élisabeth (hp)—see ORCHESTRAS & ENSEMBLES Gioccarpa

Colbers, Ron (perc)—see ORCHESTRAS & ENSEMBLES Ives Ensemble members

Colburn, Janet (pno)
Mozart, F.X.W.:Con Pno, Op. 14, w. N. Marriner (cnd), Academy of St. Martin in the Fields Audiofon ▲ CD 72038
Mozart, W.A.:Con 23 Pno, w. N. Marriner (cnd), Academy of St. Martin in the Fields Audiofon ▲ CD 72038

Colburn, Michael (eup)
The Golden Age of Brass, Vol. 3, w. M. Colburn (eup), American Serenade Band [cnd:H.C. Smith] Summit ▲ DCD 150 [DDD]

Cole, Graham (perc)
Jolivet, A.:Suite en concert, w. Anna Noakes (fl), Kate Eyre (perc), Rachel Gledhill (perc), Gary Kettel (perc) ASV ("French Chamber Music" series) ▲ ASV 948

Cole, Maggie (hpd)
Bach, J.S.:Goldberg Vars Virgin Classics ("Veritas" series) ▲ CDC 59045-2 [DDD]
Boccherini, L.:Sons (34) Vc, w. S. Isserlis (vc)—Nos. 6 in C, 2 in c & 5 in G Virgin Classics ▲ CDC 59015
Scarlatti, D.:Sons Kbd—K.27, 141, 263, 264, 318, 319, 380, 381, 417, 446, 550, 551 Amon Ra ▲ CD-SAR 27 [DDD]
Soler, P.A.:Fandango Virgin Classics ▲ 59624 [DDD]

Cole, Maggie (pno)
Guitar Collection, w. N. North (gtr) Amon Ra ▲ CDSAR 18 [DDD]

Cole, Maurice (pno)
Soler, P.A.:Sons Hpd—Sonata Nos. 84, 85, 86, 88, 90 Virgin Classics ▲ 59624 [DDD]
Soler, P.A.:Sons Pno—Sonata Nos. 18, 19, 41, 72, 78, 87 Virgin Classics ▲ 59624 [DDD]

Cole, Peter (va)
Britten, H.:Young Apollo, w. P. Donohoe (pno), F. Kok (vn), J. Ballard (vn), M. Kaznowski (vc), S. Rattle (cnd), City of Birmingham SO *(rec 4/82)* EMI Classics 2-▲ CDCB 54270 [DDD]

Cole, Robert (bn)—see ORCHESTRAS & ENSEMBLES New York Woodwind Soloists

Cole, Roger (ob)
The Expressive Oboe, w. Linda Lee Thomas (pno) Musica Viva ▲ MVCD 1070 [DDD]

Cole, Steve (cl)—see ORCHESTRAS & ENSEMBLES Rhythm & Bluefield Band

Cole, Warwick (pno)
Dussek, J.L.:Hp Music, w. Danielle Perrett (hp), James Ellis (vn), Helen Verney (vc), Gillian Jones (hand-hn)—A Favorite Duet for Hp & Pno, Op. 11; Son in E♭ for Hp, Op. 34/1; Favorite Son for Hp, Vn & Vc, Op. 37; Son in B♭ for Hp, Op. 34/2; Duo for Hp, Pno & Hand-Horn, Op. 38 Meridian ▲ MER 84244 [DDD]

Coleman, Anthony (kbd)
Zorn, J.:Kristallnacht, w. David Krakauer (cl/b cl), Frank London (tpt), Mark Feldman (vn), Marc Ribot (gtr), Mark Dresser (electric bass), William Winant (perc) Tzadik ▲ TZA 7301 [ADD]

Coleman, Anthony (pno)
Gisberg:Music of, w. Gisburg (sgr/fl), Jeff O'Malley (nar), Midori Seiler (vn), Ron Lawrence (va), Guy Tyler (db), Christine Bard (perc)—Low-End; Since You Have Left; The Woman Is Perfected; Sharks; Night & Wind; Saturnspacemonsters Walking on a Sandy Surface; Old Moon in Winter; Never Saw the Stars So Bright; Habe Die Liebe Verschlafen; W.A.L.S.H. Tzadik ▲ TZA CD 7019 [DDD]

Coleman, Anthony (toy pno/org)
Sharp, E.:20 Below, w. Wayne Horvitz (syn), Zeena Parkins (org/syn), Joseph Paul Taylor (elec/syn), Gwen Toth (reed org), David Weinstein (org/syn) Newport Classics ▲ NPD 85504

Coleman, Cy (pno)
Suesse, D.:Music of, w. Dana Suesse (pno), Robert Barlow (hp), F. Fennell (cnd), American SO, All City Concert Choir—Con Romantico for Pno & Orch; A Little Light Music; Young Man with Harp for Hp & Orch; The Blues [from Con in 3 Rhythms]; Coronach for Hp & Orch; Jazz Con for Combo & Orch; The Night Is Young & You're So Beautiful for Orch & Chorus *(rec Carnegie Hall, Dec 1974)* Premier ▲ PRCD 1055
Suesse, D.:Music of, w. Dana Suesse (pno)—Coctail Suite; Jazz Concerto in D for Combo & Orch (arr for 2 pnos); plus others *(rec 1940–56)* Pearl ▲ PEA 9202 [ADD]

Coleman, Donna (pno)
Perlongo, D.:Con Pno, w. R. Black (cnd), Slovak RSO Bratislava *(rec Slovak Radio & Television Studios, Slovak National Republic)* Master Musicians Collective ▲ MMC 2020 [DDD]

Coleman, Elizabeth (pno)
Schubert, Franz:Songs (misc), w. Elisabeth Schumann (sop) Gerald Moore (pno), Leo Rosenek (pno)—An die Nachtigall, D.497; Die Forelle, D.550; Ave Maria (Ellens Gesang III), D.839; An die Musik, D.547; Auf dem Wasser zu singen, D.774; Des Fischers Liebesglück, D.933; Der Musensohn, D.764; Fischerweise, D.881; Gretchen am Spinrade, D.118; Liebesbotschaft ("Schwanegesang" No. 1), D.957; Nacht und Träume, D.827; Seligkeit, D.433; Nähe des Geliebten, D.162; Lachen und Weinen, D.777; Frühlingstraum ("Winterreise" No. 11), D.911; Der Einsame, D.800; Nachtviolen, D.752; An die Geliebte, D.303; Wiegenlied (Schlafe, Schlafe), D.498; Der Schmetterling, D.633; Des Baches Wiegenlied (Die Schöne Müllerin" No. 20), D.957; Der Jüngling und der Tod, D.545; Das Heimweh, D.456; Dass sie hier gewesen, D.775; Der Vollmond strahlt ("Rosamunde" Romanze), D.797; Der Junge Nonne, D.828 *(rec 1933–1945)* Minerva ▲ MN-A22 [ADD]

Coleman, Ira (elec bass)
So Many Stars, w. K. Battle (sop), Antonio Hart (sax), Grover Washington Jr (sax), Tom Harrell (flgl), James Carter (b cl), Cyrus Chestnut (pno), Jon Herrington (gtr), Romero Lubambo (gtr), Christian McBride (elec bass), Cyro Baptista (perc), Steven Berrios (perc) *(rec Hit Factory, Clinton Recording Studios, R.P.M. Sound Studios, Unique Recording Studios, Power Station)* Sony Classical ▲ SK 68473 [DDD]

Coleman, Tom (db)
Something for Recorder & Strings, w. J. Tyson (rcr), Frances Conover Fitch (hpd), Jane Starkman (vn), Katheryn Shaw (vn), Jann Cosart (va), Alice Robbins (vc) Titanic ▲ Ti 169 [DDD]

Colemann, Steve (sax)
Sato, M.:Improvs, w. Michihiro Sato (tsugaru shamisen), Bill Frisell (elec gtr), Fred Frith (elec gtr), Tenko (sgr), Mark Miller (elec bass), Nicolas Collins (elec), Christian Marclay (turntables), Tom Cora (vc), Joey Baron (perc), Mark Dresser (elec bass), Gerry Hemingway (perc), Toh Ban Djan [Ikue Mori (perc), Luli Shioi (elec bass/sgr)], Semantics—23 improvisations with various accompaniment combinations *(rec Baby Monster Studio, NY, Apr. 11–16, 1988)* Hat Hut ▲ hat ART CD 6015 [ADD]

Coles, Samuel (fl)
Mozart, W.A.:Cons Fl, w. Y. Menuhin (cnd), English CO Virgin Classics ▲ 59075 [DDD]
Mozart, W.A.:Con Fl Hp, w. N. Yoshino (hp), Y. Menuhin (cnd), English CO Virgin Classics ▲ 59075 [DDD]
Mozart, W.A.:Con Fl Hp, w. N. Yoshino (hp), Y. Menuhin (cnd), English CO Virgo ▲ CDZ 61108 [DDD]

Coletti, Paul (va)—see also ORCHESTRAS & ENSEMBLES Menuhin Festival Piano Quartet
Brahms, J.:Son 2 Cl, w. F. Rieger (pno) Ars Produktion ▲ FCD 368308 [DDD]
Bruch, M.:Romanze Va, w. P. Bush (pno) Ars Produktion ▲ FCD 368316 [DDD]
English Music for Viola, w. L. Howard (pno) Hyperion ▲ CDA 66687
Herzogenberg, H. von:Legenden, w. F. Rieger (pno) Ars Produktion ▲ FCD 368308 [DDD]
International Menuhin Music Academy, w. International Menuhin Music Academy, Nora Chastain (vn), Hu-Kun (vn), Mi-Kyung Lee (vn), Alberto Lysy (vn) Arcobaleno ▲ SBCD 4700 [DDD]
Schubert, Franz:Son Arpeggione, w. P. Bush (pno) Ars Produktion ▲ FCD 368316 [DDD]
Schumann, R.:Märchenbilder, w. F. Rieger (pno) Ars Produktion ▲ FCD 368308 [DDD]
Shostakovich, D.:Son Va, w. P. Bush (pno) Ars Produktion ▲ FCD 368316 [DDD]
Turina, J.:Escena andaluza, w. F. Rieger (pno), N. Chastain (vn), C. Busch (vn), A. B. Deutschler (va), F. Goutou (vc) *(rec May 25–28, 1993)* Claves ▲ CD 9403 [DDD]

Colgan, J. (gtr)—see ORCHESTRAS & ENSEMBLES San Francisco Guitar Quartet

Colgrass, Michael (instrs)
Cage, J.:Music of, w. John Cage, Xenia Cage, Don Butterfield, Merce Cunningham, et al.—6 Short Inventions for 7 Instruments; First Construction in Metal; Imaginary Landscape No. 1; The Wonderful Widow of 18 Springs; She Is Asleep; Son. & Interludes; Music for Carillon; Williams Mix; Con. for Piano & Orch. Wergo 3-▲ WER 6247-2

Colin, Lois (hp)
Franzetti, C.:Concertino Bass Trbn, w. David Taylor (b trbn), Carlos Franzetti (pno), C. Franzetti (cnd), Modus Chamber Ensemble *(rec Hip Pocket Studios, New York)* Premier ▲ PRCD 1044 [DDD]

Cóll, Ramon (pno)
Brahms, J.:Con 2 Pno, w. V. Sinaisky (cnd), Moscow PO *(rec studio 1991)* Russian Disc ▲ RC CD 10 013 [DDD]

▲ = CD ♦ = Enhanced CD Δ = MD ■ = Cassette Tape □ = DCC

Cóll, Ramon (pno) (cont.)
Fauré, G.:Ballade Pno, w. V. Sinaisky (cnd), Moscow PO *(rec 1991)* Russian Disc ▲ RC CD 10 013 [DDD]

Coll, Xavier (gtr)
Tangos & Habaneras for Flute & Guitar, w. M. Gascón (fl) *(rec Capilla de la Esperanza de Barcelona, Sept 4–6 & 25–26, 1995)* PROdigital ▲ PRO 1113 [DDD]

Colladant, Laure (pno)
Benda, G.A.:Sons Pno—in F, G & a Accord ▲ ACD 202622
Mozart, W.A.:Son 10 Pno Accord ▲ ACD 205162 [DDD]
Mozart, W.A.:Son 11 Pno Accord ▲ ACD 205162 [DDD]
Mozart, W.A.:Son 12 Pno Accord ▲ ACD 205162 [DDD]
Mozart, W.A.:Son 13 Pno Accord ▲ ACD 205162 [DDD]

Collard, André (pno)
Honegger, A.:Songs, w. Irma Kolassi (mez)—Un grand sommeil noir Memoire Vive ▲ CD 262024
Honegger, A.:Songs, w. Irma Kolassi (mez)—La Douceur de tes yeux; Derrière Murcie en fleurs; Un grand sommeil noir; Trois Psaumes *(rec 1957)* Mémoire Vive ▲ 262014 (m)

Collard, Catherine (pno)
Debussy, C.:Ariettes oubliées, w. N. Stutzmann (cta) [F] RCA Red Seal ▲ 09026–60899–2
Debussy, C.:Chansons de Bilitis, w. N. Stutzmann (cta) [F] RCA Red Seal ▲ 09026–60899–2
Debussy, C.:Poèmes (5) de Baudelaire, w. N. Stutzmann (cta) [F] RCA Red Seal ▲ 09026–60899–2
Fauré, G.:Songs, w. N. Stutzmann (cta)—28 songs RCA Red Seal ▲ 09026–61439–2
Indy, V. d':Sym on a French Mountain Air, w. M. Janowski (cnd), Radio France PO Erato ("Musifrance" series) ▲ 2292–45821–2–ZK
Ravel, M.:Histoires naturelles, w. N. Stutzmann (cta) [F] RCA Red Seal ▲ 09026–60899–2
Schumann, R.:Dichterliebe, w. N. Stutzmann (cta) [G] RCA Red Seal ▲ 09026–61187–2
Schumann, R.:Frauenliebe und –leben, w. N. Stutzmann (cta) [G] RCA Red Seal ▲ 09026–61187–2
Schumann, R.:Liederkreis, Op. 39, w. N. Stutzmann (cta) RCA Red Seal ▲ 09026–61728–2
Schumann, R.:Songs, w. N. Stutzmann (cta)—6 songs from Dem Liederbuch eines Malers [G] RCA Red Seal ▲ 09026–61187–2
Schumann, R.:Songs, w. N. Stutzmann (cta)—Opp. 27, 51, 77 & 96 RCA Red Seal ▲ 09026–61728–2

Collard, Jean-Philippe (pno)
Bizet, G.:Jeux d'enfants, w. Michel Béroff (pno) EMI Classics ▲ CDC 55347
Debussy, C.:Prélude à l'après–midi d'un faune, w. Michel Béroff (pno) [arr 2 pianos] EMI Classics ▲ CDC 55347
Dukas, P.:L'Apprenti sorcier, w. Michel Béroff (pno) [arr 2 pianos] EMI Classics ▲ CDC 55347
Fauré, G.:Ballade Pno [solo piano ver.] EMI Classics (Studio) 2–▲ CDMB 69149
Fauré, G.:Nocturnes (13) Pno EMI Classics (Studio) 2–▲ CDMB 69149
Fauré, G.:Préludes, Op. 103 EMI Classics (Studio) 2–▲ CDMB 69149
Fauré, G.:Qts Pno, Opp. 15 & 45, w. A. Dumay (vn), B. Pasquier (va), F. Lodeon (vc) EMI Classics 2–▲ ZDMB 62548
Fauré, G.:Son 1 Vc, w. F. Lodeon (vc) EMI Classics 2–▲ CDC 62545
Fauré, G.:Son 2 Vc, w. F. Lodeon (vc) EMI Classics 2–▲ CDC 62545
Fauré, G.:Son 1 Vn, w. A. Dumay (vn) EMI Classics 2–▲ CDC 62545
Fauré, G.:Theme & Vars Pno EMI Classics (Studio) 2–▲ CDMB 69149
Fauré, G.:Trio, w. A. Dumay (vn), F. Lodeon (vc) EMI Classics 2–▲ CDC 62545
Franck, C.:Symphonic Vars, w. M. Plasson (cnd), Toulouse Capitole Orch EMI Classics ("Studio DDD" series) ▲ CDD 63889 [DDD]
Gounod, C.:Songs, w. J. Van Dam (b–bar)—Medjé; Envoi de fleurs; Si la mort est le but; Crépuscule; Hymne à la nuit EMI Classics ▲ CDC 54818
Massenet, J.:Songs, w. J. Van Dam (b–bar)—Les mains; Berceuse; La mort de la cigale; Elégie [w. G. Rouge (cello)] EMI Classics ▲ CDC 54818
Ravel, M.:Rapsodie espagnole, w. Michel Béroff (pno) [arr 2 pianos] EMI Classics ▲ CDC 55347
Saint–Saëns, C.:Africa, w. A. Previn (cnd), Royal PO EMI Classics ▲ CDC 49757
Saint–Saëns, C.:Allegro appassionato, w. A. Previn (cnd), Royal PO EMI Classics ▲ CDC 49757
Saint–Saëns, C.:Cons Pno (comp), w. A. Previn (cnd), Royal PO—No. 1 in D EMI Classics ▲ CDC 49757
Saint–Saëns, C.:Con 2 Pno, w. A. Previn (cnd), Royal PO EMI Classics ▲ CDC 47816
Saint–Saëns, C.:Con 3 Pno, w. A. Previn (cnd), Royal PO EMI Classics ▲ CDC 49051
Saint–Saëns, C.:Con 4 Pno, w. A. Previn (cnd), Royal PO EMI Classics ▲ CDC 47816
Saint–Saëns, C.:Con 5 Pno, w. A. Previn (cnd), Royal PO EMI Classics ▲ CDC 49051
Saint–Saëns, C.:Rapsodie d'Auvergne, w. A. Previn (cnd), Royal PO EMI Classics ▲ CDC 49757
Saint–Saëns, C.:Songs, w. J. Van Dam (b–bar)—Rêverie; Clair de lune; Sonnet; Si vous n'avez rien à me dire; Le lever de la lune; Extase; Les cloches de la mer; Danse macabre; Le pas d'armes du roi Jean EMI Classics ▲ CDC 54818
Saint–Saëns, C.:Wedding Cake, w. A. Previn (cnd), Royal PO EMI Classics ▲ CDC 49757

Collet, P. (sax)
Vuataz, R.:Destin, w. E. Guibentif (hp), Y. Brustaux (perc)—3rd movt. *(rec Nov. 1980)* Grammont ▲ CTSP 7–2 [ADD]

Colliard, Gilles (vn)
Bach, J.S.:Cons Vn (comp), w. C. Meister (cnd), Brixi CO Prague *(rec Studio Martinek, Prague, Sept 5–8, 1994)* Doron ▲ DRC 5005 [DDD]
Bach, J.S.:Con Vn & Ob, w. Isaac Duarte (ob), C. Meister (cnd), Brixi CO Prague *(rec Studio Martinek, Prague, Sept 5–8, 1994)* Doron ▲ DRC 5005 [DDD]
Bach, J.S.:Con for 2 Vns, w. Saskia Lethiec (vn), C. Meister (cnd), Brixi CO Prague *(rec Studio Martinek, Prague, Sept 5–8, 1994)* Doron ▲ DRC 5005 [DDD]
Haydn, J.:Con 1 Vn, w. C. Meister (cnd), Prague Brixi CO *(rec Oct. 5–7, 1993)* Doron ▲ DRC 5003 [DDD]
Haydn, J.:Con 3 Vn, w. C. Meister (cnd), Prague Brixi CO *(rec Oct. 5–7, 1993)* Doron ▲ DRC 5003 [DDD]
Haydn, J.:Con 4 Vn, w. C. Meister (cnd), Prague Brixi CO *(rec Oct. 5–7, 1993)* Doron ▲ DRC 5003 [DDD]
Tartini, G.:L'arte del arco *(rec June 29–30, 1992)* Doron ▲ DRC 3007 [DDD]

Collier, Katherine (pno)
Bloch, E.:Suite Va & Pno, w. Y. Schotten (va) Crystal ▲ CD 637
Clarke, R.:Son Va, w. Y. Schotten (va) Crystal ▲ CD 637
Hindemith, P.:Son Va & Pno, Op. 11/4, w. Y. Schotten (va) Crystal ▲ CD 637
Schubert, Franz:Son Arpeggione, w. Y. Schotten (va) Crystal ▲ CD 635

Collins, Geoffrey (fl)—see also ORCHESTRAS & ENSEMBLES Australia Ensemble
Brumby, C.:Exotic Dances, w. Alice Giles (hp) *(rec Studio 200, ABC Sydney, Jan 1993)* Tall Poppies ▲ TP 31 [DDD]
Butterly, N.:The Wind Stirs Gently, w. David Pereira (vc) *(rec Studios 200 & 227, ABC Ultimo Centre, Jan–Feb 1995)* Tall Poppies ▲ TP 069 [DDD]
Conyngham, B.:Streams, w. Patricia Pollett (va), Marshall McGuire (hp) *(rec Studio 200, ABC Ultimo Centre, Sydney, 1994)* Tall Poppies ▲ TP 071 [DDD]
Edwards, R.:Ecstatic Dances Fls *(rec Studios 200 & 227, ABC Ultimo Centre, Jan–Feb 1995)* Tall Poppies ▲ TP 069 [DDD]
Ford, A.:Spinning *(rec Studios 200 & 227, ABC Ultimo Centre, Jan–Feb 1995)* Tall Poppies ▲ TP 069 [DDD]
Humble, K.:Son Fl, w. David Miller (pno) *(rec Studios 200 & 227, ABC Ultimo Centre, Jan–Feb 1995)* Tall Poppies ▲ TP 069 [DDD]
Jongen, J.:Danse lente, w. Alice Giles (hp) *(rec Studio 200, ABC Sydney, Jan 1993)* Tall Poppies ▲ TP 31 [DDD]
Piazzolla, A.:Histoire du tango, w. Alice Giles (hp) *(rec Studio 200, ABC Sydney, Jan 1993)* Tall Poppies ▲ TP 31 [DDD]
Rochberg, G.:Slow Fires of Autumn, w. Alice Giles (hp) *(rec Studio 200, ABC Sydney, Jan 1993)* Tall Poppies ▲ TP 31 [DDD]
Shankar, R.:L'Aube enchantée, w. Alice Giles (hp) *(rec Studio 200, ABC Sydney, Jan 1993)* Tall Poppies ▲ TP 31 [DDD]

Collins, Geoffrey (fl) (cont.)
Smalley, R.:Ceremony III *(rec Studios 200 & 227, ABC Ultimo Centre, Jan–Feb 1995)* Tall Poppies ▲ TP 069 [DDD]
Smalley, R.:Ceremony III Tall Poppies ▲ TP 69 [DDD]
Takemitsu, T.:Toward the Sea III, w. Alice Giles (hp) *(rec Studio 200, ABC Sydney, Jan 1993)* Tall Poppies ▲ TP 31 [DDD]
Vine, C.:Son Fl, w. David Miller (pno) *(rec Studios 200 & 227, ABC Ultimo Centre, Jan–Feb 1995)* Tall Poppies ▲ TP 069 [DDD]
Wesley–Smith, M.:Balibo *(rec Studios 200 & 227, ABC Ultimo Centre, Jan–Feb 1995)* Tall Poppies ▲ TP 069 [DDD]

Collins, Keith (perc)
Paredes, R.:Small Writing, w. Craig Hultgren (vc) Innova ▲ 502

Collins, M. (pno)
Arnold, M.:Con Pno 4–Hands, w. M. Stephenson (cnd), London Musici Conifer Classics ▲ 75605–51228–2

Collins, Michael (b cl)
Matthews, C.:Suns Dance, w. Sebastian Bell (pic), Gareth Hulse (ob), John Orford (ctbn), Michael Thompson (hn), Nona Liddell (vn), Joan Atherton (vn), Paul Silverthorne (va), Christopher van Kampen (vc), Robin McGee (db) *(rec All Saint's Church, Petersham, Oct 1992)* Deutsche Grammophon ▲ 447067–2 [DDD]

Collins, Michael (cl)
Arnold, M.:Con 2 Cl, w. M. Stephenson (cnd), London Musici Conifer Classics ▲ 75605–51228–2
Knussen, O.:"...upon one note", w. Clio Gould (vn), Paul Silverthorne (va), Christopher van Kampen (vc), John Constable (pno) *(rec Henry Wood Hall & All Hollows Gospel Oak, London, Oct & Dec 1995)* Deutsche Grammophon ▲ 449 572–2 [DDD]
Schubert, Franz:Der Hirt auf dem Felsen, w. F. Lott (sop), I. Brown (pno) [G] IMP Classics ▲ PCD 868 [DDD]

Collins, Peter (pno)
Dankner, S.:Trio Cl, w. Steven Cohen (cl), Allen Nisbet (vc) Albany ▲ TROY 144 [DDD]

Collins, Phillip (tpt)
Copland, A.:Quiet City, w. William Harrod (E hn), E. Kunzel (cnd), Cincinnati Pops Orch *(rec Cincinatti Music Hall, 1989–95)* Telarc ▲ CD 80339 [DDD]

Collot, Serge (va)—see ORCHESTRAS & ENSEMBLES French String Trio, Parrenin String Quartet

Collum, Christian (org)
Christian Collum, w. Collum, Christian (org) MD + G ▲ L 3276 [DDD]

Colombain, P. (ob)—see ORCHESTRAS & ENSEMBLES Stanislas Ensemble

Colson, David (perc)
Harrison, L.:Con Vn, w. Janna Lower (vn), R. Brown (cnd), Continuum Percussion Quartet New World ▲ NW 382–2 [AAD]

Colton, Martin (org)
Schubert, Franz:Mass 2, w. Peter Crowther (cnd), Sheffield Cathedral Choir Herald ▲ HAVPCD 130

Columbie, Douglas Vistel (vc)
Schwaen, K.:Concertino Vc, w. Almuth Krausser–Vistel (pno) *(rec Oct 4, 1995)* Thorofon ▲ CTH 2284 [ADD/DDD]
Schwaen, K.:Curious Waltzes, w. Almuth Krausser–Vistel (pno) *(rec Oct 4, 1995)* Thorofon ▲ CTH 2284 [ADD/DDD]

Colvig, William (sheng/fang–hsiang)
Harrison, L.:Music for Vn, w. William Bouton (vn), Richard Dee (cheng), Lou Harrison (piri), Helen Rifas (hp) Phoenix ▲ PHCD 118 [AAD]

Combelle, François (sax)
"Le Patron" of the Saxophone, w. M. Mule (sax), Guy Chauvet (ten), G. Charon (sgr), F. l'Homme (sgr), P. Romby (sgr), Eugène Bozza (cnd), Francis Çebron (cnd), Phillipe Gaubert (cnd), *(orchs unknown)*, Joseph Benvenutti (pno), Marcel Gaveau (pno), Marthe Pellas–Lenom (pno) *(rec 1930–1940)* Clarinet Classics ▲ CC 0013 [AAD]

Comberti, Micaela (vn)—see also ORCHESTRAS & ENSEMBLES L'École d'Orphée, Salomon String Quartet
Bach, J.S.:Con for 2 Vns, w. Simon Standage (vn), S. Standage (cnd), Collegium Musicum 90 Chandos ("Chaconne" series) ▲ CHAN 0594
Bach, J.S.:Con for 3 Vns, w. Miles Golding (vn), Simon Standage (vn), S. Standage (cnd), Collegium Musicum 90 Chandos ("Chaconne" series) ▲ CHAN 0594
Telemann, G.P.:Con in G for 2 Vns, w. S. Standage (vn), S. Standage (cnd), Collegium Musicum 90 Chandos ("Chaconne" series) ▲ CHAN 0512 [DDD]
Vivaldi, A.:Con Ob Vns, w. A. Robson (ob), S. Standage (vn), S. Standage (cnd), Collegium Musicum 90 Chandos ("Chaconne" series) ▲ CHAN 0528 [DDD]

Comberti, Sebastian (vc)
Donizetti, G.:Songs, w. I. Caddy (bass–bar), A. Halstead (hn), M. Tan (pno)—Canto d'Ugolino; L'amor funesto; Trovatore in caricatura; Spirito di Dio; Viva il matrimonio; Le renégat; Noé—scène du Déluge; Le départ pour la chasse; On coeur pour abri; La hart [I, F] *(rec 8/84 & 12/85)* Meridian ▲ CDE 84183
Vivaldi, A.:Cons Diverse Instrs, w. M. Verbruggen (rcr), P. Goodwin (ob), J. Holloway (vn), D. Godburn (bn), J. Toll (hpd)—7 Concerti—in D, RV.84; in a, RV.86; in D, RV.94; in D, "Las Pastorella," RV.95; in F, RV.99; in g, RV.103; in g, RV.105 Harmonia Mundi USA ▲ HMU 907046

Combs, Larry (cl)
Argento, D.:To Be Sung Upon The Water, w. Patrice Michaels Bedi (sop), Elizabeth Buccheri (pno) *(rec Mandel Hall, Univ of Chicago, June 17–21, 1996)* Cedille ▲ CDR 90000029 [DDD]
Beethoven, L. van:Qnt Pno, Ob, Cl, Hn & Bn, w. D. Barenboim (pno), H. Schellenberger (ob), D. Damiano (bn), D. Clevenger (hn) Erato ▲ 96359–2
Bernstein, L.:Son Cl, w. Deborah Sobol (pno) *(rec Bennett Hall, Highland Park, IL, Jan. 18, 24 & 25, 1994)* Summit ▲ DCD 172 [DDD]
Brahms, J.:Son 2 Vn, w. D. Sobol (pno) [clarinet & piano trans. Kent Kennan] Summit ▲ DCD 125 [DDD]
Copland, A.:Son Vn & Pno, w. Deborah Sobol (pno) [trans. for clarinet] *(rec Bennett Hall, Highland Park, IL, Jan. 18, 24 & 25, 1994)* Summit ▲ DCD 172 [DDD]
Falla, M. de:Con Hpd, w. Rembrandt Chamber Players Cedille ▲ CDR 90000 011 [DDD]
Gould, M.:Benny's Gig, w. Bradley Opland (db) *(rec Bennett Hall, Highland Park, IL, Jan. 18, 24 & 25, 1994)* Summit ▲ DCD 172 [DDD]
Larry Combs:Clarinet, w. Deborah Sobol (pno) Summit ▲ DCD 125 [DDD]
Mozart, W.A.:Qnt Pno, K.452, w. D. Barenboim (pno), H. Schellenberger (ob), D. Damiano (bn), D. Clevenger (hn) Erato ▲ 96359–2
Orchestral Excepts for Clarinet, w. *(rec Aug. 6 & 7, 1993)* Summit ▲ DCD 161 [DDD]
Prokofiev, S.:Son Vn, Op. 94bis, w. D. Sobol (pno) [clarinet & piano trans. by Kent Kennan] Summit ▲ DCD 125 [DDD]
Rochberg, G.:Trio Cl, w. G. Williams (hn), M. A. Covert (pno) Crystal ■ C 731
Rózsa, M.:Sonatina Cl Crystal ■ C 731
Schuller, G.:Romantic Son Cl, w. G. Williams (hn), M. A. Covert (pno) Crystal ■ C 731
Scriabin, A.:Preludes Pno (misc), w. D. Sobol (pno) [clarinet & piano transcriptions by Willard Elliot]—Op. 11, No. 23; Op. 15, No. 2; Op. 16, Nos. 1–5 Summit ▲ DCD 125 [DDD]
Vaughan Williams, R.:Vocalises, w. Patrice Michaels Bedi (sop) *(rec Mandel Hall, Univ of Chicago, June 17–21, 1996)* Cedille ▲ CDR 90000029 [DDD]

Comentale, Guy (vn)
Ligeti, G.:Trio Hn, Vn & Pno, w. A. Cazalet (hn), C. Huvé (pno) Montaigne ▲ MO 782006 [DDD]

Comet, Catherine (fl)
Colgrass, M.:Light Spirit, w. *(ensemble unknown)* New World ▲ NW 318–2 [ADD]

Comita, William (vc)
The Classical Banjo, w. J. Bullard (banjo), John Patykula (gtr), Steve Bennett (hp gtr), Greg Giannascoli (vib) *(rec Big Audio, Richmond, VA, May–July 1992, Oct. 1994)* Dargason Music ▲ DM 115 [DDD]; ■ DM 115

Comparone, E. (hpd)
Bach, J.S.:Inventions (30) Hpd, w. D. Bogdonovič (gtr) *(rec Aug 2-4, 1993)* ESS.A.Y ▲ CD 1039 [DDD]
Bach, J.S.:Trio Sons Org, BWV 525-530, w. D. Bogdonovič (gtr) [trans performers for gtr & hpd] ESS.A.Y ▲ CD 1023 [DDD]
Christmas in the New World, w. Western Wind, Albert de Ruiter (bass), Louise Schulman (vn), Wendy Gillespie (vl), Joseph Karpienia (gtr) MusicMasters ▲ 01612-67176-2
McKinley, W.T.:Fant Variazioni, w. R. Stankovsky (cnd), Slovak RSO Bratislava *(rec Slovak Radio & TV Studios, Slovak National Republic)* MMC ▲ MMC 2016 [DDD]
Persichetti, V.:Sons Hpd—Nos. 2-5 Laurel ▲ LR 838CD [AAD]
Scarlatti, D.:Sons Kbd—K.48, 107, 109, 132, 222, 258 & 363 Laurel ▲ LR 838CD [AAD]

Comparone, Elaine (hpd)—see ORCHESTRAS & ENSEMBLES Bell'Arte Trio

Compton, Jane (va)
Vivaldi, A.:Cons Rcr, w. Piers Adams (rcr), Ray Goodman (vn), Miles Golding (vn), Jane Coe (vc), Mandy MacNamara (db), David Miller (archlt), Robert King (hpd/org)—in F for Treble Rcr, Op. 10/1; in a for Sopranino Rcr, RV.440; in c for Treble Rcr, RV.441; in D for Sopranino Rcr, Op. 10/3; in g for Treble Rcr, Op. 10/2; in C for Sopranino Rcr, RV.443 *(rec Radley College, Abingdon, Oxon)* United ▲ CAL 88015 [DDD]

Comuzzi, Demetrio (va)—see ORCHESTRAS & ENSEMBLES Giovane Quartetto Italiano

Conable, William (vc)
Mathias, W.:Trio Pno, w. Nelson Harper (pno), Michael Davis (vn) Koch International Classics ▲ KIC 7326

Conger, C. (pno)
Mahin, B.:Shadows, w. E. Curtis (sop), A. Wojtera (perc) Capstone ▲ CPS 8061
Mahin, B.:Shadows, w. Elizabeth Curtis (sop), Al Wojtera (perc) Capstone ▲ CPS 8611
Mahin, B.:Time Chants II. Monhegan Island, August 1992, w. Bruce Mahin (digital delay) *(rec Radford University's Preston Hall, May 8-9, 1994)* Capstone ♦ CPS 8624 [DDD]

Conil, Roland (pno)
Ohana, M.:Cantigas, w. M. Quercia (sop), F. Atlan (mez), R. Hayrabedian (cnd), Strasbourg Percussion Ensemble, Choeur Contemporain [Sp] Pierre Verany ▲ PV 787032 [DDD]
Stravinsky, I.:Les Noces, w. M. Quercia (sop), S. Cooper (mez), P. Capelle (ten), P. Marinov (bass), Vieuxtemps (pno), Arzoumanian (pno), Raynaut (pno), R. Hayrabedian (cnd), Strasbourg Percussion Ensemble, Contemporary Choir Pierre Verany ▲ PV 787032 [DDD]

Conn, Michael (gtr)
Arnold, M.:Con Gtr, w. J. Lubbock (cnd), St. John's Smith Square Orch IMP ("Classic" series) ▲ IMP 2035
Arnold, M.:Con Gtr, w. J. Lubbock (cnd), St. John's Smith Square Orch IMP Classics ▲ PCD 859 [DDD]
Rodrigo, J.:Concierto de Aranjuez, w. J. Lubbock (cnd), St. John's Smith Square Orch IMP ("Classic" series) ▲ IMP 2035
Rodrigo, J.:Concierto de Aranjuez, w. J. Lubbock (cnd), St. John's Smith Square Orch IMP Classics ▲ PCD 859 [DDD]
Spanish Fiesta, w. London SO, Rafael Frühbeck de Burgos (cnd), Xalapa SO [cnd:H. de la Fuente] Pickwick ("The Orchid" series) ▲ PICORCD 11014

Connell, Andy (cl)
Tailleferre, G.:Chansons populaires françaises, w. Patrice Maginnis (sop), John Fairweather (vn), David Ryther (vn), Jill Cohen (va), Karen Andrie (vc), Elizabeth Bodine (ob), Gordon Mumma (hn), June Orzel (bn), N. Paiement (cnd) *(rec UC, Santa Cruz, May 1992)* Helicon Classics ▲ HE 1008
Tailleferre, G.:Image, w. John Fairweather (vn), David Ryther (vn), Jill Cohen (va), Karen Andrie (vc), Elizabeth Bodine (ob), Gordon Mumma (hn), June Orzel (bn), N. Paiement (cnd) *(rec UC, Santa Cruz, May 1992)* Helicon Classics ▲ HE 1008

Connelly, Brian (pno/syn)—see also ORCHESTRAS & ENSEMBLES Duo Vivo
Schultz, Arthur:T-Rex, w. T. Bacon (hn) Summit ▲ DCD 135 [DDD]

Connors, Clare (vn)—see also ORCHESTRAS & ENSEMBLES Balanescu String Quartet
Bryars, G.:The Last Days, w. Alexander Balanescu (vn) Argo ▲ 448175-2 [DDD]

Conquer, Jeanne-Marie (vn)
Saint-Saëns, C.:Trio 1 Pno, w. Angéline Pondepeyre (pno), Philippe Bary (vc) REM ▲ REM 311273 [DDD]
Saint-Saëns, C.:Trio 2 Pno, w. Angéline Pondepeyre (pno), Philippe Bary (vc) REM ▲ REM 311273 [DDD]

Conrad, Ferdinand (rcr)
Telemann, G.P.:Kleine Kammermusik, w. Hans-Martin Linde (fl), Helmut Winschermann (ob), Susanne Lautenbacher (vn), Johannes Koch (vl), Hugo Ruf (hpd) *(rec Südwest-Tonstudio H. Jansen, Stuttgart, Jan. 1966)* Musicaphon ▲ 51539 [ADD]

Console, Hector (db)—see also ORCHESTRAS & ENSEMBLES New Tango Sex-tet
Piazzolla, A.:Music of, w. F.S. Paz (vn), Horacio Malivicino (elec gtr), A. Piazolla (band), Pablo Ziegler (pno)—Verano porteño; Lunfardo; Milonga del angel; Muerte del angel; Astor's Speech; La camorra; Mumuki; Adios Nonino; Contra bajissmo; Michelangelo; Concierto para quinteto *(rec Sept. 6, 1987)* Chesky ▲ JD 107 [DDD]

Constable, John (pno)
Berlioz, H.:Songs, w. Jill Gomez (sop)—Le Coucher de soleil; L'Origine de la harpe; La Belle voyageuse Saga Classics ▲ EC 3333
Bizet, G.:Songs, w. Jill Gomez (sop)—Chanson d'avril; Adieux de l'hôtesse arabe; Vous ne priez pas; La Chanson de la rose Saga Classics ▲ EC 3333
Cabaret Classics, w. J. Gomez (sop) Unicorn-Kanchana ▲ DKPCD 9055
Debussy, C.:Proses lyriques, w. Jill Gomez (sop) Saga Classics ▲ EC 3333
Debussy, C.:Songs, w. Jill Gomez (sop)—Noël des enfants qui n'ont plus de maisons Saga Classics ▲ EC 3333
Honegger, A.:Antigone, w. Aurèle Nicolet (fl), Heinz Holliger (E hn)—sels. [arr. for flute, English horn & piano] *(rec St. John's, London, Oct. 8-11, 1991)* Philips ▲ 434105-2
Honegger, A.:Petite Suites, w. Aurèle Nicolet (fl), Heinz Holliger (E hn) *(rec St. John's, London, Oct. 8-11, 1991)* Philips ▲ 434105-2
Knussen, O.:"...upon one note", w. Michael Collins (cl), Clio Gould (vn), Paul Silverthorne (va), Christopher van Kampen (vc) *(rec Henry Wood Hall & All Hollows Gospel Oak, London, Oct & Dec 1995)* Deutsche Grammophon ▲ 449 572-2 [DDD]
Lewis, R.H.:Kantaten, w. R.H. Lewis (cnd), London Sinfonietta Chorus New World ▲ 80444-2
Liszt, F.:Songs, w. Philip Langridge (ten)—Die Macht der Musik; Ihr Glocken von Marling; Im Rhein, im schönen Strome; Bist du!; Vergiftet sind meine Lieder; Jugendglück; Freudvoll und leidvoll; Der Fischerknabe; Der Hirt; Der Alpenjäger; Die drei Zigeuner; Der Glückliche; Kling leise, mein Lied; Wer nie sein Brot mit Tränen ass; Ich möchte hingehn; Die Vätergruft; Ich Scheide; Wanderers Nachtlied II Unicorn-Kanchana ▲ DKP CD 9162
Martin, F.:Petite complainte, w. Heinz Holliger (ob) *(rec St. John's, London, Oct. 8-11, 1991)* Philips ▲ 434105-2
A Spanish Songbook, w. J. Gomez (sop) Conifer Classics ▲ 75605-51243-2 [DDD]

Constable, Robert (prepared pno)
Wesley-Smith, M.:VENCEREMOS, w. Michael Askill (perc), Martin Wesley-Smith (elec) *(rec Electronic Music Studio, Sydney Conservatorium of Music)* Tall Poppies ▲ TP 072 [DDD]

Constantin, Anne (vn)
Bonis, M.:Son Vn, w. A. Rojdestvenski (pno) Thésis ▲ THC 82058
Debussy, C.:Son Vn, w. A. Rojdestvenski (pno) Thésis ▲ THC 82058
Franck, C.:Son Vn, w. A. Rojdestvenski (pno) Thésis ▲ THC 82058

Conti, Diego (vn)
Bottesini, G.:Gran Duo Concertant, w. M. Giorgi (db), V. Antonellini (cnd), I Solisti Aquilani Nuova Era ▲ 6810 [DDD]
Bottesini, G.:Passioni Amorose, w. M. Giorgi (db), V. Antonellini (cnd), I Solisti Aquilani Nuova Era ▲ 6810 [DDD]

Conti, M. (pno)
Zyman, S.:Con Pno, w. S. Zyman (cnd), Chelsea Chamber Ensemble Antilles/New Directions ▲ 91055-2 ■ 91055-4

Conti, M. (pno) (cont.)
Zyman, S.:Qnt Pno, w. S. Zyman (cnd), Chelsea Chamber Ensemble Antilles/New Directions ▲ 91055-2 ■ 91055-4

Conti, M. T. (hpd)
Sacchini, A.:La contandina in corte, w. S. Rigacci (sop—Tancia), E. Palacio (ten—Ruggiero), G. Gatti (bar—Berto), C. Boersma (vc), M. Clavenna (db), G. Catalucci (cnd), Sassari SO *(rec Dec. 17-18, 1991)* Bongiovanni 2-▲ GB 2145/46 [DDD]

Conti, Marzio (fl)
Albinoni, T.:Sinf (6) e con (6) à 5, Op. 2, w. I Solisti Aquilani—Sinfs. in G & A Nuova Era ▲ 7066
Bach, C.P.E.:Trio Sons (misc), w. A. Marion (fl), D. Roi (hpd)—in B♭ & in d Fonè ▲ 89F04-28 [DDD]
Cambini, G.M.:Trio 1 for 2 Fls & Hpd, w. A. Marion (fl), D. Roi (hpd) Fonè ▲ 89 F 03-27 [DDD]
Nardini, P.:Cons Fl, w. I Solisti Aquilani—in D & G Nuova Era ▲ 7066
Nardini, P.:Son Terza, w. A. Marion (fl), D. Roi (hpd) Fonè ▲ 89 F 03-27 [DDD]
Platti, G.B.:Trio Fls, w. A. Marion (fl), D. Roi (hpd) Fonè ▲ 89 F 03-27 [DDD]
Sammartini, G.B.:Son terza Fls, w. A. Marion (fl), D. Roi (hpd) Fonè ▲ 89 F 03-27 [DDD]
Tartini, G.:Con in F Fl, w. I Solisti Aquilani Nuova Era ▲ 7066

Conti, Mirian (pno)
Turina, J.:Cuentos de España—Book II Koch International Classics ▲ KIC 7322 [DDD]
Turina, J.:Niñerias—Book 1 Koch International Classics ▲ KIC 7322 [DDD]
Turina, J.:Sanlucar de Barrameda Koch International Classics ▲ KIC 7322 [DDD]

Contiguglia, John (pno)
Bolcom, W.:The Garden of Eden, w. Richard Contiguglia (pno)—The Serpent's Kiss; Through Eden's Gates [trans Bolcom for 2 pnos] Helicon Classics ▲ HE 1004
Bolcom, W.:Recuerdos, w. Richard Contiguglia (pno) Helicon Classics ▲ HE 1004
Corigliano, J.:Gazebo Dances Pno 4-Hands, w. Richard Contiguglia (pno) *(rec Merkin Concert Hall, New York City, Nov 3, 1992)* CRI ▲ CD 659 [DDD]
Corigliano, J.:Kaleidoscope, w. Richard Contiguglia (pno) *(rec Merkin Concert Hall, NYC, Nov 3, 1992)* CRI ▲ CD 659 [DDD]
Gershwin, G.:Music of, w. R. Contiguglia (pno) MCA Classics ▲ MCAD 6626; ■ MCAC 6626
Grainger, P.:Children's March, w. Richard Contiguglia (pno) [arr Grainger for 2 pnos, 1915-18] Helicon Classics ▲ HE 1004
Grainger, P.:Hill Songs 1 & 2, w. Richard Contiguglia (pno)—No. 1 [arr Grainger for 2 pnos, 1921] Helicon Classics ▲ HE 1004
Grainger, P.:Lincolnshire Posy, w. Richard Contiguglia (pno) Helicon Classics ▲ HE 1004
Grainger, P.:Pno Music (arrs, transcriptions & paraphrases), w. R. Contiguglia (pno)—Cuban Overture; Embraceable you; Fantasy on Porgy & Bess; Love walked in; The man I love; Rhapsody in Blue MCA Classics ▲ MCAD 6626; ■ MCAC 6626

Contiguglia, R. (pno)
Bolcom, W.:The Garden of Eden, w. John Contiguglia (pno)—The Serpent's Kiss; Through Eden's Gates [trans Bolcom for 2 pnos] Helicon Classics ▲ HE 1004
Bolcom, W.:Recuerdos, w. John Contiguglia (pno) Helicon Classics ▲ HE 1004
Corigliano, J.:Gazebo Dances Pno 4-Hands, w. John Contiguglia (pno) *(rec Merkin Concert Hall, New York City, Nov 3, 1992)* CRI ▲ CD 659 [DDD]
Corigliano, J.:Kaleidoscope, w. John Contiguglia (pno) *(rec Merkin Concert Hall, NYC, Nov 3, 1992)* CRI ▲ CD 659 [DDD]
Gershwin, G.:Music of, w. J. Contiguglia (pno) MCA Classics ▲ MCAD 6626; ■ MCAC 6626
Grainger, P.:Children's March, w. John Contiguglia (pno) [arr Grainger for 2 pnos, 1915-18] Helicon Classics ▲ HE 1004
Grainger, P.:Hill Songs 1 & 2, w. John Contiguglia (pno)—No. 1 [arr Grainger for 2 pnos, 1921] Helicon Classics ▲ HE 1004
Grainger, P.:Lincolnshire Posy, w. John Contiguglia (pno) Helicon Classics ▲ HE 1004
Grainger, P.:Pno Music (arrs, transcriptions & paraphrases), w. J. Contiguglia (pno)—Cuban Overture; Embraceable you; Fantasy on Porgy & Bess; Love walked in; The man I love; Rhapsody in Blue MCA Classics ▲ MCAD 6626; ■ MCAC 6626

Còntini, Luciano (lt)—see also ORCHESTRAS & ENSEMBLES Clemencic Consort
Zamboni, G.:Sons Lt—Nos. 1-4, & 6-8 Symphonia ▲ SY 92S16

Contini, Luciano (lt/chit)
Piccinini, A.:Intavolature Tactus ▲ TC 561601 [DDD]

Conway, C. (vn)
Beethoven, L. van:Serenade Strs, Op. 8, w. P. Silverthorne (va), G. Garcia (vc) [flute, viola, guitar arr.] Meridian ▲ CDE 84199

Conway, Clive (fl)
Haydn, J.:Qts Fl, w. Nona Liddell (vn), Paul Silverthorne (va), Charles Tunnell (vc) Meridian ▲ CDE 84118
Hummel, J.N.:Adagio, Vars & Rondo on "Schöne Minka", w. C. Croshaw (pno), C. Tunnell (vc) Meridian ▲ MER 84217
Hummel, J.N.:Rondo brillant Vn & Pno, w. C. Croshaw (pno) Meridian ▲ MER 84217
Kreutzer, J.:Grand Trio, w. P. Silverthorne (va), G. Garcia (gtr) Meridian ▲ CDE 84199
Molino, F.:Trio Fl, Op. 45, w. P. Silverthorne (va), G. Garcia (gtr) Meridian ▲ CDE 84199
Schubert, Franz:Qt Fl, w. P. Silverthorne (va), G. Garcia (gtr), C. Tunnell (vc) Meridian ▲ CDE 84118
Weber, C.M. von:Son 2 Pno, w. Christine Croshaw (pno) [arr for fl & pno] Meridian ▲ MER 84260 [DDD]
Weber, C.M. von:Trio Fl, w. Christina Shillito (vc), Christine Croshaw (pno) Meridian ▲ MER 84260 [DDD]

Conway, Robert (pno)
Bassett, L.:Dialogues, w. H. Sargous (ob) Crystal ▲ CD326 [DDD]
Cowell, H.:Ostinati (3) with Chorales, w. H. Sargous (ob) Crystal ▲ CD326 [DDD]

Conway, William (vc)
Haydn, J.:Con 1 Vc, w. W. Conway (cnd), Goldberg Ensemble Meridian ▲ CDE 84177

Cook, Alex (hn)—see ORCHESTRAS & ENSEMBLES Old Fairfield Academy Orch members

Cook, Barbara (ob)
Rutter, J.:Requiem, w. Karyn List (sop), Kathy Farmer (fl), Julie Albertson (hp), Mary Alice Swope (vc), Tom Alderman (org), Jennifer Mautz (timp), Mike Del Campo (perc), Michael O'Neal (cnd), Michael O'Neal Singers *(rec Roswell United Methodist Church, Atlanta, GA, Mar 27, 1995)* ACA Digital Recording ▲ CM 20048 [DDD]

Cook, Martha (hpd)
Bach, J.S.:A Musical Offering, w. D. Moroney (hpd), J. See (fl), J. Holloway (vn), J. ter Linden (vc) Harmonia Mundi France ▲ HMC 901260 [DDD]

Cook, Susan Lamb (vc)
Kingman, D.:Scénario musical 1, w. James Een (va), Richard Cionco (pno) Innova ▲ INNOVA 504

Cooke, Antony (vc)
Bartók, B.:Romanian Folk Dances Pno, w. Armin Watkins (pno)—Joc Cu Bâtă; Brâul; Pe Loc; Buciumeana; Poarcă Românească; Măruntel [all arr Luigi Silva for Vc & Pno] *(rec Capitol Records, Hollywood, CA)* PROdigital ▲ PRO 7192 [DDD]
Dohnányi, E. von:Son Vc, w. Armin Watkins (pno) *(rec Capitol Records, Hollywood, CA)* PROdigital ▲ PRO 7192 [DDD]
Hubay, J.:Hullámzó Balaton, w. Armin Watkins (pno) [arr Antony Cooke & Armin Watkins for Vc & Pno] *(rec Capitol Records, Hollywood, CA)* PROdigital ▲ PRO 7192 [DDD]
Kodály, Z.:Chorale Preludes, w. Armin Watkins (pno) *(rec Capitol Records, Hollywood, CA)* PROdigital ▲ PRO 7192 [DDD]

Coolen, Saskia (fl/rcr/vl)—see ORCHESTRAS & ENSEMBLES Camerata Trajectina, La Fontegara Amsterdam, Senario Ensemble

Cooley, Carlton (va)
Berlioz, H.:Harold in Italy, w. A. Toscanini (cnd), NBC SO RCA Gold Seal ▲ 60275-2-RG ■ 60275-4-RG

Cooley, Floyd (tuba)
Bach, J.S.:Sons Fl, BWV 1030-35, w. Naomi Chaitkin Nimmo (hpd)—in E♭, BWV 1031 [trans. Cooley] Crystal ▲ CD 120

Cooley, Floyd (tuba) (cont.)
Brahms, J.:Ernste Gesänge, w. Naomi Chaitkin Nimmo (pno) [trans. John Elwood Williams] Crystal ▲ CD 120
Russell, A.:Suite Concertante, w. Janet Ketchum (fl), James Kanter (cl), Earle Dumler (ob), Arthur David Krehbiel (hn), Charles Ullery (bn) Crystal ▲ CD 120
Schumann, R.:Adagio & Allegro Hn, w. R. Sutherland (pno) [trans. for tuba] Summit ▲ DCD 156 [DDD]
Schumann, R.:Fantasiestücke Cl, w. R. Sutherland (pno) [trans. for tuba] Summit ▲ DCD 156 [DDD]
Schumann, R.:Märchenbilder, w. R. Sutherland (pno) [trans. for tuba] Summit ▲ DCD 156 [DDD]
Schumann, R.:Romances Ob, w. R. Sutherland (pno) [trans. for tuba] Summit ▲ DCD 156 [DDD]
Zindars, E.:Trigon Crystal ▲ CD 120

Coombs, Stephen (pno)
Arensky, A.:Con Pno, w. J. Maksymiuk (cnd), BBC Scottish SO Hyperion ▲ CDA 66624
Arensky, A.:Fant on Themes of Ryabinin, w. J. Maksymiuk (cnd), BBC Scottish SO Hyperion ▲ CDA 66624
Arensky, A.:Suite 1 for 2 Pnos, w. Ian Munro (pno) Hyperion ▲ CDA 66755
Arensky, A.:Suite 2 for 2 Pnos, "Silhouettes", w. Ian Munro (pno) Hyperion ▲ CDA 66755
Arensky, A.:Suite 3 for 2 Pnos, "Vars", w. Ian Munro (pno) Hyperion ▲ CDA 66755
Arensky, A.:Suite 4 for 2 Pnos, w. Ian Munro (pno) Hyperion ▲ CDA 66755
Bortkiewicz, S.:Con 1 Pno, w. J. Maksymiuk (cnd), BBC Scottish SO Hyperion ▲ CDA 66624
Glazunov, A.:Con 1 Pno, w. M. Brabbins (cnd), BBC Scottish SO Hyperion ▲ CDA 66877
Glazunov, A.:Con 2 Pno, w. M. Brabbins (cnd), BBC Scottish SO Hyperion ▲ CDA 66877
Glazunov, A.:Pno Music—Etudes; Theme & Vars, Op. 72; Two Pieces, Op. 22; Trois Morceaux (1894); Nocturne, Op. 37; Miniature in C; Easy Sonata; Sonatina; Two Prelude-Improvisations Hyperion ▲ CDA 66844
Glazunov, A.:Pno Music—Suite on the Name "Sascha", Op. 2; Three Miniatures, Op. 42; Valse de Salon (1893); Grande Valse de Concert; Waltzes on the Theme "Sabela", Op. 23; Petite valse, Op. 36 Hyperion ▲ CDA 66833
Glazunov, A.:Pno Music—Barcarolle sur les touches noires; Characteristic Dance in G; Idylle for Pno, Op. 103; Impromptus for Pno, Op. 54; In modo religioso; Prelude & Fugue in e; Prelude & Fugue, Op. 62; Prelude & 2 Mazurkas, Op. 25; Preludes & Fugues, Op. 101; Son No. 2 in E; Song of the Volga Boatmen; Triumphal March Hyperion ▲ CDA 66866
Goedicke, A.:Con Pno, w. M. Brabbins (cnd), BBC Scottish SO Hyperion ▲ CDA 66877
Mendelssohn, F.:Cons (2) for 2 Pnos, w. I. Munro (pno), J. Maksymiuk (cnd), BBC Scottish SO Hyperion ▲ CDA 66567 [DDD]
Ravel, M.:Entre cloches, w. C. Scott (pno) Gamut Classics ▲ GAM CD 517 [DDD]
Ravel, M.:Frontispiece, w. C. Scott (pno) Gamut Classics ▲ GAM CD 517 [DDD]
Ravel, M.:Intro & Allegro, w. C. Scott (pno) [Ravel's two-piano arr.] Gamut Classics ▲ GAM CD 517 [DDD]
Ravel, M.:Rapsodie espagnole, w. C. Scott (pno) [Ravel's two-piano arr.] Gamut Classics ▲ GAM CD 517 [DDD]
Ravel, M.:Shéhérazade Pno, w. C. Scott (pno) Gamut Classics ▲ GAM CD 517 [DDD]
Ravel, M.:La Valse, w. C. Scott (pno) [Ravel's 1921 two-piano arr.] Gamut Classics ▲ GAM CD 517 [DDD]

Coon, Kenneth (sax)—see also ORCHESTRAS & ENSEMBLES Rascher Saxophone Quartet
Bach, J.S.:Cant 190, w. Rascher Saxophone Quartet—Prelude & Fugue [arr for sax qt] Cala ▲ CAL CACD 77003 [DDD]
Glazunov, A.:Qt Saxes, w. Rascher Saxophone Quartet Cala ▲ CAL CACD 77003 [DDD]
Grainger, P.:Shepherd's Hey, w. Rascher Saxophone Quartet [arr for sax qt] Cala ▲ CAL CACD 77003 [DDD]
Keuris, T.:Music for Saxs, w. Rascher Saxophone Quartet Cala ▲ CAL CACD 77003 [DDD]
Koch, E. von:Cantilena, w. Rascher Saxophone Quartet Cala ▲ CAL CACD 77003 [DDD]
Reich, S.:Manhatan Counterpoint, w. Rascher Saxophone Quartet Cala ▲ CAL CACD 77003 [DDD]
Starer, R.:Light & Shadow, w. Rascher Saxophone Quartet Cala ▲ CAL CACD 77003 [DDD]

Coonrod, Michael (pno)
Hurley, S.:Wind River Songs, w. Nicole Philibosian (sop), Crispin Campbell (vc) *(rec Interlochen Center for the Arts)* Capstone ▲ CPS 8618

Coop, Jane (pno)
Bartók, B.:Con 3 Pno, w. M. Bernardi (cnd), Calgary PO CBC ("SM 5000" series) ▲ SMCD 5124 [DDD]
Beethoven, L. van:Son 30 Pno Skylark ▲ 8802 CD [AAD]
Beethoven, L. van:Son 32 Pno Skylark ▲ 8802 CD [AAD]
Beethoven, L. van:Vars & Fugue Pno, Op. 35, "Eroica" Skylark ▲ 8802 CD [AAD]
Chopin, F.:Mazurkas—'A Emile Gaillard', Opp. 7/4, 30/4, 56/1 & 3, 59/1 & 3, 63/2, 67/4, 68/4 Skylark ▲ 9601 [DDD]
Chopin, F.:Nocturnes—Opp. 9/3, 32/1, 37/2, 48/1, 62/1 & 2 Skylark ▲ 9601 [DDD]
Chopin, F.:Pno Music (misc)—Études in E, Op. 10/3 & in e, Op. 25/5; Mazurka in a, Op. 17/4; Nocturne in Db, Op. 27/2 CBC ("Musica Viva" series) ▲ MVCD 1015 [DDD]
Debussy, C.:Pno Music (misc)—Clair de lune; L'isle joyeuse CBC ("Musica Viva" series) ▲ MVCD 1015 [DDD]
Forsyth, M.:Con Pno, w. M. Bernardi (cnd), Calgary PO CBC ("SM 5000" series) ▲ SMCD 5124 [DDD]
Haydn, J.:Sons Pno—H.XVI/20, 34, 41, 42, 51; H.XVII/4 Skylark ▲ SKY 8501 [ADD/DDD]
Liszt, F.:Pno Music (misc)—Liebesträume; Un sospiro CBC ("Musica Viva" series) ▲ MVCD 1015 [DDD]
Mendelssohn, F.:Pno Music (misc)—Venetian boat song, Op. 30/6; Etude in f CBC ("Musica Viva" series) ▲ MVCD 1015 [DDD]
Mozart, W.A.:Adagio Pno, K.540 Skylark ▲ 9002 CD [DDD]
Mozart, W.A.:Pno Music (misc)—Fant., K.397 & 475; Gigue, K.574; Minuet, K.355; Rondos, K.485 & 511; Vars., K.455 Skylark ▲ 8801 CD [DDD]
Mozart, W.A.:Qts Pno, w. Orford String Quartet members Skylark ▲ 9002 CD [DDD]
Mozart, W.A.:Son 4 Pno Skylark ▲ 8801CD [DDD]
Prokofiev, S.:Con 1 Pno, w. M. Bernardi (cnd), Calgary PO CBC ("SM 5000" series) ▲ SMCD 5124 [DDD]
Rachmaninoff, S.:Pno Music (misc)—Étude-Tableau, Op. 39/8; Prelude in c, Op. 23/7 CBC ("Musica Viva" series) ▲ MVCD 1015 [DDD]
The Romantic Piano Musica Viva ▲ MVCD 1015 [DDD]
The Romantic Piano, Vol. 2 *(rec Glenn Gould Studio, CBC Toronto, Ontario, April 28–30, 1994)* CBC Records ("Musica Viva" series) ▲ MVCD 1083 [DDD]
Schumann, R.:Pno Music (misc)—Träumerei CBC ("Musica Viva" series) ▲ MVCD 1015 [DDD]

Cooper, D. (tpt)—see ORCHESTRAS & ENSEMBLES Wisconsin Brass Quintet
Cooper, Deirdre (vc)—see ORCHESTRAS & ENSEMBLES Smith String Quartet
Cooper, Gary (org)—see also ORCHESTRAS & ENSEMBLES Sonnerie Ensemble
Boyce, W.:Anthems & Voluntaries, w. E. Higginbottom (cnd), New College Choir Oxford—By the waters of Babylon; I have surely built thee an house; The Lord is King; O give thanks; O praise the Lord; O where shall wisdom be found?; Turn thee unto me; Voluntaries I, IV & VII; Wherewithal shall a young man [E] *(rec 4/91)* CRD ▲ 3483
Motets en espace, w. Gervais (cnd), Versailles National Masters, New College Choir Oxford [cnd:Edward Higginbottom] K617 ▲ 7010 [DDD]
Weelkes, T.:Anthems, w. Jeremy Summerly (org), Oxford Camerata—Hosanna to the son of David; Give ear, O Lord; All people clap your hands; What joy so true; O Lord, grant the king a long life; Lord, to thee I make my mooan; All laud and praise; Lachrimae Pavan (Morley); A remembrance of my friend Thomas Morley; Passymeasures Pavan (Morley); Gloria in excelsis Deo; When David hear; Give the king thy judgements; O Lord, arise; O how amiable are thy dwellings; Most mighty and all-knowing Lord; Alleluia, I heard a voice *(rec Chapel of Hertford College, Oxford, Jan 3–4, 1995)* Naxos ▲ 8.553209 [DDD]

Cooper, Imogen (pno)
Brahms, J.:Fants Pno, Op. 116 Ottavo ▲ 39027 [DDD]
Haydn, J.:Pno Music, w. Alfred Brendel (pno), N. Marriner (cnd), Academy of St. Martin in the Fields—Andante w. Vars (H.XVII/6); Sons Nos. 49, 50 & 52 Philips 25-▲ 446920-2
Mozart, W.A.:Pno Music (misc), w. Alfred Brendel (pno), N. Marriner (cnd), Academy of St. Martin in the Fields—Adagio K.540; Cons for Pno Nos. 10, 14, 15, 19, 21, 26, 27; Fant K.475; Rondo K.511; Sons Nos. 8, 11, 13, 14 Philips 25-▲ 446920-2

Cooper, Imogen (pno) (cont.)
Mozart, W.A.:Pno Music 4-Hands, w. A. Queffélec (pno)—Fant., K.608:Allegro & Andante; Son., K.521; Son., K.497; Adagio & Allegro in F, K.594 Ottavo ▲ OTT 129242 [DDD]
Schubert, Franz:Allegretto Pno, D.915 *(rec 8/88)* Ottavo ▲ OTR C88821 [DDD]
Schubert, Franz:German Dances Pno, D.783 Ottavo ▲ OTR C78923 [DDD]
Schubert, Franz:Impromptus Pno, D.899 Ottavo ▲ OTR C78923 [DDD]
Schubert, Franz:Impromptus Pno, D.935 Ottavo ▲ OTR C88817 [DDD]
Schubert, Franz:Pieces Pno, D.946 *(rec 8/88)* Ottavo ▲ OTR C88821 [DDD]
Schubert, Franz:Schwanengesang, w. Wolfgang Holzmair (bar) *(rec Vienna Konzerthaus, Austria, Jan. 10–12, 1994)* Philips ▲ 442460-2
Schubert, Franz:Son Pno, D.845 Ottavo ▲ OTR C88817 [DDD]
Schubert, Franz:Son Pno, D.958 Ottavo ▲ OTR C78923 [DDD]
Schubert, Franz:Son Pno, D.960 *(rec 8/88)* Ottavo ▲ OTR C88821 [DDD]
Schubert, Franz:Songs (misc), w. Wolfgang Holzmair (bar)—Widerspruch; Der Wanderer an den Mond; Sehnsucht; Irdisches Glück; Lebensmut; Herbst *(rec Vienna Konzerthaus, Austria, Jan. 10–12, 1994)* Philips ▲ 442460-2
Schubert, Franz:Winterreise, w. Wolfgang Holzmair (bar) Philips ▲ 446407-2
Schumann, R.:Davidsbündlertänze Ottavo ▲ 39027 [DDD]
Schumann, R.:Vars on A-B-E-G-G Ottavo ▲ 39027 [DDD]

Cooper, Jessica (ob)
Brooke, N.:Obomobile, w. Brandon Adrien, Jennifer Baker, Karen Birch, Daniel Cate, Judy Christy, Richard Cochran, Leslie Dominguez, Erin Hannigan, Dorothy Knight, Jason Lichtenwalter, Jay Moore, Hwa-Ling Russell, Toyin Spellman, Sarah Weiner, Jay Weinland Opus One ▲ CD 160

Cooper, Kenneth (hpd)
Bach, J.S.:Sons VI, BWV 1027-1029, w. Yo-Yo Ma (vc) CBS ▲ MK 37794 [DDD] ■ IMT 37794 (D)

Cooper, N. (vc)—see ORCHESTRAS & ENSEMBLES Balanescu String Quartet

Cooper, Peter (ob)
Encore, w. [cnd:Duain Wolfe], Colorado Children's Chorale, Rick Chinski (gtr), Robert Davine (acc), Laurie Kahler (pno), Samuel Lancaster (pno), Barry Oliver (pno), Marylin Preston (fl), Karen Yonovitz (fl), Andy Stevens (cl), Lionel Young (vn), Basil Vendreys (va), Wayne Templeman (vc), Charle *(rec Denver Center Media)* Colorado Children's Chorale ▲ 001

Cooperstock, Andrew (pno)
Starer, R.:Duo Vn, w. William Terwilliger (vn) Albany ▲ TROY 152 [DDD]

Cope, Mei Chen Liao (vn)
Musgrave, T.:Orfeo III, w. Pamela Guidetti (fl), Igor Szwec (vn), Michael Strauss (va), Lori Barnett (vc), Miles B. Davis (db), J. Freeman (cnd) *(rec Lang Concert Hall, Swarthmore College)* CRI ▲ CD 723 [DDD]

Copes, Ronald (pno)
Hartke, S.:Oh Them Rats Is Mean in My Kitchen, w. Michelle Makarski (vn) New World ▲ 80391-2 [DDD]

Copes, Ronald (va)
Kraft, William:Gallery 4-5, w. Diane Heffner (cl), Nancy Cirillo (vn), Ronald Lowry (vc), Hugh Hinton (pno) Albany ▲ TROY 218 [DDD]

Copes, Ronald (vc)
Hartke, S.:Son-Vars, w. James Bonn (pno) *(rec Hancock Auditorium, USC, Los Angeles, CA, Nov. 25–27, 1994)* New World ▲ 80461-2

Copes, Ronald (vn)—see also ORCHESTRAS & ENSEMBLES Dunsmuir Piano Quartet
Kraft, William:Episodes, w. Jeremy Haladyna (pno) Albany ▲ TROY 218 [DDD]

Copes, Steve (vn)
Rorem, N.:Studies for 11, w. E. Ostling (fl), K. Lord (ob), G. Raden (cl), J. Sutte (tpt), S. Copes (vn), C.-J. Chang (va), J. Lastrapes (vc), K. Englichova (hp), R. Uchida (pno), A. LaFargue (perc), R. Laveille (perc), R. Milanov (cnd) New World ▲ 80445-2

Copland, Aaron (pno)
Copland, A.:Con Pno, w. L. Bernstein (cnd), New York PO *(rec 1964)* Sony Classical 2-▲ SM2K 47232 [ADD]

Copley, Michael (ww)
The Classic Buskers, w. Ian Moore (acc) Newport Classic ▲ NPD 85559 [DDD]

Coppens, Claude (pno)
Stravinsky, I.:Pno Music—Scherzo; 4 Studies, Op. 7; Souvenir d'une marche boche; Valse pour les enfants; Pno-rag-music; Les 5 doigts, 8 Easy Pieces; Son; Serenade *(rec Steurbaut Sound Recording Centre)* René Gailly ▲ CD 87079 [DDD]

Coppey, Marc (vc)
Beethoven, L. van:Qts Pno, WoO 36, w. Philippe Cassard (pno), Raphael Oleg (vn), Miguel da Siva (va) Valois 2-▲ V 4715
Beethoven, L. van:Qt Pno, Op. 16, w. Philippe Cassard (pno), Raphael Oleg (vn), Miguel da Siva (va) Valois 2-▲ V 4715
Britten, H.:Phantasy Qt, w. François Leleux (ob), Guillaume Sutre (vn), Miguel Da Silva (va) Harmonia Mundi France ("Les Nouveaux Interprètes" series) ▲ HMN 911556
Debussy, C.:Son Vc, w. E. Le Sage (pno) *(rec Feb. 2–6, 1993)* K617 ▲ 7031 [DDD]
Emmanuel, M.:Son Vc, w. E. Le Sage (pno) *(rec Feb. 2–6, 1993)* K617 ▲ 7031 [DDD]
Grieg, E.:Son Vc, w. Eric Le Sage (pno) Harmonia Mundi France ▲ HMN 911550
Music at the Time of Beaumarchais, w. Montserrat Figueras (sop), Lawrence Monteyro (sop), Raphel Oleg (vn), Miguel da Silva (va), Christophe Coin (vc), José Miguel Moreno (gtr), Paul Badura-Skoda (pno), Philippe Cassard (pno), Eric Le Sage (pno), Bob Van Asperen (h Valois ▲ V 4767
Strauss, R.:Son Vc, w. Eric Le Sage (pno) Harmonia Mundi France ▲ HMN 911550

Coppieters, Frank (db)
Salon-Music for a Double Bass, w. H. Eeman (pno) René Gailly ▲ CD 86006 [ADD]

Coppock, Bruce (vc)
Foote, A.:Nocturne, w. F. Smith (fl), L. Chang (vn), V. Uritzky (vn), K. Murdock (va) Northeastern ("Classical Arts" series) ▲ NR 227-CD

Coquillat, Willy (perc)—see ORCHESTRAS & ENSEMBLES Le Cercle Trio

Cora, Tom (vc)
Kinney, M.:You Are So Stingingly Demure, w. M. Kinney (vc), M. Anderson (perc), S. Mensah (perc) Innova ▲ MN 107
Sato, M.:Improvs, w. Michihiro Sato (tsugaru shamisen), Bill Frisell (elec gtr), Fred Frith (elec gtr), Tenko (sgr), Mark Miller (elec bass), Nicolas Collins (elec), Christian Marclay (turntables), Steve Colemann (sax), Joey Baron (perc), Mark Dresser (elec bass), Gerry Hemingway (perc), Toh Ban Djan [Ikue Mori (perc), Luli Shioi (elec bass/sgr)], Semantics [Elliott Sharp (electric gtr/bass), Samm Bennett (perc), Ned Rothenberg (sax)]—23 improvisations with various accompaniment combinations *(rec Baby Monster Studio, NY, Apr. 11–16, 1988)* Hat Hut ▲ hat ART CD 6015 [ADD]

Coray, Curdin (vc)
Bruch, M.:Adagio on a Celtic Theme, w. H. Griffiths (cnd), Royal PO Gallo ▲ CD 692
Bruch, M.:Canzone Vc, w. H. Griffiths (cnd), Royal PO Gallo ▲ CD 692
Bruch, M.:Kol Nidrei, w. H. Griffiths (cnd), Royal PO Gallo ▲ CD 692
Mieg, P.:Triple Con, w. Gunars Larsens (vn), Wilhelm Gerlach (va), M. Venzago (cnd), Lucerne Festival Strings *(rec 1979)* Jecklin ▲ JS 314-2 [DDD]

Corbolini, Lorenzo (vc)—see ORCHESTRAS & ENSEMBLES I Filarmonici

Cordelette, Claude (perc)
Bolcom, W.:Sons (2) for 2 Pnos, Bass & Perc, w. E. Ax (pno), C. Bolling (pno), C. Sorin (db) CBS ▲ MK 45646 [DDD]
Bolling, C.:Suite 2 Fl, w. J.-P. Rampal (fl), C. Bolling (pno), C. Sorin (db) CBS ▲ MK 42318 [DDD] ■ FMT 42318 (D)

Cordes, Manfred (org)
Schütz, H.:Cantiones sacrae, w. Mona Spägele (sop), Ralf Popken (alt), Rogers Covey-Crump (ten), John Potter (ten), Peter Kooj (bass), Thomas Ihlenfeldt (chit)—complete 40 motets CPO 2-▲ 999405-2 [DDD]

Cordes, Manfred (trbn/org)—see ORCHESTRAS & ENSEMBLES Weser-Renaissance Ensemble

Cordovana, Miachael (pno)
Burleigh, H.T.:Art Songs, w. Regina McConnell (sop)—You Ask Me If I Love You?; The Prayer I Make for You; One Day; Elysium; The Prayer; And as the Gulls Soar; Heigh-Ho!; The Man in White; Now Sleeps the Crimson Petal; I Hear His Footstep, Music sweet; Just You; He Sent Me You; Were I a Star; Oh Love of a Day; Adoration; Tide; The Grey Wolf; The Dove and the Lily; Oh, My Love!; Why Art Thou Not Near Me!; The Sailor's Wife; Carry Me Back to the Pine Wood; Lovely Dark and Lonely One *(rec Harmony Hall, Fort Washington, MD, Feb 23-24, 1995)* Centaur ▲ CRC 2252 [DDD]
Pfitzner, H.:Songs, w. M. Busching (mez)—24 songs [G] Centaur ▲ CRC 2136

Corea, Chick (pno)
Mozart, W.A.:Con 20 Pno, w. Bobby McFerrin (sgr), B. McFerrin (cnd), St. Paul CO—Prelude [a capella voc & pno improvisation] *(rec Donald Benson Great Hall, Bethel College, St. Paul & Masonic Grand Lodge, New York, Feb 5-7, 1996 & May 21, 1)* Sony Classical ▲ SK 62601 [DDD] ■ ST 62601
Mozart, W.A.:Con 23 Pno, w. Bobby McFerrin (sgr), B. McFerrin (cnd), St. Paul CO—Prelude [a capella voc & pno improvisation] *(rec Donald Benson Great Hall, Bethel College, St. Paul & Masonic Grand Lodge, New York, Feb 5-7, 1996 & May 21, 1)* Sony Classical ▲ SK 62601 [DDD] ∆ SM 62601 ■ ST 62601
Mozart, W.A.:Son 2 Pno, w. Bobby McFerrin (sgr), B. McFerrin (cnd), St. Paul CO [Voc & Pno improvisation based on Adagio] *(rec Donald Benson Great Hall, Bethel College, St. Paul & Masonic Grand Lodge, New York, Feb 5-7, 1996 & May 21, 1)* Sony Classical ▲ SK 62601 [DDD] ■ ST 62601

Corigliano Sr., John (vn)
Beethoven, L. van:Con Vn, Vc & Pno, "Triple Con", w. Leonard Rose (vc), Walter Hendl (pno), B. Walter (cnd), New York PO Sony Classical ("Bruno Walter:The Edition" series) ▲ SMK 64479
Corigliano, J.:Son Vn & Pno, w. Ralph Votapek (pno) *(rec Steinway Hall, NYC, Mar 1, 1966)* CRI ▲ CD 659 [ADD]
Mozart, W.A.:Sinf Concertante, w. William Lincer (va), B. Walter (cnd), New York PO Enterprise ("The Radio Years" series) ▲ ENT RY 69
Three Tenors of the Golden Age, w. J. Björling (ten), Mario Lanza (ten), Jan Peerce (ten), Constantine Callinicos (pno), Frederick Schauwecker (pno), RCA Victor Orch [cnd:Renato Cellini, Constantine Callinicos, Erich Leinsdorf, Sylvan Levin, Maximilian Pilzer, Frieder Weissmann], Rome Opera Orch, Rome Opera Chorus, et al. RCA Gold Seal ▲ 09026-68531-2 [ADD] ■ 09026-68531-4

Corkhill, David (perc)
Bartók, B.:Son for 2 Pnos, w. M. Perahia (pno), G. Solti (pno), E. Glennie (perc) CBS ▲ MK 42625 [DDD]

Cornil, Dominique (pno)
Joplin, S.:Pno Music GHA ▲ CD 126.004
Nazareth, E.:Pno Music—Odeon; Ouro sobre azul; Expansiva; Apanhel-te cavaquinho; Nove de julho; Helena; Nenê; Batuque; Fon-fon; Dirce; Sarambeque; Improviso; Tenebroso; Julietta; Esta chumbado; Belja-flor; Carioca; Eponina; Duvidoso; Elegantissima; Talisma GHA ▲ GHA 126.028
Prokofiev, S.:Peter & the Wolf [original version for pno] René Gailly ▲ 87098
Prokofiev, S.:Pieces Pno, Op. 12 René Gailly ▲ 87098
Prokofiev, S.:Son 2 Pno René Gailly ▲ 87098
Uy, P.:Choral pour la Paix, w. Dinah Bryant (sop), Zeger Vandersteene (ten), Philippe Huttenlocher (bar), Alain Carré (nar), G. Octors (cnd), Wallonie Royal CO, Denis Menier (cnd), Namur Chamber Choir *(rec Aulne, Belgium, 1995)* Cypres ▲ 2611 [DDD]

Cornoldi, C. (vn)
Scarlatti, D.:Sons Vn, w. G. Catalucci (hpd) *(rec live, 1988)* Bongiovanni ▲ GB 2026 [DDD]

Corostola, Pedro (vc)
Beethoven, L. van:Con Vn, Vc & Pno, "Triple Con", w. P. León (vn), L. Milà (pno), H. Zongjie (cnd), Chinese Central PO Regis Tro ▲ RTAC 003 [DDD]

Corré, Philippe (pno)
Blanc, A.:Sonatine concertante, w. E. Exerjean (pno) Pierre Verany ▲ PV.790041 [DDD]
Chabrier, E.:España, w. E. Exerjean (pno) *(rec 6/85)* Pierre Verany ▲ PV.786031 [DDD]
Chabrier, E.:Pas redoublé, w. E. Exerjean (pno) *(rec 6/85)* Pierre Verany ▲ PV.786031 [DDD]
Chabrier, E.:Valses romantiques (3), w. E. Exerjean (pno) *(rec 6/85)* Pierre Verany ▲ PV.786031 [DDD]
Dvořák, A.:Slavonic Dances (comp), w. E. Exerjean (pno) [piano 4-hands] Pierre Verany ▲ PV.790091 [DDD]
Dvořák, A.:Slavonic Dances (comp), w. Edouard Exerjean (pno) Pierre Verany ("Favourites" series) ▲ PVY 730011 [DDD]
Gouvy, T.:Scherzo, Op. 60, w. E. Exerjean (pno) Pierre Verany ▲ PV.790041 [DDD]
Infante, M.:Danzas andaluzas, w. E. Exerjean (pno) *(rec 6/85)* Pierre Verany ▲ PV.786031 [DDD]
Infante, M.:Spanish Music, w. E. Exerjean (pno) *(rec 6/85)* Pierre Verany ▲ PV.786031 [DDD]
Lefébure-Wély, L.J.A.:Duo symphonique 1, w. E. Exerjean (pno) Pierre Verany ▲ PV.790041 [DDD]
Pierné, G.:Tarantella Pnos, w. E. Exerjean (pno) Pierre Verany ▲ PV.790041 [DDD]
Saint-Saëns, C.:Variations on a Theme of Beethoven, w. E. Exerjean (pno) Pierre Verany ▲ PV.790041 [DDD]
Weber, C.M. von:Qt Pno, w. Carl Stamitz Ensemble Pierre Verany ▲ PV.792021 [DDD]

Correa, Riccardo (lt)—see also ORCHESTRAS & ENSEMBLES Lautentrio Riccardo Correa
Lute Music from the Renaissance, w. Hans Michael Koch (lt) Entrée ▲ 0046 [ADD]

Cortazzo, Jeff (b trbn)
O'Rourke, J.:Terminal Pharmacy, w. Tony Burr (cl), Jeff Cortazzo (b trbn), John McEntire (dr), Rob Prosser (acc), Isha Suftin (acc), Mike Dockter (vc), Hattie Franck (vc), Robert Keck (vc), Mary LaBreque (vc), Dan Loch (vc), Stan Saderk (vc), Lisa Hemmer (fl), Sue Oberg (fl), Wendi Lev (fl), Jim Vanden (fl), Jim O'Rourke (gtr), Steve Braack (elec) Tzadik ▲ TZA 7011 [DDD]

Cortese, Paul (va)
Bergsma, W.:Fantastic Vars on a Theme from Tristan, w. J. Klibonoff (pno) *(rec 6/91)* Crystal ▲ CD 636
Carter, E.:Elegy Va, w. J. Klibonoff (pno) *(rec 6/91)* Crystal ▲ CD 636
Currier, N.:A Sambuca Son, w. Maarika Järvi (fl), Marie-Pierre Langlamet (hp) Chandos ▲ CHAN 9395 [DDD]
Debussy, C.:Son Fl, w. Maarika Järvi (fl), Marie-Pierre Langlamet (hp) Chandos ▲ CHAN 9395 [DDD]
Genzmer, H.:Trio Fl, Va & Hp, w. Maarika Järvi (fl), Marie-Pierre Langlamet (hp) Chandos ▲ CHAN 9395 [DDD]
Hindemith, P.:Kammermusik 5, w. M. Brabbins (cnd), Philharmonia Orch ASV ▲ ASV 931 [DDD]
Hindemith, P.:Konzertmusik Va, w. M. Brabbins (cnd), Philharmonia Orch ASV ▲ ASV 931 [DDD]
Hindemith, P.:Der Schwanendreher, w. M. Brabbins (cnd), Philharmonia Orch ASV ▲ ASV 931 [DDD]
Hindemith, P.:Sons Va ASV ▲ ASV 947
Hovhaness, A.:Chahagir *(rec 6/91)* Crystal ▲ CD 636
Jolivet, A.:Petite suite, w. Maarika Järvi (fl), Marie-Pierre Langlamet (hp) Chandos ▲ CHAN 9395 [DDD]
Persichetti, V.:Infanta marina, w. J. Klibonoff (pno) Crystal ▲ CD 636
Persichetti, V.:Parable 16 Crystal ▲ CD 636
Reger, M.:Son Cl, Op. 107 *(rec Barcelona, Dec. 1993)* Posh Boy ▲ 8167-2
Reger, M.:Suites Va *(rec Barcelona, Dec. 1993)* Posh Boy ▲ 8167-2

Cortesi, Raphaele (pno)
Rossini, G.:Petite messe solennelle, w. Livia Aghova (sop), Marta Benackova (mez), Gil Manuel Beltran (ten), Peter Mikulas (bass), Peter Toperczer (pno), Josef Ksica (harm), Romano Gandolfi (cnd), Prague Chamber Choir *(rec Domovina Studios, Prague, Sept. 10-12, 1994)* Discover International 2-▲ DI 920324-5 [DDD]

Cortet, Roger (fl)
Bach, J.S.:Brandenburg Con 5, w. A. Cortot (pno), J. Thibaud (vn), Paris Conservatory Societé des Concerts Orch *(rec May 16, 1932)* Biddulph ▲ LAB 028 [ADD]

Corti, Daniel (va)—see also ORCHESTRAS & ENSEMBLES Euler String Quartet
Müller-Zurich, P.:Trio Strs, w. B. Langbein (vn), R. Altwegg (vc) Grammont ▲ CTSP 20-2

Corti, Guido (cnt)
Battiato, F.:Haiku, w. Franco Battiato (voc), Pouran Ghaffarpour (voc), Antonio Ballista (pno), Marco Boni (vc), Guido Corti (cnt), Filippo Destrieri (kbd/computer), John Giblin (bass), Gavin Harrison (dr/perc), Jakko Jakszyk (gtr), Roberto Mazza (ob), Fabrizio Merlini (va), Angelo Privitera (kbd/computer), Mino Bordignon (cnd), Milan Chamber Music Choir Hemisphere ▲ 837234-2
Battiato, F.:Ricerca sul Terzo, w. Franco Battiato (voc), Alessio Alba (tamboura), Antonio Ballista (pno), Marco Boni (vc), Debendra Kanti Chakraborty (tabla), Guido Corti (cnt), Filippo Destrieri (kbd/computer), John Giblin (bass), Buddhadeu Das Gupta (sarod), Gavin Harrison (dr/perc), Jakko Jakszyk (gtr), Roberto Mazza (ob), Fabrizio Merlini (va), Angelo Privitera (kbd/computer), Mino Bordignon (cnd), Milan Chamber Music Choir Hemisphere ▲ 837234-2

Corti, Guido (hn)
Rossini, G.:Chamber Music, w. Sergio Lamberto (vn), Sergio del Mastro (cl), Ricardo Caramella (pno) Nuova Era ▲ NUO 7245

Cortman, Stan (hn)
Scelsi, G.:Anahit, w. Paul Zukofsky (vn), Julie Bogorad (fl), Peggy Russell (fl), Courtney Westcott (fl), Lawrence McDonald (cl), Joan Waryha (cl), Jean Hansen (b cl), Bill Suite (e hn), Nita VanPelt (sax), Bob Zobal (tpt), John Carter (trbn), Martin Lydecker (trbn), Stan Cortman (hn), Robert Ward (hn), William Curry (va), Jody Rowitsch (va), Irene Wade (va), Anne Fagerburg (vc), John Gockel (vc), Sue Manz (bass), Steven Stearman (bass) *(rec Oberlin Conservatory of Music, Oct 8, 1973)* CP² ▲ CP2 108 [AAD]

Cortot, Alfred (pno)
Bach, J.S.:Brandenburg Con 5, w. Jacques Thibaud (vn), A. Cortot (cnd), Paris Ecole Normale CO *(rec 1930)* Music Memoria ▲ 30321
Bach, J.S.:Brandenburg Con 5, w. J. Thibaud (vn), R. Cortet (fl), Paris Conservatory Societé des Concerts Orch *(rec May 16, 1932)* Biddulph ▲ LAB 028 [ADD]
Beethoven, L. van:Son 9 Vn, "Kreutzer", w. J. Thibaud (vn) *(rec 5/27-28/29)* Biddulph ▲ LAB 028 [ADD]
Beethoven, L. van:Son 9 Vn, "Kreutzer", w. J. Thibaud (vn) *(rec May 1929)* EMI Classics 3-▲ 64057 (m) [ADD]
Beethoven, L. van:Trio 7 Pno, w. J. Thibaud (vn), P. Casals (vc) *(rec Nov.-Dec. 1928)* EMI Classics 3-▲ 64057-2 (m) [ADD]
Beethoven, L. van:Trio 9 Pno, "Kakadu", w. J. Thibaud (vn), P. Casals (vc) *(rec July 6, 1926)* EMI Classics 3-▲ 64057 (m) [ADD]
Beethoven, L. van:Vars on "Bei Männern" from Mozart's *Die Zauberflöte*, w. P. Casals (vc) *(rec June 21, 1927)* EMI Classics 3-▲ 64057-2 (m) [ADD]
Beethoven, L. van:Vars on "Bei Männern" from Mozart's *Die Zauberflöte*, w. P. Casals (vc) *(rec 1927 for HMV)* Pearl 2-▲ PEAS 9461 (m) [ADD]
Beethoven, L. van:Vars on "Bei Männern" from Mozart's *Die Zauberflöte*, w. P. Casals (vc) Pearl 4-▲ PEAS 9935 (m) [ADD]
The 1922-23 HMV & 1924 Victor Recordings, w. J. Thibaud (vn), Harold Craxton (pno), Jesús-Maria Sanromà (pno) Biddulph ▲ LAB 014 [ADD]
Chausson, E.:Con Vn, Pno & Str Qt, w. J. Thibaud (vn), *(string quartet unknown)* *(rec 1931)* Biddulph ▲ LAB 029 [ADD]
Chausson, E.:Con Vn, Pno & Str Qt, w. Jaques Thibaud (vn), *(ensemble unknown)* Memories ▲ MEM CD 4605
Chopin, F.:Ballades Pno (comp) Biddulph ▲ LHW 001 [ADD]
Chopin, F.:Ballades Pno (comp) Enterprise ("The Piano Library" series) ▲ ENT 184
Chopin, F.:Con 2 Pno, w. J. Barbirolli (cnd), *(orch unknown)*, *(orch. unknown)* *(rec 1933 & 1935)* Grammofono 2000 ▲ GRM 78516 [ADD]
Chopin, F.:Con 2 Pno, w. J. Barbirolli (cnd), *(orch unknown)* *(rec 1935 for Victor)* Pearl ▲ PEA 9491 (m) [AAD]
Chopin, F.:Fant *(rec 1933 & 1935)* Grammofono 2000 ▲ GRM 78516 [ADD]
Chopin, F.:Nocturnes—Op. 9, No. 2 *(rec 1929 for HMV)* Biddulph ▲ LHW 001 [ADD]
Chopin, F.:Pno Music (misc)—Son 3 in b, Op. 58; Fant in f, Op. 49; 4 Ballades; Son 2 in bb, Op. 35; Con 2 for Pno, Op. 21 [w. John Barbirolli (cnd) *(orch unknown)*]; 24 Preludes, Op. 28; 14 Waltzes, Opp. 18, 34/1-3, 42, 64/1-3, 69/1-2, 70/1-3 & Op. posth. in e Enterprise ("Piano Library" series) 3-▲ ENT PL 206
Chopin, F.:Pno Music (misc) *(rec 1954-57)* Arkadia ▲ 510 (m) [AAD]
Chopin, F.:Pno Music (misc)—Berceuse, Op. 57; 2 Etudes, Opp. 10/11 & 25/9; 2 Nocturnes, Opp. 9/2 & 15/2; 4 Waltzes, Opp. 64/1 & 2, 69/1 & 70/1 *(rec 1950s)* Melodram ▲ CD 18018 (m)
Chopin, F.:Preludes, Op. 28 Enterprise ("The Piano Library" series) ▲ ENT 184
Chopin, F.:Preludes, Op. 28—No. 15 *(rec 1900-10)* Adès ▲ ADE 203932 [AAD]
Chopin, F.:Preludes, Op. 28 *(rec 7/26)* Musica Memoria ▲ 30268 (m)
Chopin, F.:Preludes, Op. 28 *(rec 1954-57)* Arkadia ▲ 510 (m) [AAD]
Chopin, F.:Son Pno, Op. 35 *(rec 1933 & 1935)* Grammofono 2000 ▲ GRM 78516 [ADD]
Chopin, F.:Son Pno, Op. 35 *(rec 1928 for HMV)* Biddulph ▲ LHW 001 [ADD]
Chopin, F.:Son Pno, Op. 35 *(rec 1950s)* Melodram ▲ MEL 18018 (m)
Chopin, F.:Son Pno, Op. 58 *(rec London, May 12, 1931)* Iron Needle ▲ IN 1341 (m) [ADD]
Chopin, F.:Son Pno, Op. 58, w. A. Cortot *(rec 1931 for HMV)* Biddulph ▲ LHW 001 [ADD]
Chopin, F.:Son Pno, Op. 58 Enterprise ("Sirio" series) ▲ ENT SO 530014
Chopin, F.:Waltzes—14 sels Enterprise ("Sirio" series) ▲ ENT SO 530014
Chopin, F.:Waltzes—Opp. 18, 34/1-3, 42, 64/1-3, 69/1-2, 70/1-3 & Op. posth. *(rec Paris, May 24, 1943)* Iron Needle ▲ IN 1341 (m) [ADD]
Debussy, C.:Children's Corner *(rec 1928 for HMV)* Biddulph ▲ LHW 006 [ADD]
Debussy, C.:Music of, w. J. Thibaud (vn)—Minstrels EMI Classics ▲ CDH 63032
Debussy, C.:Preludes Pno (sels), Book 1 *(rec 1928-31 from HMV original)* Biddulph ▲ LHW 006 [ADD]
Debussy, C.:Son Vn, w. J. Thibaud (vn) *(rec 1929 for HMV)* Biddulph ▲ LHW 006 [ADD]
Debussy, C.:Son Vn, w. J. Thibaud (vn) EMI Classics ▲ CDH 63032
Debussy, C.:Son Vn, w. J. Thibaud (vn) *(rec 1929 for HMV)* Music Memoria ▲ 30321
Debussy, C.:Son Vn, w. J. Thibaud (vn) *(rec 1929 for HMV)* Pearl ▲ PEA 9348 (m) [AAD]
Fauré, G.:Berceuse Vn, w. Jaques Thibaud (vn) Memories ▲ MEM CD 4605
Fauré, G.:Berceuse Vn, w. J. Thibaud (vn) *(rec 1931, from HMV DB1653)* Biddulph ▲ LAB 029 [ADD]
Fauré, G.:Berceuse Vn, w. J. Thibaud (vn) EMI Classics ▲ CDH 63032
Fauré, G.:Son 1 Vn, w. Jacques Thibaud (vn) *(rec ca 1928)* Symposium ▲ 1156
Fauré, G.:Son 1 Vn, w. J. Thibaud (vn) EMI Classics ▲ CDH 63032
Franck, C.:Prélude, aria et final Biddulph ▲ LHW 027
Franck, C.:Prélude, choral et fugue Biddulph ▲ LHW 027
Franck, C.:Qnt Pno, w. International String Quartet *(rec 1927)* Pearl ▲ PEA 9396 (m) [AAD]
Franck, C.:Son Vn, w. Jacques Thibaud (vn) Biddulph ▲ LHW 027
Franck, C.:Son Vn, w. J. Thibaud (vn) EMI Classics ▲ CDH 63032
Franck, C.:Symphonic Vars, *(orch unknown)* Biddulph ▲ LHW 027
Great Pianists of the Golden Era:Cortot & Horowitz, w. Cortot, Alfred (pno), Vladimir Horowitz (pno) Foné ▲ FON 90F12 [DDD]
Haydn, J.:Trios Pno, Vn & Vc, w. Jacques Thibaud (vn), Pablo Casals (vc)—No. 25 only *(rec 6/20/27)* Biddulph ▲ LAB 028 [ADD]
Liszt, F.:Pno Music (misc)—Hungarian Rhapsody No. 11; Etude de concert, "Le leggierezza" (two versions); 2 Chopin song transcriptions, "Spring" & "The Betrothal [or The Ring]" *(78 rpm studio rec'gs, new transfers)* Music & Arts ▲ CD 662 (m) [AAD]
Liszt, F.:Pno Music (misc) [from 78 rpm Victor & HMV discs]—Au bord d'une source [Victor 982-A]; La leggierezza (2 versions, acoustic [Victor 74589] & electric [HMV DB 1535]); Legend No. 2 (St. François de Paule marchant sur les flots) [HMV DB 3269]; Hungarian Rhapsodies Nos. 2, 11 (2 versions, both electric [Victor matr. CE 32175, unpub.; Victor 1277]; Rigoletto Paraphrase [Victor 6641]; Chopin-Liszt:Spring; The Ring [HMV DA 1682] Pearl ▲ PEA 9396 (m) [AAD]
Liszt, F.:Son Pno Music & Arts ▲ CD 662 (m) [AAD]
Liszt, F.:Son Pno Pearl ▲ PEA 9396 (m) [AAD]

Cortot, Alfred (pno) (cont.)
Mendelssohn, F.:Lieder ohne Worte Pno—Op. 19/1 *(rec 1937 for HMV)* Biddulph ▲ LHW 002 [ADD]
Mendelssohn, F.:Trio 1 Pno, w. J. Thibaud (vn), P. Casals (vc) *(rec 1927 for HMV)* Biddulph ▲ LHW 002 [ADD]
Mendelssohn, F.:Trio 1 Pno, w. Jacques Thibaud (vn), Pablo Casals (vc) *(rec June 1927)* Iron Needle 2-▲ IN 1342/43 (m) [ADD]
Mendelssohn, F.:Trio 1 Pno, w. J. Thibaud (vn) , P. Casals (vc) *(rec June 1927)* EMI Classics 3-▲ 64057-2 (m) [ADD]
Mendelssohn, F.:Vars sérieuses *(rec 1937 for HMV)* Biddulph ▲ LHW 002 [ADD]
Ravel, M.:Con Pno (left hand), w. C. Munch (cnd), Paris Conservatory Societé des Concerts Orch *(rec 1939 for Victor)* Pearl ▲ PEA 9491 (m) [AAD]
Ravel, M.:Jeux d'eau *(rec 1931)* Biddulph ▲ LHW 006 [ADD]
Ravel, M.:Sonatine Pno *(rec 1931 for HMV)* Biddulph ▲ LHW 006 [ADD]
Saint-Saëns, C.:Con 4 Pno, w. C. Munch (cnd), Paris Conservatory Societé des Concerts Orch *(rec 1935 for Victor)* Pearl ▲ PEA 9491 (m) [AAD]
Saint-Saëns, C.:Étude Pno, Op. 52/6 *(rec 1900–10)* Adès ▲ ADE 203932 [AAD]
Saint-Saëns, C.:Étude Pno, Op. 52/6 *(rec 1931 for Victor)* Pearl ▲ PEA 9491 (m) [AAD]
Schubert, Franz:Trio 1 Pno, w. J. Thibaud (vn), P. Casals (vc) *(rec 1926)* EMI Classics 3-▲ 64057-2 (m) [ADD]
Schubert, Franz:Trio 1 Pno, w. Jaques Thibaud (vn), Pablo Casals (vc) Memories ▲ MEM CD 4605
Schumann, R.:Carnaval Pno *(rec 1928 for HMV)* Biddulph ▲ LHW 004 [ADD]
Schumann, R.:Con Pno, w. F. Fricsay (cnd), Berlin RSO *(rec in concert, 1950s)* Melodram ▲ MEL 18018 (m)
Schumann, R.:Con Pno, w. L. Ronald (cnd), London SO *(rec 1927 for HMV)* Biddulph ▲ LHW 003 [ADD]
Schumann, R.:Davidsbündlertänze *(rec 1937 for HMV)* Biddulph ▲ LHW 003 [ADD]
Schumann, R.:Dichterliebe, w. C. Panzéra (bar) *(rec 1934 for HMV)* Biddulph ▲ LHW 005 [ADD]
Schumann, R.:Dichterliebe, w. C. Panzéra (bar) *(rec 1934 for HMV)* Pearl ▲ PEA 9919 (m) [AAD]
Schumann, R.:Fantasiestücke Pno, Op. 12—No. 1, "Des Abends" *(rec 1937 for HMV)* Biddulph ▲ LHW 005 [ADD]
Schumann, R.:Kinderszenen *(rec 1935 for HMV)* Biddulph ▲ LHW 005 [ADD]
Schumann, R.:Kreisleriana *(rec 1935 for HMV)* Biddulph ▲ LHW 005 [ADD]
Schumann, R.:Papillons *(rec 1935 for HMV)* Biddulph ▲ LHW 003 [ADD]
Schumann, R.:Pno Music (misc)—Symphonic Etudes, Opp. 13 & posth.; Carnaval, Op. 9; Kreisleriana, Op. 16; Des Abends, Op. 12; Papillons, Op. 2; Kinderszenen, Op. 15; Davidsbündlertänze, Op. 6 *(rec 1928–48)* Music & Arts 2-▲ CD 858 [ADD]
Schumann, R.:Sym Etudes *(rec 1929 for HMV)* Biddulph ▲ LHW 004 [ADD]
Schumann, R.:Trio 1 Pno, w. J. Thibaud (vn), P. Casals (vc) *(rec 1928 for HMV)* Biddulph ▲ LHW 004 [ADD]
Schumann, R.:Trio 1 Pno, w. J. Thibaud (vn), P. Casals (vc) *(rec 1928 for HMV)* EMI Classics 3-▲ 64057-2 (m) [ADD]
Victor Recordings (1919–1926), w. Cortot, Alfred (pno) Pearl ▲ PEA 9386 (m) [AAD]
Weber, C.M. von:Invitation to the Dance Pno *(rec 1926 for Victor)* Biddulph ▲ LHW 002 [ADD]
Weber, C.M. von:Sons Pno—No. 2 *(rec 78 rpm, in studio)* Music & Arts ▲ CD 662 (m) [AAD]
Weber, C.M. von:Son 2 Pno *(rec 1939 for Victor)* Biddulph ▲ LHW 002 [ADD]

Cortvrint, Yves (va)—see ORCHESTRAS & ENSEMBLES Brussels String Quartet

Corver, Ellen (pno)
Adams, J.:Grand Pianola Music, w. Kym Amps (sop), Ruth Holton (sop), Lyndsay Wagstaff (sop), Sepp Grotenhuis (pno), S. Mosko (cnd), Netherlands Wind Ensemble Chandos ▲ CHAN 9363 [DDD]
Lang, D.:Orpheus Over & Under, w. Sepp Grotenhuis (pno)—Under Orpheus Chandos ▲ CHAN 9363 [DDD]

Coryell, Larry (gtr)
3 Guitars 3, w. Isbin, Sharon (gtr), Laurindo Almeida (gtr) Pro Arte ▲ CDD 235 ■ PCD 235

Coryn, Franck (db)
Rossini, G.:Tancredi, w. Sumi Jo (sop—Amenaide), Lucretia Lendi (mez—Roggiero), Anna Maria di Micco (mez—Isaura), Ewa Podles (cta—Tancredi), Stanford Olsen (ten—Argirio), Pietro Spagnoli (bar—Orbazzano), Ewald Demeyere (hpd), Lieven Baert (vc), A. Zedda (cnd), Collegium Instrumentale Brugense, Capella Brugensis *(rec Poissy Theatre & Centre Musical-Lyrique-Phonographique, Ile de France, Jan. 26–31, 1994)* Naxos ("Opera Classics" series) 2-▲ 8.660037/38 [DDD]

Corzon, C. (pno)
Mozart, W.A.:Con 21 Pno, w. R. Kubelik (cnd), Bavarian RSO *(rec 1975)* Artists ▲ FED 51 [ADD]
Mozart, W.A.:Con 23 Pno, w. R. Kubelik (cnd), Bavarian RSO *(rec 1975)* Artists ▲ FED 51 [ADD]

Cosachov, Monica (hpd)
Sammartini, G.B.:Con Hpd, Camerata Bariloche CO Argentina FSM-Adagio ▲ FCD 91118 [DDD]
Sammartini, G.:Giuseppe St. Martini's Cons Hpd, Camerata Bariloche, No. 1 in A FSM-Adagio ▲ FCD 91118 [DDD]

Cosand, Walter (pno)
Aschaffenburg, W.:Conversations *(rec June 20–21, 1993)* Summit ▲ DCD 154 [DDD]
Cohen, David:Son Pno *(rec June 20–21, 1993)* Summit ▲ DCD 154 [DDD]
Creston, P.:Son Sax, w. J. Wytko (sax) ACA Digital Recording ▲ CM 20012
Matthews, H.:Preludes—7 sels. *(rec June 20–21, 1993)* Summit ▲ DCD 154 [DDD]
Maurice, P.:Tableaux de Provence, w. J. Wytko (sax) ACA Digital Recording ▲ CM 20012
Rorem, N.:Etudes Pno *(rec June 20–21, 1993)* Summit ▲ DCD 154 [DDD]

Cosart, Jann (h-g/rebec)—see ORCHESTRAS & ENSEMBLES Altramar Medieval Music Ensemble

Cosart, Jann (va)
Hovhaness, A.:Sextet Rcr, w. J. Tyson (rcr), J. Starkman (vn), K. Shaw (vn), A. Robbins (vc), F. Conover Fitch (hpd) Titanic ▲ Ti 169 [DDD]
Purcell, H.:Come Ye Sons of Art, w. Laura Goetz (ob), Sarah Weiner (ob), Davis Brooks (vn), Lisa Brooks (vn), Mary Burke (vl), Vance Reese (db), Thomas Gerber (hpd), Henry H. Leck (cnd), Indianapolis Children's Choir [arr. Maurice Blower] *(rec The Lodge, May & June 1995)* VAI Audio ▲ VAIA 1130 [DDD]
Purcell, H.:Fly, Bold Rebellion (sels), w. Laura Goetz (ob), Sarah Weiner (ob), Davis Brooks (vn), Lisa Brooks (vn), Mary Burke (vl), Vance Reese (db), Thomas Gerber (hpd), Henry H. Leck (cnd), Indianapolis Children's Choir—Be Welcome Then, Great Sir [arr. Steven Rickards] *(rec The Lodge, May & June 1995)* VAI Audio ▲ VAIA 1130 [DDD]
Purcell, H.:King Arthur (sels), w. Laura Goetz (ob), Sarah Weiner (ob), Davis Brooks (vn), Lisa Brooks (vn), Mary Burke (vl), Vance Reese (db), Thomas Gerber (hpd), Henry H. Leck (cnd), Indianapolis Children's Choir—Fairest Isle [arr. Steven Rickards] *(rec The Lodge, May & June 1995)* VAI Audio ▲ VAIA 1130 [DDD]
Something for Recorder & Strings, w. J. Tyson (rcr), Frances Conover Fitch (hpd), Jane Starkman (vn), Katheryn Shaw (vn), Alice Robbins (vc), Tom Coleman (db) Titanic ▲ Ti 169 [DDD]

Cosma, Sofia (pno)
Beethoven, L. van:Vars Pno, WoO 80 Town Hall ▲ THCD 29
Brahms, J.:Pieces Pno, Op. 76—Nos. 1 [Carpiccio in f#] & 5 [Capriccio in c#] Town Hall ▲ THCD 29
Brahms, J.:Pieces Pno, Op. 118—Nos. 1 [Intermezzo in a] & 2 [Intermezzo in A] Town Hall ▲ THCD 29
Busoni, F.:Bach Transcriptions—Chaconne in d Town Hall ▲ THCD 29
Chopin, F.:Mazurkas—Op. 7/1 & 3; Op. 24/4; Op. 63/2 & 3; Op. 67/4 Town Hall ▲ THCD 29
Chopin, F.:Waltzes—Op. 34/1 Town Hall ▲ THCD 29

Costa, Daniela (pno)
Giuliani, M.:Music for Gtr & Pno, w. Francesco Romano (gtr)—Gran Duo Concertante; Due Rondo, Op. 68; Grandi Variazzioni Concertanti sul tema; Grand Pot-pourri National, Op. 93; Variazioni sul tema, Op. 104 Nuova Era ("Ancient Music" series) 2-▲ NUO 7227

Costa, E. (db)—see ORCHESTRAS & ENSEMBLES Stanislas Ensemble

Costa, Jean (org)
Recital d'orgue en corse Musidisc ▲ MUS 290292 [DDD]

Costa, Raie de (pno)
Mayerl, W.J.:Music of, w. Billy Mayerl (pno), R. Noble (cnd), New Mayfair Orch, Fred Hartley Quintet—Marigold; Pianolettes (6); Pno Exaggerations (4); 4 aces Suite; plus others Happy Days Nostalgia ▲ CDHD 205

Costa, Sequeira (pno)
A Musical Snuff-Box:Sequeira Costa Plays Encores *(rec Tamamura-machi Bunka Center, Japan, Nov. 24, 1994)* Camerata ▲ 30CM 369 [DDD]
Rachmaninoff, S.:Con 1 Pno, w. C. Seaman (cnd), Royal PO RPO ▲ RPO 7024 [DDD]
Rachmaninoff, S.:Con 3 Pno, w. C. Seaman (cnd), Royal PO RPO ▲ RPO 7006 [DDD]
Rachmaninoff, S.:Rhapsody on a Theme of Paganini, w. C. Seaman (cnd), Royal PO RPO ▲ RPO 7006 [DDD]
Rachmaninoff, S.:Suite 1 for 2 Pnos, w. Artur Pizzaro (pno) RPO ▲ RPO 7024 [DDD]
Schumann, R.:Con Pno, w. S. Gunzenhauser (cnd), Lisbon Gulbenkian Foundation Orch Naxos ▲ 8.550277 [DDD]
Schumann, R.:Intro & Allegro appassionato, Op. 92, w. S. Gunzenhauser (cnd), Lisbon Gulbenkian Foundation Orch Naxos ▲ 8.550277 [DDD]
Schumann, R.:Intro & Allegro, Op. 134, w. S. Gunzenhauser (cnd), Lisbon Gulbenkian Foundation Orch Naxos ▲ 8.550277 [DDD]

Costanzi, Rita (hp)
Pastorales de Noël, w. V. Costanzi (vn), K. Rudolph (fl), Jesse Read (bn) Skylark ▲ 9400 [DDD]

Costanzi, V. (vn)
Pastorales de Noël, w. R. Costanzi (hp), K. Rudolph (fl), Jesse Read (bn) Skylark ▲ 9400 [DDD]

Costanzo, Silva (pno)
Menotti, G.C.:Canti della lontananza, w. A. V. Banks (mez) [I] Nuova Era ▲ 7122 [DDD]
Menotti, G.C.:Ricercare & Toccata on a Theme from *The Old Maid & the Thief* Nuova Era ▲ 7122 [DDD]

Costea, Gavril (fl)
Dittersdorf, K.D. von:Con Fl, w. M. Cristescu (cnd), Cluj-Napoca PO Olympia (Explorer) ▲ OCD 405 [AAD]
Salieri, A.:Con Fl, w. F. Ionoaia (ob), M. Cichirdan (cnd), Craiova PO Gallo ▲ CD 601 [AAD]
Terényi, E.:Gallant Dances, w. *(other artists unknown)* Electrecord ▲ ELCD 124 [AAD]
Terényi, E.:Vivaldiana, w. E. Botár, C. Mandeal, Cluj-Napoca CO *(Vivaldiana, Gallant Dances)* Electrecord ▲ ELCD 124 [AAD]

Costello, Marilyn (hp)
Debussy, C.:Danses sacrée et profane, w. E. Ormandy (cnd), Philadelphia Orch CBS 2-■ MGT 30950
Mozart, W.A.:Con Fl Hp, w. Elaine Shaffer (fl), Y. Menuhin (cnd), Philharmonia Orch Royal Classics ▲ ROY 6450

Cottet, Jean-Marie (pno)
Arma, P.:Music of, w. Josette Morata (nar), Fabrice Moretti (sax), Régis Poulain (bn), Alain Béghin (perc), Francis Petit (perc), J.-L. Petit (cnd), Avray Atelier Musique—Phases contre phases for S Sax & Pno; Celui qui dort et dort for Nar, Bn, Xyl & Perc [after poems by Max Jacob]; 5 esquisses for Pno [from a Hungarian Theme]; Divertissement 1600 for Fls [w. Jean-Noël Catrice (fl), Béatrice Delpierre (fl), Pascale Haarscher (fl), Marie-Aude Menou (fl)]; 3 Regards for solo Ob [w. Jacques Vandeville (ob)]; Divert No. 6 for Cl & Pno [w. Dominique Vidal (cl)]; Parlando for solo Fl [w. Patrice Bocquillon (fl)] REM ▲ REM 311266 [DDD]

Cottin, Nelly (pno)
Arban, J.-B.:Cavatina & Vars, w. Guy Touvron (cnt) *(rec Feb 1996)* Ligia Digital ▲ 0105040 [DDD]
Arban, J.-B.:Fants Verdi, w. Guy Touvron (cnt)—Fant No. 1 on Il Trovatore; Fant brillante on Don Carlos; Fant brillante on I vespri siciliani; Fant on La forza del destino; Fant on Rigoletto; Fant on La traviata *(rec Feb 1996)* Ligia Digital ▲ 0105040 [DDD]

Cotutiù, Radu (fl)
Bach, J.S.:Trio Sons Org, BWV 525–530, w. R. Vuataz (pno) [trans Cotutiù & Vataz for fl & pno] Gallo ▲ CD 611 [ADD]
Schulé, B.:Gin No Nami *(rec 1990)* Jecklin-Disco ▲ JS 284-2 [DDD]
Schulé, B.:In Memoriam Dinu Lipatti, w. J.M. Roig (gtr) *(rec 1990)* Jecklin-Disco ▲ JS 284-2 [DDD]
Schulé, B.:Petit livre des formes musicales, w. J.M. Roig (gtr) *(rec 1990)* Jecklin-Disco ▲ JS 284-2 [DDD]
Schulé, B.:Triptyque, w. J.M. Roig (gtr) *(rec 1990)* Jecklin-Disco ▲ JS 284-2 [DDD]

Couëffé, Paul (org)
Légendes 2, w. P. Husser (fl) Pavane ▲ ADW 7350

Coughlin, Steve (instrs)
Riley, T.:In C, w. Bruce Ackley, Steve Adams, Don R. Baker, Chris Brown, George Brooks, Blake Derby, Bill Douglass, Mihr'un'Nisa Douglass, Hank Dutt, David Harrington, Don Howe, Joan Jeanrenaud, Alden Jenks, Warner Jepson, Henry Kaiser, Jaron Lanier, Bill Maginnis, George Marsh, Shabda Owens, Jon Raskin, Gyan Riley, Terry Riley, Gino Robair, John Sackett, Ramón Sender, John Sherba, Toyji Tomita, Danny Tunick, William Winant, Evan Ziporyn *(rec Jan. 14, 1990)* New Albion ▲ NA 071

Coull, R. (vn)—see ORCHESTRAS & ENSEMBLES Coull String Quartet

Council, Elizabeth (va)—see ORCHESTRAS & ENSEMBLES Cincinnati Contemporary Music Ensemble

Coursier, Gilbert (hn)
Corrette, M.:Cons Comiques, w. Georges Barboteu (hn), Michel Berges (hn), Daniel Dubar (hn), J.-F. Paillard (cnd), Jean-François Paillard CO—No. 14 for Hns & Orch [La Choisy] Erato ▲ 94801-2

Courtin, N. (gtr)—see ORCHESTRAS & ENSEMBLES Versailles Guitar Quartet

Courtois, Alain (hn)
Schumann, R.:Konzertstück Hns, w. Jean-Claude Barro (hn), Jean-Paul Gantiez (hn), Jean-Jacques Justafre (hn), *(orch unknown)*—Lebhaft; Romanze Erato ▲ 94801-2

Cousu, Philippe (ob)
Indy, V. d':Fant sur des thèmes populaires français, w. J.-M. Burfin (cnd), Württemberg PO *(rec Baden-Baden, 1992–93)* Marco Polo ▲ 8.223659 [DDD]

Covelli, John (pno)
Achron, J.:Vn & Pno Music, w. A. Rosand (vn)—Hebrew Melody, Op. 33; Stimmungen, Op. 32/1; Hebrew Lullaby, Op. 35/2 Audiofon ▲ CD 72033
Bloch, E.:Baal Shem, "3 Pictures of Chassidic Life", w. A. Rosand (vn) Audiofon ▲ CD 72033
Bloch, E.:Son 1 Vn, w. A. Rosand (vn) Audiofon ▲ CD 72033
Bruch, M.:Kol Nidrei, w. A. Rosand (vn) Audiofon ▲ CD 72033
Respighi, O.:Son Vn, w. A. Rosand (vn) Audiofon ▲ CD 72020
Sibelius, J.:Sonatina Vn, w. A. Rosand (vn) Audiofon ▲ CD 72020
Walton, W.:Son Vn & Pno, w. A. Rosand (vn) Audiofon ▲ CD 72020

Cover, David (org)
On This Day Earth Shall Ring!, w. Rooke Chapel Choir, Rooke Chapel Ringers, D'Anna Fortunato (mez), Elizabeth Etters-Asmus (hp), William Payn (cnd) *(rec Rooke Chapel, Bucknell Univ, Feb & May 1995)* Albany ▲ TROY 177 [DDD]

Covert, Mary Ann (pno)
Bach, J.S.:Music of, w. Steven Mauk (s sax)— Suite 2, BWV 1067 [Bandinerie; arr Mauk/Covert]; Pastorale in F, BWV 590 [Aria; arr M. Brown]; Son in g, BWV 1020 [arr J. Harle]; Suite 3, BWV 1068 [Air; arr N. Ramsay]; Cant 147, Jesu, Joy of Man's Desiring [arr Mauk/Covert]; Son in C, BWV 1033 [arr C. F. Peters] Cant 156 [Sinf; arr H. Voxman]; Prelude in C [Ave maria; arr Mauk/Covert]; Partita Fl in A, BWV 1013 [arr P. G. Buffardin] *(rec Ithaca, NY, May 1994)* Open Loop ▲ 029
Classical Bouquet:Music for Soprano Saxophone & Piano, w. S. Mauk (s sax) Open Loop ▲ OL 008
Distances within Me:Contemporary Classics for Alto Saxophone, w. S. Mauk Open Loop ▲ OL 012
Rochberg, G.:Trio Cl, w. L. Combs (cl), G. Williams (hn) Crystal ■ C 731
Schuller, G.:Romantic Son Cl, w. L. Combs (cl), G. Williams (hn) Crystal ■ C 731
Tenor Excursions, w. S. Mauk (t sax) *(rec Walter Ford Hall Auditorium, Ithaca College, Ithaca, New York, June 1–3, 1993)* Open Loop ▲ OL 019 [DDD]

Covington, Forrest (hammered dlc/cimbalom)
Veeneman, C.:The Wiry Concord, w. Susan Werner (banjo), Georganne Assat (hp), Donald Martin Jenni (hpd), Mark Johnson (hpd), Barbara Phillips Farley (pno), James Austin (pno), Marta Soderberg (va), James Knutson (perc), Patrick Doyle (perc), Steven Butters (perc), James Popejoy (perc), M. Geary (cnd) Capstone ▲ SCI 6

Cowan, Carole (vn)
Starer, R.:Elegy for a Woman Who Died Too Young, w. Susan Seligman (vc) Albany ▲ TROY 152 [DDD]
Cowan, Robert (pno)
Britten, H.:Introduction & Rondo alla burlesca & Mazurka elegiaca, w. J. Yarbrough (pno)—No. 1 Centaur ▲ CRC 2095 [DDD]
Britten, H.:Scottish Ballad, w. J. Yarbrough (pno), P. Freeman (cnd), Berlin RSO Centaur ▲ CRC 2095 [DDD]
Bruch, M.:Con for 2 Pnos, w. Joan Yarbrough (pno), P. Freeman (cnd), Moscow PO *(rec Moscow Radio Union, Feb 28, 1994)* Centaur ▲ CRC 2227 [DDD]
Milhaud, D.:Con for 2 Pnos, w. Joan Yarbrough (pno), P. Freeman (cnd), Royal PO *(rec Henry Wood Hall, London, Sept 26, 1977)* Centaur ▲ CRC 2227 [DDD]
Milhaud, D.:Scaramouche for 2 Pnos, w. Joan Yarbrough (pno) *(rec Moscow Radio Union, Mar 2, 1994)* Centaur ▲ CRC 2227 [DDD]
Vaughan Williams, R.:Con Pno, w. J. Yarbrough (pno), P. Freeman (cnd), Berlin RSO Centaur ▲ CRC 2095 [DDD]
Cowell, Henry (pno)
Cowell, H.:Pno Music—The tides of Manaunaun; Exultation; Harp of Life; Lilt of the Reel; Advertisement; Antinomy; Aeolian Harp & sinister Resonance; Anger Dance; The Banshee; Fabric; What's This; Amiable Conversation; Fairy answer; Jig; Snow of Fujiyama; Voice of Lir; Dynamic Motion; The Trumpet of Angus Og; Tiger; Henry Cowell's Comments *(rec 1958)* Smithsonian/Folkways ▲ SF 40801
Cowell, H.:Pno Music—"Tone Cluster" pieces CRI ■ ACS 6005
Cowell, John (tpt)
The Baroque Album, w. A. Davis (cnd), Toronto CO, J. Baxtresser (fl), O. Harnoy (vc) Mastersound ▲ MST 19 [DDD]
Trumpet Concertos, w. J. Cowell (tpt), Toronto SO IMP ("Classics" series) ▲ IMP 6700602
Wagner, R.:Siegfried Idyll, w. T. Holowach (vn), M. Skazinetsky (vn), L. Toman (va), R. Laurie (vc), C. Elliott (db), S. Shulman (fl), T. Maloney (cl), J. Valdepenas (cl), J. Fetherston (cl), S. Mosher (bn), S. Wilson (hn), R. Cohen (hn), G. Gould (cnd) *(rec July 27–29 & Sept. 8, 198)* Sony Classical ▲ SMK 52650 [ADD]
Cowley, David (ob)
Mathias, W.:Con Ob, w. G. Llewellyn (cnd), BBC Welsh National SO Nimbus ▲ NI 5343
Cox, Alan (fl)
Liebman, D.:Remembrance, w. David Taylor (b trbn), Bill Blount (cl), Stephen Taylor (ob), Dennis Godburn (bn) New World ▲ 80494–2
Cox, Cindy Annice (pno)
Cox, C.A.:Studies of Light & Dark (4), w. Kay Stonefelt (perc) Capstone ▲ SCI 6
Cox, John (hn)
Chopin, F.:Intro & Polonaise, "Polonaise brilliante", w. K. George (pno) *(rec 8/91)* Centaur ▲ CRC 2122 [DDD]
Gieseking, W.:Qnt Hn, w. F. Korman (ob), Y. Nakao (cl), B. Fillmore (bn), K. George (pno) *(rec 8/91)* Centaur ▲ CRC 2122 [DDD]
Schumann, R.:Adagio & Allegro Hn, w. K. George (pno) Centaur ▲ CRC 2122 [DDD]
Cox, Michael (fl)
Elgar, E.:Harmony Music I–V, w. Paul Edmund-Davies (fl), Roy Carter (ob), Nicholas Rodwell (cl), Martin Gatt (bn)—No. 4, "The Farmyard" EMI Classics ("Anglo-American Chamber Music" series) ▲ CDC 55403
Cox, Nicholas (cl)
Brahms, J.:Sons Cl (comp), w. V. Latarche (pno) *(rec All Saints, Petersham, UK, Oct 12–14, 1993)* United ▲ UNI 88012 [DDD]
Reger, M.:Son Cl, Op. 107, w. V. Latarche (pno) *(rec All Saints, Petersham, UK, Oct 12–14, 1993)* United ▲ UNI 88012 [DDD]
Coyle, B. (pno)
Weill, K.:Songs, w. H. Schneider (sop), L. Fast (elec) CBS ▲ MK 45703 [DDD] ■ FMT 45703 (D)
Cozzolino, Giorgio (pno)
Clementi, M.:Sons Pno, w. Pietro Spada (pno)—Op.7/1–3; Op. 8/1–3 *(rec Rome, Italy, 1981–83)* Arts ▲ 447225–2 [DDD]
Clementi, M.:Sons Pno, w. Pietro Spada (pno)—Op. 9/1–3; Op. 10/1–3; Op. 11/1 *(rec Rome, Italy, 1981–83)* Arts ▲ 447226–2 [DDD]
Clementi, M.:Sons Pno, w. Pietro Spada (pno)—Op. 12/1–5 *(rec Rome, Italy, 1981–83)* Arts ▲ 47227–2 [DDD]
Clementi, M.:Sons Pno 4-Hands, w. Pietro Spada (pno)—Op. 3/1–3 & Op. 6/1 *(rec Rome, Italy, Jan 1981 & Mar 1983)* Arts Music ▲ 447224–2 [DDD]
Clementi, M.:Sons Pno 4-Hands, w. Pietro Spada (pno)—Op. 1/6 *(rec Rome, Italy, Jan 1981 & Mar 1983)* Arts Music ▲ 447223–2 [DDD]
Field, J.:Pno Music (comp), w. Pietro Spada (pno)—Waltzer; Polonaise; Marche triomphale; Prelude; Largo; 3 Valses; 2 Quadrilles; Anglaise; 4 Exercises; Poco Adagio (from Con 2 Pno); Andante inédite; Rondeau; Air russe varié; Grande valse en forme de Rondeau; Andante; Danse des ours *(rec Rome, Italy, Apr 1989–Apr 1990)* Arts ▲ 47183–2 [DDD]
Martucci, G.:Pno Music, w. Pietro Spada (pno)—Fant in d, Op. 32; Fant on Un Ballo in Maschera, Op. 8; Theme & Vars in E♭, Op. 58 ASV ▲ ASVCD 956
Crabtree, Richard (va)
Bax, A.:Fant Son, w. Charles Matthew (pno) Olympia ▲ OLY 454 [DDD]
Bax, A.:Legend Va, w. Charles Matthew (pno) Olympia ▲ OLY 454 [DDD]
Cracknell, Graham (vn)—see also ORCHESTRAS & ENSEMBLES Revolutionary Drawing Room String Quartet
Bach, Joh. Christian:Sinf concertante, T.284/1, w. Anna McDonald (vn), Angela East (vc), A. Halstead (cnd), Hanover Band *(rec Rosslyn Hill Chapel, London, Dec 1995)* CPO ▲ CPO 999348–2 [DDD]
Bach, Joh. Christian:Sinf concertante, T.288/4, w. Anna McDonald (vn), Angela East (vc), A. Halstead (cnd), Hanover Band *(rec Rosslyn Hill Chapel, London, Dec 1995)* CPO ▲ CPO 999348–2 [DDD]
Bach, Joh. Christian:Sinf concertante, T.284/6, w. Anna McDonald (vn), Anthony Robson (ob), A. Halstead (cnd), Hanover Band *(rec Rosslyn Hill Chapel, London, Dec 1995)* CPO ▲ CPO 999348–2 [DDD]
Craeynest, Stefaan (vc)
Berkeley, M.:For the Savage Messiah, w. Kristof van Gryspeere (pno), Dirk Lievens (vn), Kaat De Cock (va), Jan Verheye (db) *(rec Steurbaut Sound Recording Ctr)* René Gailly ▲ CD87 118 [DDD]
Crafoord, Gert (vn)—see ORCHESTRAS & ENSEMBLES Crafoord String Quartet
Crafoord, Henrik (va)—see ORCHESTRAS & ENSEMBLES Bern String Quartet
Craig, Phebe (hpd)
Bach, J.S.:Con for 4 Hpds, w. John Butt (hpd), Johathan Dimmock (hpd), Jeffrey Thomas (hpd), J. Thomas (cnd), American Bach Soloists Koch International Classics ▲ KIC 7237 [DDD]
Burns, R.:Songs, w. Susan Rode Morris (sop)—When rosy May comes wi' Flowers; Sweet are the Banks; Last May a braw Woaer; O saw ye bonie Lesley ; Oran gaoil; Thine am I; Weary fa' you Duncan Gray; My Harry was a gallant Gay; Lament for Abercairney; What shall I do with an auld Man?; Auld Lang Syne; Whare are ye gaun my bonie Lass?; I'll ay ca' in by yon Town; Her Daddie forbad; First when Maggie; O wha my Babie-Clouts will buy?; I hae a Wife o' my ain; Over the Water to Charlie; She's fair & fause; Peggy's Lament; Ye Banks & Braes o' bonie Doon; O whar gat ye that hauvermeal Bannock?; Now Nature hangs her Mantle green; Saw ye my Father?; Wae is my Heart?; Out over the Forth; O leave Novéls ye Mauchline Belles; My Love she's but a Lassie; Sir John Cope; McPherson's Rant; The Bairns gat out wi' an unco Shout; Corn Rigs; Jamie come try me *(rec Pony Tracks Ranch, Portola Valley, CA, Jan. 9–10, 1994)* Donsuemor ▲ DSM 40601 [DDD]

Craig, Phebe (hpd) (cont.)
Burns, R.:Songs, w. Susan Rode Morris (sop)—Dainty Davie; There Was a Lad; Ca' the Yowes; John Anderson; How Pleasant the Banks; Blew Bonnetts; Tam Glen; A Rosebud; Laddie Lie Near Me; Ettrick Banks; My Jo Janet; Willie Wastle; Lasly's March; Fareweel to a' our Scottish Fame [Parcel of Rogues]; Cauld Blaws the Wind; Turn Again Fair Eliza; The Birks of Aberfeldy; Roslin Castle; No Cold Approach, No Alter'd Mien; Castle Swien; The Winter it is Past; Peggie's Dream; Rattlin, Roarin Willie; A.A. Cameron Strathspey; I hae Been at Crookieden; By Yon Castle Wa'; Green Grow the Rashes O! *(rec Pony Tracks Ranch, Portola Valley, CA, Nov 27–28, 1994)* Donsuemor ▲ DSM 51201
Purcell, H.:Songs, w. Susan Rode Morris (sop)—Prelude; Chacone; Minuet; Almand; Courante [all from Suite No. 8 in F]; Bess of Bedlam; I Lov'd Fair Celia; Who can from Joy Refrain; A Dialogue; The Fatal Hour; The Blessed Virgin's Expostulation; Ye Gentle Spirits of the Air; Dear Pritty Youth; We Sing to Him; Let Us Dance; Oh! Lead Me; On the Brow of Richmond Hill; Fairest Isle; Love in their Little Veins inspires; Hornpipe [from Suite No. 7]; The Rich Rival; Man is for the Woman made; A Mad Song [Beneath a Popular]; Musick for Awile *(rec Pony Tracks Rach, Portola Valley, CA, Nov. 2–4, 1991)* Donsuemor ▲ DSM 20601 [DDD]
Craig, Richard (a sax)
Andriessen, L.:Hoketus, w. Katherine Pendry (panpipes), James Poke (panpipes), Evan Ziporyn (a sax), Richard Craig (a sax), Steven Schick (congas), Amy Knoles (congas), Lisa Moore (Fender Rhodes), Damian LeGassick (Fender Rhodes), Cees van Zeeland (pno), Gerard Bouwhuis (pno), Robert Black (bass gtr), Mark Stewart (bass gtr) *(rec Air Recording Studios, Lyndhurst Hall, Hampstead, London, June 29–July 3, 1994)* Sony Classical ▲ SK 66483 [DDD]
Craighead, David (org)
Albright, W.:Organbooks 1 & 2 Gothic ▲ G 58627 [DDD]
Hanson, H.:Con Org, w. E. Malone (hp), D. Fetler (cnd), Rochester CO Albany ▲ TROY 129 [ADD]
Harrison, L.:Con Org, w. W. Kraft (cnd), Los Angeles Percussion Ensemble *(rec 1977)* Crystal ▲ CD850
The Last Rose of Summer, & Other Things They Played Gothic ▲ GOT 49021 [DDD]
Reger, M.:Son 2 Org Delos ▲ DE 3096 [DDD]
Sowerby, L.:Medieval Poem, w. J. Welsh (cnd), Fairfield Orch *(rec St. Bartholomew's Church, New York City, May 3–5, 1994)* Marco Polo ▲ 8.223725 [DDD]
Sowerby, L.:Pageant of Autumn *(rec live, St. Bartholomew's Church, New York City, May 4, 1994)* Marco Polo ▲ 8.223725 [DDD]
Vierne, L.:Sym 6 Org Delos ▲ DE 3096 [DDD]
Cram, Robert (fl)
Cherney, B.:Doppelgänger Centrediscs ▲ CMC 5094 [DDD]
Mather, B.:Elegy, w. David Hutchenreuther (vc), Charlotte Sheng (pno), Jonathan Wade (perc) Centrediscs ▲ CMC 5094 [DDD]
Tremblay, G.:Aubes—or Initial, w. Pierre Béluse (perc), René Gosselin (db) Centrediscs ▲ CMC 5094 [DDD]
Tremblay, G.:Envol Centrediscs ▲ CMC 5094 [DDD]
Tremblay, G.:le sifflement des vents porteurs de l'amour, w. Pierre Béluse (perc) Centrediscs ▲ CMC 5094 [DDD]
Cramer, Browning (vn)—see ORCHESTRAS & ENSEMBLES Bronx Arts Ensemble
Cramer, Craig (org)
Cochereau, P.:Vars (3) sur un theme chromatique [Beuchet Org, St Pierre Cathedral, Angoulême, France] Arkay ▲ ARK 6146
Demessieux, J.:Org Music [Beuchet Org, St Pierre Cathedral, Angoulême, France]—Prelude & Fugue in C Arkay ▲ ARK 6146
Grunenwald, J.-J.:Pièce en mosaïque [Beuchet Org, St Pierre Cathedral, Angoulême, France] Arkay ▲ ARK 6146
Henry, J.-C.:Chaconne Org [Beuchet Org, St Pierre Cathedral, Angoulême, France] Arkay ▲ ARK 6146
Langlais, J.:Essai [Beuchet Org, St Pierre Cathedral, Angoulême, France] Arkay ▲ ARK 6146
Langlais, J.:Sonate en trio [Beuchet Org, St Pierre Cathedral, Angoulême, France] Arkay ▲ ARK 6146
Litaize, G.:Org Music [Beuchet Org, St Pierre Cathedral, Angoulême, France]—Prelude et danse fuguee Arkay ▲ ARK 6146
Messiaen, O.:Verset pour la fête de la dédicace [Beuchet Org, St Pierre Cathedral, Angoulême, France] Arkay ▲ ARK 6146
Cranck, E. de (pno)
Rodrigo, J.:Canciones Valencianas, w. L. Ara (vn) CPO ▲ CPO 999186 [DDD]
Rodrigo, J.:2 Esbozos, w. L. Ara (vn) CPO ▲ CPO 999186 [DDD]
Rodrigo, J.:Rumaniana, w. L. Ara (vn) CPO ▲ CPO 999186 [DDD]
Rodrigo, J.:Son pimpante, w. L. Ara (vn) CPO ▲ CPO 999186 [DDD]
Crandall, Dean (db)—see ORCHESTRAS & ENSEMBLES Bronx Arts Ensemble
Craven, Leslie (cl)
Jolivet, A.:Sonatine Fl, w. Anna Noakes (fl) ASV ("French Chamber Music" series) ▲ ASV 948
Crawford, Lisa Goode (hpd)
Rameau, J.P.:Pièces de clavecin avec une méthode sur la mécanique des doigts Gasparo Gallante ▲ GS 1006 [DDD]
Rameau, J.P.:Pièces de clavecin en concert—Premier concert Gasparo Gallante ▲ GS 1006 [DDD]
Royer, J.-N.-P.:Pièces de clavecin Gasparo Gallante ▲ GS 1006 [DDD]
Crawford, P. (pno)
Mozart, W.A.:Fant Pno, K.475 Titanic ▲ Ti 206 [DDD]
Mozart, W.A.:Rondo Pno, K.511 Titanic ▲ Ti 206 [DDD]
Mozart, W.A.:Son 6 Pno Titanic ▲ Ti 206 [DDD]
Mozart, W.A.:Son 14 Pno Titanic ▲ Ti 206 [DDD]
Craxton, Harold (pno)
The 1922–23 HMV & 1924 Victor Recordings, w. J. Thibaud (vn), Alfred Cortot (pno), Jesús-María Sanromá (pno) Biddulph ▲ LAB 014 [ADD]
Delius, F.:Son Vc & Pno, w. Beatrice Harrison (vc) *(rec Feb & Mar 1926)* Symposium ▲ SYM 1140
Craxton, Janet (ob)
Bach, J.S.:Con 8 Hpd, w. I. Kipnis (hpd), N. Marriner (cnd), London Strings *(rec 1967–1970)* Sony Classical 2–▲ SB2K 53243 [ADD]
Reizenstein, F.:Sonatina Ob, w. L. Crowson (pno) Continuum ▲ CCD 1024
Crayford, Marcia (vn)—see also ORCHESTRAS & ENSEMBLES Nash Ensemble
Debussy, C.:Son Vn, w. I. Brown (pno) Virgin Classics ▲ 59604 [DDD]
Saint-Saëns, C.:Trio 1 Pno, w. C. Van Kampen (vc), I. Brown (pno) Virgin Classics ▲ 59514 [DDD]
Creaser-Rumley, Evelyn (vn)
Classic Elektra, w. [cnd:Morna Edmundson, Diane Loomer], Elektra Women's Choir, Eric Hominich (pno), Nancy DiNovo (vn), Brenda Fedoruk (fl) Skylark ▲ 9402 [DDD]
Creed, Marcus (pno)
Brahms, J.:Liebeslieder Waltzes SATB, w. R. Stelzner (pno), U. Gronostay (cnd), Berlin RIAS Chamber Choir [G] *(rec March 1984)* Koch Treasure ▲ 31616–2 [ADD]
Creitz, James (va)
Britten, H.:Lachrymae, w. M. Sarbu (pno) Dynamic ▲ CD 61 [DDD]
Enescu, G.:Concertpiece Va, w. M. Sarbu (pno) Dynamic ▲ CD 61 [DDD]
Penderecki, K.:Cadenza Dynamic ▲ CD 61 [DDD]
Shostakovich, D.:Son Va, w. M. Sarbu (pno) Dynamic ▲ CD 61 [DDD]
Stravinsky, I.:Elégie Va Dynamic ▲ CD 61 [DDD]
20th Century Viola, w. Mihail Sarbu (pno) Dynamic ▲ CD 61 [DDD]
Crellin, Jeffrey (ob)
Fauré, G.:Pavane Orch, w. P. Davis (fl), P. Lynch (gtr) [flute-oboe-guitar arr. Peter Lynch] Move ▲ MD 3090 [DDD]
Formosa, R.:Dedica, w. P. Thomas (cnd), Melbourne SO *(rec studio)* Vox Australis ▲ VAST 015–2 [AAD]
Ravel, M.:Pavane pour une infante défunte, w. P. Davis (fl), P. Lynch (gtr) [flute-oboe-guitar arr. by Peter Lynch] Move ▲ MD 3090 [DDD]
Cremonesi, Attilio (hpd)
Pasquini, B.:Sons for 2 Hpds, w. A. de Marchi (hpd) Symphonia ▲ SYM 91S26 [DDD]

▲ = CD ♦ = Enhanced CD Δ = MD ■ = Cassette Tape □ = DCC

Cremonesi, Attilio (org)
Frescobaldi, G.:Missa sopra l'aria della monica, w. A. de Marchi (cnd), Armonico Theater Ensemble — Symphonia ▲ SYM 91S08 [DDD]

Crenne, Christian (vn)—see also ORCHESTRAS & ENSEMBLES Ravel Trio
Bach, J.S.:Con for 2 Vns, w. Philip Bride (vn), French Instrumental Ensemble *(rec Nov 5 & 6, 1988)* — Pierre Verany ▲ PVY 730020 [DDD]
Mozart, W.A.:Concertone Vns, w. Philip Bride (vn), K. Redel (cnd), French Instrumental Ensemble *(rec Apr. 9 & 10, 1990)* — Pierre Verany ▲ PVY 730024 [DDD]

Crespo, Carlos (hn)
Baur, J.:Ostinato senza fine, "Pour rien", w. H. Fischer (cl), A. Münten (cl), *(not advised of 2nd hn)*, F. Effmann (bn), S. Fasang (bn) *(rec May 13, 1981)* — Koch Schwann ▲ SCH 311982 [ADD/DDD]

Cresswell, Pamela (ten vl)—see ORCHESTRAS & ENSEMBLES English Fantasy

Crewe, Philip (perc)
Songs of War & Peace, w. [cnd:Diane Loomer], Leoni Men's Chorus, Christopher Gaze (nar), Stephen Smith (pno), Salvador Ferreras (perc) — Skylark ▲ 9501 [DDD]

Crisafulli, E. (bn)
Milesi, P.:Modi 2, w. L. M. Pickova (sop), Françoise Goddard (alt), M. Ferradini (ten), B. Andersen (bass), D. Cassamagnaghi (fl), S. Scanziani (ob), A. Bianchi (cl/b cl), C. Gazzola (hn), F. Gualandris (tuba), A. Girardi (celtic hp), R. Anedda (vn), E. Groppo (vn), M. Pagani (vn), M. Ravasio (va), S. Righini (vc), P. Rizzi (db), J. Scully (perc), P. Milesi (cnd) — Cuneiform ▲ RUNE 63

Crisafulli, R. (vn)—see ORCHESTRAS & ENSEMBLES Concerto Rococo

Crisimani, Claudio (pno)
Beethoven, L. van:Bagatelles (24) — RS Applausi ▲ 6367-45
Beethoven, L. van:Bagatelle, WoO 60 — RS Applausi ▲ 6367-45
Beethoven, L. van:Ecossaises, WoO 83 — RS Applausi ▲ 6367-45
Beethoven, L. van:German Dances, WoO 42—2 sels (unknown) — RS Applausi ▲ 6367-45

Crispell, Marilyn (pno)
Kabat, J.:Poems by H. D., w. J. Kabat (voice/glass hmc/saw/African drums/kalimba), B. Hudson (vn), A. Adzenyah (African drums/conga) [E] — Leonarda ■ LE 319 (D)

Crispell, Marilyn (toy pno)
Cage, J.:Music Amplified Toy Pnos, w. Joe Kubera (toy pno), Joshua Pierce (toy pno) [3 toy pno version] *(rec 1976–89)* — Wergo ▲ WER 6158-2 [ADD]

Crissante, Isabella (pno)
Tosti, P.F.:Canti populari e romanze abruzzesi, w. C. Di Censo (sop), M. Gentile (mez), W. Omaggio (ten), P. Speca (sgr) — Nuova Era ▲ NUO 7166 [DDD]

Cristiano, Antonella (hpd)
Ragazzi, A.:Con Grosso, w. Marco Rogliano (vn), Andrea Guerrini (vn), Eduardo Pitone (va), Aurelio Bertucci (vc), I. Caiazza (cnd), I Solisti Partenopei *(rec Mar 1996)* — Kicco Classics ▲ 396 [DDD]

Cristiano, Antonella (pno)
Durante, F.:Con Pno, w. I. Caiazza (cnd), I Solisti Partenopei *(rec Mar 1996)* — Kicco Classics ▲ 396 [DDD]
Prati, A.:Con Pno, w. I. Caiazza (cnd), I Solisti Partenopei *(rec Mar 1996)* — Kicco Classics ▲ 396 [DDD]

Crittenden, David (gtr)—see ORCHESTRAS & ENSEMBLES Minneapolis Guitar Quartet

Croitoru, Gabriel (vn)
Sarasate, P. de:Airs espagnols, w. J. Bodmer (cnd), Málaga City Orch [orchd] — Regis Tro ▲ RTAC 010/1 [DDD]
Sarasate, P. de:Barcarolle vénitienne, w. J. Bodmer (cnd), Málaga City Orch [orchd] — Regis Tro ▲ RTAC 010/3 [DDD]
Sarasate, P. de:El canto del ruiseñor, w. J. Bodmer (cnd), Málaga City Orch [orchd Édouard Lalo] — Regis Tro ▲ RTAC 010/2 [DDD]
Sarasate, P. de:Carmen Fant, w. J. Bodmer (cnd), Málaga City Orch — Regis Tro ▲ RTAC 010/2 [DDD]
Sarasate, P. de:Chansons russe, w. J. Bodmer (cnd), Málaga City Orch [orchd] — Regis Tro ▲ RTAC 010/3 [DDD]
Sarasate, P. de:La Chasse, w. J. Bodmer (cnd), Málaga City Orch [orchd] — Regis Tro ▲ RTAC 010/3 [DDD]
Sarasate, P. de:Faust Fant, w. J. Bodmer (cnd), Málaga City Orch [orchd] — Regis Tro ▲ RTAC 010/1 [DDD]
Sarasate, P. de:Freischütz Fant, w. J. Bodmer (cnd), Málaga City Orch [orchd] — Regis Tro ▲ RTAC 010/1 [DDD]
Sarasate, P. de:Intro & Tarantella, w. J. Bodmer (cnd), Málaga City Orch [orchd] — Regis Tro ▲ RTAC 010/3 [DDD]
Sarasate, P. de:Intro et caprice-jota, w. J. Bodmer (cnd), Málaga City Orch [orchd] — Regis Tro ▲ RTAC 010/3 [DDD]
Sarasate, P. de:Jota de Pablo, w. J. Bodmer (cnd), Málaga City Orch [orchd] — Regis Tro ▲ RTAC 010/3 [DDD]
Sarasate, P. de:Jota de Pamplona, w. J. Bodmer (cnd), Málaga City Orch [orchd] — Regis Tro ▲ RTAC 010/3 [DDD]
Sarasate, P. de:Jota de San Fermín, w. J. Bodmer (cnd), Málaga City Orch [orchd] — Regis Tro ▲ RTAC 010/2 [DDD]
Sarasate, P. de:Miramar, w. J. Bodmer (cnd), Málaga City Orch [orchd] — Regis Tro ▲ RTAC 010/3 [DDD]
Sarasate, P. de:Muiñeira, w. J. Bodmer (cnd), Málaga City Orch [orchd] — Regis Tro ▲ RTAC 010/2 [DDD]
Sarasate, P. de:Navarra, w. Manuel Guillén Navarro (vn), J. Bodmer (cnd), Málaga City Orch [orchd] — Regis Tro ▲ RTAC 010/2 [DDD]
Sarasate, P. de:Nocturne-sérénade, w. J. Bodmer (cnd), Málaga City Orch — Regis Tro ▲ RTAC 010/3 [DDD]
Sarasate, P. de:Peteneras, w. J. Bodmer (cnd), Málaga City Orch [orchd] — Regis Tro ▲ RTAC 010/2 [DDD]
Sarasate, P. de:Viva Sevilla!, w. J. Bodmer (cnd), Málaga City Orch [orchd] — Regis Tro ▲ RTAC 010/2 [DDD]
Sarasate, P. de:Zapateado, w. J. Bodmer (cnd), Málaga City Orch [orchd] — Regis Tro ▲ RTAC 010/1 [DDD]
Sarasate, P. de:Zigeunerweisen, w. J. Bodmer (cnd), Málaga City Orch [orchd] — Regis Tro ▲ RTAC 010/1 [DDD]

Crommelynck, Patrick (pno)—see ORCHESTRAS & ENSEMBLES Crommelynck Duo

Crommelynck, Taeko (pno)—see ORCHESTRAS & ENSEMBLES Crommelynck Duo

Cronin, Tim (baroque vn)
Insalata, w. I Fagiolini, E. Kenny (theorbo), D. Burchell (hpd/org), Riona D.(baroque vn), D. Clasen (bar) — Metronome ▲ METCD 1004

Cronin, Tim (va)
Biber, H. von:Sonatae tam aris quam aulis servientes, w. Mark Bennett (tpt), Michael Laird (tpt), Katherine McGillvray (va), Jane Rogers (va), Purcell Quartet — Chandos ▲ CHAN 0591

Croscet, Bruno (vl)
Clérambault, L.N.:Cants, w. Noémi Rime (sop), Jean-Paul Fouchécourt (ten), Nicolas Rivenq (bass), Hiro Kurosaki (vn), Ryo Terakado (vn), Marc Hantaï (fl), Eric Bellocq (thb), Elisabeth Matiffa (b vl), W. Christie (cnd), Les Arts Florissants—Pyrame et Tisbé, La Muse de l'opéra ou les Caractères Lyriques, La Mort d'Hercule, Orphée — Musique d'Abord ▲ HMA 1901329

Cros Dich, Arne de (pno)
Stolarczyk, W.:Earth Air Fire Water, w. Amalie Malling (pno), John Damgaard (pno), Anne Øland (pno), Teddy Teirup (pno), Friedrich Gürtler (pno), Rosalind Bevan (pno), Poul Rosenbaum (pno), Rodolfo Llambias (pno), Bella Horn-Ribera (pno), Anders Riber (pno), Elisabeth Sigurdsson (pno), Thomas Tronheim (pno), Elsebeth Broderson (pno), Erik Kaltoft (pno), Jørgen Hald Nielsen (pno), Aino Gilemann (pno), Birgit Kjær (pno), Jørgen Thomsen (pno), Gunhild Donslund (pno), Henrik Bo Hansen (pno), Lone Karlsson (pno), Erik Fessel (pno), Lasse Nilsson (pno), Janos Ferenczi (pno), Erik Bach (pno), Axel Momme (pno), Sven Micha Slot (pno), Hanne Bramsen Buhl (pno), Lili Olesen (pno), Susannah Carlsson (pno), Ulla Erml (pno), Vagn Sørensen (pno), Leif Greibe (pno), Bodil Krogh (pno), Kirsten Ottosen (pno), Inger Bergenholz (pno), Karsten Gylendorf (pno), Bjønr Elkjær (pno), Jacob Bjørn Jensen (pno), Jørgen Kaad (pno), Anne Marie Hjelm (pno), Carl Ulrik Munk Andersen (pno), Poul Lumbye (pno), Oluf Hildebrandt Nielsen (pno), Joachim Olsson (pno), Peter Pade Ramsøe Jacobsen (pno), Astrid Pollmann (pno), Jette Borsch (pno), Kirsten Karlshøj (pno), Maria Teresa Assing (pno), Allan Dahl Hansen (pno), Johan Hugossen (pno), Tine Fenger Pederson (pno), Arne Jørgen Fæø (pno), Anja Høgsted (pno), Anne Sophie Parbo (pno), Inga Lindmark (pno), Teresa Drabik Stathakis (pno), Anne Ruth Ferenczi (pno), Irene Hasager (pno), Yuka Ichikawa (pno), Birgitte Baur (pno), Malene Thastum (pno), Jens E. Rasmussen (pno), Birgitte Zielke (pno), Claus Zielke (pno), Stefan Kasch (pno), Bin Qiao (pno), Inger Johanne Teirup (pno), Lindy Rosborg (pno), Liisa Heininen (pno), David Højer (pno), Ellen Refstrup (pno), Thomas K. Søorensen (pno), Erik Kure (pno), Michael Rauff (pno), Jan beck Eriksson (pno), Tanja Zapolski (pno), Vibeke Skagbo (pno), Pål Eide Lindtner (pno), Ha-Young Sul (pno), Benedicte Palko (pno), Inke Kesseler (pno), Anne Marie Meineche (pno), Sverre Larsen (pno), Kasper Peter Bach (pno), Elisabetta Eliseo (pno), Olga Magieres (pno), Carl Erik Kühl (pno), Thorkild Borup Nielsen (pno), Valeria Zanini (pno), Lars Stenhoft (perc), Dennis Boel (perc), Winnie Dahlgren (perc), Susanne Vind (perc), Claus Byrith (elec), Anne Marie Storm (elec), J. Ribera (cnd) *(rec live, Koldinghaus Castle, Denmark, May 2, 1996)* — Danica ▲ DCD 1996

Croshaw, Christine (pno)
Hummel, J.N.:Adagio, Vars & Rondo on "Schöne Minka", w. C. Conway (fl), C. Tunnell (vc) — Meridian ▲ MER 84217
Hummel, J.N.:Rondo brillant Pno — Meridian ▲ MER 84217
Hummel, J.N.:Rondo brillant Vn & Pno, w. C. Conway (fl) — Meridian ▲ MER 84217
Hummel, J.N.:Son Vc, w. C. Tunnell (vc) — Meridian ▲ MER 84217
Weber, C.M. von:Son 2 Pno, w. Clive Conway (fl) [arr for fl & pno] — Meridian ▲ MER 84260 [DDD]
Weber, C.M. von:Trio Fl, w. Clive Conway (fl), Christina Shillito (vc) — Meridian ▲ MER 84260 [DDD]
Weber, C.M. von:Vars on a Theme from *Silvana* Cl, w. David Campbell (cl) — Meridian ▲ MER 84260 [DDD]
Weber, C.M. von:Vars on an Original Theme Pno, J.55 — Meridian ▲ MER 84260 [DDD]

Cross, Fiona (b cl)
Simpson, R.:Qnt Cl, w. J. Farrall (cl), Vanbrugh String Quartet — Hyperion ▲ CDA 66626

Crossan, Jack Richard (hpd)
Bach, J.S.:Das wohltemperierte Klavier—[Book 1] Prelude No. 22; [Book 2] Preludes & Fugues Nos. 6, 7, 12, 17 & 19 — Janus ■ JAN 1109 (CrO2)

Crossan, Jack Richard (kbds)
Keyboard Excursions — Janus Recordings ■ JAN 1105

Crossan, Jack Richard (pno)
The Bach Album — Janus Recordings ■ JAN 1109 (CrO2)
Bach, J.S.:Toccatas Hpd, BWV 910–16—Nos. 2 & 7 — Janus ■ JAN 1109 (CrO2)
Busoni, F.:Bach Transcriptions—Wachet auf, ruft uns die Stimme; Ich ruf zu Dir, Herr [Andante]; Toccata & Fugue in d, BWV 565 — Janus ■ JAN 1109 (CrO2)
Chopin, F.:Nocturnes—in E♭, Op. 55/2; in e, Op. 72/1; in f♯, Op. 48/2; in F, Op. 15/1; in D♭, Op. 27/2; in c♯, Op. 27/1; in c, Op. 48/1 *(rec 1st Congregational Church, Los Angeles, CA, Sept. 6 & 13, 1993)* — Cambria ▲ CMB 1073 [DDD]
Chopin, F.:Nocturnes—Nos. 1–19 — Janus 2-■ JAN 1101-2 (CrO2)
Chopin, F.:Son Pno, Op. 35 — Janus ■ JAN 1108-1 (CrO2)
Chopin's Nocturnes Nos. 1–19 — Janus Recordings 2-■ JAN 1101-2 (CrO2)
Copland, A.:El salón México, w. A. Dominguez (pno) — Janus ■ JAN 1110 (CrO2)
Crossan in Recital, w. Crossan, Jack Richard (pno) — Janus Recordings ■ JAN 1108-1 (CrO2)
Crossan in Unique Live Performances — Janus Recordings ■ JAN 1107-1 (CrO2)
Franck, C.:Prélude, choral et fugue — Janus ■ JAN 1103 (CrO2)
Great Piano Duos, w. Albert Dominguez (pno) — Janus Recordings ■ JAN 1110 (CrO2)
Griffes, C.T.:The White Peacock [composer's original piano version] — Janus ■ JAN 1108-1 (rO2)
Keyboard Excursions
Kohs, E.:Suite for 2 Pnos, w. A. Dominguez (pno) — Janus ■ JAN 1110 (CrO2)
Kohs, E.:Vars Pno — Janus ■ JAN 1102 (CrO2)
Liszt, F.:Pno Music (misc)—Legend II [St. Francis Walking on the Waves]; Nocturne II; Valse oubliée; Valse-Impromptu; Consolation No. 3; Ballade II *(rec 1st Congregational Church, Los Angeles, CA, Sept. 6 & 13, 1993)* — Cambria ▲ CMB 1073 [DDD]
Mozart, W.A.:Rondo Pno, K.511 — Janus ■ JAN 1108-1 (CrO2)
Piano Masterworks, Vol. 1 — Janus Recordings ■ JAN 1102 (CrO2)
Piano Masterworks, Vol. 2 — Janus Recordings ■ JAN 1103 (CrO2)
Poulenc, F.:Con for 2 Pnos, w. J. Nesleny (pno), M. Perriere (cnd), Festival SO — Janus ■ JAN 1104 (CrO2)
Poulenc's Concerto for 2 Pianos & Orchestra — Janus Recordings ■ JAN 1104 (CrO2)
Rachmaninoff, S.:Rhapsody on a Theme of Paganini, w. Lillian Steuber (pno) [two-piano arr.] — Janus ■ JAN 1107-1 (CrO2)
Rachmaninoff, S.:Suite 2 for 2 Pnos, w. A. Dominguez (pno) — Janus ■ JAN 1110 (CrO2)
Ravel, M.:Alborada del gracioso [composer's solo piano version] — Janus ■ JAN 1107-1 (CrO2)
Ravel, M.:La Valse, w. A. Dominguez (pno) [2-piano version] — Janus ■ JAN 1110 (CrO2)
Saint-Saëns, C.:Variations on a Theme of Beethoven, w. A. Dominguez (pno) — Janus ■ JAN 1110 (CrO2)
Schubert, Franz:Son Pno, D.784 — Janus ■ JAN 1107-1 (CrO2)
Schumann, R.:Fant Pno — Janus ■ JAN 1102 (CrO2)

Crossland, Anthony (org)
The Psalms of David, Vol. 2:O Praise the Lord of Heaven, w. [cnd:Anthony Crossland], Wells Cathedral Choir — Priory ▲ PRCD 337 [DDD]

Crossley, Paul (pno)
Debussy, C.:Children's Corner — Sony Classical ▲ SK 53111
Debussy, C.:Estampes — Sony Classical ▲ SK 53111
Debussy, C.:Etudes *(rec Nov. 23–27, 1992)* — Sony Classical ▲ SK 53281 [DDD]
Debussy, C.:Images (3) Pno—Nos. 1 & 2 — Sony Classical ▲ SK 52583
Debussy, C.:Music of, w. Cho-Liang Lin (vn)—works for vn & pno; sels unknown — Sony Classical ▲ SK 66839
Debussy, C.:Pno Music (complete solo)—Suite bergamasque; Images; Pour le piano; Deux Arabesques; Ballade; Rêverie; Valse romantique; Nocturne in D♭; Mazurka; Danse bohemienne; Danse (Tarentelle styrienne); Morceau de concours — Sony Classical ▲ SK 53973
Debussy, C.:Pno Music (misc)—Masques; D'un cahier d'esquisses; L'isle joyeuse; Berceuse heroique; Page d'album; Elegie; Hommage à Haydn; Le petit negre *(rec Nov. 23–27, 1992)* — Sony Classical ▲ SK 53281 [DDD]
Debussy, C.:Preludes Pno—Book 2 — Sony Classical ▲ SK 53111
Fauré, G.:Ballade Pno — CRD ▲ CD 3426
Fauré, G.:Barcarolles (13) — CRD ▲ 3422 [ADD]
Fauré, G.:Impromptus Pno, Opp. 25, 31, 34, 91 & 102 — CRD ▲ 3423
Fauré, G.:Mazurka Pno — CRD ▲ 3426
Fauré, G.:Nocturnes (13) Pno—Nos. 8–13 — CRD ▲ 3407 [ADD]
Fauré, G.:Nocturnes (13) Pno—Nos. 1–7 — CRD ▲ 3406 [ADD]
Fauré, G.:Pièces brèves — CRD ▲ 3407 [ADD]
Fauré, G.:Préludes, Op. 103 — CRD ▲ 3423
Fauré, G.:Romances sans paroles, Op. 17 — CRD ▲ CD 3426
Fauré, G.:Theme & Vars Pno — CRD ▲ 3423

Crossley, Paul (pno) (cont.)
Fauré, G.:Valses-caprices (4) CRD ▲ 3426
Franck, C.:Symphonic Vars, w. C.M. Giulini (cnd), Vienna PO *(rec Musikverein, Grosser Saal, Vienna, Austria, June 12 & 13, 1993)* Sony Classical ▲ S2K 58958 [DDD]
Gruber, H.K.:Bossa Nova, w. E. Kovacic (vn) *(rec Apr. 29, 1993)* Largo ▲ 5124 [DDD]
Gruber, H.K.:Episoden, Op. 20 *(rec Apr. 29, 1993)* Largo ▲ 5124 [DDD]
Lutoslawski, W.:Con Pno, w. E.-P. Salonen (cnd), Los Angeles PO *(rec Los Angeles, Nov 14, 17 & 18, 1994)* Sony Classical ▲ SK 67189 [DDD]
Messiaen, O.:Des Canyons aux étoiles, w. E.-P. Salonen (cnd), London Sinfonietta—sels. Sony Classical ▲ SMK 53473
Messiaen, O.:Des Canyons aux étoiles, w. E.-P. Salonen (cnd), London Sinfonietta CBS 2-▲ M2K 44762 [DDD]
Messiaen, O.:Couleurs de la cité céleste, w. E.-P. Salonen (cnd), London Sinfonietta CBS 2-▲ M2K 44762 [DDD]
Messiaen, O.:Oiseaux exotiques, w. E.-P. Salonen (cnd), London Sinfonietta CBS 2-▲ M2K 44762 [DDD]
Poulenc, F.:Music of, w. Cho-Liang Lin (vn)—works for vn & pno; sels unknown Sony Classical ▲ SK 66839
Poulenc, F.:Pno Music (comp)—Feuillets d'album; 5 Impromptus; 15 Improvisations; Napoli; 8 Nocturnes; 10 Promenades; Les Soirées de Nazelles; Suite in C; Suite française (d'après Claude Gervaise); Theme & 11 Variations; Trois intermezzi; Trois pièces; Trois mouvements perpétuels; Trois novelettes; Villageoises; & nine shorter works CBS 3-▲ M3K 44921 [DDD]
Ravel, M.:Music of, w. Cho-Liang Lin (vn)—works for vn & pno; sels unknown Sony Classical ▲ SK 66839
Ravel, M.:Pno Music—Gaspard de la nuit; Le tombeau de Couperin; Jeux d'eau; Sérénade grotesque; Menuet sur le nom de Haydn; Prélude; A la manière...de Borodine & de Chabrier CRD ▲ 3384 [DDD]
Ravel, M.:Pno Music—Miroirs; Sonatine; Menuet Antique; Valses nobles et sentimentales; Pavane pour une infane défunte CRD ▲ 3383 [DDD]
Stravinsky, I.:Capriccio, w. E.-P. Salonen (cnd), London Sinfonietta [1949 version] Sony Classical ▲ SK 45797 [DDD]
Stravinsky, I.:Con Pno Ww, w. E.-P. Salonen (cnd), London Sinfonietta [1950 version] Sony Classical ▲ SK 45797 [DDD]
Stravinsky, I.:Movts Pno, w. E.-P. Salonen (cnd), London Sinfonietta Sony Classical ▲ SK 45797 [DDD]
Takemitsu, T.:riverrun, w. O. Knussen (cnd), London Sinfonietta Virgin Classics ▲ CDC 59020
Tippett, M.:Sons Pno (comp) *(rec 1984-85)* CRD 2-▲ 34301 [DDD]
Crosta, Beppe (vn)
Zimmermann, B.A.:Son Vn Stradivarius ▲ STR 33340
Croton, Peter (lt)
Italian Lute Songs, w. D. L. Ragin (ct) Channel Classics ▲ CCS 4092 [DDD]
Croucher, Sonia (fl)
Schultz, Andrew:Mephisto, w. Karen Schaupp (gtr), Michele Walsh (vn), Belinda Kendall-Smith (bass), G. Roberts (cnd), Perihelion Ensemble members *(rec Nickson Room, Music Dept, Univ of Queensland, Australia, Dec 1994)* Tall Poppies ▲ TP 065 [DDD]
Crouse, Wayne (va)—see ORCHESTRAS & ENSEMBLES Lyric Art String Quartet, Shepherd String Quartet
Crow, R. (instr)
Caprioli, A.:Serenata per Francesca, w. V. Fuchsberger (sgr), G. Schneider (vn), S. Winiarczyk (ob), A. Aigmüller (dr), R. Huber (instr), K. Ager (cnd), Austrian Ensemble for New Music *(rec 1987)* Pro Viva ▲ ISPV 148 CD [ADD]
Crow, Todd (pno)
Liszt, F.:Con 1 Pno, w. Percussion All Stars *(rec live, Purchase Univ, Theater C, White Plains, NY, Sept 23, 1995)* Golden String ▲ GSCD 027 [DDD]
Mozart, W.A.:Con 21 Pno, w. Percussion All Stars *(rec live, Purchase Univ, Theater C, White Plains, NY, Sept 23, 1995)* Golden String ▲ GSCD 027 [DDD]
Schubert, Franz:Son Pno, D.784 Bridge ▲ BCD 9018 [DDD]
Schubert, Franz:Son Pno, D.959 Bridge ▲ BCD 9018 [DDD]
Crowley, Andrew (tpt)
Vivaldi, A.:Con for 2 Tpts, w. M. Bennett (tpt), L. Friedman (cnd), St. Andrew Camerata Omega ▲ OCD 1012 [DDD]
Crowson, Lamar (pno)
Benjamin, A.:Concertino Pno, w. A. Benjamin (cnd), London SO *(rec Walhamstow Assembly Hall, London)* Everest ▲ EVC 9029 [AAD]
Benjamin, A.:Con quasi una fantasia, w. A. Benjamin (cnd), London SO *(rec Walhamstow Assembly Hall, London)* Everest ▲ EVC 9029 [AAD]
Klatzow, P.:Chamber Con, w. Beat Wenger (fl), Jimmy Reinders (cl), Robert Grishkoff (hn), Uliano Marchio (gtr), Barry Jordan (elec org), Peter Hamblin (perc), P. Klatzow (cnd) Claremont ▲ GSE 1524
Reizenstein, F.:Sonatina Ob, w. J. Craxton (ob) Continuum ▲ CCD 1024
Crozier, Catharine (org)
Alain, J.:Danses (3) [on the Rosales Organ, Trinity Episcopal Church, Portland, OR] *(rec May 18-21, 1993)* Delos ▲ DE 3147 [DDD]
Catherine Crozier at Grace Cathedral, San Francisco Delos ▲ 13491 3090 2 [DDD]
In Recital Gothic ▲ GOT 49041 [ADD]
Langlais, J.:Paraphrases grégoriennes [Rosales Organ, Trinity Episcopal Church, Portland, OR] *(rec May 18-21, 1993)* Delos ▲ DE 3147 [DDD]
Liszt, F.:Prelude & Fugue on the name B-A-C-H Delos ▲ DE 3090 [DDD]
Mendelssohn, F.:Sons Org—No. 6 Delos ▲ DE 3090 [DDD]
Messiaen, O.:Messe de la Pentecôte [Rosales Organ, Trinity Episcopal Church, Portland, OR] *(rec May 18-21, 1993)* Delos ▲ DE 3147 [DDD]
Reubke, J.:Son Org Delos ▲ DE 3090 [DDD]
Rorem, N.:A Quaker Reader Delos ▲ DCD 3076 [DDD]
Rorem, N.:Views from the Oldest House Delos ▲ DCD 3076 [DDD]
Schumann, R.:Fugues on B-A-C-H—Nos. 1 & 5 Delos ▲ DE 3090 [DDD]
Sowerby, L.:Fant for Fl Stops Delos ▲ DCD 3075 [DDD]
Sowerby, L.:Requiescat in pace Delos ▲ DCD 3075 [DDD]
Sowerby, L.:Sym Org Delos ▲ DCD 3075 [DDD]
Crozier, Philip (org)
Organ Duets, w. S. Poirier (org) REM ▲ 335603 [DDD]
Crudeli, Marcella (pno)
Cimarosa, D.:Sons (32) Kbd Arcobaleno 2-▲ SBCD 1509
Cimarosa, D.:Sons (31) Kbd Arcobaleno 2-▲ SBCD 1509
Glinka, M.:Vars on Themes from Bellini's "La Sonnambula", w. J. Stárek (cnd), RIAS Sinfonietta *(rec 1977)* Koch Treasure ▲ 31611-2 [ADD]
Cruickshank, Andrew (pno)
Grové, S.:Nonyana, the Ceremonial Dancer Claremont ▲ GSE 1546 [DDD]
Grové, S.:Songs & Dances from Africa Claremont ▲ GSE 1546 [DDD]
Crum, A. (vl)—see ORCHESTRAS & ENSEMBLES Spectre de la Rose
Crumb, V. (hp)—see ORCHESTRAS & ENSEMBLES Griffin Music Ensemble
Csaba, Péter (vn)
Brahms, J.:Qt 1 Pno, w. Ralf Gothoni (pno), Matti Hirvikangas (va), Frans Helmerson (vc) Ondine ▲ ODE 843
Brahms, J.:Qt 3 Pno, w. Ralf Gothoni (pno), Matti Hirvikangas (va), Frans Helmerson (vc) Ondine ▲ ODE 843
Enescu, G.:Son 2 Vn, w. A. Satukangas (pno) Ondine ▲ ODE 789-2 [DDD]
Enescu, G.:Son 3 Vn, w. A. Satukangas (pno) Ondine ▲ ODE 789-2 [DDD]
Haydn, J.:Con Org, Vn & Strs, H.XVIII/6, w. Ralf Gothoni (pno), Kuhmo Virtuosi Ondine ODE 810
Mendelssohn, F.:Con in d Vn, Pno & Strs, w. R.A. Gothoni (pno), Kuhmo Virtuosi Ondine ▲ ODE 810 [DDD]

Csánky, Emilia (ob)
Bach, Joh. Christian:Sinf concertante, T.287/2, w. Lajos Lencsés (ob), Károly Botvay (vc), B. Bánfalvi (cnd), Budapest Strings Capriccio ▲ 10509 [DDD]
Bach, J.S.:Con Vn & Ob, w. Béla Bánfalvi (vn), Budapest Strings *(rec Unitarian Church, Budapest, Nov 1991)* Naxos ▲ 8.553028 [DDD]
Bach, J.S.:Easter Oratorio, w. Béla Bánfalvi (vn), Budapest Strings—Adagio *(rec Unitarian Church, Budapest, Nov 1991)* Naxos ▲ 8.553028 [DDD]
Vivaldi, A.:Cons Ob, w. Budapest Strings—in a, RV.461 *(rec Unitarian Church, Budapest, Nov. 1991)* Naxos ▲ 8.553028 [DDD]
Cser (perc)
Bartók, B.:Son for 2 Pnos, w. Kocsis (pno), Ránki (pno), Rácz (perc) *(rec 9/11/81)* Hungaroton ▲ HCD 12400
Csury, Lajos (vn)
Sarasate, P. de:Caprice basque, w. Béla Simon (pno) Classical Diamonds ▲ 4007 [DDD]
Sarasate, P. de:Carmen Fant, w. Béla Simon (pno) [arr for vn & pno] Classical Diamonds ▲ 4007 [DDD]
Sarasate, P. de:Spanish Dances, w. Béla Simon (pno) Classical Diamonds ▲ 4007 [DDD]
Sarasate, P. de:Zigeunerweisen, w. Béla Simon (pno) Classical Diamonds ▲ 4007 [DDD]
Cuckston, Alan (hpd)
Couperin, F.:Pièces de clavecin (sels)—Books 3 & 4 (sels.) *(rec 10/90)* Naxos ▲ 8.550461 [DDD]
Couperin, F.:Pièces de clavecin (sels)—Book 4:Suites 22, 23, 25 & 26 *(rec Oct. 21, 1990)* Naxos ▲ 8.550462 [DDD]
Handel, G.F.:Hpd Music—Capriccio in F; Sonatina in d; Sonata in g; Toccata in g; Air & Variations *(rec April 1990)* Naxos ▲ 8.550416 [DDD]
Handel, G.F.:Suites Hpd—Nos. 1-5 in A, F, d, e & E *(rec Apr. 1990)* Naxos ▲ 8.550415 [DDD]
Handel, G.F.:Suites Hpd—Nos. 4, 6-8 *(rec April 1990)* Naxos ▲ 8.550416 [DDD]
Cuckston, Alan (org)
Handel, G.F.:The Harmonious Blacksmith—Capriccio; Sonatinas in d & g; Toccata in g *(rec Apr. 1990)* Naxos ▲ 8.550416 [DDD]
Cuckston, Alan (pno)
German, E.:Pno Music—Concert Study in A♭; Elegy in c; Graceful Dance in F; Humoresque in E; Impromptu No. 1 in e; Intermezzo in a; Mazurka in E; Melody in D♭; Melody in E♭; Polish Dance in E; Reverie in a; Tarantella in a; Valse-Caprice in A; Valse fantastique; Valsette in e Marco Polo ▲ 8.223370
Cudd, Patti (perc)
Cage, J.:But What About The Noise...?, w. Craig Bitterman, Eberhard Blum, Thomas Furminger, Erik Oña, Christopher Swist *(rec Slee Concert Hall, Univ. at Buffalo, NY, May 28 - June 1, 1995)* Hat Art ("Hat Now" series) ▲ 6179 [DDD]
Cuerda, Gloria (vc)
Falla, M. de:Psyché, w. Elena Montaña (sop), Conchi Vacas (fl), Zoraida Avila (hp), Wen-Yu Ku (vn), Alison Montoya (va) *(rec Madrid, Oct 1-3 1990)* RNE/Spanish National Radio ▲ M3/06 [DDD]
Guibert, A.:The Bath Tub, w. Elena Montaña (sop), Conchi Vacas (fl), Wen-Yu Ku (vn), Alison Montoya (va), Zoraida Avila (hp) *(rec Madrid, Oct 1-3 1990)* RNE/Spanish National Radio ▲ M3/06 [DDD]
Roussel, A.:Sérénade, w. Conchi Vacas (fl), Wen-Yu Ku (vn), Alison Montoya (va), Zoraida Avila (hp) *(rec Madrid, Oct 1-3 1990)* RNE/Spanish National Radio ▲ M3/06 [DDD]
Cueto, José (vn)
Bach, J.S.:Cant 20, w. Yuval Waldman (vn), Jennifer Rende (va), Gail Kruvand (db), Maryland Bach Aria Group members—Wacht auf Crystal ▲ CD 705 [DDD]
Bach, J.S.:Cant 82, w. Yuval Waldman (vn), Jennifer Rende (va), Gail Kruvand (db), Maryland Bach Aria Group members *(rec St. Peter's Church, Hale, Cheshire, Mar 14, 1994)* Naxos ▲ 8.550763 [DDD]
Bach, J.S.:Cant 110, w. Yuval Waldman (vn), Jennifer Rende (va), Gail Kruvand (db), Maryland Bach Aria Group members—Wachtet auf Crystal ▲ CD 705 [DDD]
Stradella, A.:Sinf alla Serenata, w. Yuval Waldman (vn), Jennifer Rende (va), Gail Kruvand (db), Maryland Bach Aria Group members Crystal ▲ CD 705 [DDD]
Torelli, G.:Son Tpt, G.1, w. Yuval Waldman (vn), Jennifer Rende (va), Gail Kruvand (db), Maryland Bach Aria Group members Crystal ▲ CD 705 [DDD]
Vivaldi, A.:Cons Bn, w. Yuval Waldman (vn), Jennifer Rende (va), Gail Kruvand (db), Maryland Bach Aria Group members—in B♭, RV.501, "La notte" Crystal ▲ CD 705 [DDD]
Cuiller, Daniel (vn)—see also ORCHESTRAS & ENSEMBLES Pariser Quartet
Leclair, J.-M.:Cons Vn, Op. 7, w. Stradivaria Ensemble—Nos. 1-3 & 5 Accord ▲ ACD 242552 [DDD]
Cuiller, Jocelyn (hpd)—see ORCHESTRAS & ENSEMBLES Pariser Quartet
Culley, James (perc)
Handel, D.:The Poems of Our Climate, w. Sheryl Woods (sop), Pamela Watson (fl), Brian Delay (gtr), Val Griffen (vc), Anton Nel (pno), Jack Brennan (perc), Allen Otte (perc), G. Samuel (cnd) Vienna Modern Masters ▲ VMM 2019 [DDD]
Culp, James (pno)
Sowerby, L.:Dialogue, w. Lorenz Maycher (org) [1949 Aeolian-Skinner Org, 1st Presbyterian Church, Kilgore, TX] *(rec Oct. 21, 1994)* Raven ▲ OAR 310 [DDD]
Culp, Jennifer (vc)—see ORCHESTRAS & ENSEMBLES Dunsmuir Piano Quartet
Culshaw, Andy (tpt)—see ORCHESTRAS & ENSEMBLES Fine Arts Brass Ensemble
Cumming, Richard (pno)
Love's Secrets & Other Songs By American Composers, w. E. Steber (sop), Milldred Miller (mez), John McCollum (ten), Donald Gramm (bass-bar), Edwin Biltcliffe (pno) Vox Box ("The American Composers" series) 2-▲ CDX 5129
Rorem, N.:Dialogues, w. Anita Darian (sop), John Stewart (ten), Ned Rorem (pno) Phoenix ▲ PHCD 116 [AAD]
Cummings, Douglas (vc)
Schubert, Franz:Qnt Strs, D.956, w. Lindsay String Quartet ASV ▲ ASV 537 [DDD]
Cummings, Laurence (hpd)
Couperin, F.:Hpd Music—Premier Ordre (book 1); Premier Concert [w. Reiko Ichise (vl)]; Deuxième Concert [w. Reiko Ichise (vl)] *(rec St. Martin's Church, Hampshire, Oct 1994)* Naxos ▲ 8.550961 [DDD]
Cummings, Laurence (org)
Couperin, L.:Suites Hpd—in D, a, C & f *(rec June 13-15, 1993)* Naxos ▲ 8.550922 [DDD]
Couperin, L.:Tombeau de M. de Blancrocher *(rec June 13-15, 1993)* Naxos ▲ 8.550922 [DDD]
Gibbons, O.:Org Music (misc)—Prelude in G; Prelude in d; Fantazia of 4 parts *(rec Chapel of Hertford College, Oxford, July 29-30, 1994)* Naxos ▲ 8.553130 [DDD]
Purcell, H.:Anthems & Services, w. Jeremy Summerly (cnd), Oxford Camerata—Jehova, quam multi sunt hostes mei, Z.135 [w. Andrew Carwood (ten), Michael McCarthy (bass)]; Remember not, Lord, our offences, Z.50; I will sing unto the Lord, as long as I live, Z.22; Voluntary in d, Z.718; O God, thou art my God, Z.35; O God, the King of glory, Z.34; Voluntary in G, Z.720; Lord, how long wilt thou be angry?, Z.25; Hear my prayer, O Lord, Z.15; Voluntary in C, Z.717; Blow up the trumpet in Sion, Z.10; O God, thou hast cast us out, Z.36 *(rec Chapel of Hertford College, Oxford, June 9-10, 1994)* Naxos ▲ 8.553129 [DDD]
Purcell, H.:Music for the Funeral of Queen Mary, w. Jeremy Summerly (cnd), Oxford Camerata—March, Z.860a; Man that is born of a woman, Z.27; In the midst of life we are in death, Z.17a; Thou knowest, Lord, the secrets of our hearts, Z.58b; Incassum, Lesbia...The Queen's Epicedium, Z.383 [w. Carys-Anne Lane (sop)], Canzona, Z.860b; Thou knowest, Lord, the secrets of our hearts, Z.58c *(rec Chapel of Hertford College, Oxford, June 9-10, 1994)* Naxos ▲ 8.553129 [DDD]
Schein, J.H.:Suites Instrs—Suite 12 in d (1617) [Pavan]; Suite 17 in a (1617) [Pavan] *(rec Hertford College Chapel, Oxford, Sept 5-6, 1994)* Naxos ▲ 8.553044 [DDD]
Schütz, H.:Deutsches Magnificat, w. J. Summerly (cnd), Oxford Camerata *(rec Hertford College Chapel, Oxford, Sept 5-6, 1994)* Naxos ▲ 8.553044 [DDD]
Schütz, H.:Motets (misc), w. J. Summerly (cnd), Oxford Camerata—Erhöre mich, wenn ich rufe (SWV.289); Ich liege und schlafe (SWV.310); Das ist je gewisslich wahr (SWV.277) *(rec Hertford College Chapel, Oxford, Sept 5-6, 1994)* Naxos ▲ 8.553044 [DDD]

Cummings, Laurence (org) (cont.)
Schütz, H.:Psalmen Davids, w. J. Summerly (cnd), Oxford Camerata—An den Wassern zu Babel [SWV 37]; Ach Herr, straf mich nicht mit deinem Zorn [SWV 24]; Singet dem Herrn ein neues Lied [SWV 35]; Wohl dem, der nicht wandelt im Rat der Gottlosen [SWV 28]; Wie lieblich sind deine Wohnungen [SWV 29]; Lobe den Herren, meine Seele [SWV 39] *(rec Hertford College Chapel, Oxford, Sept 5–6, 1994)* Naxos ▲ 8.553044 [DDD]
Cundick, Robert (org)
A Tabernacle Organ Duo Extravaganza, w. John Longhurst (org) Argo ▲ 430426-2 ZH [DDD]
Cune, Arthur (vib)
Andriessen, L.:Anachrony 1, w. Nico de Rooij (pno), Sepp Grotenhuis (cel), Douceline Aleven (hp), Nicolette Heerema (org), H. Williams (cnd), Netherlands Ballet Orch *(rec Amsterdam Music Theater, Oct 3–6, 1994)* Donemus ▲ CV 54 [DDD]
Cunningham, Sarah (b vl)
Purcell, H.:Ayres & Songs, w. Jill Feldman (sop), Nigel North (lt) Arcana ▲ ACA 2 [DDD]
Cunningham, Sarah (vc)—see ORCHESTRAS & ENSEMBLES Sonnerie Ensemble
Cunningham, Sarah (vl)
Bach, J.S.:Sons Fl, BWV 1030–35, w. James Galway (fl), Phillip Moll (hpd)—BWV 1032 RCA Red Seal ▲ 0902-668182-2 [DDD]
Bach, J.S.:Son Fl, BWV 1079, w. James Galway (fl), Monica Huggett (vn), Phillip Moll (hpd) RCA Red Seal ▲ 0902-668182-2 [DDD]
Bach, J.S.:Trio Son, BWV 1038, w. James Galway (fl), Monica Huggett (vn), Phillip Moll (hpd) RCA Red Seal ▲ 0902-668182-2 [DDD]
Bach, J.S.:Trio Son for 2 Fls, BWV 1039, w. James Galway (fl), Jeanne Galway (fl), Phillip Moll (hpd) RCA Red Seal ▲ 0902-668182-2 [DDD]
Play This Passionate Virgin Classics ▲ CDC 59050
Telemann, G.P.:Con in F Rcr, B Vl, w. M. Verbruggen (rcr), M. Huggett (cnd), Orch of the Age of Enlightenment *(rec Nov. 2–4, 1992)* Harmonia Mundi USA ▲ HMU 907093
Telemann, G.P.:Con in a for Rcr, Vl, w. M. Verbruggen (rcr), M. Huggett (cnd), Orch of the Age of Enlightenment *(rec Nov. 2–4, 1992)* Harmonia Mundi USA ▲ HMU 907093
Telemann, G.P.:Suite Vl, w. M. Huggett (cnd), Orch of the Age of Enlightenment *(rec Nov. 2–4, 1992)* Harmonia Mundi USA ▲ HMU 907093
Cuper, Philippe (cl)
Copland, A.:Con Cl, w. Bretagne Orch Accord ▲ ACD 243852 [DDD]
Françaix, J.:Con Cl, w. Bretagne Orch Accord ▲ ACD 243852 [DDD]
Nielsen, C.:Con Cl, w. Bretagne Orch Accord ▲ ACD 243852 [DDD]
Cupples, Audrey (b sax)—see ORCHESTRAS & ENSEMBLES East Coast Saxophone Quartet
Curl, Jennifer (va)
Lim, L.:Amulet Vox Australis ▲ VAST 0192
Curley, Carlo (org)
Bach, J.S.:Org Music (misc)—Toccata & Fugue in d, BWV 565; Toccata, Adagio & Fugue in C, BWV 564; Fugue in g, BWV 578; Prelude & Fugue in a, BWV 543; Air on a G string; Jesu, joy of man's desiring; Wachet auf, ruft uns die stimme; etc. London ("Jubilee" series) ▲ 430746-2 [DDD]
Cererols, J.:Vespers, w. Guillemette Laurens (mez), Currende, E. van Nevel (cnd) *(rec May 1994)* Accent ▲ 94106 [DDD]
Elgar, E.:Org Music Argo ▲ 433450-2 [DDD]
The Finest Hour Pro Arte ▲ CDD 353
Live at Royal Festival Hall Pro Arte ▲ CDD 354
Organ Imperial Argo ▲ 433450-2 ZH [DDD]
Widor, C.M.:Sym 6 Org Pro Arte ▲ CDD 354
Curnow, Jeffrey (tpt)—see also ORCHESTRAS & ENSEMBLES Empire Brass Quintet, New York Trumpet Ensemble
Christmas in Dallas, w. C. Harmon (org), Adam Gordon (tpt), Gregory Hustis (hn), Clarece Candamio (org) *(rec Lover's Lane United Methodist Church, Dallas)* Hester Park ▲ 7706 [DDD]
Curran, Alvin (instrs/syn)
Curran, A.:Music of—From a Room on the Piazza; Crystal Aires; Walked the Way Home; Gil Scariolanti; On My Satin Harp; At Harmony Ranch Catalyst ▲ 09026-61823-2
Curran, Alvin (pno)
Curran, A.:Why Is This Night Different Than All Other Nights?, w. Roy Malan (vn), Donald Haas (acc), Peter Wahrhaftig (tuba), William Winant (perc) Tzadik ("The Composers" series) ▲ TZA 7001 [DDD]
Curry, M. (vc)
Sowerby, L.:Songs, w. D'Anna Fortunato (mez), Veronica Macchia-Kadlubkiewicz (vn), Tessa van Buskirk (vn), Virginia Christensen (va)—Premonition; Kisses; Midnight; Reassurance; Adventure [all text L. E. Thomas] Gasparo ▲ GSCD 315 [DDD]
Curry, William (va)
Scelsi, G.:Anahit, w. Paul Zukofsky (vn), Julie Bogorad (fl), Peggy Russell (fl), Courtney Westcott (fl), Lawrence McDonald (cl), Joan Waryha (cl), Jean Hansen (b cl), Bill Suite (e hn), Nita VanPelt (sax), Bob Zobal (tpt), John Carter (trbn), Martin Lydecker (trbn), Stan Cortman (hn), Robert Ward (hn), Jody Rowitsch (va), Irene Wade (va), Anne Fagerburg (vc), John Gockel (vc), Sue Manz (bass), Steven Stearman (bass) *(rec Oberlin Conservatory of Music, Oct 8, 1973)* CP² ▲ CP2 108 [AAD]
Curtis, Alan (hpd)
Bach, C.P.E.:Con doppio, w. G. Leonhardt (hpd), Collegium Aureum Editio Classica ▲ 77061-2 [ADD]
Bach, J.S.:Cons for 3 Hpds (comp), w. G. Leonhardt (hpd), A. Uittenbosch (hpd), G. Leonhardt (cnd), Leonhardt Consort Teldec 3-▲ 2292-42726-2 [ADD]
The Chromatic Harpsichord in Naples Nuova Era ("Ancient Music" series) ▲ NUO 7177 [DDD]
Veracini, F.M.:Sons Fl, w. Giorgio Bernabò (fl)—Nos. 1-5 & 11-12 *(rec Villa Trissino-Marzotto, Vicenza, Italy, Jan. 15–17, 1994)* Dynamic ▲ CDS 114 [DDD]
Curtis, D. (va)—see ORCHESTRAS & ENSEMBLES Coull String Quartet
Curtis, Henry Adam (instrs)
Mozart, W.A.:Music of, w. Philip Aaberg, Todd Boekelheide, Chris Botti, Steve Erquiaga, Béla Fleck, Eugene Friesen, Paul McCandless, Tim Story, Richard Schönherz, Tracy Scott Silverman, Thea Suits-Silverman, ValGardena, Modern Mandolin Quartet Imaginary Road ▲ 314534065-2 ■ 314534065-4
Curtis, John (gtr)
Pinkham, D.:Intro, Nocturne & Rondo, w. W. Buonocore (mand) *(rec Dec. 1992)* Koch International Classics ▲ KIC 7180 [DDD]
Curtis, Paul (fl)
Lemmoné, J.:Fl Music, w. David Miller (pno)—Graceful Dance; Fant on Scottish Melodies; Wind Amongst the Trees; Dainty Dance; Serenade; Valse de Concert; A Fant; Danse Romantique; The Elves; La Danseuse; Minuet; Fant Caprice; Aria *(rec Newcastle Conservatorium of Music Concert Hall, Nov 1994–Feb 1995)* Tall Poppies ▲ TP 68 [DDD]
Curtiss, S. (va)
Russo, J.:Largetto, w. J. Russo (cl), L. Walton Ignacio (pno) CRS ▲ 9255
Curtis-Smith, Curtis (pno)
Curtis-Smith, C.:Fant Pieces, w. Renata Artman Knific (vn) Albany ▲ TROY 148 [DDD]
Curzon, Clifford (pno)
Brahms, J.:Con 1 Pno, w. G. Szell (cnd), London SO London ("The Classic Sound" series) ▲ 425082-2
Brahms, J.:Intermezzos Pno, Op. 117—No. 1 In E♭ London ("The Classic Sound" series) ▲ 448578-2
Brahms, J.:Pieces Pno, Op. 119—No. 3 in C London ("The Classic Sound" series) ▲ 448578-2
Brahms, J.:Son 3 Pno London ("The Classic Sound" series) ▲ 448578-2
Britten, B.:Introduction & Rondo alla burlesca & Mazurka elegiaca, w. Benjamin Britten (pno) *(rec 1941–44)* Pearl ▲ PEA 9177 [ADD]
Franck, C.:Symphonic Vars, w. G. Szell (cnd), London SO London ("The Classic Sound" series) ▲ 425082-2
Mozart, W.A.:Con 23 Pno, w. I. Kertész (cnd), London SO London ("Weekend Classics" series) ▲ 433086-2 [AAD]
Mozart, W.A.:Con 24 Pno, w. I. Kértesz (cnd), London SO London ("Weekend Classics" series) ▲ 433086-2 [AAD]
Schubert, Franz:Qnt Pno, D.667, w. Vienna Octet members London ▲ 417459-2 [ADD]

Curzon, Clifford (pno) (cont.)
Schubert, Franz:Son Pno, D.960 *(rec Aug 24, 1974)* Orfeo d'or ("Festspiel Dokumente" series) ▲ 401951
Schubert, Franz:Son Pno, D.960 London ("The Classic Sound" series) ▲ 448578-2
Schumann, R.:Adagio & Allegro Hn, w. Pablo Casals (vc) Andromeda ▲ ANR 2524
Schumann, R.:Fant Pno *(rec Aug 24, 1974)* Orfeo d'or ("Festspiel Dokumente" series) ▲ 401951
Custer, Laurenz (pno)
Koussevitzky, S.:Concert Db Pno, w. Yoan Goilav (db) *(rec 1972)* Tuxedo ▲ TUXCD 1090 [ADD]
Cút, Ján (va)
Romberg, A.:Qnts Fl, w. V. Brunner (fl), V. Simcisko (vn), M. Telecky (va), J. Alexander (vc) Trevak ▲ TRE 40007 [DDD]
Cutler, Sara (hp)
Serenades for Flute & Harp Cantilena ▲ C 660082
Cuturello, Stefano (vn)—see ORCHESTRAS & ENSEMBLES Consort Fontegara
Czapczynski, Z. (vn)
Martin, F.:Polyptyque (6 images de la Passion du Christ), w. E. de Stoutz (cnd), Zurich CO Gallo ▲ CD 713 [ADD]
Czapski, Jutta (pno)
Eisler, H.:Songs, w. Roswitha Trexler (sop) Berlin Classics ("Hanns Eisler Edition" series) 2-▲ BER 9229
Czelusta, W. (trbn)—see ORCHESTRAS & ENSEMBLES Stuttgart Philharmonia Ensemble
Czernicka, Ida (pno)
Chopin, F.:Pno Music (misc)—Ballade No. 1; 2 Mazurkas, Op. 68/2 & 3; Nocturne, Op. 9/1; Polonaise, Op. 26/1; 3 Waltzes, Opp. 34/2, 64/1, 70/2 PMG (Vienna Master) ▲ CD 160207 [DDD]
Chopin, F.:Preludes, Op. 28—Nos. 3,6,7,8,14,15,17 & 19 PMG (Vienna Master) ▲ CD 160207 [DDD]
Czerny-Stefanska, Halina (pno)
Chopin, F.:Andante Spianato & Grande Polonaise, w. W. Rowicki (cnd), Warsaw PO *(rec Warsaw, 1959)* Polskie Nagrania ▲ PNCD 306 B
Chopin, F.:Andante Spianato & Grande Polonaise, w. W. Rowicki (cnd), Warsaw PO *(rec Warsaw, 1959–60)* Polskie Nagrania ▲ PNCD 308
Chopin, F.:Andante Spianato & Grande Polonaise, w. K. Kord (cnd), Warsaw PO *(rec Warsaw Philharmonic Hall, June 27–30, 1994)* Canyon Classics ▲ CD 248
Chopin, F.:Con 1 Pno, w. W. Rowicki (cnd), Narodowej PO *(rec Warsaw, 1959)* Polskie Nagrania ▲ PNCD 305
Chopin, F.:Con 2 Pno, w. W. Rowicki (cnd), Narodowej PO *(rec Warsaw, 1959)* Polskie Nagrania ▲ PNCD 305
Chopin, F.:Mazurkas—Nos. 26–43 & 48–58, Opp. 41/1–4, 50/1–3, 56/1–3, 59/1–3, 63/1–3, 68/1–4 & opp. posth. *(rec June 11–13, 1990)* Canyon ▲ EC 3644-2 [DDD]
Chopin, F.:Mazurkas—Nos. 1–25 & 42–45, Opp. 6/1–4, 7/1–5, 17/1–4, 24/1–4, 30/1–4, 33/1–4, 67/1–4 *(rec Nov. 15–17, 1989 & June 1)* Canyon ▲ EC 3643-2 [DDD]
Chopin, F.:Pno Music (misc), w. Martha Argerich (pno), Vladimir Ashkenazy (pno), Stanislav Bunin (pno), Jan Ekier (pno), Yuval Fichman (pno), Kemal Gekic (pno), Adam Harasiewicz (pno), Krzysztof Jablonski (pno), Louis Kentner (pno), Jean-Marc Luisada (pno), Garrick Ohlsson (pno), Ivo Pogorelich (pno), Maurizio Pollini (pno), Dang Thai Son (pno)—includes Ballade (Nos. 1 & 2); Barcarolle, Op. 60; Concerto Nos. 1 & 2; Études (Op. 10, Nos. 1, 5, 8, 10 & 12 & Op. 25, No. 10, 18 & 25); Grand valse brillante; Impromptus (Nos. 3 & 4); Mazurkas (Op. 24, Nos. 1–4; Op. 30, Nos. 1–4; Op. 50, No. 32; Op. 59, Nos. 1–3); Nocturnes (Op. 9, No. 3; Op. 37, No. 12; Op. 48, No. 13; Op. 55, No. 16)Polonaise (Op. 40, Nos. 3 & 4; Op. 44, No. 5; Op. 53, No. 6; Op. 61, No. 7); Preludes (Op. 28 Nos. 13–18, 21–24 & Op. 45, No. 25); Scherzos (Nos. 1–3); Sonatas (Nos. 2 & 3); Waltzes (No. 1 & 6) LaserLight 5-▲ 15 961 [ADD/DDD]
Chopin, F.:Polonaises—Opp. 26, 40, 44, 53 & 61 *(rec Warsaw, 1959)* Polskie Nagrania ▲ PNCD 306 B
Chopin, F.:Polonaises, w. Ludwik Stefanski (pno)—Youthful Polonaises [in g, B, A, g♯, B♭ & G♭]; Polonaises, Op. 71 [in d, B♭ & f] *(rec Warsaw, 1960)* Polskie Nagrania ▲ PNCD 306 A
Chopin, F.:Preludes, Op. 28 *(rec Warsaw, 1959)* Polskie Nagrania ▲ PNCD 303
Chopin, F.:Rondos Pno & 4-Hands, w. Ludwik Stefanski (pno) *(rec Warsaw, 1960)* Polskie Nagrania ▲ PNCD 310
Mozart, W.A.:Con 20 Pno, w. E. Chakarov (cnd), Festival Sinfonietta Vivace 2-▲ G 217 [ADD]
Mozart, W.A.:Con 23 Pno, w. K. Ančerl (cnd), Czech PO *(rec 1952–1966)* Supraphon ▲ CD 111935 [AAD]
Czidra, László (rcr)
Handel, G.F.:Trio Sons, w. Zsolt Harsányi (rcr/bn), Pál Kelemen (vc), Zsursa Pertis (clvd)—in F, H.405 *(rec May 4–7, 1992)* Naxos ▲ 8.550700 [DDD]
Telemann, G.P.:Con in F Rcr Bn, w. J. Vajda (bn), J. Rolla (cnd), Franz Liszt CO White Label ▲ HRC 042
Cziffra, György (pno)
Beethoven, L. van:Son 21 Pno, "Waldstein" *(rec Dec. 19, 1963)* Ermitage ▲ ERM 143 [ADD]
Busoni, F.:Bach Transcriptions—Prelude & Fugue in D, BWV 532 *(rec Dec. 19, 1963)* Ermitage ▲ ERM 143 [ADD]
Chopin, F.:Pno Music (misc)—Polonaise-Fant, Op. 61; Fant-Impromptu, Op. 66; Intro & Vars, Op. 12; Polonaise, Op. 53 *(rec Nov 5, 1978 & Apr 12, 198)* APR ▲ APR 5554 [ADD]
Chopin, F.:Pno Music (misc)—Ballade No. 4 in f, Op. 52; 4 Etudes (Op. 10, Nos. 3,10 & 12; Op. 25, No. 1); Fantaisie-impromptu in c♯, Op. 66; Waltzes in A♭, Op. 42 & in D♭, Op. 64/1 *(rec 1969)* Ermitage ▲ ERM 103 [ADD]
Chopin, F.:Polonaises—in e♭, Op. 26/2; in A♭, Op. 53, "Héroique" *(rec Dec. 19, 1963)* Ermitage ▲ ERM 143 [ADD]
Cziffra, G.:Transcriptions & Paraphrases—Verdi:Il Trovatore; Brahms:Hungarian Dance No. 5 *(rec Budapest, 1954–56)* Hungaroton ▲ HCD 31596 [ADD]
Liszt, F.:Hungarian Rhaps—No. 19 *(rec Budapest, 1954–56)* Hungaroton ▲ HCD 31596 [ADD]
Liszt, F.:Pno Music (misc)—Funérailles; Gnomenreigen; Hungarian Rhapsody No. 2; Liebestraum No. 3; Transcendental Etude No. 10 *(rec 1969)* Ermitage ▲ ERM 103 [ADD]
Liszt, F.:Pno Music (misc)—Leibstraum 3; Trancendental Study 10; Gnomenreigen; Les Jeux d'eau à la Villa d'Este *(rec Nov 5, 1978 & Apr 12, 198)* APR ▲ APR 5554 [ADD]
Liszt, F.:Transcriptions & Paraphrases—Wagner:Tannhäuser; Verdi:Rigoletto; Mendelssohn:Wedding March & Funeral Music [from A Midsummer Night's Dream]; Auber:La muette de Portici *(rec Budapest, 1954–56)* Hungaroton ▲ HCD 31596 [ADD]
Liszt, F.:Valse impromptu *(rec Dec. 19, 1963)* Ermitage ▲ ERM 143 [ADD]
Ravel, M.:Jeux d'eau *(rec Nov 5, 1978 & Apr 12, 198)* APR ▲ APR 5554 [ADD]
Saint-Saëns, C.:Étude Pno, Op. 52/6 *(rec Nov 5, 1978 & Apr 12, 198)* APR ▲ APR 5554 [ADD]
Schumann, R.:Carnaval Pno *(rec Dec. 19, 1963)* Ermitage ▲ ERM 143 [ADD]
Czifra, Andras (vn)—see also ORCHESTRAS & ENSEMBLES Ophir Trio
Brahms, J.:Qnt Cl, w. W. Boeykens (cl), J.-J. Kantarow (vn), V. Mendelssohn (va), H.-J. Stegenga (vc) Erasmus ▲ WVH 017 [DDD]
Dabelsteen, Michael (db)
Roussel, A.:Chamber Music, w. Majken Bjerno (sop), Toke Lund Christiansen (fl), Bjørn Carl Nielsen (ob), Niels Thomsen (cl), Per Jacobsen (hn), Asger Svendsen (bn), Ketil Christensen (tpt), Anne Søe Hansen (vn), Zwi Carmelli (va), Piotr Zelazny (va), Niels Ullner (vc), Tine Rehling (hp), Morten Mogensen (pno), Per Salo (pno), Per Jensen (perc)—Divertissement, Op. 6; Trio, Op. 40; Joueurs de Flute, Op. 27; Serenade, Op. 30; Le marchand de sable qui passe, Op. 13; Andante et scherzo, Op. 13; 2 poèmes de ronsard, Op. 26; Aria; Elpenor, Op. 59; Pipe Kontrapunkt 2-▲ KPT 32218 [DDD]
Dabney, Denise C. (bar sax)—see ORCHESTRAS & ENSEMBLES Resounding Winds Saxophone Quartet
Dacosta, Paulinho (perc)
Duke, G.:Muir Woods Suite, w. George Duke (pno), Stanley Clarke (bass), Chester Thompson (dr), E. Stratta (cnd), Lille National Orch *(rec live, Montreaux Music Festival, Montreaux, Switzerland, July 12, 1993)* Warner Bros ▲ 9 46132-2 [DDD]

INSTRUMENT.

Dadelsen, Anne de (pno)
Gerber, R.:Chamber Music, w. Fränzi Badertscher-Jaquiéry (fl), Gunhard Mattes (ob), Dimitri Ashkenazy (cl), Claude Delley (cl), Pierre-Yves Dubois (cl)—Pièce lente; Habanera; Berceuse [all for Cl & Pno]; Trio for Fl, Ob & Pno; Son for Fl & Pno; Ballet for Fl & Pno; Sonatine for 3 Cl; Pavane for Fl & Pno; Suite for Fl & Pno; Prélude et fugue sur le nom de Bach for Cl — Gallo ▲ CD 788 [DAD]
Wehrli, W.:Son Vc, w. Gerhard Pawlica (vc) *(rec 1989)* — Jecklin ▲ JS 301-2 [ADD]
Wehrli, W.:Trio 3 Vn, w. Gunar Larsens (vn), Jakob Hefti (hn) *(rec 1989)* — Jecklin ▲ JS 301-2 [ADD]

Dael, Lucy van (va)
Mozart, W.A.:Qts Fl, w. B. Kuijken (fl), S. Kuijken (vn), W. Kuijken (vc) — Accent ▲ 48225

Dael, Lucy van (vn)—see ORCHESTRAS & ENSEMBLES L'Archibudelli

Daelen, Ulla van (hp)
Rush Hour — New Classic Colours ♦ NCC 8003 [DDD]
Shalimar — New Classic Colours ▲ NCC 8701 [DDD]

Daellenbach, Charles (tuba)—see ORCHESTRAS & ENSEMBLES Canadian Brass

Daeublin, Friederike (vl)—see ORCHESTRAS & ENSEMBLES Isabella D'Este

Daffagni, C. (lt/sgr/perc)—see ORCHESTRAS & ENSEMBLES La Reverdie

Dagon, R. (cl)
Foss, L.:Paradigm, w. J. Williams (perc), J. Grassel (electric gtr), S. Basson (bn), L. Anderson (vn) *(rec 1989–90)* — Koss Classics ▲ KC 1006 [DDD]

Dahinden, Clemens (vn)
Brahms, J.:Qnt Pno, w. Clara Haskil (pno), Peter Rybar (vn), Heinz Wigand (va), Antonio Tusa (vc) — Doron 2-▲ DRC 4007/8 [ADD]
Brahms, J.:Sextet Strs, Op. 36, w. Peter Rybar (vn), Heinz Wigand (va), Oskar Kromer (va), Carl-Heinz Jucker (vc), Antonio Tusa (vc) — Doron 2-▲ DRC 4007/8 [ADD]

Dahinden, Roland (ten trbn)
Cage, J.:Two⁵, w. Hildegard Kleeb (pno) *(rec Studio DRS, Zurich, Jan. 4–5, 1993)* — Hat Hut ("NOW." series) ▲ hat ART CD 6129 [DDD]

Dahinden, Roland (trbn)
Cage, J.:Ryoanji Trbn *(rec Studio DRS, Zurich, Jan. 4–5, 1993)* — Hat Hut ("NOW." series) ▲ hat ART CD 6129 [DDD]
Wolff, C.:Exercises, w. Eberhard Blum (fl), Steffen Schleiermacher (pno), Jan Williams (perc) *(rec Hessischer Radio, Frankfurt, Aug 6–7, 1994)* — Hat Hut ("Now" series) ▲ CD 6167 [DDD]

Dahl, Christine (pno)
Macy, C.:Ostinato Studies, w. John Jensen (pno) *(rec Macalester College, Mar 11–12, 1994)* — Innova ▲ 503

Dahl, David (org)
Brombaugh Organ at Christ Church, Tacoma, Washington — Organ Historical Society ■ OHSC 2

Dahle, Kjersti (ob/E hn)
Saeverud, H.:Peer Gynt Suites, w. Sveinung Sand (vn), Anna Dolezych (va), Gyrid Erlandsen (cl), Bohumil Maliska (hn), A. Dmitriev (cnd), Stavanger SO *(rec Stavanger Konserthus, Stavanger, Norway, Nov 13–17, 1995)* — BIS ▲ CD 762 [DDD]

Dähler, Jörg Ewald (hpd)
Albinoni, T.:Cons à 5 Obs, Op. 7, w. I. Gortizki (ob), J. Müller-Brincken (ob), H. L. Hirsch (cnd), Accademia Instrumentalis Claudio Monteverdi—Nos. 1,2 & 4 — Claves ■ C 601
Bach, J.S.:Inventions (30) Hpd *(rec Berne, Apr. 1968 & Thun, Aug 1971)* — Claves ("Favor Collection" series) ▲ CLF 170
Bach, J.S.:Preludes & Fugues Hpd—(12) in C, BWV 924; in D, BWV 925 [doubtful]; in d, BWV 926; in F, BWV 927; in F, BWV 928; in g, BWV 929; in g, BWV 930; in C, BWV 939; in d, BWV 940; in e, BWV 941; in a, BWV 942; in c, BWV 999 *(rec Berne, Apr. 1968 & Thun, Aug 1971)* — Claves ("Favor Collection" series) ▲ CLF 170 [ADD]
Galuppi, B.:Sons (6) Hpd, w. P. Angerer (cnd), English CO—Son in F *(rec St. Mary's Parish Church, London, Apr 1983)* — Claves ▲ CD 508306 [DDD]
Galuppi, B.:Sons (12) Hpd—Nos. I-VI *(rec Munich, 1976)* — Claves ▲ CD 500603 [ADD]
Handel, G.F.:Sons Fl, w. Peter-Lukas Graf (fl), Manfred Sax (bn)—4 Sons—Op. 1, Nos. 1a,1b,5 & 9 — Claves ▲ CD 238 [ADD]
Purcell, H.:Songs, w. P. Huttenlocher (bar)—18 songs [E] — Claves ▲ CD 705 [ADD]

Dähler, Jörg Ewald (pno)
Musiche Veneziene per Voce e Strumenti, w. Berganza, Teresa (mez), Yasunori Imamura (lt/thb/gtr), Pere Ros (vl), Lynn Dickinson (vl), Carol Lewis (vl), Silvie Mocquet (vl), Jörg Ewald Dähler (cnd) *(rec Kirche Saanen, Feb 1982)* — Claves ▲ CD 508206 [DDD]
Schubert, Franz:Impromptus Pno (comp) *(rec Basle Ethnological Museum, July 1975)* — Claves ▲ CD 50509 [ADD]
Schubert, Franz:Die Schöne Müllerin, w. Ernst Haefliger (ten) *(rec Kirche Seon, June 1982)* — Claves ▲ CD 508301 [DDD]
Schubert, Franz:Die Schöne Müllerin, w. Ernst Haefliger (ten) — Claves ▲ 50-8301
Schubert, Franz:Schwanengesang, w. Ernst Haefliger (ten) — Claves ▲ 50-8506
Schubert, Franz:Songs (misc), w. Ernst Haefliger (ten)—23 songs — Claves ▲ 50-8611
Schubert, Franz:Winterreise, w. Ernst Haefliger (ten) — Claves ▲ 50-8008
Schubert, Franz:Winterreise, w. Ernst Haefliger (ten) *(rec Kirche Saanen, Sept 1980)* — Claves ▲ CD 508008 [DDD]

Dähler, Jürg (va)—see ORCHESTRAS & ENSEMBLES Winterthur String Quartet

Dähler, Jürg (vn)—see ORCHESTRAS & ENSEMBLES Zurich Chamber Players

Dähler-Mulet, Valérie (va)—see ORCHESTRAS & ENSEMBLES Zurich Chamber Players

Dahlman, Barbro (pno)
Crumb, G.:Music For A Summer EveningMusic for a Summer Evening (Makrokosmos III), w. I. Lindgren (pno), S. Asikainen (perc), R. Kuisma (perc) *(rec analog)* — BIS ▲ CD 261

Dahmen, Andreas (fl)—see ORCHESTRAS & ENSEMBLES VIF Flute Quartet

Dalberto, Michel (pno)
Brahms, J.:Sons Vn (comp), w. Boris Belkin (vn) *(rec Musica Théâtre, La Chaux-de-Fonds, Switzerland, May 24–29, 1994)* — Denon ▲ DEN 78962 [DDD]
Fauré, G.:La bonne chanson, w. B. Hendricks (sop) — EMI Classics ▲ CDC 49841
Fauré, G.:Songs, w. B. Hendricks (sop)—Trois poèmes d'un jour & 16 (sels.) — EMI Classics ▲ CDC 49841
Franck, C.:Symphonic Vars, w. J.-B. Pommier (cnd), Philharmonia Orch *(rec Jan. 29–31, 1992)* — Denon ▲ CO 75258 [DDD]
Grieg, E.:Con Pno, Op. 16, w. J.-B. Pommier (cnd), Philharmonia Orch *(rec June 19, 1992)* — Denon ▲ CO 75258 [DDD]
Liszt, F.:Années de pèlerinage 2 — Denon ▲ CO 75500 [DDD]
Mozart, W.A.:Fant Pno, K.475 *(rec Salle de Châtonneyre, Corseaux Switzerland, Nov. 29–Dec. 1, 1993)* — Denon ▲ CO 78909 [DDD]
Mozart, W.A.:Son 11 Pno *(rec Salle de Châtonneyre, Corseaux Switzerland, Nov. 29–Dec. 1, 1993)* — Denon ▲ CO 78909 [DDD]
Mozart, W.A.:Vars Pno, K.353 *(rec Salle de Châtonneyre, Corseaux Switzerland, Nov. 29–Dec. 1, 1993)* — Denon ▲ CO 78909 [DDD]
Mozart, W.A.:Vars Pno, K.455 *(rec Salle de Châtonneyre, Corseaux Switzerland, Nov. 29–Dec. 1, 1993)* — Denon ▲ CO 78909 [DDD]
Plaisir d'Amour - Mélodies Françaises, w. Hendricks, Barbara (sop), Cherubini Quartet — EMI Classics ▲ CDC 55388
Schubert, Franz:Adagio Pno, D.178 *(rec Salle de Chatonneyre, Corseaux, Switzerland, Jan. 1994)* — Denon ▲ CO 78914 [DDD]
Schubert, Franz:Allegretto Pno, D.346 — Denon ▲ CO 76865 [DDD]
Schubert, Franz:Cotillon, D.976 *(rec Salle de Chatonneyre, Corseaux, Switzerland, Jan. 1994)* — Denon ▲ CO 78914 [DDD]
Schubert, Franz:Ecossaises Pno, D.529 — Denon ▲ CO 74499 [DDD]
Schubert, Franz:Ecossaises Pno, D.529 *(rec Salle de Chatonneyre, Corseaux, Switzerland, Jan. 1994)* — Denon ▲ CO 78914 [DDD]
Schubert, Franz:Galop & Ecossaises *(rec Salle de Châtonneyre, Corseaux, Switzerland, July 11–14, 1994)* — Denon ▲ DEN 78803 [DDD]

Dalberto, Michel (pno) (cont.)
Schubert, Franz:Impromptus Pno (comp) *(rec Sept. 19–20 1991 & Feb. 2)* — Denon ▲ CO 75071 [DDD]
Schubert, Franz:Minuet & Trio Pno — Denon ▲ CO 74499 [DDD]
Schubert, Franz:Moments musicaux — Denon ▲ CO 74499 [DDD]
Schubert, Franz:Originaltänze—Nos. 1, 2, 14, 20, 22, 26, 29, 30, 31, 32, 33, 34, 35 & 36 *(rec Salle de Chatonneyre, Corseaux, Switzerland, Jan. 1994)* — Denon ▲ CO 78914 [DDD]
Schubert, Franz:Pno Music (comp)—Sons., D.784, D.566, D.790, D.593, D.781 *(rec Feb. 25–28, 1992 & Jan. 1)* — Denon/PCM Digital ▲ DEN 75757 [DDD]
Schubert, Franz:Pno Music (misc)—Fant. in C, D.760; Deutsche und 2 Ecossaisen, D.783; Walzer, Anh I-14; Son. in C, D.613; Marsch in E, D.606 *(rec Salle de Châtonneyre, Corseaux, Switzerland, Jan. 1993, Jan. 1994 & Ju)* — Denon ▲ CO 78955 [DDD]
Schubert, Franz:Pno Music (misc)—Impromptus; Sonata in E; Minuets (3) with Two Trios; Allegretto *(rec Sept. 3–6, 1991)* — Denon ▲ CO 79730 [DDD]
Schubert, Franz:Pno Music (misc)—Hungarian Melody in b, D.817; Son in f♯; 3 German Dances, D.971; Var on a Waltz by Diabelli, D.718; Son in E♭, D.568 — Denon ▲ DEN 78845
Schubert, Franz:Pno Music (misc)—Andante in C, D.29; Deutsche Tänze, D.841, Nos. 1 & 2; Ecossaise, D.158; Waltz in G, "Albumblatt," D.844 — Denon ▲ CO 76330 [DDD]
Schubert, Franz:Sons Pno (comp)—Sonatas in E (unfinished), D.157 & in a, D.845 — Denon ▲ CO 73787 [DDD]
Schubert, Franz:Sons Pno (comp)—Sonata in a, D.537 — Denon ▲ CO 74499 [DDD]
Schubert, Franz:Sons Pno (comp)—Sonata in C, "Reliquie," D.840 — Denon ▲ CO 76330 [DDD]
Schubert, Franz:Sons Pno (comp)—Sonata in C, D.279; Sonata in G, D.894 — Denon ▲ CO 76865 [DDD]
Schubert, Franz:Sons Pno (comp)—in f, D.625; in D, D.850 (Op. 53) *(rec Salle de Châtonneyre, Corseaux, Switzerland, July 11–14, 1994)* — Denon ▲ DEN 78803 [DDD]
Schubert, Franz:Son Pno, D.557 *(rec Sept. 19–20 1991 & Feb. 2)* — Denon ▲ CO 75071 [DDD]
Schubert, Franz:Son Pno, D.575 *(rec Salle de Chatonneyre, Corseaux, Switzerland, Jan. 1994)* — Denon ▲ CO 78914 [DDD]
Schubert, Franz:Son Pno, D.664 *(rec Salle de Chatonneyre, Corseaux, Switzerland, Jan. 1994)* — Denon ▲ CO 78914 [DDD]
Schumann, R.:Con Pno, w. E. Inbal (cnd), Vienna SO — Denon/PCM Digital ▲ DEN 75859 [DDD]
Schumann, R.:Gedichte, Op. 135, w. Nathalie Stutzmann (cta) — Erato ("Recital" series) ▲ 98505-2
Schumann, R.:Intro & Allegro appassionato, Op. 92, w. E. Inbal (cnd), Vienna SO — Denon/PCM Digital ▲ DEN 75859 [DDD]
Schumann, R.:Intro & Allegro, Op. 134, w. E. Inbal (cnd), Vienna SO — Denon/PCM Digital ▲ DEN 75859 [DDD]
Schumann, R.:Myrthen, w. Nathalie Stutzmann (cta) — Erato ("Recital" series) ▲ 98505-2
Strauss, R.:Burleske, w. J.-B. Pommier (cnd), Philharmonia Orch *(rec Jan. 29–31, 1992)* — Denon ▲ CO 75258 [DDD]

Dale, C. (vn)
Bach, J.S.:Con Vn, BWV 1058, w. J. Rees (cnd), Scottish Ensemble — Virgin Classics ▲ CDZ 59641
Bach, J.S.:Con for 2 Vns, w. J. Murdoch (vn), J. Rees (cnd), Scottish Ensemble — Virgin Classics ▲ CDZ 59641
Virgo Collections, w. J. Murdoch (vn), S. Heath (vc), Scottish Ensemble [cnd:J. Rees (vn)] — Virgin Classics ▲ CDZ 59652

Dalglish, M. (hammer dlc/sgr)
Dalglish, M.:Hymnody of Earth, w. G. Velez (perc), J. Litton (cnd), American Boychoir — MusicMasters ▲ 7058-2 [DDD] ■ 01612-67058-4 (D)

Dalheim, Eric (pno)
David Hickman, w. D. Hickman (tpt) — Crystal ■ C368
Dello Joio, N.:Son Tpt & Pno, w. D. Hickman (tpt) — Crystal ■ C368
Kennan, K.W.:Son Tpt, w. D. Hickman (tpt) — Crystal ■ C368

Dalitz, Joachim (org)
Poulenc, F.:Con Org, w. C.P. Flor (cnd), Berlin SO — Berlin Classics ▲ BER 2138 [DDD]
Saint-Saëns, C.:Sym 3, w. C.P. Flor (cnd), Berlin SO — Berlin Classics ▲ BER 2138 [DDD]

Dallapè, Adriano (org)—see ORCHESTRAS & ENSEMBLES Academy of Ancient Music Instumental Ensemble

Dalley, John (vn)—see ORCHESTRAS & ENSEMBLES Guarneri String Quartet

Dall'Olio, Gabriella (hp)
Turina, J.:Theme & Vars, Op. 100, w. J. de Udaeta (cnd), Granada City Orch — Claves ▲ CD 9215 [DDD]

Dalsgarò, E. (fl)
Rasmussen, S.:Music of, w. W. Gaffron (vn), A. Turner (vc), A. Klett (cl), P. Sõlstein (hn), J. Andreasen (pno), S.A. Johansen (cnd), *(orch unknown)*—"Warnings I"—The Naked Destruction — Tutl ▲ FKT 4

Dalton, James (org)
Bach, J.S.:Preludes & Fugues, BWV 531–552 [Frobenius Organ, Queen's College, Oxford] *(rec Aug. 1991 & 1992)* — Studio SM 2-▲ D 2447 [DDD]
Bach, J.S.:Toccata, Adagio & Fugue Org, BWV 564 [Frobenius Organ, Queen's College, Oxford] *(rec Aug. 1991 & 1992)* — Studio SM 2-▲ D 2447 [DDD]
Buxtehude, D.:Org Music (misc) [Frobenius Organ, Queen's College, Oxford] *(rec Aug. 1991 & 1992)* — Studio SM 2-▲ D 2447 [DDD]
Froberger, J.J.:Org Music [Frobenius Organ, Queen's College, Oxford] *(rec Aug. 1991 & 1992)* — Studio SM 2-▲ D 2447 [DDD]
Tunder, F.:Org Music [Frobenius Organ, Queen's College, Oxford] *(rec Aug. 1991 & 1992)* — Studio SM 2-▲ D 2447 [DDD]

Dambreville, Philippe (tpt)
Trumpet & Organ in St. Wandrille Abbey, w. Father M. Baumel (org) — Studio SM ▲ 12 18 58 [DDD]

Damerini, Massimiliano (pno)
Berecuse Lullaby Wiegenlied, w. Bima, Jeanne Marie (sop), Georg Mönch (vn) *(rec Roma, Italy, Feb 1987)* — Arts ▲ 447282-2 [DDD]
Franck, C.:Son Vn, w. Georg Mönch (vn) *(rec Rome, Italy, May 21–25, 1989)* — Arts Music ▲ 447106-2 [DDD]
Gershwin, G.:The George Gershwin Songbook — Musikstrasse 2-▲ 2106
Gershwin, G.:London Solos (10) — Musikstrasse 2-▲ 2106
Gershwin, G.:Preludes (3) Pno — Musikstrasse 2-▲ 2106
Gershwin, G.:Rhap in Blue [solo pno version] — Musikstrasse 2-▲ 2106
Gershwin, G.:Three-Quarter Blues — Musikstrasse 2-▲ 2106
Schubert, Franz:Minuet Pno, D.277a — Arts ▲ 47173-2 [DDD]
Schubert, Franz:Son Pno, D.279 — Arts ▲ 47173-2 [DDD]
Schubert, Franz:Son Pno, D.568 — Arts ▲ 47173-2 [DDD]
Sciarrino, S.:Pno Music (comp) — Dynamic ▲ CD 82 [DDD]

▲ = CD ♦ = Enhanced CD Δ = MD ■ = Cassette Tape □ = DCC

Damgaard, John (pno)—see also ORCHESTRAS & ENSEMBLES Tre Musici members, Tre Musici

Stolarczyk, W.:Earth Air Fire Water, w. Amalie Malling (pno), Anne Øland (pno), Teddy Teirup (pno), Friedrich Gürtler (pno), Rosalind Bevan (pno), Poul Rosenbaum (pno), Rodolfo Llambias (pno), Bella Horn–Ribera (pno), Anders Riber (pno), Elisabeth Sigurdsson (pno), Thomas Tronheim (pno), Elsebeth Broderson (pno), Erik Kaltoft (pno), Jørgen Hald Nielsen (pno), Aino Gilemann (pno), Birgit Kjær (pno), Jørgen Thomsen (pno), Gunhild Donslund (pno), Henrik Bo Hansen (pno), Lone Karlsson (pno), Erik Fessel (pno), Lasse Nilsson (pno), Janos Ferenczi (pno), Erik Bach (pno), Axel Momme (pno), Arne de Cros Dich (pno), Sven Micha Slot (pno), Hanne Bramsen Buhl (pno), Lili Olesen (pno), Susannah Carlsson (pno), Ulla Erml (pno), Vagn Sørensen (pno), Leif Greibe (pno), Bodil Krogh (pno), Kirsten Ottosen (pno), Inger Bergenholz (pno), Karsten Gylendorf (pno), Bjønr Elkjær (pno), Jacob Bjørn Jensen (pno), Jørgen Kaad (pno), Anne Marie Hjelm (pno), Carl Ulrik Munk Andersen (pno), Poul Lumbye (pno), Oluf Hildebrandt Nielsen (pno), Joachim Olsson (pno), Peter Pade Ramsøe Jacobsen (pno), Astrid Pollmann (pno), Jette Borsch (pno), Kirsten Karlshøj (pno), Maria Teresa Assing (pno), Allan Dahl Hansen (pno), Johan Hugossen (pno), Tine Fenger Pederson (pno), Arne Jørgen Fæø (pno), Anja Høgsted (pno), Anne Sophie Parbo (pno), Inga Lindmark (pno), Teresa Drabik Stathakis (pno), Anne Ruth Ferenczi (pno), Irene Hasager (pno), Yuka Ichikawa (pno), Birgitte Baur (pno), Malene Thastum (pno), Jens E. Rasmussen (pno), Birgitte Zielke (pno), Claus Zielke (pno), Stefan Kasch (pno), Bin Qiao (pno), Inger Johanne Teirup (pno), Lindy Rosborg (pno), Liisa Heininen (pno), David Højer (pno), Ellen Refstrup (pno), Thomas K. Søorensen (pno), Erik Kure (pno), Michael Rauff (pno), Jan beck Eriksson (pno), Tanja Zapolski (pno), Vibeke Skagbo (pno), Pål Eide Lindtner (pno), Ha–Young Sul (pno), Benedicte Palko (pno), Inke Kesseler (pno), Anne Marie Meineche (pno), Sverre Larsen (pno), Kasper Peter Bach (pno), Elisabetta Eliseo (pno), Olga Magieres (pno), Carl Erik Kühl (pno), Thorkild Borup Nielsen (pno), Valeria Zanini (pno), Lars Stenhoft (perc), Dennis Boel (perc), Winnie Dahlgren (perc), Susanne Vind (perc), Claus Byrith (elec), Anne Marie Storm (elec), J. Ribera (cnd) *(rec live, Koldinghaus Castle, Denmark, May 2, 1996)* Danica ▲ DCD 1996

Dami, Magali (rcr)—see ORCHESTRAS & ENSEMBLES Isabella D'Este

Damiano, Daniele (bn)—see ORCHESTRAS & ENSEMBLES Berlin Philharmonic Wind Ensemble

Beethoven, L. van:Qnt Pno, Ob, Cl, Hn & Bn, w. D. Barenboim (pno), H. Schellenberger (ob), L. Combs (cl), D. Clevenger (hn) Erato ▲ 96359–2

Mozart, W.A.:Qnt Pno, K.452, w. D. Barenboim (pno), H. Schellenberger (ob), L. Combs (cl), D. Clevenger (hn) Erato ▲ 96359–2

Damien, Marie–Noelle (pno)

Prokofiev, S.:Sarcasms Masters of Art ▲ AAOC–9379

Prokofiev, S.:Son 2 Pno Masters of Art ▲ AAOC–9379

Prokofiev, S.:Son 6 Pno Masters of Art ▲ AAOC–9379

Damiens, Alain (cl)

Amy, G.:Trio Cl, w. Maryvonne Le Dizes (vn), Pierre–Laurent Aimard (pno) Adda ▲ ADD 581142 [DDD]

Bartók, B.:Contrasts, w. Maryvonne Le Dizes (vn), Pierre–Laurent Aimard (pno) Adda ▲ ADD 581142 [DDD]

Berg, A.:Adagio, w. Maryvonne Le Dizes (vn), Pierre–Laurent Aimard (pno) Adda ▲ ADD 581142 [DDD]

Boulez, P.:Dialogue de l'ombre double Erato ▲ 2292–45648–2 [DDD]

Lachenmann, H.:Allegro sostenuto, w. Pierre–Laurent Aimard (pno), Pierre Strauch (vc) Accord ▲ ACD 202082 [DDD]

Lachenmann, H.:Dal niente Accord ▲ ACD 202082 [DDD]

Stravinsky, I.:L'Histoire du soldat Suite Vn, w. Maryvonne Le Dizes (vn), Pierre–Laurent Aimard (pno) Adda ▲ ADD 581142 [DDD]

Damm, Peter (hn)

Brahms, J.:Trio Hn, w. J. Suk (vn), W. Genuit (pno) Acanta ▲ CD 43270 [DDD]

Mozart, W.A.:Cons Hn, w. N. Marriner (cnd), Academy of St. Martin in the Fields Philips ▲ 422330–2 [DDD]

Schumann, R.:Konzertstück Hns, w. H. Märker (hn), W. Pilz (hn), G. Böhner (hn), F. Konwitschny (cnd), Leipzig Gewandhaus Orch *(rec 1960–61)* Berlin Classics ("Eterna" series) 3–▲ BER 2016 [ADD]

Strauss, R.:Con 1 Hn, w. R. Kempe (cnd), Dresden Staatskapelle EMI Classics 3–▲ CDZC 64342

Strauss, R.:Con 2 Hn, w. R. Kempe (cnd), Dresden Staatskapelle EMI Classics 3–▲ CDZC 64342

Damonico, C. (db)

Bolling, C.:California Suite, w. H. Laws (fl), C. Bolling (pno), S. Manne (perc) CBS ▲ MK 36691

Damsté, Marjan (db)

Andriessen, L.:Ittrospezione 3, w. Gerard Bouwhuis (pno), Sepp Grotenhuis (pno), Peter van Bergen (sax), H. Williams (cnd), Netherlands Ballet Orch *(rec Amsterdam Music Theater, Oct 3–6, 1994)* Donemus ▲ CV 54 [DDD]

Damzel, Hans (cl)

Togni, C.:Gesang zur Nacht, w. Carla Henius (alt), Saschko Gawriloff (vn), Werner Heider (pno), Mariolina de Robertis (pno) Stradivarius ▲ STV DTM 90002 [ADD]

Dan, P. (pno)

Bacewicz, G.:Son 4 Vn & Pno, w. W. Wilkomiska (vn) *(rec 1988)* Ambitus ▲ 97830 [DDD]

Bargielski, Z.:Neo–Sonatina, w. W. Wilkomiska (vn) *(rec 1988)* Ambitus ▲ 97830 [DDD]

Padorowski, I.J.:Son Vn, w. W. Wilkomiska (vn) *(rec 1988)* Ambitus ▲ 97830 [DDD]

Zarycki, A.:Mazurka Vn, w. W. Wilkomiska (vn) *(rec 1988)* Ambitus ▲ 97830 [DDD]

Danby, Nicholas (org)

Buxtehude, D.:Org Music (misc)—Canzonetta in a, BuxWV 225; Passacaglia in d, BuxWV 161; Ten Chorales (BuxWV 178, 186, 189, 197, 201, 204, 208, 211, 217, 220); Four Preludes (in C, BuxWV 138; in D, BuxWV 139; in g, BuxWV 148; in a, BuxWV 153); Toccata in F, BuxWV 156; Toccata in G, BuxWV 164 Virgin Classics ▲ 59212 [DDD]

Franck, C.:Org Music (misc) Virgin Classics ▲ CDC 59010

Danchev, Dimiter (vn)—see ORCHESTRAS & ENSEMBLES Academic Chamber Ensemble

Danczowska, Kaja (vn)—see ORCHESTRAS & ENSEMBLES Wawelskie Trio

Dandolo, Andrea (gtr)

Giardini, F.:Chamber Music, w. Pian e Forte Ensemble—Sons. & Trios w. Guitar Nuova Era ("Ancient Music" series) ▲ NUO 7186 [DDD]

Noferi, G.B.:Chamber Music, w. Pian e Forte Ensemble—Sons. & Trios w. Guitar Nuova Era ("Ancient Music" series) ▲ NUO 7186 [DDD]

Danel, Guy (vc)—see ORCHESTRAS & ENSEMBLES Danel String Quartet

Danel, Juliette (va)—see ORCHESTRAS & ENSEMBLES Danel String Quartet

Danel, Marc (vn)—see also ORCHESTRAS & ENSEMBLES Danel String Quartet

de Clerck, P.:Già, w. Jean–Marie Bardèche (pno) *(rec Ravenstein Hall, May & June 1994)* Megadisc ▲ 7866

Dangain, Guy (cl)

Debussy, C.:Première rapsodie, w. J. Martinon (cnd), French National RSO EMI Classics ▲ CDM 69668

Dangain, Serge (cl)

Debussy, C.:Première rapsodie, w. L. de Froment (cnd), Luxembourg RSO *(rec 1972)* Vox Box 2–▲ CDX 5053 [ADD]

Weber, C.M. von:Con 1 Cl, w. L. de Froment (cnd), Luxembourg Radio–TV SO Forlane ▲ FRL 9 [AAD]

Weber, C.M. von:Con 2 Cl, w. L. de Froment (cnd), Luxembourg Radio–TV SO Forlane ▲ FRL 9 [AAD]

Dangel, Ronald (db)

Mieg, P.:Septet, w. Peter Solomon (hpd), Günter Rumpel (fl), Simon Fuchs (ob), Primroz Novsak (vn), Marius Ungareanu (va), Carolyn Hopkins Marti (vc) *(rec 1993)* Jecklin ▲ JS 314–2 [DDD]

Daniel, Nicholas (E hn)

Alwyn, W.:Autumn Legend, w. R. Hickox (cnd), City of London Sinfonia Chandos ▲ CHAN 9065 [DDD]

Alwyn, W.:Con Ob, w. R. Hickox (cnd), City of London Sinfonia Chandos ▲ CHAN 8866 [DDD]

Daniel, Nicholas (ob)—see also ORCHESTRAS & ENSEMBLES Daniel Trio

Debussy, C.:Chamber Music, w. William Bennett (fl), David Campbell (cl), James Campbell (cl), Robert Makell (hn), Richard Watkins (hn), Robin Kennard (bn), Rachel Gough (bn), Simon Haram (sax), Ieuan Jones (hp), Clifford Benson (pno), Julius Drake (pno), John York (pno), Roger Tapping (va)—Rapsodie for Eng hn; Syrinx; Première rapsodie; Son for Fl, Va & Hp; Le petit nègre; Petite pièce; Rapsodie for Sax *(rec All Saints' Church, East Finchley, London, Jan 12–20, 1994)* Cala 2–▲ CACD 1017 [DDD]

Daniel, Nicholas (ob) (cont.)

Mozart, W.A.:Qt Ob, w. Lindsay String Quartet ASV ▲ ASV CD 968

Oboe Alone Léman Classics ▲ LC 42801 [DDD]

Poulenc, F.:Chamber Music, w. Peter Sidhom (bar), William Bennett (fl), David Campbell (cl), James Campbell (cl), Richard Watkins (hn), Rachel Gough (bn), Peter Carter (vn), Chris West (db), Ieuan Jones (hp), Clifford Benson (pno), Julius Drake (pno), John York (pno)—Son for Ob; L'invitation au château; Villanelle; Son 2 Cls; Trio; Sxt; Son for Cl & Bn; Rapsodie nègre; Son for Cl; Mouvements perpétuels; Son for Fl *(rec All Saints' Church, East Finchley, London, Jan 12–20, 1994)* Cala ▲ CACD 1018 [DDD]

Saint–Saëns, C.:Chamber Music, w. W. Bennett (fl), D. Campbell (cl), J. Campbell (cl), R. Makell (hn), R. Watkins (hn), R. Kennard (bn), R. Gough (bn), S. Haram (sax), I. Jones (hp), C. Benson (pno), J. Drake (pno), J. York (pno), R. Tapping (va)—Odelette, Op. 162; Son for Cl, Op. 167; Feuillet d'album, Op. 81; Son for Bn, Op. 168; Caprice on Danish & Russian Airs, Op. 79; Son for Ob, Op. 166; Romance in D♭, Op. 37; Tarantelle, Op. 6 *(rec All Saints' Church, East Finchley, London, Jan 12–20, 1994)* Cala 2–▲ CACD 1017 [DDD]

Strauss, R.:Con Ob, w. R. Hickox (cnd), City of London Sinfonia Chandos ▲ CHAN 9286 [DDD]

Daniels, David (vc)—see ORCHESTRAS & ENSEMBLES Lyric String Quartet

Daniels, Eddie (cl)—see also ORCHESTRAS & ENSEMBLES Trio di Clarone

Brahms, J.:Qnt Cl, w. Composers String Quartet Reference ▲ RR 40CD [DDD]

Gershwin, G.:Music of, w. D. Grusin, G. Burton (cl), L. Ritenour, J. Pattitucci— instrumental jazz improvisations on 14 Gershwin tunes:That certain feeling; Soon; Fascinating rhythm; Prelude II; How long has this been going on?; There's a boat dat's leavin' soon for New York; My man's gone now; Maybe; Our love is here to stay; 'S Wonderful; I've got plenty o' nuthin; Nice work if you can get it; Medley (Bess, you is my woman now/I loves you, Porgy) GRP ▲ GRD 2005 [ADD]

Vivaldi, A.:Cons Vn, Op. 8/1–4, "The Four Seasons", w. Peter Erskine (dr), Alan Broadbent (pno), Dave Carpenter (db) *(rec California State University, Long Beach, CA, Mar 15, 1996)* Shanachie ▲ SHA 5017 ■ SHA 5017

Weber, C.M. von:Qnt Cl, w. Composers String Quartet Reference ▲ RR 40CD [DDD]

Danielson, Glen (E hn)

Piston, W.:Fant E Hn, w. T. E. Wunrow (hp), G. Schwarz (cnd), Seattle SO *(rec Jan. 27–28, 1992)* Delos ▲ DE 3126 [DDD]

Danilina, Natalia (fl)

Ustvolskaya, G.:Composition 3, w. Maria Osipova (fl), Inna Rodina (fl), Michail Tokarev (fl), Kirill Sokolov (bn), Dmitrii Krasnik (bn), Arsenii Makarov (bn), Konstantin Shevchuk (bn), Galina Sandovskaya (pno), O. Malov (cnd) *(rec St. Petersburg Radio House, Jan. 1994)* Megadisc ▲ 7867

Danilow, Marji (db)—see ORCHESTRAS & ENSEMBLES Mozzafiato

Dankworth, Alec (db)

Ellington, D.:Mainly Black, w. N. Kennedy (vn) [arr Kennedy] EMI Classics ▲ CDC 47621 [ADD]

Dann, Klaus–Ulrich (tpt)

Orgel & Trompete in Landsberg, w. Dann, Klaus–Ulrich (tpt), Johannes Skudlik (org) Ambitus ▲ AMB 97870 [DDD]

Dann, Steven (va)

Hatzis, C.:The Mega4 Meta4 *(rec 1993)* Centrediscs ▲ CMCCD 4693 [DDD]

Mozart, W.A.:Sinf concertante Vn, K.364, w. J. Israelievitch (vn), M. Bernardi (cnd), CBC Vancouver SO CBC ("SM 5000" series) ▲ SMCD 5133 [DDD]

Portriat of the Viola, w. Bruce Vogt (pno) Musica Viva ▲ MVCD 1072 [DDD]

Ridout, G.:Orch Music, w. V. Feldbrill (cnd), Toronto SO—Ballade No. 1 for Violin & String Orchestra; Cantiones Mysticae No. 1; Music for a Young Prince; No Mean City—Scenes from Childhood; La Prima Ballerina Suite No. 1 CBC ▲ CMCCD 3890 [DDD]

Schubert, Franz:Qnt Strs, D.956, w. L. Rautenberg (vn), J. Gatwood (vn), A. Bylsma (vc), K. Slowick (vc) Sony Classical ("Vivarte" series) ▲ SK 46669

Weinzweig, J.:Tremologue *(rec live, Walter Hall, Univ. of Toronto, Mar. 11, 1993)* Centrediscs ▲ CMC 5295 [DDD]

Danovitch, Gerald (sax)

The Gerald Danovitch Saxophone Quartet Musica Viva ▲ MVCD 1018 [DDD]

Dantone, Ottavio (hpd)

Bach, J.S.:Sons Fl, BWV 1030–35, w. S. Bagliano (rcr)—in c, BWV 1030 [trans. Dantone & Bagliano]; in C, BWV 1032 [trans. Reinhald Gerlach & Dantone] *(rec June 1993)* Dynamic ▲ CDS 77 [DDD]

Bach, J.S.:Trio Sons Org, BWV 525–530, w. S. Bagliano (rcr)—in d, BWV 527 & in F, BWV 527 [trans. Dantone & Bagliano] *(rec June 1993)* Dynamic ▲ CDS 77 [DDD]

Derasse, Xavier (org)

Albinoni, T.:Adagio Org, w. L. Auriacombe (cnd), Toulouse CO *(rec Chapelle des Italiens, Toulouse, Jan 1968)* EMI Classics ▲ CDK 65337 [ADD]

Darden, George (pno)

Sings Favorite Spirituals, w. W. Fernandez (sop) Kem–Disc ▲ 1010 [DDD]

Dardyikin, Alexander (vc)

Tchaikovsky, P.:Ballet Music, w. Olga Vedernikova (vn), Anna Verkholanzeva (hp), A. Vedernikov (cnd), Russian Philharmonia—ballet suites from Swan Lake; Sleeping Beauty; Nutcracker *(rec Moscow Conservatory Large Hall, Feb 1996)* Arts ▲ 47372–2 [DDD]

Darling, D. (vc/elec vc/syn/sgr)

Darling, D.:Blessings:A Prayer for the Planet, w. P.E. Clark (sop), C.B. Rowe (sop), W. Zukof (ct), L. Bennett (ten), W.L. Lee (ten), E. Levine (bar) Western Wind ▲ WW 2001

Darling, D.:Blessings (sels), w. P.E. Clark (sop), C.B. Rowe (sop), W. Zukof (ct), L. Bennett (ten), W.L. Lee (ten), E. Levine (bar) Western Wind ▲ WW 2001

Darling, James S. (org)

At the Huguenot Church, Charleston, South Carolina Organ Historical Society ■ OHSC 7

Historic Organs of New Orleans, w. George Bozeman (org), Jesse E. Eschbach (org), Gerald D. Frank (org), John Gearhart (org), James Hammann (org), Frederick Hohman (org), Lenora McCroskey (org), Mary Gifford Matthys (org), Lorenz Maycher (org), Donald Messer (org) *(rec June 1989)* Organ Historical Society 2–▲ OHS 89

Darlington, Mahlon (vn)—see also ORCHESTRAS & ENSEMBLES Ames Piano Quartet

Strauss, R.:Qt Pno, w. W. David (pno), L. Burkhalter (va), G. Work (vc) *(rec Oct. 1991)* Dorian ▲ DOR 90167 [DDD]

Widor, C.M.:Qt Pno, w. W. David (pno), L. Burkhalter (va), G. Work (vc) *(rec Oct. 1991)* Dorian ▲ DOR 90167 [DDD]

Darré, Jeanne–Marie (pno)

Chopin, F.:Berceuse *(rec Palais Schönburg, Vienna, June 24 & 25, 1965)* Vanguard Classics ▲ OVC 8092 [ADD]

Chopin, F.:Fant *(rec Palais Schönburg, Vienna, June 24 & 25, 1965)* Vanguard Classics ▲ OVC 8092 [ADD]

Chopin, F.:Preludes, Op. 28 *(rec Palais Schönburg, Vienna, June 24 & 25, 1965)* Vanguard Classics ▲ OVC 8092 [ADD]

The Early Recordings, w. J.–M. Darré (pno), Paris Conservatory Orch [cnd:A. Cluytens], Colonne Concerts Orch [cnd:P. Paray] *(rec between 1922 & 1947)* VAI Audio 2–▲ VAIA/IPA 1065 (m) [ADD]

Dartel, Norman van (perc)—see ORCHESTRAS & ENSEMBLES Percussive Rotterdam

Dartigolles, Jean–Bernard (pno)

Debussy, C.:Songs, w. Francis Dudziak (bar)—Trois chansons de France [Le temps a laissé son manteau; La grotte; Pour ce que plaisance est morte]; Mandoline; Fêtes galantes II [Les ingénus; Le faune; Colloque sentimental]; Trois mélodies de Paul Verlaine [La mer est plus belle; Le son du cor s'afflige; L'échelonnement des haies]; Huit d'étoiles; Aimons–nous et dormons; Trois ballades de François Villon [Villon à sa mie; Prière à Nostre Dame; Des femmes de Paris]; La belle au bois dormant; Beau soir; Le cloches; Romance; Le promenoir des deux amants [Auprès de cette grotte sombre; Crois mon conseil, Chère Climène; Je tremble en voyant ton visage]; Le Noël des enfants qui n'ont plus de maison Accord ▲ ACD 202302

Dartigolles, Jean-Bernard (pno) (cont.)
Massenet, J.:Songs, w. Catherine Dubosc (sop), Francis Dudziak (bar), Syrille Lacrouts (vc)—Quelques chansons mauves; Dans le sentier, parmi les roses; Tu l'as bien dit; Roses d'Octobre; A Colombine [Sérénade d'Arlequin]; Sérénade de Molière [Musique du temps]; Marquise! [Menuet pour chant]; Les alcyons; Voic que les grands lys; Poème d'amour; L'improvisateur [Souvenir du Transtévère]; Nuit d'Espagne; Elégie; Déclaration; A mignonne; Souhait; Un adieu; Sérénade d'automne; Sonnet; Si tu veux, mignonne; Pensée d'automne; Soir de rêve; On dit; Souvenez-vous, Vierge Marie! Accord ▲ ACD 201632 [DDD]

Ascoli, Bernard d' (pno)
Chopin, F.:Andante Spianato & Grande Polonaise Nimbus ▲ NI 5249 [DDD]
Chopin, F.:Ballades Pno (comp) Nimbus ▲ NI 5249 [DDD]
Chopin, F.:Berceuse Nimbus ▲ NI 5249 [DDD]
Chopin, F.:Pno Music (misc)—Nocturne in c#, Op. posth.; Tarantelle in Ab, Op. 43 Nimbus ▲ NI 5249 [DDD]
Schumann, R.:Carnaval Pno Nimbus ▲ NI 5170 [DDD]
Schumann, R.:Fantasiestücke Pno, Op. 111 Nimbus ▲ NI 5170 [DDD]
Schumann, R.:Papillons Nimbus ▲ NI 5170 [DDD]

Dash, Patricia (perc)
Cahn, W.:Partita Nexus ▲ 10339 [DDD]

Datyner, Harry (pno)
Marescotti, A.-F.:Fantasque Grammont ▲ CTSP 13-2

Daucher, Elmar (steinklänge)
Stahmer, K.H.:Hommage à Daidalos, w. Dietburg Spohr (cnd), Belcanto Ensemble Frankfurt *(rec Munich, Oct 1989)* Pro Viva ▲ ISPV 159 [DDD]
Vetter, M.:Music of, w. Dietburg Spohr (cnd), Belcanto Ensemble Frankfurt—Music aus Stein [improvisation]; Steinklänge *(rec Munich, Oct 1989)* Pro Viva ▲ ISPV 159 [DDD]

Daugareil, Roland (vn)
Chausson, E.:Con Vn, Pno & Str Qt, w. R. Pasquier (vn), G. Simonot (vn), B. Pasquier (va), R. Pidoux (vc), J.-C. Pennetier (pno) Harmonia Mundi Plus ▲ HMP 3901135
Chausson, E.:Poème Vn, w. A. Lombard (cnd), Bordeaux-Aquitaine National Orch Forlane ▲ FRL 16723 [DDD]
Ladmirault, P.:Son Vn, w. Robert Plantard (pno) *(rec Nantes National Conservatory Auditorium, 1980)* Skarbo ▲ SK 4952 [ADD]
Lalo, E.:Sym espagnole, w. A. Lombard (cnd), Bordeaux-Aquitaine National Orch Forlane ▲ FRL 16723 [DDD]

Daugherty, M. (syn/sampling kbds)
Daugherty, M.:Celestial Hoops IV Opus One ▲ 138

Dauppinen, Pekka (vn)
Sibelius, J.:Adagio Vn, Folkwang CO Koch Schwann ▲ SCH 317862
Sibelius, J.:Suite Vn Strs, Folkwang CO Koch Schwann ▲ SCH 317862

Dautricourt, Jean-Pierre (fl)
Tcherepnin, I.:Songs Cta, w. Marion Dry (cta), Ivan Tcherepnin (elecs) *(rec Harvard University Electronic Music Studio, Oct. & Dec. 1981)* CRI ▲ CD 684 [ADD]

David, E.-J. (hp)
Saint-Saëns, C.:Fant Vn, w. N. Mastero (hp) *(rec 1988)* FSM-Adagio ▲ FCD 97722 [DDD]

David, Nima Ben (vl)
Marais, M.:Tombeau pour Monsieur de Ste Colombe, w. Maurice Buraglia (thb) Astrée ▲ E 8592

David, W. (pno)—see also ORCHESTRAS & ENSEMBLES Ames Piano Quartet
Strauss, R.:Qt Pno, w. M. Darlington (vn), L. Burkhalter (va), G. Work (vc) *(rec Oct. 1991)* Dorian ▲ DOR 90167 [DDD]
Widor, C.M.:Qt Pno, w. M. Darlington (vn), L. Burkhalter (va), G. Work (vc) *(rec Oct. 1991)* Dorian ▲ DOR 90167 [DDD]

Davidoff, Judith (trb vl/b vl)—see ORCHESTRAS & ENSEMBLES New York Consort of Viols

Davidovich, Bella (pno)
Grieg, E.:Con Pno, Op. 16, w. G. Schwarz (cnd), Seattle SO Delos ▲ DE 3091 [DDD]
Grieg, E.:Sons Vn, Opp. 8, 13 & 45, w. D. Sitkovetsky (vn) Orfeo ▲ 047831 [DDD]
Rachmaninoff, S.:Rhapsody on a Theme of Paganini, w. N. Järvi (cnd), Royal Concertgebouw Orch Philips ▲ 410052-2 [DDD]
Ravel, M.:Berceuse sur le nom de Gabriel Fauré, w. D. Sitkovetsky (vn) Orfeo ▲ 108841 [DDD] ■ M 108841A (D)
Ravel, M.:Son Vn Pno, w. D. Sitkovetsky (vn) Orfeo ▲ 108841 [DDD] ■ M 108841A (D)
Ravel, M.:Sonate posthume, w. D. Sitkovetsky (vn) Orfeo ▲ 108841 [DDD] ■ M 108841A (D)
Ravel, M.:Tzigane, w. D. Sitkovetsky (vn) [violin-piano version] Orfeo ▲ 108841 [DDD] ■ M 108841A (D)
Saint-Saëns, C.:Con 2 Pno, w. N. Järvi (cnd), Royal Concertgebouw Orch Philips ▲ 410052-2 [DDD]

Davidovici, Robert (vn)
Aitken, H.:Partita Vn New World ▲ 80334-2 [DDD]
Austin, L.:Montage:Themes & Vars Centaur ▲ CRC 2110 [DDD]
Conyngham, B.:Southern Cross, w. Tamás Ungár (pno), G. Simon (cnd), London SO *(rec St Jude-on-the-Hill, Hampstead Garden Suburb, London, Apr 2-4, 1990)* Cala ▲ CACD 1008 [DDD]
Copland, A.:Nocturne, w. S. de Groote (pno) New World ▲ NW 334-2 [DDD]
Piston, W.:Sonatina Vn, w. de Groote (pno) New World ▲ NW 334-2 [DDD]
Schoenfield, P.:Country Fiddle Pieces, w. P. Schoenfield (pno) New World ▲ NW 334-2 [DDD]
Schuller, G.:Recitative & Rondo, w. A. De Groote (pno) New World ▲ NW 334-2 [DDD]
Subotnick, M.:Trembling, w. A. Wodnicki (pno), J. La Barbara (recorded voc), L. Austin ("Ghost" elec) *(rec Dec. 1992)* Centaur ▲ CRC 2170 [DDD]

Davidson, Beverly (vc)
Bourland, R.:Sax Qnt, w. Al Regni (s sax), Laura Seton (vn), Mark Feldman (vn), Lois Martin (va) Open Loop ▲ 034 [DDD]

Davidson, D. (vn)
Rorem, N.:Hearing, w. R. Rees (sop), K. Wheeler (mez), M. Galloway (ten), R. Hilley (bar), R. Wagner (cl), J. Hamlin (tpt), D. Starobin (mand), K. Askew (va), J. Babich (db), P. Suits (pno), D. Druckman (perc), G. Smith (cnd) Premier ▲ PRCD 1035 [ADD]

Davidson, Jerry (pno)
Etler, A.:Son Bn, w. David DeBolt (bn) Crystal ▲ CD 347
Garfield, B.:Poème, w. David DeBolt (bn) Crystal ▲ CD 347

Davidson, Kevin (va)
Johnson, Roger:Invention II Opus One ▲ CD 169

Davidson-Kelly, K. (pno)—see ORCHESTRAS & ENSEMBLES Piano Circus

Davidsson, Christian (bn)
Danzi, F.:Con Bn, w. N. Willén (cnd), Sundsvall CO *(rec Tonhallen, Sundsvall, Sweden, Dec. 5-10, 1994)* BIS ▲ CD 705 [DDD]
Hummel, J.N.:Con Bn, w. N. Willén (cnd), Sundsvall CO *(rec Tonhallen, Sundsvall, Sweden, Dec. 5-10, 1994)* BIS ▲ CD 705 [DDD]
Jolivet, A.:Fl Music (comp), w. Manuela Wiesler (fl), Erica Goodman (hp), Patrik Swedrup (vn), Håkan Olsson (va), Helena Nilsson (vc), Roland Pöntinen (pno), P. Järvi (cnd), Tapiola Sinfonietta, Kroumata Percussion Ensemble—Alla rustica for Fl & Hp; Chant de Linos for Fl, Hp & Str Trio; Pastorales de Noël for Fl, Bn & Hp; Con for Fl & Str; Suite en concert for Fl & 4 Perc Players; Fant-Caprice for Fl & Pno; Cabrioles for Fl & Pno *(rec Danderyd Grammar School, Sweden, Tapiola Hall, Tapiola, Finland, Gothenburg Concert Hall, Sweden & Studio 2, Radiohuset, Stockholm, Sweden)* BIS ▲ CD 739 [DDD]
Puteanus, E.:Quintetto Bn, w. N. Willén (cnd), Sundsvall CO *(rec Tonhallen, Sundsvall, Sweden, Dec. 5-10, 1994)* BIS ▲ CD 705 [DDD]
Schnittke, A.:Hymns Vc, w. Torleff Thedéen (vc), Entcho Rdoukanov (db), Ingegerd Fredlund (hp), M. Kamata (hpd), Anders Holdar (tubular bells/timp), Anders Loguin (tubular bells) BIS ("BIS Twins" series) 2-▲ CD 437/507
Schnittke, A.:Hymns Vc, w. T. Thedéen (vc), E. Radoukanov (db), I. Fredlund (hp), M. Kamata (hpd), A. Holdar (tubular bells / timp), A. Loguin (tubular bells) BIS ▲ CD 507 [DDD]

Davidsson, Christian (bn) (cont.)
Weber, C.M. von:Andante & Rondo ungarese Bn, w. N. Willén (cnd), Sundsvall CO *(rec Tonhallen, Sundsvall, Sweden, Dec. 5-10, 1994)* BIS ▲ CD 705 [DDD]

Davidsson, Hans (org)
Weckmann, M.:Org Music [reconstructed Arp Schnitger organ in Norden, Germany; performances are based on a critical study of all manuscript sources]—Chorale Settings, 4 Canzoni, 2 Preludes, Fantasia, Fugue & Toccata Motette 2-▲ DCD 11461 [DDD] ■ DCD 114

Davies, Dennis Russell (pno)
Copland, A.:Qt Pno, w. R. Tecco (vn), K. Harrison (va), L. Duckles (vc) MusicMasters ▲ 7026-2-C [DDD]
Copland, A.:Son Vn & Pno, w. R. Tecco (vn) MusicMasters ▲ 7026-2-C [DDD]
Copland, A.:Vitebsk:Study on a Jewish Theme, w. R. Tecco (vn), L. Duckles (vc) MusicMasters ▲ 7026-2-C [DDD]
Curtis-Smith, C.:Sextet Pno, w. Stuttgart Wind Quintet Albany ▲ TROY 148 [DDD]
Haas, P.:The Chosen One, w. Jörg Dürmüller (ten), Willy Freivogel (fl), Friedhelm Pütz (hn), Monika Hölszky-Wiedemann (vn) Orfeo ("Musica Rediviva" series) ▲ 386961 [DDD]
Haas, P.:Suite Ob, w. Sigurd Michael (ob) [rev František Suchy] Orfeo ("Musica Rediviva" series) ▲ 386961 [DDD]
Haas, P.:Suite Pno [rev Bernard Kaff] Orfeo ("Musica Rediviva" series) ▲ 386961 [DDD]
Harrison, L.:Grand Duo, w. Romuald Tecco (vn) *(rec. Cabrillo Music Festival, Santa Cruz, CA, 1988)* MusicMasters ▲ 7073-2-C [DDD]

Davies, Fanny (pno)
Schumann, R.:Con Pno, w. E. Ansermet (cnd), Royal PO Pearl 6-▲ PEA 99049 (m) [AAD]

Davies, Harriet (vn)—see ORCHESTRAS & ENSEMBLES Lyric String Quartet

Davies, Marion (vc)—see ORCHESTRAS & ENSEMBLES Lyric Art String Quartet

Davies, Oliver (pno)
The Art of the Clarinettist:Fantaisies & Paraphrases for Clarinet & Piano, w. C. Bradbury (cl) Clarinet Classics 2-▲ CC 0008
The Bel Canto Clarinettist, w. C. Bradbury (cl) *(rec St. George's Brandon Hill, Bristol)* Clarinet Classics ▲ CC 0014 [DDD]

Davies, Philippa (fl)
Debussy, C.:Son Fl, w. R. Chase (va), Marisa Robles (hp) Virgin Classics ▲ 59604 [DDD]
Debussy, C.:Syrinx Virgin Classics ▲ 59604 [DDD]
Mozart, W.A.:Con Fl, K.313, w. J. Glover (cnd), London Mozart Players ASV ▲ ASV 795 [DDD]
Mozart, W.A.:Con Fl Hp, w. Rachel Masters (hp), R. Hickox (cnd), City of London Sinfonia IMP ▲ IMP 2011

Davies, Richard (fl)
Fauré, G.:Fant Fl, w. Y. P. Tortelier (cnd), BBC PO Chandos ▲ CHAN 9416 [DDD]

Davies, William (org)
Johnson, Laurie:Music of, w. L. Johnson (cnd), London PO, London Jazz Orch, London Studio SO, Coldstream Guards Regimental Band, Fanfare Trumpeters of the Scots Guards, London Brass Chorale—Royal Tour (suite); Symphony (Synthesis) for Combined Jazz & Symphony Orchestras (1969); Three Paintings by Lautrec; The Wind In the Willows (1985) *(rec 1969-82)* Unicorn-Kanchana ▲ UKCD 2057 [DDD/ADD]

Davine, Robert (acc)
Encore, w. Colorado Children's Chorale [cnd:Duain Wolfe], Rick Chinski (gtr), Laurie Kahler (pno), Samuel Lancaster (pno), Barry Oliver (pno), Marylin Preston (fl), Karen Yonovitz (fl), Peter Cooper (ob), Andy Stevens (cl), Lionel Young (vn), Basil Vendreys (va), Wayne Templeman (vc), et al. *(rec Denver Center Media)* Colorado Children's Chorale ▲ 001

Davis (pno)
Grieg, E.:Ballade Pno Audiofon ▲ CD 72022
Grieg, E.:Holberg Suite [original piano version] Audiofon ▲ CD 72022
Grieg, E.:Lyric Pieces—Op. 12/1; Op. 43/1,4,5; Op. 62/4 Audiofon ▲ CD 72022
Plog, A.:Animal Ditties 2, w. Smith (spkr), A. Plog (tpt) Crystal ▲ CD 663 [DDD]
Stevens, H.:Son Tpt, w. A. Plog (tpt) Crystal ▲ CD 663 [DDD]

Davis, A. (org)
Holst, G.:The Planets, w. A. David (cnd), BBC SO, BBC Sym Women's Chorus *(rec London, Dec. 1993)* Teldec ▲ 94541-2 [DDD]

Davis, Andrew (org)
At Roy Thomson Hall [Toronto, Canada], w. Davis, Andrew (org) Marquis Classics ▲ ERAD 109 [DDD]
Bach, J.S.:Chorale Preludes Org—Wachet Auf, Ruft uns Die Stimme, BWV 645 [org at Roy Thompson Hall, Toronto] IMP ("IMP Classics" series) ▲ IMP 6700942
Bach, J.S.:Toccata & Fugue Org, BWV 565 [org at Roy Thompson Hall, Toronto] IMP ("IMP Classics" series) ▲ IMP 6700942
Franck, C.:Prélude, fugue et var [org at Roy Thompson Hall, Toronto] IMP ("IMP Classics" series) ▲ IMP 6700942
Handel, G.F.:Chandos Anthems (11), w. April Cantelo (sop), Ian Partridge (ten), D. Willcocks (cnd), Academy of St. Martin in the Fields, King's College Choir Cambridge—No. 10 only *(rec Chapel of King's College, Cambridge, 1967)* London 2-▲ 443470-2 [ADD]
Ives, C.:Vars on *America* [org at Roy Thompson Hall, Toronto] IMP ("IMP Classics" series) ▲ IMP 6700942
Messiaen, O.:Ascension—Transports de Joie d'une Âme Devant la Gloire du Christ Qui Est Sienne [org at Roy Thompson Hall, Toronto] IMP ("IMP Classics" series) ▲ IMP 6700942
Purcell, H.:Cortege Academique [org at Roy Thompson Hall, Toronto] IMP ("IMP Classics" series) ▲ IMP 6700942
Purcell, H.:Tpt Tune [org at Roy Thompson Hall, Toronto] IMP ("IMP Classics" series) ▲ IMP 6700942

Davis, Andrew (pno)
The Art of Maureen Forrester, w. M. Forrester (cta) Mastersound ▲ DFCDI 212 [DDD]
Duets:Ofra Harnoy & Friends, w. O. Harnoy (vc), Michael Dussek (pno), Orford String Quartet, Maureen Forrester (cta), Jeanne Baxtresser (fl), Catherine Wilson (pno), Paul Brodie (sax), Shauna Rolston (vc), Armin Strings, Canadian Piano Trio, Adele Armin (vn) Mastersound ▲ MST 30 [DDD]

Davis, Anthony (pno)
Davis, A.:Wayang 5, w. W. McGlaughlin (cnd), Kansas City SO Gramavision ▲ R2-79429 [DDD]

Davis, Barry (ob)
Vivaldi, A.:Cons for 2 Obs, w. C. Nicklin (ob), N. Marriner (cnd), Academy of St. Martin in the Fields—RV.536 Philips ▲ 412892-2 [DDD]

Davis, Deborah (fl)
Vivaldi, A.:Cons Diverse Instrs, w. Joanna Graham (bn), Ruth McDowall (cl), David Rix (ct), Duke Dobing (fl), Tim Caister (hn), Stephen Stirling (hn), Christopher Hooker (ob), Helen McQueen (ob), Michael Meekes (tpt), Crispian Steele-Perkins (tpt), Nicholas Kraemer (hpd), N. Kraemer (cnd), London Sinfonietta—Cons. in F, RV.539; in C, RV.533; in D, RV.122; in C, RV.537; in C, RV.560; in F, RV.538; in G, RV.545 *(rec All Saints Church, East Finchley, Oct. 1994 & Jan. 1995)* Naxos ("Vivaldi Collection" series) ▲ 8.553204 [DDD]

Davis, Douglas (vc)
Dvořák, A.:Silent Woods, w. G. Schwarz (cnd), Los Angeles CO Delos ▲ DCD 3011 [DDD]
Egilsson:Contemplation, w. Endeé Granat (vn), Richard Altenbach (vn), Janet Lakatos (va), Árni Egilsson (db) Cambria ▲ CD 1033
Egilsson:Get Down!, w. Endeé Granat (vn), Richard Altenbach (vn), Janet Lakatos (va), Árni Egilsson (db) Cambria ▲ CD 1033
Egilsson:Is It?, w. Endeé Granat (vn), Richard Altenbach (vn), Janet Lakatos (va), Árni Egilsson (db) Cambria ▲ CD 1033
Egilsson:What If?, w. Endeé Granat (vn), Richard Altenbach (vn), Janet Lakatos (va), Árni Egilsson (db) Cambria ▲ CD 1033
Egilsson:Why?, w. Endeé Granat (vn), Richard Altenbach (vn), Janet Lakatos (va), Árni Egilsson (db) Cambria ▲ CD 1033

Davis, Gregory (pno)
Mason, D.G.:Son Cl (or Vn), w. D. Wright (cl) Centaur ▲ CRC 2067 [DDD]
Reger, M.:Sons Cl, Op. 49, w. D. Wright (cl)—No. 1 Centaur ▲ CRC 2067 [DDD]
Saint-Saëns, C.:Son Cl, w. D. Wright (cl) Centaur ▲ CRC 2067 [DDD]

▲ = CD ♦ = Enhanced CD Δ = MD ■ = Cassette Tape □ = DCC

Davis, Gregory (pno) (cont.)
Weber, C.M. von:Grand duo concertant Cl, w. D. Wright (cl) Centaur ▲ CRC 2067 [DDD]

Davis, Ivan (pno)
Czerny, C.:Vars on "La Ricordanza" Audiofon ▲ CD 72004
Gershwin, G.:Rhap in Blue, w. L. Maazel (cnd), Cleveland Orch London ▲ 417716–2 [ADD]
Grieg, E.:Peer Gynt Suite 1 Audiofon ▲ CD 72022
In Recital, w. M. Olivero (sop) *(rec Dallas, Dec 13, 1977)* Standing Room Only ▲ SRO 815–1 [ADD]
Liszt, F.:Fant on Hungarian Folk Tunes, w. E. Ormandy (cnd), Philadelphia Orch CBS ▲ MLK 39450 ■ MT 39450
Liszt, F.:Polonaises Pno—No. 1 in c Audiofon ▲ CD 72004
Liszt, F.:Réminiscences de Norma Audiofon ▲ 72004
Schumann, R.:Faschingsschwank aus Wien Audiofon ▲ CD 72004
The Wind Demon & Other 19th Century Piano Music, w. Davis, Ivan (pno) *(rec Columbia Recording Studios, 30th Street, NYC)* New World ▲ 80257–2

Davis, L. (vn)—see ORCHESTRAS & ENSEMBLES Valcour String Quartet

Davis, M. (va)
Van De Vate, N.:Etudes Va Vienna Modern Masters ▲ VMM 2003 [DDD]
Van De Vate, N.:Son Va, w. R. Platt (pno) Vienna Modern Masters ▲ VMM CD 2001 [ADD]

Davis, Mark (gtr)—see ORCHESTRAS & ENSEMBLES Mair–Davis Duo

Davis, Michael (vn)
Baker, M.C.:The Flight of Aphrodite, w. T. Russell (cnd), Pro Musica CO *(rec Ohio State Univ., Weigel Hall, 1995)* Summit ▲ SMT 182 [DDD]
Berkeley, L.:Intro & Allegro Vn Vienna Modern Masters ▲ VMM 2013 [DDD]
Berkeley, L.:Sonatina Vn & Pno, w. Nelson Harper (pno) Vienna Modern Masters ▲ VMM 2013 [DDD]
Berkeley, L.:Theme & Vars Vn *(rec Weigel Hall, Columbus, Ohio, Dec 20–21, 1994)* Vienna Modern Masters ▲ VMM 2015 [DDD]
Berkeley, L.:Toccata Vn, w. Nelson Harper (pno) *(rec Weigel Hall, Columbus, Ohio, Dec 20–21, 1994)* Vienna Modern Masters ▲ VMM 2015 [DDD]
Bloch, E.:Baal Shem, "3 Pictures of Chassidic Life", w. Nelson Harper (pno) *(rec Los Angeles & Columbus, 1969 & 1979)* Orion ▲ 7813–2 [AAD]
Bloch, E.:Son 2 Vn, "Poème mystique", w. Nelson Harper (pno) *(rec Los Angeles & Columbus, 1969 & 1979)* Orion ▲ 7813–2 [AAD]
Frankel, B.:Son 1 Vn Vienna Modern Masters ("Distinguished Performers III" series) ▲ VMM 2016 [DDD]
Ireland, J.:Bagatelle Vn & Pno, w. N. Harper (pno) Vienna Modern Masters ▲ VMM 2009
Ireland, J.:Son 1 Vn, w. N. Harper (pno) Vienna Modern Masters ▲ VMM 2009
Ireland, J.:Son 2 Vn, w. N. Harper (pno) Vienna Modern Masters ▲ VMM 2009
Josephs, W.:Siesta, w. N. Harper (pno) Vienna Modern Masters ▲ VMM 2004 [DDD]
Josephs, W.:Son Vn, Op. 15 Vienna Modern Masters ▲ VMM 2004 [DDD]
Josephs, W.:Son 1 Vn & Pno, w. N. Harper (pno) Vienna Modern Masters ▲ VMM 2004 [DDD]
Josephs, W.:Son 3 Vn & Pno, w. N. Harper (pno) Vienna Modern Masters ▲ VMM 2004 [DDD]
Mathias, W.:Sons Vn Koch International Classics ▲ KIC 7326
Mathias, W.:Trio Pno, w. Nelson Harper (pno), William Conable (vc) Koch International Classics ▲ KIC 7326
Reznicek, E.N. von:Con Vn, w. G. Wright (cnd), Philharmonia Hungarica *(rec 1984)* Koch Schwann ▲ CD 311 128 [ADD]
Van De Vate, N.:Suite Vn Vienna Modern Masters ▲ VMM 2006 [DDD]
Vaughan Williams, R.:The Lark Ascending, w. B. Thomson (cnd), London SO Chandos ▲ CHAN 8554 [DDD]

Davis, Miles B. (db)
Musgrave, T.:Orfeo III, w. Pamela Guidetti (fl), Mei Chen Liao Cope (vn), Igor Szwec (vn), Michael Strauss (va), Lori Barnett (vc), J. Freeman (cnd) *(rec Lang Concert Hall, Swarthmore College)* CRI ▲ CD 723 [DDD]

Davis, P. (fl)
Fauré, G.:Pavane Orch, w. J. Crellin (ob), P. Lynch (gtr) [flute–oboe–guitar arr. Peter Lynch] Move ▲ MD 3090 [DDD]
Ravel, M.:Pavane pour une infante défunte, w. J. Crellin (ob), P. Lynch (gtr) [flute–oboe–guitar arr. by Peter Lynch] Move ▲ MD 3090 [DDD]
Vivaldi, A.:Cons Fl (misc), w. L. Friedman (cnd), St. Andrew Camerata—RV.428, "Il Gardellino" Omega ▲ OCD 1012 [DDD]

Davis, Ronald (tuba)
Solo Pro:Contest Music for Tuba, w. T. Lichtmann (pno) Summit ■ DCD 106

Davis, S. (pno)
Still, W.G.:Miniatures, w. G. Shanley (fl), P. Christ (ob) Crystal ■ C 321
Still, W.G.:Miniatures, w. G. Shanley (fl), P. Christ (ob) Crystal ▲ CD 321

Davis, T. L. (perc)
Bartók, B.:Son for 2 Pnos, w. J. Simms (pno), J. Avery (pno), S. Schick (perc) Music & Arts ▲ CD 648 [AAD/ADD]

Davis, William (bn)—see ORCHESTRAS & ENSEMBLES Georgia Woodwind Quintet

Davison, B. (vn)
Gough, O.:Currulao, w. Roger Heaton (cl), Bruce Nockles (tpt), John Pigneguy (hn), David Stewart (trbn), Tracey Goldsmith (acc), Orlando Gough (kbd), Paul Clarvis (perc) *(rec London, 1995)* Catalyst ▲ 0902–668332–2 [DDD]
Vivaldi, A.:Cons for 4 Vns, w. C. Warren–Green (vn), R. Furniss (vn), T. Bowes (vn), C. Warren–Green (cnd), London CO—RV.580 in b Virgin Classics ▲ 59609 [DDD]

Davison, John (pno)
Davison, J.:Pno Music—Prelude; Fugue; Prelude; Lullaby; Passacaglia Albany ▲ TROY 199 [DDD]

Dawes, A. (vn)—see also ORCHESTRAS & ENSEMBLES Orford String Quartet
Glick, S.I.:Suite Hébraïque 5, w. S. Shulman (fl), J. Campbell (cl), D. Domb (vc) CBC ("Musica Viva" series) ▲ MVCD 1046 [DDD]

Dawson, Lucy (hn)
Van Appledorn, M.J.:Patterns, w. A. Brittin (hn), J. Whitaker (hn), M. Walzel (hn), H. Landers (hn) Opus One ▲ CD 162

Daykin, Frank (pno)—see ORCHESTRAS & ENSEMBLES Alexander & Daykin Piano Duo

Daza, Nicolás (gtr)—see also ORCHESTRAS & ENSEMBLES Arlequin Trio
Schubert, Franz:Songs (misc), w. Pura Maria Martinez (sop)—Nachtstück, D.672; Greisengesang, D.778; Hänflings Liebeswerbung, D.552; Meeres Stille, D.216; Heidenröslein, D.257; Jägers Abendlied, D.368; Schäfers Klagelied, D.121b; Frühlingsglaube, D.686b; Wehmut, D.772; Gesänge Des Harfners 1, D.478b RNE/Spanish National Radio ▲ 650001 [AAD]
Weber, C.M. von:Songs, w. Pura Maria Martinez (sop)—5 Lieder, Op. 13; Lied, Op. 25; 3 Canzonette, Op. 29 RNE/Spanish National Radio ▲ 650001 [AAD]

Deak, John (db)
Seasons Remembered 2, w. J. L. Stillman (pno), Toby Appel (va), Eliot Porter (db), Diaz Trio, Lutz Rath (vc), Fenwick Smith (fl), Ruth Waterman (vn) North Star ▲ 9837–40052–2 ■ 9837–40052–4

Deakin, R. (vn)—see ORCHESTRAS & ENSEMBLES Deakin Piano Trio

DeAlmeida, Cynthia Koledo (ob)
Balada, L.:Lament, w. L. Maazel (cnd), Pittsburgh SO *(rec Pittsburgh, May 10–12, 1996)* New World ▲ 805032 [DDD]

Dean, Allan (tpt)—see ORCHESTRAS & ENSEMBLES Calliope

Dean, Allen (tpt)
Fine, V.:Qt Brass, w. Ronald Anderson (tpt), David Jolley (hn), Lawrence Benz (b trbn) CRI ▲ CD 692 [ADD]
Rzewski, F.:Moonrise with Memories, w. David Taylor (b trbn), David Carp (kazoo), Bill Blount (cl), Louise Schulman (vn), Robert Wolinsky (gtr), Bill Moersch (mar/dlc) *(rec RCA Studios, NYC, June 4, 1981)* New World ▲ 80494–2
Schwartz, E.:Cycles & Gongs, w. L. Raver (org), E. Schwartz (tape) CRI ▲ CD 598 [ADD]

Dean, Amanda (perc)—see ORCHESTRAS & ENSEMBLES Nova Ensemble

Dean, Brett (va)—see also ORCHESTRAS & ENSEMBLES Berlin Spectrum Ensemble members
Brahms, J.:Qnt 2 Strs, w. Brandis String Quartet *(rec Teldec–Studio, Berlin, Feb 23–26, 1996)* Nimbus ▲ NI 5488 [DDD]
Bruckner, A.:Qnt Strs, w. Brandis String Quartet *(rec Teldec–Studio, Berlin, Feb 23–26, 1996)* Nimbus ▲ NI 5488 [DDD]

Dean, Geoffrey (vc)
Nikolov, L.:Qt 3 Strs, w. A. Ilchev (vn), K. Mikaelian (vn), V. Gerov (va) Gega ▲ GD 149 [DDD]

Dean, Laurence (trns fl)
Amor ist mein Lied:Music of the Age of Sentimentalism for Flute & Harp, w. Andrew Lawrence–King (hp/hpd/org) Christophorus ▲ CHR 77182 [DDD]

Dean, Roger (db)—see ORCHESTRAS & ENSEMBLES austraLYSIS members

Dean, Roger (pno)—see ORCHESTRAS & ENSEMBLES austraLYSIS members

Dearing, Erica (vn)—see ORCHESTRAS & ENSEMBLES Double Image members

Dearman, John (gtr)—see ORCHESTRAS & ENSEMBLES Los Angeles Guitar Quartet

Dearnley, C. (org)
Howells, H.:Pieces Org—No. 3, "Master Tallis's Testament" Hyperion ▲ CDA 66260 [DDD]
Howells, H.:Psalm–Preludes, Set II—No. 1, "Out of the depths have I called unto thee, O Lord" Hyperion ▲ CDA 66260 [DDD]
Organ:The Magnificent, w. B. Rose (org), Francis Jackson (org) Pickwick ("The Orchid" series) ▲ PICORCD 11009

Dearnley, Caroline (vc)—see also ORCHESTRAS & ENSEMBLES Joachim Trio
Brahms, J.:Son 2 Vc, w. J. Drake (pno) Meridian ▲ MER 84223 [DDD]
Brahms, J.:Son in D Vc, w. J. Drake (pno) Meridian ▲ MER 84223 [DDD]
Ravel, M.:Trio Pno, w. Joachim Trio *(rec Conway Hall, London, Oct. 5–7, 1993)* Naxos ▲ 8.550934 [DDD]
Saint–Saëns, C.:Trio 1 Pno, w. Rebecca Hirsch (vn), John Lenehan (pno) *(rec Conway Hall, London, Oct. 11 & 12, 1993)* Naxos ▲ 8.550935 [DDD]
Saint–Saëns, C.:Trio 2 Pno, w. Rebecca Hirsch (vn), John Lenehan (pno) *(rec Conway Hall, London, Oct. 11 & 12, 1993)* Naxos ▲ 8.550935
Schmitt, F.:Très lent, w. Joachim Trio *(rec Conway Hall, London, Oct. 5–7, 1993)* Naxos ▲ 8.550934 [DDD]
Simpson, R.:Qt Hn, w. R. Watkins (hn), P. Lowbury (vn), C. Green Armytage (pno) Hyperion ▲ CDA 66695

Death, Stewart (pno)
Fascinating Rhythm, w. S. Rebello (perc), Edwards Jazz Quartet, Brittania Building Society Brass Band [cnd:Howard Snell] Doyen ▲ CD 024 [DDD]

Debast, Michel (fl)
Nelson, G.L.:Moreso Opus One ▲ CD 160

DeBolt, David (bn)
Etler, A.:Son Bn, w. Jerry Davidson (pno) Crystal ▲ CD 347
Farago, M.:Vars on a folia theme of Corelli Crystal ▲ CD 347
Garfield, B.:Poème, w. Jerry Davidson (pno) Crystal ▲ CD 347
Heiden, B.:Serenade, w. Stephanie Sant'Ambrogio (vn), Katherine DeBolt (va), Richard Aaron (vc) Crystal ▲ CD 347
Osborne, W.:Rhap Bn Crystal ▲ CD 347

DeBolt, Katherine (va)
Heiden, B.:Serenade, w. David DeBolt (bn), Stephanie Sant'Ambrogio (vn), Richard Aaron (vc) Crystal ▲ CD 347

Debost, Michel (fl)
Boehm, T.:Compositions Fl, w. A. Adorján (fl), W. Bennett (fl), U. Burkhard (fl), I. Grafenauer (fl), A. Nicolet (fl), B. Weber (pno)—works for Flute & Piano *(Andante pastorale, from Souvenir des Alpes; Elegie in A♭, Op. 47; Fantaisie sur un air allemand, Op. 22; Fantaisie in A♭ on a Theme by Schubert; Grande Polonaise in D, Op. 16; Variations on Nel cor più non mi sento)*; works for Flute Ensemble *(Duettino in D, Pièce facile in C & Romanza in F [Nos. 66–68]; plus a six–flute ensemble performance of the 2nd movt. from Boismortier's Flute Concerto No. 1 in G)* *(rec live, Cuvilliés Theater, Munich 11/27/81)* Orfeo ▲ 018821 [DDD]
Entr'acte, w. Toke Lund Christiansen (fl), Tine Rehling (hp) Kontrapunkt ▲ 32043 [DDD]
Flûte Panorama, w. Christian Ivaldi (pno) Skarbo 2–▲ D SK 4963–4 [DDD]
Hindemith, P.:Son Fl, w. Christian Ivaldi (pno) Arion ▲ ARN 68319
Telemann, G.P.:Sons Fl, w. James Galway (fl)—in b for 2 Fl, Op. 2/4 *(rec Salle Wagram, Paris, July 1974)* EMI Classics ▲ CDK 65340 [ADD]

Debost, Michel (fl/pic)
Schoenberg, A.:Pierrot lunaire, w. Y. Minton (speaker), P. Zukerman (vn/va), L. Harrell (vc), D. Barenboim (pno), A. Pay (cl/b cl), P. Boulez (cnd) *(rec June 20–21, 1977)* Sony Classical ▲ SMK 48466 [ADD]

Debrus, Alexandre (vc)
Vivaldi, A.:Cons Vc, w. G. Boucher (cnd), Arpeggio CO—RV.413 & 417 *(rec Studio Métamorphoses d'orphée)* Pavane ▲ ADW 7352 [DDD]
Vivaldi, A.:Con for 2 Vcs, w. G. Boucher (cnd), Arpeggio CO *(rec Studio Métamorphoses d'orphée)* Pavane ▲ ADW 7352 [DDD]

DeCarli, M. I. (org/cembalo)—see ORCHESTRAS & ENSEMBLES Milan Solisti

Dechenne, Danielle (pno)
Schubert, Franz:Qnt Pno, D.667, w. E. Verhey (vn), F. Erblich (va), J. DeCroos (vc), P. Jansen (db) Laserlight ▲ 15 522 [DDD]
Schubert, Franz:Qnt Pno, D.667, w. E. Verhey (vn), F. Erblich (va), J. DeCroos (vc), P. Jansen (db) Vivace ▲ E 561 [DDD]

Decimo, Marco (vc)—see also ORCHESTRAS & ENSEMBLES Stauffer String Quartet
Platti, G.B.:Sons Vc, w. Marco Mosca (vc)—in D, G, A, c, B♭ & F *(rec Santuario dell'Addolorata, Ceceglio, Turin, Oct 28–30, 1995)* Agora Musica ▲ AG 016.1 [DDD]
Tosti, P.F.:Songs, w. E. Palacio (ten), M. Rapattoni (pno), H. Liviabella (vn), G. Scabbia (fl), B. Giuffredi (gtr), C. Passerini (hp) [arr. Massimo de Bernart for instrumental accompaniment]—La serenata; Sogno; 'A vucchella; Segreto; Ideale; 2ème Aubade; Anima mia; Donna, vorrei morir; Aprile; Ancora!; Mattinata; L'ultima canzone; Malìa; Non t'amo più; Il pescatore canta!; Tristezza; O falce di luna calante; L'abla separa dalla luce l'ombra; Mi guitarra dice "Te amo!"; Ricordati di me; Vuol note o banconote? Arkadia–Akademia ▲ 125 [DDD]

Deck, Warren (tuba)
Bernstein, L.:Waltz for Mippy III, w. John McNeely (pno) Cala Records ("New York Legends" series) ▲ CAL CACD 508 [DDD]

Decker, Laurent (ob)
Alain, J.:Music of, w. Delphine Collot (sop), Bruno Boterf (ten), Jacques Bona (bar), Françoise Gyps (fl), Bruno Pazqueir (va), Philippe Muller (vc), Georges Guillard (org), Ludwig String Quartet, Georges Guillard (cnd), St. Louis Camerata Vocal Ensemble—2 Melodies for Sop & Pno; Nuptial Song for Bar, Bass, Vc & Org; Post–Scriptum for 3 Female Voices & Pno; Canticle in Phrygian Mode for 4 Mixed–Voice, Sop & Strs; Invention for Fl, Ob & Cl; Monody for solo Fl; Prelude for Str Qnt; Adagio for Str Qnt; Funerals for Str Qnt; March of the Horiaces & the Curiaces for 2 Bugles, Drum & Org Arion ▲ ARN 68321
Landowski, M.:Music of, w. Nadine Sautereau (sop), Jean–Christophe Benoit (bar), Xavier Depraz (bass), Michel Bouquet (spkr), Gilbert Audin (bn), Evelyne Aïello, Didier Bouture, Ludovic Chevalier, Françoise Deslogères, Landowski, Tzipine (cnd), Colonne Association des Concerts Orch, Boulogne–Billancourt Orch Conservatory, Paris Conservatory Société des Concerts Orch, L'Itinéraire Ensemble, Harmonia Nova Orch Ensemble—Con Bn; Con pour ondes Martenot; Femme sans passé; Hauts de Hurlevent; Horologe; Mouvement; Notes de Nuit; Souvenir d'un jardin d'enfance; Ventriloque Chamade 3–▲ 5639/40/41 [AAD/DDD]

Decker, P. (org)
Albright, W.:Chasm, w. D. Robbins (echo timp) Albany ▲ TROY 140 [DDD]
Albright, W.:Flights of Fancy Albany ▲ TROY 140 [DDD]
Bielawa, H.:Undertones Albany ▲ TROY 140 [DDD]
Decker, P.:Nightsong & Ostinato Dances Albany ▲ TROY 140 [DDD]

Decreus, Camille (pno)
Eugène Ysaÿe, w. E. Ysaÿe (vn) Symposium ▲ SYM 1045
Decroos, Jean (vc)
Martin, F.:Con Vc, w. B. Haitink (cnd), Royal Concertgebouw Orch *(rec live, Radio Hilversum, Dec 9, 1970)* Preludio ▲ PRL 2147 [ADD]
Schubert, Franz:Qnt Pno, D.667, w. D. Dechene (pno), E. Verhey (vn), F. Erblich (va), P. Jansen (db) Laserlight ▲ 15 522 [DDD]
Schubert, Franz:Qnt Pno, D.667, w. D. Dechene (pno), E. Verhey (vn), F. Erblich (va), P. Jansen (db) Vivace ▲ E 561 [DDD]
Decuyper, Ginette (vn)
Orrego-Salas, J.:Glosas, w. Feliu Gasuli i Altisent (gtr) *(rec Musical Arts Ctr, Bloomington, IN, Dec 2, 1988)* Indiana Univ School of Music ▲ IUSM 02
Dederich-Pejovich, Susan (hp)—see ORCHESTRAS & ENSEMBLES Dallas Tryptych Players
Dedieu-Vidal, Marcelle (pno)
Romance & Dances for Violin, w. Bushkov, Yevgheny (vn) Valois ▲ V 4727
Dedyukhin, Alexander (pno)
The Voices of Living Stereo, Vol. 2, w. E. Farrell (sop), Birgit Nilsson (sop), Roberta Peters (sop), Leontyne Price (sop), Galina Vishnevskaya (sop), Rosalind Elias (mez), Shirley Verrett (mez), Marian Anderson (cta), Maureen Forrester (cta), Sergio Franchi (ten), Mario Lanza (ten), Richard Lewis (ten), Jan Pee, Franz Rupp (pno), Leo Taubman (pno), George Trovillo (pno), Charles Wadsworth (pno), Boston Pops Orch [cnd:Arthur Fiedler], Boston SO [cnd:Charles Munch], Chicago SO [cnd:Fritz Reiner], RCA Victor Orch, RCA Victor Chorus, et al. *(rec Boston & Chicago & New York & Rome, 1957-1964)* RCA Living Stereo ▲ 09026-68167-2 [ADD]
The Young Rostropovich:Rare Recordings from the 1950/1952 Years, w. M. Rostropovich (vc) Enterprise ("Palladio" series) ▲ ENTPD 4157 [ADD]
Dee, John (E hn)
McAlister, C.:Elegía para Quijote y Quijana, w. Lucas Drew (db) *(rec Miami Beach, Feb 1996)* Albany ▲ TROY 212 [DDD]
Dee, John (ob)
Gibson, R.:November Field, w. Lucas Drew (db) Capstone ▲ CPS 8621
Dee, Richard (cheng)
Harrison, L.:Music for Vn, w. William Bouton (vn), William Colvig (sheng/fang-hsiang), Lou Harrison (piri), Helen Rifas (hp) Phoenix ▲ PHCD 118 [AAD]
Defalque, Jean-Michel (vn)
Villette, P.:Qts Strs, w. L. Bobesco (vn), D. Huybrechts (va), S. Mariage (vc)—Nos. 1-6 in A, C, F, B♭, E♭ & E Talent ▲ DOM 2910 46 [DDD]
Deferne, Sylviane (pno)
Franck, C.:Son Vn, w. Anne Robert (vn) REM ▲ REM 311260 [DDD]
Pierné, G.:Son Vn, w. Anne Robert (vn) REM ▲ REM 311260 [DDD]
Poulenc, F.:Con for 2 Pnos, w. P. Rogé (pno), C. Dutoit (cnd), Philharmonia Orch *(rec Feb. 24-28, 1992)* London ▲ 436546-2
Tournemire, C.:Sonate-poème, w. Anne Robert (vn) REM ▲ REM 311260 [DDD]
Deforce, Arne (vc)
Crumb, G.:Black Angels (Images I), w. Filip Suys (vn), Marleen Ydiers (vn), Annemarie Vercauteren (va), Johan Vandermaelen (elec) *(rec Steurbaut Sound Recording Ctr)* René Gailly ▲ CD87 118 [DDD]
Mozetich, M.:Qt Strs, w. Filip Suys (vn), Marleen Ydiers (vn), Annemarie Vercauteren (va) *(rec Steurbaut Sound Recording Ctr)* René Gailly ▲ CD87 118 [DDD]
Degen, Johannes (vc)
Dussek, J.L.:Son Fl, w. Brigitte Kronjäger (fl), André Desponds (pno) *(rec June 1994)* Jecklin ▲ JEC 303 [DDD]
Hummel, J.N.:Adagio, Vars & Rondo on "Schöne Minka", w. André Desponds (pno), Brigitte Kronjäger (fl) *(rec June 1994)* Jecklin ▲ JEC 303 [DDD]
Ries, F.:Trio Pno, w. André Desponds (pno), Brigitte Kronjäger (fl) *(rec June 1994)* Jecklin ▲ JEC 303 [DDD]
Degenhardt, Peter (pno)
Gruenberg, L.:Jazzberries Ars Musici ▲ AM 1100-2 [DDD]
Hindemith, P.:Suite "1922" Ars Musici ▲ AM 1100-2 [DDD]
Ibert, J.:Concertino da camera, w. H. Read (alt sax) [arr. alto saxophone & piano] Ars Musici ▲ AM 1100-2 [DDD]
Milhaud, D.:Scaramouche (transcriptions), w. H. Read (a sax) Ars Musici ▲ AM 1100-2 [DDD]
Schulhoff, E.:Hot Son Sax, w. H. Read (a sax) Ars Musici ▲ AM 1100-2 [DDD]
Degenne, Pierre (vc)
Ravel, M.:Chansons madécasses, w. J. Herbillon (bar), C. Lardé (fl), T. Paraskivesco (pno) [F] Calliope ▲ CAL 9893 [ADD]
Degtjarenko, A. (bn)—see ORCHESTRAS & ENSEMBLES Collegium dell'Arte
Deinzer, Hans (cl)
Henze, H.-W.:Le Miracle de la rose, w. H. W. Henze (cnd), Ensemble Modern Ars Musici ▲ 0859
Messiaen, O.:Quatuor pour la fin du temps, w. Saschko Gawrilov (vn), Siegfried Palm (vc), Alfons Kontarsky (pno) EMI Classics 2-▲ CDCB 47463 [DDD]
Schubert, Franz:Songs (misc), w. E. Ameling (sop), J. Demus (pno) Editio Classica ▲ 77085-2-RG [ADD]
Dejean, G. (bn/ctbn)
Wilson, R.:Persuasions, w. A. Burton (sop), B. Uribe (pno), J. Solum (alt fl), M. Schachman (ob/E hn) Albany ▲ TROY 074 [DDD]
Dekany, Béla (vn)—see ORCHESTRAS & ENSEMBLES Dekany String Quartet
Dekker, Henk (hpd)
Focking, H. von:Sons Fl, w. P. van Houwelingen (trns fl), N. Hirschfeld (vl)—in C, G & D Erasmus ▲ WVH 078 [DDD]
Van Wassenaer, U.:Sons Rcr, w. P. van Houwelingen (fl), N. Hirschfeld (vl) Erasmus ▲ WVH 078 [DDD]
Dekkers, Maarten (acc)
Saint-Saëns, C.:Carnival of the Animals, w. D. Wayenberg (vn), H. Oudenaarden (vn), J. Hagen (fl), H. de Fraaf (cl), H. Krul (db), W. Vos (xyl), Daniel String Quartet *(rec Rotterdam, May 28, 1985)* Erasmus ▲ WHV 001 [DDD]
Dekkers, Miny (acc)—see ORCHESTRAS & ENSEMBLES Duo Novair
Dekov, Emil (vn)
Christoskov, P.:Suite 1 Vn *(rec 1971 & 1974)* BIS ▲ CD 9 [AAD]
Goleminov, M.:Little Suite BIS ▲ CD 9 [AAD]
Holewa, H.:Duettino 1, w. Magnus Andersson (gtr) Phono Suecia ▲ PHN 49 [ADD]
Linde, B.:Son Vn, w. C. Gille-Rybrant (pno) BIS ▲ CD 9 [AAD]
Pergament, M.:Chaconne Vn *(rec June 24, 1974)* BIS ▲ CD 37 [AAD]
Pergament, M.:Chaconne Vn BIS ▲ CD 9 [AAD]
Shostakovich, D.:Songs Sop, Op. 127, w. J. Delman (sop), A. Olofsson (vc), L. Negro (pno) [R] BIS ▲ CD 26 [AAD]
Delafontaine, Christian (fl)
Amirov, F.:Pieces (6) Fl, w. Marina Mourtazine-Chapochnikova (pno) Gallo ▲ CD 894 [DDD]
Bach, C.P.E.:Trio Sons (misc), w. F. Sarnau (vn), P. Mermoud (vc), M. Jordan (hpd)—in b, a, d, B♭ & D *(rec Jan 4, 5 & 6, 1988)* Gallo ▲ CD 541
Glière, R.:Pieces Fl & Pno, Op. 35, w. Marina Mourtazine-Chapochnikova (pno)—Melody; Waltz Gallo ▲ CD 894 [DDD]
Liadov, A.:Prelude Fl & Pno, w. Marina Mourtazine-Chapochnikova (pno) Gallo ▲ CD 894 [DDD]
Rachmaninoff, S.:Vocalise, w. Marina Mourtazine-Chapochnikova (pno) [trans fl & pno] Gallo ▲ CD 894 [DDD]
Taktakishvili, O.:Son Fl, w. Marina Mourtazine-Chapochnikova (pno) Gallo ▲ CD 894 [DDD]
Delafontaine, Christian (pic)
The Lausanne Vocal Ensemble Euterpe in Concert, w. [cnd:Christophe Gesseney], Euterpe, Christine Sortoretti (hpd), Yves Rechsteiner (org), Marianne Amrein (fl douce/perc) Gallo ▲ CD 766 [DDD]

Delahunt, Walter (pno)
Korte, O.:Philosophical Dialogues, w. Ivan Štraus (vn) *(rec Martinů Hall of Liechtenstein Palace in Prague, Mar 11 & 12, 1995)* Panton ▲ 811398-2 [DDD]
DeLancie, John (ob)
Haydn, J.:Sinf concertante, w. Bernard Garfield (bn), Jacob Krachmalnick (vn), Lorne Munroe (vc), E. Ormandy (cnd), Philadelphia Orch Sony Classical ("Essential Classics" series) ▲ SBK 62649 ■ SBT 62649
Mozart, W.A.:Con Ob, w. E. Ormandy (cnd), Philadelphia Orch Sony Classical ("Essential Classics" series) ▲ SBK 62652 ■ SBT 62652
Russo, J.:Elegy CRS ▲ CD 9052
Delangle, Claude (a sax)
Berio, L.:Sequenza IXb BIS ▲ CD 640 [DDD]
Denisov, E.:Con piccolo, w. G. van Gucht (cnd), Strasbourg Percussion Ensemble *(rec Jan. 1990)* Pierre Verany ▲ PV.790112 [DDD]
Denisov, E.:Son A Sax & Vc, w. Vérène Westphal (vc) *(rec Paris, July 1995)* BIS ▲ CD 765 [DDD]
Denisov, E.:Son A Sax *(rec Jan. 1990)* Pierre Verany ▲ PV.790112 [DDD]
Denisov, E.:Son A Sax, w. Odile Delangle (pno) *(rec Paris, July 11, 1995)* BIS ▲ CD 665 [DDD]
Denisov, E.:Son A Sax, w. Odile Delangle (pno) *(rec Paris, July 1995)* BIS ▲ CD 765 [DDD]
Jolas, B.:Episode Quatrième BIS ▲ CD 640 [DDD]
Karasikov, V.:Casus in terminus, w. Vérène Westphal (vc), Odile Delangle (pno) *(rec Paris, July 1995)* BIS ▲ CD 765 [DDD]
Scelsi, G.:Ixor BIS ▲ CD 640 [DDD]
Scelsi, G.:Maknongan BIS ▲ CD 640 [DDD]
Scelsi, G.:Pezzi Sop Sax BIS ▲ CD 640 [DDD]
Delangle, Claude (bar sax)
Gubaidulina, S.:Duo-Son, w. Damien Royannais (bar sax) *(rec Paris, July 1995)* BIS ▲ CD 765 [DDD]
Delangle, Claude (s sax)
Berio, L.:Sequenza VIIb BIS ▲ CD 640 [DDD]
Stockhausen, K.:In Freundschaft BIS ▲ CD 640 [DDD]
Takemitsu, T.:Distance BIS ▲ CD 640 [DDD]
Delangle, Claude (s sax/t sax)
Constant, M.:Concertante Sax, w. J. Kaltenbach (cnd), Nancy SO *(rec Salle Poirel, Nancy, Apr. 4, 1990)* Erato ▲ 94815-2 [DDD]
Denisov, E.:Con A Sax, w. T. Otaka (cnd), BBC Welsh National SO *(rec Brangwyn Hall, Swansea, Wales, Jan 31, 1994 & Feb 1, 199)* BIS ▲ CD 665 [DDD]
Escaich, T.:Le chant des ténèbres, w. J. Béreau (cnd), *(orch unknown)* *(rec Apr 16-17, Nov 4 & 26, 19)* Chamade ▲ CHCD 5638 [DDD]
Grisey, G.:Chamber Music, w. Gérard Caussé (va), Rophé, Foster (cnd), Itinéraire Ensemble—Talea for ensemble; Prologue for Va & Ww; Anubis for Sax; Jour Contre Jour Accord ▲ ACD 201952 [DDD]
Raskatov, A.:Pas de deux, w. Elena Vassilieva (sop), Elena Vassilieva (chimes) *(rec Paris, July 1995)* BIS ▲ CD 765 [DDD]
Delangle, Claude (t sax)
Vustin, A.:Musique pour l'ange, w. Vérène Westphal (vc), Jean Geoffroy (vib) *(rec Paris, July 1995)* BIS ▲ CD 765 [DDD]
Delangle, Odile (pno)
Denisov, E.:Pieces (3) Pno 4-Hands, w. J.-L. Haguenauer (pno), M. Soveral (pno) *(rec Jan. 1990)* Pierre Verany ▲ PV.790112 [DDD]
Denisov, E.:Son A Sax, w. Claude Delangle (alt sax) *(rec Paris, July 11, 1995)* BIS ▲ CD 665 [DDD]
Denisov, E.:Son A Sax, w. Claude Delangle (a sax) *(rec Paris, July 1995)* BIS ▲ CD 765 [DDD]
Karasikov, V.:Casus in terminus, w. Claude Delangle (a sax), Vérène Westphal (vc) *(rec Paris, July 1995)* BIS ▲ CD 765 [DDD]
Delaunay, Catherine (cl)
Mozart, W.A.:Adagio Bas Hns, K.484d, w. Jean Jeltsch (bas hn), Trio di Bassetto *(rec Chapelle Notre-Dame de l'Hor, Moselle, June 29 - July 1, 1995)* K617 ▲ 7060 [DDD]
Mozart, W.A.:Adagio Cl, K.Anh.93, w. Jean Jeltsch (bas hn), Trio di Bassetto *(rec Chapelle Notre-Dame de l'Hor, Moselle, June 29 - July 1, 1995)* K617 ▲ 7060 [DDD]
Mozart, W.A.:Adagio Cl, K.Anh.94, w. Jean Jeltsch (bas hn), Trio di Bassetto *(rec Chapelle Notre-Dame de l'Hor, Moselle, June 29 - July 1, 1995)* K617 ▲ 7060 [DDD]
Mozart, W.A.:Adagio Cls, K.411, w. Jean Jeltsch (bas hn), Trio di Bassetto *(rec Chapelle Notre-Dame de l'Hor, Moselle, June 29 - July 1, 1995)* K617 ▲ 7060 [DDD]
Mozart, W.A.:Nozze di Figaro (winds), w. Jean Jeltsch (bas hn), Trio di Bassetto *(rec Chapelle Notre-Dame de l'Hor, Moselle, June 29 - July 1, 1995)* K617 ▲ 7060 [DDD]
Stadler, A.:Trios Bas Hns, w. Jean Jeltsch (bas hn), Trio di Bassetto *(rec Chapelle Notre-Dame de l'Hor, Moselle, June 29 - July 1, 1995)* K617 ▲ 7060 [DDD]
Delay, Brian (gtr)
Handel, D.:The Poems of Our Climate, w. Sheryl Woods (sop), Pamela Watson (fl), Val Griffen (vc), Anton Nel (pno), Jack Brennan (perc), James Culley (perc), Allen Otte (perc), G. Samuel (cnd) Vienna Modern Masters ▲ VMM 2019 [DDD]
Delfino, Riccardo (va da rota)
Vivaldi, A.:Sons Vn, w. Marco Ambrosini (va d'amore), Thomas Wimmer (va da gamba)—RV.23, 53 & 58 Preiser ▲ PRE 90276
Vivaldi, A.:Sons for 2 Vns, Op. 1, w. Marco Ambrosini (va d'amore), Thomas Wimmer (va da gamba)—No. 12 [La Follia] Preiser ▲ PRE 90276
Delft, M. van (hpd)
Bach, J.S.:Sons Vn, w. J. Leertouwer (vn)—BWV 1014-1019; in G, BWV 1019a [2 older versions] *(rec Jan 1992)* Globe 2-▲ GLO 6008 [DDD]
Delgado, Imelda (pno)—see also ORCHESTRAS & ENSEMBLES Aguilar-Delgado Duo
Doran, M.:Sonatina Ob, w. Evelyn McCarty (ob) *(rec Chorus Room of Symphony Hall, Boston, MA, Feb 26-27, 1994)* Boston Records ▲ BR 1012
Gems for Oboe & Piano, w. E. McCarty (ob) *(rec Chorus Room of Symphony Hall, Boston, MA Feb. 26-27, 1994)* Boston Records ▲ BR 1012
Madden, J.:Songes of Sadness & Pitie, w. Evelyn McCarty (ob) *(rec Chorus Room of Symphony Hall, Boston, MA, Feb 26-27, 1994)* Boston Records ▲ BR 1012
Rediscovering... Boston Records ▲ BR 1009 CD [DDD]
Rubbra, E.:Son Ob, w. Evelyn McCarty (ob) *(rec Chorus Room of Symphony Hall, Boston, MA, Feb 26-27, 1994)* Boston Records ▲ BR 1012
Schelling, E.:Impressions from an Artist's Life, w. Evelyn McCarty (ob)—Nocturne for Ob & Pno [Var No. 7] *(rec Chorus Room of Symphony Hall, Boston, MA, Feb 26-27, 1994)* Boston Records ▲ BR 1012
Sinigaglia, L.:Variations (12) on a theme of Schubert, w. Evelyn McCarty (ob) *(rec Chorus Room of Symphony Hall, Boston, MA, Feb 26-27, 1994)* Boston Records ▲ BR 1012
Widerkehr, J.:Duo Ob, w. Evelyn McCarty (ob) *(rec Chorus Room of Symphony Hall, Boston, MA, Feb 26-27, 1994)* Boston Records ▲ BR 1012
DeLibero, Kim (hp)—see ORCHESTRAS & ENSEMBLES Sierra Winds
Dell'Agnello, Caterina (vc)—see ORCHESTRAS & ENSEMBLES Ricordanze String Quartet
Dellanoy, M. (db)
Suter, R.:Musikalisches Tagesbuch 1, w. B. Geiser-Payer (alt), H. Haldemann (pic/fl), H. Holliger (ob), H. Bochet (bn), J. Joubert (vn), J. Semper (va), W. Eugster (vc) *(rec 1962)* Grammont ▲ CSTP 6-2 [AAD]
Dell'Aquila (hp)
Bavicchi, J.:Trio 4 Cl, w. D. Glazer (cl), M. Raimondi (vn) CRI ■ C 138
dell'Atti, Salvatore (fl)—see ORCHESTRAS & ENSEMBLES Consort Fontegara
Delle-Vigne, Aquiles (pno)
Liszt, F.:Etudes d'exécution transcendante, S.139 Arcobaleno ▲ AAOC 9360
Liszt, F.:La Lugubre gondola Pno Arcobaleno ▲ AAOC 9360
Ravel, M.:Berceuse sur le nom de Gabriel Fauré, w. A. Lysy (vn) Arcobaleno ▲ SBCD 6400 [DDD]
Ravel, M.:Son Vn Pno, w. A. Lysy (vn) Arcobaleno ▲ SBCD 6400 [DDD]
Ravel, M.:Sonate posthume, w. A. Lysy (vn) Arcobaleno ▲ SBCD 6400 [DDD]

528 ▲ = CD ♦ = Enhanced CD Δ = MD ■ = Cassette Tape □ = DCC

Delle-Vigne, Aquiles (pno) (cont.)
Ravel, M.:Tzigane, w. A. Lysy (vn) — Arcobaleno ▲ SBCD 6400 [DDD]
Delley, Claude (cl)
Gerber, R.:Chamber Music, w. Fränzi Badertscher-Jaquiéry (fl), Gunhard Mattes (ob), Dimitri Ashkenazy (cl), Pierre-Yves Dubois (cl), Anne de Dadelsen (pno)—Pièce lente; Habanera; Berceuse [all for Cl & Pno]; Trio for Fl, Ob & Pno; Son for Fl & Pno; Ballet for Fl & Pno; Sonatine for 3 Cl; Pavane for Fl & Pno; Suite for Fl & Pno; Prélude et fugue sur le nom de Bach for Cl — Gallo ▲ CD 788 [DAD]
Delly, Alison (vn)—see ORCHESTRAS & ENSEMBLES Pro Arte String Trio
Delmoni, Arturo (vn)
Bach, J.S.:Sons & Partitas Vn, BWV 1001–1006—Partita No. 2 in d, BWV 1004 — John Marks ▲ JMR 14
Beach, A.M.C.:Son Vn, w. Yuri Funahashi (pno) — John Marks ▲ JMR 2
Beethoven, L. van:Folksong Arrs, w. Fred Sherry (vc), New York Vocal Arts Ensemble—Highlander's Lament; Chase of the Wolf; The Soldier in a Foreign Land; The Pulse of an Irishman; Lochnagar; O Swiftly Glides the Bonny Boat; O Might I but my Patrick Love; Kak Pashli; Bolero; Ridder Stigs Runekast; When Mortals all to Rest Retire; Faithful Johnie; Charlie is my Darling; Glencoe; Come Fill, Fill, my Good Fellow; Auld Lang Syne *(rec SUNY Purchase Performing Arts Center, Theatre C, Sept 11–13, 1995)* — Arabesque ▲ Z6672 [DDD]
Brahms, J.:Son 1 Vn, w. Yuri Funahashi (pno) — John Marks ▲ JMR 2
(compact disc version), w. Delmoni, Arturo (vn) — Mobile Fidelity ▲ MFCD 877
Fauré, G.:Après un rêve, w. Meg Bachman Vas (pno) — John Marks ▲ JMR 8
Fauré, G.:Après un rêve, w. M. Bachman Vas (pno) [violin-piano arr.] — Mobile Fidelity ▲ MFCD 781 [AAD]
Fauré, G.:Son 1 Vn, w. Meg Bachman Vas (pno) — John Marks ▲ JMR 8
Fauré, G.:Son 1 Vn, w. M. Bachman Vas (pno) — Mobile Fidelity ▲ MFCD 781 [AAD]
Franck, C.:Son Vn, w. Meg Bachman Vas (pno) — John Marks ▲ JMR 8
Franck, C.:Son Vn, w. M. Bachman Vas (pno) — Mobile Fidelity ▲ MFCD 781 [AAD]
Kreisler, F.:Recitativo & Scherzo-caprice — John Marks ▲ JMR 14
Music for Violin & Guitar, w. D. Burgess (gtr) — Athena ▲ ACSC 10006 [ADD]
Orientale:Romantic Music for Cello, w. N. Rosen (vc), Doris Stevenson (pno) — North Star ▲ NS 0027
Reverie:Romantic Music for Quiet Times, w. N. Rosen (vc), Kaaren Erickson (sop), Doris Stevenson (pno) — John Marks Records ▲ JMR 10
Schubert, Franz:Sonatinas Vn, w. E. Auer (pno)—1 Sonatina *(rec Dec. 1993)* — Clarity ▲ CCP 1007
Schubert, Franz:Trio 2 Pno, w. E. Auer (pno), N. Rosen (vc) *(rec Dec. 1993)* — Clarity ▲ CCD 1007
Songs My Mother Taught Me, w. M. Bachman Vas (pno) *(rec 1982)* — John Marks Records ▲ JMR 1
Songs My Mother Taught Me, w. Meg Bachman Vas (pno) — North Star ■ DS 0004
Tchaikovsky, P.:Souvenir de Florence, w. L. Chang (vn), M. Thompson (va), S. Ansel (va), R. Thomas (vc), M. Reynolds (vc) *(rec Weston, MA, Jan. 1993)* — Northeastern ▲ NOR 249 [DDD]
Ysaÿe, E.:Sons Vn — John Marks ▲ JMR 14
Delmotte, Roger (tpt)
Ibert, J.:Impromptu Tpt & Pno, w. Raphaël Beaufort (pno) — Adès ▲ ADE 203462 [AAD]
Delony, Willis (pno)
Barber, S.:Son Pno — Centaur ▲ CRC 2064 [DDD]
Prokofiev, S.:Son 6 Pno — Centaur ▲ CRC 2064 [DDD]
Deloria, Deborah (db)—see also ORCHESTRAS & ENSEMBLES New Performance Group of the Cornish Institute
Giteck, J.:Callin' Home Coyote, w. John Duykers (ten), Andy Narell (perc) [E] — Mode ▲ 14 ■ 14CS (CrO2)
Delpriora, Mark (gtr)
Second Renaissance — Koch International Classics ▲ 3-7089-2 [DDD]
Delvallée, Georges (org)
Tournemire, C.:Fant symphonique [Grand Org of Saint-Quentin Basilica] — Adda ▲ ADD 581276 [DDD]
Tournemire, C.:Fioretti Org [Grand Org of Saint-Quentin Basilica] — Adda ▲ ADD 581276 [DDD]
Tournemire, C.:L'orgue mystique—sels from Op. 57 — Arion 2-▲ ARN 268105 [AAD]
Tournemire, C.:Poèmes Org—No. 3 — Adda ▲ ADD 581276 [DDD]
Tournemire, C.:Suite évocatrice [Grand Org of Saint-Quentin Basilica] — Adda ▲ ADD 581276 [DDD]
Delvallée, Georges (pno)
Tournemire, C.:Cloches de Châteauneuf-du-Faou — Accord 2-▲ ACD 204772 [DDD]
Tournemire, C.:Etudes de chaque jour — Accord 2-▲ ACD 204772 [DDD]
Tournemire, C.:Poème mystique — Accord 2-▲ ACD 204772 [DDD]
Tournemire, C.:Préludes-poèmes — Accord 2-▲ ACD 204772 [DDD]
Tournemire, C.:Rhap Pno — Accord 2-▲ ACD 204772 [DDD]
Vierne, L.:Pno Music (comp)—Suite bourguignonne, Op. 17; Solitude, Op. 44; Ainsi parlait Zarathoustra, Op. 49; Le glas, Op. 39; 2 pièces, Op. 7 — Arion ▲ ARN 68312 [DDD]
Vierne, L.:Silhouettes d'enfants — Arion ▲ ARN 68270 [DDD]
Delz, Christoph (pno)
Delz, C.:Con Pno, w. M. Bamert (cnd), Southwest German RSO Baden-Baden *(rec 9/26/88 & 8/29/86)* — FSM ▲ FCD 97743 [ADD]
Delz, C.:Qt Pno, w. F. Gauwerky (pno), A. Hempel (pno), J. Krist (pno), N. Shirato (pno) — Grammont ▲ CTSP 18-2 [ADD]
Delz, C.:Sils *(rec 9/26/88 & 8/29/86)* — FSM ▲ FCD 97743 [ADD]
Liszt, F.:Pno Music (misc) *(rec 9/26/88 & 8/29/86)* — FSM ▲ FCD 97743 [ADD]
DeMare, A. (pno)
Moravec, P.:Music Remembers — CRI ▲ CD 641 [DDD]
Demarquette, Henri (vc)—see ORCHESTRAS & ENSEMBLES Phillips String Quartet
DeMart, Jean (fl)
Korde, S.:Tenderness of Cranes — Neuma ▲ 450-85 [DDD]
Dembinsky, G. (cl)
Rossini, G.:Fant Cl, w. J. Zak (pno) — PWK Classics ▲ PWK 1142 [DDD]
Schumann, R.:Fantasiestücke Cl, w. J. Zak (pno) — PWK Classics ▲ PWK 1142 [DDD]
Weber, C.M. von:Grand duo concertant Cl, w. J. Zak (pno) — PWK Classics ▲ PWK 1142 [DDD]
Weber, C.M. von:Vars on a Theme from *Silvana* Cl, w. J. Zak (pno) — PWK Classics ▲ PWK 1142 [DDD]
Demenga, C. (vn)
Holliger, H.:Duo Vn & Vc, w. T. Demenga (vc) — ECM New Series ▲ 78118-21340-2 [DDD]
Demenga, Patrick (vc)
Beethoven, L. van:Sons Vc (comp), w. Paul Coker (pno) — Accord 2-▲ ACD 204302 [DDD]
Beethoven, L. van:Vars on "Ein Mädchen oder Weibchen" from Mozart's *Die Zauberflöte*, w. Paul Coker (pno) — Accord ▲ ACD 204302 [DDD]
Beethoven, L. van:Vars on "See, the Conquering Hero Comes" from Handel's *Judas Maccabaeus*, w. Paul Coker (pno) — Accord ▲ ACD 204302 [DDD]
Dutilleux, H.:Strophes (3) sur le nom Sacher *(rec Switzerland, June 1993)* — ECM New Series 2-▲ 78118-21520-2 [DDD]
Keller, A.:Der enthüllte Stern, w. D. Fueter (sop), K. Graf (sop), A. K. Graf (fl), L. Pellerin (ob), E. Schmid (cl), U. Walker (vn), C. Schiller (va), P. Demenga (vc), P. Hug-Rutti (hp), F. Eberle (dr) [G] — Grammont ▲ CTSP 19-2 [ADD]
Keller, A.:Ewiger Augenblick, w. D. Fueter (sop), K. Graf (sop), A. K. Graf (fl), E. Schmid (cl), D. Isler (cel), P. Hug-Rutti (hp), U. Walker (vn) [G] — Grammont ▲ CTSP 19-2 [ADD]
Koechlin, C.:Paysages et marines, w. Kiyoshi Kasai (fl), Elmar Schmid (cl), Alexandru Gavrilovici (vn), Urs Walker (vn), Christoph Schiller (va) — Accord ▲ ACD 201092 [DDD]
Scelsi, G.:Elegia per Thy, w. Christoph Schiller (va) — Accord ▲ ACD 200622 [DDD]
Scelsi, G.:Trio Strs, w. Robert Zimansky (vn), Christoph Schiller (va) — Accord ▲ ACD 200622 [DDD]
Demenga, Thomas (vc)
Bach, J.S.:Suites Vc, BWV 1007–1012—No. 4 — ECM New Series ▲ 78118-21340-2 [DDD]
Bach, J.S.:Suites Vc, BWV 1007–1012—BWV.1007 *(rec Dec 1991)* — ECM New Series ▲ 78118-21477-2 [DDD]
Bach, J.S.:Suites Vc, BWV 1007–1012 *(rec Feb & July 1995)* — ECM New Series ▲ ECM 1571 [DDD]
Berio, L.:Les Mots sont allés *(rec Switzerland, June 1993)* — ECM New Series 2-▲ 78118-21520-2 [DDD]

Demenga, Thomas (vc) (cont.)
Britten, H.:Tema "Sacher" *(rec Switzerland, June 1993)* — ECM New Series 2-▲ 78118-21520-2 [DDD]
Carter, E.:Enchanted Preludes, w. P. Racine (fl) — ECM New Series ▲ 78118-21391-2 [DDD]
Carter, E.:Triple Duo, w. P. Racine (fl), E. Molinari (cl), H. Schneeberger (vn), P. Cleeman (va), G. Huber (perc) — ECM New Series ▲ 78118-21391-2 [DDD]
Holliger, H.:Chaconne Vc *(rec Switzerland, June 1993)* — ECM New Series 2-▲ 78118-21520-2 [DDD]
Holliger, H.:Duo Vn & Vc, w. C. Demenga (vn) — ECM New Series ▲ 78118-21340-2 [DDD]
Holliger, H.:Trema — ECM New Series ▲ 78118-21340-2 [DDD]
Lutoslawski, W.:Sacher Variationen *(rec Switzerland, June 1993)* — ECM New Series 2-▲ 78118-21520-2 [DDD]
Magnard, A.:Trio Pno, w. Christoph Keller (pno), Adelina Oprean (vn) — Accord ▲ ACD 200102 [DDD]
Shostakovich, D.:Movts Str Qt, w. G. Kremer (vn), A. Bik (vn), V. Hagen (va) *(rec Lockenhaus Festival, 1986)* — ECM New Series 2-▲ 78118-21347-2 [DDD]
Veress, S.:Son Vc — ECM New Series ▲ 78118-21477-2 [DDD]
Veress, S.:Trio, w. H. Schneeberger (vn), T. Zimmermann (va) — ECM New Series ▲ 78118-21477-2 [DDD]
Wyttenbach, J.:Encore!, w. J. Keller (sgr) [F] *(rec May 19–20, 1990)* — Grammont ▲ CTSP 37-2 [ADD]
Zimmermann, B.A.:Son Vc *(rec Feb & July 1995)* — ECM New Series ▲ ECM 1571 [DDD]
Demer, Thomas (va)—see ORCHESTRAS & ENSEMBLES Dallas Tryptych Players
Demeterová, Gabriela (vn)
Biber, H. von:Mystery (or Rosary) Sons, w. Jaroslav Tuma (org) — Supraphon ▲ SUP CD 3155
Demetriades, Anastase (rcr)
Mosaïque:Works for Recorder & Harpsichord, w. George Kiss (hpd) *(rec Mar. 25, 1995)* — Bongiovanni ▲ GB 5045 [DDD]
Demeyere, Ewald (hpd)
Rossini, G.:Tancredi, w. Sumi Jo (sop—Amenaide), Lucretia Lendi (mez—Roggiero), Anna Maria di Micco (mez—Isaura), Ewa Podles (cta—Tancredi), Stanford Olsen (ten—Argirio), Pietro Spagnoli (bar—Orbazzano), Lieven Baert (vc), Franck Coryn (db), A. Zedda (cnd), Collegium Instrumentale Brugense, Capella Brugensis *(rec Poissy Theatre & Centre Musical-Lyrique-Phonographique, Ile de France, Jan. 26–31, 1994)* — Naxos ("Opera Classics" series) 2-▲ 8.660037/38 [DDD]
Demidenko, Nikolai (pno)
Back to the Earth, w. I. Tomita (cnd), Plasma SO, Clamma Dale (sop), et al. *(rec live, NYC, 1986)* — RCA Red Seal ▲ 7717-2-RC [DDD]
Busoni, F.:Bach Transcriptions—Six Chorale Preludes—BWV 552, 564, 565, 639, 659 & 734; Capriccio in B, BWV 992 — Hyperion ▲ CDA 66566 [DDD]
Chopin, F.:Allegro de concert — Hyperion ▲ CDA 66597
Chopin, F.:Con 1 Pno, w. H. Schiff (cnd), Philharmonia Orch — Hyperion ▲ CDA 66647
Chopin, F.:Con 2 Pno, w. H. Schiff (cnd), Philharmonia Orch — Hyperion ▲ CDA 66647
Chopin, F.:Intro & Vars on a German National Air "Der Schweizerbub" — Hyperion ▲ CDA 66514 [DDD]
Chopin, F.:Polonaises—6 Polonaises, Op. posth. — Hyperion ▲ CDA 66597
Chopin, F.:Polonaise-fant — Hyperion ▲ CDA 66597
Chopin, F.:Scherzos — Hyperion ▲ CDA 66514 [DDD]
Chopin, F.:Son Pno, Op. 58 — Hyperion ▲ CDA 66577
Chopin, F.:Vars on Mozart's *La ci darem la mano* — Hyperion ▲ CDA 66514 [DDD]
Clementi, M.:Sons Pno—in f#, Op. 25/5 [Op. 26/2]; in b, Op. 40/2; in D, Op. 40/3; in bb, Op. 41/2 [Op. 47/2] — Hyperion ▲ CDA 66808
Live at the Wigmore Hall, w. Demidenko, Nikolai (pno) — Hyperion 2-▲ CDA 66781/2
Medtner, N.:Con 2 Pno, w. J. Maksymiuk (cnd), BBC Scottish SO — Hyperion ▲ CDA 66580 [DDD]
Medtner, N.:Con 3 Pno, w. J. Maksymiuk (cnd), BBC Scottish SO — Hyperion ▲ CDA 66580 [DDD]
Medtner, N.:Knight Errant, w. D. Alexeev (pno) — Hyperion ▲ CDA 66654 [DDD]
Medtner, N.:Pno Music (misc)—Canzona Serenata, Op. 38/6; Fairy Tale, Op. 20/1; Sonata Elegia in d, Op. 11/2; Canzona Matinata, Op. 39/4; Sonata Tragica in c, Op. 39/5; Theme & Variations in c#, Op. 55; Dithyrambe, Op. 10/2; Sonata Reminiscenza in a, Op. 38/1 — Hyperion ▲ CDA 66636
Medtner, N.:Russian Round Dance (A Tale), w. D. Alexeev (pno) — Hyperion ▲ CDA 66654 [DDD]
Mussorgsky, M.:Nursery, w. Anatoli Safiulin (bass) — Hyperion ▲ CDA 66775
Mussorgsky, M.:Peepshow, w. Anatoli Safiulin (bass) — Hyperion ▲ CDA 66775
Mussorgsky, M.:Songs & Dances, w. Anatoli Safiulin (bass) — Hyperion ▲ CDA 66775
Mussorgsky, M.:Sunless, w. Anatoli Safiulin (bass) — Hyperion ▲ CDA 66775
Prokofiev, S.:Con 2 Pno, w. A. Lazarev (cnd), London PO — Hyperion ▲ CDA 66858
Prokofiev, S.:Con 3 Pno, w. A. Lazarev (cnd), London PO — Hyperion ▲ CDA 66858
Rachmaninoff, S.:Pno Music (misc)—Etudes-tableaux, Op. 33/2 & 8 & Op. 39/3, 4 & 5; Preludes, Op. 23/1, 3, 5, 7, & 10; Morceaux de fantaisie, Op. 3 (original version); Preludes, Op. 23/6, 8, 10 & 12 — Hyperion ▲ CDA 66713
Rachmaninoff, S.:Russian Rhap, w. D. Alexeev (pno) — Hyperion ▲ CDA 66654 [DDD]
Rachmaninoff, S.:Suite 2 for 2 Pnos, w. D. Alexeev (pno) — Hyperion ▲ CDA 66654 [DDD]
Rachmaninoff, S.:Symphonic Dances, w. D. Alexeev (pno) — Hyperion ▲ CDA 66654 [DDD]
The Romantic Piano Concerto, Vol. 2, w. BBC Scottish SO [cnd:J. Maksymiuk] — Hyperion ▲ CDA 66580 [DDD]
Schubert, Franz:Fant Pno, D.760, "Wandererfantasie" — Hyperion 2-▲ CDA 67091/92
Schubert, Franz:Impromptus Pno (comp) — Hyperion 2-▲ CDA 67091/92
Schubert, Franz:Moments musicaux — Hyperion 2-▲ CDA 67091/92
Schubert, Franz:Pieces Pno, D.946 — Hyperion 2-▲ CDA 67091/92
Schumann, R.:Son Pno, Op. 14—also includes an extra Scherzo & 2 Vars on Op. 14 — Hyperion ▲ CDA 66864
Schumann, R.:Son 1 Pno — Hyperion ▲ CDA 66864
Scriabin, A.:Con Pno, w. A. Lazarev (cnd), BBC SO — Hyperion ▲ CDA 66680
Tchaikovsky, P.:Con 1 Pno, w. A. Lazarev (cnd), BBC SO — Hyperion ▲ CDA 66680
Weber, C.M. von:Con 1 Pno, w. C. Mackerras (cnd), Scottish CO — Hyperion ▲ CDA 66680
Weber, C.M. von:Con 2 Pno, w. C. Mackerras (cnd), Scottish CO — Hyperion ▲ CDA 66680
Weber, C.M. von:Konzertstück Pno, w. C. Mackerras (cnd), Scottish CO — Hyperion ▲ CDA 66680
Demierre-Baruchet, Aline (pno)
Daetwyler, J.:Chants lunaires — Gallo ▲ CD 578 [DAD]
Daetwyler, J.:Livre pour Toi seul, w. M. Sébastien (alt)—[F] — Gallo ▲ CD 578 [DAD]
de'Mircovich, Elisabetta (sgr/rebec/medieval hp/portitive org)—see ORCHESTRAS & ENSEMBLES La Reverdie
Demirev, Vesselin (vn)
Sargon, S.:Music of, w. Lila Deis (sop), Stephen Dubov (ten), Stephen Girko (cl), Christopher Adkins (vc), Deborah Baron (fl), Simon Sargon (pno)—Shemà [Hear] for Sop, Fl, Cl, Vc & Pno; Before the Ark for Vn & Pno; Wedding Dance for Vn & Pno; Klezmuzik for Cl & Pno; At Gradmother's Knee [5 Yiddish Folk Songs] for Ten & Pno; Meditation for Vc & Pno; At Grandfather's Knee [5 Judeo-Spanish Folk Songs] for Sop & Pno *(rec Caruth Auditorium, SMU, Dallas, TX, Jan 1996)* — Gasparo ▲ GAS 318
Demmler, Jürgen (a sax)
Dessau, P.:Suite Sax, w. Peter Grabinger (pno) — Bayer ▲ CD 100100 [DDD]
Holcombe, B.:Blues Con — Bayer ▲ CD 100100 [DDD]
Huang, A.:Chinese Rhap 3, w. Peter Grabinger (pno) — Bayer ▲ CD 100100 [DDD]
Jolivet, A.:Fantaisie-Impromptu, w. Peter Grabinger (pno) — Bayer ▲ CD 100100 [DDD]
Mayer, Wolf:Inner Voices, w. Peter Grabinger (pno) — Bayer ▲ CD 100100 [DDD]
Rosenthal, M.:Sax-Marmalade, w. Peter Grabinger (pno) — Bayer ▲ CD 100100 [DDD]
Demottaz, B. (fl)
Bizet, G.:Jeux d'enfants, w. B. Schenkel (ob), R. Meyer (cl), G. Cass (hn), R. Birnstingl (bn) *(rec June 1987)* — Gallo ▲ CD 527
Demottaz, B. (instr)
Ibert, J.:Pièces brèves, w. R. Birnstingl (bn), G. Cass (hn), B. Demottaz, R. Meyer, B. Schenkel *(rec June 1987)* — Gallo ▲ CD 527
Demottaz, B. (ob)
Berio, L.:Opus Number Zoo, w. B. Schenkel (fl), R. Meyer (cl), G. Cass (hn), R. Birnstingl (bn) *(rec June 1987)* — Gallo ▲ CD 527

Demottaz, B. (ob) (cont.)
Saint-Saëns, C.:Carnival of the Animals, w. B. Schenkel (inst), R. Meyer (cl), G. Cass (horn), R. Birnstingl (bn) *(rec June 1987)* Gallo ▲ CD 527

Dempster, Stuart (trbn)—see also ORCHESTRAS & ENSEMBLES New Performance Group of the Cornish Institute
Deep Listening Band:Troglodyte's Delight, w. Pauline Oliveros (acc/voc/whistles), Panaiotis (voc), Julie Lyon Balliett (voc), Fritz Hauser (perc) *(rec Tarpaper Cave, Rosendale, NY, June 1989)* ¿What Next? ▲ WN 003 ■ WN 0003
Dempster, S.:Didjeridervish New Albion ▲ NA 013 [ADD]
Dempster, S.:Standing Waves 78/87 New Albion ▲ NA 013 [ADD]
Dresher, P.:Channels Passing, w. P. Taub (fl), B. Shapiro (ob), C. Sereque (cl), R. Pressley (tpt), E.M. Gray (vn), W. Gray (vc) *(rec 1983–84)* New Albion ▲ NA 053
Erb, D.:And then Toward the End New World ▲ 80457-2
Suderburg, R.:Night Set, w. R. Suderburg (pno) Delfon ▲ DRS 2127 [DDD]

Dempster, Stuart (trbn/didjeridu/conch)
Dempster, S.:Music of, w. Jay Bulen (trbn), Jeff Domoto (trbn), Moc Escobedo (trbn/didjeridu/conch), Scott Higbee (trbn), Gretchen Hopper (trbn), Nathaniel Irby-Oxford (trbn), Chad Kirby (trbn/conch), Dave Marriott (trbn), Greg Powers (trbn), Debra Sykes (cym)—Conch Calling; Morning Light; Didjerilayover; Secret Currents; Melodic Communion; Shell Shock; Cloud Landings *(rec Fort Worden, Port Townsend, WA, June 18, 1994)* New Albion ▲ NA 076

Dempster, Stuart (trbn/didjeridu/garden hose)
Deep Listening Band:Music of Deep Listening Band, w. Pauline Oliveros (acc/elec), David Gamper (org/fl/elec)—Invocation; Processional [both w. Julie Lyon Balliet (sgr)]; Hi Bali, Hi; Sanctuary; Non-Stop Flight [w. Thomas Buckner (sgr), Julie Lyon Balliet (sgr), Joe McPhee (b cl/tpt), Margarit Shenker (acc/sgr), Nego Gato (perc), Carol Chappell (perc), Jason Finkleman (perc), Women Who Drum (perc)] *(rec Trinity United Methodist Church Sanctuary, 1993–94)* Mode ▲ mode 46

Dempster, Stuart (trbn/didjeridu/voc)
Deep Listening Band:Deep Listening, w. P. Oliveros (voc/acc), Panaiotis (voc/whistling) New Albion ▲ NA 022 [DDD]

Demsey, David (s sax)
Morrill, D.:Sketches *(rec Bailey Hall, cornell Univ., Ithaca, NY)* Centaur ▲ CRC 2214 [DDD]

Demsey, David (t sax)
Morrill, D.:Getz Vars *(rec Wellin Hall, Hamilton College, Clinton, NY, June 26–27, 1993)* Centaur ▲ CRC 2214 [DDD]
Morrill, D.:Studies & Improv *(rec Wellin Hall, Hamilton College, Clinton, NY, June 26–27, 1993)* Centaur ▲ CRC 2214 [DDD]

Demus, Jörg (pno)
Beethoven, L. van:Bagatelle, WoO 59, "Für Elise" Intercord ▲ INT 892.934 [AAD]
Beethoven, L. van:Sons Vc (comp), w. Antonio Janigro (vc) *(rec Vienna, 1964)* Vanguard Classics 2-▲ SVC 56/57 [AAD]
The Best of Beethoven, w. E. Leinsdorf (cnd), C. Munch (cnd), Boston SO, et al. Victrola ("Victrola Best of" series) ▲ 60769-2-RV [ADD] ■ 60769-4-RV
Debussy, C.:Clair de lune Intercord ▲ INT 892.934 [AAD]
Dvořák, A.:Biblical Songs, Op. 99, w. Dietrich Fischer-Dieskau (bar) Deutsche Grammophon ("Double" series) 2-▲ 437377-2
Liszt, F.:Liebesträume—in A♭ Interchord ▲ INT 892.923 [AAD]
Mozart, W.A.:Complete Mozart Edition, w. Ingrid Haebler (pno), Ludwig Hoffmann (pno), Paul Badura-Skoda (pno) Philips 2-▲ 422516-2 [ADD]
Schmidt, F.:Pno Music—Romanze in A (1922); Intermezzo in f# (1938); Toccata in d (1938); Weinachtspastorale in A [piano arr. by Demus of the composer's Organ Prelude in A of 1934] *(rec 1964)* Preiser ▲ 93063 [ADD]
Schmidt, F.:Qnt Cl, w. A. Prinz (cl), A. Kamper (vn), F. Stangler (va), W. Resel (vc) *(rec 1965)* Preiser ▲ 93383 [ADD]
Schmidt, F.:Qnt Pno, w. A. Kamper (vn), W. Hink (vn), F. Stangler (va), W. Resel (vc) *(rec 1965)* Preiser ▲ 93383 [ADD]
Schubert, Franz:Der Hirt auf dem Felsen, w. E. Ameling (sop), I. Gage (pno) EMI Classics ▲ CDM 65179
Schubert, Franz:Die Schöne Müllerin, w. W. Holzmair (bar) [G] *(rec 1983)* Preiser ▲ 93337 [ADD]
Schubert, Franz:Schwanngesang, w. Theo Adam (bass), Rudolf Dunckel (pno) Berlin Classics 2-▲ BER CD 9216
Schubert, Franz:Songs (misc), w. E. Ameling (sop), H. Deinzer (cl) Editio Classica ▲ 77085-2-RG [ADD]
Schubert, Franz:Winterreise, w. Dietrich Fischer-Dieskau (bar) *(rec 1965)* Deutsche Grammophon ("The Originals" series) ▲ 447421-2
Schubert, Franz:Winterreise, w. Julius Patzak (ten) *(rec 1964)* Preiser ▲ PRE 93067 [ADD]
Schubert, Franz:Winterreise, w. Theo Adam (bass), Rudolf Dunckel (pno) Berlin Classics 2-▲ BER CD 9216
Schumann, R.:Dichterliebe, w. Theo Adam (bass), Rudolf Dunckel (pno) Berlin Classics 2-▲ BER CD 9216
Schumann, R.:Songs, w. E. Ameling (sop) Editio Classica ▲ 77085-2-RG [ADD]
Wolf, H.:Michelangelo-Lieder, w. Theo Adam (bass), Rudolf Dunckel (pno), ' Berlin Classics 2-▲ BER CD 9216

Dénes, István (org)
Bach, J.S.:Cant 147, w. Gergely Sárközy (va bastarda/lt), Péter Ella (hpd/lt hpd)—chorale *(rec 1980, 1984 & 1991)* Hungaroton 2-▲ HCD 31616/17 [ADD/DDD]
Bach, J.S.:Sons Vl, BWV 1027–1029, w. Gergely Sárközy (va bastarda), Péter Ella (hpd/lt hpd) *(rec 1980, 1984 & 1991)* Hungaroton 2-▲ HCD 31616/17 [ADD/DDD]

Dengel, Eugenie (va)—see ORCHESTRAS & ENSEMBLES Kohon String Quartet

Dengler, Gudrun (hpd)
Haydn, J.:Capriccio on *Acht Sauschneider müssen sein* Koch Schwann ▲ 311712 [ADD]

Denis, J. M. (vn)
Eccles, H.:Son Db, w. B. Cazauran (db), A. Loger (vn), N. Carles (va), E. Petit (vc) *(rec Aug. 29–30, 1992)* Gallo ▲ CD 753 [ADD]

Denk, Jeremy (pno)
Encore:Pieces for Violin & Piano, w. I. Shapira (vn) Meridian ▲ MER 84314 [DDD]

Denley, Jim (fl/sax/sgr)—see ORCHESTRAS & ENSEMBLES Machine for Making Sense

Denman, John (cl)
Spohr, L.:Con 3 Cl, w. R. Bernhardt (cnd), Royal PO IMP ("Masters" series) ▲ IMP 6600082
Spohr, L.:Con 4 Cl, w. R. Bernhardt (cnd), Royal PO IMP ("Masters" series) ▲ IMP 6600082
Spohr, L.:Potpourri, w. R. Bernhardt (cnd), Royal PO IMP ("Masters" series) ▲ IMP 6600082
Spohr, L.:Vars in B♭ on a Theme from *Alruna*, w. R. Bernhardt (cnd), Royal PO IMP ("Masters" series) ▲ IMP 6600082

Dennemarck, Rudolf (pno)
Furtwängler, W.:Son 2 Vn, w. Wolfgang Müller-Nishio (vn) Bayer ▲ 100268 [ADD]

Dent, John (tpt)
Kernis, A.J.:America(n) (Day) Dreams, w. Kim Barber (mez), Mary Rowell (vn), Leslie Tomkins (va), Tonya Tomkins (vc), Robert Black (db), Kathleen Nester (fl), Larry Guy (cl/b cl), Anthony Cecere (hn), Leslie Stifelman (pno), Susan Jolles (hp), Jeffrey Milarsky (perc), M. Barrett (cnd)—A Navajo Blanket; Wednesday at the Waldorf; The Pregnant Dream; The Blue Bottle; "So Long" to the Moon from the Men of Apollo; Epilogue:The Pure Suit of Happiness *(rec Manhattan Center Studios, New York, May 31–June 3, 1995)* New Albion ♦ NA 083CD
Kernis, A.J.:Nocturne, w. Nancy Allen Lundy (sop), Jeff Milarsky (glock), Benjamin Herman (glock), Leslie Stifelman (pno), Lisa Moore (pno), M. Barrett (cnd) *(rec Manhattan Center Studios, New York, May 31–June 3, 1995)* New Albion ♦ NA 083CD

Dent, S. (cl)
Crusell, B.H.:Divert Ob, w. V. Czarnecki (cnd), Southwest German CO Pforzheim Amati ▲ 9103 [DDD]

Dent, Simon (ob d'amore)
Bach, J.S.:Con Ob d'amore, w. V. Czarnecki (cnd), Southwest German CO Pforzheim Amati ▲ 9103 [DDD]

Dent, Simon (ob)
Albinoni, T.:Cons à 5 Obs, Op. 9, w. V. Czarnecki (cnd), Southwest German CO Pforzheim—No. 2 in d Amati ▲ 9103 [DDD]
Cimarosa, D.:Con in C Ob, w. V. Czarnecki (cnd), Southwest German CO Pforzheim Amati ▲ 9103 [DDD]
Mozart, W.A.:Con Ob, K.314, w. V. Czarnecki (cnd), Southwest German CO Pforzheim Amati ▲ 9103 [DDD]
Strauss, R.:Con Ob, Polish Chamber PO Amati ▲ 9205

Dent, Susan (baroque hn)
The Early Clarinet Family, w. K. Puddy (cl), Gary Brodie (cl/bass chalumeaux), P. Price (bass chalumeaux), Alastair Mitchell (8-keyed bn), Malcolm Martineau (pno) Clarinet Classics ▲ CC 0004

Dentan, M. (org)
Frischknecht, H.E.:Fant Vn, w. H. Glamsch (perc), H. E. Frischknecht (org) *(rec Feb. 26, 1989)* Pro Viva ▲ ISPV 161 CD [DDD]
Frischknecht, H.E.:Org Music, w. E. Frischknecht (org), H. E. Frischknecht (org), H. Glamsch (perc)—3 pieces *(rec Sept. 7, 1989)* Pro Viva ▲ ISPV 161 CD [DDD]

Denyer, Frank (pno)
Ustvolskaya, G.:Sons Pno *(rec Hilversum Conservatorium, Jan 23 & 31, 1995)* Conifer Classics ▲ 75605-51262-2 [DDD]

Deoriti, Maurizio (pno)
Brahms, J.:Sons Cl (comp), w. G. Trinicanti (cl) *(rec June 1993)* Sipario Dischi ▲ CS 27 C
Brahms, J.:Sons Cl (comp), w. Gaspare Tirincanti (cl) Stradivarius ▲ STV SIP 27 [DDD]
Brahms, J.:Trio Cl, w. Gaspare Tirincanti (cl), Marco Boni (vc) Stradivarius ▲ STV SIP 27 [DDD]
Brahms, J.:Trio Cl, w. G. Trinicanti (cl), M. Boni (vc) *(rec June 1993)* Sipario Dischi ▲ CS 27 C

Depetris, Philippe (fl)
Giuliani, G.F.:Grand Son, w. P. Polidori (gtr) *(rec July 1993)* Pavane ▲ ADW 7298 [DDD]
Gragnani, F.:Son Fl, w. P. Polidori (gtr) *(rec July 1993)* Pavane ▲ ADW 7298 [DDD]
Legnani, L.:Duetto concertante, w. P. Polidori (gtr) *(rec July 1993)* Pavane ▲ ADW 7298 [DDD]
Paganini, N.:Son concertata, w. P. Polidori (gtr) [arr fl & gtr] *(rec July 1993)* Pavane ▲ ADW 7298 [DDD]

Deplus, Guy (cl)
Weber, C.M. von:Grand duo concertant Cl, w. Martine Joste (pno) Accord ▲ ACD 202782 [AAD]

Deppe, François (vc)
Schoenberg, A.:The Cabaret Songs, w. Yumi Nara (sop), Izumi Okubo (vn/va), Machiko Takahashi (fl/pic), Vincent Jacquemin (cl/b cl), Brigitte Foccroulle (pno), J.-P. Peuvion (cnd), Liège New Music Ensemble [arr Patrick Davin for Salon Orch] Adda ▲ ADD 581273 [DDD]
Schoenberg, A.:Pierrot lunaire, w. Yumi Nara (sop), Izumi Okubo (vn/va), Machiko Takahashi (fl/pic), Vincent Jacquemin (cl/b cl), Brigitte Foccroulle (pno), J.-P. Peuvion (cnd), Liège New Music Ensemble Adda ▲ ADD 581273 [DDD]

Dequeker, Eric (fl)
Benda, F.:Con in e Fl & Orch, w. P. Peire (cnd), Collegium Instrumentale Brugense Eufoda ▲ 1172 [DDD]

Dequeker, Eric (rcr)
Danzi, F.:Cons (4) Fl, w. P. Peire (cnd), Collegium Instrumentale Brugense—Op. 31 Eufoda ▲ 1172 [DDD]
Devienne, F.:Con 4 Fl, w. P. Peire (cnd), Collegium Instrumentale Brugense Eufoda ▲ 1172 [DDD]

Derewecki, Mariusz (vn)—see ORCHESTRAS & ENSEMBLES Tutti e solo

Déri, A. (pno)
Rossini, G.:Il barbiere di Siviglia, w. I. Kertesi (sop—Berta), S. Ganassi (mez—Rosina), R. Vargas (ten—Almaviva), A. Romero (bar—Dr. Bartolo), R. Servile (bar—Figaro), F. de Grandis (bass—Basilio), K. Sárkány (bass—Fiorello), B. Sztankovits (gtr), W. Humburg (cnd), Failoni CO, Hungarian Radio Chorus *(rec Nov. 16–28, 1992)* Naxos 3-▲ 8.660027/29 [DDD]

Déri, György (vc)—see ORCHESTRAS & ENSEMBLES Duo Ongarese

Dermota, Hilda (pno)
Schumann, R.:Frauenliebe und -leben, w. J. Dermota (sop) Preiser ▲ CD 90955 [DDD]

Derolez, Béatrice (va)—see ORCHESTRAS & ENSEMBLES Gaggini String Quartet

Deroote, S. (pno)
Bartók, B.:Qnt Pno & Strs, w. Chilingirian String Quartet Chandos ▲ CHAN 8660 [DDD]

DeRosa, G. (hmc)
Lansky, P.:Guy's Harp New Albion ▲ NA 030 [DDD]

Derouin, J. (vn)
Matson, S.:Steel Chords, w. D. Livingston (gtr), P. Kent (vn), M. Newman (vn), C. Moussas (vn), R. Tischer (va), E. Duke-Kirkpatrick (vc), B. Morgenthaler (db), S. Matson (cnd) *(rec Aug. 29–30, 1992)* Audioquest ▲ AQCD 1013

Derungs, Martin (hpd)
Haydn, J.:Con Vn, Hpd & Strs, w. Václav Hudecek (vn), L. Sagrestano (cnd), Prague Musici Accord ▲ ACD 220462 [DDD]

Derwinger, Love (pno)
Danzi, F.:Qnt Ob, w. Berlin Philharmonic Wind Quintet members BIS ▲ CD 552 [DDD]
Danzi, F.:Qnt Pno, Op. 53, w. Berlin Philharmonic Wind Quintet members BIS ▲ CD 532 [DDD]
Danzi, F.:Qnt Pno, Op. 54, w. Berlin Philharmonic Wind Quintet *(rec 1991 & 1992)* BIS ▲ CD 592 [DDD]
Danzi, F.:Qnts Ww, Op. 56, w. Berlin Philharmonic Wind Quintet *(rec 1991 & 1992)* BIS ▲ CD 592 [DDD]
Dutilleux, H.:Sonatine Fl, w. Áshildur Haraldsdóttir (fl) Intim Musik ▲ INT 9 [DDD]
Eliasson, A.:Qnt Hpd, w. Tale String Quartet *(rec Sept. 26–27, 1992)* BIS ▲ CD 603 [DDD]
Fauré, G.:Fant Fl, w. Áshildur Haraldsdóttir (fl) Intim Musik ▲ INT 9 [DDD]
Fauré, G.:Morceau de concours Fl & Pno, w. Áshildur Haraldsdóttir (fl) Intim Musik ▲ INT 9 [DDD]
Gaubert, P.:Nocturne et Allegro scherzando, w. Áshildur Haraldsdóttir (fl) Intim Musik ▲ INT 9 [DDD]
Grieg, E.:Con Pno, Op. 16, w. J. Hirokami (cnd), Norrköping SO BIS ("BIS Twins" series) 2-▲ CD 200/619
Grieg, E.:Con Pno, Op. 16, w. J. Hirokami (cnd), Norrköping SO [original version] *(rec Mar. 28, 1993)* BIS ▲ CD 619
Grieg, E.:Peer Gynt *(rec May 5–6, 1993)* BIS ▲ CD 620 [DDD]
Grieg, E.:Pno Music (sels)—Small Piano Pieces (23); Larvikspolka *(rec May 4, 1993)* BIS ▲ CD 619
Grieg, E.:Pno Music (sels)—23 Small Pno Pieces; Larviks-Polka BIS ("BIS Twins" series) 2-▲ CD 200/619
Grieg, E.:Pno Music (sels)—3 Piano Pieces; Agitato; At Halfdan Kjerulf's Memorial; 10 Song Arrangements from "Norwegian Melodies"; Albumblad; Entry of the Boyars *(rec May 5–6, 1993)* BIS ▲ CD 620 [DDD]
Grieg, E.:Songs, w. M. Groop (mez)—Sex digte [6 Poems], Op. 4/1–6; Hjertets melodier [The Heart's Melody], Op. 5/1–4; Sex digte of Ibsen, Op. 25/1–6; Songs from Rolfsen's Laesebog, Op. 61/1–7; Haugtussa (song cycle), Op. 67/1–8 BIS ▲ CD 637 [DDD]
Larsson, M.:Clockworks, w. Rolan Pöntinen (pno), Johan Silvmark (perc), Stockholm Chamber Brass *(rec Studio 2, Swedish Radio, Nov. 13, 1994)* BIS ▲ CD 699 [DDD]
Linde, B.:Music of, w. Ulf Wallin (vn)—DansFantasi for Vn & Pno, Op. 7; Danse for Vn & Xyl [w. Johan Silvmark (xyl)]; Son for Vn & Pno, Op. 15/2; 2 Duets for 2 Vns [w. Ulf Johansson (vn)]; Son for Vn & Pno, Op. 10; Romantic Melody for Vn & Pno *(rec Musikaliska Akademien, Stockholm, Sweden, Apr 1994)* BIS ▲ CD 631 [DDD]
Mendelssohn, F.:Cons (2) for 2 Pnos, w. Roland Pöntinen (pno), L. Markiz (cnd), Amsterdam New Sinfonietta *(rec Concertgebouw, Haarlem, Holland, Sept 20–22, 1994)* BIS ▲ CD 688 [DDD]
Orff, C.:Carmina burana, w. Lena Nordin (sop), Hans Dornbusch (ten), Peter Mattei (bar), Roland Pöntinen (pno), Kroumata Percussion Ensemble, Cecilia Rydinger Alin (cnd), Allmänna Sången, Uppsala Choir School Children's Chorus [chamber version] *(rec Uppsala Univ Hall, Uppsala, Sweden, June 9–11, 1995)* BIS ▲ CD 734 [DDD]
Pärt, A.:Fratres I, w. Tallinn String Quartet BIS ▲ CD 574 [DDD]
Poulenc, F.:Capriccio Pnos, w. R. Pöntinen (pno) *(rec Apr. 1–2, 1993)* BIS ▲ CD 593 [DDD]

▲ = CD ♦ = Enhanced CD Δ = MD ■ = Cassette Tape □ = DCC

Derwinger, Love (pno) (cont.)
Poulenc, F.:Con for 2 Pnos, w. R. Pöntinen (pno), O. Vänskä (cnd), Malmö SO *(rec Nov. 6–7, 1992)* BIS ▲ CD 593 [DDD]
Poulenc, F.:Élégie Pnos, w. R. Pöntinen (pno) *(rec Apr. 1–2, 1993)* BIS ▲ CD 593 [DDD]
Poulenc, F.:L'Embarquement pour Cythère, w. R. Pöntinen (pno) *(rec Apr 1–2, 1993)* BIS ▲ CD 593 [DDD]
Poulenc, F.:Son Fl, w. Áshildur Haraldsdóttir (fl) Intim Musik ▲ INT 9 [DDD]
Poulenc, F.:Son Pno 4–Hands, w. R. Pöntinen (pno) *(rec Apr. 1–2, 1993)* BIS ▲ CD 593 [DDD]
Poulenc, F.:Son for 2 Pnos, w. R. Pöntinen (pno) *(rec Apr. 1–2, 1993)* BIS ▲ CD 593 [DDD]
Reger, M.:Con Pno, w. L. Segerstam (cnd), Norrköping SO *(rec Louis De Geer Concert Hall, Norrköping, Dec 13–14, 1994)* BIS ▲ CD 711 [DDD]
Roussel, A.:Joueurs de flûte, w. Áshildur Haraldsdóttir (fl) Intim Musik ▲ INT 9 [DDD]
Sancan, P.:Sonatine Fl, w. Áshildur Haraldsdóttir (fl) Intim Musik ▲ INT 9 [DDD]
Sibelius, J.:Songs, w. M. Groop (mez)—The Fool's Song of the Spider, Op. 27/4 [from *King Christian I*]; 5 Christmas Songs, Op. 1; 8 Songs, Op. 57; Hymn to Thaïs; 6 Songs, Op. 72; 6 Songs, Op. 86; The Little Girls BIS ▲ CD 657 [DDD]
Tubin, E.:Music of, w. Tallinn String Quartet—String Qt.; Elegy; Piano Quartet BIS ▲ CD 574 [DDD]

Desbaillet, François (org)
Bach, J.S.:Org Music (misc)—Fugue in g; Trio Son No. 1 in B♭; Partita; O Mensch bewein' dein' Sünde gross; Herr Jesu Christ Dich zu uns wend'; Mit Fried' und Freud' ich fahr darin; Dies sind die heil'gen zehn Gebot; Es ist das Heil und kommen her; Herr Christ der ein'ge Gottes Sohn; Herr Gott nun schleuss den Himmel auf; Prelude & Fugue in C *(rec St. Pierre Cathedral, Geneva)* Gallo ▲ CD 706

Désert, Claire (pno)—see also ORCHESTRAS & ENSEMBLES Kandinsky Quartet
Brahms, J.:Son for 2 Pnos, w. Emmanuel Strosser (pno) FNAC Music ▲ 592351
Brahms, J.:Vars on a Theme of Robert Schumann, Op. 23, w. Emmanuel Strosser (pno) FNAC Music ▲ 592351
Chausson, E.:Duos, "La nuit" & "Le réveil", w. D. Collot (sop), B. Vinson (mez), J. Bouillat (ten), G. Wieclaw (bass), E. Strosser (pno), J. Sourisse (cnd), Jean Sourisse Ensemble, Audite Nova Vocal Ensemble FNAC Music ▲ 592224 [DDD]
Debussy, C.:Songs, w. D. Collot (sop), B. Vinson (mez), J. Bouillat (ten), G. Wieclaw (bass), E. Strosser (pno), J. Sourisse (cnd), Jean Sourisse Ensemble, Audite Nova Vocal Ensemble—3 chansons de Chateau D'Orleans FNAC Music ▲ 592224 [DDD]
Dvořák, A.:Con Pno, w. T. Guschlbauer (cnd), Strasbourg PO *(rec Strasbourg, July 10–12, 1995)* FNAC Music ▲ CD 592008 [DDD]
Fauré, G.:Madrigal, w. D. Collot (sop), B. Vinson (mez), J. Bouillat (ten), G. Wieclaw (bass), E. Strosser (pno) FNAC Music ▲ 592224 [DDD]
Fauré, G.:Pavane Orch, w. D. Collot (sop), B. Vinson (mez), J. Bouillat (ten), G. Wieclaw (bass), E. Strosser (pno), J. Sourisse (cnd), Jean Sourisse Ensemble, Audite Nova Vocal Ensemble FNAC Music ▲ 592224 [DDD]
Fauré, G.:Songs, w. D. Collot (sop), B. Vinson (mez), J. Bouillat (ten), G. Wieclaw (bass), E. Strosser (pno), J. Sourisse (cnd), Jean Sourisse Ensemble, Audite Nova Vocal Ensemble—Le Ruisseau, Op. 22; Puisqu'ici bas, Op. 10/1, Les Djinns, Op. 12 FNAC Music ▲ 592224 [DDD]
Ravel, M.:Songs, w. D. Collot (sop), B. Vinson (mez), J. Bouillat (ten), G. Wieclaw (bass), E. Strosser (pno), J. Sourisse (cnd), Jean Sourisse Ensemble, Audite Nova Vocal Ensemble—3 a capella songs FNAC Music ▲ 592224 [DDD]
Saint-Saëns, C.:Choral Music, w. D. Collot (sop), B. Vinson (mez), J. Bouillat (ten), G. Wieclaw (bass), E. Strosser (pno), J. Sourisse (cnd), Jean Sourisse Ensemble , Vocal Audite Nova Ensemble—Calme des nuits, Op. 68/1; Les fleurs et les arbres, Op. 68/2; Salterelle, Op. 74 FNAC Music ▲ 592224 [DDD]
Scriabin, A.:Con Pno, w. T. Guschlbauer (cnd), Strasbourg PO *(rec Strasbourg, July 10–12, 1995)* FNAC Music ▲ CD 592008 [DDD]

Desjardins, Christophe (va)
Lekeu, G.:Qt Pno, Vn, Va & Vc, w. D. Blumenthal (pno), T. Adamopoulos (vn), G. Zanlonghi (vc) Koch Schwann ▲ CD 310185 [DDD]

Desponds, André (pno)
Dussek, J.L.:Son Fl, w. Brigitte Kronjäger (fl), Johannes Degen (vc) *(rec June 1994)* Jecklin ▲ JEC 303 [DDD]
Hummel, J.N.:Adagio, Vars & Rondo on "Schöne Minka", w. Brigitte Kronjäger (fl), Johannes Degen (vc) *(rec June 1994)* Jecklin ▲ JEC 303 [DDD]
Ries, F.:Trio Pno, w. Brigitte Kronjäger (fl), Johannes Degen (vc) *(rec June 1994)* Jecklin ▲ JEC 303 [DDD]

Despont, Philippe (org)
Granato, D.:Motets, w. Marie-Hélène Dupard (sop), Lausanne Ensemble of Female Voices—Crux, moments de la Passion (1990); Homo Quidam (1960); Récitatifs pour la fin du jour (1978); Messe brève (1994); Improvisations rolloises (1958); Rosa vernans (1960); Mariale (1955); Ex Libro Job (1984); Solfeggio sopra'l Jubilate (1968); Petit Magnificat (1980) Gallo ▲ CD 895 [DDD]

DesRoches, R. (perc)
Crumb, G.:Music For A Summer Evening, w. J. Freeman (pno), G. Kalish (pno), R. Fitz (perc) Elektra/Nonesuch ▲ 79149-2 [AAD]
Davidovsky, M.:Synchronism 5, w. R. Fitz (perc), Holdrich (perc), D. Marcone (perc), van Hyning (perc), H. Sollberger (cnd) CRI ▲ CD 611 [ADD]
New Jersey Percussion Ensemble, Desroches, w. New Jersey Percussion Ensemble Elektra/Nonesuch ▲ 79150-2
Ronsheim, J.:Bitter-Sweet, w. DeGaetani, DesRoches CRI ■ C 301
Ronsheim, J.:Easter-Wings, w. J. De Gaetani (mez) CRI ■ C 301
Stravinsky, I.:L'Histoire du soldat Suite Vn, w. G. Tarack (vn), C. Russo (cl), T. Weis (tpt), J. Levine (db), Loren Glickman (bn), J. Swallow (trbn), L. Stokowski (cnd) Vanguard Classics ▲ SVC 1 [AAD]

Destefano, Dario (vc)—see ORCHESTRAS & ENSEMBLES Turin Piano Trio

Destrieri, Filippo (kbd/cmpt)
Battiato, F.:Haiku, w. Franco Battiato (voc), Pouran Ghaffarpour (voc), Antonio Ballista (pno), Marco Boni (vc), Guido Corti (cnt), John Giblin (bass), Gavin Harrison (dr/perc), Jakko Jakszyk (gtr), Roberto Mazza (ob), Fabrizio Merlini (va), Angelo Privitera (kbd/computer), Mino Bordignon (cnd), Milan Chamber Music Choir Hemisphere ▲ 837234-2
Battiato, F.:Messa Arcaica, w. Akemi Sakamoto (mez), Franco Battiato (voc), Carlo Guaitoli (pno), Angelo Privitera (kbd/cmpt), A. Ballista (cnd), Italian Virtuosi, Filippo Maria Bressan (cnd), Athestis Chorus Hemisphere ▲ 837234-2
Battiato, F.:L'Ombra della Luce, w. Franco Battiato (voc), Antonio Ballista (pno), Roger Chase (va), Anthony Pleeth (vc), Gavin Wright (vn), G. Pio (cnd), London Astarte Orch Hemisphere ▲ 837234-2
Battiato, F.:Povera Patria, w. Franco Battiato (voc), Antonio Ballista (pno), Roger Chase (va), Anthony Pleeth (vc), Gavin Wright (vn), G. Pio (cnd), London Astarte Orch Hemisphere ▲ 837234-2
Battiato, F.:Ricerca sul Terzo, w. Franco Battiato (voc), Alessio Alba (tamboura), Antonio Ballista (pno), Marco Boni (vc), Debendra Kanti Chakraborty (tabla), Guido Corti (cnt), John Giblin (bass), Buddhadeu Das Gupta (sarod), Gavin Harrison (dr/perc), Jakko Jakszyk (gtr), Roberto Mazza (ob), Fabrizio Merlini (va), Angelo Privitera (kbd/computer), Mino Bordignon (cnd), Milan Chamber Music Choir Hemisphere ▲ 837234-2
Battiato, F.:Le Sacre Sinfonie del Tiempo, w. Franco Battiato (voc), Antonio Ballista (pno), Roger Chase (va), Anthony Pleeth (vc), Gavin Wright (vn), G. Pio (cnd), London Astarte Orch Hemisphere ▲ 837234-2

Destro, Massimiliano (vn)
Setaccioli, G.:Romances Vn, w. Maurizio Aschelter (pno) *(rec Audiovisivi S. Paolo–Albano Laziale, 1995)* Bongiovanni ▲ 5560 [DDD]

Desurmont, Claude (cl)
Messiaen, O.:Quatuor pour la fin du temps, w. L. Yordanoff (vn), A. Tetard (vc), D. Barenboim (pno) Deutsche Grammophon ("20th Century Classics" series) ▲ 423247-2 [ADD]

Detering, Heinz (db)
Haydn, J.:Die Schöpfung, w. Jeannette van Dijck (sop), Peter Schreier (ten), Theo Adam (bass), Hans Plumacher (vc), Fritz Lehan (hpd), G. Wand (cnd), Cologne Gürzenich Orch, Cologne Gürzenich Chorus Accord 2–▲ ACD 200422 [AAD]

Deuren, Erik van (b cl)—see ORCHESTRAS & ENSEMBLES Ives Ensemble members

Deurungs, Martin (hpd)
Bach, J.S.:Cons solo Hpd, BWV 972–987—BWV 972–978 & 980 Accord ▲ ACD 220492 [DDD]

Deuter, F. (vn)—see ORCHESTRAS & ENSEMBLES Invocation

Deutsch, Helmut (pno)
Brahms, J.:Liebeslieder Waltzes SATB, w. Barbara Bonney (sop), Anne Sofie von Otter (mez), Kurt Streit (ten) Olaf Bär (bar), Bengt Forsberg (pno) EMI Classics ▲ CDC 55430
Brahms, J.:Neue Liebeslieder Waltzes, w. Barbara Bonney (sop), Anne Sofie von Otter (mez), Kurt Streit (ten) Olaf Bär (bar), Bengt Forsberg (pno) EMI Classics ▲ CDC 55430
Brahms, J.:Romanzen aus Tieck's *Magelone*, w. H. Prey (bar), Annette Prey (nar) [G] Orfeo 2–▲ 116842 [DDD]
Mendelssohn, F.:Songs, w. J. Protschka (ten)—31 songs [G] Capriccio ▲ CD 10 363 [DDD]
Schubert, Franz:Die Schöne Müllerin, w. J. Protschka (ten) [G] Capriccio ▲ 10082 [DDD]
Schubert, Franz:Winterreise, w. Bernd Weikl (bar) Nightingale Classics ▲ NIG CD 70960
Schumann, C.:Songs, w. Bo Skovhus (bar)—Liebeszauber; Der Mond kommt still gegangen; Die stille Lotosblume; Liebst du um Schönheit; Warum willst du and're fragen; Ich hab' in deinem Auge; Die gute Nacht; Ich stand in dunklen Träumen; Sie Liebten sich beide; Volkslied; Lorelei Sony Classical ▲ SK 62372
Schumann, R.:Dichterliebe, w. J. Protschka (ten) [G] Capriccio ▲ 10215 ■ 27215
Schumann, R.:Dichterliebe, w. Bo Skovhus (bar) Sony Classical ▲ SK 62372
Schumann, R.:Liederkreis, Op. 24, w. Bo Skovhus (bar) Sony Classical ▲ SK 62372
Schumann, R.:Liederkreis, Op. 39, w. J. Protschka (ten) [G] Capriccio ▲ 10215 ■ 27215
Schumann, R.:Spanisches Liederspiel, w. Barbara Bonney (sop), Anne Sofie von Otter (mez), Kurt Streit (ten), Olaf Bär (bar), Bengt Forsberg (pno) EMI Classics ▲ CDC 55430
Wolf, H.:Italienische Liederbücher (comp), w. Dawn Upshaw (sop), Olaf Bär (bar) EMI Classics ▲ CDC 55618
Zemlinsky, A. von:Songs, w. Bo Skovhus (bar)—Under Blooming Trees; In the Current; Last Request; In Spring; Welcome, Op. 7/2; Blissful Hour, Op. 10/2 *(rec Hannover, Dec 10–11, 1994)* RCA Red Seal ▲ 09026-68111-2 [DDD]

Deutsch, N. (pno)
Ives, C.:Pno Music—March in G & D, "Here's to Good Old Yale"; The Bells of Yale [arr. Deutsch]; The Seen & Unseen Vox Box 2–▲ CDX 5089 [ADD]
Ives, C.:Son 1 Pno Vox Box 2–▲ CDX 5089 [ADD]
Ives, C.:Son 2 Pno Vox Box 2–▲ CDX 5089 [ADD]
Ives, C.:Three-Page Son Vox Box 2–▲ CDX 5089 [ADD]
Ives, C.:Transcriptions from Emerson Vox Box 2–▲ CDX 5089 [ADD]
Schumann, R.:Spanische Liebeslieder, w. M. Shirai (mez), M. Lipovsek (mez), J. Protschka (ten), M. Hölle (bass), N. Shetler (pno) [G] Capriccio ▲ CDC 10079

Deutschler, A. B. (va)
Turina, J.:Escena andaluza, w. P. Coletti (va), F. Rieger (pno), N. Chastain (vn), C. Busch (vn), F. Goutou (vc) *(rec May 25–28, 1993)* Claves ▲ CD 9403 [DDD]

Deutschler, U. (hpd)
Bach, J.S.:Con Fl, Vn & Hpd, w. J. Galway (fl), R. Wolters (vn), J. Faerber (cnd), Württemberg CO RCA Red Seal ▲ 09026-60900-2 ■ 09026-60900-4 □ 09026-60900-5
Bach, J.S.:Sons Fl, BWV 1030–35, w. J. Galway—BWV 1032 RCA Red Seal ▲ 09026-60900-2 ■ 09026-60900-4 □ 09026-60900-5
Tartini, G.:Sons Vn & Continuo, w. I. Turban (vn), Y. Savary (vc)—Sonata in A, "Pastorale" (B A16); Sonata in C (B C11); Sonata in E (B E6); Sonata in g, "Devil's Trill" (B G5); Sonata in g, "Didone abbandonata" (B G10) Claves ▲ CD 9110 [DDD]

Devaere, Hannelore (hp)—see ORCHESTRAS & ENSEMBLES Romanesque

Deveau, David (pno)
Liszt, F.:Pno Music (misc)—Ab Irato; Ballade No. 2 in b; Berceuse; Consolation No. 3; Hungarian Rhapsodies Nos. 5 & 13; Reminiscenses de Bellini's Norma Centaur ▲ CRC 2115
Schumann, R.:Carnaval Pno EcoClassics ▲ ECOCD 002
Schumann, R.:Kreisleriana EcoClassics ▲ ECOCD 002

Devendra, Anand (cl)
Martino, D.:Triple Con, w. Dennis Smylie (cl), Leslie Thimmig (cl), H. Sollberger (cnd), Group for Contemporary Music *(rec Dec 1978)* Albany ▲ TROY 168 [DDD]
Schoenberg, A.:Pierrot lunaire, w. Maureen McNalley (nar), Dwight Peltzer (pno), Eric Rosenblith (vn/va), Chris Finckel (vc), Sue Ann Kahn (fl), J. Thome (cnd), Orch of Our Time Vox Box 2–▲ CDX 5144

Devenny, Ward (pno)
Bloch, E.:Son 2 Vn, "Poème mystique", w. S. Harth (vn) Crystal ▲ CD634
Gamer, C.:Son Vn, w. S. Harth (vn) Crystal ▲ CD634
Janácek, L.:Son Vn, w. S. Harth (vn) Crystal ▲ CD634

Dévérité, Michèle (hpd)—see also ORCHESTRAS & ENSEMBLES Fitzwilliam Ensemble members, Fitzwilliam Ensemble
Telemann, G.P.:Son Hpd in C Astrée ▲ E 8561

Deviatov, Boris (va)—see ORCHESTRAS & ENSEMBLES Leontóvych String Quartet

Devich, János (vc)—see ORCHESTRAS & ENSEMBLES Kodály String Quartet

Devos, Luc (pno)—see also ORCHESTRAS & ENSEMBLES Grumiaux Piano Trio
Benoit, P.:Symphonic Poem Pno, w. F. Devreese (cnd), Royal Flanders PO *(rec Elisabeth Hall, Antwerp, Belgium, Apr 1995)* Marco Polo ("Anthology of Flemish Music" series) ▲ 8.223827 [DDD]
Brahms, J.:Liebeslieder Waltzes SATB, w. Greta De Reyghere (sop), Lucienne Van Deyck (mez), Guy De Mey (ten), Huub Claessens (bass), Jean-Claude Vanden Eynden (pno) *(rec Consevatoire Royal, Liège, 1994)* Ricercar ▲ 153138
Brahms, J.:Neue Liebeslieder Waltzes, w. Greta De Reyghere (sop), Lucienne Van Deyck (mez), Guy De Mey (ten), Huub Claessens (bass), Jean-Claude Vanden Eynden (pno) *(rec Consevatoire Royal, Liège, 1994)* Ricercar ▲ 153138
Brahms, J.:Waltzes Pno, Op. 39, w. Jean-Claude Vanden Eynden (pno) *(rec Consevatoire Royal, Liège, 1994)* Ricercar ▲ 153138
Chopin, F.:Albumleaf Ricercar ▲ 145143
Chopin, F.:Berceuse Ricercar ▲ 145143
Chopin, F.:Nocturnes—in e, Op. posth. 72/1; No. 20 in c♯; No. 21 in c; Op. 48/1 & 2; Op. 55/1 & 2; Op. 62/1 & 2 Ricercar ▲ 145143
Chopin, F.:Nocturnes—Opp. 9/1-3, 15/1-3, 27/1-2, 32/1-2 & 37/1-2 *(rec July 1993)* Ricercar ▲ 132116
Chopin, F.:Waltzes—Op. 64/1-3 Ricercar ▲ 145143
Durlet, E.:Pno Music—Le Legends de tours hallucinces; Chrysanthemes; Jacques; La Valee des bonnes penseés; Teniers pinxit; La Source dans les ruines du temple; Inquieto; La Fourmi allée; Tu es poussiere; Tango tragique Koch Schwann ▲ SCH CD 317752
Janácek, L.:Son Vn, w. A. Hardy (vn) Olympia ▲ OLY 355 [DDD]
Mozart, W.A.:Sons Vn Pno (misc), w. S. Kuijken (vn)—K.379, 380 & 526 Accent ▲ 9175 [DDD]
Mozart, W.A.:Sons Vn Pno (misc), w. S. Kuijken (vn)—K.306, 378, 481 Accent ▲ ACC 9292 D [DDD]
Prokofiev, S.:Son Vn, Op. 94bis, w. A. Hardy (vn) Olympia ▲ OLY 355 [DDD]
Prokofiev, S.:Son 1 Vn, w. A. Hardy (vn) Olympia ▲ OLY 355 [DDD]
Vieuxtemps, H.:Va Pno Music, w. P. Koch (va)—Ballade et Polonaise, Op. 38; Feuilles d'Album, Op. 40; Rêverie, Op. 22; Romances sans paroles, Op. 7 & Op. 8; Souvenir d'Amérique sur "Yankee Doodle," Op. 17 Ricercar ▲ RIS 108094 [DDD]

Devoyon, Pascal (pno)—see also ORCHESTRAS & ENSEMBLES Arion Trio
Debussy, C.:Son Vc, w. Steven Isserlis (vc) Virgin Classics ("Ultraviolet" series) ▲ CUV 61198
Debussy, C.:Son Vn, w. D.-S. Kang (vn) *(rec 4/89)* Naxos ▲ 8.550276 [DDD]
Fauré, G.:Andante Vn, w. Dong-Suk Kang (vn) *(rec Temple Saint Marcel, Paris, Jan 18–20, 1995)* Naxos ▲ 8.550906 [DDD]
Fauré, G.:Berceuse Vn, w. Dong-Suk Kang (vn) *(rec Temple Saint Marcel, Paris, Jan 18–20, 1995)* Naxos ▲ 8.550906 [DDD]
Fauré, G.:Vc Music, w. Steven Isserlis (vc)—Son. 1 [Allegretto moderato]; Son. 2 [Andante]; Papillon RCA Red Seal ▲ 09026-68049-2
Fauré, G.:Elégie, w. Steven Isserlis (vc) RCA Red Seal ▲ 09026-68049-2

INSTRUMENT.

Devoyon, Pascal (pno) (cont.)
Fauré, G.:Elégie, w. S. Isserlis (vc) Hyperion ▲ CDA 66235 [DDD]
Fauré, G.:Music for Vc & Pno, w. S. Isserlis (vc)—Après un rêve, Op. 7/1; Berceuse, Op. 16; Papillon, Op. 77; Romance, Op. 69; Sicilienne, Op. 78 Hyperion ▲ CDA 66235 [DDD]
Fauré, G.:Romance Vc, w. Steven Isserlis (vc) RCA Red Seal ▲ 09026-68049-2
Fauré, G.:Romance Vn, w. Dong-Suk Kang (vn) *(rec Temple Saint Marcel, Paris, Jan 18-20, 1995)* Naxos ▲ 8.550906 [DDD]
Fauré, G.:Sérénade, w. Steven Isserlis (vc) RCA Red Seal ▲ 09026-68049-2
Fauré, G.:Son 2 Vc, w. S. Isserlis (vc) Hyperion ▲ CDA 66235 [DDD]
Fauré, G.:Son 1 Vn, w. Dong-Suk Kang (vn) *(rec Temple Saint Marcel, Paris, Jan 18-20, 1995)* Naxos ▲ 8.550906 [DDD]
Fauré, G.:Son 2 Vn, w. Dong-Suk Kang (vn) *(rec Temple Saint Marcel, Paris, Jan 18-20, 1995)* Naxos ▲ 8.550906 [DDD]
Franck, C.:Son Vn, w. Steven Isserlis (vc) [trans. Jules Delsart] Virgin Classics ("Ultraviolet" series) ▲ CUV 61198
Grieg, E.:Con Pno, Op. 16, w. J. Maksymiuk (cnd), London PO Classics For Pleasure ▲ CDCFP4574 [DDD]
Honegger, A.:Chamber Music (comp), w. D.-S. Kang (vn), J.-P. Audoli (vn), P.-H. Xuereb (va), R. Wallfisch (vc), J. Rossi (db)—Sonatine for 2 Violins (1920); Sonatine for Violin & Cello (1932); Sonata for Cello & Piano (1920); Sonata for Viola & Piano (1920); Trio in f for Violin, Cello & Piano (1914); Paduana for Solo Cello (1945); Prelude for Double Bass & Piano (1932) Timpani ▲ IC1009 [DDD]
Honegger, A.:Chamber Music (comp), w. D.-S. Kang (vn)—Sonata in d for Violin & Piano (1912); Sonata Nos. 1 & 2 for Violin & Piano (1916-18; 1919); Arioso for Violin & Piano (ca. 1927/29); Sonata for Solo Violin (1940); Morceau de concours for Violin & Piano (1945) Timpani ▲ IC1008 [DDD]
Honegger, A.:Chamber Music (comp), w. D.-S. Kang (vn), P.-H. Xuereb (va), R. Wallfisch (vc), M. Arrignon (cl), A. Marion (fl), A. Haraldsdottir (fl), C. Moreaux (ob), T. Caens (tpt), M. Becquet (trbn), P. Zanlonghi (hp), P. Devoyon (pno), F. Kondo (mez), Ludwig String Quartet—Sonatine for Clarinet & Piano (1921-22); Rapsodie for 2 Flutes, Clarinet & Piano (1917); Danse de la Chèvre for Solo Flute (1921); Romance for Flute & Piano (1953); Petite Suite for 2 Flutes & Piano (1934); Trois Contrepoints for Piccolo, Oboe, Violin & Cello (1922); Intrada for Trumpet & Piano (1947); Hommage du trombone exprimant la tristesse de l'auteur absent for Trombone & Piano (1925); J'avais un fidèle amant for String Quartet (1929); Chanson de Ronsard & 3 Chansons de la petite Sirène for Mezzo, Flute & String Quartet (1924); Introduction et Danse for Flute, Harp & String Trio [undated]; Colloque for Flute, Celesta, Violin & Viola [undated] Timpani ▲ IC1010 [DDD]
Honegger, A.:Sonatina Cl, w. M. Arrignon (cl) Timpani ▲ IC1010 [DDD]
Poulenc, F.:Son Vc, w. Steven Isserlis (vc) Virgin Classics ("Ultraviolet" series) ▲ CUV 61198
Poulenc, F.:Son Vn, w. Dong-Suk Kang (vn) *(rec 4/89)* Naxos ▲ 8.550276 [DDD]
Ravel, M.:Son Vn Pno, w. D.-S. Kang (vn) *(rec 4/89)* Naxos ▲ 8.550276 [DDD]
Saint-Saëns, C.:Son 1 Vn, w. D.-S. Kang (vn) Naxos ▲ 8.550276 [DDD]
Schubert, Franz:Fant Vn, D.934, w. D.-S. Kang (vn) Naxos ▲ 8.550420 [DDD]
Schubert, Franz:Sonatinas Vn, w. D. Kang (vn) Naxos ▲ 8.550420 [DDD]
Schumann, R.:Con Pno, w. J. Maksymiuk (cnd), London PO Classics For Pleasure ▲ CDCFP4574 [DDD]
Tchaikovsky, P.:Con 1 Pno, w. C. Dutoit (cnd), Philharmonia Orch Erato ▲ 92865-2

Devries, G. (vn)
Wissmer, P.:Con 2 Vn, w. E. Appia (cnd), Swiss Romande Orch *(rec 1959)* Quantum ▲ QM 6918

Dewar, Ron (t sax)—see ORCHESTRAS & ENSEMBLES Univ of Illinois Contemporary Chamber Players

Dewey, Thomas (pno)
Mahler, G.:Des Knaben Wunderhorn, w. Margaret Price (sop)—Des Antonius von Padua Fischpredigt; Rheinlegendchen; Wo die schönen Trompeten blasen; Lob des hohen Verstandes; Das irdische Leben; Urlicht Forlane ▲ FRL 16744 [DDD]
Mahler, G.:Lieder eines fahrenden Gesellen, w. Margaret Price (sop)—Wenn mein Schatz Hochzeit macht; Ging heut' Morgen über's Feld; Ich hab' ein glühend Messer; Die zwei blauen Augen Forlane ▲ FRL 16744 [DDD]
Mahler, G.:Songs from Rückert, w. Margaret Price (sop)—Blicke mir nicht in die Lieder; Ich atmet' einen linden Duft; Um Mitternacht; Liebst du um Schönheit; Ich bin der Welt abhanden gekommen Forlane ▲ FRL 16744 [DDD]
Schumann, R.:Frauenliebe und -leben, w. M. Price (sop) Forlane ▲ FOR 16711 [DDD]
Schumann, R.:Gedichte, Op. 36, w. M. Price (sop) Forlane ▲ FOR 16711 [DDD]
Schumann, R.:Lieder-Album (sels), w. M. Price (sop) Forlane ▲ FOR 16711 [DDD]
Schumann, R.:Myrthen, w. M. Price (sop) Forlane ▲ FOR 16711 [DDD]
Schumann, R.:Songs, w. Margaret Price (sop)—Der Sandmann; Marienwörmchen; Zigeunerliedchen 1 & 2; Die wandelnde Glocke; Schneeglöckchen; Des Sennen Abschied; Er ist's [all from Liederalbum für die Jugend, Op. 79]; Widmung, Op. 25/1; Aus den östlichen Rosen, Op. 25/25; Volksliedchen, Op. 51/2; Rose, Meer und Sonne, Op. 37/9; Lied der Braut 1 & 2, Op. 25/11 & 12; Frauenliebe und Leben, Op. 42; Aus dem Liederbuch eines Malers, Op. 36 Forlane ▲ FRL 16711 [DDD]

Dewez, L. (vc)—see ORCHESTRAS & ENSEMBLES Grumiaux Piano Trio

Dewez, Luc (vc)—see also ORCHESTRAS & ENSEMBLES Brussels String Quartet
Biarent, A.:Sonnets, w. P. Bartholomée (cnd), Liège PO *(rec Conservatoire Royal de Liège, Oct 16-19, 1995)* Cypres ▲ CYPRES 3601

Dexter, J. (va)
Newman, Anthony:Con Va, w. A. Newman (cnd), New York Arts Orch Newport Classic ▲ NCD 60140 [DDD]

Dexter, John (va)—see ORCHESTRAS & ENSEMBLES Manhattan String Quartet

Deyanova, Marta (pno)
Chopin, F.:Impromptus Nimbus ▲ NI 5297 [ADD/DDD]
Chopin, F.:Scherzos Nimbus ▲ NI 5297 [ADD/DDD]
Mozart, W.A.:Sons Pno *(rec Wyastone Leys, Monmouth, Apr 26-27 & June 8 & Dec)* Nimbus 6-▲ NI 1775 [DDD]
Prokofiev, S.:Tales of an Old Grandmother Nimbus ▲ NI 5176 [DDD]
Prokofiev, S.:Visions fugitives Nimbus ▲ NI 5176 [DDD]
Rachmaninoff, S.:Prelude Pno, Op. 3/2 Nimbus ▲ NI 5094 [DDD]
Rachmaninoff, S.:Preludes Pno, Opp 23 & 32 Nimbus ▲ NI 5094 [DDD]
Schubert, Franz:Moments musicaux Nimbus ▲ NI 5293 [ADD]
Schubert, Franz:Son Pno, D.568 Nimbus 3-▲ NI 1779 [DDD]
Schubert, Franz:Son Pno, D.613 Nimbus ▲ NI 1779 [DDD]
Schubert, Franz:Son Pno, D.625 [w. slow movt D.505] Nimbus ▲ NI 1779 [DDD]
Schubert, Franz:Son Pno, D.664 Nimbus ▲ NI 1779 [DDD]
Schubert, Franz:Son Pno, D.894 Nimbus ▲ NI 1779 [DDD]
Schubert, Franz:Son Pno, D.960 Nimbus ▲ NI 1779 [DDD]
Scriabin, A.:Mazurkas Pno, Op. 3 *(rec Concert Hall of the Nimbus Foundation, July 1993)* Nimbus ▲ NI 5446 [DDD]
Scriabin, A.:Mazurkas Pno, Op. 25 *(rec Concert Hall of the Nimbus Foundation, July 1993)* Nimbus ▲ NI 5446 [DDD]
Scriabin, A.:Mazurkas Pno, Op. 40 *(rec Concert Hall of the Nimbus Foundation, July 1993)* Nimbus ▲ NI 5446 [DDD]
Scriabin, A.:Pno Music (misc)—Etudes (Opp. 2,8 & 65); Poèmes (Opp. 32 & 52) Nimbus ▲ NI 5176 [DDD]
Scriabin, A.:Preludes Pno, Op. 11 Nimbus ▲ NI 5026
Scriabin, A.:Son 5 Pno Nimbus ▲ NI 5176 [DDD]
Shostakovich, D.:Preludes Pno, Op. 34 (complete) Nimbus ▲ NI 5026

Dhavernas, Vincent (perc)—see ORCHESTRAS & ENSEMBLES La Nef

Diakoyiorgis, Tassos (santouri)
Karaindrou, E.:Film Music, w. Jan Garbarek (t sax), Vangelis Christopoulos (ob), Anthis Sokratis (tpt), Nikos Guinos (cl), Vangelis Skouras (hn), Petros Protopapas (fl), Andreas Tsekouras (acc), Christos Sfetsas (vc), Eleni Karaindrou (pno/voc), L. Chalkiadakis (cnd), *(ensemble unknown)*—Farewell Theme; Scream; Improv. On Farewell & Waltz Theme; Farewell Theme II [all from The Beekeeper; w. Jan Garbarek (ten sax), Tassos Diakoyiorgis (satouri), Vassilis Dertilis (kbd), Eleni Karaindrou (pno), Lefteris Chalkiadakis (cnd)]; Elegy for Rosa; Rosa's Song (text:Christofis) [both from Rosa; w. Vangelis Skouras (Fr hn), Petros Protopapas (fl), Alekos Christidis (timp), Eleni Karaindrou (voc), Lefteis Chalkiadakis (cnd)]; Fairytale; Parade; Return; Song [all from Happy Homecoming, Comrade; w. Vangelis Skouras (Fr hn), Christos Sfetsas (vc), Aliki Krithari (hp), Andreas Tsekouras (acc), Eleni Karaindrou (pno), Nelli Semitekolo (pno), Anthis Sokratis (tpt), Lefteris Chalkiadakis (cnd)]; Wandering in Alexandria (2 vers) [both from Wandering; w. Tassos Diakoyiorgis (santouri), Nelli Semitekolo (prepared pno), Anthis Sokratis (tpt), Nikos Guinos (cl), Katerina Ktona (hpd), Christos Sfetsas (vc)]; The Journey [from Voyage to Cythera]; Adagio [from Landscape in the Mist] [both w. Vangelis Christopoulos (ob), str orch, Lefteris Chalkiadakis (cnd)] ECM ▲ 78118-21429-2 [AAD]

Dias, Kirstine Heyde (vn)
Heyde, O.:Songs, w. Margrehte Heyde (sgr), Ole Heyde (sgr/gtr), Knud Erik Jørgensen (va), Lars Gram (db)—44 songs from texts by Piet Hein Danica ▲ DCD 8175

Diatto, M. (va)—see ORCHESTRAS & ENSEMBLES Aglàia Ensemble

Diaz, Alirio (gtr)
Boccherini, L.:Qnts Gtr, G.445-453, w. A. Schneider (vn), F. Galimir (vn), M. Tree (va), D. Soyer (vc)—in C, G.446 *(rec 1965)* Vanguard Classics ▲ OVC 8006 [ADD]
Castelnuovo-Tedesco, M.:Con 1 Gtr, w. A. Janigro (cnd), Zagreb Solisti *(rec Grossesaal, Musikverein, Vienna, June 1965)* Vanguard Classics ▲ OVC 8069 [ADD]
Four Centuries of Spanish Guitar *(rec 1965)* Vanguard Classics ("Everyman" series) ▲ OVC 5006 [ADD]
Four Centuries of Spanish Guitar *(rec Judson Hall, New York, Apr 1965)* Vanguard Classics ▲ SVC 49 [AAD]
Kohaut, K.:Cons Lt & Strs, w. A. Janigro (cnd), Zagreb Solisti—in F *(rec Grossesaal, Musikverein, Vienna, June 1965)* Vanguard Classics ▲ OVC 8069 [ADD]
Masterpieces of the Spanish Guitar *(rec 1961)* Vanguard Classics ("Everyman" series) ▲ OVC 5004 [ADD]
Masterpieces of the Spanish Guitar *(rec Judson Hall, New York, Oct 4-6, 1961)* Vanguard Classics ▲ SVC 48 [AAD]

Diaz, Andrés (vc)
Brahms, J.:Sons Vc (comp), w. S. Sanders (pno) *(rec 1991)* Dorian ▲ DOR 90165 [DDD]
The Cantorial Voice of the Cello, w. C. Bloemendal (vc), Valerie Tryon (pno), Andrew Mark (vc) *(rec Troy Savings Bank Music Hall, Troy, NY, May 1994)* Dorian ▲ DOR 90208 [DDD]
Dvořák, A.:Silent Woods, w. S. Sanders (pno) [Brahms's version for cello & piano] *(rec 1991)* Dorian ▲ DOR 90165 [DDD]
Finzi, G.:Interlude Ob & Strs, w. W. Rapier (ob), R. Diaz (va), T. Dimitriades (str), J. Shames (pno) *(rec live Oct. 1, 1989)* Boston Records ▲ BR 1001
McLennan, J.S.:Qnt Vn, Va, Vc, Cl & Pno, w. A. Levy (vn), B. Fine (va), P. Hancock (cl), R. Hodgkinson (pno) CRI ▲ CD 594 [DDD]
Russian Romantics for Cello & Piano, w. Samuel Sanders (pno) *(rec Apr. 1993)* Dorian ▲ DOR 90188 [DDD]
Seasons Remembered 2, w. J. L. Stillman (pno), Toby Appel (va), John Deak (db), Eliot Porter (db), Diaz Trio, Lutz Rath (vc), Fenwick Smith (fl), Ruth Waterman (vn) North Star ▲ 9837-40052-2 ■ 9837-40052-4
Villa-Lobos, H.:Con 2 Vc, w. E. Diemecke (cnd), Simón Bolívar SO *(rec Aula Magna of the Universidad Central de Venezuela, Caracas, July & Aug 1995)* Dorian ▲ DOR 90228 [DDD]

Diaz, James (org)
Schuller, G.:Con Org, w. M. Bernardi (cnd), Calgary PO *(rec live, Jack Singer Concert Hall, Calgary, Alberta, Oct. 14, 1994)* New World ▲ 80492-2

Diaz, Roberto (va)
Finzi, G.:Interlude Ob & Strs, w. W. Rapier (ob), A. Diaz (vc), T. Dimitriades (str), J. Shames (pno) *(rec live Oct. 1, 1989)* Boston Records ▲ BR 1001
Seasons Remembered 2, w. J. L. Stillman (pno), Toby Appel (va), John Deak (db), Eliot Porter (db), Diaz Trio, Lutz Rath (vc), Fenwick Smith (fl), Ruth Waterman (vn) North Star ▲ 9837-40052-2 ■ 9837-40052-4

Dichter, Mischa (pno)
Addinsell, R.:Warsaw Con, w. N. Marriner (cnd), Philharmonia Orch Philips ▲ 411123-2 [DDD]
Beethoven, L. van:Son 8 Pno, "Pathétique" Philips ("Concert Classics" series) ▲ 422475-2 [ADD]
Beethoven, L. van:Son 14 Pno, "Moonlight Son" Philips ("Concert Classics" series) ▲ 422475-2 [ADD]
Beethoven, L. van:Son 28 Pno Philips ("Concert Classics" series) ▲ 422475-2 [ADD]
Brahms, J.:Fants Pno, Op. 116 *(rec June 1-3, 1993)* MusicMasters ▲ 01612-67126-2 [DDD]
Brahms, J.:Vars & Fugue on a Theme by Handel *(rec June 1-3, 1993)* MusicMasters ▲ 01612-67126-2 [DDD]
Brahms, J.:Waltzes Pno, Op. 39 *(rec June 1-3, 1993)* MusicMasters ▲ 01612-67126-2 [DDD]
Gershwin, G.:Rhap in Blue, w. N. Marriner (cnd), Philharmonia Orch Philips ▲ 411123-2 [DDD]
Gershwin, G.:Rhap in Blue, w. J. Williams (cnd), Boston Pops Orch Philips ("Digital Classics" series) ▲ 426404-2 [DDD]
Liszt, F.:Hungarian Rhaps Philips ("Digital Classics" series) 2-▲ 416463-2
Liszt, F.:Polonaises Pno, w. N. Marriner (cnd), Philharmonia Orch Philips ▲ 411123-2 [DDD]
Tchaikovsky, P.:Con 1 Pno, w. E. Leinsdorf (cnd), Boston SO RCA Gold Seal ("Papillon Collection" series) ▲ 6526-2-RG [ADD] ■ 6526-4-RG

Dick, James (pno)
Chopin, F.:Con 1 Pno, w. H. Ohyama (cnd), Texas Festival Orch Round Top ▲ RTR 002
Prokofiev, S.:Con 3 Pno, w. P. Verrot (cnd), Texas Festival Orch Round Top ▲ RTR 002
Saint-Saëns, C.:Con 2 Pno, w. P. Verrot (cnd), Texas Festival Orch *(rec Festival Concert Hall, Round Top, TX)* Round Top ▲ RTR 003 [DDD]
Welcher, D.:Con 1 Pno, w. P. Verrot (cnd), Texas Festival Orch *(rec Festival Concert Hall, Round Top, TX)* Round Top ▲ RTR 003 [DDD]

Dick, Robert (bass fl)
Dick, R.:Sea of Holes, w. S. Gorn (Amazonas fl/Lakota fl/Balinese suling/Indian penny whistle) O.O. Discs ▲ OO 12 [DDD]

Dick, Robert (fl)
Asia, D.:Dreamsequence II, "Plum" [all parts, overdubbed] Attacca ▲ BABEL 9158-1 [DDD]
Berio, L.:Sequenza I Attacca ▲ BABEL 9158-1 [DDD]
Biscardi, C.:Tenzone, w. Keith Underwood (fl), Robert Weirich (pno) *(rec Sprague Hall, Yale Univ., New Haven, CT, 1978)* CRI ▲ CD 686 [ADD]
Debussy, C.:Syrinx Attacca ▲ BABEL 9158-1 [DDD]
Dick, R.:Bassbamboo, w. S. Gorn (fl) O.O. Discs ▲ OO 7 [DDD]
Dick, R.:Calaveras Jump, w. S. Gorn (fl) O.O. Discs ▲ OO 12 [DDD]
Dick, R.:DTR, w. S. Gorn (fl) O.O. Discs ▲ OO 12 [DDD]
Dick, R.:Lapis Blues, w. S. Gorn (fl) O.O. Discs ▲ OO 12 [DDD]
Dick, R.:Light, w. S. Gorn (fl) O.O. Discs ▲ OO 12 [DDD]
Dick, R.:Piece in Gamelan Style O.O. Discs ▲ OO 12 [DDD]
Dick, R.:Solo Fl Music—Concert Etudes Vol. 2, "Flying Lessons" (1987); Anamnesis (1990); Flames must not encircle sides (1980); Lookout (1989) Attacca ▲ BABEL 9158-2 [DDD]
Dick, R.:Solo Fl Music—Afterflight (1973); News? (1983); Flying Lessons (6 Contemporary Concert Etudes) (1984) GM ▲ 2013CD [DDD]
Dolphy, E.:Gazzelloni GM ▲ 2013CD [DDD]
Fukushima, K.:Mei Attacca ▲ BABEL 9158-1 [DDD]
Kim, J.H.:Tchong, w. Hong Jong-Jin (daegum) O. O. Discs ▲ OO24
Ladder of Escape, Vol. 5 Attacca ▲ BABEL 9158-1 [DDD]
Morris, R.:Raudra Attacca ▲ BABEL 9158-1 [DDD]
Paganini, N.:Caprices Vn [No. 15; arr Dick for solo fl] GM Recordings ▲ GM 2013

▲ = CD ♦ = Enhanced CD Δ = MD ■ = Cassette Tape ▯ = DCC

Dick, Robert (fl) (cont.)
Rolnick, N.B.:Blowing — O.O. Discs ▲ OO 8 [ADD]
Varèse, E.:Density 21.5 — GM ▲ 2013CD [DDD]
Dick, Robert (pic)
Dick, R.:Tongue & Groove, w. S. Gorn (fl) — O.O. Discs ▲ OO 12 [DDD]
Dickey, Bruce (cnt)—see ORCHESTRAS & ENSEMBLES Sonnerie Ensemble
Dickey, Bruce (cornetto)
Virtuoso Solo Music for Cornetto, w. Stephen Stubbs (chit/vih), Erin Headley (vl), Andrew Lawrence-King (double hp/Renaissance hp) — Accent ▲ 9173 [DDD]
Dickey, Bruce (sackbut)
Cavalli, P.F.:Vespero della beata Vergine Maria, w. Barbara Borden (sop), Emily van Evera (sop), Markus Brutscher (ten), Mark Padmore (ten), Rodrigo del Pozo (ten), Gerd Türk (ten), Harry van der Kamp (bass), Peter Zimpel (sgr), Charles Toet (sackbut), Concerto Palatino, Schola Cantorum Basiliensis — Harmonia Mundi France ("Documenta" series) 2-▲ HMC 905219/20
Dickie, Brendan (didgeridu)
McLean, B.:Rainforest Images, w. Panaiotis (sgr), I. Troselj (sgr), K. Ryan (sgr), P. McLean (sgr/rcr/vn), B. McLean (rcr/clariflute) — Capstone ▲ CPS 8617n
Dickinson, Lynn (vl)
Musiche Veneziene per Voce e Strumenti, w. T. Berganza (mez), Yasunori Imamura (lt/thb/gtr), Pere Ros (vl), Carol Lewis (vl), Silvie Mocquet (vl), Jörg Ewald Dähler (pno), Jörg Ewald Dähler (cnd) *(rec Kirche Saanen, Feb 1982)* — Claves ▲ CD 508206 [DDD]
Dickstein, M. (hp)—see ORCHESTRAS & ENSEMBLES Debussy Trio
Dicterow, Glenn (vn)
Copland, A.:Qt Pno, w. Israela Margalit (pno), Rebecca Young (va), Alan Stepansky (vc) — EMI Classics ("Anglo-American Chamber Music" series) ▲ CDC 55405
Holdridge, L.:Albinoni, w. L. Holdridge (cnd), London SO [arr. Holdridge] *(rec St. Giles Church, Cripplegate, London, Sept. & Oct. 1973)* — Citadel ▲ CTD 88104 [ADD]
Holdridge, L.:Con 2 Vn, w. L. Holdridge (cnd), London SO *(rec St. Barnabas Church, Woodside Park, London, Jan. 4 & 5, 1980)* — Citadel ▲ CTD 88104 [DDD]
Ives, C.:Largo, w. Stanley Drucker (cl), Israela Margalit (pno) — EMI Classics ("Anglo-American Chamber Music" series) ▲ CDC 55406
Ives, C.:Son 2 Vn, w. Israela Margalit (pno) — EMI Classics ("Anglo-American Chamber Music" series) ▲ CDC 55406
Ives, C.:Son 4 Vn, w. Israela Margalit (pno) — EMI Classics ("Anglo-American Chamber Music" series) ▲ CDC 55406
Korngold, E.W.:Son Vn, w. Israela Margalit (pno) — EMI Classics ("Anglo-American Chamber Music" series) ▲ CDC 55401
Korngold, E.W.:Trio Pno, w. Israela Margalit (pno), Alan Stepansky (vc) — EMI Classics ("Anglo-American Chamber Music" series) ▲ CDC 55401
Rimsky-Korsakov, N.:Scheherazade, w. Y. Temirkanov (cnd), New York PO — RCA Red Seal ▲ 09026-61173-2 ■ 09026-61173-4
Dieci, Andrea (gtr)
Ponce, M.:Gtr Music—24 Preludes; Sonata III; Prelude in A; Homenaje a Tarrega; Mazurka; Valse; plus other sels — Nuova Era ▲ NUO CD 7267
Dieckmann, Ulrich (trbn)—see ORCHESTRAS & ENSEMBLES Triton Trombone Quartet
Diedrichsen, Annegret (vn)
Haydn, J.:Divert for 2 E Hns, Hns, Vns & Bns, H.II/16, w. Divertimento Salzburg [arr fl, ob, 2 vns, vc, bn & db] — Orfeo ▲ 310941 [DDD]
Haydn, J.:Divert Fl, Ob, Vns, Vc, Bn & Db, H.II/11, "Der Geburtstag", w. Divertimento Salzburg — Orfeo ▲ 310941 [DDD]
Diefes, Edwin (tuba)—see ORCHESTRAS & ENSEMBLES New World Brass
Diehl, Brian (trbn)—see ORCHESTRAS & ENSEMBLES New World Brass
Dieltiens, Roel (vc)—see also ORCHESTRAS & ENSEMBLES Ensemble 415
Bach, J.S.:Suites Vc, BWV 1007-1012 *(rec Jan 1991)* — Accent 2-▲ 9171/72 [DDD]
Bruch, M.:Pieces Cl, Op. 83/1-8, w. Walter Boeykens (cl), Thérèse-Marie Gilissen (va), Robert Groslot (pno) *(rec 1991)* — Musique d'Abord ▲ HMA 1901371
Bruch, M.:Pieces Cl, Op. 83/1-8, w. Walter Boeykens (cl), Thérèse-Marie Gilissen (va), Robert Groslot (pno) *(rec 1991)* — Musique D'Abord ▲ HMA 1901371
Gabrielli, D.:Vc Music, w. Richte van der Meer (vc), Konrad Junghänel (thb), Robert Kohnen (hpd)—music by Bononcini *(Son in a for 2 Vcs)*, Willem De Fesch *(Son in a for Vc & Cont, Op. 13/6)*, D. Gabrieli *(Sons (2) in A & G for Vc & Cont; Ricercare I-VII; Canon for 2 Vcs)* — Accent ▲ 9070 [DDD]
Geminiani, F.:Sons Vc & Continuo, Op. 5, w. R. van der Meer (vc), R. Kohnen (hpd)—Sonata in d; Sonata No. 3 in C; Sonata No. 6 in a — Accent ▲ 9181 [DDD]
Haydn, J.:Trios Pno, Fl & Vc, w. Guy Penson (hpd), Jan de Winne (fl) — Eufoda ▲ EUF 1185 [DDD]
Italian Cello Music, w. Richte van der Meer (vc), K. Junghänel (thb), R. Kohnen (hpd) — Accent ▲ 9070 [DDD]
Kodály, Z.:Duo Vn & Vc, w. Sergiu Luca (vn) — Harmonia Mundi France ▲ HMC 901560
Kodály, Z.:Son Vc, Op. 8 — Harmonia Mundi France ▲ HMC 901560
Reicha, A.:Qts Fl, w. Konrad Hünteler (fl), Rainer Kussmaul (vn), Jürgen Kussmaul (va) — MD + G ▲ MDG 3110630
Vivaldi, A.:Sons Vc, w. A. Woodrow (db), R. Kohnen (hpd)—(3) in b♭ & g (from Op. 14); in e — Accent ▲ 9181 [DDD]
Zemlinsky, A. von:Trio Cl, w. Walter Boeykens (cl), Thérèse-Marie Gilissen (va), Robert Groslot (pno) *(rec 1991)* — Musique d'Abord ▲ HMA 1901371
Dieltjens, Thomas (pno)
Brotons, S.:Rebroll, w. N. Nozy (cnd), Belgian Guides Symphonic Band — René Gailly ▲ CD 87107 [DDD]
Falla, M. de:El sombrero de tres picos, w. N. Nozy (cnd), Belgian Guides Symphonic Band — René Gailly ▲ CD 87107 [DDD]
Granados, E.:Danzas españolas (10), w. N. Nozy (cnd), Belgian Guides Symphonic Band — René Gailly ▲ CD 87107 [DDD]
Diemecke, Pablo (vn)—see also ORCHESTRAS & ENSEMBLES McPherson Trio
Dvořák, A.:Con Vn, w. P. Freeman (cnd), Slovak National Orch *(rec Concert Hall of Radio Bratislava, Slovakia, Dec 1994)* — Intersound ▲ 3538
Dvořák, A.:Sonatina Vn, w. May-Ling Kwok (pno) *(rec Concert Hall of Radio Bratislava, Slovakia, Dec 1994)* — Intersound ▲ 3538
Prokofiev, S.:Con 1 Vn, w. P. Freeman (cnd), Moscow PO *(rec MoscFilm Studio Concert Hall, Moscow)* — Fanfare ▲ CDS 3479 [DDD]
Prokofiev, S.:Son Vn, Op. 94bis, w. May-Ling Kwok (pno) *(rec MoscFilm Studio Concert Hall, Moscow)* — Fanfare ▲ CDS 3479 [DDD]
Diesselhorst, Jan (vc)—see ORCHESTRAS & ENSEMBLES Philharmonia String Quartet, Berlin Philharmonia String Quartet
Dietrich, Marie (triangle)
Clementi, M.:Waltzes, Op. 38, w. V. de Col (pno), K. Künstler (tambourine) — Entrée ▲ 0038 [ADD]
Digney, John (ob)
Eller, H.:Dawn, w. N. Järvi (cnd), Scottish National Orch — Chandos ▲ CHAN 8525 [DDD]
Dijk, Louis van (pno)
Gershwin, G.:Rhap in Blue—version for 2 pnos — Erasmus ▲ WVH 117
Dijk, Pieter van (org)
Andriessen, H.:Intermezzi Org (5) — NM Classics ▲ NM 92034
Recital by Pieter van Dijk at the Organ of the Reformed Church, Oosthuizen, w. Dijk, Pieter van (org) *(rec Apr. 9, 1992)* — Emergo ▲ EC 3995 [DDD]
Dikmen, Mustafa Dogan (voc/fl/dr)—see ORCHESTRAS & ENSEMBLES Ensemble Saraband
Dikov, Anton (pno)
Beethoven, L. van:Con 1 Pno, w. E. Tabakov (cnd), Sofia PO — LaserLight ▲ 15 626 [DDD]
Beethoven, L. van:Con 2 Pno, w. E. Tabakov (cnd), Sofia PO — LaserLight ▲ 15 626 [DDD]
Beethoven, L. van:Con 3 Pno, w. E. Tabakov (cnd), Sofia PO — LaserLight ▲ 15 627 [DDD]
Beethoven, L. van:Con 4 Pno, w. E. Tabakov (cnd), Sofia PO — LaserLight ▲ 15 627 [DDD]
Beethoven, L. van:Con 5 Pno, "Emperor", w. E. Tabakov (cnd), Sofia PO — LaserLight ▲ 15 628 [DDD]

Dikov, Anton (pno) (cont.)
Beethoven, L. van:Con 5 Pno, "Emperor", w. E. Tabakov (cnd), Sofia PO — Laserlight ▲ 15 523 [DDD]
Beethoven, L. van:Con 5 Pno, "Emperor", w. E. Tabakov (cnd), Sofia PO — Capriccio ▲ 10 911 [DDD]
Beethoven, L. van:Fant Pno, Op. 80, "Choral Fant", w. E. Tabakov (cnd), Sofia PO — Capriccio ▲ 10 911 [DDD]
Dill, Tom (tpt)
Brown, C.:Lava, w. William Winant (perc), Toyoji Tomita (trbn), Peter Wahrhaftig (tuba), Chris Brown (elecs)—Crack; Eruption; Fountain; River; Crest; Pahoehoe — Tzadik ("The Composers" series) ▲ TZA 7002 [DDD]
Diller, Clemens (vc)
Eisler, H.:Chamber Music, w. Rudolf Ulbrich (vn), Joachim Zindler (va) — Berlin Classics ▲ BER CD 9231
Dillon, G. B. (tpt)
Petrassi, G.:Fanfare for 3 Tpts, w. R. Karon (tpt), A. Plog (tpt) — Crystal ▲ CD 663 [DDD]
Dilworth-Leslie, S. (pno)
Fauré, G.:Pno Music—Ballade in F#, Op. 19; Barcarolles, Nos. 3, 5 & 8; Impromptus, Nos. 2 & 5; Nocturne No. 6; Preludes (9), Op. 103; Theme & Variations in c#, Op. 73 — CRS ▲ 9154
DiMeola, Al (gtr)
Pavarotti & Friends for War Child, w. L. Pavarotti (ten), Eric Clapton (sgr), Sheryl Crow (sgr), Elton John (sgr), Liza Minelli (sgr), Joan Osborne (sgr), Jon Secada (sgr), Eric Clapton (gtr), John McLaughlin (gtr), Marco Armiliato, Edoardo Bennato, José Molina, Kelly Family, Ligabue, Litfiba, et al. *(rec Modena, Italy, 1996)* — London ▲ 452900-2 ■ 452900-4
Dimigen, Christiane (ob)—see also ORCHESTRAS & ENSEMBLES Albert Schweitzer Wind Quintet
Yun, I.:Rondell, w. D. Schneider (cl), E. Hübner (bn) *(rec Dec. 1991)* — CPO ▲ CPO 999184 [DDD]
Dimitriades, Tatiana (strs)
Bach, J.S.:Con Ob, BWV 1053, w. W. Rapier (ob), Diaz-Shames-Diaz Trio *(rec live in concert, Oct 1, 1989)* — Boston Records ▲ BR 1001 ■ BR 1001 CT
Bach, J.S.:Con Ob d'amore, w. W. Rapier (ob d'amore), Diaz-Shames-Diaz Trio *(rec live in concert, Oct 1, 1989)* — Boston Records ▲ BR 1001 ■ BR 1001 CT
Finzi, G.:Bagatelles, Op. 23, w. W. Rapier (ob), Diaz-Shames-Diaz Trio *(rec live 10/1/89)* — Boston Records ▲ BR 1001 ■ BR 1001 CT
Finzi, G.:Interlude Ob & Strs, w. W. Rapier (ob), R. Diaz (va), A. Diaz (vc), J. Shames (pno) *(rec live Oct. 1, 1989)* — Boston Records ▲ BR 1001
Wayne Rapier:Oboe, w. W. Rapier (ob), Diaz-Shames-Diaz Trio — Boston Records ▲ BR1001CD ■ BR1001CT
Dimmock, Johathan (hpd)
Bach, J.S.:Con for 4 Hpds, w. John Butt (hpd), Phebe Craig (hpd), Jeffrey Thomas (hpd), J. Thomas (cnd), American Bach Soloists — Koch International Classics ▲ KIC 7237 [DDD]
Dimmock, Johathan (org)
French Masterworks from St. John the Divine [New York City] — Arkay ▲ ARK 6114 [DDD]
Dimond, V. (va)—see ORCHESTRAS & ENSEMBLES Amelite Consortium
Dindo, Andrea (pno)
Bassi, L.:Divert on Verdi's *Il Trovatore*, w. Alessandro Carbonare (cl) *(rec Jungle Studios, Milan, July 29-31, 1995)* — Agora Musica ▲ AG 017.1 [DDD]
Bassi, L.:Fant di concerto on Verdi's *Rigoletto*, w. Alessandro Carbonare (cl) *(rec Jungle Studios, Milan, July 29-31, 1995)* — Agora Musica ▲ AG 017.1 [DDD]
Carulli, B.:Fant on Verdi's *Macbeth*, w. Alessandro Carbonare (cl) *(rec Jungle Studios, Milan, July 29-31, 1995)* — Agora Musica ▲ AG 017.1 [DDD]
Leonesi, G.:Capriccio on Verdi's *Un ballo in maschera*, w. Alessandro Carbonare (cl) *(rec Jungle Studios, Milan, July 29-31, 1995)* — Agora Musica ▲ AG 017.1 [DDD]
Lovreglio, D.:Fant da concerto on Motifs of Verdi's *La traviata*, w. Alessandro Carbonare (cl) *(rec Jungle Studios, Milan, July 29-31, 1995)* — Agora Musica ▲ AG 017.1 [DDD]
Poulenc, F.:Élégie Hn, w. Stefano Pignatelli (hn) *(rec Sala Maffeiana dell'Accademia Filarmonica di Verona, May 7-9, 1995)* — Agorá ▲ 021 [DDD]
Poulenc, F.:Sxt Pno, w. Gianpaolo Pretto (fl), Paolo Grazia (ob), Alessandro Carbonare (cl), Roberto Giaccaglia (bn), Stefano Pignatelli (hn) *(rec Sala Maffeiana dell'Accademia Filarmonica di Verona, May 7-9, 1995)* — Agorá ▲ 021 [DDD]
Poulenc, F.:Son Cl Pno, w. Alessandro Carbonare (cl) *(rec Sala Maffeiana dell'Accademia Filarmonica di Verona, May 7-9, 1995)* — Agorá ▲ 021 [DDD]
Poulenc, F.:Son Fl, w. Gianpaolo Pretto (fl) *(rec Sala Maffeiana dell'Accademia Filarmonica di Verona, May 7-9, 1995)* — Agorá ▲ 021 [DDD]
Poulenc, F.:Trio Ob, w. Paolo Grazia (ob), Roberto Giaccaglia (bn) *(rec Sala Maffeiana dell'Accademia Filarmonica di Verona, May 7-9, 1995)* — Agorá ▲ 021 [DDD]
Serafini, M.:Fantasia on Verdi's *Aida*, w. Alessandro Carbonare (cl) *(rec Jungle Studios, Milan, July 29-31, 1995)* — Agora Musica ▲ AG 017.1 [DDD]
Verdi, G.:Music of, w. Alessandro Carbonare (cl)—melodies from Ballo in Maschera; Aida; Macbeth; Il Trovatore; La Traviata; Rigoletto — Agorá ▲ 017
Dindo, E. (vc)—see ORCHESTRAS & ENSEMBLES La Scala String Trio
Dine, Matthew (ob)
Cohn, J.:Music of, w. M. Piccinini (fl), J. Manasse (cl), M. Finn (bn), J. Tarpley (hn), N. Akamatsu (db), S. Alderking (pno)—Wind Quintet, Op. 36b (1981); Little Overture for Wind Quintet, Op. 59 (1982); Sonatina for Clarinet & Piano, Op. 56 (1981); Sonata Romantica for Double Bass & Piano, Op. 18 (1952); Sonata Robusta for Bassoon & Piano, Op. 55 (1980); Sonata for Flute & Piano, Op. 52 (1974); Goldfinch Variations for Three Treble Instruments, Op. 61 (1984) *(rec 1985)* — XLNT ▲ CD 18006 [ADD]
Cohn, J.:Music of, w. M. Piccinini (fl), J. Manasse (cl), M. Finn (bn), J. Tarpley (hn), N. Akamatsu (db), S. Alderking (pno)—Wind Quintet, Op. 36b (1981); Goldfinch Variations for Wind Trio, Op. 61 (1984); Little Overture for Wind Quartet, Op. 59 (1982); Suite Champêtre for Wind Quintet (after Rameau), Op. 47 (1968) — XLNT ■ C 2
Dingfelder, Ingrid (fl)
Rorem, N.:Romeo & Juliet, w. Levine (gtr) — CRI ■ ACS 6007
Dinion, S. (perc)
Glazer, S.:Duo Cl, w. J. Russo (cl) — CRS ▲ CD 9153
Dinitzen, Kim Bak (vc)
Brahms, J.:Son 1 Vc, w. E. Westenholz (pno) — Kontrapunkt ▲ KPT 32172 [DDD]
Britten, H.:Son Vc, w. P. Salo (pno) — Kontrapunkt 2-▲ KPT 32101 [DDD]
Britten, H.:Suites Vc (comp) — Kontrapunkt 2-▲ KPT 32101 [DDD]
Britten, H.:Tema "Sacher" — Kontrapunkt 2-▲ KPT 32101 [DDD]
Fauré, G.:Music for Vc & Pno, w. Elisabeth Westenholz (pno)—Son No. 1, Op. 109; Elégie, Op. 24; Son No. 2, Op. 117; Après un rêve, Op. 7; Sicilienne, Op. 78; Papillon, Op. 77; Sérénade, Op. 98; Romance, Op. 69; Berceuse, Op. 16 — Kontrapunkt ▲ KPT 32220 [DDD]
Prokofiev, S.:Son Vc, w. P. Coker (pno) — Kontrapunkt ▲ KPT 32146 [DDD]
Schnittke, A.:Klingende Buchstaben — Kontrapunkt ▲ KPT 32146 [DDD]
Schumann, R.:Adagio & Allegro Hn, w. E. Westenholz (pno) — Kontrapunkt ▲ KPT 32172 [DDD]
Strauss, R.:Son Vc, w. E. Westenholz (pno) — Kontrapunkt ▲ KPT 32172 [DDD]
Dinkel, Philippe (pno)
Dvořák, A.:Qnt Pno, Op. 81, w. Sine Nomine String Quartet — Cascavelle ▲ CVL 1018 [DDD]
Dinkin, Alvin (va)—see ORCHESTRAS & ENSEMBLES Hollywood String Quartet members, Hollywood String Quartet
DiNovo, Nancy (va)
Davies, V.:Qt 1 Strs, "Fun for 4", w. Arthur Polson (vn), Mark Ferris (vn), Ian Hampton (vc) — Campion ▲ RRCD 1339 [DDD]
DiNovo, Nancy (vn)
Classic Elektra, w. [cnd:Morna Edmundson, Diane Loomer], Elektra Women's Choir, Eric Hominich (pno), Evelyn Creaser-Rumley (vn), Brenda Fedoruk (fl) — Skylark ▲ 9402 [DDD]

INSTRUMENT.

Dionisio, Paolo (vl)
Sui Palchi Delle Stelle:Sacred Music in the Neapolitan Conservatories at the Time of Francesco Provenzale, w. [cnd:Antonio Florio], Cappella Pietà de Turchini, Antonella Ippolito (sop), Jane Haughton (sop), Daniela del Monaco (alt), Sebastiano Cassarà (vn), Rosario Di Meglio (vn), Antonella Bologna (va), Antonio Florio (vc), Pierluigi Ciappareli (thb), Enrico Baiano (org/hpd) Symphonia ▲ SY 93S20 [DDD]

Dirani, Paolo (pno)
Donizetti, G.:Sons Pno 4-Hands, w. F. Amelotti (pno)—7 Sonatas—in F ("La solita Suonata"), in B♭ ("Per Dolci e Donizetti"), in E♭ ("L'inaspettata"), in F ("Sonata a quattro sanfe"), in D, in C, & in F *(rec 7/90)* Fonè ▲ 91F21 [DDD]

Dirlam, R. (a sax)
Aubart, M.J.:Hanblecheyapi:Crying for a Vision Innova ▲ MN 109
Stokes, E.:Tag Innova ▲ MN 109

Dispa, Michel (vc)
Dietrich, A.:Trio 1 Pno, w. Aldo Orvieto (pno), Dora Bratchkova (vn) *(rec Dynamic's, Genova, May 17–19, 1994)* Dynamic ▲ CD 121 [DDD]
Dietrich, A.:Trio 2 Pno, w. Aldo Orvieto (pno), Dora Bratchkova (vn) *(rec Dynamic's, Genova, May 17–19, 1994)* Dynamic ▲ CD 121 [DDD]
Klein, I.:Iris, w. L. Vis (cnd), Netherlands Ballet Orch Donemus ▲ CV 27

Disselhorst, D. (org)
Pinkham, D.:Org Music—Proverbs (1979–80) Arkay ▲ ARK 6123 [DDD]
Rorem, N.:Orgbooks Arkay ▲ ARK 6123 [DDD]

Dittmann, Friedwart (vc)
Mozart, W.A.:Sons Pno Vn Vc, w. A. Zenziper (pno), E. Haupt (fl)—K.15 LaserLight ▲ 15 878 [DDD]

DiTullio, L. (fl)
Badings, H.:Cavatina A Fl & Hp, w. S. McDonald (hp) Klavier ▲ KCD 11019 [ADD]
Debussy, C.:Prélude à l'après-midi d'un faune, w. J. Mauceri (cnd), Hollywood Bowl Orch *(rec Culver City, CA, Sept 1992)* Philips ▲ 438867-2 [DDD]
Imbrie, A.W.:Serenade Fl, w. W. Trampler (va), L. Brandwynne (pno) *(rec Aug. 17, 1971; originally)* CRI ▲ CD 632 [ADD]

Divoký, Zdenek (hn)
Mozart, W.A.:Sinf concertante Ob, K.Anh.9, w. Jan Adamus (ob), Frantisek Bláha (cl), Svatopluk Cech (bn), J. Belohlávek (cnd), Dvořák CO Panton ▲ PAN 811206
Reicha, A.:Trios Hns, Op. 82, w. B. Tylšar (hn), Z. Tylšar (hn) Supraphon ▲ 11 1446-2 [DDD]

Dixon, Peter (vc)
Fauré, G.:Elégie, w. Y. P. Tortelier (cnd), BBC PO Chandos ▲ CHAN 9416 [DDD]
Martin, F.:Ballade Vc, w. M. Bamert (cnd), London PO Chandos ▲ CHAN 9380 [DDD]

Dizhur, Sergey (pno)
Bortnyansky, D.:Qnt Vn, Vl, w. Nina Barshay (vn), Boris Dobrokhotov (vl), Vladimir Berlinsky (vc), Olga Erdeli (hp) *(rec 1950)* Multisonic ("Russian Treasures" series) ▲ 31 0253
Bortnyansky, D.:Sinf concertante, w. Nina Barshay (vn), Boris Dobrokhotov (vl), Vladimir Berlinsky (vc), Olga Erdeli (hp), Moscow CO *(rec 1984)* Multisonic ("Russian Treasures" series) ▲ 31 0253

Djokic, M. (vc)
Schoenberg, A.:Verklärte Nacht, w. S. Chase (vn), L. Chang (vn), M. Thompson (va), S. Ansel (va), R. Thomas (vc) *(rec Methuen, MA, Dec. 1990)* Northeastern ▲ NOR 249 [DDD]

Djokic, Philippe (vn)
Delius, F.:Con Vn, w. G. Tintner (cnd), Nova Scotia Sym CBC ("SM 5000" series) ▲ SMCD 5134 [DDD]

Djupsjöbacka, Gustav (pno)
Schubert, Franz:Winterreise, w. T. Krause (bar) Finlandia ▲ 4509-95876-2 [DDD]
Sibelius, J.:Songs, w. R. Auvinen (sop)—27 songs [Fin,Sw] Ondine ▲ ODE 728-2 [DDD]

Dlouhy, L. (va)—see ORCHESTRAS & ENSEMBLES Czech String Trio

Dlugoszewski, Lucia (pno)
Dlugoszewski, L.:Duende Quidditas, w. David Taylor (b trbn) *(rec live, Solomon R. Guggenheim Museum, Oct 23, 1983)* New World ▲ 80494-2

Dmiterko, Leonora (vn)
Mosolov, A.:Con Vn, w. A. Vinogradov (cnd), Moscow Contemporary Music Ensemble *(rec Mosfilm Studio, Jan 1995)* Triton ▲ 17004 [DDD]

Dmitriev, A. (vc)
Vivaldi, A.:Sons Vc, w. S. Akopov (db)—(6) R.40, 41, 43, 45–47 Arkadia-Akademia ▲ 119 [DDD]

Dnizhinin, Fyodor (va)
Schnittke, A.:Qt 2 Strs, w. A. Krysa (vn), N. Zabavnikov (vn), Y. Altman (vc) Vox Box 2-▲ CDX 5121 [ADD]

Doane, Steven (vc)
Benson, W.:Moon Rain & Memory Jane, w. L. Shelton (sop), S. Isserlis (vc) [E] Gasparo ▲ GS 261
Bland, W.:Trio 2, "Elegy & Consolation", w. D. Phillips (vn), A. Feinberg (pno) Bridge ▲ BCD 9013 [DDD]
Britten, H.:Son Vc, w. Barry Snyder (pno) *(rec Eastman Theater, Rochester, NY, Jan 14–15 & Apr 10–11, 19)* Bridge ▲ BCD 9056 [DDD]
Bridge, F.:Mélodie Vn, w. Barry Snyder (pno) *(rec Eastman Theater, Rochester, NY, Jan 14–15 & Apr 10–11, 19)* Bridge ▲ BCD 9056 [DDD]
Bridge, F.:Scherzetto Vc, w. Barry Snyder (pno) *(rec Eastman Theater, Rochester, NY, Jan 14–15 & Apr 10–11, 19)* Bridge ▲ BCD 9056 [DDD]
Bridge, F.:Son Vc, w. Barry Snyder (pno) *(rec Eastman Theater, Rochester, NY, Jan 14–15 & Apr 10–11, 19)* Bridge ▲ BCD 9056 [DDD]
Bridge, F.:Spring Song, w. Barry Snyder (pno) *(rec Eastman Theater, Rochester, NY, Jan 14–15 & Apr 10–11, 19)* Bridge ▲ BCD 9056 [DDD]
Dotzauer, F.:Pieces Vc, Op. 104, w. Anner Bylsma (vc), Kenneth Slowik (vc) *(rec New York City, Jan. 19–22, 1994)* Sony Classical ("Vivarte" series) ▲ SK 64307 [DDD]
Fauré, G.:Music for Vc & Pno, w. B. Snyder (pno)—Sérénade, Op. 98; Sicilienne, Op. 78; Élégie, Op. 24; Sonatas, Opp. 109 & 117; Romance, Op. 69; Mourceau de lecture (w. Kurt Fowler, 2nd cello); Papillon, Op. 77; Après un rêve, Op. 7/1 Bridge ▲ BCD 9038 [DDD]

Dobal, Juan Pablo (pno)
Piazzolla, A.:Music of, w. Gustavo Toker (band), Aurelia Saxophone Quartet—Escualo; Adio Nonino; Caliente; Astor que Estas en Los Cielos; Contrabajeando; Cuatro Estaciones Porteñas; Vayamos al Diablo; Four, for Tango; Milonga del Angel; Contrabajissimo; Michelangelo 70; Fuga y Misterio; Variaciones de la Fuga *(rec live, De Rode Hoed, Amsterdam, June 26, 1994)* Etcetera ▲ KTC 1186

Dobbs, Wendell (fl)
Stevens, H.:Qnt Fl, w. Leslie Petteys (pno), Montclaire String Quartet Koch International Classics ▲ KIC 7147 [DDD]

Dober, L. (vn)
Vogel, W.:Sonances, w. H. Peter-Indermühle (fl), H. Elhorst (ob), K. Weber (cl), I. Backer (bn), K. Hanke (hn), U. Lehmann (vn), H. Forster (va), M. Liechti (vc), R. Tschupp (cnd) Grammont ▲ CTSP 14-2 [ADD]

Dobey, Robert Benjamin (org)
Howells, H.:Pieces Org [Roosevelt/Schantz org, Cathedral, Syracuse, NY] Pro Organo ▲ CD 7005
Howells, H.:Son Org [Roosevelt/Schantz org, Cathedral, Syracuse, NY] Pro Organo ▲ CD 7005

Dobiásová, Marica (hpd)
Purcell, H.:Sons (12) Vns, Z.790–801, w. Elisabeth Selig-Plaskurova (vn), Viktor Simcisko (vn), Dusan Dockal (vc)—Nos. 1–3 *(rec Bratislava, 1994)* Discover International ▲ DI 920251 [DDD]
Purcell, H.:Sons (10) Vns, Z.802–811, w. Elisabeth Selig-Plaskurova (vn), Viktor Simcisko (vn), Dusan Dockal (vc)—Nos. 2, 3, 5, 6 & 9 *(rec Bratislava, 1994)* Discover International ▲ DI 920251 [DDD]
Zimmermann, A.:Con Hpd, w. P. Zajícek (cnd), Bratislava Musica Aeterna Trevak ▲ TRE 40010 [DDD]
Zimmermann, A.:Grand Con Hpd, w. P. Zajícek (cnd), Bratislava Musica Aeterna Trevak ▲ TRE 40010 [DDD]

Dobing, Duke (fl)
Vivaldi, A.:Cons Diverse Instrs, w. Joanna Graham (bn), Ruth McDowall (cl), David Rix (ct), Deborah Davis (fl), Tim Caister (hn), Stephen Stirling (hn), Christopher Hooker (ob), Helen McQueen (ob), Michael Meekes (tpt), Crispian Steele-Perkins (tpt), Nicholas Kraemer (hpd), N. Kraemer (cnd), London Sinfonietta—Cons. in F, RV.539; in C, RV.533; in D, RV.122; in C, RV.537; in C, RV.560; in F, RV.538; in G, RV.545 *(rec All Saints Church, East Finchley, Oct. 1994 & Jan. 1995)* Naxos ("Vivaldi Collection" series) ▲ 8.553204 [DDD]

Dobler, Charles (pno)
Bloch, E.:Con grosso 1, w. C. Meister (cnd), Prague Brixi CO Gallo ▲ CD 728 [DDD]
Keller, A.:Flageolett Grammont ▲ CTSP 19-2 [ADD]
Meier, J.:Esquisses, w. J. Meier (cnd), Prague Brixi CO Gallo ▲ CD 728 [DDD]
Moeschinger, A.:Suite Pno Grammont ▲ CTSP 1-2 [ADD]
Zbinden, J.-F.:Con da camera Pno, w. C. Meister (cnd), Prague Brixi CO Gallo ▲ CD 728 [DDD]

Dobos, Rose (pno)
Hugues Cuenod, w. H. Cuénod (ten), Joel Cohen (lt) Memoire Vive ▲ CD 262020 [ADD]

Dobrea, Marlène (pno)
Brahms, J.:Sons Vc (comp), w. Catalin Ilea (vc) Arcobaleno ▲ AAOC 93932

Dobrée, Georgina (bas hn)
Bennett, Richard Rodney:Crosstalk, w. Thea King (bas hn) Clarinet Classics ▲ CC 0012 [AAD]
Lutyens, E.:This Green Tide, w. Morris Pert (pno) Clarinet Classics ▲ CC 0012 [AAD]

Dobrée, Georgina (cl)
Cooke, A.:Suite for 3 Cls, w. London Clarinet Consort members Clarinet Classics ▲ CC 0012 [AAD]
Lutyens, E.:Valediction, w. Morris Pert (pno) Clarinet Classics ▲ CC 0012 [AAD]
Mayer, J.:Dance Suite, w. Susan Bradshaw (pno) Clarinet Classics ▲ CC 0012 [AAD]
Mayer, J.:Raga Music Clarinet Classics ▲ CC 0012 [AAD]
Mendelssohn, F.:Concert Pieces, w. Thea King (cl) Hyperion ▲ CDA 66022
Pert, M.:Eoastrion Clarinet Classics ▲ CC 0012 [AAD]
Solère, E.:Sinf concertante Cls, w. T. King (cl), A. Litton (cnd), English CO Hyperion ▲ CDA 66300 [DDD]
Wellesz, E.:Pieces Cl, w. Susan Bradshaw (pno) Clarinet Classics ▲ CC 0012 [AAD]

Dobrokhotov, Boris (vl)
Bortnyansky, D.:Qnt Vn, Vl, w. Nina Barshay (vn), Vladimir Berlinsky (vc), Olga Erdeli (hp), Sergey Dizhur (pno) *(rec 1950)* Multisonic ("Russian Treasures" series) ▲ 31 0253
Bortnyansky, D.:Sinf concertante, w. Nina Barshay (vn), Vladimir Berlinsky (vc), Olga Erdeli (hp), Sergey Dizhur (pno), Moscow CO *(rec 1984)* Multisonic ("Russian Treasures" series) ▲ 31 0253

Dockal, Dusan (vc)
Purcell, H.:Sons (12) Vns, Z.790–801, w. Elisabeth Selig-Plaskurova (vn), Viktor Simcisko (vn), Marica Dobiasova (hpd)—Nos. 1–3 *(rec Bratislava, 1994)* Discover International ▲ DI 920251 [DDD]
Purcell, H.:Sons (10) Vns, Z.802–811, w. Elisabeth Selig-Plaskurova (vn), Viktor Simcisko (vn), Marica Dobiasova (hpd)—Nos. 2, 3, 5, 6 & 9 *(rec Bratislava, 1994)* Discover International ▲ DI 920251 [DDD]

Dockter, Mike (vc)
O'Rourke, J.:Terminal Pharmacy, w. Tony Burr (cl), Jeff Cortazzo (b trbn), John McEntire (dr), Rob Prosser (acc), Isha Suftin (acc), Hattie Franck (vc), Robert Keck (vc), Mary LaBreque (vc), Dan Loch (vc), Stan Saderk (vc), Lisa Hemmer (fl), Sue Oberg (fl), Wendi Lev (fl), Jim Vanden (fl), Jim O'Rourke (gtr), Steve Braack (elec) Tzadik ▲ TZA 7011 [DDD]

Doctor, Paul (va)
Telemann, G.P.:Con Va, w. F. Brüggen (cnd), Concerto Amsterdam Teldec ▲ 77620-2 [ADD]

Dodd (fl)
Sutherland, M.:Little Suite, w. Swift (cl), G. Dreyfus (bn) Move ▲ MD 3071

Dodge, Baird (va)
Dodge, C.:Va Elegy New Albion ▲ NA 043

Dodge, F. (vc)—see ORCHESTRAS & ENSEMBLES Berlin Spectrum Ensemble members

Doering, Susan (vn)—see also ORCHESTRAS & ENSEMBLES Hawthorne Trio
Dankner, S.:Son Vn, w. Logan Skelton (pno) *(rec Loyola Univ.)* Centaur ▲ CRC 2247

Dogadin, Andrei (va)—see ORCHESTRAS & ENSEMBLES St. Petersburg String Quartet

Doherty, D. (ob)
Haydn, J.:Con Ob, w. O. Henzold (cnd), Lucerne SO Pan Classics ▲ 510090 [DDD]
Martinů, B.:Con Ob, w. O. Henzold (cnd), Lucerne SO Pan Classics ▲ 510090 [DDD]
Mozart, W.A.:Con Ob, K.314, w. O. Henzold (cnd), Lucerne SO Pan Classics ▲ 510090 [DDD]
Pfiffner, E.:Cambiamenti concertanti, w. T. Waldner (dr), Basel Serenata *(rec March 1992)* Pro Viva ▲ ISPV 170 [DDD]
Zimmermann, B.A.:Con Ob, w. O. Henzold (cnd), Lucerne SO Pan Classics ▲ 510090 [DDD]

Dohn, R. (ob)
Richter, F.X.:Con Ob, w. B. Warchal (cnd), Slovak CO CPO ▲ CPO 999117 [DDD]

Dohn, Robert (fl)
Haydn, J.:Cons for 2 Lire organizzata, w. Lajos Lencsés (ob), B. Warchal (cnd), Slovak CO CPO ▲ CPO 999182 [DDD]
Haydn, J.:Notturni (8), w. Lajos Lencsés (ob), B. Warchal (cnd), Slovak CO CPO 2-▲ CPO 999121-2 [DDD]
Lutoslawski, W.:Die Strohkette, w. Barbara Miller (sop), Oksana Sowiak (mez), Willy Schnell (ob), Martin Klose (cl), Hartmut Stute (cl), Karl Steinbrecher (bn), A. Grüber (cnd) Vox Box 2-▲ CDX 5133
Richter, F.X.:Cons Fl, w. B. Warchal (cnd), Slovak CO—in D & e CPO ▲ CPO 999117 [DDD]

Dohnányi, Ernst von (pno)
Dohnányi, E. von:Vars on a Nursery Song, w. L. Collingwood (cnd), London SO *(rec 1928–1937)* EMI Classics ▲ CDC 55031
Dohnányi, E. von:Vars on a Nursery Song, w. L. Collingwood (cnd), London SO *(rec 1931 for HMV)* Koch Schwann ▲ CD 311136 (m) [ADD]
Ernő Dohnányi Hungaroton ▲ HCD 12085 (m) [ADD]
Mozart, W.A.:Con 17 Pno, w. E. Dohnányi (cnd), Budapest PO *(rec 1928 for Columbia Records)* Koch Schwann ▲ CD 311136 (m) [ADD]

Dokoupil, Hans (pno)
Sings Lieder, w. H. Hotter (bar) *(rec 1968–69)* Preiser ▲ PRE 93390 [ADD]

Dokovska, Pavlina (pno)
Couperin, F.:Pièces de clavecin (sels)—Forlane; Les graces-naturèles; La ténébreuse; L'adolescente; Le dodo, ou l'amour au berceau; L'etincelante ou la bontems; La muse-plantine; Les baricades mistérieuses; La favorite; Soeur Monique; Les petits moulins à vent; Les charmes; Passacaille; Désordre, et déroute de toute la troupe:causés par les yvrognes, les singes et les ours *(rec Dec. 27–29, 1992)* Arcadia ▲ ARC 2000-2 [DDD]
Prokofiev, S.:Son Vc, w. N. Rosen (vc) Élan ▲ CD 2226 [DDD]
Rachmaninoff, S.:Son Vc, w. N. Rosen (vc) Élan ▲ CD 2226 [DDD]
Ravel, M.:Le Tombeau de Couperin *(rec Dec. 27–29, 1992)* Arcadia ▲ ARC 2002
Russian Romances, w. N. Ghiaurov (bass) RCA Red Seal ▲ 09026-62501-2
Schumann, R.:Fant Pno Gega ▲ GD 131 [DDD]
Schumann, R.:Faschingsschwank aus Wien Gega ▲ GD 131 [DDD]
Schumann, R.:Vars on an Original Theme Gega ▲ GD 131 [DDD]

Dokshitser, Timofei (tpt)
Arutiunian, A.:Con Tpt, w. G. Rozhdestvensky (cnd), Bolshoi Theater Orch *(rec 1968)* RCA Gold Seal ▲ 74321-32045-2 [ADD]
Biber, H. von:Son a 6 Tpt, w. R. Barshaï (cnd), Moscow CO *(rec 1968)* RCA Gold Seal ▲ 74321-32045-2 [ADD]
Gershwin, G.:Rhap in Blue, w. A. Lazarev (cnd), Bolshoi Theater Orch *(rec 1978)* RCA Gold Seal ▲ 74321-32045-2 [ADD]
Glazunov, A.:Album Leaf, w. G. Rozhdestvensky (cnd), Bolshoi Theater Orch *(rec 1968)* RCA Gold Seal ▲ 74321-32045-2 [ADD]
Glière, R.:Con Coloratura Sop, w. A. Maltsev (cnd), USSR Ministry of Defense Orch *(rec 1981)* RCA Gold Seal ▲ 74321-32045-2 [ADD]

Dokshitser, Timofei (tpt) (cont.)
Hummel, J.N.:Con in E♭ Tpt, S.49, w. R. Barshaï (cnd), Moscow CO *(rec 1968)*
RCA Gold Seal ▲ 74321-32045-2 [ADD]
Tchaikovsky, P.:Swan Lake (sels), w. G. Rozhdestvensky (cnd), Bolshoi Theater Orch—Neapolitan Dance *(rec 1968)*
RCA Gold Seal ▲ 74321-32045-2 [ADD]
Vainberg, M.:Con Tpt, w. A. Zhuraitis (cnd), Moscow PO
Russian Disc ▲ RUS 11006 [AAD]

Doktor, K. (va)—see ORCHESTRAS & ENSEMBLES Busch String Quartet

Doktor, P. (va)
Palmer, R.:Qnt Cl, w. A. Bloom (cl), K. Kooper (vn), Fred Sherry (vc), Mary Louise Boehm (pno)
Albany ▲ TROY 153

Dolezal, Fritz (vc)—see ORCHESTRAS & ENSEMBLES Vienna String Quartet

Dolezal, Fritz (vc)
Schubert, Franz:Trio Pno, D.28, w. Werner Hink (vn), Jasminka Stancul (pno) *(rec Apr & June 1995)*
Camerata ▲ 30 CM 342 [DDD]
Schubert, Franz:Trio 1 Pno, w. Jasminka Stancul (pno), Werner Hink (vn) *(rec Apr & June 1995)*
Camerata ▲ 30 CM 342 [DDD]

Dolezal, Kamil (cl)
Barton, H.:Qnt Con, w. Martinů String Quartet *(rec Martínek Studio, Prague, Jan 13, 16, 17, 24 & Feb)*
Panton ▲ 811397-2 [DDD]
Graham, P.:Different Geometry *(rec Martínek Studio, Prague, Jan 13, 16, 17, 24 & Feb)*
Panton ▲ 811397-2 [DDD]
Havelka, S.:Dialogues of the Soul with God, w. Svatopluk Havelka (pno) *(rec Martínek Studio, Prague, Jan 13, 16, 17, 24 & Feb)*
Panton ▲ 811397-2 [DDD]
Kopelent, M.:Canto espansivo *(rec Martínek Studio, Prague, Jan 13, 16, 17, 24 & Feb)*
Panton ▲ 811397-2 [DDD]
Matejů, Z.:Stele of Forbiddance, w. Barbora Váchalová (hp) *(rec Martínek Studio, Prague, Jan 13, 16, 17, 24 & Feb)*
Panton ▲ 811397-2 [DDD]
Pokorny, P.:Summer Evening in the Mountains, w. Ludmila Peterková (cl) *(rec Martínek Studio, Prague, Jan 13, 16, 17, 24 & Feb)*
Panton ▲ 811397-2 [DDD]

Dolezal, Karel (va)—see also ORCHESTRAS & ENSEMBLES Dolezalovo String Quartet
Bloch, E.:Suite hébraïque, w. Kyoko Hashimoto (pno) *(rec Covenent of St. Agnes of Bohemia, Prague, Mar 1995)*
Arta ▲ 0062 [DDD]
Hindemith, P.:Son Va, Op. 25/1 *(rec Covenent of St. Agnes of Bohemia, Prague, Mar 1995)*
Arta ▲ 0062 [DDD]
Matoušek, L.:Intimate Music *(rec Covenent of St. Agnes of Bohemia, Prague, Mar 1995)*
Arta ▲ 0062 [DDD]
Rubinstein, A.:Son Va, w. *(pianist unknown) (rec Covenent of St. Agnes of Bohemia, Prague, Mar 1995)*
Arta ▲ 0062 [DDD]

Dolezych, Anna (va)
Saeverud, H.:Peer Gynt Suites, w. Sveinung Sand (vn), Kjersti Dahle (ob/E hn), Gyrid Erlandsen (cl), Bohumil Maliska (hn), A. Dmitriev (cnd), Stavanger SO *(rec Stavanger Konserthus, Stavanger, Norway, Nov 13–17, 1995)*
BIS ▲ CD 762 [DDD]

Dolgin, Michail (va)
Beethoven, L. van:Qnt Fl, Vn, 2 Vas & Vc, w. T. L. Christiansen (fl), J. Søe Hansen (vn), H. Olsen (va), T.S. Hermansen (vc)
Kontrapunkt 2-▲ 32160/61 [DDD]
Kuhlau, F.:Qnts Fl, w. T.L. Christiansen (fl), J. Søe Hansen (vn), H. Olsen (va), T.S. Hermansen (vc)
Kontrapunkt 2-▲ 32160/61 [DDD]

Dolin, Elizabeth (vc)—see ORCHESTRAS & ENSEMBLES Montreal Chamber Group

Döling, Waldemar (hpd)
Bach, J.S.:Sons Fl, BWV 1030–35, w. G. Schmalfuss (ob)—BWV 1030 & 1031
MD + G ▲ L 3461 [DDD]
Bach, J.S.:Sons Vn, w. G. Schmalfuss (ob)—BWV 1013 & 1020 [trans. for oboe & continuo; BWV 1020 doubtful]
MD + G ▲ L 3461 [DDD]

Doll, Barbara (vn)—see ORCHESTRAS & ENSEMBLES Westphalia PO Chamber Ensemble

Dolmetsch, Arnold (vir)
The Arnold Dolmetsch Years
Program 1, w. Wieland Kuijken (vl), Robert Kohnen (hpd)
IMP Allegro ▲ PCD 989 [DDD]
Program 2, w. Frank Preuss (vn), Marguerite Dolmetsch (vl), Carl Dolmetsch (rec), Nigel Foster (hpd)
IMP Allegro ▲ PCD 990 [DDD]
Program 3, w. François (trb rcr), Jeanne Dolmetsch (trb rcr), Marguerite Dolmetsch (vl), Nigel Foster (hpd), Kathleen Livingstone (sop), John Hancorn (bass), Jennifer Bate (org), et al.
IMP Allegro ▲ PCD 995 [DDD]
Program 4, w. Carl Dolmetsch (rcr), François Dolmetsch (rcr), Marguerite Dolmetsch (rcr), Virginia Black (hpd), et al.
IMP Allegro ▲ PCD 1010 [DDD]

Dolmetsch, Carl (rcr)—see also ORCHESTRAS & ENSEMBLES Dolmetsch-Schoenfeld Ensemble
Program 4, w. A. Dolmetsch (vir), François Dolmetsch (rcr), Marguerite Dolmetsch (rcr), Virginia Black (hpd), et al.
IMP Allegro ▲ PCD 1010 [DDD]

Dolmetsch, François (rcr)
Program 4, w. A. Dolmetsch (vir), Carl Dolmetsch (rcr), Marguerite Dolmetsch (rcr), Virginia Black (hpd), et al.
IMP Allegro ▲ PCD 1010 [DDD]

Dolmetsch, Jeanne (rcr)
Bach, J.S.:Cons Hpd, BWV 1052–1058, w. I. Kipnis (hpd), Marguerite Dolmetsch (rcr), N. Marriner (cnd), London Strings—BWV 1057 *(rec 1967–1970)*
Sony Classical 2-▲ SB2K 53243 [ADD]
Program 3, w. A. Dolmetsch (vir), François (trb rcr), Marguerite Dolmetsch (vl), Nigel Foster (hpd), Kathleen Livingstone (sop), John Hancorn (bass), Jennifer Bate (org), et al.
IMP Allegro ▲ PCD 995 [DDD]

Dolmetsch, Marguerite (rcr)
Bach, J.S.:Cons Hpd, BWV 1052–1058, w. I. Kipnis (hpd), Jeanne Dolmetsch (rcr), N. Marriner (cnd), London Strings—BWV 1057 *(rec 1967–1970)*
Sony Classical 2-▲ SB2K 53243 [ADD]
Program 4, w. A. Dolmetsch (vir), Carl Dolmetsch (rcr), François Dolmetsch (rcr), Virginia Black (hpd), et al.
IMP Allegro ▲ PCD 1010 [DDD]

Dolmetsch, Marguerite (vl)
Program 2, w. A. Dolmetsch (vir), Frank Preuss (vn), Carl Dolmetsch (rec), Nigel Foster (hpd)
IMP Allegro ▲ PCD 990 [DDD]
Program 3, w. A. Dolmetsch (vir), François (trb rcr), Jeanne Dolmetsch (trb rcr), Nigel Foster (hpd), Kathleen Livingstone (sop), John Hancorn (bass), Jennifer Bate (org), et al.
IMP Allegro ▲ PCD 995 [DDD]

Domanico, Chuck (elec bass)
Kellaway, R.:Music of, w. Roger Kellaway (pno/perc), Fred Seykora (vc), Emil Richards (mar/perc), Joe Porcaro (perc), Bob Zimmitti (perc)—Thinking of You; Un canto per la pace [A Song for Peace]; Love of my Life; Eleventide; In My Heart; Eve; Windows; Winter [Parts 1–3] *(rec Ocean Way Recording Studio, Los Angeles, CA, May 1–5, 1993)*
EMI Classics ▲ CDC 54903 [DDD]

Domanska, Joanna (pno)
Szymanowski, K.:Masques
Olympia ▲ OLY 344
Szymanowski, K.:Mazurkas
Olympia ▲ OLY 344

Domb, Daniel (vc)
Bach, J.S.:Suites Vc, BWV 1007–1012—BWV 1007, 1009 & 1011
Mastersound ▲ MST 25 [DDD]
Bach, J.S.:Suites Vc, BWV 1007–1012—BWV 1008, 1010 & 1012
Mastersound ▲ MST 26 [DDD]
Glick, S.I.:Suite Hébraïque 5, w. S. Shulman (fl), J. Campbell (cl), A. Dawes (vn)
CBC ("Musica Viva" series) ▲ MVCD 1046 [DDD]
Meditations, w. D. Domb (vc), Judy Loman (hp)
Pro Arte ▲ CDD 3414

Dombrecht, Paul (ob)—see also ORCHESTRAS & ENSEMBLES Fitzwilliam Ensemble
Kalliwoda, J.W.:Morceau de Salon, w. J. van Immerseel (pno)
Accent ▲ 78330
Pixis, J.P.:Grand Son Ob, w. J. van Immerseel (pno)
Accent ▲ 78330
Schumann, R.:Liederkreis, Op. 39, w. J. van Immerseel (pno)—No. 5
Accent ▲ 78330
Schumann, R.:Romances Ob, w. J. van Immerseel (pno)
Accent ▲ 78330
Telemann, G.P.:Sons Ob, w. W. Kuijken (vc), R. Kohnen (hpd)—Sonata in B♭ (from *Essercizii musici*); Sonata in g (from *Musique de table*); Suite in g (from *Getreue Music-Meister*); Partita II in G (from *Kleine Kammer-Music*)
Accent ▲ 48013

Dombrecht, Paul (ob) (cont.)
Zelenka, J.D.:Trio Sons Obs, w. D. Bond (bn), et al.
Accent 2-▲ 8848

Domenica, Leona di (pno)
di Domenica, R.:The Art of the Row
GM Recordings 2-▲ GM 2001
di Domenica, R.:Improvisations
GM Recordings 2-▲ GM 2001
di Domenica, R.:Movts (4) Pno
GM Recordings 2-▲ GM 2001
di Domenica, R.:Pno Music—Son. after Essays for Piano, w. Soprano, Baritone, Flute, Alto Flute & Tape (1977) [rec. New England Conservatory, Boston, Nov. 20, 1978]; Improvisations (1974) [rec. New England Conservatory, Boston, Mar. 18, 1975]; 11 Short Pieces (1973) [rec. New England Conservatory, Boston, Mar. 18, 1975]; 4 Movts. (1959) [rec. Donnell Library, New York City, Dec. 19, 1959]; Sonatina (1958) [rec. Donnell Library, New York City, Dec. 19, 1959]; The Art of the Row (1989) [rec. New England Conservatory, Boston, Dec. 12, 1990]
GM 2-▲ GM 2001
di Domenica, R.:Short Pieces (11)
GM Recordings 2-▲ GM 2001
di Domenica, R.:Son after Essays [w. Sop, Bar, Fl, Alto Fl & Tape *(performers unknown)*]
GM Recordings 2-▲ GM 2001
di Domenica, R.:Sonatina Pno
GM Recordings 2-▲ GM 2001

Dominguez, Albert (pno)
Copland, A.:El salón México, w. J. R. Crossan (pno)
Janus ■ JAN 1110 (CrO2)
Great Piano Duos, w. J. R. Crossan (pno)
Janus Recordings ■ JAN 1110 (CrO2)
Indy, V. d':Son Vn, w. Henri Temianka (vn) *(rec Loas Angeles, CA, 1973)*
Orion ▲ 7820-2 [AAD]
Kohs, E.:Suite for 2 Pnos, w. J. R. Crossan (pno)
Janus ■ JAN 1110 (CrO2)
Prokofiev, S.:Mélodies, w. A. Belnick (vn)
Cambria ▲ CMB 1096 [DDD]
Prokofiev, S.:Son Vn, Op. 94bis, w. A. Belnick (vn)
Cambria ▲ CMB 1096 [DDD]
Prokofiev, S.:Son 1 Vn, w. A. Belnick (vn)
Cambria ▲ CMB 1096 [DDD]
Rachmaninoff, S.:Suite 2 for 2 Pnos, w. J. R. Crossan (pno)
Janus ■ JAN 1110 (CrO2)
Ravel, M.:La Valse, w. J. R. Crossan (pno) [2-piano version]
Janus ■ JAN 1110 (CrO2)
Saint-Saëns, C.:Variations on a Theme of Beethoven, w. J. R. Crossan (pno)
Janus ■ JAN 1110 (CrO2)

Domini, Marco (vn)
Handel, G.F.:Con for 2 Vns & Vc, w. A. Reale (vn), N. Chirivi (vc), M. Peca (cnd), Rome Stradivari Ensemble
Bongiovanni ▲ GB 2100 [DDD]

Dominique, Carl-Axel (pno)
Jacob, G.:Sextet Pno & Wind Qnt, w. Sundsvall Wind Quartet
Caprice ▲ CAP 21497
Messiaen, O.:Catalogue d'oiseaux *(rec July 1–7 & Dec. 10–12, 19)*
BIS 3-▲ CD 594/96 [DDD]
Messiaen, O.:La Fauvette des jardins *(rec July 1–7 & Dec. 10–12, 19)*
BIS 3-▲ CD 594/96 [DDD]
Messiaen, O.:Harawi, w. D. Dorow (sop) [F]
BIS ▲ CD 86
Messiaen, O.:Petites esquisses d'oiseaux *(rec July 1–7 & Dec. 10–12, 19)*
BIS 3-▲ CD 594/96 [DDD]
Schnittke, A.:Sym 1, w. B. Kallenberg (vn), A. Lännerholm (trbn), L. Segerstam (cnd), Royal Stockholm PO *(rec Oct. 14, 1992)*
BIS ▲ CD 577 [DDD]
Thuille, L.:Sxt Pno, w. Sundsvall Wind Quartet
Caprice ▲ CAP 21497

Domonkos, Judit Kis (vc)
Truscott, H.:Meditation Vc *(rec Alpha-Line Studio, Festetich Castle, Budapest, 1994)*
Marco Polo ▲ 8.223727 [DDD]
Truscott, H.:Son Vc, w. Melinda Lugossy (pno) *(rec Alpha-Line Studio, Festetich Castle, Budapest, 1994)*
Marco Polo ▲ 8.223727 [DDD]
Vivaldi, A.:Cons Ob, w. S. Schilli (ob), D. Jonas (ob), G. Thomas (hpd), G. Kósa (hpd), Nagy, Morandi (cnd), Failoni CO—RV 450, 452, 453, 454, 534, 535 & 536 *(rec Dec. 1992)*
Naxos ▲ 8.550859 [DDD]
Vivaldi, A.:Cons Ob, w. S. Schilli (ob), G. Kósa (hpd), Nagy, Morandi (cnd), Failoni CO—RV 447, 451, 455, 457, 461 & 463 *(rec Apr. 1993)*
Naxos ▲ 8.550860 [DDD]

Domoto, Jeff (trbn)
Dempster, S.:Music of, w. Stuart Dempster (trbn/didjeridu/conch), Jay Bulen (trbn), Moc Escobedo (trbn/didjeridu/conch), Scott Higbee (trbn), Gretchen Hopper (trbn), Nathaniel Irby-Oxford (trbn), Chad Kirby (trbn/conch), Dave Marriott (trbn), Greg Powers (trbn), Debra Sykes (cym)—Conch Calling; Morning Light; Didjerilayover; Secret Currents; Melodic Communion; Shell Shock; Cloud Landings *(rec Fort Worden, Port Townsend, WA, June 18, 1994)*
New Albion ▲ NA 076

Donald, Jon (perc)
Festival of Organ & Brass, w. Missouri Brass Quintet, John Obetz (org) *(rec RLDS Peace Temple, Independence, MO)*
RBW ▲ RBWCD 008

Donaruma, Nancy (vc)
Hand, F.:Music of, w. Donald York (synth), Jazzantiqua—Cantigas de Santa Maria; Rose Liz; Bachiaras; Tourdion; Lady Carey's Fant; Chaconne; Toby & Lynn
MusicMasters ▲ 01612-65150-2

Donath, K. (pno)
Divas in Song:Marylin Horne, a 60th Birthday Celebration, w. Montserrat Caballé (sop), H. Donath (sop), R. A. Swenson (sop), F. von Stade (mez), R. Fleming (mez), S. Ramey (bass), J. Levine (cnd), M. Katz (pno), W. Jones (pno), Manuel Burgueras (pno)
RCA Red Seal ▲ 09026-62547-2
Kalliwoda, J.W.:Heimatlied, "Treues, stilles Friedensthal", w. H. Donath (sop), D. Klöcker (cl) [G]
Acanta ▲ 43508
Schubert, Franz:Der Hirt auf dem Felsen, w. H. Donath (sop), D. Klöcker (cl) [G]
Acanta ▲ 43508
Spohr, L.:German Songs , Op. 103, w. H. Donath (sop), D. Klöcker (cl) [G]
Acanta ▲ 43508

Donath, Klaus (cl)
Lachner, F.P.:Songs Sop, w. H. Donath (sop), D. Klöcker (cl)—Seit ich ihn gesehen, Op. 82; Auf Flügeln Gesanges [G]
Acanta ▲ 43508

Donato, Dominic (perc)
Partch, H.:Daphne of the Dunes, w. Frank Cassara (boo/spoils of war/kithara 2), Dean Drummond (harmonic canons/kithara 2/spoils of war/kithara), Nina Kellman (kithara 2/harmonic canon/surrogate kithara), Michael Lipsey (cloud-chamber bowls), Ted Mook (vc/gourd tree/cone gongs), James Pugliese (diamond mar), Elizabeth Rodgers (chromelodeon/harmonic canon) *(rec Queens, NY, Mar. 12, 1991)*
Mode ▲ MODE 33

Donato, Dominic (perc/elec)
Drummond, D.:Different Drums for Different Strokes *(rec Glen Cove, NY, Jan. 26, 1991)*
Mode ▲ MODE 33

Donato, Dominic (zmz)
Monk, T.:Round Midnight, w. Ted Mook (vc), Dean Drummond (zmz), Frank Cassara (zmz) [arr. Drummond for cello & 3 zoomoozophones] *(rec The Magic Shop, New York City, Jan. 31, 1993)*
Mode ▲ MODE 33
Pugliese, J.:Freeze, w. Stefani Starin (alt fl), Dean Drummond (zmz), James Pugliese (Yamaha DX711) *(rec New York City, May 29, 1992)*
Mode ▲ MODE 33

Donato, Jacques di (b cl)
Rebotier, J.:Soif d'aujourd'hui
Adès ▲ ADE 204472 [DDD/AAD]

Donato, Jacques di (cl)
Chen, Q.:Yi, w. Ville d'Avray Instrumental Ensemble
REM ▲ REM 311223 [DDD]
Poulenc, F.:Son Cl Pno, w. Kun Woo Paik (pno)
Accord ▲ ACD 205192 [DDD]
Poulenc, F.:Son for 2 Cls, w. Lucien Aubert (cl)
Accord ▲ ACD 205192 [DDD]

Donderer, George (vc)
Stephan, R.:Music for 7 Stringed Instrs, w. B. Hartog (vn), I. Schliephake (vn), S. Passaggio (va), A. Akahoshi (db), C. Tainton (pno), M. Schmidt (hp) *(rec 1983)*
Koch Schwann ▲ CD 311 122 [ADD]

Dongois, William (cnt)—see ORCHESTRAS & ENSEMBLES Weser-Renaissance Ensemble

Donn, Richard A. (pno/hpd)
Elegance, w. R. Behrend (eup)
Coronet ▲ COR 400-0

Donnington, Robert (vl)
Corelli, A.:Sons Vn, Op. 5, w. Yehudi Menuhin (vn), George Malcolm (hpd)—Nos. 1 in D, 5 in g & 12 in d
EMI Classics ("Baroque" series) ▲ CDK 65731

Donohoe, Peter (pno)
Bartók, B.:Con 1 Pno, w. S. Rattle (cnd), City of Birmingham SO
EMI Classics ▲ CDC 54871
Bartók, B.:Con 3 Pno, w. S. Rattle (cnd), City of Birmingham SO
EMI Classics ▲ CDC 54871
Beethoven, L. van:Qnt Pno, Ob, Cl, Hn & Bn, w. Netherlands Wind Ensemble members
Chandos ▲ CHAN 9470

Donohoe, Peter (pno) (cont.)
Britten, H.:Diversions Pno, w. S. Rattle (cnd), City of Birmingham SO *(rec 7/90)* EMI Classics 2-▲ CDCB 54270 [DDD]
Britten, H.:Scottish Ballad, w. P. Fowke (pno), S. Rattle (cnd), City of Birmingham SO *(rec 4/82)* EMI Classics 2-▲ CDCB 54270 [DDD]
Britten, H.:Young Apollo, w. F. Kok (vn), J. Ballard (vn), P. Cole (va), M. Kaznowski (vc), S. Rattle (cnd), City of Birmingham SO *(rec 4/82)* EMI Classics 2-▲ CDCB 54270 [DDD]
Gershwin, G.:Con Pno, w. S. Rattle (cnd), City of Birmingham SO EMI Classics ▲ CDC 54280
Gershwin, G.:Con Pno, w. S. Rattle (cnd), City of Birmingham SO EMI Classics ("American Composer" series) ▲ CDM 64305
Gershwin, G.:The George Gershwin Songbook EMI Classics ▲ CDC 54280
Gershwin, G.:Rhap in Blue, w. S. Rattle (cnd), London Sinfonietta EMI Classics ▲ CDC 54280
Macmillan, J.:The Berserking, w. M. Stenz (cnd), Royal Scottish National Orch *(rec Glasgow City Hall, Jan 29–31, 1995)* RCA Red Seal ▲ 09026-68328-2 [DDD]
Messiaen, O.:Couleurs de la cité céleste, w. R. de Leeuw (cnd), Netherlands Wind Ensemble Chandos ("New Direction" series) ▲ CHAN 9301/02 [DDD]
Messiaen, O.:Haïkaï, w. R. de Leeuw (cnd), Netherlands Wind Ensemble Chandos ("New Direction" series) ▲ CHAN 9301/02 [DDD]
Messiaen, O.:Oiseaux exotiques, w. R. de Leeuw (cnd), Netherlands Wind Ensemble Chandos ("New Direction" series) ▲ CHAN 9301/02 [DDD]
Messiaen, O.:La Ville d'en-haut, w. R. de Leeuw (cnd), Netherlands Wind Ensemble Chandos ("New Direction" series) ▲ CHAN 9301/02 [DDD]
Messiaen, O.:Un Vitrail et des oiseaux, w. R. de Leeuw (cnd), Netherlands Wind Ensemble Chandos ("New Direction" series) ▲ CHAN 9301/02 [DDD]
Shostakovich, D.:Con 2 Pno, w. M. Shostakovich (cnd), BBC SO IMP ("BBC Radio Classics" series) ▲ IMP 5691702

Donovetsky, Greg (ob)
Levitch, L.:Fant Ob, w. Alexander Treger (vn), Kenneth Burward-Hoy (va), Janice Foy (vc) Cambria ▲ CD 1059 [ADD]
Levitch, L.:Ricordo di Mario Pno, w. Leon Levitch (pno) [trans. for ob & Pno] Cambria ▲ CD 1059 [ADD]

Donslund, Gunhild (pno)
Stolarczyk, W.:Earth Air Fire Water, w. Amalie Malling (pno), John Damgaard (pno), Anne Øland (pno), Teddy Teirup (pno), Friedrich Gürtler (pno), Rosalind Bevan (pno), Poul Rosenbaum (pno), Rodolfo Llambias (pno), Bella Horn-Ribera (pno), Anders Riber (pno), Elisabeth Sigurdsson (pno), Thomas Tronheim (pno), Elsebeth Broderson (pno), Erik Kaltoft (pno), Jørgen Hald Nielsen (pno), Aino Gilemann (pno), Birgit Kjær (pno), Jørgen Thomsen (pno), Henrik Bo Hansen (pno), Lone Karlsson (pno), Erik Fessel (pno), Lasse Nilsson (pno), Janos Ferenczi (pno), Erik Bach (pno), Axel Momme (pno), Arne de Cros Dich (pno), Sven Micha Slot (pno), Hanne Bramsen Buhl (pno), Lili Olesen (pno), Susannah Carlsson (pno), Ulla Erml (pno), Vagn Sørensen (pno), Leif Greibe (pno), Bodil Krogh (pno), Kirsten Ottosen (pno), Inger Bergenholz (pno), Karsten Gylendorf (pno), Bjønr Elkjær (pno), Jacob Bjørn Jensen (pno), Jørgen Kaad (pno), Anne Marie Hjelm (pno), Carl Ulrik Munk Andersen (pno), Poul Lumbye (pno), Oluf Hildebrandt Nielsen (pno), Joachim Olsson (pno), Peter Pade Ramsøe Jacobsen (pno), Astrid Pollmann (pno), Jette Borsch (pno), Kirsten Karlshøj (pno), Maria Teresa Assing (pno), Allan Dahl Hansen (pno), Johan Hugossen (pno), Tine Fenger Pederson (pno), Arne Jørgen Fæø (pno), Anja Høgsted (pno), Anne Sophie Parbo (pno), Inga Lindmark (pno), Teresa Drabik Stathakis (pno), Anne Ruth Ferenczi (pno), Irene Hasager (pno), Yuka Ichikawa (pno), Birgitte Baur (pno), Malene Thastum (pno), Jens E. Rasmussen (pno), Birgitte Zielke (pno), Claus Zielke (pno), Stefan Kasch (pno), Bin Qiao (pno), Inger Johanne Teirup (pno), Lindy Rosborg (pno), Liisa Heininen (pno), David Højer (pno), Ellen Refstrup (pno), Thomas K. Sørensen (pno), Erik Kure (pno), Michael Rauff (pno), Jan beck Eriksson (pno), Tanja Zapolski (pno), Vibeke Skagbo (pno), Pål Eide Lindtner (pno), Ha-Young Sul (pno), Benedicte Palko (pno), Inke Kesseler (pno), Anne Marie Meineche (pno), Sverre Larsen (pno), Kasper Peter Bach (pno), Elisabetta Eliseo (pno), Olga Magieres (pno), Carl Erik Kühl (pno), Thorkild Borup Nielsen (pno), Valeria Zanini (pno), Lars Stenhoft (perc), Dennis Boel (perc), Winnie Dahlgren (perc), Susanne Vind (perc), Claus Byrith (elec), Anne Marie Storm (elec), J. Ribera (cnd) *(rec live, Koldinghaus Castle, Denmark, May 2, 1996)* Danica ▲ DCD 1996

Doppmann, William (pno)
Bartók, B.:Contrasts, w. D. Shifrin (cl), Ik-Hwan Bae (vn) Delos ▲ CD 3043 [DDD]
Messiaen, O.:Quatuor pour la fin du temps, w. D. Shifrin (cl), Ik-Hwan Bae (vn), W. Lash (vc) Delos ▲ CD 3043 [DDD]

Dora, Claudia (vn)—see ORCHESTRAS & ENSEMBLES Aria String Quartet

Dorati, Antál (hpd)
Haydn, J.:Die Schöpfung, w. Helena Döse (sop—Eva), Lucia Popp (sop—Gabriel), Werner Hollweg (ten—Uriel), Benjamin Luxon (bar—Adam), Kurt Moll (bass—Raphael), Jack McCormack (db), David Strange (vc), A. Dorati (cnd), Royal PO, Brighton Festival Chorus *(rec Kingsway Hall, London, Dec 1976)* London 2-▲ 443027-2 [ADD]

Dorer, Sally Gibson (vc)
Gibson, R.:Haiku (4), w. Naoko Takao (pno) Capstone ▲ CPS 8621

Dörfler, S. (vc)
Lachner, F.P.:Qnt 2 Pno, w. H. Göbel (pno), O. Duliba (vn), T. Jahnel (vn), S. Clark (va) *(rec June 10, 1991)* Thorofon ▲ CTH 2132 [DDD]

Dorfman, Ania (pno)
Beethoven, L. van:Con 1 Pno, w. A. Toscanini (cnd), NBC SO RCA Gold Seal ▲ 60268-2-RG ■ 60268-4-RG
Beethoven, L. van:Con Vn, Vc & Pno, "Triple Con", w. Mishel Piastro (vn), Joseph Schuster (vc), A. Toscanini (cnd), New York PO Grammofono 2000 ▲ GRM 78636
Beethoven, L. van:Fant Pno, Op. 80, "Choral Fant", w. A. Toscanini (cnd), NBC SO, Westminster Choir [G] *(rec live 12/2/39)* Melodram 2-▲ MEL 28031 (m) [AAD]
Beethoven, L. van:Fant Pno, Op. 80, "Choral Fant", w. A. Toscanini (cnd), NBC SO, Westminster Choir *(rec New York City, 1939)* Grammofono 2000 ▲ GRM 78524 (m)

Dørge, P. (gtr)—see ORCHESTRAS & ENSEMBLES Antifonale Chamber Ensemble

Dornenburg, John (vl)
Handel, G.F.:Cants, w. J. Baird (sop), M. Proud (hpd)—Occhi miei, che faceste?; Quel fior che all'alba ride; Solitudini care, amata liberata; Udite il mil consiglio [I] *(rec 6/90)* Meridian ▲ CDE 84189
Handel, G.F.:Son VI, w. Malcolm Proud (hpd) *(rec 6/90)* Meridian ▲ CDE 84189
Telemann, G.P.:Son VI in e, w. Music's Re-Creation Meridian ▲ CDE 84159

Dorsch, Kenneth (hpd)
Songs, Dances & Fantasy, w. J. Fuller (db), Frederick Ockwell (pno), William Ferris (pno), Steve Hartman (hp), Thomas Potter (bar), John Vorrasi (ten), Anne Waller (gtr) Musical Arts Society ▲ CD 41589 [AAD] ■ CS 41589

Dorsey, Don (syn)
Bach, J.S.:Music of Telarc ▲ CD 80123 [DDD] ■ CS 30123 (D)

Dosaka, Kiyotaka (bn)
Vivaldi, A.:Cons Bn, w. Bach-Mozart Ensemble Tokyo *(rec June 22–26, 1992)* Denon ▲ CO 75198 [DDD]
Vivaldi, A.:Con Fl Ob, RV.107, w. M. Arita (fl), M. Homma (ob), N. Wakamatsu (vn), Bach-Mozart Ensemble Tokyo *(rec June 22–26, 1992)* Denon ▲ CO 75198 [DDD]

Dosse, Marylene (pno)
Debussy, C.:Fant Pno, w. L. de Froment (cnd), Luxembourg RSO *(rec 1972)* Vox Box 2-▲ CDX 5053 [ADD]
Granados, E.:Pno Music (comp)—Allegro di concierto; Aparición; Barcarola; Capricho español; Cuentos de la juventúd; Danza lenta; Estudio; Estudios expresivos; Goyescas; Impromptus; Piezas sobre cantos populares españoles Vox Box 2-▲ CDX 5075 [ADD]
Granados, E.:Pno Music (comp)—A la pradera; Carezza; Cartas de amor; Danzas españolas; Escenas poeticas; Escenas romanticas; Moreque; Paisaje; El pelele; Rapsodia aragonesa; Valses poeticos Vox Box 2-▲ CDX 5076

Dosso, Leonardo (bn)—see also ORCHESTRAS & ENSEMBLES Arnold Quintet
Cambini, G.M.:Trios Fl, Ob & Bn, w. R. Rivolta (fl), F. Pomarico (ob) Stradivarius ▲ STR 33310 [DDD]

Dosso, Leonardo (bn) (cont.)
Milesi, P.:Modi 1, w. D. Cassamagnaghi (fl), F. Pomarico (ob), A. Bianchi (cl), G. Govi (vn), D. Tellini (vn), M. Ravasio (va), S. Righini (vc), P. Rizzi (db), C. Vignani (hpd), J. Scully (perc), P. Milesi (cnd) Cuneiform ▲ RUNE 63

Dossow, M. (gtr)
Sor, F.:Divert militaire, w. B. Ahlert (gtr) Ambitus ▲ 97860 [ADD]
Sor, F.:Sons Gtr, Opp. 15 & 22—Op. 22 Ambitus ▲ 97860 [ADD]

Dostal, M. (org)
Mozart, W.A.:Arias, w. A. Raunig (ct), K. F. Schmid (cl), W. Kobera (cnd), Vienna Amadeus Ensemble, Vienna Landstrasse Church Choir—Il padre adorato [from Idomneo]; Cara, lontano ancora [from Ascanio in Alba]; Parto, ma tu ben mio [from La clemenza di Tito] Divertimento ▲ DIV 31013 [DDD]
Mozart, W.A.:Exsultate, w. A. Raunig (ct), K. F. Schmid (cl), W. Kobera (cnd), Vienna Amadeus Ensemble, Vienna Landstrasse Church Choir Divertimento ▲ DIV 31013 [DDD]
Salieri, A.:Arias, w. A. Raunig (ct), K. F. Schmid (cl), W. Kobera (cnd), Vienna Amadeus Ensemble, Vienna Landstrasse Church Choir—Perdermi? [from Axur, Re d'ormus]; Lungi da te [from Armida]; A fulminas m'invita [from Anibale] Divertimento ▲ DIV 31013 [DDD]
Salieri, A.:Songs, w. A. Raunig (ct), K. F. Schmid (cl), W. Kobera (cnd), Vienna Amadeus Ensemble, Vienna Landstrasse Church Choir—Fremat Thyrannus (motet) Divertimento ▲ DIV 31013 [DDD]

Dotzauer, Sibylle (pno)
Austin, E.:An Die Nachgeborenen, w. Alex Bassermann (sgr), Kirsten Grünenpült (sgr), Veronika Winter (sgr), Gerald Kegelmann (cnd), Heidelberg-Mannheim State Univ Chamber Choir Capstone ▲ CPS 8625
Austin, E.:Music of, w. Jeanannе Albee (pno), Jerome Reed (pno), Mary Lou Rylands (vc), Ursula Trede-Boettcher (hpd), Markus Lücke (cl), Constitution Brass, Gerald Kegelmann (cnd), Heidelberg State Music School Chamber Choir—To Begin for Brass Qnt; Klavier Double for Pno & Tape; Circling for Vc & Pno; Lighthouse I for solo Hpd; Gathering Threads for solo Cl; Zodiac Suite for Pno; An Die Nachgeborenen [To Those Born Later] Capstone ▲ CPS 8625

Douay, J. (trbn)
Milhaud, D.:Concertino d'hiver, w. P. Bender (cnd), Cannes-Provençe Alpes-Côte d'Azur Regional Orch Nuova Era ▲ 7130 [DDD]

Doughty, Henry (org)
Choral Evensong from Truro Cathedral, w. [cnd:David Briggs], Truro Cathedral Choir Priory ▲ PRCD 322 [DDD]

Douglas, Barry (pno)
Basic 100, Vol. 50, w. Arthur Fiedler (cnd) RCA Victor ▲ 09026-62679-2 ■ 09026-62679-4
Beethoven, L. van:Son 21 Pno, "Waldstein" RCA Red Seal ▲ 09026-61280-2
Beethoven, L. van:Son 23 Pno, "Appassionata" RCA Red Seal ▲ 09026-61280-2
Beethoven, L. van:Son 27 Pno RCA Red Seal ▲ 09026-61280-2
Berg, A.:Son Pno RCA Red Seal ▲ 09026-61221-2
Corigliano, J.:Con Pno, w. L. Slatkin (cnd), St. Louis SO *(rec Powell Symphony Hall, St. Louis, MO, Feb 11 & 13, 1994)* RCA Red Seal ▲ 09026-68100-2 [DDD]
Liszt, F.:Cons Pno, w. J. Hirokami (cnd), London SO RCA Red Seal ▲ 7916-2-RC [DDD] ■ 7916-4-RC (CrO2)
Liszt, F.:Cons Pno, w. J. Hirokami (cnd), London SO RCA Victor ▲ 09026-62679-2 ■ 09026-62679-4
Liszt, F.:Fant on Hungarian Folk Tunes, w. J. Hirokami (cnd), London SO RCA Red Seal ▲ 7916-2-RC [DDD] ■ 7916-4-RC (CrO2)
Liszt, F.:Pno Music (misc)—Zweite Elegie; Nuages gris RCA Red Seal ▲ 09026-61221-2
Liszt, F.:Son Pno RCA Red Seal ▲ 09026-61221-2
Prokofiev, S.:Cinderella Pno, Op. 97—Nos. 4,6 & 10 RCA Red Seal ▲ 60779-2-RC [DDD]
Prokofiev, S.:The Love for 3 Oranges (march) RCA Red Seal ▲ 60779-2-RC [DDD]
Prokofiev, S.:Pieces Pno, Op. 96 RCA Red Seal ▲ 60779-2-RC [DDD]
Prokofiev, S.:Son 2 Pno RCA Red Seal ▲ 60779-2-RC [DDD]
Prokofiev, S.:Son 7 Pno RCA Red Seal ▲ 60779-2-RC [DDD]
Tchaikovsky, P.:Concert Fant, w. L. Slatkin (cnd), Philharmonia Orch RCA Red Seal ▲ 09026-61632-2
Tchaikovsky, P.:Con 1 Pno, w. L. Slatkin (cnd), London SO RCA Red Seal ▲ 5708-2-RC [DDD]
Tchaikovsky, P.:Con 1 Pno, w. L. Slatkin (cnd), Philharmonia Orch RCA Red Seal ▲ 09026-61632-2
Tchaikovsky, P.:Con 2 Pno, w. L. Slatkin (cnd), Philharmonia Orch RCA Red Seal ▲ 09026-61633-2
Tchaikovsky, P.:Con 3 Pno, w. L. Slatkin (cnd), Philharmonia Orch RCA Red Seal ▲ 09026-61633-2
Webern, A.:Vars Pno RCA Red Seal ▲ 09026-61221-2

Douglas, Bill (bn)
Harkl, w. R. Stoltzman (cl), Eddie Gomez (perc), Jeremy Wall (kbd), Dave Samuels (vib), Harlem Boys Choir RCA Victor ▲ 09026-61272-2 [DDD] ■ 09026-61272-4 (CrO2)
Spirits, w. R. Stoltzman (cl), Eddie Gomez (db), David Torn (gtr), Dave Samuels (vib), King's Singers RCA Victor ▲ 09026-68416-2 ■ 09026-68416-4

Douglas, Bill (elec bass)
Riley, T.:In C, w. Bruce Ackley, Steve Adams, Don R. Baker, Chris Brown, George Brooks, Steve Coughlin, Blake Derby, Mihr'un'Nisa Douglass, Hank Dutt, David Harrington, Don Howe, Joan Jeanrenaud, Alden Jenks, Warner Jepson, Henry Kaiser, Jaron Lanier, Bill Maginnis, George Marsh, Shabda Owens, Jon Raskin, Gyan Riley, Terry Riley, Gino Robair, John Sackett, Ramón Sender, John Sherba, Toyji Tomita, Danny Tunick, William Winant, Evan Ziporyn *(rec Jan. 14, 1990)* New Albion ▲ NA 071
Waits, T.:The Black Rider:The Casting of Magic Bullets, w. Angelika Thomas (sgr—Anne), Annette Paulmann (sgr—Kätchen), Sona Cervena (sgr—Bird/Messenger/Spoonwoman), Monika Tahal (sgr—Witness/Bird/Shrink/Wilhelm's Double/Skeleton), Susi Eisenkolb (sgr—Bridesmaid/Pegleg's Double), Heinz Vossbrink (sgr—Kuno), Dominique Horwitz (sgr—Pegleg), Gerd Kunath (sgr—Bertram), Stefan Kurt (sgr—Wilhelm), Klaus Schreiber (sgr—Robert/Man on Stag/Georg Schmid), Jörg Holm (Old Uncle/Duke), Jan Moritz Steffen (sgr—Young Kuno/Bird/Shrink/Skeleton), Tom Waits (vocals/coliope/organ/chamberlain/mar/emax/guitar/train whistle), Ralph Carney (saxophone/bass clarinet/baritone horn), Kenny Wollesen (perc) Island ▲ 314518559-2

Douglas, Bonnie (vn)—see ORCHESTRAS & ENSEMBLES Los Angeles String Quartet

Douglas, P. (hn)
Lachner, F.P.:Nonet, w. A. Duisberg (fl), D. Wollenweber (ob), P. Prieditis (cl), M. Postinghel (bn), I. Grünkorn (vn), M. Gieler (va), T. Ruge (vc), F. Heidenreich (db) *(rec June 10, 1991)* Thorofon ▲ CTH 2132 [DDD]

Douglass, David (vn)
Musick for Severall Friends, w. M. Springfels (cnd), Newberry Consort, Drew Minter (ct), Kevin Mason (thb/lt) Harmonia Mundi France ("Musique d'abord" series) ▲ HMA 1907013

Dounay, Amy (pno)—see ORCHESTRAS & ENSEMBLES Bowed Piano Ensemble

Douwes, Sjef (cl)
de Leeuw, T.:Hommage à Henri, w. René Eckhardt (pno) NM Classics ▲ NM 92020

Dove, Barry (perc)
Zaimont, J.L.:Hidden Heritage, w. Karen Moratz (fl), David Krakauer (cl/b cl/t sax), David Finkel (vc), Clinton Adams (pno), D. Kosloff (cnd) *(rec SUNY Purchase, Theatre C, Jan 8–10 & Feb 20, 1995)* Arabesque ▲ ARA 6667 [DDD]

Dove-Pellito, Glenda (fl)
Morrill, D.:Roxbury Preludes, w. Ernest Lascell (cl), Tremont String Quartet *(rec June 1991 & June 1992)* Centaur ▲ CRC 2143 [DDD]

Dowdall, John (gtr)
Rossini, Mozart et al.:Serenades from the 19th Century Salon on Period Instruments, w. J. Boland (fl) Titanic ▲ Ti 182 [DDD]

Dowling, Eugene (tuba)
English Tuba, w. Edward Norman (pno), London SO [cnd:Paul Freeman] Pro Arte ▲ CDD 595 [DDD]
Jacob, G.:Suite Tuba, w. Norman (pno) Pro Arte/Fanfare ▲ CDD 595 [DDD]
Vaughan Williams, R.:Con Bass Tuba, w. P. Freeman (cnd), London SO Pro Arte/Fanfare ▲ CDD 595 [DDD]

Down, Sarah (pno)
Leigh, W.:Songs, w. E. Nash (sop)—9 Songs *(rec Aug. & Sept. 1991)* Tremula ▲ TREM 101-2

Downes, Ralph (org)
Handel, G.F.:Messiah, w. Kenneth McKellar (ten), George Malcolm (hpd), A. Boult (cnd), London SO, London Sym Chorus—And the glory of the Lord; And He shall purify; For unto us a Child is born; Glory to God in the highest; His yoke is easy; Behold the Lamb of God; Surely He hath borne our griefs; And with His stripes we are healed; All we like sheep have gone astray; All they that see Him...He trusted in God; Lift up your heads; The Lord gave the word; Their sound has gone out; Let us break the bonds asunder; Hallelujah; Since by man came death; Worthy is the Lamb...Amen London ▲ 436569-2
Holst, G.:Psalms 86 & 148, w. I. Partridge (ten), I. Holst (cnd), English CO, Purcell Singers—Psalm 86 EMI Classics ▲ CDC 49784

Downey, John (pno)
Downey, J.:A Dolphin, w. D. Nelson (ten), Bourachoff (fl), B. Zaslav (va), B. Burda (perc) Gasparo ▲ GS 276 ■ GS 276C

Doyen, Jean (pno)
Fauré, G.:Pno Music—Nocturnes; Ballade, Op. 19; Theme & Vars, Op. 73; Romances sans paroles, Op. 17; Préludes, Op. 103; Barcarolles; Valses-Caprices; Impromptus; Mazurka, Op. 32; Pièces Brèves, Op. 84 Erato 4-▲ ERA 96220 [ADD]

Doyle, Patrick (perc)
Veeneman, C.:The Wiry Concord, w. Susan Werner (banjo), Forrest Covington (hammered dlc/cimbalom), Georganne Assat (hp), Donald Martin Jenni (hpd), Mark Johnson (hpd), Barbara Phillips Farley (pno), James Austin (pno), Marta Soderberg (va), James Knutson (perc), Steven Butters (perc), James Popejoy (perc), M. Geary (cnd) Capstone ▲ SCI 6

Draeger, Christine (fl)
Broadstock, B.:Eheu Fugaces, w. Marilyn Richardson (sop), Roslyn Dunlop (cl), Fiona Ziegler (vn), Susan Blake (vc), David Miller (pno), Daryl Pratt (perc) Vox Australis ▲ VAST018-2 [DDD]
Sitsky, L.:Deep in My Hidden Country, w. Marilyn Richardson (sop), Susan Blake (vc), David Miller (pno), Daryl Pratt (perc) Vox Australis ▲ VAST018-2 [DDD]

Dráfi, Kalman (pno)
Berwald, F.:Trio Fragments, w. J. Modrian (vn), G. Kertész (vc) *(rec June 7-16, 1991)* Marco Polo ▲ 8.223430 [DDD]
Berwald, F.:Trios, w. J. Modrian (vn), G. Kertész (vc)—in C (1845); No. 4 *(rec June 7-16, 1991)* Marco Polo ▲ 8.223430 [DDD]
Liszt, F.:Pno Music (misc), w. J. Jandó (pno), I. Lantos (pno)—Harmonies poétiques et religieuses; Invocation (1st version); Hymne du matin; Hymne de la nuit; Berceuse (1st version); Klavierstück; Trois odes funèbres; Berceuse (2nd version); Urbi et orbi; Vexilla regis prodeunt; Drei Stücke aus der Legende der heiligen Elisabeth No. 1 Intro; Impromptu; Epithalam; Resignazione; Recueillement; Sancta Dorothea; In festo transfigurationis Domini nostri Jesu Christi; Ave Maria; Trübe Wolken/Nuages gris; Wiegenlied/Chant du berceau; Am Grabe Richard Wagners; En rêve; Trauervorspiel und Trauermarsch *(rec Italian Cultural Institute, Budapest, 1985-86)* Hungaroton 2-▲ HCD 31656-57 [DDD]

Drage, B. A. (org)
Grieg, E.:Lyric Pieces [Klais Organ, Hallgrim's Church, Reykjavik]—4 pieces, Op. 12; 2 pieces, Op. 43; 1 piece, Op. 47; 3 pieces, Op. 54; 2 pieces, Op. 65; 1 piece, Op. 71 *(rec Oct. 1993)* Norway Music ▲ EUCD 002
Grieg, E.:Nordic Folksongs & Dances [Klais Organ, Hallgrim's Church, Reykjavik]—Springdans *(rec Oct. 1993)* Norway Music ▲ EUCD 002
Grieg, E.:Norwegian Dances, Op. 35 [Klais Organ, Hallgrim's Church, Reykjavik] *(rec Oct. 1993)* Norway Music ▲ EUCD 002
Grieg, E.:Peer Gynt Suite 1 [Klais Organ, Hallgrim's Church, Reykjavik] *(rec Oct. 1993)* Norway Music ▲ EUCD 002

Dragon, Carmen E. (hp)
Classical Moods Acoustic Moods ▲ AM 22589-01

Dragovic, Sasa (tpt)—see ORCHESTRAS & ENSEMBLES Tickmayer Formatio

Drake, Julius (pno)—see also ORCHESTRAS & ENSEMBLES Daniel Trio
Bärmann, H.J.:Air Varié, w. V. Soames (cl) Clarinet Classics ▲ CC 0003
Brahms, J.:Son 2 Vc, w. C. Dearnley (vc) Meridian ▲ MER 84223 [DDD]
Brahms, J.:Son in D Vc, w. C. Dearnley (vc) Meridian ▲ MER 84223 [DDD]
Debussy, C.:Chamber Music, w. William Bennett (fl), David Campbell (cl), James Campbell (cl), Nicholas Daniel (ob), Robert Makell (hn), Richard Watkins (hn), Robin Kennard (bn), Rachel Gough (bn), Simon Haram (sax), Ieuan Jones (hp), Clifford Benson (pno), John York (pno), Roger Tapping (va)—Rapsodie for Eng hn; Syrinx; Première rapsodie; Son for Fl, Va & Hp; Le petit nègre; Petite pièce; Rapsodie for Sax *(rec All Saints' Church, East Finchley, London, Jan 12-20, 1994)* Cala 2-▲ CACD 1017 [DDD]
Encores 2 ASV ▲ ASV 910 [DDD]
Howells, H.:Songs, w. L. Dawson (sop), C. Pierard (mez), J.M. Ainsley (ten), B. Luxon (bar)—7 various songs; 2 South African Settings; 3 Folksongs; A Garland for De la Mare; Peacock Pie, Op. 33; 4 French Chansons, Op. 29; In Green Ways, Op. 43; 12 various songs; 3 Children's Songs; 4 Songs, Op. 22 Chandos 2-▲ CHAN 9185/86 [DDD]
Mendelssohn, F.:Concert Pieces, w. V. Soames (cl), R. Heaton (cl)—Nos. 1 & 2 Clarinet Classics ▲ CC 0003
Poulenc, F.:Chamber Music, w. Peter Sidhom (bar), William Bennett (fl), David Campbell (cl), James Campbell (cl), Nicholas Daniel (ob), Richard Watkins (hn), Rachel Gough (bn), Peter Carter (vn), Chris West (db), Ieuan Jones (hp), Clifford Benson (pno), John York (pno)—Son for Ob; L'invitation au château; Villanelle; Son 2 Cls; Trio; Sxt; Son for Cl & Bn; Rapsodie nègre; Son for Cl; Mouvements perpétuels; Son for Fl *(rec All Saints' Church, East Finchley, London, Jan 12-20, 1994)* Cala 2-▲ CACD 1018 [DDD]
Saint-Saëns, C.:Chamber Music, w. W. Bennett (fl), D. Campbell (cl), J. Campbell (cl), N. Daniel (ob), R. Makell (hn), R. Watkins (hn), R. Kennard (bn), R. Gough (bn), S. Haram (sax), I. Jones (hp), C. Benson (pno), J. York (pno), R. Tapping (va)—Odelette, Op. 162; Son for Cl, Op. 167; Feuillet d'album, Op. 81; Son for Bn, Op. 168; Caprice on Danish & Russian Airs, Op. 79; Son for Ob, Op. 166; Romance in D♭, Op. 37; Tarantelle, Op. 6 *(rec All Saints' Church, East Finchley, London, Jan 12-20, 1994)* Cala 2-▲ CACD 1017 [DDD]
Schoeck, O.:Songs (comp), w. Nathan Berg (bar), Oskar Birchmeier (org)—3 geistliche Gesänge, Op. 11; 3 Lieder, Op. 7; 2 Gesänge, Op. 9; 5 Lieder, Op. 31; 12 Eichendorff-Lieder, Op. 30 *(rec Sept 1995)* Jecklin ▲ JD 672
Schumann, R.:Myrthen, w. Lynne Dawson (sop), Ian Partridge (ten) Chandos ▲ CHAN 9307 [DDD]
Schumann, R.:Songs, w. Ian Partridge (ten)—Sag an, o lieber Vogel mein, Op. 27/1; Dem roten Röslein gleicht mein Lieb, Op. 27/2; Was soll ich sagen?, Op. 27/3; Jasminenstrauch, Op. 27/4; Nur ein lächelnder Blick, Op. 27/5; Die Löwenbraut, Op. 31/1 Chandos ▲ CHAN 9307 [DDD]
Les Six Works for Clarinet & Piano, w. V. Soame (cl) *(rec 1989)* Clarinet Classics ▲ CC 0001 [DDD]
Weber, C.M. von:Melody Cl, w. V. Soames (cl) Clarinet Classics ▲ CC 0003
Weber, C.M. von:Vars on a Theme from *Silvana* Cl, w. V. Soames (cl) Clarinet Classics ▲ CC 0003
Weitz, G.:Sym 1 Arkay ▲ AR 6109 [DDD]
Weitz, G.:Sym 2 Arkay ▲ AR 6109 [DDD]

Drake, Susan (hp)
Arabesque:Romantic Harp Music of the 19th Century Hyperion ▲ CDA 66116 [DDD]

Drake, V. (hpd)
Bach, J.S.:French Suites—BWV 815 [trans. for harp] Well-Tempered Productions ▲ WTP 5161 [AAD]
Bach, J.S.:Partitas Hpd, BWV 825-830—BWV 825 [trans. for harp] Well-Tempered Productions ▲ WTP 5161 [AAD]

Drake, V. (lt)
Bach, J.S.:Suite Lt, BWV 995 [trans for hp] Well-Tempered Productions ▲ WTP 5161 [AAD]

Drake, Victoria (hp)—see also ORCHESTRAS & ENSEMBLES Speculum Musicae
Martin, F.:Petite sym concertante, w. A. Newman (hpd), R. Hoca (pno), R. Kapp (cnd), Philharmonia Virtuosi ESS.A.Y ▲ CD 1014 [DDD]

Drake, Victoria (hp) (cont.)
Scarlatti, D.:Sons Kbd—in G, K.201; in C, K.461; in C, K.159; in d, K.9; in d, K.10; in b, K.87; in E, K.531; in A, K.208; in A, K.212; in a, K.451; in E, K.135; in g, K.476; in f, K.466; in F, K.468; in d, K.213; in B♭, K.545 Well-Tempered Productions ▲ WPT 5168 [DDD]
Spanish Gold Well-Tempered ▲ WTP 5179

Drápal, Vitezslav (fl)
Benda, F.:Sons (2) Fl, w. Hana Mullerová (hp) Panton ▲ PAN 811004
Krumpholtz, J.-B.:Sons (3) Fl & Hp, w. Hana Mullerová (hp) Panton ▲ PAN 811004
Vanhal, J.B.:Son 1 Fl, w. Hana Mullerová (hp) Panton ▲ PAN 811004

Draper, Charles (cl)
Brahms, J.:Qnt Cl, w. Léner String Quartet *(rec 1928 for Columbia Records)* Pearl ▲ PEA 9903 (m) [AAD]
Mozart, W.A.:Qnt Cl, K.581, w. Léner String Quartet *(rec 1928 for Columbia Records)* Pearl ▲ PEA 9903 (m) [AAD]

Draper, John (gtr)
Brouwer, L.:Gtr Music, w. Robert Beer (gtr), Carl Ljungstrom (gtr), Steven Patterson (gtr)—Musica Incidental Campesina; Vier Mikropiezas; Cuban Landscape with Rain; Preludios Epigrammaticos; El Decameron Negro; other works Koch Schwann ▲ SCH 311742 [DDD]

Dratsay, Ákos (fl)
Doppler, A.F.:Music Fl & Pno, w. Bea Berényi (fl), László Révész (pno)—for 2 fls & pno composed by A. Doppler:Andante et Rondeau, Op. 25; Fantasie sur des motifs hongrois, Op. 35; Duettino sur des motifs hongrois, Op. 36; Duettino sur motifs Americains, Op. 37; La Sonnambula, Op. 42; for 2 fls & pno composed by A. Doppler & K. Doppler:Souvenir de Prague, Op. 24; Valse di Bravura, Op. 33; Rigoletto-fantasie, Op. 38 *(rec Jan 22-24, 1996)* Hungaroton ▲ HCD 31648 [DDD]

Dratva, Tomas (pno)
Brennan, J.W.:Atanos, w. Andrea Formenti (a sax), Carlo Peliccione (db) *(rec Sept. 1993 & Jan. 1994)* Jecklin ▲ JS 301-2
Pflüger, A.:Tra qua e la, w. Andrea Formenti (alt sax) *(rec Sept. 1993 & Jan. 1994)* Jecklin ▲ JS 302-2
Vassena, N.:Nocturnes, w. Andrea Formenti (a sax) *(rec Sept. 1993 & Jan. 1994)* Jecklin ▲ JS 302-2

Draugsvoll, Geir (acc)
Frounberg, I.:A Dirge:Other Echos Inhabit the Garden *(rec Oct 1995-Jan 1996)* Marco Polo/Dacapo ▲ 8.224028 [DDD]
Geir Draugsvoll:Classical Accordion Simax ▲ PSC 1096
Holm, M.W.:Troglodyt *(rec Oct 1995-Jan 1996)* Marco Polo/Dacapo ▲ 8.224028 [DDD]
Jørgensen, K.I.:Cadenza *(rec Oct 1995-Jan 1996)* Marco Polo/Dacapo ▲ 8.224028 [DDD]
Kanding, E.:Winter Darkness *(rec Oct 1995-Jan 1996)* Marco Polo/Dacapo ▲ 8.224028 [DDD]
Kayser, L.:Confetti—Nos. 2, 5, 6 & 11 *(rec Oct 1995-Jan 1996)* Marco Polo/Dacapo ▲ 8.224028 [DDD]
Pape, A.:I've Never Seen A Butterfly Here, w. Lise-Lotte Nielsen (sop), Søren Kaas Claesson (vn) *(rec Oct 1995-Jan 1996)* Marco Polo/Dacapo ▲ 8.224028 [DDD]

Draxinger, Franz (hn)
Smyth, E.:Double Con, w. R. Eggebrecht-Kupsa (vn), C. Dutilly (pno) *(rec 1992)* Troubadisc ▲ TRO CD 01405 [DDD]

Dreier, Sabine (fl)
Bon Di Venezia, A.:Sons Fl, Op. 1, w. I. Hegen (pno) *(rec Sept. 1992)* CPO ▲ CPO 999181-2 [DDD]

Dreier, Sabine (trns fl)
Love Songs & Dances:Consort Music for Lute & Voices from "Pratum Musicum", w. Kirchhof, Lutz (lt), Marie-Claude Vallin (sop), Claudio Cavina (altus), Max van Egmond (bar), Petra Manz (vl) *(rec Evangelische Kirche, St Osdag, Mandelsloh, Germany, Nov 21-24, 1994)* Sony Classical ("Vivarte" series) ▲ SK 66263 [DDD]

Dreisig, Flemming (org)
Danish Christmas Carols, w. St. Annae Girls' Choir, Ketil Christensen (tpt), Erling Pedersen (org) Danica ▲ DCD 8103

Drenikov, Ivan (pno)
Brahms, J.:Con 1 Pno, w. V. Kazandjiev (cnd), Bulgarian RSO Pierre Verany ▲ PV.791012 [DDD]
Brahms, J.:Rhaps Pno, Op. 79 Pierre Verany ▲ PV.791012 [DDD]

Dreser, Pavel (acc)
Trojan, V.:Bagaja, w. Václav Hudeček (vn), Lubomir Brabec (gtr) Supraphon ▲ SUP 112203 [DDD]
Trojan, V.:The Emperor's Nightengale, w. Václav Hudeček (vn), Lubomir Brabec (gtr) Supraphon ▲ SUP 112203 [DDD]

Dresher, Paul (elec gtr/elec)
Dresher, P.:Destiny, w. Gene Reffkin (perc) Lovely Music ▲ LCD 2011 [ADD]
Dresher, P.:Liquid & Stellar Music Lovely Music ▲ LCD 2011 [ADD]

Dresher, Paul (gtr/kbd/elec)
Dresher, P.:Slow Fire, w. R. Eckert (sgr), G. Reffkin (perc) [E] Minmax ▲ CD 010

Dresser, Mark (elec bass)
Sato, M.:Improvs, w. Michihiro Sato (tsugaru shamisen), Bill Frisell (elec gtr), Fred Frith (elec gtr), Tenko (sgr), Mark Miller (elec bass), Nicolas Collins (elec), Christian Marclay (turntables), Steve Colemann (sax), Tom Cora (vc), Joey Baron (perc), Gerry Hemingway (perc), Toh Ban Djan [Ikue Mori (perc)], Luli Shioi (elec bass/sgr)], Semantics [Elliott Sharp (electric gtr/bass), Samm Bennett (perc), Ned Rothenberg (sax)]—23 improvisations with various accompaniment combinations *(rec Baby Monster Studio, NY, Apr. 11-16, 1988)* Hat Hut ▲ hat ART CD 6015 [ADD]
Zorn, J.:Kristallnacht, w. David Krakauer (cl/b cl), Frank London (tpt), Mark Feldman (vn), Marc Ribot (gtr), Anthony Coleman (kbd), William Winant (perc) Tzadik ▲ TZA 7301 [ADD]

Drew, Lucas (db)
Debussy, C.:Danses sacrée et profane, w. M. Klinko (hp), Miami String Quartet Audiofon ▲ CD 72036
Gibson, R.:November Field, w. John Dee (ob) Capstone ▲ CPS 8621
McAlister, C.:Elegia para Quijote y Quijana, w. John Dee (E hn) *(rec Miami Beach, Feb 1996)* Albany ▲ TROY 212 [DDD]
Surinach, C.:Double Con Fl, w. Christine Nield-Capote (fl), T.M. Sleeper (cnd), Univ of Miami SO *(rec Maurice Gusman Concert Hall, The University of Miami, Florida, Oct 1993 & Nov 1994)* Centaur ▲ CRC 2256 [DDD]
Surinach, C.:Sinf chica, w. Christine Nield-Capote (fl), T.M. Sleeper (cnd), Univ of Miami SO *(rec Maurice Gusman Concert Hall, The University of Miami, Florida, Oct 1993 & Nov 1994)* Centaur ▲ CRC 2256 [DDD]
Surinach, C.:Symphonic Melismas, w. Christine Nield-Capote (fl), T.M. Sleeper (cnd), Univ of Miami SO *(rec Maurice Gusman Concert Hall, The University of Miami, Florida, Oct 1993 & Nov 1994)* Centaur ▲ CRC 2256 [DDD]

Drewes, Tim (org)
At Holy Rosary Church, Edmonds, Washington Organ Historical Society ■ OHSC 1

Drexler, Jonathan (fl)
Wyner, Y.:Memorial Music, w. Susan Davenny Wyner (sop), Mary Posses (fl), Peter Standaart (fl) *(rec Dwight Chapel, Yale University, 1975)* CRI ("American Masters" series) ▲ CD 701 [ADD]

Dreyfus, George (bn)
Dreyfus, G.:The Adventures of Sebastian the Fox, w. Knappet (nar) Move ▲ MD 3071
Dreyfus, G.:Old Melbourne, w. Schubert (gtr) Move ▲ MD 3071
Dreyfus, G.:Rush, w. Schubert (gtr) Move ▲ MD 3071
Dreyfus, G.:Trio Fl, w. Ridell (fl), Swift (cl) Move ▲ MD 3071
Sutherland, M.:Little Suite, w. Dodd (fl), Swift (cl) Move ▲ MD 3071
Weiss, A.:Petite suite Fl, w. Ridell (fl), Swuft (cl) Move ▲ MD 3071

Dreyfus, Huguette (hpd)
Bach, J.S.:Chromatic Fant & Fugue Denon ▲ 7233 [DDD]
Bach, J.S.:Fants Hpd—BWV 906 Denon ▲ 7233 [DDD]
Bach, J.S.:Italian Con Denon ▲ 7233 [DDD]
Bach, J.S.:Preludium & Fugue Hpd, BWV 894 Denon ▲ 7233 [DDD]
Bach, J.S.:Das wohltemperierte Klavier—Bk. 1, BWV 846-69 *(rec Oct 3-9 1992)* Denon/PCM Digital 2-▲ DEN 75638/39 [DDD]

INSTRUMENT.

Dreyfus, Karen (va)
Bruch, M.:Romanze Va, w. R. McDonald (pno) Bridge ▲ BCD 9016 [DDD]
Debussy, C.:Beau soir, w. R. McDonald (pno)—trans. Karen Dreyfus for viola & piano Bridge ▲ BCD 9016 [DDD]
Falla, M. de:Suite populaire espagnole, w. R. McDonald (pno) [trans Paul Kochanski for vn & pno] Bridge ▲ BCD 9016 [DDD]
Hindemith, P.:Son Va & Pno, Op. 11/4, w. R. McDonald (pno) Bridge ▲ BCD 9016 [DDD]
Schumann, R.:Märchenbilder, w. R. McDonald (pno) Bridge ▲ BCD 9016 [DDD]
Dreyfus, Laurence (vl)
Bach, J.S.:Sons Vl, BWV 1027–1029, w. K. Haugsand (hpd) Simax ▲ PSC 1024 [DDD]
Marais, M.:Pièces de viole [Book 2] (sels), w. K. Haugsand (hpd)—Suites in b & e Simax ▲ PSC 1053 [DDD]
Marais, M.:Vars on *Folies d'Espagne*, w. K. Haugsand (hpd) Simax ▲ PSC 1053 [DDD]
Driever, Bertho (rcr)—see ORCHESTRAS & ENSEMBLES Amsterdam Loeki Stardust Quartet
Drinkall, R. (pno)—see ORCHESTRAS & ENSEMBLES Artaria Trio
Drinkall, R. (vc)
Duo, w. Drinkall, R. (vc), Dian Baker (pno) Klavier ▲ KCD 11043 [DDD]
Hindemith, P.:Son Vc & Pno, Op. 11/3, w. Dian Baker (pno) Pyramid ▲ PYR 13505
Kodály, Z.:Son Vc & Pno, Op. 4, w. Dian Baker (pno) Pyramid ▲ PYR 13505
Martinů, B.:Son 3 Vc, w. Dian Baker (pno) Pyramid ▲ PYR 13505
Weill, K.:Son Vc, w. Dian Baker (pno) Pyramid ▲ PYR 13505
Drobeck, Charly (fl/alt fl/pic)
Allen, J.:Brazilian Son, w. Ron Grinage (pno), Shana Norton (hp), Carol Redman (fl), Sam Lunt (perc), Tom Maguire (perc) *(rec Santuario de Guadalupe, Sante Fe, NM, Sept 29–30, 1995)* Wild Iris ▲ WI 001
Drobinsky, M. (pno)
Schmitt, F.:Hasards, w. E. Herbin (pno), A. Galpérine (pno), B. Pasquier (pno) Gallo ▲ CD 711 [ADD]
Drobinsky, Mark (vc)
Biarent, A.:Music of, w. D. Andersen (pno)—Poco lento; Presto furioso; Lamento; Un peu lent *(rec 1980; 1993)* Talent ▲ DOM 2910 14 [DDD]
Chausson, E.:Pièce Vc & Pno, w. D. Andersen (pno) *(rec 1980/1993)* Talent ▲ DOM 2910 14 [DDD]
Fuchs, R.:Fantasiestücke Vc, Op. 78, w. D. Blumenthal (pno) Marco Polo ▲ 8.223423 [DDD]
Herbin, R.:Qt Pno, w. E. Herbin (pno), Alexis Galpérine (vn), Bruno Pasquier (va) Gallo ▲ CD 711 [ADD]
Magnard, A.:Music of, w. A. Rabinovitch (pno)—Sans lenteur; Sans faiblir; Funèbre; Rondement *(rec 1980 & 1993)* Talent ▲ DOM 2910 14 [DDD]
Marc Grauwels & Friends, w. M. Grauwels (fl), Marie-Noelle de Callataÿ (sop), Hiroko Masaki (sop), Dennis James (glass hmc), Ingrid Procureur (hp), Yves Storms (gtr), Yvietta Matison (va), Alain De Rijckere (bn), Daniel Blumenthal (pno), Frank Michiels (perc), Belgian RSO, W Syrinx 2-▲ 96101 [DDD]
Schubert, Franz:Qt Fl, w. M. Grauwels (fl), Y. Matison (va), Y. Storms (gtr) Syrinx ▲ 93105 [DDD]
Drouet, Jean-Pierre (perc)—see also ORCHESTRAS & ENSEMBLES Le Cercle Trio
Bartók, B.:Con for 2 Pnos, w. K. Labeque (pno), M. Labeque (pno), S. Gualda (perc), S. Rattle (cnd), City of Birmingham SO EMI ▲ CDC 47446
Bartók, B.:Son for 2 Pnos, w. K. Labeque (pno), M. Labeque (pno), S. Gualda (perc) EMI ▲ CDC 47446
Berio, L.:Circles, w. C. Berberian (sop), F. Pierre (hp), J.-C. Casadesus (perc) *(rec 1967)* Wergo ▲ WER 6021-2 [AAD]
Bernstein, L.:West Side Story (symphonic dances), w. K. Labèque (pno), M. Labèque (pno), Sylvio Gualdo (perc), Trilok Gurtu (perc)—Overture; Scherzando; Blues; Somewhere; Scherzo; Mambo; Cha-cha; Cool; The rumble; I have a love [arr. Irwin Kostal for 2 pianos, percussion & jazz drums] CBS ▲ MK 45531 [DDD]
Boucourechliev, A.:Les Archipels, w. Brigitte Sylvestre (hp), Elisabeth Chojnacka (hpd), Françoise Rieunier (org), Roland Auzet, Hakon Austbö (pno), Françoise-Frédéric Guy (pno), Claude Helffer (pno), Georges Pludermacher (pno), Ysaÿe String Quartet, Les Pléiades Ensemble Musique Francaise d'Aujourd'hui ("Collection MFA-Radio France" series) ▲ MFA 216001
Drucker, Eugene (vn)
Hindemith, P.:Con Vn, w. L. Bernstein (cnd), New York PO Sony Classical ▲ SMK 47599
Drucker, Naomi (cl)
Babbitt, M.:Composition for 4 Instrs, w. Wummer (fl), March (vn), McCall (vc) CRI ■ C 138
Kupferman, M.:Four Double Features, w. S. Drucker (cl) Soundspells ▲ SP 102
Kupferman, M.:Qt Cl, w. Laurentian String Quartet Soundspells ▲ SP 102
Kupferman, M.:Triple Play, w. S. Drucker (cl), B. Abram (pno) Soundspells ▲ SP 102
Poulenc, F.:Son for 2 Cls, w. Stanley Drucker (cl) Cala Records ("New York Legends" series) ▲ CAL CACD 509 [DDD]
Siegmeister, E.:Prelude, Blues & Finale, w. Stanley Drucker (cl), Kazuko Hayami (pno) Cala Records ("New York Legends" series) ▲ CAL CACD 509 [DDD]
Drucker, Stanley (cl)
Barber, S.:Summer Music, w. Jeanne Baxtresser (fl), Joseph Robinson (ob), Judith LeClair (bn), Philip Myers (hn) EMI Classics ("Anglo-American Chamber Music" series) ▲ CDC 55400
Bernstein, L.:Son Cl, w. Kazuko Hayami (pno) Cala Records ("New York Legends" series) ▲ CAL CACD 509 [DDD]
Copland, A.:Con Cl, w. L. Bernstein (cnd), New York PO Deutsche Grammophon ▲ 431672-2 [DDD]
Corigliano, J.:Con Cl, w. Z. Mehta (cnd), New York PO New World ▲ NW 309-2 [ADD]
Corigliano, J.:Soliloquy, w. Kerry McDermott (vn), Lisa Kim (vn), Rebecca Young (va), Gerald Appleman (vc) Cala Records ("New York Legends" series) ▲ CAL CACD 509 [DDD]
Debussy, C.:Première rapsodie, w. Kazuko Hayami (pno) Cala Records ("New York Legends" series) ▲ CAL CACD 509 [DDD]
Debussy, C.:Première rapsodie, w. L. Bernstein (cnd), New York PO *(rec 1961)* Sony Classical ▲ SMK 47545 [ADD]
Falla, M. de:Con Hpd, w. I. Kipnis (hpd), P. Brook (fl), H. Gomberg (ob), E. Chapo (vn), L. Munroe (vc), P. Boulez (cnd), New York PO *(rec Mar. 2, 1975)* Sony Classical ▲ SBK 53264 ■ SBT 53264
Ives, C.:Largo, w. Glenn Dicterow (vn), Israela Margalit (pno) EMI Classics ("Anglo-American Chamber Music" series) ▲ CDC 55406
Kupferman, M.:Five Flings, w. K. Hayami (pno) Soundspells ▲ SP 102
Kupferman, M.:Four Double Features, w. N. Drucker (cl) Soundspells ▲ SP 102
Kupferman, M.:Soundspells Fant Soundspells ▲ SP 102
Kupferman, M.:Triple Play, w. N. Drucker (cl), B. Abram (pno) Soundspells ▲ SP 102
Nielsen, C.:Con Cl, w. L. Bernstein (cnd), New York PO *(rec 1967)* Sony Classical 4-▲ S4K 45989 [ADD]
Poulenc, F.:Son Cl Pno, w. Kazuko Hayami (pno) Cala Records ("New York Legends" series) ▲ CAL CACD 509 [DDD]
Poulenc, F.:Son for 2 Cls, w. Naomi Drucker (cl) Cala Records ("New York Legends" series) ▲ CAL CACD 509 [DDD]
Schumann, R.:Fantasiestücke Cl, w. Sandra Shapiro (pno) *(rec Performing Arts Ctr/Purchase College-State Univ of NY Recital Hall, May 8, 1995)* Elysium ▲ GRK 709 [DDD]
Schumann, R.:Märchenerzählungen, w. Dorian Rence (va), Sandra Shapiro (pno) *(rec Performing Arts Ctr/Purchase College-State Univ of NY Recital Hall, May 8, 1995)* Elysium ▲ GRK 709 [DDD]
Siegmeister, E.:Prelude, Blues & Finale, w. Naomi Drucker (cl), Kazuko Hayami (pno) Cala Records ("New York Legends" series) ▲ CAL CACD 509 [DDD]
Weigl, V.:Nature Moods, w. G. Shirley (ten), Gordon (vn) CRI ■ C 326
Weigl, V.:New England Suite, w. Sass (vc), G. Moore (pno) CRI ■ C 326
Druckman, Daniel (mar)
Wuorinen, C.:Trio Trbn, w. R. Borror (trbn), A. Feinberg (pno) *(rec Sept. 11–13, 1991)* Koch International Classics ▲ KIC 7123-2 [DDD]
Druckman, Daniel (perc)
Rorem, N.:Hearing, w. R. Rees (sop), K. Wheeler (mez), M. Galloway (ten), R. Hilley (bar), R. Wagner (cl), J. Hamlin (tpt), D. Starobin (mand), D. Davidson (vn), K. Askew (va), J. Babich (db), P. Suits (pno), G. Smith (cnd) Premier ▲ PRCD 1035 [ADD]
Drufuca, A. (vc)—see ORCHESTRAS & ENSEMBLES Matisse Trio
Druian, Rafael (vn)
Mozart, W.A.:Sinf concertante Vn, K.364, w. A. Skernick (va), G. Szell (cnd), Cleveland Orch *(rec 1963)* CBS ▲ MYK 37810 [AAD] ■ MYT 37810
Mozart, W.A.:Sons Vn Pno (misc), w. G. Szell (pno)—K.296 & 301 *(rec 1967)* Sony Masterworks ("Portrait" series) ▲ MPK 47685 [ADD]
Paine, J.K.:Son Vn, Op. 24, w. B. Pasternack (pno) GM ▲ 2021CD
Schuller, G.:Duologue, w. B. Pasternack (pno) GM ▲ GM 2021CD
Vaughan Williams, R.:The Lark Ascending, w. L. Lane (cnd), Cleveland Sinfonietta Sony Classical ("Essential Classics" series) ▲ SBK 62645 ■ SBT 62645
Drummond, Dean (harmonic canons/kithara 2/spoils of war/kithara)
Partch, H.:Daphne of the Dunes, w. Frank Cassara (boo/spoils of war/kithara 2), Dominic Donato (b mar/surrogate kithara/boo), Nina Kellman (kithara 2/harmonic canon/surrogate kithara), Michael Lipsey (cloud-chamber bowls), Ted Mook (vc/gourd tree/cone gongs), James Pugliese (diamond mar), Elizabeth Rodgers (chromelodeon/harmonic canon) *(rec Queens, NY, Mar. 12, 1991)* Mode ▲ MODE 33
Drummond, Dean (zmz)
Monk, T.:Round Midnight, w. Ted Mook (vc), Dominic Donato (zmz), Frank Cassara (zmz) [arr. Drummond for cello & 3 zoomoozophones] *(rec The Magic Shop, New York City, Jan. 31, 1993)* Mode ▲ MODE 33
Pugliese, J.:Freeze, w. Stefani Starin (alt fl), Dominic Donato (zmz), James Pugliese (Yamaha DX711) *(rec New York City, May 29, 1992)* Mode ▲ MODE 33
Drury, David (org)
Bach, J.S.:Chorale Preludes Org—4 sels Walsingham Classics ("Great Organs of Australia" series) ▲ WAL 8021 [DDD]
Bach, J.S.:Preludes & Fugues, BWV 531–552 Walsingham Classics ("Great Organs of Australia" series) ▲ WAL 8021 [DDD]
Byrd, W.:Kbd Music—3 Dances Walsingham Classics ("Great Organs of Australia" series) ▲ WAL 8021 [DDD]
David Drury Plays the Sydney Town Hall Organ, w. Drury, David (org) ABC Classics ▲ 438 881-2 [DDD]
Drury, D.:Org Music—Improvisation [Elegy in memorian Michael Dudman]; Improvisation on an original theme Walsingham Classics ("Great Organs of Australia" series) ▲ WAL 8021 [DDD]
Mendelssohn, F.:Sons Org—No. 3 in A Walsingham Classics ("Great Organs of Australia" series) ▲ WAL 8021 [DDD]
Mozart, W.A.:Andante Mechanical Org, K.616 Walsingham Classics ("Great Organs of Australia" series) ▲ WAL 8021 [DDD]
Mozart, W.A.:Fant Mechanical Org Walsingham Classics ("Great Organs of Australia" series) ▲ WAL 8021 [DDD]
Music for a Grand Organ, w. Drury, David (org) ABC Classics ▲ 432527-2 [DDD]
Valente, A.:Org Music—La romanesca Walsingham Classics ("Great Organs of Australia" series) ▲ WAL 8021 [DDD]
Vierne, L.:Pièces en style libre—3 sels Walsingham Classics ("Great Organs of Australia" series) ▲ WAL 8021 [DDD]
Drury, Stephen (kbd)
Cage, J.:Etudes Australes:Bk 1 Neuma ▲ 450-76
Drury, Stephen (pno)—see also ORCHESTRAS & ENSEMBLES Collage New Music Ensemble
Cage, J.:Music for 2 *(rec Jordan Hall, New England Conservatory, Boston, MA, Mar. 1993)* Mode ▲ mode 47
Cage, J.:Music Walk *(rec Jordan Hall, New England Conservatory, Boston, MA, Mar. 1993)* Mode ▲ mode 47
Cage, J.:One *(rec Jordan Hall, New England Conservatory, Boston, MA, Mar. 1993)* Mode ▲ mode 47
Cage, J.:One^5 *(rec Jordan Hall, New England Conservatory, Boston, MA, Mar. 1993)* Mode ▲ mode 47
Carter, E.:Night Fants Neuma ▲ 450-76
McPhee, C.:Balinese Ceremonial Music, w. Yukiko Takagi (pno), D. R. Davies (cnd), Brooklyn PO MusicMasters ("Classics" series) ▲ 01612-67159-2
McPhee, C.:Con Pno, w. D. R. Davies (cnd), Brooklyn PO MusicMasters ("Classics" series) ▲ 01612-67159-2
Rzewski, F.:The People United Will Never Be Defeated *(rec June 1992)* New Albion ▲ NA 063 [DDD]
Druyinin, Fedor (va)—see ORCHESTRAS & ENSEMBLES Beethoven String Quartet
Druzhnin, Fedor (va)
Rubinstein, A.:Son Va, w. L. Panteyeva (pno) Russian Disc ("The A. Rubinstein Edition" series) ▲ RUS 11 061 [ADD]
Drzewiecki, Jaroslav (pno)
Chopin, F.:Etudes (24) *(rec July 5–10, 1922)* Canyon Classics ▲ 3645 [DDD]
Chopin, F.:Nouvelles études *(rec July 5–10, 1922)* Canyon Classics ▲ 3645 [DDD]
Chopin, F.:Polonaises—No. 9 in B♭, Op. 71/2; No. 10 in f, Op. 71/3; in g; in B♭; in A♭; in g#; in b♭; in G♭ *(rec Dec. 2–7, 1990)* Canyon Classics ▲ 3640 [DDD]
Chopin, F.:Polonaises—No. 1 in c#, Op. 26/1; No. 2 in e♭, Op. 26/2; No. 3 in A, Op. 40/1; No. 4 in C, Op. 40/2; No. 5 in f#, Op. 44; No. 6 in A♭, Op. 53; No. 7 in A♭, Op. 61; No. 8 in d, Op. 71/1 Canyon Classics ▲ 3639 [DDD]
Duarte, Isaac (ob)
Bach, J.S.:Con Vn & Ob, w. Gilles Colliard (vn), C. Meister (cnd), Brixi CO Prague *(rec Studio Martinek, Prague, Sept 5–8, 1994)* Doron ▲ DRC 5005 [DDD]
Dubach, Alexandre (vn)
Paganini, N.:Con 2 Vn, w. L. Foster (cnd), Monte Carlo PO [Cadenza Dubach] *(rec Sept. 23–26, 1993)* Claves ▲ CD 9408 [DDD]
Paganini, N.:Con 3 Vn, w. L. Foster (cnd), Monte Carlo PO Claves ▲ CD 9503
Paganini, N.:Con 5 Vn, w. L. Foster (cnd), Monte Carlo PO [Cadenza Dubach] *(rec Sept. 23–26, 1993)* Claves ▲ CD 9408 [DDD]
Paganini, N.:Con 6 Vn, w. L. Foster (cnd), Monte Carlo PO Claves ▲ CD 9503
Dubar, Daniel (hn)
Corrette, M.:Cons Comiques, w. Georges Barboteu (hn), Michel Berges (hn), Gilbert Coursier (hn), J.-F. Paillard (cnd), Jean-François Paillard CO—No. 14 for Hns & Orch [La Choisy] Erato ▲ 94801-2
Dubeau, Angèle (vn)
Brott, A.:Con Vn, w. B. Brott (cnd), McGill CO Analekta ▲ ANC 9801
Debussy, C.:Son Vn, w. A. Tunis (pno) *(rec 1988)* Analekta Fleur de Lys ▲ FL 2 3021 [DDD] ■ AN4-8702
Falla, M. de:Canciones populares españolas (7), w. Alvaro Pierri (gtr) Analekta ▲ AN 28706
Falla, M. de:Canciones populares españolas (7), w. A. Pierri (gtr)—El paño moruno, Nana, Cancion, Jota, Asturiana, Polo Analekta Fleur de Lys ▲ FL 2 3034
Fauré, G.:Son 1 Vn, w. Andrew Tunis (pno) Analekta ▲ AN 28701
Fauré, G.:Son 1 Vn, w. A. Tunis (pno) *(rec 1988)* Analekta Fleur de Lys ▲ FL 2 3021 [DDD] ■ AN4-8702
Glazunov, A.:Con Vn, w. I. Marinov (cnd), Bulgarian RSO Analekta ▲ AN 28707
Glazunov, A.:The Seasons, w. I. Marinov (cnd), Bulgarian RSO Analekta Fleur de Lys ▲ FL 2 3045
Kabalevsky, D.:Con Vn, w. I. Blazhkov (cnd), Kiev SO Analekta ▲ AN 28702
Kabalevsky, D.:Con Vn, w. I. Blazhkov (cnd), Kiev SO *(rec 1989)* Analekta Fleur de Lys ▲ FL 2 3036 [DDD] ■ AN4-8702
Leclair, J.-M.:Sons Vn (Books 1–4), w. Andrew Tunis (pno)—Op. 9/3 Analekta ▲ AN 28701
Leclair, J.-M.:Sons Vn (Books 1–4), w. A. Tunis (pno) [arr for vn & pno]— Op. 9/3 *(rec 1988)* Analekta Fleur de Lys ▲ FL 2 3021 [DDD] ■ AN4-8702

▲ = CD ♦ = Enhanced CD Δ = MD ■ = Cassette Tape □ = DCC

Dubeau, Angèle (vn) (cont.)
Mozart, W.A.:Music of, w. Alain Marion (fl)—sels from Die Zauberflöte, Die Entführung aus dem Serail, Don Giovanni, Le Nozze di Figaro [trans for fl & vn] Analekta Fleur de Lys ▲ FL 23076 [DDD]
Paganini, N.:Centone di sonate, w. A. Pierri (gtr) Analekta Fleur de Lys ▲ FL 2 3034
Paganini, N.:Son concertata, w. A. Pierri (gtr) Analekta Fleur de Lys ▲ FL 2 3034
Prokofiev, S.:Cons Vn (comp), w. I. Blazhkov (cnd), Kiev SO—No. 1 *(rec 1989)* Analekta Fleur de Lys ▲ FL 2 3036 [DDD] ■ AN4–8702
Prokofiev, S.:Con 1 Vn, w. I. Blazhkov (cnd), Kiev SO Analekta ▲ AN 28702
La Ronde des Berceuses, w. Amati Ensemble [cnd:R. Dessaints] Analekta ▲ AN 28711 [DDD]
Schubert, Franz:Sonatinas Vn, w. A. Kuerti (pno) *(rec 1990)* Analekta Fleur de Lys ▲ FL 2 3042 ■ AN4–8703
Schubert, Franz:Sonatinas Vn, w. Anton Kuerti (pno) Analekta ▲ AN 28703
Sibelius, J.:Con Vn, w. I. Marinov (cnd), Bulgarian RSO Analekta ▲ AN 28705 [DDD]
Sibelius, J.:Con Vn, w. I. Marinov (cnd), Bulgarian RSO Analekta ("Fleur de Lys" series) ▲ FL 23045
Tchaikovsky, P.:Sérénade mélancolique, w. I. Blazhkov (cnd), Kiev SO *(rec 1989)* Analekta Fleur de Lys ▲ FL 2 3036 [DDD] ■ AN4–8702
Tchaikovsky, P.:Souvenir d'un lieu cher, w. I. Blazhkov (cnd), Kiev SO—Mélodie [arr vn & orch] Analekta ▲ AN 28702
Telemann, G.P.:Fants Vn Analekta Fleur de Lys ▲ FL 2 3048
Telemann, G.P.:Fants Hpd Analekta ▲ AN 28708

Dubinsky, Rostislav (va)
Debussy, C.:Son Vn, w. L. Edlina (pno) Chandos ▲ CHAN 8458
Mozart, W.A.:Trio Cl, K.498, w. J. Campbell (cl), L. Edlina (pno) Chandos ▲ CHAN 8655 [DDD]
Shostakovich, D.:Son Vn, w. L. Edlina (pno) Chandos ▲ CHAN 8343 [DDD]

Dubinsky, Rostislav (vn)—see also ORCHESTRAS & ENSEMBLES Borodin Trio
Arensky, A.:Trio 1 Pno, w. Edlina (pno), Turovsky (vc) Chandos ▲ CHAN 8477 [DDD]
Beethoven, L. van:Son 5 Vn, "Spring", w. L. Edlina (pno) Chandos ▲ CHAN 9297 [DDD]
Beethoven, L. van:Son 9 Vn, "Kreutzer", w. L. Edlina (pno) Chandos ▲ CHAN 9297 [DDD]
Brahms, J.:Trio Hn, w. M. Thompson (hn), L. Edlina (pno) Chandos ▲ CHAN 8606 [DDD]
Glinka, M.:Trio pathétique, w. Y. Turovsky (vc), L. Edlina (pno) Chandos ▲ CHAN 8477 [DDD]
Schnittke, A.:Suite in the Old Style, w. L. Edlina (pno) Chandos ▲ CHAN 8343 [DDD]

Dublanchet, Lionel (tuba)
Curran, A.:Crystal Psalms, An Homage to Kristallnacht, w. F. Badaloni (cl), D. Keberlee (cl), M. Riesler (cl), A. Santoloci (cl), M. Capone (acc), D. Rueff (tuba), A. Caggiano (perc), w. Ensemble Vocale Sesquialtera [cnd:E. Razzicchia], Radio France Chamber Choir [cnd:D. LaBorde]—[F] New Albion ▲ NA 067

Dublinsky, Rostislav (vn)—see ORCHESTRAS & ENSEMBLES Borodin Trio
Dubois, C. (vc)—see ORCHESTRAS & ENSEMBLES Deakin Piano Trio
Dubois, C. (pno)—see ORCHESTRAS & ENSEMBLES Deakin Piano Trio

Dubois, Pierre-Yves (cl)
Gerber, R.:Chamber Music, w. Fränzi Badertscher-Jaquiéry (fl), Gunhard Mattes (ob), Dimitri Ashkenazy (cl), Claude Delley (cl), Anne de Dadelsen (pno)—Pièce lente; Habanera; Berceuse [all for Cl & Pno]; Trio for Fl, Ob & Pno; Son for Fl & Pno; Ballet for Fl & Pno; Sonatine for 3 Cl; Pavane for Fl & Pno; Suite for Fl & Pno; Prélude et fugue sur le nom de Bach for Cl Gallo ▲ CD 788 [DAD]

Dubourg, Evelyne (pno)
Mozart, W.A.:Con 8 Pno, w. H. Stadlmair (cnd), Munich CO Tudor ▲ 703 [DDD]
Mozart, W.A.:Con 9 Pno, w. H. Stadlmair (cnd), Munich CO Tudor ▲ 703 [DDD]
Schumann, R.:Kinderszenen—No. 1, "Of Foreign Countries & People" LaserLight ▲ 14 224
Schumann, R.:Waldscenen—Abschied LaserLight ▲ 14 224
Scriabin, A.:Con Pno, w. N. Uljanov (cnd), Sofia PO Tudor ▲ TUD 7025 [DDD]
Scriabin, A.:Preludes Pno, Op. 11 Tudor ▲ TUD 793 [ADD]
Scriabin, A.:Sons Pno (comp)—Nos. 1-10 Tudor 2-▲ 726 [ADD]
Scriabin, A.:Son 2 Pno Tudor ▲ TUD 793 [ADD]
Scriabin, A.:Son 3 Pno Tudor ▲ TUD 793 [ADD]

Dubreuil, Pascal (hpd)
Bodino, S.:Sons, w. Peter Zajíček (vn), Miloš Valent (vn), Peter Királ (vc), Musica Aeterna—Sons 1–6 *(rec Castle of Tonky, Slovakia, Apr 1994)* Slovart ▲ SR 0008–2–131 [DDD]

Dubrov, Piotr (ob)
Telemann, G.P.:Cons Ob, w. Pierre Pierlot (ob), Evgeni Nepalov (ob), Andrei Abramenkov (vn), Rudolf Barshai (vn), Leonid Poleess (vn), R. Barshai (cnd), Moscow CO—in B♭ for 3 Obs, 3 Vns & Bc *(rec Salle Wagram, Paris, June 1964)* EMI Classics ▲ CDK 65340 [ADD]

Dubugnon, M. (org)
Roques, L.:Ancient Christmas Carols—33 sels Gallo ▲ CD 830

Duchable, François-René (pno)
Brahms, J.:Sons Cl (comp), w. Paul Meyer (cl)—Allegro gracioso; Vivace [both from Son 1]; Allegro amabile [from Son 2] *(rec Chateau de Châtonneyre, Corseaux, Switzerland, Oct. 1989)* Erato ▲ 94679–2
Bruch, M.:Pieces Cl, Op. 83/1–8, w. Paul Meyer (cl), Gérard Caussé (va)—No. 8 [Moderato in e♭] *(rec Studio 106, Radio France, Feb. 1989)* Erato ▲ 94679–2
Bruch, M.:Trios Cl, Va & Pno, Op. 83, w. P. Meyer (cl), G. Caussé (va) Erato ▲ 2292–45483–2 ZK [DDD]
Grieg, E.:Con Pno, Op. 16, w. T. Guschlbauer (cnd), Strasbourg PO Erato ▲ 92872–2 [DDD]
Rachmaninoff, S.:Con 2 Pno, w. T. Guschlbauer (cnd), Strasbourg PO Erato ▲ 92872–2 [DDD]
The Romantic Horn, w. J.-J. Justafré (hn) Pierre Verany ▲ 793091 [DDD]
Weber, C.M. von:Grand duo concertant Cl, w. Paul Meyer (cl)—Andante con moto *(rec Chateau de Châtonneyre, Corseaux, Switzerland, Oct. 1989)* Erato ▲ 94679–2

Duchemin, André-Gilles (fl)
French Music for Flute & Piano, w. Mario Duchemin (pno)
Ibert, J.:Pièce Fl Pavane ▲ ADW 7197
Kabalevsky, D.:Con Vn, w. M. Bélanger (cnd), Montreal Metropolitan Orch [performer's arr. for flute] Pavane ▲ ADW 7197
Kennan, K.W.:Night Soliloquy, w. M. Duchemin (pno), B. Jean (cnd), Montreal Metropolitan Orch Pavane ▲ ADW 7197
Lipsky, H.:Images, w. Helmut Lipsky Ensemble Pavane ▲ ADW 7197

Duchemin, Mario (pno)
Brahms, J.:Qnt Pno, w. Lavel String Quartet Analekta ▲ CLCD 2003
French Music for Flute & Piano, w. Duchemin, André-Gilles (fl)
Kennan, K.W.:Night Soliloquy, w. A.-G. Duchemin (fl), B. Jean (cnd), Montreal Metropolitan Orch Pavane ▲ ADW 7197

Duckles, Lee (vc)
Copland, A.:Qt Pno, w. D.R. Davies (pno), R. Tecco (vn), K. Harrison (va) MusicMasters ▲ 7026–2–C [DDD]
Copland, A.:Vitebsk:Study on a Jewish Theme, w. R. Tecco (vn), D.R. Davies (pno) MusicMasters ▲ 7026–2–C [DDD]

Ducommun, Samuel (org)
Ducommun, S.:Org Music, w. R. Märki (org), J. Molnar (hn), P.-A. Monot (tpt), P. Lehmann (tpt)—10 Invocations for Organ; Sonata da Chiesa for Horn & Organ; Sonata da Chiesa for 2 Trumpets & Organ; Variations on a Theme by François Nadler for Organ *(rec 1959, 1985 & 1991)* Gallo ▲ CD655

Dudiet, Jan (handbells)
Vees, J.:Stigmata non Grata, w. Dorian Ringers (handbells), Cammi Carteng (handbells), JoAnn Kerns (handbells), Monica McGowan (handbells), B. Mathis (cnd) CRI ("Emergency Music" series) ▲ CD 730 [DDD]

Dudley, Jo (rcr)
Edwards, R.:Ulpirra *(rec 2MBS-FM, Apr 1994)* Tall Poppies ▲ TP 51 [DDD]

Dudley, R. (pno)
Chopin, F.:Pno Music (misc)—Barcarolle Titanic ▲ Ti 209 [DDD]
Debussy, C.:Clair de lune Titanic ▲ Ti 209 [DDD]
Debussy, C.:Preludes Pno (sels)—Feux d'artifice Titanic ▲ Ti 209 [DDD]
Liszt, F.:Harmonies poétiques et religieuses—Funerailles Titanic ▲ Ti 209 [DDD]

Dudley, R. (pno) (cont.)
Liszt, F.:Mephisto Waltz 3 Pno Titanic ▲ Ti 209 [DDD]
Ravel, M.:Gaspard de la nuit Titanic ▲ Ti 209 [DDD]

Dudley, Whit (hp)
Debussy, C.:Chansons de Bilitis (recitation), w. L. Jeffrey (fl), M. Meisenbach (fl), M. Golden (hp), K. Tamagawa (cel)—no speaker *(rec 6 & 8/91)* Centaur ▲ CRC 2114 [DDD]
Debussy, C.:Prélude à l'après-midi d'un faune, w. M. Meisenbach (fl), M. Golden (hp) [arr. flute & 2 harps Whit Dudley] *(rec 6 & 8/91)* Centaur ▲ CRC 2114 [DDD]
Ravel, M.:Ma mère l'oye Pno, w. M. Golden (hp) [harp duo arr of Laideronette & Impératrice des Pagodes] Centaur ▲ CRC 2114 [DDD]

Duesing, Dale (pno)
Gershwin, G.:Songs, w. A. Oliver (ten), S. Houben (sax)—He Loves and She Loves; Somebody Loves Me; Let's Do It; How Long Has This Been Going on; By Strauss; They All Laughed; Who Cares; But Not for Me; Love Walked in Ricercar ▲ RIC 135119 [DDD]
Porter, C.:Songs, w. A. Oliver (ten), S. Houben (sax)—So in Love; Let's Do It; At Long Last Love; I Get A Kick Out of You; Every Time We Say Goodbye Ricercar ▲ RIC 135119 [DDD]

Duetschler, Anna Barbara (va)
Dittersdorf, K.D. von:Son Va, w. Ursula Duetschler (pno) *(rec Kirche Blumenstein, Oct. 10–14, 1994)* Claves ▲ CD 9502 [DDD]
Hummel, J.N.:Son Va, w. Ursula Duetschler (pno) *(rec Kirche Blumenstein, Oct. 10–14, 1994)* Claves ▲ CD 9502 [DDD]
Stamitz, C.:Son Va, w. Ursula Duetschler (pno) *(rec Kirche Blumenstein, Oct. 10–14, 1994)* Claves ▲ CD 9502 [DDD]
Vanhal, J.B.:Son Va, w. Ursula Duetschler (pno) *(rec Kirche Blumenstein, Oct. 10–14, 1994)* Claves ▲ CD 9502 [DDD]

Duetschler, Irsula (hpd)
Arie Antiche, w. M. Bayo (sop) Claves ▲ CD 9023 [DDD]

Duetschler, Ursula (hpd)—see also ORCHESTRAS & ENSEMBLES CO of Europe Soloists
Balbastre, C.-B.:Hpd Music, w. U. Duetschler—Pièces de clavecin, Book One (1759) Claves ▲ CD 9206 [DDD]
Byrd, W.:Kbd Music—13 pieces from the Fitzwilliam Virginal Book—All in a garden green; The bells; The carman's whistle; Fantasias in C & G; Pavans & Galliards in F, G & g; The Queen's alman; Ut re mi fa sol la; La volta; Walsingham; The woods so wild Claves ▲ CD 9001 [DDD]

Duetschler, Ursula (pno)
Dittersdorf, K.D. von:Son Va, w. Anna Barbara Duetschler (va) *(rec Kirche Blumenstein, Oct. 10–14, 1994)* Claves ▲ CD 9502 [DDD]
Hummel, J.N.:Son Va, w. Anna Barbara Duetschler (va) *(rec Kirche Blumenstein, Oct. 10–14, 1994)* Claves ▲ CD 9502 [DDD]
Stamitz, C.:Son Va, w. Anna Barbara Duetschler (va) *(rec Kirche Blumenstein, Oct. 10–14, 1994)* Claves ▲ CD 9502 [DDD]
Vanhal, J.B.:Son Va, w. Anna Barbara Duetschler (va) *(rec Kirche Blumenstein, Oct. 10–14, 1994)* Claves ▲ CD 9502 [DDD]

Duetschler, Ursula (positive org)
Frescobaldi, G.:Canzonas, Caprici & Ricercari, w. Novus Brass Quartet—19 sels. Claves ▲ CD 9104 [DDD]

Dufka, Vlastimi (ob)
Sperger, J.:Trios, w. M. Jukovic (fl), V. Simcisko (vn), M. Telecky (va), J. Alexander (vc), sels. unknown Trevak ▲ TRE 40002 [DDD]

Dufourcet, Marie Bernadette (org)
Hakim, N.:Fant sur "Adeste Fideles", w. N. Hakim (org) Motette ▲ CD 11171 [DDD]
Hakim, N.:Org Music, w. Naji Hakim (org) [Cavaille-Coll Org, Sacre-Coeur, Paris]—The Embrace of Fire; Mariales; Expressions; Rhap Priory ▲ PRI 465

Duftschmid, Lorenz (vl)
Schmelzer, J.H.:Ballet Suites, w. L. Duftschmid (cnd), Armonico Tributo Austria Arcana ▲ ACA 33
Schmelzer, J.H.:Sons Instrs, w. L. Duftschmid (cnd), Armonico Tributo Austria Arcana ▲ ACA 33

Duftschmid, Lorenz (vn)
Merula, T.:Arias & Capriccios, w. M. Figueras (sop), J.-P. Canihac (cnt), T. Koopman (hpd), J. Savall (vl), R. Lislevand (thb), A. Laurence-King (hp) Astrée ▲ E 8503
Ortiz, D.:Trattado de Glosas, w. J. Savall (vl), T. Koopman (hpd/org), R. Lislevand (vih), P. Pandolfo (b vl), A. Lawrence-King (hp) Astrée ▲ E 8717 [DDD]

Dugan, G. S. (db)—see ORCHESTRAS & ENSEMBLES Scott Chamber Players

Dugas, Sylvie (pno)
Chabrier, E.:España, w. G. Rabol (pno) [trans. for 2 pianos] *(rec Boulogne, France, Jan. 12–14, 1994)* Naxos ▲ 8.553080 [DDD]
Chabrier, E.:Quadrilles on themes from *Tristan und Isolde*, w. G. Rabol (pno)—Prélude et marche française; Cortège burlesque; Air de ballet; Suite de valses *(rec Boulogne, France, Jan. 12–14, 1994)* Naxos ▲ 8.553080 [DDD]
Chabrier, E.:Souvenirs de Munich, w. G. Rabol (pno) *(rec Boulogne, France, Jan. 12–14, 1994)* Naxos ▲ 8.553080 [DDD]
Chabrier, E.:Valses romantiques (3), w. G. Rabol (pno) *(rec Boulogne, France, Jan. 12–14, 1994)* Naxos ▲ 8.553080 [DDD]

Duijck, J. (pno)—see ORCHESTRAS & ENSEMBLES Hans Memling Trio

Duisberg, A. (fl)
Lachner, F.P.:Nonet, w. D. Wollenweber (ob), P. Prieditis (cl), P. Douglas (hn), M. Postinghel (bn), I. Grünkorn (vn), M. Gieler (va), T. Ruge (vc), F. Heidenreich (db) *(rec June 10, 1991)* Thorofon ▲ CTH 2132 [DDD]

Duke, George (pno)
Duke, G.:Muir Woods Suite, w. Stanley Clarke (bass), Chester Thompson (dr), Paulinho Dacosta (perc), E. Stratta (cnd), Lille National Orch *(rec live, Montreaux Music Festival, Montreaux, Switzerland, July 12, 1993)* Warner Bros ▲ 9 46132–2 [DDD]

Duke, John (pno)
Duke, J.:Songs, w. D. Boothman (bar)—22 songs [E] AFKA ▲ SK 505

Duke-Kirkpatrick, Erika (vc)—see also ORCHESTRAS & ENSEMBLES California EAR Unit
Matson, S.:i–5, w. A. Shulmann (hp), P. Kent (vn), M. Newman (vn), R. Tischer (va), B. Morgenthaler (db) *(rec Aug. 29–30, 1992)* Audioquest ▲ AQCD 1013
Matson, S.:Steel Chords, w. D. Livingston (gtr), P. Kent (vn), M. Newman (vn), J. Derouin (vn), C. Moussas (vn), R. Tischer (va), B. Morgenthaler (db), S. Matson (cnd) *(rec Aug. 29–30, 1992)* Audioquest ▲ AQCD 1013
Mosko, S.L.:for Morton Feldman, w. Dorothy Stone (fl), Gaylord Mowrey (pno) New World ▲ 80456–2
Smith, W.L.:Music of, w. Robin Lorentz (vn), Dorothy Stone (fl/pic), Martin Walker (cl), Wadada Leo Smith (tpt/flgl/fls/bells), Vicki Ray (pno/cel), Mika Noda (vib/bells/timp), David Philipson (perc/bells)—Another Wave More Waves; Double Thunderbolt; Tao-Njia; and others Tzadik ("Composer" series) ▲ TZA 7017 [DDD]

Dukes, Philip (va)
Clarke, R.:Son Va, w. S. Rahman (pno) Gamut Classics ▲ GAM 537 [DDD]
Lloyd Webber, W.S.:Sonatina Va ASV ▲ ASV 961
Maconchy, E.:Sketches, w. S. Rahman (pno) Gamut Classics ▲ GAM 537 [DDD]
Martin, F.:Ballade Va, Wind, Hpd & Hp, w. M. Bamert (cnd), London PO Chandos ▲ CHAN 9380 [DDD]
Shostakovich, D.:Son Va, w. S. Rahman (pno) Gamut Classics ▲ GAM 537 [DDD]
Vaughan Williams, R.:Flos Campi, w. R. Hickox (cnd), Northern Sinfonia of England Chandos ▲ CHAN 9392 [DDD]

Dukov, Bruce (elec vn)
Waxman, F.:Night unto Night (sels), w. J. Mauceri (cnd), Hollywood Bowl Orch—Dusk *(rec Culver City, CA, Sept 1992)* Philips ▲ 438867–2 [DDD]

Duliba, O. (vn)
Lachner, F.P.:Qnt 2 Pno, w. H. Göbel (pno), T. Jahnel (vn), S. Clark (va), S. Dörfler (vc) *(rec June 10, 1991)* Thorofon ▲ CTH 2132 [DDD]

Dullaert, Hans (hn)
Hindemith, P.:Son Hn, w. M. Bon (pno) *(rec Oct. & Dec. 1992)* CPO ▲ CPO 999229 [DDD]
Hindemith, P.:Son Alto Hn, w. M. Bon (pno) *(rec Oct. & Dec. 1992)* CPO ▲ CPO 999229 [DDD]

Dulova, Vera (hp)
Damase, J.-M.:Sonatine Hp, w. N. Shameyeva (hp) [arr for 2 harps] *(rec 1975)* Russian Compact Disc ("Talents of Russia" series) ▲ RCD 16204 [AAD]
Debussy, C.:Clair de lune, w. Y. Reentovich (cnd), Bolshoi Theater Violin Ensemble *(rec 1961)* Russian Compact Disc ("Talents of Russia" series) ▲ RCD 16204 [AAD]
Donizetti, G.:Son Fl & Hp, w. A. Korsakov (fl) *(rec 1979)* Russian Compact Disc ("Talents of Russia" series) ▲ RCD 16206 [AAD]
Jolivet, A.:Con Hp, w. A. Zhuraitis (cnd), Russian Radio-TV SO *(rec 1961)* Russian Compact Disc ("Talents of Russia" series) ▲ RCD 16204 [AAD]
Manino, F.:Canzoni per Apra *(rec 1982)* Russian Compact Disc ("Talents of Russia" series) ▲ RCD 16204 [AAD]
Mozart, W.A.:Music of, w. A. Korsakov (fl)—2 Sons for Violin & Harp in G & D *(rec 1978)* Russian Compact Disc ("Talents of Russia" series) ▲ RCD 16206 [AAD]
Pascal, C.R.G.:Con Hp, w. A. Korneiev (cnd), Moscow Radio-TV SO *(rec 1970)* Russian Compact Disc ("Talents of Russia" series) ▲ RCD 16206 [AAD]
Rameau, J.P.:Music of—Tambourin & Menuet *(rec 1962)* Russian Compact Disc ("Talents of Russia" series) ▲ RCD 16204 [AAD]
Ravel, M.:Pavane pour une infante défunte, w. Y. Tkanov (va) [arr. V. Borisovsky] *(rec 1992)* Russian Compact Disc ("Talents of Russia" series) ▲ RCD 16206 [AAD]
Saint-Saëns, C.:Fant Vn, w. A. Korsakov (vn) *(rec 1979)* Russian Compact Disc ("Talents of Russia" series) ▲ RCD 16206 [AAD]
Salzedo, C.:Preludes Hp—Whirlwind *(rec 1957)* Russian Compact Disc ("Talents of Russia" series) ▲ RCD 16204 [AAD]
Zecchi, A.:Divert Fl, w. O. Kudryachov (fl), M. Terian (cnd), Moscow Conservatory Student Orch String Group *(rec 1961)* Russian Compact Disc ("Talents of Russia" series) ▲ RCD 16204 [AAD]

Dumay, Augustin (vn)
Brahms, J.:Sons Vn (comp), w. M. J. Pires (pno) Deutsche Grammophon ▲ 435800-2
Fauré, G.:Qts Pno, Opp. 15 & 45, w. J.P. Collard (pno), B. Pasquier (va), F. Lodeon (vc) EMI Classics 2-▲ ZDMB 62548
Fauré, G.:Son 1 Vn, w. J. P. Collard (pno) EMI Classics 2-▲ CDC 62545
Fauré, G.:Trio, w. F. Lodeon (vc), J.P. Collard (pno) EMI Classics 2-▲ CDC 62545
Grieg, E.:Sons Vn, Opp. 8, 13 & 45, w. M. J. Pires (pno) Deutsche Grammophon ▲ 437525-2 [DDD]
Mozart, W.A.:Music of, w. Alban Berg Quartet, F. P. Zimmermann (vn), A. S. Mutter (vn), S. Meyer (cl), R. Vlatkovi (hn), C. Zacharias (pno), *(sels unknown)* EMI Classics ▲ CDC 54165
Petitgirard, L.:Le Légendaire, w. L. Petitgirard (cnd), Classic Polonaise PO, Cracow Polish Radio-TV Chorus Orchestre Symphonique France ▲ OSF 49013 [DDD]

Dumestre, Vincent (thb)—see ORCHESTRAS & ENSEMBLES Ricercar Consort

Dümig, Hugo (perc)—see ORCHESTRAS & ENSEMBLES Karl Peinkofer Percussion Ensemble

Dumler, Donald (org)
The Great Organ of St. Patrick's Cathedral *(rec New York)* Gothic ▲ GOT 49081 [DDD]

Dumler, Earle (ob)
Russell, A.:Suite Concertante, w. Floyd Cooley (tuba), Janet Ketchum (fl), James Kanter (cl), Arthur David Krehbiel (hn), Charles Ullery (bn) Crystal ▲ CD 120

Dumm, Thomas (va)
Mozart, W.A.:Trio Cl, K.498, w. G. Silfies (cl), P. Paul (pno) *(rec 1975-79)* Vox Box 3-▲ CD3X 3014 [ADD]

Dumond, Arnaud (gtr)
The Finest Works for the Guitar Pierre Verany ▲ 786103 [DDD]

Dumortier, André (pno)
Absil, J.:Con 1 Pno, w. F. Quinet (cnd), Belgian National Orch *(rec Brussells, Aug 20, 1952)* Cypres ▲ CYP 3602

Dumortier, Micheline (gtr)
Sor, F.:Duos, w. Peter Pieters (gtr)—Divertissement, Op. 38 *(rec Studio Steuerbaut, Gent, June 1995)* René Gailly ▲ VTP CD92027 [DDD]
Sor, F.:Fants Gtr, w. Peter Pieters (gtr)—Encouragement, Op. 34; 2 Amis, Op. 41; Fant, Op. 54bis; Souvenir de Russie, Op 63 *(rec Studio Steuerbaut, Gent, June 1995)* René Gailly ▲ VTP CD92027 [DDD]

Dumschat, Claudia (org)
Bruhns, N.:Nun komm der Heiden Heiland *(rec Sept. 16-18, 1994)* Pro Organo ▲ POCD 7054 [DDD]
Bruhns, N.:Preludes & Fugues (4) Org [von Beckerath Org of St. Michael's Episcopal Church, New York City]—in G *(rec Sept. 16-18, 1994)* Pro Organo ▲ POCD 7054 [DDD]
Buxtehude, D.:Nun komm, der Heiden Heiland [von Beckerath Org of St. Michael's Episcopal Church, New York City] *(rec Sept. 16-18, 1994)* Pro Organo ▲ POCD 7054 [DDD]
Buxtehude, D.:Praeludium Org, BuxWV 146 [von Beckerath Org of St. Michael's Episcopal Church, New York City] *(rec Sept. 16-18, 1994)* Pro Organo ▲ POCD 7054 [DDD]

Dunaway, Judy (gtr/balloons)
Exquisite Corpses from P.S. 122, w. David Watson (shears/stick vn/gtr/tpt), Anthony Coleman (sampler), Raissa St. Pierre (drums), Guy Yarden (vn/pno), Leslie Ross (bn), Linda Austin (gtr), Bruce Kaplan (gtr), Doug Henderson (peckhorn/bass/toy pno), Sue Ann Harkey (gtr), Cinnie Cole (sampler), et al. ¿What Next? ▲ WN 0002 [ADD]

Dunbar, Dan (timp)
Erickson, R.:Dunbar's Delight *(rec 1987-91)* CRI ▲ CD 616 [DDD]

Duncan, S. Blake (E hn)—see ORCHESTRAS & ENSEMBLES Wizards!

Dunckel, Rudolf (pno)
Schubert, Franz:Schwanngesang, w. Theo Adam (bass), Jorg Demus (pno) Berlin Classics 2-▲ BER CD 9216
Schubert, Franz:Winterreise, w. Theo Adam (bass), Jorg Demus (pno) Berlin Classics 2-▲ BER CD 9216
Schumann, R.:Dichterliebe, w. Theo Adam (bass), Jorg Demus (pno) Berlin Classics 2-▲ BER CD 9216
Wolf, H.:Michelangelo-Lieder, w. Theo Adam (bass), Jorg Demus (pno), ' Berlin Classics 2-▲ BER CD 9216

Dunford, Jonathan (b vl)
de Machy, S.:Music of—Suites in a, D, d & A Adda ▲ ADD 581256 [DDD]
Sainte-Colombe, M. de:Vl Music, w. Sylvia Abramowicz (b vl)—Suite in d; Concert [Le meslé]; Suite in B; Concert [Les roulades]; Concert [Le Varié]; Suite in G; Concert [Tombeau, les regret]; Vielle in D Adès ▲ ADE 204912

Dunford, Jonathan (vl)
Steffkin, T.:Vl Music—Suites in d, G, d, D & g Adès ▲ ADE 204382 [DDD]

Dunham, James (va)—see also ORCHESTRAS & ENSEMBLES Cleveland String Quartet, Sequoia String Quartet
Holst, G.:Terzetto Fl, w. Barcellona (fl), P. Christ (ob) Crystal ■ C 647
Pleyel, I.:Miniatures Va, w. Westwood Wind Quintet Crystal ■ C 647
Sapieyevski, J.:Arioso, w. Boatman (perc), Westwood Wind Quintet Crystal ■ C 647

Dunkel, Paul (fl)
Hudson, J.:Sonare, w. Rolf Schulte (vn), Laura Flax (cl), Ursula Oppens (pno), Joseph Passaro (perc) CRI ■ C 382

Dunkel, Paul Lustig (fl)—see ORCHESTRAS & ENSEMBLES Contemporary Chamber Players

Dünki, Jean-Jacques (clvd)
Dünki, J.-J.:Tétraptéron O-IV, w. P. Clemann (pno), S. Reymond (hpd), P. Sublet (cel) *(rec Sept. 18, 1992)* Jecklin ▲ JS 289-2 [ADD]

Dünki, Jean-Jacques (hammerflügel)
Schumann, R.:Son 1 Vn, w. H. Schneeberger (vn) *(rec Dec. 1991)* Jecklin-Disco ▲ JD 664-2 [DDD]

Dünki, Jean-Jacques (pno)
Berg, A.:Pno Music—17 pieces *(rec 1990)* Jecklin-Disco ▲ JD 643-2 [DDD]

Dünki, Jean-Jacques (pno) (cont.)
Grieg, E.:Sons Vn, Opp. 8, 13 & 45, w. Ingolf Turban (vn) Claves ▲ 50-8808
Reger, M.:Son Vn Pno, Op. 122, w. H. Schneeberger (vn) Jecklin-Disco ▲ JD 649-2 [DDD]
Reger, M.:Son Vn Pno, Op. 139, w. H. Schneeberger (vn) Jecklin-Disco ▲ JD 649-2 [DDD]
Stockhausen, K.:Tierkreis Pno, w. P. Sublet (sgr)—Scorpio & Pisces *(rec May 27 & Sept. 18, 1992)* Jecklin ▲ JS 289-2 [ADD]
Zemlinsky, A. von:Fant über Gedichte von Richard Dehmel *(rec 1985)* Jecklin-Disco ▲ JD 594-2 [ADD]
Zemlinsky, A. von:Ländliche Tänze *(rec 1985)* Jecklin-Disco ▲ JD 594-2 [ADD]
Zemlinsky, A. von:Songs (misc), w. K. Widmer (bass)—6 songs *(rec 1985)* Jecklin-Disco ▲ JD 594-2 [ADD]
Zimmerlin, A.:Klavierstück 2 *(rec May 28, 1992)* Jecklin ▲ JS 289-2 [ADD]

Dunlop, Roslyn (cl)
Broadstock, B.:Eheu Fugaces, w. Marilyn Richardson (sop), Christine Draeger (fl), Fiona Ziegler (vn), Susan Blake (vc), David Miller (pno), Daryl Pratt (perc) Vox Australis ▲ VAST018-2 [DDD]

Dunn, Scott (pno)
Reynolds, R.:Fant Pianist Neuma 2-▲ 450-91 [DDD]

Dunner, L.B. (cl)
Dunner, L.B.:Motherless Child Songs, w. C. Sebron (mez), J. Rubino (pno)—Motherless Child; I Gave My Love a Cherry; Nobody Knows the Trouble I've Seen; Deep River Innova ▲ MN 108

Dunnett, David (org)
Holst, G.:Choral Music, w. Winchester Cathedral Choir—Christmas Song [Personent hodie] *(rec Winchester Cathedral, Jan 10-13, 1994)* London ▲ 444130-2 [DDD]
Purcell, H.:Anthems, w. D. Hill (cnd), Brandenburg Consort, London Baroque Brass, Winchester Cathedral Choir—Funeral Sentences; Rejoice in the Lord Always; Jehova, Quam Multi Sunt Hostes; O God, Thou Art My God; Remember Not, Lord, Our Offences; Give Sentence with Me, O God; Hear My Prayer, O Lord; Voluntary in C; A Double Verse in G; O, I'm Sick of Life Argo ▲ 436833-2 [DDD]
Purcell, H.:Music for the Funeral of Queen Mary, w. D. Hill (cnd), Brandenburg Consort, London Baroque Brass, Winchester Cathedral Choir Argo ▲ 436833-2 [DDD]
Purcell, H.:My Beloved Spake, w. D. Hill (cnd), Brandenburg Consort, London Baroque Brass, Winchester Cathedral Choir Argo ▲ 436833-2 [DDD]
Vaughan Williams, R.:Fant on Christmas Carols, w. Donald Sweeney (bass), D. Hill (cnd), Bournemouth SO, Winchester Cathedral Choir, Waynflete Singers *(rec Winchester Cathedral, Jan 10-13, 1994)* London ▲ 444130-2 [DDD]

Dünschede, W. (fl)—see ORCHESTRAS & ENSEMBLES Consortium Classicum

Dünshede, Hans Wolfgang (fl)
Vivaldi, A.:Cons Pic, w. W. Güttler (db), Motoi (hpd), Berlin Philharmonia String Quartet—RV.441, 443, 444, 445 Denon ▲ 7076 [DDD]

Duphil, Monique (pno)
Debussy, C.:Son Vc, w. Peter Rejto (vc) *(rec Tuscon Winter Chamber Festival; Mar 5, 1995)* Arizona Friends of Chamber Music ▲ AFCD 19951
Debussy, C.:Son Vc, w. Peter Rejto (vc) *(rec 1994-95)* Arizona Friends of Chamber Music ▲ 1994/5 [DDD]
Villa-Lobos, H.:Son 2 Vc, w. J. Humeston (vc) Marco Polo ▲ 8.223164
Villa-Lobos, H.:Trio 1 Vn, w. A. Spiller (vn), J. Humeston (vc) Marco Polo ▲ 8.223182
Villa-Lobos, H.:Trio 2 Vn, w. A. Nuñez (vn), J. Humeston (vc) Marco Polo ▲ 8.223164
Villa-Lobos, H.:Trio 3 Vn, w. A. Spiller (vn), J. Humeston (vc) Marco Polo ▲ 8.223182

Duport, D. (pno)
Derbès, J.:Music of, w. A. Chédel (cta), V. Desarzens (cnd), Lausanne CO—Chant d'amour et de mort; Con for Pno; 7 mélodies; Adagio for Large Orch Grammont ▲ CTSP 46

Dupouy, Jean (va)
Bax, A.:Elegiac Trio, w. T. Prévost (fl), M. Geliot (hp) Quantum ▲ QM 6898 ■ QM 1993
Brahms, J.:Sextet Strs, Op. 18, w. Régis Pasquier (vn), Raphaël Oleg (vn), Bruno Pasquier (va), Roland Pidoux (vc), Etienne Péclard (vc)—No. 1 Harmonia Mundi France ("Musique d'abord" series) ▲ HMA 1901073
Debussy, C.:Son Fl, w. T. Prévost (fl), M. Geliot (hp) Quantum ▲ QM 6898 ■ QM 1993
Hommage à Martine Geliot (1948-1988), w. M. Geliot (hp), Thomas Prévost (fl) Quantum ▲ QM 6898 ■ QM 1993
Leclair, J.-M.:Trio Sons, w. T. Prévost (fl), M. Geliot (hp) [trans. for flute, viola & harp] Quantum ▲ QM 6898 ■ QM 1993
Lemeland, A.:To Holst's Memory, w. T. Prévost (fl), M. Geliot (hp) Quantum ▲ QM 6898 ■ QM 1993
Lemeland, A.:Vars Va, w. R. de Herrera (gtr) Skarbo ▲ SKR 3901 [AAD]
Porter, Q.:Duo Va, w. M. Geliot (hp) Quantum ▲ QM 6898 ■ QM 1993

Dupré, Desmond (gtr/lt)
Alfred Deller, w. A. Deller (ct), Harold Lester (hpd/org), Robert Spencer (fl) *(rec between 1965 & 1979)* Memoire Vive ▲ 262004 [ADD]
Folksongs, w. A. Deller (ct), Mark Deller (ct) Harmonia Mundi ▲ HMA 190.226
The 3 Ravens, w. A. Deller (ct) *(rec Masonic Temple, Brooklyn, NY, Oct 1955)* Vanguard Classics ("Alfred Deller Edition" series) ▲ OVC 8104 [ADD]
The 3 Ravens:Elizabethan Folk & Minstrel Songs, w. A. Deller (ct) Vanguard Classics ▲ OVC 8026 (m) [ADD]
The Wraggle Taggle Gypsies, w. A. Deller (ct), Taylor Recorder Consort *(rec Walthamstow Town Hall, London, Feb 1956)* Vanguard Classics ("Alfred Deller Edition" series) ▲ OVC 8105 [ADD]

Dupré, Desmond (lt)
Elizabethan & Jacobean Music - Airs & Instrumental Music of England, w. N. Harnoncourt (cnd), Deller Consort, Consort of Viols Vanguard Classics ▲ OVC 8102 [ADD]

Dupré, Desmond (vl)—see also ORCHESTRAS & ENSEMBLES In Nomine Players
Couperin, F.:Leçons de ténèbres (for Good Friday), w. Alfred Deller (ct), Wilfred Brown (ten), Harry Gabb (org) Vanguard Classics ("The Bach Guild" series) ▲ OVC 2525 [ADD]
Monteverdi, C.:Ballo delle ingrate, w. April Cantelo (sop—Una dell' Ingrate), Eileen McLoughlin (sop—Amore), Alfred Deller (alt—Venere), David Ward (bass—Plutone), Julian Bream (lt), A. Deller (cnd), London Chamber Players *(rec Walthamstow Hall, London)* Vanguard Classics ▲ OVC 8100 [ADD]
Purcell, H.:Music of, w. April Cantelo (sop), Alfred Deller (ct), Maurice Bevan (bar), Neville Marriner (vn), Peter Gibbs (vn), Granville Jones (vn), George Malcolm (hpd), Walter Bergmann (hpd)—15 Songs & Airs; Fantasia upon a Ground in d for 3 Violins & Continuo, Z.731; Fantasia upon One Note in F for 5 Viols, Z.745; Hornpipe in e (from The Old Bachelor); Music Lessons 1-12 from Musick's Hand-Maid, Part II; A New Irish Tune, "Lilliburlero," Z.646; Pavan in g for 3 Violins & Bass Viol, Z.752; Sonata in g for Violin & Continuo, Z.780; Sonata No. 9 in F, "Golden Sonata," Z.810 (from Ten Sonatas in Four Parts); Suite in D for Harpsichord, Z.667 Vanguard Classics ("The Bach Guild" series) 2-▲ OVC 2002/03 [ADD]

Du Pré, Jacqueline (vc)
Beethoven, L. van:Sons Vc (comp), w. D. Barenboim (pno) EMI Classics 2-▲ ZDMB 63015
Beethoven, L. van:Son 3 Vc, w. D. Barenboim (pno) EMI Classics 2-▲ ZDMB 69707
Beethoven, L. van:Trios Pno (comp), w. D. Barenboim (pno), P. Zukerman (vn) EMI Classics ("Studio" series) 3-▲ ZDMC 63124 [ADD]
Beethoven, L. van:Trio 3 Pno, w. D. Barenboim (pno), P. Zukerman (vn) *(rec live, Brighton Festival 1970)* Arkadia 2-▲ 589 [ADD]
Beethoven, L. van:Trio 5 Pno, w. D. Barenboim (pno), P. Zukerman (vn) *(rec live, Brighton Festival 1970)* Arkadia 2-▲ 589 [ADD]
Beethoven, L. van:Trio 5 Pno, w. D. Barenboim (pno), P. Zukerman (vn) EMI Classics 2-▲ ZDMB 69707
Beethoven, L. van:Trio 6 Pno, "Archduke", w. D. Barenboim (pno), P. Zukerman (vn) *(rec live, Brighton Festival 1970)* Arkadia 2-▲ 589 [ADD]
Beethoven, L. van:Trio 7 Pno, w. D. Barenboim (pno), G. De Peyer (cl) *(rec live, Brighton Festival 1970)* Arkadia 2-▲ 589 [ADD]
Beethoven, L. van:Vars on "See, the Conquering Hero Comes" from Handel's *Judas Maccabaeus*, w. D. Barenboim (pno) EMI Classics 2-▲ ZDMB 63015

Du Pré, Jacqueline (vc) (cont.)

Beethoven, L. van:Vars on "Bei Männern" from Mozart's *Die Zauberflöte,* w. D. Barenboim (pno) EMI Classics 2-▲ ZDMB 63015

Boccherini, L.:Con Vc, G.482, w. D. Barenboim (cnd), English CO EMI Classics ▲ CDC 47840

Brahms, J.:Sons Vc (comp), w. D. Barenboim (pno) EMI Classics ("Studio" series) ▲ CDM 63298 [ADD]

Chopin, F.:Son Vc, w. D. Barenboim (pno) EMI Classics ▲ CDM 63184

The Columbia Recordings, Vol. 2, w. Michael Taube (pno), Theo van der Pas (pno), Gerald Moore (pno), Wolfgang Rebner (pno) *(rec 1930–1939)* Pearl ▲ PEA 9443 (m) [AAD]

The Columbia Recordings, Vol. 3, w. Gerald Moore (pno), Myra Hess (pno), Paul Hindemith (va/cnd), Szymon Goldberg (cnd) *(rec 1930–1939)* Pearl ▲ PEA 9446 (m) [AAD]

Dvořák, A.:Con Vc, w. D. Barenboim (cnd), Chicago SO EMI Classics ▲ CDC 47614

Early German Parlophone Recordings *(rec 1921–1930)* Pearl ▲ PEA 9077 [AAD]

Elgar, E.:Con Vc, w. J. Barbirolli (cnd), London SO EMI Classics ▲ CDC 47329

Elgar, E.:Con Vc, w. M. Sargent (cnd), BBC SO *(rec live, Royal Albert Hall 1963)* Intaglio ▲ INCD 7351 [ADD]

Elgar, E.:Con Vc, w. J. Barbirolli (cnd), London SO EMI Classics 2-▲ ZDMB 69707

Franck, C.:Son Vn, w. D. Barenboim (pno) EMI Classics ▲ CDM 63184

Goehr, A.:Romanze, w. D. Barenboim (cnd), New Philharmonia Orch *(rec 1968)* Intaglio ▲ ING 767 [ADD]

Haydn, J.:Con 1 Vc, w. J. Barbirolli (cnd), London SO EMI Classics 2-▲ ZDMB 69707

Haydn, J.:Con 1 Vc, w. D. Barenboim (cnd), English CO EMI Classics ▲ CDC 47614

Haydn, J.:Con 1 Vc, w. D. Barenboim (cnd), English CO EMI Classics ▲ CDC 47840

Les introuvables de Jacqueline Du Pré EMI Classics 6-▲ CDZF 68132 [ADD]

Jacqueline Du Pré:Her Early BBC Recordings, Vol. 2, w. William Pleeth (vc), Ernest Lush (pno) EMI Classics ▲ CDM 63166

Lalo, E.:Con Vc, w. D. Barenboim (cnd), Cleveland Orch *(rec live, Severance Hall, Boston, 1973)* EMI Classics ▲ CDC 55528

Schumann, R.:Con Vc, w. D. Barenboim (cnd), New Philharmonia Orch EMI Classics ▲ CDM 64626

Strauss, R.:Don Quixote, w. A. Boult (cnd), New Philharmonia Orch *(rec 1968)* EMI Classics ▲ CDC 55528

Dupré, Marcel (org)

Dupré, M.:Préludes & Fugues, Op. 7—in g EMI Classics ▲ CDC 55037

Franck, C.:Chorals Org, M.38–40 Mercury Living Presence ▲ 434311-2 [ADD]

Franck, C.:Pièce héroïque Mercury Living Presence ▲ 434311-2 [ADD]

Messiaen, O.:L'Ascension Org EMI Classics ▲ CDC 55037

Saint-Saëns, C.:Sym 3, w. P. Paray (cnd), Detroit SO Mercury Living Presence ▲ 432719-2 [ADD]

Widor, C.M.:Salve regina Mercury Living Presence ▲ 434311-2 [ADD]

Widor, C.M.:Sym 6 Org—Allegro section Mercury Living Presence ▲ 434311-2 [ADD]

Dupree, Jillion Stopples (hpd/org)

Out of the Orient Crystall Skyes, w. N. Zylstra (sop), Margriet Tindemans (vl), Michael Sand (baroque vn/vl), Linda Melsted (baroque vn), Olga Hauptmann (baroque va), Ellen Siebert (vl), Russell Paige (vl) Wildboar ▲ WLBR 8901 [DDD]

Duquesnoy, Jean-François (bn)

Poulenc, F.:Trio Ob, w. François Leleux (ob), Emmanuel Strosser (pno) Harmonia Mundi France ("Les Nouveaux Interprètes" series) ▲ HMN 911556

Duran, Elena (fl)

Bach, J.S.:Con Fl, Vn & Hpd, w. V. Spivakov (vn), S. Bezrodny (hpd), V. Spivakov (cnd), Moscow Virtuosi RCA Red Seal ▲ 7991-2-RC [DDD]

Durand, Marc (pno)

Massenet, J.:Songs, w. France Duval (mez), Bruno Laplante (bar)—Poème d'octobre; Poème d'amour; Poème d'hiver; Poème d'un soir; Lui et Elle [all are song cycles] *(rec Chapelle historique du Bon Pasteur, Montréal, June 1992)* Analekta ▲ AN 2 9406 [DDD]

Prokofiev, S.:Romeo & Juliet (sels), w. V. Landsman (vn)—Montaigus et Capulets; La Danse des filles aux fleurs; Masques *(rec June 1990)* Analekta ▲ UMM 301

Prokofiev, S.:Son solo Vn, Op. 115, w. V. Landsman (vn) *(rec June 1990)* Analekta ▲ UMM 301

Prokofiev, S.:Son Vn, Op. 94bis, w. V. Landsman (vn) *(rec June 1990)* Analekta ▲ UMM 301

Satie, E.:Songs, w. B. Laplante (bar)—30 sels. Analekta ▲ OPCD 1002

Shchedrin, R.:In Imitation of Albéniz, w. V. Landsman (vn) [arr Tziganov] *(rec June 1990)* Analekta ▲ UMM 301

Shostakovich, D.:Preludes Pno, Op. 34, w. V. Landsman (vn) [arr Tziganov]—4 Preludes *(rec June 1990)* Analekta ▲ UMM 301

Durkó, Zsolt (pno)

Durkó, Z.:The History of the Spheres—Idioms in Free Order; Jupiter-motif; Water-drops; Post scriptum; Canto serioso; Trombone of the Despair; Bartókian Melody; Precipitando e ritardando; Improvizáció; In the Forest; Vae victis; Variante su una particella orchestrale *(rec 1995)* Hungaroton ▲ HCD 31654 [DDD]

Duron, Lusia (hpd)

Marcello, B.:Sons Vc, w. B. Slawinska (vc) Producciones Fonograficas ▲ PFCD 232

Dürr, Franziska (va)

Rihm, W.:Bratschenkonzert Bayer ▲ CAD 800886

Durran, D. (bn)—see ORCHESTRAS & ENSEMBLES Pennsylvania Wind Quintet

Durran, Katharine (pno)

Esplá, O.:Canciones playeras, w. María Dolores Campos (sop) *(rec West Road Concert Hall, Univ of Cambridge, Jan 17–19, 1995)* Herald ▲ HAVPCD 184 [DDD]

Falla, M. de:Canciones populares españolas (7), w. María Dolores Campos (sop) *(rec West Road Concert Hall, Univ of Cambridge, Jan 17–19, 1995)* Herald ▲ HAVPCD 184 [DDD]

Granados, E.:Colección de Tonadillas escritas en estilo antiguo, w. María Dolores Campos (sop)—La maja de Goya; El tra-la-l y el punteado; El majo tímido; El mirar de la maja; La maja dolorosa no. 2; Callejeo; El majo discreto; Las currutacas modestas *(rec West Road Concert Hall, Univ of Cambridge, Jan 17–19, 1995)* Herald ▲ HAVPCD 184 [DDD]

Mompou, F.:Combat del somni, w. María Dolores Campos (sop) *(rec West Road Concert Hall, Univ of Cambridge, Jan 17–19, 1995)* Herald ▲ HAVPCD 184 [DDD]

Obradors, F.:Canciones clásicas españolas, w. María Dolores Campos (sop) *(rec West Road Concert Hall, Univ of Cambridge, Jan 17–19, 1995)* Herald ▲ HAVPCD 184 [DDD]

Turina, J.:Poema en forma de canciones, w. María Dolores Campos (sop) *(rec West Road Concert Hall, Univ of Cambridge, Jan 17–19, 1995)* Herald ▲ HAVPCD 184 [DDD]

Duruflé, Maurice (org)

Poulenc, F.:Con Org, w. G. Prêtre (cnd), French National RSO EMI Classics ▲ CDC 47723 [ADD]

Dusevic, Tanya (fl)

Badings, H.:Con Fl, w. G. Price (cnd), Univ of Calgary Wind Ensemble *(rec Calgary Center for the Performing Arts)* Unical ▲ UC 9401 [DDD]

Kraft, L.:Cloud Studies, w. Lisa Maron (pic), Margaret Swinchoski (pic), Adrienne Flynn (fl), Christina Jennings (fl), Zara Lawler (fl), Joseph Piscitelli (fl), Michelle Ryang (fl), Dominique Soucy (fl), Diane Taublieb (fl), Laurel Ann Maurer (alt fl), Richard Wyton (alt fl), J. Solum (cnd) *(rec Skinner Recital Hall, Vassar College, Poughkeepsie, NY, Mar 24–26, 1994)* CRI ▲ CD 712 [DDD]

Dushkin, Samuel (vn)

Stravinsky, I.:Chants du rossignol et Marche, w. I. Stravinsky (pno) EMI Classics 2-▲ ZDCB 54607

Stravinsky, I.:Duo Concertant, w. Igor Stravinsky (pno) Memories ▲ MEM 3004

Stravinsky, I.:Jeu de cartes, w. I. Stravinsky (cnd), *(orch unknown)* Memories ▲ MEM 3004

Stravinsky, I.:Pétrouchka (russian dance), w. I. Stravinsky (pno) [arr Samuel Dushkin for Violin & Piano] EMI Classics 2-▲ ZDCB 54607

Stravinsky, I.:Suite italienne Vc, w. I. Stravinsky (pno) EMI Classics 2-▲ ZDCB 54607

Stravinsky, I.:Vn Pno Music, w. Igor Stravinsky (pno)—Berceuse de l'oiseau de feu; Scherzo de l'oiseau de feu; Dance Russe; Serenata at Scherzino de la Suite Italienne; Air du Rossignol; Marche Chinoise du Rossignol Memories ▲ MEM 3004

Dusinberre, Edward (vn)—see ORCHESTRAS & ENSEMBLES Takács String Quartet

Dussault, Michel (pno)

Chopin, F.:Pno Music (misc)—Albumblatt in E; Allegro de concert, Op. 46; Bolero, Op. 19; Cantabile in B♭; Contredanse in G♭; Largo in E♭; 6 Mazurkas (posthumous); Nocturnes 1 & 2; Polonaises, Op. 71, Nos. 1 & 3; Tarantelle, Op. 43; 4 Waltzes (posthumous) *(rec 7/88 & 6/90)* CBC ("Musica Viva" series) ▲ MVCD 1045 [DDD]

Dussaut, T. (pno)

Ravel, M.:Miroirs Pierre Verany ▲ PV 787022 [DDD]

Ravel, M.:Pavane pour une infante défunte Pierre Verany ▲ PV 787022 [DDD]

Ravel, M.:La Valse *(rec 7/86)* Pierre Verany ▲ PV 787022 [DDD]

Ravel, M.:Valses nobles et sentimentales *(rec 7/86)* Pierre Verany ▲ PV 787022 [DDD]

Dussek, Michael (pno)—see also ORCHESTRAS & ENSEMBLES Dussek Piano Trio

Beethoven, L. van:Vars on "See, the Conquering Hero Comes" from Handel's *Judas Maccabaeus,* w. Ofra Harnoy (vc) *(rec Thornhill, Ontario, Canada, 1987)* RCA Gold Seal ▲ 09026-68372-2 [DDD]

Britten, H.:Pno Music—5 Waltzes; Night Piece; Holiday Diary Hyperion ▲ CDA 66776

Duets:Ofra Harnoy & Friends, w. O. Harnoy (vc), Orford String Quartet, Maureen Forrester (cta), Andrew Davis (pno), Jeanne Baxtresser (fl), Catherine Wilson (pno), Paul Brodie (sax), Shauna Rolston (vc), Armin Strings, Canadian Piano Trio, Adele Armin (vn) Mastersound ▲ MST 30 [DDD]

Dvořák, A.:Polonaise Vc, w. Ofra Harnoy (vc) *(rec Glenn Gould Studio, Toronto, June 18–19, 1995)* RCA Red Seal ▲ 09026-68186-2 [DDD]

Dvořák, A.:Slavonic Dances (sels), w. Ofra Harnoy (vc)—Op. 46/3 & 8 *(rec Glenn Gould Studio, Toronto, June 18–19, 1995)* RCA Red Seal ▲ 09026-68186-2 [DDD]

Martin, F.:Ballade Fl, w. S. Milan (fl), R. Hickox (cnd), City of London Sinfonia Chandos ▲ CHAN 8840 [DDD]

Ofra Harnoy & Friends, w. O. Harnoy (vc), Orford String Quartet, J. Baxtresser (fl), M. Forrester (cta), P. Brodie (sax), et al. Pro Arte ▲ CDD 552 [DDD]

Prokofiev, S.:Son Vc, w. O. Harnoy (vc) RCA Red Seal ▲ 7845-2-RC [DDD]

Saint-Saëns, C.:Le Cygne, w. O. Harnoy (vc) *(rec Walter Hall, University of Toronto, Canada, Aug 25, 1985)* RCA Gold Seal ▲ 09026-68373-2 [DDD]

Salut d'Amour, w. O. Harnoy (vc), Helena Bowkun (pno), Catherine Wilson (pno) RCA Red Seal ▲ 60697-2-RC [AAD/DDD]

Schubert, Franz:Son Arpeggione, w. O. Harnoy (vc) RCA Red Seal ▲ 7845-2-RC [DDD]

Tchaikovsky, P.:Morceaux, Op. 51, w. Ofra Harnoy (vc)—No. 6, Valse sentimentale *(rec Walter Hall, University of Toronto & Timothy Eaton Memorial Church, Toronto, Aug 25, 1985)* RCA Gold Seal ▲ 09026-68373-2 [DDD]

Tchaikovsky, P.:Les Saisons, w. Ofra Harnoy (vc)—No. 10 Chant d'automne *(rec Walter Hall, University of Toronto & Timothy Eaton Memorial Church, Toronto, 1982)* RCA Gold Seal ▲ 09026-68373-2 [DDD]

Wild Classics:A Celebration of Animals & Nature, w. James Galway (fl), Ofra Harnoy (vc), Martin Hoherman (vc), Emily Mitchell (hp), Michael Dussek (pno), Samuel Lipman (pno), Leo Litwin (pno), Gerhard Oppitz (pno), Isao Tomita (synths), Boston Pops Orch [cnd:Arthur Fiedler], Chicago SO [cnd:Fritz Reiner] RCA Red Seal ▲ 09026-68483-2 ■ 09026-68483-4

Dütchler, Ursula (hpd/org)—see ORCHESTRAS & ENSEMBLES Camerata Trajectina

Dutilleux, Henri (pno)

Dutilleux, H.:Figures (2) de résonnances, w. G. Joy (pno) Erato 2-▲ 91721

Dutilly, Céline (pno)

Mendelssohn, Fanny:Qt Pno, w. Fanny Mendelssohn String Quartet members *(rec 1988/89)* Troubadisc ▲ TROCD 01408 [AAD]

Mendelssohn, Fanny:Trio Pno, w. Fanny Mendelssohn String Quartet members *(rec 1988/89)* Troubadisc ▲ TROCD 01408 [AAD]

Smyth, E.:Chamber Music, w. Fanny Mendelssohn String Quartet—Sonata in a for Cello & Piano, Op. 5 (1887); Sonata in a for Violin & Piano, Op. 7 (1887); String Quintet in E, Op. 1 (1883); String Quartet in e (1902/12) *(rec 1990)* Troubadisc 2-▲ TRO CD 03 [ADD]

Smyth, E.:Double Con, w. R. Eggebrecht-Kupsa (vn), F. Draxinger (hn) *(rec 1992)* Troubadisc ▲ TRO CD 01405 [DDD]

Dutkiewicz, Andrzej (pno)

Twentieth Century Piano Music From Poland, w. Ewa Osinka (pno) Olympia ▲ OCD 316 [AAD]

Dutt, Hank (va)—see also ORCHESTRAS & ENSEMBLES Kronos Quartet

Riley, T.:In C, w. Bruce Ackley, Steve Adams, Don R. Baker, Chris Brown, George Brooks, Steve Coughlin, Blake Derby, Bill Douglass, Mihr'un'Nisa Douglass, David Harrington, Don Howe, Joan Jeanrenaud, Alden Jenks, Warner Jepson, Henry Kaiser, Jaron Lanier, Bill Maginnis, George Marsh, Shabda Owens, Jon Raskin, Gyan Riley, Terry Riley, Gino Robair, John Sackett, Ramón Sender, John Sherba, Toyji Tomita, Danny Tunick, William Winant, Evan Ziporyn *(rec Jan. 14, 1990)* New Albion ▲ NA 071

Dutton, Jon (perc)—see ORCHESTRAS & ENSEMBLES Univ of Illinois Contemporary Chamber Players

Dutton, Lawerence (va)

Brahms, J.:Songs, w. J. DeGaetani (mez), L. Luvisi (pno)—O kühler Wald, Op. 72/3; Verzagen, Op. 72/4; Geistliches Wiegenlied, Op. 91/2 [G] *(rec Aspen Music Festival 7/7/83)* Bridge ▲ BCD 9025 [ADD]

Duven, Richard (vc)

Mozart, W.A.:Qt Pno, K.478, w. Alfred Brendel (pno), Thomas Zehetmair (vn), Tabea Zimmermann (va), Peter Riegelbauer (db) Philips ▲ 446001-2

Schubert, Franz:Qnt Pno, D.667, w. Alfred Brendel (pno), Thomas Zehetmair (vn), Tabea Zimmermann (va), Peter Riegelbauer (db) Philips ▲ 446001-2

Duz, Ryszard (va)—see ORCHESTRAS & ENSEMBLES Wilanów String Quartet

Dvořáková, Hana (pno)

Eben, Petr:Suita balladica, w. B. Pavlas (vc) *(rec 11/90)* Multisonic ▲ 31 0065-2 [DDD]

Janácek, L.:Fairy Tale, w. B. Pavlas (vc) *(rec 11/90)* Multisonic ▲ 31 0065-2 [DDD]

Martinů, B.:Son 3 Vc, w. B. Pavlas (vc) *(rec 11/90)* Multisonic ▲ 31 0065-2 [DDD]

Dwyer, Doriot Anthony (fl)

Beach, A.M.C.:Theme & Vars, w. Manhattan String Quartet Koch International Classics ▲ KIC 7001-2 [DDD] ■ 3-7001-4 (D)

Bergsma, W.:Quintet Fl, w. Manhattan String Quartet Koch International Classics ▲ KIC 7001-2 [DDD] ■ 3-7001-4 (D)

Bernstein, L.:Halil, w. J. Sedares (cnd), London SO Koch International Classics ▲ KIC 7142-2 [DDD]

Flute Salad, w. L. Gilbert (fl), Alexa Still (fl), Bradley Garner (fl), New Zealand CO, London SO Koch Schwann ▲ KIC CD 7602

Piston, W.:Qnt Fl, w. Portland String Quartet Northeastern ▲ NR 9002-CD

Tovey, D.F.:Vars on a Theme by Gluck, w. Manhattan String Quartet Koch International Classics ▲ KIC 7001-2 [DDD] ■ 3-7001-4 (D)

Villa-Lobos, H.:Assobio a Jato, w. J. Glyde (vc) Koch International Classics ▲ KIC 7001-2 [DDD] ■ 3-7001-4 (D)

Zwilich, E.T.:Con Fl, w. J. Sedares (cnd), London SO Koch International Classics ▲ KIC 7142-2 [DDD]

Dwyer, Doriot Anthony (pno)

Piston, W.:Concertino Pno, w. J. Sedares (cnd), London SO Koch International Classics ▲ KIC 7142-2 [DDD]

Dyball, Jeffery (hp)

Spratling, H.:Choral Music, w. Tracey Chadwell (sop), Susan Bullock (sop), Helen Tunstall (hp), John Hatton (org), J. Rennert (cnd), Parnassus String Ensemble, Spratling Choir—Mass of the Holy Spirit; O Salutaris Hostia; Tantum Ergo; Sinf Str Orch; Son Hp; O Magnum Mysterium; In Paradisum *(rec St. Mary Magdelene, Paddington, May 15–17, 1988)* SOMM ▲ SOMMCD 206 [ADD]

Dye, Mimi (va)

Giteck, J.:Tapasya, w. *(perc unknown)* New Albion ▲ NA 054

Dye, T. (pno)

Powell, Mel:Setting, w. B. Pezzone (pno) Harmonia Mundi USA ▲ HMU 907096

Dygert, Nancy (hp)

Serenade, w. D. Cohl (fl) PHD ▲ PHD 570004 [DDD]

Dyson, Richard (perc)
A Secret Place, w. S. Rebello (perc), Andrew Scott (a sax), Liz Gilliver (mar), Kalengo Percussion Ensemble, Eryl Roberts (perc), John Melbourne (perc), Chris Bastock (perc) *(rec Zion Institute, Manchester, 1995)* Doyen ▲ CD 040 [DDD]

Dyson, Ruth (hpd)
English Harpsichord Music, w. R. Dyson (hpd) Gamut Classics ▲ GAM CD 515 [DDD]

Dzubay, David (tpt)
Fox, F.:Time Messages, w. David McChesney (tpt), Michael Galbraith (hn), Andrew Glendenning (trbn), Andrew Oppenheim (tuba) *(rec Musical Arts Ctr, Bloomington, IN, Nov 30, 1989)* Indiana Univ School of Music ▲ 0-253-32433-5

Dzubenko, Gennady (pno)
Glinka, M.:Trio pathétique, w. V. Abramyan (vn), A. Bourikov (vc) *(rec Firma Melodiya, Big Studio, 1995)* Russian Compact Disc ▲ RCD 10401 [DDD]
Rachmaninoff, S.:Trio élégiaque 1, w. V. Abramyan (vn), A. Bourikov (vc) *(rec Firma Melodiya, Big Studio, 1995)* Russian Compact Disc ▲ RCD 10401 [DDD]
Shostakovich, D.:Trio 2 Pno, w. V. Abramyan (vn), A. Bourikov (vc) *(rec Firma Melodiya, Big Studio, 1995)* Russian Compact Disc ▲ RCD 10401 [DDD]

Dzwiza, Gerhard (db)
Böck, A.:Pieces (4), w. G. Langenstein (hn), J. Stobart (hn), K. Stoll (db) Signum ▲ X 45-00 [DDD]
Bottesini, G.:Grandi Duetti for 2 Db, w. K. Stoll (db)—Nos. 1 & 2 Signum ▲ X 45-00 [DDD]
Haydn, M.:Divert Va, Vc & Db, w. Hirofumi Fukai (va), Klaus Stoppel (vc) Signum ▲ X 46-00 [ADD]
Romberg, B.:Trios Va, w. H. Fukai (va), K. Stoppel (vc)—1 trio Signum ▲ X 46-00 [ADD]
Rossini, G.:Duet Vc, w. K. Stoppel (vc) Signum ▲ X 46-00 [ADD]
Sperger, J.:Sons Va, w. H. Fukai (va) Signum ▲ X 46-00 [ADD]
Vanhal, J.B.:Divert Strs, w. R. Mehne (vn), C. Solothurski (va), K. Stoll (db) Signum ▲ X 45-00

Eade, Mary (vn)
Albinoni, T.:Adagio Org, w. I. Watson (org), J.L. Garcia (vn), English CO Virgin Classics ▲ CDZ 59656
Albinoni, T.:Cons Obs, w. N. Black (ob), J. L. Garcia (vn), English CO—in d Virgin Classics ▲ CDZ 59656
Corelli, A.:Concerti grossi, Op. 6, w. J.L. Garcia (vn), W. Bennett (fl), N. Black (ob), I. Watson (hpd/org), English CO—No. 2 in F Virgin Classics ▲ CDZ 59656
Vivaldi, A.:Cons Vn, Op. 3/1-12, "L'estro armonico", w. J.L. Garcia (vn), I. Watson (hpd), I. Watson (cnd), English CO Virgin Classics ▲ CDZ 59656

Eagan, Michael (archlt)
Handel, G.F.:Sons Ob, w. Gonzalo X. Ruiz (ob), Shelley Taylor (vc), Kathy Shao (hpd/org)—in B♭, after HWV 365; in g, HWV 364; in d, HWV 359a; in B♭, HWV 357; in a, after HWV 367b; in F, HWV 363a; in c, HWV 366 Well-Tempered ▲ WTP 5174 [DDD]

Eagle, David (fl)
Eagle, D.:Traces New Concert Discs ▲ NCD 0294 [DDD]

Eagleston, Linda (fl)
Eastman, D.K.:Just Us, w. Lee Beaudoin (mez) Capstone ▲ CPS 8632

Eaken, John (vn)—see ORCHESTRAS & ENSEMBLES Eaken Piano Trio

Early, Robert (tpt)
Vivaldi, A.:Con for 2 Tpts, w. J.Thompson (tpt), Y. Turovsky (cnd), Montreal Musici Chandos ▲ CHAN 8651 [DDD]

East, Angela (vc)—see also ORCHESTRAS & ENSEMBLES Revolutionary Drawing Room String Quartet
Bach, Joh. Christian:Sinf concertante, T.284/1, w. Graham Cracknell (vn), Anna McDonald (vn), A. Halstead (cnd), Hanover Band *(rec Rosslyn Hill Chapel, London, Dec 1995)* CPO ▲ CPO 999348-2 [DDD]
Bach, Joh. Christian:Sinf concertante, T.288/4, w. Graham Cracknell (vn), Anna McDonald (vn), A. Halstead (cnd), Hanover Band *(rec Rosslyn Hill Chapel, London, Dec 1995)* CPO ▲ CPO 999348-2 [DDD]

Eaton, Steuart (va)
Krommer, F.:Qt Bn, Op. 46/1, w. Eckart Hbner (bn), Johannes Lüthy (va), Reinhard Latzko (vc) *(rec Hans-Rosbaud Studio, Oct 10-11, 1994)* CPO ▲ CPO 999297-2 [DDD]
Krommer, F.:Qt Bn, Op. 46/2, w. Eckart Hbner (bn), Johannes Lüthy (va), Reinhard Latzko (vc) *(rec Hans-Rosbaud Studio, Oct 10-11, 1994)* CPO ▲ CPO 999297-2 [DDD]

Eban, Eli (cl)
Beethoven, L. van:Trio 7 Pno, w. O. Volkov (pno), Marcel Bergman (vc) Meridian ▲ CDE 84122
Brahms, J.:Sons Cl (comp), w. M. Coffey (pno) Meridian ▲ CDE 84164
Brahms, J.:Trio Cl, w. Marcel Bergman (vc), A. Volkov (pno) Meridian ▲ CDE 84122

Eban, Eli (cl/E♭ cl)—see ORCHESTRAS & ENSEMBLES Indiana Trio

Ebbinge, Ku (ob)
Pisendel, J.G.:Son Ob, w. G. von der Goltz (cnd), Freiburg Baroque Orch *(rec Maria Minor Church, Utrecht, Sept. 29-Oct. 3, 1994)* Deutsche Harmonia Mundi ▲ 05472-77339-2 [DDD]

Eben, Petr (org)
Eben, Petr:Org Music—Prelude; Postlude Multisonic ▲ 31 0003-2 [ADD]

Eben, Petr (pno)
Eben, Petr:Sonatina Semplice, w. Jiří Hurník (vn) *(rec Martínek Studio in Prague, Jan 23 & 26 & Feb 13 & 14)* Panton ▲ 811398-2 [DDD]

Eberle, F. (dr)
Keller, A.:Der enthüllte Stern, w. D. Fueter (sop), K. Graf (sop), A. K. Graf (fl), L. Pellerin (ob), E. Schmid (cl), U. Walker (vn), C. Schiller (va), P. Demenga (vc), P. Hug-Rutti (hp) [G] Grammont ▲ CTSP 19-2 [ADD]

Ebert, Harry (pno)
Jussi Björling:In Song & Ballad, w. J. Björling (ten), Bertil Bokstedt (pno), Swedish Radio Orch [cnd:Sixten Ehrling], New York PO [cnd:Martti Similä] *(rec 1940, 1942 & 1957)* Bluebell ▲ BLU 050 [ADD]
Jussi Björling, Vol. 2, w. J. Björling (ten), Nils Grevillius (cnd) *(rec New York and Stockholm 1936-1941 for HMV/Victor)* Nimbus ("Prima Voce" series) ▲ NI 7842 [ADD]

Ebi, Akiko (pno)
Franck, C.:Qnt Pno, w. Paris String Quartet Adès ▲ ADE 204112 [DDD]
Oe, H.:Fl & Pno Music, w. Hiroshi Koizumi (fl)—Snow; June Lullaby; Merry Waltz; Siciliano in e; Adagio in d; Nocturne No. 2 *(rec Asahikawa City, Hokkaido, June 27, 29 & 30, 1994)* Denon ▲ CO 78953 [DDD]
Oe, H.:Fl & Pno Music, w. Hiroshi Koizumi (fl)—A Favourite Waltz; Nocturne; Magic Flute; Sad Waltz; Pied Piper; Graduation (w. vars.) *(rec Nippon Columbia Studio 1, June 8 & 9, 1992)* Denon ▲ CO 78952 [DDD]
Oe, H.:Pno Music—Forest Ballad; Birthday Waltz; Ave Maria; Bluebird March; Star; Mister Prelude; Waltz in a; Rondo; Summer in Kitakaru; Winter; Requiem for M; Lullaby for Keiko; Dance; Siciliano; Ländler; Grief; Stream; Barcarolle; Hiroshima Requiem *(rec Nippon Columbia Studio 1, June 8 & 9, 1992)* Denon ▲ CO 78952 [DDD]
Oe, H.:Pno Music—Grief No. 3; Minuet for Children; Baroque Waltz; Salzburg; Grief No. 2; Wistful Adagio; May the Plane Not Fall; Requiem for Mrs. I *(rec Asahikawa City, Hokkaido, June 27, 29 & 30, 1994)* Denon ▲ CO 78953 [DDD]
Oe, H.:Sonatina Pno *(rec Asahikawa City, Hokkaido, June 27, 29 & 30, 1994)* Denon ▲ CO 78953 [DDD]
Oe, H.:Vn & Pno Music, w. Tomoko Kato (vn)—Dream; Summer Holidays; Nocturnal Capriccio; Andante Cantabile; August Capriccio *(rec Asahikawa City, Hokkaido, June 27, 29 & 30, 1994)* Denon ▲ CO 78953 [DDD]
Pierné, G.:Qnt Pno, w. Paris String Quartet Adès ▲ ADE 204112 [DDD]
Webern, A.:Qnt Pno, w. Paris String Quartet Accord ▲ ACD 201642 [DDD]

Ebihara, Koshin (jumon)
Fujieda, M.:Music of, w. Mamoru Fujueda (cmpt), Makiko Sakurai (shomyo/Buddhist chant), Mineko Grimmer (audible sculptures), Kodo Uesugi (fukimono), Kazuko Takada (hikimono), Toshiyuki Matsukura (uchimono), Satoshi Sakai (uchimono)—The Night Chant III; Wind Chant; Cocoon Chant; Duct Chant; Falling Chant; The Night Chant I Tzadik ("The Composers" series) ▲ TZA 7003 [DDD]

Ebisuta, Reiko (pno)
Noda, T.:Ode Capricious Camerata ▲ 32CM 58

Ebienkamp, Stefan (perc)—see also ORCHESTRAS & ENSEMBLES Percussion Art Quartet
Stahmer, K.H.:Ariadnes Faden, w. Carin Levine (va) Pro Viva ▲ ISPV 167 [DDD]

Ebner, M. (fl)—see ORCHESTRAS & ENSEMBLES Les Joueurs de Flute

Eccher, Giuliano (vl)—see ORCHESTRAS & ENSEMBLES Academy of Ancient Music Instumental Ensemble

Echols, Gary (bn)—see also ORCHESTRAS & ENSEMBLES Moran Woodwind Quintet
Snyder, R.:Qnt 3 Fl, w. John Bailey (fl), William McMullen (ob), Eric Ginsberg (cl), Allen French (hn) Coronet ▲ COR 400-9

Eckert, Erika (va)
Erb, D.:Qt 2 Strs, w. A. Fullard (vn), S. Waterbury (vn), M. Peckham (vc) Albany ▲ TROY 092 [DDD]

Eckert, Marcia (pno)
Tailleferre, G.:Pno Music—Romance; Impromptu; Pastorale in D; Pastorale in A♭; Pastorale in C; Hommage à Debussy *(rec Evangelical Lutheran Church, Jersey City, NJ, Jan. 1992)* Cambria ▲ CD 1085 [DDD]
Tailleferre, G.:Son 1 Vn, w. Ruth Erlich (vn) *(rec Evangelical Lutheran Church, Jersey City, NJ, Jan. 1992)* Cambria ▲ CD 1085 [DDD]
Tailleferre, G.:Son 2 Vn, w. Ruth Erlich (vn) *(rec Evangelical Lutheran Church, Jersey City, NJ, Jan. 1992)* Cambria ▲ CD 1085 [DDD]
Tailleferre, G.:Sonatine Vn, w. Ruth Erlich (vn) *(rec Evangelical Lutheran Church, Jersey City, NJ, Jan. 1992)* Cambria ▲ CD 1085 [DDD]

Eckert, Simone (vl)
Heudelinne, L.:Suites de pièces, w. Ulrich Wedemeier (lt/Baroque gtr), Karl-Ernst Went (hpd), Hermann Hickethier (vl) Christophorus ▲ 77181 [DDD]

Eckert, Thomasa (pno)
Lam, B.-C.:After Spring, w. Bun-Ching Lam (pno) CRI ▲ CD 726 [DDD]

Eckhardt, Gábor (pno)
Satie, E.:Pno 4-Hands Music, w. Klára Körmendi (pno)—Trois morceaux en forme de poire; En habit de cheval; Trois petites pièces montées; Aperçus désagréables; La belle excentrique *(rec Unitarian Church, Budapest, Feb. 8-11, 1994)* Naxos ▲ 8.550699 [DDD]

Eckhardt, René (pno)—see also ORCHESTRAS & ENSEMBLES Het Trio
Bland, W.:Qt Fl, Cl, Vn & Pno, w. H. Starreveld (fl), C. Neidich (cl), C. Macomber (vn) Bridge ▲ BCD 9013 [DDD]
Bland, W.:Rhap on an Original Theme Pno Bridge ▲ BCD 9013 [DDD]
Bland, W.:Warm Country Night, w. H. Starreveld (fl) Bridge ▲ BCD 9013 [DDD]
de Leeuw, T.:Les Adieux NM Classics ▲ NM 92020
de Leeuw, T.:Hommage à Henri, w. Sjef Douwes (cl) NM Classics ▲ NM 92020
Harvey, J.:Nataraja, w. Harrie Starreveld (fl/pic) Bridge ▲ BCD 9031 [DDD]

Eckhardt, Violetta (vn)
Bach, Joh. Christian:Sinf concertante, T.284/6, w. Ildiko Line (vn), Marianna Kruzse (ob), H. Gmür (cnd), Budapest Camerata *(rec Festetich Castle, Budapest, Mar 1994)* Naxos ▲ 8.553085 [DDD]
Truscott, H.:Son Vn *(rec Alpha-Line Studio, Festetich Castle, Budapest, 1994)* Marco Polo ▲ 8.223727 [DDD]

Eckroth, Loran (cl)
Porter, T.:Pieces Ww Qnt, w. Linda Schmidt (fl), Deirdre Fay (ob), Leslie Peterson (hn), Holly Holm (bn) Meyer ▲ MC 0108

Economou, Nicolas (pno)
Tchaikovsky, P.:Nutcracker Suite, w. Martha Argerich (pno) [arr N. Economou for 2 pnos] *(rec Munich, Mar 1983)* Deutsche Grammophon ▲ 449816-2 [DDD]

Eddy, Hugh (trbn)—see ORCHESTRAS & ENSEMBLES Speculum Musicae

Eddy, Timothy (vc)
Bach, J.S.:Sons Fl, BWV 1030-35, w. S. Baron (fl), G. Ranck (hpd)—Sons. BWV 1030-1032, 1034 & 1035 Soundspells ▲ CD 106 [DDD]
Diamond, D.:Qnt Cl, w. Lawrence Sobol (cl), Linda Moss (va), Louise Schulman (va), Fred Sherry (vc) *(rec RCA Studio A, New York City)* New World ▲ 80508-2
Husa, K.:Evocations of Slovakia, w. L. Sobol (cl), L. Schulman (va) Grenadilla ■ GSC 1008
Searle, H.:2 Practical Cats, w. P. Mason (bar), S. Palma (fl), D. Starobin (gtr) [E] Bridge ▲ BCD 9022 [DDD]
Silver, S.:Son Vc, w. G. Kalish (pno) CRI ▲ CD 590 [DDD]

Edelberg, Joseph (vn)—see ORCHESTRAS & ENSEMBLES Earplay, Earplay members

Edelen, C. (hpd)
Boismortier, J.B. de:Sons Fl & Continuo, w. C. St. Martin (baroque fl)—(6) in D, g, G, e, A & c Focus ▲ FOCUS 936 [DDD]

Edelmann, Sergei (pno)
Mendelssohn, F.:Capriccio brillante, w. C. P. Flor (cnd), Bamberg SO RCA Red Seal ▲ 7988-2-RC [DDD]
Mendelssohn, F.:Con 1 Pno, w. C. P. Flor (cnd), Bamberg SO RCA Red Seal ▲ 7988-2-RC [DDD]
Mendelssohn, F.:Con 2 Pno, w. C. P. Flor (cnd), Bamberg SO RCA Red Seal ▲ 7988-2-RC [DDD]
Prokofiev, S.:Romeo & Juliet Pno RCA Red Seal ▲ 09026-60848-2
Prokofiev, S.:Son 8 Pno RCA Red Seal ▲ 09026-60848-2
Strauss, R.:Burleske, w. P. Berglund (cnd), Stockholm PO RCA Red Seal ▲ 60173-2-RC [DDD]

Eden, Bracha (pno)
Brahms, J.:Neue Liebeslieder Waltzes, w. A. Tamir (pno)—65a CRD ▲ 3413 [ADD]
Brahms, J.:Sym 3, w. A. Tamir (pno) [2-piano version] CRD ▲ 3414
Brahms, J.:Vars on a Theme by Haydn, w. A. Tamir (pno)—Op. 56b CRD ▲ 3413 [ADD]
Brahms, J.:Vars on a Theme of Robert Schumann, Op. 23, w. A. Tamir (pno) CRD ▲ 3414
Brahms, J.:Waltzes Pno, Op. 39, w. A. Tamir (pno) [piano duet versions] CRD ▲ 3413 [ADD]
Dances around the World, w. Eden, Bracha (pno), Alexander Tamir (pno) PWK Classics ▲ PWK 1134 [DDD]
The World's Favorite Piano Music Vol. 1 Odyssey ■ YT 44510
The World's Favorite Piano Music Vol. 2 Odyssey ■ YT 44511
The World's Favorite Piano Music Vol. 3 Odyssey ■ YT 44512

Éder, György (vc)—see ORCHESTRAS & ENSEMBLES Éder String Quartet

Eder, Lorna (pno)—see ORCHESTRAS & ENSEMBLES California EAR Unit

Éder, Pál (vn)—see ORCHESTRAS & ENSEMBLES Éder String Quartet

Edge, Jane (org)
In Search of the Lost Chord *(rec Apr 15-20, 1994)* AFKA ▲ SK 536

Edge, Kenneth (a sax)
Binge, R.:Con A Sax, w. E. Tomlinson (cnd), Slovak RSO Bratislava *(rec Oct. 1992)* Marco Polo ("British Light Music" series) ▲ 8.223515 [DDD]

Edgren, Ingemar (pno)
Wiklund, A.:Con 1 Pno, w. J. Panula (cnd), Gothenburg SO Caprice ▲ CAP 21363 [AAD]

Edinger, Christiane (vn)
Blake, H.:Con Vn, "The Leeds", w. P. Daniel (cnd), English Northern PO ASV ▲ ASV 905 [DDD]
Brandmüller, T.:Enigma, w. Theo Brandenmüller (org) MD + G ▲ MDG 6250551 [DDD]
Einem, G. von:Con Vn, w. A. Walter (cnd), North German RSO Marco Polo ▲ 8.223138 [DDD]
Penderecki, K.:Con Vn, w. K. Penderecki (cnd), Bamberg SO Orfeo ▲ 285931 [DDD]

Edlina, Luba (pno)—see also ORCHESTRAS & ENSEMBLES Borodin Trio
Arensky, A.:Trio 1 Pno, w. Dubinsky (vn), Turovsky (vc) Chandos ▲ CHAN 8477 [DDD]
Beethoven, L. van:Son 5 Vn, "Spring", w. R. Dubinsky (vn) Chandos ▲ CHAN 9297 [DDD]
Beethoven, L. van:Son 9 Vn, "Kreutzer", w. R. Dubinsky (vn) Chandos ▲ CHAN 9297 [DDD]
Beethoven, L. van:Trio 7 Pno, w. J. Campbell (cl), Y. Turovsky (vc) Chandos ▲ CHAN 8655 [DDD]
Borodin, A.:Petite Suite Chandos ▲ CHAN 9297 [DDD]
Brahms, J.:Pno Music (misc)—Op. 76/3, 4, 6 & 7; Op. 116/2, 4, 5 & 6; Op. 117/1-3; Op. 118/1, 2, 4 & 6; Op. 119/1-3 Chandos ▲ CHAN 8467 [DDD]
Brahms, J.:Trio Cl, w. J. Campbell (cl), Y. Turovsky (vc) Chandos ▲ CHAN 8606 [DDD]
Brahms, J.:Trio Hn, w. M. Thompson (hn), R. Dubinsky (vn) Chandos ▲ CHAN 8606 [DDD]

▲ = CD ♦ = Enhanced CD Δ = MD ■ = Cassette Tape □ = DCC

Edlina, Luba (pno) (cont.)
Debussy, C.:Son Vc, w. Y. Turovsky (vc) Chandos ▲ CHAN 8458
Debussy, C.:Son Vn, w. R. Dubinsky (va) Chandos ▲ CHAN 8458
Glinka, M.:Trio pathétique, w. R. Dubinsky (vn), Y. Turovsky (vc) Chandos ▲ CHAN 8477 [DDD]
Mendelssohn, F.:Lieder ohne Worte Pno Chandos 2-▲ CHAN 8948/49 [DDD]
Miaskovsky, N.:Son 2 Vc, w. E. Turovsky (vn) Chandos ▲ CHAN 8523 [DDD]
Mozart, W.A.:Trio Cl, K.498, w. J. Campbell (cl), R. Dubinsky (va) Chandos ▲ CHAN 8655 [DDD]
Prokofiev, S.:Son Vc, w. Y. Turovsky (vc) Chandos ▲ CHAN 8340 [DDD]
Rachmaninoff, S.:Son Vc, w. Y. Turovsky (vc) Chandos ▲ CHAN 8523 [DDD]
Schnittke, A.:Suite in the Old Style, w. R. Dubinsky (vn) Chandos ▲ CHAN 8343 [DDD]
Shostakovich, D.:Son Vc, w. Y. Turovsky (vc) Chandos ▲ CHAN 8340 [DDD]
Shostakovich, D.:Son Vn, w. R. Dubinsky (va) Chandos ▲ CHAN 8343 [DDD]
Tchaikovsky, P.:Les Saisons Chandos ▲ CHAN 9309 [DDD]

Edmund-Davies, Paul (fl)
Corigliano, J.:Voyage Fl, w. R. Werthen (cnd), I Fiamminghi CO *(rec Belgium, July 19–21, 1995)* Telarc ▲ CD 80421 [DDD]
Elgar, E.:Harmony Music I–V, w. Michael Cox (fl), Roy Carter (ob), Nicholas Rodwell (cl), Martin Gatt (bn)—No. 4, "The Farmyard" EMI Classics ("Anglo-American Chamber Music" series) ▲ CDC 55403
Górecki, H.–M.:Good Night, w. Elzbieta Szmytka (sop), Huub Righarts (perc), Mireille Gleizes (pno) *(rec Abbey Bonne Espérance, Vellereille-les-Brayeux, Belgium; July 17–19, 1995)* Telarc ▲ CD–80417 [DDD]
Hovhaness, A.:Tzaikerk, w. Arnold Kobyliansky (vn), Randy Max (timp), R. Werthen (cnd), I Fiamminghi CO *(rec Basilica of Bonne Espérance, Vellereille-les-Brayeux, Belgium, Aug. 18–20, 1994)* Telarc ▲ CD 80392 [DDD]

Edni, Daniel (pno)
Rare Cello Music, w. S. Heled (vc), Jonathan Feldman (pno), Michael Levin (pno), Alexander Peskanov (pno), Jonathan Zak (pno) *(rec 1976, 1982, 1983, 1985, 1)* Classico ▲ CLASSCD 153

Edouard, Odile (vn)—see also ORCHESTRAS & ENSEMBLES Aurora Ensemble
Boccherini, L.:Qnt Pno, G.407–412, w. L. Alvini (pno), E. Gatti (vn), E. Moreno (va), R. Gini (vc)—Nos. 1, 5 & 6 Tactus ▲ TC 740203
Rebel, J.–F.:Sons 2 or 3 Parts, w. Frédéric Martin (vn), Christine Plumbeau (vl), Eric Bellocq (thb), Noëlle Spieth (hpd)—Nos. 1–7 [L'immortelle; L'apollon; Tombeau de monsieur de Lully; La venus; La flore; La pallas; La junon] Adda ▲ ADD 581265 [DDD]

Edvaldsdóttir, Sigrún (vn)
Hallgrímsson, H.:Poemi, w. P. Sakari (cnd), Iceland SO Music from Iceland ▲ ITM 602 [DDD]

Edward-Kelly, J. (sax)
Contemporary Music for Saxophone, w. Bob Versteegh (pno) Col legno ▲ AU31805

Edwards, Catherine (pno)—see also ORCHESTRAS & ENSEMBLES Capricorn members, Capricorn
Chopin, F.:Intro & Polonaise, "Polonaise brilliante", w. H. Brendstrup (vc) Kontrapunkt ▲ 32026 [DDD]
Chopin, F.:Son Vc, w. H. Brendstrup (vc) Kontrapunkt ▲ 32026 [DDD]
Ireland, J.:Chamber Music, w. Paul Barritt (vn)—Bagatelle; Berceuse; Catavina; The Holy Boy Hyperion ▲ CDA 66853
Ireland, J.:Son 1 Vn, w. Paul Barritt (vn) Hyperion ▲ CDA 66853
Ireland, J.:Son 2 Vn, w. Paul Barritt (vn) Hyperion ▲ CDA 66853
Liszt, F.:Vc & Pno Music, w. H. Brendstrup (vc)—Elegies Nos. 1 & 2, S.130 & S.131; Romance oubliée, S.132; La lugubre gondola, S.134 Kontrapunkt ▲ 32026 [DDD]
Mendelssohn, F.:Lied ohne Worte Vc, w. H. Brendstrup (vc) Kontrapunkt ▲ 32007 [DDD]
Mendelssohn, F.:Son 1 Vc, w. H. Brendstrup (vc) Kontrapunkt ▲ 32007 [DDD]
Mendelssohn, F.:Son 2 Vc, w. H. Brendstrup (vc) Kontrapunkt ▲ 32007 [DDD]
Mendelssohn, F.:Vars concertantes, w. H. Brendstrup (vc) Kontrapunkt ▲ 32007 [DDD]
The Flute Album, w. K. Jones (fl), Jane Pendlebury (vc), Aline Brewer (hp) Conifer Classics 2-▲ 75605-51905-2 [DDD]

Edwards, Ryan (pno)
Rorem, N.:Ariel, w. Phyllis Curtin (sop), Joseph Rabbai (cl) Phoenix ▲ PHCD 126

Eeman, Hilde (pno)
Salon-Music for a Double Bass, w. F. Coppieters (db) René Gailly ▲ CD 86006 [ADD]

Een, James (va)
Kingman, D.:Scénario musical 1, w. Susan Lamb Cook (vc), Richard Cionco (pno) Innova ▲ INNOVA 504

Eerola, Pertti (pno)
Merikanto, O.:Music of, w. Eeva-Jiisa Saarinen (mez), Jorma Hynninen (bar), Sauli Tiilikainen (bar), Kaija Saaikettu (vn), Erkki Rautio (vc), Ralf Gothoni (pno), Raija Kerppo (pno), Izumi Tateno (pno), Tauno Satomaa (cnd), Candomino Choir—Summer Evening (waltz); Valse lente; Romance; On the Highest Tree-Top; Annina; Bye, Bye Lullabye; The Weeping Flute; At Sea; Hey My Heart; Where Rustling Birches Bend; Play Softly, the Tune of Mourning; Fairy Tale by the Fireside; Idyll; Scherzo, Op. 6/4; O Dost Thou Remember That Hymn; Lade Ladoga; Why Do I Sing; The Thunderbird; The Happy Ones; Summer Evening's Idyll Finlandia ▲ FIN 500432 [AAD/DDD]

Effmann, Fritz (bn)
Baur, J.:Ostinato senza fine, "Pour rien", w. H. Fischer (cl), A. Münten (cl), C. Crespo (hn), *(not advised of 2nd hn)*, S. Fasang (bn) *(rec May 13, 1981)* Koch Schwann ▲ SCH 311982 [ADD/DDD]

Egarr, Richard (hpd)—see also ORCHESTRAS & ENSEMBLES Cambridge Musick, London Baroque
Bach, J.S.:Sons Fl, BWV 1030–35, w. M. Root (trns fl), V. de Hoog (vc)—1030, 1034 & 1035 *(rec May 1993)* Globe ▲ GLO 5102 [DDD]
Bach, W.F.:Cons Hpd, w. C. Medlam (cnd), London Baroque—in D, F.41; in F, F.44; in a, F.45 Harmonia Mundi France ▲ HMC 901558
Blow, J.:Music for Kbd—Suites in a & d *(rec Utrecht, Aug 1995)* Globe ▲ 5145 [DDD]
Couperin, L.:Suites Hpd—Suites in F, A, D & F *(rec Utrecht, Aug 1995)* Globe ▲ GLO 5148 [DDD]
Draghi, G.B.:Hpd Music—Suite in G; Curtain Tune *(rec Utrecht, Aug 1995)* Globe ▲ 5145 [DDD]
Locke, M.:Suite Hpd *(rec Utrecht, Aug 1995)* Globe ▲ 5145 [DDD]
Purcell, H.:Hpd Music (misc)—Suites in g, Z.662 & in D, Z.667; Grounds in c, Z.D221, in d, Z.D222 & in e, Z.T682 *(rec Utrecht, Aug 1995)* Globe ▲ 5145 [DDD]

Egendal, Anne (vn)
Gade, N.W.:Octet, w. Per Lund Madsen (vn), Sune Ranmo (va), Hans Nygaard (vc), Kontra String Quartet *(rec Torpen Kapel, Humlebaek, Denmark, May, 5–8, 1992)* BIS ▲ CD 545 [DDD]

Eggebrecht, Jörg (baryton)—see ORCHESTRAS & ENSEMBLES Munich Baryton Trio

Eggebrecht, Renate (vn)—see also ORCHESTRAS & ENSEMBLES Fanny Mendelssohn String Quartet
Milhaud, D.:Catalogue de fleurs, w. Ulrike Sonntag (sop), Irmela Nolte (fl), Deborah Marshall (cl), Michael Weigel (bn), Stefan Berg (va), Friedemann Kupsa (vc), Arpat György (db) *(rec Ludwigsburg, Germany, Jan. 1995)* Troubadisc ▲ TROCD 01410 [DDD]
Milhaud, D.:Machines agricoles, w. Ulrike Sonntag (sop), Irmela Nolte (fl), Deborah Marshall (cl), Michael Weigel (bn), Stefan Berg (va), Friedemann Kupsa (vc), Arpat György (db) *(rec Ludwigsburg, Germany, Jan. 1995)* Troubadisc ▲ TROCD 01410 [DDD]
Smyth, E.:Double Con, w. F. Draxinger (hn), C. Dutilly (pno) *(rec 1992)* Troubadisc ▲ TRO CD 01405 [DDD]
Tailleferre, G.:Son 1 Vn, w. A. Gassenhuber (pno) *(rec Dec. 1992)* Troubadisc ▲ TRO 01406 [DDD]
Tailleferre, G.:Son 2 Vn, w. A. Gassenhuber (pno) *(rec Dec. 1992)* Troubadisc ▲ TRO 01406 [DDD]
Tailleferre, G.:Trio Pno, w. A. Gassenhuber (pno), F. Kupas (vc) *(rec Dec. 1992)* Troubadisc ▲ TRO 01406 [DDD]

Egger, Cynthia (gtr)
Owen, J.:Intimate Dances, w. Jan Boland (fl) *(rec Aug 10, 1991)* Centaur ▲ CRC 2233 [DDD]
Owen, J.:Studies Gtr *(rec Smithfield Studios, Cedar Rapids, IA, Aug 11, 1991)* Centaur ▲ CRC 2233 [DDD]

Egger, Georg (vn)
Bach, J.S.:Con Fl, Vn & Hpd, w. G. Höller (fl), J. Faerber (cnd), Württemberg CO *(rec 1978)* Vox Box 3-▲ CD3X 3018 [ADD]
Schaeuble, H.:Concertino Ob, w. S. Fuchs (ob), S. Lautenbacher (vn), J. Faerber (cnd), Württemberg CO Gallo ▲ CD 577 [DAD]
Schaeuble, H.:Music for 2 Vns, w. S. Lautenbacher (vn), J. Faerber (cnd), Württemberg CO Gallo ▲ CD 577 [DAD]

Egger, Georg (vn) (cont.)
Schaeuble, H.:Sym for Strs, "In Memoriam", w. S. Lautenbacher (vn), J. Faerber (cnd), Württemberg CO Gallo ▲ CD 577 [DAD]

Egholm, Per (sax)
Bentzon, N.V.:Sons Sax, Opp. 320, 471, 478 & 498, w. N. V. Bentzon (pno) *(rec 9/86)* Kontrapunkt ▲ 32017
Moser, R.:Wal, w. I. Roth (sax), B. Beaufreton (sax), M. Weiss (sax), J.–G. Koerper (sax), M. Venzago (cnd), Basel SO Grammont ▲ CTSP 12-2 [ADD]

Egilson, Gunnar (cl)
Sigurbjörnsson, T.:Intrada, w. Ingvar Jónasson (va), Thorkell Sigurbjörnsson (pno) Music from Iceland ▲ ITM 702 [ADD]

Egilsson, Árni (db)
Egilsson:Contemplation, w. Endeé Granat (vn), Richard Altenbach (vn), Janet Lakatos (va), Douglas Davis (vc) Cambria ▲ CD 1033
Egilsson:Get Down!, w. Endeé Granat (vn), Richard Altenbach (vn), Janet Lakatos (va), Douglas Davis (vc) Cambria ▲ CD 1033
Egilsson:Is It?, w. Endeé Granat (vn), Richard Altenbach (vn), Janet Lakatos (va), Douglas Davis (vc) Cambria ▲ CD 1033
Egilsson:What If?, w. Endeé Granat (vn), Richard Altenbach (vn), Janet Lakatos (va), Douglas Davis (vc) Cambria ▲ CD 1033
Egilsson:Why?, w. Endeé Granat (vn), Richard Altenbach (vn), Janet Lakatos (va), Douglas Davis (vc) Cambria ▲ CD 1033

Egler, Steven (org)—see ORCHESTRAS & ENSEMBLES Shelly/Egler Duo

Egon, Petri (pno)
Brahms, J.:Vars & Fugue on a Theme by Handel *(rec 1936–1951)* Pearl ▲ CD 9078 [AAD]
Busoni, F.:Albumblätter Pno—No. 1 *(rec 1936–1951)* Pearl ▲ CD 9078 [AAD]
Busoni, F.:Bach Transcriptions—Capriccio on the Departure of His Beloved Brother *(rec 1936–1951)* Pearl ▲ CD 9078 [AAD]
Busoni, F.:Elegies (7) Pno—All'Italia *(rec 1936–1951)* Pearl ▲ CD 9078 [AAD]
Tausig, C.:Trans & Arr—Andante & Vars. [Schubert] *(rec 1936–1951)* Pearl ▲ CD 9078 [AAD]

Egorov, Pavel (pno)
Schumann, R.:Con Pno, w. C. Croci (cnd), St. Petersburg State Academic Cappella SO Audiophile Classics ▲ 101.020 [DDD]

Egorov, Yuri (hpd)
Bach, J.S.:Chromatic Fant & Fugue *(rec Dec 16, 1978)* Globe ▲ GLO 6015 [ADD]

Egorov, Yuri (pno)
Bach, J.S.:Italian Con Pavane ▲ ADW 7029 [ADD]
Bach, J.S.:Das wohltemperierte Klavier—Preludes & Fugues in D, F# & b, BWV 850, 857 & 869 Pavane ▲ ADW 7029 [ADD]
Bartók, B.:Son 2 Vn & Pno, w. E. Verhey (vn) *(rec May 25, 1981)* Erasmus ▲ WVH 023 [ADD]
Brahms, J.:Son 3 Vn, w. E. Verhey (vn) *(rec May 25, 1981)* Erasmus ▲ WVH 023 [ADD]
Chopin, F.:Études (24)—Op. 10, No. 5 *(rec Dec. 16, 1978)* Globe ▲ GLO 6015 [ADD]
Chopin, F.:Fant *(rec Dec. 16, 1978)* Globe ▲ GLO 6015 [ADD]
Chopin, F.:Pno Music (misc)—Fantasie; Ballade 1; Scherzo 2; 3 Nocturnes Royal Classics ▲ ROY 6455
Mozart, W.A.:Fant Pno, K.475 *(rec Dec. 16, 1978)* Globe ▲ GLO 6015 [ADD]
Schubert, Franz:Son Vn, D.574, w. E. Verhey (vn) *(rec May 25, 1981)* Erasmus ▲ WVH 023 [ADD]
Schumann, R.:Carnaval Pno Royal Classics ▲ ROY 6455
Schumann, R.:Fant Pno *(rec May 1979)* Globe ▲ GLO 6015 [ADD]

Eguchi, Akira (pno)
Debussy, C.:Son Vn, w. Chee-Yun (vn) *(rec May 1990)* Denon/PCM Digital ▲ CO 75625 [DDD]
Fauré, G.:Son 1 Vn, w. Chee-Yun (vn) *(rec May 1990)* Denon/PCM Digital ▲ CO 75625 [DDD]
Franck, C.:Son Vn, w. Chee-Yun (vn) *(rec Chichibu-Muse Park, Music Hall, Saitama-prefecture, Japan, Oct. 17–20, 1994)* Denon ▲ CO 78954 [DDD]
Saint-Saëns, C.:Son 1 Vn, w. Chee-Yun (vn) *(rec May 1990)* Denon/PCM Digital ▲ CO 75625 [DDD]
Szymanowski, K.:Son Vn, w. Chee-Yun (vn) *(rec Chichibu-Muse Park, Music Hall, Saitama-prefecture, Japan, Oct. 17–20, 1994)* Denon ▲ CO 78954 [DDD]
Vocalise, w. Chee-Yun (vn) *(rec July 31–Aug. 1, 1992)* Denon ▲ CO 75118 [DDD]

Eguez, Eduardo (thb/baroque gtr)
Forqueray, A.:Suites (5) Va da Gamba, w. Guido Balestracci (vl), Paolo Pandolfo (vl), Rolf Lislevand (thb/baroque gtr), Guido Morini (clvd) Glossa 2-▲ 920401

Eguez, Eduardo (thb/lt/pandora/gtr)—see ORCHESTRAS & ENSEMBLES Labyrinto

Ehde, John (vc)—see ORCHESTRAS & ENSEMBLES LINensemble

Ehnes, James (vn)
Paganini, N.:Caprices Vn *(rec Severance Hall, Cleveland, OH, Aug 7–10, 1995)* Telarc ▲ CD 80398 [DDD]

Ehrén, Håkan (db)
Tubin, E.:Con Db, w. N. Järvi (cnd), Gothenburg SO BIS ▲ CD 337 [DDD]

Ehrhardt, Werner (vn)
Trumpet Concerti of the Italian Baroque, w. F. Immer (baroque tpt), Graham Nicholson (baroque tpt), Cologne Concerto MD + G ▲ L 3271 [DDD]
Locatelli, P.:Introduttioni teatrali & Concerti, Concerto Cologne—No. 4 Pierre Verany ▲ PV 787093 [DDD]

Ehrlich, David (vn)—see ORCHESTRAS & ENSEMBLES Audubon String Quartet

Ehrlich, Don (va)—see ORCHESTRAS & ENSEMBLES Aurora String Quartet

Ehrlich, Marth (b cl)
Jenkins, L.:Monkey on the Dragon, w. Leroy Jenkins (vn), Henry Threadgill (fl), Don Byron (cl), Janet Frice (bn), Vincent Chancey (hn), Frank Gordon (tpt), Jeff Hoyer (trbn), David Soldier (vn), Jane Henry (vn) Ron Lawrence (va), Mary Wooton (vc), Lindsey Horner (db), Thurman Barker (traps), Myra Melford (pno), T. Léon (cnd) *(rec live, Merkin Concert Hall, New York City, Apr. 9, 1992)* CRI ("eXchange" series) ▲ CD 663 [DDD]

Ehrlich, Robert (rcr)—see ORCHESTRAS & ENSEMBLES Cambridge Musick

Eichenberger, J. (pno)
Müller-Zurich, P.:Petite Sonate, w. A. Morf (cl) Grammont ▲ CTSP 20-2

Eickhorst, Konstanze (pno)
Schumann, C.:Pno Music—Pièces fugitives, Op. 15; Romance in a, Op. 21/1; Romance in b, Op. posth.; Scherzo in d, Op. 10; Scherzo in c, Op. 14; Soirées musicales, Op. 6; Variations on a Theme of Robert Schumann, Op. 20 CPO ▲ CPO 999132-2 [DDD]
Schumann, C.:Songs, w. Gabriele Fontana (sop) CPO ▲ CPO 999127 [DDD]

Eidi, Billy (pno)
Chausson, E.:Mélodies (comp), w. Sandrine Piau (sop), Brigitte Balleys (mez), Jean François Gardeil (bar), Ludwig String Quartet Timpani 2-▲ 2C 2028
Debussy, C.:Songs, w. Jean-François Gardeil (bar)—Fêtes galantes 1er cahier; Fêtes galantes 2e cahier; 3 ballades de François Villon; Le promenoir des 2 amants; 3 poèmes de Stéphanie Mallarmé Adda ▲ ADD 581307
Honegger, A.:Songs, w. Brigitte Balleys (mez), Jean-François Gardeil (bar)—Mimaamaquim; Nature morte; O Salutaris; O Temps suspends ton Vol; Panis Angelicus; Petit Cours de Morale; Quatre Chansons pour voix grave; Quatre Poèms; Saluste du Bartas; Six Poésie de Jean Cocteau; Trois Poèmes de Claudel; Trois Poèmes de Paul Fort; Trois Psaumes; Vocalise-Etude [F,L,Heb] *(rec Aug. 1992)* Timpani ▲ 1C1015 [DDD]
Milhaud, D.:Pno Music—L'Automne; Sketches; Sonata No. 1; Sonatina; Springtime 1 & 2 Arcobaleno ▲ SBCD 5400
Poulenc, F.:Banalités, w. Jean-François Gardeil (bar) Adda ▲ ADD 581210 [DDD]
Poulenc, F.:Le Bestiaire, w. Jean-François Gardeil (bar) Adda ▲ ADD 581210 [DDD]
Poulenc, F.:Poèmes, w. Jean-François Gardeil (bar) Adda ▲ ADD 581210 [DDD]
Ravel, M.:Don Quichotte à Dulcinée, w. Jean-François Gardeil (bar) Adda ▲ ADD 581210 [DDD]
Ravel, M.:Histoires naturelles, w. Jean-François Gardeil (bar) Adda ▲ ADD 581210 [DDD]
Ravel, M.:Mélodies populaires grecques, w. Jean-François Gardeil (bar) Adda ▲ ADD 581210 [DDD]
Roussel, A.:Songs, w. Jean-François Gardeil (bar)—2 mélodies, Op. 20; 2 mélodies, Op. 50; 2 mélodies, Op. 55; Odes anacréontiques, Opp. 31 & 32 Adda ▲ ADD 581307

Eidi, Billy (pno) (cont.)
Sacre, G.:Pno Music—Works for Pno; 2nd Serenade; Vars on Chopin's Mazurkas Timpani ▲ 1026
Satie, E.:Nocturnes Pno *(rec Aug. 26–27, 1993)* Timpani ▲ 1020 [DDD]
Satie, E.:Premier menuet *(rec Aug. 26–27, 1993)* Timpani ▲ 1020 [DDD]
Satie, E.:Socrate, w. J. Belliard (ten) *(rec Aug. 26–27, 1993)* Timpani ▲ 1020 [DDD]
Eifert, Otto (bn)
Hindemith, P.:Stücke (4) Bn & Vc, w. Roy Christensen (vc) Gasparo ▲ 1009
Eijk, T. van (org)
Hollander, H.:Sacred Music, w. S. van Grootel (sop), K. van der Poel (mez), J. Boswinkel (bass), P. Rikkers (vn), J. van der Meer (db), Cappella Breda—Cantabant sancti; Domine Jesu Christe; Domine Deus; Ecce vicit leo; O nomen Jesu; Recipe me; Quem vidistis pastores; Sanctus Jacobus; Quid est hoc; O vos omnes; Ecce clamo; Ave Maria; O Beatum Virum; O bone Jesu; Te gloriosus Erasmus ▲ WVH 047 [DDD]
Einem, J. von (vn)—see ORCHESTRAS & ENSEMBLES Trio Galanterie
Eiriksson, Petur (b trbn)
Cage, J.:Ryoanji for 4 Soloists, w. Anthony D'Amico (db), Fenwick Smith (fl), Michael Miller (ob), S. Drury (cnd), New England Conservatory Avant–Garde Ensemble *(rec New England Conservatory of Music, Boston, MA, Mar. 4 & 6, 1991)* Mode ▲ MODE 41
Eisenberg, Matthias (org)
Bach, J.S.:Org Music (misc)—Prelude & Fugue in c, BWV 546; Nun komm, der Heiden Heiland, BWV 659; Prelude & Fugue in b, BWV 544; Prelude & Fugue in G, BWV 541; An Wasserflüssen Babylon, BWV 653; Herr Jesu Christ, dich zu uns wend, BWV 655; Prelude & Fugue in e, BWV 548 Capriccio ▲ CDC 10038 [DDD]
Great European Organs No. 33:Matthias Eisenberg Plays the Silbermann Organ at St. Georgenkirche, Rotha Priory ▲ PRI 411 [DDD]
Eisenberg, Maurice (vc)
Beethoven, L. van:Trio 4 Pno, "Ghost", w. Hepzibah Menuhin (pno), Yehudi Menuhin (vn) *(rec 1936)* Biddulph ▲ LAB 127
Tchaikovsky, P.:Trio Pno, w. Hepzibah Menuhin (pno), Yehudi Menuhin (vn) *(rec 1936)* Biddulph ▲ LAB 127
Eisenberger, C. (vn)
Mozart, W.A.:Arias, w. U. Fiedler (sop), C. Traunfellner (cnd), Vienna CO—Exsultate, Jubilate; Voi avete un cor fedele; Misera, dove son!; Non temer, amato bene; Vedrai carino, se sei buonino; Bella mia fiamma, addio; Alma grande e nobil core; Chi sa, chi sa, qual sia Camerata ▲ 30CM–343
Eisenberger, Severin (pno)
Grieg, E.:Con Pno, Op. 16, w. A. von Kreisler (cnd), Cincinnati SO [previously unpublished] *(rec live 4/4/38)* Pearl ▲ PEA 9933 (m) [AAD]
Eisenhoffer, Catherine (hp)
Catherine Eisenhoffer, Harp Gallo ▲ CD 622 [AAD]
Daetwyler, J.:Dialogue concertant, w. B. Slokar (trbn) Gallo ▲ CD 578 [DAD]
Daetwyler, J.:Poèmes (3), w. M. Sébastien (alt)—[F] Gallo ▲ CD 578 [DAD]
Daetwyler, J.:Rêverie du Soir, w. B. Slokar (trbn) Gallo ▲ CD 578 [DAD]
Debussy, C.:Arabesques (2), w. Ursula Hölliger (hp) [arr for Hp] Claves ▲ 50–9603
Debussy, C.:Arrs for 2 Pnos, w. Ursula Hölliger (hp)—Schumann's Studies (6) in canon form for 2 Pnos [arr for 2 Hps] Claves ▲ 50–9603
Fauré, G.:Dolly, w. Ursula Hölliger (hp) [arr for 2 Hps] Claves ▲ 50–9603
Mendelssohn, F.:Evening Bell, w. Ursula Hölliger (hp) [arr for 2 Hps] Claves ▲ 50–9603
Schoeck, O.:Spielmannsweisen, w. E. Haefliger (ten) [G] Gallo ▲ CD 622 [AAD]
Viotti, G.B.:Son Hp, w. Ursula Hölliger (hp) Claves ▲ 50–9603
Eisenlohr, Ulrich (pno)
Wolf, H.:Goethe–Lieder (sels), w. R. Ziesak (sop)—Blumengruss; Gleich und Gliech; Anakreons Grab; Die Spröde; Die Bekehrte; Der Schäfer; Philine; Epiphanias; Nimmer will ich dich verlieren; Phänomen; Hochbeglückt in deiner Liebe *(rec Oct. 8–10, 1992)* Sony Classical ▲ SK 53278 [DDD]
Wolf, H.:Mörike–Lieder (sels), w. R. Ziesak (sop)—Elfenlied; Zitronenfalter im April; Auf eine Christblume I; Auf eine Christblume II; Der Gärtner; Er ist's; Denk es, O Seele; Schlanfendes Jesuskind; Auf ein altes Bild; Frage und Antwort; Im Frühling; Gesang Weylas; Die Geister am Mummelsee; Nixe Binsefuss *(rec Oct. 8–10, 1992)* Sony Classical ▲ SK 53278 [DDD]
Eisinger, Christopher (pno)—see ORCHESTRAS & ENSEMBLES Bowed Piano Ensemble
Eiso, Shigemitsu (perc)
Nishimura, A.:Kamunagi, w. Teiko Kikuchi (17–string koto) *(rec Saitama Arts Theater Concert Hall, Apr 27–28, 1995)* Camerata ▲ 30CM 267 [DDD]
Shinohara, M.:Cooperation, w. A. Nishigata (shamisen), K. Mitsuhashi (shakuhachi), M. Akao (fue), S. Yaotani (hichiriki), K. Ishikawa (sho), C. Fukunaga (koto), J. Ueda (biwa), M. Yoshizawa (kokyu), I. Tsuji (oboe), T. Takahashi (cl), G. Kitamura (tpt), A. Murata (trbn), S. Ueki (vn), S. Katsuta (vc), Y. Shibuya (pno), K. Komatsu (cnd) *(rec live Casals Hall, Tokyo, Mar. 5, 1994)* Camerata ▲ 30CM 375 [DDD]
Shinohara, M.:Tabiyuki, w. A. Ogawa (mez), M. Kakagawa (fl), I. Tsuji (ob), T. Takahashi (cl), K. Okazaki (fagotto), G. Kitamura (tpt), A. Murata (trbn), S. Ueki (vn), A. Nakakoji (va), S. Katsuta (vc), M. Komuro (contrabass), K. Komatsu (cnd) *(rec live Casals Hall, Tokyo, Mar. 5, 1994)* Camerata ▲ 30CM 375 [DDD]
Eissenberg, Judith (vn)—see ORCHESTRAS & ENSEMBLES Lydian String Quartet
Eje, Inge Mulvad (vc)—see ORCHESTRAS & ENSEMBLES Trio Rococo
Eje, Niels (ob)—see ORCHESTRAS & ENSEMBLES Trio Rococo
Ekier, Jan (pno)
Chopin, F.:Ballades Pno (comp) *(rec Warsaw, 1959–60)* Polskie Nagrania ▲ PNCD 314
Chopin, F.:Barcarolle Pno *(rec Warsaw, 1959–60)* Polskie Nagrania ▲ PNCD 314
Chopin, F.:Mazurkas Polskie Nagrania 2–▲ PLN 56 [DDD]
Chopin, F.:Pno Music (misc), w. Martha Argerich (pno), Vladimir Ashkenazy (pno), Stanislav Bunin (pno), Halina Czerny–Stefanska (pno), Yuval Fichman (pno), Kemal Gekic (pno), Adam Harasiewicz (pno), Krzysztof Jablonski (pno), Louis Kentner (pno), Jean–Marc Luisada (pno), Garrick Ohlsson (pno), Ivo Pogorelich (pno), Maurizio Pollini (pno), Dang Thai Son (pno)—includes Ballade (Nos. 1 & 2); Barcarolle, Op. 60; Concerto Nos. 1 & 2; Etudes (Op. 10, Nos. 1, 5, 8, 10 & 12 & Op. 25, No. 10, 18 & 25); Grand valse brillante; Impromptus (Nos. 3 & 4); Mazurkas (Op. 24, Nos. 1–4; Op. 30, Nos. 1–4; Op. 50, No. 32; Op. 59, Nos. 1–3); Nocturnes (Op. 9, No. 3; Op. 37, No. 12; Op. 48, No. 13; Op. 55, No. 16)Polonaise (Op. 40, Nos. 3 & 4; Op. 44, No. 5; Op. 53, No. 6; Op. 61, No. 7); Preludes (Op. 28 Nos. 13–18, 21–24 & Op. 45, No. 25); Scherzos (Nos. 1–3); Sonatas (Nos. 2 & 3); Waltzes (No. 1 & 6) LaserLight 5–▲ 15 961 [ADD/DDD]
Eklund, Niklas (tpt)
Italian Masterworks for Organ & Trumpet, w. E. Tarr (tpt), Irmtraud Krüger (org), C. Frigerio (vc) Christophorus ▲ CHR 77145 [DDD]
Molter, J.M.:Con 1 Tpt, w. N.–E. Sparf (cnd), Drottningholm Baroque Ensemble *(rec Petruskyrkan, Stockholm, Sweden, Aug 8–11, 1995)* Naxos ▲ 8.553531 [DDD]
Mozart, L.:Con Tpt, w. N.–E. Sparf (cnd), Drottningholm Baroque Ensemble *(rec Petruskyrkan, Stockholm, Sweden, Aug 8–11, 1995)* Naxos ▲ 8.553531 [DDD]
Telemann, G.P.:Con Tpt Strs in D, w. N.–E. Sparf (cnd), Drottningholm Baroque Ensemble *(rec Petruskyrkan, Stockholm, Sweden, Aug 8–11, 1995)* Naxos ▲ 8.553531 [DDD]
Torelli, G.:Son Tpt, G.1, w. N.–E. Sparf (cnd), Drottningholm Baroque Ensemble *(rec Petruskyrkan, Stockholm, Sweden, Aug 8–11, 1995)* Naxos ▲ 8.553531 [DDD]
Elaine, Karen (va)
Bartók, B.:Con Va, w. E. de Carvalho (cnd), Paraiba SO Delos ▲ DE 1018 [DDD]
Elbaek, Peder (vn)
Bach, Joh. Christian:Qts (4) for 2 Fls, w. B. Larsen (fl), B. Pedersen (fl), H. Olsen (va), B. Holst Christensen (vc) Kontrapunkt ▲ 32048 [DDD]
Bach, Joh. Christian:Trios for 2 Fls & Strs, w. B. Larsen (fl), B. Pedersen (fl), H. Olsen (va), B. Holst Christensen (vc) Kontrapunkt ▲ 32048 [DDD]
Olsen, P.R.:Concertino Cl, w. Jens Schou (cl), Verner Skovlund (va), Svend Winsløv (vc), Rosalind Bevan (pno) *(rec PAULA's Recording Hall, 1984)* Paula ▲ PACD 36 [AAD]
Olsen, P.R.:Qt 2 Strs, w. Jørgen Larsen (vn), Verner Skovlund (va), Svend Winsløv (vc) *(rec PAULA's Recording Hall, 1984)* Paula ▲ PACD 36 [AAD]

Elbaek, Peder (vn) (cont.)
Olsen, P.R.:Serenade Vn, w. Rosalind Bevan (pno) *(rec PAULA's Recording Hall, 1984)* Paula ▲ PACD 36 [AAD]
Olsen, P.R.:Trio II Pno, w. Svend Winsløv (vc), Rosalind Bevan (pno) *(rec PAULA's Recording Hall, 1984)* Paula ▲ PACD 36 [AAD]
Elbæk, Søren (vn)—see also ORCHESTRAS & ENSEMBLES Copenhagen Trio
Brahms, J.:Scherzo Vn, w. M. Mogensen (pno) Kontrapunkt ▲ KPT 32177 [DDD]
Brahms, J.:Sons Vn (comp), w. M. Mogensen (pno) Kontrapunkt ▲ KPT 32177 [DDD]
Gade, N.W.:Music of, w. E. Westenholz (pno)—Volkstanze, Op. 62; Elegie, Op. 19/1; Scherzo, 19/1; Canzonette, Op. 19/3; Abenddämmerung, Op. 34/4; Allegro Vivace in A; Fantasiestücke, Op. 43; Capriccio in a Kontrapunkt ▲ 32164 [DDD]
Hartmann, J.P.E.:Fant–Allegro *(rec Mar 1995)* Kontrapunkt ▲ KPT 32206
Hartmann, J.P.E.:Son 1 Vn, w. Morten Morgensen (pno) *(rec Mar 1995)* Kontrapunkt 2–▲ KPT 32206
Hartmann, J.P.E.:Son 2 Vn, w. Morten Morgensen (pno) *(rec Mar 1995)* Kontrapunkt ▲ KPT 32206
Hartmann, J.P.E.:Son 3 Vn, w. Morten Morgensen (pno) *(rec Mar 1995)* Kontrapunkt ▲ KPT 32206
Hartmann, J.P.E.:Suite Vn *(rec Mar 1995)* Kontrapunkt ▲ KPT 32206
Lange–Müller, P.E.:Fant Pieces, w. M. Mogensen (pno) *(rec 1991)* Kontrapunkt ▲ KPT 32208
Lange–Müller, P.E.:Romance, w. Morten Mogensen (pno) Kontrapunkt ▲ KPT 32208
Nielsen, C.:Prelude & Theme *(rec 1994)* Kontrapunkt ▲ KPT 32200
Nielsen, C.:Preludio e Presto *(rec 1994)* Kontrapunkt ▲ KPT 32200
Nielsen, C.:Son 1 Vn, w. Morten Morgensen (pno) *(rec 1994)* Kontrapunkt ▲ KPT 32200
Nielsen, C.:Son 2 Vn, w. Morten Morgensen (pno) *(rec 1994)* Kontrapunkt ▲ KPT 32200
Ravel, M.:Son Vn Vc, w. T.S. Hermansen (vc) Kontrapunkt ▲ KPT 32174 [DDD]
Ravel, M.:Son Vn Pno, w. M. Morgensen (pno) Kontrapunkt ▲ KPT 32174 [DDD]
Ravel, M.:Sonate posthume, w. M. Morgensen (pno) Kontrapunkt ▲ KPT 32174 [DDD]
Ravel, M.:Tzigane, w. M. Morgensen (pno) Kontrapunkt ▲ KPT 32174 [DDD]
Eldredge, Allison (vc)
Fauré, G.:Elégie, w. H. Vonk (cnd), Royal PO *(rec London, Aug. 9–11, 1989)* Canyon Classics ▲ 3694 [DDD]
Glazunov, A.:Chant du ménéstrel, w. H. Vonk (cnd), Royal PO *(rec London, Aug. 9–11, 1989)* Canyon Classics ▲ 3694 [DDD]
Lalo, E.:Con Vc, w. H. Vonk (cnd), Royal PO *(rec London, Aug. 9–11, 1989)* Canyon Classics ▲ 3694 [DDD]
Saint–Saëns, C.:Con 1 Vc, w. H. Vonk (cnd), Royal PO *(rec London, Aug. 9–11, 1989)* Canyon Classics ▲ 3694 [DDD]
Eldridge, Steven (pno)
Penn, W.:A Cornfield in July & the River, w. Robert Maher (bar) *(rec Carriage House, CT)* Capstone ▲ CPS 8618
Elek, Szilvia (pno)—see ORCHESTRAS & ENSEMBLES Trio Cristofori
Elekes, Zsuzsa (org)
Liszt, F.:Org Music MD + G ▲ MDG 6060567
Liszt, F.:Septam sacramenta, w. T. Takács (mez), J. Bándi (ten), G. Kallay (ten), K. Kaváts (bar), I. Zámbó (cnd), Hungarian State Orch, Hungarian People's Army Male Chorus, Jeunesses Musicales Women's Chorus [L] Hungaroton ▲ HCD 12748 [DDD]
Sulyok, I.:Partita Hungaroton ▲ HCD 31350 [DDD]
Sulyok, I.:Pieces Org Hungaroton ▲ HCD 31350 [DDD]
Sulyok, I.:Te Deum Hungaroton ▲ HCD 31350 [DDD]
Elesin, Genrich (vc)—see ORCHESTRAS & ENSEMBLES Gosteleradio String Quartet
Eley, Jennifer (pno)
Mendelssohn, Fanny:Das Jahr (sels), w. S. Stone (cnd), English CO *(rec Roslyn Hill Chapel, London)* Koch International Classics ▲ KIC 7197
Mendelssohn, F.:Con in e Pno, w. S. Stone (cnd), English CO *(rec Roslyn Hill Chapel, London)* Koch International Classics ▲ KIC 7197
Schumann, C.:Pno Music, w. S. Stone (cnd), English CO—Sonata (newly discovered) *(rec Roslyn Hill Chapel, London)* Koch International Classics ▲ KIC 7197
Schumann, R.:Konzertsatz Pno, w. S. Stone (cnd), English CO *(rec Roslyn Hill Chapel, London)* Koch International Classics ▲ KIC 7197
Elgar, Edward (pno)
Elgar, E.:Music of—Disc One:Enigma Variations, Op. 36 [w. Y. Menuhin]; Disc Two:Wand of Youth Suites 1 & 2; Nursery Suite; Severn Suite; Disc Three:Land of Hope & Glory; It Comes from the Misty Ages; National Anthem; Meditation (from the Light of Life, Op. 29); Three Characteristic Pieces for Viola & Orchestra, Op. 10; Chanson de nuit, Op. 15 No. 1; Chanson de matin, Op. 15 No. 2; Three Bavarian Dances, Op. 27; The Crown of India (suite), Op. 66; Fantasia & Fugue in c EMI Classics 3–▲ ZDCC 54564
Elgar, E.:Music of—Disc One:Carissima; Pomp & Circumstance Marches Nos. 1 & 4; Salut d'amour; Carillon; The Starlight Express [w. A. Nicholls (soprano) & C. Mott (baritone)]; Disc Two:Violin Concerto, Op. 61 [abridged version; w. M. Hall (violin)]; Three Bavarian Dances; Cockaigne Overture; Prelude/Angel's Farewell from The Dream of Gerontius; The Fringes of the Fleet (song cycle for 4 baritones & orchestra); Disc Three:The Wand of Youth (Suites 1 & 2, including all master & 6 variant takes); Polonia; Chanson de nuit; Cello Concerto, Op. 85 (abridged verson) [w. B. Harrison (cello)]; selection from ballet The Sanguine Fan; Disc Four:Enigma Variations, Op. 36; Sea Pictures, Op. 37 [w. L. Megane (contralto)]; In the South (overture); A Little Bird in the Air (from King Olaf); Disc Five:Symphony No. 2, Op. 63 (complete); Meditation from The Light of Life; Transcriptions of works by Bach (Fantasia & Fugue in c) & Handel (Overture in d) Pearl 5–▲ PEAS 9951/55 (m) [AAD]
Elgar, E.:Music of EMI Classics 3–▲ CDCC 54560
Elhorst, Hans (ob)
Vogel, W.:Sonances, w. H. Peter–Indermühle (fl), K. Weber (cl), I. Backer (bn), K. Hanke (hn), U. Lehmann (vn), L. Dober (vn), H. Forster (va), M. Liechti (vc), R. Tschupp (cnd) Grammont ▲ CTSP 14–2 [ADD]
Elias, Elianne (pno)
On the Classical Side, w. Elias, Elianne (pno) EMI Classics ▲ CDC 54826 ■ 4DS 54826
Elias, F. (vn)
Bach, J.S.:Con for 2 Vns, w. J. Brezina (vn), E. Duvier (cnd), Camerata Romana PMG ("Vienna Master" series) ▲ CD 160101 [DDD]
Elizondo, Esteban (org)
de Gamarra, M.:Son in Tone 8 [La Valenciana Organ] *(rec Apr. 1991)* Titanic ▲ Ti 201 [DDD]
de Gamarra, M.:Versos [La Valenciana Organ]—in Tones 4 & 7, "Punto vajo:Para los dias Primera Clase" *(rec Apr. 1991)* Titanic ▲ Ti 201 [DDD]
The Iberian Organ, Vol. 1, w. Elizondo, Esteban (org) Titanic ▲ Ti 153 [DDD]
Ledesma, N.:Son 6 Org [Basilica Organ] *(rec Apr. 1991)* Titanic ▲ Ti 201 [DDD]
Organs of Guanajuato, w. Elizondo, Esteban (org) Titanic ▲ Ti 201 [DDD]
Oxinaga, J. de:Fugues Org—Fuga airosa; Intento in G [La Valenciana Organ] *(rec Apr. 1991)* Titanic ▲ Ti 201 [DDD]
Soler, P.A.:Cons Kbds, w. B. Brauchli (org)—Nos. 1 & 2—2 clavichords; Nos. 3 & 6—harpsichord & organ; Nos. 4 & 5—2 organs Titanic ▲ Ti 152 [DDD]
Soler, P.A.:Versos para Te Deum [La Valenciana Organ] *(rec Apr. 1991)* Titanic ▲ Ti 201 [DDD]
Elizondo, Esteban (org/clvd)
18th Century Music for 2 Keyboard Instruments, w. Brauchli, Bernard (hpd/clvd) Titanic ▲ Ti 185 [DDD]

Elkjær, Bjørn (pno)
Stolarczyk, W.:Earth Air Fire Water, w. Amalie Malling (pno), John Damgaard (pno), Anne Øland (pno), Teddy Teirup (pno), Friedrich Gürtler (pno), Rosalind Bevan (pno), Poul Rosenbaum (pno), Rodolfo Llambias (pno), Bella Horn-Ribera (pno), Anders Riber (pno), Elisabeth Sigurdsson (pno), Thomas Tronheim (pno), Elsebeth Broderson (pno), Erik Kaltoft (pno), Jørgen Hald Nielsen (pno), Aino Gilemann (pno), Birgit Kjær (pno), Jørgen Thomsen (pno), Gunhild Donslund (pno), Henrik Bo Hansen (pno), Lone Karlsson (pno), Erik Fessel (pno), Lasse Nilsson (pno), Janos Ferenczi (pno), Erik Bach (pno), Axel Momme (pno), Arne de Cros Dich (pno), Sven Micha Slot (pno), Hanne Bramsen Buhl (pno), Lili Olesen (pno), Susannah Carlsson (pno), Ulla Erml (pno), Vagn Sørensen (pno), Leif Greibe (pno), Bodil Krogh (pno), Kirsten Ottosen (pno), Inger Bergenholz (pno), Karsten Gylendorf (pno), Jacob Bjørn Jensen (pno), Jørgen Kaad (pno), Anne Marie Hjelm (pno), Carl Ulrik Munk Andersen (pno), Poul Lumbye (pno), Oluf Hildebrandt Nielsen (pno), Joachim Olsson (pno), Peter Pade Ramsøe Jacobsen (pno), Astrid Pollmann (pno), Jette Borsch (pno), Kirsten Karlshøj (pno), Maria Teresa Assing (pno), Allan Dahl Hansen (pno), Johan Hugossen (pno), Tine Fenger Pederson (pno), Arne Jørgen Fæø (pno), Anja Høgsted (pno), Anne Sophie Parbo (pno), Inga Lindmark (pno), Teresa Drabik Stathakis (pno), Anne Ruth Ferenczi (pno), Irene Hasager (pno), Yuka Ichikawa (pno), Birgitte Baur (pno), Malene Thastum (pno), Jens E. Rasmussen (pno), Birgitte Zielke (pno), Claus Zielke (pno), Stefan Kasch (pno), Bin Qiao (pno), Inger Johanne Teirup (pno), Lindy Rosborg (pno), Liisa Heininen (pno), David Højer (pno), Ellen Refstrup (pno), Thomas K. Søorensen (pno), Erik Kure (pno), Michael Rauff (pno), Jan beck Eriksson (pno), Tanja Zapolski (pno), Vibeke Skagbo (pno), Pål Eide Lindtner (pno), Ha-Young Sul (pno), Benedicte Palko (pno), Inke Kesseler (pno), Anne Marie Meineche (pno), Sverre Larsen (pno), Kasper Peter Bach (pno), Elisabetta Eliseo (pno), Olga Magieres (pno), Carl Erik Kühl (pno), Thorkild Borup Nielsen (pno), Valeria Zanini (pno), Lars Stenhoft (perc), Dennis Boel (perc), Winnie Dahlgren (perc), Susanne Vind (perc), Claus Byrith (elec), Anne Marie Storm (elec), J. Ribera (cnd) *(rec live, Koldinghaus Castle, Denmark, May 2, 1996)* Danica ▲ DCD 1996

Ella, István (org)
Bengraf, J.:Sacred Music, w. Ingrid Kertesi (sop), Katalin Gémes (mez), Gábor Kállay (ten), Ákos Ambrus (bar), Zsolt Kovács (vc), Balázs Arnóth (bn), Vilmos Buza (db), J. Dobra (cnd), Vienna-Szász CO, Tomkins Vocal Ensemble—Te Deum; O sacrum convivium; Libera me; Gloria [from Missa solemnis in D] Hungaroton ▲ HCD 31609 [DDD]
Druschetzky, G.:Missa solemnis, w. Ingrid Kertesi (sop), Katalin Gémes (mez), Gábor Kállay (ten), Ákos Ambrus (bar), Zsolt Kovács (vc), Balázs Arnóth (bn), Vilmos Buza (db), J. Dobra (cnd), Vienna-Szász CO, Tomkins Vocal Ensemble Hungaroton ▲ HCD 31609 [DDD]
Grand Duett:Music for 2 Organs, w. János Sebestyén (org) Hungaroton ▲ HCD 31464 [DDD]
Mozart, W.A.:Alma Dei creatoris, w. Ibolya Verebics (sop), Judit Németh (cta), József Mukk (ten), József Moldvay (bar), Gábor Oláh (bar), János Reményi (cnd), Hungarian Radio-TV Children's Chorus Girls' Voices, Hungarian Radio-TV Male Chamber Choir *(rec Hungaroton Studio, June 14-16, 1991)* Hungaroton ▲ HCD 4003 [DDD]
Mozart, W.A.:Ave verum corpus, w. Ibolya Verebics (sop), Judit Németh (cta), József Mukk (ten), József Moldvay (bar), Gábor Oláh (bar), János Reményi (cnd), Hungarian Radio-TV Children's Chorus Girls' Voices, Hungarian Radio-TV Male Chamber Choir *(rec Hungaroton Studio, June 14-16, 1991)* Hungaroton ▲ HCD 4003 [DDD]
Mozart, W.A.:Miserere, w. Ibolya Verebics (sop), Judit Németh (cta), József Mukk (ten), József Moldvay (bass), Gábor Oláh (bar/Gregorian intonations), János Reményi (cnd), Hungarian Radio-TV Children's Chorus Girls' Voices, Hungarian Radio-TV Male Chamber Choir *(rec Hungaroton Studio, June 14-16, 1991)* Hungaroton ▲ HCD 4003 [DDD]
Mozart, W.A.:Misericordias Domini, w. Ibolya Verebics (sop), Judit Németh (cta), József Mukk (ten), József Moldvay (bass), Gábor Oláh (bar/Gregorian intonations), János Reményi (cnd), Hungarian Radio-TV Children's Chorus Girls' Voices, Hungarian Radio-TV Male Chamber Choir *(rec Hungaroton Studio, June 14-16, 1991)* Hungaroton ▲ HCD 4003 [DDD]
Mozart, W.A.:Missa brevis, K.65, w. Ibolya Verebics (sop), Judit Németh (cta), József Mukk (ten), József Moldvay (bass), Gábor Oláh (bar/Gregorian intonations), János Reményi (cnd), Hungarian Radio-TV Children's Chorus Girls' Voices, Hungarian Radio-TV Male Chamber Choir *(rec Hungaroton Studio, June 14-16, 1991)* Hungaroton ▲ HCD 4003 [DDD]
Mozart, W.A.:Missa brevis, K.194, w. Ibolya Verebics (sop), Judit Németh (cta), József Mukk (ten), József Moldvay (b), Gábor Oláh (bar/Gregorian intonations), János Reményi (cnd), Hungarian Radio-TV Children's Chorus Girls' Voices, Hungarian Radio-TV Male Chamber Choir *(rec Hungaroton Studio, June 14-16, 1991)* Hungaroton ▲ HCD 4003 [DDD]
Mozart, W.A.:Sancta Maria, w. Ibolya Verebics (sop), Judit Németh (cta), József Mukk (ten), József Moldvay (bass), Gábor Oláh (bar/Gregorian intonations), János Reményi (cnd), Hungarian Radio-TV Children's Chorus Girls' Voices, Hungarian Radio-TV Male Chamber Choir *(rec Hungaroton Studio, June 14-16, 1991)* Hungaroton ▲ HCD 4003 [DDD]

Ella, Péter (hpd)
Bach, J.S.:Cant 147, w. Gergely Sárközy (va bastarda/lt), István Dénes (org)—chorale *(rec 1980, 1984 & 1991)* Hungaroton 2-▲ HCD 31616/17 [ADD/DDD]
Bach, J.S.:Sons Vl, BWV 1027-1029, w. Gergely Sárközy (va bastarda), István Dénes (org) *(rec 1980, 1984 & 1991)* Hungaroton 2-▲ HCD 31616/17 [ADD/DDD]
Telemann, G.P.:Fants Hpd Hungaroton 3-▲ HCD 31536/38 [DDD]

Ellegaard, Mogens (acc)
Bentzon, N.V.:In the Zoo Point ▲ PCD 5073 [DDD]
Nørgård, P.:Intro & Toccata Point ▲ PCD 5073 [DDD]
Pade, S.:Excursion with Detours Point ▲ PCD 5073 [DDD]
Schmidt, O.:Escape of the Meat-Ball over the Fence Point ▲ PCD 5073 [DDD]
Schmidt, O.:Sym Fant & Fugue Acc, w. O. Schmidt (cnd), Danish National RSO Point ▲ PCD 5073 [DDD]
Schmidt, O.:Toccata 1 Acc Point ▲ PCD 5073 [DDD]

Ellin, Vincent (bn)
Eckhardt-Gramatté, S.-C.:Con Bn, w. S. Streatfeild (cnd), Manitoba CO *(rec St. Matthews Anglican Church, Winnipeg, Manitoba, Sept. 4-9, 1994)* BIS ▲ CD 698 [DDD]

Elliott, Anthony (vc)
Kabalevsky, D.:Son Vc, w. R. Tomfohrdè (pno) Koch International Classics ▲ KIC 7064-2 [DDD]
Martinů, B.:Son 3 Vc, w. R. Tomfohrdè (pno) Koch International Classics ▲ KIC 7064-2 [DDD]
Shostakovich, D.:Son Vc, w. R. Tomfohrdè (pno) Koch International Classics ▲ KIC 7064-2 [DDD]

Elliott, Charles (db)
Wagner, R.:Siegfried Idyll, w. T. Holowach (vn), M. Skazinetsky (vn), L. Toman (va), R. Laurie (vc), S. Shulman (fl), T. Maloney (cl), J. Valdepenas (cl), J. Fetherston (cl), S. Mosher (bn), S. Wilson (hn), R. Cohen (hn), J. Cowell (tpt), G. Gould (cnd) *(rec July 27-29 & Sept. 8, 198)* Sony Classical ▲ SMK 52650 [ADD]

Elliott, Robert (hpd)
Purcell, H.:Songs, w. A. Deller (ct), R. Skeaping (vn), W. Kuijken (vl), J. Ryan (vl), W. Christie (hpd)—An Evening Hymn; Fairest Isle; From Rosy Bow'rs; I Attempt From Love's Sickness; If Music Be the Food of Love; Not All My Torments; O Lead Me to Some Peaceful Gloom; O Solitude; The Plaint; Retired From My Dear Astrea's Sight; Sweeter Than Roses; Thrice Happy Lovers *(rec April 1979)* Harmonia Mundi ▲ HML 590249

Elliott-Goldschmid, Ann (vn)—see ORCHESTRAS & ENSEMBLES Lafayette String Quartet
Ellis, G. (vn)—see ORCHESTRAS & ENSEMBLES Vanbrugh String Quartet

Ellis, James (vn)
Dussek, J.L.:Hp Music, w. Danielle Perrett (hp), Helen Verney (vc), Warwick Cole (pno), Gillian Jones (hand-hn)—A Favorite Duet for Hp & Pno, Op. 11; Son in E♭ for Hp, Op. 34/1; Favorite Son for Hp, Vn & Vc, Op. 37; Son in B♭ for Hp, Op. 34/2; Duo for Hp, Pno & Hand-Horn, Op. 38 Meridian ▲ MER 84244 [DDD]

Ellis, John (tpt)
Solo Pro:Contest Music for Trumpet, w. T. Lichtmann (cnd) Summit ■ DCD 103

Ellis, Osian (hp)
Alwyn, W.:Lyra Angelica, w. W. Alwyn (cnd), London PO Lyrita ▲ SRCD 230 [ADD]
Britten, H.:A Ceremony of Carols, w. Uwe Christian Harrer (cnd), Vienna Boys' Choir RCA Gold Seal ▲ 09026-68150-2 [ADD]

Ellis, Osian (hp) (cont.)
Britten, H.:Folksong Arrs, w. J. Shirley-Quirk (bar)—Bird scarers' song; Bonny at morn; Dafydd y Garreg en; Lemady; Lord! I married me a wife!; She's like the swallow Meridian ▲ 84119
Britten, H.:Suite Hp Meridian ▲ 84119
Bruch, M.:Scottish Fant Vn, w. Jascha Heifetz (vn), M. Sargent (cnd), London New SO *(rec Walthamstow Town Hall, London, May 15 & 22, 1961)* RCA Red Seal ▲ 09026-61745-2 [ADD]
Mathias, W.:Con Hp, w. D. Atherton (cnd), *(orch unknown)* Lyrita ▲ SRCD 325
Mozart, W.A.:Con Fl, Hp, w. William Bennett (fl), R. Leppard (cnd), English CO ASV ▲ ASV 532

Ellis, Robert (ob)
Hanson, H.:Pastorale Ob, w. Susan Jolles (hp), G. Schwarz (cnd), Seattle SO Delos 4-▲ DE 3150 [DDD]
Hanson, H.:Pastorale Ob, w. Susan Jolles (hp), G. Schwarz (cnd), Seattle SO Delos ▲ DE 3105 [DDD]

Ellis, S. (uillean pipes)
Cage, J.:Roaratorio:An Irish Circus on Finnegans Wake, w. J. Cage (voice), J. Heaney (sgr), P. Glackin (fid), M. Mercier (bodrhan), P. Mercier (bodrhan), M. Mallory (fl) Mode 2-▲ mode 28/29
Cage, J.:Roaratorio:An Irish Circus on Finnegans Wake, w. J. Cage (voice), J. Heaney (sgr), P. Glackin (fid), M. Mercier (bodrhan), P. Mercier (bodrhan), M. Mallory (fl) Wergo ▲ WER 6303-2

Ellsasser, Richard (org)
Widor, C.M.:Sym 5 Org Elektra/Nonesuch ■ N5-71210

Ellsworth, Ann (hn)—see ORCHESTRAS & ENSEMBLES Missouri Brass Quintet

Elman, Mischa (vn)
The Acoustic Solo Recordings *(rec 1910-24)* Biddulph 4-▲ LAB 035-038 [ADD]
Bach, J.S.:Cons Vn (comp), w. V. Golschmann (cnd), Vienna State Opera CO—No. 2 *(rec June 1960)* Vanguard Classics ▲ OVC 8033 [ADD]
Bach, J.S.:Con 2 Vn, w. J. Barbirolli (cnd), *(orch unknown)* *(rec 1933)* Pearl ▲ PEA 9388 (m) [AAD]
Encore Pieces for Violin & Piano *(rec 1930-33)* Pearl ▲ PEA 9388 (m) [AAD]
Favorite Encores, w. Elman, Mischa (vn), Joseph Sieger (pno) *(rec 1959 & 1966)* Vanguard Classics ▲ OVC 8029
Grieg, E.:Albumblade, Op. 28, w. L. Mittman (pno) [trans. for violin & piano]—No. 3 in A *(rec 1947)* RCA Red Seal ▲ 09026-61826-2
Hebrew & Russian Melodies, w. Joseph Seiger (pno) *(rec 1959, 1962 & 1966)* Vanguard Classics ▲ OVC 8030 [ADD]
Khachaturian, A.:Con Vn, w. V. Golschmann (cnd), Vienna State Opera Orch *(rec 1959)* Vanguard Classics ▲ OVC 8035 [ADD]
Kreisler, F.:Vn Pieces, w. Joseph Sieger (pno)—Caprice viennois; La Gitana; Liebesfreud; Rondino on a Theme of Beethoven; Schön Rosmarin; 4 arrs. of works by Dvořák *(Slavonic Dances 1 & 2; Slavonic Fantasie in b)* & Tartini *(Variations on a Theme of Corelli)*; 7 works in the styles of other composers *(Allegretto in the style of Boccherini; La précieuse...Couperin; Sicilienne & Rigaudon...Francoeur; Malagueña...Granados; Andantino...Martini; Preghiera...Martini; Preludium & Allegro...Pugnani)* *(rec 1960 & 1966)* Vanguard Classics ▲ OVC 8028
Lalo, E.:Sym espagnole, w. V. Golschmann (cnd), Vienna State Opera Orch *(rec 1959)* Vanguard Classics ▲ OVC 8034 [ADD]
Mendelssohn, F.:Con in e Vn & Orch, Op. 64, w. V. Golschmann (cnd), Vienna State Opera Orch *(rec 1959)* Vanguard Classics ▲ OVC 8034 [ADD]
Nardini, P.:Con Vn, w. V. Golschmann (cnd), Vienna State Opera CO *(rec June 1960)* Vanguard Classics ▲ OVC 8033 [ADD]
The Recordings with Frances Alda, Enrico Caruso, & String Quartet Biddulph ▲ LAB 039 [ADD]
Saint-Saëns, C.:Introduction & Rondo capriccioso, w. V. Golschmann (cnd), Vienna State Opera Orch *(rec 1959)* Vanguard Classics ▲ OVC 8035 [ADD]
Tchaikovsky, P.:Con Vn, w. J. Barbirolli (cnd), London SO *(rec 1929 for HMV)* Pearl ▲ GEMMCD 9388 (m) [AAD]
Vivaldi, A.:Cons Vn (misc), w. V. Golschmann (cnd), Vienna State Opera CO *(rec June 1960)* Vanguard Classics ▲ OVC 8033 [ADD]

Elmassian, Jeff (cl)—see ORCHESTRAS & ENSEMBLES Viklarbo Chamber Ensemble

Elmiger, Roger (vn)
Albicastro, H.:Son Vn, Op. 5/3, w. M. Mitrani (hpd) Gallo ▲ CD 625 [ADD]
Bach, J.S.:Sons Vn, w. M. Mitrani (hpd)—BWV 1021, 1023 & 1024 Gallo ▲ CD 694 [ADD]
Bonporti, F.A.:Invenzioni (10) de camera, w. M. Mitrani (hpd)—Nos. 1, 3, 4, 8, 9, & 10 Gallo ▲ CD 693 [ADD]
Bonporti, F.A.:Invenzioni (10) de camera, w. M. Mitrani (hpd)—Nos. 2, 5, 6, & 7 Gallo ▲ CD 694 [ADD]
Burkhard, W.:Sonatine Vn, w. M. Mitrani (hpd) Gallo ▲ CD 625 [ADD]
Burkhard, W.:Suite en miniature Vn, w. M. Mitrani (hpd) Gallo ▲ CD 625 [ADD]
Fritz, G.:Son Vn, Op. 2/4, w. M. Mitrani (pno) Gallo ▲ CD 625 [ADD]
Honegger, A.:Sons Vn—Sonata for Solo Violin (1940) Gallo ▲ CD 625 [ADD]
Milhaud, D.:Sailor Song, w. M. Mitrani (hpd) Gallo ▲ CD 585 [AAD]
Milhaud, D.:Son Vn & Hpd, Op. 144, w. M. Mitrani (hpd) Gallo ▲ CD 585 [AAD]
Milhaud, D.:Son Vn & Hpd, Op. 257, w. M. Mitrani (hpd) Gallo ▲ CD 585 [AAD]
Milhaud, D.:Sonatine pastorale Gallo ▲ CD 585 [AAD]
Rieti, V.:Son breve, w. M. Mitrani (hpd) Gallo ▲ CD 585 [AAD]
Segond, P.:Petite sérénade, w. M. Mitrani (hpd) Gallo ▲ CD 625 [ADD]
Vivaldi, A.:Sons Vn, w. M. Mitrani (hpd)—RV.5, 10, 14, 15, 17a, 21, 26, & 35 *(rec July 1987)* Gallo ▲ CD 526
Vivaldi, A.:Sons Vn, w. M. Mitrani (hpd)—(6) RV.2, 3, 12, 28, 29 & 34 Gallo ▲ CD 602 [AAD]

Elms, Roderick (org)
Britten, H.:War Requiem, w. H. Harper (sop), P. Langridge (ten), J. Shirley-Quirk (bar), R. Hickox (cnd), London SO, London Sym Chorus, St. Paul's Cathedral Choristers [E,L] Chandos 2-▲ CHAN 8983/84 [DDD]

Elms, Roderick (pno)
Addinsell, R.:Music of, w. Philip Martin (pno), K. Alwyn (cnd), BBC Concert Orch—Theme from Goodbye Mr. Chips; Invitation Waltz [from Ring Round the Moon]; The Smokey Mountains (con.); The Isle of Apples; The Prince & the Showgirl (sel.); Tom Brown's Schooldays [Ov.]; Festival; Journey to Romance; Fire Over England (suite); Theme from A Tale of Two Cities *(rec Golders Green Hippodrome, London, Apr. 20 & 21, 1994)* Marco Polo ("British Light Music" series) ▲ 8.223732 [DDD]
Martin, F.:Ballade Pno, w. M. Bamert (cnd), London PO Chandos ▲ CHAN 9380 [DDD]

Els, S. van (va)
Britten, H.:Phantasy Qt, w. P. Oosternrijk (ob), M. Mars (vn), J. Insinger (vc) Channel Classics ▲ CCS 9326 [DDD]
White, J.:Poem, w. P. Oosternrijk (ob), D. Kuyken (pno) Channel Classics ▲ CCS 9326 [DDD]

Elsing, E. (vc)
Krenek, E.:Capriccio Vc, w. J. Stephens (cnd), American Camerata AmCam ▲ ACR 10305CD
Lebaron, A.:Noh Reflections, w. H. Fujiwara (vn), M. Kawasaki (va), Kennedy Center Theater Chamber Players Mode ▲ 30

Elsner, Helma (hpd)
Bach, J.S.:Chromatic Fant & Fugue Allegretto ▲ ACD 8007 [ADD] ■ ACS 8007
Bach, J.S.:Fants Hpd—BWV 906 Allegretto ▲ ACD 8007 [ADD] ■ ACS 8007
Bach, J.S.:Italian Con Allegretto ▲ ACD 8007 [ADD] ■ ACS 8007
Bach, J.S.:Preludes Hpd, BWV 933-38, "Little Preludes" Allegretto ▲ ACD 8007 [ADD] ■ ACS 8007
Bach, J.S.:Toccatas Hpd, BWV 910-16—BWV 911 Allegretto ▲ ACD 8007 [ADD] ■ ACS 8007

Elsner, K. (thb)—see ORCHESTRAS & ENSEMBLES Musica Secreta
Elson, Margret (pno)—see ORCHESTRAS & ENSEMBLES Elson-Swarthout Duo
Emanuel, Carol (hp)—see also ORCHESTRAS & ENSEMBLES Musicians' Accord members
Zorn, J.:Redbird, w. Jill Jaffee (va), Erik Friedlander (vc), Jim Pugliese (perc) Tzadik ▲ TZA 7008 [DDD]

Emelianoff, André (vc)
Levinson, G.:Dreamlight, w. P. Basquin (pno), P. Hostetter (perc), B. Ramirez (perc) CRI ▲ CD 642 [DDD]
Ran, S.:Private Game, w. L. Flax (cl) *(rec 1979-91)* CRI ▲ CD 609 [ADD/DDD]
Tower, J.:Très lent, w. Joan Tower (pno) *(rec American Academy of Arts & Letters, New York City, Sept. 26-28, 1994)* New World ▲ 80470-2

INSTRUMENT.

Emery, Deborah Dewolf (pno)
Hindemith, P.:Son Tpt, w. Charles Schlueter (tpt) *(rec Symphony Hall, Boston, MA, Sept. 1994)* Vox Classics ▲ VOX 7513 [DDD]

Emler, Andy (pno)
Constant, M.:Choruses & Interludes, w. Jean-Jacques Justafre (hn), Pierre-Marie Bonafosse (sax), François Moutin (b gtr), Pierre Guignon (dr), J. Kaltenbach (cnd), Nancy SO *(rec Salle Poirel, Nancy, Apr. 4, 1990)* Erato ▲ 94815-2 [DDD]

Emmons, Scott (trbn)
Shewan, S.:Magnificat, w. Erin Stedman (sop), Kimberly Higgins (alt), Robert Dingman (ten), Alexander Burgess (bar), Paul Shewan (tpt), Barbara Hull (tpt), Nanita Wilson (hn), Kirk Kettinger (tuba), Ann Musser Honeywell (org) Albany ▲ TROY 149 [DDD]
Shewan, S.:The Voice of the Lord in the Storm, w. Erin Stedman (sop), Kimberly Higgins (alt), Robert Dingman (ten), Alexander Burgess (bar), Paul Shewan (tpt), Barbara Hull (tpt), Nanita Wilson (hn), Kirk Kettinger (tuba), Ann Musser Honeywell (org) Albany ▲ TROY 149 [DDD]

Enderle, Matthias (vn)—see ORCHESTRAS & ENSEMBLES Carmina String Quartet

Endo, Ikuko (pno)
Yashiro, A.:Son Pno Camerata ▲ 30CM 50

Endo, Yoshiko (pno)—see ORCHESTRAS & ENSEMBLES Rogeri Trio

Endres, Michael (pno)
Schubert, Franz:Son Pno, D.537 Capriccio ▲ 10 717 [DDD]
Schubert, Franz:Son Pno, D.568 Capriccio ▲ 10 717 [DDD]
Schubert, Franz:Son Pno, D.840 Capriccio ▲ 10 717 [DDD]
Schubert, Franz:Son Pno, D.845 *(rec West German Radio, Cologne, Jan 14 & Feb 23, 1994)* Capriccio ▲ 10 707 [DDD]
Schubert, Franz:Son Pno, D.850 *(rec West German Radio, Cologne, Jan 14 & Feb 23, 1994)* Capriccio ▲ 10 707 [DDD]

Enescu, George (vn)
Chausson, E.:Poème Vn, w. Sanford Schlüssel (pno) [arr for vn & pno] *(rec ca 1928)* Symposium ▲ 1156
Chausson, E.:Poème Vn, w. Sanford Schlüssel (pno) *(rec 1929)* Biddulph ▲ LAB 066 [ADD]
The Complete Solo Columbia Recordings, w. Edward C. Harris (pno), Yehudi Menuhin (pno), Hepzibah Menuhin (pno), Sanford Schlüssel (pno) *(rec 1924 & 1929)* Biddulph ▲ LAB 066 [ADD]
Great Composers at the Keyboard, w. Sergei Prokofiev (pno), Alfredo Casella (pno) Foné ▲ FON 90F15 [DDD]

Engegard, A. (vn)—see ORCHESTRAS & ENSEMBLES Orlando String Quartet

Engel, J. (bgp)
Mozart, L.:Bauernhochzeit, w. M. Engel (h-g), H. Stadlmair (cnd), Munich CO Orfeo ▲ 033821 [DDD]

Engel, Karl (pno)
Brahms, J.:Liebeslieder Waltzes SATB, w. E. Mathis (sop), B. Fassbaender (mez), P. Schreier (ten), D. Fischer-Dieskau (bar), W. Sawallisch (pno) [G] Deutsche Grammophon ▲ 423133-2 [DDD]
Brahms, J.:Neue Liebeslieder Waltzes, w. E. Mathis (sop), B. Fassbaender (mez), P. Schreier (ten), D. Fischer-Dieskau (bar), W. Sawallisch (pno) [G] Deutsche Grammophon ▲ 423133-2 [DDD]
Brahms, J.:Son Bn, w. Milan Turkovic (bn) Camerata ▲ 32CM 66
Goethe Lieder:Songs on Texts by Johann Wolfgang von Goethe, w. D. Fischer-Dieskau (bar) *(rec live, Stockholm, 1970)* Orfeo d'or ▲ 389951 (m) [ADD]
Ibert, J.:Carignane, w. Milan Turkovic (bn) Camerata ▲ 32CM 66
Les introuvables de Dietrich Fischer-Dieskau, w. D. Fischer-Dieskau (bar), Hertha Klust (pno), Gerald Moore (pno), Aribert Reimann (pno), Robert Veyron-Lacroix (hpd) EMI Classics 6-▲ CDZF 68509
Mendelssohn, F.:Songs, w. P. Schreier (ten)—Auf Flügeln des Gesanges, Op. 34/2; Schilflied, Op. 71; Der Mond, Op. 86/5; Pagenlied; Im Frühling, Op. 9/4; Reiselied, Op. 34/6; Allnächtlich im Traume, Op. 86/4; Venezianisches Gondellied, Op. 57/5; An die Entfernte, Op. 71/3; Frühlingslied, Op. 19/1; Minnelied, Op. 34/1; Lieblingsplätzchen, Op. 99/3; Winterlied, Op. 19/3; Gruss, Op. 19/5; Das erste Veilchen, Op. 19/2; Da lieg ich unter den Bäumen, Op. 84/1; Minnelied, Op. 47/1; Morgengruss, Op. 47/2; Auf der Wanderschaft, Op. 71/5; Nachtlied, Op. 71/6; Hirtenlied, Op. 57/2; Frühlingslied, Op. 47/3; Neue Liebe, Op. 19/4; Andres Maienlied, Op. 8/8 *(rec Oct. 1993)* Berlin Classics ▲ BER 1107-2 [DDD]
Mozart, W.A.:Songs, w. Edith Mathis (sop) Novalis ▲ 150010 [DDD]
Saint-Saëns, C.:Son Bn, w. Milan Turkovic (bn) Camerata ▲ 32CM 66
Schubert, Franz:Der Hirt auf dem Felsen, w. E. Mathis (sop), K. Weber (cl) [G] Novalis ▲ 150026 [DDD]
Schubert, Franz:Songs (misc), w. D. Fischer-Dieskau (bar), G. Moore (pno)—37 songs *(rec 1958-65)* EMI Classics ("Studio" series) 2-▲ CDMB 63566 [ADD]
Schubert, Franz:Songs (misc), w. E. Mathis (sop)—18 songs [G] Novalis ▲ 150026 [DDD]
Schumann, R.:Romances Ob, w. Milan Turkovic (bn) Camerata ▲ 32CM 66

Engel, M. (h-g)
Mozart, L.:Bauernhochzeit, w. J. Engel (bgp), H. Stadlmair (cnd), Munich CO Orfeo ▲ 033821 [DDD]

Engel, Wilfrid (va)—see ORCHESTRAS & ENSEMBLES Capella Clementina

Engelman, R. (perc)—see ORCHESTRAS & ENSEMBLES Nexus

Engerer, Brigette (pno)
Beethoven, L. van:Bagatelle, WoO 59, "Für Elise" Harmonia Mundi Plus ▲ HMP 3901346
Beethoven, L. van:Rondos Pno, Op. 51 Harmonia Mundi Plus ▲ HMP 3901346
Beethoven, L. van:Son 31 Pno Harmonia Mundi Plus ▲ HMP 3901346
Beethoven, L. van:Son 7 Vn, w. Olivier Charlier (vn) Harmonia Mundi France ▲ HMC 901580
Beethoven, L. van:Son 8 Vn, w. Olivier Charlier (vn) Harmonia Mundi France ▲ HMC 901580
Beethoven, L. van:Son 9 Vn, "Kreutzer", w. Olivier Charlier (vn) Harmonia Mundi France ▲ HMC 901580
Beethoven, L. van:Vars on an Original Theme, Op. 76 Harmonia Mundi Plus ▲ HMP 3901346
Chopin, F.:Nocturnes—Opp. 9, 15, 27, 32 Harmonia Mundi ("Suite" series) ▲ 7901430
Liszt, F.:Song Transcriptions—Geheimes Flüstern; Er ist's; Frülingsnacht; Liebeslied Harmonia Mundi ▲ 901600
Mussorgsky, M.:Pictures Harmonia Mundi ("Suite" series) ▲ 7901266
Rachmaninoff, S.:Duets Pno 4-Hands, w. O. Maisenberg (pno) Harmonia Mundi France 2-▲ HMC 901301/02
Rachmaninoff, S.:Pno Music (2 pnos & pno 4- & 6-hands), w. O. Maisenberg (pno)—Polka italienne; Romance in G; *(4 hands)*; Valse; Romance *(6-hands, w. 3rd pianist Elena Bachkirova)* Harmonia Mundi France 2-▲ HMC 901301/02
Rachmaninoff, S.:Russian Rhap, w. O. Maisenberg (pno) Harmonia Mundi France 2-▲ HMC 901301/02
Rachmaninoff, S.:Suite 1 for 2 Pnos, w. O. Maisenberg (pno) Harmonia Mundi France 2-▲ HMC 901301/02
Rachmaninoff, S.:Suite 2 for 2 Pnos, w. O. Maisenberg (pno) Harmonia Mundi France 2-▲ HMC 901301/02
Rachmaninoff, S.:Symphonic Dances, w. O. Maisenberg (pno) Harmonia Mundi France 2-▲ HMC 901301/02
Ravel, M.:Berceuse sur le nom de Gabriel Fauré, w. R. Pasquier (vn) Harmonia Mundi France ▲ HMC 901364
Ravel, M.:Kaddisch, w. R. Pasquier (vn) Harmonia Mundi France ▲ HMC 901364
Ravel, M.:Pièce en forme de Habanera, w. R. Pasquier (vn) [Fritz Kreisler trans. for violin & piano] Harmonia Mundi France ▲ HMC 901364
Ravel, M.:Son Vn Pno, w. R. Pasquier (vn) Harmonia Mundi France ▲ HMC 901364
Ravel, M.:Sonate posthume, w. R. Pasquier (vn) Harmonia Mundi France ▲ HMC 901364
Ravel, M.:Tzigane, w. R. Pasquier (vn) Harmonia Mundi France ▲ HMC 901364
Schumann, R.:Carnaval Pno Harmonia Mundi ▲ 901600
Schumann, R.:Con Pno, w. E. Krivine (cnd), Royal PO *(rec Nov. 14-16, 1991)* Denon ▲ CO 75290 [DDD]
Schumann, R.:Kinderszenen Harmonia Mundi ▲ 901600
Schumann, R.:Romances Ob, w. O. Charlier (ob) [trans. for violin & piano] Harmonia Mundi France ▲ HMC 901405

Engerer, Brigette (pno) (cont.)
Schumann, R.:Son 1 Vn, w. O. Charlier (vn) Harmonia Mundi France ▲ HMC 901405
Schumann, R.:Son 2 Vn, w. O. Charlier (vn) Harmonia Mundi France ▲ HMC 901405
Tchaikovsky, P.:Con 1 Pno, w. E. Krivine (cnd), Royal PO *(rec Nov. 14-16, 1991)* Denon ▲ CO 75290 [DDD]

Englert, Carolyn (ob)
Alexander, W.:Cambridge Trio, w. J. Russo (cl), L. Walton Ignacio (pno) CRS ▲ CD 8949

Englhardt, W. (org)
French Music for Choir & 2 Organs, w. Munich Madrigal Choir [cnd:Franz Brandl], E. Sperer (org) FSM ▲ 97735 [DDD]

Englichova, Katerina (hp)
Rorem, N.:Studies for 11, w. E. Ostling (fl), K. Lord (ob), G. Raden (cl), J. Sutte (tpt), S. Copes (vn), C.-J. Chang (va), J. Lastrapes (vc), R. Uchida (pno), A. LaFargue (perc), R. Laveille (perc), R. Milanov (cnd) New World ▲ 80445-2

English, John (tpt)
Banfield, W.:Sym 6, "4 Songs for 5 American Voices", w. Jack Schantz (tpt), A. Balter (cnd), Akron SO *(rec Masonic Auditorium, Cleveland, OH, Feb 22, 1994)* Telarc ▲ CD 80409 [DDD]

Englund, Karen (hpd)
Biber, H. von:Mystery (or Rosary) Sons, w. Troels Svendsen (vn) or Wim ten Have (vn)—No. 4 *(rec Strandmarks Church, Copenhagen, Denmark, Sept 1994)* Rondo Gramophon ▲ RCD 8343 [DDD]
Biber, H. von:Son à 3 for 2 Vns, B Trbn, w. Troels Svendsen (vn), Wim ten Have (vn), Mogens Andresen (b trbn) *(rec Strandmarks Church, Copenhagen, Denmark, Sept 1994)* Rondo Gramophon ▲ RCD 8343 [DDD]
Clarke, J.:The Prince of Denmark's March *(rec Strandmarks Church, Copenhagen, Denmark, Sept 1994)* Rondo Gramophon ▲ RCD 8343 [DDD]
Marini, B.:Sons, Syms & Retornelli, w. Mogens Andresen (b trbn), Mogens Rasmussen (vl)—Son *(rec Strandmarks Church, Copenhagen, Denmark, Sept 1994)* Rondo Gramophon ▲ RCD 8343 [DDD]
Purcell, H.:Pavans, Z.748-751, w. Troels Svendsen (vn), Wim ten Have (vn)—in B♭, Z.750 *(rec Strandmarks Church, Copenhagen, Denmark, Sept 1994)* Rondo Gramophon ▲ RCD 8343 [DDD]
Purcell, H.:Suites Hpd—in g, Z.661 *(rec Strandmarks Church, Copenhagen, Denmark, Sept 1994)* Rondo Gramophon ▲ RCD 8343 [DDD]
Schmelzer, J.H.:Polish Bagpipes, w. Troels Svendsen (vn), Wim ten Have (vn) *(rec Strandmarks Church, Copenhagen, Denmark, Sept 1994)* Rondo Gramophon ▲ RCD 8343 [DDD]
Telemann, G.P.:Son Polonese, w. Troels Svendsen (vn), Wim ten Have (va) *(rec Strandmarks Church, Copenhagen, Denmark, Sept 1994)* Rondo Gramophon ▲ RCD 8343 [DDD]

Engström, Anders (bn)
Berwald, F.:Konsertstycke Bn, w. T. Svedlund (cnd), Gothenburg SO Intim Musik ▲ INT 15 [DDD]
Brendler, E.:Divertissement Bn, w. T. Svedlund (cnd), Gothenburg SO Intim Musik ▲ INT 15 [DDD]
Crusell, B.H.:Concertino Bn, w. T. Svedlund (cnd), Gothenburg SO Intim Musik ▲ INT 15 [DDD]
Fernström, J.:Concertino Bn, w. T. Svedlund (cnd), Gothenburg SO Intim Musik ▲ INT 15 [DDD]

Enoch, Naomi (vc)
Martin, F.:Sonnets à Cassandre, w. U. Mayer-Reinach (mez), A. Sella (fl), G. Lewertoff (va) Gallo ▲ CD 633 [DDD]

Enoksson, Per (vn)
Aulin, T.:Son Vn, w. A. Kilström (pno) Musica Sveciae ▲ MSCD 608

Enslow, Ridley (fid)
Foster, S.C.:Songs, w. J. Baird (sop), L. Russell (alt/mountain dulcimer), F. Urrey (ten), J. Van Buskirk (pno)—The Glendy Burke; Nelly Was a Lady; Melinda May; The Soirée Polka; The Moustache Song; O Willie, Is It You, Dear?; Mr. & Mr Albany ▲ TROY 119

Entremont, Philippe (pno)
Bartók, B.:Con 2 Pno, w. L. Bernstein (cnd), New York PO Sony Classical ▲ SMK 47511 [ADD]
Bartók, B.:Con 3 Pno, w. L. Bernstein (cnd), New York PO Sony Classical ▲ SMK 47511 [ADD]
Bartók, B.:Con for 2 Pnos, w. L. Bernstein (cnd), New York PO Sony Classical ▲ SMK 47511 [ADD]
Chopin, F.:Ballades Pno (comp) Odyssey 2-▲ MB2K 45670
Chopin, F.:Preludes, Op. 28 *(rec Switzerland, Feb 2-5, 1970)* Sony Classical ("Essential Classics" series) ▲ SBK 62415 [ADD] ■ SBT 62415
Chopin, F.:Scherzos Odyssey 2-▲ MB2K 45670
Chopin, F.:Waltzes Odyssey 2-▲ MB2K 45670
Debussy, C.:Pno Music (misc)—Children's Corner Suite; Clair de lune; Deux Arabesques; Images I & II Sony Classical (Essential Classics) ▲ SBK 48174 ■ SBT 48174
Dvořák, A.:Qnt Pno, Op. 81, w. Vienna CO Soloists Pro Arte ▲ CDD 470 [DDD]
Franck, C.:Symphonic Vars, w. C. Dutoit (cnd), Philharmonia Orch *(rec 1981)* Odyssey ▲ MBK 46276 [AAD]
Gershwin, G.:Con Pno, w. E. Ormandy (cnd), Philadelphia Orch CBS 2-▲ MGT 30073
Gershwin, G.:Con Pno, w. E. Ormandy (cnd), Philadelphia Orch Sony Classical ("Essential Classics" series) ▲ SBK 46338 [ADD] ■ SBT 46338
Gershwin, G.:Rhap in Blue, w. E. Ormandy (cnd), Philadelphia Orch CBS 2-▲ MGT 30073
Gershwin, G.:Rhap in Blue, w. E. Ormandy (cnd), Philadelphia Orch Odyssey ■ YT 35496
Grieg, E.:Con Pno, Op. 16, w. E. Ormandy (cnd), Philadelphia Orch CBS ▲ MYK 37805 [ADD] ■ MYT 37805
Grieg, E.:Con Pno, Op. 16, w. E. Ormandy (cnd), Philadelphia Orch CBS ▲ MLK 39435 [ADD] ■ MT 39435
Grieg, E.:Con Pno, Op. 16, w. E. Ormandy (cnd), Philadelphia Orch Sony Classical ("Essential Classics" series) ▲ SBK 46543 [ADD] ■ SBT 46543
Liszt, F.:Cons Pno, w. E. Ormandy (cnd), Philadelphia Orch Sony Classical ("Essential Classics" series) ▲ SBK 48167 [ADD] ■ SBT 48167
Liszt, F.:Fant on Hungarian Folk Tunes, w. S. Ozawa (cnd), New Philharmonia Orch Sony Classical ("Essential Classics" series) ▲ SBK 48167 [ADD] ■ SBT 48167
Mendelssohn, F.:Con in d Vn, Pno & Strs, w. O. Rudner (vn), Vienna CO Koch Schwann ▲ CD 311047 [DDD] ■ MC 211047 (D)
Mozart, W.A.:Con 12 Pno, w. P. Entremont (cnd), Vienna CO *(rec June 1985)* Koch Schwann ▲ 311157 G1 [DDD]
Mozart, W.A.:Con 14 Pno, w. P. Entremont (cnd), Vienna CO *(rec June 1985)* Koch Schwann ▲ 311157 G1 [DDD]
Mozart, W.A.:Fant Pno, K.397 Pro Arte ▲ CDD 469 [DDD]
Mozart, W.A.:Fant Pno, K.475 Pro Arte ▲ CDD 3411
Mozart, W.A.:Music of, w. Szell (cnd), Cleveland Orch, *(sels unknown)* CBS ▲ MLK 39436 ■ MT 39436
Mozart, W.A.:Qts Pno, w. Vienna CO Soloists Pro Arte ▲ CDD 469 [DDD]
Mozart, W.A.:Sons Pno—Nos. 4, 5, 7, 8 & 15 Pro Arte ▲ CDD 498
Mozart, W.A.:Sons Pno—Nos. 3,9,14,16 Pro Arte ▲ CDD 3411
Mozart, W.A.:Sons Pno—Nos. 10-12 & 17 Pro Arte ▲ CDD 499
Mozart, W.A.:Sons Pno—Nos. 1,2,6,13 Pro Arte ▲ CDD 3410
Rachmaninoff, S.:Con 1 Pno, w. E. Ormandy (cnd), Philadelphia Orch Sony Classical ("Essential Classics" series) ▲ SBK 46541 [ADD] ■ SBT 46541
Rachmaninoff, S.:Con 2 Pno, w. L. Bernstein (cnd), New York PO Odyssey ▲ MBK 46271 [AAD] ■ YT 46271
Rachmaninoff, S.:Con 2 Pno, w. L. Bernstein (cnd), New York PO *(rec Feb. 3, 1960)* Sony Classical ("Essential Classics" series) ▲ SBK 53512 [ADD] ■ SBT 53512
Rachmaninoff, S.:Con 4 Pno, w. E. Ormandy (cnd), Philadelphia Orch Sony Classical ("Essential Classics" series) ▲ SBK 46541 [ADD] ■ SBT 46541
Rachmaninoff, S.:Music of, w. Gary Graffman (pno), E. Ormandy (cnd), Philadelphia Orch CBS ▲ MLK 39437 ■ MT 39437
Rachmaninoff, S.:Preludes Pno, Opp 23 & 32—Nos. 2,5 & 12 Odyssey ▲ MBK 46271 [AAD] ■ YT 46271
Rachmaninoff, S.:Rhapsody on a Theme of Paganini, w. E. Ormandy (cnd), Philadelphia Orch Odyssey ▲ MBK 46271 [AAD] ■ YT 46271
Ravel, M.:Con Pno (left hand), w. P. Boulez (cnd), Cleveland Orch Sony Classical ("Essential Classics" series) ▲ SBK 46338 [ADD] ■ SBT 46338

▲ = CD ♦ = Enhanced CD △ = MD ■ = Cassette Tape □ = DCC

Entremont, Philippe (pno) (cont.)
Ravel, M.:Con in G Pno, w. P. Boulez (cnd), Cleveland Orch
Sony Classical ("Essential Classics" series) ▲ SBK 46338 [ADD] ■ SBT 46338
Ravel, M.:Pno Music—Pavane pour une Infante défunte; A la manière de...; Sonatine; Miroirs; Ma mère l'Oye; Habanera; Jeux d'eau *(rec 1974)*
Sony Classical ("Essential Classics" series) 2-▲ SB2K 53528 [ADD]
Saint-Saëns, C.:Cons Pno (comp), w. M. Plasson (cnd), Toulouse Capitole Orch
Odyssey 2-▲ MB2K 45624
Saint-Saëns, C.:Con 2 Pno, w. E. Ormandy (cnd), Philadelphia Orch
CBS ▲ MYK 37805 [ADD] ■ MYT 37805
Saint-Saëns, C.:Con 2 Pno, w. E. Ormandy (cnd), Philadelphia Orch *(rec 1964)*
Sony Classical ("Essential Classics" series) ▲ SBK 48276 [ADD] ■ SBT 48276
Saint-Saëns, C.:Con 4 Pno, w. E. Ormandy (cnd), Philadelphia Orch *(rec 1961)*
Sony Classical ("Essential Classics" series) ▲ SBK 48276 [ADD] ■ SBT 48276
Satie, E.:Pno Music (misc), w. D. Varsano (pno)
Sony Classical ("Essential Classics" series) ▲ SBK 48283 [ADD] ■ SBT 48283
Schubert, Franz:Qnt Pno, D.667, w. Vienna CO Soloists — Pro Arte ▲ CDD 470 [DDD]
Schumann, R.:Qnt Pno, w. Alban Berg String Quartet — EMI Classics ▲ CDC 55593
Viotti, G.B.:Con 3 Pno, w. O. Rudner (vn), Vienna CO
Koch Schwann ▲ CD 311047 [DDD] ■ MC 211047 (D)

Ephrikaim, Angelo (vn)
Vivaldi, A.:Sons Vn, Op. 5, w. F. Fantini (vn), M. Ferarris (vn), A. Pocaterra (vc), G. Ghetti (vc), I. De Carli (cembalo), V. Luccini (cembalo) — Rivoalto ▲ CRA 9005 [ADD]

Epp, Peter (baroque tpt)
Bach Trumpet Gala, Vol. 1, w. Arnold Mehl (baroque tpt), Rudolf Ulrich (baroque tpt), Munich Bach Trumpet Ensemble, Franz Lehrndorfer (org) — Ars Musici ▲ 0869

Epperson, Anne (pno)
Bloch, E.:Abodah, "God's Worship", w. P. Berman (vn) — Koch International Classics ▲ KIC 7116 [DDD]
Bloch, E.:Baal Shem, "3 Pictures of Chassidic Life", w. P. Berman (vn)
Koch International Classics ▲ KIC 7116 [DDD]
Brahms, J.:Son 1 Cl, w. W. Ludwig (bn) [trans for bn & pno] — Centaur ▲ CRC 2130
Prokofiev, S.:Son Fl, w. W. Ludwig (bn) [bassoon & piano trans.] — Centaur ▲ CRC 2130
Schumann, R.:Fantasiestücke Cl, w. W. Ludwig (bn) [bassoon & piano trans.] — Centaur ▲ CRC 2130
Ward, R.:Son 1 Vn, w. Vartan Manoogian (vn) — Albany ▲ TROY 204 [DDD]

Epperson, Bryan (vc)
Fossa, F. de:Trios, Op. 18, w. S. Wynberg (gtr), M. Beaver (vn) *(rec St. John's Church, Elora, Ontario, Mar. 23–25, 1993)* — Naxos ▲ 8.550760 [DDD]

Epperson, Eugenia (fl)
Constantinides, D.:Vocal Music, w. Cynthia Dewey (nar), Angela DeVerger (sop), Evelyn Petros (sop), Susan Faust Straley (sop), Richard Jernigan (cl), Kelly Smith Toney (vn), Hye-Yun Chung (hp), Stephen Brown (pno), John Raush (perc), D. Constantinides (cnd), Louisiana State Univ New Music Ensemble—Reflections IV for Sop, Fl, Hp & Pno; Intimations [1 Act Opera]; 4 Songs on Poems by Sappho; Mutability for Sop & Str Qt.; 4 Greek Songs — Vestige ▲ 04

Epperson, Gordon (vc)
Barber, S.:Son Vc, w. Frances Burnett (pno) *(rec Bryan Hall, Moore College of Musical Arts, Bowling Green State Univ, Bowling Green, OH, Aug 2–3, 1994)* — Centaur ▲ CRC 2275 [DDD]
Bartók, B.:Rhap 1 Vc, w. Frances Burnett (pno) *(rec Bryan Hall, Moore College of Musical Arts, Bowling Green State Univ, Bowling Green, OH, Aug 2–3, 1994)* — Centaur ▲ CRC 2275 [DDD]
Bavicchi, J.:Son 2 Vc, w. Frances Burnett (pno) *(rec Bryan Hall, Moore College of Musical Arts, Bowling Green State Univ, Bowling Green, OH, Aug 2–3, 1994)* — Centaur ▲ CRC 2275 [DDD]
Martinů, B.:Son 2 Vc, w. Frances Burnett (pno) *(rec Bryan Hall, Moore College of Musical Arts, Bowling Green State Univ, Bowling Green, OH, Aug 2–3, 1994)* — Centaur ▲ CRC 2275 [DDD]

Epstein, E. (pno)
Dvořák, A.:Slavonic Dances (sels), w. Igor Politkovsky (vn)—Op. 46/2 [trans F. Kreisler for vn & pno] *(rec 1974)* — Russian Compact Disc ("Talents of Russia" series) ▲ RCD 16279 [ADD]
Rubinstein, A.:Son 1 Vn, w. Igor Politkovsky (vn) *(rec 1981)*
Russian Compact Disc ("Talents of Russia" series) ▲ RCD 16279 [ADD]
Taneyev, S.:Son Vn, w. Igor Politkovsky (vn) *(rec 1982)*
Russian Compact Disc ("Talents of Russia" series) ▲ RCD 16279 [ADD]

Epstein, Frank (perc)—see also ORCHESTRAS & ENSEMBLES Collage New Music Ensemble
Bazelon, I.:Legends & Love Letters, w. J. Heller (sop), C. Oldfather (pno), R. Annis (cl), J. Scolnik (fl), J. Moerchel (vc), C. Fussell (cnd), Collage New Music Ensemble — Albany ▲ TROY 054 [DDD]
Lazarof, H.:Divert Cl, w. Collage New Music Ensemble — Delos ▲ DE 3124 [DDD]

Eras, Ernst-Martin (ob)
Telemann, G.P.:Cants, w. Barbara Schlick (sop), Manfred Harras (rcr), Richard Gwilt (vn), Brian Franklin (vl), Sally Fortino (hpd)—Hemmet den Eifer, verbannet die Rache; Jauchzt, ihr Christen, seid vergnügt; Umschlinget uns, ihr sanften Freidensbande; Die Kinder des Höchsten sind rufende Stimmen; Lauter Wonne, lauter Freude — Cantate ▲ 580003 [DDD]

Erben, Valentin (vc)
Schoenberg, A.:Verklärte Nacht, w. Thomas Kakusa (va), Arditti String Quartet
Montaigne 2-▲ MO 782025

Erber, Gerhard (pno)
Kelemen, M.:Mirabilia, w. Eckhard Rodger (ring modulator), M. Pommer (cnd), Leipzig RSO
Berlin Classics ▲ BER 1144 [ADD]

Erblich, F. (va)—see ORCHESTRAS & ENSEMBLES Orlando String Quartet

Erblich, Ferdinand (va)
Schubert, Franz:Qnt Pno, D.667, w. D. Dechene (pno), E. Verhey (vn), J. DeCroos (vc), P. Jansen (db)
Laserlight ▲ 15 522 [DDD]
Schubert, Franz:Qnt Pno, D.667, w. D. Dechene (pno), E. Verhey (vn), J. DeCroos (vc), P. Jansen (db)
Vivace ▲ E 561 [DDD]

Erdeli, Olga (hp)
Bortnyansky, D.:Qnt Vn, Vl, w. Nina Barshay (vn), Boris Dobrokhotov (vl), Vladimir Berlinsky (vc), Sergey Dizhur (pno) *(rec 1950)* — Multisonic ("Russian Treasures" series) ▲ 31 0253
Bortnyansky, D.:Sinf concertante, w. Nina Barshay (vn), Boris Dobrokhotov (vl), Vladimir Berlinsky (vc), Sergey Dizhur (pno), Moscow CO *(rec 1984)* — Multisonic ("Russian Treasures" series) ▲ 31 0253
Glière, R.:Con Hp, w. B. Khaikin (cnd), USSR Radio-TV Large SO *(rec 1968)*
Consonance ▲ 81-3001 [AAD]

Erdman, Jerzy (org)
Nowowiejski, F.:Christmas 3 — Polskie Nagrania ▲ PLN 52 [DDD]
Nowowiejski, F.:Con 2 Org—No. 2 — Polskie Nagrania ▲ PLN 52 [DDD]
Nowowiejski, F.:Con 4 Org—No. 4 — CPO 2-▲ CPO 999274
Nowowiejski, F.:Sym 3 Org — Polskie Nagrania ▲ PLN 52 [DDD]
Nowowiejski, F.:Sym 4 Org — CPO 2-▲ CPO 999274
Nowowiejski, F.:Sym 5 Org — Polskie Nagrania ▲ PLN 52 [DDD]
Nowowiejski, F.:Sym 6 Org — CPO 2-▲ CPO 999274
Nowowiejski, F.:Sym 7 Org — CPO 2-▲ CPO 999274

Erdmann, Eduard (pno)
Beethoven, L. van:Bagatelles (24)—in E♭, Op. 126/6 *(rec 1920–33)*
Enterprise ("Piano Library" series) ▲ ENT PL 215
Beethoven, L. van:Con 3 Pno, w. A. Rother (cnd), Berlin PO *(rec 1920–33)*
Enterprise ("Piano Library" series) ▲ ENT PL 215
Brahms, J.:Intermezzos Pno, Op. 117 *(rec 1920–33)*
Enterprise ("Piano Library" series) ▲ ENT PL 215
Debussy, C.:Preludes Pno (sels)—No. 12 "Minstrels" [from Book 1] & No. 8 "Ondine" [from Book 2] *(rec 1920–33)* — Enterprise ("Piano Library" series) ▲ ENT PL 215
Haydn, J.:Sons Pno—in F, H.XVII/6 *(rec 1920–33)* — Enterprise ("Piano Library" series) ▲ ENT PL 215

Erdody, Steve (vc)
Leclair, J.-M.:Trio Sons, w. Debussy Trio—in D, Op. 2/8 *(rec July 1992)*
Sierra Classical ▲ SXCD 5004

Erdody, Steve (vc) (cont.)
Locatelli, P.:Sons Fl, Op. 2, w. Debussy Trio—No. 2 in B *(rec July 1992)*
Sierra Classical ▲ SXCD 5004
Telemann, G.P.:Trio Sons, w. Debussy Trio—in g, g & b *(rec July 1992)*
Sierra Classical ▲ SXCD 5004

Erez, A. (pno)
Radzynski, J.:Music of, w. M. Beiser (vc), Aviv String Quartet, *(Qt. for Strings Y. Aloni (viola), A. Erez (Canto for Piano [rec. 1991]), M. Beiser, Z. Plesser (5 Duets for 2 Cellos [rec. 1992])*
CRI ▲ CD 649 [DDD]

Erhard, Hans-Joachim (hpd)
Bach, J.S.:The Art of the Fugue (sels), w. I. Goritzki (ob) — Hänssler Classic ▲ HAN 98987 [DDD]
Bach, J.S.:Sons Fl, BWV 1030–35, w. I. Goritzki (ob)—BWV 1030
Hänssler Classic ▲ HAN 98987 [DDD]
Bach, J.S.:Trio Sons Org, BWV 525–530—BWV 525 & 527 — Hänssler Classic ▲ HAN 98987 [DDD]

Erickson, Raymond (hpd/org)
Purcell, H.:Songs, w. S. Sanford (sop), B. Wissick (vl/baroque vc)—Tis Nature's Voice; Strike the Viol; Ye Gentle Spirits; Round O'; From Rosy Bowers; Hornpipe; Let Us Dance; Hard, the Echoing Air; Ah, How Sweet It Is — Albany ▲ TROY 127

Ericson, Bengt (vc)—see also ORCHESTRAS & ENSEMBLES Musica Holmiae
Handel, G.F.:Sons Rcr, w. Class Pehrsson (rcr), Thomas Schuback (hpd) — BIS ▲ CD 208

Ericson, Bengt (vl)
Ericson & La Fleur, w. R. la Fleur (lt) — BIS ▲ CD 22 [AAD]

Ericson, Camille (vn)—see ORCHESTRAS & ENSEMBLES Valley String Quartet

Ericsson, Hans-Ola (org)
Aho, K.:Sym 8, w. O. Vänskä (cnd), Lahti SO *(rec Lahti, Finland, May 23–25, 1994)*
BIS ▲ CD 646 [DDD]
Baltic Organ Music *(rec Mar. 16–19, 1992)* — BIS ▲ CD 561 [DDD]
Beethoven, L. van:Org Music—Adagio assai; Scherzo & Allegro [from Suite für eine mechanische Orgel]; 2 Pieces [from 5 Stücke für Flötenuhr]; 2 Praeludien für Orgel; Orgel Fuge in D *(rec Bälinge Church, Uppland, Högalid's Church, Stockholm & the Masonic Hall, Uppsala, Sweden, Feb. 11–14, 1993)* — BIS ▲ CD 609 [DDD]
Cage, J.:Some of the Harmony of Maine — BIS ▲ CD 510 [DDD]
Copland, A.:Episode — BIS ▲ CD 510 [DDD]
Copland, A.:Preamble for a Solemn Occasion — BIS ▲ CD 510 [DDD]
Feldman, Morton:Principal Sound — BIS ▲ CD 510 [DDD]
Haydn, J.:Flute-Clock Pieces—32 pieces *(rec Bälinge Church, Uppland, Högalid's Church, Stockholm & the Masonic Hall, Uppsala, Sweden, Feb. 11–14, 1993)* — BIS ▲ CD 609 [DDD]
Ives, C.:Prelude on Adeste fideles — BIS ▲ CD 510 [DDD]
Ives, C.:Vars on *America* — BIS ▲ CD 510 [DDD]
Messiaen, O.:Apparition de l'Eglise éternelle — BIS ▲ CD 409 [DDD]
Messiaen, O.:L'Ascension Org — BIS ▲ CD 409 [DDD]
Messiaen, O.:Le Banquet céleste — BIS ▲ CD 409 [DDD]
Messiaen, O.:Les Corps glorieux — BIS ▲ CD 442 [DDD]
Messiaen, O.:Diptyque — BIS ▲ CD 409 [DDD]
Messiaen, O.:Livre d'orgue — BIS ▲ CD 441 [DDD]
Messiaen, O.:Livre du Saint Sacrement — BIS 2-▲ CD 491/92 [DDD]
Messiaen, O.:Méditations sur le mystère la Sainte Trinité — BIS ▲ CD 464 [DDD]
Messiaen, O.:Messe de la Pentecôte — BIS ▲ CD 441 [DDD]
Messiaen, O.:La Nativité du Seigneur — BIS ▲ CD 410 [DDD]
Messiaen, O.:Org Music (comp)—Méditations sur le mystère de la Sainte Trinité (1969)
BIS ▲ CD 464 [DDD]
Messiaen, O.:Org Music (comp)—Apparition de l'Église éternelle (1932); L'Ascension (1934); Le banquet céleste (1928); Diptyque (1930) — BIS ▲ CD 409 [DDD]
Messiaen, O.:Org Music (comp)—Livre du Saint Sacrement (1984); The Birdsong in Messiaen's Organ Music (ornithological recordings of the songs of 26 types of both European & Israeli birds which inspired particular passages of Messiaen's music) — BIS 2-▲ CD 491/92 [DDD]
Messiaen, O.:Org Music (comp)—Livre d'orgue (1951); Messe de la Pentecôte (1950)
BIS ▲ CD 441 [DDD]
Messiaen, O.:Org Music (comp)—Les corps glorieux [Sept visions brèves de la Vie des Ressuscités] (1939); Verset pour la fête de la Dédicace (1960) — BIS ▲ CD 442 [DDD]
Messiaen, O.:Org Music (comp)—La nativité du Seigneur (1935) — BIS ▲ CD 410 [DDD]
Messiaen, O.:Verset pour la fête de la dédicace — BIS ▲ CD 442 [DDD]
Nilsson, T.:Music of, w. Ingmari Landin (alt), Lars Sjögren (ten), Lage Wedin (bass), Jerker Halldén (fl), Nils-Erik Sparf (vn), Anders Loguin (perc), Torsten Nilsson (cnd), Gustaf Sjökvist (cnd), Swedish Radio Chorus—Ordinarium Missae; Balthasar/Daniel; Drei Gedichte — Phono Suecia ▲ PHN 40 [AAD]
20th Century Music for Trumpet & Organ, w. A. Plog (tpt) *(rec Mar. 1992)* — BIS ▲ CD 565 [DDD]

Ericsson, Hans-Ola (org/hpd)
Bach, C.P.E.:Sons Fl, w. Lena Weman (baroque fl)—H.504–9; H.515; H.542–3; H.545; H.574; H.578 *(rec Masonic Hall, Uppsala, Sweden & Entrance Hall, Uppsala Cathedral, Sweden; Feb 20–25, 1995)*
BIS 2-▲ CD 755/756 [DDD]

Ericsson, Mikael (vc)—see also ORCHESTRAS & ENSEMBLES New Vlach String Quartet, Vlach String Quartet
Martinů, B.:Ariette, w. František Malý (pno) *(rec Martínek Studio, Prague, Nov. 29–30 & Dec. 1, 1993)*
Panton ("Protokol XX" series) ▲ PAN 811269 [DDD]
Martinů, B.:Nocturnes Vc, w. František Malý (pno) *(rec Martínek Studio, Prague, Nov. 29–30 & Dec. 1, 1993)* — Panton ("Protokol XX" series) ▲ PAN 811269 [DDD]
Martinů, B.:Pastorales, w. František Malý (pno) *(rec Martínek Studio, Prague, Nov. 29–30 & Dec. 1, 1993)* — Panton ("Protokol XX" series) ▲ PAN 811269 [DDD]
Martinů, B.:Vars on a Theme by Rossini, w. František Malý (pno) *(rec Martínek Studio, Prague, Nov. 29–30 & Dec. 1, 1993)* — Panton ("Protokol XX" series) ▲ PAN 811269 [DDD]
Martinů, B.:Vars on a Slovak folksong, w. František Malý (pno) *(rec Martínek Studio, Prague, Nov. 29–30 & Dec. 1, 1993)* — Panton ("Protokol XX" series) ▲ PAN 811269 [DDD]

Eriksen, E. R. (pno)
Alnaes, E.:Songs, w. B. Arnesen (sop)—The Skogsråo, Op. 38/4; Out There in the World, Op. 12/4; A Little Tune about Spring, Op. 38/2; Narcissus, Op. 28/2; The Last Voyage, Op. 17/2; February Morning by the Gulf, Op. 28/5; Longings of Spring, Op. 17/3; I Was Lying by the Sea, Op. 2/3; Northern Lights, Op. 14/4; Sun, Op. 15/1; In the Season of Lilacs, Op. 30/2; Early Summer Morning, Op. 30/3; Promenade, Op. 31/1; Rocking Song, Op. 1/4; Gonel, Op. 1/1; The Mind Young and Full of Sweetness, Op. 14/2; Old Spinster, Op. 22/3; A Summer Melody, Op. 35/4; The Hundred Violins, Op. 42/2; See, the Sun Is Setting, Op. 42/1; Happiness between Two People, Op. 26/1; Where You Lead the Way, Op. 17/1; Poet, Op. 31/3; Little Kirsten, Op. 2/4; Living , Op. 42/3; The Dress, Op. 29/3; Rain, Op. 45/3; Anne Knutsdotter, Norwegian Traditional Melody [N] — Simax ▲ PSC 1110

Erikson, Greta (pno)
Sjögren, E.:Son 1 Vn, w. L. Berlin (vn) — Swedish Society ▲ SCD 1028
Sjögren, E.:Son 2 Vn, w. L. Berlin (vn) — Swedish Society ▲ SCD 1028
Stenhammar, W.:Con 2 Pno, w. E. Svetlanov (cnd), Swedish RSO — Musica Sveciae ▲ MSCD 622
Wiklund, A.:Con 2 Pno, w. S. Westerberg (cnd), Swedish RSO — Caprice ▲ CAP 21363 [AAD]

Eriksson, Marie (hp)
Popular Music for Flute & Harp, w. Beier, Mikael (fl) — Danacord ▲ DACOCD 306 [DDD]

Erkkila, Dan (shak/ram's hn/Tibetan thighbone tpt)
Mostel, R.:Swiftly, w. John Charles Thomas (tube tpt/ram's horn), Geoffrey Gordon (perc), Tibetan Singing Bowl Ensemble *(rec live, WNYC Studios, Sept 18, 1987)* — Digital Fossils ▲ 10009-2 [DDD]

Erkkilä, Lassi (perc)
Bartók, B.:Son for 2 Pnos, w. M. Raekallio (pno), J. Lagerspätz (pno), T. Ferchen (perc)
Ondine ▲ ODE 806 [DDD]
Bergman, E.:Borealis, w. M. Raekallio (pno), J. Lagerspätz (pno), T. Ferchen (perc)
Ondine ▲ ODE 806 [DDD]

Erlandsen, Gyrid (cl)
Saeverud, H.:Peer Gynt Suites, w. Sveinung Sand (vn), Anna Dolezych (va), Kjersti Dahle (ob/E hn), Bohumil Maliska (hn), A. Dmitriev (cnd), Stavanger SO *(rec Stavanger Konserthus, Stavanger, Norway, Nov 13–17, 1995)* BIS ▲ CD 762 [DDD]

Erlendsdóttir, Edda (pno)
Leifs, J.:Music of, w. Sigrídur Ella Magnúsdóttir (mez), Ólafur Vignir Albertsson (pno), Sólveig Anna Jónsdóttir (pno), Hjálmar Ragnarsson (pno), Marteinn Hunger Fridriksson (org), Hildigunnur Halldórsdóttir (vn), Gréta Gudnadóttir (vn), Gudmundur Kristmundsson (va), Sigurdur Halldórsson (vc), Richard Korn (db), Iceland SO, Icelandic Opera Chorus, Langholts Church Graduale Choir, Hamrahlíd Choir—Icelandic Cant, Op. 13/4; Valse Lento, Op. 2/1; Icelandic Dance, Op. 11/2 [Tempo Giusto]; Requiem; Lullaby [After the Riots]; Fairy-Tale in the Wood [from Baldr, Op. 34]; Funeral March; Separation [from Elegy, Op. 53]; Galdra Loftur Ov, Op. 10; Funeral March, Op. 6; Reverie; Reunion [from Elegy, Op. 53]; Fine I, Op. 55; Andante [The Last Supper]; Preludia Organo, Op. 16/3 [In the Church]; The Tear of Stone [from Elegy, Op. 53] Music From Iceland ▲ ITM 605 [DDD]
Ragnarsson, H.:Music of, w. S. E. Magnúsdóttir (mez), H. Halldórsdóttir (vn), G. Gudnadóttir (vn), G. Kristmundsson (va), S. Halldórsson (vc), R. Korn (db), Ó. V. Albertsson (pno), S. A. Jónsdóttir (pno), H. Ragnarsson (pno), M. H. Fridriksson (org), Sakari, Wilkinson (cnd), Iceland SO, G. Cortes (cnd), J. Stefánsson (cnd), T. Ingólfsdóttir (cnd), Hamrahlíd Choir, Icelandic Opera Chorus, Langholts Church Graduale Choir—Meine kleine Freundin [In the Ballroom]; Lovers Duet; After the concert; Meine kleine Freundin [Annie listens to the Radio]; Lif's Theme [On the Beach]; Lif's Theme II [Night Prayer]; Composing Ov [Vars I, II & III] Music From Iceland ▲ ITM 605 [DDD]

Erlich, Ruth (vn)
Tailleferre, G.:Son 1 Vn, w. Marcia Eckert (pno) *(rec Evangelical Lutheran Church, Jersey City, NJ, Jan. 1992)* Cambria ▲ CD 1085 [DDD]
Tailleferre, G.:Son 2 Vn, w. Marcia Eckert (pno) *(rec Evangelical Lutheran Church, Jersey City, NJ, Jan. 1992)* Cambria ▲ CD 1085 [DDD]
Tailleferre, G.:Sonatine Vn, w. Marcia Eckert (pno) *(rec Evangelical Lutheran Church, Jersey City, NJ, Jan. 1992)* Cambria ▲ CD 1085 [DDD]

Erlih, Devy (vn)
Tournemire, C.:Sonate-poème, w. H. Puig-Roget (pno) *(rec 1973)* Memoire Vive ▲ 262006 [ADD]

Erml, Alexander (vc)—see ORCHESTRAS & ENSEMBLES Bohuslav Martinů Philharmonic String Quartet

Erml, Ulla (pno)
Stolarczyk, W.:Earth Air Fire Water, w. Amalie Malling (pno), John Damgaard (pno), Anne Øland (pno), Teddy Teirup (pno), Friedrich Gürtler (pno), Rosalind Bevan (pno), Poul Rosenbaum (pno), Rodolfo Llambias (pno), Bella Horn-Ribera (pno), Anders Riber (pno), Elisabeth Sigurdsson (pno), Thomas Tronheim (pno), Elsebeth Broderson (pno), Erik Kaltoft (pno), Jørgen Hald Nielsen (pno), Aino Gilemann (pno), Birgit Kjær (pno), Jørgen Thomsen (pno), Gunhild Donslund (pno), Henrik Bo Hansen (pno), Lone Karlsson (pno), Erik Fessel (pno), Lasse Nilsson (pno), Janos Ferenczi (pno), Erik Bach (pno), Axel Momme (pno), Arne de Cros Dich (pno), Sven Micha Slot (pno), Hanne Bramsen Buhl (pno), Lili Olesen (pno), Susannah Carlsson (pno), Vagn Sørensen (pno), Leif Greibe (pno), Bodil Krogh (pno), Kirsten Ottosen (pno), Inger Bergenholz (pno), Karsten Gylendorf (pno), Bjønr Elkjær (pno), Jacob Bjørn Jensen (pno), Jørgen Kaad (pno), Anne Marie Hjelm (pno), Carl Ulrik Munk Andersen (pno), Poul Lumbye (pno), Oluf Hildebrandt Nielsen (pno), Joachim Olsson (pno), Peter Pade Ramsøe Jacobsen (pno), Astrid Pollmann (pno), Jette Borsch (pno), Kirsten Karlshøj (pno), Maria Teresa Assing (pno), Allan Dahl Hansen (pno), Johan Hugossen (pno), Tine Fenger Pederson (pno), Arne Jørgen Fæø (pno), Anja Høgsted (pno), Anne Sophie Parbo (pno), Inga Lindmark (pno), Teresa Drabik Stathakis (pno), Anne Ruth Ferenczi (pno), Irene Hasager (pno), Yuka Ichikawa (pno), Birgitte Baur (pno), Malene Thastum (pno), Jens E. Rasmussen (pno), Birgitte Zielke (pno), Claus Zielke (pno), Stefan Kasch (pno), Bin Qiao (pno), Inger Johanne Teirup (pno), Lindy Rosborg (pno), Liisa Heininen (pno), David Højer (pno), Ellen Refstrup (pno), Thomas K. Søorensen (pno), Erik Kure (pno), Michael Rauff (pno), Jan beck Eriksson (pno), Tanja Zapolski (pno), Vibeke Skagbo (pno), Pål Eide Lindtner (pno), Ha-Young Sul (pno), Benedicte Palko (pno), Inke Kesseler (pno), Anne Marie Meineche (pno), Sverre Larsen (pno), Kasper Peter Bach (pno), Elisabetta Eliseo (pno), Olga Magieres (pno), Carl Erik Kühl (pno), Thorkild Borup Nielsen (pno), Valeria Zanini (pno), Lars Stenhoft (perc), Dennis Boel (perc), Winnie Dahlgren (perc), Susanne Vind (perc), Claus Byrith (elec), Anne Marie Storm (elec), J. Ribera (cnd) *(rec live, Koldinghaus Castle, Denmark, May 2, 1996)* Danica ▲ DCD 1996

Erni, Daniel (gtr)
Music from Spain & Latin America for 2 Guitars, w. W. Feybli (gtr) Orfeo ▲ CD 189891 [DDD] ■ MC 189891 (D)

Erni, Michael (timp)
Hauser, F.:Die Welle, w. Martin André Grütter (cym/tamtam), Roli Fischer (cym), Barbara Frey (cym), Cyril Lützelschwab (cym), Lukas Rohner (cym), Severin Steinhauser (cym), Hans Ulrich (cym), Ruud Wiener (cym), Fran Lorkovic (timp), F. Hauser (cnd) *(rec Studio DRS, Basel, Switzerland, Nov. 6, 1988)* Hat Hut ▲ hat ART CD 6017 [ADD]

Ernst, Peter (gtr)—see ORCHESTRAS & ENSEMBLES Duo Bergerac

Ernst, Siegrid (pno)
Ernst, S.:Quattro mani dentro e fuori, w. Rudolf Meister (pno) Vienna Modern Masters ▲ VMM 2018 [DDD]

Errante, F. Gerard (cl)
Electric Clarinet:Contemporary Works for Clarinet & Various Electronic Processes, w. Burton Beerman (cl) Capstone ▲ CPS 8607 [DDD]

Erskine, Peter (dr)
Vivaldi, A.:Cons Vn, Op. 8/1–4, "The Four Seasons", w. Eddie Daniels (cl), Alan Broadbent (pno), Dave Carpenter (db) *(rec California State University, Long Beach, CA, Mar 15, 1996)* Shanachie ▲ SHA 5017 ■ SHA 5017

Ertüngealp, Alpaslan (pno)
Pizzetti, I.:Canti Vn, w. Leila Rásonyi (vn) *(rec Hungaroton Studio, Rottenbiller St, Budapest, May 17–18 & June 2, 1994)* Marco Polo ▲ 8.223812 [DDD]
Pizzetti, I.:Son 1 Vn, w. Leila Rásonyi (vn) *(rec Hungaroton Studio, Rottenbiller St, Budapest, May 17–18 & June 2, 1994)* Marco Polo ▲ 8.223812 [DDD]
Pizzetti, I.:Trio Pno, w. Leila Rásonyi (vn), László Fenyő (vc) *(rec Hungaroton Studio, Rottenbiller St, Budapest, May 17–18 & June 2, 1994)* Marco Polo ▲ 8.223812 [DDD]

Erwin (trbn)
Thomson, V.:Sonata da chiesa, w. L. Fuchs (va), P. Ingraham (hn) CRI ■ ACS 6009

Erxleben, Michael (vn)
Christmas Concertos, w. M. Erxleben (cnd), New Berlin SO, Knut Zimmerman (vn), Hans-Peter Kirchberg (org) Capriccio ▲ 10442 [DDD]
Mozart, W.A.:Adagio Vn, K.261, w. M. Erxleben (cnd), New Berlin CO LaserLight ▲ 15 881 [DDD]
Mozart, W.A.:Con 6 Vn, w. M. Erxleben (cnd), New Berlin CO LaserLight ▲ 15 881 [DDD]
Mozart, W.A.:Con 7 Vn, w. M. Erxleben (cnd), New Berlin CO LaserLight ▲ 15 881 [DDD]
Mozart, W.A.:Rondo Vn, K.373, w. M. Erxleben (cnd), New Berlin CO LaserLight ▲ 15 881 [DDD]
Schoenberg, A.:Con Vn, w. M. Schønwandt (cnd), Berlin SO Berlin Classics ▲ BER 1119 [DDD]
Stravinsky, I.:Con Vn, w. M. Schønwandt (cnd), Berlin SO Berlin Classics ▲ BER 1119 [DDD]

Erxleben, Renate (hp)
Wusthoff, K.:Orchestral Music, w. Ernst-August Quelle (pno), P. Falk (cnd), Berlin RSO—A Little Harp Serenade; Concertino for Piano & Orch; 3 Russian Fants for Piano & Orch Koch Schwann ▲ SCH 318062

Esaki, Katsuko (vn)
Dvořák, A.:Terzetto, w. Richard Rood (vn), Nardo Poy (va) Music & Arts ▲ MUA CD 926

Escaich, Thierry (org)
Escaich, T.:Org Music—Noël; Pacques; Pentecote; Assomption [Grand Organ of St. Pierre de Chaillot, Paris] Chamade ▲ 5635

Escarpa, Margarita (gtr)
Britten, H.:Nocturnal Gtr *(rec Madrid, Sept 12–14, 1990)* RNE/Spanish National Radio ▲ M3/05 [DDD]
Giuliani, M.:Vars on a Theme by Handel *(rec Madrid, Sept 12–14, 1990)* RNE/Spanish National Radio ▲ M3/05 [DDD]

Escarpa, Margarita (gtr) (cont.)
Kleynjans, F.:Arabesque en forme de caprice sur le tombeau de Tarrega *(rec Madrid, Sept 12–14, 1990)* RNE/Spanish National Radio ▲ M3/05 [DDD]
Rodrigo, J.:Invocación y danza *(rec Madrid, Sept 12–14, 1990)* RNE/Spanish National Radio ▲ M3/05 [DDD]
Sor, F.:Fants Gtr—No. 1, Op. 7 *(rec Madrid, Sept 12–14, 1990)* RNE/Spanish National Radio ▲ M3/05 [DDD]

Eschbach, Jesse E. (org)
Franck, C.:Grande pièce symphonique Centaur ▲ CRC 2053 [DDD]
Guilmant, A.:Son 5 Org Centaur ▲ CRC 2053 [DDD]
Historic Organs of New Orleans, w. George Bozeman (org), James S. Darling (org), Gerald D. Frank (org), John Gearhart (org), James Hammann (org), Frederick Hohman (org), Lenora McCroskey (org), Mary Gifford Matthys (org), Lorenz Maycher (org), Donald Messer (org) *(rec June 1989)* Organ Historical Society 2-▲ OHS 89

Eschenbach, Christoph (pno)
Bach, J.S.:Con 1 for 2 Hpds, w. J. Frantz (pno), C. Eschenbach (cnd), Hamburg PO Deutsche Grammophon ▲ 415655-2 [DDD]
Bach, J.S.:Con 2 for 2 Hpds, w. J. Frantz (pno), C. Eschenbach (cnd), Hamburg PO Deutsche Grammophon ▲ 415655-2 [DDD]
Bach, J.S.:Con 1 for 3 Hpds, w. J. Frantz (pno), G. Oppitz (pno), C. Eschenbach (cnd), Hamburg PO Deutsche Grammophon ▲ 415655-2 [DDD]
Bach, J.S.:Con for 4 Hpds, w. J. Frantz (pno), G. Oppitz (pno), H. Schmidt (pno), C. Eschenbach (cnd), Hamburg PO Deutsche Grammophon ▲ 415655-2 [DDD]
Beethoven, L. van:Qnt Pno, Ob, Cl, Hn & Bn, w. A. Leek (ob), J. Moog (cl), S. Scott (hn), U. Freund (bn) Signum ▲ X 06-00
Berg, A.:Son Pno Koch International Classics ▲ KIC 7337
Brahms, J.:Qnt Pno, w. Amadeus String Quartet Deutsche Grammophon 3-▲ 419875-2 [ADD]
Mozart, W.A.:Pno Music 4-Hands, w. J. Frantz (pno)—Adagio, K.594; Andante & 5 Vars., K.501; Fantasia, K.608; Sons. in C, K.19d; K.358; in D, K.381 Deutsche Grammophon ▲ 429809-2 [ADD]
Mozart, W.A.:Qnt Pno, K.452, w. A. Leek (ob), J. Moog (cl), S. Scott (hn), U. Freund (bn) Signum ▲ X 06-00
Picker, T.:Old & Lost Rivers, w. C. Eschenbach (cnd), Houston SO [2 versions:orch. & solo piano] Virgin Classics ▲ 59007 [DDD]
Schnittke, A.:Gratulationsrondo, w. G. Kremer (vn) Teldec ▲ 94540-2
Schnittke, A.:Stille Nacht Vn, w. G. Kremer (vn) Teldec ▲ 94540-2
Schubert, Franz:Qnt Pno, D.667, w. Koeckert String Quartet Deutsche Grammophon ("Resonance" series) ▲ 427215-2 [ADD]
Webern, A.:Con Fl, w. Houston Sym Chamber Players Koch International Classics ▲ KIC 7337
Webern, A.:Little Pieces Vc, w. *(cellist unknown)* Koch International Classics ▲ KIC 7337
Webern, A.:Pieces Vn, w. *(violinist unknown)* Koch International Classics ▲ KIC 7337

Eschenburg, Hans-Jakob (vc)—see also ORCHESTRAS & ENSEMBLES Petersen String Quartet
Schulhoff, E.:Duo Vn, w. Gernot Süssmuth (vn) *(rec Berlin, June 6–8 & Nov 7–8, 1994)* Capriccio ▲ 10 539 [DDD]

Escher, Stephen (cnt/fl/rcr)—see ORCHESTRAS & ENSEMBLES The Whole Noyse

Escobedo, Moc (trbn/didjeridu/conch)
Dempster, S.:Music of, w. Stuart Dempster (trbn/didjeridu/conch), Jay Bulen (trbn), Jeff Domoto (trbn), Scott Higbee (trbn), Gretchen Hopper (trbn), Nathaniel Irby-Oxford (trbn), Chad Kirby (trbn/conch), Dave Marriott (trbn), Greg Powers (trbn), Debra Sykes (cym)—Conch Calling; Morning Light; Didjerilayover; Secret Currents; Melodic Communion; Shell Shock; Cloud Landings *(rec Fort Worden, Port Townsend, WA, June 18, 1994)* New Albion ▲ NA 076

Eselson, L. (fl)—see ORCHESTRAS & ENSEMBLES New Works Calgary Ensemble

Eser, Matthias (perc)—see ORCHESTRAS & ENSEMBLES Zurich New Music Ensemble

Eskin, Jules (vc)
Fauré, G.:Elégie, w. S. Ozawa (cnd), Boston SO Deutsche Grammophon ▲ 423089-2 [DDD]
Foote, A.:Pieces Vc & Pno, Op. 1, w. V. Eskin (pno) Northeastern ▲ NR 206-CD
Foote, A.:Trio 2, w. V. Eskin (pno), J. Silverstein (vn) Northeastern ▲ NR 206-CD

Eskin, Virginia (pno)
Bauer, M.:Son Va, w. A. Steinhardt Northeastern ■ NR 222-C
Beach, A.M.C.:Music for Vn & Pno, w. J. Silverstein (vn)—Oh Mistress Mine, Op. 37/1; Romance, Op. 23; Three Pieces, Op. 40 (La captive; Berceuse; Mazurka); Lento espressivo, Op. 125 Northeastern ▲ NR 9004-CD
Beach, A.M.C.:Pno Music—Les rêves de Colombine for Piano, Op. 65 (1907); Variations on Balkan Themes for Piano, Op. 60 (1905, rev. 1935) Northeastern ▲ NR 223-CD
Beach, A.M.C.:Pno Music—Ballad in D♭; Valse Caprice; Nocturne; Prelude & Fugue; 4 Sketches, Op. 15; Hermit Thrush at Eve; Hermit Thrush at Morn; Suite for 2 Pnos on Irish Melodies, Op. 104 [w. Kathleen Supové] Koch International Classics ▲ KIC 7254 [DDD]
Beach, A.M.C.:Pno Music—By the Still Waters, Op. 114; A Humming-bird; From Grandmother's Garden Op. 97 (Morning Glories; Heartsease; Mignonette; Rosemary and Rue; Honeysuckle) Northeastern ▲ NR 9004-CD
Beach, A.M.C.:Songs, w. D. Fortunato (mez)—Ariette, Op. 1/4; Ah, Love But a Day, Op. 44/2; Just For This!, Op. 26/2; Dearie, Op. 43/1; Ye Banks and Braes o' Bonny Doone, Op. 12/2; Hymn of Trust, Op. 13; Chanson d'amour, Op. 21/1; Juni, Op. 51/3; Dark Garden, Op. 131; Elle et moi, Op. 21/3; Ecstasy, Op. 19/2; Dark is the Night, Op. 11/11; Rendezvous, Op. 120 Northeastern ▲ NR 9004-CD
Boulanger, L.:Cortège, w. A. Steinhardt (vn) Northeastern ■ NR 222-C
Boulanger, L.:D'un matin de printemps Fl & Pno, w. K. Hoover (fl) Leonarda ■ LE 304
Boulanger, L.:Nocturne, w. K. Hoover (fl) Leonarda ■ LE 304
Boulanger, L.:Nocturne, w. A. Steinhardt (vn) Northeastern ■ NR 222-C
Chadwick, G.W.:Qnt Pno, w. Portland String Quartet Northeastern (Classical Arts) ■ NR 235-CD
Chaminade, C.:Romanza appassionata, w. A. Steinhardt (vn) Northeastern (Classical Arts) ■ NR 222-C
Chaminade, C.:Sérénade espagnole, w. A. Steinhardt (vn) Northeastern (Classical Arts) ■ NR 222-C
Clarke, R.:Passacaglia on an Old English Tune, w. P. McCarty (va) Northeastern ("Classical Arts" series) ▲ NR 212-CD
Clarke, R.:Son Va, w. P. McCarty (va) Northeastern ("Classical Arts" series) ▲ NR 212-CD
Coleridge-Taylor, S.:Ballade, w. M. Ludwig (vn) *(rec 9/90)* Koch International Classics ▲ KIC 7056-2 [DDD]
Coleridge-Taylor, S.:Negro Melodies [based on Take Nabandji]—Going Up; Deep River; Run, Mary, Run; Sometimes I Feel Like a Motherless Child; The Bamboula *(rec 9/90)* Koch International Classics ▲ KIC 7056-2 [DDD]
Coleridge-Taylor, S.:Petite Suite de Concert *(rec 9/90)* Koch International Classics ▲ KIC 7056-2 [DDD]
Dvořák, A.:Qnt Pno, Op. 81, w. Portland String Quartet *(rec Theatre C, SUNY, Purchase, Aug. 22–24, 1994)* Arabesque ▲ ARA 6660 [DDD]
Fluffy Ruffle Girls:Women in Ragtime Northeastern ("Classical Arts" series) ▲ NOR 9003
Foote, A.:Pieces Vc & Pno, Op. 1, w. J. Eskin (vc) Northeastern ▲ NR 206-CD
Foote, A.:Pieces Vn & Pno, Op. 9, w. J. Silverstein (vc) Northeastern ▲ NR 206-CD
Foote, A.:Poems Pno, Op. 41 Northeastern ▲ NR 223-CD
Foote, A.:Suite 2 Pno Northeastern ▲ NR 223-CD
Foote, A.:Trio 2, w. J. Silverstein (vn), J. Eskin (vc) Northeastern ▲ NR 206-CD
Hoover, K.:On the Betrothal of Princess Isabelle of France, Aged 6, w. K. Hoover (fl) Leonarda ■ LE 304
Kaprálová, V.:Dubnova Preludia Suite—Allegro; Andante; Andante semplice; Vivo *(rec Jan. 1992)* Northeastern ▲ NR 248-CD
Klein, G.:Son Pno Channel Classics ▲ CCS 1691 [DDD]

▲ = CD ♦ = Enhanced CD Δ = MD ■ = Cassette Tape □ = DCC

Eskin, Virginia (pno) (cont.)
Lamb, J.:Pno Music—Walper House Rag; The Alaskan Rag; Ragime Reverie; Brown Derby No. 2; Alabama Rag; Arctic Sunset; Bird–Brain Rag; Cottontail Rag; Hot Cinders; Ragtime Bobolink; The Old Home Rag; Firefly Rag; Thoroughbred Rag; Toad Stool Rag; Sensation; Ethiopia; Excelsior; American Beauty Rag; Patricia Rag; Nightingale Rag *(rec The Music Room, Cambridge, MA, January, 1995)* Northeastern ▲ NR 257
Tailleferre, G.:Pastorale, w. K. Hoover (fl) Leonarda ■ LE 304
Tailleferre, G.:Son 1 Vn, w. A. Steinhardt (vn) Northeastern ■ NR 222–C
Esmerode, Raoul (perc)
Queens of the Night, w. Yovanka Marville (hpd), Luca Antoniotti (org) Gallo ▲ CD 658 [ADD]
Espagno, Antoine (db)
Lefébure–Wély, L.J.A.:Music of, w. Sylvie de May (sop), Sophie Fournier (sop), Catherine Ravenne (alt), Vincent Genvrin (org), La Lyre Seraphique, Pythagore Vocal Ensemble—Sainte cité, demeure permanente; Récit de Hautbois ou de Trompette harmonique; L'Encens divin; Offertoire [grand choeur]; Seigneur dès ma première enfance; Verset; Pleins de ferveur; Marche; Jour heureux, sainte allégresse; Esprit divin, Dieu de lumière; Andante, choeur de voix humaines; Afin d'être docile et sage; Mon fils, pour apprendre; Andante; Motet à la Sainte–Vierge; Andante; Du Roi des cieux tout célèbre la gloire; Scène pastorale; Andantino Media 7 ▲ 004 [DDD]
Espasa, Salvador (fl)—see ORCHESTRAS & ENSEMBLES Arlequin Trio
Esperen, R. van (hpd)
Bach, C.P.E.:Con Hpd, H.190 Teldec 3–▲ 77623–2
Bach, C.P.E.:Sons Hpd, H.30–34, "Württemberg" Teldec 3–▲ 77623–2
Espino, Eugene (timp)
Strauss, R.:Burleske, w. Jeffrey Kahane (pno), J. López–Cobos (cnd), Cincinnati SO *(rec Music Hall, Cincinnati, OH, Oct. 2–3, 1994)* Telarc ▲ CD 80371 [DDD]
Espinoza, Samuel (va)—see ORCHESTRAS & ENSEMBLES Paraíba Quintet
Esser, Daniel (vc)
Diepenbrock, A.:Songs, w. Roberta Alexander (sop), Christa Pfeiler (mez), Jard Van Ness (mez), Robert Holl (bass), Rudolf Jansen (pno)—Berceuse; Clair de lune; Mandoline; L'Invitation au voyage; Les Chats; Receuillement; Puisque l'aube grandit; Incantation; En Sourdine; La Chanson de l'hypertrophique NM Classics ▲ NM 92051
Yun, I.:Novelette Fl, w. G. Ockers (hp), J. Kracht (vn) Attacca ▲ BABEL 9056–3 [DDD]
Yun, I.:Pezzo fantasioso Attacca ▲ BABEL 9056–3 [DDD]
Essex, Kenneth (va)—see ORCHESTRAS & ENSEMBLES London Chamber Players
Essmann, Fritz (bn)
Mozart, W.A.:Missa, K.427, w. S. Meinardus (sop), H.–J. Möhring (fl), G. Passin (ob), H. Müller–Brühl (cnd), Cologne CO—Et incarnatus est [L] *(rec May 1968)* Koch Treasure ▲ 316182 [ADD]
Estill, Cynthia (bn)—see ORCHESTRAS & ENSEMBLES Blair Woodwind Quintet
Estrada, Gregori (org)
Britten, H.:A Ceremony of Carols, w. S. Bardolet (trb), X. Canadell (trb), J. Pieres (alt), F. Gasa (alt), M. L. Ibañez (hp), Escolania de Montserrat, I. Segarra (cnd) *(rec 1978?)* Koch Treasure ▲ 31624–2 [ADD]
Mendelssohn, F.:Motets, Op. 39, w. S. Bardolet (trb), X. Canadell (trb), J. Pieres (alt), F. Gasa (alt), M. L. Ibañez (hp), I. Segarra (cnd), Montserrat Escolania *(rec 1978?)* Koch Treasure ▲ 31624–2 [ADD]
Viola, A.:Org Music—Organ Sonata in G; Partido for the Left Hand Koch Schwann ▲ 3–1246–2 [DDD]
Estrella, M. A. (pno)
Liszt, F.:Son Pno *(rec Nov. 14, 1991)* Gallo ▲ CD 719 [DDD]
Mozart, W.A.:Fant Pno, K.475 *(rec Nov. 14, 1991)* Gallo ▲ CD 719 [DDD]
Mozart, W.A.:Son 14 Pno *(rec Nov. 14, 1991)* Gallo ▲ CD 719 [DDD]
Estrellas, Gabriel (gtr)
Barrios, A.:Gtr Music—Sueño juvenil; Villancico granadino; Tango zapateado; Gitanos por siguiriyas; De Cádiz a La Habana; Minueto; Flor Granadina; Pitijolo; Mañanitas granadinas; Rosario de la aurora; Eloisa; Jardín granadino; Zacatín; Baile de los tontos; Viejo romance; Primorosa; Pregón de las flores; Estrellita marinera; Saeta granadina; Bambini y Chanchane; Bulerías del macaco; Arroyos de la Alhambra; Navidad en la alpujarra; Apuntes de serranas; Canción y danza del valle de Lecrín; Recuerdos de mi jardín; Sin estrella y sin cielo; Vieja canción granadina; Sal y pimienta; Nostalgia de petenera; Te llevo en el Albaicín; Estampa romántica; Zapapongo; Fandango antiguo; Saludo de mi guitarra; Cristinilla; Parador de San Francisco; Va de cuento; Gamboria; Boliche; Chiquitita y bonita; Olivaritos; Cortijo del aire Opera Tres 2–▲ 1019/20 [DDD]
Estricher, Jurek (org)
17th Century Organ Music of the Southern Low Countries Symphonia ▲ SYM 92E12 [DDD]
Estrin, H. (sax)
Walton, W.:Façade, w. J. Bookspan (nar), S. Baron (fl), C. Russon (cl), M. Broiles (tpt), K. Moore (vc), H. Harris (perc), D. Epstein (cnd) Allegretto ▲ ACD 8153 [ADD] ■ ACD 8153
Estrin, Morton (pno)
Rubinstein, A.:Etudes Pno Newport ▲ NPT 85591
Tchaikovsky, P.:Son Pno, Op. 37 Newport ▲ NPT 85591
Etienne, Daniele (trns fl)
Bach, W.F.:Duets Fls, F.54–59, w. Patrick Beukels (trns fl) *(rec 1992)* Ricercar 2–▲ 089125/26
Bach, W.F.:Trios Fls, F.47–49, w. Patrick Beukels (trns fl), Guy Penson (hpd) *(rec 1992)* Ricercar 2–▲ 089125/26
Etters–Asmus, Elizabeth (hp)
Ewazen, E.:Ballade, w. J. Russo (cl), T. Crawford (cnd), New York Society Orch members CRS ▲ CD 8840
On This Day Earth Shall Ring!, w. Rooke Chapel Choir, Rooke Chapel Ringers, D'Anna Fortunato (mez), David Cover (org), William Payn (cnd) *(rec Rooke Chapel, Bucknell Univ, Feb & May 1995)* Albany ▲ TROY 177 [DDD]
Ettori, Michel (gtr)—see ORCHESTRAS & ENSEMBLES Heldon
Ettorre, Fabio Renato d' (gtr)—see ORCHESTRAS & ENSEMBLES Trio Chitarristico
Eugster, W. (vc)
Suter, R.:Musikalisches Tagesbuch 1, w. B. Geiser–Payer (alt), H. Haldemann (pic/fl), H. Holliger (ob), H. Bochet (bn), J. Joubert (vn), J. Semper (va), M. Dellanoy (db) *(rec 1962)* Grammont ▲ CSTP 6–2 [AAD]
Eustace, Frances (bn)
Bassoon Collection, w. Andrew Watts (bn), Paul Nicholson (kbds), Jennifer Ward Clarke (vc) Amon Ra ▲ CDSAR 35 [DDD]
Vivaldi, A.:Sons Ob, w. P. Goodwin (ob), G. Hennessey (ob), J. Holloway (vn), C. Lawson (cl), N. North (archlt/gtr), S. Sheppard (vc), J. Toll (hpd/org)—RV.53, 58, 81 & 779 Harmonia Mundi USA ▲ HMU 907104
Evans, Bryan (pno)
Brahms, J.:Sons Vc (comp), w. S. Isserlis (vc) Hyperion ▲ CDA 66159 [DDD]
Rózsa, M.:Kaleidoscope Silva Classics ▲ SIL 6006 [DDD]
Evans, Ralph (vn)—see also ORCHESTRAS & ENSEMBLES Fine Arts String Quartet
Foss, L.:Vn & Pno Music, w. L. Foss (pno)—Composer's Holiday; Dedication; Early Song *(rec 1989–90)* Koss Classics ▲ KC 1006 [DDD]
Evers, Reinbert (gtr)
Bach, J.S.:Chaconne *(rec July 1987)* Ambitus ▲ 97818 [DDD]
Bach, J.S.:Lt Music—BWV 997, 998, 1006a *(rec July 1987)* Ambitus ▲ 97818 [DDD]
Dinescu, V.:Figuren II, w. Wolfgang Weigel (gtr)—2 versions *(rec SDR Studio Villa Berg, Apr 1992)* Pro Viva ▲ ISPV 165 [DDD]
Guitar Music of the 20th Century MD + G ▲ L 3292 [DDD]
Henze, H.–W.:El Cimarrón, w. P. Yoder (bar), M. Faust (fl), Mircea Ardeleanu (perc) Koch Schwann 2–▲ 314 030 [DDD]
Henze, H.–W.:Royal Winter Music MD + G ▲ L 3110 [DDD]
Jung, H.:Topografien, w. Wolfgang Weigel (gtr) *(rec SDR Studio Villa Berg, Apr 1992)* Pro Viva ▲ ISPV 165 [DDD]
Klangsa(e)iten, w. Evers, Reinbert (gtr) Ambitus ▲ AMB 97841 [DDD]
Kučera, V.:Festivals of the Imagination, w. Wolfgang Weigel (gtr) *(rec SDR Studio Villa Berg, Apr 1992)* Pro Viva ▲ ISPV 165 [DDD]

Evers, Reinbert (gtr) (cont.)
Like Fire Burning:Contemporary Music for 2 Guitars, w. Wolfgang Weigel (gtr) *(rec Apr. 1992)* DA Music U.S.A. ▲ ISPV 165 CD [DDD]
Meyer, K.:Trio Fl, w. Robert Aitken (fl), Eckart Schloifer (va) *(rec Munich, 1995)* Pro Viva ▲ ISPV 176 CD [DDD]
Nickerson, J.:Like Fire Burning, w. Wolfgang Weigel (gtr) *(rec SDR Studio Villa Berg, Apr 1992)* Pro Viva ▲ ISPV 165 [DDD]
Stahmer, K.H.:Notturni lugubri e capricciosi, w. Wolfgang Weigel (gtr) *(rec SDR Studio Villa Berg, Apr 1992)* Pro Viva ▲ ISPV 165 [DDD]
Everson, Terry (tpt)
Davison, J.:Son Tpt, w. Susan Nowicki (pno) Albany ▲ TROY 199 [DDD]
Evison, Penelope (fl)
Babell, W.:Con Fl, w. Drottningholm Baroque Ensemble BIS ▲ CD 249 [DDD]
Bach, J.S.:Suite 2 Orch, w. Drottningholm Baroque Ensemble BIS ▲ CD 249 [DDD]
Roman, J.H.:Sons Fl, w. C. Huntgeburth (fl), K. Ottesen (vc), O. Larsson (vc), E. Nordenfeldt (hpd)—Nos. 1, 2, 5, 6, 7 & 9 Proprius ▲ PRCD 9020
Roman, J.H.:Sons Fl, w. O. Larsson (vc), E. Nordenfeldt (hpd)—Nos. 3, 4, 8, 10, 11 & 12 Proprius ▲ PRCD 9019
Telemann, G.P.:Con Rcr, Fl, w. C. Pehrsson (rcr), Drottningholm Baroque Ensemble BIS ▲ CD 249 [DDD]
Telemann, G.P.:Con Rcr, Fl, w. C. Pehrsson (rcr), Drottningholm Baroque Ensemble *(rec Apr. 8–9, 1983)* BIS ▲ CD 617 [DDD]
Evrov, Nikolai (pno)
Haydn, J.:Con Hpd & Strs, H.XVIII/4, w. Y. Davov (cnd), Sofia PO Vivace ▲ E 569 [ADD]
Haydn, J.:Con Hpd, Obs, Hns & Strs, H.XVIII/11, w. Y. Davov (cnd), Sofia PO Vivace ▲ E 569 [ADD]
Evstigneev, Mikhail (ob)
Vivaldi, A.:Cons for 2 Obs, w. A. Utkin (ob), V. Spivakov (cnd), Moscow Virtuosi—RV.535 RCA Red Seal ▲ 60240–2–RC [DDD]
Ewazen, Eric (pno)
Ewazen, E.:Son Hn, w. Scott Brubaker (hn) *(rec Recital Hall, SUNY Purchase, 1993)* Well–Tempered Productions ▲ WTP 5172 [DDD]
Ewerhart, Rudolf (positiv/hpd/regal)
Biber, H. von:Mystery (or Rosary) Sons, w. Susanne Lautenbacher (vn), Johannes Koch (va) *(rec 1962)* Vox Box 2–▲ CDX 5171
Ewing, M. (va)
Polishook, M.:The Tribute, w. P. Van Dewater (vn), M. Gibson (vn), D. Assael (vc) Vienna Modern Masters ▲ VMM 2008 [DDD]
Exerjean, Edouard (pno)
Blanc, A.:Sonatine concertante, w. P. Corre (pno) Pierre Verany ▲ PV.790041 [DDD]
Chabrier, E.:España, w. P. Corre (pno) *(rec 6/85)* Pierre Verany ▲ PV.786031 [DDD]
Chabrier, E.:Pas redoublé, w. P. Corre (pno) *(rec 6/85)* Pierre Verany ▲ PV.786031 [DDD]
Chabrier, E.:Valses romantiques (3), w. P. Corre (pno) *(rec 6/85)* Pierre Verany ▲ PV.786031 [DDD]
Doppler, A.F.:Music of, w. J.–L. Beaumadier (fl), A. Marion (fl)—Souvenir, Op. 24; Sommnambula, Op. 42; Chanson d'amour, Op. 20; L'oiseau des bois; Casilda fant. [w. F. Pierre (harp)]; Duettino americain, Op. 37; Duettino hongrois, Op. 36 *(rec 1993)* Calliope ▲ CAL 9224 [DDD]
Dvořák, A.:Slavonic Dances (comp), w. P. Corre (pno) [piano 4–hands] Pierre Verany ▲ PV.790091 [DDD]
Dvořák, A.:Slavonic Dances (comp), w. Philippe Corré (pno) Pierre Verany ("Favourites" series) ▲ PVY 730011 [DDD]
Gouvy, T.:Scherzo, Op. 60, w. P. Corre (pno) Pierre Verany ▲ PV.790041 [DDD]
Infante, M.:Danzas andaluzas, w. P. Corré (pno) *(rec 6/85)* Pierre Verany ▲ PV.786031 [DDD]
Infante, M.:Spanish Music, w. P. Corré (pno) *(rec 6/85)* Pierre Verany ▲ PV.786031 [DDD]
Lefébure–Wély, L.J.A.:Duo symphonique 1, w. P. Corre (pno) Pierre Verany ▲ PV.790041 [DDD]
Pierné, G.:Tarantella Pnos, w. P. Corre (pno) Pierre Verany ▲ PV.790041 [DDD]
Saint–Saëns, C.:Variations on a Theme of Beethoven, w. P. Corre (pno) Pierre Verany ▲ PV.790041 [DDD]
Exleben, Michael (vn)
Hartmann, K.A.:Con funèbre, w. S. Weigle (cnd), New Berlin CO Berlin Classics ▲ BER 1049 [DDD]
Shostakovich, D.:Con 1 Vn, w. S. Weigle (cnd), New Berlin CO Berlin Classics ▲ BER 1049 [DDD]
Extermann, M. (org)
Briquet, M.:Org Music—Prélude pour une fête; Toccata avec interlude; Cantilène; Rhapsodie; Prière pour ceux qui vont mourir; Pastorale; Choral sur la mort de Siddhartha; "Qui al señor habla"; Fantaisie sur l'inscription de la cloche de Schiller *(rec Oct. 15–16, 1992)* Gallo ▲ CD 734 [DDD]
Eymar, Jacqueline (pno)
Fauré, G.:Qt 1 Pno, w. G. Kehr (vn), E. Sichermann (va), B. Braunholz (vc) *(rec 1966)* Vox Box 2–▲ CDX 5073 [ADD]
Fauré, G.:Qt 2 Pno, w. G. Kehr (vn), E. Sichermann (va), B. Braunholz (vc) *(rec 1966)* Vox Box 2–▲ CDX 5073 [ADD]
Fauré, G.:Qnts Pno & Strs, Opp. 89 & 115, w. G. Kehr (vn), W. Neuhaus (vn), E. Sichermann (va), B. Braunholz (vc) *(rec 1970)* Vox Box 2–▲ CDX 5073 [ADD]
Eynde, Louis Op't (ob)—see ORCHESTRAS & ENSEMBLES Belgian Wind Quintet
Eyre, Kate (perc)
Jolivet, A.:Suite en concert, w. Anna Noakes (fl), Graham Cole (perc), Rachel Gledhill (perc), Gary Kettel (perc) ASV ("French Chamber Music" series) ▲ ASV 948
Eyron, Jan (pno)
Elisabeth Söderström & Kerstin Meyer, w. E. Söderström (sop), Kerstin Meyer (mez) *(rec Nov. 1–3, 1974)* BIS ▲ CD 17 [AAD]
Fabbriciani, Roberto (fl)
Flute XX:Flute 20th Century, w. R. Fabbriciani (fl) *(rec Montevarchi, Italy, Jan 1986 & July 1994)* Arts ▲ 47167–2 [DDD]
Fabbriciani, Roberto (pic)
Vivaldi, A.:Cons Pic, w. A. Orizio (cnd), Brescia & Bergamo Festival CO—in C Fonè ▲ 87F 05–17 [DDD]
Fabbrizzi, F. (fl)
Respighi, O.:Suite Fl, w. E. Rojatti (cnd), Haydn Philharmonia Nuova Era ▲ 6876 [DDD]
Fabi, Marie (pno)
Dvořák, A.:Qnt Pno, Op. 81, w. Claudel String Quartet ISBA ▲ ISB 5015
Fábián, Marta (cimbalom)
Kurtág, G.:Scenes from a Novel, w. C. Whittlesey (sop), M. Tacke (vn), T. Fichter (db) *(rec Jan. 7–9, 1992)* Sony Classical ▲ SK 53290 [DDD]
Fabre, Josée (pno)
Berlioz, H.:Les Nuits d'été, w. Jérôme Pruett (ten) Sonpact ▲ SPT 94013 [DDD]
Massenet, J.:Songs, w. Jérôme Pruett (ten)—Voix Suprême; Poème du Souvenir; Plus Vite; Soleil Couchant; Les Alcyons; Elégie; Les Mains; Heure Vécue; Pensée d'Automne; Nuit d'Espagne; La Mort de la Cigale; Il Pleuvait; Sonnet; Soir de Rêve; Quelques Chansons Mauves Sonpact ▲ SPT 96018 [DDD]
Reyer, L.–E.–E.:Mélodies, w. Jérôme Pruett (ten)—Hylas; Sérénade; Douce harmonie; Vieille chanson du jeune temps; Comme à l'aube nouvelle; Il est un trésor plus rare que l'or; Fleur des nuits; Pourquoi ne m'aimez–vous?; Adieu, Suzon; Les larmes; J'ai dit à toute la nature; Aux étoiles Sonpact ▲ SPT 94013 [DDD]
Fabretti, Pierluigi (ob)—see ORCHESTRAS & ENSEMBLES L'Astrée Ensemble
Fabricius, Peter (va)—see ORCHESTRAS & ENSEMBLES Kontra String Quartet
Fackert, A. (vn)—see ORCHESTRAS & ENSEMBLES Arcangelo Corelli Trio
Fader, Oren (elec gtr)
Machover, T.:Bug–Mudra, w. D. Starobin (gtr), D. Kennedy (perc), T. Machover (elec) *(rec live, Tokyo)* Bridge ▲ BCD 9022 [DDD]
Fader, Oren (gtr)
Sor, F.:Souvenir de Russie, w. D. Starobin (gtr) Bridge ▲ BCD 9004 ■ BC5–7004

Fadle, Jörg (cl)—see also ORCHESTRAS & ENSEMBLES Sebon Quartet
Donizetti, G.:Concertinos (4) solo Winds, w. K.–B. Sebon (fl), G. Passin (ob/ob d'amore), J. Starek (cnd), Berlin RIAS Sinfonietta *(rec 1979)* Koch Schwann ▲ CD 311 121 [ADD/DDD]
Mercadante, S.:Con in B♭ Cl, Op. 101, w. J. Starek (cnd), RIAS Sinfonietta Koch Treasure ▲ 31626–2 [ADD]
Meyerbeer, G.:Gli amori di Teolinda, w. Julia Varady (sop), G. Albrecht (cnd), Berlin RSO, Berlin RIAS Chamber Choir [I] Orfeo ▲ 054831 [DDD]
Saint-Saëns, C.:Tarantelle Fl, w. K.–B. Sebon (fl), U. Lajovic (cnd), Berlin RSO [flute, clarinet & orchestra arr.] Koch Treasure ▲ 316132 [ADD]

Fagerburg, Anne (vc)
Scelsi, G.:Anahit, w. Paul Zukofsky (vn), Julie Bogorad (fl), Peggy Russell (fl), Courtney Westcott (fl), Lawrence McDonald (cl), Joan Waryha (cl), Jean Hansen (b cl), Bill Suite (e hn), Nita VanPelt (sax), Bob Zobal (tpt), John Carter (trbn), Martin Lydecker (trbn), Stan Cortman (hn), Robert Ward (hn), William Curry (va), Jody Rowitsch (va), Irene Wade (va), John Gockel (vc), Sue Manz (bass), Steven Stearman (bass) *(rec Oberlin Conservatory of Music, Oct 8, 1973)* CP² ▲ CP2 108 [AAD]

Fagéus, Kjell (b cl)
Brahms, J.:Qnt Cl, w. Zetterqvist String Quartet Opus 3 ▲ OP 19301
Mozart, W.A.:Qnt Cl, K.581, w. Zetterqvist String Quartet Opus 3 ▲ OP 19301

Fagéus, Kjell (cl)
Crusell, B.H.:Den Lilla Slavinnan (sels), w. E. Klas (cnd), Royal Stockholm Orch—Aria Opus 3 ▲ OP 8801
Frumerie, G. de:Con Cl, w. E. Klas (cnd), Royal Stockholm Orch—1st movt Opus 3 ▲ OP 8801
Larsson, L.–E.:Hommage à Mozart, w. E. Klas (cnd), Royal Stockholm Orch Opus 3 ▲ OP 8801
Mozart, W.A.:Con Cl, w. E. Klas (cnd), Royal Stockholm Orch Opus 3 ▲ OP 8801
The Virtuoso Clarinet, w. Kjell–Inge Stevensson (cl), Eva Knardahl (pno), Mats Persson (pno) *(rec Nacka Aula, Nacka, Sweden, June 10–12, 1976 & Sept.)* BIS ▲ CD 62 [AAD]

Fagéus, S. (ob)—see ORCHESTRAS & ENSEMBLES Frösunda Wind Quintet

Fagius, Hans (org)
Alain, J.:Vars sur un thème de Jannequin *(rec Nederluleå Church, Gammelstad, Sweden, June 18–19, 1974)* BIS ▲ CD 7 [AAD]
Bach, Joh. Christian:Duets Org, Op. 18/5 & 6, w. Sanger (org) BIS ▲ CD 273 [DDD]
Bach, J.S.:Chorale Preludes (Schübler) BIS 2–▲ CD 235/36 [DDD]
Bach, J.S.:Chorale Settings, BWV 651–668 BIS 2–▲ CD 235/36 [DDD]
Bach, J.S.:Org Music (comp)—Neumeister chorales; Preludes & Fugues, BWV 533m 549 & 550; Passacaglia in c, BWV 582; Trio Sonata in d, BWV 527; Fantasy in G, BWV 571, plus others BIS 2–▲ CD 379/80 [DDD]
Bach, J.S.:Org Music (comp)—13 Chorale Preludes & Settings, BWV 711–713, 715–718, 721, 726–728, 765 & "O Lamm Gottes, unschuldig" (a two-section setting without BWV number); Concerto in C (after Vivaldi), BWV 594; Fantasia in c, BWV 562;Fantasia & Fugue in c, BWV 537; Fugues in b (after Corelli), BWV 579 & in c, BWV 575; Partite diverse sopra, "Sei gegrüsset, Jesu gütig," BWV 768; Preludes & Fugues in b, BWV 544 & in e, BWV 548; Toccata & Fugue in d, BWV 565; Trio in G, BWV 1027a; Trio Sonata No. 4 in e, BWV 528 BIS 2–▲ CD 397/98 [DDD]
Bach, J.S.:Org Music (comp)—Preludes & Fugues, BWV 539 & BWV 541; etc. BIS 2–▲ CD 343/44
Bach, J.S.:Org Music (comp)—Canonic Variations, BWV 769; 18 Chorales, BWV 708, 720, 722–725, 729, 732, 734, 738, 739–741, 743–745, 755 & 763; Concerto No. 4 in C, BWV 595; Concerto in E♭, BWV 597; Fantaisie in G, BWV 572; Fugues (in c, BWV 574; in g, BWV 577; & in g, BWV 578); Pedal Exercise, BWV 598; Preludes (in G, BWV 568 & in C, BWV 943); Preludes & Fugues (in C, BWV 545 & in C, BWV 547); Toccatas & Fugues (in d, BWV 539, "Dorian," & in F, BWV 540); Trio in d, BWV 583 BIS 2–▲ CD 439/40 [DDD]
Bach, J.S.:Org Music (comp)—Clavierübung, Book 3, BWV 552/1, 552/2, 669–689 & 802–805; Concerto in d, BWV 596; Toccata in E, BWV 566; Trio Sonata No. 3 in C, BWV 529 BIS 2–▲ CD 443/44 [DDD]
Bach, J.S.:Org Music (comp)—6 Chorale Settings, BWV 747, 752, 754, 757, 758, 762; Fugue in D, BWV 580; Partite diverse sopra, BWV 770; Preludes & Fugues (in f, BWV 534; in a, BWV 543; in c, BWV 546); Trio Sonata No. 6 in G, BWV 530 BIS ▲ CD 445 [DDD]
Bach, J.S.:Org Music (comp)—Fantasy & Fugue in a; 8 "Little" Preludes & Fugues; Trio Sonata in c BIS 2–▲ CD 329/30
Bach, J.S.:Org Music (comp) [1728 Cahman organ at Leufsta bruk, Sweden]—Allabreve in D, BWV 589; Canzona in d, BWV 588; Chorale Preludes, BWV 653b, 690, 691, 730, 731, 733, 735, 736 & 737; Concerto in G, BWV 592; Fantasia & Fugue in g, BWV 542; Fugue in g, BWV 131a; Partite diverse sopra, BWV 766; Preludes & Fugues, BWV 531, 532, 535 & 551; Trio Sonata in E♭, BWV 525 BIS 2–▲ CD 308/09 [DDD]
Badings, H.:Dialogues Fl Org, w. G. von Bahr (fl) BIS ▲ CD 160 [AAD]
Boëllmann, L.:Suite gothique *(rec Härnösand Cathedral, Sweden, July 8, 1977)* BIS ▲ CD 7 [AAD]
Couperin, F.:Masses (2) Org—Offertoire sur les grands jeux [from No. 1] *(rec Nederluleå Church, Gammelstad, Sweden, June 18–19, 1974)* BIS ▲ CD 7 [AAD]
Daquin, L.–C.:Nouveau livre de noëls—Noël étranger; Noël en trio et en dialogue; Noël, grand jeu et duo *(rec Härnösand Cathedral, Sweden, Jan 15, 1979)* BIS ▲ CD 7 [AAD]
Dupré, M.:Ballade, w. M. Jansson (pno) *(rec July 2–5, 1992)* BIS ▲ CD 551 [DDD]
Dupré, M.:Sinf, w. M. Jansson (pno) *(rec July 2–5, 1992)* BIS ▲ CD 551 [DDD]
Dupré, M.:Vars sur un vieux Noël *(rec Härnösand Cathedral, Sweden, Jan 15, 1979)* BIS ▲ CD 7 [AAD]
Dupré, M.:Vars à deux thèmes, w. M. Jansson (pno) *(rec July 2–5, 1992)* BIS ▲ CD 551 [DDD]
Duruflé, M.:Prélude et fugue sur le nom d'Alain *(rec Nederluleå Church, Gammelstad, Sweden, June 18–19, 1974)* BIS ▲ CD 7 [AAD]
Franck, C.:Prélude, fugue et var *(rec July 2–5, 1992)* BIS ▲ CD 551 [DDD]
Fryklöf, H.:Symphonic Piece BIS ▲ CD 191 [AAD]
Handel, G.F.:Alleluja & Amen, w. R. Leanderson (bar) *(rec Johannes Church, Stockholm, Sweden, May 16 & 17, Oct 20, 1978)* BIS ▲ CD 127 [AAD]
Handel, G.F.:Dolce pur d'amor l'affanno, w. Rolf Leanderson (bar) *(rec Johannes Church, Stockholm, Sweden, May 16 & 17, Oct 20, 1978)* BIS ▲ CD 127 [AAD]
Hans Fagius:The Organ of Härösand Cathedral *(rec 1977 & 1980)* BIS ▲ CD 156/57 [AAD]
Hans Fagius Plays French Organ Music BIS ▲ CD 7 [AAD]
Hesse, A.F.:Fant Org 4–Hands, Op. 35, w. David Sanger (org) BIS ▲ CD 273 [DDD]
Karg–Elert, S.:Poesien, w. M. Jansson (pno)—2 pieces *(rec July 2–5, 1992)* BIS ▲ CD 551 [DDD]
Karg–Elert, S.:Silhouetten, w. M. Jansson (pno)—3 pieces *(rec July 2–5, 1992)* BIS ▲ CD 551 [DDD]
Kellner, J.C.:Quartetto Org 4–Hands, w. D. Sanger (org) BIS ▲ CD 273 [DDD]
Kodály, Z.:Org Music—complete:Epigrams, Pange lingua & Organoeida BIS ▲ CD 199 [AAD]
Lindberg, O.:Son Org BIS ▲ CD 191 [AAD]
Liszt, F.:Fant & Fugue on "Ad nos, ad salutarem undam" Org *(rec 1980)* BIS ▲ CD 170 [AAD]
Liszt, F.:Prelude & Fugue on the name B–A–C–H *(rec 1980)* BIS ▲ CD 170 [AAD]
Liszt, F.:Vars on "Weinen, Klagen, Sorgen, Zagen", S.179 *(rec 1980)* BIS ▲ CD 170 [AAD]
Martin, F.:Son da chiesa, w. Gunilla von Bahr (fl) *(rec Härnösand Cathedral, Sweden, Feb 29, 1980)* BIS ▲ CD 71 [AAD]
Merkel, G.A.:Son Org 4–Hands, w. David Sanger (org) BIS ▲ CD 273 [DDD]
Nilsson, T.:Concertino Trbn, w. Christer Torgé (trbn) *(rec Österåker Church, Åkersberga, Sweden, Apr 25–26, 1979)* BIS ▲ CD 138 [AAD]
Olsson, O.:Études Org, Op. 45 *(rec May 2–3, 1977)* BIS ▲ CD 85 [AAD]
Olsson, O.:Prelude & Fugue, Op. 52 BIS ▲ CD 191 [AAD]
Olsson, O.:Prelude & Fugue, Op. 52 *(rec Oct. 4, 1981)* BIS ▲ CD 85 [AAD]
Olsson, O.:Prelude & Fugue, Op. 56 *(rec June 17, 1974)* BIS ▲ CD 85 [AAD]
Olsson, O.:Romance Fl, w. G. von Bahr (fl) BIS ▲ CD 160 [AAD]
Olsson, O.:Son Org, Op. 38 *(rec May 2–3, 1977)* BIS ▲ CD 85 [AAD]
Olsson, O.:Vars (10) on "Ave Maris Stella" *(rec May 2–3, 1977)* BIS ▲ CD 85 [AAD]
Peeters, F.:Con Org Pno, w. M. Jansson (pno) *(rec July 2–5, 1992)* BIS ▲ CD 551 [DDD]
Plays the Romantic Swedish Organ BIS ▲ CD 191 [AAD]
Purcell, H.:Hail. Bright Cecilia, w. Rolf Leanderson (bar)—'Tis Nature's Voice *(rec Johannes Church, Stockholm, Sweden, May 16 & 17, Oct 20, 1978)* BIS ▲ CD 127 [AAD]

Fagius, Hans (org) (cont.)
Purcell, H.:Songs, w. Rolf Leanderson (bar)—If Music be the Food of Love; How long, Great God; The Earth Trembled *(rec Johannes Church, Stockholm, Sweden, May 16 & 17, Oct 20, 1978)* BIS ▲ CD 127 [AAD]
Rachmaninoff, S.:Vocalise, w. G. von Bahr (fl) BIS ▲ CD 175 [AAD]
Romantic & Picturesque Music for Flute with Piano or Organ, w. G. von Bahr (fl), Dag Achatz (pno) BIS ▲ CD 160 [AAD]
Saint–Saëns, C.:Bénédiction nuptiale BIS ▲ CD 556 [DDD]
Saint–Saëns, C.:Fants Org—in E♭ *(rec Härnösand Cathedral, Sweden, July 8, 1977)* BIS ▲ CD 7 [AAD]
Saint–Saëns, C.:Fant Org BIS ▲ CD 556 [DDD]
Saint–Saëns, C.:Fant Org, Op. 101 BIS ▲ CD 556 [DDD]
Saint–Saëns, C.:Fant Org, Op. 157 BIS ▲ CD 556 [DDD]
Saint–Saëns, C.:Preludes & Fugues, Op. 99 BIS ▲ CD 556 [DDD]
Saint–Saëns, C.:Preludes & Fugues, Op. 109 BIS ▲ CD 556 [DDD]
Saint–Saëns, C.:Rapsodies sur des cantiques bretons Org BIS ▲ CD 555 [DDD]
Saint–Saëns, C.:Sym 3, w. J. DePreist (cnd), Royal Stockholm PO BIS ▲ CD 555 [DDD]
Sjögren, E.:Org Music—Prelude & Fugue in C; Two Legends (Op. 46, Nos. 5 & 19) BIS ▲ CD 191 [AAD]
Telemann, G.P.:Cants, w. Rolf Leanderson (bar), Gunilla von Bahr (fl)—Kleine Kantate von Wald und Au; Ew'ge Quelle, milder Strom *(rec Johannes Church, Stockholm, Sweden, May 16 & 17, Oct 20, 1978)* BIS ▲ CD 127 [AAD]
Wesley, S.:Grand Duett Org, w. D. Sanger (org) BIS ▲ CD 273 [DDD]
Widor, C.M.:Sym 1 Org—sections 5 & 6 only, "Marche pontificale" & "Méditation" BIS ▲ CD 471 [DDD]
Widor, C.M.:Sym 3 Org BIS ▲ CD 471 [DDD]
Widor, C.M.:Sym 6 Org BIS ▲ CD 471 [DDD]

Fahrni, Stefan (pno)
Karg–Elert, S.:Sinfonische Kanzone, w. Verena Bosshart (fl) *(rec Radio Studio Bern, 1993)* Jecklin ▲ JS 302–2 [DDD]
Karg–Elert, S.:Son Vc, w. Walter Grimmer (vc) *(rec Radio Studio Bern, 1993)* Jecklin ▲ JD 686–2 [DDD]
Karg–Elert, S.:Son Fl, Op. 68, w. Verena Bosshart (fl) *(rec Radio Studio Bern, 1993)* Jecklin ▲ JD 686–2 [DDD]
Karg–Elert, S.:Suite pointillistique, w. Verena Bosshart (fl) *(rec Radio Studio Bern, 1993)* Jecklin ▲ JD 686–2 [DDD]

Faieta, John (trbn)—see ORCHESTRAS & ENSEMBLES Atlantic Brass Quintet

Faigen, Tina (pno)
Schultz, R.:Pno Music—Visions of Dunbar, Op. 25; Montage, Op. 20; Reminiscences, Op. 24/1–8; Ballade, Op. 17; Impromtus, Op. 23/3–5 *(rec Atlanta, GA, June 24–27, 1993)* ACA Digital ▲ CM 20026 ■ CM 20026
Schultz, R.:Trans Pno—Gluck's Dance of the Blessed Spirits [from *Orfeo ed Euridice*]; Fauré's Pavane, Op. 50; Rachmaninoff's Vocalise, Op. 34/14 *(rec Atlanta, GA, June 24–27, 1993)* ACA Digital ▲ CM 20026 ■ CM 20026

Failoni, Donatella (pno)
Cimarosa, D.:Sons (31) Kbd White Label ▲ HRC 149 [ADD]
Liszt, F.:Pno Music (misc)—Liebestraum No. 3 in A♭; Études de concert (Waldesrauschen & Gnomenreigen); La Campanella (No. 3 from *6 Transendental Etuides after Paganini*); Mephisto Waltz No. 1; Rakóczy March; Berceuse; Hungarian Rhapsody No. 15; Valse oubliée Capriccio ▲ CDC 10078 [DDD]

Fairweather, John (vn)
Tailleferre, G.:Chansons populaires françaises, w. Patrice Maginnis (sop), David Ryther (vn), Jill Cohen (va), Karen Andrie (vc), Elizabeth Bodine (ob), Andy Connell (cl), Gordon Mumma (hn), June Orzel (bn), N. Paiement (cnd) *(rec UC, Santa Cruz, May 1992)* Helicon Classics ▲ HE 1008
Tailleferre, G.:Image, w. David Ryther (vn), Jill Cohen (va), Karen Andrie (vc), Elizabeth Bodine (ob), Andy Connell (cl), Gordon Mumma (hn), June Orzel (bn), N. Paiement (cnd) *(rec UC, Santa Cruz, May 1992)* Helicon Classics ▲ HE 1008

Faisandier, Gerard (bn)
Jolivet, A.:Pastorale de Noël, w. Jacques Castagner (fl), Lily Laskine (hp) Adès ▲ ADE 203492 [ADD]

Fait, Lubos (double bn)
Schulhoff, E.:Bass Nightingale Supraphon ▲ SUP 112170 [DDD]

Falbe, Gerda (pno)
Brahms, J.:Liebeslieder Waltzes SATB, w. E. Berger (sop), G. Pfitzinger (alt), W. Ludwig (ten), E. Wenk (bass), E.–G. Scherzer (pno) *(rec 1959)* FNAC Music ▲ 642313
Brahms, J.:Neue Liebeslieder Waltzes, w. E. Berger (sop), G. Pfitzinger (alt), W. Ludwig (ten), E. Wenk (bass), E.–G. Scherzer (pno) *(rec 1959)* FNAC Music ▲ 642313

Falcao, Mario (hp)
Kurek, M.:Con Hp, w. K. Schermerhorn (cnd), chamber ensemble *(rec Javelina Recording Studios, Nashville, 1996)* New World ▲ 80497–2
Kurek, M.:Son Va & Hp, w. John Kochanowski (va) *(rec Blair School of Music Recital Hall, 1995)* New World ▲ 80497–2

Faldi, Paolo (ob)—see also ORCHESTRAS & ENSEMBLES L'Astrée Ensemble
Telemann, G.P.:Con in a for Rcr, Ob, w. L. Cavasanti (rcr), D. Moore (vn), C. Boersma (vc), S. Ciomei (hpd) *(rec July 23–26, 1991)* Nuova Era ("Ancient Music" series) ▲ NUO 7067 [DDD]
Telemann, G.P.:Quartet in G for Recorder, Oboe, Violin & Continuo, w. L. Cavasanti (rcr), D. Moore (vn), S. Ciomei (hpd) *(rec July 23–26, 1991)* Nuova Era ("Ancient Music" series) ▲ NUO 7067 [DDD]

Falentin, Paul (tpt)
Daetwyler, J.:Capriccio, Andante et Humoresque, w. H. Molnar (pic), J. Molnar (alphn), A. Ramirez (perc), Bern Chamber Ensemble Gallo ▲ CD 548 [AAD]
Daetwyler, J.:Con Tpt, w. A. Ramirez (perc), Bern Chamber Ensemble Gallo ▲ CD 548 [AAD]
Daetwyler, J.:Vars sur une chanson médiévale et populaire, "Le Noël des Bergers", w. B. Heiniger (org) Gallo ▲ CD 548 [AAD]
Paul Falentin, w. Craiova PO [cnd:Modest Cichirdan] Gallo ▲ CD 576 [AAD]

Falla, Manuel de (kbd)
Falla, M. de:El amor brujo, w. A. Argenta (cnd), Spanish National Orch Montilla ▲ MNT 3024
Falla, M. de:El sombrero de tres picos, w. A. Argenta (cnd), Spanish National Orch Montilla ▲ MNT 3024

Falla, Manuel de (pno)
Falla, M. de:Canciones populares españolas (7), w. M. Barrientos (sop) *(rec 1928)* Opal ▲ CD 9852 (m) [AAD]
Falla, M. de:Songs, w. M. Barrientos (sop)—Canción del fuego fatuo from *Amor brujo*; Soneto a Cordoba *(rec 1928)* Opal ▲ CD 9852 (m) [AAD]

Fallows, R. (cl)
Debussy, C.:Petite pièce, w. I. Brown (pno) Chandos ▲ CHAN 8385 [ADD]
Debussy, C.:Première rapsodie, w. I. Brown (pno) Chandos ▲ CHAN 8385 [ADD]

Falout, Joze (hn)
The Mozart Collection, w. Joze Banic (bn), Pietro Cavaliere (cl), Ruda Kosi (hp), Dubrovka Tomsic (pno), Ljubljana SO [cnd:Anton Nanut, Marko Munih, Alexander Pitamic, Mihail Glinka] Stradivari Classics ("Treasury of Great Classics" series) 5–▲ S5D 61000 [DDD] 5–■ S5C 61000 (D)
Mozart, W.A.:Cons Hn, w. A. Lizzio (cnd), Mozart Festival Orch Vivace 3–▲ E 315 [DDD]
Mozart, W.A.:Con Hn, K.412, w. K. Redel (cnd), Camerata Labacensis PMG ("Vienna Master" series) ▲ CD 160224 [DDD]
Mozart, W.A.:Con Hn, K.447, w. K. Redel (cnd), Camerata Labacensis PMG ("Vienna Master" series) ▲ CD 160224 [DDD]
Mozart, W.A.:Con Hn, K.447, w. K. Redel (cnd), Camerata Labacensis Sound 2–▲ CDN 115/116 [DDD]
Mozart, W.A.:Con Hn, K.447, w. K. Redel (cnd), Camerata Labacensis Vivace ▲ 549 [DDD]

Falvai, Sándor (pno)
Atterberg, K.:Chamber Music, w. E. Pérényi (vn), A. Kiss (vn), I. Prunyi (pno), G. Kertész (vc), D. Spikay (hp)—Son. in b for Violin, Op. 27; Höstballader, Op. 15; Valse monotone in C; Rondeau Rétrospectif, Op. 26; Trio Concertante in g, Op. 57 — Marco Polo ▲ 8.223404
Bach, J.S.:Cons for 3 Hpds (comp), w. Z. Kocsis (pno), A. Schiff (pno), A. Simon (cnd), Franz Liszt Academy Orch — Vivace ▲ E 563 [ADD]
Bach, J.S.:Con for 4 Hpds, w. Z. Kocsis (pno), A. Schiff (pno), I. Rohmann (pno), A. Simon (cnd), Franz Liszt Academy Orch — Vivace ▲ E 563 [ADD]
Beethoven, L. van:German Dances, WoO 42, w. B. Bánfalvi (vn) — Hungaroton ▲ HCD 12303
Beethoven, L. van:Qnt Pno, Ob, Cl, Hn & Bn, w. Hungarian Wind Quartet — White Label ▲ HRC 169 [ADD]
Beethoven, L. van:Vars Fl, Op. 105, w. B. Bánfalvi (vn) — Hungaroton ▲ HCD 12303
Brahms, J.:Qt 3 Pno, w. P. Kolmós (vn), G. Németh (va), K. Botvay (vc) *(rec 1972–74)* — Hungaroton 2-▲ HCD 11597/98 [ADD]
Chopin, F.:Con 1 Pno, w. Budapest PO [cnd:Andras Korodi] — Laserlight ♦ 90016 [DDD]
Chopin, F.:Con 1 Pno, w. A. Korodi (cnd), Budapest PO — LaserLight ▲ 14 003 [DDD]
Chopin, F.:Mazurkas — Lydian ▲ LYD 18108 [DDD]
Chopin, F.:Polonaises — Lydian ▲ LYD 18115 [DDD]
From Schubert to Strauss with French Horn, w. Friedrich, Ádám (hn), Ingrid Kertesi (sop), Katalin Halmai (mez) — Hungaroton ▲ HCD 31585 [DDD]
Mozart, W.A.:Qnt Pno, K.452, w. Hungarian Wind Quartet — White Label ▲ HRC 169 [ADD]

Falvay, Attila (vn)—see ORCHESTRAS & ENSEMBLES Kodály String Quartet
Fanciullacci, P. (bass vl)—see ORCHESTRAS & ENSEMBLES Modo Antiquo
Fanciullacci, P. (vn)—see ORCHESTRAS & ENSEMBLES Modo Antiquo
Fantini, Franco (vn)—see also ORCHESTRAS & ENSEMBLES Milan Solisti
Marcello, B.:Cons a cinque, w. Genunzio Ghetti (vc), A. Ephrikian (cnd), Milan Solisti—Nos. 1–6 — Rivoalto ▲ RIV 8913 [ADD]
Vivaldi, A.:Sons Vn, Op. 5, w. M. Ferarris (vn), A. Ephrikaim (vn), A. Pocaterra (vc), G. Ghetti (vc), I. De Carli (cembalo), V. Luccini (cembalo) — Rivoalto ▲ CRA 9005 [ADD]

Fantinuoli, Antonio (db)
Stanley, J.:Cons Org, Op. 10, w. A Frigé (hpd), F. Cipriani (vn), R. Pietropaolo (vn), *(w. accompaniments for 2 vn & db)* — Nuova Era ("Ancient Music" series) ▲ 7152

Fantinuoli, Antonio (vc)—see also ORCHESTRAS & ENSEMBLES Aira String Quartet, Collegium Pro Musica
Torelli, G.:Concertino per camera, w. F. Cipriani (vn)—No. 2 *(rec Feb. 17–20, 1992)* — Nuova Era ("Ancient Music" series) ▲ NUO 7128 [DDD]
Vivaldi, A.:Con for 2 Vcs, w. M. Naddeo (vc), F. Biondi (cnd), Europa Galante *(rec Apr. 1993)* — Opus 111 ▲ OPS 3086 [DDD]

Fardink, Michael (pno)
Baksa, R.:Bagatelles (12) — Capstone ▲ CPS 8610

Farina, Edoardo (hpd)
Galuppi, B.:Cons Hpd, w. C. Scimone (cnd), Venice Solisti — Erato 2-▲ ERA SEL 12984 [ADD]

Farkas, Andor (pno)
Corelli, A.:Son Vn, Op. 5/12, "La Follia", w. J. Szigeti (vn) *(rec 1940)* — Sony Masterworks (Portrait) ▲ MPK 52569 (m) [ADD]
Lalo, E.:Aubade, w. J. Szigeti (vn) *(rec 1941)* — Sony Masterworks ("Portrait" series) ▲ MPK 52569 (m) [ADD]

Farkas, Lajos (vn)
Korngold, E.W.:Der Schneemann, w. W. A. Albert (cnd), Northwest German PO—Prelude, Serenade & Entr'acte — CPO ▲ CPO 999037-2 [DDD]

Farley, Barbara Phillips (pno)
Veeneman, C.:The Wiry Concord, w. Susan Werner (banjo), Forrest Covington (hammered dlc/cimbalom), Georganne Assat (hp), Donald Martin Jenni (hpd), Mark Johnson (hpd), James Austin (pno), Marta Soderberg (va), James Knutson (perc), Patrick Doyle (perc), Steven Butters (perc), James Popejoy (perc), M. Geary (cnd) — Capstone ▲ SCI 6

Farmer, Adrian (pno)
Butterworth, G.:Songs (6) from *A Shropshire Lad*, w. S. Gehrman (bass) [E] — Nimbus ▲ NI 5033 [ADD]
Duparc, H.:Songs, w. S. Gehrman (alt)—Chanson triste; L'invitation du voyage; Extase; Lamento — Nimbus ▲ NI 5396 [DDD]
Fauré, G.:Songs, w. S. Gehrman (male alt)—L'horizon chimerique, Op. 118; Le secret; Tristesse; Au bord de l'eau; La chanson du pecheur; Automne; Les berceaux; Apres un rève, Mirages, Op. 113 — Nimbus ▲ NI 5396 [DDD]
Folk Songs Of The British Isles, w. S. Gehrman (bass) — Nimbus ▲ NI 5082 [DDD]
The Male Alto Voice, w. S. Gehrman (bass) — Nimbus ▲ NI 5395
Milhaud, D.:Soirées de Pétrograd, w. Shura Gehrman (bass) [F] — Nimbus ▲ NI 5029
Ravel, M.:Ma mère l'oye Pno, w. V. Perlemuter (pno) — Nimbus ▲ NI 5340 [DDD]
Schubert, Franz:Pno Music (4–hands), w. Nina Walker (pno)—Marches militaire in D, G & B♭, D.733; Polonaises (6) for Pno 4–Hands, D.824; Variations on a theme in B♭, D.968 — Nimbus ▲ NI-5485 [DDD]
Schubert, Franz:Polonaises Pno, D.599, w. Nina Walker (pno) *(rec Concert Hall of the Nimbus Foundation, Dec. 14–16, 1994)* — Nimbus ▲ NI 5443 [DDD]
Schubert, Franz:Rondo Pno, D.608, w. Nina Walker (pno) *(rec Concert Hall of the Nimbus Foundation, Dec. 14–16, 1994)* — Nimbus ▲ NI 5443 [DDD]
Schubert, Franz:Son Pno, D.617, w. Nina Walker (pno) *(rec Concert Hall of the Nimbus Foundation, Dec. 14–16, 1994)* — Nimbus ▲ NI 5443 [DDD]
Schubert, Franz:Vars on a French Song Pno 4–Hands, D.624, w. Nina Walker (pno) *(rec Concert Hall of the Nimbus Foundation, Dec. 14–16, 1994)* — Nimbus ▲ NI 5443 [DDD]

Farmer, Judith (bn)
del Aguila, M.:Herbsttag, w. M. Bayer St. Mary (fl), G. Mossyrsch (hp), H. Earle (cnd), American Music Ensemble Vienna — Albany ▲ TROY 066 [DDD]
del Aguila, M.:Hexen, w. H. Earle (cnd), American Music Ensemble Vienna — Albany ▲ TROY 066 [DDD]

Farmer, Kathy (fl)
Rutter, J.:Requiem, w. Karyn List (sop), Barbara Cook (ob), Julie Albertson (hp), Mary Alice Swope (vc), Tom Alderman (org), Jennifer Mautz (timp), Mike Del Campo (perc), Michael O'Neal (cnd), Michael O'Neal Singers *(rec Roswell United Methodist Church, Atlanta, GA, Mar 27, 1995)* — ACA Digital Recording ▲ CM 20048 [DDD]

Farmer, W. (pno)
Ibert, J.:Chansons de Don Quichotte, w. S. Gehrman (bass) [F] — Nimbus ▲ NI 5029
Poulenc, F.:Le Bestiarire, w. S. Gehrman (bass) [F] [arr bar & pno] — Nimbus ▲ NI 5029
Ravel, M.:Chants populaires, w. S. Gehrman (bass) — Nimbus ▲ NI 5029
Ravel, M.:Mélodies populaires grecques, w. S. Gehrman (bass) — Nimbus ▲ NI 5029
Vaughan Williams, R.:Songs of Travel, w. S. Gehrman (bass) [E] — Nimbus ▲ NI 5033 [ADD]

Farnadi, Edith (pno)
Liszt, F.:Consolations — MCA Classics ▲ MCAD 10429 (m) [AAD]
Liszt, F.:Hungarian Rhaps—Nos. 1–8 — MCA Classics ▲ MCAD 10328 (m) [AAD]
Liszt, F.:Hungarian Rhaps—Nos. 9–15 — MCA Classics ▲ MCAD 10393 (m) [AAD]
Liszt, F.:Hungarian Rhaps—Nos. 16–19 — MCA Classics ▲ MCAD 10429 (m) [AAD]

Faron, Christine (pno)
Clementi, M.:Sons Pno—Sons., Op. 2/4 in A; Op. 7/3 in g; Op. 8/3 in B♭; Op. 25/5 in f♯ — Koch Schwann ▲ CD 310 106 [DDD]
Kozeluch, L.:Sons Pno—in g, Op. 15/1; in d, Op. 20/3; in E♭, Op. 26/3; in f, Op. 38/3 — Koch Schwann ▲ SCH 310592 [DDD]

Farr, Chris (hpd)
Bach, J.S.:Sons Fl, BWV 1030–35, w. W. Barella (ob)—BWV 1030 — Channel Classics ▲ CCS 2091 [DDD]
Bach, J.S.:Sons Vn, w. W. Barella (ob)—BWV 1020 [doubtful; trans. for oboe & continuo] — Channel Classics ▲ CCS 2091 [DDD]
Bach, W.F.:Fugues, w. W. Barella (oboe)—3 fugues — Channel Classics ▲ CCS 2091 [DDD]

Farr, Chris (kbd)
Bach, C.P.E.:Son Ob, H.549, w. W. Barella (ob), V. de Hoog (vc) — Channel Classics ▲ CCS 2091 [DDD]

Farr, Stephen (org)
Alain, J.:Org Music (misc)—3 Danses; Vars. Sur un theme de Clement Jannequin; 2 Chorals; Climat; Monodie; Berceuse sur 2 notes qui cornet; Premiere fant.; Deuxieme fant.; Prelude et fugue; Postlude pour l'office de complies; Vars. sur le lucis creator *(rec Christ Church Cathedral, Oxford)* — Meridian ▲ MER 84282 [DDD]
Blow, J.:Anthems, w. Stephen Darlington (cnd), Christ Church Cathedral Choir Oxford—The Lord Even the Most Mighty; O Lord, Thou Hast Searched Me *(rec Dorchester Abbey, Oxon, Mar 13–14, 1995)* — Nimbus ▲ NI 5454 [DDD]
Humfrey, P.:Anthems, w. Stephen Darlington (cnd), Christ Church Cathedral Choir Oxford—Hear, O Heav'ns *(rec Dorchester Abbey, Oxon, Mar 13–14, 1995)* — Nimbus ▲ NI 5454 [DDD]
Locke, M.:Anthems, Motets & Ceremonial Music, w. Stephen Darlington (cnd), Christ Church Cathedral Choir Oxford—How Doth the City (anthem) *(rec Dorchester Abbey, Oxon, Mar 13–14, 1995)* — Nimbus ▲ NI 5454 [DDD]
Masters of the Royal Chapel, Lisbon, w. A Capella Portugesa [cnd:Owen Rees] — Hyperion ▲ CDA 66725
Oxford Church Anthems, w. Christ Church Cathedral Choir Oxford [cnd:Stephen Darlington] *(rec Christ Church Cathedral, Oxford, May 23–24, 1994)* — Nimbus ▲ NI 5440 [DDD]
Purcell, H.:Anthems, w. Stephen Darlington (cnd), Christ Church Cathedral Choir Oxford—I Will Love Thee; O Lord our Governor; Blessed is He Whose Righteousness; Who Hath Believed; Out of the Deep; Hear Me O Lord *(rec Dorchester Abbey, Oxon, Mar 13–14, 1995)* — Nimbus ▲ NI 5454 [DDD]
Walther, Joh. G.:Org Music—5 Chorale Preludes; Concerto del Signor Meck; Concerto del Signor Taglietti; Concerti del Signor Telemann in c & G; Concerto del Signor Torelli; Partita—Jesu meine Freude — Meridian ▲ CDE 84213

Farrall, Joy (cl)—see also ORCHESTRAS & ENSEMBLES Daniel Trio
Simpson, R.:Qnt Cl, w. F. Cross (b cl), Vanbrugh String Quartet — Hyperion ▲ CDA 66626
Strauss, R.:Duet–Concertino, w. Julie Andrews (bn), N. Cleobury (cnd), Britten Sinfonia — Classics for Pleasure ("Eminence" series) ▲ CFP 2238

Farrell, Peter (vc)—see also ORCHESTRAS & ENSEMBLES Univ of Illinois Contemporary Chamber Players, SONOR Ensemble of Univ of California San Diego members
Reynolds, R.:Whispers out of Time, w. J. Négyesy (vn), Liu (va), B. Turetzky (db), H. Sollberger (cnd), San Diego SO Ensemble — New World ▲ NW 80401-2 [DDD]

Farrell, Timothy (org)
A Choral Festival, w. Westminster Abbey Choir [cnd:Douglas Guest] — Chandos ("Collect" series) ▲ CHAN 6603 [ADD]

Farris, John (org)
Alain, J.:Deuxième fantaisie — Delos ▲ DCD 3049 [DDD]
Dupré, M.:Vars sur un vieux Noël — Delos ▲ DCD 3049 [DDD]
Duruflé, M.:Prélude et fugue sur le nom d'Alain — Delos ▲ DCD 3049 [DDD]
Franck, C.:Fant Org — Delos ▲ DCD 3049 [DDD]
Vierne, L.:Sym 6 Org—Finale — Delos ▲ DCD 3049 [DDD]
Widor, C.M.:Sym 6 Org—Allegro — Delos ▲ DCD 3049 [DDD]

Farris, Michael (org)
French Fireworks:The Symphonic Organ — Delos ▲ DCD 3049 [DDD]
Michael Farris at SMU — Gothic ▲ GOT 49065 [DDD]

Farulli, A. (va)
Paganini, N.:Serenata Va, w. A. Noferini (vc), A. Sebastiani (gtr) — Dynamic ▲ CD 76 [DDD]
Paganini, N.:Terzetto concertante Va, w. A. Noferini (vc), A. Sebastiani (gtr) — Dynamic ▲ CD 76 [DDD]

Farulli, P. (vl)
Schubert, Franz:Qnt Pno, D.667, w. F. Petracchi (db), Fiesole Trio — Fonè ▲ 90F21 [DDD]

Farulli, Piero (va)—see ORCHESTRAS & ENSEMBLES Quartetto Italiano
Farver-Sonne, Robert (db)—see ORCHESTRAS & ENSEMBLES Con Sordino Chamber Group
Fasang, Susan (bn)
Baur, J.:Ostinato senza fine, "Pour rien", w. H. Fischer (cl), A. Münten (cl), C. Crespo (hn), *(not advised of 2nd hn)*, F. Effmann (bn) *(rec May 13, 1981)* — Koch Schwann ▲ SCH 311982 [ADD/DDD]

Fasseva, Gergana (perc)—see ORCHESTRAS & ENSEMBLES Percussion Art Quartet
Fauchet, Bernard (pno)
Kurtz, E.:From Time to Time, w. A. Auviol (vn) *(rec Nov. 1992)* — CRI ▲ CD 661 [DDD]
Schwartz, E.:Memorial in 2 Parts, w. Adele Auriol (vn) — Capstone ▲ CPS 863300

Faukstad, Jon (acc)
Bibalo, A.:Son quasi una fant — Norway Music ▲ CD 7028
Grieg, E.:Holberg Suite [trans Faukstad] — Norway Music ▲ CD 7028
Kvandal, J.:Son Acc — Norway Music ▲ CD 7028
Plagge, W.:Facsimiles Acc — Norway Music ▲ CD 7028

Faulkner, Jane (vn)—see ORCHESTRAS & ENSEMBLES English Piano Trio
Faulkner, Mary Murrell (hpd)
Carlton, R.:Madrigals, w. Quentin Faulkner (hpd)—A Verse for 2 to Play on 1 Vir or Org — Pro Organo ▲ POCD 7049 [DDD]
Tomkins, T.:Instr & Voc Music, w. Quentin Faulkner (hpd)—A Fancy for 2 to Play — Pro Organo ▲ POCD 7049 [DDD]

Faulkner, Mary Murrell (kbd)
Bach, W.F.:Kbd Music, w. Quentin Faulkner (kbd)—Duetto [4–Hands] — Pro Organo ▲ POCD 7049 [DDD]

Faulkner, Mary Murrell (org)
Gabrieli, G.:Music of, w. Quentin Faulkner (org)—Canzon Sol Sol La Sol Fa Mi a 8 [arr for Kbd 4–Hands] — Pro Organo ▲ POCD 7049 [DDD]
Hassler, H.L.:Sacred Music, w. Quentin Faulkner (org)—Laudate Dominum [from Cantiones Sacrae; arr for Kbd 4–Hands] — Pro Organo ▲ POCD 7049 [DDD]
Mozart, W.A.:Adagio & Allegro Mechanical Org, w. Quentin Faulkner (org) [arr. for 4–Hands] — Pro Organo ▲ POCD 7049 [DDD]
Mozart, W.A.:Fant Mechanical Org, w. Quentin Faulkner (org) [arr. for 4–Hands] — Pro Organo ▲ POCD 7049 [DDD]
Soler, P.A.:Cons Kbds, w. Quentin Faulkner (org)—No. 2 in a — Pro Organo ▲ POCD 7049 [DDD]

Faulkner, Quentin (hpd)
Carlton, R.:Madrigals, w. Mary Murrell Faulkner (hpd)—A Verse for 2 to Play on 1 Vir or Org — Pro Organo ▲ POCD 7049 [DDD]
Tomkins, T.:Instr & Voc Music, w. Mary Murrell Faulkner (hpd)—A Fancy for 2 to Play — Pro Organo ▲ POCD 7049 [DDD]

Faulkner, Quentin (kbd)
Bach, W.F.:Kbd Music, w. Mary Murrell Faulkner (kbd)—Duetto [4–Hands] — Pro Organo ▲ POCD 7049 [DDD]

Faulkner, Quentin (org)
Gabrieli, G.:Music of, w. Mary Murrell Faulkner (org)—Canzon Sol Sol La Sol Fa Mi a 8 [arr for Kbd 4–Hands] — Pro Organo ▲ POCD 7049 [DDD]
Hassler, H.L.:Sacred Music, w. Mary Murrell Faulkner (org)—Laudate Dominum [from Cantiones Sacrae; arr for Kbd 4–Hands] — Pro Organo ▲ POCD 7049 [DDD]
Mozart, W.A.:Adagio & Allegro Mechanical Org, w. Mary Murrell Faulkner (org) [arr. for 4–Hands] — Pro Organo ▲ POCD 7049 [DDD]
Mozart, W.A.:Fant Mechanical Org, w. Mary Murrell Faulkner (org) [arr. for 4–Hands] — Pro Organo ▲ POCD 7049 [DDD]
Soler, P.A.:Cons Kbds, w. Mary Murrell Faulkner (org)—No. 2 in a — Pro Organo ▲ POCD 7049 [DDD]

Fauré, Maurice (pno)
Ravel, M.:Tzigane, w. M. Zino Francescatti (vn) *(rec ca 1928)* — Symposium ▲ 1156
Vivaldi, A.:Cons Vn, Op. 3/1–12, "L'estro armonico", w. Maurice Marechal (vc)—No. 9 in D *(rec 1929 – 1943)* — Iron Needle ▲ IN 1324 [ADD]

Faust, George (vc)
Schubert, Franz:Qt Fl, w. J. Levine (pno), G. Hetzel (vn), W. Christ (va), A. Posch (db) Deutsche Grammophon ▲ 431783–2
Schubert, Franz:Qnt Pno, D.667, w. J. Levine (pno), G. Hetzel (vn), W. Christ (va), A. Posch (db) Deutsche Grammophon ▲ 431783–2

Faust, Michael (fl)
Bach, C.P.E.:Sons Fl, w. I. Wjuniski (hpd)—in D, H.505 (W.83) *(rec May 1991)* GM ▲ GM 2037
Bach, J.C.F.:Son Fl, HW.VIII/1–2, w. I. Wjuniski (hpd)—in d *(rec May 1991)* GM ▲ GM 2037
Bach, J.S.:Sons Fl, BWV 1030–35, w. I. Wjuniski (hpd)—BWV 1030–1032 *(rec May 1991)* GM ▲ GM2036
Bach, J.S.:Trio Son Fl, BWV 529, w. I. Wjuniski (hpd) *(rec May 1991)* GM ▲ GM2036
Bach, J.S.:Sons Vn, w. I. Wjuniski (hpd)—BWV 1020 [doubtful; trans. for flute & continuo] *(rec May 1991)* GM ▲ GM 2037
Henze, H.–W.:El Cimarrón, w. P. Yoder (bar), R. Evers (gtr), Mircea Ardeleanu (perc) Koch Schwann 2–▲ 314 030 [DDD]
Mozart, W.A.:Sons Fl Hpd (misc), w. I. Wjuniski (hpd)—K.14, 57, 304 & 379 *(rec Oct. 6, 1991)* GM ▲ GM2038
Mozart, W.A.:Sons Fl Hpd (misc), w. I. Wjuniski (hpd)—in F, K.13 *(rec May 1991)* GM ▲ GM2037

Favery, Robby (gtr)
Ladder of Escape 2 Attacca ▲ BABEL 8846–1

Favre, Christian (pno)
Chopin, F.:Con 2 Pno, w. B. Mersson (cnd), Rome Festival Orch—Larghetto Intercord ▲ INT 892.923 [AAD]
Schubertiade:Rétrospective, w. Sine Nomine String Quartet, Lausanne Trio, C. Homberger (ten), S. Kanoff (pno), Choeur des XVI de Fribourg, et al. Gallo ▲ CD 631 [AAD]

Favre, P. (dr)
Pärt, A.:Sarah Was 90 Years Old, w. Hilliard Ensemble members ECM New Series ▲ 78118–21430–2 [DDD]; ■ 78118–21430–4

Favrod, Maxime (perc)
Gaudibert, E.:Feuillages, w. S. Borel (perc), J. Hostettler (perc) Gallo ▲ CD 630 [AAD]

Fawcett, W. (db)
Weisgarber, E.:Night, w. B. Pullan (bar), J. Washburn (cnd), Purcell Quartet, Vancouver Chamber Choir [E] Centrediscs ▲ CMCCD 3790 [DDD]

Fay, Deirdre (ob)
Meisner, D.:He Who Dwells, w. Lois Swenson (sop), Julie Schwartz (pno) Meyer ▲ MC 0108
Porter, T.:Pieces Ww Qnt, w. Linda Schmidt (fl), Loran Eckroth (cl), Leslie Peterson (hn), Holly Holm (bn) Meyer ▲ MC 0108

Feasley, William (gtr)—see ORCHESTRAS & ENSEMBLES D'Amore Duo

Fedi, Alfonso (hpd)—see also ORCHESTRAS & ENSEMBLES Modo Antiquo
Bach, J.S.:Adagio Clvd *(rec S. Francisco Poverino Church, Florence, Italy, Feb 1994)* Arts ▲ 472532 [DDD]
Bach, J.S.:Italian Con *(rec S. Francisco Poverino Church, Florence, Italy, Feb 1994)* Arts ▲ 472532 [DDD]
Bach, J.S.:Ov Hpd, BWV 831 *(rec S. Francisco Poverino Church, Florence, Italy, Feb 1994)* Arts ▲ 472532 [DDD]
Bach, J.S.:Sons (5) Kbd—BWV 964 *(rec S. Francisco Poverino Church, Florence, Italy, Feb 1994)* Arts ▲ 472532 [DDD]
Bach, J.S.:Sons Vl, BWV 1027–1029, w. Bettina Hoffman (vl) *(rec Florence, Italy, Jan 1994)* Arts ▲ 472522 [DDD]

Fedkov, Piotr (ob)
Mosolov, A.:Pieces Ob, w. Victor Yampolsky (pno) *(rec Mosfilm Studio, Jan 1995)* Triton ▲ 17004 [DDD]

Fedora, Diana (bn)
Macchia, S.:Chamber Con 3, w. J. Tanner (fl/alt fl), M. Sussman (cl), F. Cohen (ob/E hn), L. Klock (hn), V. Kadlubkiewicz (vn), J. Messina (db), P. Tanner (perc) *(rec July 1992)* Gasparo ▲ GS 226 [DDD]

Fedorovtsev, Vadim (pno)
Tchaikovsky, P.:Songs, w. N. Krasnaya (sop) Russian Disc ▲ RUS 11 078 [DDD]

Fedoruk, Brenda (fl)
Classic Elektra, w. Elektra Women's Choir [cnd:Morna Edmundson, Diane Loomer], Eric Hominich (pno), Evelyn Creaser–Rumley (vn), Nancy DiNovo (vn) Skylark ▲ 9402 [DDD]

Fedotov, Maxim (vn)
Shostakovich, D.:Con 1 Vn, w. A. Vedernikov (cnd), Russian State SO Triton ▲ 17006 [DDD]
Shostakovich, D.:Con 2 Vn, w. A. Vedernikov (cnd), Russian State SO Triton ▲ 17006 [DDD]
Tchaikovsky, P.:Trio Pno, w. L. Timofeyeva (pno), K. Rodin (vc) MK ▲ 417001 [DDD]

Feehan, Brian (thb/gtr)—see ORCHESTRAS & ENSEMBLES Les Cyclopes

Feghali, José (pno)
Nazareth, E.:Pno Music—Apanhei–te, Brejeiro, Cavaquinhol, Escorregando, Odeon Koss Classics ▲ KC1018
Ravel, M.:Valses nobles et sentimentales Koss Classics ▲ KC1018
Scriabin, A.:Pno Music (misc)—Mazurkas, Opp. 3/1, 25/2–3, 40/1 Koss Classics ▲ KC1018
Valse Nobles, w. J. Feghali (pno) *(rec Aug. 26–28, 1991)* Koss Classics ▲ KC 1018 [DDD]
Villa–Lobos, H.:Pno Music—Alma Brasileira, Impressoes Seresteiras, Valsa da Dor Koss Classics ▲ KC1018

Feher, Viorica (bn)
Enescu, G.:Dectet Ww, w. Virgil Francu (fl), Nicolae Maxin (fl), Valeriu Barbuceanu (cl), Leontin Boanta (cl), Adrian Petrescu (ob), Goedri Orban (bn), Florin Ionoaia (Eng hn), Dan Cinca (hn), Simon Jebeleanu (hn), H. Andreescu (cnd) Olympia ▲ OLY 445 [DDD]

Fehérvári, János (va)
Boëllmann, L.:Qt Pno & Strs, w. I. Prunyi (pno), B. Bánfalvi (vn), K. Botvay (vc) Marco Polo ▲ 8.223524
Boëllmann, L.:Trio Pno, w. I. Prunyi (pno), B. Bánfalvi (vn), K. Botvay (vc) Marco Polo ▲ 8.223524
Mozart, W.A.:Qnts Strs, w. Éder String Quartet—K. 174 & 515 *(rec Unitarian Church, Budapest, Dec. 2–5, 1993)* Naxos ▲ 8.553103 [DDD]

Fehlandt, Stefan (va)
Schoenberg, A.:Ode to Napoleon, w. Roland Hermann (nar), Rim Vogler (vn), Frank Reinecke (vn), Michael Sanderling (vc), Frank–Immo Zichner (pno) *(rec Siemensvilla, Berlin–Lankwitz, Aug. 1994)* EDA ▲ EDA 008–2 [DDD]

Fehrman, Annette (vn)—see ORCHESTRAS & ENSEMBLES Acht Ensemble

Feidman, Giora (cl)
Prokofiev, S.:Ov on Hebrew Themes, w. Yefim Bronfman (pno), Juilliard String Quartet *(rec Richardson Auditorium, Alexander Hall, Princeton Univ, Princeton, NJ, May 18, 1994)* Sony Classical ("Greatest Hits" series) ▲ MLK 69249 [DDD] ■ LT 69
Prokofiev, S.:Ov on Hebrew Themes, w. Y. Bronfman (pno), Juilliard String Quartet *(rec May 18, 1994)* Sony Classical ▲ SK 58966 [DDD]

Feige, Carlo (vn)—see also ORCHESTRAS & ENSEMBLES Stauffer String Quartet
Honegger, A.:Sons Vn, w. S. Redaelli (pno)—Sonatas 1 & 2 for Violin & Piano; Sonatine for 2 Violins; Sonata for Solo Violin Giulia ▲ GIU 201015 [DDD]
Rieti, V.:Serenata Vn, w. G. Grazioli (cnd), Harmonia Ensemble Giulia ▲ GS 201009 [DDD]

Feigenwinter, B. (vc)
Boulez, P.:Messagesquisse, w. B. Licther (vc), A. Loudos (vc), M. Keller (vc), F. Schiltknecht (vc), P. Toso (vc), J. Wyttenbach (cnd) *(rec Switzerland, June 1993)* ECM New Series 2–▲ 78118–21520–2 [DDD]

Feile, Matthias (vc)
Brahms, J.:Sextet Strs, Op. 18, w. Daniel Höxter (pno), John Harding (vn) [arr. Kirchner for Piano Trio] Koch Schwann ▲ SCH 313652 [DDD]
Brahms, J.:Sextet Strs, Op. 36, w. Daniel Höxter (pno), John Harding (vn) [arr. Kirchner for Piano Trio] Koch Schwann ▲ SCH 313652 [DDD]
Haydn, J.:Sym 102, w. L. Slatkin (cnd), Philharmonia Orch *(rec Abbey Road Studio No. 1, London, Apr & Oct 1994)* RCA Red Seal ▲ 09026–68424–2 [DDD]

Feinberg, Alan (pno)
The American Romantic Argo ▲ 430330–2 ZH [DDD]
American Virtuoso *(rec July 1991)* Argo ▲ 436121–2 [DDD]
Babbitt, M.:Con Pno, w. C. Wuorinen (cnd), American Composers Orch New World ▲ 80346 [DDD]
Babbitt, M.:The Joy of More Sextets, w. R. Schulte (vn) New World ▲ 80364–2 [DDD]
Babbitt, M.:Pno Music (sels)—About Time (1982); Playing for Time (1979); It Takes 12 to Tango (1984); Minute Waltz (1977); Partitions (1957) CRI ▲ CD 521
Babbitt, M.:Sxts Vn, w. R. Schulte (vn) New World ▲ 80364–2 [DDD]
Beach, A.M.C.:Pno Music—Dreaming; Ballade *(rec Feb. 1990)* Argo ▲ 430330–2 [DDD]
Bland, W.:Trio 2, "Elegy & Consolation", w. D. Phillips (vn), S. Doane (vc) Bridge ▲ BCD 9013 [DDD]
Bowles, P.:Con for 2 Pnos, w. Leslie Stifelman (pno), J. Sheffer (cnd), Eos Ensemble *(rec Manhattan Center Studios, New York, Sept 22 & 23, 1995)* Catalyst ▲ 09026–68409–2 [DDD]
Davison, J.:Son Hn, w. William Purvis (hn) Albany ▲ TROY 199 [DDD]
Dembski, S.:Alta, w. L. Flax (cl) CRI ▲ CD 570 [DDD]
Dembski, S.:Altamira, w. L. Flax (cl) CRI ▲ CD 570 [DDD]
Dembski, S.:Trio, w. R. Schulte (vn), F. Sherry (vc) CRI ▲ CD 570 [DDD]
Dodge, C.:Any Resemblance Is Purely Coincidental, w. E. Caruso (ten) New Albion ▲ NA 043
Fascinatin' Rhythm Argo ▲ 444457–2
Feldman, Morton:Palais de Mari Koch International Classics ▲ KIC 7308
Gottschalk, L.M.:Pno Music—La Chute des feuilles; Illusions perdues; God Save the Queen *(rec Feb. 1990)* Argo ▲ 430330–2 [DDD]
Helps, R.:Hommages *(rec Feb. 1990)* Argo ▲ 430330–2 [DDD]
Helps, R.:Nocturne *(rec Feb. 1990)* Argo ▲ 430330–2 [DDD]
Ligeti, G.:Trio Hn, Vn & Pno, w. W. Purvis (hn), R. Schulte (vn) Bridge ▲ BCD 9012 [DDD]
Ornstein, L.:Son Vn, w. Gregory Fulkerson (vn) *(rec RCA Recording Studios, New York City)* New World ▲ 80313–2
Powell, Mel:Duplicates, w. R. Taub (pno), D.A. Miller (cnd), Los Angeles PO Harmonia Mundi USA ▲ HMU 907096
Ran, S.:Apprehensions, w. J. Nicosia (sop), L. Flax (cl) *(rec 1979–91)* CRI ▲ CD 609 [ADD/DDD]
Wuorinen, C.:Pno Music—Bagatelle; Capriccio Koch International Classics ▲ KIC 7308
Wuorinen, C.:Son 3 Pno Koch International Classics ▲ KIC 7308
Wuorinen, C.:Trio Hn, w. W. Purvis (hn), B. Hudson (vn) *(rec Sept. 11–13, 1991)* Koch International Classics ▲ KIC 7123–2 [DDD]
Wuorinen, C.:Trio Trbn, w. R. Borror (trbn), D. Druckman (mar) *(rec Sept. 11–13, 1991)* Koch International Classics ▲ KIC 7123–2 [DDD]

Feinberg, Samuel (pno)
Bach, J.S.:Chorale Preludes Org—4 Chorale Preludes; [arr Feinberg for pno] Melodiya ("Russian Piano School" series) ▲ 74321–25175–2
Bach, J.S.:Das wohltemperierte Klavier Russian Disc 4–▲ RUS 15013 [AAD]
Mozart, W.A.:Prelude & Fugue Pno Melodiya ("Russian Piano School" series) ▲ 74321–25175–2
Mozart, W.A.:Son 4 Pno Melodiya ("Russian Piano School" series) ▲ 74321–25175–2
Mozart, W.A.:Son 17 Pno Melodiya ("Russian Piano School" series) ▲ 74321–25175–2
Mozart, W.A.:Vars Pno, K.500 Melodiya ("Russian Piano School" series) ▲ 74321–25175–2

Feit, Pierre W. (ob)
Haydn, J.:Con Ob, w. P. Entremont (cnd), Vienna CO Koch Schwann ▲ CD 311075
Mozart, W.A.:Con Ob, K.314, w. P. Entremont (cnd), Vienna CO Koch Schwann ▲ CD 311 075

Feitosa, Radegundis (trbn/eup)—see ORCHESTRAS & ENSEMBLES Brasil Brass Quintet

Fejér, Andrs (vc)—see ORCHESTRAS & ENSEMBLES Takács String Quartet

Fejko, Paul (org)
Incantation Arkay ▲ ARK 6104 [DDD]
On Making the Flowers Dance:Organ Improvisations Arkay ▲ ARK 6147
Outburst! Arkay ▲ ARK 6132 [DDD]

Feld, Melanie (ob)
Bach, J.S.:Arioso Ob, w. Mary Jane Newman (org) [arr ob & org] *(rec Presbyterian Church, Mt. Kisco, NY, Aug 26–27, 1995)* Helicon ▲ HE 1006 [DDD]

Feldbæk, Eva (org)
Maegaard, J.:Elegy, w. Anette Simonsen (mez), Henrik Brendstrup (vc) *(rec Copenhagen, 1995–96)* Marco Polo/Dacapo ▲ 8.224050 [DDD]

Felder, A. (vc)
Felder, A.:Ballade, w. L'Estro Armonico Gallo ▲ CD 493

Feldman, Jonathan (pno)
Moszkowski, M.:Suite 2 Vns, w. A. Kavafian (vn), I. Kavafian (vn) Elektra/Nonesuch ▲ 79117–2 [DDD]
Rare Cello Music, w. S. Heled (vc), Daniel Edni (pno), Michael Levin (pno), Alexander Peskanov (pno), Jonathan Zak (pno) *(rec 1976, 1982, 1983, 1985, 1)* Classico ▲ CLASSCD 153
Sarasate, P. de:Navarra, w. I. Kavafian (vn), A. Kavafian (vn) Elektra/Nonesuch ▲ 79117–2 [DDD]

Feldman, L. (vc)
Swack, I.:Profiles, w. S. Toulson (cl), J. Zagst (vn) Opus One ▲ 149

Feldman, Mark (vn)
Aldridge, R.:Qt for an Outdoor Festival, w. Al Regni (s sax), Beverly Lauridsen (vc), T. O. Sterrett (pno) Open Loop ▲ 034 [DDD]
Bourland, R.:Sax Qnt, w. Al Regni (s sax), Laura Seton (vn), Lois Martin (va), Beverly Davidson (vc) Open Loop ▲ 034 [DDD]
Feldman, Mark:Vn Music—Etude; Jeté; Sul G; Molly; Caprice; Fant. for the Vn; Elegy; Stalker; The Tri 5; 4 Spiker Tzadik ("The Composers" series) ▲ TZA 7006 [DDD]
Feldman, Morton:Why Patterns, w. E. Blum (fl), J. Williams (perc) *(rec 12/17/78)* CRI ▲ CD 620 [ADD]
Soldier, D.:Ultraviolet Railroad, w. Erik Frielander (vc), Neal Kirkwood (pno), R.A. Clark (cnd), Manhattan CO Newport Classic ▲ NPD 85589 [DDD]
Zorn, J.:Kristallnacht, w. David Krakauer (cl/b cl), Frank London (tpt), Marc Ribot (gtr), Mark Dresser (electric bass), Anthony Coleman (kbd), William Winant (perc) Tzadik ▲ TZA 7301 [ADD]

Feldman, Ronald (vc)
Flute Flavors, w. P. Fried (fl), Christopher O'Riley (pno), David Sussman (gtr) Golden Tone ▲ GTCD 002
Kovách, A.:Trio 2, w. C. Lieberman (vn), L. Shapiro (pno) AFKA ▲ SK 503
Mozart, W.A.:Qts Fl, w. P. Fried (fl), V. Romanul (vn), R. Barnes (va) Golden Tone ▲ GT 003

Felice, Enrico di (fl)
Albinoni, T.:Fl Music, w. Rita Peiretti (hpd), R. Peiretti (cnd), Accademia dei Solinghi—Sons. in a, Nos. 3 in E, 5 in D & 6 in b; Cons. Nos. 1 in G & 2 in G Stradivarius ▲ STV 33377 [DDD]

Felitsiant, Victor (vn)—see also ORCHESTRAS & ENSEMBLES Moscow Ancient Music Ensemble members
Berezowsky, N.:Son Vn, w. Moscow Ancient Music Ensemble MK ▲ MKA 417119 [DDD]

Fellegi, Ádám (pno)
Kodály, Z.:Pno Music—Dances of Marosszék (1927); Háry János Suite (1926); Valsette (1907); Pieces (9) for Piano (1905–09); Little Canons (24) on the Black Keys; Galanta Dances; Pieces (7) for Piano, Op. 11 (1910–18); Méditation sur un motif de Claude Debussy (1907); Children's Dances (1945) *(rec Hungaroton Studio, Budapest, July 15–18, 1992)* Hungaroton ("Classic" series) 2–▲ HCD 31540/41 [DDD]
Medtner, N.:Pno Music (misc)—Sonata in f, Op. 5; Sonata Triad, Op. 11 Marco Polo ▲ 8.223268

Fellenbaum, James (vc)—see ORCHESTRAS & ENSEMBLES Ad Hoc String Quartet

Feller, Bart (fl)
Maggio, R.:Qts for 2 Fls & 2 Vcs, w. Kathleen Nester (fl), Fred Sherry (vc), Jonathan Spitz (vc), B. Lubman (cnd) *(rec St. Peter's Church, Chelsea, New York, May 22, 1995)* CRI ▲ CD 720 [DDD]

Feller, Harald (org)
Duruflé, M.:Prélude, Adagio et Choral varié sur le thème du *Veni Creator* Calig ▲ CAL 50939
Messiaen, O.:Messe de la Pentecôte Calig ▲ CAL 50939
Messiaen, O.:La Nativité du Seigneur *(rec 1993)* Calig ▲ CAL 50924 [DDD]
Tournemire, C.:L'orgue mystique—Op. 56 Calig ▲ CAL 50939

Fellner, Till (pno)
Beethoven, L. van:Son 5 Pno *(rec live Sept. 19, 1993)* Claves ▲ CD 9328 [DDD]

Fellner, Till (pno) (cont.)
Mozart, W.A.:Con 22 Pno, w. U. Segal (cnd), Lausanne CO *(rec live Sept. 19, 1993)* Claves ▲ CD 9328 [DDD]
Mozart, W.A.:Rondo Pno, K.511 *(rec live Sept. 19, 1993)* Claves ▲ CD 9328 [DDD]

Fellows, Donald (org)
Alleluia, Song of Gladness:Ars Antiqua Choralis, Vol. 2:Choral Masterworks from the 15th-18th Centuries, w. Cathedral Singers [cnd:Richard Proulx] GIA ▲ GIA 299
Rejoice in the Lord:Ars Antiqua Choralis, Vol. 1:Choral Masterworks from the 15th-18th Centuries, w. Cathedral Singers [cnd:Richard Proulx] GIA ▲ GIA 290

Felmlee, J. (fl)
Gluck, C.W.:Ovs, w. A. Mirschel (ob), P. R. Klecka (hpd), J. Corazolla (cnd), Rhenish CO—Euristeo; Iphigénie en Aulide; Orfeo ed Euridice; Don Juan Entrée ▲ 0064

Feltsman, Vladimir (hpd)
Bach, J.S.:Das wohltemperierte Klavier—Book 1, BWV 846-869 MusicMasters ▲ 01612-67105-2

Feltsman, Vladimir (pno)
Bach, J.S.:Cons Hpd, BWV 1052-1058, w. V. Feltsman (cnd), Orch of St. Luke's—BWV 1055, 1056 & 1058 *(rec American Academy & Institution of Arts & Letters, July 12-14, 1993)* MusicMasters ▲ 01612-67143-2 [DDD]
Bach, J.S.:Con 1 Hpd, w. V. Feltsman (cnd), Orch of St. Luke *(rec July 12-14, 1993)* MusicMasters ▲ 01612-67132-2 [DDD]
Bach, J.S.:Con 2 Hpd, w. V. Feltsman (cnd), Orch of St. Luke *(rec July 12-14, 1993)* MusicMasters ▲ 01612-67132-2 [DDD]
Bach, J.S.:Con 3 Hpd, w. E. Fischer (cnd), Orch of St. Luke *(rec July 12-14, 1993)* MusicMasters ▲ 01612-67132-2 [DDD]
Bach, J.S.:Goldberg Vars MusicMasters ▲ 01612-67093-2
Bach, J.S.:Das wohltemperierte Klavier—Book 2 *(rec American Academy of Arts & Letters, NYC, June 28, 29 & July 1, 199)* Music Masters Classics 2-▲ 01612-67162-2
Beethoven, L. van:Son 30 Pno MusicMasters ▲ 01612-67098-2
Beethoven, L. van:Son 31 Pno MusicMasters ▲ 01612-67098-2
Beethoven, L. van:Son 32 Pno MusicMasters ▲ 01612-67098-2
Brahms, J.:Pieces Pno, Op. 118—sels. *(rec between 1972-1974)* Russian Disc ▲ RUS 11001 [AAD]
Chopin, F.:Preludes, Op. 28 CBS ▲ MK 39966
Liszt, F.:Légendes CBS ▲ MK 44925 [DDD]
Liszt, F.:Son Pno CBS ▲ MK 44925 [DDD]
Liszt, F.:Sonetti del Petrarca Pno CBS ▲ MK 44925 [DDD]
Prokofiev, S.:Con 1 Pno, w. M. Tilson Thomas (cnd), London SO CBS ▲ MK 44818 [DDD]
Prokofiev, S.:Con 2 Pno, w. M. Tilson Thomas (cnd), London SO CBS ▲ MK 44818 [DDD]
Prokofiev, S.:Romeo & Juliet Pno—No. 10, Romeo bids Juliet farewell CBS ▲ MK 44818 [DDD]
Rachmaninoff, S.:Con 3 Pno, w. Z. Mehta (cnd), Israel PO CBS ▲ MK 44761 [DDD] ■ MT 44761 (D)
Rachmaninoff, S.:Rhapsody on a Theme of Paganini, w. Z. Mehta (cnd), Israel PO CBS ▲ MK 44761 [DDD] ■ MT 44761 (D)
Schubert, Franz:Fant Pno, D.760, "Wandererfantasie" *(rec between 1972-1974)* Russian Disc ▲ RUS 11001 [AAD]
Schumann, R.:Son 1 Pno *(rec between 1972-1974)* Russian Disc ▲ RUS 11001 [AAD]
Tchaikovsky, P.:Con 1 Pno, w. M. Rostropovich (cnd), National SO Washington D.C. Sony Classical ▲ SK 45756 [DDD]
Tchaikovsky, P.:Con 3 Pno, w. M. Rostropovich (cnd), National SO Washington D.C. Sony Classical ▲ SK 45756 [DDD]

Felumb, Svend Christian (ob)
Nielsen, C.:Qnt Ww, w. H.G. Jespersen (fl), A. Oxenvad (cl), H. Sorensen (hn), K. Larsson (bn) *(rec Jan. 24 & 25, 1936)* Clarinet Classics ▲ CC 0002

Fenby, Eric (pno)
Delius, F.:Son Vc & Pno, w. Julian Lloyd Webber (vc) Unicorn-Kanchana ("Souvenir" series) ▲ UK 2074
Delius, F.:Son 1 Vn & Pno, w. Ralph Holmes (vn) Unicorn-Kanchana ("Souvenir" series) ▲ UK 2074
Delius, F.:Son 2 Vn & Pno, w. Ralph Holmes (vn) Unicorn-Kanchana ("Souvenir" series) ▲ UK 2074
Delius, F.:Son 3 Vn & Pno, w. Ralph Holmes (vn) Unicorn-Kanchana ("Souvenir" series) ▲ UK 2074

Fennelly, Brian (pno)
Fennelly, B.:Empirical Rag *(rec 1980)* New World ▲ 80448-2
Fennelly, B.:Scintilla Prisca, w. David Moore (vc) Capstone ▲ CPS 8631

Fennimore, Joseph (pno)
Brahms, J.:Pno Music (misc)—Rhap in b, Op. 79/1; Intermezzo in E, Op. 116/4; Capriccio in b, Op. 76/2; Intermezzo in e♭, Op. 118/6; Capriccio in f♯, Op. 76/1; Intermezzo in b♭, Op. 117/2; Rhap in g, Op. 79/2 *(rec Kiggins Hall, Emma Willard School, Troy, NY, Sept. 6 & 7, 1992)* Albany ▲ TROY 161 [DDD]
Chopin, F.:Ballades Pno (comp)—in f, Op. 52 *(rec Kiggins Hall, Emma Willard School, Troy, NY, Sept. 6 & 7, 1992)* Albany ▲ TROY 161 [DDD]
Fennimore, J.:Berlitz:Introduction to French, w. J. Castle (mez) [F] Albany ▲ TROY 023-2 [ADD]
Fennimore, J.:Inscape, w. J. Castle (mez) [E] Albany ▲ TROY 023-2 [ADD]
Fennimore, J.:Pno Music, w. P. Freeman (cnd), Royal PO Soloists—Two Pieces from Armistice; Variations on a Theme by Beethoven; Two Rags; Foxtrot; Second Romance; Calentura de Teresa [w. J. Zayas (piano)]; Concerto Piccolo Albany ▲ TROY 113 [ADD]
Fennimore, J.:Romance 4 Pno *(rec Kiggins Hall, Emma Willard School, Troy, NY, Sept. 6 & 7, 1992)* Albany ▲ TROY 161 [DDD]
Fennimore, J.:Son 3 Pno *(rec Kiggins Hall, Emma Willard School, Troy, NY, Sept. 6 & 7, 1992)* Albany ▲ TROY 161 [DDD]
Fennimore, J.:Songs (6), w. K. Williams (sop)—Winter love; Mary weeps for her child; The snow grew out of the sky last night; Infant joy; Now death has shut your eyes; My heart [E] Albany ▲ TROY 023-2 [ADD]
Granados, E.:Goyescas—Lament [Maiden & the Nightingale] *(rec Kiggins Hall, Emma Willard School, Troy, NY, Sept. 6 & 7, 1992)* Albany ▲ TROY 161 [DDD]
Griffes, C.T.:Son Pno Albany ▲ TROY 102 [ADD]
Griffes, C.T.:The White Peacock Albany ▲ TROY 102 [ADD]
Liadov, A.:Pieces Pno, Op. 11—Prelude in b Albany ▲ TROY 102 [ADD]
Schumann, R.:Carnaval Pno Albany ▲ TROY 102 [ADD]
Scriabin, A.:Etudes Pno, Op. 8—Nos. 2, 8, 10, 11 & 12 Albany ▲ TROY 102 [ADD]
Scriabin, A.:Etudes Pno, Op. 42—Nos. 3-5 Albany ▲ TROY 102 [ADD]
Sgambati, G.:Melodie Pno Albany ▲ TROY 102 [ADD]

Fenton, Paul (va)—see ORCHESTRAS & ENSEMBLES Stanislas Ensemble

Fentress, Mike (chit/gtr)—see ORCHESTRAS & ENSEMBLES Al Ayre Español

Fentress, Mike (lt)
Kapsberger, G.G.:Villanelles (misc), w. La Sfera Armoniosa—Lasciavete Pastorelle; Avrilla Mia; Voi Che Dietro; Gia Risi del Mio Mal; Alla Caccia Pastore; Ite Sospiri Miei; Pieta di Chi Si Mora; Amor Non Piangere; Passacaglia; Tu Che Pallido e Sangue; Fuggi Fuggi l'Inganno; Figlio Dormi; Sussurat'aure; Spiega, Spiega; Canzona Prima; Tu Dormi Anima Mia; No No No Non Burlar; Che Fai Tu Carlton ("Musick's Monument" series) ▲ MSK 6500092

Fentress, Mike (lt/thb)
Philidor, P.:Music of, w. W. Hazelet (trns fl), K. Clark (trns fl), T. Zwart (vl), J. Ogg (hpd)—Trios 1 & 2 in G & e for 2 Flutes & Continuo; Suite No. 3 in D for 2 Flutes; Suites Nos. 5, 6 & 12 in e, b & D for Flute & Continuo *(rec June 1993)* Globe ▲ GLO 5107 [DDD]

Fenyö, Gusztáv (pno)
Bantock, G.:Son 3 Vn, w. Susanne Stanzeleit (vn) *(rec St. Michael's Church, Highgate, London)* United ▲ CAL 88031 [DDD]
Dunhill, T.:Son Vn, w. Susanne Stanzeleit (vn) *(rec St. Michael's Church, Highgate, London)* United ▲ CAL 88031 [DDD]
Stanford, C.V.:Son 1 Vn, w. Susanne Stanzeleit (vn) *(rec St. Michael's Church, Highgate, London)* United ▲ CAL 88031 [DDD]

Fenyö, László (vc)
Pizzetti, I.:Trio Pno, w. Alpaslan Ertüngealp (pno), Leila Rásonyi (vn) *(rec Hungaroton Studio, Rottenbiller St, Budapest, May 17-18 & June 2, 1994)* Marco Polo ▲ 8.223812 [DDD]

Fenyves, Lorand (vn)
Rimsky-Korsakov, N.:Scheherazade, w. W. van Otterloo (cnd), Vienna Festival Orch FNAC Music ("Via Classics" series) ▲ 642330

Feodorov, Adil (cl)
Ustvolskaya, G.:Trio Cl, w. Alexander Shustin (vn), Oleg Malov (pno) *(rec St. Petersburg Radio House, Oct. & Nov. 1994)* Megadisc ▲ 7865

Ferarris, M. (vn)
Vivaldi, A.:Sons Vn, Op. 5, w. F. Fantini (vn), A. Ephrikaim (vn), A. Pocaterra (vc), G. Ghetti (vc), I. De Carli (cembalo), V. Luccini (cembalo) Rivoalto ▲ CRA 9005 [ADD]

Ferber, Albert (pno)
Fauré, G.:Pno Music—Theme & Vars., Op. 73; Capriccio, Op. 84/1; Barcarolle No. 2, Op. 41; Improvisation, Op. 84/4; Adagietto, Op. 84/5; 9 Preludes, Op. 105 Saga Classics ▲ 3397
Fauré, G.:Pno Music—Romance sans paroles in A♭, Op. 17/3; Barcarolle No. 1 in a, Op. 26; Nocturne No. 1 in e♭, Op. 33/1; Nocturne No. 3 in A♭, Op. 33/3; Nocturne No. 4 in E♭, Op. 36; Nocturne No. 6 in D♭, Op. 63; Barcarolle No. 6 in E♭ Saga Classics ▲ 3398

Ferchen, Timothy (perc)
Bartók, B.:Son for 2 Pnos, w. M. Raekallio (pno), J. Lagerspätz (pno), L. Erkkilä (perc) Ondine ▲ ODE 806 [DDD]
Bergman, E.:Borealis, w. M. Raekallio (pno), J. Lagerspätz (pno), L. Erkkilä (perc) Ondine ▲ ODE 806 [DDD]
Kortekangas, O.:Memoria, w. E. Pohjola (cnd), Tapiola Choir, Tapiola Children's Choir [Fin] Ondine ▲ ODE 749-2 [ADD]
Lindberg, M.:Metalwork, w. Matti Rantanen (acc) Finlandia ▲ FIN 54404 [DDD]

Ferchen, Timothy (vib/crotales)
Takemitsu, T.:Music of, w. Mikael Helasvuo (fl), Jukka Savijoki (gtr), Eero Palviainen (lt)—Sacrifice; Voice; All in Twilight; Ring; Folios; Itinerant; Toward the Sea Ondine ▲ ODE 839 [DDD]

Ferebauer, Václav (trbn)
Janácek, L.:Capriccio, w. Daniel Wiesner (pno), Jan Riedlbauch (fl/pic), Vladislav Kozderka (tpt), Jan Fišer (tpt), Jan Hynčica (trbn), Antonin Keller (trbn), Jiří Novotny (ten tuba), L. Svárovsky (cnd) *(rec Martinek Studio in Prague, Jan 9, Feb 27, Mar 20, 19)* Panton ▲ 811393-2 [DDD]

Ferencsik, János (pno)
Stolarczyk, W.:Earth Air Fire Water, w. Amalie Malling (pno), John Damgaard (pno), Anne Øland (pno), Teddy Teirup (pno), Friedrich Gürtler (pno), Rosalind Bevan (pno), Poul Rosenbaum (pno), Rodolfo Llambias (pno), Bella Horn-Ribera (pno), Anders Riber (pno), Elisabeth Sigurdsson (pno), Thomas Tronheim (pno), Elsebeth Broderson (pno), Erik Kaltoft (pno), Jørgen Hald Nielsen (pno), Aino Gilemann (pno), Birgit Kjær (pno), Jørgen Thomsen (pno), Gunhild Donslund (pno), Henrik Bo Hansen (pno), Lone Karlsson (pno), Erik Fessel (pno), Lasse Nilsson (pno), Erik Bach (pno), Axel Momme (pno), Arne de Cros Dich (pno), Sven Micha Slot (pno), Hanne Bramsen Buhl (pno), Lili Olesen (pno), Susannah Carlsson (pno), Ulla Erml (pno), Vagn Sørensen (pno), Leif Greibe (pno), Bodil Krogh (pno), Kirsten Ottosen (pno), Inger Bergenholz (pno), Karsten Gylendorf (pno), Bjørr Elkjær (pno), Jacob Bjørn Jensen (pno), Jørgen Kaad (pno), Anne Marie Hjelm (pno), Carl Ulrik Munk Andersen (pno), Poul Lumbye (pno), Oluf Hildebrandt Nielsen (pno), Joachim Olsson (pno), Peter Pade Ramsøe Jacobsen (pno), Astrid Pollmann (pno), Jette Borsch (pno), Kirsten Karlshøj (pno), Maria Teresa Assing (pno), Allan Dahl Hansen (pno), Johan Hugossen (pno), Tine Fenger Pederson (pno), Arne Jørgen Fæø (pno), Anja Høgsted (pno), Anne Sophie Parbo (pno), Inga Lindmark (pno), Teresa Drabik Stathakis (pno), Anne Ruth Ferenczi (pno), Irene Hasager (pno), Yuka Ichikawa (pno), Birgitte Baur (pno), Malene Thastum (pno), Jens E. Rasmussen (pno), Birgitte Zielke (pno), Claus Zielke (pno), Stefan Kasch (pno), Bin Qiao (pno), Inger Johanne Teirup (pno), Lindy Rosborg (pno), Liisa Heininen (pno), David Højer (pno), Ellen Refstrup (pno), Thomas K. Søorensen (pno), Erik Kure (pno), Michael Rauff (pno), Jan beck Eriksson (pno), Tanja Zapolski (pno), Vibeke Skagbo (pno), Pål Eide Lindtner (pno), Ha-Young Sul (pno), Benedicte Palko (pno), Inke Kesseler (pno), Anne Marie Meineche (pno), Sverre Larsen (pno), Kasper Peter Bach (pno), Elisabetta Eliseo (pno), Olga Magieres (pno), Carl Erik Kühl (pno), Thorkild Borup Nielsen (pno), Valeria Zanini (pno), Lars Stenhoft (perc), Dennis Boel (perc), Winnie Dahlgren (perc), Susanne Vind (perc), Claus Byrith (elec), Anne Marie Storm (elec), J. Ribera (cnd) *(rec live, Koldinghaus Castle, Denmark, May 2, 1996)* Danica ▲ DCD 1996

Ferey, Jean-Pierre (pno)
Bartók, B.:Romanian Dances Skarbo ▲ SKR 3891 [DDD]
Cras, J.:Pieces (4) Vn & Pno, w. Marie-Annick Nicolas (vn) *(rec 1993)* Skarbo ▲ SK 4941 [DDD]
Cras, J.:Poèmes Intimes *(rec 1993)* Skarbo ▲ SK 4941 [DDD]
Cras, J.:Suite en Duo, w. Marie-Annick Nicolas (vn) *(rec 1993)* Skarbo ▲ SK 4941 [DDD]
Fauré, G.:Allegro symphonique, w. J.-A. Gendille (cnd), Mans SO [arr. for Piano & Orch.] Skarbo ▲ SKR 3921 [DDD]
Franck, C.:Symphonic Vars, w. J.-A. Gendille (cnd), Mans SO Skarbo ▲ SKR 3921 [DDD]
Koechlin, C.:L'Accienne maison de campagne Skarbo ▲ SKR 3932 [DDD]
Koechlin, C.:Ballade Pno Skarbo ▲ SKR 3932 [DDD]
Koechlin, C.:Preludes Pno Skarbo ▲ SKR 3932 [DDD]
Rameau, J.P.:Nouvelles suites—Gavotte avec 6 doubles in a Skarbo ▲ SKR 3891 [DDD]
Rameau, J.P.:Pièces de clavecin avec une méthode sur la mécanique des doigts—1st rigaudon in e; 2nd rigaudon in E; Double of 2nd rigaudon in E Skarbo ▲ SKR 3891 [DDD]
Ravel, M.:Miroirs—Alborada del gracioso Skarbo ▲ SKR 3891 [DDD]
Roussel, A.:Suite Pno Skarbo ▲ SKR 3891 [DDD]

Fergus-Thompson, Gordon (pno)
Debussy, C.:Pno Music (complete solo) ASV ▲ ASV 711 [DDD]
Debussy, C.:Pno Music (complete solo)—Deux arabesques; Images oubliées; Preludes, Book 1 ASV ▲ ASV 720 [DDD]
Debussy, C.:Pno Music (complete solo)—Etudes, Books 1 & 2 ASV ▲ ASV 703 [DDD]
Debussy, C.:Pno Music (complete solo)—Preludes (Book 2) & Suite bergamasque ASV ▲ ASV 723 [DDD]
Debussy, C.:Pno Music (complete solo)—Children's Corner Suite; Estampes; Images, Books 1 & 2 ASV ▲ ASV 695 [DDD]
Rachmaninoff, S.:Études-tableaux, Opp. 33 & 39 ASV ▲ ASV 789
Ravel, M.:Pno Music—À la manière de Borodine; À la manière de Chabrier; Menuet antique; Menuet sur le nom d'Haydn; Miroirs; Pavane pour une infante défunte; Prélude; Sérénade grotesque; Sonatine ASV ▲ ASV 809 [DDD]
Reverie, w. Fergus-Thompson, Gordon (pno) ASV ("White Line" series) ▲ ASV 2066
Scriabin, A.:Etudes Pno, Op. 8 ASV ▲ ASV 882 [DDD]
Scriabin, A.:Etudes Pno, Op. 42 ASV ▲ ASV 776
Scriabin, A.:Nocturnes Pno, Op. 5 ASV ▲ ASV 882 [DDD]
Scriabin, A.:Pno Music (comp)—Etudes (8), Op. 42; Piano Sonatas 4, 5, 9 & 10 ASV ▲ ASV 776
Scriabin, A.:Pno Music (comp)—Preludes, Opp. 2/2, 9/1, 11, 13, 16 & 17 ASV ▲ ASV 919 [DDD]
Scriabin, A.:Sons Pno (comp)—Nos. 4,5,9 & 10 ASV ▲ ASV 776
Scriabin, A.:Son 2 Pno ASV ▲ ASV 882 [DDD]
Scriabin, A.:Son 3 Pno ASV ▲ ASV 882 [DDD]

Ferko, Frank (org)
Ferko, F.:The Hildegard Org Cycle—The Origin of Life; The Construction of the World; Human Nature; Articulation of the Body; Places of Purification; The Meaning of History; Preparation for Christ; The Effect of Love; Completion of the Cosmos; The End of Time [Lively-Fulcher Org] *(rec St. Patrick's Church, Washington, DC, Dec 6-7, 1994)* ARSIS ▲ CD 101 [DDD]

Fernandes, Marialena (pno)
Mišek, A.:Son 1 Db, w. Josef Niederhammer (db) Ambitus ▲ 97890 [DDD]
Mišek, A.:Son 2 Db, w. Josef Niederhammer (db) Ambitus ▲ 97890 [DDD]
Mišek, A.:Son 3 Db, w. Josef Niederhammer (db) Ambitus ▲ 97890 [DDD]

INSTRUMENT.

Fernandez, David (sax)
Colgrass, M.:Urban Requiem, w. Tom McCormick (sax), Stephen Welsh (sax), George Weremchuk (sax), G. Green (cnd), Univ of Miami Wind Ensemble *(rec Miami Beach, Feb 1996)* Albany ▲ TROY 212 [DDD]

Fernández, Eduardo (gtr)
Day's End:The Soft Sound of Spanish Guitar, w. William Gómez (gtr), Nicola Hall (gtr), Timothy Walker (gtr), John Williams (gtr) London ▲ 448 560-2

Fernandez, François (va)
Bach, W.F.:Duets (3) Vas, w. Ryo Terakado (va) *(rec 1992)* Ricercar 2-▲ 089125/26
Haydn, J.:Qts Fl, w. Barthold Kuijken (fl), Sigswald Kuijken (vn), Wieland Kuijken (vc) Accent 2-▲ 9283/84

Fernandez, François (vn)—see also ORCHESTRAS & ENSEMBLES Kuijken String Quartet
Bach, J.S.:Con Fl, Vn & Hpd, w. Marc Hantaï (fl), Pierre Hantaï (hpd), P. Hantaï (cnd), Le Concert Français Astrée ▲ E 8523
Couperin, F.:Les Nations, w. M. Hantaï (fl), B. Kuijken (fl), S. Kuijken (vn), W. Kuijken (bass vl), R. Kohnen (hpd) *(rec Mar. 1992)* Accent 2-▲ 9285/86 [DDD]
Defense de la Basse Viole contre les Enterprises du Violon et les Pretentions du Violoncelle [Defense of the Bass Viol against the Enterprise of the Violin & the Pretension of the Cello], w. P. Pierlot (b vl), Hidemi Suzuki (vc), Ricercar Consort Ricercar 3-▲ RIC 93005

Fernández, Nohema (pno)
Cervantes, I.:Danzas Cubanas Protone ▲ PRCD 1107 [DDD]
Harrison, L.:A Summerfield Set MusicMasters ▲ 7051-2-C [DDD]
Morel Campos, J.:Danzas Puertorriqueñas Protone ▲ PRCD 1107 [DDD]
Saumell, M.:Contradanzas Cubanas Protone ▲ PRCD 1107 [DDD]

Ferran, Dominique (org)
Corrette, M.:Org Music—Premier livre d'orgue Adda ▲ ADD 3 [DDD]
Zipoli, D.:Dell'offese a vendicarmi chiamo all'armi, w. Elyma Ensemble Soloists [organ at Monticello in Corsica] K617 ▲ 7037
Zipoli, D.:Mia bella Irene, w. Elyma Ensemble Soloists [organ at Monticello in Corsica] K617 ▲ 7037
Zipoli, D.:Son Vn, w. Elyma Ensemble Soloists [organ at Monticello in Corsica] K617 ▲ 7037
Zipoli, D.:Son d'intavolatura Org [organ at Monticello in Corsica] K617 ▲ 7037

Ferrari, Benito (vn)
Marcello, B.:Sons Vc, w. A. Pocaterra (vc), M.I. De Carli (cembalo) Rivoalto ▲ CRA 9008 [ADD]

Ferrari, J. (vib/perc)
Jones, D.E.:Still Life Dancing, w. J. Bluestone (dr/cym/hand perc), D. Kennedy (mar/perc) Centaur ▲ CRC 2052 [DDD]
Jones, D.E.:Still Life in Wood & Metal, w. D. Kennedy (mar/perc) Centaur ▲ CRC 2052 [DDD]

Ferrarini, Claudio (fl)
Besozzi, A.:Trio Sons (6), w. Lavard Skou Larsen (vn), Detlef Mielke (vc) Stradivarius ▲ STV 33317 [ADD]
Handel, G.F.:Royal Fireworks Music, w. Luigi Fontana (hpd) Stradivarius ▲ STV 33301 [DDD]
Handel, G.F.:Royal Fireworks Music, w. L. Fontana (hpd) Stradivarius ▲ STR 33301 [DDD]
Handel, G.F.:Water Music (comp), w. L. Fontana (hpd) Stradivarius ▲ STR 33301 [DDD]
Handel, G.F.:Water Music (comp), w. Luigi Fontana (hpd) Stradivarius ▲ STV 33301 [DDD]
Handel, G.F.:Water Music (suites), w. L. Fontana (hpd) Stradivarius ▲ STR 33301 [DDD]
Rousseau, J.-J.:Le Printemps du Vivaldi Stradivarius ▲ STV 33301 [DDD]
Sarti, G.:Sons Fl, w. Sokol Koka (vc), Christine Meyr (hpd) Stradivarius ▲ STV 33368 [DDD]
Viotti, G.B.:Qts Fl, Op. 22, w. Salisburg String Quartet members Stradivarius ▲ STV 33338 [DDD]
Vivaldi, A.:Cons Vn, Op. 8/1-12, "Il cimento dell'armonia e dell'inventione", w. L. Fontana (hpd)—Nos. 1-4 Stradivarius ▲ STR 33301 [DDD]
Vivaldi, A.:Cons Vn, Op. 8/1-4, "The Four Seasons", w. Luigi Fontana (hpd)—Summer, Autumn & Winter Stradivarius ▲ STV 33301 [DDD]

Ferraris, Benito (vn)
Marcello, B.:Sons Vc, w. Antonio Pocaterra (vc), Maria Isabella de Carli (hpd) Rivoalto ▲ RIV 9008 [ADD]

Ferraris, M. (vn)—see ORCHESTRAS & ENSEMBLES Milan Solisti

Ferras, Christian (vn)
Beethoven, L. van:Son 4 Vn, w. P. Barbizet (pno) *(rec 1971)* FNAC Music ▲ 642327
Beethoven, L. van:Son 6 Vn, w. P. Barbizet (pno) *(rec 1971)* FNAC Music ▲ 642327
Beethoven, L. van:Son 7 Vn, w. P. Barbizet (pno) *(rec 1971)* FNAC Music ▲ 642327
Chausson, E.:Con Vn, Pno & Str Qt, w. P. Barbizet (pno), Lamoureux Concerts Orch members EMI Classics ▲ CDM 64365
Tchaikovsky, P.:Con Vn, w. H. von Karajan (cnd), Berlin PO Deutsche Grammophon ("Resonance" series) ▲ 429166-2 [ADD]

Ferré, Eugène (baroque gtr)
Vivaldi, A.:Sons Vc, w. A. Zweistra (vc)—(3) in E♭, RV.39; in g, RV.42; in a, RV.44 L'Oiseau-Lyre ▲ 433052-2 [DDD]

Ferré, Eugène (lt)
Paladino, G.:Premier livre de tabulature de Lute [Renaissance 6-string lt] Arcana ▲ CD 1 [DDD]

Ferrell, J. (vn)
Lewis, P.T.:Music of, w. J. Avery (pno), S. Schick (perc), Peter Tod Lewis (elec), Center for New Music Ensemble, Columbia String Quartet—Bricolage (1979); Gestes (1973); Manestar (1970); ...of bells...and time (1967); Signs & Circuits—String Quartet No. 2 (1969) *(rec 1978-82)* CRI ▲ CD 619 [ADD]

Ferrer, Miguel Garcia (gtr)
Sor, F.:Gtr Music, w. Carmen Maria Ros (gtr)—L'Encouragement, Op. 34; Divert, Op. 38; Seis valses, Op. 39; Los dos amigos, Op. 41; Seis valses, Op. 44 bis; Divert. Militar, Op. 49; Bolero a duo la premier pas vers moi, Op. 53; Fant., Op. 54 bis; Tres duos, Op. 55; Tres Pequeños divert., Op. 61; Divert., Op. 62; Souvenir de rusia, Op. 63 Opra Tres 2-▲ 1008/09

Ferreras, S. (perc)
Louie, A.:Love Songs for a Small Planet, w. E. Goodman (hp), Vancouver Chamber Choir Centrediscs ▲ CMCCD 4893 [DDD]
Songs of War & Peace, w. Leoni Men's Chorus [cnd:Diane Loomer], Christopher Gaze (nar), Stephen Smith (pno), Philip Crewe (perc) Skylark ▲ 9501 [DDD]

Ferris, Hadley (va)
Beside Thy Cradle, w. Salt Lake Children's Choir [cnd:Ralph B. Woodward], Tamara B. Oswald (hp), Janet Peterson (hp), Kelly Parkinson (vn), Victoria Ferris (vn), Ellen Bridger (vc) *(rec Maurice Abravanel Hall, Salt Lake City)* Cherbourne ▲ CH 121

Ferris, Mark (vn)
Davies, V.:Qt 1 Strs, "Fun for 4", w. Arthur Polson (vn), Nancy DiNovo (va), Ian Hampton (vc) Campion ▲ RRCD 1339 [DDD]

Ferris, Victoria (vn)
Beside Thy Cradle, w. Salt Lake Children's Choir [cnd:Ralph B. Woodward], Tamara B. Oswald (hp), Janet Peterson (hp), Kelly Parkinson (vn), Hadley Ferris (va), Ellen Bridger (vc) *(rec Maurice Abravanel Hall, Salt Lake City)* Cherbourne ▲ CH 121

Ferris, William (pno)
Songs, Dances & Fantasy, w. J. Fuller (db), Frederick Ockwell (pno), Kenneth Dorsch (hpd), Steve Hartman (hp), Thomas Potter (bar), John Vorrasi (ten), Anne Waller (gtr) Musical Arts Society ▲ CD 41589 [AAD] ■ CS 41589

Ferro, Luigi (vn)
Vivaldi, A.:Cons Vn, Op. 8/1-4, "The Four Seasons", w. Guido Mozzato (vn), R. Fasano (cnd), Rome Virtuosi *(rec Abbey Road Studios, London, Mar. 1959)* EMI Classics ▲ CDK 65338 [ADD]
Vivaldi, A.:Cons for 4 Vns, w. Franco Gulli (vn), Edmondo Malanotte (vn), Angelo Stefanato (vn), R. Fasano (cnd), Rome Virtuosi—in b, Op. 3/10 *(rec Opéra de Rome, July & August, 1959)* EMI Classics ▲ CDK 65338 [ADD]

Ferrone, Don (db)
Matson, S.:Range, w. Catherine Robbin (mez), Susan Greenberg (fl), Joseph Stone (fl), Glen Garrett (cl), Suren Karapetyan (hn), Peter Kent (vn), Kazi Pitelka (va), Sebastian Toettcher (vc), Doug Livingston (gtr/mand), John Schneider (gtr), Amy Shulman (hp), Terry Schoenig (perc), S. Matson (cnd) *(rec Schnee Studio, Universal City, CA, Mar 12, 1995)* New Albion ▲ NA 091

Ferry, Dennis (tpt)
Melani, A.:Cants, w. J. Nelson (sop)—"All'armi, pensieri" for Soprano & Trumpet [I] Musique d'Abord ▲ HMA 1905137
Melani, A.:Sinf a 5, w. J. Nelson (sop) [I] Musique d'Abord ▲ HMA 1905137
Scarlatti, A.:Arias Sop, w. Nelson (sop), et al. [I] Musique d'Abord ▲ HMA 1905137

Ferschtman, Dimitri (vc)
Bosmans, H.:Poème, w. E. Spanjaard (cnd), Netherlands Radio CO NM Classics ▲ NM 92040
Bosmans, H.:Poème, w. E. Spanjaard (cnd), Netherlands Radio CO *(rec Concertgebouw Haarlem, Sept 1, 1993)* NM Special ▲ 92095 [DDD]
Escher, R.:Chamber Music, w. Jacques Zoon (fl), Herman De Boer (cl), Bart Schneemann (ob), Zoltan Benyacs (va), Glen Wilson (hpd)—includes Le Tombeau de Ravel; Trio for Strings; Trio for Cl, Va & Pno NM Classics ▲ NM 92026
Tchaikovsky, P.:Andante cantabile, w. L. Markiz (cnd), Amsterdam New Sinfonietta *(rec Oct. & Dec. 1990)* Globe ▲ GLO 6021 [DDD]

Ferstl, Erich (pno/gtr/perc/monochord)
Ihn Kinderlein kommet, w. [cnd:Gerhard Schmidt-Gaden], Tölz Boys' Choir Capriccio ▲ 10491 [DDD]

Fessel, Erik (pno)
Stolarczyk, W.:Earth Air Fire Water, w. Amalie Malling (pno), John Damgaard (pno), Anne Øland (pno), Teddy Teirup (pno), Friedrich Gürtler (pno), Rosalind Bevan (pno), Poul Rosenbaum (pno), Rodolfo Llambias (pno), Bella Horn-Ribera (pno), Anders Riber (pno), Elisabeth Sigurdsson (pno), Thomas Tronheim (pno), Elsebeth Broderson (pno), Erik Kaltoft (pno), Jørgen Hald Nielsen (pno), Aino Gilemann (pno), Birgit Kjær (pno), Jørgen Thomsen (pno), Gunhild Donslund (pno), Henrik Bo Hansen (pno), Lone Karlsson (pno), Lasse Nilsson (pno), Janos Ferenczi (pno), Erik Bach (pno), Axel Momme (pno), Arne de Cros Dich (pno), Sven Micha Slot (pno), Hanne Bramsen Buhl (pno), Lili Olesen (pno), Susannah Carlsson (pno), Ulla Erml (pno), Vagn Sørensen (pno), Leif Greibe (pno), Bodil Krogh (pno), Kirsten Ottosen (pno), Inger Bergenholz (pno), Karsten Gylendorf (pno), Bjørnr Elkjær (pno), Jacob Bjørn Jensen (pno), Jørgen Kaad (pno), Anne Marie Hjelm (pno), Carl Ulrik Munk Andersen (pno), Poul Lumbye (pno), Oluf Hildebrandt Nielsen (pno), Joachim Olsson (pno), Peter Pade Ramsøe Jacobsen (pno), Astrid Pollmann (pno), Jette Borsch (pno), Kirsten Karlshøj (pno), Maria Teresa Assing (pno), Allan Dahl Hansen (pno), Johan Hugossen (pno), Tine Fenger Pederson (pno), Arne Jørgen Fæø (pno), Anja Høgsted (pno), Anne Sophie Parbo (pno), Inga Lindmark (pno), Teresa Drabik Stathakis (pno), Anne Ruth Ferenczi (pno), Irene Hasager (pno), Yuka Ichikawa (pno), Birgitte Baur (pno), Malene Thastum (pno), Jens E. Rasmussen (pno), Birgitte Zielke (pno), Claus Zielke (pno), Stefan Kasch (pno), Bin Qiao (pno), Inger Johanne Teirup (pno), Lindy Rosborg (pno), Liisa Heininen (pno), David Højer (pno), Ellen Refstrup (pno), Thomas K. Søorensen (pno), Erik Kure (pno), Michael Rauff (pno), Jan beck Eriksson (pno), Tanja Zapolski (pno), Vibeke Skagbo (pno), Pål Eide Lindtner (pno), Ha-Young Sul (pno), Benedicte Palko (pno), Inke Kesseler (pno), Anne Marie Meineche (pno), Sverre Larsen (pno), Kasper Peter Bach (pno), Elisabetta Eliseo (pno), Olga Magieres (pno), Carl Erik Kühl (pno), Thorkild Borup Nielsen (pno), Valeria Zanini (pno), Lars Stenhoft (perc), Dennis Boel (perc), Winnie Dahlgren (perc), Susanne Vind (perc), Claus Byrith (elec), Anne Marie Storm (elec), J. Ribera (cnd) *(rec live, Koldinghaus Castle, Denmark, May 2, 1996)* Danica ▲ DCD 1996

Fetherston, John (cl)
Wagner, R.:Siegfried Idyll, w. T. Holowach (vn), M. Skazinetsky (vn), L. Toman (va), R. Laurie (vc), C. Elliott (db), S. Shulman (fl), T. Maloney (cl), J. Valdepenas (cl), S. Mosher (bn), S. Wilson (hn), R. Cohen (hn), J. Cowell (tpt), G. Gould (cnd) *(rec July 27-29 & Sept. 8, 198)* Sony Classical ▲ SMK 52650 [ADD]

Fetz, Günther (hpd)
Bach, C.P.E.:Sonatina for 2 Hpds, w. R. Scheidegger (hpd) Koch Schwann ▲ CD 311081 [ADD]
Bach, C.P.E.:Sonatina for 2 Hpds, w. R. Scheidegger (hpd) Koch Schwann ▲ SCH 313422 [ADD]

Feuermann, Emanuel (vc)
Albert, E. d':Con Vc, w. L. Barzin (cnd), *(orch unknown)* Arlecchino 2- ARL
Beethoven, L. van:Serenade Strs, Op. 8, w. S. Goldberg (vn), P. Hindemith (va) *(rec 1/22/34)* EMI Classics ▲ CDH 64250-2 (m) [ADD]
Beethoven, L. van:Serenade Strs, Op. 8, w. S. Goldberg (vn), P. Hindemith (va) *(rec 1934)* Pearl ▲ PEA 9443 (m) [AAD]
Beethoven, L. van:Son 3 Vc, w. M. Hess (pno) *(rec 6/37)* EMI Classics ▲ CDH 64250-2 (m) [ADD]
Beethoven, L. van:Son 3 Vc, w. M. Hess (pno) *(rec 1937)* Pearl ▲ PEA 9446 (m) [AAD]
Beethoven, L. van:Son 3 Vc, w. M. Hess (pno) *(rec 1937)* Pearl ▲ PEA 9462 (m) [AAD]
Beethoven, L. van:Trio 6 Pno, "Archduke", w. A. Rubinstein (pno), J. Heifetz (vn) RCA Gold Seal ▲ 09026-60926-2 ■ 09026-60926-4
Beethoven, L. van:Vars on "Bei Männern" from Mozart's *Die Zauberflöte*, w. T. van der Pas (pno) *(rec 7/11/34)* EMI Classics ▲ CDH 64250-2 (m) [ADD]
Beethoven, L. van:Vars on "Bei Männern" from Mozart's *Die Zauberflöte*, w. T. van der Pas (pno) *(rec 1937)* Pearl ▲ PEA 9442 (m) [AAD]
Bloch, E.:Schelomo, w. L. Barzin (cnd), *(orch unknown)* Arlecchino 2- ARL
Bloch, E.:Schelomo, w. L. Stokowski (cnd), Philadelphia Orch *(rec 1940 Victor)* Biddulph ▲ LAB 042 [ADD]
Brahms, J.:Con Vn & Vc, "Double Con", w. Jascha Heifetz (vn), E. Ormandy (cnd), Philadelphia Orch *(rec Dec 21, 1939)* Iron Needle ▲ IN 1351 [ADD]
Brahms, J.:Son 1 Vc, w. T. van der Pas (pno) *(rec 1934)* Biddulph ▲ LAB 011 [ADD]
Brahms, J.:Son 1 Vc, w. T. van der Pas (pno) *(rec 1934)* Pearl ▲ PEA 9443 (m) [AAD]
The Columbia Recordings, Vol. 1, w. Theo van der Pas (pno), Malcolm Sargent (cnd), *(orch unknown)* *(rec 1934-1937)* Pearl ▲ PEA 9442 (m) [AAD]
Dohnányi, E. von:Serenade, w. J. Heifetz (vn), W. Primrose (va) Biddulph ▲ LAB 074 [ADD]
Dvořák, A.:Con Vc, w. L. Barzin (cnd), *(orch unknown)* Arlecchino 2- ARL
Dvořák, A.:Rondo, w. L. Barzin (cnd), *(orch unknown)* Arlecchino 2- ARL
Dvořák, A.:Silent Woods, w. L. Barzin (cnd), *(orch unknown)* Arlecchino 2- ARL
Haydn, J.:Con 2 Vc, w. M. Sargent (cnd), *(orch unknown)* *(rec 1935)* Pearl ▲ PEA 9442 (m) [AAD]
Hindemith, P.:Scherzo Va & Vc, w. P. Hindemith (va) EMI Classics 2-▲ ZDCB 55032
Hindemith, P.:Scherzo Va & Vc, w. P. Hindemith (va) *(rec 1934)* Pearl ▲ PEA 9446 (m) [AAD]
Hindemith, P.:Son Vc, Op. 25/3 *(rec 1934)* Pearl ▲ PEA 9446 (m) [AAD]
Hindemith, P.:Trio 2, w. S. Goldberg (vn), P. Hindemith (va) EMI Classics 2-▲ ZDCB 55032
Hindemith, P.:Trio 2, w. S. Goldberg (vn), P. Hindemith (va) *(rec 1927-1934)* Koch Schwann ▲ CD 311342 [DDD]
Mozart, W.A.:Trio Vn, K.563, w. Jascha Heifetz (vn), William Primrose (va) *(rec RCA Studios, Hollywood, Sept 9, 1941)* RCA Gold Seal 2-▲ 09026-61740-2 (m) [ADD]
Mozart, W.A.:Trio Vn, K.563, w. J. Heifetz (vn), W. Primrose (va) Biddulph ▲ LAB 074 [ADD]
Reger, M.:Suites Vc—No. 1 *(rec 1939)* Pearl ▲ PEA 9443 (m) [AAD]
Schubert, Franz:Son Arpeggione, w. Gerald Moore (pno) *(rec 1937)* Pearl ▲ PEA 9442 (m) [AAD]
Schubert, Franz:Son Arpeggione, w. Gerald Moore (pno) *(rec 6/30/37)* EMI Classics ▲ CDH 64250-2 (m) [ADD]
Schubert, Franz:Trio 1 Pno, w. A. Rubinstein (pno), J. Heifetz (vn) RCA Gold Seal ▲ 09026-60926-2 ■ 09026-60926-4
Strauss, R.:Don Quixote, w. E. Ormandy (cnd), Philadelphia Orch *(rec 1940 for Victor)* Biddulph ▲ LAB 042 [ADD]
Strauss, R.:Don Quixote, w. A. Toscanini (cnd), NBC SO *(rec 1938)* Music & Arts ▲ CD 613 [AAD]

Feves, Julie (bn)
Fontana, G.B.:Sons, w. Gerard Schwarz (tpt), Helen Katz (hpd) Vox Box 2-▲ CDX 5124 [ADD]

▲ = CD ♦ = Enhanced CD Δ = MD ■ = Cassette Tape □ = DCC

Feves, Julie (bn) (cont.)
Frescobaldi, G.:Canzonas, Caprici & Ricercari, w. Gerard Schwarz (tpt), Helen Katz (hpd) Vox Box 2-▲ CDX 5124 [ADD]
Nielsen, C.:Qnt Ww, w. R. Wilson (fl), A. Vogel (ob), D. Shifrin (cl), D. Jolley (hn) *(rec July 1–4, 1992)* Delos ▲ DE 3136 [DDD]

Feves, Michael (vl)
Einhorn, R.:Voices of Light, w. Susan Narucki (sop), Corrie Pronk (alt), Frank Hameleers (ten), Henk van Heijnsbergen (b-bar), Ronald Hoogeveen (vn), Harm Bakker (vl), Naomi Hirschfeld (vl), S. Mercurio (cnd), Netherlands Radio PO, Martin Wright (cnd), Anonymous 4, Netherlands Radio Chorus *(rec Music Center of the Netherlands Radio & TV, Aug 23–25, 1995)* Sony Classical ▲ SK 62006 [DDD]

Février, Jacques (pno)
Favorite Piano, w. Daniel Adni (pno), A. Brownridge (pno), M. Lympany (pno), J. Ogdon (pno), G. Tacchino (pno) Classics for Pleasure ▲ CDCFP 4622 [ADD/DDD]

Fevrier, Jacques (pno)
Ravel, M.:Pno Music—Galpard de la nuit; Prelude; A la manière de...Borodine; A la maniere de...Emmanuel Chabrier; Valses nobles et sentimentales sit auriculaires Adès ▲ ADE 141072
Ravel, M.:Pno Music—Miroirs; Pavane pour une infante défunte; Menuet sur le nom de Haydn; Ma mère l'oye Adès ▲ ADE 203912 [AAD]
Satie, E.:En habit de cheval, w. Georgis Auric (pno) Adès ▲ ADE 203842 [AAD]
Satie, E.:Morceaux en forme de poire, w. Georgis Auric (pno) Adès ▲ ADE 203842 [AAD]
Satie, E.:Petites pièces montées, w. Georgis Auric (pno) Adès ▲ ADE 203842 [AAD]

Few, Guy (pno)
Alain Trudel, w. A. Trudel (trbn) Analekta ▲ CLCD 2015
Huggett, A.:Suite Acc, w. J. Petric (accord) *(rec June 12–13, 1991)* CBC ("Musica Viva" series) ▲ MVCD 1056 [DDD]
Molique, W.B.:Son Concertina, w. J. Petric (accordian) *(rec June 12–13, 1991)* CBC ("Musica Viva" series) ▲ MVCD 1056 [DDD]

Few, Guy (tpt)
Hétu, J.:Con Tpt, w. R. Armenian (cnd), Kitchener-Waterloo SO *(rec May 23, 1991 & June 1, 19)* CBC ("SM 5000" series) ▲ SMCD 5130 [DDD]
Martinů, B.:La Revue de Cuisine, w. James Campbell (cl), James McKay (bn), Moshe Hammer (vn), Tsuyoshi Tsutsumi (vc), André Laplante (pno) *(rec Glenn Gould Studio, CBC Toronto, Mar. 26–27, 1994)* CBC ("Musica Viva" series) ▲ MVV 1089 [DDD]

Feybli, Walter (gtr)
Dances from Spain & Latin America, w. K. Ragossnig (gtr) *(rec 1973)* Entrée ▲ 0022-2 [AAD]
Music from Spain & Latin America for 2 Guitars, w. Daniel Erni (gtr) Orfeo ▲ CD 189891 [DDD] ■ MC 189891 (D)

Feyer, George (pno)
Gershwin, G.:Music of—sixteen songs & song medleys *(rec 1974)* Vanguard Classics ▲ OVC 6002 [ADD]

Feyertag, Maximilian (bn)—see ORCHESTRAS & ENSEMBLES Vienna Quintet

Feyler, Pierre (db)
Beethoven, L. van:Trio Pno, Op.38, w. Thierry Ravassard (pno), Françoise Perrin (vn) Gallo ▲ CD 761
Chausson, E.:Poème Vn, w. Françoise Perrin (vn), Thierry Ravassard (pno) [arr Antoine Duhamel for trio] *(rec 1994)* Gallo ▲ CD 801 [DDD]
Duhamel, A.:Contrebasse oblige *(rec 1994)* Gallo ▲ CD 801 [DDD]
Kreisler, F.:Music of, w. Françoise Perrin (vn), Thierry Ravassard (pno)—Liebesleid Gallo ▲ CD 761
Massenet, J.:Méditation from *Thaïs*, w. Thierry Ravassard (pno), Françoise Perrin (vn) [arr for Pno, Vn & Db] Gallo ▲ CD 761
Monti, A.:Czardas, w. Thierry Ravassard (pno), Françoise Perrin (vn) Gallo ▲ CD 761
Ravel, M.:Tzigane, w. Françoise Perrin (vn), Thierry Ravassard (pno) [arr Antoine Duhamel for trio] *(rec 1994)* Gallo ▲ CD 801 [DDD]

Feyrabend, Simone (va)—see ORCHESTRAS & ENSEMBLES Elyséen String Quartet

Fiacco, Arthur (vc)
Handel, G.F.:Trio Sons, w. John Solum (trns fl), Judson Griffin (vn), Igor Kipnis (hpd)—in c, H.386a Epiphany ▲ EP 7
The Instrument of Kings:A Program of 18th Century Music for Flute & Keyboard, w. J. Solum (trns fl), Igor Kipnis (hpd/pno) *(rec Jan. 17–21, 1994)* Epiphany ▲ EP 2
Telemann, G.P.:Musique de Table, w. J. Solum (trns fl), I. Kipnis (hpd)—solo in b for Fl & Bc Epiphany ▲ EP 7

Fialkowska, Janina (pno)
Chopin, F.:Andante Spianato & Grande Polonaise, w. R. Armenian (cnd), Kitchener-Waterloo SO *(rec Centre in the Square, Kitchener, Ontario, Feb. 9 & 10, 1993)* CBC ("SM 5000" series) ▲ SMCD 5140 [DDD]
Koprowski, P.P.:Souvenirs de Pologne, w. R. Armenian (cnd), Kitchener-Waterloo SO *(rec Centre in the Square, Kitchener, Ontario, Feb. 9 & 10, 1993)* CBC ("SM 5000" series) ▲ SMCD 5140 [DDD]
Liszt, F.:Études d'exécution transcendante, S.139—No. 5, "Feux follets"; No. 9, "Ricordanza"; No. 12, "Chasse-neige") CBC ("Musica Viva" series) ▲ MVCD 1035 [DDD]
Liszt, F.:Mephisto Waltz 3 Pno—No. 1 CBC ("Musica Viva" series) ▲ MVCD 1035 [DDD]
Liszt, F.:Sonetti del Petrarca Pno—No. 104 CBC ("Musica Viva" series) ▲ MVCD 1035 [DDD]
Liszt, F.:Song Transcriptions—Chopin—Polish Song No. 1, "The maiden's wish," from Op. 74; Schubert—Hark, hark, the lark; Schumann—Liebeslied, "Widmung" CBC ("Musica Viva" series) ▲ MVCD 1035 [DDD]
Liszt, F.:Venezia e Napoli CBC ("Musica Viva" series) ▲ MVCD 1035 [DDD]
Moszkowski, M.:Con Pno, w. R. Armenian (cnd), Kitchener-Waterloo SO *(rec Centre in the Square, Kitchener, Ontario, Feb. 9 & 10, 1993)* CBC ("SM 5000" series) ▲ SMCD 5140 [DDD]
Schubert, Franz:Schwanngesang, w. Daniel Lichti (b-bar) Doremi ▲ 9302
Schubert, Franz:Songs (misc), w. Daniel Lichti (b-bar)—Frühlingsglaube; Heidenröslein; Die Forelle; Rastlose Liebe; Geheimes; Lachen und Weine; Nacht und Träume; Der Musensohn Doremi ▲ 9302
Szymanowski, K.:Masques Doremi ▲ DHR 9305 [DDD]
Szymanowski, K.:Mazurkas—2 sets Doremi ▲ DHR 9305 [DDD]
Szymanowski, K.:Metopes Doremi ▲ DHR 9305 [DDD]
Szymanowski, K.:Studies Pno Doremi ▲ DHR 9305 [DDD]
Szymanowski, K.:Vars Pno Doremi ▲ DHR 9305 [DDD]

Fian, Karl (tpt)
Rüegg, M.:Music of, w. Lauren Newton (sgr), Wolfgang Puschnig (fl/s sax), Harry Sokal (s sax), Roman Schwaller (t sax), Christian Radovan (trbn), Woody Schabata (vib)—Reflections on Aubade; Reflections on Méditation; Reflections on Sévère Réprimande; Reflections on Idylle; Reflections on Gnossiennes Nos. 1 & 2; Satie ist mir im traum 3x nicht erschienen *(rec Vienna, Sept. 20–22, 1983 & Mar.)* Hat Hut ("NOW." series) ▲ hat ART CD 6024 [ADD]

Fias, Gábor (va)—see ORCHESTRAS & ENSEMBLES Kodály String Quartet

Fichman, Yuval (pno)
Chopin, F.:Pno Music (misc), w. Martha Argerich (pno), Vladimir Ashkenazy (pno), Stanislav Bunin (pno), Halina Czerny-Stefanska (pno), Jan Ekier (pno), Kemal Gekic (pno), Adam Harasiewicz (pno), Krzysztof Jablonski (pno), Louis Kentner (pno), Jean-Marc Luisada (pno), Garrick Ohlsson (pno), Ivo Pogorelich (pno), Maurizio Pollini (pno), Dang Thai Son (pno)—includes Ballade (Nos. 1 & 2); Barcarolle, Op. 60; Concerto Nos. 1 & 2; Études (Op. 10, Nos. 1, 5, 8, 10 & 12 & Op. 25, No. 10, 18 & 25); Grand valse brillante; Impromptus (Nos. 3 & 4); Mazurkas (Op. 24, Nos. 1–4; Op. 30, Nos. 1–4; Op. 50, No. 32; Op. 59, Nos. 1–3); Nocturnes (Op. 9, No. 3; Op. 37, No. 12; Op. 48, No. 13; Op. 55, No. 16)Polonaise (Op. 40, Nos. 3 & 4; Op. 44, No. 5; Op. 53, No. 6; Op. 61, No. 7); Preludes (Op. 28 Nos. 13–18, 21–24 & Op. 45, No. 25); Scherzos (Nos. 1–3); Sonatas (Nos. 2 & 3); Waltzes (No. 1 & 6) LaserLight 5-▲ 15 961 [ADD/DDD]

Fichter, T. (db)
Kurtág, G.:Scenes from a Novel, w. C. Whittlesey (sop), M. Tacke (vn), M. Fábián (cimbalom) *(rec Jan. 7–9, 1992)* Sony Classical ▲ SK 53290 [DDD]

Fichtner, Guido (gtr)
Tárrega, F.:Gtr Music—34 Preludes; Vars on a Theme by Paganini Enterprise ("Tiziano" series) ▲ ENT TZ 96008 [DDD]

Fleisher, L. (pno)
Britten, H.:Diversions Pno, w. S. Comissiona (cnd), Baltimore SO Phoenix ▲ PHCD 122 [ADD]

Field, Elizabeth (vn)
Telemann, G.P.:Con Tpt Strs in D, w. Edward Carroll (tpt/pic tpt), Diane Bruce (vn), Annabelle Hoffman (vc), Dongsok Shin (positiv org), Edward Brewer (hpd/positiv org) *(rec Rye Presbyterian Church)* Helicon Classics ▲ HE 1009
Telemann, G.P.:Musique héroïque, w. Edward Carroll (tpt/pic tpt), Diane Bruce (vn), Annabelle Hoffman (vc), Dongsok Shin (positiv org), Edward Brewer (hpd/positiv org) *(rec Rye Presbyterian Church)* Helicon Classics ▲ HE 1009
Telemann, G.P.:Sons Tpt, w. Edward Carroll (tpt/pic tpt), Diane Bruce (vn), Annabelle Hoffman (vc), Dongsok Shin (positiv org), Edward Brewer (hpd/positiv org) *(rec Rye Presbyterian Church)* Helicon Classics ▲ HE 1009
Telemann, G.P.:Trio Sons, w. Edward Carroll (tpt/pic tpt), Diane Bruce (vn), Annabelle Hoffman (vc), Dongsok Shin (positiv org), Edward Brewer (hpd/positiv org) *(rec Rye Presbyterian Church)* Helicon Classics ▲ HE 1009

Field, Hilary (gtr)
Music of Spain & Latin America Yellow Tail ▲ YTR 10101 [DDD]

Field, Ken (sax/perc/syn/fl)
Field, K.:Music of, w. Karen Aqua (perc), Ken Winokur (perc), Mike Rivard (elec bass), John Fleagle (voice), Karen Gruber (perc)—A Space in a Place; Om on the Range; Takuskanskan; 5 Saxophones in Search of Meaning; Sanity; Perpetual Motion; Thoughts Unspoken; Berrendo; Sympathetic Magic; The Missing Soul; When I Fall in Love *(rec The Henge, Roswell, NM, Wellspring Sound, Concord, MA, The Chicken Loft, Cambridge, MA & The Basement, Cambridge, MA, 1988–1995)* O.O. Discs ▲ OO 25

Fields, Michael (lt)
The Dark Is My Delight, w. E. Tubb (sop) Musica Oscura ("Women in Song" series) ▲ MOS 70980

Fiene, Sarah (vc)—see also ORCHESTRAS & ENSEMBLES Phoenix Trio
Cowell, H.:Hymn & Fuguing Tune 9, w. Josephine Gandolfi (pno) Koch International Classics ▲ KIC 7205 [DDD]

Fierro, Charles (pno)
Copland, A.:Fant Pno Delos ▲ DCD-1013 [AAD]
Copland, A.:Night Thoughts Delos ▲ DCD-1013 [AAD]
Copland, A.:Passacaglia Delos ▲ DCD-1013 [AAD]
Copland, A.:Vars Pno Delos ▲ DCD-1013 [AAD]
Macdowell, E.:Sea Pieces Elektra/Nonesuch ■ 71411-4
Macdowell, E.:Son 2 Pno Delos ▲ DE 1019 [ADD]
Macdowell, E.:Virtuoso Etudes Delos ▲ DE 1019 [ADD]
Macdowell, E.:Woodland Sketches Elektra/Nonesuch ■ 71411-4

Fierro, Nancy (pno)
Rags & Riches:Ragtime & Classical Piano Music by Women *(rec Hancock Auditorium, Univ of Southern CA, Los Angeles, July 21–23, 1992)* Dorchester Classic ▲ DRC 1004

Fife, Kirstin (vn)
Dvořák, A.:Ballad, w. Paul da Silva (pno) *(rec Castle Oaks Studio, Calabasas, CA)* Raptoria Caam ▲ RCD 1006
Dvořák, A.:Notturno, w. Paul da Silva (pno) *(rec Castle Oaks Studio, Calabasas, CA)* Raptoria Caam ▲ RCD 1006
Janácek, L.:Dumka, w. Paul da Silva (pno) *(rec Castle Oaks Studio, Calabasas, CA)* Raptoria Caam ▲ RCD 1006
Janácek, L.:Romance Vn & Pno, w. Paul da Silva (pno) *(rec Castle Oaks Studio, Calabasas, CA)* Raptoria Caam ▲ RCD 1006
Janácek, L.:Son Vn, w. Paul da Silva (pno) *(rec Castle Oaks Studio, Calabasas, CA)* Raptoria Caam ▲ RCD 1006
Smetana, B.:From the Homeland, w. Paul da Silva (pno) *(rec Castle Oaks Studio, Calabasas, CA)* Raptoria Caam ▲ RCD 1006

Fifer, Julian (vc)
Trio, w. H. Pittel (sax), Levering Rothfuss (pno) Crystal ■ C 157

Figueiredo, Nicolau de (hpd)
Blavet, M.:Sons Trns Fl, w. Hans-Joachim Fuss (trns fl), Michael Spengler (vl)—Op. 2/2-4 & 6; Sonataterza; Son seconda [both from Op. 3] Pan Classics ▲ CD 510089 [DDD]

Filice, Elizabeth di (pno)
Chambers, W.M.:Ten Grand, w. Ursula Oppens (pno), Walter Hilse (pno), Bennett Lerner (pno), Nurit Tiles (pno), Aleck Karis (pno), Edmund Niemann (pno), Joseph Kubera (pno), Martin Goldray (pno), Allen Shawn (pno), Geisel (cnd) Newport ▲ NPD 85553

Filipová, Lenka (gtr)
Concertino Supraphon ▲ SUP 110402 [DDD]

Filippini, Rocco (vc)
Weber, C.M. von:Trio Fl, w. A. Nicolet (fl), B. Canino (pno) Novalis ▲ 150065 [DDD]

Filippis, C. de (mand)
Vivaldi, A.:Cons Diverse Instrs, w. G. Vicari (mand), J. Wummer (fl), R. Morris (fl), W. Vacchiano (tpt), N. Prager (tpt), E. Brenner (b ob), C. Stavrache (hp), A. Wurtzler (hp), J. Gorigliano (vn), L. Varga (vc), L. Bernstein (cnd), New York PO—in C, RV.558 *(rec Dec. 15, 1958)* Sony Classical ("Leonard Bernstein:The Royal Edition" series) ▲ SMK 47642 [ADD]

Filippo, E. di (perc)—see ORCHESTRAS & ENSEMBLES Seicentonovecento Ensemble

Fillmore, Bonnie (bn)
Gieseking, W.:Qnt Hn, w. J. Cox (hn), F. Korman (ob), Y. Nakao (cl), K. George (pno) *(rec 8/91)* Centaur ▲ CRC 2122 [DDD]

Filsell, Jeremy (org)
Harwood, B.:Org Music—Toccata, Op. 49; In an Old Abbey, Op. 32; In exitu Israel, Op. 46; 2 Sketches, Op. 18; Paean, Op. 15/3; Short Postlude for Ascensiontide, Op. 15/4; 3 Preludes on Anglican Chants, Op. 42; Sonata No. 1 for Organ, Op. 5 *(rec Nov. 1992)* Herald ▲ HAVPCD 162 [DDD]
Oxford Book of Wedding Music *(rec Lancing College Chapel, Sussex, Jan. 5–6, 1995)* Guild ▲ 7107 [DDD]
Tournemire, C.:Suite évocatrice Herald ▲ HAVPCD 145
Vierne, L.:Sym 3 Org Herald ▲ HAVPCD 145
Widor, C.M.:Sym 9 Org Herald ▲ HAVPCD 145

Filsell, Jeremy (pno)
Dupré, M.:Org Music—6 Antiennes pour le Temps de Noël, Op. 48; Chorale & Fugue, Op. 57; Évocation, Op. 37; Prelude & Fugue, Op. 36/2; Psalm 18, Op. 47 Gamut Classics ▲ GAM 530 [DDD]
Elgar, E.:Son Vn, w. Oliver Lewis (vn) *(rec Hillesden Church, Buckinghamshire, England)* Guild ▲ GMCD 7124 [DDD]
Ferguson, H.:Son 2 Vn, w. Oliver Lewis (vn) Guild ▲ GMCD 7120 [DDD]
Goossens, E.:Lyric Poem, w. Oliver Lewis (vn) *(rec Hillesden Church, Buckinghamshire, England)* Guild ▲ GMCD 7124 [DDD]
Goossens, E.:Old Chinese Folksong, w. Oliver Lewis (vn) *(rec Hillesden Church, Buckinghamshire, England)* Guild ▲ GMCD 7124 [DDD]
Goossens, E.:Romance, w. Oliver Lewis (vn) *(rec Hillesden Church, Buckinghamshire, England)* Guild ▲ GMCD 7124 [DDD]
Goossens, E.:Son 1 Vn, w. Oliver Lewis (vn) Guild ▲ GMCD 7120 [DDD]
Goossens, E.:Son 2 Vn, w. Oliver Lewis (vn) *(rec Hillesden Church, Buckinghamshire, England)* Guild ▲ GMCD 7124 [DDD]
Howells, H.:Gadabout Gamut ▲ GAM 541
Howells, H.:Gadabout Guild ▲ GMCD 7119 [DDD]
Howells, H.:Pieces Pno Guild ▲ GMCD 7119 [DDD]
Howells, H.:Pieces Pno Gamut ▲ GAM 541 [DDD]
Howells, H.:Sonatina Pno Gamut ▲ GAM 541 [DDD]
Howells, H.:Sonatina Pno Guild ▲ GMCD 7119 [DDD]
Ireland, J.:Son 2 Vn, w. Oliver Lewis (vn) Guild ▲ GMCD 7120 [DDD]

INSTRUMENT.

Filsell, Jeremy (pno) (cont.)
Stevens, B.:Aria Pno — Gamut ▲ GAM 541 [DDD]
Stevens, B.:Aria Pno [original version] — Guild ▲ GMCD 7119 [DDD]
Stevens, B.:Fantasy on *Giles Farnabys Dreame* — Gamut ▲ GAM 541 [DDD]
Stevens, B.:Fantasy on *Giles Farnabys Dreame* — Guild ▲ GMCD 7119 [DDD]
Stevens, B.:Son in 1 Movt — Guild ▲ GMCD 7119 [DDD]
Stevens, B.:Son in 1 Movt — Gamut ▲ GAM 541 [DDD]

Finch, D. (vc)
Dohnányi, E. von:Qnt 2 Pno, w. A. Wolf (pno), R. Lefkowitz (vn), C. Lieberman (vn), M. Thompson (va) — AFKA ▲ SK 503

Finch, Joshua (pno)—see ORCHESTRAS & ENSEMBLES Bowed Piano Ensemble

Finck, David (db)
Kern, J.:Songs, w. S. McNair (sop), A. Previn (pno)—Land Where the Good Songs Go; I Won't Dance; Nobody Else but Me; The Folks Who Live on the Hill; A Fine Romance; Remind Me; You Couldn't Be Cuter; Why Was I Born?; I'm Old Fashioned; Al — Philips ▲ 442129-2

Finckel, Chris (vc)
Cory, E.:Hemispheres, w. Christopher Oldfather (pno) — Soundspells ▲ CD 116 [DDD]
Cory, E.:Hemispheres, w. Christopher Oldfather (pno) — Soundspells ▲ CD 116 [DDD]
Cory, E.:Profiles, w. A. Blustine (cl), A. Karis (pno) *(rec 1981 & 1986; originally r)* — CRI ▲ CD 621 [ADD]
Fine, I.:Fant Str Trio, w. L. Quan (vn), L. Martin (va) — CRI ▲ CD 574 [ADD]
Rosenzweig, M.:Diptych, w. S. Palma (fl), A. Blustine (cl), B. Hudson (vn), E. Garth (pno), M. Rosenzweig — Centaur ▲ CRC 2103 [DDD]
Schoenberg, A.:Pierrot lunaire, w. Maureen McNalley (nar), Dwight Peltzer (pno), Eric Rosenblith (vn/va), Sue Ann Kahn (fl), Anand Devendra (cl/b cl), J. Thome (cnd), Orch of Our Time — Vox Box 2–▲ CDX 5144
Ung, C.:Tall Wind, w. Joan Heller (sop), Keith Underwood (fl), Robert Atherholt (ob), David Starobin (gtr), A. Weisberg (cnd) *(rec Vanguard Recording Studio, New York, 1982)* — CRI ▲ CRI 710 [DDD/ADD]

Finckel, David (vc)
Fine, V.:Missa Brevis, w. Jan DeGaetani (mez), Eric Barlett (vc), Michael Finckel (vc), Maxine Neuman (vc) — CRI ▲ CD 692 [ADD]

Finckel, M. (vc)—see also ORCHESTRAS & ENSEMBLES Jennings String Quartet
Adams, J.L.:Earth & the Great Weather, w. R. Lorentz (vn/perc), R. Lawrence (va), R. Black (db/perc), A. Knoles (perc), J. L. Adams (perc), J. Nageak (Iñupiat Eskimo performer), D. Simmonds (Iñupiat Eskimo performer), L. Tritt (Gwich'in Indian performer), A. P. Raboff (Gwich'in Indian performer), D. Hunsaker (Latin voice), J.L. Adams (cnd) *(rec Fairbanks, Mar. 8–11, 1993)* — New World ▲ 80459-2
Fine, V.:Missa Brevis, w. Jan DeGaetani (mez), Eric Barlett (vc), David Finckel (vc), Maxine Neuman (vc) — CRI ▲ CD 692 [ADD]

Findon, Andrew (sax)
Nyman, M.:Noises, w. Catherine Bott (sop), Hilary Summers (alt), Ian Bostridge (ten), David Roach (sax), D. Debart (cnd), Basse Normandie Instrumental Ensemble *(rec Caen, June 1991 & Abbey Road Studios, London, June 1993)* — Argo ▲ 440842-2 [DDD]

Fine, Burton (va)
Loeffler, C.M.:Rhaps, w. A. Genovese (ob), P. Serkin (pno) *(rec Aug. 1992)* — Boston Records ▲ BR 1004
McLennan, J.S.:Qnt Vn, Va, Vc, Cl & Pno, w. A. Levy (vn), A. Diaz (vc), P. Hancock (cl), R. Hodgkinson (pno) — CRI ▲ CD 594 [DDD]

Fine, Irving (pno)
Fine, I.:Mutability, w. E. Alberts (cta) [E] — CRI ▲ CD 630 [ADD]

Fine, Tamra Saylor (org)
Rózsa, M.:El Cid, w. J. Sedares (cnd), New Zealand SO, New Zealand Youth Choir *(rec Symphony House, Wellington, New Zealand, May 1995)* — Koch International Classics ▲ KIC 7340 [DDD] ■ KIC 7340

Fine, V. (pno)
Crawford, R.:Son Vn & Pno, w. I. Kavafian (vn) — CRI ▲ CD 658 [ADD]
Fine, I.:Son Vn, w. I. Kavafian (vn) — CRI ▲ CD 630 [ADD]

Fingerhut, Margaret (pno)
Balakirev, M.:Pno Music—In the Garden; Polka in f♯; Toccata in c♯ — Chandos ▲ CHAN 8439 [DDD]
Bax, A.:Morning Time, w. B. Thomson (cnd), London PO — Chandos ▲ CHAN 8516 [DDD]
Bax, A.:Saga Fragment, w. B. Thomson (cnd), London PO — Chandos ▲ CHAN 8484 [DDD]
Bax, A.:Symphonic Vars, w. B. Thomson (cnd), London PO — Chandos ▲ CHAN 8516 [DDD]
Bax, A.:Winter Legends, w. B. Thomson (cnd), London PO — Chandos ▲ CHAN 8484 [DDD]
Borodin, A.:Pno Music—In the Monastery & Nocturne (from *Petite Suite*); Scherzo in A♭ — Chandos ▲ CHAN 8439 [DDD]
Cui, C.:Preludes Pno, Op. 64—Nos. 2,8,9 & 10 — Chandos ▲ CHAN 8439 [DDD]
Dukas, P.:La plainte, au loin, du faune... — Chandos ▲ CHAN 8765 [DDD]
Dukas, P.:Prélude élégiaque — Chandos ▲ CHAN 8765 [DDD]
Dukas, P.:Son Pno — Chandos ▲ CHAN 8765 [DDD]
Dukas, P.:Vars, Interlude et Finale sur en thème de Rameau — Chandos ▲ CHAN 8765 [DDD]
Falla, M. de:Noches en los jardines de España, w. G. Simon (cnd), London SO — Chandos ▲ CHAN 8457 [DDD]
Grieg, E.:Con Pno, Op. 16, w. V. Handley (cnd), Ulster Orch — Chandos ▲ CHAN 7040
Grieg, E.:Con Pno, Op. 16, w. V. Handley (cnd), Ulster Orch — Chandos ▲ CHAN 8723 [DDD]
Hommages, w. Margaret Cable (mez), William Bennett (fl), Kenneth Sillito (vn), Clifford Benson (pno) — Chandos ▲ CHAN 8578 [DDD]
Howells, H.:Pno Music—Gadabout; Sarum Sketches; 3 Pieces, Op. 14; Slow Dance; Cobbler's Hornpipe; Snapshots, Op. 30; The Chosen Tune; 4 Pieces from Lambert's Clavichord; Music Sine Nomine; Sonatina — Chandos ▲ CHAN 9273 [DDD]
Moeran, E.J.:Rhap Pno, w. V. Handley (cnd), Ulster Orch — Chandos ▲ CHAN 8639 [DDD]
Mussorgsky, M.:Pno Music — Chandos ▲ CHAN 8439 [DDD]
Rimsky-Korsakov, N.:Pno Music—Scherzino, Op. 11/3; A little song; Novelette, Op. 11/2 — Chandos ▲ CHAN 8439 [DDD]
Russian Piano Music of the Mighty Handful — Chandos ▲ CHAN 8439 [DDD]
Stanford, C.V.:Concert Vars upon an English Theme, w. V. Handley (cnd), Ulster Orch — Chandos ▲ CHAN 8736 [DDD]
Stanford, C.V.:Con 2 Pno, w. V. Handley (cnd), Ulster Orch — Chandos ▲ CHAN 8736 [DDD]
Suk, J.:Pno Music—Piano Pieces Nos. 1,2,4 & 5 (from Op. 7); Spring, Op. 22a; Summer Impressions, Op. 22b; About Mother, Op. 28; Things Lived & Dreamed, Op. 30; Lullabies, Op. 33 — Chandos 2–▲ CHAN 9026/27 [DDD]
Tchaikovsky & His Friends — Chandos ▲ CHAN 9218 [DDD]

Fink, Claus (db)
Reger, M.:Cantatas, w. V. Schweizer (sop), A. Hellmann (alt), R. Julius Koch (ob), R. Hellmann, U. Soldan (vn), B. Banz (va), C. Hellmann (vc), H. Bilgram (org), D. Hellmann (cnd), Mainz Bach Choir — Entrée ▲ 0049 [ADD]

Fink, Kathy (fl)
Wigglesworth, F.:Psalm 148, w. Elizabeth Brown (fl), Jeanne Wilson (fl), Kevin James (trbn), David Taylor (trbn), D. Schuler (cnd), Church of St. Luke in the Fields Choir — CRI ▲ C 733 [DDD]

Fink, R. (sax)
Kupferman, M.:Challenger, w. L. Holkmann (mez), J. Domarkas (cnd), Lithuanian National PO — Soundspells ▲ CD 104
Kupferman, M.:Jazz Sym, w. L. Holkmann (mez), J. Domarkas (cnd), Lithuanian National PO — Soundspells ▲ CD 104

Fink, Siegfried (perc)
Praetorius, M.:Terpsichore, w. S. Behrend (gtr), Collegium Terpsichore, Ulsamer Collegium—36 sels — IMP Collectors Series ▲ IMPX 9026 [AAD]

Finkel, Christopher (vc)
Zaimont, J.L.:Sky Curtains, w. Kathleen Nester (fl), Daniel Gilbert (cl), Bob Wagner (bn), Lois Martin (va) *(rec SUNY Purchase, Theatre C, Jan 8–10 & Feb 20, 1995)* — Arabesque ▲ ARA 6667 [DDD]

Finkel, David (vc)
Zaimont, J.L.:Hidden Heritage, w. Karen Moratz (fl), David Krakauer (cl/b cl/t sax), Clinton Adams (pno), Barry Dove (perc), D. Kosloff (cnd) *(rec SUNY Purchase, Theatre C, Jan 8–10 & Feb 20, 1995)* — Arabesque ▲ ARA 6667 [DDD]

Finkenbeiner, Gerhard (glass armonica)
The Maestros Tea Party:Mr. Einstein Visits the Queen, w. Mary Jane Rupert (pno), Diana Salomon (vn), Patricia Wenzel (vn), Ella Lou Weiler (va), Fern Meyers (vc), Vera Meyer (glass armonica) *(rec Euphoria Sound Studio, Revere, MA)* — Cultured Kids ▲ unknown ■ 120012FM-4

Finley, Brian (pno)
Lullabies for Benjamin, w. D. Bennett (sop) — Marquis Classics ▲ MAR 155

Finn, Kenneth (bass tpt)—see ORCHESTRAS & ENSEMBLES New York Trumpet Ensemble

Finn, Michael (bn)
Cohn, J.:Music of, w. M. Piccinini (fl), M. Dine (ob), J. Manasse (cl), J. Tarpley (hn), N. Akamatsu (db), S. Alderking (pno)—Wind Quintet, Op. 36b (1981); Goldfinch Variations for Wind Trio, Op. 61 (1984); Little Overture for Wind Quartet, Op. 59 (1982); Suite Champêtre for Wind Quintet (after Rameau), Op. 47 (1968) — XLNT ■ C 2
Cohn, J.:Music of, w. M. Piccinini (fl), M. Dine (ob), J. Manasse (cl), J. Tarpley (hn), N. Akamatsu (db), S. Alderking (pno)—Wind Quintet, Op. 36b (1981); Little Overture for Wind Quintet, Op. 59 (1982); Sonatina for Clarinet & Piano, Op. 56 (1981); Sonata Romantica for Double Bass & Piano, Op. 18 (1952); Sonata Robusta for Bassoon & Piano, Op. 55 (1980); Sonata for Flute & Piano, Op. 52 (1974); Goldfinch Variations for Three Treble Instruments, Op. 61 (1984) *(rec 1985)* — XLNT ▲ CD 18006 [ADD]

Finney, E. (s sax)
Kallman, D.:Forecasts, w. S. Hyslop (alt sax), K. Claussen (ten sax), W. Burton (bar sax) — Innova ▲ MN 109
Macy, C.:4 Saxes, w. S. Hyslop (a sax), K. Claussen (ten sax), W. Burton (bar sax) — Innova ▲ MN 109

Finnissy, Michael (pno)
Finnissy, M.:Pno Music—Reels; Short but...; Freightrain Bruise; Autumnall; Kemp's Morris; Stanley Stokes, East Street 1836 — NM Classics ▲ NMCD 002 [DDD]
Newman, C.:Pno Music—Grooving through Old Tombs; News of My Own; Le repos sur le lit — NM Classics ▲ NMCD 002 [DDD]
Skempton, H.:Music of—Eirenicons I–IV; Even Tenor — NM Classics ▲ NMCD 002 [DDD]
Weir, J.:Pno Music—An mein Klavier; Michael's Strathspey — NM Classics ▲ NMCD 002 [DDD]

Finotti, Mario (vc)
Dragonetti, D.:Qnt Strs, w. Ubaldo Fioravanti (db), Piero Toso (vn), Giancarlo di Vacri (va), Monica Tosi (va) *(rec Sala San Bovo, Padova, Italy, Jan 17–19, 1995)* — Dynamic ▲ CD 133 [DDD]

Fioravanti, Ubaldo (db)
Dragonetti, D.:Con Db, w. C. Martignon (cnd), Padua & Venice CO *(rec Sala San Bovo, Padova, Italy, Jan 17–19, 1995)* — Dynamic ▲ CD 133 [DDD]
Dragonetti, D.:Duo Vc & Db, w. Teodora Campagnaro (vc) *(rec Sala San Bovo, Padova, Italy, Jan 17–19, 1995)* — Dynamic ▲ CD 133 [DDD]
Dragonetti, D.:Qnt Strs, w. Piero Toso (vn), Giancarlo di Vacri (va), Monica Tosi (va), Mario Finotti (vc) *(rec Sala San Bovo, Padova, Italy, Jan 17–19, 1995)* — Dynamic ▲ CD 133 [DDD]
Dragonetti, D.:Waltzes, D.370 *(rec Sala San Bovo, Padova, Italy, Jan 17–19, 1995)* — Dynamic ▲ CD 133 [DDD]

Fiorentin, Aldo (hpd)—see ORCHESTRAS & ENSEMBLES Ensemble Barocco Padua Sans Souci

Fiorentino, Sergio (pno)
Chopin, F.:Nocturnes—Opp. 37/1-2, 48/1-2, 55/1-2, 62/1-2, 72/1 & No. 20, Op. posth. — Saga Classics ▲ EC 3388
Sergio Fiorentino in Germany, w. S. Fiorentino (pno) *(rec live, 1993)* — APR 2–▲ APR 7036 [ADD]

Fiorini, M. (vn)
Rendano, A.:Qnt Pno, w. R. Caporali (pno), R. Bonucci (vn), F. Anzelmo (va), A. Bonucci (vc) *(rec Mar. 29–31, 1989)* — Ermitage ▲ ERM 409 [ADD]

Firkušný, Rudolf (pno)
Beethoven, L. van:Son 8 Pno, "Pathétique" — EMI Classics ▲ CDM 66064
Beethoven, L. van:Son 14 Pno, "Moonlight Son" — EMI Classics ▲ CDM 66064
Beethoven, L. van:Son 21 Pno, "Waldstein" — EMI Classics ▲ CDM 66064
Beethoven, L. van:Son 30 Pno — EMI Classics ▲ CDM 66064
Benda, G.A.:Son 9 Pno *(rec 1972–74)* — Vox Box 2–▲ CDX 5058 [ADD]
Brahms, J.:Fants Pno, Op. 116—No. 1 *(rec New York City, 1958–59)* — EMI Classics ▲ CDM 66065
Brahms, J.:Intermezzos Pno, Op. 117 *(rec New York City, 1958–59)* — EMI Classics ▲ CDM 66065
Brahms, J.:Pieces Pno, Op. 76—Nos. 1 & 3 *(rec New York City, 1958–59)* — EMI Classics ▲ CDM 66065
Brahms, J.:Pieces Pno, Op. 118—No. 6 *(rec New York City, 1958–59)* — EMI Classics ▲ CDM 66065
Brahms, J.:Pieces Pno, Op. 119—Nos. 1–4 *(rec New York City, 1958–59)* — EMI Classics ▲ CDM 66065
Brahms, J.:Rhaps Pno, Op. 79—No. 2 in g *(rec New York City, 1958–59)* — EMI Classics ▲ CDM 66065
Brahms, J.:Sons Cl (comp), w. William Primrose (va) *(rec New York City, 1958–59)* — EMI Classics ▲ CDM 66065
Chopin, F.:Barcarolle Pno *(rec New York City, 1957 & 1959)* — EMI Classics ▲ CDM 66066
Chopin, F.:Nocturnes—in E♭, Op. 9/2; in D♭, Op. 27/2 *(rec New York City, 1957 & 1959)* — EMI Classics ▲ CDM 66066
Chopin, F.:Pno Music (misc)—Ballade No. 3; Impromptu, Op. 36; Mazurkas, Opp. 7/3, 41/1, 50/1, 63/3; Nocturne, Op. 62/1; Scherzo, Op. 31 *(rec live 6/67)* — Fonè ▲ 91F04 [ADD]
Chopin, F.:Polonaises—in c, Op. 40/2 *(rec New York City, 1957 & 1959)* — EMI Classics ▲ CDM 66066
Chopin, F.:Scherzos—in b♭, Op. 31 *(rec New York City, 1957 & 1959)* — EMI Classics ▲ CDM 66066
Chopin, F.:Son Pno, Op. 58 *(rec New York City, 1957 & 1959)* — EMI Classics ▲ CDM 66066
Chopin, F.:Son Pno, Op. 58 *(rec live 6/67)* — Fonè ▲ 91F04 [ADD]
Chopin, F.:Waltzes—in c♯, Op. 64/2; in E♭, Op. 18 *(rec New York City, 1957 & 1959)* — EMI Classics ▲ CDM 66066
Debussy, C.:Arabesques (2) *(rec New York City, 1956 & 1958)* — EMI Classics ▲ CDM 66067
Debussy, C.:Children's Corner *(rec New York City, 1956 & 1958)* — EMI Classics ▲ CDM 66067
Debussy, C.:Estampes *(rec New York City, 1956 & 1958)* — EMI Classics ▲ CDM 66067
Debussy, C.:Images (6) Pno—Reflet dans L'eau [Reflections in the Water] *(rec New York City, 1956 & 1958)* — EMI Classics ▲ CDM 66067
Debussy, C.:Pno Music (misc)—La cathédral engloutie [The Engulfed Cathedral]; Minstrels *(rec New York City, 1956 & 1958)* — EMI Classics ▲ CDM 66067
Debussy, C.:Pno Music (misc)—La Plus que Lent; Poissons d'Or; La Fille aux cheveux de lin; Général Lavine; Rêverie; Feux d'artifice *(rec May 1957 & Jan 1958)* — EMI Classics ▲ CDM 66069
Debussy, C.:Suite bergamasque *(rec New York City, 1956 & 1958)* — EMI Classics ▲ CDM 66067
Dussek, J.L.:Son Pno, Op. 77, "L'invocation" *(rec 1972–74)* — Vox Box 2–▲ CDX 5058 [ADD]
Dvořák, A.:Bagatelles, Op. 47, w. Juilliard String Quartet members — Odyssey 2–▲ MB2K 45672
Dvořák, A.:Con Pno, w. V. Neumann (cnd), Czech PO — RCA Red Seal ▲ 09026-60781-2
Dvořák, A.:Con Pno, w. W. Susskind (cnd), St. Louis SO — Vox Box 2–▲ CDX 5015 [ADD]
Dvořák, A.:Con Pno, w. R. Kubelík (cnd), Czech PO *(rec ca. 1944)* — Multisonic (Prague Spring Collection) ▲ 31 0019-2 [ADD]
Dvořák, A.:Humoresques, Op. 101 *(rec 1972–74)* — Vox Box 2–▲ CDX 5058 [ADD]
Dvořák, A.:Mazurkas, Op. 56 *(rec 1972–74)* — Vox Box 2–▲ CDX 5058 [ADD]
Dvořák, A.:Music of, w. Frederica von Stade (mez), Itzhak Perlman (vn), Yo-Yo Ma (vc), S. Ozawa (cnd), Boston SO, Czech Phil Chorus—Carnival Ov., Op. 92; Romance in f for Vn & Orch, Op. 11; Klid [Silent Woods] for Vc & Orch, Op. 68/5; Humoresque in G♭, Op. 101/1 & 7; Mesicku na nebi hlubokém [from Rusalka, Op. 114]; Psalm 149 for Chorus & Orch, Op. 79; Gypsy Songs for Voice & Piano, Op. 55/4 & 5; Allegro [from Trio for Vn, Vc & Pno, Op. 90]; Slavonic Dances, Op. 72/2 & 7 *(rec Smetana Hall, Prague, Dec. 16, 1993)* — Sony Classical ("Front Line" series) ▲ SK 46687 [DDD]; ■ ST 46687
Dvořák, A.:Poetic Tone Pictures *(rec 1972–74)* — Vox Box 2–▲ CDX 5058 [ADD]

▲ = CD ♦ = Enhanced CD Δ = MD ■ = Cassette Tape ▯ = DCC

Firkušný, Rudolf (pno) (cont.)
Dvořák, A.:Qts Pno Strs, Opp. 23 & 87, w. Juilliard String Quartet members Odyssey 2-▲ MB2K 45672
Dvořák, A.:Qnt Pno, Op. 5, w. Ridge String Quartet RCA Red Seal ▲ 09026-60436-2
Dvořák, A.:Qnt Pno, Op. 81, w. Juilliard String Quartet Odyssey 2-▲ MB2K 45672
Dvořák, A.:Qnt Pno, Op. 81, w. Juilliard String Quartet Sony Classical (Essential Classics) ▲ SBK 48170 ■ SBT 48170
Dvořák, A.:Qnt Pno, Op. 81, w. Ridge String Quartet RCA Red Seal ▲ 09026-60436-2
Dvořák, A.:Silhouettes (12) *(rec 1972)* Allegretto ▲ ACD 8208
Dvořák, A.:Songs, w. G. Benackova (sop)—Love Songs, Op. 83; Gypsy Songs, Op. 55; In Folk Style, Op. 73; Biblical Songs, Op. 99 RCA Red Seal ▲ 09026-60823-2
Dvořák, A.:Theme with Vars *(rec 1972–74)* Vox Box 2-▲ CDX 5058 [ADD]
Franck, C.:Symphonic Vars, w. C. P. Flor (cnd), Royal PO RCA Red Seal ▲ 60146-2-RC [DDD]; ■ 60146-4-RC (CrO2)
Janácek, L.:Capriccio, w. V. Neumann (cnd), Czech PO RCA Red Seal ▲ 09026-60781-2
Janácek, L.:Concertino Pno, w. V. Neumann (cnd), Czech PO RCA Red Seal ▲ 09026-60781-2
Janácek, L.:In the Mists RCA Red Seal ▲ 60147-2-RC [DDD]
Janácek, L.:Moravian Folk Poetry, w. G. Benackova (sop) RCA Red Seal ▲ 09026-60823-2
Janácek, L.:On an Overgrown Path Deutsche Grammophon ("20th Century Classics" series) ▲ 429857-2 [ADD]
Janácek, L.:On an Overgrown Path RCA Red Seal ▲ 60147-2-RC [DDD]
Janácek, L.:Reminiscence RCA Red Seal ▲ 60147-2-RC [DDD]
Janácek, L.:Son October 1, 1905 Pno Deutsche Grammophon ("20th Century Classics" series) ▲ 429857-2 [ADD]
Janácek, L.:Son October 1, 1905 Pno RCA Red Seal ▲ 60147-2-RC [DDD]
Martinů, B.:Con 2 Pno, w. J. Belohlávek (cnd), Czech PO Supraphon ▲ SUP 111988
Martinů, B.:Con 2 Pno, w. L. Pešek (cnd), Czech PO RCA Red Seal ▲ 09026-61934-2
Martinů, B.:Con 3 Pno, w. L. Pešek (cnd), Czech PO RCA Red Seal ▲ 09026-61934-2
Martinů, B.:Con 4 Pno, w. L. Pešek (cnd), Czech PO RCA Red Seal ▲ 09026-61934-2
Martinů, B.:Sons Vc, w. J. Starker (vc) RCA Red Seal ▲ 09026-61220-2
Mendelssohn, F.:Con 1 Pno, w. L. de Froment (cnd), Luxembourg RSO *(rec 1971)* Allegretto ▲ ACD 8208
Mozart, W.A.:Con 9 Pno, w. G. Szell (cnd), Royal Concertgebouw Orch Sony Classical ("Festspiel Dokumente:Salzburger Festspiele" series) ▲ SMK 68445
Mozart, W.A.:Con 10 Pnos, w. A. Weiss (pno), D. Zinman (cnd), Rochester PO *(rec 1978)* Vox Box 3-▲ CD3X 3010 [ADD]
Mozart, W.A.:Pno Music 4-Hands, w. A. Weiss (pno)—Andante & Vars., K.501; Fugue, K.426; Sons., K.19d, 357, 358, 381, 448, 497, 521 *(rec 1978–79)* Vox Box 3-▲ CD3X 3010 [ADD]
Mozart, W.A.:Qt Pno, K.478, w. Panocha String Quartet Supraphon ▲ SUP 112242 [DDD]
Music From the Heart of Europe, w. Lubomir Brabec (gtr), Josef Suk (vn), Rudolf Firkušný (pno), Vaclav Neumann (cnd), Jiří Belohlávek (cnd), Panocha Quartet, Czech PO, Prague CO, Prague Musica Antiqua, et al. Supraphon ▲ SUP 0063 [DDD]
Schumann, R.:Con Pno, w. L. de Froment (cnd), Luxembourg RSO *(rec 1971)* Allegretto ▲ ACD 8208
Schumann, R.:Davidsbündlertänze *(rec Dec 1955 & Nov–Dec 1959)* EMI Classics ▲ CDM 66068
Schumann, R.:Kinderscenen *(rec Dec 1955 & Nov–Dec 1959)* EMI Classics ▲ CDM 66068
Schumann, R.:Sym Etudes *(rec Dec 1955 & Nov–Dec 1959)* EMI Classics ▲ CDM 66068
Smetana, B.:Czech Dances—Furiant; Little Onion; Little Hen; Lancer Bear; Stepping Dance; Stamping Dance; Grain Dance; Hop Dance; Neighbor's Dance *(rec May 1957 & Jan 1958)* EMI Classics ▲ CDM 66069
Smetana, B.:Czech Dances—10 sels. *(rec ca. 1972/74)* Vox Box 2-▲ CDX 5058 [ADD]
Smetana, B.:Polkas Pno *(rec May 1957 and Jan 1958)* EMI Classics ▲ CDM 66069
Tomášek, V.J.K.:Ecologues Pno—No. 22 *(rec ca. 1972/74)* Vox Box 2-▲ CDX 5058 [ADD]
Voříšek, J.V.:Impromptu Pno, Op. 7/4 *(rec ca. 1972/74)* Vox Box 2-▲ CDX 5058 [ADD]

First, David (gtr)—see also ORCHESTRAS & ENSEMBLES World Casio Quartet
First, D.:Distance Receives Permission to Enter, w. E. Kaplinsky (kbd controller), K. Sparke (dr) *(rec Apr. 1991)* O.O. Discs ▲ OO 5 [DDD]
First, D.:The Good Book's (Accurate) Jail of Escape Dust Coordinates 2, w. Matt Sullivan (ob), Chris Jepperson (cl), Annemarie Wiesner (vn), Gary Trosclair (tpt), Elaine Kaplinsky (kbd syn), Chad Henderson (teahouse gtr/b gtr), Kevin Sparke (perc) *(rec Baby Monster Studios, NYC, May 1992)* O. O. Discs ▲ OO 23 [DDD]
First, D.:Lens Pt 2, w. M. Bard (gtr), C. Henderson (gtr), E. Sandrof (syn) *(rec Oct. 1987)* O.O. Discs ▲ OO 5 [DDD]

Firth, Benjamin (pno)
Arnold, M.:Pno Music Koch International Classics ▲ KIC 7162 [DDD]
Mendelssohn, F.:Capriccio brillante, w. R. Stankovsky (cnd), Slovak State PO Košice Naxos ▲ 8.550681 [DDD]
Mendelssohn, F.:Con 1 Pno, w. R. Stankovsky (cnd), Slovak State PO Košice Naxos ▲ 8.550681 [DDD]
Mendelssohn, F.:Con 2 Pno, w. R. Stankovsky (cnd), Slovak State PO Košice Naxos ▲ 8.550681 [DDD]
Mendelssohn, F.:Rondo brilliant, w. R. Stankovsky (cnd), Slovak State PO Košice Naxos ▲ 8.550681 [DDD]

Firth, Rebecca (vc)
Bryars, G.:Incipit Vita Nova, w. D. James (countertenor), A. Dreyer (violin), U. Lachner (viola) ECM New Series ▲ 78118-21533-2 [DDD]
Kancheli, G.:Exil, w. Catrin Demenga (sop), Maacha Deubner (sop), Natalia Pschenitschnikova (a fl/b fl), Ruth Killius (va), Christian Sutter (db) *(rec Propstei St. Gerold, Basel, May 1994)* ECM New Series ▲ 78118-21535-2 [DDD]

Fischer, Annie (pno)
Bartók, B.:Con 3 Pno, w. I. Markevitch (cnd), Philharmonia Orch EMI Classics ("Artist Profile" series) 2-▲ CDZB 68733
Beethoven, L. van:Con 3 Pno, w. H. Esser (cnd), Budapest SO *(rec 1966)* Hungaroton ▲ HCD 31493 [ADD]
Beethoven, L. van:Con 3 Pno, w. F. Fricsay (cnd), Bavarian RSO *(rec 1957)* Enterprise ("Palladio" series) ▲ ENT PD 4213 (m)
Beethoven, L. van:Sons Pno (comp)—No. 6, Op. 10/2; No. 12, Op. 26; No. 13, Op. 27/1; No. 31, Op. 110 *(rec 1977–78)* Hungaroton ▲ HCD 31626 [ADD]
Beethoven, L. van:Sons Pno (comp)—Nos. 1, 3 & 8 *(rec 1977–78)* Hungaroton ▲ HCD 31627 [ADD]
Beethoven, L. van:Son 14 Pno, "Moonlight Son", w. I. Markevitch (cnd), Philharmonia Orch EMI Classics ("Artist Profile" series) 2-▲ CDZB 68733
Beethoven, L. van:Son 15 Pno, "Pastoral" IMP ("BBC Radio Classics" series) ▲ IMP 5691722
Beethoven, L. van:Son 19 Pno IMP ("BBC Radio Classics" series) ▲ IMP 5691722
Beethoven, L. van:Son 30 Pno IMP ("BBC Radio Classics" series) ▲ IMP 5691722
Beethoven, L. van:Son 32 Pno, w. I. Markevitch (cnd), Philharmonia Orch EMI Classics ("Artist Profile" series) 2-▲ CDZB 68733
Beethoven, L. van:Son 32 Pno IMP ("BBC Radio Classics" series) ▲ IMP 5691722
Liszt, F.:Con 1 Pno, w. O. Klemperer (cnd), Philharmonia Orch *(rec ca. 1963)* EMI Classics ▲ CDM 64144
Liszt, F.:Son Pno *(rec 1968)* Hungaroton ▲ HCD 31494
Mozart, W.A.:Con 20 Pno, w. E. Lukács (cnd), Budapest SO *(rec 1965)* Hungaroton ▲ HCD 31492
Mozart, W.A.:Con 21 Pno, w. E. Lukács (cnd), Budapest SO *(rec 1965)* Hungaroton ▲ HCD 31492
Mozart, W.A.:Con 21 Pno, w. W. Sawallisch (cnd), Philharmonia Orch EMI Classics ▲ CDE 67780
Mozart, W.A.:Con 22 Pno, w. O. Klemperer (cnd), Royal Concertgebouw Orch *(rec live July 12, 1956)* Memories 2-▲ HR 4248/49 (m) [ADD]
Mozart, W.A.:Prelude & Fugue Pno *(rec 1965)* Hungaroton ▲ HCD 31493 [ADD]
Mozart, W.A.:Rondo Pno, K.382, w. E. Lukács (cnd), Budapest SO *(rec 1965)* Hungaroton ▲ HCD 31492

Fischer, Annie (pno) (cont.)
Schubert, Franz:Impromptus Pno (comp), w. I. Markevitch (cnd), Philharmonia Orch EMI Classics ("Artist Profile" series) 2-▲ CDZB 68733
Schubert, Franz:Impromptus Pno, D.935—in f, D.935/1 *(rec 1968)* Hungaroton ▲ HCD 31493 [ADD]
Schubert, Franz:Son Pno, D.960 *(rec 1968)* Hungaroton ▲ HCD 31494
Schumann, R.:Con Pno, w. O. Klemperer (cnd), New Philharmonia Orch *(rec ca. 1963)* EMI Classics ▲ CDM 64145
Schumann, R.:Kinderszenen, w. I. Markevitch (cnd), Philharmonia Orch EMI Classics ("Artist Profile" series) 2-▲ CDZB 68733
Schumann, R.:Kreisleriana, w. I. Markevitch (cnd), Philharmonia Orch EMI Classics ("Artist Profile" series) 2-▲ CDZB 68733

Fischer, Clare (pno)
Symphonic Boleros, w. V. Lewis (cnd), Royal PO, Ettore Stratta (cnd), Ernie Watts (sax), Sal Marquez (tpt), Jorge Callandrelli (pno), Brian Monroney (gtr) Teldec ▲ 91180-2 ■ 91180-4

Fischer, Eckhard (vn)—see ORCHESTRAS & ENSEMBLES Opus 8 Trio

Fischer, Edwin (pno)
Bach, J.S.:Fants Hpd EMI Classics ▲ CDH 64928
Beethoven, L. van:Con 5 Pno, "Emperor", w. K. Böhm (cnd), Dresden State Orch Pearl ▲ PEA 9218
Beethoven, L. van:Con 5 Pno, "Emperor", w. W. Furtwängler (cnd), Philharmonia Orch EMI Classics ▲ CDH 61005 (m)
Beethoven, L. van:Son 7 Pno *(rec 1948 & 1954)* Arkadia ▲ 514 (m) [AAD]
Beethoven, L. van:Son 7 Pno EMI Classics ("Great Recordings of the Century" series) ▲ CDH 61005 (m)
Beethoven, L. van:Son 8 Pno, "Pathétique" APR ▲ APR 5502 [AAD]
Beethoven, L. van:Son 8 Pno, "Pathétique" Pearl ▲ PEA 9218
Beethoven, L. van:Son 8 Pno, "Pathétique" *(rec 1952 & 1954)* Arkadia ▲ 513 (m) [AAD]
Beethoven, L. van:Son 14 Pno, "Moonlight Son" *(rec 1948–54)* Music & Arts 2-▲ CD 880 [ADD]
Beethoven, L. van:Son 15 Pno, "Pastoral" *(rec 1948 & 1954)* Arkadia ▲ 514 (m) [AAD]
Beethoven, L. van:Son 15 Pno, "Pastoral" *(rec 1948–54)* Music & Arts 2-▲ CD 880 [ADD]
Beethoven, L. van:Son 21 Pno, "Waldstein" *(rec 1948–54)* Music & Arts 2-▲ CD 880 [ADD]
Beethoven, L. van:Son 21 Pno, "Waldstein" *(rec 1952 & 1954)* Arkadia ▲ 513 (m) [AAD]
Beethoven, L. van:Son 23 Pno, "Appassionata" APR ▲ APR 5502 [AAD]
Beethoven, L. van:Son 30 Pno *(rec 1952 & 1954)* Arkadia ▲ 513 (m) [AAD]
Beethoven, L. van:Son 30 Pno *(rec 1948–54)* Music & Arts 2-▲ CD 880 [ADD]
Beethoven, L. van:Son 31 Pno APR ▲ APR 5502 [AAD]
Beethoven, L. van:Son 31 Pno *(rec 1938)* Pearl ▲ PEA 9481 (m) [AAD]
Beethoven, L. van:Son 32 Pno *(rec 1948 & 1954)* Arkadia ▲ 514 (m) [AAD]
Beethoven, L. van:Son 32 Pno *(rec 1948–54)* Music & Arts 2-▲ CD 880 [ADD]
Beethoven, L. van:Trio 4 Pno, "Ghost", w. W. Schneiderhan (vn), E. Mainardi (vc) *(rec 1954)* Arkadia 2-▲ 568 (m) [ADD]
Beethoven, L. van:Trio 4 Pno, "Ghost", w. Wolfgang Schneiderhan (vn), Enrico Mainardi (vc) *(rec Salzburg, 1952–53)* Music & Arts 2-▲ CD 840 [AAD]
Beethoven, L. van:Trio 6 Pno, "Archduke", w. Wolfgang Schneiderhan (vn), Enrico Mainardi (vc) *(rec Salzburg, 1952–53)* Music & Arts 2-▲ CD 840 [AAD]
Brahms, J.:Con 2 Pno, w. W. Furtwängler (cnd), Berlin PO Music & Arts 4-▲ CD 804 [ADD]
Brahms, J.:Qt 1 Pno, w. V. Brero (vn), R. Nel (va), T. Schürgers (vc) *(rec Berlin, ca. 1939/41, Electrola DB)* Koch Historic ▲ 7701-2 [AAD]
Brahms, J.:Trios (3) Pno, w. W. Schneiderhan (vn), E. Mainardi (vc) *(rec 1954)* Arkadia 2-▲ 568 (m) [ADD]
Brahms, J.:Trio 1 Pno, w. W. Schneiderhan (vn), E. Mainardi (vc) *(rec 1953)* Music & Arts ▲ CD 739 (m)
Brahms, J.:Trio 2 Pno, w. W. Schneiderhan (vn), E. Mainardi (vc) *(rec 1951)* Music & Arts ▲ CD 739 (m)
Edwin Fischer Pearl ▲ PEA 9481 (m) [AAD]
Handel, G.F.:Chaconne Hpd APR ▲ APR 5502 [AAD]
Handel, G.F.:Suites Hpd APR ▲ APR 5502 [AAD]
Mozart, W.A.:Con 22 Pno, w. E. Fischer (cnd), Royal Danish Orch *(rec 1954)* Music & Arts ▲ CD 872 [ADD]
Mozart, W.A.:Con 24 Pno, w. E. Fischer (cnd), Royal Danish Orch *(rec 1954)* Music & Arts ▲ CD 872 [ADD]
Mozart, W.A.:Fant Pno, K.396 Enterprise ("The Piano Library" series) ▲ ENT 191
Mozart, W.A.:Minuet Pno, K.1 Enterprise ("The Piano Library" series) ▲ ENT 191
Mozart, W.A.:Rondo Pno Orch, K.382, w. E. Fischer (cnd), Royal Danish Orch *(rec 1954)* Music & Arts ▲ CD 872 [ADD]
Mozart, W.A.:Son 11 Pno Enterprise ("The Piano Library" series) ▲ ENT 191
Mozart, W.A.:Son 11 Pno *(rec 1933)* Pearl ▲ PEA 9481 (m) [AAD]
Mozart, W.A.:Trio Pno, K.548, w. Wolfgang Schneiderhan (vn), Enrico Mainardi (vc) *(rec Salzburg, 1952–53)* Music & Arts 2-▲ CD 840 [AAD]
Schubert, Franz:Fant Pno, D.760, "Wandererfantasie" Pearl ▲ PEA 9216
Schubert, Franz:Impromptus Pno (comp) Enterprise ("The Piano Library" series) ▲ ENT 191
Schubert, Franz:Impromptus Pno (comp) Pearl ▲ PEA 9216
Schubert, Franz:Songs (misc), w. E. Schwarzkopf (sop)—21 songs, including—An die Musik; An Sylvia; Ganymed; Gretchen am Spinnrade [G] *(rec 1952)* Angel ("Great Recordings of the Century" series) ▲ CDH 64026
Schumann, R.:Trio 1 Pno, w. Wolfgang Schneiderhan (vn), Enrico Mainardi (vc) *(rec Salzburg, 1952–53)* Music & Arts 2-▲ CD 840 [AAD]
Schumann, R.:Trio 1 Pno, w. Wolfgang Schneiderhan (vn), Enrico Mainardi (vc) *(rec 1954)* Arkadia 2-▲ 568 (m) [ADD]

Fischer, György (pno)
Caccini, G.:Amarilli mia bella, w. Cecilia Bartoli (mez) *(rec 1990)* London ▲ 448300-2 [DDD]; ■ 448300-4
Giordano, U.:Arias, w. Cecilia Bartoli (mez)—Caro mio ben *(rec 1990)* London ▲ 448300-2 [DDD] ■ 448300-4
Parisotti, A.:Se tu m'ami, w. Cecilia Bartoli (mez) *(rec 1990)* London ▲ 448300-2 [DDD]; ■ 448300-4
Se tu m'ami [If You Love Me]:18th Century Italian Songs, w. Bartoli, Cecilia (mez) London ▲ 436267-2 [DDD] ■ 436267-4

Fischer, Hans (cl)
Baur, J.:Ostinato senza fine, "Pour rien", w. A. Münten (cl), C. Crespo (hn), *(not advised of 2nd hn)*, F. Effmann (bn), S. Fasang (bn) *(rec May 13, 1981)* Koch Schwann ▲ SCH 311982 [ADD/DDD]

Fischer, J. (perc)—see ORCHESTRAS & ENSEMBLES Griffin Music Ensemble

Fischer, Jeanne Kierman (pno)—see also ORCHESTRAS & ENSEMBLES Fischer Duo
York, W.:Native Songs, w. N. Armstrong (sop), S. Sylvan (bar), S. Downey (sgr), R. Woodhouse (sgr), P. Friedland (fl), J. Russell Smith (perc) *(rec May 1987)* New World ▲ 80439-2

Fischer, Kenneth (a sax)
Anderson, Tommy Joe:Son 3 Sax, w. R. Zimdars (pno) *(rec 1988)* ACA Digital Recording ▲ CM 20003
Bassett, L.:Duo Concertante, w. R. Zimdars (pno) *(rec 1988)* ACA Digital Recording ▲ CM 20003
Heiden, B.:Diversion, w. Richard Zimdars (pno) *(rec 1988)* ACA Digital Recording ▲ CM 20003
Nielson, L.:Fants S Sax *(rec 1988)* ACA Digital Recording ▲ CM 20003

Fischer, Norman (vc)—see also ORCHESTRAS & ENSEMBLES Fischer Duo, Concord String Quartet
Finney, R.L.:Narrative Vc, w. E. London (cnd), Cleveland Chamber SO Albany ▲ TROY 208 [DDD]
Read Thomas, A.:Vigil, w. E. London (cnd), Cleveland Chamber SO GM ▲ GM 2045
Rochberg, G.:Duo Concertante, w. M. Sokol (vn) CRI ■ ACS 6013
Rochberg, G.:Ricordanza, w. G. Rochberg (pno) CRI ■ ACS 6013

Fischer, P. (gtr)
Rautavaara, E.:Monologues of the Unicorn *(rec May 3, 1982)* BIS ▲ CD 66 [AAD]

INSTRUMENT.

Fischer, Roli (cym)
Hauser, F.:Die Welle, w. Martin André Grütter (cym/tamtam), Roli Fischer (cym), Barbara Frey (cym), Cyril Lützelschwab (cym), Lukas Rohner (cym), Severin Steinhauser (cym), Hans Ulrich (cym), Ruud Wiener (cym), Michael Erni (timp), Fran Lorkovic (timp), F. Hauser (cnd) *(rec Studio DRS, Basel, Switzerland, Nov. 6, 1988)* Hat Hut ▲ hat ART CD 6017 [ADD]

Fischer, Vilmos (pno)
Liszt, F.:Sonetti del Petrarca Pno—No. 123 LaserLight ▲ 14 224
Mozart, W.A.:Con 17 Pno, w. H. Kraus (cnd), Vienna Mozart Ensemble LaserLight ▲ 15 618 [DDD]
Mozart, W.A.:Con 21 Pno, w. H. Kraus (cnd), Vienna Mozart Ensemble Laserlight ▲ 15 618 [DDD]

Fischer-Dieskau, Manuel (vc)
Messiaen, O.:Quatuor pour la fin du temps, w. Wolfgang Meyer (cl), Christoph Poppen (vn), Y. Loriod (pno) EMI Classics ▲ CDC 54395

Fišer, Jan (tpt)
Janácek, L.:Capriccio, w. Daniel Wiesner (pno), Jan Riedlbauch (fl/pic), Vladislav Kozderka (tpt), Václav Ferebauer (trbn), Jan Hynčica (trbn), Antonín Keller (trbn), Jiří Novotný (ten tuba), L. Svárovský (cnd) *(rec Martinek Studio in Prague, Jan 9, Feb 27, Mar 20, 19)* Panton ▲ 811393-2 [DDD]

Fišer, Jiří (vn)
Krček, J.:Songs of Love, w. L. Vraspír (ten), J. Krček (cnd), Musica Bohemica Panton ▲ 81 1030-2

Fišer, Jiří (vn)—see ORCHESTRAS & ENSEMBLES Dolezalovo String Quartet

Fisher, H. (dr)
Gershwin, G.:Rhap in Blue, w. B. Griffiths (vn), P. Whittaker (cl), R. Simmons (tpt), D. James (trbn), A. Litton (pno), A. Litton (cnd), Royal PO [original big band orchestration] RPO ▲ RPO 5011 [DDD]

Fisher, Mark (eup)
Arban, J.-B.:Fant, Theme & Vars on "The Carnival of Venice", w. Mark Lawson (pno) [arr. Eric Leidzen] *(rec Boutell Concert Hall, Northern Illinois Univ., June 6–7 & Nov. 26–27, 19)* Albany ▲ TROY 162 [DDD]
Bach, Jan:Concert Vars, w. Mark Lawson (pno) *(rec Boutell Concert Hall, Northern Illinois Univ., June 6–7 & Nov. 26–27, 19)* Albany ▲ TROY 162 [DDD]
Bach, J.S.:Sons Fl, BWV 1030–35, w. Mark Lawson (pno)—BWV 1031 *(rec Boutell Concert Hall, Northern Illinois Univ., June 6–7 & Nov. 26–27, 19)* Albany ▲ TROY 162 [DDD]
Brahms, J.:Songs, w. Mark Lawson (pno)—Es Rauschet Das Wasser; Der Jäger Und Sein Liebchen [both Op. 28]; Weg der Liebe, Op. 20; So Lass Uns Wandern, Op. 75 *(rec Boutell Concert Hall, Northern Illinois Univ., June 6–7 & Nov. 26–27, 19)* Albany ▲ TROY 162 [DDD]
Jacob, G.:Fant Eup, w. Mark Lawson (pno) *(rec Boutell Concert Hall, Northern Illinois Univ., June 6–7 & Nov. 26–27, 19)* Albany ▲ TROY 162 [DDD]
Telemann, G.P.:Son Bn, w. Mark Lawson (pno) *(rec Boutell Concert Hall, Northern Illinois Univ., June 6–7 & Nov. 26–27, 19)* Albany ▲ TROY 162 [DDD]

Fisher, Roger (org)
Bach, J.S.:Fant & Fugue Org, BWV 542 *(rec St. Peter's Church, Budleigh Salterton Aug 1993)* Mirabilis ▲ MMSCD2 [DDD]
Bach, J.S.:Jesu bleibet meine Freude *(rec St. Peter's Church, Budleigh Salterton Aug 1993)* Mirabilis ▲ MMSCD2 [DDD]
Bach, J.S.:Org Music (misc)—Fugue alla Gigue *(rec St. Peter's Church, Budleigh Salterton, Aug 1993)* Mirabilis ▲ MMSCD2 [DDD]
Bach, J.S.:Toccata & Fugue Org, BWV 565 *(rec St. Peter's Church, Budleigh Salterton, Aug 1993)* Mirabilis ▲ MMSCD2 [DDD]
Cocker, N.:Tuba Tune *(rec St. Peter's Church, Budleigh Salterton Aug 1993)* Mirabilis ▲ MMSCD2 [DDD]
Elgar, E.:Org Music—Sonata in G for Organ, Op. 28; Vesper Voluntaries; Cantique, Op. 3/1; Pomp & Circumstance March No. 1 [solo organ arrangement by Edwin H. Lemare, 1902]; Sonata No. 2 in B♭, Op. 87a [1933 solo organ arrangement by Sir Ivor Atkins of Elgar's Severn Suite for Brass Band] Motette ▲ CD 11501 [DDD]
Elgar, E.:Son Org Motette ▲ CD 11501 [DDD]
Guilmant, A.:Son 1 Org *(rec St. Peter's Church, Budleigh Salterton, Aug 1993)* Mirabilis ▲ MMSCD2 [DDD]
Harwood, B.:Org Music—Son No. 1 in c#, Op. 5; Son No. 2 in f#, Op. 26; Dithyramb, Op. 7; Interlude, Op. 15/2; Paean, Op. 15/3; Quiet Voluntary for Evensong, Op. 70; Reverie [Chester Cathedral Organ] *(rec Feb.–Mar. 1991)* Mirabilis ▲ MRCD 906
Saint-Saëns, C.:Fant Org *(rec St. Peter's Church, Budleigh Salterton, Aug 1993)* Mirabilis ▲ MMSCD2 [DDD]
Whitlock, P.:Org Music—3 Reflections *(rec St. Peter's Church, Budleigh Salterton, Aug 1993)* Mirabilis ▲ MMSCD2 [DDD]

Fisk, Charles (pno)
Brody, M.:Apparitions CRI ▲ CD 594 [DDD]
Brody, M.:Moments musicaux, w. D. Evans (elecs) CRI ▲ CD 594 [DDD]

Fisk, Eliot (gtr)
Baroque Guitar, w. Fisk, Eliot (gtr) MusicMasters ▲ 01612-67130-2 [DDD]
Bell'Italia:Four Centuries of Italian Music, w. Fisk, Eliot (gtr) MusicMasters ▲ 01612-67079-2 [DDD]
The Best of Eliot Fisk, w. Fisk, Eliot (gtr) MusicMasters ▲ 01612-67151-2 [ADD/DDD]
Guitar Fantasies, w. Fisk, Eliot (gtr) MusicMasters ▲ 7008-2-C [DDD]
Guitar Virtuoso, w. Fisk, Eliot (gtr) MusicMasters ▲ 01612-67128-2 [AAD]
Latin American Guitar, w. Fisk, Eliot (gtr) MusicMasters ▲ 01612-67127-2 [AAD]
Segovia, w. Fisk, Eliot (gtr) *(rec Parish Church, Weston, Hertfordshire, England, May 17–20, 1996)* MusicMasters ▲ 01612-67174-2 [DDD]

Fisk, Elliott (gtr)
Bach, J.S.:Cons solo Hpd, BWV 972–987, w. F. Hand (gtr)—BWV 972 *(rec July 27 & Aug 4, 1992)* MusicMasters ▲ 01612-67097-2 [DDD]
Bach, J.S.:Sons & Partitas Vn, BWV 1001–1006 [arr. for guitar]—Partita No. 2 in d, BWV 1004, Ciaccona MusicMasters ▲ 01612-67130-2 [DDD]
Bach, J.S.:Suite Lt, BWV 996 MusicMasters ▲ 01612-67128-2 [DDD]
Beaser, R.:Mountain Songs, w. P. Robison (fl) MusicMasters ▲ 7038-2-C [DDD]
Beethoven, L. van:Vars on Paisiello's duet "Nel cor più non mi sento", WoO 70 [trans Fisk] *(rec Parish Church of the Holy Trinity, Weston, Hertfordshire, England, May 2–3 & Sept. 18–20, 19)* MusicMasters ▲ 01612-67150-2 [DDD]
Berio, L.:Brin [trans Fisk] *(rec Parish Church of the Holy Trinity, Weston, Hertfordshire, England, May 2–3 & Sept. 18–20, 19)* MusicMasters ▲ 01612-67150-2 [DDD]
Berio, L.:Duets for 2 Vns [trans Fisk] *(rec Parish Church of the Holy Trinity, Weston, Hertfordshire, England, May 2–3 & Sept. 18–20, 19)* MusicMasters ▲ 01612-67150-2 [DDD]
Berio, L.:Sequenza XI *(rec Parish Church of the Holy Trinity, Weston, Hertfordshire, England, May 2–3 & Sept. 18–20, 19)* MusicMasters ▲ 01612-67150-2 [DDD]
Frescobaldi, G.:Balletto MusicMasters ▲ 01612-67130-2 [DDD]
Froberger, J.J.:Hpd Music—Suite XV in a MusicMasters ▲ 01612-67128-2 [AAD]
Martin, F.:Guitare *(rec 1982)* GSP ▲ GSP 1008
Mendelssohn, F.:Lieder ohne Worte Pno [trans Fisk] *(rec Parish Church of the Holy Trinity, Weston, Hertfordshire, England, May 2–3 & Sept. 18–20, 19)* MusicMasters ▲ 01612-67150-2 [DDD]
Mountain Songs:A Cycle of American Folk Music, w. Robison, Paula (fl) MusicMasters ▲ 7038-2-C [DDD]
Paganini, N.:Caprice d'adieux [trans Fisk] *(rec Parish Church of the Holy Trinity, Weston, Hertfordshire, England, May 2–3 & Sept. 18–20, 19)* MusicMasters ▲ 01612-67150-2 [DDD]
Paganini, N.:Caprices Vn [arr. for solo guitar] MusicMasters ▲ 01612-67092-2 [DDD]
Paganini, N.:Caprices Vn—Nos. 7, 9, 13 & 21 *(rec 1982)* GSP ▲ GSP 1008
Paganini, N.:Caprices Vn MusicMasters ▲ 01612-67139-2
Paganini, N.:Intro & Vars on "Nel cor più" [trans Fisk] *(rec Parish Church of the Holy Trinity, Weston, Hertfordshire, England, May 2–3 & Sept. 18–20, 19)* MusicMasters ▲ 01612-67150-2 [DDD]
Paganini, N.:Sons Vn & Gtr—No. 23 [trans Fisk] *(rec Parish Church of the Holy Trinity, Weston, Hertfordshire, England, May 2–3 & Sept. 18–20, 19)* MusicMasters ▲ 01612-67150-2 [DDD]
Ponce, M.:Gtr Music—Valse; Thème, Varié et Finale *(rec 1982)* GSP ▲ GSP 1008
Raffman, R.:Für Eliot *(rec 1982)* GSP ▲ GSP 1008

Fisk, Elliott (gtr) (cont.)
Rochberg, G.:Paganini Vars—Vars. 1–51 MusicMasters ▲ 01612-67133-2 [DDD]
Scarlatti, D.:Sons Kbd—K.27 [Allegro]; K.164 [Andante Moderato]; K.96 [Allegrissimo] *(rec 1982)* GSP ▲ GSP 1008
Scarlatti, D.:Sons Kbd—in E, K 380; in E, K.531; in A, K.322; in A, K.323; in d, K.213, in C, K.159 MusicMasters ▲ 01612-67130-2 [DDD]
Scarlatti, D.:Sons Kbd—(3) in G, K.146, 390 & 391 MusicMasters ▲ 01612-67128-2 [AAD]
Scarlatti, D.:Sons Kbd—Sons, K.175, 481 & 482 *(rec Parish Church of the Holy Trinity, Weston, Hertfordshire, England, May 2–3 & Sept. 18–20, 19)* MusicMasters ▲ 01612-67150-2 [DDD]
Vivaldi, A.:Con Mand, RV.425, Orch of St. Luke *(rec July 27 & Aug. 4, 1992)* MusicMasters ▲ 01612-67097-2 [DDD]
Vivaldi, A.:Con for 2 Mands, w. F. Hand (gtr), Orch of St. Luke *(rec July 27 & Aug. 4, 1992)* MusicMasters ▲ 01612-67097-2 [DDD]
Vivaldi, A.:Con Va d'amore Lt, w. L. Schulman (vn), Orch of St. Luke *(rec July 27 & Aug. 4, 1992)* MusicMasters ▲ 01612-67097-2 [DDD]
Vivaldi, A.:Sons Vc, w. A. Fuller (hpd)—in g, RV.42 [trans for gtr & hpd] *(rec July 27 & Aug. 4, 1992)* MusicMasters ▲ 01612-67097-2 [DDD]
Vivaldi, A.:Trio Sons Vn Lt, w. F. Hand (gtr), A. Fuller (hpd) *(rec July 27 & Aug. 4, 1992)* MusicMasters ▲ 01612-67097-2 [DDD]

Fitch, Frances Conover (hpd)
Hovhaness, A.:Sextet Rcr, w. J. Tyson (rcr), J. Starkman (vn), K. Shaw (vn), J. Cosart (va), A. Robbins (vc) Titanic ▲ Ti 169 [DDD]
Something for Recorder & Strings, w. Tyson, John (rcr), Jane Starkman (vn), Katheryn Shaw (vn), Jann Cosart (va), Alice Robbins (vc), Tom Coleman (db) Titanic ▲ Ti 169 [DDD]

Fitkin, Graham (kbd)
Fitkin, G.:Frame, w. S. Sutherland (kbd), Smith String Quartet Argo ▲ 433690-2 [DDD]
Fitkin, G.:Huah, w. S. Sutherland (kbd), Smith String Quartet Argo ▲ 433690-2 [DDD]
Fitkin, G.:Slow, w. S. Sutherland (kbd), Smith String Quartet Argo ▲ 433690-2 [DDD]

Fitkin, Graham (pno)
Fitkin, G.:Music of—Arract [w. Eleanor Alberga (pno)]; Fervent; Pno Piece 91; Pno Piece very early 92; Pno Piece early 92; Hard Fairy [w. John Harle (sax), John Lenehan (pno)]; Blue; Pno Piece mid 92; Pno Piece late 92; Pno Piece very late 92; Pno Piece 93; Fract [w. Eleanor Alberga (pno)] *(rec Walthamstow Assembly Hall, London, Feb 8–9 & May 10, 1994)* Argo ▲ 444112-2 [DDD]

Fitz, Richard (perc)
Bartók, B.:Son for 2 Pnos, w. G. Kalish (pno), L. Luvisi (pno), Gottlieb (perc) *(rec Feb. 1, 1993)* Delos ▲ DE 3151 [DDD]
Crumb, G.:Music For A Summer EveningMusic for a Summer Evening (Makrokosmos III), w. J. Freeman (pno), G. Kalish (pno), R. DesRoches (perc) Elektra/Nonesuch ▲ 79149-2 [AAD]
Davidovsky, M.:Synchronism 5, w. R. DesRoches (perc), Heldrich (perc), D. Marcone (perc), van Hyning (perc), H. Sollberger (cnd) CRI ▲ CD 611 [ADD]

Fitzmaurice, Mike (db)
A Colorado Kind of Christmas, w. [cnd:Duain Wolfe], Colorado Children's Chorale, Rod Garnet (fl), William Hill (perc), Deborah Schmit-Lobis (pno), Brett Walace (vc), Mary Louise Burke (pno), Laurie Kahler (pno), Helen Hope (hp) *(rec Denver Center Media)* Colorado Children's Chorale ▲ XMAS

Fitzpatrick, M. (vn)—see ORCHESTRAS & ENSEMBLES Mobius

Fix-Keller, Bronwyn (hpd)
Bach, J.S.:Magnificat, BWV 243, w. Julianne Baird (sop), Lorie Gratis (mez), David Price (ten), Kevin Deas (bass-bar), V. Radu (cnd), Ama Deus Ensemble Vox Classics ▲ VOX 7531

Fizdale, Robert (pno)
Poulenc, F.:Con for 2 Pnos, w. A. Gold (pno), L. Bernstein (cnd), New York PO *(rec Dec. 23, 1961)* Sony Classical ▲ SMK 47618 [ADD]
Rieti, V.:Con Pnos, w. A. Gold (pno), E. Ansermet (cnd), Swiss Romande Orch Premier ▲ PRCD 1033 [ADD]
Rieti, V.:2nd Ave Waltzes, w. A. Gold (pno) Premier ▲ PRCD 1033 [ADD]

Flagel, Claude (h-g)
Baroque Music for Recorder, w. Steinmann, Conrad (rcr), Monica Huggett (baroque vn), Hopkinson Smith (lt/thb/gtr), Jordi Savall (vl), Pere Ros (vl), Johann Sonnleitner (hpd) Claves ▲ CD 508103 [ADD]

Flaksman, Michael (vc)
Fortner, J.:Concertpiece, w. S. Kawalla (cnd), Koszalin State PO Vienna Modern Masters ▲ VMM 3024 [DDD]

Flammer, Amy (vn)
Cage, J.:Two[6], w. Martine Joste (pno) *(rec Radio France, Paris, Jan. 18–4, 1994)* Mode ▲ mode 44
Dvořák, A.:Qnt Pno, Op. 81, w. Roberte Mamou (pno), Silvia Marcovici (vn), Gerard Causse (va), Robert Cohen (vc) *(rec Mozart Festival, Lille, France, 1994)* Verdi Classics ▲ AU 32 250
Dvořák, A.:Terzetto, w. Silvia Marcovici (vn), Gerard Causse (va) *(rec Mozart Festival, Lille, France, 1994)* Verdi Classics ▲ AU 32 250

Flammer, Amy (vn/rainsticks)
Cage, J.:Four[3], w. Dominique Alchourroun (pno/rainsticks), Martine Joste (pno/rainsticks), Jean Michaut (rainsticks) *(rec Radio France, Paris, Jan. 18–4, 1994)* Mode ▲ mode 44

Flanders, Katharine (fl/pic)—see ORCHESTRAS & ENSEMBLES Musicians' Accord

Flath, Edwin (org)
Bach, J.S.:Cant 118, w. E. Flath (cnd), California Bach Society CO, California Bach Society Chorus, Valley Choral Society [G] Bainbridge ▲ BCD 2502 [DDD]
Bach, J.S.:Preludes & Fugues, BWV 531–552—BWV 548 Bainbridge ▲ BCD 2502 [DDD]
Kobialka, D.:Antiphony Across..., w. E. Flath (cnd), California Bach Society CO, California Bach Society Chorus, Valley Choral Society Bainbridge ▲ BCD 2502 [DDD]

Flax, Laura (cl)
Dembski, S.:Alta, w. A. Feinberg (pno) CRI ▲ CD 570 [DDD]
Dembski, S.:Altamira, w. A. Feinberg (pno) CRI ▲ CD 570 [DDD]
Dembski, S.:Digit CRI ▲ CD 570 [DDD]
Hudson, J.:Sonare, w. Rolf Schulte (vn), Paul Dunkel (fl), Ursula Oppens (pno), Joseph Passaro (perc) CRI ■ C 382
Olan, D.:Composition Cl CRI ▲ CD 565 [AAD/DDD]
Ran, S.:Apprehensions, w. J. Nicosia (sop), A. Feinberg (pno) *(rec 1979–91)* CRI ▲ CD 609 [ADD/DDD]
Ran, S.:Private Game, w. A. Emelianoff (vc) *(rec 1979–91)* CRI ▲ CD 609 [ADD/DDD]
Tower, J.:Black Topaz, w. Stephen Gosling (pno), Patricia Spencer (fl), Chris Gekker (tpt), Mike Powell (trbn), Jonathan Haas (perc), Deborah Moore (perc) *(rec American Academy of Arts & Letters, New York City, Sept. 26–28, 1994)* New World ▲ 80470-2
Tower, J.:Wings CRI ▲ CD 582 [DDD]

Fleagle, John (gothic hp/lt/fid/sinfonia/bodhran/sgr)
World's Bliss:Medieval Songs of Love & Death, w. Shira Kammen (vielle/fid) *(rec 1st & 2nd Church, Marlborough St., Boston, MA; Church of the Redeemer, Chestnut Hill, MA; July 27 & 28, 1995 & Jan)* Archetype ▲ 60103 [DDD]

Fleagle, John (sgr)—see ORCHESTRAS & ENSEMBLES Project Ars Nova Ensemble

Fleck, Béla (banjo)
Mozart, W.A.:Music of, w. Philip Aaberg, Todd Boekelheide, Chris Botti, Henry Adam Curtis, Steve Erquiaga, Eugene Friesen, Paul McCandless, Tim Story, Richard Schönherz, Tracy Scott Silverman, Thea Suits-Silverman, ValGardena, Modern Mandolin Quartet Imaginary Road ▲ 314534065-2 ■ 314534065-4

Flederman (pno)
Vine, C.:Elegy *(rec Dec. 1986)* Tall Poppies ▲ TP013 [DDD]
Vine, C.:Miniature III *(rec Dec. 1983)* Tall Poppies ▲ TP013 [DDD]

Fleezanis, Jorja (vn)
Bolle, J.:Pieces (8), w. Basil Reeve (ob) Gasparo ▲ GSCD 317 [DDD]
Wolpe, S.:Son Vn, w. G. Ohlsson (pno) *(rec Nov. 9–10, 1991)* Koch ▲ KIC 7112 [DDD]

558 ▲ = CD ♦ = Enhanced CD Δ = MD ■ = Cassette Tape □ = DCC

Fleischmann, Christine (hp)
Concert de musique liturgique Juive á la synagogue de Lausanne, w. Lausanne Israeli Community Male Chorus, Alain Blum, Antoine D., André Stora, Gueorgui Popov, Jean Akiba, J. Rubin (lt), Oleg Kogan (hp) Doron ▲ DRC 3003 [DDD]
Gounod, C.:Requiem, w. M. Veillon (db), F. Margot (org), A. Charlet (cnd), Romande Chamber Choir *(rec 1992 & 1993)* Claves ▲ CD 9326 [DDD]

Fleisher, Leon (pno)
Beethoven, L. van:Cons Pno (comp), w. G. Szell (cnd), Cleveland Orch CBS 3–▲ M3K 42445
Beethoven, L. van:Cons Pno (comp), w. G. Szell (cnd), Cleveland Orch Sony Classical ("Essential Classics" series) 3–▲ SB3K 48397
Beethoven, L. van:Con 1 Pno, w. G. Szell (cnd), Cleveland Orch Odyssey ■ YT 35928
Beethoven, L. van:Con 1 Pno, w. G. Szell (cnd), Cleveland Orch Sony Classical ("Essential Classics" series) ▲ SBK 47658 ■ SBT 47658
Beethoven, L. van:Con 2 Pno, w. G. Szell (cnd), Cleveland Orch Sony Classical ("Essential Classics" series) ▲ SBK 48165 ■ SBT 48165
Beethoven, L. van:Con 2 Pno, w. G. Szell (cnd), Cleveland Orch Odyssey ■ YT 35928
Beethoven, L. van:Con 3 Pno, w. G. Szell (cnd), Cleveland Orch Sony Classical ("Essential Classics" series) ▲ SBK 47658 ■ SBT 47658
Beethoven, L. van:Con 4 Pno, w. G. Szell (cnd), Cleveland Orch Odyssey ■ YT 35490
Beethoven, L. van:Con 4 Pno, w. G. Szell (cnd), Cleveland Orch CBS ▲ MYK 37762 [ADD] ■ MYT 37762
Beethoven, L. van:Con 4 Pno, w. G. Szell (cnd), Cleveland Orch Sony Classical ("Essential Classics" series) ▲ SBK 48165 ■ SBT 48165
Beethoven, L. van:Con 4 Pno, w. O. Klemperer (cnd), Bavarian RSO, Berlin RSO, Cologne RSO Enterprise ("Palladio" series) ▲ ENT 4189 [ADD]
Beethoven, L. van:Con 5 Pno, "Emperor", w. E. Ormandy (cnd), Philadelphia Orch Sony Classical ("Essential Classics" series) ▲ SBK 46549 [ADD] ■ SBT 46549
Beethoven, L. van:Con 5 Pno, "Emperor", w. G. Szell (cnd), Cleveland Orch Odyssey ■ YT 35491
Brahms, J.:Con 1 Pno, w. G. Szell (cnd), Cleveland Orch Odyssey ■ YT 31273
Brahms, J.:Con 2 Pno, w. G. Szell (cnd), Cleveland Orch Odyssey ■ YT 32222
Brahms, J.:Liebeslieder Waltzes SATB, w. B. Valente (sop), M. Kleinman (cta), W. Conner (ten), M. Singher (bar), R. Serkin (pno) [G] Sony Classical ("Essential Classics" series) ▲ SBK 48176 ■ SBT 48176
Britten, H.:Diversions Pno, w. S. Ozawa (cnd), Boston SO Sony Classical ▲ SK 47188 [DDD]
Franck, C.:Symphonic Vars, w. G. Szell (cnd), Cleveland Orch *(rec 1956)* CBS ▲ MYK 37812 (m) [ADD] ■ MYT 37812 (m)
Mozart, W.A.:Con 25 Pno, w. G. Szell (cnd), Cleveland Orch CBS 3–▲ M3K 42445
Mozart, W.A.:Con 25 Pno, w. G. Szell (cnd), Cleveland Orch CBS ▲ MYK 37762 [ADD] ■ MYT 37762
Prokofiev, S.:Con 4 Pno, w. S. Ozawa (cnd), Boston SO Sony Classical ▲ SK 47188 [DDD]
Rachmaninoff, S.:Rhapsody on a Theme of Paganini, w. G. Szell (cnd), Cleveland Orch *(rec 1956)* CBS ▲ MYK 37812 (m) [ADD]
Ravel, M.:Alborada del gracioso *(rec 1958)* CBS ▲ MYK 37812 (m) [ADD]
Ravel, M.:Con Pno (left hand), w. S. Ozawa (cnd), Boston SO Sony Classical ▲ SK 47188 [DDD]
Ravel, M.:Con Pno (left hand), w. S. Comissiona (cnd), Baltimore SO Vanguard Classics ▲ OVC 4002 [ADD]
Recital:Piano Works for the Left Hand *(rec June 21–24, 1992)* Sony Classical ▲ SK 48081
Schubert, Franz:Son Pno, D.664 Sony Classical ("Essential Classics" series) ▲ SBK 47667 ■ SBT 47667
Schumann, R.:Con Pno, w. G. Szell (cnd), Cleveland Orch Odyssey ■ YT 30668

Fleková, Hana (t vl)—see ORCHESTRAS & ENSEMBLES Pro Arte Antiqua Prague

Fiello, David (tpt)
Zwilich, E.T.:Clarino Qt, w. Christopher Lane (tpt), David Michaux (tpt), Louis Ranger (tpt) *(rec Univ of Victoria, May 1994)* Crystal ▲ CD 669

Fleming, C. (fl)
Harty, H.:In Ireland, w. Denise Kelley (hp), B. Thomson (cnd), Ulster Orch Chandos ▲ CHAN 8321 [DDD]
Harty, H.:In Ireland, w. Denise Kelley (hp), B. Thomson (cnd), Ulster Orch Chandos ("Collect" series) ▲ CHAN 6583 [ADD]

Fleming, Jenni (pno)
Schultz, Andrew:Sea-Change *(rec Nickson Room, Music Dept, Univ of Queensland, Australia, Dec 1994)* Tall Poppies ▲ TP 065 [DDD]

Flemming, Jenni (pno)—see ORCHESTRAS & ENSEMBLES Perihelion Ensemble members

Flemming, Jenni (pno/sgr/whirly instr)—see ORCHESTRAS & ENSEMBLES Perihelion

Flemström, Per (fl)
Nielsen, C.:Con Fl, w. E.-P. Salonen (cnd), Swedish RSO *(rec Sept. 16–18, 1991)* Sony Classical ▲ SK 53276 [DDD]

Flesch, Carl (vn)
Bach, J.S.:Con for 2 Vns, w. J. Szigeti (vn), W. Goehr (cnd), *(orch unknown)* *(rec 1937)* Pearl ▲ PEA 9938 (m) [AAD]
Carl Flesch, 1873–1944 Symposium 3–▲ SYM 1032/4
The Complete HMV Recordings, w. J. Hubay (vn) Biddulph ▲ LAB 045 [ADD]

Fletcher, Andrew (org)
St. Mary's Collegiate Church, Warwick Organ Mirabilis ▲ MRCD 903 [DDD]

Fletcher, John (tuba)
Vaughan Williams, R.:Con Bass Tuba, w. A. Previn (cnd), London SO RCA Gold Seal ▲ 60586–2–RG [ADD]

Fleur, R. la (lt)
Ericson & La Fleur, w. B. Ericson (vl) BIS ▲ CD 22 [AAD]

Flexer, Marie (vn)—see ORCHESTRAS & ENSEMBLES Stratos

Flieder, Johannes (va)
Tchaikovsky, P.:Souvenir de Florence, w. W. Schulz (vc), Franz Schubert String Quartet *(rec Nov. 9–12, 1993)* Nimbus ▲ NI 5399 [DDD]

Fliegel, Raphael (va)—see ORCHESTRAS & ENSEMBLES Shepherd String Quartet

Flieger, Jiri (bn)
Magnard, A.:Qnt Pno, w. Christoph Keller (pno), Anna-Katharina Graf (fl), Roman Schmid (ob), Elmar Schmid (cl) Accord ▲ ACD 200102 [DDD]

Flier, Yakov (pno)
Busoni, F.:Chaconne Pno *(rec 1947)* Russian Compact Disc ("Talents of Russia" series) ▲ RCD 16284 [ADD]
Debussy, C.:Preludes Pno (sels)—Nos. 10, 12 & 17 *(rec 1952)* Russian Compact Disc ("Talents of Russia" series) ▲ RCD 16284 [ADD]
Debussy, C.:Suite bergamasque—Nos. 1, 3 & 4 *(rec 1954)* Russian Compact Disc ("Talents of Russia" series) ▲ RCD 16284 [ADD]
Liszt, F.:Pno Music (misc)—Nocturne [No. 3 from Romance Oubliée]; Funeral Procession [No. 7 from Harmonies poetiques & religieuses]; Etude in f [No. 10 from Etudes d'execution]; Consolation in D♭ [No. 3 from Consolations] *(rec 1946–52)* Russian Compact Disc ("Talents of Russia" series) ▲ RCD 16284 [ADD]
Mendelssohn, F.:Lieder ohne Worte Pno—Opp. 19/2; 30/4; 53/2; 102/3 & 4 *(rec 1951–52)* Russian Compact Disc ("Talents of Russia" series) ▲ RCD 16284 [ADD]
Rachmaninoff, S.:Son Vc, w. Daniil Shafran (vc) Multisonic ▲ MUL 310354

Flissler, Eileen (pno)
Beethoven, L. van:Sons Vn (comp), w. Aaron Rosand (vn) *(rec 1961)* Vox Box ("Legends" series) 3–▲ CDX3 3503 [ADD]
Beethoven, L. van:Son 5 Vn, "Spring", w. A. Rosand (vn) Allegretto ▲ ACD 8082 [ADD] ■ ACS 8082
Beethoven, L. van:Son 9 Vn, "Kreutzer", w. A. Rosand (vn) Allegretto ▲ ACD 8082 [ADD] ■ ACS 8082
Sarasate, P. de:Caprice basque, w. A. Rosand (vn) Allegretto ▲ ACD 8160 [ADD] ■ ACS 8160

Flissler, Eileen (pno) (cont.)
Sarasate, P. de:Navarra, w. A. Rosand (vn) [Rosand plays both vn parts] Allegretto ▲ ACD 8160 [ADD] ■ ACS 8160
Sarasate, P. de:Spanish Dances, w. A. Rosand (vn) Allegretto ▲ ACD 8160 [ADD] ■ ACS 8160
The Violinist, w. A. Rosand (vn) Allegretto ▲ ACD 8149 [ADD] ■ ACS 8149

Flood, David (org)
Tallis, T.:Church Music, w. Canterbury Cathedral Choir—Ave Dei patris filia; Ave rosa sine spinis; Salve intermerata virgo *(rec Canterbury Cathedral nave)* Metronome ▲ 1014 [DDD]
Tallis, T.:Mass "Salve intemerata", w. Canterbury Cathedral Choir *(rec Canterbury Cathedral nave)* Metronome ▲ 1014 [DDD]

Florentin, Aldo (hpd)—see ORCHESTRAS & ENSEMBLES Ensemble Barocco Padua Sans Souci

Florio, Antonio (vc)
Sui Palchi Delle Stelle:Sacred Music in the Neapolitan Conservatories at the Time of Francesco Provenzale, w. Cappella Pietà de Turchini [cnd:Antonio Florio], Antonella Ippolito (sop), Jane Haughton (sop), Daniela del Monaco (alt), Sebastiano Cassarà (vn), Rosario Di Meglio (vn), Antonella Bologna (va), Paolo Dionisio (vl), Antonio Florio (vc), Pierluigi Ciappareli (thb), Enrico Baiano (org/hpd) Symphonia ▲ SY 93S20 [DDD]

Florio, Lorena di (pno)
Clementi, M.:Pno Music (comp), w. Federico Aldao (pno), Aldo Antognazzi (pno), Ana Chavez (pno), Marcela Paludi (pno), Ricardo Zanon (pno)—Sons (6) for Pno, Op. 1, Nos. 4–6; Sons (6) for Pno, Op. 2, Nos. 2, 4 & 6 Aura Classics ▲ AU 32072

Flower, Edward (gtr)
Chords & Thyme:English Folksongs for Guitar, w. J. Brown (gtr) *(rec Troy, NY, Apr. 1994)* Dorian ▲ DOR 90204 [DDD]

Fluhr, P. (ob)
Villa-Lobos, H.:Duo Ob, w. Ulrich Freund (bn) Bayer ▲ BR 100117 [DDD]
Villa-Lobos, H.:Qt Fl, w. Joachim Schmitz (fl), Johannes Moog (cl), Ulrich Freund (bn) Bayer ▲ BR 100117 [DDD]
Villa-Lobos, H.:Trio Ob, w. Johannes Moog (cl), Ulrich Freund (bn) Bayer ▲ BR 100117 [DDD]

Flury, Dieter (fl)
Fahrbach, P.:Music of, w. Peter Schmidl (cl), Vienna Biedermeier Soloists—Die Schwärmer, Op. 43; Talmi-Polka, Op. 304; Lerchenfelder-Polka, Op. 178; Vienna Polka, Op. 109; S'Schwarzblatl Aus'n Weanerwald, Op. 61; Wiener-Feuerwehr, Op. 280; Marien-Polka, Op. 164; Wiener Polka, Op. 109 *(rec Studio Baumgarten, Vienna, 1991–95)* Camerata ▲ 30CM 411 [DDD]
Fahrbach (Jr.), P.:Music of, w. Peter Schmidl (cl), Vienna Biedermeier Soloists—Der Klapperstorch, Op. 149; Wiener Lebensbilder, Op. 213; Reissausl, Op. 121; Pester Offiziers Casino Polka, Op. 83; Landsturm-Galopp, Op. 250; Erinnerung An Josef Strauss, Op. 53; Im Kahlenbergerdörfel, Op. 340 *(rec Studio Baumgarten, Vienna, 1991–95)* Camerata ▲ 30CM 411 [DDD]

Flury, Urs Joseph (vn)
Flury, U.J.:Concertino veneziano, w. R. Baumgartner (cnd), Lucerne Festival Strings *(rec Phonag Tonstudio, Dec. 5, 1978)* Gallo ▲ CD 802 [ADD]
Flury, U.J.:Con Vn, w. T. Hug (cnd), Bern Radio Chamber Ensemble *(rec Phonag Tonstudio, March 4, 1977)* Gallo ▲ CD 802 [ADD]
Flury, U.J.:Suite nostalgique, w. G. Wyss (pno) *(rec Radio Studio, Bern, Apr. 29, 1977)* Gallo ▲ CD 802 [ADD]

Flyer, Nina (vc)
Boulanger, N.:Pieces (3) Vc & Pno, w. Chi-Fun Lee (pno) Koch International Classics ▲ KIC 7280 [DDD]
Ran, S.:Fant Movts, w. J. Falletta (cnd), English CO Koch International Classics ▲ KIC 7280 [DDD]

Flynn, Adrienne (fl)
Kraft, L.:Cloud Studies, w. Lisa Maron (pic), Margaret Swinchoski (pic), Tanya Dusevic (fl), Christina Jennings (fl), Zara Lawler (fl), Joseph Piscitelli (fl), Michelle Ryang (fl), Dominique Soucy (fl), Diane Taublieb (fl), Laurel Ann Maurer (alt fl), Richard Wyton (alt fl), J. Solum (cnd) *(rec Skinner Recital Hall, Vassar College, Poughkeepsie, NY, Mar 24–26, 1994)* CRI ▲ CD 712 [DDD]

Flynn, Jane (org)
Tomorrow Shall Be My Dancing Day:Christmas at Emory University, w. Emory Univ Concert Choir [cnd:Alfred Calabrese], Timothy Albrecht (org), Nella Rigell (hp) *(rec Cathedral of St. Philip, Atlanta, GA, Apr. 30 & May 1, 1994)* ACA Digital ▲ CM 20035

Foccardi, P. (vn)—see ORCHESTRAS & ENSEMBLES Modo Antiquo

Foccroulle, Bernard (org)
Lohet, S.:Org Music—Fuga 4, 14 & 16; Nun welche Hofnung; Media vita in morte *(rec St. Lambert à Mozet, Nov 1994)* Ricercar ▲ 155141

Foccroulle, Brigitte (pno)
Schoenberg, A.:The Cabaret Songs, w. Yumi Nara (sop), Izumi Okubo (vn/va), Machiko Takahashi (fl/pic), Vincent Jacquemin (cl/b cl), François Deppe (vc), J.-P. Peuvion (cnd), Liège New Music Ensemble [arr Patrick Davin for Salon Orch] Adda ▲ ADD 581273 [DDD]
Schoenberg, A.:Pierrot lunaire, w. Yumi Nara (sop), Izumi Okubo (vn/va), Machiko Takahashi (fl/pic), Vincent Jacquemin (cl/b cl), François Deppe (vc), J.-P. Peuvion (cnd), Liège New Music Ensemble Adda ▲ ADD 581273 [DDD]

Fodor, Eugene (vn)
Mendelssohn, F.:Con in e Vn & Orch, Op. 64, w. P. Maag (cnd), New Philharmonia Orch RCA Silver Seal ▲ 09026-60910-2 ■ 09026-60910-4
Nanes, R.:Rhap Pathétique, w. K. Clark (cnd), London PO Delfon ▲ CDR 2422 [DDD] ■ DRS 2422C (D)

Fodoreanu, Dorel (vc)—see ORCHESTRAS & ENSEMBLES Enesco String Quartet

Fojta, Josef (perc)—see ORCHESTRAS & ENSEMBLES Prague Percussion Project

Földes, Andor (pno)
Bartók, B.:Con 2 Pno, w. E. Bigot (cnd), Lamoureux Orch *(rec 1948)* Jecklin-Disco ▲ JD 648-2 [ADD]
Bartók, B.:Rhap Pno, w. E. Bigot (cnd), Lamoureux Orch *(rec 1948)* Jecklin-Disco ▲ JD 648-2 [ADD]
Debussy, C.:Clair de lune, w. J. Szigeti (vn) *(rec 1942)* Sony Masterworks (Portrait) ▲ MPK 52569 (m) [ADD]
Ives, C.:Sons Vn, w. J. Szigeti (vn), No. 4 *(rec 1942)* CRI ■ ACS 6014
Schubert, Franz:Sonatina Vn, D.384, w. J. Szigeti (vn) *(rec 1942; from Columbia LP ML)* Sony Masterworks ("Portrait" series) ▲ MPK 52538 (m) [ADD]

Földesi, Lajos (vn)—see ORCHESTRAS & ENSEMBLES Haydn String Quartet Budapest

Folena, Mario (trns fl)—see also ORCHESTRAS & ENSEMBLES Ensemble Barocco Padua Sans Souci
Albinoni, T.:Trattenimenti armonici per camera, w. Barocco Padovano Sans Souci Ensemble—Nos. 1, 2 & 6–9 [trans anon in early 1700's] *(rec Chiesa della Natività della B.V. Maria ai Servi, Padova, Italy, Apr 24–25 & May 1, 1995)* Dynamic ▲ CD 139 [DDD]

Foley, J. Damian (tpt)—see ORCHESTRAS & ENSEMBLES Atlantic Brass Quintet

Foley, Joseph (tpt)—see ORCHESTRAS & ENSEMBLES Atlantic Brass Quintet

Foley, Madeline (vc)
Brahms, J.:Sextet Strs, Op. 18, w. I. Stern (vn), A. Schneider (vn), M. Katims (va), M. Thomas (va), P. Casals (vc) *(rec 1952)* Sony Masterworks ("Portrait" series) ▲ MPK 44851 [ADD]
Brahms, J.:Sextet Strs, Op. 18, w. I. Stern (vn), A. Schneider (vn), M. Katims (va), M. Thomas (va), P. Casals (vc) *(rec Prades, France, June 23–July 3, 1952)* Sony Classical ("The Casals Edition" series) ▲ SMK 58994 [ADD]
Mozart, W.A.:Trio Pno, K.502, w. R. Serkin (pno), J. Laredo (vn) *(rec 1968)* Sony Classical ▲ SMK 46255 [ADD]

Folio, C. (fl)
Folio, C.:Developing Hues, w. L. R. Thompson (b cl) Capstone ▲ CPS 8615

Follari, Susan (va)—see ORCHESTRAS & ENSEMBLES Bronx Arts Ensemble

Follows, A. (vc)
Van Appledorn, M.J.:Duos Va, w. S. Schoenfeld (va) Opus One ▲ 147

Foltyn, Pavel (fl)
Schulhoff, E.:Concertino Fl, w. Pavel Perina (va), Emanuel Kumpera (db) Supraphon ▲ SUP 112170 [DDD]
Schulhoff, E.:Son Fl, w. Jan Cech (pno) Supraphon ▲ SUP 112169 [DDD]

INSTRUMENT.

Fonda, Jean (pno)
Brahms, J.:Sons Vc (comp), w. P. Fournier (vc) Stradivarius ▲ STR 33320 [ADD]
Grieg, E.:Son Vc, w. P. Fournier (vc) Stradivarius ▲ STR 33320 [ADD]

Fontaine, Bruno (pno)
Quand on n'a que l'amour, w. F. Pollet (sop), Lamoureux Concert Orch [cnd:Yutaka Sado] Accord ▲ ACD 205522 [DDD]

Fontaine, Robert (cl)
Lemeland, A.:Fant Cl & Gtr, w. R. de Herrera (gtr) Skarbo ▲ SKR 3901 [AAD]
Lemeland, A.:Pieces Cl Skarbo ▲ SKR 3901 [AAD]

Fontana, Luigi (hpd)
Handel, G.F.:Royal Fireworks Music, w. Claudio Ferrarini (fl) Stradivarius ▲ STR 33301 [DDD]
Handel, G.F.:Royal Fireworks Music, w. Claudio Ferrarini (fl) Stradivarius ▲ STV 33301 [DDD]
Handel, G.F.:Water Music (comp), w. Claudio Ferrarini (fl) Stradivarius ▲ STR 33301 [DDD]
Handel, G.F.:Water Music (comp), w. Claudio Ferrarini (fl) Stradivarius ▲ STV 33301 [DDD]
Handel, G.F.:Water Music (suites), w. Claudio Ferrarini (fl) Stradivarius ▲ STR 33301 [DDD]
Vivaldi, A.:Cons Vn, Op. 8/1-12, "Il cimento dell'armonia e dell'inventione", w. C. Ferrarini (fl)—Nos. 1-4 Stradivarius ▲ STR 33301 [DDD]
Vivaldi, A.:Cons Vn, Op. 8/1-4, "The Four Seasons", w. Claudio Ferrarini (fl)—Summer, Autumn & Winter Stradivarius ▲ STV 33301 [DDD]

Fontanarosa, Patrice (vn)
The Art of the Violin, w. Jean-Jacques Kantorow (vn), Régis Pasquier (vn), Gérard Poulet (vn) Arion ▲ ARN 60262

Fontan-Binoche, Elisabeth (hp)
Ibert, J.:Entr'Acte, w. Jacques Castagner (fl) Adès ▲ ADE 203462 [AAD]

Fonteneau, Jean-Michel (vc)—see ORCHESTRAS & ENSEMBLES Ravel String Quartet

Fonville, John (fl)—see also ORCHESTRAS & ENSEMBLES Tone Road Ramblers, SONOR Ensemble of Univ of California San Diego members
Delio, T.:Music of, w. Steven Schick (perc), Aleck Karis (pno), Jacques Linder (pno), Sandra Sprecher (pno)—anti-paysage for Fl, Perc, Pno & Tape; Of for Tape; Though for solo Pno; so again for Tape; on again for Tape; of again for Tape *(rec Univ of CA, San Diego, Univ of Maryland, Catonsville & Washington D.C.)* Neuma ▲ 45090 [DDD]
Erickson, R.:Quoq *(rec 1987-91)* CRI ▲ CD 616 [DDD]
Reynolds, R.:Transfigured Wind 2, w. H. Sollberger (cnd), San Diego SO Ensemble New World ▲ NW 80401-2 [DDD]
Smith, S.S.:Here & There, w. D. Savage (bn), D. Yoken (pno) O.O. Discs ▲ OO 11 [DDD]
Smith, S.S.:Notebook, w. E. Harkins (tpt), P. Hoffmann (pno), B. Turetzky (db) O.O. Discs ▲ OO 11 [DDD]

Fonville, John (fl/pic)—see ORCHESTRAS & ENSEMBLES SONOR Ensemble of Univ of California San Diego members

Fonville, John (pic)
Reynolds, R.:The Ivanov Suite, w. P. Larson (bar), E. Harkins (tpt), J. Ngyesy (vn), R. Mushabec (vc), S. Schick (perc) New World ▲ 80431-2
Reynolds, R.:Versions/Stages, w. P. Larson (bar), E. Harkins (tpt), J. Ngyesy (vn), R. Mushabec (vc), S. Schick (perc) New World ▲ 80431-2

Forbes, Charles (vc)—see also ORCHESTRAS & ENSEMBLES New York Camerata
Cory, E.:Pas de Quatre, w. Jayn Rosenfeld (fl), Diane Bruce Sinclair (vn), Meg Bachman Vas (pno), New York Camerata Soundspells ▲ CD 116 [DDD]

Forbes Somerville, Murray (org)
Bach, J.S.:Das Orgelbüchlein [Flentrop Org, Adolphus Busch Hall, Harvard Univ] Titanic ▲ TI 221 [DDD]

Forchert, Walter (vn)
Reger, M.:Con Vn, w. H. Stein (cnd), Bamberg SO Koch Schwann ▲ CD 311 186 [DDD]

Ford, Linda (org)
Ward, R.:Choral Music, w. Sherry Hill Kelly (cnd), Belmont Chorale—In His Last Days; Let Us Heed the Voice Within [both from Images of God]; Earth Shall Be Fair; When Christ Rode Into Jerusalem; Concord Hymn; Sweet Freedom's Song; Ballad of Boston Bay; Epitaphs; Let Music Swell the Breeze Gasparo ▲ GS 303

Foreman, Charles (pno)
Archer, V.:Son 2 Pno *(rec Calgary Center for the Performing Arts)* Unical ▲ UC 9501 [DDD]
Archer, V.:Theme & Vars on Là-Haut *(rec 1984)* Centrediscs ▲ CMCCD 1684 [DDD]
Ballade *(rec 1984)* Centrediscs ▲ CMCCD 1684 [DDD]
Barber, S.:Son Pno *(rec Calgary Center for the Performing Arts)* Unical ▲ UC 9501 [DDD]
Beckwith, J.:Love Songs (4), w. D. Bell (sgr) Unical ▲ UCCD 9101
Beckwith, J.:Novelette *(rec 1984)* Centrediscs ▲ CMC CD 1684 [DDD]
Copland, A.:Son Pno *(rec Calgary Center for the Performing Arts)* Unical ▲ UC 9501 [DDD]
Hawkins, J.:Pieces (5) Pno *(rec 1984)* Centrediscs ▲ CMC CD 1684 [DDD]
Johnston, B.:Folk Love, Canadian Style, w. D. Bell (bar) Unical ▲ UCCD 9101
Jordan, W.:Son 2 Pno *(rec Calgary Center for the Performing Arts)* Unical ▲ UC 9501 [DDD]
Kálmán, I.:Folk Love, Canadian Style, w. D. Bell (bar) Unical ▲ UCCD 9101
A Little Romance, w. E. Agopian (vn) *(rec Calgary Center for the Performing Arts)* Unical ▲ UC 9502 [DDD]
Morawetz, O.:Ballade Pno Centrediscs ▲ CMC CD 1684 [DDD]
Schumann, R.:Dichterliebe, w. D. Bell (bar) Unical ▲ UCCD 9101

Forest, René (vc)—see also ORCHESTRAS & ENSEMBLES Göbel Trio Berlin
Boccherini, L.:Syms, w. S. Prunnbauer (gtr), Jürgen Hollerbuhl (ob), B. Vestre (ob), Jörn Maatz (ob), H. Maile (vn), H. Ganz (vn), J. Stárek (cnd), Berlin RIAS Sinfonietta—in C, G.495 (Op. 21/3) *(rec Dec. 1979)* Koch Treasure ▲ 31612-2 [ADD]
Tchaikovsky, P.:Andante cantabile, w. J. Stárek (cnd), RIAS Sinfonietta *(rec 1977)* Koch Treasure ▲ 31611-2 [ADD]
Tchaikovsky, P.:Nocturne Vc, w. J. Stárek (cnd), RIAS Sinfonietta—Entr'act & Elégie *(rec 1977)* Koch Treasure ▲ 31611-2 [ADD]

Forger, J. (sax)
Lennon, J.A.:Distances Within Me, w. D. Moriarty (pno) CRI ▲ CD 599 [ADD/DDD]

Forget, N. (ob)—see ORCHESTRAS & ENSEMBLES Pentaèdre Ensemble

Forgione, Michele (hpd)
Martin Y Soler, V.:Il Tutore Burlato, w. Liliana Marzano (sop—Menica), Maria Angeles Peters (sop—Violante), Juan Diego Florez (ten—Anselmo), Ernesto Palacio (ten—Il Cavaliere), Marcello Lippi (bar—Pippo), Giancarlo Tosi (bass—Don Fabrizio), M. Harth-Bedoya (cnd), Dianopolis Bulgarian CO *(rec VI Festival Internazionale di Gerace nella Chiesa di San Francesco, Aug 16, 1994)* Bongiovanni 2-▲ GB 2175/76-2 [DDD]

Forman, William (tpt)
Arutiunian, A.:Music of, w. V. Válek (cnd), Prague RSO—Trumpet Con. Supraphon ▲ 11 1409 [DDD]
Baroque Trumpet Concertos, w. Flandria Baroque Soloists Vivace ▲ E 557 [DDD]
Goedicke, A.:Music of, w. V. Válek (cnd), Prague RSO—Con Tpt Supraphon ▲ 11 1409 [DDD]
Hummel, B.:Music of, w. V. Válek (cnd), Prague RSO—Trumpet Con. Supraphon ▲ 11 1409 [DDD]
Tomasi, H.:Con Tpt, w. V. Válek (cnd), Prague RSO Supraphon ▲ 11 1409 [DDD]

Formenti, Andrea (a sax)
Brennan, J.W.:Atanos, w. Tomas Dratva (pno), Carlo Peliccione (db) *(rec Sept. 1993 & Jan. 1994)* Jecklin ▲ JS 301-2
Cesarini, F.:Aubade, w. Milan Quartet *(rec Sept. 1993 & Jan. 1994)* Jecklin ▲ JS 302-2
Pflüger, A.:Tra qua e la, w. Tomas Dratva (pno) *(rec Sept. 1993 & Jan. 1994)* Jecklin ▲ JS 302-2
Vassena, N.:Nocturnes, w. Tomas Dratva (pno) *(rec Sept. 1993 & Jan. 1994)* Jecklin ▲ JS 302-2
Wildberger, J.:Portrait *(rec Sept. 1993 & Jan. 1994)* Jecklin ▲ JS 302-2

Fornaciari, Marco (va)
Beethoven, L. van:Notturno, w. I. Barontini (pno) Fonè ▲ FON 93F 20 [DDD]

Fornaciari, Marco (vn)
Bartók, B.:Son Vn Fonè ▲ 83F 01 [ADD]
Bazzini, A.:Pieces (3) in the form of a Son, w. D. Roi (pno) *(rec 5/88)* Fonè ▲ 88 F 02-22 [DDD]

Fornaciari, Marco (vn) (cont.)
Beethoven, L. van:Son 9 Vn, "Kreutzer", w. I. Barontini (pno) Fonè ▲ FON 93F 20 [DDD]
Bettinelli, B.:Monologo Fonè ▲ 83F 01 [ADD]
Fauré, G.:Trio, w. Hayashi Duo Fonè ▲ 86F 05-11
Gragnani, F.:Gtr Music, w. M. Annunziati (gtr), R. Bini (gtr), C. Mascilli Migliorini (gtr)—3 Sonatas for Violin & Guitar; 3 Duets for 2 Guitars Fonè ▲ FON 93F 18 [DDD]
Lipinski, K.J.:Capriccio Vn Fonè ▲ 83F 01 [ADD]
Martucci, G.:Son Vn, w. D. Roi (pno) *(rec 5/88)* Fonè ▲ 88 F 02-22 [DDD]
Paganini, N.:Intro & Vars on "Nel cor più" Fonè ▲ FON 93F 20 [DDD]
Paganini, N.:Son large Va Fonè ▲ FON 93F 20 [DDD]
Ravel, M.:Trio Pno, w. Hayashi Duo Fonè ▲ 86F 05-11 [DDD]
Respighi, O.:Son Vn, w. D. Roi (pno) *(rec 5/88)* Fonè ▲ 88 F 02-22 [DDD]
Schubert, Franz:Ländler Vn, D.374—6 sels Fonè ▲ 83F 01 [ADD]
Schumann, R.:Son 1 Vn, w. L. Palmieri (pno) Fonè ▲ 86 F 02-8 [ADD]
Schumann, R.:Son 2 Vn, w. L. Palmieri (pno) Fonè ▲ 86 F 02-8 [ADD]
Tartini, G.:Sons solo Vn—No. 13 Fonè ▲ 83F 01 [ADD]

Forno, Anton del (gtr)
Christmas Gifts Juston Records ▲ JRS 1077CD ■ JRC 1077
In Concert, Part I Juston Records ■ JRC 1078

Forsberg, Bengt (pno)
Aulin, T.:Four Watercolors, w. N.-E. Sparf (vn) Musica Sveciae ▲ MSV 616 [DDD]
Boëllmann, L.:Morceaux Vc, OP. 31, w. Mats Lidström (vc) Hyperion ▲ CDA 66888
Boëllmann, L.:Son Vc, w. Mats Lidström (vc) Hyperion ▲ CDA 66888
La Bonne Chanson:French Chamber Songs, w. A. S. von Otter (mez), *(chamber ensemble unknown)* Deutsche Grammophon ▲ 447752-2
Brahms, J.:Gypsy Songs (8), w. A. Sofie von Otter (mez) [G] Deutsche Grammophon ▲ 429727-2 [DDD]
Brahms, J.:Liebeslieder Waltzes SATB, w. Barbara Bonney (sop), Anne Sofie von Otter (mez), Kurt Streit (ten) Olaf Bär (bar), Helmut Deutsch (pno) EMI Classics ▲ CDC 55430
Brahms, J.:Neue Liebeslieder Waltzes, w. Barbara Bonney (sop), Anne Sofie von Otter (mez), Kurt Streit (ten) Olaf Bär (bar), Helmut Deutsch (pno) EMI Classics ▲ CDC 55430
Brahms, J.:Songs, w. A. Sofie von Otter (mez)—14 songs [G] Deutsche Grammophon ▲ 429727-2 [DDD]
Chausson, E.:Chanson perpétuelle, w. Anne Sofie von Otter (mez), Nils-Erik Sparf (vn), Ulf Forsberg (vn), Matti Hirvikangas (va), Mats Lindström (vc) *(rec Stockholm, Nov 1994)* Deutsche Grammophon ▲ 447 752-2 [DDD]
Fauré, G.:La bonne chanson, w. Anne Sofie von Otter (mez), Nils-Erik Sparf (vn), Ulf Forsberg (vn), Matti Hirvikangas (va), Mats Lindström (vc), Tomas Gertonsson (db) *(rec Stockhom, Nov 1994)* Deutsche Grammophon ▲ 447 752-2 [DDD]
Godard, B.:Aubade et scherzo, w. Mats Lidström (vc) Hyperion ▲ CDA 66888
Godard, B.:Son Vc, w. Mats Lidström (vc) Hyperion ▲ CDA 66888
Grieg, E.:Songs, w. A. S. von Otter (mez)—features various sels. including Haugtussa Deutsche Grammophon ▲ 437521-2
Martin, F.:Chants de Noël, w. Anne Sofie von Otter (mez), Andreas Alin (fl) *(rec Stockholm, Nov 1994)* Deutsche Grammophon ▲ 447 752-2 [DDD]
Poulenc, F.:Rapsodie nègre, w. Anne Sofie von Otter (mez), Andreas Alin (fl), Lars Paulsson (cl), Nils-Erik Sparf (vn), Ulf Forsberg (vn), Matti Hirvikangas (va), Mats Lindström (vc) *(rec Stockhom, Nov 1994)* Deutsche Grammophon ▲ 447 752-2 [DDD]
Ravel, M.:Trois poèmes de Stéphane Mallarmé, w. Anne Sofie von Otter (mez), Peter Rydström (fl/pic), Andreas Alin (fl), Lars Paulsson (cl), Per Billman (cl/b cl), Nils-Erik Sparf (vn), Ulf Forsberg (vn), Matti Hirvikangas (va), Mats Lindström (vc), Bengt Forsberg (pno) *(rec Stockholm, Nov 1994)* Deutsche Grammophon ▲ 447 752-2 [DDD]
Saint-Saëns, C.:Une Flûte invisible, w. Anne Sofie von Otter (mez), Andreas Alin (fl) *(rec Stockhom, Nov 1994)* Deutsche Grammophon ▲ 447 752-2 [DDD]
Schumann, R.:Frauenliebe und -leben, w. Anne Sofie von Otter (mez) Deutsche Grammophon ▲ 445881-2
Schumann, R.:Spanisches Liederspiel, w. Barbara Bonney (sop), Anne Sofie von Otter (mez), Kurt Streit (ten) Olaf Bär (bar), Helmut Deutsch (pno) EMI Classics ▲ CDC 55430
Sibelius, J.:Danses champêtres, w. N.-E. Sparf (vn) *(rec Danderyd Grammar School, Sweden, May 21-23, 1993)* BIS ▲ CD 625 [DDD]
Sibelius, J.:Music for Vn Pno, w. N.-E. Sparf (vn)—Two Pieces, Op. 2 (original version); Two Pieces, Op. 2 (revised version); Scène d'amour from Scaramouche, Op. 71; Two Pieces (Serious Melodies), Op. 77; Four Pieces, Op. 78; Six Pieces, Op. 79 BIS ▲ CD 525 [DDD]
Sibelius, J.:Novelette, w. N.-E. Sparf (vn) *(rec Danderyd Grammar School, Sweden, May 21-23, 1993)* BIS ▲ CD 625 [DDD]
Sibelius, J.:Pieces Vn Pno, Op. 81, w. N.-E. Sparf (vn) *(rec Danderyd Grammar School, Sweden, May 21-23, 1993)* BIS ▲ CD 625 [DDD]
Sibelius, J.:Pieces Vn Pno, Op. 115, w. N.-E. Sparf (vn) *(rec Danderyd Grammar School, Sweden, May 21-23, 1993)* BIS ▲ CD 625 [DDD]
Sibelius, J.:Pieces Vn Pno, Op. 116, w. N.-E. Sparf (vn) *(rec Danderyd Grammar School, Sweden, May 21-23, 1993)* BIS ▲ CD 625 [DDD]
Sibelius, J.:Sonatina Vn, w. N.-E. Sparf (vn) BIS ▲ CD 525 [DDD]
Sibelius, J.:Songs, w. A. S. van Otter (mez)— *four song groups*—Seven Songs, Op. 17; Six Songs, Op. 36; Five Songs, Op. 37; Six Songs, Op. 88; *four individual songs*—Arioso, Op. 3; Souda, souda, sinisorsa (1899); Les trois soeurs aveugles, Op. 46/4; Narciss (1918) [Fin,F,Sw] BIS ▲ CD 457 [DDD]
Sibelius, J.:Songs, w. Anne Sofie von Otter (mez)—7 Songs, Op. 13; 6 Songs, Op. 50; 6 Songs, Op. 90; Skogsrået; Den judiska flickans sång; Likhet; En visa; Serenade; Tanken [w. Monica Groop (mez)] *(rec Musikaliska Akademien, Stockholm, Sweden, 1994-95)* BIS ▲ CD 757 [DDD]
Stenhammar, W.:Son Vn, w. N.-E. Sparf (vn) Musica Sveciae ▲ MSV 616 [DDD]
Stenhammar, W.:Songs, w. A. S. von Otter (mez), H. Hagegard (bar), T. Schuback (pno) Musica Sveciae ▲ MSCD 623

Forsberg, Seven (vc)
Berg, A.:Adagio, w. Hans-Udo Heinzmann (fl), Malte Lammers (ob), Walter Hermann (cl), Heinrich Horlein (vn), Jaap Zeijl (va), Willi Beyer (db), Jurgen Lamke (pno), Werner Hagen (pno), Volker Kneip (perc) [arr chamber ensemble] Koch Schwann ▲ SCH CD 311912
Busoni, F.:Berceuse élégiaque, w. Hans-Udo Heinzmann (fl), Malte Lammers (ob), Walter Hermann (cl), Heinrich Horlein (vn), Jaap Zeijl (va), Willi Beyer (db), Jurgen Lamke (pno), Werner Hagen (pno), Volker Kneip (perc) [arr Stein for chamber ensemble] Koch Schwann ▲ SCH CD 311912
Debussy, C.:Prélude à l'après-midi d'un faune, w. Hans-Udo Heinzmann (fl), Malte Lammers (ob), Walter Hermann (cl), Heinrich Horlein (vn), Jaap Zeijl (va), Willi Beyer (db), Jurgen Lamke (pno), Werner Hagen (pno), Volker Kneip (perc) [arr Sachs for chamber ensemble] Koch Schwann ▲ SCH CD 311912
Schoenberg, A.:Chamber Sym 1, w. Hans-Udo Heinzmann (fl), Malte Lammers (ob), Walter Hermann (cl), Heinrich Horlein (vn), Jaap Zeijl (va), Willi Beyer (db), Jurgen Lamke (pno), Werner Hagen (pno), Volker Kneip (perc) [arr Webern for chamber ensemble] Koch Schwann ▲ SCH CD 311912

Forsberg, Ulf (vn)
Chausson, E.:Chanson perpétuelle, w. Anne Sofie von Otter (mez), Nils-Erik Sparf (vn), Matti Hirvikangas (va), Mats Lindström (vc), Bengt Forsberg (pno) *(rec Stockholm, Nov 1994)* Deutsche Grammophon ▲ 447 752-2 [DDD]
Delage, M.:Poèmes hindous, w. Anne Sofie von Otter (mez), Andreas Alin (fl), Peter Rydström (fl/pic), Ulf Bjurenhed (ob/E hn), Lars Paulsson (cl), Per Billman (cl/b cl), Nils-Erik Sparf (vn), Matti Hirvikangas (va), Mats Lindström (vc), Lisa Viguier (hp) *(rec Stockholm, Nov 1994)* Deutsche Grammophon ▲ 447 752-2 [DDD]
Fauré, G.:La bonne chanson, w. Anne Sofie von Otter (mez), Nils-Erik Sparf (vn), Matti Hirvikangas (va), Mats Lindström (vc), Tomas Gertonsson (db), Bengt Forsberg (pno) *(rec Stockhom, Nov 1994)* Deutsche Grammophon ▲ 447 752-2 [DDD]
Poulenc, F.:Rapsodie nègre, w. Anne Sofie von Otter (mez), Andreas Alin (fl), Lars Paulsson (cl), Nils-Erik Sparf (vn), Matti Hirvikangas (va), Mats Lindström (vc), Bengt Forsberg (pno) *(rec Stockhom, Nov 1994)* Deutsche Grammophon ▲ 447 752-2 [DDD]

▲ = CD ♦ = Enhanced CD Δ = MD ■ = Cassette Tape □ = DCC

Forsberg, Ulf (vn) (cont.)
Ravel, M.:Trois poèmes de Stéphane Mallarmé, w. Anne Sofie von Otter (mez), Peter Rydström (fl/pic), Andreas Alin (fl), Lars Paulsson (cl), Per Billman (cl/b cl), Nils-Erik Sparf (vn), Matti Hirvikangas (va), Mats Lindström (vc), Bengt Forsberg (pno) *(rec Stockholm, Nov 1994)* Deutsche Grammophon ▲ 447 752-2 [DDD]

Forsblom, E. (org)
Bach, J.S.:Org Music (misc)—Prelude & Fugue in b; Pièce d'Orgue (Fantasia) in G; Prelude & Fugue in C; Chorale Preludes [performed on the Christensen Organ in St. Catherine Church at Ribe, Denmark] Proprius ▲ PRCD 9962

Forsman, Folke (org)
Stenius, T.:Partita on a Finnish Sacred Folk-Tune [the organ of the Olaus Petri Church, Helsinki, Finland] *(rec Nov. 17, 1973)* BIS ▲ CD 207 [AAD/DDD]

Forssén, S. (pno)
Taube, E.:Där blaser, w. G. Taube (vn), Gothenburg Chamber Choir Prophone ▲ PCD 003

Forster, H. (va)
Vogel, W.:Sonances, w. H. Peter-Indermühle (fl), H. Elhorst (ob), K. Weber (cl), I. Backer (bn), K. Hanke (hn), U. Lehmann (vn), L. Dober (vn), M. Liechti (vc), R. Tschupp (cnd) Grammont ▲ CTSP 14-2 [ADD]

Forsyth, A. (vc)—see ORCHESTRAS & ENSEMBLES Chinook Trio

Forsyth, Lorene (pno)
Ashford, R.:A Musical Joke Nigel Classics ▲ NC 10101

Fortino, Sally (hpd)
Boismortier, J.B. de:Chamber Music, w. Manfred Harras (rcr), Marianne Lüthi (rcr), Richard Gwilt (baroque vn), Arno Jochem (vl), Brian Franklin (vl)—Con. in C, "Zampogna"; Son. in F, Op. 91/1; Son. in A, Op. 10/2; Trio Son. in D, Op. 37/3; Son. in e, Op. 34/3; Con. in A, Op. 38/4; Suite No. 1, Op. 59; Balet de village en trio, Op. 52/4 *(rec Reformed Church, Bubendorf, Switzerland, Feb. 9-11, 1989)* Musicaphon ▲ 56812 [DDD]
Telemann, G.P.:Cants, w. Barbara Schlick (sop), Manfred Harras (rcr), Ernst-Martin Eras (ob), Richard Gwilt (vn), Brian Franklin (vl)—Hemmet den Eifer, verbannet die Rache; Jauchzt, ihr Christen, seid vergnügt; Umschlinget uns, ihr sanften Freidensbande; Die Kinder des Höchsten sind rufende Stimmen; Lauter Wonne, lauter Freude Cantate ▲ 580003 [DDD]

Forward, Fast (instrs)
Forward, F.:Panhandling—Pomp & Circumstance; Craftmatic; Rollerball; The Dream State; Red Dance; Precious Metals; Harpo; The Big Wind; Waterball; Crusader in the Groove (Once Back); Stix; Flip Flop; The Bullroarers Lovely Music ▲ LCD 2091 [ADD]

Fosdal, Björn (hn)
Nielsen, C.:Qnt Ww, w. James Galway (fl), Björn Carl Nielsen (ob), Niels Thomsen (cl), Jens Tofte-Hansen (bn) *(rec Vangede Church, Copenhagen, Mar 16, 1985)* RCA Red Seal ▲ 07863-56359-2 [ADD]

Foss, Harry (org)
Kol Nidre:Sacred Music of the Synagogue, w. Leo Roth (ten), Rudolf Wiebel (bar), Werner Buschnakowski (org), Leipzig RSO members, Jewish Congregation Choir Berlin, Leipzig Synagogue Choir EMI Classics ▲ CDM 65457

Foss, Hubert (pno)
Copland, A.:Danzón Cubano, w. J. Tocco (pno) Pro Arte ▲ CDD-183
Walton, W.:Façade, w. D. Stevens (sop)—(3 songs) Daphne; Through Gilded Trellises; Old Sir Faulk *(rec Mar. 20, 1940)* Dutton Laboratories ▲ CDAX 8003 [ADD]

Foss, Lukas (pno)
Bernstein, L.:Sym 2, "Age of Anxiety", w. L. Bernstein (cnd), Israel PO Deutsche Grammophon 2-▲ 445245-2 [ADD]
Foss, L.:Airs (3) for Frank O'Hara's Angel, w. Judith Kellock (sop) Koch International Classics ▲ KIC 7209 [DDD]
Foss, L.:Early Song, w. Z. Zeitlin (vn) Gasparo ▲ GS 279
Foss, L.:Songs (4), w. Judith Kellock (sop) Koch International Classics ▲ KIC 7209 [DDD]
Foss, L.:Thirteen Ways of Looking at a Blackbird, w. Judith Kellock (sop) Koch International Classics ▲ KIC 7209 [DDD]
Foss, L.:Vn & Pno Music, w. R. Evans (vn)—Composer's Holiday; Dedication; Early Song *(rec 1989-90)* Koss Classics ▲ KC 1006 [DDD]

Fossà, A. (vc)
Bononcini, G.:Italian Cants, w. C. Miatello (sop), G. Morini (hpd)—Ah, non avesse, no, permesso il fato; Che tirannia di stelle; Cieco nume, tiranno spietato; Vidi in cimento due vaghi amori [I] Tactus ▲ TC 660002
Scarlatti, A.:Cants, w. C. Miatello (sop), G. Morini (hpd)—Andante, o miei sospiri; Per un momento solo; Lascia più di tormentarmi; Lontan dalla sua Clori [I] Tactus ▲ TC 660002

Foster, D. (va)
Van Appledorn, M.J.:Ayre, w. G.J. Schenk (vn), J. Ingolfsson (vn), C.-J. Chang (va), M. Ingolfsson (vc), S. Shao (vc) CRS ▲ CD 9257

Foster, Donald (hpd)
Handel, G.F.:Arias, w. B. Norden (sop), B. Haley (tpt), Alexander String Quartet—Destro dall' empia dite (from *Amadigi di Gaula*); Alle voci del bronzo guerriero (from Cantata No. 19, *O come chiare e belle*) [I] Crystal ▲ CD 952 [DDD] ■ C 952
Scarlatti, A.:Arias Sop, w. Betsy Norden (sop), Bob Haley (tpt), Alexander String Quartet—Con voce festiva; Mio tesoro [I] Crystal ▲ CD 952 [DDD] ■ C 952

Foster, Donald (org)
Bach, J.S.:Arias, w. Betsy Norden (sop), Bob Haley (tpt), Alexander String Quartet—(2) from Cantatas 21 & 36 [G] Crystal ▲ CD 952 [DDD] ■ C 952
Bach, J.S.:Cant 51, w. Betsy Norden (sop), Bob Haley (tpt), Alexander String Quartet [G] Crystal ▲ CD 952 [DDD] ■ C 952
Clarke, J.:Tpt Voluntary, w. Bob Haley (tpt) Crystal ▲ CD 952 [DDD] ■ C 952

Foster, Martin (vn)
Guarnieri, C.M.:Coletanea, w. Eugene Plawutsky (pno) SNE ▲ SNE-593-CD
Miguez, L.:Son Vn, w. Eugene Plawutsky (pno) SNE ▲ SNE-593-CD
Nobre, M.:Desafio III, w. Eugene Plawutsky (pno) [arr. vn & pno] SNE ▲ SNE-593-CD
Villa-Lobos, H.:Son 2 Vn, w. Eugene Plawutsky (pno) SNE ▲ SNE-593-CD

Foster, Nigel (hpd)
Program 2, w. A. Dolmetsch (vir), Frank Preuss (vn), Marguerite Dolmetsch (vl), Carl Dolmetsch (rec) IMP Allegro ▲ PCD 990 [DDD]
Program 3, w. A. Dolmetsch (vir), François (trb rcr), Jeanne Dolmetsch (trb rcr), Marguerite Dolmetsch (vl), Kathleen Livingstone (sop), John Hancorn (bass), Jennifer Bate (org), et al. IMP Allegro ▲ PCD 995 [DDD]

Fotherby, Karen (cl)
Gregson, E.:Metamorphoses, w. Owain Bailey (fl), E. Gregson (cnd), Royal Northern College of Music Wind Orch Doyen ▲ CD 043 [DDD]

Foucheux, A. (va)
Koechlin, C.:Son Va, w. M.-M. Petit (pno) *(rec 1976)* Skarbo ▲ SKR 3924

Fourichon, J. F. (gtr)—see ORCHESTRAS & ENSEMBLES Versailles Guitar Quartet

Fournier, Carmen (vn)
Scelsi, G.:Duo Vn, w. David Simpson (vc) Accord ▲ ACD 200742 [DDD]
Scelsi, G.:Xnoybis Accord ▲ ACD 200742 [DDD]

Fournier, E. (vc)
Schubert, Franz:Trio 1 Pno, w. A. Rubinstein (pno), H. Szeryng (vn) RCA Gold Seal ▲ 6262-2-RG [ADD]

Fournier, P. (vn)
Mendelssohn, F.:Trio 1 Pno, w. A. Grumiaux (pno), N. Magaloff (vc) Arkadia ▲ 606

Fournier, Pierre (vc)
Bach, J.S.:Suites Vc, BWV 1007-1012 Deutsche Grammophon 2-▲ 419359-2 [ADD]
Bach, J.S.:Suites Vc, BWV 1007-1012 Deutsche Grammophon ("The Originals" series) ▲ 449 711-2
Beethoven, L. van:Sons Vc (comp), w. Wilhelm Kempff (pno) Deutsche Grammophon ("2CD" series) 2-▲ 453 013-2

Fournier, Pierre (vc) (cont.)
Beethoven, L. van:Trios Pno (comp), w. W. Kempff (pno), H. Szerying (vn)—Opp. 1,70 & 97 Deutsche Grammophon 3-▲ 415879-2 [ADD]
Beethoven, L. van:Trio 4 Pno, "Ghost", w. W. Kempff (pno), H. Szeryng (vn) Deutsche Grammophon ("Galleria" series) ▲ 429712-2 [ADD]
Beethoven, L. van:Trio 6 Pno, "Archduke", w. W. Kempff (pno), H. Szeryng (vn) Deutsche Grammophon ("Galleria" series) ▲ 429712-2 [ADD]
Beethoven, L. van:Vars on "Ein Mädchen oder Weibchen" from Mozart's *Die Zauberflöte*, w. Wilhelm Kempff (pno) Deutsche Grammophon ("2CD" series) 2-▲ 453 013-2
Beethoven, L. van:Vars on "See, the Conquering Hero Comes" from Handel's *Judas Maccabaeus*, w. Wilhelm Kempff (pno) Deutsche Grammophon ("2CD" series) 2-▲ 453 013-2
Beethoven, L. van:Vars on "Bei Männern" from Mozart's *Die Zauberflöte*, w. Wilhelm Kempff (pno) Deutsche Grammophon ("2CD" series) 2-▲ 453 013-2
Bloch, E.:Schelomo, w. A. Wallenstein (cnd), Berlin PO Deutsche Grammophon ("Resonance" series) ▲ 429155-2 [ADD]
Boccherini, L.:Con Vc, G.482, w. R. Baumgartner (cnd), Lucerne Festival Strings Deutsche Grammophon ("Musikfest" series) ■ 413682-4
Brahms, J.:Con Vn & Vc, "Double Con", w. Zino Francescatti (vn), B. Walter (cnd), Columbia SO Sony Classical ("Bruno Walter:The Edition" series) ▲ SMK 64479
Brahms, J.:Con Vn & Vc, "Double Con", w. Z. Francescatti (vn), B. Walter (cnd), Columbia SO CBS ▲ MYK 37237 [ADD] ■ MYT 37237
Brahms, J.:Con Vn & Vc, "Double Con", w. Z. Francescatti (vn), B. Walter (cnd), Columbia SO CBS ▲ MK 42024
Brahms, J.:Con Vn & Vc, "Double Con", w. David Oistrakh (vn), A. Galliera (cnd), Philharmonia Orch EMI Classics 2-▲ CDFB 69331
Brahms, J.:Sons Vc (comp), w. J. Fonda (pno) Stradivarius ▲ STR 33320 [ADD]
Brahms, J.:Trio 1 Pno, w. A. Rubinstein (pno), H. Szeryng (vn) *(rec 1972)* RCA Red Seal ▲ 6260-2-RC [ADD]
Brahms, J.:Trio 2 Pno, w. A. Rubinstein (pno), H. Szeryng (vn) *(rec 1972)* RCA Red Seal ▲ 6260-2-RC [ADD]
Bruch, M.:Kol Nidrei, w. J. Martinon (cnd), Lamoureux Orch Deutsche Grammophon ("Resonance" series) ▲ 429155-2 [ADD]
Dvořák, A.:Con Vc, w. S. Celibidache (cnd), *(orch unknown)* *(rec 1971)* Arlecchino ARL
Dvořák, A.:Con Vc, w. S. Celibidache (cnd), ORTF National Orch *(rec live, Paris, 1974)* Arkadia ▲ 615
Dvořák, A.:Con Vc, w. S. Celibidache (cnd), *(orch unknown)* *(rec 1945)* Pearl ▲ PEA 9198
Dvořák, A.:Con Vc, w. G. Sébastian (cnd), Czech PO *(rec live, Prague 1949)* Melodram ▲ CDM 18037 [ADD]
Dvořák, A.:Con Vc, w. G. Szell (cnd), Berlin PO Deutsche Grammophon ("Resonance" series) ▲ 429155-2 [ADD]
Fauré, G.:Qt 2 Pno, w. Marguerite Long (pno), Jacques Thibaud (vn), Maurice Vieux (va) *(rec June 10, 1940)* Iron Needle 2-▲ IN 1342/43 (m) [ADD]
Fauré, G.:Qt 2 Pno, w. Marguerite Long (pno), Jacques Thibaud (vn), Maurice Vieux (va) *(rec June 10, 1940)* Enterprise ("Strings" series) ▲ ENT QT 99302
Grieg, E.:Son Vc, w. J. Fonda (pno) Stradivarius ▲ STR 33320 [ADD]
Kodály, Z.:Adagio Vn, w. Josef Suk (vn), André Navarra (vc), Tatjana Sadovskaja (pno) Praga ▲ PR 250065
Kodály, Z.:Duo Vn & Vc, w. Josef Suk (vn), André Navarra (vc) Praga ▲ PR 250065
Kodály, Z.:Son Vc, Op. 8, w. André Navarra (vc) Praga ▲ PR 250065
Kodály, Z.:Sonatina Vc & Pno, w. André Navarra (vc), Tatjana Sadovskaja (pno) Praga ▲ PR 250065
Lalo, E.:Con Vc, w. J. Martinon (cnd), Lamoureux Orch Deutsche Grammophon ("Double" series) 2-▲ 437371-2
Mendelssohn, F.:Trio 2 Pno, w. N. Magaloff (pno), A. Grumiaux (vn) Arkadia ▲ 606
Schubert, Franz:Son Arpeggione Pearl ▲ PEA 9198
Schubert, Franz:Trio 2 Pno, w. N. Magaloff (pno), A. Grumiaux (vn) Arkadia ▲ 598
Schumann, R.:Trio 1 Pno, w. A. Rubinstein (pno), I. Szerying (vn) RCA Gold Seal ▲ 6262-2-RG [ADD] ■ 6262-4-RG (CrO2)
Tchaikovsky, P.:Vars on a Rococo Theme, *(cnd & orch unknown)* Pearl ▲ PEA 9198

Fournier, Suzanne (pno)
Scelsi, G.:Illustrazioni Pno Accord ▲ ACD 200742 [DDD]
Scelsi, G.:Incantations Pno Accord ▲ ACD 200742 [DDD]

Fouter, Arkady (vn)
Vivaldi, A.:Con for 2 Vns Vc, R.565, w. V. Spivakov (vn), M. Milman (vc), V. Spivakov (cnd), Moscow Virtuosi RCA Red Seal ▲ 60240-2-RC [DDD]

Fowke, Philip (pno)
Bliss, A.:Piano Music—'Bliss' (A One-step) (1923); The Rout Trot (1927); Study (1927); Das alte Jahr vergangen ist (1932); Miniature Scherzo (1969) Chandos ▲ CHAN 8979 [DDD]
Bliss, A.:Son Pno Chandos ▲ CHAN 8979 [DDD]
Bliss, A.:Suite Pno Chandos ▲ CHAN 8979 [DDD]
Bliss, A.:Triptych Chandos ▲ CHAN 8979 [DDD]
Britten, H.:Scottish Ballad, w. P. Donohoe (pno), S. Rattle (cnd), City of Birmingham SO *(rec 4/82)* EMI Classics 2-▲ CDCB 54270 [DDD]
Finzi, G.:Grand Fant & Toccata, w. R. Hickox (cnd), Royal Liverpool PO EMI Classics ▲ CDM 64720
Rachmaninoff, S.:Con 2 Pno, w. Y. Temirkanov (cnd), Royal PO Classics for Pleasure ("Eminence" series) ▲ CFP-9509 [DDD]
Ravel, M.:Con Pno (left hand), w. S. Baudo (cnd), London PO Classics for Pleasure ▲ CDCFP 4667
Ravel, M.:Con in G Pno, w. S. Baudo (cnd), London PO Classics for Pleasure ▲ CDCFP 4667
Ravel, M.:Valses nobles et sentimentales Classics for Pleasure ▲ CDCFP 4667
Saint-Saëns, C.:Carnival of the Animals, w. P. Katin (pno), A. Gibson (cnd), Scottish National Orch Classics for Pleasure ▲ CDCFP 4086 [ADD]

Fox, Deborah (vn)
Chopin, F.:Trio Pno, w. Leslie Howard (pno), William Howard (vc) United ▲ CAL 88038
Liszt, F.:Music for Pno Trio, w. Leslie Howard (pno), William Howard (vc)—Vallée d'Obermann; Orphee [poeme symphonique]; Tristia; Rapsodie hongrois No. 9 [Le carnaval de pest] United ▲ CAL 88038

Fox, Tim (tpt)—see ORCHESTRAS & ENSEMBLES Rhythm & Bluefield Band

Fox, Timothy (gtr)—see also ORCHESTRAS & ENSEMBLES San Francisco Guitar Quartet
Orbón, J.:Prelude & Toccata Klavier ▲ KCD 11028

Fox, Virgil (org)
The Art of Virgil Fox EMI Classics ("Full Dimensional Sound" series) ▲ CDM 65426
Bach, J.S.:Jesu bleibet meine Freude RCA ■ ALK1-4467
Bach, J.S.:Org Music (misc) MCA ■ MCAC 28
Bach, J.S.:Org Music (misc)—Toccata & Fugue in d, BWV 565; Fugue in g, BWV 578; Air on a G string; etc. RCA Victrola ▲ 7736-2-RV [ADD] ■ 7736-4-RV (CrO2)
Bach, J.S.:Trio Sons Org, BWV 525-530—BWV 530 RCA ■ ALK1-4467
Basic 100, Vol. 42, w. Eugene Ormandy (cnd), Arthur Fiedler (cnd) RCA Victor ▲ 09026-62562-2 ■ 09026-62562-4
The Best of Bach, w. Lucerne Festival Strings [cnd:Rudolf Baumgartner] Victrola ("Victrola Best of" series) ▲ 60768-2-RV [ADD] ■ 60768-4-RV
Encores Victrola ■ ALK1-4467
Encores RCA Living Stereo ▲ 09026-61251-2 ■ 09026-61251-4
Here Comes the Bride, w. Fox, Virgil (org) *(rec 7-68)* MCA Classics 2-■ MCAC2-4058
Jongen, J.:Symphonie Concertante, w. G. Prêtre (cnd), Paris Opera Orch EMI Classics ▲ CDM 65075
Saint-Saëns, C.:Sym 3, w. E. Ormandy (cnd), Philadelphia Orch RCA Victrola ▲ 7737-2-RV [ADD] ■ 7737-4-RV (CrO2)
Saint-Saëns, C.:Sym 3, w. E. Ormandy (cnd), Philadelphia Orch RCA Victor ▲ 09026-61269-2 [ADD] ■ 09026-61269-4 (CrO2)
Virgil Fox LaserLight ▲ 15313
A Virgil Fox Christmas *(rec Riverside Church, New York City)* EMI Classics ▲ CDM 66088
Virgil Fox 1912-1980:Sole Deo Gloria Bainbridge 2-▲ BCD 8005 [AAD] ■ BBR 8005

Fox, Virgil (org) (cont.)
Virgil Fox Plays the Wanamaker Organ, Phildelphia, PA — Bainbridge ▲ BCD 2501 [AAD]
Widor, C.M.:Sym 5 Org—5th movement, Toccata — RCA ■ ALK1-4467

Foy, Janice (vc)
Levitch, L.:Fant Ob, w. Greg Donovetsky (ob), Alexander Treger (vn), Kenneth Burward-Hoy (va) — Cambria ▲ CD 1059 [ADD]

Fraaf, H. de (cl)
Saint-Saëns, C.:Carnival of the Animals, w. D. Wayenberg (vn), H. Oudenaarden (vn), J. Hagen (fl), H. Krul (db), W. Vos (xyl), M. Dekkers (acc), Daniel String Quartet *(rec Rotterdam, May 28, 1985)* — Erasmus ▲ WHV 001 [DDD]

Frager, Malcolm (pno)
Chopin, F.:Andante Spianato & Grande Polonaise — Telarc ▲ CD 80280 [DDD]
Chopin, F.:Pno Music (misc)—Contredanse in G♭; Intro. & Variations on a theme from Hérold's *Ludovic*, Op. 12; Mazurkas, Op. 6; Polonaise in A♭, Op. 53; Tarantelle, Op. 43 — Telarc ▲ CD 80280 [DDD]
Chopin, F.:Son Pno, Op. 58 — Telarc ▲ CD 80280 [DDD]
Donizetti, G.:Son Fl & Pno, w. E. Talmi (fl) — Stradivari Classics ▲ SCD 6042 [DDD]
Kabalevsky, D.:Son Vc, w. L. Parnas (vc) — Arcadia ▲ ARC 1992-2 [DDD]
Moscheles, I.:Son Fl, w. E. Talmi (fl) — Stradivari Classics ▲ SCD 6042 [DDD]
Mozart, W.A.:Con 17 Pno, w. E. Chakarov (cnd), Festival Sinfonietta — Vivace ▲ E 515 [ADD]
Mozart, W.A.:Con 23 Pno, w. E. Chakarov (cnd), Festival Sinfonietta — Vivace 2-▲ G 217 [ADD]
Schubert, Franz:Intro & Vars Fl on "Tröckne Blumen", w. E. Talmi (fl) — Stradivari Classics ▲ SCD 6042 [DDD]
Schumann, R.:Con Pno, w. J. Horenstein (cnd), Royal PO *(rec , Walthamstow Town Hall, London, 2/2/67)* — Chesky ▲ CD52 [ADD]
Shostakovich, D.:Son Vc, w. L. Parnas (vc) — Arcadia ▲ ARC 1992-2 [DDD]
Strauss, R.:Burleske, w. R. Kempe (cnd), Dresden Staatskapelle — EMI Classics 3-▲ CDZC 64342

Fragnito, Mario (gtr)
Duo Guitarists, w. Lucio Matarazzo (gtr) — Ducale ▲ DUC 9 [DDD]

Fraioli, Franco (db)
Petrassi, G.:Serenata Fls, w. M. Berni (fl), A. Vismara (va), V. de Vita (pno), M. Vinci (perc) — Bongiovanni ▲ GB 5534 [DDD]

Frame, Pamela (vc)
Beach, A.M.C.:Pieces Vn, Op. 40, w. Robert Weirich (pno) — Koch International Classics ▲ KIC 7281 [DDD]
Beach, A.M.C.:Son Vn, w. Robert Weirich (pno) [arr. Frame] — Koch International Classics ▲ KIC 7281 [DDD]
Clarke, R.:Epilogue — Koch International Classics ▲ KIC 7281 [DDD]
Clarke, R.:Son Vc, w. Barry Snyder (pno) — Koch International Classics ▲ KIC 7281 [DDD]

Frampton, Roger (pno)
Frampton, R.:Pno Music—10 pieces for piano & prepared piano *(rec June 1989)* — Tall Poppies ▲ TP 006 [DDD]
Frampton, R.:Pno Music—10 pieces *(rec June 1989)* — Tall Poppies ▲ TP 019 [DDD]
Frampton, R.:Pno Music—10 pieces for prepared piano *(rec June 1989)* — Tall Poppies ▲ TP 005 [DDD]

Frampton, Roger (sax)
Whiticker, M.:Man, Skin Cancer of the Earth, w. Clive Birch (nar), Jane Edwards (nar), Matthew Glasgow (nar), David Hewitt (perc), R. Peelman (cnd) *(rec Studio 200, ABC Ultimo Centre, Apr 1993)* — Tall Poppies ▲ TP 064 [DDD]

Françaix, Jean (pno)
Beethoven, L. van:Vars on "Ein Mädchen oder Weibchen" from Mozart's *Die Zauberflöte*, w. M. Gendron (vc) — Philips ("Duo" series) 2-▲ 442565-2
Beethoven, L. van:Vars on "See, the Conquering Hero Comes" from Handel's *Judas Maccabaeus*, w. M. Gendron (vc) — Philips ("Duo" series) 2-▲ 442565-2
Beethoven, L. van:Vars on "Bei Männern" from Mozart's *Die Zauberflöte*, w. M. Gendron (vc) — Philips ("Duo" series) 2-▲ 442565-2
Debussy, C.:Son Vc, w. M. Gendron (vc) — Philips ▲ 422839-2 [ADD]
Françaix, J.:Concertino, w. A. Dorati (cnd), London SO *(rec London, Aug. 4-6, 1965)* — Mercury Living Presence ▲ 434335-2

Francescatti, Zino (vn)
Bach, J.S.:Cons Vn (comp), w. R. Baumgartner (cnd), Lucerne Festival Strings — Deutsche Grammophon ("Musikfest" series) ▲ 429151-2 [ADD]
Bach, J.S.:Con for 2 Vns, w. R. Pasquier (vn), R. Baumgartner (cnd), Lucerne Festival Strings — Deutsche Grammophon ("Musikfest" series) ▲ 429151-2 [ADD]
Beethoven, L. van:Con Vn, Op. 61, w. D. Mitropoulos (cnd), New York PO *(rec live 1956)* — Melodram ▲ MEL 18030
Beethoven, L. van:Son 4 Vn, w. R. Casadesus (pno) *(rec 1961)* — Sony Masterworks ("Portrait" series) ▲ MPK 52534 [ADD]
Beethoven, L. van:Son 5 Vn, "Spring", w. Casadesus (pno) — Sony Classical ("Essential Classics" series) ▲ SBK 46342 [ADD] ■ SBT 46342
Beethoven, L. van:Son 5 Vn, "Spring", w. R. Casadesus (pno) — Odyssey ▲ MBK 42528
Beethoven, L. van:Son 6 Vn, w. R. Casadesus (pno) *(rec 1961)* — Sony Masterworks ("Portrait" series) ▲ MPK 52534 [ADD]
Beethoven, L. van:Son 7 Vn, w. R. Casadesus (pno) *(rec 1961)* — Sony Masterworks ("Portrait" series) ▲ MPK 52534 [ADD]
Beethoven, L. van:Son 8 Vn, w. R. Casadesus (pno) *(rec 1961)* — Sony Masterworks ("Portrait" series) ▲ MPK 52534 [ADD]
Beethoven, L. van:Son 9 Vn, "Kreutzer", w. Casadesus (pno) — Odyssey ▲ MBK 42528
Beethoven, L. van:Son 9 Vn, "Kreutzer", w. R. Casadesus (pno) — Sony Classical ("Essential Classics" series) ▲ SBK 46342 [ADD] ■ SBT 46342
Beethoven, L. van:Son 10 Vn, w. R. Casadesus (pno) — Sony Classical ("Essential Classics" series) ▲ SBK 46342 [ADD] ■ SBT 46342
Brahms, J.:Con Vn, w. L. Bernstein (cnd), New York PO — Sony Classical ▲ SMK 47540 [ADD]
Brahms, J.:Con Vn, w. D. Mitropoulos (cnd), Vienna PO *(rec live, Salzburg 8/24/58)* — Intaglio ▲ IND 706-1 [ADD]
Brahms, J.:Con Vn & Vc, "Double Con", w. Pierre Fournier (vc), B. Walter (cnd), Columbia SO — Sony Classical ("Bruno Walter:The Edition" series) ▲ SMK 64479
Brahms, J.:Con Vn & Vc, "Double Con", w. P. Fournier (vc), B. Walter (cnd), Columbia SO — CBS ▲ MK 42024
Brahms, J.:Con Vn & Vc, "Double Con", w. P. Fournier (vc), B. Walter (cnd), Columbia SO — CBS ▲ MYK 37237 [ADD] ■ MYT 37237
Brahms, J.:Sons Vn (comp), w. R. Casadesus (pno) *(rec 1949 & 1952)* — Library of Congress ▲ LOC 3 [ADD]
Bruch, M.:Con 1 Vn, w. D. Mitropoulos (cnd), New York PO *(rec Feb 1952)* — Sony Classical ("Masterworks Heritage" series) 2-▲ MH2K 62339 [ADD]
Chausson, E.:Poème Vn, w. L. Bernstein (cnd), New York PO *(rec 1964)* — Sony Classical ▲ SMK 47548 [ADD]
Chausson, E.:Poème Vn, w. E. Ormandy (cnd), Philadelphia Orch *(rec Nov 1950)* — Sony Classical ("Masterworks Heritage" series) 2-▲ MH2K 62339 [ADD]
The HMV Recordings *(rec 1922-28)* — Biddulph ▲ LAB 030 [ADD]
Mendelssohn, F.:Con in e Vn & Orch, Op. 64, w. D. Mitropoulos (cnd), New York PO *(rec Nov 1954)* — Sony Classical ("Masterworks Heritage" series) 2-▲ MH2K 62339 [ADD]
Mozart, W.A.:Con 2 Vn, w. E. de Stoutz (cnd), Zurich CO *(rec 1968; from CBS Masterwork)* — Sony Masterworks ("Portrait" series) ▲ MPK 52526 [ADD]
Mozart, W.A.:Con 3 Vn, w. B. Walter (cnd), Columbia SO *(rec 1958; from CBS Masterwork)* — Sony Masterworks ("Portrait" series) ▲ MPK 52526 [ADD]
Mozart, W.A.:Con 3 Vn, w. B. Walter (cnd), Columbia SO *(rec Hollywood, CA, Dec. 10-17, 1958)* — Sony Classical ("Bruno Walter Edition, Vol. 2" series) ▲ SMK 64468 [ADD]
Mozart, W.A.:Con 4 Vn, w. B. Walter (cnd), Columbia SO *(rec Hollywood, CA, Dec. 10-17, 1958)* — Sony Classical ("Bruno Walter Edition, Vol. 2" series) ▲ SMK 64468 [ADD]

Francescatti, Zino (vn) (cont.)
Mozart, W.A.:Con 5 Vn, w. E. de Stoutz (cnd), Zurich CO *(rec 1968; from CBS Masterwork)* — Sony Masterworks ("Portrait" series) ▲ MPK 52526 [ADD]
Paganini, N.:Con 1 Vn, w. E. Ormandy (cnd), Philadelphia Orch — Sony Classical ("Essential Classics" series) ▲ SBK 47661 ■ SBT 47661
Paganini, N.:Con 4 Vn, w. E. Ormandy (cnd), Philadelphia Orch — Sony Classical ("Essential Classics" series) ▲ SBK 47661 ■ SBT 47661
Prokofiev, S.:Con 2 Vn, w. D. Mitropoulos (cnd), New York PO *(rec Oct 1952)* — Sony Classical ("Masterworks Heritage" series) 2-▲ MH2K 62339 [ADD]
Ravel, M.:Tzigane, w. L. Bernstein (cnd), New York PO *(rec 1964)* — Sony Classical ▲ SMK 47548 [ADD]
Ravel, M.:Tzigane, w. M. Faure (pno) *(rec ca 1928)* — Symposium ▲ 1156
Saint-Saëns, C.:Con 3 Vn, w. D. Mitropoulos (cnd), New York PO *(rec Jan 1950)* — Sony Classical ("Masterworks Heritage" series) 2-▲ MH2K 62339 [ADD]
Saint-Saëns, C.:Introduction & Rondo capriccioso, w. L. Bernstein (cnd), New York PO — Sony Classical ▲ SMK 47608
Sibelius, J.:Con Vn, w. L. Bernstein (cnd), New York PO — Sony Classical ▲ SMK 47540 [ADD]
Tchaikovsky, P.:Con Vn, w. D. Mitropoulos (cnd), New York PO *(rec Jan 1950)* — Sony Classical ("Masterworks Heritage" series) 2-▲ MH2K 62339 [ADD]

Francesch, Homero (pno)
Henze, H.-W.:Pno Music—Une petite phrase [from the film Un amour de Swann]; Lucy Escott Vars.; Cherubino; 6 Pieces for Young Pianists [from Pollicino]; Vars., Op. 13; Son. — Wergo ▲ WER 6239-2
Mozart, W.A.:Allegro & Andante & Rondo — Kontrapunkt 5-▲ 32092/96 [DDD]
Mozart, W.A.:Cons 1-4 Pno, w. K. Weise (cnd), Nice PO — Kontrapunkt ▲ KPT 32109 [DDD]
Mozart, W.A.:Con 9 Pno, w. K. Weise (cnd), Nice PO — Kontrapunkt ▲ KPT 32209
Mozart, W.A.:Con 14 Pno, w. K. Weise (cnd), Nice PO *(rec live 1991)* — Kontrapunkt ▲ KPT 32139 [DDD]
Mozart, W.A.:Con 15 Pno, w. K. Weise (cnd), Nice PO *(rec live 1991)* — Kontrapunkt ▲ KPT 32139 [DDD]
Mozart, W.A.:Con 16 Pno, w. K. Weise (cnd), Nice PO *(rec live 1991)* — Kontrapunkt ▲ KPT 32139 [DDD]
Mozart, W.A.:Con 17 Pno, w. K. Weise (cnd), Nice PO — Kontrapunkt ▲ KPT 32159 [DDD]
Mozart, W.A.:Con 18 Pno, w. K. Weise (cnd), Nice PO — Kontrapunkt ▲ KPT 32159 [DDD]
Mozart, W.A.:Con 21 Pno, w. K. Weise (cnd), Nice PO — Kontrapunkt ▲ KPT 32189 [DDD]
Mozart, W.A.:Con 22 Pno, w. K. Weise (cnd), Nice PO — Kontrapunkt ▲ KPT 32189 [DDD]
Mozart, W.A.:Con 25 Pno, w. K. Weise (cnd), Nice PO — Kontrapunkt ▲ KPT 32209
Mozart, W.A.:Fant Pno, K.396 — Kontrapunkt 5-▲ 32092/96 [DDD]
Mozart, W.A.:Fant Pno, K.397 — Kontrapunkt 5-▲ 32092/96 [DDD]
Mozart, W.A.:Fant Pno, K.475 — Kontrapunkt 5-▲ 32092/96 [DDD]
Mozart, W.A.:Sons Pno — Kontrapunkt 5-▲ 32092/96 [DDD]
Ravel, M.:À la manière de Borodine & de Chabrie — Tudor ▲ TUD 781 [DDD]
Ravel, M.:Gaspard de la nuit — Tudor ▲ TUD 781 [DDD]
Ravel, M.:Jeux d'eau — Tudor ▲ TUD 781 [DDD]
Ravel, M.:Menuet antique — Tudor ▲ TUD 781 [DDD]
Ravel, M.:Miroirs — Tudor ▲ TUD 781 [DDD]
Ravel, M.:Pno Music—Le tombeau de Couperin; Prélude; Menuet sur le nom d'Haydn; Sérénade grotesque; Sonatine; Valses nobles et sentimentales; Pavane pour une infante défunte — Tudor ▲ TUD 777 [DDD]
Stravinsky, I.:Les Noces, w. A. Mory (sop), P. Parker (mez), J. Mitchinson (ten), P. Hudson (bass), M. Argerich (pno), K. Zimerman (pno), C. Katsaris (pno), L. Bernstein (cnd), English Bach Festival Orch, English Bach Festival Chorus [R] — Deutsche Grammophon ("20th Century Classics" series) ▲ 423251-2 [ADD]

Franceschi, W. De (ob)—see ORCHESTRAS & ENSEMBLES Venice New Quintet

Francesconi, C. (fl)
Blumer, T.:The Animal Kingdom, w. F. Rieger (pno) — Ars Produktion ▲ FCD 368306 [DDD]
Blumer, T.:From Floral Realm, w. F. Rieger (pno) — Ars Produktion ▲ FCD 368306 [DDD]
Guastavino, C.:Intro & Allegro, w. F. Rieger (pno) — Ars Produktion ▲ FCD 368306 [DDD]
Komma, K.M.:Lauda, w. F. Rieger (pno) — Ars Produktion ▲ FCD 368306 [DDD]
Komma, K.M.:Threnos, w. F. Rieger (pno) — Ars Produktion ▲ FCD 368306 [DDD]

Francis, David (hpd)
Haydn, J.:Con Org, Vn & Strs, H.XVIII/6, w. Malcolm Layfield (vn), M. Layfield (cnd), Goldberg Ensemble — Meridian ▲ CDE 84177

Francis, Sarah (ob)
Albinoni, T.:Cons à 5 Obs, Op. 7, w. London Harpsichord Ensemble—Nos. 3, 6, 9 & 12 — Unicorn-Kanchana ▲ DKP CD 9088 [DDD]
Albinoni, T.:Cons à 5 Obs, Op. 9, w. London Harpsichord Ensemble—Nos. 2, 5, 8 & 11 — Unicorn-Kanchana ▲ DKP CD 9088 [DDD]
Boccherini, L.:Qnts Fl, G.431-436, w. Allegri String Quartet — London ("Serenata" series) ▲ 433173-2 [ADD]
Britten, H.:Metamorphoses Ob — Hyperion ▲ CDA 66776
Britten, H.:Phantasy Qt, w. Delmé String Quartet members — Hyperion ▲ CDA 66776
Handel, G.F.:Cons (3) Ob, w. London Harpsichord Ensemble — Unicorn-Kanchana ▲ DKP CD 9153
Handel, G.F.:Sons Ob, w. London Harpsichord Ensemble—Malmesbury Son.; Son. in c, B♭, F & g — Unicorn-Kanchana ▲ DKP CD 9153
Telemann, G.P.:Cons (misc), w. London Harpsichord Ensemble—Concerto in E♭; Concerto in c; Concerto in G for Oboe d'amore; Concerto in E; "Concerto gratioso" in D; Concerto in F *(rec Jan. 13-15, 1992)* — Unicorn-Kanchana ▲ DKP CD 9128 [DDD]

Franck, Hattie (vc)
O'Rourke, J.:Terminal Pharmacy, w. Tony Burr (cl), Jeff Cortazzo (b trbn), John McEntire (dr), Rob Prosser (acc), Isha Suftin (acc), Mike Dockter (vc), Robert Keck (vc), Mary LaBreque (vc), Dan Loch (vc), Stan Saderk (vc), Lisa Hemmer (fl), Sue Oberg (fl), Wendi Lev (fl), Jim Vanden (fl), Jim O'Rourke (gtr), Steve Braack (elec) — Tzadik ▲ TZA 7011 [DDD]

Franck, Pierre (va)
Onslow, G.:Sons Vc, w. François-Joël Thiollier (pno) — Pierre Verany ▲ PVY 796032 [DDD]

François, Jean-Charles (perc)
Cage, J.:Ryoanji Fl & Octobass, w. P.-Y. Artaud (fl) — Neuma ▲ 450-77 [DDD]
Contemporary Flute Music, w. P.-Y. Artaud (fl) — Neuma ▲ 450-77 [DDD]

François, Jean-Charles (rcr)
Program 3, w. A. Dolmetsch (vir), Jeanne Dolmetsch (trb rcr), Marguerite Dolmetsch (vl), Nigel Foster (hpd), Kathleen Livingstone (sop), John Hancorn (bass), Jennifer Bate (org), et al. — IMP Allegro ▲ PCD 995 [DDD]

François, Michel (vc)
Schumann, R.:Andante & Vars Hn, w. Marie-Josèphe Jude (pno), Laurent Cabasso (pno), Roland Pidoux (vc), Hervé Joulain (hn) — Harmonia Mundi France ("Les Nouveaux Interprètes" series) ▲ HMN 911559
Schumann, R.:Songs, w. Marie-Josèphe Jude (pno), Laurent Cabasso (pno), Roland Pidoux (vc), Hervé Joulain (hn)—Abendlied, Op. 107/6 — Harmonia Mundi France ("Les Nouveaux Interprètes" series) ▲ HMN 911559

Francois, Renaud (instrs)
Bayer, F.:Music of, w. Donatienne Michel-Dansac (sop), Alain Meunier (vc), Jean-Louis Haguenauer (pno), Renaud Francois, Francesca Paderni, Tetra Ensemble — Pierre Verany ▲ PVY 796093

François, Samson (pno)
Debussy, C.:Children's Corner *(rec 1968)* — EMI (Pathé Marconi) ▲ 7473742
Debussy, C.:Estampes *(rec 1969)* — EMI (Pathé Marconi) ▲ 7473742
Debussy, C.:Pour le piano *(rec 1968)* — EMI (Pathé Marconi) ▲ 7473742
Debussy, C.:Suite bergamasque *(rec 1968)* — EMI (Pathé Marconi) ▲ 7473742

▲ = CD ♦ = Enhanced CD Δ = MD ■ = Cassette Tape □ = DCC

Francu, Virgil (fl)
Enescu, G.:Dectet Ww, w. Nicolae Maxin (fl), Valeriu Barbuceanu (cl), Leontin Boanta (cl), Adrian Petrescu (ob), Viorica Feher (bn), Goedri Orban (bn), Florin Ionoaia (Eng hn), Dan Cinca (hn), Simon Jebeleanu (hn), H. Andreescu (cnd) Olympia ▲ OLY 445 [DDD]
Franesch, H. (pno)
Mozart, W.A.:Con 19 Pno, w. K. Weise (cnd), Nice PO Kontrapunkt ▲ KPT 32179 [DDD]
Mozart, W.A.:Con 20 Pno, w. K. Weise (cnd), Nice PO Kontrapunkt ▲ KPT 32179 [DDD]
Frank (vc)
Handel, G.F.:Sons Vn & Kbd, w. György Pauk (vn), Sebestyén (pno)—Op. 1, Nos. 1b, 3, 6, 10, 12, 13, 14 Hungaroton ▲ HCD 12657 [DDD]
Frank, Claude (pno)
Beethoven, L. van:Sons Pno (comp)—Sons. 1-32 Music & Arts 10-▲ CD 640
Beethoven, L. van:Son 6 Vn, w. Pamela Frank (vn) *(rec American Academy of Arts & Letters, New York, Aug 10 & 14, 1992 & June)* MusicMasters ▲ 01612-67106-2 [DDD]
Beethoven, L. van:Son 7 Vn, w. Pamela Frank (vn) *(rec American Academy of Arts & Letters, New York, Aug 10 & 14, 1992 & June)* MusicMasters ▲ 01612-67106-2 [DDD]
Beethoven, L. van:Son 8 Vn, w. Pamela Frank (vn) *(rec American Academy of Arts & Letters, New York, Aug 10 & 14, 1992 & June)* MusicMasters ▲ 01612-67106-2 [DDD]
Saint-Saëns, C.:Carnival of the Animals, w. Lilian Kallir (pno), E. Ormandy (cnd), Philadelphia Orch Sony Classical ("Essential Classics" series) ▲ SBK 62638 ■ SBT 62638
Frank, Evelyn (fl)
Matiegka, W.T.:Serenade Fl, Va & Gtr, w. R. Smissen (va), D. Chivers (gtr) Erasmus ▲ WVH 086
Frank, Gerald D. (org)
Historic Organs of New Orleans, w. George Bozeman (org), James S. Darling (org), Jesse E. Eschbach (org), John Gearhart (org), James Hammann (org), Frederick Hohman (org), Lenora McCroskey (org), Mary Gifford Matthys (org), Lorenz Maycher (org), Donald Messer (org) *(rec June 1989)* Organ Historical Society 2-▲ OHS 89
Frank, Pamela (vn)
Beethoven, L. van:Son 6 Vn, w. Claude Frank (pno) *(rec American Academy of Arts & Letters, New York, Aug 10 & 14, 1992 & June)* MusicMasters ▲ 01612-67106-2 [DDD]
Beethoven, L. van:Son 7 Vn, w. Claude Frank (pno) *(rec American Academy of Arts & Letters, New York, Aug 10 & 14, 1992 & June)* MusicMasters ▲ 01612-67106-2 [DDD]
Beethoven, L. van:Son 8 Vn, w. Claude Frank (pno) *(rec American Academy of Arts & Letters, New York, Aug 10 & 14, 1992 & June)* MusicMasters ▲ 01612-67106-2 [DDD]
Chopin, F.:Trio Pno, w. Emanuel Ax (pno), Yo-Yo Ma (vc) *(rec Jordan Hall, New England Conservatory, Boston, MA, June 8-10, 1992)* Sony Classical ▲ SK 53112 [DDD]
Herrmann, B.:Souvenirs de Voyage, w. D. Schifrin (cl), T. Arm (vn), W. Trampler (va), W. Lash (vc) *(rec 6 & 7/90)* Delos ▲ 3088 [DDD]
Kernis, A.J.:Still Movement with Hymn, w. Paul Neubauer (va), Carter Brey (vc), Christopher O'Riley (pno) *(rec Florence Gould Auditorium, Seiji Ozawa Hall, Tanglewood, June 19 & 20, 1995)* Argo ▲ 448174-2 [DDD]
Prokofiev, S.:Qnt Ob, w. A. Vogel (ob), D. Shifrin (cl), S. Tenebom (va), E. Meyer (db) *(rec July 1-4, 1992)* Delos ▲ DE 3136 [DDD]
Schubert, Franz:Qnt Strs, D.956, w. F. Galimir (vn), S. Tenenbom (va), P. Wiley (vc), J. Lichten (vc) Sony Classical ▲ SMK 45901 [ADD/DDD] ■ SMT 45901
Frank, Susanne (vn)—see ORCHESTRAS & ENSEMBLES Carmina String Quartet
Franke, Jerome (vn)
Vivaldi, A.:Cons Vn, Op. 8/1-4, "The Four Seasons", w. Karine Garibova (vn), Pasquale Laurino (vn), Olga Miliaeva (va), Roza Borisova (vc), Mika Hennessy (db), Melanie Panush (ham dlc), Stanislav Venglevski (bayan), Mike Kashou (arabic tabla), Daryl Stuermer (gtr), Ed Paloucek (celtic fid), Gary Bottoni (highland pipe), Dubuffet String Quartet *(rec July-Sept 1995)* EarthBeat! ▲ 35270-2 [DDD]
Frankenberg, Peter (ob)—see also ORCHESTRAS & ENSEMBLES Senario Ensemble
Vivaldi, A.:Con Ob Bn, w. G. van der Wulp (bn), M. Haselböck (cnd), Vienna Academy [period instrs] Novalis ▲ 150074 [DDD]
Frankl, Peter (pno)
Bartók, B.:Dance Suite ASV ▲ ASV 860
Brahms, J.:Qnt Pno, w. Lindsay String Quartet ASV ▲ ASV 728 [DDD]
Chopin, F.:Andante Spianato & Grande Polonaise ASV ▲ ASV 781
Chopin, F.:Ballades Pno (comp) Allegretto ▲ ACD 8151 [ADD]
Chopin, F.:Barcarolle Pno ASV ▲ ASV 781
Chopin, F.:Fant Allegretto ▲ ACD 8151 [ADD]
Chopin, F.:Impromptus ASV ▲ ASV 781
Chopin, F.:Pno Music (misc)—selected Preludes, Nocturnes & Waltzes ASV ▲ ASV 781
Debussy, C.:Arabesques (2)—No. 2 Allegretto ▲ ACD 8041 [ADD] ■ ACS 8041
Debussy, C.:Clair de lune Allegretto ▲ ACD 8041 [ADD] ■ ACS 8041
Debussy, C.:Images (6) Pno Vox Box 2-▲ CDX 5062 [ADD]
Debussy, C.:Pno Music (misc)—Danse Bohémienne; Deux Arabesques; D'un cahier d'esquisses; Hommage à Haydn; Mazurka; La petit Nègre; Rêverie; Valse romantique Vox Box 2-▲ CDX 5062 [ADD]
Debussy, C.:Pno Music (misc)—Estampes; Ballade; Masques; Children's Corner; Berceuse héroique; Danse:Tarantelle Styrienne; Nocturne; Pour le piano; La plus que lente; Etudes (12); L'isle joyeuse; La boîte à joujoux Vox Box 2-▲ CDX 5063 [ADD]
Debussy, C.:Preludes Pno Vox Box 2-▲ CDX 5062 [ADD]
Debussy, C.:Suite bergamasque Vox Box 2-▲ CDX 5062 [ADD]
Dvořák, A.:Qnt Pno, Op. 81, w. Lindsay String Quartet ASV ▲ ASV 889 [DDD]
The Hungarian Anthology ASV ▲ CD DCA 860
Liszt, F.:Csárdás macabre ASV ▲ ASV 860
Martinů, B.:Qnt 2 Pno, w. Lindsay String Quartet ASV ▲ ASV 889 [DDD]
Mozart, W.A.:Fant Mechanical Org, w. T. Vásáry (pno) [arr. for piano duet] ASV ▲ ASV 799 [DDD]
Mozart, W.A.:Fugue Pno, K.401, w. T. Vásáry (pno) [duet version] ASV ▲ ASV 799 [DDD]
Mozart, W.A.:Pno Music 4-Hands, w. T. Vásáry (pno)—Sons., K.357, 358 & 521; & 2 shorter works ASV ▲ ASV 792
Mozart, W.A.:Son Pno 4-Hands, K.19d, w. T. Vásáry (pno) ASV ▲ ASV 799 [DDD]
Mozart, W.A.:Son Pno 4-Hands, K.381, w. T. Vásáry (pno) ASV ▲ ASV 799 [DDD]
Mozart, W.A.:Son Pno 4-Hands, K.497, w. T. Vásáry (pno) ASV ▲ ASV 799 [DDD]
Schubert, Franz:Fant Pno, D.760, "Wandererfantasie" *(rec 1974-75)* Vox Box 3-▲ CD3X 3011 [ADD]
Schubert, Franz:Impromptus Pno (comp) *(rec 1974-75)* Vox Box 3-▲ CD3X 3011 [ADD]
Schubert, Franz:Moments musicaux *(rec 1974-75)* Vox Box 3-▲ CD3X 3011 [ADD]
Schubert, Franz:Pno Music (misc)—Adagio, D.612; Allegretto, D.915; March, D.606; Scherzi, D.593; Variation, D.718 *(rec 1974-75)* Vox Box 3-▲ CD3X 3011 [ADD]
Schubert, Franz:Pieces Pno, D.946 *(rec 1974-75)* Vox Box 3-▲ CD3X 3011 [ADD]
Schumann, R.:Andante & Vars Hn, w. A. Schiff (pno), L. Varga (vc), O. Hegedüs (vc), A. Halstead (hn) Vox Box 3-▲ CD3X 3001 [ADD]
Schumann, R.:Ballszenen, w. A. Schiff (pno) Vox Box 3-▲ CD3X 3001 [ADD]
Schumann, R.:Bilder aus Osten, w. A. Schiff (pno) Vox Box 3-▲ CD3X 3001 [ADD]
Schumann, R.:Con Pno, w. J. Fürst (cnd), Bamberg SO Vox Box 2-▲ CDX 5027 [ADD]
Schumann, R.:Con Pno, w. J. Fürst (cnd), Bamberg SO Allegretto ▲ ACD 8166 [ADD] ■ ACS 8166
Schumann, R.:Etudes after Paganini's Caprices, Op. 3 Vox Box 3-▲ CD3X 3020 [ADD]
Schumann, R.:Intro & Allegro appassionato, Op. 92, w. J. Fürst (cnd), Bamberg SO Allegretto ▲ ACD 8166 [ADD] ■ ACS 8166
Schumann, R.:Intro & Allegro appassionato, Op. 92, w. J. Fürst (cnd), Bamberg SO Vox Box 2-▲ CDX 5027 [ADD]
Schumann, R.:Intro & Allegro, Op. 134, w. J. Fürst (cnd), Bamberg SO Vox Box 2-▲ CDX 5027 [ADD]
Schumann, R.:Intro & Allegro, Op. 134, w. J. Fürst (cnd), Bamberg SO Allegretto ▲ ACD 8166 [ADD] ■ ACS 8166
Schumann, R.:Kinderball, w. A. Schiff (pno) Vox Box 3-▲ CD3X 3001 [ADD]

Frankl, Peter (pno) (cont.)
Schumann, R.:Klavierstücke, Op. 85, w. A. Schiff (pno) Vox Box 3-▲ CD3X 3001 [ADD]
Schumann, R.:Polonaises Pno 4-Hands, w. A. Schiff (pno) Vox Box 3-▲ CD3X 3001 [ADD]
Schumann, R.:Qnt Pno, w. Lindsay String Quartet ASV ▲ ASV 728 [DDD]
Schumann, R.:Sketches Pedal Pno, w. A. Schiff Vox Box 3-▲ CD3X 3001 [ADD]
Schumann, R.:Studies Canon Form Vox Box 3-▲ CD3X 3001 [ADD]
Franklin, Brian (vl)
Blavet, M.:Recueil de pièces, w. Manfred Harras (rcr), Marianne Lüthi (rcr), Rudolf Scheidegger (hpd)—Prélude de Mr. Blavet; Pourquoi doux Rossignols; Entrée de chasse *(rec Reformierte Kirche, Arlesheim, Schweiz, May 18-19, 1987)* Musicaphon ▲ 56802 [DDD]
Boismortier, J.B. de:Chamber Music, w. Manfred Harras (rcr), Marianne Lüthi (rcr), Richard Gwilt (baroque vn), Arno Jochem (vl), Sally Fortino (hps)—Con. in C, "Zampogna"; Son. in F, Op. 91/1; Son. in A, Op. 10/2; Trio Son. in D, Op. 37/3; Son. in e, Op. 34/3; Con. in A, Op. 38/4; Suite No. 1, Op. 59; Balet de village en trio, Op. 52/4 *(rec Reformed Church, Bubendorf, Switzerland, Feb. 9-11, 1989)* Musicaphon ▲ 56812 [DDD]
Dornel, L.-A.:Concert 1, w. Manfred Harras (rcr), Marianne Lüthi (rcr), Rudolf Scheidegger (hpd) *(rec Reformierte Kirche, Arlesheim, Schweiz, May 18-19, 1987)* Musicaphon ▲ 56802 [DDD]
Marais, M.:Ballet in rondeau *(rec Reformierte Kirche, Arlesheim, Schweiz, May 18-19, 1987)* Musicaphon ▲ 56802 [DDD]
Philidor, P.:Music of, w. Manfred Harras (rcr), Marianne Lüthi (rcr), Rudolf Scheidegger (hpd)—Première suite in C; Deuxième suite in B; Septième suite in b *(rec Reformierte Kirche, Arlesheim, Schweiz, May 18-19, 1987)* Musicaphon ▲ 56802 [DDD]
Telemann, G.P.:Cants, w. Barbara Schlick (sop), Manfred Harras (rcr), Ernst-Martin Eras (ob), Richard Gwilt (vn), Sally Fortino (hpd)—Hemmet den Eifer, verbannet die Rache; Jauchzt, ihr Christen, seid vergnügt; Umschlinget uns, ihr sanften Freidensbande; Die Kinder des Höchsten sind rufende Stimmen; Lauter Wonne, lauter Freude Cantate ▲ 580003 [DDD]
Franklin, Harry (pno)
Balada, L.:Con Pno, w. R. Strange (cnd), Carnegie Mellon Concert Winds New World ▲ 80442-2
Franklin, Ian (ob)
Biscogli, F.:Con in D, w. E. Schultz (tpt), D. Haward (bn), V. Czarnecki (cnd), Southwest German CO Pforzheim ebs ▲ ebs 6054 [DDD]
Hertel, J.W.:Con à 6, w. E. Schultz (tpt), V. Czarnecki (cnd), Southwest German CO Pforzheim ebs ▲ ebs 6054 [DDD]
Franklin, Rachel (pno)
Chopin, F.:Ballades Pno (comp)—in f, Op. 52 Endeca ▲ EN/RF 199401 [DDD]
Chopin, F.:Son Pno, Op. 35 Endeca ▲ EN/RF 199401 [DDD]
Grieg, E.:Son 3 Vn, w. Sergiu Schwartz (vn) *(rec Feb 1988)* Allegretto ▲ ACD 8199
Zarebski, J.:Pno Music—Novellette caprice, Op. 19; Grande polonaise, Op. 6; Sérénade Burlesque, Op. 20; Suite polonaise, Op. 16 Endeca ▲ EN/RF 199401 [DDD]
Franová, Tatjana (pno)
Glazunov, A.:Pno Music—4 Preludes & Fugues, Op. 101; Idylle, Op. 103; Fant. for 2 Pnos, Op. 104 [w. Silvia Čáprová (pno)] *(rec Moyzes Hall of the Slovak PO, Bratislava, Apr.-May, 1993)* Marco Polo ▲ 8.223154 [DDD]
Glazunov, A.:Pno Music—Valse de Salon (1893); Trois Morceaux (1894); Prelude & Fugue (1899); Theme & Vars. (1900); Impromptus (1895); Deux Poèmes-improvisations Marco Polo ▲ 8.223152
Glazunov, A.:Pno Music—Suite on the name 'Sacha', Op. 2; Two Pieces, Op. 22; Waltzes on the name 'Sabela', Op. 23; Prelude & Two Mazurkas, Op. 25; Etudes; Petite valse, Op. 36; Nocturne, Op. 37; Grand valse de concert, Op. 41; Three Miniatures, Op. 42 *(rec July-Nov. 1990)* Marco Polo ▲ 8.223151 [DDD]
Glazunov, A.:Prelude & Fugue, Op. 62 *(rec Feb. & Apr., 1991)* Marco Polo ▲ 8.223153 [DDD]
Glazunov, A.:Sons Pno, Opp. 74 & 75 *(rec Feb. & Apr. 1991)* Marco Polo ▲ 8.223153 [DDD]
Franssen, Hein (pno)
Burgmüller, J.F.F.:Etudes Pno, "25 Easy & Progressive Studies" Partridge ▲ 1117-2 [DDD]
Frantz, Justin (pno)
Bach, J.S.:Con 1 for 2 Hpds, w. C. Eschenbach (pno), C. Eschenbach (cnd), Hamburg PO Deutsche Grammophon ▲ 415655-2 [DDD]
Bach, J.S.:Con 2 for 2 Hpds, w. C. Eschenbach (pno), C. Eschenbach (cnd), Hamburg PO Deutsche Grammophon ▲ 415655-2 [DDD]
Bach, J.S.:Con 1 for 3 Hpds, w. C. Eschenbach (pno), G. Oppitz (pno), C. Eschenbach (cnd), Hamburg PO Deutsche Grammophon ▲ 415655-2 [DDD]
Bach, J.S.:Con for 4 Hpds, w. C. Eschenbach (pno), G. Oppitz (pno), H. Schmidt (pno), C. Eschenbach (cnd), Hamburg PO Deutsche Grammophon ▲ 415655-2 [DDD]
Beethoven, L. van:Son 8 Pno, "Pathétique" Eurodisc ▲ 69139-2-RC [DDD]
Beethoven, L. van:Son 8 Pno, "Pathétique" Acanta ▲ CD 43804
Beethoven, L. van:Son 14 Pno, "Moonlight Son" Eurodisc ▲ 69139-2-RC [DDD]
Boothoven, L. van:Son 23 Pno, "Appassionata" Acanta ▲ CD 43804
Beethoven, L. van:Son 23 Pno, "Appassionata" Eurodisc ▲ 69139-2-RC [DDD]
Beethoven, L. van:Son 26 Pno, "Les Adieux" Acanta ▲ CD 43804
Dvořák, A.:Con Pno, w. J. Belohlávek (cnd), Prague SO *(rec live)* Eurodisc ▲ 69072-2-RG [DDD]
Mozart, W.A.:Pno Music 4-Hands, w. C. Eschenbach (pno)—Adagio, K.594; Andante & 5 Vars., K.501; Fantasia, K.608; Sons. in C, K.19d; K.358; in D, K.381 Deutsche Grammophon ▲ 429809-2 [ADD]
Ruzicka, P.:Approach & Peace, w. G. Herbig (cnd), Southwest German RSO Baden-Baden *(rec Nov 1984)* Thorofon ▲ CTH 2220
Franzetti, Allison Brewster (pno)
Franzetti, C.:Con Ob, w. Blair Tindall (ob), C. Franzetti (cnd), Modus Chamber Ensemble *(rec Hip Pocket Studios, New York)* Premier ▲ PRCD 1044 [DDD]
South American Landscapes Premier ▲ PRCD 1036 [DDD]
Franzetti, Carlos (pno)
Franzetti, C.:Concertino Bass Trbn, w. David Taylor (b trbn), Lois Colin (hp), C. Franzetti (cnd), Modus Chamber Ensemble *(rec Hip Pocket Studios, New York)* Premier ▲ PRCD 1044 [DDD]
Franzetti, C.:Suite Fl, w. Jorge de la Vega (fl), C. Franzetti (cnd), Modus Chamber Ensemble *(rec Hip Pocket Studios, New York)* Premier ▲ PRCD 1044 [DDD]
Franzetti, Giulio (vn)
Vivaldi, A.:Cons Vn, Op. 8/1-12, "Il cimento dell'armonia e dell'inventione", w. R. Muti (cnd), La Scala Orch Soloists—Nos. 1-5 EMI Classics ▲ CDC 55183
Frasca-Colombier, Monique (vn)
Franck, C.:Son Vn, w. Michelle Langot (pno) Pierre Verany ▲ PVY 730068 [DDD]
Magnard, A.:Son Vn, w. Michelle Langot (pno) Pierre Verany ▲ PVY 730068 [DDD]
Modern Favourites, w. M. Frasca-Colombier (vn), Pual Kuentz Orch [cnd:Paul Kuentz] Pierre Verany ▲ PVY 730072
Vivaldi, A.:Cons Diverse Instrs, w. Sylvia Ochi (man), Takashi Ochi (man), Jean-Marc Labylle (pic), Laurence Paugam (vn), P. Kuentz (cnd), Paul Kuentz Orch—in G for 2 Man; in C for Rcr; in B♭ for Bn [La notte]; in d for Vl; in a for Bn; in A for Vn & other Vns in echo Pierre Verany ▲ PVY 730052 [DDD]
Vivaldi, A.:Con Va d'amore Lt, w. N. Yepes (gtr), P. Kuentz (cnd), Kuentz CO Deutsche Grammophon ("Resonance" series) ▲ 429528-2 [ADD] ■ 429528-4
Frazier, Ivan (pno)
Songs with a Touch of Bass, w. D. Stoffel (b-bar), Milton Masciadri (db) *(rec Central Presbyterian Church, Athens, GA 1995)* ACA Digital Recording ▲ CM 20030
Fredericks, J. D. (fl)
York, W.:Reminiscence 2, w. I. Greitzer (cl), K. Supové (pno) *(rec May 1987)* New World ▲ 80439-2
Frederico, A. (elecs/pno)
Amendola, F.:Ricercari, w. D. Patumi (db), A. Flore (voc), G. Lanzini (cl), L. Ciolfi (vn), C. Cavalieri (vn), C. Sanzo (vc), O. Mangiavacchi (perc), Donizetti Ensemble Bongiovanni ▲ GB 5519 [DDD]

INSTRUMENT.

Frederiksen, J. E. (pno)
Wagner, R.:Songs, w. L. Koppel (sop), B. Asker (bar), Hymnia Chamber Choir—Seven Faust-Lieder (1832); Der Tannenbaum; Geburtsangrüss an Cosima; Kraft-lied; Adieux de Marie Stuart; Dors mon enfant; Attente; Mignonne; Tout n'est qu'images fugitives; Les deux grenadiers *(rec 1988)* Classico ▲ CLASSCD 102
Frederiksen, Tim (va)
Maegaard, J.:Labirinto I *(rec Copenhagen, 1995–96)* Marco Polo/Dacapo ▲ 8.224050 [DDD]
Fredin, Thorvald (db)
Bottesini, G.:Con 2 Db, w. J.-O. Wedin (cnd), Oskarshamn Ensemble Opus 3 ▲ OP 8502
Bottesini, G.:Elegy & Tarantella, w. J.-O. Wedin (cnd), Oskarshamn Ensemble—Elegy Opus 3 ▲ OP 8502
Koch, E. von:Serenade Db, w. J.-O. Wedin (cnd), Oskarshamn Ensemble Opus 3 ▲ OP 8502
Larsson, L.-E.:Concertinos, w. J.-O. Wedin (cnd), Oskarshamn Ensemble—Concertino for Db Opus 3 ▲ OP 8502
Fredlund, Ingegerd (hp)
Schnittke, A.:Hymns Vc, w. T. Thedéen (vc), E. Radoukanov (db), C. Davidsson (bn), M. Kamata (hpd), A. Holdar (tubular bells / timp), A. Loguin (tubular bells) BIS ▲ CD 507 [DDD]
Schnittke, A.:Hymns Vc, w. Torleff Thedéen (vc), Entcho Rdoukanov (db), Christian Davidsson (bn), M. Kamata (hpd), Anders Holdar (tubular bells/timp), Anders Loguin (tubular bells) BIS ("BIS Twins" series) 2-▲ CD 437/507
Fredrickson, Thomas (db)—see ORCHESTRAS & ENSEMBLES Univ of Illinois Contemporary Chamber Players
Freed, Paul (pno)
Boulanger, L.:Cortège, w. J. Roche (vn) Vox Box 2-▲ CDX 5029 [ADD]
Boulanger, L.:Nocturne, w. J. Roche (vn) Vox Box 2-▲ CDX 5029 [ADD]
Tailleferre, G.:Son 1 Vn, w. J. Roche (vn) Vox Box 2-▲ CDX 5029 [ADD]
Freedman, L. (cl)
Berg, O.:Peter Quince at the Clavier, w. J. Relyea (bass), J. Hess (pno), T. Tureski (perc) Centaur ▲ CRC 2167 [DDD]
Freeman, J. (pno)
Crumb, G.:Music For A Summer EveningMusic for a Summer Evening (Makrokosmos III), w. G. Kalish (pno), R. DesRoches (perc), R. Fitz (perc) Elektra/Nonesuch ▲ 79149-2 [AAD]
Levinson, G.:Bronze Music, w. C. Abramovic (pno) CRI ▲ CD 642 [DDD]
Levinson, G.:Morning Star, w. C. Abramovic (pno) CRI ▲ CD 642 [DDD]
Stiller, A.:Music of, w. Orch 2001, Maelström Percussion Ensemble—The Mouse Singer; A Periodic Table of the Elements; A Descent into the Maelstrom; Son a 3 Pulsatoribus, with Gargoyle; The Water is Wide, Daisy Bell MMC ▲ MMC 2014
Stiller, A.:The Water Is Wide, Daisy Bell MMC ▲ 2014
Freeman, James (sitar)
Crumb, G.:Lux Aeterna, w. Freda Herseth (mez), Pamela Guidetti (b fl/sop rcr), Susan Jones (perc), William Kerrigan (perc) *(rec Lang Concert Hall, Swarthmore College)* CRI ▲ CD 723 [DDD]
Frehner, Hans Peter (fl)—see ORCHESTRAS & ENSEMBLES Zurich New Music Ensemble
Frei, Rudolf (db)
Holzbauer, I.:Nocturni Fl, w. R. Weber (va), Winterthur Baroque Quintet *(rec 1969)* Jecklin-Disco ▲ JD 4406-2 [ADD]
Onslow, G.:Grand Septuor Fl, w. W. Bärtschi (pno), Stalder Wind Quintet *(rec 1979)* Jecklin-Disco ▲ JD 554-2 [ADD]
Freiberg, Gottfried von (hn)
Strauss, R.:Con 2 Hn, w. K. Böhm (cnd), Vienna PO *(rec 1943)* Orfeo ▲ 376941 (m)
Freiberg, Sarah (baroque vc)—see ORCHESTRAS & ENSEMBLES American Baroque
Freiberg, Sarah (vc)—see ORCHESTRAS & ENSEMBLES Streicher Trio
Freiberger, Rupert Gottfried (org)
Duello a Due Organi, Vol. 1, w. I. Melchersson (org) Christophorus ▲ 77141 [DDD]
Historic Organs in Undine & Florence Entrée ▲ 0082
Freimuth, Michael (thb)
Krieger, J.P.:Trio Sons, w. Mihoko Kimura (vn), Peter Wendland (vl), Siebe Henstra (hpd/org)—Nos. 1–6 Prezioso ▲ 840.402
Visée, R. de:Pieces Thb—for Thb in g Ars Produktion ▲ ARS 368337
Freire, Joaquim (gtr)—see also ORCHESTRAS & ENSEMBLES Linhares Guitar Quartet
Chopin, F.:Pno Music (misc)—Impromptu No. 2, Op. 36; Mazurkas No. 17 in b♭, Op. 24/4 & No. 26 in c♯, Op. 41/1; Scherzo No. 2, Op. 31 Audiofon ▲ CD 72023
Freire, Nelson (pno)
Chopin, F.:Ballades Pno (comp) *(rec New York City, Apr 22–25, 1970)* Sony Classical ("Essential Classics" series) ▲ SBK 62415 [ADD] ■ SBT 62415
Debussy, C.:Images (6) Pno Alphée ▲ 9502003
Grieg, E.:Con Pno, Op. 16, w. R. Kempe (cnd), Munich PO *(rec 1968)* Odyssey ▲ MBK 46269 [AAD]
In Recital *(rec Gusman Cultural Center, Miami, Florida, 12/13/84)* Audiofon ▲ CD 72023
Liszt, F.:Con 1 Pno, w. M. Plasson (cnd), Dresden PO Berlin Classics ▲ BER 1130 [DDD]
Liszt, F.:Con 2 Pno, w. M. Plasson (cnd), Dresden PO Berlin Classics ▲ BER 1130 [DDD]
Liszt, F.:Totentanz, w. M. Plasson (cnd), Dresden PO Berlin Classics ▲ BER 1130 [DDD]
Mozart, W.A.:Son 11 Pno Audiofon ▲ CD 72023
Mozart, W.A.:Son 12 Pno *(rec Toronto)* Alphée ▲ 9502003
Saint-Saëns, C.:Carnival of the Animals, w. M. Argerich (pno), G. Kremer (vn), I. van Keulen (vn), T. Zimmermann (va), M. Maisky (vc), et al. Philips ("Digital Classics" series) ▲ 416841-2 [DDD]
Schubert, Franz:Impromptus Pno, D.899 Sony Classical ("Essential Classics" series) ▲ SBK 47667 ■ SBT 47667
Schumann, R.:Con Pno, w. R. Kempe (cnd), Munich PO *(rec 1968)* Odyssey ▲ MBK 46269 [AAD]
Schumann, R.:Fant Pno *(rec Toronto)* Alphée ▲ 9502003
Scriabin, A.:Son 4 Pno Alphée ▲ 9502003
Tchaikovsky, P.:Con 1 Pno, w. R. Kempe (cnd), Munich PO *(rec 1968)* Odyssey ▲ MBK 46268 [ADD] ■ YT 46268
Villa-Lobos, H.:A Lenda do Caboclo Audiofon ▲ CD 72023
Villa-Lobos, H.:As tres Marias Alphée ▲ 9502003
Villa-Lobos, H.:Bachianas brasileiras (comp), w. Leila Guimaraes (sop), I. Karabtchevsky (cnd), Brazil SO *(rec June–Sept 1987)* Iris 3-▲ 143/3 [ADD]
Villa-Lobos, H.:A Lenda do Caboclo Alphée ▲ 9502003
Villa-Lobos, H.:Próle do bébé—sels. Audiofon ▲ CD 72023
Freivogel, Willy (fl)—see also ORCHESTRAS & ENSEMBLES Stuttgart Wind Quintet
Haas, P.:The Chosen One, w. Jörg Dürmüller (ten), Friedhelm Pütz (hn), Monika Hölszky-Wiedemann (vn), Dennis Russell Davies (pno) Orfeo ("Musica Rediviva" series) ▲ 386961 [DDD]
Frejdlich, Pawel (vc)—see ORCHESTRAS & ENSEMBLES Chopin Trio
Frémy, Gérard (pno)
Stockhausen, K.:Kontakte, w. Florent Jodelet (perc) Accord ▲ ACD 202742 [DDD]
Stockhausen, K.:Refrain, w. Jean-Efflam Bavouzet (cel), Florent Jodelet (perc) Accord ▲ ACD 202742 [DDD]
French, Allen (hn)—see also also ORCHESTRAS & ENSEMBLES Moran Woodwind Quintet
Snyder, R.:Qnt 3 Fl, w. John Bailey (fl), William McMullen (ob), Eric Ginsberg (cl), Gary Echols (bn) Coronet ▲ COR 400-9
Fresno, Alba (vl)—see ORCHESTRAS & ENSEMBLES Labyrinto
Fresno, Jorge (gtr)—see also also ORCHESTRAS & ENSEMBLES Meister Consort
Giuliani, M.:Music for Fl & Gtr (sels), w. E. Casularo (fl)—Rondeau, Op. 68; Divertimento in G; Qual mesto gemito, 3 Pièces, Op. 74 *(rec 1989)* Jecklin-Disco ▲ JD 624-2 [ADD]
Sanz, G.:Gtr Music MP Classics 2-▲ 3-11022/23
Freund, Etelka (pno)
Bach, J.S.:Kbd Music (misc) Pearl 2-▲ PEA 9193
Bartók, B.:Pno Music Pearl 2-▲ PEA 9193
Brahms, J.:Pno Music (misc) Pearl 2-▲ PEA 9193
Kodály, Z.:Pno Music Pearl 2-▲ PEA 9193
Freund, Etelka (pno) (cont.)
Liszt, F.:Pno Music (misc) Pearl 2-▲ PEA 9193
Mendelssohn, F.:Pno Music (misc) Pearl 2-▲ PEA 9193
Freund, Ulrich (hn)
Beethoven, L. van:Qnt Pno, Ob, Cl, Hn & Bn, w. C. Eschenbach (pno), A. Leek (ob), J. Moog (cl), S. Scott (hn) Signum ▲ X 06-00
Mozart, W.A.:Qnt Pno, K.452, w. C. Eschenbach (pno), A. Leek (ob), J. Moog (cl), S. Scott (hn) Signum ▲ X 06-00
Villa-Lobos, H.:Bachiana brasileira 6, w. Joachim Schmitz (fl) Bayer ▲ BR 100117 [DDD]
Villa-Lobos, H.:Duo Ob, w. Petra Fluhr (ob) Bayer ▲ BR 100117 [DDD]
Villa-Lobos, H.:Qt Fl, w. Joachim Schmitz (fl), Petra Fluhr (ob), Johannes Moog (cl) Bayer ▲ BR 100117 [DDD]
Villa-Lobos, H.:Trio Ob, w. Petra Fluhr (ob), Johannes Moog (cl) Bayer ▲ BR 100117 [DDD]
Freundlich, Douglas (lt)—see ORCHESTRAS & ENSEMBLES Renaissonics
Frey, Alexander (pno)
Korngold, E.W.:Between 2 Worlds, w. J. Mauceri (cnd), Berlin RSO *(rec Berlin, Apr. 1995)* London ("Entartete Musik" series) ▲ 444170-2 [DDD]
Frey, Barbara (cym)
Hauser, F.:Die Welle, w. Martin André Grütter (cym/tamtam), Roli Fischer (cym), Cyril Lützelschwab (cym), Lukas Rohner (cym), Severin Steinhauser (cym), Hans Ulrich (cym), Ruud Wiener (cym), Michael Erni (timp), Fran Lorkovic (timp), F. Hauser (cnd) *(rec Studio DRS, Basel, Switzerland, Nov. 6, 1988)* Hat Hut ▲ hat ART CD 6017 [ADD]
Frey, Mischa (vc)
Vivaldi, A.:Sons Vc, w. C. Starck (vc), I. Ahlgrimm (hpd)—Op. 14/1–5; Son in a, RV.44; Sons in B♭, E♭ & g Tudor 2-▲ 709 [ADD]
Frice, Janet (bn)
Jenkins, L.:Monkey on the Dragon, w. Leroy Jenkins (vn), Henry Threadgill (fl), Don Byron (cl), Marth Ehrlich (b cl), Vincent Chancey (hn), Frank Gordon (tpt), Jeff Hoyer (trbn), David Soldier (vn), Jane Henry (vn) Ron Lawrence (va), Mary Wooton (vc), Lindsey Horner (db), Thurman Barker (traps), Myra Melford (pno), T. Léon (cnd) *(rec live, Merkin Concert Hall, New York City, Apr. 9, 1992)* CRI ("eXchange" series) ▲ CD 663 [DDD]
Fridriksson, Marteinn Hunger (org)
Leifs, J.:Music of, w. Sigridur Ella Magnúsdóttir (mez), Ólafur Vignir Albertsson (pno), Sólveig Anna Jónsdóttir (pno), Hjálmar Ragnarsson (pno), Edda Erlendsdóttir (pno), Hildigunnur Halldórsdóttir (vn), Gréta Gudnadóttir (vn), Gudmundur Kristmundsson (va), Sigurdur Halldórsson (vc), Richard Korn (db), Iceland SO, Icelandic Opera Chorus, Langholts Church Graduale Choir, Hamrahlid Choir—Icelandic Cant, Op. 13/4; Valse Lento, Op. 2/1; Icelandic Dance, Op. 11/2 [Tempo Giusto]; Requiem; Lullaby [After the Riots]; Fairy-Tale in the Wood [from Baldr, Op. 34]; Funeral March; Separation [from Elegy, Op. 53]; Galdra Loftur Ov, Op. 10; Funeral March, Op. 6; Reverie; Reunion [from Elegy, Op. 53]; Fine I, Op. 55; Andante [The Last Supper]; Preludia Organo, Op. 16/3 [In the Church]; The Tear of Stone [from Elegy, Op. 53] Music From Iceland ▲ ITM 605 [DDD]
Ragnarsson, H.:Music of, w. S. E. Magnúsdóttir (mez), H. Halldórsdóttir (vn), G. Gudnadóttir (vn), G. Kristmundsson (va), S. Halldórsson (vc), R. Korn (db), Ó. V. Albertsson (pno), S. A. Jónsdóttir (pno), H. Ragnarsson (pno), E. Erlendsdóttir (pno), Sakari, Wilkinson (cnd), Iceland SO, G. Cortes (cnd), J. Stefánsson (cnd), T. Ingólfsdóttir (cnd), Hamrahlid Choir, Icelandic Opera Chorus, Langholts Church Graduale Choir—Meine kleine Freundin [In the Ballroom]; Lovers Duet; After the concert; Meine kleine Freundin [Annie listens to the Radio]; Lif's Theme [On the Beach]; Lif's Theme II [Night Prayer]; Composing Ov [Vars I, II & III] Music From Iceland ▲ ITM 605 [DDD]
Fried, Miriam (vn)
Erb, D.:Con Vn, w. C. Comet (cnd), Grand Rapids SO *(rec DeVos Hall, Grand Rapids, MI, Apr. 18, 1993)* Koss Classics ▲ KC 3002 [DDD]
Sibelius, J.:Con Vn, w. O. Kamu (cnd), Helsinki PO *(rec Oct. 9–10 1987)* Finlandia ▲ 4509-95856-2 [DDD]
Sibelius, J.:Karelia Suite, w. O. Kamu (cnd), Helsinki PO *(rec Oct. 9–10 1987)* Finlandia ▲ 4509-95856-2 [DDD]
Fried, Paul (fl)
Bach, J.S.:Sons Fl, BWV 1030–35, w. M. Kroll (hpd), D. Sussman (vc) Golden Tone ▲ GTCD 001 ■ GTC 001
Flute Flavors, w. Christopher O'Riley (pno), Ronald Feldman (vc), David Sussman (gtr) Golden Tone ▲ GTCD 002
Mozart, W.A.:Don Giovanni (sels), w. Allan Vogel (ob)—sels [arr. for fl & ob] *(rec Shadow Mountain Studios, Jan.–Feb. 1995)* Golden Tone ▲ GTCD 004
Mozart, W.A.:Entführung (sels), w. Allan Vogel (ob)—How anxious Serail; With tenderness Serail; What Rapture Serail [arr. for fl & ob] *(rec Shadow Mountain Studios, Jan.–Feb. 1995)* Golden Tone ▲ GTCD 004
Mozart, W.A.:Nozze di Figaro (sels), w. Allan Vogel (ob)—Tell me fair ladies; Say goodbye; How delightful; Non so piu [arr. for fl & ob] *(rec Shadow Mountain Studios, Jan.–Feb. 1995)* Golden Tone ▲ GTCD 004
Mozart, W.A.:Qts Fl, w. V. Romanul (vn), R. Barnes (va), R. Feldman (vc) Golden Tone ▲ GT 003
Mozart, W.A.:Zauberflöte (sels), w. Allan Vogel (ob)—Vogelfänger; Loveliness beyond; All the world; Till love; How Strong; Du feines; In diesen...; Kindly Voice; Act 1 Finale; Bewahret euch; I'll have revenge [all arr. for Fl & Ob] *(rec Shadow Mountain Studios, Jan.–Feb. 1995)* Golden Tone ▲ GTCD 004
Friedheim, Arthur (pno)
The Complete Recordings Pearl ▲ PEA 9993 (m) [AAD]
Friedland, Peggy (fl)—see also also ORCHESTRAS & ENSEMBLES Griffin Music Ensemble
York, W.:Native Songs, w. N. Armstrong (sop), S. Sylvan (bar), S. Downey (sgr), R. Woodhouse (sgr), J. Fischer (pno), J. Russell Smith (perc) *(rec May 1987)* New World ▲ 80439-2
Friedlander, Erik (vc)
Hersch, F.:Tango Bittersweet, w. F. Hersch (pno) *(rec Aug. 31, 1993)* Catalyst ▲ 09026-61979-2 ■ 09026-61979-4
Red Square Blue Russian Composers, w. F. Hersch (pno), James Newton (fl), Toots Thielemans (hmc), Phil Woods (a sax), Steve La Spina (bass), Jeff Hirshfield (drums) Angel ▲ CDC 54743
Soldier, D.:Duo Son, w. L. Seaton (vn) Newport Classic ▲ NPB 85549 [ADD]
Zorn, J.:Redbird, w. Carol Emanuel (hp), Jill Jaffee (va), Jim Pugliese (perc) Tzadik ▲ TZA 7008 [DDD]
Friedli, Thomas (cl)—see also ORCHESTRAS & ENSEMBLES Zemlinsky Trio
French Music for Clarinet, w. U. Koella (pno) Claves ▲ 9322 [DDD]
Krommer, F.:Con Cl, w. A. Pay (cnd), English CO Claves ▲ CD 8602 [DDD]
Krommer, F.:Con for 2 Cls, Op. 35, w. A. Pay (cl), A. Pay (cnd), English CO Claves ▲ CD 8602 [DDD]
Krommer, F.:Con Fl, Op. 86, w. A. Pay (cnd), English CO Claves ▲ CD 8602 [DDD]
Mercadante, S.:Con in B♭ Cl, Op. 101, w. P. Angerer (cnd), Southwest German CO Pforzheim Claves ▲ CD 813
Molter, J.M.:Con in D Cl, w. P. Angerer (cnd), Southwest German CO Pforzheim Claves ▲ CD 813
Mozart, W.A.:Con Cl, w. E. de Stoutz (cnd), Zurich CO *(rec Kirche Altstetten/ZH, June 1982)* Claves ▲ CD 508205 [DDD]
Pleyel, I.:Con in C Cl, w. P. Angerer (cnd), Southwest German CO Pforzheim Claves ▲ CD 813
Rogg, L.:Music of, w. M. Larrieu (fl), J.-P. Goy (ob), M. Kameda (pno), J.-J. Balet (pno), L. Rogg (syn), M. Kameda (piano) *(8 Études [1990]; Jazzic J.-J. Balet (piano) (Cinq petites pièces lyriques [1952]; Trois pièces [1952]; Valse [1952]; Cinq petites géométries [1958]),* Kameda, Balet *(Face à face for 2 Pianos [1987]),* J.-P. Goy, L. Rogg *(Pièce for Oboe & Synthesizer [1991]),* T. Friedli *(Pièce for solo Clarinet [1986]); M. Larrieu (Suite for solo Flute [1991])* BIS ▲ CD 546 [DDD]
Schnyder von Wartensee, X.:Con for 2 Cls, w. H. R. Stalder (cl), Capriccio Ensemble Tudor ▲ 757 [DDD]
Schumann, R.:Fantasiestücke Cl, w. Ricardo Requejo (pno) *(rec Gstaad, Mar 1981)* Claves ▲ CD 508201 [ADD]
Schumann, R.:Märchenerzählungen, w. Hirofumi Fukai (va), Ricardo Requejo (pno) *(rec Gstaad, Mar 1981)* Claves ▲ CD 508201 [ADD]
Strauss, R.:Duet-Concertino, w. K. Thunemann (bn), M. Aeschbacher (cnd), Lausanne CO Claves ▲ CD 9010 [DDD]
Veress, S.:Con Cl, w. H. Holliger (cnd), Bern Camerata Grammont ▲ CTSP 16-2 [ADD]

Friedman, Aloysia (vn)
Summerdays:From the Musical Masterworks Festival at Old Lyme, w. S. Greenawald (sop), Beverly Hoch (sop), John Koch (ten), Michele Sidener (va), Norman Krieger (cnd), Norman Krieger (pno) Well-Tempered Productions ▲ WTP 5173 [DDD]

Friedman, Erik (vn)
Bach, J.S.:Con for 2 Vns, w. J. Heifetz (vn), M. Sargent (cnd), London New SO RCA Red Seal ▲ 6778-2-RC [ADD]
Chausson, E.:Poème Vn, w. M. Sargent (cnd), London SO RCA Silver Seal ▲ 09026-61210-2 ■ 09026-61210-4
Ravel, M.:Tzigane, w. M. Sargent (cnd), London SO RCA Silver Seal ▲ 09026-61210-2 ■ 09026-61210-4
Saint-Saëns, C.:Havanaise Vn, w. M. Sargent (cnd), London SO RCA Silver Seal ▲ 09026-61210-2 ■ 09026-61210-4
Saint-Saëns, C.:Introduction & Rondo capriccioso, w. W. Hendl (cnd), Chicago SO RCA Silver Seal ▲ 09026-61210-2 ■ 09026-61210-4
Sarasate, P. de:Zigeunerweisen, w. M. Sargent (cnd), London SO RCA Silver Seal ▲ 09026-61210-2 ■ 09026-61210-4
Tchaikovsky, P.:Con Vn, w. S. Ozawa (cnd), London SO RCA Silver Seal ▲ 60491-2-RV [ADD] ■ 60491-4-RV (CrO2)
Wieniawski, H.:Légende, w. M. Sargent (cnd), London SO RCA Silver Seal ▲ 09026-61210-2 ■ 09026-61210-4

Friedman, Ignaz (pno)
Bach, J.S.:Music of, w. Harold Bauer (pno), Percy Grainger (pno), Myra Hess (pno), Harold Samuel (pno)—Toccata No. 3 in G; Toccata & Fugue in d for Org [trans Tausig]; Well-Tempered Clavier Book 1, Nos. 5 & 21; Chorale [from Cant 147; trans Bauer]; Chromatic Fant & Fugue [trans von Bülow]; 2-Part Inventions Nos. 1, 6 & 8; Fant & Fugue in g for Org [trans Liszt]; Toccata & Fugue in g; French Suite No. 6; Gigue [from Partita in B♭, Book 1, No. 1] [all pno rolls] Nimbus ("Grand Piano" series) ▲ NI 8808 [DDD]
Bach, J.S.:Toccata & Fugue Org, BWV 538, "Dorian" [trans Tausig] Nimbus ("Grand Piano" series) ▲ NI 8808
Beethoven, L. van:Son 14 Pno, "Moonlight Son"—the complete master recording [rec. 9/7/26]; alternate take versions of movts. 2 & 3 [rec. 3/1/27] Pearl 4-▲ IF 2000 (m) [AAD]
Chopin, F.:Ballades Pno (comp)—No. 4, Op. 52 Nimbus ("Grand Piano" series) ▲ NI 8805 [DDD]
Chopin, F.:Nocturnes—Op. 37/1; Op. 62/1 Nimbus ("Grand Piano" series) ▲ NI 8805 [DDD]
Chopin, F.:Pno Music (misc)—Ballade in A♭, Op. 47—two versions, from 1925 & 1933; Berceuse in D♭, Op. 57; 5 Études—Op. 10/ 5,7 & 12 & Op. 25/6 & 9; Impromptu in F♯, Op. 36; 18 Mazurkas—Opp. 7/1-3 including two versions of No. 1, 24/4, 33/2 & 4 including three versions of No. 2 & two of No. 4, 41/1 in two versions, 50/2, 63/2 & 3 including two versions of No. 3, & 67/3 & 4; Nocturne in E♭, Op. 55/2; 2 Polonaises—in A♭, Op. 53 & in B♭, Op. 71/2; 2 Preludes—Op. 28, Nos. 15 & 19; Sonata in b♭, Op. 35—Funeral March movement only; 2 Waltzes—in a, Op. 34/2 & in D♭, Op. 64/1 Pearl 4-▲ IF 2000 (m) [AAD]
Chopin, F.:Polonaises—Op. 71/2 Nimbus ("Grand Piano" series) ▲ NI 8805 [DDD]
Chopin, F.:Waltzes—Op. 64/1 [Minute] Nimbus ("Grand Piano" series) ▲ NI 8805 [DDD]
The Complete Solo Recordings:1923–1936 Pearl 4-▲ PEA 2000 (m) [AAD]
Grieg, E.:Con Pno, Op. 16, w. P. Gaubert (cnd), *(orch unknown)* *(rec 1928)* Pearl 4-▲ IF 2000 (m) [AAD]
Liszt, F.:Fant on Themes from Mozart's *Don Juan* Nimbus ("Grand Piano" series) ▲ NI 8805 [DDD]
Liszt, F.:Grandes études de Paganini, S.141—No. 3 Nimbus ("Grand Piano" series) ▲ NI 8805 [DDD]
Liszt, F.:Hungarian Rhaps—No. 14 Nimbus ("Grand Piano" series) ▲ NI 8805 [DDD]
Liszt, F.:Transcriptions & Paraphrases—Paraphrase on Tannhäuser Ov Nimbus ("Grand Piano" series) ▲ NI 8805 [DDD]

Friedman, Leonard (vn)
Bloch, E.:Baal Shem, "3 Pictures of Chassidic Life", w. Allan Schiller (pno) ASV ▲ ASV 714
Bloch, E.:Son 1 Vn, w. A. Schiller (pno) ASV ▲ ASV 714
Bloch, E.:Son 2 Vn, "Poème mystique", w. A. Schiller (pno) ASV ▲ ASV 714
Vivaldi, A.:Cons for 2 Vns, w. R. Friedman (vn), L. Friedman (cnd), St. Andrew Camerata Omega ▲ OCD 1012 [DDD]

Friedman, Richard (vn)
Damase, J.-M.:Qnt Fl, Hp & Strs, w. Anna Noakes (fl), Gillian Tingay (hp), Jane Atkins (vl), Ferenc Szucs (vc) ASV ▲ ASV 898 [DDD]
Vaughan Williams, R.:The Lark Ascending, w. R. Pople (cnd), London Festival Orch ASV ▲ ASV 779
Vivaldi, A.:Cons for 2 Vns, w. L. Friedman (vn), L. Friedman (cnd), St. Andrew Camerata Omega ▲ OCD 1012 [DDD]

Friedman, Stanley (tpt)
Freund, D.W.:Silverling, w. McDonald (pno) Ode/New Zealand ▲ ODE 1327 [DDD]
Friedman, S.:She Walks in Beauty Ode/New Zealand ▲ ODE 1327 [DDD]
Friedman, S.:Solus Ode/New Zealand ▲ ODE 1327 [DDD]
The Lyric Trumpet, w. Bruce Greenfield (pno), Judith McDonald (pno), Elizabeth Biggs (sop), et al. Ode/New Zealand ▲ ODE 1327 [DDD]

Friedmann, I. (pno)
Beethoven, L. van:Son 9 Vn, "Kreutzer", w. B. Huberman (vn) *(rec ca. 1930)* EMI Classics ("Great Recordings of the Century" series) ▲ CDH 63194 (m) [ADD]

Friedrich, Ádám (hn)
From Schubert to Strauss with French Horn, w. Ingrid Kertesi (sop), Katalin Halmai (mez), Sándor Falvai (pno) Hungaroton ▲ HCD 31585 [DDD]

Friedrich, Andreas (vn)—see ORCHESTRAS & ENSEMBLES Novanta Trio, Universal Ensemble

Friedrich, Felix (org)
Bach, J.S.:Chorale Preludes Org, w. F. Friedrich (org) [the historic Bach organs at Altenburg & Störmthal] Motette 2-▲ DCD 11621 [DDD]
Bach, J.S.:Org Music (misc)—Prelude & Fugue in G, BWV 545; In dulci jubilo, BWV 751; Allein Gott in der Höh', BWV 711; Wie schön leuchtet der Morgenstern, BWV 739; Canonic Variations, BWV 769; Prelude & Fugue in E♭, BWV 552; Wir glauben all an einen Gott, BWV 680 & BWV 437; Fantasia & Fugue in c, BWV 537 Capriccio ▲ CDC 10036 [DDD]
Music for Trumpet & Organ, w. L. Güttler (tpt), Christoph Kircheis (org) Capriccio ▲ CDC 10057 [DDD]

Friedrich, H. (vc)
Jochen Kowalski:Aria from Berlin's Operatic History, w. J. Kowalski (ct), C. Schornsheim (hpd), R. Alpermann (hpd), Markus Stauch (db), Berlin CO [cnd:M. Pommer] Berlin Classics ▲ BER 1050 [DDD]

Friedrich, Hans (fl)
Mozart, W.A.:Con Fl Hp, w. A. Berger (hp), H. Kraus (cnd), Vienna Mozart Ensemble LaserLight ▲ 15 873 [DDD]

Friedrich, Nikolaus (cl)
Bassi, L.:Fant di concerto on Verdi's *Rigoletto,* w. T. Palm (pno) Bayer ▲ 100131
Bassi, L.:Melodies from *I Puritani,* w. T. Palm (pno) Bayer ▲ 100131
Cavallini, E.:Fant on Motifs from Bellini's *I somnambula* , w. T. Palm (pno) Bayer ▲ 100131
Labanchi, G.:Fant on Verdi's *Aida,* w. T. Palm (pno) Bayer ▲ 100131
Lovreglio, D.:Fant da concerto on Motifs of Verdi's *La traviata,* w. T. Palm (pno) Bayer ▲ 100131

Friedrich, Reinhold (tpt)
Endler, J.S.:Sinf, w. Budapest Strings Capriccio ▲ 10 529 [DDD]
Fasch, J.F.:Cons (68) Var Instrs, w. Budapest Strings—Concerto in D; Concerto à 8 in D Capriccio ▲ 10 529 [DDD]
Haydn, J.:Con Tpt, w. M. Haselböck (cnd), Vienna Academy *(rec Sofiensäle, Vienna, Oct 17–20, 1994)* Capriccio ▲ 10 598 [DDD]
Hummel, J.N.:Con in E♭ Tpt, S.49, w. M. Haselböck (cnd), Vienna Academy *(rec Sofiensäle, Vienna, Oct 17–20, 1994)* Capriccio ▲ 10 598 [DDD]
Puccini, M.:Concertone Fl, w. Christian Gurtner (fl), Lisa Klevit-Ziegler (cl), Hector McDonald (nat hn), M. Haselböck (cnd), Vienna Academy *(rec Sofiensäle, Vienna, Oct 17–20, 1994)* Capriccio ▲ 10 598 [DDD]

Friedrich, Reinhold (tpt) (cont.)
Telemann, G.P.:Con Tpt Strs in D, w. Budapest Strings Capriccio ▲ 10 529 [DDD]

Friedrichs, John (cl)
Liptak, D.:Rhaps, w. L. Greene (fl), D. Gerikh (vn), W. Bass (vc), S. Heyman (pno) Opus One ▲ CD 168 [DDD]

Frielander, Erik (vc)
Soldier, D.:Ultraviolet Railroad, w. Mark Feldman (vn), Neal Kirkwood (pno), R.A. Clark (cnd), Manhattan CO Newport Classic ▲ NPD 85589 [DDD]

Friend, Rodney (vn)—see also ORCHESTRAS & ENSEMBLES Solomon Trio
Mozart, W.A.:Qts Fl, w. R. Siebert (fl), W. Trampler (va), G. Neikrug (vc) Vox Box 3-▲ CD3X 3003 [ADD]

Friesen, Eugene (instrs)
Mozart, W.A.:Music of, w. Philip Aaberg, Todd Boekelheide, Chris Botti, Henry Adam Curtis, Steve Erquiaga, Béla Fleck, Eugene Friesen, Paul McCandless, Tim Story, Richard Schönherz, Tracy Scott Silverman, Thea Suits-Silverman, ValGardena, Modern Mandolin Quartet Imaginary Road ▲ 314534065-2 ■ 314534065-4

Frigé, Antonio (hpd)
Milanese Instrumental Songs of the 17th Century, w. G. Cassone (nat tpt), C. Frigerio (vc) Nuova Era ▲ NUO 7184 [DDD]
Stanley, J.:Cons Org, Op. 10, w. F. Cipriani (vn), R. Pietropaolo (vn), A. Fantinuoli (db), *(w. accompaniments for 2 vn & db)* Nuova Era ("Ancient Music" series) ▲ 7152

Frigé, Antonio (org)
Ives, C.:Vars on *America* Nuova Era ▲ 7042 [DDD]
The Joyful Organist Nuova Era ▲ NUO 7042 [DDD]
Mozart, W.A.:Church Sons, w. Pian e Forte Ensemble *(rec St. Francis of Paola Church, Milan, Aug. 1994)* Agora Music ▲ 002
Stanley, J.:Cons Strs, w. Pian e Forte Ensemble Nuova Era ("Ancient Music" series) ▲ 7019 [DDD]
Telemann, G.P.:Con Fl, Hpd, w. V. Balssa (fl) Nuova Era ("Ancient Music" series) ▲ NUO 7135 [DDD]
Telemann, G.P.:Fants Kbd—5 fants from each book Nuova Era ("Ancient Music" series) ▲ 7134 [DDD]

Frigerio, C. (vc)—see ORCHESTRAS & ENSEMBLES Quartetto Modì
Italian Masterworks for Organ & Trumpet, w. E. Tarr (tpt), Irmtraud Krüger (org), N. Eklund (tpt) Christophorus ▲ CHR 77145 [DDD]
Milanese Instrumental Songs of the 17th Century, w. G. Cassone (nat tpt), Antonio Frigé (hpd) Nuova Era ▲ NUO 7184 [DDD]

Friis, Morten (perc)—see ORCHESTRAS & ENSEMBLES Safri Duo

Friis, Søren (vc)—see ORCHESTRAS & ENSEMBLES Con Sordino Chamber Group

Friman, Per (vn)
Vesth, T.:Music of, w. Jan Sommer (gtr), Nils Sylvest Jeppesen (vc), Gert-Inge Andersson (va), Berit Spaelling (hp), Bent Larsen (fl), Bjorn Nielsen (ob), Svend Rasmussen (cl), Henrik Simonsen (db)—Cuddling Rain; Waltz the Blue Sea; Kaspers Lullaby; Autumn Sunshine; Red Fox Hunting Tea Party; Off White Eternity; Tartan Fl Danica ▲ DCD 8142

Frimout-hei, Inge (hp)
Maric, L.:Ostinato super thema octoicha, w. Gordana Marjanovic (pno), Camerata Academica Novi Sad Emergo ▲ EC 3951 [DDD]

Frisch, Jean-Christophe (fl)
Mozart, W.A.:Sons Fl Hpd (misc), w. Olivier Baumont (hpd), Antoine Ladrette (vc)—No. 1 in B♭, K.10; No. 2 in G, K.11; No. 3 in A, K.12; No. 4 in F, K.13; No. 5 in C, K.14; No. 6 in B♭, K.15 Adda ▲ ADD 581229 [DDD]
Vivaldi, A.:Sons Fl, w. Christine Plubeau (vl), Pascale Boquet (archlt), Claude Wassmer (bn), Alessandro de Marchi (hpd)—in F, d, e, g, c, D & g Adda ▲ ADD 241882

Frisch, Nikolaus (hn)—see ORCHESTRAS & ENSEMBLES Sabine Meyer Wind Ensemble
Lachner, F.P.:Octet, w. S. Meyer (cl), J. Steinbrecher (bn), Chalumeau Quintet Ambitus ▲ 97825 [DDD]

Frischknecht, H. E. (org)
Frischknecht, H.E.:Composition, w. F. Schmidhäusler (tpt), R. Schmidhäusler (tpt) *(rec July 2, 1990)* Pro Viva ▲ ISPV 161 CD [DDD]
Frischknecht, H.E.:Fant Vn, w. M. Dentan (org), H. Glamsch (perc) *(rec Feb. 26, 1989)* Pro Viva ▲ ISPV 161 CD [DDD]
Frischknecht, H.E.:Farbschimmerungen *(rec Sept. 7, 1989)* Pro Viva ▲ ISPV 161 CD [DDD]
Frischknecht, H.E.:Interweaving *(rec Aug. 15, 1985)* Pro Viva ▲ ISPV 161 CD [DDD]
Frischknecht, H.E.:Org Music, w. M. Dentan (org), H. Glamsch (perc)—3 pieces *(rec Sept. 7, 1989)* Pro Viva ▲ ISPV 161 CD [DDD]

Frisell, Bill (elec gtr)
Bryars, G.:After the Requiem, w. A. Balanescu, G. Bryars, R. Heaton, et al. ECM New Series ▲ 78118-21424-2 [DDD]
Bryars, G.:Alaric I or II, w. A. Balanescu, G. Bryars, R. Heaton, et al. ECM New Series ▲ 78118-21424-2 [DDD]
Bryars, G.:Allegrasco, w. A. Balanescu, G. Bryars, R. Heaton, et al. ECM New Series ▲ 78118-21424-2 [DDD]
Bryars, G.:The Old Tower of Löbenicht, w. A. Balanescu (vn), R. Heaton (cl), G. Bryars (db), et al. ECM New Series ▲ 78118-21424-2 [DDD]
Sato, M.:Improvs, w. Michihiro Sato (tsugaru shamisen), Fred Frith (elec gtr), Tenko (sgr), Mark Miller (elec bass), Nicolas Collins (elec), Christian Marclay (turntables), Steve Colemann (sax), Tom Cora (vc), Joey Baron (perc), Mark Dresser (elec bass), Gerry Hemingway (perc), Toh Ban Djan [Ikue Mori (perc), Luli Shioi (elec bass/sgr)], Semantics [Elliott Sharp (electric gtr/bass), Samm Bennett (perc), Ned Rothenberg (sax)]—23 improvisations with various accompaniment combinations *(rec Baby Monster Studio, NY, Apr. 11–16, 1988)* Hat Hut ▲ hat ART CD 6015 [ADD]

Frith, Benjamin (pno)
Arnold, M.:Children's Suite Koch International Classics ▲ KIC 7607
Beethoven, L. van:Vars on a waltz by Diabelli, Op. 120 ASV ("Quicksilva" series) ▲ ASQ 6155 [DDD]
Mendelssohn, F.:Capriccio brillante *(rec St. Martin's Church, East Woodhay, Mar. 7 & 8, 1994)* Naxos ▲ 8.550939 [DDD]
Mendelssohn, F.:Con 2 Pno, w. R. Stankovsky (cnd), Slovak State PO Košice *(rec House of Arts, Košice, Apr 27–30, 1992)* Naxos ▲ 8.553267 [DDD]
Mendelssohn, F.:Cons 2 Pnos, w. Hugh Tinney (pno), P. Ó. Duinn (cnd), RTE Sinfonietta *(rec Dublin, Oct 1995)* Naxos ▲ 8.553416 [DDD]
Mendelssohn, F.:Perpetuum mobile *(rec St. Martin's Church, East Woodhay, Mar. 7 & 8, 1994)* Naxos ▲ 8.550939 [DDD]
Mendelssohn, F.:Preludes & Fugues Pno, Op. 35 *(rec St. Martin's Church, East Woodhay, Mar. 7 & 8, 1994)* Naxos ▲ 8.550939 [DDD]
Schumann, R.:Davidsbündlertänze *(rec Nov. 27–29, 1991)* Naxos ▲ 8.550493 [DDD]
Schumann, R.:Fantasiestücke Pno, Op. 12 *(rec Nov. 27–29, 1991)* Naxos ▲ 8.550493 [DDD]
Stravinsky, I.:Con Pnos, w. Peter Hill (pno) *(rec St. Silas Church, London, May 9–11, 1995)* Naxos ▲ 8.553386 [DDD]
Stravinsky, I.:Le Sacre du printemps Pno, w. Peter Hill (pno) *(rec St. Silas Church, London, May 9–11, 1995)* Naxos ▲ 8.553386 [DDD]
Stravinsky, I.:Son Pnos, w. Peter Hill (pno) *(rec St. Silas Church, London, May 9–11, 1995)* Naxos ▲ 8.553386 [DDD]

Frith, Fred (elec gtr)
Sato, M.:Improvs, w. Michihiro Sato (tsugaru shamisen), Bill Frisell (elec gtr), Tenko (sgr), Mark Miller (elec bass), Nicolas Collins (elec), Christian Marclay (turntables), Steve Colemann (sax), Tom Cora (vc), Joey Baron (perc), Mark Dresser (elec bass), Gerry Hemingway (perc), Toh Ban Djan [Ikue Mori (perc), Luli Shioi (elec bass/sgr)], Semantics [Elliott Sharp (electric gtr/bass), Samm Bennett (perc), Ned Rothenberg (sax)]—23 improvisations with various accompaniment combinations *(rec Baby Monster Studio, NY, Apr. 11–16, 1988)* Hat Hut ▲ hat ART CD 6015 [ADD]

Fritsch, Thomas (vc)
Benda, F.:Son Fl, Vc & Hpd, w. A. Kröpper (transverse fl), B. Gillitzer (hpd) Supraphon ▲ SUP 111597 [DDD]

Fritz, Reto (harm)
Marti, H.:Échos de Détresse, w. W. Bärtschi (pno) Grammont ▲ CTS P 22-2 [ADD]

Fritze, Ulrich (va)
Holewa, H.:Trio Vn, Va & Vc, w. Leon Spierer (vn), Jörg Baumann (vc) Phono Suecia ▲ PHN 49 [ADD]

Fritzsch, Thomas (vc)
Haydn, J.:Trios Pno, Fl & Vc, w. Bernhard Gillitzer (pno), Andreas Kröper (fl) *(rec Evangelic Church, Korunní, Prague, Sept 1993)* Arta ▲ CD 0052 [DDD]
Mysliveček, J.:Trio Fl, w. Andreas Kröper (fl), Simon Standage (vn) *(rec Evangelic Church, Korunní, Prague, Jan 1994)* Arta ▲ LC 4789 [DDD]
Pichl, V.:Divert Fl, w. Andreas Kröper (fl), Simon Standage (vn) *(rec Evangelic Church, Korunní, Prague, Jan 1994)* Arta ▲ LC 4789 [DDD]
Reicha, A.:Grand Trio Fl, w. Andreas Kröper (fl), Simon Standage (vn) *(rec Evangelic Church, Korunní, Prague, Jan 1994)* Arta ▲ LC 4789 [DDD]

Fröhlich, Joseph (vn)
Bach, J.S.:Con Vn & Ob, w. J. Girdwood (ob), R. Haydon Clark (cnd), Consort of London Collins Quest ▲ 30182 [DDD]

Froidebise, Anne (org)
Fétis, F.J.:Fant symphonique, w. B. Priestman (cnd), Belgian RSO Koch Schwann ▲ CD 311097 [DDD]

Frölich, Andrea (pno)
Brahms, J.:Hungarian Dances Pno 4-Hands, w. Ramon Jaffé (vc)—Nos. 2, 4 & 7 [arr vc & pno] Koch Schwann ▲ SCH CD 317282
Brahms, J.:Son 1 Vn, w. Ramon Jaffé (vc) [arr Klengel vc & pno in D] Koch Schwann ▲ SCH CD 317282
Brahms, J.:Songs, w. Ramon Jaffé (vc)—6 songs Koch Schwann ▲ SCH CD 317282

Frolov, Igor (vn)
Raickovich, M.:Romances, w. M. Raickovich (cnd), Moscow SO *(rec Mosfilm Studios, Moscow, Aug 24–25, 1993)* Mode ▲ mode 45

Fromanger, Benoît (fl)
Carulli, F.:Fantasy on Themes from Bellini's *Il pirata*, w. I. Suzuki (gtr) Forlane ▲ FOR 16635 [DDD]
Diabelli, A.:Pieces (3) Fl & Gtr, w. I. Suzuki (gtr) Forlane ▲ FOR 16635 [DDD]
Giuliani, M.:Grand Son Fl, w. I. Suzuki (gtr) Forlane ▲ FOR 16635 [DDD]
Paganini, N.:Sons Fl, w. I. Suzuki (gtr)—Centone di Sonate (Sonate 1), Op. 64; Sonata No. 4 in A Forlane ▲ FOR 16635 [DDD]

Fromm, Armin (vc)—see ORCHESTRAS & ENSEMBLES Mannheim String Quartet

Frost, Julie (pno)
Songs from the Heart *(rec Studio P, Bala Cynwyd, Pennsylvania, Oct. 31, Dec. 12, 1994, J)* Albany ▲ TROY 165 [DDD]

Fröst, Martin (cl)
Penderecki, K.:Prelude Cl *(rec Feb. 18–20, 1994)* BIS ▲ CD 652 [DDD]
Penderecki, K.:Qt Cl, w. P. Swedrup (vn), I. Kierkegaard (va), H. Nilsson (vc) *(rec Feb. 18–20, 1994)* BIS ▲ CD 652 [DDD]

Frost, Rachel (ob)—see ORCHESTRAS & ENSEMBLES CO of Europe Soloists

Fry, Tristan (perc)
Contemporary Trumpet Music, w. G. Ashton (tpt/flgl), I. Watson (pno) Virgin Classics ▲ CDC 45003

Fryberger-Vote, Jeanne (hpd)—see ORCHESTRAS & ENSEMBLES Maryland Bach Aria Group members

Frydén, Lars (baroque vn)—see ORCHESTRAS & ENSEMBLES Musica Holmiae

Frydén, Lars (vn)
Rameau, J.P.:Pièces de clavecin en concert, w. G. Leonhardt (hpd), N. Harnoncourt (vl) Vanguard Classics ("The Bach Guild" series) ▲ OVC 2520 [ADD]

Frydman, Sylvain (cl)
Escaich, T.:Intermezzi (3), w. Jean-Pierre Baraglioli (sax), Yves Queyroux (fl) *(rec Apr 16–17, Nov 4 & 26, 19)* Chamade ▲ CHCD 5638 [DDD]
Rebotier, J.:D'ailleurs Adès ▲ ADE 204472 [DDD/AAD]

Frykholm, Lars (vc)
Lindblad, A.F.:Qnt Strs, w. Peter Olofsson (vn), Patrik Swedrup (vn), Tony Bauer (va), Jonal Lindgård (va) Musica Sveciae ▲ MSV 522 [DDD]
Randel, A.:Qt Strs, w. Peter Olofsson (vn), Patrik Swedrup (vn), Tony Bauer (va), Jonal Lindgård (va) Musica Sveciae ▲ MSV 522 [DDD]

Fuchs, Daniel (org)
Böhm, G.:Org Music [the organ at St. Paul of Lausanne]—Prelude and Fuge in C, a and d; Partita über Freu dich sehr, o meine Seele (12); Vater unser im Himmelreich; Vom Himmel hoch da komm ich her; Partita über Wer nur den lieben Gott lässt walten (7); Num bitten wir den heilgen Geist; Christe, der du bist Tag und Licht (3 Verse) Gallo ▲ CD 494

Fuchs, Daniel (pno)
Weber, C.M. von:Grand duo concertant Cl, w. L. Fuchs (cl) Gallo ▲ CD 570 [DDD]
Weber, C.M. von:Vars on a Theme from *Silvana* Cl, w. L. Fuchs (cl) Gallo ▲ CD 570 [DDD]

Fuchs, Ellen (vc)—see ORCHESTRAS & ENSEMBLES Alorian String Quartet

Fuchs, Joseph (vn)
Beethoven, L. van:Trio 1 Pno, w. E. Istomin (pno), P. Casals (vc) *(rec Prades, France, July 5, 1953)* Sony Classical ("The Casals Edition" series) ▲ SMK 58988 [ADD]
Beethoven, L. van:Trio 4 Pno, "Ghost", w. E. Istomin (pno), P. Casals (vc) *(rec Prades, France, July 6–9, 1953)* Sony Classical ("The Casals Edition" series) ▲ SMK 58991 [ADD]
Hindemith, P.:Con Vn, w. E. Goossens (cnd), London SO Everest ▲ EVC 9009 [AAD]

Fuchs, Lillian (va)
Thomson, V.:Sonata da chiesa, w. P. Ingraham (hn), Erwin (trbn) CRI ▮ ACS 6009

Fuchs, Luc (cl)
Weber, C.M. von:Grand duo concertant Cl, w. D. Fuchs (pno) Gallo ▲ CD 570 [DDD]
Weber, C.M. von:Qnt Cl, w. M. Solms (vn), O. Sipahi (vn), D. Morice (va), P. Caldwell (vc) Gallo ▲ CD 570 [DDD]
Weber, C.M. von:Vars on a Theme from *Silvana*, w. D. Fuchs (pno) Gallo ▲ CD 570 [DDD]

Fuchs, P. (ob)
Lehmann, H.U.:Tractus, w. U. Burkhard (fl), H. R. Stalder (cl) *(rec Jan. 13, 1978)* Grammont ▲ CTS P 4–2

Fuchs, S. (ob)
Fiala, J.:Qts Ob, w. Novsak Trio Tudor ▲ TUD 7022 [DDD]
Krommer, F.:Qts Ob, w. Novsak Trio Tudor ▲ TUD 7022 [DDD]
Mieg, P.:Septet, w. Peter Solomon (hpd), Günter Rumpel (fl), Primroz Novsak (vn), Marius Ungareanu (va), Carolyn Hopkins Marti (vc), Ronald Dangel (db) *(rec 1993)* Jecklin ▲ JS 314–2 [DDD]
Schaeuble, H.:Concertino Ob, w. S. Lautenbacher (vn), G. Egger (vn), J. Faerber (cnd), Württemberg CO Gallo ▲ CD 577 [DAD]

Fuchs, Ulrich (vc)
Hasse, J.A.:Trio Sons Fls, Op. 3, w. Elisabeth Weinzierl (fl), Edmund Wächter (fl)—Trio Son No. 6 in D Entrée ▲ 0081 [DDD]
Haydn, J.:Trios Fls & Vc, "London Trios", w. Elizabeth Weinzier (fl), Edmund Wächter (fl) Christophorus ▲ CHR 77146 [DDD]
Hoffmeister, F.A.:Trios for 2 Fls & Vc, w. E. Weinzierl (fl), E. Wächter (fl) Christophorus ▲ CHR 77146 [DDD]
Lotti, A.:Trio Son Fl, w. Elisabeth Weinzierl (fl), Eva Schieferstein (hpd) Entrée ▲ 0081 [DDD]
Quantz, J.J.:Trio Son Fls, w. Elisabeth Weinzierl (fl), Edmund Wächter (fl) Entrée ▲ 0081 [DDD]
Vivaldi, A.:Trio Son Fls, w. Elisabeth Weinzierl (fl), Edmund Wächter (fl) Entrée ▲ 0081 [DDD]

Fuchs, Wenzel (cl)
del Aguila, M.:Con Cl, w. H. Earle (cnd), American Music Ensemble Vienna Albany ▲ TROY 066 [DDD]

Fuga, Giacomo (pno)—see ORCHESTRAS & ENSEMBLES Turin Piano Trio

Fuhuda, R. (pno)
Dussek, J.L.:Son Pno, Op. 24 Partridge ▲ 1135–2 [DDD]
Dussek, J.L.:Son Pno, Op. 44, "The Farewell" Partridge ▲ 1135–2 [DDD]
Dussek, J.L.:Son Pno, Op. 69/3 Partridge ▲ 1135–2 [DDD]

Fujikawa, Mayumi (vn)
Fauré, G.:Andante Vn, w. Jorge Federico Osorio (pno) ASV ("Quicksilva" series) ▲ ASQ 6170
Fauré, G.:Berceuse Vn, w. Jorge Federico Osorio (pno) ASV ("Quicksilva" series) ▲ ASQ 6170

Fujikawa, Mayumi (vn) (cont.)
Prokofiev, S.:Mélodies, w. Craig Sheppard (pno) ASV ▲ ASV 667
Prokofiev, S.:Son Vn, Op. 94bis, w. Craig Sheppard (pno) ASV ▲ ASV 667
Prokofiev, S.:Son 1 Vn, w. Craig Sheppard (pno) ASV ▲ ASV 667

Fujimoto, Futomi (koto)
Miyagi, M.:Kazo-uta hensokyoku Ambitus ▲ 97851 [DDD]
Miyagi, M.:Rondon Ambitus ▲ 97851 [DDD]
Music for Koto Ambitus ▲ AMB 97851 [DDD]
Nakanoshima, K.:Mittsu no dansho Ambitus ▲ 97851 [DDD]
Yatsuhashi, K.:Rokudan Ambitus ▲ 97851 [DDD]
Yoshizawa, K.:Chidori no kyoku Ambitus ▲ 97851 [DDD]

Fujita, Toshi (koto)
Noda, T.:Mutation, w. Katsuya Yokoyama (shak), Mikiko Haga (koto), Chieko Mori (koto), T. Otaka (cnd), Tokyo Metropolitan SO *(rec live, Tokyo Bunka-Kaikan, Large Hall, May 24, 1980)* Camerata ▲ 32CM-292 [AAD]

Fujiwara, Hamao (vn)
Lebaron, A.:Noh Reflections, w. M. Kawasaki (va), E. Elsing (vc), Kennedy Center Theater Chamber Players Mode ▲ 30

Fujiwara, Mari (vc)—see also ORCHESTRAS & ENSEMBLES Mozart String Trio
Bach, Joh. Christian:Con Vn & Vc, w. J.-J. Kantorow (vn), J.-J. Kantorow (cnd), Netherlands CO Denon ▲ 7867 [DDD]
Bach, J.S.:Sons Fl, BWV 1030–35, w. A. Nicolet (fl), C. Jaccottet (hpd)—BWV 1030, 1032, 1034, 1035 Denon ▲ 7331 [DDD]
Bloch, E.:Schelomo, w. J. Hirokami (cnd), Norrköping SO Denon ▲ DEN 78830
Dvořák, A.:Con Vc, w. J. Hirokami (cnd), Norrköping SO Denon ▲ DEN 78830
Haydn, J.:Con 1 Vc, w. J.-J. Kantorow (cnd), Netherlands CO Denon ▲ 7867 [DDD]
Haydn, J.:Con 2 Vc, w. J.-J. Kantorow (cnd), Netherlands CO Denon ▲ 7867 [DDD]
Mozart, W.A.:Sons Vn Vc, w. J.-J. Kantorow (vn)—in C, K.46d & in F, K.46e Denon ▲ 7867 [DDD]
Strauss, R.:Romanze Vc, w. H. Wakasugi (cnd), Tokyo Metropolitan SO Denon/PCM Digital ▲ DEN 75860 [DDD]

Fukačová, Michaela (vc)
Brahms, J.:Sons Vc (comp), w. I. Klánský (pno) Kontrapunkt ▲ 32027 [DDD]
Brahms, J.:Son in D Vc, w. I. Klánský (pno) Kontrapunkt ▲ 32027 [DDD]
Cantos de España, w. Christensen, Jacob (gtr) Kontrapunkt ▲ 32044 [DDD]
Dvořák, A.:Con Vc, w. J. Belohlávek (cnd), Prague SO Panton ▲ PAN 810706
Dvořák, A.:Rondo, w. I. Klánský (pno) Kontrapunkt ▲ 32013 [DDD]
Elgar, E.:Con Vc, w. L. Pešek (cnd), Brno State PO *(rec 6/89)* Supraphon ▲ 110390–2 [DDD]
Franck, C.:Son Vn, w. I. Klánský (pno) Kontrapunkt ▲ 32013 [DDD]
Grieg, E.:Son Vc, w. I. Klánský (pno) Kontrapunkt ▲ 32013 [DDD]
Martinů, B.:Vc Music (complete), w. I. Klánský (pno)—7 Arabesques; Ariette; 4 Nocturnes; 6 Pastorales; Rossini Variations; Sonatas 1–3; Suite Miniature; Variations On a Theme from a Slovak Folk Song *(rec 6/91)* Kontrapunkt 3-▲ 32084/86 [DDD]
Prokofiev, S.:Son Vc, w. Ivan Klansky (pno) Kontrapunkt ▲ KPT 32216 [DDD]
Reger, M.:Suites Vc Kontrapunkt ▲ KPT 32142 [DDD]
Shostakovich, D.:Son Vc, w. Ivan Klansky (pno) Kontrapunkt ▲ KPT 32216 [DDD]
Stravinsky, I.:Suite italienne Vc, w. Ivan Klansky (pno) Kontrapunkt ▲ KPT 32216 [DDD]
Suk, J.:Qt Pno, w. J. Panenka (pno), J. Suk (vn), J. Talich (va) Supraphon ▲ SUP 111532 [DDD]
Tchaikovsky, P.:Pezzo capriccioso, w. I. Klánský (pno) [Tchaikovsky's cello & piano version] Kontrapunkt ▲ 32013 [DDD]
Tchaikovsky, P.:Pezzo capriccioso, w. L. Pešek (cnd), Brno State PO Supraphon ▲ 110390–2 [DDD]
Tchaikovsky, P.:Vars on a Rococo Theme, w. L. Pešek (cnd), Brno State PO Supraphon ▲ 110390–2 [DDD]

Fukai, Hirofumi (va)
Beethoven, L. van:Duet, WoO 32, "Mit 2 obligaten Augengläsern", w. K. Stoppel (vc) Signum ▲ X 46–00 [ADD]
Haydn, M.:Divert Va, Vc & Db, w. Klaus Stoppel (vc), G. Dzwiza (db) Signum ▲ X 46–00 [ADD]
Hindemith, P.:Son Va & Pno, Op. 25/4 Signum ▲ X 38–00 [ADD]
Reger, M.:Suites Va Signum ▲ X 38–00 [ADD]
Romberg, B.:Trios Va, w. K. Stoppel (vc), G. Dzwiza (db)—1 trio Signum ▲ X 46–00 [ADD]
Schumann, R.:Märchenbilder, w. Ricardo Requejo (pno) *(rec Gstaad, Mar 1981)* Claves ▲ CD 508201 [ADD]
Schumann, R.:Märchenerzählungen, w. Thomas Friedli (cl), Ricardo Requejo (pno) *(rec Gstaad, Mar 1981)* Claves ▲ CD 508201 [ADD]
Sperger, J.:Sons Va, w. G. Dzwiza (db) Signum ▲ X 46–00 [ADD]
Suter, R.:Nocturnes Va, w. J. Meier (cnd), Basel SO Jecklin ▲ JD 690
Yun, I.:Son Ob, w. Heinz Holliger (ob), Ursula Holliger (hp) *(rec March 25, 1976)* Camerata ▲ 30CM 22

Fukuda, Shin-ichi (gtr)
Aguado, D.:Gtr Music—Rondo brilliant, Op. 2/2 *(rec Chichibu Muse Park, Nov. 24–26, 1994)* Denon ▲ DEN 78950 [DDD]
Copper, L.:Grande sérénade *(rec Fukushima City Music Hall, May 9–12, 1995)* Denon ▲ CO 78978 [DDD]
Copper, L.:Gtr Music—Rêverie, Op. 53/1; Andante, Op. 38/14; Caprice sur L'Air Espagnol; La Cachucha, Op. 13 *(rec Chichibu Muse Park, Nov. 24–26, 1994)* Denon ▲ DEN 78950 [DDD]
Mertz, K.J.:Gtr Music—Fant. Hongroise, Op. 65/1; Abendlied [from Bardenklänge, Op. 13] *(rec Chichibu Muse Park, Nov. 24–26, 1994)* Denon ▲ DEN 78950 [DDD]
Mertz, K.J.:Gtr Music—Liebeslied [from Bardenklänge, Op. 13] & arrs of Schubert [Ständchen; Aufenthalt; Liebesbothschaft; Das Fischermädchen; Loss Der Thränen; Die Post] & Abt [Agathe, Op. 22/1] *(rec Fukushima City Music Hall, May 9–12, 1995)* Denon ▲ CO 78978 [DDD]
Sor, F.:Fant elégiaque *(rec Fukushima City Music Hall, May 9–12, 1995)* Denon ▲ CO 78978 [DDD]
Sor, F.:Gtr Music—Studies in A, Op. 6/12; in C, Op. 29/17; Exercise in b, Op. 35/22; Leçon in E, Op. 31/23; Vars. on a Theme of Mozart, Op. 9; Valse in E, Op. 32/2 *(rec Chichibu Muse Park, Nov. 24–26, 1994)* Denon ▲ DEN 78950 [DDD]

Fukuhara, Mayuki (vn)—see ORCHESTRAS & ENSEMBLES St. Luke's Chamber Ensemble

Fukunaga, C. (koto)
Shinohara, M.:Cooperation, w. A. Nishigata (shamisen), K. Mitsuhashi (shakuhachi), M. Akao (fue), S. Yaotani (hichiriki), K. Ishikawa (sho), C. Fukunaga (koto), J. Ueda (biwa), M. Yoshizawa (kokyu), I. Tsuji (oboe), T. Takahashi (cl), G. Kitamura (tpt), A. Murata (trbn), S. Eiso (perc), S. Ueki (vn), S. Katsuta (vc), Y. Shibuya (pno), K. Komatsu (cnd) *(rec live Casals Hall, Tokyo, Mar. 5, 1994)* Camerata ▲ 30CM 375 [DDD]

Fülemile, Tibor (bn)
Haydn, J.:Diverts for 2 Obs, Hns & Bns, H.II/7, 15, D18, 23 & deest, w. P Pongrácz (ob), B. Hock (ob), A. Medveczky (hn), D. Mesterházy (hn), A. Nagy (bn) White Label ▲ HRC 155 [ADD]

Fulkerson, Gregory (vn)
Black, R.:Pieces (3) Vn, w. Charles Abramovic (pno) Bridge ▲ BCD 9061 [DDD]
Copland, A.:Duo Fl, w. Robert Shannon (pno) *(rec RCA Recording Studios, New York City)* New World ▲ 80313–2
Cory, E.:Ehre Soundspells ▲ CD 116 [DDD]
Cory, E.:Ehre Soundspells ▲ CD 116 [DDD]
Glass, Philip:Einstein on the Beach, w. Philip Glass Ensemble Elektra/Nonesuch ▲ 79323–2 ▮ 79323–4
Glass, Philip:Einstein on the Beach (sels)—violin solo music *(rec RCA Recording Studios, New York City)* New World ▲ 80313–2
Harris, R.:Con Vn, w. L. Leighton Smith (cnd), Louisville Orch Albany ▲ AR 012–2 [AAD]
Ives, C.:Sons Vn, w. R. Shannon (pno) Bridge 2-▲ BCD 9024 [DDD]
Miller, E.J.:Beyond the Wheel, w. L. Rachleff (cnd), Oberlin Wind Ensemble Opus One ▲ 138
Ornstein, L.:Son Vn, w. Alan Feinberg (pno) *(rec RCA Recording Studios, New York City)* New World ▲ 80313–2
Wernick, R.:Cadenzas & Vars 2 *(rec RCA Recording Studios, New York City)* New World ▲ 80313–2

Fulkerson, Jim (trbn)—see ORCHESTRAS & ENSEMBLES austraLYSIS members

Fullard, Annie (vn)
Erb, D.:Qt 2 Strs, w. S. Waterbury (vn), E. Eckert (va), M. Peckham (vc) Albany ▲ TROY 092 [DDD]

Fullbrook, Charles (bells)
Tavener, J.:Innocence, w. Patricia Rozario (sop), Leigh Nixon (ten), Graham Titus (bass), Alice Neary (vc), Martin Baker (org), Martin Neary (cnd), Westminster Abbey Choir *(rec Westminster Abbey, May 1-5, 1995)* Sony Classical ▲ SK 66613 [DDD]

Fullbrook, Charles (perc)
Bryars, G.:Three Viennese Dances, w. Pascal Porgy (hn), Arditti String Quartet ECM New Series ▲ 78118-21323-2 [DDD]

Fuller, Albert (hpd)
Bach, J.S.:Anna Magdalena Bach Notebook—(6) Wer nur den lieben Gott lässt walten; Polonaise; Aria; Menuet; Polonaise; Bist du bei mir *(rec 1992)* Reference ▲ RR 51 CD [DDD]
Bach, J.S.:French Suites—BWV 817 *(rec 1992)* Reference ▲ RR 51 CD [DDD]
Bach, J.S.:Italian Con *(rec 1992)* Reference ▲ RR 51 CD [DDD]
Bach, J.S.:Sons Vn, w. S. Luca (vn)—BWV 1019 Facet ▲ FCD 8005 [AAD]
Bach, J.S.:Trio Son for 2 Vns, w. J. Schröder (vn), S. Ritchie (vn) *(rec June 6-8, 1986)* Reference ▲ RR 23 CD [DDD]
Bach, J.S.:Das wohltemperierte Klavier—[Book 2] Prelude & Fugue in D; Prelude & Fugue in f *(rec 1992)* Reference ▲ RR 51 CD [DDD]
Bach, J.S.:Das wohltemperierte Klavier *(rec June 6-8, 1986)* Reference ▲ RR 2 3CD [DDD]
Rameau, J.P.:Nouvelles suites—Suite in A Reference ▲ RR 27 CD [DDD]
Rameau, J.P.:Pièces de clavecin avec une méthode sur la mécanique des doigts—9 sels. from various collections:La Dauphine; 2 Menuets; La Cupis; Les Sauvages; L'entretien des Muses; La Livri; L'enharmonique; Les Cyclopes Reference ▲ RR 27 CD [DDD]
Vivaldi, A.:Cons for 2 Vns, w. J. Schröder (vn), S. Ritchie (vn), N. TeBrake (vn), R. Brown (vn), J. Griffin (va), M. Lutszke (vc), M. Willems (db) *(rec June 6-8, 1986)* Reference ▲ RR 23 CD [DDD]
Vivaldi, A.:Sinf, RV.116, w. J. Schröder (vn), S. Ritchie (vn), J. Griffin (va), M. Lutszke (vc), M. Willems (db) *(rec June 6-8, 1986)* Reference ▲ RR 23 CD [DDD]
Vivaldi, A.:Sons Vc, w. E. Fisk (gtr)—in g, RV.42 [trans for gtr & hpd] *(rec July 27 & Aug. 4, 1992)* MusicMasters ▲ 01612-67097-2 [DDD]
Vivaldi, A.:Trio Sons Vn Lt, w. E. Fisk (gtr), F. Hand (gtr) *(rec July 27 & Aug. 4, 1992)* MusicMasters ▲ 01612-67097-2 [DDD]
Vivaldi, A.:Trio Sons 2 Vns & Bc, w. J. Schröder (vn), S. Ritchie (vn), M. Lutszke (vc)—RV.73 *(rec June 6-8, 1986)* Reference ▲ RR 23 CD [DDD]

Fuller, G. (elec gtr/elec bass)
Thorne, F.:Liebesrock, w. J. Dixon (cnd), Royal PO CRI ▲ CD 586 [ADD]

Fuller, Jerry (db)
Dittersdorf, K.D. von:Son Va, w. Li-Kuo Chang (va) Musical Arts Society ▲ CD 41592 [DDD] ■ CS 41592 (D)
Duets, w. Fuller, Jerry (db) Musical Arts Society ▲ CD 41592 [DDD] ■ CS 41592 (D)
Guillemant, B.:Son Bn, w. B. Grainger (bn) Musical Arts Society ▲ CD 41592 [DDD] ■ CS 41592 (D)
Haydn, M.:Divert Vn, Vc & Db, w. David Taylor (vn), Gary Stucka (vc) *(rec WTMT Studio 1, Jan 24, 1993)* Musical Arts Society ▲ MAS 41595 [DDD]
Romberg, B.:Son Vc, w. *(soloist unkown)* Musical Arts Society ▲ CD 41592 [DDD] ■ CS 41592 (D)
Romberg, B.:Trios Va, w. Li-Kuo Chang (va), Gary Stucka (vc)—No. 1 in e *(rec WTMT Studio 1, Jan 24, 1993)* Musical Arts Society ▲ MAS 41595 [DDD]
Songs, Dances & Fantasy, w. Fuller, Jerry (db), Frederick Ockwell (pno), Kenneth Dorsch (hpd), William Ferris (pno), Steve Hartman (hp), Thomas Potter (bar), John Vorrasi (ten), Anne Waller (gtr) Musical Arts Society ▲ CD 41589 [AAD] ■ CS 41589
Vanhal, J.B.:Divert Strs, w. David Taylor (vn), Li-Kuo Chang (va) *(rec WTMT Studio 1, Jan 24, 1993)* Musical Arts Society ▲ MAS 41595 [DDD]

Fuller, Louisa (vn)—see ORCHESTRAS & ENSEMBLES Duke String Quartet

Fuller, Richard (pno)
Mozart, W.A.:Fant Pno, K.397 *(rec 1988)* Ambitus ▲ 97827 [DDD]
Mozart, W.A.:Son 4 Pno *(rec 1988)* Ambitus ▲ 97827 [DDD]
Mozart, W.A.:Son 5 Pno *(rec 1988)* Ambitus ▲ 97827 [DDD]
Mozart, W.A.:Son 10 Pno *(rec 1988)* Ambitus ▲ 97827 [DDD]
Mozart, W.A.:Son 15 Pno *(rec 1988)* Ambitus ▲ 97827 [DDD]
Mozart, W.A.:Sons Vn Pno (misc), w. T. Pietsch (vn)—K.301, 302, 303 & 304 Ambitus ▲ 97816 [DDD]

Fulton, Cheryl Ann (hp)
The Airs of Wales, w. Fulton, Cheryl Ann (Welsh triple hp) Koch International Classics ▲ KIC 7071 [DDD]
Lo Gai Saber:Troubadours and Minstrels, 1100-1300, w. J. Cohen (cnd), Camerata Mediterranea, Anne Azema (voc), François Harismendy (voc), Jean-Luc Madier (voc), Joel Cohen (instr), Shira Kammen (instr) Erato ▲ 2292-45647-2 [DDD]

Fulton, Cheryl Ann (hps)
The Unicorn:Myth & Miracle in Medieval France (1200-1300), w. Azema, Anne (sop), Shira Kammen (rebec/vielle/hp), Jesse Lepkoff (fl) Erato ▲ 94380 [DDD]

Fulton, Cheryl Ann (triple hp)—see ORCHESTRAS & ENSEMBLES American Baroque

Funahashi, Yuri (pno)
Beach, A.M.C.:Son Vn, w. Arturo Delmoni (vn) John Marks ▲ JMR 2
Brahms, J.:Son 1 Vn, w. Arturo Delmoni (vn) John Marks ▲ JMR 2

Fung, Lam (pipa)
Chen, G.:Wang Zhaojun Con, w. Takako Nishizaki (vn), Y.W. Sie (cnd), Hong Kong PO *(rec Shatin Town Hall, Hong Kong, June 23, 1987)* Marco Polo ("Chinese Composers" series) ▲ 8.223908 [DDD]

Funke, Christian (vn)
Beethoven, L. van:Con Vn, Vc & Pno, "Triple Con", w. J. Timm (vc), Rösel (pno), H. Kegel (cnd), Dresden PO Capriccio ▲ 10150 [DDD]
Schumann, R.:Son 2 Vn, w. Peter Rösel (pno) Berlin Classics ▲ BER 9189

Füri, Thomas (vn)—see also ORCHESTRAS & ENSEMBLES Aria String Quartet
Ponchielli, A.:Paolo et Virginia, w. Antony Morf (cl), Gérard Wyss (pno) Accord ▲ ACD 220682 [AAD]
Spohr, L.:Son 3 Vn, w. U. Holliger (hp) *(rec 1982)* Jecklin-Disco ▲ JD 573-2 [ADD]
Spohr, L.:Son 4 Vn, w. U. Holliger (hp) *(rec 1982)* Jecklin-Disco ▲ JD 573-2 [ADD]

Furini, Stefano (vn)
Dragonetti, D.:Qt 4 Strs, w. Pietro Juvarra (vn), Giancarlo di Vacri (va), Teodora Campagnaro (vc) *(rec Sala San Bovo, Padova, Italy, Jan 17-19, 1995)* Dynamic ▲ CD 133 [DDD]

Furlanetto, Bruno (cl)
Ponchielli, A.:Qt Fl, w. Heinrich Keller (fl), Omar Zoboli (ob), Antony Morf (cl), Gérard Wyss (pno) Accord ▲ ACD 220682 [AAD]

Furlanetto, Giuliano (trns fl)—see ORCHESTRAS & ENSEMBLES Ensemble Barocco Padua Sans Souci

Furman, M. (vn)—see ORCHESTRAS & ENSEMBLES Daniel String Quartet

Furminger, Thomas (perc)
Cage, J.:But What About The Noise...?, w. Craig Bitterman, Eberhard Blum, Patti Cudd, Thomas Furminger, Erik Oña, Christopher Swist *(rec Slee Concert Hall, Univ. at Buffalo, NY, May 28 - June 1, 1995)* Hat Art ("Hat Now" series) ▲ 6179 [DDD]

Furniss, Peter (bas hn)
Mendelssohn, F.:Concert Pieces, w. Dimitri Ashkenazy (cl), Karl-Andreas Kolly (pno) Pan ▲ 510 070 [DDD]

Furniss, Rosemary (vn)
Vivaldi, A.:Cons for 2 Vns, w. C. Warren-Green (vn), C. Warren-Green (cnd), London CO—RV.522 in a Virgin Classics ▲ 59609 [DDD]
Vivaldi, A.:Cons for 4 Vns, w. C. Warren-Green (vn), T. Bowes (vn), B. Davison (vn), C. Warren-Green (cnd), London CO—RV.580 in b Virgin Classics ▲ 59609 [DDD]

Furstner, Carl (pno)
Paganini, N.:Moto perpetuo Vn & Orch, w. R. Ricci (vn) [arr. for Violin & Piano] One-Eleven ▲ EPR 94010

Furtwängler, Wilhelm (pno)
Wolf, H.:Songs (misc), w. Elisabeth Schwarzkopf (sop) *(rec live, Salzburg Festival, 1954)* EMI Classics ▲ CDM 65749

Fusco, Randall (pno)
Beethoven, L. van:Son Hn, w. W. Slocum (hn) Dana Recording Project ▲ DRP 2
Brown, N.K.:Déjeuner sur l'herbe, w. D. Orhenstein (sop), J. Umble (a sax), K. Thomas Umble (fl) Dana Recording Project ▲ DRP 5 [DDD]
Dukas, P.:Villanelle, w. W. Slocum (hn) Dana Recording Project ▲ DRP 2
Hindemith, P.:Son Hn, w. W. Slocum (hn) Dana Recording Project ▲ DRP 2
Turok, P.:Improvisations Vn, w. S. Warner (vn), J. Umble (sax) Dana Recording Project ▲ DRP 5 [DDD]

Fuss, Hans-Joachim (trns fl)
Blavet, M.:Sons Trns Fl, w. Michael Spengler (vl), Nicolau de Figueiredo (hpd)—Op. 2/2-4 & 6; Sonataterza; Son seconda [both from Op. 3] Pan Classics ▲ CD 510089 [DDD]

Futer, Arkady (vn)
Bach, J.S.:Con for 2 Vns, w. V. Spivakov (vn), V. Spivakov (cnd), Moscow Virtuosi RCA Red Seal ▲ 7991-2-RC [DDD]
Bach, J.S.:Con for 3 Vns, w. V. Spivakov (vn), B. Garlitsky (vn), V. Spivakov (cnd), Moscow Virtuosi RCA Red Seal ▲ 7991-2-RC [DDD]

Futtrup, Mikkel (vn)
Holmboe, V.:Chamber Con 2, w. Eva Østergaard (fl), H. Koivula (cnd), Danish Radio Concert Orch *(rec Danish Radio Studio 2, June & Sept 1996)* Marco Polo/Dacapo ▲ 8.224038 [DDD]

Fuxon, Sarah (pno)—see also ORCHESTRAS & ENSEMBLES Duo Beersheva
Martin, F.:Esquisses [arr for pno] Gallo ▲ CD 633 [DDD]

Gaál, Ágnes (pno)
Cantemus 2:An International Choral Collection, w. Adolf Fredriks Girls' Choir [cnd:Bo Johansson] Caprice ▲ CAP 21498

Gabb, Harry (org)
Couperin, F.:Leçons de ténèbres (for Good Friday), w. Alfred Deller (ct), Wilfred Brown (ten), Desmond Dupré (vl) Vanguard Classics ("The Bach Guild" series) ▲ OVC 2525 [ADD]

Gabel, Bernard (tpt)
Telemann, G.P.:Musique de Table, w. J. Chambon (ob), J.-F. Paillard (cnd), Jean-François Paillard CO—sels. Erato ▲ 92868-2

Gaber, George (perc)
Baker, D.:Singers of Songs/Weavers of Dreams, w. Janos Starker (vc) *(rec Indiana Univ Opera House, Bloomington, 1980)* Laurel ▲ LR 817

Gabinsky, Viktor (mar)
Schnittke, A.:Suite in the Old Style, w. Igor Boguslavsky (va), Alla Litvinenko (hpd), Viktor Grishin (vib), Vadim Vasilykov (bells) [arr. unknown] *(rec 1989)* Consonance ▲ 81-0009 [DDD]

Gabos, Gábor (pno)
Bartók, B.:Dance Suite Hungaroton ▲ HCD 31051
Bartók, B.:Improvs (8) on Hungarian Peasant Songs Hungaroton ▲ HCD 31051
Bartók, B.:Studies, Op. 18 Hungaroton ▲ HCD 31051

Gabriel, M. (ob)
Mozart, W.A.:Con Fl, K.314, w. J. Wildner (cnd), Vienna Mozart Academy *(rec Oct. 1989)* Naxos ▲ 8.550345 [DDD]

Gabrilowitsch, Ossip (pno)
His Issued & Unissued Recordings (1923-1929) VAI Audio ▲ VAIA/IPA 1018 (m) [ADD]
Schumann, R.:Qnt Pno, w. Flonzaley String Quartet *(rec Dec. 21, 1927)* Biddulph 2-▲ LAB 072/73 [ADD]
Schumann, R.:Qnt Pno, w. Flonzaley String Quartet [abridged version] *(rec 1923-4)* VAI Audio ▲ VAIA/IPA 1018 (m) [ADD]

Gabunia, Nodar (pno)
Beethoven, L. van:Music of, w. Ekaterina Murina (pno), A. Titov (cnd), New Classical Orch—Allegro con brio [from Sym No. 5]; Adagio sostenuto [from Son No. 14 for Pno]; Scherzo; Allegro vivace [both from Sym No. 3]; Adagio cantabile [from Son No. 8 for Pno]; Egmont Ov; Allegro ma non troppo [from Son No. 23 for Pno]; Adagio un poco moto; Rondo; Allegro [all from Con No. 5 for Pno]; Leonore Ov No. 3 Infinity Digital ▲ QK 61975 [DDD]

Gadd, Charmian (vn)
Martinů, B.:Qt Ob, w. Joel Marangella (ob), Kathryn Selby (pno), Alexander Ivashkin (vc) *(rec Australian Festival of Chamber Music, July 1994)* Naxos ▲ 8.553916 [DDD]
Martinů, B.:Qnt Strs, w. Solomia Soroka (vn), Rainer Moog (va), Theodore Kuchar (va), Young-Chang Cho (vc) *(rec Australian Festival of Chamber Music, July 1994)* Naxos ▲ 8.553916 [DDD]

Gade, Nina (pno)
Glass, L.:Fant Pno *(rec Copenhagen, Nov. 17-21, 1993)* Marco Polo/Dacapo ▲ DC 9306 [DDD]
Glass, L.:Son 1 Pno *(rec Copenhagen, Nov. 17-21, 1993)* Marco Polo/Dacapo ▲ DC 9306 [DDD]
Glass, L.:Son 2 Pno *(rec Copenhagen, Nov. 17-21, 1993)* Marco Polo/Dacapo ▲ DC 9306 [DDD]

Gadzina, Tadeusz (vn)—see also ORCHESTRAS & ENSEMBLES Wilanów String Quartet
Lutoslawski, W.:Partita Vn & Pno, w. Maciej Paderewski (pno) Accord ▲ ACD 201142 [DDD]
Szymanowski, K.:Myths, w. M. Paderewski (pno) Koch Schwann ▲ 311552 [DDD]
Szymanowski, K.:Notturno e Tarantella, w. M. Paderewski (pno) Koch Schwann ▲ 311552 [DDD]

Gaffron, W. (vn)
Rasmussen, S.:Music of, w. A. Turner (vc), E. Dalsgarò (fl), A. Klett (cl), P. Sólstein (hn), J. Andreasen (pno), S.A. Johansen (cnd), *(orch unknown)*—"Warnings I"—The Naked Destruction Tutl ▲ FKT 4

Gäfvert, B. (org/hpd)
Roman, J.H.:Songs, w. S. Rydén (sop), N. E. Sparf (vn), K. Ottesen (vc), S. Úberg (thb/lt/gtr)—Thet är en kostelig ting; 4 Songs from *Vårbetraktelser* [text by Jacob Freese]:Mit hierta rörs af frögd/I foglar, vilde djur/Min andagt/Gud, alla härars Gud; Ihr Augen worzu nutzt ihr mir [w. E. Nordenfelt (harpsichord)]; Sein eigen Hertze fressen [w. Nordenfelt]; Kom tysta enslighet; La Ragion gli affetti ascolta; The Happy Man; For the Few Hours; Herren lofver af Himlen hög [Ps. 148]; 5 Songs by Olof von Dalin:Ata litet, dricka vatten/At ju mången har idag/Födas, gråta dij och lindas/Af hela tidsfördrifvet/Den är lycklig född til Verlden; Herre när jag tig hafver; Jag förtröstar på Herran; Gud, jag will sjunga om din makt *(rec May 9-11 & July 10, 1994)* Swedish Society ▲ SCD 1066

Gage, Irwin (pno)
Berg, A.:Early Songs, w. L. Popp (sop) RCA Red Seal ▲ 09026-60950-2
Berg, A.:Schliesse mir die Augen beide, w. E. Speiser (sop)—both versions [G] Jecklin ▲ JD 561-2 [ADD]
Berg, A.:Songs, Op. 2, w. E. Speiser (sop) [G] Jecklin ▲ JD 561-2 [ADD]
Brahms, J.:Songs, w. B. Fassbaender (mez)—18 songs [G] Acanta ▲ 43507
Brahms, J.:Songs, w. T. Krause (bar) *(rec Dec. 2-5, 1990)* Finlandia ▲ 4509-95862-2 [DDD]
Debussy, C.:Songs, w. J. Kaufmann (sop)—Pantomime; Claire de lune; Pierrot; Apparition; Mandoline Orfeo ▲ 305931 [DDD]
Hindemith, P.:Das Marienleben, w. G. Janowitz (sop) [G] *(rec 1982)* Jecklin-Disco ▲ JD 574-2 [ADD]
In Salzburg, w. Cheryl Studer (sop) Deutsche Grammophon ▲ 437784-2
Jugendstil:Lieder, w. Popp, Lucia (sop) RCA Red Seal ▲ 09026-60950-2
Kilpinen, Y.:Songs, w. M. Talvela (bass)—kirkkorannassa, Op. 54/2; Kesäyö, Op. 23/3; Laululle, Op. 52/3; Tunturille, Op. 52/4; Vanha Kirkko, Op. 54/1; Suvilaulu, Op. 54/3; Jänkä, Op. 52/1; Rannalta, Op. 23/1 Finlandia ▲ 4509-95846-2 [DDD]
Mussorgsky, M.:Songs & Dances, w. T. Krause (bar)—4 sels. *(rec Dec. 2-5, 1990)* Finlandia ▲ 4509-95862-2 [DDD]
Schoenberg, A.:Book of the Hanging Gardens, w. J. Kaufmann (sop) Orfeo ▲ 305931 [DDD]
Schoenberg, A.:Songs, Op. 2, w. E. Speiser (sop) [G] *(rec 1981)* Jecklin-Disco ▲ JD 561-2 [ADD]
Schubert, Franz:Der Hirt auf dem Felsen, w. E. Ameling (sop), J. Demus (pno) EMI Classics ▲ CDM 65179
Schubert, Franz:Songs (misc), w. C. Studer (sop)—Die Forelle; Nacht und Träume; Im Frühling; Klage der Ceres; etc. [G] Deutsche Grammophon ▲ 431773-2 [DDD]
Schubert, Franz:Songs (misc), w. Gundala Janowitz (sop) Deutsche Grammophon 2-▲ 437943-2 [ADD]

INSTRUMENT.

Gage, Irwin (pno) (cont.)
Schumann, R.:Dichterliebe, w. T. Krause (bar) *(rec Dec. 2-5, 1990)* Finlandia ▲ 4509-95862-2 [DDD]
Schumann, R.:Frauenliebe und -leben, w. J. Norman (sop) [G] Philips ▲ 420784-2 [ADD]
Schumann, R.:Liederkreis, Op. 39, w. J. Norman (sop) [G] Philips ▲ 420784-2 [ADD]
Strauss, R.:Songs, w. J. Kaufmann (sop)—Ich wollt' ein Sträusslein binden, Op. 68/2; Wasserrose, Op. 22/4; Malven; Säusle, liebe Myrte, Op. 68/3; Wir beide wollen springen; Amor, Op. 68/5; Waldesfahrt, Op. 69/4; Das ist ein schlechtes Wetter, Op. 69/5; Als mir dein Lied erklang, Op. 68/4; Glückes genug Orfeo ▲ 305931 [DDD]
Wolf, H.:Goethe-Lieder (sels), w. A. Auger (sop)—Agnes; An eine Äolsharfe; Auf ein altes Bild; Er ist's; Erstes Liebeslied eines Mädchens; Im Frühling; In der Frühe; Lied vom Winde; Neue Liebe; Schlafendes Jesukind; Das verlassene Mägdlein; Wo find' ich Trost?; Zitronenfalter im April [G] Hyperion ▲ CDA 66590 [DDD]
Wolf, H.:Mörike-Lieder (sels), w. A. Auger (sop)—Die Bekehrte; Frühling übers Jahr; Ganymed; Heiss mich nicht reden; Nur wer die Sehnsucht kennt; Phänomen; Die Spröde [G] Hyperion ▲ CDA 66590 [DDD]

Gagelmann, Jens (perc)
Barockmusik für Posaunen und Gesang, w. Datura Trombone Quartet, A. Scharinger (db), C. Weigel (baroque vc), T. Strauss (org), R. Haeger (perc) Ars Musici ▲ AM 1094 [DDD]
Markevitch, I.:L'Envol d'Icare, w. K. Lessing (pno), C. Lyndon-Gee (pno), R. Haeger (perc), F. Lang (perc) *(rec July 10-11, 1993)* Largo ▲ 5127 [DDD]

Gagelmann, Stefan (perc)
Hummel, B.:Music of, w. F. Bach (perc), E. Guggeis (perc), Peter Sadlo (perc)—Tempo di valse, Op. 76c; 5 Szenen für 2 Schlagzeuger, Op. 58; Marimbana, Op. 95d; 5 Aspekte für Schlagzeuger, Op. 88d; Quattro pezzi für Schlagzeuger, Op. 92; Freken 70 für vier Schlagzeuger, Op. 38 *(rec Gasteig Munich, Dec. 1993)* Thorofon ▲ CTH 2233 [DDD]

Gagnepain, Xavier (vc)—see ORCHESTRAS & ENSEMBLES Rosamunde String Quartet

Gagov, Nikolai (vn)
Bond, V.:Dreams of Flying, w. Georgy Valtchev (vn), Valentin Gerov (va), Christo Tanev (vc) Gega ▲ GD 197 [DDD]

Gajdošová, Marie (vn)
Janácek, L.:Schluck und Jau, w. J. Beneš, F. Jílek (cnd), Brno State PO *(rec Jan. 22-25, 1992)* Supraphon ▲ 111522-2 [DDD]

Gál, László (hn)—see ORCHESTRAS & ENSEMBLES Budapest Festival Horn Quartet

Gál, Zoltán (va)—see ORCHESTRAS & ENSEMBLES Keller String Quartet

Galán, Carlos (pno)—see ORCHESTRAS & ENSEMBLES Grupo Cosmos

Galard, Jean (org)
Schubert, Ferdinand:Requiem, w. D. Degos (trb), K. Markus (ten), R. Soyer (bass), J.-P. Lore (cnd), French Oratorio Orch, J.-P. Lore Vocal Ensemble, Petits Chanteurs de Notre Dame de la Joie *(rec Nov. 9-11, 1980 & Jan. 25)* Esoldun ▲ MOS 1003 [ADD]
Schubert, Franz:Requiem, w. D. Degos (trb), K. Markus (ten), R. Soyer (bass), J.-P. Lore (cnd), French Oratorio Orch, J.-P. Lore Vocal Ensemble, Petits Chanteurs de Notre Dame de la Joie *(rec Nov. 9-11, 1980 & Jan. 25)* Esoldun ▲ MOS 1003 [ADD]

Galasso, Ugo (fl)—see ORCHESTRAS & ENSEMBLES Consort Fontegara, Modo Antiquo

Galbraith, Michael (hn)
Fox, F.:Time Messages, w. David Dzubay (tpt), David McChesney (tpt), Andrew Glendenning (trbn), Andrew Oppenheim (tuba) *(rec Musical Arts Ctr, Bloomington, IN, Nov 30, 1989)* Indiana Univ School of Music ▲ 0-253-32433-5

Gales, Carl (pno)
Gottschalk, L.M.:Pno Music—The Dying Poet; Le Bananier Mastersound ▲ MST 223 [DDD]
Liszt, F.:Con 1 Pno, w. P. Freeman (cnd), National Czech SO Mastersound ▲ MST 223 [DDD]
Liszt, F.:Harmonies poétiques et religieuses—Funérailles Mastersound ▲ MST 223 [DDD]

Galimir, Felix (vn)
Boccherini, L.:Qnts Gtr, G.445-453, w. A. Diaz (gtr), A. Schneider (vn), M. Tree (va), D. Soyer (vc)—in C, G.446 *(rec 1965)* Vanguard Classics ▲ OVC 8006 [ADD]
Boccherini, L.:Qnts Strs, w. A. Schneider (vn), M. Tree (va), D. Soyer (vc), L. Harrell (vc)—Op. 13, No. 5 *(rec 1965)* Vanguard Classics ▲ OVC 8006 [ADD]
Dvořák, A.:Qnt Pno, Op. 81, w. P. Serkin (pno), A. Schneider (vn), M. Tree (va), D. Soyer (vc) *(rec 1965)* Vanguard Classics ▲ OVC 8003 [ADD]
Schubert, Franz:Qnt Strs, D.956, w. P. Frank (vn), S. Tenenbom (va), P. Wiley (vc), J. Lichten (vc) Sony Classical ▲ SMK 45901 [ADD/DDD] ■ SMT 45901

Galkovsky, A. (va)—see ORCHESTRAS & ENSEMBLES Shostakovich String Quartet

Gallagher, Evan (perc/junk/toys/pno)
Exquisite Corpses from P.S. 122, w. Watson, David (shears/stick vn/gtr/tpt), Judy Dunaway (gtr/balloons), Anthony Coleman (sampler), Raissa St. Pierre (drums), Guy Yarden (vn/pno), Leslie Ross (bn), Linda Austin (gtr), Bruce Kaplan (gtr), Doug Henderson (peckhorn/bass/toy pno), Sue Ann Harkey (gtr), Cinnie Cole (sampler), et al. ¿What Next? ▲ WN 0002 [ADD]

Gallagher, Maureen (va)
Riley, D.:Apparitions, w. M. Kaufman (fl), B. Allen (hp) CRI ▲ CD 595 [DDD]

Gallant, Julian (pno)
Górecki, H.-M.:Con Pno, w. S. Asbury (cnd), Oxford Camerata Medici Quartet ▲ MQT 4003 [DDD]
Hindemith, P.:The Four Temperaments, w. S. Asbury (cnd), Oxford Camerata Medici Quartet ▲ MQT 4003 [DDD]
Shostakovich, D.:Con 1 Pno, w. S. Asbury (cnd), Oxford Camerata Medici Quartet ▲ MQT 4003 [DDD]
Williamson, M.:Con 2 Pno, w. S. Asbury (cnd), Oxford Camerata Medici Quartet ▲ MQT 4003 [DDD]

Gallardo, Ricardo (perc)—see ORCHESTRAS & ENSEMBLES Tambuco Camerata

Gallaway, P. (vn)—see ORCHESTRAS & ENSEMBLES Coull String Quartet

Gallet, Anne (hpd)
Bach, J.S.:Das wohltemperierte Klavier—Book 2 Gallo ▲ CD 524/525 [ADD]

Galli, Claudia (bn)—see ORCHESTRAS & ENSEMBLES Rara Ensemble

Galli, T. (baroque vn/va)—see ORCHESTRAS & ENSEMBLES Musica Holmiae

Galli, T. (va)
Vivaldi, A.:Con Lt, w. N.-E. Sparf (vn), J. Lindberg (cnd), Drottningholm Baroque Ensemble BIS ▲ CD 290 [DDD]

Galling, Martin (hpd)
Bach, J.S.:Cant 202, "Wedding Cant", w. Ursula Buckel (sop), Willy Schnell (ob), Werner Keltsch (vn), Peter Buck (vc), R. Ewerhart (cnd), Württemberg CO *(rec 1965)* Vox Box 3-▲ CD3X 3039
Bach, J.S.:Cant 203, w. Claus Ocker (bass), Dieter Messlinger (vc), R. Ewerhart (cnd) *(rec 1966)* Vox Box 3-▲ CD3X 3039
Bach, J.S.:Cant 209, w. Elisabeth Speiser (sop), Helmuth Steinkraus (fl), R. Ewerhart (cnd), Württemberg CO *(rec 1966)* Vox Box 3-▲ CD3X 3039
Bach, J.S.:Cant 212, "Peasant Cant", w. Ursula Buckel (sop), Claus Ocker (bass), Gabriele Zimmerman (fl), Peter Buck (vc), R. Ewerhart (cnd), Württemberg CO *(rec 1965)* Vox Box 3-▲ CD3X 3039
Bach, J.S.:Cons for 3 Hpds (comp), w. H. Bilgram (hpd), F. Lehrndorfer (hpd), G. Kehr (cnd), Mainz CO Vox Box 2-▲ CDX 5040
Bach, J.S.:Con for 4 Hpds, w. H. Bilgram (hpd), F. Lehrndorfer (hpd), K.-H. Stolze (hpd), G. Kehr (cnd), Mainz CO Vox Box 2-▲ CDX 5040
Bach, J.S.:Inventions (30) Hpd Allegretto ▲ ACD 8028 [ADD] ■ ACS 8028
Boccherini, L.:Sons (34) Vc, w. J. Berger (vc)—Sonatas in A, F & c; Sonata in E♭ for 2 Cellos (w. Hyun-Jung Sung) ebs ▲ ebs 6031 [DDD]

Galling, Martin (pno)
Boccherini, L.:Fugues, G.73, w. J. Berger (vc), H.-J. Sung (vc) ebs ▲ EBS 6032 [DDD]
Boccherini, L.:Sons (34) Vc, w. J. Berger (vc), H.-J. Sung (vc)—G.6, 565, 571 & 572 ebs ▲ EBS 6032 [DDD]
Hummel, J.N.:Con Pno, Op. 85, w. A. Paulmüller (cnd), Stuttgart PO Preiser ▲ 90167 [ADD]

Gallo, Paul (cl)—see also ORCHESTRAS & ENSEMBLES Bronx Arts Ensemble
Brings, A.:Concert Piece for 4 Cls, w. M. Abt-Greenfield (E♭ cl), E. Gilmore (cl), B. Hysong (b cl) *(rec 1989-90)* Centaur ▲ CRC 2079 [ADD]

Gallois, Patrick (fl)
Desbrière, J.:Pièces Etranges (5), w. E. Sombart (pno) Thésis ▲ THC 82012 [DDD]
Fauré, G.:Fant Fl, w. E. Sombart (pno) Thésis ▲ THC 82012 [DDD]
Fauré, G.:Sicilienne, w. E. Sombart (pno) [flute-piano version] Thésis ▲ THC 82012 [DDD]
Flute Concertos from Sansoucci, w. Gallois, Patrick (fl), C.P.E. Bach CO [cnd:Peter Schreier] Deutsche Grammophon ▲ 439895-2
Messiaen, O.:La Merle noir, w. E. Sombart (pno) Thésis ▲ THC 82012 [DDD]
Nielsen, C.:Con Fl, w. M.-W. Chung (cnd), Gothenburg SO BIS ▲ CD 454 [DDD]
Nielsen, C.:Con Fl, w. M.-W. Chung (cnd), Gothenburg SO BIS ▲ CD 616 [DDD]
Poulenc, F.:Sxt Pno, w. P. Rogé (pno), M. Bourgue (ob), M. Portal (cl), A. Wallez (bn), A. Cazalet (hn) London ▲ 421581-2 [DDD]
Poulenc, F.:Son Fl, w. P. Rogé (pno) London ▲ 421581-2 [DDD]
Poulenc, F.:Son Fl, w. E. Sombart (pno) Thésis ▲ THC 82012 [DDD]
Roussel, A.:Joueurs de flûte, w. E. Sombart (pno) Thésis ▲ THC 82012 [DDD]
Vivaldi, A.:Cons Fl, Op. 10, Orpheus CO Deutsche Grammophon ▲ 437839-2

Galpérine, Alexis (vn)—see also ORCHESTRAS & ENSEMBLES Stanislas Ensemble
Bloch, E.:Son 1 Vn, w. Frédéric Aguessy (pno) Accord ▲ ACD 240132 [DDD]
Bloch, E.:Son 2 Vn, "Poème mystique", w. Frédéric Aguessy (pno) Accord ▲ ACD 240132 [DDD]
Furtwängler, W.:Son 2 Vn, w. F. Kerdoncuff (pno) *(rec 1989)* Timpani ▲ 1C1001 [DDD]
Herbin, R.:Qt Pno, w. E. Herbin (pno), Bruno Pasquier (va), Mark Drobinsky (vc) Gallo ▲ CD 711 [ADD]
Schmitt, F.:Hasards, w. E. Herbin (pno), B. Pasquier (va), M. Drobinsky (vc) Gallo ▲ CD 711 [ADD]

Galway, James (fl)
Bach, C.P.E.:Cons Fl, w. J. Faerber (cnd), Württemberg CO—in F, H.426, in A, H.438 (W.168) & in G, H.445 (W.169) RCA Red Seal ▲ 60244-2-RC [DDD] ■ 60244-4-RC (CrO2)
Bach, Joh. Christian:Sinf concertante Fl, w. D. Wickens (ob), W. Armon (vn), N. Jones (vc), L. Jones (cnd), London Little Orch Elektra/Nonesuch ■ 71165-4
Bach, J.S.:Con in e Fl, w. Zagreb Solisti RCA Red Seal ("Papillon Collection" series) ▲ 6517-2-RG [ADD] ■ 6517-4-RG
Bach, J.S.:Con Fl, Vn & Hpd, w. R. Wolters (vn), U. Deutschler (hpd), J. Faerber (cnd), Württemberg CO RCA Red Seal ▲ 09026-60900-2 ■ 09026-60900-4 □ 09026-60900-5
Bach, J.S.:Con 8 Hpd, w. Zagreb Solisti [arr for fl & orch in a] RCA Gold Seal ("Papillon Collection" series) ▲ 6517-2-RG [ADD] ■ 6517-4-RG
Bach, J.S.:A Musical Offering, w. Kyung-Wha Chung (vn), P. Moll (hpd)—Trio Sonata Section RCA Red Seal ("Papillon Collection" series) ▲ 6517-2-RG [ADD] ■ 6517-4-RG
Bach, J.S.:Partita Fl, BWV 1013 RCA Red Seal ▲ 0902-668182-2 [DDD]
Bach, J.S.:Sons Fl, BWV 1030-35, w. Sarah Cunningham (vl), Phillip Moll (hpd)—BWV 1032 RCA Red Seal ▲ 0902-668182-2 [DDD]
Bach, J.S.:Sons Fl, BWV 1030-35 U. Deutschler (hpd)—BWV 1032 RCA Red Seal ▲ 09026-60900-2 ■ 09026-60900-4 □ 09026-60900-5
Bach, J.S.:Son Fl, BWV 1079, w. K.-W. Chung (vn), P. Moll (hpd), M. Welsh (vc) RCA Gold Seal ("Papillon Collection" series) ▲ 6517-2-RG [ADD] ■ 6517-4-RG
Bach, J.S.:Son Fl, BWV 1079, w. Monica Huggett (vn), Sarah Cunningham (vl), Phillip Moll (hpd) RCA Red Seal ▲ 0902-668182-2 [DDD]
Bach, J.S.:Suite 2 Orch, w. Zagreb Solisti RCA Gold Seal ("Papillon Collection" series) ▲ 6517-2-RG [ADD] ■ 6517-4-RG
Bach, J.S.:Suite 2 Orch, w. J. Faerber (cnd), Württemberg CO RCA Red Seal ▲ 09026-60900-2 ■ 09026-60900-4 □ 09026-60900-5
Bach, J.S.:Trio Son, BWV 1038, w. Monica Huggett (vn), Sarah Cunningham (vl), Phillip Moll (hpd) RCA Red Seal ▲ 0902-668182-2 [DDD]
Bach, J.S.:Trio Son for 2 Fls, BWV 1039, w. Sarah Cunningham (vl), Phillip Moll (hpd) RCA Red Seal ▲ 0902-668182-2 [DDD]
Bach, J.S.:Trio Son for 2 Fls, BWV 1039, w. Sarah Cunningham (vl), Phillip Moll (hpd) RCA Red Seal ▲ 0902-668182-2 [DDD]
Bach, J.S.:Trio Son for 2 Fls, BWV 1039, w. K.-W. Chung (vn), P. Moll (hpd), M. Welsh (vc) RCA Gold Seal ("Papillon Collection" series) ▲ 6517-2-RG [ADD] ■ 6517-4-RG
Basic 100, Vol. 55, w. Richard Stoltzman (cl), Marisa Robles (hp) RCA Victor ▲ 09026-68024-2 ■ 09026-68024-4
Beethoven, L. van:Serenade Fl, Op. 25, w. J. Swensen (vn), P. Neubauer (va) RCA Red Seal ▲ 7756-2-RC [DDD] ■ 7756-4-RC
Beethoven, L. van:Serenade Strs, Op. 8, w. et al. RCA Red Seal ▲ 7756-2-RC [DDD] ■ 7756-4-RC
Beethoven, L. van:Son Fl, w. P. Moll (pno) RCA Red Seal ▲ 7756-2-RC [DDD] ■ 7756-4-RC
The Bells of St. Genevieve & Other Baroque Favorites, w. J. Levine (cnd), English CO, Vladimir Spivakov (vn), Pinchas Zukerman (vn), Canadian Brass, et al. RCA Victor ▲ 09026-61002-2 [DDD] ■ 09026-61002-4 (CrO2) □ 09026-61002-5
Carol of the Drum, w. Chieftains, Emily Mitchell (hp), Richard Stoltzman (cl), Michala Petri (rcr), Hampton String Quartet, Royal PO, Boys' Choir of Harlem RCA Victor ▲ 09026-61839-2 ■ 09026-61839-4
Christmas Sampler, w. Plácido Domingo (ten), Vienna Boys' Choir, Boston Pops Orch [cnd:Arthur Fiedler] RCA Victor ▲ 09026-61840-2 ■ 09026-61840-4
Cimarosa, D.:Serenade Fl & Gtr, w. K. Yamashita (gtr) *(rec CBS Studios, London, June 23-25, 1986)* RCA Gold Seal ▲ 61448-2
The Concerto Collection RCA Red Seal 4-▲ 60450-2-RC [ADD/DDD]
Corigliano, J.:Pied Piper Fant, w. D. Effron (cnd), Eastman Philharmonia RCA Red Seal ▲ 6602-2-RC [DDD]
Corigliano, J.:Voyage Fl, w. D. Effron (cnd), Eastman Philharmonia RCA Red Seal ▲ 6602-2-RC [DDD]
Dances for Flute RCA Red Seal ▲ 09026-60917-2 ■ 09026-60917-4
Danzi, F.:Concertante Fl, w. S. Meyer (cl), J. Faerber (cnd), Württemberg CO RCA Red Seal ▲ 09026-61976-2; ■ 09026-61976-4
Danzi, F.:Con 2 Fl, w. J. Faerber (cnd), Württemberg CO RCA Red Seal ▲ 09026-61976-2; ■ 09026-61976-4
Debussy, C.:La Fille aux cheveaux de lin for Voice, w. Christopher O'Riley (pno) [trans Galway for flute & piano] *(rec Meggen, Switzerland, Dec 6 & 7, 1994)* RCA Red Label ▲ 09026-68351-2 [DDD] ■ 09026-68351-4
Debussy, C.:Petite suite, w. Christopher O'Riley (pno)—En bateau [trans Galway for flute & piano] *(rec Meggen, Switzerland, Dec 6 & 7, 1994)* RCA Red Label ▲ 09026-68351-2 [DDD] ■ 09026-68351-4
Debussy, C.:La Plus que lente, w. Christopher O'Riley (pno) [trans Galway for flute & piano] *(rec Meggen, Switzerland, Dec 6 & 7, 1994)* RCA Red Label ▲ 09026-68351-2 [DDD] ■ 09026-68351-4
Debussy, C.:Prélude à l'après-midi d'un faune, w. Christopher O'Riley (pno) [trans Galway for flute & piano] *(rec Meggen, Switzerland, Dec 6 & 7, 1994)* RCA Red Label ▲ 09026-68351-2 [DDD] ■ 09026-68351-4
The Enchanted Forest:Melodies of Japan RCA Victor ▲ 7893-2-RC [DDD] ■ 7893-4-RC (CrO2)
Fauré, G.:Son 1 Vn, w. Christopher O'Riley (pno) [trans Galway for flute & piano] *(rec Meggen, Switzerland, Dec 6 & 7, 1994)* RCA Red Label ▲ 09026-68351-2 [DDD] ■ 09026-68351-4
Flying Dreams:A Lullaby Album, w. Emily Mitchell (hp) RCA Victor ▲ 09026-61188-2 [DDD] ■ 09026-61188-4
Galuppi, B.:Con Fl, w. C. Scimone (cnd), Venice Solisti RCA Red Seal ▲ 09026-61164-2; ■ 09026-61164-4
Galway at the Movies RCA Victor ▲ 09026-61326-2 ■ 09026-61326-4
Gianella, L.:Cons Fl (comp), w. C. Scimone (cnd), Venice Solisti—Concerto lugubre RCA Red Seal ▲ 09026-61164-2; ■ 09026-61164-4
Giuliani, M.:Grand Duo Concertant, Op. 52, w. K. Yamashita (gtr) RCA Red Seal ▲ 09026-60237-2
Giuliani, M.:Grand Duo Concertant Fl, w. K. Yamashita (gtr) *(rec CBS Studios, London, June 23-25, 1986)* RCA Gold Seal ▲ 61448-2
Giuliani, M.:Grand Son Fl, w. K. Yamashita (gtr) RCA Red Seal ▲ 09026-60237-2
Golden Galway, w. National PO London [cnd:Charles Gerhardt] RCA Gold Seal ▲ 09026-60924-2 ■ 09026-60924-4
Greatest Hits RCA Victor ▲ 7778-2-RC [DDD] ■ 7778-4-RC (CrO2)

▲ = CD ♦ = Enhanced CD Δ = MD ■ = Cassette Tape □ = DCC

Galway, James (fl) (cont.)
Greatest Hits, Vol. 2
RCA Victor ▲ 09026-61178-2 [DDD] ■ 09026-61178-4 (CrO2) □ 09026-61178-5
In Dulci Jubilo, w. Munich Radio Orch, Domspatzen Boys' Choir [cnd:John Georgiadis]
RCA Red Seal ▲ 60736-2-RC [DDD] ■ 60736-4-RC
James Galway & Friends RCA Victor 4-▲ 60114-2-RC
James Galway & The Chieftains:In Ireland RCA Victor ▲ 5798-2-RC [DDD] ■ 5798-4-RC (CrO2)
James Galway & The Chieftains:Over the Sea to Skye (The Celtic Connection)
RCA Victor ▲ 60424-2-RC [DDD] ■ 60424-4-RC (CrO2)
James Galway:Seasons, w. Chieftans, Emily Mitchell (sgr)
RCA Victor ▲ 09026-61915-2 ■ 09026-61915-4 (CrO2)
Khachaturian, A.:Con Vn, w. M.-W. Chung (cnd), Royal PO RCA Red Seal ▲ 57010-2
Khachaturian, A.:Masquerade (sels), w. M.-W. Chung (cnd), Royal PO—Waltz
RCA Red Seal ▲ 57010-2
Khachaturian, A.:Spartacus (sels), w. M.-W. Chung (cnd), Royal PO—Adagio of Spartacus & Phrygia
RCA Red Seal ▲ 57010-2
Lazarof, H.:Cadence V *(rec 1973)* CRI ▲ CD 631
Lazarof, H.:Con Fl, w. H. Lazarof (cnd), New Philharmonia Orch CRI ▲ CD 588 [ADD]
The Magic Flute of James Galway, w. National PO of London [cnd:Charles Gerhardt]
RCA Gold Seal ▲ 09026-60918-2 ■ 09026-60918-4
Mercadante, S.:Cons in D, e & E for Fl, w. C. Scimone (cnd), Venice Solisti
RCA Red Seal ▲ 09026-61447-2
Mozart, W.A.:Andante Fl, K.315/285a, w. J. Galway (cnd), CO of Europe
RCA Red Seal 2-▲ 7861-2-RC [DDD]
Mozart, W.A.:Andante Fl, K.315/285a, w. R. Baumgartner (cnd), Lucerne Festival Strings
RCA Victor ▲ 09026-68024-2; ■ 09026-68024-2
Mozart, W.A.:Andante Fl, K.315/285a, w. R. Baumgartner (cnd), Lucerne Festival Strings
RCA Gold Seal ▲ 6723-2-RG [ADD] ■ 6723-4-RG (CrO2)
Mozart, W.A.:Cons Fl, w. J. Galway (cnd), CO of Europe RCA Red Seal 2-▲ 7861-2-RC [DDD]
Mozart, W.A.:Con Fl, K.313, w. R. Baumgartner (cnd), Lucerne Festival Strings
RCA Gold Seal ▲ 6723-2 [ADD] ■ 6723-4 (CrO2)
Mozart, W.A.:Con Fl, K.313, w. A. Blau (fl), F. Helmis (hp), H. von Karajan (cnd), Berlin PO
EMI Classics ▲ CDM 69187
Mozart, W.A.:Con Fl Hp, w. A. Blau (fl), F. Helmis (hp), H. von Karajan (cnd), Berlin PO
EMI Classics ▲ CDM 69187
Mozart, W.A.:Con Fl Hp, w. M. Robles (hp), J. Galway (cnd), CO of Europe
RCA Red Seal 2-▲ 7861-2-RC [DDD]
Mozart, W.A.:Con Fl Hp, w. Marisa Robles (hp), E. Mata (cnd), London SO
RCA Gold Seal ▲ 09026-68113-2 [ADD]
Mozart, W.A.:Con Fl Hp, w. M. Robles (hp), E. Mata (cnd), London SO
RCA Gold Seal ▲ 6723-2 [ADD] ■ 6723-4 (CrO2)
Mozart, W.A.:Con Fl Hp, w. Marisa Robles (hp), E. Mata (cnd), London SO
RCA Victor ▲ 09026-68024-2; ■ 09026-68024-2
Mozart, W.A.:Divert Hns Strs, K.334, w. J. Galway (cnd), CO of Europe—Menuetto
RCA Red Seal 2-▲ 7861-2 [DDD]
Mozart, W.A.:Qt Ob, K.370, w. Tokyo String Quartet members
RCA Red Seal ▲ 09026-60442-2 ■ 09026-60442-4
Mozart, W.A.:Son 11 Pno, w. J. Galway (cnd), CO of Europe—Rondo
RCA Red Seal 2-▲ 7861-2-RC [DDD]
Nielsen, C.:Children Are Playing *(rec CBS Studios, London, Feb 25, 1986)*
RCA Red Seal ▲ 07863-56359-2 [ADD]
Nielsen, C.:Con Fl, w. J. Galway (cnd), Danish National RSO *(rec Danish Radio Concert Hall, Copenhagen, Mar 17, 1985)* RCA Red Seal ▲ 07863-56359-2 [ADD]
Nielsen, C.:Faith & Hope, w. Brian Hawkins (va) *(rec CBS Studios, London, Feb 25, 1986)*
RCA Red Seal ▲ 07863-56359-2 [ADD]
Nielsen, C.:Fants Ob, w. Phillip Moll (pno) *(rec CBS Studios, London, Feb 25, 1986)*
RCA Red Seal ▲ 07863-56359-2 [ADD]
Nielsen, C.:Fog is Lifting, w. Sioned Williams (hp) *(rec Wilshire United Church, Hollywood, CA, Dec 2, 1986)* RCA Red Seal ▲ 07863-56359-2 [ADD]
Nielsen, C.:Qnt Ww, w. Björn Carl Nielsen (ob), Niels Thomsen (cl), Jens Tofte-Hansen (bn), Björn Fosdal (hn) *(rec Vangede Church, Copenhagen, Mar 16, 1985)*
RCA Red Seal ▲ 07863-56359-2 [ADD]
Nocturne, w. National PO of London [cnd:David Measham] RCA Victor ▲ RCD1-4810 ■ ARK1-4810
Noël, w. Canadian Brass, Canadian Brass Jazz All-Stars, Angel Romero (gtr), *(children's choir unknown)*, Richard Stoltzman (cl), Harolyn Blackwell (sop), Jerry Hadley (ten), King's Singers *(rec Apr. 17-20, 1994)* RCA Victor ▲ 09026-62683-2 ■ 09026-62683-4
O Holy Night:Christmas Favorites, w. Richard Stoltzman (cl), Michala Petri (rcr), Emily Mitchell (hp), Canadian Brass, Boston Pops Orch [cnd:Arthur Fiedler]
RCA Victor ▲ 09026-61836-2 ■ 09026-61836-4
Pachelbel Canon & other Baroque Favorites
RCA Red Seal ▲ 09026-61928-2 [DDD] ■ 09026-61928-4
Pachelbel Canon & Other Baroque Hits, w. A. Fiedler (cnd), Leopold Stokowski (cnd), et al.
RCA Victor ▲ 60840-2-RG ■ 60840-4-RG
The Pachelbel Canon & Other Favorites, w. Sydney SO
RCA Victor ▲ 4063-2-RG [ADD] ■ AFK1-4063
Paganini, N.:Son concertata, w. K. Yamashita (gtr) *(rec CBS Studios, London, June 23-25, 1986)*
RCA Gold Seal ▲ 61448-2
Pergolesi, G.B.:Con Fl, w. C. Scimone (cnd), Venice Solisti
RCA Red Seal ▲ 09026-61164-2; ■ 09026-61164-4
Piacentino, R.A.:Con Fl, w. C. Scimone (cnd), Venice Solisti
RCA Red Seal ▲ 09026-61164-2; ■ 09026-61164-4
A Portrait RCA Victor Red Seal 2-▲ 0902-668412-2 [DDD]
Quantz, J.J.:Cons Fl & Orch, w. J. Faerber (cnd), Württemberg CO
RCA Red Seal ▲ 60247-2-RC [DDD] ■ 60247-4-RC (CrO2)
Ravel, M.:Intro & Allegro, w. Hedi Lehwalder (hp), Richard Stoltzman (cl), Tokyo String Quartet
RCA Red Seal ▲ 09026-62552-2
Rodrigo, J.:Concierto de Aranjuez, w. Kazuhito Yamashita (gtr), J.-F. Paillard (cnd), Jean-François Paillard CO RCA Gold Seal ▲ 09026-68428-2 ■ 09026-68428-4
Rodrigo, J.:Concierto pastorale, w. E. Mata (cnd), Philharmonia Orch
RCA Gold Seal ▲ 09026-68428-2
Rodrigo, J.:Fant para un gentilhombre, w. E. Mata (cnd), Philharmonia Orch [arr Galway for flute & orchestra] RCA Gold Seal ▲ 09026-68428-2
Rossini, G.:Andante con variazioni Va, w. K. Yamashita (gtr) *(rec CBS Studios, London, June 23-25, 1986)* RCA Gold Seal ▲ 61448-2
Serenade RCA Victor ▲ 60033-2-RC [ADD] ■ 60033-4-RC (CrO2)
Sometimes When We Touch, w. Cleo Laine (sgr) RCA Victor ▲ RCD1-3628 ■ ARK1-3628
Song of the Seashore & Other Melodies of Japan RCA Victor ▲ RCD1-3534 ■ ARK1-3534
Tartini, G.:Con in G Fl, w. C. Scimone (cnd), Venice Solisti
RCA Red Seal ▲ 09026-61164-2 ■ 09026-61164-4
Telemann, G.P.:Sons Fl, w. Michel Debost (fl)—in b for 2 Fl, Op. 2/4 *(rec Salle Wagram, Paris, July 1974)* EMI Classics ▲ CDK 65340 [ADD]
Vivaldi, A.:Cons Fl (misc), w. C. Scimone (cnd), Venice Solisti—6 concerti—in a, RV.108; in D, RV.427; in D, RV.429; in G, RV.436; in G, RV.438; in a, RV.440
RCA Red Seal ▲ 7928-2-RC [DDD] ■ 7928-4-RC (CrO2)
Vivaldi, A.:Cons Fl, Op. 10, New Irish CO RCA Gold Seal ▲ 09026-61351-2 ■ 09026-61351-4
Vivaldi, A.:Cons Vn, Op. 8/1-4, "The Four Seasons", w. J. Galway (cnd), Zagreb Solisti
RCA Gold Seal ▲ 60748-2 [ADD] ■ 60748-4 (CrO2)
The Wayward Wind RCA Victor ▲ RCD1-4222 ■ AFK1-4222

Galway, James (fl) (cont.)
Widor, C.M.:Suite Fl, w. Christopher O'Riley (pno) *(rec Meggen, Switzerland, Dec 6 & 7, 1994)*
RCA Red Label ▲ 09026-68351-2 [DDD] ■ 09026-68351-4
Wild Classics:A Celebration of Animals & Nature, w. Ofra Harnoy (vc), Martin Hoherman (vc), Emily Mitchell (hp), Michael Dussek (pno), Samuel Lipman (pno), Leo Litwin (pno), Gerhard Oppitz (pno), Isao Tomita (synths), Boston Pops Orch [cnd:Arthur Fiedler], Chicago SO [cnd:Fritz Reiner]
RCA Red Seal ▲ 09026-68483-2 ■ 09026-68483-4
The Wind Beneath My Wings
RCA Victor ▲ 60862-2-RC [DDD] ■ 60862-4-RC (CrO2) □ 09026-60862-5

Galynin, Dmitri (pno)
Medtner, N.:Music for Vn & Pno, w. A. Shirinsky (vn)—Sonata No. 1 in b, Op. 21; Sonata No. 2 in G, Op. 44; Sonata No. 3 in e, Op. 57; Nocturnes, Op. 16; Canzonas, Op. 43; Danzas, Op. 43
MK 2-▲ MKA 417109 [DDD]

Gamard, Jean-Marie (vc)
Saint-Saëns, C.:Allegro appassionato, w. P. Kuentz (cnd), Paul Kuentz Orch
Pierre Verany ▲ PVY 730053 [DDD]
Saint-Saëns, C.:Con 1 Vc, w. P. Kuentz (cnd), Paul Kuentz Orch Pierre Verany ▲ PVY 730053 [DDD]
Schumann, R.:Con Vc, w. P. Kuentz (cnd), Paul Kuentz Orch Pierre Verany ▲ PVY 730053 [DDD]

Gambini, Gianfranco (ob)
Boccherini, L.:Qnts Fl, G.431-436, w. Rome Solisti—No. 1 in G *(rec Rome, 1996)*
musicaimmagine ▲ MR 10031

Gambini, Maurizio (vc)—see also ORCHESTRAS & ENSEMBLES Rome Solisti
Haydn, J.:Lo Speziale, w. Gil Manuel Beltran (ten—Sempronio), Daniela Broganelli (sgr—Volpino), Cinzia Forte (sgr—Grilletta), Paolo Pellegrini (sgr—Mengone), Marco Tinarelli (db), Gabriele Catalucci (hpd), F. Maestri (cnd), In Canto CO *(rec 1993)* Bongiovanni 2-▲ GB 2171/72 [DDD]

Gamper, David (org/fl/elec)
Deep Listening Band:Music of Deep Listening Band, w. Stuart Dempster (trbn/didjeridu/garden hose), Pauline Oliveros (acc/elec)—Invocation; Processional [both w. Julie Lyon Balliet (sgr)]; Hi Bali, Hi; Sanctuary; Non-Stop Flight [w. Thomas Buckner (sgr), Julie Lyon Balliet (sgr), Joe McPhee (b cl/tpt), Margarit Shenker (acc/sgr), Nego Gato (perc), Carol Chappell (perc), Jason Finkleman (perc), Women Who Drum (perc)] *(rec Trinity United Methodist Church Sanctuary, 1993-94)* Mode ▲ mode 46

Ganchini, C. (vn)
Schobert, J.:Music of, w. L. Sgrizzi (pno), V. Méjean (vn), Philipp Bosbach (vc)—Qts. in f, Op. 7/2 & in E♭, Op. 14/1; Sons. in d & A, Op. 14/4 & 5; Trios in D & B♭, Op. 16/1 & 4
Musique d'Abord ▲ HMA 1901294

Gandini, Gerardo (pno)—see ORCHESTRAS & ENSEMBLES New Tango Sex-tet
Gandolfi, Josephine (pno)—see also ORCHESTRAS & ENSEMBLES Phoenix Trio
Cowell, H.:Hymn & Fuguing Tune 9, w. Sarah Fiene (vc) Koch International Classics ▲ KIC 7205 [DDD]
Cowell, H.:Set of 5, w. Kay Stern (vn), Rick Kvistad (perc)
Koch International Classics ▲ KIC 7205 [DDD]
Gandolfi, M.:Il Ventaglio di Josephine *(rec 1992)* CRI ▲ CD 661 [DDD]

Gandolfo, C. (pno)
Cilea, F.:Adriana Lecouvreur (sels), w. M. Olivero (sop—Adriana), M. Moretto (mez—Princess di Bouillon), A. Cupido (ten—Maurizio), O. Mori (bar—Michonnet) *(rec Apr. 1993)*
Bongiovanni ▲ GB 2515 [DDD]
Omaggio a Magda Olivero, w. Magda Olivero (sop), Marco Montanari (org)
Great Opera Performances 2-▲ GOP 795

Geneva, Daniella (perc)
Abe, K.:Dream of the Cherry Blossom Cala ▲ CAL 77002
Miki, M.:Mar Spiritual Cala ▲ CAL 77002
Miki, M.:Time Cala ▲ CAL 77002
Takemitsu, T.:Rain Tree Cala ▲ CAL 77002
Tanaka, T.:Movts Cala ▲ CAL 77002
Yuyama, A.:Divert Perc Cala ▲ CAL 77002

Gangler, A (ob)—see ORCHESTRAS & ENSEMBLES Cologne Divitia Ensemble
Gangler, Alison (shms/WX7-MIDI wind controller)—see ORCHESTRAS & ENSEMBLES Vox
Gangolfi, D. (instr)—see ORCHESTRAS & ENSEMBLES Present Music
Ganoci, Anton (mand)
Vivaldi, A.:Con for 2 Mands, w. F. Pavlinek (mand), A. Janigro (cnd), Zagreb Solisti *(rec 1964)*
Vanguard Classics ("The Bach Guild" series) ▲ OVC 2006 [ADD]

Gantiez, Jean-Paul (hn)
Schumann, R.:Konzertstück Hns, w. Jean-Claude Barro (hn), Alain Courtois (hn), Jean-Jacques Justafre (hn), *(orch unknown)*—Lebhaft; Romanze Erato ▲ 94801-2

Gantolea, Elena (hpd)
Constantinescu, P.:Con Hp, w. I. Conta (cnd), Romanian Radio-TV Orch *(rec 1981)*
Olympia ▲ OCD 415 [AAD]

Gantvarg, Mikhail (vn)
Bach, J.S.:Con 1 Vn, w. M. Gantvarg (cnd), St. Petersburg Soloists Audiophile Classics ▲ 101.021
Bach, J.S.:Con 2 Vn, w. M. Gantvarg (cnd), St. Petersburg Soloists Audiophile Classics ▲ 101.021
Bach, J.S.:Con Vn & Ob, w. Chanjafi Tchinakajev (ob), M. Gantvarg (cnd), St. Petersburg Soloists
Audiophile Classics ▲ 101.021
Bach, J.S.:Con for 2 Vns, w. Olga Martinova (vn), M. Gantvarg (cnd), St. Petersburg Soloists
Audiophile Classics ▲ 101.021
Haydn, J.:Con 1 Vn, w. R. Martynov (cnd), St. Petersburg State SO, St. Petersburg Soloists
Audiophile Classics ▲ 101.023

Ganz, Brian (pno)
Bach, J.S.:Cons for 3 Hpds (comp), w. F. Braley (pno), S. Prutsman (pno), P. Peire (cnd), Collegium Instrumentale Brugense René Gailly ▲ CD 87065 [DDD]
Dutilleux, H.:Preludes Pno—D'ombre et de silence; Sur un même accord; Le jeu des contraires
Accord ▲ ACD 202442 [DDD]
Dutilleux, H.:Résonances Accord ▲ ACD 202442 [DDD]
Dutilleux, H.:Son Pno Accord ▲ ACD 202442 [DDD]
Mozart, W.A.:Con 7 Pnos, w. F. Braley (pno), S. Prutsman (pno), P. Peire (cnd), Collegium Instrumentale Brugense René Gailly ▲ CD 87065 [DDD]
Rachmaninoff, S.:Pno Music (pno 6-hands), w. Frank Braley (pno), Stephen Prutsman (pno)—Romance; Valse René Gailly ▲ CD 87065 [DDD]
Schumann, R.:Son 1 Vn, w. S. Tran Ngoc (vn) REM ▲ REM 311218 [DDD]
Schumann, R.:Son 2 Vn, w. S. Tran Ngoc (vn) REM ▲ REM 311218 [DDD]

Ganz, Heidrun (va)
Gragnani, F.:Qt for 2 Gtrs, w. S. Prunnbauer (gtr), I. Turnagoel (gtr), D. Klöcker (cl) *(rec Sept. 1984)*
Koch Treasure ▲ 31612-2 [ADD]
Tal, J.:Else-Hommage, w. C. Gayer (sop), J. Bliese (nar), G. Teutsch (vc), N. Hauptmann (hn), K. Helwig (pno), J. Tal (cnd) Academy ▲ ACA 8506 [ADD]

Ganz, Heidrun (vn)
Boccherini, L.:Syms, w. S. Prunnbauer (gtr), Jürgen Hollerbuhl (ob), B. Vestre (ob), Jörn Maatz (ob), H. Maile (vn), R. Forest (vc), J. Stárek (cnd), Berlin RIAS Sinfonietta—in C, G.495 (Op. 21/3) *(rec Dec. 1979)* Koch Treasure ▲ 31612-2 [ADD]
Spohr, L.:Con Str Qt, w. E. Sebestyen (vn), H. Beyerle (va), M. Ostertag (vc), G. Albrecht (cnd), Berlin RSO Koch Schwann ▲ CD 311088 [DDD] ■ MC 211088 (D)
Spohr, L.:Var, Op. 6, w. E. Sebestyen (vn), H. Beyerle (va), M. Ostertag (vc)
Koch Schwann ▲ CD 311088 [DDD] ■ MC 211088 (D)

Ganz, M. (pno)
Mozart, W.A.:Sons Vn Pno (misc), w. P. Coehand (vn)—in C, K.296 & in G, K.301 Gallo ▲ CD 701
Schubert, Franz:Sonatina Vn, D.408, w. P. Coehand (vn) Gallo ▲ CD 701

Garay, M. (perc)
Blanchard, P.:Music of, w. P. Blanchard (vn), V. Pagliarin (vn), C. Mouton (bass), C. Terranova (kbd), L. Robin (dr)—Isidora; Koid'9; Perdoname; Folklores; Train de sables; Lithops; Marguesas Keys; Bodas de sangue *(rec Nov. 1992)* OMD ▲ CD 1538 [DDD]

Garbarek, Jan (t sax)
Karaindrou, E.:Film Music, w. Vangelis Christopoulos (ob), Anthis Sokratis (tpt), Nikos Guinos (cl), Tassos Diakoyiorgis (santouri), Vangelis Skouras (hn), Petros Protopapas (fl), Andreas Tsekouras (acc), Christos Sfetsas (vc), Eleni Karaindrou (pno/voc), L. Chalkiadakis (cnd), *(ensemble unknown)*—Farewell Theme; Scream; Improv. On Farewell & Waltz Theme; Farewell Theme II [all from The Beekeeper; w. Jan Garbarek (ten sax), Tassos Diakoyiorgis (satouri), Vassilis Dertilis (kbd), Eleni Karaindrou (pno), Lefteris Chalkiadakis (cnd)]; Elegy for Rosa; Rosa's Song (text:Christofis) [both from Rosa; w. Vangelis Skouras (Fr hn), Petros Protopapas (fl), Alekos Christidis (timp), Eleni Karaindrou (voc), Lefteis Chalkiadakis (cnd)]; Fairytale; Parade; Return; Song [all from Happy Homecoming, Comrade; w. Vangelis Skouras (Fr hn), Christos Sfetsas (vc), Aliki Krithari (hp), Andreas Tsekouras (acc), Eleni Karaindrou (pno), Nelli Semitekolo (pno), Anthis Sokratis (tpt), Lefteris Chalkiadakis (cnd)]; Wandering in Alexandria (2 vers) [both from Wandering; w. Tassos Diakoyiorgis (santouri), Nelli Semitekolo (prepared pno), Anthis Sokratis (tpt), Nikos Guinos (cl), Katerina Ktona (hpd), Christos Sfetsas (vc)]; The Journey [from Voyage to Cythera]; Adagio [from Landscape in the Mist] [both w. Vangelis Christopoulos (ob), str orch, Lefteris Chalkiadakis (cnd)] ECM ▲ 78118-21429-2 [AAD]

Garben, Cord (pno)
Cornelius, P.:Duets, Op. 6, w. Edith Mathis (sop), Hidenori Komatsu (bar) CPO ▲ CPO 999262 [DDD]
Cornelius, P.:Duets, Op. 16, w. Edith Mathis (sop), Hidenori Komatsu (bar) CPO ▲ CPO 999262 [DDD]
Loewe, C.:Songs, w. Edith Mathis (sop)—Des Bettlers Tochter von Bednall Green; Der Freibeuter; Meine Ruh'ist hin; Szene aus Faust; Der Fischer; Gesang der Königin Maria Stuart auf den Tod Franz II; In die Ferne; Jephtas's Tochter; Die Zugvögel; Brautlied; Die engste Nähe; Frülingsweihe; Taubenpost; An den Wassern zu Babel; Die schlanke Wasserlilie *(rec Studio Villa Berg, Mar 1995)* CPO ▲ 999334-2 [DDD]
Loewe, C.:Songs, w. Kurt Moll (bass)—Kleiner Haushalt; Die Heinzalmännchen; Heinrich der Vogler; Das Vaterland; Der Nöck; Liederkranz for Bass, Op. 145; Prinz Eugen; Archibald Douglas *(rec Radio Berlin, Nov 1994)* CPO ▲ 999306-2 [DDD]
Schubert, Franz:Songs (misc), w. K. Moll (bass)—18 songs [G] Orfeo ▲ 021821 [DDD]
Schubert, Franz:Songs (misc), w. B. Fassbaender (mez)—19 songs—D.138, 149, 216, 224, 225, 226, 257, 259, 295, 321, 328, 478, 544, 558, 719, 764, 766, 768, 877 [G] Sony Classical ▲ SK 53104 [DDD]
Schubert, Franz:Winterreise, w. K. Moll (bass) [G] Orfeo 2-▲ 042832 2-■ 042832
Schumann, R.:Songs, w. Edith Mathis (sop), Hidenori Komatsu (bar)—Duets from Opp. 37, 43, 74, 78 & 79 CPO ▲ CPO 999262 [DDD]
Weill, K.:Songs, w. B. Fassbaender (mez)—Complainte de la Seine; Youkali; Es regnet; Wie lange noch?; Nanna's Lied; Berlin im Licht Harmonia Mundi France ▲ HMC 901420
Zemlinsky, A. von:Songs (misc), w. S. Kimbrough (bar)—(23) from Opp. 2, 5, 6, 7, 8, 10, 13, 22 & 27 [G] Acanta ▲ 43509 [DDD]
Zemlinsky, A. von:Songs (misc), w. B. Bonney (sop), A.-S. von Otter (mez), H.-P. Blochwitz (ten), A. Schmidt (bar)—Lieder, Op. 2; Gesänge, Op. 5; Walzer-Gesänge nach toskanischen Volksliedern, Op. 6; Irmelin Rose und andere Gesänge, Op. 7; Turmwächterlied und andere Gesänge, Op. 8; Ehetanzlied und andere Gesänge, Op. 10; Schlummerlied; 6 Gesänge, Op. 13; 6 Lieder, Op. 22; Ahnung Beatricens; 12 Lieder, Op. 27 [G] Deutsche Grammophon 2-▲ 427348-2 [DDD]
Zemlinsky, A. von:Songs (misc), w. Ruth Ziesak (sop), Iris Vermillion (mez), Hans Peter Blochwitz (ten), Andreas Schmidt (bar)—Die schlanke Wasserlilie; Gute Nacht; Liebe und Frühling; Ich sah mein eigen Angesicht; In der Ferne; Waldgespräch; Der Rosenband; Abendstern; Des Mädchens Klage; Der Morgenstern; Wandl' ich im Wald des Abends; Orientalisches Sonett; Süsse, süsse Sommernacht; Herbsten; Nun schwillt der See so bang; In der Sonnengasse; Herr Bombardil; Es war ein alter König; Uber eine Wiege; Mädel, kommst du mit zum Tanz?; Jane Grey; Der verlorene Haufen; Vorspiel; Ansturm; Auf See; Noch spür ich ihren Atem; Hörtest du denn nicht hinein; Die Beiden; Harmonie des Abends; Und einmal gehst du *(rec Stuttgart & Berlin, Germany, Mar. 30–June 8, 1993)* Sony Classical ▲ SK 57960

Garcia, G. (vc)
Beethoven, L. van:Serenade Strs, Op. 8, w. C. Conway (vn), P. Silverthorne (va) [arr.] Meridian ▲ CDE 84199

Garcia, Gerald (gtr)
Albéniz, I.:Gtr Music, w. P. Breiner (cnd), Czech State PO—Asturias; Zamba Granadina [orchd Breiner] Naxos ▲ 8.550220 [DDD]
Bach, J.S.:Con 1 Hpd, w. P. Breiner (cnd), Camerata Cassovia [arr. Garcia from Con. 1 for Harpsichord, BWV 1052] June 6-8, 1990) Naxos ▲ 8.550274 [DDD]
Brazilian Portrait Naxos ▲ 8.550226 [DDD]
Falla, M. de:Gtr Music, w. P. Breiner (cnd), Czech State PO—Aragonesa [arr guitar & orchestra Breiner] Naxos ▲ 8.550220 [DDD]
Granados, E.:Pno Music (misc), w. P. Breiner (pno), Czech State PO [arranged by cond. for guitar & orch.]—Spanish Dances Nos. 2,6,8 & 11; Zapateado Naxos ▲ 8.550220 [DDD]
Kreutzer, J.:Grand Trio, w. C. Conway (fl), P. Silverthorne (va) Meridian ▲ CDE 84199
Latin American Guitar Festival Naxos ▲ 8.550273 [DDD]
The Latin Guitar Collection *(rec Tonstudio van Geest, Heidelberg, June 30–July 2, 1989)* Naxos 4-▲ 8.504008 [DDD]
Molino, F.:Trio Fl, Op. 45, w. C. Conway (fl), P. Silverthorne (va) Meridian ▲ CDE 84199
Rodrigo, J.:Concierto de Aranjuez, w. P. Breiner (cnd), Czech State PO Naxos ▲ 8.550220 [DDD]
The Romance Collection *(rec Tonstudio van Geest, Heidelberg, Dec 1989)* Naxos 4-▲ 8.504005 [DDD]
Romantic French Music For Guitar & Orchestra, w. CSFR State PO Košice [cnd:P. Breiner] Naxos ▲ 8.550480 [DDD]
Romantic Guitar Favorites Naxos ▲ 8.550296 [DDD]
Schubert, Franz:Qt Fl, w. C. Conway (fl), P. Silverthorne (va), C. Tunnell (vc) Meridian ▲ CDE 84118
Vivaldi, A.:Cons Gtr, w. P. Breiner (cnd), Camerata Cassovia [all arr. Garcia]—in D, RV.93; in e, RV.277; in C, RV.425; in d, RV.540 (w. Karol Petroczi [viol]) *(rec June 6-8 & Dec. 10-13, 19)* Naxos ▲ 8.550274 [DDD]

Garcia, Gustavo (vn)
Tubin, E.:Ballade Vn, w. N. Järvi (cnd), Gothenburg SO BIS ▲ CD 337 [DDD]

Garcia, José-Luis (vn)
Albinoni, T.:Adagio Org, w. I. Watson (org), M. Eade (vn), English CO Virgin Classics ▲ CDZ 59656
Albinoni, T.:Cons Obs, w. N. Black (ob), M. Eade (vn), English CO—in d Virgin Classics ▲ CDZ 59656
Bach, J.S.:Con for 2 Vns, w. P. Zukerman (vn), P. Zukerman (cnd), English CO RCA Red Seal ▲ 60718-2-RC [DDD] ■ 60718-4-RC (CrO2) ▯ 09026-60718-5
Bach, J.S.:Con for 2 Vns, w. H. Szeryng (vn), H. Szeryng (cnd), English CO *(rec live, Queen Elizabeth Hall, London Feb 26, 1972)* Intaglio ▲ INCD 7201 [ADD]
Bottesini, G.:Gran Duo Concertant, w. T. Martin (db) ASV ▲ ASV 563 [DDD]
Corelli, A.:Concerti grossi, Op. 6, w. M. Eade (vn), W. Bennett (fl), N. Black (ob), I. Watson (hpd/org), English CO—No. 2 in F Virgin Classics ▲ CDZ 59656
Reindl, C.:Sinf concertante, w. H. Griffiths (cnd), English CO Novalis ▲ 150031 [DDD]
Schubert, Franz:Adagio & Rondo concertante Vn, w. Y. Menuhin (cnd), English CO [in A] Start Classics ▲ SCD 13
Vaughan Williams, R.:The Lark Ascending, w. Y. Menuhin (cnd), English CO Arabesque ▲ Z 6568
Vivaldi, A.:Cons Vn (misc), English CO ASV ("Quicksilva" series) ▲ ASQ 6148 [DDD]
Vivaldi, A.:Cons Vn, Op. 3/1-12, "L'estro armonico", w. M. Eade (vn), I. Watson (hpd), I. Watson (cnd), English CO Virgin Classics ▲ CDZ 59656
Vivaldi, A.:Cons Vn, Op. 8/1-4, "The Four Seasons", English CO ASV ("Quicksilva" series) ▲ ASQ 6148 [DDD]
Vivaldi, A.:Cons Vn, Op. 8/1-4, "The Four Seasons", w. Maurice Hasson (vn), Manoug Parikian (vn), Daniel Phillips (vn), Y. Menuhin (cnd), English CO [each movt. w. different vn soloist] Start Classics ▲ SCD 13

Garcia, Luiz (hn)—see ORCHESTRAS & ENSEMBLES Empire Brass Quintet
Garcia, Russell (hn)—see ORCHESTRAS & ENSEMBLES Los Angeles Horn Club

Garcia, Serge (vn)
Garcia & Geliot, w. Huguette Geliot (hp) Quantum ▲ QM 6938 [DDD]
Klein, G.:Duo in Quarter Tones, w. Françoise Gnéri (va) Arion ▲ ARN 68272 [DDD]

Garcia, Serge (vn) (cont.)
Klein, G.:Duo Vn & Vc, w. David Simpson (vc) Arion ▲ ARN 68272 [DDD]
Klein, G.:Four Movements, w. Sona Khochafian (vn), Françoise Gnéri (va), David Simpson (vc) Arion ▲ ARN 68272 [DDD]
Klein, G.:Movements Str Qt, w. Sona Khochafian (vn), Françoise Gnéri (va), David Simpson (vc) Arion ▲ ARN 68272 [DDD]

Garcin-Marrou, Michel (alphn)
Mozart, L.:Sinf pastorella, w. J. Malgoire (cnd), La Grande Écurie et la Chambre du Roy Sony Classical ("Essential Classics" series) ▲ SBK 62639 ■ SBT 62639

Gardon, Olivier (pno)
Alkan, C.-V.:Chamber Music, w. Dong-Suk Kang (vn), Y. Chiffoleau (vc)—Grand Duo concertant for Violin & Piano, Op. 21; Sonate de Concert for Cello & Piano, Op. 47; Trio for Piano, Violin & Cello, Op. 30 Timpani ▲ 1C 1013 [DDD]

Gareis, Ute (pno)
Wyshnegradsky, I.:Chant nocturne, w. Martin Gelland (vn), Klaus-Georg Pohl (pno) *(rec Tonhallen, Sundsvall/Sweden & Holmsund Church, Aug 24-27 & Sept 8, 1995)* Vienna Modern Masters ▲ VMM 2017 [DDD]

Garfield, Bernard (bn)
Haydn, J.:Sinf concertante, w. John DeLancie (ob), Jacob Krachmalnick (vn), Lorne Munroe (vc), E. Ormandy (cnd), Philadelphia Orch Sony Classical ("Essential Classics" series) ▲ SBK 62649 ■ SBT 62649
Mozart, W.A.:Con Bn, w. E. Ormandy (cnd), Philadelphia Orch Sony Classical ("Essential Classics" series) ▲ SBK 62652 ■ SBT 62652
Weber, C.M. von:Andante & Rondo ungarese Bn, w. E. Ormandy (cnd), Philadelphia Orch Sony Classical ("Essential Classics" series) ▲ SBK 62652 ■ SBT 62652

Garibova, Karine (vn)
Vivaldi, A.:Cons Vn, Op. 8/1-4, "The Four Seasons", w. Jerome Franke (vn), Karine Garibova (vn), Pasquale Laurino (vn), Olga Miliaeva (va), Roza Borisova (vc), Mika Hennessy (db), Melanie Panush (ham dlc), Stanislav Venglevski (bayan), Mike Kashou (arabic tabla), Daryl Stuermer (gtr), Ed Paloucek (celtic fid), Gary Bottoni (highland pipe), Dubuffet String Quartet *(rec July-Sept 1995)* EarthBeat! ▲ 35270-2 [DDD]

Garlick, Glenn (vc)
Corigliano, J.:Sym 1, w. David Hardy (vc), Lambert Orkis (pno), L. Slatkin (cnd), National SO Washington D.C. *(rec J. F. K. Center for the Performing Arts, Washington, D. C., Nov 9–11, 1995 & Apr 19 &)* RCA Red Seal ▲ 09026-68450-2 [DDD]

Garlitski, Boris (vn)
Bach, J.S.:Con for 3 Vns, w. V. Spivakov (vn), A. Futer (vn), V. Spivakov (cnd), Moscow Virtuosi RCA Red Seal ▲ 7991-2-RC [DDD]
Mozart, W.A.:Concertone Vns, w. V. Spivakov (vn), Moscow Virtuosi RCA Red Seal ▲ 09026-60467-2

Garlöv, Maria (fl)—see ORCHESTRAS & ENSEMBLES Sundsvall Wind Quartet
Garner, B. (instr)—see ORCHESTRAS & ENSEMBLES Atlantic Sinfonietta members

Garner, Bradley (fl)
Baksa, R.:Son Fl, w. A. Kim (pno) Capstone ▲ CPS 8608 [DDD]
Flute Salad, w. Gilbert, Laura (fl), Alexa Still (fl), Doriot Dwyer (fl), New Zealand CO, London SO Koch Schwann ▲ KIC CD 7602
Handel, D.:Barge Music, w. Rodney Studky (gtr), Jon Pascolini (db), Russell Burge (perc), Allen Otte (perc) Vienna Modern Masters ▲ VMM 2019 [DDD]
Handel, D.:Fl City, w. Frank Weinstock (pno) Vienna Modern Masters ▲ VMM 2019 [DDD]

Garner, Sue (elec bass)
Exquisite Corpses from P.S. 122, w. D. Watson (shears/stick vn/gtr/tpt), Judy Dunaway (gtr/balloons), Anthony Coleman (sampler), Raissa St. Pierre (drums), Guy Yarden (vn/pno), Leslie Ross (bn), Linda Austin (gtr), Bruce Kaplan (gtr), Doug Henderson (peckhorn/bass/toy pno), Sue Ann Harkey (gtr), Cinnie Cole (sampler), Mike Sap ¿What Next? ▲ WN 0002 [ADD]

Garnet, Rod (fl)
A Colorado Kind of Christmas, w. [cnd:Duain Wolfe], Colorado Children's Chorale, Mike Fitzmaurice (db), William Hill (perc), Deborah Schmit-Lobis (pno), Brett Walace (vc), Mary Louise Burke (pno), Laurie Kahler (pno), Helen Hope (hp) *(rec Denver Center Media)* Colorado Children's Chorale ▲ XMAS

Garnier, Catherine (pno)
Sauguet, H.:Sonatine bucolique, w. Didier Vadrot (sax) Sonpact ▲ SPT 96017 [DDD]

Garnier, O. (pno)
Debussy, C.:Images (3) Pno, w. J.-L. Pouchet (vn)—Poisson d'or [arr. for violin & piano] Analekta ▲ ATM 29725 [DDD]
Franck, C.:Son Vn, w. J.-L. Pouchet (vn) Analekta ▲ ATM 29725 [DDD]
Lafond, R.:À l'Aube, w. J.-L. Pouchet (vn) Analekta ▲ ATM 29725 [DDD]
Massenet, J.:Méditation from *Thaïs*, w. J.-L. Pouchet (vn) Analekta ▲ ATM 29725 [DDD]
Ravel, M.:Une Barque sur l'océan Analekta ▲ ATM 29725 [DDD]
Ravel, M.:Oiseaux Tristes Vn, w. J.-L. Pouchet (vn) Analekta ▲ ATM 29725 [DDD]
Ravel, M.:Tzigane, w. J.-L. Pouchet (vn) Analekta ▲ ATM 29725 [DDD]

Garosi, Alessandra (pno)—see ORCHESTRAS & ENSEMBLES Harmonia Ensemble

Garret, Jennifer (pno)
Van Appledorn, M.J.:Incantations, w. W. Strieder (tpt) Opus One ▲ CD 162

Garrett, David (vc)
Holmes, R.:Cat's Cradle 3 Opus One ▲ CD 162

Garrett, Glen (cl)
Matson, S.:Range, w. Catherine Robbin (mez), Susan Greenberg (fl), Joseph Stone (fl), Suren Karapetyan (hn), Peter Kent (vn), Kazi Pitelka (va), Sebastian Toettcher (vc), Don Ferrone (db), Doug Livingston (gtr/mand), John Schneider (gtr), Amy Shulman (hp), Terry Schoenig (perc), S. Matson (cnd) *(rec Schnee Studio, Universal City, CA, Mar 12, 1995)* New Albion ▲ NA 091

Garrett, Margo (pno)
Aitken, H.:Soledades, Cantata VII, w. I. Gubrud (sop) CRI ▲ CD 595 [DDD]
At Carnegie Hall, w. K. Battle (sop) *(rec Carnegie Hall debut concert, 1991)* Deutsche Grammophon ▲ 435440-2 GH [DDD]
Bland, W.:Rhap Vc & Pno, w. S. Robinson (vc) Bridge ▲ BCD 9013 [DDD]
Debussy, C.:Son Vc, w. S. Robinson (vc) Grenadilla ■ 1065
Fauré, G.:Elégie, w. S. Robinson (vc) Grenadilla ■ 1065
In Concert, w. K. Battle (sop), Jean-Pierre Rampal (fl), Anthony Newman (hpd), Myron Lutzke (vc), John Steel Ritter (pno) *(rec Feb. 24, 1991)* Sony Classical ▲ SK 53106 [ADD] ■ ST 53106
Virtuosol:A Treasury of Favorite Violin Encores, w. J. Laredo (vn) Dorian ▲ DOR 90153 [DDD]
Ward, R.:Arioso & Tarantelle, w. Mark Ward (vc) Albany ▲ TROY 204 [DDD]

Garrison, Leonard (fl)
Still, W.G.:Folk Suites, w. Robert Umiker (cl), Samuel Magill (vc), Arthur Tollefson (pno) Cambria ▲ CD 1060 [ADD]

Garritson, Paul (cl)—see ORCHESTRAS & ENSEMBLES Missouri Quintet

Garson, Heidi (hn)
Rosner, A.:Son Hn, w. Yolanda Liepa (pno) *(rec SUNY, Stony Brook)* Albany ▲ TROY 163 [DDD]

Garth, Eliza (pno)
Froom, D.:Down To A Sunless Sea, w. *(strings unknown)* Centaur ▲ CRC 2103 [DDD]
Froom, D.:Qt Piano, w. *(strings unknown)* Centaur ▲ CRC 2103 [DDD]
Froom, D.:Son Pno Centaur ▲ CRC 2103 [DDD]
Martino, D.:Fants & Impromptus Centaur ▲ CRC 2173
Martino, D.:Pianississimo Centaur ▲ CRC 2173
Moravec, P.:Open Secret, w. R. Schulte (vn), E. Bartlett (vc) CRI ▲ CD 641 [DDD]
Rosenzweig, M.:Diptych, w. S. Palma (fl), A. Blustine (cl), B. Hudson (vn), C. Finckel (vc), M. Rosenzweig Centaur ▲ CRC 2103 [DDD]

Gartmann, Luzius (vc)—see ORCHESTRAS & ENSEMBLES Kammermusik Ensemble Chamäleon

▲ = CD ♦ = Enhanced CD Δ = MD ■ = Cassette Tape ▯ = DCC

Gärtner, Susanne (fl)
Burkhard, W.:Serenade Fl, Op. 77, w. W. Meienberg (cl), J. Stavicek (bn), M. Gugel (hn), M. Paccagnella (hp), H. Schneeberger (vn), C. Schiller (va), B. Wyganth (db) *(rec between 1985 & 1989)* Jecklin-Disco ▲ JD 647-2 [ADD]

Garvelmann, D. (pno)
Field, J.:Pno Music, w. B. Posner (pno)—complete piano duets Koch International Classics ▲ KIC 7287 [DDD]
Osborne, G.A.:Duo Brilliant, w. B. Posner (pno) Koch International Classics ▲ KIC 7287 [DDD]
Trimble, J.:Pno Music, w. B. Posner (pno)—complete piano duets Koch International Classics ▲ KIC 7287 [DDD]

Garvey, David (pno)
A Program of Song, w. L. Price (sop) *(rec 1959)* RCA Living Stereo ▲ 09026-61499-2 ■ 09026-61499-4
Return to Carnegie Hall, w. L. Price (sop) *(rec Carnegie Hall, New York, Jan 26, 1991)* RCA Red Seal ▲ 09026-68435-2 [DDD]

Garvey, Evelyn (pno)
Bach, C.P.E.:Fants Kbd—W.58/6 & 7, 59/5 & 6, 61/3 & 6, 63/6, 67, 112/2, 8, & 15, 113/3, 114/7, 117/4, 11, 12, 13, & 15, 119/7 Elan ▲ 2214 [ADD]

Garzón, María (pno)
Albéniz, I.:Suite española
Falla, M. de:Fant bética ASV ▲ ASV 798 [DDD]
Piano Music of Spain ASV ▲ ASV 798 [DDD]
Soler, P.A.:Sons Pno—Nos. 45, 84 & 90 ASV ▲ ASV 798 [DDD]

Garzuly, Anna (fl)
Bartók, B.:Hungarian Peasant Songs, w. Dorian Keilhack (pno) [arr Arma for fl & pno] *(rec July 9–11, 1995 & Feb 12–)* Hungaroton ▲ HCD 31655 [DDD]
Berio, L.:Sequenza I *(rec July 9–11, 1995 & Feb 12–)* Hungaroton ▲ HCD 31655 [DDD]
Geszler, G.:Vision, w. Dorian Keilhack (pno) *(rec July 9–11, 1995 & Feb 12–)* Hungaroton ▲ HCD 31655 [DDD]
Hindemith, P.:Son Fl, w. Dorian Keilhack (pno) *(rec July 9–11, 1995 & Feb 12–)* Hungaroton ▲ HCD 31655 [DDD]
Kurtág, G.:Hommage à J. S. B. *(rec July 9–11, 1995 & Feb 12–)* Hungaroton ▲ HCD 31655 [DDD]
Muczynski, R.:Son Fl, w. Dorian Keilhack (pno) *(rec July 9–11, 1995 & Feb 12–)* Hungaroton ▲ HCD 31655 [DDD]

Gascoigne, Brian (mar/vib)
John Williams & Friends, w. J. Williams (gtr), J. Williams (gtr), Carlos Bonell (gtr), Morris Pert (mar/vib), Keith Marjoram (db) CBS ▲ MK 35108 [AAD]

Gascón, Montserrat (fl)
Tangos & Habaneras for Flute & Guitar, w. Xavier Coll (gtr) *(rec Capilla de la Esperanza de Barcelona, Sept 4–6 & 25–26, 1995)* PROdigital ▲ PRO 1113 [DDD]

Gaskell, Helen (ob)
Warlock, P.:Songs Bar, w. S. Austin (bar), M. Harrison (vn), C. Lynch (pno)—(2) Ha'Nacker Mill; Away to Twiver *(rec live 2/3/36)* Symposium ▲ 1075

Gassenhuber, Angela (pno)
Boulanger, N.:Pieces (3) Vc & Pno, w. F. Kupsa (vc) Troubadisc ▲ TROCD 01407
Boulanger, N.:Songs, w. M. Paulsen (mez)—5 Songs; 7 Songs; Les heures claires Troubadisc ▲ TROCD 01407
Boulanger, N.:Vers la vie nouvelle Troubadisc ▲ TROCD 01407
Smyth, E.:Songs (3) Mez, w. M. Petersen (mez) *(rec 1992)* Troubadisc ▲ TRO CD 01405 [DDD]
Tailleferre, G.:Arabesque, w. D. Marshall (cl) *(rec Dec. 1992)* Troubadisc ▲ TRO 01406 [DDD]
Tailleferre, G.:Forlane, w. U. Siebler (fl) *(rec Dec. 1992)* Troubadisc ▲ TRO 01406 [DDD]
Tailleferre, G.:Image, w. U. Siebler (fl), D. Marshall (cl), H. Stralendorf (cel), Fanny Mendelssohn String Quartet *(rec Dec. 1992)* Troubadisc ▲ TRO 01406 [DDD]
Tailleferre, G.:Son 1 Vn, w. R. Eggebrecht (vn) *(rec Dec. 1992)* Troubadisc ▲ TRO 01406 [DDD]
Tailleferre, G.:Son 2 Vn, w. R. Eggebrecht (vn) *(rec Dec. 1992)* Troubadisc ▲ TRO 01406 [DDD]
Tailleferre, G.:Trio Pno, w. R. Eggebrecht (vn), F. Kupas (vc) *(rec Dec. 1992)* Troubadisc ▲ TRO 01406 [DDD]

Gassman, B. (ob)
Foss, L.:Con Ob, w. A. Endo (cnd), Crystal CO, Los Angeles PO members [string quintet version] Crystal ▲ CD871
Music for Double-Reed Ensemble, w. A. Endo (cnd), Los Angeles PO members, Crystal CO Crystal ▲ CD871

Gast, Arvid (org)
Bach, J.S.:Cant 143, w. Joachim Pliquett (tpt) [excerpt for tpt & org] Entrée ▲ 0071
Bach, J.S.:Cons Org, BWV 592–597, w. Joachim Pliquett (tpt)—in G, BWV 592 Entrée ▲ 0071
Bach, J.S.:Toccata & Fugue Org, BWV 565, w. Joachim Pliquett (tpt) Entrée ▲ 0071
Baldassare, P.:Son 1 Tpt, w. Joachim Pliquett (tpt) Entrée ▲ 0071
400 Years of Music for Trumpet & Organ, w. J. Pliquett (tpt) Classic Studio Berlin ▲ CS 11808 [DDD]
Krebs, J.L.:Org Music, w. Joachim Pliquett (tpt)—Fant in C for Org & Tpt Entrée ▲ 0071
Loeillet, J.-B.:Son Tpt, w. Joachim Pliquett (tpt) Entrée ▲ 0071
Purcell, H.:Org Music, w. Joachim Pliquett (tpt)—Son in D; Suite in C Entrée ▲ 0071
Stanley, J.:Voluntaries Org, w. Joachim Pliquett (tpt)—Tpt Voluntary Entrée ▲ 0071
Trumpet & Organ, w. A. Lange (tpt), Joachim Pliquett (tpt), Ulrich Bremsteller (org) Classic Studio Berlin ▲ CS 12 208 [DDD]

Gastinel, Anne (vc)
Debussy, C.:Son Vc, w. S. Bossard (pno) *(rec 7/90)* Ottavo ▲ OTR C79032 [DDD]
Debut Recital, w. Suzy Bossard (pno) Ottavo ▲ 79032 [DDD]
Fauré, G.:Elégie, w. S. Bossard (pno) *(rec 7/90)* Ottavo ▲ OTR C79032 [DDD]
Fauré, G.:Elégie, w. E. Krivine (cnd), Lyon National Orch Valois ▲ V 4754
Fauré, G.:Son 2 Vc, w. S. Bossard (pno) *(rec 7/90)* Ottavo ▲ OTR C79032 [DDD]
Gastinel, G.:Marutz, w. S. Bossard (pno) *(rec 7/90)* Ottavo ▲ OTRC 79032 [DDD]
Janácek, L.:Fairy Tale, w. Pierre-Laurent Aimard (pno) Valois ▲ V 4748
Kodály, Z.:Son Vc & Pno, Op. 4, w. Pierre-Laurent Aimard (pno) Valois ▲ V 4748
Lalo, E.:Con Vc, w. E. Krivine (cnd), Lyon National Orch Valois ▲ V 4754
Liszt, F.:Elegie 1, w. Pierre-Laurent Aimard (pno) Valois ▲ V 4748
Liszt, F.:Elegie 2, w. Pierre-Laurent Aimard (pno) Valois ▲ V 4748
Liszt, F.:La Lugubre gondola Vn & Pno, w. Pierre-Laurent Aimard (pno) Valois ▲ V 4748
Marais, M.:La Folia, w. S. Bossard (pno) *(rec 7/90)* Ottavo ▲ OTR C79032 [DDD]
Merlet, M.:Une Soirée à Nohant, w. S. Bossard (pno) *(rec 7/90)* Ottavo ▲ OTR C79032 [DDD]
Saint-Saëns, C.:Con 1 Vc, w. E. Krivine (cnd), Lyon National Orch Valois ▲ V 4754
Strauss, R.:Son Vc, w. P.-L. Aimard (pno) Valois ▲ V 4692

Gates, Marcia (fl)
Kupferman, M.:O Harlequin Soundspells ▲ CD 108 [DDD]

Gatt, Martin (bn)
Elgar, E.:Harmony Music I-V, w. Michael Cox (fl), Paul Edmund-Davies (fl), Roy Carter (ob), Nicholas Rodwell (cl)—No. 4, "The Farmyard" EMI Classics ("Anglo-American Chamber Music" series) ▲ CDC 55403
Elgar, E.:Romance Bn, w. D. Barenboim (cnd), English CO *(rec Oct. 24, 1973–June 26, 19)* Sony Classical (Essential Classics) ▲ SBK 53510 [ADD] ■ SBT 53510

Gatti, Enrico (vn)—see also ORCHESTRAS & ENSEMBLES Ensemble 415, Fitzwilliam Ensemble, La Real Camera, Aurora Ensemble
Boccherini, L.:Qnt Pno, G.407–412, w. L. Alvini (pno), O. Edouard (vn), E. Moreno (va), R. Gini (vc)—Nos. 1, 5 & 6 Tactus ▲ TC 740203
Boccherini, L.:Trio Sons Hpd, G.143–148, w. L. Alvini (hpd), R. Gini (vc) *(rec June 27–30, 1991)* Tactus ▲ TC 740202
The Piemontese School of the 18th Century, w. Antonio Mosca (vc), Giorgio Tabacco (hpd) Symphonia ▲ SYM 92S13 [DDD]

Gatti, Enrico (vn) (cont.)
Veracini, F.M.:Sons Vn, Op. 1, w. Alain Gervreau (vc), Guido Morini (hpd)—Nos. 1 & 8 Arcana ▲ ACA 27
Veracini, F.M.:Sonate accademiche, w. Alain Gervreau (vc), Guido Morini (hpd)—Nos. 6 & 12 Arcana ▲ ACA 27

Gatti, Marcello (fl)—see also ORCHESTRAS & ENSEMBLES Modo Antiquo
Cimarosa, D.:Con for 2 Fls, w. Federico Maria Sardelli (fl), R. Cirri (cnd), Ars Cantus *(rec Sept 7–10, 1995)* Bongiovanni ▲ GB 2184 [DDD]

Gatwood, Jody (vn)
Dotzauer, F.:Qt Strs, w. Vera Beths (vn), Lisa Rautenberg (va), Anner Bylsma (vc) *(rec New York City, Jan. 19–22, 1994)* Sony Classical ▲ SK 66259 [DDD]
Dotzauer, F.:Qnt Strs, w. Vera Beths (vn), Lisa Rautenberg (va), Anner Bylsma (vc), Kenneth Slowik (vc) *(rec New York City, Jan. 19–22, 1994)* Sony Classical ("Vivarte" series) ▲ SK 64307 [DDD]
Schubert, Franz:Qnt Strs, D.956, w. L. Rautenberg (vn), S. Dann (va), A. Bylsma (vc), K. Slowick (vc) Sony Classical ("Vivarte" series) ▲ SK 46669

Gauce, Jean-Louis (bas hn)—see ORCHESTRAS & ENSEMBLES Trio di Bassetto

Gaudard, Line (hp)
Gerber, R.:Con 2 Hp, w. T. Loosli (cnd), Neuchâtelois SO Gallo ▲ CD 862 [ADD]

Gaudi, Patrick (gtr)
Sor, F.:Gtr Music—Etudes, Op. 29/17, 23; Leçon in F, Op. 31/21; Etude in A, Op. 6/6; Intro & Allegro, Op. 14; 3 Menuets, Op. 11; Son, Op. 15b; Intro, Thème & Vars on a Theme of Mozart, Op. 9; Fant sur un air favori écossais, Op. 40; Valses Nos. 4 & 5, Op. 17 Accord ▲ ACD 220782 [AAD]

Gaudibert, Eric (pno)
Gaudibert, E.:Syzygy, w. A. Magnin (fl) *(rec Jan. 20, 1971)* Grammont ▲ CTSP 8-2 [ADD]

Gauger, Thomas (perc)
In The Family, w. Ronald Barron (trbn), Marianne Gedigian (fl), Ann Hobson Pilot (hp), Douglas Yeo (trbn), Edwin Barker (bass) *(rec Morse Auditorium, Boston Univ, Dec 1995)* Boston Brass ▲ BB 1004

Gaugué, Christophe (va)
Fervers, A.:Paronomases Accord ▲ ACD 205552 [DDD]

Gaugué, Emmanuel (vc)
Saint-Saëns, C.:Allegro appassionato, w. Erik Berchot (pno) [arr for vc & pno] Chamade ▲ 5628
Saint-Saëns, C.:Le Cygne, w. Erik Berchot (pno) Chamade ▲ 5628
Saint-Saëns, C.:Romance Vc, w. Erik Berchot (pno) Chamade ▲ 5628
Saint-Saëns, C.:Son 1 Vc, w. Erik Berchot (pno) Chamade ▲ 5628
Saint-Saëns, C.:Son 2 Vc, w. Erik Berchot (pno) Chamade ▲ 5628

Gauk, Rachel (gtr)
Brouwer, L.:Paisaje cubano con campanas Marquis Classics ▲ MAR 191
Brouwer, L.:Sencillos—Nos. XI, XII & XV Marquis Classics ▲ MAR 191
Daniel:After the Panorama Marquis Classics ▲ MAR 191
Danzas y Canciones Marquis Classics ▲ ERAD 137 [DDD]
Histoire du Tango, w. Susan Hoeppner (fl) Marquis ▲ MAR 177 [DDD]
Lauro, A.:Suite Venezolano Marquis Classics ▲ MAR 191
Ponce, M.:Piezas Marquis Classics ▲ MAR 191
Torroba:Pieces Caractéristiques Marquis Classics ▲ MAR 191
Toward the Sea, w. S. Hoeppner (fl) Marquis Classics ▲ MAR 147 [DDD]

Gauntlett, Ambrose (vl)
Butterworth, G.:Songs (6) from *A Shropshire Lad*, w. John Shirley-Quirk (bar), Nona Liddell (vn), Ivor McMahon (vn), Martin Isepp (hpd/pno) Saga Classics ▲ EC 3336
Humfrey, P.:Anthems, w. John Shirley-Quirk (bar), Nona Liddell (vn), Ivor McMahon (vn), Martin Isepp (hpd/pno)—A Hymne to God the Father Saga Classics ▲ EC 3336
Moeran, E.J.:Songs, w. John Shirley-Quirk (bar), Martin Isepp (hpd/pno), Nona Liddell (vn), Ivor McMahon (vn)—When Smoke Stood Up from Ludlow; Say, Lad, Have You Things to Do?; Farewell to Barn & Stack & Trees [all from Ludlow Town] Saga Classics ▲ EC 3336
Purcell, H.:Chamber Music, w. Alberto Lysy (vn), Robert Masters (vn), Yehudi Menuhin (vn), Cecil Arnowitz (va), Walter Gerhard (va), Derek Simpson (vc), Roy Jesson (hpd/org)—Trio Sons Nos. 2 in C, 6 in G & 8 in G; Fants Nos. 4 in g, 7 in c, 8 in d & 13 in F, "Upon One Note" EMI Classics ("Baroque" series) ▲ CDK 65734
Purcell, H.:Fants, w. Alberto Lysy (vn), Robert Masters (vn), Yehudi Menuhin (vn), Cecil Aronowitz (va), Walter Gerhard (va), Derek Simpson (vc), Roy Jesson (hpd/org)—Nos. 4 in g, 7 in c, 8 in d, 13 in F EMI Classics ▲ CDK 65734
Purcell, H.:Sons (22) Vns, w. Alberto Lysy (vn), Robert Masters (vn), Yehudi Menuhin (vn), Cecil Aronowitz (va), Walter Gerhard (va), Derek Simpson (vc), Roy Jesson (hpd/org)—Nos. 2, 6, & 8 EMI Classics ▲ CDK 65734
Purcell, H.:Songs, w. John Shirley-Quirk (bar), Martin Isepp (hpd/pno), Nona Liddell (vn), Ivor McMahon (vn)—Man Is for the Woman Made; Music for a While; Twas within a Furlong of Edinborough Town; When Night her Purple Veil Saga Classics ▲ EC 3336

Gauthier, Patrick (syn)
East/West, w. Richard Pinhas (syns/gtr), Norman Spinrad (voc), Dominique E. (voc), G. Grunblatt (syn), François Auger (perc), Steve Shehan (perc), Didier Batard (bass gtr) Cuneiform ▲ Rune 31
Rhizosphere/Live, Paris 1982, w. Richard Pinhas (syns/gtr), Bernard Paganotti (bass), François Auger (perc), Clement Bailly (perc) Cuneiform ▲ Rune 61

Gauthier, Patrick (syn/bass)
L'Ethique, w. Richard Pinhas (syns/gtr), Gilles Deleuze (voc), J. P. Goude (syn/perc), G. Grunblatt (syn), Bernard Paganotti (bass), François Auger (drums), Clément Bailly (drums) Cuneiform ▲ Rune 36X

Gauthier, Patrick (syns/pno)—see ORCHESTRAS & ENSEMBLES Heldon

Gauthier, Patrick (syns/pno/drums)
D.W.W., w. Richard Pinhas (syns/gtr), J. Philippe Goude (syn programming/drums/gtr), Bernard Paganotti (bass gtr), Alain Bellaich (synthesized gtr) Cuneiform ▲ Rune 40

Gautier, Annick (vc)—see ORCHESTRAS & ENSEMBLES Zemlinsky Trio

Gautier, J.-F. (org)
Albinoni, T.:Adagio Org, w. Amati Ensemble *(rec Aug 1993)* Analekta ▲ AN 29504

Gautier, Stéphane (bn)—see ORCHESTRAS & ENSEMBLES Tickmayer Formatio

Gauwerky, Friedrich (pno)
Delz, C.:Qt Pno, w. C. Delz (pno), A. Hempel (pno), J. Krist (pno), N. Shirato (pno) Grammont ▲ CTSP 18-2 [ADD]

Gaveau, Marcel (pno)
"Le Patron" of the Saxophone, w. Marcel Mule (sax), Guy Chauvet (ten), G. Charon (sgr), F. l'Homme (sgr), P. Romby (sgr), Eugène Bozza (cnd), Francis Çebron (cnd), Phillipe Gaubert (cnd), *(orchs unknown)*, Joseph Benvenutti (pno), Marthe Pellas-Lenom (pno), et al. *(rec 1930–1940)* Clarinet Classics ▲ CC 0013 [AAD]

Gaver, Elizabeth (fid)—see ORCHESTRAS & ENSEMBLES Sequentia

Gavoty, Bernard (org)
Saint-Saëns, C.:Syms (comp), w. J. Martinon (cnd), ORTF National Orch EMI Classics ("Studio" series) 2-▲ CDMB 62643 [ADD]
Saint-Saëns, C.:Sym 3, w. J. Martinon (cnd), ORTF National Orch EMI Classics ("Studio" series) 2-▲ CDMB 62643 [ADD]

Gavrilov, André (pno)
Bach, J.S.:Cons Hpd, BWV 1052–1058, w. N. Marriner (cnd), Academy of St. Martin in the Fields—Nos. 1, 2, 4 & 5 EMI Classics ▲ CDD 64055-2 [DDD]
Bach, J.S.:Cons Hpd, BWV 1052–1058, w. N. Marriner (cnd), Academy of St. Martin in the Fields—Nos. 1, 6 & 7 EMI Classics ▲ CDD 64293-2 [DDD]
Bach, J.S.:Cons Hpd, BWV 1052–1058, w. N. Marriner (cnd), Academy of St. Martin in the Fields—Nos. 1, 2, 4 & 5 EMI Classics ▲ CDM 65173
Bach, J.S.:Cons Hpd, BWV 1052–1058, w. N. Marriner (cnd), Academy of St. Martin in the Fields—Nos. 3, 6 & 7 EMI Classics ▲ CDM 65174
Bach, J.S.:French Suites EMI Classics 2-▲ CDFB 69479
Bach, J.S.:French Suites, w. N. Marriner (cnd), Academy of St. Martin in the Fields—BWV 816 EMI Classics ▲ CDD 64293-2 [DDD]

Gavrilov, André (pno) (cont.)
Bach, J.S.:French Suites, w. N. Marriner (cnd), Academy of St. Martin in the Fields—No. 5 EMI Classics ▲ CDM 65174
Balakirev, M.:Islamey EMI Classics ▲ CDM 64329-2
Chopin, F.:Ballades Pno (comp) Deutsche Grammophon ▲ 435622-2 [DDD]
Chopin, F.:Son Pno, Op. 35 Deutsche Grammophon ▲ 435622-2 [DDD]
Grieg, E.:Lyric Pieces Deutsche Grammophon ▲ 437522-2
Handel, G.F.:Suites Hpd—Nos. 1, 4, 6 & 7 EMI Classics ("Doubleforte" series) 2-▲ CDFB 69337
Hindemith, P.:Son Vn & Pno, Op. 11/1, w. Gidon Kremer (vn) EMI Classics 2-▲ CDFB 69334
Prokofiev, S.:Con 1 Pno, w. S. Rattle (cnd), London SO EMI Classics ▲ CDM 64329
Prokofiev, S.:Pieces Pno, Op. 4 EMI Classics ▲ CDM 64329
Prokofiev, S.:Son 3 Pno Deutsche Grammophon ▲ 435439-2 [DDD]
Prokofiev, S.:Son 7 Pno Deutsche Grammophon ▲ 435439-2 [DDD]
Prokofiev, S.:Son 8 Pno Deutsche Grammophon ▲ 435439-2 [DDD]
Rachmaninoff, S.:Con 2 Pno, w. R. Muti (cnd), Philadelphia Orch EMI Classics ▲ CDC 49966
Rachmaninoff, S.:Rhapsody on a Theme of Paganini, w. R. Muti (cnd), Philadelphia Orch EMI Classics ▲ CDC 49966
Ravel, M.:Con Pno (left hand), w. S. Rattle (cnd), London SO EMI ▲ CDM 69026
Ravel, M.:Gaspard de la nuit Deutsche Grammophon ▲ 437532-2
Ravel, M.:Gaspard de la nuit EMI ▲ CDM 69026
Ravel, M.:Pavane pour une infante défunte Deutsche Grammophon ▲ 437532-2
Schnittke, A.:Son 2 Vn, w. Gidon Kremer (vn) EMI Classics 2-▲ CDFB 69334
Stravinsky, I.:Con Pnos, w. V. Ashkenazy (pno) London ▲ 433829-2 [DDD]
Stravinsky, I.:Le Sacre du printemps Orch, w. V. Ashkenazy (pno) [2-pno trans.] London ▲ 433829-2 [DDD]
Stravinsky, I.:Scherzo à la russe, w. V. Ashkenazy (pno) [2-pno trans.] London ▲ 433829-2 [DDD]
Stravinsky, I.:Son Pnos, w. V. Ashkenazy (pno) London ▲ 433829-2 [DDD]
Tchaikovsky, P.:Con 1 Pno, w. R. Muti (cnd), Philharmonia Orch EMI Classics ▲ CDM 64329
Tchaikovsky, P.:Pno Music—Theme & Variations, Op. 19/6 EMI Classics ▲ CDM 64329
Weber, C.M. von:Grand duo concertant Cl, w. Gidon Kremer (vn) [arr for vn & pno] EMI Classics 2-▲ CDFB 69334

Gavrilovici, Alexandru (vn)
Koechlin, C.:Paysages et marines, w. Kiyoshi Kasai (fl), Elmar Schmid (cl), Urs Walker (vn), Christoph Schiller (va), Patrick Demenga (vc) Accord ▲ ACD 201092 [DDD]

Gawriloff, Saschko (vn)
Berg, A.:Chamber Con, w. Daniel Barenboim (pno), P. Boulez (cnd), London SO Sony Classical ("Pierre Boulez Edition" series) ▲ SMK 68331
Françaix, J.:Trio Vn, Vc & Pno, w. J. Goritzki (vc), R. Havenith (pno) *(rec 12/13/89)* Wergo ▲ WER 6198-2 [AAD]
Janácek, L.:Pno Music, w. Gilead Mishory (pno), András Adorján (pic), Wen-Sinn Yang (vc)—Son. for Vn & Pno; Allegro for Vn & Pno; Romance for Vn & Pno; Dumka for Vn & Pno; Tema Con Vars. for Pno; Fairy Tale for Vc & Pno; Presto for Vc & Pno; March of the Bluebreasts for Pic & Pno; Music for Excercises w. Clubs for Pno; In Memoriam for Pno; Reminiscence for Pno Tudor ▲ TUD 7003 [DDD]
Kagel, M.:An Tasten, w. Bruno Canino (pno), Siegfried Palm (vc) Montaigne ▲ MO 782043
Kagel, M.:Klangwölfe, w. Bruno Canino (pno), Siegfried Palm (vc) Montaigne ▲ MO 782043
Kagel, M.:Trio Pno, w. Siegfried Palm (vc), Bruno Canino (pno) Montaigne ▲ MO 782043
Kagel, M.:Unguis incarnatus est, w. Bruno Canino (pno), Siegfried Palm (vc) Montaigne ▲ MO 782043
Ligeti, G.:Con Vn, w. P. Boulez (cnd), Ensemble InterContemporain Deutsche Grammophon ▲ 439808-2
Ligeti, G.:Trio Hn, Vn & Pno, w. H. Baumann (hn), E. Besch (pno) Wergo ▲ WER 60100-50 [DDD]
Messiaen, O.:Quatuor pour la fin du temps, w. Hans Deinzer (cl), Siegfried Palm (vc), Alfons Kontarsky (pno) EMI Classics 2-▲ CDCB 47463 [DDD]
Pfitzner, H.:Con Vn, w. W.A. Albert (cnd), Bamberg SO CPO ▲ CPO 999079-2 [DDD]
Pfitzner, H.:Duo Vn, w. J. Berger (vc), W.A. Albert (cnd), Bamberg SO CPO ▲ CPO 999079-2 [DDD]
Togni, C.:Gesang zur Nacht, w. Carla Henius (alt), Hans Damzel (cl), Werner Heider (pno), Mariolina de Robertis (pno) Stradivarius ▲ STV DTM 90002 [ADD]

Gay, Claude (org)
Saint Benedict, w. St. Peter's Abbey of Solesmes Monastic Choir [cnd:Jean Claire] Paraclete ▲ PCL 820 ■ PCL 620

Gay, Margaret (vc)
Clarke, J.:Songs, w. Carolyn Sinclair (sop), Michael Jarvis (hpd)—Celia is Soft; Long Has Pastora Rul'd the Plain; So Sweets the Charms of Love; Alas, Here Lies the Poor Alonzo Slain; Divine Astrea Hither Flew; Lord, What's Come to My Mother; I'se No More to Shady Coverts; Jockey Was a Dawdy Lad; The Bonny Grey Ey'd Morn; Jockey Was as Brisk & Blith a Lad *(rec St. Lawrence the Martyr Church, Hamilton, Ontario)* Hungaroton ▲ HCD 31602 [DDD]
Eccles, J.:Songs, w. Carolyn Sinclair (sop), Michael Jarvis (hpd)—Stay, Ah Turn; Love is An Empty, Airy Name; If I Hear Orinda Swear; E'er Since You Came into My Sight; My Lover Has An Inconstant Mind; I'll Hurry Thee Hence; I Burn, My Brain Consumes to Ashes *(rec St. Lawrence the Martyr Church, Hamilton, Ontario)* Hungaroton ▲ HCD 31602 [DDD]
Purcell, H.:Songs, w. Carolyn Sinclair (sop), Michael Jarvis (hpd)—Ah! How Sweet It is to Love; I Sigh'd & Owned My Love; Sweeter Than Roses; Whilst I with Grief Did on You Look; Oh! How You Protest; 'Twas Within a Furlong of Edinborough Town; Man is For the Woman Made; Ah Me! To Many Deaths Decreed; Oh! Lead Me to Some Peaceful Gloom; Lads & Lasses, Blith & Gay *(rec St. Lawrence the Martyr Church, Hamilton, Ontario)* Hungaroton ▲ HCD 31602 [DDD]

Gayer, Ferenc (db/bass gtr)
Cornologia, w. Budapest Festival Horn Quartet, Zoltán Varga (timp/perc), Dimitris Politis (gtr), János Weszely (dr), Sándor Balogh (pno) *(rec Hungaroton Classic Studio, Feb 15–16, 1996)* Hungaroton ▲ HCD 31652 [ADD/DDD]

Gaylord, Monica (pno)
Black Piano:A Treasury of Works for Solo Piano by Black Composers Music & Arts ▲ MUA 737 [DDD]
Coleridge-Taylor, S.:Three-fours Music & Arts ▲ CD 737-1 [DDD]
Still, W.G.:Sahdji—Seven Traceries; Three Visions Music & Arts ▲ CD 737-1 [DDD]

Gazeau, Sylvie (va)
Beethoven, L. van:Qnt Strs, Op. 29, w. S. Accardo (vn), M. Batjer (vn), T. Hoffman (va), G. Hoffman (vc) Nuova Era ▲ 6870 [DDD]
Mendelssohn, F.:Qnt 2 Strs, w. S. Accardo (vn), M. Batjer (vn), T. Hoffman (va), G. Hoffman (db) Nuova Era ▲ 6870 [DDD]

Gazeau, Sylvie (vn)
Norman, L.:Qt Pno, Op. 10, w. Christian Ivaldi (pno), Gérard Caussé (vn), Alain Meunier (vc) Musica Sveciae ▲ MSV 518 [DDD]

Gazzelloni, Severino (fl)
Handel, G.F.:Con Fl, w. M. Peca (cnd), Rome Stradivari Ensemble Bongiovanni ▲ GB 2100 [DDD]
Ibert, J.:Pièce Fl Adès ▲ ADE 203462 [AAD]
Mercadante, S.:Duets for 2 Fls, w. Gian-Luca Petrucci (fl) Bongiovanni ▲ GB 5543 [DDD]
Rota, N.:Film Music, w. L. Michelini (pno) [trans. L. Michelini]—La Strada; La dolce vita; Rocco e I suoi fratelli; Amarcord; Il Padrino II; Il Gattopardo; Il Padrino; G. Degli Spiriti; Romeo e Giulietta; Otto e Mezzo CAM ▲ CVS 006 [AAD]
Severino Gazzelloni Ermitage ▲ ERM 130 [ADD]
Togni, C.:Son Fl, w. Camillo Togni (pno) Stradivarius ▲ STV DTM 90002 [ADD]
Vivaldi, A.:Cons Fl (misc), I Musici—includes Con in F, "La tempesta di mare"; Con in g, "La Notte"; Con in D, "Il Gardellino" Philips ("Duo" series) 2-▲ 454 256-2

Gazzola, C. (hn)
Milesi, P.:Modi 2, w. L. M. Pickova (sop), Françoise Goddard (alt), M. Ferradini (ten), B. Andersen (bass), D. Cassamagnaghi (fl), S. Scanziani (ob), A. Bianchi (cl/b cl), E. Crisafulli (bn), F. Gualandris (tuba), A. Girardi (celtic hp), R. Anedda (vn), E. Groppo (vn), M. Pagani (vn), M. Ravasio (va), S. Righini (vc), P. Rizzi (db), J. Scully (perc), P. Milesi (cnd) Cuneiform ▲ RUNE 63

Gearhart, Fritz (vn)—see also ORCHESTRAS & ENSEMBLES Arman Ensemble
Copland, A.:Duo Vn, w. Paul Tardiff (pno) Koch International Classics ▲ KIC 7268

Gearhart, Fritz (vn) (cont.)
Cowell, H.:Suite Vn, w. Paul Tardiff (pno) Koch International Classics ▲ KIC 7268
Dello Joio, N.:Vars & Capriccio, w. Paul Tardiff (pno) Koch International Classics ▲ KIC 7268
Fuchs, R.:Trio Vn, Va & Pno, w. Jonathan Bagg (va), Jane Hawkins (pno) *(rec Baldwin Audit., Durham, NC, Dec 16–18, 1994)* Centaur ▲ CRC 2278 [DDD]
Still, W.G.:Suite Vn, w. Paul Tardiff (pno) Koch International Classics ▲ KIC 7268

Gearhart, John (org)
Historic Organs of New Orleans, w. George Bozeman (org), James S. Darling (org), Jesse E. Eschbach (org), Gerald D. Frank (org), James Hammann (org), Frederick Hohman (org), Lenora McCroskey (org), Mary Gifford Matthys (org), Lorenz Maycher (org), Donald Messer (org) *(rec June 1989)* Organ Historical Society 2-▲ OHS 89

Geary, Michael (perc)
Nielson, L.:Valentine Mechanique, w. Craig Hultgren (vc) Innova ▲ 502

Geber, David (vc)—see also ORCHESTRAS & ENSEMBLES American String Quartet
Cacioppo, C.:Wolf, w. Janice Fiore (sop), Curt Cacioppo (pno) Capstone ▲ CPS 8632

Geber, Stephen (vc)—see also ORCHESTRAS & ENSEMBLES Cleveland Orch String Quartet
Mozart, W.A.:Qt Ob, K.370, w. J. Mack (ob), D. Majeske (vn), A. Skernick (va) Crystal ▲ CD323 ■ C 323

Gedigian, Marianne (fl)
In The Family, w. Ronald Barron (trbn), Ann Hobson Pilot (hp), Douglas Yeo (trbn), Edwin Barker (bass), Thomas Gauger (perc) *(rec Morse Auditorium, Boston Univ, Dec 1995)* Boston Brass ▲ BB 1004

Geem, Jack van (perc)
Lewis, P.S.:Delicate Sky, w. Nadya Tichman (vn), Robin Sutherland (pno) *(rec St. Stephen's Church, Belvedere, CA, Oct 1994 & June 1995)* New Albion ▲ NA 079

Geeting, Daniel (cl)
Jacob, G.:Concertino Cl & Pno, w. Theodora Carras Primes (pno) *(rec Memorial Chapel, Univ. of Redlands, Redlands, CA, Mar. 5, Apr. 30 & June 30)* PROdigital ▲ PRO 9226 [DDD]
Jacob, G.:Pieces Cl *(rec Memorial Chapel, Univ. of Redlands, Redlands, CA, Mar. 5, Apr. 30 & June 30)* PROdigital ▲ PRO 9226 [DDD]
Jacob, G.:Qnt Cl, w. Melissa Phelps-Beckstead (vn), David Stenske (vn), Richard Rintoul (va), Joyce Geeting (vc) *(rec Memorial Chapel, Univ. of Redlands, Redlands, CA, Mar. 5, Apr. 30 & June 30)* PROdigital ▲ PRO 9226 [DDD]
Jacob, G.:Songs Sop & Cl, w. Samela Aird Beasom (sop) *(rec Memorial Chapel, Univ. of Redlands, Redlands, CA, Mar. 5, Apr. 30 & June 30)* PROdigital ▲ PRO 9226 [DDD]

Geeting, Joyce (vc)
Jacob, G.:Qnt Cl, w. Daniel Geeting (cl), Melissa Phelps-Beckstead (vn), David Stenske (vn), Richard Rintoul (va) *(rec Memorial Chapel, Univ. of Redlands, Redlands, CA, Mar. 5, Apr. 30 & June 30)* PROdigital ▲ PRO 9226 [DDD]

Gefe, U. (pno)
Schumann, R.:Liederkreis, Op. 39, w. L. Goetz (sop) [G] Ars Produktion ▲ FCD 368302
Wolf, H.:Italienische Liederbücher (sels), w. L. Goetz (sop)—19 songs [G] Ars Produktion ▲ FCD 368302

Geffert, Johannes (org)
Liszt, F.:Pno Music (misc)—Variations on "Weinen, Klagen"; La lugubre gondola II; Legende de St. François I, La prédication aux oiseaux; Bénédiction de Dieu dans la solitude MITRA ▲ CD 16191 [DDD]

Gehann, H. (org)
Handel, G.F.:Cons (16) Org, Collegium Musicum LaserLight ▲ 15502 [ADD]

Gehring, Wolfram (org)
Dupré, M.:Le Chemin de la croix [organ of the Abbey Marienstatt] Entrée ▲ 0076

Geibel, Steve (fl)—see ORCHESTRAS & ENSEMBLES Missouri Quintet

Geiger, György (tpt)
Classical Gems on Trumpet & Harp, w. Éva Maros (hp) Hungaroton ▲ HCD 31542 [DDD]

Geiger, S. (trbn)—see ORCHESTRAS & ENSEMBLES Datura Trombone Quartet

Geiger, Susanne (pno)
Ernst, S.:Seven Miniatures on Japanese Haiku, w. Barbara Stein (alt), Hertha Rosa-Herseni (vc) Vienna Modern Masters ▲ VMM 2018 [DDD]

Geiser, J.-C. (org)
Mendelssohn, F.:Sacred Pieces, w. H-J. Rickenbacher (ten), Michel Corboz (cnd), Lausanne Vocal Ensemble *(rec Lausanne Cathedral, Jan. 29–31, 1994)* FNAC Music ▲ 592298 [DDD]

Geisler, Peter (cl)—see also ORCHESTRAS & ENSEMBLES Berlin Philharmonic Wind Ensemble
Mozart, W.A.:Adagio Cls, K.411, w. K. Leister (cl), H.R. Stalder (bas hn), H. Hofer (bas hn), E. Schmid (bas hn) *(rec 1978)* Jecklin-Disco ▲ JD 549-2 [ADD]

Geiss, P. (tpt)
Guyonnet, J.:La Cantate interrompue, w. F. Rochaix (nar), S. Stenhammar (sop), S. Seban (pno), G. Calame (pno), E. Séjourne (perc), E. Tarr (tpt), B. Nilsson (tpt), H. Ries (trbn), H. Rückert (trbn), J.-M. Collet, J. Guyonnet (cnd), Geneva Collegium Academicum [F] *(rec Nov. 15, 1986)* Grammont ▲ CTSP 30-2

Geiss, Wolfram (vc)—see also ORCHESTRAS & ENSEMBLES Pallas Trio
Spohr, L.:Adagio, w. Rolf Plagge (pno) Musicaphon ▲ M 56822 [DDD]

Gekic, Kemal (pno)
Chopin, F.:Pno Music (misc), w. Martha Argerich (pno), Vladimir Ashkenazy (pno), Stanislav Bunin (pno), Halina Czerny-Stefanska (pno), Jan Ekier (pno), Yuval Fichman (pno), Adam Harasiewicz (pno), Krzysztof Jablonski (pno), Louis Kentner (pno), Jean-Marc Luisada (pno), Garrick Ohlsson (pno), Ivo Pogorelich (pno), Maurizio Pollini (pno), Dang Thai Son (pno)—includes Ballade (Nos. 1 & 2); Barcarolle, Op. 60; Concerto Nos. 1 & 2; Etudes (Op. 10, Nos. 1, 5, 8, 10 & 12 & Op. 25, No. 10, 18 & 25); Grand valse brillante; Impromptus (Nos. 3 & 4); Mazurkas (Op. 24, Nos. 1–4; Op. 30, Nos. 1–4; Op. 50, No. 32; Op. 59, Nos. 1–3); Nocturnes (Op. 9, No. 3; Op. 37, No. 12; Op. 48, No. 13; Op. 55, No. 16)Polonaise (Op. 40, Nos. 3 & 4; Op. 44, No. 5; Op. 53, No. 6; Op. 61, No. 7); Preludes (Op. 28 Nos. 13–18, 21–24 & Op. 45, No. 25); Scherzos (Nos. 1–3); Sonatas (Nos. 2 & 3); Waltzes (No. 1 & 6) LaserLight 5-▲ 15 961 [ADD/DDD]

Gekker, Chris (tpt)—see also ORCHESTRAS & ENSEMBLES American Brass Quintet
Amram, D.:Travels, w. R.A. Clark (cnd), Manhattan CO Newport Classic ▲ NPD 85546 [DDD]
Ewazen, E.:Qnt Tpt, w. St. Luke's Chamber Ensemble *(rec Recital Hall, SUNY Purchase, 1993)* Well-Tempered Productions ▲ WTP 5172 [DDD]
Ewazen, E.:"...to cast a shadow again", w. William Sharp (bar), Colette Valentine (pno) *(rec Recital Hall, SUNY Purchase, 1993)* Well-Tempered Productions ▲ WTP 5172 [DDD]
Hovhaness, A.:Haroutiun, w. R.A. Clark (cnd), Manhattan CO Koch International Classics ▲ KIC 7221 [DDD]
Hovhaness, A.:Prayer of St. Gregory, w. R.A. Clark (cnd), Manhattan CO Koch International Classics ▲ KIC 7221 [DDD]
Hovhaness, A.:Return & Rebuild the Desolate Places, w. R.A. Clark (cnd), Manhattan CO Koch International Classics ▲ KIC 7221 [DDD]
Previn, A.:Honey & Rue, w. Kathleen Battle (sop), James Pugh (trbn), Rufus Reid (bass), Grady Tate (dr), A. Previn (cnd), Orch of St. Luke's Deutsche Grammophon ▲ 437787-2 ■ 437 787-4
Stravinsky, I.:Octet, w. M. Parloff (fl), D. Schiffrin (cl), F. Morelli (bn), S. Heinneman (bn), R. Mase (tpt), R. Borror (trbn), D. Taylor (trbn), G. Schuller (cnd) *(rec Sep. 1991)* GM ▲ GM 2030
Tower, J.:Black Topaz, w. Stephen Gosling (pno), Patricia Spencer (fl), Laura Flax (cl), Mike Powell (trbn), Jonathan Haas (perc), Deborah Moore (perc) *(rec American Academy of Arts & Letters, New York City, Sept. 26–28, 1994)* New World ▲ 80470-2

Gekker, Chris (tpts/flgl)—see ORCHESTRAS & ENSEMBLES American Brass Quintet

Gelber, Bruno-Leonardo (pno)
Beethoven, L. van:Son 1 Pno Denon ▲ DEN 78849 [DDD]
Beethoven, L. van:Son 6 Pno Denon ▲ DEN 78849 [DDD]
Beethoven, L. van:Son 7 Pno Denon ▲ DEN 78849 [DDD]
Beethoven, L. van:Son 13 Pno Denon ▲ CO 72539 [DDD]
Beethoven, L. van:Son 14 Pno, "Moonlight Son" Denon ▲ CO 72539 [DDD]
Beethoven, L. van:Son 15 Pno, "Pastoral" Denon ▲ CO 72539 [DDD]
Beethoven, L. van:Son 17 Pno, "Tempest" Denon/PCM Digital ▲ CO 75245 [DDD]

Gelber, Bruno-Leonardo (pno) (cont.)
Beethoven, L. van:Son 18 Pno Denon ▲ CO 73006 [DDD]
Beethoven, L. van:Son 23 Pno, "Appassionata" Denon ▲ CO 73006 [DDD]
Beethoven, L. van:Son 25 Pno Denon/PCM Digital ▲ CO 75245 [DDD]
Beethoven, L. van:Son 26 Pno, "Les Adieux", w. Gelber Denon ▲ CO 73006 [DDD]
Beethoven, L. van:Son 28 Pno Denon/PCM Digital ▲ CO 75245 [DDD]
Beethoven, L. van:Vars & Fugue Pno, Op. 35, "Eroica" Orfeo ▲ 040841 [DDD]
Beethoven, L. van:Vars on an Original Theme, WoO 77 Orfeo ▲ 040841 [DDD]
Beethoven, L. van:Vars Pno, WoO 80 Orfeo ▲ 040841 [DDD]

Gele, Geert Van (rcr)—see ORCHESTRAS & ENSEMBLES Flanders Recorder Quartet

Gelenbe, Deniz Arman (pno)—see ORCHESTRAS & ENSEMBLES Arman Ensemble

Geliot, Huguette (hp)
Garcia & Geliot, w. Serge Garcia (vn) Quantum ▲ QM 6938 [DDD]

Geliot, Martine (hp)
Bax, A.:Elegiac Trio, w. T. Prévost (fl), J. Dupouy (va) Quantum ▲ QM 6898 ■ QM 1993
Debussy, C.:Son Fl, w. T. Prévost (fl), J. Dupouy (va) Quantum ▲ QM 6898 ■ QM 1993
Hommage à Martine Geliot (1948–1988), w. Thomas Prévost (fl), Jean Dupouy (va) Quantum ▲ QM 6898 ■ QM 1993
Leclair, J.-M.:Trio Sons, w. T. Prévost (fl), J. Dupouy (va) [trans. for flute, viola & harp] Quantum ▲ QM 6898 ■ QM 1993
Lemeland, A.:To Holst's Memory, w. T. Prévost (fl), J. Dupouy (va) Quantum ▲ QM 6898 ■ QM 1993
Porter, Q.:Duo Va, w. J. Dupouy (va) Quantum ▲ QM 6898 ■ QM 1993
Recital Quantum ▲ QM 6903 ■ QM 1997

Gelland, Cecilia (vn)—see ORCHESTRAS & ENSEMBLES Gelland Duo

Gelland, Martin (vn)—see also ORCHESTRAS & ENSEMBLES Gelland Duo
Acker, D.:Son Vn *(rec Tonhallen, Sundsvall/Sweden & Holmsund Church, Aug 24–27 & Sept 8, 1995)* Vienna Modern Masters ▲ VMM 2017 [DDD]
Burkhard, W.:Son Vn, w. Lennart Wallin (pno) *(rec Tonhallen, Sundsvall/Sweden & Holmsund Church, Aug 24–27 & Sept 8, 1995)* Vienna Modern Masters ▲ VMM 2017 [DDD]
Jelinek, H.:Zahme Xenien, w. Lennart Wallin (pno) *(rec Tonhallen, Sundsvall/Sweden & Holmsund Church, Aug 24–27 & Sept 8, 1995)* Vienna Modern Masters ▲ VMM 2017 [DDD]
Sapp, A.D.:And the Bombers Went Home, w. Lennart Wallin (pno) *(rec Tonhallen, Sundsvall/Sweden & Holmsund Church, Aug 24–27 & Sept 8, 1995)* Vienna Modern Masters ▲ VMM 2017 [DDD]
Schoeck, O.:Son Vn, Op. 22, w. Lennart Wallin (pno) *(rec Tonhallen, Sundsvall/Sweden & Holmsund Church, Aug 24–27 & Sept 8, 1995)* Vienna Modern Masters ▲ VMM 2017 [DDD]
Strauss, R.:Allegretto Vn, w. Lennart Wallin (pno) *(rec Tonhallen, Sundsvall/Sweden & Holmsund Church, Aug 24–27 & Sept 8, 1995)* Vienna Modern Masters ▲ VMM 2017 [DDD]
Wyshnegradsky, I.:Chant douloureux et étude, w. Lennart Wallin (pno) *(rec Tonhallen, Sundsvall/Sweden & Holmsund Church, Aug 24–27 & Sept 8, 1995)* Vienna Modern Masters ▲ VMM 2017 [DDD]
Wyshnegradsky, I.:Chant nocturne, w. Ute Gareis (pno), Klaus-Georg Pohl (pno) *(rec Tonhallen, Sundsvall/Sweden & Holmsund Church, Aug 24–27 & Sept 8, 1995)* Vienna Modern Masters ▲ VMM 2017 [DDD]

Gelmini, Anna Alessandra (vn)
Segoviana:Duets for Violin & Guitar, w. Michele Manuguerra (gtr) Kicco Classic ▲ 295

Gemmell, James (pno)
Crumb, G.:Vox balaenae, w. Z. Mueller (fl), F. Sherry (vc) New World ▲ NW 357-2
Zwilich, E.T.:Son in 3 Movts, w. J. Zwilich (vn) CRI ▲ CD 621 [ADD]

Gendron, Maurice (vc)
Bach, J.S.:Suites Vc, BWV 1007–1012 Philips ("Duo" series) 2-▲ 442293-2
Beethoven, L. van:Vars on "Ein Mädchen oder Weibchen" from Mozart's *Die Zauberflöte*, w. J. Françaix (pno) Philips ("Duo" series) 2-▲ 442565-2
Beethoven, L. van:Vars on "See, the Conquering Hero Comes" from Handel's *Judas Maccabaeus*, w. J. Françaix (pno) Philips ("Duo" series) 2-▲ 442565-2
Beethoven, L. van:Vars on "Bei Männern" from Mozart's *Die Zauberflöte*, w. J. Françaix (pno) Philips ("Duo" series) 2-▲ 442565-2
Chopin, F.:Intro & Polonaise, "Polonaise brilliante", w. Keiko Toyama (pno) *(rec Iruma-shi Shimin Kaikan, June 1981)* Camerata ▲ 25CM 366
Chopin, F.:Son Vc, w. Keiko Toyama (pno) *(rec Iruma-shi Shimin Kaikan, June 1981)* Camerata ▲ 25CM 366
Debussy, C.:Son Vc, w. J. Françaix (pno) Philips ▲ 422839-2 [ADD]
Dvořák, A.:Con Vc, w. W. Mengelberg (cnd), *(orch unknown)* Archive Documents ("The Mengelberg Edition" series) ▲ ADCD 116
Dvořák, A.:Con Vc, w. W. Mengelberg (cnd), Paris RSO *(rec live, Paris, Jan 16, 1944)* Arkadia ▲ 627 [ADD]
Lalo, E.:Son Vc, w. Keiko Toyama (pno) *(rec Honjo Bunka-kaikan, Sept 1985)* Camerata ▲ 25CM 366

Genet, Patrick (vn)—see ORCHESTRAS & ENSEMBLES Sine Nomine String Quartet, Musiviva Trio

Genovese, Alfred (ob)
Bach, J.S.:Con 1 for 2 Hpds, w. Andrew Kohji Taylor (vn), P. van Haeren (cnd), New England CO [orig Bach version for Ob & Vn] *(rec Campion Center, Weston, MA, Feb 1993)* Boston Records ▲ BR 1007
Barlow, W.:The Winter's Past, w. P. van Haeren (cnd), New England CO *(rec Campion Center, Weston, MA, Feb 1993)* Boston Records ▲ BR 1007
Loeffler, C.M.:Rhaps, w. B. Fine (va), P. Serkin (pno) *(rec Aug. 1992)* Boston Records ▲ BR 1004
Mozart, W.A.:Qnt Pno, K.452, w. P. Serkin (pno), H. Wright (cl), R. Sebring (hn), F. Svoboda (bn) *(rec Aug. 1992)* Boston Records ▲ BR 1004
Poulenc, F.:Son Ob, w. P. Serkin (pno) *(rec Aug. 1992)* Boston Records ▲ BR 1004
Schumann, R.:Romances Ob, w. Peter Serkin (pno) *(rec Aug. 1992)* Boston Records ▲ BR 1004

Gentili, Massimo (trns fl)—see ORCHESTRAS & ENSEMBLES L'Astrée Ensemble

Genty, Jacques (pno)
Fauré, G.:Andante Vn, w. L. Bobesco (vn) *(rec 1980)* Pavane 2-▲ ADW 7292/93
Fauré, G.:Berceuse Vn, w. L. Bobesco (vn) *(rec 1980)* Pavane 2-▲ ADW 7292/93
Fauré, G.:Son 1 Vn, w. L. Bobesco (vn) *(rec 1980)* Pavane 2-▲ ADW 7292/93
Fauré, G.:Son 2 Vn, w. L. Bobesco (vn) *(rec 1980)* Pavane 2-▲ ADW 7292/93
Franck, C.:Son Vn, w. L. Bobesco (vn) *(rec 1980)* Pavane 2-▲ ADW 7292/93
Lekeu, G.:Son Vn, w. L. Bobesco (vn) *(rec 1980)* Pavane 2-▲ ADW 7292/93

Genuit, Werner (pno)
Brahms, J.:Sons Cl (comp), w. D. Klöcker (cl) Acanta ▲ CD 43270 [DDD]
Brahms, J.:Trio Hn, w. P. Damm (hn), J. Suk (vn) Acanta ▲ CD 43270 [DDD]
Daelli, G.:Fantasia on Verdi's *Rigoletto*, w. Thomas Indermühle (ob) *(rec Studio Baumgarten, Vienna, Jan 31 & Feb 1, 1994)* Camerata ▲ 30CM 403 [DDD]
Donizetti, G.:Chamber Music, w. Thomas Indermühle (ob)—Andante sostenuto in f [arr Thomas Indermühle] *(rec Studio Baumgarten, Vienna, Jan 31 & Feb 1, 1994)* Camerata ▲ 30CM 403 [DDD]
Donizetti, G.:Son Ob, w. Thomas Indermühle (ob) *(rec Studio Baumgarten, Vienna, Jan 31 & Feb 1, 1994)* Camerata ▲ 30CM 403 [DDD]
Dutilleux, H.:Son Ob, w. Thomas Indermühle (ob) *(rec Studio Baumgarten, Vienna, Feb 10–12, 1993)* Camerata ▲ 25CM 282 [DDD]
Farrenc, J.-L.:Trio Cl, w. D. Klöcker (cl), Hoerr (vc) Divox ▲ CDX 29205 [DDD]
Jolivet, A.:Sérénade Ob, w. Thomas Indermühle (ob) *(rec Studio Baumgarten, Vienna, Feb 10–12, 1993)* Camerata ▲ 25CM 282 [DDD]
Lovreglio, D.:Fant on themes from Verdi's *Un ballo in maschera*, w. Thomas Indermühle (ob) *(rec Studio Baumgarten, Vienna, Jan 31 & Feb 1, 1994)* Camerata ▲ 30CM 403 [DDD]
Milhaud, D.:Sonatina Ob, w. Thomas Indermühle (ob) *(rec Studio Baumgarten, Vienna, Feb 10–12, 1993)* Camerata ▲ 25CM 282 [DDD]
Pasculli, A.:Concerto on Themes from Donizetti's *La Favorita*, w. Thomas Indermühle (ob) *(rec Studio Baumgarten, Vienna, Jan 31 & Feb 1, 1994)* Camerata ▲ 30CM 403 [DDD]
Pasculli, A.:Fantaisie on Themes from Donizetti's *Poliuto*, w. Thomas Indermühle (ob) *(rec Studio Baumgarten, Vienna, Jan 31 & Feb 1, 1994)* Camerata ▲ 30CM 403 [DDD]

Genuit, Werner (pno) (cont.)
Pasculli, A.:Grand Con Ob, w. Thomas Indermühle (ob) *(rec Studio Baumgarten, Vienna, Jan 31 & Feb 1, 1994)* Camerata ▲ 30CM 403 [DDD]
Ponchielli, A.:Capriccio Ob, w. Thomas Indermühle (ob) *(rec Studio Baumgarten, Vienna, Jan 31 & Feb 1, 1994)* Camerata ▲ 30CM 403 [DDD]
Ravel, M.:Le Tombeau de Couperin, w. Thomas Indermühle (ob)—Suite [arr Werner Genuit for ob & pno] *(rec Studio Baumgarten, Vienna, Feb 10–12, 1993)* Camerata ▲ 25CM 282 [DDD]
Skalkottas, N.:Concertino Ob, w. Thomas Indermühle (ob) *(rec Studio Baumgarten, Vienna, Feb 10–12, 1993)* Camerata ▲ 25CM 282 [DDD]

Genvrin, Vincent (org)
Bach, J.S.:Chorale Preludes Org—13 Chorals for Christmas Studio SM ▲ 121892
Lefébure-Wély, L.J.A.:Music of, w. Sylvie de May (sop), Catherine Ravenne (alt), Xavier Bisaro (org), La Lyre Seraphique, L'Accent Grave Vocal Ensemble—Adoremus et procidamus; Marche en mib majeur; Adoro te [alterné]; Tantum ergo; Sacris solemnis; Elévation en la mineur; Marche en ut majeur; Noël varié, offertoire pour le jour de Noël; Sanctus; O Salutaris; Pastorale en sol majeur; Agnus Dei; Communion en fa majeur; Domine salvum; Missum redemptorem; Sortie en sib majeur et Cloches Media 7 ▲ 005 [DDD]
Lefébure-Wély, L.J.A.:Music of, w. Sylvie de May (sop), Sophie Fournier (sop), Catherine Ravenne (alt), Antoine Espagno (db), La Lyre Seraphique, Pythagore Vocal Ensemble—Sainte cité, demeure permanente; Récit de Hautbois ou de Trompette harmonique; L'Encens divin; Offertoire [grand choeur]; Seigneur dès ma première enfance; Verset; Pleins de ferveur; Marche; Jour heureux, sainte allégresse; Esprit divin, Dieu de lumière; Andante, choeur de voix humaines; Afin d'être docile et sage; Mon fils, pour apprendre; Andante; Motet à la Sainte-Vierge; Andante; Du Roi des cieux tout célèbre la gloire; Scène pastorale; Andantino Media 7 ▲ 004 [DDD]

Geoffray, Nathalie (vn)—see ORCHESTRAS & ENSEMBLES Ravel String Quartet

Geoffroy, Jean (perc)
Campana, J.L.:Je est un autre..., w. F. della Valle (vn) Skarbo ▲ SKR3923 [DDD]
Malec, I.:Attacca, w. F. della Valle (vn) Skarbo ▲ SKR3923 [DDD]
Tanguy, E.:Towards, w. F. della Valle (vn) Skarbo ▲ SKR3923 [DDD]
Tosi, D.:Phonic Design, w. F. della Valle (vn) Skarbo ▲ SKR3923 [DDD]

Geoffroy, Jean (vib)
Vustin, A.:Musique pour l'ange, w. Claude Delangle (t sax), Vérène Westphal (vc) *(rec Paris, July 1995)* BIS ▲ CD 765 [DDD]

Geoffroy-Dechaume, Antoine (hpd)
Couperin, F.:Les Nations, w. J. Roussel (cnd), Antiqua Musica CO EMI Classics ("Baroque" series) ▲ CDK 65732
Couperin, F.:Les Nations (sels), w. J. Roussel (cnd), Antiqua Musica CO EMI Classics ▲ CDK 65732
Couperin, F.:La Pucelle, w. J. Roussel (cnd), Antiqua Musica CO EMI Classics ▲ CDK 65732

George, Katherine (pno)
Chopin, F.:Intro & Polonaise, "Polonaise brilliante", w. J. Cox (hn) *(rec 8/91)* Centaur ▲ CRC 2122 [DDD]
Gieseking, W.:Qnt Hn, w. J. Cox (hn), F. Korman (ob), Y. Nakao (cl), B. Fillmore (bn) *(rec 8/91)* Centaur ▲ CRC 2122 [DDD]
Schumann, R.:Adagio & Allegro Hn, w. J. Cox (hn) Centaur ▲ CRC 2122 [DDD]

Georgi, Olaf (fl)
Berlinski, H.:Das Gebet Bonhoeffers, w. Nancy Gibson (sop), Matthias Weichert (bass), Bernhard Hentrich (vc), Herman Berlinski (org), Holger Miersch (cel), Martin Homann (perc), Hans-Christoph Rademann (cnd), Dresden Chamber Choir Vienna Modern Masters ▲ VMM 3027 [DDD]

Georgian, Karina (vc)
Brahms, J.:Trio Cl, w. T. King (cl), C. Benson (pno) Hyperion ▲ CDA 66107
Ireland, J.:The Holy Boy, w. Ian Brown (pno) Chandos ▲ CHAN 9377/8 [DDD]
Ireland, J.:Phantasie Trio, w. Ian Brown (pno), Lydia Mordkovitch (vn) Chandos ▲ CHAN 9377/8 [DDD]
Ireland, J.:Son Vc, w. Ian Brown (pno) Chandos ▲ CHAN 9377/8 [DDD]
Ireland, J.:Trio 2 Pno, w. Ian Brown (pno), Lydia Mordkovitch (vn) Chandos ▲ CHAN 9377/8 [DDD]
Ireland, J.:Trio 3 Pno, w. Ian Brown (pno), Lydia Mordkovitch (vn) Chandos ▲ CHAN 9377/8 [DDD]

Georgieva, Velislava (pno)
Bruch, M.:Fant for 2 Pnos, w. K. Taskov (pno) Gega ▲ GD 139 [DDD]
Busoni, F.:Fant contrappuntistica Pno, w. K. Taskov (pno) Gega ▲ GD 139 [DDD]
Martinů, B.:Fant for 2 Pnos, w. K. Taskov (pno) Gega ▲ GD 139 [DDD]
Mozart, W.A.:Fant Pno, K.396, w. K. Taskov (pno) Gega ▲ GD 139 [DDD]
Taskov, K.:Fant for 2 Pnos, w. K. Taskov (pno) Gega ▲ GD 139 [DDD]

Geraldo, Tino di (perc)—see ORCHESTRAS & ENSEMBLES Al Ayre Español

Gerard, D. (pno)
Mozart, W.A.:Con 9 Pno, w. H. Kraus (cnd), Vienna Mozart Ensemble LaserLight ▲ 15 632 [DDD]
Mozart, W.A.:Con 23 Pno, w. H. Kraus (cnd), Vienna Mozart Ensemble LaserLight ▲ 15 632 [DDD]
Mozart, W.A.:Con 23 Pno, w. H. Kraus (cnd), Vienna Mozart Ensemble LaserLight ▲ 15 649 [DDD]

Gérard, Jean-Claude (fl)
Dutilleux, H.:Sonatine Fl, w. F. Killian (pno) *(rec May 1987)* Signum ▲ X 21-00 [DDD]
Franck, C.:Son Vn, w. F. Killian (pno) *(rec May 1987)* Signum ▲ X 21-00 [DDD]
Hindemith, P.:Son Fl, w. Kalle Randalu MD + G ▲ MDG CD 3040695
Mozart, W.A.:Qts Fl, w. Villa Musica Ensemble *(rec Aug. 29–30, 1990)* Naxos ▲ 8.550438 [DDD]
Poulenc, F.:Son Fl, w. F. Killian (pno) *(rec May 1987)* Signum ▲ X 21-00 [DDD]
Reicha, A.:Sinf concertante, w. Ida Bieler (vn), P. Gülke (cnd), Wuppertal SO MD + G ▲ MDG 3350661

Gerber, Thomas (hpd)
Purcell, H.:Come Ye Sons of Art, w. Laura Goetz (ob), Sarah Weiner (ob), Davis Brooks (vn), Lisa Brooks (vn), Jann Cosart (va), Mary Burke (vl), Vance Reese (db), Henry H. Leck (cnd), Indianapolis Children's Choir [arr. Maurice Blower] *(rec The Lodge, May & June 1995)* VAI Audio ▲ VAIA 1130 [DDD]
Purcell, H.:Fly, Bold Rebellion (sels), w. Laura Goetz (ob), Sarah Weiner (ob), Davis Brooks (vn), Lisa Brooks (vn), Jann Cosart (va), Mary Burke (vl), Vance Reese (db), Henry H. Leck (cnd), Indianapolis Children's Choir—Be Welcome Then, Great Sir [arr. Steven Rickards] *(rec The Lodge, May & June 1995)* VAI Audio ▲ VAIA 1130 [DDD]
Purcell, H.:King Arthur (sels), w. Laura Goetz (ob), Sarah Weiner (ob), Davis Brooks (vn), Lisa Brooks (vn), Jann Cosart (va), Mary Burke (vl), Vance Reese (db), Henry H. Leck (cnd), Indianapolis Children's Choir—Fairest Isle [arr. Steven Rickards] *(rec The Lodge, May & June 1995)* VAI Audio ▲ VAIA 1130 [DDD]

Gerbi, A. (cl)
Vivaldi, A.:Cons Obs Cls, w. A. Caroldi (ob), A. Alvarosi (ob), E. Schiani (cl), P. Santi (cnd), Milan Virtuosi Allegretto ▲ ACD 8036 [ADD] ■ ACS 8036

Gergely, Ferenc (org)
Silent Night, w. Imre Kovacs (fl), Hedy Lubik (hp), Frigyes Hidas (org), Gabor Lehotka (org), Hungarian State Orch CO, Csanyi (cnd), Szekeres (cnd), Budapest Children's Choir Madrigal Choir Hungaroton ▲ HCD 16598

Gergieva, Larissa (pno)
Balakirev, M.:Songs, w. Olga Borodina (mez)—When I but Hear Your Voice; The Pleasure You Bring Is Enthralling; The Crescent Moon; Over the Lake; My Restless Heart; Selim's Song; Spanish Song; I Loved Him Philips ▲ 442780-2
Borodin, A.:Songs, w. Olga Borodina (mez)—A Note of Insincerity; The Princess of the Sea Philips ▲ 442780-2
Cui, C.:Songs, w. Olga Borodina (mez)—I Remember an Evening; You & Thou; A Statue in Tsarskoye; My Desire; Here the Lilac Blossom Fades So Quickly; I Touched the Bloom Lightly; It's Over Philips ▲ 442780-2
Mussorgsky, M.:Songs (misc), w. Olga Borodina (mez)—What Are Love's Words to You?; In the Night Philips ▲ 442780-2
Rimsky-Korsakov, N.:Songs, w. Olga Borodina (mez)—The Octave; The Swift Parade of Clouds; My Dreams; The Nightingale; 'Twas Not the Wind; The Lark's Song Philips ▲ 442780-2

INSTRUMENTALISTS 573

Gergieva, Larissa (pno) (cont.)
Tchaikovsky, P.:Songs, w. O. Borodina (mez)—None but the Lonely Heart; Night; Once Again, Alone; The Frightening Moment; Gypsy Girl's Song; Serenade; Lullaby; Heed Not, My Love; Spirit My Heart away; This, Our First Reunion; Indoors, the Light Philips ▲ 442013-2

Gerhard, Walter (va)
Purcell, H.:Chamber Music, w. Alberto Lysy (vn), Robert Masters (vn), Yehudi Menuhin (vn), Cecil Arnowitz (va), Derek Simpson (vc), Ambrose Gauntlett (vl), Roy Jesson (hpd/org)—Trio Sons Nos. 2 in C, 6 in G & 8 in G; Fants Nos. 4 in g, 7 in c, 8 in d & 13 in F, "Upon One Note" EMI Classics ("Baroque" series) ▲ CDK 65734
Purcell, H.:Fants, w. Alberto Lysy (vn), Robert Masters (vn), Yehudi Menuhin (vn), Cecil Aronowitz (va), Derek Simpson (vc), Ambrose Gauntlett (vl), Roy Jesson (hpd/org)—Nos. 4 in g, 7 in c, 8 in d, 13 in F EMI Classics ▲ CDK 65734
Purcell, H.:Sons (22) Vns, w. Alberto Lysy (vn), Robert Masters (vn), Yehudi Menuhin (vn), Cecil Aronowitz (va), Derek Simpson (vc), Ambrose Gauntlett (vl), Roy Jesson (hpd/org)—Nos. 2, 6, & 8 EMI Classics ▲ CDK 65734

Gerikh, Dmitri (vn)
Liptak, D.:Rhaps, w. L. Greene (fl), J. Friedrichs (cl), W. Bass (vc), S. Heyman (pno) Opus One ▲ CD 168 [DDD]

Geringas, David (baryton)—see ORCHESTRAS & ENSEMBLES Geringas Baryton Trio

Geringas, David (vc)
Beethoven, L. van:Trio 6 Pno, "Archduke", w. G. Oppitz (pno), D. Sitkovetsky (vn) Novalis ▲ 150008 [DDD]
Beethoven, L. van:Trio 9 Pno, "Kakadu", w. G. Oppitz (pno), D. Sitkovetsky (vn) Novalis ▲ 150008 [DDD]
Boccherini, L.:Cons Vc (comp), w. B. Giuranna (cnd), Padua & Venice CO Claves 3-▲ CD 8814/16 [DDD]
Brahms, J.:Songs, w. M. Lipovsek (mez), C. Spencer (pno)—Gestillte Sehnsucht; Geistliches Wiegenlied; Wie Melodien zieht es; Immer leiser wird mein Schlummer; Klage; Auf den Kirchhofe; Der Tod, das ist die kühle Nacht; Wir wandelten; Es schauen die Blumen; Von ewiger Liebe; Die Mainacht; Wie bist du, mein Königin; Wenn du nur zuweilen lächelst; Es träumte mir; Unbewegte laue luft; Im Garten am Seegestade; Lerchengesang; Serenade; Abendregen; Dort in den Weiden steht ein Haus; Da unten im Tale; Och Moder, ich well en Ding han *(rec Apr. 29–May 1, 1992)* Sony Classical ▲ SK 52490 [DDD]
Dutilleux, H.:Strophes (3) sur le nom Sacher Erato 2-▲ 91721
Gubaidulina, S.:In Croce, w. E. Krapp (org) Koch Schwann ▲ CD 310091 [DDD]
Haydn, J.:Con 1 Vc, w. D. Geringas (cnd), Czech Phil CO *(rec Domovina Studio, Prague, Nov 19–21, 1993)* Canyon Classics ▲ 242
Haydn, J.:Con 2 Vc, w. D. Geringas (cnd), Czech Phil CO *(rec Domovina Studio, Prague, Nov 19–21, 1993)* Canyon Classics ▲ 242
Haydn, J.:Sym 13, w. D. Geringas (cnd), Czech Phil CO [andante] *(rec Domovina Studio, Prague, Nov 19–21, 1993)* Canyon Classics ▲ 242
Pärt, A.:Spiegel im Spiegel, w. T. Schatz (pno) Koch Schwann ▲ CD 310091 [DDD]
Pfitzner, H.:Con 1 Vc, w. W.A. Albert (cnd), Bamberg SO CPO ▲ CPO 999135 [DDD]
Pfitzner, H.:Con 2 Vc, w. W.A. Albert (cnd), Bamberg SO CPO ▲ CPO 999135 [DDD]
Pfitzner, H.:Con 3 Vc, w. W.A. Albert (cnd), Bamberg SO CPO ▲ CPO 999135 [DDD]
Schnittke, A.:Son Vc, w. T. Schatz (pno) Koch Schwann ▲ CD 310091 [DDD]
Schoenberg, A.:Chamber Sym 1, w. A. Andorjan (fl), E. Brunner (cl), D. Sitkovetzky (vn), G. Oppitz (pno) [Webern's 1923 arr. for Flute, Clarinet, Violin, Cello & Piano] Tudor ▲ 717 [DDD]
Schubert, Franz:Trio 1 Pno, w. G. Oppitz (pno), D. Sitkovetsky (vn) Novalis ▲ 150002
Schubert, Franz:Trio 2 Pno, w. G. Oppitz (pno), D. Sitkovetsky (vn) Novalis ▲ 150003
Schulhoff, E.:Duo Vn, w. P. Hirschhorn (vn) *(rec Lockenhaus Festival, 1986)* ECM New Series 2-▲ 78118-21347-2 [DDD]
Schulhoff, E.:Sxt Strs, w. G. Kremer (vn), P. Hirschhorn (vn), N. Imai (va), K. Kashkasian (va), J. Berger (vc) *(rec Lockenhaus Festival, 1986)* ECM New Series 2-▲ 78118-21347-2 [DDD]
Shostakovich, D.:Qt 14 Strs, w. G. Kremer (vn), Y. Horigome (vn), K. Kashkashian (va) *(rec Lockenhaus Festival, 1986)* ECM New Series 2-▲ 78118-21347-2 [DDD]
Vasks, P.:Con Vc, w. J. Aleksa (cnd), Riga PO, *(Riga, Latvia, Dec 1995)* Conifer Classics ▲ 75605-51271-2 [DDD]
Zemlinsky, A. von:Trio Cl, w. E. Brunner (cl), G. Oppitz (pno) Tudor ▲ 717 [DDD]

Gerlach, Alexis Pia (vc)—see ORCHESTRAS & ENSEMBLES Clementi Quartet

Gerlach, Wilhelm (va)
Mieg, P.:Triple Con, w. Gunars Larsens (vn), Curdin Coray (vc), M. Venzago (cnd), Lucerne Festival Strings *(rec 1979)* Jecklin ▲ JS 314-2 [DDD]

Gerle, Robert (vn)
Lewis, R.H.:Duetto da Camera, w. Marilyn Neeley (pno) Albany ▲ TROY 166 [ADD/DDD]

Germani, Fernando (org)
Bach, J.S.:Cons Org, BWV 592-597—in a, BWV 593 & in d, BWV 596 EMI Classics ("Doublefforte" series) 2-▲ CDFB 69328
Bach, J.S.:Passacaglia & Fugue Org EMI Classics ("Doublefforte" series) 2-▲ CDFB 69328
Bach, J.S.:Toccata, Adagio & Fugue Org, BWV 564 EMI Classics ("Doublefforte" series) 2-▲ CDFB 69328
Bach, J.S.:Toccata & Fugue Org, BWV 565 EMI Classics ("Doublefforte" series) 2-▲ CDFB 69328
Franck, C.:Chorals Org, M.38-40 EMI Classics ("Doublefforte" series) 2-▲ CDFB 69328
Franck, C.:Pastorale EMI Classics ("Doublefforte" series) 2-▲ CDFB 69328
Franck, C.:Pièce héroïque EMI Classics ("Doublefforte" series) 2-▲ CDFB 69328
Widor, C.M.:Sym 5 Org—5th movement, Toccata EMI Classics ("Doublefforte" series) 2-▲ CDFB 69328

Gerogiev, L. (vc)
Paganini, N.:Terzetto Vn, w. M. Minchev (vn), M. Sao Marcos (gtr) Vivace ▲ E 534 [ADD]

Gerov, Valentin (va)
Bond, V.:Dreams of Flying, w. Georgy Valtchev (vn), Nikolai Gagov (vn), Christo Tanev (vc) Gega ▲ GD 197 [DDD]
Nikolov, L.:Qt 3 Strs, w. A. Ilchev (vn), K. Mikaelian (vn), G. Dean (vc) Gega ▲ GD 149 [DDD]

Gerschwitz, Peter (vc)
Dauprat, L.-F.:Qnt Hn & Strs, w. P. Arnold (hn), A. Grötzinger (vn), A. Henschke (vn/va), H.-B. Henscke (va) Bayer ▲ BR 100236 [DDD]
Mozart, W.A.:Qnt Hn, K.407, w. P. Arnold (hn), A. Grötzinger (vn), A. Henschke (vn/va), H.-B. Henscke (va) Bayer ▲ BR 100236 [DDD]
Stamitz, A.:Qnt Hn, w. P. Arnold (hn), A. Grötzinger (vn), A. Henschke (vn/va), H.-B. Henscke (va) Bayer ▲ BR 100236 [DDD]

Gershwin, George (pno)
George Gershwin Plays Rhapsody in Blue Klavier ■ KC 122
Gershwin, G.:Con Pno, w. G. Gershwin (cnd), *(orch unknown)*—3rd movt., plus a song medley with chorus & orchestra, I got rhythm/Of thee I sing *(rec live broadcast of the Rudy Vallee Show from an 11/9/33)* Pearl 2-▲ PEAS 9483 (m) [AAD]
Gershwin, G.:Music of, w. A. Astaire (sgr), F. Astaire (sgr)—Hang on to me; Fascinatin' rhythm; The half of it dearie blues; I'd rather Charleston; solo piano rec'gs by Gershwin—Sweet & low down; That certain feeling; Looking for a boy; Then do we dance?; Do-do-do; Someone to watch over me; Clap yo' hands; Maybe; My one & only; Andante from Rhapsody in Ble; S' wonderful/Funny face *(rec 1926 & 1928 Columbia rec')* Pearl 2-▲ PEAS 9483 (m) [AAD]
Gershwin, G.:Music of RCA ■ ALK1-7114 (m)
Gershwin, G.:Pno Music—Kickin' the Clouds Away; Swanee; Sweet & Low-Down; So am I; Drifting Along with the Tide; I'll Build a Stairway to Paradise; Do It Again; Yankee Doodle Blues; I Was So Young; That Certain Feeling; Rhapsody in Blue Klavier ▲ KC 133

Gershwin, George (pno) (cont.)
Gershwin, G.:Pno Music—Rhapsody in Blue; Swanee; That Certain Feeling; Tee-Oodle-Um-Bum-Bo (from La La Lucille); Kickin' The Clouds Away; Sweet & Low-down (from Tip-toes); So am I (from Lady Be Good); Drifting Along With The Tide; I Was So Young, You Were So Beautiful; Left All Alone Blues (from The Night Boat); Whip-Poor-Will (from Sally); Whose Baby Are You (from The Night Boat); Rock-a-Bye Lullaby land (from Mammy); For Your Country and My Country; Land Where the Good Songs Go; Some Sunday Morning; Ain't You Coming Back to Dixie Klavier ▲ KCD 11001 [ADD]
Gershwin, G.:Pno Music—Swanee [w. Fred Van Eps Trio]; Sweet & Low Down; That Certain Feeling; Looking for a Boy; When Do We Dance? [from Tiptoes]; Do-Do-Do; Someone to Watch over Me; Clap Yo' Hands; Maybe [from O, Kay!]; My One & Only; S'Wonderful/Funny Face [from Funny Face]; Rhap in Blue [w. Paul Whiteman Concert Orch]; 3 Preludes; Andante [from Rhap in Blue]; An American in Paris Mastersound ▲ MST 116 [ADD]
Gershwin, G.:Pno Music—Sweet & Low-Down; Kickin' the Clouds Away;I Was So Young; Too-Oodle-Um-Bum-Bo; Drifting Along With The Tide; So Am I; Left All Alone Blues; Whip-Poor-Will; Whose Baby Are You; Rock-a-bye Lullaby Land Klavier ■ KC 122
Gershwin, G.:Pno Music—Clap Yo' Hands; Do-Do-Do; Looking for a Boy; Maybe; My One & Only; Rhapsody in Blue—Andante; Someone to Watch Over Me; Swanee; Sweet & Low Down; S'Wonderful/Funny Face; That Certain Feeling; Three Preludes; When Do We Dance? Pro Arte ▲ CDD 433 (m)
Gershwin, G.:Pno Music—Sweet & Lowdown; Novelette in Fourths; That Certain Feeling; So Am I; Rhap. in Blue; Swanee; When You Want 'Em, You Can't Get 'Em; Kick'n the Clouds; Idol Dreams; On My Mind the Whole Night Long; Scandal Walk; American in Paris Elektra/Nonesuch ▲ 79287-2 ■ 79287-4
Gershwin, G.:Preludes (3) Pno *(rec 6/8/28 for Columbia)* Pearl 2-▲ PEAS 9483 (m) [AAD]
Gershwin, G.:Preludes (3) Pno RCA ■ ALK1-7114 (m)
Gershwin, G.:Rhap in Blue, w. M. Tilson Thomas (cnd), Columbia Jazz Band [1925 piano roll] CBS ▲ MK 42516 ■ FMT 42516
Gershwin, G.:Rhap in Blue, w. M. Tilson Thomas (cnd), Columbia Jazz Band [1925 piano roll] CBS ▲ MK 42240 [ADD]
Gershwin, G.:Rhap in Blue, w. N. Wayland (cnd), Denver Sym Pops [1925 piano roll] Pro Arte ▲ CDS 574 [DDD]
Gershwin, G.:Rhap in Blue, w. P. Whiteman (cnd), Paul Whiteman Orch *(rec 4/21/27 for Victor)* Pearl 2-▲ PEAS 9483 (m) [AAD]
Gershwin, G.:Rhap in Blue, w. P. Whiteman (cnd), Paul Whiteman Orch Pro Arte ▲ CDD 433 (m)
Gershwin, G.:Rhap in Blue, w. P. Whiteman (cnd), Paul Whiteman Orch RCA ■ ALK1-7114 (m)
Gershwin, G.:Rhap in Blue, Paul Whiteman Orch Claremont ▲ CDGSE 785065

Gershwin, George (pno/cel)
Gershwin, G.:An American in Paris, w. N. Shilkret (cnd), RCA Victor SO Pro Arte ▲ CDD 433 (m)
Gershwin, G.:An American in Paris, w. N. Shilkret (cnd), RCA Victor SO *(rec 2/4/29 for Victor)* Pearl 2-▲ PEAS 9483 (m) [AAD]
Gershwin, G.:Pno Music—Kicking the clouds away; Drifting along with the tide; Twee-oodle-um-bum-bo; So am I; That certain feeling; Sweet & low down Pro Arte ▲ CDS 574 [DDD]

Gertler, André (vn)
Bach, J.S.:Con 1 Vn, w. G. Lehel (cnd), Budapest SO Hungaroton ▲ HCD 31635
Bartók, B.:Con 1 Vn, w. J. Ferencsik (cnd), Brno State PO Supraphon Collection ▲ 11 0632-2 [ADD]
Bartók, B.:Con 2 Vn, w. K. Ančerl (cnd), Czech PO Supraphon Collection ▲ 11 0632-2 [ADD]
Bartók, B.:Con 2 Vn, w. K. Ančerl (cnd), Czech PO Supraphon ▲ SUP 111956 [AAD]
Bartók, B.:Duos (44), w. J. Suk (vn) Sound ▲ CD 3444
Bartók, B.:Son Vn Hungaroton ▲ HCD 31635
Berg, A.:Con Vn, w. P. Kletzki (cnd), Philharmonia Orch Hungaroton ▲ HCD 31635
Hartmann, K.A.:Con funèbre, w. K. Ančerl (cnd), Czech PO Supraphon ▲ SUP 111955 [AAD]
Hindemith, P.:Con Vn, w. K. Ančerl (cnd), Czech PO Supraphon ▲ SUP 111955 [AAD]
Tartini, G.:Cons Vn (misc), w. E. de Stoutz (cnd), Zurich CO—(5) in D, D.24; in D, D.30; in F, D.68; in G, D.83; in A, D.95 *(rec 1962-63)* Hungaroton ▲ HCD 31529 [ADD]

Gertonsson, Tomas (db)
Fauré, G.:La bonne chanson, w. Anne Sofie von Otter (mez), Nils-Erik Sparf (vn), Ulf Forsberg (vn), Matti Hirvikangas (va), Mats Lindström (vc), Bengt Forsberg (pno) *(rec Stockhom, Nov 1994)* Deutsche Grammophon ▲ 447 752-2 [DDD]

Gertschen, Hilmar (org)
Daetwyler, J.:Dialogue Tpt, w. D. Sieber (tpt) Gallo ▲ CD 548 [AAD]

Gertschen, Sabine (dlc)
Holliger, H.:Alb-Chehr, w. Oswald Brumann (bass), Edmund Volken (dlc), Elmar Schmid (cl), Klaus Schmid (cl), Markus Tenisch (Swiss org), Marcel Volken (Swiss org), Paul Locher (vn), Franziskus Abgottspon (nar) ECM New Series ▲ 78118-21540-2 [DDD]

Gervreau, Alain (vc)—see also ORCHESTRAS & ENSEMBLES Aurora Ensemble
Veracini, F.M.:Sons Vn, Op. 1, w. Enrico Gatti (vn), Guido Morini (hpd)—Nos. 1 & 8 Arcana ▲ ACA 27
Veracini, F.M.:Sonate accademiche, w. Enrico Gatti (vn), Guido Morini (hpd)—Nos. 6 & 12 Arcana ▲ ACA 27

Geselbracht, Charlotte (va)—see ORCHESTRAS & ENSEMBLES Pellegrini String Quartet

Gessi, P. (vc)
Lemeland, A.:American Epitaph (à la mémoire de Aaron Copland), w. A. Kapchiev (vn), F. Jeandet (va) *(rec 1991)* Skarbo ▲ SKR 3913 [ADD]

Gester, Martin (org)
Bach, J.S.:Sons Vn, w. Alice Pierot (vn)—BWV 1014-1019 Accord 2-▲ ACD 205322 [DDD]

Gevers, Cas (trbn)—see ORCHESTRAS & ENSEMBLES Weser-Renaissance Ensemble

Gevers, Frédéric (pno)
Schumann, R.:Arabeske Pno *(rec Barcelona, Sept 1995)* Edicions Albert Moraleda ▲ 6134 [DDD]
Schumann, R.:Blumenstück *(rec Barcelona, Sept 1995)* Edicions Albert Moraleda ▲ 6134 [DDD]
Schumann, R.:Fant Pno *(rec Barcelona, Sept 1995)* Edicions Albert Moraleda ▲ 6134 [DDD]
Schumann, R.:Kinderszenen *(rec Barcelona, Sept 1995)* Edicions Albert Moraleda ▲ 6134 [DDD]
Schumann, R.:Romances Pno *(rec Barcelona, Sept 1995)* Edicions Albert Moraleda ▲ 6134 [DDD]

Gheorghiu, Valentin (pno)
Mendelssohn, F.:Con 1 Pno, w. H. Kegel (cnd), Leipzig RSO Berlin Classics ▲ BER 9027 [ADD]
Mendelssohn, F.:Con 2 Pno, w. H. Kegel (cnd), Leipzig RSO Berlin Classics ▲ BER 9027 [ADD]

Ghetti, Genunzio (vc)
Marcello, B.:Cons a cinque, w. Franco Fantini (vn), A. Ephrikian (cnd), Milan Solisti—Nos. 1-6 Rivoalto ▲ RIV 8913 [ADD]
Vivaldi, A.:Sons Vn, Op. 5, w. F. Fantini (vn), M. Ferarris (vn), A. Ephrikaim (vn), A. Pocaterra (vc), I. De Carli (cembalo), V. Luccini (cembalo) Rivoalto ▲ CRA 9005 [ADD]

Ghidoni, Antonello (gtr)—see ORCHESTRAS & ENSEMBLES Duo Chitarristico

Ghidoni, P. (vn)—see ORCHESTRAS & ENSEMBLES Matisse Trio

Ghielmi, Lorenzo (hpd)
Frescobaldi, G.:Aria detta "La Frescobalda" Nuova Era ("Ancient Music" series) ▲ 6799 [DDD]
Frescobaldi, G.:Toccatas (11) Hpd—Nos. 1,2,7,9,10 & 11; organ—Nos. 3-6 & 8 Nuova Era ("Ancient Music" series) ▲ 6799 [DDD]

Ghielmi, Lorenzo (org)
Bach, J.S.:Aria variata alla maniera italiana [Ahrend organ, Deutsches Museum, Munich] *(rec Munich, June 3-4, 1996)* Ars Musici ▲ AM 1176-2 [DDD]
Bach, J.S.:Cons Org, BWV 592-597—in G, BWV 592 [Ahrend organ, Deutsches Museum, Munich] *(rec Munich, June 3-4, 1996)* Ars Musici ▲ AM 1176-2 [DDD]
Bach, J.S.:Fugue on a Theme by Corelli [Ahrend organ, Deutsches Museum, Munich] *(rec Munich, June 3-4, 1996)* Ars Musici ▲ AM 1176-2 [DDD]
Bach, J.S.:Fugue Org, BWV 578 [Ahrend organ, Deutsches Museum, Munich] *(rec Munich, June 3-4, 1996)* Ars Musici ▲ AM 1176-2 [DDD]
Bach, J.S.:Pastorale Org, BWV 590 [Ahrend organ, Deutsches Museum, Munich] *(rec Munich, June 3-4, 1996)* Ars Musici ▲ AM 1176-2 [DDD]
Bach, J.S.:Preludes & Fugues, BWV 531-552—in G, BWV 541 [Ahrend organ, Deutsches Museum, Munich] *(rec Munich, June 3-4, 1996)* Ars Musici ▲ AM 1176-2 [DDD]

▲ = CD ♦ = Enhanced CD Δ = MD ■ = Cassette Tape ▯ = DCC

Ghielmi, Lorenzo (org) (cont.)
Bach, J.S.:Trio Sons Org, BWV 525–530—in E♭ BWV 525 [Ahrend organ, Deutsches Museum, Munich] *(rec Munich, June 3–4, 1996)* Ars Musici ▲ AM 1176–2 [DDD]
Frescobaldi, G.:Fiori musicali, w. Christoph Erkens (cnd), Canticum—Toccata avanti la Messa; Kyrie; Gloria; Canzon dopo la Pistola; Credo IV; Recercar dopo il Credo; Sanctus; Toccata per le Levatione; Agnus Dei; Tocatta avanti il Ricercar; Recercar con obligato di cantare; Ite Missa est; Toccata Sesta; Invitatorium:Deus in auditorium; Canzon detta la Pesenti; Antiphon:Jam heims Psalm 112; Capriccio sopra la Bassa Fiamenga; Responsorium breve:Ave Maria, gratia plena; Hymnus:Ave Maris stella; Antiphon:Ave Maria, gratia plena Magnificat primi toni; Benedicamus Domino; Marianische Antiphon:Ave Regina; Capriccio sopra la Girolmeta *(Milan, Oct 1994)* Deutsche Harmonia Mundi ▲ 05472–77345–2 [DDD]
Pasquini, B.:Kbd Music—Partite diverse di follia, Bergamasca, Bizzarria, Sonatas, etc.; harpsichord—Variazione capricciose; Toccata & Scherzo del cucco; etc. Nuova Era ("Ancient Music" series) ▲ 6890 [DDD]

Ghirardi, Marie-Thérèse (gtr)
Paganini, N.:Cantabile, w. Maryvonne le Dizès (vn) Adès ▲ ADE 204732 [DDD]
Paganini, N.:Sons Vn & Gtr, w. Maryvonne le Dizès (vn)—Opp. 2 & 3 Adès ▲ ADE 204732 [DDD]

Ghisa, Marian (cl)
Hollós, M.:Dúli-dúli, w. Zoltán Rémann (cl), Marius Lupsa (cl) *(rec Academy of Music G. Dima in Cluj)* Hungaroton ("Classic" series) ▲ HCD 31572 [DDD]

Ghitalla, A. (tpt)
Albrechtsberger, J.G.:Concertino 5 Instrs, w. Robert Shermont (vn), Jean Cauhape (va), Alfred Zighera (vc), James Weaver (pno) *(rec Dec 1963 & Jan 1964)* Crystal ▲ CD 760
Böhme, O.:Con Tpt, w. W. Perry (cnd), Slovak PO Premier ▲ PRCD 1027 [DDD]
Haydn, M.:Con in C Tpt, w. J. Moriarty (cnd), Copenhagen CO *(rec 1969)* Crystal ▲ CD 760
Hummel, J.N.:Con in E Tpt, w. P. Monteux (cnd), Boston Chamber Ensemble *(rec Dec 1963 & Jan 1964)* Crystal ▲ CD 760
Molter, J.M.:Con in D Tpt, w. W. Perry (cnd), Capella Istropolitana Premier ▲ PRCD 1027 [DDD]
Molter, J.M.:Con 3 Tpt, w. H. Farberman (cnd), Boston Chamber Ensemble *(rec Dec 1963 & Jan 1964)* Crystal ▲ CD 760
Perry, W.:Con Tpt, w. W. Perry (cnd), Slovak PO Premier ▲ PRCD 1027 [DDD]
Ponchielli, A.:Con Tpt, w. W. Perry (cnd), Slovak PO Premier ▲ PRCD 1027 [DDD]
Sapieyevski, J.:Mercury Con, w. J. Stephens (cnd), American Camerata AmCam ▲ ACR 10305CD

Ghough, Helen (vc)
Vivaldi, A.:Sons Vc, w. David Miller (archlt/gtr/thb), Robert King (hpd/org), David Watkin (vc)—Sonatas in E♭, RV.39; e, RV.40; F, RV.41; g, RV.42; a, RV.43; a, RV.44; B♭, RV.45; B♭, RV.46; B♭, RV.47 Hyperion 2–▲ CDA 66881/82

Giaccaglia, Roberto (bn)
Poulenc, F.:Sxt Pno, w. Andrea Dindo (pno), Gianpaolo Pretto (fl), Paolo Grazia (ob), Alessandro Carbonare (cl), Stefano Pignatelli (hn) *(rec Sala Maffeiana dell'Accademia Filarmonica di Verona, May 7–9, 1995)* Agorá ▲ 021 [DDD]
Poulenc, F.:Trio Ob, w. Paolo Grazia (ob), Andrea Dindo (pno) *(rec Sala Maffeiana dell'Accademia Filarmonica di Verona, May 7–9, 1995)* Agorá ▲ 021 [DDD]

Giacobassi, Julie Ann (E hn)
Kernis, A.J.:Colored Field, w. A. Neale (cnd), San Francisco SO *(rec Davies Symphony Hall, San Francisco, May 14, 1994)* Argo ▲ 448174–2 [DDD]

Giacomazzi, Claudio (vc)—see ORCHESTRAS & ENSEMBLES Flautarte Quartet

Giacometti, Paolo (pno)
Reger, M.:Caprice & Kleine Romanze, w. Pieter Wispelwey (vc) Channel Classics ▲ CCS 9596
Reger, M.:Suite Vn Pno, w. Pieter Wispelwey (vc)—3rd movt. Channel Classics ▲ CCS 9596
Reger, M.:Wiegenlied, Capriccio & Burla, w. Pieter Wispelwey (vc)—Wiegenlied Channel Classics ▲ CCS 9596
Schubert, Franz:Son Arpeggione, w. Pieter Wispelwey (vc) Channel Classics ▲ CCS 9696
Schubert, Franz:Sonatinas Vn, w. Pieter Wispelwey (vc) [trans P. Wispelwey for vc & pno] Channel Classics ▲ CCS 9696

Giacosa, Franco (pno)
Sivori, C.:Music for Pno Trio, w. B. Pignata (vn), R. Agosti (vc)—Mira la bianca luna on Rossini's Soirées musicales; La Pesca e La Promessa on Rossini's Soirées musicales; Il coro delle sirene on Weber's Oberon *(rec Jan. 12–14, 1994)* Dynamic ▲ CDS 115 [DDD]

Gianattosio, R. (pno)
Gold, E.:Music of, w. H. Dilworth (sop), G. Nestor (gtr), F. Benedetti (gtr), Holmby String Quartet—Sonata for Piano (1980); Songs of Love & Parting (1963); Quartet No. 1 for Strings (1948) *(rec 1983 & 1990)* Cambria ▲ CD 1062 [DDD/ADD]

Giangiulio, Richard (tpt)
Hertel, J.W.:Con à 6, w. R. Barr (ob), R. Neal (cnd), Dallas CO Crystal ▲ CD 512
Music for Ceremony & Celebration, w. Paul Riedo (org), Dallas Sym Trumpets Crystal ▲ CD234
Music for Festive Occasions, w. Paul Riedo (org) Crystal ▲ CD 232 [DDD] ■ C 232 (D)
Pistons & Pipes, w. Paul Riedo (org) Crystal ▲ CD 666
Roman, J.H.:Drottningholmsmusiquen Suite, w. P. Riedo (org) Crystal ▲ CD234
Treasures for Horn & Trumpet, w. Gregory Hustis (hn), Dallas CO [cnd:Ronald Neal] *(rec 11/88)* Crystal ▲ CD 512

Giani, Ugo (fl)
Sarro, D.N.:Son Fl, w. E. Rohrmann (vc), M. Tinarelli (db), G. Catalucci (hpd) *(rec Dec. 8, 1992)* Bongiovanni ▲ GB 2147 [DDD]

Giannascoli, Greg (vib)
The Classical Banjo, w. John Bullard (banjo), John Patykula (gtr), Steve Bennett (hp gtr), William Comita (vc) *(rec Big Audio, Richmond, VA, May–July 1992, Oct. 1994)* Dargason Music ▲ DM 115 [DDD]; ■ DM 115

Gianoli, Reine (pno)
Schumann, R.:Pno Music (comp)—Carnival, Op. 9; Blumenstück, Op. 19; Kinderszenen, Op. 15; Clavierstücke in Fughettenform (7), Op. 126 Adès ▲ ADE 203192 [AAD]
Schumann, R.:Pno Music (comp)—Papillons; Son No. 1; Waldscenen Adès ▲ ADE 203172
Schumann, R.:Pno Music (comp)—Fant, Op. 17; 3 Romances, Op. 28; Intermezzi, Op. 4 Adès ▲ ADE 203202 [AAD]
Schumann, R.:Pno Music (comp)—Son No. 2 in g, Op. 22; 4 Pièces, Op. 32; Impromptus on a Theme by Clara Wieck, Op. 5; Presto, Op. posth.; 4 Fugues, Op. 72 Adès ▲ ADE 203212
Schumann, R.:Pno Music (comp)—Kreisleriana, Op. 16; Bunte Blätter, Op. 99 Adès ▲ ADE 203222 [AAD]
Schumann, R.:Pno Music (comp)—Scenes de la foret, Op. 82 [Waldszenen]; Son No. 1 in f#, Op. 11; Papillons, Op. 2 Adès ▲ ADE 132412
Schumann, R.:Pno Music (comp)—Son, Op. 14; Etudes, Op. 10; Scherzo Adès ▲ ADE 203252 [AAD]

Giaquinta, Anna Maria (cl)
Gragnani, F.:Gtr Music, w. Marco Riboni (gtr), Leopoldo Saracino (gtr), Andrea Pecola (vn), Emilio Vapi (fl), Andrea Bellato (vc)—Qt in A for Vn, Cl & 2 Gtrs, Op. 8; Duet No. 1 in A for Vn & Gtr; Trio in D for Fl, Vn & Gtr, Op. 13; Duet No. 2 in A for Vn & Gtr; Sxt in A for Fl, Cl, Vn, 2 Gtrs & Vc, Op. 9 Stradivarius ▲ STV 33385 [DDD]

Giardelli, Catherine (vn)—see also ORCHESTRAS & ENSEMBLES Elyséen String Quartet
Jacquet De La Guerre, E.:Trio Sons for 2 Vns, w. B. Charbonnier (vn), Claire Giardelli (vc), G. Guillard (hpd)—No. 4 Arion 2–▲ ARN 268012 [AAD]

Giardelli, Claire (vc)—see also ORCHESTRAS & ENSEMBLES Elyséen String Quartet, Il Divertimento, Les Nièces de Rameau
Jacquet De La Guerre, E.:Trio Sons for 2 Vns, w. B. Charbonnier (vn), Catherine Giardelli (vn), G. Guillard (hpd)—No. 4 Arion 2–▲ ARN 268012 [AAD]

Giardelli, Mirella (hpd)—see ORCHESTRAS & ENSEMBLES Il Divertimento

Giarmanà, Pinuccia (pno)
Busoni, F.:Fant contrappuntistica Pno 4–Hands, w. A. Luccheti (pno) Nuova Era ▲ NUO 7161 [DDD]
Busoni, F.:Finnländische Volksweisen, w. A. Luccheti (pno) Nuova Era ▲ NUO 7161 [DDD]
Busoni, F.:Improvisation on Bach's *Wie wohl ist mir*, w. A. Luccheti (pno) Nuova Era ▲ NUO 7161 [DDD]

Giarmanà, Pinuccia (pno) (cont.)
Chabrier, E.:Pno Music 4–Hands, w. A. Lucchetti (pno)—España; 3 Valses romantiques [both for 2 Pnos]; Cortège burlesque; Bourrée fantasque; Prélude et marche française; Souvenirs de Munich [Quadrille sur les themes favoris de Tristan et Isolde] [all for Pno 4–Hands] *(rec RSI studio Auditorio, Lugano, 1994)* Gallo ▲ CD 818 [DDD]
Liszt, F.:Pno Music (misc), w. A. Lucchetti (pno)—Rhap Hongroise No. 2; Gaudeamus Igitur; Fest Polonaise; Weihnachtsbaum Gallo ▲ CD 817

Giaux, Baudoin (fl)
Mahaut, A.:Cons Fl, w. H. Schoonbroot (cnd), Camerata Leodiensis—(2) in d & e Koch Schwann ▲ CD 311100 [DDD]

Gibbons, Jack (hpd)
Bach, J.S.:Capriccio Departure Elektra/Nonesuch ▲ 79132–2 [DDD] ■ 79132–4 (D)
Bach, J.S.:Chromatic Fant & Fugue Elektra/Nonesuch ▲ 79132–2 [DDD] ■ 79132–4 (D)
Bach, J.S.:Fants Hpd—BWV 906 & Ricercare BWV 1079 Elektra/Nonesuch ▲ 79132–2 [DDD] ■ 79132–4 (D)
Bach, J.S.:Preludium & Fugue Hpd, BWV 894 Elektra/Nonesuch ▲ 79132–2 [DDD] ■ 79132–4 (D)
Bach, J.S.:Preludium, Fugue & Allegro Hpd, BWV 998 Elektra/Nonesuch ▲ 79132–2 [DDD] ■ 79132–4 (D)
Bach, J.S.:Sons Vn, w. J. Swensen (vn)—not advised of selections RCA Red Seal ▲ 09026–60563–2
Bach, J.S.:Toccatas Hpd, BWV 910–16—BWV 914 Elektra/Nonesuch ▲ 79132–2 [DDD] ■ 79132–4 (D)
Scarlatti, D.:Sons Kbd—K. 56, 69, 107, 141, 144, 145, 201, 206, 501, 502, 544, 545, 546, 547 *(rec Pilgrim Congregational Church, Lexington, MA, Aug 1–3, 1992)* Centaur ▲ CRC 2177 [DDD]

Gibbons, Jack (pno)
Alkan, C.-V.:Etudes (12) in minor keys ASV 2–▲ ASV 227 [DDD]
Alkan, C.-V.:Pno Music—Nocturne in B; Allegro Barbaro; Assez vivement; J'etait endormie, mai mon coeur veillait; Le Staccatissimo; Les Cloches; Les Soupirs; En songe; Gros temps; Barcarolle; Le Chanson de la folle au bord de la mer; Le Temps qui n'est plus ASV 2–▲ ASV 227 [DDD]
Gershwin, G.:Pno Music—Cuban Ov.; Rhap. No. 2; Porgy & Bess Suite; For You, for Me, Forevermore; Isn't It a Pity?; Jilted; Let's Call the Whole Thing off; Of Thee I Sing Ov.; Our Love Is Here to Stay ASV ("White Line" series) ▲ ASV 2082 [DDD]
Gershwin, G.:Pno Music—Come to the Moon, Concerto in F (slow movement), Drifting Along With the Tide, Fascinating Rhythm, I Was So Young, The Man I Love, Nobody But You, Oh Lady Be Good!, Rhapsody in Blue, Swanee, Tee-Oodle-Um-Bum-Bo ASV ("White Line" series) ▲ WHL 2074
Gershwin, G.:Pno Music—[Vol. 1, 1918–25] Rhap in Blue; Come to the Moon; Drifting along with the Tide; Fascinating Rhythm; Hang on to Me; Kickin' the Clouds away; Swanee; others; [Vol. 2, 1925–30] An American in Paris; 3 Preludes; Embraceable You; I Got Rhythm; Do, Do, Do; Someone to Watch over Me; others; [Vol. 3, 1931–37] Cuban Ov; Catfish Row Suite; I Got Rhythm Vars; 2nd Rhap; Let's Call the Whole Thing off; Isn't It a Pity?; others ASV 3–▲ ASV 328 [DDD]
Gershwin, G.:Songs—Embraceable you; I got rhythm; Someone to watch over me; S'Wonderful, plus others ASV ("White Line" series) ▲ ASV 2077 [DDD]
Lambert, C.:The Rio Grande, w. S. Burgess (mez), D. Lloyd-Jones (cnd), English Northern Philharmonia [E] Hyperion ▲ CDA 66565 [DDD]
Milhaud, D.:Le Carnaval d'Aix, w. R. Corp (cnd), New London Orch Hyperion ▲ CDA 66594 [DDD]

Gibbons, John (hpd)—see ORCHESTRAS & ENSEMBLES Boston Museum Trio, Boston Museum Trio members

Gibbs, Norman (bgl)
Portsmouth, w. Heming (cnd), Her Majesty's Royal Marines Band Corps of Drums Bandleader ▲ BND 5020 [DDD]

Gibbs, Peter (vn)—see also ORCHESTRAS & ENSEMBLES London Chamber Players
Purcell, H.:Music of, w. April Cantelo (sop), Alfred Deller (ct), Maurice Bevan (bar), Neville Marriner (vn), Granville Jones (vn), Desmond Dupré (vl), George Malcolm (hpd), Walter Bergmann (hpd)—15 Songs & Airs; Fantasia upon a Ground in d for 3 Violins & Continuo, Z.731; Fantasia upon One Note in F for 5 Viols, Z.745; Hornpipe in e (from The Old Bachelor); Music Lessons 1–12 from Musick's Hand-Maid, Part II; A New Irish Tune, "Lilliburlero," Z.646; Pavan in g for 3 Violins & Bass Viol, Z.752; Sonata in g for Violin & Continuo, Z.780; Sonata No. 9 in F, "Golden Sonata," Z.810 (from Ten Sonatas in Four Parts); Suite in D for Harpsichord, Z.667 Vanguard Classics ("The Bach Guild" series) 2–▲ OVC 2002/03 [ADD]

Gibellato, Stefano (pno)
Rubinstein, A.:Pieces, Op. 11, w. Carlo Lazari (vn) Enterprise ("Tiziano" series) ▲ ENT TZ 96001 [DDD]
Rubinstein, A.:Son 1 Vn, w. C. Lazari (vn) *(rec July 21, 1991)* Nuova Era ▲ 7148 [DDD]
Rubinstein, A.:Son 2 Vn, w. C. Lazari (vn) *(rec Aug. 10, 1991)* Nuova Era ▲ 7148 [DDD]
Rubinstein, A.:Son 3 Vn, w. Carlo Lazari (vn) Enterprise ("Tiziano" series) ▲ ENT TZ 96001 [DDD]

Giblin, John (elec bass)
Battiato, F.:Haiku, w. Franco Battiato (voc), Pouran Ghaffarpour (voc), Antonio Ballista (pno), Marco Boni (vc), Guido Corti (cnt), Filippo Destrieri (kbd/computer), Gavin Harrison (dr/perc), Jakko Jakszyk (gtr), Roberto Mazza (ob), Fabrizio Merlini (va), Angelo Privitera (kbd/computer), Mino Bordignon (cnd), Milan Chamber Music Choir Hemisphere ▲ 837234–2
Battiato, F.:Ricerca sul Terzo, w. Franco Battiato (voc), Alessio Alba (tamboura), Antonio Ballista (pno), Marco Boni (vc), Debendra Kanti Chakraborty (tabla), Guido Corti (cnt), Filippo Destrieri (kbd/computer), Buddhadeu Das Gupta (sarod), Gavin Harrison (dr/perc), Jakko Jakszyk (gtr), Roberto Mazza (ob), Fabrizio Merlini (va), Angelo Privitera (kbd/computer), Mino Bordignon (cnd), Milan Chamber Music Choir Hemisphere ▲ 837234–2

Gibson, David (vc)
Behrman, D.:Figure in a Clearing, w. David Behrman (elec), Kim–1 (cmpt) *(rec State Univ of New York, Albany, June 9, 1977)* Lovely Music ▲ LCD 1041 [ADD]

Gibson, Jon (didjeridu)
Lockwood, A.:Thousand Year Dreaming, w. Art Baron (conch shell/trbn/didjerido), Liby Van Cleve (ob/E hn), J.D. Parran (cl), Michael Publiese (perc), Scott Robinson (conch shell/perc), John Snyder (didjeridu/waterphone), Charles Wood (tam-tam, stones), Peter Zummo (trbn/didjeridu) ¿What Next? ▲ WN 0010

Gibson, Jon (sax)—see ORCHESTRAS & ENSEMBLES Philip Glass Ensemble
Gibson, Jon:Running Commentary, w. T. Buckner (bar), J. Kubera (pno), Bill Ruyle (perc) Lovely Music ▲ LCD 3022 [DDD]

Gibson, M. (vn)
Polishook, M.:The Tribute, w. P. Van Dewater (vn), M. Ewing (va), D. Assael (vc) Vienna Modern Masters ▲ VMM 2008 [DDD]

Gibson, P. (pno)
Mozart, W.A.:Con 21 Pno, w. P. Gibson (cnd), London SO—2nd movt Vox Cameo Classics ("Sketches" series) ▲ ACD 8776 [DDD] ■ ACS 8776

Gicquel, Annie (pno)
Schubert, Franz:Son Pno 4–Hands, D.812, w. Gregor Weichert (pno) Accord ▲ ACD 200212 [AAD]
Schubert, Franz:Vars on an Original Theme Pno 4–Hands, w. Gregor Weichert (pno) Accord ▲ ACD 200212 [AAD]

Gieler, M. (va)
Lachner, F.P.:Nonet, w. A. Duisberg (fl), D. Wollenweber (ob), P. Prieditis (cl), P. Douglas (hn), M. Postinghel (bn), I. Grünkorn (vn), T. Ruge (vc), F. Heidenreich (db) *(rec June 10, 1991)* Thorofon ▲ CTH 2132 [DDD]

Gieseking, Walter (pno)
Bach, J.S.:English Suites—BWV 811 *(rec 1953)* Forlane ▲ FOR 16590 [AAD]
Bach, J.S.:English Suites—BWV 807, 808, 809 & 811 *(rec from a broadcast recital 1950)* Music & Arts 4–▲ CD 743 [AAD]
Bach, J.S.:French Suites—BWV 813 & 816 *(rec broadcast recital 1950)* Music & Arts 4–▲ CD 743 [AAD]
Bach, J.S.:Inventions (30) Hpd—BWV 772–791 & 792–801) *(rec 1950)* Music & Arts 4–▲ CD 743 [AAD]
Bach, J.S.:Italian Con *(rec Berlin, ca 1944/45)* Melodram ▲ MEL 18023 (m) [AAD]

INSTRUMENT.

Gieseking, Walter (pno) (cont.)
Bach, J.S.:Kbd Music (misc)—Partitas (6); Fant in c, BWV 906; Toccata in c, BWV 911; Fant & Fugue in a; Ov nach Französischer Art; Con Hpd, BWV 971; English Suite No. 6 — Music & Arts 2-▲ MUA CD 947
Bach, J.S.:Partitas Hpd, BWV 825–830—No. 1 in B♭, BWV 825 *(rec Vienna, Sept. 10, 1934)* — APR ▲ APR 5512 [ADD]
Bach, J.S.:Partitas Hpd, BWV 825–830—BWV 825 *(rec live, Dec 2, 1950)* — Arkadia ▲ 907 [ADD]
Bach, J.S.:Partitas Hpd, BWV 825–830—No. 1 in B♭, BWV 825 — Enterprise ("Piano Library" series) ▲ ENT PL 203
Bach, J.S.:Das wohltemperierte Klavier — Deutsche Grammophon ("Dokumente" series) 3-▲ 429929-2 (m) [ADD]
Beethoven, L. van:Bagatelles (24)—in E♭, Op. 33/1 *(rec Aug. 11, 1938)* — VAI Audio ▲ VAIA 1088
Beethoven, L. van:Con 1 Pno, w. H. Rosbaud (cnd), Berlin State Opera Orch *(rec 1930's)* — APR ▲ APR 5511
Beethoven, L. van:Con 1 Pno, Philharmonia Orch — Theorema ▲ TH 121215
Beethoven, L. van:Con 1 Pno, w. H. Rosbaud (cnd), Berlin State Opera Orch *(rec Berlin 8/28/37)* — The Classical Collector ▲ FDC 2008 [AAD]
Beethoven, L. van:Con 4 Pno, w. K. Böhm (cnd), Saxon State Orch — Enterprise ("The Radio Years" series) ▲ ENT RY 61
Beethoven, L. van:Con 4 Pno, w. K. Böhm (cnd), Saxon State Orch *(rec Berlin, Jan. 3, 1939)* — APR ▲ APR 5512 [ADD]
Beethoven, L. van:Con 4 Pno, w. K. Böhm (cnd), Saxon State Orch *(rec 1934)* — Grammofono 2000 ▲ GRM 78506 [ADD]
Beethoven, L. van:Con 5 Pno, "Emperor", w. A. Rother (cnd), Berlin RSO *(rec 1944)* — Arkadia ▲ 588 [ADD]
Beethoven, L. van:Con 5 Pno, "Emperor", w. A. Rother (cnd), Berlin Large RSO — Enterprise ("The Radio Years" series) 2-▲ ENT RY 66
Beethoven, L. van:Con 5 Pno, "Emperor", w. A. Rother (cnd), Berlin RSO *(rec 1944, Berlin)* — Melodram ▲ MEL 18023 (m) [AAD]
Beethoven, L. van:Con 5 Pno, "Emperor", w. A. Rother (cnd), Berlin RSO *(rec Berlin, 1944)* — Music & Arts ▲ CD 815 [AAD]
Beethoven, L. van:Con 5 Pno, "Emperor", w. B. Walter (cnd), Vienna PO *(rec Vienna, Sept. 10 & 11, 1934)* — APR ▲ APR 5512 [ADD]
Beethoven, L. van:Con 5 Pno, "Emperor", w. B. Walter (cnd), Vienna PO — Enterprise ("The Radio Years" series) ▲ ENT RY 61
Beethoven, L. van:Con 5 Pno, "Emperor", w. B. Walter (cnd), Vienna PO *(rec 1939)* — Grammofono 2000 ▲ GRM 78506 [ADD]
Beethoven, L. van:Con 5 Pno, "Emperor", w. A. Rother (cnd), Berlin Large RSO *(rec Sept 1944)* — Enterprise ("The Piano Library" series) ▲ ENT 185
Beethoven, L. van:Con 5 Pno, "Emperor", w. G. Cantelli (cnd), New York PO — Stradivarius ▲ STV 13594 [AAD]
Beethoven, L. van:Qnt Pno, Ob, Cl, Hn & Bn, w. Philharmonia Wind Quartet *(rec London, 1955)* — Testament ▲ SBT 1091
Beethoven, L. van:Son 8 Pno, "Pathétique" — Theorema ▲ TH 121215
Beethoven, L. van:Son 16 Pno *(rec 1949, from a broadcast re)* — Music & Arts 4-▲ CD 743 [AAD]
Beethoven, L. van:Son 17 Pno, "Tempest" *(rec live, Berlin 9/29/55)* — Arkadia ▲ 907 [ADD]
Beethoven, L. van:Son 17 Pno, "Tempest" *(rec Berlin ca. 1944/5)* — Melodram ▲ MEL 18023 (m) [AAD]
Beethoven, L. van:Son 17 Pno, "Tempest" *(rec Mar. 13, 1931)* — VAI Audio ▲ VAIA 1088
Beethoven, L. van:Son 21 Pno, "Waldstein" *(rec Aug. 11, 1938)* — VAI Audio ▲ VAIA 1088
Beethoven, L. van:Son 23 Pno, "Appassionata" *(rec May 1939)* — Enterprise ("The Piano Library" series) ▲ ENT 185
Beethoven, L. van:Son 23 Pno, "Appassionata" *(rec May 1939)* — VAI Audio ▲ VAIA 1088
Beethoven, L. van:Son 24 Pno *(rec 1949, from a broadcast re)* — Music & Arts 4-▲ CD 743 [AAD]
Beethoven, L. van:Son 25 Pno *(rec 1949, from a broadcast re)* — Music & Arts 4-▲ CD 743 [AAD]
Beethoven, L. van:Son 26 Pno, "Les Adieux" *(rec 1949, from a broadcast re)* — Music & Arts 4-▲ CD 743 [AAD]
Beethoven, L. van:Son 27 Pno *(rec 1949, from a broadcast re)* — Music & Arts 4-▲ CD 743 [AAD]
Beethoven, L. van:Son 28 Pno *(rec 1949, from a broadcast re)* — Music & Arts 4-▲ CD 743 [AAD]
Beethoven, L. van:Son 28 Pno *(rec May 1939)* — VAI Audio ▲ VAIA 1088
Beethoven, L. van:Son 29 Pno, "Hammerklavier" *(rec 1949, from a broadcast re)* — Music & Arts 4-▲ CD 743 [AAD]
Beethoven, L. van:Son 30 Pno *(rec ca. 1939/40)* — Pearl ▲ PEA 9930 (m) [AAD]
Beethoven, L. van:Son 32 Pno *(rec 1949, from a broadcast re)* — Music & Arts 4-▲ CD 743 [AAD]
Brahms, J.:Con 2 Pno, w. R. Heger (cnd), Berlin PO—movts 1 & 2 *(rec 1939–56)* — Arbiter ▲ CD 103 [ADD]
Brahms, J.:Fants Pno, Op. 116 — Theorema 2-▲ TH 121187/188
Brahms, J.:Pieces Pno, Op. 76 — Theorema 2-▲ TH 121187/188
Brahms, J.:Pieces Pno, Op. 118—No. 5, Romance in F *(rec 1924–1955)* — Pearl ▲ PEA 9038
Brahms, J.:Pieces Pno, Op. 118 — Theorema 2-▲ TH 121187/188
Brahms, J.:Pieces Pno, Op. 119 — Theorema 2-▲ TH 121187/188
Brahms, J.:Rhaps Pno, Op. 79—No. 2 in g — Enterprise ("Piano Library" series) ▲ ENT PL 203
Brahms, J.:Rhaps Pno, Op. 79—No. 2 in g *(rec 1924–1955)* — Pearl ▲ PEA 9038
Brahms, J.:Son 3 Pno *(rec 1939–56)* — Arbiter ▲ CD 103 [ADD]
Brahms, J.:Sym 2, w. A. Rother (cnd), Berlin Large RSO — Enterprise ("The Radio Years" series) 2-▲ ENT RY 66
Casella, A.:Sonatina Pno *(rec 1924–1955)* — Pearl ▲ PEA 9038
Chopin, F.:Ballades Pno (comp)—in A♭, Op. 47 *(rec 1924–1955)* — Pearl ▲ PEA 9038
Chopin, F.:Barcarolle Pno *(rec Berlin 8/10/38 for Columbia Reco)* — The Classical Collector ▲ FDC 2008 [AAD]
Chopin, F.:Études (24)—Op. 25/1 & 2 — Enterprise ("Piano Library" series) ▲ ENT PL 203
Chopin, F.:Études (24)—in A♭ & f, Op. 25/1 & 2 *(rec 1924–1955)* — Pearl ▲ PEA 9038
Chopin, F.:Nocturnes—Opp. 9/3 & 15/2 — Enterprise ("Piano Library" series) ▲ ENT PL 203
Chopin, F.:Nocturnes—in B, Op. 9/3; in F#, Op. 15/2 *(rec 1924–1955)* — Pearl ▲ PEA 9038
Chopin, F.:Polonaises—in A♭, Op. 53 *(rec 1924–1955)* — Pearl ▲ PEA 9038
Chopin, F.:Polonaises (misc)—in A♭, Op. 53 — Enterprise ("Piano Library" series) ▲ ENT PL 203
Debussy, C.:Estampes—No. 2, "Soirée dans Grenade" *(rec live, Monaco, 12/2/50)* — Arkadia ▲ 907 [ADD]
Debussy, C.:Estampes—No. 1, "Pagodes" & No. 3, "Jardins sous la pluie" *(rec from European Columbia 78 rpm discs mid–1930s)* — Pearl ▲ PEA 9449 (m) [AAD]
Debussy, C.:Images (6) Pno—Reflets dans l'eau — Enterprise ("Piano Library" series) ▲ ENT PL 203
Debussy, C.:L'Isle joyeuse *(rec from European Columbia 78 rpm disc rec. mid–1930s)* — Pearl ▲ PEA 9449 (m) [AAD]
Debussy, C.:Pno Music (misc)—Suite Bergamasque; Valse, la plus que lente; Images, Sets I & II; Rêverie; Préludes, Books I & II; Children's Corner Suite; Estampes; Deux Arabesques; L'isle joyeuse *(rec London, Berlin, & NY, Apr 1927; Aug 11, 1938; J)* — VAI Audio 2-▲ VAIA 1117-2 [ADD]
Debussy, C.:Preludes Pno — EMI Classics (Great Recordings of the Century) ▲ CDH 61004
Debussy, C.:Preludes Pno—Book 1 *(rec from European Columbia 78)* — Pearl ▲ PEA 9449 (m) [AAD]
Franck, C.:Symphonic Vars, w. A. Cluytens (cnd), French National Orch *(rec live, Paris, 7/18/55)* — Arkadia ▲ 588 [ADD]
Franck, C.:Symphonic Vars, w. H. Wood (cnd), London PO *(rec London, Oct 31, 1932)* — APR ▲ APR 5513 [ADD]
Gieseking, W.:Kinderleider, w. E. Schwarzkopf (sop)—Cantata 199, Mein Herze schwimmt in Blut *(rec 1955)* — EMI Classics ▲ CDM 63655
Grieg, E.:Con Pno, Op. 16, Berlin PO — Music & Arts ▲ CD 925
Grieg, E.:Con Pno, Op. 16, w. W. Furtwängler (cnd), Berlin PO *(rec July 30, 1944)* — Iron Needle 3-▲ IN 1348/50 [ADD]
Grieg, E.:Con Pno, Op. 16, w. H. von Karajan (cnd), Philharmonia Orch *(rec 1951)* — Enterprise ("Palladio" series) ▲ ENT 4178 [ADD]

Gieseking, Walter (pno) (cont.)
Grieg, E.:Con Pno, Op. 16, w. H. Rosbaud (cnd), Berlin State Opera Orch *(rec Berlin, Apr 28–Oct 13, 1937)* — APR ▲ APR 5513 [ADD]
Grieg, E.:Lyric Pieces—Book II *(rec 1953)* — Enterprise ("Palladio" series) ▲ ENT 4178 [ADD]
Grieg, E.:Lyric Pieces—At the Cradle; French Serenade *(rec Berlin, Apr 29, 1937)* — APR ▲ APR 5513 [ADD]
Liszt, F.:Con 1 Pno, w. H. Heimans (cnd), Maastricht Municipal Orch — Enterprise ("The Piano Library" series) ▲ ENT PL 202
Liszt, F.:Con 1 Pno, w. H. Wood (cnd), London PO *(rec London, Oct 31, 1932)* — APR ▲ APR 5513 [ADD]
Liszt, F.:Con 1 Pno, w. H. Wood (cnd), London PO *(rec London, 10/31/32 for Columbia)* — The Classical Collector ▲ FDC 2008 [AAD]
Liszt, F.:Hungarian Rhaps—No. 12 — Enterprise ("Piano Library" series) ▲ ENT PL 203
Mendelssohn, F.:Lieder ohne Worte Pno—Op. 19/1 & 6; Op. 30/6; Op. 38/4 & 6; Op. 53/2–4; Op. 62/1, 5 & 6; Op. 67/3 & 4; Op. 85/4 & 6; Op. 102/3 & 5 *(rec 1957)* — Theorema ▲ TH 121181
Mozart, W.A.:Con 9 Pno, *(cnd & orch unknown) (rec 1924–1955)* — Pearl ▲ PEA 9038
Mozart, W.A.:Con 9 Pno, w. H. Rosbaud (cnd), Berlin State Opera Orch *(rec Berlin, Sept. 29, 1936)* — APR ▲ APR 5511 [ADD]
Mozart, W.A.:Con 9 Pno, w. H. Rosbaud (cnd), Berlin State Opera Orch *(rec Berlin, Sept 29, 1936)* — Iron Needle ▲ IN 1316 [ADD]
Mozart, W.A.:Con 21 Pno, w. G. Cantelli (cnd), New York Philharmonic SO *(rec live, 1948–1956)* — Pearl ▲ PEA 9236
Mozart, W.A.:Con 21 Pno, w. G. Cantelli (cnd), New York PO *(rec 1953 & 1955)* — Legend ▲ LGD 130 [ADD]
Mozart, W.A.:Con 27 Pno, w. V. Desarzens (cnd), Lausanne CO *(rec live, 1948–1956)* — Pearl ▲ PEA 9236
Mozart, W.A.:Pno Music (comp) — EMI Classics ("Great Recordings of the Century" series) 8-▲ CDHH 63688 (m) [ADD]
Mozart, W.A.:Qnt Pno Wnds, w. Philharmonia Wind Quartet *(rec London, 1955)* — Testament ▲ SBT 1091
Mozart, W.A.:Son 16 Pno *(rec Berlin, Sept 30, 1936)* — Iron Needle ▲ IN 1316 [ADD]
Mozart, W.A.:Son 17 Pno *(rec Berlin, Sept. 30, 1936)* — APR ▲ APR 5511 [ADD]
Mozart, W.A.:Son 17 Pno *(rec live, 1948–1956)* — Pearl ▲ PEA 9236
Mozart, W.A.:Songs, w. E. Schwarzkopf (sop) — EMI Classics ▲ CDH 63702
Pfitzner, H.:Con Pno, Hamburg PO — Music & Arts ▲ CD 925
Rachmaninoff, S.:Con 2 Pno, w. W. Mengelberg (cnd), Royal Concertgebouw Orch *(rec 1940)* — Music & Arts ▲ CD 250 (m)
Rachmaninoff, S.:Con 3 Pno, w. W. Mengelberg (cnd), Royal Concertgebouw Orch *(rec 1940)* — Music & Arts ▲ CD 250 (m)
Ravel, M.:Gaspard de la nuit — Pearl ▲ PEA 9449 (m) [AAD]
Ravel, M.:Jeux d'eau — Enterprise ("Piano Library" series) ▲ ENT PL 203
Ravel, M.:Jeux d'eau *(rec 1924–1955)* — Pearl ▲ PEA 9038
Ravel, M.:Miroirs—No. 4, "Alborada del gracioso" & No. 5, "La vallée des cloches" *(rec mid–1930s)* — Pearl ▲ PEA 9449 (m) [AAD]
Ravel, M.:Pno Music—Menuet sur le nom de Haydn; A la manière de Chabrier; Jeux d'eau; Gaspard de la nuit; Le tombeau de Couperin; Prélude; A la manière de Borodine; Miroirs; Pavane pour une infante défunte; Sonatina; Valses nobles et sentimentales; Menuet antique *(rec 1951)* — Theorema 2-▲ TH 121163/64
A Retrospective, Vol. 1 — Pearl ▲ PEA 9930 (m) [AAD]
Vol. 2 *(rec 1931–51)* — Pearl ▲ PEA 9011 [AAD]
Schubert, Franz:Moments musicaux — Theorema 2-▲ TH 121187/188
Schubert, Franz:Pieces Pno, D.946 — Theorema 2-▲ TH 121187/188
Schumann, R.:Con Pno, w. W. Furtwängler (cnd), Berlin PO — Enterprise ("The Piano Library" series) ▲ ENT PL 202
Schumann, R.:Con Pno, w. W. Furtwängler (cnd), Berlin PO *(rec Berlin, Mar. 1–3, 1942)* — Music & Arts ▲ CD 815 [AAD]
Schumann, R.:Con Pno, w. G. Wand (cnd), Cologne RSO *(rec live, Essen 1/8/51)* — Arkadia ▲ 588 [ADD]
Schumann, R.:Davidsbündlertänze *(rec 1953)* — Forlane ▲ FOR 16590 [AAD]
Schumann, R.:Kreisleriana *(rec 1953)* — Forlane ▲ FOR 16590 [AAD]
Schumann, R.:Romances Pno *(rec 1951)* — Music & Arts 4-▲ CD 743 [AAD]
Schumann, R.:Sym Etudes *(rec 1951)* — Music & Arts 4-▲ CD 743 [AAD]

Giesen, Hubert (pno)
Beethoven, L. van:Son 1 Vn, w. Y. Menuhin (vn) *(rec 1929)* — Biddulph ▲ LAB 032 [ADD]
Beethoven, L. van:Songs, w. Fritz Wünderlich (ten)—Adelaide, Op. 46; Resignation, WoO 149; Mailied, Op. 52/4; Der Kuss, Op. 128 *(rec Hannover, Mar 24, 1966)* — Bella Voce ▲ 7003 [AAD]
Beethoven, L. van:Songs, w. F. Wunderlich (ten) *(rec Salzburg August 1965)* — Acanta ▲ CD 43529
Beethoven, L. van:Songs, w. F. Wunderlich (ten)—Adelaide, Op. 46; Resignation; Der Wachtelschlag; Mailied, Op. 52, No. 4; Der Küss, Op. 128 [G] *(rec Mar. 24, 1966)* — Myto ▲ MCD 93278
Beethoven, L. van:Songs, w. Fritz Wunderlich (ten)—Adelaide, Op. 46; Mailied, Op. 52/4; Der Wachtelschlag; Resignation; Der Kuss, Op. 128 *(rec Salzburg, Aug 19, 1965)* — Orfeo d'or ("Festspiel Dikumente" series) ▲ C 432961 (m) [ADD]
Beethoven, L. van:Songs, w. F. Wunderlich (ten)—Ich liebe dich; Adelaide; Resignation; Der Kuss — Deutsche Grammophon ("Dokumente" series) ▲ 429933-2 [ADD]
Fritz Wunderlich's Last Concert, w. Fritz Wunderlich (ten) *(rec Edinburgh, Sept 17, 1966)* — Myto ▲ MCD 890.11 (m) [ADD]
Schubert, Franz:Die Forelle, w. Fritz Wunderlich (ten) *(rec Hochschule for Music, Munich, Nov 1965)* — Deutsche Grammophon ("The Originals" series) ▲ 447452-2 [ADD]
Schubert, Franz:Frühlingsglaube, w. Fritz Wunderlich (ten) *(rec Hochschule for Music, Munich, Nov 1965)* — Deutsche Grammophon ("The Originals" series) ▲ 447452-2 [ADD]
Schubert, Franz:Heidenröslein, w. Fritz Wunderlich (ten) *(rec Hochschule for Music, Munich, Nov 1965)* — Deutsche Grammophon ("The Originals" series) ▲ 447452-2 [ADD]
Schubert, Franz:Die Schöne Müllerin, w. Fritz Wunderlich (ten) *(rec Acad. der Wissenschaften, Munich, July 1966)* — Deutsche Grammophon ("The Originals" series) ▲ 447452-2 [ADD]
Schubert, Franz:Die Schöne Müllerin, w. F. Wunderlich (ten) [G] *(rec 1965 broadcast)* — Verona ▲ 2701 [AAD]
Schubert, Franz:Songs (misc), w. Fritz Wunderlich (ten)—Der Einsame, D.800; Nachtstück, D.672; An die Laute, D.905; Lied eines Schiffers an die Dioskuren, D.360; An Sylvia, D.891; Der Musensohn, D.764; Im Abendrot, D.799; Ungeduld aus Die schöne Müllerin, D.795 *(rec Salzburg, Aug 19, 1965)* — Orfeo d'or ("Festspiel Dikumente" series) ▲ C 432961 (m) [ADD]
Schubert, Franz:Songs (misc), w. F. Wunderlich (ten) *(rec Salzburg, 8/65)* — Acanta ▲ CD 43529
Schubert, Franz:Songs (misc), w. F. Wunderlich (ten)—9 songs — Deutsche Grammophon ("Dokumente" series) ▲ 429933-2 [ADD]
Schubert, Franz:Songs (misc), w. F. Wunderlich (ten)—6 songs [G]—D.360, 672, 764, 795/7, 891, 905 *(rec live, Salzburg 8/19/65)* — Myto 2-▲ 2 MCD 91544 [ADD]
Schubert, Franz:Songs (misc), w. F. Wunderlich (ten)—4 songs—D.360, 672, 800, 905 [G] *(rec live, Salzburg, 8/19/65)* — Myto 2-▲ 2 MCD 91648 [ADD]
Schubert, Franz:Songs (misc), w. F. Wunderlich (ten)—Der Einsame, Op. 41; Nachtstuck, Op. 36, No. 2; An die Laute, Op. 81, No. 2; Lied eines Schiffers an die Dioskuren, Op. 65, No. 1; An Silvia, Op. 106, No. 4; Der Musensohn, Op. 92, No. 1; Frühlingsglaube, Op. 20, No. 2; An die Musik, Op. 88, No. 4 [G] *(rec Mar. 24, 1966)* — Myto ▲ MCD 93278
Schumann, R.:Dichterliebe, w. F. Wunderlich (ten) [G] *(rec live, 9/17/66)* — Myto ▲ 1 MCD 89011 (m) [ADD]
Schumann, R.:Dichterliebe, w. F. Wunderlich (ten) — Deutsche Grammophon ("Dokumente" series) ▲ 429933-2 [ADD]
Schumann, R.:Dichterliebe, w. F. Wunderlich (ten) *(rec Salzburg, 8/65)* — Acanta ▲ CD 43529
Schumann, R.:Dichterliebe, w. F. Wunderlich (ten) [G] *(rec live, Salzburg 8/19/65)* — Myto 2-▲ 2 MCD 91544 [ADD]

▲ = CD ♦ = Enhanced CD Δ = MD ■ = Cassette Tape □ = DCC

Giesen, Hubert (pno) (cont.)
Schumann, R.:Dichterliebe, w. Fritz Wunderlich (ten) *(rec Salzburg, Aug 19, 1965)* Orfeo d'or ("Festspiel Dikumente" series) ▲ C 432961 (m) [ADD]
Schumann, R.:Dichterliebe, w. F. Wunderlich (ten) [G] *(rec Mar. 24, 1966)* Myto ▲ MCD 93278
The Young Yehudi Menuhin:The 1929–30 HMV Recordings, w. Menuhin, Yehudi (vn) Biddulph ▲ LAB 032 [ADD]

Gifford, Anthea (gtr)
Dodgson, S.:Duo Con, w. Jean-Jacques Kantorow (vn), R. Zollman (cnd), Northern Sinfonia of England *(rec St Nicholas Hospital, Newcastle-upon-Tyne, Oct 23–24, 1992)* Biddulph ▲ LAW 013 [DDD]
Giuliani, M.:Vars Vn, w. J.-J. Kantorow (vn) *(rec Aug. 24–5, 1992)* Biddulph ▲ NT CD 003 [DDD]
Leclair, J.-M.:Sons Vn (Books 1–4), w. J.-J. Kantorow (vn) [arr. by Anthea Gifford for violin & guitar]—Sonata in D, Op. 9/3 Biddulph ▲ NTCD 003 [DDD]
Paganini, N.:Cantabile & Waltz, w. J.-J. Kantorow (vn) Biddulph ▲ NT CD 003 [DDD]
Paganini, N.:Centone di sonate, w. J.-J. Kantorow (vn)—No. 11 in a Biddulph ▲ NT CD 003 [DDD]
Paganini, N.:Sons Vn & Gtr, Op. 2, w. J.-J. Kantorow (vn)—Sonata Nos. 3 & 4 Biddulph ▲ NT CD 003 [DDD]
Tartini, G.:Son Vn "Devil's Trill", w. J.-J. Kantorow (vn) [arr. Anthea Gifford for violin & guitar] Biddulph ▲ NT CD 003 [DDD]

Gifford, Gerald (hpd/org)
Krebs, J.L.:Kbd Music—Suite in b; Chorales [Jesus, meine Zuversicht; Allein Gott in der Höh sei ehr; Christ lag in Todesbanden; Warum betrübst du dich, mein Herz; Auf meinen lieben Gott; Vater unser im Himmelreich; Jesu, meine Freude; Von Gott will ich nicht lassen; Was Gott tut, das ist wohlgetan]; Preludes Nos. 2, 3, 5 & 6; Suite in c Meridian ▲ MER 84306 [DDD]

Gifford, Gerald (org)
Bach, C.P.E.:Kbd Music—Präludium in D; Sons in F, a, D & g; 6 Vars; Fant & Fugue in c; Fugue in d Meridian ▲ MER 84318 [DDD]
A Choral Festival, w. Ely Cathedral Choir [cnd:Arthur Wills] Chandos ("Collect" series) ▲ CHAN 6603 [ADD]
Trumpet Voluntary, w. Stephen Burns (tpt), Crispian Steele-Perkins (tpt) ASV ("Quicksilva" series) ▲ ASV 6081 [ADD/DDD]

Giger, Paul (vn)
Giger, P.:Bay ECM New Series ▲ 78118-21487-2
Giger, P.:Bombay ECM New Series ▲ 78118-21487-2
Giger, P.:Chartres *(rec Chartres Cathedral crypt & upper church, Chartres, France)* ECM New Series ("New" series) ▲ 78118-21386-2 [DDD]
Giger, P.:Labyrinthos—(7 Scenes) No. 1. Dancing with the Stars; No. 2. Crane; No. 3. Crating the Labyrinth; No. 4. Birth of the bull; No. 5. 14 Virgins; No. 6. Death; No. 7. Dancing in the World of Shadows ECM New Series ▲ 78118-21487-2

Giger, Walther (gtr)—see also ORCHESTRAS & ENSEMBLES Orches Trio
Maggini, E.:Disegni, w. Werner Zumsteg (fl) *(rec RTSI, Rete 2, Dec 1993)* Jecklin ▲ JS 311-2 [DDD]

Giger, Werner (pno)
Brahms, J.:Sons Vc (comp), w. Rama Jucker (vc) Accord ▲ ACD 220382

Gignac, Claire (rcr)—see ORCHESTRAS & ENSEMBLES La Nef

Gil, Jean-Louis (org)
Fauré, G.:Cantique de Jean Racine, w. E. Krivine (cnd), Lyon National Chorus Denon ▲ CO 77527 2 [DDD]
Musiques Nuptiales, w. André Bernard (tpt), Jean-Louis Gil (org) *(various orchs & cnds)* Forlane ▲ FRL 16754 [DDD]

Gilad, Kimaree (E hn)
Bernstein, C.H.:Dimensions, w. Thomas Raney (perc) Arcobaleno 2-▲ AAOC 93922

Gilardi, S. (vn)—see ORCHESTRAS & ENSEMBLES Aglàia Ensemble

Gilbert, Beverly (pno)
Ravel, M.:Pièce en forme de Habanera, w. Patrick McFarland (E hn) Arundax ▲ 21339
Tchaikovsky, P.:Les Saisons, w. Patrick McFarland (E hn) [trans Renate Rosenblatt] Arundax ▲ 21339

Gilbert, Daniel (cl)
Zaimont, J.L.:Sky Curtains, w. Kathleen Nester (fl), Bob Wagner (bn), Lois Martin (va), Christopher Finkel (vc) *(rec SUNY Purchase, Theatre C, Jan 8–10 & Feb 20, 1995)* Arabesque ▲ ARA 6667 [DDD]

Gilbert, Geoffrey (fl)
Ravel, M.:Daphnis et Chloé (suite 1), w. G. Prêtre (cnd), Royal PO, Beecham Choral Society *(rec Apr. 8 & 9, 1963)* Chesky ▲ CD 101 [ADD]
Ravel, M.:Daphnis et Chloé (suite 2), w. G. Prêtre (cnd), Royal PO, Beecham Choral Society *(rec Apr. 8 & 9, 1963)* Chesky ▲ CD 101 [ADD]

Gilbert, Kenneth (hpd)
Anglebert, J.-H. d':Kbd Music—6 pieces in g, G, C, d, D & g [all trans. from works by Jean-Baptiste Lully] Musique d'Abord ▲ HMA 1901267
Anglebert, J.-H. d':Kbd Music—4 Suites in D, d, G & g Musique d'Abord ▲ HMA 190941
Bach, J.S.:The Art of the Fugue Archiv ▲ 427673-2 [DDD]
Bach, J.S.:Con 1 Hpd, English CO Novalis ▲ 150034 [DDD]
Bach, J.S.:Con 2 Hpd, English CO Novalis ▲ 150034 [DDD]
Bach, J.S.:Con 4 Hpd, English CO Novalis ▲ 150034 [DDD]
Bach, J.S.:Con 5 Hpd, English CO Novalis ▲ 150034 [DDD]
Bach, J.S.:Das wohltemperierte Klavier Archiv 4-▲ 413439-2 [DDD]
Chambonnières, J.C. de:Hpd Music—Chaconne in F; Rondeau in F *(rec Aug 1969)* Musique d'Abord ▲ HMA 190941
Couperin, F.:Music of, w. René Jacobs (alt), Gérard Lesne (alt), Christophe Rousset (hpd), W. Christie (cnd), Les Arts Florissants, Phillippe Herreweghe (cnd), Chapelle Royale Choir—Hpd pieces; Tenebeae Lessons [sels] Harmonia Mundi ("Great Baroque Composers" series) 3-▲ HMX 390870.72
Couperin, F.:Pièces de clavecin (comp)—Book 1 Musique d'Abord 3-▲ HMA 190351/53
Couperin, F.:Pièces de clavecin (comp)—Book 2 Musique d'Abord 3-▲ HMA 190354/56
Couperin, F.:Pièces de clavecin (comp)—Book 3 Musique d'Abord 3-▲ HMA 190357/58
Couperin, F.:Pièces de clavecin (comp)—Book 4 Musique d'Abord 2-▲ HMA 190359/60
Couperin, L.:Hpd Music—Passacaille in C; La Piémontoise Musique d'Abord ▲ HMA 190941
du Mont, H.:Pavane Hpd *(rec Aug 1969)* Musique d'Abord ▲ HMA 190941
Handel, G.F.:Music of, w. Lorraine Hunt (sop), et al., D. Mintner (cnd), Philharmonia Baroque Orch, Ensemble 415, Concerto Vocale—sels. from Duetto "Tanti strali"; Flavio; Giulio Cesare; Harpsichord Suite No. 5; Nisi Dominus; Susanna; Water Music *(rec 1976–79)* Harmonia Mundi Plus ▲ HMP 390804
Handel, G.F.:Suites Hpd—Nos. 1–8 Musique d'Abord 2-▲ HMA 190447.48
Kenneth Gilbert Plays Novalis ▲ 150018
Lully, J.-B.:Music of, w. René Jacobs (alt), Gérard Lesne (alt), Christophe Rousset (hpd), W. Christie (cnd), Les Arts Florissants, Phillippe Herreweghe (cnd), Chapelle Royale Choir—Hpd Pieces; 'Atys' excerpts; Dies Israe; Petits Motets Harmonia Mundi ("Great Baroque Composers" series) 3-▲ HMX 390870.72
Purcell, H.:Suites Hpd Harmonia Mundi France ▲ HMC 901496
Rameau, J.P.:Les Indes Galantes (airs) Musique d'Abord ▲ HMA 1901028
Rameau, J.P.:Music of, w. René Jacobs (alt), Gérard Lesne (alt), Christophe Rousset (hpd), W. Christie (cnd), Les Arts Florissants, Phillippe Herreweghe (cnd), Chapelle Royale Choir—Pieces; Les Indes Gallantes (sels) Harmonia Mundi ("Great Baroque Composers" series) 3-▲ HMX 390870.72

Gilbert, Laura (fl)—see also ORCHESTRAS & ENSEMBLES Auréole
Debussy, C.:Épigraphes antiques, w. B. Allen (hp) [trans. V. Drake for flute & harp] Koch International Classics ▲ KIC 7055-2 [DDD]
Flute Salad, w. Alexa Still (fl), Doriot Dwyer (fl), Bradley Garner (fl), New Zealand CO, London SO Koch Schwann ▲ KIC CD 7602
Prokofiev, S.:Mélodies, w. E. Tahmizian (pno) [arr. Gilbert] *(rec Jan. 1991)* Koch International Classics ▲ KIC 7105 [DDD]
Prokofiev, S.:Son Fl, w. E. Tahmizian (pno) *(rec Jan. 1991)* Koch International Classics ▲ KIC 7105 [DDD]
Prokofiev, S.:Visions fugitives, w. E. Tahmizian (pno) [arr. Howard Harrison for Flute & Piano] *(rec Jan. 1991)* Koch International Classics ▲ KIC 7105 [DDD]

Gilby, B. J. (vn)
18th Century Virtuoso String Music, w. Geoffrey Lancaster (pno), Tasmanian Sym Chamber Players ABC Classics ▲ 432530-2 [DDD]

Gilels, Elena (pno)
Beethoven, L. van:Cons Pno (comp), w. K. Sanderling (cnd), Czech PO *(rec Nov. 19, 1958)* Multisonic ("Prague Spring Collection" series) 3-▲ 31 0106-2 [ADD]
Beethoven, L. van:Con 1 Pno, w. G. Szell (cnd), Cleveland Orch EMI Classics ("Doubleforte" series) 2-▲ CDFB 69506
Beethoven, L. van:Con 2 Pno, w. G. Szell (cnd), Cleveland Orch EMI Classics ("Doubleforte" series) 2-▲ CDFB 69506
Beethoven, L. van:Con 3 Pno, w. G. Szell (cnd), Cleveland Orch EMI Classics ("Doubleforte" series) 2-▲ CDFB 69506
Beethoven, L. van:Con 4 Pno, w. M. Pradella (cnd), Naples Alessandro Scarlatti RAI Orch *(rec live 12/18/65)* Melodram 2-▲ CDM 28034 [AAD]
Beethoven, L. van:Con 4 Pno, w. G. Szell (cnd), Cleveland Orch EMI Classics ("Doubleforte" series) 2-▲ CDFB 69506
Beethoven, L. van:Con 5 Pno, "Emperor", w. B. Martinotti (cnd), Milan RAI SO *(rec live 4/24/70)* Melodram 2-▲ CDM 28034 [AAD]
Beethoven, L. van:Con 5 Pno, "Emperor", w. G. Szell (cnd), Cleveland Orch EMI Classics ("Doubleforte" series) 2-▲ CDFB 69509
Beethoven, L. van:Son 5 Pno Deutsche Grammophon ▲ 419172-2 [DDD]
Beethoven, L. van:Son 8 Pno, "Pathétique" Deutsche Grammophon ▲ 400036-2 [DDD]
Beethoven, L. van:Son 10 Pno Deutsche Grammophon ▲ 419172-2 [DDD]
Beethoven, L. van:Son 12 Pno, "Funeral March" *(rec live in recital, Moscow)* Music & Arts ▲ CD 746-1 [AAD]
Beethoven, L. van:Son 13 Pno Deutsche Grammophon ▲ 400036-2 [DDD]
Beethoven, L. van:Son 14 Pno, "Moonlight Son" Deutsche Grammophon ▲ 400036-2 [DDD]
Beethoven, L. van:Son 19 Pno Deutsche Grammophon ▲ 419172-2 [DDD]
Beethoven, L. van:Son 20 Pno Deutsche Grammophon ▲ 419172-2 [DDD]
Beethoven, L. van:Son 21 Pno, "Waldstein" Deutsche Grammophon ▲ 419162-2 [ADD]
Beethoven, L. van:Son 21 Pno, "Waldstein" *(rec July 20, 1966)* Music & Arts ▲ CD 759 [AAD]
Beethoven, L. van:Son 23 Pno, "Appassionata" Deutsche Grammophon ▲ 419162-2 [ADD]
Beethoven, L. van:Son 23 Pno, "Appassionata" *(rec live, Czechoslovakia Radio Prague 1954)* Multisonic ("Prague Spring Collection" series) ▲ 31 0091-2 [ADD]
Beethoven, L. van:Son 26 Pno, "Les Adieux", w. Gilels Deutsche Grammophon ▲ 419162-2 [ADD]
Beethoven, L. van:Son 28 Pno *(rec July 20, 1966)* Music & Arts ▲ CD 759 [AAD]
Beethoven, L. van:Son 30 Pno Deutsche Grammophon ▲ 419174-2 [DDD]
Beethoven, L. van:Son 31 Pno Deutsche Grammophon ▲ 419174-2 [DDD]
Beethoven, L. van:Trio 6 Pno, "Archduke", w. L. Kogan (vn), M. Rostropovich (vc) Monitor ■ 55010
Beethoven, L. van:Vars on an Original Theme, Op. 76 EMI Classics ("Doublefforte" series) 2-▲ CDFB 69509
Beethoven, L. van:Vars on a Russian Dance from P. Wranitzky's ballet "Das Waldmachen", WoO 71 EMI Classics ("Doubleforte" series) 2-▲ CDFB 69509
Beethoven, L. van:Vars Pno, WoO 80 EMI Classics ("Doubleforte" series) 2-▲ CDFB 69509
Borodin, A.:Trio Pno, w. Dmitry Tsyganov (vn), Sergey Shirinsky (vc) Multisonic ▲ MUL 310266
Brahms, J.:Ballades, Op. 10 Deutsche Grammophon ▲ 431595-2 [ADD]
Brahms, J.:Ballades, Op. 10 Deutsche Grammophon ("The Originals" series) ▲ 447407-2
Brahms, J.:Ballades, Op. 10 *(rec live 1968, 1973 & 1978)* Praga ▲ PR 250 039
Brahms, J.:Con 1 Pno, w. E. Jochum (cnd), Berlin PO Deutsche Grammophon 2-▲ 419158-2 [ADD]
Brahms, J.:Con 1 Pno, w. E. Jochum (cnd), Berlin PO Deutsche Grammophon ▲ 431595-2 [ADD]
Brahms, J.:Con 1 Pno, w. E. Jochum (cnd), Berlin PO *(rec Jesus-Christus Church, Berlin, June 1972)* Deutsche Grammophon ("The Originals" series) 2-▲ 447446-2 [ADD]
Brahms, J.:Con 2 Pno, w. E. Jochum (cnd), Berlin PO Deutsche Grammophon 2-▲ 419158-2 [ADD]
Brahms, J.:Con 2 Pno, w. E. Jochum (cnd), Berlin PO Deutsche Grammophon ("Galleria" series) ▲ 435588-2 [ADD]
Brahms, J.:Con 2 Pno, w. E. Jochum (cnd), Berlin PO *(rec Jesus-Christus Church, Berlin, June 1972)* Deutsche Grammophon ("The Originals" series) 2-▲ 447446-2 [ADD]
Brahms, J.:Con 2 Pno, w. F. Reiner (cnd), Chicago SO RCA Silver Seal ▲ 60536-2-RV [ADD] ■ 60536-4-RV
Brahms, J.:Fants Pno, Op. 116 Deutsche Grammophon 2-▲ 419158-2 [ADD]
Brahms, J.:Fants Pno, Op. 116 Deutsche Grammophon ("Galleria" series) ▲ 435588-2 [ADD]
Brahms, J.:Fants Pno, Op. 116 *(rec Concert Hall, Turku, Finland, Sept 1975)* Deutsche Grammophon ("The Originals" series) 2-▲ 447446-2 [ADD]
Brahms, J.:Fants Pno, Op. 116 *(rec live, 1968, 1973 & 1978)* Praga ▲ PR 250 039
Brahms, J.:Qt 1 Pno, w. Amadeus String Quartet Deutsche Grammophon ("The Originals" series) ▲ 447407-2
Chopin, F.:Ballades Pno (comp)—Op. 23 *(rec live in recital, 1960s)* Music & Arts ▲ CD 747-1 [AAD]
Chopin, F.:Con 1 Pno, w. E. Ormandy (cnd), Philadelphia Orch CBS ▲ MYK 37804 [ADD] ■ MYT 37804
Chopin, F.:Con 1 Pno, w. E. Ormandy (cnd), Philadelphia Orch Odyssey ■ YT 32369
Chopin, F.:Con 1 Pno, w. E. Ormandy (cnd), Philadelphia Orch Sony Classical (Essential Classics) ▲ SBK 46336 [ADD] ■ SBT 46336
Chopin, F.:Nocturnes—Op. 55/2 *(rec live in recital, 1960s)* Music & Arts ▲ CD 747-1
Chopin, F.:Son Pno, Op. 35 *(rec live, Czechoslovakia Radio Prague 1954)* Multisonic (Prague Spring Collection) ▲ 31 0091-2 [ADD]
Chopin, F.:Son Pno, Op. 35 *(rec 1961)* Theorema ▲ TH 121126
Chopin, F.:Vars on Mozart's *La ci darem la mano* *(rec live in recital, 1960s)* Music & Arts ▲ CD 747-1 [AAD]
Debussy, C.:Images (6) Pno—Set 1 *(rec live in recital, 1960s)* Music & Arts ▲ CD 747-1 [AAD]
Grieg, E.:Lyric Pieces—20 sels. Deutsche Grammophon ▲ 419749-2 [ADD]
Haydn, J.:Sons Pno—Sonata No. 36 in c, H.XVI/20 *(rec live, Czechoslovakia Radio Prague, 1962)* Multisonic ("Prague Spring Collection" series) ▲ 31 0091-2 [ADD]
Liszt, F.:Son Pno *(rec July 20, 1966)* Music & Arts ▲ CD 759 [AAD]
Liszt, F.:Son Pno RCA Living Stereo ▲ 09026-61614-2
Liszt, F.:Son Pno *(rec 1961)* Theorema ▲ TH 121126
Mozart, W.A.:Con 27 Pno, w. K. Böhm (cnd), Vienna PO Deutsche Grammophon ▲ 429810-2 [ADD]
Mozart, W.A.:Fant Pno, K.397 *(rec 1960)* Memories ▲ MEM 4603
Prokofiev, S.:Prelude Pno *(rec live in recital, Moscow)* Music & Arts ▲ CD 746-1 [AAD]
Prokofiev, S.:Son 3 Pno *(rec live in recital, Moscow)* Music & Arts ▲ CD 746-1 [AAD]
Prokofiev, S.:Son 8 Pno Vox Box 2-▲ CDX 5122 [ADD]
Prokofiev, S.:Visions fugitives—8 sels *(rec live in recital, Moscow)* Music & Arts ▲ CD 746-1 [AAD]
Prokofiev, S.:Visions fugitives Vox Box 2-▲ CDX 5122 [ADD]
Rachmaninoff, S.:Con 3 Pno, w. A. Cluytens (cnd), Paris Conservatory Societé des Concerts Orch Testament ▲ TES SBT 1029 [ADD]
Rachmaninoff, S.:Pno Music (misc)—Four Preludes (from Opp. 23 & 32); Daisies, Op. 38/3; etc. *(rec live in recital, Moscow)* Music & Arts ▲ CD 746-1 [AAD]
Ravel, M.:Alborada del gracioso *(rec live in recital, 1960s)* Music & Arts ▲ CD 747-1 [AAD]
Ravel, M.:Valses nobles et sentimentales *(rec live, Czechoslovakia Radio Prague, 1958)* Multisonic ("Prague Spring Collection" series) ▲ 31 0091-2 [ADD]
Saint-Saëns, C.:Con 2 Pno, w. A. Cluytens (cnd), Paris Conservatory Societé des Concerts Orch Testament ▲ TES SBT 1029 [ADD]
Schubert, Franz:Moments musicaux Vox Box 2-▲ CDX 5122 [ADD]
Schubert, Franz:Son Pno, D.850 RCA Living Stereo ▲ 09026-61614-2
Schumann, R.:Arabeske Pno *(rec 1959)* Memories ▲ MEM 4603
Schumann, R.:Arabeske Pno *(rec live in recital, 1960s)* Music & Arts ▲ CD 747-1 [AAD]
Schumann, R.:Klavierstücke, Op. 32 *(rec live in recital, 1960s)* Music & Arts ▲ CD 747-1 [AAD]
Schumann, R.:Nachtstücke Vox Box 2-▲ CDX 5122 [ADD]
Shostakovich, D.:Preludes & Fugues Pno Testament ▲ TES SBT 1029 [ADD]

Gilels, Elena (pno) (cont.)

Tchaikovsky, P.:Con 1 Pno, w. L. Maazel (cnd), New Philharmonia Orch EMI Classics ("Doublefforte" series) 2–▲ CDFB 68637

Tchaikovsky, P.:Con 1 Pno, w. Z. Mehta (cnd), New York PO Sony Classical ("Essential Classics" series) ▲ SBK 46339 [ADD] ■ SBT 46339

Tchaikovsky, P.:Con 1 Pno, w. E. Mravisnky (cnd), Leningrad PO Russian Disc ▲ RUS 11170 [ADD]

Tchaikovsky, P.:Con 2 Pno, w. L. Maazel (cnd), New Philharmonia Orch EMI Classics ("Doublefforte" series) 2–▲ CDFB 68637

Tchaikovsky, P.:Con 3 Pno, w. L. Maazel (cnd), New Philharmonia Orch EMI Classics ("Doublefforte" series) 2–▲ CDFB 68637

Tchaikovsky, P.:Son Pno, Op. 80 Russian Disc ▲ RUS 11170 [ADD]

Weber, C.M. von:Sons Pno—No. 2 *(rec live 1968, 1973 & 1978)* Praga ▲ PR 250 039

Gilels, Elizaveta (vn)

Telemann, G.P.:Canonic Sons, w. Leonid Kogan (vn)—in G *(rec Salle Wagram, Paris, May 1962)* EMI Classics ▲ CDK 65340 [ADD]

Gilemann, Aino (pno)

Stolarczyk, W.:Earth Air Fire Water, w. Amalie Malling (pno), John Damgaard (pno), Anne Øland (pno), Teddy Teirup (pno), Friedrich Gürtler (pno), Rosalind Bevan (pno), Poul Rosenbaum (pno), Rodolfo Llambias (pno), Bella Horn–Ribera (pno), Anders Riber (pno), Elisabeth Sigurdsson (pno), Thomas Tronheim (pno), Elsebeth Broderson (pno), Erik Kaltoft (pno), Jørgen Hald Nielsen (pno), Birgit Kjær (pno), Jørgen Thomsen (pno), Gunhild Donslund (pno), Henrik Bo Hansen (pno), Lone Karlsson (pno), Erik Fessel (pno), Lasse Nilsson (pno), Janos Ferenczi (pno), Erik Bach (pno), Axel Momme (pno), Arne de Cros Dich (pno), Sven Micha Slot (pno), Hanne Bramsen Buhl (pno), Lili Olesen (pno), Susannah Carlsson (pno), Ulla Erml (pno), Vagn Sørensen (pno), Leif Greibe (pno), Bodil Krogh (pno), Kirsten Ottosen (pno), Inger Bergenholz (pno), Karsten Gylendorf (pno), Bjønr Elkjær (pno), Jacob Bjørn Jensen (pno), Jørgen Kaad (pno), Anne Marie Hjelm (pno), Carl Ulrik Munk Andersen (pno), Poul Lumbye (pno), Oluf Hildebrandt Nielsen (pno), Joachim Olsson (pno), Peter Pade Ramsøe Jacobsen (pno), Astrid Pollmann (pno), Jette Borsch (pno), Kirsten Karlshøj (pno), Maria Teresa Assing (pno), Allan Dahl Hansen (pno), Johan Hugossen (pno), Tine Fenger Pederson (pno), Arne Jørgen Fæø (pno), Anja Høgsted (pno), Anne Sophie Parbo (pno), Inga Lindmark (pno), Teresa Drabik Stathakis (pno), Anne Ruth Ferenczi (pno), Irene Hasager (pno), Yuka Ichikawa (pno), Birgitte Baur (pno), Malene Thastum (pno), Jens E. Rasmussen (pno), Birgitte Zielke (pno), Claus Zielke (pno), Stefan Kasch (pno), Bin Qiao (pno), Inger Johanne Teirup (pno), Lindy Rosborg (pno), Liisa Heininen (pno), David Højer (pno), Ellen Refstrup (pno), Thomas K. Søorensen (pno), Erik Kure (pno), Michael Rauff (pno), Jan beck Eriksson (pno), Tanja Zapolski (pno), Vibeke Skagbo (pno), Pål Eide Lindtner (pno), Ha–Young Sul (pno), Benedicte Palko (pno), Inke Kesseler (pno), Anne Marie Meineche (pno), Sverre Larsen (pno), Kasper Peter Bach (pno), Elisabetta Eliseo (pno), Olga Magieres (pno), Carl Erik Kühl (pno), Thorkild Borup Nielsen (pno), Valeria Zanini (pno), Lars Stenhoft (perc), Dennis Boel (perc), Winnie Dahlgren (perc), Susanne Vind (perc), Claus Byrith (elec), Anne Marie Storm (elec), J. Ribera (cnd) *(rec live, Koldinghaus Castle, Denmark, May 2, 1996)* Danica ▲ DCD 1996

Giles, Alice (hp)

Brown, R.:Concertino, w. Budapest Brass Quintet Koch Schwann ▲ SCH 311732

Brumby, C.:Exotic Dances, w. Geoffrey Collins (fl) *(rec Studio 200, ABC Sydney, Jan 1993)* Tall Poppies ▲ TP 31 [DDD]

Caplet, A.:Conte fantastique, w. R. Kaminkovsky (vn), R. Mozes (vn), Y. Kaminkovsky (va), Y. Alperin (vc) PWK Classics ▲ PWK 1141 [DDD]

Debussy, C.:Preludes Pno (sels) [solo harp arr. of "Danseuses de Delphes" & "La fille aux cheveux e lin"] Koch Schwann ▲ CD 310179 [DDD]

Debussy, C.:Son Fl, w. E. Talmi (fl), G. Levertov (vn) PWK Classics ▲ PWK 1141 [DDD]

Fauré, G.:Impromptu Hp Koch Schwann ▲ CD 310179 [DDD]

Ichiyanagi, T.:Flowers Blooming in Summer, w. Arnan Wiesel (pno) Koch Schwann ▲ SCH 317652

Jongen, J.:Danse lente, w. Geoffrey Collins (fl) *(rec Studio 200, ABC Sydney, Jan 1993)* Tall Poppies ▲ TP 31 [DDD]

Koch, J.:Toccata Hp & Pno, w. Arnan Wiesel (pno) Koch Schwann ▲ SCH 317652

Mogot, G.:Prélude, w. Arnan Wiesel (pno) Koch Schwann ▲ SCH 317652

Piazzolla, A.:Histoire du tango, w. Geoffrey Collins (fl) *(rec Studio 200, ABC Sydney, Jan 1993)* Tall Poppies ▲ TP 31 [DDD]

Ravel, M.:Intro & Allegro, w. E. Talmi (fl), A. Arnheim (cl), R. Kaminkovsky (vn), R. Mozes (vn), Y. Kaminkovsky (va), Y. Alperin (vc) PWK Classics ▲ PWK 1141 [DDD]

Rochberg, G.:Slow Fires of Autumn, w. Geoffrey Collins (fl) *(rec Studio 200, ABC Sydney, Jan 1993)* Tall Poppies ▲ TP 31 [DDD]

Salzedo, C.:Hp Music—Whirlwind Koch Schwann ▲ SCH 313392 [ADD/DDD]

Salzedo, C.:Morceaux Hp—Ballade Koch Schwann ▲ SCH 312232 [DDD]

Salzedo, C.:Poetical Studies Koch Schwann ▲ SCH 312232 [DDD]

Salzedo, C.:Preludes Hp Koch Schwann ▲ CD 310179 [DDD]

Salzedo, C.:Scintillation Koch Schwann ▲ SCH 312232 [DDD]

Salzedo, C.:Son Hp, w. Arnan Wiesel (pno) Koch Schwann ▲ SCH 317652

Salzedo, C.:Suite Hp Koch Schwann ▲ SCH 312232 [DDD]

Salzedo, C.:Vars on a Theme in the Olden Style Koch Schwann ▲ SCH 312232 [DDD]

Schmidt, W.:Music for Scrimshaws, w. Budapest Brass Quintet Koch Schwann ▲ SCH 311732

Shankar, R.:L'Aube enchantée, w. Geoffrey Collins (fl) *(rec Studio 200, ABC Sydney, Jan 1993)* Tall Poppies ▲ TP 31 [DDD]

Takemitsu, T.:Toward the Sea III, w. Geoffrey Collins (fl) *(rec Studio 200, ABC Sydney, Jan 1993)* Tall Poppies ▲ TP 31 [DDD]

Tournier, M.:Mouvementé Hp Koch Schwann ▲ SCH 313392 [ADD/DDD]

Tournier, M.:Sonatine Hp Koch Schwann ▲ CD 310179 [DDD]

Turina, J.:Theme & Vars, Op. 100, w. Arnan Wiesel (pno) Koch Schwann ▲ SCH 317652

Zagwijn, H.:Van de Jaargetijden, w. Arnan Wiesel (pno) Koch Schwann ▲ SCH 317652

Gilgore, Elisha (pno)

Stravinsky, S.S.:Son Vc, w. C. Pegis (vc) *(rec May 1992)* Centaur ▲ CRC 2141 [DDD]

Gililov, Pavel (pno)

Debussy, C.:Music of, w. Boris Pergamenschikov (vc)—Golliwogg's Cake–Walk; Beau soir; Menuet; Minstrels *(rec Walchstadt, Studio Kraus, Mar 1–3, 1994)* Orfeo ▲ 349951 [DDD]

Fauré, G.:Music for Vc & Pno, w. Boris Pergamenschikov (vc)—Elegie; Romance; Serenade; Papillon; Après un rêve; Sicilienne; Berceuse *(rec Walchstadt, Studio Kraus, Mar 1–3, 1994)* Orfeo ▲ 349951 [DDD]

Hummel, J.N.:Adagio, Vars & Rondo on "Schöne Minka", w. A. Adorján (fl), B. Pergamenschikow (vc) *(rec Apr. 23–25, 1991)* Orfeo ▲ 252931 [DDD]

Hummel, J.N.:Son Vc, w. B. Pergamenschikow (vc) *(rec Apr. 23–25, 1991)* Orfeo ▲ 252931 [DDD]

Hummel, J.N.:Son 5 Pno *(rec Apr. 23–25, 1991)* Orfeo ▲ 252931 [DDD]

Ibert, J.:Music of, w. Boris Pergamenschikov (vc)—La meneuse de tortues d'or; La cage de cristal; La vieux mendiant; Le petit âne blanc *(rec Walchstadt, Studio Kraus, Mar 1–3, 1994)* Orfeo ▲ 349951 [DDD]

Prokofiev, S.:Adagio Vc, w. B. Pergamenschikow (vc) Orfeo ▲ 249921 [DDD]

Prokofiev, S.:Ballade Vc, w. B. Pergamenschikow (vc) Orfeo ▲ 249921 [DDD]

Prokofiev, S.:Mélodies, w. D. Sitkovetsky (vn) Virgin Classics ▲ CDC 59023

Prokofiev, S.:Son Vc, w. B. Pergamenschikow (vc) Orfeo ▲ 249921 [DDD]

Prokofiev, S.:Son Vn, Op. 94bis, w. D. Sitkovetsky (vn) Virgin Classics ▲ CDC 59023

Prokofiev, S.:Son 1 Vn, w. D. Sitkovetsky (vn) Virgin Classics ▲ CDC 59023

Ravel, M.:Pièce en forme de Habanera, w. Boris Pergamenschikov (vc) *(rec Walchstadt, Studio Kraus, Mar 1–3, 1994)* Orfeo ▲ 349951 [DDD]

Roslavets, N.:Chamber Music, w. B. Pergamenschikow (vc)—Méditation for Cello & Piano (1921); Sonata for Cello & Piano (1921) Orfeo ▲ 249921 [DDD]

Saint–Saëns, C.:Allegro appassionato, w. B. Pergamenschikov (vc) *(rec Walchstadt, Studio Kraus, Mar 1–3, 1994)* Orfeo ▲ 349951 [DDD]

Saint–Saëns, C.:Le Cygne, w. B. Pergamenschikov (vc) *(rec Walchstadt, Studio Kraus, Mar 1–3, 1994)* Orfeo ▲ 349951 [DDD]

Gilissen, Thérèse–Maria (va)

Bruch, M.:Pieces Cl, Op. 83/1–8, w. Walter Boeykens (cl), Roel Dieltiens (vc), Robert Groslot (pno) *(rec 1991)* Musique d'Abord ▲ HMA 1901371

Bruch, M.:Pieces Cl, Op. 83/1–8, w. Walter Boeykens (cl), Roel Dieltiens (vc), Robert Groslot (pno) *(rec 1991)* Musique D'Abord ▲ HMA 1901371

Jongen, J.:Allegro appassionata, w. B. Priestman (cnd), RTBF SO Koch Schwann ▲ CD 315012 [ADD]

Jongen, J.:Suite Va, w. B. Priestman (cnd), RTBF SO Koch Schwann ▲ CD 315012 [ADD]

Jongen, J.:Suite Va, w. B. Priestman (cnd), RTBF SO Koch Schwann ▲ SCH 313372 [ADD/DDD]

Rogister, J.:Con Va, w. M. Trautmann (cnd), Pécs SO Koch Schwann ▲ SCH 317182

Rogister, J.:Fant concertante, w. M. Trautmann (cnd), Pécs SO Koch Schwann ▲ SCH 317182

Vieuxtemps, H.:Duo concertant on themes from Weber's Oberon, w. Jean–Claude Vanden Eynden (pno) [arr va & pno] *(rec Studio 2 Flagey RTBF, Brussels, June 1985)* Pavane ▲ ADW 7340 [DDD]

Vieuxtemps, H.:Elégie, w. Jean–Claude Vanden Eynden (pno) *(rec Studio 2 Flagey RTBF, Brussels, June 1985)* Pavane ▲ ADW 7340 [DDD]

Vieuxtemps, H.:Son Va *(rec Studio 2 Flagey RTBF, Brussels, June 1985)* Pavane ▲ ADW 7340 [DDD]

Zemlinsky, A. von:Trio Cl, w. Walter Boeykens (cl), Roel Dieltiens (vc), Robert Groslot (pno) *(rec 1991)* Musique d'Abord ▲ HMA 1901371

Gill, Tim (vc)—see ORCHESTRAS & ENSEMBLES Chagall Trio, Chagall Trio members

Gill, Timothy (vc)

Britten, H.:Son Vc, w. Fali Pavri (pno) Guild ▲ GMCD 7114 [DDD]

Mayer, J.:Prabhanda, w. Fali Pavri (pno) Guild ▲ GMCD 7114 [DDD]

Rubbra, E.:Son Vc, w. Fali Pavri (pno) [arr vc & pno] Guild ▲ GMCD 7114 [DDD]

Gillaspie, Jon (pno)

Jane Austen Songs, w. Patricia Wright (sop) Pearl ▲ PEA 9613 [DDD]

Gille–Rybrant, Carin (pno)

Linde, B.:Son Vn, w. E. Dekov (vn) BIS ▲ CD 9 [AAD]

Gillespie, Wendy (bowed instrs)—see ORCHESTRAS & ENSEMBLES Echos Muse

Gillespie, Wendy (vl)

Christmas in the New World, w. Western Wind, Albert de Ruiter (bass), Louise Schulman (vn), Joseph Karpienia (gtr), Elaine Comparone (hpd) MusicMasters ▲ 01612–67176–2

Dance Songs of Renaissance England, w. Folger Consort, M. Bleeke, T. Chancey, W. Gillespie, M. Springfels, B. Wissick *(rec Jan. 24, 1988)* Folger Consort ▲ BDCD1 9004 [DDD]

Gilliam, J. (pno)

Beethoven, L. van:Son 9 Vn, "Kreutzer", w. R. Ricci (vn) One–Eleven ▲ URS 93050 [ADD]

Strauss, R.:Son Vn, w. R. Ricci (vn) One–Eleven ▲ URS 93050 [ADD]

Gillieron, Agnès (pno)

Mozart, W.A.:Adagio Pno, K.540 Arkadia–Akademia ▲ 134 [DDD]

Mozart, W.A.:Capriccio Pno, K.395/300g Arkadia–Akademia ▲ 134 [DDD]

Mozart, W.A.:Fant Pno, K.475 Arkadia–Akademia ▲ 134 [DDD]

Mozart, W.A.:Prelude & Fugue Pno Arkadia–Akademia ▲ 134 [DDD]

Mozart, W.A.:Son 10 Pno Arkadia–Akademia ▲ 134 [DDD]

Mozart, W.A.:Son 15 Pno Arkadia–Akademia ▲ 134 [DDD]

Schubert, Franz:Impromptus Pno, D.899—No. 3 in G♭ Arkadia–Akademia ▲ 135 [DDD]

Schubert, Franz:Moments musicaux Arkadia–Akademia ▲ 135 [DDD]

Schubert, Franz:Son Pno, D.157 Arkadia–Akademia ▲ 135 [DDD]

Schubert, Franz:Son Pno, D.557 Arkadia–Akademia ▲ 135 [DDD]

Gillitzer, Bernhard (hpd)

Benda, F.:Son Fl, Vc & Hpd, w. A. Kröpper (transverse fl), T. Fritsch (vc) Supraphon ▲ SUP 111597 [DDD]

Benda, F.:Sons (2) Fl, w. A. Kröpper (transverse fl)—in C Supraphon ▲ SUP 111597 [DDD]

Benda, G.A.:Son in G Fl & Hpd, w. A. Kröpper (transverse fl) Supraphon ▲ SUP 111597 [DDD]

Gillitzer, Bernhard (pno)

Benda, F.:Son Fl & Pno, w. A. Kröpper (transverse fl) Supraphon ▲ SUP 111597 [DDD]

Haydn, J.:Trios Pno, Fl & Vc, w. Andreas Kröper (fl), Thomas Fritzsch (vc) *(rec Evangelic Church, Korunní, Prague, Sept 1993)* Arta ▲ CD 0052 [DDD]

Gilliver, Liz (mar)

A Secret Place, w. Simone Rebello (perc), Andrew Scott (a sax), Kalengo Percussion Ensemble, Eryl Roberts (perc), John Melbourne (perc), Chris Bastock (perc), Richard Dyson (perc) *(rec Zion Institute, Manchester, 1995)* Doyen ▲ CD 040 [DDD]

Gillock, Jon (org)

Bach, J.S.:Con 1 for 2 Hpds, w. Kathleen Bride (hp)—Adagio [arr for org & hp] *(rec Church of the Ascension, New York, Nov 1995)* Milan ▲ 73138–35764–2 [DDD]

Bach, J.S.:Preludes & Fugues, BWV 531–552—BWV 552 *(rec Church of the Ascension, New York, Nov 1995)* Milan ▲ 73138–35764–2 [DDD]

Grandjany, M.:Aria in Classic Style, w. Kathleen Bride (hp) *(rec Church of the Ascension, New York, Nov 1995)* Milan ▲ 73138–35764–2 [DDD]

Messiaen, O.:Les Corps glorieux *(rec Trinity Church, Paris, Mar 16 & 17, 1995)* Milan ▲ 73138 35752–2 [DDD]

Messiaen, O.:Diptyque *(rec Trinity Church, Paris, Mar 16 & 17, 1995)* Milan ▲ 73138 35752–2 [DDD]

Soler, P.A.:Cons Kbds—Nos. 3 & 6 [arr for org] *(rec Church of the Ascension, New York, Nov 1995)* Milan ▲ 73138–35764–2 [DDD]

Tournemire, C.:Te Deum Org [improv by Gillock] *(rec Church of the Ascension, New York, Nov 1995)* Milan ▲ 73138–35764–2 [DDD]

White, L.:Suite Hp, w. Kathleen Bride (hp)—Aria; Fugue *(rec Church of the Ascension, New York, Nov 1995)* Milan ▲ 73138–35764–2 [DDD]

Gilmore, Edward (cl)

Brings, A.:Concert Piece for 4 Cls, w. M. Abt–Greenfield (E♭ cl), P. Gallo (a cl), B. Hysong (b cl) *(rec 1989–90)* Centaur ▲ CRC 2079 [ADD]

Brings, A.:Eclogue Cl *(rec 1989–90)* Centaur ▲ CRC 2079 [ADD]

Brings, A.:Inventions (3) for 2 Cls, w. M. Abt–Greenfield (cl) *(rec 1989–90)* Centaur ▲ CRC 2079 [ADD]

Brings, A.:Son Cl, w. A. Brings (pno) Centaur ▲ CRC 2156

Brings, A.:Trio Cl, Vc & Pno, w. A. Kouguell (vc), G. Chinn (pno) *(rec 1989–90)* Centaur ▲ CRC 2079 [ADD]

Kraft, L.:Episodes, w. E. Charlston (perc) *(rec 1989–1990)* Centaur ▲ CRC 2079 [ADD]

Kraft, L.:Inventions & Airs, w. E. Wyrick (vn), A. Karis (pno) *(rec 1989–1990)* Centaur ▲ CRC 2079 [ADD]

Kraft, L.:O Primavera, w. R. Stallman (fl), R. Roseman (ob) *(rec 1989–1990)* Centaur ▲ CRC 2079 [ADD]

Ran, S.:Con da Camera II, w. C. Colnot (cnd), Univ of Chicago Contemporary Chamber Players *(rec 1979–91)* CRI ▲ CD 609 [ADD/DDD]

Van Appledorn, M.J.:Sonatine Cl, w. K. Inoue (pno) Opus One ▲ 147

Gimpel, Bronislaw (vn)

Bruch, M.:Con 1 Vn, w. R. Reinhardt (cnd), Southwest German RSO Baden–Baden Vox Legends 2–▲ CDX 5523

Dvořák, A.:Con Vn, w. R. Reinhardt (cnd), Southwest German RSO Baden–Baden Vox Legends 2–▲ CDX 5523

Goldmark, K.:Con 1 Vn, w. R. Reinhardt (cnd), Southwest German RSO Baden–Baden Vox Legends 2–▲ CDX 5523

Kreisler, F.:Vn Pieces, w. C. Cremer (cnd), Stuttgart Pro Musica Orch—Tartini:Fugue in A; La Gitana; Old Viennese Dance Melodies (3); Polichinelle – Serenade; Rimsky–Korsakov:Arab Song from Scheherazade; Perlude & Allegro (in the Style of Gaetano Pugnani); La Précieuse (in the Style of Louis Couperin); Caprice Viennois; Tambourin Chinois; Rachmaninoff:Marguerite; Falla:Danse Espagnole Vox Legends ▲ CDX 5523

Gimpel, Jakob (pno)
Chopin, F.:Ballades Pno (comp)—No. 1, Op. 23 *(rec live, Ambassador Auditorium, May 11, 1978)* Cambria 2-▲ CD 1070
Chopin, F.:Barcarolle Pno *(rec live, Ambassador Auditorium, May 11, 1978)* Cambria 2-▲ CD 1070
Chopin, F.:Etudes (24)—Etudes in A♭ Op. 25/1 & in a Op. 25/11 *(rec live, Ambassador Auditorium, May 11, 1978)* Cambria 2-▲ CD 1070
Chopin, F.:Impromptus—No. 2 in F# *(rec live, Ambassador Auditorium, May 11, 1978)* Cambria 2-▲ CD 1070
Chopin, F.:Intro & Vars on "Je vends des scalpulaines" *(rec live, Ambassador Auditorium, May 11, 1978)* Cambria 2-▲ CD 1070
Chopin, F.:Mazurkas—Opp. 30/3, 50/3 & 56/2 *(rec live, Ambassador Auditorium, May 11, 1978)* Cambria 2-▲ CD 1070
Chopin, F.:Nocturnes—Nocturne in E, Op. 62/2 *(rec live, Ambassador Auditorium, May 11, 1978)* Cambria 2-▲ CD 1070
Chopin, F.:Scherzos, Scherzo in b, Op. 20 *(rec live, Ambassador Auditorium, May 11, 1978)* Cambria 2-▲ CD 1070
Chopin, F.:Son Pno, Op. 35 *(rec live, Ambassador Auditorium, May 11, 1978)* Cambria 2-▲ CD 1070
Debussy, C.:Etudes—Etude pour les 5 doigts *(rec live, Ambassador Auditorium, May 11, 1978)* Cambria 2-▲ CD 1070
Liszt, F.:Valses oubliées— 1 waltz *(rec live, Ambassador Auditorium, May 11, 1978)* Cambria 2-▲ CD 1070

Gimse, Havard (pno)
Grieg, E.:Intermezzo, w. Ø. Birkeland (vc) *(rec May & Aug. 1993)* Naxos ▲ 8.550878 [DDD]
Grieg, E.:Son Vc, w. Ø. Birkeland (vc) *(rec May & Aug. 1993)* Naxos ▲ 8.550878 [DDD]
Grieg, E.:Son Pno *(rec May & Aug. 1993)* Naxos ▲ 8.550878 [DDD]

Gingold, Josef (vn)
Fauré, G.:Son 1 Vn, w. W. Robert (pno) *(rec 1966)* Music & Arts ▲ CD 286 [AAD]
Kodály, Z.:Duo Vn & Vc, w. J. Starker (vc) Delos ▲ DCD 1015
Kreisler, F.:Short Pieces Vn, w. W. Robert (pno) *(rec 1966)* Music & Arts ▲ CD 286 [AAD]
Kreisler, F.:Vn Pieces, w. Charles H. Webb (pno) *(rec 1976)* Music & Arts ▲ CD 286 [AAD]

Gini, R. (vc)
Boccherini, L.:Qnt Pno, G.407–412, w. L. Alvini (pno), E. Gatti (vn), O. Edouard (vn), E. Moreno (va)—Nos. 1, 5 & 6 Tactus ▲ TC 740203
Boccherini, L.:Trio Sons Hpd, G.143–148, w. L. Alvini (hpd), E. Gatti (vn) *(rec June 27–30, 1991)* Tactus ▲ TC 740202
Frescobaldi, G.:Sonetto spirituale:Maddalena all Croce, w. C. Calvi (cta) [I] *(rec 5/91)* Nuova Era ("Ancient Music" series) ▲ 7030 [DDD]
Sances, G.F.:Stabat mater dolorosa, w. C. Calvi (cta) [L] *(rec 5/91)* Nuova Era ("Ancient Music" series) ▲ 7030 [DDD]

Gini, R. (vl)
Bach, J.S.:Sons Vl, BWV 1027–1029, w. L. Alvini (hpd) Tactus ▲ TC 680201

Gini, Roberto (kbd/cnd)—see ORCHESTRAS & ENSEMBLES Concerto Ensemble

Ginot, Eugène (va)
Debussy, C.:Son Fl, w. M. Moyse (fl), L. Laskine (hp) *(rec ca. 1927)* Pearl ▲ PEA 9348 (m) [AAD]

Ginsberg, Eric (cl)—see also ORCHESTRAS & ENSEMBLES Moran Woodwind Quintet
Snyder, R.:Enneagram Studies, w. Stephen Krahn (pno), Chris Casart (perc), Rick Schaefer (perc), Kelly Scheef (perc), Jason Varga (perc), Scott Zimmerman (perc) Coronet ▲ COR 400-9
Snyder, R.:Qnt 3 Fl, w. John Bailey (fl), William McMullen (ob), Allen French (hn), Gary Echols (bn) Coronet ▲ COR 400-9

Ginzburg, Grigori (pno)
Rachmaninoff, S.:Suite 2 for 2 Pnos, w. Alexander Goldenweiser (pno) Melodiya ("Russian Piano School" series) ▲ 74321-25173-2
Schumann, R.:Sym Etudes Multisonic ▲ MUL 310265

Ginzel, Reiner (vc)—see ORCHESTRAS & ENSEMBLES German String Trio

Giorgi, Massimo (db)
Bottesini, G.:Allegretto capriccio Db, w. V. Antonellini (cnd), I Solisti Aquilani Nuova Era ▲ 6810 [DDD]
Bottesini, G.:Elegy & Tarantella, w. V. Antonellini (cnd), I Solisti Aquilani Nuova Era ▲ 6810 [DDD]
Bottesini, G.:Gran Duo Cl, w. V. Mariozzi (cl), V. Antonellini (cnd), I Solisti Aquilani Nuova Era ▲ 6810 [DDD]
Bottesini, G.:Gran Duo Concertant, w. D. Conti (vn), V. Antonellini (cnd), I Solisti Aquilani Nuova Era ▲ 6810 [DDD]
Bottesini, G.:Introduction & Gavotte, w. V. Antonellini (cnd), I Solisti Aquilani Nuova Era ▲ 6810 [DDD]
Bottesini, G.:Passioni Amorose, w. D. Conti (vn), V. Antonellini (cnd), I Solisti Aquilani Nuova Era ▲ 6810 [DDD]
Bottesini, G.:Vars on *La Sonnambula*, w. V. Antonellini (cnd), I Solisti Aquilani Nuova Era ▲ 6810 [DDD]

Giot, Claude (perc)
Chaynes, C.:Oginoha, "Lights from Japanese Poetry", w. Y. Nara (sop), P.–Y. Artaud (fl), D. Megévand (celtic hp) REM ▲ REM 311194 [DDD]

Giovaninetta, C. (vn)—see ORCHESTRAS & ENSEMBLES Ysaÿe String Quartet

Giovannetti, Geralyn (ob)—see ORCHESTRAS & ENSEMBLES Essex Winds Woodwind Quintet

Gippo, Jan (pic)
Erb, D.:Drawing down the Moon, w. K. Brundage (perc) New World ▲ 80457-2

Giradot, Marc (ophicleide/tuba)
Damaré, E.:Music of, w. Jean-Louis Beaumadier (petite fl), Christophe Poiget (vn), Circe Wind Quintet, La Follia Instrumental Ensemble—La Capricieuse, Op. 270; Feux follets, Op. 378; Les Échos des bois, Op. 220; Le Merle blanc, Op. 161; Tarentelle, Op. 391; L'Oiseau et les roses, Op. 153; Le Tourbillon, Op. 212; L'Alouette, Op. 172; Pizzicato, Op. 426; La Danse des grillons, Op. 380 *(rec 1996)* Calliope ▲ CAL 9869 [DDD]

Girardi, A. (celtic hp)
Milesi, P.:Modi 2, w. L. M. Pickova (sop), Françoise Goddard (alt), M. Ferradini (ten), B. Andersen (bass), D. Cassamagnaghi (fl), S. Scanziani (ob), A. Bianchi (cl/b cl), E. Crisafulli (bn), C. Gazzola (hn), F. Gualandris (tuba), A. Girardi (celtic hp), R. Anedda (vn), E. Groppo (vn), M. Pagani (vn), M. Ravasio (va), S. Righini (vc), P. Rizzi (db), J. Scully (perc), P. Milesi (cnd) Cuneiform ▲ RUNE 63

Girardi, P. (pno)
Dvořák, A.:Sonatina Vn, w. Raffaele Trevisani (fl) Stradivarius ▲ STV 33321 [DDD]
Franck, C.:Son Vn, w. R. Trevisani (fl) Stradivarius ▲ STR 33321
Franck, C.:Son Vn, w. Raffaele Trevisani (fl) Stradivarius ▲ STV 33321 [DDD]
Prokofiev, S.:Son Fl, w. Raffaele Trevisani (fl) Stradivarius ▲ STV 33321 [DDD]

Girdwood, Julia (ob)
Bach, J.S.:Con Vn & Ob, w. J. Fröhlich (vn), R. Haydon Clark (cnd), Consort of London Collins Quest ▲ 30182 [DDD]
Barber, S.:Canzonetta, w. J. Serebrier (cnd), Scottish CO Phoenix ▲ PHCD 111 [DDD]
Fiorillo, F.:Sinf concertante, w. Anthony Camden (ob), N. Ward (cnd), City of London Sinfonia—in F *(rec East Finchley, England, Apr 1995)* Naxos ▲ 8.553433 [DDD]
Handel, G.F.:Ottone, Rè di Germania (ov), w. Anthony Camden (ob), N. Ward (cnd), City of London Sinfonia *(rec All Saints Church, East Finchley, Apr 24 & 27, 1995)* Naxos ▲ 8.553430 [DDD]
Handel, G.F.:Suites Hpd, w. Anthony Camden (ob), N. Ward (cnd), City of London Sinfonia—in g [trans by A. Camden] *(rec All Saints Church, East Finchley, Apr 24 & 27, 1995)* Naxos ▲ 8.553430 [DDD]
Vaughan Williams, R.:Con Ob, w. R. Haydon Clark (cnd), Consort of London Collins Classics ▲ 11402 [DDD]

Girko, Stephen (cl)
Sargon, S.:Music of, w. Lila Deis (sop), Stephen Dubov (ten), Christopher Adkins (vc), Vesselin Demirev (vn), Deborah Baron (fl), Simon Sargon (pno)—Shemà [Hear] for Sop, Fl, Cl, Vc & Pno; Before the Ark for Vn & Pno; Wedding Dance for Vn & Pno; Klezmuzik for Cl & Pno; At Gradmother's Knee [5 Yiddish Folk Songs] for Ten & Pno; Meditation for Vc & Pno; At Grandfather's Knee [5 Judeo-Spanish Folk Songs] for Sop & Pno *(rec Caruth Auditorium, SMU, Dallas, TX, Jan 1996)* Gasparo ▲ GAS 318

Giró, Jordi (pno)
Cercós, J.:Hinamatsuri *(rec Albert Moraleda Studio, 1993–95)* Edicions Albert Moraleda 2-▲ 032D [DDD]

Girod, Marie-Catherine (pno)
Emmanuel, M.:Songs, w. Florence Katz (mez) Timpani ▲ 1030
Le Flem, P.:Fantaisie Pno, w. C. Schnitzler (cnd), Bretagne Orch *(rec Oct. 22 & 25, 1993)* Timpani ▲ 1C 1021 [DDD]
Lourié, A.:Pno Music—5 Préludes, Op. 1 [Préludes fragiles]; Synthèses; Pno gosse; Nocturne en b; 4 Pièces; A Phoenix Park Nocturne; Emploi du temps Accord ▲ ACD 201072 [DDD]
Tournemire, C.:Etudes de chaque jour Accord ▲ ACD 201312 [DDD]
Tournemire, C.:Préludes-poèmes Accord ▲ ACD 201312 [DDD]

Girolamo (cl)
Puccini, M.:Concertone Fl, w. Mencarelli (fl), G. Bodanza (tpt), Caproni (hn), G. Cosmi (cnd), Lucca Teatro Comunale del Giglio Orch Bongiovanni ▲ GB 2048 [DDD]

Girollet, Miguel Angel (gtr)
Bach, J.S.:Suite Lt, BWV 995 [trans. M.A. Girollet] Opera tres ▲ 1006 [DDD]
Dowland, J.:Lt Music—Fantasie; Robert Earle of Essex, his Galliard; Captain Piper's Galliard; Sir John Smith, his Almaine; Melancholy Galliard; Fantasie [trans. M.A. Girollet] Opera tres ▲ 1006 [DDD]
Frescobaldi, G.:Aria detta "La Frescobalda" [trans. M.A. Girollet] Opera tres ▲ 1006 [DDD]
Praetorius, M.:Terpsichore [trans. M.A. Girollet] Opera tres ▲ 1006 [DDD]
Weiss, S.L.:Lt Music—Fantasie [trans. M.A. Girollet] Opera tres ▲ 1006 [DDD]

Girshenko, Sergei (vn)
Petukhov, M.:Élégie romantique, w. Sergei Kalyanov (vc), Mikhaïl Petukhov (pno) *(rec Great Hall of Moscow Conservatory, July 25 & Aug 10, 1995)* Pavane ▲ ADW 7365 [DDD]

Gisburg (fl/cpsr/voc)
Gisberg:Music of, w. Christine Bard (perc), Christina Sun (erhu), Jeff O'Malley (nar), Jacqueline Leclair (ob), Quentin Chiappetta (sampler/pno/cpsr), Reuben Radding (bass instrument)—Opening; No Stranger Not At All; Imaginary Movielandscape 1; Portrait; "Jowohl"; Mein Herz hat nicht vergessen [tango]; Ritual; Dying Takes Its Time; Fruits; Mic' N Drums Tzadik ("The Composers" series) ▲ TZA 7007 [DDD]

Gisburg (fl/sgr)
Gisberg:Music of, w. Jeff O'Malley (nar), Midori Seiler (vn), Ron Lawrence (va), Guy Tyler (db), Anthony Coleman (pno), Christine Bard (perc)—Low-End; Since You Have Left; The Woman Is Perfected; Sharks; Night & Wind; Saturnspacemonsters Walking on a Sandy Surface; Old Moon in Winter; Never Saw the Stars So Bright; Habe Die Liebe Verschlafen; W.A.L.S.H. Tzadik ▲ TZA CD 7019 [DDD]

Gisler-Haase, Barbara (fl)—see also ORCHESTRAS & ENSEMBLES Vienna Flautists
Dvořák, A.:Sonatina Vn, w. Mika Mori (pno) *(rec Studio Baumgarten, Vienna, Feb. 2 & 3, 1994)* Camerata ▲ 30CM 393 [DDD]
Hindemith, P.:Son Fl, w. Mika Mori (pno) *(rec Studio Baumgarten, Vienna, Feb. 2 & 3, 1994)* Camerata ▲ 30CM 393 [DDD]
Hindemith, P.:Son Fl, w. Mika Mori (pno) Camerata ▲ 30CM 358 [DDD]
Hummel, J.N.:Son Vn & Pno, Op. 50, w. Mika Mori (pno) *(rec Studio Baumgarten, Vienna, Feb. 2 & 3, 1994)* Camerata ▲ 30CM 393 [DDD]
Martinů, B.:Son Fl & Pno, w. Mika Mori (pno) *(rec Studio Baumgarten, Vienna, Feb. 2 & 3, 1994)* Camerata ▲ 30CM 393 [DDD]

Gislinge, F. (ob)—see ORCHESTRAS & ENSEMBLES Vestjysk Chamber Ensemble

Gislinge, Katrine (pno)
Bartók, B.:Rhap 1 Vc, w. Henrik Brendstrup (vc) Kontrapunkt ▲ KPT 32217
Janácek, L.:Fairy Tale, w. Henrik Brendstrup (vc) Kontrapunkt ▲ KPT 32217
Janácek, L.:Presto, w. Henrik Brendstrup (vc) Kontrapunkt ▲ KPT 32217
Kodály, Z.:Adagio Vn, w. Henrik Brendstrup (vc) Kontrapunkt ▲ KPT 32217
Kodály, Z.:Son Vc & Pno, Op. 4, w. Henrik Brendstrup (vc) Kontrapunkt ▲ KPT 32217
Kodály, Z.:Sonatina Vc & Pno, w. Henrik Brendstrup (vc) Kontrapunkt ▲ KPT 32217

Gislinge, Sonja (hp)
Jersild, J.:Con Hp, w. O. Vänskä (cnd), Copenhagen PO Paula ▲ PACD 75 [DAD]
Jersild, J.:Fant e canto affetuoso, w. Lena Bust Nielsen (fl), Jesper Helmuth Madsen (cl), Hege Waldeland (vc) Paula ▲ PACD 75 [DAD]

Gitlis, Ivry (vn)
Bartók, B.:Con 2 Vn, w. J. Horenstein (cnd), Vienna SO *(rec 1954–57)* Vox Box ("Legends" series) 2-▲ CDX2 5505 [ADD]
Bartók, B.:Son Vn *(rec 1954–57)* Vox Box ("Legends" series) 2-▲ CDX2 5505 [ADD]
Bernstein, C.H.:Rhap Israélienne Arcobaleno 2-▲ AAOC 93922
Bernstein, C.H.:Romantic Suite Arcobaleno 2-▲ AAOC 93922
Bruch, M.:Con 1 Vn, w. J. Horenstein (cnd), Vienna SO *(rec 1954–57)* Vox Box ("Legends" series) 2-▲ CDX2 5505 [ADD]
Hindemith, P.:Con Vn, w. H. Rosbaud (cnd), Southwest German RSO Baden-Baden *(rec live, 1962)* Music & Arts ▲ CD 627 (m) [AAD]
Mendelssohn, F.:Con in e Vn & Orch, Op. 64, w. H. Swarowsky (cnd), Vienna SO *(rec ca. 1954–57)* Vox Box ("Legends" series) 2-▲ CDX2 5505 [ADD]
Mendelssohn, F.:Con in e Vn & Orch, Op. 64, w. D. Josefowitz (cnd), Japan PO *(rec 1968)* FNAC Music ("Via Classique" series) ▲ 642305
Sibelius, J.:Con Vn, w. J. Horenstein (cnd), Vienna SO *(rec ca. 1954–57)* Vox Box ("Legends" series) 2-▲ CDX2 5505 [ADD]
Tchaikovsky, P.:Con Vn, w. J. Horenstein (cnd), Vienna SO *(rec ca. 1954–57)* Vox Box ("Legends" series) 2-▲ CDX2 5505 [ADD]

Giudici, G. (pno)
Napoli, J.:Other Vars Zuma Records ▲ ZMA 102

Giuffredi, Bruno (gtr)
Giuliani, M.:Rossiniana—Opp. 119–123 Arkadia-Akademia ▲ 128 [DDD]
Tosti, P.F.:Songs, w. E. Palacio (ten), M. Rapattoni (pno), H. Liviabella (vn), G. Scabbia (fl), C. Passerini (hp), M. Decimo (vc) [arr. Massimo de Bernart for instrumental accompaniment]—La serenata; Sogno; 'A vucchella; Segreto; Ideale; 2ème Aubade; Anima mia; Donna, vorrei morir; Aprile; Ancora!; Mattinata; L'ultima canzone; Malìa; Non t'amo più; Il pescatore canta!; Tristezza; O falce di luna calante; L'abla separa dalla luce l'ombra; Mi guitarra dice "Te amo!"; Ricordati di me; Vuol note o banconote? Arkadia-Akademia ▲ 125 [DDD]

Giuffredi, C. (cl)—see ORCHESTRAS & ENSEMBLES Rossini Wind Quartet

Giuffredi, Corrado (cl)—see ORCHESTRAS & ENSEMBLES Italiano Octet

Giuliani, Luciano (hn)
Cherubini, L.:Sons (2) Hn, w. V. Antonellini (cnd), I Solisti Aquilani Nuova Era ▲ 6910 [DDD]
Cherubini, L.:Sons (2) Hn, w. Rome Solisti—No. 2 *(rec Rome, 1996)* musicaimmagine ▲ MR 10031
Mercadante, S.:Con Hn, w. V. Antonellini (cnd), I Solisti Aquilani Nuova Era ▲ 6910 [DDD]

Giulini, A. (pno)
Mozart, W.A.:Con 20 Pno, w. A. Lizzio (cnd), Mozart Festival Orch Sound 2-▲ E 219 [DDD]
Mozart, W.A.:Con 20 Pno, w. A. Giulini, A. Lizzio, Mozart Festival Orch Vivace 3-▲ E 313 [DDD]
Mozart, W.A.:Con 21 Pno, w. A. Lizzio (cnd), Mozart Festival Orch Vivace ▲ E 552 [DDD]
Mozart, W.A.:Con 21 Pno, w. A. Lizzio (cnd), Mozart Festival Orch Vivace 2-▲ G 117/118 [DDD]
Mozart, W.A.:Con 21 Pno, w. A. Lizzio (cnd), Mozart Festival Orch Sound 2-▲ E 219 [DDD]
Mozart, W.A.:Con 21 Pno, w. A. Lizzio (cnd), Mozart Festival Orch Vivace 3-▲ E 313 [DDD]
Mozart, W.A.:Con 21 Pno, w. A. Lizzio (cnd), Mozart Festival Orch Vivace 3-▲ E 323 [DDD]
Mozart, W.A.:Con 23 Pno, w. A. Lizzio (cnd), Mozart Festival Orch Sound 2-▲ E 219 [DDD]
Mozart, W.A.:Con 23 Pno, w. A. Lizzio (cnd), Mozart Festival Orch Vivace 3-▲ E 313 [DDD]
Mozart, W.A.:Con 26 Pno, w. A. Lizzio (cnd), Mozart Festival Orch Vivace 3-▲ E 313 [DDD]

INSTRUMENT.

Giulini, A. (pno) (cont.)
Mozart, W.A.:Con 26 Pno, w. A. Lizzio (cnd), Mozart Festival Orch Vivace 3–▲ E 323 [DDD]
Mozart, W.A.:Con 26 Pno, w. A. Lizzio (cnd), Mozart Festival Orch Sound 2–▲ E 219 [DDD]
Mozart, W.A.:Con 26 Pno, w. A. Lizzio (cnd), Mozart Festival Orch Vivace ▲ E 552 [DDD]

Giullou, J. (org)
Mussorgsky, M.:Pictures at an Exhibition [performer's trans. for organ] Dorian ▲ DOR 90117 [DDD]
Stravinsky, I.:Pétrouchka (sels) [performing his own trans. for organ]—3 Dances Dorian ▲ DOR 90117 [DDD]

Giuranna, Bruno (pno)
Mozart, W.A.:Con 7 Pnos, w. Padua & Venice CO, Crommelynck Duo Claves ▲ CD 9022 [DDD]

Giuranna, Bruno (va)
Beethoven, L. van:Trio Strs, Op. 3, w. A.–S. Mutter (vn), M. Rostropovich (vc) Deutsche Grammophon 2–▲ 427687–2 [DDD]
Beethoven, L. van:Trios Strs, Op. 9, w. A.–S. Mutter (vn), M. Rostropovich (vc) Deutsche Grammophon 2–▲ 427687–2 [DDD]
Berlioz, H.:Harold in Italy, w. M. Shostakovich (cnd), BBC SO IMP ("BBC Radio Classics" series) ▲ IMP 5691532
Mozart, W.A.:Qts Pno, w. Beaux Arts Trio Philips ▲ 410391–2 [DDD]
Mozart, W.A.:Sinf concertante Vn, K.364, w. A.–S. Mutter (vn), N. Marriner (cnd), Academy of St. Martin in the Fields EMI Classics ▲ CDC 54302

Giuranna, Bruno (vn)
Beethoven, L. van:Serenade Strs, Op. 8, w. A.–S. Mutter (vn), M. Rostropovich (vc) Deutsche Grammophon 2–▲ 427687–2 [DDD]

Giussani, Ermes (trbn)—see ORCHESTRAS & ENSEMBLES Academy of Ancient Music Instumental Ensemble

Givens, Charlotte (va)
Banfield, W.:Cone Tone, w. Velda Kelly (vn), Linda Trotter (vn), Tim Holley (vc) Innova ▲ 510 [DDD]

Givskov, Tutter (vn)—see ORCHESTRAS & ENSEMBLES Copenhagen String Quartet

Glab, Elisabeth (vn)
Mozart, W.A.:Qnt Hn & Strs, w. Hervé Joulain (hn), Françoise Gnéri (va), Pascal Robault (va), Nadine Pierre (vc) Arion ▲ ARN 68311 [DDD]
Weill, K.:Con Vn, w. P. Herreweghe (cnd), Musique Oblique Ensemble *(rec May 1992)* Harmonia Mundi France ▲ HMC 901422

Glackin, Paddy (fid)
Cage, J.:Roaratorio:An Irish Circus on Finnegans Wake, w. J. Cage (voice), J. Heaney (sgr), M. Mercier (bodrhan), P. Mercier (bodrhan), M. Mallory (fl), S. Ellis (uillean pipes) Mode 2–▲ mode 28/29
Cage, J.:Roaratorio:An Irish Circus on Finnegans Wake, w. J. Cage (voice), J. Heaney (sgr), M. Mercier (bodrhan), P. Mercier (bodrhan), M. Mallory (fl), S. Ellis (uillean pipes) Wergo ▲ WER 6303–2

Gladkov, Eugene (dlc)
Smolsky, D.:Con 1 Dlc, Belarussian State Radio–TV Orch Olympia ▲ OCD 551 [AAD]

Gladstone, A. (pno)
Sibelius, J.:Qnt Pno, w. Gabrieli String Quartet Chandos ▲ CHAN 8742 [DDD]

Glaetzner, Burkhard (ob)
Bach, C.P.E.:Con Ob, H.466, w. M. Pommer (cnd), Leipzig New Bach Collegium Musicum Capriccio ▲ 10069
Bach, C.P.E.:Con Ob, H.468, w. M. Pommer (cnd), Leipzig New Bach Collegium Musicum Capriccio ▲ 10069
Berio, L.:Sequenza VII Berlin Classics ▲ BER 1172
Devienne, F.:Sons Ob, Op. 70, w. C. Shornsheim (hpd), S. Pank (vc) Berlin Classics ▲ BER 1017 [DDD]
Devienne, F.:Sons Ob, Op. 71, w. C. Shornsheim (hpd), S. Pank (vc) Berlin Classics ▲ BER 1017 [DDD]
Fasch, J.F.:Trio Sons, w. I. Goritzki (ob), T. Reinhardt (bn), S. Pank (vl), A. Beyer (vle), C. Schornsheim (hpd) Berlin Classics ▲ BER 1069 [DDD]
Ferlendis, G.:Con 1 Ob, w. H. Haenchen (cnd), C.P.E. Bach CO Capriccio ▲ 10087 [DDD]
Hertel, J.W.:Cons Various Solo Instruments & Orch, w. B. Glaetzner (cnd), New Bach Collegium Musicum—Cons. for Oboe Nos. 6–9 Berlin Classics ▲ BER 1009 [DDD]
Lombardi, L.:Einklang Berlin Classics ▲ BER 1172
Mozart, W.A.:Con Ob, K.314, w. H. Haenchen (cnd), C.P.E. Bach CO Capriccio ▲ 10087 [DDD]
Mozart, W.A.:Con Ob, K.314, w. H. Haenchen (cnd), C.P.E. Bach CO LaserLight ▲ 15 875 [DDD]
Rosetti, F.A.:Cons Ob, w. H. Haenchen (cnd), C.P.E. Bach CO—Con. in F Capriccio ▲ 10087 [DDD]
Schenker, F.:Horstuck Berlin Classics ▲ BER 1172
Schumann, R.:Romances Ob, w. Peter Rösel (pno) Berlin Classics ▲ BER 9189
Telemann, G.P.:Cons Ob Orch, w. H. Haenchen (cnd), Berlin CO *(rec 1978)* Berlin Classics ▲ BER 9210
Vivaldi, A.:Cons Diverse Instrs, w. L. Mayer (mand), Güttler (tpt), Sandau (tpt), Botvay, Pommer (cnd), New Bach Collegium Musicum, Budapest Strings LaserLight ▲ 15518 [DDD]
Vivaldi, A.:Cons Ob, w. K. Botvay (cnd), Budapest Strings—RV.454 Laserlight ▲ 15 518
Vivaldi, A.:Cons Ob, w. H. Haenchen (cnd), Berlin CO *(rec 1978)* Berlin Classics ▲ BER 9210
Vivaldi, A.:Sons Ob, w. I. Goritzki (ob), K. Suske (vn), A. Bayer (vn), T. Reinhardt (bn), S. Pank (vl), C. Schornsheim (org/hpd)—RV.28, 34, 53, 81 & 779 Capriccio ▲ CD 10143 [DDD] ■ CAS 27153 (CrO2)
Xenakis, I.:Dmaathen, w. *(ensemble unknown)* Berlin Classics ▲ BER 1172
Yun, I.:Piri Ob Berlin Classics ▲ BER 1172
Zelenka, J.D.:Confitebor, w. L. Güttler (cnd), Virtuosi Saxoniae, Thüringian Academic Sing Circle Berlin Classics 4–▲ BER 1150 [DDD]
Zelenka, J.D.:Trio Sons Obs, w. Ingo Goritzki (ob), Knut Sønstevold (bn), Achim Beyer (vn), Siegfried Pank (va), Walter–Heinz Bernstein (hpd) Berlin Classics 4–▲ BER 1150 [DDD]
Zelenka, J.D.:Trio Sons Obs, w. I. Goritzki (ob), K. Sønstevold (bn), A. Beyer (vn), S. Pank (vl), W. H. Bernstein (hpd) Berlin Classics 2–▲ BER 1070 [DDD]

Glak, K. (pno)—see ORCHESTRAS & ENSEMBLES Antifonale Chamber Ensemble

Glamsch, H. (perc)
Frischknecht, H.E.:Fant Vn, w. M. Dentan (org), H. E. Frischknecht (org) *(rec Feb. 26, 1989)* Pro Viva ▲ ISPV 161 CD [DDD]
Frischknecht, H.E.:Org Music, w. E. Frischknecht (org), H. E. Frischknecht (org), M. Dentan (org)—3 pieces *(rec Sept. 7, 1989)* Pro Viva ▲ ISPV 161 CD [DDD]

Glass, Elisabeth (vn)
Mozart, W.A.:Con 5 Vn, w. R. König (cnd), Bayreuth Festival Orch members Platz ▲ PLZ 629

Glass, Philip (kbds)—see ORCHESTRAS & ENSEMBLES Philip Glass Ensemble

Glass, Philip (org)
Glass, Philip:Dances (5), w. M. Riesman (org), Philip Glass Ensemble CBS 2–▲ M2K 44765 [ADD]

Glass, Philip (pno)
Glass, Philip:Pno Music—Metamorphosis 1–5; Mad Rush; Wichita Sutra Vortex CBS ▲ MK 45576 [DDD] ■ FMT 45576 (D)

Glasscock, Lynn (perc)
Kouneva, P.:Aeon, w. Terry Rhodes (sop), Ellen Williams (mez), Penka Kouneva (pno), Robbie Link (gtr) Albany ▲ TROY 172 [DDD]

Glat, A. (vl)—see ORCHESTRAS & ENSEMBLES Kuijken Consort

Glazer, David (cl)—see also ORCHESTRAS & ENSEMBLES New York Woodwind Quintet
Bavicchi, J.:Trio 4 Cl, w. M. Raimondi (vn), Dell'Aquila (hp) CRI ■ C 138
Krommer, F.:Con Cl, w. J. Faerber (cnd), Württemberg CO Preiser ▲ 90167 [ADD]
Mozart, W.A.:Con Cl, w. G. Simon (cnd), English CO LaserLight ▲ 15 875 [DDD]
Ward–Steinman, D.:Fragments from Sappho, w. P. Curtin (sop), D. Baron (fl), D. Ward–Steinman (pno) [E] CRI ■ C 238
Weber, C.M. von:Concertino Cl, w. R. Wagner (cnd), Innsbruck SO *(rec 1963)* Allegretto ▲ ACD 8189
Weber, C.M. von:Con 1 Cl, w. J. Faerber (cnd), Württemberg CO *(rec 1967)* Allegretto ▲ ACD 8189
Weber, C.M. von:Qnt Cl, w. Kohon String Quartet *(rec 1962)* Allegretto ▲ ACD 8189

Glazer, Frank (pno)
Busoni, F.:Konzertstück Pno, w. C.A. Bunte (cnd), Berlin SO Vox Box 2–▲ CDX 5133
Poulenc, F.:Sxt Pno, w. New York Woodwind Quintet Boston Skyline ▲ BSD 141 [AAD]

Glazer, Frank (pno) (cont.)
Satie, E.:Pno Music (misc) Vox Box 2–▲ CDX 5011 [ADD]

Glazer, Robert (va)
Gould, M.:Con Va, w. L. Leighton Smith (cnd), Louisville Orch Albany 2–▲ TROY 013–14–2 [AAD]

Glazier, Richard (pno)
Gershwin, G.:Pno Music—Promenade; 3/4 Blues; Jilted [from Of Thee I Sing]; Meadow Serenade [from Strike up the Band]; Love Walked in [trans Grainger]; The Man I Love [trans Grainger]; Impromptu in 2 Keys; Sleepless Nights; They Can't Take that away from Me; Balle Music [from Primrose]; 16 Bars without a Name; Melody No. 40 [arr Sylvia Rabinof] *(rec Christel DeHaan Fine Arts Center, University of Indianapolis, May 2–4, 1995)* Centaur ▲ CRC 2271 [DDD]
Gershwin, G.:Preludes (3) Pno *(rec Christel DeHaan Fine Arts Center, University of Indianapolis, May 2–4, 1995)* Centaur ▲ CRC 2271 [DDD]
Rubinstein, B.:Concert Trans *(rec Christel DeHaan Fine Arts Center, University of Indianapolis, May 2–4, 1995)* Centaur ▲ CRC 2271 [DDD]
Wild, E.:Etudes on Gershwin Songs *(rec Christel DeHaan Fine Arts Center, University of Indianapolis, May 2–4, 1995)* Centaur ▲ CRC 2271 [DDD]

Gledhill, Rachel (perc)
Jolivet, A.:Suite en concert, w. Anna Noakes (fl), Graham Cole (perc), Kate Eyre (perc), Gary Kettel (perc) ASV ("French Chamber Music" series) ▲ ASV 948

Gleghorn, Arthur (fl)
Ravel, M.:Intro & Allegro, w. Ann Mason Stockton (hp), Mitchell Lurie (cl), Hollywood String Quartet Testament ▲ TESSBT 1053 (m) [ADD]

Gleizes, Mireille (pno)
Górecki, H.–M.:Good Night, w. Elzbieta Szmytka (sop), Paul Edmund–Davies (a fl), Huub Righarts (perc) *(rec Abbey Bonne Espérance, Vellereille–les–Brayeux, Belgium; July 17–19, 1995)* Telarc ▲ CD–80417 [DDD]
Górecki, H.–M.:Kleines Requiem für eine Polka, w. R. Werthen (cnd), I Fiamminghi CO *(rec Abbey Bonne Espérance, Vellereille–les–Brayeux, Belgium; July 17–19, 1995)* Telarc ▲ CD–80417 [DDD]

Glemser, Bernd (pno)
Le Grand Tango & Other Dances for Cello & Piano, w. Maria Kliegel (vc) *(rec May 3–4, 1993)* Naxos ▲ 8.550785 [DDD]
Hindemith, P.:Son Fl, w. P.–L. Graf (fl) *(rec Dec. 9–12, 1992)* Claves ▲ CD 9307 [DDD]
The Love Collection, w. Maria Kliegel (vc) *(rec Clara Wieck Auditorium, Heidelberg, May 3–4, 1993)* Naxos 4–▲ 8.504004 [DDD]
Martin, F.:Ballade Fl, w. P.–L. Graf (fl) *(rec Dec. 9–12, 1992)* Claves ▲ CD 9307 [DDD]
Milhaud, D.:Sonatina Fl, w. P.–L. Graf (fl) *(rec Dec. 9–12, 1992)* Claves ▲ CD 9307 [DDD]
Prokofiev, S.:Son Fl, w. P.–L. Graf (fl) *(rec Dec. 9–12, 1992)* Claves ▲ CD 9307 [DDD]
Prokofiev, S.:Son 2 Pno *(rec Lugano, Switzerland, Jan. 3–5, 1994)* Naxos ▲ 8.553021 [DDD]
Prokofiev, S.:Son 7 Pno *(rec Lugano, Switzerland, Jan. 3–5, 1994)* Naxos ▲ 8.553021 [DDD]
Prokofiev, S.:Son 8 Pno *(rec Lugano, Switzerland, Jan. 3–5, 1994)* Naxos ▲ 8.553021 [DDD]
Rachmaninoff, S.:Con 3 Pno, w. J. Maksymiuk (cnd), Irish National SO *(rec National Concert Hall, Dublin, Dec. 17–18, 1992)* Naxos ▲ 8.550666 [DDD]
Rachmaninoff, S.:Prince Rostislav, w. J. Maksymiuk (cnd), Irish National SO *(rec National Concert Hall, Dublin, Dec. 17–18, 1992)* Naxos ▲ 8.550666 [DDD]
Reinecke, C.:Son Fl, w. P.–L. Graf (fl) *(rec Dec. 9–12, 1992)* Claves ▲ CD 9307 [DDD]
Scriabin, A.:Fant Pno *(rec Radio Concert Hall, Lugano, May 25–27, 1994)* Naxos ▲ 8.553158 [DDD]
Scriabin, A.:Sons Pno (comp)—Nos. 2, 5–7 & 9 *(rec Radio Concert Hall, Lugano, May 25–27, 1994)* Naxos ▲ 8.553158 [DDD]
Tchaikovsky, P.:Andante & Finale, w. A. Wit (cnd), Polish National RSO Katowice *(rec Polish Radio Concert Hall, Mar 1995)* Naxos ▲ 8.550819 [DDD]
Tchaikovsky, P.:Concert Fant, w. A. Wit (cnd), Polish National RSO Katowice *(rec Polish Radio Concert Hall, Katowice, Mar 20–24, 1995)* Naxos ▲ 8.550820 [DDD]
Tchaikovsky, P.:Con 1 Pno, w. A. Wit (cnd), Polish National RSO Katowice *(rec Polish Radio Concert Hall, Mar 1995)* Naxos ▲ 8.550819 [DDD]
Tchaikovsky, P.:Con 2 Pno, w. A. Wit (cnd), Polish National RSO Katowice *(rec Polish Radio Concert Hall, Katowice, Mar 20–24, 1995)* Naxos ▲ 8.550820 [DDD]
Tchaikovsky, P.:Con 3 Pno, w. A. Wit (cnd), Polish National RSO Katowice *(rec Polish Radio Concert Hall, Mar 1995)* Naxos ▲ 8.550819 [DDD]

Glendenning, Andrew (trbn)
Fox, F.:Time Messages, w. David Dzubay (tpt), David McChesney (tpt), Michael Galbraith (hn), Andrew Oppenheim (tuba) *(rec Musical Arts Ctr, Bloomington, IN, Nov 30, 1989)* Indiana Univ School of Music ▲ 0–253–32433–5

Glenn, C. (vn)
Harrison, L.:Con Vn, w. J. Beck (cnd), Eastman Percussion Ensemble members *(rec 1972)* Vox Box ("The American Composers" series) 2–▲ CDX 5158
Hummel, J.N.:Con Pno, Vn & Orch, Op. 17, w. Eugene List (pno), E. Märzendorfer (cnd), Vienna CO Monitor ■ 55002
Tchaikovsky, P.:Sérénade mélancolique, w. E. Rachlin (cnd), Cambridge SO Vox Box 3–▲ CD3X 3026 [ADD]
Tchaikovsky, P.:Souvenir d'un lieu cher, w. E. Rachlin (cnd), Cambridge SO [orch. Glazunov] Vox Box 3–▲ CD3X 3026 [ADD]
Tchaikovsky, P.:Valse–Scherzo Vn, w. E. Rachlin (cnd), Cambridge SO Vox Box 3–▲ CD3X 3026 [ADD]

Glennie, Evelyn (mar)
Abe, K.:Michi *(rec Whitfield Street Studios, London, Sept. 22–29, 1994)* Catalyst ▲ 09026–68193–2 [DDD]
Abe, K.:Vars on Japanese Children's Songs *(rec Whitfield Street Studios, London, Sept. 22–29, 1994)* Catalyst ▲ 09026–68193–2 [DDD]
Abe, K.:Wind in the Bamboo Grove *(rec Whitfield Street Studios, London, Sept. 22–29, 1994)* Catalyst ▲ 09026–68193–2 [DDD]
Last Night of the Proms, w. Bryn Terfel (bar), Andrew Davis (cnd), BBC SO, BBC Sym Chorus, BBC Singers *(rec Royal Albert Hall, Sep. 10, 1994)* Teldec ▲ 97868–2 [DDD]
Miki, M.:Mar Spiritual, w. Stephen Henderson (perc), Gary Kettel (perc), Greg Knowles (perc) *(rec Whitfield Street Studios, London, Sept. 22–29, 1994)* Catalyst ▲ 09026–68193–2 [DDD]
Miyoshi, A.:Con Mar, w. P. Daniel (cnd), Scottish CO RCA Red Seal ▲ 09026–61277–2 ■ 09026–61277–4
Rosauro, N.:Con Mar, w. P. Daniel (cnd), Scottish CO RCA Red Seal ▲ 09026–61277–2 ■ 09026–61277–4
Yoshioka, T.:Rhap Mar, w. Edward Beckett (fl), Roy Howitt (cl), Chris Laurence (db), Ralph Salmins (dr) *(rec Whitfield Street Studios, London, Sept. 22–29, 1994)* Catalyst ▲ 09026–68193–2 [DDD]
Yuyama, A.:Divert Mar, w. John Harle (a sax) *(rec Whitfield Street Studios, London, Sept. 22–29, 1994)* Catalyst ▲ 09026–68193–2 [DDD]

Glennie, Evelyn (perc)
Bartók, B.:Son for 2 Pnos, w. M. Perahia (pno), G. Solti (pno), D. Corkhill (perc) CBS ▲ MK 42625 [DDD]
Bennett, Richard Rodney:Con Perc, w. P. Daniel (cnd), Scottish CO RCA Red Seal ▲ 09026–61277–2 ■ 09026–61277–4
Drumming, w. Philip Smith (pno) *(rec Whitfield Street Studios, London, Dec 11–15, 1994)* Catalyst ▲ 09026–68195–2 [DDD]
Light in Darkness RCA Red Seal ▲ 60557–2–RC [DDD]
Macmillan, J.:Music of, w. J. MacMillan (cnd), Scottish CO—Veni, veni, Emannuel; After the Tryst; "...as others see us..."; 3 Dawn Rituals; Untold Catalyst ▲ 09026–61916–2
Milhaud, D.:Con Perc, w. P. Daniel (cnd), Scottish CO RCA Red Seal ▲ 09026–61277–2 ■ 09026–61277–4
Rebounds:Concertos for Percussion, w. Scottish CO [cnd:Paul Daniel] RCA Red Seal ▲ 09026–61277–2
Rhythm Song, w. National PO [cnd:Barry Wordsworth] RCA Victor ▲ 60242–2–RC [DDD]

▲ = CD ♦ = Enhanced CD Δ = MD ■ = Cassette Tape ◻ = DCC

Glenton, Robert (vc)
Vivaldi, A.:Beatus vir, R.597, w. Carys-Anne Lane (sop), Jayne Whitaker (sop), Christine Swain (ob), Christopher Stokes (org), N. Ward (cnd), Northern CO, Oxford Schola Cantorum *(rec St. Peter's Church, Hale, Cheshire, Mar. 14, 1994)* Naxos ▲ 8.550767 [DDD]
Vivaldi, A.:Gloria, RV.589, w. Anna Crookes (sop), Jayne Whitaker (sop), Caroline Trevor (alt), Christine Swain (ob), Christopher Stokes (org), N. Ward (cnd), Northern CO, Oxford Schola Cantorum *(rec St. Peter's Church, Hale, Cheshire, Dec. 3, 1993)* Naxos ▲ 8.550767 [DDD]

Glick, Jacob (va)—see also ORCHESTRAS & ENSEMBLES Contemporary Chamber Players, Jennings String Quartet
Pousseur, H.:Chants sacrés, w. Valarie Lamoree (sop), Eric Rosenblith (vn), Michael Rudiakov (vc) Vox Box 2–▲ CDX 5144

Glickman, Loren (bn)—see also ORCHESTRAS & ENSEMBLES New York Woodwind Soloists
Stravinsky, I.:L'Histoire du soldat Suite Vn, w. G. Tarack (vn), C. Russo (cl), T. Weis (tpt), J. Levine (db), J. Swallow (trbn), R. Desroches (perc), L. Stokowski (cnd) Vanguard Classics ▲ SVC 1 [AAD]

Glickman, Sylvia (pno)
Reinagle, A.:Sons Pno—in D, E, F & C *(rec Ensemble Room, Mills College, CA, Mar 23, 1982)* Orion ▲ 7807-2 [AAD]

Glise, Anthony (gtr)
Diabelli, A.:Sons Gtr, Op. 29—Sons. in F, A & C Dorian Discovery ▲ DIS 80113 [DDD]
Brescianello, G.A.:Partitas Gtr—In A, d, A, e, C, a, D & A *(rec Alabama Shakespeare Theatre, Aug. 16–17, 1994)* Dorian Discovery ▲ DIS 80127 [DAD]
Glise, A.L.:Son 2 Gtr, "The Canonization" E.R.M. ▲ CCC 6659 [DDD]
Winstin, R.I.:Episodes, w. R. I. Winstin (pno) E.R.M. ▲ CCC 6659 [DDD]

Globokar, Vinko (trbn)
Berio, L.:Sequenza V *(rec 1967)* Wergo ▲ WER 6021-2 [AAD]
Wyttenbach, J.:D'Hommage oder "Freunde! Nicht diese Töne..." *(rec May 19–20, 1990)* Grammont ▲ CTSP 37-2 [ADD]

Gluck, David (dr/perc)
Bernstein, L.:Dance Suite Chamber Ensemble, w. Will Rudd (tpt/flgl), Bob Thompson (tpt/flgl), Alex Shuhan (hn/pno), Mark Kellogg (trbn/eup), Charles Villarrubia (tuba) *(rec Cliff Temple Baptist Church, Dallas, TX)* D'Note Classics ▲ DND 1007 [DDD]
Corea, C.:Children's Songs, w. Will Rudd (tpt/flgl), Bob Thompson (tpt/flgl), Alex Shuhan (hn/pno), Mark Kellogg (trbn/eup), Charles Villarrubia (tuba)—Nos 6 & 11 [arr Gluck/Shuhan] *(rec Cliff Temple Baptist Church, Dallas, TX)* D'Note Classics ▲ DND 1007 [DDD]
Gershwin, G.:Porgy & Bess (sels), w. Will Rudd (tpt/flgl), Bob Thompson (tpt/flgl), Alex Shuhan (hn/pno), Mark Kellogg (trbn/eup), Charles Villarrubia (tuba)—Summertime [arr Thompson] *(rec Cliff Temple Baptist Church, Dallas, TX)* D'Note Classics ▲ DND 1007 [DDD]
Gluck, C.W.:Nicole, w. Will Rudd (tpt/flgl), Bob Thompson (tpt/flgl), Alex Shuhan (hn/pno), Mark Kellogg (trbn/eup), Charles Villarrubia (tuba) *(rec Cliff Temple Baptist Church, Dallas, TX)* D'Note Classics ▲ DND 1007 [DDD]
Khachaturian, A.:Gayane (suites), w. Will Rudd (tpt/flgl), Bob Thompson (tpt/flgl), Alex Shuhan (hn/pno), Mark Kellogg (trbn/eup), Charles Villarrubia (tuba)—Sabre Dance [arr Gluck]; Lullaby; Dance of the Rose Maidens [both arr Villarrubia] *(rec Cliff Temple Baptist Church, Dallas, TX)* D'Note Classics ▲ DND 1007 [DDD]
McCarthy, D.:American Dance Music, w. Will Rudd (tpt/flgl), Bob Thompson (tpt/flgl), Alex Shuhan (hn/pno), Mark Kellogg (trbn/eup), Charles Villarrubia (tuba) *(rec Cliff Temple Baptist Church, Dallas, TX)* D'Note Classics ▲ DND 1007 [DDD]
Scheidt, S.:Instr Music, w. Will Rudd (tpt/flgl), Bob Thompson (tpt/flgl), Alex Shuhan (hn/pno), Mark Kellogg (trbn/eup), Charles Villarrubia (tuba)—Centone No. 5 [trans Verne Reynolds] *(rec Cliff Temple Baptist Church, Dallas, TX)* D'Note Classics ▲ DND 1007 [DDD]

Gluz, Vladislav (vn)
Vivaldi, A.:Cons Vn, Op. 3/1–12, "L'estro armonico", w. I. Romanyuk (vn), A. Titov (cnd), St. Petersburg Classical Music Studio Orch—No. 8 in a, RV.522; No. 11 in d, RV.565 Infinity Digital ▲ QK 57243 [DDD]
Vivaldi, A.:Cons Vn, Op. 8/1–4, "The Four Seasons", w. A. Titov (cnd), St. Petersburg Classical Music Studio Orch Infinity Digital ▲ QK 57243 [DDD]
Vivaldi, A.:Cons Vn, Op. 8/1–4, "The Four Seasons", w. A. Titov (cnd), St. Petersburg Classical Music Studio Orch—Winter Infinity Digital ▲ QK 69255 [DDD]
Vivaldi, A.:Cons for 2 Vns, w. I. Romanyuk (vn), A. Titov (cnd), St. Petersburg Classical Music Studio Orch—in G, RV.516 Infinity Digital ▲ QK 57243 [DDD]
Vivaldi, A.:Cons for 2 Vns, w. Igor Romanyuk (vn), A. Titov (cnd), St. Petersburg New Classical Orch Infinity Digital ▲ QK 66725 [DDD]

Gluzman, Vadim (vn)
Bennett, Richard Rodney:Con Vn, w. J. DePreist (cnd), Monte Carlo PO Koch International Classics ▲ KIC 7341

Glyde, Judith (vc)—see also ORCHESTRAS & ENSEMBLES Manhattan String Quartet
Villa-Lobos, H.:Assobio a Jato, w. D. Anthony Dwyer (fl) Koch International Classics ▲ KIC 7001-2 [DDD] ■ 3-7001-4 (D)

Gmeinder, P. (instr)—see ORCHESTRAS & ENSEMBLES Present Music

Gmür, R. (cl)
Schmid, E.:Rhap Cl, w. J. Wyttenbach (pno) *(rec Dec. 16, 1986)* Grammont ▲ CTSP 33-2 [ADD]

Gnéri, Françoise (va)
Klein, G.:Duo in Quarter Tones, w. Serge Garcia (vn) Arion ▲ ARN 68272 [DDD]
Klein, G.:Four Movements, w. Serge Garcia (vn), Sona Khochafian (vn), David Simpson (vc) Arion ▲ ARN 68272 [DDD]
Klein, G.:Movements Str Qt, w. Serge Garcia (vn), Sona Khochafian (vn), David Simpson (vc) Arion ▲ ARN 68272 [DDD]
Mozart, W.A.:Qnt Hn & Strs, w. Hervé Joulain (hn), Élisabeth Glab (vn), Pascal Robault (va), Nadine Pierre (vc) Arion ▲ ARN 68311 [DDD]

Gniewek, Raymond (vn)
Strauss, R.:Don Quixote, w. Jerry Grossman (vc), Michael Ouzounian (va), J. Levine (cnd), Metropolitan Opera Orch *(rec Manhattan Ctr, NY, May 1995)* Deutsche Grammophon ▲ 447762-2 [DDD]

Göbel, Horst (pno)—see also ORCHESTRAS & ENSEMBLES Göbel Trio Berlin
Blacher, B.:Con 1 Pno, w. R. Alberth (cnd), Bavarian RSO *(rec 1978)* Thorofon ▲ CTH 2167 [ADD/DDD]
Blacher, B.:Songs, w. Katharina Richter (sop), Cornella Wosnitza (sop), Markus Köhler (bar), Chatschatur Kanajan (vn), Piotr Prysiasnik (vn), Fred Günther (va), Ithay Khen (vc), Christian Peters (sax), Markus Weidmann (bn)—3 Chansons; Ungereimtes; 4 Lieder; Nebel; 13 Ways of Looking at a Blackbird; 5 Sinnsprüche Omars des Zeitmachers; 3 Psalmen; Aprèslude; Francesca da Rimini; Jazz-Koloraturen Signum ▲ SIG X73-00 [DDD]
Copland, A.:Duo Fl, w. M.-U. Senn (fl) Thorofon ▲ CTH 2012 [DDD]
Copland, A.:Sextet Cl, Pno & Strs, w. Berlin Philharmonic Academy Orch members Thorofon ▲ CTH 2012 [DDD]
Copland, A.:Son Vn & Pno, w. H. Maile (vn) Thorofon ▲ CTH 2012 [DDD]
Czerny, C.:Con Pno 4-Hnds, w. Liu Xiao Ming (pno), N. Athinäos (cnd), Frankfurt on the Oder State Orch *(rec Frankfurt, June 24–28, 1996)* Signum ▲ X 78-00 [DDD]
Dessau, P.:Les Voix, w. Ksenija Lukic (sop), N. Athinäos (cnd), Frankfurt State Orch Signum ▲ X65-00 [DDD]
Lachner, F.P.:Qnt 2 Pno, w. O. Duliba (vn), T. Jahnel (vn), S. Clark (va), S. Dörfler (vc) *(rec June 10, 1991)* Thorofon ▲ CTH 2132 [DDD]
Louis Ferdinand, Prince:Octet Fl, w. T. Ukigaya (cnd), Philharmonia Pomorska Thorofon ▲ CTH 2088 [DDD]
Louis Ferdinand, Prince:Rondos, Berlin Phil Academy Orch Thorofon ▲ CTH 2088 [DDD]
Rheinberger, J.:Improv on a Theme from Mozart's "Die Zauberflöte" *(rec 1990)* Thorofon ▲ CTH 2157 [DDD]
Rheinberger, J.:Qt Pno, w. Berlin Philharmonic Academy Orch members Thorofon ▲ CTH 2108 [DDD]
Rheinberger, J.:Qt Pno, w. Z. Almasi (vn), D. Cofré (vc) *(rec 1989)* Thorofon 6–▲ BCTH 2161/6
Rheinberger, J.:Qnt Pno, w. Sonare String Quartet Thorofon ▲ CTH 2060 [DDD]

Göbel, Horst (pno) (cont.)
Rheinberger, J.:Qnt Pno, w. Yumiko Noda (va), Sonare String Quartet *(rec 1989)* Thorofon 6–▲ BCTH 2161/6
Rheinberger, J.:Sxt Fl, w. Berlin Philharmonic Academy Orch members Thorofon ▲ CTH 2078 [ADD/DDD]
Rheinberger, J.:Son Vc, w. T. Ruge (vc) Thorofon 6–▲ BCTH 2161/6
Rheinberger, J.:Son Vc, w. T. Ruge (vc) Thorofon ▲ CTH 2108 [DDD]
Rheinberger, J.:Son Hn, w. B. Krug (hn) Thorofon 6–▲ BCTH 2161/6
Rheinberger, J.:Son Hn, w. B. Krug (hn) Thorofon ▲ CTH 2108 [DDD]
Rheinberger, J.:Son 2 Pno *(rec 1990)* Thorofon ▲ CTH 2157 [DDD]
Rheinberger, J.:Sons Vn, w. H. Maile (vn) Thorofon 6–▲ BCTH 2161/6
Rheinberger, J.:Theme & Vars Pno *(rec 1990)* Thorofon ▲ CTH 2157 [DDD]

Gobet, Françoise (pno)
Jolivet, A.:Mana Adès ▲ ADE 203492 [ADD]

Gockel, John (vc)
Scelsi, G.:Anahit, w. Paul Zukofsky (vn), Julie Bogorad (fl), Peggy Russell (fl), Courtney Westcott (fl), Lawrence McDonald (cl), Joan Waryha (cl), Jean Hansen (b cl), Bill Suite (e hn), Nita VanPelt (sax), Bob Zobal (tpt), John Carter (trbn), Martin Lydecker (trbn), Stan Cortman (hn), Robert Ward (hn), William Curry (va), Jody Rowitsch (va), Irene Wade (va), Anne Fagerburg (vc), Sue Manz (bass), Steven Stearman (bass) *(rec Oberlin Conservatory of Music, Oct 8, 1973)* CP² ▲ CP2 108 [AAD]

Godburn, Dennis (bn)—see also ORCHESTRAS & ENSEMBLES Old Fairfield Academy Orch members, Mozzafiato
Liebman, D.:Remembrance, w. David Taylor (b trbn), Bill Blount (cl), Stephen Taylor (ob), Alan Cox (fl) New World ▲ 80494-2
Mozart, W.A.:Con Bn, w. T. Crawford (cnd), Old Fairfield Academy Orch MusicMasters ▲ 01612-67157-2 [DDD]
Poulenc, F.:Sxt Pno, w. André Previn (pno), Elizabeth Mann (fl), Steve Taylor (ob), David Shifrin (cl), Richard Todd (hn) *(rec Manhattan Center Studios, New York City, Apr. 7–8, 1993)* RCA Red Seal ▲ 09026-68181-2 [DDD]
Vivaldi, A.:Cons Diverse Instrs, w. M. Verbruggen (rcr), P. Goodwin (ob), J. Holloway (vn), J. Toll (hpd), S. Comberti (vc)—7 Concerti—in D, RV.84; in a, RV.86; in D, RV.94; in D, "Las Pastorella," RV.95; in F, RV.99; in g, RV.103; in g, RV.105 Harmonia Mundi USA ▲ HMU 907046
Vivaldi, A.:Con Fl Bn, w. M. Verbruggen (rcr), N. McGegan (cnd), Philharmonia Baroque Orch Harmonia Mundi USA ▲ HMU 907040

Godeck, Andrzej (cl)
Arnaud, L.:Midinette, w. M. Mitsumoto (cnd), Cracow RSO *(rec Krakow, Poland, Sept. 20–22, 1993)* Cambria ▲ CMB 1074 [DDD]

Godhoff, Burkhard (vn)
Vieuxtemps, H.:Va Pno Music, w. E. Ingwersen (pno)—Morceau brillant de Salon, Air varié, Rêverie (Op. 22, Nos. 1–3); Variations on the Last Rose of Summer, Op. 33/5; Romance, Regrets (Op. 40, Nos. 1 & 2); Rêve, Op. 53/5; Désespoir Koch Schwann ▲ CD 310042 [DDD]

Godowsky, Leopold (pno)
Beethoven, L. van:Son 26 Pno, "Les Adieux" APR 2–▲ APR 7010
Chopin, F.:Nocturnes APR 2–▲ APR 7010
Grieg, E.:Ballade Pno Pearl ▲ PEA 9933 (m) [AAD]
Grieg, E.:Ballade Pno APR 2–▲ APR 7010
The Pianist's Pianist, Vol. APR ▲ APR 7011 [AAD]
Schumann, R.:Carnaval Pno APR 2–▲ APR 7010

Godwin, Paul (vn)—see ORCHESTRAS & ENSEMBLES Alma Musica Ensemble

Godziszewski, Jerzy (pno)
Chopin, F.:Prelude in A♭ *(rec Warsaw, Oct 1979)* Polskie Nagrania ▲ PNCD 014
Chopin, F.:Preludes, Op. 28 *(rec Warsaw, Oct 1979)* Polskie Nagrania ▲ PNCD 014
Chopin, F.:Prelude, Op. 45 *(rec Warsaw, Oct 1979)* Polskie Nagrania ▲ PNCD 014
Prokofiev, S.:Son Vn, Op. 94bis, w. Krzysztof Jakowicz (vn) *(rec National Philharmonic Concert Hall, Warsaw, May 26–28, 1991)* Polskie Nagrania ▲ PNCD 114
Prokofiev, S.:Son 1 Vn, w. Krzysztof Jakowicz (vn) *(rec National Philharmonic Concert Hall, Warsaw, May 26–28, 1991)* Polskie Nagrania ▲ PNCD 114

Goemer, Stephan (vc)—see ORCHESTRAS & ENSEMBLES Carmina String Quartet

Goeres, Nancy (bn)
Zwilich, E.T.:Con Bn, w. L. Maazel (cnd), Pittsburgh SO *(rec Pittsburgh, May 10–12, 1996)* New World ▲ 805032 [DDD]

Goerner, Stephan (vc)—see ORCHESTRAS & ENSEMBLES Carmina String Quartet

Goeser, Amy K. (ob)
Hölszky, A.:Quasi una Fant Koch Schwann ▲ 3-1062-2 [DDD]

Goethem, F. van (va)
Glière, R.:Duets Vn, Op. 39, w. H. Raudales (vn) *(rec Mar. 1993)* Pavane ▲ ADW 7308 [DDD]
Halvorsen, J.:Passacaglia & Sarabande con variazioni, w. H. Raudales (vn) *(rec Mar. 1993)* Pavane ▲ ADW 7308 [DDD]
Rolla, A.:Duo 3 Vn, w. H. Raudales (vn) *(rec Mar. 1993)* Pavane ▲ ADW 7308 [DDD]

Goethem, Joris Van (rcr)—see ORCHESTRAS & ENSEMBLES Flanders Recorder Quartet

Goetz, Laura (ob)
Purcell, H.:Come Ye Sons of Art, w. Sarah Weiner (ob), Davis Brooks (vn), Lisa Brooks (vn), Jann Cosart (va), Mary Burke (vl), Vance Reese (db), Thomas Gerber (hpd), Henry H. Leck (cnd), Indianapolis Children's Choir [arr. Maurice Blower] *(rec The Lodge, May & June 1995)* VAI Audio ▲ VAIA 1130 [DDD]
Purcell, H.:Fly, Bold Rebellion (sels), w. Sarah Weiner (ob), Davis Brooks (vn), Lisa Brooks (vn), Jann Cosart (va), Mary Burke (vl), Vance Reese (db), Thomas Gerber (hpd), Henry H. Leck (cnd), Indianapolis Children's Choir—Be Welcome Then, Great Sir [arr. Steven Rickards] *(rec The Lodge, May & June 1995)* VAI Audio ▲ VAIA 1130 [DD]
Purcell, H.:King Arthur (sels), w. Sarah Weiner (ob), Davis Brooks (vn), Lisa Brooks (vn), Jann Cosart (va), Mary Burke (vl), Vance Reese (db), Thomas Gerber (hpd), Henry H. Leck (cnd), Indianapolis Children's Choir—Fairest Isle [arr. Steven Rickards] *(rec The Lodge, May & June 1995)* VAI Audio ▲ VAIA 1130 [DDD]

Goff, Scott (fl)
Creston, P.:Partita Fl, w. I. Talvi (vn), G. Schwarz (cnd), Seattle SO *(rec 3/1/91)* Delos ▲ DE 3114 [DDD]
Drattell, D.:The Fire Within, w. G. Schwarz (cnd), Seattle SO *(rec Seattle Opera House, June 17, 1994)* Delos ▲ DE 3159 [DDD]
Griffes, C.T.:Poem Fl, w. G. Schwarz (cnd), Seattle SO Delos ▲ DE 3099 [DDD]
Hovhaness, A.:Celestial Canticle, w. Hinako Fujihara (sop), A. Hovhaness (cnd), Northwest Sinfonia *(rec St Thomas Center Chapel, Bothell, WA, Jan 1995)* Crystal ▲ CD 811 [DDD]
Hovhaness, A.:Starry Night, w. Ronald Johnson (xyl), John Carrington (hp) *(rec St Thomas Center Chapel, Bothell, WA, Jan 1995)* Crystal ▲ CD 811 [DDD]
Hovhaness, A.:Tale of the Sun Goddess Going into the Stone House (sels), w. Hinako Fujihara (sop), A. Hovhaness (cnd), Northwest Sinfonia—O, Joy at the Dawn of Spring *(rec St Thomas Center Chapel, Bothell, WA, Jan 1995)* Crystal ▲ CD 811 [DDD]
Piston, W.:The Incredible Flutist [arr fl] *(rec Jan. 27–28, 1992)* Delos ▲ DE 3126 [DDD]

Gohl, Käthi (vc)—see also ORCHESTRAS & ENSEMBLES Ensemble 415
Schumann, R.:Andante & Vars Hn, w. Robert Majek (pno), Mario Venzago (pno), Rama Jucker (vc), Francesco Raselli (hn) Accord ▲ ACD 201572 [AAD]

Gohl, Käthi (vn)
Handel, G.F.:German Arias, H.202–210, w. Elisabeth Speiser (sop), Jap Schröder (vn), Johann Sonnleitner (hpd) [G] *(rec 1984)* Jecklin-Disco ▲ JD 589-2 [ADD]

Gohl, Michael (cl)
Mäder, U.:Mit Nacht beladen, w. Verena-Barbara Gohl (alt), P. Siegwart (cnd), Zurich Collegium Musicum *(rec 1996)* Jecklin ▲ JS 3072 [DDD]

Goïlav, Yoan (db)
Bottesini, G.:Music for Db—Fant on Bellini's *La Sonnambula*; Melody in e; Tarantella in a *(rec 1980)* Tuxedo ▲ TUXCD 1090 [ADD]

INSTRUMENT.

Goïlav, Yoan (db) (cont.)
Dimitrescu, C.:Danse Taranesc [trans Yoan Goilav] *(rec 1972)* Tuxedo ▲ TUXCD 1090 [ADD]
Eccles, H.:Son Va *(rec 1972)* Tuxedo ▲ TUXCD 1090 [ADD]
Koussevitzky, S.:Concert Db Pno, w. Laurenz Custer (pno) *(rec 1972)* Tuxedo ▲ TUXCD 1090 [ADD]
Koussevitzky, S.:Valse miniature *(rec 1972)* Tuxedo ▲ TUXCD 1090 [ADD]
Madensky, E.:Tarantella *(rec 1972)* Tuxedo ▲ TUXCD 1090 [ADD]
Les Plus belles transcriptions pour contrebass et piano, w. Heinz Börlin (pno) Gallo ▲ CD 675 [DDD]
Ravel, M.:Pièce en forme de Habanera [trans Koussevitzky] *(rec 1972)* Tuxedo ▲ TUXCD 1090 [ADD]

Goimard, Magali (pno)
Castro, J.J.:Tangos Pno—Evocation; Lloron; Compadron; Milonguero; Nostalgico *(rec Aug 22–24, 1995)* Pavane ▲ ADW 7353 [DDD]
Ginastera, A.:Danzas argentinas—Danza del Viejo Boyero; Danza de la Moza Donosa; Danza del Gaucho Matrero *(rec Aug 22–24, 1995)* Pavane ▲ ADW 7353 [DDD]
Guastavino, C.:Cantilenas Argentinas (10)—No. 2 (Abelarda Olmos); No. 10 (La casa) *(rec Aug 22–24, 1995)* Pavane ▲ ADW 7353 [DDD]
Lopez Buchardo, C.:Bailecito Pno *(rec Aug 22–24, 1995)* Pavane ▲ ADW 7353 [DDD]
Lopez Buchardo, C.:Sonatina Pno *(rec Aug 22–24, 1995)* Pavane ▲ ADW 7353 [DDD]
Piazzolla, A.:Preludes Pno—Leijia's Game; Flora's Game; Sunny's Game *(rec Aug 22–24, 1995)* Pavane ▲ ADW 7353 [DDD]
Pignoni, R.:Dances Pno—En Septima (chacarera); Como Queriendo (zamba); Chumbeao (gato); Por el sur (huella) *(rec Aug 22–24, 1995)* Pavane ▲ ADW 7353 [DDD]

Golabek, Mona (pno)
Arensky, A.:Trio 1 Pno, w. A. Cardenes (vn), J. Solow (vc) Delos ▲ DE 3056 [DDD]
Poulenc, F.:Babar, w. Meryl Streep (nar), René Golabek (pno) [E] Koch Schwann ▲ KIC CD 7368 ■ KIC MC 4368; 7371 (blister pack)
Ravel, M.:Ma mère l'oye suite, w. Meryl Streep (nar), René Golabek (pno), J. Falletta (cnd), New Zealand SO [E] Koch Schwann ▲ KIC CD 7368 ■ KIC MC 4368; 7371 (Blister Pack)
Tchaikovsky, P.:Trio Pno, w. A. Cardenes (vn), J. Solow (vc) Delos ▲ DE 3056 [DDD]

Golabek, R. (pno)
Poulenc, F.:Babar, w. Meryl Streep (nar), Mona Golabek (pno) [E] Koch Schwann ▲ KIC CD 7368 ■ KIC MC 4368; 7371 (blister pack)
Ravel, M.:Ma mère l'oye suite, w. Meryl Streep (nar), Mona Golabek (pno), J. Falletta (cnd), New Zealand SO [E] Koch Schwann ▲ KIC CD 7368 ■ KIC MC 4368; 7371 (Blister Pack)

Golan, Jeanne (pno)
Beethoven, L. van:Son 30 Pno Albany ▲ TROY 211 [DDD]
Cardew, C.:Pno Album—The Croppy Boy; Father Murphy; Sailing the Seas Depends upon the Helmsman Albany ▲ TROY 211 [DDD]
Curran, A.:For Cornelius [Cardew] Albany ▲ TROY 211 [DDD]
Granados, E.:Goyescas—Lament, or the Maiden and the Nightingale; Fandango by Lamplight Albany ▲ TROY 211 [DDD]
Nancarrow, C.:Canons Albany ▲ TROY 211 [DDD]

Golani, Rivka (va)
Arnold, M.:Con Va, w. M. Stephenson (cnd), London Musici Conifer Classics ▲ 75605–51211–2 [DDD]
Bach, J.S.:Sons Vl, BWV 1027–1029, w. Judy Loman (hpd)—BWV 1028 [trans. for viola & harp] *(rec St. Timothy's Church, Toronto)* Marquis Classics ▲ MAR 131 [DDD]
Bax, A.:Fant Son, w. Judy Loman (harp) *(rec St. Timothy's Church, Toronto)* Marquis Classics ▲ MAR 131 [DDD]
Berlioz, H.:Harold in Italy, w. Y. Talmi (cnd), San Diego SO *(rec Copley Symphony Hall, San Diego, May 13–14, 1995)* Naxos ▲ 8.553034 [DDD]
Bloch, E.:Suite hébraïque, w. A. Davis (cnd), Toronto SO CBC ("SM 5000" series) ▲ SMCD 5087 [DDD] ■ 4–5087 (D)
Brahms, J.:Qts Pno (comp), w. Borodin Trio Chandos 2–▲ CHAN 8809/10 [DDD]
Britten, H.:Lachrymae, w. Y. Turovsky (cnd), Montreal Musici Chandos ▲ CHAN 8817 [DDD]
Britten, H.:Lachrymae, w. A. Davis (cnd), Toronto SO CBC ("SM 5000" series) ▲ SMCD 5087 [DDD] ■ 4–5087 (D)
Cherney, B.:Seven Miniatures in the Form of a Mobile Centrediscs ▲ CMC CD 0883
Colgrass, M.:Chaconne Va, w. A. Davis (cnd), Toronto SO CBC ("SM 5000" series) ▲ SMCD 5087 [DDD] ■ 4–5087 (D)
Hindemith, P.:Trauermusik, w. A. Davis (cnd), Toronto SO CBC ("SM 5000" series) ▲ SMCD 5087 [DDD] ■ 4–5087 (D)
Joachim, O.:Requiem Va Centrediscs ▲ CMCCD 0883
Morawetz, O.:Son Va, w. Judy Loman (hp) *(rec St. Timothy's Church, Toronto)* Marquis Classics ▲ MAR 131 [DDD]
Prokofiev, S.:Ov on Hebrew Themes, w. E. Turovsky (vn), J. Campbell (cl), Borodin Trio [orig. chamber version] Chandos ▲ CHAN 8924 [DDD]
Rubbra, E.:Con Va, w. V. Handley (cnd), Royal PO *(rec All Saints' Church, Petersham, Surrey, Dec. 10–11, 1993)* Conifer Classics ▲ 75605–51225–2 [DDD]

Gold, Arthur (pno)
Poulenc, F.:Con for 2 Pnos, w. R. Fizdale (pno), L. Bernstein (cnd), New York PO *(rec Dec. 23, 1961)* Sony Classical ▲ SMK 47618 [ADD]
Rieti, V.:Con Pnos, w. R. Fizdale (pno), E. Ansermet (cnd), Swiss Romande Orch Premier ▲ PRCD 1033 [ADD]
Rieti, V.:2nd Ave Waltzes, w. R. Fizdale (pno) Premier ▲ PRCD 1033 [ADD]

Gold, D. (fl)—see ORCHESTRAS & ENSEMBLES Huntingdon Trio

Goldberg, Loretta (kbd)
Hays, S.:Music of—Past Present; 90's–A Calendar Bracelet Opus One ▲ 00152
Lockwood, A.:Music of—Red Mesa Opus One ▲ 00152
Semegan, D.:Music of—Rhapsody Opus One ▲ 00152
Tucker, T.S.G.:Music of—Son. 2 "The Peyote"; My Melancholy Baby–Fantasy on Ernie Burnett's Famous Theme Opus One ▲ 00152

Goldberg, Loretta (pno)
Boziwick, G.:Boats Against the Current Opus One ▲ CD 162
Boziwick, G.:First Dance, w. K. Grossman (mar) Opus One ▲ CD 162
First, D.:The Laws of Gambling Gold *(rec Apr. 1990)* O.O. Discs ▲ OO 5 [DDD]
Tone over Tone Opus One ▲ OO 135

Goldberg, Michael (gtr)—see ORCHESTRAS & ENSEMBLES Alma Duo

Goldberg, Szyman (va)
Milhaud, D.:Son 1 Va, w. R. Hairgrove (pno) Koch Schwann ▲ 3–1310–2 [DDD]

Goldberg, Szyman (vn)
Beethoven, L. van:Serenade Strs, Op. 8, w. P. Hindemith (va), E. Feuermann (vc) *(rec 1/22/34)* EMI Classics ▲ CDH 64250–2 (m) [ADD]
Beethoven, L. van:Serenade Strs, Op. 8, w. P. Hindemith (va), E. Feuermann (vc) *(rec 1934)* Pearl ▲ PEA 9443 (m) [AAD]
Beethoven, L. van:Son 5 Vn, "Spring", w. L. Kraus (pno) *(rec ca. 1938/40)* Music & Arts 3–▲ CD 665 (m) [AAD]
Beethoven, L. van:Son 9 Vn, "Kreutzer", w. L. Kraus (pno) *(rec ca. 1938/40)* Music & Arts 3–▲ CD 665 (m) [AAD]
Beethoven, L. van:Son 10 Vn, w. L. Kraus (pno) *(rec ca. 1938/40)* Music & Arts 3–▲ CD 665 (m) [AAD]
Beethoven, L. van:Trio 4 Pno, "Ghost", w. R. Serkin (pno), P. Casals (vc) *(rec live June 18, 1954)* Music & Arts 4–▲ CD 688 (m) [AAD]
Beethoven, L. van:Trio 5 Pno, w. R. Serkin (pno), P. Casals (vc) *(rec live, June 18, 1954)* Music & Arts 4–▲ CD 688 (m) [AAD]
Beethoven, L. van:Trio 9 Pno, "Kakadu", w. R. Serkin (pno), P. Casals (vc) Music & Arts 4–▲ CD 688 (m) [AAD]
Hindemith, P.:Trio 2, w. P. Hindemith (va), E. Feuermann (vc) EMI Classics 2–▲ ZDCB 55032

Goldberg, Szyman (vn) (cont.)
Hindemith, P.:Trio 2, w. P. Hindemith (va), E. Feuermann (vc) *(rec 1927–1934)* Koch Schwann ▲ CD 311342 [DDD]
Milhaud, D.:Le Printemps, w. R. Hairgrove (pno) Koch Schwann ▲ 3–1310–2 [DDD]
Mozart, W.A.:Con 3 Vn, w. W. Susskind (cnd), Philharmonic Orch Testament ▲ TES SBT 1028 [ADD]
Mozart, W.A.:Con 4 Vn, w. W. Susskind (cnd), Philharmonic Orch Testament ▲ TES SBT 1028 [ADD]
Mozart, W.A.:Con 5 Vn, w. P. Kletzki (cnd), Berlin PO—Adagio Symposium ▲ SYM 1141
Mozart, W.A.:Con 5 Vn, w. W. Susskind (cnd), Philharmonia Orch Testament ▲ TES SBT 1028 [ADD]
Mozart, W.A.:Duos Vn, K.423 [w. F. Riddle (va)]; –K.424 [w. P Hindemith (va)] Music & Arts 3–▲ CD 665 (m) [AAD]
Mozart, W.A.:Sons Vn Pno (misc), w. L. Kraus (pno)—K.296, 377, 378 & 379 Pearl ▲ PEA 9454 (m) [AAD]
Mozart, W.A.:Sons Vn Pno (misc), w. L. Kraus (pno)—K.296, 377, 378, 379, 380, 404 & 481 Music & Arts 3–▲ CD 665 (m) [AAD]

Goldblatt, David (kbd)
Passage, 138 B.C.–A.D. 1611, w. Empire Brass Quintet, Laurie Monahan (sgr), M. Collver (sgr), Pete Maunu (acoustic/elec/12string gtr), Doug Lunn (fretless bass), K. Wortman (elec/acoustic perc) *(rec Lenox, MA & Los Angeles, CA May 27–29 & June 28–July)* Telarc ▲ CD 80355 [DDD]

Golden, Mary (hp)
Bax, A.:Elegiac Trio, w. M. Meisenbach (fl), B. Williams (va) *(rec 6 & 8/91)* Centaur ▲ CRC 2114 [DDD]
Debussy, C.:Chansons de Bilitis (recitation), w. L. Jeffrey (fl), M. Meisenbach (fl), W. Dudley (hp), K. Tamagawa (cel)—no speaker *(rec 6 & 8/91)* Centaur ▲ CRC 2114 [DDD]
Debussy, C.:Music of, w. M. Meisenbach (fl) [arr. for flute & harp of En Bateau; Clair de Lune; Golliwogg's Cakewalk; Rêverie *(rec 6 & 8/91)* Centaur ▲ CRC 2114 [DDD]
Debussy, C.:Prélude à l'après-midi d'un faune, w. M. Meisenbach (fl), W. Dudley (hp) [arr. flute & 2 harps Whit Dudley] *(rec 6 & 8/91)* Centaur ▲ CRC 2114 [DDD]
Ravel, M.:Intro & Allegro, w. M. Meisenbach (fl), R. McDowall (cl), R. Neal (vn), D. Pettys (vn), D. Hermann (va), G. Manasjan (vc) Centaur ▲ CRC 2114 [DDD]
Ravel, M.:Ma mère l'oye Pno, w. W. Dudley (hp) [harp duo arr of Laideronette & Impératrice des Pagodes] Centaur ▲ CRC 2114 [DDD]

Goldenweiser, Alexander (pno)
Arensky, A.:Essais sur les rythmes oubliés—Sari Melodiya ("Russian Piano School" series) ▲ 74321–25173–2
Borodin, A.:Pno Music—Mazurka in C Melodiya ("Russian Piano School" series) ▲ 74321–25173–2
Goldenweiser, A.:Song & Dance Melodiya ("Russian Piano School" series) ▲ 74321–25173–2
Medtner, N.:Novelles Pno—in c Melodiya ("Russian Piano School" series) ▲ 74321–25173–2
Rachmaninoff, S.:Morceaux de salon—Barcarolle in g Melodiya ("Russian Piano School" series) ▲ 74321–25173–2
Rachmaninoff, S.:Suite 2 for 2 Pnos, w. Grigori Ginzburg (pno) Melodiya ("Russian Piano School" series) ▲ 74321–25173–2
Tchaikovsky, P.:Pno Music—Romance; Dialogue; Meditation; Valse sentimentale Melodiya ("Russian Piano School" series) ▲ 74321–25173–2

Golding, Miles (vn)
Arne, T.:Songs, w. John Mark Ainsley (ten), Roy Goodman (vn), Anthony Robson (sop rcr), Jane Coe (vc), Robert King (hpd/org)—Under the Greenwood Tree; Come Away Death; Where the Bee Sucks *(rec St Jude–on–the–Hill, London, Dec 20–21, 1968)* United ▲ CAL 88002 [DDD]
Bach, J.S.:Con for 3 Vns, w. Micaela Comberti (vn), Simon Standage (vn), S. Standage (cnd), Collegium Musicum 90 Chandos ("Chaconne" series) ▲ CHAN 0594
Vivaldi, A.:Cons Rcr, w. Piers Adams (rcr), Ray Goodman (vn), Jane Compton (va), Jane Coe (vc), Mandy MacNamara (db), David Miller (archlt), Robert King (hpd/org)—in F for Treble Rcr, Op. 10/1; in a for Sopranino Rcr, RV.440; in c for Treble Rcr, RV.441; in D for Sopranino Rcr, Op. 10/3; in g for Treble Rcr, Op. 10/2; in C for Sopranino Rcr, RV.443 *(rec Radley College, Abingdon, Oxon)* United ▲ CAL 88015 [DDD]

Goldmann, Dieter (pno)
Chopin, F.:Pno Music (misc)—Berceuse in D♭, Op. 57; two Études—in G♭ & f, Op. 10/5 & 9; four Mazurkas—Opp. 7/1 & 3, 24/2 & Op. 57; Polonaise–fantaisie in A♭, Op. 61; Polonaise in A, Op. 40/1; two Nocturnes—in F, Op. 15/1 & in c♯, Op. posth.; three Preludes—Op. 28, Nos. 20–22; Scherzo No. 2 in b♭, Op. 31; Waltz in E♭, Op. posth. Vivace ▲ E 529 [DDD]
Rachmaninoff, S.:Con 2 Pno, w. A. Lizzio (cnd), London Festival Orch Vivace ▲ 550 [ADD]
Tchaikovsky, P.:Con 1 Pno, w. A. Lizzio (cnd), London Festival Orch Vivace ▲ 550 [ADD]

Goldray, Martin (kbd)—see ORCHESTRAS & ENSEMBLES Philip Glass Ensemble

Goldray, Martin (pno)
Chambers, W.M.:Ten Grand, w. Ursula Oppens (pno), Walter Hilse (pno), Bennett Lerner (pno), Nurit Tiles (pno), Aleck Karis (pno), Edmund Niemann (pno), Joseph Kubera (pno), Allen Shawn (pno), Elizabeth di Filice (pno), Geisel (cnd) Newport ▲ NPD 85553
Imbrie, A.W.:Roethke Songs, w. Susan Narucki (sop) *(rec SUNY Purchase, NY, Sept. 13, 1994)* New World ▲ 80441–2

Goldschmidt, B. (vn)—see ORCHESTRAS & ENSEMBLES Cleveland Orch String Quartet
Goldschmidt, H. (ob)—see ORCHESTRAS & ENSEMBLES Danish Wind Octet

Goldsmith, Harris (pno)
Schumann, R.:Fantasiestücke Cl, w. H. Wright (cl) Music & Arts ▲ CD 690–1 [AAD]
Schumann, R.:Fantasiestücke Pno, Op. 12/9 Music & Arts ▲ CD 690–1 [AAD]
Schumann, R.:Märchenbilder, w. N. Imai (va) Music & Arts ▲ CD 690–1 [AAD]
Schumann, R.:Märchenerzählungen, w. H. Wright (cl), N. Imai (va) Music & Arts ▲ CD 690–1 [AAD]
Schumann, R.:Marches Pno Music & Arts ▲ CD 690–1 [AAD]

Goldsmith, Kenneth (vn)—see also ORCHESTRAS & ENSEMBLES Mirecourt Trio
Cowell, H.:Cleistogamy (sels), w. T. King (vc) Music & Arts ▲ CD 635 [AAD]
Harrison, L.:Double Con, w. Terry King (vc), Mills College Gamelan Ensemble Music & Arts ▲ CD 635 [AAD]
Sowash, R.:Street Suite, w. C. Olzenak (cl) Gasparo ▲ GS 285

Goldsmith, Tracey (acc)
Gough, O.:Currulao, w. Beverly Davison (vn), Roger Heaton (cl), Bruce Nockles (tpt), John Pigneguy (hn), David Stewart (trbn), Orlando Gough (kbd), Paul Clarvis (perc) *(rec London, 1995)* Catalyst ▲ 0902–668332–2 [DDD]

Goldstein, Lauren (bn)
Ibert, J.:Music of, w. C. Schadeberg (sop), Sue Ann Kahn (fl), E. Lawrence (fl), P. Schechter (fl), R. Schmidt (fl), David Krakauer (cl), Curtis Macomber (vn), Susan Jolles (hp), Frederick Hand (gtr), Arthur Willis (pno)—Entr'acte; Jeux; Sonatine; 2 Movements; 2 Interludes; Aria; Pièce for solo Fl; Histoires; 2 Stèles orientées; Pastoral; Aria; Entr'acte Albany ▲ TROY 145

Goldstein, Malcolm (gam)
Corner, P.:The Gold Stone *(rec July 1991)* ¿What Next? ▲ WN 0005 ■ WN 0005

Goldstein, Malcolm (vn)
Cage, J.:Eight Whiskus for Vn *(rec July 1991)* ¿What Next? ▲ WN 0005
Celli, J.:Vn & Video O.O. Discs ▲ OO 22
Coleman, O.:Trinity *(rec July 1991)* ¿What Next? ▲ WN 0005 ■ WN 0005
Goldstein, M.:Sounding the Fragility of Line *(rec July 1991)* ¿What Next? ▲ WN 0005 ■ F751018000529
Oliveros, P.:Portrait of Malcolm *(rec July 1991)* ¿What Next? ▲ WN 0005 ■ WN 0005
Tenney, J.:Koan *(rec July 1991)* ¿What Next? ▲ WN 0005 ■ WN 0005

Goldstein, Thomas (perc)
Smith, S.S.:Tunnels O.O. Discs ▲ OO 11 [DDD]

Goldstone, Anthony (pno)
Alkan, C.–V.:Cons (2) de camera, w. Morhange Ensemble Symposium ▲ 1062
Bainton, E.:Miniature Suite, w. Caroline Clemmow (pno) *(rec 1996)* Albany ▲ TROY 198 [DDD]
The Britten Connection Gamut Classics ▲ GAM CD 526 [DDD]
Bury, F.:Prelude & Fugue, w. Caroline Clemmow (pno) *(rec 1996)* Albany ▲ TROY 198 [DDD]
Elgar, E.:Serenade Strs, w. Caroline Clemmow (pno) [arr Elgar for 2 Pnos] *(rec 1996)* Albany ▲ TROY 198 [DDD]

▲ = CD ♦ = Enhanced CD Δ = MD ■ = Cassette Tape □ = DCC

Goldstone, Anthony (pno) (cont.)
German, E.:Pno Music, w. Caroline Clemmow (pno)—Suite for Pno 4-Hands (1896) *(rec St. John the Baptist Church, Alkborough, South Humberside, Aug. 1994)* Amphion ▲ PHI 129 [DDD]
Holst, G.:Pno Music—Arpeggio Study; 2 pièces; Toccata; A Piece for Yvonne; Chrissemas Day in the Morning; 2 Folk Song fragments; Nocturne; Jig; Dances for Pno Duet [w. Caroline Clemmow (pno)] Chandos ▲ CHAN 9382 [DDD]
Holst, G.:The Planets, w. Caroline Clemmow (pno) [arr Holst for 2 Pnos] *(rec 1996)* Albany ▲ TROY 198 [DDD]
Holst, G.:Qnt Pno, Ob, Cl, Hn & Bn, w. Elysian Wind Quintet members Chandos ▲ CHAN 9077 [DDD]
Holst, G.:Sym, "The Cotswolds", w. Caroline Clemmow (pno)—Elegy, In Memoriam William Morris [arr Holst for 2 Pnos] *(rec 1996)* Albany ▲ TROY 198 [DDD]
Jacob, G.:Sextet Pno & Wind Qnt, w. Elysian Wind Quintet Chandos ▲ CHAN 9077 [DDD]
Lambert, C.:Elegiac Blues Chandos ▲ CHAN 9382 [DDD]
Lambert, C.:Elegy Pno Chandos ▲ CHAN 9382 [DDD]
Lambert, C.:Son Pno Chandos ▲ CHAN 9382 [DDD]
Massenet, J.:Pièces Pno 4-Hands, w. Caroline Clemmow (pno) *(rec St. John the Baptist Church, Alkborough, South Humberside, Aug. 1994)* Amphion ▲ PHI 129 [DDD]
Mendelssohn, F.:Son in F Vc, w. Y. Zivoni (vc) Meridian ▲ MER 84229 [DDD]
Mendelssohn, F.:Son Vn (1820), w. Y. Zivoni (vn) Meridian ▲ MER 84229 [DDD]
Mendelssohn, F.:Son Vn, Op. 4, w. Y. Zivoni (vn) Meridian ▲ MER 84229 [DDD]
Parry, H.:Adagissimo *(rec 1994)* Albany ▲ TROY 132
Parry, H.:Charakterbilder *(rec 1994)* Albany ▲ TROY 132 ▲ ■ □
Parry, H.:Son 1 Pno *(rec 1994)* Albany ▲ TROY 132 ▲ ■ □
Parry, H.:Son 2 Pno *(rec 1994)* Albany ▲ TROY 132 ▲ ■ □
Parry, H.:Theme & 19 Vars *(rec 1994)* Albany ▲ TROY 132 ▲ ■ □
Play Virtuoso Variations for Piano Duet, w. Caroline Clemmow (pno) Symposium ▲ SYM 1037
Rachmaninoff, S.:Duets Pno 4-Hands, w. Caroline Clemmow (pno) *(rec St. John the Baptist Church, Alkborough, South Humberside, Aug. 1994)* Amphion ▲ PHI 129 [DDD]
Saint-Saëns, C.:Carnival of the Animals, w. I. Brown (pno), O.A. Hughes (cnd), Royal PO ASV Quicksilva ▲ CD QS 6017 [ADD]
Sinding, C.:Suite Pno 4-Hands, w. Caroline Clemmow (pno) *(rec St. John the Baptist Church, Alkborough, South Humberside, Aug. 1994)* Amphion ▲ PHI 129 [DDD]

Goldsworthy, James (pno)
Biscardi, C.:The Gift of Life, w. Judith Bettina (sop) *(rec SUNY Purchase Recital Hall, Feb. 12, 1993)* CRI ▲ CD 686 [DDD]

Golebiowski, Karol (org)
Brahms, J.:Org Musc (comp) [at the Frobenius Organ of the Heliga Trefaldighets Kyrka, Kristianstad, Sweden] *(rec Oct. 1993)* Pavane ▲ ADW 7315 [DDD]

Golovin, Alexis (pno)
Brahms, J.:Son 1 Vn, w. T. Bozok (vn) Gallo ▲ CD 609 [AAD]
Strauss, R.:Son Vn, w. T. Bozok (vn) Gallo ▲ CD 609 [AAD]

Goltz, Gottfried von der (vn)
Pisendel, J.G.:Cons Vn, w. G. von der Goltz (cnd), Freiburg Baroque Orch—in D *(rec Maria Minor Church, Utrecht, Sept. 29–Oct. 3, 1994)* Deutsche Harmonia Mundi ▲ 05472-77339-2 [DDD]
Zavateri, L.G.:Cons Strs (comp), w. G. von der Goltz (cnd), Freiburg Baroque Orch—Nos. 2, 4, 6 & 8 also require an obligatto vn *(rec Festsaal des Maximilian-Parks, Hamm, Germany, 1995)* Deutsche Harmonia Mundi 2-▲ 05472-77352-2 [DDD]

Golub, David (pno)—see also ORCHESTRAS & ENSEMBLES Golub/Kaplan/Carr Trio
Brahms, J.:Trio Cl, w. D. Shifrin (cl), C. Carr (vc) Arabesque ▲ Z 6608
Brahms, J.:Trio Hn, w. D. Jolley (hn), M. Kaplan (vn) Arabesque ▲ Z 6607
Brahms, J.:Trio 1 Pno, w. M. Kaplan (vn), C. Carr (vc) Arabesque ▲ Z 6607
Brahms, J.:Trio 2 Pno, w. M. Kaplan (vn), C. Carr (vc) Arabesque ▲ Z 6608
Brahms, J.:Trio 3 Pno, w. M. Kaplan (vn), C. Carr (vc) Arabesque ▲ Z 6608
Elgar, E.:Concert Allegro *(rec SUNY Purchase Recital Hall, Oct 1–3, 1994)* Arabesque ▲ ARA 6664 [DDD]
Elgar, E.:Dream Children *(rec SUNY Purchase Recital Hall, Oct 1–3, 1994)* Arabesque ▲ ARA 6664 [DDD]
Elgar, E.:In Smyrna *(rec SUNY Purchase Recital Hall, Oct 1–3, 1994)* Arabesque ▲ ARA 6664 [DDD]
Elgar, E.:Skizze *(rec SUNY Purchase Recital Hall, Oct 1–3, 1994)* Arabesque ▲ ARA 6664 [DDD]
Mendelssohn, F.:Trio 1 Pno, w. M. Kaplan (vn), C. Carr (vc) Arabesque ▲ Z 6599
Mendelssohn, F.:Trio 2 Pno, w. M. Kaplan (vn), C. Carr (vc) Arabesque ▲ Z 6599
Rachmaninoff, S.:Con 2 Pno, w. W. Morris (cnd), London SO IMP Classics ("LSO Classic Masterpieces" series) ▲ IMPPCD 903 [DDD]
Rachmaninoff, S.:Rhapsody on a Theme of Paganini, w. W. Morris (cnd), London SO IMP Classics ▲ PCD 903 [DDD]
Rachmaninoff, S.:Rhapsody on a Theme of Paganini, w. W. Morris (cnd), London SO IMP Classics ("LSO Classic Masterpieces" series) ▲ IMPPCD 903 [DDD]
Schubert, Franz:Fant Pno, D.760, "Wandererfantasie" *(rec American Academy of Arts & Letters, June 7–9, 1993)* Arabesque ▲ ARA 6647 [DDD]
Schubert, Franz:Nocturne Pno, w. M. Kaplan (vn), C. Carr (vc) Arabesque 2-▲ Z 6580-2
Schubert, Franz:Pieces Pno, D.946 *(rec American Academy of Arts & Letters, June 7–9, 1993)* Arabesque ▲ ARA 6647 [DDD]
Schubert, Franz:Rondo Vn, D.895, w. M. Kaplan (vn) Arabesque ▲ ARA 6636 [DDD]
Schubert, Franz:Son Pno, D.840 *(rec American Academy of Arts & Letters, June 7–9, 1993)* Arabesque ▲ ARA 6647 [DDD]
Schubert, Franz:Sonatinas Vn, w. M. Kaplan (vn) Arabesque ▲ ARA 6636 [DDD]
Schubert, Franz:Trio Pno, D.28, w. M. Kaplan (vn), C. Carr (vc) Arabesque 2-▲ Z 6580-2
Schubert, Franz:Trio 1 Pno, w. M. Kaplan (vn), C. Carr (vc) Arabesque 2-▲ Z 6580-2
Schubert, Franz:Trio 2 Pno, w. M. Kaplan (vn), C. Carr (vc)—includes both the traditional finale as well as the first recording of the original finale, which contains 100 bars cut by Schubert prior to publication Arabesque 2-▲ Z 6580-2
Strauss, R.:Son Pno *(rec SUNY Purchase Recital Hall, Oct 1–3, 1994)* Arabesque ▲ ARA 6664 [DDD]
Strauss, R.:Stimmungsbilder *(rec SUNY Purchase Recital Hall, Oct 1–3, 1994)* Arabesque ▲ ARA 6664 [DDD]

Golub, Elliot (vn)
Vaughan Williams, R.:Along The Field, w. Patrice Michaels Bedi (sop)—Along the Field; Goodbye; Fancy's Knell; With Rue My Heart is Laden *(rec Mandel Hall, Univ of Chicago, June 17–21, 1996)* Cedille ▲ CDR 90000029 [DDD]

Golub, Ludmila (org)
Gretchaninoff, A.:Mass "Et in terra pax", w. Anatoly Obraztsov (bass), Valéri Polianski (cnd), Russian State Symphonic Cappella Chandos ▲ CHAN 9486

Golub, Ludmila (pno)
Busoni, F.:Son 2 Vn, w. S. Luca (vn) Facet ▲ FCD 8005 [AAD]

Golubovskaya, Nadezhda (pno)
Bortnyansky, D.:Son 2 Pno *(rec 1951)* Multisonic ("Russian Treasures" series) ▲ 31 0253

Goluses, Nicholas (gtr)
Bach, J.S.:Sons & Partitas Vn, BWV 1001–1006—Sons 1–3, BWV 1001, 1003 & 1005 [trans for gtr] *(rec St. John Chrysostom Church, Newmarket, Canada, Oct. 4–7, 1994)* Naxos ▲ 8.553193 [DDD]
de Blasio, C.:God is Our Righteousness, w. H. Huff (org) *(rec Aug. 26, 1993)* Catalyst ▲ 09026-61979-2 ■ 09026-61979-4
Sor, F.:Gtr Music—Fant, Op. 58; Fant elégiaque, Op. 59; 25 Progressive Studies, Op. 60 *(rec St. John's Chrysostom Church, Newmarket, Canada, May 15–20, 1995)* Naxos ▲ 8.553342 [DDD]

Gomberg, Harold (ob)
Bach, J.S.:Con Vn & Ob, w. I. Stern (vn), L. Bernstein (cnd), New York PO CBS ▲ MK 42258
Bach, J.S.:Con Vn & Ob, w. I. Stern (vn), L. Bernstein (cnd), New York PO CBS ■ MGT 39798
Bach, J.S.:Con Vn & Ob, w. Isaac Stern (vn), *(orch unknown)* Sony Classical ▲ SMK 66471
Falla, M. de:Con Hpd, w. I. Kipnis (hpd), P. Brook (fl), S. Drucker (cl), E. Chapo (vn), L. Munroe (vc), P. Boulez (cnd), New York PO *(rec Mar. 2, 1975)* Sony Classical ▲ SBK 53264 ■ SBT 53264

Gomberg, Harold (ob) (cont.)
Vivaldi, A.:Cons Ob, w. L. Bernstein (cnd), New York PO—in d, RV.454 *(rec Dec. 15, 1958)* Sony Classical ("Leonard Bernstein:The Royal Edition" series) ▲ SMK 47642 [ADD]

Gomez, Eddie (db)
Brasil, w. Richard Stoltzman (cl), Gary Burton (vib), Danny Gottlieb (perc) RCA Victor ▲ 60708-2-RC [DDD] ■ 60708-4-RC (CrO2)
Spirits, w. Richard Stoltzman (cl), David Torn (gtr), Dave Samuels (vib), Bill Douglas (bn), King's Singers RCA Victor ▲ 09026-68416-2 ■ 09026-68416-4

Gomez, Eddie (perc)
Hark!, w. Richard Stoltzman (cl), Jeremy Wall (kbd), Dave Samuels (vib), Bill Douglas (bn), Harlem Boys Choir RCA Victor ▲ 09026-61272-2 [DDD] ■ 09026-61272-4 (CrO2)

Gómez, William (gtr)
Day's End:The Soft Sound of Spanish Guitar, w. Eduardo Fernández (gtr), Nicola Hall (gtr), Timothy Walker (gtr), John Williams (gtr) London ▲ 448 560-2

González, Guillermo (pno)
Abril, A.G.:Con Pno, w. E. G. Asensio (cnd), Madrid SO *(rec live, National Music Auditorium, Madrid, Dec 10, 1994)* Marco Polo ▲ 8.223849 [DDD]

Gonzalez-Espinosa, David (pno)
Enriquez, M.:Hoy de ayer Gallo ▲ CD 550 [AAD]
Enriquez, M.:Movil I Gallo ▲ CD 550 [AAD]
Galindo, B.:Pieces (7) Pno Gallo ▲ CD 550 [AAD]
Moncayo Garcia, J.P.:Pieces Pno Gallo ▲ CD 550 [AAD]
Velazquez, L.:Bagatelles Gallo ▲ CD 550 [AAD]
Velazquez, L.:Dances Gallo ▲ CD 550 [AAD]
Velazquez, L.:Toccata Gallo ▲ CD 550 [AAD]

Goode, David (org)
Britten, H.:A Boy Was Born, w. Susan Gritton (sgr), Catherine Wyn-Rogers (sgr), Stephen Layton (cnd), Holst Singers Hyperion ▲ CDA 66825
Britten, H.:Choral Music, w. Susan Gritton (sgr), Catherine Wyn-Rogers (sgr), Stephen Layton (cnd), Holst Singers—Christ's Nativity; A Shepherd's Carol; Jubilate in C Hyperion ▲ CDA 66825
Britten, H.:A Hymn to the Virgin, w. Susan Gritton (sgr), Catherine Wyn-Rogers (sgr), Stephen Layton (cnd), Holst Singers Hyperion ▲ CDA 66825
Britten, H.:Te Deum, w. Susan Gritton (sgr), Catherine Wyn-Rogers (sgr), Stephen Layton (cnd), Holst Singers Hyperion ▲ CDA 66825

Goode, Richard (pno)
Bartók, B.:Contrasts, w. R. Stoltzman (cl), L. C. Stoltzman (vn) RCA Red Seal ▲ 60170-2-RC [DDD]
Beethoven, L. van:Son 8 Pno, "Pathétique" BOMR 2-▲ 31-7510 [DDD] 2-■ 81-7507 (D)
Beethoven, L. van:Son 14 Pno, "Moonlight Son" BOMR 2-▲ 31-7510 [DDD] 2-■ 81-7507 (D)
Beethoven, L. van:Son 15 Pno, "Pastoral" BOMR 2-▲ 31-7510 [DDD] 2-■ 81-7507 (D)
Beethoven, L. van:Son 16 Pno Elektra/Nonesuch ▲ 79212-2 [DDD] ■ 79212-4 (D)
Beethoven, L. van:Son 17 Pno, "Tempest" BOMR 2-▲ 31-7510 [DDD] 2-■ 81-7507 (D)
Beethoven, L. van:Son 17 Pno, "Tempest" Elektra/Nonesuch ▲ 79212-2 [DDD] ■ 79212-4 (D)
Beethoven, L. van:Son 18 Pno Elektra/Nonesuch ▲ 79212-2 [DDD] ■ 79212-4 (D)
Beethoven, L. van:Son 25 Pno BOMR 2-▲ 31-7510 [DDD] 2-■ 81-7507 (D)
Beethoven, L. van:Son 26 Pno, "Les Adieux", w. Goode BOMR 2-▲ 31-7510 [DDD] 2-■ 81-7507 (D)
Beethoven, L. van:Son 27 Pno BOMR 2-▲ 31-7510 [DDD] 2-■ 81-7507 (D)
Beethoven, L. van:Sons 28–32 Pno, "The Late Sons" Elektra/Nonesuch 2-▲ 79211-2 [DDD] 2-■ 79211-4 (D)
Beethoven, L. van:Son 28 Pno Elektra/Nonesuch 2-▲ 79211-2 2-■ 79211-4
Beethoven, L. van:Son 29 Pno, "Hammerklavier" Elektra/Nonesuch 2-▲ 79211-2 2-■ 79211-4
Beethoven, L. van:Son 30 Pno Elektra/Nonesuch 2-▲ 79211-2 2-■ 79211-4
Beethoven, L. van:Son 31 Pno Elektra/Nonesuch 2-▲ 79211-2 2-■ 79211-4
Beethoven, L. van:Son 32 Pno Elektra/Nonesuch 2-▲ 79211-2 2-■ 79211-4
Brahms, J.:Fants Pno, Op. 116 Elektra/Nonesuch ▲ 79154-2 [DDD] ■ 79154-4 (D)
Brahms, J.:Pieces Pno, Op. 119 Elektra/Nonesuch ▲ 79154-2 [DDD] ■ 79154-4 (D)
Brahms, J.:Sons Cl (comp), w. R. Stoltzman (cl) RCA Gold Seal ▲ 60036-2-RG [DDD]
Brahms, J.:Songs, w. B. Valente (sop) [G] InSync ■ C 4150
Brahms, J.:Trio Hn, w. W. Purvis (hn), D. Phillips (vn) Bridge ▲ BCD 9012 [DDD]
Ives, C.:Largo, w. L. Chapman Stoltzman (vn), R. Stoltzman (cl) RCA Red Seal ▲ 60170-2-RC [DDD]
Ives, C.:Songs, w. R. Stoltzman (cl) [arr. for clarinet & piano]—The things our fathers loved; Walking; Like a sick eagle; Ann Street - Broadway; The cage; The see'r; The Housatonic at Stockbridge; In the mornin'; Serenity RCA Red Seal ▲ 60170-2-RC [DDD]
Mozart, W.A.:Con 17 Pno, Orpheus CO Elektra/Nonesuch ▲ 79042-2 [DDD]
Mozart, W.A.:Con 23 Pno, Orpheus CO Elektra/Nonesuch ▲ 79042-2 [DDD]
Mozart, W.A.:Songs, w. B. Valente (sop) [G,I] InSync ■ C 4150
Perle, G.:Ballade Pno Elektra/Nonesuch ▲ 79108-2 [DDD]
Perle, G.:Concertino Pno, w. G. Schwarz (cnd), Music Today Ensemble Elektra/Nonesuch ▲ 79108-2 [DDD]
Perle, G.:Serenade 3 Pno, w. G. Schwarz (cnd), Music Today Ensemble Elektra/Nonesuch ▲ 79108-2 [DDD]
Schubert, Franz:Allegretto Pno, D.915 Elektra/Nonesuch ▲ 79124-2
Schubert, Franz:German Dances Pno, D.790 Elektra/Nonesuch ▲ 79064-2 ■ 79064-4 (D)
Schubert, Franz:Impromptus Pno, D.935—No. 2 in A♭ Elektra/Nonesuch ▲ 79124-2
Schubert, Franz:Pieces Pno, D.946—No. 1 Elektra/Nonesuch ▲ 78028-2 [ADD] ■ 78028-4
Schubert, Franz:Son Pno, D.845 Elektra/Nonesuch ▲ 79271-2 ■ 79271-4
Schubert, Franz:Son Pno, D.850 Elektra/Nonesuch ▲ 79271-2 ■ 79271-4
Schubert, Franz:Son Pno, D.958 Elektra/Nonesuch ▲ 79064-2 ■ 79064-4 (D)
Schubert, Franz:Son Pno, D.959 Elektra/Nonesuch ▲ 78028-2 [ADD] ■ 78028-4
Schubert, Franz:Son Pno, D.960 Elektra/Nonesuch ▲ 79124-2
Schubert, Franz:Sonatinas Vn, w. R. Stolzman (cl)—D.384 & D.385 RCA Red Seal ▲ 6772-2-RC [DDD]
Schubert, Franz:Songs (misc), w. B. Valente (sop) [G] InSync ■ C 4150
Schumann, R.:Fant Pno Elektra/Nonesuch ▲ 79014-2 [DDD]
Schumann, R.:Fantasiestücke Cl, w. R. Stoltzman (cl) RCA Red Seal ▲ 6772-2-RC [DDD]
Schumann, R.:Humoreske Pno Elektra/Nonesuch ▲ 79014-2 [DDD]
Schumann, R.:Romances Ob, w. R. Stoltzman (cl) RCA Red Seal ▲ 6772-2-RC [DDD]
Stravinsky, I.:L'Histoire du soldat Suite Vn, w. R. Stoltzman (cl), L. Chapman Stoltzman (vn) RCA Red Seal ▲ 60170-2-RC [DDD]
Wolf, H.:Italienische Liederbücher (sels), w. B. Valente (sop) [G] InSync ■ C 4150

Goodearl, N. (hn)
Gottschalk, A.:Section for 4 Hns, w. T. Bacon (hn), J. Wilson (hn), J. Graber (hn), R. Brown (timp) Summit ▲ DCD 135 [DDD]
Pinkston, R.:Qt for 4 Hns, w. T. Bacon (hn), J. Landsman (hn), J. Horrocks (hn) Summit ▲ DCD 135 [DDD]

Goodenough, David (org)
Wood, C.:Music of, w. David Cooper (cnd), Blackburn Cathedral Choir—Magnificat in E♭; O Most Merciful; God Omnipotent Reigneth; I Will Arise; Father All-Holy; Nunc Dimittis in c; Prelude & Fugue in g; Summer Ended; Haec Dies; Tis The Day of Resurrection; An Easter Carol; Prelude on the Hymn Tune St. Mary; Great Lord of Lords; Oculi Omnium; Prelude on the Hymn Tune York; Expectans Expectavi; Magnificat in F [Collegium Regale] Priory ▲ PRI 484 [DDD]

Goodman, Benny (cl)
Bartók, B.:Contrasts, w. Szigeti (vn), Bartók (pno) CBS ▲ MK 42227 ■ MYT 42227
Bartók, B.:Contrasts, w. Szigeti (vn), Bartók (pno) *(rec 1940)* Hungaroton 6-▲ HCD 12326/31 (m) [ADD]
Bartók, B.:Contrasts, w. Szigeti (vn), Bartók (pno) *(rec 1940)* Sony Masterworks ("Portrait" series) ▲ MPK 47676 [ADD]

INSTRUMENT.

Goodman, Benny (cl) (cont.)

Bartók, B.:Pno Music, w. B. Bartók (pno), V. Medgyaszay (sop), M. Basilides (cta), F. Székelyhidy (ten), J. Szigeti (vn), D. Bartók Pásztory (pno), H. J. Baker, E. J. Rubsam (perc)—studio, broadcast & piano roll recordings of music by Bartók, Kodály, Beethoven, Debussy, Liszt & Scarlatti, chronologically arranged from ca. 1920 through 1945—Sonatina; 6 Romanian Folk Dances; Evening in Transylvania; 8 sels. from 15 Hungarian Peasant Songs; Suite, Op. 14 (both the issued & test recordings); Allegro barbaro; 5 sels. from 2 Romanian Dances, 3 Burlesques, 10 Easy Pieces & 14 Bagatelles; 4 Sons. by D. Scarlatti (test recordings); 8 sels. from 15 Hungarian Peasant Songs; 4 sels. from 9 Little Piano Pieces, Petite Suite & 3 Rondos on Folk Melodies; 4 "Sursum corda" from Liszt's Années de pèlerinage; 20 Hungarian Folk Songs; 5 Hungarian Folk Tunes; 8 Hungarian Folksongs; Hungarian Folk Tunes; 6 Romanian Folk Dances; Rhap. 1 Violin & Piano; Contrasts for Clarinet, Violin & Piano; 2 sels. from Mikrokosmos; 32 sels. from Mikrokosmos; Rhap. 1; Son. No. 2; Beethoven's "Kreutzer" Son.; Debussy's Son. 3; Son. 2 Pianos & Percussion; Petite Suite; 3 Hungarian Folk Tunes; 11 sels. from Improvs. on Hungarian Peasant Songs; Mikrokosmos; 3 Rondos on Folk Melodies; 9 Little Piano Pieces; 14 Bagatelles; 15 sels. from For Children & 2 sels. from 10 Easy Pieces
Hungaroton 6—▲ HCD 12326/31 (m) [ADD]
Bernstein, L.:Prelude, Fugue & Riffs Cl, w. L. Bernstein (cnd), Columbia Jazz Combo
CBS ▲ MK 42227 ■ MYT 42227
Copland, A.:Con Cl, w. A. Copland (cnd), Columbia SO CBS ▲ MK 42227 ■ MYT 42227
Copland, A.:Con Cl, w. F. Reiner (cnd), NBC SO (rec 1951) Legend ▲ LGD 122
Gershwin, G.:An American in Paris, w. A. Toscanini (cnd), NBC SO Iron Needle ▲ 1306
Gershwin, G.:An American in Paris, w. Earl Wild (pno), A. Toscanini (cnd), NBC SO
Enterprise ("The Radio Years" series) ▲ ENT RY 60
Gershwin, G.:Rhap in Blue, w. Earl Wild (pno), A. Toscanini (cnd), NBC SO Iron Needle ▲ 1306
Gershwin, G.:Rhap in Blue, w. Earl Wild (pno), A. Toscanini (cnd), NBC SO (rec Nov. 1, 1942)
Vintage Jazz Classics ▲ VJC 1034
Gershwin, G.:Rhap in Blue, w. Earl Wild (pno), A. Toscanini (cnd), NBC SO
Enterprise ("The Radio Years" series) ▲ ENT RY 60
Gould, M.:Derivations, w. M. Gould (cnd), Columbia Jazz Combo CBS ▲ MK 42227 ■ MT 42227
Mozart, W.A.:Qnt Cl, K.581, w. Budapest String Quartet (rec 1938)
EMI Classics ("Great Recordings of the Century" series) ▲ CDH 63697 (m) [ADD]
Mozart, W.A.:Qnt Cl, w. Budapest String Quartet Biddulph ▲ LAB 140
Mozart, W.A.:Qnt Cl & Strs, w. Budapest String Quartet
Enterprise ("The Radio Years" series) ▲ ENT RY 60
Mozart, W.A.:Qnt Cl, K.581, w. Budapest String Quartet Iron Needle ▲ 1306
The Recordings with Béla Bartók & Andor Foldes, w. Joseph Szigeti (vn), Bela Bartok (son) (rec 1940-41) Biddulph ▲ BID LAB 070 [ADD]
Rodgers, R.:Music of, w. S. Bass (sgr), J. Andrews (sgr), P. Como (sgr), D. Reese (sgr), J. Jones (sgr), N. Luboff (sgr), M. Gold (sgr), N. Walker (sgr), H. Bowen (sgr), V. Damone (sgr), P. Nero (pno), J. P. Morgan (sgr), E. Fisher (sgr), Ann-Margaret (sgr), Shorty Rogers (sgr), D. Shore (sgr), T. Martin (sgr), M. King (sgr), A. Newley (sgr) RCA ▲ 8590-2 R ■ 8590-4 R
Stravinsky, I.:Ebony Con, w. I. Stravinsky (cnd), Columbia Jazz Combo CBS ▲ MK 42227 ■ MT 42227

Goodman, Erica (hp)

Andrés, B.:Chants d'arreère-saison, w. Sören Hermansson (hn) (rec Länna Church, Sweden, Mar 30–Apr 2, 1996) BIS ▲ CD 793 [DDD]
Barnes, M.:Divert Hp, w. Amadeus Ensemble members CBC ("Musica Viva" series) ▲ MVCD 1054 [DDD]
Cherney, B.:River of Fire, w. Lawrence Cherney (ob) (rec St Martin-in-the-Fields Church, Toronto, July 1995) Centrediscs ▲ CMC 5395 [DDD]
Damase, J.-M.:Son Fl & Hp, w. Robert Aitken (fl) (rec Elora, Ontario, Canada, Sept–Oct, 1993) BIS ▲ CD 650 [DDD]
Donizetti, G.:Son Fl & Hp, w. Robert Aitken (fl) (rec Castle Wik, Sweden, June 2–4, 1979)
BIS ▲ CD 143 [AAD]
Dussek, J.L.:Sons Vn, Op. 2 BIS ▲ CD 319 [DDD]
Erica Goodman Plays Canadian Harp Music (rec Oct. 4–6, 1993) BIS ▲ CD 649 [DDD]
Fauré, G.:Impromptu Hp BIS ▲ CD 319 [DDD]
Flagello, N.:Son Hp BIS ▲ CD 319 [DDD]
Flute & Harp, w. Robert Aitken (fl) BIS ▲ CD 320
Hoffmann, E.T.A.:Qnt Hp, w. Amadeus Ensemble members
CBC ("Musica Viva" series) ▲ MVCD 1054 [DDD]
Horn & Harp Soirée:19th Century French & Italian Duos, w. Sören Hermansson (hn) (rec Sept. 20–23, 1993) BIS ▲ CD 648 [DDD]
Hovhaness, A.:The Garden of Adonis, w. Robert Aitken (fl) (rec Castle Wik, Sweden, June 2–4, 1979) BIS ▲ CD 143 [AAD]
Inghelbrecht, D.-E.:Sonatina en trois parties, w. Robert Aitken (fl) (rec Elora, Ontario, Canada, Sept–Oct, 1993) BIS ▲ CD 650 [DDD]
Jeux à Deux, w. Robert Aitken (fl) Marquis Classics ▲ ERAD 101 [DDD]
Jolivet, A.:Fl Music (comp), w. Manuela Wiesler (fl), Patrik Swedrup (vn), Håkan Olsson (va), Helena Nilsson (vc), Christian Davidsson (bn), Roland Pöntinen (pno), P. Järvi (pno), Tapiola Sinfonietta, Kroumata Percussion Ensemble—Alla rustica for Fl & Hp; Chant de Linos for Fl, Hp & Str Trio; Pastorales de Noël for Fl, Bn & Hp; Con for Fl & Strs; Suite en concert for Fl & 4 Perc Players; Fant-Caprice for Alto Fl & Pno; Cabrioles for Fl & Hp (rec Danderyd Grammar School, Tapiola Hall, Tapiola, Finland, Gothenburg Concert Hall, Sweden & Studio 2, Radiohuset, Stockholm, Sweden)
BIS ▲ CD 739 [DDD]
Klein, L.:AOIDOI, w. Sören Hermansson (hn) (rec Länna Church, Sweden, Mar 30–Apr 2, 1996)
BIS ▲ CD 793 [DDD]
Koch, E. von:Nocturne, w. Sören Hermansson (hn) (rec Länna Church, Sweden, Mar 30–Apr 2, 1996) BIS ▲ CD 793 [DDD]
Koetsier, J.:Son Hn & Hp, w. Sören Hermansson (hn) (rec Länna Church, Sweden, Mar 30–Apr 2, 1996) BIS ▲ CD 793 [DDD]
Krumpholtz, J.-B.:Son Fl & Hp, w. Robert Aitken (fl) (rec Castle Wik, Sweden, June 2–4, 1979)
BIS ▲ CD 143 [AAD]
Lauber, J.:Medieval Dances, w. Robert Aitken (fl) (rec Elora, Ontario, Canada, Sept–Oct, 1993)
BIS ▲ CD 650 [DDD]
Louie, A.:Love Songs for a Small Planet, w. S. Ferreras (perc), Vancouver Chamber Choir
Centrediscs ▲ CMCCD 4893 [DDD]
Louie, A.:Refuge, w. Joseph Macerollo (acc), Beverley Johnston (perc) (rec Glenn Gould Studio, CBC Toronto, Mar 17, 1994 & Mar 13 & 2) CBC ▲ MVCD 1096 [DDD]
Mather, B.:Vouvray, w. Lawrence Cherney (ob) (rec St Martin-in-the-Fields Church, Toronto, July 1995) Centrediscs ▲ CMC 5395 [DDD]
Molique, W.B.:Songs without Words, w. J. Petric (accordian) (rec June 12–13, 1991)
CBC ("Musica Viva" series) ▲ MVCD 1056 [DDD]
Mozetich, M.:El Dorado, w. Amadeus Ensemble CBC ("Musica Viva" series) ▲ MVCD 1038 [DDD]
Petra-Basacopol, C.:Son Fl Hp, w. Robert Aitken (fl) (rec Elora, Ontario, Canada, Sept–Oct, 1993)
BIS ▲ CD 650 [DDD]
Procaccini, T.:Serenata, w. Sören Hermansson (hn) (rec Länna Church, Sweden, Mar 30–Apr 2, 1996) BIS ▲ CD 793 [DDD]
Prokofiev, S.:Prelude Pno [arr for hp] BIS ▲ CD 319 [DDD]
Ravel, M.:Intro & Allegro, w. S. Shulman (fl), S. McCartney (cl), Amadeus Ensemble members
CBC ("Musica Viva" series) ▲ MVCD 1054 [DDD]
Salzedo, C.:Scintillation BIS ▲ CD 319 [DDD]
Samuel-Rousseau, M.:Pastoral Vars on an Old Christmas Carol, w. Amadeus Ensemble members
CBC ("Musica Viva" series) ▲ MVCD 1054 [DDD]
Singer, J.:Suite Hn, w. Sören Hermansson (hn) (rec Länna Church, Sweden, Mar 30–Apr 2, 1996)
BIS ▲ CD 793 [DDD]
Spohr, L.:Son 3 Vn, w. Robert Aitken (fl) [trans. fl & hp] (rec Castle Wik, Sweden, June 2–4, 1979)
BIS ▲ CD 143 [AAD]
Spohr, L.:Son 4 Vn, w. Robert Aitken (fl) [trans. fl & hp] (rec Castle Wik, Sweden, June 2–4, 1979)
BIS ▲ CD 143 [AAD]

Goodman, Erica (hp) (cont.)

Spohr, L.:Son 5 Vn, w. Robert Aitken (fl) [trans. fl & hp] (rec Castle Wik, Sweden, June 2–4, 1979)
BIS ▲ CD 143 [AAD]
Takemitsu, T.:Toward the Sea III, w. Robert Aitken (fl) (rec Elora, Ontario, Canada, Sept–Oct, 1993)
BIS ▲ CD 650 [DDD]
Tournier, M.:Images, w. Amadeus Ensemble members
CBC ("Musica Viva" series) ▲ MVCD 1054 [DDD]
Tournier, M.:Sonatine Hp BIS ▲ CD 319 [DDD]
Virtuoso Harp BIS ▲ CD 319

Goodman, Isador (pno)

Addinsell, R.:Warsaw Con, w. P. Thomas (cnd), Melbourne SO
Philips ("Concert Classics" series) ▲ 422471-2 [ADD]
Gershwin, G.:Rhap in Blue, w. P. Thomas (cnd), Melbourne SO
Philips ("Concert Classics" series) ▲ 422471-2 [ADD]
Litolff, H.C.:Con Symphonique 4, w. P. Thomas (cnd), Melbourne SO—Scherzo
Philips ("Concert Classics" series) ▲ 422471-2

Goodman, Lanie (fl)

Redolfi, M.:Underwater Music, w. Melissa Morgan (hp), Michel Redolfi (syn), Ricercar Ensemble—Effractions (1988); Sunny Afternoon at Bird Rock Beach (1983); Full Scale Ocean (1989) (rec Pacific Ocean, CA & Nice, France, 1983 & 1989)
Hat Hut ("NOW." series) ▲ hat ART CD 6026 [ADD]

Goodman, Roy (org)

Bach, J.S.:Cant 82, w. Nathalie Stutzmann (cta), Anthony Robson (ob), R. Goodman (cnd), Hanover Band (rec Watford Town Hall, Hertfordshire, U.K, Jan 31–Feb 3, 1994)
RCA Red Seal ▲ 09026-62655-2 [DDD]
Bach, J.S.:Cant 170, w. Nathalie Stutzmann (cta), Anthony Robson (ob), Alistair Ross (cnd), R. Goodman (cnd), Hanover Band (rec Watford Town Hall, Hertfordshire, U.K, Jan 31–Feb 3, 1994)
RCA Red Seal ▲ 09026-62655-2 [DDD]
Pergolesi, w. Stutzmann, Nathalie (cta), Elizabeth Norberg-Schulz (sop), Hanover Band
RCA Red Seal ▲ 09026-61215-2

Goodman, Roy (vn)

Arne, T.:Songs, w. John Mark Ainsley (ten), Miles Golding (vn), Anthony Robson (sop rcr), Jane Coe (vc), Robert King (hpd/org)—Under the Greenwood Tree; Come Away Death; Where the Bee Sucks (rec St Jude-on-the-Hill, London, Dec 20–21, 1968) United ▲ CAL 88002 [DDD]
Bach, J.S.:Cant 54, w. Nathalie Stutzmann (cta), R. Goodman (cnd), Hanover Band (rec Watford Town Hall, Hertfordshire, U.K, Jan 31–Feb 3, 1994) RCA Red Seal ▲ 09026-62655-2 [DDD]
Corbett, W.:Le Bizzarie universali, w. A. Manze (vn), R. Goodman (cnd), European Community Baroque Orch—9 concerti Channel Classics ▲ CCS 1391 [DDD]
Hellendaal, P.:Concerti grossi, w. A. Manze (vn), R. Goodman (cnd), European Community Baroque Orch—complete Channel Classics ▲ CCS 3492 [DDD]
Vivaldi, A.:Cons Rcr, w. Piers Adams (rcr), Miles Golding (vn), Jane Compton (va), Jane Coe (vc), Mandy MacNamara (db), David Miller (archlt), Robert King (hpd/org)—in F for Treble Rcr, Op. 10/1; in a for Sopranino Rcr, RV.440; in c for Treble Rcr, RV.441; in D for Sopranino Rcr, Op. 10/3; in g for Treble Rcr, Op. 10/2; in C for Sopranino Rcr, RV.443 (rec Radley College, Abingdon, Oxon)
United ▲ CAL 88015 [DDD]

Goodrich, Joseph (kbd)

Moran, R.:Rocky Road, w. Kevin Hanson (gtr), Erik Johnson (perc), Andrew Morrell (perc) (rec Chapel of Girard College, Philadelphia & Henry Wood Hall, London, Mar 17, 1994 & Dec 13, 19)
Argo ▲ 444540-2 [DDD]

Goodwin, Paul (ob d'amore)

Bach, J.S.:Con Ob d'amore, w. R. King (cnd), King's Consort Hyperion ▲ CDA 66267 [DDD]

Goodwin, Paul (ob)

Bach, C.P.E.:Con Ob H.468, w. T. Pinnock (cnd), English Concert Archiv ▲ 431821-2 [DDD]
Bach, J.S.:Con Ob, BWV 1053, w. R. King (cnd), King's Consort Hyperion ▲ CDA 66267 [DDD]
Handel, G.F.:Sons Solo Instrs, w. Rachel Beckett (fl), Lisa Beznosiuk (rcr), Locatelli Trio
Hyperion 3—▲ CDA 66921/23
Haydn, J.:Con Ob, w. T. Pinnock (cnd), English Concert Archiv ▲ 431678-2 [DDD]
Lebrun, L.A.:Con 1 Ob, w. T. Pinnock (cnd), English Concert Archiv ▲ 431821-2 [DDD]
Mozart, W.A.:Con Ob, K.314, w. T. Pinnock (cnd), English Concert Archiv ▲ 431821-2 [DDD]
Telemann, G.P.:Con in A Ob d'amore, w. R. King (cnd), King's Consort Hyperion ▲ CDA 66267 [DDD]
Telemann, G.P.:Cons Ob Orch, w. R. King (cnd), King's Consort—1—in d
Hyperion ▲ CDA 66267 [DDD]
Telemann, G.P.:Cons Tpts, w. Mark Bennett (tpt), Michael Harrison (tpt), Nicholas Thompson (tpt), Lorraine Wood (ob), T. Pinnock (cnd), English Concert—in D (rec Henry Wood Hall, London, Mar 1993) Archiv Produktion ▲ 439893-2 [DDD]
Telemann, G.P.:Sons Ob, w. John Toll (hpd), Susan Sheppard (vc), Nigel North (thb/archlt)
Harmonia Mundi ▲ HMU 907152
Vivaldi, A.:Cons Diverse Instrs, w. M. Verbruggen (rcr), J. Holloway (vn), D. Godburn (bn), J. Toll (hpd), S. Comberti (vc)—7 Concerti—in D, RV.84; in a, RV.86; in D, RV.94; in D, "Las Pastorella", in F, RV.99; in g, RV.103; in g, RV.105 Harmonia Mundi USA ▲ HMU 907046
Vivaldi, A.:Sons Ob, w. J. Holloway (vn), C. Lawson (cl), N. North (archlt/gtr), S. Sheppard (vc), F. Eustace (bn), J. Toll (hpd/org)—RV.53, 58, 81 & 779
Harmonia Mundi USA ▲ HMU 907104

Goodyear, Stewart (pno)

Anderson, L.:Con Pno, w. E. Kunzel (cnd), Cincinnati Pops Orch Telarc ▲ CD 80112 [DDD]
Gershwin, G.:Second Rhap, w. E. Kunzel (cnd), Cincinnati Pops Orch Telarc ▲ CD 80112 [DDD]

Goraieb, Henri (pno)

Djabadary, H.:Con Pno, w. L. de Froment (cnd), Luxembourg RSO (rec 1980) Quantum ▲ QM 6915
Schumann, R.:Con Pno, w. L. de Froment (cnd), Luxembourg Radio-TV SO Forlane ▲ FRL 14 [AAD]
Schumann, R.:Intro & Allegro appassionato, Op. 92, w. L. de Froment (cnd), Luxembourg Radio-TV SO Forlane ▲ FRL 14 [AAD]

Gordon (vn)

Weigl, V.:Nature Moods, w. G. Shirley (ten), S. Drucker (cl) CRI ▲ C 326

Gordon, A. (org)

Wagner, R.:Die Walküre (ride of the valkyries), w. B. Jones (org) [organ duet arr.] AFKA ▲ SK 506

Gordon, A. (pno)

Clokey, J.:Symphonic Piece, w. B. Jones (org) AFKA ▲ SK 506
Demarest, C.:Fant Org, w. B. Jones (org) AFKA ▲ SK 506
Dupré, M.:Vars à deux thèmes, w. B. Jones (org) AFKA ▲ SK 506
Grasse, E.:Festival Ov, w. B. Jones (org) AFKA ▲ SK 506

Gordon, Adam (tpt)

Christmas in Dallas, w. Christina Harmon (org), Jeffery Curnow (tpt), Gregory Hustis (hn), Clarece Candamio (org) (rec Lover's Lane United Methodist Church, Dallas) Hester Park ▲ 7706 [DDD]

Gordon, Derek (org)

Sunday Masterworks Arkay ▲ ARK 6151 [DDD]

Gordon, Frank (tpt)

Jenkins, L.:Monkey on the Dragon, w. Leroy Jenkins (vn), Henry Threadgill (fl), Don Byron (cl), Marth Ehrlich (b cl), Janet Frice (hn), Vincent Chancey (hn), Jeff Hoyer (trbn), David Soldier (vn), Jane Henry (vn) Ron Lawrence (va), Mary Wooton (vc), Lindsey Horner (db), Thurman Barker (traps), Myra Melford (pno), T. Léon (cnd) (rec live, Merkin Concert Hall, New York City, Apr. 9, 1992)
CRI ("eXchange" series) ▲ CD 663 [DDD]

Gordon, Geoffrey (perc)

Mostel, R.:River Tibetan Singing Bowls, w. Tibetan Singing Bowl Ensemble (rec live, WNYC Studios, Sept 18, 1987) Digital Fossils ▲ 10009-2 [DDD]
Mostel, R.:Swiftly, w. Dan Erkkila (shakuhachi/ram's horn/Tibetan thighbone trumpets), John Charles Thomas (tube tpt/ram's horn), Tibetan Singing Bowl Ensemble (rec live, WNYC Studios, Sept 18, 1987) Digital Fossils ▲ 10009-2 [DDD]

Gordon, J. (vc)—see ORCHESTRAS & ENSEMBLES Group for Contemporary Music String Quartet

▲ = CD ♦ = Enhanced CD △ = MD ■ = Cassette Tape □ = DCC

Gordon, Judith (pno)
Bärmann, H.J.:Qnt 3 Cl, w. J. Cohler (cl) [arr. for Clarinet & Piano]—Adagio *(rec May 29-30, 1992)*
  Ongaku ▲ 024-101 [DDD]
Brahms, J.:Son 1 Cl, w. J. Cohler (cl) *(rec May 29-30, 1992)*
  Ongaku ▲ CTD 88101 [DDD]
Harbison, J.:Son 1 Pno, "Roger Sessions In Memoriam" *(rec Kresge Auditorium, between 1988 & 1994)*
  Archetype ▲ 60104 [DDD]
Moonflowers, Babyl, w. Jonathan Cohler (cl) *(rec Aug. 23-24, 1993)*
  Crystal ▲ CD 733 [DDD]
Sargon, S.:Deep Ellum Nights, w. J. Cohler (cl) *(rec May 29-30, 1992)*
  Ongaku ▲ 024-101 [DDD]
Weber, C.M. von:Grand duo concertant Cl, w. J. Cohler (cl) *(rec May 29-30, 1992)*
  Ongaku ▲ 024-101 [DDD]

Gordon, M. (instr)—see ORCHESTRAS & ENSEMBLES Icebreaker
Gordon, Nadia (pno)
Chopin, F.:Suite 1, w. S. Gordon (pno) Klavier ■ KC 549
Rachmaninoff, S.:Suite 1 for 2 Pnos, w. S. Gordon (pno) Citadel ▲ CTD 88101 [ADD]
Ravel, M.:Pno Music, w. S. Gordon (pno)—La Valse; Frontispiece; Sites; Auriculaires; Bolero; Fanfare
  Klavier ■ KC 563

Gordon, Steven (pno)
Chopin, F.:Ballades Pno (comp) Klavier ■ KC 7027
Chopin, F.:Barcarolle Pno Klavier ■ KC 7027
Chopin, F.:Suite 1, w. N. Gordon (pno) Klavier ■ KC 549
Rachmaninoff, S.:Suite 1 for 2 Pnos, w. N. Gordon (pno) Citadel ▲ CTD 88101 [ADD]
Ravel, M.:Pno Music, w. N. Gordon (pno)—La Valse; Frontispiece; Sites; Auriculaires; Bolero; Fanfare
  Klavier ■ KC 563

Gordy, L. (pno)—see ORCHESTRAS & ENSEMBLES Thamyris
Górecka, A. (pno)
Górecki, H.-M.:Con Pno, w. A. Duczmal (cnd), Amadeus CO *(rec Concert Hall of Adam Mickiewicz Univ, May-June 1992)* Conifer Classics ▲ CDCF 246 [DDD]

Gorelic, Leo (vn)
Smolsky, D.:Con Vn, Belarussian State Radio-TV Orch Olympia ▲ OCD 551 [AAD]

Gorigliano, J. (vn)
Vivaldi, A.:Cons Diverse Instrs, w. G. Vicari (mand), C. de Filippis (mand), J. Wummer (fl), R. Morris (fl), W. Vacchiano (tpt), N. Prager (tpt), E. Brenner (ob), C. Stavrache (hp), A. Wurtzler (hp), L. Varga (vc), L. Bernstein (cnd), New York PO—in C, RV.558 *(rec Dec. 15, 1958)*
  Sony Classical ("Leonard Bernstein:The Royal Edition" series) ▲ SMK 47642 [ADD]
Vivaldi, A.:Cons Vn, Op. 8/1-4, "The Four Seasons", w. L. Bernstein (cnd), New York PO members [arr. Alceo Toni] *(rec Dec. 15, 1958)*
  Sony Classical ("Leonard Bernstein:The Royal Edition" series) ▲ SMK 47642 [ADD]

Gorini, Gino (pno)
Hindemith, P.:Kammermusik 2, w. S. Celibidache (cnd), Naples Alessandro Scarlatti RAI Orch *(rec live, 1959)* Originals ▲ ORI 864

Gorisek, Bojan (pno)
Satie, E.:Pno Music (comp)—Pièces froides: Poudre d'or; Le Piccadilly; Rêverie du pauvre; Petite ouv. à danser; Petite musique de clown triste; Verset laïque et somptueux; Le poisson rêveur; Trois morceaux en forme de poire Audiophile Classics ▲ 101.017
Satie, E.:Pno Music (comp)—Musiques intimes et secrètes; 6 Pièces de la periode; Aperçus désagréables; Nouvelles pièces froides; Deux rêveries nocturnes; Carnet d'esquisses et de croquis; En habit de cheval [pno 4-hands; w. Aleksandar Madzar]; Préludes flasques [Pour un chien]; Véritable préludes flasques [Pour un chien]; Le piège de méduse; Descriptions automatiques
  Audiophile Classics ▲ 101.018
Satie, E.:Pno Music (comp)—Messe des pauvres; Pages mystiques; Gnossienne Nos. 6 & 7; Danse de travers; Je te veux; Caresse Audiophile Classics ▲ 101.016
Satie, E.:Pno Music (comp)—Embryons desséchés; Croquis et agaceries d'un gros bonhomme en bois; Chapitres tournés en tous sens; Vieux sequins et vielles cuirasses enfantines; 3 nouvelles enfantines; Les pantins dansent; Sports et divertissements; Heures séculaires et instantanées; Les trois valses distinguées du précieux dégoûté; Cinq grimaces pour le songe d'une nuit d'été; Avant-dernières pensées Audiophile Classics ▲ 101.019
Satie, E.:Pno Music (comp) Audiophile Classics 10-▲ 101.391 [DDD]
Satie, E.:Songs, w. Jane Manning (sop) Audiophile Classics ▲ 101.391 [DDD]

Goritzki, Deinhart (va)—see ORCHESTRAS & ENSEMBLES Munich Baryton Trio
Goritzki, Ingo (E hn)
Hindemith, P.:Son Ob, w. Kalle Randalu (pno) MD + G ▲ MDG CD 3040695

Goritzki, Ingo (ob)
Albinoni, T.:Cons à 5 Obs, Op. 7, w. J. Müller-Brincken (ob), J. E. Dähler (hpd), H. L. Hirsch (cnd), Accademia Instrumentalis Claudio Monteverdi—Nos. 1,2 & 4 Claves ▲ C 601
Bach, J.S.:The Art of the Fugue (sels), w. H.-J. Erhard (hpd) Hänssler Classic ▲ HAN 98987 [DDD]
Bach, J.S.:Sons Fl, BWV 1030-35, w. H.-J. Erhard (hpd)—BWV 1030
  Hänssler Classic ▲ HAN 98987 [DDD]
Fasch, J.F.:Trio Sons, w. B. Glaetzner (ob), T. Reinhardt (bn), S. Pank (vl), A. Beyer (vle), C. Schornsheim (hpd) Berlin Classics ▲ BER 1069 [DDD]
Fiala, J.:Con Ob, w. W. Rajski (cnd), Polish Chamber PO Claves ▲ CD 9018 [DDD]
Haydn, J.:Con Ob, w. P. Angerer (cnd), Southwest German CO Pforzheim *(rec Pforzheim, 1975)* Claves ("Favor Collection" series) ▲ CLF 606 [ADD]
Herzogenberg, H. von:Trio Pno, Ob & Hn, w. Barry Tuckwell (hn), Ricardo Requejo (pno)
  Claves ▲ CD 803
Hindemith, P.:Son Ob, w. Kalle Randalu (pno) MD + G ▲ MDG CD 3040695
Kalliwoda, J.W.:Concertino Ob, w. W. Rajski (cnd), Polish Chamber PO Claves ▲ CD 9018 [DDD]
Krommer, F.:Con Ob, Op. 37, w. W. Rajski (cnd), Polish Chamber PO Claves ▲ CD 9018 [DDD]
Martinů, B.:Con Ob, w. W. Rajski (cnd), Polish Chamber PO Claves ▲ CD 9018 [DDD]
Mozart, W.A.:Andante Fl, K.315/285a, w. W. Rajski (cnd), Polish Chamber PO [arr. for oboe] *(rec Apr. 21-25, 1992)* Claves ▲ CD 9302 [DDD]
Mozart, W.A.:Con Fl, K.313, w. W. Rajski (cnd), Polish Chamber PO [arr for oboe] *(rec Apr. 21-25, 1992)* Claves ▲ CD 9302 [DDD]
Mozart, W.A.:Con Ob, K.314, w. W. Rajski (cnd), Polish Chamber PO *(rec Apr. 21-25, 1992)*
  Claves ▲ CD 9302 [DDD]
Mozart, W.A.:Con Ob, K.314, w. P. Angerer (cnd), Southwest German CO Pforzheim *(rec Pforzheim, 1975)* Claves ("Favor Collection" series) ▲ CLF 606 [ADD]
Poulenc, F.:Son Ob, w. R. Requejo (pno) Claves ▲ CD 9020 [DDD]
Poulenc, F.:Trio Ob, w. K. Thunemann (bn), R. Requejo (pno) Claves ▲ CD 9020 [DDD]
Reinecke, C.:Trio Ob, w. B. Tuckwell (hn), R. Requejo (pno) Claves ▲ CD 803
Saint-Saëns, C.:Son Ob, w. R. Requejo (pno) Claves ▲ CD 9020 [DDD]
Schumann, R.:Romances Ob, w. Ricardo Requejo (pno) *(rec Gstaad, Mar 1981)*
  Claves ▲ CD 508201 [ADD]
Strauss, R.:Son Ob, w. M. Aeschbacher (cnd), Lausanne CO Claves ▲ CD 9010 [DDD]
Vivaldi, A.:Sons Ob, w. B. Glaetzner (ob), K. Suske (vn), A. Beyer (vn), T. Reinhardt (bn), S. Pank (vl), C. Schornsheim (org/hpd)—RV.28, 34, 53, 81 & 779
  Capriccio ▲ CD 10143 [DDD] ■ CAS 27153 [CrO2]
Zelenka, J.D.:Trio Sons Obs, w. B. Glaetzner (ob), K. Sønstevold (bn), A. Beyer (vn), S. Pank (vl), W. H. Bernstein (hpd) Berlin Classics 2-▲ BER 1070 [DDD]
Zelenka, J.D.:Trio Sons Obs, w. Burkhard Glaetzer (ob), Knut Sønstevold (bn), Achim Beyer (vn), Siegfried Pank (va), Walter-Heinz Bernstein (hpd) Berlin Classics 4-▲ BER 1150 [DDD]

Goritzki, Johannes (vc)
Françaix, J.:Trio Vn, Vc & Pno, w. S. Gawriloff (vn), R. Havenith (pno) *(rec 12/13/89)*
  Wergo ▲ WER 6198-2 [AAD]

Gorn, Steve (fl)
Dick, R.:Bassbamboo, w. R. Dick (fl) O.O. Discs ▲ OO 7 [DDD]
Dick, R.:Calaveras Jump, w. R. Dick (fl) O.O. Discs ▲ OO 12 [DDD]
Dick, R.:DTR, w. R. Dick (fl) O.O. Discs ▲ OO 12 [DDD]
Dick, R.:Lapis Blues, w. R. Dick (fl) O.O. Discs ▲ OO 12 [DDD]

Gorn, Steve (fl) (cont.)
Dick, R.:Light, w. R. Dick (fl) O.O. Discs ▲ OO 12 [DDD]
Dick, R.:Tongue & Groove, w. R. Dick (fl) O.O. Discs ▲ OO 12 [DDD]
Gorn, S.:Seven Cranes O.O. Discs ▲ OO 12 [DDD]

Gorodetzky, Jac (vn)—see ORCHESTRAS & ENSEMBLES Budapest String Quartet
Gorokhov, Leonid (vc)
Haydn, J.:Con 1 Vc, w. R. Martynov (cnd), St. Petersburg State SO, St. Petersburg Soloists
  Audiophile Classics ▲ 101.023
Haydn, J.:Con 2 Vc, w. R. Martynov (cnd), St. Petersburg State SO, St. Petersburg Soloists
  Audiophile Classics ▲ 101.023
Prokofiev, S.:Son Vc, w. Alexander Melnikov (pno) *(rec 1995)* Supraphon ▲ SUP 3243
Shostakovich, D.:Son Vc, w. Alexander Melnikov (pno) *(rec 1995)* Supraphon ▲ SUP 3243
Stravinsky, I.:Suite italienne Vc, w. Alexander Melnikov (pno) *(rec 1995)* Supraphon ▲ SUP 3243

Gorsch, Achim (pno)
Kagel, M.:Nah und Fern, w. Andreas Adam (tpt), Marco Blaauw (tpt), Markus Stockhausen (tpt), Arie Abbenes (car), M. Kagel (cnd) Montaigne ▲ MO 782062

Goršek, Bojan (pno)
Satie, E.:Pno Music (comp)—Valse-ballet, Op. 62; Fant.-valse; 4 Ogives; 3 Sarabandes; 3 Gymnopédies; Gnossiennes Nos. 1-5; Première pensée Rose + Croix; Le Fils des étoiles
  Audiophile Classics ▲ 101.014 [DDD]
Satie, E.:Pno Music (comp)—Sonneries de la Rose + Croix; 4 Préludes; Uspud "Ballet Chrétien en 3 Actes"; Danses Gothiques; Prélude de La Porte héroïque du ciel
  Audiophile Classics ▲ 101.015 [DDD]

Gortler, Daniel (pno)
Dvořák, A.:Sonatina Vn, w. Yossi Arnheim (fl) Meridian ▲ MER 84320 [DDD]
Reinecke, C.:Son Fl, w. Yossi Arnheim (fl) Meridian ▲ MER 84320 [DDD]
Schubert, Franz:Intro & Vars Fl on "Trockne Blumen", w. Yossi Arnheim (fl)
  Meridian ▲ MER 84320 [DDD]

Goryachev, Vitalii (db)
Ustvolskaya, G.:Composition 2, w. Igo Propischin (db), Leonid Kolosov (db), Vladimir Vulih (db), Vyacheslav Kovalenko (db), Alexei Peresipkin (db), Dmitrii Sokolov (db), Vladimir Nefedov (db), Valerii Javnertchik (perc), Galina Sandovskaya (pno), O. Malov (cnd) *(rec St. Petersburg Radio House, Jan. 1994)* Megadisc ▲ 7867

Gosling, Stephen (pno)
Tower, J.:Black Topaz, w. Patricia Spencer (fl), Laura Flax (cl), Chris Gekker (tpt), Mike Powell (trbn), Jonathan Haas (perc), Deborah Moore (perc) *(rec American Academy of Arts & Letters, New York City, Sept. 26-28, 1994)* New World ▲ 80470-2

Gosselin, René (db)
Tremblay, G.:Aubes—or Initial, w. Robert Cram (fl), Pierre Béluse (perc)
  Centrediscs ▲ CMC 5094 [DDD]

Gothóni, Ralf (pno)
Brahms, J.:Ernste Gesänge, w. J. Hynninen (bar) [G] Ondine ▲ ODE 738-2 [DDD]
Brahms, J.:Qt 1 Pno, w. Peter Csaba (vn), Matti Hirvikangas (va), Frans Helmerson (vc)
  Ondine ▲ ODE 843
Brahms, J.:Qt 3 Pno, w. Peter Csaba (vn), Matti Hirvikangas (va), Frans Helmerson (vc)
  Ondine ▲ ODE 843
Brahms, J.:Romanzen aus Tieck's *Magelone*, w. W. Grönroos (bar) *(rec Nacka Aula, Nacka Sweden, July 26-27, 1976)* BIS ▲ CD 70 [AAD]
Brahms, J.:Romanzen aus Tieck's *Magelone*, w. J. Hynninen (bar) [G] Ondine ▲ ODE 755-2 [DDD]
Britten, B.:Con Pno, w. O. Kamu (cnd), Helsingborg SO Ondine ▲ ODE 825 [DDD]
Collan, K.:Songs, w. Jorma Hynninen (bar), Pentti Koskimies (pno)—Ihr Bildnis; Erster Verlust; To Emma; At the Burn-beating; Old Man Hurtti; On the Shores of Lake Roine
  Finlandia ▲ FIN 500282 [ADD]
Haydn, J.:Concertino Hpd, Finlandia Sinfonietta Ondine ▲ ODE 732-2 [DDD]
Haydn, J.:Con Hpd, Obs, Hns & Strs, H.XVIII/11, Finlandia Sinfonietta Ondine ▲ ODE 732-2 [DDD]
Haydn, J.:Con Org, Vn & Strs, H.XVIII/6, w. Péter Csaba (vn), Kuhmo Virtuosi Ondine ODE 810
Janáček, L.:On an Overgrown Path Ondine ▲ ODE 753-2 [DDD]
Kilpinen, Y.:Songs, w. J. Hynninen (bar)—Hans Fritz von Zwehl Songs; Lakeus; Lieder un den Tod; Spielmannslieder [G] *(rec 1/91)* Ondine ▲ ODE 772-2 [DDD]
Kuula, T.:Songs, w. Jorma Hynninen (bar), Pentti Koskimies (pno)—Beat, My Heart; Ave Maria, Op. 23/2; Fate; Night on the Moor Finlandia ▲ FIN 500282 [ADD]
Mahler, G.:Qt Pno [comp Schnittke], w. Mark Lubotsky (vn), Matti Hirvikangas (va), Martti Rousi (vc)
  Ondine ▲ ODE 840 [DDD]
Mendelssohn, F.:Con in d Vn, Pno & Strs, w. P. Csaba (vn), Kuhmo Virtuosi Ondine ▲ ODE 810 [DDD]
Merikanto, O.:Music of, w. Eeva-Jiisa Saarinen (mez), Jorma Hynninen (bar), Sauli Tiilikainen (bar), Kaija Saikkettu (at), Erkki Rautio (vc), Pertti Eerola (pno), Raija Kerppo (pno), Izumi Tateno (pno), Tauno Satomaa (cnd), Candomino Choir—Summer Evening (waltz); Valse lente; Romance; On the Highest Tree-Top; Annina; Bye, Bye Lullabye; The Weeping Flute; At Sea; Hey My Heart; Where Rustling Birches Bend; Play Softly, the Tune of Mourning; Fairy Tale by the Fireside; Idyll; Scherzo, Op. 6/4; O Dost Thou Remember That Hymn; Lade Ladoga; Why Do I Sing; The Thunderbird; The Happy Ones; Summer Evening's Idyll Finlandia ▲ FIN 500432 [AAD/DDD]
Mozart, W.A.:Qts Pno, w. Munich String Trio Calig ▲ CAL 50 897 [DDD]
Mussorgsky, M.:Pictures at an Exhibition Ondine ▲ ODE 753-2 [DDD]
Mussorgsky, M.:Songs & Dances, w. M. Talvela (bass) Finlandia ▲ 4509-95846-2 [ADD]
Nummi, S.:Songs, Margaret Haverinen (sop) [Songs of the Western Palace, Autumn days, et al.], Matti Juhani Pipponen (ten) [Mountain shepherd, Songs from a deserted place, et al.], Jorma Hynninen (bar) [From spring roads, et al.] BIS ▲ CD 279
Nummi, S.:Wilderness, w. Jorma Hynninen (bar) *(rec Studio BIS, Djursholm, Sweden, May 18-19, 1984)*
  BIS ▲ CD 207 [AAD/DDD]
Rachmaninoff, S.:Songs, w. M. Talvela (bass)—A Dream, Op. 8/5; The harvest of Sorrow, Op. 4/5; Night is Mournful, Op. 26/12; Oh, Never Sing to Me Again, Op. 4/4; Christ Is Risen, Op. 26/6
  Finlandia ▲ 4509-95846-2 [ADD]
Rangström, T.:Ur kung Eriks visor, w. Walton Grönroos (bar) *(rec Nacka Aula, Nacka, Sweden, July 26-27, 1976)* BIS ▲ CD 43 [AAD]
Rautavaara, E.:Con 1 Pno, w. M. Pommer (cnd), Leipzig RSO Ondine ▲ ODE 757-2 [DDD]
Rautavaara, E.:Con 2 Pno, w. J.-P. Saraste (cnd), Bavarian RSO Ondine ▲ ODE 800
Schnittke, A.:Suite in the Old Style, w. M. Lubotsky (vn) Ondine ▲ ODE 763-2 [DDD]
Schubert, Franz:Adagio & Rondo concertante Vn, w. Munich String Trio Ondine ▲ ODE 734 [DDD]
Schubert, Franz:Fant Pno, D.760, "Wandererfantasie" Ondine ▲ ODE 734 [DDD]
Schubert, Franz:German Dances Pno, D.783 Ondine ▲ ODE 718 [DDD]
Schubert, Franz:Qnt Pno, D.667, w. E. Laine (db), Munich String Trio Ondine ▲ ODE 763-2 [DDD]
Schubert, Franz:Die Schöne Müllerin, w. J. Hynninen (bar) Ondine ▲ ODE 719-2 [DDD]
Schubert, Franz:Son Pno, D.537 Ondine ▲ ODE 797 [DDD]
Schubert, Franz:Son Pno, D.840 Ondine ▲ ODE 797 [DDD]
Schubert, Franz:Son Pno, D.845 Ondine ▲ ODE 734 [DDD]
Schubert, Franz:Son Pno, D.960 Ondine ▲ ODE 718 [DDD]
Schubert, Franz:Son Vn, D.574, w. A. Chumachenco (vn) Ondine ▲ ODE 746-2 [DDD]
Schubert, Franz:Sonatinas Vn, w. A. Chumachenco (vn) Ondine ▲ ODE 746-2 [DDD]
Schubert, Franz:Winterreise, w. M. Talvela (bass) [G] BIS ▲ CD 253 [DDD]
Schumann, R.:Dichterliebe, w. W. Grönroos (bar) *(rec 1977)* BIS ▲ CD 92 [AAD]
Schumann, R.:Dichterliebe, w. J. Hynninen (bar) Ondine ▲ ODE 738-2 [DDD]
Schumann, R.:Liederkreis, op. 24, w. W. Grönroos (bar) *(rec 1977)* BIS ▲ CD 92 [AAD]
Segerstam, L.:3 Moments Painting, w. H. Segerstam (vn) BIS ▲ CD 84 [AAD]
Sibelius, J.:Pno Music—3 Lyric Pieces, Op. 41; Barcarola, Op. 24/10; 5 Pieces, Op. 75; Bagatelles, Op. 34; 5 Esquisses, Op. 114; Valse Triste [arr. Sibelius]; Finlandia [arr. Sibelius]
  Ondine ▲ ODE 847 [DDD]
Sibelius, J.:Songs, w. Walton Grönroos (bar)—Diamond on the March Snow, Op. 36/6; The Young Huntsman, Op. 13/7; Astray, Op. 17/4; Sunrise, Op. 38/3; Romeo, Op. 61/4 *(rec Nacka Aula, Nacka, Sweden, July 26-27, 1976)* BIS ▲ CD 43 [AAD]

Gothóni, Ralf (pno)

Gothóni, Ralf (pno) (cont.)
Sibelius, J.:Songs, w. J. Hynninen (bar)—7 Songs, Op. 13; 6 Songs, Op. 50; 2 Songs from Shakespeare's *Twelfth Night*, Op. 60; 8 Songs, Op. 57; Kaiutar; Norden
  Finlandia ▲ 4509-95848-2 [ADD]
Strauss, R.:Qt Pno, w. Mark Lubotsky (vn), Matti Hirvikangas (va), Martti Rousi (vc)
  Ondine ▲ ODE 840 [DDD]
Strauss, R.:Songs, w. B. Hendricks (sop)—22 songs
  EMI Classics ▲ CDC 54381
Stravinsky, I.:The Firebird (arr piano)
  Ondine ▲ ODE 753-2 [DDD]
Wolf, H.:Mörike-Lieder (sels), w. Jorma Hynninen (bar), Pentti Koskimies (pno)
  Finlandia ▲ FIN 500282 [ADD]

Gotlieb, Jay (pno)
Messiaen, O.:Harawi, w. Yumi Nara (sop)
  Adda ▲ ADD 581139 [DDD]

Gotkovsky, Ivar (pno)—see also ORCHESTRAS & ENSEMBLES Artaria Trio
Beethoven, L. van:Sons Vn (comp), w. N. Gotkovsky (vn)
  Pyramid 3-▲ PYR 13490/92 [AAD]
Brahms, J.:Sons Vn (comp), w. N. Gotkovsky (vn)
  Pyramid ▲ PYR 13487
Haydn, J.:Sons Pno—Nos. 30,33,47,53 & 58
  Pyramid ▲ PYR 13488
Kabalevsky, D.:Preludes Pno, Op. 38 (rec Provo, Utah, Mar 1993)
  Pyramid ▲ 13514 [DDD]
Prokofiev, S.:Son 1 Vn, w. N. Gotkovsky (vn)
  Pyramid 4-▲ PYR 13496 [DDD]
Schoenberg, A.:Phantasy Vn, w. N. Gotkovsky (vn)
  Pyramid ▲ PYR 13496 [DDD]
Schubert, Franz:Son Vn, D.574, w. Nell Gotkovsky (vn)
  Pyramid ▲ PYR 13506 [DDD]
Schubert, Franz:Sonatinas Vn, w. Nell Gotkovsky (vn)
  Pyramid ▲ PYR 13506 [DDD]
Stravinsky, I.:Duo Concertant, w. N. Gotkovsky (vn)
  Pyramid ▲ PYR 13496 [DDD]
Webern, A.:Pieces Vn, w. N. Gotkovsky (vn)
  Pyramid ▲ PYR 13496 [DDD]

Gotkovsky, Nell (vn)—see also ORCHESTRAS & ENSEMBLES Artaria Trio
Bartók, B.:Con 1 Vn, w. C. Gerhardt (cnd), National PO London
  Pyramid ▲ PYR 13486
Bartók, B.:Con 2 Vn, w. C. Gerhardt (cnd), National PO London
  Pyramid ▲ PYR 13486
Beethoven, L. van:Con Vn, Op. 61, w. V. Yampolsky (cnd), Sofia PO
  Pyramid ▲ PYR 13499 [DDD]
Beethoven, L. van:Sons Vn (comp), w. I. Gotkovsky (pno)
  Pyramid 3-▲ PYR 13490/92 [AAD]
Berg, A.:Con Vn, w. V. Yampolsky (cnd), Sofia PO
  Pyramid ▲ PYR 13499 [DDD]
Brahms, J.:Sons Vn (comp), w. I. Gotkovsky (pno)
  Pyramid ▲ PYR 13487
Prokofiev, S.:Son solo Vn, Op. 115
  Pyramid ▲ PYR 13496 [DDD]
Prokofiev, S.:Son 1 Vn, w. I. Gotkovsky (pno)
  Pyramid ▲ PYR 13496 [DDD]
Schoenberg, A.:Phantasy Vn, w. I. Gotkovsky (pno)
  Pyramid ▲ PYR 13496 [DDD]
Schubert, Franz:Son Vn, D.574, w. Ivar Gotkovsky (pno)
  Pyramid ▲ PYR 13506 [DDD]
Schubert, Franz:Sonatinas Vn, w. Ivar Gotkovsky (pno)
  Pyramid ▲ PYR 13506 [DDD]
Shostakovich, D.:Con 1 Vn, w. V. Kazandjiev (cnd), Bulgarian National RSO
  Pyramid ▲ PYR 13493
Shostakovich, D.:Con 2 Vn, w. V. Kazandjiev (cnd), Bulgarian National RSO
  Pyramid ▲ PYR 13493
Stravinsky, I.:Duo Concertant, w. I. Gotkovsky (pno)
  Pyramid ▲ PYR 13496 [DDD]
Webern, A.:Pieces Vn, w. I. Gotkovsky (pno)
  Pyramid ▲ PYR 13496 [DDD]

Götting, Tobias (org)
Duruflé, M.:Requiem, w. C. Guber (mez), P. Sefcik (bar), C. O. Beyer (vc), H. Hennig (cnd), Kammerorchester, Hanover Youth Choir
  Ars Musici ▲ AM 1098-2 [DDD]
Kodály, Z.:Pange lingua, w. Heinz Hennig (cnd), Hanover Boys' Choir
  Ars Musici ▲ 1129 [DDD]
Liszt, F.:Missa choralis, w. Heinz Hennig (cnd), Hanover Boys' Choir
  Ars Musici ▲ 1129 [DDD]
Vierne, L.:Messe solennelle, w. C. Guber (mez), P. Sefcik (bar), H. Hennig (cnd), Hanover CO, Hanover Youth Choir
  Ars Musici ▲ AM 1098-2 [DDD]
Widor, C.M.:Mass, w. Heinz Hennig (cnd), Hanover Boys' Choir
  Ars Musici ▲ 1129 [DDD]

Gottlieb, Marc (vn)—see ORCHESTRAS & ENSEMBLES Claremont String Quartet

Gottlieb, Danny (perc)
Bartók, B.:Son for 2 Pnos, w. G. Kalish (pno), L. Luvisi (pno), R. Fitz (perc) (rec Feb. 1, 1993)
  Delos ▲ DE 3151 [DDD]
Brasil, w. Stoltzman, Richard (cl), Gary Burton (vib), Eddie Gomez (db)
  RCA Victor ▲ 60708-2-RC [DDD] ■ 60708-4-RC (CrO2)

Gottlieb, F. (pno)
Schubert, Franz:Intro & Vars Fl on "Tröckne Blumen", w. S. Stadler (fl) (violin & piano)
  Art & Electronics ▲ AED 10478 [DDD]
Schumann, R.:Son 1 Vn, w. S. Stadler (vn)
  Art & Electronics ▲ AED 10478 [DDD]
Strauss, R.:Son Vn, w. S. Stadler (vn)
  Art & Electronics ▲ AED 10478 [DDD]

Gottlieb, G. (vc)—see ORCHESTRAS & ENSEMBLES Amelite Consortium

Gottlieb, Gordon (perc)
Rolnick, N.B.:Ever-Livin' Rhythm
  O.O. Discs ▲ OO 8 [ADD]
Siegmeister, E.:Sextet Brass, w. American Brass Quintet
  Premier ("Composer" series) ▲ PRCD 1010 [ADD]

Gottlieb, Gordon (timp)
Crumb, G.:An Idyll for the Misbegotten, w. Z. Mueller (fl), B. Herman (perc), S. Paysen (perc)
  New World ▲ NW 357-2
Wuorinen, C.:Variations Bn, w. Donald MacCourt (bn), Susan Jolles (hp)
  New World ▲ 80517-2

Gottlieb, Jay (pno)
Kolb, B.:Appello
  CRI ▲ CD 576 [ADD]

Gottlieb, Karen (hp)
Harrison, L.:La Koro Sutro, w. William Winant (gamelan cnd), Agnes Sauerbeck (org), P. Brett (cnd), Univ of California at Berkeley Chamber Chorus (Esperanto)
  New Albion ▲ NA 015 [ADD];

Gottraux, F. (vn)—see also ORCHESTRAS & ENSEMBLES Sine Nomine String Quartet
Balissat, J.:Vars (7), w. P. Genet, N. Pache (va), M. Jaermann (vc), R. Birnstigl (db), F. Rapin (cl), F. Schmocker (bn), M. Veillon (hn), J. Balissat (pno)
  Grammont ▲ CTSP 17-2 [ADD]

Götzel, Peter (va)—see ORCHESTRAS & ENSEMBLES Vienna Ring Ensemble

Götzel, Peter (vn)—see ORCHESTRAS & ENSEMBLES Vienna Ring Ensemble

Gouat, Simone (pno)
Fauré, G.:La bonne chanson, w. Renée Doria (sop), Berthe Monmart (sop), Pierre Mollet (bar)
  Accord ▲ ACD 204262 [AAD]
Fauré, G.:La Chanson d'Eve, w. Renée Doria (sop), Berthe Monmart (sop), Pierre Mollet (bar)
  Accord ▲ ACD 204262 [AAD]
Fauré, G.:L'Horizon chimérique, w. Renée Doria (sop), Berthe Monmart (sop), Pierre Mollet (bar)
  Accord ▲ ACD 204262 [AAD]
Fauré, G.:Le Jardin clos, w. Renée Doria (sop), Berthe Monmart (sop), Pierre Mollet (bar)
  Accord ▲ ACD 204262 [AAD]
Fauré, G.:Songs, w. Renée Doria (sop), Berthe Monmart (sop), Pierre Mollet (bar)—Chanson du pêcheur; Lydia; Tristesse; Au bord de l'eau; Puisqu'ici bas; Automne; Poême d'un jour; Les berceaux; Le secret; Aurore; Les roses d'ispahan; Nocturne; Clair de lune; Spleen; En prière; Mandoline; Green; En sourdine; A Clymène; C'est l'extase; Pleurs d'or; Arpège; Le parfum impérissable; Soir; Dans la forêt de septembre; Le don silencieux; Chanson
  Accord ▲ ACD 204602 [AAD]

Goude, Jean-Phillippe (syn programming/drums/gtr)
D.W.W., w. Richard Pinhas (syns/gtr), Patrick Gauthier (syns/pno/drums), Bernard Paganotti (bass gtr), Alain Bellaich (synthesized gtr)
  Cuneiform ▲ Rune 40

Goude, Jean-Phillippe (syn)
Iceland, w. Richard Pinhas (syns/gtr), François Auger (perc)
  Cuneiform ▲ Rune 44X

Goude, Jean-Phillippe (syn/perc)
L'Ethique, w. Richard Pinhas (syns/gtr), Gilles Deleuze (voc), G. Grunblatt (syn), Patrick Gauthier (syn/bass), Bernard Paganotti (bass), François Auger (drums), Clément Bailly (drums)
  Cuneiform ▲ Rune 36X

Gough, Helen (baroque vc)
A Banquet of Voices:Music for Mulitple Choirs, w. Cambridge Singers [cnd:John Rutter], W. Hunt (violone), M. Warshall (chamber org) (rec London, Feb. 1993)
  Collegium ▲ COLCD 123

Gough, Orlando (kbd)
Gough, O.:Currulao, w. Beverly Davison (vn), Roger Heaton (cl), Bruce Nockles (tpt), John Pigneguy (hn), David Stewart (trbn), Tracey Goldsmith (acc), Paul Clarvis (perc) (rec London, 1995)
  Catalyst ▲ 0902-668332-2 [DDD]
Gough, O.:Late, w. Roger Heaton (cl), Melinda Maxwell (ob), Smith String Quartet (rec London, 1995)
  Catalyst ▲ 0902-668332-2 [DDD]

Gough, Orlando (kbd) (cont.)
Gough, O.:Saeta, w. Pepe de la Matrona (voc), Bruce Nockles (tpt), Michael Thompson (hn), John Pigneguy (hn), David Purser (trbn) (rec London, 1995)
  Catalyst ▲ 0902-668332-2 [DDD]

Gough, Rachel (bn)
Debussy, C.:Chamber Music, w. William Bennett (fl), David Campbell (cl), James Campbell (cl), Nicholas Daniel (ob), Robert Makell (hn), Richard Watkins (hn), Robin Kennard (hn), Simon Haram (sax), Ieuan Jones (hp), Clifford Benson (pno), Julius Drake (pno), John York (pno), Roger Tapping (va)—Rapsodie for Eng hn; Syrinx; Première rapsodie; Son for Fl, Va & Hp; Le petit nègre; Petite pièce; Rapsodie for Sax (rec All Saints' Church, East Finchley, London, Jan 12-20, 1994)
  Cala 2-▲ CACD 1017 [DDD]
Poulenc, F.:Chamber Music, w. Peter Sidhom (bar), William Bennett (fl), David Campbell (cl), James Campbell (cl), Nicholas Daniel (ob), Richard Watkins (hn), Peter Carter (vn), Chris West (db), Ieuan Jones (hp), Clifford Benson (pno), Julius Drake (pno), John York (pno)—Son for Ob; L'invitation au château; Villanelle; Son 2 Cls; Trio; Sxt; Son for Cl & Bn; Rapsodie nègre; Son for Cl; Mouvements perpétuels; Son for Fl (rec All Saints' Church, East Finchley, London, Jan 12-20, 1994)
  Cala 2-▲ CACD 1018 [DDD]
Saint-Saëns, C.:Chamber Music, w. W. Bennett (fl), D. Campbell (cl), J. Campbell (cl), N. Daniel (ob), R. Makell (hn), R. Watkins (hn), R. Kennard (bn), S. Haram (sax), I. Jones (hp), C. Benson (pno), J. Drake (pno), J. York (pno), R. Tapping (va)—Odelette, Op. 162; Son for Cl, Op. 167; Feuillet d'album, Op. 81; Son for Bn, Op. 168; Caprice on Danish & Russian Airs, Op. 79; Son for Ob, Op. 166; Romance in Db, Op. 37; Tarantelle, Op. 6 (rec All Saints' Church, East Finchley, London, Jan 12-20, 1994)
  Cala 2-▲ CACD 1017 [DDD]

Gould, Clio (vn)
Knussen, O.:"...upon one note", w. Michael Collins (cl), Paul Silverthorne (va), Christopher van Kampen (vc), John Constable (pno) (rec Henry Wood Hall & All Hallows Gospel Oak, London, Oct & Dec 1995)
  Deutsche Grammophon ▲ 449 572-2 [DDD]

Gould, Glenn (hpd)
Bach, J.S.:Preludes & Fugues Hpd—Fugues, BWV 952, 953 & 961; Preludes, BWV 924-928, 930 & 902A; Preludes & Fugues in d, BWV 900; in a, BWV 895; in d, BWV 899; Prelude & Fughetta in G, BWV 902
  Sony Classical 2-▲ SM2K 52597
Bach, J.S.:Preludes Hpd, BWV 933-38, "Little Preludes"
  Sony Classical 2-▲ SM2K 52597
Bach, J.S.:Sons Vn, w. Y. Menuhin (vn)—BWV 1017 (rec Oct 25-26, 1965)
  Sony Classical ▲ SMK 52688 [ADD]

Gould, Glenn (kbd)
Sweelinck, J.P.:Kbd Music—Fantasia in d (rec Apr. 23-24, 1964)
  Sony Classical ▲ SMK 52589 [ADD]

Gould, Glenn (org)
Bach, J.S.:The Art of the Fugue (sels)—Contrapunctus Nos. 1-9 (rec 1962)
  CBS 2-▲ M2K 42270 [AAD]

Gould, Glenn (pno)
Bach, J.S.:Cons Hpd, BWV 1052-1058, w. V. Golschmann (cnd), Columbia SO [Nos. 2-5 & 7], L. Bernstein (cnd), Columbia SO [No. 1] (rec 1957-69)
  Sony Classical ("Glenn Gould Edition" series) 2-▲ SM2K 52591 [ADD]
Bach, J.S.:Con 1 Hpd, w. L. Slovák (cnd), Leningrad Conservatory Academic SO (rec 1957)
  CBS 2-▲ M2K 42270 (m) [AAD]
Bach, J.S.:Con 1 Hpd, w. D. Mitropoulos (cnd), Royal Concertgebouw Orch (rec live, Salzburg, Oct 10, 1958)
  Memories 2-▲ HR 4415/16 (m) [ADD]
Bach, J.S.:Con 1 Hpd, w. L. Slovák (cnd), Leningrad Conservatory Academic SO (rec May 18, 1957)
  Sony Classical ▲ SMK 52686 [ADD]
Bach, J.S.:Con 1 Hpd, w. L. Bernstein (cnd), Columbia SO (rec 1957)
  CBS ▲ MYK 38524 (m) [ADD] ■ MYT 38524
Bach, J.S.:Con 1 Hpd, w. E. MacMillan (cnd), Toronto SO
  CBC ("Perspective" series) ▲ PSCD 2005 (m) [ADD]
Bach, J.S.:Con 2 Hpd, w. V. Golschmann (cnd), Columbia SO (rec 1969)
  CBS 2-▲ M2K 42270 [AAD]
Bach, J.S.:Con 3 Hpd, w. V. Golschmann (cnd), Columbia SO (rec 1967)
  CBS 2-▲ M2K 42270 [AAD]
Bach, J.S.:Con 4 Hpd, w. V. Golschmann (cnd), Columbia SO (rec stereo, 1959)
  CBS ▲ MYK 38524 [ADD] ■ MYT 38524
Bach, J.S.:Con 4 Hpd, w. V. Golschmann (cnd), Columbia SO (rec 1969)
  CBS 2-▲ M2K 42270 [AAD]
Bach, J.S.:Con 5 Hpd, w. V. Golschmann (cnd), Columbia SO (rec 1958)
  CBS 2-▲ M2K 42270 [AAD]
Bach, J.S.:Con 5 Hpd, w. V. Golschmann (cnd), Columbia SO (rec stereo, 1958)
  CBS ▲ MYK 38524 [ADD] ■ MYT 38524
Bach, J.S.:Con 7 Hpd, w. V. Golschmann (cnd), Columbia SO (rec 1967)
  CBS 2-▲ M2K 42270 [AAD]
Bach, J.S.:English Suites
  CBS 2-▲ M2K 42268 [AAD]
Bach, J.S.:French Suites
  CBS ▲ MK 42267 [AAD]
Bach, J.S.:Goldberg Vars (rec June 21, 1954)
  CBC ("Perspective" series) ▲ PSCD 2007 (m) [ADD]
Bach, J.S.:Goldberg Vars (rec 1981)
  CBS ▲ MK 37779 [DDD] ■ IMT 37779 (D)
Bach, J.S.:Goldberg Vars (rec 1955)
  CBS ▲ MYK 38479 (m) [ADD] ■ MYT 38479 (m)
Bach, J.S.:Goldberg Vars
  Sony Classical □ MM 52619
Bach, J.S.:Goldberg Vars (rec 1955)
  Sony Classical ("Glenn Gould Edition" series) ▲ SMK 52685 [ADD]
Bach, J.S.:Goldberg Vars (rec Aug 25, 1957)
  Sony Classical ▲ SMK 52685 [ADD]
Bach, J.S.:Inventions (30) Hpd
  CBS ■ MPT 38766
Bach, J.S.:Inventions (30) Hpd
  CBS 2-▲ M2K 42269 [AD]
Bach, J.S.:Inventions (30) Hpd—3-Part, BWV 788-800 (rec May 7, 1957)
  Sony Classical ▲ SMK 52685 [ADD]
Bach, J.S.:Italian Con
  CBC ("Perspective" series) ▲ PSCD 2005 (m) [ADD]
Bach, J.S.:Italian Con (rec 1959)
  CBS 2-▲ M2K 42269 [AAD]
Bach, J.S.:Italian Con
  Odyssey ▲ MBK 42527 ♦ YT 42527
Bach, J.S.:Partitas Hpd, BWV 825-830—No. 5 in G, BWV 829
  CBC ("Perspective" series) ▲ PSCD 2005 (m) [ADD]
Bach, J.S.:Partitas Hpd, BWV 825-830
  CBS 2-▲ M2K 42402 [AAD]
Bach, J.S.:Partitas Hpd, BWV 825-830—BWV 828
  Odyssey ▲ MBK 42527 ♦ YT 42527
Bach, J.S.:Partitas Hpd, BWV 825-830
  Sony Classical 2-▲ SM2K 52597
Bach, J.S.:Partita Hpd, BWV 831, "Ov nach französischer Art"
  CBS 2-▲ M2K 42268 [AAD]
Bach, J.S.:Preludes & Fugues Hpd—14
  CBS ■ MT 35891
Bach, J.S.:Preludes & Fugues Hpd—Preludes, Fugues & Fughettas, BWV 895, 899, 900, 902, 902a, 924-928, 930, 952, 953, 961
  CBS 2-▲ M2K 42402 [AAD]
Bach, J.S.:Preludes Hpd, BWV 933-38, "Little Preludes"
  CBS 2-▲ M2K 42402 [AAD]
Bach, J.S.:Preludes Hpd, BWV 933-38, "Little Preludes"
  CBS ■ MT 35891
Bach, J.S.:Sinfs—15 3-Part Inventions, BWV 787-801
  CBC ("Perspective" series) ▲ PSCD 2005 (m) [ADD]
Bach, J.S.:Sons VI, BWV 1027-1029, w. L. Rose (vc)
  CBS 2-▲ M2K 42414 [AAD]
Bach, J.S.:Sons Vn, w. J. Laredo (vn)—BWV 1014-1019
  CBS 2-▲ M2K 42414 [AAD]
Bach, J.S.:Toccatas Hpd, BWV 910-16, BWV 910,912 & 913
  CBS ■ MT 35144
Bach, J.S.:Toccatas Hpd, BWV 910-16—BWV 914
  Odyssey ▲ MBK 42527 ♦ YT 42527
Bach, J.S.:Toccatas Hpd, BWV 910-16
  CBS 2-▲ M2K 42269 [AAD]
Bach, J.S.:Toccatas Hpd, BWV 910-16 (rec 1963-1979)
  Sony Classical 2-▲ SM2K 52612 [ADD]
Bach, J.S.:Das wohltemperierte Klavier—BWV 878 & 883 (rec Feb 18, 1970)
  Sony Classical ▲ SMK 52590 [ADD]
Bach, J.S.:Das wohltemperierte Klavier—Préludes & Fugues, BWV 876, 878, 883 & 891 [from book 2] (rec CBC Concert Hall, Oct 21, 1952 & Feb 28, 19)
  CBC ("Perspective" series) ▲ PSCD 2007 (m) [ADD]
Bach, J.S.:Das wohltemperierte Klavier
  CBS 3-▲ M3K 42266 [AAD] 4-■ M4T 42042
Bach, J.S.:Das wohltemperierte Klavier—Book 1 (rec 1962-65)
  Sony Classical 2-▲ SM2K 52600 [ADD]
Bach, J.S.:Das wohltemperierte Klavier—Book 2 (rec 1966-71)
  Sony Classical 2-▲ SM2K 52603 [ADD]
Bach, J.S.:Das wohltemperierte Klavier—[Book 2] Fugues in E & f# (rec 1957)
  Sony Classical ("Glenn Gould Edition" series) ▲ SMK 52594 (m) [ADD]

---

586   ▲ = CD   ♦ = Enhanced CD   △ = MD   ■ = Cassette Tape   □ = DCC

Gould, Glenn (pno) (cont.)
Beethoven, L. van:Bagatelles (24)—Opp. 33 & 126 *(rec 1974)* Sony Classical ("Glenn Gould Edition" series) 2-▲ SM2K 52646 [ADD]
Beethoven, L. van:Con 1 Pno, w. V. Golschmann (cnd), Columbia SO CBS 3-▲ M3K 39036
Beethoven, L. van:Con 2 Pno, w. G.L. Jochum (cnd), Swedish RSO BIS 2-▲ CD 323/24
Beethoven, L. van:Con 2 Pno, w. L. Slovák (cnd), Leningrad Conservatory Academic SO CBS 3-▲ M3K 39036
Beethoven, L. van:Con 2 Pno, w. L. Slovák (cnd), Leningrad Conservatory Academic SO *(rec May 18., 1957)* Sony Classical ▲ SMK 52686 [ADD]
Beethoven, L. van:Con 3 Pno, w. H. von Karajan (cnd), Berlin PO *(rec live, Berlin 1957)* Memories 2-▲ HR 4415/16 (m) [ADD]
Beethoven, L. van:Con 3 Pno, w. H. Unger (cnd), CBC Vancouver SO CBC ("Perspective" series) ▲ PSCD 2004 (m) [ADD]
Beethoven, L. van:Con 5 Pno, "Emperor", w. K. Ančerl (cnd), Toronto SO Sony Classical ("Glen Gould Edition" series) ▲ SMK 52687
Beethoven, L. van:Sons Pno (comp)—Nos. 15–18 & 23; plus various Bagatelles & Variations Odyssey 3-▲ MB3K 45822
Beethoven, L. van:Sons Pno (comp)—Nos. 1, 2, 3, 5, 6, 7, 8, 9, 10, 13 & 14 *(rec between 1964 & 1981)* Sony Classical 3-▲ SM3K 52638 [ADD]
Beethoven, L. van:Sons Pno (comp)—Nos. 15, 16, 17, 18, 23, 30, 31 & 32 *(rec between 1956 & 1979)* Sony Classical 3-▲ SM3K 52642 [ADD]
Beethoven, L. van:Sons Pno (comp)—Nos. 1–3, 5–10 & 12–14 Odyssey 3-▲ MB3K 45821
Beethoven, L. van:Son 8 Pno, "Pathétique" CBS ■ MT 7413
Beethoven, L. van:Son 14 Pno, "Moonlight Son" CBS ■ MT 7413
Beethoven, L. van:Son 23 Pno, "Appassionata" CBS ■ MT 7413
Beethoven, L. van:Son 24 Pno Sony Classical ▲ SMK 52645
Beethoven, L. van:Son 29 Pno, "Hammerklavier" Sony Classical ▲ SMK 52645
Beethoven, L. van:Son 30 Pno CBS 3-▲ M3K 39036
Beethoven, L. van:Son 31 Pno BIS 2-▲ CD 323/24
Beethoven, L. van:Son 31 Pno CBS 3-▲ M3K 39036
Beethoven, L. van:Son 32 Pno CBS 3-▲ M3K 39036
Beethoven, L. van:Son 10 Vn, w. Y. Menuhin (vn) *(rec Oct. 25–26, 1965)* Sony Classical ▲ SMK 52688 [ADD]
Beethoven, L. van:Sym 5 [Liszt's solo piano trans.] *(rec 1967)* Sony Classical ("Glenn Gould Edition" series) ▲ SMK 52636 [ADD]
Beethoven, L. van:Sym 6, "Pastorale" [Liszt's solo piano trans.] *(rec 1968)* Sony Classical ("Glenn Gould Edition" series) ▲ SMK 52636 [ADD]
Beethoven, L. van:Vars on an Original Theme, Op. 34 *(rec 1967)* Sony Classical ("Glenn Gould Edition" series) 2-▲ SM2K 52646 [ADD]
Beethoven, L. van:Vars on an Original Theme, Op. 34 CBC ("Perspective" series) ▲ PSCD 2004 (m) [ADD]
Beethoven, L. van:Vars & Fugue Pno, Op. 35, "Eroica" CBC ("Perspective" series) ▲ PSCD 2004 (m) [ADD]
Beethoven, L. van:Vars & Fugue Pno, Op. 35, "Eroica" *(rec 1970)* Sony Classical ("Glenn Gould Edition" series) 2-▲ SM2K 52646 [ADD]
Beethoven, L. van:Vars Pno, WoO 80 *(rec 1966)* Sony Classical ("Glenn Gould Edition" series) 2-▲ SM2K 52646 [ADD]
Berg, A.:Son Pno BIS 2-▲ CD 323/24
Berg, A.:Son Pno *(rec Oct. 14, 1952)* CBC ("Perspective" series) ▲ PSCD 2008 (m) [ADD]
Berg, A.:Son Pno Sony Classical ("Glen Gould Edition" series) ▲ SMK 52661
Bizet, G.:Nocturne *(rec 1972)* Sony Classical ("Glenn Gould Edition" series) 2-▲ SM2K 52654 [ADD]
Bizet, G.:Vars chromatiques de concert *(rec 1971)* Sony Classical ("Glenn Gould Edition" series) 2-▲ SM2K 52654 [ADD]
Brahms, J.:Ballades, Op. 10—Nos. 1–4 CBS ▲ MK 37800 [DDD]
Brahms, J.:Qnt Pno, w. Montreal String Quartet Sony Classical ▲ SMK 52684
Brahms, J.:Rhaps Pno, Op. 79 *(rec 1982)* Odyssey 3-▲ MB3K 45828
Brahms, J.:Rhaps Pno, Op. 79 CBS ▲ MK 37800 [DDD]
Byrd, W.:Kbd Music—1st & 6th Pavan & Galliard; Hughe Ashton's Ground; A Voluntary; Sellinger's Round *(rec 1967 & 1971)* Sony Classical ▲ SMK 52589 [ADD]
Chopin, F.:Son Pno, Op. 58 Sony Classical ("Glen Gould Edition" series) 2-▲ SM2K 52622
Debussy, C.:Première rapsodie, w. James Campbell (cl) Sony Classical ("Glen Gould Edition" series) ▲ SMK 52661
Gibbons, O.:Kbd Music—Allemande; Lord of Salisbury Pavan & Galliard *(rec Aug. 1, 1968)* Sony Classical ▲ SMK 52589 [ADD]
Grieg, E.:Son Pno *(rec 1971)* Sony Classical ("Glenn Gould Edition" series) 2-▲ SM2K 52654 [ADD]
Handel, G.F.:Suites Hpd—H.426–429 *(rec Mar. 26, Apr. 30, May 1 &)* Sony Classical ▲ SMK 52590 [ADD]
Haydn, J.:Sons Pno—H.XVI/49 *(rec 1958)* Sony Classical ("Glenn Gould Edition" series) ▲ SMK 52626 [ADD]
Haydn, J.:Sons Pno—No. 59 CBS 3-▲ M3K 39036
Haydn, J.:Sons Pno—Nos. 56 & 58–62 CBS 2-▲ M2K 36947 [DDD]
Haydn, J.:Sons Pno—No. 49 in E♭ BIS 2-▲ CD 323/24
Haydn, J.:Sons Pno—in D, H.XVI/42; in C, H.XVI/48; in E♭, H.XVI/49; in C, H.XVI/50; in D, H.XVI/51; in E♭, H.XVI/52 *(rec 1980–1981)* Sony Classical 2-▲ SM2K 52623 [DDD]
Hétu, J.:Vars Pno *(rec 1967)* Sony Classical ("Glenn Gould Edition" series) ▲ SMK 52677 [ADD]
Hindemith, P.:Das Marienleben, w. Roxolana Roslak (sop) or Lois Marshall (sop) Sony Classical ("Glen Gould Edition" series) 2-▲ SM2K 52674
Hindemith, P.:Son Hn, w. M. Jones (hn) *(rec 1975)* Sony Classical ("Glenn Gould Edition" series) 2-▲ SM2K 52671 [ADD]
Hindemith, P.:Son Alto Hn, w. M. Jones (hn) *(rec 1976)* Sony Classical ("Glenn Gould Edition" series) 2-▲ SM2K 52671 [ADD]
Hindemith, P.:Son Trbn, w. H. C. Smith (trbn) *(rec 1976)* Sony Classical ("Glenn Gould Edition" series) 2-▲ SM2K 52671 [ADD]
Hindemith, P.:Son Tpt, w. G. Johnson (tpt) *(rec 1975)* Sony Classical ("Glenn Gould Edition" series) 2-▲ SM2K 52671 [ADD]
Hindemith, P.:Son Bass Tuba, w. Abe Torchinsky (tuba) *(rec 1975)* Sony Classical ("Glenn Gould Edition" series) 2-▲ SM2K 52671 [ADD]
Images Sony Classical 2-▲ SX2K 62588
Krenek, E.:Sons Pno—No. 3, Op. 92 Sony Classical ("Glen Gould Edition" series) ▲ SMK 52661
Krenek, E.:Songs, w. *(sop unknown)*—Wanderlied im Herbst Sony Classical ("Glen Gould Edition" series) 2-▲ SM2K 52674
Mendelssohn, F.:Lieder ohne Worte Pno Sony Classical ("Glen Gould Edition" series) 2-▲ SM2K 52622
Morawetz, O.:Fant Pno *(rec 1966)* Sony Classical ("Glenn Gould Edition" series) ▲ SMK 52677 [ADD]
Mozart, W.A.:Allegro & Andante & Rondo *(rec ca. 1972/73)* Odyssey 2-▲ MB2K 45613
Mozart, W.A.:Con 24 Pno, w. W. Susskind (cnd), CBC Vancouver SO *(rec 1961)* Sony Classical ("Glenn Gould Edition" series) ▲ SMK 52626 [ADD]
Mozart, W.A.:Con 24 Pno, w. G.L. Jochum (cnd), Swedish RSO BIS 2-▲ CD 323/24
Mozart, W.A.:Fant Pno, K.397 *(rec 1972)* Odyssey 2-▲ MB2K 45613
Mozart, W.A.:Prelude & Fugue Pno CBS 3-▲ M3K 39036
Mozart, W.A.:Prelude & Fugue Pno *(rec 1958)* Sony Classical ("Glenn Gould Edition" series) ▲ SMK 52626 [ADD]
Mozart, W.A.:Sons Pno—Nos. 1–10 *(rec 1967–70)* Odyssey 2-▲ MB2K 45612
Mozart, W.A.:Sons Pno—Nos. 11–17 *(rec 1965–74)* Odyssey 2-▲ MB2K 45613
Mozart, W.A.:Son 10 Pno *(rec 1958)* Sony Classical ("Glenn Gould Edition" series) ▲ SMK 52626 [ADD]
Mozart, W.A.:Son 10 Pno CBS 3-▲ M3K 39036
Pentland, B.:Ombres *(rec 1967)* Sony Classical ("Glenn Gould Edition" series) ▲ SMK 52677 [ADD]
Prokofiev, S.:Son 7 Pno *(rec live 1962; monophonic)* Memories 2-▲ HR 4415/16 (m) [ADD]

Gould, Glenn (pno) (cont.)
Prokofiev, S.:Visions fugitives Sony Classical ("Glen Gould Edition" series) 2-▲ SM2K 52622
Ravel, M.:La Valse Sony Classical ("Glen Gould Edition" series) ▲ SMK 52661
Schoenberg, A.:Con Pno, w. D. Mitropoulos (cnd), New York PO *(rec live, New York, 3/16/58)* Memories 2-▲ HR 4415/16 (m) [ADD]
Schoenberg, A.:Con Pno, w. J.-M. Beaudet (cnd), CBC Vancouver SO *(rec Dec. 21, 1953)* CBC ("Perspective" series) ▲ PSCD 2008 (m) [ADD]
Schoenberg, A.:Phantasy Vn, w. Y. Menuhin (vn) *(rec Oct. 25–26, 1965)* Sony Classical ▲ SMK 52688 [ADD]
Schoenberg, A.:Pieces Pno, Op. 11 *(rec Oct. 4, 1952)* CBC ("Perspective" series) ▲ PSCD 2008 (m) [ADD]
Schoenberg, A.:Songs, w. Ellen Faull (sop), Helen Vanni (mez), Donald Gramm (b-bar)—Zwei Gesange, Op. 1; Vier Lieder, Op. 2; Das Buch der hängenden Gärten; Sechs Lieder, Op. 3; Zwei Balladen, Op. 12; Drei Lieder, Op. 48; Zwei Lieder, Op. 14; Zwei Lieder, Op. Posth.; Acht Lieder, Op. 6 Sony Classical ("Glen Gould Edition" series) 2-▲ SM2K 52667
Schoenberg, A.:Suite Pno, Op. 25 *(rec Oct. 14, 1952)* CBC ("Perspective" series) ▲ PSCD 2008 (m) [ADD]
Schumann, R.:Qt Pno, Op. 47, w. Juilliard String Quartet members Sony Classical ▲ SMK 52684
Scriabin, A.:Pno Music (misc)—Preludes in C & in F; Feuillet d'album; Sons. Nos. 3 & 5; 2 Morceaux Sony Classical ("Glen Gould Edition" series) 2-▲ SM2K 52622
Sibelius, J.:Kyllikki *(rec 1977)* Sony Classical ("Glenn Gould Edition" series) 2-▲ SM2K 52654 [ADD]
Sibelius, J.:Sonatinas Pno *(rec 1976–77)* Sony Classical ("Glenn Gould Edition" series) 2-▲ SM2K 52654 [ADD]
Strauss, R.:Burleske, w. V. Golschmann (cnd), Toronto SO Sony Classical ("Glen Gould Edition" series) ▲ SMK 52687
Strauss, R.:Burleske, *(orch unknown)* *(rec live, Canada, 1960)* Memories 2-▲ HR 4415/16 (m) [ADD]
Strauss, R.:Enoch Arden, w. C. Rains (nar) *(rec 1961)* Sony Classical ("Glenn Gould Edition" series) 2-▲ SM2K 52657 [ADD]
Strauss, R.:4 Last Songs, w. Roxolana Roslak (sop), Lois Marshall (sop)—Beim Schlafengehen Sony Classical ("Glen Gould Edition" series) 2-▲ SM2K 52674
Strauss, R.:Pieces Pno CBS ▲ MK 38659 [DDD]
Strauss, R.:Pieces Pno *(rec 1979)* Sony Classical ("Glenn Gould Edition" series) 2-▲ SM2K 52657 [ADD]
Strauss, R.:Son Pno CBS ▲ MK 38659 [DDD]
Strauss, R.:Son Pno *(rec 1982)* Sony Classical ("Glenn Gould Edition" series) 2-▲ SM2K 52657 [ADD]
Strauss, R.:Songs, w. Roxolana Roslak (sop), Lois Marshall (sop)—Songs for Orphelia, Op. 67/1–3 Sony Classical ("Glen Gould Edition" series) 2-▲ SM2K 52674
Strauss, R.:Songs, w. E. Schwarzkopf (sop)—Ophelia Lieder [3 songs after Shakespeare], Op. 67, Nos. 1–3 [G] *(rec 1966)* Sony Classical ("Glenn Gould Edition" series) 2-▲ SM2K 52657 [ADD]
Thirty-Two Short Films about Glenn Gould Sony Classical ▲ SK 46686
Valen, F.:Son 2 Pno *(rec 1972)* Sony Classical ("Glenn Gould Edition") ▲ SMK 52677 [ADD]
Wagner, R.:Götterdämmerung (sels) [arr. Gould]—Dawn; Siegfried's Rhine Journey *(rec May 14, 1973)* Sony Classical ▲ SMK 52650 [ADD]
Wagner, R.:Die Meistersinger von Nürnberg (prelude/act 1) [arr. Gould] *(rec June 30, 1973)* Sony Classical ▲ SMK 52650 [ADD]
Webern, A.:Con Fl, w. B. Brott (cnd), *(ensemble unknown)* Sony Classical ("Glen Gould Edition" series) ▲ SMK 52661
Webern, A.:Vars Pno *(rec Jan. 9, 1954)* CBC ("Perspective" series) ▲ PSCD 2008 (m) [ADD]
Webern, A.:Vars Pno Sony Classical ("Glen Gould Edition" series) ▲ SMK 52661
The Young Glenn Gould 1947–53 Mastersound ▲ MST 24 [ADD]

Gould, Jean (b cl)—see ORCHESTRAS & ENSEMBLES Kalamos Clarinet Quartet

Gould, Morton (pno)
The Little Drummer Boy:Christmas Favorites, w. New Philharmonia Orch, Boston Pops Orch [cnd:Arthur Fiedler], et al. RCA Victor ▲ 09026-61837-2 ■ 09026-61837-4

Goutet, Elise (hpd)
Geoffroy, J.-N.:Pieces de clavecin (sels)—Tombeau in c; Suites in c, a, F & a; Allemande [La rêveuse in F]; Passacaille in a; Chaconne sur 4 notes in D Accord ▲ ACD 205262 [DDD]

Goutou, Francis (vc)—see also ORCHESTRAS & ENSEMBLES Menuhin Festival Piano Quartet
Turina, J.:Escena andaluza, w. P. Coletti (va), F. Rieger (pno), N. Chastain (vn), C. Busch (vn), A. B. Deutschler (va) *(rec May 25–28, 1993)* Claves ▲ CD 9403 [DDD]

Govi, G. (vn)
Milesi, P.:Modi 1, w. D. Cassamagnaghi (fl), F. Pomarico (ob), A. Bianchi (cl), L. Dosso (bn), D. Tellini (vn), M. Ravasio (va), S. Righini (vc), P. Rizzi (db), C. Vignani (hpd), J. Scully (perc), P. Milesi (cnd) Cuneiform ▲ RUNE 63

Govier, Geoffrey (pno)
Dussek, J.L.:Sons Pno—in C, Op. 9/2; in g, Op. 10/2; in B♭, G & c, Op. 35/1–3 Olympia ▲ OLY 430 [DDD]
Haydn, J.:Fant Pno Olympia ▲ OLY 390 [DDD]
Haydn, J.:Sons Pno—Nos. 33, 52 & 59 Olympia ▲ OLY 390 [DDD]
Haydn, J.:Son Pno, H.XVII/6, "Andante with Vars"—Vars. only Olympia ▲ OLY 390 [DDD]

Gowen, Rhonda (cl)
Hoffman, D.:Son Cl, w. Julie Schwartz (pno) Meyer ▲ MC 0108
Hoffman, D.:Trio Cl, Vn & Pno, w. Kathleen Clothier-Angeroth (vn), Julie Schwartz (pno) Meyer ▲ MC 0108

Gower, Robert (org)
Whitlock, P.:Reflections ASV ▲ ASV 957
Whitlock, P.:Rustic Cavalry March ASV ▲ ASV 957
Whitlock, P.:Short Pieces Org ASV ▲ ASV 957
Whitlock, P.:Son Org ASV ▲ ASV 957

Gower, Robert (pno)
Voices & Light, w. [cnd:Jo-Michael Scheibe], Univ of Miami Chorale Albany ▲ TROY 215 [DDD]

Goy, Jean-Paul (ob)
Bellini, V.:Con in E♭ Ob, w. A. Jordan (cnd), Lausanne CO Gallo ▲ CD 129
Benjamin, A.:Con Ob Strs, w. A. Jordan (cnd), Lausanne CO Gallo ▲ CD 129
Cimarosa, D.:Con in G Ob, w. A. Jordan (cnd), Lausanne CO Gallo ▲ CD 129
Marcello, A.:Con Ob & Strs, w. A. Jordan (cnd), Lausanne CO Gallo ▲ CD 129
Rogg, L.:Music of, w. M. Larrieu (fl), T. Friedli (cl), M. Kameda (pno), J.-J. Balet (pno), L. Rogg (syn), M. Kameda (piano) *(8 Etudes [1990]; Jazzic J.-J. Balet (piano) (Cinq petites pièces lyriques [1952]; Trois pièces [1952]; Valse [1952]; Cinq petites géométries [1958]),* Kameda, Balet *(Face à face for 2 Pianos [1987]),* J.-P. Goy, L. Rogg *(Pièce for Oboe & Synthesizer [1991]),* T. Friedli *(Pièce for solo Clarinet [1986]); M. Larrieu (Suite for solo Flute [1991])* BIS ▲ CD 546 [DDD]
Vivaldi, A.:Cons Ob, w. A. Jordan (cnd), Lausanne CO—RV.454 Gallo ▲ CD 129

Graber, J. (hn)
Gottschalk, A.:Section for 4 Hns, w. T. Bacon (hn), J. Wilson (hn), N. Goodearl (hn), R. Brown (timp) Summit ▲ DCD 135 [DDD]

Graber, M. (pno)
Zappa, E.A.:Hydra Son, w. P. Call (fl) CRS ▲ CD 9257

Grabinger, P. (pno)
Dessau, P.:Suite Sax, w. Jürgen Demmler (a sax) Bayer ▲ CD 100100 [DDD]
Huang, A.:Chinese Rhap 3, w. Jürgen Demmler (sax) Bayer ▲ CD 100100 [DDD]
Jolivet, A.:Fantaisie-Impromptu, w. Jürgen Demmler (a sax) Bayer ▲ CD 100100 [DDD]
Mayer, Wolf:Inner Voices, w. Jürgen Demmler (a sax) Bayer ▲ CD 100100 [DDD]
Rosenthal, M.:Sax-Marmalade, w. Jürgen Demmler (a sax) Bayer ▲ CD 100100 [DDD]

Grabinger, Werner (perc)
Bartók, B.:Son for 2 Pnos, w. M. Bergmann (pno), H. Rosbaud (pno), E. Seiler (perc) *(rec live, 1953)* Music & Arts ▲ CD 627 (m) [AAD]

Grabois, Daniel (hn)—see ORCHESTRAS & ENSEMBLES Meridian Arts Ensemble, Continuum Chamber Ensemble

Grabowski, Thomas (hpd)
Mozart, W.A.:Clemenza, w. L. Popp (sop), R. Ziesack (sop), A. Murray (mez), D. Ziegler (mez), P. Langridge (ten), L. Polgar (bass), C. Hermann (vc), N. Harnoncourt (cnd), Zurich Opera Orch, Zurich Opera House Chorus — Teldec 2-▲ 90857-2

Grace, Susan (pno)
Alwyn, W.:Son Cl, w. Charles West (cl) *(rec Concert Hall, Virginia Commonwealth University, Richmond, VA)* — Klavier ▲ KCD 11073 [DDD]
Delmas, M.:Fant italienne, w. Charles West (cl) *(rec Concert Hall, Virginia Commonwealth Univ, Richmond, VA)* — Klavier ▲ KCD 11073 [DDD]
Faith, R.:Sea Pieces (2), w. Charles West (cl) *(rec Concert Hall, Virginia Commonwealth Univ, Richmond, VA)* — Klavier ▲ KCD 11073 [DDD]
Genzmer, H.:Sonatine Cl & Pno, w. Charles West (cl) *(rec Concert Hall, Virginia Commonwealth Univ, Richmond, VA)* — Klavier ▲ KCD 11073 [DDD]
Lutoslawski, W.:Dance Preludes Cl & Pno, w. Charles West (cl) *(rec Concert Hall, Virginia Commonwealth Univ, Richmond, VA)* — Klavier ▲ KCD 11073 [DDD]
Muczynski, R.:Time Pieces, w. Charles West (cl) *(rec Concert Hall, Virginia Commonwealth Univ, Richmond, VA)* — Klavier ▲ KCD 11073 [DDD]

Grach, Eduard (vn)
Brahms, J.:Con Vn, w. K. Kondrashin (cnd), Moscow State SO *(rec 1961)* — Rondo Grammofon ▲ RCD 16211 [AAD]

Grady, John (org)
Christmas with Renata Scotto at St. Patrick's Cathedral, w. Renata Scotto (sop), Lorenzo Anselmi (cnd), St. Patrick's Cathedral Choir *(rec St. Patrick's Cathedral, New York City, June 1981)* — VAI Audio ▲ VAIA 1013 [AAD]
Christmas with the Canadian Brass, w. Canadian Brass — RCA Gold Seal ▲ RCD1-4132 ■ ARK1-4132

Graef, Friedemann (sax)—see ORCHESTRAS & ENSEMBLES Berlin Saxophone Quartet

Graef, Richard (fl)
Ives, C.:Son 2 Pno, w. E. Blackwood (pno) — Cedille ▲ CDR 90000 005 [DDD]

Graf, Anna-Katharina (fl)—see also ORCHESTRAS & ENSEMBLES Les Joueurs de Flute
Keller, A.:Der enthüllte Stern, w. D. Fueter (sop), K. Graf (sop), L. Pellerin (ob), E. Schmid (cl), U. Walker (vn), C. Schiller (va), P. Demenga (vc), P. Hug-Rutti (hp), F. Eberle (dr) [G] — Grammont ▲ CTSP 19-2 [ADD]
Keller, A.:Ewiger Augenblick, w. D. Fueter (sop), K. Graf (sop), E. Schmid (cl), D. Isler (cel), P. Hug-Rutti (hp), U. Walker (vn), P. Demenga (vc) [G] — Grammont ▲ CTSP 19-2 [ADD]
Lehmann, H.U.:Kammermusik, w. K. Graf (sop), E. Schmid (cl), W. Grimmer (vc), I. Nakamura (perc) — Jecklin ▲ JD 689
Magnard, A.:Qnt Pno, w. Christoph Keller (pno), Roman Schmid (ob), Elmar Schmid (cl), Jiri Flieger (bn) — Accord ▲ ACD 200102 [DDD]

Graf, Enrique (pno)
Bach, J.S.:English Suites—BWV 807 — Centaur ▲ CRC 2125
Bach, J.S.:French Suites—BWV 817 — Centaur ▲ CRC 2125
Bach, J.S.:Partitas Hpd, BWV 825-830—BWV 826 — Centaur ▲ CRC 2125
Beethoven, L. van:Con 1 Pno, w. D. Burkh (cnd), Janáček PO — Centaur ▲ CRC 2175 [DDD]
Beethoven, L. van:Con 2 Pno, w. D. Burkh (cnd), Janáček PO — Centaur ▲ CRC 2175 [DDD]
Grieg, E.:Con Pno, Op. 16, w. K. Won (cnd), Moscow PO *(rec Great Hall of Moscow Radio Union, Dec 1994)* — Intersound ▲ 3539
Liszt, F.:Son Pno, w. K. Won (cnd), Moscow PO *(rec Great Hall of Moscow Radio Union, Dec 1994)* — Intersound ▲ 3539

Graf, Hans (pno)
Saxophone Colors, w. Eugène Rousseau (sax) — Delos ▲ DE 1007 [AAD]

Graf, Maria (hp)
Lutoslawski, W.:Con Ob, w. E. Brunner (ob), L. Zagrosek (cnd), Bamberg SO — Koch Schwann ▲ CD 311065 [DDD]
Mozart, W.A.:Con Fl Hp, w. I. Grafenauer (fl), N. Marriner (cnd), Academy of St. Martin in the Fields — Philips ▲ 422339-2 [DDD]
Recital, w. Graf, Maria (hp) — Philips ▲ 432103-2 PH [DDD]
Reichardt, J.F.:Lieder, w. D. Fischer-Dieskau (bar)—20 lieder, most set to texts by Goethe or Schiller [G] *(rec 1990)* — Orfeo ▲ 245921 [DDD]
Strauss, R.:Duet-Concertino, w. E. Brunner (cl), M. Turkovič (bn), L. Zagrosek (cnd), Bamberg SO — Koch Schwann ▲ CD 311065 [DDD]

Graf, Peter-Lukas (fl)
Bach, J.S.:Arias, w. Kathrin Graf (sop), Raffaele Altwegg (vc), Michio Kobayashi (hpd/pno)—Meine Seele sie vergnügt [from Cantata No. 204, Von der Vergnügsamkeit] *(rec Protestant Chuch Seon, 1976)* — Claves ("Favor Collection" series) ▲ CD 604 [ADD]
Bach, J.S.:A Musical Offering, w. Hansheinz Schneeberger (vn), et al., J.E. Dähler (cnd) — Claves ▲ CD 198 [ADD]
Bach, J.S.:Partita Fl, BWV 1013, w. H. Barbé (hpd), J. Koch (vl) [trans. for additional instrs.] — Jecklin-Disco 2-▲ JEC CD 4400 [ADD]
Bach, J.S.:Sons Fl, BWV 1030-35, w. H. Barbé (hpd), J. Koch (vl) [trans. for additional instr.] — Jecklin-Disco 2-▲ JEC CD 4400 [ADD]
Bach, J.S.:Sons Vl, BWV 1027-1029 [arr. for solo flute] *(rec 1967)* — Jecklin-Disco 2-▲ JEC CD 4400 [ADD]
Boccherini, L.:Con in D Fl [attrib.], w. R. Tschupp (cnd), Camerata Zurich *(rec 1968)* — Jecklin-Disco ▲ JD 506-2 [ADD]
Burkhard, W.:Serenade Fl, Op. 71/3, w. K. Ragossnig (gtr) — Claves ▲ CD 408 [ADD]
Carulli, F.:Serenade Fl & Gtr, w. K. Ragossnig (gtr) — Claves ▲ CD 408 [ADD]
Cimarosa, D.:Con for 2 Fls, w. G. Guéneux (fl), R. Tschupp (cnd), Zurich Camerata *(rec 1968)* — Jecklin-Disco ▲ JD 506-2 [ADD]
Czerny, C.:Intro, Vars & Finale, w. Zsuzsanna Sirokay (pno) — Jecklin ▲ JEC 577 [ADD]
Czerny, C.:Rondoletto concertant, w. Zsuzsanna Sirokay (pno) — Jecklin ▲ JEC 577 [ADD]
Debussy, C.:Son Fl, w. Serge Collot (trb), Ursula Holliger (hp) [arr for fl, alt & hp] — Claves ▲ CD 50280 [ADD]
Devienne, F.:Con 2 Fl, w. R. Leppard (cnd), English CO *(rec EMI Studio London, 1975)* — Claves ▲ CD 50501 [ADD]
Donizetti, G.:Larghetto & Allegro, w. Ursula Holliger (hp) [arr for fl & hp] *(rec Kirche Seon, 1977)* — Claves ▲ CD 50708 [ADD]
Fauré, G.:Fant Fl, w. Ursula Holliger (hp) [arr for fl & hp] *(rec Kirche Seon, 1977)* — Claves ▲ CD 50708 [ADD]
Giuliani, M.:Grand Duo Concertant, Op. 25, w. K. Ragossnig (gtr) — Claves ▲ CD 408 [ADD]
Gluck, C.W.:Con Fl, w. R. Tschupp (cnd), Zurich Camerata *(rec 1968)* — Jecklin-Disco ▲ JD 506-2 [ADD]
Handel, G.F.:Arias, w. K. Graf (sop), R.Altwegg (vc), M. Kobayashi (hpd/pno)—Meine Seele hört im Sehen [from 9 German Arias] *(rec Protestant Chuch Seon, 1976)* — Claves ("Favor Collection" series) ▲ CD 604 [ADD]
Handel, G.F.:Sons Fl, w. Manfred Sax (bn), Jörg Ewald Dähler (hpd)—4 Sons—Op. 1, Nos. 1a,1b,5 & 9 — Claves ▲ CD 238 [ADD]
Handel, G.F.:Sons Fl, "Halle Sons", w. Manfred Sax (bn), J.E. Dähler (cnd) — Claves ▲ CD 238 [ADD]
Hindemith, P.:Son Fl, w. B. Glemser (pno) *(rec Dec. 9-12, 1992)* — Claves ▲ CD 9307 [DDD]
Ibert, J.:Con Fl, w. R. Leppard (cnd), English CO *(rec EMI Studio London, 1975)* — Claves ▲ CD 50501 [ADD]
Ibert, J.:Entracte, w. K. Ragossnig (gtr) — Claves ▲ CD 408 [ADD]
Joueurs de Flûte, w. Michio Kobayashi (pno) *(rec 1973)* — Claves ▲ CD 500704 [ADD]
Krommer, F.:Concertino Fl, Op. 65, w. H. Holliger (cnd), English CO — Claves ▲ CD 8203 [DDD]
Krommer, F.:Con Fl, Op. 30, w. H. Holliger (cnd), English CO — Claves ▲ CD 8203 [DDD]
Krommer, F.:Con Ob, Op. 52, w. H. Holliger (cnd), English CO — Claves ▲ CD 8203 [DDD]

Graf, Peter-Lukas (fl) (cont.)
Krommer, F.:Sinf Concertante, w. H. R. Stalder (cl), T. Wicky (vn), Capriccio Ensemble — Tudor ▲ 757 [DDD]
Kuhlau, F.:Intro & Rondo on "Ahl quand il gèle" from *Le Colporteur*, w. Zsuzsanna Sirokay (pno) *(rec 1982)* — Jecklin ▲ JEC 577 [ADD]
Lauber, J.:Medieval Dances, w. Ursula Holliger (hp) *(rec Kirche Seon, 1977)* — Claves ▲ CD 50708 [ADD]
Martin, F.:Ballade Fl, w. B. Glemser (pno) *(rec Dec. 9-12, 1992)* — Claves ▲ CD 9307 [DDD]
Martin, F.:Chants de Noël, w. Kathrin Graf (sop), Michio Kobayashi (pno) *(rec Protestant Chuch Seon, 1976)* — Claves ("Favor Collection" series) ▲ CD 604 [ADD]
Mieg, P.:Morceau élégant, w. Ursula Holliger (hp) *(rec 1976)* — Jecklin ▲ JS 314-2 [DDD]
Milhaud, D.:Sonatina Fl, w. B. Glemser (pno) *(rec Dec. 9-12, 1992)* — Claves ▲ CD 9307 [DDD]
Molique, W.B.:Intro, Andante & Polonaise, w. Zsuzsanna Sirokay (pno) — Jecklin ▲ JEC 577 [ADD]
Mozart, W.A.:Con Fl Hp, w. Ursula Holliger (hp), P.-L. Graf (cnd), Lausanne CO *(rec EMI Studio London, 1970)* — Claves ▲ CD 50208 [ADD]
Paganini, N.:Vars di bravura, w. Ursula Holliger (hp) [arr for fl & hp] *(rec Kirche Seon, 1977)* — Claves ▲ CD 50708 [ADD]
Peter-Lukas Graf — Claves ▲ CD 8005 [ADD]
Prokofiev, S.:Son Fl, w. B. Glemser (pno) *(rec Dec. 9-12, 1992)* — Claves ▲ CD 9307 [DDD]
Rameau, J.P.:Music of, w. Kathrin Graf (sop), Alexander van Wijnkoop (vn), Michio Kobayashi (hpd/pno)—Rossignols amoureux *(rec Protestant Chuch Seon, 1976)* — Claves ("Favor Collection" series) ▲ CD 604 [ADD]
Ravel, M.:Chansons madécasses, w. Kathrin Graf (sop), Raffaele Altwegg (vc), Michio Kobayashi (hpd/pno) *(rec Protestant Chuch Seon, 1976)* — Claves ("Favor Collection" series) ▲ CD 604 [ADD]
Ravel, M.:Intro & Allegro, w. Ursula Holliger (hp), Hans Rudolf Stalder (cl), Zurich CO — Claves ▲ CD 50280 [ADD]
Ravel, M.:Pavane pour une infante défunte, w. K. Ragossnig (gtr) — Claves ▲ CD 408 [ADD]
Ravel, M.:Pièce en forme de Habanera, w. K. Ragossnig (gtr) — Claves ▲ CD 408 [ADD]
Reger, M.:Serenades Fl Vn Va, w. Sandor Vegh (vn), Rainer Moog (va) *(rec Kirche Reutigen, Dec 1980)* — Claves ▲ CD 508104 [ADD]
Reinecke, C.:Son Fl, w. B. Glemser (pno) *(rec Dec. 9-12, 1992)* — Claves ▲ CD 9307 [DDD]
Ries, F.:Fant on themes from "Mosè in Egitto", w. Zsuzsanna Sirokay (pno) — Jecklin ▲ JEC 577 [ADD]
Rossini, G.:Andante con variazioni Fl, w. Ursula Holliger (hp) *(rec Kirche Seon, 1977)* — Claves ▲ CD 50708 [ADD]
Roussel, A.:Poèmes de Ronsard, w. Kathrin Graf (sop) *(rec Protestant Chuch Seon, 1976)* — Claves ("Favor Collection" series) ▲ CD 604 [ADD]
Scarlatti, A.:Solitudini amene, apriche collinette, w. Kathrin Graf (sop), Raffaele Altwegg (vc), Michio Kobayashi (hpd/pno) *(rec Protestant Chuch Seon, 1976)* — Claves ("Favor Collection" series) ▲ CD 604 [ADD]
Spohr, L.:Potpourri 2, w. Ursula Holliger (hp) [arr for fl & hp] *(rec Kirche Seon, 1977)* — Claves ▲ CD 50708 [ADD]
Spohr, L.:Son Vn Hp, Op. 113, w. Ursula Holliger (hp) [arr for fl & hp] *(rec Kirche Seon, 1977)* — Claves ▲ CD 50708 [ADD]
Works for Solo Flute *(rec Johanneskirche, 1973)* — Claves ▲ CD 508005 [ADD]

Graf, V. (pno)
Martin, F.:Petite sym concertante, w. C. Mathieu (hp), C. Rütti (hpd), E. de Stoutz (cnd), Zurich CO — Gallo ▲ CD 713 [ADD]

Grafenauer, Irena (fl)
Boehm, T.:Compositions Fl, w. A. Adorján (fl), W. Bennett (fl), U. Burkhard (fl), M. Debost (fl), A. Nicolet (fl), B. Weber (pno)—works for Flute & Piano *(Andante pastorale, from Souvenir des Alpes; Elegie in A♭, Op. 47; Fantaisie sur un air allemand, Op. 22; Fantaisie in A♭ on a Theme by Schubert; Grande Polonaise in D, Op. 16; Variations on Nel cor più non mi sento)*; works for Flute Ensemble *(Duettino in D, Pièce facile in C & Romanza in F [Nos. 66-68]; plus a six-flute ensemble performance of the 2nd movt. from Boismortier's Flute Concerto No. 1 in G)* *(rec live, Cuvilliés Theater, Munich 11/27/81)* — Orfeo ▲ 018821 [DDD]
Mozart, W.A.:Andante Fl, K.315/285a, w. N. Marriner (cnd), Academy of St. Martin in the Fields — Philips ▲ 422339-2 [DDD]
Mozart, W.A.:Con Fl, K.313, w. N. Marriner (cnd), Academy of St. Martin in the Fields — Philips ▲ 422339-2 [DDD]
Mozart, W.A.:Con Fl Hp, w. M. Graf (hp), N. Marriner (cnd), Academy of St. Martin in the Fields — Philips ▲ 422339-2 [DDD]
Mozart, W.A.:Qts Fl, w. Gidon Kremer (vn), Veronika Hagen (va), Clemens Hagen (vc) — Sony Classical ▲ SK 66240

Graff, S. (pno)
Kirby, P.:Son Tpt, w. R. Lee (tpt) *(rec Brooklyn College, Apr. 1993 & May 1994)* — Capstone ▲ CPS 8620 [DDD]

Graffman, Gary (pno)
Prokofiev, S.:Con 1 Pno, w. G. Szell (cnd), Cleveland Orch — CBS ▲ MYK 37806 [ADD] ■ MYT 37806
Prokofiev, S.:Con 3 Pno, w. G. Szell (cnd), Cleveland Orch — CBS ▲ MYK 37806 [ADD] ■ MYT 37806
Prokofiev, S.:Son 3 Pno — CBS ▲ MYK 37806 [ADD] ■ MYT 37806
Rachmaninoff, S.:Con 2 Pno, w. L. Bernstein (cnd), New York PO — CBS ▲ MLK 39437 ■ MT 39437
Rachmaninoff, S.:Con 2 Pno, w. L. Bernstein (cnd), New York PO — CBS ■ MT 31813
Rachmaninoff, S.:Con 2 Pno, w. L. Bernstein (cnd), New York PO — CBS ▲ MYK 36722 ■ MYT 36722
Rachmaninoff, S.:Con 2 Pno, w. L. Bernstein (cnd), New York PO *(rec May 26, 1964)* — Sony Classical ▲ SMK 47630 [ADD]
Rachmaninoff, S.:Music of, w. Philippe Entremont (pno), E. Ormandy (cnd), Philadelphia Orch — CBS ▲ MLK 39437 ■ MT 39437
Rachmaninoff, S.:Preludes Pno, Opp 23 & 32—Op. 23, No. 5 & Op. 32, Nos. 8 & 12 — CBS ▲ MYK 37263 [ADD] ■ MYT 37263
Rachmaninoff, S.:Rhapsody on a Theme of Paganini, w. L. Bernstein (cnd), New York PO — CBS ■ MT 31813
Rachmaninoff, S.:Rhapsody on a Theme of Paganini, w. L. Bernstein (cnd), New York PO — CBS ▲ MYK 36722 ■ MYT 36722
Rachmaninoff, S.:Rhapsody on a Theme of Paganini, w. L. Bernstein (cnd), New York PO *(rec 1964)* — Sony Classical ("Bernstein:The Royal Edition" series) ▲ SMK 47571 [ADD]
Rorem, N.:Con Pno Left Hand, w. A. Previn (cnd), Curtis Institute of Music SO — New World ▲ 80445-2
Saint-Saëns, C.:Carnival of the Animals, w. Lillie (nar), Katchen (pno), S. Henderson (cnd), London SO [E] — London ■ 411650-4
Tchaikovsky, P.:Con 1 Pno, w. G. Szell (cnd), Cleveland Orch — CBS ▲ MYK 37263 [ADD] ■ MYT 37263

Graham, Janice (vn)
Delius, F.:Son 1 Vn & Pno, w. Israela Margalit (pno) — EMI Classics ("Anglo-American Chamber Music" series) ▲ CDC 55399
Delius, F.:Son 2 Vn & Pno, w. Israela Margalit (pno) — EMI Classics ("Anglo-American Chamber Music" series) ▲ CDC 55399
Elgar, E.:Qnt Pno Strs, w. Israela Margalit (pno), Alexander Barantschick (vn), Paul Silverthorne (va), Moray Welsh (vc) — EMI Classics ("Anglo-American Chamber Music" series) ▲ CDC 55403
Walton, W.:Qt Pno, w. *(pianist unknown)*, Paul Silverthorne (va), Moray Welsh (vc) — EMI Classics ("Anglo-American Chamber Music" series) ▲ CDC 55404
Walton, W.:Son Vn & Pno, w. *(pianist unknown)* — EMI Classics ("Anglo-American Chamber Music" series) ▲ CDC 55404

Graham, Joanna (bn)
Vivaldi, A.:Cons Bn, w. L. Friedman (cnd), St. Andrew Camerata—RV.495 — Omega ▲ OCD 1012 [DDD]
Vivaldi, A.:Cons Diverse Instrs, w. Ruth McDowall (cl), David Rix (ct), Deborah Davis (fl), Duke Dobing (fl), Tim Caister (hn), Stephen Stirling (hn), Christopher Hooker (ob), Helen McQueen (ob), Michael Meekes (tpt), Crispian Steele-Perkins (tpt), Nicholas Kraemer (hpd), N. Kraemer (cnd), London Sinfonietta—Cons. in F, RV.539; in C, RV.533; in D, RV.122; in C, RV.537; in C, RV.560; in F, RV.538; in G, RV.545 *(rec All Saints Church, East Finchley, Oct. 1994 & Jan. 1995)* — Naxos ("Vivaldi Collection" series) ▲ 8.553204 [DDD]

▲ = CD ♦ = Enhanced CD Δ = MD ■ = Cassette Tape □ = DCC

Graham, John (va)
Babbitt, M.:Composition Va, w. R. Black (pno) CRI ■ ACS 6016 (CrO2)
Bassett, L.:Sxt Vns, w. Gilbert Kalish (pno), Concord String Quartet *(rec Baltimore, MD, May 19, 1975* CRI ▲ CD 677 [ADD]
Bergsma, W.:Fantastic Vars on a Theme from Tristan, w. T. Muraco (pno) CRI ■ ACS 6018 (CrO2)
Ghent, E.:Entelechy, w. R. Black (pno) CRI ■ ACS 6016 (CrO2)
John Graham CRI ■ ACS 6017 (CrO2)
Persichetti, V.:Parable 16 CRI ■ ACS 6016 (CrO2)
Pollock, R.:Violament, w. Black (pno) CRI ■ ACS 6016 (CrO2)
Schiff, D.:Joycesketch II CRI ■ ACS 6017 (CrO2)
Shapey, R.:Evocation 3 Va, w. T. Muraco (pno) CRI ■ ACS 6016 (CrO2)
Shostakovich, D.:Son Va, w. T. Muraco (pno) CRI ■ ACS 6018 (CrO2)
Subotnick, M.:An Arsenal of Defense CRI ■ ACS 6017 (CrO2)
Viola Anthology, Vols. 1–3, w. Graham, John (va) CRI ■ ACS6016, 6017, 6018 (CrO2)
Wolpe, S.:Piece Va CRI ■ ACS 6017 (CrO2)
Zimmermann, B.A.:Son Va CRI ■ ACS 6017 (CrO2)

Graham, Robin (hn)
Beethoven, L. van:Qnt Pno, Ob, Cl, Hn & Bn, w. C. Rosenberger (pno), A. Vogel (ob), D. Shifrin (cl), K. Munday (bn) Delos ▲ DCD 3024 [DDD]
Mozart, W.A.:Qnt Pno, K.452, w. C. Rosenberger (pno), A. Vogel (ob), D. Shifrin (cl), K. Munday (bn) Delos ▲ DCD 3024 [DDD]

Grainger, Bruce (bn)
Boutry, R.:Interferences, w. Gail Niwa (pno) *(rec DePaul Univ. Concert Hall, Chicago, Sept 1992)* Centaur ▲ CRC 2244 [DDD]
Cascarino, R.:Son Bn, w. Gail Niwa (pno) *(rec DePaul Univ. Concert Hall, Chicago, Sept 1992)* Centaur ▲ CRC 2244 [DDD]
Elgar, E.:Romance Bn, w. Gary Stucka (vc), Gail Niwa (pno) *(rec DePaul Univ. Concert Hall, Chicago, Sept 1992)* Centaur ▲ CRC 2244 [DDD]
Etler, A.:Son Bn, w. Gail Niwa (pno) *(rec DePaul Univ. Concert Hall, Chicago, Sept 1992)* Centaur ▲ CRC 2244 [DDD]
Guillemant, B.:Son Bn, w. J. Fuller (db) Musical Arts Society ▲ CD 41592 [DDD] ■ CS 41592 (D)
Hindemith, P.:Son Bn, w. Gail Niwa (pno) *(rec DePaul Univ. Concert Hall, Chicago, Sept 1992)* Centaur ▲ CRC 2244 [DDD]
Mozart, W.A.:Duo Bn Vc, w. Gary Stucka (vc) *(rec DePaul Univ. Concert Hall, Chicago, Sept 1992)* Centaur ▲ CRC 2244 [DDD]
Saint-Saëns, C.:Son Bn, w. G. Niwa (pno) *(rec DePaul Univ. Concert Hall, Chicago, Sept 1992)* Centaur ▲ CRC 2244 [DDD]

Grainger, Percy (pno)
Bach, J.S.:Fant & Fugue Org, BWV 542 [trans. Liszt] Nimbus ("Grand Piano" series) ▲ NI 8808
Bach, J.S.:Music of, w. Harold Bauer (pno), Ignaz Friedman (pno), Myra Hess (pno), Harold Samuel (pno)—Toccata No. 3 in G; Toccata & Fugue in d for Org [trans Tausig]; Well-Tempered Clavier Book 1, Nos. 5 & 21; Chorale [from Cant 147; trans Bauer]; Chromatic Fant & Fugue [trans von Bülow]; 2-Part Inventions Nos. 1, 6 & 8; Fant & Fugue in g for Org [trans Liszt]; Toccata & Fugue in g; French Suite No. 6; Gigue [from Partita in B♭, Book 1, No. 1] [all pno rolls] Nimbus ("Grand Piano" series) ▲ NI 8808 [DDD]
Bach, J.S.:Org Music (misc) [trans. for piano]—Prelude & Fugue in a; Toccata & Fugue in d; Fant. & Fugue in g *(rec Oct 13 & 15, 1931)* Biddulph ▲ LHW 010 [ADD]
Brahms, J.:Son 3 Pno *(rec 1926 Columbia recording)* Biddulph ▲ LHW 008 [ADD]
Brahms, J.:Waltzes Pno, Op. 39—No. 15 in A♭ *(rec 1926)* Biddulph ▲ LHW 008 [ADD]
Byrd, W.:Kbd Music—Carman's Whistle [arr. Grainger] *(rec between 1908–48)* Pearl ▲ PEA 9013 [AAD]
Chopin, F.:Études (24)—in b, Op. 25/10 *(rec Oct. 13 & 15, 1931)* Biddulph ▲ LHW 010 [ADD]
Chopin, F.:Son Pno, Op. 35 *(rec Oct. 13 & 15, 1931)* Biddulph ▲ LHW 010 [ADD]
Chopin, F.:Son Pno, Op. 35 *(rec between 1908–48)* Pearl ▲ PEA 9013 [AAD]
Chopin, F.:Son Pno, Op. 58 *(rec Oct. 13 & 15, 1931)* Biddulph ▲ LHW 010 [ADD]
Chopin, F.:Son Pno, Op. 58 *(rec between 1908–48)* Pearl ▲ PEA 9013 [AAD]
Chopin, F.:Son Pno, Op. 58 Symposium ▲ SYM 1145
Grainger, P.:Pno Music (arrs, transcriptions & paraphrases), w. Lotta Mills Hough (pno)—Shepherd's Hey; Country Gardens; Sussex Mummers' Christmas Carol; Jutish Medley; Molly on the Shore; One More Day My John; Spoon River; The Warriors; Ramble [on love-duet from Der Rosenkavalier]; March-Jig; The Leprechaun's Dance; A Reel; Sheep & Goat Walkin' to the Pasture; Turkey in the Straw; Gay but Wistful; The Gum-suckers March; Zanzibar Boat-Song; Colonial Song; Walking Tune; Over the Hills & Far Away [all pno rolls] Nimbus ("Grand Piano" series) ▲ NI 8809 [DDD]
Percy Grainger Plays Pearl ▲ PEA 9957 (m) [AAD]
Schumann, R.:Fantasiestücke Pno, Op. 12—No. 3, "Warum" *(rec 1924 Columbia)* Biddulph ▲ LHW 008 [ADD]
Schumann, R.:Romances Pno *(rec between 1908–48)* Pearl ▲ PEA 9013 [AAD]
Schumann, R.:Son 2 Pno *(rec 1927 for Columbia)* Biddulph ▲ LHW 008 [ADD]
Schumann, R.:Son 2 Pno Nimbus ("Grand Piano" series) ▲ NI 8804
Schumann, R.:Son 2 Pno Pearl ▲ PEA 9957 (m) [AAD]
Schumann, R.:Sym Etudes *(rec 1928 for Columbia)* Biddulph ▲ LHW 008 [ADD]
Schumann, R.:Sym Etudes *(rec between 1908–48)* Pearl ▲ PEA 9013 [AAD]
Schumann, R.:Sym Etudes Nimbus ("Grand Piano" series) ▲ NI 8804
Stanford, C.V.:Irish Dances [arr. Grainger]—No. 1 *(rec between 1908–48)* Pearl ▲ PEA 9013 [AAD]

Gram, Lars (db)
Heyde, O.:Songs, w. Margrethe Heyde (sgr), Ole Heyde (sgr/gtr), Kirstine Heyde Dias (vn), Knud Erik Jørgensen (va)—44 songs from texts by Piet Hein Danica ▲ DCD 8175

Gramstrup, Helge (org)
Malling, O.:Paulus *(rec St. Markus church, Arhus, Oct 1995)* Marco Polo/Dacapo ▲ 8.224023 [DDD]
Malling, O.:Seven Last Words, w. Mogens Dahl (cnd), Jjyske Choir *(rec St. Markus church, Arhus, Oct 1995)* Marco Polo/Dacapo ▲ 8.224023 [DDD]

Granados, Daniel (cl)—see ORCHESTRAS & ENSEMBLES Quintet of the Americas

Granados, Enrique (pno)
Great Composers at the Keyboard, w. Camille Saint-Saëns (pno), Maurice Ravel (pno) Foné ▲ FON 90F14 [DDD]

Granados, Marco (fl)—see also ORCHESTRAS & ENSEMBLES Quintet of the Americas
Cohn, J.:Serenade, w. E. Kiesewetter (vn), J. Spitz (vc) *(rec Sept. 1992)* XLNT ▲ CD 18007 [DDD]
Gary Schocker:Flutist, w. Gary Schocker (fl), Dennis Helmrich (hpd), Ted Hoyle (vc) Chesky ▲ CD 46 [DDD]

Granat, Endre (vn)
Á. Egilsson:Contemplation, w. Richard Altenbach (vn), Janet Lakatos (va), Douglas Davis (vc), Árni Egilsson (db) Cambria ▲ CD 1033
Á. Egilsson:Get Down!, w. Richard Altenbach (vn), Janet Lakatos (va), Douglas Davis (vc), Árni Egilsson (db) Cambria ▲ CD 1033
Á. Egilsson:Is It?, w. Richard Altenbach (vn), Janet Lakatos (va), Douglas Davis (vc), Árni Egilsson (db) Cambria ▲ CD 1033
Á. Egilsson:What If?, w. Richard Altenbach (vn), Janet Lakatos (va), Douglas Davis (vc), Árni Egilsson (db) Cambria ▲ CD 1033
Á. Egilsson:Why?, w. Richard Altenbach (vn), Janet Lakatos (va), Douglas Davis (vc), Árni Egilsson (db) Cambria ▲ CD 1033

Granat, Tamara (pno)
Chopin, F.:Intro, Theme & Vars, w. Waldemar Malicki (pno)—Vars *(rec Warsaw Philharmonic Hall, June 27–30, 1994)* Canyon Classics ▲ CD 248

Granberg, Maria (hn)—see ORCHESTRAS & ENSEMBLES Sundsvall Wind Quartet

Granert, Nancy B. (org)
Alleluia! Sacred Choral Music in New England, w. Harvard Univ Choir [cnd:Murray Forbes Somerville] Northeastern ("Classical Arts" series) ▲ NOR 247

Granger, Lawrence (vc)
Barati, G.:Trio Cl, w. William Wohlmacher (cl), Stacy Phelps-Wetzel (vn) *(rec Emeryville Recording Company, Emeryville, CA, 1994)* Centaur ▲ CRC 2286 [DDD]
Lewis, P.S.:Little Trio, w. J. McKenzie (fl), M. Shapiro (pno) New Albion ▲ NA 060 [DDD]
Lewis, P.S.:Through the Mountain, w. M. Shapiro (pno) New Albion ▲ NA 060 [DDD]

Grant, Cameron (pno)—see also ORCHESTRAS & ENSEMBLES Leonardo Trio
Cohn, J.:Con da Camera, w. E. Kiesewetter (vn), Quintet of the Americas *(rec Sept. 1992)* XLNT ▲ CD 18007 [DDD]
King David's Lyre, w. Zina Schiff (vn) *(rec SUNY, Mar 7–8, 1995)* 4-Tay ▲ 4002

Grante, Carlo (pno)
Busoni, F.:Sonatina 6 Pno, w. C. Grante Altarus ▲ AIR 9098
Clementi, M.:Sons Pno—Op. 2/ 2, 4 & 6; Op. 7/1; Op. 24/2 Altarus ▲ CD 9101
Godowsky, L.:Studies (53) after Chopin's Etudes—Nos. 21–43 Altarus ▲ CD 9093
Godowsky, L.:Studies (53) after Chopin's Etudes Altarus ▲ CD 9092
Liszt, F.:Réminiscences de Don Juan Altarus ▲ AIR 9098
Liszt, F.:Réminiscences de Norma Altarus ▲ AIR 9098
Sorabji, K.S.:Pastiches—No. 2 [after the Habanera from Bizet's Carmen] Altarus ▲ AIR 9098

Grappelli, Stéphane (vn)
Anything Goes, w. Yo-Yo Ma (vc) CBS ▲ MK 45574 [DDD]
Just One of Those Things, w. Martin Taylor (gtr) EMI Classics ▲ CDM 69172

Grappelli, Stéphane (vn/pno)
Menuhin & Grappelli Play, w. Yehudi Menuhi (vn) EMI Classics ▲ CDM 69219
Menuhin & Grappelli Play Jalousie & Other Great Standards, w. Yehudi Menuhin (vn) EMI Classics ▲ CDM 69220

Gräsbeck, Manfred (vn)
Aho, K.:Con Vn, w. O. Vänskä (cnd), Lahti SO BIS ▲ CD 396 [DDD]
Aho, K.:Silence, w. O. Vänskä (cnd), Lahti SO BIS ▲ CD 396 [DDD]

Gräsle, Barbara (gtr)—see ORCHESTRAS & ENSEMBLES Duo Favori

Grassel, J. (elec gtr)
Foss, L.:Paradigm, w. J. Williams (perc), S. Basson (bn), R. Dagon (cl), L. Anderson (vn) *(rec 1989–90)* Koss Classics ▲ KC 1006 [DDD]

Grasser, Christophe (pno)
Chopin, F.:Songs Sop (comp), w. Y.-H. Choi (sop) [Pol] Quantum ▲ QM 6900 [DDD] ■ QM 1995 (D)
Herz, H.:Pno Music—Grande Fant, Op. 47; Rondo, Op. 37; Vars brillantes, Op. 77; Cavatine de Séminaris, Op. 68; Grande Fant sur des motifs de Sémiramide, Op. 130 Quantum ▲ QM 6928
Liszt, F.:Song Transcriptions—Chopin:6 Polish Songs, G.274 Quantum ▲ QM 6900 [DDD] ■ QM 1995 (D)

Grassman, Walter (dr)
Zawinul, J.:Stories of the Danube, w. Bruhan Ocal (voc/perc), Joe Zawinul (kbd), C. Richter (cnd), Brno State PO Philips ▲ 454143-2

Gratovich, Eugene (vn)
Baley, V.:Figments Titanic ▲ Ti 199 [DDD]
Blank, A.:Toccatina & Mixtures Titanic ▲ Ti 199 [DDD]
Flynn, G.:Fant Etudes (3) Titanic ▲ Ti 199 [DDD]
Shapey, R.:Etudes Vn Titanic ▲ Ti 199 [DDD]

Grau, Andreas (pno)
Stockhausen, K.:Mantra, w. Götz Schumacher (pno) Wergo ▲ WER 6267-2

Grauwels, Marc (fl)
Beethoven, L. van:Vars on Grétry's romance "Un fièvre brûlante", WoO 72, w. B. Bessler (vn), C. Springuel (va), G. H. (hp), Y. Stormes (gtr) Syrinx ▲ 94101 [DDD]
Bréval, J.B.:Sym concertante, w. A. De Rijckere (bn), B. Labadie (cnd), Walloon CO Syrinx ▲ 92101 [DDD]
Chopin, F.:Vars on Rossini's *Non più mesta*, w. C. Michel (hp) Marco Polo ▲ 8.220441 [DDD]
Devienne, F.:Con 2 Fl, w. B. Labadie (cnd), Walloon CO Syrinx ▲ 92101 [DDD]
Devienne, F.:Con 7 Fl, w. B. Labadie (cnd), Walloon CO Syrinx ▲ 92101 [DDD]
Donizetti, G.:Larghetto & Allegro, w. C. Michel (hp) Marco Polo ▲ 8.220441 [DDD]
Drouet, L.:Intro & Vars on an English Theme, w. C. Michel (hp) Marco Polo ▲ 8.220441 [DDD]
Hindemith, P.:Echo Fl & Pno, w. Daniel Blumenthal (pno) Syrinx ▲ 95101
Hindemith, P.:Die junge Magd, w. Lucienne Van Deyck (mez), Ronald Van Spaendonck (cl), Gaggini String Quartet Syrinx ▲ 95101
Hindemith, P.:Kanonische Sonatine, w. *(2nd fl unknown)* Syrinx ▲ 95101
Hindemith, P.:Kleine Kammermusik, w. Juris van den Hauwe (ob), Ronald Van Spaendonck (cl), et al. Syrinx ▲ 95101
Hindemith, P.:Pieces (8) Fl & Pno Syrinx ▲ 95101
Hindemith, P.:Son Fl, w. Daniel Blumenthal (pno) Syrinx ▲ 95101
Marc Grauwels & Friends, w. Marc Grauwels (fl), Marie-Noelle de Callataÿ (sop), Hiroko Masaki (sop), Dennis James (glass hmc), Ingrid Procureur (hp), Yves Storms (gtr), Yvietta Matison (va), Mark Drobinsky (vc), Alain De Rijckere (bn), Daniel Blumenthal (pno), Frank Michiels (perc), Belgian RSO, W Syrinx 2-▲ 98101 [DDD]
Operatic Fantasies for Flute & Orchestra, w. Marc Grauwels (fl) Syrinx ▲ CSR 93101 [DDD]
Piazzolla...Shanker, w. Marc Grauwels (fl), Yves Storms (gtr) Syrinx ▲ CSR 91103 [DDD]
Le Rossignol de l'Opéra:Musique Française de la Belle Epoque, w. Marc Grauwels (fl), Waterloo CO [cnd:U. Waterlot] Syrinx ▲ 93102 [DDD]
Rossini, G.:Andante con variazioni Hp, w. C. Michel (hp) Marco Polo ▲ 8.220441 [DDD]
Schubert, Franz:Intro & Vars Fl on "Tröckne Blumen", w. D. Blumenthal (pno) Syrinx ▲ 93105 [DDD]
Schubert, Franz:Qt Fl, w. Y. Matison (va), Y. Storms (gtr), M. Drobinsky (vc) Syrinx ▲ 93105 [DDD]
Spohr, L.:Son 1 Vn, w. C. Michel (hp) [arr for fl & hp] Marco Polo ▲ 8.220441 [DDD]
Spohr, L.:Son 4 Vn, w. B. Bessler (vn), C. Springuel (va), G. H. (hp), Y. Stormes (gtr) Syrinx ▲ 94101 [DDD]
Traeg, A.:Son Fl, w. Y. Stormes (gtr) Syrinx ▲ 94101 [DDD]

Graves, Marlon (perc)
So Many Stars, w. Kathleen Battle (sop), Antonio Hart (sax), Grover Washington Jr (sax), Tom Harrell (flgl), James Carter (b cl), Cyrus Chestnut (pno), Jon Herrington (gtr), Romero Lubambo (gtr), Ira Coleman (elec bass), Christian McBride (elec bass), Cyro Baptista (perc), Steven Berrios (perc) *(rec Hit Factory, Clinton Recording Studios, R.P.M. Sound Studios, Unique Recording Studios, Power Station)* Sony Classical ▲ SK 68473 [DDD]

Graves, Terry (gtr)—see ORCHESTRAS & ENSEMBLES Falla Trio

Graviers, Raphaëlle des (vn)
Haydn, J.:Con 1 Vn, w. B. Dupaquier (cnd), Jura CO Gallo ▲ CD 623 [DDD]

Gravill, Alan (pno)
Elgar, E.:Pno Music—Adieu (ca. 1901); Concert Allegro (1901); In Smyrna (1905); Skizze (1901) Gamut Classics ▲ GAM CD 516 [DDD]
Gurney, I.:Pno Music—Nine Preludes (1919–20); Two Nocturnes, Revery, A Picture, & To E.M.R. (1908–09) Gamut Classics ▲ GAM CD 516 [DDD]

Gräwe, Georg (pno)
Gräwe, G.:East Coker, w. G. Gräwe (cnd), Grubenklang Orch *(rec Cologne, Dec. 2, 1988 & May 7, 198)* Hat Hut ▲ hat ART CD 6028 [ADD]
Gräwe, G.:Lookin' for Work, w. G. Gräwe (cnd), Grubenklang Orch *(rec Cologne, Dec. 2, 1988 & May 7, 198)* Hat Hut ▲ hat ART CD 6028 [ADD]
Gräwe, G.:Vars, w. G. Gräwe (cnd), Grubenklang Orch *(rec Cologne, Dec. 2, 1988 & May 7, 198)* Hat Hut ▲ hat ART CD 6028 [ADD]

Gray, Ella Marie (vn)
Dresher, P.:Channels Passing, w. P. Taub (fl), B. Shapiro (ob), C. Sereque (cl), R. Pressley (tpt), S. Dempster (trbn), W. Gray (vc) *(rec 1983–84)* New Albion ▲ NA 053
Lam, B.-C.:Last Spring, w. Bun-Ching Lam (pno), John Weller (vn), Melissa Hamilton (va), Walter Gray (vc) CRI ▲ CD 726 [DDD]

INSTRUMENT.

Gray, Gary (cl)
Arnold, Bernstein, Debussy, Martinů, Poulenc, Saint-Saëns, w. Gary Gray (cl), C. Benson (pno) *(rec June 1992)* Centaur ▲ CRC 2165 [DDD]
Lazarof, H.:Trio Wind Instruments, w. S. Stokes (fl), J. Winter (ob) Laurel ▲ LR 845CD [AAD]
Thow, J.:Qt Cl, w. Francesco Trio Music & Arts ▲ CD 915

Gray, Julian (gtr)—see also ORCHESTRAS & ENSEMBLES Classical Guitar Duo
Homages & Evocations, w. Ronald Pearl (gtr) *(rec Troy Savings Bank Music Hall, Troy, NY, Sept 1995)* Dorian ▲ DOR 90230 [DDD]
The Magic Circle:Music for 2 Guitars, w. Ronald Pearl (gtr) Dorian Discovery ▲ DIS 80111

Gray, Walter (vc)
Dresher, P.:Channels Passing, w. P. Taub (fl), B. Shapiro (ob), C. Sereque (cl), R. Pressley (tpt), S. Dempster (trbn), E.M. Gray (vn) *(rec 1983–84)* New Albion ▲ NA 053
Lam, B.-C.:Another Spring, w. Paul Taub (fl), Bun-Ching Lam (pno) CRI ▲ CD 726 [DDD]
Lam, B.-C.:Last Spring, w. Bun-Ching Lam (pno), Ella Marie Gray (vn), John Weller (vn), Melissa Hamilton (va) CRI ▲ CD 726 [DDD]

Graybeal, M. (va)
Mozart, W.A.:Qnt Hn, K.407, w. L. Greer (hn), J. Schröder (vn), J. Griffin (vn), K. Slowik (vc) [period instrs] Smithsonian Collection ▲ ND 039
Mozart, W.A.:Qnt Hn, K.407, w. L. Greer (hn), J. Schröder (vn), J. Griffin (vn), K. Slowik (vc) [period instrs] Smithsonian Collection 5-▲ ND 031

Grazia, Paolo (ob)
Poulenc, F.:Sxt Pno, w. Andrea Dindo (pno), Gianpaolo Pretto (fl), Alessandro Carbonare (cl), Roberto Giaccaglia (bn), Stefano Pignatelli (hn) *(rec Sala Maffeiana dell'Accademia Filarmonica di Verona, May 7–9, 1995)* Agorá ▲ 021 [DDD]
Poulenc, F.:Trio Ob, w. Roberto Giaccaglia (bn), Andrea Dindo (pno) *(rec Sala Maffeiana dell'Accademia Filarmonica di Verona, May 7–9, 1995)* Agorá ▲ 021 [DDD]

Grazioli, G. (pno)
Lambert, C.:Con Pno, w. Harmonia Ensemble *(rec 1/89)* Giulia ▲ GS 201009 [DDD]

Grazzi, Paolo (ob)—see ORCHESTRAS & ENSEMBLES Al Ayre Español

Grebanier, Michael (vc)
Prokofiev, S.:Son Vc, w. Janet Guggenheim (pno) *(rec Fisher Hall, Santa Rosa, CA, Feb. 9–12, 1994)* Naxos ▲ 8.553136 [DDD]

Grebanier, Sharon (vn)—see ORCHESTRAS & ENSEMBLES Aurora String Quartet

Greco, L. A. (vc)
Bach, J.S.:Music of, w. M. M. Zeyen—arr. by Silto/Casals for cello & piano:Jesu, meine Freude; Andante from Son. Violin in A, BWV 1003; Adagio from Organ Toccata in C; Air from Orchestral Suite in D Orion ▲ CDA 8901 [AAD] ■ OC 8802
Barber, S.:Son Vc, w. M. M. Zeyen (pno) Orion ▲ CDA 8901 [AAD] ■ OC 8802
Casals, P.:Song of the Birds, w. V. Di Tullio (pno) Orion ▲ CDA 8901 [AAD] ■ OC 8802
Riddle, N.:Son Vc, w. V. di Tullio (pno) Orion ▲ CDA 8901 [AAD] ■ OC 8802

Greef, Arthur de (pno)
Beethoven, L. van:Son 9 Vn, "Kreutzer", w. I. Menges (gtr) *(rec 1925)* Biddulph ▲ BID LAB 076
Chopin, F.:Nocturnes—Op. 15/2 Pearl ▲ PEA 9974
Grieg, E.:Lyric Pieces—Op. 65, No. 6, "Wedding Day at Troldhaugen" Pearl ▲ PEA 9974 (m) [AAD]
Grieg, E.:Lyric Suite, Op. 54 Pearl ▲ PEA 9974 (m) [AAD]
Grieg, E.:Pno Music (sels)—Humoresque, Op. 6 Pearl ▲ PEA 9974 (m) [AAD]
Liszt, F.:Hungarian Rhaps Pearl ▲ PEA 9974 (m) [AAD]
Liszt, F.:Polonaises Pno—No. 2 in E Pearl ▲ PEA 9974 (m) [AAD]
Saint-Saëns, C.:Con 2 Pno, w. L. Ronald (cnd), London New SO Pearl ▲ PEA 9974 (m) [AAD]
Schumann, R.:Arabeske Pno Pearl ▲ PEA 9974 (m) [AAD]
Schumann, R.:Faschingsschwank aus Wien Pearl ▲ PEA 9974 (m) [AAD]

Green, Gareth (org)
Elgar, E.:Son Org Naxos ▲ 8.550582 [DDD]
English Organ Music, w. Green, Gareth (org) Naxos ▲ 8.550582 [DDD]
Howells, H.:Psalm-Preludes, Set I Naxos ▲ 8.550582 [DDD]

Green, Gordon (pno)
Green, G.:Trans Digital Pno—Ovs. [Rossini:Il barbiere di Seviglia; Guillaume Tell]; Raga [Amer. Trad.:Amazing Grace]; Vars. [Anon:Greensleeves]; Lullaby [Beethoven:Ode to Joy]; Marches [Sousa:The Thunderer; Semper Fidelis; The Washington Post; The Stars & Stripes Forever]; Anthemonium *(rec Sept. 1993)* Centaur ▲ CRC 2187 [DDD]

Green, Nancy (vc)
Britten, H.:Son Vc, w. F. Moyer (pno) Jupiter ■ J102
Debussy, C.:Son Vc, w. F. Moyer (pno) Jupiter ■ J102
Fuchs, R.:Fantasiestücke Vc, Op. 78, w. C. Palmer (pno) Biddulph ▲ LAW 005 [DDD]
Fuchs, R.:Son 1 Vc & Pno, w. C. Palmer (pno) Biddulph ▲ LAW 005 [DDD]
Fuchs, R.:Son 2 Vc & Pno, w. C. Palmer (pno) Biddulph ▲ LAW 005 [DDD]
Mendelssohn, F.:Son 2 Vc, w. F. Moyer (pno) Jupiter ■ J102
Schumann, R.:Fantasiestücke Cl, w. F. Moyer (pno) [arr. cello & piano] Jupiter ■ J102

Green, R. (vl)
Herrmann, B.:Night Digger:Scenario Macbre, w. T. R. Herrmann (hmc), Sessions of London Label "X" ▲ LXCD 12 [AAD]

Green, Robert (h-g)
French Music for Hurdy-Gurdy Focus ▲ FOCUS 932

Greenbank, Kathryn (vn)
Holst, G.:A Fugal Con, w. J. Bogorad (vn), R. Tecco (vn), L. Shank (vn), J. Koestenbaum (vc), C. Hogwood (cnd), St. Paul CO *(rec May 1992)* London ▲ 440376-2

Greenberg, Susan (fl)
Matson, S.:Range, w. Catherine Robbin (mez), Joseph Stone (fl), Glen Garrett (cl), Suren Karapetyan (hn), Peter Kent (vn), Kazi Pitelka (va), Sebastian Toettcher (vc), Don Ferrone (db), Doug Livingston (gtr/mand), John Schneider (gtr), Amy Shulman (hp), Terry Schoenig (perc), S. Matson (cnd) *(rec Schnee Studio, Universal City, CA, Mar 12, 1995)* New Albion ▲ NA 091

Greene, K. (va)—see ORCHESTRAS & ENSEMBLES Debussy Trio

Greene, Linda (fl)
Ashford, R.:Beauty, w. David Sabin (pno) Nigel Classics ▲ NC 10101
Liptak, D.:Rhaps, w. J. Friedrichs (cl), D. Gerikh (vn), W. Bass (vc), S. Heyman (pno) Opus One ▲ CD 168 [DDD]
Willey, J.:Society Music, w. G. Coble (tpt), W. Harris (trbn), D. Resue (hn), S. Heyman (pno), E. Gustafson (via), G. Macero (vc), E. Castilano (db), L. Luttinger (perc), E. Murray (cnd) Opus One ▲ CD 168 [DDD]

Greene, Linda (fl/pic)
Caltabiano, R.:Torched Liberty, w. N. Pilgrim (sop), V. Pritsker (vn), G. Macero (vc), K. Schempf (E♭/A/B♭ cl), G. Coble (tpt), S. Heyman (pno), L. Luttinger (perc), R. Caltabiano (cnd) Opus One ▲ CD 168 [DDD]

Greenfield, Bruce (pno)
The Lyric Trumpet, w. Stanley Friedman (tpt), Judith McDonald (pno), Elizabeth Biggs (sop), et al. Ode/New Zealand ▲ ODE 1327 [DDD]

Greenhouse, Bernard (vc)—see also ORCHESTRAS & ENSEMBLES Beaux Arts Trio
Schubert, Franz:Qnt Strs, D.956, w. Guarneri String Quartet Philips ▲ 432108-2
Schubert, Franz:Qnt Strs, D.956, w. Juilliard String Quartet CBS ▲ MK 42383 [DDD]

Greenslade, Hubert (pno)
Rich & Rare:The Voice of Margaret Sheridan, w. Margaret Sheridan (sop), Aureliano Pertile (ten), Renato Zanelli (ten), Carlo Sabajno (cnd), La Scala Orch, Queens Hall Orch *(rec 1926–29)* Time Machine ▲ 0100

Greer, John (pno)
Britten, H.:Folksong Arrs, w. K. McMillan (bar)—The Salley Gardens; The plough boy; Come you not from Newcastle?; The ash grove; The brisk young widow [E] Marquis ▲ ERAD 127 [DDD]
Britten, H.:Songs & Proverbs of William Blake, w. K. McMillan (bar) [E] Marquis ▲ ERAD 127 [DDD]

Greer, John (pno) (cont.)
Vaughan Williams, R.:Songs, w. K. McMillan (bar), M. Hammer (vn)—Rolling in the dew; Searching for lambs; How cold the wind doth blow [E] Marquis ▲ ERAD 127 [DDD]

Greer, Lowell (hn)
Krufft, N. von:Son Hn & Pno, w. S. Lubin (pno) Harmonia Mundi USA ▲ HMU 907037
Mozart, W.A.:Cons Hn, w. N. McGegan (cnd), Philharmonia Baroque Orch Harmonia Mundi USA ▲ HMU 907012 [AAD]
Mozart, W.A.:Qnt Hn, K.407, w. J. Schröder (vn), J. Griffin (vn), M. Graybeal (va), K. Slowik (vc) [period instrs] Smithsonian Collection 5-▲ ND 031
Mozart, W.A.:Qnt Hn, K.407, w. J. Schröder (vn), J. Griffin (vn), M. Graybeal (va), K. Slowik (vc) [period instrs] Smithsonian Collection ▲ ND 039

Greer, Lowell (nat hn)
Beethoven, L. van:Son Hn, w. S. Lubin (pno) Harmonia Mundi USA ▲ HMU 907037
Brahms, J.:Trio Hn, w. S. Chase (vn), S. Lubin (pno) Harmonia Mundi USA ▲ HMU 907037
Mozart, W.A.:Rondo Hn, K.371, w. N. McGegan (cnd), Philharmonia Baroque Orch Harmonia Mundi USA ▲ HMU 907012 [AAD]
Mozart, W.A.:Rondo Hn, K.514 (compl'd Jeurissen), w. N. McGegan (cnd), Philharmonia Baroque Orch Harmonia Mundi USA ▲ HMU 907012 [AAD]

Gref, W. (hn)—see ORCHESTRAS & ENSEMBLES SONOR Ensemble of Univ of California San Diego members

Gregor-Smith, Bernard (vc)
Bax, A.:Folk Tale, w. Y. Wrigley (pno) ASV ▲ ASV 896 [DDD]
Bax, A.:Legend-Son, w. Y. Wrigley (pno) ASV ▲ ASV 896 [DDD]
Bax, A.:Son Vc & Pno, w. Y. Wrigley (pno) ASV ▲ ASV 896 [DDD]
Bax, A.:Sonatina Vc & Pno, w. Y. Wrigley (pno) ASV ▲ ASV 896 [DDD]
Bridge, F.:Son Vc, w. Y. Wrigley (pno) ASV ▲ ASV 796
Chopin, F.:Son Vc, w. Yolande Wrigley (pno) ASV Quicksilva ▲ ASQ 6178
Debussy, C.:Son Vc, w. Y. Wrigley (pno) ASV ▲ ASV 796
Dohnányi, E. von:Son Vc, w. Y. Wrigley (pno) ASV ▲ ASV 796
Rachmaninoff, S.:Son Vc, w. Yolande Wrigley (pno) ASV Quicksilva ▲ ASQ 6178

Greibe, Leif (pno)
Stolarczyk, W.:Earth Air Fire Water, w. Amalie Malling (pno), John Damgaard (pno), Anne Øland (pno), Teddy Teirup (pno), Friedrich Gürtler (pno), Rosalind Bevan (pno), Poul Rosenbaum (pno), Rodolfo Llambias (pno), Bella Horn-Ribera (pno), Anders Riber (pno), Elisabeth Sigurdsson (pno), Thomas Tronheim (pno), Elsebeth Broderson (pno), Erik Kaltoft (pno), Jørgen Hald Nielsen (pno), Aino Gilemann (pno), Birgit Kjær (pno), Jørgen Thomsen (pno), Gunhild Donslund (pno), Henrik Bo Hansen (pno), Lone Karlsson (pno), Erik Fessel (pno), Lasse Nilsson (pno), Janos Ferenczi (pno), Erik Bach (pno), Axel Momme (pno), Arne de Cros Dich (pno), Sven Micha Slot (pno), Hanne Bramsen Buhl (pno), Lili Olesen (pno), Susannah Carlsson (pno), Ulla Erml (pno), Vagn Sørensen (pno), Bodil Krogh (pno), Kirsten Ottosen (pno), Inger Bergenholz (pno), Karsten Gylendorf (pno), Bjønr Elkjær (pno), Jacob Bjørn Jensen (pno), Jørgen Kaad (pno), Anne Marie Hjelm (pno), Carl Ulrik Munk Andersen (pno), Poul Lumbye (pno), Oluf Hildebrandt Nielsen (pno), Joachim Olsson (pno), Peter Pade Ramsøe Jacobsen (pno), Astrid Pollmann (pno), Jette Borsch (pno), Kirsten Karlshøj (pno), Maria Teresa Assing (pno), Allan Dahl Hansen (pno), Johan Hugossen (pno), Tine Fenger Pederson (pno), Arne Jørgen Fæø (pno), Anja Høgsted (pno), Anne Sophie Parbo (pno), Inga Lindmark (pno), Teresa Drabik Stathakis (pno), Anne Ruth Ferenczi (pno), Irene Hasager (pno), Yuka Ichikawa (pno), Birgitte Baur (pno), Malene Thastum (pno), Jens E. Rasmussen (pno), Birgitte Zielke (pno), Claus Zielke (pno), Stefan Kasch (pno), Bin Qiao (pno), Inger Johanne Teirup (pno), Lindy Rosborg (pno), Liisa Heininen (pno), David Højer (pno), Ellen Refstrup (pno), Thomas K. Søorensen (pno), Erik Kure (pno), Michael Rauff (pno), Jan beck Eriksson (pno), Tanja Zapolski (pno), Vibeke Skagbo (pno), Pål Eide Lindtner (pno), Ha-Young Sul (pno), Benedicte Palko (pno), Inke Kesseler (pno), Anne Marie Meineche (pno), Sverre Larsen (pno), Kasper Peter Bach (pno), Elisabetta Eliseo (pno), Olga Magieres (pno), Carl Erik Kühl (pno), Thorkild Borup Nielsen (pno), Valeria Zanini (pno), Lars Stenhoft (perc), Dennis Boel (perc), Winnie Dahlgren (perc), Susanne Vind (perc), Claus Byrith (elec), Anne Marie Storm (elec), J. Ribera (cnd) *(rec live, Koldinghaus Castle, Denmark, May 2, 1996)* Danica ▲ DCD 1996

Greif, Haridas (pno)
Varèse, E.:Un Grand sommeil noir, w. Jean-Paul Fouchécourt (ten) Memoire Vive ▲ CD 262024

Greif, Matthew (gtr)
Aguila, M. del:Tennessee *(rec Mission San Luis Rey)* Metro ▲ MCD 59601
Bogdanovic, D.:Gtr Music—Improvisations on Funk in E, A Little Story, Shards of Blue & Good Stuff; 2 improvisations on Chameleon [by Herbie Hancock] [all w. Dusan Bogdanovic (gtr)]; Diferencias Diferentes; Intro & Passacaglia for the Golden Flower *(rec Mission San Luis Rey)* Metro ▲ MCD 59601
Davis, M.:Blue in Green [arr Greif] *(rec Mission San Luis Rey)* Metro ▲ MCD 59601
Domeniconi, C.:Koyunbaba *(rec Mission San Luis Rey)* Metro ▲ MCD 59601
Greif, M.:Clear Day, w. Andrew York (gtr) *(rec Mission San Luis Rey)* Metro ▲ MCD 59601

Greiner, Gottfried (vc)
Rossini, G.:Tancredi, w. Veronica Cangemi (sop—Roggiero), Eva Mei (sop—Amenaide), Vasselina Kasarova (mez—Tancredi), Melinda Paulsen (cta—Isaura), Ramón Vargas (ten—Argirio), Harry Peeters (bass—Orbazzano), Janos Maté (vn), Ingo Nawra (db), David Syrus (hpd), R. Abbado (cnd), Munich RSO, Bavarian Radio Chorus *(rec Studio 1, Munich, July 17–30, 1995)* RCA Red Seal 3-▲ 09026-68349-2 [DDD]

Greitzer, Deborah (bn)—see ORCHESTRAS & ENSEMBLES Maryland Bach Aria Group members

Greitzer, Ian (cl)
Martino, D.:Canzone e Tarantella, w. Andrew Mark (vc) *(rec Jordan Hall, New England Conservatory of Music, Boston, MA, June 1996)* New World ▲ 80518-2
York, W.:Reminiscence 2, w. J. D. Fredericks (fl), K. Supové (pno) *(rec May 1987)* New World ▲ 80439-2

Greitzer, Pamela (vc)—see ORCHESTRAS & ENSEMBLES Maryland Bach Aria Group members

Gremelle, Daniel (a sax)
Ibert, J.:Concertino da camera, w. B. Desgraupes (cnd), Erwartung Ensemble Adda ▲ ADD 581263 [DDD]

Grenacher, Karl (pno)
Schoeck, O.:Der Postillon, w. E. Haefliger (ten), Wettinger CO, Wettinger Chamber Chorus, Seminarchor Wettingen [G] *(rec 1967)* Jecklin-Disco ▲ JD 504-2 [ADD]
Schoeck, O.:Songs (misc), w. E. Haefliger (ten), Wettinger CO, Wettinger Chamber Chorus, Seminarchor Wettingen [G] *(rec 1967)* Jecklin-Disco ▲ JD 504-2 [ADD]
Schoeck, O.:Songs (misc), w. A. Loosli (bass), T. Loosli (cnd), Bern Radio Chamber Ensemble—9 songs *(rec 1968)* Jecklin-Disco ▲ JD 535-2 [ADD]
Schubert, Franz:Winterreise, w. A. Loosli (bass) [G] *(rec 1973)* Jecklin-Disco ▲ JS 268-2 [ADD]

Gresham, David (cl)—see ORCHESTRAS & ENSEMBLES Continuum Chamber Ensemble

Gresko, R. (pno)
Kabalevsky, D.:Pieces for Children—Waltz; Little Song; Etude; Moonlight on the River; Playing Ball; Sad Little Tale; Old Dance; A Little Fairy Tale; Joking; Toccatina; Having Fun; Rondino; Scherzo; Ballad; Fairy Tale; Sonatina; Soldiers' Dance; Dancing on the Lawn; Novelette; Dark Forest; Dance; Cradle Song Analekta ▲ ATM 29723
Prokofiev, S.:Music for Children—Morning; Promenade; Fairy Tale; Tarantella; Regrets; Waltz; Grasshopper's Parade; Rain & the Rainbow; Tag; March; Evening; Moonlight Meadows Analekta ▲ ATM 29723

Grettie, Amanda (va)—see ORCHESTRAS & ENSEMBLES Alorian String Quartet

Grevesmühl, D. (vn)—see ORCHESTRAS & ENSEMBLES Berlin String Quintet

Grey, Julian (gtr)
Paganini, N.:Cantabile, w. *(violinist unknown)* Dorian ▲ DOR 90237
Paganini, N.:Qts (15) Vn Dorian ▲ DOR 90237
Paganini, N.:Son concertata, w. *(violinist unknown)* Dorian ▲ DOR 90237
Paganini, N.:Terzetto concertante Va Dorian ▲ DOR 90237

Gridenko, Tatian (vn)
Artyomov, V.:Gurian Hymn, w. Y. Smirnov (vn), Y. Adjemova (vn), D. Kitayenko (cnd), Moscow PO Olympia ▲ OLY 515 [DDD]

▲ = CD ♦ = Enhanced CD Δ = MD ■ = Cassette Tape □ = DCC

Gridenko, Tatian (vn) (cont.)
Glazunov, A.:Mazurka-oberek, w. A. Zhuraitis (cnd), USSR Radio-TV Orch
Russian Disc ▲ RUS 11 024 [ADD]

Grier, Francis (org)
Franck, C.:Prélude, fugue & var [Christ Church Cathedral, Oxford Org] ASV Quicksilva ▲ ASQ 6175
Grier, F.:Choral Music, w. Ralph Allwood (cnd), Rodolfus Choir—A Sequence for the Ascension
Herald ▲ HAVPCD 158
Messiaen, O.:La Nativité du Seigneur IMP ("BBC Radio Classics" series) ▲ IMP 5691602
Scarlatti, D.:Sons Kbd—K.254, 255, 287, 288, 328 Hyperion ▲ CDA 66182 [DDD]

Grier, Francis (org/hpd)
Monteverdi, C.:Vespro della Beata Vergine, w. Elly Ameling (sop), Norma Burrowes (sop), Charles Brett (ct), Martyn Hill (ten), Anthony Rolfe-Johnson (ten), Robert Tear (ten), Peter Knapp (bass), John Noble (bass), James Lancelot (org/hpd), Andrew Leach (org/hpd), P. Ledger (cnd), London Early Music Consort, King's College Choir Cambridge—Nigra sum [con.]; Laudate pueri [psalm]; Sancta Maria [son. sopra]; Magnificat *(rec Chapel of King's College, Cambridge, July & Aug. 1975)*
EMI Classics ▲ CDK 65339 [ADD]

Grierson, Ralph (pno)
Bobissimo!, w. Roger Bobo (tuba) Crystal ▲ CD 125
Galliard, J.E.:Son 5 Tuba, w. R. Bobo (tuba) *(rec 1969)* Crystal ▲ CD 125
Grierson, R.:Sometimes...Not Always Town Hall ▲ THCD 24
Hindemith, P.:Son Bass Tuba, w. R. Bobo (tuba) *(rec 1969)* Crystal ▲ CD 125
Joplin, S.:Music of, w. G. Schuller (cnd), New England Conservatory Ragtime Ensemble *(The Red Back Book)*, Sponhaltz, Southland Stingers *(Elite Syncopations)* EMI Classics ▲ CDC 47193
Kraft, William:Requiescat Town Hall ▲ THCD 24
Lesemann, F.:Nataraja Town Hall ▲ THCD 24
Subotnick, M.:Liquid Strata Town Hall ▲ THCD 24
Wilder, A.:Children's Suite:Effie the Elephant, w. R. Bobo (tuba) *(rec 1969)* Crystal ▲ CD 125

Grierson, Ralph (pno/cel)
Feldman, Morton:Pnos & Voices, w. Joan La Barbara (sop) *(rec Fantasy Studios, Berkeley, CA, O'Henry Studios, Burbank, CA & Metamusic Productions, Los Angeles, CA, Jan 18, Aug 25-26 & Dec 1)*
New Albion ▲ NA 085

Griese, Christof (sax)—see ORCHESTRAS & ENSEMBLES Berlin Saxophone Quartet

Griffen, Val (vc)
Handel, D.:The Poems of Our Climate, w. Sheryl Woods (sop), Pamela Watson (fl), Brian Delay (gtr), Anton Nel (pno), Jack Brennan (perc), James Culley (perc), Allen Otte (perc), G. Samuel (cnd)
Vienna Modern Masters ▲ VMM 2019 [DDD]

Griffin, Dennis (timp)
Gawthrop, D.:This Child, This King, w. Rebecca Parkinson (org), Tamara Bischoff-Oswald (hp), Will Kesling (cnd), Utah State Univ Chamber Singers *(rec Kent Concert Hall, USU Chase Fine Arts Center, Logan, UT, Feb. 4-5, 1995)* Integra Classic ▲ IMCD 951 [DDD]

Griffin, Judson (va)
Bach, J.S.:Cons Vn (comp), w. J. Schröder (vn), S. Ritchie, N. TeBrake, R. Brown, M. Lutszke, M. Willems, A. Fuller *(rec June 6-8, 1986)* Reference ▲ RR 23 CD [DDD]
Mozart, W.A.:Qt Fl, K.285, w. Cristopher Krueger (fl), J. Schröder (vn), K. Slowik (vc) [period instrs]
Smithsonian Collection 5-▲ ND 031
Mozart, W.A.:Qts Pno, w. J. Weaver (pno), J. Schröder (vn), K. Slowik (vc) [period instrs]
Smithsonian Collection 5-▲ ND 031
Mozart, W.A.:Trio Cl, K.498, w. L. McDonald (cl), J. Weaver (pno) [period instrs]
Smithsonian Collection 5-▲ ND 031
Vivaldi, A.:Cons for 2 Vns, w. J. Schröder (vn), S. Ritchie (vn), N. TeBrake (vn), R. Brown (vn), M. Lutszke (vc), M. Willems (db), A. Fuller (hpd) *(rec June 6-8, 1986)* Reference ▲ RR 23 CD [DDD]
Vivaldi, A.:Sinf, RV.116, w. J. Schröder (vn), S. Ritchie (vn), M. Lutszke (vc), M. Willems (db), A. Fuller (hpd) *(rec June 6-8, 1986)* Reference ▲ RR 23 CD [DDD]

Griffin, Judson (vn)
Handel, G.F.:Trio Sons, w. John Solum (trns fl), Arthur Fiacco (vc), Igor Kipnis (hpd)—in c, H.386a
Epiphany ▲ EP 7
Mozart, W.A.:Qnt Hn, K.407, w. L. Greer (hn), J. Schröder (vn), M. Graybeal (va), K. Slowik (vc) [period instrs] Smithsonian Collection ▲ ND 039
Mozart, W.A.:Qnt Hn, K.407, w. L. Greer (hn), J. Schröder (vn), M. Graybeal (va), K. Slowik (vc) [period instrs] Smithsonian Collection 5-▲ ND 031

Griffiths, Barry (vn)
Gershwin, G.:Rhap in Blue, w. P. Whittaker (cl), R. Simmons (tpt), D. James (trbn), A. Litton (pno), H. Fisher (dr), A. Litton (cnd), Royal PO [original big band orchestration] RPO ▲ RPO 5011 [DDD]
Vaughan Williams, R.:The Lark Ascending, w. A. Previn (cnd), Royal PO Telarc ▲ CD 80138 [DDD]

Griffiths, J. (lt/gtr morisca)
Codax, M.:Cantigas d'amigo (7), w. H. Newnham (ct/perc), R. Wilkinson (vielle/rcr), R. Bandt (rcr/fl/psalter/perc) Vox Australis ▲ VAST 005-2
Codax, M.:Music of, w. H. Newnham (ct/perc), R. Wilkinson (vielle/rcr), R. Bandt (rcr/fl/psalter/perc)—L'Autrier Jost' una Sebissa; Istanpitta Gaetta; Bel m'es Quant Son Li Fruit Madur; Slatarello Vox Australis ▲ VAST 005-2

Griffiths, K. (pno)
Schoenberg, A.:Ode to Napoleon, w. LaSalle String Quartet
Deutsche Grammophon ("20th Century Classics" series) ▲ 437036-2 [DDD]

Griggs, Whitney (vc)—see ORCHESTRAS & ENSEMBLES Cincinnati Contemporary Music Ensemble

Grigorov, S. (hn)
Brahms, J.:Trio Hn, w. D. Milanova (pno) Monitor 2-■ 55005/06

Grigoryan, Slava (gtr)
Spirit of Spain Sony Classical ▲ SK 62627

Grijp, L.P. (lt/cither)—see ORCHESTRAS & ENSEMBLES Camerata Trajectina

Grimaud, Hélène (pno)
Brahms, J.:Pieces Pno, Op. 118 *(rec Dec. 12-14, 1991)* Denon ▲ CO 79782 [DDD]
Brahms, J.:Son 3 Pno *(rec Dec. 12-14, 1991)* Denon ▲ CO 79782 [DDD]
Chopin, F.:Ballades Pno (comp)—Op. 23 Denon ▲ CO 1786 [DDD]
Liszt, F.:Années de pèlerinage 2—No. 7, "Dante Sonata" Denon ▲ CO 1786 [DDD]
Rachmaninoff, S.:Con 2 Pno, w. J. López-Cobos (cnd), Royal PO
Denon/PCM Digital ▲ CO 75368 [DDD]
Rachmaninoff, S.:Études-tableaux, Opp. 33 & 39—Op. 33 *(rec 1985)* Denon ▲ CO 1054 [DDD]
Rachmaninoff, S.:Preludes Pno, Opp 23 & 32—Op. 32, Nos. 2 & 12 *(rec 1985)*
Denon ▲ CO 1054 [DDD]
Rachmaninoff, S.:Son 2 Pno Denon ▲ CO 1054 [DDD]
Ravel, M.:Con in G Pno, w. J. López-Cobos (cnd), Royal PO Denon/PCM Digital ▲ CO 75368 [DDD]
Schumann, R.:Con Pno, w. D. Zinman (cnd), Berlin German SO *(rec Paris 1995)*
Erato ▲ 11727-2 [DDD]
Strauss, R.:Burleske, w. D. Zinman (cnd), Berlin German SO *(rec Paris 1995)* Erato ▲ 11727-2 [DDD]

Grimes, Jan (pno)
Hayden, P.:Grand Mamou, w. Katherine Kemler (fl) *(rec 1992)* Centaur ▲ CRC 2146 [DDD]
Muczynski, R.:Son Fl, w. K. Kemler (fl) *(rec 1992)* Centaur ▲ CRC 2146 [DDD]

Griminelli, Andrea (fl)—see also ORCHESTRAS & ENSEMBLES Rossini Wind Quartet
Villa-Lobos, H.:Bachiana brasileira 6, w. Rino Vernizzi (bn) *(rec Chiesa della Misericordia, Torino, Italy, Feb 1987)* Arts Music ▲ 447200-2 [DDD]
Villa-Lobos, H.:Chôro 2, w. Michele Carulli (cl) *(rec Chiesa della Misericordia, Torino, Italy, Feb 1987)*
Arts Music ▲ 447200-2 [DDD]
Villa-Lobos, H.:Qt Fl, w. Pietro Borgonovo (ob), Michele Carulli (cl), Rino Vernizzi (bn) *(rec Chiesa della Misericordia, Torino, Italy, Feb 1987)* Arts Music ▲ 447200-2 [DDD]
Villa-Lobos, H.:Qnten forme de chôros, w. Pietro Borgonovo (ob), Michele Carulli (cl), Francesco Pomarico (E hn), Rino Vernizzi (bn) *(rec Chiesa della Misericordia, Torino, Italy, Feb 1987)*
Arts Music ▲ 447200-2 [DDD]

Grimmer, Walter (vc)—see also ORCHESTRAS & ENSEMBLES Bern String Quartet, Arion Trio
Karg-Elert, S.:Son Vc, w. Stefan Fahrni (pno) *(rec Radio Studio Bern, 1993)*
Jecklin ▲ JD 686-2 [DDD]
Lehmann, H.U.:Kammermusik, w. K. Graf (sop), A.-K. Graf (fl), E. Schmid (cl), I. Nakamura (perc)
Jecklin ▲ JD 689
Schubert, Franz:Son Arpeggione, w. I. von Alpenheim (pno) BIS 4-▲ CD 521/24 [DDD]
Yun, I.:Duo Vc, w. Marion Hofmann (hp) Col Legno ▲ AU 31808
Yun, I.:Recontre, w. Eduard Brunner (cl), Marion Hofmann (hp) Col Legno ▲ AU 31808

Grinage, Ron (pno)
Allen, J.:Brazilian Son, w. Shana Norton (hp), Carol Redman (fl), Charly Drobeck (fl/alt fl/pic), Sam Lunt (perc), Tom Maguire (perc) *(rec Santuario de Guadalupe, Sante Fe, NM, Sept 29-30, 1995)*
Wild Iris ▲ WI 001
Allen, J.:In Memory of a Once New World, w. Sam Lunt (mar), Tom Maguire (perc) *(rec Santuario de Guadalupe, Sante Fe, NM, Sept 29-30, 1995)* Wild Iris ▲ WI 001

Grinberg, Maria (pno)
Beethoven, L. van:Son 2 Pno *(rec 1965-66)* Arlecchino ▲ ARLA 62
Beethoven, L. van:Son 3 Pno *(rec 1965-66)* Arlecchino ▲ ARLA 62

Grindenko, Tatjana (vn)
Nono, L.:Hay que caminar, w. G. Kremer (vn) Deutsche Grammophon ▲ 435870-2 [DDD]
Nono, L.:Lontananza, w. G. Kremer (vn) Deutsche Grammophon ▲ 435870-2 [DDD]
Pärt, A.:Tabula rasa, w. G. Kremer (vn), S. Sondeckis (cnd), Lithuanian CO
ECM New Series ▲ 78118-21275-2 [DDD]; ■ 78118-21275-4
Schnittke, A.:Con grosso 1, w. Gidon Kremer (vn), Yuri Smirnov (hpd/pno), H. Schiff (cnd), CO of Europe Deutsche Grammophon ("Digital Midprice" series) ▲ 445520-2
Schnittke, A.:Moz-Art à la Haydn, w. Gidon Kremer (vn), H. Schiff (cnd), CO of Europe
Deutsche Grammophon ("Digital Midprice" series) ▲ 445520-2

Grinhauz, Léo (vc)—see ORCHESTRAS & ENSEMBLES Montreal Musica Camerata, Montreal Musica Camerata members

Grinhauz, Luis (vn)—see ORCHESTRAS & ENSEMBLES Montreal Musica Camerata members, Montreal Musica Camerata

Gripp, Louis Peter (lt/thb/cittern)—see ORCHESTRAS & ENSEMBLES Camerata Trajectina

Gripp, Neal (va)—see ORCHESTRAS & ENSEMBLES Montreal Chamber Group

Grishin, N. (perc/bells)
Schnittke, A.:Hymns Vc, w. A. Ivashkin (vc), Y. Rudometkin (bn), I. Pashinskaya (hp), V. Barsalkin (db), V. Chasovennaya (hpd), V. Grishin (perc)—No. 1 for Cello, Harp & Timpani [Quasi andante]; No. 2 for Cello & Double *(rec National Radio House, Moscow, 1987)* Vox Box 2-▲ CDX 5121 [ADD]

Grishin, Viktor (perc)
Schnittke, A.:Hymns Vc, w. A. Ivashkin (vc), Y. Rudometkin (bn), I. Pashinskaya (hp), V. Barsalkin (db), V. Chasovennaya (hpd), V. Grishin, N. Grishin (perc/bells)—No. 1 for Cello, Harp & Timpani [Quasi andante]; No. 2 for Cello & Double *(rec National Radio House, Moscow, 1987)*
Vox Box 2-▲ CDX 5121 [ADD]

Grishin, Viktor (vib)
Schnittke, A.:Suite in the Old Style, w. Igor Boguslavsky (va), Alla Litvinenko (hpd), Viktor Gabinsky (mar), Vadim Vasilykov (bells) [arr. unknown] *(rec 1989)* Consonance ▲ 81-0009 [DDD]

Grishkoff, Robert (hn)
Klatzow, P.:Chamber Con, w. Beat Wenger (fl), Jimmy Reinders (cl), Uliano Marchio (gtr), Lamar Crowson (pno), Barry Jordan (elec org), Peter Hamblin (perc), P. Klatzow (cnd)
Claremont ▲ GSE 1524
Klatzow, P.:Mass, w. Di Maris (mar), Barry Smith (cnd), St. Georges Singers Claremont ▲ GSE 1524

Grodner, Murray (db)—see ORCHESTRAS & ENSEMBLES Baroque Chamber Players

Groethuysen, Andreas (pno)—see also ORCHESTRAS & ENSEMBLES Tal & Groethuysen Duo
Czerny, C.:Pno Music (4-Hands), w. Y. Tal (pno)—Grand Sonate brillante, Op. 10; Ouverture caracteristique et brillante, Op. 54; Grand Sonate, Op. 178; Fantaisie, Op. 226
Sony Classical ▲ SK 45936 [DDD]
Gouvy, T.:Aubade, w. Y. Tal (pno) Sony Classical ▲ SK 53110
Gouvy, T.:Ghiribizzi, w. Y. Tal (pno) Sony Classical ▲ SK 53110
Gouvy, T.:Morceaux, Op. 59, w. Y. Tal (pno)—Nos. 1 & 2 Sony Classical ▲ SK 53110
Gouvy, T.:Scherzo, Op. 77/1, w. Y. Tal (pno) Sony Classical ▲ SK 53110
Gouvy, T.:Son Pno 4-Hands, Op. 36, w. Y. Tal (pno) Sony Classical ▲ SK 53110
Gouvy, T.:Son Pno 4-Hands, Op. 49, w. Y. Tal (pno) Sony Classical ▲ SK 53110
Gouvy, T.:Son Pno 4-Hands, Op. 51, w. Y. Tal (pno) Sony Classical ▲ SK 53110
Hummel, J.N.:Nocturne, w. Y. Tal (pno) Koch Schwann ▲ CD 310017 [DDD]
Hummel, J.N.:Sons Pno 4-Hands, w. Y. Tal (pno) Koch Schwann ▲ CD 310017 [DDD]

Grogan, Robert (org)
In Dulci Jubilo:Christmas Music for the Organ Gothic ▲ GOT 49069 [DDD]
Times & Seasons:Organ Music for the Liturgy by 20th Century Composers *(rec Basilica of the National Shrine of the Immaculate Conception, Washington, D.C.)* Gothic ▲ GOT 49070 [DDD]

Gron, Anders (vc)
Cello Favorites, Vol. 3, w. J. Nielsen (pno) Danica ▲ DCD 8158

Grønbech, Bo (org)
Duruflé, M.:Requiem, w. Ebbe Munk (cnd), Vox Danica Chamber Choir *(rec Jesus Church, Copenhagen, Spring 1990)* Danica ▲ DCD 8140
Gounod, C.:Sacred Music, w. Ebbe Munk (cnd), Vox Danica Chamber Choir—Te Deum *(rec Jesus Church, Copenhagen, Spring 1990)* Danica ▲ DCD 8140

Groot, Frank de (vn)
Schat, P.:Canto general, w. Lucia Meeuwsen (sop), Gerard Bouwhuis (pno) Donemus ▲ CV 19

Groote, André de (pno)
Camilleri, C.:Con 1 Pno, w. M. Laus (cnd), Bournemouth SO Unicorn-Kanchana ▲ DKP CD 9150
Camilleri, C.:Con 2 Pno, w. M. Laus (cnd), Bournemouth SO Unicorn-Kanchana ▲ DKP CD 9150
Camilleri, C.:Con 3 Pno, w. M. Laus (cnd), Bournemouth SO Unicorn-Kanchana ▲ DKP CD 9150
de Greef, A.:Con 1 Pno, w. F. Devreese (cnd), Moscow SO *(rec Mosfilm Studio, Moscow, Feb 1995)*
Marco Polo ("Anthology of Flemish Music" series) ▲ 8.223810 [DDD]
de Greef, A.:Con 2 Pno, w. F. Devreese (cnd), Moscow SO *(rec Mosfilm Studio, Moscow, Feb 1995)*
Marco Polo ("Anthology of Flemish Music" series) ▲ 8.223810 [DDD]
Devreese, F.:Film Music—Country Dance; Chorale; Butterfly; Waltz I; Moviola; Waltz II; The Other Waltz; Concertina Waltz; Danza Mobile; Ballade for Damien; Danse Sacrée; Four a.m.; The Third Waltz; Children's Portraits; Children's Games; Nocturne; Divert. I; Divert. II; March; Rotations; Intermezzo; Prélude; French Can-Can *(rec Brussels, Dec. 1992 & June 1993)* Marco Polo ▲ 8.223651 [DDD]
Jongen, J.:Son Vc, w. Viviane Spanoghe (vc) *(rec Brussels Royal Conservatory Concert Hall, Aug 1995)*
Talent ▲ DOM 291035 [DDD]
Schuller, G.:Recitative & Rondo, w. R. Davidovici (vn) New World ▲ NW 334-2 [DDD]
Tournemire, C.:Poème Vc, w. Viviane Spanoghe (vc) *(rec Brussels Royal Conservatory Concert Hall, Aug 1995)* Talent ▲ DOM 291035 [DDD]
Vierne, L.:Son Vc, w. Viviane Spanoghe (vc) *(rec Brussels Royal Conservatory Concert Hall, Aug 1995)*
Talent ▲ DOM 291035 [DDD]

Groote, Philip de (vc)—see also ORCHESTRAS & ENSEMBLES Chilingirian String Quartet
Tippett, M.:Triple Con, w. Levon Chilingirian (vn), Simon Rowland-Jones (va), R. Hickox (cnd), Bournemouth SO Chandos ▲ CHAN 9384 [DDD]

Groote, Steven de (pno)
Beethoven, L. van:Con 2 Pno, w. O. Hadari (cnd), Cape Town SO *(rec City Hall, Cape Town, Aug. 21, 1988)* Claremont ▲ GSE 1536 [ADD]
Beethoven, L. van:Con 4 Pno, w. D. de Villiers (cnd), Cape Town SO Vivace 3-▲ E 322 [DDD]
Beethoven, L. van:Son 2 Pno Finlandia 2-▲ FIN 577032 [ADD]
Beethoven, L. van:Son 21 Pno, "Waldstein" Finlandia 2-▲ FIN 577032 [ADD]
Brahms, J.:Con 2 Pno, w. D. de Villiers (cnd), Cape Town SO Vivace 3-▲ E 323 [DDD]
Brahms, J.:Con 2 Pno, w. D. de Villiers (cnd), Cape Town SO Vivace ▲ 592 [DDD]
Chopin, F.:Con 1 Pno, w. E. Bergel (cnd), Cape Town SO *(rec City Hall, Cape Town, Aug. 7, 1986)*
Claremont ▲ GSE 1536 [ADD]

INSTRUMENT.

Groote, Steven de (pno) (cont.)
Copland, A.:Nocturne, w. R. Davidovici (vn) New World ▲ NW 334-2 [DDD]
Korngold, E.W.:Con Pno Left-Hand, w. W. A. Albert (cnd), Northwest German PO CPO ▲ CPO 999046-2 [DDD]
Piston, W.:Sonatina Vn, w. R. Davidovici (vn) New World ▲ NW 334-2 [DDD]
Prokofiev, S.:Romeo & Juliet Pno Finlandia 2-▲ FIN 577032 [ADD]
Prokofiev, S.:Son 8 Pno Finlandia 2-▲ FIN 577032 [ADD]
Rachmaninoff, S.:Con 2 Pno, w. D. de Villiers (cnd), Cape Town SO Vivace 3-▲ E 322 [DDD]

Groppo, E. (vn)
Milesi, P.:Modi 2, w. L. M. Pickova (sop), Françoise Goddard (alt), M. Ferradini (ten), B. Andersen (bass), D. Cassamagnaghi (fl), S. Scanziani (ob), A. Bianchi (cl/b cl), E. Crisafulli (bn), C. Gazzola (hn), F. Gualandris (tuba), A. Girardi (celtic hp), R. Anedda (vn), M. Pagani (vn), M. Ravasio (va), S. Righini (vc), P. Rizzi (db), J. Scully (perc), P. Milesi (cnd) Cuneiform ▲ RUNE 63

Grosgurin, D. (vc)
Vuataz, R.:Nocturnes Vc *(rec Dec. 12, 1991)* Grammont ▲ CTSP 7-2 [ADD]

Groslot, Robert (pno)
Arensky, A.:Children's Suite, w. D. Blumenthal (pno) [arr. for 2 pnos] *(rec Heidelberg, Aug 1992)* Marco Polo ▲ 8.223497 [DDD]
Arensky, A.:Suite 1 for 2 Pnos, w. D. Blumenthal (pno) *(rec Heidelberg, Aug 1992)* Marco Polo ▲ 8.223497 [DDD]
Arensky, A.:Suite 2 for 2 Pnos, "Silhouettes", w. D. Blumenthal (pno) *(rec Heidelberg, Aug 1992)* Marco Polo ▲ 8.223497 [DDD]
Arensky, A.:Suite 3 for 2 Pnos, "Vars", w. D. Blumenthal (pno) *(rec Heidelberg, Aug 1992)* Marco Polo ▲ 8.223497 [DDD]
Arensky, A.:Suite 4 for 2 Pnos, w. D. Blumenthal (pno) *(rec Heidelberg, Aug 1992)* Marco Polo ▲ 8.223497 [DDD]
Bruch, M.:Pieces Cl, Op. 83/1-8, w. Walter Boeykens (cl), Roel Dieltiens (vc), Thérèse-Marie Gilissen (va) *(rec 1991)* Musique d'Abord ▲ HMA 1901371
Bruch, M.:Pieces Cl, Op. 83/1-8, w. Walter Boeykens (cl), Thérèse-Marie Gilissen (va), Roel Dieltiens (vc) *(rec 1991)* Musique D'Abord ▲ HMA 1901371
Debussy, C.:Arrs for 2 Pnos, w. D. Blumenthal (pno)—Saint-Saëns:Introduction & Rondo Capriccioso; Etienne Marcel; Tchaikovsky:Swan Lake; Gluck/Saint-Saëns:Caprice; Schumann:6 Etudes, Op. 56; Wagner:The Flying Dutchman:Overture *(rec Mar. 18-20, 1991)* Marco Polo ▲ 8.223378 [DDD]
Glorieux, F.:Movts Pno, w. N. Nozy (cnd), Belgian Guides Symphonic Band René Gailly ▲ CD 87057 [DDD]
Zemlinsky, A. von:Trio Cl, w. Walter Boeykens (cl), Thérèse-Marie Gilissen (va), Roel Dieltiens (vc) *(rec 1991)* Musique d'Abord ▲ HMA 1901371

Gross, David (pno)
Lalo, E.:Con Pno, w. N. Athinäos (cnd), Frankfurt State Orch Signum ▲ X66-00 [DDD]

Gross, M. (vc)—see ORCHESTRAS & ENSEMBLES Parnassus Trio

Gross, Steve (hn)
Bozza, E.:En forêt, w. B. Hillmer (pno) *(rec Aug.-Sept. 1988)* ACA Digital Recording ■ CM20005-5 (CrO2)
Dukas, P.:Villanelle, w. B. Hillmer (pno) *(rec Aug.-Sept. 1988)* ACA Digital Recording ■ CM20005-5 (CrO2)
Music for Horn & Organ, w. Robert Simpson (org) *(rec 1987)* ACA Digital ■ CM20002-2
Poulenc, F.:Élégie Hn, w. B. Hillmer (pno) *(rec Aug.-Sept. 1988)* ACA Digital Recording ■ CM20005-5 (CrO2)
Saint-Saëns, C.:Morceau de concert Hn, w. B. Hillmer (pno) *(rec Aug.-Sept. 1988)* ACA Digital Recording ■ CM20005-5 (CrO2)
Saint-Saëns, C.:Romance Hn, Op. 67, w. B. Hillmer (pno) *(rec Aug.-Sept. 1988)* ACA Digital Recording ■ CM20005-5 (CrO2)
Tomasi, H.:Con Hn, w. B. Hillmer (pno) [arr. for horn & piano] *(rec Aug.-Sept. 1988)* ACA Digital Recording ■ CM20005-5 (CrO2)

Grossman, Jerry (vc)
Kodály, Z.:Duo Vn & Vc, w. D. Phillips (vn) Elektra/Nonesuch ▲ 79074-2
Kodály, Z.:Son Vc, Op. 8 Elektra/Nonesuch ▲ 79074-2
Strauss, R.:Don Quixote, w. Raymond Gniewek (vn), Michael Ouzounian (va), J. Levine (cnd), Metropolitan Opera Orch *(rec Manhattan Ctr, NY, May 1995)* Deutsche Grammophon ▲ 447762-2 [DDD]

Grossman, Kathy (mar)
Boziwick, G.:Beyond the Last Thought, w. C. Pelton (sop), G. Reuter (ob), C. Iverson (bn) Opus One ▲ CD 162
Boziwick, G.:First Dance, w. L. Goldberg (pno) Opus One ▲ CD 162

Grossman, Kathy (perc)
Cage, J.:Music for 4 for Perc, w. C. Nappi (perc), M. Pugliese (perc), W. Trigg (perc) *(rec in concert at Merkin Concert Hall, New York City, 4/4/89)* Mode ▲ 25
Harrison, L.:Ariadne, w. Rachel Rudich (fl) CRI ▲ CD 568 [DDD]
Harrison, L.:Con 1 Fl, w. Rachel Rudich (fl) CRI ▲ CD 568 [DDD]
Sollberger, H.:Double Triptych, w. R. Rudich (fl) CRI ▲ CD 568 [DDD]
Sueyoshi, Y.:Correspondence V, w. R. Rudich (fl) CRI ▲ CD 568 [DDD]
Trombly, P.:Duo Fl, w. R. Rudich (fl) CRI ▲ CD 568 [DDD]
Trombly, P.:Trio in 3 Mvts, w. R. Rudich (fl), S. Macchia (db) CRI ▲ CD 568 [DDD]

Grossman, Michael (vn)—see ORCHESTRAS & ENSEMBLES Stratos

Grotenhuis, Sepp (cel)
Andriessen, L.:Anachrony 1, w. Nico de Rooij (pno), Douceline Aleven (hp), Arthur Cune (vib), Nicolette Heerema (org), H. Williams (cnd), Netherlands Ballet Orch *(rec Amsterdam Music Theater, Oct 3-6, 1994)* Donemus ▲ CV 54 [DDD]

Grotenhuis, Sepp (pno)
Adams, J.:Grand Pianola Music, w. Kym Amps (sop), Ruth Holton (sop), Lyndsay Wagstaff (sop), Ellen Corver (pno), S. Mosko (cnd), Netherlands Wind Ensemble Chandos ▲ CHAN 9363 [DDD]
Andriessen, L.:Contra tempus, w. Gerard Bouwhuis (pno), Tomoko Mukaiyama (elec pno), Nico de Rooij (elec pno) *(rec Amsterdam Music Theater, Oct 3-6, 1994)* Donemus ▲ CV 54 [DDD]
Andriessen, L.:Ittrospezione 3, w. Gerard Bouwhuis (pno), Peter van Bergen (sax), Marjan Damsté (db), H. Williams (cnd), Netherlands Ballet Orch *(rec Amsterdam Music Theater, Oct 3-6, 1994)* Donemus ▲ CV 54 [DDD]
Lang, D.:Orpheus Over & Under, w. Ellen Corver (pno)—Under Orpheus Chandos ▲ CHAN 9363 [DDD]
Mozart, W.A.:Con 10 Pnos, w. M. Leonhard (pno), J. Kussmaul (cnd), Amsterdam Mozart Players *(rec Aug. 1990)* Channel Classics ▲ CCS 1190 [DDD]

Grötzinger, Andreas (vn)
Dauprat, L.-F.:Qnt Hn & Strs, w. P. Arnold (hn), A. Henschke (vn/va), H.-B. Henscke (va), P. Gerschwitz (vc) Bayer ▲ BR 100236 [DDD]
Mozart, W.A.:Qnt Hn, K.407, w. P. Arnold (hn), A. Henschke (vn/va), H.-B. Henscke (va), P. Gerschwitz (vc) Bayer ▲ BR 100236 [DDD]
Stamitz, A.:Qnt Hn, w. P. Arnold (hn), A. Henschke (vn/va), H.-B. Henscke (va), P. Gerschwitz (vc) Bayer ▲ BR 100236 [DDD]

Gruber, Emanuel (vc)
Barber, S.:Son Vc, w. Uriel Tsachor (pno) Arcobaleno ▲ AAOC 9326
Britten, H.:Son Vc, w. Uriel Tsachor (pno) Arcobaleno ▲ AAOC 9326
Heart of the Cello, w. Herut Israeli (pno) PWK Classics ▲ PWK 1135 [DDD]
Schnittke, A.:Son Vc, w. Uriel Tsachor (pno) Arcobaleno ▲ AAOC 9326

Gruber, Herbert (cl)
Stravinsky, I.:Elegy for J.F.K., w. D. Fischer-Dieskau (bar), K. T. Adler (cl), K. Berger (cl) [E] Orfeo ▲ 015821 [DDD]

Gruber, Karen (perc)
Field, K.:Music of, w. Ken Field (sax/perc/syn/fl), Karen Aqua (perc), Ken Winokur (perc), Mike Rivard (elec bass), John Fleagle (voice)—A Space in a Place; Om on the Range; Takuskanskan; 5 Saxophones in Search of Meaning; Sanity; Perpetual Motion; Thoughts Unspoken; Berrendo; Sympathetic Magic; The Missing Soul; When I Fall in Love *(rec The Henge, Roswell, NM, Wellspring Sound, Concord, MA, The Chicken Loft, Cambridge, MA & The Basement, Cambridge, MA, 1988-1995)* O.O. Discs ▲ OO 25

Grüber, M. (hpd)
Abel, C.F.:Son Fl, Vc & Hpd, w. Claude Arimany (fl), A. Schmöller (vc) Motette ▲ MOT CD 30141 [DDD]
Bach, C.P.E.:Trio Son Fl, H.586, w. C. Arimany (fl), A. Schmöller (vc) Motette ▲ MOT CD 30141 [DDD]
Kirnberger, J.P.:Son Fl, w. C. Arimany (fl), A. Schöller (vc) Motette ▲ MOT CD 30141 [DDD]
Müthel, J.G.:Son Fl, w. C. Arimany (fl), A. Schöller (vc) Motette ▲ MOT CD 30141 [DDD]

Grubert, Ilya (vn)
Bruch, M.:Con 1 Vn, w. I. Golovshin (cnd), Russian State SO Russian Disc ▲ RUS 10012 [DDD]
Paganini, N.:Con 1 Vn, w. C. Orbelian (cnd), Moscow CO Chandos ▲ CHAN 9492
Paganini, N.:Con 2 Vn, w. C. Orbelian (cnd), Moscow CO Chandos ▲ CHAN 9492
Sibelius, J.:Con Vn, w. I. Golovshin (cnd), Russian State SO Russian Disc ▲ RUS 10012 [DDD]

Grubert, Naum (pno)
Mussorgsky, M.:Pictures at an Exhibition *(rec 1992)* Emergo ▲ EC 3993 [DDD]
Rachmaninoff, S.:Études-tableaux, Opp. 33 & 39—Op. 33/2 & 4; Op. 39/2, 5 & 6 *(rec 1992)* Emergo ▲ EC 3993 [DDD]
Rachmaninoff, S.:Morceaux de fant—No. 1 in E♭, "Elégie" *(rec 1992)* Emergo ▲ EC 3993 [DDD]
Rachmaninoff, S.:Preludes Pno, Opp 23 & 32—Op. 23/1 & 2; Op. 32/5 & 10 *(rec 1992)* Emergo ▲ EC 3993 [DDD]
Schubert, Franz:Son Pno, D.784 Ottavo ▲ 78926 [DDD]
Schubert, Franz:Son Pno, D.960 Ottavo ▲ 78926 [DDD]

Grubich, Joachim (org)
Anthologie de la musique d'orgue en pologne sous la renaissance Accord ▲ ACD 200522 [DDD]

Grudin-Brandt, Inger (clvd)
Bach, J.S.:Suites Kbd, BWV 818a & 819a BIS ▲ CD 142 [AAD]

Grudin-Brandt, Inger (kbd)
Bach, C.P.E.:Kbd Music—7 sels. from the Sonatas, Rondos & Fantasias publ. 1779-1787 [performed on clvd & fortepno] *(rec 1976 & 1979)* BIS ▲ CD 142 [AAD]

Gruel, M. von Annette (lt)
Mudarra, A.:Music of, w. Lautentrio Ricardo Correa—Fantasia VII; "Fantasia que contrehaze la harpa en la manera de Luduvico" Christophorus ▲ CHR 74527 [ADD]
Pacoloni, G.:Music of, w. Lautentrio Ricardo Correa—La Bataglia; La Desperata Christophorus ▲ CHR 74527 [ADD]
Piccinini, A.:Intavolature, w. Lautentrio Ricardo Correa—Toccata IX; Toccata; Canzone Christophorus ▲ CHR 74527 [ADD]
Valderrábano, E. de:Music of, w. Lautentrio Ricardo Correa—"Contrapunto sobre el tenor de la baxa"; "Para discanto" Christophorus ▲ CHR 74527 [ADD]

Gruenberg, Erich (vn)
Bax, A.:Son 1 Vn & Pno, w. J. McCabe (pno) [1945 version] Chandos ▲ CHAN 8845 [DDD]
Bax, A.:Son 2 Vn & Pno, w. J. McCabe (pno) Chandos ▲ CHAN 8845 [DDD]
Beethoven, L. van:Con Vn, Op. 61, w. J. Horenstein (cnd), New Philharmonia Orch *(rec Walthamstow Town Hall, London 3/31/67)* Chesky ▲ CD52 [ADD]
Holloway, R.:Romanza, w. R. Hickox (cnd), City of London Sinfonia Chandos ▲ CHAN 9228 [DDD]
Reizenstein, F.:Son Vn, w. D. Wilde (pno) Continuum ▲ CCD 1024

Gruenberg, Joanna (pno)
Wieniawski, H.:Vn & Pno Music, w. R. Ricci (vn)—Kuyawiak; Légende; Obertass Mazurka; Polonaise in A; Polonaise in D; Scherzo Souvenir de Moscow; Tarantelle; Variations on an Original Theme Unicorn-Kanchana ▲ UKCD 2048 [DDD]

Gruesser, Eva (vn)—see ORCHESTRAS & ENSEMBLES Lark String Quartet

Gruithuyzen, Jan (pno)
Brahms, J.:Ernste Gesänge, w. G. Geijsen (mez) Erasmus ▲ WVH 041 [DDD]
Duparc, H.:Songs, w. G. Geijsen (mez)—La Vie antérieure; La Manoir de Rosemonde; Au pays où se fait la Guerre Erasmus ▲ WVH 041 [DDD]
Granados, E.:Songs, w. G. Geijsen (mez)—La maja Dolorosa, Nos. 1-3 Erasmus ▲ WVH 041 [DDD]
Sibelius, J.:Songs, w. G. Geijsen (mez)—Till Kvällen; Den första Kyssen; Flickan kom ifrån sin Alsklings möte; se'n har jag ej frågat mera; Svarta Rosor; Kom nu hit, död Erasmus ▲ WVH 041 [DDD]
Turina, J.:Songs, w. G. Geijsen (mez)—cantares Erasmus ▲ WVH 041 [DDD]

Grumiaux, Arthur (vn)
Bach, J.S.:Cons Vn (comp), w. E. de Waart (cnd), Philharmonia Orch Philips ("Silver Line" series) ▲ 420700-2 [ADD]
Bach, J.S.:Cons Vn (comp), w. R. Leppard (cnd), English CO Philips ("Solo" series) ▲ 442386-2
Bach, J.S.:Con Vn & Ob, w. H. Holliger (ob), E. de Waart (cnd), Philharmonia Orch Philips ("Silver Line" series) ▲ 420700-2 [ADD]
Bach, J.S.:Con for 2 Vns, w. E. de Waart (cnd), Philharmonia Orch Philips ("Silver Line" series) ▲ 420700-2 [ADD]
Bach, J.S.:Sons & Partitas Vn, BWV 1001-1006 Philips ("Duo" series) 2-▲ 438736-2
Bach, J.S.:Sons Vn, w. C. Jaccottet (hpd), P. Mermoud (vc)—BWV 1014-1019, 1021 & 1023; BWV 1020 & 1022 [doubtful] Philips 2-▲ 426452-2 [ADD]
Bach, J.S.:Sons Vn, w. Philippe Mermoud (vc), Christiane Jaccottet (hpd)—BWV 1014-1023 Philips 2-▲ 454011-2
Beethoven, L. van:Con Vn, Op. 61, w. C. Davis (cnd), Royal Concertgebouw Orch Philips ▲ 420348-2 [ADD]
Beethoven, L. van:Romances Vn, w. B. Haitink (cnd), Royal Concertgebouw Orch Philips ("Duo" series) 2-▲ 442577-2
Beethoven, L. van:Romances Vn, w. E. de Waart (cnd), New Philharmonia Orch Philips ▲ 420348-2 [ADD]
Beethoven, L. van:Son 1 Vn, w. William Kapell (pno) Stradivarius ▲ STV 10020 [ADD]
Beethoven, L. van:Son 2 Vn, w. Claudio Arrau (pno) Philips ("Solo" series) ▲ 442651-2
Beethoven, L. van:Son 3 Vn, w. C. Haskil (pno) *(rec live in performance)* Melodram ▲ MEL 18001
Beethoven, L. van:Son 4 Vn, w. Claudio Arrau (pno) Philips ("Solo" series) ▲ 442651-2
Beethoven, L. van:Son 4 Vn, w. C. Haskil (pno) *(rec Aug. 22, 1960)* Ermitage ▲ ERM 112 [ADD]
Beethoven, L. van:Son 5 Vn, "Spring", w. Claudio Arrau (pno) Philips ("Solo" series) ▲ 442651-2
Beethoven, L. van:Son 5 Vn, "Spring", w. Clara Haskil (pno) *(rec Sept. 18, 1957)* Music & Arts ▲ CD 860 [AAD]
Beethoven, L. van:Son 8 Vn, w. Claudio Arrau (pno) Philips ("Solo" series) ▲ 442651-2
Beethoven, L. van:Son 10 Vn, w. C. Haskil (pno) *(rec Aug. 22, 1960)* Ermitage ▲ ERM 112 [ADD]
Beethoven, L. van:Son 10 Vn, w. Clara Haskil (pno) *(rec Sept. 18, 1957)* Music & Arts ▲ CD 860 [AAD]
Debussy, C.:Son Vn, w. I. Hajdu (gtr) Philips ▲ 422839-2 [ADD]
Mendelssohn, F.:Con in e Vn & Orch, Op. 64, w. C.M. Giulini (cnd), Hessian RSO Originals ▲ ORISH 818 [ADD]
Mendelssohn, F.:Trio 1 Pno, w. P. Fournier (vn), N. Magaloff (vc) Arkadia ▲ 606
Mendelssohn, F.:Trio 2 Pno, w. N. Magaloff (pno), P. Fournier (vc) Arkadia ▲ 606
Mozart, W.A.:Cons Vn, w. C. Davis (cnd), London SO Philips 2-▲ 438323-2
Mozart, W.A.:Qts Pno, w. W. Kapell (pno), M. Thomas (va), P. Tortelier (vc)—K.493 *(rec live June 1, 1953)* Music & Arts 4-▲ CD 689 (m) [AAD]
Mozart, W.A.:Sons Vn Pno (misc), w. C. Haskil (pno)—K.378 *(rec Aug. 22, 1960)* Ermitage ▲ ERM 112 [ADD]
Mozart, W.A.:Sons Vn Pno (misc), w. C. Haskil (pno)—K.304 & 454 *(rec live)* Melodram ▲ MEL 18001

▲ = CD ♦ = Enhanced CD Δ = MD ■ = Cassette Tape □ = DCC

Grumiaux, Arthur (vn) (cont.)
Mozart, W.A.:Sons Vn Pno (misc), w. Clara Haskil (pno)—Nos. 5 & 10 *(rec Sept. 18, 1957)* Music & Arts ▲ CD 860 [AAD]
Mozart, W.A.:Sons Vn Pno (misc), w. C. Haskil (pno)—K.301, 304, 376 & 378 Philips ▲ 412253-2 [ADD]
Schubert, Franz:Trio 2 Pno, w. N. Magaloff (pno), P. Fournier (vc) Arkadia ▲ 598
Stravinsky, I.:Con Vn, w. F. Fricsay (cnd), Cologne RSO Originals ▲ ORISH 818 [AAD]

Grünbacher, G. (cl)
Mozart, W.A.:Music of, w. D. Robin (sop), A. Martin (bar), K. Leitner (pno), K. Leitner (cnd), Vienna Mozart Orch—features selections from Die Entführung aus dem Serail, K.384; Don Giovanni, K.527; Serenade No. 13, K.525, "Eine kleine Nachtmusik"; Con. No. 21 in C for Piano & Orch., K.467; Symphony No. 41 in C, K.551, "Jupiter"; Con. No. 5 in A for Violin & Orch., K.219; Die Zauberflöte, K.620; Alla turca [arr. for orch.] *(rec Feb. 9–13, 1990)* Naxos ▲ 8.550866 [DDD]
Mozart, W.A.:Music of, w. D. Robin (sop), A. Martin (bar), K. Leitner (pno), K. Leitner (cnd), Vienna Mozart Orch—features selections from Le nozze di Figaro, K.492; Con. No. 23 in A for Piano & Orch., K.488; Sym. No. 40 in g, K.550; Die Zauberflöte, K.620; Posthorn Serenade, K.320; Con. in A for Clarinet & Orch., K.622; Sym. No. 35 in in D, K.385 "Haffner" *(rec Feb. 9–13, 1990)* Naxos ▲ 8.550867 [DDD]

Grunblatt, George (syn)
East/West, w. Richard Pinhas (syns/gtr), Norman Spinrad (voc), Dominique E. (voc), Patrick Gauthier (syn), François Auger (perc), Steve Shehan (perc), Didier Batard (bass gtr) Cuneiform ▲ Rune 31
L'Ethique, w. Richard Pinhas (syns/gtr), Gilles Deleuze (voc), J. P. Goude (syn/perc), Patrick Gauthier (syn/bass), Bernard Paganotti (bass), François Auger (drums), Clément Bailly (drums) Cuneiform ▲ Rune 36X

Grunblatt, George (syns/gtr)—see ORCHESTRAS & ENSEMBLES Heldon

Grund, Paul (mand)
Music for Lute, Guitar & Mandolin, w. Konrad Ragossnig (gtr), Anton Stingl (lt), Michael Schäffer (lt), Karl Scheit (gtr), Leo Witoszinskyj (gtr), William Matthews (gtr), Artur Rumetsch (mand), Edith Bauer-Slais (mand), Elfriede Kunschak (mand) Vox Box 3-▲ CD3X 3022

Grund, Wenzel (cl)
Honegger, A.:Sonatina Cl, w. N. Popov (pno) Gallo ▲ CD 573 [DAD]
Milhaud, D.:Caprice, w. N. Popov (pno) Gallo ▲ CD 573 [DAD]
Milhaud, D.:Duo concertante Cl & Pno, w. N. Popov (pno) Gallo ▲ CD 573 [DAD]
Milhaud, D.:Sonatina Cl, w. N. Popov (pno) Gallo ▲ CD 573 [DAD]
Poulenc, F.:Son Cl Pno, w. N. Popov (pno) Gallo ▲ CD 573 [DAD]
Tailleferre, G.:Arabesque, w. N. Popov (pno) Gallo ▲ CD 573 [DAD]
Tailleferre, G.:Son Cl Gallo ▲ CD 573 [DAD]

Grunenwald, J. J. (org)
Boulanger, L.:Du fond de l'abîme, w. Oralia Dominguez (ct), Raymond Amade (ten), I. Markevitch (cnd), Lamoureux Orch, Elisabeth Brasseur Chorale *(rec Salle Pleyel, Paris)* Everest ▲ EVC 9034 [AAD]
Boulanger, L.:Pie Jesu, w. Alain Fauqueur (boy sop), I. Markevitch (cnd), Lamoureux Orch members *(rec Salle Pleyel, Paris)* Everest ▲ EVC 9034 [AAD]
Boulanger, L.:Psalm 24, w. I. Markevitch (cnd), Lamoureux Orch, Elisabeth Brasseur Chorale *(rec Salle Pleyel, Paris)* Everest ▲ EVC 9034 [AAD]

Grünfarb, Josef (vn)
Pettersson, G.A.:Sons for 2 Vns, w. Karl-Ove Mannberg (vn) Caprice ▲ CAP 21401 [AAD]

Grünfeld, Alfred (pno)
Alfred Grünfeld Opal ▲ 9850 [AAD]

Grünkorn, I. (vn)
Lachner, F.P.:Nonet, w. A. Duisberg (fl), D. Wollenweber (ob), P. Prieditis (cl), P. Douglas (hn), M. Postinghel (bn), M. Gieler (va), T. Ruge (vc), F. Heidenreich (db) *(rec June 10, 1991)* Thorofon ▲ CTH 2132 [DDD]

Grunschlag, Rosi (pno)
Ballou, E.W.:Son for 2 Pnos, w. T. Grunschlag (pno) CRI ▲ CD 606 [ADD]
Dello Joio, N.:Aria & Toccata, w. T. Grunschlag (pno) CRI ■ ACS 6012
Dello Joio, N.:Aria & Toccata, w. T. Grunschlag (pno) CRI ▲ CD 606 [ADD]
Grunschlag & Grunschlag, w. Toni Grunschlag (pno) *(rec 1981 & 1991)* CRI ▲ CRI 606 [ADD/DDD]
Hindemith, P.:Son for 2 Pnos, w. T. Grunschlag (pno) CRI ▲ CD 606 [ADD]
Luening, O.:Coal-Scuttle Blues, w. T. Grunschlag (pno) CRI ▲ CD 606 [DDD]
Martinů, B.:Fant for 2 Pnos, w. T. Grunschlag (pno) CRI ▲ CD 606 [ADD]
Milhaud, D.:Les Songes, Op. 124, w. T. Grunschlag (pno) CRI ▲ CD 606 [ADD]
Starer, R.:Son Pnos, w. T. Grunschlag (pno) CRI ▲ CD 606 [DDD]

Grunschlag, Toni (pno)
Ballou, E.W.:Son for 2 Pnos, w. R. Grunschlag (pno) CRI ▲ CD 606 [ADD]
Dello Joio, N.:Aria & Toccata, w. R. Grunschlag (pno) CRI ■ ACS 6012
Dello Joio, N.:Aria & Toccata, w. R. Grunschlag (pno) CRI ▲ CD 606 [ADD]
Grunschlag & Grunschlag, w. Rosi Grunschlag (pno) *(rec 1981 & 1991)* CRI ▲ CRI 606 [ADD/DDD]
Hindemith, P.:Son for 2 Pnos, w. R. Grunschlag (pno) CRI ▲ CD 606 [ADD]
Luening, O.:Coal-Scuttle Blues, w. R. Grunschlag (pno) CRI ▲ CD 606 [DDD]
Martinů, B.:Fant for 2 Pnos, w. R. Grunschlag (pno) CRI ▲ CD 606 [ADD]
Milhaud, D.:Les Songes, Op. 124, w. R. Grunschlag (pno) CRI ▲ CD 606 [ADD]
Starer, R.:Son Pnos, w. R. Grunschlag (pno) CRI ▲ CD 606 [DDD]

Grunth, Lars (va)—see also ORCHESTRAS & ENSEMBLES Molino Trio
Molino, F.:Trio Fl, Op. 4/1, w. B. Larsen (fl), J. Sommer (gtr) *(rec Feb. 22–23, 1993)* Classico ▲ CLASSCD 106
Molino, F.:Trio Fl, Op. 45, w. B. Larsen (fl), J. Sommer (gtr) *(rec Feb. 22–23, 1993)* Classico ▲ CLASSCD 106

Gruppman, Igor (vn)
Arnold, M.:Con for 2 Vns, w. V. Gruppman (vn), D. Barra (cnd), San Diego CO *(rec Nov 29, 1991)* Koch International Classics ▲ KIC 7134-2 [DDD]
Berlioz, H.:Rêverie et caprice, w. Y. Talmi (cnd), San Diego SO *(rec Copley Symphony Hall, San Diego, May 13–14, 1995)* Naxos ▲ 8.553034 [DDD]
Respighi, O.:Poema autunnale, w. D. Barra (cnd), San Diego CO Koch International Classics ▲ KIC 7215 [DDD]
Rózsa, M.:Sinf concertante, w. Richard Boch (vc), J. Sedares (cnd), New Zealand SO Koch International Classics ▲ KIC 7304 [DDD]

Gruppman, V. (vn)
Arnold, M.:Con for 2 Vns, w. I. Gruppman (vn), D. Barra (cnd), San Diego CO *(rec Nov 29, 1991)* Koch International Classics ▲ KIC 7134-2 [DDD]

Grütter, Martin André (cym/tamtam)
Hauser, F.:Die Welle, w. Roli Fischer (cym), Barbara Frey (cym), Cyril Lützelschwab (cym), Lukas Rohner (cym), Severin Steinhauser (cym), Hans Ulrich (cym), Ruud Wiener (cym), Michael Erni (timp), Fran Lorkovic (timp), F. Hauser (cnd) *(rec Studio DRS, Basel, Switzerland, Nov. 6, 1988)* Hat Hut ▲ hat ART CD 6017 [ADD]

Grützmann, Susanne (pno)
Khachaturian, A.:Spartacus, w. J. Schwab (vc), J. Tuggle (cnd), Brandenburg PO *(rec Jan. 1993)* Divox ▲ CDX 39307 [DDD]

Grychtolówna, Lidia (pno)
Beethoven, L. van:Con Vn, Vc & Pno, "Triple Con", w. H. Szeryng (pno), J. Starker (vc), H. Dressel (cnd), Folkwang CO Philips ("Duo" series) 2-▲ 442580-2
Chopin, F.:Impromptus *(rec Warsaw, 1960)* Polskie Nagrania ▲ PNCD 312
Chopin, F.:Scherzos *(rec Warsaw, 1960)* Polskie Nagrania ▲ PNCD 312

Gryn, Roman (tpt)
Stachowicz, D.:Veni Consolator, w. Benigna Jaskulska (sop), Tutti e solo *(rec Grand Ballroom, Rydzyna Castle, Poland, Sept 1994)* Dorian Discovery ▲ DIS 80136 [DDD]

Gryspeere, Kristof van (pno)
Berkeley, M.:For the Savage Messiah, w. Dirk Lievens (vn), Kaat De Cock (va), Stefaan Craeynest (vc), Jan Verheye (db) *(rec Steurbaut Sound Recording Ctr)* René Gailly ▲ CD87 118 [DDD]

Gu, W.-F. (va)
Debussy, C.:Danses sacrée et profane, w. Y. Kondonassis (hp), F. Cohen (cl), M. Chalifour (vn), S. Konopka (va), R. Weiss (vc), T. Sperl (db), J. Smith (instr) *(rec Nov. 23–25, 1992)* Telarc ▲ CD 80361 [DDD]
Ravel, M.:Intro & Allegro, w. Y. Kondonassis (hp), J. Smith (fl), F. Cohen (cl), M. Chalifour (vn), S. Konopka (va), R. Weiss (vc), T. Sperl (db) *(rec Nov. 23–25, 1992)* Telarc ▲ CD 80361 [DDD]
Ravel, M.:Pavane pour une infante défunte, w. Y. Kondonassis (hp), J. Smith (fl), F. Cohen (cl), M. Chalifour (vn), S. Konopka (va), R. Weiss (vc), T. Sperl (db) [arr. by Kondonassis] *(rec Nov. 23–25, 1992)* Telarc ▲ CD 80361 [DDD]

Guaitoli, Carlo (pno)
Battiato, F.:Messa Arcaica, w. Akemi Sakamoto (mez), Franco Battiato (voc), Filippo Destrieri (kbd/cmpt), Angelo Privitera (kbd/cmpt), A. Ballista (cnd), Italian Virtuosi, Filippo Maria Bressan (cnd), Athestis Chorus Hemisphere ▲ 837234-2

Gualandris, F. (tuba)
Milesi, P.:Modi 2, w. L. M. Pickova (sop), Françoise Goddard (alt), M. Ferradini (ten), B. Andersen (bass), D. Cassamagnaghi (fl), S. Scanziani (ob), A. Bianchi (cl/b cl), E. Crisafulli (bn), C. Gazzola (hn), F. Gualandris (tuba), A. Girardi (celtic hp), R. Anedda (vn), E. Groppo (vn), M. Pagani (vn), M. Ravasio (va), S. Righini (vc), P. Rizzi (db), J. Scully (perc), P. Milesi (cnd) Cuneiform ▲ RUNE 63

Gualda, Sylvio (perc)
Bartók, B.:Con for 2 Pnos, w. K. Labeque (pno), M. Labeque (pno), J.-P. Drouet (perc), S. Rattle (cnd), City of Birmingham SO EMI ▲ CDC 47446
Bartók, B.:Son for 2 Pnos, w. K. Labeque (pno), M. Labeque (pno), J.-P. Drouet (perc) EMI ▲ CDC 47446
Xenakis, I.:Oresteïa, w. Spiros Sakkas (bar), Strasbourg Univ Chorus Salabert ▲ SCD 8906

Gualdo, Sylvio (perc)
Bernstein, L.:West Side Story (symphonic dances), w. K. Labèque (pno), M. Labèque (pno), Jean-Pierre Drouet (perc), Trilok Gurtu (perc)—Overture; Scherzando; Blues; Somewhere; Scherzo; Mambo; Cha-cha; Cool; The rumble; I have a love [arr. Irwin Kostal for 2 pianos, percussion & jazz drums] CBS ▲ MK 45531 [DDD]

Gudel, Irene (vc)
Il Flauto Dolce, w. Benedikta Bonitz (rcr), Yoma Appenheimer (hpd) Arcadia ▲ ARC 1993-2 [DDD]

Gudmundsdóttir, Gudny (vn)
Eirlksdottlr, Karolina:In vultus solis Music from Iceland ▲ ITM 701 [ADD]
Ragnarsson, H.:Music of, w. S. E. Magnúsdóttir (mez), H. Halldórsdóttir (vn), G. Gudnadóttir (vn), G. Kristmundsson (va), S. Halldórsson (vc), R. Korn (db), Ó. V. Albertsson (pno), S. A. Jónsdóttir (pno), H. Ragnarsson (pno), E. Erlendsdóttir (pno), M. H. Fridriksson (org), Sakari, Wilkinson (cnd), Iceland SO, G. Cortes (cnd), J. Stefánsson (cnd), T. Ingólfsdóttir (cnd), Hamrahlíd Choir, Icelandic Opera Chorus, Langholts Church Graduale Choir—Meine kleine Freundin [In the Ballroom]; Lovers Duet; After the concert; Meine kleine Freundin [Annie listens to the Radio]; Lif's Theme [On the Beach]; Lif's Theme II [Night Prayer]; Composing Ov [Vars I, II & III] Music From Iceland ▲ ITM 605 [DDD]

Gudmundsson, Hafsteinn (bn)—see ORCHESTRAS & ENSEMBLES Reykjavik Wind Quintet

Gudnadóttir, Gréta (vn)
Leifs, J.:Music of, w. Sigrídur Ella Magnúsdóttir (mez), Ólafur Vignir Albertsson (pno), Sólveig Anna Jónsdóttir (pno), Hjálmar Ragnarsson (pno), Edda Erlendsdóttir (pno), Marteinn Hunger Fridriksson (org), Hildigunnur Halldórsdóttir (vn), Gudmundur Kristmundsson (va), Sigurdur Halldórsson (vc), Richard Korn (db), Iceland SO, Icelandic Opera Chorus, Langholts Church Graduale Choir, Hamrahlid Choir—Icelandic Cant, Op. 13/4; Valse Lento, Op. 2/1; Icelandic Dance, Op. 11/2 [Tempo Giusto]; Requiem; Lullaby [After the Riots]; Fairy-Tale in the Wood [from Baldr, Op. 34]; Funeral March; Separation [from Elegy, Op. 53]; Galdra Loftur Ov, Op. 10; Funeral March, Op. 6; Reverie; Reunion [from Elegy, Op. 53]; Fine I, Op. 55; Andante [The Last Supper]; Preludia Organo, Op. 16/3 [In the Church]; The Tear of Stone [from Elegy, Op. 53] Music From Iceland ▲ ITM 605 [DDD]

Gueit, Philippe (org)
Boëllmann, L.:Offertoire sur des noëls Sonpact ▲ SPT 92005
Franck, C.:L'Organiste—[sels] Messe de Noël:Premier verset du Kyrie, Deuxieme verset, Troisieme verset, Sortie sur "Venz divin Messie," Noël angevin en sol majeur, Noël angevin en sol mineur, Vieux Noël en sol mineur, Vieux Noël en re mineur, Grand Choeur sur des Noëls Sonpact ▲ SPT 92005
Gigout, E.:Rhapsodie sur des Noëls Sonpact ▲ SPT 92005
Guilmant, A.:Noëls—Noël expagnol [offertoire], Noël brabançon "alla Haydn" [élévation], "Puer nobis nascitur" [variations], Noël polonais "Accourez bergers fidèles" [introduction et variations], Noël "Nuit sombre" [offertoire], Noël écossais [communion], Noël "J. est bien marié" [offertoire] Sonpact ▲ SPT 92005

Guéneux, Georges (fl)
Cimarosa, D.:Con for 2 Fls, w. P.-L. Graf (fl), R. Tschupp (cnd), Zurich Camerata *(rec 1968)* Jecklin-Disco ▲ JD 506-2 [ADD]

Guéneux, R. (pno)
Ringger, R.U.:Pieces Pno Grammont ▲ CTSP 29-2 [ADD]

Guerda, Gloria (vc)
Tournier, M.:Nocturno, w. Zoraida Avila (hp) *(rec Madrid, Oct 1–3 1990)* RNE/Spanish National Radio ▲ M3/06 [DDD]

Guerguerian, P. (perc)
Dun, T.:Silk Road, w. S. Botti (sop) *(rec June 4, 1992)* CRI ▲ CD 655 [DDD]
Lebaron, A.:Rite of the Black Sun, w. W.A. Trigg (perc), F. Cassara (zoomoozophone), M. Pugliese (perc), C. Heldrich (cnd), New Music Consort Mode ▲ 30

Guerguerian, Paul (perc)—see ORCHESTRAS & ENSEMBLES New Music Consort

Guerrero, J. A. (vc)—see ORCHESTRAS & ENSEMBLES Aglàia Ensemble

Guerrini, Andrea (vn)
Ragazzi, A.:Con Grosso, w. Marco Rogliano (vn), Eduardo Pitone (va), Aurelio Bertucci (vc), Antonella Cristiano (hpd), I. Caiazza (cnd), I Solisti Partenopei *(rec Mar 1996)* Kicco Classics ▲ 396 [DDD]

Guerrini, M. (pno)
Puccini, D.:Con Pno, w. G. Cosmi (cnd), Lucca Teatro Comunale del Giglio Orch Bongiovanni ▲ GB 2048 [DDD]

Guest, George (org)
Duruflé, M.:Motets on Gregorian Chants, Op. 10, w. G. Guest (cnd), St. John's College Choir Cambridge London ("Double Decca" series) 2-▲ 436486-2
Duruflé, M.:Requiem, w. George Guest (cnd), St. John's College Choir Cambridge London ("Double Decca" series) 2-▲ 436486-2
Fauré, G.:Cantique de Jean Racine, w. G. Guest (cnd), St. John's College Choir Cambridge London ("Double Decca" series) 2-▲ 436486-2
Fauré, G.:Messe basse, w. G. Guest (cnd), St. John's College Choir Cambridge London ("Double Decca" series) 2-▲ 436486-2

Gugel, Matthias (hn)
Burkhard, W.:Serenade Fl, Op. 77, w. S. Gärtner (fl), W. Meienberg (cl), J. Stavicek (bn), M. Paccagnella (hp), H. Schneeberger (vn), C. Schiller (va), B. Wyganth (db) *(rec between 1985 & 1989)* Jecklin-Disco ▲ JD 647-2 [ADD]

Guggeis, Edgar (perc)
Hummel, B.:Music of, w. F. Bach (perc), S. Gagelmann (perc), Peter Sadlo (perc)—Tempo di valse, Op. 76c; 5 Szenen für 2 Schlagzeuger, Op. 58; Marimbana, Op. 95d; 5 Aspekte für Schlagzeuger, Op. 88d; Quattro pezzi für Schlagzeuger, Op. 92; Freken 70 für vier Schlagzeuger, Op. 38 *(rec Gasteig Munich, Dec. 1993)* Thorofon ▲ CTH 2233 [DDD]

Guggenberger, P. (vn)
Schubert, Franz:Con Vn, w. Vienna Ensemble Sony Classical ▲ SK 48386 [DDD]
Schubert, Franz:Rondo Vn, D.438, w. Vienna Ensemble Sony Classical ▲ SK 48386 [DDD]

Guggenberger, Paul (vn)—see ORCHESTRAS & ENSEMBLES Vienna Ring Ensemble

Guggenheim, Janet Goodman (pno)
Encores, w. Itzhak Perlman (vn) EMI Classics ▲ CDC 54108 ■ 4DS 54108
Prokofiev, S.:Son Vc, w. Michael Grebanier (vc) *(rec Fisher Hall, Santa Rosa, CA, Feb. 9–12, 1994)* Naxos ▲ 8.553136 [DDD]

Guglielmo, Federico (vn)—see ORCHESTRAS & ENSEMBLES L'Arte dell'Arco

Guglielmo, Giovanni (vn)—see ORCHESTRAS & ENSEMBLES L'Arte dell'Arco

Gugoltz (pno)
Debussy, C.:Première rapsodie, w. Robert (cl), E. Ansermet (cnd), Swiss Romande Orch *(rec 1964)* London ▲ 433711-2 [ADD]

Guibbory, Shem (vn)
Davis, A.:Ghost Factory—MAPS, w. W. McGlaughlin (cnd), Kansas City SO Gramavision ▲ R2-79429 [DDD]

Guibentif, Eva (hp)
Vuataz, R.:Destin, w. P. Collet (sax), Y. Brustaux (perc)—3rd movt. *(rec Nov. 1980)* Grammont ▲ CTSP 7-2 [ADD]

Guichard, J. (ob)—see ORCHESTRAS & ENSEMBLES Stanislas Ensemble

Guidetti, N. (fl)
Martini, G.B.:Music for Fls, w. M. Mercelli (fl), G. Perrucci (fl), M. Vangi (fl)—(2 works for 2 Flutes) Sonata in C; Sonata in D; (3 works for 2 Flutes & Continuo) Allegro in C; Allegro & Rondo in C; Pastorale in C Bongiovanni ▲ GB 5517 [DDD]

Guidetti, Pamela (b fl/s rcr)
Crumb, G.:Lux Aeterna, w. Freda Herseth (mez), James Freeman (sitar), Susan Jones (perc), William Kerrigan (perc) *(rec Lang Concert Hall, Swarthmore College)* CRI ▲ CD 723 [DDD]

Guidetti, Pamela (fl)
Musgrave, T.:Orfeo III, w. Mei Chen Liao Cope (vn), Igor Szwec (vn), Michael Strauss (va), Lori Barnett (vc), Miles B. Davis (db), J. Freeman (cnd) *(rec Lang Concert Hall, Swarthmore College)* CRI ▲ CD 723 [DDD]

Guido, Verena (Medieval fls)—see ORCHESTRAS & ENSEMBLES Vox

Guignon, Pierre (dr)
Constant, M.:Choruses & Interludes, w. Jean-Jacques Justafre (hn), Pierre-Marie Bonafosse (sax), François Moutin (b gtr), Andy Emler (pno), J. Kaltenbach (cnd), Nancy SO *(rec Salle Poirel, Nancy, Apr. 4, 1990)* Erato ▲ 94815-2 [DDD]

Guijarro, Ana (pno)
Castillo, M.:Pno Music—Sonatina (1949); Toccata (1952); Preludio, Diferencias Y Toccata (1959); Tres Piezas (1959); Sonata (1972); Tempus (1980); Nocturno en Sanlúcar (1985); Intimus (1986); Perpetuum (1992) Almaviva ("Musical Heritage of Andalusia" series) ▲ 119 [DDD]

Guilels, Elena (pno)
Tchaikovsky, P.:Music of, w. K. Nagata (vn)—Méditation; Scherzo; Mélody; Sérénade Méloncolique; Valse-Scherzo; Romance; Feuillet d'Album; Chant sans paroles; Valse sentimentale; Chanson d'automne; Andante cantabile; Barcarolle; Chanson Triste Talent ▲ DOM 2910 25 [DDD]

Guilet, D. (vn)—see ORCHESTRAS & ENSEMBLES Beaux Arts Trio

Guiliani, Alberto (trbn)—see ORCHESTRAS & ENSEMBLES Academy of Ancient Music Instumental Ensemble

Guillard, Georges (hpd)
Jacquet De La Guerre, E.:Pièces de clavecin qui peuvent se jouer sur le viollon, w. B. Charbonnier (baroque vn) Arion 2-▲ ARN 268012 [AAD]
Jacquet De La Guerre, E.:Le Raccomondement comique de Pierrot et de Nicole, w. I. Poulenard (sop), M. Verschaeve (bass), *(ensemble unknown)* [F] Arion 2-▲ ARN 268012 [AAD]
Jacquet De La Guerre, E.:Trio Sons for 2 Vns, w. B. Charbonnier (vn), Catherine Giardelli (vn), Claire Giardelli (vc)—No. 4 Arion 2-▲ ARN 268012 [AAD]

Guillard, Georges (org)
Alain, J.:Music of, w. Delphine Collot (sop), Bruno Boterf (ten), Jacques Bona (bar), Françoise Gyps (fl), Laurent Decker (ob), Bruno Pazqueir (va), Philippe Muller (vc), Ludwig String Quartet, Georges Guillard (cnd), St. Louis Camerata Vocal Ensemble—2 Melodies for Sop & Pno; Nuptial Song for Bar, Bass, Vc & Org; Post-Scriptum for 3 Female Voices & Pno; Canticle in Phrygian Mode for 4 Mixed-Voice, Sop & Strs; Invention for Fl, Ob & Cl; Monody for solo Fl; Prelude for Str Qnt; Adagio for Str Qnt; Funerals for Str Qnt; March of the Horiaces & the Curiaces for 2 Bugles, Drum & Org Arion ▲ ARN 68321
Alain, O.:Souvenances, w. Françoise Gyps (fl) Arion ▲ ARN 68321

Guillou, Jean (org)
The Art of Improvisation Dorian ▲ DOR 90101 [DDD]
Bach, J.S.:Cons Org, BWV 592-597—playing the 3 Vivaldi arr., BWV 593, 594 & 596 Dorian ▲ DOR 90118 [DDD]
Bach, J.S.:Goldberg Vars—transd. Guillou; [the Kleuker Organ of Notre-Dame des Neiges, Alpe d'Huez, France] Dorian ▲ DOR 90110 [DDD]
Bach, J.S.:Org Music (comp)—8 Chorale Preludes from Orgelbüchlein (BWV 599-606); Fantasia & Fugue in g, BWV 542; Fugue on a theme by Corelli, BWV 579; Partita on "O Gott, du frommer Gott," BWV 767; Preludes & Fugues in g, BWV 542 & in a, BWV 543; Trio Sonata No. 1 in E♭, BWV 525 Dorian ▲ DOR 90111 [DDD]
Bach, J.S.:Org Music (comp)—Chorale Preludes, BWV.645, 646, 647, 653b, 659 & 660; Chorale Settings, BWV.714, 715 & 716; Fantasia, BWV.570; Fugue in c, BWV.574; Pastorella, BWV.590; Prelude & Fugue, BWV.539, 547 & 566 *(rec Aug 1990)* Dorian ▲ DOR 90152 [DDD]
Bach, J.S.:Org Music (misc)—Allabreve, BWV 589; Chorale Preludes, BWV 607-610, 651, 653, 654, 702 & 703; Partita, BWV 768; Prelude, BWV 569; Toccata & Fugue, BWV 538 *(rec Aug 1990)* Dorian ▲ DOR 90149 [DDD]
Bach, J.S.:Org Music (misc)—Chorale Preludes, BWV 611, 612, 652, 655, 656, 690-695 & 701; Prelude, BWV 568; Prelude & Fugue, BWV 544; Toccata & Fugue, BWV 565; Trio Sonata, BWV 526 *(rec Aug 1990)* Dorian ▲ DOR 90150 [DDD]
Bach, J.S.:Org Music (misc)—Chorale Preludes, BWV 657, 658a, 704-706, 708, 709, 710-713; Fantasy, BWV 562; Preludes & Fugues, BWV 548 & 549; Toccata & Fugue, BWV 540 *(rec Aug 1990)* Dorian ▲ DOR 90151 [DDD]
Bach, J.S.:Prelude & Fugue Org, BWV 566 *(rec Nov 1984)* Pierre Verany ▲ PV.785021 [DDD]
Bach, J.S.:Toccata, Adagio & Fugue Org, BWV 564 *(rec Cathedrale de Breda, Netherlands, Nov. 15-17, 1984)* Pierre Verany ▲ PVY 730001 [DDD]
Bach, J.S.:Toccata, Adagio & Fugue Org, BWV 564 *(rec Nov 1984)* Pierre Verany ▲ PV.785021 [DDD]
Bach, J.S.:Toccata & Fugue Org, BWV 538, "Dorian" *(rec Nov 1984)* Pierre Verany ▲ PV.785021 [DDD]
Bach, J.S.:Toccata & Fugue Org, BWV 538, "Dorian" *(rec Cathedrale de Breda, Netherlands, Nov. 15-17, 1984)* Pierre Verany ▲ PVY 730001 [DDD]
Bach, J.S.:Toccata & Fugue Org, BWV 540 *(rec Nov 1984)* Pierre Verany ▲ PV.785021 [DDD]
Bach, J.S.:Toccata & Fugue Org, BWV 540 *(rec Cathedrale de Breda, Netherlands, Nov 15-17, 1984)* Pierre Verany ▲ PVY 730001 [DDD]
Bach, J.S.:Toccata & Fugue Org, BWV 565 *(rec Nov 1984)* Pierre Verany ▲ PV.785021 [DDD]
Bach, J.S.:Toccata & Fugue Org, BWV 565 *(rec Cathedrale de Breda, Netherlands, Nov 15-17, 1984)* Pierre Verany ▲ PVY 730001 [DDD]
Bach, J.S.:Toccata & Fugue Org, BWV 566 *(rec Cathedrale de Breda, Netherlands, Nov 15-17, 1984)* Pierre Verany ▲ PVY 730001 [DDD]
Franck, C.:Org Music (comp) [Great Organ of St. Eustache, Paris] [Disc 1:]—Pièce héroïque; Pastorale; Fantaisie in A; Choral No. 1 in E; Choral No. 2 in B; Choral No. 3 in a; [Disc 2:] Final in B♭; Fantaisie in C; Prélude, Fugue et Variation; Cantabile; Prière; Grande pièce symphonique *(rec 1989)* Dorian 2-▲ DOR 90135 [DDD]
The Great Organ of Saint Eustache, Paris:Inaugural Recording, 1989 Dorian ▲ DOR 90135 [DDD]
Guillou, J.:Hyperion, or The Rhetoric of Fire Dorian ▲ DOR 90134 [DDD]
Improvisations for Christmas Dorian ▲ DOR 90119 [DDD]
Jongen, J.:Symphonie Concertante, w. E. Mata (cnd), Dallas SO *(rec Jan. 1994)* Dorian ▲ DOR 90200 [DDD]
Organ Encores Dorian ▲ DOR 90112 [DDD]
Reubke, J.:Son Org Dorian ▲ DOR 90106 [DDD]
Saint-Saëns, C.:Sym 3, w. E. Mata (cnd), Dallas SO *(rec Jan. 1994)* Dorian ▲ DOR 90200 [DDD]
Vivaldi, A.:Cons Org [arr Guillou]—2 concerti Dorian ▲ DOR 90118 [DDD]

Guillou, Jean (pno)
Reubke, J.:Son Pno Dorian ▲ DOR 90106 [DDD]

Guimarães, Maria Inês (pno)
Oswald, H.:Pno Music—Feuilles d'Album, Op. 20; Valse Lente; Três Peças, Op. 23; Nocturnes, Op. 6/1 & 2; Il Neige; Seis Peças, Op. 14 *(rec Clara-Wieck-Auditorium, Sandhausen, Sept 13-14 & Nov 7-8, 199)* Marco Polo ("Latin American Classics" series) ▲ 8.223639 [DDD]

Guimond, C. (baroque fl)—see ORCHESTRAS & ENSEMBLES Arion Ensemble

Guimond, Claire (fl)
Boismortier, J.B. de:Sons Fl & Continuo, w. Luc Beauséjour (hpd)—Nos. 1-6 Analekta ▲ ATM 29730
Boismortier, J.B. de:Sons Fl, Op. 91, w. L. Beauséjour (hpd)—in D, g, G, e, A, c *(rec Aug. 22-24, 1994)* Analekta Fleur de Lys ▲ FL 2 3008 [DDD]
Telemann, G.P.:Fants Fl *(rec St-Joseph-de-Rivière-des-Prairies Church, Aug 1995)* Analekta ▲ AN 2 8053 [DDD]

Guimond, Claire (trns fl)
Gluck, C.W.:Orfeo ed Euridice (dance of the blessed spirits), w. Barthold Kuijken (trns fl), J. Lamon (cnd), Tafelmusik Sony Classical ▲ MLK 62369 [ADD/DDD]

Guindin, Alexander (pno)
Rachmaninoff, S.:Moments musicaux Russian Season ▲ RUS 288122
Rachmaninoff, S.:Pno Transcriptions—J.S. Bach:Prelude, Gavotte & Gigue [from Vn Part in E]; Bizet:Minuet [from L'Arlésienne]; Kreisler:Liebeslied; Mendelssohn:Scherzo [from A Midsummer Night's Dream]; Mussorgsky:Hopak [from The Sorochintsy Fair]; Rachmaninoff:Lilacs; Daisies; Rimsky-Korsakov:The Flight of the Bumblebee; Schubert:Wohin?; Tchaikovsky:Lullaby Russian Season ▲ RUS 288122

Guinos, Nikos (cl)
Karaindrou, E.:Film Music, w. Jan Garbarek (t sax), Vangelis Christopoulos (ob), Anthis Sokratis (tpt), Tassos Diakoyiorgis (santouri), Vangelis Skouras (hn), Petros Protopapas (fl), Andreas Tsekouras (acc), Christos Sfetsas (vc), Eleni Karaindrou (pno/voc), L. Chalkiadakis (cnd), *(ensemble unknown)*—Farewell Theme; Scream; Improv. On Farewell & Waltz Theme; Farewell Theme II [all from The Beekeeper; w. Jan Garbarek (ten sax), Tassos Diakoyiorgis (satouri), Vassilis Dertilis (kbd), Eleni Karaindrou (pno), Lefteris Chalkiadakis (cnd)]; Elegy for Rosa; Rosa's Song (text:Christofis) [both from Rosa; w. Vangelis Skouras (Fr hn), Petros Protopapas (fl), Alekos Christidis (timp), Eleni Karaindrou (voc), Lefteis Chalkiadakis (cnd)]; Fairytale; Parade; Return; Song [all from Happy Homecoming, Comrade; w. Vangelis Skouras (Fr hn), Christos Sfetsas (vc), Aliki Krithari (hp), Andreas Tsekouras (acc), Eleni Karaindrou (pno), Nelli Semitekolo (pno), Anthis Sokratis (tpt), Lefteris Chalkiadakis (cnd)]; Wandering in Alexandria (2 vers) [both from Wandering; w. Tassos Diakoyiorgis (santouri), Nelli Semitekolo (prepared pno), Anthis Sokratis (tpt), Nikos Guinos (cl), Katerina Ktona (hpd), Christos Sfetsas (vc)]; The Journey [from Voyage to Cythera]; Adagio [from Landscape in the Mist] [both w. Vangelis Christopoulos (ob), str orch, Lefteris Chalkiadakis (cnd)] ECM ▲ 78118-21429-2 [AAD]

Guinovart, Albert (pno)
Turina, J.:Danzas andaluzas Harmonia Mundi ▲ HMI 987009
Turina, J.:Danzas fantásticas Harmonia Mundi ▲ HMI 987009
Turina, J.:Danzas gitanes Harmonia Mundi ▲ HMI 987009
Turina, J.:Danzas sobre temas populares españolas Harmonia Mundi ▲ HMI 987009

Guiomar, Erika (pno)
Fauré, G.:songs, w. Thierry Félix (bar)—Arpège, Op. 76/2; L'horizon chimérique, Op. 118; La bonne chanson, Op. 61; Le parfum impérissable, Op. 76/1; Mélodies de Venise, Op. 58; Mirages, Op. 113; Prison, Op. 83/1; Soir, Op. 83/2 Arcana ▲ ACA 28 [DDD]

Gulbransen, Ørnulf (fl)
Braein, E.F.:Concertino, w. K. Andersen (cnd), Bergen PO Simax ▲ PSC 3117

Gulda, Friedrich (pno)
Beethoven, L. van:Con 4 Pno, w. A. Cluytens (cnd), Swiss-Italian RSO *(rec Switzerland, 1965)* Ermitage ▲ ERM 155
Beethoven, L. van:Con 5 Pno, "Emperor", w. H. Stein (cnd), Vienna PO *(rec ca. 1971)* PWK Classics ▲ PWK 1146 [AAD]
Beethoven, L. van:Son 14 Pno, "Moonlight Son" London ("Double Decker" series) 2-▲ 443012-2
Beethoven, L. van:Son 15 Pno, "Pastoral" London ("Double Decker" series) 2-▲ 443012-2
Beethoven, L. van:Son 17 Pno, "Tempest" London ("Double Decker" series) 2-▲ 443012-2
Beethoven, L. van:Son 21 Pno, "Waldstein" *(rec live, Lugano 1/19/68)* Ermitage ▲ ERM 115 [ADD]
Beethoven, L. van:Son 21 Pno, "Waldstein" London ("Double Decker" series) 2-▲ 443012-2
Beethoven, L. van:Son 22 Pno London ("Double Decker" series) 2-▲ 443012-2
Beethoven, L. van:Son 23 Pno, "Appassionata" London ("Double Decker" series) 2-▲ 443012-2
Beethoven, L. van:Son 24 Pno London ("Double Decker" series) 2-▲ 443012-2
Beethoven, L. van:Son 31 Pno *(rec live 1959)* Artists ▲ FED 58 [ADD]
Beethoven, L. van:Son 32 Pno London ("Double Decker" series) 2-▲ 443012-2
Beethoven, L. van:Vars on a waltz by Diabelli, Op. 120 Musique d'Abord ▲ HMA 1905127 [ADD]
Gulda, F.:Gegenwart, w. U. Anders (perc) *(rec Jan. 1976)* Celestial Harmonies ▲ 19003-2
Gulda, F.:"Non-Stop Gulda" *(rec live, Munich, Nov. 19, 1990)* Sony Classical ▲ SK 52499 [DDD]
Haydn, J.:Sons Pno—Son. in E♭, H.XVI/52 *(rec live, 1959)* Artists ▲ FED 58 [ADD]
Haydn, J.:Son Pno, H.XVII/6, "Andante with Vars" *(rec live, 1959)* Artists ▲ FED 58 [ADD]
Haydn, J.:Son Pno, H.XVII/6, "Andante with Vars" *(rec live, Lugano, Jan. 19, 1968)* Ermitage ▲ ERM 115 [ADD]
Mozart, W.A.:Con 23 Pno, w. N. Harnoncourt (cnd), Royal Concertgebouw Orch Teldec ▲ 2292-42997-2
Mozart, W.A.:Con 23 Pno, w. N. Harnoncourt (cnd), Royal Concertgebouw Orch Teldec ▲ 92150
Mozart, W.A.:Con 26 Pno, w. N. Harnoncourt (cnd), Royal Concertgebouw Orch Teldec ▲ 2292-42997-2
Mozart, W.A.:Con 26 Pno, w. N. Harnoncourt (cnd), Royal Concertgebouw Orch Teldec ▲ 92150
Mozart, W.A.:Music of Sony Classical 2-▲ SX2K 48082
Mozart, W.A.:Son 8 Pno *(rec live, Lugano Jan. 19, 1968)* Ermitage ▲ ERM 115 [ADD]
Schubert, Franz:Impromptus Pno, D.899 *(rec live, Lugano 1/19/68)* Ermitage ▲ ERM 115 [ADD]

Gulda, Paul (pno)
Brahms, J.:Qnt Pno, w. Hagen String Quartet Deutsche Grammophon ▲ 437804-2
Schoenberg, A.:Chamber Sym 1, w. Hagen String Quartet [arr. Webern] Deutsche Grammophon ▲ 437804-2
Schumann, R.:Blumenstück *(rec Oct. 26-29, 1990)* Naxos ▲ 8.550401 [DDD]
Schumann, R.:Kreisleriana *(rec Oct. 26-29, 1990)* Naxos ▲ 8.550401 [DDD]

Guller, Youra (pno)
The Art of Youra Guller, 1895-1980, w. Youra Guller (pno) *(rec late 1970s)* Nimbus ▲ NI 5030
Beethoven, L. van:Son 31 Pno Nimbus ▲ NI 5061 [AAD]
Beethoven, L. van:Son 32 Pno Nimbus ▲ NI 5061 [AAD]

Gulli, Franco (vn)
Mendelssohn, F.:Con in d Vn, Pno & Strs, w. Enrica Cavallo (pno), P. Urbini (cnd), Milano Angelicum Orch Sarx ▲ SRX 2027 [ADD]
Mendelssohn, F.:Con in d Vn, Pno & Strs, w. E. Cavallo (pno), P. Urbini (cnd), Angelicum CO Koch Treasure ▲ 31622-2 [ADD]
Mendelssohn, F.:Son Vn (1838), w. E. Cavallo (pno) Koch Treasure ▲ 31622-2 [ADD]
Mendelssohn, F.:Son Vn (1838), w. Enrica Cavallo (pno) Sarx ▲ SRX 2027 [ADD]
Orrego-Salas, J.:Con Vn, w. T. Baldner (cnd), Indiana Univ SO *(rec Musical Arts Ctr, Bloomington, IN, Oct 4, 1984)* Indiana Univ School of Music ▲ IUSM 02
Paganini, N.:Cantabile, w. E. Cavallo (pno) [arr for vn & pno] *(rec 1963)* Dynamic ▲ CD 30U [AAD]
Paganini, N.:Caprices Vn—Nos. 16 & 17 *(rec 1963)* Dynamic ▲ CD 30U [AAD]
Paganini, N.:Con 5 Vn, w. L. Rosado (cnd), Orch dell'Angelicum *(rec 1963)* Dynamic ▲ CD 30U [AAD]
Paganini, N.:I palpiti, w. E. Cavallo (pno) [arr vn & pno] *(rec 1963)* Dynamic ▲ CD 30U [AAD]
Paganini, N.:Sons Vn & Gtr, Op. 3, w. E. Cavallo (pno)—No. 6 *(rec 1963)* Dynamic ▲ CD 30U [AAD]
Vivaldi, A.:Cons for 4 Vns, w. Luigi Ferro (vn), Edmondo Malanotte (vn), Angelo Stefanato (vn), R. Fasano (cnd), Rome Virtuosi—in b, Op. 3/10 *(rec Opéra de Rome, July & August, 1959)* EMI Classics ▲ CDK 65338 [ADD]

Gullickson, Andrea (ob/ob d'amore)—see ORCHESTRAS & ENSEMBLES Wizards!

594 ▲ = CD ♦ = Enhanced CD Δ = MD ■ = Cassette Tape □ = DCC

Gulyás, Márta (pno)
Bartók, B.:Son in e Vn & Pno, w. Vilmos Szabadi (vn) *(rec 1993)* Hungaroton ▲ HCD 31558 [DDD]
The Virtuoso Violin, w. Vilmos Szabadi (vn) White Label ▲ HRC 180 [ADD]
Günes, Rusen (va)
Saygun, A.A.:Con Va, w. G. Aykal (cnd), London PO Koch Schwann ▲ CD 311002 [DDD]
Gunji, Maya (perc)
Hays, S.:Dreaming the World, w. Thomas Bruckner (bar), Sal Basile (voc), Jennifer López (voc), John Schaffer (voc), Sorrel Hays (voc), Joseph Kubera (pno), John Kennedy (perc), Charles Wood (perc), Eric Kivnick (perc), Jai Smith (perc) New World ▲ 805202 [DDD]
Gunning, Adrian (org)
Demessieux, J.:Chorale Preludes (12) on Gregorian Themes [St John the Evangelist Org, Islington] Herald ▲ HLRCD 1572
Hakim, N.:Org Music [St John the Evangelist Org, Islington]—Mariales Herald ▲ HLRCD 1572
Langlais, J.:Paraphrases grégoriennes [St John the Evangelist Org, Islington] Herald ▲ HLRCD 1572
Langlais, J.:Suite médévale [St John the Evangelist Org, Islington] Herald ▲ HLRCD 1572
Tournemire, C.:L'orgue mystique [St John the Evangelist Org, Islington] Herald ▲ HLRCD 1572
Günther, Fred (va)
Blacher, B.:Songs, w. Katharina Richter (sop), Cornelia Wosnitza (sop), Markus Köhler (bar), Horst Göbel (pno), Chatschatur Kanajan (vn), Piotr Prysiasnik (vn), Ithay Khen (vc), Christian Peters (sax), Markus Weidmann (bn)—3 Chansons; Ungereimtes; 4 Lieder; Nebel; 13 Ways of Looking at a Blackbird; 5 Sinnsprüche Omars des Zeitmachers; 3 Psalmen; Apréslude; Francesca da Rimini; Jazz-Koloraturen Signum ▲ SIG X73-00 [DDD]
Gunther, Thomas (pno)
Kahn, E.I.:Adagio, w. J. Prelle (vn) CRI ▲ CD 563 [DDD]
Kahn, E.I.:Bagatelles CRI ▲ CD 563 [DDD]
Kahn, E.I.:Inventions (3), Op. 7/4, 7 & 8 CRI ▲ CD 563 [DDD]
Kahn, E.I.:Nenia judaeis qui hac aetate perierunt, w. J. Sessions (vc) CRI ▲ CD 563 [DDD]
Guntner, K. (vn)
Spohr, L.:Son 1 Vn, w. H. Storck (hp) Calig ▲ CAL 50887 [DDD]
Spohr, L.:Trio Hp, w. H. Storck (hp), K. Storck (vc) Calig ▲ CAL 50887 [DDD]
Gupta, Buddhadeu Das (sarod)
Battiato, F.:Ricerca sul Terzo, w. Franco Battiato (voc), Alessio Alba (tamboura), Antonio Ballista (pno), Marco Boni (vc), Debendra Kanti Chakraborty (tabla), Guido Corti (cnt), Filippo Destrieri (kbd/computer), John Giblin (bass), Gavin Harrison (dr/perc), Jakko Jakszyk (gtr), Roberto Mazza (ob), Fabrizio Merlini (va), Angelo Privitera (kbd/computer), Mino Bordignon (cnd), Milan Chamber Music Choir Hemisphere ▲ 837234-2
Guralnick, Tom (sax/elec)
Guralnick, T.:Broken Dances—Broken Dance; Whirled Weary; Tone Farm; Memory Link; Sides Peak; Blown Logic; Mobile Motive; In Different Version; Different Version; Foam Tones; In the Out-Take; Spoken Pedals; Reading Sample; Invisible on It *(rec Outpost Performance Space, Albuquerque, NM, Jan 25-27, 1994)* ¿What Next? ▲ WN0017
Guralnik, Robert (pno)
Shostakovich, D.:Qnt Pno, w. Leontóvych String Quartet *(rec May 1994)* Greystone ▲ GS 521 [DDD]
Gurch, T. (cl/b cl)—see ORCHESTRAS & ENSEMBLES Thamyris
Gurch, Ted (sax)
Kodály, Z.:Háry János (suite), w. James Barnes (cimbalom), Reid Harris (va), Y. Levi (cnd), Atlanta SO *(rec Atlanta, 1995-96)* Telarc ▲ CD 80413 [DDD]
Gürke, A. (fid)—see ORCHESTRAS & ENSEMBLES Estampie
Gurlitt, Manfred (pno)
Franck, C.:Son Vn, w. Shin-Ichi Suzuki (vn) *(rec ca 1928)* Symposium ▲ 1156
Schubert, Franz:Songs (misc), w. H. Rehkemper (bar)—21 Lieder—fourteen song cycle selections *(Die schöne Müllerin—Nos. 2, 6, 11, 15, 17; Schwanengesang—Nos. 7 & 13; Winterreise—Nos. 1, 5, 7, 13, 15, 23, 24)*; seven individual songs—Das Rosenband, D.280; Erlkönig, D.328; Am, Bach im Frühling, D.361; Orpheus, D.474; Sei mir gegrüsst, D.741; Der Musensohn, D.764; Auf dem Wasser zu singen, D.774 *(rec 1924-28 for Grammophon)* Preiser ("Lebendige Vergangenheit" series) ▲ 89058 (m) [AAD]
Gurt, Joseph (pno)
Bolcom, W.:Qt Pno, w. Charles Avshalian (vn), David Ireland (va), Jerome Jelinek (vc) *(rec Univ of Michigan, May 1979)* CRI ▲ CD 711 [ADD]
Finney, R.L.:Son 2 Vc, w. Jerome Jelinek (vc) CRI ▲ CD 711 [ADD]
Finney, R.L.:Trio 2 Pno, w. Charles Avshalian (vn), Jerome Jelinek (vc) *(rec Univ of Michigan, Oct 1980)* CRI ▲ CD 711 [ADD]
Gürtler, Friedrick (pno)
Grieg, E.:Songs, w. K. Dolberg (alt)—While I Wait; The First Meeting; With a Water Lily; Two Brown Eyes; I Love You; A Swan Point ▲ PCD 5106
Lange-Müller, P.E.:Songs, w. K. Dolberg (alt)—Shulamite's Song in the Wine Garden; Shulamite's Song in the Grove of the Wood-Pigeons; Soloman's song with the Homing Pigeon; Shulamite's Song at the Top of the Mountain; Shulamit'es Song on the Mountains; Shulamite's Song in the Queen's Garden; Shulamite's Song in the Bridal Doorway Point ▲ PCD 5106
Rangström, T.:Songs, w. K. Dolberg (alt)—The Wind and the Tree; The Rain Song; Serenade; The Farewell Point ▲ PCD 5106
Sibelius, J.:Songs, w. K. Dolberg (alt)—The First Kiss; The Girl Came Home from her Lover's Tryst; The Diamond in the March Snow; Little Lasse; Spring Takes Flight Hastily; Reed, Reed, Rustle; Black Roses Point ▲ PCD 5106
Stolarczyk, W.:Earth Air Fire Water, w. Amalie Malling (pno), John Damgaard (pno), Anne Øland (pno), Teddy Teirup (pno), Rosalind Bevan (pno), Poul Rosenbaum (pno), Rodolfo Llambias (pno), Bella Horn-Ribera (pno), Anders Riber (pno), Elisabeth Sigurdsson (pno), Thomas Tronheim (pno), Elsebeth Broderson (pno), Erik Kaltoft (pno), Jørgen Hald Nielsen (pno), Aino Gilemann (pno), Birgit Kjær (pno), Jørgen Thomsen (pno), Gunhild Donslund (pno), Henrik Bo Hansen (pno), Lone Karlsson (pno), Erik Fessel (pno), Lasse Nilsson (pno), Janos Ferenczi (pno), Erik Bach (pno), Axel Momme (pno), Arne de Cros Dich (pno), Sven Micha Slot (pno), Hanne Bramsen Buhl (pno), Lili Olesen (pno), Susannah Carlsson (pno), Ulla Erml (pno), Vagn Sørensen (pno), Leif Greibe (pno), Bodil Krogh (pno), Kirsten Ottosen (pno), Inger Bergenholz (pno), Karsten Gylendorf (pno), Bjørr Elkjær (pno), Jacob Bjørn Jensen (pno), Jørgen Kaad (pno), Anne Marie Hjelm (pno), Carl Ulrik Munk Andersen (pno), Poul Lumbye (pno), Oluf Hildebrandt Nielsen (pno), Joachim Olsson (pno), Peter Pade Ramsøe Jacobsen (pno), Astrid Pollmann (pno), Jette Borsch (pno), Kirsten Karlshøj (pno), Maria Teresa Assing (pno), Allan Dahl Hansen (pno), Johan Hugossen (pno), Tine Fenger Pederson (pno), Arne Jørgen Fæø (pno), Anja Høgsted (pno), Anne Sophie Parbo (pno), Inga Lindmark (pno), Teresa Drabik Stathakis (pno), Anne Ruth Ferenczi (pno), Irene Hasager (pno), Yuka Ichikawa (pno), Birgitte Baur (pno), Malene Thastum (pno), Jens E. Rasmussen (pno), Birgitte Zielke (pno), Claus Zielke (pno), Stefan Kasch (pno), Bin Qiao (pno), Inger Johanne Teirup (pno), Lindy Rosborg (pno), Liisa Heininen (pno), David Højer (pno), Ellen Refstrup (pno), Thomas K. Søorensen (pno), Erik Kure (pno), Michael Rauff (pno), Jan beck Eriksson (pno), Tanja Zapolski (pno), Vibeke Skagbo (pno), Pål Eide Lindtner (pno), Ha-Young Sul (pno), Benedicte Palko (pno), Inke Kesseler (pno), Anne Marie Meineche (pno), Sverre Larsen (pno), Kasper Peter Bach (pno), Elisabetta Eliseo (pno), Olga Magieres (pno), Carl Erik Kühl (pno), Thorkild Borup Nielsen (pno), Valeria Zanini (pno), Lars Stenhoft (perc), Dennis Boel (perc), Winnie Dahlgren (perc), Susanne Vind (perc), Claus Byrith (elec), Anne Marie Storm (elec), J. Ribera (cnd) *(rec live, Koldinghaus Castle, Denmark, May 2, 1996)* Danica ▲ DCD 1996
Gürtler, Wolfgang (db)—see ORCHESTRAS & ENSEMBLES Vienna String Quintet
Gurtner, Christian (fl)
Handel, G.F.:Sons Fl, w. Balázs Maté (vc), Martin Haselböck (hpd/org)—Op. 1, Nos. 1, 4 & 5 *(rec Lutheran City Church, Vienna, Oct 1995)* Novalis ▲ 150120 [DDD]
Handel, G.F.:Sons Fl, "Halle Sons", w. Balázs Maté (vc), Martin Haselböck (hpd/org) *(rec Lutheran City Church, Vienna, Oct 1995)* Novalis ▲ 150120 [DDD]
Handel, G.F.:Son Fl, HWV 378, w. Balázs Maté (vc), Martin Haselböck (hpd/org) *(rec Lutheran City Church, Vienna, Oct 1995)* Novalis ▲ 150120 [DDD]
Handel, G.F.:Son Fl, HWV 379, w. Balázs Maté (vc), Martin Haselböck (hpd/org)—excerpt *(rec Lutheran City Church, Vienna, Oct 1995)* Novalis ▲ 150120 [DDD]

Gurtner, Christian (fl) (cont.)
Mozart, W.A.:Con Fl, K.314, w. M. Haselböck (cnd), Vienna Academy [period instrs] Novalis ▲ 150113 [DDD]
Puccini, M.:Concertone Fl, w. Lisa Klevit-Ziegler (cl), Reinhold Friedrich (tpt), Hector McDonald (nat hn), M. Haselböck (cnd), Vienna Academy *(rec Sofiensäle, Vienna, Oct 17-20, 1994)* Capriccio ▲ 10 598 [DDD]
Vivaldi, A.:Con for 2 Fls, w. L. Brunmayr (fl), M. Haselböck (cnd), Vienna Academy [period instrs] Novalis ▲ 150074 [DDD]
Gurtner, Heinrich (org)
Bach, J.S.:Trio Sons Org, BWV 525-530 *(rec Klosterkirche Muri/AG, May 10-13, 1973)* Claves 2-▲ CD 500405/6 [DDD]
Müller-Zurich, P.:Toccata IV Grammont ▲ CTSP 20-2
Gurtu, Trilok (perc)
Bernstein, L.:West Side Story (symphonic dances), w. K. Labèque (pno), M. Labèque (pno), Jean-Pierre Drouet (perc), Sylvio Gualdo (perc)—Overture; Scherzando; Blues; Somewhere; Scherzo; Mambo; Cha-cha; Cool; The rumble; I have a love [arr. Irwin Kostal for 2 pianos, percussion & jazz drums] CBS ▲ MK 45531 [DDD]
Gusak-Grin, Marina (pno)
Franck, C.:Son Vn, w. L. Mordkovitch (vn) Chandos ▲ CHAN 9109 [DDD]
Glazunov, A.:Grand Waltz, w. L. Mordkovitch (vn) Chandos ▲ CHAN 8500 [DDD]
Messiaen, O.:Thème et vars, w. L. Mordkovitch (vn) Chandos ▲ CHAN 9109 [DDD]
Poème:Lyrical Encore Pieces for Violin & Piano, w. Lydia Mordkovitch (vn) Chandos ▲ CHAN 8748 [DDD]
Prokofiev, S.:Mélodies, w. L. Mordkovitch (vn) Chandos ▲ CHAN 8500 [DDD]
Rachmaninoff, S.:Romance Vn, w. Lydia Mordkovitch (vn) Chandos ▲ CHAN 8500 [DDD]
Russian Music for Violin & Piano, w. Mordkovitch, Lydia (vn) Chandos ▲ CHAN 8500 [DDD]
Saint-Saëns, C.:Son 1 Vn, w. L. Mordkovich (vn) Chandos ▲ CHAN 9109 [DDD]
Stravinsky, I.:Parasha's Song, w. L. Mordkovitch (vn) Chandos ▲ CHAN 8500 [DDD]
Szymanowski, K.:Myths, w. L. Mordkovitch (vn) Chandos ▲ CHAN 8747 [DDD]
Szymanowski, K.:Notturno e Tarantella, w. L. Mordkovitch (vn) Chandos ▲ CHAN 8747 [DDD]
Szymanowski, K.:Son Vn, w. L. Mordkovitch (vn) Chandos ▲ CHAN 8747 [DDD]
Tchaikovsky, P.:Sérénade mélancolique, w. L. Mordkovitch Chandos ▲ CHAN 8500 [DDD]
Tchaikovsky, P.:Souvenir d'un lieu cher, w. L. Mordkovitch (vn) Chandos ▲ CHAN 8500 [DDD]
Tchaikovsky, P.:Valse-Scherzo Vn, w. L. Mordkovitch (vn) Chandos ▲ CHAN 8500 [DDD]
Guschlbauer, Theodore (pno)
Parish Alvars, E.:Concertino Hp, w. M. Nordmann (hp) *(rec June 22 & 30, 1992)* FNAC Music ▲ 592266 [DDD]
Parish Alvars, E.:Fant Hp, w. M. Nordmann (hp) *(rec June 22 & 30, 1992)* FNAC Music ▲ 592266 [DDD]
Gustafson, E. (va)
Willey, J.:Society Music, w. L. Greene (fl), G. Coble (tpt), W. Harris (trbn), D. Resue (hn), S. Heyman (pno), G. Macero (vc), E. Castilano (db), L. Luttinger (perc), E. Murray (cnd) Opus One ▲ CD 168 [DDD]
Gustafsson, Jan-Erik (vc)
Kodály, Z.:Son Vc & Pno, Op. 4, w. Heini Kärkkäinen (pno) Ondine ▲ ODE 827 [DDD]
Merikanto, A.:Con 2 Vc, w. S. Oramo (cnd), Finnish RSO Ondine ▲ ODE 861 [DDD]
Prokofiev, S.:Sym-Con Vc, w. S. Oramo (cnd), Finnish RSO Ondine ▲ ODE 861 [DDD]
Schnittke, A.:Son Vc, w. Heini Kärkkäinen (pno) Ondine ▲ ODE 827 [DDD]
Szymanowski, K.:Son Vn, w. Heini Kärkkäinen (pno) [arr Wilkomirski for vc & pno] Ondine ▲ ODE 827 [DDD]
Gustafsson, R. (org)
Gade, N.W.:Org Music (comp) [Menzel Organ of Sabra Church, Harnosand, Sweden]—sixteen works (Andantes, Trios, Chorale Preludes, etc.) BIS ▲ CD 496 [DDD]
Guthrie, Robert (gtr)
Almeida, L.:Gtr Music—Batuque; Crepusculo em Copacabana; Serenata; Braziliance *(rec Holy Nativity Episcopal Church, Plano, TX, Aug 13 & 14 & Sept 3 & 10)* EPR ▲ EPR 9509 [DDD]
Guimarães, J.:Gtr Music—Sounds of Bells; Pó de Mico; Graúna *(rec Holy Nativity Episcopal Church, Plano, TX, Aug 13 & 14 & Sept 3 & 10)* EPR ▲ EPR 9509 [DDD]
Lauro, A.:Gtr Music—Adiós a Ocumare; Triptico; Vals Venezolano; El Marabino *(rec Holy Nativity Episcopal Church, Plano, TX, Aug 13 & 14 & Sept 3 & 10)* EPR ▲ EPR 9509 [DDD]
Ponce, M.:Gtr Music—Mazurka; Trópico; Valz; Rumba *(rec Holy Nativity Episcopal Church, Plano, TX, Aug 13 & 14 & Sept 3 & 10)* EPR ▲ EPR 9509 [DDD]
Silva, J.:Gtr Music—Salmo de David; Soledad; Mascara Dorada; Estrella; Interludio de la Esperanza *(rec Holy Nativity Episcopal Church, Plano, TX, Aug 13 & 14 & Sept 3 & 10)* EPR ▲ EPR 9509 [DDD]
Villa-Lobos, H.:Preludes Gtr *(rec Holy Nativity Episcopal Church, Plano, TX, Aug 13 & 14 & Sept 3 & 10)* EPR ▲ EPR 9509 [DDD]
Gutiérrez, Horacio (pno)
Brahms, J.:Con 1 Pno, w. A. Previn (cnd), Royal PO Telarc ▲ CD 80252 [DDD]
Brahms, J.:Con 2 Pno, w. A. Previn (cnd), Royal PO Telarc ▲ CD 80197 [DDD]
Prokofiev, S.:Cons Pno (comp), w. B. Berman (pno), N. Järvi (cnd), Royal Concertgebouw Orch Chandos 2-▲ CHAN 8938 [DDD]
Prokofiev, S.:Con 2 Pno, w. N. Järvi (cnd), Royal Concertgebouw Orch Chandos ▲ CHAN 8889 [DDD]
Prokofiev, S.:Con 3 Pno, w. N. Järvi (cnd), Royal Concertgebouw Orch Chandos ▲ CHAN 8889 [DDD]
Rachmaninoff, S.:Con 2 Pno, w. L. Maazel (cnd), Pittsburgh SO Telarc ▲ CD 80259 [DDD]
Rachmaninoff, S.:Con 3 Pno, w. L. Maazel (cnd), Pittsburgh SO Telarc ▲ CD 80259 [DDD]
Rachmaninoff, S.:Rhapsody on a Theme of Paganini, w. D. Zinman (cnd), Baltimore SO Telarc ▲ CD 80193 [DDD]
Tchaikovsky, P.:Con 1 Pno, w. D. Zinman (cnd), Baltimore SO Telarc ▲ CD 80193 [DDD]
Gutman, Monica (pno)
Schulhoff, E.:Double Con Fl, w. Jacque Zoon (fl), I. Yinon (cnd), Bavarian Chamber PO Koch Schwann ▲ SCH 313712 [DDD]
Gutman, Natalia (vc)
Bach, J.S.:Suites Vc, BWV 1007-1012—No. 3, BWV 1009 *(rec Kreuth Musikfest, July 9/16, 1992)* Live Classics ▲ 621
Beethoven, L. van:Serenade Strs, Op. 8, w. Oleg Kagan (vn), Yuri Bashmet (va) *(rec Hohenems Schubertiade, June 22, 1988)* Live Classics ("Kagan Edition" series) ▲ 142
Beethoven, L. van:Son 3 Vc, w. Elisso Wirssaladze (pno) *(rec Schliersee, July 9, 1992)* Live Classics ▲ LCL 622 [DDD]
Beethoven, L. van:Trio 7 Pno, w. Elisso Wirssaladze (pno), Eduard Brunner (cl) *(rec Wildbad Kreuth, July 3, 1992)* Live Classics ▲ LCL 622 [DDD]
Beethoven, L. van:Trios Strs, Op. 9, w. Oleg Kagan (vn), Yuri Bashmet (va)—Nos. 1 & 3 *(rec Hohenems Schubertiade & Kuhmo Chamber Festival)* Live Classics ("Kagan Edition" series) ▲ 141
Brahms, J.:Qt 1 Pno, w. Vassily Lobanov (pno), Oleg Kagan (vn), Diemuth Poppen (va) *(rec Chamber Music Festival Kuhmo, Finland, July, 19, 1989)* Live Classics ▲ LCL 124 [DDD]
Brahms, J.:Son 1 Vc, w. Elisso Wirssaladze (pno) *(rec Kreuth Musikfest, July 9/16, 1992)* Live Classics ▲ 621
Britten, H.:Son Vc, w. Sviatoslav Richter (pno) *(rec Kur- und Kongresszentrum, Rottach-Egern, July 12, 1992)* Live Classics ▲ LCL 641 [DDD]
Dvořák, A.:Con Vc, w. W. Sawallisch (cnd), Philadelphia Orch EMI Classics ▲ CDC 54320
Grieg, E.:Son Vc, w. Elisso Wirssaladze (pno) *(rec Kreuth Musikfest, July 9/16, 1992)* Live Classics ▲ 621
Gubaidulina, S.:Rejoice, w. Oleg Kagan (vn) *(rec Chamber Music Festival Kuhmo, Finland, July 27, 1988)* Live Classics ▲ LCL 121 [DDD]
Prokofiev, S.:Son Vc, w. Sviatoslav Richter (pno) *(rec Kur- und Kongresszentrum, Rottach-Egern, July 12, 1992)* Live Classics ▲ LCL 641 [DDD]
Ravel, M.:Son Vn Vc, w. Oleg Kagan (vn) *(rec Chamber Music Festival Kuhmo, Finland, July 21, 1989)* Live Classics ▲ LCL 121 [DDD]
Saint-Saëns, C.:Son 1 Vc, w. S. Richter (pno) *(rec Kur- und Kongresszentrum, Rottach-Egern, July 12, 1992)* Live Classics ▲ LCL 641 [DDD]

Gutman, Natalia (vc) (cont.)
Schnittke, A.:Con 1 Vc, w. K. Masur (cnd), London PO EMI Classics ▲ CDC 54443
Schubert, Franz:Trio Strs, D.471, w. Oleg Kagan (vn), Yuri Bashmet (va) *(rec Hohenems Schubertiade, June 22, 1988)* Live Classics ("Kagan Edition" series) ▲ 142
Schubert, Franz:Trio Strs, D.581, w. Oleg Kagan (vn), Yuri Bashmet (va) *(rec Hohenems Schubertiade, June 22, 1988)* Live Classics ("Kagan Edition" series) ▲ 142
Schumann, R.:Con Vc, w. K. Masur (cnd), London PO EMI Classics ▲ CDC 54443
Shostakovich, D.:Con 1 Vc, w. Y. Temirankov (cnd), Royal PO RCA Red Seal ▲ 7918-2-RC [DDD]
Shostakovich, D.:Con 2 Vc, w. Y. Temirankov (cnd), Royal PO RCA Red Seal ▲ 7918-2-RC [DDD]
Vieru, A.:Con Vn Vc, w. O. Kagan (vn), A. Vieru (cnd), Romanian National RSO Olympia ▲ OCD 409 [AAD]

Güttler, Ludwig (corno da caccia)
Fasch, J.F.:Con Tpt & Strs, w. M. Pommer (cnd), Leipzig New Bach Collegium Musicum Capriccio ▲ CDC 10008 [DDD]
Heinichen, J.D.:Con Tpt, w. M. Pommer (cnd), Leipzig New Bach Collegium Musicum Capriccio ▲ CDC 10008 [DDD]

Güttler, Ludwig (tpt)
Albinoni, T.:Con in D Tpt, w. L. Güttler (cnd), Leipzig Bach Collegium Capriccio ▲ 10166 [DDD]
Bach, J.S.:Music of, w. M. Lorenz (ten), A. Reiss (ten), P. Schreier (ten), H.-C. Polster (b-bar), M. Pommer (cnd), Leipzig New Bach Collegium Musicum, Leipzig Choirs—arias, choruses & chorales Capriccio ▲ CDC 10039 [DDD]
Classical Trumpet Concertos Capriccio Δ 80051 □ 70051
Concertos for Trumpet & Corno da caccia, w. Virtuosi Saxoniae Berlin Classics ▲ BER 1102 [DDD]
Haydn, J.:Con Tpt, w. M. Pommer (cnd), New Bach Collegium Musicum Capriccio ▲ CDC 10010 [DDD]
Hindemith, P.:Con Tpt, Bn & Strs, w. Eckard Königstedt (bn), H. Kegel (cnd), Dresden PO Berlin Classics 2-▲ BER 9054
Italian Trumpet Concertos Capriccio Δ 80141
Ludwig Güttler:Trompete, Corno da Caccia, Posthorn, w. Virtuosi Saxoniae, F. Kircheis (hpd), J. Bischof (vc), W. Zeibig (db) *(rec 1988–92)* Berlin Classics ▲ BER 1053 [DDD]
Molter, J.M.:Con 1 Tpt, w. M. Pommer (cnd), Leipzig New Bach Collegium Musicum Capriccio ▲ CDC 10010 [DDD]
Mozart, L.:Con Tpt, w. M. Pommer (cnd), Leipzig New Bach Collegium Musicum—& Anon.:Con. in E♭ Capriccio ▲ CDC 10010 [DDD]
Music for Trumpet & Organ, w. Friedrich (org), Christoph Kircheis (org) Capriccio ▲ CDC 10057 [DDD]
Music for Trumpet, Corno da caccia & Organ from St. Thomas Church in Leipzig, w. Friedrich Kircheis (org) *(rec 1990)* Berlin Classics ▲ BER 1005 [DDD]
Neruda, J.B.G.:Con Tpt, w. M. Pommer (cnd), Leipzig New Bach Collegium Musicum Capriccio ▲ CDC 10008
Telemann, G.P.:Con Tpt Strs in D, w. M. Pommer (cnd), New Bach Collegium Musicum Capriccio ▲ CDC 10008 [DDD]
Vivaldi, A.:Cons Diverse Instrs, w. L. Mayer (mand), B. Glaetzner (ob), Sandau (tpt), Botvay, Pommer (cnd), New Bach Collegium Musicum, Budapest Strings LaserLight ▲ 15518 [DDD]
Vivaldi, A.:Con for 2 Tpts, w. K. Sandau (tpt), M. Pommer (cnd), New Bach Collegium Musicum Laserlight ▲ 15 518

Güttler, Ludwig (tpt/corno da caccia)
Ludwig Güttler Plays Music for Trumpet & Organ, w. Friedrich Kircheis (org) Berlin Classics ▲ BER 1110 [DDD]

Güttler, Ludwig (tpt/hunting hn)
The Golden Trumpet, w. Virtuosi Saxoniae Berlin Classics 2-▲ BER 9053

Güttler, Wolfgang (db)
Bottesini, G.:Duo Concertant on Themes from Bellini's *I Puritani*, w. M. Ostertag (vc), M. Bamert (cnd), Berlin RSO Koch Schwann ▲ CD 311042 [DDD]
Bottesini, G.:Gran Duetto 2 Db & Va, w. E. Sebestyen (va) Koch Schwann ▲ CD 311042 [DDD]
Bottesini, G.:Gran Duo Concertant, w. E. Sebestyen (vn), M. Bamert (cnd), Berlin RSO Koch Schwann ▲ CD 311042 [DDD]
Bottesini, G.:Grande con for 2 Dbs, w. K. Stoll (db), M. Bamert (cnd), Berlin RSO Koch Schwann ▲ CD 311042 [DDD]
Bottesini, G.:Grande con for 2 Dbs, w. M. Bamert (cnd), Berlin RSO Koch Schwann ▲ SCH 313382 [ADD/DDD]
Mozart, W.A.:Kleine Nachtmusik, w. M. Klier (hn), Berlin Philharmonia String Quartet Denon/PCM Digital ▲ DEN 7229 [DDD]
Vivaldi, A.:Cons Pic, w. H. W. Dünshede (fl), Motoi (hpd), Berlin Philharmonia String Quartet—RV.441, 443, 444, 445 Denon ▲ 7076 [DDD]

Guttman, Michaël (vn)—see also ORCHESTRAS & ENSEMBLES Arriaga String Quartet
Bloch, E.:Baal Shem, "3 Pictures of Chassidic Life", w. J. Serebrier (cnd), Royal PO ASV ▲ ASV 785
Bloch, E.:Con Vn, w. J. Serebrier (cnd), Royal PO ASV ▲ ASV 785
Chaminade, C.:Automne, w. J. Serebrier (cnd), Royal PO [orchd for solo vn by Paul Uy] ASV ▲ ASV 855 [DDD]
Dvořák, A.:Con Vn, w. J. Serebrier (cnd), Royal PO *(rec St. Barnabas Church, Mitcham, Jan 12 & Mar 4, 1994)* IMP ("Classics" series) ▲ IMP PCD 1110
Dvořák, A.:Mazurek, w. J. Serebrier (cnd), Royal PO *(rec St. Barnabas Church, Mitcham, Jan 12 & Mar 4, 1994)* IMP ("Classics" series) ▲ IMP PCD 1110
Dvořák, A.:Romance Vn, w. J. Serebrier (cnd), Royal PO *(rec St. Barnabas Church, Mitcham, Jan 12 & Mar 4, 1994)* IMP ("Classics" series) ▲ IMP PCD 1110
Hindemith, P.:Con Vn, w. J. Serebrier (cnd), Philharmonia Orch ASV ▲ ASV 945 [DDD]
Hindemith, P.:Kammermusik 4, w. J. Serebrier (cnd), Philharmonia Orch ASV ▲ ASV 945 [DDD]
Milhaud, D.:Concertino de printemps, w. J. Serebrier (cnd), Royal PO ASV ▲ ASV 855 [DDD]
Rodrigo, J.:Concierto de estío, w. J. Serebrier (cnd), Royal PO ASV ▲ ASV 855 [DDD]
Serebrier, J.:Winter Con Vn, w. J. Serebrier (cnd), Royal PO ASV ▲ ASV 855 [DDD]
Tchaikovsky, P.:Music of, w. J. Serebrier (cnd), Royal PO, Czech State PO—Waltzes [from Sleeping Beauty; Eugene Onegin; Swan Lake; Nutcracker (Waltz of the Flowers)]; Marches [from Nutcracker; Coronation March for Alexander III; Solennelle; Marche Slave, Op. 31]; Méditation in d, Op. 42/1; Mélodie in E♭, Op. 42/3; Elegy in G for Strs; Andante Cantabile, Op. 11 IMG/Pickwick ▲ PIC IMG 1617
Vivaldi, A.:Cons Vn, Op. 8/1–4, "The Four Seasons", w. J. Serebrier (cnd), Scottish National Orch Pickwick ("IMG" series) ▲ PIC IMG 1602 [DDD]

Gutu, Alexandra (vc)
Constantinescu, P.:Outlaw Ballad, w. R. Georgescu (cnd), Timisoara Banatul PO *(rec 1983)* Olympia ▲ OCD 415 [AAD]

Gutzwiller, Andreas Fuyû (shak)
The Flute of the Misty Sea:From the Classical Repertoire of the Kinko-School, w. Gutzwiller, Andreas Fuyû (shak) *(rec Aug 1994)* Jecklin ▲ JD 699-2 [DDD]

Guy, Guy (pno)
Boucourechliev, A.:Les Archipels, w. Brigitte Sylvestre (hp), Elisabeth Chojnacka (hpd), Françoise Rieunier (org), Roland Auzet, Jean-Pierre Drouet (perc), Hakon Austbö (pno), Claude Helffer (pno), Georges Pludermacher (pno), Ysaÿe String Quartet, Les Pléiades Ensemble Musique Francaise d'Aujourd'hui ("Collection MFA-Radio France" series) ▲ MFA 216001

Guy, Larry (cl/b cl)
Kernis, A.J.:America(n) (Day) Dreams, w. Kim Barber (mez), Mary Rowell (vn), Leslie Tomkins (va), Tonya Tomkins (vc), Robert Black (db), Kathleen Nester (fl), Larry Guy (cl/b cl), John Dent (tpt), Anthony Cecere (hn), Leslie Stifelman (pno), Susan Jolles (hp), Jeffrey Milarsky (perc), M. Barrett (cnd)—A Navajo Blanket; Wednesday at the Waldorf; The Pregnant Dream; The Blue Bottle; "So Long" to the Moon from the Men of Apollo; Epilogue:The Pure Suit of Happiness *(rec Manhattan Center Studios, New York, May 31–June 3, 1995)* New Albion ♦ NA 083CD

Guy, R. (pno)
From a Woman's Perspective:Art Songs by Women Composers, w. Eberle, K. (mez), Kristin Pederson Thelander (hn) Vienna Modern Masters ▲ VMM 2005 [DDD]

Guye, François (vc)
Honegger, A.:Son Vc, w. David Lively (pno) Gallo ▲ CD 468 [DDD]
Honegger, A.:Sonatina Cl, w. David Lively (pno) Gallo ▲ CD 468 [DDD]
Strauss, R.:Son Vc, w. D. Lively (pno) Gallo ▲ CD 468 [DDD]

Guymer, Sheila (pno)
Partch, H.:Bitter Music, w. Warren Burt (voc) [prepared by Warren Burt] *(rec Melbourne, Australia, Jan 24, 1992)* Innova 4-▲ 401

Guzelimian, Armen (pno)
Brahms, J.:Liebeslieder Waltzes SATB, w. Herrera (pno), Los Angeles Vocal Arts Ensemble [G] Elektra/Nonesuch ▲ 79008-2 [DDD]
Brahms, J.:Neue Liebeslieder Waltzes, w. Herrera (pno), Los Angeles Vocal Arts Ensemble [G] Elektra/Nonesuch ▲ 79008-2 [DDD]
Getty, G.:The White Election, w. K. Erickson (sop) [E] Delos ▲ DCD 3057 [DDD]
Griffes, C.T.:Songs, w. T. Hampson (bar)—17 songs—An den Wind; Am Kreuzweg wird begraben; Meeres Stille; Auf geheimem Waldespfade; Wohl lag ich einst in Gram und Schmerz; So halt' ich endlich dich umfangen; Mein Herz ist wie die dunkle Nacht; Der träumende See; Mit schwarzen Segeln; Das ist ein Brausen und Heulen; Wo ich bin, mich rings umdunkelt; Auf ihrem Grab; Das sterbende Kind; Elfe; Zwei Könige sassen auf Orkadal; Des Müden Abendlied; Nachtlied [G] Teldec ▲ 9031-72168-2 [DDD]
Ives, C.:Songs, w. T. Hampson (bar)—Minnelied; Gruss; Frühlingslied; Du bist wie eine Blume; Ballad from Rosamunde; Ein Ton; Widmung; Marie; Rosenzweige; Wiegenlied; Feldeinsamkeit; Ich grolle nicht; Weil' auf mir; Ilmenau (Wanderers Nachtlied) [G] Teldec ▲ 9031-72168-2 [DDD]
Macdowell, E.:Songs, w. T. Hampson (bar)—5 songs (Op. 11, Nos. 1–3 & Op. 12, Nos. 1 & 2)—Mein Liebchen, wir sassen beisammen; Du liebst mich nicht; Oben, wo die Sterne glühen; Nachtlied; Das Rosenband [G] Teldec ▲ 9031-72168-2 [DDD]
An Old Song Re-sung, American Concert Songs, w. Hampson, Thomas (bar) EMI Classics ▲ CDC 54051

Guzmán, María Esther (gtr)
Arcas, J.:Gtr Music—Fant. on El Paño; El Sueño de Rosellén; Polaca fantástica; Fant on La Favorita; Rondo Andante; Visperas Sicilianas; Andante & Etude de Prudent; El Delirio Almaviva ▲ 0103 [DDD]

Gwiazda, Henry (elec gtr/cmpt/elec/voc)
Gwiazda, H.:Music of—MANEATINGCHIIPSLISTENINGTOAVIOLIN; whErEyoulivE; wM; afterglоW; themythofAcceptAnce [w. Jeffery Kreiger (elec vc)]; theflLuteintheworLdtheflLuteistheworLd [w. Ann LaBerge (elec fl)]; buzzingreynold'sdreamland Innova ▲ Innova 505 [DDD]

Gwilt, Richard (baroque vn)
Boismortier, J.B. de:Chamber Music, w. Manfred Harras (rcr), Marianne Lüthi (rcr), Arno Jochem (vl), Brian Franklin (vl), Sally Fortino (hps)—Con. in C, "Zampogna"; Son. in F, Op. 91/1; Son. in A, Op. 10/2; Trio Son. in D, Op. 37/3; Son. in e, Op. 34/3; Con. in A, Op. 38/4; Suite No. 1, Op. 59; Balet de village en trio, Op. 52/4 *(rec Reformed Church, Bubendorf, Switzerland, Feb. 9–11, 1989)* Musicaphon ▲ 56812 [DDD]

Gwilt, Richard (vn)—see also ORCHESTRAS & ENSEMBLES London Baroque
Telemann, G.P.:Cants, w. Barbara Schlick (sop), Manfred Harras (rcr), Ernst-Martin Eras (ob), Brian Franklin (vl), Sally Fortino (hpd)—Hemmet den Eifer, verbannet die Rache; Jauchzt, ihr Christen, seid vergnügt; Umschlinget uns, ihr sanften Freidensbande; Die Kinder des Höchsten sind rufende Stimmen; Lauter Wonne, lauter Freude Cantate ▲ 580003 [DDD]

Gwozdz, Lawrence (sax)
An American Tribute to Sigurd Rascher, w. Gwozdz, Lawrence (sax) *(rec Mannoni Performing Arts Center, Univ. of Southern Mississippi, Dec. 20–22, 1993 & Jan. 9)* Crystal ▲ CD 652

Gylendorf, Karsten (pno)
Stolarczyk, W.:Earth Air Fire Water, w. Amalie Malling (pno), John Damgaard (pno), Anne Øland (pno), Teddy Teirup (pno), Friedrich Gürtler (pno), Rosalind Bevan (pno), Poul Rosenbaum (pno), Rodolfo Llambias (pno), Bella Horn-Ribera (pno), Anders Riber (pno), Elisabeth Sigurdsson (pno), Thomas Tronheim (pno), Elsebeth Broderson (pno), Erik Kaltoft (pno), Jørgen Hald Nielsen (pno), Aino Gilemann (pno), Birgit Kjær (pno), Jørgen Thomsen (pno), Gunhild Donslund (pno), Henrik Bo Hansen (pno), Lone Karlsson (pno), Erik Fessel (pno), Lasse Nilsson (pno), Janos Ferenczi (pno), Erik Bach (pno), Axel Momme (pno), Arne de Cros Dich (pno), Sven Micha Slot (pno), Hanne Bramsen Buhl (pno), Lili Olesen (pno), Susannah Carlsson (pno), Ulla Erml (pno), Vagn Sørensen (pno), Leif Greibe (pno), Bodil Krogh (pno), Kirsten Ottosen (pno), Inger Bergenholz (pno), Karsten Gylendorf (pno), Bjønr Elkjær (pno), Jacob Bjørn Jensen (pno), Jørgen Kaad (pno), Anne Marie Hjelm (pno), Carl Ulrik Munk Andersen (pno), Poul Lumbye (pno), Oluf Hildebrandt Nielsen (pno), Joachim Olsson (pno), Peter Pade Ramsøe Jacobsen (pno), Astrid Pollmann (pno), Jette Borsch (pno), Kirsten Karlshøj (pno), Maria Teresa Assing (pno), Allan Dahl Hansen (pno), Johan Hugossen (pno), Tine Fenger Pederson (pno), Arne Jørgen Fæø (pno), Anja Høgsted (pno), Anne Sophie Parbo (pno), Inga Lindmark (pno), Teresa Drabik Stathakis (pno), Anne Ruth Ferenczi (pno), Irene Hasager (pno), Yuka Ichikawa (pno), Birgitte Baur (pno), Malene Thastum (pno), Jens E. Rasmussen (pno), Birgitte Zielke (pno), Claus Zielke (pno), Stefan Kasch (pno), Bin Qiao (pno), Inger Johanne Teirup (pno), Lindy Rosborg (pno), Liisa Heininen (pno), David Højer (pno), Ellen Refstrup (pno), Thomas K. Søorensen (pno), Erik Kure (pno), Michael Rauff (pno), Jan beck Eriksson (pno), Tanja Zapolski (pno), Vibeke Skagbo (pno), Pål Eide Lindtner (pno), Ha-Young Sul (pno), Benedicte Palko (pno), Inke Kesseler (pno), Anne Marie Meineche (pno), Sverre Larsen (pno), Kasper Peter Bach (pno), Elisabetta Eliseo (pno), Olga Magieres (pno), Carl Erik Kühl (pno), Thorkild Borup Nielsen (pno), Valeria Zanini (pno), Lars Stenhoft (perc), Dennis Boel (perc), Winnie Dahlgren (perc), Susanne Vind (perc), Claus Byrith (elec), Anne Marie Storm (elec), J. Ribera (cnd) *(rec live, Koldinghaus Castle, Denmark, May 2, 1996)* Danica ▲ DCD 1996

Gylfadóttir, Bryndís Halla (vc)
Cello, w. Gylfadóttir, Bryndís Halla (vc), Snorri Sigfús Birgisson (pno), Marta Guthrún Halldórsdóttir (sop) Music from Iceland ▲ ITM 804

Gyöngyössy, Z. (fl)
Ravel, M.:Intro & Allegro, w. É. Maros (hp), B. Kovács (cl), Kodály String Quartet *(rec Dec. 6–8, 1988)* Naxos ▲ 8.550249 [DDD]

György, Arpat (db)
Milhaud, D.:Catalogue de fleurs, w. Ulrike Sonntag (sop), Irmela Nolte (fl), Deborah Marshall (cl), Michael Weigel (bn), Renate Eggebrecht (vn), Stefan Berg (va), Friedemann Kupsa (vc) *(rec Ludwigsburg, Germany, Jan. 1995)* Troubadisc ▲ TROCD 01410 [DDD]
Milhaud, D.:Machines agricoles, w. Ulrike Sonntag (sop), Irmela Nolte (fl), Deborah Marshall (cl), Michael Weigel (bn), Renate Eggebrecht (vn), Stefan Berg (va), Friedemann Kupsa (vc) *(rec Ludwigsburg, Germany, Jan. 1995)* Troubadisc ▲ TROCD 01410 [DDD]

Gyps, Françoise (fl)
Alain, J.:Music of, w. Delphine Collot (sop), Bruno Boterf (ten), Jacques Bona (bar), Laurent Decker (ob), Bruno Pazqueir (va), Philippe Muller (vc), Georges Guillard (org), Ludwig String Quartet, Georges Guillard (cnd), St. Louis Camerata Vocal Ensemble—2 Melodies for Sop & Pno; Nuptial Song for Bar, Bass, Vc & Org; Post-Scription for 3 Female Voices & Pno; Canticle in Phrygian Mode for 4 Mixed-Voice, Sop & Strs; Invention for Fl, Ob & Cl; Monody for solo Fl; Prelude for Str Qnt; Adagio for Str Qnt; Funerals for Str Qnt; March of the Horiaces & the Curiaces for 2 Bugles, Drum & Org Arion ▲ ARN 68321
Alain, O.:Souvenances, w. Georges Guillard (org) Arion ▲ ARN 68321

Gyr, Suzanne (pno)
Schubert, Franz:Winterreise, w. M. Rothmüller (bar) *(rec 1954)* Symposium 2-▲ 1098-1099

Gyurik, Michael (va)
Dankner, S.:Sextet, w. L. Skelton (pno), V. Poullette (vn), E. Tanner (vn), A. Nisbet (vc), R. Kassinger (db) Albany ▲ TROY 067

Haag, Bernd (va)—see ORCHESTRAS & ENSEMBLES Kammermusik Ensemble Chamäleon

Haag, Gudrun (hp)
Schoeck, O.:Spielmannsweisen, w. Kurt Streit (ten) *(rec Pere Casulleras, Christine Rosse, CH-Waldenburg, Apr, 1995)* Jecklin ▲ JD 679-2 [DDD]

Haag, Ivo (pno)
Debussy, C.:L'Enfant prodigue, w. Adrienne Soós (pno)—Symphonie [arr for 2 Pnos] Pan Classics ▲ 510076 [DDD]

596 ▲ = CD ♦ = Enhanced CD Δ = MD ■ = Cassette Tape □ = DCC

Haag, Ivo (pno) (cont.)
Debussy, C.:Épigraphes antiques, w. Adrienne Soós (pno) [arr for 2 Pnos] Pan Classics ▲ 510076 [DDD]
Debussy, C.:Petite suite, w. Adrienne Soós (pno) [arr for 2 Pnos] Pan Classics ▲ 510076 [DDD]
Debussy, C.:Triomphe de Bacchus, w. Adrienne Soós (pno) [arr for 2 Pnos] Pan Classics ▲ 510076 [DDD]
Koechlin, C.:Sonatines françaises, w. Adrienne Soós (pno)—No. 1 Pan Classics ▲ 510076 [DDD]
Koechlin, C.:Suite for 2 Pnos, w. Adrienne Soós (pno) Pan Classics ▲ 510076 [DDD]

Haak, S. (vn)
de Fesch, W.:Sons Vn, Op. 8a, w. H. Herrmann (tpt), E. Schloter (org)—No. 10 *(rec Nov. 18–21, 1991)* Koch Schwann ▲ SCH 310252 [DDD]

Haan, Remco de (gtr)—see ORCHESTRAS & ENSEMBLES Groningen Guitar Duo

Haar, Job Ter (vc)—see ORCHESTRAS & ENSEMBLES Ives Ensemble members, Affetti Musicali members, Ives Ensemble members

Haar, Josje ter (vn)—see also ORCHESTRAS & ENSEMBLES Ives Ensemble members, Ives Ensemble members
Cage, J.:Two^4, w. Mayumi Miyata (shô) *(rec Theater Romein, Leeuwarden, the Netherlands, Jan 14–17, 1996)* Hat Art ("Hat NOW." series) 2–▲ 6192 [DDD]
Cage, J.:Two^6, w. John Snijders (pno) *(rec Theater Romein, Leeuwarden, the Netherlands, Jan 14–17, 1996)* Hat Art ("Hat NOW." series) 2–▲ 6192 [DDD]

Haas, Andy (didjeridu)—see ORCHESTRAS & ENSEMBLES Gangster Band

Haas, Arthur (hpd)
Barney, N.:Strs of Light, w. D. Bastian (gtr) Neuma ▲ 450–72 [DDD]
Forqueray, J.–B.:Pièces de clavecin Wildboar ▲ WLBR 9201

Haas, Arthur (hpd/org)
A Baroque Christmas from the Metropolitan Museum of Art Concerts, w. Julianne Baird (sop), Aulos Ensemble MusicMasters ▲ 01612–67119–2 ■ 01612–67119–4

Haas, Donald (acc)
Curran, A.:Why Is This Night Different Than All Other Nights?, w. Roy Malan (vn), Peter Wahrhaftig (tuba), Alvin Curran (pno), William Winant (perc) Tzadik ("The Composers" series) ▲ TZA 7001 [DDD]

Haas, Douglas (org)
Albinoni, T.:Adagio Org, w. J. Faerber (cnd), Württemberg CO Allegretto ▲ ACD 8098 [ADD] ■ ACS 8098

Haas, George (ob)—see ORCHESTRAS & ENSEMBLES Contemporary Chamber Ensemble

Haas, Jonathan (perc)
Druckman, J.:Dark Upon the Harp, w. J. DeGaetani (mez), B. Herman (perc), J. Druckman (cnd), American Brass Quintet [E] *(rec Aspen Music Festival 8/6/88)* Bridge ▲ BCD 9023 [ADD]
Hamilton, T.:Off–Hour Wait State, w. Thomas Buckner (voc), Roscoe Mitchell (a sax), Ralph Samuelson (shak), Peter Zummo (trbn), Tom Hamilton (syn/elec) O.O. Discs ▲ OO 26 [DDD]
Tower, J.:Black Topaz, w. Stephen Gosling (pno), Patricia Spencer (fl), Laura Flax (cl), Chris Gekker (tpt), Mike Powell (trbn), Deborah Moore (perc) *(rec American Academy of Arts & Letters, New York City, Sept. 26–28, 1994)* New World ▲ 80470–2

Haas, Jonathan (timp)
Druschetzky, G.:Con Ob & Timp, w. G. Hunt (oboe), H. Farberman (cnd), Bournemouth Sinfonietta CRD ▲ 3449 [ADD]
Druschetzky, G.:Partita, w. H. Farberman (cnd), Bournemouth Sinfonietta CRD ▲ 3449 [ADD]
Fischer, J.C. Christian:Sym for 8 Timp, w. H. Farberman (cnd), Bournemouth Sinfonietta CRD ▲ 3449 [ADD]

Haas, Jonathan (vib)
Kolb, B.:Solitaire, w. E. Niemann (pno) New World ▲ 80422–2 [DDD]

Haas, Polo de (pno)
Holt, S. ten:Horizon, w. Yoko Abe (pno), Margaret Krill (pno), Fred Oldenburg (pno) Donemus 2–▲ CV 5/6
Pasternak, B.:Pno Music—Preludes in d# & g#; Son. in b Erasmus ▲ WVH 091 [DAD]
Prokofiev, S.:Visions fugitives Erasmus ▲ WVH 091 [DAD]
Scriabin, A.:Pieces Pno, Op. 51 Erasmus ▲ WVH 091 [DAD]

Haas, Rosalinde (org)
Reger, M.:Bach Transcriptions—Fants.; Sons.; Inventions; 10 sels. from Das wohltemperierte Klavier MD + G ("Gold" series) 2–▲ MDG 3150484 [DDD]
Reger, M.:Org Music (comp)—Fantasy on Freu dich sehr; Suite in g, Op. 92; Pieces (12), Op. 59; Chorale Preludes MD + G ▲ L 3356 [DDD]
Reger, M.:Org Music (comp)—Fantasy & Fugue, Op. 7, Nos. 2 & 3; Fantasy & Fugue in c, Op. 29; Sonata No. 1 in f#, Op. 33; Prelude & Fugue in E, Op. 56, No. 1; Six Chorale Preludes; Six Trios, Op. 47 MD + G ▲ L 3355 [DDD]
Reger, M.:Org Music (comp)—Symphonic Fantasy & Fugue, Op. 57; Prelude & Fugue in C; Variations & Fugue on Heil dir siegerkranz; Trauerode; Siegesfeier; Chorale Preludes MD + G ▲ L 3357 [DDD]
Reger, M.:Org Music (comp)—Fantasy, Op. 40, No. 2; Fantasy & Fugue in d, Op. 135b; Suite No. 1 in e on B–A–C–H, Op. 16; Three Chorale Preludes MD + G ▲ L 3354 [DDD]
Reger, M.:Org Music (comp)—12 Pieces, Op. 65; 8 Chorale Preludes MD + G ▲ L 3358 [DDD]
Reger, M.:Org Music (comp)—10 Pieces, Op. 69; Preludes & Fugues, Op. 85; Chorale Preludes MD + G ▲ L 3359 [DDD]
Reger, M.:Org Music (comp)—12 Pieces, Op. 80; Fantasy on Alle menschen müssen sterben, Op. 52/1; 18 Chorale Preludes MD + G ▲ L 3360 [DDD]
Reger, M.:Org Music (comp)—Monologe, Op. 63 (twelve pieces); 8 Chorale Preludes; Fantaisie on "Hallelujah! Gott zu loben," Op. 52/3; Ostern, Op. 145/5 MD + G ▲ L 3353 [DDD]
Reger, M.:Org Music (comp)—Introduction, Passacaglia & Fugue in e, Op. 127; Sonata No. 2 in d, Op. 60; Prelude & Fugue in G, Op. 56, No. 3; Weihnachten, Op. 145, No. 3; Nine Chorale Preludes MD + G ▲ L 3352 [DDD]
Reger, M.:Org Music (comp)—Introduction, Variations & Fugue on an Original Theme, Op. 73; Romance in a; Intro. & Passacaglia in d; etc. MD + G ▲ L 3351 [DDD]
Reger, M.:Org Music (comp)—Fantasy & Fugue on B–A–C–H, Op. 46; Twelve Pieces, Op. 58; etc. MD + G ▲ L 3350 [DDD]
Reger, M.:Org Music (comp)—9 Pieces, Op. 129; 9 Chorale Preludes; etc. MD + G ▲ L 3361 [DDD]

Haas, Werner (pno)
Debussy, C.:Pno Music (complete solo)—Préludes; Images; Children's Corner; others Philips 2–▲ 438718–2
Debussy, C.:Pno Music (complete solo), w. Noel Lee (pno)—Etudes; Suite Bergamasque; En blanc et noir; Petite Suite; others Philips 2–▲ 438721–2
Rachmaninoff, S.:Con 2 Pno, w. E. Inbal (cnd), Frankfurt RSO Philips ("Concert Classics" series) ▲ 422465–2
Ravel, M.:Pno Music—complete solo piano music Philips 2–▲ 438353–2
Tchaikovsky, P.:Con 1 Pno, w. E. Inbal (cnd), Frankfurt RSO Philips ("Concert Classics" series) ▲ 422465–2

Haase, Erika (pno)
Chopin, F.:Études (24) *(rec 1992 & 1993)* Thorofon ▲ CTH 2195 [DDD]
Chopin, F.:Nouvelles études *(rec 1992 & 1993)* Thorofon ▲ CTH 2195 [DDD]
Ligeti, G.:Kbd Music—Etudes, Book I; Invention; Capriccios Nos. 1 & 2; Musica Ricercata; 3 Works for Harpsichord Col Legno ▲ AU 31815

Habel–Thormé, T. (rcr)—see also ORCHESTRAS & ENSEMBLES Bonn Telemann Ensemble
Rosier, N.–C.:Son Vn, w. N. Scheer (vn), B. Wicke (org) *(rec 1992)* FSM ▲ FCD 97759 [DDD]

Häberli, Mariann (vn)—see ORCHESTRAS & ENSEMBLES Euler String Quartet

Habermann, Michael (pno)
Habermann, M.:Au clair de la lune Elan ▲ CD 2264
Sorabji, K.S.:Pno Music—Gulistan [The Rose Garden]; Quaere reliqua hujus materiei inter secretiora; Fantasiettina sul nome illustre dell'egregio poeta Christopher Grieve ossia Hugh M'Diarmid; Djâmî [Nocturne] Elan ▲ CD 2264

Hacke, Cordula (pno)
A Distant Mirror, w. Cornelia Thorspecken (fl) Bayer ▲ 100246 [DDD]

Hacken, Huub ten (org)
Bruynèl, T.:Relief Donemus ▲ NEAR 01 [DDD]

Hacker, Alan (cl)
Brahms, J.:Sons Cl (comp), w. R. Burnett (pno) [period instrs] Amon Ra ▲ CD–SAR 37 [DDD]
Brahms, J.:Trio Cl, w. J. Ward Clarke (vc), R. Burnett (pno) [period instrs] Amon Ra ▲ CD–SAR 37 [DDD]
Clarinet Collection, w. Alan Hacker (cl), Richard Burnett (chamber org/spinet/hpd/pno) Amon Ra ▲ CDSAR 10
Finzi, G.:Con Cl, w. W. Boughton (cnd), English String Orch Nimbus 4–▲ NI 5210/13 [DDD]
Finzi, G.:Con Cl, w. W. Boughton (cnd), English String Orch Nimbus ▲ NI 5101 [DDD]
Mendelssohn, F.:Concert Pieces, w. L. Schatzberger (bas hn), R. Burnett (pno) [period instrs] Amon Ra ▲ CD–SAR 38 [DDD]
Mendelssohn, F.:Son Cl, w. R. Burnett (pno) [period instrs] Amon Ra ▲ CD–SAR 38 [DDD]
Mozart, W.A.:Qnt Cl, K.581, w. Salomon String Quartet Amon Ra ▲ CD–SAR 17 [DDD]
Mozart, W.A.:Qnts Cl Bas Hn, w. Lesley Schatzberger (bas hn), Salomon String Quartet members Amon Ra ▲ CD–SAR 17 [DDD]

Hadcock, Peter (cl)
Clarke, R.:Prelude, Allegro & Pastorale, w. P. McCarty (va) Northeastern ("Classical Arts" series) ▲ NR 212–CD

Hadden, Frances Roots (pno)—see ORCHESTRAS & ENSEMBLES Haddens

Hadden, Nancy (fl)
Hasse, J.A.:Sons (12) Fl, w. Malcolm Proud (hpd)—No. 6 in b *(rec May 30–June 1, 1991)* CRD ▲ CRD 3488 [DDD]

Hadden, R. (pno)—see ORCHESTRAS & ENSEMBLES Haddens

Hadjaje, P. (va)
Bach, J.S.:Con for 2 Vas, w. J. Roudin (va), D. Rouits (cnd), Massy CO *(rec Mar 1990)* Quantum ▲ QM 6906 [DDD] ■ QM 2000
Vivaldi, A.:Cons for 2 Vas, w. J. Roudin (va), D. Rouits (cnd), Massy CO *(rec 3/90)* Quantum ▲ QM 6906 [DDD] ■ QM 2000

Hadjinikos, G. (pno)
Skalkottas, N.:Con 2 Pno, w. H. Scherchen (cnd), North German RSO *(rec 1953)* Arkadia ▲ 768 [ADD]

Hadulla, Markus (pno)
Wolf, H.:Goethe–Lieder (sels), w. Locky Chung (bar), Stephan Genz (bar), Claar Ter Horst (pno)—24 sels Claves ▲ 50–9517

Haebler, Ingrid (pno)
Bach, Joh. Christian:Cons Hpd, T.292/1, w. E. Melkus (cnd), Capella Academica Vienna Philips 2–▲ 438712–2
Bach, Joh. Christian:Semi Cons Hpd, w. E. Melkus (cnd), Capella Academica Vienna Philips 2–▲ 438712–2
Beethoven, L. van:Sons Vn (comp), w. Henryk Szeryng (vn)—Nos. 1–5 Philips ▲ 446521–2
Beethoven, L. van:Sons Vn (comp), w. Henryk Szeryng (vn)—Nos. 6–10 Philips ▲ 446524–2
Chopin, F.:Life & Music of—narration & selected excerpts from Con. No. 1 for Piano, Op. 11; Scherzo No. 2, Op. 31; Polonaise, Op. 53; Mazurka No. 39, Op. 63/1; Vars. on a German Theme; Valse brillante, Op. 18; Mazurka No. 23, Op.33/2; Ballade No. 4, Op. 52; Prelude, Op. 28/20; Con. No. 1 for Piano, Op. 11; Polonaise, Op. 44; Etude No. 12, Op. 10; Valse No. 7, Op. 64/2; Nocturne No. 2, Op. 9/2; Valse No. 6, Op. 64/1; Fant. Impromptu No. 4, Op. 66; Etude No. 3, Op. 10; Nocturne No. 5, Op. 15; Polonaise No. 3, Op. 40/1; Ballade No. 1, Op. 23; Con. No. 2 for Piano, Op. 21; Son. No. 2, Op. 35; Son. No. 3, Op. 58; Waltzes, Opp. 34/2 & 3, 42, 64/1–3, 69/1 & 2, 70/1–3 Vox Music Masters (Music Masters) ▲ MMD 8502 [ADD] ■ MMC 8502
Chopin, F.:Waltzes—17 waltzes Allegretto ▲ ACD 8027 [ADD] ■ ACS 8027
Haydn, J.:Sons Pno—Nos. 35–39 Philips ("Solo" series) ▲ 442659–2
Mozart, W.A.:Allegro & Andante & Rondo Denon ▲ CO 73087 [DDD]
Mozart, W.A.:Complete Mozart Edition, w. Ludwig Hoffmann (pno), Paul Badura–Skoda (pno), Jörg Demus (pno) Philips 2–▲ 422516–2 [ADD]
Mozart, W.A.:Complete Mozart Edition, w. Ton Koopman (hpd), Mitsuko Uchida (pno) Philips 5–▲ 422518–2 [ADD]
Mozart, W.A.:Con 18 Pno, w. K. Melles (cnd), Vienna SO Allegretto ▲ ACD 8011 [ADD] ■ ACS 8011
Mozart, W.A.:Con 19 Pno, w. K. M. Helles (cnd), Vienna SO Allegretto ▲ ACD 8011 [ADD] ■ ACS 8011
Mozart, W.A.:Con 20 Pno, w. K. Melles (cnd), Vienna SO Allegretto ▲ ACD 8011 [ADD] ■ ACS 8011
Mozart, W.A.:Fant Pno, K.475 Denon 5–▲ CO 79426/30 [DDD]
Mozart, W.A.:Sons Pno—Nos. 12 & 13, K.332 & K.333 Denon ▲ CO 1848 [DDD]
Mozart, W.A.:Sons Pno—Nos. 8, 10 & 11, K.310, 330, 331 Denon ▲ CO 1517 [DDD]
Mozart, W.A.:Sons Pno—No. 15, K.545 & No. 17, K.576 Denon ▲ CO 73087 [DDD]
Mozart, W.A.:Sons Pno—No. 6 in D, K.284; No. 9 in D, K.211 Denon ▲ CO 79399 [DDD]
Mozart, W.A.:Sons Pno Denon 5–▲ CO 79426/30 [DDD]
Mozart, W.A.:Sons Pno—No. 1 in C, K.279; No. 3 in B♭, K.281; No. 5 in G, K.283 Denon ▲ 76689–2 [DDD]
Schubert, Franz:Qnt Pno, D.667, w. J. Cazauran (db), Grumiaux Trio Philips ▲ 422838–2 [ADD]

Haefliger, Andreas (pno)
Boulez, P.:Sonatine Fl & Pno, w. M. Piccinini (fl) Connoisseur Society ▲ CD 4183 [DDD]
Jolivet, A.:Chant de Linos, w. M. Piccinini (fl) Connoisseur Society ▲ CD 4183 [DDD]
Mozart, W.A.:Fant Pno, K.475 Sony Classical ▲ SK 46748
Mozart, W.A.:Son 12 Pno Sony Classical ▲ SK 46748
Mozart, W.A.:Son 13 Pno Sony Classical ▲ SK 46748
Mozart, W.A.:Son 14 Pno Sony Classical ▲ SK 46748
Prokofiev, S.:Son Fl, w. M. Piccinini (fl) Connoisseur Society ▲ CD 4183 [DDD]
Schubert, Franz:Impromptus Pno (comp) Sony Classical ▲ SK 53108
Schumann, R.:Davidsbündlertänze Sony Classical ▲ SK 48036
Schumann, R.:Waldscenen Sony Classical ▲ SK 48036

Haeger, Raphael (perc)
Barockmusik für Posaunen und Gesang, w. Datura Trombone Quartet, A. Scharinger (db), C. Weigel (baroque vc), T. Strauss (org), J. Gagelmann (perc) Ars Musici ▲ AM 1094 [DDD]
Markevitch, I.:L'Envol d'Icare, w. K. Lessing (pno), C. Lyndon–Gee (pno), J. Gagelmann (perc), F. Lang (perc) *(rec July 10–11, 1993)* Largo ▲ 5127 [DDD]

Haendel, Ida (vn)
Bach, J.S.:Sons & Partitas Vn, BWV 1001–1006 Testament ▲ 2090
Beethoven, L. van:Con Vn, Op. 61, w. R. Kubelik (cnd), Philharmonia Orch *(rec 1951)* Testament ▲ SBT 1083
Britten, H.:Con Vn, w. P. Berglund (cnd), Bournemouth SO EMI Classics ▲ CDM 64202
Bruch, M.:Con 1 Vn, w. R. Kubelik (cnd), Philharmonia Orch *(rec 1948)* Testament ▲ SBT 1083
Lalo, E.:Sym espagnole, w. K. Ančerl (cnd), Czech PO Supraphon ("Czech Philharmonic" series) ▲ SUP 111936 [AAD]
The 1940 Recordings, w. Ida Haendel (vn), Josef Hassid (vn) Pearl ▲ PEA 9939 (m) [AAD]
Pettersson, G.A.:Con 2 Vn Orch, w. H. Blomstedt (cnd), Swedish RSO Caprice ▲ CAP 21359 [AAD]
Ravel, M.:Tzigane, w. K. Ančerl (cnd), Czech PO Supraphon ("Czech Philharmonic" series) ▲ SUP 111936 [AAD]
Walton, W.:Con Vn, w. P. Berglund (cnd), Bournemouth SO EMI Classics ▲ CDM 64202

Haenni, Regina (vl)—see ORCHESTRAS & ENSEMBLES Isabella D'Este

Haertel, Rob (perc)
Bizet, G.:Carmen (sels), w. Carmen Oprisanu (mez), Daniel Speer Trombone Consort [arr Gerard de Krom] World Wind ▲ CD KK 9618 [DDD]
Gervaise, C.:French Dances of the 16th Century, w. Daniel Speer Trombone Consort [arr Hans Mooren, 1961] World Wind ▲ CD KK 9618 [DDD]

Haffner, Caroline (pno)
Weber, C.M. von:Sons Vn, w. Luigi Alberto Bianchi (vn) *(rec Dynamic's, Genova, May 23–25, 1995)* Dynamic ▲ CDS 149 [DDD]

Haffner, Caroline (pno) (cont.)
Weber, C.M. von:Vars on a Norwegian Air Vn, w. Luigi Alberto Bianchi (vn) *(rec Dynamic's, Genova, May 23-25, 1995)* Dynamic ▲ CDS 149 [DDD]

Haffner, J. (va)
Vivaldi, A.:Con Lt, w. P. Press (gtr), P. Peabody (vn), E. Lim (vn), T. Mook (vc), E. Brewer (hpd) ESS.A.Y ▲ CD 1004 [DDD] ■ C 1004 (D)

Hafsteindóttir, Audur (vn)
Blak, K.:Álvarann *(rec Listasafn Sigurjóns Ólafssonar, Reykjavik, May 1995)* Tutl ▲ FKT 8

Haga, Mikiko (koto)
Noda, T.:Mutation, w. Katsuya Yokoyama (shak), Toshi Fujita (koto), Chieko Mori (koto), T. Otaka (cnd), Tokyo Metropolitan SO *(rec live, Tokyo Bunka-Kaikan, Large Hall, May 24, 1980)* Camerata ▲ 32CM-292 [AAD]

Hagao, Hiroshi (pno)
French Trumpet in Japan, w. Eric Aubier (tpt) *(rec Hiroshima, Oct. 1990)* Maguelone ▲ 351.006 [DDD]

Hagberg, Anders (fl/perc/sgr)
Blak, K.:Con Grotto, w. John Tchicai (t sax/sgr/perc), Lennart Kullgren (gtr/fl/sgr/perc), Kristian Blak (pno/perc/sgr), Anders Jormin (bass instr/perc/sgr), Karin Korpelainen (perc/sgr), Sharon Weiss (perc/kaval) *(rec Lídargjógv, Sandoy, Aug. 1984)* Tutl ▲ HJF 33

Hagberg, Anders (fl/s sax/perc)
Blak, K.:Drangar, w. Tore Brunborg (s sax/t sax/perc), Lennart Kullgren (gtr/sgr), Kristian Blak (pno/sgr), Anda Kuitse (sgr/perc), Anders Jormin (bass instr/perc), Karin Korpelainen (dr/perc) *(rec Nordic House, Tórshavn, Jan. 1995)* Tutl ▲ HJF 33

Hagberg, Anders (fl/t sax)—see ORCHESTRAS & ENSEMBLES Antifonale Chamber Ensemble

Hagberg, Eva (rcr)
Pergament, M.:Little Suite, w. L. Åkerlund (rcr) *(rec Dec. 17-18, 1976)* BIS ▲ CD 37 [AAD]

Hagedorn, Joseph (gtr)—see ORCHESTRAS & ENSEMBLES Minneapolis Guitar Quartet

Hagen, Clemens (vc)
Franck, C.:Qnt Pno, w. A Rabinovitch (pno), K. Bennion (vn), L. Hagen (vn), T. Zimmerman (va) *(rec Lockenhaus Fest, 1984)* ▲
Mozart, W.A.:Qts Fl, w. Irena Grafenauer (fl), Gidon Kremer (vn), Veronika Hagen (va) Sony Classical ▲ SK 66240

Hagen, J. (fl)
Saint-Saëns, C.:Carnival of the Animals, w. D. Wayenberg (vn), H. Oudenaarden (vn), H. de Fraaf (cl), H. Krul (db), W. Vos (xyl), M. Dekkers (acc), Daniel String Quartet *(rec Rotterdam, May 28, 1985)* Erasmus ▲ WHV 001 [DDD]

Hagen, L. (vn)
Franck, C.:Qnt Pno, w. A Rabinovitch (pno), K. Bennion (vn), T. Zimmerman (va), C. Hagen (vc) *(rec Lockenhaus Fest, 1984)* ▲

Hagen, Veronika (va)
Mozart, W.A.:Qts Fl, w. Irena Grafenauer (fl), Gidon Kremer (vn), Clemens Hagen (vc) Sony Classical ▲ SK 66240
Shostakovich, D.:Movts Str Qt, w. G. Kremer (vn), A. Bik (vn), T. Demenga (vc) *(rec Lockenhaus Festival, 1986)* ECM New Series 2-▲ 78118-21347-2 [DDD]

Hagen, Werner (pno)
Berg, A.:Adagio, w. Hans-Udo Heinzmann (fl), Malte Lammers (ob), Walter Hermann (cl), Heinrich Horlein (vn), Jaap Zeijl (va), Seven Forsberg (vc), Willi Beyer (db), Jurgen Lamke (pno), Volker Kneip (perc) [arr chamber ensemble] Koch Schwann ▲ SCH CD 311912
Busoni, F.:Berceuse élégiaque, w. Hans-Udo Heinzmann (fl), Malte Lammers (ob), Walter Hermann (cl), Heinrich Horlein (vn), Jaap Zeijl (va), Seven Forsberg (vc), Willi Beyer (db), Jurgen Lamke (pno), Volker Kneip (perc) [arr Stein for chamber ensemble] Koch Schwann ▲ SCH CD 311912
Debussy, C.:Prélude à l'après-midi d'un faune, w. Hans-Udo Heinzmann (fl), Malte Lammers (ob), Walter Hermann (cl), Heinrich Horlein (vn), Jaap Zeijl (va), Seven Forsberg (vc), Willi Beyer (db), Jurgen Lamke (pno), Volker Kneip (perc) [arr Sachs for chamber ensemble] Koch Schwann ▲ SCH CD 311912
Schoenberg, A.:Chamber Sym 1, w. Hans-Udo Heinzmann (fl), Malte Lammers (ob), Walter Hermann (cl), Heinrich Horlein (vn), Jaap Zeijl (va), Seven Forsberg (vc), Willi Beyer (db), Jurgen Lamke (pno), Volker Kneip (perc) [arr Webern for chamber ensemble] Koch Schwann ▲ SCH CD 311912

Hager, L. (hpd)
Honegger, A.:La Tempête (suite), w. M. Kemmer (cnd), RTL SO *(rec Nov. 16-20, 1992)* Timpani ▲ 1C 1016 [DDD]

Hagström, L. (fl)—see ORCHESTRAS & ENSEMBLES Frösunda Wind Quintet

Haguenauer, Jean-Louis (pno)—see also ORCHESTRAS & ENSEMBLES Stanislas Ensemble
Bayer, F.:Music of, w. Donatienne Michel-Dansac (sop), Alain Meunier (vc), Renaud Francois, Francesca Paderni, Tetra Ensemble Pierre Verany ▲ PVY 796093
Debussy, C.:Pno Music (complete solo)—Estampes; Masques; D'un cahier d'esquisses; L'isle joyeuse; Images [Book I]; Images [Book II] *(rec Apr. 1993)* Ligia Digital ▲ 0103006 [DDD]
Debussy, C.:Preludes Pno Ligia Digital 2-▲ 0103023-24
Denisov, E.:Pieces (3) Pno 4-Hands, w. O. Delangle (pno), M. Soveral (pno) *(rec Jan. 1990)* Pierre Verany ▲ PV.790112 [DDD]
Liszt, F.:Transcriptions & Paraphrases—Jean-Louis Haguenauer [Beethoven's Syms Nos. 1 & 2], Georges Pludermacher [Beethoven's Sym No. 3], Alain Planès [Beethoven's Syms Nos. 4 & 8], Paul Badura-Skoda [Beethoven's Sym No. 5], Michel Dalberto [Beethoven's Sym No. 6], Jean-Claude Pennetier [Beethoven's Sym No. 7], Georges Pludermacher & Alain Planès [Beethoven's Sym No. 9] Harmonia Mundi France 7-▲ HMX 2901192.98

Hahn, Detlef (vn)
Lekeu, G.:Son Vn, w. John York (pno) ASV ("Quicksilva" series) ▲ ASQ 6158 [DDD]
Ravel, M.:Son Vn Pno, w. John York (pno) ASV ("Quicksilva" series) ▲ ASQ 6158 [DDD]
Saint-Saëns, C.:Son 1 Vn, w. J. York (pno) ASV ("Quicksilva" series) ▲ ASQ 6158 [DDD]

Haider, Friedrich (pno)
Songs of Mendelssohn, Schubert & Brahms, w. Edita Gruberova (sop), Peter Schmidl (cl) Nightingale Classics ▲ NIG CD 70860
Strauss (II), Joh.:Songs, w. Gösta Winbergh (ten) Nightingale Classics ▲ NIG 948

Haimovitz, Matt (vc)
Bach, C.P.E.:Con Vc, H.439, w. A. Davis (cnd), English CO Deutsche Grammophon ▲ 429219-2 [DDD]
Boccherini, L.:Con Vc, G.482, w. A. Davis (cnd), English CO Deutsche Grammophon ▲ 429219-2 [DDD]
Britten, H.:Suite 1 Vc Deutsche Grammophon ▲ 431813-2 [DDD]
Crumb, G.:Son Vc Deutsche Grammophon ▲ 431813-2 [DDD]
Haydn, J.:Con 1 Vc, w. A. Davis (cnd), English CO Deutsche Grammophon ▲ 429219-2 [DDD]
Ligeti, G.:Son Vc Deutsche Grammophon ▲ 431813-2 [DDD]
Reger, M.:Suites Vc—No. 1 Deutsche Grammophon ▲ 431813-2 [DDD]

Hairgrove, Robert (pno)
Bach, J.S.:Sons Fl, BWV 1030-35, w. A. Magnin (fl)—BWV 1030-1032 Gallo ▲ CD 566 [DDD]
Bach, J.S.:Sons Vn, w. A. Magnin (vn)—BWV 1020 [doubtful; trans. for flute & continuo] Gallo ▲ CD 566 [DDD]
Milhaud, D.:Caprice, w. H. Mätzener (cl) Koch Schwann ▲ 3-1310-2 [DDD]
Milhaud, D.:Duo concertante Cl & Pno, w. H. Mätzener (cl) Koch Schwann ▲ 3-1310-2 [DDD]
Milhaud, D.:Petit Concert, w. H. Mätzener (cl) Koch Schwann ▲ 3-1310-2 [DDD]
Milhaud, D.:Le Printemps, w. S. Goldberg (vn) Koch Schwann ▲ 3-1310-2 [DDD]
Milhaud, D.:Son 1 Va, w. S. Goldberg (va) Koch Schwann ▲ 3-1310-2 [DDD]
Milhaud, D.:Sonatina Cl, w. H. Mätzener (cl) Koch Schwann ▲ 3-1310-2 [DDD]

Hajdu, Ildikó (vn)—see ORCHESTRAS & ENSEMBLES Duo Ongarese

Hajdu, István (pno)
Debussy, C.:Son Vn, w. A. Grumiaux (vn) Philips ▲ 422839-2 [ADD]

Hakim, Naji (org)
Boston Debut Recital AFKA ■ SK 323
Great European Organs, Vol. 22, w. Cleobury, Stephen (org) Priory ▲ PRCD 327 [DDD]

Hakim, Naji (org) (cont.)
Hakim, N.:Fant sur "Adeste Fideles", w. M.-B. Dufourcet (org) Motette ▲ CD 11171 [DDD]
Hakim, N.:Org Music, w. Marie Bernadette Dufourcet (org) [Cavaille-Coll Org, Sacre-Coeur, Paris]—The Embrace of Fire; Mariales; Expressions; Rhap Priory ▲ PRI 465
Hakim, N.:Symphonie en Trois Mouvements Motette ▲ CD 11171 [DDD]
Langlais, J.:Hommage à Rameau Motette ▲ CD 11171 [DDD]
Langlais, J.:Incantation pour un jour saint Motette ▲ CD 11171 [DDD]
Langlais, J.:Te Deum Motette ▲ CD 11171 [DDD]

Hakkila, Tuija (pno)
Beethoven, L. van:Son 3 Vc, w. Anssi Karttunen (vc) Finlandia ▲ FIN 99955 [DDD]
Beethoven, L. van:Son 4 Vc, w. Anssi Karttunen (vc) Finlandia ▲ FIN 99955 [DDD]
Beethoven, L. van:Son 5 Vc, w. Anssi Karttunen (vc) Finlandia ▲ FIN 99955 [DDD]
Haydn, J.:Trios Pno, Fl & Vc, w. Mikael Helasvuo (fl), Anssi Karttunen (vc) [period instrs] *(rec Oct. 7-9, 1991)* Finlandia ▲ 4509-95869-2 [DDD]
Mozart, W.A.:Sons Pno—No. 3 in B♭, K.281; No. 9 in D, K.311; No. 12 in F, K.332; No. 15 in C, K.545 *(rec Nov. 4-6, 1992)* Finlandia ▲ 4509-95879-2 [DDD]
Mozart, W.A.:Sons Pno—Nos. 4, 10 & 13 Finlandia ▲ FIN 99954 [DDD]
Mozart, W.A.:Sons Pno—Nos. 5, 11 & 16 Finlandia ▲ FIN 99953 [DDD]

Hála, Josef (hpd)
Benda, F.:Cons Hpd, w. Ars Rediviva—4 cons in G, D, g & C *(rec 1978)* Supraphon ▲ 11 1001-2 [AAD]
Benda, G.A.:Sons for 2 Vns, w. Shizuka Ishikawa (vn), Josef Suk (vn), Jitka Vlasankova (vc) Lotos ▲ CD 0027 [DDD]
The Harpsichord in Czech Music of the 18th Century, w. Vaclav Jan Sykora (hpd) Panton ▲ PAN 811038
Locatelli, P.:Sons Vn, Op. 8, w. Shizuka Ishikawa (vn), Josef Suk (vn), Jitka Vlasankova (vc)—Trio Son Lotos ▲ CD 0027 [DDD]
Tartini, G.:Trio Sons, w. Shizuka Ishikawa (vn), Josef Suk (vn), Jitka Vlasankova (vc)—Op. 3/2; Op. 8/1 & 3; Son in D Lotos ▲ CD 0027 [DDD]

Hála, Josef (pno)
Bruch, M.:Trios Cl, Va & Pno, Op. 83, w. Ludmila Peterková (cl), Josef Suk (va) Supraphon ▲ SUP 3014
Dvořák, A.:Ballad, w. Josef Suk (vn) Supraphon ▲ SUP 111466
Dvořák, A.:Notturno, w. Josef Suk (vn) [arr vn & pno] Supraphon ▲ SUP 111466
Dvořák, A.:Qts Pno Strs, Opp. 23 & 87, w. Josef Suk (vn), J. Kodousek (va), J. Chuchro (vc)—Op. 23 & Op. 87 Supraphon ▲ 11 1464-2 [DDD]
Dvořák, A.:Romantic Pieces, Op. 75, w. Josef Suk (vn) Supraphon ▲ SUP 111466
Dvořák, A.:Son Vn, w. Josef Suk (vn) Supraphon ▲ SUP 111466
Dvořák, A.:Sonatina Vn, w. Josef Suk (vn) Supraphon ▲ SUP 111466
Fauré, G.:Son 2 Vn, w. Josef Suk (vn) *(rec Domovina Studio, Prague, Sept. 23-24, 1994)* Discover International ▲ DI 920306 [DDD]
Franck, C.:Son Vn, w. Josef Suk (vn) *(rec Domovina Studio, Prague, Sept. 23-24, 1994)* Discover International ▲ DI 920306 [DDD]
Hindemith, P.:Son Fl, w. Jiří Válek (fl) Supraphon ▲ SUP 0096 [DDD]
Josef Suk Plays Famous Violin Encores, w. Josef Suk (vn) Supraphon ▲ SUP 111311 [DDD]
Korte, O.:Con grosso, w. Miroslav Kejmar (tpt), Zdenek Šedivý (tpt), J. Belohlávek (cnd), Czech PO *(rec House of Artists, Prague, Dec. 2-4, 1987)* Panton ▲ PAN 811257 [DDD]
Lovely Time, w. Josef Suk (vn) Lotos ▲ CD 0026 [DDD]
Martinů, B.:Madrigal Stanzas, w. J. Suk (vn) Supraphon ▲ 11 0099-2 [DDD]
Martinů, B.:Sons Vc, w. J. Chuchro (vc) Supraphon ▲ SUP 110992 [DDD]
Martinů, B.:Son Fl & Pno, w. Jiří Válek (fl) Supraphon ▲ SUP 0096 [DDD]
Martinů, B.:Son 2 Vn, w. J. Suk (vn) Supraphon ▲ 11 0099-2 [DDD]
Martinů, B.:Son 3 Vn, w. J. Suk (vn) Supraphon ▲ 11 0099-2 [DDD]
Milhaud, D.:Son 2 Vn, w. V. Snítil (vn) *(rec 1987)* Supraphon ▲ 110103-2 [DDD]
Mozart, W.A.:Trio Cl, K.498, w. Ludmila Peterková (cl), Josef Suk (va) Supraphon ▲ SUP 3014
Paganini, N.:Sons Vn & Gtr, w. Shizuka Ishikawa (vn)—Sons II, IV & Op. posth.; 6 Sons, Op. 2 Lotos ▲ CD 0028 [DDD]
Poulenc, F.:Sxt Pno, w. Prague Wind Quintet Supraphon ▲ 11 0372-2 [DDD]
Poulenc, F.:Son Fl, w. Jiří Válek (fl) Supraphon ▲ SUP 0096 [DDD]
Prokofiev, S.:Son Fl, w. Jiří Válek (fl) Supraphon ▲ SUP 0096 [DDD]
Ravel, M.:Son Vn Pno, w. V. Snítil (vn) *(rec 1987)* Supraphon ▲ 110103-2 [DDD]
Ravel, M.:Sonate posthume, w. Josef Suk (vn) *(rec Domovina Studio, Prague, Sept. 23-24, 1994)* Discover International ▲ DI 920306 [DDD]
Roussel, A.:Son 1 Vn, w. V. Snítil (vn) *(rec 1987)* Supraphon ▲ 110103-2 [DDD]
Schulhoff, E.:Melody Vn, w. Ivan Zenaty (vn) Supraphon ▲ SUP 112168 [DDD]
Schulhoff, E.:Son 1 Vn, w. Ivan Zenaty (vn) Supraphon ▲ SUP 112168 [DDD]
Schulhoff, E.:Son 2 Vn, w. Ivan Zenaty (vn) Supraphon ▲ SUP 112168 [DDD]
Schulhoff, E.:Suite Vn, w. Ivan Zenaty (vn) Supraphon ▲ SUP 112168 [DDD]
Smetana, B.:From the Homeland, w. Petr Messiereur (vn), Václav Snítil (vn), Jarmila Kozderková (pno) Panton ▲ PAN 811202
Suk, J.:Ballade Vn, w. Petr Messiereur (vn), Václav Snítil (vn), Jarmila Kozderková (pno) Panton ▲ PAN 811202
Szymanowski, K.:Caprices, w. Shizuka Ishikawa (vn) Lotos ▲ CD 0028 [DDD]

Haladyna, Jeremy (pno)
Kraft, William:Episodes, w. Ronald Copes (vn) Albany ▲ TROY 218 [DDD]

Halász, Débora (pno)
Brouwer, L.:Danzas concertantes (3), w. F. Halász (gtr) [arr. for guitar & piano] *(rec Dortmund, Germany, Mar. 21-25, 1994)* BIS ▲ CD 671 [DDD]
Castelnuovo-Tedesco, M.:Fant Gtr & Pno, w. Franz Halász (gtr) *(rec Musikaliska Akademien, Stockholm, Sweden, Jan 22-25, 1995)* BIS ▲ CD 717 [DDD]
Ginastera, A.:Son 1 Pno *(rec Dortmund, Germany, Mar. 21-25, 1994)* BIS ▲ CD 671 [DDD]
Haug, H.:Fant Gtr & Pno, w. Franz Halász (gtr) *(rec Musikaliska Akademien, Stockholm, Sweden, Jan 22-25, 1995)* BIS ▲ CD 717 [DDD]
Ponce, M.:Son Gtr Pno(1931), w. F. Halász (gtr) *(rec Dortmund, Germany, Mar. 21-25, 1994)* BIS ▲ CD 671 [DDD]
Santórsola, G.:Son a duo Gtrs, w. Franz Halász (gtr) *(rec Musikaliska Akademien, Stockholm, Sweden, Jan 22-25, 1995)* BIS ▲ CD 717 [DDD]
Shostakovich, D.:Preludes Vn, w. Franz Halász (gtr) *(rec Musikaliska Akademien, Stockholm, Sweden, Jan 22-25, 1995)* BIS ▲ CD 717 [DDD]
Villa-Lobos, H.:Bachiana brasileira 4 BIS ▲ CD 712
Villa-Lobos, H.:Carnaval das crianças brasileiras BIS ▲ CD 712
Villa-Lobos, H.:Chôro 5 BIS ▲ CD 712
Villa-Lobos, H.:A Lenda do Caboclo BIS ▲ CD 712
Villa-Lobos, H.:Rudepoema BIS ▲ CD 712
Villa-Lobos, H.:Suite floral BIS ▲ CD 712

Halász, Franz (gtr)
Brouwer, L.:Danzas concertantes (3), w. D. Halász (pno) [arr. for guitar & piano] *(rec Dortmund, Germany, Mar. 21-25, 1994)* BIS ▲ CD 671 [DDD]
Castelnuovo-Tedesco, M.:Fant Gtr & Pno, w. Débora Halász (pno) *(rec Musikaliska Akademien, Stockholm, Sweden, Jan 22-25, 1995)* BIS ▲ CD 717 [DDD]
Falla, M. de:Homenaje 'Le tombeau de Debussy' *(rec Schloss Hirschberg, Beilngriess, Germany, May 1-4, 1995)* BIS ▲ CD 736 [DDD]
Gerhard, R.:Fant Gtr *(rec Schloss Hirschberg, Beilngriess, Germany, May 1-4, 1995)* BIS ▲ CD 736 [DDD]
Ginastera, A.:Son Gtr *(rec Dortmund, Germany, Mar. 21-25, 1994)* BIS ▲ CD 671 [DDD]
Haug, H.:Fant Gtr & Pno, w. Débora Halász (pno) *(rec Musikaliska Akademien, Stockholm, Sweden, Jan 22-25, 1995)* BIS ▲ CD 717 [DDD]
José Martinez Palacios, A.:Son Gtr *(rec Schloss Hirschberg, Beilngriess, Germany, May 1-4, 1995)* BIS ▲ CD 736 [DDD]

Halász, Franz (gtr) (cont.)
Ponce, M.:Son Gtr Pno(1931), w. D. Halász (pno) *(rec Dortmund, Germany, Mar. 21-25, 1994)* BIS ▲ CD 671 [DDD]
Santórsola, G.:Son a duo Gtrs, w. Débora Halász (pno) *(rec Musikaliska Akademien, Stockholm, Sweden, Jan 22-25, 1995)* BIS ▲ CD 717 [DDD]
Shostakovich, D.:Preludes Vn, w. Débora Halász (pno) *(rec Musikaliska Akademien, Stockholm, Sweden, Jan 22-25, 1995)* BIS ▲ CD 717 [DDD]
Turina, J.:Gtr Music—Ráfaga, Op. 53; Son for Gtr, Op. 61; Fandanguillo, Op. 36; Homenaje a Tárrega, Op. 69; Sevillana-fant, Op. 29 *(rec Schloss Hirschberg, Beilngriess, Germany, May 1-4, 1995)* BIS ▲ CD 736 [DDD]

Haldemann, H. (pic/fl)
Suter, R.:Musikalisches Tagesbuch 1, w. B. Geiser-Payer (alt), H. Holliger (ob), H. Bochet (bn), J. Joubert (vn), J. Semper (va), W. Eugster (vc), M. Dellanoy (db) *(rec 1962)* Grammont ▲ CSTP 6-2 [AAD]

Haley, Bob (tpt)
Bach, J.S.:Arias, w. Betsy Norden (sop), Donald Foster (org), Alexander String Quartet—(2) from Cantatas 21 & 36 [G] Crystal ▲ CD 952 [DDD] ■ C 952
Bach, J.S.:Cant 51, w. Betsy Norden (sop), Donald Foster (org), Alexander String Quartet [G] Crystal ▲ CD 952 [DDD] ■ C 952
Clarke, J.:Tpt Voluntary, w. Donald Foster (org) Crystal ▲ CD 952 [DDD] ■ C 952
Handel, G.F.:Arias, w. B. Norden (sop), D. Foster (hpd), Alexander String Quartet—Destro dall' empia dite (from *Amadigi di Gaula*); Alle voci del bronzo guerriero (from Cantata No. 19, *O come chiare e belle*) [I] Crystal ▲ CD 952 [DDD] ■ C 952
Scarlatti, A.:Arias Sop, w. Betsy Norden (sop), Donald Foster (hpd), Alexander String Quartet—Con voce festiva; Mio tesoro [I] Crystal ▲ CD 952 [DDD] ■ C 952

Hali̇̌r, Jaroslav (tpt)
Albinoni, T.:Cons Tpt, w. L. Svárovský (cnd), Brno State PO—in B♭ Panton ▲ PAN 811368
Albinoni, T.:Con Tpt & Org, w. Pavel Černý (org) *(rec Mirror Chapel of the Prague Klementinum, Mar 31, 1995)* Panton ▲ 811368-2 [DDD]
Enescu, G.:Légende, w. Daniel Wiesner (pno) *(rec Martínek Studio, Prague, Jan 23 & 26, 1995)* Panton ▲ 811368-2 [DDD]
Françaix, J.:Sonatine Tpt & Pno, *(pianist unknown)* Panton ▲ PAN 811368
Françaix, J.:Sonatine Tpt & Pno, w. Daniel Wiesner (pno) *(rec Martínek Studio, Prague, Jan 23 & 26, 1995)* Panton ▲ 811368-2 [DDD]
Hummel, J.N.:Con in E♭ Tpt, S.49, w. L. Svárovský (cnd), Brno State PO Panton ▲ PAN 811368
Hummel, J.N.:Con in E Tpt, w. L. Svárovský (cnd), Czech Chamber Soloists *(rec Stadion-Hall, Brno, Mar 12, 1995)* Panton ▲ 811368-2 [DDD]
Purcell, H.:Son Tpt, w. Marek Vajo (tpt), Radek Nemec (tpt), Jan Vobořil (hn), Jiří Nauš (trbn), Lubomír Maryška (tuba), Pavel Černý (org), Oldřich Šatava (timp) [trans. F. Antonín Vaigl] *(rec Mirror Chapel of the Prague Klementinum, Mar 26, 1995)* Panton ▲ 811368-2 [DDD]
Tomasi, H.:Con Tpt, w. L. Svárovský (cnd), Czech State PO *(rec Stadion-Hall, Brno, Mar 2 & 3, 1995)* Panton ▲ 811368-2 [DDD]

Hališka, Jan (vc)
Stamitz, C.:Con 2 Vc, w. Z. Dejmek (cnd), Ostrava Janáček CO *(rec Ostrava Church Studio, June 3-11, 1986)* Panton ▲ PAN 811307 [AAD]

Hall, C. (fl)
Messiaen, O.:La Merle noir, w. D. Thoreson (pno) ACA Digital Recording ▲ CM 20024

Hall, David (org)
Anthems for America, w. Salisbury Cathedral Choir [cnd:Richard Seal] Meridian ▲ 84180

Hall, Dimity (vn)—see ORCHESTRAS & ENSEMBLES Australia Ensemble

Hall, G. (pno)
Barber, S.:Son Pno *(rec Bedales School, Hampshire, England, July 8, 1994)* Posh Boy ▲ 8172-2 [DDD]
Bartók, B.:Out of Doors *(rec Bedales School, Hampshire, England, July 8, 1994)* Posh Boy ▲ 8172-2 [DDD]
Busoni, F.:Sonatina 6 Pno *(rec Bedales School, Hampshire, England, July 8, 1994)* Posh Boy ▲ 8172-2 [DDD]
Rachmaninoff, S.:Son 2 Pno *(rec Bedales School, Hampshire, England, July 8, 1994)* Posh Boy ▲ 8172-2 [DDD]

Hall, Jim (gtr)
A Different Kind of Blues, w. Itzhak Perlman (vn), Andre Previn (pno), Shelly Manne (drums), Red Mitchell (bass) Angel ▲ CDM 64319 [DDD]
It's a Breeze, w. Itzhak Perlman (vn), Andre Previn (pno), Shelly Manne (drums), Red Mitchell (bass) Angel ▲ CDM 64318 [DDD]

Hall, Judith (fl)
Images & Impressions:Music for Flute & Harp, w. Elinor Bennett (hp) Nimbus ▲ NI 5247 [DDD]
Mozart, W.A.:Cons Fl, w. P. Thomas (cnd), Philharmonia Orch IMP ("Classic" series) ▲ IMP 2036
Mozart, W.A.:Qts Fl, w. P. Barritt (vn), G. Clarkson (va), J. Horder (vc) Collins Quest ▲ 3044 [DDD]
Vivaldi, A.:Cons Fl, Op. 10, w. P. Barritt (cnd), London Divertimenti IMP ("Classics" series) ▲ IMP 6700212

Hall, Linda (pno)
Elgar, E.:Music of, w. W. Bouton (vn)—includes Chanson de nuit, Chanson de matin, Salute d'amour, Sospiri, La Capricieuse, Sonata in e for Violin & Piano, & others IMP Classics 2-▲ IMP 1039 [DDD]
The Now & Present Flute, w. Patricia Spencer (fl) *(rec SUNY Purchase, June 3-5, 20, 1993)* Neuma ▲ 450-88

Hall, Lucia (vn)
Vivaldi, A.:Con for 2 Vns Vcs, w. C. Prevost (vn), A. Aubut (vc), B. Hurtubise (vc), Y. Turovsky (cnd), Montreal Musici—RV.542 in F Chandos ▲ CHAN 8651 [DDD]

Hall, Nicola (gtr)
Day's End:The Soft Sound of Spanish Guitar, w. Eduardo Fernández (gtr), William Gómez (gtr), Timothy Walker (gtr), John Williams (gtr) London ▲ 448 560-2
Virtuoso Guitar Transcriptions London ▲ 430839-2 [DDD]

Hall, Stephen (perc)
Gibson, R.:Faces Capstone ▲ CPS 8621

Hall, Steven (pno)
Bach, J.S.:Chromatic Fant & Fugue ACA Digital Recording ▲ CM 20006
Beethoven, L. van:Son 16 Pno *(rec Oct. 1986)* ACA Digital Recording ▲ CM 20001
Beethoven, L. van:Vars Pno, WoO 80 ACA Digital Recording ▲ CM 20006
Chopin, F.:Ballades Pno (comp)—in f, Op. 52 ACA Digital Recording ▲ CM 20006
Chopin, F.:Nocturnes—in D♭, Op. 27/2 ACA Digital Recording ▲ CM 20006
Chopin, F.:Pno Music (misc)—Ecossaise, Op. 72/3; Polonaise-fantasie, Op. 61 *(rec 10/86)* ACA Digital Recording ▲ CM 20001
Classic Piano *(rec Atlanta, GA, Dec. 1988)* ACA Digital ▲ CM 20006
Clementi, M.:Sons Pno—in f♯, Op. 26/2 ACA Digital Recording ▲ CM 20006
Liszt, F.:Hungarian Rhaps—No. 2 ACA Digital Recording ▲ CM 20006
Mendelssohn, F.:Rondo capriccioso ACA Digital Recording ▲ CM 20006
Rachmaninoff, S.:Son 2 Pno—Ecossaise, Op. 72/3; Polonaise-fantasie, Op. 61 *(rec 10/86)* ACA Digital Recording ▲ CM 20001
Scarlatti, D.:Sons Kbd—in d, K.32; in d, K.444 ACA Digital Recording ▲ CM 20006

Hall, W. (cl)—see ORCHESTRAS & ENSEMBLES Relâche Ensemble

Halldén, Jerker (fl)
Nilsson, T.:Music of, w. Ingmari Landin (alt), Lars Sjögren (ten), Lage Wedin (bass), Nils-Erik Sparf (vn), Hans-Ola Ericsson (org), Anders Loguin (perc), Torsten Nilsson (cnd), Gustaf Sjökvist (cnd), Swedish Radio Chorus—Ordinarium Missae; Balthasar/Daniel; Drei Gedichte Phono Suecia ▲ PHN 40 [AAD]

Halldórsdóttir, Hildigunnur (vn)
Leifs, J.:Music of, w. Sigrídur Ella Magnúsdóttir (mez), Ólafur Vignir Albertsson (pno), Sólveig Anna Jónsdóttir (pno), Hjálmar Ragnarsson (pno), Edda Erlendsdóttir (pno), Marteinn Hunger Fridriksson (org), Gréta Gudnadóttir (vn), Gudmundur Kristmundsson (va), Sigurdur Halldórsson (vc), Richard Korn (db), Iceland SO, Icelandic Opera Chorus, Langholts Church Graduale Choir, Hamrahlid Choir—Icelandic Cant, Op. 13/4; Valse Lento, Op. 2/1; Icelandic Dance, Op. 11/2 [Tempo Giusto]; Requiem; Lullaby [After the Riots]; Fairy-Tale in the Wood [from Baldr, Op. 34]; Funeral March; Separation [from Elegy, Op. 53]; Galdra Loftur Ov, Op. 10; Funeral March, Op. 6; Reverie; Reunion [from Elegy, Op. 53]; Fine I, Op. 55; Andante [The Last Supper]; Preludia Organo, Op. 16/3 [In the Church]; The Tear of Stone [from Elegy, Op. 53] Music From Iceland ▲ ITM 605 [DDD]
Ragnarsson, H.:Music of, w. S. E. Magnúsdóttir (mez), G. Gudnadóttir (vn), G. Kristmundsson (va), S. Halldórsson (vc), R. Korn (db), Ó. V. Albertsson (pno), S. A. Jónsdóttir (pno), H. Ragnarsson (pno), E. Erlendsdóttir (pno), M. H. Fridriksson (org), Sakari, Wilkinson (cnd), Iceland SO, G. Cortes (cnd), J. Stefánsson (cnd), T. Ingólfsdóttir (cnd), Hamrahlíd Choir, Icelandic Opera Chorus, Langholts Church Graduale Choir—Meine kleine Freundin [In the Ballroom]; Lovers Duet; After the concert; Meine kleine Freundin [Annie listens to the Radio]; Lif's Theme [On the Beach]; Lif's Theme II [Night Prayer]; Composing Ov [Vars I, II & III] Music From Iceland ▲ ITM 605 [DDD]

Halldórsson, Sigurdur (vc)
Leifs, J.:Music of, w. Sigrídur Ella Magnúsdóttir (mez), Ólafur Vignir Albertsson (pno), Sólveig Anna Jónsdóttir (pno), Hjálmar Ragnarsson (pno), Edda Erlendsdóttir (pno), Marteinn Hunger Fridriksson (org), Hildigunnur Halldórsdóttir (vn), Gréta Gudnadóttir (vn), Gudmundur Kristmundsson (va), Richard Korn (db), Iceland SO, Icelandic Opera Chorus, Langholts Church Graduale Choir, Hamrahlid Choir—Icelandic Cant, Op. 13/4; Valse Lento, Op. 2/1; Icelandic Dance, Op. 11/2 [Tempo Giusto]; Requiem; Lullaby [After the Riots]; Fairy-Tale in the Wood [from Baldr, Op. 34]; Funeral March; Separation [from Elegy, Op. 53]; Galdra Loftur Ov, Op. 10; Funeral March, Op. 6; Reverie; Reunion [from Elegy, Op. 53]; Fine I, Op. 55; Andante [The Last Supper]; Preludia Organo, Op. 16/3 [In the Church]; The Tear of Stone [from Elegy, Op. 53] Music From Iceland ▲ ITM 605 [DDD]
Ragnarsson, H.:Music of, w. S. E. Magnúsdóttir (mez), H. Halldórsdóttir (vn), G. Gudnadóttir (vn), G. Kristmundsson (va), R. Korn (db), Ó. V. Albertsson (pno), S. A. Jónsdóttir (pno), H. Ragnarsson (pno), E. Erlendsdóttir (pno), M. H. Fridriksson (org), Sakari, Wilkinson (cnd), Iceland SO, G. Cortes (cnd), J. Stefánsson (cnd), T. Ingólfsdóttir (cnd), Hamrahlíd Choir, Icelandic Opera Chorus, Langholts Church Graduale Choir—Meine kleine Freundin [In the Ballroom]; Lovers Duet; After the concert; Meine kleine Freundin [Annie listens to the Radio]; Lif's Theme [On the Beach]; Lif's Theme II [Night Prayer]; Composing Ov [Vars I, II & III] Music From Iceland ▲ ITM 605 [DDD]

Halleux, Laurent (vn)—see ORCHESTRAS & ENSEMBLES Pro Arte String Quartet

Hallgren, Ingvar (perc)—see ORCHESTRAS & ENSEMBLES Kroumata Percussion Ensemble

Hallgrímsson, Haflidi (vc)
Sigurbjörnsson, T.:Mild und leise Music from Iceland ▲ ITM 702 [ADD]

Halliday, Malcolm (pno)
Sowerby, L.:Songs, w. Robert Osborne (b-bar)—Songs on Poems of John Masefield (3); Songs on Poems of John Galsworthy (3); American Folksong Arrs (3); Songs for Donna Harrison (3); British Folksong Arrs (2); Songs on Poems of Jeanne Delamarter (2); Late Songs; From the Hillcrest (2) *(rec Patrych Studios, NY, Mar 1995)* Albany ▲ TROY 196 [DDD]

Halska, Barbara (pno)
Polish Piano Music, w. Teresa Rutkowska (pno), Marian Brokowski (pno), Maria Nosowska (pno) Olympia ▲ OLY 394 [AAD]

Halstead, Anthony (hn)
Britten, H.:Serenade, Op. 31, w. J. Hadley (ten), W. Boughton (cnd), English String Orch Nimbus ▲ 5234-2 [DDD]
Donizetti, G.:Songs, w. I. Caddy (b-bar), S. Comberti (vc), M. Tan (pno)—Canto d'Ugolino; L'amor funesto; Trovatore in caricatura; Spirito di Dio; Viva il matrimonio; Le renégat; Noé—scène du Déluge; Le départ pour la chasse; On coeur pour abri; La hart [I, F] *(rec 8/84 & 12/85)* Meridian ▲ CDE 84183
Haydn, J.:Con 1 Hn, w. R. Goodman (cnd), Hanover Band Nimbus 3-▲ NI 1789
Haydn, J.:Con 1 Hn, w. R. Goodman (cnd), Hanover Band Nimbus ▲ NI 5190 [DDD]
Haydn, M.:Con 2 Hn, w. R. Goodman (cnd), Hanover Band Nimbus 3-▲ NI 1789
Mozart, W.A.:Cons Hn, w. C. Hogwood (cnd), Academy of Ancient Music L'Oiseau-Lyre ▲ 443216-2 [DDD]
Mozart, W.A.:Cons Hn, w. R. Goodman (cnd), Hanover Band [period instrs] Nimbus 4-▲ NI 1791 [DDD]
Mozart, W.A.:Cons Hn, w. R. Goodman (cnd), Hanover Band [period instrs] Nimbus ▲ NI 5104 [DDD]
Mozart, W.A.:Con Hn, K.495, w. R. Goodman (cnd), Hanover Band *(rec All Saints', Tooting, London, July 1987)* Nimbus ▲ NI 7023 [DDD]
Mozart, W.A.:Con Movt Hn, K.494a, w. R. Goodman (cnd), Hanover Band [period instrs] Nimbus 4-▲ NI 1791 [DDD]
Mozart, W.A.:Con Movt Hn, K.494a, w. R. Goodman (cnd), Hanover Band [period instruments; different orchestration than above] Nimbus ▲ NI 5104 [DDD]
Mozart, W.A.:Music of, w. Gundula Janowitz (sop), Julia Bernheimer (mez), Martyn Hill (ten), David Thomas (bass), Colin Lawson (b cl), Christopher Kite (pno), R. Goodman (cnd), Hanover Band—Cons for Hn, K.412, 417, 447, 494a & 495; Sym No. 40; Con for Cl; Eine kleine Nachtmusik; Requiem; Sym No. 41; Con No. 20 for Pno; Serenata Notturna Nimbus 4-▲ NI 1791 [DDD]
Mozart, W.A.:Rondo Hn, K.514, w. C. Hogwood (cnd), Academy of Ancient Music L'Oiseau-Lyre ▲ 443216-2 [DDD]
Schumann, R.:Andante & Vars Hn, w. P. Frankl (pno), A. Schiff (pno), L. Varga (vc), O. Hegedüs (vc) Vox Box 3-▲ CD3X 3001 [ADD]

Halstead, Anthony (hpd)
Bach, Joh. Christian:Cons Hpd, T.292/1, w. A. Halstead (cnd), Hanover Band CPO ▲ CPO 999299

Halstead, Anthony (hpd/org)
Vivaldi, A.:Cons Diverse Instrs, w. A. Halstead (cnd), Hanover Band—for Ob, RV.463; for Strs & Bc, RV.129 & 156; for Vn, RV.308; for Fl, RV.439; for 4 Vns & Vc, RV.580 Classics for Pleasure ("Eminence" series) ▲ CDEMX 2210 [DDD]

Halstead, Anthony (nat hn)
Haydn, M.:Con 2 Hn, w. R. Goodman (cnd), Hanover Band Nimbus ▲ NI 5190 [DDD]
Weber, C.M. von:Concertino Hn, w. R. Goodman (cnd), Hanover Band [period instrs] Nimbus ▲ NI 5180 [DDD]

Halstead, Anthony (pno)
Bottesini, G.:Music for Db, w. T. Martin (db)—Capriccio di Bravura; Elegia; Fant. on Beatrice di Tenda; Fant. on Lucia di Lammermoor; Grand Allegro di Concerto; Romanza drammatica [w. J. Fugelle (soprano)]; Intro. & Bolero ASV ▲ ASV 626 [DDD]

Hamada, Mitsuhiko (lt)
Takemitsu, T.:Music of, w. Tashi Y. Nagano (mez), H. Ibe (gtr), M. Nagasako (hp), K. Abe (vib), Y. Takahashi (pno), R. Noguchi (fl), M. Hamada (lt), T. Koizumi (picc), S. Ueki (vn), Y. Hattori (vc), R. Stoltzman (cl), P. Serkin (pno), Ozawa, Wakasugi (cnd), Boston SO—Quatrain; Stanza I; Sacrifice; Ring; Valeria; A Flock Descends into the Pentagonal Garden Deutsche Grammophon ("20th Century Classics" series) ▲ 423253-2 [ADD]

Hämäläinen, Kati (hpd)—see ORCHESTRAS & ENSEMBLES Les Goûts-Réünis

Hamberger, Clemens (org)
Guilmant, A.:Son 1 Org *(rec Abteikirche Münsterschwarzach, 1979)* Calig ▲ CAL 50494 [ADD]
Vierne, L.:Sym 3 Org *(rec Abteikirche Münsterschwarzach, 1981)* Calig ▲ CAL 50494 [ADD]

Hamblin, Peter (perc)
Klatzow, P.:Chamber Con, w. Beat Wenger (fl), Jimmy Reinders (cl), Robert Grishkoff (hn), Uliano Marchio (gtr), Lamar Crowson (pno), Barry Jordan (elec org), P. Klatzow (cnd) Claremont ▲ GSE 1524

Hamelin, Clode
Hamelin, C.:Archangelus Gabriel, w. J. Blake Horizon ▲ HOCD 7003

Hamelin, Marc-André (pno)
Alkan, C.-V.:Cons (2) de camera, w. M. Brabbins (cnd), BBC Scottish SO Hyperion ▲ CDA 66717
Alkan, C.-V.:Etudes (12) in minor keys—No. 12 Hyperion ▲ CDA 66794

Hamelin, Marc-André (pno) (cont.)
Alkan, C.-V.:Etudes (12) in minor keys—Nos. 8, 9 & 10, "Concerto" Music & Arts ▲ CD 724-1 [DDD]
Alkan, C.-V.:Grande son [Les quatre âges] Hyperion ▲ CDA 66794
Alkan, C.-V.:Sonatina Pno Hyperion ▲ CDA 66794
Alkan, C.-V.:Troisième recueil de chants—No. 6 Hyperion ▲ CDA 66794
Bolcom, W.:Cabaret Songs, w. J. K. Applebaum (sop) Music & Arts ▲ CD 729-1 [DDD]
Bolcom, W.:New Etudes (12) New World ▲ NW 354-2 [DDD]
Britten, H.:Cabaret Songs, w. J. K. Applebaum (sop) Music & Arts ▲ CD 729-1 [DDD]
Chopin, F.:Son Pno, Op. 35 ISBA ▲ ISB 5016
Chopin, F.:Son Pno, Op. 35 *(rec Sept 1994)* ISBA ▲ ISBCD 5016 [DDD]
Eckhardt-Gramatté, S.-C.:Sons (6) Pno Altarus ▲ CD 9052
Grainger, P.:Pno Music (arrs, transcriptions & paraphrases)—Jutish Medley; Colonial Song; Molly on the Shore; Harvest Hymn; A Reel; Spoon River; Country Gardens; Walking Tune; Mock Morris; Ramble on Love [from Der Rosenkavalier]; Shepherd's Hey; Irish Tune from County Derry; Handel in the Strand; A March Jig; The Hunter in His Career; Scotch Strathspey & Reel; The Gum Suckers March [from In a Nutshell Suite]; The Merry King; In Dahomey [Cakewalk Smasher] Hyperion ▲ CDA 66884
Henselt, A. von:Con Pno, w. M. Brabbins (cnd), BBC Scottish SO Hyperion ▲ CDA 66717
Henselt, A. von:Vars de concert, w. M. Brabbins (cnd), BBC Scottish SO Hyperion ▲ CDA 66717
Ives, C.:Son 2 Pno New World ▲ NW 378-2 [DDD]
Liszt, F.:Études de concert (3) Pno—La leggierezza; Un sospiro Music & Arts ▲ CD 723-1 [DDD]
Liszt, F.:Harmonies poétiques et religieuses—Bénédiction de Dieu dans la solitude Music & Arts ▲ CD 723-1 [DDD]
Liszt, F.:Pno Music (misc)—Apparition No. 1; En rêve; Hungarian Rhaps 2, 10 & 13; Nuages gris; Réminiscences de Don Juan; Un sospiro; Waldesrauschen; *(rec Wigmore Hall, Jan 14, 1996)* Hyperion ▲ CDA 66874
Liszt, F.:Polonaises Pno—No. 2 in E Music & Arts ▲ CD 723-1 [DDD]
Liszt, F.:Réminiscences de Don Juan Music & Arts ▲ CD 723-1 [DDD]
Liszt, F.:Réminiscences de Norma Music & Arts ▲ CD 723-1 [DDD]
Marc-Andre Hamelin live at Wigmore Hall Hyperion ▲ CDA 66765
Martinů, B.:Music of, w. Alain Marion (fl) *(violinist unknown)*—Son for Fl, Vn & Pno; Promenades for Fl, Vn & Hpd; Son for Fl & Pno; 5 Madrigal Stanzas for Fl, Vn & Pno; Scherzo for Fl & Pno; Madrigal Son for Fl, Vn & Pno Analekta ▲ AN 28709
Rachmaninoff, S.:Son 2 Pno ISBA ▲ ISB 5016
Rachmaninoff, S.:Son 2 Pno *(rec Sept 1994)* ISBA ▲ ISBCD 5016 [DDD]
Schoenberg, A.:The Cabaret Songs, w. J. K. Applebaum (sop) Music & Arts ▲ CD 729-1 [DDD]
Schoenberg, A.:Ode to Napoleon, w. K. McMillan (bar), Y. Turovsky (cnd), Montreal Musici [orchestral version] [G] Chandos ▲ CHAN 9116 [DDD]
Schulz-Evler, A.:Arabesque on Themes from Johann Strauss' *The Beautiful Blue Danube* ISBA ▲ ISB 5016
Schulz-Evler, A.:Arabesque on Themes from Johann Strauss' *The Beautiful Blue Danube (rec Sept 1994)* ISBA ▲ ISBCD 5016 [DDD]
Scriabin, A.:Fant Pno Hyperion ▲ CDA 67131/32
Scriabin, A.:Sons Pno (comp) Hyperion ▲ CDA 67131/32
Scriabin, A.:Son-fant Pno Hyperion ▲ CDA 67131/32
Sorabji, K.S.:Son 1 Pno Altarus ▲ CD 9050
Strauss, R.:Son Vc, w. Sophie Rolland (vc) ASV ▲ ASV 913 [DDD]
Thuille, L.:Son Vc, w. Sophie Rolland (vc) ASV ▲ ASV 913 [DDD]
Villa-Lobos, H.:Rudepoema ISBA ▲ ISB 5016
Villa-Lobos, H.:Rudepoema *(rec Sept 1994)* ISBA ▲ ISBCD 5016 [DDD]
Wolpe, S.:Battle Piece New World ▲ NW 354-2 [DDD]
Wright, M.:Chamber Sym Pno CRI ▲ CD 660 [DDD]
Wright, M.:Night Watch, w. J. Applebaum (sop) CRI ▲ CD 660 [DDD]
Wright, M.:Son Pno New World ▲ NW 378-2 [DDD]
Wright, M.:Son 2 Pno CRI ▲ CD 660 [DDD]
Wright, M.:Suite Pno CRI ▲ CD 660 [DDD]

Hamilton, D. (trbn)
Pepping, E.:Suite Tpt, w. G. Malvern (tpt), C. Leaman (sax) CRS ▲ 9051

Hamilton, Laura (vn)—see ORCHESTRAS & ENSEMBLES Manchester Chamber Players

Hamilton, Malcom (hpd)
Handel, G.F.:Chaconne Hpd Delos ▲ DE 1001 [AAD]
Handel, G.F.:Suites Hpd—No. 7 Delos ▲ DE 1001 [AAD]
Scarlatti, D.:Sons Kbd—L.12, 23, 49, 104, 132, 203, 257, 281, 338, 352, 387, 415, 449, 500 Delos ▲ DE 1001 [AAD]

Hamilton, Melissa (va)
Lam, B.-C.:Last Spring, w. Bun-Ching Lam (pno), Ella Marie Gray (vn), John Weller (vn), Walter Gray (vc) CRI ▲ CD 726 [DDD]

Hamilton, Robert (pno)
Ung, C.:Spiral II, w. Judy May Sellheim (mez), Daniel Perantoni (tuba), A. Weisberg (cnd) *(rec Kerr Center, Tempe, AZ, Jan 29, 1991)* CRI ▲ CRI 710 [DDD/ADD]

Hamilton, S. (org)
Dupré, M.:Le Chemin de la croix Arkay ▲ AR 6115 [DDD]

Hamlin, J. (tpt)
Rorem, N.:Hearing, w. R. Rees (sop), K. Wheeler (mez), M. Galloway (ten), R. Hilley (bar), R. Wagner (cl), D. Starobin (mand), D. Davidson (vn), K. Askew (va), J. Babich (db), P. Suits (pno), D. Druckman (perc), G. Smith (cnd) Premier ▲ PRCD 1035 [ADD]

Hammann, James (org)
Dubois, T.:Org Music [1894 Farrand & Votey Org, St Martin of Tours Roman Catholic Church, Louisville, KY]—Toccata in G Raven ▲ OAR 330 [DDD]
Guilmant, A.:Org Music—Caprice, Op. 20/3; Fugue in D, Op. 25/3; Intermezzo, Op. 90; Marche nuptiale, Op. 25/1; Marche religieuse on Lift Up Your Heads, Op. 15/2 Raven ▲ OAR 160 CD [DDD]
Guilmant, A.:Org Music [1894 Farrand & Votey Org, St Martin of Tours Roman Catholic Church, Louisville, KY]—Marche funèbre et chant séraphique; Invocation in B♭; Final in E♭ Raven ▲ OAR 330 [DDD]
Guilmant, A.:Son 1 Org Raven ▲ OAR 160 CD [DDD]
Guilmant, A.:Son 3 Org Raven ▲ OAR 160 CD [DDD]
Historic Organs of New Orleans, w. George Bozeman (org), James S. Darling (org), Jesse E. Eschbach (org), Gerald D. Frank (org), John Gearhart (org), Frederick Hohman (org), Lenora McCroskey (org), Mary Gifford Matthys (org), Lorenz Maycher (org), Donald Messer (org) *(rec June 1989)* Organ Historical Society 2-▲ OHS 89
Lemmens, N.J.:Org Music [1894 Farrand & Votey Org, St Martin of Tours Roman Catholic Church, Louisville, KY]—Son No. 1 [Pontificale] Raven ▲ OAR 330 [DDD]
Mendelssohn, F.:Sons Org [1894 Farrand & Votey Org, St Martin of Tours Roman Catholic Church, Louisville, KY]—No. 3 in A Raven ▲ OAR 330 [DDD]
Schumann, R.:Studies Canon Form [1894 Farrand & Votey Org, St Martin of Tours Roman Catholic Church, Louisville, KY]—No. 5 in b Raven ▲ OAR 330 [DDD]

Hammann, Mary (va)—see also ORCHESTRAS & ENSEMBLES Auréole
Mozart, W.A.:Qts Fl, w. Laurel Zucker (fl), Shirien Taylor (vn), Sam Magill (vc)—K.285, 285b & 298 *(rec Academy of Arts & Letters, New York City, June 11, 1994)* Cantilena ▲ C 660072 [DDD]

Hammel, Bruce (bn)
Glinka, M.:Trio pathétique, w. Charles West (cl), Landon Bilyeu (pno) Klavier ▲ KCD 11072 [DDD]
Mozart, W.A.:Qnt Pno, K.452, w. Landon Bilyeu (pno), Philip Teachey (ob), Charles West (cl), Alan Paterson (hn) Klavier ▲ KCD 11072 [DDD]

Hammer, Alvin (hn)
Glazunov, A.:Idyll, w. J. Stárek (cnd), RIAS Sinfonietta *(rec 1977)* Koch Treasure ▲ 31611-2 [ADD]
Glazunov, A.:Serenade 2 Hn, w. J. Stárek (cnd), RIAS Sinfonietta *(rec 1977)* Koch Treasure ▲ 31611-2 [ADD]

Hammer, Christoph (org)
Brixi, F.X.:Con 1 for 2 Tpts, w. W. Kelber (cnd), Monteverdi Orch *(rec 1993)* Calig ▲ CAL 50927 [DDD]
Brixi, F.X.:Missa di Gloria, w. F. Wagner (sop), R. Schneider-Waterberg (alt), B. Hirtreiter (ten), M. Mantaj (bass), W. Kelber (cnd), Munich Monteverdi Orch, Munich Concerto Vocale *(rec 1993)* Calig ▲ CAL 50927 [ADD]

Hammer, E.-L. (vl)
Schütz, H.:Psalmen Davids, w. H. Otto (org), W. Jaroslawski (vl), R. Mauersberger (cnd), Dresden Church Choir—Singet dem Herrn ein neues Lied, denn er tut Wunder, Psalm 98; Wohl dem, der nicht wandelt im Rat der Gottlosen, Psalm 1; Warum toben die Heiden, Psalm 2; Jauchzet dem Herrn, alle Welt, dienet dem Herren mit Freuden, Psalm 100; Der Herr ist mein Hirt, mir wird nichts mangeln, Psalm 23; Wie lieblich sind deine Wohnungen, Herr Zebaoth, Psalm 84; Aus der Tiefe ruf' ich, Herr, zu dir, Psalm 130; Ach Herr, Straf mich nicht in deinem Zorn, Psalm 6; Ich hebe meine Augen auf zu den Bergen, Psalm 121; Nun lob, mein Seel, den Herren, SWV 41; Ich danke dem Herrn von ganzem Herzen, Psalm 111 [w. Dresden State Orch. members] *(rec Oct. 1965)* Berlin Classics ▲ BER 2070-2 [ADD]

Hammer, M. (fl)
Mozart, W.A.:Adagio & Rondo Glass Armonica, w. J. Petric (acc), M. Berard (ob), D. Perry (va), D. Hetherington (vc) [trans. for accordion & string quartet] *(rec June 12-13, 1991)* CBC ("Musica Viva" series) ▲ MVCD 1056 [DDD]

Hammer, Moshe (vn)
Dances & Romances for Violin, w. Valerie Tryon (pno), William Beauvais (gtr) Musica Viva ▲ MVCD 1071 [DDD]
Martinů, B.:La Revue de Cuisine, w. James Campbell (cl), James McKay (bn), Guy Few (tpt), Tsuyoshi Tsutsumi (vc), André Laplante (pno) *(rec Glenn Gould Studio, CBC Toronto, Mar. 26-27, 1994)* CBC ("Musica Viva" series) ▲ MVV 1089 [DDD]
Milhaud, D.:Suite Vn, w. James Campbell (cl), André Laplante (pno) *(rec Glenn Gould Studio, CBC Toronto, Mar. 26-27, 1994)* CBC ("Musica Viva" series) ▲ MVV 1089 [DDD]
Miniatures, w. Tsuyoshi Tsutsumi (vc), William Tritt (pno) CBC Records ("Musica Viva" series) ▲ MVCD 1043 [DDD]
Paganini, N.:Centone di sonate, w. Norbert Kraft (gtr)—Nos. 7-12 *(rec St. John Chrysostom Church, Newmarket, Canada, Sept. 24-26, 1994)* Naxos ("Guitar Collection" series) ▲ 8.553142 [DDD]
Paganini, N.:Centone di sonate, w. Norbert Kraft (gtr)—Nos. 13-18 *(rec Newmarket, Canada, Nov 1995)* Naxos ▲ 8.553143 [DDD]
Vaughan Williams, R.:Songs, w. K. McMillan (bar), J. Greer (pno)—Rolling in the dew; Searching for lambs; How cold the wind doth blow [E] Marquis ▲ ERAD 127 [DDD]

Hammer, Stephen (ob)
Vivaldi, A.:Cons for 2 Obs, w. F. de Bruine (ob), C. Hogwood (cnd), Academy of Ancient Music—RV.535 London ▲ 433674-2
Vivaldi, A.:Cons Obs Cls, w. F. de Bruine (ob), E. Hoeprich (cl), A. Pay (cl), C. Hogwood (cnd), Academy of Ancient Music—RV.559 London ▲ 433674-2

Hammond, Frederick (hpd)
Telemann, G.P.:Sons Vn, Op. 2, w. Louis Kaufman (vn) Music & Arts ▲ CD 905 [ADD]

Hamon, Pierre (rcr)
Lucente Stella:Middle Ages to the 20th Century Opus 111 ▲ OPS 30-122

Hampton, Allison (hp)
Yule, w. Barnes, Linn (gtr/lt) *(rec Inner Ear Studios, Arlington, VA)* Oak Leaf ▲ OL 2110

Hampton, Bonnie (vc)—see ORCHESTRAS & ENSEMBLES Francesco Trio, Hampton-Schwartz Duo

Hampton, Calvin (org)
Digital Pipes:The Splendor of the Organ, w. Hampton, Calvin (org) Kem-Disc ▲ 1005 [DDD]

Hampton, Ian (vc)
Davies, V.:Qt 1 Strs, "Fun for 4", w. Arthur Polson (vn), Mark Ferris (vn), Nancy DiNovo (va) Campion ▲ RRCD 1339 [DDD]
Davies, V.:Trio 1 Pno, "Silhouettes", w. Melinda Coffey (pno), Arthur Polson (vn) Campion ▲ RRCD 1339 [DDD]

Han, Derek (pno)
Macdowell, E.:Con 1 Pno, w. P. Freeman (cnd), Chicago Sinfonietta Pro Arte/Fanfare ▲ CDS 3412 [DDD]
Macdowell, E.:Con 2 Pno, w. P. Freeman (cnd), Chicago Sinfonietta Pro Arte/Fanfare ▲ CDS 3412 [DDD]
Mozart, W.A.:Cons Pno, w. P. Freeman (cnd), Philharmonia Orch—Nos. 1, 21 & 25 Pro Arte ▲ CDS 3445
Mozart, W.A.:Cons Pno, w. P. Freeman (cnd), Philharmonia Orch—Nos. 11, 15 & 23 Pro Arte/Fanfare ▲ CDS 3434 [DDD]
Mozart, W.A.:Cons Pno, w. P. Freeman (cnd), Philharmonia Orch—Nos. 3, 13 & 24 Pro Arte/Fanfare ▲ CDS 593 [DDD]
Shostakovich, D.:Con 1 Pno, w. J. Henes (tpt), P. Freeman (cnd), Chicago Sinfonietta Pro Arte ▲ CDD 551 [DDD]
Tchaikovsky, P.:Con 2 Pno, w. P. Freeman (cnd), St. Petersburg PO Pro Arte ▲ CDS 3441

Hanani, Yehuda (vc)
Barber, S.:Son Vc, w. M. Levin (pno) *(rec May 1990)* Koch International Classics ▲ KIC 7070 [DDD]
Foss, L.:Capriccio, w. M. Levin (pno) *(rec May, 1990)* Koch International Classics ▲ KIC 7070 [DDD]
Ornstein, L.:Son Vc, w. M. Levin (pno) *(rec May 1990)* Koch International Classics ▲ KIC 7070 [DDD]

Hancock, Carolyn Toll (vn)—see ORCHESTRAS & ENSEMBLES Atlanta Chamber Players

Hancock, David (pno)
Grieg, E.:Sons Vn, Opp. 8, 13 & 45, w. G. Tarack (vn) Bridge ▲ BCD 9026 [ADD]

Hancock, David (vc)—see ORCHESTRAS & ENSEMBLES Atlanta Chamber Players

Hancock, Fralia (db canon)
Partch, H.:US Highball, w. William Wendlandt (bar), Harry Partch (adapted gtr/voc), Christine Charnstrom (chromelodeon), Lee Hoiby (kitara) *(rec 1946)* Innova 4-▲ 401

Hancock, Fralia (perc)
Partch, H.:Dark Brother, w. William Wendlandt (bar), Christine Charnstrom (chromelodeon), Lee Hoiby (kithara), Harry Partch (adapted va) *(rec 1945)* Innova 4-▲ 401

Hancock, Gerre (org)
Evensong, w. St. Thomas Church Men & Boys' Choir New York Koch International Classics ▲ KIC 7285 [DDD]
Fanfare *(rec St. Thomas Church, Fifth Avenue, New York City)* Gothic ▲ GOT 49038 [DDD]

Hancock, Judith (org)
Duruflé, M.:Motets on Gregorian Chants, Op. 10, w. Gerre Hancock (cnd), St. Thomas Men & Boys' Choir Koch International Classics ▲ KIC 7228
Franck, C.:Psalm 150, w. Gerre Hancock (cnd), St. Thomas Men & Boys' Choir Koch International Classics ▲ KIC 7228
Langlais, J.:Messe solenelle, w. Gerre Hancock (cnd), St. Thomas Men & Boys' Choir Koch International Classics ▲ KIC 7228
Messiaen, O.:O sacrum conviviuml, w. Gerre Hancock (cnd), St. Thomas Men & Boys' Choir Koch International Classics ▲ KIC 7228
Poulenc, F.:Exultate Deo, w. Gerre Hancock (cnd), St. Thomas Men & Boys' Choir Koch International Classics ▲ KIC 7228
Tournemire, C.:Org Music—Petite rapsodie improviesée Koch International Classics ▲ KIC 7228

Hancock, Peter (cl)
McLennan, J.S.:Qnt Vn, Va, Vc, Cl & Pno, w. A. Levy (vn), B. Fine (va), A. Diaz (vc), R. Hodgkinson (pno) CRI ▲ CD 594 [DDD]

Hancock, R. (cl)
Ravel, M.:Intro & Allegro, w. M. Klinko (hp), C. Nield (fl), Miami String Quartet Audiofon ▲ CD 72036

Hancock-Child, Rosemary (pno)
Gibbs, C.A.:Songs, w. N. Hancock-Child (bar)—The Bells; Araby; Ann's Cradle Song; Beggar's Song; Candlestick Maker's Song; 5 Eyes; As I Lay in the Early Sun; Silver; The Tiger Lily; The Sleeping Beauty; The Wanderer; Take Heed, Young Heart; Proud Maisie; Jenny Jones; The Ballad of Semmerwater; Padraic the Fiddler; Down in Yonder Meadow; Dream Song Midnight; A Ballad Maker; The Witch; The Splendour Falls; The Cherry Tree; Hypochondriacus; Dusk *(rec July 1990 & July 1991)* Marco Polo ▲ 8.223458 [DDD]

Hand, Frederic (gtr)—see also ORCHESTRAS & ENSEMBLES Calliope
Bach, J.S.:Cons solo Hpd, BWV 972–987, w. E. Fisk (gtr)—BWV 972 *(rec July 27 & Aug 4, 1992)* MusicMasters ▲ 01612-67097-2 [DDD]
Ibert, J.:Chamber Music, w. Sue Ann Kahn (fl), Eleanor Lawrence (fl), Peggy Schecter (fl), Rie Schmidt (fl), David Krakauer (cl), Lauren Goldstein (bn), Curtis Macomber (vn), Susan Jolles (hp), Andrew Willis (pno)—2 Mouvements; Aria; Histoires; Pastoral; Aria; Entr'acte Albany ▲ TROY 145 [DDD]
Ibert, J.:Entracte, w. Sue Ann Kahn (fl) Albany ▲ TROY 145 [DDD]
Ibert, J.:Music of, w. C. Schadeberg (sop), Sue Ann Kahn (fl), E. Lawrence (fl), P. Schechter (fl), R. Schmidt (fl), David Krakauer (cl), L. Goldstein (bn), Curtis Macomber (vn), Susan Jolles (hp), Arthur Willis (pno)—Entr'acte; Jeux; Sonatine; 2 Movements; 2 Interludes; Aria; Pièce for solo Fl; Histoires; 2 Stèles orientées; Pastoral; Aria; Entr'acte Albany ▲ TROY 145
Vivaldi, A.:Con for 2 Mands, w. E. Fisk (gtr), Orch of St. Luke *(rec July 27 & Aug. 4, 1992)* MusicMasters ▲ 01612-67097-2 [DDD]
Vivaldi, A.:Trio Sons Vn Lt, w. E. Fisk (gtr), A. Fuller (hpd) *(rec July 27 & Aug. 4, 1992)* MusicMasters ▲ 01612-67097-2 [DDD]

Hand, Frederic (gtr/lt/vih)—see ORCHESTRAS & ENSEMBLES Jazzantiqua

Handsworth, Peter (cl)—see ORCHESTRAS & ENSEMBLES Trio di Clarone

Handy, Lionel (vc)—see ORCHESTRAS & ENSEMBLES Hartley Piano Trio

Hanke, K. (hn)
Vogel, W.:Sonances, w. H. Peter-Indermühle (fl), H. Elhorst (ob), K. Weber (cl), I. Backer (bn), U. Lehmann (vn), L. Dober (vn), H. Forster (va), M. Liechti (vc), R. Tschupp (cnd) Grammont ▲ CTSP 14-2 [ADD]

Hanke, S. (pno)
Respighi, O.:Preludes on Gregorian Melodies Marco Polo ▲ 8.220176

Hanna, J. F. (va)—see ORCHESTRAS & ENSEMBLES Valcour String Quartet

Hannan, Peter (rcr)
Baroque Sonatas & Canzonas for Recorder, Harpsichord & Gamba, w. Hannan, Peter (rcr), Colin Tilney (hpd), Christel Thielmann (va da gamba) CBC Records ("SM 5000" series) ▲ SMCD 5049 [DDD]
Hannan, Peter:Generic Music, w. Colin Tilney (hpd) CBC ("Musica Viva" series) ▲ MVCD 1055 [DDD]
Hatzis, C.:Nadir, w. D. Perry (va) CBC ("Musica Viva" series) ▲ MVCD 1055 [DDD]

Hannecart-Jakes, Miriam (E hn)
Honegger, A.:Con da camera, w. Emile Biessen (fl), J. Fournet (cnd), Netherlands Radio PO *(rec Hilversum Music Center, Netherlands, May & Dec, 1993)* Denon ▲ CO 78831 [DDD]

Hannevold, Per (bn)
Bozza, E.:Recit, Sicilienne et Rondo, w. Geir Henning Braaten (pno) Norway Music ▲ 0096-0038 [DDD]
Chagrin, F.:Pieces (2) Bn Norway Music ▲ 0096-0038 [DDD]
Jolivet, A.:Sonatine Ob, w. Steinar Hannevold (ob) Norway Music ▲ 0096-0038 [DDD]
Poulenc, F.:Trio Ob, w. Steinar Hannevold (ob), Geir Henning Braaten (pno) Norway Music ▲ 0096-0038 [DDD]
Saint-Saëns, C.:Son Bn, w. Geir Henning Braaten (pno) Norway Music ▲ 0096-0038 [DDD]

Hannevold, Steinar (E hn)
Bozza, E.:Divertissement Sax, w. Geir Henning Braaten (pno) [arr for E hn & pno] Norway Music ▲ 0096-0038 [DDD]

Hannevold, Steinar (ob)
Bozza, E.:Fant pastoral, w. Geir Henning Braaten (pno) Norway Music ▲ 0096-0038 [DDD]
Jolivet, A.:Sonatine Ob, w. Per Hannevold (bn) Norway Music ▲ 0096-0038 [DDD]
Poulenc, F.:Trio Ob, w. Per Hannevold (bn), Geir Henning Braaten (pno) Norway Music ▲ 0096-0038 [DDD]
Saint-Saëns, C.:Son Ob, w. Geir Henning Braaten (pno) Norway Music ▲ 0096-0038 [DDD]

Hannibal, Lars (gtr)
Souvenir, w. Michala Petri (rcr) RCA Red Seal ▲ 09026-62530-2

Hannigan, Barry (pno)
Hill, J.:Rhap Fl & Pno, w. Mary Hannigan (fl) Capstone ▲ CPS 8631

Hannigan, Erin (instr)
Brooke, N.:Obomobile, w. Brandon Adrien, Jennifer Baker, Karen Birch, Daniel Cate, Judy Christy, Richard Cochran, Jessica Cooper, Leslie Dominguez, Dorothy Knight, Jason Lichtenwalter, Jay Moore, Hwa-Ling Russell, Toyin Spellman, Sarah Weiner, Jay Weinland Opus One ▲ CD 160

Hannigan, Mary (fl)
Hill, J.:Rhap Fl & Pno, w. Barry Hannigan (pno) Capstone ▲ CPS 8631

Hannisdal, Per (bn)
Poulenc, F.:Trio Ob, w. G. Zubicky (ob), M. Hirvonen (pno) Simax ▲ PSC 1057 [DDD]

Hanousek, Jiri (vc)
Martinů, B.:Sons Vc, w. Paul Kaspar (pno) Centaur ▲ CRC 2207

Hans, Thomas (pno)
Bizet, G.:Songs, w. Y. Jänicke (mez)—Tarentelle; Ma vie a son secret; Guitare; Pastel; La coccinelle; Rose d'amour; Ouvre ton coeur; Rêve dala bien-aimée; A une fleur; Si vous aimez!; Pastorale; Vieille chanson; L'Esprit saint; Chanson d'avril; Adieux de l'hôtesse arabe; Absence; Douce mer; L'abandonnée; Vous ne priez pas!; Chant d'amour Orfeo ▲ 309931 [DDD]
Rachmaninoff, S.:Songs, w. A. Pusar (sop)—Oh, Never Sing to Me again, Op. 4/4; The Harvest of Sorrow, Op. 4/5; So Many Hours, So Many Fancies, Op. 4/6; For a Life of Pain I Have Giv'n My Love, Op. 8/4, Dream, Op. 8/5; A Prayer, Op. 8/6; I Wait for Thee, Op. 14/1; The Isle, Op. 14/2; Believe It Not!, Op. 14/7; Love's Flame, Op. 14/10; Twilight, Op. 21/3; The Answer, Op. 21/4; The Lilacs, Op. 21/5; Fragment from Musset, Op. 21/6; How Fair This Spot, Op. 21/7; Melody, Op. 21/9; No Prophet I, Op. 21/11; Sorrow in Springtime, Op. 21/12; To the Children, Op. 26/7; Before My Window, Op. 26/10; Day to Night Comparing, Op. 34/4; So Dread a Fate I'll Ne'er Believe!, Op. 34/7; The Morn of Life, Op. 34/10; In My Garden at Night, Op. 38/1; Daisies, Op. 38/3 [Cz] *(rec Nov. 12–15, 1992)* Orfeo ▲ 340941 [DDD]

Hansen, Anne Søe (vn)
Roussel, A.:Chamber Music, w. Majken Bjerno (sop), Toke Lund Christiansen (fl), Bjørn Carl Nielsen (ob), Niels Thomsen (cl), Per Jacobsen (hn), Asger Svendsen (bn), Ketil Christensen (tpt), Zwi Carmelli (va), Piotr Zelazny (va), Niels Ullner (vc), Michael Dabelsteen (db), Tine Rehling (hp), Morten Mogensen (pno), Per Salo (pno), Per Jensen (perc)—Divertissement, Op. 6; Trio, Op. 40; Joueurs de Flute, Op. 27; Serenade, Op. 30; Le marchand de sable qui passe, Op. 13; Andante et scherzo, Op. 13; 2 poèmes de ronsard, Op. 26; Aria; Elpenor, Op. 59; Pipe Kontrapunkt 2-▲ KPT 32218 [DDD]

Hansen, Bjarne (vn)—see also ORCHESTRAS & ENSEMBLES Con Sordino Chamber Group
Bentzon, N.V.:Qt Cl, w. John Kruse (cl), Rastko Roknic (va), Svend Winsløw (vc) *(rec Det Fynske Musikkonservatorium, 1993)* Paula ▲ PACD 78 [DAD]

Hansen, Christoph (t sax)
Ernst, S.:e...staremo freschi! Vienna Modern Masters ▲ VMM 2018 [DDD]

Hansen, Conrad (pno)
Beethoven, L. van:Con 4 Pno, w. W. Furtwängler (cnd), Berlin PO *(rec Oct.–Nov. 1943)* Music & Arts ▲ CD 839 [ADD]

Hansen, E. (gtr)—see ORCHESTRAS & ENSEMBLES Antifonale Chamber Ensemble

Hansen, Finn (db)—see also ORCHESTRAS & ENSEMBLES Vestjysk Chamber Ensemble
Cima, G.P.:Sons 1 & 2 Rcr, w. V. Boeckman (rcr), L. U. Mortensen (hpd) *(rec 9/90)* Kontrapunkt ▲ 32059 [DDD]
Frescobaldi, G.:Canzona detta la Bernadinia, w. V. Boeckman (rcr), L. U. Mortensen (hpd) *(rec 9/90)* Kontrapunkt ▲ 32059 [DDD]
Frescobaldi, G.:Canzona quatra, w. V. Boeckman (rcr), L. U. Mortensen (hpd) *(rec 9/90)* Kontrapunkt ▲ 32059 [DDD]

Hansen, Finn (vl)
Castello, D.:Sons (3) Rcr, w. V. Boeckman (rcr), L. U. Mortensen (hpd) *(rec 9/90)* Kontrapunkt ▲ 32059 [DDD]
Fontana, G.B.:Sons 2, 3 & 4 Rcr, w. V. Boeckman (rcr), L. U. Mortensen (hpd) *(rec 9/90)* Kontrapunkt ▲ 32059 [DDD]
Merula, T.:Music for Rcr, w. V. Boeckman (rcr), L. U. Mortensen (hpd)—La Merula; L'Arisia; La Dada; & La Pighetta *(rec 9/90)* Kontrapunkt ▲ 32059 [DDD]
Telemann, G.P.:Sons (6) Rcr, w. V. Boeckman (rcr), L.U. Mortensen (hpd) *(rec 9/88)* Kontrapunkt ▲ 32014 [DDD]

Hansen, Heidi (acc)
Werner, S.E.:Tango Studies, w. Majken Bell (acc), Carsten Holbek (acc), Hans Jorgen Holbek (acc), Lelo Nika (acc), Morten Rossen (acc), Anders Vesterdahl (acc) *(rec Danish Accordian Academy, Oct. 1994)* Marco Polo ("dacapo" series) ▲ 8.224006 [DDD]

Hansen, Henning (hn)—see ORCHESTRAS & ENSEMBLES Royal Danish Brass

Hansen, Henrik Bo (pno)
Stolarczyk, W.:Earth Air Fire Water, w. Amalie Malling (pno), John Damgaard (pno), Anne Øland (pno), Teddy Teirup (pno), Friedrich Gürtler (pno), Rosalind Bevan (pno), Poul Rosenbaum (pno), Rodolfo Llambias (pno), Bella Horn-Ribera (pno), Anders Riber (pno), Elisabeth Sigurdsson (pno), Thomas Tronheim (pno), Elsebeth Broderson (pno), Erik Kaltoft (pno), Jørgen Hald Nielsen (pno), Aino Gilemann (pno), Birgit Kjær (pno), Jørgen Thomsen (pno), Gunhild Donslund (pno), Lone Karlsson (pno), Erik Fessel (pno), Lasse Nilsson (pno), Janos Ferenczi (pno), Erik Bach (pno), Axel Momme (pno), Arne de Cros Dich (pno), Sven Micha Slot (pno), Hanne Bramsen Buhl (pno), Lili Olesen (pno), Susannah Carlsson (pno), Ulla Erml (pno), Vagn Sørensen (pno), Leif Greibe (pno), Bodil Krogh (pno), Kirsten Ottosen (pno), Inger Bergenholz (pno), Karsten Gylendorf (pno), Bjønr Elkjær (pno), Jacob Bjørn Jensen (pno), Jørgen Kaad (pno), Anne Marie Hjelm (pno), Carl Ulrik Munk Andersen (pno), Poul Lumbye (pno), Oluf Hildebrandt Nielsen (pno), Joachim Olsson (pno), Peter Pade Ramsøe Jacobsen (pno), Astrid Pollmann (pno), Jette Borsch (pno), Kirsten Karlshøj (pno), Maria Teresa Assing (pno), Allan Dahl Hansen (pno), Johan Hugossen (pno), Tine Fenger Pederson (pno), Arne Jørgen Fæø (pno), Anja Høgsted (pno), Anne Sophie Parbo (pno), Inga Lindmark (pno), Teresa Drabik Stathakis (pno), Anne Ruth Ferenczi (pno), Irene Hasager (pno), Yuka Ichikawa (pno), Birgitte Baur (pno), Malene Thastum (pno), Jens E. Rasmussen (pno), Birgitte Zielke (pno), Claus Zielke (pno), Stefan Kasch (pno), Bin Qiao (pno), Inger Johanne Teirup (pno), Lindy Rosborg (pno), Liisa Heininen (pno), David Højer (pno), Ellen Refstrup (pno), Thomas K. Søorensen (pno), Erik Kure (pno), Michael Rauff (pno), Jan beck Eriksson (pno), Tanja Zapolski (pno), Vibeke Skagbo (pno), Pål Eide Lindtner (pno), Ha-Young Sul (pno), Benedicte Palko (pno), Inke Kesseler (pno), Anne Marie Meineche (pno), Sverre Larsen (pno), Kasper Peter Bach (pno), Elisabetta Eliseo (pno), Olga Magieres (pno), Carl Erik Kühl (pno), Thorkild Borup Nielsen (pno), Valeria Zanini (pno), Lars Stenhoft (perc), Dennis Boel (perc), Winnie Dahlgren (perc), Susanne Vind (perc), Claus Byrith (elec), Anne Marie Storm (elec), J. Ribera (cnd) *(rec live, Koldinghaus Castle, Denmark, May 2, 1996)* Danica ▲ DCD 1996

Hansen, J. Søe (vn)
Beethoven, L. van:Qnt Fl, Vn, 2 Vas & Vc, w. T. L. Christiansen (fl), H. Olsen (va), M. Dolgin (va), T.S. Hermansen (vc) Kontrapunkt 2-▲ 32160/61 [DDD]
Kuhlau, F.:Qnts Fl, w. T.L. Christiansen (fl), M. Dolgin (va), H. Olsen (va), T.S. Hermansen (vc) Kontrapunkt 2-▲ 32160/61 [DDD]

Hansen, Jean (b cl)
Scelsi, G.:Anahit, w. Paul Zukofsky (vn), Julie Bogorad (fl), Peggy Russell (fl), Courtney Westcott (fl), Lawrence McDonald (cl), Joan Waryha (cl), Jean Hansen (b cl), Bill Suite (e hn), Nita VanPelt (sax), Bob Zobal (tpt), John Carter (trbn), Martin Lydecker (trbn), Stan Cortman (hn), Robert Ward (hn), William Curry (va), Jody Rowitsch (va), Irene Wade (va), Anne Fagerburg (vc), John Gockel (vc), Sue Manz (bass), Steven Stearman (bass) *(rec Oberlin Conservatory of Music, Oct 8, 1973)* CP² ▲ CP2 108 [AAD]

Hansen, Jennie (va d'amore)
Loeffler, C.M.:La Mort de Tintagiles, w. J. Nelson (cnd), Indianapolis SO New World ▲ NW 332-2 [DDD]

Hansen, Jennie (va)—see ORCHESTRAS & ENSEMBLES Hudson River String Trio

Hansen, Johannes Soe (vn)—see ORCHESTRAS & ENSEMBLES Danish Duo

Hansen, Jørgen Ernst (org)
Bach, J.S.:Org Music (misc), w. H. Otto (org), H. Rilling (org), K. Vad (org)—Toccata & Fugue in d, BWV 565; Fugue in g, BWV 578; Passacaglia & Fugue in c, BWV 582; Fantasia & Fugue in g, BWV 542; Chorales, BWV 147, 583, 608, 622, 645 Denon ▲ CO 8009 [DDD]
Nielsen, C.:Songs, w. Elisabeth Rehling (sop), Peder Severin (ten), Dorte Kirkeskov (pno)—Strange to Say...; Maria Sat on Hay & Straw; God's Angels Sing in Chorus; Now the Sun in the East...; Alas, My Rose...; Standing in Pain under the Cross...; It Is a Wonder...; Jesus Mine, Let My Heart Savour... [all from Hymns & Sacred Songs]; Jens the Road-Mender; The 1st Lark [both from Strophic Songs, Op. 21]; Vibeke's Song [I Came Upon a Song...]; Song of the Sea [The Sea Around Denmark] [both from the play Willemoes]; We Sons of the Plains; The Bird-Catcher's Song, The Tiny Forest Birds are Hiding...; Tove's Song [An Angel Stood Beside Me...]; The Hunter's Song [The Kite Swoops from the Mountain Crest...] [all from the play Tove]; Gulnare's Song [Zither, Let My Prayer Move You...]; Aladdin's Lullaby [Lullalullaby, Tiny Babe...]; Fatima's Song [The Moon is Already Risen...] [all from the play Aladdin]; Music to 5 Poems by J.P. Jacobsen, Op. 4; 10 Little Danish Songs *(rec West Jutland Academy of Music, Sept 1989)* Rondo Grammofon ▲ RCD 8327

Hansen, Leo (vn)
Nørholm, I.:Con Vn, w. H. Blomstedt (cnd), Danish National RSO BIS ▲ CD 80 [AAD]

Hanskov, Mette (db)
Lady Plays the Bass, w. T. Lønskov (pno), N. E. Aggesea (orgn) *(rec Apr. 1991)* Danacord ▲ DACOCD 378 [DDD]

Hanson, Kevin (gtr)
Moran, R.:Rocky Road, w. Joseph Goodrich (kbd), Erik Johnson (perc), Andrew Morrell (perc) *(rec Chapel of Girard College, Philadelphia & Henry Wood Hall, London, Mar 17, 1994 & Dec 13, 19)* Argo ▲ 444540-2 [DDD]

Hans-Peter (pno)—see ORCHESTRAS & ENSEMBLES Stenzl Piano Duo

Hanstedt, Katharina (hp)
Mozart, W.A.:Concertone Vns, w. Werner Tast (fl), H. Haenchen (cnd), C.P.E. Bach CO Berlin Classics ▲ BER 2004

Hantaï, Jérome (vl)—see also ORCHESTRAS & ENSEMBLES Orlando Gibbons Viol Ensemble
Handel, G.F.:Sons Rcr, w. Pascal Monteilhet (thb), Pierre Hantaï (hpd/org), H. Reyne (cnd)—HWV 358, 360, 362, 365, 367, 369, 377 (complete) Harmonia Mundi France ▲ HMC 905211

Hantaï, Marc (fl)
Bach, J.S.:Con Fl, Vn & Hpd, w. François Fernandez (vn), Pierre Hantaï (hpd), P. Hantaï (cnd), Le Concert Français Astrée ▲ E 8523
Bach, J.S.:Trio Son for 2 Fls, BWV 1039, w. B. Kuijken (fl), G. Leonhardt (hpd), W. Kuijken (bass vl) [period instrs] Deutsche Harmonia Mundi 2-▲ 77026-2-RC [ADD]
Clérambault, L.N.:Cants, w. Noémi Rime (sop), Jean-Paul Fouchécourt (ten), Nicolas Rivenq (bass), Hiro Kurosaki (vn), Ryo Terakado (vn), Eric Bellocq (thb), Elisabeth Matiffa (b vl), Bruno Croscet (basse de vn), W. Christie (cnd), Les Arts Florissants—Pyrame et Tisbé, La Muse de l'opéra ou les Caractères Lyriques, La Mort d'Hercule, Orphée Musique d'Abord ▲ HMA 1901329
Couperin, F.:Les Nations, w. B. Kuijken (fl), F. Fernandez (vn), S. Kuijken (vn), W. Kuijken (bass vl), R. Kohnen (hpd) *(rec Mar. 1992)* Accent 2-▲ 9285/86 [DDD]
Haydn, J.:Trios Fls & Vc, "London Trios", w. Barthold Kuijken (fl), Wieland Kuijken (vc) Accent 2-▲ 9283/84

Hantaï, Pierre (hpd)
Bach, J.S.:Con Fl, Vn & Hpd, w. Marc Hantaï (fl), François Fernandez (vn), P. Hantaï (cnd), Le Concert Français Astrée ▲ E 8523
Bach, J.S.:Con 1 Hpd, w. P. Hantaï (cnd), Le Concert Français Astrée ▲ E 8523
Bach, J.S.:Con 3 Hpd, w. P. Hantaï (cnd), Le Concert Français Astrée ▲ E 8523
Bach, J.S.:Goldberg Vars Opus 111 ▲ OPS 3084
Bach, J.S.:Preludes & Fugues Hpd Astrée ▲ E 8523

Hantaï, Pierre (hpd) (cont.)

Bull, J.:Kbd Music—In nomine; Pavan in the 2nd tone; Galliard; The King's hunt; Germain's alman; English toy; Why aske you; Fant; Melancholy galliard; In nomine; Dutch dance; Pavan fantastic; Galliard to the pavan; In nomine; Fant; Doctor Bull's goodnight; Lord Lumley's galliard; Salvator mundi; Irish toy; Chromatic pavan; Chromatic gaillard; The Duke of Brunswick's Alman Astrée ▲ E 8543

Colonel Chabert, w. Pasquier, Régis (vn), Lluís Claret (vc), Philippe Cassard (pno) Travelling ▲ K 1013

Frescobaldi, G.:Toccate e partite d'intavolatura Astrée ▲ E 8585

Mozart, W.A.:Con Pno, K.107, w. Le Concert Français Opus 111 ▲ OPS 30-9003

Telemann, G.P.:Con Tpt 2 Obs, w. Per-Olev Lindeke (tpt), Taka Kitazato (ob), Marcel Ponseele (ob), Fred Jacobs (thb), Richte Van Der Meer (vc) *(rec St. Stefanus, Melsen, Belgium, June 1995)* Accent ▲ 95110 [DDD]

Telemann, G.P.:Essercizii musici (sels), w. Taka Kitazato (ob), Marcel Ponseele (ob), Per-Olev Lindeke (tpt), Fred Jacobs (thb), Richte Van Der Meer (vc)—Trio Son in E♭ for Ob, Hpd & Continuo *(rec St. Stefanus, Melsen, Belgium, June 1995)* Accent ▲ 95110 [DDD]

Telemann, G.P.:Der Getreue Music-Meister (sels), w. Taka Kitazato (ob), Marcel Ponseele (ob), Per-Olev Lindeke (tpt), Fred Jacobs (thb), Richte Van Der Meer (vc)—Son in a *(rec St. Stefanus, Melsen, Belgium, June 1995)* Accent ▲ 95110 [DDD]

Telemann, G.P.:Kleine Kammermusik, w. Taka Kitazato (ob), Marcel Ponseele (ob), Per-Olev Lindeke (tpt), Fred Jacobs (thb), Richte Van Der Meer (vc)—Partita IV in g *(rec St. Stefanus, Melsen, Belgium, June 1995)* Accent ▲ 95110 [DDD]

Telemann, G.P.:Musique de Table, w. Taka Kitazato (ob), Marcel Ponseele (ob), Per-Olev Lindeke (tpt), Fred Jacobs (thb), Richte Van Der Meer (vc)—Son in g *(rec St. Stefanus, Melsen, Belgium, June 1995)* Accent ▲ 95110 [DDD]

Telemann, G.P.:Son 2 Ob, w. Taka Kitazato (ob), Marcel Ponseele (ob), Per-Olev Lindeke (tpt), Fred Jacobs (thb), Richte Van Der Meer (vc) *(rec St. Stefanus, Melsen, Belgium, June 1995)* Accent ▲ 95110 [DDD]

Hantaï, Pierre (hpd/org)

Handel, G.F.:Sons Rcr, w. Jérôme Hantaï (vl), Pascal Monteilhet (thb), H. Reyne (cnd)—HWV 358, 360, 362, 365, 367, 369, 377 (complete) Harmonia Mundi France ▲ HMC 905211

Hantaï, Pierre (kbd)

Farnaby, G.:Kbd Music—For 2 Virginals; Muscadin; Fant; Meridian Alman; Mal Sims; Alman; Rosseter's Galliard; Wooddy-Cock; A Maske; Pawles Wharfe; The Old Spagnioletta; Fant; His Humour; A Maske; The King's Hunt; Fant; A Gigge; Galiarda; Tell Mee Daphne; Spagnioletta; Fant; A Maske; Alman; Fant; Pavana; Why Aske You; Giles Farnabys; Dreame; Quodling's Delight; Lachrymae Pavan; A Toye Adda ▲ ADD 581172 [DDD]

Hantaï, Pierre (org)

Bach, J.S.:Cant 49, w. N. Argenta (sop), K. Mertens (bass), M. Ponseele (ob), S. Kuijken (vn), H. Suzuki (vc), La Petite Bande Accent ▲ ACC 9395 D [DDD]

Bach, J.S.:Cant 58, w. N. Argenta (sop), K. Mertens (bass), M. Ponseele (ob), S. Kuijken (vn), H. Suzuki (vc), La Petite Bande Accent ▲ ACC 9395 D [DDD]

Bach, J.S.:Cant 82, w. N. Argenta (sop), K. Mertens (bass), M. Ponseele (ob), S. Kuijken (vn), H. Suzuki (vc), La Petite Bande Accent ▲ ACC 9395 D [DDD]

Hanták, František (ob)

Handel, G.F.:Cons (3) Ob, w. V. Talich (cnd), Czech PO—No. 3 *(rec 1954–55)* Supraphon ▲ SUP 11 1906 [AAD]

Mozart, W.A.:Sinf concertante Ob, K.Anh.9, w. Milos Kopecky (cl), Miroslav Stefek (hn), Karel Vacek (bn), *(orch unknown)* Supraphon ▲ SUP 3053

Hanzel, Peter (bn)

Mozart, W.A.:Con Bn, w. R. Edlinger (cnd), Mozart Academy *(rec Concert Hall of the Slovak PO, Bratislava, July 1987)* Lydian ▲ 18058 [DDD]

Hara, László (bn)

Crusell, B.H.:Concertino Bn, w. O. Vänskä (cnd), Tapiola Sinfonietta BIS ▲ CD 495 [DDD]

Danzi, F.:Con Bn, w. E. Lukács (cnd), Franz Liszt CO Hungaroton ▲ HCD 31139 [DDD]

Rosetti, F.A.:Con Bn, w. E. Lukács (cnd), Franz Liszt CO Hungaroton ▲ HCD 31139 [DDD]

Weber, C.M. von:Con Bn, w. E. Lukács (cnd), Franz Liszt CO Hungaroton ▲ HCD 31139 [DDD]

Winter, P. von:Concertino Bn, w. E. Lukács (cnd), Franz Liszt CO Hungaroton ▲ HCD 31139 [DDD]

Harada, Koichiro (vn)—see ORCHESTRAS & ENSEMBLES Tokyo String Quartet

Harada, Sadao (vc)—see ORCHESTRAS & ENSEMBLES Tokyo String Quartet

Harada, Takashi (ondes martenot)

Peebles, S.:Aqua Babble, w. Kazue Mizushima (perc), Sarah Peebles (shô/elec/perc) *(rec live, Studio Kinshicho, Japan, June 11, 1993)* Innova ▲ 506

Harada, Takashi (pno)

Messiaen, O.:Turangalîla-sym, w. J.-Y. Thibaudet (ondes Martenot), R. Chailly (cnd), Royal Concertgebouw Orch *(rec March 1992)* London ▲ 436626-2 [DDD]

Haraldsdóttir, Áshildur (fl)

Bach, C.P.E.:Cons Fl, w. T. Svedlund (cnd), Umeå SO—in G Intim Musik ▲ INT 38

Benda, F.:Con in e Fl & Orch, w. T. Svedlund (cnd), Umeå SO Intim Musik ▲ INT 38

Dutilleux, H.:Sonatine Fl, w. Love Derwinger (pno) Intim Musik ▲ INT 9 [DDD]

Fauré, G.:Fant Fl, w. Love Derwinger (pno) Intim Musik ▲ INT 9 [DDD]

Fauré, G.:Morceau de concours Fl & Pno, w. Love Derwinger (pno) Intim Musik ▲ INT 9 [DDD]

Gaubert, P.:Nocturne et Allegro scherzando, w. Love Derwinger (pno) Intim Musik ▲ INT 9 [DDD]

Haydn, J.:Con Fl, H.VIIf/D1, w. T. Svedlund (cnd), Umeå SO Intim Musik ▲ INT 38

Honegger, A.:Chamber Music (comp), w. D.-S. Kang (vn), P.-H. Xuereb (va), R. Wallfisch (vc), M. Arrignon (cl), A. Marion (fl), C. Moreaux (ob), T. Caens (tpt), M. Becquet (trbn), P. Zanlonghi (hp), P. Devoyon (pno), F. Kondo (mez), Ludwig String Quartet—Sonatine for Clarinet & Piano (1921–22); Rapsodie for 2 Flutes, Clarinet & Piano (1917); Danse de la Chèvre for Solo Flute (1921); Romance for Flute & Piano (1953); Petite Suite for 2 Flutes & Piano (1934); Trois Contrepoints for Piccolo, Oboe, Violin & Cello (1922); Intrada for Trumpet & Piano (1947); Hommage du trombone exprimant la tristesse de l'auteur absent for Trombone & Piano (1925); J'avais un fidèle amant for String Quartet (1929); Chanson de Ronsard & 3 Chansons de la petite Sirène for Mezzo, Flute & String Quartet (1924); Introduction et Danse for Flute, Harp & String Trio [undated]; Colloque for Flute, Celesta, Violin & Viola [undated] Timpani ▲ 1C1010 [DDD]

Poulenc, F.:Son Fl, w. Love Derwinger (pno) Intim Musik ▲ INT 9 [DDD]

Roussel, A.:Joueurs de flûte, w. Love Derwinger (pno) Intim Musik ▲ INT 9 [DDD]

Sancan, P.:Sonatine Fl, w. Love Derwinger (pno) Intim Musik ▲ INT 9 [DDD]

Tómasson, H.:Eco del passato, w. A. Magnúsdóttir (hpd) Music from Iceland ▲ ITM 707

Haram, Simon (sax)

Debussy, C.:Chamber Music, w. William Bennett (fl), David Campbell (cl), James Campbell (cl), Nicholas Daniel (ob), Robert Makell (hn), Richard Watkins (hn), Robin Kennard (bn), Rachel Gough (bn), Ieuan Jones (hp), Clifford Benson (pno), Julius Drake (pno), John York (pno), Roger Tapping (va)—Rapsodie for Eng hn; Syrinx; Première rapsodie; Son for Fl, Va & Hp; Le petit nègre; Petite pièce; Rapsodie for Sax *(rec All Saints' Church, East Finchley, London, Jan 12–20, 1994)* Cala 2-▲ CACD 1017 [DDD]

Saint-Saëns, C.:Chamber Music, w. W. Bennett (fl), D. Campbell (cl), J. Campbell (cl), N. Daniel (ob), R. Makell (hn), R. Watkins (hn), R. Kennard (bn), R. Gough (bn), I. Jones (hp), C. Benson (pno), J. Drake (pno), J. York (pno), R. Tapping (va)—Odelette, Op. 162; Son for Cl, Op. 167; Feuillet d'album, Op. 81; Son for Bn, Op. 168; Caprice on Danish & Russian Airs, Op. 79; Son for Ob, Op. 166; Romance in D♭, Op. 37; Tarantelle, Op. 6 *(rec All Saints' Church, East Finchley, London, Jan 12–20, 1994)* Cala 2-▲ CACD 1017 [DDD]

Haran, Michael (vc)

Ravel, M.:Chansons madécasses, w. M. Zakai (cta), A. Biron (fl), Y. Zak (pno) [F] Koch International Classics ▲ KIC 7021-2 [DDD] ■ 3-7021-4 (D)

Harand, R. (vc)

Haydn, J.:Mass 10, "Kriegsmesse", "Paukenmesse", w. Netania Davrath (sop), Hilde Rössl-Majdan (alt), Anton Dermota (ten), W. Bery (bass), Anton Heiller (org), M. Wöldike (cnd), Vienna State Opera Orch, Vienna State Opera Chorus *(rec May 14–16, 1960)* Vanguard Classics ("The Bach Guild" series) ▲ OVC 2518 [ADD]

Harasiewicz, Adam (pno)

Brahms, J.:Pno Music (misc), w. Stephen Bishop Kovacevich (pno), Dinorah Varsi (pno)—Opp. 79, 116, 117, 118 & 119; Vars. on themes by Handel, Op. 24 & Paganini, Op. 35 Philips ("Duo" series) 2-▲ 442589-2

Chopin, F.:Con 2 Pno, w. K. Kord (cnd), Warsaw PO LaserLight ▲ 14 003 [DDD]

Chopin, F.:Concerto No. 2 in f for Piano & Orchestra, Op. 21 (1829–30), w. Warsaw PO [cnd:Kazimierz Kord] Laserlight ♦ 90017 [DDD]

Chopin, F.:Nocturnes Philips ("Duo" series) 2-▲ 442266-2

Chopin, F.:Pno Music (misc), w. Martha Argerich (pno), Vladimir Ashkenazy (pno), Stanislav Bunin (pno), Halina Czerny-Stefanska (pno), Jan Ekier (pno), Yuval Fichman (pno), Kemal Gekic (pno), Krzysztof Jablonski (pno), Louis Kentner (pno), Jean-Marc Luisada (pno), Garrick Ohlsson (pno), Ivo Pogorelich (pno), Maurizio Pollini (pno), Dang Thai Son (pno)—includes Ballade (Nos. 1 & 2); Barcarolle, Op. 60; Concerto Nos. 1 & 2; Études (Op. 10, Nos. 1, 5, 8, 10 & 12 & Op. 25, No. 10, 18 & 25); Grand valse brillante; Impromptus (Nos. 3 & 4); Mazurkas (Op. 24, Nos. 1–4; Op. 30, Nos. 1–4; Op. 50, No. 32; Op. 59, Nos. 1–3); Nocturnes (Op. 9, No. 3; Op. 37, No. 12; Op. 48, No. 13; Op. 55, No. 16)Polonaise (Op. 40, Nos. 3 & 4; Op. 44, No. 5; Op. 53, No. 6; Op. 61, No. 7); Preludes (Op. 28 Nos. 13–18, 21–24 & Op. 45, No. 25); Scherzos (Nos. 1–3); Sonatas (Nos. 2 & 3); Waltzes (No. 1 & 6) LaserLight 5-▲ 15 961 [ADD/DDD]

Chopin, F.:Pno Music (misc)—Vars brillantes, Op. 12; Vars sur un air national allemand, Op. posth; Vars sur un thème de Paganini, Op. posth; Hexaméron vars; Allegro de concert, Op. 46; Mazurkas, Op. 6/1–4; Mazurkas, Op. 24/1–2; Polonaise, Op. 53 "Héroïque" *(rec Polish Radio S-1 Hall, Nov 13–26, 1992)* Canyon Classics ▲ 193

Chopin, F.:Pno Music (misc)—Barcarolle in F♯; Berceuse in D♭; Fantasie-Impromptu; Grand valse brillante; Mazurkas 5 & 37; Minute Waltz; Nocturnes 5 & 13; Polonaises 3 & 6; Scherzos 2 & 3 Philips ("Miniature" series) ▲ 422282-2 [ADD] ■ 422282-4

Chopin, F.:Polonaises—Nos. 3 & 6 Philips ("Miniature" series) ▲ 422282-2 [ADD] ■ 422282-4

Chopin, F.:Prelude in A♭ Philips ("Duo" series) 2-▲ 442266-2

Chopin, F.:Preludes, Op. 28 Philips ("Duo" series) 2-▲ 442266-2

Chopin, F.:Prelude, Op. 45 Philips ("Duo" series) 2-▲ 442266-2

Harbach, Barbara (hpd)

Adler, S.:Bridges to Span Adversity Gasparo ▲ GS 280 ■ GS 280

Adler, S.:Son 2 Vn, w. C. Castleman (vn) Albany ▲ TROY 041

Auenbrugg, M. von:Son in E♭ Hpd Gasparo ▲ GS 272 [DDD]

Bach, J.S.:Goldberg Vars Gasparo 3-▲ GS 282/83 3-■ GS 282C

Barbara Harbach Gasparo ▲ GSCD 281 ■ GS 281C

Barthélémon, C.M.:Son Hpd, Op. 1/3 Gasparo ▲ GAS 272 [DDD]

Barthélémon, C.M.:Son Hpd, Op. 3 Gasparo ▲ GS 281 ■ GS 281C

Billington, E.:Sons Hpd, Op. 1 Hester Park ▲ CD 7703 [DDD]

Billington, E.:Sons Hpd, Op. 2 Hester Park ▲ CD 7703 [DDD]

Borroff, E.:Metaphors Gasparo ▲ GS 266 ■ GS 266C

Fine, V.:Toccatas & Arias Gasparo ▲ GS 266 ■ GS 266C

Gambarini, E. de:Pieces Hpd, Op. 2 Gasparo ▲ GS 272 [DDD]

Gambarini, E. de:Sets of Lessons (6) Hester Park ▲ CD 7702 [DDD]

Harbach, B.:Spaindango Gasparo ▲ GS 266 ■ GS 266C

Hardin, E.:Lessons (6) Hester Park ▲ CD 7702 [DDD]

Jones, S.:Movts Hpd Gasparo ▲ GS 280 ■ GS 280C

Locklair, D.:The Breakers Pound Gasparo ▲ GS 266 ■ GS 266C

Locklair, D.:Fant Brings the Day Gasparo ▲ GS 280 ■ GS 280C

Locklair, D.:Org Music—Ayre for the Dance (1984); Inventions (1978); Pageant for Sally (1975); Rubrics (1988) Gasparo ▲ GS 277 ■ GS 277C

Martinez, M.:Son in A Hpd Gasparo ▲ GAS 272 [DDD]

Martinez, M.:Son in E Hpd Gasparo ▲ GAS 272 [DDD]

Martinů, B.:Promenades, w. C. Castleman (vn), B. Boyd (fl) Albany ▲ TROY 041-2

Milhaud, D.:Son Vn & Hpd, Op. 257, w. C. Castleman (vn) Albany ▲ TROY 041-2

Mozart, W.A.:Pno Music (misc)—Allegro in C, K.6/1; Andante in F, K.6/2; Menuett I in C, K.6/Menuett I; Allegro in B♭, K.8/1; Menuett & Trio in G, K.1; Klavierstück in C, K.9a; 8 Vars in G, K.24; Untitled in F, K.15hh; 7 Variations in D, K.25 Hester Park ▲ CD 7703 [DDD]

Park, M.H.:Con Hpd Gasparo ▲ GS 281 ■ GS 281C

Park, M.H.:Son Hpd, Op. 4 Gasparo ▲ GS 272 [DDD]

Park, M.H.:Son Hpd, Op. 7 Gasparo ▲ GS 281 ■ GS 281C

Pinkham, D.:Part Hpd Gasparo ▲ GS 280 ■ GS 280C

Piston, W.:Sonatina Vn, w. C. Castleman (vn) Albany ▲ TROY 041-2

Read, G.:Chamber Music, w. Janet Packer (vn), Gerald Berthiaume (cel), Leslie Stratton Norris (hp), Joseph Holt (pno), Howard Karp (pno), Boston Composers String Quartet—5 Aphorisms, Op. 150; Son. da Chiesa, Op. 61; Sonoric Fant. No. 1, Op. 102; Qt. 1 Strings, Op. 100 Northeastern ▲ NOR 253 [DDD]

Read, G.:Sonoric Fantasia 1, w. Gerald Berthiaume (cel), Leslie Stratton Norris (hp) *(rec KWSU-TV Studios, Pullman, WA, Nov. 1993)* Northeastern ("Classical Arts, Contemporary" series) ▲ NR 253

Rosner, A.:Music de clavecin Gasparo ▲ GS 266 ■ GS 266C

Rosner, A.:Sonatine d'Amour Gasparo ▲ GS 280 ■ GS 280C

Rubbra, E.:Cant Pastorale, w. B. Boyd (fl), et al. Albany ▲ TROY 041-2

Rubbra, E.:Fant on a Theme of Machaut, w. B. . Boyd (fl), et al. Albany ▲ TROY 041-2

Schuman, W.:When Jesus Wept [arr for hpd] Gasparo ▲ GS 258 ■ GS 258C

Thompson, R.:Inventions Hpd Gasparo ▲ GS 266 ■ GS 251C

Turner, E.:Lesson I Hpd Gasparo ▲ GS 281 ■ GS-281C

Turner, E.:Lesson II Hpd Gasparo ▲ GS 281 ■ GS 281C

20th Century Harpsichord Music, Vol. 2 Gasparo ▲ GSCD 266 ■ GS 275C

Harbach, Barbara (org)

Adler, S.:Hymnset Gasparo ▲ GS 258 ■ GS 258C

Adler, S.:Meditations (2) Gasparo ▲ GS 277 ■ GS 277C

Adler, S.:Reflections Gasparo ▲ GS 277 ■ GS 277C

Adler, S.:Toccata, Recitation & Postlude Gasparo ▲ GS 277 ■ GS 277C

Adler, S.:Wind Songs Gasparo ▲ GS 277 ■ GS 277C

Bach, J.S.:The Art of the Fugue Gasparo 3-▲ GS 282/83 3-■ GS 283C

Hanson, H.:Pieces (4) Bar, w. T. Sipes (bar), R. Shewan (cnd), Roberts Wesleyan College Chorale Albany ▲ TROY 129 [ADD]

Höller, K.:Fant Vn & Org, w. William Preucil (vn) Gasparo ▲ GS 278 ■ GS 278C

Höller, K.:Improvisationen über "Schönster Herr Jesu", w. Birthe Holst Christensen (vc) Gasparo ▲ GS 278 ■ GS 278C

Höller, K.:Triptychon Gasparo ▲ GS 278 ■ GS 278C

Summershimmer:Women Composers for Organ Hester Park ▲ CD 7704 [DDD]

Women Composers for Organ:Music Spanning 5 Centuries Gasparo ▲ GSCD 294

Harbaugh, R. (vc)—see ORCHESTRAS & ENSEMBLES New World String Quartet

Harbison, Rose Mary (vn)

Harbison, J.:Fant Duo, w. Robert Levin (pno) *(rec Kresge Auditorium, between 1988 & 1994)* Archetype ▲ 60104 [DDD]

Wolpe, S.:Piece in 2 Parts *(rec Rutgers Presbyterian Church, New York City)* New World ▲ 80308-2

Harden, Wolf (pno)

Bach, J.S.:Partitas Hpd, BWV 825–830—BWV 827–829 *(rec Dec 1985)* Naxos ▲ 8.550312 [DDD]

Pfitzner, H.:Con Pno, w. H. Beissel (cnd), Slovak RSO Bratislava Marco Polo ▲ 8.223162 [DDD]

Reger, M.:Vars & Fugue on a Theme of J. S. Bach Naxos ▲ 8.550469 [DDD]

The Romance Collection, w. Takako Nishizaki (vn) *(rec Festeburgkirche, Frankfurt, 1982–84)* Naxos 4-▲ 8.504005 [DDD]

Romantic Violin Favorites, w. Takako Nishizaki (vn) Naxos ▲ 8.550125 [DDD]

Schumann, R.:Humoreske Pno Naxos ▲ 8.550469 [DDD]

Hardenberger, Håkan (cnt)

Arban, J.-B.:Vars on a Theme from Bellini's *Norma*, w. R. Pöntinen (pno) BIS ▲ CD 287 [DDD]

Hardenberger, Håkan (tpt)
Davies, P.M.:Son Tpt, w. R. Pöntinen (pno) BIS ▲ CD 287 [DDD]
Françaix, J.:Sonatine Tpt & Pno, w. R. Pöntinen (pno) BIS ▲ CD 287 [DDD]
Hartmann, J.:Vars on Rule Britannia, w. Roland Pöntinen (pno) BIS ▲ CD 287 [DDD]
Haydn, J.:Con Tpt, w. N. Marriner (cnd), Academy of St. Martin in the Fields Philips ▲ 420203-2 [DDD] ■ 420203-4
Henze, H.-W.:Requiem, w. U. Wiget (pno), I. Metzmacher (cnd), Ensemble Modern *(rec Sept. 11, 1993)* Sony Classical ▲ SK 58972 [DDD]
Hertel, J.W.:Con Tpt, w. N. Marriner (cnd), Academy of St. Martin in the Fields Philips ▲ 420203-2 [DDD] ■ 420203-4
Honegger, A.:Intrada Tpt & Pno, w. R. Pöntinen (pno) BIS ▲ CD 287 [DDD]
Hummel, J.N.:Con in E♭ Tpt, S.49, w. N. Marriner (cnd), Academy of St. Martin in the Fields Philips ▲ 420203-2 [DDD] ■ 420203-4
Rabe, F.:Shazam BIS ▲ CD 287 [DDD]
Stamitz, C.:Con Tpt, w. N. Marriner (cnd), Academy of St. Martin in the Fields Philips ▲ 420203-2 [DDD] ■ 420203-4
Telemann, G.P.:Cons Tpt, w. M. Laird (tpt), W. Houghton (tpt), I. Brown (cnd), Academy of St. Martin in the Fields—Concerto for 2 Trumpets & Strings; Concerto for Trumpet, 2 Oboes & Strings; Concerto for 3 Trumpets & Strings; Concerto for Trumpet & Strings Philips ("Digital Classics" series) ▲ 420954-2 [DDD]
Tisné, A.:Héraldiques, w. R. Pöntinen (pno) BIS ▲ CD 287 [DDD]
Trumpet & Organ Spectacular, w. Simon Preston (org) Philips ▲ 434074-2 PH [DDD]
The Virtuoso Trumpet, w., Roland Pöntinen (pno) BIS ▲ CD 287 [DDD]

Harding, David (va)—see also ORCHESTRAS & ENSEMBLES Chester String Quartet
Kernis, A.J.:Mozart en Route, w. Aaron Berofsky (vn), Tom Rosenberg (vc) *(rec Manhattan Center Studios, New York, May 31-June 3, 1995)* New Albion ♦ NA 083CD

Harding, John (vn)
Brahms, J.:Sextet Strs, Op. 18, w. Daniel Höxter (pno), Matthias Feile (vc) [arr. Kirchner for Piano Trio] Koch Schwann ▲ SCH 313652 [DDD]
Brahms, J.:Sextet Strs, Op. 36, w. Daniel Höxter (pno), Matthias Feile (vc) [arr. Kirchner for Piano Trio] Koch Schwann ▲ SCH 313652 [DDD]

Hardy, Andrew (vn)
Janácek, L.:Son Vn, w. L. Devos (pno) Olympia ▲ OLY 355 [DDD]
Kabalevsky, D.:Con Vn, w. V. Dudarova (cnd), Russian SO Olympia ▲ OLY 573
Prokofiev, S.:Son Vn, Op. 94bis, w. L. Devos (pno) Olympia ▲ OLY 355 [DDD]
Prokofiev, S.:Son 1 Vn, w. L. Devos (pno) Olympia ▲ OLY 355 [DDD]
Rakov, N.:Con 1 Vn, w. V. Dudarova (cnd), Russian SO Olympia ▲ OLY 573
Reger, M.:Son Vn Pno, Op. 139, w. U. Tsachor (pno) Olympia ▲ OLY 357 [DDD]
Shebalin, V.Y.:Con Vn, w. V. Dudarova (cnd), Russian SO Olympia ▲ OLY 573
Strauss, R.:Son Vn, w. U. Tsachor (pno) Olympia ▲ OLY 357 [DDD]

Hardy, David (vc)
Corigliano, J.:Sym 1, w. Glenn Garlick (vc), Lambert Orkis (pno), L. Slatkin (cnd), National SO Washington D.C. *(rec J. F. K. Center for the Performing Arts, Washington, D. C., Nov 9-11, 1995 & Apr 19 &)* RCA Red Seal ▲ 09026-68450-2 [DDD]

Harel, Michaela (pno)
Elgar, E.:Pno Music—In Smyrna *(rec New York City, Aug. 1990)* M Records ▲ MCD 001 [DDD]
Ravel, M.:Sonatine Pno *(rec New York City, Aug. 1990)* M Records ▲ MCD 001 [DDD]
Ravel, M.:La Vallée des cloches *(rec New York City, Aug. 1990)* M Records ▲ MCD 001 [DDD]
Schumann, R.:Son 2 Pno *(rec New York City, Aug. 1990)* M Records ▲ MCD 001 [DDD]
Scriabin, A.:Etude Pno, Op. 2/1 *(rec New York City, Aug. 1990)* M Records ▲ MCD 001 [DDD]
Scriabin, A.:Etudes Pno, Op. 8—Nos. 2, 8 & 11 *(rec New York City, Aug. 1990)* M Records ▲ MCD 001 [DDD]
Shostakovich, D.:Preludes & Fugues Pno—Nos. 3-5, 7, 20, 22 & 24 *(rec New York City, Feb. 1991 & June 1992)* M Records ▲ MCD 003 [DDD]

Hargitai, G. (vn)—see ORCHESTRAS & ENSEMBLES Bartók String Quartet

Harjanne, Jouko (tpt)
Hauta-Aho, T.:Fant Tpt, w. L. Segerstam (cnd), Finnish RSO *(rec Nov. 1989 & Dec. 1990)* Finlandia ▲ 4509-95863-2 [DDD]
Linkola, J.:Con Tpt, w. L. Segerstam (cnd), Finnish RSO *(rec Nov. 1989 & Dec. 1990)* Finlandia ▲ 4509-95863-2 [DDD]
Segerstam, L.:Con 2 Tpt, w. L. Segerstam (cnd), Finnish RSO *(rec Nov. 1989 & Dec. 1990)* Finlandia ▲ 4509-95863-2 [DDD]
Wessman, H.:Con Tpt, w. L. Segerstam (cnd), Finnish RSO *(rec Nov. 1989 & Dec. 1990)* Finlandia ▲ 4509-95863-2 [DDD]

Harkey, Sue Ann (gtr)
Exquisite Corpses from P.S. 122, w. David Watson (shears/stick vn/gtr/tpt), Judy Dunaway (gtr/balloons), Anthony Coleman (sampler), Raissa St. Pierre (drums), Guy Yarden (vn/pno), Leslie Ross (bn), Linda Austin (gtr), Bruce Kaplan (gtr), Doug Henderson (peckhorn/bass/toy pno), Cinnie Cole (sampler), et al. ¿What Next? ▲ WN 0002 [ADD]

Harkins, Edwin (tpt)
Erickson, R.:Kryl *(rec 1987-91)* CRI ▲ CD 616 [DDD]
Reynolds, R.:The Ivanov Suite, w. P. Larson (bar), J. Fonville (pic), J. Ngyesy (vn), R. Mushabec (vc), S. Schick (perc) New World ▲ 80431-2
Reynolds, R.:Versions/Stages, w. P. Larson (bar), J. Fonville (pic), J. Ngyesy (vn), R. Mushabec (vc), S. Schick (perc) New World ▲ 80431-2
Smith, S.S.:Notebook, w. J. Fonville (fl), P. Hoffmann (pno), B. Turetzky (db) O.O. Discs ▲ OO 11 [DDD]

Harlander, Rudolf (db)
Mozart, W.A.:Kleine Nachtmusik, w. Salzburg String Quartet Preiser ▲ 93387 [ADD]

Harle, John (a sax)
Bennett, Richard Rodney:Con A Sax, w. N. Marriner (cnd), Academy of St. Martin in the Fields EMI Classics ▲ CDC 54301
Yuyama, A.:Divert Mar, w. Evelyn Glennie (mar) *(rec Whitfield Street Studios, London, Sept. 22-29, 1994)* Catalyst ▲ 09026-68193-2 [DDD]

Harle, John (sax)
Bennett, Richard Rodney:Con for Stan Getz, w. B. Wordsworth (cnd), BBC Concert Orch *(rec BBC Hippodrome, Golders Green, London, Mar. 11, 1993)* Argo ▲ 443529-2
Bryars, G.:The Green Ray, w. I. Bolton (cnd), Bournemouth Sinfonietta Argo ▲ 433847-2 [DDD]
Dahl, I.:Con A Sax, w. M. Tilson Thomas (cnd), New World SO *(rec Au-Rene Theatre, Broward Centre for the Performing Arts, Miami, Jan 30-31, 1994)* Argo ▲ 444459-2 [DDD]
Debussy, C.:Rapsodie, w. N. Marriner (cnd), Academy of St. Martin in the Fields EMI Classics ▲ CDC 54301
Glazunov, A.:Con Sax, w. N. Marriner (cnd), Academy of St. Martin in the Fields EMI Classics ▲ CDC 54301
John Harle's Saxophone Songbook Unicorn-Kanchana ▲ DKP 9160
Myers, S.:Con Sop Sax, w. J. Judd (cnd), Argo SO *(rec Studio 1, EMI, Abbey Road, London, July 21-22, 1993)* Argo ▲ 443529-2
Nyman, M.:Where the Bee Dances, w. I. Bolton (cnd), Bournemouth Sinfonietta Argo ▲ 433847-2 [DDD]
Saxophone Concertos, w. Academy of St. Martin in the Fields [cnd:Neville Marriner] EMI Classics ▲ CDC 54301
Torke, M.:Con Sax, w. D.A. Miller (cnd), Albany SO *(rec Troy Savings Bank Music Hall, Troy, NY, Jan. 16, 1994)* Argo ▲ 443529-2
Villa-Lobos, H.:Fant Sop Sax, w. N. Marriner (cnd), Academy of St. Martin in the Fields EMI Classics ▲ CDC 54301
Westbrook, M.:Bean Rows & Blues Shots, w. I. Bolton (cnd), Bournemouth Sinfonietta Argo ▲ 433847-2 [DDD]

Harlos, Steven (pno)
Hindemith, P.:Son Bass Tuba, w. M. Lind (tuba) *(rec Nacka, Sweden, Aug. 12, 1977)* BIS ▲ CD 159 [AAD]

Harman, D. (cl)
Liptak, D.:Illusions, w. A. Nel (pno) Gasparo ▲ GS 286

Harmon, Christina (org)
Christmas in Dallas, w. Jeffery Curnow (tpt), Adam Gordon (tpt), Gregory Hustis (hn), Clarece Candamio (org) *(rec Lover's Lane United Methodist Church, Dallas)* Hester Park ▲ 7706 [DDD]

Harms, Ben (timp)—see also ORCHESTRAS & ENSEMBLES Calliope
Baroque Trumpetissimo, w. David Bilger (tpt), Stephen Burns (tpt), Edward Carroll (tpt), Alex Holton (tpt), Raymond Mase (tpt), Timothy Morrison (tpt), Lee Soper (tpt), Atsuko Sato (bn), Edward Brewer (org/hpd), Philharmonia Virtuosi [cnd:Richard Kapp] ESS.A.Y ▲ ESS 1035 [DDD]
The Joy of Christmas, w. Anthony Newman (org), Chestnut Brass Company [cnd:William Noll], Choral Guild of Atlanta, Choral Guild of Atlanta Brass & Percussion, Walter Huff (org) Sony Classical ▲ SFK 62698 ■ SFT 62698

Harnoncourt, Alice (vn)
Vivaldi, A.:Cons Vn, Op. 8/1-12, "Il cimento dell'armonia e dell'inventione", w. N. Harnoncourt (cnd), Vienna Concentus Musicus—Nos. 1-6 Teldec ▲ 91851-2

Harnoncourt, Nicholas (b-vl)—see ORCHESTRAS & ENSEMBLES Deller Consort

Harnoncourt, Nikolaus (vl)
Rameau, J.P.:Pièces de clavecin en concert, w. G. Leonhardt (hpd), L. Frydén (vn) Vanguard Classics ("The Bach Guild" series) ▲ OVC 2520 [ADD]

Harnoy, Ofra (vc)
The Art of Ofra Harnoy, Vol. 1, w. Helena Bowkun (pno), William Aide (pno) Mastersound ▲ DFCD1-012
Bach, J.S.:Cant 156, w. Michael Bloss (org)—Arioso [arr for vc & org] *(rec Church of the Blessed Sacrament, Toronto, 1981)* RCA Gold Seal ▲ 09026-68368-2 [ADD]
Bach, J.S.:Con 2 Vn, w. Michael Bloss (org)—Adagio [arr for vc & org] *(rec Church of the Blessed Sacrament, Toronto, 1981)* RCA Gold Seal ▲ 09026-68368-2 [ADD]
Bach, J.S.:Toccata, Adagio & Fugue Org, BWV 564, w. Michael Bloss (org)—Adagio [arr for vc & org] *(rec Church of the Blessed Sacrament, Toronto, 1981)* RCA Gold Seal ▲ 09026-68368-2 [ADD]
The Baroque Album, w. A. Davis (cnd), Toronto CO, J. Baxtresser (fl), J. Cowell (tpt) Mastersound ▲ MST 19 [DDD]
Basic 100, Vol. 61, w. Lynn Harrell (vc), James Levine (cnd), Charles Mackerras (cnd), London SO, London PO RCA Victor ▲ 09026-68086-2 ■ 09026-68086-4
Beethoven, L. van:Son 2 Vc RCA Gold Seal ▲ 09026-68372-2
Beethoven, L. van:Son 3 Vc RCA Gold Seal ▲ 09026-68372-2
Beethoven, L. van:Vars on "See, the Conquering Hero Comes" from Handel's *Judas Maccabaeus*, w. Michael Dussek (pno) *(rec Thornhill, Ontario, Canada, 1987)* RCA Gold Seal ▲ 09026-68372-2 [DDD]
Bloch, E.:Schelomo, w. C. Mackerras (cnd), London PO RCA Red Seal ▲ 60757-2-RC [DDD] ■ 60757-4-RC
Boccherini, L.:Con Vc, G.482, w. C. Scimone (cnd), Venice Solisti RCA Red Seal ▲ 09026-61228-2 ■ 09026-61228-4
Brahms, J.:Son 1 Vc, w. William Aide (pno) RCA Gold Seal ▲ 09026-68371-2
Brahms, J.:Son 2 Vc, w. William Aide (pno) RCA Gold Seal ▲ 09026-68371-2
Bruch, M.:Adagio on a Celtic Theme, w. C. Mackerras (cnd), London PO RCA Red Seal ▲ 60757-2-RC [DDD] ■ 60757-4-RC (CrO2)
Bruch, M.:Ave Maria Vc, w. C. Mackerras (cnd), London PO RCA Red Seal ▲ 60757-2-RC [DDD] ■ 60757-4-RC (CrO2)
Bruch, M.:Canzone Vc, w. C. Mackerras (cnd), London PO RCA Red Seal ▲ 60757-2-RC [DDD] ■ 60757-4-RC (CrO2)
Bruch, M.:Kol Nidrei, w. C. Mackerras (cnd), London PO RCA Red Seal ▲ 60757-2-RC [DDD] ■ 60757-4-RC (CrO2)
Bruch, M.:Kol Nidrei, w. Michael Bloss (org) [arr for vc & org] *(rec Church of the Blessed Sacrament, Toronto, 1981)* RCA Gold Seal ▲ 09026-68368-2 [ADD]
Casals, P.:El Cant dels ocells, w. Michael Bloss (org) [arr for vc & org] *(rec Church of the Blessed Sacrament, Toronto, 1981)* RCA Gold Seal ▲ 09026-68368-2 [ADD]
Corelli, A.:Sons Vn, Op. 5, w. Michael Bloss (org)—No. 8 [arr for vc & org] *(rec Church of the Blessed Sacrament, Toronto, 1981)* RCA Gold Seal ▲ 09026-68368-2 [ADD]
Duets:Ofra Harnoy & Friends, w. Michael Dussek (pno), Orford String Quartet, Maureen Forrester (cta), Andrew Davis (pno), Jeanne Baxtresser (fl), Catherine Wilson (pno), Paul Brodie (sax), Shauna Rolston (vc), Armin Strings, Canadian Piano Trio, Adele Armin (vn) Mastersound ▲ MST 30 [DDD]
Dvořák, A.:Con Vc, w. C. Mackerras (cnd), Prague SO *(rec Smetana Hall, Prague, Sept 24-25, 1994)* RCA Red Seal ▲ 09026-68186-2 [DDD]
Dvořák, A.:Polonaise Vc, w. Michael Dussek (pno) *(rec Glenn Gould Studio, Toronto, June 18-19, 1995)* RCA Red Seal ▲ 09026-68186-2 [DDD]
Dvořák, A.:Rondo, w. C. Mackerras (cnd), Prague SO *(rec Smetana Hall, Prague, Sept 24-25, 1994)* RCA Red Seal ▲ 09026-68186-2 [DDD]
Dvořák, A.:Silent Woods, w. C. Mackerras (cnd), Prague SO *(rec Smetana Hall, Prague, Sept 24-25, 1994)* RCA Red Seal ▲ 09026-68186-2 [DDD]
Dvořák, A.:Slavonic Dances (sels), w. Michael Dussek (pno)—Op. 46/3 & 8 *(rec Glenn Gould Studio, Toronto, June 18-19, 1995)* RCA Red Seal ▲ 09026-68186-2 [DDD]
An Evening with Ofra Harnoy, w. Orford String Quartet Pro Arte ▲ CDD 418 [DDD]
Franck, C.:Son Vn, w. W. Aide (pno) [cello-piano arr.] Mastersound ▲ DFCD1-012
Haydn, J.:Con 1 Vc, w. P. Robinson (cnd), Toronto CO *(rec Massey Hall, Toronto, Canada, 1983)* RCA Gold Seal ▲ 09026-60722-2 [DDD]
Haydn, J.:Con 2 Vc, w. P. Robinson (cnd), Toronto CO *(rec Massey Hall, Toronto, Canada, 1983)* RCA Gold Seal ▲ 09026-60722-2 [DDD]
Lalo, E.:Con Vc, w. A. de Almeida (cnd), Bournemouth SO *(rec Wessex Hall, Dorset, England, May 11-12, 1995)* RCA Red Seal ▲ 09026-68420-2 [DDD]
Mozart, W.A.:Ave verum corpus, w. Michael Bloss (org) [arr for vc & org] *(rec Church of the Blessed Sacrament, Toronto, 1981)* RCA Gold Seal ▲ 09026-68368-2 [ADD]
Mysliveček, J.:Con Vc, w. C. Scimone (cnd), Venice Solisti RCA Red Seal ▲ 09026-61228-2 ■ 09026-61228-4
Offenbach, J.:Andante Vc, w. A. de Almeida (cnd), Bournemouth SO *(rec Wessex Hall, Dorset, England, May 11-12, 1995)* RCA Red Seal ▲ 09026-68420-2 [DDD]
Offenbach, J.:Con militaire, w. A. de Almeida (cnd), Bournemouth SO *(rec Wessex Hall, Dorset, England, Jan 16-17, 1995)* RCA Red Seal ▲ 09026-68420-2 [DDD]
Offenbach, J.:Con militaire, w. E. Kunzel (cnd), Cincinnati Pops Orch Vox Box 2-▲ CDX 5131
Ofra Harnoy & Friends:Duets IMP ("Classics" series) ▲ IMP 6700622
Ofra Harnoy & Friends, w. Orford String Quartet, J. Baxtresser (fl), M. Forrester (cta), P. Brodie (sax), M. Dussek (pno), et al. Pro Arte ▲ CDD 552 [DDD]
Ofra Harnoy Collection, Vol. 4, w. William Aide (pno) *(rec Timothy Eaton Memorial Church, Toronto, Canada, 1982)* RCA Gold Seal ▲ 09026-68369-2 [ADD]
Out Classics, w. Richard Stoltzman (cl), Peter Serkin (pno), Leonard Slatkin (cnd), London PO, et al. RCA Red Seal ▲ 09026-68261-2 ■ 09026-68261-4
Prokofiev, S.:Son Vc, w. M. Dussek (pno) RCA Red Seal ▲ 7845-2-RC [DDD]
Saint-Saëns, C.:Con 1 Vc, w. P. Freeman (cnd), Victoria SO *(rec University of Victoria, British Columbia, 1983)* RCA Gold Seal ▲ 09026-68373-2 [DDD]
Saint-Saëns, C.:Le Cygne, w. M. Dussek (pno) *(rec Walter Hall, University of Toronto, Canada, Aug 25, 1985)* RCA Gold Seal ▲ 09026-68373-2 [DDD]
Salut d'Amour, w. Helena Bowkun (pno), Michael Dussek (pno), Catherine Wilson (pno) RCA Red Seal ▲ 60697-2-RC [AAD/DDD]
Schubert, Franz:Qnt Strs, D.956, w. Orford String Quartet Pro Arte ▲ CDD 418 [DDD]
Schubert, Franz:Son Arpeggione, w. M. Dussek (pno) RCA Red Seal ▲ 7845-2-RC [DDD]

Harnoy, Ofra (vc) (cont.)
Tchaikovsky, P.:Morceaux, Op. 51, w. Michael Dussek (pno)—No. 6, Valse sentimentale *(rec Walter Hall, University of Toronto & Timothy Eaton Memorial Church, Toronto, Aug 25, 1985)* RCA Gold Seal ▲ 09026-68373-2 [DDD]
Tchaikovsky, P.:Music of, w. C. Mackerras (cnd), London PO—Chant d'automne, Op. 37b/10; Lensky's Aria (from Eugene Onegin); Nocturne, Op. 19/4; Valse sentimentale, Op. 51/6 RCA Red Seal ▲ 09026-60758-2 ■ 09026-60758-4 (CrO2) ▯ 09026-60758-5
Tchaikovsky, P.:Nocturne Vc, w. Helena Bowkun (pno) *(rec Walter Hall, University of Toronto & Timothy Eaton Memorial Church, Toronto, 1980)* RCA Gold Seal ▲ 09026-68373-2 [DDD]
Tchaikovsky, P.:Pezzo capriccioso, w. C. Mackerras (cnd), London PO RCA Red Seal ▲ 09026-60758-2 ■ 09026-60758-4 (CrO2) ▯ 09026-60758-5
Tchaikovsky, P.:Les Saisons, w. Michael Dussek (pno)—No. 10 Chant d'automne *(rec Walter Hall, University of Toronto & Timothy Eaton Memorial Church, Toronto, 1982)* RCA Gold Seal ▲ 09026-68373-2 [DDD]
Tchaikovsky, P.:Sérénade mélancolique, w. C. Mackerras (cnd), London PO RCA Red Seal ▲ 09026-60758-2 ■ 09026-60758-4 (CrO2) ▯ 09026-60758-5
Tchaikovsky, P.:Songs, w. P. Domingo (ten)—None but the Lonely Heart EMI Classics ▲ CDC 55018 ■ 4DS 55018
Tchaikovsky, P.:Vars on a Rococo Theme, w. P. Freeman (cnd), Victoria SO *(rec University of Victoria, British Columbia, 1983)* RCA Gold Seal ▲ 09026-68373-2 [DDD]
Tchaikovsky, P.:Vars on a Rococo Theme, w. C. Mackerras (cnd), London PO RCA Red Seal ▲ 09026-60758-2 ■ 09026-60758-4 (CrO2) ▯ 09026-60758-5
Viotti, G.B.:Con Vc, w. C. Scimone (cnd), Venice Solisti RCA Red Seal ▲ 09026-61228-2 ■ 09026-61228-4
Vitali, T.A.:Chaconne Vn, w. Michael Bloss (org) [arr for vc] *(rec Church of the Blessed Sacrament, Toronto, 1981)* RCA Gold Seal ▲ 09026-68368-2 [ADD]
Vivaldi, A.:Cons Vc, w. R. Stamp (cnd), Toronto CO—Cons RV.408, 413, 416, 418 & 419 *(Toronto, Feb 1994)* RCA Victor Red Seal ▲ 09026-68228-2 [DDD]
Vivaldi, A.:Cons Vc, w. P. Robinson (cnd), Toronto CO—5 concerti—RV.399, 410, 405, 423, 538 RCA Red Seal ▲ 7774-2-RC [DDD] ■ 7774-4-RC (CrO2)
Vivaldi, A.:Cons Vc, w. P. Robinson (cnd), Toronto CO—7 concerti—RV.402, 403, 406, 412, 414, 422, 424 RCA Red Seal ▲ 60155-2-RC [DDD] ■ 60155-4-RC (CrO2) ▯ 60155-5
Vivaldi, A.:Cons Vc, w. P. Robinson (cnd), Toronto CO—in D, RV.404; in d, RV.407; in F, RV.411; in g, RV.417; in a, RV.420 RCA Red Seal ▲ 09026-61578-2; ■ 09026-61578-4
Vivaldi, A.:Con Vc, RV.409, w. J. McKay (bn), P. Robinson (cnd), Toronto CO RCA Red Seal ▲ 7774-2-RC [DDD] ■ 7774-4-RC (CrO2)
Vivaldi, A.:Con Vn Vc, RV.544, w. P. Robinson (cnd), Toronto CO RCA Red Seal ▲ 09026-61578-2; ■ 09026-61578-4
Vivaldi, A.:Con Vn Vc, RV.547, w. Igor Oistrakh (vn), P. Robinson (cnd), Toronto CO, *(Toronto, Feb 1992)* RCA Victor Red Seal ▲ 09026-68228-2 [DDD]
Vivaldi, A.:Sons Vc, w. C. Tilney (hpd)—RV.40, 41, 43, 45, 46, 47 RCA Red Seal ▲ 09026-60430-2 ■ 09026-60430-4
Wild Classics:A Celebration of Animals & Nature, w. James Galway (fl), Martin Hoherman (vc), Emily Mitchell (hp), Michael Dussek (pno), Samuel Lipman (pno), Leo Litwin (pno), Gerhard Oppitz (pno), Isao Tomita (synths), Boston Pops Orch [cnd:Arthur Fiedler], Chicago SO [cnd:Fritz Reiner] RCA Red Seal ▲ 09026-68483-2 ■ 09026-68483-4

Haroutunian, Ronald (bn)
Thomson, V.:Portraits, w. A. Tommasini (pno), S. Leventhal (vn), J. Miller (vc), F.T. Cohen (ob)—Selected Portraits (13) for Pno (1935–42); Five Ladies for Vn & Pno (1930; 1940; 1983); A Portrait of 2, for Ob, Bn & Pno (1984); 3 Portraits for Pno (1940; arr Samuel Dushkin in 1947 for Vn & Pno); Etude for Vc & Pno:A Portrait of Frederic James (1966); Lili Hastings for Vc & Pno (1983) Northeastern ▲ NR 240-CD

Haroz, A. (hp)
Fleischer, T.:Lamentation, w. C. Grossmeyer (sop), E. Lavry (hp), D. Kovalsky (perc), Zimrat Women's Chorus Opus One ▲ Cd 158 [DDD]

Harper, Celia (hp)
Melgaz, D.D.:Motets, w. R. Aldwinckle (org), M. Brown (cnd), Pro Cantione Antiqua Hyperion ▲ CDA 66715
Morago, E.L.:Motets, w. R. Aldwinckle (org), M. Brown (cnd), Pro Cantione Antiqua Hyperion ▲ CDA 66715

Harper, Nelson (hpd)
Telemann, G.P.:Qt Bn Fls, w. Christopher Weait (bn), Katherine Borst (fl), Craig J. Kirchhoff (fl) D'Note Classics ▲ DND 1008 [DDD]
Telemann, G.P.:Son Bn, w. Christopher Weait (bn) D'Note Classics ▲ DND 1008 [DDD]
Telemann, G.P.:Trio Sons, w. *(artist unknown)* Christopher Weait (bn)—in F for Fl, Bn & Bc D'Note Classics ▲ DND 1008 [DDD]

Harper, Nelson (pno)
Berkeley, L.:Sonatina Vn & Pno, w. Michael Davis (vn) Vienna Modern Masters ▲ VMM 2013 [DDD]
Berkeley, L.:Toccata Vn, w. Michael Davis (vn) *(rec Weigel Hall, Columbus, Ohio, Dec 20–21, 1994)* Vienna Modern Masters ▲ VMM 2015 [DDD]
Bloch, E.:Baal Shem, "3 Pictures of Chassidic Life", w. Michael Davis (vn) *(rec Los Angeles & Columbus, 1969 & 1979)* Orion ▲ 7813-2 [AAD]
Bloch, E.:Son 2 Vn, "Poème mystique", w. Michael Davis (vn) *(rec Los Angeles & Columbus, 1969 & 1979)* Orion ▲ 7813-2 [AAD]
Ireland, J.:Bagatelle Vn & Pno, w. M. Davis (vn) Vienna Modern Masters ▲ VMM 2009
Ireland, J.:Son 1 Vn, w. M. Davis (vn) Vienna Modern Masters ▲ VMM 2009
Ireland, J.:Son 2 Vn, w. M. Davis (vn) Vienna Modern Masters ▲ VMM 2009
Josephs, W.:Siesta, w. M. Davis (vn) Vienna Modern Masters ▲ VMM 2004 [DDD]
Josephs, W.:Son 1 Vn & Pno, w. M. Davis (vn) Vienna Modern Masters ▲ VMM 2004 [DDD]
Josephs, W.:Son 3 Vn & Pno, w. M. Davis (vn) Vienna Modern Masters ▲ VMM 2004 [DDD]
Mathias, W.:Little Suite Koch International Classics ▲ KIC 7326
Mathias, W.:Toccata alla danza Koch International Classics ▲ KIC 7326
Mathias, W.:Trio Pno, w. Michael Davis (vn), William Conable (vc) Koch International Classics ▲ KIC 7326

Harras, Manfred (rcr)
Blavet, M.:Recueil de pièces, w. Marianne Lüthi (rcr), Brian Franklin (vl), Rudolf Scheidegger (hpd)—Prélude de Mr. Blavet; Pourquoi doux Rossignols; Entrée de chasse *(rec Reformierte Kirche, Arlesheim, Schweiz, May 18–19, 1987)* Musicaphon ▲ 56802 [DDD]
Boismortier, J.B. de:Chamber Music, w. Marianne Lüthi (rcr), Richard Gwilt (baroque vn), Arno Jochem (vl), Brian Franklin (vl), Sally Fortino (hps)—Con. in C, "Zampogna"; Son. in F, Op. 91/1; Son. in A, Op. 10/2; Trio Son. in D, Op. 37/3; Son. in e, Op. 34/3; Con. in A, Op. 38/4; Suite No. 1, Op. 59; Balet de village en trio, Op. 52/4 *(rec Reformed Church, Bubendorf, Switzerland, Feb. 9–11, 1989)* Musicaphon ▲ 56812 [DDD]
Dornel, L.-A.:Concert 1, w. Marianne Lüthi (rcr), Brian Franklin (vl), Rudolf Scheidegger (hpd) *(rec Reformierte Kirche, Arlesheim, Schweiz, May 18–19, 1987)* Musicaphon ▲ 56802 [DDD]
Philidor, P.:Music of, w. Marianne Lüthi (rcr), Brian Franklin (vl), Rudolf Scheidegger (hpd)—Première suite in C; Deuxième suite in B; Septième suite in b *(rec Reformierte Kirche, Arlesheim, Schweiz, May 18–19, 1987)* Musicaphon ▲ 56802 [DDD]
Telemann, G.P.:Cants, w. Barbara Schlick (sop), Ernst-Martin Eras (ob), Richard Gwilt (vn), Brian Franklin (vl), Sally Fortino (hpd)—Hemmet den Eifer, verbannet die Rache; Jauchzt, ihr Christen, seid vergnügt; Umschlinget uns, ihr sanften Freidensbande; Die Kinder des Höchsten sind rufende Stimmen; Lauter Wonne, lauter Freude Cantate ▲ 580003 [DDD]

Harrell, Lynn (vc)
Bach, C.P.E.:Con Vc, H.439, w. P. Zukerman (cnd), English CO EMI Classics ("Baroque" series) ▲ CDK 65733
Basic 100, Vol. 61, w. Ofra Harnoy (vc), James Levine (cnd), Charles Mackerras (cnd), London SO, London PO RCA Victor ▲ 09026-68086-2 ■ 09026-68086-4
Beethoven, L. van:Serenade Strs, Op. 8, w. I. Perlman (vn), P. Zukerman (va) EMI Classics 2-▲ ZDCB 54198

Harrell, Lynn (vc) (cont.)
Beethoven, L. van:Sons Vc (comp), w. V. Ashkenazy (pno) London 2-▲ 417628-2 [DDD]
Beethoven, L. van:Trio 6 Pno, "Archduke", w. V. Ashkenazy (pno), I. Perlman (vn) EMI Classics ▲ CDC 47010 [DDD]
Beethoven, L. van:Trio 10 Pno, w. Ashkenazy, Perlman, Harrell EMI Classics ▲ CDC 47010 [DDD]
Beethoven, L. van:Trio Strs, Op. 3, w. I. Perlman (vn), P. Zukerman (va) EMI Classics 2-▲ ZDCB 54198
Beethoven, L. van:Trios Strs, Op. 9, w. I. Perlman (vn), P. Zukerman (va) EMI Classics 2-▲ ZDCB 54198
Boccherini, L.:Qnts Strs, w. A. Schneider (vn), F. Galimir (vn), M. Tree (va), D. Soyer (vc)—Op. 13, No. 5 *(rec 1965)* Vanguard Classics ▲ OVC 8006 [ADD]
Brahms, J.:Con Vn & Vc, "Double Con", w. P. Zukerman (vn), Z. Mehta (cnd), New York PO Odyssey 3-▲ MB3K 45828
Brahms, J.:Trios (3) Pno, w. V. Ashkenazy (pno), I. Perlman (vn) EMI Classics ▲ CDCB 54725
Brahms, J.:Trio in A Pno (posth), w. V. Ashkenazy (pno), I. Perlman (vn) EMI Classics ▲ CDCB 54725
Bruch, M.:Kol Nidrei, w. G. Levine (cnd), Royal PO *(rec Apr. 7, 1994)* Justice ▲ JR 1801 [DDD]
Debussy, C.:Son Vc, w. Vladimir Ashkenazy (pno) *(rec Henry Wood Hall, London, May 1994)* London ▲ 444318-2 [DDD]
Dvořák, A.:Con Vc, w. V. Ashkenazy (cnd), Philharmonia Orch London ("Jubilee" series) ▲ 430743-2 [DDD]
Dvořák, A.:Con Vc, w. J. Levine (cnd), London SO RCA Gold Seal ("Papillon Collection" series) ▲ 6531-2-RG [ADD]
Dvořák, A.:Con Vc, w. J. Levine (cnd), London SO RCA Victor ▲ 09026-68086-2; ■ 09026-68086-4
Erb, D.:Orchestral Music, w. L. Slatkin (cnd), St. Louis SO—Concerto for Brass & Orchestra (1987); Concerto for Cello & Orchestra (1976); Ritual Observances (1992) *(rec 1991–92)* New World ▲ 80415-2
Haydn, J.:Con 1 Vc, w. N. Marriner (cnd), Academy of St. Martin in the Fields EMI Classics ▲ CDM 64326
Haydn, J.:Con 2 Vc, w. N. Marriner (cnd), Academy of St. Martin in the Fields EMI Classics ▲ CDM 64326
Hindemith, P.:Kammermusik (comp), w. R. Brautigam (pno), K. Kulka (vn), K. Kashkashian (va), N. Blume (va d'amore), L. van Doeselaar (org), R. Chailly (cnd), Royal Concertgebouw Orch—No. 1 for Small Orchestra, Op. 24/1 (1922); No. 2 (Piano Concerto) for Piano & 12 Instruments, Op. 36/1 (1924); No. 3 (Cello Concerto), foe Cello & 10 Instruments, Op. 36/2 (1925); No. 4 (Violin Concerto) for Violin & Large Orchestra, Op. 36/3 (1925); No. 5 (Viola Concerto) for Viola & Large Chamber Orchestra, Op. 36/4 (1927); No. 6 (Viola d'amore Concerto) for Viola d'amore & Chamber Orchestra, Op. 46/1 (1927); No. 7 (Organ Concerto) for Organ & Chamber Orchestra, Op. 46/2 (1927) London 2-▲ 433816-2 [DDD]
Mendelssohn, F.:Lied ohne Worte Vc, w. B. Canino (pno) London ▲ 430198-2 [DDD]
Mendelssohn, F.:Lieder ohne Worte Pno, w. B. Canino (pno)—Op. 19/1 [trans for vc & pno] London ▲ 430198-2 [DDD]
Mendelssohn, F.:Son 1 Vc, w. B. Canino (pno) London ▲ 430198-2 [DDD]
Mendelssohn, F.:Son 2 Vc, w. B. Canino (pno) London ▲ 430198-2 [DDD]
Mendelssohn, F.:Vars concertantes, w. B. Canino (pno) London ▲ 430198-2 [DDD]
Ravel, M.:Trio Pno, w. Vladimir Ashkenazy (pno), Itzhak Perlman (vn) *(rec Henry Wood Hall, London, May 1994)* London ▲ 444318-2 [DDD]
Schoenberg, A.:Pierrot lunaire, w. Y. Minton (speaker), P. Zukerman (vn/va), D. Barenboim (pno), M. Debost (fl/pic), A. Pay (cl/b cl), P. Boulez (cnd) *(rec June 20–21, 1977)* Sony Classical ▲ SMK 48466 [ADD]
Schubert, Franz:Son Arpeggione, w. J. Levine (pno) RCA Gold Seal ("Papillon Collection" series) ▲ 6531-2-RG [ADD] ■ 6531-4-RG
Schumann, R.:Con Vc, w. L. Maazel (cnd), Bavarian RSO Artists ▲ FED 54 [ADD]
Schumann, R.:Con Vc, w. N. Marriner (cnd), Cleveland Orch London ("Jubilee" series) ▲ 430743-2 [DDD]
Tchaikovsky, P.:Trio Pno, w. V. Ashkenazy (pno), I. Perlman (vn) EMI Classics ▲ CDC 47988 [ADD]
Tchaikovsky, P.:Vars on a Rococo Theme, w. J. Levine (cnd), London SO RCA Victor ▲ 09026-68086-2; ■ 09026-68086-4
Tchaikovsky, P.:Vars on a Rococo Theme, w. J. Levine (cnd), London SO RCA ▲ 09026-68086-2 ■ 09026-68086-4
Tower, J.:Music for Vc, w. L. Slatkin (cnd), St. Louis SO Elektra/Nonesuch ▲ 79245-2-ZK ■ 79245-4-AW
Villa-Lobos, H.:Bachiana brasileira 5, w. Kiri Te Kanawa (sop), Lynn Harrell (vc) *(other cellists unknown) (rec Walthamstow Town Hall, June 24, 1984)* London ("Double Decker" series) 2-▲ 444995-2 [DDD]
Vivaldi, A.:Cons Vc, w. P. Zukerman (cnd), English CO—RV.413 & 417 EMI Classics ▲ CDM 64326
Walton, W.:Con Vc, w. S. Rattle (cnd), City of Birmingham SO EMI Classics ▲ CDC 54572

Harrell, Tom (flgl)
So Many Stars, w. Kathleen Battle (sop), Antonio Hart (sax), Grover Washington Jr (sax), James Carter (b cl), Cyrus Chestnut (pno), Jon Herrington (gtr), Romero Lubambo (gtr), Ira Coleman (elec bass), Christian McBride (elec bass), Cyro Baptista (perc), Steven Berrios (perc) *(rec Hit Factory, Clinton Recording Studios, R.P.M. Sound Studios, Unique Recording Studios, Power Station)* Sony Classical ▲ SK 68473 [DDD]

Harrer, Ralph (perc)—see ORCHESTRAS & ENSEMBLES Karl Peinkofer Percussion Ensemble

Harrer, Wolfgang (db)
Bottesini, G.:Con 2 Db, w. G. Meditz (cnd), New Vienna Soloists Koch Schwann ▲ SCH 313382 [ADD/DDD]
Bottesini, G.:Con 2 Db, w. G. Meditz (cnd), New Vienna Soloists Koch Schwann ▲ CD 311112 [DDD] ■ MC 211112 (D)
Bottesini, G.:Gran Duo Concertant, w. C. Altenburger (vn), G. Meditz (cnd), New Vienna Soloists Koch Schwann ▲ CD 311112 [DDD] ■ MC 211112 (D)
Bottesini, G.:Introduction & Gavotte, w. G. Meditz (cnd), New Vienna Soloists Koch Schwann ▲ CD 311112 [DDD] ■ MC 211112 (D)
Bottesini, G.:Melody in e, w. G. Meditz (cnd), New Vienna Soloists Koch Schwann ▲ CD 311112 [DDD] ■ MC 211112 (D)
Bottesini, G.:Music for Db, w. G. Meditz (cnd), New Vienna Soloists—Melody in e Koch Schwann ▲ SCH 313382 [ADD/DDD]

Harrild, Patrick (tuba)
Vaughan Williams, R.:Con Bass Tuba, w. B. Thomson (cnd), London SO Chandos ▲ CHAN 8740 [DDD]

Harrington, David
Riley, T.:In C, w. Bruce Ackley, Steve Adams, Don R. Baker, Chris Brown, George Brooks, Steve Coughlin, Blake Derby, Bill Douglass, Mihr'un'Nisa Douglass, Hank Dutt, Don Howe, Joan Jeanrenaud, Alden Jenks, Warner Jepson, Henry Kaiser, Jaron Lanier, Bill Maginnis, George Marsh, Shabda Owens, Jon Raskin, Gyan Riley, Terry Riley, Gino Robair, John Sackett, Ramón Sender, John Sherba, Toyji Tomita, Danny Tunick, William Winant, Evan Ziporyn *(rec Jan. 14, 1990)* New Albion ▲ NA 071

Harrington, David (vn)—see ORCHESTRAS & ENSEMBLES Kronos Quartet

Harrington, John (va)
Brahms, J.:Songs, Op. 91, w. L. Finnie (mez), A. Legge (pno) [G] Chandos ▲ CHAN 8786 [DDD]

Harris, Edward C. (pno)
The Complete Solo Columbia Recordings, w. Georges Enescu (vn), Yehudi Menuhin (pno), Hepzibah Menuhin (pno), Sanford Schlüssel (pno) *(rec 1924 & 1929)* Biddulph ▲ LAB 066 [ADD]

Harris, H. (perc)
Walton, W.:Façade, w. J. Bookspan (nar), S. Baron (fl), C. Russon (cl), H. Estrin (sax), M. Broiles (tpt), K. Moore (vc), D. Epstein (cnd) Allegretto ▲ ACD 8153 [ADD] ■ ACD 8153

Harris, Johana (pno)
Debussy, C.:Children's Corner—excluding section No. 4, "The Snow is Dancing" *(rec 1987)* MCA Classics ■ MCAC 6260
Debussy, C.:Images (3) Pno—No. 1 MCA Classics ■ MCAC 6260
Debussy, C.:Preludes Pno (sels)—Book 1, Nos. 4,6,8,10 & 11; Book 2, Nos. 5,6 & 10 MCA Classics ■ MCAC 6260

▲ = CD ♦ = Enhanced CD Δ = MD ■ = Cassette Tape ▯ = DCC

Harris, Johana (pno) (cont.)
Debussy, C.:Rêverie MCA Classics ■ MCAC 6260
Debussy, C.:Suite bergamasque—Prélude & Menuet MCA Classics ■ MCAC 6260
Harris, R.:Con Amplified Pno, w. R. Harris (cnd), International String Congress Orch, United States Air Force Academy Band members *(rec Colorado Springs, CO, 1971)* Citadel ▲ CTD 88114
Harris, R.:Qnt Pno, w. R. Harris (cnd), International String Congress Orch *(rec live, San German, Puerto Rico, 1960)* Citadel ▲ CTD 88114
Johana Harris:A Living Legacy
Harris, Michael (chl)
Telemann, G.P.:Con for 2 Chls, w. Colin Lawson (chl), S. Standage (cnd), Collegium Musicum 90 *(rec Goldsmiths' College, Apr 24-26, 1995)* Chandos ("Chaconne" series) ▲ CHAN 0593
Telemann, G.P.:Son 2 Chls, w. Colin Lawson (chl), S. Standage (cnd), Collegium Musicum 90 *(rec Goldsmiths' College, Apr 24-26, 1995)* Chandos ("Chaconne" series) ▲ CHAN 0593
Harris, Michael (cl)
Bach, Joh. Christian:Sinf concertante, T.290/9, w. Colin Lawson (cl), P. Holman (cnd), Parley of Instruments Hyperion ▲ CDA 66896
Mahon, J.:Duet 1 Cls, w. Colin Lawson (cl) Hyperion ▲ CDA 66896
Mahon, J.:Duet 4 Cls, w. Colin Lawson (cl) Hyperion ▲ CDA 66896
Harris, R. (pno)—see ORCHESTRAS & ENSEMBLES Piano Circus
Harris, Reid (va)
Kodály, Z.:Háry János (suite), w. James Barnes (cimbalom), Ted Gurch (sax), Y. Levi (cnd), Atlanta SO *(rec Atlanta, 1995-96)* Telarc ▲ CD 80413 [DDD]
Harris, Sophie (vc)—see ORCHESTRAS & ENSEMBLES Smith String Quartet
Harris, William (trbn)
Willey, J.:Society Music, w. L. Greene (fl), G. Coble (tpt), D. Resue (hn), S. Heyman (pno), E. Gustafson (vla), G. Macero (vc), E. Castilano (db), L. Luttinger (perc), E. Murray (cnd) Opus One ▲ CD 168 [DDD]
Harris-Heggie, Johana (pno)
Harris, R.:Duo Vc & Pno, w. Terry King (vc) Music & Arts ▲ CD 603 [AAD/DDD]
Harrison, Beatrice (vc)
Bach, J.S.:Suites Vc, BWV 1007-1012—Prelude & Gigue [from Suite in C, BWV 1009] *(rec 1920)* Symposium ▲ SYM 1140
Bax, A.:Con Vc (1925), w. H. Wood (cnd), BBC SO Symposium ▲ SYM 1150
Brahms, J.:Son 1 Vc, w. Gerald Moore (pno) *(rec 1926 & 27)* Symposium ▲ SYM 1140
Delius, F.:Hassan, w. Margaret Harrison (pno)—Serenade Symposium ▲ SYM 1140
Delius, F.:Son Vc & Pno, w. Harold Craxton (pno) *(rec Feb & Mar 1926)* Symposium ▲ SYM 1140
Elgar, E.:Music of—Con. in e for Cello & Orch., Op. 85 (1919); Pomp & Circumstance, No. 1 (1911); Froissart, op. 19 (1890); Cockaigne, Op. 40 (1901); In the South, Op. 50 (1904); The Kingdom Prelude, Op. 51 (1906); Serenade in e for Strings EMI Classics ▲ ZDCC 54568
Popper, D.:Vc & Pno Music—Gavotte, Op. 23/2 [w. Margaret Harrison (pno)]; Vito-Spanish Dance, Op. 54/5 [w. May Harrison (pno)] *(rec June 1919)* Symposium ▲ SYM 1140
Harrison, Gavin (dr/perc)
Battiato, F.:Haiku, w. Franco Battiato (voc), Pouran Ghaffarpour (voc), Antonio Ballista (pno), Marco Boni (vc), Guido Corti (cnt), Filippo Destrieri (kbd/computer), John Giblin (bass), Jakko Jakszyk (gtr), Roberto Mazza (ob), Fabrizio Merlini (va), Angelo Privitera (kbd/computer), Mino Bordignon (cnd), Milan Chamber Music Choir Hemisphere ▲ 837234-2
Battiato, F.:Ricerca sul Terzo, w. Franco Battiato (voc), Alessio Alba (tamboura), Antonio Ballista (pno), Marco Boni (vc), Debendra Kanti Chakraborty (tabla), Guido Corti (cnt), Filippo Destrieri (kbd/computer), John Giblin (bass), Buddhadeu Das Gupta (sarod), Jakko Jakszyk (gtr), Roberto Mazza (ob), Fabrizio Merlini (va), Angelo Privitera (kbd/computer), Mino Bordignon (cnd), Milan Chamber Music Choir Hemisphere ▲ 837234-2
Harrison, Kenneth (va)
Copland, A.:Qt Pno, w. D.R. Davies (pno), R. Tecco (vn), L. Duckles (vc) MusicMasters ▲ 7026-2-C [DDD]
Harrison, Lou (piri)
Harrison, L.:Music for Vn, w. William Bouton (vn), Richard Dee (cheng), William Colvig (sheng/fang-hsiang), Helen Rifas (hp) Phoenix ▲ PHCD 118 [AAD]
Harrison, Lou (psaltery)
Harrison, L.:Pieces Psaltery Phoenix ▲ PHCD 118 [AAD]
Harrison, Lou (suling)
Harrison, L.:Pieces (3) Gamelan, w. Scott L. Hartman (hn), S. Bates (va) CRI ■ ACS 6006
Harrison, L.:Pieces (3) Gamelan, w. Sekar Kembar (gamelan), Scott L. Hartman (hn—Main), S. Bates (vn—Threnody), L. Harrison (suling—Serenade) *(rec 1979)* CRI ▲ CD 613 [ADD]
Harrison, Margaret (vn)
Bax, A.:Son 3 Vn & Pno, w. C. Lynch (pno) *(rec live 2/3/36)* Symposium ▲ 1075
Burleigh, H.T.:Songs, w. Reginald Paul (pno)—Southland Sketches Symposium ▲ SYM 1140
Delius, F.:Con Vn, w. R. Austin (cnd), Bournemouth Municipal Orch *(rec live, 5/13/37)* Symposium ▲ 1075
Delius, F.:Son 1 Vn & Pno, w. Arnold Bax (pno) *(rec 1929)* Symposium ▲ SYM 1140
Delius, F.:Son 3 Vn & Pno, w. A. Bax (pno) *(rec private recording, ca. 1937)* Symposium ▲ 1075
Moeran, E.J.:Son Vn Symposium ▲ 1075
Warlock, P.:Songs Bar, w. S. Austin (bar), H. Gaskell (ob), C. Lynch (pno)—(2) Ha'Nacker Mill; Away to Twiver *(rec live 2/3/36)* Symposium ▲ 1075
Harrison, May (pno)
Delius, F.:Hassan, w. Beatrice Harrison (vc)—Serenade Symposium ▲ SYM 1140
Harrison, Michael (tpt)
Telemann, G.P.:Cons Tpts, w. Mark Bennett (tpt), Nicholas Thompson (tpt), Paul Goodwin (ob), Lorraine Wood (ob), T. Pinnock (cnd), English Concert—in D *(rec Henry Wood Hall, London, Mar 1993)* Archiv Produktion ▲ 439893-2 [DDD]
Harrison, Stephen (vc)—see ORCHESTRAS & ENSEMBLES San Francisco Contemporary Music Players
Harrod, William (E hn)
Copland, A.:Quiet City, w. Phillip Collins (tpt), E. Kunzel (cnd), Cincinnati Pops Orch *(rec Cincinatti Music Hall, 1989-95)* Telarc ▲ CD 80339 [DDD]
Harsányi, Zsolt (rcr)
Handel, G.F.:Sons Rcr, w. Zsursa Pertis (clvd)—Op. 1, Nos. 2 in g, 4 in a, 7 in C, 11 in F; H.367a in d *(rec May 4-7, 1992)* Naxos ▲ 8.550700 [DDD]
Harsányi, Zsolt (rcr/bn)
Handel, G.F.:Trio Sons, w. László Czidra (rcr), Pál Kelemen (vc), Zsursa Pertis (clvd)—in F, H.405 *(rec May 4-7, 1992)* Naxos ▲ 8.550700 [DDD]
Harshman, Allan (va)
Spohr, L.:Double Qt 1, w. J. Heifetz (vn), I. Baker (vn), P. Amoyal (vn), P. Rosenthal (vn), M. Thomas (va), G. Piatigorsky (vc), L. Lesser (vc) RCA Gold Seal ▲ 7870-2-RG (m/s) [ADD]
Hart, Antonio (sax)
So Many Stars, w. Kathleen Battle (sop), Grover Washington Jr (sax), Tom Harrell (flgl), James Carter (b cl), Cyrus Chestnut (pno), Jon Herrington (gtr), Romero Lubambo (gtr), Ira Coleman (elec bass), Christian McBride (elec bass), Cyro Baptista (perc), Steven Berrios (perc) *(rec Hit Factory, Clinton Recording Studios, R.P.M. Sound Studios, Unique Recording Studios, Power Station)* Sony Classical ▲ SK 68473 [DDD]
Härtelová, Lydie (hp)
Janácek, L.:Our Father, w. Josef Ksica (org), Josef Pancík (cnd), Prague Chamber Choir [arr for hp, org & mixed chorus] *(rec Dvořák Hall, Prague, Nov 1993)* ECM New Series ▲ 78118-21539-2 [DDD]
Hartenberger, Russell. (perc)—see also ORCHESTRAS & ENSEMBLES Nexus
Cahn, W.:Nara Nexus ▲ 10339 [DDD]
Hui, M.:San Rocco, w. Lawrence Cherney (ob), Noel Edison (cnd), Elora Festival Singers *(rec St Martin-in-the-Fields Church, Toronto, July 1995)* Centrediscs ▲ CMC 5395 [DDD]
Reich, S.:Clapping Music, w. S. Reich Elektra/Nonesuch ▲ 79169-2 [DDD] ■ 79169-4 (D)
Hartenstein, István (bn)
Janácek, L.:Concertino Pno, w. Thomas Hlawatsch (pno), Béla Nagy (vn), Vilmos Oláh (vn), Csaba Babácsi (va), Géza Bánhegyi (cl), Károly Ambrus (hn) *(rec Budapest, May 1995)* Naxos ▲ 8.553587 [DDD]
Harth, Sidney (vn)
Bloch, E.:Son 2 Vn, "Poème mystique", w. W. Devenny (pno) Crystal ▲ CD634
Gamer, C.:Son Vn, w. W. Devenny (pno) Crystal ▲ CD634
Janácek, L.:Son Vn, w. W. Devenny (pno) Crystal ▲ CD634
Rimsky-Korsakov, N.:Scheherazade, w. F. Reiner (cnd), Chicago SO *(rec Orchestra Hall, Chicago, Feb 8, 1960)* RCA Living Stereo ▲ 09026-68168-2 [ADD]
Hartig (vc)—see ORCHESTRAS & ENSEMBLES Cologne Divitia Ensemble
Hartig, Julija (vn)
Maric, L.:Archaia, w. Hans Rijkmans (va), Ivana Poparic (vc) Emergo ▲ EC 3951 [DDD]
Harting-Ware, Lynn (gtr)
Bach, J.S.:Goldberg Vars—Nos. 1, 2, 4, 7, 9, 13, 15, 19, 27, 30; 2 Arias [arr Harting-Ware for gtr] Acoma ▲ GXD 5734 [DDD]
Harting-Ware, L.:Reverie & March Acoma ▲ GXD 5734 [DDD]
The Many Moods of the Guitar *(rec Acoma Studio)* Acoma ▲ GXD 5732 [DDD]
Rollin, R.:Hebraic Contrasts Acoma ▲ GXD 5734 [DDD]
Smoot, R.J.:Con Gtr, "Drone" [arr. from 3rd mvmt by Harting-Ware] Acoma ▲ GXD 5734 [DDD]
Smoot, R.J.:Con Gtr, w. G. Samuel (cnd), CCM Contemporary Music Ensemble *(rec Corbett Auditorium, Cincinnati Conservatory, OH)* Acoma ▲ GXD 5733 [DDD]
Ware, P.:Forest Scenes Acoma ▲ GXD 5734 [DDD]
Hartley, Jacqueline (vn)—see ORCHESTRAS & ENSEMBLES Hartley Piano Trio
Hartlieb, Jessica (vn)
Suder, J.:Festival Mass, w. Natalia Kornewa (sop), Maria Neilau (alt), Vladimir Mostomoi (ten), Juri Dobrowolski (bass), Marlene Hinterberger (org), W.A. Albert (cnd), Bavarian State Youth Orch, St. Petersburg Chamber Choir Calig ▲ CAL 50945 [DDD]
Hartman, Scott A. (trbn)—see also ORCHESTRAS & ENSEMBLES Empire Brass Quintet
Four of a Kind:Music for Trombone Quartet, w. Joseph Allessi (trbn), Blair Bollinger (trbn), Mark H. Lawrence (trbn) Summit ▲ DCD 123 [DDD] ■ DCD 123
Hartman, Scott L. (hn)
Harrison, L.:Pieces (3) Gamelan, w. S. Bates (va), L. Harrison (suling) CRI ■ ACS 6006
Harrison, L.:Pieces (3) Gamelan, w. Sekar Kembar (gamelan), Scott L. Hartman (hn—Main), S. Bates (vn—Threnody), L. Harrison (suling—Serenade) *(rec 1979)* CRI ▲ CD 613 [ADD]
Hartman, Steve (hp)
Songs, Dances & Fantasy, w. Jerry Fuller (db), Frederick Ockwell (pno), Kenneth Dorsch (hpd), William Ferris (pno), Thomas Potter (bar), John Vorrasi (ten), Anne Waller (gtr) Musical Arts Society ▲ CD 41589 [AAD] ■ CS 41589
Sowerby, L.:Con Hp, w. J. Bolle (cnd), Monadnock Music Festival Orch Gasparo ▲ GSCD 315 [DDD]
Hartmann, Arno (org)
Schubert, Franz:Mass 1, w. Alexander Nader (sop), Thomas Puchegger (sop), Georg Leskovich (alto), Jörg Hering (ten), Kurt Azesberger (ten), Harry van der Kamp (bass), B. Weil (cnd), Orch of the Age of Enlightenment, Vienna Boys' Choir *(rec Vienna, Austria, Sept 1995)* Sony Classical ("Vivarte" series) ▲ SK 68247 [DDD]
Schubert, Franz:Mass 2, w. Thomas Puchegger (sop), Jörg Hering (ten), Harry van der Kamp (bass), B. Weil (cnd), Orch of the Age of Enlightenment, Vienna Boys' Choir *(rec Vienna, Austria, Sept 1995)* Sony Classical ("Vivarte" series) ▲ SK 68247 [DDD]
Schubert, Franz:Mass 3, w. Alexander Nader (sop), Thomas Puchegger (sop), Belá Fischer (alt), Georg Leskovich (alt), Jörg Hering (ten), Harry Van der Kamp (bass), B. Weil (cnd), Orch of the Age of Enlightenment, Chorus Viennensis, Vienna Boys' Choir Sony Classical ("Vivarte" series) ▲ SK 68248
Schubert, Franz:Mass 4, w. Alexander Nader (sop), Thomas Puchegger (sop), Belá Fischer (alt), Georg Leskovich (alt), Jörg Hering (ten), Harry Van der Kamp (bass), B. Weil (cnd), Orch of the Age of Enlightenment, Chorus Viennensis, Vienna Boys' Choir Sony Classical ("Vivarte" series) ▲ SK 68248
Hartmann, Christian (ob)
Mozart, W.A.:Don Giovanni, w. Gernot Schmalfub (ob), Dieter Klöcker (cl), Waldemar Wandel (cl), Sara Willis (hn), Christian Auer (hn), Karl-Otto Hartmann (bn), Eberhard Buschmann (bn), Jürgen Normann (db), Consortium Classicum Bayer ▲ BR 100 135 [DDD]
Hartmann, G. (vn)
Paganini, N.:Serenata Vns, w. D. Bratchkova (vn), A. Sebastiani (gtr) Dynamic ▲ CD 76 [DDD]
Paganini, N.:Terzetto Vns, w. D. Bratchkova (vn), A. Sebastiani (gtr) Dynamic ▲ CD 76 [DDD]
Hartmann, Karl-Otto (bn)—see also ORCHESTRAS & ENSEMBLES Consortium Classicum
Bach, C.P.E.:Duo Cl, w. D. Klöcker (cl), J. Normann (db) MD + G ▲ L 3365 [DDD]
Danzi, F.:Sinf concertante, w. D. Klöcker (cl), P. Škvor (cnd), Suk CO MD + G ▲ L 3365 [DDD]
Mozart, W.A.:Arias, w. Helen Donath (sop), Dieter Klöcker (cl), Josef Suk (vn), K. Donath (cnd), Suk CO—Cor Sincerum; Jesus Amor Meus; Mens Sancta Deo [2 versions]; Jesu Dulcis Memoria; Salve Regina; Domine Deus Salutis Meae; Plasmator Deus; Die Hoffnung dient zum Stabo *(rec Cultural House, Prague, June 3-10, 1987)* Panton ▲ PAN 810860
Mozart, W.A.:Concertone Vns, w. D. Klöcker (cl), P. Škvor (cnd), Suk CO [arr. Anton Hoffmeister for clarinet & bassoon] MD + G ▲ L 3365 [DDD]
Mozart, W.A.:Don Giovanni, w. Gernot Schmalfub (ob), Christian Hartmann (ob), Dieter Klöcker (cl), Waldemar Wandel (cl), Sara Willis (hn), Christian Auer (hn), Eberhard Buschmann (bn), Jürgen Normann (db), Consortium Classicum Bayer ▲ BR 100 135 [DDD]
Schubert, J.F.:Con Cl, w. D. Klöcker (cl), P. Škvor (cnd), Suk CO MD + G ▲ L 3366 [DDD]
Tausch, F.W.:Duo, w. D. Klöcker (cl), J. Normann (db) MD + G ▲ L 3366 [DDD]
Winter, P. von:Concertino Cl, w. D. Klöcker (cl), P. Škvor (cnd), Suk CO MD + G ▲ L 3366 [DDD]
Hartmann, Nicolas (vc)
Daetwyler, J.:Divert Fl, Vn & Vc, w. Verena Bosshart (fl), Hans-Walter Hirzel (vn) Grammont ▲ CTSP 15-2
Hartmann, S. (cl)—see ORCHESTRAS & ENSEMBLES Boehme Quintet
Hartog, Bernhard (vn)
Stephan, R.:Music for 7 Stringed Instrs, w. I. Schliephake (vn), S. Passaggio (va), G. Donderer (vc), A. Akahoshi (db), C. Tainton (pno), M. Schmidt (hp) *(rec 1983)* Koch Schwann ▲ CD 311 122 [ADD]
Hartog, Jacques (vn)—see ORCHESTRAS & ENSEMBLES Dekany String Quartet
Harty, Hamilton (pno)
Lambert, C.:The Rio Grande, w. A.H. Whitehead (alt), C. Lambert (cnd), Hallé Orch, St. Michaels' Singers Claremont ▲ CDGSE 785065
Harvan, Jarolslav (fl)
Holst, G.:A Fugal Con, w. M. Šintàl (ob), G. Brand (cnd), European Winds Albany ▲ TROY 120 [DDD]
Harvey, M. K. (pno)
Vine, C.:Son Pno *(rec Nov. 1991)* Tall Poppies ▲ TP013 [DDD]
Harvey, Richard (rcr)
Sammartini, G.:Cons Rcr, w. M. Huggett (vn), London Vivaldi Orch—in F ASV ("Gaudeamus" series) ▲ CDGAU 111
Scarlatti, A.:Sinf 3, w. M. Huggett (cnd), London Vivaldi Orch ASV ("Gaudeamus" series) ▲ CDGAU 111
Vivaldi, A.:Cons Rcr, w. M. Huggett (rcr), London Vivaldi Orch—RV.441 & RV.444 ASV ("Gaudeamus" series) ▲ CDGAU 111
Hašek, Ludek (vn)—see ORCHESTRAS & ENSEMBLES Suk String Quartet
Hasel, Michael (fl)—see ORCHESTRAS & ENSEMBLES Berlin Philharmonic Wind Quintet
Haselböck, Franz (org)
Bach, J.S.:Chorale Preludes Org [the organ of the Dom zu Eisenstadt]—Chorale Preludes BWV 1090-1120 Hänssler Classic ▲ 98.573 [DDD]
Handel, G.F.:Cons (16) Org, w. P. Németh (cnd), Capella Savaria—5 sels. Hänssler Classic ▲ 98940 [DDD]
Handel, G.F.:Cons (16) Org, w. K. Münchinger (cnd), Stuttgart CO—No. 13 London ▲ 411973-2 [DDD]
Haydn, J.:Con Org & Strs, H.XVIII/2, w. Divertimento Salzburg [period instrs] Orfeo ▲ 158871 [DDD]
Haydn, J.:Con Org, Vn & Strs, H.XVIII/6, w. Divertimento Salzburg Orfeo ▲ 310941 [DDD]

INSTRUMENT.

Haselböck, Franz (org) (cont.)
Haydn, J.:Con Org, Vns & Bass Instrument, H.XVIII/7, w. Divertimento Salzburg [period instrs] Orfeo ▲ 158871 [DDD]
Haydn, J.:Con Org, Vns & Bass Instrument, H.XVIII/8, w. Divertimento Salzburg [period instrs] Orfeo ▲ 158871 [DDD]
Intradas & Choral Settings for Organ & Brass, w. Militärmusik Burgenland Wind Ensemble [cnd:Rudolf Schrumpf] Hänssler Classic ▲ 98.544 [AAD]
Liszt, F.:Fant & Fugue on "Ad nos, ad salutarem undam" for Org Orfeo ▲ 125901 [DDD] ■ M 125901 (D)
Organ Concertos of the Classical Era, w. Capella Academica Vienna [cnd:Eduard Melkus] Hänssler Classic ▲ 98.575 [DDD]
Organ Music by Famous Opera Composers Koch Schwann ▲ SCH 315017 [DDD]
Organs in Southern Tyrol *(rec Parish Church of St. John the Baptist, Toblach; Parish and Convent Church of St. Augustine, Bozen–Gries; Bolzano (Brixen) Cathedral; and Priory Church, Bolzano, 1984)* Koch Schwann ▲ SCH 312832 [ADD]
Die schönsten Orgelwerke [The Most Beautiful Organ Works] Hänssler Classic ▲ 98.559 [DDD]

Haselböck, Martin (hpd/org)
Handel, G.F.:Sons Fl, w. Christian Gurtner (fl), Balázs Maté (vc)—Op. 1, Nos. 1, 4 & 5 *(rec Lutheran City Church, Vienna, Oct 1995)* Novalis ▲ 150120 [DDD]
Handel, G.F.:Sons Fl, "Halle Sons", w. Christian Gurtner (fl), Balázs Maté (vc) *(rec Lutheran City Church, Vienna, Oct 1995)* Novalis ▲ 150120 [DDD]
Handel, G.F.:Son Fl, HWV 378, w. Christian Gurtner (fl), Balázs Maté (vc) *(rec Lutheran City Church, Vienna, Oct 1995)* Novalis ▲ 150120 [DDD]
Handel, G.F.:Son Fl, HWV 379, w. Christian Gurtner (fl), Balázs Maté (vc)—excerpt *(rec Lutheran City Church, Vienna, Oct 1995)* Novalis ▲ 150120 [DDD]

Haselböck, Martin (org)
Haydn, J.:Concertino Org, w. Divertimento Salzburg Orfeo ▲ 310941 [DDD]
Liszt, F.:Ora pro nobis Orfeo ▲ 125901 [DDD] ■ M 125901 (D)
Liszt, F.:Prelude & Fugue on the name B–A–C–H Orfeo ▲ 125901 [DDD] ■ M 125901 (D)
Liszt, F.:Vars on "Weinen, Klagen, Sorgen, Zagen", S.179 Orfeo ▲ 125901 [DDD] ■ M 125901 (D)
Mozart, W.A.:Org Music—Fantaisie in f, K.594; Fantaisie in f, K.608; Adagio in C, K.356; Andante in F, K.616; Adagio & Rondo in C, K.617; Adagio & Fugue in c, K.546; Allegro in G, K.443; Eine kleine Gigue, K.574; Fugues in E♭ g & g, K.153 154 & 401; Ov. in C from K.399; Ave verum [Mozart/arr. Liszt] & Benedictus [Mozart/arr. Novello] Koch Schwann ▲ 317003 [ADD]
Reger, M.:Chorale Fants, Op. 52—No. 2, Wachet auf, ruft uns die Stimme Preiser ▲ PRE 90173 [ADD]
Reger, M.:Vars & Fugue on an Original Theme Preiser ▲ PRE 90173 [ADD]
Schmidt, F.:Das Buch mit sieben Siegeln, w. Gabriele Fontana (sop), Margareta Hintermeier (alt), Kurt Azesberger (ten), Eberhard Büchner (ten—Johannes), Robert Holl (bass—Voice of the Lord), Robert Holzer (bass), H. Stein (cnd), Vienna SO, Vienna Sym Chorus *(rec live, Vienna Music Hall, May 1996)* Calig 2–▲ CAL 50978/9 [DDD]
Vivaldi, A.:Con Vn Org, RV.542, w. I. Kertész (vn), M. Haselböck (cnd), Vienna Academy [period instrs] Novalis ▲ 150074 [DDD]

Hasenöhrl, Jan (tpt)
Telemann, G.P.:Cons Tpt, w. O. Vlček (cnd), Prague Virtuosi—Con. in D Trumpet; Son. in D for Trumpet; Con. in B for 2 Trumpets [w. J. Burian]; Con. in D for 3 Trumpets [J. Burian & U. F. Walser]; Con. in G for 4 Trumpets [J. Burian, U. F. Walser & F. Vlasák (trumpets)], J. Tuma (organ), J. Kolár (oboe)] Emergo ▲ EC 3982 [DDD]
Vejvanovsky, P.J.:Sons & Serenades, w. Vaclav Jirovec (vc), Jiri Pribyl (trbn), Frantisek Xaver (hpd), Milan Hruby (brass), Oldrich Vlcek (vn), O. Vlček (cnd), Prague Virtuosi—Intrada; Harmonia romana; Serenada; Offertur ad duos chorus; Son à 4 be mollis; Son paschalis; Son tribus quadrantibus; Son campanarum; Serenada *(rec Lobochovice castle, July 26–28, 1992)* Discover International ▲ DI 920243 [DDD]
Vivaldi, A.:Cons for 2 Obs, w. J. Kolár (ob), R. Hrabé (ob), F. Vlasák (tpt), O. Vlček (cnd), Prague Virtuosi—Con. in C, RV.559 *(rec 1991)* Emergo ▲ EC 3981 [DDD]
Vivaldi, A.:Con for 2 Tpts, w. F. Vlasák (tpt), O. Vlček (cnd), Prague Virtuosi *(rec 1991)* Emergo ▲ EC 3981 [DDD]

Hashimoto, Eiji (hpd)
Bach, C.P.E.:Sinfs, H.657–662, "Hamburg Syms", w. E. Hashimoto (cnd), Ensemble for 18th Century Music—H.659 in C *(rec Corbett Auditorium, College–Conservatory of Music, Univ. of Cincinnati)* Klavier ▲ KCD 11054 [DDD]
Bach, C.P.E.:Sinfs, H.663–666, w. E. Hashimoto (cnd), Ensemble for 18th Century Music—H.663 in D *(rec Corbett Auditorium, College–Conservatory of Music, Univ. of Cincinnati)* Klavier ▲ KCD 11054 [DDD]
Bach, Joh. Christian:Sinfs, Op. 6, w. E. Hashimoto (cnd), Ensemble for 18th Century Music—Nos. 3 in E♭ & 6 in g *(rec Corbett Auditorium, College–Conservatory of Music, Univ. of Cincinnati)* Klavier ▲ KCD 11054 [DDD]
Bach, J.C.F:Sinf, HW.I/3, w. E. Hashimoto (cnd), Ensemble for 18th Century Music *(rec Corbett Auditorium, College–Conservatory of Music, Univ. of Cincinnati)* Klavier ▲ KCD 11054 [DDD]
Bach, W.F.:Sinf in d, w. E. Hashimoto (cnd), Ensemble for 18th Century Music *(rec Corbett Auditorium, College–Conservatory of Music, Univ. of Cincinnati)* Klavier ▲ KCD 11054 [DDD]
Haydn, J.:Con Org, Vn & Strs, H.XVIII/6, w. H. Schneeberger (vn), K. Toyoda (cnd), Tchikashi Tanaka Ensemble Camerata ▲ 30CM 376
Scarlatti, D.:Sons Kbd—in A, K.26 [Presto]; in c, K.99 [Allegro]; in C, K.100 [Allegrissimo]; in A, K.211 [Andantino]; in A, K.212 [Allegro molto]; in B♭, K.248 [Allegro]; in B♭, K.249 [Allegro]; in D, K.298 [Allegro]; in D, K.299 [Allegro]; in E, K.380 [Andante Commodo]; in E, K.381 [Allegro]; in G, K.424 [Allegro]; in G, K.425 [Allegro molto]; in F, K.468 [Allegro]; in F, K.469 [Allegro molto]; in C, K.485 [Allegro è Cantabile]; in C, K.486 [Allegro]; in C, K.487 [Allegro] *(rec Fisher Auditorium, Indiana University of Pennsylvania, Indiana, PA)* Klavier ▲ KCD 11061 [DDD]

Hashimoto, Kyoko (pno)
Bloch, E.:Suite hébraïque, w. Karel Dolezal (va) *(rec Covenent of St. Agnes of Bohemia, Prague, Mar 1995)* Arta ▲ 0062 [DDD]

Haskil, Clara (pno)
Beethoven, L. van:Con 4 Pno, w. M. Rossi (cnd), Turin RAI SO *(rec Turin, Apr. 22, 1960)* Emozioni ▲ CDAR 2027 [ADD]
Bach, J.S.:Con 5 Hpd, w. P. Casals (cnd), Prades Festival Orch *(rec June 6, 1950)* Sony Classical ("The Casals Edition" series) ▲ SMK 58982 [ADD]
Beethoven, L. van:Con 3 Pno, w. H. Swoboda (cnd), Winterthur SO *(rec 1950)* Enterprise ("Palladio" series) ▲ ENTPD 4179 [ADD]
Beethoven, L. van:Con 4 Pno, w. A. Cluytens (cnd), French National Orch *(rec Dec. 8, 1955)* Music & Arts ▲ CD 863 [ADD]
Beethoven, L. van:Son 18 Pno *(rec live, 1956)* Music & Arts ▲ CD 542 (m)
Beethoven, L. van:Son 3 Vn, w. A. Grumiaux (vn) *(rec live in performance)* Melodram ▲ MEL 18001
Beethoven, L. van:Son 4 Vn, w. A. Grumiaux (vn) *(rec Aug. 22, 1960)* Ermitage ▲ ERM 112 [ADD]
Beethoven, L. van:Son 5 Vn, "Spring", w. Arthur Grumiaux (vn) *(rec Sept. 18, 1957)* Music & Arts ▲ CD 860 [AAD]
Beethoven, L. van:Son 10 Vn, w. A. Grumiaux (vn) *(rec Aug. 22, 1960)* Ermitage ▲ ERM 112 [ADD]
Beethoven, L. van:Son 10 Vn, w. Arthur Grumiaux (vn) *(rec Sept. 18, 1957)* Music & Arts ▲ CD 860 [AAD]
Brahms, J.:Qnt Pno, w. Peter Rybar (vn), Clemens Dahinden (vn), Heinz Wigand (va), Antonio Tusa (vc) Doron 2–▲ DRC 4007/8 [ADD]
Busoni, F.:Son 2 Vn, w. Peter Rybar (vn) Doron 2–▲ DRC 4007/8 [ADD]
Busoni, F.:Son 2 Vn, w. Joseph Szigeti (vn) Music & Arts 4–▲ CD 720–4 [AAD]
Chopin, F.:Con 2 Pno, w. A. Cluytens (cnd), National Orch *(rec Apr 1954)* Music & Arts ▲ CD 922
Clara Haskil at the Ludwigsburg Festival *(rec Apr. 11, 1953)* Music & Arts ▲ MUA 859 [AAD]
Falla, M. de:Noches en los jardines de España, w. I. Markevitch (cnd), Lamoureux Concerts Orch *(rec 1960)* Philips ("Spanish" series) ▲ 432829–2 [ADD]
Hindemith, P.:The Four Temperaments, w. P. Hindemith (cnd), French National Orch *(rec Montreux, 1957)* Music & Arts ▲ CD 864 [ADD]

Haskil, Clara (pno) (cont.)
Mozart, W.A.:Con 9 Pno, w. C. Schuricht (cnd), Stuttgart RSO *(rec live, 1952)* Originals ▲ ORI SH 867
Mozart, W.A.:Con 19 Pno, w. C. Schuricht (cnd), Stuttgart RSO *(rec live, 1956)* Originals ▲ ORI SH 867
Mozart, W.A.:Con 20 Pno, w. F. Fricsay (cnd), Berlin RSO *(rec Europa–Palast, Berlin, Jan. 10, 1954)* Myto 2–▲ 2 MCD 92361 [ADD]
Mozart, W.A.:Con 20 Pno, w. P. Hindemith (cnd), French National Orch *(rec Montreux, 1957)* Music & Arts ▲ CD 864 [ADD]
Mozart, W.A.:Con 20 Pno, w. O. Klemperer (cnd), Cologne Gürzenich Orch Legend ▲ LGD 113 [ADD]
Mozart, W.A.:Con 20 Pno, w. H. Swoboda (cnd), Winterthur SO *(rec 1950)* Enterprise ("Palladio" series) ▲ ENTPD 4179 [ADD]
Mozart, W.A.:Con 23 Pno, w. C. Munch (cnd), National Orch *(rec Sept 1959)* Music & Arts ▲ CD 922
Mozart, W.A.:Con 24 Pno, w. A. Cluytens (cnd), French National Orch *(rec Dec. 8, 1955)* Music & Arts ▲ CD 863 [ADD]
Mozart, W.A.:Con 27 Pno, w. O. Klemperer (cnd), Cologne Gürzenich Orch Legend ▲ LGD 113 [ADD]
Mozart, W.A.:Sons Vn Pno (misc), w. A. Grumiaux (vn)—K.304 & 454 *(rec live)* Melodram ▲ MEL 18001
Mozart, W.A.:Sons Vn Pno (misc), w. A. Grumiaux (vn)—K.378 *(rec Aug. 22, 1960)* Ermitage ▲ ERM 112 [ADD]
Mozart, W.A.:Sons Vn Pno (misc), w. Arthur Grumiaux (vn)—Nos. 5 & 10 *(rec Sept. 18, 1957)* Music & Arts ▲ CD 860 [AAD]
Mozart, W.A.:Sons Vn Pno (misc), w. A. Grumiaux (vn)—K.301, 304, 376 & 378 Philips ▲ 412253–2 [ADD]
Mozart, W.A.:Son Vn Pno, K.454, w. Peter Rybar (vn) Doron 2–▲ DRC 4007/8 [ADD]
Mozart, W.A.:Vars Pno, K.573 *(rec live, 1956)* Music & Arts ▲ CD 542 (m)
Schubert, Franz:Son Pno, D.845 *(rec live, 1956)* Music & Arts ▲ CD 542 (m)
Schumann, R.:Kinderszenen *(rec live, 1956)* Music & Arts ▲ CD 542 (m)

Haskins, Dan (timp)
Sowerby, L.:Festival Musick, w. Carl Albach (tpt), Susan Radcliff (tpt), Jeffrey Caswell (trbn), Tom Hutchinson (trbn), David Mulbury (org), J. Welsh (cnd), Fairfield Orch *(rec St. Bartholomew's Church, New York City, May 5, 1994)* Marco Polo ▲ 8.223725 [DDD]

Haslam, M. (pno)—see ORCHESTRAS & ENSEMBLES Piano Circus

Haslop, Clayton (vn)
Bartók, B.:Romanian Folk Dances Pno, w. J. Sanders (gtr) [arr. for violin & guitar]—6 dances Centaur ▲ CRC 2061 [DDD]
Giuliani, M.:Grand Son Fl, w. J. Sanders (gtr) [arr. for violin–guitar] Centaur ▲ CRC 2061 [DDD]
Kohn, K.:Concords, w. J. Sanders (gtr) Centaur ▲ CRC 2061 [DDD]
Leisner, D.:Dances in the Madhouse, w. J. Sanders (gtr) Centaur ▲ CRC 2061 [DDD]
Sarasate, P. de:Carmen Fant, w. J. Sanders (gtr) [violin–guitar arr.] Centaur ▲ CRC 2061 [DDD]
Sarasate, P. de:Spanish Dances, w. J. Sanders (pno) [arr. for violin & guitar]—Op. 22/1, "Romanza andaluza" Centaur ▲ CRC 2061 [DDD]

Hass, W. (pno)
Brahms, J.:Qnt Pno, w. Berlin Philharmonic Octet members Philips ("Duo" series) 2–▲ 446172–2
Ravel, M.:Con Pno (left hand), w. A. Galliera (cnd), Monte Carlo Opera Orch Philips 2–▲ 438353–2
Ravel, M.:Con in G Pno, w. A. Galliera (cnd), Monte Carlo Opera Orch Philips 2–▲ 438353–2

Hassard, Donald (pno)
Argento, D.:To Be Sung Upon The Water, w. John Stewart (ten), Charles Russo (cl/b cl) Phoenix ▲ PHCD 129

Hassell, Jon (tpt)
Hassell, J.:Vernal Equinox, w. Fender Rhodes (pno), Nana Vasconcelos, et al. (perc) Lovely Music ▲ LCD 1021 [ADD]

Hasselmann, Knut (nat hn)
Haydn, J.:Lauda Sion, w. Ab Koster (nat hn), Bob Van Asperen (org), B. Weil (cnd), L'Archibudelli, Tölz Boys' Choir *(rec Bad Tolz, Germany, Jan. 2–4, 1993)* Sony Classical ("Vivarte" series) ▲ SK 53368 [DDD]

Hassid, Josef (vn)
The 1940 Recordings, w. Haendel, Ida (vn) Pearl ▲ PEA 9939 (m) [AAD]

Hasson, Maurice (vn)
Bach, J.S.:Con for 2 Vns, w. H. Szeryng (vn), N. Marriner (cnd), Academy of St. Martin in the Fields—Air & Suite No. 3, BWV 1068 Philips ▲ 422250–2 [ADD]
Bach, J.S.:Con for 2 Vns, w. H. Szeryng (vn), N. Marriner (cnd), Academy of St. Martin in the Fields Philips 2–▲ 426462–2 [ADD]
Chausson, E.:Poème Vn, w. J. Lubbock (cnd), Orch of St. John ASV Quicksilva ▲ QS 6051 [ADD/DDD]
Debussy, C.:Son Vn, w. C. Ivaldi (pno) IMP Masters ▲ MCD 37 [DDD]
Fauré, G.:Son 1 Vn, w. C. Ivaldi (pno) IMP Masters ▲ MCD 37 [DDD]
Franck, C.:Son Vn, w. C. Ivaldi (pno) IMP Masters ▲ MCD 37 [DDD]
Virtuoso Violin, w. Hasson, Maurice (vn), St. John's Smith Square Orch [cnd:John Lubbock], Ian Brown (pno) ASV ("Quicksilva" series) ▲ ASV 6034 [ADD]
Vivaldi, A.:Cons Vn, Op. 8/1–4, "The Four Seasons", w. Jose–Luis Garcia (vn), Manoug Parikian (vn), Daniel Phillips (vn), Y. Menuhin (cnd), English CO [each movt. w. different vn soloist] Start Classics ▲ SCD 13

Hatch, P. (vc)
Brahms, J.:Son in D Vc, w. D. Stevens (pno) PROdigital ▲ VM 5308 [DDD]

Hatch, Peter (va)
Brahms, J.:Sons Cl (comp), w. Michel Wagemans (pno) *(rec Elder Forest Studios, Elder Forest, CA)* PROdigital ▲ PRO 6215 [DDD]
Enescu, G.:Concertpiece Va, w. D. Stevens (pno) PROdigital ▲ VM 5308 [DDD]
Joachim, J.:Hebrew Melodies, w. D. Stevens (pno) PROdigital ▲ VM 5308 [DDD]
19th Century Viola Music, w. Delores Stevens (pno) PROdigital ▲ PROVM 5308 [DDD]
Sitt, H.:Album Leaves Va, w. D. Stevens (pno) PROdigital ▲ VM 5308 [DDD]

Hatfield, L. (instr)—see ORCHESTRAS & ENSEMBLES Capricorn members

Hathaway, Norman (va)
Catherine Wilson & Friends:Classical Potpourri, w. Wilson, Catherine (pno), Mark Skazinetsky (vn), Jack Mendelsohn (vc), Joel Quarrington (db) Doremi ▲ DHR 71111

Hatton, Jean–François (harm)
Rossini, G.:Petite messe solennelle, w. E. Schmitt (sop), S. Gregoire (cta), R. Garin (ten), A. Golven (bass), F. Maciocchi (pno) J.–F. Hatton (harm), Paris Opéra–Comique Chorus IMP Masters ▲ IMP MCD61

Hatton, Jean–François (org)
Fauré, G.:Choral Music, w. Hervé Lamy (ten), F. Polgár (cnd), Paris Opera Soloists, Neuilly St–Croix Youth Chorus—Requiem, Op. 48 [1893 Version]; Salve Regina, Op. 67/1; Ave Maria, Op. 67/2; Tantum Ergo, Op. 65/2; Ave Verum, Op. 65/1; Cantique de Jean Racine, Op. 11 Adès ▲ ADE 202982
Saint–Saëns, C.:Choral Music, w. H. Lamy (ten), Paris Opera Orch Soloists, F. Polgár (cnd), Neuilly St–Croix Youth Chorus—Pie Jesu; Ave Verum Adès ▲ ADE 202982

Hatton, John (org)
Spratling, H.:Choral Music, w. Tracey Chadwell (sop), Susan Bullock (sop), Jeffery Dyball (hp), Helen Tunstall (hp), J. Rennert (cnd), Parnassus String Ensemble, Spratling Choir—Mass of the Holy Spirit; O Salutaris Hostia; Tantum Ergo; Sinf Str Orch; Son Hp; O Magnum Mysterium; In Paradisum *(rec St. Mary Magdelene, Paddington, May 15–17, 1988)* SOMM ▲ SOMMCD 206 [ADD]

Hattori, Yoshio (vc)
Takemitsu, T.:Music of, w. Tashi, Y. Nagano (mez), H. Ibe (gtr), M. Nagasako (hp), K. Abe (vib), Y. Takahashi (pno), R. Noguchi (fl), M. Hamada (lt), T. Koizumi (picc), S. Ueki (vn), R. Stoltzman (cl), P. Serkin (pno), Ozawa, Wakasugi (cnd), Boston SO—Quatrain; Stanza I; Sacrifice; Ring; Valeria; A Flock Descends into the Pentagonal Garden Deutsche Grammophon ("20th Century Classics" series) ▲ 423253–2 [ADD]

Hauber, Michael (pno)—see ORCHESTRAS & ENSEMBLES Opus 8 Trio

606 ▲ = CD ♦ = Enhanced CD Δ = MD ■ = Cassette Tape ◻ = DCC

Haubold, Rudolf (tpt)
Vivaldi, A.:Con for 2 Tpts, w. A. Scherbaum (tpt), Hamburg Scherbaum Baroque Ensemble Deutsche Grammophon ("Musikfest" series) ▲ 413256-2 ■ 413256-4
Hauck, B. (va)—see ORCHESTRAS & ENSEMBLES Apple Hill Chamber Players
Haudebourg, Brigitte (hpd)
Boutmy, J.:Second livre de pièces—6 suites Arcobaleno ▲ AAOC 9366
Couperin, L.:Pavan Hpd Arion ▲ ARN 68027 [AAD]
Couperin, L.:Pièces de clavecin (sels)—24 selections from Suites I, III, V, IX, XII, XIII & XV, all but one in F major Arion ▲ ARN 68027 [AAD]
Haudebourg, Brigitte (pno)
Méhul, E.-N.:Sons Hpd, Opp. 1/1-3 & 2/1-3 Arcobaleno ▲ SBCD 1504 [DDD]
Schobert, J.:Sons Hpd, Op. 14 Arion ▲ ARN 68287
Haudenschild, Emilie (vn)—see also ORCHESTRAS & ENSEMBLES Erato String Quartet
Messiaen, O.:Quatuor pour la fin du temps, w. Fabio di Casola (cl), Emeric Kostyak (vc), Ricardo Castro (pno) Accord ▲ ACD 201772 [AAD]
Haudenschild, H. (va)—see ORCHESTRAS & ENSEMBLES Erato String Quartet
Haugland, S. (bn)—see ORCHESTRAS & ENSEMBLES Boreas Wind Quintet, Danish Wind Octet
Haugsand, Ketil (hpd)
Bach, J.S.:Sons Vl, BWV 1027-1029, w. L. Dreyfus (vl) Simax ▲ PSC 1024 [DDD]
Marais, M.:Pièces de viole [Book 2] (sels), w. L. Dreyfus (vl)—Suites in b & e Simax ▲ PSC 1053 [DDD]
Marais, M.:Vars on *Folies d'Espagne*, w. L. Dreyfus (vl) Simax ▲ PSC 1053 [DDD]
Hauk, Franz (org)
Boëllmann, L.:Fant dialoguée, w. O. Koch (cnd), Leipzig SO IMP ("Classics" series) ▲ IMP 6701092
Fétis, F.J.:Fant symphonique, w. O. Koch (cnd), Leipzig SO IMP ("Classics" series) ▲ IMP 6701092
Guilmant, A.:Org Music, w. O. Koch (cnd), Leipzig SO—Allegro for Org & Orch, Op. 81; Marche fantasie sur deux chantes d'eglise for Org, Hp & Orch, Op. 44; Meditation sur le stabat mater for Org & Orch, Op. 63; Final all Schumann sur un Noël languedocien, Op. 83; Sym No. 1 for Org & Orch, Op. 42 IMP ("Classics" series) ▲ IMP 6701092
Haupt, Eckart (fl)
Bach, C.P.E.:Cons Fl, w. H. Haenchen (cnd), C.P.E. Bach CO—in d, H.425 (W.22); in a, H.431 (W.166); in A, H.438 (W.168) Capriccio ▲ 10104
Bach, C.P.E.:Cons Fl, w. H. Haenchen (cnd), C.P.E. Bach CO—in B♭, H.435 (W.167) & in G, H.445 (W.169) Capriccio ▲ 10105
Bach, C.P.E.:Cons Fl, w. H. Haenchen (cnd), C.P.E. Bach CO—in d LaserLight ▲ 14036 [DDD]
Bach, C.P.E.:Cons Fl, w. H. Haenchen (cnd), C.P.E. Bach CO—W.169 LaserLight ▲ 15634 [DDD]
Bach, J.S.:Partita Fl, BWV 1013 *(rec 1989-90)* Berlin Classics 2-▲ BER 1007 [DDD]
Bach, C.P.E.:Sons Fl, w. Thalheim (hpd), Pank (vl)—in e, H.551 (W.124); in G, H.554 (W.127); in a, H.555 (W.128); in D, H.556 (W.129); in G, H.564 (W.133); in G, H.548 (W.134) Capriccio ▲ 10101
Bach, J.S.:Sons Fl, BWV 1030-35, w. S. Pank (vl), C. Schornsheim (hpd)—BWV 1030-1035 & 1033 [reconstruction after Marshall] *(rec June 1989 & Jan 1990)* Berlin Classics 2-▲ BER 1007 [DDD]
Bach, J.S.:Trio Son Fl, Vn & Hpd, w. P. Mirring (vn), C. Schornsheim (hpd) *(rec June 1989 & 1990)* Berlin Classics 2-▲ BER 1007 [DDD]
Bach, J.S.:Trio Son for 2 Fls, BWV 1039, w. W. Loebner (fl), S. Pank (vl) *(rec June 1989 & Jan 1990)* Berlin Classics 2-▲ BER 1007 [DDD]
Mozart, W.A.:Qt Fl, K.285, w. P. Mirring (vn), P. Schikora (va), G. Pluskwik (vc) LaserLight ▲ 15 878 [DDD]
Mozart, W.A.:Sons Pno Vn Vc, w. A. Zenziper (pno), F. Dittmann (vc)—K.15 LaserLight ▲ 15 878 [DDD]
Vivaldi, A.:Cons Fl (misc), w. P. Schreier (cnd), Dresden Baroque Soloists—RV.104, 106, 108, 428, 433, 443 & 441 Berlin Classics ▲ BER 1002 [DDD]
Hauptmann, Norbert (hn)—see also ORCHESTRAS & ENSEMBLES Berlin Philharmonic Wind Ensemble
Mozart, W.A.:Musikalischer Spass, w. M. Klier (hn), Berlin Philharmonia String Quartet Denon/PCM Digital ▲ DEN 7229 [DDD]
Mozart, W.A.:Qnt Hn, K.407, w. Berlin Philharmonia String Quartet Denon/PCM Digital ▲ DEN 8003 [DDD]
Mozart, W.A.:Qnt Hn, K.407, w. Berlin Philharmonia String Quartet Denon/Pcm Digital ▲ DEN 7229 [DDD]
Strauss, R.:Con 2 Hn, w. Z. Mehta (cnd), Berlin PO Sony Classical ▲ SK 53267
Tal, J.:Else-Hommage, w. C. Gayer (sop), J. Bliese (nar), H. Ganz (va), G. Teutsch (vc), K. Helwig (pno), J. Tal (cnd) Academy ▲ ACA 8506 [ADD]
Hauptmann, Olga (baroque va)
Out of the Orient Crystall Skyes, w. Nancy Zylstra (sop), Margriet Tindemans (vl), Jillion Stopples Dupree (hpd/org), Michael Sand (baroque vn/vl), Linda Melsted (baroque vn), Ellen Siebert (vl), Russell Paige (vl) Wildboar ▲ WLBR 8901 [DDD]
Hauschild, Wolf-Dieter (hpd)
Telemann, G.P.:Don Quichotte (suite), w. W.-D. Hauschild (cnd), Leipzig RSO Berlin Classics ▲ BER 9262
Hauser, Adrienne (pno)
Bartók, B.:The Miraculous Mandarin Pno 4-Hands, w. Zoltán Kocsis (pno) Musique D'Abord ▲ HMA 1903021
Schoenberg, A.:Chamber Sym 1, w. Zoltán Kocsis (pno), *(pno 4-hands)* Musique d'Abord ▲ HMA 1903021
Hauser, Fritz (perc)
Deep Listening Band:Troglodyte's Delight, w. Pauline Oliveros (acc/voc/whistles), Stuart Dempster (trbn), Panaiotis (voc), Julie Lyon Balliett (voc) *(rec Tarpaper Cave, Rosendale, NY, June 1989)* ¿What Next? ▲ WN 003 ■ WN 0003
Hauser, F.:Music for Perc—Tic Tac; Traumbilder; Tutguri; Kangwolke I-III; Labyrinth; Skizzen, Gedenken, Gesten I-V; Der Pendler *(rec Berlin, Apr. 4-7, 1985)* Hat Hut ▲ hat ART CD 6023 [DDD]
Hauser, F.:Die Trommel *(rec Studio DRS, Basel, Switzerland, Nov. 1987)* Hat Hut ▲ hat ART CD 6017 [AAD]
Häusler, Regula (vc)
Reger, M.:Trio Vn Vc, w. C. Ragaz (vn), J. Buttrick (pno) *(rec 1985)* Jecklin-Disco ▲ JD 604-2 [ADD]
Hausmann, Ib (cl)
Feldman, Morton:Qt Cl, w. Pellegrini String Quartet *(rec Church Blumenstein, Thun, Switzerland, June 20-21, 1994)* Hat Hut ("Now." series) ▲ ART CD 6166 [DDD]
Goldschmidt, B.:Qt Cl, w. Mandelring String Quartet members *(rec 1991)* Largo ▲ 5117 [DDD]
Hausmann, Iven (trbn)
Cage, J.:Ryoanji, w. John Patrick Thomas (voc), Gudrun Reschke (ob), Eberhard Blum (fl), Robert Black (db), Jan Williams (perc) *(rec Akademie der Künste, Berlin, June 22, 1995)* Hat Hut ("Now" series) ▲ hat ART CD 6183 [DDD]
Hauta-aho, Teppo (db/vc)
Braxton, A.:Composition 144, w. Anthony Braxton (fl/s sax/a sax), Seppo Baron Paakkunainen (fl/t sax/br sax), Pentti Lahti (fl/s sax/a sax), Pepa Päivinen (fl/t sax/sop sax/b cl), Mircea Stan (trbn), Mikko-Ville Luolajan-Mikkola (vn), Jukka Wasama (dr) *(rec Järvenpää House, Järvenpää, Finland, Nov 7, 1988)* Leo ▲ LR 233
Braxton, A.:Composition 145, w. Anthony Braxton (fl/s sax/a sax), Seppo Baron Paakkunainen (fl/t sax/br sax), Pentti Lahti (fl/s sax/a sax), Pepa Päivinen (fl/t sax/sop sax/b cl), Mircea Stan (trbn), Mikko-Ville Luolajan-Mikkola (vn), Jukka Wasama (dr) *(rec Järvenpää House, Järvenpää, Finland, Nov 7, 1988)* Leo ▲ LR 233
Hautzig, Walter (pno)
Schubert, Franz:Moments musicaux Connoisseur Society ▲ CD 4209
Schubert, Franz:Son Pno, D.960 Connoisseur Society ▲ CD 4209
Schubert, Franz:Waltzes Pno—D.365/1, 2, 14, 17, 26, 29, 32 & 35; D.799/13; D.969/9 Connoisseur Society ▲ CD 4209

Hauwe, Joris van den (ob)
Bellini, V.:Con in E♭ Ob, w. R. Werthen (cnd), I Fiamminghi CO Koch Schwann ▲ SCH 310822 [DDD]
Cimarosa, D.:Con for 2 Fls, w. R. Werthen (cnd), I Fiamminghi CO [trans. for solo oboe & orch.] Koch Schwann ▲ SCH 310822 [DDD]
Corelli, A.:Concerti grossi, Op. 6, w. R. Werthen (cnd), I Fiamminghi CO—[arr. Barbirolli] Koch Schwann ▲ SCH 310822
Ferlendis, G.:Con 1 Ob, w. D. Vermeulen (cnd), Flanders CO Sinfonia Eufoda ▲ 1154 [DDD]
Hindemith, P.:Kleine Kammermusik, w. Marc Grauwels (fl), Ronald Van Spaendonck (cl), et al. Syrinx ▲ 95101
Hummel, J.N.:Vars Ob, w. D. Vermeulen (cnd), Flanders CO Sinfonia Eufoda ▲ 1154 [DDD]
Krommer, F.:Con Ob, Op. 52, w. D. Vermeulen (cnd), Flanders CO Sinfonia Eufoda ▲ 1154 [DDD]
Lebrun, L.A.:Con 1 Ob, w. D. Vermeulen (cnd), Flanders CO Sinfonia Eufoda ▲ 1154 [DDD]
Marcello, A.:Con Ob Bass Cl, w. R. Werthen (cnd), I Fiamminghi CO Koch Schwann ▲ SCH 310822 [DDD]
Rimsky-Korsakov, N.:Vars on a Theme of Glinka, w. N. Nozy (cnd), Belgian Guides Symphonic Band René Gailly ▲ CD 87075 [DDD]
Vivaldi, A.:Con Ob, RV.456, w. R. Werthen (cnd), I Fiamminghi CO Koch Schwann ▲ SCH 310822 [DDD]
Hauwe, Walter van (fl)
Telemann, G.P.:Sonate metodiche, w. B. Van Asperen (hpd), W. Möller (vc)—Son No. 10 in B♭ for voice flute & continuo Globe ▲ GLO 5016 [ADD]
Hauwe, Walter van (rcr)—see also ORCHESTRAS & ENSEMBLES Little Consort
Bach, J.S.:Partita Fl, BWV 1013, w. W. Möller (vc), T. Satoh (lt), G. Wilson (hpd)—in c *(rec 1988)* Channel Classics ▲ CCS 4492 [DDD]
Blockflutes 3:The Early 17th Century, w. Van Hauwe, Walter (rcr), Toyohiko Satoh (lt) Channel Classics ▲ CCS 3392 [DDD]
Ladder of Escape 3, w. Van Hauwe, Walter (rcr) Attacca ▲ BABEL 8847-5
Telemann, G.P.:Fants Fl—Nos. 5,9 & 12 Globe ▲ GLO 5016 [ADD]
Telemann, G.P.:Der Getreue Music-Meister (sels), w. B. Van Asperen (hpd), W. Möller (vc)—Sonata in f for recorder & continuo Globe ▲ GLO 5016 [ADD]
Telemann, G.P.:Kleine Kammermusik, w. B. Van Asperen (hpd)—Partita No. 4 in g Globe ▲ GLO 5016 [ADD]
Telemann, G.P.:Rcr Music (misc), w. W. Möller (vc), T. Satoh (lt), G. Wilson (hpd)—Fantasies Nos. 1 & 8; Partita No. 5 in e; Son. d; Son. D; Trio Son. in B♭ *(rec 1988)* Channel Classics ▲ CCS 4492 [DDD]
Have, Wim ten (va)—see also ORCHESTRAS & ENSEMBLES Ensemble 415
Telemann, G.P.:Son Polonese, w. Troels Svendsen (vn), Karen Englund (hpd) *(rec Strandmarks Church, Copenhagen, Denmark, Sept 1994)* Rondo Gramophon ▲ RCD 8343 [DDD]
Vivaldi, A.:Music of, w. Anthony Bailes (lt), Raymond Leppard (hpd), Hans-Martin Linde (fl/rcr), Leppard, Linde (cnd), English CO, Prague CO, Danske Strings members—Concertino in D, RV.121; Cons. in f, RV.156; in G, RV.435 [Op. 10/4]; in D, RV.429; in F, RV.434 [Op. 10/5]; in D, RV.93; in d, RV.540; Son. in E♭, RV.130 [Al Santo Sepolcro] Classics for Pleasure ▲ CDCFP 4656 [ADD]
Have, Wim ten (vn)
Biber, H. von:Mystery (or Rosary) Sons, w. Troels Svendsen (vn) Karen Englund (hpd)—No. 4 *(rec Strandmarks Church, Copenhagen, Denmark, Sept 1994)* Rondo Gramophon ▲ RCD 8343 [DDD]
Biber, H. von:Son à 3 for 2 Vns, B Trbn, w. Troels Svendsen (vn), Mogens Andresen (b trbn), Karen Englund (hpd) *(rec Strandmarks Church, Copenhagen, Denmark, Sept 1994)* Rondo Gramophon ▲ RCD 8343 [DDD]
Purcell, H.:Pavans, Z.748-751, w. Troels Svendsen (vn), Karen Englund (hpd)—in B♭, Z.750 *(rec Strandmarks Church, Copenhagen, Denmark, Sept 1994)* Rondo Gramophon ▲ RCD 8343 [DDD]
Schmelzer, J.H.:Polish Bagpipes, w. Troels Svendsen (vn), Karen Englund (hpd) *(rec Strandmarks Church, Copenhagen, Denmark, Sept 1994)* Rondo Gramophon ▲ RCD 8343 [DDD]
Havelka, Svatopluk (pno)
Havelka, S.:Dialogues of the Soul with God, w. Kamil Dolezal (cl) *(rec Martínek Studio, Prague, Jan 13, 16, 17, 24 & Feb)* Panton ▲ 811397-2 [DDD]
Havenith, Raymund (pno)
Brahms, J.:Choral Music, w. A. Ickstadt (cnd), Hesse Radio Chorus, Frankfurt Choir—4 Quartets for SATB Choir & Piano, Op. 92 [G] Koch Treasure ▲ 31616-2 [ADD]
Françaix, J.:Trio Vn, Vc & Pno, w. S. Gawriloff (vn), J. Goritzki (vc) *(rec 12/13/89)* Wergo ▲ WER 6198-2 [AAD]
Schnittke, A.:Stille Musik Vc, w. M. Kliegel (vc) Marco Polo ▲ 8.223334
Virtuoso Cello Encores, w. Maria Kliegel (vc) Marco Polo ▲ 8.223403 [DDD]
Havlikova, Klara (pno)
Martinů, B.:Con 4 Pno, w. O. Lenárd (cnd), Slovak Radio Sym CO Campion ▲ 1321 [DDD]
Martinů, B.:Con 5 Pno, w. T. Koutník (cnd), Slovak Radio Sym CO Campion ▲ 1321 [DDD]
Havran, Vladimír (fl)
Respighi, O.:Liriche su parole di poeti armeni, w. Denisa Šlepkovská (mez), Michal Sintál (ob), Gabriel Koncer (cl), Ivan Viskup (b cl), Ivan Paulicka (bn), Frantisek Kovács (trbn), Katarína Vavreková (hp), M. Adriano (cnd) [arr. for chamber group by Adriano] *(rec Slovak Radio Concert Hall, Bratislava, Jan. 4-9, Feb. 19 & June)* Marco Polo ▲ 8.223595 [DDD]
Haward, David (bn)
Biscogli, F.:Con in D, w. E. Schultz (tpt), I. Franklin (ob), V. Czarnecki (cnd), Southwest German CO Pforzheim ebs ▲ ebs 6054 [DDD]
Pezel, J.C.:Son Tpt, w. E. Schultz (tpt), V. Czarnecki (cnd), Southwest German CO Pforzheim ebs ▲ ebs 6054 [DDD]
Hawk-Burt, Debra (ob/E hn)
A Double Reed Consort, w. Wizardsl, Iowa Double Reed Consort [Lissa Stolz (ob), Ronald Tyree (bn), Ronald Snitker (bn/ctbn), Trevor Johnson (hpd)] *(rec Clapp Recital Hall, Univ. of Iowa, Iowa City, Jan. 1993 & May 1994)* CRS Master ▲ CRS 9460
Hawkes, Brian (va)—see ORCHESTRAS & ENSEMBLES Balanescu String Quartet
Hawkins, Brian (va)
Nielsen, C.:Faith & Hope, w. James Galway (fl) *(rec CBS Studios, London, Feb 25, 1986)* RCA Red Seal ▲ 07863-56359-2 [ADD]
Hawkins, Jane (pno)
Fuchs, R.:Fantstücke Va, w. Jonathan Bagg (va) *(rec Baldwin Audit., Durham, NC, Dec 16-18, 1994)* Centaur ▲ CRC 2278 [DDD]
Fuchs, R.:Son Va, w. Jonathan Bagg (va) *(rec Baldwin Audit., Durham, NC, Dec 16-18, 1994)* Centaur ▲ CRC 2278 [DDD]
Fuchs, R.:Trio Vn, Va & Pno, w. Fritz Gearhart (vn), Jonathan Bagg (va) *(rec Baldwin Audit., Durham, NC, Dec 16-18, 1994)* Centaur ▲ CRC 2278 [DDD]
Ward, R.:Serenade for Mallarmé, w. Anna Wilson (fl), Jonathan Bagg (va), Fred Raimi (vc) Albany ▲ TROY 204 [DDD]
Hawthorne, Kelvin (va)
Hawthorne, D.:Night:Near the Wind's Eye, w. R. Stankovsky (cnd), Slovak RSO Bratislava MMC ▲ MMC 2023
Hayachi, Mineo (vc)
Haydn, J.:Trios Cl, Vn & Vc, H.IV/Es1, Es2 & B1, w. Eduard Brunner (cl), Hiroaki Ozeki (vn) *(rec Maebashi Shimin Bunka Kaikan, Aug 31-Sept 2, 1984)* Camerata ▲ 25CM 356 [DDD]
Hayami, K. (pno)
Bernstein, L.:Son Cl, w. Stanley Drucker (cl) Cala Records ("New York Legends" series) ▲ CAL CACD 509 [DDD]
Debussy, C.:Première rapsodie, w. Stanley Drucker (cl) Cala Records ("New York Legends" series) ▲ CAL CACD 509 [DDD]
Kupferman, M.:Five Flings, w. S. Drucker (cl) Soundspells ▲ SP 102
Kupferman, M.:A Little Ivory Con, w. L. Botstein (cnd), Hudson Valley Philharmonic String Quartet, Hudson Valley Wind Quintet Soundspells ▲ SP 101
Kupferman, M.:The Moor's Con, w. K. Krimets (cnd), Moscow SO Soundspells ▲ CD 110 [DDD]
Kupferman, M.:Qnt Pno, w. Laurentian String Quartet Soundspells ▲ SP 101

Hayami, K. (pno) (cont.)
Poulenc, F.:Son Cl Pno, w. Stanley Drucker (cl)
Cala Records ("New York Legends" series) ▲ CAL CACD 509 [DDD]
Siegmeister, E.:Prelude, Blues & Finale, w. Stanley Drucker (cl), Naomi Drucker (cl)
Cala Records ("New York Legends" series) ▲ CAL CACD 509 [DDD]

Hayashi, Mariko (pno)
Devienne, F.:Son 1 Cl, w. Eduard Brunner (cl) *(rec Maebashi Shimin Bunka Kaikan, Aug 31–Sept 2, 1984)* Camerata ▲ 25CM 356 [DDD]
Devienne, F.:Son 2 Cl, w. Eduard Brunner (cl) *(rec Maebashi Shimin Bunka Kaikan, Aug 31–Sept 2, 1984)* Camerata ▲ 25CM 356 [DDD]
Weber, C.M. von:Grand duo concertant Cl, w. Karl Leister (cl) Camerata 2-▲ 25CM71-2 [DDD]
Weber, C.M. von:Vars on a Theme from *Silvana* Cl, w. Karl Leister (cl)
Camerata 2-▲ 25CM71-2 [DDD]

Hayashi, Mineo (vc)
Cassadó, G.:Suite Vc Pavane ▲ ADW 7221 [DDD]
Kodály, Z.:Son Vc, Op. 8 Pavane ▲ ADW 7221 [DDD]
Mayuzumi, T.:Bunkaru Pavane ▲ ADW 7221 [DDD]

Hayden, Seymour (hpd)
Bach, J.S.:Goldberg Vars Boston Skyline ▲ BSD 126 [ADD]
Scarlatti, D.:Sons Kbd—K.1, 6, 87, 146, 208, 248, 249, 262, 377, 443, 462, 525, 551
Boston Skyline ▲ BSD 112 [DDD/ADD] ■ BSC 112

Haydock, Geoffery (cl)—see ORCHESTRAS & ENSEMBLES Classic Trio

Hayes, Jane (pno)
The French Oboe, w. A. Pohran (ob) Mastersound ▲ MST 23 [DDD]

Haym, Y. (ob)
Rossé, F.:Music of, w. P. Ruby (gtr), M. Michalakakos (va), C. Roy (vc), I. Assayag (hpd)—Zembrocordal; Digitales; Lance du Souvenant; Impromptu 0990; For a Little Hot Quaint Time
Quantum ▲ QM 6949

Hayman, Richard (hmc)
Perry, W.:Film Music, w. W. Perry (cnd), Rome PO, Slovak PO, Vienna SO, Slovak Phil Chorus, Vienna Boys' Choir [scores for 6 Mark Twain films originally produced for PBS in the 1980s]—Adventures of Huckleberry Finn; The Innocents Abroad; Life on the Mississippi; The Mysterious Stranger; The Private History of a Campaign That Failed; Pudd'head Wilson Premier ▲ PRCD 1015 [DDD]

Haynes, Bruce (ob)
Handel, G.F.:Cons (3) Ob, w. N. McGegan (cnd), Philharmonia Baroque Orch—in g
Harmonia Mundi France ("Musique d'abord" series) ▲ HMA 1905157

Hays (pno)
Cowell, H.:Pno Music Finnadar ■ CS 9016

Hays, Marian Rian (hp)
Menotti, G.C.:Cantilena e scherzo, w. D. Barra (cnd), San Diego CO
Koch International Classics ▲ KIC 7215 [DDD]

Hayward, Donald (b trbn)—see ORCHESTRAS & ENSEMBLES New Music Consort

Hazelzet, Wilbert (fl)
Bach, C.P.E.:Fl & Pno Music, w. J. Ogg (pno)—Duettos in C, W.73 (H.504) & in E, W.84 (H.506); (Trio) Sonata in B♭, W.161/2 Channel Classics ▲ CCS 0790 [DDD]
Bach, C.P.E.:Son Fl, H.562 *(rec Oct 1992)* Globe ▲ GLO 5091 [DDD]
Bach, C.P.E.:Sons Fl, w. J. Ogg (pno)—in D, H.505 (W.83) Channel Classics ▲ CCS 0790 [DDD]
Bach, C.P.E.:Sons Fl, w. J. Ogg (pno), Christian Norde (vl)—W. 124, 128, 130, 131 & 134 *(rec Oct 1992)* Globe ▲ GLO 5091 [DDD]
Bach, C.P.E.:Trio Son Fl, H.367, w. Alda Stuurop (vn), Richte van der Meer (vc), Jacques Ogg (hpd) *(rec Utrecht, Sept 1993)* Globe ▲ GLO 5110 [DDD]
Bach, C.P.E.:Trio Son Fl, H.371, w. Alda Stuurop (vn), Richte van der Meer (vc), Jacques Ogg (hpd) *(rec Utrecht, Sept 1993)* Globe ▲ GLO 5110 [DDD]
Bach, C.P.E.:Trio Son Fl, H.570, w. Alda Stuurop (vn), Richte van der Meer (vc), Jacques Ogg (hpd) *(rec Utrecht, Sept 1993)* Globe ▲ GLO 5110 [DDD]
Bach, C.P.E.:Trio Son Fl, H.574, w. Alda Stuurop (vn), Richte van der Meer (vc), Jacques Ogg (hpd) *(rec Utrecht, Sept 1993)* Globe ▲ GLO 5110 [DDD]
Bach, C.P.E.:Trio Son for 2 Fls, H.580, w. Kate Clarke (fl), Alda Stuurop (vn), Richte van der Meer (vc), Jacques Ogg (hpd) *(rec Utrecht, Sept 1993)* Globe ▲ GLO 5110 [DDD]
Telemann, G.P.:Qts Vn, w. Sonnerie Trio—Quartets 8 & 12, & the Concerto Primo in G & Sonata Primo in A from the first six quartets Virgin Classics ▲ 59049 [DDD]

Hazelzet, Wilbert (trns fl)
de Fesch, W.:Trio Sons, Op. 7, w. M. Huggett (vn), T. Koopman (hpd)—No. 4 in g
Erasmus ▲ WVH 010 [ADD]
Focking, H. von:Sons Fl, w. T. Koopman (hpd)—in D, Op. 1/5 Erasmus ▲ WVH 010 [ADD]
Hotteterre, J.:Music of, w. Jaap ter Linden (vl), Konrad Junghänel (thb), Jacques Ogg (hpd)—5 Airs; Passacaille; 8 Preludes in b, c, C, D, g, g, G, G; 3 Suites in c, g, G *(rec San Miguel Church, Cuenca, Spain, May 1996)* Glossa ▲ GCD 920801 [DDD]
Philidor, P.:Music of, w. K. Clark (trns fl), M. Fentross (lt/thb), T. Zwart (vl), J. Ogg (hpd)—Trios 1 & 2 in G & e for 2 Flutes & Continuo; Suite No. 3 in D for 2 Flutes; Suites Nos. 5, 6 & 12 in e, b & D for Flute & Continuo *(rec June 1993)* Globe ▲ GLO 5107 [DDD]

Hazleton, Tom (org)
The Pipes of the Mighty Wurlitzer Klavier ▲ KCD 77014 [DDD]
Ragtime's Greatest Hits Pro Arte ▲ CDD 445 [DDD]

He, Qiu Xia (pipa)
Armanini, M.:Of Wind, w. J. Zoltek (cnd), Bohuslav Martinů PO Chroma ▲ CHR CD 10001 [DDD]

Headley, Erin (h-g)
Proensa, w. Paul Hillier (bass), Stephen Stubbs (lt/voc), Andrew Lawrence-King (hp/voc)
ECM New Series ▲ 78118-21368-2 [DDD]

Headley, Erin (vl)—see also ORCHESTRAS & ENSEMBLES Tragicomedia
Hasse, J.A.:Arias, w. Malcolm Proud (hpd)—Ah Dio, ritornate [from *La conversione di Sant'Agostino*] *(rec May 30–June 1, 1991)* CRD ▲ CRD 3488 [DDD]
Hasse, J.A.:Cants, w. Julianne Baird (sop), Malcolm Proud (hpd)—Quel vago seno, O Fille; Fille dolce, mio bene *(rec May 30–June 1, 1991)* CRD ▲ CRD 3488 [DDD]
Virtuoso Solo Music for Cornetto, w. Bruce Dickey (cornetto), Stephen Stubbs (chit/vih), Andrew Lawrence-King (double hp/Renaissance hp) Accent ▲ 9173 [DDD]

Heagney, Robert (hpd)
Bach, J.S.:Sons Fl, BWV 1030–35, w. V. Hill (fl), J. Johnson (vc)—BWV 1030, 1032 & 1033 *(rec 1989)* Move ▲ MD 3118 [DDD]
Bach, J.S.:Sons Vn, w. V. Hill (vn), J. Johnson (vc)—BWV 1020 [doubtful; trans. for flute & continuo] *(rec 1989)* Move ▲ MD 3118 [DDD]

Heard, Cornelia (vn)—see ORCHESTRAS & ENSEMBLES Blair String Quartet
Hearn, Steven (cl)—see ORCHESTRAS & ENSEMBLES Kalamos Clarinet Quartet
Heath, K. (pno)—see ORCHESTRAS & ENSEMBLES Piano Circus

Heath, Kenneth (vc)
Vivaldi, A.:Cons Vc, w. N. Marriner (cnd), Academy of St. Martin in the Fields—in c
London ■ 417100-4

Heath, S. (hpd)
Bach, J.S.:Con 4 Hpd, w. J. Rees (cnd), Scottish Ensemble Virgin Classics ▲ CDZ 59641

Heath, S. (vc)
Virgo Collections, w. Jane Murdoch (vn), C. Dale (vn), Scottish Ensemble [cnd:J. Rees (vn)]
Virgin Classics ▲ CDZ 59652

Heaton, Roger (cl)—see also ORCHESTRAS & ENSEMBLES Gavin Bryars Ensemble
Bryars, G.:After the Requiem, w. A. Balanescu, G. Bryars, B. Frisell, R. Heaton, et al.
ECM New Series ▲ 78118-21424-2 [DDD]
Bryars, G.:Alaric I or II, w. A. Balanescu, G. Bryars, B. Frisell, et al.
ECM New Series ▲ 78118-21424-2 [DDD]
Bryars, G.:Allegrasco, w. A. Balanescu, G. Bryars, B. Frisell, et al.
ECM New Series ▲ 78118-21424-2 [DDD]

Heaton, Roger (cl) (cont.)
Bryars, G.:Four Elements, w. Large Chamber Ensemble ECM New Series ▲ 78118-21533-2 [DDD]
Bryars, G.:The Old Tower of Löbenicht, w. A. Balanescu (vn), B. Frisell (elec gtr), G. Bryars (db), et al.
ECM New Series ▲ 78118-21424-2 [DDD]
Gough, O.:Currulao, w. Beverly Davison (vn), Bruce Nockles (tpt), John Pigneguy (hn), David Stewart (trbn), Tracey Goldsmith (acc), Orlando Gough (kbd), Paul Clarvis (perc) *(rec London, 1995)*
Catalyst ▲ 0902-668332-2 [DDD]
Gough, O.:Late, w. Melinda Maxwell (ob), Orlando Gough (kbd), Smith String Quartet *(rec London, 1995)*
Catalyst ▲ 0902-668332-2 [DDD]
Mendelssohn, F.:Concert Pieces, w. V. Soames (cl), J. Drake (pno)—Nos. 1 & 2
Clarinet Classics ▲ CC 0003
New Music for Multi-Tracked Clarinets, w. S. Limbrick (perc), D. Smith (pno)
Clarinet Classics ▲ CC 0009

Heavner, T. (perc)
Belden, G.:Gilgamesh, w. S. D. Belden (cta), M. Stratman (pno) [E] Capstone ▲ CPS 8613

Hebb, Bernard (gtr)—see also ORCHESTRAS & ENSEMBLES Duo Geminiani
Granados, E.:Danzas españolas (10), w. G. Ribke (vc) [arr vc & gtr] Ambitus ▲ 97880
Music for 2 Guitars, w. Klaus Wollny (gtr) Entrée ▲ 0054 [ADD]
Tchaikovsky, P.:Morceaux, Op. 51, w. G. Ribke (vc) [trans. for string] Ambitus ▲ 97880

Hecher, Gert (pno)
Clementi, M.:Sons Pno—in B♭, Op. 12/1; in f♯, Op. 25/5; in b, Op. 40/2 *(rec Marble Hall of the Neue Burg, Vienna, Mar 1994)* Dorian Discovery ▲ DIS 80134 [DDD]

Hecht, Thomas (pno)
Schumann, R.:Adagio & Allegro Hn, w. L. William Kuyper (hn) *(rec Performing Arts Ctr/Purchase College–State Univ of NY Recital Hall, May 8, 1995)* Elysium ▲ GRK 709 [DDD]
Schumann, R.:Andante & Vars Hn, w. Sandra Shapiro (pno), Gerald Appleman (vc), Alan Stepansky (vc), L. William Kuyper (Fr hn) *(rec Performing Arts Ctr/Purchase College–State Univ of NY Recital Hall, May 8, 1995)* Elysium ▲ GRK 709 [DDD]
Schumann, R.:Romances Ob, w. Joseph Robinson (ob) *(rec Performing Arts Ctr/Purchase College–State Univ of NY Recital Hall, May 8, 1995)* Elysium ▲ GRK 709 [DDD]

Hector, William (vn)—see ORCHESTRAS & ENSEMBLES Valley String Quartet

Hedinger, Christine (pno)
Martinů, B.:Son 1 Vc, w. M. Brady (vc) Koch Schwann ▲ 310 107 [DDD]
Martinů, B.:Son Fl & Pno, w. F. Renggli (fl) Koch Schwann ▲ 310 107 [DDD]
Martinů, B.:Trio Fl, w. F. Renggli (fl), M. Brady (vc) Koch Schwann ▲ 310 107 [DDD]

Hedrich, Christian (va)—see ORCHESTRAS & ENSEMBLES German String Trio

Heerema, Nicolette (org)
Andriessen, L.:Anachrony 1, w. Nico de Rooij (pno), Sepp Grotenhuis (cel), Douceline Aleven (hp), Arthur Cune (vib), H. Williams (cnd), Netherlands Ballet Orch *(rec Amsterdam Music Theater, Oct 3–6, 1994)* Donemus ▲ CV 54 [DDD]

Heffernan, James (cl)—see ORCHESTRAS & ENSEMBLES Kalamos Clarinet Quartet

Heffner, Diane (cl)
Kraft, William:Con Perc, w. Dean Anderson (perc), Renee Krimsier (fl), Nancy Cirillo (vn/va), Ronald Lowry (vc), Hugh Hinton (pno) Albany ▲ TROY 218 [DDD]
Kraft, William:Gallery 4–5, w. Nancy Cirillo (vn), Ronald Copes (va), Ronald Lowry (vc), Hugh Hinton (pno) Albany ▲ TROY 218 [DDD]
Kraft, William:Settings from Pierrot Lunaire, w. Jane Manning (sop), Renee Krimsier (fl), Nancy Cirillo (vn/va), Ronald Lowry (vc), Dean Anderson (perc), Hugh Hinton (pno) Albany ▲ TROY 218 [DDD]

Hefti, Jakob (hn)
Reinecke, C.:Trio Pno, Op. 274, w. H.R. Stalder (cl), J. von Vintschger (pno) *(rec 1987)*
Jecklin-Disco ▲ JD 602-2 [ADD]
Wehrli, W.:Trio 3 Vn, w. Gunar Larsens (vn), Anne de Dadelsen (pno) *(rec 1989)*
Jecklin ▲ JS 301-2 [ADD]

Hegedüs, Endre (pno)
Liszt, F.:Operatic Paraphrases & Transcriptions—Réminiscences de Lucrezia Borgia:Grand fantaisie, S.400; Lucie de Lammermoor:Funeral March & Cavatine, S.398; Réminiscences de Lucia di Lammermoor, S.397; Valse à capriccio on 2 motifs from Lucia et Parisina, S.401; I puritani:Introduction et polonaise, S.391; Divertissement on the Cavatine "I tuoi frequenti palpiti", S.419 Hungaroton ▲ HCD 31547 [DDD]
Miaskovsky, N.:Sons Pno—No. 2 in f♯, Op. 13; No. 3 in c, Op. 19; No. 5 in B, Op. 64/1
Marco Polo ▲ 8.223156
Miaskovsky, N.:Sons Pno—No. 6 in A♭, Op. 64/2; No. 7 in C, Op. 82; No. 8 in d, Op. 83; No. 9 in F, Op. 84 Marco Polo ▲ 8.223178
Miaskovsky, N.:Sons Pno—Nos. 1 in d, Op. 6 & No. 4 in c, Op. 27 *(rec Aug. 3–11, Dec. 27–28, 1991)*
Marco Polo ▲ 8.223469 [DDD]

Hegedüs, M. (fl)
Mercadante, S.:Cons (6) Fl (1819), w. K. Botvay (cnd), Budapest Strings—in e
LaserLight ▲ 15634 [DDD]
Mercadante, S.:Con in e Fl, Op. 57, w. K. Botvay (cnd), Budapest Strings LaserLight ▲ 14037 [DDD]

Hegedüs, Olga (vc)
Schumann, R.:Andante & Vars Hn, w. P. Frankl (pno), A. Schiff (pno), L. Varga (vc), A. Halstead (hn)
Vox Box 3-▲ CD3X 3001 [ADD]

Hegen, Irene (pno)
Bon Di Venezia, A.:Sons Fl, Op. 1, w. S. Dreier (fl) *(rec Sept. 1992)* CPO ▲ CPO 999181-2 [DDD]

Heger, Simonetta (pno)
Finzi, A.:Lyrics, w. Laura Crescini (sop) Nuova Era ▲ NUO 7249
Finzi, A.:Pavane Nuova Era ▲ NUO 7249
Finzi, A.:Son Vn, w. Giambattista Pianezzola (vn) Nuova Era ▲ NUO 7249

Hegner, Louis (db)
Nielsen, C.:Serenata in vano, w. A. Oxenvad (cl), K. Larsson (bn), H. Sorensen (hn), L. Jensen (vc) *(rec Feb. 2, 1937)* Clarinet Classics ▲ CC 0002

Hegyi, Ildikó (vn)
Beethoven, L. van:Septet Strs, w. Győző Máthé (va), Péter Szabó (vc), István Tóth (db), Jozsef Balogh (cl), Jenő Keveházi (hn), József Vajda (bn) *(rec Scottish Church, Budapest, Apr. 21–23 & May 29–31, 1)* Naxos ▲ 8.553090 [DDD]
Beethoven, L. van:Sxt Hns, Op. 81b, w. Jenő Keveházi (hn), János Keveházi (hn), Péter Popa (vn), Győző Máthé (va), Péter Szabó (vc) *(rec Scottish Church, Budapest)* Naxos ▲ 8.553090 [DDD]
Hadley, H.:Scherzo diabolique, Albany SO New World ▲ NW 321-2 [DDD]

Heidenreich, F. (db)
Lachner, F.P.:Nonet, w. A. Duisberg (fl), D. Wollenweber (ob), P. Prieditis (cl), P. Douglas (hn), M. Postinghel (bn), I. Grünkorn (vn), M. Gieler (va), T. Ruge (vc) *(rec June 10, 1991)*
Thorofon ▲ CTH 2132 [DDD]

Heider, Werner (pno)
Togni, C.:Gesang zur Nacht, w. Carla Henius (alt), Saschko Gawriloff (vn), Hans Damzel (cl), Mariolina de Robertis (pno) Stradivarius ▲ STV DTM 90002 [ADD]

Heidsieck, Eric (pno)
Hommage à Rouget de Lisle Arb ▲ DOM 1404

Heifetz, Daniel (vn)
Hoiby, L.:Son Vn, w. Lee Hoiby (pno) Master Muscians Collective ▲ MMC 2038 [DDD]
Richter, M.:Landscapes of the Mind II, w. M. Skelly (pno) Leonarda ▲ LE 337

Heifetz, E. (cl)
Avni, T.:Leda & the Swan, w. E. Berendsen (sgr) Symposium ▲ 1110

Heifetz, Galina (vn)
Prokofiev, S.:Cinderella (sels), w. Arnold Kaplan (pno)—Var of the Winter Fairy; Gavotte; Grand Waltz [all trans Mikhail Fikhtengoltz] *(rec Music Hall, Tarrytown, NY, May 28–30, 1994)*
Connoisseur Society ▲ CD 4204
Prokofiev, S.:Son Vn, Op. 94bis, w. Arnold Kaplan (pno) *(rec Music Hall, Tarrytown, NY, May 28–30, 1994)* Connoisseur Society ▲ CD 4204

Heifetz, Galina (vn) (cont.)
Prokofiev, S.:Son 1 Vn, w. Arnold Kaplan (pno) *(rec Music Hall, Tarrytown, NY, May 28–30, 1994)* Connoisseur Society ▲ CD 4204
Russian Music for Violin & Piano, w. A. Kaplan (pno) Connoisseur Society ▲ CD 4196

Heifetz, Inna (pno)
Bach, J.S.:Con 1 Hpd, w. E. Blank (cnd), Russian CO Sonora ▲ SO 22564CD [DDD]
Bach, J.S.:Con 1 for 2 Hpds, w. N. Zusman (pno), E. Blank (cnd), Russian CO Sonora ▲ SO 22564CD [DDD]
Bach, J.S.:Italian Con Sonora ▲ SO 22564CD [DDD]
Borodin, A.:Tarantella, w. Natalia Zusman (pno) *(rec Tsai Performance Center, Boston)* Sonora ▲ SO 22566 [DDD]
Glière, R.:Pieces for 2 Pnos, Op. 41, w. Natalia Zusman (pno) *(rec Tsai Performance Center, Boston)* Sonora ▲ SO 22566 [DDD]
Liszt, F.:Consolations Sonora ▲ SO 22561
Liszt, F.:Consolations—Nos. 1-5 Sonora ▲ SO 22565
Liszt, F.:Consolations—Nos. 1-5 Sonora ▲ SON 565 [DDD]
Liszt, F.:Hungarian Rhaps—Nos. 6 & 12 Sonora ▲ SO 22561
Liszt, F.:Mephisto Waltz 3 Pno Sonora ▲ SO 22561
Liszt, F.:Operatic Paraphrases & Transcriptions—Verdi:Rigoletto Fant Sonora ▲ SO 22561
Liszt, F.:Pno Music (misc)—Mephisto-Waltz; Consolations (6); Hungarian Rhaps. No. 6 & 12; Polish Songs (6); Rigoletto Fant. Sonora ▲ SO 22561 ■ SO 22561
Liszt, F.:Song Transcriptions—The Maiden's Wish; Spring; My Darling Sonora ▲ SO 22565
Liszt, F.:Song Transcriptions—Chopin:6 Polish Songs Sonora ▲ SO 22561
Liszt, F.:Transcriptions & Paraphrases—Chopin:The Maiden's Wish; Spring; My Darling Sonora ▲ SON 565 [DDD]
Prokofiev, S.:Music for Children Sonora ▲ SO 22563 [DDD] ■ SO 22563
Prokofiev, S.:Pno Music (misc)—Regrets; Evening Sonora ▲ SON 565 [DDD]
Prokofiev, S.:Pno Music (misc)—Regrets; Evening Sonora ▲ SO 22565
Prokofiev, S.:Son 3 Pno Sonora ▲ SO 22562
Prokofiev, S.:Toccata Pno Sonora ▲ SO 22562
Rachmaninoff, S.:Moments musicaux—Nos. 1, 4 & 5 Sonora ▲ SO 22562
Rachmaninoff, S.:Moments musicaux—Nos. 1 & 5 Sonora ▲ SO 22565
Rachmaninoff, S.:Morceaux de fant—No. 4 [Polichinelle] Sonora ▲ SO 22562
Schnittke, A.:The Revisionist's Tale, w. Natalia Zusman (pno) *(rec Tsai Performance Center, Boston)* Sonora ▲ SO 22566 [DDD]
Scriabin, A.:Etudes Pno, Op. 8—Nos. 11 & 12 Sonora ▲ SO 22562 ■ SO 22562
Scriabin, A.:Etudes Pno, Op. 8—No. 11 Sonora ▲ SO 22565
Scriabin, A.:Etudes Pno, Op. 8—No. 11 Sonora ▲ SON 565 [DDD]
Shostakovich, D.:Concertino for 2 Pnos, w. Natalia Zusman (pno) *(rec Tsai Performance Center, Boston)* Sonora ▲ SO 22566 [DDD]
Shostakovich, D.:Dances of the Dolls Sonora ▲ SO 22563 [DDD] ■ SO 22563
Tchaikovsky, P.:Album pour enfants Sonora ▲ SO 22563 [DDD] ■ SO 22563
Tchaikovsky, P.:Album pour enfants—No. 21, Douce rêverie in C; No. 23, A l'église in e Sonora ▲ SON 565 [DDD]
Tchaikovsky, P.:Dumka:Russian Rustic Scene Sonora ▲ SO 22562
Tchaikovsky, P.:Morceaux, Op. 19—No. 4 Sonora ▲ SO 22565
Tchaikovsky, P.:Morceaux, Op. 19—No. 4 in c# [nocturne] Sonora ▲ SO 22562
Tchaikovsky, P.:Pno Music—Sweet Dreams; At Church Sonora ▲ SO 22565
Tchaikovsky, P.:Pieces Pno, Op. 1—No. 1 Sonora ▲ SO 22562 ■ SO 22562

Heifetz, Jascha (vn)
The Acoustic Recordings *(rec 1917–24)* RCA Gold Seal 3-▲ 0942-2-RG [ADD]
Bach, J.S.:Con for 2 Vns, w. E. Friedman (vn), M. Sargent (cnd), London New SO RCA Red Seal ▲ 6778-2-RC [ADD]
Bach, J.S.:English Suites—BWV 808 arr. Heifetz for solo violin EMI Classics ▲ CDH 64494-2
Bach, J.S.:Sinfs, w. E. Bay (pno)—Nos. 3 in D, 4 in d & 9 in f RCA Gold Seal ▲ 7964-2-RG [ADD] ■ 7964-4-RG (CrO2)
Bach, J.S.:Sons & Partitas Vn, BWV 1001-1006—BWV 1002, 1003, 1004 & 1006 EMI Classics ▲ CDH 64494-2
Bach, J.S.:Sons & Partitas Vn, BWV 1001-1006—No. 2, BWV 1004 *(rec London, 1935 & 1937)* Grammofono 2000 ▲ GRM 78511 [ADD]
Bach, J.S.:Sons & Partitas Vn, BWV 1001-1006—Son 1, BWV 1001 *(rec Dec 11, 1935)* Iron Needle ▲ IN 1351 [ADD]
Bach, J.S.:Sons & Partitas Vn, BWV 1001-1006 RCA Gold Seal 2-▲ 7708-2 RG (m) [ADD] 2-■ 7708-4 RRG13 (CrO2)
Beethoven, L. van:Con Vn, Op. 61, w. A. Toscanini (cnd), NBC SO RCA Gold Seal ▲ 60261-2-RG (m) [ADD] ■ 60261-4-RG
Beethoven, L. van:Con Vn, Op. 61, w. A. Rodzinski (cnd), New York PO *(rec live, Jan. 14, 1945)* As Disc ▲ ASD 2500 (m)
Beethoven, L. van:Con Vn, Op. 61, w. C. Munch (cnd), Boston SO RCA Red Seal ▲ RCD1-5402
Beethoven, L. van:Con Vn, Op. 61, w. A. Rodzinski (cnd), New York PO *(rec 1945)* Legend ▲ LGD 123 [ADD]
Beethoven, L. van:Con Vn, Op. 61, w. D. Mitropoulos (cnd), New York PO *(rec live, Feb 12, 1956)* Prelude ▲ PRE 2160 [ADD]
Beethoven, L. van:Con Vn, Op. 61, w. C. Munch (cnd), Boston SO RCA ■ AGK1-5242
Beethoven, L. van:Con Vn, Op. 61, w. C. Munch (cnd), Boston SO *(rec Symphony Hall, Boston, Nov 27–28, 1955)* RCA Red Seal ▲ 09026-61742-2 [ADD]
Beethoven, L. van:Serenade Strs, Op. 8, w. W. Primrose (va), G. Piatigorsky (vc) RCA Gold Seal ▲ 7870-2-RG (m/s) [ADD]
Beethoven, L. van:Sons Vn (comp), w. E. Bay (pno)—Nos. 1–4 RCA Gold Seal ▲ 7704-2 RC (m) [ADD] ■ 7704-4 RC (m)
Beethoven, L. van:Sons Vn (comp), w. E. Bay (pno)—Nos. 5-7 RCA Gold Seal ▲ 7705-2 RC (m) [ADD] ■ 7705-4 RC (m)
Beethoven, L. van:Sons Vn (comp), w. E. Bay (pno)—Nos. 8-10 RCA Gold Seal ▲ 7706-2 RC (m) [ADD] ■ 7706-4 RC (m)
Beethoven, L. van:Trio 6 Pno, "Archduke", w. A. Rubinstein (pno), E. Feuermann (vc) RCA Gold Seal ▲ 09026-60926-2 ■ 09026-60926-4
Beethoven, L. van:Trios Strs, Op. 9, w. W. Primrose (va), G. Piatigorsky (vc)—No. 2 RCA Gold Seal ▲ 7873-2-RG [ADD] ■ 7873-4-RG
Brahms, J.:Con Vn, w. S. Koussevitzky (cnd), Boston SO *(rec 1935–41)* Pearl 2-▲ PEA 9167 [ADD]
Brahms, J.:Con Vn, w. S. Koussevitzky (cnd), Boston SO *(rec Symphony Hall, Boston, Apr 11, 1939)* RCA Gold Seal 2-▲ 09026-61735-2 [ADD]
Brahms, J.:Con Vn, w. F. Reiner (cnd), Chicago SO *(rec Orchestra Hall, Chicago, Feb 21–22, 1955)* RCA Red Seal ▲ 09026-61742-2 [ADD]
Brahms, J.:Con Vn, w. F. Reiner (cnd), Chicago SO *(rec 1955 & 1957)* RCA Gold Seal ▲ 09026-61495-2 ■ 09026-61495-4
Brahms, J.:Con Vn, w. F. Reiner (cnd), Chicago SO RCA Red Seal ▲ RCD1-5402
Brahms, J.:Con Vn, w. G. Szell (cnd), New York PO *(rec live, Dec 9, 1951)* Prelude ▲ PRE 2160 (m) [ADD]
Brahms, J.:Con Vn & Vc, "Double Con", w. Emanuel Feuermann (vc), E. Ormandy (cnd), Philadelphia Orch *(rec Dec 21, 1939)* Iron Needle ▲ IN 1351 [ADD]
Brahms, J.:Con Vn & Vc, "Double Con", w. G. Piatigorsky (vc), A. Wallenstein (cnd), RCA Victor SO RCA Red Seal ▲ 6778-2-RC [ADD]
Brahms, J.:Hungarian Dances Pno 4-Hands, w. B. Smith (pno)—Nos. 11,17 & 20 [arr. violin & piano] RCA Gold Seal ▲ 7965-2-RG [ADD]
Brahms, J.:Qt 3 Pno, w. J. Lateiner (pno), S. Schonbach (va), G. Piatigorsky (vc) RCA Gold Seal ▲ 7873-2-RG [ADD] ■ 7873-4-RG
Brahms, J.:Sextet Strs, Op. 36, w. I. Baker (vn), W. Primrose (va), V. Majewski (va), G. Piatigorsky (vc), G. Rejto (vc) RCA Gold Seal ▲ 7965-2-RG [ADD]
Brahms, J.:Son 2 Vn, w. E. Bay (pno) *(rec 1936)* Biddulph ▲ LAB 011 [ADD]

Heifetz, Jascha (vn) (cont.)
Brahms, J.:Son 2 Vn, w. Emanuel Bay (pno) *(rec RCA Studio 3, New York, Jan 31, 1936)* RCA Gold Seal 2-▲ 09026-61735-2 [ADD]
Bruch, M.:Con 1 Vn, w. M. Sargent (cnd), London New SO *(rec Walthamstow Town Hall, London, May 14 & 16, 1962)* RCA Red Seal ▲ 09026-61745-2 [ADD]
Bruch, M.:Con 2 Vn, w. I. Solomon (cnd), RCA Victor SO RCA Gold Seal ▲ 09026-60927-2 ■ 09026-60927-4
Bruch, M.:Scottish Fant Vn, w. Osian Ellis (hp), M. Sargent (cnd), London New SO *(rec Walthamstow Town Hall, London, May 15 & 22, 1961)* RCA Red Seal ▲ 09026-61745-2 [ADD]
Castelnuovo-Tedesco, M.:Con 2 Vn, "The Prophets", w. A. Wallenstein (cnd), Los Angeles PO RCA Gold Seal ▲ 7872-2-RG (m/s) [ADD]
Chausson, E.:Poème Vn, w. I. Solomon (cnd), RCA Victor SO RCA Gold Seal ▲ 7709-2 RG [ADD] ■ 7709-4 RG6 (CrO2)
Conus, J.:Con Vn, w. I. Solomon (cnd), RCA Victor SO RCA Gold Seal ▲ 09026-60927-2 ■ 09026-60927-4
Debussy, C.:Preludes Pno (sels), w. E. Bay (pno) [arr. for violin & piano]—Book 1, No. 8, "La fille aux cheveux de lin" RCA Gold Seal ▲ 7871-2-RG (m) [ADD]
Debussy, C.:Son Vn, w. E. Bay (pno) RCA Gold Seal ▲ 7871-2-RG (m/s) [ADD]
The Decca Masters, Vol. 1, w. Emanuel Bay (pno), Milton Kaye (pno) *(rec 1944–46)* MCA Classics ▲ MCAD 42211 (m) [ADD]
The Decca Masters, Vol. 2 (1944–1946), w. Emanuel Bay (pno), Milton Kaye (pno), Bing Crosby (sgr) *(rec 1944–46)* MCA Classics ▲ MCAD 42212 (m) [ADD]
Dohnányi, E. von:Serenade, w. W. Primrose (va), E. Feuermann (vc) Biddulph ▲ LAB 074 [ADD]
Dvořák, A.:Qnt Pno, Op. 81, w. J. Lateiner (pno), M. Baker (va), J. de Pasquale (va), G. Piatigorsky (vc) RCA Gold Seal ▲ 7965–2–RG [ADD]
The Early Victor Recordings *(rec 1917–18)* Biddulph ▲ LAB 015 [ADD]
Elgar, E.:Con Vn, w. M. Sargent (cnd), London SO RCA Gold Seal ▲ 7966–2–RG (m) [ADD]
Fauré, G.:Son 1 Vn, w. E. Bay (pno) *(rec 1936)* Biddulph ▲ LAB 065 [ADD]
Fauré, G.:Son 1 Vn, w. Emanuel Bay (pno) *(rec RCA Studio 3, New York, Feb 10, 1936)* RCA Gold Seal 2-▲ 09026-61735-2 [ADD]
Ferguson, H.:Son 1 Vn, w. L. Steuber (pno) RCA Gold Seal ▲ 7872–2–RG (m/s) [ADD]
Françaix, J.:Trio Vn, Va & Vc, w. J. de Pasquale (va), G. Piatigorsky (vc) RCA Gold Seal ▲ 7872–2–RG (m/s) [ADD]
Franck, C.:Son Vn, w. A. Rubinstein (pno) *(rec 4/3/37; from HMV DB 3206/)* Biddulph ▲ LAB 025 [ADD]
Gershwin, G.:Porgy & Bess (suite) Vn & Pno, w. *(pianist unknown)* RCA Gold Seal ▲ 09026-60928-2; ■ 09026-60928-4
Glazunov, A.:Con Vn, w. W. Hendl (cnd), RCA Victor SO RCA Red Seal ▲ RCD1-7019
Glazunov, A.:Con Vn, *(cnd & orch unknown)* Memories 2-▲ MEM CD 3011
Glazunov, A.:Con Vn, w. J. Barbirolli (cnd), London PO *(rec 1934)* Biddulph ▲ LAB 026 [ADD]
Glazunov, A.:Con Vn, w. W. Hendl (cnd), RCA Victor SO *(rec Santa Monica Civic Auditorium, CA, June 3 & 4, 1963)* RCA Red Seal ▲ 09026-61744-2 [ADD]
Glazunov, A.:Con Vn, w. J. Barbirolli (cnd), London PO *(rec 1934)* EMI Classics ("Great Recordings of the Century" series) ▲ CDH 64030
Glazunov, A.:Con Vn, w. J. Barbirolli (cnd), London PO *(rec Mar 28, 1934)* Iron Needle ▲ IN 1351 [ADD]
Glazunov, A.:Con Vn, w. J. Barbirolli (cnd), London PO *(rec 1934–40)* Pearl ▲ PEA 9157 [ADD]
Grieg, E.:Sons Vn, Opp. 8, 13 & 45, w. E. Bay (pno)—Sonata No. 2, Op. 13 *(rec 1936)* Biddulph ▲ LAB 065 [ADD]
Grieg, E.:Son 2 Vn, w. Brooks Smith (pno) *(rec Radio Recorders, Hollywood, Dec 15, 1955)* RCA Gold Seal 2-▲ 09026-61740-2 (m) [ADD]
Halvorsen, J.:Passacaglia & Sarabande con variazioni, w. W. Primrose (va) Biddulph ▲ LAB 074 [ADD]
Handel, G.F.:Sons Vn & Kbd, w. Emanuel Bay (pno)—No. 15 in E *(rec Radio Recorders, Hollywood, Nov 30, 1953)* RCA Gold Seal 2-▲ 09026-61740-2 (m) [ADD]
Handel, G.F.:Suites Hpd, w. William Primrose (va)—No. 7 in g [Passacaglia; trans Halvorsen for vn & va] *(rec RCA Studio 2, New York City, May 22, 1941)* RCA Gold Seal 2-▲ 09026-61740-2 (m) [ADD]
The Heifetz Collection RCA Gold Seal 66-▲ 09026-61778-2
Heifetz Plays Gershwin (& Encores) RCA Gold Seal ▲ 09026-60928-2
Khachaturian, K.:Son Vn, w. L. Steuber (pno) RCA Gold Seal ▲ 7872–2–RG (m/s) [ADD]
Korngold, E.W.:Con Vn, w. A. Wallenstein (cnd), Los Angeles PO RCA Gold Seal ▲ 7963–2–RG [ADD]
Martinů, B.:Duo Vn & Vc, w. G. Piatigorsky (vc) RCA Gold Seal ▲ 7871–2–RG (m/s) [ADD]
Mendelssohn, F.:Con in e Vn & Orch, Op. 64, w. G. Cantelli (cnd), New York PO *(rec live, Mar. 14, 1954)* As Disc ▲ ASD 2500 (m)
Mendelssohn, F.:Con in e Vn & Orch, Op. 64, w. C. Munch (cnd), Boston SO RCA Red Seal ▲ 5933–2–RC
Mendelssohn, F.:Con in e Vn & Orch, Op. 64, w. A. Toscanini (cnd), NBC SO *(rec live)* Melodram ▲ MEL 18013
Mendelssohn, F.:Con in e Vn & Orch, Op. 64, w. C. Munch (cnd), Boston SO *(rec Symphony Hall, Boston, Feb 23–25, 1959)* RCA Red Seal ▲ 09026-61743-2 [ADD]
Mendelssohn, F.:Trio 1 Pno, w. A. Rubenstein (pno), G. Piatigorsky (vc) RCA Gold Seal ▲ 7768–2–RG (m) [ADD]
Mozart, W.A.:Con 4 Vn, w. T. Beecham (cnd), Royal PO *(rec 1947)* EMI Classics ("Great Recordings of the Century" series) ▲ CDH 63820
Mozart, W.A.:Con 5 Vn, w. J. Barbirolli (cnd), London PO *(rec 1934–40)* Pearl ▲ PEA 9157 [ADD]
Mozart, W.A.:Con 5 Vn, w. M. Sargent (cnd), London SO RCA Gold Seal ▲ 7869–2 (m/s) [ADD] ■ 7869–4 (m/s)
Mozart, W.A.:Con 5 Vn, w. J. Barbirolli (cnd), London PO *(rec Feb. 23, 1934 for HMV)* Biddulph ▲ LAB 012 [AAD]
Mozart, W.A.:Con 5 Vn, *(orch unknown)* Memories ("Golden" series) 2-▲ MEM 3007
Mozart, W.A.:Duo Vn, K.424, w. W. Primrose (va) Biddulph ▲ LAB 074 [ADD]
Mozart, W.A.:Duo Vn, K.424, w. William Primrose (va) *(rec RCA Studio 2, New York City & RCA Studios, Hollywood, May 22 & Aug 29, 1941)* RCA Gold Seal 2-▲ 09026-61740-2 (m) [ADD]
Mozart, W.A.:Qnt Strs, K.516, w. I. Baker (vn), W. Primrose (va), V. Majewski (va), G. Piatigorsky (vc) RCA Gold Seal ▲ 7869–2 (m/s) [ADD] ■ 7869–4 (m/s)
Mozart, W.A.:Sinf concertante Vn, K.364, w. W. Primrose (va), I. Solomon (cnd), RCA Victor SO RCA Red Seal ▲ 6778–2 [ADD]
Mozart, W.A.:Sons Vn Pno (misc), w. E. Bay (pno)—K.378 & 454 *(rec 1936 for HMV)* Biddulph ▲ LAB 012 [AAD]
Mozart, W.A.:Sons Vn Pno (misc), w. Emanuel Bay (pno)—in B♭, K.378; in B♭, K.454 *(rec RCA Studio 3, New York City, Feb 10, 1936)* RCA Gold Seal 2-▲ 09026-61740-2 (m) [ADD]
Mozart, W.A.:Sons Vn Pno (misc), w. Smith (pno)—K.378 RCA Gold Seal ▲ 7869–2 (m/s) [ADD] ■ 7869–4 (m/s)
Mozart, W.A.:Trio Vn, K.563, w. William Primrose (va), Emanuel Feuermann (vc) *(rec RCA Studios, Hollywood, Sept 9, 1941)* RCA Gold Seal 2-▲ 09026-61740-2 (m) [ADD]
Mozart, W.A.:Trio Vn, K.563, w. W. Primrose (va), E. Feuermann (vc) Biddulph ▲ LAB 074 [ADD]
Music of France, w. Brooks Smith (pno) RCA Gold Seal ▲ 7707-2 RC [ADD]
Prokofiev, S.:Con 2 Vn, w. S. Koussevitzky (cnd), Boston SO *(rec 12/20/37)* Biddulph ▲ LAB 018 [ADD]
Prokofiev, S.:Con 2 Vn, w. S. Koussevitzky (cnd), Boston SO *(rec Symphony Hall, Boston, Dec 20, 1937)* RCA Gold Seal 2-▲ 09026-61735-2 [ADD]
Prokofiev, S.:Con 2 Vn, w. C. Munch (cnd), Boston SO *(rec Symphony Hall, Boston, Feb. 24, 1959)* RCA Red Seal ▲ 09026-61744-2 [ADD]
Prokofiev, S.:Con 2 Vn, w. C. Munch (cnd), Boston SO RCA Red Seal ▲ RCD1-7019
Prokofiev, S.:Con 2 Vn, w. S. Koussevitzky (cnd), Boston SO *(rec 1935–41)* Pearl ▲ PEA 9167 [ADD]
Ravel, M.:Trio Pno, w. A. Rubinstein (pno), G. Piatigorsky (vc) RCA Gold Seal ▲ 7871–2–RG (m/s) [ADD]
Respighi, O.:Son Vn, w. E. Bay (pno) RCA Gold Seal ▲ 7871–2–RG (m/s) [ADD]
Rózsa, M.:Con Vn, w. W. Hendl (cnd), Dallas SO RCA Gold Seal ▲ 7963–2–RG [ADD]

Heifetz, Jascha (vn) (cont.)
Rózsa, M.:Theme & Vars Vn, w. G. Piatigorsky (vc) RCA Gold Seal ▲ 7963-2-RG [ADD]
Saint-Saëns, C.:Havanaise Vn, w. J. Barbirolli (cnd), London SO *(rec London, 1935 & 1937)* Grammofono 2000 ▲ GRM 78511 [ADD]
Saint-Saëns, C.:Havanaise Vn, w. J. Barbirolli (cnd), London SO *(rec 1937)* EMI Classics ▲ CDH 64251-2 (m) [ADD]
Saint-Saëns, C.:Havanaise Vn, w. J. Barbirolli (cnd), London SO *(rec EMI Studios, Abbey Road, London, Apr 9, 1937)* RCA Gold Seal 2-▲ 09026-61735-2 [ADD]
Saint-Saëns, C.:Havanaise Vn, w. P. Steinberg (cnd), RCA Victor SO RCA Gold Seal ▲ 7709-2-RG [ADD] ■ 7709-4-RG (CrO2)
Saint-Saëns, C.:Havanaise Vn, w. J. Barbirolli (cnd), London SO *(rec 1937; mats 2EA 4744/5, HM)* Biddulph ▲ LAB 025 [ADD]
Saint-Saëns, C.:Introduction & Rondo capriccioso, w. J. Barbirolli (cnd), London PO *(rec 1935; mats 2EA 1450/1, HM)* Biddulph ▲ LAB 025 [ADD]
Saint-Saëns, C.:Introduction & Rondo capriccioso, w. J. Barbirolli (cnd), London PO *(rec 1935)* EMI Classics ▲ CDH 64251-2 (m) [ADD]
Saint-Saëns, C.:Introduction & Rondo capriccioso, w. J. Barbirolli (cnd), London SO *(rec London, 1935 & 1937)* Grammofono 2000 ▲ GRM 78511 [ADD]
Saint-Saëns, C.:Introduction & Rondo capriccioso, w. J. Barbirolli (cnd), London PO *(rec EMI Studios, Abbey Road, London, Mar 18, 1935)* RCA Gold Seal 2-▲ 09026-61735-2 [ADD]
Saint-Saëns, C.:Introduction & Rondo capriccioso, w. P. Steinberg (cnd), RCA Victor SO RCA Gold Seal ▲ 7709-2-RG [ADD] ■ 7709-4-RG (CrO2)
Sarasate, P. de:Zigeunerweisen, w. W. Steinberg (cnd), RCA Victor SO RCA Gold Seal ▲ 7709-2-RG [ADD] ■ 7709-4-RG (CrO2)
Sarasate, P. de:Zigeunerweisen, w. J. Barbirolli (cnd), London SO *(rec EMI Studios, Abbey Road, London, Apr 9, 1937)* RCA Gold Seal 2-▲ 09026-61735-2 [ADD]
Sarasate, P. de:Zigeunerweisen, w. J. Barbirolli (cnd), London SO *(rec 1937)* EMI Classics ▲ CDH 64251-2 (m) [ADD]
Sarasate, P. de:Zigeunerweisen, w. J. Barbirolli (cnd), London SO *(rec 1937 HMV recording)* Biddulph ▲ LAB 026 [ADD]
Schubert, Franz:Ave Maria! Jungfrau mild!, w. E. Bay (pno) RCA Gold Seal ▲ 7964-2-RG [ADD] ■ 7964-4-RG (CrO2)
Schubert, Franz:Fant Vn, D.934, w. J. Lateiner (pno) RCA Gold Seal ▲ 7873-2-RG [ADD] ■ 7873-4-RG
Schubert, Franz:Qnt Strs, D.956, w. I. Baker (vn), W. Primrose (va), G. Piatigorsky (vc), G. Rejto (vc) RCA Gold Seal ▲ 7964-2-RG [ADD] ■ 7964-4-RG (CrO2)
Schubert, Franz:Trio 1 Pno, w. A. Rubinstein (pno), E. Feuermann (vc) RCA Gold Seal ▲ 09026-60926-2 ■ 09026-60926-4
Schubert, Franz:Trio Strs, D.581, w. W. Primrose (va), G. Piatigorsky (vc) RCA Gold Seal ▲ 7964-2-RG [ADD] ■ 7964-4-RG (CrO2)
Selections from the Heifetz Collection RCA Gold Seal ▲ 09026-62645-2
Showpieces, w. Heifetz, Jascha (vn) RCA Gold Seal ▲ 7709-2-RG [ADD]
Sibelius, J.:Con Vn, w. T. Beecham (cnd), London PO *(rec 11/26 & 12/14, 1935)* Biddulph ▲ LAB 018 [ADD]
Sibelius, J.:Con Vn, w. T. Beecham (cnd), London PO *(rec 11/26 & 12/14, 1935)* EMI Classics ("Great Recordings of the Century" series) ▲ CDH 64030
Sibelius, J.:Con Vn, w. D. Mitropoulos (cnd), Philharmonic SO *(rec Mar. 11, 1951)* Music & Arts 2-▲ CD 766 [AAD]
Sibelius, J.:Con Vn, w. W. Hendl (cnd), Chicago SO RCA Red Seal ▲ RCD1-7019
Sibelius, J.:Con Vn, w. W. Hendl (cnd), Chicago SO *(rec Orchestra Hall, Chicago, Jan. 10 & 12, 1959)* RCA Red Seal ▲ 09026-61744-2 [ADD]
Sibelius, J.:Con Vn, w. T. Beecham (cnd), London PO *(rec 1934-40)* Pearl ▲ PEA 9157 [ADD]
Sinding, C.:Suite im alten Stil, w. A. Wallenstein (cnd), Los Angeles PO [orchd Sinding] *(rec Republic Studios Sound Stage 9, Hollywood, Dec 9, 1953)* RCA Gold Seal 2-▲ 09026-61740-2 (m) [ADD]
Spohr, L.:Con 8 Vn, w. I. Solomon (cnd), RCA Victor SO RCA Gold Seal ▲ 7870-2-RG (m/s) [ADD]
Spohr, L.:Double Qt 1, w. I. Baker (vn), P. Amoyal (vn), P. Rosenthal (vn), M. Thomas (va), A. Harshman (va), G. Piatigorsky (vc), L. Lesser (vc) RCA Gold Seal ▲ 7870-2-RG (m/s) [ADD]
Strauss, R.:Son Vn, w. A. Sandor (pno) *(rec 2/6/34)* Biddulph ▲ LAB 018 [ADD]
Tchaikovsky, P.:Con Vn, w. J. Barbirolli (cnd), London PO *(rec 1937 for HMV)* EMI Classics ("Great Recordings of the Century" series) ▲ CDH 64030
Tchaikovsky, P.:Con Vn, w. F. Reiner (cnd), Chicago SO *(rec Orch Hall, Chicago, Apr 19, 1957)* RCA Red Seal ▲ 09026-61743-2 [ADD]
Tchaikovsky, P.:Con Vn, w. F. Reiner (cnd), Chicago SO RCA Red Seal ▲ 5933-2-RC
Tchaikovsky, P.:Con Vn, w. F. Reiner (cnd), Chicago SO *(rec 1955 & 1957)* RCA Gold Seal ▲ 09026-61495-2 ■ 09026-61495-4
Tchaikovsky, P.:Con Vn, w. J. Barbirolli (cnd), London PO *(rec 1934-40)* Pearl ▲ PEA 9157 [ADD]
Tchaikovsky, P.:Con Vn, w. J. Barbirolli (cnd), London PO *(rec 1937 for HMV)* Biddulph ▲ LAB 026 [ADD]
Tchaikovsky, P.:Sérénade mélancolique RCA Red Seal ▲ 5933-2-RC
Tchaikovsky, P.:Sérénade mélancolique, w. A. Wallenstein (cnd), Los Angeles PO RCA Gold Seal ▲ 09026-60927-2 ■ 09026-60927-4
Tchaikovsky, P.:Sérénade mélancolique, chamber orch *(rec RCA Studio A, Hollywood, July 8-10, 1970)* RCA Red Seal ▲ 09026-61743-2 [ADD]
Tchaikovsky, P.:Trio Pno, w. A. Rubinstein (pno), G. Piatigorsky (vc) RCA Gold Seal ▲ 7768-2-RG (m) [ADD]
Vieuxtemps, H.:Con 4 Vn, w. J. Barbirolli (cnd), London PO *(rec 3/14/35)* EMI Classics ▲ CDH 64251-2 (m) [ADD]
Vieuxtemps, H.:Con 4 Vn, w. J. Barbirolli (cnd), London PO *(rec 3/14/35)* Biddulph ▲ LAB 025 [ADD]
Vieuxtemps, H.:Con 4 Vn, w. J. Barbirolli (cnd), London PO *(rec 1935-41)* Pearl ▲ PEA 9167 [ADD]
Vieuxtemps, H.:Con 5 Vn, w. M. Sargent (cnd), London New SO RCA Red Seal ▲ 6214-2-RC [ADD]
Vieuxtemps, H.:Con 5 Vn, w. M. Sargent (cnd), London New SO *(rec Walthamstow Town Hall, London, May 15 & 22, 1961)* RCA Red Seal ▲ 09026-61745-2 [ADD]
The Virtuoso Jascha Heifetz Pearl ▲ PEA 9023
Walton, W.:Con Vn, w. W. Walton (cnd), Philharmonia Orch RCA Gold Seal ▲ 7966-2-RG (m) [ADD]
Walton, W.:Con Vn, w. E. Goossens (cnd), Cincinnati SO *(rec 1935-41)* Pearl ▲ PEA 9167 [ADD]
Waxman, F.:Carmen Fant, w. D. Vorhees (cnd), RCA Victor SO RCA Gold Seal ▲ 7963-2-RG (m) [ADD]
Wieniawski, H.:Con 2 Vn, w. J. Barbirolli (cnd), London PO *(rec 1935-41)* Pearl ▲ PEA 9167 [ADD]
Wieniawski, H.:Con 2 Vn, w. J. Barbirolli (cnd), London PO *(rec 3/18/35)* EMI Classics ▲ CDH 64251-2 (m) [ADD]
Wieniawski, H.:Con 2 Vn, w. I. Solomon (cnd), RCA Victor SO RCA Gold Seal ▲ 09026-60927-2 ■ 09026-60927-4
Wieniawski, H.:Con 2 Vn, w. J. Barbirolli (cnd), London PO *(rec London, 1935 & 1937)* Grammofono 2000 ▲ GRM 78511 [ADD]
Wieniawski, H.:Con 2 Vn, w. J. Barbirolli (cnd), London PO *(rec 1935 for HMV)* Biddulph ▲ LAB 026 [ADD]

Heifetz, B. (va)—see ORCHESTRAS & ENSEMBLES Kolisch String Quartet
Heikkilä, Eeva (fl)—see ORCHESTRAS & ENSEMBLES Sinfonia Lahti Chamber Ensemble members

Heiller, Anton (hpd)
Bach, J.S.:Con 1 Hpd, w. M. Caridis (cnd), Vienna State Opera Orch *(rec Brahmsall, Vienna, May 1958)* Vanguard Classics ("The Bach Guild" series) 2-▲ OVC 2523/24 [ADD]
Bach, J.S.:Con 4 Hpd, w. M. Caridis (cnd), Vienna State Opera Orch *(rec Brahmsall, Vienna, May 1958)* Vanguard Classics ("The Bach Guild" series) 2-▲ OVC 2523/24 [ADD]
Bach, J.S.:Con 5 Hpd, w. M. Caridis (cnd), Vienna State Opera Orch *(rec Brahmsall, Vienna, May 1958)* Vanguard Classics ("The Bach Guild" series) 2-▲ OVC 2523/24 [ADD]

Heiller, Anton (hpd) (cont.)
Gabrieli, G.:Music of, w. R. Clemenic (rcr), H. Tachezi (pno), E. Appia (cnd), Gabrieli Festival Orch, Gabrieli Festival Chorus—Processional & Ceremonial Music from Sacrae Symphoniae [1597, 1615] & Concerti [1587]; originally released as Bach Guild BGS 5004)—Sancta et immaculata virginitas; O magnum mysterium; Nunc dimittis; Angelus ad pastores; O Jesu mi dulcissime; Exaudi Deus; Hodie completi sunt; O Domine Jesu Christe; Canzona Quarti Toni a 15 (ricercar); Inclina Domine *(rec Vienna, Feb. 1958)* Vanguard Classics ("The Bach Guild" series) ▲ OVC 2007 [ADD]

Heiller, Anton (org)
Bach, J.S.:Org Music (misc)—various undisclosed organ works *(rec live, 1967)* Ermitage ▲ ERM 135
Bach, J.S.:Org Music (misc)—Fantasia in G, BWV 572; Fantasia & Fugue in g, BWV 542; Passacaglia & Fugue in c, BWV 582; Prelude & Fugue in A, BWV 536; Prelude & Fugue in e, BWV 548; Toccata & Fugue in d, BWV 565 *(rec 1964)* Vanguard Classics ("The Bach Guild" series) ▲ OVC 2005 [ADD]
Haydn, J.:Mass 10, "Kriegsmesse", "Paukenmesse", w. Netania Davrath (sop), Hilde Rössl-Majdan (alt), Anton Dermota (ten), W. Bery (bass), R. Harand (vc), M. Wöldike (cnd), Vienna State Opera Orch, Vienna State Opera Chorus *(rec May 14-16, 1960)* Vanguard Classics ("The Bach Guild" series) ▲ OVC 2518 [ADD]

Heimovitz, M. (vc)
Bruch, M.:Kol Nidrei, w. J. Levine (cnd), Chicago SO Deutsche Grammophon ▲ 427323-2 [DDD]
Lalo, E.:Con Vc, w. J. Levine (cnd), Chicago SO Deutsche Grammophon ▲ 427323-2 [DDD]
Saint-Saëns, C.:Con 1 Vc, w. J. Levine (cnd), Chicago SO Deutsche Grammophon ▲ 427323-2 [DDD]

Heindel, Kim (lt)
Dowland, J.:Lt Music Gasparo ▲ GS 275 ■ GS 275C
Duphly, J.:La Damanzy Gasparo ▲ GS 276 ■ GS 275C

Heindel, Kim (lt/hpd)
The Art of the Lautenwerk Gasparo ▲ GSCD 275 ■ GS 275C

Heindel, Kim (org)
Bach, J.S.:Org Music (misc)—Fant in G, BWV 572; Son No. 4 in e, BWV 528; Das alte Jahr vergangen ist, BWV 614; Herr Gott, nun schleuss den Himmel auf, BWV 617; Con in C after Vivaldi, BWV 594; An Wasserflüssen Babylon, BWV 653; Nun danket alle Gott, BWV 657; Prelude & Fugue in Eb, BWV 552 [St. Anne] *(rec Steinfeld, Germany, Oct 5-7, 1992)* Gasparo ▲ GSCD 321

Heineman, S. (bn)—see ORCHESTRAS & ENSEMBLES Aspen Wind Quintet

Heiniger, Bernard (org)
Daetwyler, J.:Vars sur une chanson médiévale et populaire, "Le Noël des Bergers", w. P. Falentin (tpt) Gallo ▲ CD 548 [AAD]

Heinneman, S. (bn)
Stravinsky, I.:Octet, w. M. Parloff (fl), D. Schiffrin (cl), F. Morelli (bn), R. Mase (tpt), C. Gekker (tpt), R. Borror (trbn), D. Taylor (trbn), G. Schuller (cnd) *(rec Sep. 1991)* GM ▲ GM 2030

Heinonen, Eero (pno)
Englund, S.E.:Pno Music (comp) BIS ▲ CD 277
Kuula, T.:Pno Music—Kolme Satukuvaa (3 Fairy Tale Pictures), Op. 19; Kolme kappaletta (3 Pieces), Op. 3b *(rec Jan. 25-26, 1982)* BIS ▲ CD 198 [AAD]
Merikanto, O.:From the World of Children *(rec Jan. 25-26, 1982)* BIS ▲ CD 198 [AAD]
Palmgren, S.:Cons Pno (comp), w. E. Heinonen (pno—No. 1), J. Lagerspetz (pno—Nos. 2 & 4), M. Raekallio (pno—No. 3), R. Kerppo (pno—No. 5), J. Mercier (cnd), Turku PO Finlandia 2-▲ 4509-95852-2 [DDD]
Sibelius, J.:Music for Vn Pno, w. Y. Arai (vn) Ondine ▲ ODE 756-2 [DDD]
Sibelius, J.:Music for Vn Pno, w. Y. Arai (vn)—2 Pieces, Op. 2; 2 Pieces, Op. 77; 4 Pieces, Op. 78; 6 Pieces, Op. 79 Ondine ▲ ODE 720-2 [DDD]
Sibelius, J.:Novelette, w. Y. Arai (vn) Ondine ▲ ODE 756-2 [DDD]
Sibelius, J.:Pieces Vn Pno, Op. 81, w. Y. Arai (vn) Ondine ▲ ODE 756-2 [DDD]
Sibelius, J.:Pieces Vn Pno, Op. 115, w. Y. Arai (vn) Ondine ▲ ODE 756-2 [DDD]
Sibelius, J.:Pieces Vn Pno, Op. 116, w. Y. Arai (vn) Ondine ▲ ODE 756-2 [DDD]

Heinrich, Susanne (vl)—see ORCHESTRAS & ENSEMBLES Palladian Ensemble

Heintze, Hans (org)
Pachelbel, J.:Org Music Berlin Classics ▲ BER 9213
Walther, Joh. G.:Org Music Berlin Classics ▲ BER 9213

Heinz, Bettina (pno)—see ORCHESTRAS & ENSEMBLES Chalumeau Trio
Heinze, Sheryl (fl)—see ORCHESTRAS & ENSEMBLES Boehme Quintet

Heinzmann, Hans-Udo (fl)
Berg, A.:Adagio, w. Malte Lammers (ob), Walter Hermann (cl), Heinrich Horlein (vn), Jaap Zeijl (va), Seven Forsberg (vc), Willi Beyer (db), Jurgen Lamke (pno), Werner Hagen (pno), Volker Kneip (perc) [arr chamber ensemble] Koch Schwann ▲ SCH CD 311912
Busoni, F.:Berceuse élégiaque, w. Malte Lammers (ob), Walter Hermann (cl), Heinrich Horlein (vn), Jaap Zeijl (va), Seven Forsberg (vc), Willi Beyer (db), Jurgen Lamke (pno), Werner Hagen (pno), Volker Kneip (perc) [arr Stein for chamber ensemble] Koch Schwann ▲ SCH CD 311912
Debussy, C.:Prélude à l'après-midi d'un faune, w. Malte Lammers (ob), Walter Hermann (cl), Heinrich Horlein (vn), Jaap Zeijl (va), Seven Forsberg (vc), Willi Beyer (db), Jurgen Lamke (pno), Werner Hagen (pno), Volker Kneip (perc) [arr Sachs for chamber ensemble] Koch Schwann ▲ SCH CD 311912
Schoenberg, A.:Chamber Sym 1, w. Malte Lammers (ob), Walter Hermann (cl), Heinrich Horlein (vn), Jaap Zeijl (va), Seven Forsberg (vc), Willi Beyer (db), Jurgen Lamke (pno), Werner Hagen (pno), Volker Kneip (perc) [arr Webern for chamber ensemble] Koch Schwann ▲ SCH CD 311912

Heiser, Bernd (hn)
Mozart, W.A.:Con Hn, K.412, w. H. Kraus (cnd), Vienna Mozart Ensemble LaserLight ▲ 15 624 [DDD]
Mozart, W.A.:Con Hn, K.447, w. H. Kraus (cnd), Vienna Mozart Ensemble LaserLight ▲ 15 624 [DDD]

Heisser, Jean-François (pno)
Bartók, B.:Son for 2 Pnos, w. G. Pludermacher (pno), G.-J. Cipriana (perc), G. Perotin (perc) Erato ▲ 2292-45861-2
Bartók, B.:Suite for 2 Pnos, w. G. Pludermacher (pno) Erato ▲ 2292-45861-2
Berlioz, H.:Harold in Italy, w. B. Pasquier (pno) [Liszt's va-pno trans] Musique d'Abord ▲ HMA 1901246
Debussy, C.:Images Orch, w. G. Pludermacher (pno) [2-piano trans. André Caplet] Erato ▲ 2292-45698-2 ZK
Debussy, C.:La Mer, w. G. Pludermacher (pno) [2-piano trans. André Caplet] Erato ▲ 2292-45698-2 ZK
Debussy, C.:Nocturnes, w. G. Pludermacher (pno) [2-piano trans. Mauruice Ravel]—Nuages & Fêtes Erato ▲ 2292-45698-2 ZK
Debussy, C.:Transcriptions for 2 Pnos, w. G. Pludermacher (pno)—Wagner:Der fliegende Holländer Ov.; Schumann:6 Studies in Canon Form, Op. 56; Saint-Saëns:Introduction & Rondo capriccioso; Gluck:Caprice on airs [from *Alceste*]; Tchaikovsky:3 Dances [from *Swan Lake*]; Debussy:Prélude à l'après-midi d'un faune Erato ▲ 93209
Falla, M. de:El amor brujo (sels)—5-movt. piano suite Erato ▲ 2292-45481-2 ZK [DDD]
Falla, M. de:Fant bética Erato ▲ 2292-45481-2 ZK [DDD]
Falla, M. de:Homenaje 'Le tombeau de Debussy' Erato ▲ 2292-45481-2 ZK [DDD]
Falla, M. de:Pno Music Erato ▲ 2292-45481-2 ZK [DDD]
Falla, M. de:Pièces espagnoles (4) Erato ▲ 2292-45481-2 ZK [DDD]
Falla, M. de:Pour le tombeau de Paul Dukas Erato ▲ 2292-45481-2 ZK [DDD]
Falla, M. de:El sombrero de tres picos (dances)—3 dances Erato ▲ 2292-45481-2 ZK [DDD]
Granados, E.:Danzas españolas (10) Erato ▲ 2292-45803-2 ZK
Granados, E.:Escenas romanticas (6) Erato ▲ 2292-45803-2 ZK
Martinů, B.:Double Con Pno, Tim, w. A. Planès (pno), J. Camosi (perc), J. Conlon (cnd), French National Orch Erato ▲ 2292-45499-2 ZK
Martinů, B.:Sinfonietta Pno, w. J. Conlon (cnd), French National Orch Erato ▲ 2292-45794-2 ZK
Mompou, F.:Cançons i dansas Erato ▲ ERA 98540 [DDD]
Mompou, F.:Cants magics Erato ▲ ERA 98540 [DDD]
Mompou, F.:Suburbis Erato ▲ ERA 98540 [DDD]
Schumann, R.:Märchenbilder, w. B. Pasquier (va) Musique d'Abord ▲ HMA 1901246

Heitzler, Micheal (cl)
Clarinet & Orchestra, w. Dieter Klöcker (cl), Czech-Slovak RSO Bratislava [cnd:Gernot Schmalfuss] *(rec Jan. 1990)* Marco Polo ▲ 8.223431 [DDD]

Hejný, Petr (va)
Telemann, G.P.:Cons Rcr, Vl, w. Jiří Stivi (rcr), Pro Arte Antiqua Prague—in a Arta ▲ ARTA 0058 [DDD]
Telemann, G.P.:Suite Vl, w. Pro Arte Antiqua Prague Arta ▲ ARTA 0058 [DDD]
Telemann, G.P.:Trio Sons, w. Jiří Stivi (rcr), Pro Arte Antiqua Prague—in g & F for Rcr, Vl & Bc Arta ▲ ARTA 0058 [DDD]

Hejný, Petr (vc)—see also ORCHESTRAS & ENSEMBLES Dolezalovo String Quartet
Kozeluch, L.:Original Scottish Airs, w. J. Griffett (ten), J. Krejci (vn), R. Zelenka (pno) [arr. J. Griffett; lyrics by Robert Burns]—Nae gentle dames; Here's a health to ane I lo'e dear; Ye banks and braes of bonie Doon; Blythe, blythe and merry was she; Lord Gregory; My Nannie's awa'; And ye shall walk in silk attire; Turn again, thou fair Eliza; Contented wi' little; The day returns; On a bank of flowers; Adieu ye streams; All Water; My love she's but a lassie yet; True hearted was he, the sad swain o' the Yarrow; She's fair and fause; O this is no my aine lassie; The Tears of Scotland Campion ▲ 1322 [DDD]

Helasvuo, Mikael (baroque fl)—see ORCHESTRAS & ENSEMBLES Les Goûts-Réünis

Helasvuo, Mikael (fl)—see also ORCHESTRAS & ENSEMBLES Helsinki Wind Quintet
Benda, F.:Con in e Fl & Orch, w. J.-P. Saraste (cnd), Helsinki CO BIS ▲ CD 268 [DDD]
Bergman, E.:Birds in the Morning, w. L. Segerstam (cnd), Finnish RSO *(rec May & Oct. 1988 & Jan. 19)* Finlandia ▲ 4509-95861-2 [DDD]
Englund, S.E.:Con Fl, w. L. Segerstam (cnd), Finnish RSO *(rec May & Oct. 1988 & Jan. 19)* Finlandia ▲ 4509-95861-2 [DDD]
Giuliani, M.:Music for Fl & Gtr (comp), w. J. Savijoki (gtr)—Duettino facile, Op. 77; Duo (1810-11); Grand Duetto Concertant, Op. 52; Grand Duo Concertant, Op. 85; Twelve Ländler, Op. 75 BIS ▲ CD 411 [DDD]
Giuliani, M.:Music for Fl & Gtr (comp), w. J. Savijoki (gtr)—Divertimenti Notturni, Op. 86; Grande Sérénade, Op. 82; Serenade, Op. 127; Variations, Op. 84 BIS ▲ CD 412 [DDD]
Giuliani, M.:Music for Fl & Gtr (comp), w. J. Savijoki (gtr)—Gran Pot-Pourri, Op. 126; Grand Potpourri, Op. 53; Pièces faciles et agréables, Op. 74; Potpourri tiré de l'Opéra Tancredi, Op. 76; Six Variations, Op. 81 BIS ▲ CD 413 [DDD]
Haydn, J.:Trios Pno, Fl & Vc, w. Tuija Hakkila (pno), Anssi Karttunen (vc) [period instrs] *(rec Oct. 7-9, 1991)* Finlandia ▲ 4509-95869-2 [DDD]
Merilainen, U.:Visions & Whispers, w. L. Segerstam (cnd), Finnish RSO *(rec May & Oct. 1988 & Jan. 19)* Finlandia ▲ 4509-95861-2 [DDD]
Piazzolla, A.:Études tanguistiques Ondine ▲ ODE 781-2 [DDD]
Piazzolla, A.:Histoire du tango, w. J. Savijoki (gtr) Ondine ▲ ODE 781-2 [DDD]
Stamitz, C.:Con Fl, Op. 29, w. J.-P. Saraste (cnd), Helsinki CO BIS ▲ CD 268 [DDD]
Takemitsu, T.:Music of, w. Jukka Savijoki (gtr), Eero Palviainen (lt), Timothy Ferchen (vib/crotales)—Sacrifice; Voice; All in Twilight; Ring; Foloios; Itinerant; Toward the Sea Ondine ▲ ODE 839 [DDD]

Held, Barbara (fl)
Held, B.:Upper Air Observations Lovely Music ▲ LCD 3031 [DDD]
Lucier, A.:Self-Portrait Lovely Music ▲ LCD 3031 [DDD]
Tone, Y.:Music of—Lyrictron for Fl & Elec; Trio for a Fl Player Lovely Music ▲ LCD 3031 [DDD]
Vigeland, N.:Vara, w. J. Kubera (pno) Lovely Music ▲ LCD 3031 [DDD]

Held, J. (bc)
Lanzetti, S.:Sons Vc, w. C. Ronco (vc), S. Veggetti (vc), D. Petech (hpd)—Nos. 5-9, 11 & 12 *(rec 5/91)* Nuova Era ("Ancient Music" series) ▲ 7048 [DDD]

Helden, Johan van (va)—see ORCHESTRAS & ENSEMBLES Alma Musica Ensemble

Heldrich (perc)
Davidovsky, M.:Synchronism 5, w. R. DesRoches (perc), R. Fitz (perc), D. Marcone (perc), van Hyning (perc), H. Sollberger (cnd) CRI ▲ CD 611 [ADD]

Heled, Simca (vc)
Bazelaire, P.:Suite française, w. J. Zak (pno) InSync ■ C 4154
Boëllmann, L.:Son Vc, w. J. Zak (pno) InSync ■ C 4153
Castelnuovo-Tedesco, M.:Notturno sull'acqua & Scherzino, w. J. Zak (pno) InSync ■ C 4153
Castelnuovo-Tedesco, M.:Toccata, w. J. Zak (pno) InSync ■ C 4153
Cilea, F.:Son Vc, w. J. Zak (pno) InSync ■ C 4154
Milhaud, D.:Elégie, w. J. Zak (pno) InSync ■ C 4154
Rare Cello Music, w. Heled, Simca (vc), Daniel Edni (pno), Jonathan Feldman (pno), Michael Levin (pno), Alexander Peskanov (pno), Jonathan Zak (pno) *(rec 1976, 1982, 1983, 1985, 1)* Classico ▲ CLASSCD 153
Tcherepnin, A.:Son Vc, w. J. Zak (pno) InSync ■ C 4154

Helffer, Claude (pno)
Bartók, B.:Improvs (8) on Hungarian Peasant Songs Musique d'Abord ▲ HMA 1901094
Bartók, B.:Out of Doors Musique d'Abord ▲ HMA 1901094
Bartók, B.:Romanian Folk Dances Pno Musique d'Abord ▲ HMA 1901094
Bartók, B.:Son Pno Musique d'Abord ▲ HMA 1901094
Bartók, B.:Suito Pno Musique d'Abord ▲ HMA 1901094
Boucourechliev, A.:Les Archipels, w. Brigitte Sylvestre (hp), Elisabeth Chojnacka (hpd), Françoise Rieunier (org), Roland Auzet, Jean-Pierre Drouet (perc), Hakon Austbö (pno), Françoise-Frédéric Guy (pno), Georges Pludermacher (pno), Ysaÿe String Quartet, Les Pléiades Ensemble Musique Francaise d'Aujourd'hui ("Collection MFA-Radio France" series) ▲ MFA 216001
Debussy, C.:Arabesques (2) Musique d'Abord ▲ HMA 190954 [ADD]
Debussy, C.:Children's Corner Musique d'Abord ▲ HMA 190954 [ADD]
Debussy, C.:En blanc et noir, w. H. Austbö (pno) Musique d'Abord ▲ HMA 190957
Debussy, C.:Epigraphes antiques, w. H. Austbö (pno) Musique d'Abord ▲ HMA 190957
Debussy, C.:Images (6) Pno Musique d'Abord ▲ HMA 190954 [ADD]
Debussy, C.:Lindaraja, w. H. Austbö (pno) Musique d'Abord ▲ HMA 190957
Debussy, C.:Marche écossaise sur un thème populaire, w. H. Austbö (pno) Musique d'Abord ▲ HMA 190957
Debussy, C.:Petite suite, w. H. Austbö (pno) Musique d'Abord ▲ HMA 190957
Debussy, C.:Suite bergamasque Musique d'Abord ▲ HMA 190954 [ADD]
Ravel, M.:Gaspard de la nuit Musique d'Abord ▲ HMA 190922
Ravel, M.:Jeux d'eau Musique d'Abord ▲ HMA 190922
Ravel, M.:Menuet antique Musique d'Abord ▲ HMA 190922
Schoenberg, A.:Pno Music—3 Pieces, Op. 11; 5 Pieces, Op. 23; 2 Pieces, Opp. 33a & 33b; 6 Miniatures, Op. 19; Suite, Op. 25 Musique d'Abord ▲ HMA 190752
Xenakis, I.:Chamber Music, w. Arditti String Quartet—Akea, Quintet for Piano & Strings (1986); À R. (Hommage to Ravel) for Piano (1987); Dikthas for Violin & Piano (1979); Embellie for Viola (1981); Evryali for Piano (1973); Herma for Piano (1960-61); Ikhoor for String Trio (1978); Kottos for Cello (1977); Mikka for Violin (1971); Mikka "S," for Violin (1976); Mists for Piano (1980); Nomos Alpha for Cello (1966); St/4 for String Quartet (1955-62); Tetora for String Quartet (1990); Tetras for String Quartet (1983) Montaigne 2-▲ MO 782005 [DDD]

Helfgott, David (pno)
Rachmaninoff, S.:Con 3 Pno, w. M. Horvat (cnd), Copenhagen PO *(rec live, Tivoli Concert Hall, Copenhagen, Nov 2, 1995)* RCA Red Seal ▲ 7432-140378-2 [DDD]
Rachmaninoff, S.:Preludes Pno—Opp. 23/5; 32/5 & 12 RCA Red Seal ▲ 7432-140378-2 [DDD]
Rachmaninoff, S.:Prelude Pno, Op. 3/2 RCA Red Seal ▲ 7432-140378-2 [DDD]
Rachmaninoff, S.:Son 2 Pno RCA Red Seal ▲ 7432-140378-2 [DDD]

Helin, Jacquelyn (pno)
Thomson, V.:Parson Weems & the Cherry Tree *(rec 1992)* New World ▲ 80429-2
Thomson, V.:Portraits—9 Portraits for Pno (1930-42, 1958);17 Portraits for Pno (1982-84) *(rec 1992)* New World ▲ 80429-2

Hell, Josef (vn)—see also ORCHESTRAS & ENSEMBLES Vienna Chamber Ensemble members
Schmidt, F.:Qnt Cl, w. E. Ottensamer (cl), R. Keuschnig (pno), P. Wächter (vn), P. Pecha (va), R. Wallfisch (vc) *(rec Jan. 7, 1991)* Orfeo ▲ 287921 [DDD]
Schmidt, F.:Qnt Pno, w. R. Keuschnig (pno), P. Wächter (vn), P. Pecha (va), G. Iberer (vc) *(rec Jan. 7, 1991)* Orfeo ▲ 287921 [DDD]

Hell, Michael (vc)—see ORCHESTRAS & ENSEMBLES Vienna String Quintet

Heller, Alfred (pno)
Sondheim, S.:Songs, w. Marc Heller (ten), Martin Ormandy (vc)—The Hills of Tomorrow; Take Me to the World; Another 100 People; Not While I'm Around; You Must Meet My Wife; Send in the Clowns; Comedy Tonight; Love I Hear; Later; Anyone Can Whistle; Pretty Women; Losing My Mind; Johanna; Good Thing Going; Silly People; Ev'rybody Says Don't; Loving You; Green Finch & Linnet Bird; Being Alive; One More Kiss; Sunday Etcetera ▲ KTC 1185

Heller, Arthur (bn)
Mozart, W.A.:Duo Bn Vc, w. Yo-Yo Ma (vc) Sony Classical ▲ SMK 46248 [ADD]

Heller, Barbara (pno)
Mendelssohn, Fanny:Songs, w. I. Lippitz (sop)—23 songs in four groups:Op. 1, Op. 7, Op. 9 & Op. 10 [G] CPO ▲ CPO 999011-2 [DDD]
Werfel, A.M.:Songs, w. I. Lippitz (sop)—Licht in der Nacht; Waldseligkeit; Ansturm; Erntelied; Hymne; Ekstase; Der Erkennende; Lobgesang; Hymne an die Nacht; Die stille Stadt; In meines Vaters Garten; Laue Sommernacht; Bei dir ist es traut; Ich wandle unter Blumen [G] CPO ▲ CPO 999018-2 [DDD]

Heller, Camilla (vc)
Carreño, T.:Qt Strs, w. J. Roche (vn), R. Zelnick (vn), T. Strasser (va) Vox Box 2-▲ CDX 5029 [ADD]

Heller, Marsha (ob)—see ORCHESTRAS & ENSEMBLES Bell'Arte Trio

Hellgren, Jan (perc)—see ORCHESTRAS & ENSEMBLES Kroumata Percussion Ensemble

Hellmann, Christoph (vc)
Reger, M.:Cantatas, w. V. Schweizer (sop), A. Hellmann (alt), R. Julius Koch (ob), R. Hellmann, U. Soldan (vn), B. Banz (va), C. Fink (db), H. Bilgram (org), D. Hellmann (cnd), Mainz Bach Choir Entrée ▲ 0049 [ADD]
Schubert, Franz:Trio 1 Pno, w. M. Schäfer (pno), I. Then-Bergh (vn) *(rec Studio 3 des BR, Mar. 28-31, 1994)* Calig ▲ CAL 50931 [DDD]
Schubert, Franz:Trio 2 Pno, w. M. Schäfer (pno), I. Then-Bergh (vn) *(rec Studio 3 des BR, Mar. 28-31, 1994)* Calig ▲ CAL 50931 [DDD]

Hellmann, Klaus (bn)
Mozart, W.A.:Con Bn, w. H. Kraus (cnd), Vienna Mozart Ensemble LaserLight ▲ 15 875 [DDD]

Hellsten, H. (org)
Hambreus, B.:Music of—Interferenzen; Toccata; Monumentum per Max Reger; Livre d'orgue MAP ▲ MAPCD 9136
Hambreus, B.:Music of, w. W. Jacob (org), E. Bour (cnd), Southwest RSO—Candenza; Canvas with mirrors; Continuo MAP ▲ MAPCD 9131

Hellweg, Wilhelm (pno)
Arcas, J.:Gtr Music, w. Pepe Romero (gtr)—Fant on Themes from Verdi's *La Traviata* Philips ▲ 446090-2
Ferrer, J.:Gtr Music, w. Pepe Romero (gtr)—Fant on Verdi's *Rigoletto* Philips ▲ 446090-2
Gounod, C.:Waltzes, w. Pepe Romero (gtr) [arr Hellweg] Philips ▲ 446090-2
Mertz, K.J.:Gtr Music, w. Pepe Romero (gtr)—Fants on themes from Verdi's *Rigoletto* & *Trovatore* & Mozart's *Don Giovanni* Philips ▲ 446090-2
Tárrega, F.:Gtr Music, w. Pepe Romero (gtr)—Fant on themes from Arriete's *Marina* Philips ▲ 446090-2

Hellwig, Klaus (pno)
Hummel, J.N.:Pno Music—Rondo ongarese; La Contemplazione [Fantasie]; Rondeau, Op. 11; La Bella Capricciosa [Polonaise] Koch Schwann ▲ SCH 311082 [DDD]
Milhaud, D.:Le Carnaval d'Aix, w. P. Gülke (cnd), Berlin RSO Koch Schwann ▲ 3-1034-2 [DDD]
Mozart, F.X.W.:Cons Pno, w. R. Bader (cnd), Cologne RSO Koch Schwann ▲ CD 311004 [ADD]
Mozart, F.X.W.:Polonaises—6 sels Koch Schwann ▲ SCH 310282 [DDD]
Mozart, F.X.W.:Vars on Romance Koch Schwann ▲ SCH 310282 [DDD]
Tal, J.:Else-Hommage, w. C. Gayer (sop), J. Bliese (nar), H. Ganz (va), G. Teutsch (vc), N. Hauptmann (hn), J. Tal (cnd) Academy ▲ ACA 8506 [ADD]

Helmer, T. (va)—see ORCHESTRAS & ENSEMBLES Orford String Quartet

Helmers, William (b cl)
Sierra, R.:Piezas Características, w. Catherine Schubilske (vn), Scott Tisdel (vc), Dennis Najoom (tpt), Stefanie Jacob (pno), Thomas Wetzel (perc), N. Gittleman (cnd) CRI ▲ CD 724 [DDD]

Helmers, William (cl)
Sierra, R.:Bocetos—Preludio; Canción del campo; Interludio nocturno; Canción de la montaña; Final con pájaros CRI ▲ CD 724 [DDD]
Sierra, R.:Con Tres, w. Shawn Mauser (bn), Stefanie Jacob (pno) CRI ▲ CD 724 [DDD]
Sierra, R.:Fantasías, w. Scott Tisdel (vc), Stefanie Jacob (pno) CRI ▲ CD 724 [DDD]
Sierra, R.:Ritmorroto CRI ▲ CD 724 [DDD]

Helmerson, Frans (vc)
Bach, J.S.:Suites Vc, BWV 1007-1012—Nos. 2, 3 & 5 *(rec 1974-77)* BIS ▲ CD 5 [AAD]
Brahms, J.:Qt 1 Pno, w. Ralf Gothoni (pno), Peter Csaba (vn), Matti Hirvikangas (va) Ondine ▲ ODE 843
Brahms, J.:Qt 3 Pno, w. Ralf Gothoni (pno), Peter Csaba (vn), Matti Hirvikangas (va) Ondine ▲ ODE 843
Britten, H.:Suite 1 Vc BIS ▲ CD 31 [AAD]
Crumb, G.:Son Vc *(rec 1975-77)* BIS ▲ CD 25 [AAD]
Debussy, C.:Son Vc, w. Hans Pålsson (pno) *(rec Nacka Aula, Nacka, Sweden, July 22, 1975)* BIS ▲ CD 28 [AAD]
Dvořák, A.:Con Vc, w. N. Järvi (cnd), Gothenburg SO BIS ▲ CD 245 [DDD]
Dvořák, A.:Silent Woods, w. N. Järvi (cnd), Gothenburg SO BIS ▲ CD 245 [DDD]
Fauré, G.:Trio, w. A. Tellefsen (vn), H. Pålsson (pno) *(rec Apr. 26-27, 1975)* BIS ▲ CD 35 [AAD]
Hindemith, P.:Son Vc, Op. 25/3 *(rec 1975-77)* BIS ▲ CD 25 [AAD]
Kodály, Z.:Son Vc, Op. 8 *(rec 1975-77)* BIS ▲ CD 25 [AAD]
Pärt, A.:Pro et contra, w. N. Järvi (cnd), Bamberg SO BIS ▲ CD 434 [DDD]
Prokofiev, S.:Son Vc, w. A. Tellefsen (vn), H. Pålsson (pno) *(rec June 13, 1975)* BIS ▲ CD 35 [AAD]
Sallinen, A.:Elegy for Sebastian Knight *(rec 1975-77)* BIS ▲ CD 25 [AAD]
Sallinen, A.:Elegy for Sebastian Knight BIS ▲ CD 41 [AAD]
Shostakovich, D.:Trio 2 Pno, w. H. Palsson (pno), A. Tellefsen (vn) BIS ▲ CD 26 [AAD]

Helmis, Fritz (hp)
Mozart, W.A.:Con Fl, K.313, w. A. Blau (fl), J. Galway (fl), H. von Karajan (cnd), Berlin PO EMI Classics ▲ CDM 69187
Mozart, W.A.:Con Fl Hp, w. A. Blau (fl), J. Galway (fl), H. von Karajan (cnd), Berlin PO EMI Classics ▲ CDM 69187

Helmrich, Dennis (hpd)
Gary Schocker:Flutist, w. Schocker, Gary (fl), Ted Hoyle (vc), Marco Granados (fl) Chesky ▲ CD 46 [DDD]

Helmrich, Dennis (pno)
Donaudy, S.:Airs de style ancien, w. Robert Guarino (ten) *(rec Trenton State College, Spring 1996)* Newport Classic ▲ NPD 85607 [DDD]
Permit Me Voyage:Songs by American Composers, w. Mary Ann Hart (mez) Albany ▲ TROY 118

Helmschrott, Robert M. (org)
Helmschrott, R.:Cross & Freedom, w. Helmut Schatz, Nancy Gibson (sop), Frieder Aurich (ten), Matthias Weichert (bass), Manfred Ball (nar), Anett Baumann (vn), Frank Phillipisch, Linda Robbins, Gerhard Wolf, Martin Homann (perc), H.-C. Rademann (cnd), Munich Trombone Quartet, Dresden Chamber Choir Vienna Modern Masters ▲ VMM 3027 [DDD]
Zimmermann, H.W.:Neujahrslied Db, w. Matthias Bohrig (db), Hans-Christoph Rademann (cnd), Dresden Chamber Choir Vienna Modern Masters ▲ VMM 3027 [DDD]

Helneman, S. (bn)—see ORCHESTRAS & ENSEMBLES Continuum Chamber Ensemble

Helps, Robert (pno)
But Yesterday Is Not Today:The American Art Song 1927-1972, w. Bethany Beardslee (sop) *(rec Columbia Recording Studios, 30th St, New York)* New World ▲ 80243-2
Debussy, C.:Ariettes oubliées, w. B. Beardslee (sop) [F] GM ▲ GM2029CD [DDD]
Debussy, C.:Proses lyriques, w. B. Beardslee (sop) [F] GM ▲ GM2029CD [DDD]
del Tredici, D.:Scherzo, w. David Del Tredici (pno) CRI ("American Masters" series) ▲ CD 689 [DDD]

Helps, Robert (pno) (cont.)
Fine, V.:Sinf & Fugato CRI ▲ CD 692 [ADD]
Helps, R.:Hommages—Hommages à Fauré; Rachmaninoff; Ravel *(rec 1989)* CRI ("American Masters" series) ▲ CD 717 [ADD]
Ravel, M.:Histoires naturelles, w. B. Beardslee (sop) [F] GM ▲ GM2029CD [DDD]

Helton, James (pno)
Kurek, M.:Matisse Impressions, w. Blair Woodwind Quintet *(rec Blair School of Music Recital Hall, 1995)* New World ▲ 80497-2

Helton, Pamela (cl)—see ORCHESTRAS & ENSEMBLES Kalamos Clarinet Quartet

Hemingway, Gerry (perc)
Sato, M.:Improvs, w. Michihiro Sato (tsugaru shamisen), Bill Frisell (elec gtr), Fred Frith (elec gtr), Tenko (sgr), Mark Miller (elec bass), Nicolas Collins (elec), Christian Marclay (turntables), Steve Colemann (sax), Tom Cora (vc), Joey Baron (perc), Mark Dresser (elec bass), Toh Ban Djan [Ikue Mori (perc), Luli Shioi (elec bass/sgr)], Semantics [Elliott Sharp (electric gtr/bass), Samm Bennett (perc), Ned Rothenberg (sax)]—23 improvisations with various accompaniment combinations *(rec Baby Monster Studio, NY, Apr. 11-16, 1988)* Hat Hut ▲ hat ART CD 6015 [ADD]

Hemmer, Lisa (fl)
O'Rourke, J.:Terminal Pharmacy, w. Tony Burr (cl), Jeff Cortazzo (b trbn), John McEntire (dr), Rob Prosser (acc), Isha Suftin (acc), Mike Dockter (vc), Hattie Franck (vc), Robert Keck (vc), Mary LaBreque (vc), Dan Loch (vc), Stan Saderk (vc), Sue Oberg (fl), Wendi Lev (fl), Jim Vanden (fl), Jim O'Rourke (gtr), Steve Braack (elec) Tzadik ▲ TZA 7011 [DDD]

Hempel, A. (pno)
Delz, C.:Qt Pno, w. C. Delz (pno), F. Gauwerky (pno), J. Krist (pno), N. Shirato (pno) Grammont ▲ CTSP 18-2 [ADD]

Henck, Herbert (pno)
Boulez, P.:Son 1 Pno Wergo ▲ WER 60121-50 [DDD]
Boulez, P.:Son 2 Pno Wergo ▲ WER 60121-50 [DDD]
Boulez, P.:Son 3 Pno Wergo ▲ WER 60121-50 [DDD]
Cage, J.:Cheap Imitation Wergo ▲ WER 6186-2 [DDD]
Cage, J.:Music of Changes Wergo ▲ WER 60099-50
Ives, C.:Pno Music Wergo ▲ WER 60112-50
Ives, C.:Three-Page Son Wergo ▲ WER 60112-50
Mompou, F.:Música callada ECM New Series ▲ 78118-21523-2
Mosolov, A.:Nocturnes Pno ECM ▲ 21569-2
Mosolov, A.:Nocturnes Pno *(rec Frankfurt, Germany, Mar 1995)* ECM New Series ▲ 78118-21569-2 [DDD]
Mosolov, A.:Son 2 Pno ECM ▲ 21569-2
Mosolov, A.:Son 2 Pno *(rec Frankfurt, Germany, Mar 1995)* ECM New Series ▲ 78118-21569-2 [DDD]
Mosolov, A.:Son 5 Pno ECM ▲ 21569-2
Mosolov, A.:Son 5 Pno *(rec Frankfurt, Germany, Mar 1995)* ECM New Series ▲ 78118-21569-2 [DDD]
Schoenberg, A.:Pno Music—Pno Pieces, Opp. 11, 19, 23 & 33/a & b; Suite for Pno, Op. 25; Fragments of 17 Pno Pieces from the estate Wergo ▲ WER 6268-2
Stockhausen, K.:Klavierstücke I-XI Wergo 2-▲ WER 60135/36-50 [DDD]

Hendel, Georg Friedrich (vn)
Bach, J.S.:Con Vn & Ob, w. Helmut Winschermann (ob), H. Winschermann (cnd), German Bach Soloists Musicaphon ▲ 51357 [AAD]

Hendel, Marianne (fl)
Mercadante, S.:Serenate for 3 Fls, w. Andras Adorjan (fl), Aurèle Nicolet (fl) Tudor ▲ TUD 763 [DDD]

Henderson, Chad (gtr)
First, D.:Lens Pt 2, w. M. Bard (gtr), D. First (gtr), E. Sandrof (syn) *(rec Oct. 1987)* O.O. Discs ▲ OO 5 [DDD]

Henderson, Chad (teahouse gtr/b gtr)
First, D.:The Good Book's (Accurate) Jail of Escape Dust Coordinates 2, w. Matt Sullivan (ob), Chris Jepperson (cl), Annemarie Wiesner (vn), Gary Trosclair (tpt), Elaine Kaplinsky (kbd syn), Kevin Sparke (perc), David First (e-bow gtr/teahouse gtr/Distortion gtr/kbd syn/programming) *(rec Baby Monster Studios, NYC, May 1992)* O. O. Discs ▲ OO 23 [DDD]

Henderson, Doug (peckhorn/bass/toy pno)
Exquisite Corpses from P.S. 122, w. David Watson (shears/stick vn/gtr/tpt), Judy Dunaway (gtr/balloons), Anthony Coleman (sampler), Raissa St. Pierre (drums), Guy Yarden (vn/pno), Leslie Ross (bn), Linda Austin (gtr), Bruce Kaplan (gtr), Sue Ann Harkey (gtr), Cinnie Cole (sampler), et al. ¿What Next? ▲ WN 0002 [ADD]

Henderson, Luther (kbd)
Brass on Broadway, w. Canadian Brass, Edward Metz (perc), Star of Indiana Drummers Philips ▲ 442133-2

Henderson, Stephen (perc)
Miki, M.:Mar Spiritual, w. Evelyn Glennie (mar), Gary Kettel (perc), Greg Knowles (perc) *(rec Whitfield Street Studios, London, Sept. 22-29, 1994)* Catalyst ▲ 09026-68193-2 [DDD]

Henderson, Veronica (vc)
Rütti, C.:Choral Music, w. Ian Moore (cnd), Cambridge Voices—O magnum mysterium; Lieder; Der Liebe; Fortis ut mors; Osculetur; Que tu es belle, ma bien-aimée; Ich schlief, doch mein Herz; Behold; Thou Hast Ravished My Heart; In meinem Garten; Vater Unser; Gloria (Missa Angelorum) *(rec St. Cyriac's Church, Swaffham Prior, Mar, 1995)* Herald ▲ HAVPCD 183 [DDD]

Henderson, W. (pno)
Goosen, F.:Clausulae, w. M. Karman (vn) CRI ▲ CD 665 [ADD]
Goosen, F.:Temple Music, w. M. Karman (vn) CRI ▲ CD 665 [ADD]

Hendl, Walter (pno)
Beethoven, L. van:Con Vn, Vc & Pno, "Triple Con", w. John Corigliano (vn), Leonard Rose (vc), B. Walter (cnd), New York PO Sony Classical ("Bruno Walter:The Edition" series) ▲ SMK 64479

Hendrick, Wayne (fl)
Musical Colors, w. Hye Yun Chung Bennett (hp) Klavier ▲ KCD 11063 [DDD]

Hendry, Linn (pno)
Bloch, E.:From Jewish Life, w. R. Wallfisch (vc) Chandos ("Collect" series) ▲ CHAN 6552 [DDD]
Dvořák, A.:Pieces (5) Vc, w. R. Wallfisch (vc)—Polonaise in A; Rondo in g; Silent Woods; Slavonic Dances, Op. 46/3 & 8 Chandos ("Collect" series) ▲ CHAN 6552 [DDD]
Medtner, N.:Son 1 Vn, w. Mateja Marinkovic (vn) ASV ▲ ASV CD 951
Medtner, N.:Son 3 Vn, w. Mateja Marinkovic (vn) ASV ▲ ASV CD 951
Schnittke, A.:Chamber Music, w. Mateja Marinkovic (vn), et al.—Suite in the Old Style; À Paganini; Gratulations Rondo; Madrigal in Memoriam Oleg Kagan; Mozart; Praeludium in Memoriam Shostakovich; Stille Musik; Stille Nacht ASV ▲ ASV 877 [DDD]

Henegar, Gregg (ctbn)
Erb, D.:Con Ctbn, w. H. Farberman (cnd), London PO Leonarda ■ LE 302 (CrO2)
Erb, D.:Con Ctbn, w. H. Farberman (cnd), London PO Leonarda ▲ LE 331 [DDD]

Henegouwen, Peter Beijersbergen van (pno)
Andriessen, L.:Elegie, w. Quirijn van Regteren Altena (db) Olympia ▲ OLY 467 [DDD]
Desenclos, A.:Aria & Rondo, w. Quirijn van Regteren Altena (db) Olympia ▲ OLY 467 [DDD]
Ginastera, A.:Pampeana 2, w. Quirijn van Regteren Altena (db) Olympia ▲ OLY 467 [DDD]
Hindemith, P.:Son Db, w. Quirijn van Regteren Altena (db) Olympia ▲ OLY 467 [DDD]
Mendelssohn, F.:Assai tranquillo, w. W. Mijnders (vc) Partridge ▲ 1137-2 [DDD]
Mendelssohn, F.:Lied ohne Worte Vc, w. W. Mijnders (vc) Partridge ▲ 1137-2 [DDD]
Mendelssohn, F.:Son 1 Vc, w. W. Mijnders (vc) Partridge ▲ 1137-2 [DDD]
Mendelssohn, F.:Son 2 Vc, w. W. Mijnders (vc) Partridge ▲ 1137-2 [DDD]
Mendelssohn, F.:Vars concertantes, w. W. Mijnders (vc) Partridge ▲ 1137-2 [DDD]
Pijper, W.:Son 1 Vc, w. Wouter Mijnders (vc) Donemus ▲ CV 15
Pijper, W.:Trio 2 Pno, w. Ronald Hoogeveen (vn), Wouter Mijnders (vc) Donemus ▲ CV 15
Thilman, J.P.:Charaktere, w. Quirijn van Regteren Altena (db) Olympia ▲ OLY 467 [DDD]
Wilder, A.:Small Suite, w. Quirijn van Regteren Altena (db) Olympia ▲ OLY 467 [DDD]

Henes, J. (tpt)
Shostakovich, D.:Con 1 Pno, w. D. Han (pno), P. Freeman (cnd), Chicago Sinfonietta Pro Arte ▲ CDD 551 [DDD]

Henkel, Christophe (vc)—see also ORCHESTRAS & ENSEMBLES Arion Trio
Brahms, J.:Sons Vc (comp), w. E. Westenholz (pno) BIS ▲ CD 192
Brahms, J.:Trio Cl, w. Dieter Klöcker (cl), Claudius Tanski (pno) MD + G ▲ MDG 3010595 [DDD]
Hindemith, P.:Son Vc & Pno, Op. 11/3, w. Georges Pludermacher (pno) Signum ▲ X64-00 [DDD]
Pfitzner, H.:Son Vc, w. Georges Pludermacher (pno) Signum ▲ X64-00 [DDD]
Saint-Saëns, C.:Fant Vn, w. I. Moretti (hp) Valois ("Musique Française" series) ▲ V 4657
Strauss, R.:Son Vc, w. Georges Pludermacher (pno) Signum ▲ X64-00 [DDD]

Henking, Monika (org)
Pfiffner, E.:Componimento Org, w. M. Atzmon (cnd), Basel SO *(rec Dec. 1980)* Pro Viva ▲ ISPV 170 [ADD]

Henneberger, Jürg (pno)—see ORCHESTRAS & ENSEMBLES Zurich New Music Ensemble

Hennessey, Gail (ob)
Vivaldi, A.:Sons Ob, w. P. Goodwin (ob), J. Holloway (vn), C. Lawson (cl), N. North (archlt/gtr), S. Sheppard (vc), F. Eustace (bn), J. Toll (hpd/org)—RV.53, 58, 81 & 779 Harmonia Mundi USA ▲ HMU 907104

Hennessy, Mika (db)
Vivaldi, A.:Cons Vn, Op. 8/1-4, "The Four Seasons", w. Jerome Franke (vn), Karine Garibova (vn), Pasquale Laurino (vn), Olga Miliaeva (va), Roza Borisova (vc), Melanie Panush (ham dlc), Stanislav Venglevski (bayan), Mike Kashou (arabic tabla), Daryl Stuermer (gtr), Ed Paloucek (celtic fid), Gary Bottoni (highland pipe), Dubuffet String Quartet *(rec July-Sept 1995)* EarthBeat! ▲ 35270-2 [DDD]

Henning, Geir (pno)
Thommessen, O.A.:Gratia agimus, w. Marianne Willumsen (sop) Caprice ▲ CAP 21403

Henrich, Isabelle (pno)
Sauguet, H.:Suite Cl, w. Eric Perrier (cl) Sonpact ▲ SPT 96017 [DDD]

Henriot-Schweitzer, Nicole (pno)
Indy, V. d':Sym on a French Mountain Air, w. C. Munch (cnd), Boston SO RCA Gold Seal ▲ 09026-62582-2

Henry, J. (trbn)—see also ORCHESTRAS & ENSEMBLES Quatror de cuivres Novus
Ducommun, S.:Petit Concert, w. P. Lehmann (tpt), D. Streit (cnt) Gallo ▲ CD 654 [DDD]

Henry, J. (vn/elec)
Hunt, J.:Chimanzzi, w. J. Hunt (elec) O.O. Discs ▲ OO 9 [DDD]

Henry, Jane (vn)
Jenkins, L.:Monkey on the Dragon, w. Leroy Jenkins (vn), Henry Threadgill (fl), Don Byron (cl), Marth Ehrlich (b cl), Janet Frice (bn), Vincent Chancey (hn), Frank Gordon (tpt), Jeff Hoyer (trbn), David Soldier (vn), Ron Lawrence (va), Mary Wooton (vc), Lindsey Horner (db), Thurman Barker (traps), Myra Melford (pno), T. Léon (cnd) *(rec live, Merkin Concert Hall, New York City, Apr. 9, 1992)* CRI ("eXchange" series) ▲ CD 663 [DDD]

Henry, Paul (gtr)
The Virtuoso Guitar of Spain & Latin America Centaur ▲ CRC 2113 [DDD]

Henschke, Andrea (vn/va)
Dauprat, L.-F.:Qnt Hn & Strs, w. P. Arnold (hn), A. Grötzinger (vn), H.-B. Henscke (va), P. Gerschwitz (vc) Bayer ▲ BR 100236 [DDD]
Mozart, W.A.:Qnt Hn, K.407, w. P. Arnold (hn), A. Grötzinger (vn), H.-B. Henscke (va), P. Gerschwitz (vc) Bayer ▲ BR 100236 [DDD]
Stamitz, A.:Qnt Hn, w. P. Arnold (hn), A. Grötzinger (vn), H.-B. Henscke (va), P. Gerschwitz (vc) Bayer ▲ BR 100236 [DDD]

Henscke, H.-B. (va)
Dauprat, L.-F.:Qnt Hn & Strs, w. P. Arnold (hn), A. Grötzinger (vn), A. Henschke (vn/va), P. Gerschwitz (vc) Bayer ▲ BR 100236 [DDD]
Mozart, W.A.:Qnt Hn, K.407, w. P. Arnold (hn), A. Grötzinger (vn), A. Henschke (vn/va), P. Gerschwitz (vc) Bayer ▲ BR 100236 [DDD]
Stamitz, A.:Qnt Hn, w. P. Arnold (hn), A. Grötzinger (vn), A. Henschke (vn/va), P. Gerschwitz (vc) Bayer ▲ BR 100236 [DDD]

Hensel, Lothar (band)
Piazzolla, A.:Con Band, w. J. Goritzki (cnd), German Chamber Academy Orch Capriccio ▲ CD 10565 [DDD]

Henstra, Siebe (hpd)
Frescobaldi, G.:Hpd Music—Toccata seconda in g; Partita sopra l'Aria di Follia; Canzona sesta detta La presenti; Cento Partite sopra Passacagli Ricercar ▲ RIC 167136
Gabrieli, A.:Kbd Music—Canzon francese detta Petit Jacquet; Canzon francese detta Le bergier; Canzon francese detta Je ne diray moy bergière Ricercar ▲ RIC 167136
Luzzaschi, L.:Kbd Music—Toccata in e Ricercar ▲ RIC 167136
Merula, T.:Kbd Music—Toccata in g; Capriccio Cromatico; Capriccio in g Ricercar ▲ RIC 167136
Merulo, C.:Kbd Music—Toccata X del decimo tono Ricercar ▲ RIC 167136
Picchi, G.:Kbd Music—Toccata in d; Pass'e Mezzo in d Ricercar ▲ RIC 167136
Storace, B.:Kbd Music—Ciaccona in C; Passacaglia in a Ricercar ▲ RIC 167136

Henstra, Siebe (hpd/org)
Biber, H. von:Mystery (or Rosary) Sons, w. Ryo Terakado (baroque vn), Kaori Uemura (vl)—Passacaglia; Son. 6 *(rec Oud-Katholieke Kerk, The Hague, Netherlands, Aug. 11-12, 15-17, 1994)* Denon ▲ CO 78946 [DDD]
Biber, H. von:Sons Vn & Continuo, w. Ryo Terakado (baroque vn), Kaori Uemura (vl)—V in e [from 8 vn sons.]; VI in c; VIII in a *(rec Oud-Katholieke Kerk, the Hague, Netherlands, Aug. 11-12, 15-17, 1994)* Denon ▲ CO 78946 [DDD]
Biber, H. von:Son violino solo representativa, w. Ryo Terakado (baroque vn), Kaori Uemura (vl) *(rec Oud-Katholieke Kerk, the Hague, Netherlands, Aug. 11-12, 15-17, 1994)* Denon ▲ CO 78946 [DDD]
Corelli, A.:Sons Vn, Op. 5, w. Ryo Terakado (baroque vn), Lucia Swarts (baroque vc)—Nos. 7-12 *(rec Oud-Katholieke Kerk, The Hague, Netherlands, Aug 8-10, 1994)* Denon ▲ CO 78820 [DDD]
Krieger, J.P.:Trio Sons, w. Mihoko Kimura (vn), Peter Wendland (vl), Michael Freimuth (thb)—Nos. 1-6 Prezioso ▲ 840.402

Henstra, Siebe (org)—see ORCHESTRAS & ENSEMBLES Ricercar Consort

Hentrich, Bernhard (vc)
Berlinski, H.:Das Gebet Bonhoeffers, w. Nancy Gibson (sop), Matthias Weichert (bass), Olaf Georgi (fl), Herman Berlinski (org), Holger Miersch (cel), Martin Homann (perc), Hans-Christoph Rademann (cnd), Dresden Chamber Choir Vienna Modern Masters ▲ VMM 3027 [DDD]

Henze, Sheryl (fl)—see ORCHESTRAS & ENSEMBLES Flute Force

Herák, Miroslav (vc)
Scarmolin, A.L.:Sym 2, w. Stanislav Bicák (bn), Peter Sivanič (hn), J. E. Suben (cnd), Slovak RSO Bratislava *(rec Bratislava, Jan 23-25, 1995)* New World ▲ 80502-2

Herbert, Giselle (hp)
Beethoven, L. van:Vars on Grétry's romance "Un fièvre brûlante", WoO 72, w. M. Grauwels (fl), B. Bessler (vn), C. Springuel (va), Y. Stormes (gtr) Syrinx ▲ 94101 [DDD]
Glinka, M.:Vars on a Theme of Mozart Syrinx ▲ 94101 [DDD]
Spohr, L.:Son 4 Vn, w. M. Grauwels (fl), B. Bessler (vn), C. Springuel (va), Y. Stormes (gtr) Syrinx ▲ 94101 [DDD]
Spohr, L.:Son Vn Hp, Op. 113, w. Philipp Naegele (vn) Bayer ▲ 100264 [DDD]
Spohr, L.:Son Vn Hp, Op. 115, w. Philipp Naegele (vn) Bayer ▲ 100264 [DDD]

Herbin, E. (pno)
Herbin, R.:Qt Pno, w. Alexis Galpérine (vn), Bruno Pasquier (va), Mark Drobinsky (vc) Gallo ▲ CD 711 [ADD]
Schmitt, F.:Hasards, w. A. Galpérine (pno), B. Pasquier (pno), M. Drobinsky (pno) Gallo ▲ CD 711 [ADD]

Herder, Hermann (bn)—see ORCHESTRAS & ENSEMBLES Stuttgart Wind Quintet

▲ = CD ♦ = Enhanced CD Δ = MD ■ = Cassette Tape □ = DCC

Hering, Ekkehard (rcr)
Telemann, G.P.:Con Rcr, Fl, w. E.–B. Hilse (fl), Academy for Old Music — LaserLight ▲ 15634 [DDD]

Heringman, Jacob (Renaissance lt)
Dowland, J.:Lachrimae, or Seaven Teares, w. Caroline Trevor (alt), Rose Consort of Viols — Amon Ra ▲ CD-SAR 55 [DDD]

Herman, Benjamin (glock)
Kernis, A.J.:Nocturne, w. Nancy Allen Lundy (sop), John Dent (tpt), Jeff Milarsky (glock), Leslie Stifelman (pno), Lisa Moore (pno), M. Barrett (cnd) *(rec Manhattan Center Studios, New York, May 31–June 3, 1995)* — New Albion ♦ NA 083CD

Herman, Benjamin (perc)
Crumb, G.:An Idyll for the Misbegotten, w. Z. Mueller (fl), G. Gottlieb (timp), S. Paysen (perc) — New World ▲ NW 357-2
Druckman, J.:Dark Upon the Harp, w. J. DeGaetani (mez), J. Haas (perc), J. Druckman (cnd), American Brass Quintet [E] *(rec Aspen Music Festival 8/6/88)* — Bridge ▲ BCD 9023 [ADD]

Herman, František (bn)
Beethoven, L. van:Qnt Ob, 3 Hns & Bn, w. J. Mihule (ob), Z. Tylšar (hn), B. Tylšar (hn), R. Beránek (hn) — Supraphon ▲ 11 1445-2 [DDD]
Beethoven, L. van:Sxt Winds, Op. 71, w. V. Kyzivát (cl), Z. Tesař (cl), Z. Tylšar (hn), B. Tylšar (hn), V. Horák (bn) — Supraphon ▲ 11 1445-2 [DDD]
Mozart, W.A.:Con Bn, w. V. Neumann (cnd), Czech PO — Supraphon Collection ▲ 11 0636-2 [ADD]
Reicha, A.:Trios Hns, Op. 93, w. B. Tylšar (hn), Z. Tylšar (hn) [arr Fr hns & bn] — Supraphon ▲ 11 1445-2 [DDD]
Vivaldi, A.:Cons Bn, w. B. Warchal (cnd), Slovak CO—5 concerti—RV.472, 481, 484, 497, 501 — Supraphon ▲ 110109-2 [DDD]

Hermann, Claudius (vc)
Mozart, W.A.:Clemenza, w. L. Popp (sop), R. Ziesack (sop), A. Murray (mez), D. Ziegler (mez), P. Langridge (ten), L. Polgar (bass), T. Grabowski (hpd), N. Harnoncourt (cnd), Zurich Opera Orch, Zurich Opera House Chorus — Teldec 2-▲ 90857-2

Hermann, D. (va)
Ravel, M.:Intro & Allegro, w. M. Golden (hp), M. Meisenbach (fl), R. McDowall (cl), R. Neal (vn), D. Pettys (vn), G. Manasjan (vc) — Centaur ▲ CRC 2114 [DDD]

Hermann, Josef (db)
Pfitzner, H.:Sxt Cl, w. L. Wlach (cl), A. Kamper (vn), E. Weis (va), F. Kvarda (vc), W. Kamper (pno) — Preiser ▲ 93111 (m) [AAD]

Hermann, Walter (cl)
Berg, A.:Adagio, w. Hans–Udo Heinzmann (fl), Malte Lammers (ob), Heinrich Horlein (vn), Jaap Zeijl (va), Seven Forsberg (vc), Willi Beyer (db), Jurgen Lamke (pno), Werner Hagen (pno), Volker Kneip (perc) [arr chamber ensemble] — Koch Schwann ▲ SCH CD 311912
Busoni, F.:Berceuse élégiaque, w. Hans–Udo Heinzmann (fl), Malte Lammers (ob), Heinrich Horlein (vn), Jaap Zeijl (va), Seven Forsberg (vc), Willi Beyer (db), Jurgen Lamke (pno), Werner Hagen (pno), Volker Kneip (perc) [arr Stein for chamber ensemble] — Koch Schwann ▲ SCH CD 311912
Debussy, C.:Prélude à l'après-midi d'un faune, w. Hans–Udo Heinzmann (fl), Malte Lammers (ob), Heinrich Horlein (vn), Jaap Zeijl (va), Seven Forsberg (vc), Willi Beyer (db), Jurgen Lamke (pno), Werner Hagen (pno), Volker Kneip (perc) [arr Sachs for chamber ensemble] — Koch Schwann ▲ SCH CD 311912
Schoenberg, A.:Chamber Sym 1, w. Hans–Udo Heinzmann (fl), Malte Lammers (ob), Heinrich Horlein (vn), Jaap Zeijl (va), Seven Forsberg (vc), Willi Beyer (db), Jurgen Lamke (pno), Werner Hagen (pno), Volker Kneip (perc) [arr Webern for chamber ensemble] — Koch Schwann ▲ SCH CD 311912

Hermans, J. (org)
Saxophone & Organ, Vol. 3, w. Jean–Pierre Rorive (sax) — Pavane ▲ ADW 7320 [DDD]

Hermansen, T. S. (vc)—see ORCHESTRAS & ENSEMBLES Copenhagen Trio

Hermansen, Troels Svane (vc)
Beethoven, L. van:Qnt Fl, Vn, 2 Vas & Vc, w. T. L. Christiansen (fl), J. Søe Hansen (vn), H. Olsen (va), M. Dolgin (va) — Kontrapunkt 2-▲ 32160/61 [DDD]
Kuhlau, F.:Qnts Fl, w. T.L. Christiansen (fl), J. Søe Hansen (vn), M. Dolgin (va), H. Olsen (va) — Kontrapunkt 2-▲ 32160/61 [DDD]
Ravel, M.:Son Vn Vc, w. S. Elbæk (vn) — Kontrapunkt ▲ KPT 32174 [DDD]

Hermansson, Sören (hn)—see also ORCHESTRAS & ENSEMBLES Wisconsin Brass Quintet
Andrés, B.:Chants d'arreère-saison, w. Erica Goodman (hp) *(rec Länna Church, Sweden, Mar 30–Apr 2, 1996)* — BIS ▲ CD 793 [DDD]
Atterberg, K.:Con Hn, w. E. Chivzhel (cnd), Umeå Sinfonietta — BIS ▲ CD 376 [DDD]
Eliasson, A.:Con Hn, w. Ostrobothnian CO — Caprice ▲ CAP 21422
Horn & Harp Soirée:19th Century French & Italian Duos, w. Erica Goodman (hp) *(rec Sept. 20–23, 1993)* — BIS ▲ CD 648 [DDD]
Horn & Organ Recital, w. Per–Ove Larsson (org) *(rec Adolf Fredrik Church, Stockholm, Feb 1995)* — Opus 3 ▲ OP 19501 [AAD]
Jacob, G.:Con Hn, w. E. Chivzhel (cnd), Umeå Sinfonietta — BIS ▲ CD 376 [DDD]
Klein, L.:AOIDOI, w. Erica Goodman (hp) *(rec Länna Church, Sweden, Mar 30–Apr 2, 1996)* — BIS ▲ CD 793 [DDD]
Koch, E. von:Nocturne, w. Erica Goodman (hp) *(rec Länna Church, Sweden, Mar 30–Apr 2, 1996)* — BIS ▲ CD 793 [DDD]
Koetsier, J.:Son Hn & Hp, w. Erica Goodman (hp) *(rec Länna Church, Sweden, Mar 30–Apr 2, 1996)* — BIS ▲ CD 793 [DDD]
Larsson, L.–E.:Concertino Hn, w. E. Chivzhel (cnd), Umeå Sinfonietta — BIS ▲ CD 376 [DDD]
Procaccini, T.:Serenata, w. Erica Goodman (hp) *(rec Länna Church, Sweden, Mar 30–Apr 2, 1996)* — BIS ▲ CD 793 [DDD]
Reger, M.:Scherzino, w. E. Chivzhel (cnd), Umeå Sinfonietta — BIS ▲ CD 376 [DDD]
Seiber, M.:Notturno Hn, w. E. Chivzhel (cnd), Umeå Sinfonietta — BIS ▲ CD 376 [DDD]
Singer, J.:Suite Hn, w. Erica Goodman (hp) *(rec Länna Church, Sweden, Mar 30–Apr 2, 1996)* — BIS ▲ CD 793 [DDD]

Herojnová, Jana (vn)
Martinů, B.:Les Rondes, w. Jurij Likin (ob), Vlastimil Mareš (cl), Lumír Vanek (bn), Vladislav Kozderka (tpt), Pavel Kutman (vn), Ivan Klánsky (pno) *(rec Studio Martínek, Prague, Mar 3, 1995)* — Panton ("Protokol XX" series) ▲ 811348-2 [DDD]

Herr, John (kbd)—see ORCHESTRAS & ENSEMBLES Plymouth Trio

Herrera (pno)
Brahms, J.:Liebeslieder Waltzes for SATB, w. A. Guzelimian (pno), Los Angeles Vocal Arts Ensemble [G] — Elektra/Nonesuch ▲ 79008-2 [DDD]
Brahms, J.:Neue Liebeslieder Waltzes, w. A. Guzelimian (pno), Los Angeles Vocal Arts Ensemble [G] — Elektra/Nonesuch ▲ 79008-2 [DDD]

Herrera, R. de (gtr)
Lemeland, A.:Fant Cl & Gtr, w. R. Fontain (cl) — Skarbo ▲ SKR 3901 [AAD]
Lemeland, A.:Gtr Music—YS, Op. 47; Hommage à Albert Roussel, Op. 6; Vars., Op. 58 — Skarbo ▲ SKR 3901 [AAD]
Lemeland, A.:Vars Va, w. J. Dupouy (va) — Skarbo ▲ SKR 3901 [AAD]

Herrick, Christopher (org)
At Westminster Abbey — Hyperion ▲ CDA 66121
Bach, J.S.:Canonic Vars on "Von Himmel hoch..." [Metzler organ, St. Nikolaus Church, Bremgarten, Switzerland] *(rec May 1991)* — Hyperion ▲ CDA 66455 [DDD]
Bach, J.S.:Chorale Preludes Org—BWV 653, 690, 691, 694–713 [Metzler Org Jesuitenkirche, Lucerne] — Hyperion 2-▲ CDA 67071/72
Bach, J.S.:Chorale Preludes (Schübler) [Metzler Org Jesuitenkirche, Lucerne] — Hyperion 2-▲ CDA 67071/72
Bach, J.S.:Chorale Settings, BWV 651–668 [Metzler Org Jesuitenkirche, Lucerne] — Hyperion 2-▲ CDA 67071/72

Herrick, Christopher (org) (cont.)
Bach, J.S.:Org Music (misc)—Fantasia & Fugue in g, BWV 542; Fantasia in c, BWV 562; Fantasia in G, BWV 572; Fantasia & Fugue in c, BWV 537; Preludes & Fugues:in a, BWV 543, in b, BWV 544, in G, BWV 541, in E♭, BWV 552, in c, BWV 546, in e, BWV 548, in C, BWV 547, in f, BWV 534, in A, BWV 536 & in C, BWV 545 — Hyperion 2-▲ CDA 66791/92
Bach, J.S.:Partitas Org, "Chorale Partitas" [Metzler organ, St. Nikolaus Church, Bremgarten, Switzerland] *(rec May 1991)* — Hyperion ▲ CDA 66455 [DDD]
Bach, J.S.:Toccata & Fugue Org, BWV 565 — Meridian ▲ CDE 84148
Daquin, L.–C.:Nouveau livre de noëls [Org of St. Rémy de Dieppe, France] — Hyperion ▲ CDA 66816
Guilmant, A.:Org Music—Deuxième Offertoire sur des Noëls; Introduction et variations sur un ancien noël polonais; Noël Brabançon; Sonata No. 1 — Meridian ▲ CDE 84148
Organ Fireworks, Vol. 5 — Hyperion ▲ CDA 66676 [DDD]
Popular Organ Music from Westminster Abbey — Meridian ▲ 84148
Rheinberger, J.:Suite Vn, Op. 150, w. Paul Barritt (vn) — Hyperion ▲ CDA 66883
Rheinberger, J.:Suite Vn Vc, w. Paul Barritt (vn), Richard Lester (vc) — Hyperion ▲ CDA 66883

Herrington, Benjamin (trbn)—see ORCHESTRAS & ENSEMBLES Meridian Arts Ensemble

Herrington, Jon (gtr)
So Many Stars, w. Kathleen Battle (sop), Antonio Hart (sax), Grover Washington Jr (sax), Tom Harrell (flgl), James Carter (b cl), Cyrus Chestnut (pno), Romero Lubambo (gtr), Ira Coleman (elec bass), Christian McBride (elec bass), Cyro Baptista (perc), Steven Berrios (perc) *(rec Hit Factory, Clinton Recording Studios, R.P.M. Sound Studios, Unique Recording Studios, Power Station)* — Sony Classical ▲ SK 68473 [DDD]

Herrmann, Claudius (vc)
Reinecke, C.:Sons Vc, w. Saiko Sasaki (pno) — CPO ▲ CPO 999342

Herrmann, Heiko (tpt)
de Fesch, W.:Sons Vn, Op. 8a, w. S. Haak (vn), E. Schloter (org)—No. 10 *(rec Nov. 18–21, 1991)* — Koch Schwann ▲ SCH 310252 [DDD]

Herrmann, Irene (pno)
Bowles, P.:Canciones (4) de Garcia Lorca — Koch International Classics ▲ KIC 7343 [DDD]
Bowles, P.:Miniatures (4) — Koch International Classics ▲ KIC 7343 [DDD]
Bowles, P.:Nocturne for 2 Pnos, w. Michael McGushin (pno) — Koch International Classics ▲ KIC 7343 [DDD]
Bowles, P.:Scènes d'Anabase, w. Brian Staufenbiel (ten), Roger Weismeyer (ob) — Koch International Classics ▲ KIC 7343 [DDD]
Bowles, P.:Son Fl, w. Susan Waller (fl) — Koch International Classics ▲ KIC 7343 [DDD]
Bowles, P.:Songs, w. Brian Staufenbiel (ten) — Koch International Classics ▲ KIC 7343 [DDD]
Tailleferre, G.:Forlane, w. Leta Miller (fl) *(rec UC, Santa Cruz, May 1992)* — Helicon Classics ▲ HE 1008
Tailleferre, G.:Waltzes, w. Michael McGuishin (pno) *(rec UC, Santa Cruz, May 1992)* — Helicon Classics ▲ HE 1008

Herrmann, T. R. (hmc)
Herrmann, B.:Night Digger:Scenario Macbre, w. R. Green (va d'amore), Sessions of London — Label "X" ▲ LXCD 12 [AAD]

Hersch, Fred (pno)
Hersch, F.:Tango Bittersweet, w. E. Friedlander (vc) *(rec Aug. 31, 1993)* — Catalyst ▲ 09026-61979-2 ■ 09026-61979-4
Red Square Blue Russian Composers, w. James Newton (fl), Toots Thielemans (hmc), Phil Woods (a sax), Erik Friedlander (vc), Steve La Spina (bass), Jeff Hirshfield (drums) — Angel ▲ CDC 54743

Hersh, Paul (pno)
Great Ragtime Classics, w. David Montgomery (pno) — Victrola ■ ALK1-9543

Hertz, Friedmann (org)
Contemporary Organ Music — Koch Schwann ▲ SCH 313892 [DDD]
Neue russische Orgelmusik — Koch Schwann ▲ SCH 313832 [DDD]

Herz, Otto (pno)
Live at Carnegie Hall, w. Kenneth Lane (ten) — Valhalla ▲ VRCD 1594
Wagner, R.:Arias & Scenes, w. Kenneth Lane (ten), Martin Kalmanoff (pno), Levering Rothfuss (pno)—Rienzi's Prayer [from Rienzi]; In fernem Land, Mein Liebe Schwan [from Lohengrin]; Siegmund heiss' ich! [from Die Walküre]; Nothung! Nothung!, Schmiede mein Hammer! [from Siegfried]; O König!, Die alte Weise, O diese Sonne! [from Tristan und Isolde]; Prize Song [from Die Meistersinger]; Siegfried's Narration, Brünnhilde! Heilige Braut! [from Götterdämmerung]; Amfortas! Die Wunde!, Nur eine Waffe taugt [from Parsifal] — Valhalla VRCD 1595 [ADD]

Herza, Lubomír (vc)—see also ORCHESTRAS & ENSEMBLES Quartetto con Flauto
Jirásek, J.:Katharsis, w. Václav Slivansky (fl), Ada Silvanská (vn), Renata Jelínková (hpd) *(rec St. Virgin Mary Church, Strahov)* — Arta ▲ 0054 [DDD]

Herzbaum, Nestor (fl)
Clementi, M.:Pno Music (comp), w. Aldo Antognazzi (pno), Christian Badian (pno), Eduardo Cazaban (pno), Cristina Da Souza (pno), Dao Di Renzo (pno), Pablo Lavandera (pno), Yi Fang Huang (vn), Silvina Cardenas (fl)—Sons (6) for Pno, Op. 2, Nos. 1, 3 & 5 (w. flutes); Duets (3) for Piano 4–Hands, Op. 3, Nos. 2 & 3; Sons (3) for Pno & Vn, Op. 3, No. 4 — Aura Classics ▲ AU 32287

Herzfeld, Günther (pno)
Schoenberg, A.:Little Pieces Pno *(rec Siemensvilla, Berlin–Lankwitz, Aug. 1994)* — EDA ▲ EDA 008-2 [DDD]
Ullmann, V.:Vars & Double Fugue *(rec Siemensvilla, Berlin–Lankwitz, Aug. 1994)* — EDA ▲ EDA 008-2 [DDD]

Herzl, H. (vn)—see ORCHESTRAS & ENSEMBLES Pro Arte String Quartet

Herzog, Gerty (pno)
Blacher, B.:Con 2 Pno, w. H. Kegel (cnd), Dresden PO — Berlin Classics ▲ BER 9015 [ADD]

Heschke, Richard (org)
Richard Heschke at the Hradetsky in Red Bank, NJ — Arkay ▲ ARK 6127 [DDD]

Hess, Alyssa (hp)
Fine, I.:Notturno, w. J. Lyman Hill (va), L. Foss (cnd), Brooklyn PO — CRI ▲ CD 574 [ADD]

Hess, John (pno)
Berg, O.:Peter Quince at the Clavier, w. J. Relyea (bass), L. Freedman (E♭ & B♭ cl), T. Tureski (perc) — Centaur ▲ CRC 2167 [DDD]

Hess, Katharina (fl)—see ORCHESTRAS & ENSEMBLES Cologne Flautando

Hess, Myra (pno)
Bach, J.S.:Jesu bleibet meine Freude *(rec 1928)* — Pearl ▲ PEA 9462 (m) [AAD]
Bach, J.S.:Music of, w. Harold Bauer (pno), Ignaz Friedman (pno), Percy Grainger (pno), Harold Samuel (pno)—Toccata No. 3 in G; Toccata & Fugue in d for Org [trans Tausig]; Well–Tempered Clavier Book 1, Nos. 5 & 21; Chorale [from Cant 147; trans Bauer]; Chromatic Fant & Fugue [trans von Bülow]; 2–Part Inventions Nos. 1, 6 & 8; Fant & Fugue in g for Org [trans Liszt]; Toccata & Fugue in g; French Suite No. 6; Gigue [from Partita in B♭, Book 1, No. 1] [all pno rolls] — Nimbus ("Grand Piano" series) ▲ NI 8808 [DDD]
Bach, J.S.:Toccatas Hpd, BWV 910–16—BWV 916 in G — Nimbus ("Grand Piano" series) ▲ NI 8808
Beethoven, L. van:Con 3 Pno, w. A. Toscanini (cnd), NBC SO *(rec live 11/24/46)* — Melodram 2-▲ MEL 28031 (m) [AAD]
Beethoven, L. van:Con 4 Pno, w. A. Boult (cnd), BBC SO *(rec 1952)* — Music & Arts 3-▲ CD 779 [AAD]
Beethoven, L. van:Con 5 Pno, "Emperor", w. E. Kurtz (cnd), Philharmonic SO *(rec Feb. 6, 1953)* — Music & Arts 3-▲ CD 779 [AAD]
Beethoven, L. van:Son 3 Vc, w. E. Feuermann (vc) *(rec 1937)* — Pearl ▲ PEA 9462 (m) [AAD]
Beethoven, L. van:Son 3 Vc, w. E. Feuermann (vc) *(rec 6/37)* — EMI Classics ▲ CDH 64250-2 (m) [ADD]
Beethoven, L. van:Son 3 Vc, w. E. Feuermann (vc) *(rec 1937)* — Pearl ▲ PEA 9446 (m) [AAD]
Beethoven, L. van:Son 10 Vn, w. I. Stern (vn) *(rec 14th Edinburgh Festival, Aug. 28, 1960)* — Music & Arts 3-▲ CD 779 [AAD]
Beethoven, L. van:Die Weihe des Hauses (ov), w. A. Toscanini (cnd), NBC SO *(rec live 3/16/47)* — Melodram 2-▲ MEL 28031 (m) [AAD]
Brahms, J.:Con 2 Pno, w. B. Walter (cnd), Philharmonic SO *(rec Feb. 11, 1951)* — Music & Arts 3-▲ CD 779 [AAD]

Hess, Myra (pno) (cont.)
Brahms, J.:Son 2 Vn, w. I. Stern (vn) *(rec 14th Edinburgh Festival, Aug. 28, 1960)* Music & Arts 3-▲ CD 779 [AAD]
Brahms, J.:Trio 1 Pno, w. I. Stern (vn), P. Casals (vc) *(rec Prades, France, June 23–July 3, 1952)* Sony Classical ("The Casals Edition" series) ▲ SMK 58994 [ADD]
Brahms, J.:Trio 2 Pno, w. Joseph Szigeti (vn), Pablo Casals (vc) *(rec Prades, June 16, 1952)* Sony Classical ▲ SMK 66571 [ADD]
Brahms, J.:Trio 2 Pno, w. J. Szigeti (vn), P. Casals (vc) *(rec 1952)* Sony Masterworks ("Portrait" series) ▲ MPK 52535 (m) [ADD]
A Cameo *(rec 1928–1950)* Pearl ▲ PEA 9114 [ADD]
The Columbia Recordings, Vol. 3, w. Jacqueline Du Pré (vc), Gerald Moore (pno), Paul Hindemith (va/cnd), Szymon Goldberg (cnd) *(rec 1930–1939)* Pearl ▲ PEA 9446 (m) [AAD]
Dame Myra Hess, Vol. 1 Pearl ▲ PEA 9462 (m) [AAD]
Debussy, C.:Pno Music (misc) *(rec 1928)* Pearl ▲ PEA 9462 (m) [AAD]
Haydn, J.:Sons Pno—H.XVI/37 APR 2-▲ APR 7012 [AAD]
Mozart, W.A.:Con 9 Pno, w. P. Casals (cnd), Perpignan Festival Orch *(rec live 1952)* Melodram ▲ MEL 18024 (m) [AAD]
Mozart, W.A.:Con 12 Pno, w. R. Scholz (cnd), American CO *(rec March 20, 1956)* Music & Arts 3-▲ CD 779 [AAD]
Mozart, W.A.:Con 14 Pno, w. B. Walter (cnd), New York PO Historical Performers ▲ HPS 9 [ADD]
Mozart, W.A.:Con 20 Pno, w. B. Walter (cnd), New York PO Historical Performers ▲ HPS 9 [ADD]
Mozart, W.A.:Con 21 Pno, w. L. Stokowski (cnd), Philharmonic SO *(rec Feb. 6, 1949)* Music & Arts 3-▲ CD 779 [AAD]
Mozart, W.A.:Con 27 Pno, w. R. Scholz (cnd), American CO *(rec March 20, 1956)* Music & Arts 3-▲ CD 779 [AAD]
Schubert, Franz:Son Pno, D.664 APR 2-▲ APR 7012 [AAD]
Schubert, Franz:Son Pno, D.664 *(rec 1928)* Pearl ▲ PEA 9462 (m) [AAD]
Schubert, Franz:Sonatinas Vn, w. I. Stern (vn) *(rec 14th Edinburgh Festival, Aug. 28, 1960)* Music & Arts 3-▲ CD 779 [AAD]
Schumann, R.:Con Pno, w. D. Mitropoulos (cnd), New York PO *(rec live, Carnegie Hall, 2/10/58)* Melodram ▲ MEL 18024 (m) [AAD]

Hesse-Bukowska, Barbara (pno)
Chopin, F.:Allegro de concert *(rec Warsaw, 1960)* Polskie Nagrania ▲ PNCD 310
Chopin, F.:Bolero *(rec Dec. 1991)* Canyon ▲ EC 3634-2 [DDD]
Chopin, F.:Prelude in A♭ *(rec Warsaw, 1961)* Polskie Nagrania ▲ PNCD 303
Chopin, F.:Rondos Pno & 4-Hands, w. M. Piotrovski (pno) *(rec Dec. 1991)* Canyon ▲ EC 3634-2 [DDD]
Rozycki, L.:Ballade, w. J. Krenz (cnd), Polish National RSO Katowice Olympia ▲ OCD 306 [AAD]
Szymanowski, K.:Mazurkas—Nos. 1, 2, 4, 7, 13, 15, 18, 19 & 20 *(rec Warsaw, 1960)* Polskie Nagrania ▲ PLN 066 [ADD]

Hessova, Sylvie (vn)
Biber, H. von:Son Tpt, 2 Vns, Vc, w. Richard Steuart (tpt), Oldrich Vlcek (vn), Ivo Anyz (va), Vaclav Jirovec (vc) *(rec Prague, Nov. 1994)* Discover International ▲ DI 920244 [DDD]
Finger, G.:Son Tpt, Vn & Ob, w. Richard Steuart (tpt), Oldrich Vlcek (vn), Milan Hruby (ob) *(rec Prague, Nov. 1994)* Discover International ▲ DI 920244 [DDD]

Hester, Timothy (pno)
Barber, S.:Canzone Fl & Pno, w. P. Robison (fl) MusicMasters ▲ 7019-2-C [DDD]
Barber, S.:Mélodies passagères, w. P. Robison (fl) MusicMasters ▲ 7019-2-C [DDD]
Beaser, R.:Vars Fl, w. P. Robison (fl) MusicMasters ▲ 7019-2-C [DDD]
Copland, A.:Duo Fl, w. P. Robison (fl) MusicMasters ▲ 7019-2-C [DDD]
Harris, R.:Lyric Study, w. Paula Robison (fl) MusicMasters ▲ 7019-2-C [DDD]
Martinů, B.:Son 1 Vn, w. Fredell Lack (vn) *(rec Dudley Recital Hall, Univ of Houston School of Music, Aug 18–20, 1993)* Centaur ▲ CRC 2276 [DDD]
Martinů, B.:Son 2 Vn, w. Fredell Lack (vn) *(rec Dudley Recital Hall, Univ of Houston School of Music, Aug 18–20, 1993)* Centaur ▲ CRC 2276 [DDD]
Martinů, B.:Son 3 Vn, w. Fredell Lack (vn) *(rec Dudley Recital Hall, Univ of Houston School of Music, Aug 18–20, 1993)* Centaur ▲ CRC 2276 [DDD]
Martinů, B.:Sonatina for 2 Vns, w. Fredell Lack (vn), Leon Spierer (vn) *(rec Dudley Recital Hall, Univ of Houston School of Music, Aug 18–20, 1993)* Centaur ▲ CRC 2276 [DDD]
Rosner, A.:Nightstone, w. Randolph Lacy (ten) *(rec Dudley Recital Hall, Univ of Houston)* Albany ▲ TROY 163 [DDD]
Rosner, A.:Of Numbers & of Bells, w. Nancy Weems (pno) *(rec Dudley Recital Hall, Univ. of Houston)* Albany ▲ TROY 163 [DDD]

Hetherington, David (vc)—see also ORCHESTRAS & ENSEMBLES Amici Quartet
Mozart, W.A.:Adagio & Rondo Glass Armonica, w. J. Petric (acc), M. Hammer (fl), M. Berard (ob), D. Perry (va) [trans. for accordion & string quartet] *(rec June 12–13, 1991)* CBC ("Musica Viva" series) ▲ MVCD 1056 [DDD]

Hetzel, Gerhard (vn)—see also ORCHESTRAS & ENSEMBLES Vienna Chamber Ensemble members
Schubert, Franz:Qt Fl, w. J. Levine (pno), W. Christ (va), G. Faust (vc), A. Posch (db) Deutsche Grammophon ▲ 431783-2
Schubert, Franz:Qnt Pno, D.667, w. J. Levine (pno), W. Christ (va), G. Faust (vc), A. Posch (db) Deutsche Grammophon ▲ 431783-2

Heumann, Friederike (va)
Deutsche Barocklieder, w. Andreas Scholl (ct), Alix Verzier (vc), Markus Markl (hpd), Karl Ernst Schroder (lt), Juan Manuel Quintana (va), Stephanie Pfister (vn), Pable Valetti (vn) Harmonia Mundi France ▲ HMC 901505

Heurtematte, Aude (org)
Scheidt, S.:Org Music—Cantio sacra; Variationen über eine Gagliardo von Dowland; Magnificat 9; Toni; Modus Ludendi Pleno Organo Pedaliter Studio SM ▲ 12 20 80
Sweelinck, J.P.:Org Music—Allein Goot in Der Höh Sei Ehr; Onder Een Linde Groen; Engelsche Fortuyn; Malle Sijmen; Echo fantasia; Fant. Studio SM ▲ 12 20 80

Heward, Leslie (bc)
Handel, G.F.:Concerti grossi, Op. 6, w. E. Ansermet (cnd), Decca String Orch *(rec London, England, Sept 1929)* Koch International Classics ▲ KIC 7708

Hewig-Tröscher, S. (vn)—see ORCHESTRAS & ENSEMBLES Orfeo Trio

Hewig-Tröscher, Sylvia (pno)
Suder, J.:Arietta Vn, w. B. Lenz (vn) *(rec Jan. 4–8 & July 12, 1993)* Calig ▲ CAL 50926 [DDD]
Suder, J.:Son 1 Vn, w. B. Lenz (vn) *(rec Jan. 4–8 & July 12, 1993)* Calig ▲ CAL 50926 [DDD]
Suder, J.:Son 2 Vn, w. B. Lenz (vn) *(rec Jan. 4–8 & July 12, 1993)* Calig ▲ CAL 50926 [DDD]

Hewitt, Angela (pno)
Bach, J.S.:Con 1 Hpd, w. M. Bernardi (cnd), CBC Vancouver SO CBC ("SM 5000" series) ▲ SMCD 5065 [DDD] ■ SMC 5065 (D)
Bach, J.S.:Con 2 Hpd, w. M. Bernardi (cnd), CBC Vancouver SO CBC ("SM 5000" series) ▲ SMCD 5065 [DDD] ■ SMC 5065 (D)
Bach, J.S.:Con 5 Hpd, w. M. Bernardi (cnd), CBC Vancouver SO CBC ("SM 5000" series) ▲ SMCD 5065 [DDD] ■ SMC 5065 (D)
Bach, J.S.:French Suites Hyperion 2-▲ CDA 67121/22
Bach, J.S.:Kbd Music (misc)—Fant. in c, BWV 906; 15 Two-Part Inventions, BWV 772–786; 15 Three-Part Inventions, BWV 787–801; Chromatic Fant. & Fugue in d, BWV 903 Hyperion ▲ CDA 66746
Bach, J.S.:Preludes & Fugues Hpd—in a, BWV 894 Hyperion 2-▲ CDA 67121/22
Bach, J.S.:Preludes Hpd (misc)—18 Little Preludes, BWV 924–928, 930, 933–943, 999 Hyperion 2-▲ CDA 67121/22
Bach, J.S.:Sons (5) Kbd—in d, BWV 964 Hyperion 2-▲ CDA 67121/22
Granados, E.:Danzas españolas (10) *(rec Feb. 23–24, 1994)* CBC ("Musica Viva" series) ▲ MVCD 1074 [DDD]
Granados, E.:Goyescas—La maja y el ruiseñor, No. 4; El Pelele, No. 7 *(rec Feb. 23–24, 1994)* CBC ("Musica Viva" series) ▲ MVCD 1074 [DDD]

Hewitt, D. (perc)
Edwards, R.:Flower Songs, w. Philip South (perc), Roland Peelman (cnd), Song Company *(rec Studio 200, ABC Ultimo Centre, Apr 1993)* Tall Poppies ▲ TP 064 [DDD]
Vine, C.:Con Perc *(rec Nov. 1991)* Tall Poppies ▲ TP013 [DDD]
Whiticker, M.:Man, Skin Cancer of the Earth, w. Clive Birch (nar), Jane Edwards (nar), Matthew Glasgow (nar), Roger Frampton (sax), R. Peelman (cnd) *(rec Studio 200, ABC Ultimo Centre, Apr 1993)* Tall Poppies ▲ TP 064 [DDD]

Hewitt, Peter (pno)
Leigh, W.:Pno Music—Klavieralbum; Eclogue; Polka; Music for 3 Pianos (w. Robert Douglas, Philip Mountford); 5 Playtime Pieces; Piano Album; 3 Waltzes for 2 Pianos (w. Robert Douglas) *(rec Aug. & Sept. 1991)* Tremula ▲ TREM 101-2

Heyerick, Florian (hpd)
Bach, W.F.:Con in F for 2 Hpds, w. Guy Penson (hpd) Ricercar 2-▲ 089125/26

Heyman, Steven (pno)
Caltabiano, R.:Torched Liberty, w. N. Pilgrim (sop), V. Pritsker (vn), G. Macero (vc), L. Greene (pic/fl/alt fl), K. Schempf (E♭/A/B♭ cl), G. Coble (tpt), L. Luttinger (perc), R. Caltabiano (cnd) Opus One ▲ CD 168 [DDD]
Lindenfeld, H.:From the Grotte des Combarelles, w. G. Macero (vc), V. Pritsker (vn) Opus One ▲ CD 168 [DDD]
Liptak, D.:Rhaps, w. L. Greene (fl), J. Friedrichs (cl), D. Gerikh (vn), W. Bass (vc) Opus One ▲ CD 168 [DDD]
Willey, J.:Society Music, w. L. Greene (fl), G. Coble (tpt), W. Harris (trbn), D. Resue (hn), E. Gustafson (vla), G. Macero (vc), E. Castilano (db), L. Luttinger (perc), E. Murray (cnd) Opus One ▲ CD 168 [DDD]

Heymann, Karsten (vn)
Fuchs, R.:Qt Pno, w. K. Schilde (pno), J. Rieber (va), U. Bode (vc) MD + G ▲ L 3165
Mahler, G.:Qt Pno [1 movt], w. K. Schilde (pno), J. Rieber (va), U. Bode (vc) MD + G ▲ L 3165

Heyndrickx, F. (instr)—see ORCHESTRAS & ENSEMBLES Quintessens

Hickethier, Hermann (vl)—see ORCHESTRAS & ENSEMBLES Royal Consort

Hickethier, Hermann (vl)
Heudelinne, L.:Suites de pièces, w. Simone Eckert (treble vl), Ulrich Wedemeier (lt/Baroque gtr), Karl-Ernst Went (hpd) Christophorus ▲ 77181 [DDD]

Hickey, Mary (fl)
In Sweet Rejoicing Music for Christmas:Ars Antique Choralis, Vol 3, w. Cathedral Singers [cnd:Richard Proulx], Jeri-Lou Aike (vn), Elizabeth Anderson (vc), Samuel Soria Jr. (org) *(rec Oct. 17–19 & 24–26, 1993)* GIA ▲ CD 323 ■ CS 323

Hickman, David (cnt)
The Golden Age of Brass:Virtuoso Solos, Vol. 1, w. Mark H. Lawrence (trbn), American Serenade Band [cnd:Henry Charles Smith] Summit ▲ DCD 114 [DDD]
The Golden Age of Brass:Virtuoso Solos, Vol. 2, w., Mark H. Lawrence (trbn) Summit ▲ DCD 121 [DDD] ■ DCD 121

Hickman, David (tpt)
Bach, J.S.:Brandenburg Con 2, w. P. Bowman (ob), T. Rolston (cnd), Banff Festival Strings *(rec Aug 6–8, 1990)* Summit ▲ DCD 118 [DDD] ■ DCD 118
Baker, M.C.:Summit Con, w. T. Russell (cnd), Pro Musica CO *(rec Ohio State Univ., Weigel Hall, 1995)* Summit ▲ SMT 182 [DDD]
David Hickman, w., Eric Dalheim (pno) Crystal ■ C368
David Hickman, Trumpet Crystal ▲ CD 668
Dello Joio, N.:Son Tpt & Pno, w. E. Dalheim (pno) Crystal ■ C368
Hertel, J.W.:Con à 6, w. P. Bowman (ob), T. Rolston (cnd), Banff Festival Strings *(rec Aug. 6–8, 1990)* Summit ▲ DCD 118 [DDD] ■ DCD 118
Kennan, K.W.:Son Tpt, w. E. Dalheim (pno) Crystal ■ C368
Persichetti, V.:The Hollow Men, w. T. Russell (cnd), Naples PO D'Note Classics ▲ DND 1002
Planel, R.:Con Tpt, w. T. Russell (cnd), Naples PO D'Note Classics ▲ DND 1002
Telemann, G.P.:Con Tpt Strs in D, w. T. Rolston (cnd), Banff Festival Strings *(rec Aug. 6–8, 1990)* Summit ▲ DCD 118 [DDD] ■ DCD 118
Vivaldi, A.:Con for 2 Tpts, w. D. Carlsen (tpt), T. Rolston (cnd), Banff Festival Strings *(rec Aug. 6–8, 1990)* Summit ▲ DCD 118 [DDD] ■ DCD 118

Hidas, Frigyes (org)
Silent Night, w. Imre Kovacs (fl), Hedy Lubik (hp), Ferenc Gergely (org), Gabor Lehotka (org), Hungarian State Orch CO, Csanyi (cnd), Szekeres (cnd), Budapest Children's Choir Madrigal Choir Hungaroton ▲ HCD 16598

Higbee, Scott (trbn)
Dempster, S.:Music of, w. Stuart Dempster (trbn/didjeridu/conch), Jay Bulen (trbn), Jeff Domoto (trbn), Moc Escobedo (trbn/didjeridu/conch), Gretchen Hopper (trbn), Nathaniel Irby-Oxford (trbn), Chad Kirby (trbn/conch), Dave Marriott (trbn), Greg Powers (trbn), Debra Sykes (cym)—Conch Calling; Morning Light; Didjerilayover; Secret Currents; Melodic Communion; Shell Shock; Cloud Landings *(rec Fort Worden, Port Townsend, WA, June 18, 1994)* New Albion ▲ NA 076

Higdon, James (org)
Alain, J.:Org Music (comp), w. Mary Posses (fl) *(rec 1988)* RBW ▲ RBWCD 005
Saint-Saëns, C.:Improvs Org, Op. 150—Nos. 1 & 5 Arkay ▲ AR 6107 [DDD]
Saint-Saëns, C.:Preludes & Fugues, Op. 99 Arkay ▲ AR 6107 [DDD]
Saint-Saëns, C.:Preludes & Fugues, Op. 109 Arkay ▲ AR 6107 [DDD]

Higginbottom, Edward (org)
Howells, H.:Org Music—De La Mare's Pavane; Walton's Toye; Flourish for a Bidding; St. Louis comes to Clifton; Jacob's Brawl CRD ▲ 3454 [DDD]
Howells, H.:Org Music—Psalm Prelude, Set 1 No. 1 (1915); Preludio 'Sine nomine' & Paean (from Six Pieces for Organ, 1940) CRD ▲ 3455 [DDD]
Wesley, S.S.:Anthems, w. E. Higginbottom (cnd), New College Choir Oxford—(6 choral anthems & 3 solo organ selections) Ascribe unto the Lord; Blessed be the God and Father; Choral Song & Fugue; Thou will keep him in perfect peace; Wash me thoroughly from my wickedness; Andante in E minor; Cast me not away; Larghetto; The Wilderness [E] CRD ▲ 3463 [DDD]

Higginson, Kit (rcr)
Jewels of the Sephardim, Vol. 1:Songs from Medieval Spain, w. L. Pomerantz. (vocs/period dlc), P. Maund (perc) Songbird ▲ AEACD 1401
Jewels of the Sephardim, Vol. 2:Wings of Time—The Sephardic Legacy of Multi-Cultural Medieval Spain, w. L. Pomerantz, (vocs/period dlc), P. Maund (perc), S. Kammen (vielle/rebec) Songbird ▲ AEACD 1405

Higgs, David (org)
Bach, Joh. Christian:Sons & Duets Kbd 4-Hands, w. Todd Wilson (org)—No. 6 [National City Christian Church organs, Washington D.C.] *(rec Jan 11–13, 1995)* Delos ▲ DE 3175 [DDD]
Bach, J.S.:Org Music (misc) [Rieger Organ, Bryn Mawr Presbyterian Church]—Preludes & Fugues in D, BWV 532 & in G, BWV 541; Fantasia & Fugue in g, BWV 542; Concerto in a (after Vivaldi), BWV 593; Trio Sonata No. 5 in C, BWV 529 Delos ▲ DE 3048 [DDD]
Hampton, C.:Alexander Vars, w. Todd Wilson (org) [National City Christian Church Orgs, Washington D.C.] *(rec Jan 11–13, 1995)* Delos ▲ DE 3175 [DDD]
Inaugural Recital *(rec Jan. 4–5, 1993)* Delos ▲ DE 3148 [DDD]
Mozart, W.A.:Adagio & Allegro Mechanical Org, w. Todd Wilson (org) [National City Christian Church Orgs, Washington D.C.] *(rec Jan 11–13, 1995)* Delos ▲ DE 3175 [DDD]
Mozart, W.A.:Adagio & Fugue Strs, w. Todd Wilson (org)—Adagio [trans David Fuller for 2 orgs; National City Christian Church organs, Washington D.C.] *(rec Jan 11–13, 1995)* Delos ▲ DE 3175 [DDD]
Saint-Saëns, C.:Danse macabre, w. Todd Wilson (org) [trans C. Dikinson & C. Mathewson Lockwood for 2 orgs; National City Christian Church organs, Washington D.C.] *(rec Jan 11–13, 1995)* Delos ▲ DE 3175 [DDD]
Wagner, R.:Die Walküre (ride of the valkyries), w. Todd Wilson (org) [trans C. Dikinson & C. Mathewson Lockwood for 2 orgs; National City Christian Church organs, Washington D.C.] *(rec Jan 11–13, 1995)* Delos ▲ DE 3175 [DDD]

Hii, Philip (gtr)
Bach, J.S.:Chromatic Fant & Fugue [trans. Philip Hii for gtr] *(rec Dec. 1992)* GSP ▲ GSP 1012
Bach, J.S.:Chromatic Fant & Fugue [trans. Hii] Eclat ▲ 88-001
Bach, J.S.:Ich ruf' zu dir, Herr Jesu Christ [trans. Philip Hii for gtr] *(rec Dec. 1992)* GSP ▲ GSP 1012
Bach, J.S.:Ich ruf' zu dir, Herr Jesu Christ [trans. Hii] Eclat ▲ 88-001
Bach, J.S.:Nun komm, der Heiden Heiland, BWV 659 [trans. Hii] Eclat ▲ 88-001
Bach, J.S.:Nun komm, der Heiden Heiland, BWV 659 [trans. Philip Hii for gtr] *(rec Dec. 1992)* GSP ▲ GSP 1012
Bach, J.S.:Preludium, Fugue & Allegro Hpd, BWV 998 Eclat ▲ 88-001
Bach, J.S.:Preludium, Fugue & Allegro Hpd, BWV 998 [trans. Philip Hii for gtr] *(rec Dec. 1992)* GSP ▲ GSP 1012
Bach, J.S.:Sons Vn—in e, BWV 1023 [trans. Hii] Eclat ▲ 88-001
Bach, J.S.:Sons Vn—in e, BWV 1023 [trans. Philip Hii for gtr] *(rec Dec. 1992)* GSP ▲ GSP 1012
Bach, J.S.:Toccata & Fugue Org, BWV 565 [trans. Hii] Eclat ▲ 88-001
Bach, J.S.:Toccata & Fugue Org, BWV 565 [trans. Philip Hii for gtr] *(rec Dec. 1992)* GSP ▲ GSP 1012

Hildebrandt, G. (vn)—see ORCHESTRAS & ENSEMBLES Sancoussi Ensemble Hamburg

Hill, David (org)
Bach, J.S.:Toccata & Fugue Org, BWV 565 [Rosales Org, Trinity Cathedral, Portland, OR] *(rec May 1994)* Herald ▲ HAVPCD 190 [DDD]
Bridge, F.:Adagio Org [Rosales Org, Trinity Cathedral, Portland, OR] *(rec May 1994)* Herald ▲ HAVPCD 190 [DDD]
Dupré, M.:Les vêpres de la Vierge, w. Philippe Lefebvre (org), Mary Berry (cnd), Schola Gregoriana Herald ▲ HAVPCD 170
Franck, C.:Chorals Org, M.38-40—Nos. 1 & 3 [Rosales Org, Trinity Cathedral, Portland, OR] *(rec May 1994)* Herald ▲ HAVPCD 190 [DDD]
Guilmant, A.:Org Music—March on Hanel's "Lift Up Your Heads" [Rosales Org, Trinity Cathedral, Portland, OR] *(rec May 1994)* Herald ▲ HAVPCD 190 [DDD]
Karg-Elert, S.:Org Music [Rosales Org, Trinity Cathedral, Portland, OR]—Chorale-Improvisation on "Nun danket alle Gott", Op. 65 *(rec May 1994)* Herald ▲ HAVPCD 190 [DDD]
Music for Ceremonial Occasions, w. London SO, Westminster Abbey Choir, Francis Jackson (org) Pickwick ("The Orchid" series) ▲ PICORCD 11016
Organ Spectacular, Vol. 2 IMP Classics ▲ PCD 945
Pergolesi, G.B.:Stabat mater, w. Felicity Palmer (sop), Alfreda Hodgson (cta), G. Guest (cnd), Argo CO, St. John's College Choir Cambridge *(rec 1978)* London 2-▲ 443868-2 [ADD]
Vierne, L.:Org Music [Rosales Org, Trinity Cathedral, Portland, OR]—Clair de lune; Carillon de Westminster *(rec May 1994)* Herald ▲ HAVPCD 190 [DDD]

Hill, Eric (gtr)
The Classical Guitar Saga ▲ EC 3386
Villa-Lobos, H.:Etudes Gtr Saga Classics ▲ 3396
Villa-Lobos, H.:Preludes Gtr Saga Classics ▲ 3396
Villa-Lobos, H.:Suite populaire brésilienne Saga Classics ▲ 3396

Hill, J. Lyman (va)
Bolcom, W.:Fant Concertante, w. E. Moye (vc), D. R. Davies (cnd), American Composers Orch Argo ▲ 433077-2 [DDD]
Fine, I.:Notturno, w. A. Hess (hp), L. Foss (cnd), Brooklyn PO CRI ▲ CD 574 [ADD]

Hill, Nicholas (hn)
Telemann, G.P.:Cons Hns, w. H. Baumann (hn), T. Brown (hn), I. Brown (cnd), Academy of St. Martin in the Fields Philips ▲ 412226-2 [DDD]
Vivaldi, A.:Cons for 2 Hns, w. T. Brown (hn), N. Marriner (cnd), Academy of St. Martin in the Fields—RV.539 Philips ▲ 412892-2 [DDD]

Hill, Peter (pno)
Messiaen, O.:Catalogue d'oiseaux—Books 1-3 Unicorn-Kanchana ▲ DKP CD 9062 [DDD]
Messiaen, O.:Regards sur l'Enfant Jésus Unicorn-Kanchana 2-▲ DKP CD 9122/23
Schubert, Franz:Songs (misc), w. Lynda Russell (sop), David Campbell (cl)—Ganymed, D.544; Liebhaber in allen Gestalten, D.558; Nacht und Träume, D.827; Geheimes, D.719; Abendstern, D.806; Der Hirt auf dem Felsen, D.965; Suleika, D.720; Seligkeit, D.433; Wiegenlied, D.498; Gretchen am Spinnrade, D.118; An die Entfernte, D.765; Im Frühling, D.882; Suleikas zweiter Gesang, D.717; Du bist die Ruh, D.776; Lied der Mignon, D.877/4; Nachtviolen, D.752; Der Musensohn, D.764; Die Forelle, D.550 *(rec St. Martin's Church, East Woodhay, Hampshire, England, Nov 7-9, 1994)* Naxos ▲ 8.553113 [DDD]
Stravinsky, I.:Con Pnos, w. Benjamin Frith (pno) *(rec St. Silas Church, London, May 9-11, 1995)* Naxos ▲ 8.553386 [DDD]
Stravinsky, I.:Le Sacre du printemps Pno, w. Benjamin Frith (pno) *(rec St. Silas Church, London, May 9-11, 1995)* Naxos ▲ 8.553386 [DDD]
Stravinsky, I.:Son Pnos, w. Benjamin Frith (pno) *(rec St. Silas Church, London, May 9-11, 1995)* Naxos ▲ 8.553386 [DDD]

Hill, R. (fl)
Iannaccone, A.:Trio Fl, w. A. Abramson (cl), E. Jacobson (pno) Opus One ▲ CD 154

Hill, Robert (cl)—see also ORCHESTRAS & ENSEMBLES Michael Thompson Wind Quintet
Danzi, F.:Sextet Ob, w. Richard Berry (hn), Michael Thompson (hn), John Bradburg (cl), John Price (bn), Philip Tarlton (bn)—version for Harmonie ensemble *(rec St. Paul's Church, Rusthall, Kent, England, June 1994)* Naxos ▲ 8.553076 [DDD]
Doyle, P.:Sense & Sensibility, w. Jane Eaglen (sop), Jonathan Snowdon (fl), Richard Morgan (ob), Tony Hymas (pno), R. Ziegler (cnd), *(orch unknown)* *(rec Air Studios, Lyndhurst Hall)* Sony Classical ▲ SK 62258 [DDD]
Herrmann, B.:Qnt Cl, w. Amici String Quartet Unicorn-Kanchana ▲ UKCD 2069

Hill, Robert (hpd)
Bach, J.S.:The Art of the Fugue, w. Bradley Brookshire (hpd) Music & Arts ▲ CD 279
Bach, J.S.:Kbd Music (misc)—Suites in c, BWV 818a; in E♭, BWV 819a; in f, BWV 823; in A, BWV 832; in c, BWV 997 Music & Arts ▲ CD 874 [DDD]
Haydn, J.:Con Org, Vn & Strs, H.XVIII/6, w. R. Kussmaul (cnd), Amsterdam Bach Soloists Olympia ▲ OLY 428 [DDD]
Volans, K.:White Man Sleeps Hpds, w. Kevin Volans (hpd), Margriet Tindemans (vl), Robyn Schulkowsky (perc) *(rec West German Radio, Cologne & Watershed Recording Studio, London, Apr 20, 1984 & July 27, 1)* United ▲ CAL 88034 [ADD]

Hill, Robert (pno)
Carulli, F.:Grand Duo, Op. 70, w. Sonja Prunnbauer (gtr) MD + G ▲ MDG 6030616
Carulli, F.:Grand Duo, Op. 86, w. Sonja Prunnbauer (gtr) MD + G ▲ MDG 6030616
Carulli, F.:Music for Gtr, w. Sonja Prunnbauer (gtr)—Op. 134 MD + G ▲ MDG 6030616
Carulli, F.:Valses, Op. 32, w. Sonja Prunnbauer (gtr) MD + G ▲ MDG 6030616
Carulli, F.:Vars on Theme by Beethoven, w. Sonja Prunnbauer (gtr) MD + G ▲ MDG 6030616

Hill, Robin (gtr)—see ORCHESTRAS & ENSEMBLES Hill/Wiltschinsky Guitar Duo

Hill, Vernon (fl)
Bach, J.S.:Partita Fl, BWV 1013 Move ▲ MD 3118 [DDD]
Bach, J.S.:Sons Fl, BWV 1030-35, w. R. Heagney (hpd), J. Johnson (vc)—BWV 1030, 1032 & 1033 *(rec 1989)* Move ▲ MD 3118 [DDD]
Bach, J.S.:Sons Vn, w. R. Heagney (hpd), J. Johnson (vc)—BWV 1020 [doubtful; trans. for flute & continuo] *(rec 1989)* Move ▲ MD 3118 [DDD]

Hill, William (perc)
A Colorado Kind of Christmas, w. Colorado Children's Chorale [cnd:Duain Wolfe], Mike Fitzmaurice (db), Rod Garnet (fl), Deborah Schmit-Lobis (pno), Brett Walace (vc), Mary Louise Burke (pno), Laurie Kahler (pno), Helen Hope (hp) *(rec Denver Center Media)* Colorado Children's Chorale ▲ XMAS

Hiller, Carl-Amadeus (perc)—see ORCHESTRAS & ENSEMBLES Karl Peinkofer Percussion Ensemble

Hiller, Wilfried (perc)—see ORCHESTRAS & ENSEMBLES Karl Peinkofer Percussion Ensemble

Hiller, Wilfried (perc/mar)
Orff, C.:Schulwerk (complete), w. Godela Orff (nar), Carolin Widmann (vn), Sonja Korkeala (vn), Markus Zahnhausen (rcr), Karl Peinkofer (perc), Andreas Schumacher (perc), Martin Ruhland (mar), Munich Hochschule Madrigal Choir—Wessobrun Prayer for a capella Choir; 2 Pieces for a capella Choir; 8 Pieces for 2 Vns; Mater et filia for women's a capella Choir; Devotional Yodel for male a capella Choir; 5 Pieces for Sop, Rcr & Perc; Death for Nar., Wood Bells, Bass Xyl & Tam-Tam; Omnia tempus habent for mixed Choir, Timp & Little Dr; Rubato, molto allegro, rubato; Abenlied for Nar, Bass Metallophon, Bass Xyl, Large Dr & Wine Glass; 5 Pieces for Fl & Perc; Devotional Yodel for male Choir [version 2]; 7 Pieces for 2 Xyl *(rec Munich, 1994-95)* Celestial Harmonies ▲ 13105-2

Hillerud, Ingalill (db)
Larsson, L.-E.:Concertinos, w. Jan Stigmer (vn), Per-Ola Lindberg (va), Bjøorg Vaernes (vc), Joakim Kallhed (pno), Camerata Romana—Nos. 8-12 Intim Musik ▲ INT 31

Hillesland, Steve (vc)
Hoffman, D.:Fant on *Black is the Color of My True Love's Hair*, w. Teri Fay Storhaug (rcr), Britt Swenson (vn), Annette Wellin (pno) Meyer ▲ MC 0108

Hillmer, B. (pno)
Bozza, E.:En forêt, w. S. Gross (hn) *(rec Aug.-Sept. 1988)* ACA Digital Recording ■ CM20005-5 (CrO2)
Dukas, P.:Villanelle, w. S. Gross (hn) *(rec Aug.-Sept. 1988)* ACA Digital Recording ■ CM20005-5 (CrO2)
Poulenc, F.:Élégie Hn, w. S. Gross (hn) *(rec Aug.-Sept. 1988)* ACA Digital Recording ■ CM20005-5 (CrO2)
Saint-Saëns, C.:Morceau de concert Hn, w. S. Gross (hn) *(rec Aug.-Sept. 1988)* ACA Digital Recording ■ CM20005-5 (CrO2)
Saint-Saëns, C.:Romance Hn, Op. 67, w. S. Gross (hn) *(rec Aug.-Sept. 1988)* ACA Digital Recording ■ CM20005-5 (CrO2)
Tomasi, H.:Con Hn, w. S. Gross (hn) [arr. for horn & piano] *(rec Aug.-Sept. 1988)* ACA Digital Recording ■ CM20005-5 (CrO2)

Hills, Tom (dr/perc)—see ORCHESTRAS & ENSEMBLES Rhythm & Bluefield Band

Hillyer, Raphael (va)
Bartók, B.:Con Va, w. A. Watanabe (cnd), Japan PO Albany ▲ TROY 076 [AAD]
Hindemith, P.:Der Schwanendreher, w. A. Watanabe (cnd), Japan PO Albany ▲ TROY 076 [AAD]
Stravinsky, I.:Elégie Va Koch Schwann ▲ SCH 311612 [DDD]

Hilse, Ernst-Burghard (fl)
Telemann, G.P.:Con Rcr, Fl, w. E. Hering (rcr), Academy for Old Music LaserLight ▲ 15634 [DDD]

Hilse, Walter (pno)
Chambers, W.M.:Ten Grand, w. Ursula Oppens (pno), Bennett Lerner (pno), Nurit Tiles (pno), Aleck Karis (pno), Edmund Niemann (pno), Joseph Kubera (pno), Martin Goldray (pno), Allen Shawn (pno), Elizabeth di Filice (pno), Geisel (cnd) Newport ▲ NPD 85553

Hiltawsky, Kurt (cl)
Gershwin, G.:Rhap in Blue, w. Siegfried Stockigt (pno), K. Masur (cnd), Dresden PO Berlin Classics ("Masur Edition" series) ▲ BER 9158

Hilton, Janet (cl)
Bax, A.:Son Cl & Pno, w. K. Swallow (pno) Chandos ▲ CHAN 8683 [DDD]
Bliss, A.:Qnt Cl, w. Lindsay String Quartet Chandos ▲ CHAN 8683 [DDD]
Bruch, M.:Trios Cl, Va & Pno, Op. 83, w. N. Imai (va), R. Vignoles (pno) Chandos ▲ CHAN 8776 [DDD]
Copland, A.:Con Cl, w. M. Bamert (cnd), Scottish National Orch Chandos ▲ CHAN 8618 [DDD]
Debussy, C.:Première rapsodie, w. K. Swallow (pno), clarinet & piano Chandos ("Collect" series) ▲ CHAN 6589 [DDD]
Ferguson, H.:Short Pieces Cl, Op. 6, w. Clifford Benson (pno) Chandos ▲ CHAN 9316 [DDD]
Leighton, K.:Fant on an American Hymn-tune, w. R. Wallfisch (vc), P. Wallfisch (pno) *(rec May 14 & 15, 1992)* Chandos ▲ CHAN 9132 [DDD]
Lutoslawski, W.:Dance Preludes Cl, Hp, Pno, Perc & Strs, w. M. Bamert (cnd), Scottish National Orch Chandos ▲ CHAN 8618 [DDD]
Milhaud, D.:Duo concertante Cl & Pno, w. K. Swallow (pno) Chandos ("Collect" series) ▲ CHAN 6589 [DDD]
Mozart, W.A.:Trio Cl, K.498, w. N. Imai (va), R. Vignoles (pno) Chandos ▲ CHAN 8776 [DDD]
Nielsen, C.:Con Cl, w. M. Bamert (cnd), Scottish National Orch Chandos ▲ CHAN 8618 [DDD]
Poulenc, F.:Son Cl Pno, w. K. Swallow (pno) Chandos ("Collect" series) ▲ CHAN 6589 [DDD]
Ravel, M.:Pièce en forme de Habanera, w. K. Swallow (pno) Chandos ("Collect" series) ▲ CHAN 6589 [DDD]
Roussel, A.:Aria Cl, w. K. Swallow (pno) Chandos ("Collect" series) ▲ CHAN 6589 [DDD]
Saint-Saëns, C.:Son Cl, w. K. Swallow (pno) Chandos ("Collect" series) ▲ CHAN 6589 [DDD]
Schumann, R.:Märchenerzählungen, w. N. Imai (va), R. Vignoles (pno) Chandos ▲ CHAN 8776 [DDD]
Stanford, C.V.:Con Cl, w. V. Handley (cnd), Ulster Orch Chandos ▲ CHAN 8991 [DDD]
Vaughan Williams, R.:Studies in English Folk-Song, w. K. Swallow (pno) Chandos ▲ CHAN 8683 [DDD]
Weber, C.M. von:Concertino Cl, w. N. Järvi (cnd), City of Birmingham SO Chandos ▲ CHAN 8305 [DDD]
Weber, C.M. von:Con 1 Cl, w. N. Järvi (cnd), City of Birmingham SO Chandos ▲ CHAN 8305 [DDD]
Weber, C.M. von:Con 2 Cl, w. N. Järvi (cnd), City of Birmingham SO Chandos ▲ CHAN 8305 [DDD]
Weber, C.M. von:Grand duo concertant Cl, w. K. Swallow (pno) Chandos ▲ CHAN 8366 [DDD]
Weber, C.M. von:Qnt Cl, w. Lindsay String Quartet Chandos ▲ CHAN 8366 [DDD]
Weber, C.M. von:Vars on a Theme from *Silvana* Cl, w. K. Swallow (pno) Chandos ▲ CHAN 8366 [DDD]

Himo, L. (vc)
Falla, M. de:Suite populaire espagnole, w. N. Himo (pno) [trans for vc & pno by Maurice Maréchal] Arcobaleno ▲ SBCD 1508
Miaskovsky, N.:Son 2 Vc, w. N. Himo (pno) Arcobaleno ▲ SBCD 1508
Prokofiev, S.:Son Vc, w. N. Himo (pno) Arcobaleno ▲ SBCD 1508

Himo, Nadia (pno)
Falla, M. de:Suite populaire espagnole, w. L. Himo (vc) [trans for vc & pno by Maurice Maréchal] Arcobaleno ▲ SBCD 1508
Miaskovsky, N.:Son 2 Vc, w. L. Himo (vc) Arcobaleno ▲ SBCD 1508
Prokofiev, S.:Son Vc, w. L. Himo (vc) Arcobaleno ▲ SBCD 1508

Hind, Rolf (pno)
Hoyland, V.:The Other Side of the Air NMC ▲ NMC 20 [DDD]
Messiaen, O.:Catalogue d'oiseaux—Le traquet rieur; Le courlis cendré Cala ▲ CAL CACD 88019 [DDD]
Messiaen, O.:Études (4) de Rhythme—Ile de feu 2; Cantéyodjayâ Cala ▲ CAL CACD 88019 [DDD]
Messiaen, O.:Preludes Pno—La colombre; Cloches d'angoisse et larmes d'adieu; Le nombre léger Cala ▲ CAL CACD 88019 [DDD]
Messiaen, O.:Regards sur l'Enfant Jésus—Regard du père; Regard des prophètes, des bergers et des mages; Par lui tout a été fait Cala ▲ CAL CACD 88019 [DDD]
Sawyer, D.:The Melancholy of Departure NMC ▲ NMC 20 [DDD]

Hindar, Johs (va)
Braein, E.F.:The Merry Musicians, w. R. Kjelstrup (cl), L. Jørgensen (vn), L. Hindar (vc) Simax ▲ PSC 3117

Hindar, Levi (vc)
Braein, E.F.:The Merry Musicians, w. R. Kjelstrup (cl), L. Jørgensen (vn), J. Hindar (va) Simax ▲ PSC 3117

Hindart, K. (pno)—see ORCHESTRAS & ENSEMBLES Röhn Trio

Hindart, Kerstin (pno)
Koch, E. von:Music of, w. Sigurd Rascher (a sax), Andreas Röhn (vn), S. Westerberg (cnd), Munich PO, Swedish RSO—Nordiskt Capriccio; Skandinaviska Danser; Saxofonkonsert; Svensk Dansrapsodi; Karaktärer Föor Vn Och Pno Phono Suecia ▲ PHN 55 [ADD]
Martinů, B.:Son Fl & Pno, w. G. von Bahr (fl) *(rec 4/73)* BIS ▲ CD 234 [AAD]
Pergament, M.:Son Fl Pno, w. G. von Bahr (fl) *(rec Apr. 15, 1973)* BIS ▲ CD 37 [AAD]

Hindemith, Paul (va)
Beethoven, L. van:Serenade Strs, Op. 8, w. S. Goldberg (vn), E. Feuermann (vc) *(rec 1934)* Pearl ▲ PEA 9443 (m) [AAD]
Beethoven, L. van:Serenade Strs, Op. 8, w. S. Goldberg (vn), E. Feuermann (vc) *(rec 1/22/34)* EMI Classics ▲ CDH 64250-2 (m) [ADD]
Hindemith, P.:Scherzo Va & Vc, w. E. Feuermann (vc) *(rec 1934)* Pearl ▲ PEA 9446 (m) [AAD]
Hindemith, P.:Scherzo Va & Vc, w. E. Feuermann (vc) EMI Classics 2-▲ ZDCB 55032
Hindemith, P.:Son Va & Pno, Op. 25/4 EMI Classics 2-▲ ZDCB 55032
Hindemith, P.:Trio 2, w. S. Goldberg (vn), E. Feuermann (vc) *(rec 1927–1934)* Koch Schwann ▲ CD 311342 [DDD]
Hindemith, P.:Trio 2, w. S. Goldberg (vn), E. Feuermann (vc) EMI Classics 2-▲ ZDCB 55032

Hindemith, Paul (va/cnd)
The Columbia Recordings, Vol. 3, w. Jacqueline Du Pré (vc), Gerald Moore (pno), Myra Hess (pno), Szymon Goldberg (cnd) *(rec 1930–1939)* Pearl ▲ PEA 9446 (m) [AAD]

Hinderas, Natalie (pno)
Dett, R.N.:In the Bottoms CRI 2-▲ CD 629 [ADD]
Hakim, T.R.:Sound Gone CRI 2-▲ CD 629 [ADD]
Piano Music by African-American Composers, w. Natalie Hinderas (pno) *(rec Sept.-Oct. 1970)* CRI ▲ CRI 629 [ADD]
Still, W.G.:Sahdji—Three Visions CRI 2-▲ CD 629 [ADD]
Walker, G.:Son 1 Pno CRI 2-▲ CD 629 [ADD]
Wilson, O.:Pno Piece CRI 2-▲ CD 629 [ADD]
Work (II), J.W.:Scuppernong CRI 2-▲ CD 629 [ADD]

Hindler, J. (cl)—see ORCHESTRAS & ENSEMBLES Vienna Ring Ensemble

Hink, Werner (vn)—see also ORCHESTRAS & ENSEMBLES Vienna String Quartet
Beethoven, L. van:Son 7 Vn, w. Keiko Toyama (pno) *(rec Japan, Oct 6, 1994)* Camerata ▲ 30 CM 416 [DDD]
Beethoven, L. van:Son 10 Vn, w. Keiko Toyama (pno) *(rec Japan, Oct 6, 1994)* Camerata ▲ 30 CM 416 [DDD]
Schmidt, F.:Qnt Pno, w. J. Demus (pno), A. Kamper (vn), F. Stangler (va), W. Resel (vc) *(rec 1965)* Preiser ▲ 93383 [ADD]
Schubert, Franz:Sonatinas Vn, w. Keiko Toyama (pno) *(rec Higashimatsuyama City Hall, Saitama, Japan & Baumgartner Studio, Vienna)* Camerata ▲ 32CM 42
Schubert, Franz:Trio Pno, D.28, w. Fritz Dolezal (vc), Jasminka Stancul (pno) *(rec Apr & June 1995)* Camerata ▲ 30 CM 342 [DDD]
Schubert, Franz:Trio 1 Pno, w. Jasminka Stancul (pno), Fritz Dolezal (vc) *(rec Apr & June 1995)* Camerata ▲ 30 CM 342 [DDD]

Hinshaw, H. (hpd)
Snyder, R.:The Book of Imaginary Beings Coronet ▲ COR 400-2

Hinshaw, H. (pno)
Ives, C.:Son 1 Pno Coronet ▲ COR 400-2

Hinterberger, Marlene (org)
Suder, J.:Festival Mass, w. Natalia Kornewa (sop), Maria Neilau (alt), Vladimir Mostomoi (ten), Juri Dobrowolski (bass), Jessica Hartlieb (vn), W.A. Albert (cnd), Bavarian State Youth Orch, St. Petersburg Chamber Choir Calig ▲ CAL 50945 [DDD]

Hinton, Hugh (pno)—see also ORCHESTRAS & ENSEMBLES Core Ensemble
Kraft, William:Con Perc, w. Dean Anderson (perc), Renee Krimsier (fl), Diane Heffner (cl), Nancy Cirillo (vn/va), Ronald Lowry (vc) Albany ▲ TROY 218 [DDD]
Kraft, William:Gallery 4-5, w. Diane Heffner (cl), Nancy Cirillo (vn), Ronald Copes (va), Ronald Lowry (vc) Albany ▲ TROY 218 [DDD]
Kraft, William:Settings from Pierrot Lunaire, w. Jane Manning (sop), Renee Krimsier (fl), Diane Heffner (cl), Nancy Cirillo (vn/va), Ronald Lowry (vc), Dean Anderson (perc) Albany ▲ TROY 218 [DDD]
Martino, D.:Preludes *(rec Houghton Chapel, Wellesley College, MA, June 1995)* New World ▲ 80518-2

Hirashima, M. (pno)
Van De Vate, N.:Con Pno, w. S. Kawalla (cnd), Koszalin State PO Vienna Modern Masters ▲ VMM 3025 [DDD]
Van De Vate, N.:Son 2 Pno Vienna Modern Masters ▲ VMM 2006 [DDD]

Hironaka, Takashi (pno)
Brahms, J.:Sons Cl (comp), w. Mazumi Tanamura (va) Camerata ▲ 30CM 377
Dietrich, A.:Allegro, w. Mazumi Tanamura (va) [trans Tanamura for Va & Pno] Camerata ▲ 30CM 377

Hirons, Christopher (vn)
Bach, J.S.:Con for 2 Vns, w. J. Schröder (vn), C. Hogwood (cnd), Academy of Ancient Music L'Oiseau-Lyre ▲ 400080-2 [DDD]

Hirsch, Hans Ludwig (hpd)
Bach, J.S.:Cons Hpd, BWV 1052-1058 Divox 2-▲ CDX 29206 [DDD]
Bach, J.S.:Con 8 Hpd Divox 2-▲ CDX 29206 [DDD]
Carissimi, G.:Cants Sop Kbd, w. E. Speiser (sop)—Lamento della Maria Stuarda *(rec 1979)* Jecklin-Disco ▲ JD 5004-2 [ADD]
Haydn, J.:Arianna a Naxos, w. Jeanne Marie Bima (sop) *(rec Venice, Italy, June 1990)* Arts ▲ 47286-2 [DDD]
Haydn, J.:Canzonettas, w. Jeanne Marie Bima (sop)—6 sels *(rec Venice, Italy, June 1990)* Arts ▲ 47286-2 [DDD]
Marcello, B.:Cons a cinque [No. 1 adapted for hpd] *(rec 1980)* Jecklin-Disco ▲ JD 5001-2 [ADD]
Marcello, B.:Sons Hpd—Sons. in F, d, D, c *(rec 1980)* Jecklin-Disco ▲ JD 5001-2 [ADD]

Hirsch, Hans Ludwig (pno)
Cimarosa, D.:Il Matrimonio segreto, w. Susan Patterson (sop—Carolina), Janet Williams (mez—Elisseta), Gloria Banditelli (cta—Fidalma), William Matteuzzi (ten—Paolino), Alfonso Antoniozzi (bass—Geronimo), Petteri Salomaa (bass—Count Robinson), G. Bellini (cnd), Eastern Netherlands Orch *(rec Muziekcentrum Enschede, Holland, Aug 26-Sept 8, 1991)* Arts 3-▲ 471172 [DDD]
Haydn, J.:Sons Pno—H.XVI/21-26 *(rec Munich, Germany, Oct 24-27, 1989)* Arts ▲ 471242 [DDD]

Hirsch, Rebecca (vn)—see also ORCHESTRAS & ENSEMBLES Joachim Trio
Ruders, P.:Con 2 Vn, w. M. Schønwandt (cnd), Copenhagen Collegium Musicum *(rec Odd Fellow Palaeet, Copenhagen, Feb. 2, 1992)* Marco Polo ("dacapo" series) ▲ DC 9308 [DDD]
Saint-Saëns, C.:Trio 1 Pno, w. Caroline Dearnley (vc), John Lenehan (pno) *(rec Conway Hall, London, Oct. 11 & 12, 1993)* Naxos ▲ 8.550935 [DDD]
Saint-Saëns, C.:Trio 2 Pno, w. Caroline Dearnley (vc), John Lenehan (pno) *(rec Conway Hall, London, Oct. 11 & 12, 1993)* Naxos ▲ 8.550935
Sørensen, B.:Con Vn, w. L. Segerstam (cnd), Danish National RSO *(rec live, Danish Radio Concert Hall, 1992 & 1994)* Marco Polo/Dacapo ▲ 8.224039 [DDD]

Hirschfeld, Naomi (vl)—see also ORCHESTRAS & ENSEMBLES New Consort
Einhorn, R.:Voices of Light, w. Susan Narucki (sop), Corrie Pronk (alt), Frank Hameleers (ten), Henk van Heijnsbergen (b-bar), Ronald Hoogeveen (vn), Harm Bakker (vl), Michael Feves (vl), S. Mercurio (cnd), Netherlands Radio PO, Martin Wright (cnd), Anonymous 4, Netherlands Radio Chorus *(rec Music Center of the Netherlands Radio & TV, Aug 23-25, 1995)* Sony Classical ▲ SK 62006 [DDD]
Focking, H. von:Sons Fl, w. P. van Houwelingen (trns fl), H. Dekker (hpd)—in C, G & D Erasmus ▲ WVH 078 [DDD]
Van Wassenaer, U.:Sons Rcr, w. P. van Houwelingen (fl), H. Dekker (hpd) Erasmus ▲ WVH 078 [DDD]

Hirschhorn, Philip (vn)
Lekeu, G.:Son Vn, w. J.-C. Vanden Eynden (pno) Ricercar ▲ RIS 104091 [DDD]
Schulhoff, E.:Duo Vn, w. D. Geringas (vc) *(rec Lockenhaus Festival, 1986)* ECM New Series 2-▲ 78118-21347-2 [DDD]
Schulhoff, E.:Sxt Strs, w. G. Kremer (vn), N. Imai (va), K. Kashkasian (va), D. Geringas (vc), J. Berger (vc) *(rec Lockenhaus Festival, 1986)* ECM New Series 2-▲ 78118-21347-2 [DDD]

Hirsh, Albert (pno)
Ives, C.:Songs, w. M. Bauman (sgr)—6 songs *(rec 1938)* CRI ■ ACS 6014
Szymanowski, K.:Son Vn, w. Fredell Lack (vn) Vox Box 2-▲ CDX 5133

Hirshfield, Jeff (drums)
Red Square Blue Russian Composers, w. Fred Hersch (pno), James Newton (fl), Toots Thielemans (hmc), Phil Woods (a sax), Erik Friedlander (vc), Steve La Spina (bass) Angel ▲ CDC 54743

Hirt, Al (tpt)
Basic 100, Vol. 39, w. Guy Touvron (tpt) RCA Victor ▲ 09026-61857-2 ■ 09026-61857-4
Haydn, J.:Con Tpt, w. A. Fiedler (cnd), Boston Pops Orch RCA Victor ▲ 09026-61857-2; ■ 09026-61857-4

Hirvikangas, Matti (va)
Brahms, J.:Qt 1 Pno, w. Ralf Gothoni (pno), Peter Csaba (vn), Frans Helmerson (vc) Ondine ▲ ODE 843
Brahms, J.:Qt 3 Pno, w. Ralf Gothoni (pno), Peter Csaba (vn), Frans Helmerson (vc) Ondine ▲ ODE 843
Chausson, E.:Chanson perpétuelle, w. Anne Sofie von Otter (mez), Nils-Erik Sparf (vn), Ulf Forsberg (vn), Mats Lindström (vc), Bengt Forsberg (pno) *(rec Stockholm, Nov 1994)* Deutsche Grammophon ▲ 447 752-2 [DDD]
Delage, M.:Poèmes hindous, w. Anne Sofie von Otter (mez), Andreas Alin (fl), Peter Rydström (fl/pic), Ulf Bjurenhed (ob/E hn), Lars Paulsson (cl), Per Billman (cl/b cl), Nils-Erik Sparf (vn), Ulf Forsberg (vn), Mats Lindström (vc), Lisa Viguier (hp) *(rec Stockholm, Nov 1994)* Deutsche Grammophon ▲ 447 752-2 [DDD]
Fauré, G.:La bonne chanson, w. Anne Sofie von Otter (mez), Nils-Erik Sparf (vn), Ulf Forsberg (vn), Mats Lindström (vc), Tomas Gertonsson (db), Bengt Forsberg (pno) *(rec Stockhom, Nov 1994)* Deutsche Grammophon ▲ 447 752-2 [DDD]
Mahler, G.:Qt Pno [comp Schnittke], w. Ralf Gothoni (pno), Mark Lubotsky (vn), Martti Rousi (vc) Ondine ▲ ODE 840 [DDD]
Poulenc, F.:Rapsodie nègre, w. Anne Sofie von Otter (mez), Andreas Alin (fl), Lars Paulsson (cl), Nils-Erik Sparf (vn), Ulf Forsberg (vn), Mats Lindström (vc), Bengt Forsberg (pno) *(rec Stockhom, Nov 1994)* Deutsche Grammophon ▲ 447 752-2 [DDD]
Ravel, M.:Trois poèmes de Stéphane Mallarmé, w. Anne Sofie von Otter (mez), Peter Rydström (fl/pic), Andreas Alin (fl), Lars Paulsson (cl), Per Billman (cl/b cl), Nils-Erik Sparf (vn), Ulf Forsberg (vn), Mats Lindström (vc), Bengt Forsberg (pno) *(rec Stockholm, Nov 1994)* Deutsche Grammophon ▲ 447 752-2 [DDD]
Strauss, R.:Qt Pno, w. Ralf Gothoni (pno), Mark Lubotsky (vn), Martti Rousi (vc) Ondine ▲ ODE 840 [DDD]

Hirvonen, Matti (pno)
Bozza, E.:Fant pastoral, w. G. Zubicky (ob) Simax ▲ PSC 1057 [DDD]
Deslandres, A.E.M.:Intro et Polonaise, w. G. Zubicky (ob) Simax ▲ PSC 1057 [DDD]
Dutilleux, H.:Son Ob, w. G. Zubicky (ob) Simax ▲ PSC 1057 [DDD]
Grovlez, G.:Sarabande et Allegro, w. G. Zubicky (ob) Simax ▲ PSC 1057 [DDD]
Poulenc, F.:Trio Ob, w. G. Zubicky (ob), P. Hannisdal (bn) Simax ▲ PSC 1057 [DDD]
Saint-Saëns, C.:Son Ob, w. G. Zubicky (ob) Simax ▲ PSC 1057 [DDD]

Hirzel, Hans-Walter (vn)
Daetwyler, J.:Divert Fl, Vn & Vc, w. Verena Bosshart (fl), Nicolas Hartmann (vc) Grammont ▲ CTSP 15-2

Hiscock, Stephen (perc)—see ORCHESTRAS & ENSEMBLES Ensemble Bash

Hiseki, Hisako (pno)
Albéniz, I.:Iberia Suite Edicions Albert Moreleda ▲ 1094-1 [DDD]
Falla, M. de:El sombrero de tres picos [arr for piano] Ediciones Albert Moraleda ▲ 6136 [DDD]
Ginastera, A.:Son 1 Pno Ediciones Albert Moraleda ▲ 6136 [DDD]
Turina, J.:Danzas fantásticas Ediciones Albert Moraleda ▲ 6136 [DDD]

Hitzlberger, Thomas (pno)
Liszt, F.:A Faust Sym, w. G. Schütz (cnd), *(orch unknown)* [Liszt's 1860 two-piano arr.] CPO ▲ CPO 999056-2 [DDD]
Raff, J.:Chaconne 2 Pnos, w. G. Shütz (pno) CPO ▲ CPO 999106 [DDD]
Reinecke, C.:Pno Music, w. G. Shütz (pno)—La belle Griseldis in F, Op. 94; Andante & Variations in Eb, Op. 6; Impromptu in A, Op. 66 CPO ▲ CPO 999106 [DDD]
Rheinberger, J.:Duo Pnos, w. G. Shütz (pno) CPO ▲ CPO 999106 [DDD]

Hjelm, Anne Marie (pno)
Stolarczyk, W.:Earth Air Fire Water, w. Amalie Malling (pno), John Damgaard (pno), Anne Øland (pno), Teddy Teirup (pno), Friedrich Gürtler (pno), Rosalind Bevan (pno), Poul Rosenbaum (pno), Rodolfo Llambias (pno), Bella Horn-Ribera (pno), Anders Riber (pno), Elisabeth Sigurdsson (pno), Thomas Tronheim (pno), Elsebeth Broderson (pno), Erik Kaltoft (pno), Jørgen Hald Nielsen (pno), Aino Gilemann (pno), Birgit Kjær (pno), Jørgen Thomsen (pno), Gunhild Donslund (pno), Henrik Bo Hansen (pno), Lone Karlsson (pno), Erik Fessel (pno), Lasse Nilsson (pno), Janos Ferenczi (pno), Erik Bach (pno), Axel Momme (pno), Arne de Cros Dich (pno), Sven Micha Slot (pno), Hanne Bramsen Buhl (pno), Lili Olesen (pno), Susannah Carlsson (pno), Ulla Erml (pno), Vagn Sørensen (pno), Leif Greibe (pno), Bodil Krogh (pno), Kirsten Ottosen (pno), Inger Bergenholz (pno), Karsten Gylendorf (pno), Bjønr Elkjær (pno), Jacob Bjørn Jensen (pno), Jørgen Kaad (pno), Carl Ulrik Munk Andersen (pno), Poul Lumbye (pno), Oluf Hildebrandt Nielsen (pno), Joachim Olsson (pno), Peter Pade Ramsøe Jacobsen (pno), Astrid Pollmann (pno), Jette Borsch (pno), Kirsten Karlshøj (pno), Maria Teresa Assing (pno), Allan Dahl Hansen (pno), Johan Hugossen (pno), Tine Fenger Pederson (pno), Arne Jørgen Fæø (pno), Anja Høgsted (pno), Anne Sophie Parbo (pno), Inga Lindmark (pno), Teresa Drabik Stathakis (pno), Anne Ruth Ferenczi (pno), Irene Hasager (pno), Yuka Ichikawa (pno), Birgitte Baur (pno), Malene Thastum (pno), Jens E. Rasmussen (pno), Birgitte Zielke (pno), Claus Zielke (pno), Stefan Kasch (pno), Bin Qiao (pno), Inger Johanne Teirup (pno), Lindy Rosborg (pno), Liisa Heininen (pno), David Højer (pno), Ellen Refstrup (pno), Thomas K. Søorensen (pno), Erik Kure (pno), Michael Rauff (pno), Jan beck Eriksson (pno), Tanja Zapolski (pno), Vibeke Skagbo (pno), Pål Eide Lindtner (pno), Ha-Young Sul (pno), Benedicte Palko (pno), Inke Kesseler (pno), Anne Marie Meineche (pno), Sverre Larsen (pno), Kasper Peter Bach (pno), Elisabetta Eliseo (pno), Olga Magieres (pno), Carl Erik Kühl (pno), Thorkild Borup Nielsen (pno), Valeria Zanini (pno), Lars Stenhoft (perc), Dennis Boel (perc), Winnie Dahlgren (perc), Susanne Vind (perc), Claus Byrith (elec), Anne Marie Storm (elec), J. Ribera (cnd) *(rec live, Koldinghaus Castle, Denmark, May 2, 1996)* Danica ▲ DCD 1996

Hjelm, Jan-Olov (tpt)
Britten, H.:Fanfare for St. Edmundsbury, w. B. Nilsson (tpt), R. Tilly (tpt) BIS ▲ CD 31 [AAD]

Hjelset, Sigmund (pno)
Grieg, E.:Songs, w. P. Vollestad (bar)—Op. 5, Nos. 1, 2, 3 & 4; Op. 15, No. 2; Op. 18, Nos. 1, 2, 3 & 7; Op. 21, Nos. 1 & 3; Op. 25, Nos. 1, 2, 3, 4, 5 & 6; Op. 26, Nos. 3, 4 & 5; Op. 39, No. 2; Op. 44, Nos. 3 & 5; Op. 48, Nos. 1, 2, 3, 5 & 6; Op. 49, Nos. 4 & 6; Op. 58, No. 2; Op. 59, Nos. 3 & 4; Op. 70, No. 3 [N, G] Simax ▲ PSC 1089 [DDD]

Hlaváč, Jiří (cl)
Bernstein, L.:Prelude, Fugue & Riffs for Orch, w. S. Bogunia (cnd), Solist Band *(rec ZK Motorlet Prague Studio, Sept 4-6 & 14-15, 1986)* Panton ▲ PAN 810884
Copland, A.:Con Cl, w. Hana Müllerová (hp), Ivan Klánský (pno), S. Bogunia (cnd), Suk CO *(rec ZK Motorlet Prague Studio, Sept 4-6 & 14-15, 1986)* Panton ▲ PAN 810884
Stravinsky, I.:Ebony Con, w. S. Bogunia (cnd), Solist Band *(rec ZK Motorlet Prague Studio, Sept 4-6 & 14-15, 1986)* Panton ▲ PAN 810884

Hlaváč, Jiří (sax)
Milhaud, D.:Scaramouche Sax, w. P. Altrichter (cnd), Solist Band *(rec ZK Motorlet Prague Studio, March 21, 1989)* Panton ▲ PAN 810884

Hlawatsch, Thomas (pno)
Janácek, L.:Concertino Pno, w. Béla Nagy (vn), Vilmos Oláh (vn), Csaba Babácsi (va), Géza Bánhegyi (cl), Károly Ambrus (hn), István Hartenstein (bn) *(rec Budapest, May 1995)* Naxos ▲ 8.553587 [DDD]
Janácek, L.:On an Overgrown Path *(rec Festetich Castle, Budapest, May 1995)* Naxos ▲ 8.553586 [DDD]
Janácek, L.:Pno Music—Thema con vars "Zdenka"; Moravian Dances; Reminiscence; Music for Exercise Gymnastique; In the Mist *(rec Budapest, May 1995)* Naxos ▲ 8.553587 [DDD]
Janácek, L.:Son October 1, 1905 Pno *(rec Festetich Castle, Budapest, May 1995)* Naxos ▲ 8.553586 [DDD]
Schumann, R.:Con Pno, w. J. Wildner (cnd), Philharmonia Cassovia *(rec House of Arts, Kosice, Nov. 13-14, 1990)* Lydian ▲ 18106 [DDD]

▲ = CD ◆ = Enhanced CD Δ = MD ■ = Cassette Tape ◻ = DCC

Höbarth, Erich (va)
Mozart, W.A.:Trio Cl, w. Elmar Schmid (cl), András Schiff (pno) Teldec ▲ TEL 99205 [DDD]
Höbarth, Erich (vn)—see also ORCHESTRAS & ENSEMBLES Mosaïques String Quartet
Beethoven, L. van:Trio 1 Pno, w. Patrick Cohen (pno), Christophe Coin (vc) Harmonia Mundi France ("Musique d'abord" series) ▲ HMA 1901361
Beethoven, L. van:Trio 2 Pno, w. Patrick Cohen (pno), Christophe Coin (vc) Harmonia Mundi France ("Musique d'abord" series) ▲ HMA 1901361
Beethoven, L. van:Trio 3 Pno, w. P. Cohen (pno), C. Coin (vc) Harmonia Mundi France ▲ HMC 901475
Haydn, J.:Trios Pno, Vn & Vc, w. Arnaldo Cohen (pno), Christophe Coin (vc)—H.XV/12–14 Harmonia Mundi France ▲ HMC 901277 [DDD]
Haydn, J.:Trios Pno, Vn & Vc, w. Partick Cohen (pno), Christophe Coin (vc)—Nos. 32–34, H.XV/18–20 Harmonia Mundi France ▲ HMC 901314
Haydn, J.:Trios Pno, Vn & Vc, w. Partick Cohen (pno), Christophe Coin (vc)—H.XV/35–37 Harmonia Mundi France ▲ HMC 901400
Haydn, J.:Trios Pno, Vn & Vc, w. Patrick Cohen (pno), Christophe Coin (vc) Harmonia Mundi France ▲ HMC 901514
Haydn, J.:Trios Pno, Vn & Vc, w. Patrick Cohen (pno), Christophe Coin (vc) Harmonia Mundi France ▲ HMC 901572
Mozart, W.A.:Sons Vn Pno (misc), w. Patrick Cohen (pno) [period instrs] Auvidis Astrée ▲ E 8581
Mozart, W.A.:Sons Vn Pno (misc), w. Patrick Cohen (pno)—K.301–305 Astrée ▲ E 8542
Mozart, W.A.:Vars Vn, K.360/374b, w. Patrick Cohen (pno) [period instrs] Auvidis Astrée ▲ E 8581
Hobday, Alfred (va)
Brahms, J.:Qnt 1 Strs, w. Budapest Quartet Biddulph 2-▲ LAB 120–21
Brahms, J.:Qnt 2 Strs, w. Budapest Quartet Biddulph 2-▲ LAB 120–21
Brahms, J.:Sextet Strs, Op. 36, w. Budapest Quartet, Anthony Pini (vc) Biddulph 2-▲ LAB 120–21
Hobson, Claude (pno)
Brahms, J.:Vars Pno (comp), w. Ian Hobson (pno) [w. C. Hobson on Opp. 23 & 56b] *(rec Foellinger Great Hall of the Krannert Center for the Performing Arts, Urbana, IL, Nov. 1–3, 1993, Feb. 14 &)* Arabesque 2-▲ ARA 6654–2
Milhaud, D.:Scaramouche for 2 Pnos, w. I. Hobson (pno) Arabesque ▲ Z 6569 [DDD]
Strauss, R.:Burleske, w. N. del Mar (cnd), Philharmonia Orch Arabesque ▲ Z 6567 [DDD]
Strauss, R.:Parergon zur Symphonia domestica, w. N. del Mar (cnd), Philharmonia Orch Arabesque ▲ Z 6567 [DDD]
Hobson, Ian (pno)
Bach, Joh. Christian:Sons Kbd—Op. 17/2 Arabesque ▲ Z 6594
Beethoven, L. van:Sons Pno (comp)—Opp. 7 & 10/1–3 Arabesque ▲ ARA 6645
Beethoven, L. van:Sons Pno (comp)—Opp. 13, 14/1 & 2 & 22 Arabesque ▲ ARA 6648
Beethoven, L. van:Sons Pno (comp)—Nos. 12–15 Arabesque ▲ ARA 6659
Beethoven, L. van:Sons Pno (comp)—Sons. 1–3 *(rec June 1992)* Arabesque ▲ Z 6637
Bennett, W.S.:Pno Music—Sonata in A♭ for Piano, "Die Jungfrau von Orleans," Op. 46; Three Romances, Op. 14 Arabesque ▲ Z 6596
Brahms, J.:Theme & Vars Pno Arabesque ▲ ARA 6654 [DDD]
Brahms, J.:Vars Pno (comp), [w. C. Hobson on Opp. 23 & 56b] *(rec Foellinger Great Hall of the Krannert Center for the Performing Arts, Urbana, IL* Arabesque 2-▲ ARA 6654–2
Burton, J.:Son 1 Pno Arabesque ▲ Z 6594
Busby, T.:Son Pno, Op. 1/4 Arabesque ▲ Z 6594
Chipp, E.T.:Twilight Fancies Arabesque ▲ Z 6596
Clementi, M.:Capriccio Arabesque ▲ Z 6595
Clementi, M.:Sons Pno—Op. 13/6 in f Arabesque ▲ Z 6594
Cramer, J.B.:Son Pno, Op. 27/1 Arabesque ▲ Z 6595
Cramer, J.B.:Studio per il Pianoforte (sels)—Nos. 1,16,19,21,29 & 30 Arabesque ▲ Z 6596
Dussek, J.L.:Son Pno, Op. 44, "The Farewell" Arabesque ▲ Z 6594
Field, J.:Son Pno, Op. 1/1 Arabesque ▲ Z 6595
Godowsky, L.:Studies (53) after Chopin's Etudes—Nos. 1, 4, 5, 13, 15, 17, 22, 25, 27, 32, 34, 36, 38, 42, 45, 46, 47, 48 Arabesque ▲ Z 6537 [DDD]
Hindemith, P.:Son Db, w. Michael Cameron (db) Zuma Records ▲ ZMA 304
Hobson's Choice, w. Hobson, Ian (pno) Arabesque ▲ ARA 6639 [DDD]
Hummel, J.N.:Son 1 Pno Arabesque ▲ Z 6564
Hummel, J.N.:Son 2 Pno Arabesque ▲ Z 6565
Hummel, J.N.:Son 3 Pno Arabesque ▲ Z 6566
Hummel, J.N.:Son 4 Pno Arabesque ▲ Z 6566
Hummel, J.N.:Son 5 Pno Arabesque ▲ Z 6565
Hummel, J.N.:Son 6 Pno Arabesque ▲ Z 6564
Johnston, B.:Progression, w. Michael Cameron (db) Zuma Records ▲ ZMA 304
The London Piano School, Vol. 1 Arabesque ▲ Z 6594
The London Piano School, Vol. 2:Romantic Pioneers Arabesque ▲ Z 6595
The London Piano School, Vol. 3:Early Victorian Masters Arabesque ▲ Z 6596
Milhaud, D.:Rag-Caprices Arabesque ▲ Z 6569 [DDD]
Milhaud, D.:Scaramouche for 2 Pnos, w. C. Hobson (pno) Arabesque ▲ Z 6569 [DDD]
Milhaud, D.:Suite Vn, w. C. Tait (vn), King (cl) Arabesque ▲ Z 6569 [DDD]
Moscheles, I.:Romance et Tarantelle brilliante Arabesque ▲ Z 6596
Oldham, K.:Con Pno, w. W. McGlaughlin (cnd), Kansas City SO *(rec Mar. 27, 1993)* Catalyst ▲ 09026–61979–2 ■ 09026–61979–4
Pinto, G.F.:Son Pno Arabesque ▲ Z 6595
Rachmaninoff, S.:Études-tableaux, Opp. 33 & 39 Arabesque ▲ Z 6609
Rachmaninoff, S.:Pno Music (misc)—The Star Spangled Banner [Smith]; Suite from the Partita in E for Vn [Bach]; The Flight of the Bumblebee [Rimsky-Korsakov]; Hopak [Mussorgsky]; Wohin? [Schubert]; Minuet [Bizet]; Lullaby [Tchaikovsky]; Scherzo [Mendelssohn]; Liebesleid; Liebesfreud [both Kreisler]; Serenade, Op. 3; Lilacs; Daisies; Polka of V.R.; Melodie, Op. 3; Humoreske, Op. 10; Moment Musical [all Rachmaninoff] *(rec Stude Concert Hall of Rice Univ., Houston, TX & Great Hall of the Krannert Center for the Performing Arts, Urbana, IL, Sept. 9 & 10, 1994 & Jan.)* Arabesque ▲ ARA 6663
Saint-Saëns, C.:Allegro appassionato Arabesque ▲ Z 6570
Saint-Saëns, C.:Bagatelles Pno Arabesque ▲ Z 6570
Saint-Saëns, C.:Spt Tpt, w. I. Hobson (cnd), Sinfonia da Camera Arabesque ▲ Z 6570
Schumann, R.:Impromptus on a Theme by Clara Wieck Pno, Op. 5 Arabesque 2-▲ ARA 6621 [DDD]
Schumann, R.:Presto passionato Arabesque 2-▲ ARA 6621 [DDD]
Schumann, R.:Son Pno, Op. 14 Arabesque 2-▲ ARA 6621 [DDD]
Schumann, R.:Son 1 Pno Arabesque 2-▲ ARA 6621 [DDD]
Schumann, R.:Son 2 Pno Arabesque 2-▲ ARA 6621 [DDD]
Schumann, R.:Vars on A–B–E–G–G Arabesque 2-▲ ARA 6621 [DDD]
Segall, A.J.:Fant Db, w. Michael Cameron (db) Zuma Records ▲ ZMA 304
Shostakovich, D.:Night, w. Michael Cameron (db) Zuma Records ▲ ZMA 304
Strauss, R.:Stimmungsbilder Arabesque ▲ Z 6567 [DDD]
Weber, C.M. von:Adagio patetico Arabesque ▲ Z 6595
Wesley, S.:March & Rondo Arabesque ▲ Z 6596
Wesley, S.:Rondo on *God Rest Ye Merry, Gentlemen* Pno Arabesque ▲ Z 6594
Hobson, Richard (org)
Bach, J.S.:Org Music (misc) [William Drake Org, Mayfair, England]—Sei gregwilsser, Jesu gutig Herald ▲ HAVPCD 156
Guilain, J.-A.:Pièces d'orgue pour le Magnificat [William Drake Org, Mayfair, England]—Suite du 2nd ton Herald ▲ HAVPCD 156
Mendelssohn, F.:Sons Org [William Drake Org, Mayfair, England] Herald ▲ HAVPCD 156
Purcell, H.:Org Music [William Drake Org, Mayfair, England]—Voluntary in G Herald ▲ HAVPCD 156
Stanley, J.:Voluntaries Org [William Drake Org, Mayfair, England]—Voluntary in A Herald ▲ HAVPCD 156
Walond, W.:Org Music [William Drake Org, Mayfair, England]—Voluntary in d Herald ▲ HAVPCD 156

Hoca, Claudia (pno)
Martin, F.:Petite sym concertante, w. V. Drake (hp), A. Newman (hpd), R. Kapp (cnd), Philharmonia Virtuosi ESS.A.Y ▲ CD 1014 [DDD]
Hoch, Bertalan (org)
Wedding Music, w. I. Bogár (cnd), Budapest Strauss Ensemble *(rec 1992)* Naxos ▲ 8.550790 [DDD]
Hochscheid, Susanne (fl)—see ORCHESTRAS & ENSEMBLES Cologne Flautando
Hochuli, Felix (gtr/pno)
Distel, H.:Die Reise, w. Pietrina Cavazzini (sgr) *(rec Bern, Switzerland & Toscana, Italy, 1984–85)* Hat Hut ("NOW." series) ▲ hat ART CD 6001 [AAD]
Hock, Bertalan (ob)
Haydn, J.:Diverts for 2 Obs, Hns & Bns, H.II/7, 15, D18, 23 & deest, w. P Pongrácz (ob), A. Medveczky (hn), D. Mesterházy (hn), T. Fülemile (bn), A. Nagy (bn) White Label ▲ HRC 155 [ADD]
Hocmuth, Reiner (vc)
Wagenseil, G.C.:Con in C Vc, w. J. M. Händler (cnd), Dall'Arco CO Thorofon ▲ CTH 2068 [DDD]
Wagenseil, G.C.:Con in A Vc, w. J. M. Händler (cnd), Dall'Arco CO Thorofon ▲ CTH 2068 [DDD]
Hodges, Janice Kay (pno)
Creston, P.:Fant Trbn, w. J. Kitzman (trbn) Crystal ■ C 386
Hindemith, P.:Son Trbn, w. John Kitzman (trbn) Crystal ■ C 386
Hodgkinson, Randall (pno)—see also ORCHESTRAS & ENSEMBLES Castleman/Hodgkinson Violin–Piano Duo
Brahms, J.:Son 2 Cl, w. J. Cohler (cl) *(rec Aug. 28–29, 1993)* Ongaku ▲ 024–102 [DDD]
Copland, A.:Duo Fl, w. F. Smith (fl) Northeastern ("Classical Arts" series) ▲ NR 227–CD
Copland, A.:Vocalise, w. F. Smith (fl) Northeastern ("Classical Arts" series) ▲ NR 227–CD
Foote, A.:Pieces Ob & Pno, Op. 31, w. F. Smith (fl) Northeastern ("Classical Arts" series) ▲ NR 227–CD
Foote, A.:Sarabande & Rigaudon, w. F. Smith (fl), M. Thompson (va) Northeastern ("Classical Arts" series) ▲ NR 227–CD
Griffes, C.T.:Poem Fl, w. S. Jutt (fl) [arr. G. Barrère] GM ▲ GM2026CD
Harbison, J.:Duo Fl & Pno, w. Fenwick Smith (fl) *(rec Kresge Auditorium, between 1988 & 1994)* Archetype ▲ 60104 [DDD]
Jolivet, A.:Chant de Linos, w. S. Jutt (fl) GM ▲ GM2026CD
McKinley, W.T.:Romances, w. S. Jutt (fl) GM ▲ GM2026CD
McLennan, J.S.:Qnt Vn, Va, Vc, Cl & Pno, w. A. Levy (vn), B. Fine (va), A. Diaz (vc), P. Hancock (cl) CRI ▲ CD 594 [DDD]
Milhaud, D.:Sonatina Cl, w. J. Cohler (cl) *(rec Aug. 28–29, 1993)* Ongaku ▲ 024–102 [DDD]
Piazzolla, A.:Études tanguistiques, w. S. Jutt (fl) GM ▲ GM2026CD
Poulenc, F.:Son Cl Pno, w. J. Cohler (cl) *(rec Aug. 28–29, 1993)* Ongaku ▲ 024–102 [DDD]
Schumann, R.:Fantasiestücke Cl, w. J. Cohler (cl) *(rec Aug. 28–29, 1993)* Ongaku ▲ 024–102 [DDD]
Shostakovich, D.:Trio 2 Pno, w. S. Chase (vn), R. Thomas (vc) *(rec Methuen, MA, Jan. 1990)* Northeastern ▲ NOR 245 [DDD]
Stravinsky, I.:Pieces Cl, w. J. Cohler (cl) *(rec Aug. 28–29, 1993)* Ongaku ▲ 024–102 [DDD]
Hodgson, Gwyn (org)
A Recital of 17th & 18th Century Organ Music Point ▲ PCD 5114
Hödl, Helmut (cl)—see ORCHESTRAS & ENSEMBLES Vienna Quintet
Hoebig, Desmond (vc)
Rachmaninoff, S.:Son Vc, w. Andrew Tunis (pno) CBC ▲ MVCD 1093 [DDD]
Rachmaninoff, S.:Vocalise, w. Andrew Tunis (pno) [trans Leonard Rose for vc & pno] CBC ▲ MVCD 1093 [DDD]
Shostakovich, D.:Son Vc, w. Andrew Tunis (pno) CBC ▲ MVCD 1093 [DDD]
Hoekman, Timothy (pno)
Hoekman, T.:Margarets, w. Terry Rhodes (sop), Ellen Williams (mez) Albany ▲ TROY 172 [DDD]
Hoelbling, A. (vn)
Telemann, G.P.:Cons (misc), w. L. Kyselak (va), Z. Tylšar (hn), B. Tylšar (hn), O. Hoelbling (vn), A. Jablokov (vn), R. Edlinger (cnd), Capella Istropolitana—Viola Con. in G; Concerto in F for 3 Violins; Concerto for 2 Horns Naxos ▲ 8.550156 [DDD] ∆ 7.550156 [DDD]
Hoelbling, O. (vn)
Telemann, G.P.:Cons (misc), w. L. Kyselak (va), Z. Tylšar (hn), B. Tylšar (hn), A. Hoelbling (vn), A. Jablokov (vn), R. Edlinger (cnd), Capella Istropolitana—Viola Con. in G; Concerto in F for 3 Violins; Concerto for 2 Horns Naxos ▲ 8.550156 [DDD] ∆ 7.550156 [DDD]
Hoelscher, Ludwig (vc)
Pfitzner, H.:Duo Vn, w. M. Strub (vn), H. Pfitzner (cnd), Berlin State Opera Orch Preiser ▲ 90029 (m) [AAD]
Hoelscher, Ulf (vn)
Beethoven, L. van:Con Vn, Vc & Pno, "Triple Con", w. H. Schiff (vc), C. Zacharias (pno), K. Masur (cnd), Leipzig Gewandhaus Orch EMI Classics ▲ ZDMC 63937
Bloch, A.:Duet Vn & Vc, w. Wolfgang Boettcher (vc) Pro Viva ▲ ISPV 172
Bloch, A.:Duet Vn & Org, w. Peter Schwarz (org) Pro Viva ▲ ISPV 172
Pettersson, G.A.:Con 1 Vn Str Qt, w. Mandelring String Quartet CPO ▲ CPO 999169 [DDD]
Schoeck, O.:Concerto quasi una fantasia, w. H. Griffiths (cnd), English CO Novalis ▲ 150070 [DDD]
Spohr, L.:Con 2 Vn, w. C. Fröhlich (cnd), Berlin RSO CPO ▲ CPO 999067 [DDD]
Spohr, L.:Con 3 Vn, w. C. Fröhlich (cnd), Berlin RSO CPO ▲ CPO 999145 [DDD]
Spohr, L.:Con 4 Vn, w. C. Fröhlich (cnd), Berlin RSO CPO ▲ CPO 999196 [DDD]
Spohr, L.:Con 5 Vn, w. C. Fröhlich (cnd), Berlin RSO CPO ▲ CPO 999067 [DDD]
Spohr, L.:Con 6 Vn, w. C. Fröhlich (cnd), Berlin RSO CPO ▲ CPO 999145 [DDD]
Spohr, L.:Con 7 Vn, w. C. Fröhlich (cnd), Berlin RSO CPO ▲ CPO 999232 [DDD]
Spohr, L.:Con 8 Vn, w. C. Fröhlich (cnd), Berlin RSO CPO ▲ CPO 999187 [DDD]
Spohr, L.:Con 9 Vn, w. C. Fröhlich (cnd), Berlin RSO CPO ▲ CPO 999232 [DDD]
Spohr, L.:Con 10 Vn, w. C. Fröhlich (cnd), Berlin RSO CPO ▲ CPO 999232 [DDD]
Spohr, L.:Con 11 Vn, w. C. Fröhlich (cnd), Berlin RSO CPO ▲ CPO 999196 [DDD]
Spohr, L.:Con 12 Vn, w. C. Fröhlich (cnd), Berlin RSO CPO ▲ CPO 999145 [DDD]
Spohr, L.:Con 12 Vn, w. C. Fröhlich (cnd), Berlin RSO CPO ▲ CPO 999187 [DDD]
Spohr, L.:Con 13 Vn, w. C. Fröhlich (cnd), Berlin RSO CPO ▲ CPO 999187 [DDD]
Strauss, R.:Con Vn, w. R. Kempe (cnd), Dresden Staatskapelle EMI Classics 3-▲ CDZC 64346
Szymanowski, K.:Caprices, w. Michel Béroff (pno) *(rec West German Radio Studio 2, Cologne, May 18–20, 1982)* EMI Classics ▲ CDC 55169 [DDD]
Szymanowski, K.:Myths, w. Michel Béroff (pno) *(rec West German Radio Studio 2, Cologne, May 18–20, 1982)* EMI Classics ▲ CDC 55169 [DDD]
Szymanowski, K.:Notturno e Tarantella, w. Michel Béroff (pno) *(rec West German Radio Studio 2, Cologne, May 18–20, 1982)* EMI Classics ▲ CDC 55169 [DDD]
Szymanowski, K.:Romance, w. Michel Béroff (pno) *(rec West German Radio Studio 2, Cologne, May 18–20, 1982)* EMI Classics ▲ CDC 55169 [DDD]
Wagner, S.:Con Vn, w. W. A. Albert (cnd), Rhineland-Palatinate State PO *(rec Apr 1996)* CPO ▲ 999427–2 [DDD]
Hoener, C. (vn)
Kirchner, L.:Qt 1 Strs, w. M. Beaulieu (vn), S. Woolweaver (va), A. Mark (vc) Albany ▲ TROY 137 [DDD]
Kirchner, L.:Qt 2 Strs, w. M. Beaulieu (vn), S. Woolweaver (va), A. Mark (vc) Albany ▲ TROY 137 [DDD]
Kirchner, L.:Qt 3 Strs, w. M. Beaulieu (vn), S. Woolweaver (va), A. Mark (vc) Albany ▲ TROY 137 [DDD]
Hoeppner, Susan (fl)—see also ORCHESTRAS & ENSEMBLES Chinook Trio
Histoire du Tango, w., Rachel Gauk (gtr) Marquis ▲ MAR 177 [DDD]
Toward the Sea, w. Hoeppner, Susan (fl), Rachel Gauk (org) Marquis Classics ▲ MAR 147 [DDD]
Hoeprich, Eric (b cl)
Mozart, W.A.:Con Cl, w. F. Brüggen (cnd), Orch of the 18th Century Philips ▲ 420242–2 [DDD]
Mozart, W.A.:Con Cl, w. T. Crawford (cnd), Old Fairfield Academy Orch MusicMasters ▲ 01612–67157–2 [DDD]
Hoeprich, Eric (bas hn)—see ORCHESTRAS & ENSEMBLES New World Basset Horn Trio

INSTRUMENT.

Hoeprich, Eric (chl)
Telemann, G.P.:Cons (misc), w. Masahiro Arita (trns fl/pic), Hans Peter Westermann (ob), Dane Roberts (db), David Sinclair (db), La Stravaganza Cologne—in E for Transverse Flute, Oboe d'amore, Viola d'amore, Strings & Continuo; in e for Transverse Flute, Violin, Strings & Continuo; in D for Transverse Flute, Strings & Continuo; in E♭ for Strings & Continuo; in G for Transverse Flute, Chalumeau, Oboe, 2 Double Basses, Strings & Continuo *(rec Cologne, May 30–June 3, 1994)* Denon ("Aliare" series) ▲ CO 78933 [DDD]

Hoeprich, Eric (cl)—see also ORCHESTRAS & ENSEMBLES Biedermeier Quintet members, Biedermeier Quintet
Beethoven, L. van:Trio Pno, Op.38, w. S. Hoogland (pno), T. Tomkins (vc) Koch International Classics ▲ KIC 7015-2 [DDD] ■ 3-7015-4 (D)
Glinka, M.:Trio pathétique, w. T. Tomkins (vc), S. Hoogland (fortepno) Koch International Classics ▲ KIC 7015-2 [DDD] ■ 3-7015-4 (D)
Vivaldi, A.:Cons Obs Cls, w. S. Hammer (ob), F. de Bruine (ob), A. Pay (cl), C. Hogwood (cnd), Academy of Ancient Music—RV.559 London ▲ 433674-2

Hoeren, Harald (hpd)
Caix D'Hervelois, L. de:Pièces Trns Fl, w. Ursula Schmidt-Laukamp (rcr)—2nd Suite in F [from Premier livre] Ars Produktion ▲ ARS 368337
Couperin, A.-L.:Pièces de clavecin—from the G/g and B♭/b♭ sections:La Victoire; Allemande; Courante La De Croissy; La Grégoire; L'Intrépide [Rondeau]; Menuets I & II; L'Arlequine ou la Adam [Rondeau]; La Blanchet; La de Boisgelou; La Focquet; La Semillante ou la Joly; La Turpin; Gavottes I & II; Menuets I & II; La du Breüil; La Chéron; L'Affligée; L'Enjouée; Les Tendres Sentiments *(rec Cologne, Sept 27–29, 1994)* CPO ▲ CPO 999312-2 [DDD]
Couperin, F.:Nouveaux Concerts, "Les Goûts-réunis", w. Ursula Schmidt-Laukamp (rcr)—Nos. 7 & 8 Ars Produktion ▲ ARS 368337
Marais, M.:Pièces en trio, w. Ursula Schmidt-Laukamp (rcr), Peter Wendland (vl)—No. 3 in D Ars Produktion ▲ ARS 368337
Rameau, J.P.:1e livre de pièces de clavecin—in a Ars Produktion ▲ ARS 368337

Hoerr (vc)
Farrenc, J.-L.:Trio Cl, w. D. Klöcker (cl), W. Genuit (pno) Divox ▲ CDX 29205 [DDD]

Hoetzl, E. (hpd)—see ORCHESTRAS & ENSEMBLES Il Parnaso Musicale

Hoever, Herbert (vn)
The Viola d'Amore:In Numerous Voices, w. Dorothea Jappe (va d'amore), Konrad Hünteler (trns fl), Hans-Rudolf Stalder (chl), Michael Jappe (vl/vc), Rolf Junghanns (hpd/pno) Adagio ▲ ADG 91016

Hofer, Heinz (bas hn)
Mozart, W.A.:Adagio Cls, K.411, w. K. Leister (cl), P. Geisler (cl), H.R. Stalder (bas hn), E. Schmid (bas hn) *(rec 1978)* Jecklin-Disco ▲ JD 549-2 [ADD]
Mozart, W.A.:Adagio E Hn, w. K. Leister (cl), H.R. Stalder (bas hn), E. Schmid (bas hn) [arr. Raymond Meylan for clarinet & basset horn] *(rec 1978)* Jecklin-Disco ▲ JD 549-2 [ADD]

Hofer, Heinz (cl)
Crusell, B.H.:Duos (3) for 2 Cls, w. H.-R. Stalder (cl)—No. 2 *(rec 1975)* Jecklin-Disco ▲ JD 578-2 [ADD]
Mozart, W.A.:Diverts Bas Hns, K.Anh.229, w. H.-R. Stalder (cl), H. Leuthold (bas hn) [arr. for 3 basset horns]—No. 1 *(rec 1978)* Jecklin-Disco ▲ JD 549-2 [ADD]

Hofer, Thomas (vn)—see ORCHESTRAS & ENSEMBLES Pellegrini String Quartet

Hoff, Brynjar (ob)
Bach, J.S.:Cant 82, w. Knut Skram (bass), A. Ardal (cnd), Canticum Novum CO *(rec Greverud Church, Oslo, Norway, June 8 & 9 & Sept 23, 197)* BIS ▲ CD 101 [AAD]
Britten, H.:Metamorphoses Ob Norway Music ▲ LCD 1004
Mozart, W.A.:Qt Ob, K.370, w. Hindar String Quartet members Norway Music ▲ LCD 1004
Reizenstein, F.:Sonatina Ob, w. Kaare Ornung (pno) Norway Music ▲ LCD 1004
Schumann, R.:Romances Ob, w. Kaare Ornung (pno) Norway Music ▲ LCD 1004

Hoffman, Annabelle (vc)
Telemann, G.P.:Con Tpt Strs in D, w. Edward Carroll (tpt/pic tpt), Diane Bruce (vn), Elizabeth Field (vn), Dongsok Shin (positiv org), Edward Brewer (hpd/positiv org) *(rec Rye Presbyterian Church)* Helicon Classics ▲ HE 1009
Telemann, G.P.:Musique héroïque, w. Edward Carroll (tpt/pic tpt), Diane Bruce (vn), Elizabeth Field (vn), Dongsok Shin (positiv org), Edward Brewer (hpd/positiv org) *(rec Rye Presbyterian Church)* Helicon Classics ▲ HE 1009
Telemann, G.P.:Sons Tpt, w. Edward Carroll (tpt/pic tpt), Diane Bruce (vn), Elizabeth Field (vn), Dongsok Shin (positiv org), Edward Brewer (hpd/positiv org) *(rec Rye Presbyterian Church)* Helicon Classics ▲ HE 1009
Telemann, G.P.:Trio Sons, w. Edward Carroll (tpt/pic tpt), Diane Bruce (vn), Elizabeth Field (vn), Dongsok Shin (positiv org), Edward Brewer (hpd/positiv org) *(rec Rye Presbyterian Church)* Helicon Classics ▲ HE 1009

Hoffman, Bettina (vl)—see also ORCHESTRAS & ENSEMBLES L'Homme Armé
Bach, J.S.:Sons Vl, BWV 1027–1029, w. Alfonso Fedi (hpd) *(rec Florence, Italy, Jan 1994)* Arts ▲ 472522 [DDD]

Hoffman, Gary (db)
Mendelssohn, F.:Qnt 2 Strs, w. S. Accardo (vn), M. Batjer (vn), T. Hoffman (va), S. Gazeau (vc) Nuova Era ▲ 6870 [DDD]

Hoffman, Gary (vc)
Aho, K.:Con Vc, w. O. Vänskä (cnd), Lahti SO *(rec Ristinkirkko, Lahti, Finland, Sept. 7–8, 1993)* BIS ▲ CD 706 [DDD]
Arensky, A.:Trio 1 Pno, w. Y. Bronfman (pno), C.-L. Lin (vn) *(rec Aug 25–27, 1992)* Sony Classical ▲ SK 53269 [DDD]
Beethoven, L. van:Qnt Strs, Op. 29, w. S. Accardo (vn), M. Batjer (vn), T. Hoffman (va), S. Gazeau (va) Nuova Era ▲ 6870 [DDD]
Debussy, C.:Trio Pno, w. André Previn (pno), Julie Rosenfeld (vn) RCA Red Seal ▲ 09026-68062-2
Dohnányi, E. von:Serenade, w. J. Silverstein (vn), P. Neubauer (va) *(rec Apr. 14, 1993)* Delos ▲ DE 3151 [DDD]
Janácek, L.:Conte, w. Charles Mackerras (pno) EMI Classics ▲ CDC 55585
Janácek, L.:Presto, w. Mikhail Rudy (pno) EMI Classics ▲ CDC 55585
Mozart, W.A.:Qts Pno, w. A. Previn (pno), Y. U. Kim (vn), H. Ohyama (va) RCA Red Seal ▲ 09026-60713-2
Ravel, M.:Trio Pno, w. André Previn (pno), Julie Rosenfeld (vn) RCA Red Seal ▲ 09026-68062-2
Schumann, R.:Qt Pno in c, w. A. Previn (pno), Young Uck Kim (vn), H. Ohyama (va) RCA Red Seal ▲ 09026-61384-2
Schumann, R.:Qt Pno, Op. 47, w. A. Previn (pno), Young Uck Kim (vn), H. Ohyama (va) RCA Red Seal ▲ 09026-61384-2
Tchaikovsky, P.:Trio Pno, w. Y. Bronfman (pno), C.-L. Lin (vn) *(rec Aug. 25–27, 1992)* Sony Classical ▲ SK 53269 [DDD]

Hoffman, Joel (pno)
Hoffman, J.:Duo Vn & Pno, w. T. Hoffman (va) CRI ▲ CD 590 [DDD]

Hoffman, Miles (va)—see also ORCHESTRAS & ENSEMBLES American Chamber Players
Saylor, B.:Songs from Water St, w. C. Beavon (mez), D. Abramowitz (pno) [E] CRI ▲ CD 578 [DDD]

Hoffman, Toby (va)
Beethoven, L. van:Qnt Strs, Op. 29, w. S. Accardo (vn), M. Batjer (vn), S. Gazeau (va), G. Hoffman (vc) Nuova Era ▲ 6870 [DDD]
Hoffman, J.:Duo Vn & Pno, w. J. Hoffman (pno) CRI ▲ CD 590 [DDD]
Mendelssohn, F.:Qnt 2 Strs, w. S. Accardo (vn), M. Batjer (vn), S. Gazeau (vc), G. Hoffman (db) Nuova Era ▲ 6870 [DDD]
Milhaud, D.:La Création du monde (suite), w. André Previn (pno), Ani Kavafian (vn), Julie Rosenfeld (vn), Carter Brey (vc) *(rec Manhattan Center Studios, New York City, May 25–26, 1993)* RCA Red Seal ▲ 09026-68181-2 [DDD]
Mozart, W.A.:Sinf concertante Vn, K.364, w. S. Accardo (vn), S. Accardo (cnd), Prague CO Nuova Era ▲ 6949 [DDD]

Hoffman, Toby (va) (cont.)
Saint-Saëns, C.:Spt Tpt, w. André Previn (pno), Thomas Stevens (tpt), Julie Rosenfeld (vn), Ani Kavafian (vn), Carter Brey (vc), Jack Kulowitsch (db) *(rec Manhattan Center Studios, New York City, May 25–26, 1993)* RCA Red Seal ▲ 09026-68181-2 [DDD]

Hoffmann, B. (vc)—see ORCHESTRAS & ENSEMBLES Modo Antiquo

Hoffmann, Bruno (glass hmc)
Mozart, W.A.:Complete Mozart Edition, w. Alfred Brendel (pno), Stephen Bishop Kovacevich (pno), Beaux Arts Trio Philips 5-▲ 422514-2 [ADD]
Naumann, J.G.:Qt Glass Hmc, w. K.H. Ulrich (fl), E. Nippes (va), H. Plumacher (vc) Allegretto ▲ ACD 8174 [ADD] ■ ACS 8174
Reichardt, J.F.:Rondeau, w. H. Anrath (vn), W. Albers (vn), E. Nippes (va), H. Plumacher (vc), G. Nose (db) Allegretto ▲ ACD 8174 [ADD] ■ ACS 8174
Röllig, K.L.:Qnt Glass Hmc, w. W. Albers (vn), H. Anrath (vn), E. Nippes (va), H. Plumacher (vc) Allegretto ▲ ACD 8174 [ADD] ■ ACS 8174
Schulz, J.A.P.:Largo Allegretto ▲ ACD 8174 [ADD] ■ ACS 8174

Hoffmann, Karl (bn)
Vivaldi, A.:Con Fl Bn, w. Julius Baker (fl), A. Janigro (cnd), Zagreb Solisti *(rec Baumgarten Hall, Vienna, May 5–7, 1962)* Vanguard Classics ▲ SVC 42 [AAD]

Hoffmann, Ludwig (pno)
Mozart, W.A.:Complete Mozart Edition, w. Ingrid Haebler (pno), Paul Badura-Skoda (pno), Jörg Demus (pno) Philips 2-▲ 422516-2 [ADD]

Hoffmann, M. (ob)
Lorentzen, B.:Con Ob, w. F. Rasmussen (cnd), Aarhus SO *(rec May 4–5 1992)* Marco Polo/Dacapo ▲ DCCD 9314 [DDD]

Hoffmann, M. (tpt)
Lorentzen, B.:Regenbogen, w. F. Rasmussen (cnd), Aarhus SO *(rec May 4–5 1992)* Marco Polo/Dacapo ▲ DCCD 9314 [DDD]

Hoffmann, M. (wind instr)
Kelterborn, R.:Songs for 4 Winds & Chorus, w. T. Jones (trbn), W. Mittelbach (wind instr), G. Pettinger (wind instr), G. Kember (cnd), Bavarian Radio Chorus *(rec May 13, 1983)* Grammont ▲ CTSP 35-2 [ADD]

Hoffmann, Paul (pno)
Crawford, R.:Songs (3), w. P. Berlin (mez), J. Ostryniec (ob), D.C. Armstrong (perc) CRI ▲ CD 658 [ADD]
Kershner, B.:Son Bn, w. Brian Kershner (bn) Vienna Modern Masters ("Distinguished Performers III" series) ▲ VMM 2016 [DDD]
Smith, S.S.:Notebook, w. J. Fonville (fl), E. Harkins (tpt), B. Turetzky (db) O.O. Discs ▲ OO 11 [DDD]

Hoffmann, Rainer (pno)
Yasunori Kawahara, w. Yasunori Kawahara (db) Largo ▲ 5105 [DDD]

Hoffner, Alice (vl)—see ORCHESTRAS & ENSEMBLES Deller Consort

Hofmann, Josef (pno)
Beethoven, L. van:Turkish March *(rec 1900–10)* Adès ▲ ADE 203932 [AAD]
Chopin, F.:Con 1 Pno, *(orch unknown)* *(rec live, Long Beach, California 1/21/56)* VAI Audio ▲ VAIA/IPA 1002 (m) [ADD]
Chopin, F.:Con 2 Pno, *(orch unknown)* *(rec live, Long Beach, California 1/21/56)* VAI Audio ▲ VAIA/IPA 1002 (m) [ADD]
Chopin, F.:Pno Music (misc) VAI Audio 2-▲ VAIA/IPA 1020 (m) [ADD]
Chopin, F.:Polonaises—Op. 53 *(rec 1900–10)* Adès ▲ ADE 203932 [AAD]
The Complete Josef Hofmann, Vol. 1 VAI Audio ▲ VAIA/IPA 1002 (m) [ADD]
The Complete Josef Hofmann, Vol. 2 *(rec live, Metropolitan Opera House, New York City, Nov 28, 1937)* VAI Audio 2-▲ VAIA/IPA 1020 (m) [ADD]
The Complete Josef Hofmann, Vol. 3 *(rec 1903, 1912–1918)* VAI Audio 2-▲ VAIA/IPA 1036-2 [ADD]
The Complete Josef Hofmann, Vol. 4 *(rec 1922–23)* VAI Audio ▲ VAIA/IPS 1047 [ADD]
Hoffmann, Giovanni:Chromaticon, w. F. Reiner (cnd), Curtis Institute Student Orch VAI Audio 2-▲ VAIA/IPA 1020 (m) [ADD]
Mendelssohn, F.:Rondo capriccioso *(rec 1900–10)* Adès ▲ ADE 203932 [AAD]
Moszkowski, M.:Caprice Espagnole *(rec live Nov. 28, 1937)* VAI Audio 2-▲ VAIA/IPA 1020 (m) [ADD]
Rachmaninoff, S.:Prelude Pno, Op. 3/2 *(rec 1900–10)* Adès ▲ ADE 203932 [AAD]
Rubinstein, A.:Con 4 Pno, w. F. Reiner (cnd), Curtis Institute Student Orch *(rec live Nov. 28, 1937)* VAI Audio 2-▲ VAIA/IPA 1020 (m) [ADD]

Hofmann, Marion (hp)
Yun, I.:Duo Vc, w. Walter Grimmer (vc) Col Legno ▲ AU 31808
Yun, I.:Recontre, w. Eduard Brunner (cl), Walter Grimmer (vc) Col Legno ▲ AU 31808

Hofmann-Engel, Ludger (pno)
Hofmann-Engl, L.:Son 1 Pno Vienna Modern Masters ("Distinguished Performers III" series) ▲ VMM 2016 [DDD]

Hofstetter, Robert (org)
Lewkovitch, B.:Org Music—The Liturgical Year [sequence] Point ▲ PCD 5109

Hogan, David (pno)
Bruch, M.:Con for 2 Pnos, w. M. Berkofsky (pno), L. Herbig (cnd), Berlin SO *(rec 1977)* Allegretto ▲ ACD 8169 [ADD] ■ ACS 8169
Bruch, M.:Fant for 2 Pnos, w. M. Berkofsky (pno) Allegretto ▲ ACD 8169 [ADD] ■ ACS 8169
Bruch, M.:Swedish Dances, w. M. Berkofsky (pno) Allegretto ▲ ACD 8169 [ADD] ■ ACS 8169

Hogan, Moses (pno)
Ev'ry Time I Feel the Spirit:Spirituals, w. Derek Lee Ragin (male alt), New World Ensemble, Chamber Choir New Orleans, Moses Hogan (cnd) Channel Classics ▲ CCS 2991 [DDD]

Hogerheijde, Reiner (cl)
Crusell, B.H.:Qts (3) Cl, w. V. Liberman (vn), G. Oldeman (va), Dora Mintcheva (vc) Erasmus ▲ WVH 103

Hogg, Simon (trbn)—see ORCHESTRAS & ENSEMBLES Fine Arts Brass Ensemble

Höglund, Ola (org)
Organ Improvisations Swedish Society ▲ SCD 1044

Högner, Günter (hn)—see also ORCHESTRAS & ENSEMBLES Vienna Ring Ensemble
Hindemith, P.:Kleine Kammermusik, w. Wolfgang Schulz (fl), Hansjörg Schellenberger (ob), Karl Leister (cl), Milan Turkovic (bn) Sony Classical ▲ SK 64400
Hindemith, P.:Son Hn, w. Ferenc Bognár (pno) Sony Classical ▲ SK 64400

Hogwood, Christopher (bc)
Bach, J.S.:Con 2 Hpd, w. Neil Black (ob), Nicholas Kraemer (bc), N. Marriner (cnd), Academy of St. Martin in the Fields [trans for ob] *(rec St. John's, Smith Square, London, Aug 1974 & Feb 1975)* Boston Skyline ▲ BSD 127 [ADD]
Bach, J.S.:Con 4 Hpd, w. Neil Black (ob d'amore), Nicholas Kraemer (bc), N. Marriner (cnd), Academy of St. Martin in the Fields [trans for ob d'amore] *(rec St. John's, Smith Square, London, Aug 1974 & Feb 1975)* Boston Skyline ▲ BSD 127 [ADD]
Bach, J.S.:Con 1 for 2 Hpds, w. Carmel Kaine (vn), Tess Miller (ob), Nicholas Kraemer (bc), N. Marriner (cnd), Academy of St. Martin in the Fields [trans for vn & ob] *(rec St. John's, Smith Square, London, Aug 1974 & Feb 1975)* Boston Skyline ▲ BSD 127 [ADD]
Bach, J.S.:Con 2 for 3 Hpds, w. Carmel Kaine (vn), Ronald Thomas (vn), Richard Studt (vn), Nicholas Kraemer (bc), N. Marriner (cnd), Academy of St. Martin in the Fields [trans for 3 vn] *(rec St. John's, Smith Square, London, Aug 1974 & Feb 1975)* Boston Skyline ▲ BSD 127 [ADD]

Hogwood, Christopher (hpd)
Bach, J.S.:Con for 4 Hpds, w. C. Tilney (hpd), C. Rousset (hpd), D. Moroney (hpd), C. Hogwood (cnd), Academy of Ancient Music L'Oiseau-Lyre ▲ 433053-2 [DDD]
Vivaldi, A.:Sons Vc, Op. 14, w. C. Coin (vn) L'Oiseau-Lyre ▲ 421060-2 [DDD]

Hogwood, Christopher (kbd)
Bach, C.P.E.:Kleine Duetten (4), w. Christophe Rousset (kbd) London ▲ 440649-2
Bach, Joh. Christian:Duet Kbd, Op. 15, w. Christophe Rousset (kbd) London ▲ 440649-2

Hogwood, Christopher (kbd) (cont.)
Bach, J.S.:The Art of the Fugue (sels), w. Christophe Rousset (kbd)—Contrpuntus 13 London ▲ 440649-2
Bach, J.S.:Con 2 for 2 Hpds, w. Christophe Rousset (kbd) London ▲ 440649-2
Bach, W.F.:Con for 2 Hpds, Op. 46, w. Christophe Rousset (kbd) London ▲ 440649-2
Pleasures of the Royal Court, w. D. Munrow (cnd), London Early Music Consort Elektra/Nonesuch ▲ 71326-2 [ADD]

Hogwood, Christopher (org)
Haydn, J.:Con Org, Obs & Strs, H.XVIII/1, w. C. Hogwood (cnd), Academy of Ancient Music L'Oiseau-Lyre ▲ 417610-2 [DDD]
Purcell, H.:Sons (12) Vns, Z.790-801, w. Pavlo Beznosiuk (vn), Rachel Podger (vn), Christophe Coin (b vl) *(rec Emmanuel College, Cambridge, Feb-Aug 1994)* L'Oiseau-Lyre ▲ 444449-2 [DDD]

Hogwood, Christopher (org/spinet)
Couperin, F.:Leçons de ténèbres (for Good Friday), w. E. Kirkby (sop), J. Nelson (mez), J. Ryan (vl) L'Oiseau-Lyre ▲ 430283-2 [ADD]
Couperin, F.:Motets, w. E. Kirkby (sop), J. Nelson (mez), J. Ryan (vl) L'Oiseau-Lyre ▲ 430283-2 [ADD]
Purcell, H.:Sons (10) Vns, Z.802-811, w. C. Mackintosh (vn), M. Huggett (vn), C. Coin (b vl) L'Oiseau-Lyre ▲ 433190-2 [ADD]

Höh, Volker (gtr)
Asmus, B.:Lieder (3), w. Christina Ascher (mez) *(rec Altensteig, July 18-20, 1996)* Signum ▲ X 74-00 [DDD]
Brandmüller, T.:Despedida, w. Christina Ascher (mez), Christina Ascher (perc) *(rec Altensteig, July 18-20, 1996)* Signum ▲ X 74-00 [DDD]
Heyn, V.:I(-na), w. Christina Ascher (mez), Christina Ascher (perc) *(rec Altensteig, July 18-20, 1996)* Signum ▲ X 74-00 [DDD]
Jung, H.:Lieder, w. Christina Ascher (mez) *(rec Altensteig, July 18-20, 1996)* Signum ▲ X 74-00 [DDD]
Liberda, B.:Berenice, w. Christina Ascher (mez) *(rec Altensteig, July 18-20, 1996)* Signum ▲ X 74-00 [DDD]
Rosenfeld, G.:Quasi un madrigale, w. Christina Ascher (mez) *(rec Altensteig, July 18-20, 1996)* Signum ▲ X 74-00 [DDD]
Spassov, B.:Calliope, w. Christina Ascher (mez), Christina Ascher (perc) *(rec Altensteig, July 18-20, 1996)* Signum ▲ X 74-00 [DDD]

Höhenrieder, Margarita (pno)
Compositions for Clarinet & Piano, w. Eduard Brunner (cl) Calig ▲ CAL 50907 [DDD]
Suder, J.:Arietta & Burlesque, w. E. Brunner (cl) Calig ▲ CAL 50888 [DDD]
Suder, J.:Con Pno, w. J. Hirokami (cnd), Bavarian RSO Calig ▲ CAL 50888 [DDD]
Suder, J.:Pno Music—4 Dances in Traditional Style; 4 Pno Pieces 1951; Scherzo; 2 Lyric Pieces Calig ▲ CAL 50888 [DDD]

Hoherman, Martin (vc)
Saint-Saëns, C.:Carnival of the Animals, w. Leo Litwin (pno), Samuel Lipman (pno), Hugh Downs (nar), A. Fiedler (cnd), Boston Pops Orch [verses rec. June 12, 1963] *(rec Symphony Hall, Boston, June 14, 1961)* RCA Living Stereo ▲ 09026-68131-2 [ADD]; ▮ 09026-68131-4
Wild Classics:A Celebration of Animals & Nature, w. James Galway (fl), Ofra Harnoy (vc), Emily Mitchell (hp), Michael Dussek (pno), Samuel Lipman (pno), Leo Litwin (pno), Gerhard Oppitz (pno), Isao Tomita (synths), Boston Pops Orch [cnd:Arthur Fiedler], Chicago SO [cnd:Fritz Reiner] RCA Red Seal ▲ 09026-68483-2 ▮ 09026-68483-4

Hohman, Frederick (org)
Bach, J.S.:Chorale Preludes Org—(5) BWV 653, 666, 679, 712, 736 Pro Organo ▲ CD 7103
Bach, J.S.:Preludes & Fugues, BWV 531-552—BWV 536, 539, 541 Pro Organo ▲ CD 7103
Bach, J.S.:Trio Sons Org, BWV 525-530—BWV 530 Pro Organo ▲ CD 7103
The English Connection, w. Hohman, Frederick (org) Pro Organo ▲ POCD 7029 [DDD]
Historic Organs of New Orleans, w. George Bozeman (org), James S. Darling (org), Jesse E. Eschbach (org), Gerald D. Frank (org), John Gearhart (org), James Hammann (org), Lenora McCroskey (org), Mary Gifford Matthys (org), Lorenz Maycher (org), Donald Messer (org) *(rec June 1989)* Organ Historical Society 2-▲ OHS 89
Hollins, A.:Org Music [Mighty Kotzschmar Memorial Organ, Portland City Hall, Portland, Maine]—allegretto grazioso; Morceau de Concert en Forme De Valse *(rec 1992)* Pro Organo ▲ CD 7018 [DDD]
Lemare, E.H.:Andantino Pro Organo ▲ CD 7007
Lemare, E.H.:Org Music—Concertstücke No. 1 (polonaise), Op. 80; Rondo capriccio (A Study in Accents), Op. 64; Toccata & Fugue in d, Op. 98; Lullaby, Op. 81; Sonata No. 1 in F, Op. 95; Bell Scherzo, Op. 89; Concertstücke No. 2 (tarantella), Op. 90; Andantino in D♭ (1892); Fantasia & Fugue in e, Op. 99 Pro Organo ▲ CD 7007
Lemare, E.H.:Org Music [Mighty Kotzschmar Memorial Organ, Portland City Hall, Portland, Maine]—Con. Fantasia & vars. on "Hanover", Op. 4; Fantaisie Fugue, Op. 48; Marche Heroïque, Op. 74; "O Star of Eve" from R. Wagner's opera "Tannhäuser" arr. by E.H. Lemare; Rhapsody, Op. 43; Scherzo Fugue, Op. 102 *(rec 1992)* Pro Organo ▲ CD 7018 [DDD]
Tchaikovsky, P.:Marche slave [the Reuter Organ in the Grand Chancel, Augustana Lutheran Church, Denver, Colorado] *(rec 1991)* Pro Organo ▲ CD 7012 [DDD]
Tchaikovsky, P.:Romeo & Juliet [the Reuter Organ in the Grand Chancel, Augustana Lutheran Church, Denver, Colorado] *(rec 1991)* Pro Organo ▲ CD 7012 [DDD]
Tchaikovsky, P.:Sym 5 [the Reuter Organ in the Grand Chancel, Augustana Lutheran Church, Denver, Colorado]—Andante cantabile, con alcuna licenza *(rec 1991)* Pro Organo ▲ CD 7012 [DDD]
Vierne, L.:Sym 5 Org [Schantz Organ, Cathedral of the Sacred Heart, Newark, New Jersey] *(rec 1992)* Pro Organo ▲ CD 7021 [DDD]
Widor, C.M.:Sym 5 Org [Schantz Organ, Cathedral of the Sacred Heart, Newark, New Jersey] *(rec 1992)* Pro Organo ▲ CD 7021 [DDD]
Wolstenholme, W.:Org Music [Mighty Kotzschmar Memorial Organ, Portland City Hall, Portland, Maine]—Le Carillon; The Seraph's Strain; The Question & The Answer *(rec 1992)* Pro Organo ▲ CD 7018 [DDD]

Hohman, Frederick (pno)
Tchaikovsky, P.:Romance, Op. 5 [the Reuter Organ in the Grand Chancel, Augustana Lutheran Church, Denver, Colorado] *(rec 1991)* Pro Organo ▲ CD 7012 [DDD]

Hohorst, Claudia (vn)—see ORCHESTRAS & ENSEMBLES Mannheim String Quartet

Hoiby, Lee (pno)
Hoiby, L.:Narrative Master Musicians Collective ▲ MMC 2038 [DDD]
Hoiby, L.:Schubert Vars Master Musicians Collective ▲ MMC 2038 [DDD]
Hoiby, L.:Son Vn, w. Daniel Heifetz (vn) Master Musicians Collective ▲ MMC 2038 [DDD]
Hoiby, L.:Songs, w. Peter Stewart (bar)—I Was There [Beginning My Studies/I Was There/A Clear Midnight/O Captain! My Captain!/Joy, Shipmate, Joy!; poems by Whitman]; 2 Songs of Innocence [The Lamb/The Shepherd; poems by Blake]; An Immorality [by Pound]; O Florida [Floral Decorations for Bananas/Gubbinal/Continual Conversation With A Silent Man/Before My Door/O Florida, Venereal Soil; poems by Stevens]; Why Don't You? [by Beers]; Night [Anon]; What if... [by Coleridge]; Investiture at Cecconi's [by James Merrill]; Where the Music Comes From [by Lee Hoiby] *(rec Rutgers Church, NYC, Sept. 13-14, 1993)* CRI ▲ CD 685 [DDD]
Partch, H.:Barstow, w. William Wendlant (voc), Harry Partch (adapted gtr/voc), Christine Charnstrom (chromelodeon) *(rec 1945)* Innova 4-▲ 401
Partch, H.:By the Rivers of Babylon, w. William Wendlandt (bar), Christine Charnstrom (chromelodeon), Harry Partch (adapted va) *(rec 1945)* Innova 4-▲ 401
Partch, H.:Dark Brother, w. William Wendlandt (bar), Christine Charnstrom (chromelodeon), Harry Partch (adapted va), Fralia Hancock (Indian dr) *(rec 1945)* Innova 4-▲ 401
Partch, H.:San Francisco, w. Harry Partch (adapted va/ voc), Christine Charnstrom (chromelodeon) *(rec 1945)* Innova 4-▲ 401
Partch, H.:US Highball, w. William Wendlandt (bar), Harry Partch (adapted gtr/voc), Christine Charnstrom (chromelodeon), Fralia Hancock (db canon) *(rec 1946)* Innova 4-▲ 401
Partch, H.:Yankee Doodle Fant, w. Lola Harding (sop), Hilmar Luckhardt (tin whistle), Don Thompson (tin whistle/ob), Harry Partch (chromelodeon) *(rec 1945)* Innova 4-▲ 401

Hoitenga, Camilla (fl)
Electro Accoustic Music III, w. William Buonocore (gtr), Maria Tegzes (sop), Jacques Linder (pno), Robert McCormick (perc) Neuma ▲ 450-87 [DDD]

Höjer, Olof (pno)
Alfvén, H.:Hanserlinagoransson, w. E. Saeden (bar) Swedish Society ▲ SCD 1036
Alfvén, H.:A Tale from the Archipelago Swedish Society ▲ SCD 1036
Hägg, J.A.:Pno Music Musica Sveciae ▲ MSV 502 [DDD]

Højlund, Rene (cl)
Koppel, H.D.:Variazioni Libère, w. John Kruse (cl), Kenneth Larsen (b cl), Søren Monrad (perc) *(rec Det Fynske Musikkonservatorium, 1993)* Paula ▲ PACD 78 [DAD]

Hokanson, Leonard (pno)
Classics Go to the Movies, Vol. 3, w. Hungarian State Orch, Lajos Meyer, Budapest Strings, Carmerata Labacensis, Budapest SO, Prague Festival Orch LaserLight ▲ 15 643
Liebeslieder, w. Prey, Hermann (bar) Denon ▲ CO 1254 [DDD]
Mozart, W.A.:Con 9 Pno, w. K. Redel (cnd), Camerata Labacensis Vivace 3-▲ E 313 [DDD]
Mozart, W.A.:Con 9 Pno, w. K. Redel (cnd), Camerata Labacensis PMG ("Vienna Master" series) ▲ CD 160212 [DDD]
Mozart, W.A.:Con 17 Pno, w. K. Redel (cnd), Camerata Labacensis PMG ("Vienna Master" series) ▲ CD 160212 [DDD]
Mozart, W.A.:Con 17 Pno, w. K. Redel (cnd), Camerata Labacensis Vivace 3-▲ E 313 [DDD]
Piston, W.:Improv Pno Northeastern ▲ NR 232-CD
Piston, W.:Passacaglia Pno Northeastern ▲ NR 232-CD
Piston, W.:Qnt Pno, w. Portland String Quartet Northeastern ▲ NR 232-CD
Piston, W.:Son Pno Northeastern ▲ NR 232-CD
Schubert, Franz:Pno Music (misc)—Sonata in E, D.157; Adagio in G, D.178; Sonata in C, D.279; Fantasy in c, D.2E; Andante in C, D.29; Menuet & Trio, D.600 & D.610; 10 Variations in F, D.156 Northeastern ▲ NR 233-CD
Schubert, Franz:Son Pno, D.157 Northeastern ▲ NR 233-CD
Schubert, Franz:Son Pno, D.279 Northeastern ▲ NR 233-CD
Schumann, R.:Dichterliebe, w. H. Prey (bar) [G] Denon ▲ 7720 [DDD]
Schumann, R.:Liederkreis, Op. 39, w. H. Prey (bar) [G] Denon ▲ CO 1518 [DDD]

Holbek, Carsten (acc)
Werner, S.E.:Tango Studies, w. Majken Bell (acc), Heidi Hansen (acc), Hans Jorgen Holbek (acc), Lelo Nika (acc), Morten Rossen (acc), Anders Vesterdahl (acc) *(rec Danish Accordian Academy, Oct. 1994)* Marco Polo ("dacapo" series) ▲ 8.224006 [DDD]

Holbek, Hans Jorgen (acc)
Werner, S.E.:Tango Studies, w. Majken Bell (acc), Heidi Hansen (acc), Carsten Holbek (acc), Lelo Nika (acc), Morten Rossen (acc), Anders Vesterdahl (acc) *(rec Danish Accordian Academy, Oct. 1994)* Marco Polo ("dacapo" series) ▲ 8.224006 [DDD]

Hölbling, Anna (vn)
Corelli, A.:Sons 2 Vns, Opp. 1-4 (sels), w. Q. Hölbling (vn), J. Slávik (vc), D. Ruso (hpd)—Op. 1, No. 6; Op. 2, No. 4; Op. 4, No. 9 *(rec Oct. 21-23, 1990)* Naxos ▲ 8.550619 [DDD]
Geminiani, F.:Sons (12) Vn, Vne & Hpd, w. Q. Hölbling (vn), J. Slávik (vc), D. Ruso (hpd) *(rec Oct. 21-23, 1990)* Naxos ▲ 8.550619 [DDD]
Porpora, N.A.:Sinf da camera, w. Q. Hölbling (vn), J. Slávik (vc), D. Ruso (pno)—No. 6 only *(rec Oct. 21-23, 1990)* Naxos ▲ 8.550619 [DDD]
Pugnani, G.:Trio Sons, Op. 1, w. Q. Hölbling (vn), J. Slávik (vc), D. Ruso (pno)—No. 3 *(rec Oct. 21-23, 1990)* Naxos ▲ 8.550619 [DDD]
2 Violins & 1 Guitar II, w. Quido Hölbling (vn), Jozef Zsapka (gtr), Ján Slávik (vc) *(rec 1992)* Naxos ▲ 8.550645 [DDD]
Vivaldi, A.:Son Vn Ob, RV.779, w. Q. Hölbling (vn), V. Rusó (org) *(rec Oct. 21-23, 1990)* Naxos ▲ 8.550619 [DDD]

Hölbling, Quido (vn)
Corelli, A.:Sons 2 Vns, Opp. 1-4 (sels), w. A. Hölbling (vn), J. Slávik (vc), D. Ruso (hpd)—Op. 1, No. 6; Op. 2, No. 4; Op. 4, No. 9 *(rec Oct. 21-23, 1990)* Naxos ▲ 8.550619 [DDD]
Geminiani, F.:Sons (12) Vn, Vne & Hpd, w. A. Hölbling (vn), J. Slávik (vc), D. Ruso (hpd) *(rec Oct. 21-23, 1990)* Naxos ▲ 8.550619 [DDD]
Porpora, N.A.:Sinf da camera, w. A. Hölbling (vn), J. Slávik (vc), D. Ruso (pno)—No. 6 only *(rec Oct. 21-23, 1990)* Naxos ▲ 8.550619 [DDD]
Pugnani, G.:Trio Sons, Op. 1, w. A. Hölbling (vn), J. Slávik (vc), D. Ruso (pno)—No. 3 *(rec Oct. 21-23, 1990)* Naxos ▲ 8.550619 [DDD]
2 Violins & 1 Guitar II, w. Anna Hölbling (vn), Jozef Zsapka (gtr), Ján Slávik (vc) *(rec 1992)* Naxos ▲ 8.550645 [DDD]
Vivaldi, A.:Son Vn Ob, RV.779, w. A. Hölbling (vn), V. Rusó (org) *(rec Oct. 21-23, 1990)* Naxos ▲ 8.550619 [DDD]

Holdar, Anders (perc)—see also ORCHESTRAS & ENSEMBLES Kroumata Percussion Ensemble
Schnittke, A.:Hymns Vc, w. T. Thedéen (vc), E. Radoukanov (db), C. Davidsson (bn), I. Fredlund (hp), M. Kamata (hpd), A. Loguin (tubular bells) BIS ▲ CD 507 [DDD]

Holdar, Anders (tubular bells/timp)
Schnittke, A.:Hymns Vc, w. Torleif Thedéen (vc), Entcho Rdoukanov (db), Christian Davidsson (bn), Ingegerd Fredlund (hp), M. Kamata (hpd), Anders Loguin (tubular bells) BIS ("BIS Twins" series) 2-▲ CD 437/507

Holdeman, Charles (bn)—see also ORCHESTRAS & ENSEMBLES Relâche Ensemble
Davidson, T.:Blue Dawn (The Promised Fruit), w. Carol Brown (fl), Lloyd Shorter (E hn), Charles Abramovic (pno) CRI ▲ CD 681 [DDD]
Davidson, T.:Lullaby, w. Marshall Taylor (sax), Carol Brown (fl), Lloyd Shorter (E hn), Charles Abramovic (pno) CRI ▲ CD 681 [DDD]

Holden, Dorothy (fl)
Partch, H.:Settings (2) from "Finnegan's Wake", w. Lola Harding (sop), Hilmar Luckhardt (fl), Harry Partch (kithara) *(rec 1945)* Innova 4-▲ 401

Holder, Albrecht (bn)
Kalliwoda, J.W.:Vars et Rondo Bn, w. N. Pasquet (cnd), Stuttgart PO *(rec Stuttgart Phil Hall, June 1995)* Naxos ▲ 8.553456 [DDD]
Kreutzer, C.:Fant Bn, w. N. Pasquet (cnd), Stuttgart PO *(rec Stuttgart Phil Hall, June 1995)* Naxos ▲ 8.553456 [DDD]
Lindpaintner, P.J. von:Con Bn, w. N. Pasquet (cnd), Stuttgart PO *(rec Stuttgart Phil Hall, June 1995)* Naxos ▲ 8.553456 [DDD]
Molter, J.M.:Con Bn, w. N. Pasquet (cnd), Stuttgart PO *(rec Stuttgart Phil Hall, June 1995)* Naxos ▲ 8.553456 [DDD]

Holding, Ella Ann (pno)
Johnson, H.:Emily Dickinson Songs, w. D. Stephenson (mez)—I. Exultation (1957), II. Mortal my friend (1956), III. If pain for peace prepares (1959) Albany ▲ TROY 061 [DDD]
Johnson, H.:Trio Fl, Ob & Pno, w. R. Troxler (fl), M. W. McCracken (ob) Albany ▲ TROY 061 [DDD]

Holeček, Alfréd (pno)
Dvořák, A.:Zigeunermelodien, Op. 55, w. Jindrich Jindrák (bar) Supraphon ▲ SUP 0206 [AAD]
Haas, P.:Songs (4) to the Texts of Chinese Poetry, w. K. Berman (bass) [Cz] *(rec 2-3/85)* Channel Classics ▲ CCS 3191 [ADD]

Holeček, Josef (gtr)
Britten, H.:Nocturnal Gtr BIS ▲ CD 31 [AAD]
Britten, H.:Songs from the Chinese, w. M. Schéle (sop) [E] BIS ▲ CD 31 [AAD]
Britten, H.:Songs from the Chinese, w. Märta Schéle (sop) *(rec Castle Wik, Sweden, Sept 12 & 13, 1975)* BIS ▲ CD 34 [AAD]
Castelnuovo-Tedesco, M.:Son Gtr, "Homage to Boccherini" *(rec Studio BIS, Djursholm, Sweden, Jan. 30-31, 1982)* BIS ▲ CD 203 [AAD]
Castelnuovo-Tedesco, M.:Songs (6) from *The Divan of Moses-ibn-Ezra*, w. Märta Schéle (sop) *(rec Castle Wik, Sweden, Oct 4 & 5, 1975)* BIS ▲ CD 34 [AAD]
Holeček, J.:Aquarelles *(rec Studio BIS, Djursholm, Sweden, Jan. 30-31, 1982)* BIS ▲ CD 203 [AAD]
Holeček, J.:Serenade *(rec Studio BIS, Djursholm, Sweden, Jan. 30-31, 1982)* BIS ▲ CD 203 [AAD]

INSTRUMENT.

Holeček, Josef (gtr) (cont.)
Holeček, J.:Smoke Rings *(rec Studio BIS, Djursholm, Sweden, Jan. 30–31, 1982)* BIS ▲ CD 203 [AAD]
Holeček, J.:Swedish Romance *(rec Studio BIS, Djursholm, Sweden, Jan. 30–31, 1982)* BIS ▲ CD 203 [AAD]
Koch, E. von:Monologue 10 Gtr *(rec Studio BIS, Djursholm, Sweden, Jan. 30–31, 1982)* BIS ▲ CD 203 [AAD]
Sörenson, T.:Sonatina Gtr *(rec Studio BIS, Djursholm, Sweden, Jan. 30–31, 1982)* BIS ▲ CD 203 [AAD]

Holek, V. (vn)—see ORCHESTRAS & ENSEMBLES Prazak String Quartet

Holenko, J. (oud/chitarra/psaltery/saz–lt/perc)
Sonus Chanterai:Music of Medieval France, w. James Carrier (shm/rcrs/oud/hp/gemshn), Hazel Ketchum (sgr/saz–lt/perc), Will Mason (saz–lt/chitarra/vih/ham dlc/perc) *(rec St. John's Episcopal Church, Columbia, MD, Sept. 1993)* Dorian Discovery ▲ DIS 80123 [DDD]

Höll, Hartmut (pno)
Boulanger, L.:Songs (4), w. M. Shirai (mez)—Attente (1910); Reflets (1911); La Retour (1912); Dans l'immense Tristesse (1916) [F] Bayer ▲ 100041 [DDD]
Brahms, J.:Songs, w. D. Fischer–Dieskau (bar)—Opp. 19/5; 32/1,2,4,5 & 9; 48/1; 49/5; 59/2; 69/5; 70/3 & 4; 71/1 & 3; 72/5; 86/1 & 2; 95/2; 96/3 & 4; 105/4; 107/4 [G] Bayer ▲ 100006 [DDD]
Brahms, J.:Songs, w. M. Shirai (mez)—21 songs Capriccio ▲ 10 204 [DDD]
Debussy, C.:Songs, w. Dietrich Fischer–Dieskau (bar) (19) Claves ▲ 50–8809
Debussy, C.:Songs, w. D. Fischer–Dieskau (bar)—Beau soir; Mandoline; Le jet d'eau; Chevaux de bois; Green; Les cloches; Dans le jardin; La mer est plus belle; Le son du cor; L'échelonnement des haies; En sourdine; Clair de lune; Fantoches; Fleur des blés; Recueillement; De soir; Les ingénus; Le faune; Colloque sentimental [F] *(rec 1988)* Claves ▲ CD 8809 [DDD]
Haydn, J.:Arianna a Naxos, w. M. Shirai (sop) Camerata ▲ 32CM 123
Haydn, J.:Canzonettas, w. M. Shirai (sop) Camerata ▲ 32CM 123
Lieder der Romantik, w. Fischer–Dieskau, Dietrich (bar), Dieter Klöcker (cl), Klaus Wallendorf (hn) Orfeo ▲ 153861
Mahler, G.:Des Knaben Wunderhorn, w. Mitsuko Shirai (mez)—9 sels Capriccio ▲ CD 10712 [DDD]
Mahler, G.:Lieder und Gesänge aus der Jugendzeit, w. Mitsuko Shirai (mez)—3 sels Capriccio ▲ CD 10712 [DDD]
Mendelssohn, F.:Songs, w. D. Fischer–Dieskau (bar)—Der Verlassene; Ich weiss mir 'n Mädchen; Mary's dream; We've a bonnie wee flower; Minnelied im Mai; Pilgerspruch; Maienlied; Im Grünen; Abendlied; Wartend; Im Frühling; Im Herbst; Frühlingsglaue; Das Schifflein; Lieblingsplätzchen; Altdeutsches Frühlingslied; Minnelied; Meerfahrt; Weiter, rastlos; Der Blumenstrauss; Frühlingslied; Herbstlied; Erntelied *(rec 1989 & 1991)* Claves ▲ CD 9009 [DDD]
Mozart, W.A.:Songs, w. M. Shirai (mez)—21 songs [F,G,I] Capriccio ▲ 10098 [DDD]
Mozart, W.A.:Songs, w. M. Shirai (mez)—Abendempfindung, K.523; Als Luise die Briefe ihres ungetreuen Liebhabers verbrannte, K.520; An Chloe, K.524; Dans un bois solitaire, K.308; Einsam bin ich, meine Liebe, K.475a (fragment); Der Frühling, K.597; Ich würd' auf meinem Pfad, K.390; Die kleine Spinnerin, K.531; Komm, liebe Zither, komm, K.351; Das Lied der Trennung, K.519; Lied zur Gesellenreise, K.468; Oiseaux, si tous les ans, K.307; Ridente la calma, K.152; Sehnsucht nach dem Frühling, K.596; Sei du mein Trost, K.391; Das Traumbild, K.530; Das Veilchen, K.476; Die Verschweigung, K.518; Der Zauberer, K.472; Die Zufriedenheit, K.349; Die Zufriedenheit, K.473 [F,G,I] LaserLight ▲ 15 876 [DDD]
Pfitzner, H.:Songs, w. D. Fischer–Dieskau (bar) [G] Orfeo ▲ 036821 [DDD]
Ravel, M.:Chants populaires, w. D. Fischer–Dieskau (bar) Orfeo ▲ 061831 [DDD]
Ravel, M.:Épigrammes de Clément Marot, w. D. Fischer–Dieskau (bar) Orfeo ▲ 061831 [DDD]
Ravel, M.:Histoires naturelles, w. D. Fischer–Dieskau (bar) Orfeo ▲ 061831 [DDD]
Ravel, M.:Mélodies populaires grecques, w. D. Fischer–Dieskau (bar) Orfeo ▲ 061831 [DDD]
Ravel, M.:Songs, w. D. Fischer–Dieskau (bar) [F] Orfeo ▲ 061831 [DDD]
Schoeck, O.:Das holde Bescheiden, w. M. Shirai (mez), D. Fischer–Dieskau (bar) *(rec Jan.–Feb. 1991; March 199)* Claves 2–▲ CD 9308/9 [DDD]
Schoeck, O.:Das stille Leuchten, w. Dietrich Fischer–Dieskau (bar) Claves ▲ 50–8910
Schoeck, O.:Unter Sternen, w. Dietrich Fischer–Dieskau (bar) Claves ▲ 50–8606
Schumann, R.:Liederkreis, Op. 39, w. M. Shirai (mez) [G] Capriccio ▲ 10099 [DDD]
Schumann, R.:Songs, w. M. Shirai (mez)—4 Lieder der Mignon, Op. 98a; 5 Lieder der Maria Stuart, Op. 135; 5 Lieder nach Justinus Kerner, Op. 35 [G] Capriccio ▲ 10099 [DDD]
Spohr, L.:German Songs , Op. 103, w. J. Varady (sop), H. Schöneberger (cl) [G] Orfeo ▲ 103841 [DDD] ■ M 103841A
Spohr, L.:Songs (misc), w. D. Fischer–Dieskau (bar) [G] Orfeo ▲ 103841 [DDD] ■ M 103841A
Spohr, L.:Songs Bar, Op. 154, w. D. Fischer–Dieskau (bar), D. Sitkovetzky (vn) [G] Orfeo ▲ 103841 [DDD] ■ M 103841A
Weber, C.M. von:Songs, w. D. Fischer–Dieskau (bar)—Meine Lieder, meine Sänge; Klage; Der kleine Fritz; Was zieht zu deinem Zauberkreise; Ich sah ein Röschen am Wege steh'n; Er an Sie; Meine Farben; Liebe–Glühen; Über die Berge mit Ungestüm; Es stürmt auf der Flur; Minnelied; Reigen; Sind es Schmerzen; Mein Verlangen; Wenn ich ein Vöglein wär'; Mein Schatzerl ist hübsch; Liebesgruss aus der Ferne; Herzchen, mein Schätzchen; Das Veilchen im Thale; Ich denke dein; Serenade:Horch'! Leise horch', Geliebte!; Romanze:Sie war so hold *(rec Mar. 27–28 & Sept. 11, 19)* Claves ▲ CD 9118 [DDD]
Weber, C.M. von:Songs, w. Dietrich Fischer–Dieskau (bar)—22 sels Claves ▲ 50–9118
Wolf, H.:Songs (misc), w. Dietrich Fischer–Dieskau (bar)—21 songs [texts Heinrich Heine & Joseph von Eichendorff] Claves ▲ 50–8706

Holland, Dulcie (pno)
Holland, Dulcie:Pno Music, w. T. Birnie (pno)—A Scattering of Leaves; Nocturne; Asterisk; A Night for Ghosts; Son.; Mini–Toccata; Asterisk; other solo pieces Southern Cross ▲ SCCD 1028 [DDD]

Holland, James (vc)
Thofanidis, C.:Qt 1 Strs, w. Adrian Justus (vn), Maria Lin (vn), Timothy Lees (va) Albany ▲ TROY 158 [DDD]

Holland, Thomas (org)
at Cathedral Church of St. Paul, Worcester, Mass. *(rec AGO/OHSConvention 1983)* Organ Historical Society ■ OHSC 5

Hollander, Berten d' (fl)
Bréval, J.B.:Sym concertante, w. Luc Loubry (bn), F. Heyerick (cnd), Collegium Instrumentale Brugense Arcobaleno ▲ AAOC 9324
Vivaldi, A.:Con Fl Bn, w. Luc Loubry (bn), F. Heyerick (cnd), Collegium Instrumentale Brugense Arcobaleno ▲ AAOC 9324

Hollander, Geert d' (car)
Carillon of the Antwerp Cathedral René Gailly ▲ CD 88902 [DDD]
Carillon of the Belfry of Ghent, w. Jos D'hollander (car) René Gailly ▲ CD 88901 [DDD]
The Carillon of the St. Rombouts Cathedral at Malines, w. Jos D'hollander (car), Eddy Marien (car), Carlo van Luft (car) René Gailly ▲ CD 88903 [DDD]

Hollander, Jos d' (car)
Carillon of the Belfry of Ghent, w. D'hollander, Geert (car) René Gailly ▲ CD 88901 [DDD]
The Carillon of the St. Rombouts Cathedral at Malines, w. D'hollander, Geert (car), Eddy Marien (car), Carlo van Luft (car) René Gailly ▲ CD 88903 [DDD]

Hollander, Lorin (pno)
Copland, A.:Con Pno, w. G. Schwarz (cnd), Seattle SO *(rec Seattle Opera House, May 26, 1993)* Delos ▲ DE 3154 [DDD]

Höller, Günther (fl)
Bach, J.S.:Con Fl, Vn & Hpd, w. G. Egger (vn), J. Faerber (cnd), Württemberg CO *(rec 1978)* Vox Box 3–▲ CD3X 3018 [ADD]

Höller, Günther (rcr)
Telemann, G.P.:Con Rcr, w. K. Hünteler (trns fl), G. Fischer (cnd), Cappella Coloniensis LaserLight ▲ 14036 [DDD]

Holler, Hermann (perc)—see ORCHESTRAS & ENSEMBLES Karl Peinkofer Percussion Ensemble

Hollerbuhl, Jürgen (ob)
Boccherini, L.:Syms, w. S. Prunnbauer (gtr), B. Vestre (ob), Jörn Maatz (ob), H. Maile (vn), H. Ganz (vn), R. Forest (vc), J. Stárek (cnd), Berlin RIAS Sinfonietta—in C, G.495 (Op. 21/3) *(rec Dec. 1979)* Koch Treasure ▲ 31612–2 [ADD]

Holletschek, Franz (hpd)
Haydn, J.:Die Schöpfung, w. Anny Felbermayer (sop—Eve), Teresa Stich–Randall (sop—Gabriel), Anton Dermota (ten—Uriel), Paul Schöffler (b–bar—Adam), Frederick Guthrie (bass—Raphael), M. Wöldike (cnd), Vienna State Opera Orch, Vienna State Opera Chorus *(rec Musikverein, Vienna, Austria, May 1955)* Vanguard Classics 2–▲ SVC 34/35 [AAD]

Holleville, Christelle (pno)
Sauguet, H.:Les Jeux de l'amour et du hasard, w. Fabrice Lanoë (pno) Sonpact ▲ SPT 96017 [DDD]

Holley, Tim (vc)
Banfield, W.:Cone Tone, w. Velda Kelly (vn), Linda Trotter (vn), Charlotte Givens (va) Innova ▲ 510 [DDD]

Hollick, Douglas (org)
Bach, J.S.:Fant & Fugue Org, BWV 542 Supraphon ▲ SUP 3015
Bach, J.S.:Fugue on "Meine Seele erhebet den Herren" Supraphon ▲ SUP 3015
Bach, J.S.:Org Music (misc)—Herr Jesu Christ, dich zu uns wend, BWV 726; Vater unser im Himmelreich, BWV 737; Von Himmel hoch, da komm ich her, BWV 701 Supraphon ▲ SUP 3015
Böhm, G.:Preludes & Fugues Supraphon ▲ SUP 3015
Buxtehude, D.:Magnificat primi toni, BuxWV 204 Supraphon ▲ SUP 3015
Pachelbel, J.:Toccata & Fugue Supraphon ▲ SUP 3015

Holliger, Heinz (E hn)
Honegger, A.:Antigone, w. Aurèle Nicolet (fl), John Constable (pno)—sels. [arr. for flute, English horn & piano] *(rec St. John's, London, Oct. 8–11, 1991)* Philips ▲ 434105–2
Honegger, A.:Con da camera, w. Aurèle Nicolet (fl), N. Marriner (cnd), Academy of St. Martin in the Fields *(rec St. John's, London, Oct. 8–11, 1991)* Philips ▲ 434105–2
Honegger, A.:Petite Suites, w. Aurèle Nicolet (fl), John Constable (pno) *(rec St. John's, London, Oct. 8–11, 1991)* Philips ▲ 434105–2
Mozart, W.A.:Adagio E Hn, w. Orlando String Quartet Philips ▲ 412618–2 [DDD]

Holliger, Heinz (bas hn)
Backofen, J.G.:Concertante Hp, w. H. R. Stalder (hp), A. Schmid (vc) *(rec 1981)* Jecklin–Disco ▲ JD 560–2 [ADD]

Holliger, Heinz (ob d'amore)
Bach, J.S.:Con Ob d'amore, w. I. Brown (cnd), Academy of St. Martin in the Fields Philips ▲ 412851–2 [DDD]

Holliger, Heinz (ob)
Albinoni, T.:Cons Obs, I Musici—6 Concertos Philips ("Insignia" series) ▲ 434157–2 [DDD]
Albinoni, T.:Cons à 5 Obs, Op. 7, w. M. Bourgue (ob), I Musici Philips ▲ 432115–2 [DDD]
Albinoni, T.:Cons à 5 Obs, Op. 9, I Musici—No. 8 Philips ▲ 420189–2 [DDD]
Albinoni, T.:Sinf (6) e con (6) à 5, Op. 2, w. K. Thunemann (bn), I Musici—Nos. 5 & 6 Philips ▲ 432115–2 [DDD]
Bach, C.P.E.:Con Ob, H.466, w. Leppard, Zinman (cnd), Netherlands CO, English CO Philips ("Classics" series) 2–▲ 442592–2
Bach, C.P.E.:Con Ob, H.468, w. Leppard, Zinman (cnd), Netherlands CO, English CO Philips ("Classics" series) 2–▲ 442592–2
Bach, C.P.E.:Son Ob, H.549, w. Rama Jucker (vc), Leppard, Zinman (cnd), Netherlands CO, English CO Philips ("Classics" series) 2–▲ 442592–2
Bach, Joh. Christian:Qt Ob, w. et al. Denon ▲ CO 8006 [DDD]
Bach, J.S.:Con 8 Hpd, w. I. Brown (cnd), Academy of St. Martin in the Fields Philips ▲ 412851–2 [DDD]
Bach, J.S.:Con Ob, BWV 1053, w. I. Brown (cnd), Academy of St. Martin in the Fields Philips ▲ 412851–2 [DDD]
Bach, J.S.:Con in d Ob, w. I. Brown (cnd), Academy of St. Martin in the Fields Philips ▲ 412851–2 [DDD]
Bach, J.S.:Con Vn & Ob, w. A. Grumiaux (vn), E. de Waart (cnd), Philharmonia Orch Philips ("Silver Line" series) ▲ 420700–2 [ADD]
Bach, J.S.:Con Vn & Ob, w. G. Kremer (vn), N. Marriner (cnd), Academy of St. Martin in the Fields Philips 2–▲ 426462–2 [ADD]
Bach, J.S.:Con Vn & Ob, w. G. Kremer (vn), N. Marriner (cnd), Academy of St. Martin in the Fields Philips ▲ 434730–2
Bach, J.S.:A Musical Offering, w. et al.—section 5, "Ricarcare à 6 Denon ▲ CO 8006 [DDD]
Beethoven, L. van:Qnt Pno, Ob, Cl, Hn & Bn, w. A. Brendel (pno), E. Brunner (cl), K. Thunemann (bn), H. Baumann (hn) Philips ▲ 420182–2 [DDD]
Cimarosa, D.:Con in C Ob, I Musici Philips ▲ 420189–2 [DDD]
Globokar, V.:Atemstudie Harmonia Mundi France ▲ HMC 90933
Handel, G.F.:Cons (3) Ob, w. R. Leppard (cnd), English CO Philips ▲ 426082–2 [ADD]
Holliger, H.:Studie über Mehrklänge ECM New Series ▲ 78118–21340–2 [DDD]
Keller, A.:Pastorella Ob Grammont ▲ CTSP 19–2 [ADD]
Lehmann, H.U.:Dis–Cantus I, w. A. van Wijnkoop (cnd), Bern Camerata *(rec Nov. 1, 1972)* Grammont ▲ CTS P 4–2
Lutoslawski, W.:Con Ob, w. Ursula Holliger (hp), M. Gielen (cnd), Cincinnati SO *(rec 1983)* Vox Box 2–▲ CDX 5136 [DDD]
Marcello, A.:Con Ob & Strs, I Musici Philips ▲ 420189–2 [DDD]
Martin, F.:Danses, w. Ursula Holliger (hp), N. Marriner (cnd), Academy of St. Martin in the Fields *(rec St. John's, London, Oct. 8–11, 1991)* Philips ▲ 434105–2
Martin, F.:Petite complainte, w. John Constable (pno) *(rec St. John's, London, Oct. 8–11, 1991)* Philips ▲ 434105–2
Martin, F.:Pièce brève Fl, w. Aurèle Nicolet (fl), Ursula Holliger (hp) *(rec St. John's, London, Oct. 8–11, 1991)* Philips ▲ 434105–2
Martinů, B.:Con Ob, w. N. Marriner (cnd), Academy of St. Martin in the Fields *(rec St. John's, London, Oct. 8–11, 1991)* Philips ▲ 434105–2
Messiaen, O.:Concert à Quatre, w. Catherine Cantin (fl), Yvonne Loriod (pno), Mstislav Rostropovich (vc), M.–W. Chung (cnd), Bastille Opera Orch Deutsche Grammophon ("4D Audio" series) ▲ 445947–2
Milhaud, D.:Son Fl, Cl, Ob & Pno, w. O. Maisenberg (pno), A. Nicolet (fl), E. Brunner (cl) Orfeo ▲ 060831
Milhaud, D.:Sonatina Ob, w. O. Maisenberg (pno) Orfeo ▲ 060831
Mozart, W.A.:Con Ob, K.314, w. N. Marriner (cnd), Academy of St. Martin in the Fields Philips ▲ 411134–2 [DDD]
Mozart, W.A.:Divert Ob, K.251, w. H. Baumann (hn), Orlando String Quartet Philips ▲ 412618–2 [DDD]
Mozart, W.A.:Qt Ob, K.370, w. Orlando String Quartet Philips ▲ 412618–2 [DDD]
Mozart, W.A.:Qnt Pno, K.452, w. A. Brendel (pno), E. Brunner (cl), K. Thunemann (bn), H. Baumann (hn) Philips ▲ 420182–2 [DDD]
Sammartini, G.:Con in D Ob, I Musici Philips ▲ 420189–2 [DDD]
Strauss, R.:Con Ob, w. E. de Waart (cnd), New PO, Netherlands Wind Ensemble Philips 2–▲ 438733–2
Suter, R.:Musikalisches Tagesbuch 1, w. B. Geiser–Payer (alt), H. Haldemann (pic/fl), H. Bochet (bn), J. Joubert (vn), J. Semper (va), W. Eugster (vc), M. Dellanoy (db) *(rec 1962)* Grammont ▲ CSTP 6–2 [AAD]
Telemann, G.P.:Cons Ob Orch, w. I. Brown (cnd), Academy of St. Martin in the Fields—Nos. 2–4, 6 & 8 Philips ("Digital Classics" series) ▲ 412879–2 [DDD]
Telemann, G.P.:Fants Fl—Nos. 1 & 3 Denon ▲ CO 8006 [DDD]
Telemann, G.P.:Suite Ob Denon ▲ CO 8006 [DDD]
Veress, S.:Passacaglia concertante, w. H. Holliger (cnd), Bern Camerata ECM New Series ▲ 78118–21555–2 [DDD]

Holliger, Heinz (ob) (cont.)
Vivaldi, A.:Cons Ob, w. K. Thunemann (cnd), I Musici—RV.446, 447, 452, 454, 463, 545 Philips ("Digital Classics" series) ▲ 411480-2 [ADD]
Vivaldi, A.:Music of, w. Salvatore Accardo (vn), Frederico Agostini (vn), Ida Levin (vn), Aurele Nicolet (fl), Massimo Paris (va d'amore), Angel Romero (gtr), Celedonio Romero (gtr), Celine Romero (gtr), Henryk Szeryng (vn), Pinchas Zukerman (vn), Academy of St. Martin in the Fields, English CO, I Musici, Naples Weekly International Soloists, St. Paul CO, Dresden Staatskapelle—The Four Seasons [Winter]; Con in D for Gtr [Largo]; Con in D for Fl, "Il gardellino" [Cantabile]; Con in C for Diverse Insts [Andante molto]; Con in g for Strs [Andante molto]; Con in D for 2 Vns & 2 Vcs [Largo]; Con in g for Ob, Vn, Ww & Strs [Larghetto]; Con in a for Gtr, "L'estro armonico" [Largo]; Con in F for 3 Vns [Andante]; Con in F for Fl [Largo]; Con in d for Va D'Amore [Largo]; Con in E for Vn & Strs, "Il riposo" [Allegro]; Con in G for Ob, Bn & Strs [Largo]; Con in B♭ for Vn & Strs [Largo]; Con in A for Gtr & Strs [Larghetto]; Con in E for Vn & Strs, "L'amoroso" [Allegro]; Con in G for Fl [Largo]; Con in A for Vn [Larghetto]; Con in c for Vn & Strs, "Il sospetto" [Andante]; Con in a for 2 Obs & Strs [Largo]; Con in g for Orch [Largo non molto]; Con in a for Vn [Largo]; Con in C for Ob [Adagio]; Con in g for Fl, "La notte" [Largo] Philips ▲ 454051-2 ■ 454 051-4
Yun, I.:Son Ob, w. Ursula Holliger (hp), Hirofumi Fukai (va) *(rec March 25, 1976)* Camerata ▲ 30CM 22

Holliger, Ursula (hp)
Bach, C.P.E.:Hp Music, w. Leppard, Zinman (cnd), Netherlands CO, English CO—Son. in g, W.139 Philips ("Classics" series) 2-▲ 442592-2
Caplet, A.:Conte fantastique, Zurich CO Claves ▲ CD 50280 [ADD]
Caplet, A.:Divertissements (2) Hp Claves ▲ CD 50280 [ADD]
Debussy, C.:Arabesques (2), w. Catherine Eisenhoffer (hp) [arr for Hp] Claves ▲ 50-9603
Debussy, C.:Arrs for 2 Pnos, w. Catherine Eisenhoffer (hp)—Schumann's Studies (6) in canon form for 2 Pnos [arr for 2 Hps] Claves ▲ 50-9603
Debussy, C.:Son Fl, w. Peter-Lukas Graf (fl), Serge Collot (trb) [arr for fl, alt & hp] Claves ▲ CD 50280 [ADD]
Donizetti, G.:Larghetto & Allegro, w. Peter-Lukas Graf (fl) [arr for fl & hp] *(rec Kirche Seon, 1977)* Claves ▲ CD 50708 [ADD]
Fauré, G.:Dolly, w. Catherine Eisenhoffer (hp) [arr for 2 Hps] Claves ▲ 50-9603
Fauré, G.:Fant Fl, w. Peter-Lukas Graf (fl) [arr for fl & hp] *(rec Kirche Seon, 1977)* Claves ▲ CD 50708 [ADD]
Fauré, G.:Impromptu Hp *(rec Kirche Seon, 1977)* Claves ▲ CD 50708 [ADD]
Holliger, H.:Präludium, Arioso et Passacaglia Accord ▲ ACD 201922 [DDD]
Lauber, J.:Medieval Dances, w. Peter-Lukas Graf (fl) *(rec Kirche Seon, 1977)* Claves ▲ CD 50708 [ADD]
Lutoslawski, W.:Con Ob, w. Heinz Holliger (ob), M. Gielen (cnd), Cincinnati SO *(rec 1983)* Vox Box 2-▲ CDX 5136 [DDD]
Martin, F.:Danses, w. Heinz Holliger (ob), N. Marriner (cnd), Academy of St. Martin in the Fields *(rec St. John's, London, Oct. 8-11, 1991)* Philips ▲ 434105-2
Martin, F.:Pièce brève Fl, w. Aurèle Nicolet (fl), Heinz Holliger (ob) *(rec St. John's, London, Oct. 8-11, 1991)* Philips ▲ 434105-2
Mendelssohn, F.:Evening Bell, w. Catherine Eisenhoffer (hp) [arr for 2 Hps] Claves ▲ 50-9603
Mieg, P.:Morceau élégant, w. Peter-Lukas Graf (fl) *(rec 1976)* Jecklin ▲ JS 314-2 [DDD]
Mozart, W.A.:Con Fl Hp, w. Peter-Lukas Graf (fl), P.-L. Graf (cnd), Lausanne CO *(rec EMI Studio London, 1970)* Claves ▲ CD 50208 [ADD]
Paganini, N.:Vars di bravura, w. Peter-Lukas Graf (fl) [arr for fl & hp] *(rec Kirche Seon, 1977)* Claves ▲ CD 50708 [ADD]
Ravel, M.:Intro & Allegro, w. Perter-Lukas Graf (fl), Hans Rudolf Stalder (cl), Zurich CO Claves ▲ CD 50280 [ADD]
Rossini, G.:Andante con variazioni Fl, w. Peter-Lukas Graf (fl) *(rec Kirche Seon, 1977)* Claves ▲ CD 50708 [ADD]
Spohr, L.:Con 1 Vn Hp, w. Hansheinz Schneeberger (vn), P.-L. Graf (cnd), English CO *(rec EMI Studio London, 1970)* Claves ▲ CD 50208 [ADD]
Spohr, L.:Fant 2 Hp *(rec 1982)* Jecklin-Disco ▲ JD 573-2 [ADD]
Spohr, L.:Potpourri 2, w. Peter-Lukas Graf (fl) [arr for fl & hp] *(rec Kirche Seon, 1977)* Claves ▲ CD 50708 [ADD]
Spohr, L.:Son 3 Vn, w. T. Füri (vn) *(rec 1982)* Jecklin-Disco ▲ JD 573-2 [ADD]
Spohr, L.:Son 4 Vn, w. T. Füri (vn) *(rec 1982)* Jecklin-Disco ▲ JD 573-2 [ADD]
Spohr, L.:Son Vn Hp, Op. 113, w. Peter-Lukas Graf (fl) [arr for fl & hp] *(rec Kirche Seon, 1977)* Claves ▲ CD 50708 [ADD]
Spohr, L.:Var set No. 1 on Méhul's "Je suis encore dans mon printemps" *(rec 1982)* Jecklin-Disco ▲ JD 573-2 [ADD]
Viotti, G.B.:Son Hp, w. Catherine Eisenhoffer (hp) Claves ▲ 50-9603
Yun, I.:Gong-Hu, w. H. Holliger (cnd), Bern Camerata String Ensemble *(rec Bremen Radio Studio, June 1985)* Camerata ▲ 30CM 109 [AAD]
Yun, I.:In Balance *(rec Bremen Radio Studio, June 1985)* Camerata ▲ 30CM 109 [AAD]
Yun, I.:Son Ob, w. Heinz Holliger (ob), Hirofumi Fukai (va) *(rec March 25, 1976)* Camerata ▲ 30CM 22

Hollingworth, R. (instr)—see ORCHESTRAS & ENSEMBLES I Fagiolini

Hollmann, Gregor (hpd)
Bach, J.S.:Con for 4 Hpds, w. Rudolf Innig (hpd), Bernward Lohr (hpd), Ludger Rémy (hpd), Musica Alta Ripa MD + G ▲ MDG CD 3090681
Clavier Music of the Bach School MD + G ▲ L 3318 [DDD]
Petrassi, G.:Son da camera Hpd, w. A. Molino (cnd), Compania Stradivarius ▲ STR 33347

Holloway, John (vn)—see also ORCHESTRAS & ENSEMBLES L'École d'Orphée, Veracini Trio
Bach, J.S.:A Musical Offering, w. D. Moroney (hpd), J. See (fl), J. ter Linden (vc), M. Cook (hpd) Harmonia Mundi France ▲ HMC 901260 [DDD]
Biber, H. von:Mystery (or Rosary) Sons, w. D. Moroney (chamber org/hpd), Tragicomedia Virgin Classics ("Veritas" series) 2-▲ 59551 [DDD]
Biber, H. von:Passacaglia Vn Virgin Classics ("Veritas" series) 2-▲ 59551 [DDD]
Buxtehude, D.:Sons Vn, Vl & Continuo, w. Ursula Weiss (vn), Jaap ter Linden (vl), Mogens Rasmussen (vl), Lars Ulrik Mortensen (hpd/org)—BuxWV 266, 267, 269 & 271-273 *(rec Radio House, Studio 2, Sept 25-28, 1994)* Marco Polo ("dacapo" series) ▲ 8.224005 [DDD]
Buxtehude, D.:Sons for 2 Vns, Op. 1, w. Jaap ter Linden (vl), Lars Ulrik Mortensen (hpd) *(rec Kastelskirken, Copenhagen, June 29-July 1, 1994)* Marco Polo ▲ 8.224003 [DDD]
Buxtehude, D.:Sons for 2 Vns, Op. 2, w. Jaap ter Linden (vl), Lars Ulrik Mortensen (hpd) *(rec Kastelskirken, Copenhagen)* Marco Polo ("dacapo" series) ▲ 8.224004 [DDD]
Three Parts upon a Ground, w. Stanley Ritchie (vn), Andrew Manze (vn), Mary Springfels (vl), Nigel North (lt), John Toll (hpd/org) Harmonia Mundi USA ▲ HMU 907091
Vivaldi, A.:Cons Diverse Instrs, w. M. Verbruggen (rcr), P. Goodwin (ob), D. Godburn (bn), J. Toll (hpd), S. Comberti (vc)—7 Concerti—in D, RV.84; in a, RV.86; in D, RV.94; in D, "Las Pastorella," RV.95; in F, RV.99; in g, RV.103; in g, RV.105 Harmonia Mundi USA ▲ HMU 907046
Vivaldi, A.:Cons Vn, Op. 8/1-4, "The Four Seasons", w. A. Parrott (cnd), Taverner Players Denon ▲ 7283 [DDD]
Vivaldi, A.:Cons Vn, Op. 8/1-4, "The Four Seasons", w. J.-C. Malgoire (cnd), La Grande Écurie et la Chambre du Roy Sony Classical ("Essential Classics" series) ▲ SBK 47662 ■ SBT 47662
Vivaldi, A.:Sons Ob, w. P. Goodwin (ob), G. Hennessey (ob), C. Lawson (cl), N. North (archlt/gtr), S. Sheppard (vc), F. Eustace (bn), J. Toll (hpd/org)—RV.53, 58, 81 & 779 Harmonia Mundi USA ▲ HMU 907104

Holly, Timothy (vc)
Banfield, W.:Spiritual Songs, w. Lee Melvin (ten) Innova ▲ 510 [DDD]

Holm, Holly (bn)
Porter, T.:Pieces Ww Qnt, w. Linda Schmidt (fl), Deirdre Fay (ob), Loran Eckroth (cl), Leslie Peterson (hn) Meyer ▲ MC 0108

Holm, Torleif (vc)—see ORCHESTRAS & ENSEMBLES Musica Domestica

Holmes, Ralph (vn)
Beethoven, L. van:Son 5 Vn, "Spring", w. R. Burnett (pno) Amon Ra ▲ CD-SAR 9

Holmes, Ralph (vn) (cont.)
Beethoven, L. van:Son 7 Vn, w. R. Burnett (pno) Amon Ra ▲ CD-SAR 9
Beethoven, L. van:Son 8 Vn, w. R. Burnett (pno) [1820 Graf fortepiano] Amon Ra ▲ CD-SAR 16 [DDD]
Beethoven, L. van:Son 9 Vn, "Kreutzer", w. R. Burnett (pno) [1820 Graf fortepiano] Amon Ra ▲ CD-SAR 16 [DDD]
Delius, F.:Légende, w. E. Fenby (cnd), Royal PO Unicorn-Kanchana ▲ UK 2076
Delius, F.:Son 1 Vn & Pno, w. Eric Fenby (pno) Unicorn-Kanchana ("Souvenir" series) ▲ UK 2074
Delius, F.:Son 2 Vn & Pno, w. Eric Fenby (pno) Unicorn-Kanchana ("Souvenir" series) ▲ UK 2074
Delius, F.:Son 3 Vn & Pno, w. Eric Fenby (pno) Unicorn-Kanchana ("Souvenir" series) ▲ UK 2074
Delius, F.:Suite Vn, w. V. Handley (cnd), Royal PO Unicorn-Kanchana ▲ UK 2076
Harty, H.:Con Vn, w. B. Thomson (cnd), Ulster Orch Chandos ▲ CHAN 7032
Harty, H.:Con Vn, w. B. Thomson (cnd), Ulster Orch Chandos ▲ CHAN 8386
Harty, H.:Vars on a Dublin Air, w. B. Thomson (cnd), Ulster Orch Chandos ▲ CHAN 8386
Hummel, J.N.:Nocturne, w. Richard Burnett (pno) Amon Ra ▲ CD-SAR 12
Hummel, J.N.:Son Va, w. Burnett (piano) Amon Ra ▲ CD-SAR 12
Hummel, J.N.:Son Vn & Pno, Op. 50, w. Richard Burnett (pno) Amon Ra ▲ CD-SAR 12
Sibelius, J.:Music for Vn Orch, w. V. Handley (cnd), Berlin RSO—Serenades in D & g, Op. 69, Nos. 1 & 2; Cantique & Devotion, Op. 77, Nos. 1 & 2; Six Humoresques, Op. 87/1 & 2 & Op. 89/1-4 Koch Schwann ▲ CD 311003 [ADD]

Holmquist, Joseph (perc)
Rzewski, F.:The Lost Melody, w. Zeitgeist *(rec Studio M, St. Paul, MN, Mar. 1994)* O.O. Discs ▲ OO 15
Rzewski, F.:Spots, w. Zeitgeist *(rec Studio M, St. Paul, MN, Mar. 1994)* O.O. Discs ▲ OO 15
Rzewski, F.:Wails, w. Zeitgeist *(rec Studio M, St. Paul, MN, Mar. 1994)* O.O. Discs ▲ OO 14

Holowach, Terry (vn)
Wagner, R.:Siegfried Idyll, w. M. Skazinetsky (vn), L. Toman (va), R. Laurie (vc), C. Elliott (db), S. Shulman (fl), T. Maloney (cl), J. Valdepenas (cl), J. Fetherston (cl), S. Mosher (bn), S. Wilson (hn), R. Cohen (hn), J. Cowell (tpt), G. Gould (cnd) *(rec July 27-29 & Sept. 8, 198)* Sony Classical ▲ SMK 52650 [ADD]

Holroyd, Dwana (pno)
Schuman, W.:Orpheus & His Lute, w. Rosalind Rees (sop), Gregg Smith (cnd), Gregg Smith Singers Vox Box ("The American Composers" series) 3-▲ CDX 3037

Hölscher, G. (ob)
Mozart, W.A.:Cassation, K.63, w. S. Winiarczyk (ob), R. Schnepps (hn), H. Nerat (hn), Salzburg CO *(rec March 28-30, 1992)* Naxos ▲ 8.550609 [DDD]
Mozart, W.A.:Cassation, K.99/63a, w. S. Winiarczyk (ob), R. Schnepps (hn), H. Nerat (hn), Salzburg CO *(rec March 28-30, 1992)* Naxos ▲ 8.550609 [DDD]
Mozart, W.A.:Cassation, K.100/62a, w. S. Winiarczyk (ob), R. Schnepps (hn), H. Nerat (hn), Salzburg CO *(rec March 28-30, 1992)* Naxos ▲ 8.550609 [DDD]

Holshouser, Scott (pno)
Chausson, E.:Poème Vn, w. P. Clarke (vn) [trans. for violin & piano] Classic Jewel ▲ CJL 0101-2
Kreisler, F.:Vn Pieces, w. P. Clarke (vn)—Recitativo & Scherzo-caprice, Op. 6 Classic Jewel ▲ CJL 0101-2
Saint-Saëns, C.:Son 1 Vn, w. P. Clarke (vn) Classic Jewel ▲ CJL 0101-2
Tchaikovsky, P.:Valse-Scherzo Vn, w. P. Clarke (vn) Classic Jewel ▲ CJL 0101-2
Waxman, F.:Carmen Fant, w. P. Clarke (vn) [trans. for violin & piano] Classic Jewel ▲ CJL 0101-2

Holst, Henry (vn)
Beethoven, L. van:Trio 6 Pno, "Archduke", w. Solomon (pno), A. Pini (vc) APR ▲ APR 5503 [ADD]
Beethoven, L. van:Trio 7 Pno, w. Solomon (pno), Anthony Pini (vc) *(rec Abbey Road, Studio No. 3)* Dutton Laboratories ▲ DUT 7015 [ADD]

Holst Christensen, Birthe (vc)
Bach, Joh. Christian:Qts (4) for 2 Fls, w. B. Larsen (fl), B. Pedersen (fl), P. Elbaek (vn), H. Olsen (va) Kontrapunkt ▲ 32048 [DDD]
Bach, Joh. Christian:Trios for 2 Fls & Strs, w. B. Larsen (fl), B. Pedersen (fl), P. Elbaek (vn), H. Olsen (va) Kontrapunkt ▲ 32048 [DDD]
Höller, K.:Improvisationen über "Schönster Herr Jesu", w. Barbara Harbach (org) Gasparo ▲ GS 278 ■ GS 278C

Hölszky-Wiedemann, Monika (vn)
Haas, P.:The Chosen One, w. Jörg Dürmüller (ten), Willy Freivogel (fl), Friedhelm Pütz (hn), Dennis Russell Davies (pno) Orfeo ("Musica Rediviva" series) ▲ 386961 [DDD]

Holt, Joseph (pno)
Read, G.:Chamber Music, w. Janet Packer (vn), Gerald Berthiaume (cel), Leslie Stratton Norris (hp), Barbara Harbach (hpd), Howard Karp (pno), Boston Composers String Quartet—5 Aphorisms, Op. 150; Son. da Chiesa, Op. 61; Sonoric Fant. No. 1, Op. 102; Qt. 1 Strings, Op. 100 Northeastern ▲ NOR 253 [DDD]
Read, G.:Son da Chiesa *(rec Arlington, VA, Mar. 1993)* Northeastern ("Classical Arts, Contemporary" series) ▲ NR 253
Vainberg, M.:Trio Pno, w. George Marsh (vn), Steven Honigberg (vc) Albany ▲ TROY 157 [DDD]

Holt, Rebecca (pno)
French Flute Music, w. Peter Lloyd (fl) IMP Classics ▲ PCD 991 [DDD]

Holthe, Kolbjørn (vn)—see ORCHESTRAS & ENSEMBLES Busoni String Quartet

Holtmann, Heidrun (pno)
Mozart, W.A.:Pno Music (misc)—Adagio, K.540; Son., K.310; Vars., K.265, 398 & 573 *(rec 1990)* Ambitus ▲ 97846 [DDD]
Schumann, R.:Carnaval Pno Ambitus ▲ 97819 [DDD]
Schumann, R.:Kreisleriana Ambitus ▲ 97819 [DDD]

Holton, Alex (tpt)
Baroque Trumpetissimo, w. David Bilger (tpt), Stephen Burns (tpt), Edward Carroll (tpt), Alex Holton (tpt), Raymond Mase (tpt), Timothy Morrison (tpt), Lee Soper (tpt), Atsuko Sato (bn), Ben Harms (timp), Edward Brewer (org/hpd), Philharmonia Virtuosi [cnd:Richard Kapp] ESS.A.Y ▲ ESS 1035 [DDD]

Holtrop, Mariette (vn)—see ORCHESTRAS & ENSEMBLES New Consort

Holtslag, Peter (rcr)—see also ORCHESTRAS & ENSEMBLES La Fontegara Amsterdam
Telemann, G.P.:Fants Fl *(rec Jan. 1994)* Globe ▲ GLO 5117 [DDD]

Hötzel, Michael (hn)
Mozart, L.:Con for 2 Hns, w. Herman Jeurissen (hn), H. Friesen (cnd), Concerto Rotterdam MD + G ▲ MDG 3210085

Holub, Petr (side dr)
Martinů, B.:Qt Cl, Hn, Vc & Side Drum, w. Vlastimil Mareš (cl), Vladimíra Klánská (hn), Jitka Vlašánková (vc) *(rec Studio Martinek, Prague, Mar 3, 1995)* Panton ("Protokol XX" series) ▲ 811348-2 [DDD]

Hölzer, Barbara (gtr)—see ORCHESTRAS & ENSEMBLES Tedesco Duo

Hölzer, Eugène (gtr)—see ORCHESTRAS & ENSEMBLES Tedesco Duo

Holzman, Adam (gtr)
Sor, F.:Divert *(rec St. John Chrysostom Church, Newmarket, Canada, Dec 17-20, 1994)* Naxos ▲ 8.553340 [DDD]
Sor, F.:Gtr Music—Fant solo Gtr; Fant Villageoise; Morceau de Concert; Souveniers d'une Soirée à Berlin; Valses (6) et un Gallop *(rec Newmarket, Canada, June 1995)* Naxos ▲ 8.553450 [DDD]
Sor, F.:Short Pieces *(rec St. John Chrysostom Church, Newmarket, Canada, Dec 17-20, 1994)* Naxos ▲ 8.553340 [DDD]
Sor, F.:Sons Gtr, Opp. 15 & 22—Op. 22 *(rec St. John Chrysostom Church, Newmarket, Canada, Dec 17-20, 1994)* Naxos ▲ 8.553340 [DDD]
Sor, F.:Son Gtr, Op. 25 *(rec St. John Chrysostom Church, Newmarket, Canada, Dec 17-20, 1994)* Naxos ▲ 8.553340 [DDD]

Holzman, David (pno)
Davies, P.M.:Farewell to Stromness *(rec 1990)* Centaur ▲ CRC 2102 [DDD]
Davies, P.M.:Son Pno *(rec 1990)* Centaur ▲ CRC 2102 [DDD]
Davies, P.M.:Yesnaby Ground *(rec 1990)* Centaur ▲ CRC 2102 [DDD]
Martino, D.:Fants & Impromptus *(rec Paine Hall, Harvard Univ, 1994)* Albany ▲ TROY 169 [DDD]
Martino, D.:Fant Pno *(rec Paine Hall, Harvard Univ, 1994)* Albany ▲ TROY 169 [DDD]

Holzman, David (pno) (cont.)
Martino, D.:Impromptu for Roger *(rec Paine Hall, Harvard Univ, 1994)* Albany ▲ TROY 169 [DDD]
Martino, D.:Pianississimo *(rec Paine Hall, Harvard Univ, 1991)* Albany ▲ TROY 168 [DDD]
Martino, D.:Preludes *(rec Paine Hall, Harvard Univ, 1994)* Albany ▲ TROY 169 [DDD]
Pleskow, R.:Son Pno *(rec 1990)* Centaur ▲ CRC 2102 [DDD]
Wolpe, S.:Music of *(rec 1990)* Centaur ▲ CRC 2102 [DDD]
Homann, Martin (perc)
Berlinski, H.:Das Gebet Bonhoeffers, w. Nancy Gibson (sop), Matthias Weichert (bass), Olaf Georgi (fl), Bernhard Hentrich (vc), Herman Berlinski (org), Holger Miersch (cel), Hans-Christoph Rademann (cnd), Dresden Chamber Choir Vienna Modern Masters ▲ VMM 3027 [DDD]
Helmschrott, R.:Cross & Freedom, w. Helmut Schatz, Nancy Gibson (sop), Frieder Aurich (ten), Matthias Weichert (bass), Manfred Ball (nar), Anett Baumann (vn), Frank Philliptsch, Linda Robbins, Gerhard Wolf, Robert M. Helmschrott (org), H.-C. Rademann (cnd), Munich Trombone Quartet, Dresden Chamber Choir Vienna Modern Masters ▲ VMM 3027 [DDD]
Homatas, J.-E. (va)—see ORCHESTRAS & ENSEMBLES Arte del Suono String Quartet
Hominich, Eric (pno)
Classic Elektra, w. Elektra Women's Choir [cnd:Morna Edmundson, Diane Loomer], Evelyn Creaser-Rumley (vn), Nancy DiNovo (vn), Brenda Fedoruk (fl) Skylark ▲ 9402 [DDD]
Hominick, Ian (pno)
Thalberg, S.:Pno Music—Scherzo in c#, Op. 31; Nocturnes in Ab, Op. 21/1 & in E, Op. 28; Tarantelle in c, Op. 65 *(rec Bowling Green, OH, Dec 15-17, 1993)* Titanic ▲ TI 227 [DDD]
Thalberg, S.:Son Pno *(rec Bowling Green, OH, Dec 15-17, 1993)* Titanic ▲ TI 227 [DDD]
Homma, Masashi (ob)
Vivaldi, A.:Con Fl Ob, RV.107, w. M. Arita (fl), N. Wakamatsu (vn), K. Dosaka (bn), Bach-Mozart Ensemble Tokyo *(rec June 22-26, 1992)* Denon ▲ CO 75198 [DDD]
Vivaldi, A.:Cons Ob, w. Bach-Mozart Ensemble Tokyo—RV.457 & 461 *(rec June 22-26, 1992)* Denon ▲ CO 75198 [DDD]
Hommel, Carlo (org)
Bach, J.S.:Clavier-Übung III [Westfelder Organ of Luxemburg Cathedral] K617 ▲ 7061
Hommel, Christian (ob)
Mozart, W.A.:Sons Vn Pno (misc), w. Christian Köhn (pno)—K.10-15 [The London Sons] Ars Musici ▲ 1134 [DDD]
Homs, J.-L. (E hn)
Lemeland, A.:L'Automne et sens envols d'etourneaux, w. Sabine Chefson (hp), M. Tardue (cnd), Grenoble Instrumental Ensemble Skarbo ▲ SKR 3913 [DDD]
Hóna, Gusztáv (bn)
Bogár, I.:Con Tuba, w. József Bazsinka (tuba), L. Marosi (cnd), Budapest Symphonic Band *(rec Jul 3-7, 1995)* Hungaroton ▲ HCD 31612 [DDD]
Dubrovay, L.:Buzzing - Polka, w. József Bazsinka (tuba), L. Marosi (cnd), Budapest Symphonic Band *(rec Jul 3-7, 1995)* Hungaroton ▲ HCD 31612 [DDD]
Hidas, F.:Folksongs of Békés County, w. József Bazsinka (tuba), L. Marosi (cnd), Budapest Symphonic Band *(rec Jul 3-7, 1995)* Hungaroton ▲ HCD 31612 [DDD]
Hidas, F.:Folksongs of the Balaton, w. József Bazsinka (tuba), L. Marosi (cnd), Budapest Symphonic Band *(rec Jul 3-7, 1995)* Hungaroton ▲ HCD 31612 [DDD]
Lendvay, K.:The Last Message from Maestro Tchaikovsky, w. József Bazsinka (tuba), L. Marosi (cnd), Budapest Symphonic Band *(rec Jul 3-7, 1995)* Hungaroton ▲ HCD 31612 [DDD]
Ránki, G.:The Magic Potion, w. József Bazsinka (tuba), L. Marosi (cnd), Budapest Symphonic Band *(rec Jul 3-7, 1995)* Hungaroton ▲ HCD 31612 [DDD]
Ránki, G.:The Tales of Father Goose, w. József Bazsinka (tuba), L. Marosi (cnd), Budapest Symphonic Band *(rec Jul 3-7, 1995)* Hungaroton ▲ HCD 31612 [DDD]
Honda, Mariko (vn)
Bruch, M.:Con 1 Vn, w. K. Clark (cnd), Slovak PO *(rec Concert Hall of Slovak PO, Bratislava, May 11-16, 1988)* Lydian ▲ 18026 [DDD]
Dvořák, A.:Con Vn, w. K. Clark (cnd), Slovak PO *(rec Moyzes Hall of the Slovak PO, Bratislava, Mar. 1988)* Lydian ▲ 18084 [DDD]
Mendelssohn, F.:Con in e Vn & Orch, Op. 64, w. K. Clark (cnd), Slovak PO *(rec Concert Hall of Slovak PO, Bratislava, May 11-16, 1988)* Lydian ▲ 18026 [DDD]
Honeywell, Ann Musser (org)
Harris, R.:Easter Cant, w. R. Shewan (cnd), Roberts Wesleyan College Brass Ensemble, Wesleyan College Chorale—Alleluia *(rec St. Louis Roman Catholic Church, Pittsford, NY)* Albany ▲ TROY 164 [DDD]
Harris, R.:Mass, w. R. Shewan (cnd), Roberts Wesleyan College Chorale *(rec St. Louis Roman Catholic Church, Pittsford, NY)* Albany ▲ TROY 164 [DDD]
Shewan, S.:Magnificat, w. Erin Stedman (sop), Kimberly Higgins (alt), Robert Dingman (ten), Alexander Burgess (bar), Paul Shewan (tpt), Barbara Hull (tpt), Nanita Wilson (hn), Scott Emmons (trbn), Kirk Kettinger (tuba) Albany ▲ TROY 149 [DDD]
Shewan, S.:The Voice of the Lord in the Storm, w. Erin Stedman (sop), Kimberly Higgins (alt), Robert Dingman (ten), Alexander Burgess (bar), Paul Shewan (tpt), Barbara Hull (tpt), Nanita Wilson (hn), Scott Emmons (trbn), Kirk Kettinger (tuba) Albany ▲ TROY 149 [DDD]
Hong, Jong-Jin (daegum)
Kim, J.H.:Tchong, w. Robert Dick (fls) O. O. Discs ▲ 0024
Hongne, Paul (bn)
Beethoven, L. van:Trio Fl, WoO 37, w. J.-P. Rampal (fl), R. Veyron-Lacroix (pno) Vox Box 2-▲ CDX 5000 [ADD]
Honigberg, Carol (pno)
Beethoven, L. van:Son 2 Vc, w. S. Honigberg (vc) Albany ▲ TROY 116 [DDD]
Beethoven, L. van:Son 3 Vc, w. S. Honigberg (vc) Albany ▲ TROY 116 [DDD]
Beethoven, L. van:Vars on "See, the Conquering Hero Comes" from Handel's *Judas Maccabaeus*, w. S. Honigberg (vc) Albany ▲ TROY 116 [DDD]
Beethoven, L. van:Vars on "Bei Männern" from Mozart's *Die Zauberflöte*, w. S. Honigberg (vc) Albany ▲ TROY 116 [DDD]
Ben-Haim, P.:Sonatina Pno Albany ▲ TROY 157 [DDD]
Berlinski, H.:From the World of My Father, w. Steven Honigberg (vc) Albany ▲ TROY 157 [DDD]
Honigberg, Steven (vc)
Barber, S.:Son Vc, w. K. Brake (pno) Albany ▲ TROY 082 [DDD]
Beethoven, L. van:Son 2 Vc, w. C. Honigberg (pno) Albany ▲ TROY 116 [DDD]
Beethoven, L. van:Son 3 Vc, w. C. Honigberg (pno) Albany ▲ TROY 116 [DDD]
Beethoven, L. van:Vars on "See, the Conquering Hero Comes" from Handel's *Judas Maccabaeus*, w. C. Honigberg (pno) Albany ▲ TROY 116 [DDD]
Beethoven, L. van:Vars on "Bei Männern" from Mozart's *Die Zauberflöte*, w. C. Honigberg (pno) Albany ▲ TROY 116 [DDD]
Berlinski, H.:From the World of My Father, w. Carol Honigberg (pno) Albany ▲ TROY 157 [DDD]
Bernstein, L.:Mass (sels), w. K. Brake (pno)—Three Meditations Albany ▲ TROY 082 [DDD]
Diamond, D.:Kaddish, w. K. Brake (pno) Albany ▲ TROY 082 [DDD]
Foss, L.:Capriccio, w. K. Brake (pno) Albany ▲ TROY 082 [DDD]
Perle, G.:Hebrew Melodies Albany ▲ TROY 157 [DDD]
Schuller, G.:Fant Vc Albany ▲ TROY 082 [DDD]
Starer, R.:Elegy for a Woman Who Died Too Young, w. Jan Stewart (vn) Albany ▲ TROY 157 [DDD]
Vainberg, M.:Trio Pno, w. Joseph Holt (pno), George Marsh (vn) Albany ▲ TROY 157 [DDD]
Honma, Masashi (ob)
Takemitsu, T.:Gémeaux, w. Christian Lindberg (trbn), Numajiri, Wakasugi (cnd), Tokyo Metropolitan SO *(rec Tokyo Metropolitan Art Space, July 25-29, 1994)* Denon ▲ CO 78944 [DDD]
Honneger, Claire (pno)
Miniatures, w. Lazarevitch, Vojkan (vn) *(rec Jan 1996)* Gallo ▲ CD 877 [ADD]
Honnens, P. R. (vc)—see ORCHESTRAS & ENSEMBLES Pro Arte Piano Trio
Honsho, Reiko (pno)
Fine, V.:Concertante Pno, w. A. Watanabe (cnd), Japan PO CRI ▲ CD 692 [ADD]
Hood, Joanna (va)—see ORCHESTRAS & ENSEMBLES Lafayette String Quartet
Hood, P. (pno)
Goosen, F.:Son Cl, w. S. Bridges (cl) CRI ▲ CD 665 [ADD]
Hoog, Viola de (vc)—see also ORCHESTRAS & ENSEMBLES Schönbrunn Ensemble Amsterdam
Bach, C.P.E.:Son Ob, H.549, w. W. Barella (ob), C. Farr (kbd) Channel Classics ▲ CCS 2091 [DDD]
Bach, J.S.:Sons Fl, BWV 1030-35, w. M. Root (trns fl), R. Egarr (hpd)—1030, 1034 & 1035 *(rec May 1993)* Globe ▲ GLO 5102 [DDD]
Haydn, J.:Diverts Fl, Vn & Vc, w. Marten Root (fl), Johannes Leertouwer (vn)—H.IV/6-11; Op. 11/2 & 5 *(rec Utrecht, Nov. 1994)* Globe ▲ GLO 5131 [DDD]
Schubert, Franz:Qt Fl, w. M. Root (fl), S. Swierstra (va), F. Jacobs (gtr) Globe ▲ GLO 5040 [DDD]
Hoogendoorn, Clementine (fl)
Salieri, A.:Con Fl, w. Pietro Borgonovo (ob), C. Scimone (cnd), Venice Solisti Erato ▲ ERA SEL 12987 [DDD]
Hoogeveen, Godfried (vc)
Enescu, G.:Symphonie concertante, w. A. Lascae (cnd), Moldova Philharmonia Ottavo ▲ OTT 69449 [DDD]
Lazarof, H.:Oct Strs, w. Yukiko Kamei (vn), Peter Marsh (vn), Yoko Matsuda (vn), Miwako Watanabe (vn), Paul Silverthorne (va), Milton Thomas (va), David Speltz (vc), H. Lazarof (cnd) Laurel ▲ LR 843 [DDD]
Hoogeveen, Ronald (vn)
Einhorn, R.:Voices of Light, w. Susan Narucki (sop), Corrie Pronk (alt), Frank Hameleers (ten), Henk van Heijnsbergen (b-bar), Harm Bakker (vl), Michael Feves (vl), Naomi Hirschfeld (vl), S. Mercurio (cnd), Netherlands Radio PO, Martin Wright (cnd), Anonymous 4, Netherlands Radio Chorus *(rec Music Center of the Netherlands Radio & TV, Aug 23-25, 1995)* Sony Classical ▲ SK 62006 [DDD]
Grieg, E.:Andante con moto, w. H. Lambooij (vc), J. Röling (pno) Olympia ▲ OLY 432 [DDD]
Grieg, E.:Fugue, w. H. Lambooij (vc), J. Röling (pno) [arr for pno trio] Olympia ▲ OLY 432 [DDD]
Grieg, E.:Qt Strs (unfinished), w. H. Lambooij (vc), J. Röling (pno) [arr for pno trio] Olympia ▲ OLY 432 [DDD]
Grieg, E.:Qt Strs, Op. 27, w. H. Lambooij (vc), J. Röling (pno) Olympia ▲ OLY 432 [DDD]
Pijper, W.:Son Vn Donemus ▲ CV 15
Pijper, W.:Trio 2 Pno, w. Peter Beijersbergen van Henegouwen (pno), Wouter Mijnders (vc) Donemus ▲ CV 15
Hoogewerf, Wim (gtr)
Sigurbjörnsson, T.:Fiori, w. Thora Johansen (hpd) Music from Iceland ▲ ITM 702 [ADD]
Hoogland, Stanley (pno)
Beethoven, L. van:Folksong Arrs, w. M. Kweksilber (sop), V. Beths (vn), A. Bijlsma (vc)—Irish Songs, WoO 152, Nos. 1,5,8 & 11; Scottish Songs, Op. 108, Nos. 2,3,5,7,8,17,20 & 24 [E] *(rec 6/90)* Channel Classics ▲ CCS 1491 [DDD]
Beethoven, L. van:Trio Pno, Op.38, w. E. Hoeprich (cl), T. Tomkins (vc) Koch International Classics ▲ KIC 7015-2 [DDD] ■ 3-7015-4 (D)
Beethoven, L. van:Trio 10 Pno, w. V. Beths, A. Bijlsma *(rec June 1990)* Channel Classics ▲ CCS 1491 [DDD]
Escher, R.:Son Vn, w. Vera Beths (vn) *(rec Sept 4, 1984)* Donemus ▲ CV 47 [ADD]
Glinka, M.:Trio pathétique, w. E. Hoeprich (cl), T. Tomkins (vc) Koch International Classics ▲ KIC 7015-2 [DDD] ■ 3-7015-4 (D)
Schubert, Franz:Der Hirt auf dem Felsen, w. D. Aalbers (sop), F. van den Brink (cl) [G] Partridge ▲ 1132-2 [DDD]
Schubert, Franz:Pieces Pno, D.946—No. 1 Partridge ▲ 1132-2 [DDD]
Schubert, Franz:Songs (misc), w. D. Aalbers (sop)—10 songs (D.118, 136 [w. van den Brink (cl)], 342, 367, 433, 564, 762, 787 [w. van den Brink (cl)], 800, 828) [G] Partridge ▲ 1132-2 [DDD]
Hooker, Christopher (ob)
Vivaldi, A.:Cons Diverse Instrs, w. Joanna Graham (bn), Ruth McDowall (cl), David Rix (ct), Deborah Davis (fl), Duke Dobing (fl), Tim Caister (hn), Stephen Stirling (hn), Helen McQueen (ob), Michael Meekes (tpt), Crispian Steele-Perkins (tpt), Nicholas Kraemer (hpd), N. Kraemer (cnd), London Sinfonietta—Cons. in F, RV.539; in C, RV.533; in D, RV.122; in C, RV.537; in C, RV.560; in F, RV.538; in G, RV.545 *(rec All Saints Church, East Finchley, Oct. 1994 & Jan. 1995)* Naxos ("Vivaldi Collection" series) ▲ 8.553204 [DDD]
Hooper, Nick (gtr)
Portrait of a Concertina, w. Dave Townsend (Eng conc) Saydisc ■ SDLC 351 (D)
Hoover, Katherin (fl)
Boulanger, L.:D'un matin de printemps Fl & Pno, w. V. Eskin (pno) Leonarda ■ LE 304
Boulanger, L.:Nocturne, w. V. Eskin (pno) Leonarda ■ LE 304
Farrenc, J.-L.:Trio Vn, w. C. Brey (vc), B. Weintraub (pno) Leonarda ■ LE 304
Hoover, K.:On the Betrothal of Princess Isabelle of France, Aged 6, w. V. Eskin (pno) Leonarda ■ LE 304
Tailleferre, G.:Pastorale, w. V. Eskin (pno) Leonarda ■ LE 304
For the Flute Leonarda ■ LE 304
Ulehla, L.:Elegy, w. C. Brey (vc), B. Weintraub (pno) Leonarda ■ LE 304
Hope, Helen (hp)
A Colorado Kind of Christmas, w. Colorado Children's Chorale [cnd:Duain Wolfe], Mike Fitzmaurice (db), Rod Garnet (fl), William Hill (perc), Deborah Schmit-Lobis (pno), Brett Walace (vc), Mary Louise Burke (pno), Laurie Kahler (pno) *(rec Denver Center Media)* Colorado Children's Chorale ▲ XMAS
Encore, w. Colorado Children's Chorale [cnd:Duain Wolfe], Rick Chinski (gtr), Robert Davine (acc), Laurie Kahler (pno), Samuel Lancaster (pno), Barry Oliver (pno), Marylin Preston (fl), Karen Yonovitz (fl), Peter Cooper (ob), Andy Stevens (cl), Lionel Young (vn), Basil Vendreys (va), Wayne Templeman (vc), Charle *(rec Denver Center Media)* Colorado Children's Chorale ▲ 001
Hopf, Dieter (gtr)
Castelnuovo-Tedesco, M.:Sérénade, w. M. Tröster (gtr), J. Przybylski (cnd), Warsaw SO *(rec Aug. 1992)* Thorofon ▲ CTH 2171 [DDD]
Hopkins, Fred (elec bass)
Lebaron, A.:The E. & O. Line (sels), w. Louise Cloutier (mez—Eurydice/Vendors), Hugh Panero (ten—Hermes), Lawrence Hamilton (bar—Orpheus/Men), Frank London (tpt), Marcus Rojas (tuba), Myra Melford (pno/kbd), Davey Williams (gtr), Thurman Barker (dr), A. LeBaron (cnd)—Juke Joint Jam Session; Eurydice Meets Hermes; Eurydice's Death [Funeral Band]; Eurydice's River Journey; Orpheus Laments [Looked Away] *(rec Coolidge Auditorium, Library of Congress, 1987)* Mode ▲ Mode 42
Hopkins Marti, Carolyn (vc)
Mieg, P.:Septet, w. Peter Solomon (hpd), Günter Rumpel (fl), Simon Fuchs (ob), Primroz Novsak (vn), Marius Ungareanu (va), Ronald Dangel (db) *(rec 1993)* Jecklin ▲ JS 314-2 [DDD]
Hopman, David (gtr)
Beaser, R.:Mountain Songs, w. V. Pettys (fl) Gajo ▲ GR 1002 [DAD]
Beethoven, L. van:Serenade Strs, Op. 8, w. D. Pettys (vn), C. Brubaker (va) [violin-viola-guitar arr.] Gajo ▲ GR 1002 [DAD]
Hoppe, Michael (pno)
The Dreamer:Romances for Alto Flute, Vol. 2, w. Wheater, Tim (fl) Bainbridge ▲ BBR 6300 ■ BBR 6300
Hopper, Gretchen (trbn)
Dempster, S.:Music of, w. Stuart Dempster (trbn/didjeridu/conch), Jay Bulen (trbn), Jeff Domoto (trbn), Moc Escobedo (trbn/didjeridu/conch), Scott Higbee (trbn), Nathaniel Irby-Oxford (trbn), Chad Kirby (trbn/conch), Dave Marriott (trbn), Greg Powers (trbn), Debra Sykes (cym)—Conch Calling; Morning Light; Didjerilayover; Secret Currents; Melodic Communion; Shell Shock; Cloud Landings *(rec Fort Worden, Port Townsend, WA, June 18, 1994)* New Albion ▲ NA 076
Hoppstock, Tilman (gtr)
Bach, J.S.:French Suites—BWV 812 [trans. for guitar] Signum ▲ X 42-00 [DDD]
Bach, J.S.:Partitas Hpd, BWV 825-830 [trans. for guitar]—BWV 825 Signum ▲ X 42-00 [DDD]
Bach, J.S.:Preludes & Fugues Hpd [trans. for guitar]—in c Signum ▲ X 42-00 [DDD]
Brouwer, L.:Estudios Sencillos—(12) Nos. 1-10, 13 & 16 Signum ▲ X 41-00 [DDD]
Brouwer, L.:Tarantos Entrée ▲ 0072
Brouwer, L.:Temas populares Cubanos Entrée ▲ 0072
Buxtehude, D.:Suite Kbd, BuxWV 236 [trans. for guitar] Signum ▲ X 42-00 [DDD]

▲ = CD ♦ = Enhanced CD Δ = MD ■ = Cassette Tape □ = DCC

Hoppstock, Tilman (gtr) (cont.)
Froberger, J.J.:Suites de clavecin [trans. for guitar]—in E♭ Signum ▲ X 42-00 [DDD]
Martin, F.:Pièces brèves Gtr Entrée ▲ 0072
Paganini, N.:Caprices Vn [trans. for guitar]—No. 5 in a; No. 17 in E♭ Signum ▲ X 41-00 [DDD]
Ponce, M.:Preludes Gtr—Nos. 1-12 Signum ▲ X 41-00 [DDD]
Sor, F.:Etudes—Opp. 6, 29, 31, 35, 60 (sels.) Signum ▲ X 14-00 [DDD]
Sor, F.:Gtr Music—Bagatelle in A & Etude in D, Op. 43/35; Sicilienne & Allegretto in d, Op. 33/35; Intro. & Vars. on *Nel cor piu non mi sento*, Op. 16 Signum ▲ X 14-00 [DDD]
Sor, F.:Vars on a Theme of Mozart Signum ▲ X 14-00 [DDD]
El Ultimo Tremolo:Guitar Music of the 19th & 20th Centuries, w. Tilman Hoppstock (gtr) Entrée ▲ 0055 [ADD]
Villa-Lobos, H.:Etudes Gtr Signum ▲ X 41-00 [DDD]

Hora, Jan (org)
Brixi, F.X.:Cons Org (comp), w. F. Vajnar (cnd), Prague CO—3 Concerti—in D, C & C *(rec 1982)* Supraphon ▲ 10 3029-2 [AAD]
Janácek, L.:Amarus, w. Kvetoslava Nemeckova (sop), Leo Marian Vodicka (ten), Vaclav Zitek (bar), C. Mackerras (cnd), Czech PO, Lubomír Mátl (cnd), Czech Phil Chorus *(rec 1984)* Supraphon ▲ SUP CD 3045
Martinů, B.:Mount of 3 Lights, w. V. Dolezal (ten), R. Novák (bass), P. Haničinec (nar), P. Kühn (cnd), Prague Radio Men's Chorus, Kühn Chorus [Cz] *(rec 2-3/88)* Supraphon ▲ 11 0751-2 [DDD]
Saint-Saëns, C.:Sym 3, w. V. Válek (cnd), Prague RSO *(rec 1986)* Supraphon ▲ 11 0971-2 [DDD]
Slavicky, K.:Psalmi, w. Salome Losová (sop), Dagmar Pecková (cta), Vladimir Dolezal (ten), Ludek Vele (bass), P. Kühn (cnd), Kühn Chorus *(rec Dvořák Hall of Rudolfinum, Prague, Mar. 14-16, 1989)* Panton ("Protokol XX" series) ▲ PAN 811142 [DDD]

Horák, Josef (b cl)
Janácek, L.:Youth, w. Foerster Woodwind Quintet Panton ▲ PAN 811203

Horák, Vilém (bn)
Beethoven, L. van:Sxt Winds, Op. 71, w. V. Kyzivát (cl), Z. Tesař (cl), Z. Tylšar (hn), B. Tylšar (hn), F. Herman (bn) Supraphon ▲ 11 1445-2 [DDD]

Horder, Josephine (vc)
Mozart, W.A.:Qts Fl, w. J. Hall (fl), P. Barritt (vn), G. Clarkson (va) Collins Quest ▲ 3044 [DDD]

Höricke, Friedrich (pno)
Rachmaninoff, S.:Pno Transcriptions MD + G ("Scene" series) ▲ MDG 6110547 [DDD]
Rachmaninoff, S.:Son 2 Pno MD + G ("Scene" series) ▲ MDG 6110547 [DDD]

Horigome, Yozuko (vn)
Beethoven, L. van:Trio 9 Pno, "Kakadu", w. R. Serkin (pno), P. Wiley (vc) Sony Classical ▲ SMK 47296 [ADD]
Shostakovich, D.:Qt 14 Strs, w. G. Kremer (vn), K. Kashkashian (va), D. Geringas (vc) *(rec Lockenhaus Festival, 1986)* ECM New Series 2-▲ 78118-21347-2 [DDD]

Horlein, Heinrich (vn)
Berg, A.:Adagio, w. Hans-Udo Heinzmann (fl), Malte Lammers (ob), Walter Hermann (cl), Jaap Zeijl (va), Seven Forsberg (vc), Willi Beyer (db), Jurgen Lamke (pno), Werner Hagen (pno), Volker Kneip (perc) [arr chamber ensemble] Koch Schwann ▲ SCH CD 311912
Busoni, F.:Berceuse élégiaque, w. Hans-Udo Heinzmann (fl), Malte Lammers (ob), Walter Hermann (cl), Jaap Zeijl (va), Seven Forsberg (vc), Willi Beyer (db), Jurgen Lamke (pno), Werner Hagen (pno), Volker Kneip (perc) [arr Stein for chamber ensemble] Koch Schwann ▲ SCH CD 311912
Debussy, C.:Prélude à l'après-midi d'un faune, w. Hans-Udo Heinzmann (fl), Malte Lammers (ob), Walter Hermann (cl), Jaap Zeijl (va), Seven Forsberg (vc), Willi Beyer (db), Jurgen Lamke (pno), Werner Hagen (pno), Volker Kneip (perc) [arr Sachs for chamber ensemble] Koch Schwann ▲ SCH CD 311912
Schoenberg, A.:Chamber Sym 1, w. Hans-Udo Heinzmann (fl), Malte Lammers (ob), Walter Hermann (cl), Jaap Zeijl (va), Seven Forsberg (vc), Willi Beyer (db), Jurgen Lamke (pno), Werner Hagen (pno), Volker Kneip (perc) [arr Webern for chamber ensemble] Koch Schwann ▲ SCH CD 311912

Horn, Erwin (org)
Bruckner, A.:Org Music (comp) [the Klais Organ in the Nürnberg Frauenkirche]; trans. by Horn of the Scherzo from the Symphony in f (Study Symphony), the Andante from Symphony No. 0 in d, & the Adagio from Symphony No. 6; eleven original works—Four Preludes in E♭; Prelude in C; Prelude in c; Fugue in d; Prelude in E♭; Improvisationsskizze Bad Ischi; Vorspiel in d; Nachspiel in d Novalis ▲ 150071 [DDD]

Horn, Paul (fl)
Paul Horn Music Celestial Harmonies ▲ 11101-2 ■ 11101-4

Horner, Jerry (va)—see also ORCHESTRAS & ENSEMBLES Fine Arts String Quartet
Shostakovich, D.:Qnt Pno, w. M. Zweig (vn), Borodin Trio Chandos ▲ CHAN 8342 [DDD]

Horner, Lindsey (db)
Jenkins, L.:Monkey on the Dragon, w. Leroy Jenkins (vn), Henry Threadgill (fl), Don Byron (cl), Marth Ehrlich (b cl), Janet Frice (bn), Vincent Chancey (hn), Frank Gordon (tpt), Jeff Hoyer (trbn), David Soldier (vn), Jane Henry (vn) Ron Lawrence (va), Mary Wooton (vc), Thurman Barker (traps), Myra Melford (pno), T. Léon (cnd) *(rec live, Merkin Concert Hall, New York City, Apr. 9, 1992)* CRI ("eXchange" series) ▲ CD 663 [DDD]

Hornibrook, Wallace (hpd)—see ORCHESTRAS & ENSEMBLES Baroque Chamber Players
Hornibrook, Wallace (pno)—see ORCHESTRAS & ENSEMBLES Musica Sonora

Horn-Ribera, Bella (pno)
Stolarczyk, W.:Earth Air Fire Water, w. Amalie Malling (pno), John Damgaard (pno), Anne Øland (pno), Teddy Teirup (pno), Friedrich Gürtler (pno), Rosalind Bevan (pno), Poul Rosenbaum (pno), Rodolfo Llambias (pno), Anders Riber (pno), Elisabeth Sigurdsson (pno), Thomas Tronheim (pno), Elsebeth Broderson (pno), Erik Kaltoft (pno), Jørgen Hald Nielsen (pno), Aino Gilemann (pno), Birgit Kjær (pno), Jørgen Thomsen (pno), Gunhild Donslund (pno), Henrik Bo Hansen (pno), Lone Karlsson (pno), Erik Fessel (pno), Lasse Nilsson (pno), Janos Ferenczi (pno), Erik Bach (pno), Axel Momme (pno), Arne de Cros Dich (pno), Sven Micha Slot (pno), Hanne Bramsen Buhl (pno), Lili Olesen (pno), Susannah Carlsson (pno), Ulla Erml (pno), Vagn Sørensen (pno), Leif Greibe (pno), Bodil Krogh (pno), Kirsten Ottosen (pno), Inger Bergenholz (pno), Karsten Gylendorf (pno), Bjønr Elkjær (pno), Jacob Bjørn Jensen (pno), Jørgen Kaad (pno), Anne Marie Hjelm (pno), Carl Ulrik Munk Andersen (pno), Poul Lumbye (pno), Oluf Hildebrandt Nielsen (pno), Joachim Olsson (pno), Peter Pade Ramsøe Jacobsen (pno), Astrid Pollmann (pno), Jette Borsch (pno), Kirsten Karlshøj (pno), Maria Teresa Assing (pno), Allan Dahl Hansen (pno), Johan Hugossen (pno), Tine Fenger Pederson (pno), Arne Jørgen Fæø (pno), Anja Høgsted (pno), Anne Sophie Parbo (pno), Inga Lindmark (pno), Teresa Drabik Stathakis (pno), Anne Ruth Ferenczi (pno), Irene Hasager (pno), Yuka Ichikawa (pno), Birgitte Baur (pno), Malene Thastum (pno), Jens E. Rasmussen (pno), Birgitte Zielke (pno), Claus Zielke (pno), Stefan Kasch (pno), Bin Qiao (pno), Inger Johanne Teirup (pno), Lindy Rosborg (pno), Liisa Heininen (pno), David Højer (pno), Ellen Refstrup (pno), Thomas K. Søorensen (pno), Erik Kure (pno), Michael Rauff (pno), Jan beck Eriksson (pno), Tanja Zapolski (pno), Vibeke Skagbo (pno), Pål Eide Lindtner (pno), Ha-Young Sul (pno), Benedicte Palko (pno), Inke Kesseler (pno), Anne Marie Meineche (pno), Sverre Larsen (pno), Kasper Peter Bach (pno), Elisabetta Eliseo (pno), Olga Magieres (pno), Carl Erik Kühl (pno), Thorkild Borup Nielsen (pno), Valeria Zanini (pno), Lars Stenhoft (perc), Dennis Boel (perc), Winnie Dahlgren (perc), Susanne Vind (perc), Claus Byrith (elec), Anne Marie Storm (elec), J. Ribera (cnd) *(rec live, Koldinghaus Castle, Denmark, May 2, 1996)* Danica ▲ DCD 1996

Horowitz, Jason (vn)
Lovenstein, J.:Music of, w. Mary Brockenbrough (sop), Laura Sanders (sop), Barton Green (ten), Rockland Osgood (ten), David Murray (bar), Benjamin Sears (bar), Jonathan Lovenstein (pno), Heather O'Donnell (pno), James Silvers (pno), Rocy Reider (fl), Adrianna Hulscher (vn), James Johnston (vn), Mimi Ragson (vn), Peter Landeen (vc), Reinmar Seidler (vc)—Blake Songs; other works Titanic ▲ Ti 221 [DDD]

Horowitz, Vladimir (pno)
At the Met RCA Gold Seal ▲ 09026-61416-2 ■ 09026-61416-4
Barber, S.:Son Pno *(rec 1950)* RCA Gold Seal ▲ 60377-2-RG (m) [ADD] ■ 60377-4-RG (CrO2)
Beethoven, L. van:Con 5 Pno, "Emperor", w. F. Reiner (cnd), RCA Victor SO *(rec Carnegie Hall 1952)* RCA Gold Seal ▲ 7992-2-RG (m) [ADD] ■ 7992-4-RG
Beethoven, L. van:Sons Pno (comp) *(rec 1930-1951)* EMI Classics 3-▲ ZDHC 63538
Beethoven, L. van:Son 7 Pno RCA Gold Seal ▲ 09026-60986-2 ■ 09026-60986-4

Horowitz, Vladimir (pno) (cont.)
Beethoven, L. van:Son 14 Pno, "Moonlight Son" RCA Gold Seal ▲ 60461-2-RG (m) [ADD] ■ 60461-4-RG
Beethoven, L. van:Son 14 Pno, "Moonlight Son" *(rec Apr. 20-27, 1972)* Sony Classical ▲ SK 53467 [ADD]
Beethoven, L. van:Son 14 Pno, "Moonlight Son" CBS ▲ MK 44797 [ADD]
Beethoven, L. van:Son 14 Pno, "Moonlight Son" RCA Gold Seal ▲ 60375-2-RG [ADD] ■ 60375-4-RG
Beethoven, L. van:Son 21 Pno, "Waldstein" *(rec Apr. 20-27, 1972)* Sony Classical ▲ SK 53467 [ADD]
Beethoven, L. van:Son 21 Pno, "Waldstein" RCA Gold Seal ▲ 60375-2-RG [ADD] ■ 60375-4-RG
Beethoven, L. van:Son 23 Pno, "Appassionata" RCA Gold Seal ▲ 60375-2-RG [ADD] ■ 60375-4-RG
Beethoven, L. van:Son 23 Pno, "Appassionata" *(rec Apr. 20-27, 1972)* Sony Classical ▲ SK 53467 [ADD]
Beethoven, L. van:Son 28 Pno *(rec New York, Oct. 22 & Nov. 26, 1967)* Sony Classical ▲ SK 53466 [ADD]
Brahms, J.:Con 1 Pno, w. B. Walter (cnd), Royal Concertgebouw Orch *(rec live, Feb. 20, 1936)* As Disc ▲ ASD 2400 (m)
Brahms, J.:Con 1 Pno, w. B. Walter (cnd), Royal Concertgebouw Orch *(rec 1936)* Legend ▲ LGD 105 [ADD]
Brahms, J.:Con 2 Pno, w. A. Toscanini (cnd), NBC SO *(rec live, New York 10/23/48)* Arkadia ▲ 454 [ADD]
Brahms, J.:Con 2 Pno, w. A. Toscanini (cnd), NBC SO RCA Gold Seal ▲ 60319-2-RG ■ 60319-4-RG
Brahms, J.:Con 2 Pno, w. A. Toscanini (cnd), NBC SO *(rec live, Carnegie Hall)* RCA Gold Seal ▲ 60523-2-RG [ADD] ■ 60523-4-RG (CrO2)
Brahms, J.:Con 2 Pno, w. A. Toscanini (cnd), NBC SO Stradivarius ▲ STV 13595 [AAD]
Brahms, J.:Intermezzos Pno, Op. 117—No. 2 in b♭ RCA Gold Seal ▲ 60523-2-RG [ADD] ■ 60523-4-RG (CrO2)
Brahms, J.:Son 3 Vn, w. N. Milstein (vn) RCA Gold Seal ▲ 60461-2-RG (m) [ADD] ■ 60461-4-RG (CrO2)
Busoni, F.:Bach Transcriptions—Ich ruf' zu dir, Herr Jesu Christ [from Orgelbüchlein, BWV 599-644] *(rec New York, June 12, 1969)* Sony Classical ▲ SK 53466 [ADD]
Chopin, F.:Ballades Pno (comp)—Op. 23 RCA Gold Seal ▲ 09026-61414-2 ■ 09026-61414-4
Chopin, F.:Ballades Pno (comp) RCA Gold Seal ▲ 09026-61416-2 ■ 09026-61416-4
Chopin, F.:Ballades Pno (comp)—Op. 23 *(rec Jan. 2-Feb. 1, 1968)* Sony Classical ▲ SK 53465 [ADD]
Chopin, F.:Études (24)—Op. 25/7 *(rec 1963)* CBS ▲ MK 42412 [AAD]
Chopin, F.:Études (24)—Op. 10/4, 5 & 8; Op. 25/3 Enterprise ("The Piano Library" series) ▲ ENT 188
Chopin, F.:Études (24) Iron Needle ▲ 1303 (m) [ADD]
Chopin, F.:Impromptus Iron Needle ▲ 1303 (m) [ADD]
Chopin, F.:Impromptus—No. 1, Op. 29 Enterprise ("The Piano Library" series) ▲ ENT 188
Chopin, F.:Mazurkas Iron Needle ▲ 1303 (m) [ADD]
Chopin, F.:Mazurkas—Nos. 2, 3, 7 [Op. 7], 27 [Op. 41] & 32 [Op. 50] Enterprise ("The Piano Library" series) ▲ ENT 188
Chopin, F.:Mazurkas—Op. 33/4 & Op. 50/3 *(rec 1966 & 1973)* CBS ▲ MK 42412 [AAD]
Chopin, F.:Nocturnes—Op. 72/1 *(rec 1966)* CBS ▲ MK 42412
Chopin, F.:Nocturnes—No. 19, Op. 72/1 Enterprise ("The Piano Library" series) ▲ ENT 188
Chopin, F.:Nocturnes—in f, Op. 55/1 *(rec Jan. 2-Feb. 1, 1968)* Sony Classical ▲ SK 53465 [ADD]
Chopin, F.:Pno Music (misc) CBS ■ MT 30643
Chopin, F.:Pno Music (misc) RCA Gold Seal ▲ 09026-60986-2 ■ 09026-60986-4
Chopin, F.:Pno Music (misc)—Mazurka No. 1, Op. 41; Mazurka No. 2, Op. 63; Mazurkas Nos. 3, Opp. 59/50/63/7; Ballade No. 4, Op. 52; Nocturne No. 1, Opp. 72/15; Nocturne No. 3, Op. 9; Polonaise-fantaisie, Op. 61; Scherzo No. 1, Op. 20; Scherzo No. 2, Op. 31; Waltz No. 3, Op. 34 RCA Gold Seal ▲ 09026-60987-2 ■ 09026-60987-4
Chopin, F.:Pno Music (misc)—Ballade No. 1 in g, Op. 23; 4 Études—Op. 10, Nos. 3,4,5 & 12; 6 Mazurkas—Opp. 7/3, 17/4, 30/3, 33/2, 41/2 & 59/3; Nocturne in f, Op. 55/1; 2 Polonaises—in A, Op. 40/1 & in A♭, Op. 53; Prelude in b, Op. 28/6; Scherzo No. 1 in b, Op. 20; 2 Waltzes—in a, Op. 34/2 & in c♯, Op. 64/2 CBS ▲ MK 42306 [AAD]
Chopin, F.:Pno Music (misc)—Ballade No. 1 in g, Op. 23; 2 Études, Op. 10/3 & 4; Impromptu in A♭, Op. 29; Mazurka in c♯, Op. 30/4; 2 Nocturnes, Op. 9/2 & Op. 55/1; Scherzo No. 1 in b, Op. 20 RCA Gold Seal ▲ 60376-2-RG [ADD] ■ 60376-4-RG (CrO2)
Chopin, F.:Pno Music (misc) CBS ▲ MK 42412 [AAD]
Chopin, F.:Pno Music (misc)—Andante spianato & Grande Polonaise, Op. 22 [rec. 1945]; Ballades No. 1, Op. 23 & No. 4, Op. 52; Barcarolle, Op. 60; Études in G♭, Op. 10/5 & in c♯, Op. 25/7; Polonaise-Fantaisie in A♭, Op. 61; Waltz in A♭, Op. 69/1 [save for the Op. 22, all sels. recorded 1979-1982] RCA Gold Seal ▲ 7752-2-RG (m/s) [ADD/DDD] ■ 7752-4-RG (CrO2)
Chopin, F.:Pno Music (misc)—Études, Op. 10/3-6, 12; Étude in A♭ from Trois Nouvelles Études; Introduction & Rondo in E♭, Op. 16; Mazurkas:in f, Op. 7/3; in a, Op. 17/4; in D♭, Op. 30/3; in D, Op. 33/2; in e, Op. 41/2; in c♯, Op. 50/3; in f♯, Op. 59/3; Polonaises:in A♭, Op. 53; in A, Op. 40/1; Préludes:in b, Op. 28/6; in D, Op. 28/15; Waltzes:in a, Op. 34/2, in c♯, Op. 64/2 *(rec New York, Apr. 14 & May 4, 1971, Ju)* Sony Classical 2-▲ S2K 53468
Chopin, F.:Polonaises—Op. 44 *(rec 1968)* CBS ▲ MK 42412 [AAD]
Chopin, F.:Polonaises—Op. 53 Deutsche Grammophon ▲ 419045-2 [DDD]
Chopin, F.:Polonaises—in f♯, Op. 44 *(rec Jan. 2-Feb. 1, 1968)* Sony Classical ▲ SK 53465 [ADD]
Chopin, F.:Polonaise-fant *(rec 1966)* CBS ▲ MK 42412 [AAD]
Chopin, F.:Polonaise-fant RCA Gold Seal ▲ 09026-61414-2 ■ 09026-61414-4
Chopin, F.:Polonaise-fant CBS ■ MT 30643
Chopin, F.:Scherzos—No. 1 Deutsche Grammophon ▲ 419045-2 [DDD]
Chopin, F.:Scherzos—No. 4, Op. 54 Enterprise ("The Piano Library" series) ▲ ENT 188
Chopin, F.:Scherzos Iron Needle ▲ 1303 (m) [ADD]
Chopin, F.:Son Pno, Op. 35 *(rec 1962)* CBS ▲ MK 42412 [AAD]
Chopin, F.:Son Pno, Op. 35 CBS ▲ MK 44797 [ADD]
Chopin, F.:Son Pno, Op. 35 RCA Gold Seal ▲ 60376-2-RG [ADD] ■ 60376-4-RG (CrO2)
Chopin, F.:Waltzes RCA Gold Seal ▲ 09026-61416-2
Clementi, M.:Sons Pno—Sons., Opp. 14/3, 26/2, 33/3, 34/2 & 47/2 RCA Gold Seal ▲ 7753-2-RC [ADD]
Clementi, M.:Sons Pno—in E♭, Op. 12/2; in B♭, Op. 25/3; in A, Op. 50/1 *(rec New York, June 4 & Sept. 16-23, 196)* Sony Classical ▲ SK 53466 [ADD]
The Complete Masterworks Recordings, Vol. 1:The Studio Recordings 1962-63 *(rec New York, Apr. 18-May 14 & Nov. 6-D)* Sony Classical 2-▲ S2K 53457 [ADD]
Vol. 3:The Historic Return Carnegie Hall 1965/The 1966 Concerts Sony Classical 3-▲ S3K 53461
The Complete RCA Recordings RCA Gold Seal 22-▲ 09026-61655-2
Czerny, C.:Vars on "La Ricordanza" RCA Gold Seal ▲ 60451-2-RG [ADD] ■ 60451-4-RG (CrO2)
Debussy, C.:Etudes—No. 11 *(rec New York, Jan. 7, 1965)* Sony Classical ▲ SK 53471
Debussy, C.:Preludes Pno (sels)—Book 2, No. 7, La terrasse des audiences du clair de lune *(rec New York, Dec. 10, 1966)* Sony Classical ▲ SK 53471
Discovered Treasures Sony Classical ▲ SK 48093 [ADD] ■ ST 48093
Fauré, G.:Nocturnes (13) Pno—No. 13 in b, Op. 119 RCA Gold Seal ▲ 60377-2-RG (m) [ADD] ■ 60377-4-RG (CrO2)
Favorite Encores CBS ▲ MK 42305 [AAD]
Great Musicians In Copenhagen, w. Rudolf Serkin (pno), Wanda Landowska (hpd), Nathan Milstein (vn), Gregor Piatigorsky (vc), Fritz Busch (cnd), Nicolai Malko (cnd) Danacord ▲ DACOCD 303
Great Pianists of the Golden Era:Cortot & Horowitz, w. Cortot, Alfred (pno) Foné ▲ FON 90F12 [DDD]
Haydn, J.:Sons Pno—Sonata in E♭, H.XVI/52 RCA Gold Seal ▲ 60461-2-RG (m) [ADD] ■ 60461-4-RG (CrO2)
Haydn, J.:Sons Pno—Son. in C, H.XVI/48 *(rec Philadelphia, Dec. 1, 1968)* Sony Classical ▲ SK 53466 [ADD]
Horowitz at Home Deutsche Grammophon ▲ 427772-2 GH [DDD] ■ 427772-4 GH (D)

INSTRUMENT.

Horowitz, Vladimir (pno) (cont.)
Horowitz Encores RCA Gold Seal ▲ 7755-2-RG (m) [ADD] ■ 7755-4-RG
Horowitz:The Solo Recordings Deutsche Grammophon 3-▲ 427269-2 GH3 [DDD]
Horowitz the Poet Deutsche Grammophon ▲ 435025-2 GH [DDD]
Horowitz, V.:Vars on a Theme from Bizet's *Carmen* *(rec Jan. 2-Feb. 1, 1968)* Sony Classical ▲ SK 53465 [ADD]
In Moscow Deutsche Grammophon ▲ 419499-2 GH [DDD] ■ 419499-4 GH (D)
Kabalevsky, D.:Son 3 Pno RCA Gold Seal ▲ 60377-2-RG (m) [ADD] ■ 60377-4-RG (CrO2)
The Last Recording:Oct. 20–Nov. 1, 1989 Sony Classical ▲ SK 45818 [DDD] Δ SM 45818 [DDD]; ■ ST 45818 (CrO2)
Liszt, F.:Ballades Pno—No. 2 RCA Red Seal ▲ 09026-61415-2
Liszt, F.:Ballade 2 Pno RCA Gold Seal ▲ 09026-61416-2 ■ 09026-61416-4
Liszt, F.:Consolations—No. 2 *(rec New York, May 9, 1962)* Sony Classical ▲ SK 53471
Liszt, F.:Consolations—No. 3 RCA Red Seal ▲ 09026-61415-2
Liszt, F.:Harmonies poétiques et religieuses—Funérailles Enterprise ("The Piano Library" series) ▲ ENT 188
Liszt, F.:Harmonies poétiques et religieuses—Funérailles RCA Red Seal ▲ 09026-61415-2
Liszt, F.:Mephisto Waltz 3 Pno RCA Red Seal ▲ 09026-61415-2
Liszt, F.:Pno Music (misc)—Au bord d'une source; Hungarian Rhapsody No. 2; Sonata No. 104 del Petrarca RCA Gold Seal ▲ 60523-2-RG [ADD] ■ 60523-4-RG (CrO2)
Liszt, F.:Scherzo & March *(rec New York, Oct. 22, 1967)* Sony Classical ▲ SK 53471
Liszt, F.:Son Pno RCA Red Seal ▲ 09026-61415-2
Liszt, F.:Son Pno Iron Needle ▲ 1303 (m) [ADD]
Liszt, F.:Son Pno Enterprise ("The Piano Library" series) ▲ ENT 188
Liszt, F.:Sonetti del Petrarca Pno—No. 104 Deutsche Grammophon ▲ 419499-2 [DDD] ■ 419499-4
Medtner, N.:Fairy Tales, Op. 51—No. 3, Fairy Tale in A *(rec New York, June 12, 1969)* Sony Classical ▲ SK 53472
Mendelssohn, F.:Etudes Pno—No. 3 *(rec New York, Nov. 26, 1967)* Sony Classical ▲ SK 53471
Mendelssohn, F.:Vars sérieuses RCA Gold Seal ▲ 60451-2-RG [ADD] ■ 60451-4-RG (CrO2)
Mozart, W.A.:Adagio Pno, K.540 Deutsche Grammophon ("Masters" series) ▲ 445517-2 [DDD]
Mozart, W.A.:Con 23 Pno, w. A. Giulini (cnd), La Scala Orch Deutsche Grammophon ▲ 423287-2 [DDD] ■ 423287-4
Mozart, W.A.:Rondo Pno, K.485 Deutsche Grammophon ("Masters" series) ▲ 445517-2 [DDD]
Mozart, W.A.:Son 3 Pno Deutsche Grammophon ("3D Classics" series) ▲ 431274-2 [DDD]
Mozart, W.A.:Son 3 Pno Deutsche Grammophon ("Masters" series) ▲ 445517-2 [DDD]
Mozart, W.A.:Son 10 Pno Deutsche Grammophon ▲ 419499-2 [DDD] ■ 419499-4
Mozart, W.A.:Son 10 Pno Deutsche Grammophon ▲ 419045-2 [DDD]
Mozart, W.A.:Son 10 Pno Deutsche Grammophon ("3D Classics" series) ▲ 431274-2 [DDD]
Mozart, W.A.:Son 10 Pno Deutsche Grammophon ("Masters" series) ▲ 445517-2 [DDD]
Mozart, W.A.:Son 11 Pno CBS ▲ MK 44797 [ADD]
Mozart, W.A.:Son 12 Pno RCA Gold Seal ▲ 60451-2 [ADD] ■ 60451-4 (CrO2)
Mozart, W.A.:Son 13 Pno Deutsche Grammophon ("Masters" series) ▲ 445517-2 [DDD]
Mozart, W.A.:Son 13 Pno Deutsche Grammophon ("3D Classics" series) ▲ 431274-2 [DDD]
Mozart, W.A.:Son 13 Pno Deutsche Grammophon ▲ 423287-2 [DDD] ■ 423287-4
Mussorgsky, M.:Pictures at an Exhibition [performer's solo piano arr.] RCA Gold Seal ▲ 60449-2-RG (m) [ADD] ■ 60449-4-RG (CrO2)
Mussorgsky, M.:Pictures at an Exhibition [performer's solo piano arr.] RCA Gold Seal ▲ 60321-2-RG ■ 60321-4-RG
Mussorgsky, M.:Pictures at an Exhibition RCA Gold Seal ▲ 09026-60526-2 ■ 09026-60526-4
Plays Bach, w. Nathan Milstein (vn) RCA Gold Seal ▲ 60461-2-RG (m) [ADD]
A Portrait of Vladimir Horowitz *(rec 1962-72)* CBS ▲ MK 44797 [ADD]
Poulenc, F.:Presto Pno RCA Gold Seal ▲ 60377-2-RG (m) [ADD] ■ 60377-4-RG (CrO2)
Prokofiev, S.:Son 7 Pno RCA Gold Seal ▲ 60377-2-RG (m) [ADD] ■ 60377-4-RG (CrO2)
Prokofiev, S.:Toccata Pno RCA Gold Seal ▲ 60377-2-RG (m) [ADD] ■ 60377-4-RG (CrO2)
Rachmaninoff, S.:Con 3 Pno, w. E. Ormandy (cnd), New York PO RCA Red Seal ▲ 09026-61564-2
Rachmaninoff, S.:Con 3 Pno, w. F. Reiner (cnd), RCA Victor SO RCA Gold Seal ▲ 7754-2-RC [ADD] ■ 7754-4-RC (CrO2)
Rachmaninoff, S.:Pno Music (misc)—Moment musical, Op. 16, No. 2; Polka; Prelude, Op. 32, No. 5; Piano Con. 3; Piano Son. 2 RCA Gold Seal ▲ 7754-2-RC [ADD] ■ 7754-4-RC (CrO2)
Rachmaninoff, S.:Pno Music (misc)—Études-Tableau:in C, Op. 33/2; in e♭, Op. 33/5; in D, Op. 39; Moments musicaux in b, Op. 16/3; Prélude in g#, Op. 32/12; Son. for Piano No. 2 in b♭, Op. 36 *(rec Washington D.C. & New York)* Sony Classical ▲ SK 53472
Rachmaninoff, S.:Preludes Pno, Opp 23 & 32 RCA Gold Seal ▲ 09026-61416-2 ■ 09026-61416-4
Rachmaninoff, S.:Son 2 Pno RCA Gold Seal ▲ 7754-2-RC [ADD] ■ 7754-4-RC (CrO2)
Recital Deutsche Grammophon ▲ 419045-2 GH [DDD]
Rossini, G.:Sons Str Qt, w. A. Toscanini (cnd), NBC SO—No. 3 [arr unknown] Stradivarius ▲ STV 13595 [AAD]
Scarlatti, D.:Sons Kbd—in E, K.380 *(rec Jan. 2-Feb. 1, 1968)* Sony Classical ▲ SK 53465 [ADD]
Scarlatti, D.:Sons Kbd—in d, K.33; in a, K.54; in F, K.525; in f, K.466; in G, K.146; in D, K.96 [Allegro]; in E, K.162 [Andante e cantabile]; in E♭, K.474 [Andante e cantabile]; in e, K.198 [Allegro]; in D, K.491 [Allegro]; in f, K.481 [Andante e cantabile]; in A, K Sony Classical ▲ SK 53460 [ADD]
Scarlatti, D.:Sons Kbd—in G, K.260; in F#, K.319 *(rec New York, Nov. 6-Dec. 18, 1962)* Sony Classical ▲ SK 53466 [ADD]
Schubert, Franz:Impromptus Pno (comp)—Op. 90/2, 4; Op. 142/1-2 *(rec New York, Jan. 10-24, 1973)* Sony Classical ▲ SK 53471
Schubert, Franz:Impromptus Pno, D.899—No. 3 in G♭ RCA Gold Seal ▲ 60523-2-RG [ADD] ■ 60523-4-RG (CrO2)
Schubert, Franz:Son Pno, D.960 RCA Gold Seal ▲ 60451-2-RG [ADD] ■ 60451-4-RG (CrO2)
Schubert, Franz:Son Pno, D.960 *(rec studio, New York 1986)* Deutsche Grammophon ▲ 435025-2 [DDD] □ 435025-5
Schumann, R.:Arabeske Pno *(rec Jan. 2-Feb. 1, 1968)* Sony Classical ▲ SK 53465 [ADD]
Schumann, R.:Arabeske Pno *(rec 1968)* CBS ▲ MK 42409 [AAD]
Schumann, R.:Blumenstück *(rec 1966)* CBS ▲ MK 42409 [AAD]
Schumann, R.:Fantasiestücke Pno, Op. 111 RCA Gold Seal ▲ 6680-2-RC [ADD] ■ 6680-4-RC (CrO2)
Schumann, R.:Humoreske Pno RCA Gold Seal ▲ 6680-2-RC [ADD] ■ 6680-4-RC (CrO2)
Schumann, R.:Kinderszenen CBS ▲ MK 42409 [AAD]
Schumann, R.:Kinderszenen *(rec live, Vienna 1987)* Deutsche Grammophon ▲ 435025-2 [DDD] □ 435025-5
Schumann, R.:Kinderszenen RCA Gold Seal ▲ 09026-61414-2 ■ 09026-61414-4
Schumann, R.:Kinderszenen—No. 7, "Träumerei" *(rec Jan. 2-Feb. 1, 1968)* Sony Classical ▲ SK 53465 [ADD]
Schumann, R.:Kreisleriana *(rec 1969)* CBS ▲ MK 42409 [AAD]
Schumann, R.:Kreisleriana *(rec New York, Dec. 1, 1969)* Sony Classical 2-▲ S2K 53468
Schumann, R.:Kreisleriana Deutsche Grammophon ▲ 419217-2 [DDD]
Schumann, R.:Son Pno, Op. 14—Vars. on a theme by Clara Wieck *(rec New York, Feb. 5, 1969)* Sony Classical 2-▲ S2K 53468
Schumann, R.:Son Pno, Op. 14 RCA Gold Seal ▲ 6680-2-RC [ADD] ■ 6680-4-RC (CrO2)
Schumann, R.:Toccata Pno Odyssey ▲ MBK 42534
Schumann, R.:Toccata Pno CBS ▲ MK 42409 [AAD]
Scriabin, A.:Etudes Pno, Op. 8—No. 12 in d# *(rec Jan. 2-Feb. 1, 1968)* Sony Classical ▲ SK 53465 [ADD]
Scriabin, A.:Etudes Pno, Op. 8—Nos. 7 & 12 RCA Gold Seal ▲ 6215-2-RG [ADD] ■ 6215-4-RG
Scriabin, A.:Etudes Pno, Op. 8—No. 12 RCA Gold Seal ▲ 09026-61414-2 ■ 09026-61414-4
Scriabin, A.:Etudes Pno, Op. 42—No. 5 RCA Gold Seal ▲ 6215-2-RG [ADD] ■ 6215-4-RG
Scriabin, A.:Pno Music (misc)—Etudes:Op. 8/2, 8, 10, 11; Op. 42/3-5; Op. 65/3; Feuillett d'album in E♭, Op. 45/1; Feuillet d'album, Op. 58; 2 Poèmes, Op. 69; Vers la flamme, Op. 72 *(rec New York, Apr. 27-May 31, 1972)* Sony Classical ▲ SK 53472

Horowitz, Vladimir (pno) (cont.)
Scriabin, A.:Pno Music (misc)—3 Etudes—Op. 8/7 & 12; Op. 42/5; 16 Preludes—Op. 11/1,3,9,10,13,14 & 16; Op. 13/6; Op. 15/2; Op. 16/1 & 4; Op. 27/1; Op. 48/3; Op. 51/2; Op. 59/2; Op. 67/1 RCA Gold Seal ▲ 6215-2-RG [ADD] ■ 6215-4-RG (CrO2)
Scriabin, A.:Preludes Pno (misc)—Op. 11, Nos. 1,3,9,10,13,14 & 16; Op. 13/6; Op. 15/2; Op. 16/1 & 4; Op. 27/1; Op. 48/3; Op. 51/2; Op. 59/2; Op. 67/1 RCA Gold Seal ▲ 6215-2-RG [ADD] ■ 6215-4-RG
Scriabin, A.:Son 3 Pno RCA Gold Seal ▲ 6215-2-RG [ADD] ■ 6215-4-RG (CrO2)
Scriabin, A.:Son 5 Pno RCA Gold Seal ▲ 6215-2-RG [ADD] ■ 6215-4-RG (CrO2)
Scriabin, A.:Son 9 Pno RCA Gold Seal ▲ 09026-60526-2 ■ 09026-60526-4
Sousa, J.P.:Stars & Stripes Forever (arr pno) *(rec studio, late 1940s)* RCA Gold Seal ▲ 7755-2-RG (m) [ADD] ■ 7755-4-RG (CrO2)
Studio Recordings, 1985 Deutsche Grammophon ▲ 419217-2 GH [DDD]
Tchaikovsky, P.:Con 1 Pno, w. A. Toscanini (cnd), NBC SO *(rec Carnegie Hall, 4/25/43)* Melodram ▲ MEL 18014
Tchaikovsky, P.:Con 1 Pno, w. A. Toscanini (cnd), NBC SO RCA Gold Seal ▲ 60319-2-RG ■ 60319-4-RG
Tchaikovsky, P.:Con 1 Pno, w. A. Toscanini (cnd), NBC SO *(rec 1943 broadcast performanc)* RCA Gold Seal ▲ 60321-2-RG ■ 60321-4-RG
Tchaikovsky, P.:Con 1 Pno, w. A. Toscanini (cnd), NBC SO RCA Gold Seal ▲ 60449-2-RG (m) [ADD] ■ 60449-4-RG (CrO2)
Tchaikovsky, P.:Con 1 Pno, w. A. Toscanini (cnd), NBC SO *(rec Carnegie Hall, 4/25/43)* RCA Gold Seal ▲ 7992-2-RG (m) [ADD] ■ 7992-4-RG (CrO2)
Tchaikovsky, P.:Con 1 Pno, w. B. Walter (cnd), New York PO *(rec live, Apr. 11, 1948)* As Disc ▲ ASD 2400 (m)
Vladimir Horowitz RCA Gold Seal ▲ 09026-60986-2
Vladimir Horowitz RCA Gold Seal ▲ 09026-60526-2
Vladimir Horowitz RCA Gold Seal ▲ 09026-60463-2
Vladimir Horowitz at La Scala *(rec live)* Artists ▲ ART FED 62 [ADD]
Vladimir Horowitz:The Complete Masterworks Recordings, 1962-73 Sony Classical 13-▲ SX13K 53456 [ADD]
Vladimir Horowitz:The Private Collection RCA Red Seal ▲ 09026-62643-2

Hörr, Peter (vc)—see also ORCHESTRAS & ENSEMBLES Ravinia Trio
Brahms, J.:Son 2 Vc, w. S. Sasaki (pno) Divox ▲ CDX 29106 [DDD]
Jenner, G.:Son Vc Divox ▲ CDX 29106 [DDD]

Horrocks, J. (hn)
Pinkston, R.:Qt for 4 Hns, w. T. Bacon (hn), J. Landsman (hn), N. Goodearl (hn) Summit ▲ DCD 135 [DDD]

Horsley, Colin (pno)
Debussy, C.:Son Vn, w. M. Rostal (vn) *(rec 1957 EMI recording)* Symposium ▲ 1076
Schubert, Franz:Fant Vn, D.934, w. M. Rostal (vn) *(rec 1957 for EMI)* Symposium ▲ 1076
Schubert, Franz:Rondo Vn, D.895, w. M. Rostal (vn) *(rec 1957)* Symposium ▲ 1068
Schubert, Franz:Son Vn, D.574, w. M. Rostal (vn) *(rec 1957)* Symposium ▲ 1068
Schubert, Franz:Sonatinas Vn, w. M. Rostal (vn) *(rec 1957)* Symposium ▲ 1068
Schumann, R.:Son 1 Vn, w. M. Rostal (vn) *(rec 1957 for EMI)* Symposium ▲ 1076
Stravinsky, I.:Duo Concertant, w. M. Rostal (vn) *(rec 1957 EMI)* Symposium ▲ 1076

Horst, Claar Ter (pno)
Wolf, H.:Goethe-Lieder (sels), w. Locky Chung (bar), Markus Hadulla (pno), Stephan Genz (bar)—24 sels Claves ▲ 50-9517

Horstmann, Thomas (gtr)—see ORCHESTRAS & ENSEMBLES LTD Trio

Horszowski, Mieczyslav (pno)
Bach, J.S.:English Suites—BWV 810 Elektra/Nonesuch ▲ 79232-2
Bach, J.S.:French Suites—BWV 817 *(rec recital at the Théâtre des Champs-Elysées, Oct 8, 1989)* Thésis ▲ THC 82039 [DDD]
Bach, J.S.:Sons Vl, BWV 1027-1029, w. P. Casals (vc)—BWV 1027 *(rec live, July 8, 1956)* Music & Arts 4-▲ CD 689 (m) [AAD]
Bach, J.S.:Sons Vl, BWV 1027-1029, w. Pablo Casals (vc)—No. 1 in G; No. 2 in D Andromeda ▲ ANR 2524
Bach, J.S.:Das wohltemperierte Klavier—[Book 2] sels. *(rec live, 1956)* Music & Arts 4-▲ CD 689 (m) [AAD]
Bach, J.S.:Das wohltemperierte Klavier—Book 1 *(rec 1979-80)* Vanguard Classics 2-▲ OVC 8046/47 [ADD]
Beethoven, L. van:Qt Pno, Op. 16, w. Budapest String Quartet members *(rec Apr 7, 1955)* Bridge ("Great Performances from the Library of Congress" series) ▲ BRI 9067
Beethoven, L. van:Son 4 Vc, w. Pablo Casals (vc) *(rec London, 1936)* Iron Needle ▲ IN 1308
Beethoven, L. van:Son 5 Vc, w. P. Casals (vc) *(rec live June 1953)* Music & Arts 4-▲ CD 688 (m) [AAD]
Beethoven, L. van:Son 5 Vc, w. Pablo Casals (vc) *(rec 1953)* Historical Performers ▲ HPS 31
Beethoven, L. van:Son 2 Pno Elektra/Nonesuch ▲ 79160-2 [DDD]
Beethoven, L. van:Son 6 Pno Elektra/Nonesuch ▲ 79232-2
Beethoven, L. van:Son 6 Pno *(rec in recital at the Théâtre des Champs-Elysées, 10/8/89)* Thésis ▲ THC 82039 [DDD]
Beethoven, L. van:Son 26 Pno, "Les Adieux" Relief 4-▲ CR 911020-23
Beethoven, L. van:Sons 28-32 Pno, "The Late Sons" Relief 4-▲ CR 911020-23
Beethoven, L. van:Son 29 Pno, "Hammerklavier" Vox Box ("Legends" series) 2-▲ CDX2 5500 (m) [ADD]
Beethoven, L. van:Son 30 Pno Vox Box ("Legends" series) 2-▲ CDX2 5500 (m) [ADD]
Beethoven, L. van:Son 31 Pno *(rec live 1958)* Pearl 2-▲ PEA 9979 (m/s) [AAD]
Beethoven, L. van:Son 32 Pno Vox Box ("Legends" series) 2-▲ CDX2 5500 (m) [ADD]
Beethoven, L. van:Son 5 Vn, "Spring", w. J. Szigeti (vn) *(rec 1953)* Sony Masterworks ("Portrait" series) ▲ MPK 52536 (m) [AAD]
Beethoven, L. van:Son 6 Vn, w. J. Szigeti (vn) *(rec 1953)* Sony Masterworks ("Portrait" series) ▲ MPK 52569 (m) [ADD]
Beethoven, L. van:Trio 6 Pno, "Archduke", w. Sandor Végh (vn), Pablo Casals (vc) *(rec 1956)* Historical Performers ▲ HPS 31
Beethoven, L. van:Vars on "Ein Mädchen oder Weibchen" from Mozart's *Die Zauberflöte*, w. P. Casals (vc) AS Disc (Notes) ▲ ASDPGP 11032 [ADD]
Beethoven, L. van:Vars on a waltz by Diabelli, Op. 120 *(rec live 1982)* Pearl 2-▲ PEA 9979 (m/s) [AAD]
Beethoven, L. van:Vars on a waltz by Diabelli, Op. 120 Vox Box ("Legends" series) 2-▲ CDX2 5511 [ADD]
Beethoven, L. van:Vars on a waltz by Diabelli, Op. 120 Relief 4-▲ CR 911020-23
Brahms, J.:Sons Vc (comp), w. P. Casals (vc) Pearl 4-▲ PEAS 9935 (m) [AAD]
Brahms, J.:Son 2 Vc, w. P. Casals (vc) *(rec 1936 for HMV)* Pearl ▲ PEA 9363 (m) [AAD]
Brahms, J.:Son 2 Vc, w. Pablo Casals (vc) *(rec 1936)* Iron Needle ▲ IN 1308
Busoni, F.:Son 2 Vn, w. J. Szigeti (vn) *(rec 1956)* Sony Masterworks ("Portrait" series) ▲ MPK 52537 (m) [ADD]
Chopin, F.:Con 1 Pno, w. H. Swarowsky (cnd), Vienna State Opera Orch Relief 4-▲ CR 911020-23
Chopin, F.:Con 1 Pno, w. H. Swarowsky (cnd), Vienna SO Vox Box ("Legends" series) 2-▲ CDX2 5511 [ADD]
Chopin, F.:Fant Relief 4-▲ CR 911020-23
Chopin, F.:Impromptus Vox Box ("Legends" series) 2-▲ CDX2 5511 [ADD]
Chopin, F.:Impromptus Relief 4-▲ CR 911020-23
Chopin, F.:Nocturnes—Opp. 15/2, 27/2 Elektra/Nonesuch ▲ 79160-2 [DDD]
Chopin, F.:Nocturnes—Op. 9/2 & Op. 32/1 Elektra/Nonesuch ▲ 79232-2
Chopin, F.:Pno Music (misc)—Fantaisie in f, Op. 49; Nouvelle Etude in f; Polonaise in c, Op. 40/1 Pearl 2-▲ PEA 9979 (m/s) [AAD]

▲ = CD ♦ = Enhanced CD Δ = MD ■ = Cassette Tape □ = DCC

Horszowski, Mieczyslav (pno) (cont.)
Chopin, F.:Pno Music (misc)—Impromptu No. 2 in F#, Op. 36; Nocturne in E♭, Op. 9/2; "Raindrop" Prelude in D♭, Op. 28/15; Waltz in c#, Op. 64/2 *(rec in recital at the Théâtre des Champs-Elysées, 10/8/89)* Thésis ▲ THC 82039 [DDD]
Chopin, F.:Polonaises—Op. 40/2 Relief 4–▲ CR 911020–23
Debussy, C.:Children's Corner Elektra/Nonesuch ▲ 79160–2 [DDD]
Haydn, J.:Trios Pno, Vn & Vc, w. Budapest String Quartet members—Rondo all'Ongarese [from Trio in G] *(rec Apr 7, 1955)* Bridge ("Great Performances from the Library of Congress" series) ▲ BRI 9067
The Horszowski Collection Pearl 2–▲ PEA 9979 (m/s) [AAD]
Horszowski in Concert *(rec Comédie des Champs-Elysées 6/1/87 & 10/5/87)* Thésis ▲ THC 82008 [DDD]
In Recital at the Théâtre des Champs-Elysées *(rec Oct 8, 1989)* Thésis ▲ THC 82039 [DDD]
Mendelssohn, F.:Trio 1 Pno, w. Alexander Schneider (vn), Pablo Casals (vc) *(rec White House, Washington, D.C., Nov 13, 1961)* Sony Classical ▲ SMK 66571 [ADD]
Mozart, W.A.:Ch'io mi scordi di te, w. J. Tourel (mez), P. Casals (cnd), Perpignan Festival Orch *(rec Perpignan, France, July 15–16, 1951)* Sony Classical ("The Casals Edition" series) ▲ SMK 58984 [ADD]
Mozart, W.A.:Con 9 Pno, w. F. Waldman (cnd), Musica Aeterna *(rec 1962–72)* Pearl 2–▲ PEA 9138 [ADD]
Mozart, W.A.:Con 12 Pno, w. F. Waldman (cnd), Musica Aeterna *(rec 1962–72)* Pearl 2–▲ PEA 9138 [ADD]
Mozart, W.A.:Con 13 Pno, w. F. Waldman (cnd), Musica Aeterna *(rec 1962–72)* Pearl 2–▲ PEA 9138 [ADD]
Mozart, W.A.:Con 14 Pno, w. F. Waldman (cnd), Musica Aeterna *(rec 1962–72)* Pearl 2–▲ PEA 9138 [ADD]
Mozart, W.A.:Con 17 Pno, w. F. Waldman (cnd), Musica Aeterna Pearl 2–▲ PEA 9153 [ADD]
Mozart, W.A.:Con 18 Pno, w. F. Waldman (cnd), Musica Aeterna Pearl 2–▲ PEA 9153 [ADD]
Mozart, W.A.:Con 19 Pno, w. F. Waldman (cnd), Musica Aeterna *(rec 1962–72)* Pearl 2–▲ PEA 9138 [ADD]
Mozart, W.A.:Con 20 Pno, w. F. Waldman (cnd), Musica Aeterna Pearl 2–▲ PEA 9153 [ADD]
Mozart, W.A.:Con 22 Pno, w. F. Waldman (cnd), Musica Aeterna Pearl 2–▲ PEA 9153 [ADD]
Mozart, W.A.:Con 27 Pno, w. P. Casals (cnd), Perpignan Festival Orch *(rec Perpignan, France, July 10–17, 1951)* Sony Classical ("The Casals Edition" series) ▲ SMK 58984 [ADD]
Mozart, W.A.:Fant Pno, K.397 Elektra/Nonesuch ▲ 79160–2 [DDD]
Mozart, W.A.:Fant Pno, K.475, w. F. Waldman (cnd), Musica Aeterna Pearl 2–▲ PEA 9153 [ADD]
Mozart, W.A.:Qts Pno, w. Budapest String Quartet members—K.478 Sony Classical 3–▲ SM3K 46527
Mozart, W.A.:Qt Pno, K.493, w. Y. Menuhin (vn), W. Wallfisch (va), P. Casals (vc) *(rec live, Prades Festival, July 7, 1956)* Music & Arts 4–▲ CD 688 (m) [AAD]
Mozart, W.A.:Sons Pno—Nos 1–8 Arbiter 2–▲ 101 [ADD]
Mozart, W.A.:Son 15 Pno *(rec 1962–72)* Pearl 2–▲ PEA 9138 [ADD]
Mozart, W.A.:Vars Pno, K.455 *(rec live 1969)* Pearl 2–▲ PEA 9979 (m/s) [AAD]
The 1940 Vatican Radio Recordings & Live USA Recordings, 1957–79 Pearl 2–▲ PEA 9108 [ADD]
Schubert, Franz:Qnt Pno, D.667, w. J. Levine (db), Budapest String Quartet members Sony Classical ("Essential Classics" series) ▲ SBK 46343 [ADD] ■ SBT 46343
Schubert, Franz:Son Pno, D.958 *(rec live 1971)* Pearl 2–▲ PEA 9979 (m/s) [AAD]
Schubert, Franz:Trio 2 Pno, w. A. Schneider (vn), P. Casals (vc) *(rec Prades, France, July 5–6, 1952)* Sony Classical ("The Casals Edition" series) ▲ SMK 58988 [ADD]
Schumann, R.:Papillons *(rec in recital at the Théâtre des Champs-Elysées, 10/8/89)* Thésis ▲ THC 82039 [DDD]
Schumann, R.:Trio 1 Pno, w. A. Schneider (vn), P. Casals (vc) *(rec Prades, France, July 4, 1952)* Sony Classical ("The Casals Edition" series) ▲ SMK 58993 [ADD]
Schumann, R.:Trio 1 Pno, w. J. Szigeti (vn), R. von Tobel (vc) *(rec live 1956)* Music & Arts 4–▲ CD 689 (m) [AAD]
Schumann, R.:Trio 2 Pno, w. Y. Menuhin (vn), P. Casals (vc) *(rec live 1950s)* Music & Arts 4–▲ CD 689 (m) [AAD]

Hörth, Harald (ob)—see ORCHESTRAS & ENSEMBLES Vienna Quintet

Hörtnagel, Georg (db)
Schubert, Franz:Qnt Pno, D.667, w. E. Leonskaja (pno), Alban Berg String Quartet EMI Classics ▲ CDC 47448
Schubert, Franz:Qnt Pno, D.667, w. S. Rhodes (va), Beaux Arts Trio Philips ▲ 420716–2 [ADD]

Horváth, Anikó (hpd)
Albero, S.:Sons (30) Hpd *(rec Nov 23–25, 1995)* Hungaroton ▲ HCD 31621 [DDD]

Horváth, János (vn)—see ORCHESTRAS & ENSEMBLES Haydn String Quartet Budapest, New Haydn String Quartet

Horváth, László (cl)
Molter, J.M.:Cons Cl, Erkel CO—Nos. 1–5 *(rec 1990)* Hungaroton ▲ HCD 31370 [DDD]

Horvitz, Wayne (syn)
Sharp, E.:20 Below, w. Anthony Coleman (toy pno/org), Zeena Parkins (org/syn), Joseph Paul Taylor (elec/syn), Gwen Toth (reed org), David Weinstein (org/syn) Newport Classics ▲ NPD 85504

Hošek, Jiří (vc)
Kraft, A.:Con Vc, Op 4, w. J. Hrnčíř (cnd), Prague SO *(rec Smetana Hall of Prague's City House, Apr 11, 12 & 28, 1989)* Panton ▲ 811024–2 [DDD]
Kraft, A.:Con Vc, "Seydel's Con", w. J. Hrnčíř (cnd), Prague SO *(rec Smetana Hall of Prague's City House, Apr 11, 12 & 28, 1989)* Panton ▲ 811024–2 [DDD]
Kraft, N.:Polonaise Strs, w. J. Hrnčíř (cnd), Prague SO *(rec Smetana Hall of Prague's City House, Apr 11, 12 & 28, 1989)* Panton ▲ 811024–2 [DDD]

Hosford, Richard (cl)
Mozart, W.A.:Trio Cl, K.498, w. Domus Chamber Ensemble Virgin Classics ▲ 59063 [DDD]

Hoshido, Mikio (gtr)
Miyoshi, A.:Music of, w. Okada Percussion Ensemble—Constellation Noire for Gtr & Str Qt; Protase de Loin a Rien for 2 Gtrs; 5 Poems for Gtr; Epitase for Gtr on IXTACCHIHUATL Camerata ▲ 32CM 105

Hoskin, Paul (b cl)
Exquisite Corpses from P.S. 122, w. David Watson (shears/stick vn/gtr/tpt), Judy Dunaway (gtr/balloons), Anthony Coleman (sampler), Raissa St. Pierre (drums), Guy Yarden (vn/pno), Leslie Ross (bn), Linda Austin (gtr), Bruce Kaplan (gtr), Doug Henderson (peckhorn/bass/toy pno), Sue Ann Harkey (gtr), Cinnie Cole (sampler), et al. ¿What Next? ▲ WN 0002 [ADD]

Hoskovec, Václav (db)
Mysliveček, J.:Sons en Trio, w. Jan Sirc (vc), Radomír Sirc (vc), Robert Hugo (hpd) Studio Matous ▲ MAT 19 [DDD]
Zelenka, J.D.:Trio Sons Obs, w. Jana Brozková (ob), Vojtech Jouza (ob), Jan Jouza (vn), Jaroslav Kubita (bn), Frantisek Xaver Thuri (hpd)—Nos. 1–3 Studio Matous ▲ MAT 8 [DDD]
Zelenka, J.D.:Trio Sons Obs, w. Jana Brozková (ob), Vojtech Jouza (ob), Jaroslav Kubita (bn), Frantisek Xaver Thuri (hpd)—Nos. 4–6, ZWV 181 Studio Matous ▲ MAT 9 [DDD]

Hosley, Kenneth (perc)—see ORCHESTRAS & ENSEMBLES Contemporary Chamber Ensemble

Hospach-Martini, Mario (org)
Basilika Birnau:Duette für Orgel, w. S. J. Bleicher (org) *(rec June 7–8, 1993)* Orfeo ▲ 341941 [DDD]

Host, František (vc)—see also ORCHESTRAS & ENSEMBLES Duo di Basso, Suk String Quartet
Haydn, J.:Con 1 Vc, w. P. Škvor (cnd), Dvořák CO Panton ▲ PAN 810829
Haydn, J.:Con 2 Vc, w. P. Škvor (cnd), Dvořák CO Panton ▲ PAN 810829

Hostetter, P. (perc)
Levinson, G.:Dreamlight, w. A. Emelianoff (vc), P. Basquin (pno), B. Ramirez (perc) CRI ▲ CD 642 [DDD]

Hostettler, J. (perc)
Gaudibert, E.:Feuillages, w. S. Borel (perc), M. Favrod (perc) Gallo ▲ CD 630 [AAD]

Hostettler, Nicole (hpd)
Bach, J.S.:Cons Hpd, BWV 1052–1058, w. C. Jaccottet (hpd), C. Sartoretti (hpd), L. Klinckerfus (hpd), J. Faerber (cnd), Württemberg CO *(rec 1978)* Vox Box 3–▲ CD3X 3018 [ADD]

Hostettler, Nicole (hpd) (cont.)
Bach, J.S.:Cons for 2 Hpds (comp), w. C. Jaccottet (hpd), C. Sartoretti (hpd), L. Klinckerfus (hpd), J. Faerber (cnd), Württemberg CO *(rec 1978)* Vox Box 3–▲ CD3X 3018 [ADD]
Bach, J.S.:Cons for 3 Hpds (comp), w. C. Jaccottet (hpd), C. Sartoretti (hpd), L. Klinckerfus (hpd), J. Faerber (cnd), Württemberg CO *(rec 1978)* Vox Box 3–▲ CD3X 3018 [ADD]

Høst-Madsen, Ulrikke (vc)—see ORCHESTRAS & ENSEMBLES Tre Musici

Hotéev, Andréi (pno)
Tchaikovsky, P.:Con 3 Pno, w. R. Martynov (cnd), St. Petersburg State SO Accord ▲ ACD 202752 [DDD]
Tchaikovsky, P.:Dumka:Russian Rustic Scene Accord ▲ ACD 202752 [DDD]

Houbart, François-Henri (hpd)
Bach, J.S.:Org Music (misc)—Chorales from BWV 599, 602, 614, 686, 688; Prelude & Fugue, BWV 546–548 *(rec Feb 1984)* Pierre Verany ▲ PV.784061 [DDD]
Poulenc, F.:Concert champêtre for Hpd, w. M. Soustrot (cnd), Loire PO Pierre Verany ▲ PV.791011 [DDD]

Houbart, François-Henri (org)
Bach, J.S.:Passacaglia & Fugue Org Forlane 2–▲ FRL 16686 [DDD]
Bach, J.S.:Trio Sons Org, BWV 525–530 Forlane 2–▲ FRL 16686 [DDD]
Brass & Organ at the Church of the Madeleine, w. Concert Arban Brass Quintet, Francis Petit (perc) Pierre Verany ▲ 785096 [DDD]
Franck, C.:Pièce héroïque *(rec 10/84)* Pierre Verany ▲ PV.785031 [DDD]
Gervaise, C.:Danceries, w. Bernard Soustrot (tpt)—7 sels Forlane ▲ FRL 16732 [DDD]
Great Heroic Pieces, w. Concert Arban Pierre Verany ("Favourites" series) ▲ 730015 [DDD]
Handel, G.F.:Cons (16) Org, w. B. Soustrot (tpt)—No. 13 in F [The Cuckoo & the Nightingale] Forlane ▲ FRL 16732 [DDD]
Liszt, F.:Psalm 129, w. Lionel Peintre (bar), Yves Parmentier (cnd), French Army Chorus Adès ▲ ADE 203032
Liszt, F.:Requiem, w. Jacques Maresch (ten), Daniel Galvez-Vallejo (ten), Lionel Peintre (bar), Bertrand Bontoux (bass), Y. Parmentier (cnd), Republican Guard Brass & Percussion, French Army Chorus Adès ▲ ADE 203032
Loeillet, J.-B.:Sons (misc), w. Bernard Soustrot (tpt)—in d for Tpt & Org Forlane ▲ FRL 16732 [DDD]
Nivers, G.G.:Motets, w. Fanjat (sop), J. Nicolas (sop), Boraly (sgr), Malardenti (sgr), Maréchal (sgr)—Motet a la Sainte Vierge pour le temps de Paques; Motet pour L'Elévation; Motet pour le Saint Sacrament; Motet du temps de carême pour le Saint Sacrement; Motet du temps de Noël pour le Saint Sacrement; Motet final du tout office pour le Roy [L] Pierre Verany ▲ PV.791101 [DDD]
Nivers, G.G.:Org Music—Litanies a la Vierge Marie; Suites from Books 1 & 3 Pierre Verany ▲ PV.791101 [DDD]
Omourtet, J.-J.:Première Suite, w. Bernard Soustrot (tpt) Forlane ▲ FRL 16732 [DDD]
Poulenc, F.:Con Org, w. M. Soustrot (cnd), Loire PO Pierre Verany ▲ PV.791011 [DDD]
Ropartz, G.:Messe in the Honor of St. Anne, w. Michel Piquemal (cnd), French Vittoria Regional Choir Accord ▲ ACD 205132 [DDD]
Telemann, G.P.:Musique héroïque, w. Bernard Soustrot (tpt) Forlane ▲ FRL 16732 [DDD]
Trumpet & Organ, w. Bernard Soustrot (tpt) Pierre Verany ("Favourites" series) ▲ 730012 [DDD]
Trumpet & Organ, w. Bernard Soustrot (tpt) Pierre Verany ▲ 789103 [DDD]
Vierne, L.:Carillon de Westminster Pierre Verany ▲ PV.784041 [DDD]
Vierne, L.:Pièces de fant (sels)—Suite No. 2, Op. 53:Hymne au soleil; Clair de lune; Toccata Pierre Verany ▲ PV 788013 [DDD]

Houben, Steve (sax)
Gershwin, G.:Songs, w. A. Oliver (ten), D. Duesing (pno)—He Loves and She Loves; Somebody Loves Me; Let's Do It; How Long Has This Been Going on; By Strauss; They All Laughed; Who Cares; But Not for Me; Love Walked in Ricercar ▲ RIC 135119 [DDD]
Porter, C.:Songs, w. A. Oliver (ten), D. Duesing (pno)—So in Love; Let's Do It; At Long Last Love; I Get A Kick Out of You; Every Time We Say Goodbye Ricercar ▲ RIC 135119 [DDD]

Hough, Lotta Mills (pno)
Grainger, P.:Pno Music (arrs, transcriptions & paraphrases), w. Percy Grainger (pno)—Shepherd's Hey; Country Gardens; Sussex Mummers' Christmas Carol; Jutish Medley; Molly on the Shore; One More Day My John; Spoon River; The Warriors; Ramble [on love-duet from Der Rosenkavalier]; March-Jig; The Leprechaun's Dance; A Reel; Sheep & Goat Walkin' to the Pasture; Turkey in the Straw; Gay but Wistful; The Gum-suckers March; Zanzibar Boat-Song; Colonial Song; Walking Tune; Over the Hills & Far Away [all pno rolls] Nimbus ("Grand Piano" series) ▲ NI 8809 [DDD]

Hough, Stephen (pno)
Bowen, Y.:Ballade 2 Hyperion ▲ CDA 66838
Bowen, Y.:Berceuse Hyperion ▲ CDA 66838
Bowen, Y.:Moto perpetuo Hyperion ▲ CDA 66838
Bowen, Y.:Preludes, OP. 102—13 Preludes Hyperion ▲ CDA 66838
Bowen, Y.:Romance 1 Hyperion ▲ CDA 66838
Bowen, Y.:Romance 2 Hyperion ▲ CDA 66838
Bowen, Y.:Son Pno Hyperion ▲ CDA 66838
Bowen, Y.:Toccata Hyperion ▲ CDA 66838
Brahms, J.:Sons Vn (comp), w. Robert Mann (vn) *(rec Rectial Hall, Music Division, SUNY, Purchase, NY, June 22–23, 1993)* Music Masters Classics ▲ 01612–67165–2
Britten, H.:Holiday Diary, w. R. O'Hora (pno) Virgin Classics ▲ CDC 59027
Grieg, E.:Son Vc, w. Steven Isserlis (vc) *(rec EMI Studio 1, Abbey Road, London, Dec 12–13, 1994)* RCA Red Seal ▲ 09026–68290–2 [DDD]
Hummel, J.N.:Con Pno, Op. 85, w. B. Thomson (cnd), English CO Chandos ▲ CHAN 8507 [DDD]
Hummel, J.N.:Con Pno, Op. 89, w. B. Thomson (cnd), English CO Chandos ▲ CHAN 8507 [DDD]
Liszt, F.:Elegie 1, w. Steven Isserlis (vc) *(rec EMI Studio 1, Abbey Road, London, Dec 12–13, 1994)* RCA Red Seal ▲ 09026–68290–2 [DDD]
Liszt, F.:Elegie 2, w. Steven Isserlis (vc) *(rec EMI Studio 1, Abbey Road, London, Dec 12–13, 1994)* RCA Red Seal ▲ 09026–68290–2 [DDD]
Liszt, F.:La Lugubre gondola Vn & Pno, w. Steven Isserlis (vc) *(rec EMI Studio 1, Abbey Road, London, Dec 12–13, 1994)* RCA Red Seal ▲ 09026–68290–2 [DDD]
Liszt, F.:Pno Music (misc) Virgin Classics ▲ CDC 59222
Liszt, F.:Romance oubliée, w. Steven Isserlis (vc) *(rec EMI Studio 1, Abbey Road, London, Dec 12–13, 1994)* RCA Red Seal ▲ 09026–68290–2 [DDD]
Liszt, F.:Die Zelle in Nonnenwerth, w. Steven Isserlis (vc) *(rec EMI Studio 1, Abbey Road, London, Dec 12–13, 1994)* RCA Red Seal ▲ 09026–68290–2 [DDD]
My Favorite Things:Virtuoso Encores MusicMasters ▲ 7046–2–C [DDD]
The Piano Album Vol. 1 Virgin Classics ▲ CDC 59509
The Piano Album Vol. 2 Virgin Classics ▲ CDC 59304
Sauer, E. von:Con 1 Pno, w. L. Foster (cnd), Birmingham SO Hyperion ▲ CDA 66790
Scharwenka, X.:Con 4 Pno, w. L. Foster (cnd), Birmingham SO Hyperion ▲ CDA 66790

Houghton, Robert (pno)
Britten, H.:The Birds, w. Henry H. Leck (cnd), Indianapolis Children's Choir *(rec The Lodge, May & June 1995)* VAI Audio ▲ VAIA 1130 [DDD]
Purcell, H.:Now That the Sun Hath Veiled His Light, w. Henry H. Leck (cnd), Indianapolis Children's Choir [arr. W.G. Whitaker] *(rec The Lodge, May & June 1995)* VAI Audio ▲ VAIA 1130 [DDD]
Purcell, H.:Pausanias, the Betrayer of His Country, w. Steven Rickards (ct)—Sweeter Than Roses [arr. Benjamin Britten] *(rec The Lodge, May & June 1995)* VAI Audio ▲ VAIA 1130 [DDD]

Houghton, Steve (perc)
Childs, W.:Con Perc Klavier ▲ KCD 11079 [DDD]

Houghton, William (tpt)
Telemann, G.P.:Cons Tpt, w. H. Hardenberger (tpt), M. Laird (tpt), I. Brown (cnd), Academy of St. Martin in the Fields—Concerto for 2 Trumpets & Strings; Concerto for Trumpet, 2 Oboes & Strings; Concerto for 3 Trumpets & Strings; Concerto for Trumpet & Strings Philips ("Digital Classics" series) ▲ 420954–2 [DDD]
Vivaldi, A.:Con Vn Obs, RV.563, w. I. Brown (vn), M. Laird (tpt), N. Marriner (cnd), Academy of St. Martin in the Fields Philips ▲ 412892–2 [DDD]

Houle, Arthur (pno)
Fry, J.:Pierrot's Fancy CRS ▲ CD 8949
Houlik, James (sax)
Peck, R.:The Upward Stream, w. P.A. McRae (cnd), London SO Albany ▲ TROY 040–2 [DDD]
Rendelman Jr., R.:Concertino T Sax, w. L. Muti (cnd), St. Stephen's CO Albany ▲ TROY 111 [DDD]
Ward, R.:Con Sax, w. G. Zimmermann (cnd), North Carolina SO
Albany ▲ AR 001–2 [DDD] ■ AR 001–4 (D)
Houten, Kees van (org)
Organs of the Netherlands, Vol. 5 Emergo ▲ 3996
Houwelingen, P. van (fl)
Van Wassenaer, U.:Sons Rcr, w. H. Dekker (hpd), N. Hirschfeld (vl) Erasmus ▲ WVH 078 [DDD]
Houwelingen, P. van (trns fl)
Focking, H. von:Sons Fl, w. N. Hirschfeld (vl), H. Dekker (hpd)—in C, G & D
Erasmus ▲ WVH 078 [DDD]
Hove, Carolyn (E hn)
Carter, E.:Pastoral E hn, w. Gloria Cheng (pno) *(rec Little Bridges Auditorium, Pomona College, Dec 1994 & Jan 1996)* Crystal ▲ CD 328 [DDD]
Hindemith, P.:Son E Hn, w. Gloria Cheng (pno) *(rec Little Bridges Auditorium, Pomona College, Dec 1994 & Jan 1996)* Crystal ▲ CD 328 [DDD]
Marvin, J.:Pieces E hn & Pno, w. Gloria Cheng (pno) *(rec Little Bridges Auditorium, Pomona College, Dec 1994 & Jan 1996)* Crystal ▲ CD 328 [DDD]
Persichetti, V.:Parable 15 *(rec Little Bridges Auditorium, Pomona College, Dec 1994 & Jan 1996)*
Crystal ▲ CD 328 [DDD]
Hove, Carolyn (E hn/ob)
Stevens, T.:Triangles 4 *(rec Little Bridges Auditorium, Pomona College, Dec 1994 & Jan 1996)*
Crystal ▲ CD 328 [DDD]
Hove, Carolyn (ob)
Salonen, E.-P.:Second Meeting, w. Gloria Cheng (pno) *(rec Little Bridges Auditorium, Pomona College, Dec 1994 & Jan 1996)* Crystal ▲ CD 328 [DDD]
Hovhaness, Alan (pno)
Hovhaness, A.:Komachi *(rec 1987)* Fortuna ▲ 17062–2 ■ 17062–4
Hovhaness, A.:Pno Music—Ghazal No. 1, Op. 36/1; Love Song Vanishing into Sounds of Crickets, Op. 327; To Hiroshige's Cat (1st movt.), Op. 366 *(rec 1987)* Fortuna ▲ 17062–2 ■ 17062–4
Hovhaness, A.:Shalimar *(rec 1987)* Fortuna ▲ 17062–2 ■ 17062–4
Hovhaness, A.:Son Pno, "Prospect Hill" *(rec 1987)* Fortuna ▲ 17062–2 ■ 17062–4
Hovora, Daria (pno)
Cellissimo, w. Mischa Maisky (vc) Deutsche Grammophon ▲ 439863–2
Schubert, Franz:Son Arpeggione, w. Mischa Maisky (vc) *(rec Rittersaal, Rapperswil Palace, Jan 1996)*
Deutsche Grammophon ▲ 449817–2 [DDD]
Schubert, Franz:Songs (misc), w. Mischa Maisky (vc)—Der Neugierige, D.795/6; Der Müller & der Bach, D.795/19 [both from Die schöne Müllerin]; Lied der Mignon, D.877/4 [from Gesänge aus Wilhelm Meister]; Täuschung, D.911/19; Der Leiermann, D.911/24 [both from Winterreise]; Nacht & Träume, D.827; Am Meer, D.957/12; Ständchen, D.957/4 [both from Schwanengesang]; An die Musik, D.547; Die Forelle, D.550; Der Einsame, D.800; Heidenröslein, D.257; Litanei auf das Fest Allerseelen, D.343; Du bist die Ruh, D.776 *(rec Rittersaal, Rapperswil Palace, Jan 1996)*
Deutsche Grammophon ▲ 449817–2 [DDD]
Howald, Caroline (vl/rcr)—see ORCHESTRAS & ENSEMBLES Isabella D'Este
Howard (vc)
Bach, J.S.:Brandenburg Con 5, w. E. Zukerman (fl), P. Zukerman (vn), A. Newman (hpd)
BOMR 3–▲ 617505 [DDD] 2–■ 517504 (D)
Bach, J.S.:Con Fl, Vn & Hpd, w. E. Zukerman (fl), P. Zukerman (vn), A. Newman (hpd)
BOMR 3–▲ 617505 [DDD] 2–■ 517504 (D)
Bach, J.S.:A Musical Offering, w. E. Zukerman (fl), P. Zukerman (vn), A. Newman (pno)
BOMR 3–▲ 617505 [DDD] 2–■ 517504 (D)
Howard, Al (perc)
Wolpe, S.:Qt Tpt, w. Bob Nagel (tpt), Al Cohn (t sax), Jack Maxin (pno), S. Baron (cnd) *(rec Esoteric Studios, NY, 1954)* Hat Hut ▲ CD 6182 [AAD]
Howard, Brian (cnt/fl/rcr)—see ORCHESTRAS & ENSEMBLES The Whole Noyse
Howard, D. (timp)
Linek, J.:Intradas, w. G. Hustis (hn), D. Battey (hn), Dallas SO Trumpet Section Crystal ▲ CD234
Howard, David (cl)
Bernstein, L.:Son Cl, w. Z. Carno (pno) *(rec Aug. 6–7 & 9, 1991)* Centaur ▲ CRC 2201 [DDD]
Hindemith, P.:Son Cl, w. Z. Carno (pno) *(rec Aug. 6–7 & 9, 1991)* Centaur ▲ CRC 2201 [DDD]
Lutoslawski, W.:Dance Preludes Cl, Hp, Pno, Perc & Strs, w. Z. Carno (pno), *(other soloists unknown) (rec Aug. 6–7 & 9, 1991)* Centaur ▲ CRC 2201 [DDD]
Poulenc, F.:Son Cl Pno, w. Z. Carno (pno) *(rec Aug. 6–7 & 9, 1991)* Centaur ▲ CRC 2201 [DDD]
Sutermeister, H.:Capriccio Cl *(rec Aug. 6–7 & 9,1991)* Centaur ▲ CRC 2201 [DDD]
Howard, Leslie (pno)
Chopin, F.:Trio Pno, w. Deborah Fox (vn), William Howard (vc) United ▲ CAL 88038
English Music for Viola, w. Coletti, Paul (va) Hyperion ▲ CDA 66687
Liszt at the Opera, Vol. IV Hyperion 2–▲ 67101/2
Liszt, F.:Album d'un voyageur—Book 3 Hyperion ▲ CDA 67026
Liszt, F.:Années de pèlerinage 1 Hyperion ▲ CDA 67026
Liszt, F.:Episodes Hyperion ▲ CDA 67015
Liszt, F.:Études de concert (3) Pno Hyperion ▲ CDA 67015
Liszt, F.:Grandes études, S.137—12 etudes Hyperion ▲ CDA 66973
Liszt, F.:Hungarian Rhaps—sels. Hyperion 2–▲ CDA 66851/52
Liszt, F.:Hungarian Themes & Rhaps Hyperion 2–▲ CDA 66851/52
Liszt, F.:Music for Pno Trio, w. Deborah Fox (vn), William Howard (vc)—Vallée d'Obermann; Orphee [poeme symphonique]; Tristia; Rapsodie hongrois No. 9 [Le carnaval de pest] United ▲ CAL 88038
Liszt, F.:Operatic Paraphrases & Transcriptions—fifteen works after operas by Auber, Bellini, Donizetti, Glinka, Gounod, Handel, Meyerbeer, Mozart, Tchaikovsky, Verdi, Wagner, Weber
Hyperion 2–▲ CDA 66371/72 [DDD]
Liszt, F.:Pno Music (comp) Hyperion 2–▲ CDA 66771/72 [DDD]
Liszt, F.:Pno Music (comp) Hyperion ▲ CDA 66694 [DDD]
Liszt, F.:Pno Music (comp)—transcriptions of music by Beethoven *(Capriccio alla turca; Fantasie über "ruinen von Athen"; Turkish March),* Hebbel *(sels. from Faust; & Nibelungen),* Lassen *(Symphonisches Zwischenspiel zu Calderons Schauspiel "über allen Zauber Liebe"),* Mendelssohn *(Midsummer Night's Dream—"Dance of the Elves" & "Wedding March"),* Weber *(La Preciosa—"Einsam bin ich, nicht alleine")* Hyperion ▲ CDA 66575 [DDD]
Liszt, F.:Pno Music (comp)—Album d'un voyageur; Chanson du Béarn; Fantasie romantique sur deux mélodies suisses; Faribolo Pastour Hyperion 2–▲ CDA 66601/02
Liszt, F.:Pno Music (comp)—Liszt's piano transcriptions of Ferdinand David's violin pieces *Bunte Reihe, Op. 30* Hyperion ▲ CDA 66506
Liszt, F.:Pno Music (comp)—sels. from Christus & St. Elizabeth; Polonaises de St. Stanislaus; Salve Polonia Hyperion ▲ CDA 66466
Liszt, F.:Pno Music (comp)—Fants.; Paraphrases & Transcriptions of National Songs & Anthems
Hyperion ▲ CDA 66787
Liszt, F.:Pno Music (comp)—Scherzo & March; Petite valse favorite; Mazurka brillante; Grand galop chromatique; Galop in a; Festive polonaise; Csárdás obstinée; Csárdás macabre; Mephisto polka; Festive Ov.; Heroic March in Hungarian Style Hyperion 2–▲ CDA 66811/12
Liszt, F.:Pno Music (comp)—Gaudeamus Igitur - Paraphrase; Una stella amica; La marche pour le Sultan; Seconda Mazurka di Tirindelli; Seconde Marche hongroise; Nocturne (Impromptu); Festmarsch zur Säkularfeier von Goethes Geburstag; 'Solovei' - Air Russe; Galop russe; 'Lyubila ya'; Gaudeamus igitur - Humoresque; Ballade 2 Hyperion ▲ CDA 67034

Howard, Leslie (pno) (cont.)
Liszt, F.:Pno Music (comp)—Excelsior!—Preludio [to The Bells of Strasburg Cathedral], S.500; Die Zelle in Nonnenwerth, S.534bis (2nd version); Consolations, S.171a; Die Zelle in Nonnenwerth, S.534bis (2nd version, alt text); Geharnischte Lieder, S.511; Rosario, S.670; Schlummerlied im Grabe (Première Élégie, 1st version), S.195a; Entwurf der Ramann–Elegie (Zweite Elegie, 1st draft), S.196a; Weimars Volkslied (No. 2 in F), S.542a; National Hymne:Kaiser Wilhelm!, S.197b; Fanfare zur Enthüllung des Carl–Augusts Monument, S.542b; Weimars Volkslied (No. 1 in C), S.542 Hyperion ▲ CDA 66995
Liszt, F.:Pno Music (comp)—Lenore; Der traurige Mönch; Helge's Treue [all w Wolf Kahler (nar)]; A holt költ szerelme [w Sandor Eles (nar)]; Slyepoi [w Yuri Stepanov (nar)] Hyperion ▲ CDA 67045
Liszt, F.:Pno Music (comp)—Ballade aus Der fliegende Holländer, S.441; Fantasie & Fugue über den Choral Ad nos, ad salutarem undam, S.624 [w Geoffery Parsons (pno)]; Fantasie sur l'opéra hongrois Szép Ilonka, S.417; Feierlicher Marsch zum heiligen Gral aus Parsifal, S.450; Illustrations du Prophète, S.414; Marche funègre de Dom Sébastien, S.402; O du, mein holder Abendstern, S.444; Pilgerchor aus Tannhäuser, S.443; Die Rose, S.571; Les Sabéenes, S.407; Spinnerlied aus Der fliegende Holländer, S.440; Spirto gentil, S.400a; Walhall aus Der Ring des Nibelungen, S.449
Hyperion 2–▲ CDA 66571/72 [DDD]
Liszt, F.:Pno Music (comp) Hyperion ▲ CDA 66357
Liszt, F.:Pno Music (comp) Hyperion ▲ CDA 66445
Liszt, F.:Pno Music (comp)—A la Chapelle Sixtine [a meditation on Allegri's *Miserere* & Mozart's *Ave verum corpus*], S.461 (1862); Bach Organ Music transcribed for Solo Piano—Fantasia & Fugue in g [BWV 542], S.463 (1863; rev. 1872) & Six Preludes & Fugues [BWV 543–548], S.462 (1842–50)
Hyperion ▲ CDA 66438 [DDD]
Liszt, F.:Pno Music (comp) Hyperion 2–▲ CDA 66421/22
Liszt, F.:Pno Music (comp) Hyperion ▲ CDA 66388
Liszt, F.:Pno Music (comp) Hyperion 2–▲ CDA 66371/72
Liszt, F.:Pno Music (comp) Hyperion ▲ CDA 66346
Liszt, F.:Pno Music (comp) Hyperion ▲ CDA 66302
Liszt, F.:Pno Music (comp) Hyperion ▲ CDA 66301
Liszt, F.:Pno Music (comp) Hyperion ▲ CDA 66201
Liszt, F.:Pno Music (comp) Hyperion ▲ CDA 66448 [DDD]
Liszt, F.:Les Préludes [arr piano] Hyperion ▲ CDA 67015
Liszt, F.:Soirées de Vienne Hyperion ▲ CDA 66090
Liszt, F.:Song Transcriptions—Schubert:Soirées de Vienne, Valses–caprices d'après, S.427; Mélodies hongroises d'après, S.425; Die Rose, S.556i; Der Gondelfahrer, S.559; 2 Transcriptions for Sophie Menter, S.427/6ii, S.425/2iv; Märsche das Pno übertragen, S.426; Marche Militaire, S.426; Marche Hongroise, S.425/2ii; Ave Maria, S.557d; La Sérénade ('Leise flehen'), S.426; Erlkönig, S.557a
Hyperion ▲ CDA 66951/53
Liszt, F.:Song Transcriptions—The nightingale [Alyabiev]; Bohemian Song [Bulakhov]; Romance [Wielhorsky]; Tarantella [Dargomizhsky]; Russian Gallop [Bulakhov]; Mazurka; Prelude to a Polka [Borodin]; Polka [Borodin]; Tarantella [Cui]; Rakóczi March; Song of the Flowers [Abranyi]; Spanish Serenade [Festetics]; Adele's Waltz [Zichy]; Revive Szegedin! [Szabadi/Massenet]; Concert Waltz [Vegh]; Bevestés és magyar induló [Scéchényi] Hyperion ▲ CDA 66984
Liszt, F.:Song Transcriptions—Tanzmomente; Löse, Himmel, meine Seele; Dantes Sonett; Die Gräberinsel der Fürstin zu Gotha; Elégie sur des motifs du Prince Ferdinand de Prusse; Tanzmomente No. 4; Drei Lieder aus Julius Wolffs Tannhäuser; Ziegeuner–Polka; Löse, Himmel, meine Seele (2nd version); Ich weil' in tiefer Einsamkeit Hyperion ▲ CDA 67004
Liszt, F.:Transcriptions & Paraphrases—Weber:Oberon & Ov.; Mozart:Fant. on themes from Figaro & Don Giovanni; Verdi:Ernani, Miserere du Trovatore, Rigoletto; Reminiscences de (Simon) Boccanegra; Donizetti:Valse de concert sur deux motifs de Lucia; Meyerbeer:Reminiscences de Robert le Diable, Cavatine, Valse infernale; Gounod:Les Adieux (Rêverie sur un motif de Romeo et Juliette); Erkel:Schwanengesang und Marsch aus Hunyadi Laszló; Wagner:Elsas Brautzug zum Munster [from Lohengrin], Festspiel und Brautlied, Elsas Traum, Lohengrins Verweis an Elsa; Phantasiestück über Motive aus Rienzi Hyperion 2–▲ CDA 66861/62
Liszt, F.:Transcriptions & Paraphrases—Beethoven:Syms. 1–9 Hyperion 5–▲ CDA 66671/75
Liszt, F.:Transcriptions & Paraphrases—[CD 1] 4 Geistliche Lieder; Ungarische Melodien; Six Melodic Favorites; [CD 2] Schwanengesang; [CD 3] 12 Lieder von Franz Schubert; 6 Melodien von Franz Schubert Hyperion 3–▲ CDA 66954/56
Liszt, F.:Transcriptions & Paraphrases—Harold in Italy; Romance Oubliée; Gounod—Hymne á Sainte Cecile; Meyerbeer—Le Moine; Festmarche Hyperion ▲ CDA 66683
Liszt, F.:Valse à Capriccio sur deux motifs de Lucia et Parisina Hyperion ▲ CDA 66090
Poulenc, F.:L'Histoire de Babar, w. J. Amis (nar) [recited in English] Nimbus ▲ NI 5342 [DDD]
Rare Piano Encores Hyperion ▲ CDA 66090
Rubinstein, A.:Sons Pno Hyperion 2–▲ CDD 22007
Howard, Michael (org)
Bach, J.S.:Org Music (misc)—Preludes & Fugues in b & C; Chorale Preludes; Fuga Parvula in g; Toccata & Fugue in d [Cavillé–Coll Org, St Michael's Abbey, Farnborough] Herald ▲ HAVPCD 154
Franck, C.:Cantabile [Cavillé–Coll Org, St Michael's Abbey, Farnborough] Herald ▲ HAVPCD 147
Franck, C.:Chorals Org, M.38–40 [Cavillé–Coll Org, St Michael's Abbey, Farnborough]
Herald ▲ HAVPCD 147
Franck, C.:Org Music (misc) [Cavaillé–Coll Org, St. Michael's Abbey, Farnborough]—Fants in A & C; Choral No. 1; Offertoire & Sortie sur des Noëls; Pastorale Herald ▲ HAVPCD 125
Howard, Peter (pno)
Arlen, H.:Americanegro Suite, w. J. Kaye, Premierospel Quartet—plus ten Arlen songs from stage & screen [w. J. Kaye (sop)] Premier ▲ PRCD 1004 [DDD]
Let My Song Fill Your Heart:A Remembrance of the American Concert Song, w. Maryanne Telese (sop), Arthur Woodley (bass), Joseph Smith (pno) Premier ▲ PR 1002
Howard, Peter (vc)
Schoenfield, P.:Cafe Music, w. P. Schoenfield (pno), Y. N. Kim (vn) Innova ▲ MN 108
Howard, William (pno)—see also ORCHESTRAS & ENSEMBLES Schubert Ensemble of London
Dvořák, A.:Dumka & Furiant Chandos ▲ CHAN 9044 [DDD]
Dvořák, A.:Poetic Tone Pictures (sels)—Nos. 1,7,9 & 13 Chandos ▲ CHAN 9044 [DDD]
Dvořák, A.:Theme with Vars Chandos ▲ CHAN 9044 [DDD]
Dvořák, A.:Waltzes Pno, Op. 54 Chandos ▲ CHAN 9044 [DDD]
Fibich, Z.:Moods, Impressions & Reminiscences—Moods, Op. 41/Part 1 [Nos. 4, 8, 13–15, 19, 21, 24, 25, 36 & 44]; Impressions, Op. 41/Part 2 [Nos. 49–52, 54, 74, 78 & 85]; Impressions, Op. 41/Part 3 [Nos. 88, 94, 98, 99, 103, 106, 108, 109, 122–124]; Souvenirs, Op. 41/Part 4 [Nos. 127, 134, 135, 139, 143, 146, 149, 154, 158, 161] Chandos ▲ CHAN 9381 [DDD]
Matthews, D.:Son Pno NMC ▲ NMC 21 [DDD]
Powers, A.:The Memory Room NMC ▲ NMC 21 [DDD]
Weir, J.:Chamber Music, w. Susan Tomes (pno), Petra Casen (hpd), Domus Chamber Ensemble, Schubert Ensemble—Distance & Enchantment; The Bagpiper's Trio; I Broke Off a Golden Branch; El Rey de Francia; The Art of Touching the Keyboard; The King of France; Ardnamurchan Point
Collins Classics ▲ COL 1453
Howard, William (vc)
Chopin, F.:Trio Pno, w. Leslie Howard (pno), Deborah Fox (vn) United ▲ CAL 88038
Liszt, F.:Music for Pno Trio, w. Leslie Howard (pno), Deborah Fox (vn)—Vallée d'Obermann; Orphee [poeme symphonique]; Tristia; Rapsodie hongrois No. 9 [Le carnaval de pest] United ▲ CAL 88038
Howe, Don
Riley, T.:In C, w. Bruce Ackley, Steve Adams, Don R. Baker, Chris Brown, George Brooks, Steve Coughlin, Blake Derby, Bill Douglass, Mihr'un'Nisa Douglass, Hank Dutt, David Harrington, Joan Jeanrenaud, Alden Jenks, Warner Jepson, Henry Kaiser, Jaron Lanier, Bill Maginnis, George Marsh, Shabda Owens, Jon Raskin, Gyan Riley, Terry Riley, Gino Robair, John Sackett, Ramón Sender, John Sherba, Toyji Tomita, Danny Tunick, William Winant, Evan Ziporyn *(rec Jan. 14, 1990)*
New Albion ▲ NA 071
Howell, Christopher (pno)
Scott, C.:Pno Music—6 Pieces; 2 Pierrot Pieces; Sea–Marge–Meditation; Impressions from the Jungle Book; Rainbow Trout; Butterfly Waltz; A Little Russian Suite; First Bagatelle; Moods; Inclination À la danse; Valse sentimentale Tremula ▲ TREM 104

Howitt, Roy (cl)
Yoshioka, T.:Rhap Mar, w. Evelyn Glennie (mar), Edward Beckett (fl), Chris Laurence (db), Ralph Salmins (dr) *(rec Whitfield Street Studios, London, Sept. 22–29, 1994)* Catalyst ▲ 09026-68193-2 [DDD]
Höxter, Daniel (pno)
Beethoven, L. van:Polonaise Pno Ambitus ▲ 97838 [DDD]
Beethoven, L. van:Vars on a waltz by Diabelli, Op. 120 Ambitus ▲ 97838 [DDD]
Brahms, J.:Sextet Strs, Op. 18, w. John Harding (vn), Matthias Feile (vc) [arr. Kirchner for Piano Trio] Koch Schwann ▲ SCH 313652 [DDD]
Brahms, J.:Sextet Strs, Op. 36, w. John Harding (vn), Matthias Feile (vc) [arr. Kirchner for Piano Trio] Koch Schwann ▲ SCH 313652 [DDD]
Hoyer, Jeff (trbn)
Jenkins, L.:Monkey on the Dragon, w. Leroy Jenkins (vn), Henry Threadgill (fl), Don Byron (cl), Marth Ehrlich (b cl), Janet Frice (bn), Vincent Chancey (hn), Frank Gordon (tpt), David Soldier (vn), Jane Henry (vn) Ron Lawrence (va), Mary Wooton (vc), Lindsey Horner (db), Thurman Barker (traps), Myra Melford (pno), T. Léon (cnd) *(rec live, Merkin Concert Hall, New York City, Apr. 9, 1992)* CRI ("eXchange" series) ▲ CD 663 [DDD]
Höylä, Veikko (vc)—see also ORCHESTRAS & ENSEMBLES Segerstam String Quartet, Voces Intimae String Quartet
Segerstam, L.:Divert Vns, w. J. Rahkonen (vn), H. Louhivuori (vn), E. Kamu (va), L. Segerstam (cnd), Helsinki CO BIS ▲ CD 84 [AAD]
Hoyle, Robert (hn)
Barker, T.E.:Pieces (3) F Hn *(rec Nov. 1992)* CRI ▲ CD 661 [DDD]
Hoyle, W. Ted (vc)—see also ORCHESTRAS & ENSEMBLES Kohon String Quartet
Baksa, R.:Qnt Ob & Strs, w. B. Lucarelli (ob), N. Tanaka (vn), M. Yanagita (vn), S. Winterbottom (va) Capstone ▲ CPS 8610
Gary Schocker:Flutist, w. Gary Schocker (fl), Dennis Helmrich (hpd), Marco Granados (fl) Chesky ▲ CD 46 [DDD]
Hoznedr, Ivan (perc)—see ORCHESTRAS & ENSEMBLES Prague Percussion Project
Hrabě, Radek (ob)
Vivaldi, A.:Cons for 2 Obs, w. J. Kolár (ob), J. Hasenöhrl (tpt), F. Vlasák (tpt), O. Vlček (cnd), Prague Virtuosi—Con. in C, RV.559 *(rec 1991)* Emergo ▲ EC 3981 [DDD]
Hron, Karel (org)
Trumpet & Organ, w. Josef Svejkovsky (tpt) Multisonic ▲ MUL 310192 [DDD]
Hruby, Milan (brass)
Vejvanovsky, P.J.:Sons & Serenades, w. Vaclav Jirovec (vc), Jan Hasenöhrl (tpt), Jiri Pribyl (trbn), Frantisek Xaver (hpd), Oldrich Vlcek (vn), O. Vlček (cnd), Prague Virtuosi—Intrada; Harmonia romana; Serenada; Offertur ad duos chorus; Son à 4 be mollis; Son paschalis; Son tribus quadrantibus; Son campanarum; Serenada *(rec Lobochovice castle, July 26–28, 1992)* Discover International ▲ DI 920243 [DDD]
Hruby, Milan (ob)
Finger, G.:Son Tpt, Vn & Ob, w. Richard Steuart (tpt), Sylvie Hessova (vn), Oldrich Vlcek (vn) *(rec Prague, Nov. 1994)* Discover International ▲ DI 920244 [DDD]
Hrynkiv, Thomas (pno)
Sings Songs of Ukraine, w. Paul Plishka (bass) Forlane ▲ FOR 16645 [DDD]
Hsu, John (baryton)—see ORCHESTRAS & ENSEMBLES Haydn Baryton Trio
Hu, Nai-Yuan (vn)
Bruch, M.:Con 2 Vn, w. G. Schwarz (cnd), Seattle SO Delos ▲ DE 3156 [DDD]
Chausson, E.:Poème Vn, w. C. Chen (cnd), Royal PO *(rec St. Barnabas Church, England, Sept 22, 1986)* Sunrise ▲ 8516
Goldmark, K.:Con 1 Vn, w. G. Schwarz (cnd), Seattle SO Delos ▲ DE 3156 [DDD]
Ravel, M.:Tzigane, w. C. Chen (cnd), Royal PO *(rec St. Barnabas Church, England, Sept 22, 1986)* Sunrise ▲ 8516
Saint-Saëns, C.:Introduction & Rondo capriccioso, w. C. Chen (cnd), Royal PO *(rec St. Barnabas Church, England, Sept 22, 1986)* Sunrise ▲ 8516
Sarasate, P. de:Carmen Fant, w. C. Chen (cnd), Royal PO *(rec St. Barnabas Church, England, Sept 22, 1986)* Sunrise ▲ 8516
Sarasate, P. de:Zigeunerweisen, w. C. Chen (cnd), Royal PO *(rec St. Barnabas Church, England, Sept 22, 1986)* Sunrise ▲ 8516
Huang, Alicia (vn)—see ORCHESTRAS & ENSEMBLES Alorian String Quartet
Huang, Eileen (pno)
Ancient & Modern Chinese Music:Folk & Dance Songs *(rec Oct. 1992)* Appass ▲ ACD 69306 [DDD]
Huang, Si-Jing (vn)—see also ORCHESTRAS & ENSEMBLES Hawthorne String Quartet
Klein, G.:Duo Vn & Vc, w. S. Knudsen (vc)—Allegro con fuoco; Lento *(rec Jan. 1992)* Northeastern ▲ NR 248-CD
Huang, Yi Fang (vn)
Clementi, M.:Pno Music (comp), w. Aldo Antognazzi (pno), Christian Badian (pno), Eduardo Cazaban (pno), Cristina Da Souza (pno), Dao Di Renzo (pno), Pablo Lavandera (pno), Silvina Cardenas (fl), Nestor Herzbaum (fl)—Sons (6) for Pno, Op. 2, Nos. 1, 3 & 5 (w. flutes); Duets (3) for Piano 4-Hands, Op. 3, Nos. 2 & 3; Sons (3) for Pno & Vn, Op. 3, No. 4 Aura Classics ▲ AU 32287
Clementi, M.:Pno Music (comp), w. Aldo Antognazzi (pno), Augusto Miravalle (pno)—Sons (3) for Pno & Vn, Op. 3, Nos. 5 & 6; Sons (6) for Pno & Vn, Op. 4 Aura Classics ▲ AU 32288
Hubay, Jenö (vn)
The Complete HMV Recordings, w. Carl Flesch (vn) Biddulph ▲ LAB 045 [ADD]
Hubbard, Brad (br sax)—see ORCHESTRAS & ENSEMBLES New Century Saxophone Quartet
Hubeau, Jean (pno)
Dukas, P.:Villanelle, w. Pierre del Vescovo (hn) Erato ▲ 94801-2
Fauré, G.:Qts Pno, Opp. 15 & 45, w. Via Nova String Quartet members Erato ▲ ERA 96953 [ADD]
Fauré, G.:Qnts Pno & Strs, Opp. 89 & 115, w. Via Nova String Quartet Erato 3-▲ ERA 96953 [ADD]
Fauré, G.:Trio, w. Via Nova String Quartet members Erato ▲ ERA 96953 [ADD]
Pierné, G.:Qnt Pno, w. Viotti String Quartet Erato ("Musifrance" series) ▲ 2292-45525-2 [AAD/DDD]
Pierné, G.:Son Vn, w. O. Charlier (vn) Erato ("Musifrance" series) ▲ 2292-45525-2 [AAD/DDD]
Saint-Saëns, C.:Son 1 Vn, w. O. Charlier (vn) Erato ("Musifrance" series) ▲ 2292-45017-2-ZK
Saint-Saëns, C.:Son 2 Vn, w. O. Charlier (vn) Erato ("Musifrance" series) ▲ 2292-45017-2-ZK
Huber, Gerhard (perc)—see also ORCHESTRAS & ENSEMBLES Basel Perc Trio
Bartók, B.:Son for 2 Pnos, w. Siegfried Schmid (perc), Janka & Jürg Piano Duo Accord ▲ ACD 220372
Carter, E.:Triple Duo, w. P. Racine (fl), E. Molinari (cl), H. Schneeberger (vn), P. Cleeman (va), T. Demenga (vc) ECM New Series ▲ 78118-21391-2 [DDD]
Huber, R. (instr)
Caprioli, A.:Serenata per Francesca, w. V. Fuchsberger (sgr), G. Schneider (vn), S. Winiarczyk (ob), A. Aigmüller (dr), R. Crow (instr), K. Ager (cnd), Austrian Ensemble for New Music *(rec 1987)* Pro Viva ▲ ISPV 148 CD [ADD]
Huberman, Bronislaw (vn)
Bach, J.S.:Cons Vn (comp), w. I. Dobrowen (cnd), Vienna PO *(rec 1934)* Pearl ▲ PEA 9341 (m)
Beethoven, L. van:Con Vn, Op. 61, w. G. Szell (cnd), Vienna PO *(rec June 18–20, 1934)* APR ("Signature" series) ▲ APR 5506 [ADD]
Beethoven, L. van:Con Vn, Op. 61, Vienna PO *(rec 1934)* EMI Classics ("Great Recordings of the Century" series) ▲ CDH 63194 (m) [ADD]
Beethoven, L. van:Con Vn, Op. 61, w. G. Szell (cnd), Vienna PO—Allegro ma non troppo; Larghetto; Rondo *(rec 1934)* Preiser ▲ 90118 (m)
Beethoven, L. van:Son 9 Vn, "Kreutzer", w. I. Friedmann (pno) *(rec ca. 1930)* EMI Classics ("Great Recordings of the Century" series) ▲ CDH 63194 (m) [ADD]
Bruch, M.:Kol Nidrei, w. S. Schultze (pno) [arr. violin-piano] *(rec 1930)* The Classical Collector ▲ FDC 2003 (m) [AAD]
Chopin, F.:Waltzes, w. S. Schultze (pno) [violin-piano arr. by Huberman of the Waltz in c#, Op. 64, No. 2 *(rec 1932 for Columbia Records)* The Classical Collector ▲ FDC 2003 (m) [AAD]
The Complete Brunswick Recordings Biddulph 2-▲ LAB 077
Lalo, E.:Sym espagnole, w. G. Szell (cnd), Vienna PO *(rec June 20 & 22, 1934)* APR ("Signature" series) ▲ APR 5506 [ADD]

Huberman, Bronislaw (vn) (cont.)
Lalo, E.:Sym espagnole, w. G. Szell (cnd), Vienna PO *(rec 1934 for Columbia Records)* The Classical Collector ▲ FDC 2003 (m) [AAD]
Lalo, E.:Sym espagnole, w. G. Szell (cnd), Vienna PO—Allegro non troppo; Scherzando; Andante; Rondo *(rec 1934)* Preiser ▲ 90118 (m)
Mendelssohn, F.:Con in e Vn & Orch, Op. 64, w. S. Schultze (pno) [violin-piano arr.]—2nd & 3rd movts. *(rec 1923)* Pearl ▲ GEMMCD 9332 [AAD]
Mozart, W.A.:Con 3 Vn, w. I. Dobrowen (cnd), Vienna PO *(rec 1934)* Pearl ▲ PEA 9341 (m) [AAD]
Mozart, W.A.:Con 4 Vn, w. B. Walter (cnd), New York PO *(rec 1945)* Music & Arts ▲ CD 299 [AAD]
The Romantic Violin The Classical Collector ▲ FDC 2003 (m) [AAD]
Sarasate, P. de:Carmen Fant, w. S. Schultze (pno) [violin-piano arr.] *(rec 1926 for Polydor)* The Classical Collector ▲ FDC 2003 (m) [AAD]
Sarasate, P. de:Spanish Dances, w. S. Schultze (pno)—"Romanza andlauza," Op. 22, No. 1 *(rec 1926 for Polydor)* The Classical Collector ▲ FDC 2003 (m) [AAD]
Tchaikovsky, P.:Con Vn, w. E. Ormandy (cnd), Philadelphia Orch *(rec 1946)* Music & Arts ▲ CD 299 [AAD]
Tchaikovsky, P.:Con Vn, w. W. Steinberg (cnd), Berlin State Opera Orch *(rec 8/16/29)* InSync ■ C 4166 (CrO2)
Tchaikovsky, P.:Con Vn, w. W. Steinberg (cnd), Berlin State Opera Orch *(rec 1929)* Pearl ▲ GEMMCD 9332 (m) [AAD]
Tchaikovsky, P.:Con Vn, w. W. Steinberg, Berlin State Opera Orch *(rec 1929 for Columbia Records)* The Classical Collector ▲ FDC 2003 (m) [AAD]
Hubert, Brother (fl)
Flute & Organ, w. Jacques Berthier (org) Studio SM ▲ 12 17 48
Hubert, Marcel (vc)
Rachmaninoff, S.:Son Vc, w. Shura Cherkassky (pno) Biddulph ▲ LHW 034
Hübner, Eckart (bn)—see also ORCHESTRAS & ENSEMBLES Albert Schweitzer Wind Quintet
Devienne, F.:Cons (4) Bn, w. B. Warchal (cnd), Slovak CO CPO ▲ CPO 999120 [DDD]
Krommer, F.:Qt Bn, Op. 46/1, w. Johannes Lüthy (va), Steuart Eaton (va), Reinhard Latzko (vc) *(rec Hans-Rosbaud Studio, Oct 10–11, 1994)* CPO ▲ CPO 999297-2 [DDD]
Krommer, F.:Qt Bn, Op. 46/2, w. Johannes Lüthy (va), Steuart Eaton (va), Reinhard Latzko (vc) *(rec Hans-Rosbaud Studio, Oct 10–11, 1994)* CPO ▲ CPO 999297-2 [DDD]
Mozart, W.A.:Son Bn, w. Reinhard Latzko (vc) *(rec Hans-Rosbaud Studio, Oct 10–11, 1994)* CPO ▲ CPO 999297-2 [DDD]
Reicha, A.:Qnt Bn, w. Nomos String Quartet CPO ▲ CPO 999061-2 [DDD]
Reicha, A.:Son Bn, w. *(pianist unknown)* CPO ▲ CPO 999061-2 [DDD]
Reicha, A.:Vars Bn, w. Nomos String Quartet CPO ▲ CPO 999061-2 [DDD]
Yun, I.:Rondell, w. C. Dimigen (ob), D. Schneider (cl) *(rec Dec. 1991)* CPO ▲ CPO 999184 [DDD]
Hübscher, Jürgen (lt)
Erickson, R.:Postcards, w. C. Plantamura (sop) *(rec 1987–91)* CRI ▲ CD 616 [DDD]
Hübscher, Jürgen (lt/gtr)
Boismortier, J.B. de:Suites Fl, Op. 35, w. B. Böhm (trns fl/rcr), A. Weigel (gamba) CPO ▲ CPO 999048-2 [DDD]
Hübscher, Jürgen (renaissance lt/vih/perc)—see ORCHESTRAS & ENSEMBLES Hedos Ensemble
Huckaby, William (pno)
Argento, D.:The Andrée Expedition, w. W. Parker (bar) [E] *(rec 1988)* Centaur ▲ CRC 2092 [DDD]
Argento, D.:From the Diary of V. Woolf, w. L. Maxwell (mez) [E] *(rec 1988)* Centaur ▲ CRC 2092 [DDD]
Brahms, J.:Songs, w. Wm. Parker (bar)—8 songs [G] Centaur ▲ CRC 2022 [DAD]
Cadman, C.W.:American Indian Songs, w. William Parker (bar) *(rec Columbia Recording Studios, New York City)* New World ▲ 80463-2
Copland, A.:Songs (misc), w. William Parker (bar)—8 songs [E] Centaur ▲ CRC 2022 [DAD]
Farwell, A.:Indian Songs (3), w. William Parker (bar) *(rec Columbia Recording Studios, New York City)* New World ▲ 80463-2
Griffes, C.T.:Songs, w. William Parker (bar)—Das ist ein Brausen und Heulen; Wo ich bin, mich rings umdunkelt; Des Müden Abendlied; Zwei Könige sassen auf Orkadel; The 1st Snowfall; An Old Song Re-sung *(rec Columbia Recording Studios, New York City)* New World ▲ 80463-2
Hucke, Helmut (ob)
Bach, C.P.E.:Con Ob, H.468, Collegium Aureum Editio Classica ▲ 77061-2-RG [ADD]
Mozart, W.A.:Adagio & Rondo Glass Armonica, w. B. Hoffmann (glass armonica), K.H. Ulrich (fl), E. Nippes (va), H. Plumacher (vc) Allegretto ▲ ACD 8174 [ADD] ■ ACS 8174
Hudeč, Jiří (db)—see also ORCHESTRAS & ENSEMBLES Duo di Basso
Dvořák, A.:Qnt Strs, Op. 77, w. Stamitz String Quartet Bayer ▲ 100184 [DDD]
Hudeček, Václav (vn)
Bach, J.S.:Cons Vn (comp), w. Dmitry Sitkovetsky (vn), D. Sitkovetsky (cnd), Prague Virtuosi Supraphon ▲ SUP 3085
Bach, J.S.:Con Vn & Ob, w. Dmitry Sitkovetsky (vn), D. Sitkovetsky (cnd), Prague Virtuosi Supraphon ▲ SUP 3085
Bach, J.S.:Con for 2 Vns, w. Dmitry Sitkovetsky (vn), D. Sitkovetsky (cnd), Prague Virtuosi Supraphon ▲ SUP 3085
Dvořák, A.:Con Vn, w. J. Belohlávek (cnd), Czech PO Supraphon ▲ SUP 3187
Dvořák, A.:Con Vn, w. J. Belohlávek (cnd), Czech PO Panton ▲ PAN 810855
Dvořák, A.:Con Vn, w. V. Smetáček (cnd), Prague Musici Panton ▲ PAN 811211
Dvořák, A.:Mazurek, w. J. Belohlávek (cnd), Czech PO Supraphon ▲ SUP 3187
Dvořák, A.:Romance Vn, w. J. Belohlávek (cnd), Czech PO Supraphon ▲ SUP 3187
Dvořák, A.:Romance Vn, w. J. Belohlávek (cnd), Czech PO Panton ▲ PAN 810855
Haydn, J.:Con Vn, Hpd & Strs, w. Martin Derungs (hpd), L. Sagrestano (cnd), Prague Musici Accord ▲ ACD 220462 [DDD]
Mendelssohn, F.:Con in e Vn & Orch, Op. 64, w. V. Smetáček (cnd), Prague RSO Panton ▲ PAN 811209
Mozart, W.A.:Con 3 Vn, w. I. Oistrakh (cnd), Prague Virtuosi Supraphon ▲ SUP 112240 [DDD]
Mozart, W.A.:Con 4 Vn, w. I. Oistrakh (cnd), Prague Virtuosi Supraphon ▲ SUP 112240 [DDD]
Mozart, W.A.:Con 5 Vn, w. I. Oistrakh (cnd), Prague Virtuosi Supraphon ▲ SUP 112240 [DDD]
Prokofiev, S.:Romeo & Juliet (sels), w. D. Oistrakh (cnd), Czech PO *(rec live, Prague Spring Festival, May 20, 1972)* Supraphon ▲ SUP 0216
Sibelius, J.:Con Vn, w. J. Belohlávek (cnd), Prague RSO Panton ▲ PAN 811209
Tchaikovsky, P.:Con Vn, w. D. Oistrakh (cnd), Czech PO *(rec live, Prague Spring Festival, May 20, 1972)* Supraphon ▲ SUP 0216
Tchaikovsky, P.:Con Vn, w. J. Belohlávek (cnd), Prague RSO Panton ▲ PAN 811208
Trojan, V.:Bagaja, w. Pavel Dreser (acc), Lubomír Brabec (gtr) Supraphon ▲ SUP 112203 [DDD]
Trojan, V.:The Emperor's Nightengale, w. Pavel Dreser (acc), Lubomir Brabec (gtr) Supraphon ▲ SUP 112203 [DDD]
Vivaldi, A.:Cons Diverse Instrs, w. Jiří Stivín (va), Ludomír Brabec (pno), G. Delogu (cnd), Janáček CO, Prague CO—in C for 2 Rcrs, 2 Bns, 2 Vns, 2 Gtrs, Vc, Strings & Cont, RV.558; in d for Vn, Gtr, Strs & Cont, RV.540; in F for Vn, Gtr, Strs & Cont, RV.542; in a for Rcr, Strs & Cont, RV.108; in C for 2 Vns, 2 Gtrs, 2 Fls, 2 Rcrs, 2 Strs & 2 Conts, RV.565 Supraphon ▲ SUP 3023
Hudson, Benjamin (vn)—see also ORCHESTRAS & ENSEMBLES Group for Contemporary Music String Quartet
Jemnitz, S.:Trio Gtr, Vn & Va, w. D. Starobin (gtr), K. Kashkashian (va) Bridge ▲ BCD 9004 ■ BC5-7004
Kabat, J.:Poems by H. D., w. J. Kabat (voice/glass hmc/saw/African drums/kalimba), M. Crispell (pno), A. Adzenyah (African drums/conga) [E] Leonarda ■ LE 319 (D)
Karchin, L.:Capriccio, w. H. Sollberger (cnd), Group for Contemporary Music [E] New World ▲ 80425-2 [DDD]
Mendelssohn, F.:Con in e Vn & Orch, Op. 64, w. R. Goodman (cnd), Hanover Band Nimbus ▲ NI 5158 [DDD]
Picker, T.:Rhap Vn, w. T. Picker (pno) *(rec 1979)* CRI ▲ CD 589 [ADD]
Rosenzweig, M.:Diptych, w. S. Palma (fl), A. Blustine (cl), C. Finckel (vc), E. Garth (pno), M. Rosenzweig Centaur ▲ CRC 2103 [DDD]

Hudson, Benjamin (vn) (cont.)
Wuorinen, C.:Archangel, w. D. Taylor (trbn), C. Zeavin (vn), L. Schulman (va), F. Sherry (vc) *(rec March 31, 1981)* Koch International Classics ▲ KIC 7110-2 [DDD]
Wuorinen, C.:Double Solo, w. W. Purvis (hn), J. Winn (pno) *(rec Oct. 17, 1991)* Koch International Classics ▲ KIC 7123-2 [DDD]
Wuorinen, C.:Fant Vn, w. G. Ohlsson (pno) Bridge ▲ BCD 9008 [DDD]
Wuorinen, C.:The Long & the Short Bridge ▲ BCD 9008 [DDD]
Wuorinen, C.:Pieces Vn, w. G. Ohlsson (pno) Bridge ▲ BCD 9008 [DDD]
Wuorinen, C.:Qt 3 Strs, w. C. Zeavin (vn), L. Martin (va), F. Sherry (vc) New World ▲ NW 385-2 [DDD]
Wuorinen, C.:Son Vn, w. G. Ohlsson (pno) New World ▲ NW 385-2 [DDD]
Wuorinen, C.:Spinoff, w. D. Palma (db), J. Passaro (perc) Bridge ▲ BCD 9008 [DDD]
Wuorinen, C.:Trio Hn, w. W. Purvis (hn), A. Feinberg (pno) *(rec Sept. 11-13, 1991)* Koch International Classics ▲ KIC 7123-2 [DDD]
Wuorinen, C.:Trio Hn Continued, w. W. Purvis (hn), J. Winn (pno) *(rec Sept. 11-13, 1991)* Koch International Classics ▲ KIC 7123-2 [DDD]
Wuorinen, C.:Variations Vn Koch International Classics ▲ KIC 7242-2 [DDD]

Hue, Sylvie (cl)
La Clarinette de la Belle Epoque, w. Roger Boutry (pno) REM ▲ 311209 [DDD]

Huff, Harry (org)
de Blasio, C.:God is Our Righteousness, w. N. Goluses (gtr) *(rec Aug. 26, 1993)* Catalyst ▲ 09026-61979-2 ■ 09026-61979-4
Hampton, C.:Music of [Chancel and Gallery Organs of Calvary Church, Gramercy Park, New York City]—Fanfare of the New Year; In Praise of Humanity; In Paradisum; Concerto for Solo Organ; Lullaby; Voluntary on "Engelberg"; Alexander Vars. *(w. D. Higgs)* Pro Organo ▲ CD 7014 [DDD]
Hampton, C.:Vars on "Amazing Grace", w. T. Stacy (E hn) *(rec Aug. 26, 1993)* Catalyst ▲ 09026-61979-2 ■ 09026-61979-4

Huff, Walter (org)
The Joy of Christmas, w. Anthony Newman (org), Chestnut Brass Company [cnd:William Noll], Choral Guild of Atlanta, Choral Guild of Atlanta Brass & Percussion, Benjamin Harms (timp) Sony Classical ▲ SFK 62698 ■ SFT 62698

Hug, M. (org)—see ORCHESTRAS & ENSEMBLES Stuttgart Philharmonia Ensemble

Huge, Stefan (perc)
Lieberson, P.:King Gesar, w. Yo-Yo Ma (vc), Emanuel Ax (pno), Peter Serkin (pno), Omar Ebrahim (nar), Andras Adorjan (fl), Deborah Marshall (cl), William Purvis (hn), David Taylor (trbn) Sony Classical ▲ SK 57971

Huggett, Fiona (trb vl)—see ORCHESTRAS & ENSEMBLES English Fantasy

Huggett, Monica (baroque vn)
Baroque Music for Recorder, w. Conrad Steinmann (rcr), Hopkinson Smith (lt/thb/gtr), Jordi Savall (vl), Pere Ros (vl), Claude Flagel (h-g), Johann Sonnleitner (hpd) Claves ▲ CD 508103 [ADD]
The Early Guitar, w. James Tyler (lt/baroque gtr/mand), Paul Elliott (ten), Jane Ryan (b vl/baroque vc), Robert Spencer (thb/baroque gtr) Saga Classics ▲ 3356 [ADD]

Huggett, Monica (vn)—see also ORCHESTRAS & ENSEMBLES Sonnerie Ensemble, Hausmusik, London Fortepiano Trio
Bach, J.S.:Cant 51, w. N. Argenta (sop), M. Huggett (cnd), Sonnerie Ensemble Virgin Classics ▲ CDC 45038
Bach, J.S.:Cant 82, w. N. Argenta (sop), M. Huggett (cnd), Sonnerie Ensemble Virgin Classics ▲ CDC 45038
Bach, J.S.:Cant 199, w. N. Argenta (sop), M. Huggett (cnd), Sonnerie Ensemble Virgin Classics ▲ CDC 45038
Bach, J.S.:Son Fl, BWV 1079, w. James Galway (fl), Sarah Cunningham (vl), Phillip Moll (hpd) RCA Red Seal ▲ 0902-668182-2 [DDD]
Bach, J.S.:Trio Son, BWV 1038, w. James Galway (fl), Sarah Cunningham (vl), Phillip Moll (hpd) RCA Red Seal ▲ 0902-668182-2 [DDD]
Beethoven, L. van:Con Vn, Op. 61, w. C. Mackerras (cnd), Orch of the Age of Enlightenment Classics for Pleasure ("Eminence" series) ▲ CDEMX 2217 [DDD]
Biber, H. von:Battalia, European Community Baroque Orch *(rec Nov. 1991)* Channel Classics ▲ CCS 4392 [DDD]
de Fesch, W.:Trio Sons, Op. 7, w. W. Hazelzet (transverse fl), T. Koopman (hpd)—No. 4 in g Erasmus ▲ WVH 010 [ADD]
Giuliani, M.:Grand Duo Concertant, Op. 25, w. Richard Savino (gtr) Harmonia Mundi France ▲ HMU 907116
Hellendaal, P.:Solos Vn & Continuo, w. Ton Koopman (hpd)—No. 3 in d Erasmus ▲ WVH 010 [ADD]
Lawes, W.:Royall Consort Suites, w. Greate Consort—Nos. 1, 3, 6, 7 & 9 ASV ("Gaudeamus" series) ▲ ASV 146 [DDD]
Mendelssohn, F.:Con in e Vn & Orch, Op. 64, w. C. Mackerras (cnd), Orch of the Age of Enlightenment Classics for Pleasure ("Eminence" series) ▲ CDEMX 2217 [DDD]
Mozart, W.A.:Con 1 Vn, w. M. Huggett (cnd), Orch of the Age of Enlightenment Virgin Classics ▲ CDC 45010
Mozart, W.A.:Con 2 Vn, w. M. Huggett (cnd), Orch of the Age of Enlightenment Virgin Classics ▲ CDC 45010
Mozart, W.A.:Con 5 Vn, w. M. Huggett (cnd), Orch of the Age of Enlightenment Virgin Classics ▲ CDC 45010
Paganini, N.:Grand Son Vn, w. Richard Savino (gtr) Harmonia Mundi France ▲ HMU 907116
Paganini, N.:Son concertata, w. Richard Savino (gtr) Harmonia Mundi France ▲ HMU 907116
Purcell, H.:Music of, w. Catherine Bott (sop), Emma Kirkby (sop), James Bowman (alt), Anthony Rooley (lt), Catherine Mackintosh (vn), Christophe Coin (vc), Paula Chateauneuf (gtr), Hill, Hogwood (cnd), Brandenburg Consort, Academy of Ancient Music, Anthony Lewis (cnd), David Hill (cnd), St. Anthony Singers, Taverner Choir, Winchester Cathedral Choir—The Double Dealer; Come Ye Sons of Art; The Old Bachelor; Birthday Song for Queen Mary; Oedipus; King Arthur; Bonduca; The Fairy Queen; Son. No. 9 in F; Dido & Aeneas; Abdelazer; Bess of Bedlam; The Married Beau; Hear My Prayer, O Lord; Rejoice in the Lord Always L'Oiseau-Lyre ▲ 444620-2
Purcell, H.:Music of, w. Catherine Bott (sop), Emma Kirkby (sop), James Bowman (alt), Anthony Rooley (lt), Paula Chateauneuf (gtr), Catherine Mackintosh (vn), Christophe Coin (vc), Hill, Hogwood (cnd), Academy of Ancient Music, Brandenburg Consort, David Hill (cnd), Anthony Lewis (cnd), St. Anthony Singers, Taverner Choir, Winchester Cathedral Choir—The Double Dealer; Come Ye Sons of Art; The Old Bachelor; Birthday Song for Queen Mary; Oedipus; King Arthur; Bonduca; The Fairy Queen; Son. No. 9 in F; Dido & Aeneas; Abdelazer; Bess of Bedlam; The Married Beau; Hear My Prayer, O Lord; Rejoice in the Lord Always London ("Editions de l'oiseau-lyre" series) ▲ 444620-2
Purcell, H.:Sons (10) Vns, Z.802-811, w. C. Mackintosh (vn), C. Coin (b vl), C. Hogwood (chamber org/spinet) L'Oiseau-Lyre ▲ 433190-2 [ADD]
Ruloffs, B.:Sons Hpd, w. T. Mothot (hpd), R. van der Meer (vc)—No. 1 in G Erasmus ▲ WVH 010 [ADD]
Ruppe, C.F.:Duets Vn, w. T. Mothot (hpd)—No. 2 in G Erasmus ▲ WVH 010 [ADD]
Sammartini, G.:Cons Rcr, w. R. Harvey (rcr), London Vivaldi Orch—in F ASV ("Gaudeamus" series) ▲ CDGAU 111
Vivaldi, A.:Cons Rcr, w. R. Harvey (rcr), London Vivaldi Orch—RV.441 & RV.444 ASV ("Gaudeamus" series) ▲ CDGAU 111
Vivaldi, A.:Con Va d'amore Lt, w. J. Lindberg (lt), Drottningholm Baroque Ensemble BIS ▲ CD 290 [DDD]
Vivaldi, A.:Cons Vn (misc), w. R. Goodman (cnd), London Vivaldi Orch—RV.253, 271, 277, 353 ASV ("Gaudeamus" series) ▲ CDGAU 105
Vivaldi, A.:Cons Vn (misc), European Community Baroque Orch—"Il Grosso Mogul" Concerto, Op. 7 *(rec Nov. 1991)* Channel Classics ▲ CCS 4392 [DDD]
Vivaldi, A.:Cons Vn, Op. 4, "La stravaganza", w. C. Hogwood (cnd), Academy of Ancient Music L'Oiseau-Lyre 2-▲ 417502-2 [DDD]
Vivaldi, A.:Cons Vn, Op. 8/1-12, "Il cimento dell'armonia e dell'inventione", w. N. Kraemer (cnd), Raglan Baroque Players Veritas 2-▲ VCD 7 90803-2 [DDD] 2-■ VCD 7 90803-4 (D)
Vivaldi, A.:Con Vn Vc, RV.546, w. T. Mason (vc), N. Kraemer (cnd), Raglan Baroque Players Veritas 2-▲ VCD 7 90803-2 [DDD] 2-■ VCD 7 90803-4 (D)

Huggett, Monica (vn) (cont.)
Vivaldi, A.:Cons for 2 Vns, w. E. Wallfisch (vn), N. Kraemer (cnd), Raglan Baroque Players—Concerto in G, RV.516 Veritas 2-▲ VCD 7 90803-2 [DDD] 2-■ VCD 7 90803-4 (D)

Hugh, Timothy (vc)
Beethoven, L. van:Son 1 Vc, w. Y. Solomon (pno) IMP Masters ▲ IMPMCD 80 [DDD]
Beethoven, L. van:Son 2 Vc, w. Y. Solomon (pno) IMP Masters ▲ IMPMCD 80 [DDD]
Beethoven, L. van:Son 3 Vc, w. Y. Solomon (pno) IMP Masters ▲ IMPMCD 80 [DDD]
Bliss, A.:Con Vc, w. D. Lloyd-Jones (cnd), English Northern Philharmonia *(rec Leeds Town Hall, England, July 10-11, 1995)* Naxos ▲ 8.553383 [DDD]
Britten, H.:Suites Vc (comp) Hyperion ▲ CDA 66274 [DDD]
Grieg, E.:Son Vc, w. Y. Solomon (pno) IMP Masters ▲ IMPMCD 72 [DDD]
Grieg, E.:Songs, w. Y. Solomon (pno)—Jeg elsker dig, Op. 5/3 IMP Masters ▲ IMPMCD 72 [DDD]
Schnittke, A.:Trio Strs, w. M. Marinkovic (vn), P. Silverthorne (va) ASV ▲ ASV 868 [DDD]

Hughes, Carys (org)
Lewandowksi, L.L.:Choral Music, w. Sandra Lee (sop), Ann Sadan (alt), Don Carter (ten), Adam Cohn (b-bar), Michael Morris (bass), Robert Max (cnd), Zemel Choir—Ma Towu in F; Ma Towu in B♭; L'cho Dodi; Tow L'hodoss; Adoshem Moloch; W'hogen Ba'adenu [Uw'tsel]; W'schomru; L'icho Adoshem; J'Halahu [Hodo Al Erez]; Ladoshem Ho'orets; Uw'nucho Jomar; Adon Olom; Ki K'schimcho; Hajom Harass Olom; Kol Nidre; Schuwi Nafschi; Enosch, K'chozir Jomow; Halalujoh; Preise, Meine Seele Olympia ▲ OLY 347 [DDD]

Hughes, Christopher (org)
Grier, F.:Anthems, w. James Bowman (ct), Ralph Allwood (cnd), Rodolfus Choir—Let us invoke Christ; Great is the Power of Thy Cross; God, Who Made the Earth & Sky; Proclaim His Triumph; Day After Day; Salve Regina; Corpus Christi Carol; O King of the Friday; Christ's Love-Song; The Voice of My Beloved; Dilectus Meus Mihi; Thou, O God, Art Praised in Sion *(rec Eton College Chapel, Dec 1994)* Herald ▲ HAVPCD 177 [DDD]
Ives, C.:Choral Music, w. S. Cleobury (cnd), Duke String Quartet, New London Orch members, BBC Singers—Psalms 54, 67, 90 & 135; Easter Carol; Crossing the Bar; The Celestial Country Collins Classics ▲ COL 1479

Hughes, Clive (vn)—see ORCHESTRAS & ENSEMBLES Smith String Quartet

Hughes, Janet (org)
Franck, C.:Prière Pavane ▲ ADW 7242 [DDD]
Jongen, J.:Mass, Op. 130, w. T. Cunningham (cnd), Luc Capouillez Brass Ensemble, Brussels Choral Society [L] Pavane ▲ ADW 7242 [DDD]
Peeters, F.:Org Music—Entrata Festiva, Op. 93 (1959) Pavane ▲ ADW 7242 [DDD]

Hugo, Robert (hpd)
Myslivecek, J.:Sons en Trio, w. Jan Sirc (vc), Radomír Sirc (vc), Václav Hoskovec (db) Studio Matous ▲ MAT 19 [DDD]

Hugo, Robert (org)
Zielenski, M.:Communiones totius anni, w. Kira Borescko (sop), Marcin Borus-Szczycinski (alt), Ryszard Minkiewicz (ten), M. Bornus-Szczycinski (cnd), Bornus Consort, Tallinn Linnamussikud Instrumental Ensemble, Tallin Linnamussikud Vocal Ensemble Urtext ▲ ACD 202662 [DDD]
Zielenski, M.:Offertoria totius anni, w. Kira Borescko (sop), Marcin Borus-Szczycinski (alt), Ryszard Minkiewicz (ten), M. Bornus-Szczycinski (cnd), Bornus Consort, Tallinn Linnamussikud Instrumental Ensemble, Tallin Linnamussikud Vocal Ensemble Urtext ▲ ACD 202662 [DDD]

Hugonnard-Roche, C. (pno)
Prokofiev, S.:Romeo & Juliet Pno Quantum ▲ QM 6913 [DDD] ■ QM 2008 (D)
Prokofiev, S.:Son 9 Pno Quantum ▲ QM 6913 [DDD] ■ QM 2008 (D)
Prokofiev, S.:Tales of an Old Grandmother Quantum ▲ QM 6913 [DDD] ■ QM 2008 (D)
Schumann, R.:Fant Pno Quantum ▲ QM 6893 [DDD] ■ QM 1988 (D)
Schumann, R.:Fantasiestücke Pno, Op. 111 Quantum ▲ QM 6893 [DDD] ■ QM 1988 (D)
Schumann, R.:Intermezzos Quantum ▲ QM 6893 [DDD] ■ QM 1988 (D)

Hug-Rutti, Praxedis (hp)
Keller, A.:Der enthüllte Stern, w. D. Fueter (sop), K. Graf (sop), A. K. Graf (fl), L. Pellerin (ob), E. Schmid (cl), U. Walker (vn), C. Schiller (va), P. Demenga (vc), F. Eberle (dr) [G] Grammont ▲ CTSP 19-2 [ADD]
Keller, A.:Ewiger Augenblick, w. D. Fueter (sop), K. Graf (sop), A. K. Graf (fl), E. Schmid (cl), D. Isler (cel), U. Walker (vn), P. Demenga (vc) [G] Grammont ▲ CTSP 19-2 [ADD]

Hui-Man, Ku (P'i P'a)
Wut, M.-C.:Ambush on All Sides, w. C.-S. Chen (cnd), Yomiuri Nippon SO Sunrise ▲ 8515

Hu-Kun (vn)
International Menuhin Music Academy, w. International Menuhin Music Academy, Nora Chastain (vn), Paul Coletti (vn), Mi-Kyung Lee (vn), Alberto Lysy (vn) Arcobaleno ▲ SBCD 4700 [DDD]

Hula, Pavel (vn)
Bériot, C.-A. de:Music of, w. B. Kotmel (vn) Supraphon ▲ CD 111868 [DDD]
Leclair, J.-M.:Sons for 2 Vns, Op. 3, w. B. Kotmel (vn) Supraphon ▲ CD 111868 [DDD]
Spohr, L.:Duets Vns, Op. 3, w. B. Kotmel (vn) Supraphon ▲ CD 111868 [DDD]
Viotti, G.B.:Sym Concertante 2, w. B. Kotmel (vn), *(orch unknown)* Supraphon ▲ CD 111868 [DDD]

Hull, Barbara (tpt)
Shewan, S.:Magnificat, w. Erin Stedman (sop), Kimberly Higgins (alt), Robert Dingman (ten), Alexander Burgess (bar), Paul Shewan (tpt), Nanita Wilson (hn), Scott Emmons (trbn), Kirk Kettinger (tuba), Ann Musser Honeywell (org) Albany ▲ TROY 149 [DDD]
Shewan, S.:The Voice of the Lord in the Storm, w. Erin Stedman (sop), Kimberly Higgins (alt), Robert Dingman (ten), Alexander Burgess (bar), Paul Shewan (tpt), Nanita Wilson (hn), Scott Emmons (trbn), Kirk Kettinger (tuba), Ann Musser Honeywell (org) Albany ▲ TROY 149 [DDD]

Hulliger, Annerös (org)
Festal Music for 3 Organs & for Organ 4-Hands, w. A. Marcon (org), Philip Swanton (org) Koch Schwann ▲ SCH 310472 [DDD]
Festliche Musik für zwei Orgeln, w. Philip Swanton (org) Koch Schwann ▲ SCH 312842 [DDD]

Hulscher, Adrianna (vn)
Lovenstein, J.:Music of, w. Mary Brockenbrough (sop), Laura Sanders (sop), Barton Green (ten), Rockland Osgood (ten), David Murray (bar), Benjamin Sears (bar), Jonathan Lovenstein (pno), Heather O'Donnell (pno), James Silvers (pno), Rocy Reider (fl), Jason Horowitz (vn), James Johnston (vn), Mimi Ragson (vn), Peter Landeen (vc), Reinmar Seidler (vc)—Blake Songs; other works Titanic ▲ Ti 221 [DDD]

Hulse, Gareth (ob)
Matthews, C.:Suns Dance, w. Sebastian Bell (pic), Michael Collins (b cl), John Orford (ctbn), Michael Thompson (hn), Nona Liddell (vn), Joan Atherton (vn), Paul Silverthorne (va), Christopher van Kampen (vc), Robin McGee (db) *(rec All Saint's Church, Petersham, Oct 1992)* Deutsche Grammophon ▲ 447067-2 [DDD]
Takemitsu, T.:Music of, w. J. Williams (gtr), S. Bell (fl), E.-P. Salonen (cnd), London Sinfonietta—To the Edge of Dream (for Guitar & Orchestra); Vers, L'arc-en-ciel, Palma (for Guitar & Oboe); Toward the Sea (for Alto Flute & Guitar); Folios (for solo Guitar); 12 Songs for Guitar (selections) Sony Classical ▲ SK 46720
Takemitsu, T.:Tree Line, w. O. Knussen (cnd), London Sinfonietta Virgin Classics ▲ CDC 59020

Hulsmann, Kees (vn)
Lewis, P.S.:Con Vn, w. K. Hulsmann (cnd), Berkeley SO *(rec Berkeley, CA, June 1995)* New Albion ▲ NA 079

Hultgren, Craig (vc)
Burrier, M.:II Innova ▲ 502
Hultgren, C.:The Chained Vc Improvisation Innova ▲ 502
Hultgren, C.:The Double Bow Improvisation Innova ▲ 502
Marth, M.:They're Still Running to the West, Rex Innova ▲ 502
Mason, C.N.:The Artist & His Model Innova ▲ 502
Nielson, L.:Valentine Mechanique, w. Michael Geary (perc) Innova ▲ 502
Paredes, H.:Small Writing, w. Keith Collins (perc) Innova ▲ 502
Ross, J.C.:Encore Vc, w. Rene Lecuona (pno) Innova ▲ 502

Humberger, Janet (voc/hpd)—see ORCHESTRAS & ENSEMBLES Echos Muse

628 ▲ = CD ♦ = Enhanced CD Δ = MD ■ = Cassette Tape □ = DCC

Humeston, Jay (vc)
Villa-Lobos, H.:Son 2 Vc, w. M. Duphil (pno) Marco Polo ▲ 8.223164
Villa-Lobos, H.:Trio 1 Vn, w. A. Spiller (vn), M. Duphil (pno) Marco Polo ▲ 8.223182
Villa-Lobos, H.:Trio 2 Vn, w. A. Nuñez (vn), M. Duphil (pno) Marco Polo ▲ 8.223164
Villa-Lobos, H.:Trio 3 Vn, w. A. Spiller (vn), M. Duphil (pno) Marco Polo ▲ 8.223182
Hummel, Franz (org)
Hummel, F.:Tantalus lächelt Col legno ▲ AU 31802 [DDD]
Hummel, George (fl)
Gibson, R.:Sketches (3), w. Jeffrey Meyerriecks (gtr) Capstone ▲ CPS 8621
Humphreys, Sydney (vn)—see also ORCHESTRAS & ENSEMBLES Aeolian String Quartet
Spohr, L.:Duets Vns, Op. 3, w. R. Ricci (vn)—No. 2 in F One-Eleven ▲ URS 92010
Wieniawski, H.:Etudes-caprices, w. R. Ricci (vn)—No. 4 One-Eleven ▲ URS 92010
Humphreys, Wendy (Celtic hp)
Opening Day, w. Humphreys, Wendy (sop), Stuart Laughton (tpt), Peter Tiefenbach (org/pno), William O'Meara (org) Doremi ▲ 9301 [DDD]
Humphries, Ian (vn)—see ORCHESTRAS & ENSEMBLES Smith String Quartet
Hunger, Helmut (tpt)
Trumpet Concertos, w. André Bernard (tpt), et al., English CO [cnd:George Malcolm], Venice Soloists [cnd:Claudio Scimone] Sony Classical ("Essential Classics" series) ▲ SBK 47663 ■ SBT 47663
Hungerford, Bruce (pno)
Beethoven, L. van:Son 30 Pno *(rec 1967)* Vanguard Classics ("Everyman" series) ▲ OVC 5001 [ADD]
Beethoven, L. van:Son 31 Pno *(rec 1969)* Vanguard Classics ("Everyman" series) ▲ OVC 5001 [ADD]
Beethoven, L. van:Son 32 Pno *(rec 1967)* Vanguard Classics ("Everyman" series) ▲ OVC 5001 [ADD]
Hunt, Colin (org)
Tučapsky, A.:The Sacrifice, w. Stephen Foulkes (bar), Nigel Perrin (cnd), Bath Camerata *(rec Wells Cathedral, Jan 27, 1996)* SOMM ▲ SOMMCD 205 [DDD]
Hunt, Donald (org)
English Organ Music 2 *(rec Oct. 29, 1991)* Naxos ▲ 8.550773 [DDD]
Hunt, Gordon (ob)
Druschetzky, G.:Con Ob & Timp, w. J. Haas (timp), H. Farberman (cnd), Bournemouth Sinfonietta CRD ▲ 3449 [ADD]
Mozart, W.A.:Qt Ob, K.370, w. Chilingirian String Quartet Classics for Pleasure ▲ CDCFP 4377 [ADD]
Music for Trumpet & Organ, w. Graham Ashton (tpt), Leslie Pearson (org), John Orford (bn), Denis Vigay (vc) IMP Classics ▲ PCD 986 [DDD]
Strauss, R.:Con Ob, w. V. Ashkenazy (cnd), Berlin RSO London ▲ 436415-2 [DDD]
Trumpet & Organ:Sonatas & Suites, w. Graham Ashton (tpt), Leslie Pearson (org), John Orford (bn), Denis Vigay (vc) IMP ("Classics" series) ▲ IMP 6700922
Vivaldi, A.:Cons Ob, w. C. Warren-Green (cnd), London CO—RV.447 in C Virgin Classics ▲ 59609 [DDD]
Hunt, Jerry (perc/pno/elec)
Hunt, J.:Bitom O.O. Discs ▲ OO 9 [DDD]
Hunt, Jerry (pno/elec)
Hunt, J.:Lattice O.O. Discs ▲ OO 9 [DDD]
Hunt, Jerry (synclavier)
Hunt, J.:Fluud Centaur ▲ CRC 2029 [DDD]
Hunt, P. (trbn)
Schindler, A.:Eternal Winter Capstone ▲ CPS 8603
Hunt, W. (vle)
A Banquet of Voices:Music for Mulitple Choirs, w. [cnd:John Rutter], Cambridge Singers, H. Gough (baroque vc), W. Marshall (chamber org) *(rec London, Feb. 1993)* Collegium ▲ COLCD 123
Hünteler, Konrad (fl)
Frederick II:Con Fl, w. U. Björlin (cnd), Cappella Coloniensis LaserLight ▲ 14036 [DDD]
Haydn, J.:Trios Pno, Fl & Vc, w. Patrick Cohen (pno), Christophe Coin (vc) Harmonia Mundi France ▲ HMC 901521
Reicha, A.:Qts Fl, w. Rainer Kussmaul (vn), Jürgen Kussmaul (va), Roel Dieltiens (vc) MD + G ▲ MDG 3110630
Telemann, G.P.:Fants Fl MD + G ▲ L 3486 [DDD]
Vivaldi, A.:Cons Fl, Op. 10, w. K. Hünteler (cnd), Camerata of the 18th Century [Denner fl] MD + G ▲ MDG 3110640
Hünteler, Konrad (trns fl)
Telemann, G.P.:Con Rcr, w. G. Höller (rcr), G. Fischer (cnd), Cappella Coloniensis LaserLight ▲ 14036 [DDD]
The Viola d'Amore:In Numerous Voices, w. Dorothea Jappe (va d'amore), Hans-Rudolf Stalder (chl), Herbert Hoever (vn), Michael Jappe (vl/vc), Rolf Junghanns (hpd/pno) Adagio ▲ ADG 91016
Hunter, Desmond (org)
Stanford, C.V.:Sons Org (comp) [Organ of the Guildhall, Londonderry] Priory 2-▲ PRI 445 [DDD]
Hunter, L. (sax)—see ORCHESTRAS & ENSEMBLES Duo Vivo
Hunter, Matthew (va)—see ORCHESTRAS & ENSEMBLES Montreal Musica Camerata
Huntgeburth, Christoph (fl)
Leclair, J.-M.:Sons Vn (Books 1-4), w. Mitzi Meyerson (hpd), Hildegard Perl (vl)—Op. 2/1, 3 & 11; Op. 9/2 & 7 ASV ("Gaudeamus" series) ▲ ASV CD 158
Mozart, F.X.W.:Rondo Fl, w. R. Junghanns (pno) FSM-Adagio ▲ FCD 91638 [ADD]
Roman, J.H.:Sons Fl, w. P. Evison (fl), K. Ottesen (vc), O. Larsson (vc), E. Nordenfeldt (hpd)—Nos. 1, 2, 5, 6, 7 & 9 Proprius ▲ PRCD 9020
Hunziker, D. (fl)—see ORCHESTRAS & ENSEMBLES Les Joueurs de Flute
Hunziker, Eva (hp)
Martin, F.:Petite sym concertante, w. G. Vaucher-Clerc (hpd), D. Rosslaud (pno), F. Martin (cnd), Swiss-Italian Orch *(rec Sept. 3, 1970)* Jecklin-Disco ▲ JD 645-2 [ADD]
Hurford, Peter (org)
Bach, J.S.:Fant Org, BWV 572 London ("Double Decker" series) 2-▲ 443473-2
Bach, J.S.:Org Music (misc) London ("Jubilee" series) 3-▲ 421337-2 [ADD]
Bach, J.S.:Toccata & Fugue Org, BWV 565 London ("Double Decker" series) 2-▲ 443473-2
Handel, G.F.:Cons (16) Org, w. A. Rifkin (cnd), Royal Concertgebouw CO—Op. 4/1-6, 13 & 14 London ("Serenata" series) 2-▲ 430569-2
Organ Spectacular London ▲ 430710-2 LM [DDD]
Poulenc, F.:Con Org, w. C. Dutoit (cnd), Philharmonia Orch *(rec Feb. 24-28, 1992)* London ▲ 436546-2
Saint-Saëns, C.:Sym 3, w. C. Dutoit (cnd), Montreal SO London ▲ 430720-2 [DDD]
Hurnik, I. (pno)
Saint-Saëns, C.:Carnival of the Animals, w. P. Stepan (pno), M. Turnovsky (cnd), Prague SO Supraphon Collection ▲ 11 0646-2 [ADD]
Hurnik, Jiří (vn)—see also ORCHESTRAS & ENSEMBLES Antonín Dvořák Trio
Eben, Petr:Sonatina Semplice, w. Petr Eben (pno) *(rec Martínek Studio in Prague, Jan 23 & 26 & Feb 13 & 14)* Panton ▲ 811398-2 [DDD]
Shostakovich, D.:Son Vn, w. Jaromír Klepác (pno) Panton ▲ PAN 811013
Stravinsky, I.:Divert Vn, w. Jaromír Klepác (pno) Panton ▲ PAN 811013
Hurton, Amanda (pno)
Amirov, F.:Pieces (6) Fl, w. Lesley Newman (fl) Cala ▲ CAL CACD 88026 [DDD]
Feld, J.:Son Fl, w. Lesley Newman (fl) Cala ▲ CAL CACD 88026 [DDD]
Gubaidulina, S.:Allegro rustico, w. Lesley Newman (fl) Cala ▲ CAL CACD 88026 [DDD]
Gubaidulina, S.:Sounds of the Forest, w. Lesley Newman (fl) Cala ▲ CAL CACD 88026 [DDD]
Martinů, B.:Son Fl & Pno, w. Lesley Newman (fl) Cala ▲ CAL CACD 88026 [DDD]
Taktakishvili, O.:Son Fl, w. Lesley Newman (fl) Cala ▲ CAL CACD 88026 [DDD]
Hurtubise, Benoit (vc)
Vivaldi, A.:Con for 2 Vns Vcs, w. C. Prevost (vn), L. Hall (vn), A. Aubut (vc), Y. Turovsky (cnd), Montreal Musici—RV.542 in F Chandos ▲ CHAN 8651 [DDD]
Husser, Philippe (fl)
Légendes 2, w. Philippe Husser (fl), Paul Couëffé (org) Pavane ▲ ADW 7350

Hussla, M. (db)—see ORCHESTRAS & ENSEMBLES Berlin String Quintet
Husson, S. (pno)
Debussy, C.:Estampes Fonè ▲ 87F 02-14 [DDD]
Ginastera, A.:Danzas argentinas Fonè ▲ 87F 02-14 [DDD]
Ravel, M.:Gaspard de la nuit Fonè ▲ 87F 02-14 [DDD]
Ravel, M.:Jeux d'eau Fonè ▲ 87F 02-14 [DDD]
Scarlatti, D.:Sons Kbd—K.20 & K.141 Fonè ▲ 87F 02-14 [DDD]
Vuataz, R.:Con Pno, w. W. Sawallisch (cnd), Swiss Romande Orch *(rec Feb. 13, 1974)* Grammont ▲ CTSP 7-2 [ADD]
Hussong, Stefan (acc)
Bach, J.S.:English Suites—BWV 807, 808 & 811 *(rec Aobadai Philia Hall, Yokohama, Japan, Dec 26-28, 1994)* Denon ▲ CO 78836 [DDD]
Gubaidulina, S.:In Croce, w. Julius Berger (vc) Wergo ▲ WER 6263-2
Gubaidulina, S.:The Seven Last Words, w. Julius Berger (vc), F. Rosensteiner (cnd), CO Diagonal Wergo ▲ WER 6263-2
Whose Song, w. Hussong, Stefan (acc) *(rec Dec. 1992)* Thorofon ▲ CTH 2184 [DDD]
Hussu, V. (ob)
Handel, G.F.:Cons (3) Ob, w. V. Alexeiev (cnd), Collegium Musicum Infinity Digital ▲ QK 64293 [DDD]
Hustis, Gregory (hn)—see also ORCHESTRAS & ENSEMBLES Dallas Chamber Players
Bach, W.F.:Zerbrecht, zerreist, Aria, w. N. Keith, S. Sargon [G] *(rec Mar-July 1991)* Crystal ▲ CD675
Beethoven, L. van:Sxt Hns, Op. 81b, w. D. Battey (hn), R. Neal (cnd), Dallas CO Crystal ▲ CD 512
Berlioz, H.:Songs, w. N. Keith (sop), S. Sargon (pno)—Le jeune pâtre breton [F] *(rec 3-7/91)* Crystal ▲ CD675
Christmas in Dallas, w. Christina Harmon (org), Jeffery Curnow (tpt), Adam Gordon (tpt), Clarece Candamio (org) *(rec Lover's Lane United Methodist Church, Dallas)* Hester Park ▲ 7706 [DDD]
"Huntsman, What Quarry?", w. Nancy Keith (sop), Simon Sargon (pno) Crystal ▲ CD675
Leclaire, D.:Qt Hns, w. T. Bacon (hn), W. Caballero (hn), Erik Ralske (hn) Summit ▲ DCD 135 [DDD]
Linek, J.:Intradas, w. D. Battey (hn), D. Howard (timp), Dallas SO Trumpet Section Crystal ▲ CD234
Mozart, L.:Con Hn, w. R. Neal (cnd), Dallas CO Crystal ▲ CD 512
Nicolai, O.:Variazioni concertanti, w. N. Keith (sop), S. Sargon (pno) [I] Crystal ▲ CD675
Schubert, Franz:Songs (misc), w. N. Keith (sop), S. Sargon (pno)—Auf dem Strom, D.943 [G] Crystal ▲ CD675
Strauss, R.:Das Alphorn, w. N. Keith (sop), S. Sargon (pno) [G] Crystal ▲ CD675
Treasures for Horn & Trumpet, w. Richard Giangiulio (tpt), Dallas CO [cnd:Ronald Neal] *(rec 11/88)* Crystal ▲ CD 512
Hutchenreuther, David (vc)
Mather, B.:Elegy, w. Robert Cram (fl), Charlotte Sheng (pno), Jonathan Wade (perc) Centrediscs ▲ CMC 5094 [DDD]
Hutchins, Timothy (fl)
Vivaldi, A.:Cons Fl (misc), w. Y. Turovsky (cnd), Montreal Musici—RV.433 Chandos ▲ CHAN 8444 [DDD]
Hutchins, Timothy (rcr)
Vivaldi, A.:Cons Rcr, w. Y. Turovsky (cnd), Montreal Musici—Concerto in C, RV.444 Chandos ▲ CHAN 8444 [DDD]
Hutchinson, Nigel (org)
Duruflé, M.:Sacred Choral Music, w. Anthony Noble (cnd), Farnborough Abbey Choir—Offertory [Veritas mea]; Communion [Beatus servus] *(rec St. Michael's Abbey, Farnborough, May 1994)* Herald ▲ HAVPCD 179 [DDD]
Duruflé, M.:Suite Org—Toccata *(rec St. Michael's Abbey, Farnborough, May 1994)* Herald ▲ HAVPCD 179 [DDD]
Langlais, J.:Sacred Choral Music, w. Anthony Noble (cnd), Farnborough Abbey Choir—Kyrie [Missa in simplicitate]; Gloria [Missa in simplicitate]; Gradual [Iustus ut palma]; Alleluia [Beatus vir]; Sequence [Laetabunda]; Gospel [plainsong]; Credo [Plainsong III]; Offertory [Veritas mea]; Sanctus [Missa in simplicitate]; Benedictus [Missa in simplicitate]; Pater Noster [Plainsong]; Agnus Dei [Missa in simplicitate] *(rec St. Michael's Abbey, Farnborough, May 1994)* Herald ▲ HAVPCD 179 [DDD]
Hutchinson, Roland (vl)
Bach, C.P.E.:Sons Fl, w. L. Miller (baroque fl), L. Burman-Hall (hpd)—in G, H.548 (W.134); in G, H.550 (W.123); in e, H.551 (W.124); in B♭, H.552 (W.125); in D, H.553 (W.126); in G, H.554 (W.127) Centaur ▲ CRC 2087 [DDD]
Hutchinson, Thomas (trbn)
Chambers, W.M.:A Mass for Mass Trbns, w. D. Gilbert (cnd), *(orch unknown)* *(rec Cathedral of St. John, New York City, Jun 18, 1994)* Centaur ▲ CRC 2263 [DDD]
Sowerby, L.:Festival Musick, w. Carl Albach (tpt), Susan Radcliff (tpt), Jeffrey Caswell (trbn), Dan Haskins (timp), David Mulbury (org), J. Welsh (cnd), Fairfield Orch *(rec St. Bartholomew's Church, New York City, May 5, 1994)* Marco Polo ▲ 8.223725 [DDD]
Huter, S. (pno)
Franck, C.:Son Vn, w. L. Pantillon (vn) Gallo ▲ CD 632 [AAD]
Lekeu, G.:Son Vn, w. L. Pantillon (vn) Gallo ▲ CD 632 [AAD]
Hůla, P. (vn)—see ORCHESTRAS & ENSEMBLES Kocian String Quartet
Huvé, Cyril (pno)
Ligeti, G.:Trio Hn, Vn & Pno, w. A. Cazalet (hn), G. Commentale (vn) Montaigne ▲ MO 782006 [DDD]
Huvenne, B. (hp)—see ORCHESTRAS & ENSEMBLES Stanislas Ensemble
Huybrechts, Dominique (va)
Mahaut, A.:Sinfs Strs, w. H. Schoonbroot (cnd), Camerata Leodiensis—No. 1 in F, No. 2 in D & Op. 2, No. 4 in c; Sinfonia in A for Viola, Strings & Continuo, Op. 2, No. 6 Koch Schwann ▲ CD 311100 [DDD]
Villette, P.:Qts Strs, w. L. Bobesco (vn), J.-M. Defalque (vn), S. Mariage (vc)—Nos. 1-6 in A, C, F, B♭, E♭ & E Talent ▲ DOM 2910 46 [DDD]
Huybregts, Pierre (pno)
Albéniz, I.:Cantos de España *(rec Ghent, Belgium, Dec 1993)* Centaur ▲ CRC 2231 [DDD]
Albéniz, I.:España Centaur ▲ CRC 2026 [ADD]
Albéniz, I.:Pno Music—Cadiz-Gaditana; Mallorca; Rumores de la Caleta; Gavotte; Torre Bermejo *(rec Ghent, Belgium, Dec 1993)* Centaur ▲ CRC 2231 [DDD]
Albéniz, I.:Suite española *(rec Ghent, Belgium, Dec 1993)* Centaur ▲ CRC 2231 [DDD]
Gershwin, G.:Music of, w. C. W. Payne (pno)—Fant. "An Afternoon with Gershwin" Love Is Here to Stay, Mine & A Foggy Day; Nice Work If You Can Get It; They Can't Take That away from Me; Oh, Lady Be Good; Somebody Loves Me; Love Walked in; Strike up the Band; 'S Wonderful; I Got Rhythm; Soon Let's Call the Whole Thing Off; Fant. "An Evening with Gershwin" Of Thee I Sing; Who Cares; Embraceable You; Fascinating Rhythm [all arr. Huybregts] *(rec Nov. 1992)* Centaur ▲ CRC 2178 [DDD]
Gershwin, G.:Pno Music, w. C. Wallace Payne (pno)—The Man I Love, 2-piano arr. by Huybregts Centaur ▲ CRC 2117 [DDD]
Grainger, P.:Fant on Gershwin's *Porgy & Bess*, w. C. Wallace Payne (pno) Centaur ▲ CRC 2117 [DDD]
Granados, E.:Pno Music (misc)—Quejas o la Maja y el Ruiseñor (from Goyescas); Andaluza (Spanish Dance No. 5) Centaur ▲ CRC 2026 [ADD]
Halffter, E.:Habanera Centaur ▲ CRC 2026 [ADD]
Mompou, F.:Cançons i dansas Centaur ▲ CRC 2055 [ADD]
Mompou, F.:Cants magics Centaur ▲ CRC 2026 [ADD]
Mompou, F.:Charmes Centaur ▲ CRC 2055 [ADD]
Mompou, F.:Fêtes lointaines Centaur ▲ CRC 2055 [ADD]
Mompou, F.:Pessebres Centaur ▲ CRC 2026 [ADD]
Poulenc, F.:Élégie Pnos, w. C. Wallace Payne (pno) Centaur ▲ CRC 2117 [DDD]
Poulenc, F.:L'Embarquement pour Cythère, w. C. Wallace Payne (pno) Centaur ▲ CRC 2117 [DDD]
Poulenc, F.:Son Pno 4-Hands, w. C. Wallace Payne (pno) Centaur ▲ CRC 2117 [DDD]
Poulenc, F.:Son for 2 Pnos, w. C. Wallace Payne (pno) Centaur ▲ CRC 2117

INSTRUMENT.

Huybregts, Pierre (pno) (cont.)
Rodgers, R.:Music of, w. Carol Wallace Payne (pno)—Oklahoma Suite; My Funny Valentine; The Lady Is a Tramp; Bewitched; Where or When; Blue Moon; The Sweetest Sounds; You Are Too Beautiful; Falling in Love with Love; With a Song in My Heart; If I Loved You; Lover [all arr Huybregts for Pno Duo] *(rec Recital Hall, Pensacola, FL, Feb 1994)* Centaur ▲ CRC 2264 [DDD]
Schumann, R.:Arabeske Pno Centaur ▲ CRC 2135 [DDD]
Schumann, R.:Blumenstück Centaur ▲ CRC 2135 [DDD]
Schumann, R.:Carnaval Pno Centaur ▲ CRC 2135 [DDD]
Schumann, R.:Kinderszenen Centaur ▲ CRC 2065 [ADD]
Schumann, R.:Papillons Centaur ▲ CRC 2065 [ADD]
Spanish Piano Music Centaur ▲ CRC 2026 [ADD]
Turina, J.:Album de viaje Centaur ▲ CRC 2026 [ADD]
Turina, J.:Sacro-Monte Pno Centaur ▲ CRC 2026 [ADD]

Hwang, Byungki (kayagum)
Hwang, B.:Music of—Silk Road (1977); The Forest (1963); Spring (1963); Pomegranate House (1965); Fall (1967); Kara Town (1967); Dance in the Perfume of Aloes (1974) Arcadia ▲ ARC 1996-2 [ADD]
Hwang, B.:Music of, w. et al.—The Haunted Tree (1979) & Legend (1979) for Kayagum [12-string Korean zither] & Changgo [Korean hourglass drum]; The Labyrinth for Kayagum & Female Voice (1975); Beside a Chrysanthemum [lyric song] for Male Voice & Instruments (1962); Mountain Rhyme for Komungo [6-string fretted zither] & Taegum [bamboo flute]; Aibogaue (Children's Dances) for Kayagum, Taegum & Drum Arcadia ▲ ARC 1994-2 [ADD]

Hwang, J. K. (5 str elec vn/elec processing/bird whistles)—see ORCHESTRAS & ENSEMBLES Far East Side Band

Hyde, Dan (org)
Let All the World, w. Oakham School Chapel Choir [cnd:David Woodcock] Symposium ▲ SYM 1181

Hyde, George (hn)—see ORCHESTRAS & ENSEMBLES Los Angeles Horn Club

Hyde, Miriam (pno)
Hyde, M.:Pno Music—Fantasia on Waltzing Matilda; Magpies at Sunrise; Son. in g; Reflected Reeds; Scherzo Fantastico; Evening in Cordoba; Valley of Rocks; The Ring of New Bells Southern Cross ▲ SCCD 1027 [DDD]

Hyde-Smith, Christopher (fl)
Robertson, E.:The Namia Suite, w. M. Robles (hp), Marisa Robles Harp Ensemble ASV ("White Line" series) ▲ WHL 2068 [DDD]

Hyde-Smith, Christopher (fl/pic)
Jeux d'Enfants, w. Emma Johnson (cl), George MacDonald (cl), Gordon Back (pno), Academy of St. Martin in the Fields [cnd:Neville Marriner], Mexico City PO, Mexico State SO, Royal PO [cnd:Enrique Bátiz], et al. ASV Quicksilva ▲ ASQ 6182

Hyla, L. (dr)
Ives, C.:Halloween, w. S. Pinkas (pno), Lydian String Quartet Centaur ▲ CRC 2069 [DDD]

Hyla, Lee (pno)
Hyla, L.:The Dream of Innocent III, w. Rhonda Rider (va), James Pugliese (perc) CRI ▲ CD 564 [DDD]

Hyman, Dick (pno)
Joplin, S.:Pno Music RCA Gold Seal ▲ 7993-2-RG [ADD] ■ 7993-4-RG (CrO2)
Scott Joplin:Greatest Hits, w. James Levine (pno) RCA Victor ▲ 60842-2-RG ■ 60842-4-RG

Hymas, Tony (pno)
Doyle, P.:Sense & Sensibility, w. Jane Eaglen (sop), Jonathan Snowdon (fl), Richard Morgan (ob), Robert Hill (cl), R. Ziegler (cnd), *(orch unknown)* *(rec Air Studios, Lyndhurst Hall)* Sony Classical ▲ SK 62258 [DDD]

Hynčica, Jan (trbn)
Janácek, L.:Capriccio, w. Daniel Wiesner (pno), Jan Riedlbauch (fl/pic), Vladislav Kozderka (tpt), Jan Fišer (tpt), Václav Ferebauer (trbn), Antonin Keller (trbn), Jiří Novotný (ten tuba), L. Svárovsky (cnd) *(rec Martinek Studio in Prague, Jan 9, Feb 27, Mar 20, 19)* Panton ▲ 811393-2 [DDD]

Hyning, van (perc)
Davidovsky, M.:Synchronism 5, w. R. DesRoches (perc), R. Fitz (perc), Heldrich (perc), D. Marcone (perc), H. Sollberger (cnd) CRI ▲ CD 611 [ADD]

Hyslop, S. (a sax)
Kallman, D.:Forecasts, w. E. Finney (sop sax), K. Claussen (ten sax), W. Burton (bar sax) Innova ▲ MN 109
Macy, C.:4 Saxes, w. E. Finney (sop sax), K. Claussen (ten sax), W. Burton (bar sax) Innova ▲ MN 109

Hysong, Brian (b cl)
Brings, A.:Concert Piece for 4 Cls, w. M. Abt-Greenfield (E♭ cl), P. Gallo (a cl), E. Gilmore (cl) *(rec 1989-90)* Centaur ▲ CRC 2079 [ADD]

Hyuang, Hsin-Yun (va)—see ORCHESTRAS & ENSEMBLES Windham String Quartet

Iadone, Joseph (lt)
The Art of the Lute *(rec 1980-94)* Lyrichord ("Early Music" series) ▲ LYR 8020 [ADD]
Dowland, J.:Lt Songs, w. Russell Oberlin (ct)—Come Again! Sweet Love Doth Now Invite; Thou Mighty God; Can She Excuse My Wrongs?; Sempre Douland, Sempre Dolens; Flow So Fast, Ye Fountain; I Saw My Lady Weep; Weep You No More, Sad Fountains; Shall I Sue?; Flow My Tears; Lachrimae antiquae pavan; Far from Triumphing Court; Lady, If You So Spite Me; In Darkness Let Me Dwell Lyrichord ▲ LEM 8011

Iamamura, Yasunori (lt)—see ORCHESTRAS & ENSEMBLES August Wenzinger Ensemble

Iandiorio, Regis (vn)
Flowering of Vocal Music in America, 1767-1823, w. Susan Belling (sop), Cynthia Clarey (sop), Barbara Wallace (sop), Debra Vanderlinde (sop), D'Anna Fortunato (mez), Evelyn Petros (mez), Charles Bressler (ten), Richard Anderson (bar), James Tyeska (bar), Joseph McKee (bass), Cynthia Otis (hp), et al. New World ▲ 80467-2

Ibanez, Geneviève (pno)
Castérède, J.:Feux Croisés, w. J. Castérède (pno) REM ▲ 311092 [DDD]

Ibbott, Daphne (pno)
Elgar, E.:The Shepherd's Song, w. J. Carol Case (bar) Saga Classics ▲ 3353 [ADD]

Ibe, Harumi (gtr)
Takemitsu, T.:Music of, w. Tashi, Y. Nagano (mez), M. Nagasako (hp), K. Abe (vib), Y. Takahashi (pno), R. Noguchi (fl), M. Hamada (lt), T. Koizumi (picc), S. Ueki (vn), Y. Hattori (vc), R. Stoltzman (cl), P. Serkin (pno), Ozawa, Wakasugi (cnd), Boston SO—Quatrain; Stanza I; Sacrifice; Ring; Valeria; A Flock Descends into the Pentagonal Garden Deutsche Grammophon ("20th Century Classics" series) ▲ 423253-2 [ADD]

Iberer, Gerhard (vc)
Schmidt, F.:Qnt Pno, w. R. Keuschnig (pno), J. Hell (vn), P. Wächter (vn), P. Pecha (va) *(rec Jan. 7, 1991)* Orfeo ▲ 287921 [DDD]

Ibañez, Maria Lluisa (hp)
Britten, H.:A Ceremony of Carols, w. S. Bardolet (trb), X. Canadell (trb), J. Pieres (alt), F. Gasa (alt), G. Estrada (org), Escolania de Montserrat, I. Segarra (cnd) *(rec 1978?)* Koch Treasure ▲ 31624-2 [ADD]
Mendelssohn, F.:Motets, Op. 39, w. S. Bardolet (trb), X. Canadell (trb), J. Pieres (alt), F. Gasa (alt), G. Estrada (org), I. Segarra (cnd), Montserrat Escolania *(rec 1978?)* Koch Treasure ▲ 31624-2 [ADD]

Ichinohe, Atsushi (fl)—see ORCHESTRAS & ENSEMBLES Orphée Piano & Wind Quintet

Ichise, Reiko (b vl)—see ORCHESTRAS & ENSEMBLES English Fantasy

Ichiyanagi, Toshi (pno)
Ichiyanagi, T.:Two Existence, w. K. Kimura (pno) Camerata ▲ 32CM 52

Idenstam, Gunnar (org)
Bach, J.S.:Org Music (misc)—Canzona, BWV 588; Chorales, BWV 658 & 684; Fugues, BWV 575 & 577; Prelude & Fugue, BWV 541 & 548 Opus 111 ▲ OPS 51-9115
The Sacred Trombone, w. Christian Lindberg (trbn) BIS ▲ CD 488 [DDD]

Ienei, Aurora (pno)
Enescu, G.:Suites Pno—Op. 3/1; Op. 10; Op. 10 *(rec 1981)* Olympia ▲ OCD 414 [AAD]

Ieriomine, Alexéi (pno)
Rabinovitch, A.:Music for Pnos, w. A. Rabinovitch (pno), M. Argerich (pno), M. Adamovitch (pno), A. Batagov (pno)—Musique Populaire for 2 Pianos; La Belle Musique for 4 Pianos; Liebliches Lied for Piano 4-hands; Musique triste, parfois tragique *(rec 1990 & 1992)* Valois ▲ V 4694 [DDD]

Iglesia, Gérard (gtr)
Ravier, C.:Liturgie pour un Dieu mort, w. Guillemette Laurens (mez), C. Ravier (cnd), *(ensemble unknown)*, Maurice Bourbon Male Chorus Ensemble Memoire Vive ▲ 262023

Igloi, Thomas (vc)
Fauré, G.:Elégie, w. C. Benson (pno) CRD ▲ 3316
Fauré, G.:Sicilienne, w. C. Benson (pno) CRD ▲ 3316
Fauré, G.:Son 1 Vc, w. C. Benson (pno) CRD ▲ 3316
Fauré, G.:Son 2 Vc, w. C. Benson (pno) CRD ▲ 3316

Ignacio, Lydia Walton (pno)
Alexander, W.:Cambridge Trio, w. C. Englert (ob), J. Russo (cl) CRS ▲ CD 8949
Aubert, O.:Solo de Concours 1, w. J. Russo (cl) CRS ▲ CD 8949
Bernstein, L.:Son Cl, w. J. Russo (cl) CRS ▲ CD 8949
Bozza, E.:Caprice-Improvisation, w. J. Russo (cl) CRS ▲ CD 9257
Carter, E.:Pastoral E Hn, w. J. Russo (cl) CRS ▲ 9255
Contemporary/Classic Masters, w. John Russo (cl), Mirjam Ingolfsson (vc), et al. CRS ▲ 9255
Devienne, F.:Son 1 Cl, w. J. Russo (cl) CRS ▲ 9255
Hindemith, P.:Son Cl, w. J. Russo (cl) CRS ▲ 9051
Ibert, J.:Aria Cl & Pno, w. J. Russo (cl) CRS ▲ CD 9153
Masterworks for Clarinet & Piano, w. John Russo (cl) CRS Master ▲ CD 9561
Russo, J.:Largetto, w. J. Russo (cl), S. Curtiss (va) CRS ▲ 9255
Russo, J.:Son 1 Cl, w. J. Russo (cl) CRS ▲ CD 9153
Russo, J.:Son 4 Cl, w. J. Russo (cl) CRS ▲ 9255
Russo, J.:Son 1 Fl, w. L. Lind (fl) CRS ▲ CD 9257

Ignat, Filip (fl)
Borza, A.:Desintegration *(rec Academy of Music G. Dima in Cluj)* Hungaroton ("Classic" series) ▲ HCD 31572 [DDD]

Igolinsky, V. (vn)
Dmitriev, G.:Fant Vn & Pno, "Warsaw", w. Tatiana Sergeyeva (pno) *(rec Large Hall, Moscow Conservatory, 1990)* Russian Compact Disc ▲ RD CD 10003 [AAD]
Ekimovsky, V.:Stanzas, w. S. Kravchenko (vn) MCA Classics ▲ MLD 32131 [AAD] ■ MLC 32131
Gagnidze, M.:Poem MCA Classics ▲ MLD 32131 [AAD] ■ MLC 32131
Ryabov, V.:Con da passacaglia, w. S. Kravchenko (vn), V. Zhuk (vn), T. Sergeyeva (kbd) MCA Classics/Melodiya ▲ MLD 32131 [AAD] ■ MLC 32131

Ihlenfeldt, Thomas (chit)
Schütz, H.:Cantiones sacrae, w. Mona Spägele (sop), Ralf Popken (alt), Rogers Covey-Crump (ten), John Potter (ten), Peter Kooj (bass), Manfred Cordes (org)—complete 40 motets CPO 2-▲ 999405-2 [DDD]

Ihlenfeldt, Thomas (lt)—see ORCHESTRAS & ENSEMBLES Weser-Renaissance Ensemble

Ikeda, Kikuei (vn)—see ORCHESTRAS & ENSEMBLES Tokyo String Quartet

Ilchev, Alexander (vn)
Nikolov, L.:Qt 3 Strs, w. K. Mikaelian (vn), V. Gerov (va), G. Dean (vc) Gega ▲ GD 149 [DDD]

Ilea, Catalin (vc)—see also ORCHESTRAS & ENSEMBLES Amati Ensemble
Albert, E. d':Con Vc, w. W. A. Albert (cnd), Philharmonia Hungarica Arcobaleno ▲ AAOC 9390
Brahms, J.:Sons Vc (comp), w. Marlène Dobrea (pno) Arcobaleno ▲ AAOC 93932
Enescu, G.:Symphonie concertante, w. U. Mund (cnd), Philharmonia Hungarica Arcobaleno ▲ AAOC 9390

Ilg, Arnold (vc)—see ORCHESTRAS & ENSEMBLES Sikorsi String Quartet

Ilika, John (trbn)
Joan Lippincott & Philadelphia Brass, w. Joan Lippincott (org), Philadelphia Brass [Brian Kuszyk (tpt), Lawrence Wright (tpt), Martin Webster (hn), Grant Moore II (tuba)] Gothic ▲ GOT 49072 [DDD]

Ilio, Luigi di (pno)
Casella, A.:Scarlattiana, w. F. Biondi (vn)—Minuet [arr. for violin & piano] *(rec July 1991)* Opus 111 ▲ OPS 44-9202 [DDD]
Malipiero, G.F.:Vn & Pno Music, w. F. Biondi (vn) *(rec July 1991)* Opus 111 ▲ OPS 44-9202 [DDD]
Pizzetti, I.:Canti Vn, w. F. Biondi (vn) *(rec July 1991)* Opus 111 ▲ OPS 44-9202 [DDD]
Respighi, O.:Vn Pno Music, w. F. Biondi (vn)—Aubade; Berceuse; Humoresque; Madrigale; Melodia; Romanza *(rec July 1991)* Opus 111 ▲ OPS 44-9202 [DDD]
Schumann, C.:Romances Vn, w. F. Biondi (vn) [period instrs] Opus 111 ▲ OPS 30-77
Schumann, R.:Son 1 Vn, w. F. Biondi (vn) [period instrs] Opus 111 ▲ OPS 30-77
Schumann, R.:Son 2 Vn, w. F. Biondi (vn) [period instrs] Opus 111 ▲ OPS 30-77

Ille, Georghe (vn)
Haydn, M.:Con Vn, P.53, w. E. Acél (cnd), Oradea PO Olympia ("Explorer" series) ▲ OCD 406 [AAD]

Illenberger, Anton (pno)
Serenade:Song & Aria Recital, w. Dieter Schnerring (ten) Ars Musici ▲ 8003

Ilmer, Irving (va)—see ORCHESTRAS & ENSEMBLES Fine Arts String Quartet, Fine Arts String Quartet members

Ilves, J. (vn)—see ORCHESTRAS & ENSEMBLES Tapiola Trio

Imai, Nobuko (va)
Beethoven, L. van:Notturno, w. R. Vignoles (pno) Chandos ▲ CHAN 8664 [DDD]
Berlioz, H.:Harold in Italy, w. C. Davis (cnd), London SO Philips ▲ 416431-2 [ADD]
Brahms, J.:Sons Cl (comp), w. R. Vignoles (pno) Chandos ▲ CHAN 8550 [DDD]
Bruch, M.:Trios Cl, Va & Pno, Op. 83, w. J. Hilton (cl), R. Vignoles (pno) Chandos ▲ CHAN 8776 [DDD]
Denisov, E.:Chamber Music Va, w. A. de Man (hpd), L. Markiz (cnd), Amsterdam New Sinfonietta *(rec 6/91)* BIS ▲ CD 518 [DDD]
Denisov, E.:Con for 2 Vas, w. P. Vahle (va), A. de Man (hpd), L. Markiz (cnd), Amsterdam New Sinfonietta *(rec 6/91)* BIS ▲ CD 518 [DDD]
Franck, C.:Son Vn, w. R. Vignoles (pno) [trans. for viola & piano] Chandos ▲ CHAN 8873 [DDD]
Glinka, M.:Son Va, w. R. Pöntinen (pno) BIS ▲ CD 358
Hindemith, P.:Meditation, w. R. Pöntinen (pno) *(rec Oct. 7-9, 1993)* BIS ▲ CD 651 [DDD]
Hindemith, P.:Sons Va, w. R. Pöntinen (pno)—Op. 11/5 (1919); Op. 25/1 (1922); Op. 31/4 (1924); Sonata (1937) *(rec Oct. 7-9, 1993)* BIS ▲ CD 651 [DDD]
Hindemith, P.:Son Va & Pno, Op. 25/4 BIS ▲ CD 571 [DDD]
Martinů, B.:Rhap-Con Va, w. J. DePreist (cnd), Malmö SO BIS ▲ CD 501 [DDD]
Mozart, W.A.:Qnts Strs, w. Orlando String Quartet—K.516 & K.614 BIS ▲ CD 432 [DDD]
Mozart, W.A.:Qnts Strs, w. Orlando String Quartet—K.515 & K.593 BIS ▲ CD 431 [DDD]
Mozart, W.A.:Qnts Strs, w. Orlando String Quartet—K.174 in B♭ & K.406 in c BIS ▲ CD 433 [DDD]
Mozart, W.A.:Trio Cl, K.498, w. J. Hilton (cl), R. Vignoles (pno) Chandos ▲ CHAN 8776 [DDD]
Nystroem, G.:Con Va, w. P. Järvi (cnd), Malmö SO *(rec Malmö Concert Hall, Sweden, May 14, 1994)* BIS ▲ CD 682 [DDD]
Pettersson, G.A.:Con Va, w. L. Markiz (cnd), Malmö SO BIS ▲ CD 480 [DDD]
Rubinstein, A.:Nocturne, w. R. Pöntinen (pno) BIS ▲ CD 358
Schnittke, A.:Con Va, w. L. Markiz (cnd), Malmö SO BIS ▲ CD 447 [DDD]
Schubert, Franz:Son Arpeggione, w. R. Vignoles (pno) Chandos ▲ CHAN 8664 [DDD]
Schulhoff, E.:Sxt Strs, w. G. Kremer (vn), P. Hirschhorn (vn), K. Kashkasian (va), D. Geringas (vc), J. Berger (vc) *(rec Lockenhaus Festival, 1986)* ECM New Series 2-▲ 78118-21347-2 [DDD]
Schumann, R.:Märchenbilder, w. R. Vignoles (pno) Chandos ▲ CHAN 8550 [DDD]
Schumann, R.:Märchenbilder, w. H. Goldsmith (pno) Music & Arts ▲ CD 690-1 [AAD]
Schumann, R.:Märchenerzählungen, w. J. Hilton (cl), R. Vignoles (pno) Chandos ▲ CHAN 8776 [DDD]
Schumann, R.:Märchenerzählungen, w. H. Wright (cl), H. Goldsmith (pno) Music & Arts ▲ CD 690-1 [AAD]
Shostakovich, D.:Qt 13 Strs, w. G. Kremer (vn), T. Zehetmair (vn), B. Pergamentschikow (vc) *(rec Lockenhaus Festival, 1985)* ECM New Series 2-▲ 78118-21347-2 [DDD]
Shostakovich, D.:Son Va, w. R. Pöntinen (pno) BIS ▲ CD 358

Imai, Nobuko (va) (cont.)
Stravinsky, I.:Elégie Va BIS ▲ CD 358
Takemitsu, T.:Con Va, w. S. Ozawa (cnd), Saito Kinen Orch Philips ▲ 432176-2 [DDD]
Vaughan Williams, R.:Flos Campi, w. M. Best (cnd), English CO, Corydon Singers Hyperion ▲ CDA 66420 [DDD]
Vieuxtemps, H.:Va Pno Music, w. R. Vignoles (pno)—(complete) Capriccio in c, Op. posth.; Elégie, Op. 30; Sonata in B♭, Op. 36 Chandos ▲ CHAN 8873 [DDD]
Viola Bouquet, w. Roland Pöntinen (pno) Philips ▲ 446 103-2
Walton, W.:Con Va, w. J. Latham-König (cnd), London PO Chandos ▲ CHAN 9106 [DDD]
Imamura, Yasunori (lt/thb/gtr)
Musiche Veneziene per Voce e Strumenti, w. Teresa Berganza (mez), Pere Ros (vl), Lynn Dickinson (vl), Carol Lewis (vl), Silvie Mocquet (vl), Jörg Ewald Dähler (pno), Jörg Ewald Dähler (cnd) *(rec Kirche Saanen, Feb 1982)* Claves ▲ CD 508206 [DDD]
Imamura, Yasunori (thb)
Scarlatti, A.:Cants & Duets, w. Véronique Dietschy (sop), Alain Zaepffel (ct), Marianne Muller (vl), Macha Yanuchevskaia (vc), Aline Zylberajch (hpd/org)—Il Sonno; Clori e Mirtillo; Marcantonio e Cleopatra; Doralbo e Niso Adès ▲ ADE 202172 [DDD]
Imbert, J.-P. (org)
Chamouard, P.:Opalescence Skarbo ▲ SKR 3925 [DDD]
Messiaen, O.:Apparition de l'Eglise éternelle Skarbo ▲ SKR 3925 [DDD]
Messiaen, O.:Le Banquet céleste Skarbo ▲ SKR 3925 [DDD]
Messiaen, O.:Diptyque Skarbo ▲ SKR 3925 [DDD]
Messiaen, O.:La Nativité du Seigneur—Les enfants de Dieu; Dieu parmi nous Skarbo ▲ SKR 3925 [DDD]
Imholz, John (mandocello)—see ORCHESTRAS & ENSEMBLES Modern Mandolin Quartet
Imietowski, Dorota (vc)
Penderecki, K.:Sinfonietta, w. R. Kabara (vn), E. Szczepanska (va), Cracow Chamber Players Vienna Modern Masters ▲ VMM 3023 [DDD]
Immelman, Neil (pno)
Suk, J.:Pno Music Meridian ▲ MER 84269 [DDD]
Immer, Friedemann (baroque tpt)
Trumpet Concerti of the Italian Baroque, w. Graham Nicholson (baroque tpt), Werner Ehrhard (vn), Cologne Concerto MD + G ▲ L 3271 [DDD]
Immer, Friedemann (tpt)
Haydn, J.:Con Tpt, w. C. Hogwood (cnd), Academy of Ancient Music L'Oiseau-Lyre ▲ 417610-2 [DDD]
Immerseel, Jos van (hpd)
Duphly, J.:Pièces de clavecin (4 books)—La de vaucanson; La forqueray; Menuet; La de drummond; Chaconne; Medée; Rondeau; La victoire; La félix; La de redemond; La pothouin Erato ▲ ERA SEL 12983 [ADD]
Renotte, H.:Pièce de clavecin Koch Schwann ▲ SCH 315602
Immerseel, Jos van (kbd)
Early Music of the Netherlands, 1600-1700, w. Currende Vocal Ensemble, Ensemble dell'Anima Eterna Emergo ▲ 3986
Immerseel, Jos van (pno)
Beethoven, L. van:Con 1 Pno, w. B. Weil (cnd), Tafelmusik Sony Classical ("Vivarte" series) ▲ SK 68250
Beethoven, L. van:Con 2 Pno, w. B. Weil (cnd), Tafelmusik Sony Classical ("Vivarte" series) ▲ SK 68250
Clementi, M.:Sons Pno—Sons., Opp. 13/6, 24/2, 25/5 & 37/2 Accent ▲ 67911
Debussy, C.:Images (3) Pno *(rec June 2-4, 1992)* Channel Classics ▲ CCS 4892 [DDD]
Debussy, C.:Preludes Pno (sels)—Book 1 *(rec June 2-4, 1992)* Channel Classics ▲ CCS 4892 [DDD]
Fauré, G.:La bonne chanson, w. Max van Egmond (bar) Channel Classics ▲ CCS 8295
Franck, C.:Harm Music (misc), w. J. Verdin (harm)—12 pieces for solo harmonium, 1 for solo piano, 2 for harmonium & piano *(rec 2/90)* Ricercar ▲ RIC 75057 [DDD]
Kalliwoda, J.W.:Morceau de Salon, w. P. Dombrecht (ob) Accent ▲ 78330
Mozart, W.A.:Cons Pno, w. Anima Eterna Orch—Nos. 11, 13 & 14 *(rec July 1990)* Channel Classics ▲ CCS 0990 [DDD]
Mozart, W.A.:Cons Pno, w. Anima Eterna Orch—Nos. 15 & 16 *(rec Sept.-Oct. 1990)* Channel Classics ▲ CCS 1791 [DDD]
Mozart, W.A.:Cons Pno, w. Anima Eterna Orch—Nos. 6 & 17 *(rec Sept.-Oct. 1990)* Channel Classics ▲ CCS 1891 [DDD]
Mozart, W.A.:Cons Pno, w. Anima Eterna Orch—Nos. 8 & 12 *(rec Mar. 1990)* Channel Classics ▲ CCS 0690 [DDD]
Mozart, W.A.:Cons Pno, w. Anima Eterna Orch—Nos. 18 & 19 *(rec Oct. 1990)* Channel Classics ▲ CCS 1991 [DDD]
Mozart, W.A.:Cons Pno, w. Anima Eterna Orch—Nos. 22 & 23 *(rec Feb. 1991)* Channel Classics ▲ CCS 2491 [DDD]
Mozart, W.A.:Cons Pno, w. Anima Eterna Orch—Nos. 20 & 21 *(rec Oct. 1990 & Feb. 1991)* Channel Classics ▲ CCS 2391 [DDD]
Mozart, W.A.:Cons Pno, w. Anima Eterna Orch—Nos. 5 & 9 *(rec Mar. 1990)* Channel Classics ▲ CCS 0590 [DDD]
Mozart, W.A.:Cons Pno, w. Anima Eterna Orch Channel Classics 10-▲ CCS 0010 [DDD]
Mozart, W.A.:Cons Pno, w. Anima Eterna Orch—Nos. 24 & 25 *(rec Feb. 1991)* Channel Classics ▲ CCS 2591 [DDD]
Mozart, W.A.:Cons Pno, w. Anima Eterna Orch—Nos. 26 & 27 *(rec Mar. 1991)* Channel Classics ▲ CCS 2691 [DDD]
Mozart, W.A.:Rondo Pno Orch, K.382, w. Anima Eterna Orch *(rec Mar. 1990)* Channel Classics ▲ CCS 0690 [DDD]
Mozart, W.A.:Sons Vn Pno (misc), w. J. Schroeder (vn)—K.378, 379 & 380 RCA Victrola ▲ 77556-2 [ADD]
Pixis, J.P.:Grand Son Ob, w. P. Dombrecht (ob) Accent ▲ 78330
Schubert, Franz:Trio 1 Pno, w. Vera Beths (vn), Anner Blysma (vc) Sony Classical ("Vivarte" series) ▲ SK 62695
Schubert, Franz:Trio 2 Pno, w. Vera Beths (vn), Anner Blysma (vc) Sony Classical ("Vivarte" series) ▲ SK 62695
Schubert, Franz:Winterreise, w. M. van Egmond (bar) [G] Channel Classics ▲ CCS 0190 [DDD]
Schumann, R.:Liederkreis, Op. 39, w. P. Dombrecht (ob)—No. 5 Accent ▲ 78330
Schumann, R.:Romances Ob, w. P. Dombrecht (ob) Accent ▲ 78330
Imreh, Gabriela (pno)
Bach, J.S.:Chaconne *(rec Music Hall, Tarrytown, NY, Sept 26, 27 & 28, 1994)* Connoisseur Society ▲ CD 4207
Bach, J.S.:Chromatic Fant & Fugue *(rec Music Hall, Tarrytown, NY, Sept 26, 27 & 28, 1994)* Connoisseur Society ▲ CD 4207
Bach, J.S.:Italian Con *(rec Music Hall, Tarrytown, NY, Sept 26, 27 & 28, 1994)* Connoisseur Society ▲ CD 4207
Bach, J.S.:Partitas Hpd, BWV 825-830 *(rec Music Hall, Tarrytown, NY, Sept 26, 27 & 28, 1994)* Connoisseur Society ▲ CD 4207
Bach, J.S.:Toccatas Hpd, BWV 910-16 *(rec Music Hall, Tarrytown, NY, Sept 26, 27 & 28, 1994)* Connoisseur Society ▲ CD 4207
Ince, K. (instr)—see ORCHESTRAS & ENSEMBLES Present Music
Indermühle, Thomas (E hn)
Hindemith, P.:Son E Hn, w. Kalle Randalu (pno) Camerata ▲ 30CM 358 [DDD]
Indermühle, Thomas (ob)
Bach, J.S.:Cons (3) Ob, w. S. Preston (cnd), English CO *(rec May 1991)* Novalis ▲ 150077 [DDD]
Daelli, G.:Fantasia on Verdi's *Rigoletto*, w. Werner Genuit (pno) *(rec Studio Baumgarten, Vienna, Jan 31 & Feb 1, 1994)* Camerata ▲ 30CM 403 [DDD]
Donizetti, G.:Chamber Music, w. Werner Genuit (pno)—Andante sostenuto in f [arr Thomas Indermühle] *(rec Studio Baumgarten, Vienna, Jan 31 & Feb 1, 1994)* Camerata ▲ 30CM 403 [DDD]

Indermühle, Thomas (ob) (cont.)
Donizetti, G.:Son Ob, w. Werner Genuit (pno) *(rec Studio Baumgarten, Vienna, Jan 31 & Feb 1, 1994)* Camerata ▲ 30CM 403 [DDD]
Dutilleux, H.:Son Ob, w. Werner Genuit (pno) *(rec Studio Baumgarten, Vienna, Feb 10-12, 1993)* Camerata ▲ 25CM 282 [DDD]
Hindemith, P.:Son Ob, w. Kalle Randalu (pno) Camerata ▲ 30CM 358 [DDD]
Jolivet, A.:Sérénade Ob, w. Werner Genuit (pno) *(rec Studio Baumgarten, Vienna, Feb 10-12, 1993)* Camerata ▲ 25CM 282 [DDD]
Lovreglio, D.:Fant on themes from Verdi's *Un ballo in maschera*, w. Werner Genuit (pno) *(rec Studio Baumgarten, Vienna, Jan 31 & Feb 1, 1994)* Camerata ▲ 30CM 403 [DDD]
Martinů, B.:Con Ob, w. C. Schnitzler (cnd), Bretagne Orch Camerata ▲ 30CM 346
Martinů, B.:Con Ob, w. C. Schnitzler (cnd), Brittany Orch *(rec Rennes Opéra, France)* Camerata ▲ ACC 120 [DDD]
Milhaud, D.:Sonatina Ob, w. Werner Genuit (pno) *(rec Studio Baumgarten, Vienna, Feb 10-12, 1993)* Camerata ▲ 25CM 282 [DDD]
Mozart, W.A.:Sons Vn Pno (misc), w. Kalle Randalu (pno)—in G, K.379; in B♭, K.454; in A, K.526 [all arr for Ob & Pno] Camerata ▲ 30CM 334 [DDD]
Pasculli, A.:Concerto on Themes from Donizetti's *La Favorita*, w. Werner Genuit (pno) *(rec Studio Baumgarten, Vienna, Jan 31 & Feb 1, 1994)* Camerata ▲ 30CM 403 [DDD]
Pasculli, A.:Fantaisie on Themes from Donizetti's *Poliuto*, w. Werner Genuit (pno) *(rec Studio Baumgarten, Vienna, Jan 31 & Feb 1, 1994)* Camerata ▲ 30CM 403 [DDD]
Pasculli, A.:Grand Con Ob, w. Werner Genuit (pno) *(rec Studio Baumgarten, Vienna, Jan 31 & Feb 1, 1994)* Camerata ▲ 30CM 403 [DDD]
Ponchielli, A.:Capriccio Ob, w. Werner Genuit (pno) *(rec Studio Baumgarten, Vienna, Jan 31 & Feb 1, 1994)* Camerata ▲ 30CM 403 [DDD]
Ravel, M.:Le Tombeau de Couperin, w. Werner Genuit (pno)—Suite [arr Werner Genuit for ob & pno] *(rec Studio Baumgarten, Vienna, Feb 10-12, 1993)* Camerata ▲ 25CM 282 [DDD]
Skalkottas, N.:Concertino Ob, w. Werner Genuit (pno) *(rec Studio Baumgarten, Vienna, Feb 10-12, 1993)* Camerata ▲ 25CM 282 [DDD]
Strauss, R.:Con Ob, w. C. Schnitzler (cnd), Bretagne Orch Camerata ▲ 30CM 346
Strauss, R.:Con Ob, w. C. Schnitzler (cnd), Brittany Orch *(rec Rennes Opéra, France)* Camerata ▲ ACC 120 [DDD]
Telemann, G.P.:Con in A Ob d'amore, w. T. Indermühle (cnd), English CO Novalis ▲ 150126 [DDD]
Telemann, G.P.:Con in G Ob d'amore, w. T. Indermühle (cnd), English CO Novalis ▲ 150126 [DDD]
Telemann, G.P.:Cons Ob Orch, w. T. Indermühle (cnd), English CO—No. 16 in c; No. 17 in D; No. 18 in d; No. 20 in e Novalis ▲ 150126 [DDD]
Vaughan Williams, R.:Con Ob, w. C. Schnitzler (cnd), Brittany Orch *(rec Rennes Opéra, France)* Camerata ▲ ACC 120 [DDD]
Vaughan Williams, R.:Con Ob, w. C. Schnitzler (cnd), Bretagne Orch Camerata ▲ 30CM 346
Zimmermann, B.A.:Con Ob, w. C. Schnitzler (cnd), Bretagne Orch Camerata ▲ 30CM 346
Zimmermann, B.A.:Con Ob, w. C. Schnitzler (cnd), Brittany Orch *(rec Rennes Opéra, France)* Camerata ▲ ACC 120 [DDD]
Indjic, Eugene (pno)
Chopin, F.:Son Pno, Op. 35 Vivace ▲ E 565 [ADD]
Chopin, F.:Son Pno, Op. 58 Vivace ▲ E 565 [ADD]
Inglefield, Ruth (hp)
Baker, C.:Nightscenes Gasparo ▲ GS 286
Ingliss, R. (ob)—see ORCHESTRAS & ENSEMBLES Aspen Wind Quintet
Ingliss, Robert (E hn)—see ORCHESTRAS & ENSEMBLES New Music Consort
Ingólfsdóttir, Unnur Maria (vn)
Sigurbjörnsson, T.:Nocturnes, w. Thorkell Sigurbjörnsson (pno) Music from Iceland ▲ ITM 702 [ADD]
Ingolfsson, J. (vn)
Hush, D.:Qt 1 Strs, w. G. J. Schenk (vn), C.-J. Chang (va), M. Ingolfsson (vc) CRS ▲ CD 9257
Van Appledorn, M.J.:Ayre, w. G. J. Schenk (vn), C.-J. Chang (va), D. Foster (va), M. Ingolfsson (vc), S. Shao (vc) CRS ▲ CD 9257
Ingolfsson, Mirjam (vc)
Brings, A.:Madrigali concertati (3), w. J. Cable (sop), U. Ingolfsson (hpd) CRS ▲ CD 9153
Contemporary/Classic Masters, w. John Russo (cl), Lydia Walton Ignacio (pno), et al. CRS ▲ 9255
Hush, D.:Partita 1 Vc CRS ▲ 9255
Hush, D.:Qt 1 Strs, w. G.J. Schenk (vn), J. Ingolfsson (vn), C.-J. Chang (va) CRS ▲ CD 9257
Hush, D.:Son Vc, w. U. Ingolfsson (pno) CRS ▲ CD 9257
Van Appledorn, M.J.:Ayre, w. G.J. Schenk (vn), J. Ingolfsson (vn), C.-J. Chang (va), D. Foster (va), S. Shao (vc) CRS ▲ CD 9257
Ingolfsson, Ursala (hpd)
Brings, A.:Madrigali concertati (3), w. J. Cable (sop), M. Ingolfsson (vc) CRS ▲ CD 9153
Ingolfsson, Ursala (pno)
Hush, D.:Son Vc, w. M. Ingolfsson (vc) CRS ▲ CD 9257
Ingraham, Jeanne (vn)
Biscardi, C.:At the Still Point, w. Susan Palma (fl), Gilbert Kalish (pno), P. Dunkel (cnd), American Composers Orch *(rec Whitman Auditorium, Brooklyn College, NY, Feb. 1982)* CRI ▲ CD 686 [ADD]
Ingraham, Paul (hn)
Starer, R.:Anna Margarita's Will, w. P. Bryn-Johnson (sop), K. Kraber (fl), S. Kates (vc), D. Sutherland (pno) *(rec 1980)* CRI ▲ CD 612 [ADD]
Thomson, V.:Sonata da chiesa, w. L. Fuchs (va), Erwin (trbn) CRI ■ ACS 6009
Ingram, Robert (vn)—see ORCHESTRAS & ENSEMBLES Mozartrois
Ingwersen, Eric (pno)
Vieuxtemps, H.:Va Pno Music, w. B. Godhoff (vn)—Morceau brillant de Salon, Air varié, Rêverie (Op. 22, Nos. 1-3); Variations on the Last Rose of Summer, Op. 33/5; Romance, Regrets (Op. 40, Nos. 1 & 2); Rêve, Op. 53/5; Désespoir Koch Schwann ▲ CD 310042 [DDD]
Inhoff, Ede (tpt)
Baroque Trumpet Concertos, w. Hungarian State Opera CO Lydian ▲ LYD 18109 [DDD]
Innig, Rudolf (hpd)
Bach, J.S.:Con for 4 Hpds, w. Gregor Hollmann (hpd), Bernward Lohr (hpd), Ludger Rémy (hpd), Musica Alta Ripa MD + G ▲ MDG CD 3090681
Innig, Rudolf (org)
Mendelssohn, F.:Org Music (comp) MD + G 4-▲ L 4487 [DDD]
Messiaen, O.:Apparition de l'Eglise éternelle MD + G ("Complete Organ Works" series) ▲ MDG 3170346
Messiaen, O.:L'Ascension Org MD + G ("Complete Organ Works" series) ▲ MDG 3170346
Messiaen, O.:Le Banquet céleste MD + G ("Complete Organ Works" series) ▲ MDG 3170346
Messiaen, O.:Les Corps glorieux MD + G ("Complete Organ Works" series) ▲ MDG 3170621
Messiaen, O.:Diptyque MD + G ("Complete Organ Works" series) ▲ MDG 3170346
Messiaen, O.:La Nativité du Seigneur MD + G ("Complete Organ Works" series) ▲ MDG 3170009
Messiaen, O.:Verset pour la fête de la dédicace MD + G ("Complete Organ Works" series) ▲ MDG 3170621
Schumann, R.:Org Music (comp) MD + G ▲ MDG 3170619
Brahms, J.:Org Music (comp) MD + G ▲ MDG 3170137
Inoue, Futaba (pno)
Yashiro, A.:Son Fls, w. S. Koide (fl), R. Noguchi (fl) Camerata ▲ 30CM 50
Inoue, K. (pno)
Van Appledorn, M.J.:Sonatine Cl, w. E. Gilmore (cl) Opus One ▲ 147
Inoue, Yuko (va)
Mozart, W.A.:Sinf concertante Vn, K.364, w. Lorraine McAslan (vn), R. Pople (cnd), London Festival Orch ASV ("Quicksilva" series) ▲ ASQ 6139 [DDD]
Inouye, Mark (tpt)—see ORCHESTRAS & ENSEMBLES Empire Brass Quintet
Insell, Judith (va)—see ORCHESTRAS & ENSEMBLES Soldier String Quartet

INSTRUMENT.

Insinger, Jan (vc)
Britten, H.:Phantasy Qt, w. P. Oosternrijk (ob), M. Mars (vn), S. van Els (va) Channel Classics ▲ CCS 9326 [DDD]

Inti–Illimani (flamenco gtr)
Fragments of a Dream, w. John Williams (gtr), Paco Peña (flamenco gtr) CBS ▲ MK 44574 [ADD] ■ FMT 44574

Ionoaia, Florin (Eng hn)
Enescu, G.:Dectet Ww, w. Virgil Francu (fl), Nicolae Maxin (fl), Valeriu Barbuceanu (cl), Leontin Boanta (cl), Adrian Petrescu (ob), Viorica Feher (bn), Goedri Orban (bn), Dan Cinca (hn), Simon Jebeleanu (hn), H. Andreescu (cnd) Olympia ▲ OLY 445 [DDD]

Ionoaia, Florin (ob)
Salieri, A.:Con Fl, w. G. Costea (fl), M. Cichirdan (cnd), Craiova PO Gallo ▲ CD 601 [AAD]

Ipolyi, Istvan (va)—see ORCHESTRAS & ENSEMBLES Budapest String Quartet

Irby–Oxford, Nathaniel (trbn)
Dempster, S.:Music of, w. Stuart Dempster (trbn/didjeridu/conch), Jay Bulen (trbn), Jeff Domoto (trbn), Moc Escobedo (trbn/didjeridu/conch), Scott Higbee (trbn), Gretchen Hopper (trbn), Chad Kirby (trbn/conch), Dave Marriott (trbn), Greg Powers (trbn), Debra Sykes (cym)—Conch Calling; Morning Light; Didjerilayover; Secret Currents; Melodic Communion; Shell Shock; Cloud Landings *(rec Fort Worden, Port Townsend, WA, June 18, 1994)* New Albion ▲ NA 076

Irek, Shirley (pno)
Blumer, T.:Sextet Pno, w. Moran Woodwind Quintet Crystal ▲ CD 753 [DDD]
Chumbley, R.:Self Studies (3), w. Broyhill Chamber Ensemble *(rec Appalachian State Univ, July 1995)* MMC ▲ MMC 2041 [DDD]
Snyder, R.:Satirical Songs, w. Margaret Kennedy (sop) Coronet ▲ COR 400–9

Ireland, David (va)
Bolcom, W.:Qt Pno, w. Joseph Gurt (pno), Charles Avshalian (vn), Jerome Jelinek (vc) *(rec Univ of Michigan, May 1979)* CRI ▲ CD 711 [ADD]

Ireland, Patrick (va)—see also ORCHESTRAS & ENSEMBLES Beaux Arts Trio
Dvořák, A.:Qnt Strs, Op. 97, w. Lindsay String Quartet ASV ▲ ASV 806 [DDD]
Dvořák, A.:Terzetto, w. Lindsay String Quartet ASV ▲ ASV 806 [DDD]
Mozart, W.A.:Qnt Strs, K.516, w. Lindsay String Quartet ASV ▲ ASV 923 [DDD]

Irinsky, Tatiana (pno)
Chopin, F.:Pno Music (misc), w. I. Szekely (pno), B. Szokolay (pno), I. Zaritzkaya (pno)—includes Ballade No. 3; Barcarolle, Op. 60; Berceuse, Op. 57; Piano Con. 2 (larghetto); Etude, Op. 10/3; Fantaisie–Impromptu, Op. 66; Mazurka, Op. 33/2; Nocturne, Op. 9/2; Polonaise–Fantaisie, Op. 61; Prelude, Op. 28/15; Scherzo, Op. 31; Piano Son. 2 (finale); Waltz, Op. 64/1 Naxos ▲ 8.551104 [DDD]

Irmer, Stefan (pno)
Clementi, M.:Pno Music (comp)—3 Sons Pno, Op. 50 MD + G ▲ MDG CD 6180652
Clementi, M.:Sons Pno, Op. 40 MD + G ▲ MDG 6180651

Iruzun, Clélia (pno)
Villa–Lobos, H.:Pno Music—Bachianas Brasileiras No. 4; Choros No. 5; Ciclo Brasileiro; Prole do Bebê Duo ▲ 89017

Irving (pno)
Hindemith, P.:The Four Temperaments, w. G. Boelzner (cnd), New York City Ballet Orch Elektra/Nonesuch 2–▲ 79135–2

Isaac, Eduardo (gtr)
Asencio, V.:Suite valenciana GHA ▲ 126.008
Assad, S.:Aquarelle GHA ▲ 126.019
Bogdanovic, D.:Son Gtr GHA ▲ 126.008
Castelnuovo–Tedesco, M.:Caprichos (24) de Goya—Nos. 3, 13 & 18 GHA ▲ 126.019
Hand, F.:Trilogy GHA ▲ 126.008
Heinze, W.:Gtr Music—Dice la lianura; De aquelia luz; Milonga de Moreira; La trunca nueva GHA ▲ 126.008
Lester, B.:Jazz Fugues GHA ▲ 126.019
Piazzolla, A.:Acentuado & Romantico GHA ▲ 126.008
Piazzolla, A.:Music of—Romantico; Acentuado GHA ▲ 126.034
Rodrigo, J.:Elogio de la guitarra GHA ▲ 126.019
20th Century Guitar Music, Vol. 1 GHA ▲ 126.008
20th Century Guitar Music, Vol. 2 GHA ▲ 126.019

Isakovic, S. (hpd)
Handel, G.F.:Cons (16) Org, w. A. Nanut (cnd), Ljubljana SO—1 in F Stradivari Classics ▲ SCD 6024 [DDD] ■ SMC 6024 (D)

Isbin, Sharon (gtr)
Bach, J.S.:Lt Music—BWV 995, 996, 997 & 1006a Virgin Classics ▲ CDC 59503–2 [DDD]
Brazil with Love, w. Carlos Barbosa–Lima (gtr) Concord Picante ▲ CCD 4320 ■ CJP 320–C
Corigliano, J.:Troubadours, w. H. Wolff (cnd), St. Paul CO Virgin Classics ▲ CDC 55083
Dances for Guitar Pro Arte ▲ CDD 343
Foss, L.:American Landscapes, w. H. Wolff (cnd), St. Paul CO Virgin Classics ▲ CDC 55083
Love Songs & Lullabies, w. Benita Valente (sop), Thomas Allen (bar), Guadencio Thiago de Mello (perc), Julia Bogorad (fl) Virgin Classics ▲ 59226
Nightshade Rounds *(rec Feb. 13–14, 1991 & Apr. 1)* Virgin Classics ▲ CDC 45024 [DDD]
Rhapsody in Blue/West Side Story, w. Carlos Barbosa–Lima (gtr) Concord Concerto ▲ CCD 42012 ■ CC 2012–C
Road to the Sun:Latin Romances for Guitar Virgin Classics ▲ 59591 [DDD]
Rodrigo, J.:Concierto de Aranjuez, w. L. Foster (cnd), Lausanne CO Virgin Classics ▲ CDC 59024–2 [DDD]
Rodrigo, J.:Fant para un gentilhombre, w. L. Foster (cnd), Lausanne CO Virgin Classics ▲ CDC 59024 [DDD]
Schwantner, J.:From Afar, w. H. Wolff (cnd), St. Paul CO Virgin Classics ▲ CDC 55083
3 Guitars 3, w. Laurindo Almeida (gtr), Larry Coryell (gtr) Pro Arte ▲ CDD 235 ■ PCD 235
Tower, J.:Snow Dreams, w. Carol Wincenc (fl) *(rec American Academy of Arts & Letters, New York City, Sept. 26–28, 1994)* New World ▲ 80470–2
Vivaldi, A.:Con Lt, w. L. Foster (cnd), Lausanne CO [solo guitar & string orchestra arr. Emilio Pujol, edited by Sharon Isbin] Virgin Classics ▲ CDC 59024 [DDD]

Isepp, Martin (hpd/pno)
Butterworth, G.:Songs (6) from *A Shropshire Lad*, w. John Shirley–Quirk (bar), Nona Liddell (vn), Ivor McMahon (vn), Ambrose Gauntlett (vl) Saga Classics ▲ EC 3336
Humfrey, P.:Anthems, w. John Shirley–Quirk (bar), Nona Liddell (vn), Ivor McMahon (vn), Ambrose Gauntlett (vl)—A Hymne to God the Father Saga Classics ▲ EC 3336
Moeran, E.J.:Songs, w. John Shirley–Quirk (bar), Nona Liddell (vn), Ivor McMahon (vn), Ambrose Gauntlett (vl)—When Smoke Stood Up from Ludlow; Say, Lad, Have You Things to Do?; Farewell to Barn & Stack & Trees [all from Ludlow Town] Saga Classics ▲ EC 3336
Purcell, H.:Songs, w. John Shirley–Quirk (bar), Nona Liddell (vn), Ivor McMahon (vn), Ambrose Gauntlett (vl)—Man Is for the Woman Made; Music for a While; Twas within a Furlong of Edinborough Town; When Night her Purple Veil Saga Classics ▲ EC 3336

Isepp, Martin (pno)
An Anthology of English Songs, w. Janet Baker (cta) Saga Classics ▲ EC 3340
Butterworth, G.:Songs (6) from *A Shropshire Lad*, w. J. Shirley–Quirk (bar)—Loveliest of Trees Saga Classics ▲ 3353 [ADD]
Debussy, C.:Songs, w. H. Cuénod (ten)—Cinq poèmes de Baudelaire; Trois poèmes de Mallarmé; Nuit d'étoiles; Fleur des blés; Romance; Dans le jardin; Les angélus; L'ombre des arbres; Mandoline; Le son du cor s'afflige; L'échelonnement des haies [F] Nimbus ▲ NI 5231–2 [ADD]
Gurney, I.:Songs, w. J. Baker (cta)—I Will Go with My Father A–ploughing Saga Classics ▲ 3353 [ADD]

Iseringhausman (clvd)
Clavichord Music of the 17th & 18th Centuries MD + G ▲ L 3139 [DDD]

Ishikawa, Kô (mouth org)
Takahashi, Y.:Music of, w. Vladimir Tonkha (nar), Kazuko Takada (shamisen/sgr), Yumiko Tanaka (b shamisen), Kishiko Suzumi (va), Ayumi Shimonoto (shamisen/sgr), Yuji Takahashi (pno)—Sugagaki Kuzushi; Mimi No Ho; Kagehime No Michiyuki; Yubi–Tomyo [Finger Light] Tzadik ▲ TZA 7010 [DDD]

Ishikawa, Kô (shô)
Peebles, S.:Blue Moon Spirit *(rec Studio 246, Tokyo, Apr 4, 1995)* Innova ▲ 506
Shinohara, M.:Cooperation, w. A. Nishigata (shamisen), K. Mitsuhashi (shakuhachi), M. Akao (fue), S. Yaotani (hichiriki), C. Fukunaga (koto), J. Ueda (biwa), M. Yoshizawa (kokyu), I. Tsuji (oboe), T. Takahashi (cl), G. Kitamura (tpt), A. Murata (trbn), S. Eiso (perc), S. Ueki (vn), S. Katsuta (vc), Y. Shibuya (pno), K. Komatsu (cnd) *(rec live Casals Hall, Tokyo, Mar. 5, 1994)* Camerata ▲ 30CM 375 [DDD]

Ishikawa, Shizuka (vn)
Bartók, B.:Con 2 Vn, w. Z. Košler (cnd), Czech PO *(rec live, Czech Radio broadcasts, 1980)* Praga ▲ PR 250099
Benda, G.A.:Sons for 2 Vns, w. Josef Suk (vn), Jitka Vlasankova (vc), Josef Hala (hpd) Lotos ▲ CD 0027 [DDD]
Korte, O.:Philosophical Dialogues, w. Oldřich Korte (pno) *(rec Studio Domovina, Prague, Nov 21, 1975)* Panton ▲ PAN 811257 [DDD]
Locatelli, P.:Sons Vn, Op. 8, w. Josef Suk (vn), Jitka Vlasankova (vc), Josef Hala (hpd)—Trio Son Lotos ▲ CD 0027 [DDD]
Mysliveček, J.:Cons Vn, w. L. Pešek (cnd), Dvořák CO—in C, E, F & A Supraphon ▲ SUP 0016 [DDD]
Mysliveček, J.:Cons Vn, w. L. Pešek (cnd), Dvořák CO—4 cons Supraphon ▲ SUP CD 3259
Paganini, N.:Sons Vn & Gtr, w. Josef Hala (pno)—Sons II, IV & Op. posth.; 6 Sons, Op. 2 Lotos ▲ CD 0028 [DDD]
Szymanowski, K.:Caprices, w. Josef Hala (pno) Lotos ▲ CD 0028 [DDD]
Tartini, G.:Trio Sons, w. Josef Suk (vn), Jitka Vlasankova (vc), Josef Hala (hpd)—Op. 3/2; Op. 8/1 & 3; Son in D Lotos ▲ CD 0027 [DDD]

Isler, Dorothea (cel)
Keller, A.:Ewiger Augenblick, w. D. Fueter (sop), K. Graf (sop), A. K. Graf (fl), E. Schmid (cl), P. Hug–Rutti (hp), U. Walker (vn), P. Demenga (vc) [G] Grammont ▲ CTSP 19–2 [ADD]

Isobe, Shuhei (cl)—see also ORCHESTRAS & ENSEMBLES Orphée Piano & Wind Quintet
Busoni, F.:Concertino Cl, w. T. Ukigaya (cnd), Pomeranian PO Thorofon ▲ CTH 2159 [DDD]
Hindemith, P.:Con Cl, w. T. Ukigaya (cnd), Pomeranian PO Thorofon ▲ CTH 2159 [DDD]
Weber, C.M. von:Con 1 Cl, w. T. Ukigaya (cnd), Pomeranian PO Thorofon ▲ CTH 2159 [DDD]

Isoir, André (org)
Airs & Dances of Old Europe *(rec 4/86)* Pierre Vernay ▲ PV 787031 [DDD]
Anglebert, J.–H. d':Org Music—Quatuor *(rec 1973)* Approche ▲ CAL 6907 [ADD]
Bach, J.S.:Aria Org, BWV 587 Calliope ▲ CAL 9718 [DDD]
Bach, J.S.:Con 1 Hpd, w. M. Gester (cnd), Parlement de Musique [Westenfelder Organ of Fère–en–Tardenois] *(rec Oct 1993)* Calliope ▲ CAL 9720 [DDD]
Bach, J.S.:Con 2 Hpd, w. M. Gester (cnd), Parlement de Musique [Westenfelder Organ of Fère–en–Tardenois] *(rec Oct 1993)* Calliope ▲ CAL 9720 [DDD]
Bach, J.S.:Con 8 Hpd, w. M. Gester (cnd), Parlement de Musique [Westenfelder Organ of Fère–en–Tardenois] *(rec Oct 1993)* Calliope ▲ CAL 9720 [DDD]
Bach, J.S.:Fant & Fugue Org, BWV 542 *(rec Saint–Lambert d'Aurich, 1975)* Calliope ▲ CAL 9799
Bach, J.S.:Fant & Fugue Org, BWV 542 Calliope ▲ CAL 9718 [DDD]
Bach, J.S.:Org Music (comp)—Allabreve in D, BWV 589; 12 Chorales (BWV 55, 694, 695, 706/1, 707, 708, 714, 720, 730, 731, 747, 765; 5 Preludes & Fugues (BWV 532–535, 543); 5 Fugues (BWV 574, 579, 702, 716, 733); 5 Fughettas, BWV 696, 697, 698, 699, 703; Fantasia, BWV 713; Fantasia & Fugue in c, BWV 537; Toccata, Adagio & Fugue in C, BWV 564; Toccatas & Fugues, BWV 538,540 & 565 Calliope 3–▲ CAL 9706/08 [DDD]
Bach, J.S.:Org Music (comp)—7 Preludes & Fugues (BWV 536, 541, 544–548); Trio, BWV 583; Trio Sonatas, BWV 525–530; Fantasia, BWV 736; Chorale Settings (BWV 653b, 727 & 728); Prelude in C, BWV 943; Trio, BWV 583; Trio in G, BWV 1027a Calliope 3–▲ CAL 9712/14 [ADD]
Bach, J.S.:Org Music (comp)—Solo Organ Concerti, BWV 592–596; Canzona in d, BWV 588; Chorale Setting, "Liebster Jesu," BWV 754; Fantasia con imitazione, BWV 563; Fugue in g, BWV 578; Chorale Preludes BWV 621–644; "Schübler" Chorale Preludes, BWV 645–650; Chorale Preludes, BWV 690, 691, 701, 704, 705, 709; Partite diverse sopra, BWV 768; Passacaglia & Fugue in c, BWV 582; Trio Sonata in g, BWV 584 Calliope ▲ CAL 9709/11 [ADD/DDD]
Bach, J.S.:Org Music (comp)—Clavierübung, Part 3 (Chorales & Fughettas, BWV 669–686; Prelude in Eb, BWV 552); Chorales, Trios, Fugues (BWV 552, 653, 656, 657, 659–661, 688, 689); Four Duets, BWV 802–805; Canonic Variations on "Von Himmel Hoch," BWV 769; Chorales (BWV 651, 652, 654, 655, 657, 658, 662–668); Ricercare from A Musical Offering Calliope 3–▲ CAL 9715/17 [DDD]
Bach, J.S.:Org Music (comp) Calliope 15–▲ CAL 9703/17 [DDD/ADD]
Bach, J.S.:Org Music (comp)—29 Chorale Preludes, BWV 711, 715, 717, 718, 721, 722, 724, 726, 729, 732, 734, 737–739, 741, 742, 744, 744/b, 751, 762, 1005a, 1005b, 1090, 1091, 1093, 1094, 1096, 1105, 1110; Fantasia & Fugue in a, BWV 561; 5 Fugues (in C, Anh.90; in g, BWV 131a; in c, BWV 575; in G, BWV 576; in G, BWV 577); Pedal Exercise, BWV 598; Preludes in G, BWV 568 & in a, BWV 569; 5 Preludes & Fugues (BWV 531, 549, 550, 551, 566); Partita on "Christ der du bist der helle Tag," BWV 766; Pastorale, BWV 590; Fantasia in a, BWV 904; Partite diverse soprae, BWV 767 & BWV 770; Fantasia, BWV 735 Calliope 3–▲ CAL 9703/05 [DDD]
Bach, J.S.:Toccata, Adagio & Fugue Org, BWV 564 Calliope ▲ CAL 9718 [DDD]
Bach, J.S.:Toccata, Adagio & Fugue Org, BWV 564 *(rec Saint–Lambert d'Aurich, 1975)* Calliope ▲ CAL 9799
Bach, J.S.:Toccata & Fugue Org, BWV 538, "Dorian" *(rec Saint–Lambert d'Aurich, 1975)* Calliope ▲ CAL 9799
Bach, J.S.:Toccata & Fugue Org, BWV 540 *(rec Saint–Lambert d'Aurich, 1975)* Calliope ▲ CAL 9799
Bach, J.S.:Toccata & Fugue Org, BWV 540 Calliope ▲ CAL 9718 [DDD]
Bach, J.S.:Toccata & Fugue Org, BWV 565 *(rec Saint–Lambert d'Aurich, 1975)* Calliope ▲ CAL 9799
Bach, J.S.:Toccata & Fugue Org, BWV 565 Calliope ▲ CAL 9718 [DDD]
Bach, J.S.:Trio Org, BWV 583 Calliope ▲ CAL 9718 [DDD]
Couperin, F.:Messe à l'usage ordinaire des paroisses *(rec 1973)* Approche ▲ CAL 6907 [ADD]
Couperin, L.:Org Music—Chacone in d; Branle de Basque; Fantaisie; Passacaille (39 vars) *(rec 1973)* Approche ▲ CAL 6907 [ADD]
Grigny, N. de:Mass Org [Cathedral of Saint–Pierre de Poitiers Great Org] Approche ▲ 6911
Jewels of Early Music, w. Loïnhdana Ensemble, Musica Antiqua, John Elwes (ten), Pierre Bardon (org) *(rec 1982–86)* Pierre Verany ▲ 791051 [DDD]
Jullien, G.:Org Music—Prélude à 5 parties; Cromorne en taille; Dialogue *(rec 1973)* Approche ▲ CAL 6907 [ADD]
Lebègue, N.–A.:Org Music—Elevation in G; Symphonie for Org [Cathedral of Saint–Pierre de Poitiers Great Org] Approche ▲ 6911
Un noël en Champagne *(rec Nov. 1991)* Calliope ▲ CAL 9933 [DDD]
L'Orgue a Compiègne au Second Empire *(rec 1996)* Calliope ▲ CAL 9934 [DDD]

Isomura, Kazuhide (va)—see ORCHESTRAS & ENSEMBLES Tokyo String Quartet

Israeli, Herut (pno)
Heart of the Cello, w. Emanuel Gruber (vc) PWK Classics ▲ PWK 1135 [DDD]

Israelievitch, Jacques (vn)
Beethoven, L. van:Romances Vn, w. G. Herbig (cnd), Toronto SO *(rec Sept. 21 & 22, 1990)* Analekta ▲ AN 28201
Beethoven, L. van:Sym 3, "Eroica", w. G. Herbig (cnd), Toronto SO *(rec Sept. 21 & 22, 1990)* Analekta ▲ AN 28201
Mozart, W.A.:Sinf concertante Vn, K.364, w. S. Dann (va), M. Bernardi (cnd), CBC Vancouver SO CBC ("SM 5000" series) ▲ SMCD 5133 [DDD]
Schafer, R.M.:The Darkly Splendid Earth, w. G. Herbig (cnd), Toronto SO CBC ("SM 5000" series) ▲ SMCD 5114 [DDD]

Issakadze, Eldar (vc)
Nassidse, S.:Con Vn, w. Liana Issakadze (vn), Georgian CO Orfeo ▲ 304921 [DDD]

Issakadze, Liana (vn)
Nassidse, S.:Con Vn, w. Eldar Issakadze (vc), Georgian CO Orfeo ▲ 304921 [DDD]
Taktakishvili, O.:Con 2 Vn, Georgian CO Orfeo ▲ 304921 [DDD]
Tchaikovsky, P.:Sérénade mélancolique, Georgian CO *(rec Sept. 26–28, 1992)* Orfeo ▲ 307921 [DDD]
Tchaikovsky, P.:Valse–Scherzo Vn, Georgian CO *(rec Sept. 26–28, 1992)* Orfeo ▲ 307921 [DDD]
Isserlis, Rachel (va)
Locatelli, P.:Sons Vn, Op. 8, w. Locatelli Trio Hyperion 2–▲ CDA 67021/22
Isserlis, Steven (vc)
Barber, S.:Con Vc, w. L. Slatkin (cnd), St. Louis SO *(rec Powell Symphony Hall, St. Louis, MO, Dec 2, 1994)* RCA Red Seal ▲ 09026–68283–2 [DDD]
Benson, W.:Moon Rain & Memory Jane, w. L. Shelton (sop), S. Doane (vc) [E] Gasparo ▲ GS 261
Bloch, E.:Schelomo, w. R. Hickox (cnd), London SO Virgin Classics ▲ CDC 59511 [DDD]
Boccherini, L.:Con Vc, G.480, w. J. Kangas (cnd), Ostrobothnian CO Virgin Classics ▲ CDC 59015
Boccherini, L.:Con Vc, G.482, w. J. Kangas (cnd), Ostrobothnian CO Virgin Classics ▲ CDC 59015
Boccherini, L.:Sons (34) Vc, w. M. Cole (hpd)—Nos. 6 in C, 2 in c & 5 in G Virgin Classics ▲ CDC 59015
Brahms, J.:Sons Vc (comp), w. B. Evans (pno) Hyperion ▲ CDA 66159 [DDD]
Britten, H.:Suite 3 Vc Virgin Classics ▲ 59052 [DDD]
Debussy, C.:Son Vc, w. Pascal Devoyon (pno) Virgin Classics ("Ultraviolet" series) ▲ CUV 61198
Elgar, E.:Con Vc, w. R. Hickox (cnd), London SO Virgin Classics ▲ CDC 59511 [DDD]
Elgar, E.:Salut d'amour, w. P. Pettinger (pno) Chandos ▲ CHAN 8380 [DDD]
Fauré, G.:Vc Music, w. Pascal Devoyan (pno)—Son. 1 [Allegretto moderato]; Son. 2 [Andante]; Papillon RCA Red Seal ▲ 09026–68049–2
Fauré, G.:Elégie, w. P. Devoyon (pno) Hyperion ▲ CDA 66235 [DDD]
Fauré, G.:Elégie, w. Pascal Devoyan (pno) RCA Red Seal ▲ 09026–68049–2
Fauré, G.:Music for Vc & Pno, w. P. Devoyon (pno)—Après un rêve, Op. 7/1; Berceuse, Op. 16; Papillon, Op. 77; Romance, Op. 69; Sicilienne, Op. 78 Hyperion ▲ CDA 66235 [DDD]
Fauré, G.:Romance Vc, w. Pascal Devoyan (pno) RCA Red Seal ▲ 09026–68049–2
Fauré, G.:Sérénade, w. Pascal Devoyan (pno) RCA Red Seal ▲ 09026–68049–2
Fauré, G.:Son 2 Vc, w. P. Devoyon (pno) Hyperion ▲ CDA 66235 [DDD]
Franck, C.:Son Vn, w. Pascal Devoyon (pno) [trans. Jules Delsart] Virgin Classics ("Ultraviolet" series) ▲ CUV 61198
Grieg, E.:Son Vc, w. Stephen Hough (pno) *(rec EMI Studio 1, Abbey Road, London, Dec 12–13, 1994)* RCA Red Seal ▲ 09026–68290–2 [DDD]
Janácek, L.:Fairy Tale, w. Olli Mustonen (pno)—2 versions *(rec Great Hall, Blackheath Concert Halls, London, May 1995)* RCA Red Seal ▲ 09026–68437–2 [DDD]
Liszt, F.:Elegie 1, w. Stephen Hough (pno) *(rec EMI Studio 1, Abbey Road, London, Dec 12–13, 1994)* RCA Red Seal ▲ 09026–68290–2 [DDD]
Liszt, F.:Elegie 2, w. Stephen Hough (pno) *(rec EMI Studio 1, Abbey Road, London, Dec 12–13, 1994)* RCA Red Seal ▲ 09026–68290–2 [DDD]
Liszt, F.:La Lugubre gondola Vn & Pno, w. Stephen Hough (pno) *(rec EMI Studio 1, Abbey Road, London, Dec 12–13, 1994)* RCA Red Seal ▲ 09026–68290–2 [DDD]
Liszt, F.:Romance oubliée, w. Stephen Hough (pno) *(rec EMI Studio 1, Abbey Road, London, Dec 12–13, 1994)* RCA Red Seal ▲ 09026–68290–2 [DDD]
Liszt, F.:Die Zelle in Nonnenwerth, w. Stephen Hough (pno) *(rec EMI Studio 1, Abbey Road, London, Dec 12–13, 1994)* RCA Red Seal ▲ 09026–68290–2 [DDD]
Mendelssohn, F.:Assai tranquillo, w. Melvyn Tan (pno) RCA Red Seal ▲ 09026–62553–2
Mendelssohn, F.:Son 1 Vc, w. Melvyn Tan (pno) RCA Red Seal ▲ 09026–62553–2
Mendelssohn, F.:Son 2 Vc, w. Melvyn Tan (pno) RCA Red Seal ▲ 09026–62553–2
Mendelssohn, F.:Vars concertantes, w. Melvyn Tan (pno) RCA Red Seal ▲ 09026–62553–2
Music for Cello & Orchestra, w. CO of Europe [cnd:John Eliot Gardiner] Virgin Classics ▲ CDC 59595 [DDD]
Poulenc, F.:Son Vc, w. Pascal Devoyon (pno) Virgin Classics ("Ultraviolet" series) ▲ CUV 61198
Prokofiev, S.:Son Vc, w. Olli Mustonen (pno) *(rec Great Hall, Blackheath Concert Halls, London, May 1995)* RCA Red Seal ▲ 09026–68437–2 [DDD]
Rubinstein, A.:Son 1 Vc *(rec EMI Studio 1, Abbey Road, London, Dec 12–13, 1994)* RCA Red Seal ▲ 09026–68290–2 [DDD]
Shostakovich, D.:Son Vc, w. Olli Mustonen (pno) *(rec Great Hall, Blackheath Concert Halls, London, May 1995)* RCA Red Seal ▲ 09026–68437–2 [DDD]
Strauss, R.:Don Quixote, w. E. de Waart (cnd), Minnesota Orch Virgin Classics ▲ CDC 59234
Strauss, R.:Don Quixote, w. E. de Waart (cnd), Minnesota Orch Virgin Classics ("Ultraviolet" series) ▲ CUV 61266
Tavener, J.:The Protecting Veil, w. G. Rozhdestvensky (cnd), London SO Virgin Classics ▲ 59052 [DDD]
Tavener, J.:Thrinos Virgin Classics ▲ 59052 [DDD]
Istomin, Eugene (pno)
Bach, J.S.:Brandenburg Con 5, w. J. Szigeti (vn), J. Wummer (cl), P. Casals (cnd), Prades Festival Orch *(rec June 10–12, 1950)* Sony Classical ("The Casals Edition" series) ▲ SMK 58982 [ADD]
Beethoven, L. van:Con Vn, Vc & Pno, "Triple Con", w. Isaac Stern (vn), Leonard Rose (vc), Ormandy (cnd), *(orch unknown)* Sony Classical 2–▲ SM2K 66941
Beethoven, L. van:Con Vn, Vc & Pno, "Triple Con", w. I. Stern (vn), L. Rose (vc), E. Ormandy (cnd), Philadelphia Orch Sony Classical ("Essential Classics" series) 3–▲ SB3K 48397
Beethoven, L. van:Con Vn, Vc & Pno, "Triple Con", w. I. Stern (vn), L. Rose (vc), E. Ormandy (cnd), Philadelphia Orch Sony Classical ("Essential Classics" series) ▲ SBK 46549 [ADD] ■ SBT 46549
Beethoven, L. van:Son 14 Pno, "Moonlight Son" *(rec Highland School, White Plains, NY, June 11 & 18, 1991)* Reference ▲ RR–69CD [DDD]
Beethoven, L. van:Son 21 Pno, "Waldstein" *(rec Highland School, White Plains, NY, June 11 & 18, 1991)* Reference ▲ RR–69CD [DDD]
Beethoven, L. van:Son 31 Pno *(rec Highland School, White Plains, NY, June 11 & 18, 1991)* Reference ▲ RR–69CD [DDD]
Beethoven, L. van:Sons Vn (comp), w. Isaac Stern (vn) Sony Classical 3–▲ SM3K 64524 [ADD/DDD]
Beethoven, L. van:Sons Vn (comp), w. I. Stern (vn)—Nos. 1–4 & 9 CBS 2–▲ M2K 39680 [DDD]
Beethoven, L. van:Sons Vn (comp), w. I. Stern (vn)—Nos. 5–8 & 10 CBS 2–▲ M2K 39681 [DDD]
Beethoven, L. van:Trio 1 Pno, w. J. Fuchs (vn), P. Casals (vc) *(rec Prades, France, July 5, 1953)* Sony Classical ("The Casals Edition" series) ▲ SMK 58988 [ADD]
Beethoven, L. van:Trio 1 Pno, w. Isaac Stern (vn), Leonard Rose (vc) Sony Classical ("Isaac Stern:A Life in Music" series) 2–▲ SM2K 64510
Beethoven, L. van:Trio 2 Pno, w. A. Schneider (vn), P. Casals (vc) *(rec Perpignan, France, Aug. 1951)* Sony Classical ("The Casals Edition" series) ▲ SMK 58989 [ADD]
Beethoven, L. van:Trio 2 Pno, w. Isaac Stern (vn), Leonard Rose (vc) Sony Classical ("Isaac Stern:A Life in Music" series) 2–▲ SM2K 64510
Beethoven, L. van:Trio 3 Pno, w. Isaac Stern (vn), Leonard Rose (vc) Sony Classical ("Isaac Stern:A Life in Music" series) 2–▲ SM2K 64510
Beethoven, L. van:Trio 4 Pno, "Ghost", w. J. Fuchs (vn), P. Casals (vc) *(rec Prades, France, July 8–9, 1953)* Sony Classical ("The Casals Edition" series) ▲ SMK 58991 [ADD]
Beethoven, L. van:Trio 4 Pno, "Ghost", w. Isaac Stern (vn), Leonard Rose (vc) Sony Classical ("Isaac Stern:A Life in Music" series) 2–▲ SM2K 64513
Beethoven, L. van:Trio 4 Pno, "Ghost", w. I. Stern (vn), L. Rose (vc) Sony Classical ("Essential Classics" series) ▲ SBK 53514 ■ SBT 53514
Beethoven, L. van:Trio 5 Pno, w. A. Schneider (vn), P. Casals (vc) *(rec Perpignan, France, Aug. 1951)* Sony Classical ("The Casals Edition" series) ▲ SMK 58991 [ADD]
Beethoven, L. van:Trio 6 Pno, "Archduke", w. A. Schneider (vn), P. Casals (vc) *(rec Perpignan, France, Aug. 1951)* Sony Classical ("The Casals Edition" series) ▲ SMK 58990 [ADD]
Beethoven, L. van:Trio 6 Pno, "Archduke", w. Isaac Stern (vn), Leonard Rose (vc) Sony Classical ("Isaac Stern:A Life in Music" series) 2–▲ SM2K 64513
Beethoven, L. van:Trio 6 Pno, "Archduke", w. I. Stern (vn), L. Rose (vc) Sony Classical ("Essential Classics" series) ▲ SBK 53514 ■ SBT 53514

Istomin, Eugene (pno) (cont.)
Beethoven, L. van:Trio 7 Pno, w. A. Schneider (vn), P. Casals (vc) *(rec Perpignan, France, Aug. 1951)* Sony Classical ("The Casals Edition" series) ▲ SMK 58990 [ADD]
Beethoven, L. van:Trio 8 Pno, w. Isaac Stern (vn), Leonard Rose (vc) Sony Classical ("Isaac Stern:A Life in Music" series) 2–▲ SM2K 64510
Beethoven, L. van:Trio 9 Pno, "Kakadu", w. Isaac Stern (vn), Leonard Rose (vc) Sony Classical ("Isaac Stern:A Life in Music" series) 2–▲ SM2K 64513
Beethoven, L. van:Trio Pno, Op. 44, w. Isaac Stern (vn), Leonard Rose (vc) Sony Classical ("Isaac Stern:A Life in Music" series) 2–▲ SM2K 64510
Brahms, J.:Trio Cl, w. D. Oppenheim (cl), P. Casals (vc) *(rec live July 3, 1955)* Music & Arts 4–▲ CD 689 (m) [AAD]
Brahms, J.:Trios (3) Pno, w. Isaac Stern (vn), Leonard Rose (vc) Sony Classical ("Isaac Stern:A Life in Music" series) 3–▲ SM3K 64520
Brahms, J.:Trio 1 Pno, w. Yehudi Menuhin (vn), Pablo Casals (vc) Stradivarius ▲ STV 10020 [ADD]
Brahms, J.:Trio 1 Pno, w. Y. Menuhin (vn), P. Casals (vc) *(rec live July 13, 1955)* Music & Arts 4–▲ CD 689 (m) [AAD]
Brahms, J.:Trio 2 Pno, w. Y. Menuhin (vn), P. Casals (vc) *(rec live July 13, 1955)* Music & Arts 4–▲ CD 689 (m) [AAD]
Brahms, J.:Trio 3 Pno, w. Yehudi Menuhin (vn), Pablo Casals (vc) Stradivarius ▲ STV 10020 [ADD]
Brahms, J.:Trio 3 Pno, w. Y. Menuhin (vn), P. Casals (vc) *(rec live July 13, 1955)* Music & Arts 4–▲ CD 688 (m) [AAD]
Encores, w. Casals, Pablo (vc), Charles Baker (pno) *(rec 1915–1954)* Sony Classical ("Casals Edition" series) ▲ SMK 66573 [ADD]
Haydn, J.:Trios Pno, Vn & Vc, w. Issac Stern (vn), Leonard Rose (vc)—H.XV/10 CBS 4–▲ M4K 42003 (m/s) [ADD]
Haydn, J.:Trios Pno, Vn & Vc, w. Isaac Stern (vn), Leonard Rose (vc)—No. 20 Sony Classical ("Isaac Stern:A Life in Music" series) 2–▲ SM2K 64516
Mendelssohn, F.:Trio 1 Pno, w. Isaac Stern (vn), Leonard Rose (vc) Sony Classical ("Isaac Stern:A Life in Music" series) ▲ SMK 64519
Mendelssohn, F.:Trio 2 Pno, w. Isaac Stern (vn), Leonard Rose (vc) Sony Classical ("Isaac Stern:A Life in Music" series) ▲ SMK 64519
Mozart, W.A.:Con 21 Pno, w. G. Schwarz (cnd), Seattle SO *(rec St. Thomas Center, Bothell, WA, Oct 10, 1995)* Reference ▲ RR–68CD
Mozart, W.A.:Con 24 Pno, w. G. Schwarz (cnd), Seattle SO *(rec St. Thomas Center, Bothell, WA, Oct 10, 1995)* Reference ▲ RR–68CD
Mozart, W.A.:Qts Pno, w. Isaac Stern (vn), Milton Katims (va), Leonard Rose (vc)—No. 2 Sony Classical ("Isaac Stern:A Life in Music" series) 2–▲ SM2K 64516
Rorem, N.:War Scenes, w. Donald Gramm (b–bar) Phoenix ▲ PHCD 116 [AAD]
Schubert, Franz:Trio 1 Pno, w. A. Schneider (vn), P. Casals (vc) *(rec Perpignan, France, Aug. 1951)* Sony Classical ("Casals Edition" series) ▲ SMK 58989 [ADD]
Schubert, Franz:Trio 1 Pno, w. Isaac Stern (vn), Leonard Rose (vc) Sony Classical ("Isaac Stern:A Life in Music" series) 2–▲ SM2K 64516
Schubert, Franz:Trio 2 Pno, w. Isaac Stern (vn), Leonard Rose (vc) Sony Classical ("Isaac Stern:A Life in Music" series) 2–▲ SM2K 64516
Schumann, R.:Con Pno, w. B. Walter (cnd), Columbia SO *(rec American Legion Hall, Hollywood, CA, Jan 20 & 25, 1960)* Sony Classical ("Bruno Walter:The Edition, Vol. 4" series) ▲ SMK 64489 [ADD]
Schumann, R.:Con Pno, w. B. Walter (cnd), Columbia SO CBS ▲ MK 42024
Istomin, Sergeï (vc)
Little Notebook for Anna Magdalena Bach, w. Katrina Gauvin (sop), Luc Beauséjour (hpd) Analekta Fleur de Lys ▲ FL 23064 [DDD]
Iturbi, Amparo (pno)
Mozart, W.A.:Son Pnos, w. José Iturbi (pno) RCA Gold Seal ▲ 09026–68113–2 [ADD]
Iturbi, José (pno)
José Iturbi, w. *(rec between 1933 & 1941)* Pearl ▲ PEA 9103 [ADD]
Joseph Schmidt, w. Joseph Schmidt (ten), Berlin RSO [cnd:Rudolf Hindemith, Bruno Seidler–Winkler, Hermann Scherchen, Fritz Stiedry, Max von Schillings], unknown orchestra [cnd:Idris Lewis], General Motors SO, General Motors Sym Chorus [cnd:Erno Rapee, José Iturbi, Oscar Straus], Helen Gleas Koch Schwann ▲ SCH 312572 [ADD]
Mozart, W.A.:Son Pnos, w. Amparo Iturbi (pno) RCA Gold Seal ▲ 09026–68113–2 [ADD]
Iturri, Rafael (gtr)
Musique Espagnole Pavane ▲ ADW 7214 [DDD]
Tárrega, F.:Preludes Pavane ▲ ADW 7214 [DDD]
Villa–Lobos, H.:Chôro 1 René Gailly ▲ CD 86011 [AAD]
Villa–Lobos, H.:Etudes Gtr—Nos. 5, 6 & 8 René Gailly ▲ CD 86011 [AAD]
Villa–Lobos, H.:Preludes Gtr René Gailly ▲ CD 86011 [AAD]
Villa–Lobos, H.:Suite populaire brésilienne René Gailly ▲ CD 86011 [AAD]
Itzkoff, G. (vn)—see ORCHESTRAS & ENSEMBLES Griffin Music Ensemble
Ivaldi, Christian (pno)
Debussy, C.:Pno Music (complete duet), w. N. Lee (pno)—Andante; Diane; Divertissement; En Blanc et Noir; L'Enfant prodigue; 6 Epigraphes antiques; Intermezzo; Lindaraja; Marche écossaise; La Mer; Petite Suite; Prélude à l'après–midi d'un faune; Printemps; Symphony in b; Triomphe de Bacchus *(rec 1/90)* Arion 2–▲ ARN 268128 [DDD]
Debussy, C.:Son Vn, w. M. Hasson (vn) IMP Masters ▲ MCD 37 [DDD]
Dvořák, A.:From the Bohemian Forest, w. N. Lee (pno) Arion ▲ ARN 68014 [AAD]
Dvořák, A.:Legends, Op. 59, w. N. Lee (pno) Arion ▲ ARN 68014 [AAD]
Fauré, G.:Son 1 Vn, w. M. Hasson (vn) IMP Masters ▲ MCD 37 [DDD]
Flûte Panorama, w. Michel Debost (fl) Skarbo 2–▲ D SK 4963–4 [DDD]
Franck, C.:Son Vn, w. M. Hasson (vn) IMP Masters ▲ MCD 37 [DDD]
Hindemith, P.:Son Vc & Pno (1948), w. Alain Meunier (vc) Arion ▲ ARN 68319
Hindemith, P.:Son Fl, w. Michel Debost (fl) Arion ▲ ARN 68319
Hindemith, P.:Son for 2 Pnos, w. Noël Lee (pno) Arion ▲ ARN 68319
Hindemith, P.:Son in E Vn & Pno, w. Gérard Poulet (vn) Arion ▲ ARN 68319
Lalo, E.:Songs, w. Teresa Zylis–Gara (sop)—5 Lieder (1879); 6 mélodies [after V. Hugo], Op. 17 (1856); 3 mélodies [after A. de Musset] (?c.1870); 3 mélodies (1887); Si j'étais petit oiseau; La pauvre femme [both from 6 romances populaires]; Chant breton; Aubade; Humoresque; Marine; Ballade à la lune; Le rouge–gorge *(rec Paris, Mar 18 & 19, 1987)* Phoenix ▲ PX 904.1 [DDD]
Moniuszko, S.:Songs, w. Teresa Zylis–Gara (sop)—La filatrice; Adorazione; Le ragazze di Cracovia; Canto della follia d'Ofelia; Piccola quaglia; Il fiorellino; Conversione; L'usignolo; Lacrima; Il gattino; La rondinella; La piccola Sofia; Il ritorno della primavera; Il méssaggero d'amor piumato; La vecchia filatrice; Il violinista girovago; Le quattro stagioni; Sofia; Il pesciolino d'oro; Una fanciulla dal cuore di pietra; Sul fiume; La rosellina; Conosci il paese dove...; Il bocciuolo; Primavera *(rec Studio 107, Radio France, Paris, Dec 12–13, 1984)* Agorá Music ("Phoenix" series) ▲ 902 [DDD]
Mozart, W.A.:Songs, w. A. M. Miranda (soprano), C. Wirz (alt), M. Quillevéré (ten), U. Reinemann (bar)—K.152, 307, 308, 346, 351, 436–439, 441, 441b, 472, 473, 506, 510, 520, 523, 524, 532, 549, 561, 625, & K.Anh 5 *(rec 1979)* Arion ▲ ARN 68161 [ADD]
Mozart, W.A.:Trio Cl, K.498, w. K. Leister (cl), C. Schiller (va) Tudor ▲ TUD 798 [DDD]
Norman, L.:Qt Pno, Op. 10, w. Sylvie Gazeau (vn), Gérard Caussé (vn), Alain Meunier (vc) Musica Sveciae ▲ MSV 518 [DDD]
Reinecke, C.:Music for Fl & Pno, w. András Adorján (fl)—Son for Fl & Pno, Op. 167 [Undine]; Suite for Fl & Pno, Op. 202 [Von der Wiege bis zum Grabe]; Ballade; Sonatines Nos. 1 in F, 2 in G & 3 in B♭ Tudor ▲ TUD 792 [DDD]
Reinecke, C.:Son Fl, w. A. Adorján (fl) Tudor ▲ TUD 798 [DDD]
Reinecke, C.:Trio Pno, Op. 264, w. K. Leister (cl), C. Ivaldi (va) Tudor ▲ TUD 798 [DDD]
Saint–Saëns, C.:Caprice arabe, w. N. Lee (pno) Arion ▲ ARN 68011 [AAD]
Saint–Saëns, C.:Caprice héroïque, w. N. Lee (pno) Arion ▲ ARN 68011 [AAD]
Saint–Saëns, C.:Polonaise for 2 Pnos, w. N. Lee (pno) Arion ▲ ARN 68011 [AAD]
Saint–Saëns, C.:Scherzo for 2 Pnos, w. N. Lee (pno) Arion ▲ ARN 68011 [AAD]
Saint–Saëns, C.:Variations on a Theme of Beethoven, w. N. Lee (pno) Arion ▲ ARN 68011 [AAD]
Schubert, Franz:Allegro Pno 4–Hands, D.947, w. M. Lee (pno) Arion 2–▲ ARN 268038 [AAD]

Ivaldi, Christian (pno) (cont.)
Schubert, Franz:Divertissement sur des motifs originaux français, D.823, w. N. Lee (pno) Arion 2-▲ ARN 268038 [AAD]
Schubert, Franz:Fant Pno, D.940, w. N. Lee (pno) Arion 2-▲ ARN 268038 [AAD]
Schubert, Franz:Ländler Pno, D.814, w. N. Lee (pno) Arion 2-▲ ARN 268038 [AAD]
Schubert, Franz:Ov Pno, D.675, w. N. Lee (pno) Arion 2-▲ ARN 268038 [AAD]
Schubert, Franz:Pno Music (4-hands), w. N. Lee (pno) Arion 2-▲ ARN 268038 [AAD]
Schubert, Franz:Son Pno 4-Hands, D.812, w. N. Lee (pno) Arion 2-▲ ARN 268038 [AAD]
Schubert, Franz:Vars on an Original Theme Pno 4-Hands, w. N. Lee (pno) Arion 2-▲ ARN 268038 [AAD]
Strauss, R.:Enoch Arden, w. Rene Schirrer (nar) Adès ▲ ADE 141772
Strauss, R.:Krämerspiegel, w. Jean-Paul Fouchecourt (ten) Adès ▲ ADE 141772
Strauss, R.:Das Schloss am Meere, w. Rene Schirrer (nar) Adès ▲ ADE 141772
Stravinsky, I.:Pétrouchka, w. N. Lee (pno) [2-piano version] Arion ▲ ARN 68041 [DDD]
Stravinsky, I.:Le Sacre du printemps Orch, w. N. Lee (pno) [2-pno ver.] Arion ▲ ARN 68041 [DDD]

Ivanoff, Vladimir (lt/perc)—see ORCHESTRAS & ENSEMBLES Ensemble Saraband

Ivanoff, Vladimir (portative/perc)—see ORCHESTRAS & ENSEMBLES Vox

Ivanov, V. (vn)
Honegger, A.:Sémiramis, w. M. Kemmer (sgr), L. Hager (cnd), RTL SO, Brussels Polyphonia Choir, Namur Belgium French Community Symphonic Choir *(rec Nov. 16–20, 1992)* Timpani ▲ 1C 1016 [DDD]

Ivanova, Tsvetana (pno)
Nikolov, L.:Son 2 Pno 4-Hands, w. Dragomir Yossifov (pno) Gega ▲ GD 149 [DDD]

Ivashkin, Alexander (vc)—see also ORCHESTRAS & ENSEMBLES Canterbury Cellists
Genishta, J.:Nocturnes (3) Vc, w. I. Wahlberg (pno)—1 Nocturne Manu ▲ MAN 1426 [DDD]
Glazunov, A.:Elégie Vc, w. I. Wahlberg (pno) Manu ▲ MAN 1426 [DDD]
Glazunov, A.:Serenade espagnole, w. I. Wahlberg (pno) [trans vc & pno] Manu ▲ MAN 1426 [DDD]
Martinů, B.:Qt Ob, w. Joel Marangella (ob), Kathryn Selby (pno), Charmian Gadd (vn) *(rec Australian Festival of Chamber Music, July 1994)* Naxos ▲ 8.553916 [DDD]
Mosolov, A.:Legenda, w. I. Wahlberg (pno) Manu ▲ MAN 1426 [DDD]
Prokofiev, S.:Ballade Vc, w. Tamas Vesmas (pno) *(rec School of Music, Auckland Univ & St. Barnabas Church, Christchurch)* Manu ▲ 1517
Prokofiev, S.:Cinderella (sels), w. Tamas Vesmas (pno)—Adagio for vc & pno *(rec School of Music, Auckland Univ & St. Barnabas Church, Christchurch)* Manu ▲ 1517
Prokofiev, S.:Son Vc, w. Tamas Vesmas (pno) *(rec School of Music, Auckland Univ & St. Barnabas Church, Christchurch)* Manu ▲ 1517
Prokofiev, S.:Son solo Vc *(rec School of Music, Auckland Univ & St. Barnabas Church, Christchurch)* Manu ▲ 1517
Rimsky-Korsakov, N.:Serenade Vc, w. I. Wahlberg (pno) Manu ▲ MAN 1426 [DDD]
Roslavets, N.:Dance of the White Girls, w. I. Wahlberg (pno) Manu ▲ MAN 1426 [DDD]
Russian Elegy, w. Alexander Ivashkin (vc), Ingrid Wahlberg (pno) Manu ▲ MAN 1426 [DDD]
Schnittke, A.:Hymns Vc, w. Y. Rudometkin (bn), I. Pashinskaya (hp), V. Barsalkin (db), V. Chasovennaya (hpd), V. Grishin, N. Grishin (perc/bells)—No. 1 for Cello, Harp & Timpani [Quasi andante]; No. 2 for Cello & Double *(rec National Radio House, Moscow, 1987)* Vox Box 2-▲ CDX 5121 [ADD]
Schnittke, A.:Improv Vc *(rec School of Music, Auckland Univ)* Manu ▲ MANU 1480
Schnittke, A.:Klingende Buchstaben *(rec School of Music, Auckland Univ)* Manu ▲ MANU 1480
Schnittke, A.:Madrigal in Memoriam Oleg Kagan *(rec School of Music, Auckland Univ)* Manu ▲ MANU 1480
Schnittke, A.:Son Vc, w. Tamas Vesmas (pno) Manu ▲ MAN 1480
Schnittke, A.:Son Vc, w. T. Vesmas (pno) *(rec School of Music, Auckland Univ)* Manu ▲ MANU 1480
Shostakovich, D.:Moderato Vc, w. I. Wahlberg (pno) Manu ▲ MAN 1426 [DDD]

Iverson, Cynde (bn)
Boziwick, G.:Beyond the Last Thought, w. C. Pelton (sop), G. Reuter (ob), K. Grossman (mar) Opus One ▲ CD 162

Ives, N. (vc)
Lifchitz, M.:Canto de paz, w. L. Vardaman (sop), L. Weiss (fl), G. Kitzis (vn), M. Lifchitz (pno) Opus One ▲ 149

Ivusheikova, Olga (fl)
Tcherepnin, A.:Con da camera, w. Nazar Kozhukhar (vn), Musica Viva CO Olympia ▲ OLY 584 [DDD]

Iwaki, Hiroyuki (mar)
Ichiyanagi, T.:Paganini Personal, w. K. Kimura (pno) Camerata ▲ 32CM 52

Iwamoto, Shin-ichi (t sax)
Ikebe, S.-I.:Energeia, w. Kazuo Tomioka (s sax/a sax), H. Iwaki (cnd), New Japan PO Camerata ▲ 30CM 351 [DDD]

Iwasaki, Ko (vc)
Dvořák, A.:Con Vc, w. A. Wit (cnd), Polish National RSO Katowice *(rec Centre of Culture, Katowice, Nov 21–24, 1989)* Polskie Nagrania ▲ PNCD 059 [DDD]
Dvořák, A.:Con Vc, w. A. Wit (cnd), Polish National RSO Katowice *(rec 11/89)* Muza ▲ PNCD 059 [DDD]
Tchaikovsky, P.:Vars on a Rococo Theme, w. A. Wit (cnd), Polish National RSO Katowice *(rec Centre of Culture, Katowice, Nov 21–24, 1989)* Polskie Nagrania ▲ PNCD 059 [DDD]

Izotov, Peter (pno)
Scriabin, A.:Mysterium:Prefatory Act, w. I. Golovshin (cnd), Russian State SO, Lyudmila Ermakova (cnd), Ostankino Radio Chorus *(rec Large Hall of the Moscow Conservatory, 1995)* Triton ▲ 17001 [DDD]

Izumi, Sen (syn)
Yamash'Ta, S.:Sea & Sky, w. Takashi Kokobu (syn), Stomu Yamashta (syn/perc), Muse Orch Kuckuck ▲ CD 072 ■ MC 072

Jablokov, Alexander (vn)
Bach, J.S.:Con for 2 Vns, w. T. Nishizaki (vn), O. Dohnányi (cnd), Capella Istropolitana *(rec 1989)* Naxos ▲ 8.550194 [DDD]
Telemann, G.P.:Cons (misc), w. L. Kyselak (va), Z. Tylšar (hn), B. Tylšar (hn), A. Hoelbling (vn) O. Hoelbling (vn), R. Edlinger (cnd), Capella Istropolitana—Viola Con. in G; Concerto in F for 3 Violins; Concerto for 2 Horns Naxos ▲ 8.550156 [DDD] ▲ 7.550156 [DDD]

Jablonski, Krzysztof (pno)
Chopin, F.:Pno Music (misc), w. Martha Argerich (pno), Vladimir Ashkenazy (pno), Stanislav Bunin (pno), Halina Czerny-Stefanska (pno), Jan Ekier (pno), Yuval Fichman (pno), Kemal Gekic (pno), Adam Harasiewicz (pno), Krzysztof Jablonski (pno), Louis Kentner (pno), Jean-Marc Luisada (pno), Garrick Ohlsson (pno), Ivo Pogorelich (pno), Maurizio Pollini (pno), Dang Thai Son (pno)—includes Ballade (Nos. 1 & 2); Barcarolle, Op. 60; Concerto Nos. 1 & 2; Etudes (Op. 10, Nos. 1, 5, 8, 10 & 12 & Op. 25, No. 10, 18 & 25); Grand valse brillante; Impromptus (Nos. 3 & 4); Mazurkas (Op. 24, Nos. 1–4; Op. 30, Nos. 1–4; Op. 50, No. 32; Op. 59, Nos. 1–3); Nocturnes (Op. 9, No. 3; Op. 37, No. 12; Op. 48, no. 13; Op. 55, No. 16)Polonaise (Op. 40, Nos. 3 & 4; Op. 44, No. 5; Op. 53, No. 6; Op. 61, No. 7); Preludes (Op. 28 Nos. 13–18, 21–24 & Op. 45, No. 25); Scherzos (Nos. 1–3); Sonatas (Nos. 2 & 3); Waltzes (No. 1 & 6) LaserLight 5-▲ 15 961 [ADD/DDD]

Jablonski, Peter (pno)
Barber, S.:Ballade London ▲ 430542-2 [DDD]
Copland, A.:El salón México—solo piano arrangement by L. Bernstein London ▲ 430542-2 [DDD]
Gershwin, G.:Con Pno, w. V. Ashkenazy (cnd), Royal PO London ▲ 430542-2 [DDD]
Gershwin, G.:Preludes (3) Pno London ▲ 430542-2 [DDD]
Lutoslawski, W.:Vars on a Theme of Paganini Pno & Orch, w. V. Ashkenazy (cnd), Royal PO London ▲ 436239-2 [DDD]
Rachmaninoff, S.:Rhapsody on a Theme of Paganini, w. V. Ashkenazy (cnd), Royal PO London ▲ 436239-2 [DDD]
Scriabin, A.:Son 5 Pno London ▲ 440281-2 [DDD]
Scriabin, A.:Son 9 Pno London ▲ 440281-2 [DDD]
Shostakovich, D.:Con 1 Pno, w. V. Ashkenazy (cnd), Royal PO London ▲ 436239-2 [DDD]

Jablonski, Roman (vc)
Cresswell, L.:Con Vc, w. R. Bernas (cnd), CSR Bratislava SO Continuum ▲ CCD 1033

Jablonski, Roman (vc) (cont.)
Lutoslawski, W.:Con Vc, w. W. Lutoslawski (cnd), Polish National RSO Katowice *(rec Katowice, 1976)* Polskie Nagrania ▲ PNCD 042 [AAD]

Jaccottet, Christiane (hpd)
Bach, J.S.:Cons Hpd, BWV 1052–1058, w. C. Sartoretti (hpd), N. Hostettler (hpd), L. Klinckerfus (hpd), J. Faerber (cnd), Württemberg CO *(rec 1978)* Vox Box 3-▲ CD3X 3018 [ADD]
Bach, J.S.:Cons for 2 Hpds (comp), w. C. Sartoretti (hpd), N. Hostettler (hpd), L. Klinckerfus (hpd), J. Faerber (cnd), Württemberg CO *(rec 1978)* Vox Box 3-▲ CD3X 3018 [ADD]
Bach, J.S.:Cons for 3 Hpds (comp), w. C. Sartoretti (hpd), N. Hostettler (hpd), L. Klinckerfus (hpd), J. Faerber (cnd), Württemberg CO *(rec 1978)* Vox Box 3-▲ CD3X 3018 [ADD]
Bach, J.S.:Sons Fl, BWV 1030–35, w. A. Nicolet (fl), M. Fuijiwara (vc)—BWV 1030, 1032, 1034, 1035 Denon ▲ 7331 [DDD]
Bach, J.S.:Sons Vn, w. Arthur Grumiaux (vn), Philippe Mermoud (vc)—BWV 1014-1023 Philips 2-▲ 454011-2
Bach, J.S.:Sons Vn, w. A. Grumiaux (vn), P. Mermoud (vc)—BWV 1014-1019, 1021 & 1023; BWV 1020 & 1022 [doubtful] Philips 2-▲ 426452-2 [ADD]
Martin, F.:Con Hpd, w. F. Martin (cnd), Lausanne CO *(rec 1971)* Jecklin-Disco ▲ JD 529-2 [ADD]

Jaccottet, Christiane (pno)
Bach, C.P.E.:Fant Kbd, H.284 Capriccio ▲ 10102
Bach, C.P.E.:Sons Vl, w. Pank (vl)—in g (w. obbligato keyboard), H.510 (W.88); in C & D, H.558–559 (W.136–137) Capriccio ▲ 10102

Jackendoff, E. (pno)
Rahbee, D.G.:Son breve, w. M. S. Richter (vn) *(rec The Music Room)* Seda ▲ 333 [DDD]

Jackman, Richard (gtr)
Debussy, C.:Children's Corner, w. J. Zacek (gtr)—[trans. for guitar] Supraphon ▲ SUP 111845 [DDD]
Mussorgsky, M.:Pictures at an Exhibition, w. J. Zacek (gtr) [trans. for guitar] Supraphon ▲ SUP 111845 [DDD]

Jackson, Anthony (bass gtr)
Franzetti, C.:Images Before Dawn, w. C. Franzetti (cnd), Modus Chamber Ensemble *(rec Hip Pocket Studios, New York)* Premier ▲ PRCD 1044 [DDD]

Jackson, Bill (cl)
Welcher, D.:Con Cl, w. D. Johanos (cnd), Honolulu SO *(rec Jan. 10, 1992)* Marco Polo ▲ 8.223457 [DDD]

Jackson, Bret (tpt)
Trumpet, w. Jed Moss (pno) Summit ▲ DCD 153 [DDD]

Jackson, Christine (vc)
Arensky, A.:Trio 1 Pno, w. V. Ashkenazy (pno), R. Stamper (vn) *(rec Nov 1990)* Naxos ▲ 8.550467 [DDD]
Tchaikovsky, P.:Trio Pno, w. V. Ashkenazy (pno), R. Stamper (vn) *(rec Nov. 1990)* Naxos ▲ 8.550467 [DDD]

Jackson, Francis (org)
Bairstow, E.C.:Org Music—[York Minster organ] Prelude in C, Evening Song, Scherzo in A♭, Nocturne, Prelude on Vexilla Regis, Elegy, Toccata-Prelude on Pange Lingua, Meditation, Three Short Preludes, Legend, Organ Sonata in E♭ *(rec Apr. 1990)* Mirabilis ▲ MRCD 902 [DDD]
Music for Ceremonial Occasions, w. London SO, Westminster Abbey Choir, D. Hill (org) Pickwick ("The Orchid" series) ▲ PICORCD 11016
Organ:The Magnificent, w. Barry Rose (org), C. Dearnley (org) Pickwick ("The Orchid" series) ▲ PICORCD 11009
Pipes of Splendor:Organ Favorites, w. Michael Austin (org) Chandos ▲ CHAN 6602 [DDD]
Stanford, C.V.:Org Music—6 Short Preludes & Postludes, Set 1, Op. 101; Fant. & Fugue in d, Op. 103; Prelude & Fugue in c, Op. 193/2; Prelude [In The Form of a Minuet], Op. 88/1; Prelude [In The Form of a Toccata], Op. 88/3; 6 Short Preludes & Postludes, Set 2, Op. 105 *(rec Sledmere House Yorkshire)* Amphion ▲ PHI 126 [DDD]

Jackson, Laurence (vn)—see ORCHESTRAS & ENSEMBLES Maggini String Quartet

Jackson, Nicholas (org)
Great European Organs, No. 39 Priory ▲ PRI 423 [DDD]

Jackson, Reginald (sax)
Moss, L.:Short Pieces, w. Jessica Krash (pno) Capstone ▲ CPS 8619

Jackson, Steven (cl)
Sowerby, L.:Songs of Resignation, w. D'Anna Fortunato (mez), Veronica Macchia-Kadlubkiewicz (vn), Anthony de Mare (pno) Gasparo ▲ GSCD 315 [DDD]

Jacob, Andreas (org)
Pachelbel, J.:Magnificat, w. W. Jacob (cnd), Capella Sebaldina Nuremberg Entrée ▲ 0050 [ADD]
Pachelbel, J.:Missa brevis, w. W. Jacob (cnd), Capella Sebaldina Nuremberg Entrée ▲ 0050 [ADD]
Pachelbel, J.:Motets, w. W. Jacob (cnd), Capella Sebaldina Nuremberg—Singet dem Herrn ein neues Lied; Der Herr ist König; Nun danket alle Gott; Jauchzet dem Herrn; Exsurgat Deus; Tröste uns Gott; Gott ist unsre Zuversicht Entrée ▲ 0050 [ADD]

Jacob, Clement (org)
Les Quatre Saisons en Chant Gregorien, w. Strasbourg Cathedral Choir [cnd:M. Wackenheim] Studio SM ▲ 12 22 16 [AAD]

Jacob, Jeffrey (pno)
Barber, S.:Pno Music—Excursions, Op. 20; Piano Son., Op. 26; Souvenirs, Op. 28; Nocturne, Op. 33; Ballade, Op. 46 Centaur ▲ CRC 2162 [DDD]
Briggs, R.:Tracer, w. J. Swoboda (cnd), Silesian PO MMC ▲ MMC 2028 [DDD]
Crumb, G.:Gnomic Vars Centaur ▲ CRC 2050 [AAD]
Crumb, G.:A Little Suite for Christmas:A.D. 1979 Centaur ▲ CRC 2080 [AAD]
Crumb, G.:Makrokosmos I Centaur ▲ CRC 2050 [AAD]
Crumb, G.:Pieces (5) Pno Centaur ▲ CRC 2050 [AAD]
Crumb, G.:Processional—both the original & the revised versions Centaur ▲ CRC 2080 [AAD]
Lubet, A.:Shabbat Shalom Capstone ▲ CPS 8631
McKinley, W.T.:Con 2 Pno, w. J. Swoboda (cnd), Silesian PO MMC ▲ MMC 2028 [DDD]

Jacob, Stefanie (pno)
Sierra, R.:Con Tres, w. William Helmers (cl), Shawn Mauser (bn) CRI ▲ CD 724 [DDD]
Sierra, R.:Fantasías, w. William Helmers (cl), Scott Tisdel (vc) CRI ▲ CD 724 [DDD]
Sierra, R.:Piezas Características, w. William Helmers (b cl), Catherine Schubilske (vn), Scott Tisdel (vc), Dennis Najoom (tpt), Thomas Wetzel (perc), N. Gittleman (cnd) CRI ▲ CD 724 [DDD]

Jacob, Werner (org)
Bach, J.S.:Cons Org, BWV 592–597—Con in a, BWV 593 EMI Classics ("Baroque" series) ▲ CDK 65728
Bach, J.S.:Nun komm, der Heiden Heiland, BWV 659 EMI Classics ("Baroque" series) ▲ CDK 65728
Bach, J.S.:Passacaglia & Fugue Org EMI Classics ("Baroque" series) ▲ CDK 65728
Bach, J.S.:Toccata, Adagio & Fugue Org, BWV 564 EMI Classics ("Baroque" series) ▲ CDK 65728
Bach, J.S.:Toccata, Adagio & Fugue Org, BWV 564 EMI Classics ▲ CDK 65728
Buxtehude, D.:Org Music (misc)—Nun komm der Heiden Heiland; Prelude & Fugue in D; Puer natus est in Bethlehem; Auf meinen lieben Gott; Magnificat primi toni; Prelude, Fugue & Chaconne in C EMI Classics ("Baroque" series) ▲ CDK 65728
Denkmäler Barocker Orgelbaukunst Ambitus ▲ AMB 97891 [DDD]
Hambreus, B.:Music of, w. H. Hellsten (org), E. Bour (cnd), Southwest RSO—Cadenza; Canvas with mirrors; Continuo MAP ▲ MAPCD 9131
Pachelbel, J.:Org Music, sels. unknown Virgin Classics ▲ CDC 59197
Pachelbel, J.:Org Music [Organ of St. Sebald, Nuremberg]—Ricercare in c; Toccata in c Entrée ▲ 0050 [ADD]

Jacobi, Irene (pno)
Jacobi, F.:Ballade Vn, w. Fredell Lack (vn) CRI ("American Masters" series) ▲ CD 703 [ADD]

Jacoboni, Maria Pia (clvd)
Broschi, R.:Arias, w. Angelo Manzotti (sop), Rome Solisti—Di costanza il core armato Bongiovanni ▲ GB 5564 [DDD]
Farinelli (Carlo Broschi):Aria for la Maestà de Ferdinando VI Re cattolico, w. Angelo Manzotti (sop), Rome Solisti Bongiovanni ▲ GB 5564 [DDD]

▲ = CD ♦ = Enhanced CD Δ = MD ■ = Cassette Tape □ = DCC

Jacoboni, Maria Pia (clvd) (cont.)
Giacomelli, G.:Merope (sels), w. Angelo Manzotti (sop), Rome Solisti—Quell'usignolo che innamorato canta; Sposa non mi conosci Bongiovanni ▲ GB 5564 [DDD]
Hasse, J.A.:Artaserse (sels), w. Angelo Manzotti (sop), Rome Solisti Bongiovanni ▲ GB 5564 [DDD]

Jacobowski, Richard (gtr)
Fuenllana, M. de:Orphénica lyra—Fant. de redobles *(rec Myers Recital Hall, New York City, Sept. 1994)* Gateway Classics ▲ GC 6124
Llobet, M.:Gtr Music—5 Catalan Folksong Settings [La nit de nadal/El mestre/Canço del lladre/El testament d'Amelia/El noi de la mare] *(rec Myers Recital Hall, New York City, Sept. 1994)* Gateway Classics ▲ GC 6124
Milán, L. de:Maestro (sels)—Fants. III & X *(rec Myers Recital Hall, New York City, Sept. 1994)* Gateway Classics ▲ GC 6124
Mompou, F.:Suite compostelana *(rec Myers Recital Hall, New York City, Sept. 1994)* Gateway Classics ▲ GC 6124
Richard Jacobowski Plays Giuliani, Milano, Dowland, Carlevaro, Villa-Lobos, Falla & Berkeley *(rec Myers Recital Hall, New York City, 1993)* Gateway Classics ▲ GC 6123
Rodrigo, J.:En Los trigales *(rec Myers Recital Hall, New York City, Sept. 1994)* Gateway Classics ▲ GC 6124

Jacobs (pno)
Bolcom, W.:Three Ghost Rags Elektra/Nonesuch ▲ 79006-2 [DDD]
Copland, A.:Blues Elektra/Nonesuch ▲ 79006-2 [DDD]
Rzewski, F.:North American Ballads Elektra/Nonesuch ▲ 79006-2

Jacobs, Bert (fl)
Ives, C.:Son 2 Pno, w. Daan Vandewalle (pno), Paul Klinck (vn) *(rec Steurbaut Sound Recording Centre)* René Gailly ▲ CD 87078 [DDD]

Jacobs, F. (gtr)
Schubert, Franz:Qt Fl, w. M. Root (fl), S. Swierstra (va), V. De Hoog (vc) Globe ▲ GLO 5040 [DDD]

Jacobs, Fred (thb)
Marais, M.:Suites VI & Hpd, w. Susanne Braumann (vl)—in e; in a; in D; in e *(rec Utrecht, Oct. 1994)* Globe ▲ GLO 5122 [DDD]
Telemann, G.P.:Con Tpt 2 Obs, w. Per-Olev Lindeke (tpt), Taka Kitazato (ob), Marcel Ponseele (ob), Richte Van Der Meer (vc), Pierre Hantaï (hpd) *(rec St. Stefanus, Melsen, Belgium, June 1995)* Accent ▲ 95110 [DDD]
Telemann, G.P.:Essercizii musici (sels), w. Taka Kitazato (ob), Marcel Ponseele (ob), Pierre Hantaï (hpd), Per-Olev Lindeke (tpt), Richte Van Der Meer (vc)—Trio Son in E♭ for Ob, Hpd & Continuo *(rec St. Stefanus, Melsen, Belgium, June 1995)* Accent ▲ 95110 [DDD]
Telemann, G.P.:Der Getreue Music-Meister (sels), w. Taka Kitazato (ob), Marcel Ponseele (ob), Per-Olev Lindeke (tpt), Richte Van Der Meer (vc), Pierre Hantaï (hpd)—Son in a *(rec St. Stefanus, Melsen, Belgium, June 1995)* Accent ▲ 95110 [DDD]
Telemann, G.P.:Kleine Kammermusik, w. Taka Kitazato (ob), Marcel Ponseele (ob), Per-Olev Lindeke (tpt), Richte Van Der Meer (vc), Pierre Hantaï (hpd)—Partita IV in g *(rec St. Stefanus, Melsen, Belgium, June 1995)* Accent ▲ 95110 [DDD]
Telemann, G.P.:Musique de Table, w. Taka Kitazato (ob), Marcel Ponseele (ob), Per-Olev Lindeke (tpt), Richte Van Der Meer (vc), Pierre Hantaï (hpd)—Son in g *(rec St. Stefanus, Melsen, Belgium, June 1995)* Accent ▲ 95110 [DDD]
Telemann, G.P.:Son 2 Ob, w. Taka Kitazato (ob), Marcel Ponseele (ob), Per-Olev Lindeke (tpt), Richte Van Der Meer (vc), Pierre Hantaï (hpd) *(rec St. Stefanus, Melsen, Belgium, June 1995)* Accent ▲ 95110 [DDD]

Jacobs, Helmut C. (acc)
Karg-Elert, S.:Partita Harm CPO ▲ CPO 999051-2 [DDD]
Karg-Elert, S.:Passacaglia CPO ▲ CPO 999051-2 [DDD]
Karg-Elert, S.:Son 1 Harm CPO ▲ CPO 999051-2 [DDD]
Paganiniana CPO ▲ CPO 999057 [DDD]

Jacobs, J. (acc)
Klebe, G.:Music of, w. Christian Köhn (pno), Silke-Thora Matthies (pno), Cologne Chamber Choir—Warum hat die sonne einen Aschenrand; Der Schrei; Glockentürme Academy ▲ ACA 8509

Jacobs, Paul (hpd)
Carter, E.:Double Con, w. G. Kalish (pno), A. Weisberg (cnd), Contemporary Chamber Players Elektra/Nonesuch ▲ 79183-2
Carter, E.:Son Vc, w. J. Krosnick (vc) Elektra/Nonesuch ▲ 79183-2
Carter, E.:Son Fl, w. H. Sollberger (fl), C. Kuskin (ob), F. Sherry (vc) Elektra/Nonesuch ▲ 79183-2
Carter, E.:Son Pno Elektra/Nonesuch ▲ 79248-2-ZK ■ 79248-4-AW
Chaminade, C.:Pno Music (misc)—Automne; Autrefois; Callirhoë; Chaconne; Deuxième Waltz; Elévation in E; Etude mélodique in G♭; Etude pathétique in b; Etude scholastique; Lisonjera; L'Ondine; Pêcheurs de nuit; Romance; Scherzo in C; Sérénade in D; Solitude; Souvenance; Thème & varié in A; Valse romantique Hyperion ▲ CDA 66584
Chaminade, C.:Pno Music (misc)—Gigue; Presto; Arlequin; Tarentella; Divertissement; Libellules; Nocturne; Tristesse; Pièce romantique; 'Sous-Bois; Pastorale Hyperion ▲ CDA 66706

Jacobs, Peter (pno)
Blues, Ballads & Rags, w. Paul Jacobs (pno) Elektra/Nonesuch ▲ 79006 2
Bridge, F.:Pno Music (comp) Continuum ▲ CCD 1016
Bridge, F.:Pno Music (comp) Continuum ▲ CCD 1018
Bridge, F.:Pno Music (comp) Continuum ▲ CCD 1019
Bush, A.:Pno Music—Preludes (24); Nocturne; Letter Galliard; Corentyne Kwe-Kwe Altarus ▲ CD 9004
Chaminade, C.:Pno Music (misc)—Prelude Op. 84/3; Rigaudon Op. 55/6; Les Sylvanes Op. 60; Valse-Ballet Op. 112; Inquiétude Op. 87/3; Arabesque Op. 61; Troisième Valse Brilliante; Son Op. 21; Idylle Op. 126/1; Gavotte Op. 123/5; Rondeau Op. 123/4; Orientale Op. 123/9; Aubade Op. 126/2; Patrouille Op. 126/9; Villanelle Op. 126/10; Tarantelle Op. 123/10; Le Passé Op. 127/3; Sérenade espagnole Op. 150; Quatrième Valse Op. 91; Cortège Op. 143 Hyperion ▲ CDA 66846
Debussy, C.:En blanc et noir, w. G. Kalish (pno) *(rec public performance recording)* Elektra/Nonesuch ▲ 79161-2 [AAD]
Debussy, C.:Estampes Elektra/Nonesuch ▲ 71365-2-AW
Debussy, C.:Etudes Elektra/Nonesuch ■ 71322-4
Debussy, C.:Etudes Elektra/Nonesuch ▲ 79161-2 [AAD]
Debussy, C.:Images (6) Pno Elektra/Nonesuch ▲ 71365-2-AW
Debussy, C.:Images (3) Pno Elektra/Nonesuch ▲ 71365-2-AW
Debussy, C.:Preludes Pno Elektra/Nonesuch 2-▲ 73031-2 [ADD]
Feldman, Morton:False Relationships & the Extended Ending, w. M. Raimondi (vn), S. Barab (vc), Y. Takahashi (pno), M. Feldman (cnd) *(rec 6/8/70)* CRI ▲ CD 620 [ADD]
Foulds, J.:Pno Music—Seven Essays in the Modes; Variazioni ed Improvvisati su una Thema Originale; English Tune with Burden; Gandharva-Music; April—England Altarus ▲ CD 9001
Hold, T.:Pno Music—Kemp's Nine Daies Wonder; Ten Pieces from "The Lilford Owl"; Six Kaleidoscopes Continuum ▲ CON 1066
The Jacobs Piano Collection, Vol. 4:French Leave Continuum ▲ CON 1057
Parry, H.:Hands accross the Centuries Priory ▲ PRI 451 [DDD]
Parry, H.:Shulbrede Tunes Priory ▲ PRI 451 [DDD]
Parry, H.:Theme & 19 Vars Priory ▲ PRI 451 [DDD]
Schoenberg, A.:Pno Music—3 Pieces, Op. 11 (1908); 6 Pieces, Op. 19 (1911); 5 Pieces, Op. 23 (1920-23); Suite, Op. 25 (1923); 2 Pieces, Op. 33a & 33b (1928; 1931) Elektra/Nonesuch ▲ 71309-2 ■ 71309-4

Jacobsen, Per (hn)
Roussel, A.:Chamber Music, w. Majken Bjerno (sop), Toke Lund Christiansen (fl), Bjørn Carl Nielsen (ob), Niels Thomsen (cl), Asger Svendsen (bn), Ketil Christensen (tpt), Anne Søe Hansen (vn), Zwi Carmelli (va), Piotr Zelazny (va), Niels Ullner (vc), Michael Dabelsteen (db), Tine Rehling (hp), Morten Mogensen (pno), Per Salo (pno), Per Jensen (perc)—Divertissement, Op. 6; Trio, Op. 40; Joueurs de Flute, Op. 27; Serenade, Op. 30; Le marchand de sable qui passe, Op. 13; Andante et scherzo, Op. 13; 2 poèmes de ronsard, Op. 26; Aria; Elpenor, Op. 59; Pipe Kontrapunkt 2-▲ KPT 32218 [DDD]

Jacobson, E. (pno)
Iannaccone, A.:Trio Fl, w. R. Hill (fl), A. Abramson (cl) Opus One ▲ CD 154

Jacobson, G. (pno)
Bazelon, I.:Duo Va & Pno, w. K. Phillips (va) CRI ▲ CD 623 [ADD]

Jacobson, Julian (pno)
Brahms, J.:Sons Cl (comp), w. P. Silverthorne (va) Meridian ▲ CDE 84190
Brahms, J.:Songs, Op. 91, w. S. Walker (mez), P. Silverthorne (va) [G] Meridian ▲ CDE 84190
Dvořák, A.:Ballad, w. Susanne Stanzeleit (vn) Meridian ▲ MER 84274 [DDD]
Dvořák, A.:Humoresques, Op. 101 Meridian ▲ MER 84281 [DDD]
Dvořák, A.:Mazurek, w. Susanne Stanzeleit (vn) Meridian ▲ MER 84274 [DDD]
Dvořák, A.:Notturno, w. Susanne Stanzeleit (vn) Meridian ▲ MER 84274 [DDD]
Dvořák, A.:Romance Vn, w. Susanne Stanzeleit (vn) Meridian ▲ MER 84274 [DDD]
Dvořák, A.:Romantic Pieces, Op. 75, w. Susanne Stanzeleit (vn) Meridian ▲ MER 84281 [DDD]
Dvořák, A.:Rondo, w. Susanne Stanzeleit (vn) Meridian ▲ MER 84281 [DDD]
Dvořák, A.:Slavonic Dances (sels), w. Susanne Stanzeleit (vn) Meridian ▲ MER 84281 [DDD]
Dvořák, A.:Son Vn, w. Susanne Stanzeleit (vn) Meridian ▲ MER 84274 [DDD]
Dvořák, A.:Sonatina Vn, w. Susanne Stanzeleit (vn) Meridian ▲ MER 84281 [DDD]
Dvořák, A.:Zigeunermelodien, Op. 55, w. Susanne Stanzeleit (vn)—No. 4 [Songs My Mother Taught Me] Meridian ▲ MER 84281 [DDD]
Gerhard, R.:Alegrías, Divertissement Flamenco, w. A. Ball (pno) Largo ▲ 5119 [DDD]
Gerhard, R.:Impromptus (3) Pno Largo ▲ 5119 [DDD]
Gerhard, R.:Pandora, w. A. Ball (pno), R. Benjafield (perc) Largo ▲ 5119 [DDD]
Martin, F.:Ballade Fl, w. Manuela Wiesler (fl) *(rec Malmö Concert Hall, Sweden, Apr 1990)* BIS ▲ CD 71 [DDD]
Martinů, B.:Sinfonietta giocosa Pno, w. T. Vásáry (cnd), Bournemouth Sinfonietta Chandos ▲ CHAN 8859 [DDD]
Martinů, B.:Sinfonietta Pno, w. T. Vásáry (cnd), Bournemouth Sinfonietta Chandos ▲ CHAN 8859 [DDD]
Rózsa, M.:North Hungarian Peasant Songs & Dances, w. Paul Barritt (vn) Silva Classics ▲ SIL 6006 [DDD]
Schumann, R.:Fant Pno Meridian ▲ MER 84205
Schumann, R.:Fantasiestücke Pno, Op. 111 Meridian ▲ MER 84205
Schumann, R.:Kinderszenen Meridian ▲ MER 84205
Schumann, R.:Marches Pno Meridian ▲ MER 84205
Weber, C.M. von:Invitation to the Dance Pno Meridian ▲ MER 84251 [DDD]
Weber, C.M. von:Rondo brillante Meridian ▲ MER 84251 [DDD]
Weber, C.M. von:Sons Pno—J.199 & 206 Meridian ▲ MER 84251 [DDD]

Jacobson, Lena (org)
Court & Dance Music from the Renaissance & Early Baroque *(rec Frederiksborg Castle, Denmark, Mar 1-2, 1978)* BIS ▲ CD 126 [AAD]

Jacobson, Roxann (va)—see ORCHESTRAS & ENSEMBLES Dunsmuir Piano Quartet, Earplay

Jacowicz, K. (vn)
Lutoslawski, W.:Chain 2, w. T. Ukigaya (cnd), Pomorska PO Thorofon ▲ CTH 2041 [DDD]

Jacquemin, Vincent (cl/b cl)
Schoenberg, A.:The Cabaret Songs, w. Yumi Nara (sop), Izumi Okubo (vn/va), Machiko Takahashi (fl/pic), François Deppe (vc), Brigitte Foccroulle (pno), J.-P. Peuvion (cnd), Liège New Music Ensemble [arr Patrick Davin for Salon Orch] Adda ▲ ADD 581273 [DDD]
Schoenberg, A.:Pierrot lunaire, w. Yumi Nara (sop), Izumi Okubo (vn/va), Machiko Takahashi (fl/pic), François Deppe (vc), Brigitte Foccroulle (pno), J.-P. Peuvion (cnd), Liège New Music Ensemble Adda ▲ ADD 581273 [DDD]

Jacquon, Alain (pno)
Burgan, P.:Music of, w. Liliane Mazeron (sop), Clara Novakova (fl), Michel Arrignon (cl), Henry Trio—Jeux de femmes [6 Erotic Poems of Verlaine]; Rondes Nocturnes; Bavardage; Berceuse Maguelone ▲ 350.529
Cras, J.:Danze (4) *(rec Théâtre de Poissy, Oct 16-17, 1995)* Timpani ▲ CD 1033 [DDD]
Cras, J.:Paysages *(rec Théâtre de Poissy, Oct 16-17, 1995)* Timpani ▲ CD 1033 [DDD]
Cras, J.:Poèmes intimes *(rec Théâtre de Poissy, Oct 16-17, 1995)* Timpani ▲ CD 1033 [DDD]

Jaermann, Marc (vc)—see also ORCHESTRAS & ENSEMBLES Sine Nomine String Quartet, Musiviva Trio
Balissat, J.:Vars (7), w. P. Genet, F. Gottraux (vn), N. Pache (va), R. Birnstigl (db), F. Rapin (cl), F. Schmocker (bn), M. Veillon (hn), J. Balissat (cnd) Grammont ▲ CTSP 17-2 [ADD]

Jaffa, Max (vn)
Music for a Grand Hotel, w. Max Jaffa Trio, Jean Grayston (cta), Grand Hotel Orch Valentine ▲ VALD 8057 [DDD]

Jaffe, D. A. (mand)
Jaffe, D.A.:Ellis Island Son Well-Tempered Productions ▲ WTP 5164 [DDD]

Jaffe, Jill (va)—see ORCHESTRAS & ENSEMBLES Bronx Arts Ensemble

Jaffé, Ramon (vc)
Brahms, J.:Hungarian Dances Pno 4-Hands, w. Andrea Frölich (pno)—Nos. 2, 4 & 7 [arr vc & pno] Koch Schwann ▲ SCH CD 317282
Brahms, J.:Son 1 Vn, w. Andrea Frölich (pno) [arr Klengel vc & pno in D] Koch Schwann ▲ SCH CD 317282
Brahms, J.:Songs, w. Andrea Frölich (pno)—6 songs Koch Schwann ▲ SCH CD 317282

Jaffe, Stephen (pno)
Jaffe, S.:Fort Juniper Songs, w. Terry Rhodes (sop), Ellen Williams (mez) Albany ▲ TROY 172 [DDD]

Jaffee, Jill (va)
Zorn, J.:Redbird, w. Carol Emanuel (hp), Erik Friedlander (vc), Jim Pugliese (perc) Tzadik ▲ TZA 7008 [DDD]

Jäggin, Christoph (gtr)
Keller, M.:Erinnerungen IV *(rec June 1994-Apr 1995)* Jecklin ▲ JEC 310 [DDD]
Wildberger, J.:Los pajarillos no cantan *(rec Feb. 17, 1988)* Grammont ▲ CTSP 25-2 [ADD]

Jahn, Raimund (vn)—see ORCHESTRAS & ENSEMBLES Innsbruck Salon Quintet

Jahn, Theodore (cl)—see ORCHESTRAS & ENSEMBLES Georgia Woodwind Quintet

Jahnel, T. (vn)
Lachner, F.P.:Qnt 2 Pno, w. H. Göbel (pno), O. Duliba (vn), S. Clark (va), S. Dörfler (vc) *(rec June 10, 1991)* Thorofon ▲ CTH 2132 [DDD]

Jahren, Hèlen (ob)
Kaipainen, J.:Con Ob, w. S. Oramo (cnd), Finnish RSO Ondine ▲ ODE 855
Roman, J.H.:Con grosso, w. W. Rajski (cnd), Musica Vitae BIS ▲ CD 460 [DDD]
Schnittke, A.:Con Ob, w. K. A. Lier (hp), L. Markiz (cnd), New Stockholm CO BIS ▲ CD 377 [DDD]

Jaimes, Judit (pno)
Grieg, E.:Con Pno, Op. 16, w. E. Mata (cnd), London SO ASV Quicksilva ▲ ASQ 6176

Jakimowicz, Julia (vn)
Prokofiev, S.:Son for 2 Vns, w. Krzysztof Jakowicz (vn) *(rec National Philharmonic Concert Hall, Warsaw, May 26-28, 1991)* Polskie Nagrania ▲ PNCD 114

Jakobsen, Ó. (gtr)
Blak, K.:Dialogue, w. A. E. Klett (cl) Tutl ▲ FKT 6

Jakowicz, Krzysztof (vn)
Lutoslawski, W.:Chain 2, w. K. Kord (cnd), Warsaw PO Polskie Nagrania ▲ PNCD 044 [AAD]
Prokofiev, S.:Son Vn, Op. 94bis, w. Jerzy Godziszewski (pno) *(rec National Philharmonic Concert Hall, Warsaw, May 26-28, 1991)* Polskie Nagrania ▲ PNCD 114
Prokofiev, S.:Son 1 Vn, w. Jerzy Godziszewski (pno) *(rec National Philharmonic Concert Hall, Warsaw, May 26-28, 1991)* Polskie Nagrania ▲ PNCD 114
Prokofiev, S.:Son for 2 Vns, w. Julia Jakimowicz (vn) *(rec National Philharmonic Concert Hall, Warsaw, May 26-28, 1991)* Polskie Nagrania ▲ PNCD 114
Vivaldi, A.:Cons Vn, Op. 8/1-4, "The Four Seasons", w. J. Maksymiuk (cnd), Polish CO Classics for Pleasure ("Eminence" series) ▲ CFP 2009 [ADD]

INSTRUMENT.

Jakszyk, Jakko (gtr)

- Battiato, F.:Haiku, w. Franco Battiato (voc), Pouran Ghaffarpour (voc), Antonio Ballista (pno), Marco Boni (vc), Guido Corti (cnt), Filippo Destrieri (kbd/computer), John Giblin (bass), Gavin Harrison (dr/perc), Roberto Mazza (ob), Fabrizio Merlini (va), Angelo Privitera (kbd/computer), Mino Bordignon (cnd), Milan Chamber Music Choir — Hemisphere ▲ 837234-2
- Battiato, F.:Ricerca sul Terzo, w. Franco Battiato (voc), Alessio Alba (tamboura), Antonio Ballista (pno), Marco Boni (vc), Debendra Kanti Chakraborty (tabla), Guido Corti (cnt), Filippo Destrieri (kbd/computer), John Giblin (bass), Buddhadeu Das Gupta (sarod), Gavin Harrison (dr/perc), Roberto Mazza (ob), Fabrizio Merlini (va), Angelo Privitera (kbd/computer), Mino Bordignon (cnd), Milan Chamber Music Choir — Hemisphere ▲ 837234-2

Jakuc, Monica (pno)

- Auenbrugg, M. von:Son in e♭ Hpd — Titanic ▲ Ti 214
- Haydn, J.:Sons Pno—H.XVI/36 & 37 — Titanic ▲ Ti 214
- Martinez, M.:Son in A Hpd — Titanic ▲ Ti 214
- Martinez, M.:Son in E Hpd — Titanic ▲ Ti 214

James, Bob (pno/syn)

- Rameau, J.P.:Music of — CBS ▲ MK 39540 [DDD]

James, David (trbn)

- Gershwin, G.:Rhap in Blue, w. B. Griffiths (vn), P. Whittaker (cl), R. Simmons (tpt), A. Litton (pno), H. Fisher (dr), A. Litton (cnd), Royal PO [original big band orchestration] — RPO ▲ RPO 5011 [DDD]

James, Deborah (hpd)

- Volans, K.:Mbira, w. Kevin Volans (hpd), Robyn Schulkowsky (perc) *(rec West German Radio, Cologne, Apr 20, 1984)* — United ▲ CAL 88034 [ADD]

James, Dennis (glass hmc)

- Glass Music from Mozart's Time, w. Salzburg Soloists [cnd:Luz Leskowitz] — Syrinx ▲ CSR 91101 [DDD]
- Marc Grauwels & Friends, w. Grauwels, Marc (fl), Marie-Noelle de Callataÿ (sop), Hiroko Masaki (sop), Ingrid Procureur (hp), Yves Storms (gtr), Yvietta Matison (va), Mark Drobinsky (vc), Alain De Rijckere (bn), Daniel Blumenthal (pno), Frank Michiels (perc), Belgian RSO, W — Syrinx 2-▲ 96101 [DDD]

James, Dennis (theater org)

- Schickele, P.:Little Pickle Book *(rec Imperial Spud Theatre, Hoople, North Dakota & Commercial Recording Studio, Studio 1, Cleveland, OH, Apr. 11 & May 1, 1995)* — Telarc ▲ CD 80390 [DDD]

James, Ethan (h-g/perc/harm/dlc/sax/port org/gtr)

- The Ancient Music of Christmas, w. Catherine Edward Alexander (perc) *(rec Reptile's Cloister, Hollywood, CA)* — Hannibal ▲ HNCD 1398

James, Ifor (hn)

- Cherubini, L.:Sons (2) Hn, w. V. Czarnecki (cnd), Southwest German CO Pforzheim — ebs ▲ ebs 6052 [DDD]
- Haydn, J.:Cons Hn, w. V. Czarnecki (cnd), Southwest German CO Pforzheim — ebs ▲ ebs 6052 [DDD]
- Meditations, w. James, Ifor (hn), S. J. Bleicher (org) — ebs ▲ ebs 6040 [DDD]
- Neruda, J.B.G.:Con Hn, w. V. Czarnecki (cnd), Southwest German CO Pforzheim — ebs ▲ ebs 6052 [DDD]
- Strauss, F.:Con Hn, w. A. Wit (cnd), Polish National RSO Katowice — ebs ▲ ebs 6063 [DDD]
- Strauss, R.:Con 1 Hn, w. A. Wit (cnd), Polish National RSO Katowice — ebs ▲ ebs 6063 [DDD]
- Strauss, R.:Con 2 Hn, w. A. Wit (cnd), Polish National RSO Katowice — ebs ▲ ebs 6063 [DDD]
- Telemann, G.P.:Con Hn, w. V. Czarnecki (cnd), Southwest German CO Pforzheim — ebs ▲ ebs 6092 [DDD]
- Telemann, G.P.:Con for 2 Hns in E♭, w. T. Schnirring (hn), V. Czarnecki (cnd), Southwest German CO Pforzheim — ebs ▲ ebs 6092 [DDD]
- Telemann, G.P.:Con for 3 Horns, w. R. Teutsch (hn), T. Abramovici (hn), V. Czarnecki (cnd), Southwest German CO Pforzheim — ebs ▲ ebs 6092 [DDD]
- Telemann, G.P.:Suite for 4 Hns, w. T. Abramovici (hn), A. Lewis (hn), R. Teutsch (hn), V. Czarnecki (cnd), Southwest German CO Pforzheim — ebs ▲ ebs 6092 [DDD]

James, Kevin (trbn)

- Wigglesworth, F.:Psalm 148, w. Kathy Fink (fl), Elizabeth Brown (fl), Jeanne Wilson (fl), David Taylor (trbn), D. Schuler (cnd), Church of St. Luke in the Fields Choir — CRI ▲ C 733 [DDD]

James, Layton (org)

- Bach, J.S.:Fugue on a Theme by Corelli *(rec Jan 1993)* — London ▲ 440376-2
- Corelli, A.:Trio Sons, Op. 3, w. L. Shank (vn), R. Tecco (vn) *(rec Jan. 1993)* — London ▲ 440376-2

Jandó, Jenö (cel)

- Mozart, W.A.:Adagio & Rondo Glass Armonica, w. I. Kovács (fl), J. Kiss (ob), G. Konrád (va), T. Koó (vc) *(rec Dec. 1-4, 1990)* — Naxos ▲ 8.550511 [DDD]
- Schubert, Franz:Songs (misc), w. T. Takács (mez)—An die Musik; Heidenröslein; Die Forelle; Auf dem Wasser zu singen; Du bist die Ruh; Im Frühling; Wandrers; Nach und Träume; Der Zwerg; Gretchen am Spinnrade; Die junge Nonne; Lied der Mignon I; Lied der Mignon II; Lied der Mignon III; Suleikas Gesang I; Suleikas Gesang II; Der tod und das Mädchen; Erikönig [G] *(rec Oct. 8-11, 1991)* — Naxos ▲ 8.550476 [DDD]

Jandó, Jenö (pno)

- Bach, J.S.:Das wohltemperierte Klavier—Book 2 *(rec Unitarian Church, Budapest, Sept. 14-17 & Oct. 13-16, 1993)* — Naxos 2-▲ 8.550970/71 [DDD]
- Bartók, B.:Andante, w. György Pauk (vn) *(rec Unitarian Church, Budapest, June 27-28, 1993)* — Naxos ▲ 8.550886 [DDD]
- Bartók, B.:Con 1 Pno, w. A. Ligeti (cnd), Budapest SO *(rec Italian Institute, Budapest, Feb. 14-18, 1994)* — Naxos ▲ 8.550771 [DDD]
- Bartók, B.:Con 2 Pno, w. A. Ligeti (cnd), Budapest SO *(rec Italian Institute, Budapest, Feb. 14-18, 1994)* — Naxos ▲ 8.550771 [DDD]
- Bartók, B.:Con 3 Pno, w. A. Ligeti (cnd), Budapest SO *(rec Italian Institute, Budapest, Feb. 14-18, 1994)* — Naxos ▲ 8.550771 [DDD]
- Bartók, B.:Mikrokosmos — Koch Schwann ▲ CD 312182 [DDD]
- Bartók, B.:Qnt Pno & Strs, w. Kodály String Quartet *(rec Unitarian Church, Budapest, June 27-28, 1993)* — Naxos ▲ 8.550886 [DDD]
- Bartók, B.:Rhaps Vn & Pno, Sz.86 & 89, w. György Pauk (vn) *(rec Unitarian Church, Budapest, June 27-28, 1993)* — Naxos ▲ 8.550886 [DDD]
- Beethoven, L. van:Bagatelles (24) *(rec Aug. 26-30, 1991)* — Naxos ▲ 8.550474 [DDD]
- Beethoven, L. van:Music of, w. et al., CSR SO Bratislava, Slovak PO, Capella Istropolitana—Egmont & Fidelio Ovs.; Für Elise; sels. from Pno Son. 8 & 14; Sym. 3, 5 & 6; Pno Con. 4 & 5; Vn Con. — Naxos ▲ 8.551101 [DDD] Δ 7.551101 [DDD]
- Beethoven, L. van:Qnt Pno, Ob, Cl, Hn & Bn, w. J. Kiss (ob), B. Kovács (cl), J. Keveházi (hn), J. Vajda (bn) *(rec Dec. 1-4, 1990)* — Naxos ▲ 8.550511 [DDD]
- Beethoven, L. van:Son 1 Vc, w. C. Onczay (vc) *(rec June 25-27, 1991)* — Naxos ▲ 8.550479
- Beethoven, L. van:Son 2 Vc, w. C. Onczay (vc) — Naxos ▲ 8.550479
- Beethoven, L. van:Son 3 Vc, w. C. Onczay (vc) *(rec 12/90)* — Naxos ▲ 8.550478 [DDD]
- Beethoven, L. van:Son 4 Vc, w. C. Onczay (vc) — Naxos ▲ 8.550478 [DDD]
- Beethoven, L. van:Son 5 Vc, w. C. Onczay (vc) — Naxos ▲ 8.550478 [DDD]
- Beethoven, L. van:Sons Pno (comp)—Nos. 1-3 — Naxos ▲ 8.550150 [DDD]
- Beethoven, L. van:Sons Pno (comp)—Nos. 17, 21 & 26 — Naxos ▲ 8.550054 [DDD]
- Beethoven, L. van:Sons Pno (comp)—Nos. 5, 6, 7 & 25 *(rec 1/88)* — Naxos ▲ 8.550161 [DDD]
- Beethoven, L. van:Sons Pno (comp)—Nos. 30, 31 & 32 *(rec 12/87)* — Naxos ▲ 8.550151 [DDD]
- Beethoven, L. van:Sons Pno (comp)—Nos. 8, 14 & 23 — Naxos ▲ 8.550045 [DDD]
- Beethoven, L. van:Sons Pno (comp)—Nos. 12, 16 & 18 *(rec 2-3/88)* — Naxos ▲ 8.550166 [DDD]
- Beethoven, L. van:Sons Pno (comp)—Nos. 9, 10, 24, 27 & 28 *(rec 1/88)* — Naxos ▲ 8.550162 [DDD]
- Beethoven, L. van:Sons Pno (comp)—Nos. 4, 13, 19, 20 & 22 *(rec 2-3/88)* — Naxos ▲ 8.550167 [DDD]
- Beethoven, L. van:Sons Pno (comp)—Nos. 11 & 29 *(rec 8-9/88)* — Naxos ▲ 8.550234 [DDD]
- Beethoven, L. van:Son 15 Pno, "Pastoral" *(rec Jan. 31-Feb. 17, 1989)* — Naxos ▲ 8.550255 [DDD]
- Beethoven, L. van:Son 36 Pno *(rec Jan. 31-Feb. 17, 1989)* — Naxos ▲ 8.550255 [DDD]
- Beethoven, L. van:Sons Pno, WoO 47, "Electoral Sons" *(rec Jan. 31-Feb. 17, 1989)* — Naxos ▲ 8.550255 [DDD]

Jandó, Jenö (pno) (cont.)

- Beethoven, L. van:Son 1 Vn, w. T. Nishizaki (vn) *(rec Feb. 18-21 & Sept. 2, 199)* — Naxos ▲ 8.550284 [DDD]
- Beethoven, L. van:Son 2 Vn, w. T. Nishizaki (vn) *(rec Feb. 18-21 & Sept. 2, 199)* — Naxos ▲ 8.550284 [DDD]
- Beethoven, L. van:Son 3 Vn, w. T. Nishizaki (vn) *(rec Feb. 18-21 & Sept. 2, 199)* — Naxos ▲ 8.550284 [DDD]
- Beethoven, L. van:Son 4 Vn, w. T. Nishizaki (vn) *(rec Feb. & Sept. 1992)* — Naxos ▲ 8.550285 [DDD]
- Beethoven, L. van:Son 5 Vn, "Spring", w. T. Nishizaki (vn) *(rec 4/89)* — Naxos ▲ 8.550283 [DDD]
- Beethoven, L. van:Son 6 Vn, w. T. Nishizaki (vn) *(rec 10/89)* — Naxos ▲ 8.550286 [DDD]
- Beethoven, L. van:Son 7 Vn, w. T. Nishizaki (vn) *(rec 10/89)* — Naxos ▲ 8.550286 [DDD]
- Beethoven, L. van:Son 8 Vn, w. T. Nishizaki (vn) *(rec 10/89)* — Naxos ▲ 8.550286 [DDD]
- Beethoven, L. van:Son 9 Vn, "Kreutzer", w. T. Nishizaki (vn) *(rec 4/89)* — Naxos ▲ 8.550283 [DDD]
- Beethoven, L. van:Son 10 Vn, w. T. Nishizaki (vn) *(rec Feb. & Sept. 1992)* — Naxos ▲ 8.550285 [DDD]
- Beethoven, L. van:Sonatinas Pno—in G & F [spurious]; in 2 Movts. (ca. 1788-89) *(rec Jan. 31-Feb. 17, 1989)* — Naxos ▲ 8.550255 [DDD]
- Beethoven, L. van:Trio 4 Pno, "Ghost", w. T. Nishizaki (vn), C. Onczay (vc) *(rec May 27-30, 1991)* — Naxos ▲ 8.550442 [DDD]
- Beethoven, L. van:Trio 6 Pno, "Archduke", w. T. Nishizaki (vn), C. Onczay (vc) *(rec May 27-30, 1991)* — Naxos ▲ 8.550442 [DDD]
- Beethoven, L. van:Vars on "Ein Mädchen oder Weibchen" from Mozart's *Die Zauberflöte*, w. C. Onczay (vc) *(rec June 25-27, 1991)* — Naxos ▲ 8.550479
- Beethoven, L. van:Vars on "See, the Conquering Hero Comes" from Handel's *Judas Maccabaeus*, w. C. Onczay (vc) *(rec June 25-27, 1991)* — Naxos ▲ 8.550479
- Beethoven, L. van:Vars on "Bei Männern" from Mozart's *Die Zauberflöte*, w. C. Onczay (vc) *(rec June 25-27, 1991)* — Naxos ▲ 8.550479
- Beethoven, L. van:Vars on Mozart's, "Se vuol ballare," WoO 40, w. T. Nishizaki (vn) *(rec Feb. & Sept. 1992)* — Naxos ▲ 8.550285 [DDD]
- Brahms, J.:Con 2 Pno, w. A. Rahbari (cnd), Belgian Radio-TV PO *(rec June 3-4, 1992)* — Naxos ▲ 8.550506 [DDD]
- Brahms, J.:Ernste Gesänge, w. T. Takács (mez) [G] *(rec 1989)* — Naxos ▲ 8.550400 [DDD]
- Brahms, J.:Trio Cl, w. J. Balogh (cl), C. Onczay (vc) *(rec Oct. 16-18, 1991)* — Naxos ▲ 8.550391 [DDD]
- Classics Go to the Movies, Vol. 1, w. Hungarian State Opera Orch, Vienna Strauss Orch, Plovdiv PO, Dresden PO, New Leipzig Bach Collegium Musicum, Budapest SO — LaserLight ▲ 15 641
- Concerto No. 2 in A for Piano & Orchestra, S.125 (1839; rev 1849-61), w. Liszt, Franz, Budapest SO [cnd:András Ligeti] — Laserlight ♦ 90021 [DDD]
- Dohnányi, E. von:Humoresken — Koch Schwann ▲ SCH 312192 [DDD]
- Dohnányi, E. von:Pastorale Pno, "Hungarian Christmas Song" — Koch Schwann ▲ SCH 312192 [DDD]
- Dohnányi, E. von:Pieces Pno, Op. 2 — Koch Schwann ▲ SCH 312192 [DDD]
- Dohnányi, E. von:Rhaps, Op. 11 — Koch Schwann ▲ CD 311812 [DDD]
- Dohnányi, E. von:Ruralia hungarica Pno — Koch Schwann ▲ CD 311812 [DDD]
- Dvořák, A.:Con Pno, w. A. Wit (cnd), Polish National RSO Katowice *(rec Nov. 9-13, 1993)* — Naxos ▲ 8.550896 [DDD]
- Franck, C.:Son Vn, w. T. Nishizaki (vn) *(rec 2/90)* — Naxos ▲ 8.550417 [DDD]
- Gershwin, G.:Rhap in Blue, w. J. Sándor (cnd), Budapest PO — LaserLight ▲ 15 606 [DDD]
- Grieg, E.:Con Pno, Op. 16, w. J. Sándor (cnd), Budapest PO — LaserLight ▲ 15 617 [DDD]
- Grieg, E.:Con Pno, Op. 16, w. A. Ligeti (cnd), Budapest SO *(rec Italian Institute, Budapest, Mar 1-6, 1988)* — Naxos ▲ 8.553267 [DDD]
- Grieg, E.:Con Pno, Op. 16, w. A. Ligeti (cnd), Budapest SO — Naxos ▲ 8.550118 [DDD]
- Grieg, E.:Lyric Pieces, w. T. Nishizaki (vn) [arr. Vladimir Godar for vn & pno] *(rec 2/90)* — Naxos ▲ 8.550417 [DDD]
- Grieg, E.:Sons Vn, Opp. 8, 13 & 45, w. T. Nishizaki (vn)—No. 3 *(rec 2/90)* — Naxos ▲ 8.550417 [DDD]
- Haydn, J.:Sons Pno—Sons. Nos. 59, in E♭, H.XVI/49; 60. in C, H.XVI/50; 61 in D, H.XVI/51; 62 in E♭, H.XVI/52 *(rec Feb. 25-27, 1992)* — Naxos ▲ 8.550657 [DDD]
- Haydn, J.:Sons Pno—Nos. 36-41 *(rec Unitarian Church, Budapest, May 5-9, 1993)* — Naxos ▲ 8.553127 [DDD]
- Haydn, J.:Sons Pno—Sons. Nos. 48 in C, H.XVI/35; 49 in c#, H.XVI/36; 50 in D, H.XVI/37; 51 in E♭, H. XVI/38; 52 in G, H. XVI/39 *(rec Unitarian Church, Budapest, June 15-18, 1993)* — Naxos ▲ 8.553128 [DDD]
- Kodály, Z.:Chorale Preludes, w. Maria Kliegel (vc) *(rec Clara Wieck Auditorium, Heidelberg, July 1994 & May 1995)* — Naxos ▲ 8.553160 [DDD]
- Kodály, Z.:Son Vc & Pno, Op. 4, w. Maria Kliegel (vc) *(rec Clara Wieck Auditorium, Heidelberg, July 1994 & May 1995)* — Naxos ▲ 8.553160 [DDD]
- Kodály, Z.:Son Vc & Pno, Op. 4, w. M. Perényi (vc) — Hungaroton ▲ HCD 31046
- Liszt, F.:Années de pèlerinage (comp)—Première Année:Suisse — Naxos ▲ 8.550548 [DDD]
- Liszt, F.:Années de pèlerinage 2 *(rec 7/91)* — Naxos ▲ 8.550549 [DDD]
- Liszt, F.:Années de pèlerinage 3 *(rec 9/91)* — Naxos ▲ 8.550550 [DDD]
- Liszt, F.:Fant on Hungarian Folk Tunes, w. A. Ferencsik (cnd), Hungarian State Orch — Hungaroton ▲ HCD 12721
- Liszt, F.:Fant on Hungarian Folk Tunes, w. A. Ligeti (cnd), Budapest SO — LaserLight ▲ 15631 [DDD]
- Liszt, F.:Fant on Themes from Beethoven's *Ruins of Athens*, w. A. Ligeti (cnd), Budapest SO — LaserLight ▲ 14011 [DDD]
- Liszt, F.:Grand fantaisie symphonique on Berlioz's *Lélio*, w. A. Ligeti (cnd), Budapest SO — LaserLight ▲ 14011 [DDD]
- Liszt, F.:Malédiction, w. A. Ligeti (cnd), Budapest SO — LaserLight ▲ 14011 [DDD]
- Liszt, F.:Pno Music (misc)—Les jeux d'eau à la Villa d'Este; Vallée d'Obermann; La campanella *(rec Dec. 6-10, 1990)* — Naxos ▲ 8.550510 [DDD]
- Liszt, F.:Pno Music (misc), w. K. Dráfi (pno), I. Lantos (pno)—Harmonies poétiques et religieuses; Invocation (1st version); Hymne du matin; Hymne de la nuit; Berceuse (1st version); Klavierstück; Trois odes funèbres; Berceuse (2nd version); Urbi et orbi; Vexilla regis prodeunt; Drei Stücke aus der Legende der heiligen Elisabeth No. 1 Intro; Impromptu; Epithalam; Resignazione; Recueillement; Sancta Dorothea; In festo transfigurations Domini nostri Jesu Christi; Ave Maria; Trübe Wolken/Nuages gris; Wiegenlied/Chant du berceau; Am Grabe Richard Wagners; En rêve; Trauervorspiel und Trauermarsch *(rec Italian Cultural Institute, Budapest, 1985-86)* — Hungaroton 2-▲ HCD 31656-57 [DDD]
- Liszt, F.:Polonaise brillante, w. A. Ligeti (cnd), Budapest SO — LaserLight ▲ 15631 [DDD]
- Liszt, F.:Son Pno *(rec Dec. 6-10, 1990)* — Naxos ▲ 8.550510 [DDD]
- Liszt, F.:Son Pno *(rec Reformed Church, Budapest, Dec 6-10, 1990)* — Naxos ▲ 8.553237 [DDD]
- Liszt, F.:Totentanz, w. A. Ligeti (cnd), Budapest SO — LaserLight ▲ 15630 [DDD]
- Liszt, F.:Venezia e Napoli *(rec 7/91)* — Naxos ▲ 8.550549 [DDD]
- Liszt, F.:Wandererfantasie, w. A. Ligeti (cnd), Budapest SO — LaserLight ▲ 15630 [DDD]
- Melody in F, w. Jandó, Jenö (pno) — LaserLight ▲ 1515603 [DDD]
- Mozart, W.A.:Allegro & Andante *(rec Nov. 1990)* — Naxos ▲ 8.550445 [DDD]
- Mozart, W.A.:Cons 1-4 Pno, w. I. Hegyi (cnd), Concentus Hungaricus — Naxos ▲ 8.550212 [DDD]
- Mozart, W.A.:Con 5 Pno, w. M. Antal (cnd), Concentus Hungaricus *(rec Jan. 4-10, 1991)* — Naxos ▲ 8.550209 [DDD]
- Mozart, W.A.:Con 6 Pno, w. M. Antal (cnd), Concentus Hungaricus *(rec June & Oct. 1990)* — Naxos ▲ 8.550208 [DDD]
- Mozart, W.A.:Con 7 Pnos, w. D. Várjon (pno), M. Antal (pno), Concentus Hungaricus [arr. Mozart for 2 pianos & orch.] *(rec Jan. 7-10, 1991)* — Naxos ▲ 8.550210 [DDD]
- Mozart, W.A.:Con 8 Pno, w. M. Antal (cnd), Concentus Hungaricus *(rec June & Oct. 1990)* — Naxos ▲ 8.550208 [DDD]
- Mozart, W.A.:Con 9 Pno, w. A. Ligeti (cnd), Concentus Hungaricus *(rec July 1989)* — Naxos ▲ 8.550203 [DDD]
- Mozart, W.A.:Con 10 Pnos, w. M. Antal (pno), Concentus Hungaricus — Naxos ▲ 8.550206 [DDD]
- Mozart, W.A.:Con 10 Pnos, w. D. Várjon (pno), M. Antal (cnd), Concentus Hungaricus *(rec Jan. 7-10, 1991)* — Naxos ▲ 8.550210 [DDD]

▲ = CD ♦ = Enhanced CD Δ = MD ▮ = Cassette Tape ▯ = DCC

Jandó, Jenö (pno) (cont.)
Mozart, W.A.:Con 12 Pno, w. A. Ligeti (cnd), Concentus Hungaricus *(rec June 1989)* Naxos ▲ 8.550202 [DDD]
Mozart, W.A.:Con 13 Pno, w. A. Ligeti (cnd), Concentus Hungaricus *(rec May 1989)* Naxos ▲ 8.550201 [DDD]
Mozart, W.A.:Con 15 Pno, w. M. Antal (cnd), Concentus Hungaricus *(rec Jan. 7–10, 1991)* Naxos ▲ 8.550210 [DDD]
Mozart, W.A.:Con 16 Pno, w. M. Antal (cnd), Concentus Hungaricus *(rec June 29–July 1, 1990)* Naxos ▲ 8.550207 [DDD]
Mozart, W.A.:Con 17 Pno, w. M. Antal (cnd), Concentus Hungaricus Naxos ▲ 8.550205 [DDD]
Mozart, W.A.:Con 18 Pno, w. M. Antal (cnd), Concentus Hungaricus *(rec Sept.–Oct. 1989)* Naxos ▲ 8.550205 [DDD]
Mozart, W.A.:Con 18 Pno, w. M. Antal (cnd), Concentus Hungaricus *(rec June & Oct. 1990)* Naxos ▲ 8.550208 [DDD]
Mozart, W.A.:Con 19 Pno, w. M. Antal (cnd), Concentus Hungaricus *(rec June & Oct. 1990)* Naxos ▲ 8.550208 [DDD]
Mozart, W.A.:Con 20 Pno, w. A. Ligeti (cnd), Concentus Hungaricus *(rec May 1989)* Naxos ▲ 8.550201 [DDD]
Mozart, W.A.:Con 20 Pno, w. A. Ligeti (cnd), Concentus Hungaricus *(rec May 1989)* Naxos ▲ 8.550434 [DDD]
Mozart, W.A.:Con 22 Pno, w. M. Antal (cnd), Concentus Hungaricus Naxos ▲ 8.550206 [DDD]
Mozart, W.A.:Con 25 Pno, w. M. Antal (cnd), Concentus Hungaricus *(rec June 29–July 1, 1990)* Naxos ▲ 8.550207 [DDD]
Mozart, W.A.:Con 26 Pno, w. M. Antal (cnd), Concentus Hungaricus *(rec Jan. 4–10, 1991)* Naxos ▲ 8.550209 [DDD]
Mozart, W.A.:Con 27 Pno, w. A. Ligeti (cnd), Concentus Hungaricus *(rec June 1989)* Naxos ▲ 8.550203 [DDD]
Mozart, W.A.:Fant Pno, K.475 Naxos ▲ 8.550449 [DDD]
Mozart, W.A.:Qnt Hn, K.407, w. J. Kiss (ob), B. Kovács (cl), J. Keveházi (hn), J. Vajda (bn) *(rec Dec. 1–4, 1990)* Naxos ▲ 8.550511 [DDD]
Mozart, W.A.:Rondo Pno Orch, K.382, w. M. Antal (cnd), Concentus Hungaricus *(rec Jan. 4–10, 1991)* Naxos ▲ 8.550209 [DDD]
Mozart, W.A.:Rondo Pno Orch, K.386, w. M. Antal (cnd), Concentus Hungaricus *(rec Oct. 20, 1990)* Naxos ▲ 8.550207 [DDD]
Mozart, W.A.:Sons Pno—Nos. 1, 4, 5 & 6 *(rec Apr. 2–4 & 27–30, 1991)* Naxos ▲ 8.550447 [DDD]
Mozart, W.A.:Son 2 Pno Naxos ▲ 8.550449 [DDD]
Mozart, W.A.:Son 8 Pno *(rec Nov. 1990)* Naxos ▲ 8.550445 [DDD]
Mozart, W.A.:Son 10 Pno *(rec Nov. 1990)* Naxos ▲ 8.550445 [DDD]
Mozart, W.A.:Son 12 Pno *(rec Nov. 1990)* Naxos ▲ 8.550446 [DDD]
Mozart, W.A.:Son 13 Pno Naxos ▲ 8.550449 [DDD]
Mozart, W.A.:Son 14 Pno Naxos ▲ 8.550449 [DDD]
Mozart, W.A.:Son 15 Pno *(rec Nov. 1990)* Naxos ▲ 8.550446 [DDD]
Mozart, W.A.:Son 16 Pno *(rec Nov. 1990)* Naxos ▲ 8.550446 [DDD]
Mozart, W.A.:Trio Cl, K.498, w. B. Kovács (cl), G. Konrád (va) *(rec Sept. 16, 1991)* Naxos ▲ 8.550439 [DDD]
Music of Schubert, w. Budapest PO [cnd:János Kóvacs], Colorado String Quartet Laserlight ♦ 90032 [CD–ROM] [DDD]
Rachmaninoff, S.:Con 2 Pno, w. G. Lehel (cnd), Budapest SO *(rec Italian Institute, Budapest, Feb 9–10 & Apr 5–7, 1988)* Naxos 4–▲ 8.504011 [DDD]
Rachmaninoff, S.:Con 2 Pno, w. G. Lehel (cnd), Budapest SO Naxos ▲ 8.550117 [DDD]
Rachmaninoff, S.:Rhapsody on a Theme of Paganini, w. G. Lehel (cnd), Budapest SO Naxos ▲ 8.550117 [DDD]
Rachmaninoff, S.:Rhapsody on a Theme of Paganini, w. G. Lehel (cnd), Budapest SO *(rec Italian Institute, Budapest, Feb 9–10 & Apr 5–7, 1988)* Naxos 4–▲ 8.504011 [DDD]
Schubert, Franz:Adagio & Rondo concertante Vn, w. I. Tóth (db), Kodály String Quartet *(rec Dec. 2–4, 1991)* Naxos ▲ 8.550658 [DDD]
Schubert, Franz:Allegro Pno 4–Hands, D.947, w. I. Prunyi (pno) *(rec Nov. 5–8, 1991)* Naxos ▲ 8.550555 [DDD]
Schubert, Franz:Divertissement à l'hongroise, D.818, w. I. Prunyi (pno) *(rec Nov. 5–8, 1991)* Naxos ▲ 8.550555 [DDD]
Schubert, Franz:Fant Pno, D.760, "Wandererfantasie" *(rec Budapest, Apr. 14–17, 1993)* Naxos ▲ 8.550846 [DDD]
Schubert, Franz:Impromptus Pno (comp)—in G♭, D.899/3; in B♭, D.935/3 LaserLight ▲ 14 224
Schubert, Franz:Impromptus Pno (comp)—Op. 90/1–4; Op. 142/3 Laserlight ▲ 15 609
Schubert, Franz:Impromptus Pno (comp) LaserLight ▲ 15 609 [DDD]
Schubert, Franz:Impromptus Pno (comp) *(rec 4/89)* Naxos ▲ 8.550260 [DDD]
Schubert, Franz:Impromptus Pno, D.935—No. 3 in B♭ LaserLight ▲ 15 522 [DDD]
Schubert, Franz:Marches caractéristiques, w. I. Prunyi (pno) *(rec Nov. 5–8, 1991)* Naxos ▲ 8.550555 [DDD]
Schubert, Franz:Moments musicaux LaserLight ▲ 15 609 [DDD]
Schubert, Franz:Moments musicaux *(rec Feb. 2–17, 1989)* Naxos ▲ 8.550259 [DDD]
Schubert, Franz:Pieces Pno, D.946 *(rec Feb. 2–17, 1989)* Naxos ▲ 8.550259 [DDD]
Schubert, Franz:Qnt Pno, D.667, w. I. Tóth (db), Kodály String Quartet *(rec Dec. 2–4, 1991)* Naxos ▲ 8.550658 [DDD]
Schubert, Franz:Son Pno, D.537 *(rec Budapest, Apr. 14–17, 1993)* Naxos ▲ 8.550846 [DDD]
Schubert, Franz:Son Pno, D.664 *(rec Budapest, Apr. 14–17, 1993)* Naxos ▲ 8.550846 [DDD]
Schubert, Franz:Son Pno, D.784 *(rec July 6–8, 1992)* Naxos ▲ 8.550730 [DDD]
Schubert, Franz:Son Pno, D.894 *(rec July 6–8, 1992)* Naxos ▲ 8.550730 [DDD]
Schubert, Franz:Son Pno, D.958 *(rec Sept. 2–7, 1991)* Naxos ▲ 8.550475 [DDD]
Schubert, Franz:Son Pno, D.960 *(rec Sept. 2–7, 1991)* Naxos ▲ 8.550475 [DDD]
Schumann, R.:Adagio & Allegro Hn, w. J. Kiss (ob) [arr. for oboe & piano] *(rec Dec. 12–15, 1991)* Naxos ▲ 8.550599 [DDD]
Schumann, R.:Arabeske Pno *(rec Nov. 24–27, 1992)* Naxos ▲ 8.550783 [DDD]
Schumann, R.:Carnaval Pno *(rec Nov. 1992)* Naxos ▲ 8.550784 [DDD]
Schumann, R.:Con Pno, w. A. Ligeti (cnd), Budapest SO Naxos ▲ 8.550118 [DDD]
Schumann, R.:Fantasiestücke Cl, w. J. Kiss (ob) [arr. for oboe & piano] *(rec Dec. 12–15, 1991)* Naxos ▲ 8.550599 [DDD]
Schumann, R.:Faschingsschwank aus Wien *(rec Nov. 24–27, 1992)* Naxos ▲ 8.550783 [DDD]
Schumann, R.:Frauenliebe und –leben, w. T. Takács (mez) [G] *(rec 1989)* Naxos ▲ 8.550400 [DDD]
Schumann, R.:Intro & Allegro appassionato, Op. 92, w. A. Rahbari (cnd), Brussels BTR PO *(rec June 3–4, 1992)* Naxos ▲ 8.550506 [DDD]
Schumann, R.:Kinderszenen *(rec Nov. 1992)* Naxos ▲ 8.550784 [DDD]
Schumann, R.:Kreisleriana *(rec Nov. 24–27, 1992)* Naxos ▲ 8.550783 [DDD]
Schumann, R.:Papillons *(rec Nov. 1992)* Naxos ▲ 8.550784 [DDD]
Schumann, R.:Qnt Pno, w. Kodály String Quartet Naxos ▲ 8.550406 [DDD]
Schumann, R.:Romances Ob, w. J. Kiss (ob) [oboe & piano arr.] *(rec Dec. 12–15, 1991)* Naxos ▲ 8.550599 [DDD]
Schumann, R.:Son 1 Vn, w. J. Kiss (ob) [oboe & piano arr.] *(rec Dec. 12–15, 1991)* Naxos ▲ 8.550599 [DDD]
Schumann, R.:Stücke im Volkston, w. J. Kiss (vc) [oboe & piano arr.] *(rec Dec. 12–15, 1991)* Naxos ▲ 8.550599 [DDD]
Tchaikovsky, P.:Con 1 Pno, w. A. Ligeti (cnd), Budapest PO Laserlight ▲ 15 516 [DDD]
Tchaikovsky, P.:Con 1 Pno, w. A. Ligeti (cnd), Budapest PO—Andante semplice LaserLight ▲ 14 224
Tchaikovsky, P.:Con 1 Pno, w. A. Ligeti (cnd), Budapest PO Capriccio ▲ 10 921 [DDD]
Violin Miniatures, w. Takako Nishizaki (vn) *(rec May 21 & 27, 1989)* Naxos ▲ 8.550306 [DDD]
Wagner, R.:Wesendonck Songs, w. T. Takács (mez) [G] *(rec 1989)* Naxos ▲ 8.550400 [DDD]
Weber, C.M. von:Grand duo concertant Cl, w. Kálmán Berkes (cl) *(rec Scottish Church, Budapest, Aug. 23–27, 1994)* Naxos ▲ 8.553122 [DDD]

Jandó, Jenö (pno) (cont.)
Weber, C.M. von:Vars on a Theme from *Silvana* Cl, w. Kálmán Berkes (cl) *(rec Scottish Church, Budapest, Aug. 23–27, 1994)* Naxos ▲ 8.553122 [DDD]

Janezic, Ronald (hn)
Chabrier, E.:Larghetto, w. J.E. Gardiner (cnd), Vienna PO *(rec Vienna, Mar 1995)* Deutsche Grammophon ▲ 447 751–2 [DDD]

Janigro, Antonio (vc)
Beethoven, L. van:Sons Vc (comp), w. Jörg Demus (pno) *(rec Vienna, 1964)* Vanguard Classics 2–▲ SVC 56/57 [AAD]
Strauss, R.:Don Quixote, w. F. Reiner (cnd), Chicago SO RCA Gold Seal ▲ 09026–61796–2

Janis, Byron (pno)
Chopin, F.:Pno Music (misc)—Mazurkas in g, C, f, a, b♭, c#; Nocturnes in E♭, B, E, F#, D♭; Waltzes in a, A♭, G♭ EMI Classics ▲ CDC 56196
Liszt, F.:Cons Pno, w. Moscow PO [cnd:K. Kondrashin] (No. 1), Moscow RSO [cnd:G. Rozhdestvensky] (No. 2),—plus "Encores by Falla, Guion, Liszt, & Schumann" Mercury Living Presence ▲ 432002–2 [ADD]
Liszt, F.:Totentanz, w. F. Reiner (cnd), Chicago SO *(rec 1959)* RCA Gold Seal ▲ 09026–61250–2 ■ 09026–61250–4
Mendelssohn, F.:Lieder ohne Worte Pno—Op. 62/1 *(rec Bolshoi Hall, Tchaikovsky Conservatory, Moscow, June 10–11, 1962)* Mercury Living Presence ▲ 434333–2
Pinto, O.:Pno Music—3 Scenes from Childhood *(rec Bolshoi Hall, Tchaikovsky Conservatory, Moscow, June 10–11, 1962)* Mercury Living Presence ▲ 434333–2
Prokofiev, S.:Con 3 Pno, w. K. Kondrashin (cnd), Moscow PO *(rec Bolshoi Hall, Tchaikovsky Conservatory, Moscow, June 8–9, 1962)* Mercury Living Presence ▲ 434333–2
Prokofiev, S.:Toccata Pno *(rec Bolshoi Hall, Tchaikovsky Conservatory, Moscow, June 10–11, 1962)* Mercury Living Presence ▲ 434333–2
Rachmaninoff, S.:Con 1 Pno, w. K. Kondrashin (cnd), Moscow PO *(rec Bolshoi Hall, Tchaikovsky Conservatory, Moscow, June 13, 1962)* Mercury Living Presence ▲ 434333–2
Rachmaninoff, S.:Con 2 Pno, w. A. Dorati (cnd), Minneapolis SO Mercury Living Presence ▲ 432759–2 [ADD]
Rachmaninoff, S.:Con 3 Pno, w. C. Munch (cnd), Boston SO RCA Silver Seal ▲ 60540–2–RV [ADD] ■ 60540–4–RV
Rachmaninoff, S.:Con 3 Pno, w. A. Dorati (cnd), London SO Mercury Living Presence ▲ 432759–2 [ADD]
Rachmaninoff, S.:Prelude Pno, Op. 3/2 Mercury Living Presence ▲ 432759–2 [ADD]
Rachmaninoff, S.:Preludes Pno, Opp 23 & 32—Op. 23, No. 6 Mercury Living Presence ▲ 432759–2 [ADD]
Schumann, R.:Con Pno, w. S. Skrowaczewski (cnd), Minneapolis SO Mercury Living Presence ▲ 432011–2 [ADD]
Schumann, R.:Impromptus on a Theme by Clara Wieck Pno, Op. 5 *(rec New York, Jan. 24, 1964)* Mercury Living Presence ▲ 434333–2
Strauss, R.:Burleske, w. F. Reiner (cnd), Chicago SO RCA Gold Seal ▲ 09026–61796–2

Jankovic, Ksenija (vc)
Despic, D.:Meditations (3), Camerata Academica Novi Sad Emergo ▲ EC 3950 [DDD]
Maric, L.:Monodia octoicha Emergo ▲ EC 3951 [DDD]

Jankowska, Katarzyna (pno)
Chopin, F.:Songs Sop (comp), w. Zofia Kilanowicz (sop) *(rec Warsaw Philharmonic Hall, Jan 1993 & May 1994)* Canyon Classics ▲ CD 237

Janofsky, Bonnie (hpd)
Boccherini, L.:Fandango, w. G. Nestor (gtr) [arr. for guitar & harpsichord] Cambria ▲ CD 1049 [DDD]

Janopoulo, Tasso (pno)
Chabrier, E.:Songs, w. Renée Doria (sop), Julien Giovannetti (bar), Guy Fouché (sgr), André Rabot (bn)—Lied; Tes yeux bleus; Sommation irrespectueuse; Toutes les fleurs; Ruy blas [A quoi bon entendre...]; Credo d'amour; Romance de l'étoile; Villanelle des petits; Les cigales; Ballade des gros dindons; Pastorale des cochons roses; L'île heureuse; Chanson pour jeanne; Duo de l'ouvreuse de l'opéra–comique et de l'employé du bon–marché; L'invitation au voyage Accord ▲ ACD 201392 [AAD]

Jánoska, Aladár (cl)
Schmidt, F.:Qnt Cl, w. S. Mucha (vn), A. Lakatos (va), J. Slávik (vc), D. Ruso (pno) Marco Polo ▲ 8.223414
Schmidt, F.:Qnt Cl, w. D. Ruso (pno), F. Török (vn), A. Lakatos (va), J. Slávik (vc) Marco Polo ▲ 8.223415

Janota, Gbor (bn)
Vivaldi, A.:Cons Bn, w. J. Rolla (cnd), Franz Liszt CO—6 concerti White Label ▲ HRC 043

Janovsky, P. (fl)
Mozart, W.A.:Con Fl Hp, w. R. Zanelli (hp), A. Lizzio (cnd), Mozart Festival Orch Vivace 3–▲ E 315 [DDD]

Janowski, Piotr (vn)
Bacewicz, G.:Con 7 Vn, w. A. Markowski (cnd), Warsaw PO Olympia ▲ OLY 392 [ADD]

Jans, Carlo (fl)
Feld, J.:Son Fl, w. Daniel Blumenthal (pno) Pavane ▲ ADW 7358 [DDD]
Martinů, B.:Son 1 Fl, w. Daniel Blumenthal (pno) Pavane ▲ ADW 7358 [DDD]
Prokofiev, S.:Son Fl, w. Daniel Blumenthal (pno) Pavane ▲ ADW 7358 [DDD]
Schulhoff, E.:Son Fl, w. Daniel Blumenthal (pno) Pavane ▲ ADW 7358 [DDD]

Jansen, Jan Willem (org)
Couperin, F.:Org Music [at the historic organ of Saint–Michel en Thiérache Abbey]—Invitatoire de la fest Dieu; Fantaisie; Fantaisie; Fantaisie; Fantaisie; Fantaisie; Pange Lingua en basse [à 4]; Pange Lingua (1656) [à 3]; Pange Lingua (1656) [à 3]; Simphonie; Fantaisie [Récit de basse]; Fantaisie pour les Violes; Fantaisie de Violes; Ave Maris Stella [en basse, à 4]; Ave Maris Stella [à 3]; Fantaisie [Récit de basse]; Simphonie; Ut Queant Laxis [à 3]; Ut Queant Laxis [à 3]; Fantaisie à Paris au mois de Décembre 1656; Duo; Regina Caeli; Simphonie; Fantaisie [Récit de basse]; Fantaisie [Récit de basse]; Fantaisie; Fantaisie sur le Cromhorne; Fantaisie sur la 3ce du Gd Clavier avec le Tbt lent; Fantaisie; Iste Convessor *(rec Radio France, 1993)* FNAC Music ▲ 592291 [DDD]
Couperin, L.:Org Music [Abbey of Saint–Michel en Thierache Organ] FNAC Music ▲ 592291
Kee, C.:Phases NM Classics ▲ NM 92034

Jansen, Peter (db)
Blak, K.:Addeq, w. L. Kullgren (gtr), K. Blak (pno), M. Cissokho (perc) Tutl ▲ HJF 22
Schubert, Franz:Qnt Pno, D.667, w. D. Dechene (pno), E. Verhey (vn), F. Erblich (va), J. DeCroos (vc) Vivace ▲ E 561 [DDD]
Schubert, Franz:Qnt Pno, D.667, w. D. Dechene (pno), E. Verhey (vn), F. Erblich (va), J. DeCroos (vc) Laserlight ▲ 15 522 [DDD]

Jansen, Rudolf (pno)
Diepenbrock, A.:Songs—Entsagung; Der Fischer; Der Abend kommt gezogen [all w. Christoph Prégardien (ten)]; Mignon; Der König in Thule; Kann ich im Busen heisse Wünsche tragen?; Liebesklage [all w. Jard van Nes (mez)]; Die Liebende schreibt; Hinüber wall'ich; Lied der Spinnerin; Der Abend [all w. Roberta Alexander (sop)]; Es war ein alter König; Celebrität [both w. Rudolf Holl (bass/bar)] *(rec Singelkerk, Amsterdam, Feb 24–25, Apr 25–27, May)* NM Classics ▲ 92050 [DDD]
Diepenbrock, A.:Songs, w. Roberta Alexander (sop), Christa Pfeiler (mez), Jard Van Ness (mez), Robert Holl (bass), Daniel Esser (vc)—Berceuse; Clair de lune; Mandoline; L'invitation au voyage; Les Chats; Receuillement; Puisque l'aube grandit; Incantation; En Sourdine; La Chanson de l'hypertrophique NM Classics ▲ NM 92051
Grieg, E.:Songs, w. M. Hirsti (sop), K. M. Sandve (ten), K. Skram (bar)—Four Songs, Op. 15; 3 Songs from Peer Gynt; 5 Songs by Vilhelm Krag, Op. 60; 6 Songs by Holger Drachmann, Op. 49 [N] *(rec March & Dec. 1991)* Victoria ▲ VCD 19038 [DDD]
Grieg, E.:Songs, w. M. Hirsti (sop), C. Pfeiler (mez), K. M. Sandve (ten), K. Skram (bar)—4 Songs, Op. 2; 4 Songs by Christian Winther, Op. 10; 9 Songs, Op. 18; 6 Songs by Ibsen, Op. 25 Victoria ▲ VCD 19042

INSTRUMENT.

Jansen, Rudolf (pno) (cont.)
Grieg, E.:Songs, w. M. Hirsti (sop), K. M. Sandve (ten), K. Skram (bar)—Songs & Ballads by Munch, Op. 9; 5 Poems by Paulsen, Op. 26; Romances, Op. 39; 5 Songs by Benzon, Op. 69; 5 Songs by Benzon, Op. 70 — Victoria ▲ VCD 19043
Grieg, E.:Songs, w. M. Hirsti (sop), K. M. Sandve (ten), K. Skram (bar)—For L.M. Lindeman's Silver Wedding Anniversary; The Blueberry; Yuletide Cradle Song; Devoutest of Maidens; Little Lad; The Forgotten Maid; The White & Red, Red Roses — Victoria ▲ VCD 19044
Grieg, E.:Songs, w. M. Hirsti (sop), K. Skram (bar)—7 Children's Songs, Op. 61; Haugtussa, Op. 67; Songs from Haugtussa not included in Op. 67; Clara's Song; I Love You, Dear; The Princess; Sighs; Morning Prayer at School — Victoria ▲ VCD 19040
Grieg, E.:Songs, w. K. Skram (bar)—four songs from Melodies of the Heart Op. 5; twelve songs from Op. 33—The youth; Last spring; The wounded heart; The berry; Beside the stream; A vision; The old mother; The first thing; At Rondane; A piece on friendship; Faith; The goal; Six elegiac songs, Op. 59; The mountain thrall, Op. 32 — Victoria ▲ VCD 19039
Grieg, E.:Songs, w. M. Hirsti (sop), C. Pfeiler (mez), K. M. Sandve (ten), K. Skram (bar)—Op. 4, Nos. 1, 2, 3, 4, 5 & 6; Op. 21, Nos. 1, 2, 3 & 4; Op. 44, Nos. 1, 2, 3, 4, 5 & 6; Op. 48, Nos. 1, 2, 3, 4, 5 & 6; Op. 58, Nos. 1, 2, 3, 4 & 5 [N, G] — Victoria ▲ VCD 19041
Milhaud, D.:Songs, w. Ulrike Sonntag (sop) *(rec Sept. 1994)* — Troubadisc ▲ TROCD 01409 [DDD]
Schubert, Franz:Der Hirt auf dem Felsen, w. E. Wiens (sop), J. Valdepeñas (cl) — CBC ("Musica Viva" series) ▲ MVCD 1053 [DDD]
Schubert, Franz:Songs (misc), w. E. Ameling (sop)—18 songs [G] *(rec live, Tanglewood Theatre-Concert Hall, 7/2/87)* — Omega ▲ OCD 1001 [DDD]
Schubert, Franz:Songs (misc), w. Monica Groop (mez)—Fischerweise; Seligkeit; Lied der Mignon; Die Forelle; Romanz aus Rosamunde; Lachen und wienen; Auf dem Wasser zu singen; Schäfers Klaglied; Pax Vobiscum; Die männer sind mechant!; An die Musik; An Silvia; Du bist die Ruh; Ganymed; Wiegenlied; Der Musenshon; Meeres Stille; Ave Maria; Ständchen — Ondine ▲ ODE CD 886
Schubert, Franz:Songs (misc), w. E. Wiens (sop)—An die Musik; An Silvia; Ariette der Claudine; Auf dem Wasser zu singen; Der Einsame; Fischerweise; Frühlingsglaube; Heidenröslein; Die junge Nonne; Der Jüngling an der Quelle; Lachen und Weinen; Liebhaber in allen Gestalten; Das Lied im Grünen; Die Mutter Erde; Nacht und Träume; Seligkeit; also, Romanze, D.787, No. 2 & Der Hirt auf dem Felsen, w. Joaquin Valdepeñas (clarinet) [G] — CBC ("Musica Viva" series) ▲ MVCD 1053 [DDD]
Schubert, Franz:Winterreise, w. A. Schmidt (bar) [G] — Deutsche Grammophon ▲ 435384-2 [DDD]
Schumann, R.:Songs, w. Edith Wiens (sop)—Widmung, Op. 25/1; Schneeglöckchen, Op. 79/26; Volksliedchen, Op. 51/2; Jasminenstrauch, Op. 27/4; Lied der Braut, Op. 25/12; O ihr Herren, Op. 37/3; Aus den östlichen Rosen, Op. 25/25; Der Himmel hat eine Träne geweint, Op. 37/1; Mein schöner Stern, Op. 101/4; Zum Schluss, Op. 25/26; Aus den hebräischen Gesängen, Op. 25/15; An den Mond, Op. 95/2; Du bist wie eine Blume, Op. 25/24; Dein Angesicht, Op. 127/2 — Cascavelle ▲ CVL 1029 [DDD]
Strauss, R.:Songs, w. Edith Weins (sop)—Die Nacht, Op. 10/3; Auf ein Kind, Op. 47/1; Wiegenlied, O. Op. AV 41; Meinem Kinde, Op. 37/3; Wiegenlied, Op. 41/1; Muttertändelei, Op. 43/2; Gefunden, Op. 56/1; Blauer Sommer, Op. 31/1; Malven, O. Op.; Ein Röslein zog ich mir im Garten, O. Op. AV 49; Allerseelen, Op. 10/8; Ach Lieb, ich muss nun scheiden, Op. 21/3; Mein Herz ist stumm, Op. 19/6; Morgen, Op. 27/4; Ständchen, Op. 17/2; Freundliche Vision, Op. 48/1; Ruhe, meine Seele, Op. 27/1; Waldseligkeit, Op. 49/1; Einerlei, Op. 69/3; Schlechtes Wetter, Op. 69/5; Wir beide wollen springen, O. Op. AV 90; Zueignung, Op. 10/1 *(rec Glenn Gould Studio, CBC Toronto, Oct 31–Nov 3, 1994)* — CBC ("Musica Viva" series) ▲ MVCD 1090 [DDD]
Wolf, H.:Songs (misc), w. Elly Ameling (sop)—Die ihr schwebet; Komm, o Tod; Mögen alle bösen Zugen; Sagt, seid ihr es; Tief im Herzen trag ich Pein; In dem Schatten meiner Locken; Wer tat deinem Füsslein weh?; Ach, des Knaben Augen; Ob auch finstre Blicken glitten; Alle gingen; Herz, zur Ruh'; Bedeckt mich mit Blumen; Müh voll komm ich; Sie blasen zum Abmarsch; Geh, Geliebter; Auf ein altes Bild; Im Frühling; Elfenlied; Verborgenheit; Das verlassene Mägdlein; Lied von Winde; Nimmerstatte Liebe — Hyperion ▲ CDA 66788

Jansen, Simon C. (org)
Trumpet & Organ:Oboe & Organ, w. Alan Stringer (tpt), Koen van Slochteren (ob) — Vivace ▲ 575

Jansen, Willem (hpd)—see ORCHESTRAS & ENSEMBLES Limoges Baroque Ensemble Soloists

Janson, Thore (cl)
Bäck, S.-E.:Favola, w. Stig Arntorp (perc), Bengt Arsenius (perc), Roland Johansson (perc), Björn Liljequist (perc) — Caprice ▲ CAP 21490

Janssen, Guus (hpd)
Janssen, G.:Zoek, w. Eleonore Pameijer (fl), L. Markiz (cnd), Amsterdam New Sinfonietta — NM Classics ▲ NM 92041

Janssen, Guus (pno)
Janssen, G.:Dans van de Malic Matrijzen, w. L. Vis (cnd), Residentie Orch The Hague *(rec 1978–82)* — Olympia ▲ OCD 506 [AAD]

Janssen, Ivo (pno)
Andriessen, L.:Trepidus — NM Classics ▲ NM 92028
Brahms, J.:Vars & Fugue on a Theme by Handel *(rec Nov. 1992)* — Globe ▲ GLO 5096 [DDD]
Brahms, J.:Vars on a Theme by Paganini *(rec Nov. 1992)* — Globe ▲ GLO 5096 [DDD]
Brahms, J.:Vars on a Theme of Robert Schumann, Op. 9 *(rec Nov. 1992)* — Globe ▲ GLO 5096 [DDD]
Britten, H.:Insect Pieces (2), w. P. Oosternrijk (ob) — Channel Classics ▲ CCS 9326 [DDD]
Britten, H.:Temporal Vars Ob, w. P. Oosternrijk (ob) — Channel Classics ▲ CCS 9326 [DDD]
Charpentier, J.:Gavambodi 2, w. A. Bornkamp (sax) — Globe ▲ GLO 5032 [DDD]
de Leeuw, T.:Men Go Their Ways — NM Classics ▲ NM 92028
Denisov, E.:Son A Sax, w. A. Bornkamp (sax) — Globe ▲ GLO 5032 [DDD]
Desenclos, A.:Prélude, cadence et finale, w. A. Bornkamp (sax) — Globe ▲ GLO 5032 [DDD]
Hindemith, P.:Dance Pieces *(rec Dec. 1993)* — Globe ▲ GLO 5113 [DDD]
Hindemith, P.:Ludus Tonalis — Globe ▲ GLO 5044 [DDD]
Hindemith, P.:Sons Pno—Sons. 2 & 3 *(rec Dec. 1993)* — Globe ▲ GLO 5113 [DDD]
Hindemith, P.:Suite "1922" *(rec Dec. 1993)* — Globe ▲ GLO 5113 [DDD]
Loevendie, T.:Strides — NM Classics ▲ NM 92028
Loevendie, T.:Walk — NM Classics ▲ NM 92028
Padding, M. van:Blend — NM Classics ▲ NM 92028
Roosendael, J.R. van:Events — NM Classics ▲ NM 92028
Schmitt, F.:Légende, w. A. Bornkamp (sax) — Globe ▲ GLO 5032 [DDD]

Janssen, Wim (va)
Zimmermann, B.A.:Son Va — Stradivarius ▲ STR 33340

Janssens, S. (vn)—see ORCHESTRAS & ENSEMBLES Arte del Suono String Quartet

Jansson, Kerstin (pno)
Blomdahl, K.-B.:Chamber Con, w. Kroumata Percussion Ensemble, A. Loguin (cnd), Falu Woodwind Quintet, Omnibus Chamber Winds — Caprice ▲ CAP 21355 [DDD]
Messiaen, O.:Oiseaux exotiques, w. A. Loguin (cnd), Falu Woodwind Quintet, Kroumata Percussion Ensemble, Omnibus Chamber Winds — Caprice ▲ CAP 21355 [DDD]

Jansson, Mats (pno)
Dupré, M.:Ballade, w. H. Fagius (org) *(rec July 2–5, 1992)* — BIS ▲ CD 551 [DDD]
Dupré, M.:Sinf, w. H. Fagius (org) *(rec July 2–5, 1992)* — BIS ▲ CD 551 [DDD]
Dupré, M.:Vars à deux thèmes, w. H. Fagius (org) *(rec July 2–5, 1992)* — BIS ▲ CD 551 [DDD]
Karg-Elert, S.:Poesien, w. H. Fagius (org)—2 pieces *(rec July 2–5, 1992)* — BIS ▲ CD 551 [DDD]
Karg-Elert, S.:Silhouetten, w. H. Fagius (org)—3 pieces *(rec July 2–5, 1992)* — BIS ▲ CD 551 [DDD]
Peeters, F.:Con Org Pno, w. H. Fagius (org) *(rec July 2–5, 1992)* — BIS ▲ CD 551 [DDD]

Janus, Grazyna (hp)
Gallagher, J.:Threnody, w. S. Kawalla (cnd), Koszalin State PO — Vienna Modern Masters ▲ VMM 3028 [DDD]

Jappe, Dorothea (va)
Kreutzer, C.:Trio for 2 Cls & Va, w. E. Schmid (cl), H. R. Stalder (cl) [period instrs] *(rec 1984)* — Jecklin-Disco ▲ JD 587-2 [ADD]
The Viola d'Amore:In Numerous Voices, w. Konrad Hünteler (trns fl), Hans-Rudolf Stalder (chl), Herbert Hoever (vn), Michael Jappe (vl/vc), Rolf Junghanns (hpd/pno) — Adagio ▲ ADG 91016

Jappe, Michael (vl)
Telemann, G.P.:Rcr Music (misc), w. H. Linde (rcr), E. Müller (hpd)—Fant. for Flute in A; Partita 5 in e; Son. in B♭; Son. in d — Klavier ■ KC 511
Vivaldi, A.:Rcr Music (misc), w. H. Linde (rcr), E. Müller (hpd)—Son. 2 in C; Son. in d for Flute & Continuo; Son. in F — Klavier ■ KC 511

Jappe, Michael (vl/vc)
The Viola d'Amore:In Numerous Voices, w. Dorothea Jappe (va d'amore), Konrad Hünteler (trns fl), Hans-Rudolf Stalder (chl), Herbert Hoever (vn), Rolf Junghanns (hpd/pno) — Adagio ▲ ADG 91016

Jardon, Lydia (pno)
Granados, E.:Colección de Tonadillas escritas en estilo antiguo — Deutsche Schallplatten ▲ DS 1040
Granados, E.:Goyescas — Deutsche Schallplatten ▲ DS 1040

Jarka, Käthe (vc)—see ORCHESTRAS & ENSEMBLES Broyhill Chamber Ensemble

Jarlsfelt, Frank (pno)—see ORCHESTRAS & ENSEMBLES Danish Duo

Jaroslawski, Werner (vl)
Schütz, H.:Psalmen Davids, w. H. Otto (org), E.-L. Hammer (vl), R. Mauersberger (cnd), Dresden Church Choir—Singet dem Herrn ein neues Lied, denn er tut Wunder, Psalm 98; Wohl dem, der nicht wandelt im Rat der Gottlosen, Psalm 1; Warum toben die Heiden, Psalm 2; Jauchzet dem Herrn, alle Welt, dienet dem Herren mit Freuden, Psalm 100; Der Herr ist mein Hirt, mir wird nichts mangeln, Psalm 23; Wie lieblich sind deine Wohnungen, Herr Zebaoth, Psalm 84; Aus der Tiefe ruf' ich, Herr, zu dir, Psalm 130; Ach Herr, Straf mich nicht in deinem Zorn, Psalm 6; Ich hebe meine Augen auf zu den Bergen, Psalm 121; Nun lob, mein Seel, den Herren, SWV 41; Ich danke dem Herrn von ganzem Herzen, Psalm 111 [w. Dresden State Orch. members] *(rec Oct. 1965)* — Berlin Classics ▲ BER 2070-2 [ADD]

Jarrett, Keith (hpd)
Bach, J.S.:French Suites — ECM New Series ▲ 78118-20001-2
Bach, J.S.:Goldberg Vars — ECM New Series ▲ 78118-21395-2 [DDD]; ■ 78118-21395-4 (D)
Bach, J.S.:Sons Fl, BWV 1030–35, w. M. Petri (rcr)—BWV 1030–1035 — RCA Red Seal ▲ 09026-61274-2 ■ 09026-61274-4 □ 09026-61274-5
Bach, J.S.:Sons Vl, BWV 1027–1029, w. K. Kashkashian (vl) — ECM New Series ▲ 78118-21501-2
Bach, J.S.:Das wohltemperierte Klavier—Book 2 — ECM New Series 2-▲ 78118-21433-2 [DDD]
Handel, G.F.:Sons Rcr, w. Michala Petri (rcr) — RCA Red Seal ▲ 60441-2-RC [DDD]; ■ 60441-4-RC (CrO2) □ 09026-60441-5

Jarrett, Keith (pno)
Bach, J.S.:Das wohltemperierte Klavier—Book 1 — ECM New Series 2-▲ 78118-21362-2 [DDD]
Glanville-Hicks, P.:Etruscan Con, w. D. R. Davies (cnd), Brooklyn PO — MusicMasters ▲ 01612-67089-2
Handel, G.F.:Suites Hpd—in g, HWV 452; in d, HWV 447; in B♭, HWV 440; in f, HWV 433; in F, HWV 427; in e, HWV 429; in A, HWV 426 *(rec Purchase, NY, Sept. 1993)* — ECM New Series ▲ 78118-21530-2 [DDD]; ■ 78118-21530-4
Harrison, L.:Con Pno, w. N. Otomo (cnd), New Japan PO — New World ▲ NW 366-2 [DDD]; ■ NW 366-4 (D)
Harrison, L.:Suite Vn, Pno & Small Orch, w. Lucy Stoltzman (vn), R. Hughes (cnd), Ensemble — New World ▲ NW 366-2 [DDD]; ■ NW 366-4 (D)
Hovhaness, A.:Lousadzak, w. D. R. Davies (cnd), American Composers Orch — MusicMasters ▲ 7021-2-C
Jarrett, K.:Son Vn, w. T. Crawford (cnd), Fairfield Orch — ECM New Series ▲ 78118-21450-2
Mozart, W.A.:Con 21 Pno, w. D. R. Davies (cnd), Stuttgart CO *(rec Liederhalle, Stuttgart, Nov 1994 & Jan 1995)* — ECM New Series 2-▲ 78118-21565-2 [DDD]
Mozart, W.A.:Con 23 Pno, w. D. R. Davies (cnd), Stuttgart CO *(rec Liederhalle, Stuttgart, Nov 1994 & Jan 1995)* — ECM New Series 2-▲ 78118-21565-2 [DDD]
Mozart, W.A.:Con 27 Pno, w. D. R. Davies (cnd), Stuttgart CO *(rec Liederhalle, Stuttgart, Nov 1994 & Jan 1995)* — ECM New Series 2-▲ 78118-21565-2 [DDD]
Pärt, A.:Fratres II, w. G. Kremer (vn) [arr vn & pno] — ECM New Series ▲ 78118-21275-2 [DDD]; ■ 78118-21275-4
Shostakovich, D.:Preludes & Fugues Pno — ECM New Series 2-▲ 78118-21469-2

Jarry, Gérard (vn)—see also ORCHESTRAS & ENSEMBLES French String Trio
Ysaÿe, E.:Poème nocturne, w. Frederic Lodeon (vc), Georges Pludermarcher (pno) [arr. for piano trio] — Koch Schwann ▲ SCH 317212 [DDD]
Ysaÿe, E.:Son Vns, w. Koji Toyado (vn) — Koch Schwann ▲ SCH 317212 [DDD]

Järvi, Maarika (fl)
Currier, N.:A Sambuca Son, w. Paul Cortese (va), Marie-Pierre Langlamet (hp) — Chandos ▲ CHAN 9395 [DDD]
Debussy, C.:Son Fl, w. Paul Cortese (va), Marie-Pierre Langlamet (hp) — Chandos ▲ CHAN 9395 [DDD]
Genzmer, H.:Trio Fl, Va & Hp, w. Paul Cortese (va), Marie-Pierre Langlamet (hp) — Chandos ▲ CHAN 9395 [DDD]
Jolivet, A.:Petite suite, w. Paul Cortese (va), Marie-Pierre Langlamet (hp) — Chandos ▲ CHAN 9395 [DDD]

Järvi, Teet (vc)—see ORCHESTRAS & ENSEMBLES Tallinn String Quartet

Jarvinen, Arthur (perc)—see also ORCHESTRAS & ENSEMBLES California EAR Unit
Cage, J.:Ryoanji Fl, w. Dorothy Stone (fl) — New World ▲ 80456-2
Feldman, Morton:Why Patterns, w. D. Stone (fl), G. Mowrey (pno) *(rec 10/90)* — New Albion ▲ NA 039 [DDD]

Jarvis, Michael (hpd)
Clarke, J.:Songs, w. Carolyn Sinclair (sop), Margaret Gay (vc)—Celia is Soft; Long Has Pastora Rul'd the Plain; So Sweets the Charms of Love; Alas, Here Lies the Poor Alonzo Slain; Divine Astrea Hither Flew; Lord, What's Come to My Mother; I'se No More to Shady Coverts; Jockey Was a Dawdy Lad; The Bonny Grey Ey'd Morn; Jockey Was as Brisk & Blith a Lad *(rec St. Lawrence the Martyr Church, Hamilton, Ontario)* — Hungaroton ▲ HCD 31602 [DDD]
Clarke, J.:Suite Hpd *(rec St. Lawrence the Martyr Church, Hamilton, Ontario)* — Hungaroton ▲ HCD 31602 [DDD]
Eccles, J.:Songs, w. Carolyn Sinclair (sop), Margaret Gay (vc)—Stay, Ah Turn; Love is An Empty, Airy Name; If I Hear Orinda Swear; E'er Since You Came into My Sight; My Lover Has An Inconstant Mind; I'll Hurry Thee Hence; I Burn, My Brain Consumes to Ashes *(rec St. Lawrence the Martyr Church, Hamilton, Ontario)* — Hungaroton ▲ HCD 31602 [DDD]
Purcell, H.:Songs, w. Carolyn Sinclair (sop), Margaret Gay (vc)—Ah! How Sweet It is to Love; I Sigh'd & Owned My Love; Sweeter Than Roses; Whilst I with Grief Did on You Look; Oh! How You Protest; 'Twas Within a Furlong of Edinborough Town; Man is For the Woman Made; Ah Me! To Many Deaths Decreed; Oh! Lead Me to Some Peaceful Gloom; Lads & Lasses, Blith & Gay *(rec St. Lawrence the Martyr Church, Hamilton, Ontario)* — Hungaroton ▲ HCD 31602 [DDD]
Purcell, H.:Suites Hpd—in d *(rec St. Lawrence the Martyr Church, Hamilton, Ontario)* — Hungaroton ▲ HCD 31602 [DDD]

Jásek, Ladislav (vn)
Bach, J.S.:Con for 2 Vns, w. J. Suk (vn), V. Smetáček (cnd), Prague SO *(rec 1965)* — Supraphon Collection ▲ 11 0642-2 [ADD]

Jauniaux, Catherine (fl/voc)
Exquisite Corpses from P.S. 122, w. David Watson (shears/stick vn/gtr/tpt), Judy Dunaway (gtr/balloons), Anthony Coleman (sampler), Raissa St. Pierre (drums), Guy Yarden (vn/pno), Leslie Ross (bn), Linda Austin (gtr), Bruce Kaplan (gtr), Doug Henderson (peckhorn/bass/toy pno), Sue Ann Harkey (gtr), Cinnie Cole (sampler), et al. — ¿What Next? ▲ WN 0002 [ADD]

Javnertchik, Valerii (perc)
Ustvolskaya, G.:Composition 2, w. Igo Propischin (db), Leonid Kolosov (db), Vitalii Goryachev (db), Vladimir Vulih (db), Vyacheslav Kovalenko (db), Alexei Peresipkin (db), Dmitrii Sokolov (db), Vladimir Nefedov (db), Valerii Javnertchik (perc), Galina Sandovskaya (pno), O. Malov (cnd) *(rec St. Petersburg Radio House, Jan. 1994)* — Megadisc ▲ 7867

Jeandet, F. (va)
Lemeland, A.:American Epitaph (à la mémoire de Aaron Copland), w. A. Kapchiev (vn), P. Gessi (vc) *(rec 1991)* — Skarbo ▲ SKR 3913 [ADD]
Lemeland, A.:Con Va, w. M. Tardue (cnd), Grenoble Instrumental Ensemble *(rec 9/90)* — Quantum ▲ QM 6902 [DDD]

▲ = CD ♦ = Enhanced CD Δ = MD ■ = Cassette Tape □ = DCC

Jeanney, Hélène (pno)
Achron, J.:Vn & Pno Music, w. Yuval Yaron (vn)—Hebrew Melody, Op. 33; Hebrew Lullaby Accord ▲ ACD 205462 [DDD]
Bistritzky, Z.:Fantastic Dream, w. Yuval Yaron (vn) Accord ▲ ACD 205462 [DDD]
Bloch, E.:Abodah, "God's Worship", w. Yuval Yaron (vn) Accord ▲ ACD 205462 [DDD]
Bloch, E.:Baal Shem, "3 Pictures of Chassidic Life", w. Yuval Yaron (vn) Accord ▲ ACD 205462 [DDD]
Bruch, M.:Kol Nidrei, w. Yuval Yaron (vn) Accord ▲ ACD 205462 [DDD]
Elman, M.:Vn Arrs, w. Yuval Yaron (vn)—Eili Eili [Yiddish Melody] Accord ▲ ACD 205462 [DDD]
Ravel, M.:Kaddisch, w. Yuval Yaron (vn) Accord ▲ ACD 205462 [DDD]

Jeanrenaud, Joan (vc)—see also ORCHESTRAS & ENSEMBLES Kronos Quartet
Riley, T.:In C, w. Bruce Ackley, Steve Adams, Don R. Baker, Chris Brown, George Brooks, Steve Coughlin, Blake Derby, Bill Douglass, Mihr'un'Nisa Douglass, Hank Dutt, David Harrington, Don Howe, Alden Jenks, Warner Jepson, Henry Kaiser, Jaron Lanier, Bill Maginnis, George Marsh, Shabda Owens, Jon Raskin, Gyan Riley, Terry Riley, Gino Robair, John Sackett, Ramón Sender, John Sherba, Toyji Tomita, Danny Tunick, William Winant, Evan Ziporyn *(rec Jan. 14, 1990)* New Albion ▲ NA 071

Jebeleanu, Simon (hn)
Enescu, G.:Dectet Ww, w. Virgil Francu (fl), Nicolae Maxin (fl), Valeriu Barbuceanu (cl), Leontin Boanta (cl), Adrian Petrescu (ob), Viorica Feher (bn), Goedri Orban (bn), Florin Ionoaia (Eng hn), Dan Cinca (hn), H. Andreescu (cnd) Olympia ▲ OLY 445 [DDD]

Jedličková, Bohumila (pno)
Hartmann, J.P.E.:Fant–Allegro, w. Elisabeth Zeuthen Schneider (vn) [arr for vn & pno] *(rec Frederiksdal Castle, Lolland, Feb 6–9 & Sept 3–5, 1995)* Marco Polo/Dacapo 2–▲ 8.224021/22 [DDD]
Hartmann, J.P.E.:Sons Vn (comp), w. Elisabeth Zeuthen Schneider (vn) *(rec Frederiksdal Castle, Lolland, Feb 6–9 & Sept 3–5, 1995)* Marco Polo/Dacapo 2–▲ 8.224021/22 [DDD]
Hartmann, J.P.E.:Suite Vn, w. Elisabeth Zeuthen Schneider (vn) [arr for vn & pno] *(rec Frederiksdal Castle, Lolland, Feb 6–9 & Sept 3–5, 1995)* Marco Polo/Dacapo 2–▲ 8.224021/22 [DDD]
Weyse, C.E.F.:Études Pno, Op. 51 *(rec Copenhagen, Nov. 22–23, 1993)* Marco Polo ("dacapo" series) ▲ DC 9307 [DDD]
Weyse, C.E.F.:Études Pno, Op. 60 *(rec Copenhagen, Nov. 22–23, 1993)* Marco Polo ("dacapo" series) ▲ DC 9307 [DDD]
Weyse, C.E.F.:Grand allegro di bravura *(rec Copenhagen, Nov. 22–23, 1993)* Marco Polo ("dacapo" series) ▲ DC 9307 [DDD]

Jeffrey, Leslie (fl)
Debussy, C.:Chansons de Bilitis (recitation), w. M. Meisenbach (fl), W. Dudley (hp), M. Golden (hp), K. Tamagawa (cel)—no speaker *(rec 6 & 8/91)* Centaur ▲ CRC 2114 [DDD]

Jeffrey, Robin (mand)
Vivaldi, A.:Con for 2 Mands, w. J. Tyler (mand), T. Pinnock (cnd), English CO Archiv ▲ 415674–2 [DDD]

Jeffrey, Robin (thb/baroque gtr)
The Musical Life of Samuel Pepys, w. Richard Wistreich (voc), chamber org & strs Saydisc ▲ CDSDL 385 [DDD]

Jeffrey, Robin (thb/lt)—see ORCHESTRAS & ENSEMBLES Extempore String Ensemble

Jegorov, Pavel (pno)
Schumann, R.:Kreisleriana Infinity Digital ▲ QK 66726 [DDD]
Schumann, R.:Papillons Infinity Digital ▲ QK 64386 [DDD]
Schumann, R.:Sym Etudes Infinity Digital ▲ QK 66726 [DDD]
Schumann, R.:Waldscenen Infinity Digital ▲ QK 64386 [DDD]

Jekofsky (perc)
Gideon, M.:Questions on Nature, w. J. DeGaetani (mez), West (ob), S. Lipman (pno) CRI ■ C 343

Jelinek, Hubert (hp)
Mozart, W.A.:Con Fl Hp, w. J. Baker (fl), A. Janigro (cnd), Zagreb Solisti *(rec 1962)* Vanguard Classics ("Everyman" series) ▲ OVC 5011 [ADD]
Mozart, W.A.:Con Fl Hp, w. Julius Baker (fl), A. Janigro (cnd), Zagreb Solisti *(rec Baumgarten Hall, Vienna, May 5–7, 1962)* Vanguard Classics ▲ SVC 42 [AAD]

Jelinek, Jerome (vc)
Bolcom, W.:Qt Pno, w. Joseph Gurt (pno), Charles Avshalian (vn), David Ireland (va) *(rec Univ of Michigan, May 1979)* CRI ▲ CD 711 [ADD]
Finney, R.L.:Chromatic Fant CRI ▲ CD 711 [ADD]
Finney, R.L.:Son 2 Vc, w. Joseph Gurt (pno) CRI ▲ CD 711 [ADD]
Finney, R.L.:Trio 2 Pno, w. Joseph Gurt (pno), Charles Avshalian (vn) *(rec Univ of Michigan, Oct 1980)* CRI ▲ CD 711 [ADD]

Jelinek, Miloslav (db)
Dittersdorf, K.D. von:Sinfonia Concertante, w. Ladislav Kyselak (va), L. Svárovský (cnd), Czech Chamber Soloists *(rec 1992)* Panton ▲ PAN 811146

Jelínková, Renata (hpd)—see also ORCHESTRAS & ENSEMBLES Quartetto con Flauto
Jirásek, J.:Katharsis, w. Václav Slivanský (fl), Ada Silvanská (vn), Lubomír Herza (vc) *(rec St. Virgin Mary Church, Strahov)* Arta ▲ 0054 [DDD]

Jeltsch, Jean (bas hn)
Mozart, W.A.:Adagio Bas Hns, K.484d, w. Catherine Delaunay (cl), Trio di Bassetto *(rec Chapelle Notre–Dame de l'Hor, Moselle, June 29 – July 1, 1995)* K617 ▲ 7060 [DDD]
Mozart, W.A.:Adagio Cl, K.Anh.93, w. Catherine Delaunay (cl), Trio di Bassetto *(rec Chapelle Notre–Dame de l'Hor, Moselle, June 29 – July 1, 1995)* K617 ▲ 7060 [DDD]
Mozart, W.A.:Adagio Cl, K.Anh.94, w. Catherine Delaunay (cl), Trio di Bassetto *(rec Chapelle Notre–Dame de l'Hor, Moselle, June 29 – July 1, 1995)* K617 ▲ 7060 [DDD]
Mozart, W.A.:Adagio Cls, K.411, w. Catherine Delaunay (cl), Trio di Bassetto *(rec Chapelle Notre–Dame de l'Hor, Moselle, June 29 – July 1, 1995)* K617 ▲ 7060 [DDD]
Mozart, W.A.:Nozze di Figaro (winds), w. Catherine Delaunay (cl), Trio di Bassetto *(rec Chapelle Notre–Dame de l'Hor, Moselle, June 29 – July 1, 1995)* K617 ▲ 7060 [DDD]
Stadler, A.:Trios Bas Hns, w. Catherine Delaunay (cl), Trio di Bassetto *(rec Chapelle Notre–Dame de l'Hor, Moselle, June 29 – July 1, 1995)* K617 ▲ 7060 [DDD]

Jend, R. (ob)—see ORCHESTRAS & ENSEMBLES Bonn Telemann Ensemble

Jeney, Zoltán (fl)
Schubert, Franz:Qt Fl, w. P. Lukács (va), Szendrey–Karper (gtr), Banda (vc) White Label ▲ HRC 146 [ADD]

Jenkin, Peter (b cl)—see ORCHESTRAS & ENSEMBLES austraLYSIS members

Jenkin, Peter (cl)—see ORCHESTRAS & ENSEMBLES austraLYSIS members

Jenkins, L. (va)
Jenkins, L.:Dream of Dreams of Home, w. T. Buckner (bar), S. Starin (fl) Lovely Music ▲ LCD 3022 [DDD]

Jenkins, Leroy (vn)
Jenkins, L.:Monkey on the Dragon, w. Henry Threadgill (fl), Don Byron (cl), Marth Ehrlich (b cl), Janet Frice (bn), Vincent Chancey (hn), Frank Gordon (tpt), Jeff Hoyer (trbn), David Soldier (vn), Jane Henry (vn) Ron Lawrence (va), Mary Wooton (vc), Lindsey Horner (db), Thurman Barker (traps), Myra Melford (pno), T. Léon (cnd) *(rec live, Merkin Concert Hall, New York City, Apr. 9, 1992)* CRI ("eXchange" series) ▲ CD 663 [DDD]
Jenkins, L.:Panorama 1, w. Henry Threadgill (fl), Don Byron (cl), marty Ehrlich (b cl), Vincent Chancey (hn) *(rec live, Merkin Concert Hall, New York City, Apr. 9, 1992)* CRI ("eXchange" series) ▲ CD 663 [DDD]

Jenkins, Philip (pno)
British Music for Clarinet & Piano, w. Einar Jóhannesson (cl) Chandos ▲ CHAN 9079 [DDD]

Jenks, Alden
Riley, T.:In C, w. Bruce Ackley, Steve Adams, Don R. Baker, Chris Brown, George Brooks, Steve Coughlin, Blake Derby, Bill Douglass, Mihr'un'Nisa Douglass, Hank Dutt, David Harrington, Don Howe, Joan Jeanrenaud, Warner Jepson, Henry Kaiser, Jaron Lanier, Bill Maginnis, George Marsh, Shabda Owens, Jon Raskin, Gyan Riley, Terry Riley, Gino Robair, John Sackett, Ramón Sender, John Sherba, Toyji Tomita, Danny Tunick, William Winant, Evan Ziporyn *(rec Jan. 14, 1990)* New Albion ▲ NA 071

Jenks, P. L. (hp)
Hindemith, P.:Concert Music Pno, Brass & Hps, w. T. Lichtmann (pno), M. Walter (hp), Summit Brass Summit 2–▲ DCD 115 [DDD] 2–■ DCD 115

Jenner, J. (vn)
Shawn, A.:Winter Sketchbook, w. A. Shawn (pno) Opus One ▲ CD 157

Jennerjohn, Patricia (cel)
Harrison, L.:Con in slendro, w. Daniel Kobialka (vn), Machiko Kobialka (pno), James Barbagallo (pno), Don Marconi (perc), J. Neff (perc), R. Hughes (cnd) *(rec 1972)* CRI ▲ CD 613 [ADD]

Jenni, Donald Martin (hpd)
Veeneman, C.:The Wiry Concord, w. Susan Werner (banjo), Forrest Covington (hammered dlc/cimbalom), Georganne Assat (hp), Mark Johnson (hpd), Barbara Phillips Farley (pno), James Austin (pno), Marta Soderberg (va), James Knutson (perc), Patrick Doyle (perc), Steven Butters (perc), James Popejoy (perc), M. Geary (cnd) Capstone ▲ SCI 6

Jennings, Andrew (vn)—see ORCHESTRAS & ENSEMBLES Concord String Quartet

Jennings, Christina (fl)
Kraft, L.:Cloud Studies, w. Lisa Maron (pic), Margaret Swinchoski (pic), Tanya Dusevic (fl), Adrienne Flynn (fl), Zara Lawler (fl), Joseph Piscitelli (fl), Michelle Ryang (fl), Dominique Soucy (fl), Diane Taublieb (fl), Laurel Ann Maurer (alt fl), Richard Wyton (alt fl), J. Solum (cnd) *(rec Skinner Recital Hall, Vassar College, Poughkeepsie, NY, Mar 24–26, 1994)* CRI ▲ CD 712 [DDD]

Jennings, Patricia (pno)
Saint–Saëns, C.:Carnival of the Animals, w. V. Jennings (pno), A. Previn (cnd), Pittsburgh SO Philips ▲ 400016–2 [DDD]

Jennings, V. (pno)
Saint–Saëns, C.:Carnival of the Animals, w. P. Jennings (pno), A. Previn (cnd), Pittsburgh SO Philips ▲ 400016–2 [DDD]

Jensen, Dag (bn)
Françaix, J.:Divert Bn, w. W.A. Albert (cnd), Cologne RSO Capriccio ▲ CD 10579 [DDD]
Hummel, J.N.:Con Bn, w. W.A. Albert (cnd), Cologne RSO Capriccio ▲ CD 10579 [DDD]
Jolivet, A.:Con Bn, w. W.A. Albert (cnd), Cologne RSO Capriccio ▲ CD 10579 [DDD]
Markevitch, I.:Serenade, w. K. Lessing (vn), W. Meyer (cl) *(rec Oct. 21–22, 1993)* Largo ▲ 5127 [DDD]
Mozart, W.A.:Con Bn, w. W.A. Albert (cnd), Cologne RSO Capriccio ▲ CD 10579 [DDD]

Jensen, Jacob Bjørn (pno)
Stolarczyk, W.:Earth Air Fire Water, w. Amalie Malling (pno), John Damgaard (pno), Anne Øland (pno), Teddy Teirup (pno), Friedrich Gürtler (pno), Rosalind Bevan (pno), Poul Rosenbaum (pno), Rodolfo Llambias (pno), Bella Horn–Ribera (pno), Anders Riber (pno), Elisabeth Sigurdsson (pno), Thomas Tronheim (pno), Elsebeth Broderson (pno), Erik Kaltoft (pno), Jørgen Hald Nielsen (pno), Aino Gilemann (pno), Birgit Kjær (pno), Jørgen Thomsen (pno), Gunhild Donslund (pno), Henrik Bo Hansen (pno), Lone Karlsson (pno), Erik Fessel (pno), Lasse Nilsson (pno), Janos Ferenczi (pno), Erik Bach (pno), Axel Momme (pno), Arne de Cros Dich (pno), Sven Micha Slot (pno), Hanne Bramsen Buhl (pno), Lili Olesen (pno), Susannah Carlsson (pno), Ulla Erml (pno), Vagn Sørensen (pno), Leif Greibe (pno), Bodil Krogh (pno), Kirsten Ottosen (pno), Inger Bergenholz (pno), Karsten Gylendorf (pno), Bjønr Elkjær (pno), Jørgen Kaad (pno), Anne Marie Hjelm (pno), Carl Ulrik Munk Andersen (pno), Poul Lumbye (pno), Oluf Hildebrandt Nielsen (pno), Joachim Olsson (pno), Peter Pade Ramsøe Jacobsen (pno), Astrid Pollmann (pno), Jette Borsch (pno), Kirsten Karlshøj (pno), Maria Teresa Assing (pno), Allan Dahl Hansen (pno), Johan Hugossen (pno), Tine Fenger Pederson (pno), Arne Jørgen Fæø (pno), Anja Høgsted (pno), Anne Sophie Parbo (pno), Inga Lindmark (pno), Teresa Drabik Stathakis (pno), Anne Ruth Ferenczi (pno), Irene Hasager (pno), Yuka Ichikawa (pno), Birgitte Baur (pno), Malene Thastum (pno), Jens E. Rasmussen (pno), Birgitte Zielke (pno), Claus Zielke (pno), Stefan Kasch (pno), Bin Qiao (pno), Inger Johanne Teirup (pno), Lindy Rosborg (pno), Liisa Heininen (pno), David Højer (pno), Ellen Refstrup (pno), Thomas K. Søorensen (pno), Erik Kure (pno), Michael Rauff (pno), Jan beck Eriksson (pno), Tanja Zapolski (pno), Vibeke Skagbo (pno), Pål Eide Lindtner (pno), Ha–Young Sul (pno), Benedicte Palko (pno), Inke Kesseler (pno), Anne Marie Meineche (pno), Sverre Larsen (pno), Kasper Peter Bach (pno), Elisabetta Eliseo (pno), Olga Magieres (pno), Carl Erik Kühl (pno), Thorkild Borup Nielsen (pno), Valeria Zanini (pno), Lars Stenhoft (perc), Dennis Boel (perc), Winnie Dahlgren (perc), Susanne Vind (perc), Claus Byrith (elec), Anne Marie Storm (elec), J. Ribera (cnd) *(rec live, Koldinghaus Castle, Denmark, May 2, 1996)* Danica ▲ DCD 1996

Jensen, John (pno)—see also ORCHESTRAS & ENSEMBLES Mirecourt Trio
Barber, S.:Son Vc, w. T. King (vc) Music & Arts ▲ CD 603 [DDD]
Bloch, E.:Son Pno Music & Arts ▲ CD 757 [DDD]
Cooper, J.C.:Meditations (3), w. T. King (vc) Music & Arts ▲ CD 603 [DDD]
Copland, A.:Blues Music & Arts ▲ CD 738 [DDD]
Creston, P.:Cantilena, w. T. King (vc) Music & Arts ▲ CD 685 [DDD]
Drew, J.:Son Appassionata, w. T. King Music & Arts ▲ CD 685 [DDD]
Foss, L.:Capriccio, w. T. King (vc) Music & Arts ▲ CD 685 [DDD]
Ives, C.:Son 1 Pno Music & Arts ▲ CD 630 [DDD]
Ives, C.:Son 2 Pno Music & Arts ▲ CD 630 [DDD]
Lipkis, L.:Scaramouche Vars Pno Music & Arts ▲ CD 757 [DDD]
Macy, C.:Maria Music *(rec Macalester College, Mar 11–12, 1994)* Innova ▲ 503
Macy, C.:Ostinato Studies, w. Christine Dahl (pno) *(rec Macalester College, Mar 11–12, 1994)* Innova ▲ 503
Macy, C.:Reflections *(rec Macalester College, Mar 11–12, 1994)* Innova ▲ 503
Macy, C.:Solstice & Equinox, w. Julia Bogorad (fl), Adam Keunzel (fl) *(rec Macalester College, Mar 11–12, 1994)* Innova ▲ 503
Owen, J.:Encounters Pno *(rec Coe College, Cedar Rapids, IA, May 5, 1989)* Centaur ▲ CRC 2233 [DDD]
Owen, J.:Songs, w. Leslie Morgan (sop) *(rec July 7, 1989)* Centaur ▲ CRC 2233 [DDD]
Reale, P.V.:Salon Music Music & Arts ▲ CD 757 [DDD]
Reale, P.V.:Son Brahmsiana Music & Arts ▲ CD 757 [DDD]
Reale, P.V.:Son Vc, w. T. King (vc) Music & Arts ▲ CD 603 [DDD]
Reale, P.V.:Son 1 Pno Music & Arts ▲ CD 738 [DDD]
Reale, P.V.:Son 2 Pno Music & Arts ▲ CD 738 [DDD]
Reale, P.V.:Son 3 Pno Music & Arts ▲ CD 757 [DDD]
Riegger, W.:Whimsy, w. T. King (vc) Music & Arts ▲ CD 685 [DDD]
Ruggles, C.:Evocations Music & Arts ▲ CD 757 [DDD]

Jensen, Lars Boye (pno)
Strauss (II), Joh.:Music of—Vienna Blood; Wine, Women & Song; Fledermaus Paraphrase; Roses from the South; The Blue Danube; Kaiser Waltz; plus others [all trans for pno by Lars Boye Jensen] Classico ▲ 130

Jensen, Louis (vc)
Nielsen, C.:Serenata in vano, w. A. Oxenvad (cl), K. Larsson (bn), H. Sorensen (hn), L. Hegner (db) *(rec Feb. 2, 1937)* Clarinet Classics ▲ CC 0002

Jensen, Per (perc)
Cascade, w. Royal Danish Brass, Søren Monrad (perc) *(rec 1996)* Rondo ▲ RCD 8352
Roussel, A.:Chamber Music, w. Majken Bjerno (sop), Toke Lund Christiansen (fl), Bjørn Carl Nielsen (ob), Niels Thomsen (cl), Per Jacobsen (hn), Asger Svendsen (bn), Ketil Christensen (tpt), Anne Søe Hansen (vn), Zwi Carmelli (va), Piotr Zelazny (va), Niels Ullner (vc), Michael Dabelsteen (db), Tine Rehling (hp), Morten Mogensen (pno), Per Salo (pno)—Divertissement, Op. 6; Trio, Op. 40; Joueurs de Flute, Op. 27; Serenade, Op. 30; Le marchand de sable qui passe, Op. 13; Andante et scherzo, Op. 13; 2 poèmes de ronsard, Op. 26; Aria; Elpenor, Op. 59; Pipe Kontrapunkt 2–▲ KPT 32218 [DDD]

Jensen, Thomas (fl)
Pleyel, I.:Con in C for Fl, w. J.–P. Wallez (cnd), South Jutland SO *(rec Oct. 1992)* Talent ▲ DOM 2910 36 [DDD]
Pleyel, I.:Con in G for Fl, w. J.–P. Wallez (cnd), South Jutland SO *(rec Oct. 1992)* Talent ▲ DOM 2910 36 [DDD]

Jensen, Thomas (tpt)—see ORCHESTRAS & ENSEMBLES Royal Danish Brass

Jenson, D. (vn)
Saint-Saëns, C.:Introduction & Rondo capriccioso, w. E. Ormandy (cnd), Philadelphia Orch — RCA Victrola ▲ 7730-2-RV [DDD] ■ 7730-4-RV (CrO2)
Sibelius, J.:Con Vn, w. E. Ormandy (cnd), Philadelphia Orch — RCA Victrola ▲ 7730-2-RV [DDD] ■ 7730-4-RV (CrO2)

Jeppesen, N. F. (hn)
Blak, K.:Svabo, w. O. Røkkum (va), A. E. Klett (cl), J. Koch (pno) — Tutl ▲ FKT 6

Jepperson, Christopher (cl)—see also ORCHESTRAS & ENSEMBLES Quintet of the Americas
First, D.:The Good Book's (Accurate) Jail of Escape Dust Coordinates 2, w. Matt Sullivan (ob), Annemarie Wiesner (vn), Gary Trosclair (tpt), Elaine Kaplinsky (kbd syn), Chad Henderson (teahouse gtr/b gtr), Kevin Sparke (perc), David First (e-bow gtr/teahouse gtr/Distortion gtr/kbd syn/programming) *(rec Baby Monster Studios, NYC, May 1992)* — O. O. Discs ▲ OO 23 [DDD]

Jeppesen, Laura (vl)—see ORCHESTRAS & ENSEMBLES Boston Museum Trio

Jeppesen, N. F. (hn)—see ORCHESTRAS & ENSEMBLES Boreas Wind Quintet

Jeppesen, Nils Sylvest (vc)
Vesth, T.:Music of, w. Jan Sommer (gtr), Per Friman (vn), Gert-Inge Andersson (va), Berit Spaelling (hp), Bent Larsen (fl), Bjorn Nielsen (ob), Svend Rasmussen (cl), Henrik Simonsen (db)—Cuddling Rain; Waltz the Blue Sea; Kaspers Lullaby; Autumn Sunshine; Red Fox Hunting Tea Party; Off White Eternity; Tartan Fl — Danica ▲ DCD 8142

Jepson, Warner
Riley, T.:In C, w. Bruce Ackley, Steve Adams, Don R. Baker, Chris Brown, George Brooks, Steve Coughlin, Blake Derby, Bill Douglass, Mihr'un'Nisa Douglass, Hank Dutt, David Harrington, Don Howe, Joan Jeanrenaud, Alden Jenks, Henry Kaiser, Jaron Lanier, Bill Maginnis, George Marsh, Shabda Owens, Jon Raskin, Gyan Riley, Terry Riley, Gino Robair, John Sackett, Ramón Sender, John Sherba, Toyji Tomita, Danny Tunick, William Winant, Evan Ziporyn *(rec Jan. 14, 1990)* — New Albion ▲ NA 071

Jerie, Marek (vc)—see also ORCHESTRAS & ENSEMBLES Guarneri Trio Prague
Dvořák, A.:Rondo, w. T. Brãm (cnd), Pardubice Philharmonic CO — Panton ▲ PAN 811005
Dvořák, A.:Silent Woods, w. T. Brãm (cnd), Pardubice Philharmonic CO — Panton ▲ PAN 811005
Fauré, G.:Elégie, w. T. Brãm (cnd), Pardubice Philharmonic CO — Panton ▲ PAN 811005
Jirásek, J.:Dilema *(rec Assumtion of the Virgin Mary Church, Hradec Králové)* — Arta ▲ 0054 [DDD]
Martinů, B.:Concertino Vc, Ww, Pno & Perc, w. T. Brãm (cnd), Pardubice Philharmonic CO — Panton ▲ PAN 811005
Tchaikovsky, P.:Vars on a Rococo Theme, w. T. Brãm (cnd), Pardubice Philharmonic CO — Panton ▲ PAN 811005

Jernigan, Richard (cl)—see also ORCHESTRAS & ENSEMBLES Louisiana State Univ New Music Ensemble
Constantinides, D.:Vocal Music, w. Cynthia Dewey (nar), Angela DeVerger (sop), Evelyn Petros (sop), Susan Faust Straley (sop), Eugenia Epperson (fl), Kelly Smith Toney (vn), Hye-Yun Chung (hp), Stephen Brown (pno), John Raush (perc), D. Constantinides (cnd), Louisiana State Univ New Music Ensemble—Reflections IV for Sop, Fl, Hp & Pno; Intimations [1 Act Opera]; 4 Songs on Poems by Sappho; Mutability for Sop & Str Qt.; 4 Greek Songs — Vestige ▲ 04

Jersild, Jørgen (pno)
Jersild, J.:Duo Concertante, w. Hans Pålsson (pno) *(rec 1990–91)* — Paula ▲ PACD 61 [DAD]

Jespersen, Holger Gilbert (fl)
Nielsen, C.:Qnt Ww, w. S.C. Felumb (ob), A. Oxenvad (cl), H. Sorensen (hn), K. Larsson (bn) *(rec Jan. 24 & 25, 1936)* — Clarinet Classics ▲ CC 0002

Jessen, Niels-Jørn (tpt)—see ORCHESTRAS & ENSEMBLES Royal Danish Brass

Jesson, Roy (hpd/org)
Purcell, H.:Chamber Music, w. Alberto Lysy (vn), Robert Masters (vn), Yehudi Menuhin (vn), Cecil Arnowitz (va), Walter Gerhard (va), Derek Simpson (vc), Ambrose Gauntlett (vl)—Trio Sons Nos. 2 in C, 6 in G & 8 in G; Fants Nos. 4 in g, 7 in c, 8 in d & 13 in F, "Upon One Note" — EMI Classics ("Baroque" series) ▲ CDK 65734
Purcell, H.:Fants, w. Alberto Lysy (vn), Robert Masters (vn), Yehudi Menuhin (vn), Cecil Aronowitz (va), Walter Gerhard (va), Derek Simpson (vc), Ambrose Gauntlett (vl)—Nos. 4 in g, 7 in c, 8 in d, 13 in F — EMI Classics ▲ CDK 65734
Purcell, H.:Sons (22) Vns, w. Alberto Lysy (vn), Robert Masters (vn), Yehudi Menuhin (vn), Cecil Aronowitz (va), Walter Gerhard (va), Derek Simpson (vc), Ambrose Gauntlett (vl)—Nos. 2, 6, & 8 — EMI Classics ▲ CDK 65734

Jeurissen, Herman (hn)
Mozart, L.:Con for 2 Hns, w. Michael Holtzel (hn), H. Friesen (cnd), Concerto Rotterdam — MD + G ▲ MDG 3210085
Roussel, A.:Chamber Music, w. Paul Verhey (fl), Hans Roerade (ob), Jean-Jacques Kantorow (vn), Herre-Jan Stengenga (vc), Jet Röling (pno) — Olympia ▲ OLY 458 [DDD]

Jew, Benjamin (E hn)
Handel, D.:Trio Ob, w. Sara Lambert Bloom (ob), Frank Weinstock (pno) — Vienna Modern Masters ▲ VMM 2019 [DDD]

Jezierski, Stefan (hn)—see ORCHESTRAS & ENSEMBLES Berlin Philharmonic Wind Ensemble

Jezková, Jaromira (gtr)
Giuliani, M.:Vars on "I bin a Kohlbauern Bub" — Panton ▲ PAN 811015
Knìze, F.M.:Fant on an Original Theme — Panton ▲ PAN 811015
Matiegka, W.T.:Music of—Vars on an aria from "La molinara" — Panton ▲ PAN 811015
Paganini, N.:Gtr Music—Gran Son — Panton ▲ PAN 811015
Sor, F.:Vars on a Theme of Mozart — Panton ▲ PAN 811015

Jiang, Jing (vc)
Fetherolf, D.:Con Vc, w. R. Silva (cnd), Moravian PO — Vienna Modern Masters ▲ VMM 3031 [DDD]

Jiang, Yiwen (vn)—see ORCHESTRAS & ENSEMBLES Shanghai String Quartet

Jilek, Zdenek (pno)
Beethoven, L. van:Qnt Pno, Ob, Cl, Hn & Bn, w. Czech PO Wind Ensemble — Supraphon Collection ▲ 11 0638-2 [ADD]

Jimenez, Emma (pno)
Mendelssohn, F.:Con in d Vn, Pno & Strs, w. Felix Ayo (vn), M.B. Darman (cnd), Castilla y León SO *(rec Estudios Cinearte, Madrid, Apr 12, 1992)* — Dynamic ▲ CD 153 [DDD]

Jimenez, Rafael (gtr)
Villa-Lobos, H.:Con Gtr, w. F. Lozano (cnd), Carlos Chávez SO — Forlane ▲ FRL 16733 [DDD]
Villa-Lobos, H.:Con Gtr, w. F. Lozano (cnd), Carlos Chávez SO — Forlane ▲ FRL 16757
Villa-Lobos, H.:Con Gtr, w. F. Lozano (cnd), Carlos Chávez SO — Forlane ▲ FOR 16736 [DDD]

Jirikovsk, Petr (pno)
Smetana, B.:The Moldau, w. Daniel Wiesner (pno) [arr for Pno 4-Hands] — Studio Matou ▲ MAT 14 [DDD]

Jiroušek, Zdenek (vn)
Domazlicky, F.:Czech Folk Songs, w. J. Mráček (vn), O. Smola (va), P. Mišejka (vc), J. Karas (cnd), Disman Radio Children's Ensemble *(rec June 1992)* — Channel Classics ▲ CCS 5193 [DDD]

Jirovec, Vaclav (vc)
Biber, H. von:Son Tpt, 2 Vns, Vc, w. Richard Steuart (tpt), Oldrich Vlcek (vn), Sylvie Hessova (vn), Ivo Anyz (va) *(rec Prague, Nov. 1994)* — Discover International ▲ DI 920244 [DDD]
Vejvanovsky, P.J.:Sons & Serenades, w. Jan Hasenöhrl (tpt), Jiri Pribyl (trbn), Frantisek Xaver (hpd), Milan Hruby (brass), Oldrich Vlcek (vn), O. Vlček (cnd), Prague Virtuosi—Intrada; Harmonia romana; Serenada; Offertur ad duos chorus; Son à 4 be mollis; Son paschalis; Son tribus quadrantibus; Son campanarum; Serenada *(rec Lobochovice castle, July 26–28, 1992)* — Discover International ▲ DI 920243 [DDD]

Joachim, Heinrich (instr)—see ORCHESTRAS & ENSEMBLES New Amsterdam Trio

Joachim, Joseph (vn)
Joseph Joachim:The Complete Recordings *(rec 1903)* — Opal ▲ CD 9851 (m) [AAD]

Jochem, Arno (vl)
Boismortier, J.B. de:Chamber Music, w. Manfred Harras (rcr), Marianne Lüthi (rcr), Richard Gwilt (baroque vn), Brian Franklin (vl), Sally Fortino (hps)—Con. in C, "Zampogna"; Son. in F, Op. 91/1; Son. in A, Op. 10/2; Trio Son. in D, Op. 37/3; Son. in e, Op. 34/3; Con. in A, Op. 38/4; Suite No. 1, Op. 59; Balet de village en trio, Op. 52/4 *(rec Reformed Church, Bubendorf, Switzerland, Feb. 9–11, 1989)* — Musicaphon ▲ 56812 [DDD]

Jochum, Veronica (pno)
Busoni, F.:Pno Music—Toccata; Chaconne; Improvisation on a Bach Chorale [w. R. Hodgkinson (piano)]; Seven Short Pieces for the Cultivation of Polyphonic Playing; Prelude & Etude in Arpeggios; Perpetuum Mobile — GM ▲ GM 2042 [DDD]
Schumann, C.:Con Pno, w. J. Silverstein (cnd), Bamberg SO — Tudor ▲ TUD 788 [DDD]
Schumann, C.:Trio Pno, w. J. Silverstein (vn), C. Carr (vc) — Tudor ▲ TUD 788 [DDD]

Jodelet, Florent (perc)
Stockhausen, K.:Kontakte, w. Gérard Frémy (pno) — Accord ▲ ACD 202742 [DDD]
Stockhausen, K.:Refrain, w. Gérard Frémy (pno), Jean-Efflam Bavouzet (cel) — Accord ▲ ACD 202742 [DDD]
Stockhausen, K.:Zyklus — Accord ▲ ACD 202742 [DDD]

Jodry, Annie (vn)
Hovhaness, A.:Music of, w. Hasmig Surmélian (pno), J.-J. Werner (cnd), Léon Barzin Orch—Lousadzak [Coming of Light] for Pno & Str Orch; Saris for Vn & Pno; Oror for Vn & Pno; Shatakh for Vn & Pno; Shatakh II; Khirgiz Suite for Vn & Pno; A Khirgiz Tala; Khirgiz III; Con No. 2 for Vn & Str Orch *(rec Paris, May 1995)* — Media 7 ▲ MA 951001 [DDD]

Joeres, Dirk (pno)
Brahms, J.:Ballades, Op. 10 *(rec Nov. 1991)* — IMP Classics ▲ PCD 1044 [DDD]
Brahms, J.:Pieces Pno, Op. 118—No. 2 — IMP Classics ▲ PCD 1041 [DDD]
Brahms, J.:Pieces Pno, Op. 119—No. 1 — IMP Classics ▲ PCD 1041 [DDD]
Brahms, J.:Son 3 Pno — IMP Classics ▲ PCD 1041 [DDD]
Dietrich, A.:Klavierstück — IMP Classics ▲ PCD 1041 [DDD]
Gade, N.W.:Akvareller *(rec Nov. 1991)* — IMP Classics ▲ PCD 1044 [DDD]
Gade, N.W.:Idyller *(rec Nov. 1991)* — IMP Classics ▲ PCD 1044 [DDD]
Grimm, J.O.:Elegie — IMP Classics ▲ PCD 1041 [DDD]
Haydn, J.:Con Org & Strs, H.XVIII/2, w. D. Joeres (cnd), West German Sinfonia *(rec 3-3/91)* — IMP Classics ▲ PCD 969 [DDD]
Heller, S.:Traumbilder *(rec Nov. 1991)* — IMP Classics ▲ PCD 1044 [DDD]
Kirchner, T.:Nachtbilder *(rec Nov. 1991)* — IMP Classics ▲ PCD 1044 [DDD]
Kirchner, T.:Waltzes Pno — IMP Classics ▲ PCD 1041 [DDD]
Mozart, W.A.:Con 12 Pno, w. D. Joeres (cnd), West German Sinfonia — IMP Classics ▲ PCD 969 [DDD]
Mozart, W.A.:Rondo Pno Orch, K.386, w. D. Joeres (cnd), West German Sinfonia — IMP Classics ▲ PCD 969 [DDD]
Schubert, Franz:Allegretto Pno, D.915 — IMP Classics ▲ PCD 1002 [DDD]
Schubert, Franz:Pieces Pno, D.946 — IMP Classics ▲ PCD 1002 [DDD]
Schumann, R.:Arabeske Pno — IMP Classics ▲ PCD 1041 [DDD]
Schumann, R.:Kinderszenen *(rec Nov. 1991)* — IMP Classics ▲ PCD 1044 [DDD]
Voříšek, J.V.:Impromptus Pno, Op. 7 — IMP Classics ▲ PCD 1002 [DDD]

Joffe, Dina (pno)
Chopin, F.:Prelude in A♭ *(rec 2/88)* — MK ▲ MK 418028 [DDD]
Chopin, F.:Preludes, Op. 28 *(rec 2/88)* — MK ▲ MK 418028 [DDD]
Chopin, F.:Prelude, Op. 45 *(rec 2/88)* — MK ▲ MK 418028 [DDD]

Johannesen, Grant (pno)
Chopin, F.:Polonaises—8 polonaises — Allegretto ▲ ACD 8043 [ADD] ■ ACS 8043
Mozart, F.X.W.:Con Pno, Op. 25, w. P. Freeman (cnd), Chicago Sinfonietta — Centaur ▲ CRC 2062 [DDD]

Jóhannesson, Einar (cl)—see also ORCHESTRAS & ENSEMBLES Reykjavik Wind Quintet
British Music for Clarinet & Piano, w. Philip Jenkins (pno) — Chandos ▲ CHAN 9079 [DDD]

Johannsen, Grant (pno)
Grant Johannsen Plays French Piano Music *(rec 1972, 1974 & 1976)* — Vox Box 3-▲ CD3X 3032 [DDD]

Johansen, Aud (org)
Hakim, N.:Org Music [Schantz Organ, Cathedral of the Sacred Heart, Newark, New Jersey]—Fantaisie sur "Adeste, Fideles"; Espressions for Organ Nos. 16–30; The Embrace of Fire; Hommage à Igor Stravinski *(rec 1991)* — Pro Organo ▲ CD 7022 [DDD]

Johansen, Benedikte (hp)
Jersild, J.:For Sensitive Players, w. Torill Nielsen (hp) — Paula ▲ PACD 75 [DAD]

Johansen, Carl (va)—see ORCHESTRAS & ENSEMBLES Bronx Arts Ensemble

Johansen, G. (pno)
Liszt, F.:Pno Music (comp)—works for solo piano, substantially complete though not including all transcriptions, available on 35 single LPs or 15 cassettes — Artist Direct ■ 1-15 (m)
Liszt, F.:Pno Music (misc)—works for solo piano, substantially complete though not including all transcriptions, available on 35 single LPs or 15 cassettes — Artist Direct ■ 1-15 (m)
Reger, M.:Vars & Fugue on a Theme of J. S. Bach — Artist Direct ■ 20

Johansen, Lars Holm (vc)
Kuhlau, F.:Qnts Fl, w. Eyvind Rafn (fl), Kim Sjøgren (vn), Georg Svendsen Andersen (va), Bjarne Boye Rasmussen (va) *(rec Torpen Kapel, Humlebaek, Nordsjaelland, Denmark, Aug 1985)* — Naxos ▲ 8.553303 [DDD]

Johansen, M. (fl)—see ORCHESTRAS & ENSEMBLES Scandinavian Wind Quintet

Johansen, Niels-Ole Bo (trbn)
Trombone & Organ Music, w. Ulrik Spang-Hanssen (org) — Classico ▲ 122

Johansen, Thora (hpd)
Sigurbjörnsson, T.:Fiori, w. Wim Hoogewerf (gtr) — Music from Iceland ▲ ITM 702 [ADD]

Johanson, Emma (cl)
Carnivall, w. Enrique Bátiz (cnd), Marek Janowski (cnd), et al. — ASV ("Quicksilva" series) ▲ ASQ 6124 [DDD]

Johansson, B. (hn)—see ORCHESTRAS & ENSEMBLES Frösunda Wind Quintet

Johansson, Jan (db)
Nielsen, C.:At the Bier, w. Kontra String Quartet — BIS 2-▲ CD 503/04 [DDD]
Nielsen, C.:Qts Strs, w. Kontra String Quartet — BIS 2-▲ CD 503/04 [DDD]

Johansson, Ola (org)
Johansson, O.:Speedway Toccata *(rec Oct 1979)* — Point ▲ PCD 5118
Lindberg, O.:Requiem, w. I. Sörenson (sop), E. Thallang (alt), C. Solén (ten), E. Saedén (bass), H. Kyhle (cnd), Stockholm Univ College of Music Orch, Englebrekt Church Oratory Choir *(rec Nov. 2, 1980)* — Sterling ▲ CDS 1013

Johansson, Ola (pno)
Johansson, O.:Copenhagen's Tombstone for the City of Århus *(rec Oct 1979)* — Point ▲ PCD 5118
Johansson, O.:Great Waltz *(rec Oct 1979)* — Point ▲ PCD 5118
Johansson, O.:Polka 1 *(rec Oct 1979)* — Point ▲ PCD 5118

Johansson, Roland (perc)
Bäck, S.-E.:Favola, w. Thore Janson (cl), Stig Arntorp (perc), Bengt Arsenius (perc), Björn Liljequist (perc) — Caprice ▲ CAP 21490

John, Keith (org)
Bach, J.S.:Org Music (misc)—Concerto in G, BWV 592; Chorale Prelude, BWV 682; Toccata, Adagio & Fugue, BWV 564; Trio Sonata No.3, BWV 527 *(rec Aug 15, 1988)* — Priory ▲ PRCD 264 [DDD]
Great European Organs, Vol. 6, w. Stephen Cleobury (org) — Priory ▲ PRCD 235 [DDD]
Great European Organs, Vol. 10, w. Stephen Cleobury (org) — Priory ▲ PRCD 262 [DDD]
Great European Organs, Vol. 26, w. Stephen Cleobury (org) — Priory ▲ PRCD 370
John, K.:Time & Motion — Priory ▲ PRI 532 [DDD]
Kikta, V.:Orpheus Suite — Priory ▲ PRI 532 [DDD]
Prokofiev, S.:Romeo & Juliet (suites) — Priory ▲ PRI 532 [DDD]
Reubke, J.:Son Org *(rec 8/15/88)* — Priory ▲ PRCD 264 [DDD]

John, Keith (org) (cont.)
Tchaikovsky, P.:Nutcracker Suite — Priory ▲ PRI 532 [DDD]
Johnson (perc)
Peck, R.:Automobile, w. Ragains (sop), Middleton (fl), Calvetti (db) — CRI ■ C 367
Johnson (tuba)
Joplin, S.:Music of, w. J.-P. Rampal (fl), J. S. Ritter (pno/hpds), S. Manne (dr) — CBS ▲ MK 37818
Johnson, Alan (pno)
Kosch, M.:Highland Dances — Innova ▲ MN 107
Johnson, Brian (mar/vib/xyl/orch bells)
Celli, J.:Eight Mallets for Brian — O.O. Discs ▲ OO 22
Johnson, David (hn)—see ORCHESTRAS & ENSEMBLES American Horn Quartet
Johnson, Emma (cl)
Arnold, M.:Con 1 Cl, w. I. Bolton (cnd), English CO — ASV ▲ ASV 922 [DDD]
Arnold, M.:Con 2 Cl, w. I. Bolton (cnd), English CO — ASV ▲ ASV 922 [DDD]
Arnold, M.:Divert Fl, w. I. Bolton (cnd), English CO — ASV ▲ ASV 922 [DDD]
Arnold, M.:Fants solo Instrs, w. I. Bolton (cnd), English CO—for solo Cl — ASV ▲ ASV 922 [DDD]
Arnold, M.:Shanties, w. I. Bolton (cnd), English CO — ASV ▲ ASV 922 [DDD]
Arnold, M.:Sonatina Cl, w. I. Bolton (cnd), English CO — ASV ▲ ASV 922 [DDD]
Bärmann, H.J.:Adagio Cl Orch, w. C. Groves (cnd), English CO — ASV ▲ ASV CD 559
Bärmann, H.J.:Qnt 3 Cl, w. C. Groves (cnd), English CO—Adagio — ASV ▲ ASV 559
Bottesini, G.:Duetto Cl & Db, w. T. Martin (db) — ASV ▲ ASV 563 [DDD]
Crusell, B.H.:Con 1 Cl, w. G. Herbig (cnd), Royal PO — ASV ▲ ASV 784
Crusell, B.H.:Con 2 Cl, w. C. Groves (cnd), English CO — ASV ▲ ASV 784
Crusell, B.H.:Con 2 Cl, w. C. Groves (cnd), English CO — ASV ▲ ASV CD 559
Crusell, B.H.:Con 2 Cl, w. C. Groves (cnd), English CO — ASV ▲ ASV 559
Crusell, B.H.:Con 3 Cl, w. G. Schwarz (cnd), English CO — ASV ▲ ASV 784
Crusell, B.H.:Intro, Theme & Vars on a Swedish Air, w. Y.P. Tortelier (cnd), English CO — ASV ▲ ASV 585 [DDD]
Debussy, C.:Première rapsodie, w. Y.P. Tortelier (cnd), English CO — ASV ▲ ASV 585 [DDD]
Encores 2, w. Julius Drake (pno) — ASV ▲ ASV 910 [DDD]
Finzi, G.:Bagatelles, Op. 23, w. M. Martineau (pno) — ASV ▲ ASV 787 [DDD]
Finzi, G.:Con Cl, w. C. Groves (cnd), Royal PO — ASV ▲ ASV 787 [DDD]
Jeux d'Enfants, w. Christopher Hyde-Smith (fl/pic), George MacDonald (cl), Gordon Back (pno), Academy of St. Martin in the Fields [cnd:Neville Marriner], Mexico City PO, Mexico State SO, Royal PO [cnd:Enrique Bátiz], Northern Sinfonia of England [cnd — ASV Quicksilva ▲ ASQ 6182
Mozart, W.A.:Con Cl, w. R. Leppard (cnd), English CO — ASV ▲ ASV 532
Pastoral:Emma Johnson Plays British Clarinet Music, w. M. Martineau (pno), J. Howarth (sop) — ASV ▲ ASV 891 [DDD]
Rossini, G.:Intro, Theme & Vars Cl, w. C. Groves (cnd), English CO — ASV ▲ ASV 559
Rossini, G.:Intro, Theme & Vars Cl, w. C. Groves (cnd), English CO, ' — ASV ▲ ASV CD 559
Stanford, C.V.:Con Cl, w. C. Groves (cnd), Royal PO — ASV ▲ ASV 787 [DDD]
Stanford, C.V.:Intermezzi, w. M. Martineau (pno) — ASV ▲ ASV 787 [DDD]
Tartini, G.:Concertino Cl, w. Y.P. Tortelier (cnd), English CO — ASV ▲ ASV 585 [DDD]
Weber, C.M. von:Concertino Cl, w. C. Groves (cnd), English CO — ASV ▲ ASV CD 559
Weber, C.M. von:Concertino Cl, w. C. Groves (cnd), English CO — ASV ▲ ASV 559
Weber, C.M. von:Con 1 Cl, w. Y. P. Tortelier (cnd), English CO — ASV ▲ ASV 585 [DDD]
Johnson, Erik (perc)
Moran, R.:Rocky Road, w. Joseph Goodrich (kbd), Kevin Hanson (gtr), Andrew Morrell (perc) *(rec Chapel of Girard College, Philadelphia & Henry Wood Hall, London, Mar 17, 1994 & Dec 13, 19)* — Argo ▲ 444540-2 [DDD]
Johnson, Gilbert (tpt)
Haydn, J.:Con Tpt, w. E. Ormandy (cnd), Philadelphia Orch — Sony Classical ("Essential Classics" series) ▲ SBK 62649 ■ SBT 62649
Hindemith, P.:Son Tpt, w. G. Gould (pno) *(rec 1975)* — Sony Classical ("Glenn Gould Edition" series) 2-▲ SM2K 52671 [ADD]
Johnson, Graham (pno)
Beethoven, L. van:An die ferne Geliebte, w. L. Berkman (bar) [G] — Duo ▲ 89010
Beethoven, L. van:Songs, w. L. Berkman (bar)—Gellert-Lieder, Op. 48, Nos. 1-6; Six Goethe-Lieder (Opp. 52/4 & 7, 75/2 & 3, 83/1 & 2); Six Italian Love Songs (Op. 82/2-4; Op. 88; WoO 124; WoO 133) [G,I] — Duo ▲ 89010
Britten, H.:Canticles I-V, w. A. Rolfe-Johnson (ten)—Canticle I, "My beloved is mine" — Hyperion ▲ CDA 66209
Britten, H.:Folksong Arrs, w. A. Rolfe-Johnson (ten)—O Waly Waly; Little Sir William; The Salley Gardens; The trees they grow so high [E] — Hyperion ▲ CDA 66209
Britten, H.:The Holy Sonnets of John Donne, w. Ian Bostridge (ten) — Hyperion ▲ CDA 66823
Britten, H.:Purcell Realizations, w. Susan Gritton (sop), Felicity Lott (sop), Sarah Walker (mez), James Bowman (alto), John Mark Ainsley (ten), Anthony Rolfe Johnson (ten), Richard Jackson (bass), Simon Keenlyside (bass), Ian Bostridge (sgr) — Hyperion 2-▲ CDA 67061/62
Britten, H.:Songs, w. Ian Bostridge (ten)—The Red Cockatoo; other songs — Hyperion ▲ CDA 66823
Britten, H.:Sonnets of Michelangelo, w. A. Rolfe-Johnson (ten) — Hyperion ▲ CDA 66209
Britten, H.:Winter Words, w. A. Rolfe-Johnson (ten) — Hyperion ▲ CDA 66209
British Music on Hyperion, w. Parley of Instruments, Roy Goodman (cnd), John Mark Ainsley (ten), Salomon Quartet, BBC Scottish SO, Anthony Rolfe Johnson (ten), Royal PO, St. Paul's Cathedral Choir, Nash Ensemble, Martyn Hill (ten), Suasan Gritton (sop), Sarah Wal — Hyperion ▲ HYP 15
Cornelius, P.:Songs, w. Margaret Price (sop)—Trauer und Trost, Op. 3 — Forlane ▲ FRL 16728 [DDD]
Delius, F.:Songs, w. Marit Osnes Aambo (mez)—Slumber Song (5 Norw. Songs no. 1); Evening Mood (Evening Voices) (7 Norw. Songs no. 3); Young Venevil (Sweet Venevil) (7 NS no. 4); Hidden Love (Love Concealed) (7 NS no. 6); Softly the Forest; I Once had a Newly Cut Willow Pipe; Sing, Sing (The Nightingale) (5 NS no. 2); Longing (5 NS no. 4); Sunset (5 NS no. 5); Summer Eve (5 NS no. 3); At Rondane (The Homeward Journey) (7 NS no. 2); Fiddlers (The Minstrel) (7 NS no. 5); Cradle Song (7 NS no 1); A Birdsong (The Bird's Story) (7 NS no. 7) *(rec Eidsvoll Church, Nov 3-5, 1994)* — Simax ▲ PSC 1120 [DDD]
Dvořák, A.:Songs, w. Philip Langridge (ten)—4 Songs, Op. 73; 2 Songs, Op. 82 — Forlane ▲ FRL 16746 [DDD]
Dvořák, A.:Zigeunermelodien, Op. 55, w. Philip Langridge (ten) — Forlane ▲ FRL 16746 [DDD]
Grainger, P.:Songs, w. Marit Osnes Aambo (mez)—The Spring of Thyme; Six Dukes Went A Fishin'; Willow, Willow, Died for Love; Power of Love *(rec Eidsvoll Church, Nov 3-5, 1994)* — Simax ▲ PSC 1120 [DDD]
Grieg, E.:Songs, w. Marit Osnes Aambo (mez)—The Orphan; Morning Dew; Parting; Hunting Song; The Old Song; Where Have They Gone? [all Op. 4]; The Maid of the Mill; Closely Wrapped in Misty Billows; I Stood Before Her Portrait; What shall I say? [all Op. 2] *(rec Eidsvoll Church, Nov 3-5, 1994)* — Simax ▲ PSC 1120 [DDD]
Hahn, R.:Chansons grises, w. M. Hill (ten) [F] — Hyperion ▲ CDA 66045 [DDD]
Hahn, R.:Songs, w. M. Hill (ten)—15 early songs [F] — Hyperion ▲ CDA 66045 [DDD]
Hahn, R.:Songs, w. Felicity Lott (sop), Susan Bickley (mez), Ian Bostridge (ten), Stephen Varcoe (bar), Stephen Layton (cnd), London Choral Society—[CD 1] Si mes vers avaient des ailes; Paysage; Rêverie; Offrande; Mai; Infidelité; Seule; Les Cygnes; Nocturne; 3 jours de vendange; D'une prison; Séraphine; L'Heure exquise; Fêtes galantes; 12 Rondels; [CD 2] Quand la nuit n'est pas étoilée; Le Plus beau présent; Sur l'eau; Le Rossignol des lilas; A Chloris; Ma jeunesse; Puisque j'ai mis ma lèvre; Etudes Latines; La Nymphe de la Source; Au Rossignol; Je me souviens; Air de la lettre; C'est très vilain d'être infidèle; C'est sa banlieue; Nous avons fait un beau voyage; La Dernière Valse — Hyperion ("The Hyperion French Song Edition" series) 2-▲ CDA 67141/42
Janácek, L.:The Diary of One Who Disappeared, w. Philip Langridge (ten) — Forlane ▲ FRL 16746 [DDD]
Liszt, F.:Songs, w. Margaret Price (sop) — Forlane ▲ FOR 16728 [DDD]
Liszt, F.:Songs, w. Margaret Price (sop)—Freudvoll und Leidvoll; Über Allen Gipfeln [Wanderers Nachtlied II]; Mignons Lied; Der du von Dem Himmel Bist [Wanderers Nachtlied I] — Forlane ▲ FRL 16728 [DDD]

Johnson, Graham (pno) (cont.)
Mendelssohn, F.:Songs, w. M. Price (sop)—Frülingsglaube; Frage; Geständnis; Maienlied; Andreas Maienlied, 'Hexenlied"; Gruss; Neue Liebe; Auf Flügeln des Gesanges; Frühlingslied; Suleika:Ach, um deine feuchten Schwingen; Suleika:Was bedeutet die Bewegung?; Die Liebende schreibt; Erster Verlust; Volkslied; Minnelied; Schilflied; There Be None of Beauty's Daughter's; Sun of the Sleepless; Des Mädchens Klage; Der Mond; Das Waldschloss; Es weiss und rät es doch Keiner; Nachtlied; Wanderlied — Hyperion ▲ CDA 66666 [DDD]
Mussorgsky, M.:Nursery, w. Marjana Lipovsek (mez) — Sony Classical ▲ SK 66858
Mussorgsky, M.:Nursery, w. Ewa Podles (mez) — Forlane ▲ FRL 16683 [DDD]
Mussorgsky, M.:Songs & Dances, w. Marjana Lipovsek (mez) — Sony Classical ▲ SK 66858
Mussorgsky, M.:Songs & Dances, w. Ewa Podles (mez) — Forlane ▲ FRL 16683 [DDD]
Mussorgsky, M.:Songs (misc), w. Marjana Lipovsek (mez)—Hebrew Song; Song of the Flea [from Song of Mephistopheles]; Hopak — Sony Classical ▲ SK 66858
Mussorgsky, M.:Sunless, w. Marjana Lipovsek (mez) — Sony Classical ▲ SK 66858
On Wings of Song, w. Lott, Felicity (sop), Ann Murray (sgr) *(rec June 1991)* — EMI Classics ▲ CDC 54411-2 [DDD]
Poulenc, F.:Songs, w. F. Lott (sop), A. Murray (mez), A. Rolfe-Johnson (ten), R. Jackson (bass) [F] — Hyperion ▲ CDA 66147
Poulenc, F.:Songs, w. Felicity Lott (sop)—34 Songs — Forlane ▲ FOR 16730 [DDD]
La Procession:80 Years of French Song (1839-1919), w. Stephen Varcoe (bar) — Hyperion ▲ CDA 66248 [DDD]
Rachmaninoff, S.:Songs, w. Ewa Podles (mez)—Morning, Op. 14/2; Do Not Regret Me, Op. 14/8; I Am Waiting for You, Op. 14/1; In the Mysterious Night, Op. 4/3; Beautiful as the Day, Op. 14/9; Christ Has Risen, Op. 26/6; Springtime Waters, Op. 14/11 — Forlane ▲ FRL 16683 [DDD]
Schubert, Franz:Die Schöne Müllerin, w. Ian Bostridge (ten), Dietrich Fischer-Dieskau (reader)—5 additional poems read by Fischer-Dieskau — Hyperion ▲ CDJ 33025
Schubert, Franz:Songs (comp), w. Christoph Prégardien (ten)—Der Tod Oscars, D.375; Das Grab, D.377; Der Entfernten, D.350; Pflügerlied, D.39; Abschied von der Harfe, D.406; Der Jüngling an der Quelle, D.300; Abendlied, D.382; Stimme der Liebe, D.412; Romanze, D.144; Geist der Liebe, D.414; Klage, D.415; Julius an Theone, D.419; Der Leidende, D.432; Der Leidende, D.432b; Die frühe Liebe, D.430; Die Knabenzeit, D.400; Edone, D.445; Die Liebesgötter, D.446; An Chloen, D.363; Freude der Kinderjahre, D.455; Gesänge des Harfners aus Wilhelm Meister, D.478; Der Hirt, D.490; Am ersten Maimorgen, D.344; Bei dem Grabe meines Vaters, D.496; Mailied, D.503; Zufriedenheit, D.362; Skolie, D.507 — Hyperion ▲ CDJ 33023
Schubert, Franz:Songs (comp), w. P. Rozario (sop), J.M. Ainsley (ten), I. Bostridge (ten), M. George (bass), S. Layton (cnd), London Schubert Chorale—Winterlied; Ossians Lied nach dem Falle Nathos; Das Mädchen von Inistore; Als ich sie erröten; Schwangesang; Totenkranz für ein Kind; Die Fröhlichkeit; Der Zufriedene; Alles um Liebe; Geist der Liebe; Dei erste Liebe; Die Täuschung; Liebesrausch; Huldigung; Heidenröslein; Nachtgesang; Der Morgenstern; Der Knappenlied; Trinklied vor der Schlacht; Schwertlied; Begräbnislied; Grablied; Osterlied; Hoffnung; Punschlied; Klage um Ali Bey; Abendständchen; Tische'rlied; Wiegenlied; Die Macht der Liebe; Trinklied, D.183; Trinklied, D.267 — Hyperion ▲ CDJ 33020
Schubert, Franz:Songs (comp), w. L. Popp (sop)—24 songs from 1816, including Litanei, An mein Klavier, D.150, D.371, D.373, D.376, D.393, D.398, D.401, D.404, D.405, D.416, D.429, D.458, D.467, D.468 D.491, D.496, D.496a, D.497, D.500, D.502, D.504, D.508, D.509 [G] — Hyperion ▲ CDJ 33017
Schubert, Franz:Songs (comp), w. A. Murray (mez)—14 songs—D.222, 297, 473, 475, 476, 545, 546, 551, 573, 654, 695, 771, 786, 827 [G] — Hyperion ▲ CDJ 33003 [DDD]
Schubert, Franz:Songs (comp), w. E. Mathis (sop)—An die Musisk, D.547; Die Forelle, D.550; Schlaflied, D.527; Sehnsucht, D.516; Die Liebe, D.522; Impromptu, D.513a; Der Flug der Zeit, D.515; Trost, D.523; Die abgeblühte Linde, D514; Das Lied vom Reifen — Hyperion ▲ CDJ 33021
Schubert, Franz:Songs (comp), w. M. McLaughlin (sop), T. Hampson (bar)—soprano songs—D.312 & 542; baritone songs—D.166, 360, 396/383, 450, 540, 541, 548, 554, 677, 699, 700, 707, 737, 890 [G] — Hyperion ▲ CDJ 33014 [DDD]
Schubert, Franz:Songs (comp), w. M. McLaughlin (sop), T. Hampson (bar), New Company Singers—soprano/piano songs—D.118, 564, 623, 658, 830, 831, 837, 838, 839, 846, 866/1, 866/3, 923; baritone/piano songs—D.293 & 923; baritone & chorus—Szene aus Faust, D.126 [G] — Hyperion ▲ CDJ 33013 [DDD]
Schubert, Franz:Songs (comp), w. A. Thompson (ten)—early songs, between D.10 & D.134 [G] — Hyperion ▲ CDJ 33012 [DDD]
Schubert, Franz:Songs (comp), w. Christine Schäfer (sop), John Mark Ainsley (ten), Richard Jackson (bar), Stephen Layton (cnd), London Schubert Chorale—Der Einsame; Des Sängers Habe; Zwei Szenen aus dem Schauspiel Lacrimas (Lied der Delphine; Lied des Florio); Mondenschien (chorale); Gesänge Aus Wilhwlm Meister (Nur wer die Sehnsucht kennt; Hwiss mich nicht reden; So lasst mich scheinen); Totengräberweise; Das Echo; An Silvia; Horch, horch die Lerch'; Trinklied; Wiegenlied; Widerspruch; Der Wanderer an den Mond; Grab und Mond (chorale); Nachthelle; Abschied von der Erde — Hyperion ▲ CDJ 33026
Schubert, Franz:Songs (comp), w. Christine Schäfer (sop), Matthias Görne (bar)—22 songs including D.395, 410, 628-631, 633, 634, 646, 649, 652, 684, 690-694, 708, 711, 745, 854, 855 — Hyperion ▲ 33027
Schubert, Franz:Songs (comp), w. P. Schreier (ten)—Das Finden, D.219; Die Nacht, D.358; An den Schlaf, D.447; Abendlied, D.499; Um Mitternacht, D.862; Der Liebliche Stern, D.861; Im Walde, D.834; Im Frühling, D.882; An mein Herz, D.860 [G] — Hyperion ▲ CDJ 33018
Schubert, Franz:Songs (comp), w. S. Varcoe (bar)—13 songs—D.111, 351, 361, 525, 526, 536, 553, 562, 565, 639, 743, 766, 881 [G] — Hyperion ▲ CDJ 33002 [DDD]
Schubert, Franz:Songs (comp), w. S. Walker (mez)—18 songs—D.114, 208, 238, 259, 289, 290, 328, 418, 462, 463, 464, 465, 466, 495, 498, 614, 653, 920 [G] — Hyperion ▲ CDJ 33008 [DDD]
Schubert, Franz:Songs (comp), w. P. Langridge (ten)—14 songs—D.124, 163/165, 174, 179, 180, 206, 209, 309, 477, 539, 611, 672, 698, 749 [G] — Hyperion ▲ CDJ 33004 [DDD]
Schubert, Franz:Songs (comp), w. A. Rolfe Johnson (ten)—15 songs—D.235, 237, 521, 534, 579, 767, 806, 856, 903, 904, 905, 906, 927, 933, 939 [G] — Hyperion ▲ CDJ 33006 [DDD]
Schubert, Franz:Songs (comp), w. M. Hill (ten)—16 songs—D.149, 151, 160, 161, 177, 197, 198, 201, 207, 211, 213, 214, 271, 302, 303, 325 [G] — Hyperion ▲ CDJ 33010
Schubert, Franz:Songs (comp), w. B. Fassbaender (mez)—12 songs—D.59, 116, 433, 474, 584, 672, 744, 753, 754, 801, 871, 989 [G] — Hyperion ▲ CDJ 33011
Schubert, Franz:Songs (comp), w. E. Connell (sop)—13 songs—D.101, 291, 307, 323, 372, 381, 483, 533, 544, 772, 788, 852, 917, 989 [G] — Hyperion ▲ CDJ 33005 [DDD]
Schubert, Franz:Songs (comp), w. J. Baker (ctra)—19 songs—D.30, 73, 121, 159, 162, 195, 216, 224, 225, 226, 250, 260, 284, 296, 402, 587, 588, 636, 794 [G] — Hyperion ▲ CDJ 33001 [DDD]
Schubert, Franz:Songs (comp), w. A. Auger (sop), Thea King (cl)—D.273, 301, 510, 528, 588, 595, 631, 857, 965 (Der Hirt auf dem Felsen), etc. [G] — Hyperion ▲ CDJ 33009
Schubert, Franz:Songs (comp), w. E. Ameling (so)—23 songs [G] — Hyperion ▲ CDJ 33007 [DDD]
Schubert, Franz:Songs (misc), w. Ralph Kohn (bar)—Schwanengesang & Ausgewählte Lieder — Priory ▲ PRI 571 [DDD]
Schubert, Franz:Songs (misc), w. Felicity Lott (sop)—Die Forelle, D.550; An Silvia, D.891; Heidenröslein, D.257; Du bist die Ruh, D.776; Der Musensohn, D.764; An die Musik, D.547; Auf dem Wasser zu singen, D.774; Sei mir gegrüsst, D.741; Litanei, D.343; Die junge Nonne, D.828; Ave Maria, D.839; Im Frühling, D.882; Gretchen am Spinnrade, D.118; Nacht und Träume, D.827; Ganymed, D.544; Lied der Mignon; Seligkeit, D.433 — IMP ▲ PCD 2016
Schubert, Franz:Songs (misc), w. R. White (ten) — Virgin Classics ▲ CDZ 59650
Schubert, Franz:Songs (misc), w. Lorna Anderson (sop), Catherine Wyn-Rogers (alt), Jamie McDougall (ten) Simon Keenlyside (bar), London Schubert Chorale—Das Leben ist ein Traum; Das Grab; Trinklied; Punschlied; Vaterlandslied; Selma und Selmar; Morgenlied; An die Sonne; Hermann und Thusnelda; Cora und die Sonne; Lorna; Genugsamkeit; Der Abend; Das Mädchen aus dem Fremde; Am Rosa (I); Am Rosa (II); An Sie; Gebet während der Schlacht; Das Abendroth; Die drei Sänger; Die Sterne; Cronnan; Furcht der Geliebten; Die Erscheinung; Stolie; Das Bild; Lob des Tokayers — Hyperion ▲ CDJ 33022

INSTRUMENT.

Johnson, Graham (pno) (cont.)
Schubert, Franz:Winterreise, w. Benno Schollum (bar) IMG/Pickwick ▲ PIC IMG 1616
Schumann, R.:Frauenliebe und -leben, w. Marjana Lipovšek (mez) *(rec Konzerthaus, Mozartsaal, Vienna, Oct. 4-6, 1993)* Sony Classical ▲ SK 57972 [DDD]
Schumann, R.:Liederkreis, Op. 24, w. M. Price (sop) [G] Hyperion ▲ CDA 66596
Schumann, R.:Liederkreis, Op. 39, w. Marjana Lipovšek (mez) *(rec Konzerthaus, Mozartsaal, Vienna, Oct. 4-6, 1993)* Sony Classical ▲ SK 57972 [DDD]
Schumann, R.:Songs, w. M. Price (sop) [G] Hyperion ▲ CDA 66596
Schumann, R.:Songs, w. Christine Schäfer (sop)—Röselein, Röselein!; Mädchen-Schwermut; Die Blume der Ergebung; Melancholie; Zigeunerliedchen I; Zigeunerliedchen II; Die Meerfee; Herzeleid; Die Fensterscheibe; Der Gärtner; Die Spinnerin; Im Wald; Abendlied; Ihre Stimme; Nachtlied; Singet nicht in Trauertönen; Nur wer die Sehnsucht kennt; Heiss' mich nicht reden; So lasst mich scheinen; Mignon; Lied eines Schmiedes; Meine Rose; Kommen und Scheiden; Die Sennin; Einsamkeit; Der schwere Abend; Requiem; Das verlassene Mägdlein; Er ist's! Warnung; Sängers Trost; Aufträge Hyperion ▲ CDJ 33101
Schumann, R.:Songs, w. Marjana Lipovšek (mez)—Aus den hebräischen Gesängen; Der Nussbaum; Die Lotosblume [all from Myrthen, Op. 25/15, 3 & 7]; Er ist's; Mignon [both from Liederalbum für die Jugend, Op. 79/23 & 28]; Der Soldat [from Fünf Lieder, Op. 40/3]; Kennst du das Land?, Op. 98a/1 *(rec Konzerthaus, Mozartsaal, Vienna, Oct. 4-6, 1993)* Sony Classical ▲ SK 57972 [DDD]
The Songmakers' Almanac, w. Souvenirs de Venise, et al. Hyperion ▲ CDA 66112 [DDD]
Songs on Poems by Victor Hugo, w. Felicity Lott (sop) Harmonia Mundi ▲ HMA 1901138
Songs to Shakespeare, w. Anthony Rolfe Johnson (ten) Hyperion ▲ CDA 66480 [DDD]
Strauss, R.:songs, w. Marie McLaughlin (sop)—Die Drossel; Zueignung; Wie sollten wir geheim sie halten; In goldener Fülle; Wiegenlied; Weihnachtsgefühl; Abend-und Morgenrot; Nebel; Schlagende Herzen; Ruhe, meine Seele; Du meines Herzens Krönelein; Ach, was Kummer, Qual und Schmerzen; Das Bächlein; Las ruh'n die toten; In goldner Fülle; Nebel; Wiegenliedchen; Leises Lied; Weihnachtslied; Morgen! Wer lieben will, muss leiden; Ein Röslein zog ich mir im Garten; Die Nacht; Allerseelen; Gefunden; Ach Lieb, ich muss nun schneiden; All mein Gedanken...; Toten; Der müde Wanderer Hyperion ▲ CDA 66659
Tchaikovsky, P.:Songs, w. Ewa Podles (mez)—Was I a Blade of Grass in a Field?; Zamphira's Song; If I Had Known; If the Day Shines Forlane ▲ FRL 16683 [DDD]
Wagner, R.:Songs, w. Margaret Price (sop) Forlane ▲ FOR 16728 [DDD]
Wagner, R.:Wesendonck Songs, w. Margaret Price (sop) Forlane ▲ FRL 16728 [DDD]
Wolf, H.:Italienische Liederbücher (sels), w. Felicity Lott (sop), Peter Schreier (ten) Hyperion ▲ CDA 66760
Wolf, H.:Songs (misc), w. Margaret Price (sop)—Der Gärtner; Bei Einer Trauung; In der Frühe; Heimweh; Begegnung; Lebe Wohl; Gesang Weylas; Er ist's Forlane ▲ FRL 16728 [DDD]

Johnson, Jacqueline (vc)
Bach, J.S.:Sons Fl, BWV 1030–35, w. V. Hill (fl), R. Heagney (hpd)—BWV 1030, 1032 & 1033 *(rec 1989)* Move ▲ MD 3118 [DDD]
Bach, J.S.:Sons Vn, w. V. Hill (vn), R. Heagney (hpd)—BWV 1020 [doubtful; trans. for flute & continuo] *(rec 1989)* Move ▲ MD 3118 [DDD]

Johnson, James (org)
An American Masterpiece Titanic ▲ Ti 179 [DDD]
Bach, J.S.:Chorale Preludes Org—(5) BWV 659, 729, 738, 739, 751 Titanic ▲ Ti 162
Bach, J.S.:Cons Org, BWV 592–597—BWV 596 Titanic ▲ Ti 162
Bach, J.S.:Preludes & Fugues, BWV 531–552—BWV 532 & 544 Titanic ▲ Ti 162
Bach, J.S.:Trio Sons Org, BWV 525–530—BWV 525 Titanic ▲ Ti 162
Franck, C.:Prélude, fugue et var Titanic ▲ Ti 164 [DDD]
Joyeux Noël Titanic ▲ Ti 190 [DDD]

Johnson, James (pno)
Kabalevsky, D.:Con 3 Pno, w. P. Freeman (cnd), Slovenian RSO Centaur ▲ CRC 2089 [DDD]
Muczynski, R.:Con 1 Pno, w. P. Freeman (cnd), Slovenian RSO Centaur ▲ CRC 2089 [DDD]
Muczynski, R.:Suite Pno Centaur ▲ CRC 2089 [DDD]

Johnson, Jay (mar/perc)—see ORCHESTRAS & ENSEMBLES Zeitgeist
Johnson, Keith (gtr)—see ORCHESTRAS & ENSEMBLES Illinois Performers' Workshop Ensemble
Johnson, Laura (vn)—see ORCHESTRAS & ENSEMBLES Les Cyclopes

Johnson, Lawrence (gtr)
Sor, F.:Gtr Music—Son in C; Vars in C; 3 Minuets; 9 Etudes Elan ▲ CD 2204

Johnson, Lynette (hp)
Johnson, Lynette:Hp Music—Sonatina; 2 Ancient Airs; The Far Isle; Historical Suite [Pastourelle; Etude; The Twilight Fen]; The Star of County Down; Adagio; Old French Carol; Fant Ibérique Sierra Classical ▲ SXC 5003

Johnson, Marc (vc)—see also ORCHESTRAS & ENSEMBLES Vermeer String Quartet
Ung, C.:Khse Buon Vc *(rec DeKalb, IL, 1982)* CRI ▲ CRI 710 [DDD/ADD]

Johnson, Mark (hpd)
Veeneman, C.:The Wiry Concord, w. Susan Werner (banjo), Forrest Covington (hammered dlc/cimbalom), Georganne Assat (hp), Donald Martin Jenni (hpd), Barbara Phillips Farley (pno), James Austin (pno), Marta Soderberg (va), James Knutson (perc), Patrick Doyle (perc), Steven Butters (perc), James Popejoy (perc), M. Geary (cnd) Capstone ▲ SCI 6

Johnson, M.-K. (va)
Van De Vate, N.:Music for Va, w. W. Wiley (perc), E. Zuckerman (pno) Vienna Modern Masters ▲ VMM CD 2001 [ADD]

Johnson, P. (pno)—see ORCHESTRAS & ENSEMBLES Mobius

Johnson, Ron (mar)
Hovhaness, A.:Fant on Japanese Woodprints, w. G. Schwarz (cnd), Seattle SO *(rec Seattle Opera House, June 6-7, 1994)* Delos ▲ DE 3168 [DDD]

Johnson, Ron (xyl)
Hovhaness, A.:Starry Night, w. Scott Goff (fl), John Carrington (hp) *(rec St Thomas Center Chapel, Bothell, WA, Jan 1995)* Crystal ▲ CD 811 [DDD]

Johnson, Roy Hamlin (pno)
Powell, J.:Son Teutonica *(rec Jan, 1977)* CRI ("American Masters" series) ▲ CD 704 [ADD]
Powell, J.:Son psychologique *(rec New York, Oct, 1983)* CRI ("American Masters" series) ▲ CD 704 [ADD]

Johnson, Sarah (vn)
Beach, A.M.C.:Son Vn, w. Peter Kairoff (pno) Albany ▲ TROY 150 [DDD]
Foote, A.:Ballad, w. Peter Kairoff (pno) Albany ▲ TROY 150 [DDD]
Foote, A.:Melody, w. Peter Kairoff (pno) Albany ▲ TROY 150 [DDD]
Foote, A.:Pieces Vn & Pno, Op. 9, w. Peter Kairoff (pno) Albany ▲ TROY 150 [DDD]
Ward, R.:Con Vn, w. P. Perret (cnd), Winston-Salem Piedmont Triad SO Albany ▲ TROY 126 [DDD]

Johnson, Trevor (hpd)
A Double Reed Consort, w. Wizardsl, Iowa Double Reed Consort *(rec Clapp Recital Hall, Univ. of Iowa, Iowa City, Jan. 1993 & May 1994)* CRS Master ▲ CRS 9460

Johnson, Wayne (pno)
Hovhaness, A.:Pno Music—Macedonian Mountain Dance, Op. 144a; Mountain Dance No. 2, Op. 144b; Blue Job Mountain Sonata, Op. 340; Mystic Flute, Op. 22; Dance Ghazal, Op. 37a; Love Song Vanishing into Sounds of Crickets, Op. 327; Sonata Ananda, Op. 303; Fantasy, Op. 16 *(rec Sept. 1991)* Crystal ▲ CD813 [DDD]

Johnsson, Christer (a sax)
Larsson, L.-E.:Con Sax, w. L. Segerstam (cnd), Swedish RSO Caprice ▲ CAP 21492

Johnsson, Lars (va)—see ORCHESTRAS & ENSEMBLES Crafoord String Quartet
Johnston, Alan (gtr)—see ORCHESTRAS & ENSEMBLES Minneapolis Guitar Quartet

Johnston, Beverly (mar)
Hatch, P.:Lagtime CBC ("Musica Viva" series) ▲ MVCD 1055 [DDD]
Kulesha, G.:Angels Centrediscs ▲ CMCCD 2786

Johnston, Beverly (perc)
Arcuri, S.:Chronaxie Centrediscs ▲ CMCCD 2786
Bach, J.S.:Music of—23 sinfonias, inventions, fugues & chorales performed on solo marimba CBC ("Musica Viva" series) ▲ MVCD 1033 [DDD]

Johnston, Beverly (perc) (cont.)
Louie, A.:Cadenzas, w. J. Campbell (cl) Centrediscs ▲ CMCCD 2786
Louie, A.:Refuge, w. Joseph Macerollo (acc), Erica Goodman (hp) *(rec Glenn Gould Studio, CBC Toronto, Mar 17, 1994 & Mar 13 & 2)* CBC ▲ MVCD 1096 [DDD]
Lundquist, T.I.:Duell, w. Joseph Macerollo (acc) *(rec Glenn Gould Studio, CBC Toronto, Mar 17, 1994 & Mar 13 & 2)* CBC ▲ MVCD 1096 [DDD]
Piché, J.:Steal the Thunder, w. J. Campbell (cl) Centrediscs ▲ CMC CD 2786

Johnston, James (vn)
Lovenstein, J.:Music of, w. Mary Brockenbrough (sop), Laura Sanders (sop), Barton Green (ten), Rockland Osgood (ten), David Murray (bar), Benjamin Sears (bar), Jonathan Lovenstein (pno), Heather O'Donnell (pno), James Silvers (pno), Rocy Reider (fl), Jason Horowitz (vn), Adrianna Hulscher (vn), Mimi Ragson (vn), Peter Landeen (vc), Reinmar Seidler (vc)—Blake Songs; other works Titanic ▲ Ti 221 [DDD]

Johnston, James (vn/va)—see ORCHESTRAS & ENSEMBLES Renaissonics

Johnston, Raymond (org)
Celestial Christmas 4, w. Worcester Cathedral Choir, Robert Stringer (trb) Celestial Harmonies ▲ 13077-2

Johnstone, James (hpd)—see also ORCHESTRAS & ENSEMBLES Les Éléments
Vivaldi, A.:Cons Diverse Instrs, w. E. Aadland (cnd), European Community CO—in e for 4 Vns, R.580; for Va & Gtr, R.540; for Vc & Bn, R.409; Il Madrigalesco, R.129; La Tempesta di Mare, R.98 IMP ("Classics" series) ▲ IMP 6700222

Johsson, A.-Per (rcr)
Telemann, G.P.:Con in B♭ for 2 Rcrs, w. C. Pehrsson (rcr), Drottningholm Baroque Ensemble BIS ▲ CD 8
Telemann, G.P.:Con in B♭ for 2 Rcrs, w. C. Pehrsson (rcr), Drottningholm Baroque Ensemble BIS ▲ CD 220 [AAD]

Jokanovic, Maja (vn)
Maric, L.:Son Vn & Pno, w. Gordana Marjanovic (pno) Emergo ▲ EC 3951 [DDD]
Slavenski, J.:Slavenska son, w. Gordana Marjanovic (pno), Camerata Academica Novi Sad Emergo ▲ EC 3950 [DDD]

Jolles, Renée (vn)—see ORCHESTRAS & ENSEMBLES Continuum Chamber Ensemble

Jolles, Susan (hp)—see also ORCHESTRAS & ENSEMBLES Contemporary Chamber Ensemble
Hanson, H.:Pastorale Ob, w. Robert Ellis (ob), G. Schwarz (cnd), Seattle SO Delos ▲ DE 3105 [DDD]
Hanson, H.:Pastorale Ob, w. Robert Ellis (ob), G. Schwarz (cnd), Seattle SO Delos 4-▲ DE 3150 [DDD]
Hanson, H.:Serenade Fl, w. J. Mendenhall (fl), G. Schwarz (cnd), Seattle SO Delos ▲ DE 3105 [DDD]
Hanson, H.:Serenade Fl, w. J. Mendenhall (fl), G. Schwarz (cnd), Seattle SO Delos 4-▲ DE 3150 [DDD]
Ibert, J.:Chamber Music, w. Sue Ann Kahn (fl), Eleanor Lawrence (fl), Peggy Schecter (fl), Rie Schmidt (fl), David Krakauer (cl), Lauren Goldstein (bn), Curtis Macomber (vn), Frederic Hand (gtr), Andrew Willis (pno)—2 Mouvements; Aria; Histoires; Pastoral; Aria; Entr'acte Albany ▲ TROY 145 [DDD]
Ibert, J.:Interludes, w. Sue Ann Kahn (fl), Curtis Macomber (vn) Albany ▲ TROY 145 [DDD]
Ibert, J.:Music of, w. C. Schadeberg (sop), Sue Ann Kahn (fl), E. Lawrence (fl), P. Schechter (fl), R. Schmidt (fl), David Krakauer (cl), L. Goldstein (bn), Curtis Macomber (vn), Frederick Hand (gtr), Arthur Willis (pno)—Entr'acte; Jeux; Sonatine; 2 Movements; 2 Interludes; Aria; Pièce for solo Fl; Histoires; 2 Stèles orientées; Pastoral; Aria; Entr'acte Albany ▲ TROY 145
Kernis, A.J.:America(n) (Day) Dreams, w. Kim Barber (mez), Mary Rowell (vn), Leslie Tomkins (va), Tonya Tomkins (vc), Robert Black (db), Kathleen Nester (fl), Larry Guy (cl/b cl), John Dent (tpt), Anthony Cecere (hn), Leslie Stifelman (pno), Jeffrey Milarsky (perc), M. Barrett (cnd)—A Navajo Blanket; Wednesday at the Waldorf; The Pregnant Dream; The Blue Bottle; "So Long" to the Moon from the Men of Apollo; Epilogue:The Pure Suit of Happiness *(rec Manhattan Center Studios, New York, May 31-June 3, 1995)* New Albion ♦ NA 083CD
The Sounds of Remembered Dreams, w. Humbert Lucarelli (ob), Frank Morelli (bn) Vox ("Classics" series) ▲ VOX 7504 [DDD]
Wuorinen, C.:Variations Bn, w. Donald MacCourt (bn), Gordon Gottlieb (timp) New World ▲ 80517-2

Jolles, Susan (hp/voc)—see ORCHESTRAS & ENSEMBLES Musicians' Accord members

Jolley, David (hn)—see also ORCHESTRAS & ENSEMBLES American Brass Quintet, Bargemusic
Adagio & Allegro:German Romantic Works for Horn, w. S. Rothenberg (pno) Arabesque ▲ ARA 6641 [DDD]
Brahms, J.:Trio Hn, w. M. Kaplan (vn), D. Golub (pno) Arabesque ▲ Z 6607
Fine, V.:Qt Brass, w. Ronald Anderson (tpt), Allan Dean (tpt), Lawrence Benz (b trbn) CRI ▲ CD 692 [ADD]
Merikanto, A.:Con Vn Cl, Horn & Strs, w. O. Kagan (vn), E. Brunner (cl), et al., U. Söderblom (cnd) Ondine ▲ ODE 703-2
Mozart, W.A.:Cons Hn, Orpheus CO Deutsche Grammophon 3-▲ 431665-2 [DDD]
Mozart, W.A.:Con Hn, K.412, Orpheus CO Deutsche Grammophon ▲ 423377-2 [DDD] □ 423377-5
Mozart, W.A.:Con Hn, K.495, Orpheus CO Deutsche Grammophon ▲ 423377-2 [DDD] □ 423377-5
Nielsen, C.:Qnt Ww, w. R. Wilson (fl), A. Vogel (ob), D. Shifrin (cl), J. Feves (bn) *(rec July 1-4, 1992)* Delos ▲ DE 3136 [DDD]
Villanelle:French Masterworks for Horn, w. Joyce Guyer (sop), Nancy Allen (hp), Samuel Sanders (pno) *(rec SUNY, Purchase Recital Hall, May 24-26, 1995)* Arabesque ▲ Z 6678 [DDD]
Wilder, A.:Son 1 Hn, w. David Oei (pno) *(rec SUNY Purchase Recital Hall)* Arabesque ▲ ARA 6665 [DDD]
Wilder, A.:Son 2 Hn, w. David Oei (pno) *(rec SUNY Purchase Recital Hall)* Arabesque ▲ ARA 6665 [DDD]
Wilder, A.:Son 3 Hn, w. David Oei (pno) *(rec SUNY Purchase Recital Hall)* Arabesque ▲ ARA 6665 [DDD]
Wilder, A.:Suite Cl, w. Alan Kay (cl), David Oei (pno) *(rec SUNY Purchase Recital Hall)* Arabesque ▲ ARA 6665 [DDD]
Wilder, A.:Suite 1 Hn, w. Sam Pilafian (tuba), David Oei (pno) *(rec SUNY Purchase Recital Hall)* Arabesque ▲ ARA 6665 [DDD]

Joly, Catherine (pno)
Hahn, R.:Premières valses Accord ▲ ACD 200542 [DDD]
Hahn, R.:Le Rossignol éperdu Accord ▲ ACD 200542 [DDD]
Heller, S.:Pno Music—Caprice brillant sur "La Truite" de Schubert, Op. 33; 33 Vars on a Theme of Beethoven, Op. 130; La Chasse [Étude caractéristique], Op. 29; Dans les bois [6 Rêveries et Finale], Op. 86; L'Obstinée, Op. 81/2; Allegretto, Op. 150/16; Allegro Agitato, Op. 150/17; 4 études sur "Freishütz" de Weber, Op. 127; Tarantella in A♭, Op. 85/2 Accord ▲ ACD 201592 [DDD]

Jonas, Chris (sax)
Ziporyn, E.:Kekembangan, w. Randy McKean (sax), Dan Plonsey (sax), Evan Ziporyn (sax), Sekar Jaya Gamelan Orch New World ▲ 804302

Jonas, Dietholm (ob)—see also ORCHESTRAS & ENSEMBLES Sabine Meyer Wind Ensemble
Vivaldi, A.:Cons Ob, w. S. Schilli (ob), G. Thomas (hpd), G. Kósa (hpd), J. Kis Domonkos (vc), Nagy, Morandi (cnd), Failoni CO—RV 450, 452, 453, 454, 534, 535 & 536 *(rec Dec. 1992)* Naxos ▲ 8.550859 [DDD]

Jonas, Dorothy (pno)
Berezowsky, N.:Fant for 2 Pnos, w. J. Pierce (pno), D. Amos (cnd), Polish Radio-TV SO Albany ▲ TROY 112 [DDD]
Britten, H.:Introduction & Rondo alla burlesca & Mazurka elegiaca, w. J. Pierce (pno) Koch International Classics ▲ KIC 7013-2 [DDD] ■ 3-7013-4 (D)
Britten, H.:Scottish Ballad, w. Joshua Pierce (pno), E. Stratta (cnd), Luxembourg RSO Phoenix ▲ PHCD 104 [DDD]
Cage, J.:Pno Music, w. Joshua Pierce (pno), Borah Bergman (pno), Joseph Kubera (pno), Myra Meldorf (pno), Fumiko Miyanoo (pno)—Music Walk; Jazz Study; Experiences I & II; plus others Wergo ▲ WER 61592
Classically Broadway, w. Joshua Pierce (pno) Kem-Disc ▲ 1009 [DDD]
Copland, A.:Danzón Cubano, w. J. Pierce (pno) Koch International Classics ▲ KIC 7002-2 [DDD] ■ 3-7002-4 (D)
Copland, A.:Rodeo, w. J. Pierce (pno)—Hoedown; Saturday Night Waltz; arr. by Gold & Fizdale for two pianos Koch International Classics ▲ KIC 7002-2 [DDD] ■ 3-7002-4 (D)

▲ = CD ♦ = Enhanced CD Δ = MD ■ = Cassette Tape □ = DCC

Jones, Dorothy (pno) (cont.)
Copland, A.:El salón México, w. J. Pierce (pno)—two-piano arrangement by Leonard Bernstein
Koch International Classics ▲ KIC 7002-2 [DDD] ■ 3-7002-4 (D)
Creston, P.:Con for 2 Pnos, w. J. Pierce (pno), D. Amos (cnd), Polish Radio-TV SO
Albany ▲ TROY 112 [DDD]
Gould, M.:Dance Vars, w. J. Pierce (pno), D. Amos (cnd), Royal PO
Koch International Classics ▲ KIC 7002-2 [DDD] ■ 3-7002-4 (D)
Lopatnikoff, N.:Con for 2 Pnos, w. Joshua Pierce (pno), D. Amos (cnd), Slovak State PO Košice
Centaur ▲ CRC 2269
Lutoslawski, W.:Vars on a Theme of Paganini for 2 Pnos, w. J. Pierce (pno)
Koch International Classics ▲ KIC 7013- 2 [DDD] ■ 3-7013-4 (D)
Malipiero, G.F.:Dialogo 7, w. Joshua Pierce (pno), D. Amos (cnd), Slovak State PO Košice
Centaur ▲ CRC 2269
Martinů, B.:Con 2 Pnos, w. Joshua Pierce (pno), E. Stratta (cnd), Luxembourg RSO
Phoenix ▲ PHCD 104 [DDD]
Mendelssohn, F.:Cons 2 Pnos, w. Joshua Pierce (pno), B. Rezucha (cnd), Slovak State PO Košice *(rec House of Art, Košice, Oct & Nov 1995)* Vox Classics ▲ VOX 7538 [DDD]
Mozart, W.A.:Pno Music Pnos, w. Joshua Pierce (pno)—Con. in E♭, K.365; Son. in D, K.448; Adagio, K.546; Fugue, K.426; Larghetto & Allegro in E♭ *(rec Philharmonic Hall, Bratislava, Slovakia, June 26, 1993)* Pro Arte ▲ CDD 3475 [DDD]
Piston, W.:Con for 2 Pnos, w. J. Pierce (pno), D. Amos (cnd), Royal PO
Koch International Classics ▲ KIC 7002-2 [DDD] ■ 3-7002-4 (D)
Poulenc, F.:Con for 2 Pnos, w. J. Pierce (pno), D. Amos (cnd), Polish Radio-TV SO
Albany ▲ TROY 112 [DDD]
Rachmaninoff, S.:Russian Rhap, w. J. Pierce (pno)
Koch International Classics ▲ KIC 7013- 2 [DDD] ■ 3-7013-4 (D)
Rachmaninoff, S.:Symphonic Dances, w. J. Pierce (pno)
Koch International Classics ▲ KIC 7013- 2 [DDD] ■ 3-7013-4 (D)
Saint-Saëns, C.:Danse macabre, w. J. Pierce (pno)
Koch International Classics ▲ KIC 7013- 2 [DDD] ■ 3-7013-4 (D)
Tansman, A.:Suite 2 Pnos, w. Joshua Pierce (pno), D. Amos (cnd), Slovak State PO Košice
Centaur ▲ CRC 2269
20th Century Romantic Music for 2 Pianos, w. Joshua Pierce (pno)
Koch International Classics ▲ KIC 7013 [DDD]

Jones, Hilda (hpd)
Bach, J.S.:Goldberg Vars Sanjo Music ▲ ■ HJ 1441
Bach, J.S.:Kbd Music (misc)—Fant in c; Italian Con in F; Duet in e; Capriccio in B♭; 12 Little Preludes; Duet in F; Chromatic Fant & Fugue in d; Toccata in c; Partita in B♭ Sanjo Music ▲ ■ HJ 1008
Kuhnau, J.:Biblical Sons Sanjo Music ▲ Sanjo Music ■ HJ 1004
Listen Rebecca, The Harpsichord Sounds Sanjo ■ HJ 1001

Jónasson, Ingvar (va)
Sigurbjörnsson, T.:Intrada, w. Gunnar Egilson (cl), Thorkell Sigurbjörnsson (pno)
Music from Iceland ▲ ITM 702 [ADD]
Sveinsson, A.H.:Exploration, w. G. Emilsson (cnd), Iceland SO ITM ▲ ITM 706

Jones, Angela (fl)
Debussy, C.:Syrinx *(rec Korunni Studios, Prague, Oct. 31-Nov. 3, 1994)*
Discover International ▲ DI 920281 [DDD]
Fauré, G.:Fant Fl, w. Renie Yamahata (hp) *(rec Korunni Studios, Prague, Oct. 31-Nov. 3, 1994)*
Discover International ▲ DI 920281 [DDD]
Griffes, C.T.:Poem Fl, w. T. Briccetti (cnd), Prague Virtuosi *(rec Korunni Studios, Prague, Oct. 31-Nov. 3, 1994)* Discover International ▲ DI 920281 [DDD]
Ravel, M.:Intro & Allegro, w. Renie Yamahata (hp), T. Briccetti (cnd), Prague Virtuosi *(rec Korunni Studios, Prague, Oct. 31-Nov. 3, 1994)* Discover International ▲ DI 920281 [DDD]
Saint-Saëns, C.:Fant Vn, w. R. Yamahata (hp) *(rec Korunni Studios, Prague, Oct. 31-Nov. 3, 1994)*
Discover International ▲ DI 920281 [DDD]

Jones, Boyd (org)
Boyd Jones Performs on the Noacke Organ, Opus 105 Arkay ▲ ARK 6130 [DDD]

Jones, Brian (org)
Clokey, J.:Symphonic Piece, w. A. Gordon (pno) AFKA ▲ SK 506
Demarest, C.:Fant Org, w. A. Gordon (pno) AFKA ▲ SK 506
Dupré, M.:Vars à deux thèmes, w. A. Gordon (pno) AFKA ▲ SK 506
Grasse, E.:Festival Ov, w. A. Gordon (pno) AFKA ▲ SK 506
The Sounds of Trinity:2 Organs with Brass & Timpani, w. Ross Wood (org), *(other musicians unknown)*
Arkay ■ 4116
Wagner, R.:Die Walküre (ride of the valkyries), w. A. Gordon (org) [organ duet arr.] AFKA ▲ SK 506

Jones, Brian (perc)
An Empire Brass Christmas, w. Empire Brass Quintet, Laurie Monohan (sgr), Kurt Wortman (perc)
Telarc ▲ CD 80416 [DDD]

Jones, David Neil (pno)
Copland, A.:Pno Vars Amphion ▲ PHI 135 [DDD]
Czerny, C.:Vars on "La Ricordanza" Amphion ▲ PHI 135 [DDD]
Mozart, W.A.:Vars Pno, K.573 Amphion ▲ PHI 135 [DDD]
Rachmaninoff, S.:Variations on a Theme by Chopin Amphion ▲ PHI 135 [DDD]

Jones, Derrick (elec bass)
Heat Beat, w. Michael Pluznick (perc)
Well-Tempered Productions ("Well-Tempered World" series) ▲ WTP 5177 [DDD]

Jones, Gillian (hand hn)
Dussek, J.L.:Hp Music, w. Danielle Perrett (hp), James Ellis (vn), Helen Verney (vc), Warwick Cole (pno)—A Favorite Duet for Hp & Pno, Op. 11; Son in E♭ for Hp, Op. 34/1; Favorite Son for Hp, Vn & Vc, Op. 37; Son in B♭ for Hp, Op. 34/2; Duo for Hp, Pno & Hand-Horn, Op. 38
Meridian ▲ MER 84244 [DDD]

Jones, Gloria (db)
Rachmaninoff, S.:Vocalise, w. Patrick McFarland (E hn), David Braitberg (vn), Beth Newdome (vn), Paul Murphy (va), Dona Klein (vc), Larry LeMaster (vc) [trans John Wildermuth] Arundax ▲ 21339

Jones, Granville (vn)
Purcell, H.:Music of, w. April Cantelo (sop), Alfred Deller (ct), Maurice Bevan (bar), Neville Marriner (vn), Peter Gibbs (vn), Desmond Dupré (vl), George Malcolm (hpd), Walter Bergmann (hpd)—15 Songs & Airs; Fantasia upon a Ground in d for 3 Violins & Continuo, Z.731; Fantasia upon One Note in F for 5 Viols, Z.745; Hornpipe in e (from The Old Bachelor); Music Lessons 1-12 from Musick's Hand-Maid, Part II; A New Irish Tune, "Lilliburlero," Z.646; Pavan in g for 3 Violins & Bass Viol, Z.752; Sonata in g for Violin & Continuo, Z.780; Sonata No. 9 in F, "Golden Sonata," Z.810 (from Ten Sonatas in Four Parts); Suite in D for Harpsichord, Z.667
Vanguard Classics ("The Bach Guild" series) 2-▲ OVC 2002/03 [ADD]

Jones, Harold (fl)
Let Us Break Bread together, w. Colette Valentine Leonarda ▲ LE 333 [DDD]

Jones, Ieuan (hp)
Debussy, C.:Chamber Music, w. William Bennett (fl), David Campbell (cl), James Campbell (cl), Nicholas Daniel (ob), Robert Makell (hn), Richard Watkins (hn), Robin Kennard (bn), Rachel Gough (bn), Simon Haram (sax), Clifford Benson (pno), Julius Drake (pno), John York (pno), Roger Tapping (va)—Rapsodie for Eng hn; Syrinx; Première rapsodie; Son for Fl, Va & Hp; Le petit nègre; Petite pièce; Rapsodie for Sax *(rec All Saints' Church, East Finchley, London, Jan 12-20, 1994)*
Cala 2-▲ CACD 1017 [DDD]
Poulenc, F.:Chamber Music, w. Peter Sidhom (bar), William Bennett (fl), David Campbell (cl), James Campbell (cl), Nicholas Daniel (ob), Richard Watkins (hn), Rachel Gough (bn), Peter Carter (vn), Chris West (db), Clifford Benson (pno), Julius Drake (pno), John York (pno)—Son for Ob; L'invitation au château; Villanelle; Son 2 Cls; Trio; Sxt; Son for Cl & Bn; Rapsodie nègre; Son for Cl; Mouvements perpétuels; Son for Fl *(rec All Saints' Church, East Finchley, London, Jan 12-20, 1994)*
Cala ▲ CACD 1018 [DDD]

Jones, Ieuan (hp) (cont.)
Ravel, M.:Intro & Allegro, w. William Bennett (fl), James Campbell (cl), Allegri String Quartet *(rec All Saints' Church, East Finchley, London, Jan 12-20, 1994)* Cala 2-▲ CACD 1018 [DDD]
Saint-Saëns, C.:Chamber Music, w. W. Bennett (fl), D. Campbell (cl), J. Campbell (cl), N. Daniel (ob), R. Makell (hn), R. Watkins (hn), R. Kennard (bn), R. Gough (bn), S. Haram (sax), C. Benson (pno), J. Drake (pno), J. York (pno), R. Tapping (va)—Odelette, Op. 162; Son for Cl, Op. 167; Feuillet d'album, Op. 81; Son for Bn, Op. 168; Caprice on Danish & Russian Airs, Op. 79; Son for Ob, Op. 166; Romance in D♭, Op. 37; Tarantelle, Op. 6 *(rec All Saints' Church, East Finchley, London, Jan 12-20, 1994)*
Cala 2-▲ CACD 1017 [DDD]

Jones, J. Lind (vn)
Mozart, W.A.:Qnt Cl, K.581, w. G. Siflies (cl), J. Korman (vn), J. Korman (va), J. Sant'Ambrogio (vc) *(rec 1975-79)* Vox Box 3-▲ CD3X 3014 [ADD]

Jones, Joyce (org)
Joyce Jones Motette ▲ MOT 11491 [DDD]

Jones, Karen (fl)
Arnold, M.:Con 2 Fl, w. M. Stephenson (cnd), London Musici Conifer Classics ▲ 75605-51228-2
The Flute Album, w. Jane Pendlebury (vc), Aline Brewer (hp), Catherine Edwards (pno)
Conifer Classics 2-▲ 75605-51905-2 [DDD]

Jones, Louise (vn)
Delius, F.:Fennimore & Gerda (sels), w. Malcolm Miller (pno)—2 interludes
Meridian ▲ MER 84298 [DDD]
Delius, F.:Hassan, w. Malcolm Miller (pno)—serenade; lullaby Meridian ▲ MER 84298 [DDD]
Delius, F.:Légende, w. Malcolm Miller (pno) Meridian ▲ MER 84298 [DDD]
Delius, F.:Son Vn, w. Malcolm Miller (pno) Meridian ▲ MER 84298 [DDD]
Delius, F.:Son 1 Vn & Pno, w. Malcolm Miller (pno) Meridian ▲ MER 84298 [DDD]
Delius, F.:Son 2 Vn & Pno, w. Malcolm Miller (pno) Meridian ▲ MER 84298 [DDD]
Delius, F.:Son 3 Vn & Pno, w. Malcolm Miller (pno) Meridian ▲ MER 84298 [DDD]

Jones, Martin (pno)
Banks, D.:Trio Hn, w. B. Tuckwell (hn), B. Langbein (vn) *(rec 4/87)* Tudor ▲ 771 [DDD]
Benjamin, A.:Music of, w. R. McMahon (pno)—Jamaican Rumba, 2 Jamaican Street Songs, Caribbean Dance, From San Domingo, Jamaicalypso Pianissimo ▲ PP 11192 [DDD]
Brahms, J.:Ballades, Op. 10—Nos. 1-4 Nimbus ▲ NI 5304 [DDD]
Brahms, J.:Son 1 Pno Nimbus ▲ NI 5304 [DDD]
Brahms, J.:Trio Hn, w. B. Tuckwell (hn), B. Langbein (vn) *(rec 4/87)* Tudor ▲ 771 [DDD]
Brahms, J.:Vars & Fugue on a Theme by Handel Nimbus ▲ NI 5304 [DDD]
Britten, H.:Songs, w. J. Gomez (sop), *(ensemble unknown)*—O tell me the truth about love; Funeral Blues; Johnny; Calypso; When you're feeling like expressing your affection; As it is, plenty; The Spider and the Fly; Blues from *Paul Bunyan*; The clock on the wall; Boogie-woogie
Unicorn-Kanchana ▲ DKP CD 9138
Bridge, F.:Son Vc, w. A. Michejew (vc) Nimbus ▲ NI 5275 [ADD]
Czerny, C.:Gott erhalte Franz den Kaiser, Zurich CO Jecklin-Disco ▲ JD 608-2 [ADD]
Debussy, C.:Pno Music (complete solo)—Children's Corner Suite; Estampes; Images pour piano (Books 1 & 2); L'isle joyeuse; Le petit negre Nimbus ▲ NI 5161 [DDD]
Debussy, C.:Pno Music (complete solo)—Preludes, Books 1 & 2 Nimbus ▲ NI 5162 [DDD]
Debussy, C.:Pno Music (complete solo)—La boite à joujoux; Jeux; Khamma Nimbus ▲ NI 5163 [DDD]
Debussy, C.:Pno Music (complete solo)—Images oubliées; Valse romantique; Rêverie; Danse; Suite bergamasque; Nocturne; Ballade; Mazurka; Pour le piano; Deux arabesques; Danse bohémienne; Clair de lune Nimbus ▲ NI 5160 [DDD]
Debussy, C.:Pno Music (complete solo)—Etudes; Epigraphes antiques; Elegie; La plus que lente; Berceuse héroïque; Hommage à Haydn; Page d'album Nimbus ▲ NI 5164 [DDD]
Debussy, C.:Pno Music (complete solo)—Clair de lune; Passepied [from *Suite bergamasque*]; Jadins sous la pluie [from *Estampes*]; Reflets dans l'eau [from *Images, set 1*]; Masques; Et la lune descen sur le temple qui fût [from *Images, set 2*]; Doctor Gradus ad Parnassum; The Snow Is Dancing; Golliwogg's Cake-walk [from *Children's Corner*]; La plus que lente; Des pas sur la neige; Ce qu'a vu le vent d'ouest; La fille aux cheveaux de lin; La cathédrale engloutie; Minstrels [from *Preludes, Book 1*]; Pour les arpéges composés; Pour les accords [from *Etudes, Book 2*] *(rec Apr. & Oct. 1988)*
Nimbus ▲ NI 7702 [DDD]
Finzi, G.:Ecologue, w. W. Boughton (cnd), English String Orch Nimbus ▲ NI 5366
Grainger, P.:Fant on Gershwin's *Porgy & Bess*, w. R. McMahon (pno) Pianissimo ▲ PP 11192 [DDD]
Grainger, P.:Lincolnshire Posy, w. R. McMahon (pno) Pianissimo ▲ PP 11192 [DDD]
Grainger, P.:Pno Music (comp)—complete folk song arrs., incl. Molly on the Shore, Country Gardens, etc. Nimbus ▲ NI 5244-2 [DDD] ■ NC 5244
Grainger, P.:Pno Music (comp)—solo piano arrs. of music by Bach *(Fugue in A minor; "Blithe Bells")*, Brahms *(Cradle song)*, Delius *(Air)*, Dowland *(Now, oh Now, I needs must part)*, Foster *(Lullaby; "Tribute to Foster")*, Gershwin *(Love walkled in; The man I love)*, Rachmaninoff *(Concerto)*, Strauss *(Rosenkavalier ramble)*, Tchaikovsky *(Concerto)* Nimbus ▲ NI 5232-2 [DDD] ■ NC 5232
Grainger, P.:Pno Music (comp) [solo piano arrs.]—features music by Bach *(Toccata & Fugue in d)*, Delius *(Air & Dance)*, Fauré *(Nell; Après un reve)*, Grieg *(Piano Concerto—1st movt.)*, Handel *(Hornpipe)*, Schumann *(Piano Concerto—1st movt.)*, Stanford *(Four Irish Dances)*; plus ten original Klavierstücke, etc. Nimbus ▲ NI 5255 [DDD]
Grainger, P.:Pno Music (comp)—Andante con moto; Bridal lullaby; Children's march; Colonial song; English waltz; Handel in the Strand; Harvest hymn; In Dahomey; Mock morris; Peace & Saxon; In a Nutshell (suite); The Immovable Do; To a Nordic Princess; Walking tune
Nimbus ▲ NI 5220 [DDD] ■ NC 5220
Grainger, P.:Pno Music (comp)—one- & two-piano arr. of music by Byrd, Brahms, Delius, & Gershwin; original works (The Warriors; etc.) Nimbus ▲ NI 5286 [DDD]
Grainger, P.:Pno Music (arrs, transcriptions & paraphrases)—Handel in the Strand; Bridal Lullaby; Country Gardens; "Now, oh now, I needs must part" [by Dowland]; Blithe Bells [by Bach]; The Gum-suckers March (In a Nutshell); My Robin is to the Greenwood Gone; Molly on the Shore; A March-jig (4 Irish Dances) [by Stanford]; Irish Tune from County Derry; Con. in b♭ for Piano:Opening passage [by Tchaikovsky]; Ramble on the last love duet from Der Rosenkavalier [by Strauss]; Colonial Song; Shepherd's Hey; Near Woodstock Town; Mock Morris; Zanzibar Boat Song; Children's March—Over the Hills and Far Away; One more day my John; In Dahomey
Nimbus ▲ NI 7703 [DDD]
Hoddinott, A.:Sons Pno—Nos. 1-5 Nimbus ▲ NI 5369
Koechlin, C.:Petites Pièces, w. B. Tuckwell (hn), B. Langbein (vn) *(rec 4/87)* Tudor ▲ 771 [DDD]
Mendelssohn, F.:Pno Music (comp solo works)—6 Preludes & Fugues, Op. 35; Prelude & Fugue in e; 3 Preludes & 3 Etudes, Op. 104; Study in f Nimbus ▲ NI 5071 [AAD]
Mendelssohn, F.:Pno Music (comp solo works)—Piano Sonatas Nos. 1-3, Opp. 6, 105, 106; Six Children's Pieces, Op. 72 Nimbus ▲ NI 5070 [AAD]
Mendelssohn, F.:Pno Music (comp solo works)—Fantasy, Op. 15; 3 Fantasies, Op. 16; Fantasy in f#, Op. 28; Variations in E♭, Op. 82 & in B♭, Op. 83; Variations sérieuses, Op. 54
Nimbus ▲ NI 5072 [AAD]
Mendelssohn, F.:Pno Music (comp solo works)—Songs without Words, Books 1-5
Nimbus ▲ NI 5073 [AAD]
Mendelssohn, F.:Pno Music (comp solo works)—Songs without Words, Books 6-8; Seven Characteristic Pieces, Op. 7; Gondellied in A (1837); Albumblatt, Op. 117 Nimbus ▲ NI 5074 [AAD]
Mendelssohn, F.:Pno Music (comp solo works)—Caprice, Op. 33/1; Andante & Rondo Capriccioso, Op. 14; Prelude & Fugue in e, Op. 35/1; Study No. 2 in F; Prelude & Fugue in f, Op. 35/5; Fant., Op. 16/2; Songs without Words [Bks. I/1, 3 & 6; II/4; IV/4; V/5 & 6; VI/4; VII/1; VIII/3 & 4]; Vars. Sérieuses in d, Op. 54; Charakterstücke, Op. 7/7; Klavierstücke No. 2 Nimbus ▲ NI 7704 [AAD]
Mendelssohn, F.:Pno Music (comp solo works)—3 Caprices, Op. 33; Capriccio in f#, Op. 5; Capriccio in E, Op. 118; Scherzo in b (1829); Scherzo a capriccio in f# (ca. 1835-6); Andante & Rondo capriccioso in E, Op. 14; Perpetuum mobile, Op. 119; 4 Little Pieces (1820); Andante cantabile & Presto agitato (1838) Nimbus ▲ NI 5069 [AAD]
Porter, C.:Songs, w. J. Gomez (sop)—Let's Do It; Night and Day; My Heart Belongs to Daddy; Miss Otis Regrets; The Physician Unicorn-Kanchana ▲ DKP CD 9138
Rachmaninoff, S.:Moments musicaux Nimbus ▲ NI 5214 [DDD]
Rachmaninoff, S.:Moments musicaux Nimbus ▲ NI 5292 [ADD/DDD]

INSTRUMENT.

Jones, Martin (pno) (cont.)
Rachmaninoff, S.:Pno Music (misc)—Lilacs, Op. 21/5; Daisies, Op. 38/3; Two Kreisler transcriptions (Liebesleid & Liebesfreud) Nimbus ▲ NI 5292 [ADD/DDD]
Rachmaninoff, S.:Variations on a Theme by Corelli Nimbus ▲ NI 5292 [ADD/DDD]
Rachmaninoff, S.:Variations on a Theme by Corelli Nimbus ▲ NI 5214 [DDD]
Shostakovich, D.:Con 1 Pno, w. G. Ashton (tpt), W. Boughton (cnd), English SO *(rec 11/90)* Nimbus ▲ NI 5308 [DDD]
Shostakovich, D.:Con 2 Pno, w. W. Boughton (cnd), English SO *(rec 11/90)* Nimbus ▲ NI 5308 [DDD]
Szymanowski, K.:Pno Music (comp)—[Disc 1] 9 Preludes, Op. 1; Vars. in b♭, Op. 3; 4 Studies, Op. 4; Son. No. 1 in c, Op. 8; [Disc 2] Vars. on a Polish Folk-Theme in b, Op. 10; Fant. in C, Op. 14; Prelude & Fugue in c♯; Son. No. 2 in A, Op. 21 Nimbus 2-▲ NI 5405/6 [DDD]
Tippett, M.:Choral Music, w. Stephen Darlington (cnd), Christ Church Cathedral Choir Oxford—Bonny at Morn (Northumbrian Folksong for Unison Voices & 3 Recorders); Dance, Clarion Air (Madrigal for 5 Voices); Music (Unison Song for Voices & Piano); Plebs Angelica (Motet for Double Choir); The Weeping Babe (Motet for Soprano & Mixed Choir); Five Nwgro Spirituals (from A Child of Our Time) Nimbus ▲ NI 5266 [DDD]
Virtuoso Piano Showpieces Nimbus ▲ NI 5326 [DDD]
Weber, C.M. von:Sons Pno—Nos. 1 in C & 2 in A♭, J.199 Pianissimo ▲ PP 20792 [DDD]

Jones, Mason (hn)
Hindemith, P.:Son Hn, w. G. Gould (pno) *(rec 1975)* Sony Classical ("Glenn Gould Edition" series) 2-▲ SM2K 52671 [ADD]
Hindemith, P.:Son Alto Hn, w. G. Gould (pno) *(rec 1976)* Sony Classical ("Glenn Gould Edition" series) 2-▲ SM2K 52671 [ADD]

Jones, Norman (vc)
Bach, Joh. Christian:Sinf concertante Fl, w. J. Galway (fl), D. Wickens (ob), W. Armon (vn), L. Jones (cnd), London Little Orch Elektra/Nonesuch ■ 71165-4

Jones, Philip (tpt)
Vivaldi, A.:Con for 2 Tpts, w. Churchill (tpt), N. Marriner (cnd), Academy of St. Martin in the Fields London ■ 417100-4

Jones, Randy (dr)—see ORCHESTRAS & ENSEMBLES Dave Brubeck Quartet

Jones, Rebecca (vn)—see ORCHESTRAS & ENSEMBLES Sterling String Quartet

Jones, S. (tpt)
Schwartz, E.:Sinf Juxta, w. E. Schwartz (pno), B. Theurer (tpt), S. Barnhart (perc) Capstone ▲ CPS 8612 CD [DDD]
Theurer, B.:Music of, w. B. Theurer (tpt), G. Smart (pno)—Feste; Fant Capstone ▲ CPS 8612 CD [DDD]

Jones, Sherri (pno)
Schulhoff, E.:Pno Music—Hot Music; Suite dansante en jazz; Partita; 5 études de jazz; 5 Pittoresken Wergo ▲ WER 6281-2

Jones, Sterling (hp)
Songs around Konrad von Würzburg, w. Andrea von Ramm, Timothy C. Nelson (fl), Christian Schmid-Cadalbert (recitation) Christophorus ▲ CD 74542 [DDD]

Jones, Susan (perc)
Crumb, G.:Lux Aeterna, w. Freda Herseth (mez), Pamela Guidetti (b fl/sop rcr), James Freeman (sitar), William Kerrigan (perc) *(rec Lang Concert Hall, Swarthmore College)* CRI ▲ CD 723 [DDD]

Jones, Talitha (pno)—see ORCHESTRAS & ENSEMBLES Bowed Piano Ensemble

Jones, Trevor (trbn)
Kelterborn, R.:Songs for 4 Winds & Chorus, w. M. Hoffmann (wind instr), W. Mittelbach (wind instr), G. Pettinger (wind instr), G. Kember (cnd), Bavarian Radio Chorus *(rec May 13, 1983)* Grammont ▲ CTSP 35-2 [ADD]

Jones, Trevor (va)—see ORCHESTRAS & ENSEMBLES Salomon String Quartet

Jones, Warren (pno)
I Carry Your Heart, w. Ruth Ann Swenson (sop), Charles Neidich (cl) EMI Classics ▲ CDC 56158
Copland, A.:Old American Songs, w. S. Ramey (bass) [E] Argo ▲ 433027-2 [DDD]
Divas in Song:Marylin Horne, a 60th Birthday Celebration, w. Montserrat Caballé (sop), H. Donath (sop), R. A. Swenson (sop), F. von Stade (mez), R. Fleming (mez), S. Ramey (bass), J. Levine (cnd), M. Katz (pno), K. Donath (pno), Manuel Burgueras (pno) RCA Red Seal ▲ 09026-62547-2
Ev'ry Time We Say Goodbye, w. Samuel Ramey (bass) *(rec Champs-Elysées Theater, Paris)* Sony Classical ▲ SK 68339
Grieg, E.:Songs, w. H. Hagegard (bar) [Disc 1]—Melodies of the Heart by Hans Christian Andersen, Op. 5; 9 Songs, Op. 18; 6 Songs by Henrik Ibsen, Op. 25; Last Spring, Op. 33/2; The Mountain Thrall, Op. 32; Rocking, Rocking, Op. 49/2; Henrik Wergeland, Op. 58/3; [Disc 2]—Songs & Ballads by Andreas Munch, Op. 9; 4 Songs by Bjornstjerne Bjornson, Op. 21; 5 Songs by John Paulsen, Op. 26; Songs, Op. 39, Reminiscences from Mountain & Fjord by Holger Drachmann, Op. 44 RCA Red Seal 2-▲ 09026-61630-2
Ives, C.:Songs, w. S. Ramey (bass)—Charles Rutledge; In the Alley; Slow March; An Old Flame; Circus Band; Romanza di Central Park; Night Song; Children's Hour; At the River; He is There [E] Argo ▲ 433027-2 [DDD]
Michael Parloff, w. Michael Parloff (fl), Gerald Ranck (hpd) ESS.A.Y ▲ ESS 1027
Paulus, S.:Bittersuite, w. H. Hagegård (bar) [E] Albany ▲ TROY 036-2 [DDD]
Schubert, Franz:Die Schöne Müllerin, w. K. McMillan (bar) [G] *(rec May 1991)* Dorian ▲ DOR 90162 [DDD]

Jonge, L. de (fl)
Jolivet, A.:Fl Music (comp)—Incantation (flute); Incantation (alto flute); 5 Incantations; Ascèses *(rec 2/21/87)* Attacca ▲ Babel 9159-2 [DDD]

Jongen, Charles (vn)
Vieuxtemps, H.:Fant appassionata, w. G. Cartigny (cnd), Liège SO *(rec Conservatoire Royal de Musique, Liège, June 1972)* Pavane ▲ ADW 7340 [DDD]

Jonkers, Han (gtr)
Gagnebin, H.:Pièces (3) Gtr Bayer ▲ 800905
Haug, H.:Pièces (3) Gtr Bayer ▲ 800905
Martin, F.:Pièces brèves Gtr Bayer ▲ 800905
Widmer, E.:Stücke Gtr Bayer ▲ 800905

Jónsdóttir, Sólveig Anna (pno)
Leifs, J.:Music of, w. Sigrídur Ella Magnúsdóttir (mez), Ólafur Vignir Albertsson (pno), Hjálmar Ragnarsson (pno), Edda Erlendsdóttir (pno), Marteinn Hunger Fridriksson (org), Hildigunnur Halldórsdóttir (vn), Gréta Gudnadóttir (vn), Gudmundur Kristmundsson (va), Sigurdur Halldórsson (vc), Richard Korn (db), Iceland SO, Icelandic Opera Chorus, Langholts Church Graduale Choir, Hamrahlid Choir—Icelandic Cant, Op. 13/4; Valse Lento, Op. 2/1; Icelandic Dance, Op. 11/2 [Tempo Giusto]; Requiem; Lullaby [After the Riots]; Fairy-Tale in the Wood [from Baldr, Op. 34]; Funeral March; Separation [from Elegy, Op. 53]; Galdra Loftur Ov, Op. 10; Funeral March, Op. 6; Reverie; Reunion [from Elegy, Op. 53]; Fine I, Op. 55; Andante [The Last Supper]; Preludia Organo, Op. 16/3 [In the Church]; The Tear of Stone [from Elegy, Op. 53] Music From Iceland ▲ ITM 605 [DDD]
Ragnarsson, H.:Music of, w. S. E. Magnúsdóttir (mez), H. Halldórsdóttir (vn), G. Gudnadóttir (vn), G. Kristmundsson (va), S. Halldórsson (vc), R. Korn (db), Ó. V. Albertsson (pno), H. Ragnarsson (pno), E. Erlendsdóttir (pno), M. H. Fridriksson (org), Sakari, Wilkinson (cnd), Iceland SO, G. Cortes (cnd), J. Stefánsson (cnd), T. Ingólfsdóttir (cnd), Hamrahlid Choir, Icelandic Opera Chorus, Langholts Church Graduale Choir—Meine kleine Freundin [In the Ballroom]; Lovers Duet; After the concert; Meine kleine Freundin [Annie listens to the Radio]; Lif's Theme [On the Beach]; Lif's Theme II [Night Prayer]; Composing Ov [Vars I, II & III] Music From Iceland ▲ ITM 605 [DDD]

Joplin, Scott (pno)
Joplin, S.:Pno Music, w. H. Boulware (pno)—16 piano rolls, including 15 Joplin compositions and one by W.C. Handy; 3 selections hand-played by Joplin himself, the others from rolls produced by Hal Boulware in the 1960s:Maple leaf rag; Ole Miss rag [W.C. Handy]; Magnetic rag *(preceding three are original Joplin rolls)*; Elite syncopations; Country club; Paragon rag; Eugenia; Cleopha; A real slow drag; Scott Joplin's new rag; Leola (two-step); Lily Queen; The chrysanthemum; Heliotrope bouquet; Reflection rag; Silver swan rag (ragtime two-step) Biograph ▲ BCD 102 [DDD]
Joplin, S.:Pno Music [piano rolls] Biograph 2-■ BRC 1013

Joplin, Scott (pno) (cont.)
Joplin, S.:Pno Music, w. H. Boulware (pno)—14 piano rolls of Joplin compositions:3 hand-played by Joplin himself, the others from rolls produced by Hal Boulware in the 1960s:Maple leaf rag; Something doing; Weeping willow rag *(preceding three are original Joplin rolls)*; The entertainer; The easy winners; Pine apple rag; Solace; Gladiolus rag; The ragtime dance; Sugar cane; The crush collision march; Bethena (a concert waltz); Combination march; A breeze from Alabama Biograph ▲ BCD 101 [DDD]

Jorand, Marcel (perc)
Rossini, G.:Péchés de vieillesse (sels), w. M. Castets (sop), M. Georg (mez), J.-L. Maurette (ten), M. Brodard (bar), R. Nolte (bass), E. Kalvelage (pno), C. Spering (org), Cologne Chorus Musicus—Toast pour le nouvel an, Roméo, La Grande Coquette, Un sou, Chanson de Zora, La Nuit de Noël, Le Dodo des enfants, Le Lazzarone, Adieux à la vie!, Soupirs et sourire, L'Orpheline du Tyrol, Choeur de chasseurs démocrates; *Morceaux réservés*—Ave Maria, Les Amants de Séville, Le Chant des Titans, Chant funèbre [F] *(rec Aug. 1992)* Opus 111 ▲ OPS 30-70 [DDD]

Jordaan, Gerrit (org)
Grové, S.:Afrika Hymnus Claremont ▲ GSE 1546 [DDD]

Jordan, Barry (elec org)
Klatzow, P.:Chamber Con, w. Beat Wenger (fl), Jimmy Reinders (cl), Robert Grishkoff (hn), Uliano Marchio (gtr), Lamar Crowson (pno), Peter Hamblin (perc), P. Klatzow (cnd) Claremont ▲ GSE 1524

Jordan, D. (org)
Organ Music of America II (1868-1908), w. David Chalmers (org), J. E. Jordan, Jr. (org) Paraclete ▲ GDCD 011 ■ GDC 011

Jordan Jr., James E. (org)
Be Glad, Then America, w. [cnd:Elizabeth C. Patterson], Gloriae Dei Cantores Paraclete ▲ PCL 8 [DDD] 2-■ PCL 8
Brahms, J.:Motets (misc), w. E.C. Patterson (cnd), Gloriae Dei Cantores—Es ist das Heil uns kommen her; O Heiland reiss die Himmel auf; Ach, arme Welt, du trügest mich Paraclete ▲ GDCD 023 [DDD]
Mendelssohn, F.:Choral Music, w. E.C. Patterson (cnd), Gloriae Dei Cantores—Heilig; Zwei Geistliche Choere; Mitten wir in Leben sind; Aus tiefer Noth schrei'ich zu dir; Drei Motteten; Sechs Sprüche Paraclete ▲ GDCD 023 [DDD]
Music of the Americas, 1492-1992, w. Gloriae Dei Cantores [cnd:Elizabeth C. Patterson], David Chalmers (org) Paraclete 2-▲ PCL 10 [DDD] 2-■ PCL 10
Organ Music of America:20th Century "Romantics", w. David Chalmers (org) *(rec Church of the Advent, Boston)* Paraclete ▲ PCL 9 [DDD] ■ PCL 9
Organ Music of America (1891-1991), w. David Chalmers (org) Paraclete ▲ GDCD 009 ■ GDC 009
Organ Music of America II:The Boston Classicists, w. David Chalmers (org) *(rec Mechanics Hall, Worcester, MA)* Paraclete ▲ PCL 11 [DDD] ■ PCL 11
Organ Music of America II (1868-1908), w. David Chalmers (org), D. Jordan (org), J. E. Jordan Paraclete ▲ GDCD 011 ■ GDC 011
Organ Music of America II (1868-1908), w. David Chalmers (org), D. Jordan (org), J. E. Jordan, Jr. (org) Paraclete ▲ GDCD 011 ■ GDC 011
San Marco 1527-1740, w. . Gloriae Dei Cantores [cnd:Elizabeth C. Patterson], David Chalmers (org) Paraclete 2-▲ GDCD 014 [DDD] 2-■ GDC 014 I & II
Sowerby, L.:Choral Music, w. D. Chalmers (org), E.C. Patterson (cnd), Gloriae Dei Cantores—Great Is the Lord; Hear My Cry, O God; The Lord Is My Shepherd; How Long Wilt Thou Forget Me; Turn Thou to Thy God; Whoso Dwelleth; An Angel Stood by the Alter Of Paraclete 2-▲ GCCD 016
Sowerby, L.:Festival Musick, w. Gloriae Dei Brass Ensemble Paraclete 2-▲ GCCD 016
This Worldes Joie, w. . Gloriae Dei Cantores [cnd:Elizabeth C. Patterson], David Chalmers (pno) *(rec Mechanics Hall, Worcester, MA)* Paraclete ▲ GDCD 020

Jordan, Krassimira (pno)
Rachmaninoff, S.:Preludes Pno, Opp 23 & 32—Nos. 2, 5 & 7 *(rec Baylor Univ, Waco TX, Jan 16-20, 1995)* Albany ▲ TROY 203 [DDD]
Shchedrin, R.:Pno Music (misc)—Humoresque for Orchestra [arr. for piano]; Basso Ostintato *(rec Baylor Univ, Waco, TX, Jan 16-20, 1995)* Albany ▲ TROY 203 [DDD]
Smetana, B.:Pno Music (misc)—Dupák; Obkročák *(rec Baylor Univ, Waco, TX, Jan 16-20, 1995)* Albany ▲ TROY 203 [DDD]
Szymanowski, K.:Metopes *(rec Baylor Univ, Waco, TX, Jan 16-20, 1995)* Albany ▲ TROY 203 [DDD]
Tchaikovsky, P.:Dumka:Russian Rustic Scene *(rec Baylor Univ, Waco, TX, Jan 16-20, 1995)* Albany ▲ TROY 203 [DDD]
Vladigerov, P.:Piano Music (misc)—Norturno; Perpetuum Mobile; Prelude *(rec Baylor Univ, Waco, TX, Jan 16-20, 1995)* Albany ▲ TROY 203 [DDD]

Jordan, M. (hpd)
Bach, C.P.E.:Trio Sons (misc), w. C. Delafontaine (fl), F. Sarnau (vn), P. Mermoud (vc)—in b, a, d, B♭ & D *(rec Jan 4, 5 & 6, 1988)* Gallo ▲ CD 541

Jordan, Ronald (org)
The Joy of God:Great Hymns Across the Ages, w. Yorkminster Park Baptist Church Choir Toronto [cnd:Catherine Palmer] Marquis ▲ MAR 175 [DDD]

Jordanova, Elena (pno)—see ORCHESTRAS & ENSEMBLES Prague Chamber Ensemble

Jordanova, Victoria (hp)
Jordanova, V.:Once Upon a Time CRI ▲ CD 673 [DDD]
Jordanova, V.:Preludes Hp CRI ▲ CD 673 [DDD]
Jordanova, V.:Vars Hp CRI ▲ CD 673 [DDD]

Jordans, Wyneke (pno)
Schubert, Franz:Fant Pno, D.940, w. L. Van Doeselaar (pno) Globe ▲ GLO 5049 [DDD]
Schubert, Franz:Marches caractéristiques, w. L. Van Doeselaar (pno)—No. 1 Globe ▲ GLO 5049 [DDD]
Schubert, Franz:Rondo Pno, D.951, w. L. Van Doeselaar (pno) Globe ▲ GLO 5049 [DDD]
Schubert, Franz:Vars on an Original Theme Pno 4-Hands, w. L. Van Doeselaar (pno) Globe ▲ GLO 5049 [DDD]

Jordao, Adriano (pno)
Mozart, W.A.:Con 12 Pno, w. M. Layfield (cnd), Goldberg Ensemble Meridian ▲ 84166
Mozart, W.A.:Con 13 Pno, w. M. Layfield (cnd), Goldberg Ensemble Meridian ▲ 84166
Mozart, W.A.:Con 14 Pno, w. M. Layfield (cnd), Goldberg Ensemble Meridian ▲ 84166
Ravel, M.:Con Pno (left hand), w. D. Epstein (cnd), MIT SO MP Classics ("European" series) ▲ 3-11014
Ravel, M.:Con in G Pno, w. D. Epstein (cnd), MIT SO MP Classics ("European" series) ▲ 3-11014

Jorgensen, J. (va)
Ives, C.:Son 2 Pno, w. P. Salo (pno), T. L. Christiansen (fl) Kontrapunkt ▲ 32046 [DDD]

Jørgensen, Keld (trbn)—see ORCHESTRAS & ENSEMBLES Royal Danish Brass

Jørgensen, Knud Erik (va)
Heyde, O.:Songs, w. Margrehte Heyde (sgr), Ole Heyde (sgr/gtr), Kirstine Heyde Dias (vn), Lars Gram (db)—44 songs from texts by Piet Hein Danica ▲ DCD 8175

Jørgensen, Leif (vn)
Braein, E.F.:The Merry Musicians, w. R. Kjelstrup (cl), J. Hindar (va), L. Hindar (vc) Simax ▲ PSC 3117

Jørgensen, Ulla Miilmann (fl)
Maegaard, J.:Canon, w. Toke Lund Christiansen (fl), Henrik Svitzer (fl) *(rec Copenhagen, 1995-96)* Marco Polo/Dacapo ▲ 8.224050 [DDD]

Jörg-Wolfgang (vn)—see ORCHESTRAS & ENSEMBLES Bartholdy Piano Quartet

Jormin, Anders (bass instr/perc)
Blak, K.:Drangar, w. Anders Hagberg (fl/s sax/perc), Tore Brunborg (s sax/t sax/perc), Lennart Kullgren (gtr/sgr), Kristian Blak (pno/sgr), Anda Kuitse (sgr/perc), Karin Korpelainen (dr/perc) *(rec Nordic House, Tórshavn, Jan. 1995)* Tutl ▲ HJF 33

Jormin, Anders (bass instr/perc/sgr)
Blak, K.:Con Grotto, w. John Tchicai (t sax/sgr/perc), Lennart Kullgren (gtr/fl/sgr/perc), Anders Hagberg (fl/perc/sgr), Kristian Blak (pno/perc/sgr), Karin Korpelainen (perc/sgr), Sharon Weiss (perc/kaval) *(rec Lidargjógv, Sandoy, Aug. 1984)* Tutl ▲ HJF 33

Josefowicz, Leila (vn)
Sibelius, J.:Con Vn, w. N. Marriner (cnd), Academy of St. Martin in the Fields Philips ▲ 446131-2
Tchaikovsky, P.:Con Vn, w. N. Marriner (cnd), Academy of St. Martin in the Fields Philips ▲ 446131-2

Josel, Seth (elec gtr)
Lyon, E.:Greaseball *(rec Univ of South Florida, Sarasota, FL, Mar 24, 1994)* CRI ▲ CD 697 [DDD]
Tenney, J.:Water on the Mountain...Fire in Heaven *(rec Berlin, Germany, Dec 9 & 10, 1994)* CRI ▲ CD 697 [DDD]

Josel, Seth (gtr)
Corbett, S.:Arien IV *(rec Stuttgart, Germany, Jan 5, 1995)* CRI ▲ CD 697 [DDD]
Kernis, A.J.:Ciacona Gtr *(rec Stuttgart, Germany, Jan 5, 1995)* CRI ▲ CD 697 [DDD]

Josel, Seth (mand)
Bresnick, M.:Bag O' Tells *(rec Sprague Hall, Yale University, New Haven, CT, Mar 21, 1994)* CRI ▲ CD 697 [DDD]

Joselson, Tedd (pno)
Barber, S.:Con Pno, w. A. Schenck (cnd), London SO ASV ▲ ASV 534 [DDD]
Falla, M. de:Noches en los jardines de España, w. E. Mata (cnd), Frankfurt RSO Olympia ▲ OCD 351 [DDD]
Orbón, J.:Partita 4, w. E. Mata (cnd), Frankfurt RSO Olympia ▲ OCD 351 [DDD]
Prokofiev, S.:Cinderella Pno, Op. 97 Olympia ▲ OLY 453 [DDD]
Prokofiev, S.:The Love for 3 Oranges (scherzo & march) Olympia ▲ OLY 453 [DDD]
Prokofiev, S.:Romeo & Juliet Pno Olympia ▲ OLY 453 [DDD]

Joseph, D. N. (bn)
Pellegrini, E.:Divert a tre Bn, w. M. Schmidt (vc), V. Barton (vc) CRS ▲ CD 8949

Josheff, Peter (cl)—see ORCHESTRAS & ENSEMBLES Earplay members, Earplay

Joste, Martine (pno)
Cage, J.:One^5 *(rec Radio France, Paris, Jan. 18–4, 1994)* Mode ▲ mode 44
Cage, J.:Two^6, w. Ami Flammer (vn) *(rec Radio France, Paris, Jan. 18–4, 1994)* Mode ▲ mode 44
Weber, C.M. von:Grand duo concertant Cl, w. Guy Deplus (cl) Accord ▲ ACD 202782 [AAD]
Weber, C.M. von:Trio Fl, w. Maxence Larrieu (fl), Michel Renard (vc) Accord ▲ ACD 202782 [AAD]

Joste, Martine (pno/rainsticks)
Cage, J.:Four^3, w. Ami Flammer (vn/rainsticks), Dominique Alchourroun (pno/rainsticks), Jean Michaut (rainsticks) *(rec Radio France, Paris, Jan. 18–4, 1994)* Mode ▲ mode 44

Joubert, J. (vn)
Suter, R.:Musikalisches Tagesbuch 1, w. B. Geiser–Payer (alt), H. Haldemann (pic/fl), H. Holliger (ob), H. Bochet (bn), J. Semper (va), W. Eugster (vc), M. Dellanoy (db) *(rec 1962)* Grammont ▲ CSTP 6–2 [AAD]

Joulain, Hervé (hn)
Brahms, J.:Trio Hn, w. Jean–Jacques Kantorow (vn), Marie–Josèphe Jude (pno) Harmonia Mundi France ("Les Nouveaux Interprètes" series) ▲ HMN 911559
Glière, R.:Pieces, Op. 35, w. Denis Pascal (pno)—Intermezzo for Hn & Pno [No. 11] Arion ▲ ARN 68311 [DDD]
Haydn, J.:Con 1 Hn, w. P. Herreweghe (cnd), Radio France PO Arion ▲ ARN 68311 [DDD]
Haydn, J.:Divert Hn, Vn & Vc, H.IV/5, w. Jean–Jacques Kantorow (vn), Roland Pidoux (vc) Arion ▲ ARN 68311 [DDD]
Koechlin, C.:Little Pieces, w. Jean–Jacques Kantorow (vn), Alice Ader (pno)—2 sels Arion ▲ ARN 68311 [DDD]
Mozart, W.A.:Qnt Hn & Strs, w. Élisabeth Glab (vn), Françoise Gnéri (va), Pascal Robault (va), Nadine Pierre (vc) Arion ▲ ARN 68311 [DDD]
Schumann, R.:Andante & Vars Hn, w. Marie–Josèphe Jude (pno), Laurent Cabasso (pno), Roland Pidoux (vc), Michel François (vc) Harmonia Mundi France ("Les Nouveaux Interprètes" series) ▲ HMN 911559
Schumann, R.:Songs, w. Marie–Josèphe Jude (pno), Laurent Cabasso (pno), Roland Pidoux (vc), Michel François (vc)—Abendlied, Op. 107/6 Harmonia Mundi France ("Les Nouveaux Interprètes" series) ▲ HMN 911559
Sinigaglia, L.:Pezzi Hn & Pno, w. Denis Pascal (pno)—No. 1 Arion ▲ ARN 68311 [DDD]
Strauss, F.:Nocturne, w. Alice Ader (pno) Arion ▲ ARN 68311 [DDD]
Strauss, R.:Das Alphorn, w. Delphine Collot (sop), Denis Pascal (pno) Arion ▲ ARN 68311 [DDD]

Jouvet, Laurent (org)
Couperin, F.:Messe propre pour les couvents de religieux et religieuses, w. Ganagobie Abbey Monks' Choir Jade ▲ JAD C096

Jouza, Jan (vn)
Zelenka, J.D.:Trio Sons Obs, w. Jana Brozková (ob), Vojtech Jouza (ob), Jaroslav Kubita (bn), Václav Hoskovec (db), Frantisek Xaver Thuri (hpd)—Nos. 1–3 Studio Matous ▲ MAT 8 [DDD]

Jouza, Vojtech (ob)
Zelenka, J.D.:Trio Sons Obs, w. Jana Brozková (ob), Jan Jouza (vn), Jaroslav Kubita (bn), Václav Hoskovec (db), Frantisek Xaver Thuri (hpd)—Nos. 1–3 Studio Matous ▲ MAT 8 [DDD]
Zelenka, J.D.:Trio Sons Obs, w. Jana Brozková (ob), Jaroslav Kubita (bn), Václav Hoskovec (db), Frantisek Xaver Thuri (hpd)—Nos. 4–6, ZWV 181 Studio Matous ▲ MAT 9 [DDD]

Jouza, Vojtech (vn)—see ORCHESTRAS & ENSEMBLES Suk String Quartet

Joy, Genevieve (pno)
Dutilleux, H.:Figures (2) de résonnances, w. H. Dutilleux (pno) Erato 2–▲ 91721
Dutilleux, H.:Préludes Pno—3 Erato 2–▲ 91721
Dutilleux, H.:Son Pno Erato 2–▲ 91721
Dutilleux, H.:Sonnets (2) de Jean Cassou, w. G. Cachemaille (bar) Erato 2–▲ 91721

Joyce, Donald (org)
Bach, J.S.:Chorale Settings, BWV 651–668—Allein Gott..., BWV 664 Titanic ▲ Ti 164 [DDD]
Bach, J.S.:Org Music (misc)—Canonic Variations, "Vom Himmel hoch...," BWV 769; Chorale Partita diverse sopra, "Sei gegrüsset...," BWV 768; Prelude & Fugue in d, BWV 539; Sonata in C, BWV 529; Sonata in d, BWV 527; Toccata (Prelude) & Fugue in E, BWV 566 Titanic ▲ Ti 171 [DDD]
Bach, J.S.:Passacaglia & Fugue Org Titanic ▲ Ti 164 [DDD]
Bach, J.S.:Pastorale Org, BWV 590 Titanic ▲ Ti 164 [DDD]
Bach, J.S.:Preludes & Fugues, BWV 531–552—BWV 547 & 548 Titanic ▲ Ti 164 [DDD]
Franck, C.:Prélude, fugue et var *(rec London, for Columbia Records, 10/31/32)* The Classical Collector ▲ FDC 2008 [AAD]
Glass, Philip:Org Music—Dance IV; Mad Rush; Dance II; Contrary Motion; Satygraha; Act III Conclusion Catalyst ▲ 09026–61825–2
The Organ at La Valenciana Titanic ▲ Ti 188 [DDD]
The Organ in Santa Prisca:17th & 18th Century Music of the Spanish & Portuguese Titanic ▲ Ti 187 [DDD]
Reger, M.:Org Music (misc)—Vars & Fugue on an Original Theme, Op. 73; Benedictus, Op. 59/9; Fant & Fugue on Wachet auf, ruft; Uns Die Stimme, Op. 52/2 IMP ("Classics" series) ▲ IMP PCD 1096
Trumpet & Tuba Tunes, Toccatas & Fantasies IMP Classics ▲ PCD 1079 [DDD]

Joyce, Eileen (pno)
Arensky, A.:Trio 1 Pno, w. H. Temianka (vn), A. Sala (vc) *(rec 1938)* Biddulph 2–▲ LAB 059/60 [ADD]
Bliss, A.:Baraza, w. M. Mathieson (cnd), London SO Dutton Laboratories ▲ DUT 2501 [ADD]
Eileen Joyce:Recordings from 1933–1941 Pearl ▲ PEA 9022 [AAD]
Ireland, J.:Con Pno, w. L. Heward (cnd), Hallé Orch *(rec Jan. 14, 1942)* Dutton Laboratories ▲ CDAX 8001 [ADD]
Shostakovich, D.:Con 1 Pno, w. Arthur Lockwood (tpt), L. Heward (cnd), Hallé Orch *(rec Houldsworth Hall, Manchester, Oct. 24, 1941)* Dutton Laboratories ▲ CDAX 8010 [ADD]

Joyner, Roxanne (tpt)
Pelosi, L.:Triptych, w. Stewart Sundholm (hn), Michael Plant (trbn) Opus One ▲ CD 160

Jucker, Rama (vc)
Bach, C.P.E.:Son Ob, H.549, w. Heinz Holliger (ob), Leppard, Zinman (cnd), Netherlands CO, English CO Philips ("Classics" series) 2–▲ 442592–2
Bloch, E.:Suites (3) Vc Accord ▲ ACD 220342 [AAD]
Brahms, J.:Sextet Strs, Op. 36, w. Peter Rybar (vn), Clemens Dahinden (vn), Heinz Wigand (va), Oskar Kromer (va), Antonio Tusa (vc) Doron 2–▲ DRC 4007/8 [ADD]
Brahms, J.:Sons Vc (comp), w. Werner Giger (pno) Accord ▲ ACD 220382
Moeschinger, A.:Son in modo disinvolto, w. R. Mäser (pno) Grammont ▲ CTSP 1–2 [ADD]

Jucker, Rama (vc) (cont.)
Reger, M.:Suites Vc Accord ▲ ACD 200572 [AAD]
Schumann, R.:Andante & Vars Hn, w. Robert Majek (pno), Mario Venzago (pno), Käthi Gohl (vc), Francesco Raselli (hn) Accord ▲ ACD 201572 [AAD]
Schumann, R.:Stücke im Volkston, w. Mario Venzago (pno) Accord ▲ ACD 201572 [AAD]

Judd, Terence (pno)
Prokofiev, S.:Con 3 Pno, w. A. Lazarev (cnd), Moscow PO Chandos ("Collect" series) ▲ CHAN 6509 [ADD]
Tchaikovsky, P.:Con 1 Pno, w. A. Lazarev (cnd), Moscow PO Chandos ("Collect" series) ▲ CHAN 6509 [ADD]

Jude, Marie–Josèphe (pno)
Brahms, J.:Trio Hn, w. Hervé Joulain (hn), Jean–Jacques Kantorow (vn) Harmonia Mundi France ("Les Nouveaux Interprètes" series) ▲ HMN 911559
Dutilleux, H.:Son Pno Harmonia Mundi France ("Les Nouveaux Interprètes" series) ▲ HMN 911569
Ohana, M.:Etudes Pno—6 interpretive studies Harmonia Mundi France ("Les Nouveaux Interprètes" series) ▲ HMN 911569
Schumann, R.:Andante & Vars Hn, w. Laurent Cabasso (pno), Roland Pidoux (vc), Michel François (vc), Hervé Joulain (hn) Harmonia Mundi France ("Les Nouveaux Interprètes" series) ▲ HMN 911559
Schumann, R.:Songs, w. Laurent Cabasso (pno), Roland Pidoux (vc), Michel François (vc), Hervé Joulain (hn)—Abendlied, Op. 107/6 Harmonia Mundi France ("Les Nouveaux Interprètes" series) ▲ HMN 911559

Judge, Chris (gtr)
Gilles Apap & the Transylvanian Mountain Boys, w. Gille Apap (vn), Jean–Marc Apap (va), Brendan Statom (db) Sony Classical ▲ SK 62374

Juffinger, Andreas (org)
Bach, J.S.:Org Music (misc)—Prelude & Fugue in E♭, BWV.552; Passacaglia & Fugue in c; Schücke dich, o liebe Seele; Herr Jesu Christ dich zu uns wend *(rec Apr 28, 1991)* Koch Schwann ▲ SCH 312112 [DDD]
Mozart, W.A.:Adagio & Allegro Mechanical Org *(rec Apr. 28, 1991)* Koch Schwann ▲ SCH 312112 [DDD]
Mozart, W.A.:Andante Mechanical Org, K.616 *(rec Apr. 28, 1991)* Koch Schwann ▲ SCH 312112 [DDD]
Mozart, W.A.:Fant Mechanical Org *(rec Apr. 28, 1991)* Koch Schwann ▲ SCH 312112 [DDD]
Rheinberger, J.:Con 1 Org, w. H. Haenchen (cnd), Berlin RSO Capriccio ▲ CD 10 336 [DDD]
Rheinberger, J.:Con 2 Org, w. H. Haenchen (cnd), Berlin RSO Capriccio ▲ CD 10 336 [DDD]
Rheinberger, J.:Suite Org, w. E. Sebestyén (vn), M. Ostertag (vc), H. Haenchen (cnd), Berlin RSO Capriccio ▲ CD 10 337 [DDD]
Rheinberger, J.:Suite Vn, Op. 150, w. E. Sebestyén (vn) Capriccio ▲ CD 10 337 [DDD]
Rheinberger, J.:Suite Vn, Op. 166, w. E. Sebestyén (vn) Capriccio ▲ CD 10 336 [DDD]

Jukovic, M. (fl)
Sperger, J.:Trios, w. V. Dufka (ob), V. Simcisko (vn), M. Telecky (va), J. Alexander (vc), sels. unknown Trevak ▲ TRE 40002 [DDD]

Juliet, C. (vn)
Stravinsky, I.:Con Vn, w. C. Dutoit (cnd), Montreal SO London ▲ 436837–2 [DDD]
Szymanowski, K.:Con 1 Vn, w. C. Dutoit (cnd), Montreal SO London ▲ 436837–2 [DDD]
Szymanowski, K.:Con 2 Vn, w. C. Dutoit (cnd), Montreal SO London ▲ 436837–2 [DDD]

Jung, C. (vc)—see ORCHESTRAS & ENSEMBLES Sancoussi Ensemble Hamburg

Jung, Lars–Erik ter (vn)
Hvoslef, K.:Solo for Vn Simax ▲ PSC 1115
Penderecki, K.:Cadenza Simax ▲ PSC 1115
Schnittke, A.:Son 2 Vn, w. Einar Henning Smebye (pno) Simax ▲ PSC 1115
Szymanowski, K.:Myths, w. Einar Henning Smebye (pno) Simax ▲ PSC 1115

Junghänel, Konrad (gtr)
European Lute Music, Vol. 1:France Deutsche Harmonia Mundi ▲ 77037–2–RC [DDD]

Junghänel, Konrad (lt)—see also ORCHESTRAS & ENSEMBLES Cantus Cologne
Amarilli, mia bella, w. René Jacobs (alt) Harmonia Mundi ▲ HMA 190.1183
Bach, J.S.:Lt Music Deutsche Harmonia Mundi 2–▲ 77097–2–RC [ADD]
Monteverdi, C.:Vespro della Beata Vergine, w. K. Junghänel (cnd), Concerto Palatino, Cantus Cologne *(rec Sept 8–12, 1994)* Deutsche Harmonia Mundi 2–▲ 05472–77332–2 [DDD]
René Jacobs Recital, w. René Jacobs (ct) *(rec 1985)* Musique d'Abord ▲ HMA 1901183
Weiss, S.L.:Lt Music—Ov in B♭; Suite in d; Suite Nos. 17 in f & 21 in g Ars Musici ▲ 3025 [DDD]

Junghänel, Konrad (thb)—see also ORCHESTRAS & ENSEMBLES Smithsonian Chamber Players, Kuijken Consort
Gabrielli, D.:Vc Music, w. Roel Dieltiens (vc), Richte van der Meer (vc), Robert Kohnen (hpd)—music by Bononcini *(Son in a for 2 Vcs)*, Willem De Fesch *(Son in a for Vc & Cont, Op. 13/6)*, D. Gabrieli *(Sons (2) in A & G for Vc & Cont; Ricercare I–VII; Canon for 2 Vcs)* Accent ▲ 9070 [DDD]
Hotteterre, J.:Music of, w. Wilbert Hazelzet (trns fl), Jaap ter Linden (vl), Jacques Ogg (hpd)—5 Airs; Passacaille; 8 Preludes in b, c, C, D, g, g, G, G; 3 Suites in c, g, G *(rec San Miguel Church, Cuenca, Spain, May 1996)* Glossa ▲ GCD 920801 [DDD]
Italian Cello Music, w. Roel Dieltiens (vc), Richte van der Meer (vc), R. Kohnen (hpd) Accent ▲ 9070 [DDD]
Purcell, H.:Music for Voc & Strs, w. R. Jacobs (ct), W. Kuijken (vl)—Tis Natures's voice; Musick for a while; Retir'd from any mortal's sight, Since from my dear Astrea's sight; Pious Celinda goes to prayers; Incassum, Lesbia; Ah! Cruel nymph; The fatal hour comes on a pace; As Amoret and Thirsis lay; Sweeter than Roses; I lov'd fair Celia; Young Thirsis' fate Accent ▲ 57802

Junghanns, Rolf (clvd)
Bach, J.S.:Kbd Music (misc)—Capriccio, BWV 992; French Suite No. 5; Prelude & Fugue, BWV 846 & 866 Adagio ▲ ADG 91619 [ADD]

Junghanns, Rolf (hpd/pno)
The Viola d'Amore:In Numerous Voices, w. Dorothea Jappe (va d'amore), Konrad Hünteler (trns fl), Hans–Rudolf Stalder (chl), Herbert Hoever (vn), Michael Jappe (vl/vc) Adagio ▲ ADG 91016

Junghanns, Rolf (kbd)
Kreutzer, C.:Das Mühlrad, w. E. Speiser (sop), H.–R. Stalder (cl) [period instrs] *(rec 1984)* Jecklin–Disco ▲ JD 587–2 [ADD]
Kreutzer, C.:Trio Pno, Cl & Bn, w. H.–R. Stalder (cl), W. Stiftner (bn) [period instrs] *(rec 1984)* Jecklin–Disco ▲ JD 587–2 [ADD]

Junghanns, Rolf (pno)
Mozart, F.X.W.:Rondo Fl, w. C. Huntgeburth (fl) FSM–Adagio ▲ FCD 91638 [ADD]

Juntura, Timo (vl)—see ORCHESTRAS & ENSEMBLES Les Goûts–Réünis

Juritz, David (vn)
Vaughan Williams, R.:The Lark Ascending, w. R. Haydon Clark (cnd), Consort of London Collins Classics ▲ 11402 [DDD]

Jussila, Kari (org)
Rautavaara, E.:Annunciations, w. L. Segerstam (cnd), Helsinki PO Ondine ▲ ODE 869
Rautavaara, E.:Con Org, w. L. Segerstam (cnd), Helsinki PO *(rec Finlandia Hall, Oct 1995)* Ondine ▲ ODE 869–2 [DDD]

Justafré, Jean–Jacques (hn)
Constant, M.:Choruses & Interludes, w. Pierre–Marie Bonafosse (sax), François Moutin (b gtr), Pierre Guignon (dr), Andy Emler (pno), J. Kaltenbach (cnd), Nancy SO *(rec Salle Poirel, Nancy, Apr. 4, 1990)* Erato ▲ 94815–2 [DDD]
The Romantic Horn, w. Jean–Jacques (hn) Justafré, François–René Duchable (pno) Pierre Verany ▲ 793091 [DDD]
Schumann, R.:Konzertstück Hns, w. Jean–Claude Barro (hn), Alain Courtois (hn), Jean–Paul Gantiez (hn), *(orch unknown)*—Lebhaft; Romanze Erato ▲ 94801–2

Justus, Adrian (vn)
Thofanidis, C.:Qt 1 Strs, w. Maria Lin (vn), Timothy Lees (va), James Holland (vc) Albany ▲ TROY 158 [DDD]

Jutt, Stephanie (fl)—see also ORCHESTRAS & ENSEMBLES Present Music
Griffes, C.T.:Poem Fl, w. R. Hodgkinson (pno) [arr. G. Barrère] GM ▲ GM2026CD

Jutt, Stephanie (fl) (cont.)
Jolivet, A.:Chant de Linos, w. R. Hodgkinson (pno) GM ▲ GM2026CD
McKinley, W.T.:Romances, w. R. Hodgkinson (pno) GM ▲ GM2026CD
Piazzolla, A.:Études tanguistiques, w. R. Hodgkinson (pno) GM ▲ GM2026CD

Juvarra, Pietro (vn)
Dragonetti, D.:Qt 4 Strs, w. Stefano Furini (vn), Giancarlo di Vacri (va), Teodora Campagnaro (vc) *(rec Sala San Bovo, Padova, Italy, Jan 17–19, 1995)* Dynamic ▲ CD 133 [DDD]

Kaad, Jørgen (pno)
Stolarczyk, W.:Earth Air Fire Water, w. Amalie Malling (pno), John Damgaard (pno), Anne Øland (pno), Teddy Teirup (pno), Friedrich Gürtler (pno), Rosalind Bevan (pno), Poul Rosenbaum (pno), Rodolfo Llambias (pno), Bella Horn–Ribera (pno), Anders Riber (pno), Elisabeth Sigurdsson (pno), Thomas Tronheim (pno), Elsebeth Broderson (pno), Erik Kaltoft (pno), Jørgen Hald Nielsen (pno), Aino Gilemann (pno), Birgit Kjær (pno), Jørgen Thomsen (pno), Gunhild Donslund (pno), Henrik Bo Hansen (pno), Lone Karlsson (pno), Erik Fessel (pno), Lasse Nilsson (pno), Janos Ferenczi (pno), Erik Bach (pno), Axel Momme (pno), Arne de Cros Dich (pno), Sven Micha Slot (pno), Hanne Bramsen Buhl (pno), Lili Olesen (pno), Susannah Carlsson (pno), Ulla Erml (pno), Vagn Sørensen (pno), Leif Greibe (pno), Bodil Krogh (pno), Kirsten Ottosen (pno), Inger Bergenholz (pno), Karsten Gylendorf (pno), Bjørn Elkjær (pno), Jacob Bjørn Jensen (pno), Anne Marie Hjelm (pno), Carl Ulrik Munk Andersen (pno), Poul Lumbye (pno), Oluf Hildebrandt Nielsen (pno), Joachim Olsson (pno), Peter Pade Ramsøe Jacobsen (pno), Astrid Pollmann (pno), Jette Borsch (pno), Kirsten Karlshøj (pno), Maria Teresa Assing (pno), Allan Dahl Hansen (pno), Johan Hugossen (pno), Tine Fenger Pederson (pno), Arne Jørgen Fæø (pno), Anja Høgsted (pno), Anne Sophie Parbo (pno), Inga Lindmark (pno), Teresa Drabik Stathakis (pno), Anne Ruth Ferenczi (pno), Irene Hasager (pno), Yuka Ichikawa (pno), Birgitte Baur (pno), Malene Thastum (pno), Jens E. Rasmussen (pno), Birgitte Zielke (pno), Claus Zielke (pno), Stefan Kasch (pno), Bin Qiao (pno), Inger Johanne Teirup (pno), Lindy Rosborg (pno), Liisa Heininen (pno), David Højer (pno), Ellen Refstrup (pno), Thomas K. Søorensen (pno), Erik Kure (pno), Michael Rauff (pno), Jan beck Eriksson (pno), Tanja Zapolski (pno), Vibeke Skagbo (pno), Pål Eide Lindtner (pno), Ha–Young Sul (pno), Benedicte Palko (pno), Inke Kesseler (pno), Anne Marie Meineche (pno), Sverre Larsen (pno), Kasper Peter Bach (pno), Elisabetta Eliseo (pno), Olga Magieres (pno), Carl Erik Kühl (pno), Thorkild Borup Nielsen (pno), Valeria Zanini (pno), Lars Stenhoft (perc), Dennis Boel (perc), Winnie Dahlgren (perc), Susanne Vind (perc), Claus Byrith (elec), Anne Marie Storm (elec), J. Ribera (cnd) *(rec live, Koldinghaus Castle, Denmark, May 2, 1996)* Danica ▲ DCD 1996

Kaas, Jens (org)
Schierbeck, P.:Sorceress, w. Susanne Lange (sop), M. Schønwandt (cnd), South Jutland SO Point ▲ PCD 5085 [ADD]

Kabara, R. (vn)
Penderecki, K.:Sinfonietta, w. E. Szczepanska (va), D. Imietowski (vc), Cracow Chamber Players Vienna Modern Masters ▲ VMM 3023 [DDD]

Kadlubkiewicz, Veronica (vn)
Adler, S.:Trio 2 Pno, w. Elizabeth Wright (pno), Roy Christensen (vc) Gasparo ▲ GS 298 [DDD/DAD]
Macchia, S.:Chamber Con 3, w. J. Tanner (fl/alt fl), M. Sussman (cl), F. Cohen (ob/E hn), D. Fedora (bn), L. Klock (hn), J. Messina (db), P. Tanner (perc) *(rec July 1992)* Gasparo ▲ GS 226 [DDD]
Spratlan, L.:Night Music, w. M. Sussman (cl), J. Kelley (perc) *(rec July 1992)* Gasparo ▲ GS 226 [DDD]
Stern, R.:Fant Etude Vn *(rec July 1992)* Gasparo ▲ GS 226 [DDD]
Wheelock, D.:Partita Vn *(rec July 1992)* Gasparo ▲ GS 226 [DDD]

Kagan, Oleg (vn)
Beethoven, L. van:Serenade Strs, Op. 8, w. Yuri Bashmet (va), Natalia Gutman (vc) *(rec Hohenems Schubertiade, June 22, 1988)* Live Classics ("Kagan Edition" series) ▲ 142
Beethoven, L. van:Son 2 Vn, w. Sviatoslav Richter (pno) *(rec Large Room of the Conservatory, Moscow, Oct 27 & Nov 6, 1975)* Live Classics ▲ LCL 145 [ADD]
Beethoven, L. van:Son 3 Vn, w. Vassily Lobanov (pno) *(rec Ettlingen Palace, Stuttgart, Mar 8, 1988)* Live Classics ▲ LCL 144 [ADD]
Beethoven, L. van:Son 4 Vn, w. Sviatoslav Richter (pno) *(rec Large Room of the Conservatory, Moscow, Oct 27 & Nov 6, 1975)* Live Classics ▲ LCL 145 [ADD]
Beethoven, L. van:Son 5 Vn, "Spring", w. Sviatoslav Richter (pno) *(rec Large Room of the Conservatory, Moscow, Oct 27 & Nov 6, 1975)* Live Classics ▲ LCL 145 [ADD]
Beethoven, L. van:Son 8 Vn, w. Vassily Lobanov (pno) *(rec Chamber Music Festival Kuhmo, Finland, July 22, 1985)* Live Classics ▲ LCL 144 [DDD]
Beethoven, L. van:Son 10 Vn, w. Vassily Lobanov (pno) *(rec Chamber Music Festival Kuhmo, Finland, July 22, 1985)* Live Classics ▲ LCL 144 [DDD]
Beethoven, L. van:Trios Strs, Op. 9, w. Yuri Bashmet (va), Natalia Gutman (vc)—Nos. 1 & 3 *(rec Hohenems Schubertiade & Kuhmo Chamber Festival)* Live Classics ("Kagan Edition" series) ▲ 141
Berg, A.:Con Vn, w. T. Hannikainen (cnd), Finnish RSO *(rec Bregenzer Festspiele, Aug. 11, 1985)* Live Classics ("Kagan Edition" series) ▲ 143
Brahms, J.:Qt 1 Pno, w. Vassily Lobanov (pno), Diemuth Poppen (va), Natalia Gutman (vc) *(rec Chamber Music Festival Kuhmo, Finland, July, 19, 1989)* Live Classics ▲ LCL 124 [DDD]
Brahms, J.:Son 1 Vn, w. S. Richter (pno) MK ▲ MKA 418014 [DDD]
Brahms, J.:Son 1 Vn, w. Sviatoslav Richter (pno) Olympia 5–▲ OLY 5013 [DDD/ADD]
Dmitriev, G.:Con Vn, w. F. Glushchenko (cnd), Moscow PO *(rec Large Hall, Moscow Conservatory, Oct 18, 1981)* Russian Compact Disc ▲ RD CD 10003 [AAD]
Dvořák, A.:Romantic Pieces, Op. 75, w. Vassily Lobano (pno) *(rec Chamber Music Festival Kuhmo, Finland, July, 15, 1983)* Live Classics ▲ LCL 124 [ADD]
Gubaidulina, S.:Rejoice, w. Natalia Gutman (vc) *(rec Chamber Music Festival Kuhmo, Finland, July 27, 1988)* Live Classics ▲ LCL 121 [DDD]
Hindemith, P.:Son in C Vn & Pno, w. Sviatoslav Richter (pno) *(rec Moscow, May 7, 1978)* Live Classics ▲ LCL 161 [ADD]
Hindemith, P.:Son in E Vn & Pno, w. Sviatoslav Richter (pno) *(rec Moscow, May 7, 1978)* Live Classics ▲ LCL 161 [ADD]
Hindemith, P.:Son Vn & Pno, Op. 11/1, w. Sviatoslav Richter (pno) *(rec Moscow, May 7, 1978)* Live Classics ▲ LCL 161 [ADD]
Hindemith, P.:Son Vn & Pno, Op. 11/2, w. Sviatoslav Richter (pno) *(rec Moscow, May 7, 1978)* Live Classics ▲ LCL 161 [ADD]
Merikanto, A.:Con Vn Cl, Horn & Strs, w. E. Brunner (cl), D. Jolley (hn), et al., U. Söderblom (cnd) Ondine ▲ ODE 703–2
Mozart, W.A.:Sons Vn Pno (misc), w. Sviatoslav Richter (pno)—K.304–306 *(rec Small Room of the Conservatory, Moscow, May 16, 1975)* Live Classics ▲ LCL 122 [ADD]
Mozart, W.A.:Sons Vn Pno (misc), w. Sviatoslav Richter (pno)—in B, K.372; in E♭, K.380; in C, K.403; in C, K.404; in B, K.454 *(rec Moscow, May 20, 1975)* Live Classics ("Kagan Edition" series) ▲ 123
Mussorgsky, M.:Sunless, w. G. Vishnevskaya (sop), M. Rostropovich (pno/vc), L. Mogilevskaya (pno) *(rec Jan. 17, 1973)* Russian Disc ▲ RUS 11003 [AAD]
Ravel, M.:Son Vn Vc, w. Natalia Gutman (vc) *(rec Chamber Music Festival Kuhmo, Finland, July 21, 1989)* Live Classics ▲ LCL 121 [DDD]
Schnittke, A.:A Paganini Vn Vox Box 2–▲ CDX 5121 [ADD]
Schubert, Franz:Trio Strs, D.471, w. Yuri Bashmet (va), Natalia Gutman (vc) *(rec Hohenems Schubertiade, June 22, 1988)* Live Classics ("Kagan Edition" series) ▲ 142
Schubert, Franz:Trio Strs, D.581, w. Yuri Bashmet (va), Natalia Gutman (vc) *(rec Hohenems Schubertiade, June 22, 1988)* Live Classics ("Kagan Edition" series) ▲ 142
Shostakovich, D.:Son Vn, w. Sviatoslav Richter (pno) Olympia 5–▲ OLY 5013 [DDD/ADD]
Shostakovich, D.:Son Vn, w. S. Richter (pno) MK ▲ MKA 418014 [DDD]
Shostakovich, D.:Songs Sop, Op. 127, w. G. Vsichnevskaya (sop), M. Rostropovich (pno/vc), L. Mogilevskaya (pno) *(rec Jan. 17, 1973)* Russian Disc ▲ RUS 11003 [AAD]
Sibelius, J.:Con Vn, w. T. Hannikainen (cnd), Finnish RSO *(rec Sibelius Competition, Helsinki, Dec. 8, 1965)* Live Classics ("Kagan Edition" series) ▲ 143
Stravinsky, I.:Songs, w. G. Vsichnevskaya (sop), M. Rostropovich (pno/vc), L. Mogilevskaya (pno)—2 songs *(rec Jan. 17, 1973)* Russian Disc ▲ RUS 11003 [AAD]
Tchaikovsky, P.:Sérénade mélancolique, w. V. Lobanov (pno) Ondine ▲ ODE 733–2 [DDD]
Tchaikovsky, P.:Souvenir d'un lieu cher, w. V. Lobanov (pno) Ondine ▲ ODE 733–2 [DDD]
Tchaikovsky, P.:Valse–Scherzo Vn, w. V. Lobanov (pno) Ondine ▲ ODE 733–2 [DDD]

Kagan, Oleg (vn) (cont.)
Vieru, A.:Con Vn Vc, w. N. Gutman (vc), A. Vieru (cnd), Romanian National RSO Olympia ▲ OCD 409 [AAD]
Yun, I.:Königliches Thema Col Legno ▲ AU 31808

Kagan, Susan (pno)
Mozart, W.A.:Con 11 Pno, w. J. Suk (cnd), Suk CO *(rec Martinů Hall, Lichtenstein Palace, Prague, Jan 3–5, 1995)* Vox Classics ▲ VOX 7526 [DDD]
Mozart, W.A.:Con 12 Pno, w. J. Suk (cnd), Suk CO *(rec Martinů Hall, Lichtenstein Palace, Prague, Jan 3–5, 1995)* Vox Classics ▲ VOX 7526 [DDD]
Mozart, W.A.:Con 14 Pno, w. J. Suk (cnd), Suk CO *(rec Martinů Hall, Lichtenstein Palace, Prague, Jan 3–5, 1995)* Vox Classics ▲ VOX 7526 [DDD]
Rudolph [Archduke Of Austria]:Son Vn, w. J. Suk Koch International Classics ▲ KIC 7082–2 [DDD]

Kahan, Sylvia (pno)
Dashow, J.:Trio 4/3, w. Mia Wu (vn), Lutz Rath (vc) *(rec Studio Wonderland, Rome, June 1993)* Pro Viva ▲ ISPV 177 CD [DDD]

Kahane, Jeffrey (pno)
Bach, J.S.:Inventions (30) Hpd—3 Part, BWV 787–801 Elektra/Nonesuch ▲ 79121–2 [DDD]
Bach, J.S.:Partitas Hpd, BWV 825–830—BWV 828 Elektra/Nonesuch ▲ 79121–2 [DDD]
Bernstein, L.:Son Cl, w. Yo–Yo Ma (vc) [trans Ma for vc & pno] *(rec June 15–19, 1992)* Sony Classical ▲ SK 53126 [DDD] Δ SM 53126 [DDD]
Bernstein, L.:Sym 2, "Age of Anxiety", w. A. Litton (cnd), Bournemouth SO Virgin Classics ▲ CUV 61119
Bernstein, L.:Sym 2, "Age of Anxiety", w. A. Litton (cnd), Bournemouth SO Virgin Classics ▲ CDC 59038
Strauss, R.:Burleske, w. Eugene Espino (timp), J. López–Cobos (cnd), Cincinnati SO *(rec Music Hall, Cincinnati, OH, Oct. 2–3, 1994)* Telarc ▲ CD 80371 [DDD]

Kahler, Laurie (pno)
A Colorado Kind of Christmas, w. Colorado Children's Chorale [cnd:Duain Wolfe], Mike Fitzmaurice (db), Rod Garnet (fl), William Hill (perc), Deborah Schmit–Lobis (pno), Brett Walace (vc), Mary Louise Burke (pno), Helen Hope (hp) *(rec Denver Center Media)* Colorado Children's Chorale ▲ XMAS
Encore, w. Colorado Children's Chorale [cnd:Duain Wolfe], Rick Chinski (gtr), Robert Davine (acc), Laurie Kahler (pno), Samuel Lancaster (pno), Barry Oliver (pno), Marylin Preston (fl), Karen Yonovitz (fl), Peter Cooper (ob), Andy Stevens (cl), Lionel Young (vn), Basil Vendreys (va), Wayne Templeman (vc), Charle *(rec Denver Center Media)* Colorado Children's Chorale ▲ 001

Kahn, Eric Itor (pno)
Kahn, E.I.:Ciaconna dei tempi di guerra CRI ■ C 188
Kahn, E.I.:Inventions (8) CRI ■ C 188
Kahn, E.I.:Short Pieces Pno CRI ■ C 188

Kahn, Joseph (pno)
Brahms, J.:Liebeslieder Waltzes SATB, w. A. Balsam (pno), *(chorus unknown)* [G] *(rec Studio 8–H broadcast, Nov 27, 1948)* RCA Gold Seal 4–▲ 60325–2–RG (m) [ADD] 4–■ 60325–4–RG (CrO2)
Brahms, J.:Liebeslieder Waltzes SATB, w. A. Balsam (pno), W. Preston (cnd), *(chorus unknown)* [G] RCA Gold Seal ▲ 60260–2–RG [ADD] ■ 60260–4–RG (CrO2)

Kahn, Percy (pno)
Joseph Hislop, w. Hislop, Joseph (ten), Piero Coppola (cnd), John Barbirolli (cnd), Jacques Heuvel (cnd), et al. *(rec HMV recordings, 1923–30)* Pearl ▲ PEA 9956 (m) [AAD]
Schumann, R.:Songs, w. R. Tauber (ten)—4 songs—Widmung, Op. 25/1; Der Nussbaum, Op. 25/3; Aus den Östlichen Rosen, Op. 25/25; Mondnacht, Op. 39/5 [G] *(rec 1935/36 for Parlophone)* Pearl ▲ PEA 9370 (m) [AAD]

Kahn, Sue Ann (fl)
Ibert, J.:Chamber Music, w. Eleanor Lawrence (fl), Peggy Schecter (fl), Rie Schmidt (fl), David Krakauer (cl), Lauren Goldstein (bn), Curtis Macomber (vn), Susan Jolles (hp), Frederic Hand (gtr), Andrew Willis (pno)—2 Mouvements; Aria; Histoires; Pastoral; Aria; Entr'acte Albany ▲ TROY 145 [DDD]
Ibert, J.:Entracte, w. Frederic Hand (gtr) Albany ▲ TROY 145 [DDD]
Ibert, J.:Interludes, w. Curtis Macomber (vn), Susan Jolles (hp) Albany ▲ TROY 145 [DDD]
Ibert, J.:Jeux, w. Andrew Willis (pno) Albany ▲ TROY 145 [DDD]
Ibert, J.:Music of, w. C. Schadeberg (sop), E. Lawrence (fl), P. Schechter (fl), R. Schmidt (fl), David Krakauer (cl), L. Goldstein (bn), Curtis Macomber (vn), Susan Jolles (hp), Frederick Hand (gtr), Arthur Willis (pno)—Entr'acte; Jeux; Sonatine; 2 Movements; 2 Interludes; Aria; Pièce for solo Fl; Histoires; 2 Stèles orientées; Pastoral; Aria; Entr'acte Albany ▲ TROY 145
Ibert, J.:Pièce Fl Albany ▲ TROY 145 [DDD]
Ibert, J.:Stèles orientées, w. Christine Schadeberg (sop) Albany ▲ TROY 145 [DDD]
Kraft, L.:Fant 2 Fl & Pno, w. A. Willis (pno) Capstone ▲ CPS 8609 CD
Luening, O.:Third Short Son Fl, w. A. Willis (pno) CRI ■ C 531
Luening, O.:Third Short Son Fl, w. Andrew Willis (pno) CRI ("American Masters" series) ▲ CD 716 [ADD]
Riegger, W.:Suite Fl CRI ■ C 531
Rochberg, G.:Between 2 Worlds, w. A. Willis (pno) CRI ■ C 531
Schickele, P.:Spring Serenade, w. A. Willis (pno) CRI ■ C 531
Schoenberg, A.:Pierrot lunaire, w. Maureen McNalley (nar), Dwight Peltzer (pno), Eric Rosenblith (vn/va), Chris Finckel (vc), Anand Devendra (cl/b cl), J. Thome (cnd), Orch of Our Time Vox Box 2–▲ CDX 5144

Kain, Timothy (gtr)
The Mantis & the Moon:Guitar Duets from around the World, w. John Williams (gtr) Sony Classical ▲ SK 62007
Taylor & Kain, w. Virginia Taylor (fl) Tall Poppies ▲ TP 3 [DDD]

Kaine, Carmel (vn)
Bach, J.S.:Con 1 for 2 Hpds, w. Tess Miller (ob), Christopher Hogwood (bc), Nicholas Kraemer (bc), N. Marriner (cnd), Academy of St. Martin in the Fields [trans for vn & ob] *(rec St. John's, Smith Square, London, Aug 1974 & Feb 1975)* Boston Skyline ▲ BSD 127 [ADD]
Bach, J.S.:Con 2 for 3 Hpds, w. Ronald Thomas (vn), Richard Studt (vn), Christopher Hogwood (bc), Nicholas Kraemer (bc), N. Marriner (cnd), Academy of St. Martin in the Fields [trans for 3 vn] *(rec St. John's, Smith Square, London, Aug 1974 & Feb 1975)* Boston Skyline ▲ BSD 127 [ADD]

Kainrath, Peter Paul (pno)
Feinberg, S.:Preludes, Op. 15 Ermitage ▲ ERM 419
Feinberg, S.:Son 11 Pno Ermitage ▲ ERM 419
Mussorgsky, M.:Songs & Dances [trans Feinberg] Ermitage ▲ ERM 419
Prokofiev, S.:Son 4 Pno Ermitage ▲ ERM 419
Prokofiev, S.:Tales of an Old Grandmother Ermitage ▲ ERM 419

Kairoff, Peter (pno)
Beach, A.M.C.:Son Vn, w. Sarah Johnson (vn) Albany ▲ TROY 150 [DDD]
Foote, A.:Ballad, w. Sarah Johnson (vn) Albany ▲ TROY 150 [DDD]
Foote, A.:Melody, w. Sarah Johnson (vn) Albany ▲ TROY 150 [DDD]
Foote, A.:Pieces Vn & Pno, Op. 9, w. Sarah Johnson (vn) Albany ▲ TROY 150 [DDD]

Kaiser, Hans–Jürgen (org)
Bach, J.S.:Chorale Settings, BWV 651–668 [Jann Org of St. Peters's & Paul's at Bad Soden–Salmunster] Deutsche Schallplatten ▲ DS 1056–2
Bach, J.S.:Org Music (misc) [Jann Org, St. Peter's & Paul's, Bad Soden–Salmünster]—Toccata & Fugue, BWV 538; Triosonate, BWV 530; Toccata & Fugue, BWV 565; Chorale setting, BWV 662 Deutsche Schallplatten ▲ DS 1056–2 [DDD]
Bach, J.S.:Toccata & Fugue Org, BWV 538, "Dorian" [Jann Org of St. Peters's & Paul's at Bad Soden–Salmunster] Deutsche Schallplatten ▲ DS 1056–2
Bach, J.S.:Toccata & Fugue Org, BWV 565 [Jann Org of St. Peters's & Paul's at Bad Soden–Salmunster] Deutsche Schallplatten ▲ DS 1056–2
Bach, J.S.:Trio Sons Org, BWV 525–530 [Jann Org of St. Peters's & Paul's at Bad Soden–Salmunster]—BWV 530 Deutsche Schallplatten ▲ DS 1056–2
Couperin, F.:Messe solemnelle [Jann Org, St. Peter's & Paul's, Bad Soden–Salmünster]—Glorias 1–9 Deutsche Schallplatten ▲ DS 1056–2 [DDD]

Kaiser, Hans-Jürgen (org) (cont.)
Couperin, F.:Org Music [Jann Org of St. Peters's & Paul's at Bad Soden-Salmunster]—Gloria I-IX from the Organ Mass Deutsche Schallplatten ▲ DS 1056-2
Guilmant, A.:Son 1 Org Deutsche Schallplatten ▲ DS 1055-2 [DDD]
Liszt, F.:Prelude & Fugue on the name B-A-C-H [Klais Org of Fritzlar Cathedral] Deutsche Schallplatten ▲ DS 1055-2
Mendelssohn, F.:Sons Org—Nos 2 & 3 [Klais Org of Fritzlar Cathedral] Deutsche Schallplatten ▲ DS 1055-2
Vierne, L.:Carillon de Westminster Deutsche Schallplatten ▲ DS 1055-2 [DDD]
Kaiser, Karl (fl)
Abel, C.F.:Cons Fl, K.46-50, w. M. Schneider (cnd), La Stagione—Nos. 1 in C, 2 in e, 3 in D, 5 in G CPO ▲ CPO 999208 [DDD]
Kakagawa, M. (fl)
Shinohara, M.:Tabiyuki, w. A. Ogawa (mez), I. Tsuji (ob), T. Takahashi (cl), K. Okazaki (fagotto), G. Kitamura (tpt), A. Murata (trbn), S. Eiso (perc), S. Ueki (vn), A. Nakakoji (va), S. Katsuta (vc), M. Komuro (contrabass), K. Komatsu (cnd) *(rec live Casals Hall, Tokyo, Mar. 5, 1994)* Camerata ▲ 30CM 375 [DDD]
Kakehashi, Ikuo (perc/kbd)
Peebles, S.:Tomoé, w. Hiromi Yoshida (shô/û), Sarah Peebles (kbd/elec/perc/shô) *(rec live, Shukôji Temple, Kawasaki, Sept 25, 1993)* Innova ▲ 506
Kakehashi, Ikuo (shô)
Peebles, S.:Phoenix Calling, w. Sarah Peebles (shô), Andy Morris (perc), Bugaku Percussion Ensemble *(rec live, Shukôji Temple, Kawasaki)* Innova ▲ 506
Kakuska, Thomas (va)
Mozart, W.A.:Sinf concertante Vn, K.364, w. J. Suk (vn), J. Suk (cnd), Suk CO *(rec 1989)* Vanguard Classics ▲ OVC 7001 [DDD]
Schoenberg, A.:Verklärte Nacht, w. Valentin Erben (vc), Arditti String Quartet Montaigne 2-▲ MO 782025
Kalacheva, G. (vn)
Levina, Z.:Sons Vn & Pno, w. A. Bakhchiev (pno)—1 Son., "Poem" Russian Disc ▲ RUS 11 382 [DDD]
Kalafusz, Hans (vn)—see ORCHESTRAS & ENSEMBLES German String Trio
Kaler, Ilya (vn)
Barkauskas, V.:Partita Vn *(rec New Hope Methodist Church, Methuen, MA, May 24-25, 1995)* Ongaku ▲ 024-103 [DDD]
Brahms, J.:Con Vn & Vc, "Double Con", w. Maria Kliegel (vc), A. Constantine (cnd), Irish National SO *(rec National Concert Hall, Dublin, May 16-17, 1994)* Naxos ▲ 8.550938 [DDD]
Dvořák, A.:Con Vn, w. C. Kolchinsky (cnd), Polish National RSO Katowice *(rec Polish Radio Concert Hall, Katowice, Mar. 28-31, 1994)* Naxos ▲ 8.550758 [DDD]
Dvořák, A.:Romance Vn, w. C. Kolchinsky (cnd), Polish National RSO Katowice *(rec Polish Radio Concert Hall, Katowice, Mar. 28-31, 1994)* Naxos ▲ 8.550758 [DDD]
Glazunov, A.:Con Vn, w. C. Kolchinsky (cnd), Polish National RSO Katowice *(rec Polish Radio Concert Hall, Katowice, Mar. 28-31, 1994)* Naxos ▲ 8.550758 [DDD]
Hindemith, P.:Son Vn, Op. 31/1 *(rec New Hope Methodist Church, Methuen, MA, May 24-25, 1995)* Ongaku ▲ 024-103 [DDD]
Hindemith, P.:Son Vn, Op. 31/2 *(rec New Hope Methodist Church, Methuen, MA, May 24-25, 1995)* Ongaku ▲ 024-103 [DDD]
Martinon, J.:Sonatina 5 Vn *(rec New Hope Methodist Church, Methuen, MA, May 24-25, 1995)* Ongaku ▲ 024-103 [DDD]
Paganini, N.:Caprices Vn *(rec Oct. 19-22, 1992)* Naxos ▲ 8.550717 [DDD]
Paganini, N.:Con 1 Vn, w. S. Gunzenhauser (cnd), Polish National RSO Katowice *(rec Sept. 3-6, 1992)* Naxos ▲ 8.550649 [DDD]
Paganini, N.:Con 2 Vn, w. S. Gunzenhauser (cnd), Polish National RSO Katowice *(rec Sept. 3-6, 1992)* Naxos ▲ 8.550649 [DDD]
Prokofiev, S.:Son solo Vn, Op. 115 *(rec New Hope Methodist Church, Methuen, MA, May 24-25, 1995)* Ongaku ▲ 024-103 [DDD]
Violin Suites, w. Leonid Blok (pno) Art & Electronics ▲ AED 10527 [DDD]
Ysaÿe, E.:Sons Vn *(rec New Hope Methodist Church, Methuen, MA, May 24-25, 1995)* Ongaku ▲ 024-103 [DDD]
Kalichstein, J. (vc)—see ORCHESTRAS & ENSEMBLES Kalichstein-Laredo-Robinson Trio
Kalichstein, Joseph (pno)
Brahms, J.:Trios (3) Pno, w. J. Laredo (vn), S. Robinson (vc) Vox Box 3-▲ CD3X 3029 [DDD]
Dvořák, A.:Trio 4 Pno, "Dumky", w. J. Laredo (vn), S. Robinson (vc) Vox Box 3-▲ CD3X 3029 [DDD]
Liszt, F.:Song Transcriptions—Schumann:Widmung; Schubert:Ständchen Audiofon ▲ CD 72028
Mendelssohn, F.:Con 1 Pno, w. J. Laredo (cnd), Scottish CO Nimbus ▲ NI 5112 [DDD]
Mendelssohn, F.:Con 2 Pno, w. J. Laredo (cnd), Scottish CO Nimbus ▲ NI 5112 [DDD]
Mendelssohn, F.:Trio 1 Pno, w. J. Laredo (vn), S. Robinson (vc) Vox Box 3-▲ CD3X 3029 [DDD]
Mendelssohn, F.:Trio 2 Pno, w. J. Laredo (vn), S. Robinson (vc) Vox Box 3-▲ CD3X 3029 [DDD]
Recital Audiofon ▲ CD 72028
Schubert, Franz:Fant Vn, D.934, w. S. Luca (vn) Elektra/Nonesuch ■ 71370-4
Schubert, Franz:Rondo Vn, D.895, w. S. Luca (vn) Elektra/Nonesuch ■ 71370-4
Schubert, Franz:Sonatina Vn, D.384, w. S. Luca (vn) Elektra/Nonesuch ■ 71370-4
Schumann, R.:Son 1 Pno Audiofon ▲ CD 72028
Kalish, Gilbert (pno)—see also ORCHESTRAS & ENSEMBLES Contemporary Chamber Ensemble, Boehm Quintet members, Contemporary Chamber Players
Bartók, B.:Son for 2 Pnos, w. L. Luvisi (pno), R. Fitz (perc), Gottlieb (perc) *(rec Feb. 1, 1993)* Delos ▲ DE 3151 [DDD]
Bassett, L.:Sxt Vns, w. John Graham (va), Concord String Quartet *(rec Baltimore, MD, May 19, 1975* CRI ▲ CD 677 [ADD]
Beethoven, L. van:Sons Vc (comp), w. Joel Krosnick (vc) *(rec Recital Hall of the Staller Center, SUNY-Stony Brook, May 28-June 1, 1994)* Arabesque 2-▲ ARA 6656-2 [DDD]
Beethoven, L. van:Vars on "Ein Mädchen oder Weibchen" from Mozart's *Die Zauberflöte*, w. Joel Krosnick (vc) *(rec Recital Hall of the Staller Center, SUNY-Stony Brook, May 28-June 1, 1994)* Arabesque 2-▲ ARA 6656-2 [DDD]
Beethoven, L. van:Vars on "See, the Conquering Hero Comes" from Handel's *Judas Maccabaeus*, w. Joel Krosnick (vc) *(rec Recital Hall of the Staller Center, SUNY-Stony Brook, May 28-June 1, 1994)* Arabesque 2-▲ ARA 6656-2 [DDD]
Beethoven, L. van:Vars on "Bei Männern" from Mozart's *Die Zauberflöte*, w. Joel Krosnick (vc) *(rec Recital Hall of the Staller Center, SUNY-Stony Brook, May 28-June 1, 1994)* Arabesque 2-▲ ARA 6656-2 [DDD]
Berger, A.:Duos, w. J. Smirnoff (vn), C. Oldfather (pno), J. Krosnick (vc), P. Lanini (ob), D. Stewart (cl)—Duo No. 1 for Violin & Piano (1948); Duo for Cello & Piano (1951); Duo for Oboe & Clarinet (1952) New World ▲ NW 360-2 [DDD]
Biscardi, C.:At the Still Point, w. Jeanne Ingraham (vn), Susan Palma (fl), P. Dunkel (cnd), American Composers Orch *(rec Whitman Auditorium, Brooklyn College, NY, Feb. 1982)* CRI ▲ CD 686 [ADD]
Brahms, J.:Songs, w. J. DeGaetani (mez)—Eight Gypsy Songs; Ernste Gesänge (4), Op. 121; Fünf Gesänge, Op. 72 [G] Arabesque ▲ Z 6141
Cage, J.:Nocturne, w. Paul Zukofsky (vn) *(rec Paul Hall, Julliard School of Music, May 21, 1972)* CP² ▲ CP2 108 [AAD]
Carter, E.:Double Con, w. P. Jacobs (hpd), A. Weisberg (cnd), Contemporary Chamber Players Elektra/Nonesuch ▲ 79183-2
Carter, E.:Son Vc, w. Joel Krosnick (vc) Arabesque ▲ ARA 6682
Carter, E.:Songs, w. J. DeGaetani (mez)—2 Songs—Dust of snow; The rose family Elektra/Nonesuch ▲ 79248-2-ZK ■ 79248-4-AW
Chausson, E.:Songs, w. Jan DeGaetani (mez)—Amour d'antan, Op. 8/2; Le Charme, Op. 2/2; Le Temps des lilas, Op. 19; Les Papillons, Op. 2/3; Le Colibri, Op. 2/7; La Caravane, Op. 14 *(rec New York, Apr. 1979)* Arabesque ▲ Z 6673 [ADD]
Copland, A.:Vars Pno Elektra/Nonesuch ▲ 79168-2 [DDD] ■ 79168-4 [D]
Crumb, G.:Apparition, w. J. DeGaetani (mez)—[E] Bridge ▲ BCD 9006 [ADD]

Kalish, Gilbert (pno) (cont.)
Crumb, G.:Apparition, w. J. DeGaetani (mez) [E] *(rec 10/82)* Bridge ▲ BCD 9028 [ADD]
Crumb, G.:Music for a Summer Evening (Makrokosmos III), w. J. Freeman (pno), R. DesRoches (perc), R. Fitz (perc) Elektra/Nonesuch ▲ 79149-2 [AAD]
Debussy, C.:Chansons de Bilitis, w. Jan DeGaetani (mez) *(rec New York, Nov, 1983)* Arabesque ▲ Z 6673 [ADD]
Debussy, C.:En blanc et noir, w. P. Jacobs (pno) *(rec public performance recording)* Elektra/Nonesuch ▲ 79161-2 [AAD]
Debussy, C.:Fêtes galantes 1, w. Jan DeGaetani (mez) *(rec New York, Nov, 1983)* Arabesque ▲ Z 6673 [ADD]
Debussy, C.:Fêtes galantes 2, w. Jan DeGaetani (mez) *(rec New York, Nov, 1983)* Arabesque ▲ Z 6673 [ADD]
Debussy, C.:Songs, w. Jan DeGaetani (mez)—Fêtes galantes I & II; Chansons de Bilitis *(rec New York, Nov 1983)* Arabesque ▲ Z6673 [ADD]
Feldman, Morton:Vertical Thoughts II, w. Paul Zukofsky (vn) *(rec Paul Hall, Julliard School of Music, May 21, 1972)* CP² ▲ CP2 108 [AAD]
Foster, S.C.:Songs, w. Jan DeGaetani (mez), L. Guinn (bar) Elektra/Nonesuch ▲ 79158-2 [AAD] als
Foster, S.C.:Songs, w. Jan DeGaetani (mez), L. Guinn (bar), Washington Camerata Chorus Elektra/Nonesuch ■ 71333-4
Harbison, J.:Qnt for 2 Vns, w. Boston Sym Chamber Players Elektra/Nonesuch ▲ 79189-2 ■ 79189-4
Haydn, J.:Sons Pno—Nos. 36, 40, 41, 49, 50 Elektra/Nonesuch ▲ 79162-2 [AAD]
Ives, C.:Son 2 Pno Elektra/Nonesuch ▲ 71337-2-J
Ives, C.:Songs, w. J. DeGaetani (mez)—Down east; Two little flowers; Tom sails away; The see'r; Songs my mother taught me; The side show; The white gulls; West London; Afterglow [E] Bridge ▲ BCD 9006 [ADD]
Ives, C.:Songs, w. J. DeGaetani (mez)—The Housatonic at Stockbridge; Memories; A—Very Pleasant; B—Rather Sad; From "Paracelsus"; The Things Our Fathers Loved; Ann Street; The Innate; The Circus Band; In the Mornin'; Serenity; Majority; Thoreau; At the River; The Indians; The Cage; Like a Sick Eagle; A Christmas Carol; A Farewell to Land Elektra/Nonesuch ▲ 71325-2 ■ 71325-4
Ives, C.:Trio Pno, w. R. Lefkowitz (vn), Yo-Yo Ma (vc) *(rec June 15-19, 1992)* Sony Classical ▲ SK 53126 [DDD]
Martino, D.:Trio Cl, w. Arthur Bloom (cl), Paul Zukofsky (vn) CRI ▲ CD 693 [ADD]
Mussorgsky, M.:Nursery, w. Jan DeGaetani (mez) *(rec New York, Jan 23-25, 1984)* Arabesque ▲ Z6674 [ADD]
Poulenc, F.:Son Vc, w. Joel Krosnick (vc) Arabesque ▲ ARA 6682
Prokofiev, S.:Son Vc, w. Joel Krosnick (vc) Arabesque ▲ ARA 6682
Rachmaninoff, S.:Songs, w. Jan DeGaetani (mez)—Oh, Do Not Grieve, Op. 14/8; Lilacs, Op. 21/5; Christ Is Risen, Op. 26/6; The Answer, Op. 21/4; To the Children, Op. 26/7; A Passing Breeze, Op. 34/4; How Long Since Love, Op. 14/3; The Harvest of Sorrow, Op. 4/5 *(rec New York, Apr 1979)* Arabesque ▲ Z 6674 [ADD]
Ravel, M.:Histoires naturelles, w. Jan DeGaetani (mez) *(rec New York, Nov, 1983)* Arabesque ▲ Z 6673 [ADD]
Riegger, W.:Music of, w. New York Woodwind Quintet—Con Pno Ww; Tone Pictures Pno; Duos for 3 Winds; The New and Old; 3 Canons; Petite Etude; Qnt Ww, Op. 51 Bridge ▲ 9068
Schoenberg, A.:Book of the Hanging Gardens, w. J. DeGaetani (mez) [G] Elektra/Nonesuch ▲ 79237-2-ZK
Schubert, Franz:Pieces Pno, D.946 Elektra/Nonesuch ■ N5-71386
Schubert, Franz:Son Pno, D.840 Elektra/Nonesuch ■ N5-71386
Schubert, Franz:Songs (misc), w. J. DeGaetani (mez)—9 Songs [G] *(rec ca. 1975)* Elektra/Nonesuch ▲ 79263-2
Schumann, R.:Songs, w. J. DeGaetani (mez)—4 songs from Op. 98a [G] Elektra/Nonesuch ▲ 71364-2
Schumann, R.:Vocal Duets, w. J. DeGaetani (mez), L. Guinn (bar)—12 duets Elektra/Nonesuch ▲ 71364-2
Shapey, R.:Kroslish Son, w. J. Krosnick (vc) New World ▲ NW 355-2 [DDD]
Silver, S.:Preludes Pno—La mer à Cassis; La pendule; La descente vers l'enfers; Dans un forêt demiE brûlée; Là, tout n'est qu'ordre et beauté, luxe, calme et volupté; Vers le paradis de mes rêves *(rec Recital Hall, Staller Center, SUNY, Stony Brook, New York, June 5, 1994)* CRI ▲ CD 708 [DDD]
Silver, S.:Son Vc, w. T. Eddy (vc) CRI ▲ CD 590 [DDD]
Tchaikovsky, P.:Songs, w. Jan DeGaetani (mez)—A Summer Love Tale, Op. 6/2; Blue Eyes of Spring; The Sounds of Day Are Still, Op. 47/4; Was I Not a Blade of Grass?, Op. 47/7; From the Day That I Was Born, Op. 27/5; The Canary, Op. 25/4; It Was in the Early Spring, Op. 38/2; Invocation to Sleep, Op. 27/1; Take away My Heart; None but the Lonely Heart, Op. 6/6 *(rec American Academy of Arts & Letters, New York, Jan 23-25, 1984)* Arabesque ▲ Z 6674 [ADD]
Wolf, H.:Spanisches Liederbuch (sels), w. J. DeGaetani (mez)—16 sels. [G] *(rec ca. 1974)* Elektra/Nonesuch ▲ 79263-2
Kallaur, Barbara (fl)
Geminiani, F.:The Enchanted Forest, w. Elizabeth Wilcock (vn), Stanley Ritchie (vn), Susie Napper (vc), Janet See (fl), Patrick Wedd (hpd), J.E. Gardiner (cnd), CBC Vancouver SO CBC ▲ 5163 [DDD]
Kallenberg, Ben (vn)
Schnittke, A.:Sym 1, w. C.-A. Dominique (pno), A. Lännerholm (trbn), L. Segerstam (cnd), Royal Stockholm PO *(rec Oct. 14, 1992)* BIS ▲ CD 577 [DDD]
Kallhed, Joakim (pno)
Biscardi, C.:Son Fl & Pno, w. Göran Marcusson (fl) Intim Musik ▲ INT 34
Burton, E.:Sonatina Fl, w. Göran Marcusson (fl) Intim Musik ▲ INT 34
Copland, A.:Duo Fl, w. Göran Marcusson (fl) Intim Musik ▲ INT 34
Doppler, A.F.:Rigoletto-fant, w. Göran Marcusson (fl) Intim ▲ INT 40
Gaubert, P.:Madrigal, w. Göran Marcusson (fl) Intim ▲ INT 40
Jolivet, A.:Chant de Linos, w. Göran Marcusson (fl) Intim ▲ INT 40
Larsson, L.-E.:Concertinos, w. Jan Stigmer (vn), Per-Ola Lindberg (va), Bjøorg Vaernes (vc), Ingalill Hillerud (db), Camerata Romana—Nos. 8-12 Intim Musik ▲ INT 31
Liebermann, L.:Son Fl, w. Göran Marcusson (fl) Intim Musik ▲ INT 34
Martinů, B.:Son 1 Fl, w. Göran Marcusson (fl) Intim ▲ INT 40
Piston, W.:Son Fl, w. Göran Marcusson (fl) Intim Musik ▲ INT 34
Prokofiev, S.:Son Fl, w. Göran Marcusson (fl) Intim ▲ INT 40
Kallir, Lilian (pno)
Saint-Saëns, C.:Carnival of the Animals, w. Claude Frank (pno), E. Ormandy (cnd), Philadelphia Orch Sony Classical ("Essential Classics" series) ▲ SBK 62638 ■ SBT 62638
Kálmán, Péter (vl/vle/lt/b lt/perc/voc)—see ORCHESTRAS & ENSEMBLES Vagantes
Kalmanoff, Martin (pno)
Verdi, G.:Otello (sels), w. Kenneth Lane (ten)—Dio! mi potevi; Niun mi tema Valhalla ▲ VRCD 1595 [ADD]
Wagner, R.:Arias & Scenes, w. Kenneth Lane (ten), Otto Herz (pno), Levering Rothfuss (pno)—Rienzi's Prayer [from Rienzi]; In fernem Land, Mein Liebe Schwan [from Lohengrin]; Siegmund heiss' ich! [from Die Walküre]; Nothung! Nothung!, Schmiede mein Hammer! [from Siegfried]; O König!, Die alte Weise, O diese Sonne! [from Tristan und Isolde]; Prize Song [from Die Meistersinger]; Siegfried's Narration, Brünnhilde! Heilige Braut! [from Götterdämmerung]; Amfortas! Die Wunde!, Nur eine Waffe taugt [from Parsifal] Valhalla VRCD 1595 [ADD]
Kaltoft, Erik (pno)—see also ORCHESTRAS & ENSEMBLES LINensemble
Nielsen, T.:Paessagi, w. Frode Stangaard (pno) Point ▲ PCD 5089

Kaltoft, Erik (pno) (cont.)
Stolarczyk, W.:Earth Air Fire Water, w. Amalie Malling (pno), John Damgaard (pno), Anne Øland (pno), Teddy Teirup (pno), Friedrich Gürtler (pno), Rosalind Bevan (pno), Poul Rosenbaum (pno), Rodolfo Llambias (pno), Bella Horn-Ribera (pno), Anders Riber (pno), Elisabeth Sigurdsson (pno), Thomas Tronheim (pno), Elsebeth Broderson (pno), Jørgen Hald Nielsen (pno), Aino Gilemann (pno), Birgit Kjær (pno), Jørgen Thomsen (pno), Gunhild Donslund (pno), Henrik Bo Hansen (pno), Lone Karlsson (pno), Erik Fessel (pno), Lasse Nilsson (pno), Janos Ferenczi (pno), Erik Bach (pno), Axel Momme (pno), Arne de Cros Dich (pno), Sven Micha Slot (pno), Hanne Bramsen Buhl (pno), Lili Olesen (pno), Susannah Carlsson (pno), Ulla Erml (pno), Vagn Sørensen (pno), Leif Greibe (pno), Bodil Krogh (pno), Kirsten Ottosen (pno), Inger Bergenholz (pno), Karsten Gylendorf (pno), Bjørn Elkjær (pno), Jacob Bjørn Jensen (pno), Jørgen Kaad (pno), Anne Marie Hjelm (pno), Carl Ulrik Munk Andersen (pno), Poul Lumbye (pno), Oluf Hildebrandt Nielsen (pno), Joachim Olsson (pno), Peter Pade Ramsøe Jacobsen (pno), Astrid Pollmann (pno), Jette Borsch (pno), Kirsten Karlshøj (pno), Maria Teresa Assing (pno), Allan Dahl Hansen (pno), Johan Hugossen (pno), Tine Fenger Pederson (pno), Arne Jørgen Fæø (pno), Anja Høgsted (pno), Anne Sophie Parbo (pno), Inga Lindmark (pno), Teresa Drabik Stathakis (pno), Anne Ruth Ferenczi (pno), Irene Hasager (pno), Yuka Ichikawa (pno), Birgitte Baur (pno), Malene Thastum (pno), Jens E. Rasmussen (pno), Birgitte Zielke (pno), Claus Zielke (pno), Stefan Kasch (pno), Bin Qiao (pno), Inger Johanne Teirup (pno), Lindy Rosborg (pno), Liisa Heininen (pno), David Højer (pno), Ellen Refstrup (pno), Thomas K. Søorensen (pno), Erik Kure (pno), Michael Rauff (pno), Jan beck Eriksson (pno), Tanja Zapolski (pno), Vibeke Skagbo (pno), Pål Eide Lindtner (pno), Ha-Young Sul (pno), Benedicte Palko (pno), Inke Kesseler (pno), Anne Marie Meineche (pno), Sverre Larsen (pno), Kasper Peter Bach (pno), Elisabetta Eliseo (pno), Olga Magieres (pno), Carl Erik Kühl (pno), Thorkild Borup Nielsen (pno), Valeria Zanini (pno), Lars Stenhoft (perc), Dennis Boel (perc), Winnie Dahlgren (perc), Susanne Vind (perc), Claus Byrith (elec), Anne Marie Storm (elec), J. Ribera (cnd) *(rec live, Koldinghaus Castle, Denmark, May 2, 1996)* Danica ▲ DCD 1996

Kalvelage, Elzbieta (pno)—see also ORCHESTRAS & ENSEMBLES Cologne Piano Duo
Rossini, G.:Péchés de vieillesse (sels), w. M. Castets (sop), M. Georg (mez), J.-L. Maurette (ten), M. Brodard (bar), R. Nolte (bass), C. Spering (org), M. Jorand (perc), Cologne Chorus Musicus—Toast pour le nouvel an, Roméo, La Grande Coquette, Un sou, Chanson de Zora, La Nuit de Noël, Le Dodo des enfants, Le Lazzarone, Adieux à la vie!, Soupirs et sourire, L'Orpheline du Tyrol, Choeur de chasseurs démocrates; *Morceaux réservés*—Ave Maria, Les Amants de Séville, Le Chant des Titans, Chant funèbre [F] *(rec Aug. 1992)* Opus 111 ▲ OPS 30-70 [DDD]

Kalyanov, Sergei (vc)
Petukhov, M.:Elégie romantique, w. Sergei Girshenko (vn), Mikhail Petukhov (pno) *(rec Great Hall of Moscow Conservatory, July 25 & Aug 10, 1995)* Pavane ▲ ADW 7365 [DDD]

Kam, Dennis (pno)
Kam, D.:Fant Vars, w. Monserrat Cadiz (fl) *(rec Studio Center, Miami)* Capstone ▲ CPS 8631

Kam, Sharon (cl)
Penderecki, K.:Qt Cl, w. Christoph Poppen (vn), Kim Kashkashian (va), Boris Pergamenschikov (vc) *(rec National Philharmonic Hall, Warsaw, Poland, Nov. 23, 1993)* Sony Classical ▲ SK 66284 [DDD]

Kamal (syn)
Classics for Love Nightingale ▲ HGH 341 [DDD]

Kamasa, Stefan (va)
Penderecki, K.:Con Va, w. A. Wit (cnd), Polish National RSO Katowice Polskie Nagrania ▲ PLN 20 [AAD]

Kamata, Mayumi (hpd)
Schnittke, A.:Hymns Vc, w. T. Thedéen (vc), E. Radoukanov (db), C. Davidsson (bn), I. Fredlund (hp), A. Holdar (tubular bells / timp), A. Loguin (tubular bells) BIS ▲ CD 507 [DDD]
Schnittke, A.:Hymns Vc, w. Torleif Thedéen (vc), Entcho Rdoukanov (db), Christian Davidsson (bn), Ingegerd Fredlund (hp), Anders Holdar (tubular bells/timp), Anders Loguin (tubular bells) BIS ("BIS Twins" series) 2-▲ CD 437/507

Kamata, Yoshiaki (gtr)
Domeniconi, C.:Koyunbaba *(rec Chichibu Myuzu Park Ongaku-do, July 11-15, 1995)* Camerata ▲ 30CM 412 [DDD]
Dyens, R.:Libra Sonatine *(rec Chichibu Myuzu Park Ongaku-do, July 11-15, 1995)* Camerata ▲ 30CM 412 [DDD]
Dyens, R.:Saudade 3 *(rec Chichibu Myuzu Park Ongaku-do, July 11-15, 1995)* Camerata ▲ 30CM 412 [DDD]
Ginastera, A.:Son Gtr *(rec Chichibu Myuzu Park Ongaku-do, July 11-15, 1995)* Camerata ▲ 30CM 412 [DDD]
Kleynjans, F.:Arabesque en forme de caprice sur le tombeau de Tarrega *(rec Chichibu Myuzu Park Ongaku-do, July 11-15, 1995)* Camerata ▲ 30CM 412 [DDD]

Kameda, Mayumi (pno)
Orff, C.:Carmina burana, w. Brigitte Fournier (sop), Peter Sigrist (ten), Michel Brodard (bar), Jean-Jacques Balet (pno), Geneva Percussion Ensemble [version for 2 pnos & perc] Cascavelle ▲ CVL 1009 [DDD]
Rogg, L.:Music of, w. M. Larrieu (fl), T. Friedli (cl), J.-P. Goy (ob), J.-J. Balet (pno), L. Rogg (syn), M. Kameda (piano) *(8 Etudes [1990]; Jazzic J.-J. Balet (piano) (Cinq petites pièces lyriques [1952]; Trois pièces [1952]; Valse [1952]; Cinq petites géométries [1958]),* Kameda, Balet *(Face à face for 2 Pianos [1987]),* J.-P. Goy, L. Rogg *(Pièce for Oboe & Synthesizer [1991]),* T. Friedli *(Pièce for solo Clarinet [1986]); M. Larrieu (Suite for solo Flute [1991])* BIS ▲ CD 546 [DDD]

Kamei, Yukiko (vn)
Franck, C.:Son Vn, w. Chitose Okashiro (pno) *(rec SUNY Purchase Studio C, Aug. 15 & 16, 1994)* ProPiano ▲ PPR 224505 [DDD]
Lazarof, H.:Duo Solitaire, w. Jeffrey Solow (vc) Laurel ▲ LR 856 [DDD]
Lazarof, H.:Lyric Suite Laurel ▲ LR 843 [DDD]
Lazarof, H.:Oct Strs, w. Peter Marsh (vn), Yoko Matsuda (vn), Miwako Watanabe (vn), Paul Silverthorne (va), Milton Thomas (va), Godfried Hoogeveen (vc), David Speltz (vc), H. Lazarof (cnd) Laurel ▲ LR 843 [DDD]
Taneyev, S.:Qnt Pno Strs, w. J. Lowenthal (pno), P. Rosenthal (vn), M. Thompson (va), S. Kates (vc) Arabesque ▲ Z 6539 [DDD]
Walton, W.:Son Vn & Pno, w. C. Okashiro (pno) *(rec Purchase, NY, Aug. 15 & 16, 1994)* Pro Piano ▲ PPR 224505 [DDD]
Walton, W.:Son Vn & Pno, w. Chitose Okashiro (pno) *(rec SUNY Purchase Studio C, Aug. 15 & 16, 1994)* ProPiano ▲ PPR 224505 [DDD]
Walton, W.:Vars Vn, w. C. Okashiro (pno) *(rec Purchase, NY, Aug. 15 & 16, 1994)* Pro Piano ▲ PPR 224505 [DDD]

Kaminaga, Yoshie (pno)—see ORCHESTRAS & ENSEMBLES Orphée Piano & Wind Quintet

Kaminkovsky, Rimma (vn)
Caplet, A.:Conte fantastique, w. A. Giles (hp), R. Mozes (vn), Y. Kaminkovsky (va), Y. Alperin (vc) PWK Classics ▲ PWK 1141 [DDD]
Ravel, M.:Intro & Allegro, w. A. Giles (hp), E. Talmi (fl), A. Arnheim (cl), R. Mozes (vn), Y. Kaminkovsky (va), Y. Alperin (vc) PWK Classics ▲ PWK 1141 [DDD]

Kaminkovsky, Yuval (va)
Caplet, A.:Conte fantastique, w. A. Giles (hp), R. Kaminkovsky (vn), R. Mozes (vn), Y. Alperin (vc) PWK Classics ▲ PWK 1141 [DDD]
Ravel, M.:Intro & Allegro, w. A. Giles (hp), E. Talmi (fl), A. Arnheim (cl), R. Kaminkovsky (vn), R. Mozes (vn), Y. Alperin (vc) PWK Classics ▲ PWK 1141 [DDD]

Kamins, Benjamin (bn)
Mozart, W.A.:Con Bn, w. C. Eschenbach (cnd), Houston SO *(rec Stude Concert Hall, Shephard School of Music, Rice Univ, July 12-16, 1993)* IMP ("Masters" series) ▲ IMP MCD 91

Kamiya, Ikuyo (pno)
Noda, T.:Concerto Pno, w. T. Otaka (cnd), NHK SO Camerata ▲ 32CM 58

Kammen, Shira (h-g)—see ORCHESTRAS & ENSEMBLES Project Ars Nova Ensemble

Kammen, Shira (instr)
Lo Gai Saber:Troubadours and Minstrels, 1100-1300, w. J. Cohen (cnd), Camerata Mediterranea, Anne Azema (voc), François Harismendy (voc), Jean-Luc Madier (voc), Cheryl Ann Fulton (hp), Joel Cohen (instr) Erato ▲ 2292-45647-2 [DDD]

Kammen, Shira (rebec/vielle/hp)
The Unicorn:Myth & Miracle in Medieval France (1200-1300), w. Anne Azema (sop), C. Ann Fulton (hps), Jesse Lepkoff (fl) Erato ▲ 94380 [DDD]

Kammen, Shira (vielle/fid)
World's Bliss:Medieval Songs of Love & Death, w. John Fleagle (sgr/gothic hp/lt/fid/sinfonia/bodhran) *(rec 1st & 2nd Church, Marlborough St., Boston, MA; Church of the Redeemer, Chestnut Hill, MA; July 27 & 28, 1995 & Jan)* Archetype ▲ 60103 [DDD]

Kammen, Shira (vielle/rebec)
Jewels of the Sephardim, Vol. 2:Wings of Time—The Sephardic Legacy of Multi-Cultural Medieval Spain, w. L. Pomerantz, (vocs/period dlc), P. Maund (perc), K. Higginson (rcr) Songbird ▲ AEACD 1405

Kämmerling, Maria (gtr)
Borup-Jørgensen, A.:Für Gitarre *(rec Fruering Kirke, 1987)* Paula ▲ PACD 60 [AAD]
Borup-Jørgensen, A.:Preludes Gtr *(rec Fruering Kirke, 1987)* Paula ▲ PACD 60 [AAD]
Halffter, C.:Codex 1 *(rec Fruering Kirke, 1987)* Paula ▲ PACD 60 [AAD]
Maderna, B.:Serenata per un satellite *(rec Fruering Kirke, 1987)* Paula ▲ PACD 60 [AAD]
Maderna, B.:Y después *(rec Fruering Kirke, 1987)* Paula ▲ PACD 60 [AAD]

Kampen, Christopher van (vc)—see also ORCHESTRAS & ENSEMBLES Nash Ensemble
Debussy, C.:Son Vc, w. I. Brown (pno) Virgin Classics ▲ 59604 [DDD]
Knussen, O.:"...upon one note", w. Michael Collins (cl), Clio Gould (vn), Paul Silverthorne (va), John Constable (pno) *(rec Henry Wood Hall & All Hollows Gospel Oak, London, Oct & Dec 1995)* Deutsche Grammophon ▲ 449 572-2 [DDD]
Krauze, Z.:Quatuor pour la naissance, w. D. Campbell (cl), M. Mitchell (vn), J. MacGregor (pno) Collins Classics ▲ COL 1393 [DDD]
Matthews, C.:Suns Dance, w. Sebastian Bell (pic), Gareth Hulse (ob), Michael Collins (b cl), John Orford (ctbn), Michael Thompson (hn), Nona Liddell (vn), Joan Atherton (vn), Paul Silverthorne (va), Christopher van Kampen (vc), Robin McGee (db) *(rec All Saint's Church, Petersham, Oct 1992)* Deutsche Grammophon ▲ 447067-2 [DDD]
Saint-Saëns, C.:Trio 1 Pno, w. M. Crayford (vn), I. Brown (pno) Virgin Classics ▲ 59514 [DDD]
Schwertsik, K.:Späte Liebeslieder, w. C. Schwertsik (sgr) *(rec May 1994)* Largo ▲ 5125 [DDD]

Kamper, Anton (vn)
Pfitzner, H.:Qnt Pno, w. W. Kamper (pno), K. M. Titze (vn), E. Weis (va), F. Kvarda (vc) Preiser ▲ 93111 (m) [AAD]
Pfitzner, H.:Sxt Cl, w. L. Wlach (cl), E. Weis (va), F. Kvarda (vc), J. Hermann (db), W. Kamper (pno) Preiser ▲ 93111 (m) [AAD]
Schmidt, F.:Qnt Cl, w. A. Prinz (cl), J. Demus (pno), F. Stangler (va), W. Resel (vc) *(rec 1965)* Preiser ▲ 93383 [ADD]
Schmidt, F.:Qnt Pno, w. J. Demus (pno), W. Hink (vn), F. Stangler (va), W. Resel (vc) *(rec 1965)* Preiser ▲ 93383 [ADD]

Kamper, Walter (pno)
Pfitzner, H.:Qnt Pno, w. A. Kamper (vn), K. M. Titze (vn), E. Weis (va), F. Kvarda (vc) Preiser ▲ 93111 (m) [AAD]
Pfitzner, H.:Sxt Cl, w. L. Wlach (cl), A. Kamper (vn), E. Weis (va), F. Kvarda (vc), J. Hermann (db) Preiser ▲ 93111 (m) [AAD]

Kampmeier, Margaret (pno/syn)—see ORCHESTRAS & ENSEMBLES Musicians' Accord

Kampmeier, Margaret (pno)—see ORCHESTRAS & ENSEMBLES Musicians' Accord members

Kamrin, Phyllis (vn/va)—see ORCHESTRAS & ENSEMBLES Alma Duo

Kamu, Esa (va)
Segerstam, L.:Divert Vns, w. J. Rahkonen (vn), H. Louhivuori (vn), V. Höylä (vc), L. Segerstam (cnd), Helsinki CO BIS ▲ CD 84 [AAD]

Kan, Vassil (tpt)
Shostakovich, D.:Con 1 Pno, w. E. Kissin (pno), V. Spivakov (cnd), Moscow Virtuosi RCA Red Seal 2-▲ 60567-2-RC [DDD]
Shostakovich, D.:Con 1 Pno, w. E. Kissin (pno), V. Spivakov (cnd), Moscow Virtuosi RCA Red Seal ▲ 7947-2-RC [DDD]

Kanajan, Chatschatur (vn)
Blacher, B.:Songs, w. Katharina Richter (sop), Cornelia Wosnitza (sop), Markus Köhler (bar), Horst Göbel (pno), Piotr Prysiasnik (vn), Fred Günther (va), Ithay Khen (vc), Christian Peters (sax), Markus Weidmann (bn)—3 Chansons; Ungereimtes; 4 Lieder; Nebel; 13 Ways of Looking at a Blackbird; 5 Sinnsprüche Omars des Zeitmachers; 3 Psalmen; Aprèslude; Francesca da Rimini; Jazz-Koloraturen Signum ▲ SIG X73-00 [DDD]

Kanarek, David (hn)—see ORCHESTRAS & ENSEMBLES Briccialdi Wind Quintet

Kanazawa, Keiko (pno)
Yashiro, A.:Suite Classique, w. K. Yasukawa (pno) Camerata ▲ 30CM 50

Kanda, Masaharu (vc)—see ORCHESTRAS & ENSEMBLES Akiko Tatsumi String Quartet

Kane, M. (tpt)
Gregson, E.:Celebration, w. J. Burgess (tpt), D. Papp (tpt), E. Corporon (cnd), Cincinnati College Conservatory of Music Wind Sym Klavier ▲ KCD 11047 [DDD]

Kaneko, Takao (gtr)
Noda, T.:Rhap, w. T. Noda (cnd), NHK SO Camerata ▲ 30CM 344

Kanengiser, William (gtr)—see also ORCHESTRAS & ENSEMBLES Los Angeles Guitar Quartet
Brouwer, L.:El Decameron Negro *(rec 6/90)* GSP Recordings ▲ GSP 1004CD ■ GSP 1004C
Echoes of the Old World *(rec July 20 & 23, 1992)* GSP Recordings ▲ GSP 1006CD ■ GSP 1006C
Handel, G.F.:Suites Hpd—No. 8 *(rec 6/90)* GSP Recordings ▲ GSP 1004CD ■ GSP 1004C
Head, B.:Sketches for Friends *(rec 6/90)* GSP Recordings ▲ GSP 1004CD ■ GSP 1004C
Mozart, W.A.:Son 11 Pno *(rec June 1990)* GSP Recordings ▲ GSP 1004CD ■ GSP 1004C

Kang, Dong-Suk (vn)
Alkan, C.-V.:Chamber Music, w. Y. Chiffoleau (vc), O. Gardon (pno)—Grand Duo concertant for Violin & Piano, Op. 21; Sonate de Concert for Cello & Piano, Op. 47; Trio for Piano, Violin & Cello, Op. 30 Timpani ▲ 1C 1013 [DDD]
Debussy, C.:Son Vn, w. P. Devoyon (pno) *(rec 4/89)* Naxos ▲ 8.550276 [DDD]
Elgar, E.:Con Vn, w. A. Leaper (cnd), Polish National RSO Katowice *(rec 1989 & 1991)* Naxos ▲ 8.553233 [DDD]
Fauré, G.:Andante Vn, w. Pascal Devoyon (pno) *(rec Temple Saint Marcel, Paris, Jan 18-20, 1995)* Naxos ▲ 8.550906 [DDD]
Fauré, G.:Berceuse Vn, w. Pascal Devoyon (pno) *(rec Temple Saint Marcel, Paris, Jan 18-20, 1995)* Naxos ▲ 8.550906 [DDD]
Fauré, G.:Romance Vn, w. Pascal Devoyon (pno) *(rec Temple Saint Marcel, Paris, Jan 18-20, 1995)* Naxos ▲ 8.550906 [DDD]
Fauré, G.:Son 1 Vn, w. Pascal Devoyon (pno) *(rec Temple Saint Marcel, Paris, Jan 18-20, 1995)* Naxos ▲ 8.550906 [DDD]
Fauré, G.:Son 2 Vn, w. Pascal Devoyon (pno) *(rec Temple Saint Marcel, Paris, Jan 18-20, 1995)* Naxos ▲ 8.550906 [DDD]
Furtwängler, W.:Son 1 Vn, w. François Kerdoncuff (pno) *(rec Poissy Théâtre, Dec 20-22, 1994)* Timpani ▲ 1029 [DDD]
Grieg, E.:Sons Vn, Opp. 8, 13 & 45, w. R. Pöntinen (pno) *(rec Sept. 14-16, 1993)* BIS ▲ CD 647 [DDD]
Honegger, A.:Chamber Music (comp), w. D.-S. Kang (vn), P.-H. Xuereb (va), R. Wallfisch (vc), M. Arrignon (cl), A. Marion (fl), A. Haraldsdottir (fl), C. Moreaux (ob), T. Caens (tpt), M. Becquet (trbn), P. Zanlonghi (hp), P. Devoyon (pno), F. Kondo (mez), Ludwig String Quartet—Sonatine for Clarinet & Piano (1921-22); Rapsodie for 2 Flutes, Clarinet & Piano (1917); Danse de la Chèvre for Solo Flute (1921); Romance for Flute & Piano (1953); Petite Suite for 2 Flutes & Piano (1934); Trois Contrepoints for Piccolo, Oboe, Violin & Cello (1922); Intrada for Trumpet & Piano (1947); Hommage du trombone exprimant la tristesse de l'auteur absent for Trombone & Piano (1925); J'avais un fidèle amant for String Quartet (1929); Chanson de Ronsard & 3 Chansons de la petite Sirène for Mezzo, Flute & String Quartet (1924); Introduction et Danse for Flute, Harp & String Trio [undated]; Colloque for Flute, Celesta, Violin & Viola [undated] Timpani ▲ IC1010 [DDD]

Kang, Dong-Suk (vn) (cont.)

Honegger, A.:Chamber Music (comp), w. J.-P. Audoli (vn), P.-H. Xuereb (va), R. Wallfisch (vc), J. Rossi (db), P. Devoyon (pno)—Sonatine for 2 Violins (1920); Sonatine for Violin & Cello (1932); Sonata for Cello & Piano (1920); Sonata for Viola & Piano (1920); Trio in f for Violin, Cello & Piano (1914); Paduana for Solo Cello (1945); Prelude for Double Bass & Piano (1932) Timpani ▲ IC1009 [DDD]

Honegger, A.:Chamber Music (comp), w. P. Devoyon (pno)—Sonata in d for Violin & Piano (1912); Sonata Nos. 1 & 2 for Violin & Piano (1916–18; 1919); Arioso for Violin & Piano (ca. 1927/29); Sonata for Solo Violin (1940); Morceau de concours for Violin & Piano (1945) Timpani ▲ IC1008 [DDD]

Nielsen, C.:Con Vn, w. M.-W. Chung (cnd), Gothenburg SO BIS ▲ CD 616 [DDD]

Nielsen, C.:Con Vn, w. M.-W. Chung (cnd), Gothenburg SO BIS ▲ CD 370

Poulenc, F.:Son Vn, w. P. Devoyon (pno) *(rec 4/89)* Naxos ▲ 8.550276 [DDD]

Ravel, M.:Son Vn Pno, w. P. Devoyon (pno) *(rec 4/89)* Naxos ▲ 8.550276 [DDD]

Saint-Saëns, C.:Caprice andalous, w. A. Wit (cnd), Polish National RSO Katowice *(rec May 24–26, 1993)* Naxos ▲ 8.550752 [DDD]

Saint-Saëns, C.:Con 3 Vn, w. A. Wit (cnd), Polish National RSO Katowice *(rec May 24–26, 1993)* Naxos ▲ 8.550752 [DDD]

Saint-Saëns, C.:Introduction & Rondo capriccioso, w. A. Wit (cnd), Polish National RSO Katowice *(rec May 24–26, 1993)* Naxos ▲ 8.550752 [DDD]

Saint-Saëns, C.:Morceau de concert Vn, w. A. Wit (cnd), Polish National RSO Katowice *(rec May 24–26, 1993)* Naxos ▲ 8.550752 [DDD]

Saint-Saëns, C.:Romance Vn, w. A. Wit (cnd), Polish National RSO Katowice *(rec May 24–26, 1993)* Naxos ▲ 8.550752 [DDD]

Saint-Saëns, C.:Son 1 Vn, w. P. Devoyon (pno) Naxos ▲ 8.550276 [DDD]

Schubert, Franz:Fant Vn, D.934, w. P. Devoyon (pno) Naxos ▲ 8.550420 [DDD]

Schubert, Franz:Sonatinas Vn, w. P. Devoyon (pno) Naxos ▲ 8.550420 [DDD]

Sibelius, J.:Con Vn, w. A. Leaper (cnd), Czech-Slovak RSO Bratislava (original 1903/04 version) *(rec 1989 & 1991)* Naxos ▲ 8.553233 [DDD]

Sibelius, J.:Con Vn, w. A. Leaper (cnd), Czech-Slovak RSO Bratislava Naxos ▲ 8.550329 [DDD]

Sibelius, J.:Humoresques, w. N. Järvi (cnd), Gothenburg SO BIS ▲ CD 472 [DDD]

Sibelius, J.:Pieces Vn, w. N. Järvi (cnd), Gothenburg SO BIS ▲ CD 472 [DDD]

Sibelius, J.:Serenades Vn, w. N. Järvi (cnd), Gothenburg SO BIS ▲ CD 472 [DDD]

Sibelius, J.:Suite Vn Strs, w. O. Vänskä (cnd), Lahti SO BIS ▲ CD 575 [DDD]

Sinding, C.:Légende, w. A. Leaper (cnd), Czech-Slovak RSO Bratislava Naxos ▲ 8.550329 [DDD]

Svendsen, J.:Romance Vn, w. A. Leaper (cnd), Czech-Slovak RSO Bratislava Naxos ▲ 8.550329 [DDD]

Kang, Juliette (vn)

Juliette Kang, w. Melvin Chen (pno) *(rec Indianapolis, Nov. 1994)* Discover International ▲ DICD 920241 [DDD]

Kanga, Skaila (hp)

Bax, A.:Qnt Hp & Strs, w. English String Quartet Chandos ▲ CHAN 8391 [DDD]

Britten, H.:Choral Music, w. Alexander Wells (pno), R. Corp (cnd), New London Children's Choir—Friday Afternoons, Op. 7; Sweet was the Song; King Herod & the Cock; The Oxen; Fancie; The Birds; 3 Two-part Songs; A Walden Trio [Christmas Song of the Women]; A Ceremony of Carols *(rec All Hallows, Gospel Oak, London, Sept. 17-18, 1994)* Naxos ▲ 8.553183 [DDD]

Debussy, C.:Danses sacrée et profane, w. Academy of St. Martin in the Fields Chamber Ensemble Chandos ▲ CHAN 8621 [DDD]

Debussy, C.:Son Fl, w. W. Bennett (fl), S. Shingles (va) Chandos ▲ CHAN 8621 [DDD]

Moody, J.:Suite, w. T. Reilly (hmc) *(rec 1980)* Chandos ▲ CHAN 8802 [AAD]

Mozart, W.A.:Con Fl Hp, w. S. Milan (fl), R. Hickox (cnd), City of London Sinfonia Chandos ▲ CHAN 9051 [DDD]

Play British Folk Songs, w. Tommy Reilly (hmc) Chandos ▲ CHAN 8559 [DDD]

Ravel, M.:Intro & Allegro, w. W. Bennett (fl), A. Marriner (cl), Academy of St. Martin in the Fields Chamber Ensemble Chandos ▲ CHAN 8621 [DDD]

Roussel, A.:Sérénade, w. Academy of St. Martin in the Fields Chamber Ensemble Chandos ▲ CHAN 8621 [DDD]

Saint-Saëns, C.:Fant Vn, w. K. Sillito (vn) Chandos ▲ CHAN 8621 [DDD]

Kanji, Ricardo (fl)

de Fesch, W.:Son Voice, w. R. van der Meer (cello), J. Ogg (hpd)—No. 1 *(rec Apr. 1993)* Globe ▲ GLO 5101 [DDD]

Kanji, Ricardo (rcr)

Schenck, J.:Fant 1 Voc, w. J. Ogg (hpd), R. van der Meer (vc) *(rec Apr. 1993)* Globe ▲ GLO 5101 [DDD]

Van Wassenaer, U.:Sons Rcr, w. J. Ogg (hpd), R. van der Meer (vc)—Primata in F; Seconda in g; Terza in g *(rec Apr. 1993)* Globe ▲ GLO 5101 [DDD]

Kanka, Michel (vc)—see also ORCHESTRAS & ENSEMBLES Prazak String Quartet

Dvořák, A.:Rondo, w. V. Neumann (cnd), Czech PO *(rec Ostrava, 1992)* Praga ▲ CMX 350101

Dvořák, A.:Silent Woods, w. V. Neumann (cnd), Czech PO *(rec Ostrava, 1992)* Praga ▲ CMX 350101

Vivaldi, A.:Cons Vc, w. A. Barta (cnd), Prague CO—RV.404, 418, 421, 422, 424 & 547 Supraphon ▲ SUP 11 2121 [DDD]

Vivaldi, A.:Con for 2 Vcs, w. *(2nd cellist unknown)*, A. Barta (cnd), Prague CO Supraphon ▲ SUP 11 2121 [DDD]

Kann, H. (vn)

Kalkbrenner, F.:Con 1 Pno, w. H. Beissel (pno), Hamburg SO Preiser ▲ 90167 [ADD]

Kann, Hans (pno)

Bortnyansky, D.:Sinf concertante, w. *(bn unknown)*, I. Angerer (hp), H. Bondarenko (vn), W. Knieps (va), A. Schober (vc) Entrée ▲ 0051 [ADD]

Field, J.:Nocturnes Pno (comp) *(rec 1969)* Tuxedo ▲ TUXCD 1056

Hummel, J.N.:Con Pno, Op. 110, w. H. Beissel (cnd), Hamburg SO *(rec 1973)* Vox Box 2-▲ CDX 5064 [ADD]

Hummel, J.N.:Son Vn & Pno, Op. 5/1, w. Zlatko Topolski (vn) *(rec 1973)* Tuxedo ▲ TUXCD 1026

Kalkbrenner, F.:Con 1 Pno, w. H. Beissel (cnd), Hamburg SO *(rec 1973)* Vox Box 2-▲ CDX 5064 [ADD]

Kannar, W. (db)—see ORCHESTRAS & ENSEMBLES First Avenue

Kanoff, S. (pno)

Schubertiade:Rétrospective, w. Sine Nomine String Quartet, Lausanne Trio, C. Homberger (ten), C. Favre (pno), Choeur des XVI de Fribourg, et al. Gallo ▲ CD 631 [AAD]

Kanoff, Steven (cl)

Reger, M.:Qnt Cl, w. Anton String Quartet Accord ▲ ACD 204432 [DDD]

Reger, M.:Sons Cl, Op. 49, w. Paul Coker (pno) Accord ▲ ACD 204432 [DDD]

Kanta, L. (vc)

Boccherini, L.:Con Vc, G.482, w. P. Breiner (cnd), Capella Istropolitana *(rec 9/87)* Naxos ▲ 8.550059 [DDD]

Haydn, J.:Con 1 Vc, w. P. Breiner (cnd), Capella Istropolitana *(rec 9/87)* Naxos ▲ 8.550059 [DDD]

Haydn, J.:Con 2 Vc, w. P. Breiner (cnd), Capella Istropolitana *(rec 11/88)* Naxos ▲ 8.550059 [DDD]

Kantarjian, G. (vn)—see ORCHESTRAS & ENSEMBLES Rembrandt Trio

Kantorow, Jean-Jacques (vn)—see also ORCHESTRAS & ENSEMBLES Mozart String Trio

The Art of the Violin, w. Patrice Fontanarosa (vn), Régis Pasquier (vn), Gérard Poulet (vn) Arion ▲ ARN 60262

Bach, Joh. Christian:Con Vn & Vc, w. M. Fujiwara (vc), J.-J. Kantorow (cnd), Netherlands CO Denon ▲ 7867 [DDD]

Bach, J.S.:Cons Vn (comp), w. H. Stadlmair (cnd), Munich CO Denon ▲ CO 7096 [DDD]

Bach, J.S.:Con for 2 Vns, w. S. Cenariu (vn), H. Stadlmair (cnd), Munich CO Denon ▲ CO 7096 [DDD]

Bach, J.S.:Sons & Partitas Vn, BWV 1001–1006 Denon 2-▲ CO 74485 [DDD]

Bartók, B.:Divert, w. J.-J. Kantorow (cnd), Tapiola Sinfonietta *(rec Tapiola Concert Hall, Finland, Mar 27–30, 1995)* BIS ▲ CD 740 [DDD]

Bartók, B.:Music for Strs, Perc & Cel, w. J.-J. Kantorow (cnd), Tapiola Sinfonietta *(rec Tapiola Concert Hall, Finland, Mar 27–30, 1995)* BIS ▲ CD 740 [DDD]

Bartók, B.:Romanian Folk Dances Pno, w. J.-J. Kantorow (cnd), Tapiola Sinfonietta *(rec Tapiola Concert Hall, Finland, Mar 27–30, 1995)* BIS ▲ CD 740 [DDD]

Kantorow, Jean-Jacques (vn) (cont.)

Berens, H.:Trio Strs, w. V. Mendelssohn (va), H.-J. Stegenga (vc) Erasmus ▲ WVH 017 [DDD]

Brahms, J.:Qnt Cl, w. W. Boeykens (cl), A. Czifra (vn), V. Mendelssohn (va), H.-J. Stegenga (vc) Erasmus ▲ WVH 017 [DDD]

Brahms, J.:Trio Hn, w. Hervé Joulain (hn), Marie-Josèphe Jude (pno) Harmonia Mundi France ("Les Nouveaux Interprètes" series) ▲ HMN 911559

Bruch, M.:Con 1 Vn, w. A. Ros-Marbá (cnd), Netherlands CO Denon ▲ CO 8123 [DDD]

Canteloube, J.:Songs of Auvergne, w. M. Martin (sop), J.-J. Kantorow (cnd), Auvergne CO [trans. Jean-Guy Bailly for orch.] Denon/PCM Digital ▲ DEN 75862 [DDD]

Debussy, C.:Trio Pno, w. J. Rouvier (pno), P. Müller (vc) Denon ▲ CO 72508 [DDD]

Dodgson, S.:Duo Con, w. Anthea Gifford (gtr), R. Zollman (cnd), Northern Sinfonia of England *(rec St Nicholas Hospital, Newcastle-upon-Tyne, Oct 23–24, 1992)* Biddulph ▲ LAW 013 [DDD]

Giuliani, M.:Vars Vn, w. A. Gifford (gtr) *(rec Aug. 24–5, 1992)* Biddulph ▲ NT CD 003 [DDD]

Haydn, J.:Con 1 Vc, w. Mari Fujiwara (vc), J.-J. Kantorow (cnd), Netherlands CO Denon ▲ 7867 [DDD]

Haydn, J.:Con 2 Vc, w. Mari Fujiwara (vc), J.-J. Kantorow (cnd), Netherlands CO Denon ▲ 7867 [DDD]

Haydn, J.:Divert Hn, Vn & Vc, H.IV/5, w. Hervé Joulain (hn), Roland Pidoux (vc) Arion ▲ ARN 68311 [DDD]

Koechlin, C.:Little Pieces, w. Hervé Joulain (hn), Alice Ader (pno)—2 sels Arion ▲ ARN 68311 [DDD]

Leclair, J.-M.:Cons Vn, Op. 7, w. J.-J. Kantorow (cnd), Auvergne CO—No. 4 *(rec Basilique St. Julien de Brioude, Sept. 15–17, 1993)* FNAC Music ▲ 592317 [DDD]

Leclair, J.-M.:Cons Vn, Op. 7, w. J.-J. Kantorow (cnd), Auvergne CO—No. 4 *(rec Basilique St. Julien de Brioude, Sept. 15–17, 1993)* FNAC Music ▲ 592317 [DDD]

Leclair, J.-M.:Sons Vn (Books 1–4), w. A. Gifford (gtr) [arr. by Anthea Gifford for violin & guitar]—Sonata in D, Op. 9/3 Biddulph ▲ NTCD 003 [DDD]

Locatelli, P.:L'arte del violino, w. J.-J. Kantorow (cnd), Auvergne CO—Harmonic Labrinth *(rec Basilique St. Julien de Brioude, Sept. 15–17, 1993)* FNAC Music ▲ 592317 [DDD]

Locatelli, P.:L'arte del violino, w. J.-J. Kantorow (cnd), Auvergne CO—Harmonic Labrinth *(rec Basilique St. Julien de Brioude, Sept. 15–17, 1993)* FNAC Music ▲ 592317 [DDD]

Mendelssohn, F.:Con in d Vn & Strs, w. J.-J. Kantorow (cnd), Auvergne CO *(rec Basilique St. Julien de Brioude, Sept. 15–17, 1993)* FNAC Music ▲ 592317 [DDD]

Mendelssohn, F.:Con in d Vn & Strs, w. J.-J. Kantorow (cnd), Auvergne CO *(rec Basilique St. Julien de Brioude, Sept. 15–17, 1993)* FNAC Music ▲ 592317 [DDD]

Mendelssohn, F.:Con in e Vn & Orch, Op. 64, w. A. Ros-Marba (vn), J.-J. Kantorow (cnd), Netherlands CO Denon ▲ CO 8123 [DDD]

Mendelssohn, F.:Son Vn (1820), w. Jacques Rouvier (pno) *(rec Stadsgehoorzaal, Leiden, the Netherlands, Jan. 28–30, 1992)* Denon ▲ DEN 78964 [DDD]

Mendelssohn, F.:Son Vn, Op. 4, w. Jacques Rouvier (pno) *(rec Stadsgehoorzaal, Leiden, the Netherlands, Jan. 28–30, 1992)* Denon ▲ DEN 78964 [DDD]

Mendelssohn, F.:Son Vn (1838), w. Jacques Rouvier (pno) *(rec Stadsgehoorzaal, Leiden, the Netherlands, Jan. 28–30, 1992)* Denon ▲ DEN 78964 [DDD]

Mozart, W.A.:Concertone Vns, w. A. Adorján (flute), H. Stadlmair (cnd), Munich CO [arr. flute & violin] Denon ▲ 7804 [DDD]

Mozart, W.A.:Serenade Vn, K.250, w. L. Hager (cnd), Auvergne Orch Denon ▲ CO 73870 [DDD]

Mozart, W.A.:Sons Vn Vc, w. Mari Fujiwara (vc)—in C, K.46d & in F, K.46e Denon ▲ 7867 [DDD]

Nocturne, w. J.-J. Kantorow (cnd), Auvergne CO Denon ▲ CO 75596 [DDD]

Paganini, N.:Cantabile & Waltz, w. A. Gifford (gtr) Biddulph ▲ NT CD 003 [DDD]

Paganini, N.:Centone di sonate, w. A. Gifford (gtr)—No. 11 in a Biddulph ▲ NT CD 003 [DDD]

Paganini, N.:Con 2 Vn, w. J.-J. Kantorow (cnd), B. Thomas CO Vox Box 3-▲ CD3X 3020 [ADD]

Paganini, N.:Con 2 Vn, w. J.-J. Kantorow (cnd), B. Thomas CO Vox Box 3-▲ CD3X 3020 [ADD]

Paganini, N.:Sons Vn & Gtr, Op. 2, w. A. Gifford (gtr)—Sonata Nos. 3 & 4 Biddulph ▲ NT CD 003 [DDD]

Ravel, M.:Trio Pno, w. J. Rouvier (pno), Müller (vc) Denon ▲ CO 72508 [DDD]

Roussel, A.:Chamber Music, w. Paul Verhey (fl), Hans Roerade (ob), Herman Jeurissen (hn), Herre-Jan Stengenga (vc), Jet Röling (pno) Olympia ▲ OLY 458 [DDD]

Saint-Saëns, C.:Son 1 Vn, w. J. Rouvier (pno) *(rec March 11–12, 1991)* Denon ▲ CO 79552 [DDD]

Saint-Saëns, C.:Son 2 Vn, w. J. Rouvier (pno) *(rec March 11–12, 1991)* Denon ▲ CO 79552 [DDD]

Schoenberg, A.:Chamber Sym 1, w. J.-J. Kantorow (cnd), Tapiola Sinfonietta BIS ▲ CD 703 [DDD]

Schoenberg, A.:Qt 2 Strs, w. Christina Högman (sop), J.-J. Kantorow (cnd), Tapiola Sinfonietta BIS ▲ CD 703 [DDD]

Schoenberg, A.:Verklärte Nacht, w. J.-J. Kantorow (cnd), Tapiola Sinfonietta BIS ▲ CD 703 [DDD]

Schubert, Franz:Con Vn, w. Emmanuel Krivine (vn), J.J. Kantorow (cnd), Netherlands PO Denon ▲ CO 1666 [DDD]

Schubert, Franz:Polonaise Vn, w. E. Krivine (cnd), Netherlands PO Denon ▲ CO 1666 [DDD]

Schubert, Franz:Rondo Vn, D.438, w. E. Krivine (cnd), Netherlands PO Denon ▲ CO 1666 [DDD]

Schumann, R.:Con Vn, w. E. Krivine (cnd), Netherlands PO Denon ▲ CO 1666 [DDD]

Seduction of Violin, w. Jacques Rouvier (pno) Denon ▲ CO 77051 [DDD]

Tartini, G.:Son Vn "Devil's Trill", w. J.-J. Kantorow (cnd), Auvergne CO [trans. M. O. Dupin for Violin & Orch.] *(rec Basilique St. Julien de Brioude, Sept. 15–17, 1993)* FNAC Music ▲ 592317 [DDD]

Tartini, G.:Son Vn "Devil's Trill", w. J.-J. Kantorow (cnd), Auvergne CO [trans. M. O. Dupin for Violin & Orch.] *(rec Basilique St. Julien de Brioude, Sept. 15–17, 1993)* FNAC Music ▲ 592317 [DDD]

Tartini, G.:Son Vn "Devil's Trill", w. A. Gifford (pno) [arr. Anthea Gifford for violin & guitar] Biddulph ▲ NT CD 003 [DDD]

Kanter, James (cl)

Russell, A.:Suite Concertante, w. Floyd Cooley (tuba), Janet Ketchum (fl), Earle Dumler (ob), Arthur David Krehbiel (hn), Charles Ullery (bn) Crystal ▲ CD 120

Kantola, Erkki (vn)—see ORCHESTRAS & ENSEMBLES Sibelius Academy String Quartet

Kapchiev, A. (vn)

Lemeland, A.:American Epitaph (à la mémoire de Aaron Copland), w. F. Jeandet (va), P. Gessi (vc) *(rec 1991)* Skarbo ▲ SKR 3913 [ADD]

Kapell, William (pno)

Bach, J.S.:Partitas Hpd, BWV 825–830—BWV 828 VAI Audio ▲ VAIA/IPA 1048 [ADD]

Beethoven, L. van:Con 2 Pno *(rec 1940–53)* Pearl ▲ PEA 9194

Beethoven, L. van:Son 1 Vn, w. Arthur Grumiaux (vn) Stradivarius ▲ STV 10020 [ADD]

Brahms, J.:Con 1 Pno, w. D. Mitropoulos (cnd), New York PO *(rec live 4/12/53)* Arkadia ▲ 736 [ADD]

Brahms, J.:Con 1 Pno, w. D. Mitropoulos (cnd), New York PO *(rec live 4/12/53)* Melodram ▲ MEL 18009

Chopin, F.:Mazurkas—10 RCA Red Seal ▲ 5998-2-RC (m) [ADD]

Chopin, F.:Polonaises *(rec 1940–53)* Pearl ▲ PEA 9194

Chopin, F.:Preludes, Op. 28 *(rec 1940–53)* Pearl ▲ PEA 9194

Chopin, F.:Son Pno, Op. 35 RCA Red Seal ▲ 5998-2-RC (m) [ADD]

Chopin, F.:Son Pno, Op. 58 RCA Red Seal ▲ 5998-2-RC (m) [ADD]

Debussy, C.:Children's Corner *(rec Broadcast Performances 1942–1953)* VAI Audio ▲ VAIA/IPA 1048 [ADD]

Falla, M. de:Noches en los jardines de España, w. L. Stokowski (cnd), Philharmonic SO *(rec 1949)* Music & Arts ▲ CD 771 [AAD]

Kapell RCA Gold Seal ("Legendary Performers" series) ▲ 09026-60921-2

Khachaturian, A.:Con Pno, w. F. Black (cnd), NBC SO *(rec live, May 20, 1945)* VAI Audio ▲ VAIA/IPA 1027 [ADD]

Liszt, F.:Hungarian Rhaps—Nos. 6 & 11 VAI Audio ▲ VAIA/IPA 1048 [ADD]

Mozart, W.A.:Qts Pno, w. A. Grumiaux (vn), M. Thomas (va), P. Tortelier (vc)—K.493 *(rec live June 1, 1953)* Music & Arts 4-▲ CD 689 (m) [AAD]

Mozart, W.A.:Son 16 Pno VAI Audio ▲ VAIA/IPA 1048 [ADD]

Mussorgsky, M.:Pictures at an Exhibition VAI Audio ▲ VAIA/IPA 1048 [ADD]

Rachmaninoff, S.:Con 3 Pno, w. E. MacMillan (cnd), Toronto SO *(rec live, Apr. 13, 1948)* VAI Audio ▲ VAIA/IPA 1027 [ADD]

Rachmaninoff, S.:Rhapsody on a Theme of Paganini, *(orch unknown)* *(rec 1940–53)* Pearl ▲ PEA 9194

Schubert, Franz:Songs (misc), w. Maria Stader (sop) *(rec 1940–53)* Pearl ▲ PEA 9194

INSTRUMENT.

Kapil, Radoslav (pno)
Hindemith, P.:Concert Music Pno, Brass & Hps, w. J. Wallace (tpt), S. Wright (cnd), Philharmonia Orch, Wallace Collection Nimbus ▲ NI 5103 [DDD]
Janácek, L.:Capriccio, John Wallace (cnd), Wallace Collection, Simon Wright (cnd), Philharmonia Orch members Nimbus ▲ NI 5103 [DDD]
Vačkář, D.C.:Jazz Con, w. John Wallace (tpt), S. Wright (cnd), Wallace Collection, Philharmonia Orch members Nimbus ▲ NI 5103 [DDD]

Kapilow, Robert (pno)
Weill, K.:Songs, w. A. Réaux (sop), W. Schimmel (acc), B. Ruyle (perc)—conceived & first performed by Angelina Réaux for the 1988 New York Shakespeare Festival, this one-woman show features 21 songs composed from 1928–1946 [E,F,G] Koch International Classics 2-▲ KIC 7087-2 [DDD]

Kaplan, Arnold (pno)
Prokofiev, S.:Cinderella (sels), w. Galina Heifetz (vn)—Var of the Winter Fairy; Gavotte; Grand Waltz [all trans Mikhail Fikhtengoltz] *(rec Music Hall, Tarrytown, NY, May 28–30, 1994)* Connoiseur Society ▲ CD 4204
Prokofiev, S.:Son Vn, Op. 94bis, w. Galina Heifetz (vn) *(rec Music Hall, Tarrytown, NY, May 28–30, 1994)* Connoiseur Society ▲ CD 4204
Prokofiev, S.:Son 1 Vn, w. Galina Heifetz (vn) *(rec Music Hall, Tarrytown, NY, May 28–30, 1994)* Connoiseur Society ▲ CD 4204
Russian Music for Violin & Piano, w. Galina Heifetz (vn) Connoiseur Society ▲ CD 4196

Kaplan, Bruce (gtr)
Exquisite Corpses from P.S. 122, w. David Watson (shears/stick vn/gtr/tpt), Judy Dunaway (gtr/balloons), Anthony Coleman (sampler), Raissa St. Pierre (drums), Guy Yarden (vn/pno), Leslie Ross (bn), Linda Austin (gtr), Doug Henderson (peckhorn/bass/toy pno), Sue Ann Harkey (gtr), Cinnie Cole (sampler), Mike Sap ¿What Next? ▲ WN 0002 [ADD]

Kaplan, Esther Lee (pno)
Chopin, F.:Fant *(rec First Congregational Church, Los Angeles, Sept. 1992)* Cambria ▲ CD 1089 [DDD]
Chopin, F.:Mazurkas—in a, Op. 7/2; in A♭, Op. 24/3; in a, Op. 68/2 *(rec First Congregational Church, Los Angeles, Sept. 1992)* Cambria ▲ CD 1089 [DDD]
Chopin, F.:Nocturnes—in D♭, Op. 27/2 *(rec First Congregational Church, Los Angeles, Sept. 1992)* Cambria ▲ CD 1089 [DDD]
Chopin, F.:Waltzes—in e, Op. posth. *(rec First Congregational Church, Los Angeles, Sept. 1992)* Cambria ▲ CD 1089 [DDD]
Schumann, R.:Carnaval Pno *(rec First Congregational Church, Los Angeles, Sept. 1992)* Cambria ▲ CD 1089 [DDD]

Kaplan, Leigh (pno)
Dring, M.:Dances Fl & Pno, w. Louise Di Tullio (fl)—WIB Waltz; Sarabande; Tango Cambria ▲ CD 1084 [ADD]
Dring, M.:Pastel Panche, w. Bud Shank (fl), Bill Perkins (sax/fl), Ray Brown (bass), Shelley Manne (perc)Shank Perkins Brown—Teal for Two; Muave Mood; Lime Clash Cambria ▲ CD 1084 [ADD]
Dring, M.:Pno Duo Tour, w. Susan Pits (pno), Robin Paterson (pno)—Carribean Dance; Danza Gaya [w Susan Pits (pno)]; Tarantelle; Italian Dance [w Robin Paterson (pno)] Cambria ▲ CD 1084 [ADD]
Dring, M.:Pno Music—Moto Perpetuo; Colour Suite; Valse Française; Waltz Finale; American Dance; Jig Cambria ▲ CD 1084 [ADD]
Dring, M.:Shades of Dring, w. Bud Shank (fl), Bill Perkins (sax/fl), Ray Brown (bass), Shelley Manne (perc)—In the Pink; Hallelujah Red; Brown and Out; Hello Yellow; Saxy Blue Cambria ▲ CD 1084 [ADD]

Kaplan, Mark (vn)—see also ORCHESTRAS & ENSEMBLES Golub/Kaplan/Carr Trio
Bartók, B.:Con 2 Vn, w. L. Foster (cnd), Barcelona SO [w. original coda] Koch Schwann ▲ KIC CD 7387
Bartók, B.:Rhaps Vn & Pno, Sz.86 & 89, w. B. Canino (pno) Arabesque ▲ ARA 6649 [DDD]
Bartók, B.:Romanian Folk Dances Vn, w. B. Canino (pno) Arabesque ▲ ARA 6649 [DDD]
Bartók, B.:Son Vn Arabesque ▲ ARA 6649 [DDD]
Brahms, J.:Trio Hn, w. D. Jolley (hn), D. Golub (pno) Arabesque ▲ Z 6607
Brahms, J.:Trio 1 Pno, w. D. Golub (pno), C. Carr (vc) Arabesque ▲ Z 6607
Brahms, J.:Trio 2 Pno, w. D. Golub (pno), C. Carr (vc) Arabesque ▲ Z 6608
Brahms, J.:Trio 3 Pno, w. D. Golub (pno), C. Carr (vc) Arabesque ▲ Z 6608
Dohnányi, E. von:Con 2 Vn, w. L. Foster (cnd), Barcelona SO Koch Schwann ▲ KIC CD 7387
Mendelssohn, F.:Trio 1 Pno, w. D. Golub (pno), C. Carr (vc) Arabesque ▲ Z 6599
Mendelssohn, F.:Trio 2 Pno, w. D. Golub (pno), C. Carr (vc) Arabesque ▲ Z 6599
Sarasate, P. de:Vn & Pno Music, w. B. Canino (pno)—Navarra for 2 Violins & Piano, Op. 33 *(M. Kaplan plays both violins)*; Malagueña, Op. 21/1; Habanera, Op. 21/2; Romanza Andaluza, Op. 22/2; Jota Navarra, Op. 22/4; Playera, Op. 23/1; Zapateado, Op. 23/2; Caprice Basque, Op. 24; Spanish Dance (untitled), Op. 26/1; Spanish Dance (untitled), Op. 26/2; Bolero, Op. 30; Zortzico D'Iparaguirre, Op. 39; Miramar (Zortzico), Op. 42; Introductions & Tarantelle, Op. 43 *(rec Concordia College)* Arabesque ▲ Z 6614
Schubert, Franz:Nocturne Pno, w. D. Golub (pno), C. Carr (vc) Arabesque 2-▲ Z 6580-2
Schubert, Franz:Rondo Vn, D.895, w. D. Golub (pno) Arabesque ▲ ARA 6636 [DDD]
Schubert, Franz:Sonatinas Vn, w. D. Golub (pno) Arabesque ▲ ARA 6636 [DDD]
Schubert, Franz:Trio Pno, D.28, w. C. Carr (vc), D. Golub (pno) Arabesque 2-▲ Z 6580-2
Schubert, Franz:Trio 1 Pno, w. D. Golub (pno), C. Carr (vc) Arabesque 2-▲ Z 6580-2
Schubert, Franz:Trio 2 Pno, w. D. Golub (pno), C. Carr (vc)—includes both the traditional finale as well as the first recording of the original finale, which contains 100 bars cut by Schubert prior to publication Arabesque 2-▲ Z 6580-2
Schumann, R.:Son 1 Vn, w. Anton Kuerti (pno) *(rec SUNY, Purchase, Theatre C, Dec. 7–9, 1994)* Arabesque ▲ ARA 6662 [DDD]
Schumann, R.:Son 2 Vn, w. Anton Kuerti (pno) *(rec SUNY, Purchase, Theatre C, Dec. 7–9, 1994)* Arabesque ▲ ARA 6662 [DDD]
Schumann, R.:Son 3 Vn, w. Anton Kuerti (pno) *(rec SUNY, Purchase, Theatre C, Dec. 7–9, 1994)* Arabesque ▲ ARA 6662 [DDD]

Kaplan Solomon, N. (pno)
Lopatnikoff, N.:Pno Music—Gavotte; 5 Contrasts, Op. 16; Vars., Op. 22; Dance Piece; Intervals Laurel ▲ LR 846
Lopatnikoff, N.:Pieces Vn & Pno, w. M. Lefkowitz (vn) Laurel ▲ LR 846
Lopatnikoff, N.:Son Pno Laurel ▲ LR 846
Lopatnikoff, N.:Son 2 Vn, w. M. Lefkowitz (vn) Laurel ▲ LR 846

Kaplansky, Marian (pno)
Janácek, L.:Folk Ballads, w. Dagmar Peckova (sop), Ivan Kusnjer (bar) Supraphon ▲ SUP 112225 [DDD]
Janácek, L.:Hukvaldy Folk Poetry, w. Dagmar Peckova (mez), Ivan Kusnjer (bar) Supraphon ▲ SUP 112214 [DDD]
Janácek, L.:Moravian Folk Poetry, w. Dagmar Peckova (mez), Ivan Kusnjer (bar) Supraphon ▲ SUP 112214 [DDD]
Janácek, L.:Silesian Songs, w. Dagmar Peckova (mez), Ivan Kusnjer (bar) Supraphon ▲ SUP 112214 [DDD]

Kaplinsky, Elaine (kbd)
First, D.:Distance Receives Permission to Enter, w. D. First (gtr controller/E-bow gtr/computer & synthesizer programming), K. Sparke (dr) *(rec Apr. 1991)* O.O. Discs ▲ OO 5 [DDD]
First, D.:The Good Book's (Accurate) Jail of Escape Dust Coordinates 2, w. Matt Sullivan (ob), Chris Jepperson (cl), Annemarie Wiesner (vn), Gary Trosclair (tpt), Chad Henderson (teahouse gtr/b gtr), Kevin Sparke (perc), David First (e-bow gtr/teahouse gtr/Distortion gtr/kbd syn/programming) *(rec Baby Monster Studios, NYC, May 1992)* O. O. Discs ▲ OO 23 [DDD]

Kapp, Richard (pno)—see ORCHESTRAS & ENSEMBLES Philharmonia Virtuosi

Käppel, Hubert (gtr)
Bach, J.S.:Partitas Hpd, BWV 825–830 *(rec 1983–84)* GSP Recordings ▲ GSP 1003CD [ADD] ■ GSP 1003C
Kellner, D.:Lt Music *(rec 1983–84)* GSP Recordings ▲ GSP 1003CD [ADD] ■ GSP 1003C
Romantic Guitar Music, w. Käppel, Hubert (gtr) FSM ▲ 97760 [DDD]

Kaproff, Armand (vc)—see ORCHESTRAS & ENSEMBLES Los Angeles String Quartet

Kapustin, Nikolai (pno)
Kapustin, N.:Andante Pno MK ▲ 417051 [DDD]
Kapustin, N.:Bagatelles MK ▲ 417051 [DDD]
Kapustin, N.:Sons Pno—Nos. 4, 5 & 6 MK ▲ 417051 [DDD]

Kara, Danae (pno)
Hadjidakis, M.:For a Little White Seashell *(rec Athens Concert Hall, Aug 24, 1995)* Agora Musica ▲ AG 022 [DDD]
Hadjidakis, M.:Ionian Suite *(rec Athens Concert Hall, Aug 24, 1995)* Agora Musica ▲ AG 022 [DDD]
Hadjidakis, M.:Popular Paintings (6) *(rec Athens Concert Hall, Aug 24, 1995)* Agora Musica ▲ AG 022 [DDD]
Hadjidakis, M.:Rhythmologia *(rec Athens Concert Hall, Aug 24, 1995)* Agora Musica ▲ AG 022 [DDD]

Karajan, W. von (org)
Haydn, J.:Cons for 2 Lire organizzata, w. Berlin Instrumental Soloists Koch Schwann ▲ CD 311006 [ADD]

Karapetyan, Suren (hn)
Matson, S.:Range, w. Catherine Robbin (mez), Susan Greenberg (fl), Joseph Stone (fl), Glen Garrett (cl), Peter Kent (vn), Kazi Pitelka (va), Sebastian Toettcher (vc), Don Ferrone (db), Doug Livingston (gtr/mand), John Schneider (gtr), Amy Shulman (hp), Terry Schoenig (perc), S. Matson (cnd) *(rec Schnee Studio, Universal City, CA, Mar 12, 1995)* New Albion ▲ NA 091

Karas, Anton (zither)
Anton Karas, w. Vienna Unterhaltung Orch [cnd:Hans Hagen] Tuxedo ▲ 5003
Karas, A.:Third Man Theme, w. H. Hagen (cnd), Vienna Unterhaltung Orch Tuxedo ▲ 5003

Karas-Krasztel, Elzbieta (pno)
Chopin, F.:Vars on Mozart's *La ci darem la mano*, w. K. Kord (cnd), Warsaw PO *(rec Warsaw Philharmonic Hall, June 27–30, 1994)* Canyon Classics ▲ CD 248

Karasszon, Dezsö (org)
The Chants of the Reformation in Hungary, w. Debrecen College Cantus Hungaroton ▲ HCD 12665 [DDD]
Fauré, G.:Requiem, w. E. Maros (hp), J. Dobra (cnd), Hungarian Virtuosi CO, Budapest SO Winds, Tomkins Vocal Ensemble Hungaroton ▲ HCD 31424 [DDD]
Franck, C.:Messe solennelle, w. Attila Wendler (ten), Andrea Kocsis (hp), Zsolt Molnár (vc), Ferenc Nagy (db), Salomon Kamp (cnd), Debrecen Kodaly Choir Hungaroton ▲ HCD 31579 [DDD]
Lancaster & Valois:French & English Music, ca. 1350–1420 Hyperion ▲ CDA 66588
The Marriage of Heaven & Hell:Motets & Songs from 13th Century France Hyperion ▲ CDA 66423 [DDD]
The Medieval Romantics:French Songs & Motets, 1340–1440 Hyperion ▲ CDA 66463 [DDD]
A Song for Francesca:Music in Italy, 1330–1430 Hyperion ▲ CDA 66286

Kárászy, Szilvia (car/org/digital pno)
Jingle Bells *(rec 1995)* Hungaroton ▲ HCD 31623 [DDD]

Karcher, Éric (hn)
Klein, G.:Divert Ob, w. Jean-Pierre Arnaud (ob), Jean-Marc Liet (ob), Rémi Lerner (cl), Christian Rocca (cl), Michel Tavernier (bn), Amaury Wallez (bn), Philippe Queyraud (hn) Arion ▲ ARN 68272 [DDD]

Karel, Bidlo (bn)
Mozart, W.A.:Con Bn, w. V. Smetáček (cnd), Czech PO Supraphon ▲ SUP 3053

Karemacher, Anatol (pno)
Beethoven, L. van:Music of, w. Michel ten Houte-de Lange (ten), Peter Kranen (pno)—Sketches for a Sym; 7 Early Songs; 4 Settings of Nur wer die; Sehnsucht kennt, WoO 134; Sketches for Pno Piece in C; 9 Short Sketchbook Frags Raptus ▲ 389.02.88
Neefe, C.G.:Vars Dittersdorf, w. Michel ten Houte de Lange (ten), Peter Kranen (pno) Raptus ▲ 389.02.88
Neefe, C.G.:Vars Mozart, w. Michel ten Houte de Lange (ten), Peter Kranen (pno) Raptus ▲ 389.02.88

Karis, Aleck (pno)—see also ORCHESTRAS & ENSEMBLES SONOR Ensemble of Univ of California San Diego members
Anderson, A.:Drawn from Life CRI ▲ CD 727 [DDD]
Anderson, A.:Solfeggietti CRI ▲ CD 727 [DDD]
Babbitt, M.:Reflections *(rec American Academy of Arts & Letters, June, 1994)* CRI ▲ CD 707 [DDD]
Carter, E.:Night Fants Bridge ▲ BCD 9001 ■ BC5-7001
Chambers, W.M.:Ten Grand, w. Ursula Oppens (pno), Walter Hilse (pno), Bennett Lerner (pno), Nurit Tilles (pno), Edmund Niemann (pno), Joseph Kubera (pno), Martin Goldray (pno), Allen Shawn (pno), Elizabeth di Filice (pno), Geisel (cnd) Newport ▲ NPD 85553
Chopin, F.:Fant Bridge ▲ BCD 9001 ■ BC5-7001
Cory, E.:Apertures *(rec 1981 & 1986)* CRI ▲ CD 621 [ADD]
Cory, E.:Profiles, w. A. Blustine (cl), C. Finckel (vc) *(rec 1981 & 1986; originally r)* CRI ▲ CD 621 [ADD]
Dashow, J.:Punti di Vista 2 *(rec BMG-RCA Studios, Rome)* Neuma ▲ 45090 [DDD]
Davidovsky, M.:Synchronism 6 *(rec American Academy of Arts & Letters, June, 1994)* CRI ▲ CD 707 [DDD]
Delio, T.:Music of, w. John Fonville (fl), Steven Shick (perc), Jacques Linder (pno), Sandra Sprecher (pno)—anti-paysage for Fl, Perc, Pno & Tape; Of for Tape; Though for solo Pno; so again for Tape; on again for Tape; of again for Tape *(rec Univ of CA, San Diego, Univ of Maryland, Catonsville & Washington D.C.)* Neuma ▲ 45090 [DDD]
Hyla, L.:Con 2 Pno, w. W. Purvis (cnd), Speculum Musicae *(rec SUNY, Purchase, NY, Oct 25, 1995)* New World ▲ 80491-2
Kraft, L.:Inventions & Airs, w. E. Gilmore (cl), E. Wyrick (vn) *(rec 1989–1990)* Centaur ▲ CRC 2079 [ADD]
Kreiger, A.:Fant Pno *(rec American Academy of Arts & Letters, June, 1994)* CRI ▲ CD 707 [DDD]
Mozart, W.A.:Adagio Glass Armonica, K.356 Bridge ▲ BCD 9011 [ADD] ■ BC5 7011
Mozart, W.A.:Fant Pno, K.475 Bridge ▲ BCD 9011 [ADD] ■ BC5 7011
Mozart, W.A.:Gigue Pno, K.574 Bridge ▲ BCD 9011 [ADD] ■ BC5 7011
Mozart, W.A.:Minuet Pno, K.355 Bridge ▲ BCD 9011 [ADD] ■ BC5 7011
Mozart, W.A.:Rondo Pno, K.485 Bridge ▲ BCD 9011 [ADD] ■ BC5 7011
Mozart, W.A.:Son 8 Pno Bridge ▲ BCD 9011 [ADD] ■ BC5 7011
Mozart, W.A.:Son 12 Pno Bridge ▲ BCD 9011 [ADD] ■ BC5 7011
Mozart, W.A.:Son 17 Pno Bridge ▲ BCD 9011 [ADD] ■ BC5 7011
Picker, T.:Romance Vn, w. L. Quan (vn) *(rec 1979)* CRI ▲ CD 589 [ADD]
Primosch, J.:Secret Geometry *(rec American Academy of Arts & Letters, June, 1994)* CRI ▲ CD 707 [DDD]
Reynolds, R.:Var Pno Neuma ▲ 450-78 [DDD]
Schumann, R.:Carnaval Pno Bridge ▲ BCD 9001 ■ BC5-7001
Steiger, R.:Double Con, w. S. Schick (perc), R. Steiger (cnd), SONOR Ensemble of Univ of California San Diego *(rec May 27–June 1, 1992)* CRI ▲ CD 652 [DDD]
Stravinsky, I.:Easy Pieces Pno 4-Hands (5), w. R. Lubin (pno) *(rec Mar. 12–14, 1993)* Bridge ▲ BCD 9051 [DDD]
Stravinsky, I.:Pno Music—3 Movts. from Pétrouchka; Valse pour les enfants; Ragtime; Piano-Rag-Music; Les cinq doigts; Serenade in A; Tango; Circus Polka *(rec Mar. 12–14, 1993)* Bridge ▲ BCD 9051 [DDD]
Stravinsky, I.:Son Pnos, w. R. Lubin (pno) *(rec Mar. 12–14, 1993)* Bridge ▲ BCD 9051 [DDD]
Wolpe, S.:Qt Ob, w. S. Taylor (ob), F. Sherry (vc), D. Kennedy (perc) *(rec Nov. 9–10, 1991)* Koch ▲ KIC 7112 [DDD]
Yuasa, J.:Towards the Midnight Sun *(rec American Academy of Arts & Letters, June, 1994)* CRI ▲ CD 707 [DDD]

Kärkkäinen, Heini (pno)
Gothoni, R.:The Bull & His Herdsman:A Zen Story from Ancient China, w. Soile Isokoski (sop), Jorma Hynninen (bar), Jan Söderblom (vn), Ilari Angervo (va), Jan-Erik Kustafsson (vc), R. Gothoni (cnd) Ondine ▲ ODE 832 [DDD]
Kodály, Z.:Son Vc & Pno, Op. 4, w. Jan-Erik Gustafsson (vc) Ondine ▲ ODE 827 [DDD]

▲ = CD ♦ = Enhanced CD Δ = MD ■ = Cassette Tape ◻ = DCC

Kärkkäinen, Heini (pno) (cont.)
- Schnittke, A.:Son Vc, w. Jan-Erik Gustafsson (vc) — Ondine ▲ ODE 827 [DDD]
- Szymanowski, K.:Son Vn, w. Jan-Erik Gustafsson (vc) [arr Wilkomirski for vc & pno] — Ondine ▲ ODE 827 [DDD]

Kärkkäinen, Jaana (pno)
- Heiniö, M.:Qnt Pno, w. Avanti! String Quartet — Ondine ▲ ODE 865
- Kokkonen, J.:Qnt Pno, w. Avanti! String Quartet — Ondine ▲ ODE 865

Karlovsky, Jaroslav (va)
- Bartók, B.:Con Va, w. K. Ančerl (cnd), Czech PO — Supraphon ▲ SUP 111956 [AAD]

Karlsson, Lars (gtr)—see ORCHESTRAS & ENSEMBLES Duodecima

Karlsson, Lone (pno)
- Stolarczyk, W.:Earth Air Fire Water, w. Amalie Malling (pno), John Damgaard (pno), Anne Øland (pno), Teddy Teirup (pno), Friedrich Gürtler (pno), Rosalind Bevan (pno), Poul Rosenbaum (pno), Rodolfo Llambias (pno), Bella Horn-Ribera (pno), Anders Riber (pno), Elisabeth Sigurdsson (pno), Thomas Tronheim (pno), Elsebeth Broderson (pno), Erik Kaltoft (pno), Jørgen Hald Nielsen (pno), Aino Gilemann (pno), Birgit Kjær (pno), Jørgen Thomsen (pno), Gunhild Donslund (pno), Henrik Bo Hansen (pno), Lone Karlsson (pno), Erik Fessel (pno), Lasse Nilsson (pno), Janos Ferenczi (pno), Erik Bach (pno), Axel Momme (pno), Arne de Cros Dich (pno), Sven Micha Slot (pno), Hanne Bramsen Buhl (pno), Lili Olesen (pno), Susannah Carlsson (pno), Ulla Erml (pno), Vagn Sørensen (pno), Leif Greibe (pno), Bodil Krogh (pno), Kirsten Ottosen (pno), Inger Bergenholz (pno), Karsten Gylendorf (pno), Bjørn Elkjær (pno), Jacob Bjørn Jensen (pno), Jørgen Kaad (pno), Anne Marie Hjelm (pno), Carl Ulrik Munk Andersen (pno), Poul Lumbye (pno), Oluf Hildebrandt Nielsen (pno), Joachim Olsson (pno), Peter Pade Ramsøe Jacobsen (pno), Astrid Pollmann (pno), Jette Borsch (pno), Kirsten Karlshøj (pno), Maria Teresa Assing (pno), Allan Dahl Hansen (pno), Johan Hugossen (pno), Tine Fenger Pederson (pno), Arne Jørgen Fæø (pno), Anja Høgsted (pno), Anne Sophie Parbo (pno), Inga Lindmark (pno), Teresa Drabik Stathakis (pno), Anne Ruth Ferenczi (pno), Irene Hasager (pno), Yuka Ichikawa (pno), Birgitte Baur (pno), Malene Thastum (pno), Jens E. Rasmussen (pno), Birgitte Zielke (pno), Claus Zielke (pno), Stefan Kasch (pno), Bin Qiao (pno), Inger Johanne Teirup (pno), Lindy Rosborg (pno), Liisa Heininen (pno), David Højer (pno), Ellen Refstrup (pno), Thomas K. Søorensen (pno), Erik Kure (pno), Michael Rauff (pno), Jan beck Eriksson (pno), Tanja Zapolski (pno), Vibeke Skagbo (pno), Pål Eide Lindtner (pno), Ha-Young Sul (pno), Benedicte Palko (pno), Inke Kesseler (pno), Anne Marie Meineche (pno), Sverre Larsen (pno), Kasper Peter Bach (pno), Elisabetta Eliseo (pno), Olga Magieres (pno), Carl Erik Kühl (pno), Thorkild Borup Nielsen (pno), Valeria Zanini (pno), Lars Stenhoft (perc), Dennis Boel (perc), Winnie Dahlgren (perc), Susanne Vind (perc), Claus Byrith (elec), Anne Marie Storm (elec), J. Ribera (cnd) *(rec live, Koldinghaus Castle, Denmark, May 2, 1996)* — Danica ▲ DCD 1996

Karlsson, Ola (vc)
- Berwald, F.:Trios, w. L. Negro (pno), B. Lysell (vn)—No. 3 — Musica Sveciae ▲ MSCD 521 [DDD]
- Mozart, W.A.:Trio Pno, K.502, w. I. Wikström (pno), B. Lysell (vn) — Proprius ▲ PRCD 9054
- Mozart, W.A.:Trio Pno, K.542, w. I. Wikström (pno), B. Lysell (vn) — Proprius ▲ PRCD 9054

Karman, M. (vn)
- Goosen, F.:Clausulae, w. W. Henderson (pno) — CRI ▲ CD 665 [ADD]
- Goosen, F.:Temple Music, w. W. Henderson (pno) — CRI ▲ CD 665 [ADD]

Karolyi, J. von (pno)
- Chopin, F.:Barcarolle Pno *(rec live, Vienna 1954)* — Melodram ▲ MEL 18025 (m/s) [AAD]
- Chopin, F.:Con 2 Pno, w. L. Blech (cnd), Berlin RSO *(rec live, Berlin 6/4/50)* — Melodram ▲ MEL 18025 (m/s) [AAD]
- Chopin, F.:Preludes, Op. 28 *(rec live in Berlin, 1960)* — Melodram ▲ MEL 18025 (m/s) [AAD]

Karon, R. (tpt)
- Petrassi, G.:Fanfare for 3 Tpts, w. G. B. Dillon (tpt), A. Plog (tpt) — Crystal ▲ CD 663 [DDD]

Karp, Bess (hpd)
- Boccherini, L.:Sons Pno, Op. 5, w. Sheridon Stokes (fl) [arr for Fl & Hpd] *(rec Brentwood, CA, 1973)* — Orion ▲ 7821-2 [AAD]

Karp, Howard (pno)
- Bloch, E.:Qnt 1 Pno, w. Pro Arte String Quartet — Laurel ▲ LR 848 CD [ADD]
- Bloch, E.:Qnt 2 Pno, w. Pro Arte String Quartet — Laurel ▲ LR 848 CD [ADD]
- Read, G.:Chamber Music, w. Janet Packer (vn), Gerald Berthiaume (cel), Leslie Stratton Norris (hp), Barbara Harbach (hpd), Joseph Holt (pno), Boston Composers String Quartet—5 Aphorisms, Op. 150; Son. da Chiesa, Op. 61; Sonoric Fant. No. 1, Op. 102; Qt. 1 Strings, Op. 100 — Northeastern ▲ NOR 253 [DDD]
- Read, G.:5 Aphorisms, w. Janet Packer (vn) *(rec Tsai Performance Center, Boston Univ., May 1993)* — Northeastern ("Classical Arts, Contemporary" series) ▲ NR 253
- Rózsa, M.:Rhap Vc, w. P. Karp (vc) — Laurel ▲ LR 842CD [DDD]

Karp, Parry (vc)
- Bloch, E.:Suite 1 Vc — Laurel ▲ LR 848 CD [ADD]
- Rózsa, M.:Rhap Vc, w. H. Karp (pno) — Laurel ▲ LR 842CD [DDD]

Karpf, Juanita (vc)
- Schoenberg, A.:Pierrot lunaire, w. Leslie Boucher (nar), Julie Stone (fl/pic), Tod Kerstetter (cl/b cl), Andrew Carlson (vn), Philip Singleton (va), F. Joseph Lozier (pno) *(rec Roswell United Methodist Church, Roswell, GA, July 20, Aug. 2 & Sept. 1)* — ACA Digital ▲ CM 20027
- Zwilich, E.T.:Passages, w. Leslie Boucher (sop), Julie Stone (fl/pic), Tod Kerstetter (cl/b cl), Andrew Carlson (vn), Philip Singleton (va), F. Joseph Lozier (pno), Joanna Parks (perc), Shannon O'Kelley (perc) *(rec Roswell United Methodist Church, Roswell, GA, July 20, Aug. 2 & Sept. 1)* — ACA Digital ▲ CM 20027

Karpienia, Joseph (gtr)
- Christmas in the New World, w. Western Wind, Albert de Ruiter (bass), Louise Schulman (vn), Wendy Gillespie (vl), Elaine Comparone (hpd) — MusicMasters ▲ 01612-67176-2

Karr, Colin (vc)
- Brahms, J.:Sextet Strs, Op. 36, w. Ani Kavafian (vn), Benny Kim (vn), Randolph Kelly (va), Cynthia Phelps (va), Peter Rejto (vc) *(rec Tuscon Winter Chamber Festival; Mar 11, 1994)* — Arizona Friends of Chamber Music ▲ AFCD 19941

Karr, Gary (db)
- Downey, J.:Con Db, w. G. Simon (cnd), London SO *(rec Blackheath Concert Halls, London, Feb 27-28 & Mar 1, 1991)* — Cala ▲ CACD 1003 [DDD]
- Dvořák, A.:Qnt Strs, Op. 77, w. Portland String Quartet — Arabesque ▲ Z 6558 [DDD]
- Paganini, N.:Intro & Vars on "Dal tuo stellato soglio", w. G. Simon (cnd), London SO — LaserLight ▲ 14010 [DDD]
- Paganini, N.:Intro & Vars on "Dal tuo stellato soglio", w. U. Lajovic (cnd), Berlin RSO [arr. Karr] — Koch Schwann ▲ SCH 313382 [ADD/DDD]
- Schubert, Franz:Qnt Pno, D.667, w. E. Taussig (pno), R. Ricci (vn), M. Virizly (vc), E. Klemmstein (va) — One-Eleven ▲ URS 92010
- The Spirit of Koussevitzky, w. Harmon Lewis (pno) — VQR Digital ▲ VQR 2031 [DDD]
- We Wish You a Merry Christmas, w. Harmon Lewis (org) — VQR Digital ▲ VQR 2036 [DDD]

Karri, Harri (pno)
- Sibelius, J.:The Wood Nymph Nar, w. Lasse Pöysti (nar), O. Vänskä (cnd), Lahti SO *(rec Church of the Cross, Lahti, Finland, Jan 8-12, 1996)* — BIS ▲ CD 815 [DDD]

Karttunen, Anssi (vc)
- Beethoven, L. van:Son 3 Vc, w. Tuija Hakkila (pno) — Finlandia ▲ FIN 99955 [DDD]
- Beethoven, L. van:Son 4 Vc, w. Tuija Hakkila (pno) — Finlandia ▲ FIN 99955 [DDD]
- Beethoven, L. van:Son 5 Vc, w. Tuija Hakkila (pno) — Finlandia ▲ FIN 99955 [DDD]
- Dun, T.:Elegy:Snow in June, w. Talujon Percussion Quartet *(rec June 4, 1992)* — CRI ▲ CD 655 [DDD]
- Haydn, J.:Trios Pno, Fl & Vc, w. Tuija Hakkila (pno), Mikael Helasvuo (fl) [period instrs] *(rec Oct. 7-9, 1991)* — Finlandia ▲ 4509-95869-2 [DDD]
- Hindemith, P.:Kammermusik 3, w. E.-P. Salonen (cnd), London Sinfonietta *(rec May 8-10, 1990)* — Finlandia ▲ 4509-95865-2 [DDD]
- Lindberg, M.:Zona, w. E.-P. Salonen (cnd), London Sinfonietta *(rec May 8-10, 1990)* — Finlandia ▲ 4509-95865-2 [DDD]
- Merikanto, A.:Concert Piece Vc, w. E.-P. Salonen (cnd), London Sinfonietta *(rec May 8-10, 1990)* — Finlandia ▲ 4509-95865-2 [DDD]

Karttunen, Anssi (vc) (cont.)
- Saariaho, K.:...à la fumée, w. P. Alanko (a fl), E.-P. Salonen (cnd), Los Angeles PO — Ondine ▲ Ode 804 [DDD]
- Saariaho, K.:Petals — Neuma ▲ 450-73 [DDD]

Kasai, Kiyoshi (fl)
- Koechlin, C.:Paysages et marines, w. Elmar Schmid (cl), Alexandru Gavrilovici (vn), Urs Walker (vn), Christoph Schiller (va), Patrick Demenga (vc) — Accord ▲ ACD 201092 [DDD]

Kashkashian, Kim (va)
- Bouchard, L.:Pourtinade, w. R. Schulkowsky (perc) — ECM New Series ▲ 78118-21425-2 [DDD]
- Britten, H.:Lachrymae, w. D. R. Davies (cnd), Stuttgart CO — ECM New Series ▲ 78118-20002-2
- Britten, H.:Lachrymae, w. R. Levin (pno) — ECM New Series ▲ 78118-21316-2 [ADD]
- Carter, E.:Elegy Va, w. R. Levin (pno) — ECM New Series ▲ 78118-21316-2 [ADD]
- Chihara, P.:Redwood, w. R. Schulkowsky (perc) — ECM New Series ▲ 78118-21425-2 [DDD]
- Glazunov, A.:Elégie Vc, w. R. Levin (pno) — ECM New Series ▲ 78118-21316-2 [ADD]
- Hindemith, P.:Kammermusik (comp), w. R. Brautigam (pno), L. Harrell (vc), K. Kulka (vn), N. Blume (va d'amore), L. van Doeselaar (org), R. Chailly (cnd), Royal Concertgebouw Orch—No. 1 for Small Orchestra, Op. 24/1 (1922); No. 2 (Piano Concerto) for Piano & 12 Instruments, Op. 36/1 (1924); No. 3 (Cello Concerto), foe Cello & 10 Instruments, Op. 36/2 (1925); No. 4 (Violin Concerto) for Violin & Large Orchestra, Op. 36/3 (1925); No. 5 (Viola Concerto) for Viola & Large Chamber Orchestra, Op. 36/4 (1927); No. 6 (Viola d'amore Concerto) for Viola d'amore & Chamber Orchestra, Op. 46/1 (1927); No. 7 (Organ Concerto) for Organ & chamber Orchestra, Op. 46/2 (1927) — London 2-▲ 433816-2 [DDD]
- Hindemith, P.:Sons Va—Op. 11/5 (1919); Op. 25/1 (1922); Op. 31/4 (1924); Sonata (1937) — ECM New Series 2-▲ 78118-21330-2 [DDD]
- Hindemith, P.:Sons Va & Pno, w. R. Levin (pno)—Op. 11/4 (1919); Op. 25/4 (1922); Sonata (1939) — ECM New Series 2-▲ 78118-21330-2 [DDD]
- Hindemith, P.:Trauermusik, w. D. R. Davies (cnd), Stuttgart CO — ECM New Series ▲ 78118-20002-2
- Jemnitz, S.:Trio Gtr, Vn & Va, w. D. Starobin (gtr), B. Hudson (vn) — Bridge ▲ BCD 9004 ■ BC5-7004
- Kancheli, G.:Abii ne viderem, w. D. R. Davies (cnd), Stuttgart CO *(rec Apr. 1994)* — ECM New Series ▲ 78118-21510-2 [DDD]
- Kancheli, G.:Vom Winde beweint, w. D. R. Davies (cnd), Beethovenhalle Orch — ECM New Series ▲ 78118-21471-2 [DDD]
- Karaindrou, E.:Ulysses' Gaze — ECM New Series ▲ 78118-21570-2
- Kodály, Z.:Adagio Vn, w. R. Levin (pno) — ECM New Series ▲ 78118-21316-2 [ADD]
- Kurtág, G.:Hommage à R. Schumann, w. Eduard Brunner (cl), Robert Levin (pno) *(rec Beethovenhaus, Bonn, Aug. 1992 & May & Sept. 1)* — ECM New Series ▲ 78118-21508-2 [DDD]
- Kurtág, G.:Signs *(rec Beethovenhaus, Bonn, Aug. 1992 & May & Sept. 1)* — ECM New Series ▲ 78118-21508-2 [DDD]
- Kurtág, G.:Stücke Va *(rec Beethovenhaus, Bonn, Aug. 1992 & May & Sept. 1)* — ECM New Series ▲ 78118-21508-2 [DDD]
- Liszt, F.:Romance oubliée, w. R. Levin (pno) — ECM New Series ▲ 78118-21316-2 [ADD]
- Mozart, W.A.:Adagio & Fugue Strs, w. Gidon Kremer (vn), Jean-Marc Phillips (vn), Yo-Yo Ma (vc) — CBS ▲ MK 42134 [DDD]
- Mozart, W.A.:Sinf Concertante Vn Va Orch, w. Gidon Kremer (vn), N. Harnoncourt (cnd), Vienna PO — Deutsche Grammophon ("2CD" series) 2-▲ 453 043-2
- Mozart, W.A.:Trio Vn, K.563, w. G. Kremer (vn), Y.-Y. Ma (vc) — CBS ▲ MK 39561 [DDD]
- Orrego-Salas, J.:Mobili, w. James Tocco (pno) *(rec Musical Arts Ctr, Bloomington, IN, Apr 3, 1987)* — Indiana Univ School of Music ▲ IUSM 02
- Penderecki, K.:Con Va, w. D. R. Davies (cnd), Stuttgart CO — ECM New Series ▲ 78118-20002-2
- Penderecki, K.:Qt Cl, w. Sharon Kam (cl), Christoph Poppen (vn), Boris Pergamenschikov (vc) *(rec National Philharmonic Hall, Warsaw, Poland, Nov. 23, 1993)* — Sony Classical ▲ SK 66284 [DDD]
- Romances & Elegies for Viola & Piano, w. Robert Levin (pno) — ECM New Series ▲ 78118-21316-2 [ADD]
- Schnittke, A.:Con Va, w. D.R. Davies (cnd), Saarbrück RSO — ECM New Series ▲ 78118-21471-2 [DDD]
- Schubert, Franz:Qt 15 Strs, w. G. Kremer (vn), D. Phillips (vn), Yo Yo Ma (vc) — CBS ▲ MK 42134 [DDD]
- Schulhoff, E.:Sxt Strs, w. G. Kremer (vn), P. Hirschhorn (vn), N. Imai (va), D. Geringas (vc), J. Berger (vc) *(rec Lockenhaus Festival, 1986)* — ECM New Series 2-▲ 78118-21347-2 [DDD]
- Schumann, R.:Märchenbilder, w. Robert Levin (pno) *(rec Beethovenhaus, Bonn, Aug. 1992 & May & Sept. 1)* — ECM New Series ▲ 78118-21508-2 [DDD]
- Schumann, R.:Märchenerzählungen, w. Eduard Brunner (cl), Robert Levin (pno) *(rec Beethovenhaus, Bonn, Aug. 1992 & May & Sept. 1)* — ECM New Series ▲ 78118-21508-2 [DDD]
- Shostakovich, D.:Qt 14 Strs, w. G. Kremer (vn), Y. Horigome (vn), D. Geringas (vc) *(rec Lockenhaus Festival, 1986)* — ECM New Series 2-▲ 78118-21347-2 [DDD]
- Shostakovich, D.:Qt 15 Strs, w. G. Kremer (vn), D. Phillips (vn), Yo Yo Ma (vc) — CBS ▲ MK 44924 [DDD]
- Shostakovich, D.:Son Va, w. R. Levin (pno) — ECM New Series ▲ 78118-21425-2
- Tchaikovsky, P.:Souvenir de Florence, w. M. Perenyi (vc), Keller String Quartet — Erato ▲ 94819
- Vieuxtemps, H.:Elégie, w. R. Levin (pno) — ECM New Series ▲ 78118-21316-2 [ADD]

Kashkashian, Kim (vl)
- Bach, J.S.:Sons Vl, BWV 1027-1029, w. K. Jarrett (hpd) — ECM New Series ▲ 78118-21501-2

Kashou, Mike (arabic tabla)
- Vivaldi, A.:Cons Vn, Op. 8/1-4, "The Four Seasons", w. Jerome Franke (vn), Karine Garibova (vn), Pasquale Laurino (vn), Olga Miliaeva (va), Roza Borisova (vc), Mika Hennessy (db), Melanie Panush (ham dlc), Stanislav Venglevski (bayan), Daryl Stuermer (gtr), Ed Paloucek (celtic fid), Gary Bottoni (highland pipe), Dubuffet String Quartet *(rec July-Sept 1995)* — EarthBeat! ▲ 35270-2 [DDD]

Kasica, J. (org)
- Dvořák, A.:Mass, w. L. Mátl (cnd), Czech Phil Chorus — Supraphon ▲ SUP 11 1430 [DDD]

Kasman, Yakov (pno)
- Mussorgsky, M.:Pno Music—Hopak; Méditation; Une larme *(rec Feb. 1994)* — Calliope ▲ CAL 9228 [DDD]
- Mussorgsky, M.:Pictures at an Exhibition *(rec Feb. 1994)* — Calliope ▲ CAL 9228 [DDD]
- Prokofiev, S.:Son 1 Pno *(rec 1994 & 1995)* — Calliope ▲ CAL 9606.7 [DDD]
- Prokofiev, S.:Son 1 Pno — Calliope ▲ CAL 9607
- Prokofiev, S.:Son 2 Pno *(rec 1994 & 1995)* — Calliope ▲ CAL 9606.7 [DDD]
- Prokofiev, S.:Son 3 Pno *(rec 1994 & 1995)* — Calliope ▲ CAL 9606.7 [DDD]
- Prokofiev, S.:Son 4 Pno — Calliope ▲ CAL 9607
- Prokofiev, S.:Son 5 Pno — Calliope ▲ CAL 9607
- Prokofiev, S.:Son 5 Pno *(rec 1994 & 1995)* — Calliope ▲ CAL 9606.7 [DDD]
- Prokofiev, S.:Son 7 Pno *(rec 1994 & 1995)* — Calliope ▲ CAL 9606.7 [DDD]
- Prokofiev, S.:Son 7 Pno — Calliope ▲ CAL 9607
- Prokofiev, S.:Son 8 Pno *(rec 1994 & 1995)* — Calliope ▲ CAL 9606.7 [DDD]
- Prokofiev, S.:Son 9 Pno *(rec 1994 & 1995)* — Calliope ▲ CAL 9606.7 [DDD]
- Prokofiev, S.:Son 9 Pno — Calliope ▲ CAL 9607
- Stravinsky, I.:Pétrouchka (3 Scenes) *(rec Feb. 1994)* — Calliope ▲ CAL 9228 [DDD]
- Stravinsky, I.:Tango Pno *(rec Feb. 1994)* — Calliope ▲ CAL 9228 [DDD]

Kasmetski, Christo Todorov (ob)
- Mozart, W.A.:Adagio & Rondo Glass Armonica, w. A. Atanasov (org), L. Oshavkova (fl), Ognian Stantchev (va), N. Bespalov (vc) — Divertimento ▲ DIV 31020 [DDD]
- Mozart, W.A.:Qnt Pno, K.452, w. V. Tchutchov (pno), L. Oshavkova (fl), P. Radev (cl), S. Kunchev (hn) — Divertimento ▲ DIV 31020 [DDD]

Kašný, Miroslav (va)—see ORCHESTRAS & ENSEMBLES Bohuslav Martinů Philharmonic String Quartet

Kaspar, Paul (pno)
- Martinů, B.:Sons Vc, w. Jiri Hanousek (vc) — Centaur ▲ CRC 2207

Kaspersen, Jan (pno)
- Satie, E.:Pno Music (misc)—Gnossiennes 4-6; Pièces froides; Sarabandes 1-3; Sports & divertissements; Ogives 1-4; Descriptions automatiques; Embryons desséchés; Avant-dernières pensées *(rec Focus Recording Studio, Copenhagen, Apr, May & June 1995)* — Classico ▲ 126

INSTRUMENT.

Kaspersen, Jan (pno) (cont.)
Satie, E.:Pno Music (misc)—Gnossienne Nos 1–3; Gymnopédies 1–3; Véritables préludes flasques 1–3; Croquis et agaceries d'un gros bonhomme en bois; Heures séculaires et instantanées; 5 Portraits d'un Oiseau; Rare, Op. 5/5 *(rec Aug. 1986)* Classico ▲ CLASSCD 109
Kasprik, Ales (vc)—see ORCHESTRAS & ENSEMBLES Wilhan String Quartet
Kaspryzyk, James (sax)—see ORCHESTRAS & ENSEMBLES Chicago Saxophone Quartet
Kassai, István (pno)
Bloch, E.:Pno Music—Poems of the Sea (1922); In the Night (1922); Nirvana (poem for piano) (1923); Five Sketches in Sepia (1923); Enfantines (ten pieces for children) (1923); Four Circus Pieces Marco Polo ▲ 8.223288 [DDD]
Bloch, E.:Pno Music—Ex-voto (1914); Danse sacrée (1923); Sonata (1935); Visions & Prophecies (1936) Marco Polo ▲ 8.223289 [DDD]
Erkel, F.:Duo brillant en forme de fantaisie sur des airs hongrois concertant, w. F. Szecsődi (vn) Marco Polo ▲ 8.223317
Erkel, F.:Intro & Verbunkos, w. P. Lukács (va) Marco Polo ▲ 8.223317
Erkel, F.:Opera Transcriptions—selections from *Bánk bán, Bátori Mária, Dózsa György, Erzsébet, Hunyadi László, Sarolta* [transcr. Ferenc Erkel]; selection from *Brankovics* [transcr. Sándor Erkel] Marco Polo ▲ 8.223318
Erkel, F.:Pno Music—Albumleaves; Erinnerung an H.W. Ernst (Introduction & Capriccio); Introduction & Variations on a Theme from Endre Bartay's opera Csel; Original Ungarischer; Rákóczy March (Souvenir for Franz Liszt) Marco Polo ▲ 8.223317
Liszt, F.:Pno Music (misc)—Funeral Prelude & Funeral March; Fant. on Szép Ilonka; Funeral Procession [works inspired by Mosonyi] *(rec Festetich Castle, Budapest, Nov. 19–21, 26 & 27, 1993)* Marco Polo ▲ 8.223559 [DDD]
Mosonyi, M.:Festival Music, w. K. Körmendi (pno) *(rec Budapest, Nov. & Dec. 1992)* Marco Polo ▲ 8.223558 [DDD]
Mosonyi, M.:Grand Duo, w. K. Körmendi (pno) *(rec Budapest, Nov. & Dec. 1992)* Marco Polo ▲ 8.223558 [DDD]
Mosonyi, M.:Missa solemnis, w. K. Körmendi (pno) *(rec Budapest, Nov. & Dec. 1992)* Marco Polo ▲ 8.223558 [DDD]
Mosonyi, M.:Pno Music—Hungarian Children's World; Studies for Development in the Performance of Hungarian Music Marco Polo ▲ 8.223557 [DDD]
Mosonyi, M.:Pno Music—3 Pno Pieces; 2 Pearls; Puszta Life; Homage to the Spirit of Ferenc Kazinczy; Hungarian Musical Poem; Funeral Music for the Death of István Széchenyi *(rec Festetich Castle, Budapest, Nov. 19–21, 26 & 27, 1993)* Marco Polo ▲ 8.223559 [DDD]
Mosonyi, M.:3 Colors, w. K. Körmendi (pno) *(rec Budapest, Nov. & Dec. 1992)* Marco Polo ▲ 8.223558 [DDD]

Kassinger, Robert (db)
Dankner, S.:Sextet, w. L. Skelton (pno), V. Poullette (vn), E. Tanner (vn), M. Gyurik (va), A. Nisbet (vc) Albany ▲ TROY 067

Kastle, Richard (pno)
Streetwise Virgin Classics ▲ CVC 59225
Kästner, Hannes (org)
Bach, J.S.:Org Music (misc)—Fantasia in G, BWV 572; Wachet auf, ruft uns die Stimme, BWV 645; Fantasia & Fugue in g, BWV 542; Toccata & Fugue in d, BWV 565; Ich ruf zu dir, Herr Jesu Christ, BWV 639; Prelude & Fugue in C, BWV 547 Capriccio ▲ CDC 10035 [DDD]
Bach, J.S.:Org Music (misc), w. G. Lehotka (org)—Chorales, BWV.614, 622, 683, 703 & 727; Fantasie & Fugue, BWV.561; Fugue, BWV.578; Praeludium & Fugue, BWV.542 & 552; Toccata & Fugue, BWV.565 LaserLight ▲ 15507 [ADD]
Beethoven, L. van:Missa Solemnis, w. Anna Tomowa-Sintow (sop), Annelies Burmeister (alt), Peter Schreier (ten), Hermann Christian Polster (bass), Gerhard Bosse (vn), K. Masur (cnd), Leipzig Gewandhaus Orch, Leipzig Radio Chorus Berlin Classics ("Masur Edition" series) ▲ BER 9160
Classics Go to the Movies, Vol. 5, w. Salzburg Mozarteum Orch, Bavarian RSO, Ludovic Spiess (ten), Virginia Zeani (sop), Rumanian Opera Orch, Rumanian Radio-TV Studio Orch, Sofia PO, Budapest SO, Philharmonia Orch LaserLight ▲ 15 645
Katahn, Enid (pno)
Chaminade, C.:Pno Music (misc)—Toccata; Dragon Flies; Concert Etudes; The Fauns; Valse-caprice; Étude symphonique; Contes Bleus; Sonate Gasparo ▲ GS 247 [DDD]
Dubois, P.-M.:Pno Music—Sonata; Toccata; Pour les belles ecouteuses; Hommage a Poulenc; Etudes de Concert (10) Gasparo ▲ GS 230
Macdowell, E.:Con 2 Pno—5 sels. from New England Idyls Gasparo ▲ GS 236
Nielsen, C.:Pno Music—Chaconne, Op. 32; 5 Pieces, Op. 3; Humoresque-Bagatelles, Op. 11; Suite, Op. 45; Theme with Var., Op. 40; 3 Pieces, Op. 59 Gasparo ▲ GS 268 ■ GS 268C
Roussel, A.:L'Accueil des muses *(rec Blair School of Music Recital Hall, Vanderbilt University, Nashville, TN)* Gasparo ▲ GSCD 295
Roussel, A.:Des heures passent *(rec Blair School of Music Recital Hall, Vanderbilt University, Nashville, TN)* Gasparo ▲ GSCD 295
Roussel, A.:Pieces Pno *(rec Blair School of Music Recital Hall, Vanderbilt University, Nashville, TN)* Gasparo ▲ GSCD 295
Roussel, A.:Rustiques *(rec Blair School of Music Recital Hall, Vanderbilt University, Nashville, TN)* Gasparo ▲ GSCD 295
Roussel, A.:Sonatine Pno *(rec Blair School of Music Recital Hall, Vanderbilt University, Nashville, TN)* Gasparo ▲ GSCD 295
Roussel, A.:Suite Pno *(rec Blair School of Music Recital Hall, Vanderbilt University, Nashville, TN)* Gasparo ▲ GSCD 295

Katchen, Julius (pno)
Beethoven, L. van:Con 3 Pno, w. P. Gamba (cnd), London SO *(rec 1958)* London 2-▲ 440839-2 [ADD]
Beethoven, L. van:Con 3 Pno, w. P. Gamba (cnd), London SO *(rec 1963)* PWK Classics ▲ PWK 1153 [AAD]
Beethoven, L. van:Con 4 Pno, w. P. Gamba (cnd), London SO *(rec 1963)* London 2-▲ 440839-2 [ADD]
Beethoven, L. van:Con 4 Pno, w. P. Gamba (cnd), London SO *(rec 1959)* PWK Classics ▲ PWK 1153 [AAD]
Beethoven, L. van:Con 5 Pno, "Emperor", w. P. Gamba (cnd), London SO *(rec 1963)* London 2-▲ 440839-2 [ADD]
Beethoven, L. van:Fant Pno, Op. 80, "Choral Fant", w. P. Gamba (cnd), London SO, London Sym Chorus *(rec 1965)* London 2-▲ 440839-2 [ADD]
Brahms, J.:Con 1 Pno, w. P. Monteux (cnd), London SO London ("Double Decker" series) 2-▲ 440612-2
Brahms, J.:Con 2 Pno, w. P. Monteux (cnd), London SO London ("Double Decker" series) 2-▲ 440612-2
Brahms, J.:Trio 1 Pno, w. J. Suk (vn), J. Starker (vc) London ▲ 421152-2 [ADD]
Brahms, J.:Trio 2 Pno, w. J. Suk (vn), J. Starker (vc) London ▲ 421152-2 [ADD]
Brahms, J.:Vars & Fugue on a Theme by Handel London ("Double Decker" series) 2-▲ 440612-2
Brahms, J.:Vars on a Theme by Paganini London ("Double Decker" series) 2-▲ 440612-2
Gershwin, G.:Con Pno, w. A.P. Mantovani (cnd), Mantovani Orch London ▲ 436570-2 (m) [ADD]
Gershwin, G.:Rhap in Blue, w. I. Kertész (cnd), London SO London ▲ 436570-2 (m) [ADD]
Largo I, w. Vladimir Ashkenazy (pno), Alfred Brendel (pno), Alicia de Larrocha (pno), András Schiff (pno), Iliana Vered (pno), et al. Celestial Harmonies ▲ 35509-2 2-■ 35509-4
Largo II, w. Vladimir Ashkenazy (pno), Alfred Brendel (pno), Alicia de Larrocha (pno), András Schiff (pno), Iliana Vered (pno), et al. Celestial Harmonies ▲ 19504-2 ■ 19504-4
Mozart, W.A.:Con 23 Pno, w. P. Argento (cnd), Prague SO *(rec live 1966)* Multisonic ("Prague Spring Collection" series) ▲ 31 0079-2 [ADD]
Rachmaninoff, S.:Con 2 Pno, w. G. Solti (cnd), London SO London ("Weekend Classics" series) ▲ 417880-2 [ADD] ■ 417880-4
Rachmaninoff, S.:Rhapsody on a Theme of Paganini, w. A. Boult (cnd), London PO London ("Weekend Classics" series) ▲ 417880-2 [AAD] ■ 417880-4
Rorem, N.:Son 2 Pno CRI ■ ACS 6007

Katchen, Julius (pno) (cont.)
Saint-Saëns, C.:Carnival of the Animals, w. Lillie (nar), Graffman (pno), S. Henderson (cnd), London SO [E] London ■ 411650-4
Schumann, R.:Con Pno, w. I. Kertész (cnd), Israel PO IMP Collectors Series ▲ IMPX 9041 [ADD]
Kates, Stephen (vc)
Lewis, R.H.:Combinazioni IV, w. Ellen Mack (pno) *(rec Peabody Institute Concert Hall, Baltimore, MD, Oct 26, 1978)* Albany ▲ TROY 166 [ADD/DDD]
Rachmaninoff, S.:Son Vc, w. C. P. Kobler (pno) Bainbridge ▲ BCD 6272 [ADD]
Starer, R.:Anna Margarita's Will, w. P. Bryn-Johnson (sop), K. Kraber (fl), P. Ingraham (hn), D. Sutherland (pno) *(rec 1980)* CRI ▲ CD 612 [ADD]
Taneyev, S.:Qnt Pno Strs, w. J. Lowenthal (pno), P. Rosenthal (vn), Y. Kamei (vn), M. Thompson (va) Arabesque ▲ Z 6539 [DDD]

Katims, Milton (va)
Brahms, J.:Sextet Strs, Op. 18, w. I. Stern (vn), A. Schneider (vn), M. Thomas (va), P. Casals (vc), M. Foley (vc) *(rec Prades, France, June 23–July 3, 1952)* Sony Classical ("The Casals Edition" series) ▲ SMK 58994 [ADD]
Brahms, J.:Sextet Strs, Op. 18, w. I. Stern (vn), A. Schneider (vn), M. Thomas (va), P. Casals (vc), M. Foley (vc) *(rec 1952)* Sony Masterworks ("Portrait" series) ▲ MPK 44851 [ADD]
Debussy, C.:Son Fl, w. John Wummer (fl), Laura Newell (hp) Ambassador ▲ ARC 1013
Mozart, W.A.:Qts Pno, w. Eugene Istomin (pno), Isaac Stern (vn), Leonard Rose (vc)—No. 2 Sony Classical ("Isaac Stern:A Life in Music" series) 2-▲ SM2K 64516
Schubert, Franz:Qnt Strs, D.956, w. I. Stern (vn), A. Schneider (vn), P. Casals (vc), P. Tortelier (vc) *(rec 1952)* CBS 4-▲ M4K 42003 (m/s) [ADD]
Schubert, Franz:Qnt Strs, D.956, w. I. Stern (vn), A. Schneider (vn), P. Casals (vc), P. Tortelier (vc) *(rec Prades, France, July 1–2, 1952)* Sony Classical ("The Casals Edition" series) ▲ SMK 58992 [ADD]
Katin, Peter (pno)
Bach, J.S.:Chromatic Fant & Fugue Olympia ▲ OLY 189 [DDD]
Beethoven, L. van:Vars on an Original Theme, Op. 34 Olympia ▲ OLY 189 [DDD]
Brahms, J.:Fants Pno, Op. 116 Olympia ▲ OCD 263 [DDD]
Brahms, J.:Intermezzos Pno, Op. 117 Olympia ▲ OCD 263 [DDD]
Brahms, J.:Rhaps Pno, Op. 79 Olympia ▲ OCD 263 [DDD]
Brahms, J.:Vars & Fugue on a Theme by Handel Olympia ▲ OCD 263 [DDD]
Chopin, F.:Ballades Pno (comp)—Op. 52 Olympia ▲ OCD 186 [DDD]
Chopin, F.:Barcarolle Pno Olympia ▲ OCD 186 [DDD]
Chopin, F.:Mazurkas—Op. 59/1–3 Olympia ▲ OCD 186 [DDD]
Chopin, F.:Pno Music (misc)—Fantaisie in f, Op. 49; Nocturne in D♭, Op. 27/2; Polonaise in f♯, Op. 44 *(rec live, 1977)* PWK Classics ▲ PWK 1131 [AAD]
Chopin, F.:Polonaise-fant Olympia ▲ OCD 186 [DDD]
Chopin, F.:Son Pno, Op. 58 Olympia ▲ OCD 186 [DDD]
Chopin, F.:Son Pno, Op. 58 *(rec live, 1977)* PWK Classics ▲ PWK 1131 [AAD]
Clementi, M.:Sons Pno—in f♯, Op. 25/5; in B♭, Op. 24/2; in g, Op. 7/3; in D, Op. 25/6; in f, Op. 13/6 [Clementi Square Piano] Athene ▲ ATHCD 4
Debussy, C.:Estampes Olympia ▲ OLY 189 [DDD]
Haydn, J.:Sons Pno—No. 52 Olympia ▲ OLY 189 [DDD]
Liszt, F.:Années de pèlerinage 1—No. 6—"Vallée d'Oberman" Olympia ▲ OLY 189 [DDD]
Mathias, W.:Con 3 Pno, w. D. Atherton (cnd), London SO, New Philharmonia Orch Lyrita ▲ SRCD 325
Mozart, W.A.:Allegro & Andante & Rondo Olympia ▲ OCD 233 [DDD]
Mozart, W.A.:Fant Pno, K.475 Olympia ▲ CD 230 [DDD]
Mozart, W.A.:Sons Pno—No. 1, K.279; No. 2, K.280; No. 4, K.282; No. 7, K.309 Olympia ▲ OCD 232 [DDD]
Mozart, W.A.:Sons Pno—No. 6, K.284 & No. 16, K.570 Olympia ▲ OCD 233 [DDD]
Mozart, W.A.:Sons Pno—No. 3, K.281; No. 5, K.283; No. 13, K.333; No. 17, K.576 Olympia ▲ OCD 234 [DDD]
Mozart, W.A.:Sons Pno—No. 8, K.310; No. 9, K.311; No. 13, K.332; No. 15, K.545 Olympia ▲ OCD 231 [DDD]
Mozart, W.A.:Sons Pno Olympia 5-▲ OCD 5003 [DDD]
Mozart, W.A.:Sons Pno—No. 10, K.330; No. 11, K.331; No. 14, K.457 Olympia ▲ OCD 230 [DDD]
Piano Magic Pickwick ("The Orchid" series) ▲ PICORCD 11001
Rachmaninoff, S.:Prelude Pno, Op. 3/2 IMP Classics ▲ IMP PCD 1081 [DDD]
Rachmaninoff, S.:Preludes Pno, Opp 23 & 32 IMP Classics ▲ IMP PCD 1081 [DDD]
Saint-Saëns, C.:Carnival of the Animals, w. P. Fowke (pno), A. Gibson (cnd), Scottish National Orch Classics for Pleasure ▲ CDCFP 4086 [ADD]
Schubert, Franz:Impromptus Pno (comp) [Clementi Square Piano] Athene ▲ ATHCD 5
Schubert, Franz:Moments musicaux Athene ▲ ATH CD7 [DDD]
Schubert, Franz:Pieces Pno, D.946 Athene ▲ ATH CD7 [DDD]
Schubert, Franz:Son Pno, D.537 Olympia ▲ OCD 188 [DDD]
Schubert, Franz:Son Pno, D.960 Olympia ▲ OCD 188 [DDD]
Schubert, Franz:Valses sentimentales Athene ▲ ATH CD7 [DDD]
Schumann, R.:Carnaval Pno Olympia ▲ OCD 218
Schumann, R.:Kinderszenen Olympia ▲ OCD 218
Kato, Hideki (bass instr)
Shea, D.:Hsi-Yu Chi, w. Sim Cain (perc), Wu Man (pipa), Zeena Parkins (hp/pno/acc), Jim Pugliese (perc), Mark Ribot (gtr/banjo), David Shea (sampler/pno/turntables), Alex Tobias (celtic dr/misc.), Rebecca Wilson (screaming), John Zorn (a sax) Tzadik ("The Composers" series) ▲ TZA 7005 [DDD]
Kato, Tomoko (vn)
Oe, H.:Vn & Pno Music, w. Akiko Ebi (pno)—Dream; Summer Holidays; Nocturnal Capriccio; Andante Cantabile; August Capriccio *(rec Asahikawa City, Hokkaido, June 27, 29 & 30, 1994)* Denon ▲ CO 78953 [DDD]
Katrama, Jorma (db)
Contrabbasso con bravura, w. Margit Rahkonen (pno) *(rec Mar. 1989)* Finlandia ▲ 4509-95864-2 [DDD]

Katsaris, Cyprien (pno)
Bach, J.S.:Con 1 Hpd, w. J. Rolla (cnd), Franz Liszt CO Teldec (Digital Experience) ▲ 9031-74779-2 AW [DDD]
Bach, J.S.:Con 3 Hpd, w. J. Rolla (cnd), Franz Liszt CO Teldec (Digital Experience) ▲ 9031-74779-2 AW [DDD]
Bach, J.S.:Con 5 Hpd, w. J. Rolla (cnd), Franz Liszt CO Teldec ("Digital Experience" series) ▲ 9031-74779-2 AW [DDD]
Bach, J.S.:Con 6 Hpd, w. J. Rolla (cnd), Franz Liszt CO Teldec ("Digital Experience" series) ▲ 9031-74779-2 AW [DDD]
Beethoven, L. van:Syms (comp) [arr. Liszt] Teldec 6-▲ 9031-71619-2
Beethoven, L. van:Sym 1 [trans. Liszt] Teldec ▲ 2292-43661-2 ZK [DDD]
Beethoven, L. van:Sym 2 [transcr. Liszt] Teldec ▲ 2292-43661-2 ZK [DDD]
Beethoven, L. van:Sym 3, "Eroica" [arr. Liszt] Teldec ▲ 2292-43107-2
Beethoven, L. van:Sym 5 [Liszt's solo piano arr.] Teldec ▲ 2292-44921-2 ZK [DDD]
Beethoven, L. van:Sym 6, "Pastorale" [transcr. Liszt] Teldec ▲ 2292-42920-2
Beethoven, L. van:Sym 7 [transcr. Liszt] Teldec ▲ 2292-43065-2
Beethoven, L. van:Sym 9, "Choral Sym" [transcr. Liszt] Teldec ▲ 2292-42985-2
Beethoven, L. van:Vars & Fugue Pno, Op. 35, "Eroica" Teldec ▲ 2292-44921-2 ZK [DDD]
Brahms, J.:Con 2 Pno, w. E. Inbal (cnd), Philharmonia Orch Teldec ("Digital Experience" series) ▲ 9031-77599-2 AW [DDD]
Chopin, F.:Andante Spianato & Grande Polonaise *(rec Mar. 3–22, 1993)* Sony Classical 2-▲ S2K 53967 [DDD]
Chopin, F.:Ballades Pno (comp) Teldec (Digital Experience) ▲ 9031-74781-2 AW [DDD]
Chopin, F.:Pno Music (misc) Teldec 2-▲ 95499-2
Chopin, F.:Polonaises—in c♯ & e♭, Op. 26; in A & c, Op. 40; in f♯, Op. 44; in A♭, Op. 53; in A♭, Op. 61; in d, B♭ & f, Op. 71; in C, Op. 72/2; in g, B♭, A♭, g♯, b♭ & G♭, Opp. Post. *(rec Mar. 3–22, 1993)* Sony Classical 2-▲ S2K 53967 [DDD]

▲ = CD ♦ = Enhanced CD Δ = MD ■ = Cassette Tape □ = DCC

Katsaris, Cyprien (pno) (cont.)

Chopin, F.:Polonaise-fant—Preludes, Op. 28, in c#, Op. 45, in Ab, Op. post; Songs, Op. 74, Nos. 2 & 3; Allegretto & Mazur; 2 Bourrées; Ecossaises; Bolero in C, Op. 19; Contredanse in Gb; Galop Marquis in Ab; Feuille d'album in E; Allegretto in F#; Cantabile in Bb; Largo in Eb; Fugue in a — Sony Classical ▲ SK 53355

Chopin, F.:Scherzos — Teldec (Digital Experience) ▲ 9031-74781-2 AW [DDD] ■ 9031-74781-4

Chopin, F.:Son Pno, Op. 4 — Sony Classical ▲ SK 48483 [DDD]

Chopin, F.:Son Pno, Op. 35 — Sony Classical ▲ SK 48483 [DDD]

Chopin, F.:Son Pno, Op. 58 — Sony Classical ▲ SK 48483 [DDD]

Chopin, F.:Waltzes — Teldec ▲ 2292-43038-2

Grieg, E.:Holberg Suite — Teldec ▲ 98147

Grieg, E.:Lyric Pieces—sels. — Teldec ▲ 98147

Grieg, E.:Norwegian Dances, Op. 35 — Teldec ▲ 98147

Grieg, E.:Peer Gynt Suites, Opp. 46 & 55—Morning Mood — Teldec ▲ 98147

Mahler, G.:Das Lied von der Erde, w. B. Fassbaender (mez), T. Moser (ten)—the first recording of Mahler's original piano/vocal score version [G] — Teldec ▲ 2292-46276-2 ZK [DDD]

Mendelssohn, F.:Con in a Pno, Op. posth., w. J. Rolla (cnd), Franz Liszt CO — Teldec ("Digital Experience" series) ▲ 9031-75860-2 AW [DDD] ■ 9031-75860-4

Mendelssohn, F.:Con 1 Pno, w. K. Masur (cnd), Leipzig Gewandhaus Orch — Teldec 4-▲ 9031-71104-2

Mendelssohn, F.:Con 1 Pno, w. K. Masur (cnd), Leipzig Gewandhaus Orch — Teldec ("Digital Experience" series) ▲ 9031-75860-2 AW [DDD] ■ 9031-75860-4

Mendelssohn, F.:Con 2 Pno, w. K. Masur (cnd), Leipzig Gewandhaus Orch — Teldec 4-▲ 9031-71104-2 ZB

Mendelssohn, F.:Con 2 Pno, w. K. Masur (cnd), Leipzig Gewandhaus Orch — Teldec ("Digital Experience" series) ▲ 9031-75860-2 AW [DDD] ■ 9031-75860-4

Mozartiana — Sony Classical ▲ SK 52551 [DDD]

Schumann, R.:Albumblätter — Teldec ▲ 2292-43290-2

Schumann, R.:Kinderszenen — Teldec ▲ 2292-43290-2

Sensual Classics II, w. A. Sultanov (pno), Brodsky Quartet, London SO [cnd:M. Shostakovich], New York PO [cnd:Z. Mehta], BBC SO [cnd:A. Davis], Leipzig Gewandhaus Orch [cnd:K. Masur], 12 Cellos of the Berlin PO [cnd:A. Jordan, E. Inbal], et al. — Teldec ▲ 92014-2 ■ 92014-4

Stravinsky, I.:Les Noces, w. A. Mory (sop), P. Parker (mez), J. Mitchinson (ten), P. Hudson (bass), M. Argerich (pno), H. Francesch (pno), K. Zimerman (pno), L. Bernstein (cnd), English Bach Festival Orch, English Bach Festival Chorus [R] — Deutsche Grammophon ("20th Century Classics" series) ▲ 423251-2 [ADD]

Katsuta, S. (vc)

Shinohara, M.:Cooperation, w. A. Nishigata (shamisen), K. Mitsuhashi (shakuhachi), M. Akao (fue), S. Yaotani (hichiriki), K. Ishikawa (sho), C. Fukunaga (koto), J. Ueda (biwa), M. Yoshizawa (kokyu), I. Tsuji (oboe), T. Takahashi (cl), G. Kitamura (tpt), A. Murata (trbn), S. Eiso (perc), S. Ueki (vn), Y. Shibuya (pno), K. Komatsu (cnd) *(rec live Casals Hall, Tokyo, Mar. 5, 1994)* — Camerata ▲ 30CM 375 [DDD]

Shinohara, M.:Tabiyuki, w. A. Ogawa (mez), M. Kakagawa (fl), I. Tsuji (ob), T. Takahashi (cl), K. Okazaki (fagotto), G. Kitamura (tpt), A. Murata (trbn), S. Eiso (perc), S. Ueki (vn), A. Nakakoji (va), M. Komuro (contrabass), K. Komatsu (cnd) *(rec live Casals Hall, Tokyo, Mar. 5, 1994)* — Camerata ▲ 30CM 375 [DDD]

Katz, Helen (hpd)

Fontana, G.B.:Sons, w. Gerard Schwarz (tpt), Julie Feves (bn) — Vox Box 2-▲ CDX 5124 [ADD]

Frescobaldi, G.:Canzonas, Caprici & Ricercari, w. Gerard Schwarz (tpt), Julie Feves (bn) — Vox Box 2-▲ CDX 5124 [ADD]

Katz, Martin (pno)

Britten, H.:Canticle II, w. Ellen Shade (sop), John Stewart (ten) — Phoenix ▲ PHCD 129

Britten, H.:Sonnets of Michelangelo, w. John Stewart (ten) — Phoenix ▲ PHCD 129

Canciones Españoles, w. José Carreras (ten), English CO — Philips ("Spanish" series) ▲ 432825-2 FM [ADD]

Divas in Song:Marylin Horne, a 60th Birthday Celebration, w. Montserrat Caballé (sop), H. Donath (sop), R. A. Swenson (sop), F. von Stade (mez), R. Fleming (mez), S. Ramey (bass), J. Levine (cnd), W. Jones (pno), K. Donath (pno), Manuel Burgueras (pno) — RCA Red Seal ▲ 09026-62547-2

Italian Opera Composers' Songs, w. José Carreras (ten) — Sony Classical ▲ SK 45863 [DDD]

Mendelssohn, F.:Songs, w. F. von Stade (mez), M. Horne (mez)—4 Duets — RCA Red Seal ▲ 09026-61681-2

Renata Tebaldi alla Scala, w. Renata Tebaldi (sop) *(rec May 20, 1974)* — Myto ▲ MCD 943105

Rossini, G.:Giovanna d'Arco, w. M. Horne (mez) [I] — CBS ▲ MK 44820 [DDD]

Schumann, R.:Frauenliebe und -leben, w. F. von Stade (mez), M. Horne (mez) [sung as duet] — RCA Red Seal ▲ 09026-61681-2

Songs of the Nightingale, w. Karen Smith Emerson (sop), William Wittig (fl) *(rec Sweeney Concert Hall, Sage Hall, Smith College, Northampton, MA, Jan 3-5, 1994)* — Centaur ▲ 2232 [DDD]

Voyage à Paris, w. Frederica von Stade (mez) — RCA Red Seal ▲ 09026-62711-2

Katz, N. (va)—see ORCHESTRAS & ENSEMBLES Continuum Chamber Ensemble

Katz, Naomi (vn)—see ORCHESTRAS & ENSEMBLES Windham String Quartet

Katz, Paul (vc)—see ORCHESTRAS & ENSEMBLES Cleveland String Quartet

Kauffman, Irvin (gtr)

Kauffman, I.:D.S. al Fine, w. Brian Reagin (vn), Joen Vasquez (vn) — Alanna ▲ ALA 5552

Paganini, N.:Sons Vn & Gtr, w. Brian Reagin (vn)—in C — Alanna ▲ ALA 5552

Kauffmann, Jacques (org)

Langlais, J.:Chant grégorien, w. Schola Saint Grégoire du Mans Chorus [organ of the Dominican Church, Paris] — Skarbo ▲ SKR 1933 [DDD]

Langlais, J.:Missa in simplicitate, w. Schola Saint Grégoire du Mans Chorus [organ of the Dominican Church, Paris] — Skarbo ▲ SKR 1933 [DDD]

Kaufman, Annette (pno)

Helm, E.:Comment on 2 Spirituals, w. Louis Kaufman (vn) — Cambria ("Historical" series) ▲ CD 1078 [ADD]

Triggs, H.:Danza Braziliana, w. Louis Kaufman (vn) — Cambria ("Historical" series) ▲ CD 1078 [ADD]

Kaufman, Harry (pno)

Tchaikovsky, P.:Valse sentimentale, w. J. Szigeti (vn) *(rec 1944)* — Sony Masterworks (Portrait) ▲ MPK 52569 (m) [ADD]

Kaufman, Irvin (vc)—see ORCHESTRAS & ENSEMBLES Il Quattro

Kaufman, Louis (vn)

Barber, S.:Con Vn, w. W. Goehr (cnd), Lucerne Festival Orch *(rec 1951)* — Music & Arts ▲ CD 667 (m) [AAD]

Bennett, Robert Russell:Con Vn, w. B. Herrmann (cnd), Columbia SO — Cambria ("Historical" series) ▲ CD 1078 [ADD]

Bennett, Robert Russell:A Song Son, w. Theodore Saidenberg (pno) — Cambria ("Historical" series) ▲ CD 1078 [ADD]

Guarnieri, C.M.:Son 2 Vn, w. Arthur Balsam (pno) — Cambria ("Historical" series) ▲ CD 1078 [ADD]

Helm, E.:Comment on 2 Spirituals, w. Annette Kaufman (pno) — Cambria ("Historical" series) ▲ CD 1078 [ADD]

Khachaturian, A.:Con Vn, w. J.-M. Leconte (cnd), French National RSO *(rec 1955)* — Cambria ▲ CD 1063 [ADD]

Kreisler, F.:Vn Pieces, w. P. Ulanowsky (pno)—trans. of works by Rimsky-Korsakov *(Hymn to the Sun)*, Tchaikovsky *(Andante cantabile)*, Trad. *(Londonderry Air)* — Cambria ▲ CD 1063 [ADD]

Larsson, L.-E.:Con Vn, w. S. Frykberg (cnd), Swedish RSO *(rec Jan. 1955)* — Music & Arts ▲ CD 667 (m) [AAD]

McBride, R.:Aria & Toccata, w. B. Herrmann (cnd), Columbia SO — Cambria ("Historical" series) ▲ CD 1078 [ADD]

Martinů, B.:Con 2 Vn, w. J. Rachmilovich (cnd), Santa Monica Orch *(rec ca. 1946)* — Cambria ▲ CD 1063 [ADD]

Milhaud, D.:Saudades do Brasil, w. Theodore Saidenberg (pno)—No. 5 [Ipanema] — Cambria ("Historical" series) ▲ CD 1078 [ADD]

Spohr, L.:Son 5 Vn, w. Susann McDonald (hp) — Music & Arts ▲ CD 905 [ADD]

Kaufman, Louis (vn) (cont.)

Still, W.G.:Lenox Ave, w. B. Herrmann (cnd), Columbia SO—The Blues — Cambria ("Historical" series) ▲ CD 1078 [ADD]

Telemann, G.P.:Sons Vn, Op. 2, w. Frederick Hammond (hpd) — Music & Arts ▲ CD 905 [ADD]

Triggs, H.:Danza Braziliana, w. Annette Kaufman (pno) — Cambria ("Historical" series) ▲ CD 1078 [ADD]

Vaughan Williams, R.:Con accademico, w. C. Dahinden (cnd), Winterthur String Orch *(rec 1951)* — Music & Arts ▲ CD 667 (m) [AAD]

Kaufman, Mindy (fl)

Riley, D.:Apparitions, w. M. Gallagher (va), B. Allen (hp) — CRI ▲ CD 595 [DDD]

Kaufmann, Klaus (pno)

Mozart, W.A.:Vars Pno, K.354 — Koch Schwann ▲ 311652 [DDD]

Mozart, W.A.:Vars Pno, K.500 — Koch Schwann ▲ 311652 [DDD]

Mozart, W.A.:Vars Pno, K.613 — Koch Schwann ▲ 311652 [DDD]

Kaufmann, Manfred (perc)

Christmas with Brassissimo, w. Brassissimo Vienna, Rudolf Schmidinger (perc) *(rec MG-SOUND Studios, Vienna)* — Brassissimo ▲ BVR 5356400 [DDD]

Kaunzinger, Günter (org)

Franck, C.:Org Music (misc)—Fantasie No. 1; Grand Piéce Symphonique; Prélude, Fugue et Var.; Pastoral; Piéce Heroïque & others — Koch Schwann 2-▲ SCH 312792 [DDD]

Vierne, L.:Syms Org (comp)—Nos. 5 & 6 — Koch Schwann ▲ CD 315002 [DDD]

Widor, C.M.:Syms Org (comp) — Novalis 5-▲ 150105

Kauppinen, Pekka (vn)

Marttinen, T.:Con Vn, w. O. Vänskä (cnd), Lahti SO *(rec Ristinkirkko, Church of the Cross, Lahti, Finland, Sept. 12-15, 1994)* — BIS ▲ CD 701 [DDD]

Kavakos, Leonidas (vn)

Paganini, N.:Caprices Vn — Dynamic ▲ CD 66 [DDD]

Kavafian, Ani (vn)—see also ORCHESTRAS & ENSEMBLES Lincoln Center Chamber Music Society members

Babadjanyan, A.:Son Vn, w. S. Arzruni (pno) — Positively Armenian PA 105C

Brahms, J.:Sextet Strs, Op. 36, w. Benny Kim (vn), Cynthia Phelps (va), Randolph Kelly (va), Colin Carr (vc), Peter Rejto (vc) *(rec live, Tucson Chamber Music Festival, Mar 11, 1994)* — Arizona Friends of Chamber Music ▲ 1994 [DDD]

Brahms, J.:Sextet Strs, Op. 36, w. Benny Kim (vn), Randolph Kelly (va), Cynthia Phelps (va), Colin Karr (vc), Peter Rejto (vc) *(rec Tuscon Winter Chamber Festival; Mar 11, 1994)* — Arizona Friends of Chamber Music ▲ AFCD 19941

Hovhaness, A.:Visions of St. Mesrob, w. S. Arzruni (pno) — Positively Armenian ■ PA 105C

Khachaturian, A.:Dance Vn & Pno, w. S. Arzruni (pno) — Positively Armenian ■ PA 105C

Khachaturian, A.:Nocturne, w. S. Arzruni (pno) — Positively Armenian ■ PA 105C

Khachaturian, A.:Song-Poem, w. S. Arzruni (pno) — Positively Armenian ■ PA 105C

Kodály, Z.:Serenade for 2 Vns & Va, w. J. Silverstein (vn), P. Neubauer (va) *(rec Feb. 22, 1993)* — Delos ▲ DE 3151 [DDD]

Kosins, M.S.:Songs of the Seeker, w. J. Carradine (nar), R. Williams (bn), T. D. Barna (pno) *(rec 1980)* — Centaur ▲ CRC 2105 [ADD]

Lazarof, H.:Divert 3 Vn, w. Windham String Quartet *(rec SUNY, Purchase, Nov 1993)* — Laurel LR 856 [DDD]

Milhaud, D.:La Création du monde (suite), w. André Previn (pno), Julie Rosenfeld (vn), Toby Hoffman (va), Carter Brey (vc) *(rec Manhattan Center Studios, New York City, May 25-26, 1993)* — RCA Red Seal ▲ 09026-68181-2 [DDD]

Moszkowski, M.:Suite 2 Vns, w. I. Kavafian (vn), J. Feldman (pno) — Elektra/Nonesuch ▲ 79117-2 [DDD]

Mozart, W.A.:Duo Vn, K.424, w. I. Kavafian (va) — Elektra/Nonesuch ▲ 79117-2 [DDD]

Mozart, W.A.:Qnt Strs, K.516, w. Benny Kim (vn), Randolph Kelly (va), Cynthia Phelps (va), Colin Carr (vc) *(rec Tuscon Winter Chamber Festival; Mar 11, 1994)* — Arizona Friends of Chamber Music ▲ AFCD 19951

Mozart, W.A.:Qnt Strs, K.516, w. Benny Kim (vn), Randolph Kelley (va), Cynthia Phelps (va), Colin Carr (vc) *(rec 1994-95)* — Arizona Friends of Chamber Music ▲ 1994/5 [DDD]

Rorem, N.:Bright Music, w. M. Martin (fl), A.-M. Schub (pno), I. Kavafian (vn), F. Sherry (vc) — New World ▲ 80416-2 [DDD]

Saint-Saëns, C.:Spt Tpt, w. André Previn (pno), Thomas Stevens (tpt), Julie Rosenfeld (vn), Toby Hoffman (va), Carter Brey (vc), Jack Kulowitsch (db) *(rec Manhattan Center Studios, New York City, May 25-26, 1993)* — RCA Red Seal ▲ 09026-68181-2 [DDD]

Sarasate, P. de:Navarra, w. I. Kavafian (vn), J. Feldman (pno) — Elektra/Nonesuch ▲ 79117-2 [DDD]

Schubert, Franz:Qt 12 Strs, w. I. Kavafian (vn), P. Neubauer (va), F. Sherry (vc) — Omega ▲ OCD 1015 [DDD]

Schubert, Franz:Qnt Strs, D.956, w. I. Kavafian (vn), P. Neubauer (va), L. Parnas (vc), F. Sherry (vc) — Omega ▲ OCD 1015 [DDD]

Shostakovich, D.:Trio 2 Pno, w. James Bonn (pno), Colin Carr (vc) *(rec Tuscon Winter Chamber Festival; Mar 13, 1994)* — Arizona Friends of Chamber Music ▲ AFCD 19941

Shostakovich, D.:Trio 2 Pno, w. Colin Carr (vc), James Bonn (pno) *(rec live, Tucson Chamber Music Festival, Mar 13, 1994)* — Arizona Friends of Chamber Music ▲ 1994 [DDD]

Kavafian, Ida (vn)—see also ORCHESTRAS & ENSEMBLES Tashi, Beaux Arts Trio

Crawford, R.:Son Vn & Pno, w. V. Fine (pno) — CRI ▲ CD 658 [ADD]

Fine, I.:Son Vn, w. V. Fine (pno) — CRI ▲ CD 630 [ADD]

Moszkowski, M.:Suite 2 Vns, w. A. Kavafian (vn), J. Feldman (pno) — Elektra/Nonesuch ▲ 79117-2 [DDD]

Mozart, W.A.:Duo Vn, K.424, w. A. Kavafian (vn) — Elektra/Nonesuch ▲ 79117-2 [DDD]

Rorem, N.:Bright Music, w. M. Martin (fl), A.-M. Schub (pno), A. Kavafian (vn), F. Sherry (vc) — New World ▲ 80416-2 [DDD]

Rorem, N.:Winter Pages, w. T. Palmer (cl), F. Morelli (bn), F. Sherry (vc), C. Wadsworth (pno) — New World ▲ 80416-2 [DDD]

Sarasate, P. de:Navarra, w. A. Kavafian (vn), J. Feldman (pno) — Elektra/Nonesuch ▲ 79117-2 [DDD]

Schubert, Franz:Qt 12 Strs, w. A. Kavafian (vn), P. Neubauer (va), F. Sherry (vc) — Omega ▲ OCD 1015 [DDD]

Schubert, Franz:Qnt Strs, D.956, w. A. Kavafian (vn), P. Neubauer (va), L. Parnas (vc), F. Sherry (vc) — Omega ▲ OCD 1015 [DDD]

Kavakos, Leonidas (vn)

Kreisler, F.:Vn Pieces — Delos ▲ DE 3116 [DDD]

Leonidas Kavakos, w. Peter Nagy (pno) — Delos ▲ DE 3116 [DDD]

Sibelius, J.:Con Vn, w. O. Vänskä (cnd), Lahti SO — BIS ▲ CD 500 [DDD]

Sibelius, J.:Con Vn, w. O. Vänskä (cnd), Lahti SO (original 1903/04 version) — BIS ("BIS Twins" series) 2-▲ CD 500/581

Sibelius, J.:Humoresques, w. J. Lamminmäki (cnd), Espoo CO *(rec May-June 1989)* — Finlandia ▲ 4509-95859-2 [DDD]

Sibelius, J.:Pelléas et Mélisande, w. J. Lamminmäki (cnd), Espoo CO—Suite *(rec May-June 1989)* — Finlandia ▲ 4509-95859-2 [DDD]

Kavalovski, Charles (hn)

Krommer, F.:Con for 2 Hns, w. S. Brubaker (hn), S. Richman (cnd), Harmonie Ensemble/New York — Music & Arts ▲ CD 691-1 [DDD]

Kavanagh, Dale (gtr)

Berkeley, L.:Sonatina Gtr — FSM ▲ FCD 97761 [DDD]

Cooperman, L.:Walking on the Water — FSM ▲ FCD 97761 [DDD]

Lyrical & Virtuosic Guitar Music — FSM ▲ 97761 [DDD]

Rodrigo, J.:Invocación y danza — FSM ▲ FCD 97761 [DDD]

Rodrigo, J.:Piezas españolas — FSM ▲ FCD 97761 [DDD]

Kavtaradze, Nina (pno)

Rachmaninoff, S.:Son Vc, w. E.B. Bengtsson (vc) — Kontrapunkt ▲ 32018 [DDD]

Shostakovich, D.:Son Vc, w. E. Blöndal Bengtsson (vc) — Kontrapunkt ▲ 32018 [DDD]

INSTRUMENT.

Kavtaradze, Nina (pno) (cont.)
Wagner, R.:Pno Music—Fant; Polonaise; Züricher Vielliebchen-Walzer; Ankunft bei den schwarzen Schwänen; Polka; Schluss zum Vorspiel von; Tristan und Isolde; Notenbrief für Mathilde Wesendonck; Elegi; Albumblatt für Ernst Benedikt Kietz; Albumblatt für Frau Betty Schott; Polonaise für Klavier zu vier Händen; Son; Eine Son in das Album von Frau M.W.; Grosse Son; others — Kontrapunkt 2-▲ KPT 32235

Kawaciuk, Ivan (vn)
Paganini, N.:Caprices Vn — Supraphon 2-▲ SUP 112150 [AAD]

Kawaguchi, Masayuki (mand)
Erdmann, D.:Con Mand, w. D. Demetriades (cnd), Berlin RSO — MD + G ▲ L 3451 [DDD]

Kawahara, Yasunori (db)
Yasunori Kawahara, w. Rainer Hoffmann (pno) — Largo ▲ 5105 [DDD]

Kawalla, Bronislawa (pno)
Bach, J.S.:Chromatic Fant & Fugue *(rec National Philharmonic, Warsaw, Feb 22-23, 1989)* — Polskie Nagrania ▲ PNCD 055 [DDD]
Bach, J.S.:Fants Hpd—BWV 904 *(rec National Philharmonic, Warsaw, Feb 22-23, 1989)* — Polskie Nagrania ▲ PNCD 055 [DDD]
Bach, J.S.:Goldberg Vars *(rec National Philharmonic, Warsaw, Feb 22-23, 1989)* — Polskie Nagrania ▲ PNCD 055 [DDD]

Kawalla, J. (vn)
Van De Vate, N.:Adagio & Rondo, w. S. Kawalla (cnd), Koszalin State PO — Vienna Modern Masters ▲ VMM 3025 [DDD]
Van De Vate, N.:How Fares the Night?, w. S. Kawalla (cnd), Koszalin State PO, Silesian Univ Choir — Vienna Modern Masters ▲ VMM 3025 [DDD]

Kawasaki, M. (va)
Lebaron, A.:Noh Reflections, w. H. Fujiwara (vn), E. Elsing (vc), Kennedy Center Theater Chamber Players — Mode ▲ 30

Kay, Alan R. (cl)
Imbrie, A.W.:To a Traveler, w. Cyrus Stevens (vn), Edmund Niemann (pno) *(rec Sept. 24, 1993)* — New World ▲ 80441-2
Wilder, A.:Suite Cl, w. David Jolley (hn), David Oei (pno) *(rec SUNY Purchase Recital Hall)* — Arabesque ▲ ARA 6665 [DDD]
Wuorinen, C.:Fortune, w. C. Macomber (vn), F. Sherry (vc), J. Winn (pno) — Koch International Classics ▲ KIC 7242-2 [DDD]

Kayath, Marcelo (gtr)
Barrios, A.:Gtr Music—La Catedral; Confesion-Romanza; Danza Paraguaya; Mazurca Appassionata; Study in a "Las Abejas"; Study in b; Tango No. 2; Tremolo—Una Limosna por el Amor de Dios *(rec Apr. 1991)* — IMP Classics ▲ PCD 999 [DDD]
Guitar Favorites — IMP Classics ▲ PCD 1033 [DDD]
Ponce, M.:Gtr Music—Balletto; Gavotte; Mazurca; Preambulo & Allegro; Suite in a — IMP Classics ▲ PCD 999 [DDD]

Kaye, Milton (pno)
The Decca Masters, Vol. 1, w. Jascha Heifetz (vn), Emanuel Bay (pno) *(rec 1944–46)* — MCA Classics ▲ MCAD 42211 (m) [ADD]
The Decca Masters, Vol. 2 (1944–1946), w. Jascha Heifetz (vn), Emanuel Bay (pno), Bing Crosby (sgr) *(rec 1944–46)* — MCA Classics ▲ MCAD 42212 (m) [ADD]

Kayser, Audun (pno)
Becker, J.J.:Con arabesque, w. W. Strickland (cnd), Oslo PO — CRI ■ C 177

Kayser, David (trbn)—see ORCHESTRAS & ENSEMBLES Brass Ring

Kayser, Jan Henrik (pno)
Saeverud, H.:Con Pno, w. K. Andersen (cnd), Bergen PO — Norway Music ▲ ACD 4954
Saeverud, H.:Pno Music—Seven Easy Pieces, Op. 14; Siljuslatten, Op. 17; Suite Nos. 1 & 2, "Tunes & Dances from Siljustol," Op. 21 & Op. 22 *(rec 1976)* — BIS 2-▲ CD 173/74 [AAD]

Kazakevich, Mikhail (pno)
Bach, J.S.:Preludes & Fugues Hpd—in E♭ — Conifer Classics 2-▲ 75605-51237-2 [DDD]
Bach, J.S.:Das wohltemperierte Klavier—Prelude & Fugue in e♭ — Conifer Classics ▲ 75605-51235-2 [DDD]
Beethoven, L. van:Con 2 Pno, w. C. Mackerras (cnd), English CO — Conifer Classics ▲ 75605-51237-2 [DDD]
Beethoven, L. van:Con 4 Pno, w. C. Mackerras (cnd), English CO — Conifer Classics ▲ 75605-51237-2 [DDD]
Berg, A.:Son Pno — Conifer Classics ▲ 75605-51235-2 [DDD]
Brahms, J.:Fants Pno, Op. 116, Intermezzos in a, E, e & E — Conifer Classics ▲ 75605-51235-2 [DDD]
Brahms, J.:Intermezzos Pno, Op. 117—2 Intermezzos — Conifer Classics 2-▲ 75605-51237-2 [DDD]
Honegger, A.:Prélude, arioso et fughette sur le nom de BACH — Conifer Classics ▲ 75605-51235-2 [DDD]
Mahler, G.:Sym 1—Scherzo [arr. Kazakevich for piano] — Conifer Classics 2-▲ 75605-51237-2 [DDD]
Rachmaninoff, S.:Son 2 Pno — Conifer Classics ▲ 75605-51235-2 [DDD]
Schubert, Franz:Son Pno, D.664 *(rec All Saint's Church, Petersham, Surrey, Aug 2-8, 1994)* — Conifer Classics ▲ 75605-51254-2 [DDD]
Schubert, Franz:Son Pno, D.960 *(rec All Saint's Church, Petersham, Surrey, Aug 2-8, 1994)* — Conifer Classics ▲ 75605-51254-2 [DDD]
Schumann, R.:Intermezzos — Conifer Classics 2-▲ 75605-51237-2 [DDD]

Kazlauskas, Zigmas (lure)
Habbestad, K.:The Articles of Norwegian Christian Law, w. Ståle Bjørnhaug (nar), Adomas Kontautas (lure), Rimantas Valanctus (lure), Marius Balcytis (lure) — Norway Music ▲ 2912

Kaznowski, Michal (vc)—see also ORCHESTRAS & ENSEMBLES Maggini String Quartet
Britten, H.:Young Apollo, w. P. Donohoe (pno), F. Kok (vn), J. Ballard (vn), P. Cole (va), S. Rattle (cnd), City of Birmingham SO *(rec 4/82)* — EMI Classics 2-▲ CDCB 54270 [DDD]

Keavy, Stephen (tpt)
Vivaldi, A.:Con for 2 Tpts, w. A. Lackner (tpt), M. Haselböck (cnd), Vienna Academy [period instrs] — Novalis ▲ 150074 [DDD]

Keberlee, D. (cl)
Curran, A.:Crystal Psalms, An Homage to Kristallnacht, w. F. Badaloni (cl), M. Riesler (cl), A. Santoloci (cl), M. Capone (acc), L. Dublanchet (tuba), D. Rueff (tuba), A. Caggiano (perc), w. Ensemble Vocale Sesquialtera [cnd:E. Razzicchia], Radio France Chamber Choir [cnd:D. LaBorde]—[F] — New Albion ▲ NA 067

Keck, Robert (vc)
O'Rourke, J.:Terminal Pharmacy, w. Tony Burr (cl), Jeff Cortazzo (b trbn), John McEntire (dr), Rob Prosser (acc), Isha Suftin (acc), Mike Dockter (vc), Hattie Franck (vc), Mary LaBreque (vc), Dan Loch (vc), Stan Saderk (vc), Lisa Hemmer (fl), Sue Oberg (fl), Wendi Lev (fl), Jim Vanden (fl), Jim O'Rourke (gtr), Steve Braack (elec) — Tzadik ▲ TZA 7011 [DDD]

Kecskemethy, Stephen (vn)—see ORCHESTRAS & ENSEMBLES Portland String Quartet

Kecskés, András (lt)
Flûte à bec, Luth et Guitare, w. René Clemencic (rcr) — Harmonia Mundi ▲ HMC 90427
Lute Recital, w. András Kecskés (lt) — Harmonia Mundi Plus ▲ HMP 390766

Keda, Larissa (pno)
Russian Romances of the First Half of the 19th Century, w. Nina Sharubina (sop) — Erasmus ▲ WVH 161

Kedra, Wladyslaw (pno)
Chopin, F.:Grand Fant on Polish Airs, w. W. Rowicki (cnd), Warsaw PO *(rec Warsaw, 1959–60)* — Polskie Nagrania ▲ PNCD 308
Chopin, F.:Krakowiak, w. W. Rowicki (cnd), Warsaw PO *(rec Warsaw, 1959–60)* — Polskie Nagrania ▲ PNCD 308
Chopin, F.:Vars on Mozart's *La ci darem la mano*, w. W. Rowicki (cnd), Warsaw PO *(rec Warsaw, 1959–60)* — Polskie Nagrania ▲ PNCD 308

Kee, Piet (org)
Bach, J.S.:Org Music (comp) — Chandos ▲ CHAN 0590

Kee, Piet (org) (cont.)
Bach, J.S.:Org Music (misc)—Toccata & Fugue in d, BWV 565; 5 Chorale Preludes (BWV 659, 711, 714, 1090, 1092); Prelude & Fugue in c, BWV 549; Eight "Little" Preludes & Fugues, BWV 553–560 — Chandos ("Chaconne" series) ▲ CHAN 0527 [DDD]
Bach, J.S.:Org Music (misc)—Chorale Preludes, BWV 618, 619, 623–626, 628, 731; Preludes & Fugues, BWV 533 & BWV 546 — Chandos ("Chaconne" series) ▲ CHAN 0501 [DDD]
Bach, J.S.:Org Music (misc)—Chorale Preludes (BWV 614, 633, 636, 637, 639–642, 663, 721); Fantasia & Fugue in g, BWV 542; Preludes & Fugues, BWV 531 & BWV 544 — Chandos ("Chaconne" series) ▲ CHAN 0506 [DDD]
Bach, J.S.:Org Music (misc)—4 Chorale Preludes (BWV 690, 691, 727, 734); Passacaglia in c, BWV 582; Pastorale in F, BWV 590; Pièce d'orgue, BWV 572; Prelude & Fugue in e, BWV 548 — Chandos ("Chaconne" series) ▲ CHAN 0510 [DDD]
Buxtehude, D.:Org Music (misc)—Chorale Prelude, "Herr Christ, der einig Gottes Sohn," BuxWV.192; Fantasia on "Wie schön leuchtet der Morgenstern," BuxWV.223; Passacaglia in d, BuxWV.161; Praeludium in a, BuxWV.153 — Chandos ("Chaconne" series) ▲ CHAN 0501 [DDD]
Buxtehude, D.:Org Music (misc) [the restored 17th-cent. *Grote Kerk* organ in Alkmaar, Holland]—Magnificat primi toni, BuxWV.203; Praeludium in C, BuxWV.137; Praeludium in D, BuxWV.139; Canzona in e, BuxWV.169; Canzonetta in G, BuxWV.171; Ciacona in e, BuxWV.160; Ach Herr, mich armen Sünder, BuxWV.178; In dulci jubilo, BuxWV.197; Komm, Heiliger Geist, Herre Gott, BuxWV.199; Vater unser im Himmelreich, BuxWV.219 — Chandos ("Chaconne" series) ▲ CHAN 0514 [DDD]
Franck, C.:Andantino Org — Chandos ▲ CHAN 8891 [DDD]
Franck, C.:Cantabile — Chandos ▲ CHAN 8891 [DDD]
Franck, C.:Chorals Org, M.38–40—Nos. 2 & 3 — Chandos ▲ CHAN 8891 [DDD]
Franck, C.:Pièce héroïque — Chandos ▲ CHAN 8891 [DDD]
Franck, C.:Prélude, fugue et var — Chandos ▲ CHAN 8891 [DDD]
Hindemith, P.:Sons Org — Chandos ▲ CHAN 9097 [DDD]
Pachelbel, J.:Org Music—Ciacona in d; Ciacona in f; Fantasia in g; Praeludium in d — Chandos ("Chaconne" series) ▲ CHAN 0520 [DDD]
Piet Kee at Weingarten — Chandos ("Chaconne" series) ▲ CHAN 0520 [DDD]
Piet Kee:Concertgebouw — Chandos ▲ CHAN 9188 [DDD]
Sweelinck, J.P.:Org Music—Ballo del Granduca; Echo Fantasia; Engelsche Fortuyn; Puer nobis nascitur — Chandos ("Chaconne" series) ▲ CHAN 0514 [DDD]
Walther, Joh. G.:Vars on "Jesu, meine Freude" — Chandos ("Chaconne" series) ▲ CHAN 0520 [DDD]

Keene, Constance (pno)
An American Collage Vol. II, w. Ayke Agus (pno), Anita Swearingen (pno), Michael Lang (pno), Diane Lang Bryan (cl), James Smith (gtr), Sherry Kloss (vn), Laila Padorr (fl), Victor Morosco (a sax) — Protone ▲ PRCD 1114 [DDD]
Bach, J.S.:French Suites—BWV 816 in G — Protone ▲ PRCD 1113
Bach, J.S.:Italian Con — Protone ▲ PRCD 1113
Bach, J.S.:Partitas Hpd, BWV 825–830—BWV 825 in B♭ — Protone ▲ PRCD 1113
Bach, J.S.:Toccata & Fugue Org, BWV 565 [trans. Keene based on Tausig & Busoni] — Protone ▲ PRCD 1113
Beethoven, L. van:Son 25 Pno — Protone ▲ PRCD 1106 [ADD]
Beethoven, L. van:Vars Pno, WoO 80 — Protone ▲ PRCD 1112
Chopin, F.:Preludes, Op. 28 — Protone ▲ PRCD 1105 [AAD]
Constance Keene Plays Familiar Favorites — Protone ▲ PRCD 1102 ■ CSPR 169
Dussek, J.L.:Son Pno, Op. 61, "Elégie harmonique sur la mort du Prince Louis Ferdinand de Prusse" — Protone ▲ PRCD 1106 [ADD]
Griffes, C.T.:Son Pno — Protone ▲ PRCD 1106 [ADD]
Handel, G.F.:The Harmonious Blacksmith — Protone ▲ PRCD 1112
Haydn, J.:Sons Pno—H.XVI/52 — Protone ▲ PRCD 1106 [ADD]
Hummel, J.N.:Son 9 Pno — Protone ▲ PRCD 1106 [ADD]
Macdowell, E.:Etudes—No. 8, Shadow Dance; No. 12, Hungarian — Protone 2-▲ NRPR 2202/3
Macdowell, E.:Fancies — Protone 2-▲ NRPR 2202/3
Macdowell, E.:Fantasiestücke—No. 2, Witches Dance — Protone 2-▲ NRPR 2202/3
Macdowell, E.:Son 2 Pno — Protone 2-▲ NRPR 2202/3
Macdowell, E.:Son 3 Pno — Protone 2-▲ NRPR 2202/3
Macdowell, E.:Son 4 Pno — Protone 2-▲ NRPR 2202/3
Macdowell, E.:Son tragica — Protone 2-▲ NRPR 2202/3
Macdowell, E.:Woodland Sketches—No. 1, To a Wild Rose; No. 6, To a Water Lily — Protone 2-▲ NRPR 2202/3
Mendelssohn, F.:Etudes Pno — Protone ▲ PRCD 1105 [AAD]
Mendelssohn, F.:Fant Pno, "Sonate écossaise" — Protone ▲ PRCD 1105 [AAD]
Mendelssohn, F.:Vars sérieuses — Protone ▲ PRCD 1105 [AAD]
Mendelssohn, F.:Vars sérieuses — Protone ▲ PRCD 1112
Rachmaninoff, S.:Prelude Pno, Op. 3/2 — Protone ▲ PRCD 1101 2-■ CSPR 110/11
Rachmaninoff, S.:Preludes Pno, Opp 23 & 32 — Protone ▲ PRCD 1101 2-■ CSPR 110/11
Rachmaninoff, S.:Variations on a Theme by Corelli — Protone ▲ PRCD 1112
Schumann, R.:Vars on A-B-E-G-G — Protone ▲ PRCD 1112

Keener, Shawn (pno)—see ORCHESTRAS & ENSEMBLES Bowed Piano Ensemble

Keenlyside, R. (vn)—see ORCHESTRAS & ENSEMBLES Aeolian String Quartet

Kefer, Herbert (va)—see also ORCHESTRAS & ENSEMBLES Artis String Quartet
Magnard, A.:Qt Strs, Op. 16, w. Johannes Meissl (vn), Peter Schuhmayer (vn), Othmar Müller (vc) — Accord ▲ ACD 201982 [DDD]

Kehr, Günter (vn)
Fauré, G.:Qt 1 Pno, w. J. Eymar (pno), E. Sichermann (va), B. Braunholz (vc) *(rec 1966)* — Vox Box 2-▲ CDX 5073 [ADD]
Fauré, G.:Qt 2 Pno, w. J. Eymar (pno), E. Sichermann (va), B. Braunholz (vc) *(rec 1966)* — Vox Box 2-▲ CDX 5073 [ADD]
Fauré, G.:Qnts Pno & Strs, Opp. 89 & 115, w. J. Eymar (pno), W. Neuhaus (vn), E. Sichermann (va), B. Braunholz (vc) *(rec 1970)* — Vox Box 2-▲ CDX 5073 [ADD]

Keiding, Jakob (hn)
Brahms, J.:Choral Music, w. A. Korondi (sop), G. Mossyrsch (hp), J. Widihofer (hn), E. Ortner (cnd), Arnold Schoenberg Choir—Lieder und Romanzen, Op. 93a; 3 Gesänge, Op. 42; 7 Lieder, Op. 62; 5 Gesänge, Op. 104; 4 Gesänge, Op. 17 — Teldec ▲ 4509-92058-2 [DDD]

Keilhack, Dorian (pno)
Bartók, B.:Hungarian Peasant Songs, w. Anna Garzuly (fl) [arr Arma for fl & pno] *(rec July 9–11, 1995 & Feb 12–)* — Hungaroton ▲ HCD 31655 [DDD]
Geszler, G.:Vision, w. Anna Garzuly (fl) *(rec July 9–11, 1995 & Feb 12–)* — Hungaroton ▲ HCD 31655 [DDD]
Hindemith, P.:Son Fl, w. Anna Garzuly (fl) *(rec July 9–11, 1995 & Feb 12–)* — Hungaroton ▲ HCD 31655 [DDD]
Muczynski, R.:Son Fl, w. Anna Garzuly (fl) *(rec July 9–11, 1995 & Feb 12–)* — Hungaroton ▲ HCD 31655 [DDD]

Keinonen, Timo (vc)
Sibelius, J.:The Wood Nymph (tone poem), w. O. Vänskä (cnd), Lahti SO *(rec Church of the Cross, Lahti, Finland, Jan 8–12, 1996)* — BIS ▲ CD 815 [DDD]

Keiser, Marilyn (org)
Locklair, D.:Rubrics — Pro Organo ▲ CD 7025 [DDD]
Music of Paris in the 1920s & '30s — Gothic ▲ GOT 49037 [DDD]
The People Respond—Amen! — Pro Organo ▲ CD 7025 [DDD]

Kejmar, Miroslav (psthn)
Mozart, W.A.:Contradances, K.462, w. J. Hnyk (cnd), Czech Phil CO — Canyon Classics ▲ 3652
Mozart, W.A.:Serenade Ww, K.320, w. J. Hnyk (cnd), Czech Phil CO — Canyon Classics ▲ 3652

Kejmar, Miroslav (tpt)
Famous Trumpet Concerti, w. Capella Istropolitana [cnd:Peter Škvor] *(rec 1/89)* — Naxos ▲ 8.550243 [DDD]

Kejmar, Miroslav (tpt) (cont.)
Kabeláč, M.:Fated Dramas of Man, w. F. Maxian (pno), Prague Percussion Ensemble *(rec 1993)* Panton ▲ PAN 811143
Korte, O.:Con grosso, w. Zdenek Šedivý (tpt), Josef Hála (pno), J. Belohlávek (cnd), Czech PO *(rec House of Artists, Prague, Dec. 2-4, 1987)* Panton ▲ PAN 811257 [DDD]
Mahler, G.:Sym 5, w. Zdenek Tylsar (hn), V. Neumann (cnd), Czech PO *(rec House of Artists, Prague, Mar 1993)* Canyon Classics ▲ 3616
Martinů, B.:Field Mass, w. I. Kusnjer (bar), B. Kotmel (cnd), Czech PO, Czech Phil Chorus [Cz] Chandos ▲ CHAN 9138 [DDD]
Vejvanovsky, P.J.:Sons & Serenades, w. Z. Šedivy (tpt), L. Pešek (cnd), Prague CO—Serenades in A & C; Sonata a 4; Sonata a 5; Sonata Secunda a 6; Sonata Venatoria in D; Sonata Vespertina a 8 Supraphon ▲ 10 3593 [DDD]
Kekula, Josef (vn)—see ORCHESTRAS & ENSEMBLES Stamitz String Quartet
Kelemen, Pál (vc)
Handel, G.F.:Trio Sons, w. László Czidra (rcr), Zsolt Harsányi (rcr/bn), Zsursa Pertis (clvd)—in F, H.405 *(rec May 4-7, 1992)* Naxos ▲ 8.550700 [DDD]
Kell, Reginald (cl)
Brahms, J.:Qt 1 Strs, w. Busch String Quartet EMI Classics ▲ CDH 64932
Brahms, J.:Qnt Cl, w. Fine Arts String Quartet Boston Skyline ▲ BSD 135 [AAD]
Brahms, J.:Qnt Cl, w. Busch String Quartet EMI Classics ▲ CDH 64932
Mozart, W.A.:Qnt Cl, K.581, w. Fine Arts String Quartet Boston Skyline ▲ BSD 135 [AAD]
Kellaway, Roger (pno/perc)
Kellaway, R.:Music of, w. Fred Seykora (vc), Chuck Domanico (electric bass), Emil Richards (mar/perc), Joe Porcaro (perc), Bob Zimmitti (perc)—Thinking of You; Un canto per la pace [A Song for Peace]; Love of my Life; Eleventide; In My Heart; Eve; Windows; Winter [Parts 1-3] *(rec Ocean Way Recording Studio, Los Angeles, CA, May 1-5, 1993)* Angel ▲ CDC 54903 [DDD]
Kellaway, R.:Music of, w. Fred Seykora (vc), Chuck Domanico (elec b), Emil Richards (mar/perc), Joe Porcaro (perc), Bob Zimmitti (perc)—Thinking of You; Un canto per la pace [A Song for Peace]; Love of my Life; Eleventide; In My Heart; Eve; Windows; Winter [Parts 1-3] *(rec Ocean Way Recording Studio, Los Angeles, CA, May 1-5, 1993)* EMI Classics ▲ CDC 54903 [DDD]
Keller, András (vn)—see ORCHESTRAS & ENSEMBLES Keller String Quartet, Keller String Quartet members
Keller, Antonin (trbn)
Janáček, L.:Capriccio, w. Daniel Wiesner (pno), Jan Riedlbauch (fl/pic), Vladislav Kozderka (tpt), Jan Fišer (tpt), Václav Ferebauer (trbn), Jan Hyncica (trbn), Jiří Novotny (ten tuba), L. Svárovský (cnd) *(rec Martinek Studio in Prague, Jan 9, Feb 27, Mar 20, 19)* Panton ▲ 811393-2 [DDD]
Keller, Christoph (pno)
Bloch, E.:Baal Shem, "3 Pictures of Chassidic Life", w. Robert Zimansky (vn) Accord ▲ ACD 220342 [AAD]
Eisler, H.:Klavierstücke, Op. 3 Accord ▲ ACD 200582 [DDD]
Eisler, H.:Klavierstücke, Op. 8 Accord ▲ ACD 200582 [DDD]
Eisler, H.:Pno Music (comp) Accord 4-▲ ACD 201712 [DDD]
Eisler, H.:Pno Music (misc), w. Katharina Weber (pno)—5 frühe Klavierstücke; 2 kleine Klavierstücke; Andante; Kleine Musik zum abreagieren sentimentaler Stimmungen; Klavierstücke für Kinder, Op. 31; Sieben Klavierstücke, Op. 32; Sonatine [Gradus ad Parnassum], Op. 44; 3 Fugen; Improvisation für Ernst Bloch; Rachmaninoff Parodie; Die Mutter Ov [2 Pnos]; Ov 1940 [2 Pnos] Accord ▲ ACD 201612 [DDD]
Eisler, H.:Son 1 Pno Accord ▲ ACD 200582 [DDD]
Eisler, H.:Son 2 Pno Accord ▲ ACD 200582 [DDD]
Eisler, H.:Son 3 Pno Accord ▲ ACD 200582 [DDD]
Eisler, H.:Vars Pno Accord ▲ ACD 200582 [DDD]
Koechlin, C.:L'Accienne maison de campagne Accord ▲ ACD 202202 [DDD]
Koechlin, C.:Danses pour Ginger—No. 2 [Danse lenthe] Accord ▲ ACD 202202 [DDD]
Koechlin, C.:Nouvelles sonatines Accord ▲ ACD 202202 [DDD]
Koechlin, C.:Son Va, w. Christoph Schiller (va) Accord ▲ ACD 201092 [DDD]
Magnard, A.:Chamber Music—Son for Vn & Pno, Op. 13; 3 Pièces for Pno, Op. 1 [En dieu mon espérance]; Son for Vc & Pno, Op. 20; Promenades for Pno, Op. 7; Qt for Strs, Op. 16; Qnt for Pno & Ww, Op. 8; Trio for Pno, Vn & Vc, Op. 18; Poèmes en musique, Opp. 3 & 15; Suite in the Olden Style for Pno 4-Hands, Op. 2 Accord 5-▲ ACD 200752 [DDD]
Magnard, A.:Qnt Pno, w. Anna-Katharina Graf (fl), Roman Schmid (ob), Elmar Schmid (cl), Jiri Flieger (bn) Accord ▲ ACD 200102 [DDD]
Magnard, A.:Trio Pno, w. Adelina Oprean (vn), Thomas Demenga (vc) Accord ▲ ACD 200102 [DDD]
Reger, M.:Aus meinem Tagebuch—5 sels Accord ▲ ACD 200572 [AAD]
Reger, M.:Son Vn Pno, Op. 72, w. Robert Zimansky (vn) Accord ▲ ACD 200002 [DDD]
Reger, M.:Son Vn Pno, Op. 84, w. Robert Zimansky (vn) Accord ▲ ACD 200002 [DDD]
Schmid, E.:Bagatelles Pno *(rec April 4, 1989)* Grammont ▲ CTSP 33-2 [ADD]
Schmid, E.:Sonatine II, w. R. Zimansky (vn) *(rec Nov. 29, 1987)* Grammont ▲ CTSP 33-2 [ADD]
Schoeck, O.:Songs (comp), w. N. Tüller (bar)—16 songs *(rec March 1992)* Jecklin-Disco ▲ JD 673-2 [DDD]
Schoeck, O.:Songs (misc), w. Niklaus Tüller (bar) Eichendorff Songs, Op. 20/1-14 Accord ▲ ACD 220772 [AAD]
Schoeck, O.:Unter Sternen, w. Roman Trekel (bar) *(rec Pere Casulleras, Christine Rossi, CH-Waldenburg Jun 1995)* Jecklin ▲ JD 678-2 [DDD]
Schoenberg, A.:Nachtwandler, w. Karen Ott (sop) Nuova Era ▲ NUO 7242
Schumann, R.:Son 1 Vn, w. Robert Zimansky (vn) Accord ▲ ACD 220532 [DDD]
Schumann, R.:Son 2 Vn, w. Robert Zimansky (vn) Accord ▲ ACD 220532 [DDD]
Schumann, R.:Son 3 Vn, w. Robert Zimansky (vn) Accord ▲ ACD 220532 [DDD]
Viardot, P.G.:Songs, w. K. Ott (sop)—Madrid; Sérénade; Havanaise; Bonjour mon coeur; Grands oiseaux blancs; La petite chevrière; La chêne et le roseau; Chanson de la pluie; L'enfant et la mère; Désespoir; Adieu les beaux jours; Scène d'Hermione; Seize ans; La danse; L'oiselet; Aime-moi; La calandrina; L'espoir renait dans mon âme [F] CPO ▲ CPO 999044-2 [DDD]
Keller, Dietmar (ob)
Bach, J.S.:Cant 204, w. Elisabeth Speiser (sop), Helmuth Steinkraus (fl), Willi Schnell (ob), Susanne Lautenbacher (vn), R. Ewerhart (cnd), Württemberg CO *(rec 1966)* Vox Box 3-▲ CD3X 3039
Keller, Elizabeth (pno)—see ORCHESTRAS & ENSEMBLES Philadelphia Trio
Keller, Heinrich (fl)
Ponchielli, A.:Qt Fl, w. Omar Zoboli (ob), Bruno Furlanetto (E♭ cl), Antony Morf (cl), Gérard Wyss (pno) Accord ▲ ACD 220682 [AAD]
Keller, Helmut (vn)
Bach, J.S.:Cant 203, w. Dietrich Fischer-Dieskau (bar), Aurèle Nicolet (fl), Irmgard Poppen (vc), Edith Picht-Axenfeld (hpd) EMI Classics ("Baroque" series) ▲ CDK 65729
Telemann, G.P.:Cants, w. Dietrich Fischer-Dieskau (bar), Aurèle Nicolet (fl), Irmgard Poppen (vc), Edith Picht-Axenfeld (hpd)—Die Hoffnung ist mein Leben EMI Classics ("Baroque" series) ▲ CDK 65729
Keller, Herbert (org)
Music for Alphorn, Organ & Cello, w. Anton Wicky (alphn), Alfred Richter (vc) Koch Schwann ▲ SCH 310812 [DDD]
Keller, Lewis (pno)—see ORCHESTRAS & ENSEMBLES Bowed Piano Ensemble
Keller, M. (vc)
Boulez, P.:Messagesquisse, w. B. Licther (vc), A. Loudos (vc), B. Feigenwinter (vc), F. Schiltknecht (vc), P. Toso (vc), J. Wyttenbach (cnd) *(rec Switzerland, June 1993)* ECM New Series 2-▲ 78118-21520-2 [DDD]
Keller, Roland (pno)
Chopin, F.:Impromptus—in c#, Op. 66 Intercord ▲ INT 892.923 [AAD]
Chopin, F.:Impromptus—in c#, Op. 66 Intercord ▲ INT 892.923 [AAD]
Lachenmann, H.:Pno Music—5 Vars. on a Theme by Schubert; Echo Andante; Wiegenmusik; Guero; Ein Kinderspiel Col Legno ▲ AU 31813
Sinding, C.:Con Pno, w. J. Faerber (cnd), Berlin SO *(rec 1978)* Vox Box 2-▲ CDX 5068 [ADD]
Stavenhagen, B.:Con Pno, Op. 4, w. J. Faerber (cnd), Berlin SO *(rec 1978)* Vox Box 2-▲ CDX 5067 [ADD]

Kelley, Denise (hp)
Harty, H.:In Ireland, w. C. Fleming (fl), B. Thomson (cnd), Ulster Orch Chandos ("Collect" series) ▲ CHAN 6583 [ADD]
Harty, H.:In Ireland, w. C. Fleming (fl), B. Thomson (cnd), Ulster Orch Chandos ▲ CHAN 8321 [DDD]
Kelley, Eric Lynn (org)
Thomas Tomkins & His Contemporaries, w. T. Penrose (cnd), English Consort of Viols *(rec Honrath, Aug. 28-30, 1990)* Musicaphon ▲ 56815 [DDD]
Kelley, Frances (hp)
Carols from Christ Church, w. [cnd:Francis Grier], Christ Church Cathedral Choir Oxford, Harry Bicket (org) ASV ▲ ASV CD 2097
Kelley, John (perc)
Spratlan, L.:Night Music, w. V. Kadlubkiewicz (vn), M. Sussman (cl) *(rec July 1992)* Gasparo ▲ GS 226 [DDD]
Kelley, R. (tpt)—see ORCHESTRAS & ENSEMBLES Continuum Chamber Ensemble
Kelley, R.J. (hn)—see ORCHESTRAS & ENSEMBLES Old Fairfield Academy Orch members
Kelley, Randolph (va)
Mozart, W.A.:Qnt Strs, K.516, w. Ani Kavafian (vn), Benny Kim (vn), Cynthia Phelps (va), Colin Carr (vc) *(rec 1994-95)* Arizona Friends of Chamber Music ▲ 1994/5 [DDD]
Kelley, Richard (tpt)
Bach, J.S.:Jesu bleibet meine Freude, w. Mary Jane Newman (org) *(rec Presbyterian Church, Mt. Kisco, NY, Aug 26-27, 1995)* Helicon ▲ HE 1006 [DDD]
Clarke, J.:Tpt Voluntary, w. Mary Jane Newman (org) *(rec Presbyterian Church, Mt. Kisco, NY, Aug 26-27, 1995)* Helicon ▲ HE 1006 [DDD]
Handel, G.F.:Serse (sels), w. Mary Jane Newman (org)—Largo *(rec Presbyterian Church, Mt. Kisco, NY, Aug 26-27, 1995)* Helicon ▲ HE 1006 [DDD]
Purcell, H.:Tpt Tune, Z.t678, w. Mary Jane Newman (org) *(rec Presbyterian Church, Mt. Kisco, NY, Aug 26-27, 1995)* Helicon ▲ HE 1006 [DDD]
Telemann, G.P.:Con Tpt Strs in D, w. Collegium Brass—Adagio *(rec Presbyterian Church, Mt. Kisco, NY, Aug 26-27, 1995)* Helicon ▲ HE 1006 [DDD]
Kelley, Thomas (perc)
Childs, B.:The Distant Land, w. Carmen Lundy (mez), Billy Childs (pno), Nana Yaw Asiedu (perc) *(rec Masonic Auditorium, Cleveland, OH, Feb 27, 1995)* Telarc ▲ CD 80409 [DDD]
Kellman, N. (perc)
Lebaron, A.:Lamentation/Invocation, w. A. Shearer (sgr), R. Yamins (sgr), M. Shapiro (vc), L. Bouchard (tpt), New Music Consort [E] Mode ▲ 30
Kellman, Nina (kithara 2/harmonic canon/surrogate kithara)
Partch, H.:Daphne of the Dunes, w. Frank Cassara (boo/spoils of war/kithara 2), Dominic Donato (b mar/surrogate kithara/boo), Dean Drummond (harmonic canons/kithara 2/spoils of war/kithara), Michael Lipsey (cloud-chamber bowls), Ted Mook (vc/gourd tree/cone gongs), James Pugliese (diamond mar), Elizabeth Rodgers (chromelodeon/harmonic canon) *(rec Queens, NY, Mar. 12, 1991)* Mode ▲ MODE 33
Kellogg, Mark (trbn/eup)
Bernstein, L.:Dance Suite Chamber Ensemble, w. Will Rudd (tpt/flgl), Bob Thompson (tpt/flgl), Alex Shuhan (hn/pno), Charles Villarrubia (tuba), David Gluck (dr/perc) *(rec Cliff Temple Baptist Church, Dallas, TX)* D'Note Classics ▲ DND 1007 [DDD]
Corea, C.:Children's Songs, w. Will Rudd (tpt/flgl), Bob Thompson (tpt/flgl), Alex Shuhan (hn/pno), Charles Villarrubia (tuba), David Gluck (dr/perc)—Nos 6 & 11 [arr Gluck/Shuhan] *(rec Cliff Temple Baptist Church, Dallas, TX)* D'Note Classics ▲ DND 1007 [DDD]
Gershwin, G.:Porgy & Bess (sels), w. Will Rudd (tpt/flgl), Bob Thompson (tpt/flgl), Alex Shuhan (hn/pno), Charles Villarrubia (tuba), David Gluck (dr/perc)—Summertime [arr Thompson] *(rec Cliff Temple Baptist Church, Dallas, TX)* D'Note Classics ▲ DND 1007 [DDD]
Gluck, C.W.:Nicole, w. Will Rudd (tpt/flgl), Bob Thompson (tpt/flgl), Alex Shuhan (hn/pno), Charles Villarrubia (tuba), David Gluck (dr/perc) *(rec Cliff Temple Baptist Church, Dallas, TX)* D'Note Classics ▲ DND 1007 [DDD]
Khachaturian, A.:Gayane (suites), w. Will Rudd (tpt/flgl), Bob Thompson (tpt/flgl), Alex Shuhan (hn/pno), Charles Villarrubia (tuba), David Gluck (dr/perc)—Sabre Dance [arr Gluck]; Lullaby; Dance of the Rose Maidens [both arr Villarrubia] *(rec Cliff Temple Baptist Church, Dallas, TX)* D'Note Classics ▲ DND 1007 [DDD]
McCarthy, D.:American Dance Music, w. Will Rudd (tpt/flgl), Bob Thompson (tpt/flgl), Alex Shuhan (hn/pno), Charles Villarrubia (tuba), David Gluck (dr/perc) *(rec Cliff Temple Baptist Church, Dallas, TX)* D'Note Classics ▲ DND 1007 [DDD]
Scheidt, S.:Instr Music, w. Will Rudd (tpt/flgl), Bob Thompson (tpt/flgl), Alex Shuhan (hn/pno), Charles Villarrubia (tuba), David Gluck (dr/perc)—Centone No. 5 [trans Verne Reynolds] *(rec Cliff Temple Baptist Church, Dallas, TX)* D'Note Classics ▲ DND 1007 [DDD]
Kelly (hp)
Debussy, C.:Son Fl, w. McNicol (fl), R. Best (va) Chandos ▲ CHAN 8385 [ADD]
Kelly, Frances (hp)—see also ORCHESTRAS & ENSEMBLES Invocation
Harp Collection Amon Ra ▲ CDSAR 36 [DDD]
The Mad Lover, w. Tubb, Evelyn (sop) Musica Oscura ("The Orpheus Circle" series) ▲ MOS 70987
Mozart, W.A.:Con Fl Hp, w. L. Beznosiuk (fl), C. Hogwood (cnd), Academy of Ancient Music—No. 1 L'Oiseau-Lyre ▲ 417622-2 [DDD] ▯ 417622-5
O Tuneful Voice:Songs & Duets from Late 18th Century England, w. Emma Kirkby (sop), Rufus Müller (ten), Timothy Roberts (pno/hpd) Hyperion ▲ CDA 66497 [DDD]
Kelly, Francis (Welsh hp)—see ORCHESTRAS & ENSEMBLES Invocation
Kelly, John-Edward (sax)
Elias, B.:Pythikos Nomos, w. Bob Versteegh (pno) Col Legno ▲ AU 31817
Eliasson, A.:Poem, w. Bob Versteegh (pno) Col Legno ▲ AU 31817
Hába, A.:Suite Sax Col Legno ▲ AU 31817
John-Edward Kelly, w. John-Edward Kelly (sax), B. Versteegh (pno) Col Legno ▲ AU 31805
Kox, H.:Concertino A Sax, w. G. Oskamp (cnd), Norske Bläsere *(rec 1991)* Attacca ▲ Babel 9262-1 [ADD/DDD]
Kox, H.:Through a Glass, Darkly, w. Bob Versteegh (pno) Col Legno ▲ AU 31817
Maros, M.:Music of, w. Ilona Maros (sop), Kangas, Maros (cnd), Budapest SO, Ostrobothnian CO, Prague Radio SO, Marosensemble—Sym No. 1; 4 Songs [from Gitanjali]; Sinf concertante [Sym No. 3]; Con for A Sax & Orch Phono Suecia ▲ PHN 23 [DDD]
Reiner, K.:Dve Skladby, w. Bob Versteegh (pno) Col Legno ▲ AU 31817
Kelly, Julian (elec pno)
Howarth, E.:The Bandsman's Tale, w. H. Snell (cnd), Brittania Building Society Band *(rec BBC Studio 7, Manchester)* Doyen ▲ CD 011 [DDD]
Kelly, Randolph (va)
Brahms, J.:Sextet Strs, Op. 36, w. Benny Kim (vn), Ani Kavafian (vn), Cynthia Phelps (va), Colin Carr (vc), Peter Rejto (vc) *(rec live, Tucson Chamber Music Festival, Mar 11, 1994)* Arizona Friends of Chamber Music ▲ 1994 [DDD]
Mozart, W.A.:Qnt Strs, K.516, w. Ani Kavafian (vn), Benny Kim (vn), Cynthia Phelps (va), Colin Carr (vc) *(rec Tuscon Winter Chamber Festival; Mar 11, 1994)* Arizona Friends of Chamber Music ▲ AFCD 19951
Kelly, Thomas (cl)
Stravinsky, I.:Pastorale, w. Neville Taweel (vn), Derek Wickens (ob), Leonard Brain (E hn), John Price (bn), L. Stokowski (cnd), Royal PO *(rec Kingsway Hall, London, England, June 16-17, 1969)* London ("Phase 4 Stereo" series) ▲ 443898-2 [ADD]
Kelly, Velda (vn)
Banfield, W.:Cone Tone, w. Linda Trotter (vn), Charlotte Givens (va), Tim Holley (vc) Innova ▲ 510 [DDD]
Kelst, J. van (vc)—see ORCHESTRAS & ENSEMBLES Hans Memling Trio
Kelton, Theodore (pno)
Ravel, M.:Frontispiece, w. Bradshaw & Buono Piano Duo Connoisseur Society ▲ CD 4171 [DDD]

Keltsch, Werner (vn)
Bach, J.S.:Cant 202, "Wedding Cant", w. Ursula Buckel (sop), Willy Schnell (ob), Peter Buck (vc), Martin Galling (hpd), R. Ewerhart (cnd), Württemberg CO *(rec 1965)* Vox Box 3-▲ CD3X 3039

Kember, Sekar (gamelan)
Harrison, L.:Pieces (3) Gamelan, w. Scott L. Hartman (hn—Main), S. Bates (vn—Threnody), L. Harrison (suling—Serenade) *(rec 1979)* CRI ▲ CD 613 [ADD]

Kemler, Katherine (fl)
Hayden, P.:A Tre *(rec 1992)* Centaur ▲ CRC 2146 [DDD]
Hayden, P.:Grand Mamou, w. Jan Grimes (pno) *(rec 1992)* Centaur ▲ CRC 2146 [DDD]
Liebermann, L.:Soliloquy *(rec Louisiana State Univ., Baton Rouge, LA, June 1994)* Opus One ▲ CD 169
Liebermann, L.:Son Fl, w. K. Rountree (pno) *(rec 1992)* Centaur ▲ CRC 2146 [DDD]
Muczynski, R.:Son Fl, w. J. Grimes (pno) *(rec 1992)* Centaur ▲ CRC 2146 [DDD]
Reynolds, R.:Son Fl, w. K. Rountree (pno) *(rec 1992)* Centaur ▲ CRC 2146 [DDD]
Reynolds, V.:Son Fl, w. K. Rountree (pno) *(rec 1992)* Centaur ▲ CRC 2146 [DDD]

Kemp, A. (rcr)
Vivaldi, A.:Cons Rcr, w. R. Kapp (cnd), Philharmonia Virtuosi—RV.441 ESS.A.Y ▲ CD 1022 [DDD]

Kempe, Rudolf (pno)
Bach, J.S.:Con for 4 Hpds, w. Fritz Rieger (pno), Wolfgang Sawallisch (pno), Rafael Kubelík (pno), R. Kubelík (cnd), Bavarian RSO *(rec 1972)* Arkadia ▲ 494

Kempff, Wilhelm (pno)
Bach, J.S.:Capriccio Departure Deutsche Grammophon ("Double" series) 2-▲ 439672-2
Bach, J.S.:Chorale Preludes Org [trans. Kempff] Deutsche Grammophon ("Double" series) 2-▲ 439672-2
Bach, J.S.:Das wohltemperierte Klavier—12 Preludes & Fugues from Books 1 & 2 Deutsche Grammophon ("Double" series) 2-▲ 439672-2
Beethoven, L. van:Cons Pno (comp), w. P. van Kempen (cnd), Berlin PO Deutsche Grammophon 3-▲ 435744-2 [ADD]
Beethoven, L. van:Con 3 Pno, w. F.-P. Decker (cnd), Montreal SO Music & Arts ▲ CD 768 [ADD]
Beethoven, L. van:Con 4 Pno, w. F. Leitner (cnd), Berlin PO *(rec 1961)* Deutsche Grammophon ("The Originals" series) ▲ 447402-2
Beethoven, L. van:Con 5 Pno, "Emperor", w. F.-P. Decker (cnd), Toronto SO *(rec Nov. 13, 1966)* Music & Arts ▲ CD 768 [AAD]
Beethoven, L. van:Con 5 Pno, "Emperor", w. F. Leitner (cnd), Berlin PO *(rec 1961)* Deutsche Grammophon ("The Originals" series) ▲ 447402-2
Beethoven, L. van:Rondos Pno, Op. 51 Deutsche Grammophon 3-▲ 435744-2 [ADD]
Beethoven, L. van:Sons Vc (comp), w. Pierre Fournier (vc) Deutsche Grammophon ("2CD" series) 2-▲ 453 013-2
Beethoven, L. van:Sons Pno (comp)—Nos. 1-32 *(rec 1964-65)* Deutsche Grammophon 9-▲ 429306-2 [ADD]
Beethoven, L. van:Son 8 Pno, "Pathétique" Deutsche Grammophon ("The Originals" series) ▲ 447404-2
Beethoven, L. van:Son 14 Pno, "Moonlight Son" Deutsche Grammophon ("The Originals" series) ▲ 447404-2
Beethoven, L. van:Son 21 Pno, "Waldstein" Deutsche Grammophon ("The Originals" series) ▲ 447404-2
Beethoven, L. van:Son 23 Pno, "Appassionata" Deutsche Grammophon ("The Originals" series) ▲ 447404-2
Beethoven, L. van:Son 27 Pno Deutsche Grammophon ("2CD" series) 2-▲ 453 010-2
Beethoven, L. van:Sons 28-32 Pno, "The Late Sons" Deutsche Grammophon ("2CD" series) 2-▲ 453 010-2
Beethoven, L. van:Sons Vn (comp), w. Y. Menuhin (vn) Deutsche Grammophon 4-▲ 415874-2 [ADD]
Beethoven, L. van:Son 5 Vn, "Spring", w. Y. Menuhin (vn) Deutsche Grammophon ("Galleria" series) ▲ 427251-2 [ADD]
Beethoven, L. van:Son 9 Vn, "Kreutzer", w. Y. Menuhin (vn) Deutsche Grammophon ("Galleria" series) ▲ 427251-2 [ADD]
Beethoven, L. van:Trios Pno (comp), w. H. Szerying (vn), P. Fournier (vc)—Opp. 1,70 & 97 Deutsche Grammophon 3-▲ 415879-2 [ADD]
Beethoven, L. van:Trio 4 Pno, "Ghost", w. H. Szeryng (vn), P. Fournier (vc) Deutsche Grammophon ("Galleria" series) ▲ 429712-2 [ADD]
Beethoven, L. van:Trio 6 Pno, "Archduke", w. H. Szeryng (vn), P. Fournier (vc) Deutsche Grammophon ("Galleria" series) ▲ 429712-2 [ADD]
Beethoven, L. van:Vars on "Ein Mädchen oder Weibchen" from Mozart's *Die Zauberflöte*, w. Pierre Fournier (vc) Deutsche Grammophon ("2CD" series) 2-▲ 453 013-2
Beethoven, L. van:Vars on "See, the Conquering Hero Comes" from Handel's *Judas Maccabaeus*, w. Pierre Fournier (vc) Deutsche Grammophon ("2CD" series) 2-▲ 453 013-2
Beethoven, L. van:Vars on "Bei Männern" from Mozart's *Die Zauberflöte*, w. Pierre Fournier (vc) Deutsche Grammophon ("2CD" series) 2-▲ 453 013-2
Brahms, J.:Ballades, Op. 10 Deutsche Grammophon ("Double" series) 2-▲ 437374-2
Brahms, J.:Con 1 Pno, w. F. Konwitschny (cnd), Dresden Staatskapelle Deutsche Grammophon ("Double" series) 2-▲ 437374-2
Brahms, J.:Pno Music (misc)—Fants., Op. 116; Intermezzos, Op. 117; Pieces, Opp. 118 & 119 Deutsche Grammophon ▲ 437249-2
Brahms, J.:Pieces Pno, Op. 76—Op. 76 Deutsche Grammophon ("Double" series) 2-▲ 437374-2
Brahms, J.:Rhaps Pno, Op. 79 Deutsche Grammophon ("Double" series) 2-▲ 437374-2
Brahms, J.:Scherzo Pno, Op. 4 Deutsche Grammophon ("Double" series) 2-▲ 437374-2
Brahms, J.:Son 3 Pno Deutsche Grammophon ("Double" series) 2-▲ 437374-2
Chopin, F.:Andante Spianato & Grande Polonaise Theorema ▲ TH 121176
Chopin, F.:Ballades Pno (comp)—No. 3, Op. 47 Theorema ▲ TH 121176
Chopin, F.:Fant Theorema ▲ TH 121176
Chopin, F.:Pno Music (misc)—Son No. 2, Op. 35; Fant-Impromptu, Op. 66; Impromptu No. 1, Op. 29; Scherzo No. 3, Op. 39; Berceuse, Op. 57; Barcarolle, Op. 60 Theorema ▲ TH 121216
Chopin, F.:Polonaise-fant Theorema ▲ TH 121176
Mozart, W.A.:Con 8 Pno, w. F. Leitner (cnd), Berlin PO Deutsche Grammophon ("Double" series) 2-▲ 439699-2
Mozart, W.A.:Con 21 Pno, w. B. Klee (cnd), Bavarian RSO Deutsche Grammophon ("Musikfest" series) ■ 415920-4
Mozart, W.A.:Con 22 Pno, w. B. Klee (cnd), Bavarian RSO Deutsche Grammophon ("Musikfest" series) ■ 415920-4
Mozart, W.A.:Con 23 Pno, w. F. Leitner (cnd), Berlin PO Deutsche Grammophon ("Double" series) 2-▲ 439699-2
Mozart, W.A.:Con 24 Pno, w. F. Leitner (cnd), Berlin PO Deutsche Grammophon ("Double" series) 2-▲ 439699-2
Mozart, W.A.:Con 27 Pno, w. F. Leitner (cnd), Berlin PO Deutsche Grammophon ("Double" series) 2-▲ 439699-2
Radio Recordings, 1945-1956 Koch Schwann ▲ SCH 310292 [DDD]
Schubert, Franz:Sons Pno (comp)—in E, D.157 (Fragment); in C, D.279 (Fragment); 5 Piano Pieces ("Sonata in E"), D.459 & 459a; in a, D.537; in A♭, D.557; in e, D.566; in E♭, D.568; in B, D.575; in f, D.625; in A, D.664; in a, D.784; in C, D.840, "Reliquie" (Fragment); in a, D.845; in D, D.850; in G, D.894; in c, D.958; in A, D.959; in B♭, D.960 Deutsche Grammophon 7-▲ 423496-2 [ADD]

Kenedi, Mary (pno)
Weinzweig, J.:Refrains, w. Joel Quarrington (db) *(rec live, Walter Hall, Univ. of Toronto, Mar. 11, 1993)* Centrediscs ▲ CMC 5295 [DDD]
Weinzweig, J.:Son Vn, w. Martin Beaver (vn) *(rec live, Walter Hall, Univ. of Toronto, Mar. 11, 1993)* Centrediscs ▲ CMC 5295 [DDD]

Kennard, Robin (bn)
Debussy, C.:Chamber Music, w. William Bennett (fl), David Campbell (cl), James Campbell (cl), Nicholas Daniel (ob), Robert Makell (hn), Richard Watkins (hn), Rachel Gough (bn), Simon Haram (sax), Ieuan Jones (hp), Clifford Benson (pno), Julius Drake (pno), John York (pno), Roger Tapping (va)—Rapsodie for Eng hn; Syrinx; Première rapsodie; Son for Fl, Va & Hp; Le petit nègre; Petite pièce; Rapsodie for Sax *(rec All Saints' Church, East Finchley, London, Jan 12-20, 1994)* Cala 2-▲ CACD 1017 [DDD]
Saint-Saëns, C.:Chamber Music, w. W. Bennett (fl), D. Campbell (cl), J. Campbell (cl), N. Daniel (ob), R. Makell (hn), R. Watkins (hn), R. Gough (bn), S. Haram (sax), I. Jones (hp), C. Benson (pno), J. Drake (pno), J. York (pno), R. Tapping (va)—Odelette, Op. 162; Son for Cl, Op. 167; Feuillet d'album, Op. 81; Son for Bn, Op. 168; Caprice on Danish & Russian Airs, Op. 79; Son for Ob, Op. 166; Romance in D♭, Op. 37; Tarantelle, Op. 6 *(rec All Saints' Church, East Finchley, London, Jan 12-20, 1994)* Cala 2-▲ CACD 1017 [DDD]

Kennedy, Daniel (mar/perc)
Jones, D.E.:Still Life Dancing, w. J. Bluestone (dr/cym/hand perc), J. Ferrari (vib/perc) Centaur ▲ CRC 2052 [DDD]
Jones, D.E.:Still Life in Wood & Metal, w. J. Ferrari (vib/perc) Centaur ▲ CRC 2052 [DDD]

Kennedy, Daniel (perc)
Harrison, L.:Fugue Perc, w. William Winant (perc), D. Rosenthal (perc), T. Manley (perc) New Albion ▲ NA 055
Harrison, L.:Song of Quetzalcoatl, w. William Winant (perc), D. Rosenthal (perc), T. Manley (perc) New Albion ▲ NA 055
Machover, T.:Bug-Mudra, w. D. Starobin (gtr), O. Fader (elec gtr), T. Machover (elec) *(rec live, Tokyo)* Bridge ▲ BCD 9022 [DDD]
Wolpe, S.:Qt Ob, w. S. Taylor (ob), F. Sherry (vc), A. Karis (pno) *(rec Nov. 9-10, 1991)* Koch ▲ KIC 7112 [DDD]

Kennedy, John (perc)
Hays, S.:Dreaming the World, w. Thomas Bruckner (bar), Sal Basile (voc), Jennifer López (voc), John Schaffer (voc), Sorrel Hays (voc), Joseph Kubera (pno), Charles Wood (perc), Maya Gunji (perc), Eric Kivnick (perc), Jai Smith (perc) New World ▲ 805202 [DDD]

Kennedy, Laurie (vc)
Kreisler, F.:Qt Strs, w. F. Kreisler (vn), T. Petrie (vn), W. Primrose (va) *(rec 1935 for HMV)* Biddulph 3-▲ LAB 001-3 (m) [ADD]
Kreisler, F.:Scherzo 'in the style of Dittersdorf', w. F. Kreisler (vn), T. Petrie (vn), W. Primrose (va), 1935 for HMV] Biddulph 3-▲ LAB 001-3 (m) [ADD]
Leider Singer, w. McCormack, John (ten), E. Schneider (sgr), Grace Moore (sop), F. Kreisler (vn), V. O'Brien (pno), L. Bori (sop) Symposium ▲ 1164

Kennedy, Nigel (vn)
Bach, J.S.:Sons & Partitas Vn, BWV 1001-1006—BWV 1003 & 1006 EMI Classics ▲ CDC 54574-2 ■ 4DS 54574-4
Bartók, B.:Son Vn EMI Classics ▲ CDC 47621 [DDD]
Beethoven, L. van:Con Vn, Op. 61, w. K. Tennstedt (cnd), North German RSO EMI Classics ▲ CDC 54574 ■ 4DS 54574
Brahms, J.:Con Vn, w. K. Tennstedt (cnd), London PO EMI Classics ▲ CDC 54187 [DDD] ■ 4DS 54187
Bruch, M.:Con 1 Vn, w. J. Tate (cnd), English CO EMI Classics ▲ CDC 49663 [DDD]
Elgar, E.:Chanson de matin, w. P. Pettinger (pno) Chandos ▲ CHAN 8380 [DDD]
Elgar, E.:Chanson de nuit, w. P. Pettinger (pno) Chandos ▲ CHAN 8380 [DDD]
Elgar, E.:Con Vn, w. V. Handley (cnd), London PO EMI Classics ▲ CDM 63795
Elgar, E.:Son Vn, w. P. Pettinger (pno) Chandos ▲ CHAN 8380 [DDD]
Elgar, E.:Sospiri, w. P. Pettinger (pno) Chandos ▲ CHAN 8380 [DDD]
Elgar, E.:Vn & Pno Music, w. P. Pettinger (pno)—Mot d'amour, Op. 13; Canto popolare (In the moonlight, from *In the South*); 6 Very Easy Pieces in the First Position, Op. 22 Chandos ▲ CHAN 8380 [DDD]
Ellington, D.:Mainly Black, w. A. Dankworth (string bass) [arr Kennedy] EMI Classics ▲ CDC 47621 [DDD]
Mendelssohn, F.:Con in e Vn & Orch, Op. 64, w. J. Tate (cnd), English CO EMI Classics ▲ CDC 49663 [DDD]
Nigel Kennedy Plays Jazz, w. Peter Pettinger (pno) Chandos ("Collect" series) ▲ CHAN 6513 [DDD]
Schubert, Franz:Rondo Vn, D.438, w. J. Tate (cnd), English CO EMI Classics ▲ CDC 49663 [DDD]
Sibelius, J.:Con Vn, w. S. Rattle (cnd), City of Birmingham SO EMI Classics ▲ CDC 54559 [DDD] ■ 4DS 54559
Tchaikovsky, P.:Con Vn, w. O. Kamu (cnd), London PO EMI Classics ▲ CDC 54559 [DDD] ■ 4DS 54559
Vivaldi, A.:Cons Vn, Op. 8/1-4, "The Four Seasons", w. N. Kennedy (cnd), English CO EMI Classics ▲ CDC 49557 [DDD] ■ 4DS 49557 (D)
Walton, W.:Con Va, w. A. Previn (cnd), Royal PO EMI Classics ▲ CDC 49628 [DDD]
Walton, W.:Con Vn, w. A. Previn (cnd), Royal PO EMI Classics ▲ CDC 49628 [DDD]

Kenny, E. (thb)
Insalata, w. I Fagiolini, D. Burchell (hpd/org), Riona D.(baroque vn), T. Cronin (baroque vn), D. Clasen (bar) Metronome ▲ METCD 1004

Kent
Baroque Masterpieces for Trumpet & Organ, Vol. 1, w. E. Tarr (tpt), M. Ullrich (tpt), et al. Elektra/Nonesuch ■ 71279-4

Kent, George (org)
Courtly Trumpet Ensemble Music, w. Bengt Eklund's Baroque Ensemble [cnd.:Edward H. Tarr] *(rec 1980)* BIS ▲ CD 217 [AAD]

Kent, Peter (vn)—see also ORCHESTRAS & ENSEMBLES Amelite Consortium, Kent/Shulman Duo
Matson, S.:-5, w. A. Shulmann (hp), M. Newman (vn), R. Tischer (va), E. Duke-Kirkpatrick (vc), B. Morgenthaler (db) *(rec Aug. 29-30, 1992)* Audioquest ▲ AQCD 1013
Matson, S.:Range, w. Catherine Robbin (mez), Susan Greenberg (fl), Joseph Stone (fl), Glen Garrett (cl), Suren Karapetyan (hn), Kazi Pitelka (va), Sebastian Toettcher (vc), Don Ferrone (db), Doug Livingston (gtr/mand), John Schneider (gtr), Amy Shulman (hp), Terry Schoenig (perc), S. Matson (cnd) *(rec Schnee Studio, Universal City, CA, Mar 12, 1995)* New Albion ▲ NA 091
Matson, S.:Steel Chords, w. D. Livingston (gtr), M. Newman (vn), J. Derouin (vn), C. Moussas (vn), R. Tischer (va), E. Duke-Kirkpatrick (vc), B. Morgenthaler (db), S. Matson (cnd) *(rec Aug. 29-30, 1992)* Audioquest ▲ AQCD 1013

Kentner, Louis (pno)
Beethoven, L. van:Son 29 Pno, "Hammerklavier" *(rec 1939 for Columbia Records)* Pearl ▲ PEA 9480 (m) [AAD]
Chopin, F.:Impromptus—Op. 29 & Op. 66 *(rec 1928)* Pearl ▲ PEA 9480 (m) [AAD]
Chopin, F.:Pno Music (misc), w. Martha Argerich (pno), Vladimir Ashkenazy (pno), Stanislav Bunin (pno), Halina Czerny-Stefanska (pno), Jan Ekier (pno), Yuval Fichman (pno), Kemal Gekic (pno), Adam Harasiewicz (pno), Krzysztof Jablonski (pno), Jean-Marc Luisada (pno), Garrick Ohlsson (pno), Ivo Pogorelich (pno), Maurizio Pollini (pno), Dang Thai Son (pno)—includes Ballade (Nos. 1 & 2); Barcarolle, Op. 60; Concerto Nos. 1 & 2; Études (Op. 10, Nos. 1, 5, 8, 10 & 12 & Op. 25, No. 10, 18 & 25); Grand valse brillante; Impromptus (Nos. 3 & 4); Mazurkas (Op. 24, Nos. 1-4; Op. 30, Nos. 1-4; Op. 50, No. 32; Op. 59, Nos. 1-3); Nocturnes (Op. 9, No. 3; Op. 37, No. 12; Op. 48, No. 13; Op. 55, No. 16)Polonaise (Op. 40, Nos. 3 & 4; Op. 44, No. 5; Op. 53, No. 6; Op. 61, No. 7); Preludes (Op. 28 Nos. 13-18, 21-24 & Op. 45, No. 25); Scherzos (Nos. 1-3); Sonatas (Nos. 2 & 3); Waltzes (No. 1 & 6) LaserLight 5-▲ 15 961 [ADD/DDD]
Liszt, F.:Pno Music (misc)—Apparitions No. 1; Ballade No. 2; Benediction de Dieu dans la solitude; Elegy No. 2; 4 Little Piano Pieces; Harmonies poétiques et religieuses; 5 Hungarian Folksongs; La Lugubre gondola; Nuages gris; Reminiscences de Don Juan; Spinning Song from "The Flying Dutchman"; Valse de Concert sur deux motifs de "Lucia et Parisina"; Valse de l'opéra "Faust" de Charles Gounod; Wedding March & Elves' Dance from "Midsummer Night's Dream" *(rec 1960s & early 1970s)* Vox Box ("Legends" series) 2-▲ CDX2 5503 [ADD]

Kentner, Louis (pno) (cont.)
Liszt, F.:Pno Music (misc)—Hungarian Rhap 2; Ballade 2; Bénédiction de Dieu dans la solitude; Berecuse; Polonaise 1; Scherzo & March; Hungarian Rhap 9 *(rec 1937–41)* APR ▲ APR 5514 [ADD]
Liszt, F.:Pno Music (misc)—Hungarian Rhapsody No. 9; Bénédiction de Dieu dans le solitude, G.86/3 *(rec 1940 & 1938 for Columbia)* Pearl ▲ PEA 9480 (m) [AAD]
Mozart, W.A.:Con 12 Pno, w. T. Beecham (cnd), London PO *(rec 1940)* EMI Classics ("Great Recordings of the Century" series) ▲ CDH 63820
Mozart, W.A.:Con 12 Pno, w. T. Beecham (cnd), London PO Dutton Laboratories ▲ DUT 7019 [ADD]
Mozart, W.A.:Con 12 Pno, w. T. Beecham (cnd), London PO *(rec 1934–1940)* Pearl ▲ PEA 9081 [ADD]

Kentros, George (vn)—see ORCHESTRAS & ENSEMBLES Ferro String Quartet

Kenyon, Philip (org)
Howells, H.:Org Music [arr. Robin Wells for organ]—Six Short Pieces—Tranquillo, ma con moto; Allegro Scherzando; Aria; Allegro impetuoso; Chorale; Quasi lento; Three Pieces—Intrata (1941); Flourish for a bidding (1969); St. Louis comes to Clifton (1977); Two Slow Airs for Violin & Piano Herald ▲ HAVPCD 115 [DDD]

Keough, Miriam (hp)
Ave Maria, w. Miriam Hayward Segal (sop), K. Bower (pno) Symposium ▲ SYM 1175 [DDD]

Kerckhoven, François van (instr)—see ORCHESTRAS & ENSEMBLES Chamber Opera Quintet

Kerdoncuff, François (pno)
Furtwängler, W.:Qnt Pno, w. Sine Nomine String Quartet Timpani ▲ 1C 1018 [DDD]
Furtwängler, W.:Son 1 Vn, w. Dong-Suk Kang (vn) *(rec Poissy Théâtre, Dec 20–22, 1994)* Timpani ▲ 1029 [DDD]
Furtwängler, W.:Son 2 Vn, w. A. Galpérine (vn) *(rec 1989)* Timpani ▲ 1C1001 [DDD]

Kereskedo, Tamás (pno)—see ORCHESTRAS & ENSEMBLES Budapest Piano Duet

Kerns, JoAnn (handbells)
Vees, J.:Stigmata non Grata, w. Dorian Ringers (handbells), Cammi Carteng (handbells), Jan Dudiet (handbells), Monica McGowan (handbells), B. Mathis (cnd) CRI ("Emergency Music" series) ▲ CD 730 [DDD]

Kerppo, Raija (pno)
Finnish Violin Miniatures, w. Kaija Saarikettu (vn) Finlandia ▲ 4509–95875–2 [DDD]
Merikanto, O.:Music of, w. Eeva-Jiisa Saarinen (mez), Jorma Hynninen (bar), Sauli Tiilikainen (bar), Kaija Saarikettu (vn), Erkki Rautio (vc), Pertti Eerola (pno), Ralf Gothoni (pno), Izumi Tateno (pno), Tauno Satomaa (cnd), Candomino Choir—Summer Evening (waltz); Valse lente; Romance; On the Highest Tree-Top; Annina; Bye, Bye Lullabye; The Weeping Flute; At Sea; Hey My Heart; Where Rustling Birches Bend; Play Softly, the Tune of Mourning; Fairy Tale by the Fireside; Idyll; Scherzo, Op. 6/4; O Dost Thou Remember That Hymn; Lade Ladoga; Why Do I Sing; The Thunderbird; The Happy Ones; Summer Evening's Idyll Finlandia ▲ FIN 500432 [AAD/DDD]
Palmgren, S.:Cons Pno (comp), w. E. Heinonen (pno—No. 1), J. Lagerspetz (pno—Nos. 2 & 4), M. Raekallio (pno—No. 3), R. Kerppo (pno—No. 5), J. Mercier (cnd), Turku PO Finlandia 2–▲ 4509–95852–2 [DDD]

Kerrigan, William (perc)
Crumb, G.:Lux Aeterna, w. Freda Herseth (mez), Pamela Guidetti (b fl/sop rcr), James Freeman (sitar), Susan Jones (perc) *(rec Lang Concert Hall, Swarthmore College)* CRI ▲ CD 723 [DDD]

Kershner, Brian (bn)
Kershner, B.:Son Bn, w. Paul Hoffmann (pno) Vienna Modern Masters ("Distinguished Performers III" series) ▲ VMM 2016 [DDD]

Kerstens, Tom (gtr)
Walton, W.:Bagatelles Gtr EMI Classics ("Anglo-American Chamber Music" series) ▲ CDC 55404

Kerstetter, Tod (cl/b cl)
Schoenberg, A.:Pierrot lunaire, w. Leslie Boucher (nar), Julie Stone (fl/pic), Andrew Carlson (vn), Philip Singleton (va), Juanita Karpf (vc), F. Joseph Lozier (pno) *(rec Roswell United Methodist Church, Roswell, GA, July 20, Aug. 2 & Sept. 1)* ACA Digital ▲ CM 20027
Zwilich, E.T.:Passages, w. Leslie Boucher (sop), Julie Stone (fl/pic), Andrew Carlson (vn), Philip Singleton (va), Juanita Karpf (vc), F. Joseph Lozier (pno), Joanna Parks (perc), Shannon O'Kelley (perc) *(rec Roswell United Methodist Church, Roswell, GA, July 20, Aug. 2 & Sept. 1)* ACA Digital ▲ CM 20027

Kertész, György (vc)
Atterberg, K.:Chamber Music, w. E. Pérényi (vn), A. Kiss (vn), I. Prunyi (pno), S. Falvay (pno), D. Spikay (hp)—Son. in b for Violin, Op. 27; Höstballader, Op. 15; Valse monotone in C; Rondeau Rétrospectif, Op. 26; Trio Concertante in g, Op. 57 Marco Polo ▲ 8.223404
Berwald, F.:Trio Fragments, w. K. Drafi (pno), J. Modrian (vn) *(rec June 7–16, 1991)* Marco Polo ▲ 8.223430 [DDD]
Berwald, F.:Trios, w. K. Drafi (pno), J. Modrian (vn)—in C (1845); No. 4 *(rec June 7–16, 1991)* Marco Polo ▲ 8.223430 [DDD]
Vivaldi, A.:Cons Vc, Hungarian State Opera Orch—Nos. 1 in c, R.401; 4 in a, R.422; 7 in d, R.406; 8 in C, R.398; 9 in b, R.424; 11 in F, R.412; 12 in C, R.413 *(rec Festetich Castle, Budapest, June 1991)* Lydian ▲ 18120 [DDD]

Kertész, István (vn)—see also ORCHESTRAS & ENSEMBLES Festetics String Quartet
Vivaldi, A.:Con Vn Org, RV.542, w. M. Haselböck (org), M. Haselböck (cnd), Vienna Academy [period instrs] Novalis ▲ 150074 [DDD]

Kertész, Lajos (pno)
Bartók, B.:For Children *(rec 1995)* Hungaroton ▲ HCD 4001 [DDD]
Bartók, B.:Hungarian Folksongs from Csík *(rec 1995)* Hungaroton ▲ HCD 4001 [DDD]
Bartók, B.:Hungarian Peasant Songs *(rec 1995)* Hungaroton ▲ HCD 4001 [DDD]
Bartók, B.:Mikrokosmos *(rec 1995)* Hungaroton ▲ HCD 4001 [DDD]
Bartók, B.:Petite Suite *(rec 1995)* Hungaroton ▲ HCD 4001 [DDD]
Bartók, B.:Sonatina Pno *(rec 1995)* Hungaroton ▲ HCD 4001 [DDD]
Kodály, Z.:Pno Music *(rec 1995)* Hungaroton ▲ HCD 4001 [DDD]
Kodály, Z.:Pieces (7) Pno *(rec 1995)* Hungaroton ▲ HCD 4001 [DDD]

Kertész, Ottó (vc)—see ORCHESTRAS & ENSEMBLES Keller String Quartet, Keller String Quartet members

Kertész Jr., Otto (vc)
Borodin, A.:Qnt Vns, Va & Vcs, w. O. Kertész, Jr. (vc), New Budapest String Quartet Marco Polo ▲ 8.223172 [DDD]
Borodin, A.:Qnt Vns, Va & Vcs, w. New Budapest String Quartet Marco Polo ▲ 8.223172 [DDD]
Kraft, William:Interplay, w. W. Samples, P. Polivnick (cnd), Alabama SO Meet The Composer ▲ 79229–2 ■ 79229–4

Kesseler, Inke (pno)—see ORCHESTRAS & ENSEMBLES Con Sordino Chamber Group

Kessler, Gary (gtr)—see ORCHESTRAS & ENSEMBLES Trio Sonata

Kessler, Inke (pno)
This Is Denmark, w. Leni Voldby (mez) (rec. Dec. 1990) Danacord ▲ DACOCD 377 [DDD]

Kesting, Anno (perc)—see ORCHESTRAS & ENSEMBLES Percussion Art Quartet

Ketchum, Janet (fl)
Russell, A.:Suite Concertante, w. Floyd Cooley (tuba), James Kanter (cl), Earle Dumler (ob), Arthur David Krehbiel (hn), Charles Ullery (bn) Crystal ▲ CD 120

Kettel, Gary (perc)
Jolivet, A.:Suite en concert, w. Anna Noakes (fl), Graham Cole (perc), Kate Eyre (perc), Rachel Gledhill (perc) ASV ("French Chamber Music" series) ▲ ASV 948
Miki, M.:Mar Spiritual, w. Evelyn Glennie (mar), Stephen Henderson (perc), Greg Knowles (perc) *(rec Whitfield Street Studios, London, Sept. 22–29, 1994)* Catalyst ▲ 09026–68193–2 [DDD]

Kettelson, Robert (pno)
Tosti, P.F.:Romanzas on Italian Texts, w. Renato Bruson (bar) Nuova Era ▲ NUO 7233 [DDD]

Kettinger, Kirk (tuba)
Shewan, S.:Magnificat, w. Erin Stedman (sop), Kimberly Higgins (alt), Robert Dingman (ten), Alexander Burgess (bar), Paul Shewan (tpt), Barbara Hull (tpt), Nanita Wilson (hn), Scott Emmons (trbn), Ann Musser Honeywell (org) Albany ▲ TROY 149 [DDD]

Kettinger, Kirk (tuba) (cont.)
Shewan, S.:The Voice of the Lord in the Storm, w. Erin Stedman (sop), Kimberly Higgins (alt), Robert Dingman (ten), Alexander Burgess (bar), Paul Shewan (tpt), Barbara Hull (tpt), Nanita Wilson (hn), Scott Emmons (trbn), Ann Musser Honeywell (org) Albany ▲ TROY 149 [DDD]

Keulen, Isabelle van (va)
Henkemans, H.:Con Va, w. G. Schuller (cnd), Netherlands Radio PO Donemus ▲ CV 14
Schnittke, A.:Con Va, w. H. Schiff (cnd), Philharmonia Orch Koch Schwann ▲ SCH 315232 [DDD]

Keulen, Isabelle van (vn)
Debussy, C.:Son Vn, w. Ronald Brautigam (pno) Koch Schwann ▲ SCH 315272 [DDD]
Fauré, G.:Son 1 Vn, w. Ronald Brautigam (pno) Koch Schwann ▲ SCH 315272 [DDD]
Lutoslawski, W.:Chain 2, w. H. Schiff (cnd), Philharmonia Orch Koch Schwann ▲ SCH 315232 [DDD]
Martinů, B.:Qt 1 Pno, w. Daniel Adni (pno), Rainer Moog (va), Young-Chang Cho (vc) *(rec Australian Festival of Chamber Music, July 1994)* Naxos ▲ 8.553916 [DDD]
Mendelssohn, F.:Con in d Vn, Pno & Strs, w. Ronald Brautigam (pno), L. Markiz (cnd), Amsterdam New Sinfonietta *(rec Concertgebouw, Haarlem, Holland, July 4–5, 1995)* BIS ▲ CD 713 [DDD]
Poulenc, F.:Son Vn, w. Ronald Brautigam (pno) Koch Schwann ▲ SCH 315272 [DDD]
Saint-Saëns, C.:Carnival of the Animals, w. M. Argerich (pno), N. Freire (pno), G. Kremer (vn), T. Zimmermann (va), M. Maisky (vc), et al. Philips ("Digital Classics" series) ▲ 416841–2 [DDD]

Keuning, Dido (pno)
Wolf, H.:Songs (misc), w. Nico van der Meel (ten)—An ***; Traurige Wege; Herbstentschluss; Sie haben heut' abend Gesellschaft; Ich stand in dunkeln Träumen; Das ist ein Brausen und Heulen; Aus meinen grossen Schmerzen; Mir träumte von eimen Königskind; Mein Liebchen, wir sassen beisammen; Es blasen die blauen Husaren; Ernst ist der Frühling; Spätherbstnebel; Wo ich bin, mich rings umdunkelt; Du bist wie eine Blume; In der Fremde; Rückkehr; Die Nacht; Erwartung; Nachruf; Wohin mit der Freud; Liebchen, wo bist du?; Nachtgruss; Frühlingsglocken; Ständchen; Liebesbotschaft *(rec Utrecht, Jan 1996)* Globe ▲ GLO 5149 [DDD]

Keunzel, Adam (fl)
Macy, C.:Solstice & Equinox, w. Julia Bogorad (fl), John Jensen (pno) *(rec Macalester College, Mar 11–12, 1994)* Innova ▲ 503

Keuschnig, Rainer (pno)
Schmidt, F.:Qnt Cl, w. E. Ottensamer (cl), J. Hell (vn), P. Wächter (vn), P. Pecha (va), R. Wallfisch (vc) *(rec Jan. 7, 1991)* Orfeo ▲ 287921 [DDD]
Schmidt, F.:Qnt Pno, w. J. Hell (vn), P. Wächter (vn), P. Pecha (va), G. Iberer (vc) *(rec Jan. 7, 1991)* Orfeo ▲ 287921 [DDD]
Segerstam, L.:Con 1 Pno, w. L. Segerstam (cnd), ORF SO Kontrapunkt ▲ KPT 32184 [DDD]
Segerstam, L.:Con 3 Pno, w. L. Segerstam (cnd), Rhineland–Palatinate State PO *(rec live 2/26/89)* BIS ▲ CD 484 [DDD]
Segerstam, L.:Con-Fant Vn, w. H. Segerstam (vn), L. Segerstam (cnd), ORF SO Kontrapunkt ▲ KPT 32184 [DDD]
Segerstam, L.:Sym 13, w. L. Segerstam (cnd), Rhineland–Palatinate State PO BIS ▲ CD 484 [DDD]

Kevehäzi, Jenö (hn)
Beethoven, L. van:Qnt Ob, 3 Hns & Bn, w. Ottó Rácz (ob), Sándor Berki (hn), József Vajda (bn) Naxos ▲ 8.553090 [DDD]
Beethoven, L. van:Qnt Pno, Ob, Cl, Hn & Bn, w. J. Jandó (pno), J. Kiss (ob), B. Kovács (cl), J. Vajda (bn) *(rec Dec. 1–4, 1990)* Naxos ▲ 8.550511 [DDD]
Beethoven, L. van:Septet Strs, w. Ildikó Hegyi (vn), Győző Máthé (va), Péter Szabó (vc), István Tóth (db), József Balogh (cl), József Vajda (bn) *(rec Scottish Church, Budapest, Apr. 21–23 & May 29–31, 1)* Naxos ▲ 8.553090 [DDD]
Beethoven, L. van:Sxt Hns, Op. 81b, w. Ildikó Hegyi (vn), Péter Popa (vn), Győző Máthé (va), Péter Szabó (vc) *(rec Scottish Church, Budapest, Apr. 21–23 & May 29–31, 1)* Naxos ▲ 8.553090 [DDD]
Mozart, W.A.:Qnt Hn, K.407, w. J. Jandó (pno), J. Kiss (ob), B. Kovács (cl), J. Vajda (bn) *(rec Dec. 1–4, 1990)* Naxos ▲ 8.550511 [DDD]
Mozart, W.A.:Qnt Hn, K.407, w. Kodály String Quartet *(rec May 2–3 & 6–9, 1991)* Naxos ▲ 8.550437 [DDD]

Kevorkov, Andrei (va)—see also ORCHESTRAS & ENSEMBLES Gosteleradio String Quartet
Taneyev, S.:Trio Strs, Op. 21, w. Sergei Ryabov (vn), Lidiya Chavaukina (vn) Allegretto ▲ ACD 8178 [DDD] ■ ACS 8178

Keyes, Bayla (vn)—see ORCHESTRAS & ENSEMBLES Muir String Quartet

Keyes, I. (hpd)
Corelli, A.:Sons Vn, Op. 5, w. R. Ricci (vn), D. Nesbitt (va de gamba)—Sons. 8, 9, 10, 11 & 12 One–Eleven 2–▲ URS 92030 [ADD]

Keys, Karen (pno)
Hindemith, P.:Son Fl, w. Keith Bryan (fl) *(rec OPUS Studio 1, Bratislava, Slovak Republic, July 1989)* Premier ▲ PRCD 1053 [DDD]
La Montaine, J.:Con Pno, w. G. F. Harrison (cnd), Oklahoma City SO CRI ■ C 189
La Montaine, J.:Con Pno, w. G. F. Harrison (cnd), Oklahoma City SO *(rec 1962)* Citadel ▲ CTD 88118 [ADD]
Martinů, B.:Son Fl & Pno, w. Keith Bryan (fl) *(rec OPUS Studio 1, Bratislava, Slovak Republic, July 1989)* Premier ▲ PRCD 1053 [DDD]
Poulenc, F.:Son Fl, w. Keith Bryan (fl) *(rec OPUS Studio 1, Bratislava, Slovak Republic, July 1989)* Premier ▲ PRCD 1053 [DDD]
Prokofiev, S.:Son Fl, w. Keith Bryan (fl) *(rec OPUS Studio 1, Bratislava, Slovak Republic, July 1989)* Premier ▲ PRCD 1053 [DDD]

Khachaturian, Karen (pno)
Khachaturian, A.:Son Vn, w. Leonid Kogan (vn) Multisonic ▲ MUL 310354

Khaladj, Madjid (tombak/daf)
Persian Classical Music, w. Omoumi, Hossein (ney) *(rec 1992)* Nimbus ▲ NI 5359 [DDD]

Khanin, Michail (tpt)
Shostakovich, D.:Con 1 Pno, w. I. Margalit (pno), D. Barra (cnd), Moscow PO *(rec Sept. 1992)* Koch International Classics ▲ KIC 7159 [DDD]

Kharenko, Yuri (vn)—see ORCHESTRAS & ENSEMBLES Leontóvych String Quartet

Khen, Ithay (vc)
Blacher, B.:Songs, w. Katharina Richter (sop), Cornelia Wosnitza (sop), Markus Köhler (bar), Horst Göbel (pno), Chatschatur Kanajan (vn), Piotr Prysiasnik (vn), Fred Günther (va), Ithay Khen (vc), Christian Peters (sax), Markus Weidmann (bn)—3 Chansons; Ungereimtes; 4 Lieder; Nebel; 13 Ways of Looking at a Blackbird; 5 Sinnsprüche Omars des Zeitmachers; 3 Psalmen; Aprèslude; Francesca da Rimini; Jazz-Koloraturen Signum ▲ SIG X73–00 [DDD]

Khersonsky, Grigory (trbn)
Bloch, E.:Sym Trbn, w. V. Kozhukar (cnd), USSR SO *(rec 1988)* Consonance ▲ 81–0002 [DDD]

Khochafian, Sona (vn)
Klein, G.:Four Movements, w. Serge Garcia (vn), Françoise Gnéri (va), David Simpson (vc) Arion ▲ ARN 68272 [DDD]
Klein, G.:Movements Str Qt, w. Serge Garcia (vn), Françoise Gnéri (va), David Simpson (vc) Arion ▲ ARN 68272 [DDD]

Kholodenko, Anton (va)
Shostakovich, D.:Son Va, w. S. Milstein (pno) REM ▲ REM 311210 [DDD]

Kholodenko, Anton (vn)
Milstein, N.:Paganiniana REM ▲ REM 311210 [DDD]
Shostakovich, D.:Son Vn, w. S. Milstein (pno) REM ▲ REM 311210 [DDD]

Khoma, Natalia (vc)
Baley, V.:Duo Concertante, w. Virko Baley (pno) *(rec Longy School of Music, Cambridge, Massachusetts, June 15, 1995)* Cambria ▲ CD 1087

Khomitser, Mikhail (vc)
Schumann, R.:Con Vc, w. Y. Silantiev (cnd), Moscow RSO Multisonic ▲ MUL 310272
Tchaikovsky, P.:Vars on a Rococo Theme, w. Y. Silantiev (cnd), Moscow RSO Multisonic ▲ MUL 310272

Khonen, Robert (hpd)
Bass Viol Suites, w. Re, Bruno (b vl) Pierre Verany ▲ 788012 [DDD]

INSTRUMENT.

INSTRUMENTALISTS 657

Khoudir, Jacques (perc)
Troubador Songs of the 12th & 13th Centuries, w. Gérard Zuchetto (sgr), Patrice Brient (instr) Gallo ▲ CD 529
Troubador Songs of the 12th & 13th Centuries, Vol. 2, w. Gérard Zuchetto (sgr), Dominique Regef (rebec/israj/hurdy-gurdy) Gallo ▲ CD 684 [DDD]

Khouri, John (pno)
Chopin, F.:Pno Music (misc) (1833 Broadwood grand)—Ballade No. 2, Op. 38; Mazurkas in c#, Op. 63/3, in a, Op. 67/4 & in f, Op. 68/4; Nocturnes in E♭, Op. 9/2 & in c (1848); Polonaise in A♭, Op. 53; Scherzo No. 1, Op. 20; Waltzes in A♭, Op. 42 & in c#, Op. 64/2 Entr'acte ▲ ESCD 6506 [DDD]
Chopin, F.:Son Pno, Op. 58 (1833 Broadwood grand) Entr'acte ▲ ESCD 6506 [DDD]
Clementi, M.:Sons Pno [1812 6-octave Broadwood grand]—Op. 50/1 Entr'acte ▲ ESCD 6503 [DDD]
Cramer, J.B.:Son Pno, Op. 57 [1812 6-octave Broadwood grand] Entr'acte ▲ ESCD 6503 [DDD]
Dussek, J.L.:Son Pno, Op. 61, "Elégie harmonique sur la mort du Prince Louis Ferdinand de Prusse" [1812 6-octave Broadwood grand] Entr'acte ▲ ESCD 6503 [DDD]
Field, J.:Pno Music [1812 6-octave Broadwood grand] [Solos]—Romance in E♭; Rondo in A♭; Serenade in B♭ Entr'acte ▲ ESCD 6503 [DDD]
London Pianoforte School Entr'acte ▲ ESCD 6503 [DDD]
Mozart, W.A.:Allegro & Andante & Rondo Entr'acte ▲ EAC 6501 [DDD]
Mozart, W.A.:Allegro Pno, K.312 Entr'acte ▲ EAC 6501 [DDD]
Mozart, W.A.:Allegro Pno, K.400 Entr'acte ▲ EAC 6501 [DDD]
Mozart, W.A.:Fant Pno, K.397 Entr'acte ▲ EAC 6501 [DDD]
Mozart, W.A.:Prelude & Fugue Pno Entr'acte ▲ EAC 6501 [DDD]
Mozart, W.A.:Vars Pno, K.613 Entr'acte ▲ EAC 6501 [DDD]

Khouri, Murray (cl)
Arnold, M.:Sonatina Cl, w. P. Pettinger (pno) *(rec June 1991)* Continuum ▲ CCD 1038
Bax, A.:Son Cl & Pno, w. P. Pettinger (pno) *(rec 6/91)* Continuum ▲ CCD 1038
Brahms, J.:Sons Cl (comp), w. J. McCabe (pno) Continuum ▲ CCD 1027
Finzi, G.:Bagatelles, Op. 23, w. P. Pettinger (pno) *(rec 6/91)* Continuum ▲ CCD 1038
Gal, H.:Son Cl, w. J. McCabe (pno) Continuum ▲ CCD 1027
Horovitz, J.:Sonatina Cl, w. P. Pettinger (pno) *(rec 6/91)* Continuum ▲ CCD 1038
Ireland, J.:Fant-Son Cl & Pno, w. P. Pettinger (pno) *(rec 6/91)* Continuum ▲ CCD 1038

Khuner, F. (vn)—see ORCHESTRAS & ENSEMBLES Kolisch String Quartet

Kibbe, James (org)
Bach, J.S.:Chorale Preludes Org—Clavierübung, Bk. III AFKA 2-▲ AFK 528/29
Bach, J.S.:Clavier-Übung III [Letourneau Orgs, St. Catharines Cathedral, Ontario, Canada] Afka 2-▲ SK 528/29

Kiddle, Frederick B. (pno)
Song Recital, w. Gervase Elwes (ten) *(rec 1911-1919 for Columbia)* Opal ▲ CD 9844 (m) [ADD]
Vaughan Williams, R.:On Wenlock Edge, w. G. Elwes (ten), London String Quartet [E] *(rec 1917 for Columbia)* Opal ▲ CD 9844 (m) [AAD]

Kientzy, Daniel (sax)
Marbe, M.:Con for Daniel Kientzy & Saxes, w. H. Andreescu (cnd), Ploiesti PO Olympia ("Explorer" series) ▲ OCD 410 [AAD]
Nemescu, O.:Music of—Metabizantinirikon for Sax & Magnetic Tape (1984); Sonatu(h)r for Magnetic Tape (1986); Trisson for Magnetic Tape (1987) *(rec 1986-90)* Electrecord ▲ ELCD 130 [AAD]
Niculescu, S.:Concertante Sym 3, w. I. Conta (cnd), Romanian National RSO Olympia ("Explorer" series) ▲ OCD 410 [AAD]
The Romanian Saxophone, w. various orchs Olympia ("Explorer" series) ▲ OCD 410 [AAD]
Vieru, A.:Narration II, w. R. Georgescu (cnd), Timisoara PO Olympia ("Explorer" series) ▲ OCD 410 [AAD]

Kierkegaard, Ingegerd (va)—see also ORCHESTRAS & ENSEMBLES Tale String Quartet
Penderecki, K.:Qt Cl, w. M. Fröst (cl), P. Swedrup (vn), H. Nilsson (vc) *(rec Feb. 18-20, 1994)* BIS ▲ CD 652 [DDD]
Penderecki, K.:Trio Strs, w. T. Olsson (vn), H. Nilsson (vc) *(rec Feb. 18-20, 1994)* BIS ▲ CD 652 [DDD]

Kiesewetter, Erica (vn)—see also ORCHESTRAS & ENSEMBLES Leonardo Trio
Cohn, J.:Con da Camera, w. C. Grant (pno), Quintet of the Americas *(rec Sept. 1992)* XLNT ▲ CD 18007 [DDD]
Cohn, J.:Serenade, w. M. Granados (fl), J. Spitz (vc) *(rec Sept. 1992)* XLNT ▲ CD 18007 [DDD]

Kiezlich, Ivo (timp)
Martinů, B.:The Prophecy of Isaiah, w. N. Romanová (sop), D. Drobková (alto), R. Novák (bass), V. Kozderka (tpt), J. Peruška (va), S. Bogunia (pno), P. Kühn (cnd), Prague Radio Men's Chorus, Kühn Chorus [Cz] *(rec 2-3/88)* Supraphon ▲ 11 0751-2 [DDD]

Kikuchi, Teiko (koto)
Ikebe, S.-I.:Kageru *(rec Saitama Arts Theater Concert Hall, Apr 27-28, 1995)* Camerata ▲ 30CM 267 [DDD]
Matsumura, T.:Air of Prayer *(rec Saitama Arts Theater Concert Hall, Apr 27-28, 1995)* Camerata ▲ 30CM 267 [DDD]
Nishimura, A.:Kamunagi, w. Shigemitsu Eiso (perc) *(rec Saitama Arts Theater Concert Hall, Apr 27-28, 1995)* Camerata ▲ 30CM 267 [DDD]
Satoh, S.:Tamaogi-Koto, w. Kifu Mitsuhashi (shakuhachi fl) *(rec Saitama Arts Theater Concert Hall, Apr 27-28, 1995)* Camerata ▲ 30CM 267 [DDD]
Shinohara, M.:Birth of the Bass Koto *(rec Niiza Shimin Kaikan, Saitama, Japan, July 23, 1986)* Camerata ▲ 30CM 375 [DDD]
Yoshimatsu, T.:Nabari *(rec Saitama Arts Theater Concert Hall, Apr 27-28, 1995)* Camerata ▲ 30CM 267 [DDD]

Kilbonoff, Jon (pno)
Bolcom, W.:Son 2 Vn, w. Maria Bachman (vn) Catalyst ▲ 09026-62668-2
Copland, A.:Nocturne, w. Maria Bachman (vn) Catalyst ▲ 09026-62668-2
Dresher, P.:Double Ikat 2, w. Maria Bachman (vn) Catalyst ▲ 09026-62668-2
Macmillan, J.:Kiss on Wood, w. Maria Bachman (vn) Catalyst ▲ 09026-62668-2
Schnittke, A.:Son 1 Vn, w. Maria Bachman (vn) Catalyst ▲ 09026-62668-2

Kilcher, Erika (pno)
Boccherini, L.:Sons (34) Vc, w. André Navarra (vc)—2 sels in A & G *(rec 1981)* Approche ▲ CAL 6673 [ADD]
Falla, M. de:Suite populaire espagnole vc, w. André Navarra (vc) *(rec 1981)* Approche ▲ CAL 6673 [ADD]
Granados, E.:Goyescas (intermezzo), w. André Navarra (vc) [trans G. Cassado] *(rec 1981)* Approche ▲ CAL 6673 [ADD]
Ivan Monighetti, w. Monighetti, Ivan (vc) Calliope ▲ CAL 9673 [ADD]
Locatelli, P.:Son Vc, w. André Navarra (vc) *(rec 1981)* Approche ▲ CAL 6673 [ADD]
Nin, J.:Chants d' Espagne, w. André Navarra (vc) *(rec 1981)* Approche ▲ CAL 6673 [ADD]
Valentini, G.:Son Vc, w. André Navarra (vc) *(rec 1981)* Approche ▲ CAL 6673 [ADD]

Kilenyi, Edward (pno)
Chopin, F.:Con 1 Pno, w. D. Mitropoulos (cnd), Minneapolis SO *(rec Dec 6, 1941)* Nickson 2-▲ NN 1008/1009 (m) [ADD]
Chopin, F.:Études (24)—Op. 10 APR 2-▲ APR 7037 [ADD]
Chopin, F.:Mazurkas—No. 13, Op. 17/4 APR ▲ APR 7037 [ADD]
Chopin, F.:Son Pno, Op. 35 APR ▲ APR 7037 [ADD]
Liszt, F.:Fant on Hungarian Folk Tunes, w. S. Meyrowitz (cnd), *(orch unknown)* APR ▲ APR 7037 [ADD]
Liszt, F.:Hungarian Rhaps—Nos. 8 & 15 APR ▲ APR 7037 [ADD]
Liszt, F.:Totentanz APR ▲ APR 7037 [ADD]
Liszt, F.:Venezia e Napoli APR ▲ APR 7037 [ADD]
Liszt, F.:Wandererfantasie, w. S. Meyrowitz (cnd), *(orch unknown)* APR ▲ APR 7037 [ADD]

Killian, François (pno)
Dutilleux, H.:Sonatine Fl, w. J.-C. Gérard (fl) *(rec May 1987)* Signum ▲ X 21-00 [DDD]

Killian, François (pno) (cont.)
Franck, C.:Son Vn, w. J.-C. Gérard (vn) *(rec May 1987)* Signum ▲ X 21-00 [DDD]
Poulenc, F.:Son Fl, w. J.-C. Gérard (fl) *(rec May 1987)* Signum ▲ X 21-00 [DDD]

Killius, Ruth (va)
Kancheli, G.:Exil, w. Catrin Demenga (sop), Maacha Deubner (sop), Natalia Pschenitschnikova (a fl/b fl), Rebecca Firth (vc), Christian Sutter (db) *(rec Propstei St. Gerold, Basel, May 1994)* ECM New Series ▲ 78118-21535-2 [DDD]

Killmer, Richard (ob)
Bach, J.S.:Con Vn & Ob, w. P. Zukerman (vn), St. Paul CO CBS ▲ MK 37278 [DDD]

Kilström, Anders (pno)
Aulin, T.:Son Vn, w. P. Enoksson (vn) Musica Sveciae ▲ MSCD 608
Kreisler, F.:Vn Pieces, w. Tobias Ringborg (vn)—Romance, Op. 4; Recitativo & Scherzo-Caprice, Op. 6; Viennese Rhapsodic Fantasietta Caprice ▲ CAP 21455
Kreisleriana:The Lesser Known Works & Transcriptions of Fritz Kreisler, w. Tobias Ringborg (vn) Caprice ▲ CAP 21496
Peterson-Berger, W.:Songs, w. Gunnel Bohman (sop), Thomas Lander (bar) Musica Sveciae ▲ MSV 619 [DDD]
Poulenc, F.:Son Vn, w. Tobias Ringborg (vn) Caprice ▲ CAP 21455
Sjögren, E.:Son 2 Vn, w. Tobias Ringborg (vn) Caprice ▲ CAP 21455
Söderman, A.:Poems & Songs, w. P.-M. Nilsson (sop), A. Lundmark (bar), Eric Ericson Chamber Choir—13 songs for soprano/piano, choir, or baritone/piano [Sw] Musica Sveciae ▲ MSCD 525 [DDD]

Kim, A. (pno)
Baksa, R.:Qt Pno & Winds, w. Virtuosi Quintet members Capstone ▲ CPS 8608 [DDD]
Baksa, R.:Son Fl, w. B. Garner (fl) Capstone ▲ CPS 8608 [DDD]

Kim, Benny (vn)
Brahms, J.:Sextet Strs, Op. 36, w. Ani Kavafian (vn), Cynthia Phelps (va), Randolph Kelly (va), Colin Carr (vc), Peter Rejto (vc) *(rec live, Tucson Chamber Music Festival, Mar 11, 1994)* Arizona Friends of Chamber Music ▲ 1994 [DDD]
Mozart, W.A.:Qnt Strs, K.516, w. Ani Kavafian (vn), Randolph Kelly (va), Cynthia Phelps (va), Colin Carr (vc) *(rec Tuscon Winter Chamber Festival; Mar 11, 1994)* Arizona Friends of Chamber Music ▲ AFCD 19951 [DDD]

Kim, C. (vn)
Glazunov, A.:Con Vn, w. P. Freeman (cnd), Moscow PO *(rec Great Hall of the Moscow Radio Union, Feb. 1994)* Intersound ▲ 3535 [DDD]
Prokofiev, S.:Con 2 Vn, w. P. Freeman (cnd), St. Petersburg PO Pro Arte ▲ CDS 3442
Prokofiev, S.:Son Vn, Op. 94bis, w. P. Freeman (cnd), St. Petersburg PO [arr for vn & orch] Pro Arte ▲ CDS 3442
Tchaikovsky, P.:Con Vn, w. P. Freeman (cnd), Russian SO *(rec Great Hall of the Moscow Radio Union, Sept. 1993)* Intersound ▲ 3535 [DDD]

Kim, Chang Kook (fl)
Bach, C.P.E.:Son Fl, H.562 *(rec Casino Zögernitz, Teldec Studio, Vienna, Dec 1978)* Camerata ▲ 32CM 262
Bach, J.S.:Partita Fl, BWV 1013 *(rec Casino Zögernitz, Teldec Studio, Vienna, Dec 1978)* Camerata ▲ 32CM 262 [AAD]
Bach, J.S.:Sons Fl, BWV 1030-35, w. Edith Picht-Axenfeld (hpd), in b, BWV 1030 *(rec Iruma Shimin Kaikan, Japan, May 1979)* Camerata ▲ 32CM 262
Bach, J.S.:Sons Vn, w. Edith Picht-Axenfeld (hpd), BWV 1020 [doubtful] *(rec Iruma Shimin Kaikan, Japan, May 1979)* Camerata ▲ 32CM 262
Telemann, G.P.:Fants Fl, Nos. 10 in f# & 12 in g *(rec Casino Zögernitz, Teldec Studio, Vienna, Dec. 1978)* Camerata ▲ 32CM 262

Kim, David (vn)
Seasons Remembered 2, w. Judith Lynn Stillman (pno), Toby Appel (va), John Deak (db), Eliot Porter (db), Diaz Trio, Lutz Rath (vc), Fenwick Smith (fl), Ruth Waterman (vn) North Star ▲ 9837-40052-2 ■ 9837-40052-4

Kim, Jin Hi (komungo)
Celli, J.:Improvisations, w. J. Celli (reeds, E hn [without reeds], Mukha Veena (Yamaha WX-7 midi breath controller with TX-802)—Types of Asia for Changgo & English Horn (without reeds); Dasreng for solo Komungo; Mukhan O.O. Discs ▲ OO 2 [DDD]
Celli, J.:Improvisations, w. J. Celli (double reeds)—Triple AAA [w. A. Plack (didgeridoo)]; April One [w. Shelley Hirsh (voice)]; Baccalau Trio [w. A. Curran (synthesizer & computer samplers)]; My Friend [w. M. Thiam (African percussion) O.O. Discs ▲ OO 4 [DDD]
Celli, J.:Thirty-Six Strings O.O. Discs ▲ OO 22
Kim, J.H.:Nong Rock, w. Sirius String Quartet O. O. Discs ▲ OO24

Kim, Lisa (vn)
Corigliano, J.:Soliloquy, w. Stanley Drucker (cl), Kerry McDermott (vn), Rebecca Young (va), Gerald Appleman (vc) Cala Records ("New York Legends" series) ▲ CAL CACD 509 [DDD]

Kim, Wonmi (pno)
Dohnányi, E. von:Son Vc, w. L. Parnas (vc) *(rec 1992)* Arcadia ▲ ARC 1998-2 [DDD]
Godowsky, L.:Transcriptions & Paraphrases—Rameau:Sarabande; Rigaudon; Menuet; Elegie; Tambourin Arcadia ▲ ARC 2003
Liszt, F.:Transcriptions & Paraphrases—Mozart:Reminiscences of Don Juan; Schubert:Ständchen von Shakespeare; Erlkönig; Schumann:Liebeslied; Frühlingsnacht Arcadia ▲ ARC 2003
Porpora, N.A.:Son Vc, w. L. Parnas (vc) *(rec 1992)* Arcadia ▲ ARC 1998-2 [DDD]
Rachmaninoff, S.:Pno Transcriptions—Mendelssohn:Scherzo [from A Midsummer Night's Dream] Arcadia ▲ ARC 2003
Reger, M.:Son Vc, Op. 5, w. L. Parnas (vc) *(rec 1992)* Arcadia ▲ ARC 1998-2 [DDD]
Yun, I.:Nore Vc, w. L. Parnas (vc) *(rec 1992)* Arcadia ▲ ARC 1998-2 [DDD]

Kim, Y. N. (vn)
Schoenfield, P.:Cafe Music, w. P. Schoenfield (pno), P. Howard (vc) Innova ▲ MN 108
Ullmann, V.:Dialogues III, w. T. Strasser (va) Innova ▲ MN 108
Ultan, L.:Dialogues III, w. T. Strasser (va) Innova ▲ MN 108

Kim, Young Uck (vn)
Dvořák, A.:Trio 3 Pno, w. Yo Yo Ma (vc), E. Ax (pno) CBS ▲ MK 44527 [DDD]
Dvořák, A.:Trio 4 Pno, "Dumky", w. Yo Yo Ma (vc), E. Ax (pno) CBS ▲ MK 44527 [DDD]
Mozart, W.A.:Qts Pno, w. A. Previn (pno), H. Ohyama (va), G. Hoffman (vc) RCA Red Seal ▲ 09026-60713-2
Schumann, R.:Qt Pno in c, w. A. Previn (pno), H. Ohyama (va), G. Hoffman (vc) RCA Red Seal ▲ 09026-61384-2
Schumann, R.:Qt Pno, Op. 47, w. A. Previn (pno), H. Ohyama (va), G. Hoffman (vc) RCA Red Seal ▲ 09026-61384-2

Kimel, František (ob)
Fasch, J.F.:Con Tpt & 2 Obs, w. Zdenek Sedivy (tpt), Ivan Sequardt (ob), P. Škvor (cnd), Philharmonic CO Panton ▲ PAN 811023
Telemann, G.P.:Con Tpt 2 Obs, w. Zdenek Sedivy (tpt), Ivan Sequardt (ob), P. Škvor (cnd), Philharmonic CO Panton ▲ PAN 811023

Kimstedt, Rainer Johannes (va)
Schulhoff, E.:Sxt Strs, w. Michael Sanderling (vc), Petersen String Quartet *(rec Berlin, June 6-8 & Nov 7-8, 1994)* Capriccio ▲ 10 539 [DDD]

Kimura, Kaori (pno)
Ichiyanagi, T.:Cloud Atlas Camerata ▲ 32CM 52
Ichiyanagi, T.:Flowers Blooming in Summer, w. M. Kimura (hp) Camerata ▲ 32CM 52
Ichiyanagi, T.:Paganini Personal, w. H. Iwaki (mar) Camerata ▲ 32CM 52
Ichiyanagi, T.:Scenes II, w. K. Suzumi (vn) Camerata ▲ 32CM 52
Ichiyanagi, T.:Two Existence, w. T. Ichiyanagi (pno) Camerata ▲ 32CM 52

Kimura, Mari (hp)
Ichiyanagi, T.:Flowers Blooming in Summer, w. K. Kimura (pno) Camerata ▲ 32CM 52

▲ = CD ♦ = Enhanced CD Δ = MD ■ = Cassette Tape □ = DCC

Kimura, Mari (hp) (cont.)
Musiana 95:Electroacoustic Music from Denmark & Japan, w. Ensemble from the East, Trio Sparnaay/Kooistra/Abe, Hanne Andersen, Sofia Asunción Claro, Thomas Sandberg, Harry Sparnaay (b cl) Classico ▲ CLASSCD 139 [DDD]
Shinohara, M.:Kyudo B, w. K. Mitsuhashi (shakuhachi) *(rec live Casals Hall, Tokyo, Mar. 5, 1994)* Camerata ▲ 30CM 375 [DDD]

Kimura, Mari (vn)
Krieger, J.P.:Trio Sons, w. Peter Wendland (vl), Michael Freimuth (thb), Siebe Henstra (hpd/org)—Nos. 1–6 Prezioso ▲ 840.402

Kincaid, William (fl)
Bach, J.S.:Brandenburg Con 5, w. Fernando Valenti (hpd), Anshel Brusilow (vn), L. Stokowski (cnd), Philadelphia Orch *(rec Feb 25, 1960)* Sony Classical ("Masterworks Heritage" series) 2–▲ MH2K 62345 [ADD]

Kindalov, Ventzislav (fl)—see ORCHESTRAS & ENSEMBLES Academic Chamber Ensemble

Kinderman, William (pno)
Beethoven, L. van:Vars on a waltz by Diabelli, Op. 120 Hyperion ▲ CDA 66763

King (cl)
Milhaud, D.:Suite Vn, w. C. Tait (vn), I. Hobson (pno) Arabesque ▲ Z 6569 [DDD]

King, Andrew Lawrence (org/hp)
Gibbons, O.:Instrumental & Vocal Music, w. William Byrd Ensemble, Graham O'Reilly (cnd), The Occasional Byrd—The Eyes of All Wait upon Three; Do Not Repine, Fair Sun; Trust Not Too Much, Fair Youth; Blessed Are All They That Fear the Lord; O God, the King of Glory; In Nomine; The Cries of London; The Lord of Salisbury His Pavin; Sing unto the Lor, O Ye Saints of His; If Ye Be Risen Again with Christ; See, See, the Word is Incarnate; What is Our Life? Adda ▲ ADD 581169 [DDD]

King, Christopher (cl)
Debussy, C.:Première rapsodie, w. Y.P. Tortelier (cnd), Ulster Orch Chandos ▲ CHAN 8972 [DDD]

King, David (org)
Bach, J.S.:Org Music (misc)—An Wasserflüssen Babylon, BWV 653; Schmücke, dich, o liebe Seele, BWV 654 *(rec live, St. John's, Smith Square)* Eye of the Storm ▲ EOS 5003 [DDD]
Bach, J.S.:Toccata & Fugue Org, BWV 540 *(rec live, St. John's, Smith Square)* Eye of the Storm ▲ EOS 5003 [DDD]
Franck, C.:Chorals Org, M.38–40—No. 1 in E *(rec live, St. John's, Smith Square)* Eye of the Storm ▲ EOS 5003 [DDD]
Franck, C.:Prélude, fugue et var *(rec live, St. John's, Smith Square)* Eye of the Storm ▲ EOS 5003 [DDD]
Mendelssohn, F.:Sons Org—No. 3 in A *(rec live, St. John's, Smith Square)* Eye of the Storm ▲ EOS 5003 [DDD]
Mozart, W.A.:Fant Org *(rec live, St. John's, Smith Square)* Eye of the Storm ▲ EOS 5003 [DDD]
Rheinberger, J.:Sons Org—Intermezzo [from No. 8, Op. 132] *(rec live, St. John's, Smith Square)* Eye of the Storm ▲ EOS 5003 [DDD]

King, Larry (org)
Hoiby, L.:Choral Music, w. R. Osborne (bar), James A. Simms (cnd), Trinity Church Choir—Ascension (Holy Sonnet No. 7); At the Round Earth's Imagined Corners; Hear Us, O Hear Us Lord; Hymn to the New Age; Inherit the Kingdom; Let This Mind Be In You; Magnificat & Nunc Dimittis; The Offering Gothic ▲ G 49035 [DDD]
King, L.:Org Music, w. T. Smith (cnd), Trinity Church Choir—Fanfare to the Tongues of Fire; Introit for a Feast Day; Let Us Love in Deed & Truth; My Heart Is Ready, O God; The Lord's Prayer/And He Shall Reign as King; Benedictus es, Domine; O Gracious Light; Ressurection; The Prophet; The God-Fearing Woman Is Honoured; Revelations of St. John the Divine; The Transfiguration/The Song of Mary *(rec 1989–1990)* Gothic ▲ G 49056 [DDD]
Sowerby, L.:Choral Music, w. L. King (cnd), Trinity Church Choir Wall Street—I Will Lift Up Mine Eyes; I was glad; O Light, from age to age; Benedicte Omnia Opera; Thy word is a lantern; Magnificat & Nunc Dimittis in D; And they drew nigh; Come, Holy Ghost; Eternal light; Organ Works—Arioso; Requiescat in Pace Gothic ▲ G 49034 [DDD]

King, Peter (org)
British Organ Music from Bath Abbey Priory ▲ PRCD 335 [DDD]

King, Robert (chamber org)
Purcell, H.:Songs, w. B. Bonney (sop), S. Gritton (sop), J. Bowman (ct), R. Covey-Crump (ten), C. Daniels (ten), M. George (bass), D. Miller (archlt/thb/baroque gtr), M. Caudle (b vl)—Draw near, you lovers; While Thyrsis, wrapt in downy sleep; Love, thou canst hear, I lov'd fair Celia; What hope for us remains now he is gone; Pastora's beauties, when unblown; A thousand sev'ral ways I tried; Urge me no more; Farewell all joys; If music be the food of love [1st setting]; Amidst the shades and cool refreshing streams; They say you're angry; Let each gallant heart; This poet sings the Trojan wars; Ah, how pleasant 'tis to love; My heart whenever you appear; On the brow of Richard Hill; Rashly I swore I would disown; Since the pox or the plague; Beneath a dark and melancholy grove; Musing on cares of human fate; Whilst Cynthia sung, all angry winds lay still Hyperion ▲ CDA 66710

King, Robert (hpd/org)
Arne, T.:Songs, w. John Mark Ainsley (ten), Miles Golding (vn), Roy Goodman (vn), Anthony Robson (sop rcr), Jane Coe (vc)—Under the Greenwood Tree; Come Away Death; Where the Bee Sucks *(rec St Jude-on-the-Hill, London, Dec 20–21, 1968)* United ▲ CAL 88002 [DDD]
Humfrey, P.:Anthems, w. James Bowman (ct), Jane Coe (vc), R. King (cnd), King's Consort—A Hymn to God the Father *(rec St Jude-on-the-Hill, London, Dec 20–21, 1968)* United ▲ CAL 88002 [DDD]
Vivaldi, A.:Cons Rcr, w. Piers Adams (rcr), Ray Goodman (vn), Miles Golding (vn), Jane Compton (va), Jane Coe (vc), Mandy MacNamara (db), David Miller (archlt)—in F for Treble Rcr, Op. 10/1; in a for Sopranino Rcr, RV.440; in c for Treble Rcr, RV.441; in D for Sopranino Rcr, Op. 10/3; in g for Treble Rcr, Op. 10/2; in C for Sopranino Rcr, RV.443 *(rec Radley College, Abingdon, Oxon)* United ▲ CAL 88015 [DDD]
Vivaldi, A.:Sons Vc, w. Helen Ghough (vc), David Miller (archlt/gtr/thb), David Watkin (vc)—Sonatas in E♭, RV.39; e, RV.40; F, RV.41; g, RV.42; a, RV.43; a, RV.44; B♭, RV.45; B♭, RV.46; B♭, RV.47 Hyperion 2–▲ CDA 66881/82

King, Robert (org/hpd)
Purcell, H.:Songs, w. B. Bonney (sop), S. Gritton (sop), J. Bowman (ct), R. Covey-Crump (ten), C. Daniels (ten), M. George (bass), D. Miller (archlt/thb/baroque gtr), M. Caudle (b vl), King's Consort—Incassum Lesbia; Gentle Shepherds, you that know the charms; I love and I must; Through mournful shades and solitary groves; The Knotting Song Hyperion ▲ CDA 66720 [DDD]

King, Terry (vc)—see also ORCHESTRAS & ENSEMBLES Mirecourt Trio
Barber, S.:Son Vc, w. J. Jensen (pno) Music & Arts ▲ CD 603 [DDD]
Cello America, Vol. 1 Music & Arts ▲ MUA 603 [DDD]
Cello America, Vol. 2 Music & Arts ▲ MUA 685 [DDD]
Cooper, J.C.:Meditations (3), w. J. Jensen (pno) Music & Arts ▲ CD 603 [DDD]
Cowell, H.:Cleistogamy (sels), w. K. Goldsmith (vn) Music & Arts ▲ CD 635 [AAD]
Creston, P.:Cantilena, w. J. Jensen (pno) Music & Arts ▲ CD 685 [DDD]
Foss, L.:Capriccio, w. J. Jensen (pno) Music & Arts ▲ CD 685 [DDD]
Harris, R.:Duo Vc & Pno, w. Johana Harris-Heggie (pno) Music & Arts ▲ CD 603 [AAD/DDD]
Harrison, L.:Double Con, w. Kenneth Goldsmith (vn), Mills College Gamelan Ensemble Music & Arts ▲ CD 635 [AAD]
Reale, P.V.:Son Vc, w. J. Jensen (pno) Music & Arts ▲ CD 603 [DDD]
Riegger, W.:Whimsy, w. J. Jensen (pno) Music & Arts ▲ CD 685 [DDD]

King, Thea (b cl)
Sssmayr, F.X.:Con Movt Bas Cl, w. L. Hager (cnd), English CO Hyperion ▲ CDA 66504

King, Thea (bas hn)
Bennett, Richard Rodney:Crosstalk, w. Georgina Dobrée (bas hn) Clarinet Classics ▲ CC 0012 [AAD]

King, Thea (cl)
Blake, H.:Con Cl, w. H. Blake (cnd), English CO Hyperion ▲ CDA 66215 [DDD]
Brahms, J.:Qnt Cl, w. Gabrieli String Quartet Hyperion ▲ CDA 66107
Brahms, J.:Trio Cl, w. K. Georgian (vc), C. Benson (pno) Hyperion ▲ CDA 66107
Bruch, M.:Con Cl & Va, w. Imai, Francis (cnd), London SO Hyperion ▲ CDA 66022
The Clarinet in Concert, Vol. 1 Hyperion ▲ CDA 66022
The Clarinet in Concert, Vol. 2 Hyperion ▲ CDA 66300 [DDD] ■ KA 66300 (D)

King, Thea (cl) (cont.)
Cooke, A.:Con Cl, w. A. Francis (cnd), Northwest CO Seattle Hyperion ▲ CDA 66031 [DDD]
Cooke, A.:Qnt Cl, w. Britten String Quartet Hyperion ▲ CDA 66428 [DDD]
Crusell, B.H.:Con 1 Cl, w. A. Francis (cnd), London SO Hyperion ▲ CDA 66708 [DDD]
Crusell, B.H.:Con 2 Cl, w. A. Francis (cnd), London SO Hyperion ▲ CDA 66088
Crusell, B.H.:Con 2 Cl, w. A. Francis (cnd), London SO Hyperion ▲ CDA 66708 [DDD]
Crusell, B.H.:Con 3 Cl, w. A. Francis (cnd), London SO Hyperion ▲ CDA 66708 [DDD]
Crusell, B.H.:Intro, Theme & Vars on a Swedish Air, w. A. Francis (cnd), London SO Hyperion ▲ CDA 66022
Falla, M. de:Con Hpd, w. R. Puyana (hpd), D. Sandeman (fl), N. Black (ob), R. Cohen (vn), T. Weill (vc), C. Mackerras (cnd) *(rec 1969)* Philips ("Spanish" series) ▲ 432829–2 [ADD]
Finzi, G.:Con Cl, w. A. Francis (cnd), Philharmonia Orch Hyperion ▲ CDA 66001 [AAD]
Frankel, B.:Qnt Cl, w. Britten String Quartet Hyperion ▲ CDA 66428 [DDD]
Fuchs, R.:Qnt Cl, w. Britten String Quartet Hyperion ▲ CDA 66479 [DDD]
Heinze, G.A.:Konzertstück Cl, w. J. Judd (cnd), English CO Hyperion ▲ CDA 66300 [DDD]
Holbrooke, J.:Eilan Shona, w. Britten String Quartet Hyperion ▲ CDA 66428 [DDD]
Howells, H.:Rhapsodic Qnt, w. Britten String Quartet Hyperion ▲ CDA 66428 [DDD]
Jacob, G.:Mini-Con Cl, w. A. Francis (cnd), Northwest CO Seattle Hyperion ▲ CDA 66031 [DDD]
Lutoslawski, W.:Dance Preludes Cl, Hp, Pno, Perc & Strs, w. A. Litton (cnd), English CO Hyperion ▲ CDA 66215 [DDD]
Maconchy, E.:Qnt Cl, w. Britten String Quartet Hyperion ▲ CDA 66428 [DDD]
Mendelssohn, F.:Concert Pieces, w. Georgina Dobrée (cl) Hyperion ▲ CDA 66022
Mozart, W.A.:Con Cl, w. A. Francis (cnd), English CO Meridian ▲ CDE 84022
Mozart, W.A.:Qnt Cl, K.581, w. Aeolian String Quartet Saga Classics ▲ EC 3387
Rawsthorne, A.:Con Cl, w. A. Francis (cnd), Northwest CO Seattle Hyperion ▲ CDA 66031 [DDD]
Rietz, J.:Con Cl, w. A. Litton (cnd), English CO Hyperion ▲ CDA 66300 [DDD]
Romberg, A.:Qnt Cl, w. Britten String Quartet Hyperion ▲ CDA 66479 [DDD]
Schubert, Franz:Songs (comp), w. A. Auger (sop), G. Johnson (pno)—D.273, 301, 510, 528, 588, 595, 631, 857, 965 (Der Hirt auf dem Felsen), etc. [G] Hyperion ▲ CDJ 33009
Seiber, M.:Concertino Cl, w. A. Litton (cnd), English CO Hyperion ▲ CDA 66215 [DDD]
Solère, E.:Sinf concertante Cls, w. G. Dobrée (cl), A. Litton (cnd), English CO Hyperion ▲ CDA 66300 [DDD]
Spohr, L.:Con 4 Cl, w. A. Francis (cnd), English CO Meridian ▲ CDE 84022
Spohr, L.:Vars in B♭ on a Theme from *Alruna*, w. J. Judd (pno), English CO Hyperion ▲ CDA 66300 [DDD]
Stanford, C.V.:Con Cl, w. A. Francis (cnd), Philharmonia Orch Hyperion ▲ CDA 66001 [AAD]
Stanford, C.V.:Fants Cl, w. Britten String Quartet Hyperion ▲ CDA 66479 [DDD]
Tausch, F.W.:Concertante 2, w. N. Bucknall (cl), L. Heger (cnd), English CO Hyperion ▲ CDA 66504
Tausch, F.W.:Con 1 for 2 Cls, w. N. Bucknall (cl), L. Hager (cnd), English CO Hyperion ▲ CDA 66504
Weber, C.M. von:Con 2 Cl, w. A. Francis (cnd), London SO Hyperion ▲ CDA 66088

King, Valerie (fl)
Giuliani, M.:Grand Son Fl, w. A. Angarola (gtr) Discovery ▲ DSCD 203 [DDD]
Giuliani, M.:Serenade Fl, w. A. Angarola (gtr) Discovery ▲ DSCD 203 [DDD]

Kingstedt, Sölve (ob)
Rimsky-Korsakov, N.:Vars on a Theme of Glinka, w. G. Rozhdestvensky (cnd), Stockholm Concert Band Chandos ▲ CHAN 9444

Kinney, Michelle (vc)
Kinney, M.:You Are So Stingingly Demure, w. T. Cora (vc), M. Anderson (perc), S. Mensah (perc) Innova ▲ MN 107

Kinsela, David (org)
Butterly, N.:Fanfare for a Ceremony [Sydney Opera House organ] Southern Cross ▲ SCCD 1022 [DDD]
Butterly, N.:Westerly Prelude [Sydney Opera House organ] Southern Cross ▲ SCCD 1022 [DDD]
Carr-Boyd, A.:The Bells of Sydney Harbour [Sydney Opera House organ] Southern Cross ▲ SCCD 1022 [DDD]
Henderson, M.:Sacred Site [Sydney Opera House Organ] Southern Cross ▲ SCCD 1022 [DDD]
Koehne, G.:Toccata Aurora [Sydney Opera House Organ] Southern Cross ▲ SCCD 1022 [DDD]
Williamson, M.:Peace in Childhood [Sydney Opera House Organ] Southern Cross ▲ SCCD 1022 [DDD]
Williamson, M.:Peace in Solitude [Sydney Opera House Organ] Southern Cross ▲ SCCD 1022 [DDD]

Kinton, Leslie (pno)
Arensky, A.:Suites (4) for 2 Pnos, w. J. Anagnoson (pno) CBC ("Musica Viva" series) ▲ MVCD 1036 [DDD]
Dvořák, A.:Slavonic Dances (comp), w. James Anagnoson (pno) *(rec Glenn Gould Studio, CBC Toronto, June 28–29, 1993)* CBC ("Musica Viva" series) ▲ MVCD 1088 [DDD]
Matton, R.:Con for 2 Pnos, w. J. Anagnoson (pno), R. Armenian (cnd), Kitchener-Waterloo SO CBC ("SM 5000" series) ▲ SMCD 5120 [DDD]
Milhaud, D.:Scaramouche for 2 Pnos, w. J. Anagnoson (pno) CBC ("SM 5000" series) ▲ SMCD 5120 [DDD]
Poulenc, F.:Con for 2 Pnos, w. J. Anagnoson (pno), R. Armenian (cnd), Kitchener-Waterloo SO CBC ("SM 5000" series) ▲ SMCD 5120 [DDD]
Saint-Saëns, C.:Carnival of the Animals, w. J. Anagnoson (pno), J. Campbell (cnd), Festival of the Sound Ensemble *(rec Glenn Gould Studio, CBC Toronto, Mar. 26–27, 1994)* CBC ("Musica Viva" series) ▲ MVV 1089 [DDD]
Stravinsky, I.:Con CO, w. J. Anagnoson (pno) CBC ("SM 5000" series) ▲ SMCD 5120 [DDD]

Kioulaphides, V. (db)—see ORCHESTRAS & ENSEMBLES Continuum Chamber Ensemble

Kipnis, Igor (clvd)
Bach, J.S.:Adagio Clvd *(rec May 11, 1965)* Sony Classical ▲ SBK 53263 ■ SBT 53263
Bach, J.S.:Fants Hpd—in a, BWV 922 Sony Classical ▲ SBK 53263 ■ SBT 53263
Bach, J.S.:Das wohltemperierte Klavier—Praeludium & Fughetta, BWV 870a *(rec May 11, 1965)* Sony Classical ▲ SBK 53263 ■ SBT 53263

Kipnis, Igor (hpd)
Bach, J.S.:Brandenburg Con 2, w. H.-M. Linde (fl), N. Marriner (vn), N. Marriner (cnd), London Strings CBS ■ MGT 39802
Bach, J.S.:Brandenburg Con 5, w. H.-M. Linde (fl), N. Marriner (vn), N. Marriner (cnd), London Strings CBS ■ MGT 39802
Bach, J.S.:Chromatic Fant & Fugue Arabesque ▲ Z 6577 [DDD]
Bach, J.S.:Cons Hpd, BWV 1052–1058, w. N. Marriner (cnd), London Strings—Nos. 1–5 CBS ■ MGT 39801
Bach, J.S.:Cons Hpd, BWV 1052–1058, w. N. Marriner (cnd), London Strings Odyssey 2–▲ MB2K 45616
Bach, J.S.:Cons Hpd, BWV 1052–1058, w. Jeanne Dolmetsch (rcr), Marguerite Dolmetsch (rcr), N. Marriner (cnd), London Strings—BWV 1057 *(rec 1967–1970)* Sony Classical 2–▲ SB2K 53243 [ADD]
Bach, J.S.:Con 8 Hpd, w. N. Marriner (cnd), London Strings [reconstr. I. Kipnis] CBS ■ MGT 39802
Bach, J.S.:Con 8 Hpd, w. Janet Craxton (obligatto ob), N. Marriner (cnd), London Strings *(rec 1967–1970)* Sony Classical 2–▲ SB2K 53243 [ADD]
Bach, J.S.:English Suites—No. 2 in a BWV 807 *(rec May 28, 1965)* Sony Classical ▲ SBK 53263 ■ SBT 53263
Bach, J.S.:Fants Hpd—Fantasias & Fugues, BWV 904, 906, 944; Fantasias, BWV 917, 918; Fantasias, BWV 903a, 919, 922; Fughetta in c, BWV 961 Arabesque ▲ Z 6577 [DDD]
Bach, J.S.:French Suites—BWV 816 Elektra/Nonesuch 2–▲ 79020–2 [DDD]
Bach, J.S.:Goldberg Vars *(rec St. Matthew's Parish, Wilton, CT, May 28–31, 1996)* Epiphany ▲ EP 11
Bach, J.S.:Italian Con CBS ■ MGT 39802
Bach, J.S.:Italian Con *(rec May 27, 1965)* Sony Classical ▲ SBK 53263 ■ SBT 53263
Bach, J.S.:Preludes (12) Hpd—(12) in C, BWV 924; in d, BWV 926; in F, BWV 927; in F, BWV 928; in g, BWV 929; in g, BWV 930; in C, BWV 939; in d, BWV 940; in e, BWV 941; in a, BWV 942; in c, BWV 999 [orignally for lute]; in D, BWV 925 [spurious] *(rec May 11, 1965)* Sony Classical ▲ SBK 53263 ■ SBT 53263
Bach, J.S.:Sons Fl, BWV 1030–35, w. J. Solum (fl), B. Bogatin (vc)—BWV 1030–1035 [period instrs] Arabesque ▲ Z 6589

INSTRUMENT.

Kipnis, Igor (hpd) (cont.)
Bach, J.S.:Trio Son Fl, Vn & Hpd, w. J. Solum (fl), J.-M. Schwarz (vn), E. Potash (vc) [period instrs] Arabesque ▲ ARA 6640 [DDD]
Bach, J.S.:Trio Son for 2 Fls, BWV 1039, w. J. Solum (trns fl), R. Wyton (trns fl), E. Potash (vc) [period instrs] Arabesque ▲ ARA 6640 [DDD]
Blasco de Nebra, M.:Sons (6) Hpd & Pno—Nos. 5 & 6 *(rec May 24–25, 1967)* Sony Classical ▲ SBK 53264 ■ SBT 53264
Falla, M. de:Con Hpd, w. P. Brook (fl), H. Gomberg (ob), S. Drucker (cl), E. Chapo (vn), L. Munroe (vc), P. Boulez (cnd), New York PO *(rec Mar. 2, 1975)* Sony Classical ▲ SBK 53264 ■ SBT 53264
Falla, M. de:Con Hpd, w. P. Boulez (cnd), New York PO Sony Classical ("Pierre Boulez Edition" series) ▲ SMK 68333
Handel, G.F.:The Harmonious Blacksmith CBS ▲ MLK 39441 ■ MT 39441
Handel, G.F.:The Harmonious Blacksmith Elektra/Nonesuch ▲ 79037-2 [DDD]
Handel, G.F.:Hpd Music Elektra/Nonesuch ▲ 79037-2 [DDD]
Handel, G.F.:Music of, w. E. Ormandy (cnd), Philadelphia Orch, Mormon Tabernacle Choir—The Harmonious Blacksmith; See the conquering hero comes & Hallelujah Amen, from Judas Maccabaeus ("Handel's Greatest Hits") CBS ▲ MLK 39441 ■ MT 39441
Handel, G.F.:Suites Hpd—Bk 1, No. 5; Bk 2, No. 8 Elektra/Nonesuch ▲ 79037-2 [DDD]
Handel, G.F.:Trio Sons, w. John Solum (trns fl), Judson Griffin (vn), Arthur Fiacco (vc)—in c, H.386a Epiphany ▲ EP 7
Kolb, B.:Toccata Hpd CRI ▲ CD 576 [ADD]
Nowak, L.:Suite Fl, w. John Solum (baroque fl) *(rec Skinner Recital Hall, Vassar College, Poughkeepsie, NY, Mar 24–26, 1994)* CRI ▲ CD 712 [DDD]
Pachelbel, w. Jean-Pierre Rampal (fl), Raymond Leppard (cnd), John Williams (gtr), Canadian Brass, E. Power Biggs (org), et al. Sony Classical ("Greatest Hits" series) ▲ MLK 62680 ■ MLT 62680
Scarlatti, D.:Sons Kbd—15 Sonatas performed on five Hubbard & Broekman harpsichords after historical Flemish, German, Italian, English, & French models—Sonata in A (K.24); Sonata in d (K.141); 2 Sonatas in g & G (K.426/427); 2 Sonatas in c & C (K.158/159); 2 Sonatas in A (K.208/209); Sonata in E (K.46); Sonata in g (K.30, "The Cat's Fugue"); 2 Sonatas in E (K.380, "Cortège" & K.381); 3 Sonatas in D,D & d (K.118/119/120) Chesky ▲ CD 75 [DDD]
Scarlatti, D.:Sons Kbd—(4) in c, K.84; in D, K.490; in D, K.491; in D, K.492 *(rec May 29–30, 1967)* Sony Classical ▲ SBK 53264 ■ SBT 53264
Soler, P.A.:Fandango *(rec May 30, 1967)* Sony Classical ▲ SBK 53264 ■ SBT 53264
Soler, P.A.:Sons Hpd—in d, M.8; in B♭, M.13 *(rec May 25, 1967)* Sony Classical ▲ SBK 53264 ■ SBT 53264
Telemann, G.P.:Musique de Table, w. J. Solum (trns fl), A. Fiacco (vc)—solo in b for Fl & Bc Epiphany ▲ EP 7
Telemann, G.P.:Musique de Table, w. J. Solum (fl), E. Potash (vl) [played on period instrument] Arabesque ▲ ARA 6640 [DDD]
A Treasury of Harpsichord Favorites Music & Arts ▲ MUA 243 [DDD]
Vivaldi, A.:Cons Fl (misc), w. J. Solum (fl), I. Kipnis (cnd), Connecticut Early Music Festival Ensemble [period instrs]—Concerto in D, RV.428, "Il Gardellino" Chesky ▲ CD 78 [DDD]
Vivaldi, A.:Con Hpd, RV.780, w. I. Kipnis (cnd), Connecticut Early Music Festival Ensemble [period instrs] Chesky ▲ CD 78 [DDD]
Vivaldi, A.:Cons Vn, Op. 8/1–4, "The Four Seasons", w. J.-M. Schwarz (vn), I. Kipnis (cnd), Connecticut Early Music Festival Ensemble [period instrs] Chesky ▲ CD 78 [DDD]

Kipnis, Igor (hpd/clvd)
Bach, J.S.:Anna Magdalena Bach Notebook, w. Blegen (sop), Luxon (bar), Meinis (vl) [G] Elektra/Nonesuch 2-▲ 79020-2 [DDD]

Kipnis, Igor (hpd/pno)
The Instrument of Kings:A Program of 18th Century Music for Flute & Keyboard, w. John Solum (trns fl), Arthur Fiacco (vc) *(rec Jan. 17–21, 1994)* Epiphany ▲ EP 2

Kipnis, Igor (kbd)
Bach, C.P.E.:Kbd Music Elektra/Nonesuch 2-▲ 79020-2 [DDD]

Kipnis, Igor (pno)
Beethoven, L. van:Polonaise Pno—6 Minuets, WoO 10 [piano version]; Bagatelle in C, WoO 54, "Lustig–Traurig"; Allegretto in c, WoO 53; Rondo in C, Op. 51/1 *(rec Jan. 24–27 & Feb. 3, 1994)* Epiphany ▲ EP 1
Beethoven, L. van:Son 8 Pno, "Pathétique" *(rec Jan. 24–27 & Feb. 3, 1994)* Epiphany ▲ EP 1
Beethoven, L. van:Son 14 Pno, "Moonlight Son" *(rec Jan. 24–27 & Feb. 3, 1994)* Epiphany ▲ EP 1
Beethoven, L. van:Vars on an Original Theme, Op. 34 Epiphany ▲ EP 7
Beethoven, L. van:Vars on an Original Theme, Op. 34 *(rec Jan. 24–27 & Feb. 3, 1994)* Epiphany ▲ EP 1
Moore, T.:Irish Melodies, w. L. Shelton (sop), J. De Gaetani (mez), F. Kelley (ten), W. Sharp (bar) [E] Elektra/Nonesuch ■ 79059–4 (D)
Mozart, W.A.:Pno Music (misc)—Klavierstück in F, K.33B; Fant. in f, K.Anh.32/383c; Kleiner Trauermarsch in c, K.453a; Romance in B♭, K.Anh.205/C27.04 [reconstr. K. Marguerre, rev. I. Kipnis]; Praeludium, K.deest; Adagio K.540; Fant. K.397; Rondo K.485; Son. 11; Vars., K.265 Music & Arts ▲ CD 660 [DDD]

Királ, Peter (vc)
Bodino, S.:Sons, w. Peter Zajíček (vn), Miloš Valent (vn), Pascal Dubreuil (hpd), Musica Aeterna—Sons 1–6 *(rec Castle of Tonky, Slovakia, Apr 1994)* Slovart ▲ SR 0008-2-131 [DDD]

Kirbach, Klaus (hpd)
Mozart, W.A.:Sinf concertante Ob, K.Anh.9, w. Andreas Lorenz (ob), Sebastian Weigle (hn), Eckart Konigstedt (bn), H. Haenchen (cnd), C.P.E. Bach CO Berlin Classics ▲ BER 2004

Kirby, Chad (trbn/conch)
Dempster, S.:Music of, w. Stuart Dempster (trbn/didjeridu/conch), Jay Bulen (trbn), Jeff Domoto (trbn), Moc Escobedo (trbn/didjeridu/conch), Scott Higbee (trbn), Gretchen Hopper (trbn), Nathaniel Irby-Oxford (trbn), Dave Marriott (trbn), Greg Powers (trbn), Debra Sykes (cym)—Conch Calling; Morning Light; Didjerilayover; Secret Currents; Melodic Communion; Shell Shock; Cloud Landings *(rec Fort Worden, Port Townsend, WA, June 18, 1994)* New Albion ▲ NA 076

Kirchberg, Hans-Peter (org)
Christmas Concertos, w. M. Erxleben (cnd), New Berlin SO, Michael Erxlaben (vn), Knut Zimmerman (vn) Capriccio ▲ 10442 [DDD]

Kircheis, Christoph (org)
Music for Trumpet & Organ, w. Ludwig Güttler (tpt), Friedrich (org) Capriccio ▲ CDC 10057 [DDD]

Kircheis, Friedrich (hpd)
Ludwig Güttler:Trompete, Corno da Caccia, Posthorn, w. Ludwig Güttler (tpt), Virtuosi Saxoniae, J. Bischof (vc), W. Zeibig (db) *(rec 1988–92)* Berlin Classics ▲ BER 1053 [DDD]

Kircheis, Friedrich (org)
Ludwig Güttler Plays Music for Trumpet & Organ, w. Ludwig Güttler (tpt/corno da caccia) Berlin Classics ▲ BER 1110 [DDD]
Music for Trumpet, Corno da caccia & Organ from St. Thomas Church in Leipzig, w. Ludwig Güttler (tpt) *(rec 1990)* Berlin Classics ▲ BER 1005 [DDD]

Kircher, Ralf (perc)
Strauss (I), Joh.:Radetzky March, w. Rudolf Schmidinger (perc), Kevan Teherani (perc), Brassissimo Vienna *(rec Pfarrkirche Staatz, Nov 29–Dec 2, 1993)* Brassissimo ▲ BVR 2328517 [DDD]
Strauss (II), Joh.:Music of, w. Rudolf Schmidinger (perc), Kevan Teherani (perc), Brassissimo Vienna—Maskenball-Quadrille; Unter Donner und Blitz; Etwas Kleines; Kaiserwalzer; Annenpolka; Waldmeister-Ov; Leichtes Blut; Auf der Jagd; Pizzikato-Polka [composed w. Josef Strauss]; Elyen a Magyar; Perpetuum Mobile; Fledermaus-Ov *(rec Pfarrkirche Staatz, Nov 29–Dec 2, 1993)* Brassissimo ▲ BVR 2328517 [DDD]
Strauss, Josef:Music of, w. Rudolf Schmidinger (perc), Kevan Teherani (perc), Brassissimo Vienna—Ohne Sorgen; Moulinet-Polka; Pizzikato-Polka [composed w. Johann Strauss II]; Feuerfest *(rec Pfarrkirche Staatz, Nov 29–Dec 2, 1993)* Brassissimo ▲ BVR 2328517 [DDD]

Kirchhof, Lutz (baroque lt)
Bach, J.S.:Lt Music Sony Classical ("Vivarte" series) 2-▲ S2K 45858

Kirchhof, Lutz (baroque lt/thb)
Weiss, S.L.:Lt Music—Suite in A; Suite in B♭; Suite in d; Suite in g; Sonata in F; Praeludium, Courante, Fuga & Presto in d; Prelude in D; Preludio in E♭; Fantasia in C; Capriccio in D Sony Classical ("Vivarte" series) 2-▲ S2K 48391 [DDD]

Kirchhof, Lutz (lt)
Airs de Cour:French Court Music from the 17th Century, w. Marie-Claude Vallin (sop), Max van Egmond (bass) Sony Classical ("Vivarte" series) ▲ SK 48250 [DDD]
Baron, E.G.:Lt Music—Fant. in C; Suite in G Ars Musici ▲ 1139
Kropffganss, J.J.:Lt Music—Partita in F Ars Musici ▲ 1139
Love Songs & Dances:Consort Music for Lute & Voices from "Pratum Musicum", w. Marie-Claude Vallin (sop), Claudio Cavina (altus), Max van Egmond (bar), Sabine Dreier (trns fl), Petra Manz (vl) *(rec Evangelische Kirche, St Osdag, Mandelsloh, Germany, Nov 21–24, 1994)* Sony Classical ("Vivarte" series) ▲ SK 66263 [DDD]
The Lute in Dance & Dream Sony Classical ("Vivarte" series) ▲ SK 48068
Reusner, Esaias:Suites Lt—in a; in B♭ Ars Musici ▲ 1139

Kirchhoff, Craig J. (fl)
Telemann, G.P.:Qt Bn Fls, w. Christopher Weait (bn), Katherine Borst (fl), Nelson Harper (hpd) D'Note Classics ▲ DND 1008 [DDD]

Kirchhoff, Thomas (gtr)—see ORCHESTRAS & ENSEMBLES Albéniz Guitar Duo
Kirchner, A. (fl)—see ORCHESTRAS & ENSEMBLES Vienna Flautists
Kirchner, Jane (fl)—see ORCHESTRAS & ENSEMBLES Blair Woodwind Quintet

Kirchner, L. (pno)
Kirchner, L.:Con Vn, Vc, Winds & Perc, w. L. Kirchner (cnd), Boston Sym Chamber Players Elektra/Nonesuch ▲ 79188-2 [DDD]
Kirchner, L.:Pieces Pno Elektra/Nonesuch ▲ 79188-2 [DDD]
Kirchner, L.:Trio Vn, w. Boston Sym Chamber Players Elektra/Nonesuch ▲ 79188-2 [DDD]

Kirchner, Norbert (hpd/org)
Weichlein, R.:Encaenia musices, w. Gunar Letzbor (vn), Daniel Sepec (vn), Herbert Lindsberger (va), Christoph Bitzinger (va), Michael Oman (vl), Gaetano Nasillo (vc), Roberto Sensi (vn), Andreas Lackner (nat tpt), Herbert Walser (nat tpt), G. Letzbor (cnd), Ars Antiqua Austria—Sons. Nos. I in C, II in g, III in a, IV in E, V in C & VI in F Symphonia ▲ SY 93S23

Kirchoff, G. (pno)
Granados, E.:En la aldea, w. D. Riva (pno) Centaur ▲ CRC 2043 [DDD]

Kirichenko, Sergey (db)
Mozart, W.A.:Serenata Notturna, w. Alexander Mayorov (vn), Irina Belskaya (vn), Ilya Shpiegelman (va), A. Rudin (cnd), Musica Viva CO *(rec Moscow Conservatory Great Hall, 1996)* Russian Compact Disc ▲ RCD 30201 [DDD]

Kirkbride, J. (cl)—see ORCHESTRAS & ENSEMBLES American Brass Quintet

Kirkeskov, Dorte (pno)
Nielsen, C.:Songs, w. Elisabeth Rehling (sop), Peder Severin (ten)—I Bear My Yoke with a Smile; Now the Day is Full of Song; How Sweetly on This Summer Evening; Often I'm Happy; Spring Has Come Now; Strangest Breeze of Twilight Hours; Harken to Its Gentle Wing-Beats; Sleep Sweetly, Little Baby Mine; In Shadow We Wander; Now Leaps the Spring from Its Bed; The Snow Queen [The Meadow Lies Buried in Snow So White]; There Lived a Man in Ribe Town [all from 20 Danish Songs]; Christmas Carol [Come Yule to Earth]; To the Queen of My Heart [Shall We Roam, My Love]; Angst [Hold Me Tighter]; The Guide Sings [To the Mountains Above the Village]; Flower Songs; In the Land of Dreams; Just Bow Your Head, O Flower; Song Behind the Plough; This Evening; Greeting; It Is Autumn; *(rec West Jutland Academy of Music, Apr 1988)* Rondo Grammofon ▲ RCD 8323
Nielsen, C.:Songs, w. Elisabeth Rehling (sop), Peder Severin (ten), Jørgen Ernst Hansen (org)—Strange to Say...; Maria Sat on Hay & Straw; God's Angels Sing in Chorus; Now the Sun in the East...; Alas, My Rose...; Standing in Pain under the Cross...; It Is a Wonder...; Jesus Mine, Let My Heart Savour... [all from Hymns & Sacred Songs]; Jens the Road-Mender; The 1st Lark [both from Strophic Songs, Op. 21]; Vibeke's Song [I Came Upon a Song...]; Song of the Sea [The Sea Around Denmark] [both from the play Willemoes]; We Sons of the Plains; The Bird-Catcher's Song, The Tiny Forest Birds are Hiding...; Tove's Song [An Angel Stood Beside Me...]; The Hunter's Song [The Kite Swoops from the Mountain Crest...] [all from the play Tove]; Gulnare's Song [Zither, Let My Prayer Move You...]; Aladdin's Lullaby [Lullalullaby, Tiny Babe...]; Fatima's Song [The Moon is Already Risen...] [all from the play Aladdin]; Music to 5 Poems by J.P. Jacobsen, Op. 4; 10 Little Danish Songs *(rec West Jutland Academy of Music, Sept 1989)* Rondo Grammofon ▲ RCD 8327
Schubert, Franz:Die Schöne Müllerin, w. P. Severin (ten) *(rec Apr. 1992)* Danacord ▲ DACOCD 396 [DDD]

Kirkland, Graham (pno)
Quilter, R.:Shakespeare Songs (misc), w. Jeffrey Benton (bar), Rona Lowe (pno)—Orpheus with His Lute, Op. 32/1; When Icicles Hang by the Wall, Op. 32/2; Come away, Death, Op. 6/1; Oh Mistress Mine, Op. 6/2; Blow, Blow, Thou Winter Wind, Op. 6/3; Who Is Sylvia?, Op. 30/1; When Daffodils Begin to Peer, Op. 30/2; How Should I Your True Love Know?, Op. 30/3; Sigh No More, Ladies, Op. 30/4; Fear No More the Heat of the Sun, Op. 23/1; Under the Greenwood Tree, Op. 23/2; It Was a Lover & His Lass, Op. 23/3; Take, O Take Those Lips away, Op. 23/4; Hey, Ho, the Wind & the Rain, Op. 23/5 Symposium ▲ SYM 1184
Quilter, R.:Songs, w. Jeffrey Benton (bar), Rona Lowe (pno)—To Julia [Prelude/The Bracelet/The Maiden Blush/To Daisies/The Night Piece/Julia's Hair/Cherry Ripe; poems by Herrick], Op. 8; Weep You No More; My Life's Delight [Campion]; Damask Roses; The Faithless Shepherdess [Byrd]; Browen Is My Love; By a Fountainside [Ben Johnson]; Fair House of Joy Symposium ▲ SYM 1184

Kirkman, Steve (perc)
Bernstein, L.:West Side Story (sels), w. New Century Saxophone Quartet [arr J. Boatman for sax qt & perc] Channel Classics ▲ CCS 9896
Gershwin, G.:Porgy & Bess (sels), w. New Century Saxophone Quartet [arr J. Boatman for sax qt & perc] Channel Classics ▲ CCS 9896
Gould, M.:Main Street March, w. New Century Saxophone Quartet [arr J. Boatman for sax qt & perc] Channel Classics ▲ CCS 9896
Gould, M.:Main Street Waltz, w. New Century Saxophone Quartet [arr J. Boatman for sax qt & perc] Channel Classics ▲ CCS 9896
Gould, M.:Pavane, w. New Century Saxophone Quartet [arr J. Boatman for sax qt & perc] Channel Classics ▲ CCS 9896

Kirkpatrick, Erika Duke (vc)
Feldman, Morton:Voices & Vc, w. Joan La Barbara (sop) *(rec Fantasy Studios, Berkeley, CA, O'Henry Studios, Burbank, CA & Metamusic Productions, Los Angeles, CA, Jan 18, Aug 25–26 & Dec 1)* New Albion ▲ NA 085
Lyons, R.:Electronique, w. Robin Lorentz (vn), Amy Knoles (perc) Cambria ▲ CD 1088
Lyons, R.:Ice Cream Truck from Hell, w. Robin Lorentz (vn), Amy Knoles (perc) Cambria ▲ CD 1088

Kirkpatrick, Gary (pno)—see ORCHESTRAS & ENSEMBLES Verdehr Trio

Kirkpatrick, Gordon (hpd)
Bach, J.S.:Das wohltemperierte Klavier—[Book 1] Nos. 1/3, 5, 9, 16, 17, 21, 22; [Book 2] Nos. 12, 13, 15, 19, 24 Archiv ("Musikfest" series) 4-▲ 413419-2 [DDD]

Kirkpatrick, John (pno)
Bacon, E.:Songs from Dickenson, w. Helen Boatwright (sop), Ernst Bacon (pno)—It's All I Have to Bring; Eden; I'm Nobody; As Well as Jesus?; A Word; Weeping and Sighing; O Friend; She Went; A Threadless Way; The Imperial Hear; Summer's Lapse; Is There Such a Thing as Day?; To Make a Prairie; A Spider; The Grass So Little Has to Do; The Snake; So Bashful; Alabaster Wool; Eternity; Sunset; The Simple Days; On this Wondrous Sea *(rec 1954 & 1964)* CRI ▲ CD 675 [ADD]
Ives, C.:Songs, w. Helen Boatwright (sop), Ernst Bacon (pno)—Abide with Me; Walking; Where the Eagle; Disclosure; The White Gulls; Two Little Flowers; The Greatest Man; The Children's Hour; Berceuse; Ann Street; General William Booth Enters into Heaven; Autumn; Swimmers; Evening; Harpalus; Tarrant Moss; Serenity; At the River; The See'r; Maple Leaves; "1, 2, 3"; Tom Sails away; He Is There!; In Flanders Fields *(rec 1954 & 1964)* CRI ▲ CD 675 [ADD]

Kirkpatrick, Ralph (hpd)
Great Virtuosi of the Harpsichord, Vol. 2 Pearl ▲ PEA 9245

Kirkwood, Gordon (pno)
Horder, M.:Songs (40), w. Winifred Soutter (sop), Peter Allanson (bar), Carl Murray (bar), Stephen Betteridge (pno) Symposium ▲ 1039
Schubert, Franz:Songs (misc), w. D. Hammond-Stroud (bar)—13 songs [G] *(rec 1988–89)* Symposium ▲ 1064
Wolf, H.:Italienische Liederbücher (sels), w. D. Hammond-Stroud (bar)—8 songs [G] *(rec 1988–89)* Symposium ▲ 1064
Wolf, H.:Mörike-Lieder (sels), w. D. Hammond-Stroud (bar), 8 songs [G] *(rec 1988–89)* Symposium ▲ 1064

Kirkwood, Neal (pno)
Soldier, D.:Ultraviolet Railroad, w. Mark Feldman (vn), Erik Frielander (vc), R.A. Clark (cnd), Manhattan CO Newport Classic ▲ NPD 85589 [DDD]

Kirsch, Dieter (mandora)
Albrechtsberger, J.G.:Cons Jew's Hp, w. Mayr (jew's hp), H. Stadlmair (cnd), Munich CO Orfeo ▲ 035821 [DDD]

Kirshbaum, Ralph (vc)
Bach, J.S.:Suites Vc, BWV 1007–1012 Virgin Classics ▲ ZDCB 45086
Barber, S.:Con Vc, w. J.-P. Saraste (cnd), Scottish CO Virgin Classics ▲ 59565 [DDD]
Barber, S.:Son Vc, w. R. Vignoles (pno) Virgin Classics ▲ 59565 [DDD]
Elgar, E.:Con Vc, w. A. Gibson (cnd), Royal Scottish National Orch Chandos ("Collect" series) ▲ CHAN 6607 [DDD]
Elgar, E.:Falstaff, w. A. Gibson (cnd), Royal Scottish National Orch Chandos ("Collect" series) ▲ CHAN 6607 [DDD]
Haydn, J.:Con 2 Vc, w. P. Zukerman (cnd), English SO RCA Red Seal ▲ 09026-62696-2
Haydn, J.:Sinf concertante, w. Pinchas Zukerman (vn), P. Zukerman (cnd), English SO RCA Red Seal ▲ 09026-62696-2
Walton, W.:Con Vc, w. A. Gibson (cnd), Scottish National Orch Chandos ("Collect" series) ▲ CHAN 6547 [ADD/DDD]

Kirstein, J. Rosenblum (pno)
Schuller, G.:Con Pno, w. M. Rudolf (cnd), Cincinnati SO GM ▲ GM 2044

Kishi, Noriko (vc)
Mozart, W.A.:Adagio Rondo, w. Carol Adee (fl), Kurt Rohde (va), Roger Wiesmeyer (ob), J. Meredith (cnd), Sonos Handbell Ensemble Well-Tempered Productions ▲ WTP 5182 [DDD]

Kiss, András (vn)—see also ORCHESTRAS & ENSEMBLES New Budapest String Quartet
Atterberg, K.:Chamber Music, w. E. Pérényi (vn), I. Prunyi (pno), S. Falvay (pno), G. Kertész (vc), D. Spikay (hp)—Son. in b for Violin, Op. 27; Höstballader, Op. 15; Valse monotone in C; Rondeau Rétrospectif, Op. 26; Trio Concertante in g, Op. 57 Marco Polo ▲ 8.223404
Bartók, B.:Duos (44), w. F. Balogh (vn) Hyperion ▲ CDA 66453
Berwald, F.:Trios, w. I. Prunyi (pno), C. Onczay (vc)—Nos. 1–3 Marco Polo ▲ 8.223170
Donizetti, G.:Allegro Strs, w. Rossini Ensemble *(rec Oct. 1991)* Naxos ▲ 8.550621 [DDD]
Korngold, E.W.:Son Vn, w. I. Prunyi (pno), Danubius Quartet Marco Polo ▲ 8.223385
Liszt, F.:Music of, w. Z. Tóth (va), E. Banda (vc), M. Perényi (vc), H. Lubik (hp), I. Lantos (pno/org), S. Margittay (harm)—Angelus; La lugubre gondola; Epithalam; Am Grabe Richard Wagners; Romance oubliée; Elégies 1 & 2; Offertorium; Benedictus Hungaroton ▲ HCD 11798 [DDD]
Mozart, W.A.:Qts Fl, w. J. Szebenyi (fl), L. Bársony (va), K. Botvay (vc) White Label ▲ HRC 128 [ADD]
Rossini, G.:Sons Str Qt, w. Rossini Ensemble—Nos. 1, 2 & 3 *(rec 1991)* Naxos ▲ 8.550621 [DDD]
Rossini, G.:Sons Str Qt, w. Rossini Ensemble—Nos. 4, 5 & 6 *(rec Oct. 1991)* Naxos ▲ 8.550622 [DDD]
Sinding, C.:Trios Pno, w. T. Koó (vc), I. Prunyi (pno)—No. 1 in D, Op. 23 (1893) & No. 2 in a, Op. 64a (1902) Marco Polo ▲ 8.223283

Kiss, George (hpd)
Mosaïque:Works for Recorder & Harpsichord, w. Anastase Demetriades (rcr) *(rec Mar. 25, 1995)* Bongiovanni ▲ GB 5045 [DDD]

Kiss, Gyula (pno)
Bartók, B.:Allegro barbaro Hungaroton ▲ HCD 31604 [ADD]
Bartók, B.:Burleskes, Op. 8c Hungaroton ▲ HCD 31604 [ADD]
Bartók, B.:Pno Music—3 Hungarian Folktunes; My First Term at the Pno Hungaroton ▲ HCD 31604 [ADD]
Bartók, B.:Romanian Christmas Carols Hungaroton ▲ HCD 31604 [ADD]
Bartók, B.:Romanian Folk Dances Pno Hungaroton ▲ HCD 31604 [ADD]
Bartók, B.:Sonatina Pno Hungaroton ▲ HCD 31604 [ADD]
Bartók, B.:Suite Pno Hungaroton ▲ HCD 31604 [ADD]

Kiss, József (ob)
Bach, C.P.E.:Con Ob, H.466, Erkel CO *(rec Oct 28–Nov 1, 1991)* Naxos ▲ 8.550556 [DDD]
Bach, C.P.E.:Con Ob, H.468, Erkel CO *(rec Oct 28–Nov 1, 1991)* Naxos ▲ 8.550556 [DDD]
Bach, C.P.E.:Son Fl, H.562, Erkel CO [arr for ob] *(rec Oct 28–Nov 1, 1991)* Naxos ▲ 8.550556 [DDD]
Beethoven, L. van:Qnt Pno, Ob, Cl, Hn & Bn, w. J. Jandó (pno), B. Kovács (cl), J. Keveházi (hn), J. Vajda (bn) *(rec Dec. 1–4, 1990)* Naxos ▲ 8.550511 [DDD]
Marcello, A.:Cons Ob, Erkel CO *(rec Oct. 28–Nov. 1, 1991)* Naxos ▲ 8.550556 [DDD]
Mozart, W.A.:Adagio & Rondo Glass Armonica, w. J. Jandó (cel), I. Kovács (fl), G. Konrád (va), T. Koó (vc) *(rec Dec. 1–4, 1990)* Naxos ▲ 8.550511 [DDD]
Mozart, W.A.:Qt Ob, K.370, w. Kodály String Quartet *(rec May 2–3 & 6–9, 1991)* Naxos ▲ 8.550437 [DDD]
Mozart, W.A.:Qnt Hn, K.407, w. J. Jandó (pno), B. Kovács (cl), J. Keveházi (hn), J. Vajda (bn) *(rec Dec. 1–4, 1990)* Naxos ▲ 8.550511 [DDD]
Schumann, R.:Adagio & Allegro Hn, w. J. Jandó (pno) [arr. for oboe & piano] *(rec Dec. 12–15, 1991)* Naxos ▲ 8.550599 [DDD]
Schumann, R.:Fantasiestücke Cl, w. J. Jandó (pno) [arr. for oboe & piano] *(rec Dec. 12–15, 1991)* Naxos ▲ 8.550599 [DDD]
Schumann, R.:Romances Ob, w. J. Jandó (pno) [oboe & piano arr.] *(rec Dec. 12–15, 1991)* Naxos ▲ 8.550599 [DDD]
Schumann, R.:Son 1 Vn, w. J. Jandó (pno) [oboe & piano arr.] *(rec Dec. 12–15, 1991)* Naxos ▲ 8.550599 [DDD]
Schumann, R.:Stücke im Volkston, w. J. Jandó (pno) [oboe & piano arr.] *(rec Dec. 12–15, 1991)* Naxos ▲ 8.550599 [DDD]

Kissin, Evgeni (pno)
Beethoven, L. van:Fant Pno, Op. 80, "Choral Fant", w. C. Abbado (cnd), Berlin PO Deutsche Grammophon ▲ 435617-2 [DDD]
Brahms, J.:Fants Pno, Op. 116 Deutsche Grammophon ("Masters" series) ▲ 445562-2
Brahms, J.:Fants Pno, Op. 116 Deutsche Grammophon ◻ 435028-5
Carnegie Hall Debut Concert *(rec live, September 1990)* RCA Red Seal ▲ 60443-2-RC [DDD]
Carnegie Hall Debut Concert RCA Red Seal ▲ 09026-61202-2 [DDD] ■ 09026-61202-4 ◻ 09026-61202-5
Chopin, F.:Barcarolle Pno *(rec live 1986 & 1988)* MK ▲ 418017 [DDD]
Chopin, F.:Con 1 Pno, w. D. Kitayenko (cnd), Moscow PO *(rec live, Grand Hall of the Moscow Conservatory, Mar 27, 1984)* RCA Red Seal ▲ 09026-68378-2 [ADD]
Chopin, F.:Con 2 Pno, w. D. Kitayenko (cnd), Moscow PO *(rec live, Grand Hall of the Moscow Conservatory, Mar 27, 1984)* RCA Red Seal ▲ 09026-68378-2 [ADD]
Chopin, F.:Fant *(rec live 1986 & 1988)* MK ▲ 418016 [DDD]
Chopin, F.:Mazurkas—Opp. 24/4, 30/3, 50/3, 56/2, 63/1–3, 68/4 *(rec live 1986 & 1988)* MK ▲ 418017 [DDD]
Chopin, F.:Mazurkas RCA Red Seal ▲ 09026-62542-2; ■ 09026-62542-4
Chopin, F.:Mazurkas—Opp. 63/2 & 68/4 *(rec live, Grand Hall of the Moscow Conservatory, Mar 27, 1984)* RCA Red Seal ▲ 09026-68378-2 [ADD]
Chopin, F.:Nocturnes—Nos. 12 & 14 *(rec live 1986 & 1988)* MK ▲ 418016

Kissin, Evgeni (pno) (cont.)
Chopin, F.:Pno Music (misc)—Fant., Op. 49; Grande valse, Op. 42; Grand valse brillante, Op 34/1 & 2; Polonaise, Op. 44; Nocturnes, Op. 27/1 & 2, Op. 32/2; Scherzo, Op. 32/2 RCA Red Seal ▲ 09026-60445-2 ■ 09026-60445-4
Chopin, F.:Scherzos—Op. 31 *(rec live 1986 & 1988)* MK ▲ 418017 [DDD]
Chopin, F.:Son Pno, Op. 58 *(rec live 1986 & 1988)* MK ▲ 418016 [DDD]
Chopin, F.:Son Pno, Op. 58 RCA Red Seal ▲ 09026-62542-2; ■ 09026-62542-4
Chopin, F.:Waltzes—No. 14 in e *(rec live, Grand Hall of the Moscow Conservatory, Mar 27, 1984)* RCA Red Seal ▲ 09026-68378-2 [ADD]
Evgeny Kissin:A Musical Portrait RCA Red Seal 2-▲ 60567-2-RC [DDD]
Grieg, E.:Pno Music (sels), w. C.M. Giulini (cnd), Vienna PO Sony Classical ▲ SK 52567
Grieg, E.:Pictures from Life in the Country, w. C.M. Giulini (cnd), Vienna PO—No. 3, "Carnival Scene" Sony Classical ▲ SK 52567
Haydn, J.:Con Hpd, Obs, Hns & Strs, H.XVIII/11, w. V. Spivakov (cnd), Moscow Virtuosi RCA Red Seal ▲ 7948-2-RC [DDD] ■ 7948-4-RC (CrO2)
Kissin in Tokyo Sony Classical ▲ SK 45931 [DDD]
Kissin, E.:Inventions RCA Red Seal ▲ 60051-2-RC [DDD] ■ 60051-4-RC (CrO2)
Liszt, F.:Études d'exécution transcendante, S.139—ChassE neige; Harmonies du soir; In f; Feux follets; Wilde Jagd *(rec Freiburg, Germany, Aug 22–25, 1995)* RCA Red Seal ▲ 09026-68262-2
Liszt, F.:Hungarian Rhaps—No. 12 Deutsche Grammophon ▲ 435028-2 [DDD] ◻ 435028-5
Liszt, F.:Hungarian Rhaps—No. 12 (also, "Siciliano" from Bach's BWV.1031; & "Auld Lang Syne") *(rec live 1988)* MK ▲ 418018 [DDD]
Liszt, F.:Hungarian Rhaps—No. 12 Deutsche Grammophon ("Masters" series) ▲ 445562-2
Liszt, F.:Pno Music (misc)—Liebesträum No. 3; Rhapsodie espagnole; Song transcription [Schumann—Widmung]; Transcendental Etude No. 10 RCA Red Seal ▲ 60443-2-RC [DDD] ■ 60443-4-RC (CrO2)
Liszt, F.:Soirées de Vienne, w. C.M. Giulini (cnd), Vienna PO—Valse-caprice No. 6—First Version Sony Classical ▲ SK 52567
Liszt, F.:Song Transcriptions—Schubert:4 Songs Deutsche Grammophon ▲ 435028-2 [DDD] ◻ 435028-5
Mozart, W.A.:Con 12 Pno, w. V. Spivakov (cnd), Moscow Virtuosi RCA Red Seal ▲ 09026-60400-2 ■ 09026-60400-4
Mozart, W.A.:Con 12 Pno, w. V. Spivakov (cnd), Moscow Virtuosi RCA Red Seal 2-▲ 60567-2-RC [DDD]
Mozart, W.A.:Con 20 Pno, w. V. Spivakov (cnd), Moscow Virtuosi RCA Red Seal ▲ 09026-60400-2 ■ 09026-60400-4
Mozart, W.A.:Rondo Pno Orch, K.382, w. V. Spivakov (cnd), Moscow Virtuosi RCA Red Seal ▲ 09026-60400-2 ■ 09026-60400-4
Prokofiev, S.:Con 1 Pno, w. C. Abbado (cnd), Berlin PO Deutsche Grammophon ▲ 439898-2
Prokofiev, S.:Con 3 Pno, w. C. Abbado (cnd), Berlin PO Deutsche Grammophon ▲ 439898-2
Prokofiev, S.:Con 3 Pno, w. A. Tchistiakov (cnd), Moscow PO RCA Red Seal ▲ 60051-2-RC [DDD] ■ 60051-4-RC (CrO2)
Prokofiev, S.:Con 3 Pno, w. A. Tchistiakov (cnd), Moscow PO RCA Red Seal 2-▲ 60567-2-RC [DDD]
Prokofiev, S.:Pieces Pno, Op. 32—No. 1 Dance in f# RCA Red Seal ▲ 60051-2-RC [DDD] ■ 60051-4-RC (CrO2)
Prokofiev, S.:Son 6 Pno RCA Red Seal ▲ 60443-2-RC [DDD] ■ 60443-4-RC (CrO2)
Prokofiev, S.:Son 6 Pno Sony Classical ▲ SK 45931 [DDD]
Prokofiev, S.:Visions fugitives—Nos. 10, 11, 16 & 17 RCA Red Seal ▲ 60051-2-RC [DDD] ■ 60051-4-RC (CrO2)
Rachmaninoff, S.:Con 2 Pno, w. V. Gergiev (cnd), London SO RCA Red Seal 2-▲ 60567-2-RC [DDD]
Rachmaninoff, S.:Études-tableaux, Opp. 33 & 39—6 sels. RCA Red Seal ▲ 07863-57982-2 [DDD] ■ 7982-4-RC (CrO2) ◻ 07863-57982-5
Schnittke, A.:Suite in the Old Style, w. V. Spivakov (vn) RCA Red Seal ▲ 60370-2-RC [DDD]
Schubert, Franz:Fant Pno, D.760, "Wandererfantasie" Deutsche Grammophon ("Masters" series) ▲ 445562-2
Schubert, Franz:Fant Pno, D.760, "Wandererfantasie" Deutsche Grammophon ▲ 435028-2 [DDD] ◻ 435028-5
Schubert, Franz:Pno Music (misc)—4 Songs [arr Liszt] Deutsche Grammophon ("Masters" series) ▲ 445562-2
Schubert, Franz:Qnt Pno, D.667, w. C.M. Giulini (cnd), Vienna PO Sony Classical ▲ SK 52567
Schubert, Franz:Songs (misc), w. C.M. Giulini (cnd), Vienna PO—Erlkönig, D.328 Sony Classical ▲ SK 52567
Schumann, R.:Arabeske Pno *(rec live 1988)* MK ▲ 418018 [DDD]
Schumann, R.:Arabeske Pno Sony Classical ▲ SK 52567
Schumann, R.:Fant Pno *(rec Freiburg, Germany, Aug 22–25, 1995)* RCA Red Seal ▲ 09026-68262-2
Schumann, R.:Sym Etudes *(rec live 1988)* MK ▲ 418018 [DDD]
Schumann, R.:Sym Etudes RCA Red Seal ▲ 60443-2-RC [DDD] ■ 60443-4-RC (CrO2)
Schumann, R.:Vars on A-B-E-G-G RCA Red Seal ▲ 60443-2-RC [DDD] ■ 60443-4-RC (CrO2)
Scriabin, A.:Son 3 Pno *(rec live 1988)* MK ▲ 418018 [DDD]
Shostakovich, D.:Con 1 Pno, w. V. Kan (tpt), V. Spivakov (cnd), Moscow Virtuosi RCA Red Seal 2-▲ 60567-2-RC [DDD]
Shostakovich, D.:Con 1 Pno, w. V. Kan (tpt), V. Spivakov (cnd), Moscow Virtuosi RCA Red Seal ▲ 7947-2-RC [DDD]
Shostakovich, D.:Preludes Pno, Op. 34, w. V. Spivakov (cnd), Moscow Virtuosi [arr. by Viktor Poltoratsky for piano & string orchestra]—Nos. 5,6,10,13,14,17 & 24 RCA Red Seal ▲ 7947-2-RC [DDD]
Tchaikovsky, P.:Con 1 Pno, w. H. von Karajan (cnd), Berlin PO Deutsche Grammophon ▲ 427485-2 [DDD] ◻ 427485-5

Kitahama, Reiko (vn)—see ORCHESTRAS & ENSEMBLES Ravel String Quartet

Kitamura, G. (tpt)
Shinohara, M.:Cooperation, w. A. Nishigata (shamisen), K. Mitsuhashi (shakuhachi), M. Akao (fue), S. Yaotani (hichiriki), K. Ishikawa (sho), C. Fukunaga (koto), J. Ueda (biwa), M. Yoshizawa (kokyu), I. Tsuji (oboe), T. Takahashi (cl), A. Murata (trbn), S. Eiso (perc), S. Ueki (vn), S. Katsuta (vc), Y. Shibuya (pno), K. Komatsu (cnd) *(rec live Casals Hall, Tokyo, Mar. 5, 1994)* Camerata ▲ 30CM 375 [DDD]
Shinohara, M.:Tabiyuki, w. A. Ogawa (mez), M. Kakagawa (fl), I. Tsuji (ob), T. Takahashi (cl), K. Okazaki (fagotto), A. Murata (trbn), S. Eiso (perc), S. Ueki (vn), A. Nakakoji (va), S. Katsuta (vc), M. Komuro (contrabass), K. Komatsu (cnd) *(rec live Casals Hall, Tokyo, Mar. 5, 1994)* Camerata ▲ 30CM 375 [DDD]

Kitazato, Taka (ob)
Telemann, G.P.:Con Tpt 2 Obs, w. Per-Olev Lindeke (tpt), Marcel Ponseele (ob), Fred Jacobs (thb), Richte Van Der Meer (vc), Pierre Hantaï (hpd) *(rec St. Stefanus, Melsen, Belgium, June 1995)* Accent ▲ 95110 [DDD]
Telemann, G.P.:Essercizii musici (sels), w. Marcel Ponseele (ob), Pierre Hantaï (hpd), Per-Olev Lindeke (tpt), Fred Jacobs (thb), Richte Van Der Meer (vc)—Trio Son in E♭ for Ob, Hpd & Continuo *(rec St. Stefanus, Melsen, Belgium, June 1995)* Accent ▲ 95110 [DDD]
Telemann, G.P.:Der Getreue Music-Meister (sels), w. Marcel Ponseele (ob), Per-Olev Lindeke (tpt), Fred Jacobs (thb), Richte Van Der Meer (vc), Pierre Hantaï (hpd)—Son in a *(rec St. Stefanus, Melsen, Belgium, June 1995)* Accent ▲ 95110 [DDD]
Telemann, G.P.:Kleine Kammermusik, w. Marcel Ponseele (ob), Per-Olev Lindeke (tpt), Fred Jacobs (thb), Richte Van Der Meer (vc), Pierre Hantaï (hpd)—Partita IV in g *(rec St. Stefanus, Melsen, Belgium, June 1995)* Accent ▲ 95110 [DDD]
Telemann, G.P.:Musique de Table, w. Marcel Ponseele (ob), Per-Olev Lindeke (tpt), Fred Jacobs (thb), Richte Van Der Meer (vc), Pierre Hantaï (hpd)—Son in g *(rec St. Stefanus, Melsen, Belgium, June 1995)* Accent ▲ 95110 [DDD]
Telemann, G.P.:Son 2 Ob, w. Marcel Ponseele (ob), Per-Olev Lindeke (tpt), Fred Jacobs (thb), Richte Van Der Meer (vc), Pierre Hantaï (hpd) *(rec St. Stefanus, Melsen, Belgium, June 1995)* Accent ▲ 95110 [DDD]

Kitchen, John (hpd/vir)
Kinloch, W.:Kbd Music—Kinloche His Ground; The Quadrant Paven; Gaillart; Sussanna; Kinloche His Fantassie; A Pavion of Kinloughes; The Galliard; Kinloche His Pasmessour; Galliard; Kinloche His Pavane; Gaillard of Ye Lang Pavan; Jhonstounis Delyt; The Batell of Pavic
ASV ("Gaudeamus" series) ▲ GAU 134

Kitchen, Joseph (pno)
Ward, R.:Son 2 Vn, w. Nicholas Kitchen (vn) Albany ▲ TROY 204 [DDD]

Kitchen, Nicholas (vn)
Ward, R.:Son 2 Vn, w. Joseph Kitchen (pno) Albany ▲ TROY 204 [DDD]

Kite, Christopher (pno)
Chopin, F.:Con 1 Pno, w. R. Goodman (cnd), Hanover Band *(rec 5/90)* Nimbus ▲ NI 5291 [DDD]
Mendelssohn, F.:Con 1 Pno, w. R. Goodman (cnd), Hanover Band Nimbus ▲ NI 5158 [DDD]
Mozart, W.A.:Con 20 Pno, w. R. Goodman (cnd), Hanover Band [period instrs] Nimbus 4-▲ NI 1791 [DDD]
Mozart, W.A.:Con 20 Pno, w. R. Goodman (cnd), Hanover Band [period instrs] Nimbus ▲ NI 5259 [DDD]
Mozart, W.A.:Music of, w. Gundula Janowitz (sop), Julia Bernheimer (mez), Martyn Hill (ten), David Thomas (bass), Anthony Halstead (hn), Colin Lawson (b cl), R. Goodman (cnd), Hanover Band—Cons for Hn, K.412, 417, 447, 494a & 495; Sym No. 40; Con for Cl; Eine kleine Nachtmusik; Requiem; Sym No. 41; Con No. 20 for Pno; Serenata Notturna Nimbus 4-▲ NI 1791 [DDD]
Mozart, W.A.:Pno Music (misc)—Andantino, K.236; March, K.408/1; Funeral March, K.453a; Fant., K.396; Trios, K.498 & 548 Meridian ▲ CDE 84136
Mozart, W.A.:Son 12 Pno Meridian ▲ CDE 84113
Mozart, W.A.:Son 13 Pno Meridian ▲ CDE 84113
Mozart, W.A.:Son 15 Pno Meridian ▲ CDE 84113
Weber, C.M. von:Konzertstück Pno, w. R. Goodman (cnd), Hanover Band *(rec 5/90)* Nimbus ▲ NI 5291 [DDD]

Kitsopoulos, Maria (vc)—see also ORCHESTRAS & ENSEMBLES CELLO, Continuum Chamber Ensemble
Viñao, E.:Trio Pno, w. Ju-Ying Song (pno), Mark Steinberg (vn) *(rec Academy of Arts & Letters, New York, Nov 14–15, 1995)* Pro Piano ("Pianist's Perspective Recording" series) ▲ PPR 224511

Kitt, Loren (cl)—see also ORCHESTRAS & ENSEMBLES American Chamber Players
Adler, S.:Aeolus, God of the Winds, w. Lanier Trio Gasparo ▲ GS 298 [DDD/DAD]

Kitzinger, Fritz (pno)
Bloch, E.:Suite Va & Pno, w. W. Primrose (va) *(rec 1939)* Pearl ▲ PEA 9453 (m) [AAD]

Kitzis, G. (vn)
Lifchitz, M.:Canto de paz, w. L. Vardaman (sop), L. Weiss (fl), N. Ives (vc), M. Lifchitz (pno) Opus One ▲ 149

Kitzman, John (trbn)
Creston, P.:Fant Trbn, w. J. K. Hodges (pno) Crystal ■ C 386
Defaye, J.-M.:Danses (2) Crystal ■ C 386
Hindemith, P.:Son Trbn, w. Janice Kay Hodges (pno) Crystal ■ C 386
Pryor, A.:Air varié Crystal ■ C 386

Kiviniemi, Kalevi (org)
The Battle:Organ Music Gothic, Renaissance & Early Baroque, w. Markku Krohn (perc) Finlandia ▲ FIN 98036

Kivnick, Eric (perc)
Hays, S.:Dreaming the World, w. Thomas Bruckner (bar), Sal Basile (voc), Jennifer López (voc), John Schaffer (voc), Sorrel Hays (voc), Joseph Kubera (pno), John Kennedy (perc), Charles Wood (perc), Maya Gunji (perc), Jai Smith (perc) New World ▲ 805202 [DDD]

Kjær, Birgit (pno)
Stolarczyk, W.:Earth Air Fire Water, w. Amalie Malling (pno), John Damgaard (pno), Anne Øland (pno), Teddy Teirup (pno), Friedrich Gürtler (pno), Rosalind Bevan (pno), Poul Rosenbaum (pno), Rodolfo Llambias (pno), Bella Horn-Ribera (pno), Anders Riber (pno), Elisabeth Sigurdsson (pno), Thomas Tronheim (pno), Elsebeth Broderson (pno), Erik Kaltoft (pno), Jørgen Hald Nielsen (pno), Aino Gilemann (pno), Jørgen Thomsen (pno), Gunhild Donslund (pno), Henrik Bo Hansen (pno), Lone Karlsson (pno), Erik Fessel (pno), Lasse Nilsson (pno), Janos Ferenczi (pno), Erik Bach (pno), Axel Momme (pno), Arne de Cros Dich (pno), Sven Micha Slot (pno), Hanne Bramsen Buhl (pno), Lili Olesen (pno), Susannah Carlsson (pno), Ulla Erml (pno), Vagn Sørensen (pno), Leif Greibe (pno), Bodil Krogh (pno), Kirsten Ottosen (pno), Inger Bergenholz (pno), Karsten Gylendorf (pno), Bjønr Elkjær (pno), Jacob Bjørn Jensen (pno), Jørgen Kaad (pno), Anne Marie Hjelm (pno), Carl Ulrik Munk Andersen (pno), Poul Lumbye (pno), Oluf Hildebrandt Nielsen (pno), Joachim Olsson (pno), Peter Pade Ramsøe Jacobsen (pno), Astrid Pollmann (pno), Jette Borsch (pno), Kirsten Karlshøj (pno), Maria Teresa Assing (pno), Allan Dahl Hansen (pno), Johan Hugossen (pno), Tine Fenger Pederson (pno), Arne Jørgen Fæø (pno), Anja Høgsted (pno), Anne Sophie Parbo (pno), Inga Lindmark (pno), Teresa Drabik Stathakis (pno), Anne Ruth Ferenczi (pno), Irene Hasager (pno), Yuka Ichikawa (pno), Birgitte Baur (pno), Malene Thastum (pno), Jens E. Rasmussen (pno), Birgitte Zielke (pno), Claus Zielke (pno), Stefan Kasch (pno), Bin Qiao (pno), Inger Johanne Teirup (pno), Lindy Rosborg (pno), Liisa Heininen (pno), David Højer (pno), Ellen Refstrup (pno), Thomas K. Søorensen (pno), Erik Kure (pno), Michael Rauff (pno), Jan beck Eriksson (pno), Tanja Zapolski (pno), Vibeke Skagbo (pno), Pål Eide Lindtner (pno), Ha-Young Sul (pno), Benedicte Palko (pno), Inke Kesseler (pno), Anne Marie Meineche (pno), Sverre Larsen (pno), Kasper Peter Bach (pno), Elisabetta Eliseo (pno), Olga Magieres (pno), Carl Erik Kühl (pno), Thorkild Borup Nielsen (pno), Valeria Zanini (pno), Lars Stenhoft (perc), Dennis Boel (perc), Winnie Dahlgren (perc), Susanne Vind (perc), Claus Byrith (elec), Anne Marie Storm (elec), J. Ribera (cnd) *(rec live, Koldinghaus Castle, Denmark, May 2, 1996)* Danica ▲ DCD 1996

Kjeldsen, Eyvind Sand (vn)
Wiklander, K.:Music of, w. Kurt Wiklander (org), Mats Rondin (vc)—Toccata on the Easter Introitus for Org; 2 Chorales from Dalecarlia for Org; Fant. for Vc & Org; 4 Miniatures for Org; Meditation in Folk Style on B-A-C-H for Vn & Org; 3 Organ Chorales on Sacred Folk-Tunes in the Swedish Chorale; Fant. for Org on O Christ Who Art Light & Day; Scherzo Ostinato; Meditation for Org BIS ▲ CD 659

Kjelstrup, Richard (cl)
Braein, E.F.:The Merry Musicians, w. L. Jørgensen (vn), J. Hindar (va), L. Hindar (vc) Simax ▲ PSC 3117

Klaas, R. (pno)—see ORCHESTRAS & ENSEMBLES Alkan Trio

Kladetzky, Gotthard (pno)
Liszt, F.:Pno Music (misc)—6 Grand Etudes after Paganini; 6 Polonaises of Chopin; Totentanz FSM-Fono ▲ 97718 [DDD]

Klamand, O. (hn)—see ORCHESTRAS & ENSEMBLES Munich Residenz Quintet members

Klánská, Vladimira (hn)—see also ORCHESTRAS & ENSEMBLES Prague Wind Quintet
Martinů, B.:Qt Cl, Hn, Vc & Side Drum, w. Vlastimil Mareš (cl), Petr Holub (side dr), Jitka Vlašánková (vc) *(rec Studio Martínek, Prague, Mar 3, 1995)* Panton ("Protokol XX" series) ▲ 811348-2 [DDD]
Mozart, W.A.:Divert Ob, K.251, w. Jiří Krejčí (ob), Czech Nonet *(rec Prague, 1995)* Praga ▲ PR 250095
Mozart, W.A.:Qnt Hn, K.407, w. Prazak String Quartet *(rec Prague, 1995)* Praga ▲ PR 250095

Klánský, Ivan (pno)—see also ORCHESTRAS & ENSEMBLES Guarneri Trio Prague members, Guarneri Trio Prague
Beethoven, L. van:Son 14 Pno, "Moonlight Son" Kontrapunkt ▲ 32025 [DDD]
Beethoven, L. van:Son 23 Pno, "Appassionata" Kontrapunkt ▲ 32025 [DDD]
Beethoven, L. van:Son 27 Pno Kontrapunkt ▲ 32025 [DDD]
Beethoven, L. van:Son 32 Pno Kontrapunkt ▲ 32025 [DDD]
Brahms, J.:Sons Vc (comp), w. M. Fukacova (vc) Kontrapunkt ▲ 32027 [DDD]
Brahms, J.:Son in D Vc, w. M. Fukacova (vc) Kontrapunkt ▲ 32027 [DDD]
Copland, A.:Con Cl, w. Jiří Hlaváč (cl), Hana Müllerová (hp), S. Bogunia (cnd), Suk CO *(rec ZK Motorlet Prague Studio, Sept 4–6 & 14–15, 1986)* Panton ▲ PAN 810884
Dvořák, A.:Rondo, w. M. Fukačová (vc) Kontrapunkt ▲ 32013 [DDD]
Franck, C.:Son Vn, w. M. Fukačová (vc) Kontrapunkt ▲ 32013 [DDD]
Grieg, E.:Son Vc, w. M. Fukačová (vc) Kontrapunkt ▲ 32013 [DDD]

Klánský, Ivan (pno) (cont.)
Martinů, B.:Vc Music (complete), w. M. Fukačová (vc)—7 Arabesques; Ariette; 4 Nocturnes; 6 Pastorales; Rossini Variations; Sonatas 1–3; Suite Miniature; Variations On a Theme from a Slovak Folk Song *(rec 6/91)* Kontrapunkt 3-▲ 32084/86 [DDD]
Martinů, B.:Les Rondes, w. Jurij Likin (ob), Vlastimil Mareš (cl), Lumír Vanek (bn), Vladislav Kozderka (tpt), Jana Herojnová (vn), Pavel Kutman (vn) *(rec Studio Martínek, Prague, Mar 3, 1995)* Panton ("Protokol XX" series) ▲ 811348-2 [DDD]
Martinů, B.:Sxt Fl, Ob, Cl, 2 Bns & Pno, w. Jan Riedlbauch (fl), Jurij Likin (ob), Vlastimil Mareš (cl), Lumír Vanek (bn), Svatopluk Čech (bn) *(rec Studio Martínek, Prague, Mar 3, 1995)* Panton ("Protokol XX" series) ▲ 811348-2 [DDD]
Prokofiev, S.:Son Vc, w. Michaela Fukacova (vc) Kontrapunkt ▲ KPT 32216 [DDD]
Schubert, Franz:Moments musicaux Supraphon ▲ 11 0939-2 [DDD]
Schubert, Franz:Scherzos Pno, D.593 Supraphon ▲ 11 0939-2 [DDD]
Schubert, Franz:Valses sentimentales (sels)—Nos. 1-3, 5-7, 11-13, 15, 18-24, 26-29 Supraphon ▲ 11 0939-2 [DDD]
Shostakovich, D.:Son Vc, w. Michaela Fukacova (vc) Kontrapunkt ▲ KPT 32216 [DDD]
Smetana, B.:Bagatelles & Impromptus Kontrapunkt ▲ KPT 32226
Smetana, B.:Melodies Pno Kontrapunkt ▲ KPT 32226
Smetana, B.:Polkas Pno—3 polkas de salon Kontrapunkt ▲ KPT 32226
Smetana, B.:Reveries Kontrapunkt ▲ KPT 32226
Stravinsky, I.:Suite italienne Vc, w. Michaela Fukacova (vc) Kontrapunkt ▲ KPT 32216 [DDD]
Tchaikovsky, P.:Pezzo capriccioso, w. M. Fukačová (vc) [Tchaikovsky's cello & piano version] Kontrapunkt ▲ 32013 [DDD]

Klaus, Gerold (vn)—see ORCHESTRAS & ENSEMBLES Al Ayre Español

Klecka, P. R. (hpd)
Gluck, C.W.:Ovs, w. J. Felmlee (fl), A. Mirschel (ob), J. Corazolla (cnd), Rhenish CO—Euristeo; Iphigénie en Aulide; Orfeo ed Euridice; Don Juan Entrée ▲ 0064

Klee, Horst (gtr)
Ponce, M.:Gtr Music—24 Preludes; Alborada; Balletto; Gigue; Mazurka; 2 Preludes; Rondino; Tropica; Vespertina Koch Schwann ▲ CD 310177 [DDD]
Weiss, S.L.:Lt Music—Sonata in A; Suite in A; Capriccio; Passacaglia; Tombeau Koch Schwann ▲ CD 310 122 [DDD]

Kleeb, Hildegard (pno)
Braxton, A.:Pno Music—Compositions Nos. 1, 5, 10, 16, 33, 30, 139, 32, 31, 32 (part 2) *(rec New York City, 1995 & 1996)* Hat Hut ("Now" series) 4-▲ ART CD 46194/1-4 [DDD]
Cage, J.:Dream Pno *(rec Studio DRS, Zurich, Jan. 4–5, 1993)* Hat Hut ("NOW." series) ▲ hat ART CD 6129 [DDD]
Cage, J.:Prelude for Meditation *(rec Studio DRS, Zurich, Jan. 4–5, 1993)* Hat Hut ("NOW." series) ▲ hat ART CD 6129 [DDD]
Cage, J.:Two^5, w. Roland Dahinden (ten trbn) *(rec Studio DRS, Zurich, Jan. 4–5, 1993)* Hat Hut ("NOW." series) ▲ hat ART CD 6129 [DDD]

Klein, Dona (vc)
Mozart, W.A.:Adagio E Hn, w. Patrick McFarland (E hn), David Braitberg (vn), Beth Newdome (vn), Paul Murphy (va) [trans Renate Rosenbaltt] Arundax ▲ 21339
Rachmaninoff, S.:Vocalise, w. Patrick McFarland (E hn), David Braitberg (vn), Beth Newdome (vn), Paul Murphy (va), Larry LeMaster (vc), Gloria Jones (db) [trans John Wildermuth] Arundax ▲ 21339

Klein, Emil (vc)—see also ORCHESTRAS & ENSEMBLES Sonare String Quartet, Garingas Baryton Trio
Mendelssohn, F.:Lied ohne Worte Vc, w. C. Beldi (pno) *(rec 1988)* Ambitus ▲ 97832 [DDD]
Mendelssohn, F.:Son 1 Vc, w. C. Beldi (pno) *(rec 1988)* Ambitus ▲ 97832 [DDD]
Mendelssohn, F.:Son 2 Vc, w. C. Beldi (pno) *(rec 1988)* Ambitus ▲ 97832 [DDD]
Mendelssohn, F.:Vars concertantes, w. C. Beldi (pno) *(rec 1988)* Ambitus ▲ 97832 [DDD]

Klein, Erwin (cl)
Backofen, J.G.:Con for 2 Cls, w. F. Klein (cl), U. Schneider (cnd), Cologne RSO Koch Schwann ▲ CD 311001 [DDD]
Stamitz, C.:Con for 2 Cls, w. F. Klein (cl), U. Schneider (cnd), Cologne RSO Koch Schwann ▲ CD 311001 [DDD]

Klein, Franz (cl)
Backofen, J.G.:Con for 2 Cls, w. E. Klein (cl), U. Schneider (cnd), Cologne RSO Koch Schwann ▲ CD 311001 [DDD]
Mozart, W.A.:Qnt Cl, K.581, w. Amadeus String Quartet Koch Schwann ▲ SCH 318092
Reger, M.:Qnt Cl, w. Heutling String Quartet Koch Schwann ▲ SCH 318092
Stamitz, C.:Con for 2 Cls, w. E. Klein (cl), U. Schneider (cnd), Cologne RSO Koch Schwann ▲ CD 311001 [DDD]

Klein, Fred (hn)—see ORCHESTRAS & ENSEMBLES New York Woodwind Soloists

Klein, Gerd Uwe (vn)—see ORCHESTRAS & ENSEMBLES Euler String Quartet

Klein, H. (org)
Franck, C.:Cantabile Concerto Bayreuth ▲ CBH 16012
Franck, C.:Chorals Org, M.38-40 Concerto Bayreuth ▲ CBH 16012
Franck, C.:Pastorale Concerto Bayreuth ▲ CBH 16012

Klein, Irving (vc)—see ORCHESTRAS & ENSEMBLES Claremont String Quartet

Kleinschmidt, Michael (org)
Britten, H.:Prelude & Fugue on a Theme of Vittoria Koch International Classics ▲ KIC 7030-2 [DDD] ■ 3-7030-4 (D)
Howells, H.:Org Music—Rhapsody in c#, Op. 17/3 Koch International Classics ▲ KIC 7093-2 [DDD]

Klembala, Géza (org/hpd)—see ORCHESTRAS & ENSEMBLES Affetti Musicali

Klement, Miloslav (rcr)
Telemann, G.P.:Con in a for 2 Rcrs, w. Jiří Stivín (rcr), M. Munclinger (cnd), Prague CO Supraphon ▲ SUP 3039

Klemeyer, Herman (fl)—see also ORCHESTRAS & ENSEMBLES Munich Residenz Quintet members
Busoni, F.:Divert Fl, w. C.A. Bunte (cnd), Berlin SO Vox Box 2-▲ CDX 5133

Klemm, Joachim (bss hn)—see ORCHESTRAS & ENSEMBLES Sabine Meyer Wind Ensemble

Klemmstein, E. (va)
Schubert, Franz:Qnt Pno, D.667, w. E. Taussig (pno), R. Ricci (vn), M. Virizly (vc), G. Karr (db) One-Eleven ▲ URS 92010

Klepác, Jaromir (pno)
Shostakovich, D.:Son Vn, w. Jirí Hurník (vn) Panton ▲ PAN 811013
Stravinsky, I.:Divert Vn, w. Jirí Hurník (vn) Panton ▲ PAN 811013

Klepač, Rudolf (bn)
Vivaldi, A.:Cons Bn, w. A. Janigro (cnd), Zagreb Solisti—RV.501 in g *(rec 1964)* Vanguard Classics ("The Bach Guild" series) ▲ OVC 2006 [ADD]

Klerk, Albert de (org)
Andriessen, H.:Missa in festo assumptionis, w. M. Michielsen (cnd), Koorproject Amersterdam Erasmus ▲ WVH 076 [DDD]
Andriessen, H.:Omaggio a Marenzio, w. M. Michielsen (cnd), Koorproject Amersterdam Erasmus ▲ WVH 076 [DDD]
Andriessen, H.:Sonnet de Pierre de Ronsard, w. M. Michielsen (cnd), Koorproject Amersterdam Erasmus ▲ WVH 076 [DDD]
Andriessen, H.:Sponsa Christi, w. M. Michielsen (cnd), Koorproject Amersterdam Erasmus ▲ WVH 076 [DDD]
Bunk, G.:Symphonic Legend NM Classics ▲ NM 92034
Handel, G.F.:Cons (16) Org, w. A. Rieu (cnd), Amsterdam CO—No. 13 Sony Classical ("Essential Classics" series) ▲ SBK 47660; ■ SBT 47660
Haydn, J.:Con Org, Obs & Strs, H.XVIII/1, w. A. Rieu (cnd), Amsterdam CO Sony Classical ("Essential Classics" series) ▲ SBK 47660 ■ SBT 47660
Haydn, J.:Con Org, Vns & Bass Instrument, H.XVIII/5, w. A. Rieu (cnd), Amsterdam CO Sony Classical ("Essential Classics" series) ▲ SBK 47660 ■ SBT 47660
Haydn, J.:Con Org, Vns & Bass Instrument, H.XVIII/8, w. A. Rieu (cnd), Amsterdam CO Sony Classical ("Essential Classics" series) ▲ SBK 47660 ■ SBT 47660

Klett, A. E. (cl)—see also ORCHESTRAS & ENSEMBLES Boreas Wind Quintet
Blak, K.:Con Cl, w. P. Vronsky (cnd), Slovak RSO Bratislava *(rec Oct. 1993)* Tutl ▲ FKT 7
Blak, K.:Dialogue, w. O. Jakobsen (gtr) Tutl ▲ FKT 6
Blak, K.:Svabo, w. O. Røkkum (va), N. F. Jeppesen (hn), J. Koch (pno) Tutl ▲ FKT 6
Rasmussen, S.:Grave, w. P. Vronsky (cnd), Slovak RSO Bratislava *(rec Oct. 1993)* Tutl ▲ FKT 7
Rasmussen, S.:Music of, w. W. Gaffron (vn), A. Turner (vc), E. Dalsgarð (fl), P. Sólstein (hn), J. Andreasen (pno), S.A. Johansen (cnd), *(orch unknown)*—"Warnings I"—The Naked Destruction Tutl ▲ FKT 4

Klevit, Lisa (bas hn)—see ORCHESTRAS & ENSEMBLES New World Basset Horn Trio

Klevit-Ziegler, Lisa (cl)
Puccini, M.:Concertone Fl, w. Christian Gurtner (fl), Reinhold Friedrich (tpt), Hector McDonald (nat hn), M. Haselböck (cnd), Vienna Academy *(rec Sofiensäle, Vienna, Oct 17-20, 1994)* Capriccio ▲ 10 598 [DDD]

Klibonoff, John (pno)
Beethoven, L. van:Son 9 Vn, "Kreutzer", w. M. Bachmann (vn) Connoisseur Society ▲ CD 4178 [DDD]
Bergsma, W.:Fantastic Vars on a Theme from Tristan, w. P. Cortese (va) *(rec 6/91)* Crystal ▲ CD 636
Carter, E.:Elegy Va, w. P. Cortese (va) *(rec 6/91)* Crystal ▲ CD 636
Corigliano, J.:Son Vn & Pno, w. M. Bachmann (vn) Catalyst ▲ 09026-61824-2
Glinsky, A.:Toccata-Scherzo, w. M. Bachmann (va) Catalyst ▲ 09026-61824-2
Messiaen, O.:Quatuor pour la fin du temps, w. M. Bachmann (vn)—Praise to the Immortality of Jesus Christ [8th movt.] Catalyst ▲ 09026-61824-2
Moravec, P.:Son Vn, w. M. Bachmann (vn) Catalyst ▲ 09026-61824-2
Pärt, A.:Fratres II, w. M. Bachmann (vn) [arr vn & pno] Catalyst ▲ 09026-61824-2
Persichetti, V.:Infanta marina, w. P. Cortese (va) Crystal ▲ CD 636
Rochberg, G.:Son Vn, w. M. Bachmann (vn) Connoisseur Society ▲ CD 4178 [DDD]

Kliegel, Maria (vc)
Banter, H.:Phädra, w. M. Jurowski (cnd), Northwest German PO *(rec Cologne Phil Hall, Mar 1995)* Marco Polo ▲ 8.223860 [DDD]
Bloch, E.:Schelomo, w. G. Markson (cnd), Irish National SO *(rec National Concert Hall, Dublin, May 17-18, 1993)* Naxos ▲ 8.550519 [DDD]
Brahms, J.:Con Vn & Vc, "Double Con", w. Ilya Kaler (vn), A. Constantine (cnd), Irish National SO *(rec National Concert Hall, Dublin, May 16-17, 1994)* Naxos ▲ 8.550938 [DDD]
Brahms, J.:Sons Vc (comp), w. K. Mersher (pno) *(rec Nov. 1992)* Naxos ▲ 8.550655 [DDD]
Brahms, J.:Son in D Vc, w. K. Mersher (pno) *(rec Nov. 1992)* Naxos ▲ 8.550655 [DDD]
Bruch, M.:Kol Nidrei, w. G. Markson (cnd), Irish National SO *(rec National Concert Hall, Dublin, May 17-18, 1993)* Naxos ▲ 8.550519 [DDD]
Dvořák, A.:Con Vc, w. M. Halász (cnd), Royal PO *(rec Nov. 8-10, 1991)* Naxos ▲ 8.550503 [DDD] ▲ 7.550503 [DD
Elgar, E.:Con Vc, w. M. Halász (cnd), Royal PO *(rec Nov. 8-10, 1991)* Naxos ▲ 8.550503 [DDD] ▲ 7.550503 [DD
Le Grand Tango & Other Dances for Cello & Piano, w. Bernd Glemser (pno) *(rec May 3-4, 1993)* Naxos ▲ 8.550785 [DDD]
Kodály, Z.:Chorale Preludes, w. Jenő Jandó (pno) *(rec Clara Wieck Auditorium, Heidelberg, July 1994 & May 1995)* Naxos ▲ 8.553160 [DDD]
Kodály, Z.:Son Vc, Op. 8 *(rec Clara Wieck Auditorium, Heidelberg, July 1994 & May 1995)* Naxos ▲ 8.553160 [DDD]
Kodály, Z.:Son Vc & Pno, Op. 4, w. Jenő Jandó (pno) *(rec Clara Wieck Auditorium, Heidelberg, July 1994 & May 1995)* Naxos ▲ 8.553160 [DDD]
The Love Collection, w. Bernd Glemser (pno) *(rec Clara Wieck Auditorium, Heidelberg, May 3-4, 1993)* Naxos 4-▲ 8.504004 [DDD]
Schnittke, A.:Con 1 Vc, w. G. Markson (cnd), Saarbrück RSO Marco Polo ▲ 8.223334
Schnittke, A.:Stille Musik Vc, w. R. Havenith (pno) Marco Polo ▲ 8.223334
Schubert, Franz:Son Arpeggione, w. K. Merscher (pno) *(rec Dec. 14-15, 1991)* Naxos ▲ 8.550654 [DDD]
Schumann, R.:Adagio & Allegro Hn, w. K. Merscher (pno) *(rec Dec. 14-15, 1991)* Naxos ▲ 8.550654 [DDD]
Schumann, R.:Con Vc, w. A. Constantine (cnd), Irish National SO *(rec National Concert Hall, Dublin, May 16-17, 1994)* Naxos ▲ 8.550938 [DDD]
Schumann, R.:Fantasiestücke Cl, w. K. Merscher (pno) [arr. for cello & piano] *(rec Dec. 14-15, 1991)* Naxos ▲ 8.550654 [DDD]
Schumann, R.:Stücke im Volkston, w. K. Merscher (pno) *(rec Dec. 14-15, 1991)* Naxos ▲ 8.550654 [DDD]
Shostakovich, D.:Con 1 Vc, w. A. Wit (cnd), Polish National RSO Katowice *(rec Polish Radio Concert Hall, Katowice, Feb 27-Mar 1, 1995)* Naxos ▲ 8.550813 [DDD]
Shostakovich, D.:Con 2 Vc, w. A. Wit (cnd), Polish National RSO Katowice *(rec Polish Radio Concert Hall, Katowice, Feb 27-Mar 1, 1995)* Naxos ▲ 8.550813 [DDD]
Tchaikovsky, P.:Pezzo capriccioso, w. G. Markson (cnd), Irish National SO *(rec May 17-18, 1993)* Naxos ▲ 8.550519 [DDD]
Tchaikovsky, P.:Vars on a Rococo Theme, w. G. Markson (cnd), Irish National SO *(rec May 17-18, 1993)* Naxos ▲ 8.550519 [DDD]
Virtuoso Cello Encores, w. Raymund Havenith (pno) Marco Polo ▲ 8.223403 [DDD]

Klien, Walter (pno)
Beethoven, L. van:Fant Pno, Op. 80, "Choral Fant", w. J. Semkow (cnd), St. Louis SO, St. Louis Sym Chorus Vox Box 2-▲ CDX 5104 [ADD]
Beethoven, L. van:Rondo Pno, WoO 6, w. J. Semkow (cnd), St. Louis SO Vox Box 2-▲ CDX 5104 [ADD]
Chabrier, E.:Pno Music 4-Hands, w. R. Kyriakou (pno)—3 valses romantiques; Cortège burlesque; Souvenirs de Munich *(rec 1965)* Vox Box 2-▲ CDX 5108 [ADD]
Chopin, F.:Prelude in A♭ Allegretto ▲ ACD 8065 [ADD] ■ ACS 8065
Chopin, F.:Preludes, Op. 28 Allegretto ▲ ACD 8065 [ADD] ■ ACS 8065
Chopin, F.:Prelude, Op. 45 Allegretto ▲ ACD 8065 [ADD] ■ ACS 8065
Honegger, A.:Concertino Pno & Orch, w. H. Hollreiser (cnd), Vienna Pro Musica Orch Allegretto ▲ ACD 8157 [ADD] ■ ACS 8157
Liszt, F.:Liebesträume Special Music Co. ("Classics of the Heart" series) ▲ SCD 5197
Mozart, W.A.:Pno Music (misc)—Cons 14, 18 & 21 for Pno; 8 Vars on a Dutch Song by Christian Ernst Graf, K.208; Son Movt in B♭, K.400; Fugue in g, K.401; 7 Vars on Willem Van Nassau, K.25; Klaviersuite in C, K.399; 12 Vars on a Minuet by Johann Christian Fischer, K.179; Allegro of a Son in g, K.312; Capriccio in C, K.395; 12 Vars on Je Suis Lindor [from Beaumarchais' Barbier, K.354] Vox Box 2-▲ CDX2 5517
Mozart, W.A.:Qnt Pno, K.452, w. P. Bowman (ob), G. Silfies (cl), G. Berry (bn), R. Pandolfi (hn) *(rec 1975-79)* Vox Box 3-▲ CD3X 3014 [ADD]
Mozart, W.A.:Sons Pno—Fantasia in c, K.475; Sonatas 12-17; Son. in F, K.533 *(rec 1964)* Vox Box 2-▲ CDX 5046 [ADD]
Mozart, W.A.:Sons Pno—Nos. 1-10, K.279-284, 309-311 & 330 Vox Box 2-▲ CDX 5026 [ADD]
Strauss, R.:Songs, w. H. Hotter (b-bar)—Die Nacht; Ruhe meine Seele; Mit deinen blauen Augen; etc. [G] *(rec 1967)* Preiser ▲ 93367 [ADD]
Walter Klien Allegretto ▲ ACD 8023 [ADD] ■ ACS 8023

Klier, Manfred (hn)—see also ORCHESTRAS & ENSEMBLES Berlin PO Horns
Mozart, W.A.:Kleine Nachtmusik, w. W. Güttler (db), Berlin Philharmonia String Quartet Denon/PCM Digital ▲ DEN 7229 [DDD]
Mozart, W.A.:Musikalischer Spass, w. Hauptmann (hn), Berlin Philharmonia String Quartet Denon ▲ 7229 [DDD]
Reinecke, C.:Sextet Ww, w. Berlin Philharmonic Wind Quintet *(rec Nov. 17-22, 1992)* BIS ▲ CD 612 [DDD]

Klimkiewicz, Jacek (vn)—see ORCHESTRAS & ENSEMBLES Sonare String Quartet

Klimowicz, Wanda (pno)
Chopin, F.:Songs Sop (comp), w. Stefania Woytowicz (sop), Andrzej Bachleda (ten) *(rec Warsaw, 1960)* Polskie Nagrania ▲ PNCD 315

Klinck, Paul (vn)
Ives, C.:Son 2 Pno, w. Daan Vandewalle (pno), Bert Jacobs (fl) *(rec Steurbaut Sound Recording Centre)* René Gailly ▲ CD 87078 [DDD]

Klinckerfus, Leonore (hpd)
Bach, J.S.:Cons Hpd, BWV 1052-1058, w. C. Jaccottet (hpd), C. Sartoretti (hpd), N. Hostettler (hpd), J. Faerber (cnd), Württemberg CO *(rec 1978)* Vox Box 3-▲ CD3X 3018 [ADD]
Bach, J.S.:Cons for 2 Hpds (comp), w. C. Jaccottet (hpd), C. Sartoretti (hpd), N. Hostettler (hpd), J. Faerber (cnd), Württemberg CO *(rec 1978)* Vox Box 3-▲ CD3X 3018 [ADD]
Bach, J.S.:Cons for 3 Hpds (comp), w. C. Jaccottet (hpd), C. Sartoretti (hpd), N. Hostettler (hpd), J. Faerber (cnd), Württemberg CO *(rec 1978)* Vox Box 3-▲ CD3X 3018 [ADD]

Klinko, Markus (hp)
Debussy, C.:Arabesques (2)—solo harp arrangement of Arabesque No. 1 Audiofon ▲ CD 72036
Debussy, C.:Danses sacrée et profane, w. Lucas Drew (db), Miami String Quartet Audiofon ▲ CD 72036
Debussy, C.:Danses sacrée et profane, w. Paris Opera Orch Soloists EMI Classics ▲ CDC 54884
Debussy, C.:Petite suite, w. Paris Opera Orch Soloists—En bateau [arr. for flute & harp] EMI Classics ▲ CDC 54884
Debussy, C.:Son Fl, w. Paris Opera Orch Soloists [arr. for flute & harp] EMI Classics ▲ CDC 54884
Debussy, C.:Son Fl, w. C. Nield (fl), P. McConnell (va) Audiofon ▲ CD 72036
Fauré, G.:Berceuse Vn, w. Paris Opera Orch Soloists [arr. for flute & harp] EMI Classics ▲ CDC 54884
Fauré, G.:Impromptu Hp Audiofon ▲ CD 72036
French Impressions Audiofon ▲ CD 72036
Ibert, J.:Entracte, w. Paris Opera Orch Soloists [fl & hp] EMI Classics ▲ CDC 54884
Ravel, M.:Intro & Allegro, w. Paris Opera Orch Soloists EMI Classics ▲ CDC 54884
Ravel, M.:Intro & Allegro, w. C. Nield (fl), R. Hancock (cl), Miami String Quartet Audiofon ▲ CD 72036
Ravel, M.:Pavane pour une infante défunte, w. Paris Opera Orch Soloists [arr. for flute & harp] EMI Classics ▲ CDC 54884
Ravel, M.:Vocalise-étude en forme de habanera, w. Paris Opera Orch Soloists [arr. for flute & harp] EMI Classics ▲ CDC 54884
Recital, w. Klinko, Markus (hp) EMI Classics ▲ CDC 54467

Klocek, Jerzy (vc)—see ORCHESTRAS & ENSEMBLES Wawelskie Trio

Klock, Laura (hn)
Macchia, S.:Chamber Con 3, w. J. Tanner (fl/alt fl), M. Sussman (cl), F. Cohen (ob/E hn), D. Fedora (bn), V. Kadlubkiewicz (vn), J. Messina (db), P. Tanner (perc) *(rec July 1992)* Gasparo ▲ GS 226 [DDD]
Macchia, S.:En trouvant les tombeaux, w. Lynn Klock (sax), Salvatore Macchia (db) *(rec Eastman Theater, Eastman School of Music)* Open Loop ▲ OL 021

Klock, Lynn (a sax)
Bozza, E.:Aria Sax, w. Nadine Shank (pno) *(rec Eastman School of Music, 1993-94)* Open Loop ▲ 033 [DDD]
Glazunov, A.:Con Sax, w. Nadine Shank (pno) [arr sax & pno] *(rec Eastman School of Music, 1993-94)* Open Loop ▲ 033 [DDD]
Heiden, B.:Son A Sax, w. Nadine Shank (pno) *(rec Eastman School of Music, 1993-94)* Open Loop ▲ 033 [DDD]
Ibert, J.:Aria Cl & Pno, w. Nadine Shank (pno) [arr for sax & pno] *(rec Eastman School of Music, 1993-94)* Open Loop ▲ 033 [DDD]
Ibert, J.:Concertino da camera, w. Nadine Shank (pno) [arr for sax & pno] *(rec Eastman School of Music, 1993-94)* Open Loop ▲ 033 [DDD]
Rueff, J.:Concertino, w. Nadine Shank (pno) [arr for sax & pno] *(rec Eastman School of Music, 1993-94)* Open Loop ▲ 033 [DDD]

Klock, Lynn (b sax)
Hartley, W.S.:Son Br Sax, w. Nadine Shank (pno) *(rec Eastman Theater, Eastman School of Music)* Open Loop ▲ OL 021

Klock, Lynn (sax)
Ben-Haim, P.:Songs without Words, w. Nadine Shank (pno) *(rec Eastman Theater, Eastman School of Music)* Open Loop ▲ OL 021
Bozza, E.:Divertissement Sax *(rec Kilbourne Hall, Aug. 14, 1994)* Open Loop ▲ OL 021
Macchia, S.:En trouvant les tombeaux, w. Laura Klock (hn), Salvatore Macchia (db) *(rec Eastman Theater, Eastman School of Music)* Open Loop ▲ OL 021
Tansman, A.:Sonatine Bn, w. Nadine Shank (pno) *(rec Eastman Theater, Eastman School of Music)* Open Loop ▲ OL 021
Telemann, G.P.:Sonate metodiche, w. Nadine Shank (pno)—No. 4 in c *(rec Kilbourne Hall, Aug. 14, 1994)* Open Loop ▲ OL 021
Tomasi, H.:Chant Corse, w. Nadine Shank (pno) *(rec Eastman Theater, Eastman School of Music)* Open Loop ▲ OL 021
Vintage Flora, w. Nadine Shank (pno) Open Loop ▲ OL 007

Klöcker, Dieter (cl)—see also ORCHESTRAS & ENSEMBLES Consortium Classicum
Bach, C.P.E.:Duo Cl, w. K.-O. Hartmann (bn), J. Normann (db) MD + G ▲ L 3365 [DDD]
Bärmann, H.J.:Qnt 3 Cl, w. Berlin Philharmonia String Quartet Orfeo ▲ 213901 [DDD]
Brahms, J.:Sons Cl (comp), w. W. Genuit (pno) Acanta ▲ CD 43270 [DDD]
Brahms, J.:Trio Cl, w. Christoph Henkel (vc), Claudius Tanski (pno) MD + G ▲ MDG 3010595 [DDD]
Busoni, F.:Intro & Elegie, w. Consortium Classicum Orfeo ▲ 213901 [DDD]
Cartellieri, A.:Cons Cl, Prague CO—in B♭ & E♭ MD + G ▲ MDG 3010527
Clarinet & Orchestra, w. Micheal Heitzler (cl), Czech-Slovak RSO Bratislava [cnd:Gernot Schmalfuss] *(rec Jan. 1990)* Marco Polo ▲ 8.223431 [DDD]
Clarinet Concertos, w. Berlin RSO [cnd:Jesus Lopez-Cobos] Koch Schwann ▲ SCH 311045
Danzi, F.:Sinf concertante, w. K.-O. Hartmann (bn), P. Skvor (cnd), Suk CO MD + G ▲ L 3365 [DDD]
Eybler, J.L.E. von:Con Cl, w. W.-D. Hauschild (cnd), English CO Novalis ▲ 150061 [DDD]
Farrenc, J.-L.:Trio Cl, w. Hoerr (vc), W. Genuit (pno) Divox ▲ CDX 29205 [DDD]
Gragnani, F.:Qt for 2 Gtrs, w. S. Prunnbauer (gtr), I. Turnagoel (gtr), H. Ganz (va) *(rec Sept. 1984)* Koch Treasure ▲ 31612-2 [ADD]
Haydn, J.:Qts Cl, w. Consortium Classicum MD + G ▲ L 3315 [DDD]
Kalliwoda, J.W.:Heimatlied, "Treues, stilles Friedensthal", w. H. Donath (sop), K. Donath (pno) [G] Acanta ▲ 43508
Krommer, F.:Qts (6) Cl, w. Consortium Classicum CPO 2-▲ CPO 999141 [DDD]
Lachner, F.P.:Songs Sop, w. H. Donath (sop), K. Donath (cl)—Seit ich ihn gesehen, Op. 82; Auf Flügeln Gesanges [G] Acanta ▲ 43508
Lieder der Romantik, w. Fischer-Dieskau, Dietrich (bar), Klaus Wallendorf (hn), Hartmut Höll (pno) Orfeo ▲ 153861
Meyerbeer, G.:Qnt Cl, w. Berlin Philharmonia String Quartet Orfeo ▲ 213901 [DDD]
Mozart, W.A.:Arias, w. Helen Donath (sop), Josef Suk (vn), Karl-Otto Hartmann (bn), K. Donath (cnd), Suk CO—Cor Sincerum; Jesus Amor Meus; Mens Sancta Deo [2 versions]; Jesu Dulcis Memoria; Salve Regina; Domine Deus Salutis Meae; Plasmator Deus; Die Hoffnung dient zum Stabe *(rec Cultural House, Prague, June 3-10, 1987)* Panton ▲ PAN 810860
Mozart, W.A.:Con Cl, w. W.-D. Hauschild (cnd), English CO Novalis ▲ 150061 [DDD]
Mozart, W.A.:Concertone Vns, w. K.-O. Hartmann (bn), P. Skvor (cnd), Suk CO [arr. Anton Hoffmeister for clarinet & bassoon] MD + G ▲ L 3365 [DDD]
Mozart, W.A.:Don Giovanni, w. Gernot Schmalfub (ob), Christian Hartmann (ob), Waldemar Wandel (cl), Sara Willis (hn), Christian Auer (hn), Karl-Otto Hartmann (bn), Eberhard Buschmann (bn), Jürgen Normann (db), Consortium Classicum Bayer ▲ BR 100 135 [DDD]
Schacht, T. von:Cons Cl, w. O. Link (cl), S. Wandel (cl), H. Stadlmair (cnd), Bamberg SO—in D & B for 1 Clarinet; in B for 2 Clarinets; in B for 3 Clarinets *(rec May 11-15, 1992)* Orfeo ▲ 290931 [DDD]
Schubert, Franz:Der Hirt auf dem Felsen, w. H. Donath (sop), K. Donath (pno) [G] Acanta ▲ 43508
Schubert, J.F.:Con Cl, w. K.-O. Hartmann (bn), P. Skvor (cnd), Suk CO MD + G ▲ L 3366 [DDD]
Spohr, L.:Fant & Vars on a Theme of Danzi, w. Consortium Classicum Orfeo ▲ 213901 [DDD]
Spohr, L.:German Songs , Op. 103, w. H. Donath (sop), K. Donath (pno) [G] Acanta ▲ 43508
Spohr, L.:Notturno, w. Consortium Classicum—Andante & Variations Orfeo ▲ 213901 [DDD]
Sssmayr, F.X.:Con Cl, w. W.-D. Hauschild (cnd), English CO Novalis ▲ 150061 [DDD]
Tausch, F.W.:Duo, w. K.-O. Hartmann (bn), J. Normann (db) MD + G ▲ L 3366 [DDD]

INSTRUMENT.

Klöcker, Dieter (cl) (cont.)
Virtuoso Music for Clarinet & Guitar, w. Sonja Prunnbauer (gtr) MD + G ▲ L 3319 [DDD]
Virtuoso Operatic Arias for Soprano & Obbligato Clarinet, w. Isolde Siebert (sop), Southwest German SO [cnd:Klaus Donath] Koch Schwann ▲ SCH 314018 [DDD]
Weber, C.M. von:Concertino Cl, w. A. Tamayo (cnd), Slovak RSO Bratislava Novalis ▲ 150093
Weber, C.M. von:Con 1 Cl, w. A. Tamayo (cnd), Slovak RSO Bratislava Novalis ▲ 150093
Weber, C.M. von:Con 2 Cl, w. A. Tamayo (cnd), Slovak RSO Bratislava Novalis ▲ 150093
Weber, C.M. von:Music of, w. A. Tamayo (cnd), Slovak RSO Bratislava, Consortium Classicum Soloists—Concertino in C for Oboe & Winds; Romanza Siciliana for Flute & Orch.; Romanze Appassionata for Bassoon & Orch.; Divert. for Clarinet & Orch.; Andante & Rondo Ungarese for Bassoon & Orch., Op. 35; Concertino, Op. 45 Novalis ▲ 150100
Winter, P. von:Concertino Cl, w. K.-O. Hartmann (bn), P. Škvor (cnd), Suk CO MD + G ▲ L 3366 [DDD]

Kloft, Traud (hpd)
Bon Di Venezia, A.:Sons Fl, Op. 1, w. C. Meininger (fl) Bayer ▲ BR 100 057CD [DDD]
Jacquet De La Guerre, E.:Suites Hpd—in g; in D Bayer ▲ BR 100 056 CD [DDD]
Martinez, M.:Chaconne Hpd Bayer ▲ BR 100 056 CD [DDD]
Martinez, M.:Sons Hpd—in e; in A Bayer ▲ BR 100 056 CD [DDD]

Klopprott, Bernhard (hpd/vir)
Tomkins, T.:Instr & Voc Music MD + G ("Scene" series) ▲ MDG 6070563 [DDD]

Klos, W. (va)—see ORCHESTRAS & ENSEMBLES Vienna String Trio

Klose, Martin (cl)
Lutoslawski, W.:Die Strohkette, w. Barbara Miller (sop), Oksana Sowiak (mez), Robert Dohn (fl), Willy Schnell (ob), Hartmut Stute (cl), Karl Steinbrecher (bn), A. Grüber (cnd) Vox Box 2-▲ CDX 5133

Kloss, Sherry (vn)
An American Collage Vol. II, w. Constance Keene (pno), Ayke Agus (pno), Anita Swearingen (pno), Michael Lang (pno), Diane Lang Bryan (cl), James Smith (gtr), Laila Padorr (fl), Victor Morosco (a sax) Protone ▲ PRCD 1114 [DDD]
Sherry Kloss Plays Forgotten Gems from the Heifetz Legacy, w. Ayke Agus (pno) Protone ▲ PRCD 1104 [A/DDD] ▮ CSPR 170

Klucevsek, Guy (acc)—see also ORCHESTRAS & ENSEMBLES Relâche Ensemble
Childs, M.E.:Four of One Another, w. SoHo Quartet XI Compact Discs ▲ XI 114
Childs, M.E.:Whistling in the Dark XI Compact Discs ▲ XI 114
Coleman, A.:Below 14th St/Above 125th St CRI ▲ CD 626 [DDD]
King, J.:All Together Now CRI ▲ CD 626 [DDD]
Klucevsek, G.:Acc Music—An Air of Gathering Pipers; Samba D Hiccup CRI ▲ CD 626 [DDD]
Manhattan Cascade CRI ▲ CRI 626 [DDD]
Vierk, L.V.:Manhattan Cascade CRI ▲ CD 626 [DDD]
Zorn, J.:Road Runner CRI ▲ CD 626 [DDD]

Klucevsek, Guy (acc/melodica/pno)—see ORCHESTRAS & ENSEMBLES Bantam Orch

Klug, Howard (cl/b cl)—see ORCHESTRAS & ENSEMBLES Indiana Trio

Klugarová, Kamila (org)
Eben, Petr:Con 2 Org, "Symphonia gregoriana", w. L. Pešek (cnd), Czech PO, Czech Phil Chorus [Cz] Panton ▲ 81 1141-2911

Kluson, Josef (va)—see ORCHESTRAS & ENSEMBLES Prazak String Quartet

Klust, Hertha (pno)
Beethoven, L. van:Songs, w. Dietrich Fischer-Dieskau (bar)—7 Goethe-Lieder; 6 Lieder von Gellert, Op. 48; 14 Lieder Nach Verschiedenen Dichtern Testament ▲ TES 1057 [ADD]
Les introuvables de Dietrich Fischer-Dieskau, w. Fischer-Dieskau, Dietrich (bar), Kark Engel (pno), Gerald Moore (pno), Aribert Reimann (pno), Robert Veyron-Lacroix (hpd) EMI Classics 6-▲ CDZF 68509
Schubert, Franz:Winterreise, w. D. Fischer-Dieskau (bar) *(rec live 1953)* Melodram ▲ MEL 18016

Klütsch, Georg (bn)—see ORCHESTRAS & ENSEMBLES Sabine Meyer Wind Ensemble

Kluvetasch, Margarethe (hp)
Brahms, J.:Choral Music, w. Gunther Opitz (hn), Waldemar Markus (hn), Horst Neumann (cnd), Leipzig Radio Chorus—Opp. 17, 42, 62 & 104 Berlin Classics ▲ BER CD 9276

Knapp, Lothar (org)
Bruhns, N.:Org Music—Preludes & Fugues (4) in e, e, G & g; Nun komm der Heiden Heiland *(rec Peter und Paul Pfarrkirche, Obermarsberg, Sauerland)* Christophorus ▲ CHR 77173 [ADD]
Hanff, J.N.:Chorale Preludes (6)—Ein feste Burg ist unser Gott; Auf meinen lieben Gott; Helft mir Gott's Güte priesen; Wär Gott nicht mit uns diese Zeit; Erbarm dich mein, o Herre Gott; Ach Gott, vom Himmel sieh darein *(rec Peter und Paul Pfarrkirche, Obermarsberg, Sauerland)* Christophorus ▲ CHR 77173 [ADD]

Knappe, Lothar (org)
Herzogenberg, H. von:Org Music [at the Oberlinger Organ of St. Paul's Dominic Church, Berlin]—Chorale, "Ach Gott vom Himmel sieh darein" Op. 67; Chorale, "Meinen Jesum lass ich nicht," Op. 67; Chorale, "Es ist genug," Op. 67; Chorale Fant., "Nun komm der Heiden Heiland," Op. 39; Chorale, "Aus tiefer Not schrei ich zu dir," Op. 67; Chorale, "Erschienen ist der herrlich' Tag," Op. 67; Chorale, "Komm her zu mir, spricht Gottes Sohn," Op. 67; Chorale Fant., "Nun danket alle Gott," Op. 46 Christophorus ▲ 77162 [DDD]
Kraft, Walter:Org Music—Totentanztoccata; Fant. "Dies irae"; Fant. "Media vita"; Metaphern for Vn & Org [w. Eva-Maria Kraft (vn)]; Toccata "Ite missa est"; Partita "Nun will sich scheiden Nacht und Tag" *(rec Dominikanerkirche, St. Paulus, Berlin)* Christophorus ▲ CHR 77171 [ADD]

Knappe, Veit (bn)—see also ORCHESTRAS & ENSEMBLES Berlin German Opera Orch Soloists
Martinů, B.:La Revue de Cuisine (sels), w. T. Tomaszewski (vn), G. Lösch (vc), R. Schönemann (cl), A. Lange (tpt), S. Schubert-Weber (pno)—Suite for Violin, Cello, Clarinet, Bassoon, Trumpet & Piano FSM-Adagio ▲ FCD 97 219

Knardahl, Eva (pno)
Albéniz, I.:Cantos de España *(rec Salen Church Hall, Ski, Aug 5-7, 1991)* Simax ▲ PSC 1082 [DDD]
Barber, S.:Excursions *(rec Salen Church Hall, Ski, Aug 5-7, 1991)* Simax ▲ PSC 1082 [DDD]
Beethoven, L. van:Qnt Pno, Ob, Cl, Hn & Bn, w. E. Andersson (cl), A. Linder (hn), E. Schleiffer (bn) BIS ▲ CD 44 [AAD]
Berwald, F.:Qt Pno, Cl, Hn & Bn, w. E. Andersson (cl), A. Linder (hn), E. Schleiffer (bn) BIS ▲ CD 44 [AAD]
Bibalo, A.:Son Bn, w. R. Rønnes (bn) Simax ▲ PSC 1077 [DDD]
Braein, E.F.:Capriccio, w. S. Bruland (cnd), Bergen PO Simax ▲ PSC 3117
Copland, A.:Son Pno *(rec Nacka Aula, Nacka, Sweden, Apr 3-4, 1976)* BIS ▲ CD 52 [AAD]
Egge, K.:Con 2 Pno, w. Baekkelund (cnd), Gjovik Sinfonietta Norway Music ▲ BD 7026
Gershwin, G.:Preludes (3) Pno *(rec Salen Church Hall, Ski, Aug 5-7, 1991)* Simax ▲ PSC 1082 [DDD]
Grieg, E.:Con Pno, Op. 16, w. K. Ingebretsen (cnd), Royal PO BIS ▲ CD 113
Grieg, E.:Con Pno, Op. 16, w. T. Mikkelsen (cnd), Lithuanian National SO Simax ▲ PSC 1107
Grieg, E.:Funeral March in Memory of Rikard Nordraak *(rec Nacka Aula, Nacka, Sweden, 1977-1980)* BIS ▲ CD 51 [AAD]
Grieg, E.:Humoresker *(rec Nacka Aula, Nacka, Sweden, 1977-1980)* BIS ▲ CD 51 [AAD]
Grieg, E.:Lyric Pieces, w. T. Mikkelsen (cnd), Lithuanian National SO—18 pieces Simax ▲ PSC 1107
Grieg, E.:Lyric Pieces *(rec Nacka Aula, Nacka, Sweden, 1977-1980)* BIS ▲ CD 51 [AAD]
Grieg, E.:Nordic Folksongs & Dances—Stumping Dance; Cow-call *(rec Nacka Aula, Nacka, Sweden, 1977-1980)* BIS ▲ CD 51 [AAD]
Grieg, E.:Norwegian Peasant Dances, Op. 72—Nos. 7 & 8 *(rec Nacka Aula, Nacka, Sweden, 1977-1980)* BIS ▲ CD 51 [AAD]
Grieg, E.:Pno Music (comp)—Lyric Pieces, sets 5-7 BIS ▲ CD 105
Grieg, E.:Pno Music (comp)—Lyric Pieces, sets 1-4 BIS ▲ CD 104
♦ Grieg, E.:Pno Music (comp)—4 Norwegian Dances, Op. 35; 2 Romances, Op. 53 BIS ▲ CD 113
Grieg, E.:Pno Music (comp)—Lyric Pieces, sets 8-10 BIS ▲ CD 106
Grieg, E.:Pno Music (comp)—Poetic Tone-Pictures, Op. 3; Nordraak's Funeral March (1866); Humoresques, Op. 6; Sonata, Op. 7 BIS ▲ CD 107
Grieg, E.:Pno Music (comp)—25 Norwegian Folksongs, Op. 17; 4 Album Leaves, Op. 28; Improvisations, Op. 29 BIS ▲ CD 108
Grieg, E.:Pno Music (comp)—Peer Gynt Suites 1 & 2; Sigurd Jorsalfar; Ballade, Op. 24 BIS ▲ CD 109

Knardahl, Eva (pno) (cont.)
Grieg, E.:Pno Music (comp)—19 Norwegian Folksongs, Op. 66; 6 Song Arrangements, Op. 41; 6 Norwegian Mountain Tunes (1875) BIS ▲ CD 111
Grieg, E.:Pno Music (comp)—17 Norwegian Peasant Dances, Op. 72; Stimmungen, Op. 73; Drei Klavierstücke [published 1908] BIS ▲ CD 112
Grieg, E.:Pno Music (comp)—Holberg Suite, Op. 40; Two Elegiac Melodies, Op. 34; Walt-Caprices, Op. 37; Two Nordic Melodies, Op. 63 BIS ▲ CD 110
Grieg, E.:Pictures from Life in the Country—Wedding Procession *(rec Nacka Aula, Nacka, Sweden, 1977-1980)* BIS ▲ CD 51 [AAD]
Grieg, E.:Poetic Tone-Pictures, Op. 3 *(rec Nacka Aula, Nacka, Sweden, 1977-1980)* BIS ▲ CD 51 [AAD]
Grieg, E.:Songs, w. Knut Skram (b-bar)—Ragnhild; Ragna; Langs ei å; En Svane; Min tanke er et mægtigt fjeld *(rec Gothenburg Concert Hall, Sweden, Mar 21-23, 1976)* BIS ▲ CD 43 [AAD]
Hindemith, P.:Son Bn, w. K. Sønstevold (bn) [arr bn & pno] *(rec Nacka, Sweden, April 15, 1978)* BIS ▲ CD 159 [AAD]
Kielland, O.:Villarkorn Simax ▲ PSC 3120
Kvandal, J.:Légende, w. R. Rønnes (bn) Simax ▲ PSC 1077 [DDD]
Lerstad, T.B.:Son 2 Bn, w. R. Rønnes (bn) Simax ▲ PSC 1077 [DDD]
Liszt, F.:Liebesträume *(rec Salen Church Hall, Ski, Aug 5-7, 1991)* Simax ▲ PSC 1082 [DDD]
Plagge, W.:Son Bn, w. R. Rønnes (bn) Simax ▲ PSC 1077 [DDD]
Poulenc, F.:Sxt Pno, w. Gothenburg Wind Quintet *(rec June 6, 1976)* BIS ▲ CD 24 [AAD]
Rautavaara, E.:Sonetto Cl, w. K.-I. Stevensson (cl) *(rec June 10, 1976)* BIS ▲ CD 66 [AAD]
Rimsky-Korsakov, N.:Qnt Fl, w. E. Andersson (cl), E. Schleiffer (bn), A. Linder (hn) BIS ▲ CD 44 [AAD]
Saeverud, H.:Autumn, w. R. Rønnes (bn) Simax ▲ PSC 1077 [DDD]
Sinding, C.:Son Pno *(rec Apr. 3, 1976)* BIS ▲ CD 36 [DDD]
Sonstevold, G.:Sonatina Bn, w. R. Rønnes (bn) Simax ▲ PSC 1077 [DDD]
Strauss, E.:Songs, w. K. Skram (b-bar)—Krämerspiegel (12 songs), Op. 66 [G] *(rec March 21-23, 1976)* BIS ▲ CD 49 [AAD]
The Virtuoso Clarinet, w. Kjell Fagéus (cl), Kjell-Inge Stevensson (cl), Mats Persson (pno) *(rec Nacka Aula, Nacka, Sweden, June 10-12, 1976 & Sept.)* BIS ▲ CD 62 [AAD]

Knaub, Donald (b trbn)
Donald Knaub, w. Rex Woods (pno) Crystal ▮ C680
Hidas, F.:Rhap B Trbn & Pno, w. R. Woods (pno) Crystal ▮ C680
Jacob, G.:Cameos, w. R. Woods (pno) [bass trombone & piano arr.] Crystal ▮ C680

Knebel, C. (pno)
Mozart, W.A.:Songs, w. H. Spatzek (sop) ARS Produktion ▲ ARS 368321 [DDD]

Kneihs, Hans Maria (rcr)
Barsanti, F.:Sons Rcr, Op. 1, w. Wolfgang Zerer (hpd) *(rec Studio Baumgarten, Vienna, Jan 7-9, 1986)* Camerata ▲ 32CM 131 [DDD]
Couperin, F.:Pièces de clavecin (sels)—Le Rossignol-en-amour; Double du rossignol [both arr for fl] *(rec Studio Baumgarten, Vienna, Jan 7-9, 1986)* Camerata ▲ 32CM 131 [DDD]
Handel, G.F.:Sons Rcr, w. Michael Radulescu (org)—Op. 1/2, 4, 7 &11 Camerata ▲ 32CM 117
Loeillet, J.-B.:Sons Various Instruments, Op. 2, w. Wolfgang Zerer (hpd)—No. 5 in c *(rec Studio Baumgarten, Vienna, Jan 7-9, 1986)* Camerata ▲ 32CM 131 [DDD]
Philidor, P.:Suite Rcr, Op. 1/5, w. Wolfgang Zerer (hpd) *(rec Studio Baumgarten, Vienna, Jan 7-9, 1986)* Camerata ▲ 32CM 131 [DDD]

Kneip, Volker (perc)
Berg, A.:Adagio, w. Hans-Udo Heinzmann (fl), Malte Lammers (ob), Walter Hermann (cl), Heinrich Horlein (vn), Jaap Zeijl (va), Seven Forsberg (vc), Willi Beyer (db), Jurgen Lamke (pno), Werner Hagen (pno) [arr chamber ensemble] Koch Schwann ▲ SCH CD 311912
Busoni, F.:Berceuse élégiaque, w. Hans-Udo Heinzmann (fl), Malte Lammers (ob), Walter Hermann (cl), Heinrich Horlein (vn), Jaap Zeijl (va), Seven Forsberg (vc), Willi Beyer (db), Jurgen Lamke (pno), Werner Hagen (pno) [arr Stein for chamber ensemble] Koch Schwann ▲ SCH CD 311912
Debussy, C.:Prélude à l'après-midi d'un faune, w. Hans-Udo Heinzmann (fl), Malte Lammers (ob), Walter Hermann (cl), Heinrich Horlein (vn), Jaap Zeijl (va), Seven Forsberg (vc), Willi Beyer (db), Jurgen Lamke (pno), Werner Hagen (pno) [arr Sachs for chamber ensemble] Koch Schwann ▲ SCH CD 311912
Schoenberg, A.:Chamber Sym 1, w. Hans-Udo Heinzmann (fl), Malte Lammers (ob), Walter Hermann (cl), Heinrich Horlein (vn), Jaap Zeijl (va), Seven Forsberg (vc), Willi Beyer (db), Jurgen Lamke (pno), Werner Hagen (pno) [arr Webern for chamber ensemble] Koch Schwann ▲ SCH CD 311912

Knepper, Mary (hn)—see ORCHESTRAS & ENSEMBLES L'Astrée Ensemble

Kniazev, Alexander (vc)
Brahms, J.:Con Vn & Vc, "Double Con", w. V. Spivakov (vn), Y. Temirkanov (cnd), Royal PO RCA Red Seal ▲ 09026-61696-2

Kniejski, Turid (hp)
Tveitt, G.:Con 2 Hp, w. P. Dreier (cnd), Royal PO Simax ▲ PSC 3108 [DDD]

Knieps, Wolfgang (va)
Bortnyansky, D.:Sinf concertante, w. H. Kann (pno), *(bn unknown)*, I. Angerer (hp), H. Bondarenko (vn), A. Schober (vc) Entrée ▲ 0051 [ADD]

Knific, Renata Artman (vn)
Curtis-Smith, C.:Fant Pieces, w. Curtis Curtis-Smith (pno) Albany ▲ TROY 148 [DDD]

Knight, Dorothy
Brooke, N.:Obomobile, w. Brandon Adrien, Jennifer Baker, Karen Birch, Daniel Cate, Judy Christy, Richard Cochran, Jessica Cooper, Leslie Dominguez, Erin Hannigan, Jason Lichtenwalter, Jay Moore, Hwa-Ling Russell, Toyin Spellman, Sarah Weiner, Jay Weinland Opus One ▲ CD 160

Knight, Hyperion (pno)
The Magnificent Steinway *(rec live, Purchase Univ, Theater C, White Plains, NY, Sept 21, 1995)* Golden String ▲ GSCD 031A [DDD]

Knight, M. (baroque vn)—see ORCHESTRAS & ENSEMBLES Spectre de la Rose

Knoles, Amy (perc)—see also ORCHESTRAS & ENSEMBLES California EAR Unit
Adams, J.L.:Earth & the Great Weather, w. R. Lorentz (vn/perc), R. Lawrence (va), M. Finckel (vc), R. Black (db/perc), J. L. Adams (perc), J. Nageak (Iñupiat Eskimo performer), D. Simmonds (Iñupiat Eskimo performer), L. Tritt (Gwich'in Indian performer), A. P. Raboff (Gwich'in Indian performer), D. Hunsaker (Latin voice), J.L. Adams (cnd) *(rec Fairbanks, Mar. 8-11, 1993)* New World ▲ 80459-2
Andriessen, L.:Hoketus, w. Katherine Pendry (panpipes), James Poke (panpipes), Evan Ziporyn (a sax), Richard Craig (a sax), Steven Schick (congas), Lisa Moore (Fender Rhodes), Damian LeGassick (Fender Rhodes), Cees van Zeeland (pno), Gerard Bouwhuis (pno), Robert Black (bass gtr), Mark Stewart (bass gtr) *(rec Air Recording Studios, Lyndhurst Hall, Hampstead, London, June 29-July 3, 1994)* Sony Classical ▲ SK 66483 [DDD]
Lyons, R.:Electronique, w. Robin Lorentz (vn), Erika Duke Kirkpatrick (vc) Cambria ▲ CD 1088
Lyons, R.:Ice Cream Truck from Hell, w. Robin Lorentz (vn), Erika Duke Kirkpatrick (vc) Cambria ▲ CD 1088

Knoma, Natalia (vc)
Khudoyan, A.:Nostalgia, w. Suren Bagratuni (vc) *(rec New Hope Methodist Church, Methuen, MA, May 22-23, 1995)* Ongaku ▲ 024-104 [DDD]
Khudoyan, A.:Son for 2 Vcs, w. Suren Bagratuni (vc) *(rec New Hope Methodist Church, Methuen, MA, May 22-23, 1995)* Ongaku ▲ 024-104 [DDD]

Knowles, Alison (nar/elec)
Knowles, A.:Electronic Music—Glide Hall Banisters; Descending Clogs Event; Mechanical Saw; California Sandals; Rocky Mountain Train, 5 a.m.; On Orchard Street; Paper Pulper with Vacuum Table; Frijoles Canyon ¿What Next? ▲ WN 0007 ▮ WN 0007

Knowles, Greg (perc)
Miki, M.:Mar Spiritual, w. Evelyn Glennie (mar), Stephen Henderson (perc), Gary Kettel (perc) *(rec Whitfield Street Studios, London, Sept. 22-29, 1994)* Catalyst ▲ 09026-68193-2 [DDD]

Knox, Garth (va)—see ORCHESTRAS & ENSEMBLES Arditti String Quartet

Knox, H. (hpd)—see ORCHESTRAS & ENSEMBLES Arion Ensemble

Knudsen, Sato (vc)—see also ORCHESTRAS & ENSEMBLES Hawthorne String Quartet
Klein, G.:Duo Vn & Vc, w. S.-J. Huang (vn)—Allegro con fuoco; Lento *(rec Jan. 1992)* Northeastern ▲ NR 248-CD

Knudtsen, Celelia (vl/rcr)—see ORCHESTRAS & ENSEMBLES Isabella D'Este
Knushevitsky, Sviatoslav (vc)
Beethoven, L. van:Con Vn, Vc & Pno, "Triple Con", w. David Oistrakh (vn), Lev Oborin (pno), M. Sargent (cnd), Philharmonia Orch EMI Classics 2-▲ CDFB 69331
Beethoven, L. van:Con Vn, Vc & Pno, "Triple Con", w. D. Oistrakh (vn), L. Oborin (pno), R. Kubelik (cnd), Prague SO Multisonic ("Prague Spring" Collection) ▲ 31 0104 [ADD]
Haydn, J.:Trios Pno, Vn & Vc, w. Lev Oborin (pno), David Oistrakh (vn)—H.XV/27 *(rec live, 1961)* Multisonic ("Prague Spring Collection" series) ▲ 31 0105-2 [ADD]
Saint-Saëns, C.:Con 1 Vc, w. A. Gauk (cnd), Moscow RSO *(rec 1946)* Multisonic ("Russian Treasures" series) ▲ 31 0254
Schubert, Franz:Trio 1 Pno, w. L. Oborin (pno), D. Oistrakh (vn) *(rec live 1961)* Multisonic ("Prague Spring Collection" series) ▲ 31 0105-2 [ADD]
Shostakovich, D.:Trio 2 Pno, w. L. Oborin (pno), D. Oistrakh (vn) *(rec live 1961)* Multisonic ("Prague Spring Collection" series) ▲ 31 0105-2 [ADD]
Tchaikovsky, P.:Vars on a Rococo Theme, w. A. Gauk (cnd), All-Union RSO *(rec 1951)* Russian Disc ▲ RUS 15002 [AAD]
Tchaikovsky, P.:Vars on a Rococo Theme, w. A. Gauk (cnd), Moscow RSO *(rec 1949)* Multisonic ("Russian Treasures" series) ▲ 31 0254

Knutson, James (perc)
Veeneman, C.:The Wiry Concord, w. Susan Werner (banjo), Forrest Covington (hammered dlc/cimbalom), Georganne Assat (hp), Donald Martin Jenni (hpd), Mark Johnson (hpd), Barbara Phillips Farley (pno), James Austin (pno), Marta Soderberg (va), Patrick Doyle (perc), Steven Butters (perc), James Popejoy (perc), M. Geary (cnd) Capstone ▲ SCI 6
Ko, U Ko (pno)
Burmese Piano *(rec Chapelle historique du Bon-Pasteur, Montréal)* UMMUS ▲ UMM 203
Kobayashi, Hideko (va)—see ORCHESTRAS & ENSEMBLES Sonare String Quartet
Kobayashi, Michio (hpd/pno)
Handel, G.F.:Arias, w. K. Graf (sop), P. Graf (fl), R.Altwegg (vc)—Meine Seele hört im Sehen [from 9 German Arias] *(rec Protestant Chuch Seon, 1976)* Claves ("Favor Collection" series) ▲ CD 604 [ADD]

Kobayashi, Michio (pno)
Allusions in Moonlight:A Japanese Lieder Recital, w. Kazumichi Ohno (ten) *(rec Mannheimer Reissmuseum, Sept 1994)* Thorofon ▲ CTH 2257 [DDD]
Bach, J.S.:Arias, w. Kathrin Graf (sop), Peter-Lukas Graf (fl), Raffaele Altwegg (vc)—Meine Seele sie vergnügt [from Cantata No. 204, Von der Vergnügsamkeit] *(rec Protestant Chuch Seon, 1976)* Claves ("Favor Collection" series) ▲ CD 604 [ADD]
Joueurs de Flûte, w. Peter-Lukas Graf (fl) *(rec 1973)* Claves ▲ CD 500704 [ADD]
Martin, F.:Chants de Noël, w. Kathrin Graf (sop), Peter-Lukas Graf (fl) *(rec Protestant Chuch Seon, 1976)* Claves ("Favor Collection" series) ▲ CD 604 [ADD]
Rameau, J.P.:Music of, w. Kathrin Graf (sop), Peter-Lukas Graf (fl), Alexander van Wijnkoop (vn)—Rossignols amoureux *(rec Protestant Chuch Seon, 1976)* Claves ("Favor Collection" series) ▲ CD 604 [ADD]
Ravel, M.:Chansons madécasses, w. Kathrin Graf (sop), Peter-Lukas Graf (fl), Raffaele Altwegg (vc) *(rec Protestant Chuch Seon, 1976)* Claves ("Favor Collection" series) ▲ CD 604 [ADD]
Scarlatti, A.:Solitudini amene, apriche collinette, w. Kathrin Graf (sop), Peter-Lukas Graf (fl), Raffaele Altwegg (vc) *(rec Protestant Chuch Seon, 1976)* Claves ("Favor Collection" series) ▲ CD 604 [ADD]
Kobelt, Christoph (perc)—see ORCHESTRAS & ENSEMBLES Timporg Trio
Kobialka, Daniel (vn)
Harrison, L.:Con in slendro, w. Machiko Kobialka (pno), James Barbagallo (pno), Patricia Jennerjohn (cel), Don Marconi (perc), J. Neff (perc), R. Hughes (cnd) *(rec 1972)* CRI ▲ CD 613 [ADD]
Kobialka, Machiko (pno)
Harrison, L.:Con in slendro, w. Daniel Kobialka (vn), James Barbagallo (pno), Patricia Jennerjohn (cel), Don Marconi (perc), J. Neff (perc), R. Hughes (cnd) *(rec 1972)* CRI ▲ CD 613 [ADD]
Köbl, Ulrich (hn)
Dauprat, L.-F.:Trios Hns, Op. 4/1-3, w. K. Reitmayer (hn), E. Schmid (hn) Calig ▲ CAL 50865 [DDD]
Reicha, A.:Trios Hns, Op. 82, w. E. Schmid (hn), K. Reitmayer (hn)—6 trios—Nos. 19-24 Calig ▲ CAL 50865 [DDD]
Sacred Horn Music, w. Allgäuer Horn Ensemble, M. Neukirchner (hn), C. Wulkopf (cta), J. Skudlik (org) Ars Produktion ▲ FCD 368304
Kobler, C. P. (pno)
Rachmaninoff, S.:Son Vc, w. S. Kates (vc) Bainbridge ▲ BCD 6272 [ADD]
Kobler, Linda (hpd)
Seicento Cembalo *(rec 5/90)* Classic Masters ▲ CMCD 1023 [DDD]
Kobler, Raymond (vn)
Strauss, R.:Metamorphosen, w. D. Krehbiel (hn), H. Blomstedt (cnd), San Francisco SO *(rec Feb. 21, 24 & 25, 1992)* London ▲ 436596-2 [DDD]
Kobyayashi, Takeshi (vn)
Ifukube, A.:Son Vn, w. Yuko Umemura (pno) Camerata ▲ 32CM 290
Kobyliansky, Arnold (vn)
Hovhaness, A.:Tzaikerk, w. Paul Edmund-Davies (fl), Randy Max (timp), R. Werthen (cnd), I Fiamminghi CO *(rec Basilica of Bonne Espérance, Vellereille-les-Brayeux, Belgium, Aug. 18-20, 1994)* Telarc ▲ CD 80392 [DDD]
Koch, Hans Michael (gtr)
La Guitarra Española, 1546-1732 MD + G ▲ MDG 6050610 [DDD]
Koch, Hans Michael (lt)
Lute Music from the Renaissance, w. Riccardo Correa (lt) Entrée ▲ 0046 [ADD]
Koch, J. (pno)
Barber, S.:Prayers of Kierkegaard, w. S. Skov (pno), C. Bjørkøe (pno), Safri Duo, La Camerata Danica ▲ DCD 8154
Blak, K.:Svabo, w. O. Røkkum (va), A. E. Klett (cl), N. F. Jeppesen (hn) Tutl ▲ FKT 6
Britten, H.:Flower Songs, w. S. Skov (sop), C. Bjørkøe (pno), Safri Duo, La Camerata Danica ▲ DCD 8154
Grainger, P.:Songs, w. S. Skov (sop), C. Bjørkøe (pno), M. Bojesen (cnd), Camerata, Safri Duo—No Nighean Dhu; O Mistress Mine; 6 Dukes Went a-Fishing; Mary Thompson; Old Irish Tune Danica ▲ DCD 8154
Holmboe, V.:Songs, w. S. Skov (sop), C. Bjørkøe (pno), Safri Duo—Americana Danica ▲ DCD 8154
Nørholm, I.:Songs, w. S. Skov (sop), C. Bjørkøe (pno), Camerata, Safri Duo—Song at Sunset Danica ▲ DCD 8154
Koch, Johannes (va)
Bach, J.S.:Anna Magdalena Bach Notebook, w. E. Ameling (sop), H.-M. Linde (bar), G. Leonhardt (hpd), A. May (vc)—sels. Editio Classica ▲ 77150-2-RG [DDD]
Biber, H. von:Mystery (or Rosary) Sons, w. Susanne Lautenbacher (vn), Rudolph Ewerhart (positiv/hpd/regal) *(rec 1962)* Vox Box 2-▲ CDX 5171
Koch, Johannes (vl)
Bach, J.S.:Partita Fl, BWV 1013, w. P. Graf (fl), H. Barbé (hpd) [trans. for additional instrs.] Jecklin-Disco 2-▲ JEC CD 4400 [ADD]
Bach, J.S.:Sons Fl, BWV 1030-35, w. P. Graf (fl), H. Barbé (hpd) [trans. for additional instr.] Jecklin-Disco 2-▲ JEC CD 4400 [ADD]
Telemann, G.P.:Kleine Kammermusik, w. Hans-Martin Linde (fl), Ferdinand Conrad (rcr), Helmut Winschermann (ob), Susanne Lautenbacher (vn), Hugo Ruf (hpd) *(rec Südwest-Tonstudio H. Jansen, Stuttgart, Jan. 1966)* Musicaphon ▲ 51539 [ADD]
Koch, Lothar (ob)
Mozart, W.A.:Con Ob, K.314, w. H. von Karajan (cnd), Berlin PO EMI Classics ▲ CDM 64355 [ADD]
Mozart, W.A.:Qt Ob, K.370, w. Amadeus String Quartet members Deutsche Grammophon 2-▲ 437137-2 [ADD]
Koch, Nora (hp)
Clair de Lune Berlin Classics ▲ BER 1166

Koch, Philippe (va)
Vieuxtemps, H.:Va Pno Music, w. L. Devos (pno)—Ballade et Polonaise, Op. 38; Feuilles d'Album, Op. 40; Rêverie, Op. 22; Romances sans paroles, Op. 7 & Op. 8; Souvenir d'Amérique sur "Yankee Doodle," Op. 17 Ricercar ▲ RIS 108094 [DDD]
Koch, Philippe (vn)—see also ORCHESTRAS & ENSEMBLES Algae Trio, Grumiaux Piano Trio
Rogister, J.:Con Vn, w. M. Trautmann (cnd), Pécs SO Koch Schwann ▲ SCH 317182
Koch, Phillip (E hn)
Copland, A.:Quiet City, w. W. Marsalis (tpt), D. Hunsberger (cnd), Eastman Wind Ensemble CBS ▲ MK 44916 [DDD] ■ MT 44916 (D)
Koch, Rolf Julius (ob)
Reger, M.:Cantatas, w. V. Schweizer (sop), A. Hellmann (alt), R. Hellmann, U. Soldan (vn), B. Banz (va), C. Hellmann (vc), C. Fink (db), H. Bilgram (org), D. Hellmann (cnd), Mainz Bach Choir Entrée ▲ 0049 [ADD]
Kochanowski, John (va)—see also ORCHESTRAS & ENSEMBLES Concord String Quartet, Blair String Quartet
Kurek, M.:Son Va & Hp, w. Mario Falcao (hp) *(rec Blair School of Music Recital Hall, 1995)* New World ▲ 80497-2
Kocmieroski, Mathew (perc)—see also ORCHESTRAS & ENSEMBLES New Performance Group of the Cornish Institute
Lam, B.-C.:Lü CRI ▲ CD 726 [DDD]
Kocsis, Andrea (hp)
Franck, C.:Messe solennelle, w. Attila Wendler (ten), Dezső Karasszon (org), Zsolt Moinár (vc), Ferenc Nagy (db), Salomon Kamp (cnd), Debrecen Kodály Choir Hungaroton ▲ HCD 31579 [DDD]
Kocsis, Tamás (vn)—see ORCHESTRAS & ENSEMBLES Clementi Quartet
Kocsis, Zoltán (pno)
Bach, J.S.:The Art of the Fugue Philips 2-▲ 412729-2 [DDD]
Bach, J.S.:Con 6 Hpd, w. A. Simon (cnd), Franz Liszt Academy Orch Vivace ▲ E 563 [ADD]
Bach, J.S.:Cons for 3 Hpds (comp), w. A. Schiff (pno), S. Falvai (pno), A. Simon (cnd), Franz Liszt Academy Orch Vivace ▲ E 563 [ADD]
Bach, J.S.:Con for 4 Hpds, w. A. Schiff (pno), S. Falvai (pno), I. Rohmann (pno), A. Simon (cnd), Franz Liszt Academy Orch Vivace ▲ E 563 [ADD]
Bartók, B.:Allegro barbaro Denon ▲ 7813 [DDD]
Bartók, B.:Cons Pno (comp), w. I, Fischer (cnd), Budapest Festival Orch Philips ▲ 446368-2
Bartók, B.:For Children Hungaroton ▲ HCD 12304
Bartók, B.:Hungarian Peasant Songs & 3 Hungarin Folk Songs Denon ▲ 7813 [DDD]
Bartók, B.:The Miraculous Mandarin Pno 4-Hands, w. Adrienne Hauser (pno) Musique D'Abord ▲ HMA 1903021
Bartók, B.:Pno Music—14 Bagatelles; 2 Elegies; 6 Romanian Folk Dances; Sonatina; 3 Hungarian Folk Tunes; 2 Romanian Dances; 3 Hungarian Folk Songs [from Caik]; Allegro Barbaro; 4 Dirges; Suite; Romanian Christmas Carols; 3 Studies; 3 Rondos on Folk Tunes; 1st Term at the Pno; For Children Philips 4-▲ 446368-2
Bartók, B.:Pno Music—Bagatelles (14) for Piano, Op. 6; Two Elegies, Op. 8b; Six Romanian Folk Dances; Sonatina; Three Hungarian Folk Tunes Philips ▲ 434104-2 [DDD]
Bartók, B.:Pictures Orch, w. D. Ránki (pno) [arr. 2-piano Kocsis] *(rec 9/11/81)* Hungaroton ▲ HCD 12400
Bartók, B.:Pieces Orch, Sz.51, w. D. Ránki (pno) [2-piano arr. Kocsis]—Nos. 1 & 2, Prelude & Scherzo *(rec 9/11/81)* Hungaroton ▲ HCD 12400
Bartók, B.:Rhap 1 Vc, w. M. Perényi (vc) Hungaroton ▲ HCD 31140 [DDD]
Bartók, B.:Romanian Folk Dances Pno Denon ▲ 7813 [DDD]
Bartók, B.:Rondos (3) on Folk Tunes Denon ▲ 7813 [DDD]
Bartók, B.:Son Pno Denon ▲ 7813 [DDD]
Bartók, B.:Son for 2 Pnos, w. Ránki (pno), Cser (perc), Rácz (perc) *(rec 9/11/81)* Hungaroton ▲ HCD 12400
Bartók, B.:Suite Pno Denon ▲ 7813 [DDD]
Beethoven, L. van:Qt Pno, Op. 16, w. Keller String Quartet members Musique d'Abord Δ HMA 1903020
Beethoven, L. van:Qnt Pno, Ob, Cl, Hn & Bn, w. Budapest Wind Ensemble Musique d'Abord Δ HMA 1903020
Brahms, J.:Vars on a Theme by Haydn, w. D. Ránki (pno)—Op. 56b Hungaroton ▲ HCD 11646
Cage, J.:Amores, w. Amadinda Percussion Group Hungaroton ▲ HCD 12991 [DDD]
Debussy, C.:Arabesques (2) Philips ▲ 422404-2 [DDD]
Debussy, C.:Berceuse héroïque Philips ▲ 422404-2 [DDD]
Debussy, C.:Estampes Philips ▲ 412118-2 [DDD]
Debussy, C.:Images (6) Pno Philips ▲ 422404-2 [DDD]
Debussy, C.:L'Isle joyeuse Philips ▲ 422404-2 [DDD]
Debussy, C.:Petite suite, w. M. Perényi (vc)—performers' arrangement for cello & piano Hungaroton ▲ HCD 31140 [DDD]
Debussy, C.:Pour le piano Philips ▲ 412118-2 [DDD]
Debussy, C.:Son Vc, w. M. Perényi (vc) Hungaroton ▲ HCD 31140 [DDD]
Debussy, C.:Suite bergamasque Philips ▲ 412118-2 [DDD]
Fauré, G.:Elégie, w. M. Perényi (vc) Hungaroton ▲ HCD 31140 [DDD]
Haydn, J.:Capriccio on *Acht Sauschneider müssen sein* *(rec Dec 18, 1974)* Hungaroton 2-▲ HCD 11618-19 [ADD]
Haydn, J.:Sons Pno—Nos. 20, 28-33 Hungaroton 2-▲ HCD 11618-19 [ADD]
Haydn, J.:Vars Hpd *(rec Jan 30, 1975)* Hungaroton 2-▲ HCD 11618-19 [ADD]
Kodály, Z.:Chorale Preludes, w. M. Perényi (vc) Hungaroton ▲ HCD 31140 [DDD]
Kodály, Z.:Sonatina Vc & Pno, w. M. Perényi (vc) Hungaroton ▲ HCD 31140 [DDD]
Mozart, W.A.:Qnt Pno, K.452, w. Budapest Wind Ensemble Musique d'Abord Δ HMA 1903020
Mozart, W.A.:Sons Pno 4-Hands, w. D. Ránki (pno) Hungaroton 2-▲ HCD 11794/95
Mozart, W.A.:Son Pnos, K.448, w. D. Ránki (pno) Hungaroton ▲ HCD 11646
Rachmaninoff, S.:Con 1 Pno, w. E. de Waart (cnd), San Francisco SO Philips ▲ 412881-2 [DDD]
Rachmaninoff, S.:Con 2 Pno, w. E. de Waart (cnd), San Francisco SO Philips ▲ 412881-2 [DDD]
Ravel, M.:Ma mère l'oye Pno, w. D. Ránki (pno) Hungaroton ▲ HCD 11646
Schoenberg, A.:Chamber Sym 1, w. Adrienne Hauser (pno), *(pno 4-hands)* Musique d'Abord ▲ HMA 1903021
Schubert, Franz:Qnt Pno, D.667, w. Takács String Quartet Hungaroton 2-▲ HCD 12918/19
Koczalski, Raoul (pno)
Chopin, F.:Pno Music (misc)—Ballade No. 4 in f, Op. 52; Trois Ecossaises, Op. 72; Seven Études, Op. 10/5,10 & 12 & Op. 25/2,5,6 & 11; Trois nouvelle etudes; Fantaisie-impromptu, Op. 66; Grande valse brillante in E♭, Op. 18; Mazurka in F, Op. 68/3; Nocturne in E♭, Op. 9/2; Polonaise in A♭, Op. 53; Preludes Nos. 24 & 26; Scherzo No. 2 in b♭, Op. 31; Waltz in a, Op. 34/2 Pearl ▲ PEA 9472 (m) [AAD]
Kodama, Mari (pno)
Prokofiev, S.:Con 1 Pno, w. K. Nagano (cnd), Philharmonia Orch ASV ▲ ASV 786
Prokofiev, S.:Con 3 Pno, w. K. Nagano (cnd), Philharmonia Orch ASV ▲ ASV 786
Prokofiev, S.:Son 7 Pno ASV ▲ ASV 786
Kodinsky, Tanya (pno/org)
Angels Are Everywherel, w. [cnd:Marie Stultz], Treble Chorus of New England, Richard Stultz (pno) AFKA ▲ SK 539
Kodousek, Josef (va)
Dvořák, A.:Qts Pno Strs, Opp. 23 & 87, w. J. Hála (pno), Suk (vn), J. Chuchro (vc)—Op. 23 & Op. 87 Supraphon ▲ 11 1464-2 [DDD]
Koeckert, R. J. (vn)—see ORCHESTRAS & ENSEMBLES Koeckert String Quartet
Koehlen, Benedict (pno)
Hartmann, K.A.:Son Pno Col legno ▲ AU 31806
Hartmann, K.A.:Son:27 April 1945 Col Legno ▲ AU 31807 [DDD]
Janácek, L.:Son October 1, 1905 Pno Col Legno ▲ AU 31807 [DDD]
Janácek, L.:Son October 1, 1905 Pno Col legno ▲ AU 31806

INSTRUMENT.

Koella, Ulrich (pno)
French Music for Clarinet, w. Thomas Friedli (cl) Claves ▲ 9322 [DDD]
Kreisler, F.:Music of, w. R. Koelman (vn)—Kleiner Wiener Marsch; Tambourin Chinois; Rondino; Poupée valsante; Praeludium und Allegro im Stile von Gaetano Pugnani; Polichinelle; Liebesfreud; Liebslied; Schön Rosmarin; Caprice Viennois; Danse Espagnole; Chant Hindou; Menuet im Stile von Niccolo Popora; Marsch der Spielsoldaten; Syncopation; Tango Ars Produktion ▲ FCD 368317 [DDD]
Rossini, G.:Petite messe solennelle, w. M. Musacchio (sop), C. Bandera (alt), G. Dominguez (ten), J. Mannov (bass), N. Clayton (pno), F. Näf (cnd), *(chorus unknown)* Ars Musici ▲ AM 1091 [DDD]
Schubert, Franz:Songs (misc), w. C. Homberger (ten) Claves ▲ CD 9406

Koelman, Rudolf (vn)
Brahms, J.:Sons Vn (comp), w. A. Oomen (pno) Ars Produktion ▲ ARS 368320 [DDD]
Kreisler, F.:Music of, w. U. Koella (pno)—Kleiner Wiener Marsch; Tambourin Chinois; Rondino; Poupée valsante; Praeludium und Allegro im Stile von Gaetano Pugnani; Polichinelle; Liebesfreud; Liebslied; Schön Rosmarin; Caprice Viennois; Danse Espagnole; Chant Hindou; Menuet im Stile von Niccolo Popora; Marsch der Spielsoldaten; Syncopation; Tango Ars Produktion ▲ FCD 368317 [DDD]

Koelmans, K. (vn)—see ORCHESTRAS & ENSEMBLES Senario Ensemble

Koen, John (vc)
Maggio, R.:Barcarole, w. Scott St. John (vn), Hugh Sung (pno), Don Liuzzi (perc), J. Higdon (cnd) *(rec Settlement Music School, Germantown, PA, June 17, 1995)* CRI ▲ CD 720 [DDD]
Maggio, R.:Winter Toccata, "I Can't Believe You Want to Die" *(rec Settlement Music School, Germantown, PA, May 22, 1995)* CRI ▲ CD 720 [DDD]

Koenig, Carole (ham dlc)
After Shadows:Classics for Quiet Moods Carole Koenig Music ▲ CCD 1007 [ADD] ■ CC 1007 (CrO2)
Encore!:Rennaisance & Baroque Music on the Hammered Dulcimer Carole Koenig Music ▲ CCD 1006 [ADD] ■ CC 1006 (CrO2)
Gala:Classics from a Romantic Era Carole Koenig Music ▲ CCD 1008 [ADD] ■ CC 1008 (CrO2)
Palace Act:Baroque Music on the Hammered Dulcimer Carole Koenig Music ▲ CCD 1003 [ADD] ■ CC 1003 (CrO2)
Past Times Present:Medieval & Renaissance Music on the Hammered Dulcimer Carole Koenig Music ▲ CCD 1004 [ADD] ■ CC 1004 (CrO2)
Season's Greetings Carole Koenig Music ▲ CCD 1005 [ADD] ■ CC 1005 (CrO2)

Koenig, Robert (pno)
Gershwin, G.:Songs, w. David Chan (vn)—Summertime; A Woman Is a Sometime Thing [arr vn & pno] *(rec Joan & Irving Harris Concert Hall, Aspen, CO, May 1995)* Ambassador ▲ ARC 1017 [DDD]
Paganini, N.:Con 2 Vn, w. David Chan (vn)—3rd movt [arr for vn & pno] *(rec Joan & Irving Harris Concert Hall, Aspen, CO, May 1995)* Ambassador ▲ ARC 1017 [DDD]
Saint-Saëns, C.:Son 1 Vn, w. David Chan (vn) *(rec Joan & Irving Harris Concert Hall, Aspen, CO, May 1995)* Ambassador ▲ ARC 1017 [DDD]
Tartini, G.:Son Vn "Devil's Trill", w. David Chan (vn) *(rec Joan & Irving Harris Concert Hall, Aspen, CO, May 1995)* Ambassador ▲ ARC 1017 [DDD]
Tchaikovsky, P.:Mélodie, w. David Chan (vn) [tran for vn & pno] *(rec Joan & Irving Harris Concert Hall, Aspen, CO, May 1995)* Ambassador ▲ ARC 1017 [DDD]
Tchaikovsky, P.:Valse-Scherzo Vn, w. David Chan (vn) *(rec Joan & Irving Harris Concert Hall, Aspen, CO, May 1995)* Ambassador ▲ ARC 1017 [DDD]

Koerper, J.-G. (sax)
Moser, R.:Wal, w. I. Roth (sax), B. Beaufreton (sax), M. Weiss (sax), P. Egholm (sax), M. Venzago (cnd), Basel SO Grammont ▲ CTSP 12-2 [ADD]

Koestenbaum, Joshua (vc)
Corelli, A.:Concerti grossi, Op. 6, w. L. Shank (vn), R. Tecco (vn), C. Hogwood (cnd), St. Paul CO—No. 2 *(rec May 1992)* London ▲ 440376-2
Holst, G.:A Fugal Con, w. J. Bogorad (vn), K. Greenbank (vn), R. Tecco (vn), L. Shank (vn), C. Hogwood (cnd), St. Paul CO *(rec May 1992)* London ▲ 440376-2
Holst, G.:Savitri, w. R. Tecco (vn), L. Shank (vn), C. Hogwood (cnd), St. Paul CO *(rec May 1992)* London ▲ 440376-2
Tippett, M.:Fant Concertante on a Theme of Corelli, w. R. Tecco (vn), L. Shank (vn), C. Hogwood (cnd), St. Paul CO *(rec May 1992)* London ▲ 440376-2

Kofler, Michael Martin (fl)
Bloch, E.:Concertino, w. H. Nicolai (va), A. Duczmal (cnd), Amadeus CO *(rec 1990)* CPO ▲ CPO 999096-2 [DDD]

Kogan, Leonid (vn)
Bach, J.S.:Sons Vn, w. Vladimir Yampolsky (pno)—in b, BWV 1014 Multisonic ▲ MUL 310354
Beethoven, L van:Trio 6 Pno, "Archduke", w. E. Gilels (pno), M. Rostropovich (vc) Monitor ■ 55010
Brahms, J.:Sons Vn (comp), w. Andrei Mytnik (pno) Arlecchino ▲ ARL11
Brahms, J.:Son 1 Vn, w. Andrei Mytnik (pno) *(rec 1953-63)* Arlecchino ARL
Brahms, J.:Son 2 Vn, w. Andrei Mytnik (pno) *(rec 1953-63)* Arlecchino ARL
Bruch, M.:Con 1 Vn, w. L. Maazel (cnd), Rome RAI SO *(rec 1969)* Arlecchino ARL
Khachaturian, A.:Con Vn, w. A. Khachaturian (cnd), *(orch unknown)* Prelude ▲ PRE 2158 [ADD]
Khachaturian, A.:Gayane (sels), w. Naum Walter Mylnik (pno)—Sabre Dance [trans. for violin & piano] Russian Disc ▲ RUS 11063 [AAD]
Khachaturian, A.:Son Vn, w. Karen Khachaturian (pno) Multisonic ▲ MUL 310354
Khachaturian, A.:Son Vn, w. Nina Kogan (pno) Prelude ▲ PRE 2158 [ADD]
Khachaturian, A.:Song-Poem, w. Naum Walter Mylnik (pno) Russian Disc ▲ RUS 11063 [AAD]
Khrennikov, T.:Con 1 Vn, w. E. Svetlanov (cnd), USSR State Academy Orch Allegretto ▲ ACD 8179 [ADD] ■ ACS 8179
Mendelssohn, F.:Con Vn, Op. 64, w. L. Maazel (cnd), Rome RAI SO *(rec 1969)* Arlecchino ARL
Rachmaninoff, S.:Trio élégiaque 2, w. Evgeni Svetlanov (pno), Fedor Luzanov (vc) Russian Disc ▲ RUS 10046 [AAD]
Shostakovich, D.:Con 1 Vn, w. K. Kondrashin (cnd), Moscow PO *(rec 1962)* Russian Disc ▲ RUS 11025 [AAD]
Shostakovich, D.:Con 1 Vn, w. K. Kondrashin (cnd), Moscow PO Supraphon ▲ SUP 3005
Shostakovich, D.:Preludes Pno, Op. 34, w. D. Shostakovich (pno) [arr. w. violin]—sels. *(rec 1956)* Multisonic ("Russian Treasures" series) ▲ 31 0179
Strauss, R.:Son Vn, w. Andrei Mytnik (pno) *(rec 1953-63)* Arlecchino ARL
Telemann, G.P.:Canonic Sons, w. Elisabeth Gilels (vn)—in G *(rec Salle Wagram, Paris, May 1962)* EMI Classics ▲ CDK 65340 [ADD]
To Leonid Kogan's Memory, w. three students of Kogan MCA Classics ▲ MLD 32131 [AAD]

Kogan, Nina (pno)
Khachaturian, A.:Son Vn, w. Leonid Kogan (vn) Prelude ▲ PRE 2158 [ADD]

Kogan, Oleg (hp)
Concert de musique liturgique Juive à la synagogue de Lausanne, w. Lausanne Israeli Community Male Chorus, Alain Blum, Antoine D., André Stora, Gueorgui Popov, Jean Akiba, J. Rubin (lt), Christine Fleischmann (hp) Doron ▲ DRC 3003 [DDD]

Kogan, Oleg (vc)
Haydn, J.:Songs, w. Mhairi Lawson (sop), Rachel Podger (vn), Olga Tverskaya (pno) Opus 111 ▲ OPS 30-121

Kogosowski, Alan (pno)
Chopin, F.:Mazurkas—Opp. 7/3, 24/1, 30/2 & 4, 33/2 & 4, 67/2, 68/2 *(rec 4/4/91)* Music From Sotheby's ▲ MFS1 [DDD]
Rachmaninoff, S.:Trio élégiaque 2, w. N. Järvi (cnd), Detroit SO [orchd. A. Kogosowski] Chandos ▲ CHAN 9261 [DDD]
Rachmaninoff, S.:Variations on a Theme by Corelli, w. N. Järvi (cnd), Detroit SO Chandos ▲ CHAN 9261 [DDD]

Kohen, Robert (hpd)
Bach, J.S.:A Musical Offering, w. Barthold Kuijken (trns fl), Sigiswald Kuijken (vn), Wieland Kuijken (vl) *(rec Feb. 22-25, 1994)* Deutsche Harmonia Mundi ▲ 05472-77307-2 [DDD]

Köhler, B. (instr)
Zinsstag, G.:Wenn Zum Beispiel..., w. W. Bärtschi, A. Brunner, M. Burg, D. Dyk, R. Ericksson, M. Maassen, E. Nowak, H. Suter, W. A. Wohlgemuth [G] *(rec Aug. 27, 1976)* Grammont ▲ CTSP 36-2 [ADD]

Kohler, Christopher (hn)
Pokorny, F.X.:Con Hns, w. H. Baumann (hn), J. Schröder (cnd), Concerto Amsterdam Acanta ▲ 43278

Köhler, Johannes-Ernst (org)
Bach, J.S.:The Art of the Fugue Berlin Classics 2-▲ BER 9176
Bach, J.S.:Cons Org, BWV 592-597—Nos. 1-3 & 5 Berlin Classics 2-▲ BER 9176

Kohlhaussen, W. (vn)
Stamitz, A.:Con 8 Vn, w. W. Kohlhaussen (cnd), Fonte di Musica CO Ars Produktion ▲ FCD 368307

Köhn, Christian (pno)
Dvořák, A.:From the Bohemian Forest, w. Silke-Thora Matthies (pno) *(rec Sandhausen, Apr 1995)* Naxos ▲ 8.553137 [DDD]
Dvořák, A.:Legends, Op. 59, w. Silke-Thora Matthies (pno) *(rec Sandhausen, Apr 1995)* Naxos ▲ 8.553137 [DDD]
Dvořák, A.:Slavonic Dances (comp), w. Silke-Thora Matthies (pno) *(rec Sandhausen, Apr 1995)* Naxos ▲ 8.553138 [DDD]
Dvořák, A.:Slavonic Dances (comp), w. Silke-Thora Matthies (pno) *(rec Sandhausen, Apr 1995)* Naxos ▲ 8.553138 [DDD]
Klebe, G.:Glockentürme, w. Silke-Thora Matthies (pno) *(rec Cologne, Jan. 23-25, 1995)* Marco Polo ("WDR" series) ▲ 8.223712 [DDD]
Klebe, G.:Inventions *(rec Cologne, Jan. 23-25, 1995)* Marco Polo ("WDR" series) ▲ 8.223712 [DDD]
Klebe, G.:Klavierstücke für Sonja *(rec Cologne, Jan. 23-25, 1995)* Marco Polo ("WDR" series) ▲ 8.223712 [DDD]
Klebe, G.:Music of, w. Silke-Thora Matthies (pno), J. Jacobs (acc), Cologne Chamber Choir—Warum hat die sonne einen Aschenrand; Der Schrei; Glockentürme Academy ▲ ACA 8509
Klebe, G.:Nachklang for 2 Pnos, w. Silke-Thora Matthies (pno) *(rec Cologne, Jan. 23-25, 1995)* Marco Polo ("WDR" series) ▲ 8.223712 [DDD]
Klebe, G.:Son for 2 Pnos, w. Silke-Thora Matthies (pno) *(rec Cologne, Jan. 23-25, 1995)* Marco Polo ("WDR" series) ▲ 8.223712 [DDD]
Klebe, G.:Wiegenlieder für Christinchen *(rec Cologne, Jan. 23-25, 1995)* Marco Polo ("WDR" series) ▲ 8.223712 [DDD]
Mozart, W.A.:Sons Vn Pno (misc), w. Christian Hommel (ob)—K.10-15 [The London Sons] Ars Musici ▲ 1134 [DDD]

Kohn, Eugene (pno)
A Recital, w. Aprile Millo (sop) *(rec live, 9/14/86)* Legato Classics ▲ LCD 126-1 [AAD]

Kohnen, R. (org)—see ORCHESTRAS & ENSEMBLES Kuijken Consort

Kohnen, Robert (hpd)
Bach, C.P.E.:Trio Son Fl, H.567-71, w. B. Kuijken (fl), S. Kuijken (vn), W. Kuijken (vc)—No. 4 Accent ▲ 58019 [DDD]
Bach, J.S.:Son Fl, BWV 1038, w. B. Kuijken (fl), S. Kuijken (vn) Accent ▲ 58019 [DDD]
Boismortier, J.B. de:Sons, Op. 26, w. R. van der Meer (vc), D. Bond (bn)—Nos. 1, 2 & 3 Accent ▲ 58331 [DDD]
Boismortier, J.B. de:Suite VI & Hpd, w. B. Re (viol) *(rec 6/87)* Pierre Verany ▲ PV.788012 [DDD]
Corelli, A.:Sons Vn, Op. 5, w. S. Kuijken (vn), W. Kuijken (vc)—Nos. 1, 3, 6, 11 & 12 Accent ▲ 48433
Corrette, M.:Sons, w. R. van der Meer (vc), D. Bond (bn)—Sons. 1, 3 & 5 Accent ▲ 58331 [DDD]
Couperin, F.:Les Nations, w. M. Hantaï (fl), B. Kuijken (fl), F. Fernandez (vn), S. Kuijken (vn), W. Kuijken (bass vl) *(rec Mar. 1992)* Accent 2-▲ 9285/86 [DDD]
Couperin, F.:Nouveaux Concerts, "Les Goûts-réunis", w. W. Kuijken (vl), K. Uremura (vl)—Nos. 12 & 13 *(rec June 1992)* Accent ▲ 9288 D [DDD]
Couperin, F.:Pièces de clavecin (sels), w. Barthold Kuijken (trns fl) (Book 3:Ordes 13, 14 & 15, & Sixième Prélude) *(rec 'Vereenigde Doopsgezinde Kerk', Haarlem, Netherlands, Oct 1993)* Accent ▲ ACC 9399 [DDD]
Couperin, F.:Pièces de violes avec la bass chifrée, w. W. Kuijken (vl), K. Uremura (vl) *(rec June 1992)* Accent ▲ 9288 D [DDD]
Couperin, F.:Suite VI, w. B. Re (vl) *(rec 6/87)* Pierre Verany ▲ PV.788012 [DDD]
Devienne, F.:Trios Bn, Op. 24, w. D. Bond (bn), R. van der Meer (vc) *(rec Dec. 1992)* Accent ▲ 9290
Dollé, C.:Suite 2, w. S. Kuijken (va da gamba), W. Kuijken (va da gamba) Accent ▲ 67808
Forqueray, A.:Suite 3 Vl da Gambas, w. S. Kuijken (vn), W. Kuijken (bass vl) Accent ▲ 67808
French Flute Music of the 18th Century, w. Barthold Kuijken (trns fl), Wieland Kuijken (vl) Accent ▲ 67909
Gabrielli, D.:Vc Music, w. Roel Dieltiens (vc), Richte van der Meer (vc), Konrad Junghänel (thb)—music by Bononcini *(Son in a for 2 Vcs)*, Willem De Fesch *(Son in a for Vc & Cont, Op. 13/6)*, D. Gabrieli *(Sons (2) in A & G for Vc & Cont; Ricercare I-VII; Canon for 2 Vcs)* Accent ▲ 9070 [DDD]
Geminiani, F.:Sons Vc & Continuo, Op. 5, w. R. Dieltiens (vc), R. van der Meer (vc)—Sonata in d; Sonata No. 3 in C; Sonata No. 6 in a Accent ▲ 9181 [DDD]
Handel, G.F.:Sons Fl, w. Berthold Kuijken (trns fl), Wieland Kuijken (b vl)—Op. 1, Nos.1, 5 & 9 Accent ▲ 9180 [DDD]
Handel, G.F.:Sons Fl, "Halle Sons", w. Berthold Kuijken (trns fl), Wieland Kuijken (b vl) Accent ▲ 9180 [DDD]
Handel, G.F.:Son Fl, HWV 378, w. Berthold Kuijken (trns fl), Wieland Kuijken (b vl) Accent ▲ 9180 [DDD]
Handel, G.F.:Son Fl, HWV 379, w. Berthold Kuijken (trns fl), Wieland Kuijken (b-vl) Accent ▲ 9180 [DDD]
Italian Cello Music, w. Roel Dieltiens (vc), Richte van der Meer (vc), K. Junghänel (thb) Accent ▲ 9070 [DDD]
Italian Flute Sonatas, w. Barthold Kuijken (trns fl), Wieland Kuijken (vc) *(rec 6/91)* Accent ▲ 9177
Marais, M.:Pièces de viole [Book 5], w. W. Kuijken (vl), K. Uemura (vl)—Suite in g; Chaconne in G; Dialogue; Le Jeu du Volant; Le Tableau de l'Operation de la Taille; Suite in a; La Poitevine Accent ▲ 78744 [DDD]
Marais, M.:Suites Vl & Hpd, w. B. Re (vl) *(rec 6/87)* Pierre Verany ▲ PV.788012 [DDD]
Music for a Viol, w. Wieland Kuijken (vl), Sigiswald Kuijken (vn) Accent ▲ 68014
Program 1, w. Arnold Dolmetsch (vir), Wieland Kuijken (vl) IMP Allegro ▲ PCD 989 [DDD]
Telemann, G.P.:Qt in G Fl, w. B. Kuijken (fl), S. Kuijken (vn), W. Kuijken (bass vl) Accent ▲ 58019 [DDD]
Telemann, G.P.:Sons Fl Continuo, w. Barthold Kuijken (fl), Wieland Kuijken (vl) Accent 2-▲ 94104/05
Telemann, G.P.:Sons Ob, w. P. Dombrecht (ob), W. Kuijken (vc)—Sonata in B♭ (from *Essercizii musici*); Sonata in g (from *Musique de table*); Suite in g (from *Getreue Music-Meister*); Partita II in G (from *Kleine Kammer-Music*) Accent ▲ 48013
Telemann, G.P.:Sonate metodiche, w. Barthold Kuijken (fl) Accent 2-▲ 94104/05
Telemann, G.P.:Suites Fl & Vn, w. B. Kuijken (fl), W. Kuijken (vc) Accent ▲ 58019 [DDD]
Vivaldi, A.:Sons Vc, w. R. Dieltiens (vc), A. Woodrow (db)—(3) in b♭ & g (from Op. 14); in e Accent ▲ 9181 [DDD]

Kohon, Harold (vn)—see ORCHESTRAS & ENSEMBLES Kohon String Quartet

Kohon, Isadora (vn)—see ORCHESTRAS & ENSEMBLES Kohon String Quartet

Koide, Shinya (fl)
Yashiro, A.:Son Fls, w. R. Noguchi (fl), F. Inoue (pno) Camerata ▲ 30CM 50

Koito, Kei (org)
Bach, J.S.:Canonic Vars on "Von Himmel hoch..." [the historic Schnitger Organ, Martinikerk,roningen, Netherlands] Harmonic ▲ HAR 8828 [DDD]
Bach, J.S.:Org Music (misc) [the historic Schnitger Organ, Martinikerk, Groningen, Netherlands]—Concerti BWV 525-530 Harmonic ▲ HAR 8828 [DDD]

Koito, Kei (org) (cont.)
Bach, J.S.:Trio Sons Org, BWV 525-530 [the historic Schnitger Organ, Martinikerk, Groningen, Netherlands] Harmonic ▲ HAR 8828 [DDD]

Koizumi, Hiroshi (fl)
Oe, H.:Fl & Pno Music, w. Akiko Ebi (pno)—Snow; June Lullaby; Merry Waltz; Siciliano in e; Adagio in d; Nocturne No. 2 *(rec Asahikawa City, Hokkaido, June 27, 29 & 30, 1994)* Denon ▲ CO 78953 [DDD]
Oe, H.:Fl & Pno Music, w. Akiko Ebi (pno)—A Favourite Waltz; Nocturne; Magic Flute; Sad Waltz; Pied Piper; Graduation (w. vars.) *(rec Nippon Columbia Studio 1, June 8 & 9, 1992)* Denon ▲ CO 78952 [DDD]

Koizumi, Takeshi (pic)
Takemitsu, T.:Music of, w. Tashi, Y. Nagano (mez), H. Ibe (gtr), M. Nagasako (hp), K. Abe (vib), Y. Takahashi (pno), R. Noguchi (fl), M. Hamada (lt), S. Ueki (vn), Y. Hattori (vc), R. Stoltzman (cl), P. Serkin (pno), Ozawa, Wakasugi (cnd), Boston SO—Quatrain; Stanza I; Sacrifice; Ring; Valeria; A Flock Descends into the Pentagonal Garden Deutsche Grammophon ("20th Century Classics" series) ▲ 423253-2 [ADD]

Kojo, Kullervo (cl)
Crusell, B.H.:Intro, Theme & Vars on a Swedish Air, w. J.-P. Saraste (cnd), Finnish RSO Finlandia ▲ 4509-95873-2 [DDD]
Englund, S.E.:Con Cl, w. J.-P. Saraste (cnd), Finnish RSO Finlandia ▲ 4509-95873-2 [DDD]
Nielsen, C.:Con Cl, w. J.-P. Saraste (cnd), Finnish RSO Finlandia ▲ 4509-95873-2 [DDD]

Kok, Felix (vn)
Britten, H.:Young Apollo, w. P. Donohoe (pno), J. Ballard (vn), P. Cole (va), M. Kaznowski (vc), S. Rattle (cnd), City of Birmingham SO *(rec 4/82)* EMI Classics 2-▲ CDCB 54270 [DDD]

Koka, Sokol (vc)
Sarti, G.:Sons Fl, w. Claudio Ferrarini (fl), Christine Meyr (hpd) Stradivarius ▲ STV 33368 [DDD]

Kokinos, Nelly (pno)
World's Favorite Piano Victrola ▲ 09026-60936-2 ■ 09026-60936-4

Kokobu, Takashi (syn)
Yamash'Ta, S.:Sea & Sky, w. Sen Izumi (syn), Stomu Yamashta (syn/perc), Muse Orch Kuckuck ▲ CD 072 ■ MC 072

Kol, Bracha (rcr)
Baroque Favorites, w. A. Brodo (vc), D. Shemer (hpd) PWK Classics ▲ PWK 1138 [DDD]

Kolár, Jan (ob)
Garnier, F.-J.:Sym Concertante 1, w. C. Villevielle (ob), Talich CO Koch Schwann ▲ SCH 314752 [DDD]
Vivaldi, A.:Cons Ob, w. O. Vlček (cnd), Prague Virtuosi—Con. in F, RV.457 *(rec 1991)* Emergo ▲ EC 3981 [DDD]
Vivaldi, A.:Con Ob Bn, w. E. Polách (bn), O. Vlček (cnd), Prague Virtuosi *(rec 1991)* Emergo ▲ EC 3981 [DDD]
Vivaldi, A.:Cons for 2 Obs, w. R. Hrabé (ob), J. Hasenöhrl (tpt), F. Vlasák (tpt), O. Vlček (cnd), Prague Virtuosi—Con. in C, RV.559 *(rec 1991)* Emergo ▲ EC 3981 [DDD]

Kolbeinsson, Dadi (ob)—see ORCHESTRAS & ENSEMBLES Reykjavik Wind Quintet
Kolisch, R. (vc)—see ORCHESTRAS & ENSEMBLES Kolisch String Quartet
Koll, H. (va)—see ORCHESTRAS & ENSEMBLES Vienna Ring Ensemble
Koll, Reinhard (vn)—see ORCHESTRAS & ENSEMBLES Innsbruck Salon Quintet
Kolle, Bernard (bn)—see ORCHESTRAS & ENSEMBLES Sierra Winds

Kollegorskaya, I. (pno)
Balakirev, M.:Impromptu Vn, w. Igor Politkovsky (vn) *(rec 1957)* Russian Compact Disc ("Talents of Russia" series) ▲ RCD 16279 [ADD]
Rachmaninoff, S.:Romance Vn, w. Igor Politkovsky (vn) *(rec 1957)* Russian Compact Disc ("Talents of Russia" series) ▲ RCD 16279 [ADD]

Kollman-Sperger, Dietrich (org)
Bach, J.S.:Org Music (misc)—Prelude & Fugue, BWV 532; Fugue, BWV 577; Orgel-Büchlein, BWV 599; Herr Jesu Christ, dich zu uns wend, BWV 632; Vater unser im Himmelreich (2), BWV 636 & 737 Capriccio ▲ 10 506 [DDD]
Böhm, G.:Org Music—Partitas on "Jesu du bist allzu schöne" Capriccio ▲ 10 506 [DDD]
Brunckhorst, A.M.:Org Music—Prelude & Fugue in e Capriccio ▲ 10 506 [DDD]
Buxtehude, D.:Org Music (misc)—Prelude & Fugue in F, BuxWV 145; Magnificat BuxWV 203 Capriccio ▲ 10 506 [DDD]
Tunder, F.:Org Music—Canzona in G Capriccio ▲ 10 506 [DDD]

Kollontai, Michael (pno)
Balakirev, M.:Pno Music—Scherzo; Nocturne; Waltzes; In the Garden; Gondolier's Song; Fisherman's Song; Toccata Russian Season ▲ RUS 288110

Kollsch, R. (vn)
Berg, A.:Chamber Con, w. R. Sherman (pno), G. Schuller (cnd), New England Conservatory Ensemble GM ▲ GM 2033 CD

Kolly, Karl-Andreas (pno)—see also ORCHESTRAS & ENSEMBLES Novanta Trio
Glazunov, A.:Con 1 Pno, w. H. Griffiths (cnd), Slovak RSO Bratislava Pan Classics ▲ CD 510084 [DDD]
Glazunov, A.:Con 2 Pno, w. H. Griffiths (cnd), Slovak RSO Bratislava Pan Classics ▲ CD 510084 [DDD]
Mendelssohn, F.:Concert Pieces, w. Dimitri Ashkenazy (cl), Peter Furniss (bas hn) Pan ▲ 510 070 [DDD]
Mendelssohn, F.:Lieder ohne Worte Pno, w. Dimitri Ashkenazy (cl)—Opp. 19/1 & 4, 38/1 & 53/2 [arr. for cl & pno] Pan ▲ 510 070 [DDD]
Mendelssohn, F.:Sextet, w. Universal Ensemble Pan ▲ 510 070 [DDD]
Mendelssohn, F.:Son Cl, w. Dimitri Ashkenazy (cl) Pan ▲ 510 070 [DDD]
Mieg, P.:Double Con Pno, Vc, w. D. Riniker (vc), Southern Bohemian Chamber PO Budweis Jecklin ▲ JS 297-2 [ADD]
Mieg, P.:Son Vc, w. David Riniker (vc) *(rec 1993)* Jecklin ▲ JS 314-2 [DDD]
Schmidt, F.:Chaconne, w. H. Boeck (cnd), Vienna Youth Orch Pan Classics ▲ 510081 [DDD]
Schmidt, F.:Con Pno Left Hand, w. H. Boeck (cnd), Vienna Youth Orch Pan Classics ▲ 510081 [DDD]
Scriabin, A.:Con Pno, w. A. Jordan (cnd), Basel SO Pan Classics ▲ 510079 [DDD]
Scriabin, A.:Etudes Pno, Op. 42 Pan Classics ▲ 510079 [DDD]
Scriabin, A.:Preludes Pno, Op. 16 Pan Classics ▲ 510079 [DDD]
Scriabin, A.:Preludes Pno, Op. 74 Pan Classics ▲ 510079 [DDD]
Scriabin, A.:Son 4 Pno Pan Classics ▲ 510079 [DDD]
Scriabin, A.:Son 9 Pno Pan Classics ▲ 510079 [DDD]

Kolmós, Péter (vn)
Brahms, J.:Qt 1 Pno, w. C. Szabó (pno), G. Németh (va), K. Botvay (vc) *(rec 1972-74)* Hungaroton 2-▲ HCD 11597/98 [ADD]
Brahms, J.:Qt 2 Pno, w. I. Lantos (pno), G. Németh (va), K. Botvay (vc) *(rec 1972-74)* Hungaroton 2-▲ HCD 11597/98 [ADD]
Brahms, J.:Qt 3 Pno, w. S. Falvai (pno), G. Németh (va), K. Botvay (vc) *(rec 1972-74)* Hungaroton 2-▲ HCD 11597/98 [ADD]

Kolmstetter, Michael (gtr)
Celebrating Christmas on Guitar *(rec Blue House Productions, Baltimore, MD)* Musik Designs ▲ MD 501

Kolodenko, Anton (va)
Delibes, L.:Coppélia (sels), w. V. Vassiliev (vn), K. Nagano (cnd), Lyon Opera Orch Erato 2-▲ 91730-2

Kolosov, Leonid (db)
Ustvolskaya, G.:Composition 2, w. Igo Propischin (db), Vitalii Goryachev (db), Vladimir Vulih (db), Vyacheslav Kovalenko (db), Alexei Peresipkin (db), Dmitrii Sokolov (db), Vladimir Nefedov (db), Valerii Javnertchik (perc), Galina Sandovskaya (pno), O. Malov (cnd) *(rec St. Petersburg Radio House, Jan. 1994)* Megadisc ▲ 7867

Koman, Hollace C. (org)
Respighi, O.:Suite Org, w. D. Barra (cnd), San Diego CO Koch International Classics ▲ KIC 7215 [DDD]

Komen, Paul (pno)
Beethoven, L. van:Son 16 Pno *(rec Utrecht, Feb 1995)* Globe ▲ GLO 5136 [DDD]
Beethoven, L. van:Son 17 Pno, "Tempest" *(rec Utrecht, Feb 1995)* Globe ▲ GLO 5136 [DDD]

Komen, Paul (pno) (cont.)
Beethoven, L. van:Son 18 Pno *(rec Utrecht, Feb 1995)* Globe ▲ GLO 5136 [DDD]
Beethoven, L. van:Son 31 Pno *(rec June 1993)* Globe ▲ GLO 5106 [DDD]
Beethoven, L. van:Son 32 Pno *(rec June 1993)* Globe ▲ GLO 5106 [DDD]
Brahms, J.:Sons Vc (comp), w. P. Wispelwey (vc) *(rec Sept. 1992)* Channel Classics ▲ CCS 5493 [DDD]
Mompou, F.:Pno Music (misc)—Suburbis (1916-17); Cants màgics (1917-19); Pessebres (1914-17); Paisajes (1942-51); Four Preludes (1928); Six Preludes (1943-51); Impresiones Intimas (1911-14) Globe 2-▲ GLO 6004 [DDD]
Scriabin, A.:Preludes Pno (misc)—Prelude in B, Op. 2, No. 2; Prelude in c#, Op. 9, No. 1; Twenty-Four Preludes, Op. 11; Six Preludes, Op. 13; Five Preludes, Op. 15; Five Preludes, Op. 16 Globe ▲ GLO 5088 [DDD]
Scriabin, A.:Preludes Pno (misc)—7 Preludes, Op. 17; 4 Preludes, Op. 22; 2 Preludes, Op. 27; 4 Preludes, Op. 31; 4 Preludes Op. 33; 3 Preludes, Op. 35; 4 Preludes Op. 37; 4 Preludes, Op. 39; 4 Preludes, Op. 48; 2 Preludes, Op. 67; 5 Preludes, Op. 74 *(rec March 1993)* Globe ▲ GLO 5098 [DDD]
Styles, w. Wispelwey, Pieter (vc), Lois Shapiro (pno), Florilegium Channel Classics ▲ CCS 395

Komer, C. (hn)—see ORCHESTRAS & ENSEMBLES Aspen Wind Quintet

Komischke, Uwe (tpt)
Concerts for Corno da caccia & Strings, w. Elmar Schloter (cnd) Koch Schwann ▲ SCH 312732 [DDD]
Trumpet & Organ Music from the Altenberg Cathedral, w. Thorsten Pech (org) Koch Schwann ▲ SCH 313902 [DDD]

Komlós, P. (vn)—see ORCHESTRAS & ENSEMBLES Bartók String Quartet

Komma, Karl Michael (pno)
Komma, K.M.:Con 1 Pno, w. D. Agrafiotis (cnd), Württemberg PO Bayer ▲ 800880
Komma, K.M.:Con 2 Pno, w. S. Friedmann (cnd), Württemberg PO Bayer ▲ 800880

Kommerell, Heidi (pno)
Kinkel, J.:Songs, w. Claudia Taha (sop)—Wunsch, Op. 7/2; An den Mond, Op. 7/5; Die Zigeuner, Op. 7/6; Verlornes Glück, Op. 6/3; Vorüberfahrt, Op. 7/3; Nachtlied, Op. 7/6 Bayer ▲ 100248 [DDD]
Lang, J.:Songs, w. Claudia Taha (sop)—14 sels including Erinnerung; Den Abschied schnell genommen, Op. 15/1; An de See, Op. 14/4; Am Flusse, Op. 14/2; Frühzeitiger Frühling, Op. 6/3; In weite Ferne, Op. 15/3; Auf dem See in tausend Sterne, Op. 14/6 Bayer ▲ 100248 [DDD]

Komodore, Alex (gtr)
Passport:International Guitar Music Poco A Poco ▲ PSP1002 [DDD]

Komuro, M. (db)
Shinohara, M.:Tabiyuki, w. A. Ogawa (mez), M. Kakagawa (fl), I. Tsuji (ob), T. Takahashi (cl), K. Okazaki (fagotto), G. Kitamura (tpt), A. Murata (trbn), S. Eiso (perc), S. Ueki (vn), A. Nakakoji (va), S. Katsuta (vc), K. Komatsu (cnd) *(rec live Casals Hall, Tokyo, Mar. 5, 1994)* Camerata ▲ 30CM 375 [DDD]

Koncer, Gabriel (cl)
Respighi, O.:Liriche su parole di poeti armeni, w. Denisa Šlepkovská (mez), Vladimír Havran (fl), Michal Sintál (ob), Ivan Viskup (b cl), Ivan Paulicka (bn), Frantisek Kovács (trbn), Katarína Vavreková (hp), M. Adriano (cnd) [arr. for chamber group by Adriano] *(rec Slovak Radio Concert Hall, Bratislava, Jan. 4-9, Feb. 19 & June)* Marco Polo ▲ 8.223595 [DDD]

Kondonassis, Yolanda (hp)
Bach, J.S.:Arioso Ob *(rec Cleveland, June 13-16, 1994)* Telarc ▲ CD 80403 [DDD]
Bach, J.S.:Jesu bleibet meine Freude *(rec Cleveland, June 13-16, 1994)* Telarc ▲ CD 80403 [DDD]
Bach, J.S.:Suite Lt, BWV 996 *(rec Cleveland, June 13-16, 1994)* Telarc ▲ CD 80403 [DDD]
Bach, J.S.:Das wohltemperierte Klavier—Prelude No. 1 in C; Prelude No. 17 in A♭ *(rec Cleveland, June 13-16, 1994)* Telarc ▲ CD 80403 [DDD]
Debussy, C.:Arabesques (2)—No. 1 [arr. by Kondonassis] *(rec Nov. 23-25, 1992)* Telarc ▲ CD 80361 [DDD]
Debussy, C.:Clair de lune *(rec Mechanics Hall, Worcester, MA; Oct 2-5, 1995)* Telarc ▲ CD-80418 [DDD]
Debussy, C.:Danses sacrée et profane, w. F. Cohen (cl), M. Chalifour (vn), W.-F. Gu (va), S. Konopka (va), R. Weiss (vc), T. Sperl (db), J. Smith (instr) *(rec Nov. 23-25, 1992)* Telarc ▲ CD 80361 [DDD]
Debussy, C.:La Fille aux cheveaux de lin Pno [arr. by Kondonassis] *(rec Nov. 23-25, 1992)* Telarc ▲ CD 80361 [DDD]
Debussy, C.:Preludes Pno (sels) [arr. Kondonassis]—Book 2:Bruyéres *(rec Nov. 23-25, 1992)* Telarc ▲ CD 80361 [DDD]
Fauré, G.:Impromptu Hp *(rec Mechanics Hall, Worcester, MA; Oct 2-5, 1995)* Telarc ▲ CD-80418 [DDD]
Gershwin, G.:Preludes (3) Pno [arr. Kondonassis]—No. 2 *(rec Nov. 23-25, 1992)* Telarc ▲ CD 80361 [DDD]
Grandjany, M.:Fant Hp *(rec Nov. 23-25, 1992)* Telarc ▲ CD 80361 [DDD]
Handel, G.F.:Suites Hpd—Passacaille [from No. 7]; Sarabande [from No. 4] *(rec Cleveland, June 13-16, 1994)* Telarc ▲ CD 80403 [DDD]
Hovhaness, A.:Nocturne Hp—No. 1 *(rec Mechanics Hall, Worcester, MA; Oct 2-5, 1995)* Telarc ▲ CD-80418 [DDD]
Hovhaness, A.:Suite Hp *(rec Mechanics Hall, Worcester, MA; Oct 2-5, 1995)* Telarc ▲ CD-80418 [DDD]
Pachelbel, J.:Canon *(rec Cleveland, June 13-16, 1994)* Telarc ▲ CD 80403 [DDD]
Ravel, M.:Intro & Allegro, w. J. Smith (fl), F. Cohen (cl), M. Chalifour (vn), W.-F. Gu (va), S. Konopka (va), R. Weiss (vc), T. Sperl (db) *(rec Nov. 23-25, 1992)* Telarc ▲ CD 80361 [DDD]
Ravel, M.:Pavane pour une infante défunte, w. J. Smith (fl), F. Cohen (cl), M. Chalifour (vn), W.-F. Gu (va), S. Konopka (va), R. Weiss (vc), T. Sperl (db) [arr. by Kondonassis] *(rec Nov. 23-25, 1992)* Telarc ▲ CD 80361 [DDD]
Rorem, N.:Sky Music *(rec Mechanics Hall, Worcester, MA; Oct 2-5, 1995)* Telarc ▲ CD 80418 [DDD]
Salzedo, C.:Chansons dans la nuit *(rec Mechanics Hall, Worcester, MA; Oct 2-5, 1995)* Telarc ▲ CD-80418 [DDD]
Salzedo, C.:Scintillation *(rec Nov. 23-25, 1992)* Telarc ▲ CD 80361 [DDD]
Scarlatti, D.:Sons Kbd—in b, K.27; in A, K.208 *(rec Cleveland, June 13-16, 1994)* Telarc ▲ CD 80403 [DDD]
Telemann, G.P.:Fants pour clavecin (sels)—No. 2 in D *(rec Cleveland, June 13-16, 1994)* Telarc ▲ CD 80403 [DDD]

Kondratieva, Olga (pno)
Prokofiev, S.:Son 2 Vn, w. Yulia Krasko (vn) *(rec Moscow, July 1995)* Russian Disc ▲ RD CD 10006 [DDD]
Stravinsky, I.:Duo Concertant, w. Yulia Krasko (vn) *(rec Moscow, July 1995)* Russian Disc ▲ RD CD 10006 [DDD]

Kondratyeva, L. (pno)
Donizetti, G.:Music for Pno 4-Hands, w. R. Schmiedel (pno) CPO 2-▲ CPO 999163 [DDD]

Kong, Xiang-Dong (pno)
Grainger, P.:Paraphrase on Tchaikovsky's "Waltz of the Flowers" *(rec 1992)* Arcadia ▲ ARC 1999-2 [DDD]
Grainger, P.:Pno Music (arrs, transcriptions & paraphrases)—Paraphrase on Tchaikovsky's Flower Waltz *(rec Dec. 9-11, 1992)* Arcadia ▲ Arc 1999 [DDD]
Liszt, F.:Rhap espagnole *(rec 1992)* Arcadia ▲ ARC 1999-2 [DDD]
Muczynski, R.:Son 2 Pno *(rec 1992)* Arcadia ▲ ARC 1999-2 [DDD]
Rachmaninoff, S.:Son 2 Pno [1913 version] *(rec 1992)* Arcadia ▲ ARC 1999-2 [DDD]
Tchaikovsky, P.:Dumka:Russian Rustic Scene RCA Red Seal ▲ 09026-62520-2
Tchaikovsky, P.:Morceaux, Op. 72—No. 5 Méditation in D RCA Red Seal ▲ 09026-62520-2
Tchaikovsky, P.:Romance, Op. 5 RCA Red Seal ▲ 09026-62520-2
Tchaikovsky, P.:Les Saisons—December:Christmas-tide RCA Gold Seal ▲ 09026-68149-2 [DDD]
Tchaikovsky, P.:Les Saisons RCA Red Seal ▲ 09026-62520-2
Tchaikovsky, P.:Valse-Scherzo Pno RCA Red Seal ▲ 09026-62520-2

INSTRUMENT.

König, Gustav (rcr)
Kaufmann, D.:Heiligenlegende, w. H. M. Kneihs (speaker), E. Ortner (cnd), Austrian RSO, Austrian Radio Chorus Vienna Modern Masters ▲ VMM 3020 [AAD]

König, Heinz (perc)
Bartók, B.:Son for 2 Pnos, w. Alfons Kontarsky (pno), Aloys Kontarsky (pno), C. Caskel (perc) Deutsche Grammophon ("20th Century Classics" series) ▲ 437027-2 [ADD]

Königstedt, Eckard (bn)
Hindemith, P.:Con Tpt, Bn & Strs, w. Ludwig Güttler (tpt), H. Kegel (cnd), Dresden PO Berlin Classics 2-▲ BER 9054
Mozart, W.A.:Sinf concertante Ob, K.Anh.9, w. Andreas Lorenz (ob), Sebastian Weigle (hn), Klaus Kirbach (hpd), H. Haenchen (cnd), C.P.E. Bach CO Berlin Classics ▲ BER 2004

Konopka, Stanley (va)
Debussy, C.:Danses sacrée et profane, w. Y. Kondonassis (hp), F. Cohen (cl), M. Chalifour (vn), W.-F. Gu (va), R. Weiss (vc), T. Sperl (db), J. Smith (instr) *(rec Nov. 23–25, 1992)* Telarc ▲ CD 80361 [DDD]
Ravel, M.:Intro & Allegro, w. Y. Kondonassis (hp), J. Smith (fl), F. Cohen (cl), M. Chalifour (vn), W.-F. Gu (va), R. Weiss (vc), T. Sperl (db) *(rec Nov. 23–25, 1992)* Telarc ▲ CD 80361 [DDD]
Ravel, M.:Pavane pour une infante défunte, w. Y. Kondonassis (hp), J. Smith (fl), F. Cohen (cl), M. Chalifour (vn), W.-F. Gu (va), R. Weiss (vc), T. Sperl (db) [arr. by Kondonassis] *(rec Nov. 23–25, 1992)* Telarc ▲ CD 80361 [DDD]

Konowalow, Georghi (vn)
Jazwinski, B.:Sequenze Concertanti, w. S. Kawalla (cnd), Koszalin State PO Vienna Modern Masters ▲ VMM 3024 [DDD]

Konrád, György (va)
Brahms, J.:Qnt 1 Strs, w. Bartók String Quartet *(rec 1971–74)* Hungaroton 3-▲ HCD 11591/93 [ADD]
Brahms, J.:Qnt 2 Strs, w. Bartók String Quartet *(rec 1971–74)* Hungaroton 3-▲ HCD 11591/93 [ADD]
Brahms, J.:Sextet Strs, Op. 36, w. E. Banda (vc), Bartók String Quartet *(rec 1971–74)* Hungaroton 3-▲ HCD 11591/93 [ADD]
Kodály, Z.:Serenade for 2 Vns & Va, w. Tátrai (vn), Várkonyi (vn) Hungaroton ▲ HCD 31046
Mozart, W.A.:Adagio & Rondo Glass Armonica, w. J. Jandó (cel), I. Kovács (fl), J. Kiss (ob), T. Koó (vc) *(rec Dec. 1–4, 1990)* Naxos ▲ 8.550511 [DDD]
Mozart, W.A.:Trio Cl, K.498, w. B. Kovács (cl), J. Jandó (pno) *(rec Sept. 16, 1991)* Naxos ▲ 8.550439 [DDD]

Konstantinidi, Aristotel (pno)
Beethoven, L. van:Songs, w. A. Martynov (ten)—Adelaide; Ich liebe dich; Neue Liebe, neues Leben; Wonne der Wehmut [G] *(rec 1991)* MK ▲ 417025 [DDD]
Mendelssohn, F.:Songs, w. A. Martynov (ten)—Auf Flügeln des Gesanges; Gruss; Der Mond; Nachtlied; Schlafloser Augen Leuchte; Venetianisches Gondellied [G] MK ▲ 417025 [DDD]
Schubert, Franz:Songs (misc), w. A. Martynov (ten)—Auf dem See; Auf dem Wasser zu singen; Im Frühling; Der Schiffer; Ständchen [G] MK ▲ 417025 [DDD]
Schumann, R.:Songs, w. A. Martynov (ten)—Aufträge; Er ist's; Geisternähe; Geständnis; Meine Rose; Schneeglöckchen [G] MK ▲ 417025 [DDD]
Strauss, R.:Songs, w. A. Martynov (ten)—Morgen; Die Nacht; Ständchen; Zueignung [G] MK ▲ 417025 [DDD]
Tchaikovsky, P.:Songs, w. A. Martynov (ten)—Absence; Ah! Si vous saviez; An dem schlummernden Strom; Attends!; Cradle Song During a Storm; Dawn of Spring; Don Juan's Serenade; In trüber Stund; Je voudrais mettre dans une seule parole; Nacht; New Hopes; No, Whom I Love I Will Not Name; La Nuit; O du mondhelle Nacht; L'Oublié; Le Rossignol; A Serenade; Le Soir et le matin; Sonne ging zur Ruhe; Summer Love Tale; The Tapers Were Flashing; La Tête blanche; Unsatisfied; Warum (Op. 6); Weil ich wie einstmals allein; What Matter!; Why? (Op. 28) [R] *(rec 1991)* MK ▲ 417054 [DDD]

Kontarsky, Alfons (pno)
Bartók, B.:Son for 2 Pnos, w. Alfons Kontarsky (pno), C. Caskel (perc), H. König (perc) Deutsche Grammophon ("20th Century Classics" series) ▲ 437027-2 [ADD]
Boulez, P.:Structures, w. Aloys Kontarsky (pno) Wergo ▲ WER 6011-2 [AAD]
Dünser, R.:Tage- und Nachtbucher, w. Martin Schelling (cl), Martin Mumelter (vn), Walter Nothas (vc) Koch Schwann ▲ SCH 311882
Messiaen, O.:Quatuor pour la fin du temps, w. Hans Deinzer (cl), Saschko Gawrilov (vn), Siegfried Palm (vc) EMI Classics 2-▲ CDCB 47463 [DDD]
Messiaen, O.:Quatuor pour la fin du temps, w. Martin Schelling (cl), Martin Mumelter (vn), Walter Nothas (vc) Koch Schwann ▲ SCH 311882
Norman, L.:Songs, w. C. H. Ahnsjö (ten)—Waldlieder (song cycle—1867); Ahasverus; Blomstring; Höst; Fran sol och stjärnor; Manestralar; Pagens visa; Själens frid; Stille Sicherheit; Ungt mod [G,Sw] Musica Sveciae ▲ MSCD 525 [DDD]
Reger, M.:Allegretto grazioso, w. A. Adorján (fl) Tudor ▲ TUD 755 [DDD]
Reger, M.:Romanze Vn, w. A. Chumachenco (vn) Tudor ▲ TUD 755 [DDD]
Reger, M.:Suite Vn Pno, w. A. Chumachenco (vn) Tudor ▲ TUD 755 [DDD]
Stravinsky, I.:Con Pnos Deutsche Grammophon ("20th Century Classics" series) ▲ 437027-2 [ADD]
Stravinsky, I.:Con Pnos *(rec Nov. 1962)* Wergo ▲ WER 6228-2 [AAD]
Stravinsky, I.:Easy Pieces Pno 4-Hands (3) *(rec Nov. 1962)* Wergo ▲ WER 6228-2 [AAD]
Stravinsky, I.:Son Pnos Deutsche Grammophon ("20th Century Classics" series) ▲ 437027-2
Stravinsky, I.:Son Pnos *(rec Nov. 1962)* Wergo ▲ WER 6228-2 [AAD]
Touma, H.H.:Tagsim Gallo ▲ CD 530 [AAD]
Yun, I.:Riul, w. E. Brunner (cl) Camerata ▲ 30CM 46

Kontautas, Adomas (lure)
Habbestad, K.:The Articles of Norwegian Christian Law, w. Ståle Bjørnhaug (nar), Zigmas Kazlauskas (lure), Rimantas Valanctus (lure), Marius Balcytis (lure) Norway Music ▲ 2912

Kontra, Anton (vn)—see also ORCHESTRAS & ENSEMBLES Kontra String Quartet
Gade, N.W.:Con Vn, w. P. Järvi (cnd), Malmö SO *(rec Malmö Concert Hall, Sweden, Aug. 23–25, 1994)* BIS ▲ CD 672 [DDD]

Koó, Tamás (vc)
Mozart, W.A.:Adagio & Rondo Glass Armonica, w. J. Jandó (cel), I. Kovács (fl), J. Kiss (ob), G. Konrád (va) *(rec Dec. 1–4, 1990)* Naxos ▲ 8.550511 [DDD]
Sinding, C.:Trios Pno, w. A. Kiss (vn), I. Prunyi (pno)—No. 1 in D, Op. 23 (1893) & No. 2 in a, Op. 64a (1902) Marco Polo ▲ 8.223283

Kooiker, Anthony (pno)
Debussy, C.:Rêverie Partridge ▲ 1116-2 [DDD]
Debussy, C.:Suite bergamasque Partridge ▲ 1116-2 [DDD]
Haydn, J.:Short Pieces (12) Hpd Partridge ▲ 1122-2 [DDD]
Haydn, J.:Sons Pno—6 Sonatas—H.XVI/Nos. 4 & 7-11 Partridge ▲ 1122-2 [DDD]
Mozart, W.A.:Sonatinas Pno Partridge ▲ 1121-2 [DDD]
Rachmaninoff, S.:Morceaux de fant Partridge ▲ 1116-2 [DDD]

Kooiman, Ewald (org)
Kellner, J.C.:Fant Org *(rec May 11–12, 1992)* FSM ▲ FCD 97709 [DDD]

Kooistra, Taco (vc)
Kolb, B.:Extremes, w. H. Starreveld (fl) New World ▲ 80422-2 [DDD]
Schulhoff, E.:Sxt Strs, w. J. E. van Regteren (va), Schoenberg String Quartet Koch Schwann ▲ SCH 312332 [DDD]

Koonce, Frank (gtr)
Castelnuovo-Tedesco, M.:Platero y yo, w. Don Doyle (nar) *(rec Scottsdale, AZ, 1995)* Summit ▲ SMT 1002 [DDD]

Kooper, Kees (vn)
Cordero, R.:Qnt Fl, w. John Wion (fl), Arthur Bloom (cl), Fred Sherry (vc), Mary Louise Boehm (pno) Albany ▲ TROY 153 [DDD]
Palmer, R.:Qnt Cl, w. A. Bloom (cl), P. Doktor (va), Fred Sherry (vc), Mary Louise Boehm (pno) Albany ▲ TROY 153
Rochberg, G.:Trio Pno, w. Mary Louise Boehm (pno), Fred Sherry (vc) Albany ▲ TROY 153

Koopman, Ewald (org)
Bach, J.S.:Cons Org, BWV 592-597—BWV 596 *(Organ of Duisburg Abbey Church, Hamborn) (rec May 11–12, 1992)* FSM ▲ FCD 97709 [DDD]
Grigny, N. de:Org Music—Veni creator; Pange lingua *(rec May 11–12, 1992)* FSM ▲ FCD 97709 [DDD]

Koopman, Ton (hpd)
Bach, J.S.:The Art of the Fugue, w. T. Mathot (hpd)—2 harpsichord version *(rec Amsterdam, Nov 1993)* Erato ▲ 96387-2 [DDD]
Bach, J.S.:French Suites Erato ▲ 94805
Bach, J.S.:Sons Vl, BWV 1027–1029, w. Jordi Savall (vl) Virgin Classics ▲ CDM 61291
Couperin, F.:Pièces de violes avec la bass chifrée, w. A. Maurette (vl), J. Savall (vl) Astrée ▲ E 7744 [AAD]
de Fesch, W.:Trio Sons, Op. 7, w. W. Hazelzet (transverse fl), M. Huggett (vn)—No. 4 in g Erasmus ▲ WVH 010 [ADD]
Focking, H. von:Sons Fl, w. W. Hazelzet (trns fl)—in D, Op. 1/5 Erasmus ▲ WVH 010 [ADD]
Forqueray, A.:Pièces de clavecin (5 suites) Erato ▲ 2292-45751-2 ZK
Geminiani, F.:Sons Vc & Continuo, Op. 5, w. H. Schiff (vc), J. ter Linden (b vl)—Sonata No. 6 in a Philips ▲ 434124-2 [DDD]
Hellendaal, P.:Solos Vn & Continuo, w. Monica Huggett (vn)—No. 3 in d Erasmus ▲ WVH 010 [ADD]
Marais, M.:Pièces de viole [Book 3] (sels), w. J. Savall (bass vl), H. Smith (thb) Astrée ▲ E 8761
Marais, M.:Pièces de viole [Book 4] (sels), w. J. Savall (bass vl), H. Smith (baroque gtr)—"Suitte d'un Gout Etranger:" comprising eleven pieces from Book 4 of Pièces de viole Astrée ▲ E 7727 [AAD]
Merula, T.:Arias & Capriccios, w. M. Figueras (sop), J.-P. Canihac (cnt), J. Savall (vl), R. Lislevand (thb), A. Laurence-King (hp), L. Duftschmid (vn) Astrée ▲ E 8503
Mozart, W.A.:Complete Mozart Edition, w. Ingrid Haebler (pno), Mitsuko Uchida (pno) Philips 5-▲ 422518-2 [ADD]
Vivaldi, A.:Sons Vc, w. H. Schiff (vc), J. ter Linden (b vl)—(4) in e, RV.40; in a, RV.43; in B♭, RV.45; in B♭, RV.46 Philips ▲ 434124-2 [DDD]

Koopman, Ton (hpd/chest org)
Handel, G.F.:Sons Rcr, w. Marion Verbruggen (rec/fl), Jaap ter Linden (vc)—No. 1 in B♭; No. 2 in g, Op. 1/2; No. 4 in a, Op. 1/4; No. 7 in C, Op. 1/7; No. 9 in d, Op. 1/9; No. 11 in F, Op. 1/11 *(rec Waalse Kerk, Amsterdam, Apr 27–29, 1994)* Harmonia Mundi France ▲ HMU 907151

Koopman, Ton (hpd/org)
Monteverdi, C.:Arie e Lamenti, w. M. Figueras (sop), A. Lawrence-King (hp), R. Lislevand (thb) Astrée ▲ E 8710
Ortiz, D.:Trattado de Glosas, w. J. Savall (vl), L. Duftschmid (vn), R. Lislevand (vih), P. Pandolfo (b vl), A. Lawrence-King (hp) Astrée ▲ E 8717 [DDD]

Koopman, Ton (org)
Bach, J.S.:Chorale Preludes Org—3 chorale preludes Novalis ▲ 150005 [DDD]
Bach, J.S.:Fant & Fugue Org, BWV 542 Novalis ▲ 150005 [DDD]
Bach, J.S.:Fant Org, BWV 572 *(rec Maassluis, Grote Kerk, June 1983)* Archiv ▲ 447292-2 [DDD]
Bach, J.S.:Org Music (misc)—Chorale Preludes, BWV 682, 688; Fantasia in G, BWV 572; Partite diverse sopra, BWV 768; Prelude & Fugue in a, BWV 543; Toccata & Fugue in d, "Dorian," BWV 538; Trio Sonata in G, BWV 530 Novalis ▲ 150036 [DDD]
Bach, J.S.:Org Music (misc)—Allabreve, BWV 589; Canzona, BWV 588; Preludium, BWV 569 *(rec Maassluis, Grote Kerk, June 1983)* Archiv ▲ 447292-2 [DDD]
Bach, J.S.:Org Music (misc)—Fantasia in c, BWV 562; Fugue in g, BWV 578; Passacaglia in c, BWV 582; Pastorale in F, BWV 590; Prelude & Fugue in G, BWV 541; Four Chorale Settings, BWV 655, 656, 730/31 & 740 Novalis ▲ 150052 [DDD]
Bach, J.S.:Org Music (misc)—4 Preludes & Fugues in d, BWV 527; in e, BWV 533; in C, BWV 547; in e, BWV 548 Novalis ▲ 150078 [DDD]
Bach, J.S.:Org Music (misc)—Nun freut euch, lieben Christen g'mein, BWV 734; Liebster Jesu, wir sind hier, BWV 731; Jesus, meine Zuversicht, BWV 728; Nun komm, der Heiden Heiland, BWV 659; Herr Jesu Christ, dich zu uns wend, BWV 709; Praeludium und Fuge D, BWV 532 *(rec May 11–12, 1992)* FSM ▲ FCD 97709 [DDD]
Bach, J.S.:Partite diverse sopra *O Gott, du frommer Gott* Novalis ▲ 150005 [DDD]
Bach, J.S.:Passacaglia & Fugue Org *(rec Maassluis, Grote Kerk, June 1983)* Archiv ▲ 447292-2 [DDD]
Bach, J.S.:Pastorale Org, BWV 590 *(rec Maassluis, Grote Kerk, June 1983)* Archiv ▲ 447292-2 [DDD]
Bach, J.S.:Preludes & Fugues, BWV 531–552—BWV 552 Novalis ▲ 150005 [DDD]
Bach, J.S.:Preludes & Fugues, BWV 531–552—Prelude & Fugue in D, BWV 532 Novalis ▲ 150066 [DDD]
Bach, J.S.:Preludes & Fugues, BWV 553–60, "8 Little Preludes & Fugues" Novalis ▲ 150066 [DDD]
Bach, J.S.:Toccata, Adagio & Fugue Org, BWV 564 Novalis ▲ 150066 [DDD]
Bach, J.S.:Toccata & Fugue Org, BWV 538, "Dorian" *(rec Maassluis, Grote Kerk, June 1983)* Archiv ▲ 447292-2 [DDD]
Bach, J.S.:Toccata & Fugue Org, BWV 565 *(rec Maassluis, Grote Kerk, June 1983)* Archiv ▲ 447292-2 [DDD]
Bach, J.S.:Toccata & Fugue Org, BWV 565 Novalis ▲ 150005 [DDD]
Bach, J.S.:Trio Sons Org, BWV 525–530—BWV 525 Novalis ▲ 150066 [DDD]
Buxtehude, D.:Org Music (misc)—Fugue in C, BuxWV.174; Passacaglia in d, BuxWV.161; Prelude in D, BuxWV.139; Prelude in g, BuxWV.149; Prelude in g, BuxWV.163; Prelude & Ciacona in C, BuxWV.137; 6 Chorale Preludes—Ein feste Burg ist unser Gott, BuxWV.184; In dulci jubilo, BuxWV.197; Nun komm, der Heiden Heiland, BuxWV.211; Nun lob, mein Seel, den Herren, BuxWV.212; Puer natus in Bethlehem, BuxWV.217; Wie schön leuchtet der Morgenstern, BuxWV.223 Novalis ▲ 150048 [DDD]
Charpentier, M.-A.:Messe pour le samedi de pâques, w. H. Hennig (cnd), Hanover Boys' Choir [L] Calig ▲ CAL 50874 [ADD]

Kootz, G. (pno)
Beethoven, L. van:Fant Pno, Op. 80, "Choral Fant", w. F. Konwitschny (cnd), Leipzig Gewandhaus Orch, Leipzig Radio Chorus Berlin Classics ▲ BER 2077 [ADD]

Kopecky, Milos (cl)
Mozart, W.A.:Sinf concertante Ob, K.Anh.9, w. Frantisek Hanták (ob), Miroslav Stefek (hn), Karel Vacek (bn), *(orch unknown)* Supraphon ▲ SUP 3053

Kopelman, Jozef (vn)
Vivaldi, A.:Cons Vn, Op. 3/1-12, "L'estro armonico", w. J. Kopelman (cnd), Capella Istropolitana—Nos. 1, 2, 4, 7, 8, 10 & 11 Naxos ▲ 8.550160 [DDD]

Kopelman, M. (vn)—see ORCHESTRAS & ENSEMBLES Borodin String Quartet

Kopp, David (pno)
Berger, A.:Duos, w. R. Rider (vc)—Duo for Cello & Piano (1951) CRI ▲ CD 564 [DDD]
Webern, A.:Little Pieces Vc, w. R. Rider (vc) CRI ▲ CD 564 [DDD]
Webern, A.:Pieces Vc, w. R. Rider (vc) CRI ▲ CD 564 [DDD]
Webern, A.:Son Vc, w. R. Rider (vc) CRI ▲ CD 564 [DDD]

Köpp, G. (hn)—see ORCHESTRAS & ENSEMBLES Berlin PO Horns

Koppel, Herman (pno)
Koppel, H.D.:Music of *(other artists unknown)*—Suite for Pno, Op. 21; Ternio for Vc & Pno, Op. 53b; Qt for Pno & Strs, Op. 114; Duo for Vn & Vc, Op. 117 Point ▲ PCD 5082

Kopperud, Jeanne (cl)—see also ORCHESTRAS & ENSEMBLES New York New Music Ensemble members
Wuorinen, C.:Tashi, w. C. Macomber (vn), F. Sherry (vc), J. Winn (pno) Koch International Classics ▲ KIC 7242-2 [DDD]

Körber, Till (pno)
Brahms, J.:Songs, w. Hans Michael Beuerle (cnd), Anton Webern Choir Freiburg—In stiller Nacht; Die Wollust in den Maien; Von edler Art; Mit Lust tät ich ausreiten; Abschiedslied Ars Musici ▲ 1136 [DDD]
Schoeck, O.:Songs (comp), w. Cornelia Kallisch (mez)—3 Songs, Op. 2; 4 Songs, Op. 3; Himmelstrauer [from Op. 5]; 4 Songs, Op. 14; 5 Songs [from Op. 15]; 4 Songs [from Op. 17]; 9 Songs [from Op. 20] *(rec May 1994)* Jecklin ▲ JD 674

Korchagin, A. (vc)—see ORCHESTRAS & ENSEMBLES Shostakovich String Quartet

Körfer, Claus (db)—see ORCHESTRAS & ENSEMBLES Capella Clementina

Korhonen, Timo (gtr)
- Albéniz, I.:Gtr Music—Capricho Catalan; Cordoba; Sevilla Ondine ▲ ODE 752-2 [DDD]
- Brouwer, L.:La Espiral Eterna Ondine ▲ ODE 730-2 [DDD]
- Brouwer, L.:Paisaje cubano con campanas Ondine ▲ ODE 730-2 [DDD]
- Brouwer, L.:Tarantos Ondine ▲ ODE 730-2 [DDD]
- Donatoni, F.:Algo Ondine ▲ ODE 730-2 [DDD]
- Ginastera, A.:Son Gtr Ondine ▲ ODE 730-2 [DDD]
- Koskelin, O.:Tutte le corde Ondine ▲ ODE 730-2 [DDD]
- Moreno Torroba, F.:Gtr Music—Sonatina; Suite castellana; Torija Ondine ▲ ODE 752-2 [DDD]
- Ponce, M.:Sons Gtr—Sonata III (1927); Sonata Merdidional (1932) Ondine ▲ ODE 770-2 [DDD]
- Ponce, M.:Thème, varié et finale Ondine ▲ ODE 770-2 [DDD]
- Ponce, M.:Vars & Fugue on "Folias de España" Gtr Ondine ▲ ODE 770-2 [DDD]
- Sor, F.:Gtr Music—Fant., Op. 30; Etudes, Op. 35 (Bk. 2); Etude, Op. 31/23; Fant. Villageoise, Op. 52; Fant. Elegiaque, Op. 59 Ondine ▲ ODE 816 [DDD]
- Tárrega, F.:Gtr Music—Capricho arabe; Recuerdos de la Alhambra Ondine ▲ ODE 752-2 [DDD]
- Villa-Lobos, H.:Bachiana brasileira 5, w. Pia Freund (sop), chamber ensemble Ondine ▲ ODE 838
- Villa-Lobos, H.:Chôro 1 Ondine ▲ ODE 838
- Villa-Lobos, H.:Con Gtr, w. S. Oramo (cnd), Finnish RSO Ondine ▲ ODE 837 [DDD]
- Villa-Lobos, H.:Distribution de fleurs, w. Pia Freund (sop) Ondine ▲ ODE 838
- Villa-Lobos, H.:Etudes Gtr Ondine ▲ ODE 837 [DDD]
- Villa-Lobos, H.:Intro to Chôros, w. S. Oramo (cnd), Finnish RSO Ondine ▲ ODE 837 [DDD]
- Villa-Lobos, H.:Modinha, w. Pia Freund (sop) Ondine ▲ ODE 838
- Villa-Lobos, H.:Preludes Gtr Ondine ▲ ODE 838
- Villa-Lobos, H.:Sxt místico, w. chamber ensemble Ondine ▲ ODE 838
- Villa-Lobos, H.:Suite populaire brésilienne Ondine ▲ ODE 838

Korkeala, Sonja (vn)
- Orff, C.:Schulwerk (complete), w. Godela Orff (nar), Carolin Widmann (vn), Markus Zahnhausen (rcr), Karl Peinkofer (perc), Andreas Schumacher (perc), Wilfried Hiller (perc/mar), Martin Ruhland (mar), Munich Hochschule Madrigal Choir—Wessobrun Prayer for a capella Choir; 2 Pieces for a capella Choir; 8 Pieces for 2 Vns; Mater et filia for women's a capella Choir; Devotional Yodel for male a capella Choir; 5 Pieces for Sop, Rcr & Perc; Death for Nar., Wood Bells, Bass Xyl & Tam-Tam; Omnia tempus habent for mixed Choir, Timp & Little Dr; Rubato, molto allegro, rubato; Abenlied for Nar, Bass Metallophon, Bass Xyl, Large Dr & Wine Glass; 5 Pieces for Fl & Perc; Devotional Yodel for male Choir [version 2]; 7 Pieces for 2 Xyl *(rec Munich, 1994–95)* Celestial Harmonies ▲ 13105-2

Korman, Fred (ob)
- Gieseking, W.:Qnt Hn, w. J. Cox (hn), Y. Nakao (cl), B. Fillmore (bn), K. George (pno) *(rec 8/91)* Centaur ▲ CRC 2122 [DDD]

Korman, John (vn)
- Brahms, J.:Qnt Cl, w. G. Siflies (cl), J. Beiler (vn), D. Barnes (va), J. Sant'Ambrogio (vc) *(rec 1975–79)* Vox Box 3-▲ CD3X 3014 [ADD]
- Mozart, W.A.:Qnt Cl, K.581, w. G. Siflies (cl), J. Korman (vn), J. Lind Jones (vn), J. Sant'Ambrogio (vc) *(rec 1975–79)* Vox Box 3-▲ CD3X 3014 [ADD]
- Mozart, W.A.:Qnt Hn, K.407, w. R. Pandolfi (hn), J. Korman (vn), K. Mattis (vn), J. Sant'Ambrogio (vc) *(rec 1975–79)* Vox Box 3-▲ CD3X 3014 [ADD]

Körmendi, Klara (pno)
- Berio, L.:Rounds *(rec Hungaroton Studio, 1974–75 & 1978)* Hungaroton ▲ HCD 31606 [ADD]
- Boulez, P.:Son 1 Pno *(rec Hungaroton Studio, 1974–75 & 1978)* Hungaroton ▲ HCD 31606 [ADD]
- Boulez, P.:Son 3 Pno *(rec Hungaroton Studio, 1974–75 & 1978)* Hungaroton ▲ HCD 31606 [ADD]
- Bozay, A.:Intervalli *(rec Hungaroton Studio, 1974–75 & 1978)* Hungaroton ▲ HCD 31606 [ADD]
- Debussy, C.:Arabesques (2) *(rec Nov. 25–28, 1988)* Naxos ▲ 8.550253 [DDD]
- Debussy, C.:Images (3) Pno—Nos. 1 & 2 *(rec Nov. 25–28, 1988)* Naxos ▲ 8.550253 [DDD]
- Debussy, C.:La Plus que lente *(rec Nov. 25–28, 1988)* Naxos ▲ 8.550253 [DDD]
- Debussy, C.:Suite bergamasque *(rec Nov. 25–28, 1988)* Naxos ▲ 8.550253 [DDD]
- Holliger, H.:Elis *(rec Hungaroton Studio, 1974–75 & 1978)* Hungaroton ▲ HCD 31606 [ADD]
- Lajtha, L.:Berceuses *(rec Feb. 2–6, 1992)* Marco Polo ▲ 8.223473
- Lajtha, L.:Contes *(rec Feb. 2–6, 1992)* Marco Polo ▲ 8.223473
- Lajtha, L.:Des Ecrits d'un musicien *(rec Feb. 2–6, 1992)* Marco Polo ▲ 8.223473
- Lajtha, L.:Prélude Pno *(rec Feb. 2–6, 1992)* Marco Polo ▲ 8.223473
- Lajtha, L.:Scherzo et toccata *(rec Feb. 2–6, 1992)* Marco Polo ▲ 8.223473
- Messiaen, O.:Cantéyodjayâ *(rec Hungaroton Studio, 1974–75 & 1978)* Hungaroton ▲ HCD 31606 [ADD]
- Mosonyi, M.:Con Pno, w. R. Stankovsky (cnd), Slovak State PO Košice Marco Polo ▲ 8.223539 [DDD]
- Mosonyi, M.:Festival Music, w. I. Kassai (pno) *(rec Budapest, Nov. & Dec. 1992)* Marco Polo ▲ 8.223558 [DDD]
- Mosonyi, M.:Grand Duo, w. I. Kassai (pno) *(rec Budapest, Nov. & Dec. 1992)* Marco Polo ▲ 8.223558 [DDD]
- Mosonyi, M.:Missa solemnis, w. I. Kassai (pno) *(rec Budapest, Nov. & Dec. 1992)* Marco Polo ▲ 8.223558 [DDD]
- Mosonyi, M.:3 Colors, w. I. Kassai (pno) *(rec Budapest, Nov. & Dec. 1992)* Marco Polo ▲ 8.223558 [DDD]
- Ravel, M.:Gaspard de la nuit *(rec 11/88)* Naxos ▲ 8.550254 [DDD]
- Ravel, M.:Menuet antique *(rec 11/88)* Naxos ▲ 8.550254 [DDD]
- Ravel, M.:Pavane pour une infante défunte *(rec 11/88)* Naxos ▲ 8.550254 [DDD]
- Ravel, M.:Sonatine Pno *(rec 11/88)* Naxos ▲ 8.550254 [DDD]
- Ravel, M.:Le Tombeau de Couperin *(rec 11/88)* Naxos ▲ 8.550254 [DDD]
- Satie, E.:Pno 4-Hands Music, w. Gábor Eckhardt (pno)—Trois morceaux en forme de poire; En habit de cheval; Trois petites pièces montées; Aperçus désagréables; La belle excentrique *(rec Unitarian Church, Budapest, Feb. 8–11, 1994)* Naxos ▲ 8.550699 [DDD]
- Satie, E.:Pno Music (misc)—Musique intimes et secrètes; Caresse; 12 Petits Chorals; Danse de travers No. 1; Pièces froides; Préludes flasques; Trois nouvelles pièces enfantines; Petite musique de clown triste; Pages mystiques; Prélude et tapisserie; Les pantins dansent; Danses gothiques *(rec Mar. 1993)* Naxos ▲ 8.550697 [DDD]
- Satie, E.:Pno Music (misc)—3 Nocturnes; 2 Noctunes; Première pensée rose & croix; Sonneries de la rose & croix; Rêverie de l'enfance de Pantagruel; Rêverie du pauvre; 2 rêverie nocturnes; Prélude de la porte héroïque du ciel; Ogives; Sarabandes *(rec June 1–3, 1992)* Naxos ▲ 8.550696 [DDD]
- Satie, E.:Pno Music (misc)—Valse-ballet/Fantaisie-valse; Petite ouverture à danser; Je te veux; Premier menuet; Les 3 valses du précieux dégoûté; Avant-dernières pensées; Carnet d'esquisses et de croquis; 4 Préludes Naxos ▲ 8.550698 [DDD]
- Satie, E.:Pno Music (misc)—Le Piccadilly; Le poisson rêveur; Le piège de Méduse; La Diva de L'Empire; Jack-in-the-Box; Vieux sequins et vieilles ceirasses; Heures séculaires et instantanées; Peccadilles importunes *(rec Unitarian Church, Budapest, Feb. 8–11, 1994)* Naxos ▲ 8.550699 [DDD]
- Satie, E.:Pno Music (misc)—Enfantillages pittoresques; Chapitres tournés en tous sens; Croquis et agaceries d'un gros Bonhomme en bois; Descriptions automatiques; Embryons desséchés; Gnossiennes (6) for Piano; 3 Gymnopédies; Menu propos Enfantins; Passacaille—Pas trop vif; 6 Pièces de la période; Ragtime-Parade Naxos ▲ 8.550305 [DDD]
- Soproni, J.:Intermezzi *(rec Hungaroton Studio, 1974–75 & 1978)* Hungaroton ▲ HCD 31606 [ADD]

Korn, Richard (db)
- Leifs, J.:Music of, w. Sigrídur Ella Magnúsdóttir (mez), Ólafur Vignir Albertsson (pno), Sólveig Anna Jónsdóttir (pno), Hjálmar Ragnarsson (pno), Edda Erlendsdóttir (pno), Marteinn Hunger Fridriksson (org), Hildigunnur Halldórsdóttir (vn), Gréta Gudnadóttir (vn), Gudmundur Kristmundsson (va), Sigurdur Halldórsson (vc), Iceland SO, Icelandic Opera Chorus, Langholts Church Graduale Choir, Hamrahlid Choir—Icelandic Cant, Op. 13/4; Valse Lento, Op. 2/1; Icelandic Dance, Op. 11/2 [Tempo Giusto]; Requiem; Lullaby [After the Riots]; Fairy-Tale in the Wood [from Baldr, Op. 34]; Funeral March; Separation [from Elegy, Op. 53]; Galdra Loftur Ov, Op. 10; Funeral March, Op. 6; Reverie; Reunion [from Elegy, Op. 53]; Fine I, Op. 55; Andante [The Last Supper]; Preludia Organo, Op. 16/3 [In the Church]; The Tear of Stone [from Elegy, Op. 53] Music From Iceland ▲ ITM 605 [DDD]

Korn, Richard (db) (cont.)
- Ragnarsson, H.:Music of, w. S. E. Magnúsdóttir (mez), H. Halldórsdóttir (vn), G. Gudnadóttir (vn), G. Kristmundsson (va), S. Halldórsson (vc), Ó. V. Albertsson (pno), S. A. Jónsdóttir (pno), H. Ragnarsson (pno), E. Erlendsdóttir (pno), M. H. Fridriksson (org), Sakari, Wilkinson (cnd), Iceland SO, G. Cortes (cnd), J. Stefánsson (cnd), T. Ingólfsdóttir (cnd), Hamrahlid Choir, Icelandic Opera Chorus, Langholts Church Graduale Choir—Meine kleine Freundin [In the Ballroom]; Lovers Duet; After the concert; Meine kleine Freundin [Annie listens to the Radio]; Lif's Theme [On the Beach]; Lif's Theme II [Night Prayer]; Composing Ov [Vars I, II & III] Music From Iceland ▲ ITM 605 [DDD]

Korneyev, A. (fl)
- Vainberg, M.:Con Fl, w. R. Barshaï (cnd), Moscow CO Russian Disc ▲ RUS 11010 [AAD]

Korniszewski, Adam (vn)
- Bernstein, C.H.:Leda & the 6 Songs without Words, w. Jill Feldman (sop) Arcobaleno 2-▲ AAOC 93922

Korockin, Tamara (pno)
- Albert, E. d':Waltzes, Op. 6, w. Andreas Schonhage (pno) CPO ▲ CPO 999330
- Strauss, R.:Sym in f, w. Andreas Schonhage (pno) [arr for pno duet] CPO ▲ CPO 999330

Korokhova, Oksana (pno)—see ORCHESTRAS & ENSEMBLES Moscow Ancient Music Ensemble members

Koroliov, Evgeni (pno)
- Prokofiev, S.:Cinderella Pno, Op. 95 Tacet ▲ 32
- Prokofiev, S.:Pieces Pno, Op. 32—Dance; Gavotte Tacet ▲ 32
- Prokofiev, S.:Sarcasms Tacet ▲ 32
- Prokofiev, S.:Son 5 Pno Tacet ▲ 32
- Prokofiev, S.:Visions fugitives Tacet ▲ 32
- Schubert, Franz:Moments musicaux Tacet ▲ 46
- Schubert, Franz:Son Pno, D.960 Tacet ▲ 46
- Tchaikovsky, P.:Les Saisons Tacet ▲ 25

Koromzay, D. (va)
- Mozart, W.A.:Qnt Strs, K.593, w. Takács String Quartet Hungaroton ▲ HCD 12881 [DDD]
- Mozart, W.A.:Qnt Strs, K.614, w. Takács String Quartet Hungaroton ▲ HCD 12881 [DDD]

Korosek, Marjeta (vn)—see ORCHESTRAS & ENSEMBLES Walter Boeykens Ensemble

Korosi, György (vc)
- Wagenseil, G.C.:Con in C Vc, w. T. Pál (cnd), Salieri CO *(rec Sept. 14–15, 1993)* Arkadia-Akademia ▲ 130
- Wagenseil, G.C.:Syms à 4 parties obligées, w. T. Pál (cnd), Salieri CO *(rec Sept. 14–15, 1993)* Arkadia-Akademia ▲ 130

Korpelainen, Karin (dr/perc)
- Blak, K.:Drangar, w. Anders Hagberg (fl/s sax/perc), Tore Brunborg (s sax/t sax/perc), Lennart Kullgren (gtr/sgr), Kristian Blak (pno/sgr), Anda Kuitse (sgr/perc), Anders Jormin (bass instr/perc) *(rec Nordic House, Tórshavn, Jan. 1995)* Tutl ▲ HJF 33

Korpelainen, Karin (perc/sgr)
- Blak, K.:Con Grotto, w. John Tchicai (t sax/sgr/perc), Lennart Kullgren (gtr/fl/sgr/perc), Anders Hagberg (fl/perc/sgr), Kristian Blak (pno/perc/sgr), Anders Jormin (bass instr/perc/sgr), Sharon Weiss (perc/kaval) *(rec Lidargjógv, Sandoy, Aug. 1984)* Tutl ▲ HJF 33

Korsakov, A. (fl)
- Donizetti, G.:Son Fl & Hp, w. Vera Dulova (hp) *(rec 1979)* Russian Compact Disc ("Talents of Russia" series) ▲ RCD 16206 [AAD]
- Mozart, W.A.:Music of, w. Vera Dulova (hp)—2 Sons for Violin & Harp in G & D *(rec 1978)* Russian Compact Disc ("Talents of Russia" series) ▲ RCD 16206 [AAD]

Korsakov, Andrei (vn)
- Boiko, R.:Carpathian Rhap, w. E. Svetlanov (cnd), Russian State SO Russian Disc ▲ RUS 11020 [AAD]
- Boiko, R.:Gutsul Rhap, w. E. Svetlanov (cnd), Russian State SO Russian Disc ▲ RUS 11020 [AAD]
- Boiko, R.:Gypsy Rhap, w. E. Svetlanov (cnd), Russian State SO Russian Disc ▲ RUS 11020 [AAD]
- Boiko, R.:Volga Rhap, w. E. Svetlanov (cnd), Russian State SO Russian Disc ▲ RUS 11020 [AAD]
- Conus, J.:Con Vn Russian Disc ▲ RUS 10010 [DDD]
- Frolov, I.:Concert Fant on Themes from Porgy & Bess Russian Disc ▲ RUS 10010 [DDD]
- Khachaturian, K.:Kontsert-rapsodiya Russian Disc ▲ RUS 10010 [DDD]
- Saint-Saëns, C.:Fant Vn, w. V. Dulova (hp) *(rec 1979)* Russian Compact Disc ("Talents of Russia" series) ▲ RCD 16206 [AAD]

Korsimaa-Hursti, Anna-Maija (cl)
- Brahms, J.:Sons Cl (comp), w. M. Viitasalo (pno) *(rec Apr. 1993)* Finlandia ▲ 4509-95878-2 [DDD]
- Crusell, B.H.:Intro, Theme & Vars on a Swedish Air, w. O. Vänskä (cnd), Tapiola Sinfonietta BIS ▲ CD 495 [DDD]
- Schubert, Franz:Der Hirt auf dem Felsen, w. S. Isokoski (sop), M. Viitasalo (pno) *(rec Jan. 1993)* Finlandia ▲ 4509-95878-2 [DDD]

Korte, Oldřich (pno)
- Korte, O.:Philosophical Dialogues, w. Shizuka Ishikawa (vn) *(rec Studio Domovina, Prague, Nov 21, 1975)* Panton ▲ PAN 811257 [DDD]

Kortel, Aziz (pno)
- Schoeck, O.:Songs (comp), w. Hedwig Fassbender (mez)—Das stille Leuchten, Op. 60; Geheimnis und Gleichnis; Berg und See *(rec 1994)* Jecklin ▲ JD 680

Kortes, M. L.
- Soldier, D.:Apotheosis of John Brown, w. R. McCauley, R. A. Clark, N. Davoy, J. White, G. High, L. Seaton, et al. Newport Classic ▲ NPB 85549 [ADD]

Kortgaard, R. (pno)
- Morawetz, O.:Sonnets, w. J. Kolomyjec (sop) Centrediscs ▲ CDCCD 3589 [DDD]

Korunic, Mario (vn)—see ORCHESTRAS & ENSEMBLES Fanny Mendelssohn String Quartet

Kósa, Gábor (hpd)
- Vivaldi, A.:Cons Ob, w. S. Schilli (ob), D. Jonas (ob), G. Thomas (hpd), J. Kis Domonkos (vc), Nagy, Morandi (cnd), Failoni CO—RV 450, 452, 453, 454, 534, 535 & 536 *(rec Dec. 1992)* Naxos ▲ 8.550859 [DDD]
- Vivaldi, A.:Cons Ob, w. S. Schilli (ob), J. Kis Domonkos (vc), Nagy, Morandi (cnd), Failoni CO—RV 447, 451, 455, 457, 461 & 463 *(rec Apr. 1993)* Naxos ▲ 8.550860 [DDD]

Kosi, Mile (va)
- Ries, F.:Qnt Fl, w. W. Bennett (fl), Novsak Trio *(rec 1990)* Jecklin-Disco ▲ JD 633-2 [DDD]
- Romberg, A.:Qnts Fl, w. W. Bennett (fl), Novsak Trio—Op. 21/4-5 *(rec 1990)* Jecklin-Disco ▲ JD 633-2 [DDD]

Kosi, Ruda (hp)
- The Mozart Collection, w. Joze Banic (bn), Pietro Cavaliere (cl), Joze Falout (hn), Dubrovka Tomsic (pno), Ljubljana SO [cnd:Anton Nanut, Marko Munih, Alexander Pitamic, Mihail Glinka] Stradivari Classics ("Treasury of Great Classics" series) 5-▲ S5D 61000 [DDD] 5-■ S5C 61000 (D)

Kosina, Miroslav (vn)
- Bach, J.S.:Con for 2 Vns, w. J. Suk (vn), J. Vlach (cnd), Suk CO *(rec 1982)* Supraphon ▲ 110281-2 [AAD]

Koskimies, Pentti (pno)
- Collan, K.:Songs, w. Jorma Hynninen (bar), Ralf Gothóni (pno)—Ihr Bildnis; Erster Verlust; To Emma; At the Burn-beating; Old Man Hurtti; On the Shores of Lake Roine Finlandia ▲ FIN 500282 [ADD]
- Kuula, T.:Songs, w. Jorma Hynninen (bar), Ralf Gothóni (pno)—Beat, My Heart; Ave Maria, Op. 23/2; Fate; Night on the Moor Finlandia ▲ FIN 500282 [ADD]
- Wolf, H.:Mörike-Lieder (sels), w. Jorma Hynninen (bar), Ralf Gothóni (pno) Finlandia ▲ FIN 500282 [ADD]

Koskinen, Eeva (vn)
- Sallinen, A.:Con Vn, w. O. Vänskä (cnd), Tapiola Sinfonietta BIS ▲ CD 560 [DDD]
- Szymanowski, K.:Caprices, w. J. Lagerspetz (pno) Ondine ▲ ODE 759-2 [DDD]
- Szymanowski, K.:Lullaby, w. J. Lagerspetz (pno) Ondine ▲ ODE 759-2 [DDD]
- Szymanowski, K.:Myths, w. J. Lagerspetz (pno) Ondine ▲ ODE 759-2 [DDD]
- Szymanowski, K.:Notturno e Tarantella, w. J. Lagerspetz (pno) Ondine ▲ ODE 759-2 [DDD]
- Szymanowski, K.:Romance, w. J. Lagerspetz (pno) Ondine ▲ ODE 759-2 [DDD]
- Szymanowski, K.:Son Vn, w. J. Lagerspetz (pno) Ondine ▲ ODE 759-2 [DDD]

Koslovsky, Michel (pno)
Fauré, G.:Trio, w. H. Lipsky (vn), L. Snider (vc) Analekta ▲ ATM 29704
Granados, E.:Trio Pno, w. H. Lipsky (vn), L. Snider (vc) Analekta ▲ ATM 29704
Kosmala, Jerzy (va)
Bloch, E.:Suite Va & Pno, w. S. Kawalla (pno), Polish National RSO Cracow
Centaur ▲ CRC 2094 [ADD]
Vaughan Williams, R.:Flos Campi, w. S. Kawalla (cnd), Polish National RSO Cracow, Cracow Polish Radio–TV Chorus Centaur ▲ CRC 2094 [ADD]
Kosonen, Veikko (va)—see ORCHESTRAS & ENSEMBLES Sibelius Academy String Quartet
Kostenbader, Ginette (pno)—see ORCHESTRAS & ENSEMBLES Duo Postiglione
Koster, Ab (hn)
Mozart, W.A.:Cons Hn, w. B. Weil (cnd), Tafelmusik *(rec Sept. 11–13, 1992 & May 2)*
Sony Classical ▲ SK 53369 [DDD]
Koster, Ab (nat hn)
Haydn, J.:Cassation Hns, w. L'Archibudelli Sony Classical ▲ SK 68253
Haydn, J.:Con 1 Hn, w. L'Archibudelli Sony Classical ▲ SK 68253
Haydn, J.:Divert Hn, Vn & Vc, H.IV/5, w. L'Archibudelli Sony Classical ▲ SK 68253
Haydn, J.:Divert for 2 Hns, Vns, Va & Db, H.II/21, w. L'Archibudelli Sony Classical ▲ SK 68253
Haydn, J.:Divert for 2 Hns, Vns, Va & Db, H.II/22, w. L'Archibudelli Sony Classical ▲ SK 68253
Haydn, J.:Lauda Sion, w. Knut Hasselmann (nat hn), Bob Van Asperen (org), B. Weil (cnd), L'Archibudelli, Tölz Boys' Choir *(rec Bad Tolz, Germany, Jan. 2–4, 1993)*
Sony Classical ("Vivarte" series) ▲ SK 53368 [DDD]
Mozart, W.A.:Rondo Hn, K.371, w. B. Weil (cnd), Tafelmusik *(rec Sept. 11–13, 1992 & May 2)*
Sony Classical ▲ SK 53369 [DDD]
Koster, Rick (vn)—see ORCHESTRAS & ENSEMBLES Duke String Quartet
Kostyak, E. (vc)—see also ORCHESTRAS & ENSEMBLES Erato String Quartet
Messiaen, O.:Quatuor pour la fin du temps, w. Fabio di Casola (cl), Emilie Haudenschild (vn), Ricardo Castro (pno) Accord ▲ ACD 201772 [AAD]
Kostyanaia, T. (mand)
Vivaldi, A.:Con Mand, RV.425, w. L. Korkhin (cnd), Renaissance CO Infinity Digital ▲ QK 57244 [DDD]
Vivaldi, A.:Con for 2 Mands, w. Alina Boguk (mand), L. Korkhin (cnd), Renaissance CO
Infinity Digital ▲ QK 57244 [DDD]
Kosubek, R. (vc)—see ORCHESTRAS & ENSEMBLES Berlin String Quintet
Kosugi, Takehisa (amplified vn/live elec/bamboo fl)
Cage, J.:Five Stone Wind, w. M. Pugliese (9 clay pots/tapes), D. Tudor (live elec) Mode ▲ 24
Kosugi, Takehisa (elec vn)
Tudor, D.:Pulsers, w. David Tudor (elec) Lovely Music ▲ LCD 1601 [ADD]
Kosugi, Takehisa (vn)
Behrman, D.:Music of, w. B. Neill (tpt), R. Chatham (tpt), C. Mondshine (sound effects), Jakino (keyboard improvisation)—Interspecies Small Talk (1984); Leapday Night (1983–86); A Traveller's Dream Journal (1988–90) Lovely Music ▲ LCD 1042 [ADD]
Kosugi, T.:Vn Improvisations Lovely Music ▲ LCD 2071 [DDD]
Kotliarskaya, Polina (vn)
Guerra, J.F.:Con Vn, w. C. Halffter (cnd), Madrid Instrumental Ensemble
RNE/Spanish National Radio ▲ 650003 [AAD]
Kotmel, Bohumil (vn)
Bériot, C.–A. de:Music of, w. P. Hula (vn) Supraphon ▲ CD 111868 [DDD]
Dittersdorf, K.D. von:Con Vn, w. L. Svárovský (cnd), Czech Chamber Soloists *(rec 1992)*
Panton ▲ PAN 811144
Halvorsen, J.:Passacaglia & Sarabande con variazioni, w. Jan Perushka (va)
Supraphon ▲ SUP 0049 [DDD]
Leclair, J.–M.:Sons for 2 Vns, Op. 3, w. P. Hula (vn) Supraphon ▲ CD 111868 [DDD]
Mozart, W.A.:Duos Vn, w. Jan Perushka (va) Supraphon ▲ SUP 0049 [DDD]
Nedbal, O.:Nightingale's Waltz, w. Radomír Pivoda (fl), G. Albrecht (cnd), Czech PO *(rec House of Artists, Prague, Dec 31, 1995)* Canyon Classics 2–▲ 323
Rolla, A.:Duo 2 Vn, w. Jan Perushka (va) Supraphon ▲ SUP 0049 [DDD]
Shostakovich, D.:Con 2 Vn, w. P. Altrichter (cnd), Czech PO *(rec Feb 1996)* Supraphon ▲ SUP 3178
Spohr, L.:Duets Vns, Op. 3, w. P. Hula (vn) Supraphon ▲ CD 111868 [DDD]
Spohr, L.:Duo Vn, w. Jan Perushka (va) Supraphon ▲ SUP 0049 [DDD]
Stamitz, C.:Duos Vn Va, w. Jan Perushka (va) Supraphon ▲ SUP 0049 [DDD]
Viotti, G.B.:Sym Concertante 2, w. P. Hula (vn), *(orch unknown)* Supraphon ▲ CD 111868 [DDD]
Kotnowska, Jadwiga (fl)
Flute et Harpe en Recital, w. Joanna Kozielska (hp) Quantum ▲ QM 6937 [DDD]
Kotzia, Eleftheria (gtr)
The Blue Guitar Pearl ▲ PEA 9609
Mediterraneo:Hellenic Music for Classical Guitar *(rec July 21–23, 1993)* Pearl ▲ PEA 9634 [DDD]
Kouguell, Alexander (vc)
Brings, A.:Trio Cl, Vc & Pno, w. E. Gilmore (cl), G. Chinn (pno) *(rec 1989–90)*
Centaur ▲ CRC 2079 [ADD]
Kouneva, Penka (pno)
Kouneva, P.:Aeon, w. Terry Rhodes (sop), Ellen Williams (mez), Lynn Glasscock (perc), Robbie Link (gtr)
Albany ▲ TROY 172 [DDD]
Koutnik, Stepan (a sax)
Schulhoff, E.:Hot Son Sax, w. Jan Cech (pno) Supraphon ▲ SUP 112169 [DDD]
Koutzen, G. (vc)
Flagello, N.:Capriccio Vc, w. N. Flagello (cnd), Rome SO Phoenix ▲ PHCD 125 [ADD]
Vivaldi, A.:Cons Vn, Op. 8/1–4, "The Four Seasons", w. A. Bronne (vn), Monosoff (vn), Kwalwasser (va), M. Goberman (cnd), New York Sinfonietta Odyssey ■ YT 60132
Kováč, Pavol (pno)
Hummel, J.N.:Con Pno, Op. 34a, w. V. Horák (cnd), Bratislava Chamber Ensemble
Koch Schwann ▲ CD 311120
Kovacevich, Stephen (pno)—see also ORCHESTRAS & ENSEMBLES Beaux Arts Trio
Bartók, B.:Cons Pno (comp), w. Davis, Haitink (cnd), Royal Concertgebouw Orch, London SO, BBC SO
Philips 2–▲ 438812–2
Bartók, B.:Con 1 Pno, w. C. Davis (cnd), BBC SO Philips ("Silver Line" series) ▲ 426660–2 [ADD]
Bartók, B.:Con 2 Pno, w. C. Davis (cnd), BBC SO Philips ("Silver Line" series) ▲ 426660–2 [ADD]
Bartók, B.:Con 3 Pno, w. C. Davis (cnd), BBC SO Philips ("Silver Line" series) ▲ 426660–2 [ADD]
Beethoven, L. van:Bagatelles (24)—Op. 126 EMI Classics ▲ CDC 56148
Beethoven, L. van:Con 1 Pno, w. C. Davis (cnd), BBC SO Philips ▲ 422968–2 [ADD]
Beethoven, L. van:Con 1 Pno, w. C. Davis (cnd), BBC SO Philips ("Duo" series) 2–▲ 442577–2
Beethoven, L. van:Con 2 Pno, w. C. Davis (cnd), BBC SO Philips ▲ 422968–2 [ADD]
Beethoven, L. van:Con 2 Pno, w. C. Davis (cnd), BBC SO Philips ("Duo" series) 2–▲ 442577–2
Beethoven, L. van:Con 3 Pno, w. C. Davis (cnd), BBC SO Philips ("Duo" series) 2–▲ 442577–2
Beethoven, L. van:Con 4 Pno, w. C. Davis (cnd), BBC SO Philips ("Duo" series) 2–▲ 442577–2
Beethoven, L. van:Con 5 Pno, "Emperor", w. C. Davis (cnd), London SO
Philips ("Concert Classics" series) ▲ 422482–2 [ADD]
Beethoven, L. van:Con 5 Pno, "Emperor", w. S. Kovacevich (cnd), Australian CO
Classics for Pleasure ("Eminence" series) ▲ CFP 2184 [DDD]
Beethoven, L. van:Con Pno, WoO 4, w. C. Davis (cnd), London SO
Philips ("Duo" series) 2–▲ 442580–2
Beethoven, L. van:Son 12 Pno, "Funeral March" EMI Classics ▲ CDC 56148
Beethoven, L. van:Son 16 Pno EMI Classics ▲ CDC 55226
Beethoven, L. van:Son 17 Pno, "Tempest" EMI Classics ▲ CDC 55226
Beethoven, L. van:Son 18 Pno EMI Classics ▲ CDC 55226
Beethoven, L. van:Son 19 Pno EMI Classics ▲ CDC 56148
Beethoven, L. van:Son 20 Pno EMI Classics ▲ CDC 56148
Beethoven, L. van:Son 21 Pno, "Waldstein" EMI Classics ▲ CDC 54896
Beethoven, L. van:Son 24 Pno EMI Classics ▲ CDC 54896

Kovacevich, Stephen (pno) (cont.)
Beethoven, L. van:Son 27 Pno EMI Classics ▲ CDC 54599
Beethoven, L. van:Son 28 Pno EMI Classics ▲ CDC 54599
Beethoven, L. van:Son 29 Pno, "Hammerklavier" EMI Classics ▲ CDC 54896
Beethoven, L. van:Son 30 Pno EMI Classics ▲ CDC 56148
Beethoven, L. van:Son 30 Pno, w. C. Davis (cnd), London SO
Philips ("Concert Classics" series) ▲ 422482–2
Beethoven, L. van:Son 32 Pno EMI Classics ▲ CDC 54599
Brahms, J.:Con 1 Pno, w. C. Davis (cnd), London SO IMP ("Collectors" series) ▲ IMPX 9039 [ADD]
Brahms, J.:Con 2 Pno, w. W. Sawallisch (cnd), London PO EMI Classics ▲ CDC 55218
Brahms, J.:Con 2 Pno, w. C. Davis (cnd), London SO IMP ("Collectors" series) ▲ IMPX 9040 [ADD]
Brahms, J.:Pno Music (misc), w. Dinorah Varsi (pno), Adam Harasiewicz (pno)—Opp. 79, 116, 117, 118 & 119; Vars. on themes by Handel, Op. 24 & Paganini, Op. 35
Philips ("Duo" series) 2–▲ 442589–2
Brahms, J.:Pieces Pno, Op. 118 Philips ▲ 420750–2 [DDD]
Brahms, J.:Rhaps Pno, Op. 79—No. 1 IMP Collectors Series ▲ IMPX 9039 [ADD]
Brahms, J.:Rhaps Pno, Op. 79—No. 2 IMP Collectors Series ▲ IMPX 9040 [ADD]
Brahms, J.:Songs, w. Ann Murray (mez)—5 Lieder, Op. 105 EMI Classics ▲ CDC 55218
Brahms, J.:Waltzes Pno, Op. 39 Philips ▲ 420750–2 [DDD]
Grieg, E.:Con Pno, Op. 16, w. C. Davis (cnd), BBC SO Philips ▲ 412923–2
Mozart, W.A.:Complete Mozart Edition, w. Alfred Brendel (pno), Bruno Hoffmann (glass armonica), Beaux Arts Trio Philips 5–▲ 422514–2 [ADD]
Schubert, Franz:Allegretto Pno, D.915 *(rec Studio 1, Abbey Road, London, June 1994)*
EMI Classics ▲ CDC 55359 [DDD]
Schubert, Franz:German Dances Pno, D.790 *(rec Studio 1, Abbey Road, London, June 1994)*
EMI Classics ▲ CDC 55359 [DDD]
Schubert, Franz:Son Pno, D.960 *(rec Studio 1, Abbey Road, London, June 1994)*
EMI Classics ▲ CDC 55359 [DDD]
Schumann, R.:Con Pno, w. C. Davis (cnd), BBC SO Philips ▲ 412923–2 [ADD]
Kovacic, Ernst (vn)
Gruber, H.K.:Bossa Nova, w. P. Crossley (pno) *(rec Apr. 29, 1993)* Largo ▲ 5124 [DDD]
Gruber, H.K.:Con 1 Vn, w. H.K. Gruber (cnd), London Sinfonietta *(rec Apr. 29, 1993)*
Largo ▲ 5124 [DDD]
Gruber, H.K.:Pieces Vn, Op. 11 *(rec Apr. 29, 1993)* Largo ▲ 5124 [DDD]
The Heart of the Violin Concerto, w. Jaime Laredo (vn), Anne Akiko Meyers (vn), Elmar Oliveire (vn), Hideko Udagawa (vn) Pickwick ("The Orchid" series) ▲ PICORCD 11013
Holloway, R.:Con Vn, w. M. Bamert (cnd), Scottish CO Collins Classics ▲ COL 1439 [DDD]
Martinů, B.:Sonatina for 2 Vns, w. K. Osostowicz (vn), S. Tomes (pno) Hyperion ▲ CDA 66473 [DDD]
Milhaud, D.:Duo for 2 Vns, w. K. Osostowicz (vn) Hyperion ▲ CDA 66473 [DDD]
Milhaud, D.:Son for 2 Vns, w. K. Osostowicz (vn), S. Tomes (pno) Hyperion ▲ CDA 66473 [DDD]
Mozart, W.A.:Con 1 Vn, w. E. Kovacic (cnd), Scottish CO *(rec Aug. 1990)*
IMP Classics ▲ PCD 946 [DDD]
Mozart, W.A.:Con 3 Vn, w. E. Kovacic (cnd), Scottish CO *(rec Aug. 1990)*
IMP Classics ▲ PCD 946 [DDD]
Mozart, W.A.:Con 4 Vn, w. E. Kovacic (cnd), Scottish CO *(rec Aug. 1990)*
IMP Classics ▲ PCD 947 [DDD]
Mozart, W.A.:Con 6 Vn, w. E. Kovacic (cnd), Scottish CO *(rec Aug. 1990)*
IMP Classics ▲ PCD 947 [DDD]
Mozart, W.A.:Con 7 Vn, w. E. Kovacic (cnd), Scottish CO IMP Classics ▲ PCD 946 [DDD]
Mozart, W.A.:Rondo Vn, K.269, w. E. Kovacic (cnd), Scottish CO *(rec Aug. 1990)*
IMP Classics ▲ PCD 947 [DDD]
Mozart, W.A.:Rondo Vn, K.373, w. E. Kovacic (cnd), Scottish CO *(rec Aug. 1990)*
IMP Classics ▲ PCD 947 [DDD]
Prokofiev, S.:Son for 2 Vns, w. K. Osostowicz (vn) Hyperion ▲ CDA 66473 [DDD]
Stevens, B.:Con Vn, w. E. Downes (cnd), BBC PO Meridian ▲ CDE 84174
Tippett, M.:Con Vn Va, w. G. Caussé (va), A. Baillie (vc), M. Tippett (cnd), BBC PO
Nimbus ▲ NI 5301 [DDD]
Kovács, B. (vn)
Kocsár, M.:Movts Cl, w. Z. Pertis (hpd), M. Kocsár (cnd), Franz Liszt CO
Hungaroton ▲ HCD 31188 [DDD]
Kovács, Béla (cl)
Bartók, B.:Contrasts, w. M. Szűcs (vn), E. Tusa (pno) *(rec 1965)* Hungaroton ▲ HCD 31554 [ADD]
Beethoven, L. van:Qnt Pno, Ob, Cl, Hn & Bn, w. J. Jandó (pno), J. Kiss (ob), J. Keveházi (hn), J. Vajda (bn) *(rec Dec. 1–4, 1990)* Naxos ▲ 8.550511 [DDD]
Brahms, J.:Qnt Cl, w. Bartók String Quartet Hungaroton ▲ HCD 11596
Dohnányi, E. von:Sextet, w. E. Szegedi (pno), F. Tarjáni (hn), Tátrai String Quartet members
Hungaroton ▲ HCD 11624 [ADD]
Mozart, W.A.:Qnt Cl Bas Hn, K.580b, w. J. Balogh (bas hn), Danubius Quartet members [completed Franz Beyer] *(rec Sept. 23–25, 1991)* Naxos ▲ 8.550390 [DDD]
Mozart, W.A.:Qnt Hn, K.407, w. J. Jandó (pno), J. Kiss (ob), J. Keveházi (hn), J. Vajda (bn) *(rec Dec. 1–4, 1990)* Naxos ▲ 8.550511 [DDD]
Mozart, W.A.:Trio Cl, K.498, w. G. Konrád (va), J. Jandó (pno) *(rec Sept. 16, 1991)*
Naxos ▲ 8.550439 [DDD]
Mozart, W.A.:Trio Cl, K.498, w. G. Németh (va), F. Rados (pno) White Label ▲ HRC 128 [ADD]
Ravel, M.:Intro & Allegro, w. E. Maros (hp), Z. Gyöngyössy (fl), Kodály String Quartet *(rec Dec. 6–8, 1988)* Naxos ▲ 8.550249 [DDD]
Kovács, Dénes (vn)
Bartók, B.:Rhaps (2) Vn & Orch, w. J. Ferencsik (cnd), Budapest SO Hungaroton ▲ HCD 31050
Beethoven, L. van:Con Vn, Op. 61, w. J. Ferencsik (cnd), Hungarian State Orch
White Label ▲ HRC 147 [ADD]
Beethoven, L. van:Romances Vn, w. G. Lehel (cnd), Budapest SO White Label ▲ HRC 147 [ADD]
Beethoven, L. van:Son 5 Vn, "Spring", w. M. Bächer (pno) White Label ▲ HRC 105 [ADD]
Beethoven, L. van:Son 9 Vn, "Kreutzer", w. M. Bächer (pno) White Label ▲ HRC 105 [ADD]
Mozart, W.A.:Con 3 Vn, w. G. Németh (cnd), Budapest PO White Label ▲ HRC 154 [ADD]
Mozart, W.A.:Con 4 Vn, w. G. Lehel (cnd), Budapest SO White Label ▲ HRC 154 [ADD]
Mozart, W.A.:Con 5 Vn, w. G. Németh (cnd), Budapest PO White Label ▲ HRC 154 [ADD]
Vivaldi, A.:Cons Vn, Op. 8/1–4, "The Four Seasons", w. L. Gardelli (cnd), Budapest SO
Classical Diamonds ▲ CLD 4009 [ADD]
Kovács, Frantisek (trbn)
Respighi, O.:Liriche su parole di poeti armeni, w. Denisa Šlepkovská (mez), Vladimír Havran (fl), Michal Sintál (ob), Gabriel Koncer (cl), Ivan Viskup (b cl), Ivan Paulicka (bn), Katarína Vavreková (hp), M. Adriano (cnd) [arr. for chamber group by Adriano] *(rec Slovak Radio Concert Hall, Bratislava, Jan. 4–9, Feb. 19 & June)* Marco Polo ▲ 8.223595 [DDD]
Kovács, Imre (fl)
Haydn, M.:Con Fl, P.54, w. E. Lukács (cnd), Győr PO White Label ▲ HRC 107 [ADD]
Mozart, W.A.:Adagio & Rondo Glass Armonica, w. J. Jandó (cel), J. Kiss (ob), G. Konrád (va), T. Koó (vc) *(rec Dec. 1–4, 1990)* Naxos ▲ 8.550511 [DDD]
Silent Night, w. Kovacs, Imre (fl), Hedy Lubik (hp), Ferenc Gergely (org), Frigyes Hidas (org), Gabor Lehotka (org), Hungarian State Orch CO, Csanyi (cnd), Szekeres (cnd), Budapest Children's Choir Madrigal Choir Hungaroton ▲ HCD 16598
Truscott, H.:Trio Fl, w. Béla Nagy (vn), László Bársony (va) *(rec Alpha–Line Studio, Festetich Castle, Budapest, 1994)* Marco Polo ▲ 8.223727 [DDD]
Kovács, Kriszta (pno)
Liszt, F.:Années de pèlerinage 2—Après une lecture du Dante, No. 7 Doremi ▲ 71113 [DDD]
Liszt, F.:Années de pèlerinage 2—Après une lecture du Dante Doremi ▲ DHR 71113 [DDD]
Liszt, F.:Liebesträume Doremi ▲ 71113 [DDD]
Liszt, F.:Liebesträume Doremi ▲ DHR 71113 [DDD]
Liszt, F.:Son Pno Doremi ▲ 71113 [DDD]
Liszt, F.:Son Pno Doremi ▲ DHR 71113 [DDD]

Kovács, Lóránt (fl)
Mozart, W.A.:Cons Fl, w. E. Lukács (cnd), Hungarian State Orch — White Label ▲ HRC 107 [ADD]

Kovács, Zsolt (vc)
Bengraf, J.:Sacred Music, w. Ingrid Kertesi (sop), Katalin Gémes (mez), Gábor Kállay (ten), Ákos Ambrus (bar), István Ella (org), Balázs Arnóth (bn), Vilmos Buza (db), J. Dobra (cnd), Vienna–Szász CO, Tomkins Vocal Ensemble—Te Deum; O sacrum convivium; Libera me; Gloria [from Missa solemnis in D] — Hungaroton ▲ HCD 31609 [DDD]
Druschetzky, G.:Missa solemnis, w. Ingrid Kertesi (sop), Katalin Gémes (mez), Gábor Kállay (ten), Ákos Ambrus (bar), István Ella (org), Balázs Arnóth (bn), Vilmos Buza (db), J. Dobra (cnd), Vienna–Szász CO, Tomkins Vocal Ensemble — Hungaroton ▲ HCD 31609 [DDD]

Kovalenko, Vyacheslav (db)
Ustvolskaya, G.:Composition 2, w. Igo Propischin (db), Leonid Kolosov (db), Vitalii Goryachev (db), Vladimir Vulih (db), Alexei Peresipkin (db), Dmitrii Sokolov (db), Vladimir Nefedov (db), Valerii Javnertchik (perc), Galina Sandovskaya (pno), O. Malov (cnd) *(rec St. Petersburg Radio House, Jan. 1994)* — Megadisc ▲ 7867

Kovalsky, D. (perc)
Fleischer, T.:Lamentation, w. C. Grossmeyer (sop), A. Haroz (hp), E. Lavry (hp), Zimrat Women's Chorus — Opus One ▲ Cd 158 [DDD]

Kowalczuk, Sylvia (hp)
Albéniz, I.:Pno Music—Granada; Malagueña [both arr for hp] — Hungaroton ▲ HCD 31577 (m)
Albrechtsberger, J.G.:Partita Hp — Hungaroton ▲ HCD 31577 (m)
Grandjany, M.:Rhap Hp — Hungaroton ▲ HCD 31577 (m)
Masterpieces for Harp & Orchestra, w. Hungarian Virtuosi CO [cnd:Aristid von Würtzler] — Hungaroton ▲ HCD 31550 [DDD]
Mozart, W.A.:Adagio & Rondo Glass Armonica — Hungaroton ▲ HCD 31577 (m)
Würtzler, A. von:Modern Sketches — Hungaroton ▲ HCD 31577 (m)

Kowalski, Andrzej (vn)
Salut d'Amour, w. Rudolf Lutz (pno) *(rec Rosslyn Hill Unitarian Chapel, Hampstead, London)* — Guild ▲ GMCD 7125 [DDD]

Kowalski, Zygmunt Marek (vn)—see ORCHESTRAS & ENSEMBLES Brussels String Quartet

Koyama, Michie (pno)
Beethoven, L. van:Bagatelle, WoO 59, "Für Elise" — Sony Classical ▲ MLK 62369 [ADD/DDD]

Kozar, J. (pno)
Whithorne, E.:Pno Music—New York Days and Nights (suite in five parts), Op. 40; El Camino Real (suite in three parts), Op. 52; Valse de concert, Op. 9; The Rain, Op. 12; Sur l'eau, Op. 25; La nuit, Op. 35; The aeroplane, Op. 38; The drowsy shepherdess; Pixie frolic; Portrait — Preamble ▲ PRCD 1786 [DDD]

Kozderka, Vladimír (tpt)
Janácek, L.:Capriccio, w. Daniel Wiesner (pno), Jan Riedlbauch (fl/pic), Jan Fišer (tpt), Václav Ferebauer (trbn), Jan Hyndca (trbn), Antonin Keller (trbn), Jiří Novotny (ten tuba), L. Svárovsky (cnd) *(rec Martinek Studio in Prague, Jan 9, Feb 27, Mar 20, 19)* — Panton ▲ 811393-2 [DDD]
Martinů, B.:The Prophecy of Isaiah, w. N. Romanová (sop), D. Drobková (alto), R. Novák (bass), J. Peruška (va), I. Kiezlich (timp), S. Bogunia (pno), P. Kühn (cnd), Prague Radio Men's Chorus, Kühn Chorus [Cz] *(rec 2–3/88)* — Supraphon ▲ 11 0751-2 [DDD]
Martinů, B.:Les Rondes, w. Jurij Likin (ob), Vlastimil Mareš (cl), Lumír Vanek (bn), Jana Herojnová (vn), Pavel Kutman (vn), Ivan Klánsky (pno) *(rec Studio Martínek, Prague, Mar 3, 1995)* — Panton ("Protokol XX" series) ▲ 811348-2 [DDD]

Kozderková, Jarmila (pno)
Smetana, B.:From the Homeland, w. Petr Messiereur (vn), Václav Snítil (vn), Josef Hála (pno) — Panton ▲ PAN 811202
Suk, J.:Ballade Vn, w. Petr Messiereur (vn), Václav Snítil (vn), Josef Hála (pno) — Panton ▲ PAN 811202

Kozenko, Lisa (ob)
Zaimont, J.L.:Doubles, w. Dana Burnett (pno) *(rec SUNY Purchase, Theatre C, Jan 8–10 & Feb 20, 1995)* — Arabesque ▲ ARA 6667 [DDD]

Kozhukhar, Nazar (vn)
Tcherepnin, A.:Con da camera, w. Olga Ivusheikova (fl), Musica Viva CO — Olympia ▲ OLY 584 [DDD]

Kozielska, Joanna (hp)
Flute et Harpe en Recital, w. Jadwiga Kotnowska (fl) — Quantum ▲ QM 6937 [DDD]

Kozolupova, Marina (vn)
Beethoven, L. van:Con Vn, Op. 61, w. K. Kondrashin (cnd), Russian State SO — Multisonic ▲ MUL 310268

Kraamwinkel, Nicoline (vn)—see ORCHESTRAS & ENSEMBLES Chagall Trio members, Chagall Trio

Kraber, K. (fl)—see also ORCHESTRAS & ENSEMBLES American Brass Quintet
Starer, R.:Anna Margarita's Will, w. P. Bryn–Johnson (sop), S. Kates (vc), P. Ingraham (hn), D. Sutherland (pno) *(rec 1980)* — CRI ▲ CD 612 [ADD]

Krachmalnick, Jacob (vn)
Haydn, J.:Sinf concertante, w. John DeLancie (ob), Bernard Garfield (bn), Lorne Munroe (vc), E. Ormandy (cnd), Philadelphia Orch — Sony Classical ("Essential Classics" series) ▲ SBK 62649 ■ SBT 62649

Kracht, Johan (vn)
Yun, I.:Novelette Fl, w. *(artist unknown)* G. Ockers (hp), D. Esser (vc) — Attacca ▲ BABEL 9056–3 [DDD]

Kraemer, Manfredo (vn)—see also ORCHESTRAS & ENSEMBLES Rare Fruits Council, Capriccio Stravagante
Westhoff, J.P. von:Suite Vn *(rec Grace Rainey Rogers Auditorium, Metropolitan Museum of Art, New York City, Aug 1993)* — Deutsche Harmonia Mundi ▲ 05472–77314–2 [DDD]

Kraemer, Nicholas (bc)
Bach, J.S.:Con 2 Hpd, w. Neil Black (ob), Christopher Hogwood (bc), N. Marriner (cnd), Academy of St. Martin in the Fields [trans for ob] *(rec St. John's, Smith Square, London, Aug 1974 & Feb 1975)* — Boston Skyline ▲ BSD 127 [ADD]
Bach, J.S.:Con 4 Hpd, w. Neil Black (ob d'amore), Christopher Hogwood (bc), N. Marriner (cnd), Academy of St. Martin in the Fields [trans for ob d'amore] *(rec St. John's, Smith Square, London, Aug 1974 & Feb 1975)* — Boston Skyline ▲ BSD 127 [ADD]
Bach, J.S.:Con 1 for 2 Hpds, w. Carmel Kaine (vn), Tess Miller (ob), Christopher Hogwood (bc), N. Marriner (cnd), Academy of St. Martin in the Fields [trans for vn & ob] *(rec St. John's, Smith Square, London, Aug 1974 & Feb 1975)* — Boston Skyline ▲ BSD 127 [ADD]
Bach, J.S.:Con 2 for 3 Hpds, w. Carmel Kaine (vn), Ronald Thomas (vn), Richard Studt (vn), Christopher Hogwood (bc), N. Marriner (cnd), Academy of St. Martin in the Fields [trans for 3 vn] *(rec St. John's, Smith Square, London, Aug 1974 & Feb 1975)* — Boston Skyline ▲ BSD 127 [ADD]

Kraemer, Nicholas (hpd)
Locatelli, P.:Concerti grossi, w. Elizabeth Wallfisch (vn), Raglan Baroque Players — Hyperion 2–▲ CDA 66981/2
Vivaldi, A.:Cons Diverse Instrs, w. Joanna Graham (bn), Ruth McDowall (cl), David Rix (ct), Deborah Davis (fl), Duke Dobing (fl), Tim Caister (hn), Stephen Stirling (hn), Christopher Hooker (ob), Helen McQueen (ob), Michael Meekes (tpt), Crispian Steele–Perkins (tpt), Nicholas Kraemer (hpd), N. Kraemer (cnd), London Sinfonietta—Cons. in F, RV.539; in C, RV.533; in D, RV.122; in C, RV.537; in C, RV.560; in F, RV.538; in G, RV.545 *(rec All Saints Church, East Finchley, Oct. 1994 & Jan. 1995)* — Naxos ("Vivaldi Collection" series) ▲ 8.553204 [DDD]

Krafka, Karel (vc)—see ORCHESTRAS & ENSEMBLES Janáček String Quartet

Kraft, Norbert (gtr)
Aguado, D.:Gtr Music—Menuet; Andante; 5 Etudes *(rec Aug 1993)* — Naxos ▲ 8.553007 [DDD]
Boccherini, L.:Qnts Gtr & Strs, w. B. Silver (hpd)—in D, G.448 [arr. Kraft & Silver for guitar & harpsichord] — Chandos ▲ CHAN 8937 [DDD]
Britten, H.:Nocturnal Gtr — Chandos ▲ CHAN 8784 [DDD]
Castelnuovo–Tedesco, M.:Capriccio diabolico, "Homage to Paganini" — Chandos ▲ CHAN 9033 [DDD]
Castelnuovo–Tedesco, M.:Con 1 Gtr, w. N. Ward (cnd), Northern CO *(rec Oct. 7–9, 1992)* — Naxos ▲ 8.550729 [DDD]
Castelnuovo–Tedesco, M.:Son Cl & Pno — Chandos ▲ CHAN 9033 [DDD]

Kraft, Norbert (gtr) (cont.)
Granados, E.:Danzas españolas (10), w. P. Breiner (cnd), Razumovsky Sinfonia [arr. Peter Breiner for Gtr & Orch.] *(rec Moyzes Hall, Bratislava, Aug. 31–Sep. 2, 1994)* — Naxos ▲ 8.553037 [DDD]
Granados, E.:Escenas poeticas, w. P. Breiner (cnd), Razumovsky Sinfonia—Berceuse; Eva y Walter; Danza de la Rosa [arr. Peter Breiner for Gtr & Orch.] *(rec Moyzes Hall, Bratislava, Aug. 31–Sep. 2, 1994)* — Naxos ▲ 8.553037 [DDD]
Haydn, J.:Qts Strs, Op. 2, w. Bonnie Silver (hpd) [arr. by the performers for guitar & harpsichord]—Op. 2/2 — Chandos ▲ CHAN 8937 [DDD]
The Latin Guitar Collection *(rec St. John Chrysostom Church, Newmarket, Canada, Aug 1993)* — Naxos 4–▲ 8.504008 [DDD]
Paganini, N.:Centone di sonate, w. Moshe Hammer (vn)—Nos. 7–12 *(rec St. John Chrysostom Church, Newmarket, Canada, Sept. 24–26, 1994)* — Naxos ("Guitar Collection" series) ▲ 8.553142 [DDD]
Paganini, N.:Centone di sonate, w. Moshe Hammer (vn)—Nos. 13–18 *(rec Newmarket, Canada, Nov 1995)* — Naxos ▲ 8.553143 [DDD]
Paganini, N.:Grand Son Vn — Chandos ▲ CHAN 9033 [DDD]
Ponce, M.:Son romántica Gtr — Chandos ▲ CHAN 9033 [DDD]
Rodrigo, J.:Concierto de Aranjuez, w. N. Ward (cnd), Northern CO *(rec Oct. 7–9, 1992)* — Naxos ▲ 8.550729 [DDD]
Rodrigo, J.:Concierto de Aranjuez, w. K. Koizumi (cnd), Winnipeg SO — CBC ("SM 5000" series) ▲ SMCD 5066 [DDD] ■ SMC 5066 (D)
Rodrigo, J.:Fant para un gentilhombre, w. B. Silver (hpd) [arr. by the performers for guitar & harpsichord] — Chandos ▲ CHAN 8937 [DDD]
Schafer, R.M.:Le Cri de Merlin — Chandos ▲ CHAN 8784 [DDD]
Sor, F.:Études—6 Etudes *(rec Aug. 1993)* — Naxos ▲ 8.553007 [DDD]
Sor, F.:Minuets—No. 6 *(rec Aug. 1993)* — Naxos ▲ 8.553007 [DDD]
Spanish & South American Works for Guitar — Chandos ▲ CHAN 8857 [DDD]
Tárrega, F.:Gtr Music—Rosita; Marieta; Sueño; Adelita; Mazurka in G; Estudio brillante; Gran Vals; Endecha; Lágrima; Alborada; Recuerdos de la Alhambra; Maria; Preludios Nos. 1 & 11 *(rec Aug. 1993)* — Naxos ▲ 8.553007 [DDD]
Tippett, M.:The Blue Gtr — Chandos ▲ CHAN 8784 [DDD]
Villa–Lobos, H.:Con Gtr, w. K. Koizumi (cnd), Winnipeg SO — CBC ("SM 5000" series) ▲ SMCD 5066 [DDD] ■ SMC 5066 (D)
Villa–Lobos, H.:Con Gtr, w. N. Ward (cnd), Northern CO *(rec Oct. 7–9, 1992)* — Naxos ▲ 8.550729 [DDD]
Vivaldi, A.:Con Lt, w. B. Silver (hpd) [arr. by the performers for guitar & harpsichord] — Chandos ▲ CHAN 8937 [DDD]

Kraft, Walter (org)
Bach, J.S.:Org Music (misc)—Chorales, BWV 626, 630, 725, 728, 736 & 765; Chorale, "Fuga Magnificat"; Concerto, BWV 592, 593, 595, 596; Fantasy, BWV 562; Fugue, BWV 574; Passacaglia & Fugue, BWV 582; Prelude & Fugue, BWV 539 & 550; Toccata, Adagio & Fugue, BWV 564; Toccata & Fugue, BWV 538 & 540 *(rec 1965)* — Vox Box 2–▲ CDX 5059 [ADD]
Bach, J.S.:Org Music (misc)—Toccata & Fugue in d, BWV 565; Pastorale in F, BWV 590; Chorale Preludes (6), BWV 645, 646, 659, 711, 715, 727; Fantasy in G, BWV 572; Fugue in c, BWV 575 — Allegretto ▲ ACD 8019 [ADD] ■ ACS 8019
A Sacred Christmas, w. [cnd:Josef Schabasser], Vienna Hofburg Chapel Choir, Jean Claude Raynaud (org) — Vox 90s ■ V9–9904

Kraft, William (hn)—see ORCHESTRAS & ENSEMBLES Los Angeles Horn Club

Krahn, Stephen (pno)
Snyder, R.:Enneagram Studies, w. Eric Ginsberg (cl), Chris Casart (perc), Rick Schaefer (perc), Kelly Scheef (perc), Jason Varga (perc), Scott Zimmerman (perc) — Coronet ▲ COR 400–9

Krainev, Vladimir (pno)
Prokofiev, S.:Son 2 Pno *(rec in Moscow, 1989)* — Art & Electronics ▲ AED 68019 [DDD]
Prokofiev, S.:Son 6 Pno *(rec in Moscow, 1989)* — Art & Electronics ▲ AED 68019 [DDD]
Prokofiev, S.:Son 7 Pno *(rec in Moscow, 1989)* — Art & Electronics ▲ AED 68019 [DDD]
Rachmaninoff, S.:Choruses, Op. 15, w. Andrey Zaboronok (cnd), Bolshoi Theater Children's Choir — Russian Season ("Russian Season" series) ▲ LDC 288013 [DDD]
Schnittke, A.:Con Pno, w. V. Spivakov (vn), Moscow Virtuosi — RCA Red Seal ▲ 09026–60466–2

Krajniak, Peter (vn)
Godár, V.:Talisman, w. Eleonóra Škutová–Slaničková (pno), Jozef Lupták (vc) *(rec Residence of Slovak Composers, Apr 1996)* — Slovart ▲ SR 0018–2–131 [DDD]

Krajny, Boris (pno)
Bartók, B.:Con 3 Pno, w. J. Belohlávek (cnd), Czech PO — Panton ▲ PAN 811216
Prokofiev, S.:Con 3 Pno, w. J. Belohlávek (cnd), Czech PO — Panton ▲ PAN 811216
Ravel, M.:Pno Music—Jeux d'eau; Pavane pour une infante défunte; Sonatine; Menuet antique; Miroirs; Le tombeau de Couperin; Valses nobles et sentimentales; Gaspard de la nuit; Prélude; Menuet sur le nom d'Haydn — Supraphon 2–▲ SUP 111476 [DDD]
Voříšek, J.V.:Intro et rondeau brillant, w. I. Pařík, Prague CO — Supraphon ▲ 10 3868 [DDD]
Voříšek, J.V.:Variazione di bravura, w. I. Pařík (cnd), Prague CO — Supraphon ▲ 10 3868 [DDD]

Krakauer, David (cl)
Ibert, J.:Chamber Music, w. Sue Ann Kahn (fl), Eleanor Lawrence (fl), Peggy Schecter (fl), Rie Schmidt (fl), Lauren Goldstein (bn), Curtis Macomber (vn), Susan Jolles (hp), Frederic Hand (gtr), Andrew Willis (pno)—2 Mouvements; Aria; Histoires; Pastoral; Aria; Entr'acte — Albany ▲ TROY 145 [DDD]
Ibert, J.:Music of, w. C. Schadeberg (sop), Sue Ann Kahn (fl), E. Lawrence (fl), P. Schechter (fl), R. Schmidt (fl), L. Goldstein (bn), Curtis Macomber (vn), Susan Jolles (hp), Frederick Hand (gtr), Arthur Willis (pno)—Entr'acte; Jeux; Sonatine; 2 Movements; 2 Interludes; Aria; Pièce for solo Fl; Histoires; 2 Stèles orientées; Pastoral; Aria; Entr'acte — Albany ▲ TROY 145
Lennon, J.A.:Translations, w. R. Rosales (sop), M. Wu (vn), J. Sachs (pno) — CRI ▲ CD 599 [ADD/DDD]
Moss, L.:Songs of the Earth, w. Nan Hughes (mez), Mark Steinberg (vn), Joel Sachs (pno), Cheryl Seltzer (pno) — Capstone ▲ CPS 8619
Shawn, A.:Trio Cl, w. M. Neuman (vc), A. Shawn (pno) — Opus One ▲ CD 157

Krakauer, David (cl/b cl)
Zorn, J.:Kristallnacht, w. Frank London (tpt), Mark Feldman (vn), Marc Ribot (gtr), Mark Dresser (electric bass), Anthony Coleman (kbd), William Winant (perc) — Tzadik ▲ TZA 7301 [ADD]

Krakauer, David (cl/b cl/t sax)
Zaimont, J.L.:Hidden Heritage, w. Karen Moratz (fl), David Finkel (vc), Clinton Adams (pno), Barry Dove (perc), D. Kosloff (cnd) *(rec SUNY Purchase, Theatre C, Jan 8–10 & Feb 20, 1995)* — Arabesque ▲ ARA 6667 [DDD]

Krämer, J. (fl)—see ORCHESTRAS & ENSEMBLES Roseau Wind Quintet

Kramer, Karl (tuba)—see ORCHESTRAS & ENSEMBLES Brass Ring

Kramer, Manfred (vn)—see also ORCHESTRAS & ENSEMBLES Les Cyclopes
Mozart, W.A.:Church Sons, w. Yasuko Uyama–Bouvard (org), Maria Lindal (vn), Lucia Swarts (vc), Richard Myron (db)—K.67, 144, 145, 241, 244, 245, 274, 328 & 336 — Adda ▲ ADD 581274 [DDD]

Kramer, Thijs (org)
Kint, C.:Org Music—Fugue on B–A–C–H; Fant. on "Eine feste Burg ist unser Gott", Op. 24 — Koch Schwann ▲ SCH 312762 [DDD]
Kramer, T.:Sym Org — Koch Schwann ▲ SCH 312762 [DDD]

Kranen, Peter (pno)
Beethoven, L. van:Music of, w. Michel ten Houte–de Lange (ten), Anatol Karemacher (pno)—Sketches for a Sym; 7 Early Songs; 4 Settings of Nur wer die; Sehnsucht kennt, WoO 134; Sketches for Pno Piece in C; 9 Short Sketchbook Frags — Raptus ▲ 389.02.88
Méhul, E.–N.:Sons Hpd, Op. 1 — Raptus ▲ 395.02.89
Neefe, C.G.:Vars Dittersdorf, w. Michel ten Houte de Lange (ten), Anatol Karemacher (pno) — Raptus ▲ 389.02.88
Neefe, C.G.:Vars Mozart, w. Michel ten Houte de Lange (ten), Anatol Karemacher (pno) — Raptus ▲ 389.02.88
Séjan, N.:Recueil de pièces — Raptus ▲ 395.02.89

Kransberg–Talvi, Marjorie (vn)
Vivaldi, A.:Sinf, RV.156, w. A. Francis (cnd), Northwest CO Seattle — Ambassador ▲ ARC 1010

INSTRUMENT.

Krapp, Edgar (org)
Bach, J.S.:Preludes & Fugues, BWV 531–552 [the St. Paul's Organ in Frankfurt]—BWV 546 *(rec May 21–23, 1991)* Calig ▲ CAL 50908 [DDD]
Constant, M.:Alleluias, w. G. Touvron (tpt) RCA Red Seal ▲ 09026-61186-2
Dvořák, A.:Mass, w. D. Röschmann (sop), I. Danz (alt), C. Elsner (ten), J. Mannov (bass), W. Schäfer (cnd), Frankfurt Kantorei Ars Musici ▲ AM 1083-2 [DDD]
Dvořák, A.:Songs, w. I. Danz (alt)—Vier Geistliche Gesange [Four Spiritual Songs], Op. 19a–d Ars Musici ▲ AM 1083-2 [DDD]
Eben, Petr:Windows, w. G. Touvron (tpt) RCA Red Seal ▲ 09026-61186-2
Genzmer, H.:Son Tpt, w. G. Touvron (tpt) RCA Red Seal ▲ 09026-61186-2
Gubaidulina, S.:In Croce, w. D. Geringas (vc) Koch Schwann ▲ CD 310091 [DDD]
Hessenberg, K.:Fant Org, Op. 115 [St. Paul's Organ in Frankfurt] *(rec May 21–23, 1991)* Calig ▲ CAL 50908 [DDD]
Jolivet, A.:Arioso barocco, w. G. Touvron (tpt) RCA Red Seal ▲ 09026-61186-2
Kodály, Z.:Laudes Organi, w. U. Gronostay (cnd), Netherlands Chamber Choir *(rec October 1993)* Globe ▲ GLO 5115 [DDD]
Kodály, Z.:Missa Brevis, w. U. Gronostay (cnd), Netherlands Chamber Choir *(rec October 1993)* Globe ▲ GLO 5115 [DDD]
Langlais, J.:Chorales Tpt & Org, w. G. Touvron (tpt)—Nos. 1, 2, 4 & 7 only RCA Red Seal ▲ 09026-61186-2
Liszt, F.:Org Music [organ of Concert Hall, Bamberg]—Prelude & Fugue on B-A-C-H, S.260; transcription of J.S. Bach's Adagio in c for Violin & Organ, BWV 1017; Vars. on "Weinen, Klagen, Sorgen, Zagen"; Fant. & Fugue on "Ad nos, ad salutarum undam," S.259 *(rec Concert Hall, Bamberg, Apr. 10–12, 1994)* Calig ▲ CAL 50934 [DDD]
Mendelssohn, F.:Sons Org [St. Paul's Organ in Frankfurt]—No. 2 *(rec May 21–23, 1991)* Calig ▲ CAL 50908 [DDD]
Telemann, G.P.:Trio Sons [the St. Paul's Organ in Frankfurt]—Son. in D *(rec May 21–23, 1991)* Calig ▲ CAL 50908 [DDD]
Walther, Joh. G.:Vars on "Jesu, meine Freude" [St. Paul's Organ in Frankfurt] *(rec May 21–23, 1991)* Calig ▲ CAL 50908 [DDD]

Krarup, Henrik (va)
Lauridsen, L.:Trio Vn, Va & Pno, w. Niels Øllegaard (vn), Teddy Telrup (pno) Rondo Grammofon ▲ RCD 8316

Krasavin, Sergei (bn)
Rubinstein, A.:Qnt Pno, w. A. Nasedkin (pno), V. Zverov (fl), V. Sokolov (cl), A. Demim (hn) Russian Disc ("The A. Rubinstein Edition" series) ▲ RUS 11 061 [ADD]

Krash, Jessica (pno)
Moss, L.:Short Pieces, w. Reginald Jackson (sax) Capstone ▲ CPS 8619

Krasko, Yulia (vn)
Bartók, B.:Son Vn *(rec Moscow, July 1995)* Russian Disc ▲ RD CD 10006 [DDD]
Prokofiev, S.:Son 2 Vn, w. Olga Kondratieva (pno) *(rec Moscow, July 1995)* Russian Disc ▲ RD CD 10006 [DDD]
Stravinsky, I.:Duo Concertant, w. Olga Kondratieva (pno) *(rec Moscow, July 1995)* Russian Disc ▲ RD CD 10006 [DDD]

Krasner, Louis (vn)
Berg, A.:Con Vn, w. F. Busch (cnd), Stockholm PO *(rec live 4/20/38)* GM ▲ 2006 (m)
Schoenberg, A.:Con Vn, w. D. Mitropoulos (cnd), West German Radio Orch *(rec live 7/16/54)* GM ▲ 2006

Krasnik, Dmitry (bn)—see also ORCHESTRAS & ENSEMBLES Collegium dell'Arte
Ustvolskaya, G.:Composition 3, w. Natalia Danilina (fl), Maria Osipova (fl), Inna Rodina (fl), Michail Tokarev (fl), Kirill Sokolov (bn), Arsenii Makarov (bn), Konstantin Shevchuk (bn), Galina Sandovskaya (pno), O. Malov (cnd) *(rec St. Petersburg Radio House, Jan. 1994)* Megadisc ▲ 7867

Krasovsky, Emanuel (pno)
Dvořák, A.:Sonatina Vn, w. V. Vaidman (vn) PWK Classics ▲ PWK 1137 [DDD]
Romantic Strings, w. Vera Vaidman (vn) PWK Classics ▲ PWK 1137 [DDD]
Schubert, Franz:Sonatina Vn, D.385, w. V. Vaidman (vn) PWK Classics ▲ PWK 1137 [DDD]

Kratochvil, Jiri (va)—see ORCHESTRAS & ENSEMBLES Janáček String Quartet

Krauer, Karin (va)
Eine klingende Musikgeschichte des Kantons Luzern [A Resonant Music History of Lucerne Canton], w. R. Baumgartner (cnd), Lucerne Festival Strings, Sybille Tschopp (vn) Gallo ▲ CD 727 [ADD]

Kraus, Eberhard (hpd)
Handel, G.F.:Suites Hpd ebs ▲ 6101
Handel, G.F.:Suites Hpd ebs ▲ 6102
Handel, G.F.:Suites Hpd ebs ▲ 6103

Kraus, Eberhard (org)
Rheinberger, J.:Choral Music, w. G. Ratzinger (cnd), Regensburg Cathedral Choir—Morgenlied; Abendlied; Warum toben die Heiden; Es spricht der Tor in seinem Herzen; Adoramus te; Ave vivens hostia; Salve Regina; Dextera Domini; Eripe me Ars Musici ▲ 1063 [DDD]
Rheinberger, J.:Waldblumen, w. G. Ratzinger (cnd), Regensburg Cathedral Choir Ars Musici ▲ 1063 [DDD]

Kraus, Eberhard (pno)
Haas, P.:Suite Pno *(rec July 8 & 9, 1990)* Koch International Classics ▲ KIC 7231 [DDD]
Janácek, L.:In the Mists *(rec July 8 & 9, 1990)* Koch International Classics ▲ KIC 7231 [DDD]
Suk, J.:Things Lived & Dreamt *(rec July 8 & 9, 1990)* Koch International Classics ▲ KIC 7231 [DDD]
Ullmann, V.:Sons Pno—Nos. 1–4, Opp. 10, 19, 26 & 38 EDA ▲ EDA 005 [DDD]
Voříšek, J.V.:Impromptus Pno, Op. 7 *(rec July 8 & 9, 1990)* Koch International Classics ▲ KIC 7231 [DDD]

Kraus, Greta (pno)
Schubert, Franz:Die Schöne Müllerin, w. Lois Marshall (mez) *(rec Hart House, Univ of Toronto, Ontario, Nov 1979)* CBC ("Perspective" series) ▲ PSCD 2010 [ADD]

Kraus, Lili (pno)
Bartók, B.:Pno Music—6 Romanian Folk Dances, Sz.56; 3 Rondos on Folk Tunes, Sz.84; 3 Hungarian Folk Songs from Csík, Sz. 35a; Sonatina, Sz. 55; 15 Hungarian Peasant Songs, Sz. 71; Evening in the Country [from 10 Easy Pieces, Sz. 39]; For Children, Vol. 1 [based on Hungarian Folk Tunes] *(rec New York, Nov. 1980)* Vanguard Classics ▲ OVC 8087 [ADD]
Beethoven, L. van:Fant Pno, Op. 80, "Choral Fant", w. G. Rivoli (cnd), Amsterdam PO, Amsterdam Phil Chorus FNAC Music ("Via Classics" series) ▲ 642316
Beethoven, L. van:Son 5 Vn, "Spring", w. S. Goldberg (vn) *(rec ca. 1938/40)* Music & Arts 3–▲ CD 665 (m) [AAD]
Beethoven, L. van:Son 9 Vn, "Kreutzer", w. S. Goldberg (vn) *(rec ca. 1938/40)* Music & Arts 3–▲ CD 665 (m) [AAD]
Beethoven, L. van:Son 10 Vn, w. S. Goldberg (vn) *(rec ca. 1938/40)* Music & Arts 3–▲ CD 665 (m) [AAD]
Haydn, J.:Sons Pno—in D, H.XVI/37 *(rec 1950–51)* Vox Box 2–▲ CDX2 5516
Mozart, W.A.:Adagio Pno, K.540 *(rec 1950–51)* Vox Box 2–▲ CDX2 5516
Mozart, W.A.:Con 11 Pno, w. R. Moralt (cnd), Vienna SO Vox Box ("Legends" series) 2–▲ CDX2 5510 [ADD]
Mozart, W.A.:Con 19 Pno, w. R. Moralt (cnd), Vienna SO Vox Box ("Legends" series) 2–▲ CDX2 5510 [ADD]
Mozart, W.A.:Con 20 Pno, w. E. Jorda (cnd), Pro Musica Orch Vox Box ("Legends" series) 2–▲ CDX2 5510 [ADD]
Mozart, W.A.:Con 22 Pno, *(cnd & orch unknown)* *(rec 1950–51)* Vox Box 2–▲ CDX2 5516
Mozart, W.A.:Con 26 Pno, *(cnd & orch unknown)* *(rec 1950–51)* Vox Box 2–▲ CDX2 5516
Mozart, W.A.:Minuet Pno, K.355 Vox Box ("Legends" series) 2–▲ CDX2 5510 [ADD]
Mozart, W.A.:Pno Music (misc)—Vars on Salve tu Domine; Sons in C [Allegro], in C [Andante], in C [Allegretto], in E♭ [Adagio/Menuetto], in E♭ [Menuetto II], in E♭ [Allegro], in G [Allegro], in G [Andante] & in G [Presto] Haydn Society ▲ HSCD 9013

Kraus, Lili (pno) (cont.)
Mozart, W.A.:Rondo Pno Orch, K.382, *(cnd & orch unknown)* Vox Box ("Legends" series) 2–▲ CDX2 5510 [ADD]
Mozart, W.A.:Sons Pno Sony Classical 4–▲ SM4K 47222
Mozart, W.A.:Son 8 Pno *(rec 1950–51)* Vox Box 2–▲ CDX2 5516
Mozart, W.A.:Son 12 Pno Vox Box ("Legends" series) 2–▲ CDX2 5510 [ADD]
Mozart, W.A.:Son 17 Pno *(rec 1950–51)* Vox Box 2–▲ CDX2 5516
Mozart, W.A.:Sons Vn Pno (comp), w. W. Boskovsky (vn) EMI Classics ("Great Recordings of the Century" series) 6–▲ CDHF 63873
Mozart, W.A.:Sons Vn Pno (misc), w. S. Goldberg (vn)—K.296, 377, 378, 379, 380, 404 & 481 Music & Arts 3–▲ CD 665 (m) [AAD]
Mozart, W.A.:Sons Vn Pno (misc), w. S. Goldberg (vn)—K.296, 377, 378 & 379 Pearl ▲ PEA 9454 (m) [AAD]
Schubert, Franz:Ecossaises Pno, D.529—extracts from Opp. 18 & 33 FNAC Music ("Via Classics" series) ▲ 642328
Schubert, Franz:Fant Pno, D.760, "Wandererfantasie" *(rec Vanguard's 23rd St. Studio, NYC)* Vanguard Classics 3–▲ OVC 8200 [AAD]
Schubert, Franz:Impromptus Pno (comp) *(rec 1967)* Vanguard Classics ▲ OVC 4068 [ADD]
Schubert, Franz:Impromptus Pno (comp) *(rec Vanguard's 23rd St. Studio, NYC)* Vanguard Classics 3–▲ OVC 8200 [AAD]
Schubert, Franz:Impromptus Pno, D.899—Op. 90/2–4 FNAC Music ("Via Classics" series) ▲ 642328
Schubert, Franz:Ländler Pno—extract from D.790 (Op. 171) FNAC Music ("Via Classics" series) ▲ 642328
Schubert, Franz:Moments musicaux—Nos. 2 & 3 FNAC Music ("Via Classics" series) ▲ 642328
Schubert, Franz:Son Pno, D.664 *(rec Vanguard's 23rd St. Studio, NYC)* Vanguard Classics 3–▲ OVC 8200 [AAD]
Schubert, Franz:Son Pno, D.845 *(rec Vanguard's 23rd St. Studio, NYC)* Vanguard Classics 3–▲ OVC 8200 [AAD]
Schubert, Franz:Son Pno, D.959 FNAC Music ("Via Classics" series) ▲ 642328
Schubert, Franz:Son Pno, D.960 *(rec Vanguard's 23rd St. Studio, NYC)* Vanguard Classics 3–▲ OVC 8200 [AAD]
Schubert, Franz:Valses sentimentales—extracts FNAC Music ("Via Classics" series) ▲ 642328

Krause, Joachim (org)
Dvořák, A.:Biblical Songs, Op. 99, w. Isolde Siebert (sop) Entrée ▲ 0079 [ADD]
Lehmann, M.:A Prayer, w. Isolde Siebert (sop) Entrée ▲ 0079 [ADD]
Nilsson, T.:Consolamini popule meus, w. Isolde Siebert (sop) Entrée ▲ 0079 [ADD]

Krauss, Clemens (pno)
Strauss, R.:Songs, w. V. Ursuleac (sop)—Madrigal, Op. 15/1; Dem Herzenähnlich, Op. 15/4; Lob des Leidens, Op. 15/3; Seitdem dein Aug' in meines schaute, Op. 17/1; Muttertändelei, Op. 43/2; Blindenklage, Op. 56/2; Für fünfzehn Myto ▲ MCD 943104

Krausser-Vistel, Almuth (pno)
Schwaen, K.:Concertino Vc, w. Douglas Vistel Columbie (vc) *(rec Oct 4, 1995)* Thorofon ▲ CTH 2284 [ADD/DDD]
Schwaen, K.:Curious Waltzes, w. Douglas Vistel Columbie (vc) *(rec Oct 4, 1995)* Thorofon ▲ CTH 2284 [ADD/DDD]
Schwaen, K.:Pno Music—Spherical (1991); Toccatina No. 3 [from Movimenti] (1977); Upswing [from Reflections] (1995) *(rec Oct 4, 1995)* Thorofon ▲ CTH 2284 [ADD/DDD]

Krausz, Adrienne (pno)
Bartók, B.:Songs, w. Klára Csordás (mez)—8 Hungarian Folksongs, Sz.64; 5 Hungarian Folksongs, Sz.33; 20 Hungarian Folksongs, Sz.92; 5 Songs, Op. 15, Sz.61; Village Scenes, Sz.78 Pyramid ▲ PYR 13509
Chopin, F.:Preludes, Op. 28 *(rec Festelich Castle, Budapest, Oct 1994)* Pyramid ▲ PYR 13510 [DDD]
Shostakovich, D.:Preludes Pno, Op. 34 *(rec Festelich Castle, Budapest, Oct 1994)* Pyramid ▲ PYR 13510 [DDD]

Krautgartner, Karel (cl)
Stravinsky, I.:Ebony Con, Prague Chamber Harmony *(rec Jan. 29 to Feb. 2, 1968)* Supraphon ▲ 11 0672-2 [ADD]
Stravinsky, I.:L'Histoire du soldat Suite Ensemble, w. J. Novotný (fl), K. Zlatníková, L. Pešek (cnd), Prague Chamber Harmony *(rec May 18–22, 1964)* Supraphon ("Collection" series) ▲ 11 0672-2 [ADD]
Stravinsky, I.:Octet, w. L. Pešek (cnd), Prague Chamber Harmony *(rec Feb. 12–15, 1962)* Supraphon ("Collection" series) ▲ 11 0672-2 [ADD]

Krauze, Zygmunt (pno)
Krauze, Z.:Quatour pour la naissance, w. Miroslaw Pokrzywinski (cl), Krzysztof Bakowski (vn), Andrzej Bauer (vc) *(rec National Philharmonic, Warsaw, Mar. 1991)* Polskie Nagrania ▲ PLN 113 [DDD]

Kravchenko, S. (vn)
Ekimovsky, V.:Stanzas, w. V. Igolinsky (vn) MCA Classics ▲ MLD 32131 [AAD] ■ MLC 32131
Ryabov, V.:Con da passacaglia, w. V. Igolinsky (vn), V. Zhuk (vn), T. Sergeyeva (kbd) MCA Classics/Melodiya ▲ MLD 32131 [AAD] ■ MLC 32131

Kravtsov, Kyrill (vc)
Boccherini, L.:Con Vc, G.475, w. V. Ponkin (cnd), St. Petersburg State Academic Cappella SO Audiophile Classics ▲ 101.051
Bruch, M.:Kol Nidrei, w. V. Ponkin (cnd), St. Petersburg State Academic Cappella SO Audiophile Classics ▲ 101.051
Saint-Saëns, C.:Con 1 Vc, w. V. Ponkin (cnd), St. Petersburg State Academic Cappella SO Audiophile Classics ▲ 101.051
Tchaikovsky, P.:Vars on a Rococo Theme, w. V. Ponkin (cnd), St. Petersburg State Academic Cappella SO Audiophile Classics ▲ 101.051

Krčová, Gabriela (ob)
Marcello, A.:Cons Ob, w. J. Krček (cnd), Musica Bohemica *(rec 1989)* Supraphon ▲ 11 1290-2 [DDD]
Telemann, G.P.:Con Ob Strs, w. J. Krček (cnd), Musica Bohemica Supraphon ▲ 11 1290-2 [DDD]
Vivaldi, A.:Cons Rcr, w. J. Krček (cnd), Musica Bohemica—Concerto in F Supraphon ▲ 11 1290-2 [DDD]
Vivaldi, A.:Cons Rcr, w. O. Vlček (cnd), Prague Virtuosi—Con. in a, RV.108 *(rec 1991)* Emergo ▲ EC 3981 [DDD]

Krčová, Gabriela (rcr)
Telemann, G.P.:Con da camera, w. J. Krček (cnd), Musica Bohemica Supraphon ▲ 11 1290-2 [DDD]
Vivaldi, A.:Cons Ob, w. J. Krček (cnd), Musica Bohemica—Concerto in C Supraphon ▲ 11 1290-2 [DDD]

Krebbers, Herman (vn)
Badings, H.:Con Vns, w. T. Olof (vn), W. van Otterloo (cnd), The Hague PO Donemus ▲ CV 26
Beethoven, L. van:Con Vn, Op. 61, w. B. Haitink (cnd), Royal Concertgebouw Orch Philips ("Duo" series) 2–▲ 442580-2

Krebs, Torben (org)
Reger, M.:Son 2 Org Canzone ▲ KPTCAN 33010 [DDD]
Reubke, J.:Son Org Canzone ▲ KPTCAN 33010 [DDD]

Krech, L. (trbn)
Speach, B.:Music of, w. J. Schanzer, J. Williams (gtr), A. de Mare (pno), Michael Pugliese (perc), T. Davis (speaker), et al., B. Speach (cnd), Bowery Ensemble—Moto for Trombone, Percussion & Piano (1982); Pensées for Guitar (1983); Trajet for Trombone & Percussion (1983); Sonata for Piano (1986); Shattered Glass for Percussion (1987); Telepathy (Poetry/Music Suite) for Speaker, Contrabas Mode ▲ 16

Krecher, Andreas (vn)—see ORCHESTRAS & ENSEMBLES Mannheim String Quartet
Kreczmarsky, Klaus (sax)—see ORCHESTRAS & ENSEMBLES Berlin Saxophone Quartet

Kreger, James (vc)
Ibert, J.:Con Vc, w. S. Richman (cnd), Harmonie Ensemble/New York Music & Arts ▲ CD 649 [DDD]

672

▲ = CD ♦ = Enhanced CD Δ = MD ■ = Cassette Tape □ = DCC

Krehbiel, Arthur David (hn)
Hindemith, P.:Son for 4 Hns, w. T. Bacon (hn), L. Strieby (hn), G. Williams (hn) Summit 2-▲ DCD 115 [DDD] 2-■ DCD 115
Orchestral Excerpts for Horn, w. Lori Westin (hn) *(rec Aug. & Sept. 1992)* Summit ▲ DCD 141 [DDD]
Russell, A.:Suite Concertante, w. Floyd Cooley (tuba), Janet Ketchum (fl), James Kanter (cl), Earle Dumler (ob), Charles Ullery (bn) Crystal ▲ CD 120
Strauss, R.:Metamorphosen, w. R. Kobler (vn), H. Blomstedt (cnd), San Francisco SO *(rec Feb. 21, 24 & 25, 1992)* London ▲ 436596-2 [DDD]

Kreidler, Dieter (gtr)—see ORCHESTRAS & ENSEMBLES Duett Konzertant

Kreisler, Fritz (vn)
Archive Performances, w. Michael Raucheisen (pno) Biddulph 3-▲ LAB 001-3 (m) [ADD]
Bach, J.S.:Con for 2 Vns, w. E. Zimbalist (vn), *(orch unknown)* *(rec 1915)* Pearl 2-▲ PEA 9996 [AAD]
Beethoven, L. van:Con Vn, Op. 61, w. J. Barbirolli (cnd), London PO *(rec 1936 for HMV)* Biddulph 3-▲ LAB 001-3 (m) [ADD]
Beethoven, L. van:Con Vn, Op. 61, w. J. Barbirolli (cnd), London PO Enterprise ("Sirio" series) ▲ ENT SO 53009
Beethoven, L. van:Con Vn, Op. 61, w. J. Barbirolli (cnd), London PO *(rec 1936 for HMV)* Pearl 2-▲ PEAS 9362 (m) [AAD]
Beethoven, L. van:Con Vn, Op. 61, w. L. Blech (cnd), Berlin State Opera Orch *(rec 1926)* Biddulph 2-▲ LAB 049 [ADD]
Beethoven, L. van:Con Vn, Op. 61, w. L. Blech (cnd), Berlin State Opera Orch Grammofono 2000 ▲ GRM 78575
Beethoven, L. van:Con Vn, Op. 61, w. L. Blech (cnd), Berlin State Opera Orch *(rec 1926 for HMV)* Music & Arts 2-▲ CD 290 (m) [AAD]
Beethoven, L. van:Con Vn, Op. 61, w. L. Blech (cnd), Berlin State Opera Orch *(rec 1926)* Pearl 2-▲ PEA 9996 [AAD]
Beethoven, L. van:Sons Vn (comp), w. F. Rupp (pno)—Nos. 7 & 10 *(rec 1935 for HMV)* Pearl ▲ PEA 9400 (m) [AAD]
Beethoven, L. van:Sons Vn (comp), w. F. Rupp (pno)—Nos. 1-3 *(rec 1935 for HMV)* Pearl ▲ PEA 9330 (m) [AAD]
Beethoven, L. van:Sons Vn (comp), w. F. Rupp (pno)—Nos. 8 & 9 *(rec 1935 for HMV)* Pearl ▲ PEA 9395 (m) [AAD]
Beethoven, L. van:Sons Vn (comp), w. F. Rupp (pno)—Nos. 4-6 *(rec 1935 for HMV)* Pearl ▲ PEA 9354 (m) [AAD]
Beethoven, L. van:Son 8 Vn, w. S. Rachmaninoff (pno) *(rec March 1926 for HMV)* Biddulph 3-▲ LAB 001-3 (m) [ADD]
The Berlin HMV Recordings *(rec 1926-27)* Biddulph 2-▲ LAB 049 [ADD]
Brahms, J.:Con Vn, w. L. Blech (cnd), Berlin State Opera Orch Grammofono 2000 ▲ GRM 78579
Brahms, J.:Con Vn, *(orch unknown)* Memories ("Golden" series) 2-▲ MEM 3007
Brahms, J.:Con Vn, w. L. Blech (cnd), Berlin State Opera Orch *(rec 1926)* Pearl 2-▲ PEA 9996 [AAD]
Brahms, J.:Con Vn, w. L. Blech (cnd), Berlin State Opera Orch Music & Arts 2-▲ CD 290 (m) [AAD]
Brahms, J.:Con Vn, w. J. Barbirolli (cnd), London PO *(rec 1936 for HMV)* Biddulph 3-▲ LAB 001-3 (m) [ADD]
Brahms, J.:Con Vn, w. J. Barbirolli (cnd), London PO *(rec 1936 for HMV)* Pearl 2-▲ PEAS 9362 (m) [AAD]
Brahms, J.:Con Vn, w. L. Blech (cnd), Berlin State Opera Orch *(rec 1927)* Biddulph 2-▲ LAB 049 [ADD]
Bruch, M.:Con 1 Vn, w. E. Goossens (cnd), Royal Albert Hall Orch Grammofono 2000 ▲ GRM 78579
Bruch, M.:Con 1 Vn, w. E. Goossens (cnd), *(orch unknown)* *(rec 1924-25)* Biddulph 2-▲ LAB 009-10 (m) [AAD]
The 1926 & 1927 Victor Recordings:Favorite Short Pieces, w. Kreisler, Fritz (vn) Biddulph ▲ LAB 075 [ADD]
The 1928 Victor Recordings:Favourite Short Pieces, w. Carl Lamson (pno) Biddulph ▲ LAB 080 [ADD]
The Early Victor Recordings, Vol. 1 *(rec 1910-15)* Biddulph 2-▲ LAB 019-20 [ADD]
The Early Victor Recordings, Vol. 2 *(rec 1914-20)* Biddulph 2-▲ LAB 021-22 [ADD]
Fritz Kreisler:The Complete Recordings various artists *(rec 1910-46)* RCA Gold Seal 11-▲ 09026-61649-2 [ADD]
The Great Violinists Series One-Eleven ▲ URS 50090 [ADD]
Grieg, E.:Sons Vn, Opp. 8, 13 & 45, w. S. Rachmaninoff (pno)—No. 3 *(rec 1926 for HMV)* Biddulph 3-▲ LAB 001-3 (m) [ADD]
Grieg, E.:Son 3 Vn *(rec 1920)* RCA Red Seal ▲ 09026-61826-2
The HMV Recordings with Franz Rupp Biddulph ▲ LAB 040 [ADD]
The Kreisler Collection Biddulph 2-▲ LAB 009-10 (m) [AAD]
Kreisler, F.:Qt Strs, w. T. Petrie (vn), W. Primrose (va), L. Kennedy (vc) *(rec 1935 for HMV)* Biddulph 3-▲ LAB 001-3 (m) [ADD]
Kreisler, F.:Scherzo 'in the style of Dittersdorf', w. T. Petrie (vn), W. Primrose (va), L. Kennedy (vc), 1935 for HMV] Biddulph 3-▲ LAB 001-3 (m) [ADD]
Kreisler, F.:Scherzo 'in the style of Dittersdorf' EMI Classics ▲ CDH 64701
Legendary Performances RCA Red Seal ▲ 5910-2-RC (m)
Leider Singer, w. McCormack, John (ten), E. Schneider (sgr), Grace Moore (sop), V. O'Brien (pno), L. Bori (sop), L. Kennedy (vc) Symposium ▲ 1164
Mendelssohn, F.:Con in e Vn & Orch, Op. 64, w. L. Blech (cnd), Berlin State Opera Orch Enterprise ("Sirio" series) ▲ ENT SO 53009
Mendelssohn, F.:Con in e Vn & Orch, Op. 64, w. L. Blech (cnd), Berlin State Opera Orch Grammofono 2000 ▲ GRM 78575
Mendelssohn, F.:Con in e Vn & Orch, Op. 64, w. L. Blech (cnd), Berlin State Opera Orch *(rec 1926)* Pearl 2-▲ PEA 9996 [AAD]
Mendelssohn, F.:Con in e Vn & Orch, Op. 64, w. L. Blech (cnd), Berlin State Opera Orch *(rec 1926)* Biddulph 2-▲ LAB 049 [ADD]
Mendelssohn, F.:Con in e Vn & Orch, Op. 64, w. L. Blech (cnd), Berlin State Opera Orch *(rec 1926)* Music & Arts 2-▲ CD 290 (m) [AAD]
Mendelssohn, F.:Con in e Vn & Orch, Op. 64, w. L. Ronald (cnd), London PO *(rec 1935 HMV recording)* Biddulph ▲ LAB 047 [ADD]
Mendelssohn, F.:Con in e Vn & Orch, Op. 64, w. L. Ronald (cnd), London PO *(rec 1935 HMV recording)* Pearl 2-▲ PEAS 9362 (m) [AAD]
Mozart, W.A.:Con 4 Vn, w. L. Ronald (cnd), London SO *(rec 1924 for HMV)* Biddulph 2-▲ LAB 009-10 (m) [AAD]
Mozart, W.A.:Con 4 Vn, w. M. Sargent (cnd), London PO *(rec 1939 HMV)* Biddulph ▲ LAB 016 [ADD]
Mozart, W.A.:Con 4 Vn, w. L. Ronald (cnd), London SO *(rec 1924)* Pearl 2-▲ PEA 9996 [AAD]
Mozart, W.A.:Con 4 Vn, w. L. Ronald (cnd), London SO *(rec 1924)* Music & Arts 2-▲ CD 290 (m) [AAD]
Paganini, N.:Con 1 Vn, w. E. Ormandy (cnd), Philadelphia Orch *(rec 1938 for HMV)* Pearl 2-▲ PEAS 9362 (m) [AAD]
Schubert, Franz:Son Vn, D.574, w. S. Rachmaninoff (pno) *(rec 1926 for HMV)* Biddulph 3-▲ LAB 001-3 (m) [ADD]
Schumann, R.:Con Vn, w. F. J. Barbirolli (cnd), New York PO *(rec 1938 for HMV)* Biddulph ▲ LAB 047 [ADD]
Thomas, A.:Mignon (sels), w. Geraldine Farrar (sop), W. Rogers (cnd), *(orch unknown)*—Connais-tu le pays? *(rec May 24, 1915)* Nimbus ▲ NI 7872 [ADD]
The Victor Recordings, w. Carl Lamson (pno), John McCormack (ten) *(rec 1921-25)* Biddulph 2-▲ LAB 068-69 [ADD]

Krejci, Jan (vn)
Kozeluch, L.:Original Scottish Airs, w. J. Griffett (ten), P. Hejny (vc), R. Zelenka (pno) [arr. J. Griffett; lyrics by Robert Burns]—Nae gentle dames; Here's a health to ane I lo'e dear; Ye banks and braes of bonie Doon; Blythe, blythe and merry was she; Lord Gregory; My Nannie's awa'; And ye shall walk in silk attire; Turn again, thou fair Eliza; Contented wi' little; The day returns; On a bank of flowers; Adieu ye streams; All Water; My love she's but a lassie yet; True hearted was he, the sad swain o' the Yarrow; She's fair and fause; O this is no my aine lassie; The Tears of Scotland Campion ▲ 1322 [DDD]

Krejčí, Jiří (E hn)
Mozart, W.A.:Adagio E Hn, w. Czech Nonet *(rec Prague, 1995)* Praga ▲ PR 250095

Krejčí, Jiří (ob)—see also ORCHESTRAS & ENSEMBLES Czech String Trio
Fiala, J.:Con Ob, w. F. Vajnar (cnd), Prague CO Supraphon ▲ 10 3624-2 [DDD]
Krommer, F.:Con Ob, Op. 52, w. F. Vajnar (cnd), Prague CO Supraphon ▲ 10 3624-2 [DDD]
Mozart, W.A.:Divert Ob, K.251, w. Vladimíra Klánská (hn), Czech Nonet *(rec Prague, 1995)* Praga ▲ PR 250095
Mozart, W.A.:Qt Ob, K.370, w. Czech Nonet *(rec Prague, 1995)* Praga ▲ PR 250095
Zach, J.:Con Ob, w. F. Vajnar (cnd), Prague CO Supraphon ▲ 10 3624-2 [DDD]

Kremer, Gidon (vn)
Bach, J.S.:Cons Vn (comp), Academy of St. Martin in the Fields Philips ▲ 434730-2
Bach, J.S.:Con Vn & Ob, w. Holliger (ob), N. Marriner (cnd), Academy of St. Martin in the Fields Philips 2-▲ 426462-2 [ADD]
Bach, J.S.:Con Vn & Ob, w. Holliger (ob), N. Marriner (cnd), Academy of St. Martin in the Fields Philips ▲ 434730-2
Bach, J.S.:Con for 2 Vns, Academy of St. Martin in the Fields Philips ▲ 434730-2
Bach, J.S.:Sons & Partitas Vn, BWV 1001-1006 Philips 2-▲ 416651-2 [ADD]
Bartók, B.:Sons (2) Vn & Pno, w. E. Smirnov (pno) Hungaroton ▲ HCD 11655
Bartók, B.:Sons (2) Vn & Pno, w. D. Oistrakh (vn), G. Kremer(vn), F. Bauer (pno), O. Maisenberg (pno) *(rec 1969, 1972 & 1978)* Praga ▲ PR 250 038
Bartók, B.:Son 1 Vn & Pno, w. M. Argerich (pno) Deutsche Grammophon ▲ 427351-2 [DDD]
Beethoven, L. van:Son 1 Vn, w. M. Argerich (pno) Deutsche Grammophon ▲ 415138-2 [DDD]
Beethoven, L. van:Son 2 Vn, w. Argerich (pno) Deutsche Grammophon ▲ 415138-2 [DDD]
Beethoven, L. van:Son 3 Vn, w. M. Argerich (pno) Deutsche Grammophon ▲ 415138-2 [DDD]
Beethoven, L. van:Son 4 Vn, w. M. Argerich (pno) Deutsche Grammophon ▲ 419787-2 [DDD]
Beethoven, L. van:Son 5 Vn, "Spring", w. M. Argerich (pno) Deutsche Grammophon ▲ 419787-2 [DDD]
Beethoven, L. van:Son 6 Vn, w. Martha Argerich (pno) Deutsche Grammophon ▲ 445652-2
Beethoven, L. van:Son 7 Vn, w. Martha Argerich (pno) Deutsche Grammophon ▲ 445652-2
Beethoven, L. van:Son 8 Vn, w. Martha Argerich (pno) Deutsche Grammophon ▲ 445652-2
Beethoven, L. van:Son 9 Vn, "Kreutzer", w. Martha Argerich (pno) *(rec Auditorium Stravinski, Montreux, Mar 1994)* Deutsche Grammophon ▲ 447054-2 [DDD]
Beethoven, L. van:Son 10 Vn, w. Martha Argerich (pno) *(rec Auditorium Stravinski, Montreux, Mar 1994)* Deutsche Grammophon ▲ 447054-2 [DDD]
Berg, A.:Con Vn, w. C. Davis (cnd), Bavarian RSO Philips ▲ 412523-2 [DDD]
Bernstein, L.:Music of, w. J. Norman (sop), K. Te Kanawa (sop), J. Anderson (sop), F. von Stade (mez), C. Ludwig (mez), T. Troyanos (mez), J. Carreras (ten), D. Garrison (ten), J. Hadley (ten), T. Hampson (bar), T. Daly (sgr), G. Kremer (vn), M. Rostropovich (vc), M.T. Thomas (va), L. Bernstein (cnd), *(orch unknown)*—various popular works Deutsche Grammophon ▲ 439251-2 ■ 439251-4
Brahms, J.:Con Vn, w. L. Bernstein (cnd), Vienna PO ("Leonard Bernstein Editi Deutsche Grammophon ▲ 431031-2 [DDD]
Brahms, J.:Con Vn, w. H. von Karajan (cnd), Berlin PO EMI Classics 2-▲ CDFB 69334
Brahms, J.:Con Vn & Vc, "Double Con", w. M. Maisky (vc), L. Bernstein (cnd), Vienna PO Deutsche Grammophon ▲ 431031-2 [DDD]
Franck, C.:Son Vn, w. O. Maisenberg (pno) *(rec 1978?)* Praga ▲ PR 250 024
Glass, Philip:Con Vn, w. C. von Dohnányi (cnd), Vienna PO Deutsche Grammophon ▲ 437091-2
Gubaidulina, S.:Dancer on a Tightrope, w. Vadim Sakharov (pno) *(rec Lockenhaus Festival, Austria, 1995)* BIS ▲ CD 810 [DDD]
Gubaidulina, S.:Hommage à T. S. Eliot, w. C. Whittlesey (sop), *(other instrs unknown)* *(rec 1987 tour of "Music from)* Deutsche Grammophon ▲ 427336-2 [DDD]
Gubaidulina, S.:Offertorium, w. C. Dutoit (cnd), Boston SO Deutsche Grammophon ▲ 427336-2 [DDD]
Gubaidulina, S.:Rejoice, w. Yo-Yo Ma (vc) CBS ▲ MK 44924 [DDD]
Gubaidulina, S.:Silenzio, w. Friedrich Lips (bayan), Vladimir Tonkha (vc) *(rec Lockenhaus Festival, Austria, 1995)* BIS ▲ CD 810 [DDD]
Hindemith, P.:Son Vn & Pno, Op. 11/1, w. Andre Gavrilov (pno) EMI Classics 2-▲ CDFB 69334
Janácek, L.:Son Vn, w. M. Argerich (pno) Deutsche Grammophon ▲ 427351-2 [DDD]
Lourié, A.:Con da camera, German Chamber PO Deutsche Grammophon ▲ 437788-2
Mendelssohn, F.:Con in d Vn & Strs, Orpheus CO Deutsche Grammophon ▲ 427338-2 [DDD]
Mendelssohn, F.:Con in d Vn, Pno & Strs, w. M. Argerich (pno), Orpheus CO Deutsche Grammophon ▲ 427338-2 [DDD]
Messiaen, O.:Thème et vars, w. M. Argerich (pno) Deutsche Grammophon ▲ 427351-2 [DDD]
Mozart, W.A.:Adagio & Fugue Strs, w. Jean-Marc Phillips (vn), Kim Kashkashian (va), Yo-Yo Ma (vc) CBS ▲ MK 42134 [DDD]
Mozart, W.A.:Cons Vn Orch, w. N. Harnoncourt (cnd), Vienna PO—Nos. 1-5 Deutsche Grammophon ("2CD" series) 2-▲ 453 043-2
Mozart, W.A.:Qts Fl, w. Irena Grafenauer (fl), Veronika Hagen (va), Clemens Hagen (vc) Sony Classical ▲ SK 66240
Mozart, W.A.:Sinf Concertante Vn Va Orch, w. Kim Kashkashian (va), N. Harnoncourt (cnd), Vienna PO Deutsche Grammophon ("2CD" series) 2-▲ 453 043-2
Mozart, W.A.:Trio Vn, K.563, w. K. Kashkashian (va), Y.-Y. Ma (vc) CBS ▲ MK 39561 [DDD]
Nono, L.:Hay que caminar, w. T. Grindenko (vn) Deutsche Grammophon ▲ 435870-2 [DDD]
Nono, L.:Lontananza, w. T. Grindenko (vn) Deutsche Grammophon ▲ 435870-2 [DDD]
Pärt, A.:Chamber Music, w. *(other artists unknown)*, Stuttgart Brass Ensemble, Hilliard Ensemble—(works for brass, voice, strings & organ) Arbos; An den Wassern zu Babel; De Profundis; Es sang für langen Jahren; Summa ECM New Series ▲ 78118-21325-2 [DDD]; ■ 78118-21325-4 (D)
Pärt, A.:Fratres II, w. K. Jarrett (pno) [arr vn & pno] ECM New Series ▲ 78118-21275-2 [DDD]; ■ 78118-21275-4
Pärt, A.:Stabat Mater, w. *(other artists unknown)*, Hilliard Ensemble ECM New Series ▲ 78118-21325-2 [DDD]; ■ 78118-21325-4 (D)
Pärt, A.:Tabula rasa, w. T. Grindenko (vn), S. Sondeckis (cnd), Lithuanian CO ECM New Series ▲ 78118-21275-2 [DDD]; ■ 78118-21275-4
Prokofiev, S.:Mélodies, w. M. Argerich (pno) Deutsche Grammophon ▲ 431803-2 [DDD]
Prokofiev, S.:Son Vn, Op. 94bis, w. M. Argerich (pno) Deutsche Grammophon ▲ 431803-2 [DDD]
Prokofiev, S.:Son 1 Vn, w. M. Argerich (pno) Deutsche Grammophon ▲ 431803-2 [DDD]
Ridout, A.:Ferdinand [E] Philips ("Digital Classics" series) ▲ 416841-2 [DDD]
Rorem, N.:Con Vn, w. L. Bernstein (cnd), New York PO Deutsche Grammophon ▲ 429231-1
Saint-Saëns, C.:Carnival of the Animals, w. M. Argerich (pno), N. Freire (pno), I. van Keulen (vn), T. Zimmermann (va), M. Maisky (vc), et al. Philips ("Digital Classics" series) ▲ 416841-2 [DDD]
Schnittke, A.:Canon Vn, w. Y. Bashmet (cnd), Moscow Soloists EMI Classics ▲ CDC 55627
Schnittke, A.:Con for 3, w. Yuri Bashmet (va), Mstislav Rostropovich (vc), Y. Bashmet (cnd), Moscow Soloists EMI Classics ▲ CDC 55627
Schnittke, A.:Con grosso 1, w. Tatiana Grindenko (vn), Yuri Smirnov (hpd/pno), H. Schiff (cnd), CO of Europe Deutsche Grammophon ("Digital Midprice" series) ▲ 445520-2
Schnittke, A.:Con grosso 5, w. C. von Dohnányi (cnd), Vienna PO Deutsche Grammophon ▲ 437091-2
Schnittke, A.:Con 2 Vn, w. C. Eschenbach (cnd), CO of Europe Teldec ▲ 94540-2
Schnittke, A.:Gratulationsrondo, w. C. Eschenbach (pno) Teldec ▲ 94540-2
Schnittke, A.:Menuet Vn, w. Yuri Bashmet (va), Mstislav Rostropovich (vc) EMI Classics ▲ CDC 55627
Schnittke, A.:Moz-Art à la Haydn, w. Tatiana Grindenko (vn), H. Schiff (cnd), CO of Europe Deutsche Grammophon ("Digital Midprice" series) ▲ 445520-2

Kremer, Gidon (vn) (cont.)
Schnittke, A.:Moz-Art à la Haydn, w. H. Schiff (cnd), CO of Europe
Deutsche Grammophon ▲ 429413-2 [DDD]
Schnittke, A.:A Paganini Vn Deutsche Grammophon ("Digital Midprice" series) ▲ 445520-2
Schnittke, A.:Quasi una son, w. H. Schiff (cnd), CO of Europe
Deutsche Grammophon ▲ 429413-2 [DDD]
Schnittke, A.:Quasi una son, w. H. Schiff (cnd), CO of Europe
Deutsche Grammophon ("Digital Midprice" series) ▲ 445520-2
Schnittke, A.:Son 2 Vn, w. Andre Gavrilov (pno) EMI Classics 2-▲ CDFB 69334
Schnittke, A.:Stille Nacht Vn, w. C. Eschenbach (pno) Teldec ▲ 94540-2
Schnittke, A.:Trio Strs, w. Yuri Bashmet (va), Mstislav Rostropovich (vc) EMI Classics ▲ CDC 55627
Schubert, Franz:Qt 15 Strs, w. D. Phillips (vn), K. Kashkashian (va), Yo Yo Ma (vc)
CBS ▲ MK 42134 [DDD]
Schubert, Franz:Sonatinas Vn, w. O. Maisenberg (pno) Deutsche Grammophon ▲ 437092-2
Schulhoff, E.:Sxt Strs, w. P. Hirschhorn (vn), N. Imai (va), K. Kashkasian (va), D. Geringas (vc), J. Berger (vc) *(rec Lockenhaus Festival, 1986)* ECM New Series 2-▲ 78118-21347-2 [DDD]
Schumann, R.:Con Vn, w. N. Harnoncourt (cnd), CO of Europe *(rec Graz, Germany, July 1994)*
Teldec ▲ 90696-2 [DDD]
Schumann, R.:Con Vn, w. R. Muti (cnd), Philharmonia Orch
EMI Classics ("Studio DDD" series) ▲ CDD 63894 [DDD]
Schumann, R.:Con Vn, w. R. Muti (cnd), Philharmonic Orch EMI Classics 2-▲ CDFB 69334
Shostakovich, D.:Con Vn, Op. 125, w. S. Ozawa (cnd), Boston SO
Deutsche Grammophon ▲ 439890-2
Shostakovich, D.:Con 2 Vn, w. S. Ozawa (cnd), Boston SO Deutsche Grammophon ▲ 439890-2
Shostakovich, D.:Movts Str Qt, w. A. Bik (vn), V. Hagen (va), T. Demenga (vc) *(rec Lockenhaus Festival, 1986)* ECM New Series 2-▲ 78118-21347-2 [DDD]
Shostakovich, D.:Qt 13 Strs, w. T. Zehetmair (vn), N. Imai (va), B. Pergamentschikow (vc) *(rec Lockenhaus Festival, 1985)* ECM New Series 2-▲ 78118-21347-2 [DDD]
Shostakovich, D.:Qt 14 Strs, w. Y. Horigome (vn), K. Kashkashian (va), D. Geringas (vc) *(rec Lockenhaus Festival, 1986)* ECM New Series 2-▲ 78118-21347-2 [DDD]
Shostakovich, D.:Qt 15 Strs, w. D. Phillips (vn), K. Kashkashian (va), Yo Yo Ma (vc)
CBS ▲ MK 44924 [DDD]
Sibelius, J.:Con Vn, w. G. Rozhdestvensky (cnd), London SO RCA Gold Seal ▲ 09026-60957-2
Sibelius, J.:Con Vn, w. H. von Karajan (cnd), Berlin PO EMI Classics 2-▲ CDFB 69334
Sibelius, J.:Con Vn, w. R. Muti (cnd), Philharmonia Orch
EMI Classics ("Studio DDD" series) ▲ CDD 63894 [DDD]
The Spirit of Russia, w. Vladimir Malinin (vn), Mark Pekarsky (cymbals), Leonid Bobylev (pno), Alexander Melnikov (vn) Vox Box 2-▲ CDX 5115 [ADD]
Suslin, V.:Capriccio über die Abreise, w. Hanna Weinmeister (vn) *(rec Lockenhaus Festival, Austria, 1995)*
BIS ▲ CD 810 [DDD]
Tchaikovsky, P.:Con Vn, w. L. Maazel (cnd), Berlin PO Deutsche Grammophon ▲ 431609-2 [ADD]
Vivaldi, A.:Cons Vn, Op. 8/1–4, "The Four Seasons", w. C. Abbado (cnd), London SO
Deutsche Grammophon ("Galleria" series) ▲ 431172-2 [ADD]
Weber, C.M. von:Grand duo concertant Cl, w. Andrei Gavrilov (pno) [arr for vn & pno]
EMI Classics 2-▲ CDFB 69334

Krenberga, Dita (fl)
Vasks, P.:Landscape with Birds *(rec Riga Recording Studio, Latvia, Dec 1995)*
Conifer Classics ▲ 51272 [DDD]

Kreplin, Gordon (gtr)
Bach, J.S.:Suite Lt, BWV 995 *(rec St. John's Episcopal Church, Broad Creek, MD, Spring 1995)*
Ascención ▲ AR 103 [DDD]
Bach, J.S.:Suite Lt, BWV 996 Ascención ▲ AR 104 [DDD]
Lauro, A.:Quatro Valses Venezolanos *(rec St. John's Episcopal Church, Broad Creek, MD, Spring 1995)*
Ascención ▲ AR 103 [DDD]
Mompou, F.:Suite compostelana Ascención ▲ AR 104 [DDD]
Powell, R.:Mass Gtr Ascención ▲ AR 104 [DDD]
Villa-Lobos, H.:Preludes Gtr *(rec St. John's Episcopal Church, Broad Creek, MD, Spring 1995)*
Ascención ▲ AR 103 [DDD]

Kretz, Andreas (tpt)—see ORCHESTRAS & ENSEMBLES Brassissimo Vienna

Kretzschmar, Hermann (pno)
Antheil, G.:Music of, w. Martyn Hill (ten), Jagdish Mistry (vn), H. K. Gruber (cnd), Ensemble Modern—Printemps I; Ballet mécanique; Fighting the Waves; A Jazz Symphony; Lithuanian Night; Jazz Sonata; Concerto for CO; Son 1 Vn; Printemps II *(rec Frankfurt, Germany, June 27-30 & Dec 20-23, 1)* RCA Red Seal ▲ 09026-68066-2 [DDD]
Kurtág, G.:Quasi una fantasia, w. P. Eötvös (cnd), Ensemble Modern *(rec June 14-16, 1990)*
Sony Classical ▲ SK 53290 [DDD]
Zimmermann, B.A.:Présence, w. Peter Rundel (vn), Michael Stirling (vc) *(rec Frankfurt, May 1-4 & Oct 24-25, 1992)* RCA Red Seal ▲ 09026-61181-2 [DDD]

Krieger, Jeffrey (elec vc)
Vees, J.:Rocket Baby, w. Tony Forkush (nar) CRI ("Emergency Music" series) ▲ CD 730 [DDD]

Krieger, Jeffrey (vc)
Berger, J.:The Lead Plates of the Rom Press *(rec live, Yale Univ School of Music)*
CRI ▲ CD 680 [DDD]
Cage, J.:Ryoanji Fl *(rec Sound Situation, Glastonbury, CT)* CRI ▲ CD 680 [DDD]
Gwiazda, H.:themythofAcceptAnce *(rec Sound Situation, Glastonbury, CT)* CRI ▲ CD 680 [DDD]
Knehans, D.:Night Chains *(rec Sound Situation, Glastonbury, CT)* CRI ▲ CD 680 [DDD]
Steen, K.:Shadows & Light *(rec Sound Situation, Glastonbury, CT)* CRI ▲ CD 680 [DDD]

Krieger, Norman (pno)
Summerdays:From the Musical Masterworks Festival at Old Lyme, w. Sheir Greenawald (sop), Beverly Hoch (sop), John Koch (ten), Aloysia Friedman (vn), Michele Sidener (va), Norman Krieger (cnd)
Well-Tempered Productions ▲ WTP 5173 [DDD]

Krieger, Ulrich (sax)
Celli, J.:Video Sax O.O. Discs ▲ OO 22

Krigbaum, Charles (org)
Biber, H. von:Mystery (or Rosary) Sons, w. William Tortolano (vn) GIA 2-▲ GIA 286
Duruflé, M.:Org Music (sels)—Prélude, Adagio et Choral varié sur le thème du Veni Creator, Op. 4
Organ Historical Society 2-▲ OHS 100
Elgar, E.:Severn Suite Orch Organ Historical Society 2-▲ OHS 100
Mendelssohn, F.:Sons Org—No. 6 Organ Historical Society 2-▲ OHS 100
Messiaen, O.:L'Ascension Org Organ Historical Society 2-▲ OHS 100
Widor, C.M.:Nouvelles pièces Org AFKA ■ SK 306
Widor, C.M.:Suite latine AFKA ■ SK 305
Widor, C.M.:Sym 1 Org [Newberry Memorial Organ, Woolsey Hall, Yale Univ.] AFKA ▲ SK 521
Widor, C.M.:Sym 1 Org AFKA ■ SK 302
Widor, C.M.:Sym 2 Org [Newberry Memorial Organ, Woolsey Hall, Yale Univ.] AFKA ▲ SK 521
Widor, C.M.:Sym 2 Org AFKA ■ SK 303
Widor, C.M.:Sym 2 Org Organ Historical Society 2-▲ OHS 100
Widor, C.M.:Sym 3 Org AFKA ■ SK 302
Widor, C.M.:Sym 3 Org [Newberry Memorial Organ, Woolsey Hall, Yale Univ.] AFKA ▲ SK 522
Widor, C.M.:Sym 4 Org [Newberry Memorial Organ, Woolsey Hall, Yale Univ.] AFKA ▲ SK 522
Widor, C.M.:Sym 4 Org AFKA ■ SK 303
Widor, C.M.:Sym 5 Org AFKA ■ SK 304
Widor, C.M.:Sym 6 Org AFKA ■ SK 304
Widor, C.M.:Sym 7 Org AFKA ■ SK 305
Widor, C.M.:Sym 8 Org AFKA ■ SK 306
Widor, C.M.:Sym 9 Org AFKA ■ SK 307
Widor, C.M.:Sym 10 Org AFKA ■ SK 307

Kriikku, Kari (cl)
Crusell, B.H.:Qts (3) Cl, w. Avantil String Quartet members—comp. Ondine ▲ ODE 727-2 [DDD]

Kriikku, Kari (cl) (cont.)
Debussy, C.:Première rapsodie, w. J.-P. Saraste (cnd), Finnish RSO Ondine ▲ ODE 778-2 [DDD]
Lindberg, M.:Qnt Cl, w. Arditti String Quartet Montaigne ▲ MO 782033
Mendelssohn, F.:Concert Pieces, w. Osmo Linkola (bas hn), Arto Satukangas (pno)
Ondine ▲ ODE 820 [DDD]
Tiensuu, J.:Con Cl, w. J.-P. Saraste (cnd), Finnish RSO Ondine ▲ ODE 778-2 [DDD]
Weber, C.M. von:Grand duo concertant Cl, w. Arto Satukangas (pno) Ondine ▲ ODE 820 [DDD]
Weber, C.M. von:Qnt Cl, w. New Helsinki String Quartet Ondine ▲ ODE 820 [DDD]

Krill, Margaret (pno)
Holt, S. ten:Horizon, w. Yoko Abe (pno), Polo de Haas (pno), Fred Oldenburg (pno)
Donemus 2-▲ CV 5/6

Krimsier, Renee (fl)
Kraft, William:Con Perc, w. Dean Anderson (perc), Diane Heffner (cl), Nancy Cirillo (vn/va), Ronald Lowry (vc), Hugh Hinton (pno) Albany ▲ TROY 218 [DDD]
Kraft, William:Settings from Pierrot Lunaire, w. Jane Manning (sop), Diane Heffner (cl), Nancy Cirillo (vn/va), Ronald Lowry (vc), Dean Anderson (perc), Hugh Hinton (pno) Albany ▲ TROY 218 [DDD]

Krist, J. (pno)
Delz, C.:Qt Pno, w. C. Delz (pno), F. Gauwerky (pno), A. Hempel (pno), N. Shirato (pno)
Grammont ▲ CTSP 18-2 [ADD]

Krista, Oleh (vn)
Artyomov, V.:In Memoriam, w. D. Kitayenko (cnd), Moscow PO Olympia ▲ OLY 516 [DDD]
Artyomov, V.:Tristia, w. D. Kitayenko (cnd), Moscow PO Olympia ▲ OLY 516 [DDD]
Artyomov, V.:Way to Olympus, w. D. Kitayenko (cnd), Moscow PO Olympia ▲ OLY 516 [DDD]

Kristensen, Helle (rcr)
Christensen, M.:Birds of a Spring Night *(rec Jetsmark Kirke, Denmark, June 1993 & Dec. 1994)*
Point ▲ PCD 5116
Christensen, M.:Winter Light, w. Ricardo Odriozola (vn) *(rec Jetsmark Kirke, Denmark, June 1993 & Dec. 1994)* Point ▲ PCD 5116

Kristian, Ulrika (vn)—see ORCHESTRAS & ENSEMBLES Camerata Tallinn

Kristmundsson, Gudmundur (va)
Leifs, J.:Music of, w. Sigrídur Ella Magnúsdóttir (mez), Ólafur Vignir Albertsson (pno), Sólveig Anna Jónsdóttir (pno), Hjálmar Ragnarsson (pno), Edda Erlendsdóttir (pno), Marteinn Hunger Fridriksson (org), Hildigunnur Halldórsdóttir (vn), Gréta Gudnadóttir (vn), Sigurdur Halldórsson (vc), Richard Korn (db), Iceland SO, Icelandic Opera Chorus, Langholts Church Graduale Choir, Hamrahlíd Choir—Icelandic Cant, Op. 13/4; Valse Lento, Op. 2/1; Icelandic Dance, Op. 11/2 [Tempo Giusto]; Requiem; Lullaby [After the Riots]; Fairy-Tale in the Wood [from Baldr, Op. 34]; Funeral March; Separation [from Elegy, Op. 53]; Galdra Loftur Ov, Op. 10; Funeral March, Op. 6; Reverie; Reunion [from Elegy, Op. 53]; Fine I, Op. 55; Andante [The Last Supper]; Preludia Organo, Op. 16/3 [In the Church]; The Tear of Stone [from Elegy, Op. 53] Music From Iceland ▲ ITM 605 [DDD]
Ragnarsson, H.:Music of, w. S. E. Magnúsdóttir (mez), H. Halldórsdóttir (vn), G. Gudnadóttir (vn), S. Halldórsson (vc), R. Korn (db), Ó. V. Albertsson (pno), S. A. Jónsdóttir (pno), H. Ragnarsson (pno), E. Erlendsdóttir (pno), M. H. Fridriksson (org), Sakari, Wilkinson (cnd), Iceland SO, G. Cortes (cnd), J. Stefánsson (cnd), T. Ingólfsdóttir (cnd), Hamrahlíd Choir, Icelandic Opera Chorus, Langholts Church Graduale Choir—Meine kleine Freundin [In the Ballroom]; Lovers Duet; After the concert; Meine kleine Freundin [Annie listens to the Radio]; Lif's Theme [On the Beach]; Lif's Theme II [Night Prayer]; Composing Ov [Vars I, II & III] Music From Iceland ▲ ITM 605 [DDD]

Krivine, Emmanuel (vn)
Schubert, Franz:Con Vn, w. J. Kantorow (cnd), Netherlands PO Denon ▲ CO 1666 [DDD]

Krizanovsky, Radek (vn)—see ORCHESTRAS & ENSEMBLES Apollo String Quartet

Kroeker, B. (ob)—see ORCHESTRAS & ENSEMBLES Pennsylvania Wind Quintet

Kroeker, Christian (pno)—see also ORCHESTRAS & ENSEMBLES Trio Cantabile
Flöten Fantasien [Flute Fantasies], w. Hans-Jörg Wegner (fl) *(rec Aug. 1992)*
Thorofon ▲ CTH 2187 [DDD]

Kroft, Josef (vn)
Mozart, W.A.:Serenade Vn, K.250, w. J. Hnyk (cnd), Czech Phil CO Canyon Classics ▲ 3689

Krogh, Bodil (pno)
Stolarczyk, W.:Earth Air Fire Water, w. Amalie Malling (pno), John Damgaard (pno), Anne Øland (pno), Teddy Teirup (pno), Friedrich Gürtler (pno), Rosalind Bevan (pno), Poul Rosenbaum (pno), Rodolfo Llambias (pno), Bella Horn-Ribera (pno), Anders Riber (pno), Elisabeth Sigurdsson (pno), Thomas Tronheim (pno), Elsebeth Broderson (pno), Erik Kaltoft (pno), Jørgen Hald Nielsen (pno), Aino Gilemann (pno), Birgit Kjær (pno), Jørgen Thomsen (pno), Gunhild Donslund (pno), Henrik Bo Hansen (pno), Lone Karlsson (pno), Erik Fessel (pno), Lasse Nilsson (pno), Janos Ferenczi (pno), Erik Bach (pno), Axel Momme (pno), Arne de Cros Dich (pno), Sven Micha Slot (pno), Hanne Bramsen Buhl (pno), Lili Olesen (pno), Susannah Carlsson (pno), Ulla Erml (pno), Vagn Sørensen (pno), Leif Greibe (pno), Kirsten Ottosen (pno), Inger Bergenholz (pno), Karsten Gylendorf (pno), Bjønr Elkjær (pno), Jacob Bjørn Jensen (pno), Jørgen Kaad (pno), Anne Marie Hjelm (pno), Carl Ulrik Munk Andersen (pno), Poul Lumbye (pno), Oluf Hildebrandt Nielsen (pno), Joachim Olsson (pno), Peter Pade Ramsøe Jacobsen (pno), Astrid Pollmann (pno), Jette Borsch (pno), Kirsten Karlshøj (pno), Maria Teresa Assing (pno), Allan Dahl Hansen (pno), Johan Hugossen (pno), Tine Fenger Pederson (pno), Arne Jørgen Fæø (pno), Anja Høgsted (pno), Anne Sophie Parbo (pno), Inga Lindmark (pno), Teresa Drabik Stathakis (pno), Anne Ruth Ferenczi (pno), Irene Hasager (pno), Yuka Ichikawa (pno), Birgitte Baur (pno), Malene Thastum (pno), Jens E. Rasmussen (pno), Birgitte Zielke (pno), Claus Zielke (pno), Stefan Kasch (pno), Bin Qiao (pno), Inger Johanne Teirup (pno), Lindy Rosborg (pno), Liisa Heininen (pno), David Højer (pno), Ellen Refstrup (pno), Thomas K. Søorensen (pno), Erik Kure (pno), Michael Rauff (pno), Jan beck Eriksson (pno), Tanja Zapolski (pno), Vibeke Skagbo (pno), Pål Eide Lindtner (pno), Ha-Young Sul (pno), Benedicte Palko (pno), Inke Kesseler (pno), Anne Marie Meineche (pno), Sverre Larsen (pno), Kasper Peter Bach (pno), Elisabetta Eliseo (pno), Olga Magieres (pno), Carl Erik Kühl (pno), Thorkild Borup Nielsen (pno), Valeria Zanini (pno), Lars Stenhoft (perc), Dennis Boel (perc), Winnie Dahlgren (perc), Susanne Vind (perc), Claus Byrith (elec), Anne Marie Storm (elec), J. Ribera (cnd) *(rec live, Koldinghaus Castle, Denmark, May 2, 1996)* Danica ▲ DCD 1996

Krogh, G. (org)
Thybo, L.:Contrasti *(rec Vangede Church, Mar. 13, Apr. 11, 12 & 25)*
Marco Polo/Dacapo ▲ 8.224009 [DDD]
Thybo, L.:Sonnengesang, w. S. Lange (mez) *(rec Vangede Church, Mar. 13, Apr. 11, 12 & 25)*
Marco Polo/Dacapo ▲ 8.224009 [DDD]
Thybo, L.:Sumer is Icumen In *(rec Vangede Church, Mar. 13, Apr. 11, 12 & 25)*
Marco Polo/Dacapo ▲ 8.224009 [DDD]

Krohn, Markku (perc)
The Battle:Organ Music Gothic, Renaissance & Early Baroque, w. Kalevi Kiviniemi (org)
Finlandia ▲ FIN 98036

Kroisamer, Hubert (vn)—see ORCHESTRAS & ENSEMBLES Vienna String Quartet

Kroll, Mark (hpd)
Bach, J.S.:Sons Fl, BWV 1030–35, w. P. Fried (fl), D. Sussman (vc)
Golden Tone ▲ GTCD 001 ■ GTC 001

Kromer, Oskar (va)
Brahms, J.:Sextet Strs, Op. 36, w. Peter Rybar (vn), Clemens Dahinden (vn), Heinz Wigand (va), Carl-Heinz Jucker (vc), Antonio Tusa (vc) Doron 2-▲ DRC 4007/8 [ADD]

Krommer, K. (bn)
Mozart, W.A.:Con Bn, w. A. Lizzio (cnd), Mozart Festival Orch Vivace 3-▲ E 315 [DDD]

Kronjäger, Brigitte (fl)
Dussek, J.L.:Son Fl, w. Johannes Degen (vc), André Desponds (pno) *(rec June 1994)*
Jecklin ▲ JEC 303 [DDD]
Hummel, J.N.:Adagio, Vars & Rondo on "Schöne Minka", w. André Desponds (pno), Johannes Degen (vc) *(rec June 1994)* Jecklin ▲ JEC 303 [DDD]
Kuhlau, F.:Fl Music—3 Capricci [from Op. 10] *(rec June 1994)* Jecklin ▲ JEC 303 [DDD]
Ries, F.:Trio Pno, w. André Desponds (pno), Johannes Degen (vc) *(rec June 1994)*
Jecklin ▲ JEC 303 [DDD]

Kroon, Torbjörn (trbn)—see ORCHESTRAS & ENSEMBLES Royal Danish Brass

▲ = CD ♦ = Enhanced CD Δ = MD ■ = Cassette Tape □ = DCC

Kröper, Andreas (fl)
Haydn, J.:Trios Pno, Fl & Vc, w. Bernhard Gillitzer (pno), Thomas Fritzsch (vc) *(rec Evangelic Church, Korunní, Prague, Sept 1993)* Arta ▲ CD 0052 [DDD]
Mysliveček, J.:Trio Fl, w. Simon Standage (vn), Thomas Fritzsch (vc) *(rec Evangelic Church, Korunní, Prague, Jan 1994)* Arta ▲ LC 4789 [DDD]
Pichl, V.:Divert Fl, w. Simon Standage (vn), Thomas Fritzsch (vc) *(rec Evangelic Church, Korunní, Prague, Jan 1994)* Arta ▲ LC 4789 [DDD]
Reicha, A.:Grand Trio Fl, w. Simon Standage (vn), Thomas Fritzsch (vc) *(rec Evangelic Church, Korunní, Prague, Jan 1994)* Arta ▲ LC 4789 [DDD]
Krosnick, Joel (vc)—see also ORCHESTRAS & ENSEMBLES Juilliard String Quartet
Beethoven, L. van:Sons Vc (comp), w. Gilbert Kalish (pno) *(rec Recital Hall of the Staller Center, SUNY–Stony Brook, May 28–June 1, 1994)* Arabesque 2–▲ ARA 6656–2 [DDD]
Beethoven, L. van:Vars on "Ein Mädchen oder Weibchen" from Mozart's *Die Zauberflöte*, w. Gilbert Kalish (pno) *(rec Recital Hall of the Staller Center, SUNY–Stony Brook, May 28–June 1, 1994)* Arabesque 2–▲ ARA 6656–2 [DDD]
Beethoven, L. van:Vars on "See, the Conquering Hero Comes" from Handel's *Judas Maccabaeus*, w. Gilbert Kalish (pno) *(rec Recital Hall of the Staller Center, SUNY–Stony Brook, May 28–June 1, 1994)* Arabesque 2–▲ ARA 6656–2 [DDD]
Beethoven, L. van:Vars on "Bei Männern" from Mozart's *Die Zauberflöte*, w. Gilbert Kalish (pno) *(rec Recital Hall of the Staller Center, SUNY–Stony Brook, May 28–June 1, 1994)* Arabesque 2–▲ ARA 6656–2 [DDD]
Berger, A.:Duos, w. J. Smirnoff (vn), C. Oldfather (pno), G. Kalish (pno), P. Lanini (ob), D. Stewart (cl)—Duo No. 1 for Violin & Piano (1948); Duo for Cello & Piano (1951); Duo for Oboe & Clarinet (1952) New World ▲ NW 360–2 [DDD]
Carter, E.:Son Vc, w. Gilbert Kalish (pno) Arabesque ▲ ARA 6682
Carter, E.:Son Vc, w. P. Jacobs (hpd) Elektra/Nonesuch ▲ 79183–2
Poulenc, F.:Son Vc, w. Gilbert Kalish (pno) Arabesque ▲ ARA 6682
Prokofiev, S.:Son Vc, w. Gilbert Kalish (pno) Arabesque ▲ ARA 6682
Sessions, R.:Duo Vn & Vc, w. C. Macomber (vn) Koch International Classics ▲ KIC 7153–2 [DDD]
Shapey, R.:Kroslish Son, w. G. Kalish (pno) New World ▲ NW 355–2 [DDD]
Krotzinger, W. (vn)
Vivaldi, A.:Cons Vn, Op. 8/1–4, "The Four Seasons", w. K. Münchinger (cnd), Stuttgart CO London ("Weekend Classics" series) ▲ 417873–2 [AAD] ■ 417873–4
Kroupa, Vladimír (va)—see ORCHESTRAS & ENSEMBLES Apollo String Quartet
Kroyt, Boris (va)—see ORCHESTRAS & ENSEMBLES Budapest String Quartet, Budapest String Quartet members
Krtschil, Henry (pno)
Weill, K.:Songs, w. G. May (mez) [G] Capriccio ▲ 10180 [DDD]
Krücker, Michael (pno)—see ORCHESTRAS & ENSEMBLES Cologne Piano Duo
Kruczek, Mark (org)
Mysteries Beyond:Songs & Chants in Praise of Mary, w. [cnd:Dennis Keene], Voices of Ascension, V. Cole (ten), Kathleen Bride (hp), Patrick Stephens (pno) *(rec Apr. 17, 28–30, 1993)* Delos ▲ DE 3138 [DDD]
Krueger, Christopher (fl)
Mozart, W.A.:Qt Fl, K.285, w. J. Schröder (vn), J. Griffin (va), K. Slowik (vc) [period instrs] Smithsonian Collection 5–▲ ND 031
Telemann, G.P.:Qts, Book 4, w. Boston Museum Trio *(rec Slosberg Auditorium, Brandeis Univ, Waltham, MA, Aug 24–26, 1994)* Centaur ▲ 2260 [DDD]
Krug, B. (hn)
Rheinberger, J.:Son Hn, w. H. Göbel (pno) Thorofon 6–▲ BCTH 2161/6
Rheinberger, J.:Son Hn, w. H. Göbel (pno) Thorofon ▲ CTH 2108 [DDD]
Kruger, Anna (va)—see ORCHESTRAS & ENSEMBLES Lark String Quartet
Kruger, Erich (va)
Mozart, W.A.:Concertone Vns, w. Thorsten Rosenbusch (vn), H. Haenchen (cnd), C.P.E. Bach CO Berlin Classics ▲ BER 2003
Krüger, Irmtraud (org)
Italian Masterworks for Organ & Trumpet, w. Edward Tarr (tpt), N. Eklund (tpt), C. Frigerio (vc) Christophorus ▲ CHR 77145 [DDD]
Portuguese [Lusitanian] Organ Music, w. Irmtraud Krüger (org) MD + G ▲ O 3371/72 [DDD]
The Silver Trumpets of Lisbon & Lusitanian Organ Music, w. Edward H. Tarr (tpt), Edward Tarr Trumpet Ensemble MD + G ▲ L 3348 [DDD]
Krüger, M. M. (gtr)
Boccherini, L.:Fandango, w. K. Schilde (pno) *(rec Jan. 7–9 & 19, 1991)* Calig ▲ CAL 50912 [DDD]
Castelnuovo-Tedesco, M.:Fant Gtr & Pno, w. K. Schilde (pno) *(rec Jan. 7–9 & 19, 1991)* Calig ▲ CAL 50912 [DDD]
Giuliani, M.:Grand Duo Concertant Gtr, w. K. Schilde (pno) *(rec Jan. 7–9 & 19, 1991)* Calig ▲ CAL 50912 [DDD]
Weber, C.M. von:Divert assai facile, w. K. Schilde (pno) *(rec Jan. 7–9 & 19, 1991)* Calig ▲ CAL 50912 [DDD]
Kruglov, Vyacheslav (mand)
Hummel, J.N.:Con Mand & Strs, w. N. Maretsky (mand), Northern Crown Soloists Ensemble MK ▲ MKA 417114
Vivaldi, A.:Con Lt, w. N. Maretsky (mand), Northern Crown Soloists Ensemble MK ▲ MKA 417114
Vivaldi, A.:Con Mand, RV.425, w. N. Maretsky (mand), Northern Crown Soloists Ensemble MK ▲ MKA 417114
Vivaldi, A.:Con for 2 Mands, w. N. Maretsky (mand), Northern Crown Soloists Ensemble MK ▲ MKA 417114
Vivaldi, A.:Trio Son Vn Lt, RV. 82, w. N. Maretsky (mand), Northern Crown Soloists Ensemble MK ▲ MKA 417114
Krugmann, Heike (gtr)—see ORCHESTRAS & ENSEMBLES Rotenbeck Trio
Krükku, Kari (b cl)
Suilamo, H.:YELL Finlandia ▲ FIN 12179 [DDD]
Krükku, Kari (cl)
Nevanlinna, T.:Foto, w. Matti Rantanen (acc) Finlandia ▲ FIN 54404 [DDD]
Krul, H. (db)
Saint-Saëns, C.:Carnival of the Animals, w. D. Wayenberg (vn), H. Oudenaarden (vn), J. Hagen (fl), H. de Fraaf (cl), W. Vos (xyl), M. Dekkers (acc), Daniel String Quartet *(rec Rotterdam, May 28, 1985)* Erasmus ▲ WHV 001 [DDD]
Krumbach, Wilhelm (org)
Beethoven, L. van:Org Music [the König Organ in Schleiden]—Fugue in C; Fugues in d (6); Prelude in All Keys, Op. 39/1; Suite for Mechanical Organ, WoO 33/1–3; Prelude in f, WoO 55; Trio in e *(rec May 1967)* Koch Treasure ▲ 31609–2 [ADD]
Kruse, John (cl)
Bentzon, N.V.:Qt Cl, w. Bjarbe Hansen (vn), Rastko Roknic (va), Svend Winsløw (vc) *(rec Det Fynske Musikkonservatorium, 1993)* Paula ▲ PACD 78 [DAD]
Bentzon, N.V.:Son Cl, w. Per Salo (pno) *(rec Det Fynske Musikkonservatorium, 1993)* Paula ▲ PACD 78 [DAD]
Koppel, H.D.:Vars Cl & Pno, w. Per Salo (pno) *(rec Det Fynske Musikkonservatorium, 1993)* Paula ▲ PACD 78 [DAD]
Koppel, H.D.:Variazioni Libère, w. Rene Højlund (cl), Kenneth Larsen (b cl), Søren Monrad (perc) *(rec Det Fynske Musikkonservatorium, 1993)* Paula ▲ PACD 78 [DAD]
Ruders, P.:Tattoo for One *(rec Det Fynske Musikkonservatorium, 1993)* Paula ▲ PACD 78 [DAD]
Ruders, P.:Throne, w. Per Salo (pno) *(rec Det Fynske Musikkonservatorium, 1993)* Paula ▲ PACD 78 [DAD]
Sørensen, B.:The Songs of the Decaying Garden *(rec Det Fynske Musikkonservatorium, 1993)* Paula ▲ PACD 78 [DAD]
Sørensen, B.:Troll–Playing *(rec Det Fynske Musikkonservatorium, 1993)* Paula ▲ PACD 78 [DAD]
Krüttli, P. (tuba)—see ORCHESTRAS & ENSEMBLES Quatror de cuivres Novus

Kruvand, Gail (db)
Bach, J.S.:Cant 20, w. Yuval Waldman (vn), José Cueto (vn), Jennifer Rende (va), Maryland Bach Aria Group members—Wacht auf Crystal ▲ CD 705 [DDD]
Bach, J.S.:Cant 82, w. Yuval Waldman (vn), José Cueto (vn), Jennifer Rende (va), Maryland Bach Aria Group members *(rec St. Peter's Church, Hale, Cheshire, Mar 14, 1994)* Naxos ▲ 8.550763 [DDD]
Bach, J.S.:Cant 110, w. Yuval Waldman (vn), José Cueto (vn), Jennifer Rende (va), Maryland Bach Aria Group members—Wachtet auf Crystal ▲ CD 705 [DDD]
Stradella, A.:Sinf alla Serenata, w. Yuval Waldman (vn), José Cueto (vn), Jennifer Rende (va), Maryland Bach Aria Group members Crystal ▲ CD 705 [DDD]
Torelli, G.:Son Tpt, G.1, w. Yuval Waldman (vn), José Cueto (vn), Jennifer Rende (va), Maryland Bach Aria Group members Crystal ▲ CD 705 [DDD]
Vivaldi, A.:Cons Bn, w. Yuval Waldman (vn), José Cueto (vn), Jennifer Rende (va), Maryland Bach Aria Group members—in B♭, RV.501, "La notte" Crystal ▲ CD 705 [DDD]
Kruzse, Marianna (ob)
Bach, Joh. Christian:Sinf concertante, T.284/6, w. Ildiko Line (vn), Violetta Eckhardt (vn), H. Gmür (cnd), Budapest Camerata *(rec Festetich Castle, Budapest, Mar 1994)* Naxos ▲ 8.553085 [DDD]
Krysa, Aleg (vn)
Schnittke, A.:Qt 2 Strs, w. N. Zabavnikov (vn), F. Dnizhinin (va), Y. Altman (vc) Vox Box 2–▲ CDX 5121 [ADD]
Krysa, Oleh (vn)
Bartók, B.:Sons (2) Vn & Pno, w. Tatiana Chekina (pno) *(rec Moscow Conservatory, July 1995)* Triton ▲ 17007 [DDD]
Bloch, E.:Con Vn, w. S. Oramo (cnd), Malmö SO *(rec Malmö Concert Hall, Sweden, Apr. 23–24, 1993)* BIS ▲ CD 639 [DDD]
Gubaidulina, S.:Offertorium, w. J. DePreist (cnd), Royal Stockholm PO BIS ▲ CD 566 [DDD]
Gubaidulina, S.:Rejoice, w. T. Thedéen (vc) BIS ▲ CD 566 [DDD]
Schnittke, A.:Con grosso 2, w. T. Thedéen (vc), L. Markiz (cnd), Malmö SO BIS ▲ CD 567 [DDD]
Schnittke, A.:Con 3 Vn, w. E. Klas (cnd), Malmö SO BIS ▲ CD 517 [DDD]
Schnittke, A.:Stille Musik Vn, w. Torleif Thedéen (vc) *(rec Danderyd Grammar School, Sweden, Sept. 19, 1992)* BIS ▲ CD 697 [DDD]
Schnittke, A.:Trio Pno, w. Tatiana Tchekina (pno), Torleif Thedéen (vc) *(rec Malmö Concert Hall, Sweden, May 12–14, 1994)* BIS ▲ CD 697 [DDD]
Schulhoff, E.:Duo, w. Torleif Thedéen (vc) *(rec Malmö Concert Hall, Sweden, May 12, 1994)* BIS ▲ CD 679 [DDD]
Schulhoff, E.:Son Vn *(rec Danderyd Grammar School, Sweden, Dec 10–11, 1994)* BIS ▲ CD 679 [DDD]
Schulhoff, E.:Son 1 Vn, w. Tatiana Tchekina (pno) *(rec Danderyd Grammar School, Sweden, Dec 10–11, 1994)* BIS ▲ CD 679 [DDD]
Ksaveriyev, Eugene (vc)
Smolsky, D.:Con. Vc, Belarussian State Radio–TV Orch Olympia ▲ OCD 551 [AAD]
Kšica, Josef (harm)
Rossini, G.:Petite messe solennelle, w. Livia Aghova (sop), Marta Benackova (mez), Gil Manuel Beltran (ten), Peter Mikulas (bass), Raphaele Cortesi (pno), Peter Toperczer (pno), Romano Gandolfi (cnd), Prague Chamber Choir *(rec Domovina Studios, Prague, Sept. 10–12, 1994)* Discover International 2–▲ DI 920324–5 [DDD]
Kšica, Josef (org)
Bruckner, A.:Mass 3, w. Dagmar Masková (sgr), Vladimír Nacházel (sgr), Jiří Novotný (sgr), Jiří Seiler (sgr), Jiří Uherek (sgr), Eva Zbytovská (sgr), Jan Votava (trbn), Josef Pancík (cnd), Prague Chamber Choir Orfeo ▲ 327 951 [DDD]
Bruckner, A.:Motets, w. Dagmar Masková (sgr), Vladimír Nacházel (sgr), Jiří Novotný (sgr), Jiří Seiler (sgr), Jiří Uherek (sgr), Eva Zbytovská (sgr), Jan Votava (trbn), Josef Pancík (cnd), Prague Chamber Choir—Locus iste; Afferentur regi; Ave Maria (2); Pange lingua; Pange lingua (phrygisch); Tantum ergo (2); Libera me; Os iusti; Virga jesse; Vexilla regis; Christus factus est; Tota pulchra es Maria; Ecce sacerdos magnus Orfeo ▲ 327 951 [DDD]
Dvořák, A.:Choral Music, w. Czech Phil Chorus, L. Mátl (cnd), Czech Philharmonic Chorus—Ave Maria; Ave maris stella; Hymns ad laudes; O sanctissima Supraphon ▲ SUP 11 1430 [DDD]
Dvořák, A.:Mass, w. Dagmar Masková (sop), Marta Benacková (alt), Walter Coppola (ten), Peter Mikulás (bass), Josef Pancík (cnd), Prague Chamber Choir *(rec Dvořák Hall, Prague, Nov 1993)* ECM New Series ▲ 78118–21539–2 [DDD]
Eben, Petr:Missa cum populo, w. L. Mátl (cnd), chamber ensemble, Czech Phil Chorus [Cz] Panton ▲ 81 1141–2911
Eben, Petr:Prague Te Deum, w. Josef Pancík (cnd), Prague Chamber Choir *(rec Dvořák Hall, Prague, Nov 1993)* ECM New Series ▲ 78118–21539–2 [DDD]
Janácek, L.:Our Father, w. Lydie Härtelová (hp), Josef Pancík (cnd), Prague Chamber Choir [arr for hp, org & mixed chorus] *(rec Dvořák Hall, Prague, Nov 1993)* ECM New Series ▲ 78118–21539–2 [DDD]
Janácek, L.:Our Father, w. Walter Coppola (ten), Josef Pancík (cnd), Prague Chamber Choir ECM ▲ 21539–2
Ku, Hsiao-mei (vn)—see also ORCHESTRAS & ENSEMBLES Arman Ensemble
Hoiby, L.:Bermudas, w. Terry Rhodes (sop), Ellen Williams (mez), Jonathan Bagg (va), Fred Raimi (vc), Thomas Warburton (pno) Albany ▲ TROY 172 [DDD]
Ku, Wen-Yu (vn)
Falla, M. de:Psyché, w. Elena Montaña (sop), Conchi Vacas (fl), Zoraida Avila (hp), Alison Montoya (va), Gloria Cuerda (vc) *(rec Madrid, Oct 1–3 1990)* RNE/Spanish National Radio ▲ M3/06 [DDD]
Ginastera, A.:Cantos del Tucumán, w. Elena Montaña (sop), Conchi Vacas (fl), Zoraida Avila (hp), Conchi Sangregorio (perc) *(rec Madrid, Oct 1–3 1990)* RNE/Spanish National Radio ▲ M3/06 [DDD]
Guibert, A.:The Bath Tub, w. Elena Montaña (sop), Conchi Vacas (fl), Alison Montoya (va), Gloria Cuerda (vc), Zoraida Avila (hp) *(rec Madrid, Oct 1–3 1990)* RNE/Spanish National Radio ▲ M3/06 [DDD]
Roussel, A.:Sérénade, w. Conchi Vacas (fl), Alison Montoya (va), Gloria Cuerda (vc), Zoraida Avila (hp) *(rec Madrid, Oct 1–3 1990)* RNE/Spanish National Radio ▲ M3/06 [DDD]
Kuan, Jennifer (vn)—see ORCHESTRAS & ENSEMBLES Stratos
Kubalek, Antonin (pno)
Brahms, J.:Ernste Gesänge, w. V. Braun (bar) [G] Dorian ▲ DOR 90132 [DDD]
Brahms, J.:Fants Pno, Op. 116 *(rec Apr. 1991)* Dorian ▲ DOR 90159 [DDD]
Brahms, J.:Intermezzos Pno, Op. 117 Dorian ▲ DOR 90141 [DDD]
Brahms, J.:Pieces Pno, Op. 118 *(rec Apr. 1991)* Dorian ▲ DOR 90159 [DDD]
Brahms, J.:Pieces Pno, Op. 119 *(rec Apr. 1991)* Dorian ▲ DOR 90159 [DDD]
Brahms, J.:Rhaps Pno, Op. 79 *(rec 4/91)* Dorian ▲ DOR 90159 [DDD]
Brahms, J.:Son 3 Pno Dorian ▲ DOR 90141 [DDD]
Brahms, J.:Waltzes Pno, Op. 39 Dorian ▲ DOR 90141 [DDD]
Buczynski, W.:The August Collection Pno CBC ("Musica Viva" series) ▲ MVCD 1059 [DDD]
Chopin, F.:Ballades Pno (comp)—Op. 47 Dorian ▲ DOR 90102 [DDD]
Czech Miniature Masterpieces Dorian ▲ DOR 90121 [DDD]
Dvořák, A.:Ballad, w. I. Zenaty (vn) Dorian ▲ DOR 90171 [DDD]
Dvořák, A.:Mazurek, w. I. Zenaty (vn) Dorian ▲ DOR 90171 [DDD]
Dvořák, A.:Qnt Pno, Op. 5, w. Lafayette String Quartet *(rec Troy Savings Bank Music Hall, Troy, NY, Apr 1995)* Dorian ▲ DOR 90221 [DDD]
Dvořák, A.:Qnt Pno, Op. 81, w. Lafayette String Quartet *(rec Troy Savings Bank Music Hall, Troy, NY, Apr 1995)* Dorian ▲ DOR 90221 [DDD]
Dvořák, A.:Romantic Pieces, Op. 75, w. I. Zenatý (vn) Dorian ▲ DOR 90171 [DDD]
Dvořák, A.:Son Vn, w. I. Zenaty (vn) Dorian ▲ DOR 90171 [DDD]
Dvořák, A.:Sonatina Vn, w. I. Zenatý (vn) Dorian ▲ DOR 90171 [DDD]
Grieg, E.:Son 1 Vn, w. Ivan Zenaty (vn) *(rec Troy Savings Bank Music Hall, Troy, New York, Oct 1995)* Dorian ▲ DOR 90234 [DDD]
Grieg, E.:Son 2 Vn, w. Ivan Zenatý (vn) *(rec Troy Savings Bank Music Hall, Troy, New York, Oct 1995)* Dorian ▲ DOR 90234 [DDD]
Grieg, E.:Son 3 Vn, w. Ivan Zenatý (vn) *(rec Troy Savings Bank Music Hall, Troy, New York, Oct 1995)* Dorian ▲ DOR 90234 [DDD]

Kubalek, Antonin (pno) (cont.)
Janácek, L.:The Diary of One Who Disappeared, w. S. Love (mez), G. Hirst (ten), Columbia Pro Cantare Women's Ensemble [Cz] — Arabesque ▲ Z 6513 [DDD]
Janácek, L.:In the Mists — Dorian ▲ DOR 90185 [DDD]
Korngold, E.W.:Don Quixote — Citadel ▲ CTD 88109 [ADD]
Korngold, E.W.:Fairy Pictures *(rec Toronto, 1973)* — Citadel ▲ CTD 88109 [ADD]
Korngold, E.W.:Son 1 Pno *(rec Toronto, 1973)* — Citadel ▲ CTD 88109 [ADD]
Korngold, E.W.:Son 2 Pno — Citadel ▲ CTD 88109 [ADD]
Kymlicka, M.:Valses Pno — Dorian ▲ DOR 90102 [DDD]
Martinů, B.:Pno Music (sels)—Polkas & Etudes, Books 1-3 — CBC ("Musica Viva" series) ▲ MVCD 1059 [DDD]
Novák, V.:Memories — Dorian ▲ DOR 90185 [DDD]
Schubert, Franz:Winterreise, w. V. Braun (bar) [G] — Dorian ▲ DOR 90145 [DDD]
Schumann, R.:Carnaval Pno — Dorian ▲ DOR 90116 [DDD]
Schumann, R.:Fantasiestücke Pno, Op. 111 — Dorian ▲ DOR 90116 [DDD]
Schumann, R.:Gesänge der Frühe — Dorian ▲ DOR 90116 [DDD]
Schumann, R.:Kinderszenen — Dorian ▲ DOR 90116 [DDD]
Schumann, R.:Liederkreis, Op. 24, w. V. Braun (bar) [G] — Dorian ▲ DOR 90132 [DDD]
Schumann, R.:Liederkreis, Op. 39, w. V. Braun (bar) [G] — Dorian ▲ DOR 90132 [DDD]
Smetana, B.:Czech Dances—Furiant; The Little Hen; The Grain Dancer; The Bear; The Little Onion; The Stamping Dance; The Lancer; The Stepping Dance; The Neighbor's Dance; The Hop Dance *(rec Los Angeles, 1976)* — Citadel ▲ CTD 88112
Smetana, B.:Czech Dances — Dorian ▲ DOR 90122 [DDD]
Smetana, B.:Memories of Bohemia — Dorian ▲ DOR 90185 [DDD]
Smetana, B.:Polkas Pno—Op. 12/1 *(rec Los Angeles, 1978)* — Citadel ▲ CTD 88112
Smetana, B.:Rêves *(rec Los Angeles, 1978)* — Citadel ▲ CTD 88112
Suk, J.:About Mother — Dorian ▲ DOR 90185 [DDD]
Tchaikovsky, P.:Les Saisons — Dorian ▲ DOR 90102 [DDD]

Kubelik, Jan (vn)
The Acoustic Recordings *(rec 1902–13)* — Biddulph 2-▲ LAB 033–34 [ADD]
Great Violinists, Vol. 2 *(rec ca. 1902–1934)* — Symposium ▲ SYM 1072

Kubelik, Rafael (pno)
Bach, J.S.:Con for 4 Hpds, w. Rudolf Kempe (pno), Fritz Rieger (pno), Wolfgang Sawallisch (pno), R. Kubelik (cnd), Bavarian RSO *(rec 1972)* — Arkadia ▲ 494

Kubera, Joseph (pno)—see also ORCHESTRAS & ENSEMBLES Roscoe Mitchell New Chamber Ensemble
Ashley, R.:The Producer Speaks, w. T. Buckner (bar) — Lovely Music ▲ LCD 3022 [DDD]
Cage, J.:Atlas Eclipticalis, w. P. Kotik (cnd), S.E.M. Ensemble Orch — Wergo ▲ WER 6216–2
Cage, J.:Concert Pno, w. P. Kotik (cnd), S.E.M. Ensemble Orch — Wergo ▲ WER 6216–2
Cage, J.:Pno Music, w. Joshua Pierce (pno), Borah Bergman (pno), Dorothy Jones (pno), Myra Meldorf (pno), Fumiko Miyanoo (pno)—Music Walk; Jazz Study; Experiences I & II; plus others — Wergo ▲ WER 61592
Cage, J.:Winter Music, w. P. Kotik (cnd), S.E.M. Ensemble Orch — Wergo ▲ WER 6216–2
Chambers, W.M.:Ten Grand, w. Ursula Oppens (pno), Walter Hilse (pno), Bennett Lerner (pno), Nurit Tiles (pno), Aleck Karis (pno), Edmund Niemann (pno), Martin Goldray (pno), Allen Shawn (pno), Elizabeth di Filice (pno), Geisel (cnd) — Newport ▲ NPD 85553
First, D.:Key Lights in a Palace Balloon *(rec Apr. 1991)* — O.O. Discs ▲ OO 5 [DDD]
Gibson, Jon:Running Commentary, w. T. Buckner (bar), J. Gibson (sax), Bill Ruyle (perc) — Lovely Music ▲ LCD 3022 [DDD]
Hays, S.:Dreaming the World, w. Thomas Bruckner (bar), Sal Basile (voc), Jennifer López (voc), John Schaffer (voc), Sorrel Hays (voc), Joseph Kubera (pno), John Kennedy (perc), Charles Wood (perc), Maya Gunji (perc), Eric Kivnick (perc), Jai Smith (perc) — New World ▲ 805202 [DDD]
Smith, B.:The Panther, w. T. Buckner (bar) — Lovely Music ▲ LCD 3022 [DDD]
Vigeland, N.:Vara, w. B. Held (fl) — Lovely Music ▲ LCD 3031 [DDD]

Kubera, Joseph (toy pno)
Cage, J.:Music Amplified Toy Pnos, w. Marilyn Crispell (toy pno), Joshua Pierce (toy pno) [3 toy pno version] *(rec 1976–89)* — Wergo ▲ WER 6158–2 [ADD]

Kubian, Deryll (vn)—see ORCHESTRAS & ENSEMBLES Old Fairfield Academy Orch members

Kubiček, Jaromir (perc)—see ORCHESTRAS & ENSEMBLES Prague Percussion Project

Kubita, Jaroslav (bn)
Zelenka, J.D.:Con à 8, w. Jana Brozková (ob), Josef Suk (vn), Ludmila Vybíralová (vn), Ivo Laniar (vc), F. Vajnar (cnd), Suk CO *(rec Studio Martinek, Prague, May 15–17 & Nov. 8–13, 19)* — Panton 2-▲ PAN 811235 [DDD]
Zelenka, J.D.:Trio Sons Obs, w. Jana Brozková (ob), Vojtech Jouza (ob), Václav Hoskovec (db), Frantisek Xaver Thuri (hpd)—Nos. 4–6, ZWV 181 — Studio Matous ▲ MAT 9 [DDD]
Zelenka, J.D.:Trio Sons Obs, w. Jana Brozková (ob), Vojtech Jouza (ob), Jan Jouza (vn), Václav Hoskovec (db), Frantisek Xaver Thuri (hpd)—Nos. 1–3 — Studio Matous ▲ MAT 8 [DDD]

Kubli, Rolf (bas hn)
Mozart, W.A.:Notturnos Sops, w. E. Speiser (sop), V. Gohl (cta), K. Widmer (bass), H.R. Stalder (cl), H. Leuthold (bas hn) [I] *(rec 1968)* — Jecklin–Disco ▲ JD 549–2 [ADD]
Mozart, W.A.:Più non si trovano, w. E. Speiser (sop), V. Gohl (cta), K. Widmer (bass), H.R. Stalder (cl), H. Leuthold (bas hn) [I] *(rec 1968)* — Jecklin–Disco ▲ JD 549–2 [ADD]

Kubricht, Jaroslav (cl)
Fibich, Z.:Idyll, w. D. Bostock (cnd), Carlsbad SO *(rec Lazne III, Karlovy Vary, Czech Republic, Jan 13–15, 1996)* — Classico ▲ CLASSCD 150

Kučera, Václav (gtr)—see ORCHESTRAS & ENSEMBLES Prague Guitar Quartet

Kučera, Vladimír (vn)—see ORCHESTRAS & ENSEMBLES Dolezalovo String Quartet

Kuchar, Theodore (va)
Martinů, B.:Qnt Strs, w. Charmian Gadd (vn), Solomia Soroka (vn), Rainer Moog (va), Young-Chang Cho (vc) *(rec Australian Festival of Chamber Music, July 1994)* — Naxos ▲ 8.553916 [DDD]

Kucharsky, Boris (vn)
Zimmermann, A.:Sons Vn, w. D. Rusó (hpd) — Trevak ▲ TRE 40003 [DDD]

Küchl, Rainer (vn)—see also ORCHESTRAS & ENSEMBLES Vienna Ring Ensemble
Haydn, J.:Con 1 Vn, w. A. Fischer (cnd), Austro-Hungarian Haydn Orch — Nimbus ▲ NI 5258 [DDD]
Haydn, J.:Con 4 Vn, w. A. Fischer (cnd), Austro-Hungarian Haydn Orch — Nimbus ▲ NI 5258 [DDD]

Kůda, František (pno)
Brod, M.:Mittelmeersuite — Supraphon ▲ SUP 112188 [DDD]
Brod, M.:Qnt Pno, w. Stamic String Quartet — Supraphon ▲ SUP 112188 [DDD]
Brod, M.:Songs, Op. 32, w. Katerina Kachlikova (sop), Ivan Kusnjer (bar) — Supraphon ▲ SUP 112188 [DDD]
Schulhoff, E.:Folk Songs & Dances from the Tesin Region, w. Olga Černá (mez) — Supraphon ▲ SUP 3196
Schulhoff, E.:Mood Pictures, w. Olga Černá (mez) — Supraphon ▲ SUP 3196
Schulhoff, E.:Songs, w. Olga Černá (mez)—Songs (3), Op. 14; Songs (3), "Das Lied vom Kinde"; Songs, "Die Garbe" — Supraphon ▲ SUP 3196

Kuderna, Jerry (pno)
Babbitt, M.:Phonemena Sop & Pno, w. Lynne Webber (sop) *(rec Colombia Studios, NYC)* — New World ▲ 80466–2

Kudiak, Edward (va)—see ORCHESTRAS & ENSEMBLES Biedermeier Ensemble

Kudlicki, Marek (org)
Bach, J.S.:Toccata & Fugue Org, BWV 565 — Polskie Nagrania ▲ PNCD 151 [ADD]

Kudo, Kazue (koto)
Hirai, K.:Son Koto & Fl, w. K.F. Asawa (fl) — Crystal ▲ CD 316 [DDD]
Japanese Music for Koto & Flute, w. Madame Kazue (koto), Kazue Frances Asawa (fl) — Crystal ▲ CD 316 [DDD]
Miyagi, M.:Haru no Umi, w. K. F. Asawa (fl) — Crystal ▲ CD 316 [DDD]
Miyagi, M.:Izumi, w. K.F. Asawa (shak) — Crystal ▲ CD 316 [DDD]
Sawai, T.:Flower, w. K. F. Asawa (fl) — Crystal ▲ CD 316 [DDD]
Yamamoto, H.:Ichikotsu, w. K. F. Asawa (fl) — Crystal ▲ CD 316 [DDD]

Kudo, Shigenori (fl)
Cimarosa, D.:Con for 2 Fls, w. J.-P. Rampal (fl), J.-P. Rampal (cnd), Salzburg Mozarteum Orch — Sony Classical ▲ SK 45930 [DDD]
Duos for Flute & Harp, w. Naoko Yoshino (hp) — Sony Classical ▲ SK 48033
Haydn, J.:Trios Pno, Fl & Vc, w. R. Mamou (pno), Dominique de Williencourt (vc) — Pavane ▲ ADW 7202 [DDD]
Jean-Pierre Rampal, w. Jean-Pierre Rampal (fl), John Steele Ritter (hpd/pno) — Sony Classical ▲ SK 46482 [ADD]
Mozart, W.A.:Concertone Vns, w. J.-P. Rampal (fl), J.-P. Rampal (cnd), Salzburg Mozarteum Orch — Sony Classical ▲ SK 45930 [DDD]
Stamitz, A.:Con Fls, w. J.-P. Rampal (fl), J.-P. Rampal (cnd), Salzburg Mozarteum Orch — Sony Classical ▲ SK 45930 [DDD]
Vivaldi, A.:Con for 2 Fls, w. J.-P. Rampal (fl), J.-P. Rampal (cnd), Salzburg Mozarteum Orch — Sony Classical ▲ SK 45930 [DDD]

Kudryachov, O. (fl)
Zecchi, A.:Divert Fl, w. Vera Dulova (hp), M. Terian (cnd), Moscow Conservatory Student Orch String Group *(rec 1961)* — Russian Compact Disc ("Talents of Russia" series) ▲ RCD 16204 [AAD]

Kuehn, David (tpt)
Thomson, V.:Portraits, w. Y. Mikhashoff (pno), M. Herr (sop), J. Boudler (perc)—30 sels composed from 1926–1982 — New Albion ▲ NA 034 [ADD]

Kuehner, Heiner (org)
Moret, N.:Hymnes, w. P. Sacher (cnd), Bâle SO — Musiques Suisses ▲ CD 6103 [DDD]

Kuerti, Anton (pno)
Beethoven, L. van:Con 5 Pno, "Emperor", w. A. Davis (cnd), Toronto SO *(rec Massey Hall, Toronto, 1986)* — CBC ("SM 5000" series) ▲ SMCD 5155 [DDD]
Beethoven, L. van:Fant Pno, Op. 80, "Choral Fant", w. A. Davis (cnd), Toronto SO, Toronto Mendelssohn Choir *(rec Massey Hall, Toronto, 1986)* — CBC ("SM 5000" series) ▲ SMCD 5155 [DDD]
Beethoven, L. van:Sons Vc (comp), w. K. Bogyo (vc) — Analekta ▲ CM 2902
Beethoven, L. van:Son 14 Pno, "Moonlight Son" *(rec live 1989)* — Analekta Fleur de Lys ▲ FL 2 3007 [DDD] ■ AN4-9201
Beethoven, L. van:Son 29 Pno, "Hammerklavier" *(rec live 1989)* — Analekta Fleur de Lys ▲ FL 2 3007 [DDD] ■ AN4-9201
Brahms, J.:Son 3 Pno *(rec Academy of Arts & Letters, New York, May 1996)* — Pro Piano ▲ PPR 224512 [DDD]
Brahms, J.:Vars & Fugue on a Theme by Handel *(rec Academy of Arts & Letters, New York, May 1996)* — Pro Piano ▲ PPR 224512 [DDD]
Chopin, F.:Intro & Polonaise, "Polonaise brilliante", w. K. Bogyo (vc) — Analekta ▲ CM 2902
Falla, M. de:Suite populaire espagnole, w. K. Bogyo (vc) [trans for vc & pno by Maurice Maréchal] — Analekta ▲ CM 2902
Fauré, G.:Elégie, w. K. Bogyo (vc) — Analekta ▲ CM 2902
Glazunov, A.:Grande Valse de Concert *(rec 1982)* — Analekta Fleur de Lys ▲ FL 2 3047 [DDD] ■ AN4-9202
Glazunov, A.:Son 1 Pno — Analekta ("Fleur de Lys" series) ▲ FL 23044
Liadov, A.:Pno Music—Prelude in D, Op. 3/1; Intermezzo in F, Op. 7/2; Gigue in F, Op. 3/2; Etude in F, Op. 37; Mazurka in f, Op. 57/3; Prelude in D♭, Op. 57/1 *(rec 1982)* — Analekta Fleur de Lys ▲ FL 2 3047 [DDD] ■ AN4-9202
Mendelssohn, F.:Capriccio brillante, w. P. Freeman (cnd), London PO — IMP ("Concert Classics" series) ▲ IMP PCD 1097
Mendelssohn, F.:Capriccio brillante, w. P. Freeman (cnd), London PO *(rec 10/86)* — IMP Classics ▲ PCD 953
Mendelssohn, F.:Con 1 Pno, w. P. Freeman (cnd), London PO *(rec 10/86)* — IMP Classics ▲ PCD 953
Mendelssohn, F.:Con 2 Pno, w. P. Freeman (cnd), London PO *(rec 10/86)* — IMP Classics ▲ PCD 953
Mendelssohn, F.:Fant Pno, "Sonate écossaise" — Monitor ■ 55009
Mendelssohn, F.:Pno Music (misc) — Monitor ■ 55009
Schubert, Franz:Sons Pno (comp)—Sonatas in a, D.845 & in c, D.958 — IMP Masters ▲ MCD 20 [DDD]
Schubert, Franz:Sons Pno (comp)—Sonatas in A, D.664 & in G, D.894 — IMP Masters ▲ MCD 29 [DDD]
Schubert, Franz:Sonatinas Vn, w. A. Dubeau (vn) *(rec 1990)* — Analekta Fleur de Lys ▲ FL 2 3042 ■ AN4-8703
Schubert, Franz:Sonatinas Vn, w. Angèle Dubeau (vn) — Analekta ▲ AN 28703
Schubert, Franz:Winterreise, w. Lois Marshall (mez) — CBC ▲ CBC PSCD 2011 [ADD]
Schubert, Franz:Winterreise, w. Lois Marshall (mez) *(rec Hart House, Univ of Toronto, Ontario, Nov 1976)* — CBC ("Perspective" series) ▲ PSCD 2011 [ADD]
Schumann, R.:Carnaval Pno *(rec 1979)* — Analekta Fleur de Lys ▲ FL 2 3043 [DDD] ■ AN4-9203
Schumann, R.:Fantasiestücke Cl, w. K. Bogyo (vc) [trans. cello & piano] — Analekta ▲ CM 2902
Schumann, R.:Humoreske Pno *(rec 1979)* — Analekta Fleur de Lys ▲ FL 2 3043 [DDD] ■ AN4-9203
Schumann, R.:Son 1 Vn, w. Mark Kaplan (vn) *(rec SUNY, Purchase, Theatre C, Dec. 7–9, 1994)* — Arabesque ▲ ARA 6662 [DDD]
Schumann, R.:Son 2 Vn, w. Mark Kaplan (vn) *(rec SUNY, Purchase, Theatre C, Dec. 7–9, 1994)* — Arabesque ▲ ARA 6662 [DDD]
Schumann, R.:Son 3 Vn, w. Mark Kaplan (vn) *(rec SUNY, Purchase, Theatre C, Dec. 7–9, 1994)* — Arabesque ▲ ARA 6662 [DDD]
Schumann, R.:Vars on an Original Theme *(rec 1979)* — Analekta Fleur de Lys ▲ FL 2 3043 [DDD] ■ AN4-9203
Scriabin, A.:Etudes Pno, Op. 8 — Analekta Fleur de Lys ▲ FL 2 3044
Scriabin, A.:Etudes Pno, Op. 65 *(rec 1982)* — Analekta Fleur de Lys ▲ FL 2 3047 [DDD] ■ AN4-9202
Scriabin, A.:Preludes Pno, Op. 74 *(rec 1982)* — Analekta Fleur de Lys ▲ FL 2 3047 [DDD] ■ AN4-9202
Scriabin, A.:Son 4 Pno *(rec 1982)* — Analekta Fleur de Lys ▲ FL 2 3047 [DDD] ■ AN4-9202
Scriabin, A.:Son 6 Pno — Analekta Fleur de Lys ▲ FL 2 3044
Tchaikovsky, P.:Son Pno, Op. 37 *(rec 1982)* — Analekta Fleur de Lys ▲ FL 2 3047 [DDD] ■ AN4-9202

Kugel, M. (va)
Klein, G.:Trio Vn, w. O. Shiran (vn), F. Nemirovsky (vc) *(rec June 21, July 5 & 20, 199)* — Koch International Classics ▲ KIC 7230–2 [DDD]

Kugel, M. (vn)
Klein, G.:Fant & Fugue, w. C. Leiman (vn), O. Shiran (vn), F. Nemirovsky (vc) *(rec June 21, July 5 & 20, 199)* — Koch International Classics ▲ KIC 7230–2 [DDD]

Kugi, G. (a fl)—see ORCHESTRAS & ENSEMBLES Vienna Flautists

Kuhlman, William (org)
at S. Boniface Church, New Vienna, IA — Organ Historical Society ■ OHSC 8

Kühn, Michael (ob)
Marcello, A.:Con Ob & Strs, w. A. Orizio (cnd), Brescia & Bergamo Festival CO — Fonè ▲ 87F 05–17 [DDD]

Kuhn, Manfred (vn)—see ORCHESTRAS & ENSEMBLES Vienna Lanner Ensemble

Kühnis, Markus (org)—see ORCHESTRAS & ENSEMBLES Timporg Trio

Kuijken, Barthold (baroque fl)
Bach, J.S.:Partita Fl, BWV 1013 — Deutsche Harmonia Mundi 2-▲ 77026–2–RC [ADD]

Kuijken, Barthold (fl)
Bach, C.P.E.:Sons Fl, w. B. van Asperen (hpd)—in E♭, H.545; in G, H.509; in C, H.515; in B♭, H.578; in D, H.505; in g, H.542.5; in B♭, H.543; in C, H.504; in G, H.508; in E, H.506 *(rec Feb 24–Mar 12, 1993)* — Sony Classical 2-▲ S2K 53964 [DDD]
Bach, C.P.E.:Trio Son Fl, H.567–71, w. S. Kuijken (vn), W. Kuijken (vc), R. Kohnen (hpd)—No. 4 — Accent ▲ 58019 [DDD]
Bach, J.S.:Sons Fl, BWV 1030–35, w. G. Leonhardt (pno), W. Kuijken (vl)—BWV 1030, 1032, 1034 & 103 [period instrs] — Deutsche Harmonia Mundi 2-▲ 77026–2–RC [ADD]
Bach, J.S.:Son Fl, BWV 1038, w. S. Kuijken (vn), R. Kohnen (hpd) — Accent ▲ 58019 [DDD]

▲ = CD ◆ = Enhanced CD Δ = MD ■ = Cassette Tape □ = DCC

Kuijken, Barthold (fl) (cont.)

Bach, J.S.:Son Fl, BWV 1038, w. S. Kuijken (vn), G. Leonhardt (hpd), W. Kuijken (vl) [period instrs] Deutsche Harmonia Mundi 2-▲ 77026-2-RC [ADD]

Bach, J.S.:Trio Son for 2 Fls, BWV 1039, w. M. Hantal (fl), G. Leonhardt (hpd), W. Kuijken (bass vl) [period instrs] Deutsche Harmonia Mundi 2-▲ 77026-2-RC [ADD]

Couperin, F.:Les Nations, w. M. Hantaï (fl), F. Fernandez (vn), S. Kuijken (vn), W. Kuijken (bass vl), R. Kohnen (hpd) *(rec Mar. 1992)* Accent 2-▲ 9285/86 [DDD]

Haydn, J.:Diverts Vn, Va & Vc, H.IV/6-11, w. Sigswald Kuijken (vn), Wieland Kuijken (vc) Accent ▲ 68641 [DDD]

Haydn, J.:Qts Fl, w. Sigswald Kuijken (vn), François Fernandez (va), Wieland Kuijken (vc) Accent 2-▲ 9283/84

Haydn, J.:Trios Fls & Vc, "London Trios", w. Marc Hantaï (fl), Wieland Kuijken (vc) Accent 2-▲ 9283/84

Mozart, W.A.:Qts Fl, w. S. Kuijken (vn), L. van Dael (va), W. Kuijken (vc) Accent ▲ 48225

Telemann, G.P.:Fants Fl Accent ▲ 57803

Telemann, G.P.:Qt in G Fl, w. S. Kuijken (vn), W. Kuijken (bass vl), R. Kohnen (hpd) Accent ▲ 58019 [DDD]

Telemann, G.P.:Sons Fl Continuo, w. Wieland Kuijken (vl), Robert Kohnen (hpd) Accent 2-▲ 94104/05

Telemann, G.P.:Sonate metodiche, w. Robert Kohnen (hpd) Accent 2-▲ 94104/05

Telemann, G.P.:Suites Fl & Vn, w. W. Kuijken (vc), R. Kohnen (hpd) Accent ▲ 58019 [DDD]

Kuijken, Barthold (trns fl)

Bach, J.S.:A Musical Offering, w. Sigiswald Kuijken (vn), Wieland Kuijken (vl), Robert Kohen (hpd) *(rec Feb. 22-25, 1994)* Deutsche Harmonia Mundi ▲ 05472-77307-2 [DDD]

Couperin, F.:Pièces de clavecin (sels), w. Robert Kohnen (hpd) (Book 3:Ordes 13, 14 & 15, & Sixième Prélude) *(rec 'Vereenigde Doopsgezinde Kerk', Haarlem, Netherlands, Oct 1993)* Accent ▲ ACC 9399 [DDD]

French Flute Music of the 18th Century, w. Wieland Kuijken (vl), Robert Kohnen (hpd) Accent ▲ 67909

Gluck, C.W.:Orfeo ed Euridice (dance of the blessed spirits), w. Claire Guimond (trns fl), J. Lamon (cnd), Tafelmusik Sony Classical ▲ MLK 62369 [ADD/DDD]

Gluck, C.W.:Orfeo ed Euridice (dance of the blessed spirits), w. J. Lamon (cnd), Tafelmusik Sony Classical ("Vivarte" series) ▲ SK 48045

Handel, G.F.:Sons Fl, w. Wieland Kuijken (b vl), Robert Kohnen (hpd)—Op. 1, Nos.1, 5 & 9 Accent ▲ 9180 [DDD]

Handel, G.F.:Sons Fl, "Halle Sons", w. Wieland Kuijken (b vl), Robert Kohnen (hpd) Accent ▲ 9180 [DDD]

Handel, G.F.:Son Fl, HWV 378, w. Wieland Kuijken (b vl), Robert Kohnen (hpd) Accent ▲ 9180 [DDD]

Handel, G.F.:Son Fl, HWV 379, w. Wieland Kuijken (b-vl), Robert Kohnen (hpd) Accent ▲ 9180 [DDD]

Haydn, J.:Con Fl, H.VIIf/D1, w. J. Lamon (cnd), Tafelmusik Sony Classical ("Vivarte" series) ▲ SK 48045

Italian Flute Sonatas, w. Wieland Kuijken (vc), Robert Kohnen (hpd) *(rec 6/91)* Accent ▲ 9177

Richter, F.X.:Con in e Fl, w. J. Lamon (cnd), Tafelmusik Sony Classical ("Vivarte" series) ▲ SK 48045

Stamitz, C.:Con Fl, Op. 29, w. J. Lamon (cnd), Tafelmusik Sony Classical ("Vivarte" series) ▲ SK 48045

Kuijken, Sigiswald (vl)

Dollé, C.:Suite 2, w. W. Kuijken (va da gamba), R. Kohnen (hpd) Accent ▲ 67808

Kuijken, Sigiswald (vn)—see also ORCHESTRAS & ENSEMBLES Kuijken String Quartet

Bach, C.P.E.:Trio Son Fl, H.567-71, w. B. Kuijken (fl), W. Kuijken (vc), R. Kohnen (hpd)—No. 4 Accent ▲ 58019 [DDD]

Bach, J.S.:Cant 21, w. G. de Reyghere (mez), R. Jacobs (alt), C. Prégardien (ten), P. Lika (bass), S. Kuijken (cnd), La Petite Bande, Netherlands Chamber Choir Virgin Classics ▲ CDC 59528

Bach, J.S.:Cant 49, w. N. Argenta (sop), K. Mertens (bass), M. Ponseele (ob), H. Suzuki (vc), P. Hantaï (org), La Petite Bande Accent ▲ ACC 9395 D [DDD]

Bach, J.S.:Cant 58, w. N. Argenta (sop), K. Mertens (bass), M. Ponseele (ob), H. Suzuki (vc), P. Hantaï (org), La Petite Bande Accent ▲ ACC 9395 D [DDD]

Bach, J.S.:Cant 82, w. N. Argenta (sop), K. Mertens (bass), M. Ponseele (ob), H. Suzuki (vc), P. Hantaï (org), La Petite Bande Accent ▲ ACC 9395 D [DDD]

Bach, J.S.:Cons Vn (comp), La Petite Bande Editio Classica ▲ 77006-2-RG [DDD]

Bach, J.S.:Con for 2 Vns, La Petite Bande Editio Classica ▲ 77006-2-RG [DDD]

Bach, J.S.:Magnificat, BWV 243, w. G. de Reyghere (sop), R. Jacobs (alt), C. Prégardien (ten), P. Lika (bass), S. Kuijken (cnd), La Petite Bande, Netherlands Chamber Choir [L] Veritas ▲ VC 7 90779-2 [DDD] ■ VC 7 90779-4 (D)

Bach, J.S.:Magnificat, BWV 243, w. G. de Reyghere (sop), R. Jacobs (alt), C. Prégardien (ten), P. Lika (bass), S. Kuijken (cnd), La Petite Bande, Netherlands Chamber Choir Virgin Classics ▲ CDC 59528

Bach, J.S.:A Musical Offering, w. Barthold Kuijken (trns fl), Wieland Kuijken (vl), Robert Kohen (hpd) *(rec Feb. 22-25, 1994)* Deutsche Harmonia Mundi ▲ 05472-77307-2 [DDD]

Bach, J.S.:Sons & Partitas Vn, BWV 1001-1006 Editio Classica 2-▲ 77043-2-RG [ADD]

Bach, J.S.:Son Fl, BWV 1038, w. B. Kuijken (fl), R. Kohnen (hpd) Accent ▲ 58019 [DDD]

Bach, J.S.:Son Fl, BWV 1038, w. B. Kuijken (fl), G. Leonhardt (hpd), W. Kuijken (vl) [period instrs] Deutsche Harmonia Mundi 2-▲ 77026-2-RC [ADD]

Bach, J.S.:Sons Vn, w. G. Leonhardt (hpd)—BWV 1014-1019 Editio Classica 2-▲ 77170-2-RG [ADD]

Corelli, A.:Sons Vn, Op. 5, w. W. Kuijken (vc), R. Kohnen (hpd)—Nos. 1, 3, 6, 11 & 12 Accent ▲ 48433

Couperin, F.:Les Nations, w. M. Hantaï (fl), B. Kuijken (fl), F. Fernandez (vn), W. Kuijken (bass vl), R. Kohnen (hpd) *(rec Mar. 1992)* Accent 2-▲ 9285/86 [DDD]

Forqueray, A.:Suite 3 Vl da Gambas, w. W. Kuijken (bass vl), R. Kohnen (hpd) Accent ▲ 67808

Haydn, J.:Diverts Vn, Va & Vc, H.IV/6-11, w. Barthold Kuijken (fl), Wieland Kuijken (vc) Accent ▲ 68641 [DDD]

Haydn, J.:Qts Fl, w. Barthold Kuijken (fl), François Fernandez (va), Wieland Kuijken (vc) Accent 2-▲ 9283/84

Mozart, W.A.:Qts Fl, w. B. Kuijken (fl), L. van Dael (va), W. Kuijken (vc) Accent ▲ 48225

Mozart, W.A.:Sons Vn Pno (misc), w. L. Devos (pno)—K.379, 380 & 526 Accent ▲ 9175 [DDD]

Mozart, W.A.:Sons Vn Pno (misc), w. L. Devos (pno)—K.306, 378, 481 Accent ▲ ACC 9292 D [DDD]

Music for a Viol, w. Wieland Kuijken (vl), Robert Kohnen (hpd) Accent ▲ 68014

Music of Versailles, w. Wieland Kuijken (va), Gustav Leonhardt (hpd) Editio Classica ▲ 77145-2-RG [DDD]

Rameau, J.P.:Pièces de clavecin en concert, w. W. Kuijken (vn), G. Leonhardt (vn), Brüggen (fl) Teldec ▲ 77618-2

Telemann, G.P.:Qt in G Fl, w. B. Kuijken (fl), W. Kuijken (bass vl), R. Kohnen (hpd) Accent ▲ 58019 [DDD]

Vivaldi, A.:Cons Vn, Op. 8/1-4, "The Four Seasons", La Petite Bande Pro Arte ▲ CDD 214 [DDD] ■ PCD 214

Vivaldi, A.:Music of, w. F. Brüggen (rcr), St. Mary's Chamber Players, La Petite Bande—The 4 Seasons; Bn Con in E♭; Ob Con in F; etc. Pro Arte ▲ CDM 816 ■ PCD 816

Kuijken, Wieland (b vl)

Bach, J.S.:Trio Son for 2 Fls, BWV 1039, w. B. Kuijken (fl), M. Hantal (fl), G. Leonhardt (hpd) [period instrs] Deutsche Harmonia Mundi 2-▲ 77026-2-RC [ADD]

Couperin, F.:Les Nations, w. M. Hantaï (fl), B. Kuijken (fl), F. Fernandez (vn), S. Kuijken (vn), R. Kohnen (hpd) *(rec Mar. 1992)* Accent 2-▲ 9285/86 [DDD]

Forqueray, A.:Suite 3 Vl da Gambas, w. S. Kuijken (vn), R. Kohnen (hpd) Accent ▲ 67808

Handel, G.F.:Sons Fl, w. Berthold Kuijken (trns fl), Robert Kohnen (hpd)—Op. 1, Nos.1, 5 & 9 Accent ▲ 9180 [DDD]

Handel, G.F.:Sons Fl, "Halle Sons", w. Berthold Kuijken (trns fl), Robert Kohnen (hpd) Accent ▲ 9180 [DDD]

Handel, G.F.:Son Fl, HWV 378, w. Berthold Kuijken (trns fl), Robert Kohnen (hpd) Accent ▲ 9180 [DDD]

Handel, G.F.:Son Fl, HWV 379, w. Berthold Kuijken (trns fl), Robert Kohnen (hpd) Accent ▲ 9180 [DDD]

Kuijken, Wieland (b vl) (cont.)

Sainte-Colombe, M. de:Concerts for 2 B Vls, w. J. Savall (vl)—Concerts XXVII, "Bourrasque"; XLVIII, "Le raporté"; XLI, "Le retour"; XLIV, "Tombeau les regrets"; LIV, "[La] Dubois" Astrée ▲ E 7729 [ADD]

Sainte-Colombe, M. de:Concerts for 2 B Vls, w. J. Savall (vl)—Concerts Nos. 3, 8, 42, 47 & 51 *(rec April 1992)* Astrée ▲ E 8743 [DDD]

Telemann, G.P.:Qt in G Fl, w. B. Kuijken (fl), S. Kuijken (vn), R. Kohnen (hpd) Accent ▲ 58019 [DDD]

Kuijken, Wieland (va)

Music of Versailles, w. Sigiswald Kuijken (vn), Gustav Leonhardt (hpd) Editio Classica ▲ 77145-2-RG [DDD]

Kuijken, Wieland (vc)—see also ORCHESTRAS & ENSEMBLES Kuijken String Quartet

Bach, C.P.E.:Trio Son Fl, H.567-71, w. B. Kuijken (fl), S. Kuijken (vn), R. Kohnen (hpd)—No. 4 Accent ▲ 58019 [DDD]

Corelli, A.:Sons Vn, Op. 5, w. S. Kuijken (vn), R. Kohnen (hpd)—Nos. 1, 3, 6, 11 & 12 Accent ▲ 48433

Haydn, J.:Diverts Vn, Va & Vc, H.IV/6-11, w. Barthold Kuijken (fl), Sigswald Kuijken (vn) Accent ▲ 68641 [DDD]

Haydn, J.:Qts Fl, w. Barthold Kuijken (fl), Sigswald Kuijken (vn), François Fernandez (va) Accent 2-▲ 9283/84

Haydn, J.:Trios Fls & Vc, "London Trios", w. Marc Hantaï (fl), Barthold Kuijken (fl) Accent 2-▲ 9283/84

Italian Flute Sonatas, w. Barthold Kuijken (trns fl), Robert Kohnen (hpd) *(rec 6/91)* Accent ▲ 9177

Mozart, W.A.:Qts Fl, w. B. Kuijken (fl), S. Kuijken (vn), L. van Dael (va) Accent ▲ 48225

Telemann, G.P.:Sons Ob, w. P. Dombrecht (ob), R. Kohnen (hpd)—Sonata in B♭ (from *Essercizii musici*); Sonata in g (from *Musique de table*); Suite in g (from *Getreue Music-Meister*); Partita II in G (from *Kleine Kammer-Music*) Accent ▲ 48013

Telemann, G.P.:Suites Fl & Vn, w. B. Kuijken (fl), R. Kohnen (hpd) Accent ▲ 58019 [DDD]

Viol Solo Recital Denon ▲ CO 75659 [DDD]

Kuijken, Wieland (vl)—see also ORCHESTRAS & ENSEMBLES Kuijken Consort

Bach, J.S.:A Musical Offering, w. Barthold Kuijken (trns fl), Sigiswald Kuijken (vn), Robert Kohen (hpd) *(rec Feb. 22-25, 1994)* Deutsche Harmonia Mundi ▲ 05472-77307-2 [DDD]

Bach, J.S.:Sons Fl, BWV 1030-35, w. B. Kuijken (fl), G. Leonhardt (pno)—BWV 1030, 1032, 1034 & 103 [period instrs] Deutsche Harmonia Mundi 2-▲ 77026-2-RC [ADD]

Bach, J.S.:Sons Fl, BWV 1030-35, w. Maxence Larrieu (fl), Rafael Puyana (hpd) Philips 2-▲ 438809-2

Bach, J.S.:Son Fl, BWV 1038, w. B. Kuijken (fl), S. Kuijken (vn), G. Leonhardt (hpd) [period instrs] Deutsche Harmonia Mundi 2-▲ 77026-2-RC [ADD]

Bach, J.S.:Sons Vl, BWV 1027-1029, w. G. Leonhardt (hpd) Editio Classica ▲ 77044-2-RG [ADD]

Couperin, F.:Nouveaux Concerts, "Les Goûts-réunis", w. K. Uremura (vl), R. Kohnen (hpd)—Nos. 12 & 13 *(rec June 1992)* Accent ▲ 9288 D [DDD]

Couperin, F.:Pièces de violes avec la bass chifrée, w. K. Uremura (vl), R. Kohnen (hpd) *(rec June 1992)* Accent ▲ 9288 D [DDD]

French Flute Music of the 18th Century, w. Barthold Kuijken (trns fl), Robert Kohnen (hpd) Accent ▲ 67909

Marais, M.:Pièces de viole [Book 5], w. K. Uemura (vl), R. Kohnen (hpd)—Suite in g; Chaconne in G; Dialogue; Le Jeu du Volant; Le Tableau de l'Operation de la Taille; Suite in a; La Poitevine Accent ▲ 78744 [DDD]

Music for a Viol, w. Sigiswald Kuijken (vn), Robert Kohnen (hpd) Accent ▲ 68014

Program 1, w. Arnold Dolmetsch (vir), Robert Kohnen (hpd) IMP Allegro ▲ PCD 989 [DDD]

Purcell, H.:Music for Voc & Strs, w. R. Jacobs (ct), K. Junghanel (thb)—Tis Natures's voice; Musick for a while; Retir'd from any mortal's sight, Since from my dear Astrea's sight; Pious Celinda goes to prayers; Incassum, Lesbia; Ah! Cruel nymph; The fatal hour comes on a pace; As Amoret and Thirsis lay; Sweeter than Roses; I lov'd fair Celia; Young Thirsis' fate Accent ▲ 57802

Purcell, H.:Songs, w. A. Deller (ct), R. Skeaping (vn), J. Ryan (vl), W. Christie (hpd), R. Elliott (hpd)—An Evening Hymn; Fairest Isle; From Rosy Bow'rs; I Attempt From Love's Sickness; If Music Be the Food of Love; Not All My Torments; O Lead Me to Some Peaceful Gloom; O Solitude; The Plaint; Retired From My Dear Astrea's Sight; Sweeter Than Roses; Thrice Happy Lovers *(rec April 1979)* Harmonia Mundi ▲ HML 590249

Rameau, J.P.:Pièces de clavecin en concert, w. C. Arita (hpd), N. Wakamatsu (vn), M. Arita (trns fl/pic) Denon ▲ CO 79045 [DDD]

Telemann, G.P.:Sons Fl Continuo, w. Barthold Kuijken (fl), Robert Kohnen (hpd) Accent 2-▲ 94104/05

Kuijken, Wieland (vn)

Rameau, J.P.:Pièces de clavecin en concert, w. S. Kuijken (vn), G. Leonhardt (vn), Brüggen (fl) Teldec ▲ 77618-2

Kuisma, Rainer (mar/vib)

Virtuoso Percussion Music, w. Norrköping SO [cnd:Jorma Panula, Gustaf Sjökvist] BIS ▲ CD 149 [AAD]

Kuisma, Rainer (perc)

Bashmakov, L.:Quattro bagatelle, w. Gunilla von Bahr (fl) *(rec Castle Wik, Sweden, Oct. 22, 1974)* BIS ▲ CD 11 [AAD]

Crumb, G.:Music For A Summer Evening (Makrokosmos III), w. B. Dahlman (pno), I. Lindgren (pno), S. Asikainen (perc) *(rec analog)* BIS ▲ CD 261

Kukal, Ondřej (vn)—see ORCHESTRAS & ENSEMBLES New Vlach String Quartet

Kukorelly, G. (pno)

Mozart, W.A.:Pno Music (misc)—Rondo alla Turca from Son., K.331; Andante cantabile from Son., K.333; Menuetto, K.355; Adagio, K.540; Sons., 5, 14 & 15 Gallo ▲ CD 679 [DDD]

Kulenkampff, Georg (vn)

Aulin, T.:Con 3 Vn, w. T. Mann (cnd), Swedish RSO Bluebell ▲ BLU 3003 [ADD]

Beethoven, L. van:Romances Vn, w. P. Kletzki (cnd), Berlin PO—Op. 50 *(rec 1932 for Telefunken)* Pearl ▲ PEA 9466 (m) [AAD]

Brahms, J.:Con Vn, w. H. Schmidt-Isserstedt (cnd), Berlin PO *(rec 1936 for Telefunken)* Pearl ▲ PEA 9466 (m) [AAD]

Glazunov, A.:Con Vn, w. T. Mann (cnd), Swedish RSO Bluebell ▲ BLU 3003 [ADD]

Grieg, E.:Son 3 Vn—1st movt Bluebell ▲ BLU 3003 [ADD]

Mendelssohn, F.:Con in e Vn & Orch, Op. 64, w. H. Schmidt-Isserstedt (cnd), Berlin PO *(rec 1935 for Telefunken)* Pearl ▲ PEA 9466 (m) [AAD]

Mendelssohn, F.:Con in e Vn & Orch, Op. 64, w. H. Schmidt-Isserstedt (cnd), Berlin PO *(rec Apr. 4, 1935)* Teldec ("Historic" series) ▲ 93672

Reger, M.:Son Vn, Op. 91/1 *(rec 1936 for Telefunken)* Pearl ▲ PEA 9466 (m) [AAD]

Schumann, R.:Con Vn, w. H. Schmidt-Isserstedt (cnd), Berlin PO *(rec Dec. 20, 1937)* Teldec ("Historic" series) ▲ 93672

Sibelius, J.:Con Vn, w. W. Furtwängler (cnd), Berlin PO *(rec Feb. 7-8, 1943)* Music & Arts ▲ CD 799 [AAD]

Kuleshov, Valeri (pno)

Schumann, R.:Carnaval Pno *(rec in Moscow, 1989)* Art & Electronics ▲ AED 68021 [DDD]

Schumann, R.:Kreisleriana *(rec Moscow, 1989)* Art & Electronics ▲ AED 68021 [DDD]

Kulhan, Jaroslav (vc)—see also ORCHESTRAS & ENSEMBLES Panocha String Quartet

Dvořák, A.:Qnt Strs, Op. 77, w. J. Panocha (vn), P. Zejfart (vn), M. Sehnoutka (va), P. Nejtek (db) Supraphon ▲ SUP 11 1461 [DDD]

Kulka, Konstanty (Andrzej) (vn)

Baird, T.:Colas Breugnon, w. J. Maksymiuk (cnd), Polish CO [arr for violin & string orch] EMI Classics ▲ CDM 65418

Górecki, H.-M.:Stücke im alten Stil (3), w. J. Maksymiuk (cnd), Polish CO, Polish RSO EMI Classics ▲ CDM 65418

INSTRUMENT.

Kulka, Konstanty (Andrzej) (vn) (cont.)
Hindemith, P.:Kammermusik (comp), w. R. Brautigam (pno), L. Harrell (vc), K. Kashkashian (va), N. Blume (va d'amore), L. van Doeselaar (org), R. Chailly (cnd), Royal Concertgebouw Orch—No. 1 for Small Orchestra, Op. 24/1 (1922); No. 2 (Piano Concerto) for Piano & 12 Instruments, Op. 36/1 (1924); No. 3 (Cello Concerto), foe Cello & 10 Instruments, Op. 36/2 (1925); No. 4 (Violin Concerto) for Violin & Large Orchestra, Op. 36/3 (1925); No. 5 (Viola Concerto) for Viola & Large Chamber Orchestra, Op. 36/4 (1927); No. 6 (Viola d'amore Concerto) for Viola d'amore & Chamber Orchestra, Op. 46/1 (1927); No. 7 (Organ Concerto) for Organ & chamber Orchestra, Op. 46/2 (1927) London 2-▲ 433816-2 [DDD]
Mlynarski, E.:Con 2 Vn, w. K. Kord (cnd), Warsaw PO *(rec Concert Hall of the National Philharmonic, Warsaw, June 21-27, 1990)* Polskie Nagrania ▲ PNCD 074 [DDD]
Penderecki, K.:Con Vn, w. K. Penderecki (cnd), Polish National RSO Katowice Polskie Nagrania ▲ PLN 19 [AAD]
Szymanowski, K.:Con 1 Vn, w. J. Maksymiuk (cnd), *(orch unknown)* EMI Classics ▲ CDM 65418
Szymanowski, K.:Con 1 Vn, w. K. Stryja (cnd), Polish State PO Marco Polo ▲ 8.223291 [DDD]
Szymanowski, K.:Con 2 Vn, w. J. Maksymiuk (cnd), *(orch unknown)* EMI Classics ▲ CDM 65418
Vivaldi, A.:Cons Vn, Op. 8/1-4, "The Four Seasons", w. K. Teutsch (cnd), Warsaw Philharmonic CO *(rec Warsaw, 1970)* Polskie Nagrania ▲ PNCD 136 [ADD]

Kullgren, Lennart (gtr)
Blak, K.:Addeq, w. K. Blak (pno), P. Janson (db), M. Cissokho (perc) Tutl ▲ HJF 22

Kullgren, Lennart (gtr/fl/sgr/perc)
Blak, K.:Con Grotto, w. John Tchicai (t sax/sgr/perc), Anders Hagberg (fl/perc/sgr), Kristian Blak (pno/perc/sgr), Anders Jormin (bass instr/perc/sgr), Karin Korpelainen (perc/sgr), Sharon Weiss (perc/kaval) *(rec Lídargjógv, Sandoy, Aug. 1984)* Tutl ▲ HJF 33

Kullgren, Lennart (gtr/sgr)
Blak, K.:Drangar, w. Anders Hagberg (fl/s sax/perc), Tore Brunborg (s sax/t sax/perc), Kristian Blak (pno/sgr), Anda Kuitse (sgr/perc), Anders Jormin (bass instr/perc), Karin Korpelainen (dr/perc) *(rec Nordic House, Tórshavn, Jan. 1995)* Tutl ▲ HJF 33

Kulo, Heikki (vc)
Vuori, H.:Songs of Dreams & Death, w. Satu Kaarisola-Kulo (sop) Finlandia ▲ FIN 12179 [DDD]

Kulowitsch, Jack (db)
Saint-Saëns, C.:Spt Tpt, w. André Previn (pno), Thomas Stevens (tpt), Julie Rosenfeld (vn), Ani Kavafian (vn), Toby Hoffman (va), Carter Brey (vc) *(rec Manhattan Center Studios, New York City, May 25-26, 1993)* RCA Red Seal ▲ 09026-68181-2 [DDD]

Kumpera, Emanuel (db)
Schulhoff, E.:Concertino Fl, w. Pavel Foltyn (fl), Pavel Perina (va) Supraphon ▲ SUP 112170 [DDD]

Kun, Hu (vn)
Barber, S.:Con Vn, w. W. Boughton (cnd), English String Orch *(rec 7/2/91)* Nimbus ▲ NI 5329 [DDD]
Bernstein, L.:Serenade, w. W. Boughton (cnd), English String Orch *(rec 7/2/91)* Nimbus ▲ NI 5329 [DDD]
Khachaturian, A.:Con Vn, w. Y. Menuhin (cnd), Royal PO Nimbus ▲ NI 5277 [DDD]
Prokofiev, S.:Con 1 Vn, w. Y. Menuhin (cnd), English String Orch Nimbus ▲ NI 5192 [DDD]
Sibelius, J.:Con Vn, w. Y. Menuhin (cnd), Royal PO Nimbus ▲ NI 5277 [DDD]

Kunchev, Stefan (hn)
Mozart, W.A.:Qnt Pno, K.452, w. V. Tchutchov (pno), L. Oshavkova (fl), C. T. Kasmetski (ob), P. Radev (cl) Divertimento ▲ DIV 31020 [DDD]

Kuney, Scott (gtr)
Vivaldi, A.:Con for 2 Mands, w. P. Press (gtr), R. Kapp (cnd), Philharmonia Virtuosi ESS.A.Y ▲ CD 1004 [DDD] ■ C 1004 (D)

Kuney, Scott (mand)
Vivaldi, A.:Con for 2 Mands, w. Peter Press (mand), R. Kapp (cnd), Philharmonia Virtuosi ESS.A.Y ▲ ESS 1004 [DDD]

Kunicki, Raymond (vn)—see ORCHESTRAS & ENSEMBLES Kohon String Quartet

Kunschak, Elfriede (mand)
Music for Lute, Guitar & Mandolin, w. Konrad Ragossnig (gtr), Anton Stingl (lt), Michael Schäffer (lt), Karl Scheit (gtr), Leo Witoszinskyj (gtr), William Matthews (gtr), Paul Grund (mand), Artur Rumetsch (mand), Edith Bauer-Slais (mand) Vox Box 3-▲ CD3X 3022

Künstler, K. (tambourine)
Clementi, M.:Waltzes, Op. 38, w. V. de Col (pno), M. Dietrich (triangle) Entrée ▲ 0038 [ADD]

Kunz, B. (fl)—see ORCHESTRAS & ENSEMBLES Les Joueurs de Flute

Kupas, F. (vc)
Tailleferre, G.:Trio Pno, w. A. Gassenhuber (pno), R. Eggebrecht (vn) *(rec Dec. 1992)* Troubadisc ▲ TRO 01406 [DDD]

Kupiec, Ewa (pno)
Brahms, J.:Son 1 Vc, w. A. Bauer (vc) [arr Friedrich Grützmacher] *(rec 1990)* Koch Schwann ▲ 3-1187-2 [DDD]
Loewe, C.:Con Pno, w. J. Houtmann (cnd), Lorraine PO Koch Schwann ▲ SCH 315392 [DDD]
Mendelssohn, F.:Lied ohne Worte Vc, w. A. Bauer (vc) *(rec 1990)* Koch Schwann ▲ 3-1187-2 [DDD]
Paderewski, I.J.:Danses polonaises Koch Schwann ▲ SCH 311762
Paderewski, I.J.:Humoresques Koch Schwann ▲ SCH 311762
Paderewski, I.J.:Nocturne Pno Koch Schwann ▲ SCH 311762
Paderewski, I.J.:Tatra Album Koch Schwann ▲ SCH 311762
Paderewski, I.J.:Variations et fugue sur un thème original Koch Schwann ▲ SCH 311762
Prokofiev, S.:Son Vc, w. Andrzej Bauer (vc) Koch Schwann ▲ SCH 314362
Schubert, Franz:Son Arpeggione, w. A. Bauer (vc) *(rec 1990)* Koch Schwann ▲ 3-1187-2 [DDD]
Schumann, R.:Adagio & Allegro Hn, w. A. Bauer (vc) *(rec 1990)* Koch Schwann ▲ 3-1187-2 [DDD]
Shostakovich, D.:Son Vc, w. Andrzej Bauer (vc) Koch Schwann ▲ SCH 314362
Stravinsky, I.:Suite italienne Vc, w. Andrzej Bauer (vc) Koch Schwann ▲ SCH 314362
Weber, C.M. von:Adagio & Rondo Harm, w. A. Bauer (vc) [arr. for cello & piano by Gregor Piatigorsky] *(rec 1990)* Koch Schwann ▲ 3-1187-2 [DDD]

Kuppelwieser, Robert (org)
Mozart, W.A.:Church Sons, w. E. Hinreiner (cnd), Salzburg Mozarteum Orch—K. 328 Pro Arte ▲ CDD 471 [DDD]
Mozart, W.A.:Org Music, w. H. Scholze (org)—Fant. in f, K.608; Son. in C, K.328 LaserLight ▲ 15 884 [DDD]

Kupsa, Friedemann (vc)—see also ORCHESTRAS & ENSEMBLES Fanny Mendelssohn String Quartet
Boulanger, N.:Pieces (3) Vc & Pno, w. A. Gassenhuber (pno) Troubadisc ▲ TROCD 01407
Milhaud, D.:Catalogue de fleurs, w. Ulrike Sonntag (sop), Irmela Nolte (fl), Deborah Marshall (cl), Michael Weigel (bn), Renate Eggebrecht (vn), Stefan Berg (va), Arpat György (db) *(rec Ludwigsburg, Germany, Jan. 1995)* Troubadisc ▲ TROCD 01410 [DDD]
Milhaud, D.:Machines agricoles, w. Ulrike Sonntag (sop), Irmela Nolte (fl), Deborah Marshall (cl), Michael Weigel (bn), Renate Eggebrecht (vn), Stefan Berg (va), Arpat György (db) *(rec Ludwigsburg, Germany, Jan. 1995)* Troubadisc ▲ TROCD 01410 [DDD]

Kurosaki, Hiro (vn)
Clérambault, L.N.:Cants, w. Noémi Rime (sop), Jean-Paul Fouchécourt (ten), Nicolas Rivenq (bass), Ryo Terakado (vn), Marc Hantaï (fl), Eric Bellocq (thb), Elisabeth Matiffa (b vl), Bruno Croscet (basse de vn), W. Christie (cnd), Les Arts Florissants—Pyrame et Tisbé, La Muse de l'opéra ou les Caractères Lyriques, La Mort d'Hercule, Orphée Musique d'Abord ▲ HMA 1901329
Mozart, W.A.:Con 7 Vn, w. U. Björlin (cnd), Cappella Coloniensis Capriccio ▲ 10 620 [DDD]

Kurtág, György (cel)
Kurtág, G.:Ligatura—Message to Frances-Marie (version 1), w. Miklós Perényi (vc), Keller String Quartet members *(rec Casino Zögernitz, Vienna, Nov 1995)* ECM New Series ▲ 78118-21598-2 [DDD]
Kurtág, G.:Ligatura—Message to Frances-Marie (version 2), w. Miklós Perényi (vc), Keller String Quartet members *(rec Casino Zögernitz, Vienna, Nov 1995)* ECM New Series ▲ 78118-21598-2 [DDD]

Kurtz, Edmund (vc)
Dvořák, A.:Con Vc, w. A. Toscanini (cnd), NBC SO Grammofono 2000 ▲ GRM 78636
Prokofiev, S.:Romeo & Juliet (suites) EMI Classics ■ 4XG 60340

Kushner, Karen (pno)
Brahms, J.:Waltzes Pno, Op. 39—Nos. 1, 2, 14 & 15 Epiphany ▲ EP 7
Chopin, F.:Mazurkas—25 Mazurkas, Opp. 6, 7, 17, 24, 30 & 33 Connoisseur Society ▲ CD 4181 [DDD]
Chopin, F.:Mazurkas—26 Mazurkas, Opp. 41, 50, 56, 59, 63, 67 & 68; A son ami Émile Gaillard & Notre temps, w/o opus Connoisseur Society ▲ CD 4182 [DDD]

Kuskin, Anton (fl)—see ORCHESTRAS & ENSEMBLES Trio Sonata

Kuskin, Charles (ob)
Carter, E.:Son Fl, w. H. Sollberger (fl), F. Sherry (vc), P. Jacobs (hpd) Elektra/Nonesuch ▲ 79183-2

Kussmaul, Jürgen (va)—see also ORCHESTRAS & ENSEMBLES L'Archibudelli
Mozart, W.A.:Qts Cl, w. C. Neidich (cl), V. Beths (vn), A. Bylsma (vc)—in B♭ after K.378 Sony Classical ("Vivarte" series) ▲ SK 53366 [DDD]
Mozart, W.A.:Qnt Cl, K.581, w. C. Neidich (cl), V. Beths (vn), A. Bylsma (vc) Sony Classical ("Vivarte" series) ▲ SK 53366 [DDD]
Mozart, W.A.:Sinf concertante Vn, K.Anh.104, w. V. Beths (vn), A. Bulsma (vc) *(rec Mar. 1991)* Channel Classics ▲ CCS 3992 [DDD]
Mozart, W.A.:Sinf concertante Vn, K.364, w. R. Kussmaul (vn), Amsterdam Mozart Players *(rec Mar. 1991)* Channel Classics ▲ CCS 3992 [DDD]
Mozart, W.A.:Trio Cl, K.498, w. C. Neidich (vn), V. Beths (vn), A. Bylsma (vc) Sony Classical ("Vivarte" series) ▲ SK 53366 [DDD]
Reicha, A.:Qts Fl, w. Konrad Hünteler (fl), Rainer Kussmaul (vn), Roel Dieltiens (vc) MD + G ▲ MDG 3110630

Kussmaul, Rainer (vn)—see also ORCHESTRAS & ENSEMBLES Stuttgart Piano Trio
Chausson, E.:Con Vn, Pno & Str Qt, w. F. Meinders (pno), Schoenberg String Quartet Koch Schwann ▲ SCH 312312 [DDD]
Debussy, C.:Son Vn, w. F. Meinders (pno) Koch Schwann ▲ SCH 312312 [DDD]
Haydn, J.:Con 1 Vn, w. R. Kussmaul (cnd), Amsterdam Bach Soloists Olympia ▲ OLY 428 [DDD]
Haydn, J.:Con 3 Vn, w. R. Kussmaul (cnd), Amsterdam Bach Soloists Olympia ▲ OLY 428 [DDD]
Haydn, J.:Con 4 Vn, w. R. Kussmaul (cnd), Amsterdam Bach Soloists Olympia ▲ OLY 428 [DDD]
Mozart, W.A.:Con Vn Pno, w. M. Leonhard (pno), J. Kussmaul (cnd), Amsterdam Mozart Players *(rec Aug. 1990)* Channel Classics ▲ CCS 1190 [DDD]
Mozart, W.A.:Concertone Vns, w. V. Beths (vn), Amsterdam Mozart Players *(rec Mar. 1991)* Channel Classics ▲ CCS 3992 [DDD]
Mozart, W.A.:Sinf concertante Vn, K.364, w. J. Kussmaul (va), Amsterdam Mozart Players *(rec Mar. 1991)* Channel Classics ▲ CCS 3992 [DDD]
Mozart, W.A.:Sinf Concertante, K.364, w. Wolfram Christ (va), C. Abbado (cnd), Berlin PO Sony Classical ▲ SK 66859
Reicha, A.:Qts Fl, w. Konrad Hünteler (fl), Jürgen Kussmaul (va), Roel Dieltiens (vc) MD + G ▲ MDG 3110630
Viotti, G.B.:Con 19 Vn, w. J. Goritzki (cnd), New German Chamber Academy CPO ▲ CPO 999324
Viotti, G.B.:Con 22 Vn, w. J. Goritzki (cnd), New German Chamber Academy CPO ▲ CPO 999324

Kust, Jeffrey (gtr)
Argento, D.:Letters from Composers, w. Patrice Michaels Bedi (sop) *(rec Mandel Hall, Univ of Chicago, June 17-21, 1996)* Cedille ▲ CDR 90000029 [DDD]
Blackwood, E.:Suite in 15-note Equal Tuning Gtr *(rec 1979-81)* Cedille ▲ CDR 90000 018
Misurell-Mitchell, J.:On Thin Ice, w. Caroline Pittman (fl) Opus One ▲ CD 160

Kustafsson, Jan-Erik (vc)
Gothoni, R.:The Bull & His Herdsman:A Zen Story from Ancient China, w. Soile Isokoski (sop), Jorma Hynninen (bar), Jan Söderblom (vn), Ilari Angervo (va), Heini Kärkkäinen (pno), R. Gothoni (cnd) Ondine ▲ ODE 832 [DDD]

Kustariova, Alla (pno)
Bach, J.S.:Con 1 for 2 Hpds, w. O. Malov (pno), A. Titov (cnd), St. Petersburg Classical Music Studio Orch Infinity Digital ▲ QK 57720 [DDD]

Kuster, C. (fl)—see ORCHESTRAS & ENSEMBLES Les Joueurs de Flute

Kuszyk, Brian (tpt)—see ORCHESTRAS & ENSEMBLES Philadelphia Brass

Kutluer, Sefika (fl)
Debussy, C.:Syrinx Gallo ▲ CD 810 [DDD]
Doppler, A.F.:Fant pastorale hongroise, w. N. Sultanov (pno) Gallo ▲ CD 810 [DDD]
Genin, Pierre A.:The Carnival in Venice, w. N. Sultanov (pno) Gallo ▲ CD 810 [DDD]
Melikov, A.:Fants of Komde, w. N. Sultanov (pno) Gallo ▲ CD 810 [DDD]
Morlacchi, F.:Pastore Svizzero, w. N. Sultanov (pno) Gallo ▲ CD 810 [DDD]
Poulenc, F.:Son Fl, w. N. Sultanov (pno) Gallo ▲ CD 810 [DDD]

Kutman, Pavel (vn)
Martinů, B.:Les Rondes, w. Jurij Likin (ob), Vlastimil Mareš (cl), Lumír Vanek (bn), Vladislav Kozderka (tpt), Jana Herojnová (vn), Ivan Klánsky (pno) *(rec Studio Martínek, Prague, Mar 3, 1995)* Panton ("Protokol XX" series) ▲ 811348-2 [DDD]

Küttel, Edwin (ob)
Jenny, A.:Dialogues Ob, w. F. Schaffner (cnd), Lucerne City Wind Orch *(rec Radio Studio Zürich, Sept 15, 1995)* Gallo ▲ CD 885 [DDD]

Kutterer, Siegfried (perc)—see ORCHESTRAS & ENSEMBLES Basel Perc Trio

Kutulas, Janet (fl)—see ORCHESTRAS & ENSEMBLES Earplay, Earplay members

Kuusisto, Pekka (vn)
Sibelius, J.:Con Vn, w. L. Segerstam (cnd), Helsinki PO Ondine ▲ ODE 878
Sibelius, J.:Duo Vn Va, w. Pekka Kuusisto (vn) *(violist unknown)* Ondine ▲ ODE 850 [DDD]
Sibelius, J.:Suite Vn Pno, w. *(pianist unknown)* Ondine ▲ ODE 850 [DDD]

Kuusk, Viljar (va)—see ORCHESTRAS & ENSEMBLES Tallinn String Quartet

Kuyken, David (pno)
de Leeuw, T.:Danses sacrees, w. E. Spanjaard (cnd), Netherlands Radio CO NM Classics ▲ NM 92044
Diepenbrock, A.:Avondschemer *(rec Singelkerk, Amsterdam, Apr 4-5, 1995)* NM Classics ▲ 92049 [DDD]
Schäfer, D.:Interludes Pno *(rec Singelkerk, Amsterdam, Apr 4-5, 1995)* NM Classics ▲ 92049 [DDD]
Schäfer, D.:Klavierstukken *(rec Singelkerk, Amsterdam, Apr 4-5, 1995)* NM Classics ▲ 92049 [DDD]
Sigtenhorst Meyer, B. van den:6 Views of Fuji *(rec Singelkerk, Amsterdam, Apr 4-5, 1995)* NM Classics ▲ 92049 [DDD]
Sigtenhorst Meyer, B. van den:Son 2 Pno *(rec Singelkerk, Amsterdam, Apr 4-5, 1995)* NM Classics ▲ 92049 [DDD]
Van Baaren, K.:Concertino Pno, w. E. Spanjaard (cnd), Netherlands Radio CO NM Classics ▲ NM 92044
White, J.:Poem, w. P. Oosternrijk (ob), S. van Els (va) Channel Classics ▲ CCS 9326 [DDD]

Kuyper, L. William (hn)
Britten, H.:Serenade, Op. 31, w. Grayson Hirst (ten), K. Klein (cnd), New York Virtuosi Chamber SO Allegretto ▲ ACD 8203
Schumann, R.:Adagio & Allegro Hn, w. Thomas Hecht (pno) *(rec Performing Arts Ctr/Purchase College-State Univ of NY Recital Hall, May 8, 1995)* Elysium ▲ GRK 709 [DDD]
Schumann, R.:Andante & Vars Hn, w. Thomas Hecht (pno), Sandra Shapiro (pno), Gerald Appleman (vc), Alan Stepansky (vc) *(rec Performing Arts Ctr/Purchase College-State Univ of NY Recital Hall, May 8, 1995)* Elysium ▲ GRK 709 [DDD]

Kuyumjian, Avo (pno)
Schumann, R.:Fantasiestücke Cl, w. U. Wallin (vn) [violin & piano arr.] *(rec 1990)* Koch Schwann ▲ SCH 311852 [DDD]
Schumann, R.:Märchenbilder, w. U. Wallin (vn) [violin & piano version] *(rec 1990)* Koch Schwann ▲ SCH 311852 [DDD]

Kuzma, Janina (hpd)—see ORCHESTRAS & ENSEMBLES Trio Bariano

Kuzmin, Leonid (pno)
Beethoven, L. van:Con 5 Pno, "Emperor", w. A. Vedernikov (cnd), Moscow PO Russian Disc ▲ RUS 10023 [DDD]

▲ = CD ♦ = Enhanced CD Δ = MD ■ = Cassette Tape □ = DCC

Kuzmin, Leonid (pno) (cont.)
Chopin, F.:Pno Music (misc)—Nocturne, Op. 55/2; Mazurkas, Opp. 24/4, 33/3 & 4, 63/3; Son. No. 2, Op. 35; Barcarolle, Op. 60; Études, Opp. 10/5 & 12, 25/6; Scherzo, Op. 31 *(rec Dec. 1992)* Russian Disc ▲ RUS RD 10 022 [DDD]
Grieg, E.:Con Pno, Op. 16, w. A. Vedernikov (cnd), Moscow PO Russian Disc ▲ RUS 10023 [DDD]
Liszt, F.:Con 1 Pno, w. A. Tchistiakov (cnd), Moscow PO Russian Disc ▲ RUS 10020 [DDD]
Liszt, F.:Pno Music (misc)—Don Juan Fantasy (Busoni ed.); Feux follets; Gnomereigen; La Campanella; Hungarian Rhapsodies Nos. 2, 6 & 12 Russian Disc ▲ RUS 10021 [DDD]
Schubert, Franz:Fant Pno, D.760, "Wandererfantasie" Russian Disc ▲ RUS 10024 [DDD]
Schubert, Franz:Soirée de Vienne Russian Disc ▲ RUS 10024 [DDD]
Schubert, Franz:Son Pno, D.850 Russian Disc ▲ RUS 10024 [DDD]
Tchaikovsky, P.:Con 1 Pno, w. A. Tchistiakov (cnd), Moscow PO Russian Disc ▲ RUS 10020 [DDD]

Kuznetsoff, Alexei (pno)
Bolcom, W.:Recuerdos, w. Valentina Lisitsa (pno) Audiofon ▲ CD 72054
Chopin, F.:Rondo for 2 Pnos, w. Valentina Lisitsa (pno) *(rec Miami, FL, Aug 1995)* Audiofon ▲ CD 72053
Debussy, C.:En blanc et noir, w. Valentina Lisitsa (pno) Audiofon ▲ CD 72054
Godowsky, L.:Transcriptions & Paraphrases, w. Valentina Lisitsa (pno)—Weber's "Invitation to the Dance" Audiofon ▲ CD 72054
Liszt, F.:Réminiscences de Don Juan, w. Valentina Lisitsa (pno) *(rec Miami, FL, Aug 1995)* Audiofon ▲ CD 72053
Rachmaninoff, S.:Suite 1 for 2 Pnos, w. Valentina Lisitsa (pno) Audiofon ▲ CD 72053
Schnittke, A.:Gogol Suite, w. Valentina Lisitsa (pno) Audiofon ▲ CD 72054
Shostakovich, D.:Suite for 2 Pnos, w. Valentina Lisitsa (pno) Audiofon ▲ CD 72053

Kuznetsov, Andrey (hn)
Mozart, W.A.:Marches 2 Hns, w. Dmitry Kuznetsov (hn), A. Rudin (cnd), Musica Viva CO *(rec Moscow Conservatory Great Hall, 1996)* Russian Compact Disc ▲ RCD 30201 [DDD]

Kuznetsov, Dmitry (hn)
Mozart, W.A.:Marches 2 Hns, w. Andrey Kuznetsov (hn), A. Rudin (cnd), Musica Viva CO *(rec Moscow Conservatory Great Hall, 1996)* Russian Compact Disc ▲ RCD 30201 [DDD]

Kuznetsova, Elena (pno)
Scriabin, A.:Con Pno, w. I. Shpiller (cnd), Russian State SO *(rec Large Hall of the Moscow Conservatory, 1995)* Triton ▲ 17001 [DDD]

Kvalbein, Aage (vc)—see also ORCHESTRAS & ENSEMBLES Oslo Piano Trio
Grieg, E.:Music of, w. R. Askeland (pno), Oslo Piano Trio, Trondheim Soloists—Intermezzo for Cello & Piano; Andante con moto in c for Violin, Cello & Piano; Sonata in a for Cello & Piano, Op. 36; Holdberg Suite (sels.); Preludium; Sarabande; Gavotte; Air; Rigaudon *(rec May 1991, Jan. & Mar. 199)* Victoria ▲ VCD 19071
Haug, H.:Son elegica Victoria ▲ VCD 19049 [DDD]

Kvapil, Jan (vn)—see ORCHESTRAS & ENSEMBLES Talich String Quartet

Kvapil, Radoslav (pno)
Dvořák, A.:Con Pno, w. F. Jílek (cnd), Brno State PO Supraphon ▲ SUP 3067
Dvořák, A.:Poetic Tone Pictures Unicorn–Kanchana ▲ DKP CD 9137
Dvořák, A.:Theme with Vars Unicorn–Kanchana ▲ DKP CD 9137
Fibich, Z.:Pno Music—includes Moods, Impressions & Reminiscences, Opp. 41, 44, 47 & 57; Studies of Paintings, Opp. 16 & 56 Unicorn–Kanchana ▲ DKP CD 9149
Fibich, Z.:Qt Pno, w. Suk String Quartet *(rec Bohuslav Martinů Hall in the Lichtenstejn Pallace, Prague, Apr 8–10, 1995)* Panton ▲ 811425–2 [DDD]
Fibich, Z.:Qnt Pno, w. Suk String Quartet [arr. for pno & str quartet] *(rec Bohuslav Martinů Hall in the Lichtenstejn Pallace, Prague, Apr 8–10, 1995)* Panton ▲ 811425–2 [DDD]
Janácek, L.:Moravian Folk Poetry, w. Zdena Kloubová (sop), Leo Vodička (ten) Unicorn–Kanchana ▲ DKP CD 9154
Janácek, L.:Pno Music—Theme with Vars.; On an Overgrown Path (Books 1 & 2); Son.; In the Mists Unicorn–Kanchana ▲ DKP CD 9156
Martinů, B.:Etudes & Polkas *(rec 4/83)* BIS ▲ CD 234 [AAD]
Martinů, B.:Son Pno *(rec 4/83)* BIS ▲ CD 234 [AAD]
Smetana, B.:Czech Dances Unicorn–Kanchana ▲ DKP CD 9139
Smetana, B.:Pno Music (misc)—Bagatelles & Impromptus Unicorn–Kanchana ▲ DKP CD 9139
Smetana, B.:Pno Music (misc)—Dreams; Macbeth & the Witches; Polkas Op. 12 & 13 Unicorn–Kanchana ▲ DKP CD 9152
Smetana, B.:Polkas Pno Calliope ▲ CAL 9690 [DDD]
Suk, J.:Pno Music—About Mother, Op. 28; Piano Pieces, Op. 7; Spring, Op. 22a; Summer Impressions, Op. 22b Unicorn–Kanchana ▲ DKP CD 9159

Kvarda, Franz (vc)
Pfitzner, H.:Qnt Pno, w. W. Kamper (pno), A. Kamper (vn), K. M. Titze (vn), E. Weis (va) Preiser ▲ 93111 (m) [AAD]
Pfitzner, H.:Sxt Cl, w. L. Wlach (cl), A. Kamper (vn), E. Weis (va), J. Hermann (db), W. Kamper (pno) Preiser ▲ 93111 (m) [AAD]

Kvistad, Rick (perc)
Cowell, H.:Set of 5, w. Kay Stern (vn), Josephine Gandolfi (pno) Koch International Classics ▲ KIC 7205 [DDD]

Kwak, Eun-Joo (pno)
Boettcher, E.:Birthday Vars, w. Chiung-Ying Cheng (pno) Northwestern Univ School of Music ▲

Kwalwasser (va)
Vivaldi, A.:Cons Vn, Op. 8/1–4, "The Four Seasons", w. A. Bronne (vn), Monosoff (vn), G. Koutzen (vc), M. Goberman (cnd), New York Sinfonietta Odyssey ■ YT 60132

Kwasny, W. (vn)
Wolff, J.-C.:Sym 2, w. S. Kawalla (cnd), Polish Radio-TV SO Vienna Modern Masters ▲ VMM 3001 [DDD]

Kwast, Saskia (hp)
Mozart, W.A.:Con Fl Hp, w. M. Sandhoff (fl), Concerto Cologne Capriccio ∆ 70375

Kwok, May-Ling (pno)—see also ORCHESTRAS & ENSEMBLES McPherson Trio
Dvořák, A.:Sonatina Vn, w. Pablo Diemecke (vn) *(rec Concert Hall of Radio Bratislava, Slovakia, Dec 1994)* Intersound ▲ 3538
Prokofiev, S.:Son Vn, Op. 94bis, w. Pablo Diemecke (vn) *(rec MoscFilm Studio Concert Hall, Moscow)* Fanfare ▲ CDS 3479 [DDD]

Kyme, Katherine (vn)—see ORCHESTRAS & ENSEMBLES Streicher Trio

Kynaston, Nicolas (org)
Liszt, F.:Org Music—Excelsior; Am grabe Richard Wagners; Funerailles; Trauerode; Orpheus; Fant & Fugue [on Ad Nos, Ad Salutarem Undam] IMP ("Masters" series) ▲ IMP 6600032 [DDD]

Kyriakou, Rena (pno)
Chabrier, E.:Pno Music (misc)—Pièces pittoresques; 5 pièces pour piano; Bourrée Fantasque; Capriccio; Impromptu; Habanera; Air de ballet; Suite de valse; Marche des cipayes *(rec 1965)* Vox Box 2–▲ CDX 5108 [ADD]
Chabrier, E.:Pno Music 4-Hands, w. W. Klien (pno)—3 valses romantiques; Cortège burlesque; Souvenirs de Munich *(rec 1965)* Vox Box 2–▲ CDX 5108 [ADD]
Mendelssohn, F.:Capriccio brillante, w. H. Swarowsky (cnd), Vienna Pro Musica Orch—Andante Allegro con fuoco Tuxedo ▲ TUXCD 1011
Mendelssohn, F.:Con in a Pno, Op. posth., w. M. Lange (cnd), Vienna Pro Musica Orch—Allegro; Adagio; Finale Allegro ma non tropo Tuxedo ▲ TUXCD 1011
Mendelssohn, F.:Lieder ohne Worte Pno Vox Box 2–▲ CDX 5077 [ADD]
Mendelssohn, F.:Rondo brilliant, w. H. Swarowsky (cnd), Vienna Pro Musica Orch—Presto Tuxedo ▲ TUXCD 1011
Mendelssohn, F.:Serenade & Allegro giocoso, w. H. Swarowsky (cnd), Vienna Pro Musica Orch—Andante; Allegro giocoso Tuxedo ▲ TUXCD 1011
Mendelssohn, F.:Vars sérieuses Vox Box 2–▲ CDX 5077 [ADD]
Saint-Saëns, C.:Wedding Cake, w. H. Reichert (cnd), Westphalia SO Vivace 3–▲ E 321 [DDD]

Kyselak, Ladislav (va)
Dittersdorf, K.D. von:Sinfonia Concertante, w. Miloslav Jelinek (db), L. Svárovský (cnd), Czech Chamber Soloists *(rec 1992)* Panton ▲ PAN 811146
Mozart, W.A.:Sinf concertante Vn, K.364, w. T. Nishizaki (vn), S. Gunzenhauser (cnd), Capella Istropolitana *(rec Nov. 1989)* Naxos ▲ 8.550332 [DDD]
Telemann, G.P.:Cons (misc), w. Z. Tylšar (hn), B. Tylšar (hn), A. Hoelbling (vn) O. Hoelbling (vn), A. Jablokov (vn), R. Edlinger (cnd), Capella Istropolitana—Viola Con. in G; Concerto in F for 3 Violins; Concerto for 2 Horns Naxos ▲ 8.550156 [DDD] ∆ 7.550156 [DDD]

Kyu-Nam, Whang (kagok)
Kim, J.H.:Yoeum, w. Thomas Buckner (bar) O. O. Discs ▲ 0024

Kyzivát, Vaclav (cl)
Beethoven, L. van:Sxt Winds, Op. 71, w. Z. Tesař (cl), Z. Tylšar (hn), B. Tylšar (hn), F. Herman (bn), V. Horák (bn) Supraphon ▲ 11 1445–2 [DDD]

Labarre, R. Garreau de (org)
Alain, J.:Music of, w. A. Steyer (cnd), Maîtrise de Garçons de Colmar—12 works for organ &/or choir *(rec May 1990)* K617 ▲ 7005 [DDD]
Duruflé, M.:Prélude et fugue sur le nom d'Alain *(rec 5/90)* K617 ▲ 7005 [DDD]

Labé, Thomas (pno)
Bach, J.S.:Music of—elaborations on Bach solo string works as arranged and expanded upon by Rachmaninoff, Godowsky & Busoni Dorian Discovery ▲ DOR 80117 [DDD]
Bach, J.S.:Sons & Partitas Vn, BWV 1001–1006—BWV 1001 & 1003 [arr. Godowsky]; BWV 1004 [arr. Busoni]; BWV 1006 [arr. Rachmaninoff] *(rec June 1993)* Dorian Discovery ▲ DOR 80117 [DDD]
Bach, J.S.:Suites Vc, BWV 1007–1012—BWV 1008, 1009 & 1011 [arr. Godowsky] *(rec June 1993)* Dorian Discovery ▲ DOR 80117 [DDD]
Strauss (II), Joh.:Music of—Arabesques on "By the Beautiful Blue Danube"; Carnaval de Vienne; Die Fledermaus (Symphonic Metamorphosis); Man lebt nur einmal; Nachtfalter; Valse–Caprice in A; Wein, Weib und Gesang (Symphonic Metamorphosis); Wahlstimmen Dorian Discovery ▲ DIS 80102 [DDD]

Labèque, Katia (pno)
Bartók, B.:Con for 2 Pnos, w. M. Labèque (pno), S. Gualda (perc), J.-P. Drouet (perc), S. Rattle (cnd), City of Birmingham SO EMI ▲ CDC 47446
Bartók, B.:Son for 2 Pnos, w. M. Labèque (pno), S. Gualda (perc), J.P. Drouet (perc) EMI ▲ CDC 47446
Bernstein, L.:West Side Story (sels), w. M. Labèque (pno)—Something's coming; Maria; America; Jet song; One hand, one heart; I feel pretty; Tonight; A boy like that/I have a love CBS ▲ MK 45531 [DDD]
Bernstein, L.:West Side Story (symphonic dances), w. M. Labèque (pno), Jean-Pierre Drouet (perc), Sylvio Gualdo (perc), Trilok Gurtu (perc)—Overture; Scherzando; Blues; Somewhere; Scherzo; Mambo; Cha-cha; Cool; The rumble; I have a love [arr. Irwin Kostal for 2 pianos, percussion & jazz drums] CBS ▲ MK 45531 [DDD]
Bizet, G.:Jeux d'enfants, w. M. Labèque (pno) Philips ▲ 420159–2 [DDD]
Brahms, J.:Hungarian Dances Pno 4-Hands, w. M. Labèque (pno) Philips ▲ 416459–2 [ADD]
Dvořák, A.:Slavonic Dances (comp), w. M. Labèque (pno) [two pianos] Philips ▲ 426264–2 [DDD]
Encorel, w. Marielle Labèque (pno) Sony Classical ▲ SK 48381
Fauré, G.:Dolly, w. M. Labèque (pno) Philips ▲ 420159–2 [DDD]
Gershwin, G.:Con Pno, w. M. Labèque (pno) Philips ▲ 400022–2
Gershwin, G.:Rhap in Blue, w. M. Labèque (pno), R. Chailly (cnd), Cleveland Orch London ▲ 417326–2 [DDD]
Gershwin, G.:Rhap in Blue, w. M. Labèque (pno) Philips ▲ 400022–2 [ADD]
Gershwin, G.:Songs, w. B. Hendricks (sop), M. Labèque (pno) Philips ▲ 416460–2 [ADD]
Love of Colours, w. Marielle Labèque (pno) Sony Classical ▲ SK 47227 ∆ SM 47227
McLaughlin, J.:Duos, w. J. McLaughlin (gtr) CBS ▲ MK 45578 [DDD]
Milhaud, D.:Scaramouche for 2 Pnos, w. M. Labèque (pno) Philips ▲ 426284–2 [DDD]
Mozart, W.A.:Con 7 Pnos, w. M. Labèque (pno), S. Bychkov (pno), S. Bychkov (cnd), Berlin PO Philips ("Digital Classics" series) ▲ 426241–2
Mozart, W.A.:Con 10 Pnos, w. M. Labèque (pno), S. Bychkov (cnd), Berlin PO Philips ("Digital Classics" series) ▲ 426241–2 [DDD]
Poulenc, F.:Capriccio Pnos, w. M. Labèque (pno) Philips ▲ 426284–2 [DDD]
Poulenc, F.:Con for 2 Pnos, w. M. Labèque (pno), S. Ozawa (cnd), Boston SO Philips ▲ 426284–2 [DDD]
Poulenc, F.:L'Embarquement pour Cythère, w. M. Labèque (pno) Philips ▲ 426284–2 [DDD]
Poulenc, F.:Son for 2 Pnos, w. M. Labèque (pno) Philips ▲ 426284–2 [DDD]
Ravel, M.:Ma mère l'oye Pno, w. M. Labèque (pno) Philips ▲ 420159–2 [DDD]
Saint-Saëns, C.:Carnival of the Animals, w. I. Perlman (nar), M. Labèque (pno), Z. Mehta (cnd), Israel PO EMI Classics ▲ CDC 47067 [DDD]

Labèque, Marielle (pno)
Bartók, B.:Con for 2 Pnos, w. K. Labeque (pno), S. Gualda (perc), J.-P. Drouet (perc), S. Rattle (cnd), City of Birmingham SO EMI ▲ CDC 47446
Bartók, B.:Son for 2 Pnos, w. K. Labeque (pno), S. Gualda (perc), J.P. Drouet (perc) EMI ▲ CDC 47446
Bernstein, L.:West Side Story (sels), w. K. Labèque (pno)—Something's coming; Maria; America; Jet song; One hand, one heart; I feel pretty; Tonight; A boy like that/I have a love CBS ▲ MK 45531 [DDD]
Bernstein, L.:West Side Story (symphonic dances), w. K. Labèque (pno), Jean-Pierre Drouet (perc), Sylvio Gualdo (perc), Trilok Gurtu (perc)—Overture; Scherzando; Blues; Somewhere; Scherzo; Mambo; Cha-cha; Cool; The rumble; I have a love [arr. Irwin Kostal for 2 pianos, percussion & jazz drums] CBS ▲ MK 45531 [DDD]
Bizet, G.:Jeux d'enfants, w. K. Labèque (pno) Philips ▲ 420159–2 [DDD]
Brahms, J.:Hungarian Dances Pno 4-Hands, w. K. Labèque (pno) Philips ▲ 416459–2 [ADD]
Dvořák, A.:Slavonic Dances (comp), w. K. Labèque (pno) [two pianos] Philips ▲ 426264–2 [DDD]
Encorel, w. Katia Labèque (pno) Sony Classical ▲ SK 48381
Fauré, G.:Dolly, w. K. Labèque (pno) Philips ▲ 420159–2 [DDD]
Gershwin, G.:Con Pno, w. K. Labèque (pno) Philips ▲ 400022–2
Gershwin, G.:Rhap in Blue, w. K. Labèque (pno), R. Chailly (cnd), Cleveland Orch London ▲ 417326–2 [DDD]
Gershwin, G.:Rhap in Blue, w. K. Labèque (pno) Philips ▲ 400022–2 [ADD]
Gershwin, G.:Songs, w. B. Hendricks (sop), K. Labèque (pno) Philips ▲ 416460–2 [ADD]
Love of Colours, w. Katia Labèque (pno) Sony Classical ▲ SK 47227 ∆ SM 47227
Milhaud, D.:Scaramouche for 2 Pnos, w. K. Labèque (pno) Philips ▲ 426284–2 [DDD]
Mozart, W.A.:Con 7 Pnos, w. K. Labèque (pno), S. Bychkov (pno), S. Bychkov (cnd), Berlin PO Philips ("Digital Classics" series) ▲ 426241–2
Mozart, W.A.:Con 10 Pnos, w. K. Labèque (pno), S. Bychkov (cnd), Berlin PO Philips ("Digital Classics" series) ▲ 426241–2 [DDD]
Poulenc, F.:Capriccio Pnos, w. K. Labèque (pno) Philips ▲ 426284–2 [DDD]
Poulenc, F.:Con for 2 Pnos, w. K. Labèque (pno), S. Ozawa (cnd), Boston SO Philips ▲ 426284–2 [DDD]
Poulenc, F.:L'Embarquement pour Cythère, w. K. Labèque (pno) Philips ▲ 426284–2 [DDD]
Poulenc, F.:Son for 2 Pnos, w. K. Labèque (pno) Philips ▲ 426284–2 [DDD]
Ravel, M.:Ma mère l'oye Pno, w. K. Labèque (pno) Philips ▲ 420159–2 [DDD]
Saint-Saëns, C.:Carnival of the Animals, w. I. Perlman (nar), K. Labèque (pno), Z. Mehta (cnd), Israel PO EMI Classics ▲ CDC 47067 [DDD]

Laberge, André (hpd)
André Laberge, w. Laberge, André (hpd) REM ▲ 311156 [DDD]
Bach, J.S.:Chaconne *(rec Saint-Benoît-du-Lac Abbey, Québec, Aug 1989)* Analekta Fleur de Lys ▲ FL 2 3006
Bach, J.S.:Inventions (30) Hpd *(rec Apr 1996)* Analekta Fleur de Lys ▲ FL 23089 [DDD]
Bach, J.S.:Kbd Music (misc)—Suite in e, BWV 996; Partita in c, BWV 997; Son in d, BWV 964; Chacone in g [from Partita for Vn, BWV 1004] [all trans for Hpd] *(rec St Benoît du Lac Abbey, Aug 1989)* Analekta ▲ AN 28102 [DDD]

INSTRUMENT.

Laberge, André (hpd) (cont.)
Bach, J.S.:Prelude, Fugue & Allegro Lt, BWV 998 [arr for hpd] *(rec Apr 1996)* Analekta Fleur de Lys ▲ FL 23089 [DDD]
Böhm, G.:Hpd Music—Capriccio in D; Prelude in G; 6 Suites *(rec 4/89)* REM ▲ 311083 XCD [DDD]
Laberge, André (org)
Handel, G.F.:Cons (16) Org, w. Carl Philipp Ensemble Analekta Fleur de Lys ▲ FL 2 3028
Laberge, Angèle (hp)—see ORCHESTRAS & ENSEMBLES La Nef
La Berge, Anne (fl)
Polansky, L.:Cantillation Study 2 Centaur ▲ CRC 2133 [DDD]
Labinsky, Alexandre (pno)
Mussorgsky, M.:Songs (comp), w. B. Christoff (bass), Gerald Moore (pno), French National Radio Orch EMI Classics ("Great Recordings of the Century" series) 3-▲ CHS 63025 (m) [ADD]
Labko, Alexander (vn)
Medtner, N.:Nocturnes Vn, w. E. Svetlanov (pno)—No. 3 in c Russian Disc ▲ RUS 11017 [DDD]
Medtner, N.:Son 1 Vn, w. E. Svetlanov (pno) Russian Disc ▲ RUS 11017 [DDD]
Medtner, N.:Son 2 Vn, w. E. Svetlanov (pno) Russian Disc ▲ RUS 11019 [DDD]
Medtner, N.:Son 3 Vn, w. E. Svetlanov (pno) Russian Disc ▲ RUS 11017 [DDD]
La Breque, Mary (vc)
O'Rourke, J.:Terminal Pharmacy, w. Tony Burr (cl), Jeff Cortazzo (b trbn), John McEntire (dr), Rob Prosser (acc), Isha Suftin (acc), Mike Dockter (vc), Hattie Franck (vc), Robert Keck (vc), Dan Loch (vc), Stan Saderk (vc), Lisa Hemmer (fl), Sue Oberg (fl), Wendi Lev (fl), Jim Vanden (fl), Jim O'Rourke (gtr), Steve Braack (elec) Tzadik ▲ TZA 7011 [DDD]
Labylle, Jean-Marc (pic)
Vivaldi, A.:Cons Diverse Instrs, w. Sylvia Ochi (man), Takashi Ochi (man), Monique Frasca-Colombier (vn), Laurence Paugam (vn), P. Kuentz (cnd), Paul Kuentz Orch—in G for 2 Man; in C for Rcr; in B♭ for Bn [La notte]; in d for Vl; in a for Bn; in A for Vn & other Vns in echo Pierre Verany ▲ PVY 730052 [DDD]
Labylle, Jean-Marc (rcr)
Telemann, G.P.:Con Rcr, Fl, w. Régis Manceau (fl), P. Kuentz (cnd), Paul Kuentz Orch Pierre Verany ▲ PVY 730046
Telemann, G.P.:Suite Rcr, w. P. Kuentz (cnd), Paul Kuentz Orch Pierre Verany ▲ PVY 730046
Lachance, Janine (pno)
Gounod, C.:Songs, w. Bruno Laplante (bar)—O ma belle rebelle; Le premier jour de mai; Le vallon; Le lever; Venise; Chanson de printemps; L'absent; Sérénade; Au printemps; Les deux pigeons; Viens, les gazons sont verts; Où voulez-vous aller?; Ma belle amie est morte; Envoi de fleurs; Mignon; Prière Analekta ▲ AN 29404
Hahn, R.:Songs, w. Bruno Laplante (bar)—Si mes vers avaient des ailes; Paysage; L'Enamourée; Infidélité; Le Rossignol des Lilas; Quand je fusprís au pavillon; Offrande; L'Incrédule; D'une prison; Fêtes Galantes; A Chloris; Études Latines Analekta ▲ AN 29402
Massenet, J.:Songs, w. Bruno Laplante (bar)—Pensée d'Automne; Madrigal; Poème d'Avril; Ouvre tes yeux bleus; Elégie; A Colombine; Oh! si les fleus avaient des yeux; Sérénade de Zanetto; Automne; Roses d'octobre; Nuit d'Espagne; Si tu veux, mignonne; Fleuramye; Souvenir de Venise Analekta ▲ AN 29403
Lachenmann, Helmut (pno)
Lachenmann, H.:Pno Music, w. Rechêrche Ensemble Montaigne ▲ MO 782075
Lachner, Ulrike (va)
Bryars, G.:Incipit Vita Nova, w. D. James (ct), A. Dreyer (vn), R. Firth (vc) ECM New Series ▲ 78118-21533-2 [DDD]
Lack, Fredell (vn)—see also ORCHESTRAS & ENSEMBLES Lyric Art String Quartet
Jacobi, F.:Ballade Vn, w. Irene Jacobi (pno) CRI ("American Masters" series) ▲ CD 703 [ADD]
Martinů, B.:Son 1 Vn, w. Timothy Hester (pno) *(rec Dudley Recital Hall, Univ of Houston School of Music, Aug 18-20, 1993)* Centaur ▲ CRC 2276 [DDD]
Martinů, B.:Son 2 Vn, w. Timothy Hester (pno) *(rec Dudley Recital Hall, Univ of Houston School of Music, Aug 18-20, 1993)* Centaur ▲ CRC 2276 [DDD]
Martinů, B.:Son 3 Vn, w. Timothy Hester (pno) *(rec Dudley Recital Hall, Univ of Houston School of Music, Aug 18-20, 1993)* Centaur ▲ CRC 2276 [DDD]
Martinů, B.:Sonatina for 2 Vns, w. Leon Spierer (vn), Timothy Hester (pno) *(rec Dudley Recital Hall, Univ of Houston School of Music, Aug 18-20, 1993)* Centaur ▲ CRC 2276 [DDD]
Szymanowski, K.:Con 2 Vn, w. S. Köhler (cnd), Berlin SO Vox Box 2-▲ CDX 5133
Szymanowski, K.:Son Vn, w. Albert Hirsh (pno) Vox Box 2-▲ CDX 5133
Lackner, Andreas (nat tpt)
Weichlein, R.:Encaenia musices, w. Gunar Letzbor (vn), Daniel Sepec (vn), Herbert Lindsberger (va), Christoph Bitzinger (va), Michael Oman (vl), Gaetano Nasillo (vc), Roberto Sensi (vn), Herbert Walser (nat tpt), Norbert Kirchner (hpd/org), G. Letzbor (cnd), Ars Antiqua Austria—Sons. Nos. I in C, II in g, III in a, IV in E, V in C & VI in F Symphonia ▲ SY 93S23
Lackner, Andreas (tpt)
Vivaldi, A.:Con for 2 Tpts, w. S. Keavy (tpt), M. Haselböck (cnd), Vienna Academy [period instrs] Novalis ▲ 150074 [DDD]
Lacoste, Christine (vc)
A Century of Italian Music from Scarlatti to Paganini, w. Mark Varshavsky (vc) Ducale ▲ DUC 19 [DDD]
Lacrouts, Syrille (vc)
Massenet, J.:Songs, w. Catherine Dubosc (sop), Francis Dudziak (bar), Jean-Bernard Dartigolles (pno)—Quelques chansons mauves; Dans le sentier, parmi les roses; Tu l'as bien dit; Roses d'Octobre; A Colombine [Sérénade d'Arlequin]; Sérénade de Molière [Musique du temps]; Marquisel [Menuet pour chant]; Les alcyons; Voic que les grands lys; Poème d'amour; L'improvisateur [Souvenir du Transtévère]; Nuit d'Espagne; Elégie; Déclaration; A mignonne; Souhait; Un adieu; Sérénade d'automne; Sonnet; Si tu veux, mignonne; Pensée d'automne; Soir de rêve; On dit; Souvenez-vous, Vierge Marie! Accord ▲ ACD 201632 [DDD]
Lacy, Steve (sax)
Beck, Julian:Songs, w. Irene Aebi (sgr), Frederic Rzewski (pno)—Theatre [w. lyrics by Julian Beck]; Joy; The Hour Is Late; 1st & Last Pain; Love & Politics; I Heard the Indian Sage; Do Not Judge Me Lightly; The True & the Contrary; The Melancholy Life of Woman; Do Not Judge Me Lightly No. 2 [all w. lyrics by Judith Malina] *(rec Studio Acousti, Paris, Mar 16-17, 1995)* New Albion ▲ NA 080
Ladone, J. (lt)
Music of the Middle Ages, Vol. 3, w. Russell Oberlin (ct) Lyrichord ▲ LYR 8003 [ADD]
l'Adourek, Zbynek (vn)—see ORCHESTRAS & ENSEMBLES Prague Chamber Ensemble
Ladrette, Antoine (vc)
Mozart, W.A.:Sons Fl Hpd (misc), w. Jean-Christophe Frisch (fl), Olivier Baumont (hpd)—No. 1 in B♭, K.10; No. 2 in G, K.11; No. 3 in A, K.12; No. 4 in F, K.13; No. 5 in C, K.14; No. 6 in B♭, K.15 Adda ▲ ADD 581229 [DDD]
La Fargue, Anthony (perc)
Rorem, N.:Studies for 11, w. E. Ostling (fl), K. Lord (ob), G. Raden (cl), J. Sutte (tpt), S. Copes (vn), C.-J. Chang (va), J. Lastrapes (vc), K. Englichova (hp), R. Uchida (pno), A. LaFargue (perc), R. Laveille (perc), R. Milanov (cnd) New World ▲ 80445-2
Laforet, Marc (pno)
Chopin, F.:Preludes, Op. 28 Berlin Classics ▲ BER 1120 [DDD]
Chopin, F.:Son Pno, Op. 58 Berlin Classics ▲ BER 1120 [DDD]
La Forge, Frank (pno)
The Complete Odéon & Victor Recordings, w. Edmond Clément (ten), Geraldine Farrar (sop), Marcel Journet (bass), Rosario Bourdon (cnd) *(rec Odeon 1905; Victor 1911-1)* Romophone ▲ 82002-2
Lagacé, Bernard (org)
Bach, J.S.:Goldberg Vars *(rec Nov, 1995)* Analekta Fleur de Lys ▲ FL 23068 [DDD]
Bach, J.S.:Org Music (misc)—Christmas Cycle; Christmas Day Chorales; New Year's Chorales; Chorales for Purification Day; Chorales for the Passion of Christ; Easter Day Chorales; Whit-Sunday Cycle Analekta 2-▲ AN 28211-2
Bach, J.S.:Org Music (misc)—Toccata in d, BWV 565; Pastorale in F, BWV 590; Partita, BWV 766; Prelude & Fugue, BWV 531; Chorales, BWV 727, 730-31& 734; Fugue in g, BWV 578; Fant in g, BWV 572; Toccata in E, BWV 566 *(rec Church of the Immaculate Conception, Montreal, Mar 1996)* Analekta Fleur de Lys ▲ FL 23091 [DDD]

Lagacé, Mireille (hpd)
Bach, J.S.:Sons Vl, BWV 1027-1029, w. Robert Verebes (va) *(rec Bourcheville, Quebec)* SNE ▲ 564
Boismortier, J.B. de:Première Suite Approche ▲ 6838
Boismortier, J.B. de:Suites Hpd, Op. 59 *(rec 1978)* Approche ▲ CAL 6865 [ADD/DDD]
Rameau, J.P.:Concerts transcrits en sextuor, Caen Orch Approche ▲ 6838
Lagacé, Mireille (pno)
Dittersdorf, K.D. von:Son Va, w. Robert Verebes (va) *(rec Montreal)* SNE ▲ 569
Hummel, J.N.:Son Va, w. Robert Verebes (va) *(rec Montreal)* SNE ▲ 569
Stamitz, C.:Son Va, w. Robert Verebes (va) *(rec Montreal)* SNE ▲ 569
Vanhal, J.B.:Son Va, w. Robert Verebes (va) *(rec Montreal)* SNE ▲ 569
Laganà, Marco (pno)
Bellafronte, R.:Bankiwa, w. Adriano Paolini (pno) *(rec Villa Torano, Imola, Dec 1994)* Bongiovanni ▲ GB 5049-2 [DDD]
Lagerspetz, Juhani (pno)
Bartók, B.:Son for 2 Pnos, w. M. Raekallio (pno), T. Ferchen (perc), L. Erkkilä (perc) Ondine ▲ ODE 806 [DDD]
Bergman, E.:Borealis, w. M. Raekallio (pno), T. Ferchen (perc), L. Erkkilä (perc) Ondine ▲ ODE 806 [DDD]
Chopin, F.:Son Vc, w. M. Rousi (vc) Ondine ▲ ODE 748-2 [DDD]
Heiniö, M.:Hermes, w. Camilla Nylund (sop), J. Kangas (cnd), Ostrobothnian CO Ondine ▲ ODE 870
Heiniö, M.:In G Vc & Pno, w. Tuija Rantamäki (vc) Ondine ▲ ODE 870
Palmgren, S.:Cons Pno (comp), w. E. Heinonen (pno—No. 1), J. Lagerspetz (pno—Nos. 2 & 4), M. Raekallio (pno—No. 3), R. Kerppo (pno—No. 5), J. Mercier (cnd), Turku PO Finlandia 2-▲ 4509-95852-2 [DDD]
Rachmaninoff, S.:Son Vc, w. M. Rousi (vc) Ondine ▲ ODE 748-2 [DDD]
Stravinsky, I.:Son Pnos, w. M. Raekallio (pno) Ondine ▲ ODE 806 [DDD]
Szymanowski, K.:Caprices, w. E. Koskinen (vn) Ondine ▲ ODE 759-2 [DDD]
Szymanowski, K.:Lullaby, w. E. Koskinen (vn) Ondine ▲ ODE 759-2 [DDD]
Szymanowski, K.:Myths, w. E. Koskinen (vn) Ondine ▲ ODE 759-2 [DDD]
Szymanowski, K.:Notturno e Tarantella, w. E. Koskinen (vn) Ondine ▲ ODE 759-2 [DDD]
Szymanowski, K.:Romance, w. E. Koskinen (vn) Ondine ▲ ODE 759-2 [DDD]
Szymanowski, K.:Son Vn, w. E. Koskinen (vn) Ondine ▲ ODE 759-2 [DDD]
Lagomarsino, Marino (vn)—see ORCHESTRAS & ENSEMBLES Conserto Vago, Aira String Quartet
La Goya, Alexandre (gtr)
Bolling, C.:Con Gtr, w. Claude Bolling Trio Milan ▲ 73138-35646-2 ■ 73138-35646-4
Bolling, C.:Music of, w. C. Bolling (pno), J.-P. Rampal (fl), et al.—California Suite, Concerto for Classic Guitar & Jazz Piano, Flute & Jazz Piano Suites Nos. 1 & 2, Violin & Jazz Piano Suite, Picnic Suite, & Toot Suite CBS ▲ MK 44608 ■ FMT 44608
Bolling, C.:Picnic Suite, w. J.-P. Rampal (fl), Claude Bolling Trio CBS ▲ MK 35864 ■ PMT 35864
Carulli, F.:Con Fl, w. J.-P. Rampal (fl), J. Rolla (cnd), Franz Liszt CO CBS ▲ MK 42130 [DDD]
Rodrigo, J.:Concierto de Aranjuez, w. A. de Almeida (cnd), Monte Carlo Opera Orch Philips ("Solo" series) ▲ 442392-2
Rodrigo, J.:Fant para un gentilhombre, w. A. de Almeida (cnd), Monte Carlo Opera Orch Philips ("Solo" series) ▲ 442392-2
Lagoya, Sylavain (gtr)
Carulli, F.:Duos Fl & Gtr, Op. 104/1 & 3, w. J.-P. Rampal (fl) CBS ▲ MK 42130 [DDD]
Carulli, F.:Fantasy on Themes from Bellini's *Il pirata*, w. J.-P. Rampal (fl) CBS ▲ MK 42130 [DDD]
Carulli, F.:Nocturne Fl, w. J.-P. Rampal (fl) CBS ▲ MK 42130 [DDD]
L'Orientale Pierre Verany ▲ PVY 793105 [DDD]
Laguna, Juan Carlos (gtr)
Marco, Tomas:Tarots Urtext ▲ URT 5 [DDD]
Ponce, M.:Concierto del sur, w. F. Lozano (cnd), Carlos Chávez SO Forlane ▲ FOR 16736 [DDD]
Rodrigo, J.:Concierto de Aranjuez, w. F. Lozano (cnd), Carlos Chávez SO Forlane ▲ FRL 16757
Rodrigo, J.:Concierto de Aranjuez, w. F. Lozano (cnd), Carlos Chávez SO Forlane ▲ FRL 16733 [DDD]
Lahti, Pentti (fl/sax)
Braxton, A.:Composition 144, w. Anthony Braxton (fl/s sax/a sax), Seppo Baron Paakkunainen (fl/t sax/br sax), Pepa Päivinen (fl/t sax/sop sax/b cl), Mircea Stan (trbn), Mikko-Ville Luolajan-Mikkola (vn), Teppo Hauta-aho (db/vc), Jukka Wasama (dr) *(rec Järvenpää House, Järvenpää, Finland, Nov 7, 1988)* Leo ▲ LR 233
Braxton, A.:Composition 145, w. Anthony Braxton (fl/s sax/a sax), Seppo Baron Paakkunainen (fl/t sax/br sax), Pepa Päivinen (fl/t sax/sop sax/b cl), Mircea Stan (trbn), Mikko-Ville Luolajan-Mikkola (vn), Teppo Hauta-aho (db/vc), Jukka Wasama (dr) *(rec Järvenpää House, Järvenpää, Finland, Nov 7, 1988)* Leo ▲ LR 233
Laine, Esko (db)
Mustonen, O.:Toccata, w. O. Mustonen (pno), Orion String Quartet *(rec June 5, 1989, Aug. 8-9, 1)* Finlandia ▲ 4509-95860-2 [DDD]
Schubert, Franz:Qnt Pno, D.667, w. R. Gothoni (pno), Munich String Trio Ondine ▲ ODE 763-2 [DDD]
Laird, Michael (tpt)
Biber, H. von:Sonatae tam aris quam aulis servientes, w. Mark Bennett (tpt), Katherine McGillvray (va), Jane Rogers (va), Tim Cronin (va), Purcell Quartet Chandos ▲ CHAN 0591
Telemann, G.P.:Cons Tpt, w. H. Hardenberger (tpt), W. Houghton (tpt), I. Brown (cnd), Academy of St. Martin in the Fields—Concerto for 2 Trumpets & Strings; Concerto for Trumpet, 2 Oboes & Strings; Concerto for 3 Trumpets & Strings; Concerto for Trumpet & Strings Philips ("Digital Classics" series) ▲ 420954-2 [DDD]
Vivaldi, A.:Con Vn Obs, RV.563, w. I. Brown (vn), W. Houghton (tpt), N. Marriner (cnd), Academy of St. Martin in the Fields Philips ▲ 412892-2 [DDD]
Laivuori, Jouko (pno)
Nevanlinna, T.:Son Pno Finlandia ▲ FIN 12179 [DDD]
Suilamo, H.:...half-moon of his nails..., w. Lea Pekkala (vc) Finlandia ▲ FIN 12179 [DDD]
Lajarrige, Christine (pno)
Ropartz, G.:Choral Music, w. Christian Papis (nar), Didier Henry (bar), Vincent Le Texier (b-bar), Irène Brissot (hp), Eric Lebrun (org), M. Piquemal (cnd), Nancy SO, French Radio Chorus Soloists, Vittoria Regional French Choir—Psaume 136; Dimanche; Nocturne; Les Vêpres sonnent; Le Miracle de Saint Nicolas *(rec Salle Poirel, Nancy, Apr. 22-24, 1994)* Marco Polo ▲ 8.223774 [DDD]
Lakatoš, Alexander (va)—see also ORCHESTRAS & ENSEMBLES Moyzes String Quartet
Schmidt, F.:Qnt Cl, w. A. Janoska (cl), D. Ruso (pno), F. Török (vn), J. Slávik (vc) Marco Polo ▲ 8.223415
Schmidt, F.:Qnt Cl, w. A. Jánoska (cl), S. Mucha (vn), J. Slávik (vc), D. Ruso (pno) Marco Polo ▲ 8.223414
Lakatos, Janet (va)—see also ORCHESTRAS & ENSEMBLES Los Angeles String Quartet
Egilsson:Contemplation, w. Endeé Granat (vn), Richard Altenbach (vn), Douglas Davis (vc), Árni Egilsson (db) Cambria ▲ CD 1033
Egilsson:Get Down!, w. Endeé Granat (vn), Richard Altenbach (vn), Douglas Davis (vc), Árni Egilsson (db) Cambria ▲ CD 1033
Egilsson:Is It?, w. Endeé Granat (vn), Richard Altenbach (vn), Douglas Davis (vc), Árni Egilsson (db) Cambria ▲ CD 1033
Egilsson:What If?, w. Endeé Granat (vn), Richard Altenbach (vn), Douglas Davis (vc), Árni Egilsson (db) Cambria ▲ CD 1033
Egilsson:Why?, w. Endeé Granat (vn), Richard Altenbach (vn), Douglas Davis (vc), Árni Egilsson (db) Cambria ▲ CD 1033
Lale, P. (va)—see ORCHESTRAS & ENSEMBLES Britten String Quartet
Lam, Bun Ching (pno)—see ORCHESTRAS & ENSEMBLES New Performance Group of the Cornish Institute
Lam, Bun-Ching (pno)
Lam, B.-C.:After Spring, w. Thomasa Eckert (pno) CRI ▲ CD 726 [DDD]
Lam, B.-C.:Another Spring, w. Paul Taub (fl), Walter Gray (vc) CRI ▲ CD 726 [DDD]
Lam, B.-C.:Last Spring, w. Ella Marie Gray (vn), John Weller (vn), Melissa Hamilton (va), Walter Gray (vc) CRI ▲ CD 726 [DDD]

▲ = CD ♦ = Enhanced CD Δ = MD ■ = Cassette Tape □ = DCC

Lamandier, Esther (hp/org/vl/sgr)
Alfonso El Sabio:Cantigas de Santa Maria [Port] Astrée ▲ E 7707

Lamasse, Aleth (vc)
Haydn, J.:Con 1 Vc, w. J.–P. Wallez (cnd), French Instrumental Ensemble Forlane ▲ FRL 40 [AAD]
Haydn, J.:Con 2 Vc, w. J.–P. Wallez (cnd), French Instrumental Ensemble Forlane ▲ FRL 40 [AAD]

Lamb, A. (cl)—see ORCHESTRAS & ENSEMBLES Capricorn, Capricorn members

Lamb, Chris (perc)
Léon, T.:A la Par, w. V. Perry Lamb (pno) *(rec Oct. 21, 1992)* CRI ▲ CD 662 [DDD]
Rush, S.:Rebellion, w. Joseph Alessi (trbn), John McNeely (pno) Cala Records ("New York Legends" series) ▲ CAL CACD 508 [DDD]

Lamb, Christopher (military dr)—see ORCHESTRAS & ENSEMBLES New York Trumpet Ensemble

Lamb, V. Perry (pno)
Léon, T.:A la Par, w. C. Lamb (perc) *(rec Oct. 21, 1992)* CRI ▲ CD 662 [DDD]

Lamberto, Sergio (vn)—see also ORCHESTRAS & ENSEMBLES Turin Piano Trio
Rossini, G.:Chamber Music, w. Guido Corti (hn), Sergio del Mastro (cl), Ricardo Caramella (pno) Nuova Era ▲ NUO 7245

Lambooij, Henk (vc)
Grieg, E.:Andante con moto, w. R. Hoogeveen (vn), J. Röling (pno) Olympia ▲ OLY 432 [DDD]
Grieg, E.:Fugue, w. R. Hoogeveen (vn), J. Röling (pno) [arr for pno trio] Olympia ▲ OLY 432 [DDD]
Grieg, E.:Qt Strs (unfinished), w. R. Hoogeveen (vn), J. Röling (pno) [arr for pno trio] Olympia ▲ OLY 432 [DDD]
Grieg, E.:Qt Strs, Op. 27, w. R. Hoogeveen (vn), J. Röling (pno) Olympia ▲ OLY 432 [DDD]

Lambros, M. (va)
Hanson, H.:Con da Camera, w. B. Preston (vn), I. Swenson (vn), C. Wiersma (vn), Elizabeth Anderson (vc) Albany ▲ TROY 129 [DDD]

Lamke, Jurgen (pno)
Berg, A.:Adagio, w. Hans–Udo Heinzmann (fl), Malte Lammers (ob), Walter Hermann (cl), Heinrich Horlein (vn), Jaap Zeijl (va), Seven Forsberg (vc), Willi Beyer (db), Werner Hagen (pno), Volker Kneip (perc) [arr chamber ensemble] Koch Schwann ▲ SCH CD 311912
Busoni, F.:Berceuse élégiaque, w. Hans–Udo Heinzmann (fl), Malte Lammers (ob), Walter Hermann (cl), Heinrich Horlein (vn), Jaap Zeijl (va), Seven Forsberg (vc), Willi Beyer (db), Werner Hagen (pno), Volker Kneip (perc) [arr Stein for chamber ensemble] Koch Schwann ▲ SCH CD 311912
Debussy, C.:Prélude à l'après–midi d'un faune, w. Hans–Udo Heinzmann (fl), Malte Lammers (ob), Walter Hermann (cl), Heinrich Horlein (vn), Jaap Zeijl (va), Seven Forsberg (vc), Willi Beyer (db), Werner Hagen (pno), Volker Kneip (perc) [arr Sachs for chamber ensemble] Koch Schwann ▲ SCH CD 311912
Schoenberg, A.:Chamber Sym 1, w. Hans–Udo Heinzmann (fl), Malte Lammers (ob), Walter Hermann (cl), Heinrich Horlein (vn), Jaap Zeijl (va), Seven Forsberg (vc), Willi Beyer (db), Werner Hagen (pno), Volker Kneip (perc) [arr Webern for chamber ensemble] Koch Schwann ▲ SCH CD 311912

Lammers, Malte (ob)
Berg, A.:Adagio, w. Hans–Udo Heinzmann (fl), Walter Hermann (cl), Heinrich Horlein (vn), Jaap Zeijl (va), Seven Forsberg (vc), Willi Beyer (db), Jurgen Lamke (pno), Werner Hagen (pno), Volker Kneip (perc) [arr chamber ensemble] Koch Schwann ▲ SCH CD 311912
Busoni, F.:Berceuse élégiaque, w. Hans–Udo Heinzmann (fl), Walter Hermann (cl), Heinrich Horlein (vn), Jaap Zeijl (va), Seven Forsberg (vc), Willi Beyer (db), Jurgen Lamke (pno), Werner Hagen (pno), Volker Kneip (perc) [arr Stein for chamber ensemble] Koch Schwann ▲ SCH CD 311912
Debussy, C.:Prélude à l'après–midi d'un faune, w. Hans–Udo Heinzmann (fl), Walter Hermann (cl), Heinrich Horlein (vn), Jaap Zeijl (va), Seven Forsberg (vc), Willi Beyer (db), Jurgen Lamke (pno), Werner Hagen (pno), Volker Kneip (perc) [arr Sachs for chamber ensemble] Koch Schwann ▲ SCH CD 311912
Schoenberg, A.:Chamber Sym 1, w. Hans–Udo Heinzmann (fl), Walter Hermann (cl), Heinrich Horlein (vn), Jaap Zeijl (va), Seven Forsberg (vc), Willi Beyer (db), Jurgen Lamke (pno), Werner Hagen (pno), Volker Kneip (perc) [arr Webern for chamber ensemble] Koch Schwann ▲ SCH CD 311912

Lamon, Jeanne (vn)
Bach, J.S.:Brandenburg Cons, w. Tafelmusik Sony Classical ("Vivarte" series) 2–▲ S2K 66289
Bach, J.S.:Cons Vn (comp), Tafelmusik Sony Classical ("Vivarte" series) ▲ SK 66265
Bach, J.S.:Con for 2 Vns, Tafelmusik Sony Classical ("Vivarte" series) ▲ SK 66265
Vivaldi, A.:Cons Vn, Op. 8/1–4, "The Four Seasons", w. J. Lamon (cnd), Tafelmusik Sony Classical ("Vivarte" series) ▲ SK 48251 [DDD]

Lamond, Frederic (pno)
Frederic Lamond, 1868–1948:Liszt's Last Pupil Pearl ▲ PEA 9911 (m) [AAD]
Liszt, F.:Liebesträume—No. 3 APR ▲ APR 5504 [ADD]
Liszt, F.:Pno Music (misc)—Gnomenreigen (3 versions); Un sospiro (4 versions); Valse impromptu; Feux follets; Waldesrauschen APR ▲ APR 5504 [ADD]
Liszt, F.:Pno Music (misc) Pearl ▲ PEA 9911 (m) [AAD]
Liszt, F.:Sonetti del Petrarca Pno—No. 104 APR ▲ APR 5504 [ADD]
Liszt, F.:Transcriptions & Paraphrases—Tarantella [from Venezia e Napoli]; Schubert:Erlkönig (2 versions); Rossini:Cujus animam [from Stabat Mater]; Auber:Tarentelle di bravura [from La muette de Portici] APR ▲ APR 5504 [ADD]

La Montaine, John (kbd)
Bach, J.S.:Das wohltemperierte Klavier—Book 2 [arr Montaine for Elec Kbd] Fredonia Discs 2–▲ FDCD 13
La Montaine, J.:Of That Hallowed Season Fredonia Discs ▲ FDCD 14

Lampert, Christian (hn)—see ORCHESTRAS & ENSEMBLES Avalon Wind Quintet

Lampert, Daniel (fl)—see ORCHESTRAS & ENSEMBLES Avalon Wind Quintet

Lamprecht, P. (vl/vc)—see ORCHESTRAS & ENSEMBLES Arcangelo Corelli Trio

Lamproye, André (org)
Famous Adagios:Saxophone & Organ, Vol. 4, w. Jean–Pierre Rorive (a sax/s sax) Pavane ▲ 7333
Rêveries:Saxophone & Organ V, w. Jean–Pierre Rorive (sax) *(rec 1996)* Pavane ▲ ADW 7364 [DDD]

Lamson, Carl (pno)
The 1928 Victor Recordings:Favourite Short Pieces, w. Fritz Kreisler (vn) Biddulph ▲ LAB 080 [ADD]
The Victor Recordings, w. Fritz Kreisler (vn), John McCormack (ten) *(rec 1921–25)* Biddulph 2–▲ LAB 068–69 [ADD]

Lanaghan, Robert (pno)
Inwood, M.:Son Tpt, w. John Malazzo (tpt) Capstone ▲ CPS 8616 [DDD]

Lancaster, Geoffery (org)
Haydn, J.:Mass 7, "Kleine Orgelmesse", w. B. Weil (cnd), Tafelmusik, Tölz Boys' Choir *(rec Germany, Sept. 5, 1993)* Sony Classical ("Vivarte" series) ▲ SK 53368 [DDD]

Lancaster, Geoffrey (pno)
18th Century Virtuoso String Music, w. B. J. Gilby (vn), Tasmanian Sym Chamber Players ABC Classics ▲ 432530–2 [DDD]
Mozart, W.A.:Son 12 Pno *(rec June 4–7, 1992)* Tall Poppies ▲ TP 022 [DDD]
Mozart, W.A.:Son 13 Pno *(rec June 4–7, 1992)* Tall Poppies ▲ TP 022 [DDD]
Mozart, W.A.:Son 16 Pno *(rec June 4–7, 1992)* Tall Poppies ▲ TP022 [DDD]
Mozart, W.A.:Songs, w. J. Edwards (cta), P. Sharpe (sgr), D. Russell (sgr), D. Hamilton (ten), M. Glasgow (sgr), C. Birch (sgr), P. Hooper (sgr) *(rec July 1991)* Tall Poppies ▲ TP009 [DDD]

Lancaster, Samuel (pno)
Encore, w. Colorado Children's Chorale [cnd:Duain Wolfe], Rick Chinski (gtr), Robert Davine (acc), Laurie Kahler (pno), Barry Oliver (pno), Marylin Preston (fl), Karen Yonovitz (fl), Peter Cooper (ob), Andy Stevens (cl), Lionel Young (vn), Basil Vendreys (va), Wayne Templeman (vc), Charle *(rec Denver Center Media)* Colorado Children's Chorale ▲ 001

Lancelot, Jacques (cl)
Ladmirault, P.:Son Cl, w. Robert Plantard (pno) *(rec Nantes National Conservatory Auditorium, 1980)* Skarbo ▲ SK 4952 [ADD]
Mozart, W.A.:Con Cl, w. Jacques Lancelot (cl)., J.–F. Paillard (cnd), Jean–François Paillard CO—Adagio; Rondo Erato ▲ 94679–2
Mozart, W.A.:Con Cl, w. J.–F. Paillard (cnd), Jean–François Paillard CO Erato ▲ 45978–2 ■ 45978–4

Lancelot, James (org)
The Archbishop's Fanfare Priory ▲ PRI 346 [DDD]
Franck, C.:Cantabile [Winchester Cathedral org] ASV Quicksilva ▲ ASQ 6175
Great European Organs, Vol. 5, w. Stephen Cleobury (org) Priory ▲ PRCD 228 [DDD]

Lancelot, James (org/hpd)
Monteverdi, C.:Vespro della Beata Vergine, w. Elly Ameling (sop), Norma Burrowes (sop), Charles Brett (ct), Martyn Hill (ten), Anthony Rolfe–Johnson (ten), Robert Tear (ten), Peter Knapp (bass), John Noble (bass), Francis Grier (org/hpd), Andrew Leach (org/hpd), P. Ledger (cnd), London Early Music Consort, King's College Choir Cambridge—Nigra sum [con.]; Laudate pueri [psalm]; Sancta Maria [son. sopra]; Magnificat *(rec Chapel of King's College, Cambridge, July & Aug. 1975)* EMI Classics ▲ CDK 65339 [ADD]

Lancie, John de (ob)
Françaix, J.:L'Horloge de Flore, w. A. Previn (cnd), London SO RCA Gold Seal ▲ 7989–2–RG [ADD]
Ibert, J.:Symphonie concertante, w. A. Previn (cnd), London SO RCA Gold Seal ▲ 7989–2–RG [ADD]
Satie, E.:Gymnopédies, w. A. Previn (cnd), London SO [arr. for solo oboe & orchestra]—No. 1 RCA Gold Seal ▲ 7989–2–RG [ADD]
Strauss, R.:Con Ob, w. M. Wilcox (cnd), chamber orch RCA Gold Seal ▲ 7989–2–RG [ADD]

Landale, Susan (org)
Messiaen, O.:Apparition de l'Eglise éternelle Adda ▲ ADD 242702 [DDD]
Messiaen, O.:L'Ascension Org Adda ▲ ADD 581059 [DDD]
Messiaen, O.:Le Banquet céleste Adda ▲ ADD 242702 [DDD]
Messiaen, O.:Les Corps glorieux Adda ▲ ADD 581059 [DDD]
Messiaen, O.:La Nativité du Seigneur Adda ▲ ADD 242702 [DDD]
Paris au tournant du siécle REM ▲ 311202 [DDD]
Vierne, L.:Pièces de fant Accord ▲ ACD 204842 [DDD]

Landauer, Walter (pno)
Saint–Saëns, C.:Carnival of the Animals, w. M. Rawicz (pno), J. Barbirolli (cnd), Hallé Orch Dutton Laboratories ▲ DUT CDSJB 1002 [ADD]

Lande, Vladimir (ob)—see ORCHESTRAS & ENSEMBLES D'Amore Duo

Landeen, Peter (vc)
Lovenstein, J.:Music of, w. Mary Brockenbrough (sop), Laura Sanders (sop), Barton Green (ten), Rockland Osgood (ten), David Murray (bar), Benjamin Sears (bar), Jonathan Lovenstein (pno), Heather O'Donnell (pno), James Silvers (pno), Rocy Reider (fl), Jason Horowitz (vn), Adrianna Hulscher (vn), James Johnston (vn), Mimi Ragson (vn), Reinmar Seidler (vc)—Blake Songs; other works Titanic ▲ Ti 221 [DDD]

Landers, Harvey (hn)
Van Appledorn, M.J.:Patterns, w. A. Brittin (hn), J. Whitaker (hn), M. Walzel (hn), L. Dawson (hn) Opus One ▲ CD 162

Landes, Garah (pno)
Griffes, C.T.:Fant Pieces, Op. 6 Koch International Classics ▲ KIC 7045–2 [DDD]
Griffes, C.T.:Son Pno Koch International Classics ▲ KIC 7045–2 [DDD]
Griffes, C.T.:Tone–Pictures, Op. 5 Koch International Classics ▲ KIC 7045–2 [DDD]
Liszt, F.:Mephisto Waltz 3 Pno Stradivari Classics ▲ SCD 6069 [DDD] ■ SMC 6069 (D)
Liszt, F.:Sonetti del Petrarca Pno Stradivari Classics ▲ SCD 6069 [DDD] ■ SMC 6069 (D)
Macdowell, E.:Son 4 Pno Koch International Classics ▲ KIC 7045–2 [DDD]
Prokofiev, S.:Son 7 Pno Stradivari Classics ▲ SCD 6069 [DDD] ■ SMC 6069 (D)
Shostakovich, D.:Preludes & Fugues Pno—No. 24 Stradivari Classics ▲ SCD 6069 [DDD] ■ SMC 6069 (D)

Landgren, Peter (hn)
Pilss, K.:Pezzi (3) in forma de sonata, w. Ann Schein (pno) *(rec John Addison Concert Hall, Harmony Hall Regional Center, Fort Washington, Maryland, Dec. 1993 & Mar. 1994)* Elan ▲ CD 2260 [DDD]
Rheinberger, J.:Son Hn, w. Ann Schein (pno) *(rec John Addison Concert Hall, Harmony Hall Regional Center, Fort Washington, Maryland, Dec. 1993 & Mar. 1994)* Elan ▲ CD 2260 [DDD]
Schumann, R.:Adagio & Allegro Hn, w. Ann Schein (pno) *(rec John Addison Concert Hall, Harmony Hall Regional Center, Fort Washington, Maryland, Dec. 1993 & Mar. 1994)* Elan ▲ CD 2260 [DDD]
Schumann, R.:Fantasiestücke Cl, w. Ann Schein (pno) *(rec John Addison Concert Hall, Harmony Hall Regional Center, Fort Washington, Maryland, Dec. 1993 & Mar. 1994)* Elan ▲ CD 2260 [DDD]
Strauss, F.:Nocturne, w. Ann Schein (pno) *(rec John Addison Concert Hall, Harmony Hall Regional Center, Fort Washington, Maryland, Dec. 1993 & Mar. 1994)* Elan ▲ CD 2260 [DDD]

Landini, Gilles (pno)
Janácek, L.:Our Father, w. M. Dvorsky (ten), C. Gesseney (cnd), Lausanne Euterpe Vocal Ensemble Gallo ▲ CD 784 [DDD]

Landowska, Wanda (hpd)
Bach, J.S.:Chromatic Fant & Fugue *(rec mid 1930s)* EMI Classics (Great Recordings of the Century) ▲ CDH 61008–2 (m)
Bach, J.S.:Chromatic Fant & Fugue Enterprise ("Documents") ▲ CDLV 953 (m) [ADD]
Bach, J.S.:English Suites—BWV 807 *(rec 1936)* Pearl ▲ PEA 9490 (m) [AAD]
Bach, J.S.:French Suites—BWV 817 *(rec 1936)* Pearl ▲ PEA 9490 (m) [AAD]
Bach, J.S.:Goldberg Vars EMI Classics ("Great Recordings of the Century" series) ▲ CDH 61008–2 (m)
Bach, J.S.:Goldberg Vars RCA Gold Seal ("Legendary Performers" series) ▲ 09026–60919–2
Bach, J.S.:Italian Con *(rec mid '30s)* EMI Classics ("Great Recordings of the Century" series) ▲ CDH 61008–2 (m)
Bach, J.S.:Music of—English Suite No. 2; Gavotte & Passapieds from English Suites 3 & 5; French Suite No. 6; Fantasia in c, BWV 906; Ten Little Preludes, BWV 924, 933–939, 961 & 999; Partita No. 1 in B♭; Toccata in D *(1928–36 Victor rec'gs)*; Prelude & Fugue in c from Book 1 of the Well–tempered Clavier *(rec live, Jan 22, 1950)* Pearl ▲ PEA 9490 (m) [AAD]
Bach, J.S.:Preludes Hpd, BWV 933–38, "Little Preludes" *(rec 1935)* Pearl ▲ PEA 9490 (m) [AAD]
Bach, J.S.:Das wohltemperierte Klavier—Book 1, BWV 846–69 Enterprise ("Documents") ▲ CDLV 953 (m) [ADD]
Bach, J.S.:Das wohltemperierte Klavier—Book 1 RCA Red Seal 2–▲ 6217–2–RC (m) [ADD]
Bach, J.S.:Das wohltemperierte Klavier—Book 2 RCA Red Seal 3–▲ 7825–2–RC (m)
Couperin, F.:Pièces de clavecin (sels)—Book 1:3rd Ordre in c, "La favorite"; Book 2:11th Ordre in c, "Les fastes de la grande et ancienne ménestrandise"; Book 3:13th Ordre in b, "Les folies française"; 15th Ordre in a, "Le dodo, ou l'amour au berceau" Enterprise ("Documents") ▲ CDLV 953 (m) [ADD]
Couperin, F.:Pièces de clavecin (sels)—La Favorite; Les Moissonneurs; Les Langueurs–tendres; Le Gazouillement; La Commère; Le Moucheron; Les Bergeries; Les Tambourins; Les Fastes de la grande ménestrandise; Le Dodo, ou l'amour au berceau; Musette de taverny; Les Folies françaises ou les dominos; Les Calotins et les calotines; Les Vergers fleuris; Soeur monique; Les Ondes Enterprise ("Piano Library" series) ▲ ENT PL 204
Great Musicians In Copenhagen, w. Vladimir Horowitz (pno), Rudolf Serkin (pno), Nathan Milstein (vn), Gregor Piatigorsky (vc), Fritz Busch (cnd), Nicolai Malko (cnd) Danacord ▲ DACOCD 303
Handel, G.F.:Concerti grossi, Op. 6, w. E. Bigot (cnd), *(orch unknown)* [cadenzas by Landowska]—Concerto No. 4 in B♭ *(rec for HMV 1935)* Pearl ▲ PEA 9490 (m) [AAD]
Handel, G.F.:Suites Hpd—Suite Nos. 2,5,7,10 & 14; Air & Variations from Suite No. 15; Sarabande & Doubles from Suite No. 7 *(rec 1935–37 & live 1/22/50)* Pearl ▲ PEA 9490 (m) [AAD]
Landowska Plays Bach Pearl ▲ PEA 9489 (m) [AAD]
Landowska Plays Handel Pearl ▲ PEA 9490 (m) [AAD]
Rameau, J.P.:Pièces de clavecin en concert—Suite in g Enterprise ("Piano Library" series) ▲ ENT PL 204
Scarlatti, D.:Sons Kbd—24 sels. EMI Classics ▲ CDH 64934

Landowska, Wanda (pno)
Mozart, W.A.:Con 13 Pno, w. A. Rodzinski (cnd), New York PO *(rec New York, 1945)* Iron Needle ▲ IN 1336 (m) [ADD]
Mozart, W.A.:Con 22 Pno, w. A. Rodzinski (cnd), New York PO *(rec New York, Dec 2, 1945)* Iron Needle ▲ IN 1336 (m) [ADD]
Mozart, W.A.:Con 26 Pno, w. W. Goehr (cnd), *(orch unknown)* *(rec March 25, 1937, first iss)* Biddulph ▲ LHW 013 [ADD]
Mozart, W.A.:Fant Pno, K.397 *(rec March 1937, first issued)* Biddulph ▲ LHW 013 [ADD]

Landowska, Wanda (pno) (cont.)
Mozart, W.A.:Son 12 Pno *(rec Jan. 1938, mats. 2LA 2341)* Biddulph ▲ LHW 013 [ADD]
Mozart, W.A.:Son 17 Pno *(rec Jan. 1938)* Biddulph ▲ LHW 013 [ADD]
Musique ancienne *(rec between 1928–54)* Pearl ▲ PEA 9012 [AAD]

Landsman, J. (hn)
Pinkston, R.:Qt for 4 Hns, w. T. Bacon (hn), N. Goodearl (hn), J. Horrocks (hn) Summit ▲ DCD 135 [DDD]

Landsman, Vladimir (vn)
Chugaev, A.:Capriccio *(rec June 1990)* Analekta ▲ UMM 301
Prévost, A.:Improvisation Vn Analekta ▲ UMM 103
Prokofiev, S.:Romeo & Juliet (sels), w. M. Durand (pno)—Montaigus et Capulets; La Danse des filles aux fleurs; Masques *(rec June 1990)* Analekta ▲ UMM 301
Prokofiev, S.:Son solo Vn, Op. 115, w. M. Durand (pno) *(rec June 1990)* Analekta ▲ UMM 301
Prokofiev, S.:Son Vn, Op. 94bis, w. M. Durand (pno) *(rec June 1990)* Analekta ▲ UMM 301
Shchedrin, R.:In Imitation of Albéniz, w. M. Durand (pno) [arr Tziganov] *(rec June 1990)* Analekta ▲ UMM 301
Shostakovich, D.:Preludes Pno, Op. 34, w. M. Durand (pno) [arr Tziganov]—4 Preludes *(rec June 1990)* Analekta ▲ UMM 301

Lane, Adrian (trbn)
Bruckner, A.:motets, w. Richard Cheetham (trbn), Steven Saunders (trbn), Simon Wills (trbn), Matthew Morley (org), Robert James (cnd), James St. Bride's Church Choir—Os justi; Locus iste; Libera me [in f, 1854]; Ave maria; Ecce sacerdos; Vexilla regis; Salvum fac populum tuum [1884]; Afferentur regi; Pange lingua; Tota pulchra es [Daniel Norman (tenor)]; Virga Jesse; Inveni David; Iam lucis orto sidere [Hymnus, 1868]; Tantum ergo [in D, 1988]; Christus factus est *(rec St. Bride's Church, Fleet Street, London, Jan. 27–29, 1994)* Naxos ▲ 8.550956 [DDD]

Lane, Christopher (tpt)
Zwilich, E.T.:Clarino Qt, w. David Flello (tpt), David Michaux (tpt), Louis Ranger (tpt) *(rec Univ of Victoria, May 1994)* Crystal ▲ CD 669

Lane, Pier (pno)
Albert, E. d':Con 1 Pno, w. A. Francis (cnd), BBC Scottish SO Hyperion ▲ CDA 66747
Albert, E. d':Con 2 Pno, w. A. Francis (cnd), BBC Scottish SO Hyperion ▲ CDA 66747
Brahms, J.:Qnt Pno, w. New Budapest String Quartet Hyperion ▲ CDA 66652
Delius, F.:Con Pno, w. V. Handley (cnd), Royal Liverpool PO Classics for Pleasure ("Eminence" series) ▲ CFP 2239
Finzi, G.:Ecologue, w. V. Handley (cnd), Royal Liverpool PO Classics for Pleasure ("Eminence" series) ▲ CFP 2239
Friedman, I.:Transcriptions Pno—Frühlingsstimmen Hyperion ▲ CDA 66785
Godowsky, L.:Transcriptions & Paraphrases—Paraphrase on Johann Strauss' "Die Fledermaus" Hyperion ▲ CDA 66785
Moszkowski, M.:Con Pno, w. J. Maksymiuk (cnd), BBC Scottish SO Hyperion ▲ CDA 66452 [DDD]
Paderewski, I.J.:Con Pno, w. J. Maksymiuk (cnd), BBC Scottish SO Hyperion ▲ CDA 66452 [DDD]
The Romantic Piano Concerto, Vol. 1, w. BBC Scottish SO [cnd:J. Maksymiuk] Hyperion ▲ CDA 66452 [DDD]
Rosenthal, M.:Carnaval de Vienne Hyperion ▲ CDA 66785
Rosenthal, M.:Fant on Themes of Johann Strauss Hyperion ▲ CDA 66785
Schulz-Evler, A.:Arabesque on Themes from Johann Strauss' *The Beautiful Blue Danube* Hyperion ▲ CDA 66785
Tausig, C.:Nouvelles Soirées Hyperion ▲ CDA 66785
Vaughan Williams, R.:Con Pno, w. V. Handley (cnd), Royal Liverpool PO Classics for Pleasure ("Eminence" series) ▲ CFP 2239

Lane, Timothy (fl)—see also ORCHESTRAS & ENSEMBLES Ciosoni Trio
Gubaidulina, S.:Sounds of the Forest, w. B. Wimunc-Pearson (pno) Zuma Records ▲ ZMA 104
Ives, C.:Son 3 Vn, w. B. Wimunc-Pearson (pno) [trans. Lane] Zuma Records ▲ ZMA 104
Melby, J.:Con Fl & Sounds, w. B. Wimunc-Pearson (elec) Zuma Records ▲ ZMA 104
Nielsen, C.:Children Are Playing, w. B. Wimunc-Pearson (pno) Zuma Records ▲ ZMA 104
Nielsen, C.:Fog Is Lifting, w. B. Wimunc-Pearson (pno) Zuma Records ▲ ZMA 104

Lang (pno)
Woods, P.:Son Sax, w. V. Morosco (sax) Protone ■ CSPR 153

Lang, D. (vc)—see ORCHESTRAS & ENSEMBLES Icebreaker

Lang, Franz (perc)
Markevitch, I.:L'Envol d'Icare, w. K. Lessing (pno), C. Lyndon-Gee (pno), J. Gagelmann (perc), R. Haeger (perc) *(rec July 10–11, 1993)* Largo ▲ 5127 [DDD]
Rihm, W.:Lieder, w. R. Salter (bar), B. Wambach (pno), M. Rosenthal (drum)—Vier Gedichte aus Atemwende [text by Paul Celan] for Voice & Piano (1973); Hölderlin-Fragmente for Voice & Piano (1976–7); Neue Alexanderlieder [5 poems by Ernst Herbeck] for Baritone & Piano 1979); Wölfli-Liederbuch for Baritone, Piano & 2 Drums (1980–81) [G] CPO ▲ CPO 999049-2 [ADD]

Lang, Michael (pno)
An American Collage Vol. II, w. Constance Keene (pno), Ayke Agus (pno), Anita Swearingen (pno), Diane Lang Bryan (cl), James Smith (gtr), Sherry Kloss (vn), Laila Padorr (fl), Victor Morosco (a sax) Protone ▲ PRCD 1114 [DDD]

Lang, Peter (pno)
Mozart, W.A.:Con 20 Pno, w. C. Eberle (cnd), Capella Istropolitana *(rec Concert Hall of Czecho-Slovak Radio, Bratislava, May 3–8, 1988)* Lydian ▲ 18028 [DDD]
Mozart, W.A.:Con 21 Pno, w. C. Eberle (cnd), Capella Istropolitana *(rec Concert Hall of Czecho-Slovak Radio, Bratislava, May 3–8, 1988)* Lydian ▲ 18028 [DDD]

Lang, Teresa (vn)—see ORCHESTRAS & ENSEMBLES Sierra Winds

Langbein, Brenton (vn)
Banks, D.:Trio Hn, w. B. Tuckwell (hn), M. Jones (pno) *(rec 4/87)* Tudor ▲ 771 [DDD]
Brahms, J.:Trio Hn, w. B. Tuckwell (hn), M. Jones (pno) *(rec 4/87)* Tudor ▲ 771 [DDD]
Koechlin, C.:Petites Pièces, w. B. Tuckwell (hn), M. Jones (pno) *(rec 4/87)* Tudor ▲ 771 [DDD]
Müller-Zurich, P.:Trio Strs, w. D. Corti (va), R. Altwegg (vc) Grammont ▲ CTSP 20-2
Raff, J.:Octet Strs, w. M. Lehmann (va), R. Reichel, Zurich Chamber Players *(rec 1978)* Jecklin-Disco ▲ JD 547-2 [ADD]
Spohr, L.:Double Qt 1, w. M. Lehmann (va), R. Reichel, Zurich Chamber Players *(rec 1978)* Jecklin-Disco ▲ JD 547-2 [ADD]

Langdon, Sophie (vn)
Smyth, E.:Con Vn Hn, w. Richard Watkins (hn), O. de la Martinez (cnd), BBC PO Chandos ▲ CHAN 9449

Lange, Arno. (tpt)—see also ORCHESTRAS & ENSEMBLES Berlin German Opera Orch Soloists
Martinů, B.:La Revue de Cuisine (sels), w. T. Tomaszewski (vn), G. Lösch (vc), R. Schönemann (cl), V. Knappe (bn), S. Schubert-Weber (pno)—Suite for Violin, Cello, Clarinet, Bassoon, Trumpet & Piano FSM-Adagio ▲ FCD 97 219
Trumpet & Organ, w. Joachim Pliquett (tpt), Ulrich Bremsteller (org), Arvid Gast (org) Classic Studio Berlin ▲ CS 12 208 [DDD]

Lange, Harrie de (b trbn)—see ORCHESTRAS & ENSEMBLES Ives Ensemble members

Lange, Joanne (org)
Paine, J.K.:Mass, Op. 10, w. C. Balthrop (sop), J. Blackett (cta), V. Cole (ten), J. Cheek (bass), G. Schuller (cnd), St. Louis SO, St. Louis Sym Chorus [L] *(rec ca. mid-1970s)* New World ▲ 80262-2 [AAD]

Lange, Jos de (bn)
Roussel, A.:Chamber Music, w. Paul Verhey (fl/pic), Frank van den Brink (cl), Hans Roerade (ob), Herre-Jan Stegenga (vc), Jet Röling (pno), Schoenberg String Quartet—Trio for Fl, Va & Vc, Op. 40; Qt for Strs, Op. 45; Andante & Scherzo for Fl & Pno, Op. 51; Pipe for Pic & Pno; Trio for Strs, Op. 58; Music from Elpenor for Fl & Str Qt, Op. 59; Andante from an unfinished Ww Trio for Ob, Cl & Bn Olympia ▲ OLY 460 [DDD]

Langebo, Karin (hp)
Sun-Flute 4, w. Gunilla von Bahr (fl), Musica Vitae [cnd:Jan-Olav Wedin] BIS ▲ CD 350 [DDD]

Langenstein, Gottfried (hn)
Böck, A.:Pieces (4), w. J. Stobart (hn), G. Dzwiza (db), K. Stoll (db) Signum ▲ X 45-00 [DDD]

Langenstein, Gottfried (hn) (cont.)
Draeseke, F.:Qnt Pno, Op. 48, w. Mozart Piano Quartet MD + G ▲ MDG 6150673
Mozart, W.A.:Qnt Pno, K.452, w. Keiko Toyama (pno), Günther Passin (ob), Yuji Murai (cl), Koji Okazaki (bn) *(rec Shibukawa Shimin Kaikan, Sept 1, 1981)* Camerata ▲ 32CM 180 [DDD]

Langer, Milan (pno)
Kalabis, V.:Son Vn, w. Ivan Zenatý (vn) *(rec Martínek Studio in Prague, Jan 23 & 26 & Feb 13 & 14)* Panton ▲ 811398-2 [DDD]
Martinů, B.:Qt Ob & Pno Trio, w. Czech Nonet *(rec Nov 1995–Jan 1996)* Praga ▲ PR 250097
Martinů, B.:Son in C Vn, w. Ivan Zenaty (vn) Panton ▲ PAN 810965
Martinů, B.:Son in d Vn, w. Ivan Zenaty (vn) Panton ▲ PAN 810965
Martinů, B.:Sonatina Vn, w. Ivan Zenaty (vn) Panton ▲ PAN 810965
Shostakovich, D.:Qnt Pno, w. Talich String Quartet *(rec 1976 & 1981)* Praga ▲ PR 254 042

Langgartner, P. (va)—see ORCHESTRAS & ENSEMBLES Pro Arte String Quartet

Langlais, Jean (org)
Franck, C.:Org Music (comp) [organ of the Basilica of St. Clothilde]—First Chorale in E; Pièce Héroique; Second Chorale in b; Grande Pièce Symphonique; Prière; Prelude, Fugue & Var.; Fantaisie in A; Third Chorale in C; Final in B♭; Cantabile in B; Pastorale in E GIA 2-▲ GIA 272 [DDD]; ■ CS 272

Langlamet, Marie-Pierre (hp)
Beethoven, L. van:Leonore Prohaska, w. Sylvia McNair (sop), Karoline Eichhorn (narr), Sascha Reckert (glass hmc), C. Abbado (cnd), Berlin PO, Berlin Radio Chorus *(rec Great Hall, Philharmonie, Berlin, Sept 1993 & Feb & Dec 199)* Deutsche Grammophon ▲ 447748-2 [DDD]
Currier, N.:A Sambuca Son, w. Maarika Järvi (fl), Paul Cortese (va) Chandos ▲ CHAN 9395 [DDD]
Debussy, C.:Son Fl, w. Maarika Järvi (fl), Paul Cortese (va) Chandos ▲ CHAN 9395 [DDD]
Genzmer, H.:Trio Fl, Va & Hp, w. Maarika Järvi (fl), Paul Cortese (va) Chandos ▲ CHAN 9395 [DDD]
Jolivet, A.:Petite suite, w. Maarika Järvi (fl), Paul Cortese (va) Chandos ▲ CHAN 9395 [DDD]

Lang-Oester, Ruth (pno)
Schoeck, O.:Der Sänger, w. F. Lang (ten) Koch Schwann ▲ SCH 310912 [DDD]

Langot, Michelle (pno)
Franck, C.:Son Vn, w. Monique Frasca-Colombier (vn) Pierre Verany ▲ PVY 730068 [DDD]
Magnard, A.:Son Vn, w. Monique Frasca-Colombier (vn) Pierre Verany ▲ PVY 730068 [DDD]

Langsberg, Peter (org)
Aventure:Original Compositions for Flute & Organ, w. Bent Larsen (fl) Classico ▲ CLASSCD 111

Laniar, Ivo (vc)
Zelenka, J.D.:Con à 8, w. Jana Brozková (ob), Josef Suk (vn), Ludmila Vybíralová (vn), Jaroslav Kubita (bn), F. Vajnar (cnd), Suk CO *(rec Studio Martínek, Prague, May 15–17 & Nov. 8–13, 19)* Panton 2-▲ PAN 811235 [DDD]

Lanier, Jaron (pno)
Lanier, J.:Music of, w. *(add artists unknown)*—Come Along; Khaen Violin Duo No. 6; The Story of Water Dancing in the Night Sky; Angklung; Suite for Saxophone Ensemble; Tremolo Silence; Circular Saw; Breaking Song; The Breath of the Earth; Sentiment & Strut; Cream Soda; Khaen Violin Du Philips ▲ 442132-2 [DDD]
Riley, T.:In C, w. Bruce Ackley, Steve Adams, Don R. Baker, Chris Brown, George Brooks, Steve Coughlin, Blake Derby, Bill Douglass, Mihr'un'Nisa Douglass, Hank Dutt, David Harrington, Don Howe, Joan Jeanrenaud, Alden Jenks, Warner Jepson, Henry Kaiser, Bill Maginnis, George Marsh, Shabda Owens, Jon Raskin, Gyan Riley, Terry Riley, Gino Robair, John Sackett, Ramón Sender, John Sherba, Toyji Tomita, Danny Tunick, William Winant, Evan Ziporyn *(rec Jan. 14, 1990)* New Albion ▲ NA 071

Lanini, Phyllis (ob)—see also ORCHESTRAS & ENSEMBLES Boehme Quintet
Berger, A.:Duos, w. J. Smirnoff (vn), C. Oldfather (pno), J. Krosnick (vc), G. Kalish (pno), D. Stewart (cl)—Duo No. 1 for Violin & Piano (1948); Duo for Cello & Piano (1951); Duo for Oboe & Clarinet (1952) New World ▲ NW 360-2 [DDD]

Lännerholm, A. (trbn)
Schnittke, A.:Sym 1, w. C.-A. Dominique (pno), B. Kallenberg (vn), L. Segerstam (cnd), Royal Stockholm PO *(rec Oct. 14, 1992)* BIS ▲ CD 577 [DDD]

Lanoë, Fabrice (pno)
Sauguet, H.:Les Jeux de l'amour et du hasard, w. Christelle Holleville (pno) Sonpact ▲ SPT 96017 [DDD]

Lansky, C. (perc)
Lansky, P.:Music for Computer-Processed Natural Sounds, w. J. Lansky (perc), H. MacKay (nar), P. Lansky (hands), J. Moses (hands)—Table's Clear (percussive kitchen paraphernalia); Night Traffic (traffic sounds); Now and Then (speech-music); Quakerbridge (people in a suburban shopping mall); The Sound of Two Hands Bridge ▲ BCD 9035 [DDD]

Lansky, J. (perc)
Lansky, P.:Music for Computer-Processed Natural Sounds, w. C. Lansky (perc), H. MacKay (nar), P. Lansky (hands), J. Moses (hands)—Table's Clear (percussive kitchen paraphernalia); Night Traffic (traffic sounds); Now and Then (speech-music); Quakerbridge (people in a suburban shopping mall); The Sound of Two Hands Bridge ▲ BCD 9035 [DDD]

Lantos, I. (pno)
Brahms, J.:Qt 2 Pno, w. P. Kolmós (vn), G. Németh (va), K. Botvay (vc) *(rec 1972–74)* Hungaroton 2-▲ HCD 11597/98 [ADD]
Liszt, F.:Pno Music (misc), w. K. Dráfi (pno), J. Jandó (pno)—Harmonies poétiques et religieuses; Invocation (1st version); Hymne du matin; Hymne de la nuit; Berceuse (1st version); Klavierstück; Trois odes funèbres; Berceuse (2nd version); Urbi et orbi; Vexilla regis prodeunt; Drei Stücke aus der Legende der heiligen Elisabeth No. 1 Intro; Impromptu; Epithalam; Resignazione; Recueillement; Sancta Dorothea; In festo transfigurations Domini nostri Jesu Christi; Ave Maria; Trübe Wolken/Nuages gris; Wiegenlied/Chant du berceau; Am Grabe Richard Wagners; En rêve; Trauervorspiel und Trauermarsch *(rec Italian Cultural Institute, Budapest, 1985–86)* Hungaroton 2-▲ HCD 31656-57 [DDD]

Lantos, I. (pno/org)
Liszt, F.:Music of, w. A. Kiss (n), Z. Tóth (va), E. Banda (vc), M. Perényi (vc), H. Lubik (hp), S. Margittay (harm)—Angelus; La lugubre gondola; Epithalam; Am Grabe Richard Wagners; Romance oubliée; Elégies 1 & 2; Offertorium; Benedictus Hungaroton ▲ HCD 11798 [DDD]

Lantz, Ronald (vn)—see ORCHESTRAS & ENSEMBLES Portland String Quartet

Lanzelotte, Rosana (hpd)
Graziani, C.:Sons Vc, Op. 3, w. Antonio Meneses (vc), Gustavo Tavares (vc) Sanctus 2-▲ 002/003 [DDD]

Lanzillo, Daniela (pno)
Clementi, M.:Pno Music (comp), w. Aldo Antognazzi (pno), Christian Badian (pno), Jose Maria Brusco (pno), Federico Wiman (pno), J. Rotter (cnd), Württemberg PO—Con in C for Pno; Sons (6) for Pno, Op. 1, Nos. 1–3; "Son inedita" in A♭ Aura Classics ▲ AU 32070

Lanzini, Giovanni (cl)
Amendola, F.:Ricercari, w. D. Patumi (db), A. Frederico (elecs/pno), A. Flore (voc), L. Ciolfi (vn), C. Cavalieri (vn), C. Sanzo (vc), O. Mangiavacchi (perc), Donizetti Ensemble Bongiovanni ▲ GB 5519 [DDD]

Lanzky-Otto, Ib (hn)
Bentzon, N.V.:Son Hn, w. Wilhelm Lanzky-Otto (pno) *(rec Sweden, 1980 & 1982)* BIS ▲ CD 171 [AAD]
Britten, H.:Now Sleeps the Crimson Petal, w. C. Prégardien, Ib Lanzky-Otto, O. Vänskä, Tapiola Sinfonietta [E] *(rec 10–11/91)* BIS ▲ CD 540 [DDD]
Britten, H.:Serenade, Op. 31, w. C. Prégardien (ten), O. Vänskä (cnd), Tapiola Sinfonietta [E] *(rec 10–11/91)* BIS ▲ CD 540 [DDD]
Frumerie, G. de:Con Hn, w. S. Westerberg (cnd), Stockholm PO Caprice ▲ CAP 21400 [AAD]
Heise, P.:Fant Piece 2, w. Wilhelm Lanzky-Otto (pno) *(rec Sweden, 1980 & 1982)* BIS ▲ CD 171 [AAD]
Larsson, L.-E.:Concertino Hn, w. Stockholm Chamber Ensemble Caprice ▲ CAP 21492

Lanzky-Otto, Wilhelm (pno)
Bentzon, N.V.:Son Hn, w. Ib Lanzky-Otto (hn) *(rec Sweden, 1980 & 1982)* BIS ▲ CD 171 [AAD]
Heise, P.:Fant Piece 2, w. Ib Lanzky-Otto (hn) *(rec Sweden, 1980 & 1982)* BIS ▲ CD 171 [AAD]

▲ = CD ♦ = Enhanced CD Δ = MD ■ = Cassette Tape □ = DCC

Lapinski, Zdzislaw (vc)
- Van De Vate, N.:Concertpiece Vc, w. S. Kawalla (cnd), Polish Radio–TV SO — Vienna Modern Masters ▲ VMM 3008 [ADD]
- Van De Vate, N.:Trio Vn, w. J. Mirynski (vn), M. Mitelski (pno) — Vienna Modern Masters ▲ VMM CD 2001 [ADD]

Laplante, André (pno)
- Brahms, J.:Rhaps Pno, Op. 79 *(rec Campion Center, Boston, MA, Dec 1994)* — Analekta Fleur de Lys ▲ FL 2 3011 [DDD]
- Brahms, J.:Son 3 Pno *(rec Campion Center, Boston, MA, Dec 1994)* — Analekta Fleur de Lys ▲ FL 2 3011 [DDD]
- Françaix, J.:Heure du berger Orch, w. Suzanne Shulman (fl), James Mason (ob), James Campbell (cl), James Sommerville (hn), James McKay (bn) *(rec Glenn Gould Studio, CBC Toronto, Mar. 26–27, 1994)* — CBC ("Musica Viva" series) ▲ MVV 1089 [DDD]
- Liszt, F.:Mephisto Waltz 3 Pno *(rec Dec. 1993)* — Analekta Fleur de Lys ▲ FL 2 3030
- Liszt, F.:Pno Music (misc)—Nuages gris; En rêve; Nocturne *(rec Dec. 1993)* — Analekta Fleur de Lys ▲ FL 2 3030
- Liszt, F.:Pno Music (misc)—Sonetto del Petrarca No. 104; Mephisto Waltz No. 1; Nuages gris; En rêve; Nocturne; Son in b — Analekta ▲ AN 29273
- Liszt, F.:Son Pno *(rec Dec. 1993)* — Analekta Fleur de Lys ▲ FL 2 3030
- Liszt, F.:Sonetti del Petrarca Pno—No. 104 *(rec Dec. 1993)* — Analekta Fleur de Lys ▲ FL 2 3030
- Luedeke, R.:The Transparency of Time, w. B. Tovey (cnd), Winnipeg SO *(rec Winnipeg, Manitoba, Mar. 19–20, 1990)* — CBC ("SM 5000" series) ▲ SMCD 5141 [DDD]
- Martinů, B.:La Revue de Cuisine, w. James Campbell (cl), James McKay (bn), Guy Few (tpt), Moshe Hammer (vn), Tsuyoshi Tsutsumi (vc) *(rec Glenn Gould Studio, CBC Toronto, Mar. 26–27, 1994)* — CBC ("Musica Viva" series) ▲ MVV 1089 [DDD]
- Milhaud, D.:Suite Vn, w. Moshe Hammer (vn), James Campbell (cl) *(rec Glenn Gould Studio, CBC Toronto, Mar. 26–27, 1994)* — CBC ("Musica Viva" series) ▲ MVV 1089 [DDD]
- Ravel, M.:Gaspard de la nuit — Élan ▲ 2232 [DDD]
- Ravel, M.:Pno Music—Prélude; À la manière de Borodine; À la manière de Chabrier; Sérénade grotesque; Menuet sur le nom de Haydn; Pavane pour une infante défunte; Jeux d'eau; Miroirs *(rec Boston, Mar 1994)* — Analekta ▲ AN 29271
- Ravel, M.:Pno Music—Prélude; À la manière de Borodine; À la manière de Chabrier; Sérénade grotesque; Menuet sur le nom de Haydn; Pavane pour une infante défunte; Jeux d'eau; Miroirs, suite pour pno *(rec Campion Center, Boston, MA, Mar 1994)* — Analekta Fleur de Lys ▲ FL 2 3038 [DDD]
- Ravel, M.:Sonatine Pno — Élan ▲ 2232 [DDD]
- Ravel, M.:Valses nobles et sentimentales — Élan ▲ 2232 [DDD]

Lapointe, Bibiane (hpd)—see ORCHESTRAS & ENSEMBLES Les Cyclopes

Lapšansky, Marián (pno)
- Brahms, J.:Intermezzos Pno, Op. 117 — Supraphon ▲ SUP 3174
- Dvořák, A.:Songs, w. P. Schreier (ten)—Liebeslieder, Op. 83/1–8; Biblical Songs, Op. 99/1–10 — Berlin Classics ▲ BER 1080 [DDD]
- Dvořák, A.:Songs, w. P. Schreier (ten)—Zigeunermelodien, Op. 55; Liebeslieder, Op. 83; Biblische Lieder, Op. 99 [G] — Capriccio ▲ 10053 [DDD]
- Dvořák, A.:Suite Pno — Supraphon ▲ SUP 3174
- Dvořák, A.:Zigeunermelodien, Op. 55, w. P. Schreier (ten) — Berlin Classics ▲ BER 1080 [DDD]
- Fibich, Z.:Moods, Impressions & Reminiscences—Impressions, Op. 41 — Supraphon ▲ SUP 0189
- Fibich, Z.:Moods, Impressions & Reminiscences—Moods (44 pieces) — Supraphon ▲ SUP 0188
- Fibich, Z.:Moods, Impressions & Reminiscences—Op. 4, Vol. III (40 pieces) — Supraphon ▲ SUP CD 0190
- Fibich, Z.:Moods, Impressions & Reminiscences—Op. 41, "Reminiscences" — Supraphon ▲ SUP CD 0191
- Fibich, Z.:Scherzos Pno, Op. 4 — Supraphon ▲ SUP 3016
- Foerster, J.B.:Dreaming — Supraphon ▲ SUP 3016
- Grieg, E.:Lyric Pieces — Supraphon ▲ SUP 3174
- Janácek, L.:Intimate Sketches — Supraphon ▲ SUP 3016
- Janácek, L.:Moravian Dances Pno — Supraphon ▲ SUP 3016
- Magdalena Hajóssyova:Soprano, w. Magdalena Hajóssyova (sop) — Multisonic ▲ MUL 310195 [DDD]
- Novák, V.:Songs of a Winter Night — Supraphon ▲ SUP 3016
- Pärt, A.:Fratres I, w. Jiri Barta (vc) [arr vc & pno] — Supraphon ▲ SUP 112156 [DDD]
- Prokofiev, S.:Peter & the Wolf [pno trans Tatiana Nikolayeva] — Supraphon ▲ SUP 3174
- Rachmaninoff, S.:Son Vc, w. Jiri Barta (vc) — Supraphon ▲ SUP 112156 [DDD]
- Saint-Saëns, C.:Carnival of the Animals, w. P. Toperczer (pno), O. Lenárd (cnd), Czech–Slovak RSC Bratislava — Naxos ▲ 8.550499 [DDD]
- Schnittke, A.:Son Vc, w. Jiri Barta (vc) — Supraphon ▲ SUP 112156 [DDD]
- Suk, J.:Songs, Op. 15, w. Daniel Buranovsky (pno), Josef Pancík (cnd), Prague Chamber Choir — Chandos ▲ CHAN 9257 [DDD]
- Tomášek, V.J.K.:Songs, w. Magdaléna Hajossyová (sop)—Dauernder Frühling, Op. 77; Der Nachtigall letzter Gesang, Op. 77; Des Dichters Lied, Op. 77; Heiderösslein, Op. 53/1; Nähe des Geliebten, Op. 53/2; Mailied, Op. 53/3; Mignons Sehnsucht, Op. 54/1; Die Spröde, Op. 54/2; Die Bekehrte, Op. 54/3; Mit einem gemahlten Bande, Op. 55/4; Die Nacht, Op. 55/5; An den Mond, Op. 56/4; Das Veilchen, Op. 57/1, Rastlose Liebe, Op. 58/1; Wanderers Nachtlied, Op. 58/4; Vorschlag zur Güte, Op. 60/2; Die Erwartung; Das Lied; Das Mädchen, Op. 33; Des Pilgers Nachtlied, Op. 33; Der Knabe, Op. 33; In die Ferne, Op. 92; Mein Lieb, Op. 92; Mein Hochland, Op. 92 — Multisonic ▲ MUL 310248 [DDD]

Lara, Adelina de (pno)
- Beethoven, L. van:Vars Pno, WoO 80 [plus I. Eibenschütz playing the 2nd movt. of Sonata No. 30, Op. 109 *(rec 1950/51)* — Pearl 6–▲ PEA 99049 (m) [AAD]

Larde, C. (bn)
- Beethoven, L. van:Trio for 3 Fls, w. J.–P. Rampal (fl), A. Marion (pno) — Vox Box 2–▲ CDX 5000 [ADD]

Lardé, Christian (fl)
- Ravel, M.:Chansons madécasses, w. J. Herbillon (bar), P. Degenne (vc), T. Paraskivesco (pno) [F] — Calliope ▲ CAL 9893 [ADD]
- Stamitz, C.:Con Fl, Op. 29, w. J.–P. Berlingen (cnd), Normandy Orchestral Ensemble *(rec Kusatsu Concert Hall, Nov 2–3, 1991)* — Camerata ▲ 32CM284 [DDD]

Laredo, Jaime (va)
- Beethoven, L. van:Qt Pno, Op. 16, w. E. Ax (pno), I. Stern (vn), Y. Ma (vc) *(rec Mar. 9–12, 1992)* — Sony Classical ▲ SK 53339 [DDD]
- Boccherini, L.:Qnts Strs, w. Issac Stern (vn), Cho–Liang Lin (vn), Yo–Yo Ma (vc), Sharon Robinson (vc)—Qnt in E for Strs, Op. 13/5 — Sony Classical ▲ SK 53983
- Boccherini, L.:Qnt Strs, G.275, w. Cho–Liang Lin (vn), Isaac Stern (vn), Yo–Yo Ma (vc), Sharon Robinson (vc) — Sony Classical ▲ SK 53983
- Brahms, J.:Qts Pno (comp), w. E. Ax (pno), I. Stern (vn), Yo–Yo Ma (vc) — Sony Classical 2–▲ S2K 45846 [DDD] 2–■ S2T 45846 (D)
- Brahms, J.:Qts Pno (comp), w. Emanuel Ax (pno), Isaac Stern (vn), Yo–Yo Ma (vc) — Sony Classical ("Isaac Stern:A Life in Music" series) 3–▲ SM3K 64520
- Brahms, J.:Qt 3 Pno, w. E. Ax (pno), I. Stern (vn), Yo–Yo Ma (vc) — CBS ▲ MK 42387 [DDD]
- Brahms, J.:Sextet Strs, Op. 18, w. I. Stern (vn), C.–L. Lin (vn), M. Tree (va), Yo–Yo Ma (vc), S. Robinson (vc) — Sony Classical 2–▲ S2K 45820
- Brahms, J.:Sextet Strs, Op. 36, w. I. Stern (vn), Cho–Liang Lin (vn), M. Tree (va), Yo–Yo Ma (vc), S. Robinson (vc) — Sony Classical 2–▲ S2K 45820
- Harbison, J.:Con Va, w. H. Wolff (cnd), New Jersey SO *(rec 2/91)* — New World ▲ 80404–2 [DDD]
- Mozart, W.A.:Sinf concertante Vn, K.364, w. Cho–Liang Lin (vn), R. Leppard (cnd), English CO — Sony Classical ▲ SK 47693
- Schubert, Franz:Qnt Strs, D.956, w. Issac Stern (vn), Cho–Liang Lin (vn), Yo–Yo Ma (vc), Sharon Robinson (vc) — Sony Classical ▲ SK 53983
- Schubert, Franz:Qnt Strs, D.956, w. Cho–Liang Lin (vn), Isaac Stern (vn), Yo–Yo Ma (vc), Sharon Robinson (vc) — Sony Classical ▲ SK 53983
- Schumann, R.:Qt Pno, Op. 47, w. E. Ax (pno), I. Stern (vn), Y. Ma (vc) *(rec Mar. 9–12, 1992)* — Sony Classical ▲ SK 53339 [DDD]

Laredo, Jaime (vn)—see also ORCHESTRAS & ENSEMBLES Kalichstein–Laredo–Robinson Trio
- Bach, J.S.:Cons Vn (comp), w. J. Laredo (cnd), Scottish CO — IMP ("Classics" series) ▲ IMP 6700402
- Bach, J.S.:Con for 2 Vns, w. John Tunnell (vn), J. Laredo (cnd), Scottish CO — IMP ("Classics" series) ▲ IMP 6700402
- Bach, J.S.:Sons Vn, w. G. Gould (pno)—BWV 1014–1019 — CBS 2–▲ M2K 42414 [AAD]
- Beethoven, L. van:Con Vn, Op. 61, w. J. Laredo (cnd), Scottish CO — IMP Classics ▲ PCD 977 [DDD]
- Beethoven, L. van:Con Vn, Op. 61, w. J. Laredo (cnd), Scottish CO — IMP ("Classics" series) ▲ IMP 6700242
- Beethoven, L. van:Romances Vn, w. J. Laredo (cnd), Scottish CO — IMP ("Classics" series) ▲ IMP 6700242
- Beethoven, L. van:Romances Vn, w. J. Laredo (cnd), Scottish CO — IMP Classics ▲ PCD 977 [DDD]
- Beethoven, L. van:Romances Vn, w. J. Laredo (cnd), Scottish CO—No. 1 in G — IMP ("Concert Classics" series) ▲ IMP PCD 1099
- Brahms, J.:Sons Vn (comp), w. J. B. Pommier (pno) — Virgin Classics ▲ CDZ 59642
- Brahms, J.:Trios (3) Pno, w. J. Kalichstein (pno), S. Robinson (vc) — Vox Box 3–▲ CD3X 3029 [DDD]
- Bruch, M.:Con 1 Vn, w. J. Laredo (cnd), Scottish CO — IMP ▲ IMP 2005
- Dvořák, A.:Romance Vn, w. J. Laredo (cnd), Scottish CO — IMP ("Classics" series) ▲ IMP 6700292
- Dvořák, A.:Trio 4 Pno, "Dumky", w. S. Robinson (vc), J. Kalichstein (pno) — Vox Box 3–▲ CD3X 3029 [DDD]
- Fauré, G.:Qt 1 Pno, w. E. Ax (pno), I. Stern (vn), Y.–Y. Ma (vc) — Sony Classical ▲ SK 48066 [DDD]
- Fauré, G.:Qt 2 Pno, w. E. Ax (pno), I. Stern (vn), Y.–Y. Ma (vc) — Sony Classical ▲ SK 48066 [DDD]
- The Heart of the Violin Concerto, w. Ernst Kovacic (vn), Anne Akiko Meyers (vn), Elmar Oliveire (vn), Hideko Udagawa (vn) — Pickwick ("The Orchid" series) ▲ PICORCD 11013
- Mendelssohn, F.:Con in e Vn & Orch, Op. 64, w. J. Laredo (cnd), Scottish CO — IMP ▲ IMP 2005
- Mendelssohn, F.:Con in e Vn & Orch, Op. 64, w. J. Laredo (cnd), Scottish CO — IMP ("Concert Classics" series) ▲ IMP PCD 1097
- Mendelssohn, F.:Trio 1 Pno, w. J. Kalichstein (pno), S. Robinson (vc) — Vox Box 3–▲ CD3X 3029 [DDD]
- Mendelssohn, F.:Trio 2 Pno, w. J. Kalichstein (pno), S. Robinson (vc) — Vox Box 3–▲ CD3X 3029 [DDD]
- Mozart, W.A.:Concertone Vns, w. Cho–Liang Lin (vn), R. Leppard (cnd), English CO — Sony Classical ▲ SK 47693
- Mozart, W.A.:Trio Pno, K.502, w. R. Serkin (pno), M. Foley (vc) *(rec 1968)* — Sony Classical ▲ SMK 46255 [ADD]
- Rorem, N.:Day Music, w. R. Laredo (pno) — Phoenix ▲ PHCD 123
- Schubert, Franz:Fant Vn, D.934, w. S. Brown (pno) — Dorian 2–▲ DOR 90137 [DDD]
- Schubert, Franz:Qnt Pno, D.667, w. R. Serkin (pno), P. Naegele (va), L. Parnas (vc), J. Levine (db) *(rec 1967)* — Sony Classical ▲ SMK 46252 [ADD]
- Schubert, Franz:Rondo Vn, D.895, w. S. Brown (pno) — Dorian 2–▲ DOR 90137 [DDD]
- Schubert, Franz:Son Vn, D.574, w. S. Brown (pno) — Dorian 2–▲ DOR 90137 [DDD]
- Schubert, Franz:Sonatinas Vn, w. S. Brown (pno) — Dorian 2–▲ DOR 90137 [DDD]
- Virtuoso!:A Treasury of Favorite Violin Encores, w. Margo Garrett (pno) — Dorian ▲ DOR 90153 [DDD]
- Zwilich, E.T.:Con Vn, w. Sharon Robinson (vc), Louisville Orch — Louisville ▲ LCD 009 [ADD]

Laredo, Ruth (pno)
- Barber, S.:Nocturne, "Homage to John Field" — Elektra/Nonesuch ■ D4–79032 (D)
- Barber, S.:Son Pno — Elektra/Nonesuch ■ D4–79032 (D)
- Barber, S.:Souvenirs [arr. for solo piano] — Elektra/Nonesuch ■ D4–79032 (D)
- Falla, M. de:El amor brujo (sels)—5–movt. piano suite — MCA Classics ▲ MCAD 6265 [DDD] ■ MCAC 6265 (D)
- Falla, M. de:El sombrero de tres picos (dances)—3 dances — MCA Classics ▲ MCAD 6265 [DDD] ■ MCAC 6265 (D)
- French Masterpieces for Flute & Piano, w. Paula Robison (fl) — MusicMasters ▲ 01612–67069–2
- My First Recital — ESS.A.Y ▲ ESS 1006 [DDD]
- My Second Recital *(rec July 1991)* — ESS.A.Y ▲ ESS 1026 [DDD]
- Rachmaninoff, S.:Suite 2 for 2 Pnos, w. James Tocco (pno) *(rec St. Hugo of the Hills Catholic Church, Bloomfield Hills, MI)* — Gasparo ▲ GAS 313
- Rorem, N.:Day Music, w. J. Laredo (vn) — Phoenix ▲ PHCD 123
- Scriabin, A.:Poèmes Pno, Op. 32—No. 1 — Phoenix ▲ PHCD 114 [AAD]
- Scriabin, A.:Preludes Pno, Op. 11 — Phoenix ▲ PHCD 114 [AAD]
- Scriabin, A.:Preludes Pno, Op. 74 — Phoenix ▲ PHCD 114 [AAD]
- Stravinsky, I.:Le Sacre du printemps Pno, w. James Tocco (pno) *(rec St. Hugo of the Hills Catholic Church, Bloomfield Hills, MI)* — Gasparo ▲ GAS 313

Laredo, Teresa (hpd)
- Impressions of the Andes:Classical Music By Bolivian Composers & Alberto Ginastera — Gallo ▲ CD 590 [AAD]

Laredo, Teresa (pno)
- Schumann, C.:Pno Music—Romance [from Con No. 1]; Romance, Op. 5; Soirées Musicales, Op. 6; Valse Capriccio No. 7; Polonaises, Op. 1; Romance, Op. 11; Scherzo, Op. 14 — Gallo ▲ CD 839

Largent, Edward (pno)
- Largent, E.:Shorts, w. J. Turk (tuba) — Dana Recording Project ▲ DRP 4

Larisch, G. (vc)—see ORCHESTRAS & ENSEMBLES Trio Cantabile

Larrea, Ezequiel (va)—see ORCHESTRAS & ENSEMBLES Arriaga String Quartet

Larrieu, Maxence (fl)
- Bach, Joh. Christian:Trio for 2 Fls, Op. 2, w. M. Mercelli (fl), L. Bavaj (hpd)—in G — Bongiovanni ▲ GB 5529 [DDD]
- Bach, J.S.:Partita Fl, BWV 1013 — Philips 2–▲ 438809–2
- Bach, J.S.:Sons Fl, BWV 1030–35, w. Rafael Puyana (hpd), Wieland Kuijken (vl) — Philips 2–▲ 438809–2
- Bach, J.S.:Sons Vn, w. Rafael Puyana (hpd)—BWV 120 [doubtful; arr. flute & continuo] — Philips 2–▲ 438809–2
- Bach, W.F.:Duets Fls, F.54–59, w. M. Larrieu, M. Mercelli—Nos. 3 & 6 — Bongiovanni ▲ GB 5529 [DDD]
- Bach, W.F.:Trios Fls, F.47–49, w. M. Larrieu, M. Mercelli, L. Bavaj (harpsichord)—Nos. 1–3 — Bongiovanni ▲ GB 5529 [DDD]
- Debussy, C.:Chansons de Bilitis (recitation), w. A. Lochner (nar), A. Adorjan (fl), S. Mildonian (hp), Y. Nagae (hp), E. Sun (cel) [F] — Quantum ▲ QM 6912 [DDD]
- Duo Recital, w. Susanna Mildonian (hp) — Denon ▲ CO 7301 [DDD]
- Haydn, J.:Trios Fls & Vc, "London Trios", w. M. Mercelli (fl), C. Casadei (vc) — Bongiovanni ▲ GB 5508 [DDD]
- Rogg, L.:Music of, w. T. Friedli (cl), J.–P. Goy (ob), M. Kameda (pno), J.–J. Balet (pno), L. Rogg (syn), M. Kameda (piano) *(8 Etudes [1990]; Jazzic J.–J. Balet (piano) (Cinq petites pièces lyriques [1952]; Trois pièces [1952]; Valse [1952]; Cinq petites géométries [1958])*, Kameda, Balet *(Face à face for 2 Pianos [1987])*, J.–P. Goy, L. Rogg *(Pièce for Oboe & Synthesizer [1991])*, T. Friedli *(Pièce for solo Clarinet [1986]); M. Larrieu (Suite for solo Flute [1991])* — BIS ▲ CD 546 [DDD]
- Tambourin, w. Ichiro Suzuki (gtr) *(rec Imaichi Public Hall, Nakamichi Research Center, Kodaira city & House St. Gregorius, Higashi–Kurume city)* — Camerata ▲ 32CM 148
- Weber, C.M. von:Trio Fl, w. Michel Renard (vc), Martine Joste (pno) — Accord ▲ ACD 202782 [AAD]

Larrocha, Alicia de (pno)
- Albéniz, I.:Azulejos — EMI Classics ▲ CDM 64523
- Albéniz, I.:Cantos de España — EMI Classics ▲ CDM 64523
- Albéniz, I.:España—Malagueña — EMI Classics ▲ CDM 64523
- Albéniz, I.:Iberia Suite *(rec 1960s)* — EMI Classics 2–▲ ZDMB 64504–2
- Albéniz, I.:Iberia Suite — London 2–▲ 417887–2 [DDD]
- Albéniz, I.:Mallorca — EMI Classics ▲ CDM 64523
- Albéniz, I.:Navarra — London 2–▲ 417887–2 [DDD]
- Albéniz, I.:Pno Music—Cantos de España; Zaragoza; Malagueña; Mallorca; Zambra Granadina; La Vega; Azulejos — EMI Classics ▲ CDM 64523
- Albéniz, I.:Piezas (12) caracteristicas—Zambra — EMI Classics ▲ CDM 64523
- Albéniz, I.:Suite española — London 2–▲ 417887–2 [DDD]
- Albéniz, I.:Suite española (sels)—No. 2:Zaragoza — EMI Classics ▲ CDM 64523

Larrocha, Alicia de (pno) (cont.)
Albéniz, I.:La Vega — EMI Classics ▲ CDM 64523
Chopin, F.:Preludes, Op. 28 — London ("Weekend Classics" series) ▲ 433089-2 [AAD]
Classica de España, w. Madrid Concert Orch, National Orch of Spain, Ernesto Bitetti (gtr) — EMI Classics 2-▲ ZDMB 64241
Falla, M. de:El amor brujo (ritual fire dance) — EMI Classics ▲ CDM 64527
Falla, M. de:Fant bética *(rec Troy Savings Bank Music Hall, Troy, New York, Apr 27-29, 1992)* — RCA Red Seal ▲ 61389-2
Falla, M. de:Fant bética — EMI Classics ▲ CDM 64527
Falla, M. de:La vida breve (sels)—1st Spanish Dance *(rec Troy Savings Bank Music Hall, Troy, New York, Apr 27-29, 1992)* — RCA Red Seal ▲ 61389-2
Falla, M. de:Noches en los jardines de España, w. C. Dutoit (cnd), Montreal PO — London ▲ 430703-2 [DDD]
Falla, M. de:Pièces espagnoles (4) *(rec Troy Savings Bank Music Hall, Troy, New York, Apr 27-29, 1992)* — RCA Red Seal ▲ 61389-2
Falla, M. de:Pièces espagnoles (4) — EMI Classics ▲ CDM 64527
Falla, M. de:El retablo de maese Pedro (sels)—La sinfonía de maese Pedro *(rec Troy Savings Bank Music Hall, Troy, New York, Apr 27-29, 1992)* — RCA Red Seal ▲ 61389-2
Falla, M. de:Serenata andaluza *(rec Troy Savings Bank Music Hall, Troy, New York, Apr 27-29, 1992)* — RCA Red Seal ▲ 61389-2
Falla, M. de:El sombrero de tres picos (sels) — EMI Classics ▲ CDM 64527
Falla, M. de:La vida breve (sels) — EMI Classics ▲ CDM 64527
Granados, E.:Allegro di Concierto *(rec 1960s)* — EMI Classics ▲ CDM 64529
Granados, E.:Allegro di Concierto — RCA Red Seal ▲ 60408-2-RC [DDD] ■ 60408-4-RC (CrO2)
Granados, E.:Danza lenta — RCA Red Seal ▲ 60408-2-RC [DDD] ■ 60408-4-RC (CrO2)
Granados, E.:Danza lenta *(rec 1960s)* — EMI Classics ▲ CDM 64529
Granados, E.:Danzas españolas (10) *(rec American Academy of Arts and Letters, New York, Mar 25-28, 1994)* — RCA Red Seal ▲ 09026-68184-2 [DDD]
Granados, E.:Danzas españolas (10) *(rec 1960s)* — EMI Classics ▲ CDM 64529
Granados, E.:Goyescas *(rec 1960s)* — EMI Classics 2-▲ CDMB 65424
Granados, E.:Goyescas — RCA Red Seal ▲ 60408-2-RC [DDD] ■ 60408-4-RC (CrO2)
Granados, E.:Valses poeticos (7) *(rec American Academy of Arts and Letters, New York, Mar 25-28, 1994)* — RCA Red Seal ▲ 09026-68184-2 [DDD]
Largo I, w. Vladimir Ashkenazy (pno), Alfred Brendel (pno), Julius Katchen (pno), András Schiff (pno), Iliana Vered (pno), et al. — Celestial Harmonies ▲ 35509-2 2-■ 35509-4
Largo II, w. Vladimir Ashkenazy (pno), Alfred Brendel (pno), Julius Katchen (pno), András Schiff (pno), Iliana Vered (pno), et al. — Celestial Harmonies ▲ 19504-2 ■ 19504-4
Mendelssohn, F.:Rondo capriccioso — London ("Weekend Classics" series) ▲ 433089-2 [AAD]
Mompou, F.:Cançons i dansas—Nos. 1-12 & 14 — RCA Red Seal ▲ 09026-62554-2
Mompou, F.:Preludes (10) Pno—Nos. 5-7 — RCA Red Seal ▲ 09026-62554-2
Mompou, F.:Prelude 11 Pno — RCA Red Seal ▲ 09026-62554-2
Montsalvatge, X.:Pno Music—Divagación; Tres Divertimentos; Si, à Mompou; Berceuse a la memoria de Oscar Esplá; Sonatine pour Yvette *(rec Troy Savings Bank Music Hall, Troy, New York, Apr 27-29, 1992)* — RCA Red Seal ▲ 61389-2
Mozart, W.A.:Allegro & Andante *(rec BMG Studio A, New York, Nov 8-9, 1990)* — RCA Red Seal ▲ 09026-60867-2 [DDD]
Mozart, W.A.:Con 9 Pno, w. C. Davis (cnd), English CO — RCA Red Seal ▲ 60825-2 [DDD] ■ 60825-4 (CrO2) □ 60825-5
Mozart, W.A.:Con 10 Pnos, w. A. Previn (pno), A. Previn (cnd), Orch of St. Luke's *(rec Manhattan Center Studios, New York City, July 26-27, 1993)* — RCA Red Seal ▲ 68044-2
Mozart, W.A.:Con 20 Pno, w. C. Davis (cnd), English CO *(rec Abbey Road Studio No. 1, London, Oct 3, 7 & 8, 1993)* — RCA Red Seal ▲ 09026-68399-2 [DDD]
Mozart, W.A.:Con 21 Pno, w. C. Davis (cnd), English CO — RCA Red Seal ▲ 60825-2 [DDD] ■ 60825-4 (CrO2) □ 60825-5
Mozart, W.A.:Con 22 Pno, w. C. Davis (cnd), English CO — RCA Red Seal ▲ 09026-61698-2
Mozart, W.A.:Con 23 Pno, w. C. Davis (cnd), English CO — RCA Red Seal ▲ 09026-60989-2 [DDD] ■ 09026-60989-4 (D)
Mozart, W.A.:Con 24 Pno, w. C. Davis (cnd), English CO — RCA Red Seal ▲ 09026-60989-2 [DDD] ■ 09026-60989-4 (D)
Mozart, W.A.:Con 25 Pno, w. C. Davis (cnd), English CO *(rec Abbey Road Studio No. 1, London, Oct 3, 7 & 8, 1993)* — RCA Red Seal ▲ 09026-68399-2 [DDD]
Mozart, W.A.:Con 26 Pno, w. C. Davis (cnd), English CO — RCA Red Seal ▲ 09026-61698-2
Mozart, W.A.:Fant Pno, K.397 — RCA Red Seal ▲ 09026-60453-2 ■ 09026-60453-4
Mozart, W.A.:Fant Pno, K.475 — RCA Red Seal ▲ 09026-60453-2 ■ 09026-60453-4
Mozart, W.A.:Rondo Pno, K.485 — RCA Red Seal ▲ 09026-60453-2 ■ 09026-60453-4
Mozart, W.A.:Rondo Pno, K.511 *(rec BMG Studio A, New York, Mar 6-7, 1991)* — RCA Red Seal ▲ 09026-60867-2 [DDD]
Mozart, W.A.:Sons Pno—Nos. 7-10, K.309-311 & K.330 — RCA Red Seal ▲ 09026-60454-2 [DDD] ■ 09026-60454-4 (CrO2)
Mozart, W.A.:Sons Pno—Nos. 1, 2 & 14:K.279, 280, 457 — RCA Red Seal ▲ 09026-60453-2 ■ 09026-60453-4
Mozart, W.A.:Sons Pno—No. 5 in G, K.183; Nos. 11-13, K.331-333 — RCA Red Seal ▲ 60407-2 [DDD] ■ 60407-4 (CrO2)
Mozart, W.A.:Sons Pno—No. 3 in B♭, K.281; No. 4 in E♭, K.282; No. 6 in D, K.284; No. 15 in C, K.545 — RCA Red Seal ▲ 60709-2 [DDD] ■ 60709-4 (CrO2)
Mozart, W.A.:Son 4 Pno — London ▲ 417817-2 [ADD]
Mozart, W.A.:Son 10 Pno — London ▲ 417817-2 [ADD]
Mozart, W.A.:Son 11 Pno — RCA Gold Seal ▲ 09026-68113-2 [ADD]
Mozart, W.A.:Son 11 Pno — London ▲ 417817-2 [ADD]
Mozart, W.A.:Son 12 Pno — London ▲ 417817-2 [ADD]
Mozart, W.A.:Son 16 Pno *(rec BMG Studio A, New York, Nov 8-9, 1990)* — RCA Red Seal ▲ 09026-60867-2 [DDD]
Mozart, W.A.:Son 17 Pno *(rec BMG Studio A, New York, Mar 6-7, 1991)* — RCA Red Seal ▲ 09026-60867-2 [DDD]
Mozart, W.A.:Son 2 Pnos, w. A. Previn (pno) *(rec Manhattan Center Studios, New York City, July 12-13, 1993)* — RCA Red Seal ▲ 68044-2
Ravel, M.:Con Pno (left hand), w. L. Slatkin (cnd), St. Louis SO — RCA Red Seal ▲ 09026-60985-2
Ravel, M.:Con in G Pno, w. L. Slatkin (cnd), St. Louis SO — RCA Red Seal ▲ 09026-60985-2
Ravel, M.:Sonatine Pno, w. L. Slatkin (cnd), St. Louis SO — RCA Red Seal ▲ 09026-60985-2
Ravel, M.:Valses nobles et sentimentales, w. L. Slatkin (cnd), St. Louis SO — RCA Red Seal ▲ 09026-60985-2
Schumann, R.:Allegro Pno — London ▲ 421525-2 [DDD]
Schumann, R.:Carnaval Pno — London ▲ 421525-2 [DDD]
Schumann, R.:Con Pno, w. C. Davis (cnd), London SO — RCA Red Seal ▲ 09026-61279-2
Schumann, R.:Faschingsschwank aus Wien — London ▲ 421525-2 [DDD]
Schumann, R.:Qnt Pno, w. Tokyo String Quartet — RCA Red Seal ▲ 09026-61279-2
Spanish Encores — London ▲ 417639-2 LH [DDD/ADD]
Spanish Fireworks — London ▲ 417795-2 LM [ADD]
Turina, J.:Pno Music—Danzas fantásticas; Sacromonte; Sanlúcar de Barrameda; Zapateado *(rec 1965)* — EMI Classics ▲ CDM 64528-2 [ADD]

Larsen, Bent (fl)—see also ORCHESTRAS & ENSEMBLES Duo Musica, Molino Trio
Aventure:Original Compositions for Flute & Organ, w. Peter Langsberg (org) — Classico ▲ CLASSCD 111
Bach, Joh. Christian:Qts (4) for 2 Fls, w. B. Pedersen (fl), P. Elbaek (vn), H. Olsen (va), B. Holst Christensen (vc) — Kontrapunkt ▲ 32048 [DDD]
Bach, Joh. Christian:Trios for 2 Fls & Strs, w. B. Pedersen (fl), P. Elbaek (vn), H. Olsen (va), B. Holst Christensen (vc) — Kontrapunkt ▲ 32048 [DDD]
Hoffmeister, F.A.:Trios for 2 Fls & Vc, w. Henrik Svitzer (fl), Niels Ullner (vc) — Classico ▲ CLASSCD 119
Molino, F.:Trio Duos, Op. 16, w. J. Sommer (gtr) *(rec Feb. 22-23, 1993)* — Classico ▲ CLASSCD 106
Molino, F.:Trio Duos, Op. 61, w. J. Sommer (gtr) *(rec Feb. 22-23, 1993)* — Classico ▲ CLASSCD 106

Larsen, Bent (fl) (cont.)
Molino, F.:Trio Fl, Op. 4/1, w. L. Grunth (va), J. Sommer (gtr) *(rec Feb. 22-23, 1993)* — Classico ▲ CLASSCD 106
Molino, F.:Trio Fl, Op. 45, w. L. Grunth (va), J. Sommer (gtr) *(rec Feb. 22-23, 1993)* — Classico ▲ CLASSCD 106
Piazzolla, A.:Histoire du tango, w. J. Sommer (gtr) — Classico ▲ CLASSCD 101
Vesth, T.:Music of, w. Jan Sommer (gtr), Nils Sylvest Jeppesen (vc), Per Friman (vn), Gert-Inge Andersson (va), Berit Spaelling (hp), Bjorn Nielsen (ob), Svend Rasmussen (cl), Henrik Simonsen (db)—Cuddling Rain; Waltz the Blue Sea; Kaspers Lullaby; Autumn Sunshine; Red Fox Hunting Tea Party; Off White Eternity; Tartan Fl — Danica ▲ DCD 8142

Larsen, Christian (org)
Bach, J.S.:Preludes & Fugues, BWV 531-552 [the organ at Grundtvig Church]—BWV 548 in e — Point ▲ PCD 5092 [DAD]
Dupré, M.:Préludes & Fugues, Op. 7 [Haderslev Cathedral Org] — Point ▲ PCD 5096 [ADD]
Dupré, M.:Sym-Passion, "The World Awaiting the Saviour" [Haderslev Cathedral Org] — Point ▲ PCD 5096 [ADD]
Dupré, M.:Vars sur un vieux Noël — Point ▲ PCD 5096 [ADD]
Liszt, F.:Fant & Fugue on "Ad nos, ad salutarem undam" Org [organ at Grundtvig Church] — Point ▲ PCD 5092 [DAD]
Olsson, O.:Prelude & Fugue, Op. 56 [organ at Grundtvig Church] — Point ▲ PCD 5092 [DAD]

Larsen, Eric (pno)
Foote, A.:Ballad, w. Kevin Lawrence (vn) *(rec Crawford Hall, North Carolina School of the Arts, Sept. 6-8, 1994)* — New World ▲ 80464-2
Foote, A.:Legend, w. Kevin Lawrence (vn) *(rec Crawford Hall, North Carolina School of the Arts, Sept. 6-8, 1994)* — New World ▲ 80464-2
Foote, A.:Melody, w. Kevin Lawrence (vn) *(rec Crawford Hall, North Carolina School of the Arts, Sept. 6-8, 1994)* — New World ▲ 80464-2
Foote, A.:Pieces Vn & Pno, Op. 9, w. Kevin Lawrence (vn) *(rec Crawford Hall, North Carolina School of the Arts, Sept. 6-8, 1994)* — New World ▲ 80464-2
Foote, A.:Pieces Vn & Pno, Op. 74, w. Kevin Lawrence (vn) *(rec Crawford Hall, North Carolina School of the Arts, Sept. 6-8, 1994)* — New World ▲ 80464-2
Foote, A.:Son Vn, w. Kevin Lawrence (vn) *(rec Crawford Hall, North Carolina School of the Arts, Sept. 6-8, 1994)* — New World ▲ 80464-2

Larsen, Erik (ob)
Luening, O.:Legend, w. J. Serebrier (cnd), Oslo PO — Phoenix ▲ PHCD 101 [AAD]

Larsen, Jørgen (vn)
Olsen, P.R.:Qt 2 Strs, w. Peder Elbaek (vn), Verner Skovlund (va), Svend Winsløv (vc) *(rec PAULA's Recording Hall, 1984)* — Paula ▲ PACD 36 [AAD]

Larsen, Kenneth (b cl)
Koppel, H.D.:Variazioni Libère, w. John Kruse (cl), Rene Højlund (cl), Søren Monrad (perc) *(rec Det Fynske Musikkonservatorium, 1993)* — Paula ▲ PACD 78 [DAD]

Larsen, Lavard Skou (va)
Mozart, W.A.:Sinf concertante Vn, K.364, w. Boris Belkin (vn), Salzburg Chamber Soloists *(rec Mozarteum Grosse Saal, Salzburg, Feb. 21-23, 1994)* — Denon ▲ CO 78918 [DDD]

Larsen, Lavard Skou (vn)
Besozzi, A.:Trio Sons (6), w. Claudio Ferrarini (fl), Detlef Mielke (vc) — Stradivarius ▲ STV 33317 [ADD]

Larsen, Lyn (org)
A Bride's Book, w. M. Azzolina (cnd), Florida Symphonic Pops Orch — Pro Arte ▲ CDS 564 [DDD]
Up & away:The Paramount Theater Organ — Pro Arte ▲ CDP 4281 [DDD]
Wedding Day, w. M. Azzolina (cnd), Florida Symphonic Pops Orch, St. Louis Brass — Pro Arte ▲ CDD 569 [DDD]

Larsens, Gunars (vn)
Mieg, P.:Triple Con, w. Wilhelm Gerlach (va), Curdin Coray (vc), M. Venzago (cnd), Lucerne Festival Strings *(rec 1979)* — Jecklin ▲ JS 314-2 [DDD]
Wehrli, W.:Trio 3 Vn, w. Jakob Hefti (hn), Anne de Dadelsen (pno) *(rec 1989)* — Jecklin ▲ JS 301-2 [ADD]

Larson, JanÅke (org)
Tubin, E.:Ave Maria, w. N. Järvi (cnd), Lund's Student Choral Society — BIS ▲ CD 269 [DDD]

Larson, JanÅke (pno)
Tubin, E.:The Retreating Soldier's Song, w. Roland Rydell (bar), N. Järvi (cnd), Lund's Student Choral Society — BIS ▲ CD 269 [DDD]

Larsson, Chrichan (vc)
Carissimi, G.:Ferma lascia ch'io parli, w. Lena Nordin (sop), Maria Wieslander (org), Sven Åberg (chit), Nanette Nowels-Stenholm (pno), M. Guidarini (cnd), *(orch unknown)* — Swedish Society ▲ SCD 1076
Donizetti, G.:Maria Stuarda (sels), w. Lena Nordin (sop), Carina Morling (mez), Ingus Petterssons (ten), Anders Bergström (bar), Tord Wallström (bar), Maria Wieslander (org), Sven Åberg (chit), Nanette Nowels-Stenholm (pno), M. Guidarini (cnd), *(orch unknown)* — Swedish Society ▲ SCD 1076

Larsson, Knud (bn)
Nielsen, C.:Qnt Ww, w. H.G. Jespersen (fl), S.C. Felumb (ob), A. Oxenvad (cl), H. Sorensen (hn) *(rec Jan. 24 & 25, 1936)* — Clarinet Classics ▲ CC 0002
Nielsen, C.:Serenata in vano, w. A. Oxenvad (cl), H. Sorensen (hn), L. Jensen (vc), L. Hegner (db) *(rec Feb. 2, 1937)* — Clarinet Classics ▲ CC 0002

Larsson, Mårtin (ob)
Koch, E. von:Con Ob, Camerata Romana — Intim Musik ▲ INT 33
Larsson, L.-E.:Concertinos, Camerata Romana— for oboe [No. 2] — Intim Musik ▲ INT 33
Linde, B.:Miniature Suite, Camerata Romana — Intim Musik ▲ INT 33
Roman, J.H.:Con Ob, w. T. Svedlund (cnd), Camerata Romana — Intim Musik ▲ INT 32
Roman, J.H.:Con Ob d'Amore, Camerata Romana — Intim Musik ▲ INT 33
Söderlundh, L.B.:Concertino Ob, w. T. Svedlund (cnd), Örebro CO — Intim Musik ▲ INT 36

Larsson, Olof (vc)
Roman, J.H.:Sons Fl, w. P. Evison (fl), C. Huntgeburth (fl), K. Ottesen (vc), E. Nordenfeldt (hpd)—Nos. 1, 2, 5, 6, 7 & 9 — Proprius ▲ PRCD 9020
Roman, J.H.:Sons Fl, w. P. Evison (fl), E. Nordenfeldt (hpd)—Nos. 3, 4, 8, 10, 11 & 12 — Proprius ▲ PRCD 9019
Telemann, G.P.:Con in a for Rcr, Vl, w. C. Pehrsson (rcr), Drottningholm Baroque Ensemble *(rec Apr. 13, 1993)* — BIS ▲ CD 617 [DDD]

Larsson, Per-Ove (org)
Horn & Organ Recital, w. Sören Hermansson (hn) *(rec Adolf Fredrik Church, Stockholm, Feb 1995)* — Opus 3 ▲ OP 19501 [AAD]

Lascell, Ernest (cl)
Morrill, D.:Roxbury Preludes, w. Glenda Dove-Pellito (fl), Tremont String Quartet *(rec June 1991 & June 1992)* — Centaur ▲ CRC 2143 [DDD]

Lash, Warren (vc)
Diamond, D.:Qnt Cl, w. D. Schifrin (cl), P. Neubauer (va), W. Trampler (va), H. Cheifetz (vc) *(rec 6 & 7/90)* — Delos ▲ 3088 [DDD]
Herrmann, B.:Souvenirs de Voyage, w. D. Schifrin (cl), P. Frank (vn), T. Arm (vn), W. Trampler (va) *(rec 6 & 7/90)* — Delos ▲ 3088 [DDD]
Messiaen, O.:Quatuor pour la fin du temps, w. D. Shifrin (cl), Ik-Hwan Bae (vn), W. Doppmann (pno) — Delos ▲ CD 3043 [DDD]
Porter, Q.:Qnt Cl, w. D. Schifrin (cl), T. Arm (vn), E. Sato (vn), P. Neubauer (va) *(rec 6 & 7/90)* — Delos ▲ 3088 [DDD]

Laskine, Lily (hp)
Bochsa, N.C.:Andante sostenuto, w. Georges Barboteu (hn) — Erato ▲ 94801-2
Dauprat, L.-F.:Son Hn & Hp, w. Pierre del Vescovo (hn)—Andante — Erato ▲ 94801-2
Debussy, C.:Danses sacrée et profane, w. P. Coppola (cnd), *(orch unknown)* — Pearl ▲ PEA 9348 (m) [AAD]
Debussy, C.:Son Fl, w. M. Moyse (fl), E. Ginot (va) *(rec ca. 1927)* — Pearl ▲ PEA 9348 (m) [AAD]
Duets for Harp, w. Marielle Nordmann (hp) — Erato ▲ 92862-2
Flute & Harp, w. Jean-Pierre Rampal (fl) *(rec 1968)* — Erato ▲ 45837-2 [ADD] ■ 45837-4

684

▲ = CD ♦ = Enhanced CD Δ = MD ■ = Cassette Tape □ = DCC

Laskine, Lily (hp) (cont.)
Handel, G.F.:Con Hp, w. L. Auriacombe (cnd), Toulouse CO *(rec Chapelle des Italiens, Toulouse, July 1963)* EMI Classics ▲ CDK 65335 [ADD]
Japanese Melodies, w. J.-F. Paillard (cnd), Jean-François Paillard CO, Jacques Chambon (ob) Denon ("Repertoire" series) ▲ CO 8116 [DDD]
Japanese Melodies for Flute & Harp, w. Jean-Pierre Rampal (fl) Denon ("Repertoire" series) ▲ CO 8115 [DDD]
Jolivet, A.:Con Hp, w. A. Jolivet (cnd), Paris Opera Orch Adès ▲ ADE 203492 [ADD]
Jolivet, A.:Pastorale de Noël, w. Jacques Castagner (fl), Gerard Faisandier (bn) Adès ▲ ADE 203492 [ADD]
Mozart, W.A.:Con Fl Hp, w. R. Le Roy (fl), T. Beecham (cnd), Royal PO *(rec 1947)* EMI Classics ("Great Recordings of the Century" series) ▲ CDH 63820
Mozart, W.A.:Con Fl Hp, w. M. Moyse (fl), E. Bigot (cnd), *(orch unknown) (rec 1930–36)* Pearl ▲ PEA 9118 [ADD]
Mozart, W.A.:Con Fl Hp, w. J.-P. Rampal (fl), J.-F. Paillard (cnd), Jean-François Paillard CO *(rec 1964)* Erato ▲ 45832-2 [ADD] ■ 45832-4
Mozart, W.A.:Con Fl Hp, w. J.-P. Rampal (fl), J.-F. Paillard (cnd), Jean-François Paillard CO Erato ▲ 45978-2 ■ 45978-4
Music for Flute & Harp, w. Jean-Pierre Rampal (fl) Odyssey ■ YT 33520
Sakura:Japanese Melodies for Flute & Harp, w. Jean-Pierre Rampal (fl) CBS ▲ MK 34568 ■ MT 34568

Lasla, Anne-Marie (b vl)
Campra, A.:Motets, w. J. Nicolas (sop), W. Christie (org)—O Dulcis amor; Salve Regina; Quemadmodum desiderat cervus; Ubi es, deus meus; O Sacrum convivium; Jubilate deo Pierre Verany ▲ PV.784093 [DDD]
Sainte-Colombe, M. de:Concerts for 2 B Vls, w. Sylvie Moquet (b vl) *(rec Jan. 1993)* Alphée ▲ 9308002 [DDD]

Lasla, Anne-Marie (bass vl)—see ORCHESTRAS & ENSEMBLES Orlando Gibbons Viol Ensemble
Lasocki, Roman (vn)
Bacewicz, G.:Con 7 Vn, w. K. Stryja (cnd), Polish National RSO Katowice Olympia ▲ OCD 323 [AAD]
Meyer, K.:Con Vn, w. K. Stryja (cnd), Polish National RSO Katowice Olympia ▲ OCD 323 [AAD]
The Polish Violin, w. Polish National Radio Orch [cnd:Karol Stryja], Urszula Bozek-Musialska (pno) *(rec 1986 & 1988)* Olympia ▲ OCD 323 [AAD]
Szymanowski, K.:Con 2 Vn, w. K. Stryja (cnd), Polish State PO Marco Polo ▲ 8.223291 [DDD]
Twardowski, R.:Spanish Fant, w. U. Bozek-Musialska (pno) Olympia ▲ OCD 323 [AAD]
Lasry, Stany David (pno)
Debussy, C.:Children's Corner Arcana ▲ ACA 62
Debussy, C.:Estampes Arcana ▲ ACA 62
Debussy, C.:Images (3) Pno Arcana ▲ ACA 62
Debussy, C.:L'Isle joyeuse Arcana ▲ ACA 62
Debussy, C.:Pour le piano Arcana ▲ ACA 62
Debussy, C.:Songs, w. Thierry Félix (bar) Arcana ▲ ACA 44
Lassen, Karen (bn)—see ORCHESTRAS & ENSEMBLES Copenhagen Wind Quintet
Lastraioli, Gian Luca (lt/thb/gtr)—see ORCHESTRAS & ENSEMBLES L'Homme Armé
Lastraioli, Gian Luca (thb)—see ORCHESTRAS & ENSEMBLES Modo Antiquo
Lastrapes, Jeffrey (vc)
Rorem, N.:Studies for 11, w. E. Ostling (fl), K. Lord (ob), G. Raden (cl), J. Sutte (tpt), S. Copes (vn), C.-J. Chang (va), K. Englichova (hp), R. Uchida (pno), A. LaFargue (perc), R. Laveille (perc), R. Milanov (cnd) New World ▲ 80445-2

Latarche, Vanessa (pno)
Brahms, J.:Sons Cl (comp), w. N. Cox (cl) *(rec All Saints, Petersham, UK, Oct 12–14, 1993)* United ▲ UNI 88012 [DDD]
Reger, M.:Son Cl, Op. 107, w. N. Cox (cl) *(rec All Saints, Petersham, UK, Oct 12–14, 1993)* United ▲ UNI 88012 [DDD]
Latchem, Malcolm (vn)—see ORCHESTRAS & ENSEMBLES Academy of St. Martin in the Fields Chamber Ensemble
Lateiner, Jacob (pno)
Brahms, J.:Qt 3 Pno, w. J. Heifetz (vn), S. Schonbach (va), G. Piatigorsky (vc) RCA Gold Seal ▲ 7873-2-RG [ADD] ■ 7873-4-RG
Dvořák, A.:Qnt Pno, Op. 81, w. M. Baker (va), J. Heifetz (vn), J. de Pasquale (va), G. Piatigorsky (vc) RCA Gold Seal ▲ 7965-2-RG [ADD]
Schubert, Franz:Fant Vn, D.934, w. J. Heifetz (vn) RCA Gold Seal ▲ 7873-2-RG [ADD] ■ 7873-4-RG
Latham, Catherine (ob)
Vivaldi, A.:Cons for 2 Obs, w. A. Robson (ob), S. Standage (cnd), Collegium Musicum 90—RV.535 in d Chandos ("Chaconne" series) ▲ CHAN 0528 [DDD]

Latzko, Reinhard (vc)
Krommer, F.:Qt Bn, Op. 46/1, w. Eckart Hbner (bn), Johannes Lüthy (va), Steuart Eaton (va) *(rec Hans-Rosbaud Studio, Oct 10–11, 1994)* CPO ▲ CPO 999297-2 [DDD]
Krommer, F.:Qt Bn, Op. 46/2, w. Eckart Hbner (bn), Johannes Lüthy (va), Steuart Eaton (va) *(rec Hans Rosbaud Studio, Oct 10–11, 1994)* CPO ▲ CPO 999297-2 [DDD]
Mozart, W.A.:Son Bn, w. Eckart Hbnor (bn) *(roc Hans-Rosbaud Studio, Oct 10–11, 1994)* CPO ▲ CPO 999297-2 [DDD]

Laubach, Mark (org)
Liszt, F.:Fant & Fugue on "Ad nos, ad salutarem undam" Org [at the Reuter Organ of St. John's Evangelical Lutheran Church, Allentown, PA] *(rec St. John's Evangelical Lutheran Church, Allentown, PA, Oct. 26 & 27, 1994)* Pro Organo ▲ POCD 7045 [DDD]
Reubke, J.:Son Org [at the Reuter Organ of St. John's Evangelical Lutheran Church, Allentown, PA] *(rec St. John's Evangelical Lutheran Church, Allentown, PA, Oct. 26 & 27, 1994)* Pro Organo ▲ POCD 7045 [DDD]
Wagner, R.:Die Meistersinger von Nürnberg (prelude/act 1) [at the Reuter Organ of St. John's Evangelical Lutheran Church, Allentown, PA] [trans. E.H. Lemare] *(rec St. John's Evangelical Lutheran Church, Allentown, PA, Oct. 26 & 27, 1994)* Pro Organo ▲ POCD 7045 [DDD]
Läubin, Bernhard (tpt)
Trumpet Concertos, w. Hannes Läubin (tpt), Wolfgang Läubin (tpt), English CO [cnd:Simon Preston] Deutsche Grammophon ▲ 431817-2 GH [DDD]
Läubin, Hannes (tpt)
Trumpet Concertos, w. Wolfgang Läubin (tpt), Bernhard Läubin (tpt), English CO [cnd:Simon Preston] Deutsche Grammophon ▲ 431817-2 GH [DDD]
Läubin, Wolfgang (tpt)
Trumpet Concertos, w. Hannes Läubin (tpt), Bernhard Läubin (tpt), English CO [cnd:Simon Preston] Deutsche Grammophon ▲ 431817-2 GH [DDD]
Laubschet, Philippe (org)
Mozart, W.A.:Missa Solemnis, w. Christa Goetze (sop), Anna Schaffner (alt), Barnhard Gärtner (ten), Rudolf Rosen (bass), F. Pantillon (cnd), Bieler SO, Pro Arte Chorale, Bern Vocal Ensemble Gallo ▲ CD 893 [DDD]
Pantillon, F.:Bethlehem, w. Christa Goetze (sop), Rudolf Rosen (nar), F. Pantillon (cnd), Bieler SO, Pro Arte Chorale, Bern Vocal Ensemble Gallo ▲ CD 893 [DDD]
Pantillon, F.:Missa brevis di San Pedro, w. François Pantillon (cnd), Bern Vocal Ensemble *(rec La Salle Musica de La Chaux-de-Fonds)* Gallo ▲ CD 884 [DDD]
Pantillon, F.:Le Noël des Bergers, w. Christa Gaetze (sop), François Pantillon (cnd), Bern Vocal Ensemble *(rec La Salle Musica de La Chaux-de-Fonds)* Gallo ▲ CD 884 [DDD]
Pantillon, F.:Poème Org *(rec l'Eglise française de Berne)* Gallo ▲ CD 884 [DDD]
Suter, H.:Le Laudi di San Francesco d'Assisi, w. A. Michael (sop), J. Winklet (alt), A. Baldin (ten), J. Will (bass), Bern SO, T. Loosli (cnd), Bern Bach Choir, Sekundar School Children's Choir Ars Musici ▲ AM 1015-2 [DDD]
Lauenstein, Eva (ob)—see ORCHESTRAS & ENSEMBLES Sundsvall Wind Quartet
Lauer, Eberhard (org)
Die heitere Orgel, w. Lauer, Eberhard (org) Ambitus ▲ AMB 97864 [DDD]
Ives, C.:Vars on *America* Ambitus ▲ 97864 [DDD]

Lauer, Elizabeth (pno)
Lauer, E.:Songs on Poems of James Joyce, w. Alice Marie Nelson (mez) Capstone ▲ CPS 8632
Laufer, Daniel (vc)
Ott, David:Con for 2 Vcs, w. Wolfgang Laufer (vc), Z. Macal (cnd), Milwaukee SO *(rec Uihlein Hall, Milwaukee, Oct 4, 1992)* Koss Classics ▲ KC 1023 [DDD]
Laufer, Wolfgang (vc)—see also ORCHESTRAS & ENSEMBLES Fine Arts String Quartet
Ott, David:Con for 2 Vcs, w. Daniel Laufer (vc), Z. Macal (cnd), Milwaukee SO *(rec Uihlein Hall, Milwaukee, Oct 4, 1992)* Koss Classics ▲ KC 1023 [DDD]
Laughton, Stuart (tpt)
Franceschini, P.:Son à 7, w. William O'Meara (org), David Campion (timp/perc) Doremi ▲ DHR 9303 [DDD]
Handel, G.F.:Suite Tpt & Org, w. William O'Meara (org) Doremi ▲ DHR 9303 [DDD]
Opening Day, w. Wendy Humphreys (sop), Wendy Humphreys (Celtic hp), Peter Tiefenbach (org/pno), William O'Meara (org) Doremi ▲ 9301 [DDD]
Susato, T.:Music of, w. William O'Meara (org), David Campion (timp/perc)—Renaissance Dance Suite Doremi ▲ DHR 9303 [DDD]
Telemann, G.P.:Musique héroïque, w. William O'Meara (org), David Campion (timp/perc) Doremi ▲ DHR 9303 [DDD]

Laughton, Stuart (tpt/nat tpt/cnt)
Bach, J.S.:Music of, w. Wendy Humphreys (sop), Daniel Lichti (b-bar), William O'Meara (org), David Campion (timp/perc)—Prelude & Fugue in G; Grosser Herr [from Christmas Oratorio]; Mein gläubiges Herz [from Cant 68]; 3 Chorale Preludes; Prelude & Fugue in A Doremi ▲ DHR 9303 [DDD]
Baroque Banquet, w. Humphreys, Wendy (sop), Daniel Lichti (b-bar), William O'Meara (org), David Campion (timp/perc) Doremi ▲ 9303
Handel, G.F.:Samson (sels), w. Wendy Humphreys (sop), Daniel Lichti (b-bar), William O'Meara (org), David Campion (timp/perc)—Let the Bright Seraphim Doremi ▲ DHR 9303 [DDD]
Scarlatti, A.:Endimione e Cintia, w. Wendy Humphreys (sop), Daniel Lichti (b-bar), William O'Meara (org), David Campion (timp/perc)—Vaga Cintia Doremi ▲ DHR 9303 [DDD]
Laura, Massimo (gtr)
Neumann, H.:Schweizer Serenade, w. Luigi Magistrelli (cl) Bayer ▲ 100280 [DDD]
Neumann, H.:Serenade Bas Hn, w. Luigi Magistrelli (bas hn) Bayer ▲ 100280 [DDD]
Neumann, H.:Serenade Bas Hn, w. Luigi Magistrelli (bas hn), Rossella Perrone (gtr) Bayer ▲ 100280 [DDD]
Neumann, H.:Serenade Cl, w. Luigi Magistrelli (cl) Bayer ▲ 100280 [DDD]
Neumann, H.:Theme & Vars Paisiello, w. Luigi Magistrelli (cl) Bayer ▲ 100280 [DDD]
Neumann, H.:Theme & Vars Schubert, w. Luigi Magistrelli (cl) Bayer ▲ 100280 [DDD]
Laurence, Chris (db)
Yoshioka, T.:Rhap Mar, w. Evelyn Glennie (mar), Edward Beckett (fl), Roy Howitt (cl), Ralph Salmins (dr) *(rec Whitfield Street Studios, London, Sept. 22–29, 1994)* Catalyst ▲ 09026-68193-2 [DDD]
Lauri, David (vc)—see ORCHESTRAS & ENSEMBLES Euler String Quartet
Lauriala, Risto (pno)
Sibelius, J.:Finlandia [arr Sibelius for pno] *(rec Järvenpää Hall, Järvenpää, Finland, Oct 9–11, 1995)* Naxos ▲ 8.553661 [DDD]
Sibelius, J.:Impromptu Pno *(rec Järvenpää Hall, Järvenpää, Finland, Oct 9–11, 1995)* Naxos ▲ 8.553661 [DDD]
Sibelius, J.:Kyllikki *(rec Järvenpää Hall, Järvenpää, Finland, Oct 9–11, 1995)* Naxos ▲ 8.553661 [DDD]
Sibelius, J.:Pieces Pno, Op. 75 *(rec Järvenpää Hall, Järvenpää, Finland, Oct 9–11, 1995)* Naxos ▲ 8.553661 [DDD]
Sibelius, J.:Pieces Pno, Op. 85 *(rec Järvenpää Hall, Järvenpää, Finland, Oct 9–11, 1995)* Naxos ▲ 8.553661 [DDD]
Sibelius, J.:Pieces Pno, Op. 103 *(rec Järvenpää Hall, Järvenpää, Finland, Oct 9–11, 1995)* Naxos ▲ 8.553661 [DDD]

Lauridsen, Beverly (vc)
Aldridge, R.:Qt for an Outdoor Festival, w. Al Regni (s sax), Mark Feldman (vn), T. O. Sterrett (pno) Open Loop ▲ 034 [DDD]
Bourland, R.:Dark Paintings (3), w. Al Regni (sax), Lois Martin (va) Open Loop ▲ 034 [DDD]
Bourland, R.:Stone Qt, w. Al Regni (sax), Lois Martin (va), T. O. Sterrett (pno) Open Loop ▲ 034 [DDD]
Laurie, Ronald (vc)
Wagner, R.:Siegfried Idyll, w. T. Holowach (vn), M. Skazinetsky (vn), L. Toman (va), C. Elliott (db), S. Shulman (fl), T. Maloney (cl), J. Valdepenas (cl), J. Fetherston (cl), S. Mosher (bn), S. Wilson (hn), R. Cohen (hn), J. Cowell (tpt), G. Gould (cnd) *(rec July 27–29 & Sept. 8, 198)* Sony Classical ▲ SMK 52650 [ADD]

Laurin, Dan (rcr)
Bach, C.P.E.:Son Fl, H.562 *(rec Mar 17–19, 1994)* BIS 2-▲ CD 675 [DDD]
Bach, J.S.:Partita Fl, BWV 1013 *(rec Mar 17–19, 1994)* BIS 2-▲ CD 675 [DDD]
Blavet, M.:Sons Trns Fl, w. Mogens Rasmussen (vl), Leif Meyer (hpd)—Son Terza; Son Seconda *(rec Furuby Church, Sweden, May 8–11, 1995)* BIS ▲ CD 745 [DDD]
Braun, J.D.:Son Terza, w. Mogens Rasmussen (vl) or Leif Meyer (hpd) *(rec Furuby Church, Sweden, May 8–11, 1995)* BIS ▲ CD 745 [DDD]
Dornel, L.-A.:Sons Vn & Suites Fl, Op. 2, w. Mogens Rasmussen (vl), Leif Meyer (hpd)—Suite IIe *(rec Furuby Church, Sweden, May 8–11, 1995)* BIS ▲ CD 745 [DDD]
Hirose, R.:Hymn *(rec Nov. 27–29, 1993)* BIS ▲ CD 655 [DDD]
Hirose, R.:Meditation *(rec Nov. 27–29, 1993)* BIS ▲ CD 655 [DDD]
Ishii, M.:Black Intention *(rec Nov. 27–29, 1993)* BIS ▲ CD 655 [DDD]
Ishii, M.:east*green*spring *(rec Nov. 27–29, 1993)* BIS ▲ CD 655 [DDD]
Leclair, J.-M.:Sons Vn (Books 1–4), w. Mogens Rasmussen (vl), Leif Meyer (hpd)—Son II *(rec Furuby Church, Sweden, May 8–11, 1995)* BIS ▲ CD 745 [DDD]
Matsumoto, K.:Pastorale *(rec Nov. 27–29, 1993)* BIS ▲ CD 655 [DDD]
Shinohara, M.:Fragmente *(rec Nov. 27–29, 1993)* BIS ▲ CD 655 [DDD]
Telemann, G.P.:Con in a for 2 Rcrs, w. C. Pehrsson (rcr), Drottningholm Baroque Ensemble *(rec May 31, 1993)* BIS ▲ CD 617 [DDD]
Telemann, G.P.:Con in B♭ for 2 Rcrs, w. C. Pehrsson (rcr), Drottningholm Baroque Ensemble *(rec May 31, 1993)* BIS ▲ CD 617 [DDD]
Telemann, G.P.:Fants Fl *(rec Mar. 17–19, 1994)* BIS 2-▲ CD 675 [DDD]
Vivaldi, A.:Cons Rcr, *(orch unknown)*—Con. in F, RV.434; Con. in g, RV.439; Con. in c, RV.441; Con. in F, RV.443; Con. in C, RV.444 *(rec 1991)* BIS ▲ CD 635
Laurino, Pasquale (vn)
Vivaldi, A.:Cons Vn, Op. 8/1–4, "The Four Seasons", w. Jerome Franke (vn), Karine Garibova (vn), Olga Miliaeva (va), Roza Borisova (vc), Mika Hennessy (db), Melanie Panush (ham dlc), Stanislav Venglevski (bayan), Mike Kashou (arabic tabla), Daryl Stuermer (gtr), Ed Paloucek (celtic fid), Gary Bottoni (highland pipe), Dubuffet String Quartet *(rec July–Sept 1995)* EarthBeat! ▲ 35270-2 [DDD]
Lauten, Elodie (kbd/elec)
Lauten, E.:Tronik Involutions O.O. Discs ▲ OO 27 [DDD]
Lautenbacher, Susanne (vn)
Bach, J.S.:Cant 204, w. Elisabeth Speiser (sop), Helmuth Steinkraus (fl), Willi Schnell (ob), Dietmar Keller (ob), R. Ewerhart (cnd), Württemberg CO *(rec 1966)* Vox Box 3-▲ CD3X 3039
Bach, J.S.:Cons Vn (comp), w. G. Kehr (cnd), Mainz CO *(rec 1958)* Vox Box 3-▲ CD3X 3008 [ADD]
Bach, J.S.:Cons Vn (comp), w. G. Kehr (cnd), Mainz CO Allegretto ▲ ACD 8057 [ADD] ■ ACS 8057
Bach, J.S.:Con for 2 Vns, w. D. Vorholz (vn), G. Kehr (cnd), Mainz CO Allegretto ▲ ACD 8057 [ADD] ■ ACS 8057
Bach, J.S.:Con for 2 Vns, w. D. Vorholz (vn), G. Kehr (cnd), Mainz CO *(rec 1958)* Vox Box 3-▲ CD3X 3008 [ADD]

INSTRUMENT.

Lautenbacher, Susanne (vn) (cont.)
Bach, J.S.:Life & Music of, w. D. Vorholz (vn), G. Kehr (cnd), Mainz CO—narration with selected excerpts from Brandenburg Cons. Nos. 2, 3, 4 & 5, BWV 1047–50; Cants. Nos. 57 & 211; Chorale Prelude, BWV 645; Con. No. 2 for Violin, BWV 1042; Inventions, BWV 785; Italian Con., BWV 971; Toccata & Fugue, BWV 565; Mass in b, BWV 232; Wohltemperierte Klavier [Bk. 1], BWV 846; St. Matthew Passion, BWV 244; St. John Passion, BWV 245; Con. for 2 Violins, BWV 1043; Passacaglia & Fugue, BWV 582; Magnificat, BWV 243; plus complete versions of Con. for 2 Violins, BWV 1043 & Con. for Violin, BWV 1042 — Vox Music Masters ("Music Masters" series) ▲ MMD 8500 [ADD] ■ MMC 8500
Beethoven, L. van:Con Vn, Op. 61, w. H. Reichert (cnd), Westphalia SO — Allegretto ▲ ACD 8014 [ADD] ■ ACS 8014
Beethoven, L. van:Romances Vn, w. C. Cremer (cnd), Baden State Orch—No. 1 — Special Music Co. ("Classics of the Heart" series) ▲ SCD 5196
Beethoven, L. van:Romances Vn, w. C. Cremer (cnd), Baden State Orch — Allegretto ▲ ACD 8014 [ADD] ■ ACS 8014
Biber, H. von:Mystery (or Rosary) Sons, w. Johannes Koch (va), Rudolph Ewerhart (positiv/hpd/regal) *(rec 1962)* — Vox Box 2–▲ CDX 5171
Biber, H. von:Passacaglia Vn *(rec 1962)* — Vox Box 2–▲ CDX 5171
Brahms, J.:Con Vn, w. R. Wagner (cnd), Innsbruck SO — Allegretto ▲ ACD 8142 [ADD] ■ ACS 8142
Hartmann, K.A.:Con funèbre, w. J. Faerber (cnd), Württemberg CO — Vox Box 2–▲ CDX 5134 [ADD]
Locatelli, P.:L'arte del violino, w. G. Kehr (cnd), Mainz CO — Vox Box 2–▲ CDX 5018 [ADD]
Locatelli, P.:L'arte del violino, w. G. Kehr (cnd), Mainz CO — Vox Box 2–▲ CDX 5037 [ADD]
Locatelli, P.:Music of, w. G. Kehr (cnd), Mainz CO—Con No. 2 in c [Adagio; Allegro non troppo] — Special Music Co. ("Classics of the Heart" series) ▲ SCD 5198
Pfitzner, H.:Con Vn, w. G. Wich (cnd), Philharmonia Hungarica — Vox Box 2–▲ CDX 5134 [ADD]
Schaeuble, H.:Concertino Ob, w. S. Fuchs (ob), G. Egger (vn), J. Faerber (cnd), Württemberg CO — Gallo ▲ CD 577 [DAD]
Schaeuble, H.:Music for 2 Vns, w. G. Egger (vn), J. Faerber (cnd), Württemberg CO — Gallo ▲ CD 577 [DAD]
Schaeuble, H.:Sym for Strs, "In Memoriam", w. G. Egger (vn), J. Faerber (cnd), Württemberg CO — Gallo ▲ CD 577 [DAD]
Schumann, R.:Con Vn, w. P. Cao (cnd), Luxembourg RSO — Vox Box 2–▲ CDX 5027 [ADD]
Schumann, R.:Fant Vn, w. P. Cao (cnd), Luxembourg RSO — Vox Box 2–▲ CDX 5027 [ADD]
Telemann, G.P.:Kleine Kammermusik, w. Hans-Martin Linde (fl), Ferdinand Conrad (rcr), Helmut Winschermann (ob), Johannes Koch (vl), Hugo Ruf (hpd) *(rec Südwest-Tonstudio H. Jansen, Stuttgart, Jan. 1966)* — Musicaphon ▲ 51539 [ADD]
Vivaldi, A.:Cons Vn, Op. 8/1–4, "The Four Seasons", w. J. Faerber (cnd), Württemberg CO — Allegretto ▲ ACD 8002 [ADD] ■ ACS 8002
Vivaldi, A.:Cons Vn, Op. 8/1–4, "The Four Seasons", w. J. Faerber (cnd), Württemberg CO—Winter — Special Music Co. ▲ SCD 5200
Vivaldi, A.:Life & Music of, w. J. Faerber (cnd), Württemberg CO—narration & selected excerpts from Con. for Bassoon; Con. No. 1 for Violin, Op. 4; Con. in Bb for Flute; Con. No. 11, Op. 8; Gloria in D; The Nymph and the Shepherd; Con. No. 12, Op. 4; Con. No. 10, Op. 3; Four Seasons, Op. 8; Bach:Con. for 4 Harpsichords, BWV 1065; Con. 2, Op. 9 — Vox Music Masters ("Music Masters" series) ▲ MMD 8510 [ADD] ■ MMC 8510
Weill, K.:Con Vn, w. J. Michaels (cnd), Detmold Wind Ensemble *(rec ca. 1973)* — Vox Box 2–▲ CDX 5043 [ADD]
Zimmermann, B.A.:Con Vn, w. S. Köhler (cnd), Luxembourg RSO — Vox Box 2–▲ CDX 5134 [ADD]

Lavaillotte, Lucien (fl)
Debussy, C.:Prélude à l'après-midi d'un faune, w. M. Rosenthal (cnd), Paris Opera Orch — Adès ▲ ADE 203892 [AAD]

Laval, Danielle (pno)
Herrmann, B.:Con Macabre, w. P. Verrot (cnd), Monte Carlo PO *(rec Monte Carlo, July 1995)* — Travelling ("Music & Movies" series) ▲ K 1019 [DDD]
Hossein, A.:Con 3 Pno, w. P. Verrot (cnd), Monte Carlo PO *(rec Monte Carlo, July 1995)* — Travelling ("Music & Movies" series) ▲ K 1019 [DDD]
Legrand, M.:Concertino Pno, w. P. Verrot (cnd), Monte Carlo PO [from the film Summer of '42] *(rec Monte Carlo, July 1995)* — Travelling ("Music & Movies" series) ▲ K 1019 [DDD]
Mozart, W.A.:Vars Pno (complete)—K.25, 353, 460 & 613 — Accord ▲ ACD 201302 [DDD]
Rota, N.:Pno Music—2 Waltzes on the Theme of Bach; Vars & Fugue on the Name of Bach; 7 Difficult Pieces for Children; Ippolito Gioca; 15 Preludes — Travelling ("Music & Movies" series) ▲ K 1021
Rota, N.:Pno Music—2 Waltzes on the Name of B–A–C–H; Vars. & Fugue on the Name of B–A–C–H; 7 Difficult Pieces for Children; Ippolito Gioca; 15 préludes — Valois ▲ V 4698
Wiener, J.:Con 1 Pno, w. P. Verrot (cnd), Monte Carlo PO *(rec Monte Carlo, July 1995)* — Travelling ("Music & Movies" series) ▲ K 1019 [DDD]

Lavandera, Pablo (pno)
Clementi, M.:Pno Music (comp), w. Aldo Antognazzi (pno), Christian Badian (pno), Eduardo Cazaban (pno), Cristina Da Souza (pno), Dao Di Renzo (pno), Yi Fang Huang (vn), Silvina Cardenas (fl), Nestor Herzbaum (fl)—Sons (6) for Pno, Op. 2, Nos. 1, 3 & 5 (w. flutes); Duets (3) for Piano 4-Hands, Op. 3, Nos. 2 & 3; Sons (3) for Pno & Vn, Op. 3, No. 4 — Aura Classics ▲ AU 32287

Laveille, Ryan (perc)
Rorem, N.:Studies for 11, w. E. Ostling (fl), K. Lord (ob), G. Raden (cl), J. Sutte (tpt), S. Copes (vn), C.-J. Chang (va), J. Lastrapes (vc), K. Englichova (hp), R. Uchida (pno), A. LaFargue (perc), R. Milanov (cnd) — New World ▲ 80445–2

Lavilla, Felix (pno)
Zarzuelas y Canciones, w. Teresa Berganza (mez), various orchs — Acanta ▲ 49403

Lavoix, Claude (pno)
Collet, H.:Los Amantes de galioia, w. Rachel Yakar (sop) *(rec Théatre de Poissy, Paris, Nov. 30–Dec. 2, 1994)* — Claves ▲ CD 9506 [DDD]
Collet, H.:Canciones populares castellanas (5), w. Rachel Yakar (sop) *(rec Théatre de Poissy, Paris, Nov. 30–Dec. 2, 1994)* — Claves ▲ CD 9506 [DDD]
Collet, H.:Chansons populaires de Burgos (7), w. Rachel Yakar (sop) *(rec Théatre de Poissy, Paris, Nov. 30–Dec. 2, 1994)* — Claves ▲ CD 9506 [DDD]
Collet, H.:Chants de Castille *(rec Théatre de Poissy, Paris, Nov. 30–Dec. 2, 1994)* — Claves ▲ CD 9506 [DDD]
Collet, H.:La Pena, w. Rachel Yakar (sop) *(rec Théatre de Poissy, Paris, Nov. 30–Dec. 2, 1994)* — Claves ▲ CD 9506 [DDD]
Collet, H.:Poema de un día, w. Rachel Yakar (sop) *(rec Théatre de Poissy, Paris, Nov. 30–Dec. 2, 1994)* — Claves ▲ CD 9506 [DDD]
Collet, H.:Songs, w. Rachel Yakar (sop)—Canciones populares castellanas, Op. 69; Chansons populaires de Burgos, Op. 80; Poema de un dia, Op. 48; La Pena; Los amantes de Galicia; Songs of Castille, Op. 42/1 & 2 — Claves ▲ 50–9506

Lavotha, Elemér (vc)
Bashmakov, L.:Con da camera, w. Gunilla von Bahr (pic/fl), Paavo Pohjola (vn), Mona Nordin (vn), Zahari Tchavdarov (va) *(rec Grünewald Hall, Stockholm, Sweden, May 11, 1974)* — BIS ▲ CD 11 [AAD]
Duruflé, M.:Requiem, w. P. Hofman (ten), P. Mattei (bar), M. Wager (org), St. Jacobs Chamber Choir *(rec Nov. 9–12, 1992)* — BIS ▲ CD 602 [DDD]
Kodály, Z.:Adagio Vn, w. K. Aberg (pno) — BIS ▲ CD 172 [AAD]
Kodály, Z.:Son Vc & Pno, Op. 4, w. K. Aberg (pno) — BIS ▲ CD 172 [AAD]
Kodály, Z.:Sonatina Vc & Pno, w. K. Aberg (pno) — BIS ▲ CD 172 [AAD]
Lidholm, I.:Pieces Vc & Pno, w. K. Aberg (pno) — BIS ▲ CD 72 [AAD]
Martinů, B.:Son 1 Vc, w. K. Aberg (pno) — BIS ▲ CD 72 [AAD]
Popular & Serious Music for Cello & Piano, w. Kerstin Aberg (pno) — BIS ▲ CD 72 [AAD]
Strauss, E.:Son Vc, w. K. Aberg (pno) *(rec Feb. 24–25, 1978)* — BIS ▲ CD 49 [AAD]

Lavry, E. (hp)
Fleischer, T.:Lamentation, w. C. Grossmeyer (sop), A. Haroz (hp), D. Kovalsky (perc), Zimrat Women's Chorus — Opus One ▲ Cd 158 [DDD]

Lawler, Zara (fl)
Kraft, L.:Cloud Studies, w. Lisa Maron (pic), Margaret Swinchoski (pic), Tanya Dusevic (fl), Adrienne Flynn (fl), Christina Jennings (fl), Joseph Piscitelli (fl), Michelle Ryang (fl), Dominique Soucy (fl), Diane Taublieb (fl), Laurel Ann Maurer (alt fl), Richard Wyton (alt fl), J. Solum (cnd) *(rec Skinner Recital Hall, Vassar College, Poughkeepsie, NY, Mar 24–26, 1994)* — CRI ▲ CD 712 [DDD]

Lawless, Robert (b trbn)—see ORCHESTRAS & ENSEMBLES New World Brass

Lawlor, Lynne (perc)—see ORCHESTRAS & ENSEMBLES Peter Garland Ensemble

Lawrence, Douglas (org)
Festival of Organ Masterpieces, Vol. 1 — Move ▲ MD 3020

Lawrence, Eleanor (fl)
Ibert, J.:Chamber Music, w. Sue Ann Kahn (fl), Peggy Schecter (fl), Rie Schmidt (fl), David Krakauer (cl), Lauren Goldstein (bn), Curtis Macomber (vn), Susan Jolles (hp), Frederic Hand (gtr), Andrew Willis (pno)—2 Mouvements; Aria; Histoires; Pastoral; Aria; Entr'acte — Albany ▲ TROY 145 [DDD]
Ibert, J.:Music of, w. C. Schadeberg (sop), Sue Ann Kahn (fl), P. Schechter (fl), R. Schmidt (fl), David Krakauer (cl), L. Goldstein (bn), Curtis Macomber (vn), Susan Jolles (hp), Frederick Hand (gtr), Arthur Willis (pno)—Entr'acte; Jeux; Sonatine; 2 Movements; 2 Interludes; Aria; Pièce for solo Fl; Histoires; 2 Stèles orientées; Pastoral; Aria; Entr'acte — Albany ▲ TROY 145

Lawrence, Emily (hp)
Berio, L.:Sequenza II — Neuma ▲ 450–72 [DDD]

Lawrence, Kevin (vn)
Foote, A.:Ballad, w. Eric Larsen (pno) *(rec Crawford Hall, North Carolina School of the Arts, Sept. 6–8, 1994)* — New World ▲ 80464–2
Foote, A.:Legend, w. Eric Larsen (pno) *(rec Crawford Hall, North Carolina School of the Arts, Sept. 6–8, 1994)* — New World ▲ 80464–2
Foote, A.:Melody, w. Eric Larsen (pno) *(rec Crawford Hall, North Carolina School of the Arts, Sept. 6–8, 1994)* — New World ▲ 80464–2
Foote, A.:Pieces Vn & Pno, Op. 9, w. Eric Larsen (pno) *(rec Crawford Hall, North Carolina School of the Arts, Sept. 6–8, 1994)* — New World ▲ 80464–2
Foote, A.:Pieces Vn & Pno, Op. 74, w. Eric Larsen (pno) *(rec Crawford Hall, North Carolina School of the Arts, Sept. 6–8, 1994)* — New World ▲ 80464–2
Foote, A.:Son Vn, w. Eric Larsen (pno) *(rec Crawford Hall, North Carolina School of the Arts, Sept. 6–8, 1994)* — New World ▲ 80464–2

Lawrence, Mark (trbn)
Four of a Kind:Music for Trombone Quartet, w. Joseph Allessi (trbn), Blair Bollinger (trbn), Scott A. Hartman (trbn) — Summit ▲ DCD 123 [DDD] ■ DCD 123
The Golden Age of Brass:Virtuoso Solos, Vol. 1, w. David Hickman (cnt), American Serenade Band [cnd:Henry Charles Smith] — Summit ▲ DCD 114 [DDD]
The Golden Age of Brass:Virtuoso Solos, Vol. 2, w. David Hickman (cnt) — Summit ▲ DCD 121 [DDD] ■ DCD 121
Hindemith, P.:Son Trbn, w. T. Lichtman (pno) — Summit 2–▲ DCD 115 [DDD] 2–■ DCD 115
Trombonology, w. Robin Sutherland (pno) *(rec Little Bridges Hall, Claremont College, Pomona, CA)* — d'Note Classics ▲ DND 1012 [DDD]

Lawrence, Ron (va)—see also ORCHESTRAS & ENSEMBLES Sirius String Quartet, Soldier String Quartet
Adams, J.L.:Earth & the Great Weather, w. R. Lorentz (vn/perc), M. Finckel (vc), R. Black (db/perc), A. Knoles (perc), J. L. Adams (perc), J. Nageak (Iñupiat Eskimo performer), D. Simmonds (Iñupiat Eskimo performer), L. Tritt (Gwich'in Indian performer), A. P. Raboff (Gwich'in Indian performer), D. Hunsaker (Latin voice), J.L. Adams (cnd) *(rec Fairbanks, Mar. 8–11, 1993)* — New World ▲ 80459–2
Gisberg:Music of, w. Gisburg (sgr/fl), Jeff O'Malley (nar), Midori Seiler (vn), Guy Tyler (db), Anthony Coleman (pno), Christine Bard (perc)—Low-End; Since You Have Left; The Woman Is Perfected; Sharks; Night & Wind; Saturnspacemonsters Walking on a Sandy Surface; Old Moon in Winter; Never Saw the Stars So Bright; Habe Die Liebe Verschlafen; W.A.L.S.H. — Tzadik ▲ TZA CD 7019 [DDD]
Jenkins, L.:Monkey on the Dragon, w. Leroy Jenkins (vn), Henry Threadgill (fl), Don Byron (cl), Marth Ehrlich (b cl), Janet Frice (bn), Vincent Chancey (hn), Frank Gordon (tpt), Jeff Hoyer (trbn), David Soldier (vn), Jane Henry (vn) Mary Wooton (vc), Lindsey Horner (db), Thurman Barker (traps), Myra Melford (pno), T. Léon (cnd) *(rec live, Merkin Concert Hall, New York City, Apr. 9, 1992)* — CRI ("eXchange" series) ▲ CD 663 [DDD]

Lawrence-King, Andrew (baroque hp)
Hamburg Baroque (Songs), w. Tuula Nienstedt (mez), Stephen Stubbs (lt) *(rec 1989)* — Ambitus ▲ AMB 97837
Harp at Christmas — Ambitus ▲ AMB 97812 [DDD]
Harp Music of the Italian Renaissance — Hyperion ▲ CDA 66229 [DAD]
The Harp of Ludovico — Hyperion ▲ CDA 66518

Lawrence-King, Andrew (hp)—see also ORCHESTRAS & ENSEMBLES Tragicomedia
Corbetta, F.:Gtr Music—Fant caprice de chaconne [arr hp] *(rec St. Andrew's, Toddington, England, Jan 23–25, 1996)* — Deutsche Harmonia Mundi ▲ 05472–77371–2 [DDD]
Couperin, F.:Hpd Music—L'Auguste (allemande); Premiere Courante; La Majestueuse (sarabande); Gavotte; La Milordine (gigue); La Favourite (chaconne en rondeau) [all arr hp] *(rec St. Andrew's, Toddington, England, Jan 23–25, 1996)* — Deutsche Harmonia Mundi ▲ 05472–77371–2 [DDD]
Couperin, L.:Hpd Music—Prélude en A; La Piémontoise; Courante; Sarabande; Les Carillons de Paris; Prélude; Tombeau de M. de Blancrocher; Passacaille [all arr hp] *(rec St. Andrew's, Toddington, England, Jan 23–25, 1996)* — Deutsche Harmonia Mundi ▲ 05472–77371–2 [DDD]
Froberger, J.J.:Hpd Music—Lamento sopra la dolorosa perdità della Real Mstà di Ferdinando IV [arr hp] *(rec St. Andrew's, Toddington, England, Jan 23–25, 1996)* — Deutsche Harmonia Mundi ▲ 05472–77371–2 [DDD]
Masterpieces of Mexican Polyphony, w. [cnd:James O'Donnell], Westminster Cathedral Choir, Andrew Watts (dulcian), Iain Simcock (org) — Hyperion ▲ CDA 66330 [DDD]
Merula, T.:Arias & Capriccios, w. M. Figueras (sop), J.-P. Canihac (cnt), T. Koopman (hpd), J. Savall (vl), R. Lislevand (thb), L. Duftschmid (vn) — Astrée ▲ E 8503
Monteverdi, C.:Arie e Lamenti, w. M. Figueras (sop), T. Koopman (hpd/org), R. Lislevand (thb) — Astrée ▲ E 8710
Negri, C.:Music of—La Barriera; Brando per Quattro Pastore e Quattro Ninfe — Hyperion ▲ CDA 66229 [DAD]
Ortiz, D.:Trattado de Glosas, w. J. Savall (vl), T. Koopman (hpd/org), L. Duftschmid (vn), R. Lislevand (vih), P. Pandolfo (b vl) — Astrée ▲ E 8717 [DDD]
Stravaganze:17th Century Italian Songs & Dances, w. D. Douglass (cnd), King's Noyse *(rec Campion Center, Boston, MA, Oct 17–19, 1994)* — Harmonia Mundi France ▲ HMU 907159
Trabaci, G.M.:Music of—3 Gagliarde; Partite sopra; Ancidetemi pur; Toccata seconda — Hyperion ▲ CDA 66229 [DAD]
Visée, R. de:Gtr Music—La Royalle (allemande); Courante I & II; Sarabande; Gavotte; Chaconne; Mascarade Rondeau [all arr hp] *(rec St. Andrew's, Toddington, England, Jan 23–25, 1996)* — Deutsche Harmonia Mundi ▲ 05472–77371–2 [DDD]

Lawrence-King, Andrew (hp/hpd/org)
Amor ist mein Lied:Music of the Age of Sentimentalism for Flute & Harp, w. Laurence Dean (trns fl) — Christophorus ▲ CHR 77182 [DDD]

Lawrence-King, Andrew (hp/psaltery)
Milán, L. de:Maestro (sels), w. Jordi Savall (vl) — Astrée ▲ E 8535

Lawrence-King, Andrew (hp/psaltery/org/hpd)
Ruiz de Ribayaz, L.:Luz Y norte, w. A. Lawrence-King (cnd), Harp Consort—Spanish Dances *(rec Valkkoog, Sept 1994)* — Deutsche Harmonia Mundi ▲ 05472–77340–2 [DDD]

Lawrence-King, Andrew (hp/voc)
Proensa, w. Hillier, Paul (bass), Stephen Stubbs (lt/voc), Erin Headley (vielle) — ECM New Series ▲ 78118–21368–2 [DDD]

Lawrence-King, Andrew (hps/org/hpd)
Purcell, H.:Musick's Hand-maid, w. Ellen Hargis (sop), Ian Honeyman (ten), Rodrigo del Pozo (ten), Harry van der Kamp (bass), Paul O'Dette (thb/cittern/lt), A. Lawrence-King (cnd), Harp Consort — Astrée ▲ E 8564
Virtuoso Solo Music for Cornetto, w. Bruce Dickey (cornetto), Stephen Stubbs (chit/vih), Erin Headley (vl) — Accent ▲ 9173 [DDD]

▲ = CD ♦ = Enhanced CD △ = MD ■ = Cassette Tape ▯ = DCC

Laws, Hubert (fl)
Bolling, C.:California Suite, w. C. Bolling (pno), C. Damonico (db), S. Manne (perc) — CBS ▲ MK 36691

Lawson, Colin (b cl)
Mozart, W.A.:Con Cl, w. R. Goodman (cnd), Hanover Band [period instrs] — Nimbus 4–▲ NI 1791 [DDD]
Mozart, W.A.:Con Cl, w. R. Goodman (cnd), Hanover Band [period instrs] — Nimbus ▲ NI 5228–2 [DDD]
Mozart, W.A.:Music of, w. Gundula Janowitz (sop), Julia Bernheimer (mez), Martyn Hill (ten), David Thomas (bass), Anthony Halstead (hn), Christopher Kite (pno), R. Goodman (cnd), Hanover Band—Cons for Hn, K.412, 417, 447, 494a & 495; Sym No. 40; Con for Cl; Eine kleine Nachtmusik; Requiem; Sym No. 41; Con No. 20 for Pno; Serenata Notturna — Nimbus 4–▲ NI 1791 [DDD]

Lawson, Colin (chl)
Telemann, G.P.:Con for 2 Chls, w. Michael Harris (chl), S. Standage (cnd), Collegium Musicum 90 *(rec Goldsmiths' College, Apr 24–26, 1995)* — Chandos ("Chaconne" series) ▲ CHAN 0593
Telemann, G.P.:Son 2 Chls, w. Michael Harris (chl), S. Standage (cnd), Collegium Musicum 90 *(rec Goldsmiths' College, Apr 24–26, 1995)* — Chandos ("Chaconne" series) ▲ CHAN 0593
Vivaldi, A.:Son Fl Ob, RV.59, w. J. Toll (hpd/org) [arr rcr & va bastarda] — Harmonia Mundi USA ▲ HMU 907104

Lawson, Colin (cl)—see also ORCHESTRAS & ENSEMBLES austraLYSIS members
Bach, Joh. Christian:Sinf concertante, T.290/9, w. Michael Harris (cl), P. Holman (cnd), Parley of Instruments — Hyperion ▲ CDA 66896
Hook, J.:Con Cl, w. P. Holman (cnd), Parley of Instruments — Hyperion ▲ CDA 66896
Mahon, J.:Con 2 Cl, w. P. Holman (cnd), Parley of Instruments — Hyperion ▲ CDA 66896
Mahon, J.:Duet 1 Cls, w. Michael Harris (cl) — Hyperion ▲ CDA 66896
Mahon, J.:Duet 4 Cls, w. Michael Harris (cl) — Hyperion ▲ CDA 66896
Mozart, W.A.:Con Cl, w. R. Goodman (cnd), Hanover Band *(rec All Saints', Tooting, London, Dec. 1989)* — Nimbus ▲ NI 7023 [DDD]
Vivaldi, A.:Sons Ob, w. P. Goodwin (ob), G. Hennessey (ob), J. Holloway (vn), N. North (archlt/gtr), S. Sheppard (vc), F. Eustace (bn), J. Toll (hpd/org)—RV.53, 58, 81 & 779 — Harmonia Mundi USA ▲ HMU 907104

Lawson, Dorothy (vc)—see also ORCHESTRAS & ENSEMBLES Continuum Chamber Ensemble, Philharmonia Virtuosi
Bazelon, I.:Entre Nous, w. H. Farberman (cnd), Bournemouth SO *(rec Poole Arts Centre, Poole, Dorset, England, June 6–7, 1995)* — Albany ▲ TROY 174 [DDD]

Lawson, Mark (pno)
Arban, J.–B.:Fant, Theme & Vars on "The Carnival of Venice", w. Mark Fisher (eup) [arr. Eric Leidzen] *(rec Boutell Concert Hall, Northern Illinois Univ., June 6–7 & Nov. 26–27, 19)* — Albany ▲ TROY 162 [DDD]
Bach, Jan:Concert Vars, w. Mark Fisher (eup) *(rec Boutell Concert Hall, Northern Illinois Univ., June 6–7 & Nov. 26–27, 19)* — Albany ▲ TROY 162 [DDD]
Bach, J.S.:Sons Fl, BWV 1030–35, w. Mark Fisher (eup)—BWV 1031 *(rec Boutell Concert Hall, Northern Illinois Univ., June 6–7 & Nov. 26–27, 19)* — Albany ▲ TROY 162 [DDD]
Brahms, J.:Songs, w. Mark Fisher (eup)—Es Rauschet Das Wasser; Der Jäger Und Sein Liebchen [both Op. 28]; Weg der Liebe, Op. 20; So Lass Uns Wandern, Op. 75 *(rec Boutell Concert Hall, Northern Illinois Univ., June 6–7 & Nov. 26–27, 19)* — Albany ▲ TROY 162 [DDD]
Jacob, G.:Fant Eup, w. Mark Fisher (eup) *(rec Boutell Concert Hall, Northern Illinois Univ., June 6–7 & Nov. 26–27, 19)* — Albany ▲ TROY 162 [DDD]
Telemann, G.P.:Son Bn, w. Mark Fisher (eup) *(rec Boutell Concert Hall, Northern Illinois Univ., June 6–7 & Nov. 26–27, 19)* — Albany ▲ TROY 162 [DDD]

Lawson, Peter (pno)
Barber, S.:Son Pno — Virgin Classics ▲ 59008 [DDD]
Berners:Fant espagnole, w. Alan MacLean (pno) — Albany ▲ TROY 142 [DDD]
Berners:Morceaux (3), w. Alan MacLean (pno) — Albany ▲ TROY 142 [DDD]
Berners:Valses bourgeoises, w. Alan MacLean (pno) — Albany ▲ TROY 142 [DDD]
Carter, E.:Son Pno — Virgin Classics ▲ 59008 [DDD]
Copland, A.:Son Pno — Virgin Classics ▲ 59008 [DDD]
Griffes, C.T.:Son Pno — Virgin Classics ▲ CDC 59316
Ibert, J.:Son 1 Pno — Virgin Classics ▲ CDC 59316
Ives, C.:Three–Page Son — Virgin Classics ▲ 59008 [DDD]
Lambert, C.:Ov Pno 4–Hands, w. Alan MacLean (pno) — Albany ▲ TROY 142 [DDD]
Lambert, C.:Pièces nègres pour les touches blanches, w. Alan MacLean (pno) — Albany ▲ TROY 142 [DDD]
Lane, P.:Badinages, w. Alan MacLean (pno) — Albany ▲ TROY 142 [DDD]
Piano Sonatas, Vol. 1 — Virgin Classics ▲ 59008 [DDD]
Rawsthorne, A.:The Creel, w. Alan MacLean (pno) — Albany ▲ TROY 142 [DDD]
Satie, E.:Pno Music (misc)—Chapitres tournés en tous sens; Croquis et agaceries d'un gros bonhomme en bois; Gnossiennes Nos. 2 & 4; Heures séculaires et instantanées; Nocturnes Nos. 2 & 4; Nouvelles pièces froides; Passacaille; Le piège de Méduse; Prelude No. 2 (Le fils des etoiles); Sonatina bureaucratique; Trois Gymnopédies *(rec 1980)* — Classics for Pleasure ▲ CDCFP4329 [ADD]
Sessions, R.:Son 2 Pno — Virgin Classics ▲ CDC 59316
Walton, W.:Duets for Children, w. Alan MacLean (pno) — Albany ▲ TROY 142 [DDD]

Lawson, Rex (pnl)
Stravinsky, I.:Études Pnl *(rec SUNY Purchase, Apr. 1991)* — MusicMasters ▲ 01612–67138–2
Stravinsky, I.:Pétrouchka (reduction) *(rec SUNY Purchase, Apr. 1991)* — MusicMasters ▲ 01612–67138–2
Stravinsky, I.:Le Sacre du printemps Pno — IMP Masters ▲ MCD 25 [DDD]
Stravinsky, I.:Le Sacre du printemps Pno *(rec SUNY Purchase, Apr. 1991)* — MusicMasters ▲ 01612–67138–2

Layfield, Malcolm (vn)
Haydn, J.:Con Org, Vn & Strs, H.XVIII/6, w. David Francis (hpd), M. Layfield (cnd), Goldberg Ensemble — Meridian ▲ CDE 84177
Haydn, J.:Con 1 Vn, w. M. Layfield (cnd), Goldberg Ensemble — Meridian ▲ CDE 84177

Layton, Elizabeth (vn)—see also ORCHESTRAS & ENSEMBLES Nash Ensemble, Capricorn members
Schubert, Franz:Fant Vn, D.934, w. James Lisney (pno) — IMP ("Classics" series) ▲ IMP 6700932
Schubert, Franz:Rondo Vn, D.895, w. James Lisney (pno) — IMP ("Classics" series) ▲ IMP 6700932
Schubert, Franz:Son Vn, D.574, w. James Lisney (pno) — IMP ("Classics" series) ▲ IMP 6700932
Vivaldi, A.:Con for 3 Vns, w. C. Warren–Green (vn), A. Balanescu (vn), C. Warren–Green (cnd), London CO—RV.551 in F — Virgin Classics ▲ 59609 [DDD]

Layton, Stephen (org)
Great Cathedral Anthems, Vol. 3, w. Southwark Cathedral Choir — Priory ▲ PRI 435 [DDD]

Lazar, Adrian (vn)—see also ORCHESTRAS & ENSEMBLES New Munich Piano Trio
Arensky, A.:Trio 1 Pno, w. H. Lechler (pno), G. Zank (vc) *(rec Mar 23–26, 1992)* — Calig ▲ CAL 50913 [DDD]
Arensky, A.:Trio 2 Pno, w. H. Lechler (pno), G. Zank (vc) *(rec Mar 23–26, 1992)* — Calig ▲ CAL 50913 [DDD]

Lazarevitch, Vojkan (vn)
Miniatures, w. Claire Honneger (pno) *(rec Jan 1996)* — Gallo ▲ CD 877 [ADD]

Lazari, Carlo (vn)—see also ORCHESTRAS & ENSEMBLES L'Arte dell'Arco, Venice New Quintet
Rubinstein, A.:Pieces, Op. 11, w. Stefano Gibellato (pno) — Enterprise ("Tiziano" series) ▲ ENT TZ 96001 [DDD]
Rubinstein, A.:Son 1 Vn, w. S. Gibellato (pno) *(rec July 21, 1991)* — Nuova Era ▲ 7148 [DDD]
Rubinstein, A.:Son 2 Vn, w. S. Gibellato (pno) *(rec Aug. 10, 1991)* — Nuova Era ▲ 7148 [DDD]
Rubinstein, A.:Son 3 Vn, w. Stefano Gibellato (pno) — Enterprise ("Tiziano" series) ▲ ENT TZ 96001 [DDD]

Lea, Roberto (vn)—see ORCHESTRAS & ENSEMBLES Ensemble Barocco Padua Sans Souci

Lea, Tobias (va)—see ORCHESTRAS & ENSEMBLES Vienna String Quintet

Leach, Andrew (org/hpd)
Monteverdi, C.:Vespro della Beata Vergine, w. Elly Ameling (sop), Norma Burrowes (sop), Charles Brett (ct), Martyn Hill (ten), Anthony Rolfe–Johnson (ten), Robert Tear (ten), Peter Knapp (bass), John Noble (bass), Francis Grier (org/hpd), James Lancelot (org/hpd), P. Ledger (cnd), London Early Music Consort, King's College Choir Cambridge—Nigra sum [con.]; Laudate pueri [psalm]; Sancta Maria [son. sopra]; Magnificat *(rec Chapel of King's College, Cambridge, July & Aug. 1975)* — EMI Classics ▲ CDK 65339 [ADD]

Leach, Joanna (pno)
Bach, J.S.:Partitas Hpd, BWV 825–830—No. 1 in B♭ — Athene ▲ ATHCD 3
Field, J.:Nocturnes Pno (misc)—16 sels — Athene ▲ ATHCD 1
Haydn, J.:Sons Pno—in C, H.SVI/1 — Athene ▲ ATHCD 3
Haydn, J.:Sons Pno—in C, H.XVI/35; in E♭, H.XVI/49; in c, H.XVI/20 — Athene ▲ ATHCD 2
Haydn, J.:Son Pno, H.XVII/6, "Andante with Vars" — Athene ▲ ATHCD 2
Mendelssohn, F.:Lieder ohne Worte Pno—Op. 19/1 — Athene ▲ ATHCD 3
Mozart, W.A.:Fant Pno, K.396 — Athene ▲ ATHCD 3
Mozart, W.A.:Son 11 Pno — Athene ▲ ATHCD 3
Schubert, Franz:Impromptus Pno (comp)—in A♭, D.899/4 — Athene ▲ ATHCD 3
Soler, P.A.:Sons Kbd—No. 90 in f# — Athene ▲ ATHCD 3

Leaman, Clifford (a sax)
Brandt, H.:Con A Sax, w. M. Dickey (cnd), Michigan Chamber Players — Redwood ▲ ESCD 45

Leaman, Clifford (sax)
Pepping, E.:Suite Tpt, w. G. Malvern (tpt), D. Hamilton (trbn) — CRS ▲ 9051

Leanderson, Helene (pno)
Bartók, B.:Songs, Op. 16, w. R. Leanderson (bar) [Hun] — BIS ▲ CD 182 [ADD]
Kilpinen, Y.:Lieder der Liebe I–II, w. Rolf Leanderson (bar) *(rec Nacka Aula, Nacka, Sweden, Jan 9–10, 1976)* — BIS ▲ CD 43 [AAD]
Kilpinen, Y.:Lieder um den Tod, w. Rolf Leanderson (bar) *(rec Nacka Aula, Nacka, Sweden, Jan 9–10, 1976)* — BIS ▲ CD 43 [AAD]

Léandre, Joëlle (db)
Cage, J.:59½ — Montaigne ▲ MO 782076
Cage, J.:A Flower Db — Montaigne ▲ MO 782076
Cage, J.:Ryoanji Db, w. Ninh lê Quan (perc) — Montaigne ▲ MO 782076
Cage, J.:The Wonderful Widow of Eighteen Springs [tran db] — Montaigne ▲ MO 782076
Lándre, J.:Hommage à J... — Montaigne ▲ MO 782076

Lear, Angela (pno)
Chopin, F.:Andante Spianato & Grande Polonaise *(rec St. George's, Brandon Hill, Bristol, Nov. 24, 1993)* — APR ▲ APR 5551 [DDD]
Chopin, F.:Barcarolle Pno *(rec St. George's, Brandon Hill, Bristol, Nov. 24, 1993)* — APR ▲ APR 5551 [DDD]
Chopin, F.:Fant *(rec St. George's, Brandon Hill, Bristol, Nov. 24, 1993)* — APR ▲ APR 5551 [DDD]
Chopin, F.:Impromptus—in c#, Op. 66 *(rec St. George's, Brandon Hill, Bristol, Nov. 24, 1993)* — APR ▲ APR 5551 [DDD]
Chopin, F.:Nocturnes—in E♭, Op. 9/2; in c#, Op. 27/1; in c, Op. 48/1 *(rec St. George's, Brandon Hill, Bristol, Nov. 24, 1993)* — APR ▲ APR 5551 [DDD]
Chopin, F.:Pno Music (misc)—Ballades 1 & 3; Bolero, Op. 19; Mazurkas, Op. 17/4 & 33/4; Noct 18; Polonaise–Fant, Op. 61; Scherzos 2 & 3 *(rec St. George's, Brandon Hill, Bristol, July 27, 1994)* — APR ▲ APR 5555 [DDD]
Chopin, F.:Polonaises—in f#, Op. 44 *(rec St. George's, Brandon Hill, Bristol, Nov. 24, 1993)* — APR ▲ APR 5551 [DDD]

LeBaron, Anne (hp)
Lebaron, A.:Dog–Gone Cat Act *(rec Context Studios, 1990)* — Mode ▲ Mode 42

LeBaron, Anne (hp/elec)
Lebaron, A.:I Am an American...My Government Will Reward You *(rec Harvestworks, 1994)* — Mode ▲ Mode 42
Lebaron, A.:Planxty Bowerbird — Mode ▲ 30

Lebedev, Igor (pno)
Liszt, F.:Con 1 Pno, w. A. Anichanov (cnd), St. Petersburg State SO — Audiophile Classics ▲ 101.044
Liszt, F.:Con 2 Pno, w. A. Anichanov (cnd), St. Petersburg State SO — Audiophile Classics ▲ 101.044
Liszt, F.:Totentanz, w. A. Anichanov (cnd), St. Petersburg State SO — Audiophile Classics ▲ 101.044

Lebrun, Eric (org)
Duruflé, M.:Prélude, Adagio et Choral varié sur le thème du *Veni Creator* *(rec Eglise Saint Antoine des Quinze–Vingts Paris, June & Oct. 1994)* — Naxos ▲ 8.553197 [DDD]
Duruflé, M.:Suite Org *(rec Eglise Saint Antoine des Quinze–Vingts Paris, June & Oct. 1994)* — Naxos ▲ 8.553197 [DDD]
Ropartz, G.:Choral Music, w. Christian Papis (nar), Didier Henry (bar), Vincent Le Texier (b–bar), Christine Lajarrige (pno), Irène Brissot (hp), M. Piquemal (cnd), Nancy SO, French Radio Chorus Soloists, Vittoria Regional French Choir—Psaume 136; Dimanche; Nocturne; Les Vêpres sonnent; Le Miracle de Saint Nicolas *(rec Salle Poirel, Nancy, Apr. 22–24, 1994)* — Marco Polo ▲ 8.223774 [DDD]

Lecaudey, Jean–Pierre (org)
Bonnal, J.–E.:Noël Landais — Pavane ▲ ADW 7357 [DDD]
Bonnal, J.–E.:Paysages Euskariens—La Vallée du Béhorléguy, au matin; Le Berger d'Ahusquy; Cloches dans le Ciel — Pavane ▲ ADW 7357 [DDD]
Bonnal, J.–E.:Paysage Landais — Pavane ▲ ADW 7357 [DDD]
Bonnal, J.–E.:Petite Rhap — Pavane ▲ ADW 7357 [DDD]
Bonnal, J.–E.:Reflets Solaires — Pavane ▲ ADW 7357 [DDD]
Bonnal, J.–E.:Symphonie pour Grand Orgue D'Après "Media Vita"—Assez lent, Calme, ler Mouvt; Lent, Calme, Vif, let Mouvt; Animé, Librement, Mouvt du début, Llarge — Pavane ▲ ADW 7357 [DDD]

Lechler, Hermann (pno)—see also ORCHESTRAS & ENSEMBLES New Munich Piano Trio, Bonaventura Ensemble
Arensky, A.:Trio 1 Pno, w. A. Lazar (vn), G. Zank (vc) *(rec Mar 23–26, 1992)* — Calig ▲ CAL 50913 [DDD]
Arensky, A.:Trio 2 Pno, w. A. Lazar (vn), G. Zank (vc) *(rec Mar 23–26, 1992)* — Calig ▲ CAL 50913 [DDD]
Loewe, C.:Ballads, w. J.–H. Rootering (bass)—Herr Oluf, Op. 2/2; Elvershöh, Op. 3/2; Graf Eberstein, Op. 9/VI:5; Die wandelnde Glocke, Op. 20/3; Harald, Op. 45/1; Das Erkennen, Op. 65/2; Der Pilgrim vor St. Just, Op. 99/3; Die verfallene Mühle, Op. 109; Odins Meeresritt, Op. 118; Archibald Douglas, Op. 128; Der Nöck, Op. 129/2 [G] — Calig ▲ CAL 50900 [DDD]
Schumann, R.:Liederkreis, Op. 24, w. J.–H. Rootering (bass) [G] — Calig ▲ CAL 50892 [DDD]
Schumann, R.:Songs, w. J.–H. Rootering (bass)—11 songs (Op. 89, Nos. 1–5 & Op. 98a, Nos. 3–6,8 & 9) [G] — Calig ▲ CAL 50892 [DDD]
Strauss, R.:Songs, w. J.–H. Rootering (bass)—18 songs (Opp. 10/1–5 & 8; 21/3; 27/1–4; 29/1–3; 32/1 & 2; 36/2; 47/5; 56/3) [G] — Calig ▲ CAL 50863 [DDD]
Wolf, H.:Songs (misc), w. J.–H. Rootering (bass)—Drei Gedichte von Michelangelo; 8 Eichendorff–Lieder; 8 Mörike–Lieder [G] — Calig ▲ CAL 50870 [DDD]

Leclair, Jacqueline (ob)
Gisberg:Music of, w. Christine Bard (perc), Christina Sun (erhu), Jeff O'Malley (nar), Quentin Chiappetta (sampler/pno/cpsr), Reuben Radding (bass instrument), Gisburg (voice/fl/cpsr)—Opening; No Stranger Not At All; Imaginary Movielandscape 1; Portrait; "Jowohl"; Mein Herz hat nicht vergessen [tango]; Ritual; Dying Takes Its Time; Fruits; Mic' N Drums — Tzadik ("The Composers" series) ▲ TZA 7007 [DDD]
Reynolds, R.:Summer Island — Neuma 2–▲ 450–91 [DDD]

LeClair, Judith (bn)
Barber, S.:Summer Music, w. Jeanne Baxtresser (fl), Joseph Robinson (ob), Stanley Drucker (cl), Philip Myers (hn) — EMI Classics ("Anglo–American Chamber Music" series) ▲ CDC 55400

Leclerc, Gerard (vc)
Brahms, J.:Son 2 Vc, w. M. Slatkine (pno) — Gallo ▲ CD 509
Schubert, Franz:Son Arpeggione, w. Muriel Slatkine (pno) — Gallo ▲ CD 509

INSTRUMENT.

Leclerc, Michelle (org)
Demessieux, J.:Org Music—Andante; Twelve Chorale Preludes; Répons pour le Temps de Pâques; Te Deum, Op. 11 — Motette ▲ CD 11671 [DDD]
Dupré, M.:Préludes & Fugues, Op. 7 — Motette ▲ CD 11671 [DDD]

Leclercq, J. (sax)
Gotkovsky, I.:Con Sax, w. N. Nozy (cnd), Belgian Guides Symphonic Band — René Gailly ▲ CD 87037 [DDD]

Le Corre, Pascal (pno)
Szymanowski, K.:Lullaby, w. Annick Roussin (vn) — Accord ▲ ACD 201122 [DDD]
Szymanowski, K.:Myths, w. Annick Roussin (vn) — Accord ▲ ACD 201122 [DDD]
Szymanowski, K.:Romance, w. Annick Roussin (vn) — Accord ▲ ACD 201122 [DDD]
Szymanowski, K.:Son Vn, w. Annick Roussin (vn) — Accord ▲ ACD 201122 [DDD]

Lécot, Jean-Paul (org)
Charpentier, M.-A.:Org Music—Noëls sur les instruments, H.534; Pour un reposoir, H.508; Six Preludes du Sixieme Ton; Suite du Premier Ton; Suite du Deuxieme Ton; Suite du Cinquieme Ton — Forlane ▲ FOR 16611

Lecuona, Réne (pno)
Ross, J.C.:Encore Vc, w. Craig Hultgren (vc) — Innova ▲ 502

Lederer, Doris (va)—see also ORCHESTRAS & ENSEMBLES Audubon String Quartet
Dohnányi, E. von:Serenade, w. David Salness (vn), Clyde Shaw (vc) *(rec LSU Recital Hall, Louisiana State Univ, Baton Rouge, July 23–25, 1995)* — Centaur ▲ CRC 2309 [DDD]

Ledger, Philip (org)
Charpentier, M.-A.:Te Deum in C, w. F. Lott (sop), I. Partridge (ten), S. Roberts (bar), P. Ledger (cnd), Academy of St. Martin in the Fields, King's College Choir Cambridge — EMI Classics ▲ CDM 63135
Lloyd Webber, W.S.:Arias, w. J. Graham-Hall (ten)—Arias:The King of Love & Thou Art the King, from cantatas *The Saviour* & *The Divine Compassion*; Songs—A rent for love; Utopia; Over the bridge; The pretty washer-maiden; So lovely the rose [E] — ASV ▲ ASV 584 [DDD]

Ledger, Philip (pno)
Britten, H.:Insect Pieces (2), w. S. Watkins (ob) — Meridian ▲ 84119
Britten, H.:Tit for Tat, w. J. Shirley-Quirk (bar) — Meridian ▲ 84119
Lloyd Webber, W.S.:Songs Ten & Pno, w. J. Graham-Hall (ten)—Arias:The King of Love & Thou Art the King, from cantatas *The Saviour* & *The Divine Compassion*; Songs—A rent for love; Utopia; Over the bridge; The pretty washer-maiden; So lovely the rose [E] — ASV ▲ ASV 584 [DDD]
Schubert, Franz:Winterreise, w. R. Tear (ten) — ASV Quicksilva ▲ QS 6085 [ADD]

Le Dizès, Maryvonne (vn)
Amy, G.:Trio Cl, w. Alain Damiens (cl), Pierre-Laurent Aimard (pno) — Adda ▲ ADD 581142 [DDD]
Bartók, B.:Contrasts, w. Alain Damiens (cl), Pierre-Laurent Aimard (pno) — Adda ▲ ADD 581142 [DDD]
Berg, A.:Adagio, w. Alain Damiens (cl), Pierre-Laurent Aimard (pno) — Adda ▲ ADD 581142 [DDD]
Paganini, N.:Cantabile, w. Marie-Thérèse Ghirardi (gtr) — Adès ▲ ADE 204732 [DDD]
Paganini, N.:Sons Vn & Gtr, w. Marie-Thérèse Ghirardi (gtr)—Opp. 2 & 3 — Adès ▲ ADE 204732 [DDD]
Stravinsky, I.:L'Histoire du soldat Suite Vn, w. Alain Damiens (cl), Pierre-Laurent Aimard (pno) — Adda ▲ ADD 581142 [DDD]

Lee, Cassandra (cl)—see ORCHESTRAS & ENSEMBLES Blair Woodwind Quintet

Lee, Chi-Fun (pno)
Boulanger, N.:Pieces (3) Vc & Pno, w. Nina Flyer (vc) — Koch International Classics ▲ KIC 7280 [DDD]

Lee, Christopher Collins (vn)
Glière, R.:The Red Poppy (suite), "Russian Sailors' Dance", w. Z. Macal (cnd), New Jersey SO *(rec State Theater, New Brunswick, NJ, Oct 23, 1995)* — Delos ▲ DE 3178 [DDD]

Lee, Gee (vn)—see ORCHESTRAS & ENSEMBLES Stanislas Ensemble

Lee, Jeffrey (vn)
Söderlundh, L.B.:Allegro Concertante, w. Kerstin Svensson (vn), T. Svedlund (cnd), Örebro CO — Intim Musik ▲ INT 36

Lee, Jina (vn)
Handel, D.:The Tyger, w. Mary Henderson (sop), Sara Lambert Bloom (ob), Gabrielle Robinson (vn), Rebecca Boughton (va), Deborah Netanel (vc), Mark Butler (pno), C. Zimmerman (cnd) — Vienna Modern Masters ▲ VMM 2019 [DDD]

Lee, Josephine (pno)
A Recital of Russian & Polish Songs, w. Alfred Orda (bar), Ernest Lush (pno) — Symposium ▲ SYM 1067

Lee, M. C. (pno)
Ravel, M.:Con in G Pno, w. A. Nanut (cnd), Ljubljana RSO — PMG ("Vienna Master" series) ▲ CD 160213 [DDD]

Lee, Marjorie (pno)
Brian Bowman, w. Brian Bowman (eup), Gordon Stout (mar) — Crystal ■ C393
Ross, W.:Partita Eup, w. B. Bowman (eup) — Crystal ■ C393
Saint-Saëns, C.:Album Pno — MD + G ▲ MDG 6040590 [DDD]
Saint-Saëns, C.:Études Pno, Op. 52 — MD + G ▲ MDG 6040590 [DDD]
Saint-Saëns, C.:Études Pno, Op. 111 — MD + G ▲ MDG 6040590 [DDD]
Schubert, Franz:Allegro Pno 4-Hands, D.947, w. C. Ivaldi (pno) — Arion 2-▲ ARN 268038 [AAD]
Shostakovich, D.:Son Vc, w. R. Thomas (vc) *(rec Weston, MA, Jan. 1993)* — Northeastern ▲ NOR 245 [DDD]

Lee, Mi-Kyung (vn)
International Menuhin Music Academy, w. International Menuhin Music Academy, Nora Chastain (vn), Paul Coletti (vn), Hu-Kun (vn), Alberto Lysy (vn) — Arcobaleno ▲ SBCD 4700 [DDD]

Lee, Noël (pno)
Bartók, B.:Contrasts, w. Michel Lethiec (cl), *(violinist unknown)* — Arion ▲ ARN 68327 [DDD]
Bartók, B.:Rhap Pno, w. L. Pfaff (cnd), Turin RAI Orch — Arion ▲ ARN 68250 [DDD]
Bartók, B.:Son in e Vn & Pno, w. S. Accardo (vn) *(rec live 1968)* — Dynamic ▲ CDS 110 [ADD]
Clásicos de las Américas, w. Margot Pares-Reyna (sop), Marcel Quillevéré (ten), Jesús Castro Balbi (gtr), Georges Rabol (pno), Erwartung Ensemble [cnd:Bernard Desgraupes], Jazzogène Orch [cnd:Jean-Luc Fillon] — Opus 111 6-▲ 2000
Debussy, C.:En blanc et noir, w. Benard Ringeissen (pno) — Astrée ▲ E 8568
Debussy, C.:Épigraphes antiques, w. Benard Ringeissen (pno) — Astrée ▲ E 8568
Debussy, C.:Lindaraja, w. Benard Ringeissen (pno) — Astrée ▲ E 8568
Debussy, C.:Petite suite, w. Benard Ringeissen (pno) — Astrée ▲ E 8568
Debussy, C.:Pno Music (complete solo), w. Werner Haas (pno)—Etudes; Suite Bergamasque; En blanc et noir; Petite Suite; others — Philips 2-▲ 438721-2
Debussy, C.:Pno Music (complete duet), w. C. Ivaldi (pno)—Andante; Diane; Divertissement; En Blanc et Noir; L'Enfant prodigue; 6 Épigraphes antiques; Intermezzo; Lindaraja; Marche écossaise; La Mer; Petite Suite; Prélude à l'après-midi d'un faune; Printemps; Symphony in b; Triomphe de Bacchus *(rec 1/90)* — Arion 2-▲ ARN 268128 [DDD]
Debussy, C.:Son Vn, w. G. Poulet (vn) — Arion ▲ ARN 68228 [DDD]
Duparc, H.:Songs, w. B. Kruysen (bar)—L'Invitation au voyage; Sérénade Florentine; La Voyage et la Cloche; Extase; Chanson Triste; Lamento; Testament; Phidylé; Soupir; Le Manoir de Rosemonde; Elegie; La Vie Antérieure; Au Pays où se fait la Guerre — Valois ▲ V 4703
Duparc, H.:Songs, w. M. Mahe (mez), V. Le Texier (bar) — Pierre Verany ▲ PVY 793061 [DDD]
Dvořák, A.:From the Bohemian Forest, w. C. Ivaldi (pno) — Arion ▲ ARN 68014 [AAD]
Dvořák, A.:Legends, Op. 59, w. C. Ivaldi (pno) — Arion ▲ ARN 68014 [AAD]
French Music for Flute & Piano, w. Kurt Redel (fl) — Arion ▲ ARN 68238 [AAD]
Hindemith, P.:Son for 2 Pnos, w. Christian Ivaldi (pno) — Arion ▲ ARN 68319
Kuhlau, F.:Duos brillants, w. Kurt Redel (fl) — Etcetera ▲ KTC 1189
Kuhlau, F.:Intro & Rondo on "Ah! quand il gèle" from *Le Colporteur*, w. Kurt Redel (fl) — Etcetera ▲ KTC 1189
Massenet, J.:Songs, w. Bernard Kruysen (bar)—11 songs [F] — Arion ▲ ARN 68009 [AAD]
Pierné, G.:Son Vn, w. G. Poulet (vn) — Arion ▲ ARN 68228 [DDD]
Poulenc, F.:Songs, w. B. Kruysen (bar) — Arion ▲ ARN 68258 [DDD]
Ravel, M.:Berceuse sur le nom de Gabriel Fauré, w. Clara Bonaldi (vn) — Adda ▲ ADD 581065 [DDD]
Ravel, M.:Son Vn Pno, w. G. Poulet (vn) — Arion ▲ ARN 68228 [DDD]
Ravel, M.:Sonate posthume, w. Clara Bonaldi (vn) — Adda ▲ ADD 581065 [DDD]

Lee, Noël (pno) (cont.)
Ravel, M.:Songs, w. B. Kruysen (bar)—Histoires naturelles; Un grand sommeil noir; Ronsard à son ame; Rêves; Cinq mélodies populaires grecques; Deux mélodies hébraïques; Sainte; Don Quichotte à Dulcinée — Valois ▲ V4700
Ravel, M.:Trio Pno, w. Clara Bonaldi (vn), Yvan Chiffoleau (vc) — Adda ▲ ADD 581065 [DDD]
Saint-Saëns, C.:Caprice arabe, w. C. Ivaldi (pno) — Arion ▲ ARN 68011 [AAD]
Saint-Saëns, C.:Caprice héroïque, w. C. Ivaldi (pno) — Arion ▲ ARN 68011 [AAD]
Saint-Saëns, C.:Polonaise for 2 Pnos, w. C. Ivaldi (pno) — Arion ▲ ARN 68011 [AAD]
Saint-Saëns, C.:Scherzo for 2 Pnos, w. C. Ivaldi (pno) — Arion ▲ ARN 68011 [AAD]
Saint-Saëns, C.:Variations on a Theme of Beethoven, w. C. Ivaldi (pno) — Arion ▲ ARN 68011 [AAD]
Schnittke, A.:Madrigals Sop, w. A. Lazarev (cnd), Bolshoi Theater SO Soloists — Vox Box 2-▲ CDX 5121 [ADD]
Schubert, Franz:Divertissement sur des motifs originaux français, D.823, w. C. Ivaldi (pno) — Arion 2-▲ ARN 268038 [AAD]
Schubert, Franz:Fant Pno, D.940, w. C. Ivaldi (pno) — Arion 2-▲ ARN 268038 [AAD]
Schubert, Franz:Fant Vn, D.934, w. J.-L. Poulet (vn) — Arion 2-▲ ARN 268006 [AAD]
Schubert, Franz:Intro & Vars Fl on "Tröckne Blumen", w. Jean-Louis Beaumadier (fl) — Approche ▲ 6209
Schubert, Franz:Ländler Pno, D.814, w. C. Ivaldi (pno) — Arion 2-▲ ARN 268038 [AAD]
Schubert, Franz:Ov Pno, D.675, w. C. Ivaldi (pno) — Arion 2-▲ ARN 268038 [AAD]
Schubert, Franz:Pno Music (4-hands), w. C. Ivaldi (pno) — Arion 2-▲ ARN 268038 [AAD]
Schubert, Franz:Rondo Vn, D.895, w. G. Poulet (vn) — Arion 2-▲ ARN 268006 [AAD]
Schubert, Franz:Son Arpeggione, w. Jean-Louis Beaumadier (fl) [arr for fl & pno] — Approche ▲ 6209
Schubert, Franz:Son Pno 4-Hands, D.812, w. C. Ivaldi (pno) — Arion 2-▲ ARN 268038 [AAD]
Schubert, Franz:Son Vn, D.574, w. G. Poulet (vn) — Arion 2-▲ ARN 268006 [AAD]
Schubert, Franz:Sonatinas Vn, w. G. Poulet (vn) — Arion 2-▲ ARN 268006 [AAD]
Schubert, Franz:Sonatina Vn, D.385, w. Jean-Louis Beaumadier (fl) [arr for fl & pno] — Approche ▲ 6209
Schubert, Franz:Vars on an Original Theme Pno 4-Hands, w. C. Ivaldi (pno) — Arion 2-▲ ARN 268038 [AAD]
Stravinsky, I.:Music of, w. G. Poulet (vn) [music for vn & pno & trans. Stravinsky & others]—Danse Russe; Firebird (3 movements); Le rossignol (2 selections); Chanson Russe; Tango; Fairy's Kiss (2 selections); Pastoralle; Duo Concertant *(rec 9/88)* — Arion ▲ ARN 68062 [DDD]
Stravinsky, I.:Pétrouchka, w. C. Ivaldi (pno) [2-piano version] — Arion ▲ ARN 68041 [DDD]
Stravinsky, I.:Le Sacre du printemps Orch, w. C. Ivaldi (pno) [2-pno ver.] — Arion ▲ ARN 68041 [DDD]

Lee, P.H. (vn)
Harty, H.:The Londonderry Air — Chandos ("Collect" series) ▲ CHAN 6583 [ADD]

Lee, R. (tpt)
Baksa, R.:Earth Elegy, w. M. Vines (pno) *(rec Brooklyn College, Apr. 1993 & May 1994)* — Capstone ▲ CPS 8620 [DDD]
Baksa, R.:Son Tpt, w. M. Vines (pno) *(rec Brooklyn College, Apr. 1993 & May 1994)* — Capstone ▲ CPS 8620 [DDD]
Cohen, A.:Song of Myself, w. A. Cohen (pno) *(rec Brooklyn College, Apr. 1993 & May 1994)* — Capstone ▲ CPS 8620 [DDD]
Cohen, A.:Wings of Desire, w. A. Cohen (pno) *(rec Brooklyn College, Apr. 1993 & May 1994)* — Capstone ▲ CPS 8620 [DDD]
Kirby, P.:Son Tpt, w. S. Graff (pno) *(rec Brooklyn College, Apr. 1993 & May 1994)* — Capstone ▲ CPS 8620 [DDD]

Lee, S. Y. (fl)
Daugherty, M.:Mxyzptlk, w. J. Bogorad (fl), M. Singher (cnd), Oberlin CO — Opus One ▲ 138

Lee, Sun-Jung (pno)
Sauguet, H.:Ballade Vc, w. Sook-Jung Lee (vc) — Sonpact ▲ SPT 96017 [DDD]

Lee, Sook-Jung (vc)
Sauguet, H.:Ballade Vc, w. Sun-Jung Lee (pno) — Sonpact ▲ SPT 96017 [DDD]

Leek, Anne (ob)
Beethoven, L. van:Qnt Pno, Ob, Cl, Hn & Bn, w. C. Eschenbach (pno), J. Moog (cl), S. Scott (hn), U. Freund (bn) — Signum ▲ X 06-00
Mozart, W.A.:Qnt Pno, K.452, w. C. Eschenbach (pno), J. Moog (cl), S. Scott (hn), U. Freund (bn) — Signum ▲ X 06-00

Leenders, Christian (perc)—see ORCHESTRAS & ENSEMBLES Percussive Rotterdam
Leenders, Hans (perc)—see ORCHESTRAS & ENSEMBLES Percussive Rotterdam
Leenhouts, Paul (rcr)—see ORCHESTRAS & ENSEMBLES Amsterdam Loeki Stardust Quartet
Leertouwer, Johannes (vn)—see also ORCHESTRAS & ENSEMBLES Schönbrunn Ensemble Amsterdam, Senario Ensemble, Camerata Trajectina
Bach, J.S.:Sons Vn, w. M. van Delft (hpd)—BWV 1014–1019; in G, BWV 1019a [2 older versions] *(rec Jan 1992)* — Globe 2-▲ GLO 6008 [DDD]
Haydn, J.:Diverts Fl, Vn & Vc, w. Marten Root (fl), Viola de Hoog (vc)—H.IV/6–11; Op. 11/2 & 5 *(rec Utrecht, Nov. 1994)* — Globe ▲ GLO 5131 [DDD]
Schumann, R.:Sons Vn (comp), w. Julian Reynolds (pno) *(rec Utrecht, 1995)* — Globe ▲ GLO 5140 [DDD]

Lees, Timothy (va)
Thofanidis, C.:Qt 1 Strs, w. Adrian Justus (vn), Maria Lin (vn), James Holland (vc) — Albany ▲ TROY 158 [DDD]

Leeuw, Reinbert de (pno)
Antheil, G.:Son 1 Vn, w. Vera Beths (vn) — Montaigne ▲ MO 782022 [DDD]
Antheil, G.:Son 2 Vn, w. Vera Beths (vn) — Montaigne ▲ MO 782022 [DDD]
Antheil, G.:Son 4 Vn, w. Vera Beths (vn) — Montaigne ▲ MO 782022 [DDD]
Messiaen, O.:Visions de l'Amen, w. Maarten Bon (pno) — Montaigne ▲ MO 782050
Satie, E.:Gnossiennes Pno — Philips ▲ 446672-2
Satie, E.:Gymnopédies — Philips ▲ 446672-2
Satie, E.:Ogives Pno — Philips ▲ 446672-2
Satie, E.:Petite ouverture à danser — Philips ▲ 446672-2
Satie, E.:Pno Music (comp)—Early works — Philips ▲ 412243-2 [ADD]
Satie, E.:Pno Music (misc)—Quatre Préludes; Sonneries de la Rose-Croix; Première Pensée de la Rose-Croix; Prélude de "La Porte Héroïque du Cie"; Prière; Le Fils des Etoiles; Danses Gothiques — Philips ▲ 454 048-2
Satie, E.:Sarabandes Pno — Philips ▲ 446672-2
Ustvolskaya, G.:Duet Vn, w. Vera Beths (vn) *(rec De Vereeniging, Nijmegen, Oct. 5 & 6, 1991)* — Hat Hut ("NOW." series) ▲ hat ART CD 6115 [DDD]
Ustvolskaya, G.:Son 5 Pno *(rec De Vereeniging, Nijmegen, Oct. 5 & 6, 1991)* — Hat Hut ("NOW." series) ▲ hat ART CD 6115 [DDD]
Ustvolskaya, G.:Trio Cl, w. Vera Beths (vn), Harmen de Boer (cl) *(rec De Vereeniging, Nijmegen, Oct. 5 & 6, 1991)* — Hat Hut ("NOW." series) ▲ hat ART CD 6115 [DDD]

Leeuwen, Peter van (pno)
Scarlatti, D.:Sons Kbd—K.9, 24, 27, 69, 132, 141, 184, 185, 208, 263, 466, 476, 491, 531 — Erasmus ▲ WVH 137

Lefébure, Yvonne (pno)
Mozart, W.A.:Con 20 Pno, w. P. Casals (cnd), Perpignan Festival Orch *(rec June 17, 1951)* — Sony Classical ▲ SMK 66570 [ADD]

Lefebvre, Philippe (org)
Dupré, M.:Les vêpres de la Vierge, w. David Hill (org), Mary Berry (cnd), Schola Gregoriana — Herald ▲ HAVPCD 170

Lefevre, Alain (pno)
Corigliano, J.:Con Pno, w. C. St. Clair (cnd), Pacific SO — Koch International Classics ▲ KIC 7250 [DDD]

Lefkowitz, Mischa (vn)
Bartók, B.:Rhaps (2) Vn & Orch, w. Brent McMunn (pno)—No. 1 — Cambria ▲ 1029 [DDD]
Bloch, E.:Baal Shem, "3 Pictures of Chassidic Life", w. Brent McMunn (pno) — Cambria ▲ 1029 [DDD]
Debussy, C.:Son Vn, w. Brent McMunn (pno) — Cambria ▲ 1029 [DDD]
Diciedue, R.:Con Vn, w. D. Amos (cnd), Polish National RSO Katowice *(rec June 1990)* — Cambria ▲ CD 1064 [DDD]

Lefkowitz, Mischa (vn) (cont.)
Fauré, G.:Con Vn, w. D. Amos (cnd), Polish National RSO Katowice *(rec June 1990)* Cambria ▲ CD 1064 [DDD]
Lopatnikoff, N.:Pieces Vn & Pno, w. N. Kaplan Solomon (pno) Laurel ▲ LR 846
Lopatnikoff, N.:Son 2 Vn, w. N. Kaplan Solomon (pno) Laurel ▲ LR 846
Sibelius, J.:Con Vn, w. D. Amos (cnd), Polish National RSO Katowice *(rec June 1990)* Cambria ▲ CD 1064 [DDD]
Virtuoso Violin Classics, w. Brent McMunn (pno) *(rec 1/87)* Cambria ▲ CD 1029 [DDD]
Ysaÿe, E.:Caprice after Saint-Saëns' "Etude en forme de valse", w. B. McMunn (pno) Cambria ▲ 1029 [DDD]

Lefkowitz, Ronan (vn)—see also ORCHESTRAS & ENSEMBLES Collage New Music Ensemble, Hawthorne String Quartet
Dohnányi, E. von:Qnt 2 Pno, w. A. Wolf (pno), C. Lieberman (vn), M. Thompson (va), D. Finch (vc) AFKA ▲ SK 503
Ives, C.:Trio Pno, w. G. Kalish (pno), Yo-Yo Ma (vc) *(rec June 15–19, 1992)* Sony Classical ▲ SK 53126 [DDD]

Le Floch, Hervé (vn)
Vivaldi, A.:Cons Vn, Op. 8/1–4, "The Four Seasons", w. J.-C. Hartemann (cnd), French Soloists Calliope ▲ CAL 6629 [ADD]

Lefor, Peter (vn)
Bartók, B.:Duos (44), w. M. Mumelter (vn) Koch Schwann ▲ CD 310 054 [ADD]

LeGassick, Damian (Fender Rhodes)
Andriessen, L.:Hoketus, w. Katherine Pendry (panpipes), James Poke (panpipes), Evan Ziporyn (a sax), Richard Craig (a sax), Steven Schick (congas), Amy Knoles (congas), Lisa Moore (Fender Rhodes), Cees van Zeeland (pno), Gerard Bouwhuis (pno), Robert Black (bass gtr), Mark Stewart (bass gtr) *(rec Air Recording Studios, Lyndhurst Hall, Hampstead, London, June 29–July 3, 1994)* Sony Classical ▲ SK 66483 [DDD]

Legé, Fabienne (hp)
Gerber, R.:Son Hp Gallo ▲ CD 861 [ADD]

Legge, Anthony (pno)
Brahms, J.:Ernste Gesänge, w. L. Finnie (mez)—Nos. 1–4 [G] Chandos ▲ CHAN 8786 [DDD]
Brahms, J.:Songs, Op. 91, w. L. Finnie (mez), J. Harrington (va) [G] Chandos ▲ CHAN 8786 [DDD]
Schumann, R.:Frauenliebe und -leben, w. L. Finnie (mez) [G] Chandos ▲ CHAN 8786 [DDD]
Songs of the British Isles, w. Linda Finnie (mez) Chandos ▲ CHAN 8749 [DDD]

Legrand, Michel (hpd)
Legrand, M.:Film Music, w. Catherine Michel (hp), M. Legrand (cnd), Large SO—Suite for Hp & Orch [from The Umbrellas of Cherbourg]; Concertino for Hp & Orch [from The Summer of '42]; Suite for Hp, Hpd & Orch [from Le Messager]; Suite for Hp, Hpd & Orch [from Yentl] Travelling ("Movies & Music" series) ▲ K 1020

Legrand, Michel (pno)
Satie, E.:Pno Music (misc)—Sonatine Bureaucratique [Office Sonata]; 3 Gymnopedies; Caresse; Préludes flasques pour un chien [Really Floppy Preludes for a Dog]; Caresse; Jack in the box; 2 Reveries Nocturnes [Dreams in the Night]; 6 Pieces de la periode 1906–1913; Chapitres tourné en tous sens [Chapters in all Directions]; Avant-Dernières Pensées [Before the Last Thought]; Sports et Divertissements Erato ▲ 4509-92857-2 ■ 4509-92857-4

LeGuay, Claire Marie (pno)
L'Alto Romantique [The Romantic Viola], w. Laurent Verney (va) Pierre Verany ▲ 793121 [DDD]

LeGuin, Elisabeth (vc)—see ORCHESTRAS & ENSEMBLES Musica Pacifica

Lehan, Fritz (hpd)
Haydn, J.:Die Schöpfung, w. Jeannette van Dijck (sop), Peter Schreier (ten), Theo Adam (bass), Hans Plumacher (vc), Heinz Detering (db), G. Wand (cnd), Cologne Gürzenich Orch, Cologne Gürzenich Chorus Accord 2-▲ ACD 200422 [AAD]

Lehman, C. (org)
Handel, G.F.:Cons (16) Org, w. A. Manze (cnd), Cologne La Stravaganza *(rec Feb. 6–9, 1992)* Denon ▲ CO 79943 [DDD]

Lehmann, A.-C. (vl/rcr)—see ORCHESTRAS & ENSEMBLES Isabella D'Este

Lehmann, Jeanne (org)
Lehmann, H.U.:Son da chiesa, w. H. Schneeberger (vn) *(rec Aug. 12, 1978)* Grammont ▲ CTS P 4-2

Lehmann, M. (va)
Raff, J.:Octet Strs, w. B. Langbein (vn), R. Reichel, Zurich Chamber Players *(rec 1978)* Jecklin-Disco ▲ JD 547-2 [ADD]
Spohr, L.:Double Qt 1, w. B. Langbein (vn), R. Reichel, Zurich Chamber Players *(rec 1978)* Jecklin-Disco ▲ JD 547-2 [ADD]

Lehmann, Patrick (tpt)—see also ORCHESTRAS & ENSEMBLES Quatuor de cuivres Novus
Ducommun, S.:Org Music, w. S. Ducommun (org), R. Märki (org), J. Molnar (hn), P.-A. Monot (tpt)—10 Invocations for Organ; Sonata da Chiesa for Horn & Organ; Sonata da Chiesa for 2 Trumpets & Organ; Variations on a Theme by François Nadler for Organ *(rec 1959, 1985 & 1991)* Gallo ▲ CD655
Ducommun, S.:Petit Concert, w. D. Streit (cnt), J. Henry (trbn) Gallo ▲ CD 654 [DDD]

Lehmann, U. (vn)
Flury, R.:Con 1 Vn, w. U.J. Flury (cnd), Czech SO *(rec Filmové Studio, Prague, May 21, 1993)* Gallo ▲ CD 865 [DDD]
Vogel, W.:Sonances, w. H. Peter-Indermühle (fl), H. Elhorst (ob), K. Weber (cl), I. Backer (bn), K. Hanke (hn), L. Dober (vn), H. Forster (va), M. Liechti (vc), R. Tschupp (cnd) Grammont ▲ CTSP 14-2 [ADD]

Lehmann, V. (pno)
Stavenhagen, B.:Con 2 Pno, w. H.-R. Förster (cnd), Vogtland PO Greiz/Reichenbach ebs ▲ ebs 6079 [DDD]

Lehner, E. (vn)—see ORCHESTRAS & ENSEMBLES Kolisch String Quartet

Lehotka, Gábor (org)
Bach, J.S.:Org Music (misc), w. H. Kästner (org)—Chorales, BWV.614, 622, 683, 703 & 727; Fantasie & Fugue, BWV.561; Fugue, BWV.578; Praeludium & Fugue, BWV.542 & 552; Toccata & Fugue, BWV.565 LaserLight ▲ 15507 [ADD]
Handel, G.F.:Cons (16) Org, w. K. Botvay (cnd), Budapest Strings—Op. 4/2, 4 & 5 & Op. 7/4 LaserLight ▲ 15 629 [DDD]
Silent Night, w. Imre Kovacs (fl), Hedy Lubik (hp), Ferenc Gergely (org), Frigyes Hidas (org), Hungarian State Orch CO, Csanyi (cnd), Szekeres (cnd), Budapest Children's Choir Madrigal Choir Hungaroton ▲ HCD 16598

Lehrendorfer, Franz (org)
Baroque Trombone & Brass, w. Armin Rosin (trbn), Stuttgart Phil Brass Hänssler Classic ▲ 98.985 [AAD]
Trombone & Organ, w. Armin Rosin (trbn) Koch Schwann ▲ SCH 310992 [DDD]

Lehrer, P. A. (pno)
Rahbee, D.G.:Mosaic, w. E. B. Barton (pno) *(rec The Music Room)* Seda ▲ 333 [DDD]
Rahbee, D.G.:Son 2 Pno *(rec The Music Room)* Seda ▲ 333 [DDD]

Lehrman, Leonard (pno)
Blitzstein, M.:Songs, w. R. Edwards (ten), H. Williams (bar)—songs & scenes from Reuben, Reuben [1955], Jane Pickens Show (title theme) [1949], Goloopchik [1946], Idiots First [1962], Juno [1957], New York Opera [1941], No For An Answer [1941], Parade [1935], Sacco & Vanzetti [1959] Premier ▲ PRCD 1005 [DDD]

Lehrmann, Sabina (vc)
Orff, C.:Schulwerk (complete), w. Godela Orff (nar), Marina Koppelstetter (mez), Carolin Widmann (vn), Markus Zahnhausen (rcr), Karl Peinkofer Percussion Ensemble—4 Pieces for Xylophone; 5 Little Canons; 4 Dance Pieces; Songs & Instrumental Pieces; 3 Pieces for Fl & Perc; Songs & Dances; 2 Time Change Dances for Vn & Vc; 7 Folk Dances; Music for the Night *(rec Munich, 1994–95)* Celestial Harmonies ▲ 13104-2

Lehrndorfer, Franz (hpd)
Bach, J.S.:Cons for 3 Hpds (comp), w. M. Galling (hpd), H. Bilgram (hpd), G. Kehr (cnd), Mainz CO Vox Box 2-▲ CDX 5040
Bach, J.S.:Con for 4 Hpds, w. M. Galling (hpd), H. Bilgram (hpd), K.-H. Stolze (hpd), G. Kehr (cnd), Mainz CO Vox Box 2-▲ CDX 5040

Lehrndorfer, Franz (org)
Bach Trumpet Gala, Vol. 1, w. Peter Epp (baroque tpt), Arnold Mehl (baroque tpt), Rudolf Ulrich (baroque tpt), Munich Bach Trumpet Ensemble Ars Musici ▲ 0869
Bach, J.S.:Org Music (misc)—Prelude & Fugue in c, BWV 546; Choralvorspiel Ervarm' dich mein, o Herre Gott, BWV 721; Fugue in c, BWV 575; Fant in G, BWV 572 Calig ▲ CAL 50831
Bach, J.S.:Toccata & Fugue Org, BWV 565 [the Cathedral Organ at Munich] *(rec 1979)* Calig ▲ CAL 50472 [ADD]
Celestial Christmas 5 *(rec May & June 1994)* Celestial Harmonies ▲ 13090 [DDDD]
The Concert *(rec Dome, Munich, June & July 1994)* Celestial Harmonies ▲ 13109-2
Die heitere Orgel [The Merry Organ] *(rec 1968)* Calig ▲ CAL 50415 [ADD]
Lehrndorfer, F.:Org Music [Cathedral Organ at Munich]—Intro, Var & Fugue *(rec 1979)* Calig ▲ CAL 50472 [ADD]
Liszt, F.:Prelude & Fugue on the name B-A-C-H [Cathedral Organ at Munich] *(rec 1979)* Calig ▲ CAL 50472 [ADD]
Neufville, J.J. de:Org Music—Aria & 5 Vars Calig ▲ CAL 50831
The New Munich Cathedral Organ:Improvisations *(rec Liebfrauendom, June 1994)* Calig ▲ CAL 50944 [DDD]
Organ Music from Benedictine Abbey Calig ▲ CAL 50831
Reger, M.:Chorale Fants, Op. 52 [organ at the Eichstätt Cathedral]—No. 2 *(rec May 2–5, 1988)* Calig ▲ CAL 50877
Reger, M.:Pieces Org, Op. 59 [Organ at the Eichstätt Cathedral]—Nos. 8 & 9 *(rec May 2–5, 1988)* Calig ▲ CAL 50877
Reger, M.:Pieces Org, Op. 145 [Organ at the Eichstätt Cathedral]—No. 3 *(rec May 2–5, 1988)* Calig ▲ CAL 50877
Reger, M.:Son 2 Org [Organ at the Eichstätt Cathedral] *(rec May 2–5, 1988)* Calig ▲ CAL 50877
Spergher, I.:Son Org Calig ▲ CAL 50831

Lehtonen, Maija (org)
Bossi, M.E.:Org Music MD + G ("Gold" series) ▲ MDG 3200545 [DDD]
Organ Music in Finland MD + G ▲ O 3387 [DDD]

Lehwalder, Hedi (hp)
Ravel, M.:Intro & Allegro, w. Richard Stoltzman (cl), James Galway (fl), Tokyo String Quartet RCA Red Seal ▲ 09026-62552-2

Lei, Franklin (lt)
Weiss, S.L.:Lt Music—Sons. in C & A, Dresden Nos. 11 & 17; Partita in d [Moscow manuscript] *(rec Sept. 24–26, 1989)* Naxos ▲ 8.550470 [DDD]

Leibur, Arvo (va)
Tubin, E.:Vn & Pno Music, w. V. Rumessen (pno)—Ballade (1939); Capriccio No. 1 (1937/1971); Capriccio No. 2 (1945); The Cock's Dance (1957–8); Meditation (1938); Prelude (1944); Sonata No. 1 (1934–36/1968–9); Sonata No. 2 (1949); Suite on Estonian Dances (1943); Three Pieces (1933) BIS 2-▲ CD 541/42 [DDD]

Leibur, Arvo (vn)
Tubin, E.:Vn Music—Sonata (1962); Suite of Estonian Dance Tunes (1979) BIS 2-▲ CD 541/42 [DDD]

Leichner, Emil (pno)
Martinů, B.:Cons Pno (comp) Supraphon ▲ SUP 111313 [DDD]
Martinů, B.:Pno Music (comp)—Les Marionettes [14 miniatures for piano] (1912–14); Etudes & Polkas [16 pieces in 3 books] (1945); Sonata No. 1 (1954); Fantaisie & Toccata (1940); Les Papillons [Butterflies and Birds of Paradise] (1920); Trois Danses Tchéques; Sept Danses Tchéques (1929); Trois Esquisses (1927); Huit Préludes (1929); Les Ritournelles (1932); Esquisses de Danses (1932); Fenêtre sur le Jardin (1938) Supraphon 3-▲ 11 1010-2 [DDD]
Smetana, B.:Czech Dances Panton ▲ PAN 811337

Leifer, Lyon (fl)
Bloch, E.:Suite modale, w. D. Schrader (pno) *(rec June 2 & 3, 1992)* Centaur ▲ CRC 2140 [DDD]

Leighton, Alan (hn)—see ORCHESTRAS & ENSEMBLES Westphalia PO Chamber Ensemble

Leiman, C. (vn)
Klein, G.:Fant & Fugue, w. M. Kugel (vn), O. Shiran (vn), F. Nemirovsky (vc) *(rec June 21, July 5 & 20, 199)* Koch International Classics ▲ KIC 7230-2 [DDD]

Leiner, Peter (tpt)
Arnold, M.:Qnt Brass, w. Uwe Zaiser (tpt), Sjön Scott (hn), Jochen Scheerer (posaune), Ralf Rudolph (tuba) Bayer ▲ BR 100251 [DDD]
Crespo, E.:Suite Americana 1, w. Uwe Zaiser (tpt), Sjön Scott (hn), Jochen Scheerer (posaune), Ralf Rudolph (tuba) Bayer ▲ BR 100251 [DDD]
Ewald, V.:Qnt 1 Brass, w. Uwe Zaiser (tpt), Sjön Scott (hn), Jochen Scheerer (trbn), Ralf Rudolph (tuba) Bayer ▲ BR 100251 [DDD]
Horovitz, J.:Music Hall Suite, w. Uwe Zaiser (tpt), Sjön Scott (hn), Jochen Scheerer (posaune), Ralf Rudolph (tuba) Bayer ▲ BR 100251 [DDD]
Koetsier, J.:Qnt Brass, w. Uwe Zaiser (tpt), Sjön Scott (hn), Jochen Scheerer (posaune), Ralf Rudolph (tuba) Bayer ▲ BR 100251 [DDD]

Leisenring, John (trbn)—see ORCHESTRAS & ENSEMBLES Missouri Brass Quintet

Leister, Karl (cl)—see also ORCHESTRAS & ENSEMBLES Berlin Philharmonic Wind Ensemble
Bärmann, H.J.:Adagio Cl Str Qt, w. Vienna String Quartet Camerata ("After Hours Classics" series) ▲ 20 CM 424 [DDD]
Beethoven, L. van:Duos, WoO 27, w. Milan Turkovic (bn)—in B♭ *(rec Studio Baumgarten, Vienna, June 30–July 1, 1994)* Camerata ▲ 30CM 370 [DDD]
Brahms, J.:Qnt Cl, w. Berlin Soloists Teldec ▲ 2292-46429-2 [DDD]
Brahms, J.:Qnt Cl, w. Vermeer String Quartet Orfeo ▲ 068831 [DDD]
Brahms, J.:Qnt Cl, w. Amadeus String Quartet Deutsche Grammophon 3-▲ 419875-2 [ADD]
Brahms, J.:Qnt Cl, w. Vienna String Quartet—Adagio movt Camerata ("After Hours Classics" series) ▲ 20 CM 424 [DDD]
Brahms, J.:Sons Cl (comp), w. G. Oppitz (pno) Orfeo ▲ 086841 ■ 086841
Crusell, B.H.:Con 1 Cl, w. O. Vänskä (cnd), Lahti SO BIS ▲ CD 345
Crusell, B.H.:Con 2 Cl, w. O. Vänskä (cnd), Lahti SO BIS ▲ CD 345
Crusell, B.H.:Con 3 Cl, w. O. Vänskä (cnd), Lahti SO BIS ▲ CD 345
Crusell, B.H.:Qnt Cl, w. Prazak String Quartet Orfeo ▲ 141861 [DDD]
Crusell, B.H.:Qnt Cl, w. Vienna String Quartet—Romanze cantabile movt Camerata ("After Hours Classics" series) ▲ 20 CM 424 [DDD]
Debussy, C.:Première rapsodie, w. Ferenc Bognar (pno) *(rec Vienna, June & Dec 1995)* Camerata ▲ 30 CM 415 [DDD]
Françaix, J.:Theme & Vars Cl, w. Ferenc Bognar (pno) *(rec Vienna, June & Dec 1995)* Camerata ▲ 30 CM 415 [DDD]
Gade, N.W.:Fantasistykker, w. Ferenc Bognar (pno) Camerata ▲ 30CM 370
Glinka, M.:Trio pathétique, w. Milan Turkovic (bn), Ferenc Bognar (pno) *(rec Studio Baumgarten, Vienna, June 30–July 1, 1994)* Camerata ▲ 30CM 370 [DDD]
Hindemith, P.:Kleine Kammermusik, w. Wolfgang Schulz (fl), Hansjörg Schellenberger (ob), Günter Högner (hn), Milan Turkovic (bn) Sony Classical ▲ SK 64400
Hindemith, P.:Son Cl, w. Ferenc Bognar (pno) Camerata ▲ 30CM 358 [DDD]
Mendelssohn, F.:Concert Pieces, w. Milan Turkovic (bn)—No. 2 *(rec Studio Baumgarten, Vienna, June 30–July 1, 1994)* Camerata ▲ 30CM 370 [DDD]
Mercadante, S.:Con in B♭ Cl, Op. 101, w. K. Toyoda (cnd), Gunma SO *(rec Gunma Music Center, Takasaki, Japan, Apr 1980)* Camerata 2-▲ 25 CM 323/4 [DDD]
Milhaud, D.:Son Cl, w. Ferenc Bognar (pno) *(rec Vienna, June & Dec 1995)* Camerata ▲ 30 CM 415 [DDD]
Mozart, W.A.:Adagio Cls, K.411, w. P. Geisler (cl), H.R. Stalder (bas hn), H. Hofer (bas hn), E. Schmid (bas hn) *(rec 1978)* Jecklin-Disco ▲ JD 549-2 [ADD]
Mozart, W.A.:Adagio E Hn, w. H.R. Stalder (bas hn), H. Hofer (bas hn), E. Schmid (bas hn) [arr. Raymond Meylan for clarinet & basset horn] *(rec 1978)* Jecklin-Disco ▲ JD 549-2 [ADD]
Mozart, W.A.:Con Cl, w. H. von Karajan (cnd), Berlin PO EMI Classics ▲ CDM 64355 [ADD]

INSTRUMENT.

Leister, Karl (cl) (cont.)
Mozart, W.A.:Con Cl, w. N. Marriner (cnd), Academy of St. Martin in the Fields Philips ▲ 422390-2 [DDD]
Mozart, W.A.:Con Cl, w. K. Toyoda (cnd), Gunma SO *(rec Gunma Music Center, Takasaki, Japan, Apr 1980)* Camerata 2-▲ 25 CM 323/4 [DDD]
Mozart, W.A.:Qnt Cl, K.581, w. Berlin Soloists Teldec ▲ 2292-46429-2 [DDD]
Mozart, W.A.:Qnt Cl, K.581, w. Prazak String Quartet Orfeo ▲ 141861 [DDD]
Mozart, W.A.:Qnt Cl, K.581, w. Vienna String Quartet—Larghetto movt Camerata ("After Hours Classics" series) ▲ 20 CM 424 [DDD]
Mozart, W.A.:Qnt Cl, K.581, w. Philharmonia String Quartet *(rec Studio Baumgarten, Vienna, Mar. 1981)* Camerata ▲ 25CM 331 [DDD]
Mozart, W.A.:Qnts Cl Bas Hn, w. Philharmonia String Quartet—in B♭ *(rec Jesus Christ Church, Berlin Oct. 1988)* Camerata ▲ 25CM 331 [DDD]
Mozart, W.A.:Sons Vn Pno (misc), w. H.R. Stalder (pno)—K.378 [Duo in B for 2 Clarinets] *(rec 1978)* Jecklin-Disco ▲ JD 549-2 [ADD]
Mozart, W.A.:Trio Cl, K.498, w. C. Schiller (va), C. Ivaldi (pno) Tudor ▲ TUD 798 [DDD]
Poulenc, F.:Son Cl Bn, w. Milan Turkovic (bn) Camerata ▲ 30CM 370
Poulenc, F.:Son Cl Pno, w. Ferenc Bognar (pno) *(rec Vienna, June & Dec 1995)* Camerata ▲ 30 CM 415 [DDD]
Reger, M.:Albumblatt & Tarantella, w. A. Spiri (pno) Camerata 2-▲ 25CM-371-2
Reger, M.:Qnt Cl, w. Philharmonia String Quartet Camerata 2-▲ 25CM-371-2
Reger, M.:Qnt Cl, w. Vienna String Quartet—Largo movt Camerata ("After Hours Classics" series) ▲ 20 CM 424 [DDD]
Reger, M.:Sons Cl, Op. 49, w. A. Spiri (pno) Camerata 2-▲ 25CM-371-2
Reger, M.:Son Cl, Op. 107, w. A. Spiri (pno) Camerata 2-▲ 25CM-371-2
Reinecke, C.:Trio Pno, Op. 264, w. C. Ivaldi (pno), C. Ivaldi (va) Tudor ▲ TUD 798 [DDD]
Saint-Saëns, C.:Son Cl, w. Ferenc Bognar (pno) *(rec Vienna, June & Dec 1995)* Camerata ▲ 30 CM 415 [DDD]
Spohr, L.:Con 1 Cl, w. R. Frühbeck de Burgos (cnd), Stuttgart RSO Orfeo ▲ 088101
Spohr, L.:Con 2 Cl, w. R. Frühbeck de Burgos (cnd), Stuttgart RSO Orfeo ▲ 088201
Spohr, L.:Con 3 Cl, w. R. Frühbeck de Burgos (cnd), Stuttgart RSO Orfeo ▲ 088201
Spohr, L.:Con 4 Cl, w. R. Frühbeck de Burgos (cnd), Stuttgart RSO Orfeo ▲ 088101
Weber, C.M. von:Concertino Cl, w. A. Wit (cnd), Gunma SO *(rec Maebashi Shimin Bunka Kaikan, Japan, June 1986)* Camerata 2-▲ 25 CM 323/4 [DDD]
Weber, C.M. von:Concertino Cl, w. A. Wit (cnd), Gunma SO Camerata 2-▲ 25 CM71-2 [DDD]
Weber, C.M. von:Con 1 Cl, w. K. Toyoda (cnd), Gunma SO Camerata 2-▲ 25 CM71-2 [DDD]
Weber, C.M. von:Con 1 Cl, w. A. Wit (cnd), Gunma SO *(rec Honjo Bunka Kaikan, Japan, June 1982)* Camerata 2-▲ 25 CM 323/4 [DDD]
Weber, C.M. von:Con 2 Cl, w. K. Toyoda (cnd), Gunma SO Camerata 2-▲ 25CM71-2 [DDD]
Weber, C.M. von:Con 2 Cl, w. A. Wit (cnd), Gunma SO *(rec Honjo Bunka Kaikan, Japan, June 1982)* Camerata 2-▲ 25 CM 323/4 [DDD]
Weber, C.M. von:Divert Cl, w. K. Toyoda (cnd), Gunma SO Camerata 2-▲ 25 CM71-2 [DDD]
Weber, C.M. von:Divert Cl, w. A. Wit (cnd), Gunma SO *(rec Maebashi Shimin Bunka Kaikan, Japan, June 1986)* Camerata 2-▲ 25 CM 323/4 [DDD]
Weber, C.M. von:Grand duo concertant Cl, w. Mariko Hayashi (pno) Camerata 2-▲ 25CM71-2 [DDD]
Weber, C.M. von:Qnt Cl, w. Vienna String Quartet—Fantasia, Adagio ma non troppo movt Camerata ("After Hours Classics" series) ▲ 20 CM 424 [DDD]
Weber, C.M. von:Qnt Cl, w. Vienna String Quartet *(rec Casino Zögarnitz, TELDEC Studio, Vienna, Dec. 1982)* Camerata ▲ 25CM 331 [DDD]
Weber, C.M. von:Qnt Cl, w. Vienna String Quartet Camerata 2-▲ 25CM71-2 [DDD]
Weber, C.M. von:Vars on a Theme from *Silvana* Cl, w. Mariko Hayashi (pno) Camerata 2-▲ 25CM71-2 [DDD]
Widor, C.M.:Intro & Rondo Cl, w. Ferenc Bognar (pno) *(rec Vienna, June & Dec 1995)* Camerata ▲ 30 CM 415 [DDD]

Leitner, Ferdinand (pno)
Schubert, Franz:Winterreise, w. Karl Schmitt-Walter (bar) *(rec 1940–43)* Preiser ▲ PRE 90288

Leitner, Konrad (pno)
Mozart, W.A.:Music of, w. D. Robin (sop), A. Martin (bar), G. Grünbacher (cl), K. Leitner (cnd), Vienna Mozart Orch—features selections from Die Entführung aus dem Serail, K.384; Don Giovanni, K.527; Serenade No. 13, K.525, "Eine kleine Nachtmusik"; Con. No. 21 in C for Piano & Orch., K.467; Symphony No. 41 in C, K.551, "Jupiter"; Con. No. 5 in A for Violin & Orch., K.219; Die Zauberflöte, K.620; Alla turca [arr. for orch.] *(rec Feb. 9–13, 1990)* Naxos ▲ 8.550866 [DDD]
Mozart, W.A.:Music of, w. D. Robin (sop), A. Martin (bar), G. Grünbacher (cl), K. Leitner (cnd), Vienna Mozart Orch—features selections from Le nozze di Figaro, K.492; Con. No. 23 in A for Piano & Orch., K.488; Sym. No. 40 in g, K.550; Die Zauberflöte, K.620; Posthorn Serenade, K.320; Con. in A for Clarinet & Orch., K.622; Sym. No. 35 in in D, K.385 "Haffner" *(rec Feb. 9–13, 1990)* Naxos ▲ 8.550867 [DDD]
Schoenberg, A.:The Cabaret Songs, w. H. Zednik (ten) [G] Preiser ▲ 93401 [DDD]
Strauss, R.:Songs, w. H. Zednik (ten)—Krämerspiegel (12 songs), Op. 66 [G] Preiser ▲ 93401 [DDD]
Werfel, A.M.:Songs, w. H. Zednik (ten)—Die stille Stadt; In meines Vaters Garten; Laue Sommernacht; Bei dir ist es traut; Ich wandle unter Blumen; Der Erkennende; Ekstase [G] Preiser ▲ 93401 [DDD]

Leixner, Vladimir (vc)—see ORCHESTRAS & ENSEMBLES Stamitz String Quartet

Lejsek, Vlastimil (pno)
Mendelssohn, F.:Con in E for 2 Pnos, w. Vera Lejskova (pno), H. Rögner (cnd), Berlin RSO—in E Berlin Classics ▲ BER 9027 [ADD]

Lejskova, Vera (pno)
Mendelssohn, F.:Con in E for 2 Pnos, w. Vlastimil Lejsek (pno), H. Rögner (cnd), Berlin RSO—in E Berlin Classics ▲ BER 9027 [ADD]

Leleux, François (ob)
Britten, H.:Metamorphoses Ob Harmonia Mundi France ("Les Nouveaux Interprètes" series) ▲ HMN 911556
Britten, H.:Phantasy Qt, w. Guillaume Sutre (vn), Miguel Da Silva (va), Marc Coppey (vc) Harmonia Mundi France ("Les Nouveaux Interprètes" series) ▲ HMN 911556
Poulenc, F.:Son Ob, w. Emmanuel Strosser (pno) Harmonia Mundi France ("Les Nouveaux Interprètes" series) ▲ HMN 911556
Poulenc, F.:Trio Ob, w. Jean-François Duquesnoy (bn), Emmanuel Strosser (pno) Harmonia Mundi France ("Les Nouveaux Interprètes" series) ▲ HMN 911556

Lemahieu, Herman (hn)—see ORCHESTRAS & ENSEMBLES Belgian Wind Quintet

Lemaigre, P. (gtr)
Brouwer, L.:El Decameron Negro *(rec 6/84)* Ricercar ▲ RIC 28064 [DDD]
Brouwer, L.:Estudios Sencillos *(rec 6/84)* Ricercar ▲ RIC 28064 [DDD]
Brouwer, L.:Temas populares Cubanos *(rec 6/84)* Ricercar ▲ RIC 28064 [DDD]

Lemaire, Jean (pno)
Boulanger, L.:Songs, w. K. Ott (sop), Lugano String Quartet—Elle était descendue; Elle est gravement gaie; Parfois je suis triste; Un poète disait; Au pied de mon lit; Si tout ceci n'est qu'un pauvre rêve; Nous nous aimerons tant; Vous m'avez regardé avec toute votre; Les lilas qui avaient fleuri; Deux ancolies; Par ce que j'ai souffert; Je garde une médaille d'elle; Demain fera un an; Dans l'immense tristesse; Attente; Reflets; Le retour; Pie Jesu Signum ▲ X 39-00 [ADD]

LeMaster, Larry (vc)
Rachmaninoff, S.:Vocalise, w. Patrick McFarland (E hn), David Braitberg (vn), Beth Newdome (vn), Paul Murphy (va), Dona Klein (vc), Gloria Jones (db) [trans John Wildermuth] Arundax ▲ 21339

Lemberg, Martin (va)—see ORCHESTRAS & ENSEMBLES Vienna Phil Trio

Lemelin, Stéphane (pno)
After Hours, w. James Campbell (fl), Gene DiNovi Trio Marquis Classics ▲ MAR 153 [DDD]
Fauré, G.:Nocturnes (13) Pno *(rec Oct. 3, 1993 & Feb. 21, 1)* CBC ("Musica Viva" series) ▲ MVCD 1075 [DDD]

Lemmens, Bart (vn)—see ORCHESTRAS & ENSEMBLES Gaggini String Quartet

Lemmens, Bernard (pno)
Jolivet, A.:Danses rituelles René Gailly ▲ 87099 [ADD]

Lemmens, Bernard (pno) (cont.)
Jolivet, A.:Etude sur des modes antiques René Gailly ▲ 87099 [ADD]
Jolivet, A.:Son 1 Pno René Gailly ▲ 87099 [ADD]
Jolivet, A.:Son 2 Pno René Gailly ▲ 87099 [ADD]

Lencsés, Lajos (E hn)
Hindemith, P.:Son E Hn, w. Shoshana Rudiakov (pno) CPO ▲ CPO 999332
Honegger, A.:Con da camera, w. G. van Riet (fl), V. Czarnecki (cnd), Southwest German CO Pforzheim CPO ▲ CPO 999193-2 [ADD/DDD]
Mozart, W.A.:Adagio E hn, w. Stamitz String Quartet *(rec Bonnieux, July 1994)* Capriccio ▲ 10525 [DDD]

Lencsés, Lajos (heckelphone)
Hindemith, P.:Trio Pno, w. Shoshana Rudiakov (pno), Gunter Teuffel (va) CPO ▲ CPO 999332

Lencsés, Lajos (ob)
Bach, Joh. Christian:Sinf concertante, T.289/4, w. János Bálint (fl), Béla Bánfalvi (vn), Károly Botvay (vc), Budapest Strings Capriccio ▲ 10509 [DDD]
Bach, Joh. Christian:Sinf concertante, T.287/2, w. Emilia Csánky (ob), Károly Botvay (vc), B. Bánfalvi (cnd), Budapest Strings Capriccio ▲ 10509 [DDD]
Bach, Joh. Christian:Sinf concertante, T.284/6, w. Béla Bánfalvi (vn), Zsuzsanna Németh (vn), Budapest Strings Capriccio ▲ 10509 [DDD]
Breville, P. de:Sonatine Ob, w. Karl Bergemann (pno) Bayer ▲ BR 100227 [DDD]
Dutilleux, H.:Son Ob, w. Karl Bergemann (pno) Bayer ▲ BR 100227 [DDD]
Fiala, J.:Qts Ob, w. German String Trio—in F & E♭ Capriccio ▲ 10423 [DDD]
Françaix, J.:L'Horloge de Flore, w. U. Segal (cnd), Stuttgart RSO CPO ▲ CPO 999193-2 [ADD/DDD]
Haydn, J.:Cons for 2 Lire organizzata, w. Robert Dohn (fl), B. Warchal (cnd), Slovak CO CPO ▲ CPO 999182 [DDD]
Haydn, J.:Notturni (8), w. Robert Dohn (fl), B. Warchal (cnd), Slovak CO CPO 2-▲ CPO 999121-2 [DDD]
Hindemith, P.:Die Serenaden, w. Ruth Ziesak (sop), Gunter Teuffel (va), Ansgar Schneider (vc) CPO ▲ CPO 999332
Hindemith, P.:Son Ob, w. Shoshana Rudiakov (pno) CPO ▲ CPO 999332
Ibert, J.:Symphonie concertante, w. V. Czarnecki (cnd), Southwest German CO Pforzheim CPO ▲ CPO 999193-2 [ADD/DDD]
Indy, V. d':Fant sur des thèmes populaires français, w. H. E. Zimmer (cnd), Berlin RSO Capriccio ▲ CD 10726 [DDD]
Krommer, F.:Qts Ob, w. German String Trio—in C & F Capriccio ▲ 10423 [DDD]
Milhaud, D.:Aspen Serenade, w. G. Varga (cnd), Stuttgart RSO *(rec Jan. 1986 & Jan. 1992)* CPO ▲ CPO 999114-2 [DDD]
Milhaud, D.:Stanford Serenade, w. G. Varga (cnd), Stuttgart RSO *(rec Jan. 1986 & Jan. 1992)* CPO ▲ CPO 999114-2 [DDD]
Mozart, W.A.:Qt Ob, w. Stamitz String Quartet *(rec Bonnieux, July 1994)* Capriccio ▲ 10525 [DDD]
Mozart, W.A.:Qnt Ob, w. Stamitz String Quartet *(rec Bonnieux, July 1994)* Capriccio ▲ 10525 [DDD]
Poulenc, F.:Son Ob, w. Karl Bergemann (pno) Bayer ▲ BR 100227 [DDD]
Rimsky-Korsakov, N.:Vars on a Theme of Glinka, w. H. E. Zimmer (cnd), Berlin RSO Capriccio ▲ CD 10726 [DDD]
Rosetti, F.A.:Cons Ob, w. B. Warchal (cnd), Slovak CO—Cons. in C, D & F CPO ▲ CPO 999062-2 [DDD]
Saint-Saëns, C.:Son Ob, w. K. Bergemann (pno) Bayer ▲ BR 100227 [DDD]
Salieri, A.:Con Fl, w. D. Becker (fl), J. Faerber (cnd), Württemberg CO MD + G ▲ L 3396 [DDD]
Schwencke, C.F.G.:Con Ob, w. H. E. Zimmer (cnd), Berlin RSO Capriccio ▲ CD 10726 [DDD]
Strauss, R.:Con Ob, w. N. Marriner (cnd), Stuttgart RSO Capriccio ▲ 10231 ■ 27231
Weber, C.M. von:Concertino Ob, w. H. E. Zimmer (cnd), Berlin RSO Capriccio ▲ CD 10726 [DDD]

Lenehan, John (pno)—see also ORCHESTRAS & ENSEMBLES Joachim Trio
Brahms, J.:Scherzo Vn, w. R. Alleson (vn) *(rec 1987)* Classic Studio Berlin ▲ CS 11408 [DDD]
Brahms, J.:Sons Vn (comp), w. R. Alleson (vn) *(rec 1987)* Classic Studio Berlin ▲ CS 11408 [DDD]
Britten, H.:Son Vc, w. Moray Welsh (vc) EMI Classics ("Anglo-American Chamber Music" series) ▲ CDC 55398
Cello Song, w. Julian Lloyd Webber (vc) Philips ▲ 434917-2
Courts, E.:Son Vn & Pno, w. R. Alleson (vn) *(rec 1987)* Classic Studio Berlin ▲ CS 11408 [DDD]
Saint-Saëns, C.:Berceuse Vn, w. Y. ASV ▲ ASV 892 [DDD]
Saint-Saëns, C.:Introduction & Rondo capriccioso, w. Xue-Wei (vn) [arr. violin & piano] ASV ▲ ASV 892 [DDD]
Saint-Saëns, C.:Son 1 Vn, w. Xue-Wei (vn) ASV ▲ ASV 892 [DDD]
Saint-Saëns, C.:Son 2 Vn, w. Xue-Wei (vn) ASV ▲ ASV 892 [DDD]
Saint-Saëns, C.:Trio 1 Pno, w. Rebecca Hirsch (vn), Caroline Dearnley (vc) *(rec Conway Hall, London, Oct. 11 & 12, 1993)* Naxos ▲ 8.550935 [DDD]
Saint-Saëns, C.:Trio 2 Pno, w. Rebecca Hirsch (vn), Caroline Dearnley (vc) *(rec Conway Hall, London, Oct. 11 & 12, 1993)* Naxos ▲ 8.550935
Wieniawski, H.:Vn & Pno Music, w. M. Bisengaliev (vn)—Souvenir de Moscou, Op. 6; Capriccio-valse in E, Op. 7; Vars. on an Original Theme, Op. 15; Polonaise brillante, Op. 4; Le carnaval russe, Op. 11; Gigue in e, Op. 23; Saltarello [arr. Lenehan]; Mazurkas, Opp. 12/2 & 19/1 Naxos ▲ 8.550744 [DDD]

Lenert, Pierre (va)
Juon, P.:Chamber Music, w. Claire Vergnory-Mion (cl), Jean-François Benatar (va), Philippe Nadal (vc), Hélène Calef (pno)—Trio Miniatures for Cl, Vc & Pno; Son in D for Va & Pno, Op. 15; Divert for Cl & 2 Vas, Op. 34; Trio for Cl, Vc & Pno, Op. 17 REM ▲ REM 311267 [DDD]

Lengellé, Françoise (hpd)
Couperin, F.:Pièces de clavecin (sels), w. Laurence Boulay (hpd)—Concerts royaux pour 2 Hpds [Nos. 1–4]; Allemande à 2 Hpds [from Neuvième ordre]; Musète de choisi & musète de taverni à 2 Hpds [from Quinzième ordre] Erato ▲ ERA SEL 12982 [ADD]

Leng Tan, Margaret (pno)
Cage, J.:Four Walls, w. J. La Barbara (sop) New Albion ▲ NA 037 [DDD]
Cage, J.:In the Name of the Holocaust Mode ▲ 15
Cage, J.:The Perilous Night New Albion ▲ NA 037 [DDD]
Cage, J.:Pno Music—Bacchanale for Prepared Piano (1938); Daughters of the Lonesome Isle for Prepared Piano (1945); In a Landscape for Piano (1948); In the Name of the Holocaust for String Piano (1942); Ophelia for Piano (1946); Music for Piano 2 (1953) *(rec New York, Dec. 1993)* New Albion ▲ NA 070
Cage, J.:The Seasons *(rec New York, Dec. 1993)* New Albion ▲ NA 070
Cage, J.:Suite Toy Pno *(rec New York, Dec. 1993)* New Albion ▲ NA 070
Crumb, G.:Pieces (5) Pno Mode ▲ 15
Ge Gan-Ru:Gu Yue Mode ▲ 15
Hovhaness, A.:Jhala Mode ▲ 15
Hovhaness, A.:Orbit 2 Mode ▲ 15
Satoh, S.:Cosmic Womb Mode ▲ 15
Satoh, S.:Music of, w. Almond (vn), Messier (sop), Pugliese (perc)—Birds in Warped Time II for Violin & Piano (1980); The Heavenly Spheres are Illuminated by Lights for Soprano, Piano & Percussion (1979); Incarnation II for solo Piano with tape delay (1970); Litania for 2 Pianos with tape delay (1973); A Gate into the Stars for solo Piano (1962) New Albion ▲ NA 008 [ADD]

Leng Tan, Margaret (prepared pno)
Cage, J.:Primitive (1942) Mode ▲ 15
Raickovich, M.:Prelude & Fugue *(rec Harmonic Ranch, New York City, Apr 5, 1994)* Mode ▲ mode 45

Lengyel, Atty (pno)—see ORCHESTRAS & ENSEMBLES Lengyel Duo

Lengyel, Gabriella (vn)—see ORCHESTRAS & ENSEMBLES Lengyel Duo

Lenniger, Martin (perc)
Eben, Petr:Landscapes of Patmos, w. S. Ahrens (org) Multisonic ▲ 31 0097 [DDD]

Lenski, Kathleen (vn)
Levitch, L.:Qnt Fl, w. Sheridan Stokes (fl), Miwako Watanabe (vn), Jeffrey Solow (vc), Paul Polivnick (va) Cambria ▲ CD 1059 [ADD]

▲ = CD ♦ = Enhanced CD Δ = MD ■ = Cassette Tape □ = DCC

Lenti, Marianne (pno)
Bird, A.:Introduction & Fugue, w. T. Lenti (pno) *(rec Dec. 17, 1990)* ACA Digital Recording ▲ CM 20017
Busoni, F.:Pno Music for 2 Pnos, w. T. Lenti (pno)—Finnländische Volksweisen Nos. 1 & 2 *(rec Dec. 19, 1988)* ACA Digital Recording ▲ CM 20009
Casella, A.:Pagine di guerra, w. T. Lenti (pno) *(rec Dec. 19, 1988)* ACA Digital Recording ▲ CM 20009
Dušek, F.X.:Sons (2) Pno 4-Hands, w. T. Lenti (pno)—in E♭ *(rec Dec. 17, 1990)* ACA Digital Recording ▲ CM 20017
Gershwin, G.:Rhap in Blue, w. Tony Lenti (pno) [arr. H. Levine for piano 4-hands, 1925] ACA Digital Recording ▲ CM 20037 [DDD]
Goetz, H.:Son Pno 4-Hands, w. T. Lenti (pno) *(rec Dec. 19, 1988)* ACA Digital Recording ▲ CM 20009
Grieg, E.:Pièces symphoniques, Op. 14, w. T. Lenti (pno) *(rec Dec. 17, 1990)* ACA Digital Recording ▲ CM 20017
Grieg, E.:Waltz Caprices, w. Tony Lenti (pno) [arr. H. Levine for piano 4-hands, 1925] ACA Digital Recording ▲ CM 20037 [DDD]
Liszt, F.:Grande valse di bravura, w. T. Lenti (pno) [arr. for piano 4-hands] *(rec Dec. 17, 1990)* ACA Digital Recording ▲ CM 20017
Liszt, F.:Hungarian Rhaps, w. Tony Lenti (pno)—No. 2 [arr. for piano 4-hands] ACA Digital Recording ▲ CM 20037 [DDD]
Onslow, G.:Grand Duo Pno, w. T. Lenti (pno) *(rec Dec. 17, 1990)* ACA Digital Recording ▲ CM 20017
Respighi, O.:Little Pieces Pno, w. T. Lenti (pno) *(rec Dec. 19, 1988)* ACA Digital Recording ▲ CM 20009
Rubinstein, N.:Tarentella, w. Tony Lenti (pno) ACA Digital Recording ▲ CM 20037 [DDD]
Schubert, Franz:Fant Pno, D.940, w. Tony Lenti (pno) ACA Digital Recording ▲ CM 20037 [DDD]

Lenti, Tony (pno)
Bird, A.:Introduction & Fugue, w. M. A. Lenti (pno) *(rec Dec. 17, 1990)* ACA Digital Recording ▲ CM 20017
Busoni, F.:Pno Music for 2 Pnos, w. M. Lenti (pno)—Finnländische Volksweisen Nos. 1 & 2 *(rec Dec. 19, 1988)* ACA Digital Recording ▲ CM 20009
Casella, A.:Pagine di guerra, w. M. Lenti (pno) *(rec Dec. 19, 1988)* ACA Digital Recording ▲ CM 20009
Dušek, F.X.:Sons (2) Pno 4-Hands, w. M. A. Lenti (pno)—in E♭ *(rec Dec. 17, 1990)* ACA Digital Recording ▲ CM 20017
Gershwin, G.:Rhap in Blue, w. Marianne Lenti (pno) [arr. H. Levine for piano 4-hands, 1925] ACA Digital Recording ▲ CM 20037 [DDD]
Goetz, H.:Son Pno 4-Hands, w. M. Lenti (pno) *(rec Dec. 19, 1988)* ACA Digital Recording ▲ CM 20009
Grieg, E.:Pièces symphoniques, Op. 14, w. M. A. Lenti (pno) *(rec Dec. 17, 1990)* ACA Digital Recording ▲ CM 20017
Grieg, E.:Waltz Caprices, w. Marianne Lenti (pno) [arr. H. Levine for piano 4-hands, 1925] ACA Digital Recording ▲ CM 20037 [DDD]
Liszt, F.:Grande valse di bravura, w. M.A. Lenti (pno) [arr. for piano 4-hands] *(rec Dec. 17, 1990)* ACA Digital Recording ▲ CM 20017
Liszt, F.:Hungarian Rhaps, w. Marianne Lenti (pno)—No. 2 [arr. for piano 4-hands] ACA Digital Recording ▲ CM 20037 [DDD]
Onslow, G.:Grand Duo Pno, w. M. A. Lenti (pno) *(rec Dec. 17, 1990)* ACA Digital Recording ▲ CM 20017
Respighi, O.:Little Pieces Pno, w. M. Lenti (pno) *(rec Dec. 19, 1988)* ACA Digital Recording ▲ CM 20009
Rubinstein, N.:Tarentella, w. Marianne Lenti (pno) ACA Digital Recording ▲ CM 20037 [DDD]
Schubert, Franz:Fant Pno, D.940, w. Marianne Lenti (pno) ACA Digital Recording ▲ CM 20037 [DDD]

Lentz, Georges (vn)
Lentz, G.:Caeli enarrant...IV, w. J. Booth (vn), D. Wicks (va), P. Morrison (vc) Tall Poppies ▲ TP 35

Lenz, B. (vn)
Suder, J.:Arietta Vn, w. S. Hewig-Tröscher (pno) *(rec Jan. 4–8 & July 12, 1993)* Calig ▲ CAL 50926 [DDD]
Suder, J.:Fant Vn *(rec Jan. 4–8 & July 12, 1993)* Calig ▲ CAL 50926 [DDD]
Suder, J.:Son 1 Vn, w. S. Hewig-Tröscher (pno) *(rec Jan. 4–8 & July 12, 1993)* Calig ▲ CAL 50926 [DDD]
Suder, J.:Son 2 Vn, w. S. Hewig-Tröscher (pno) *(rec Jan. 4–8 & July 12, 1993)* Calig ▲ CAL 50926 [DDD]

Leo, M. A. Lejarza (gtr)
Garay, L.E.:Canto Koch Schwann ▲ 3-1387-2 [DDD]
Garay, L.E.:Miniatura Koch Schwann ▲ 3-1387-2 [DDD]
Hinojosa, J.:Te Lucis Ante Terminum Koch Schwann ▲ 3-1387-2 [DDD]
Navarro, J.R.:Arrabales Koch Schwann ▲ 3-1387-2 [DDD]
Navarro, J.R.:Capoeira Koch Schwann ▲ 3-1387-2 [DDD]
Ponce, M.:Gtr Music—Estrellita; Variaciones de un tema de A Cabezon Koch Schwann ▲ 3-1387-2 [DDD]

León, Eva (vn)
Grieg, E.:Son 3 Vn, w. Dagmar Muñiz (pno) *(rec Estudis Albert Moraleda de Barcelona, Mar 1995)* Edicions Albert Moraleda ▲ CD 049523 [DDD]
Sarasate, P. de:Aires bohemios, w. Dagmar Muñiz (pno) *(rec Estudis Albert Moraleda de Barcelona, Mar 1995)* Edicions Albert Moraleda ▲ CD 049523 [DDD]
Toldrá, E.:Sonnets Vn, w. Dagmar Muñiz (pno) *(rec Estudis Albert Moraleda de Barcelona, Mar 1995)* Edicions Albert Moraleda ▲ CD 049523 [DDD]
Turull, X.:Divert Vn *(rec Estudis Albert Moraleda de Barcelona, Mar 1995)* Edicions Albert Moraleda ▲ CD 049523 [DDD]

León, Pedro (vn)
Beethoven, L. van:Con Vn, Vc & Pno, "Triple Con", w. P. Corostola (vc), L. Milà (pno), H. Zongjie (cnd), Chinese Central PO Regis Tro ▲ RTAC 003 [DDD]

Leonard, Andrew (gtr)
Bach, J.S.:Sons & Partitas Vn, BWV 1001–1006—Son 2 in a [Andante; Allegro; trans Andrew Leonard] *(rec The Music Room, Cambridge, MA, May 27–29, 1996)* Archetype ▲ 60101 [DDD]
Bach, J.S.:Suites Vc, BWV 1007–1012—Suite No. 6 in D [trans Andrew Leonard] *(rec The Music Room, Cambridge, MA, May 27–29, 1996)* Archetype ▲ 60101 [DDD]
Dowland, J.:Lt Music—The Shoemaker's Wife:A Toy; Aloe; Fant [trans Andrew Leonard] *(rec The Music Room, Cambridge, MA, May 27–29, 1996)* Archetype ▲ 60101 [DDD]
Piazzolla, A.:Milonga del angel *(rec The Music Room, Cambridge, MA, May 27–29, 1996)* Archetype ▲ 60101 [DDD]
Piazzolla, A.:La muerte del angel *(rec The Music Room, Cambridge, MA, May 27–29, 1996)* Archetype ▲ 60101 [DDD]
Sor, F.:Vars Gtr—Marlborough Vars, Op. 28 *(rec The Music Room, Cambridge, MA, May 27–29, 1996)* Archetype ▲ 60101 [DDD]
York, A.:Sunburst *(rec The Music Room, Cambridge, MA, May 27–29, 1996)* Archetype ▲ 60101 [DDD]

Leonardi, R. (pno)
Rachmaninoff, S.:Suite 1 for 2 Pnos, w. M. Ponti (pno) Allegretto ▲ ACD 8162 [ADD] ■ ACS 8162
Rachmaninoff, S.:Suite 2 for 2 Pnos, w. M. Ponti (pno) Allegretto ▲ ACD 8162 [ADD] ■ ACS 8162

Leoncavallo, Ruggiero (pno)
Legendary Three Tenors, w. Enrico Caruso (ten), Beniamino Gigli (ten), John McCormack (ten), Edwin Schneider (pno), Metropolitan Opera Orch, Metropolitan Opera Chorus [cnd:Giulio Setti], Philharmonia Orch, Philharmonia Chorus [cnd:Stanford Robinson] *(rec 1904–1950)* RCA Gold Seal ▲ 09026-68534-2 [ADD] ■ 09026-68534-4

Leonhard, Monika (pno)—see also ORCHESTRAS & ENSEMBLES Stuttgart Piano Trio
Mozart, W.A.:Con 10 Pnos, w. S. Grotenhuis (pno), J. Kussmaul (cnd), Amsterdam Mozart Players *(rec Aug. 1990)* Channel Classics ▲ CCS 1190 [DDD]
Mozart, W.A.:Con Vn Pno, w. R. Kussmaul (vn), J. Kussmaul (cnd), Amsterdam Mozart Players *(rec Aug. 1990)* Channel Classics ▲ CCS 1190 [DDD]

Leonhardt, Gustav (hpd)—see also ORCHESTRAS & ENSEMBLES Amsterdam Quartet
Bach, C.P.E.:Con doppio, w. A. Curtis (hpd), Collegium Aureum Editio Classica ▲ 77061-2 [ADD]
Bach, C.P.E.:Con Hpd & Strs, H.427, Collegium Aureum Editio Classica ▲ 77061-2 [ADD]
Bach, C.P.E.:Sinfs, H.657–662, "Hamburg Syms", Orch of the Age of Enlightenment—No. 5, H.661 [period instrs] Virgin Classics ("Veritas Edition" series) ▲ CDM 61182
Bach, C.P.E.:Sinfs, H.663–666, Orch of the Age of Enlightenment [period instrs] Virgin Classics ("Veritas Edition" series) ▲ CDM 61182
Bach, J.S.:Anna Magdalena Bach Notebook, w. E. Ameling (sop), H.-M. Linde (bar), J. Koch (va), A. May (vc)—sels. Editio Classica ▲ 77150-2-RG [DDD]
Bach, J.S.:The Art of the Fugue *(rec May 1953)* Vanguard Classics ("The Bach Guild" series) 2-▲ OVC 2011/12 [ADD]
Bach, J.S.:The Art of the Fugue, w. B. van Asperen (hpd) Editio Classica 2-▲ 77013-2-RG [ADD]
Bach, J.S.:Con 8 Hpd, w. G. Leonhardt (cnd), Leonhardt Consort [reconstr. Gustav Leonhardt] Teldec 3-▲ 2292-42726-2 [ADD]
Bach, J.S.:Cons for 2 Hpds (comp), w. G. Leonhardt (cnd), Leonhardt Consort, E. Müller [2nd hpd, BWV 1060 & 1062], A. Uittenbosch [2nd hpd, BWV 1061] Teldec 3-▲ 2292-42726-2 [ADD]
Bach, J.S.:Cons for 3 Hpds (comp), w. A. Uittenbosch (hpd), A. Curtis (hpd), G. Leonhardt (cnd), Leonhardt Consort Teldec 3-▲ 2292-42726-2 [ADD]
Bach, J.S.:Con for 4 Hpds, w. E. Müller (hpd), J. van Wering (hpd), A. Uittenbosch (hpd), G. Leonhardt (cnd), Leonhardt Consort Teldec 3-▲ 2292-42726-2 [ADD]
Bach, J.S.:Goldberg Vars Editio Classica ▲ 77149-2-RG [ADD]
Bach, J.S.:Goldberg Vars, w. G. Leonhardt (hpd) *(rec 1953)* Vanguard Classics ("The Bach Guild" series) ▲ OVC 2004 [ADD]
Bach, J.S.:Italian Con Editio Classica 2-▲ 77013-2-RG [ADD]
Bach, J.S.:Partitas Hpd, BWV 825–830 Virgin Classics 2-▲ ZDMB 61292
Bach, J.S.:Partitas Hpd, BWV 825–830 Editio Classica 2-▲ 77215-2-RG [ADD]
Bach, J.S.:Partita Hpd, BWV 831, "Ov nach französischer Art" Editio Classica 2-▲ 77013-2-RG [ADD]
Bach, J.S.:Preludium, Fugue & Allegro Hpd, BWV 998 Editio Classica 2-▲ 77013-2-RG [ADD]
Bach, J.S.:Son Fl, BWV 1038, w. B. Kuijken (fl), S. Kuijken (vn), W. Kuijken (vl) [period instrs] Deutsche Harmonia Mundi 2-▲ 77026-2-RC [ADD]
Bach, J.S.:Sons Vl, BWV 1027–1029, w. W. Kuijken (vl) Editio Classica ▲ 77044-2-RG [ADD]
Bach, J.S.:Sons Vn, w. S. Kuijken (vn)—BWV 1014–1019 Editio Classica 2-▲ 77170-2-RG [ADD]
Bach, J.S.:Trio Son for 2 Fls, BWV 1039, w. B. Kuijken (fl), M. Hantal (fl), W. Kuijken (bass vl) [period instrs] Deutsche Harmonia Mundi 2-▲ 77026-2-RC [ADD]
Bach, J.S.:Das wohltemperierte Klavier—Book 1 Editio Classica 2-▲ 77011-2-RG [ADD]
Bach, J.S.:Das wohltemperierte Klavier—Book 2 Editio Classica 2-▲ 77012-2-RG [ADD]
Elizabethan & Jacobean Music - Airs & Instrumental Music of England, w. N. Harnoncourt (cnd), Deller Consort, Consort of Viols [Desmond Dupré (lt), Alfred Deller (ct)] Vanguard Classics ▲ OVC 8102 [ADD]
Forqueray, A.:Suites Hpd Sony Classical ("Vivarte" series) ▲ SK 48080
French Harpsichord Works, w. Leonhardt, Gustav (hpd) Sony Classical ("Vivarte" series) ▲ SK 48080
Masterpieces of French Harpsichord Music, w. Leonhardt, Gustav (hpd) Deutsche Harmonia Mundi ▲ 77924-2-RC [DDD]
Music of Versailles, w. Kuijken, Sigiswald (vn), Wieland Kuijken (va) Editio Classica ▲ 77145-2-RG [DDD]
Purcell, H.:Odes & Welcome Songs (misc), w. H. Cook (ten), J. Bowman (ct), C. Robson (ct), D. Wilson-Johnson (bar), G. Leonhardt (cnd), Orch of the Age of Enlightenment Virgin Classics ▲ CDC 59243
Rameau, J.P.:Pièces de clavecin en concert, w. L. Frydén (vn), N. Harnoncourt (vl) Vanguard Classics ("The Bach Guild" series) ▲ OVC 2520 [ADD]
Rameau, J.P.:Pièces de clavecin en concert, w. S. Kuijken (vn), W. Kuijken (vn), Brüggen (fl) Teldec ▲ 77618-2
Telemann, G.P.:Sons Rcr, w. Frans Brüggen (rcr), Anner Bylsma (vc)—in F, B♭, C, f, d & C [TWV 41:F2, B3, C5, f1, d4 & C2] Teldec ("Das Alte Werk" series) ▲ 93688-2 [ADD]

Leonhardt, Gustav (org)
North German Organ Music *(rec Nov. 2–6, 1992)* Sony Classical ▲ SK 53371
Organ Music in France & Southern Netherlands *(rec Falaise, Normandy & Leuven, Belgium, Sept. 13 & Mar. 2–3, 1993)* Sony Classical ("Vivarte" series) ▲ SK 57963 [DDD]
Purcell, H.:Anthems & Services, w. David Cordier (alt), John Elwes (ten), Harry van der Kamp (bass), Peter Kooy (bass), Tölz Boys' Choir—In thee, O Lord, do I put my trust; My beloved spake; O praise God in His holiness; Praise the Lord, O Jerusalem; Rejoice in the Lord always Sony Classical ("Vivarte" series) ▲ SK 53981

Leonhardt, Gustav (pno)
Bach, J.S.:Sons Fl, BWV 1030–35, w. B. Kuijken (fl), W. Kuijken (vl)—BWV 1030, 1032, 1034 & 103 [period instrs] Deutsche Harmonia Mundi 2-▲ 77026-2-RC [ADD]

Leonhardt, Gustav (vl)—see ORCHESTRAS & ENSEMBLES Paris Quartet

Leonhardt, Gustav (b-vl)—see ORCHESTRAS & ENSEMBLES Deller Consort

Leonhardt, Trudelies (pno)
Beethoven, L. van:Allegretto, WoO 53 Duo ▲ 89023
Beethoven, L. van:Bagatelles (24)—Op. 119 Duo ▲ 89023
Beethoven, L. van:Bagatelle, WoO 54, "Lustig-Traurig" Duo ▲ 89023
Beethoven, L. van:Rondos Pno, Op. 51—No. 2 Duo ▲ 89023
Beethoven, L. van:Son 13 Pno Duo ▲ 89023
Beethoven, L. van:Vars Pno, WoO 80 Duo ▲ 89023
Schubert, Franz:Adagio Pno, D.612 [pno from Benignus Seidner, Vienna, ca 1815/20] *(rec St. Sulpice, Switzerland, Oct 1993)* Globe ▲ GLO 5151 [DDD]
Schubert, Franz:Andante Pno [pno from Benignus Seidner, Vienna, ca 1815/20] *(rec St. Sulpice, Switzerland, Oct 1993)* Globe ▲ GLO 5151 [DDD]
Schubert, Franz:Ecossaises Pno, D.299 [pno from Benignus Seidner, Vienna, ca 1815/20] *(rec St. Sulpice, Switzerland, Oct 1993)* Globe ▲ GLO 5151 [DDD]
Schubert, Franz:Ecossaises Pno, D.529 [pno from Benignus Seidner, Vienna, ca 1815/20] *(rec St. Sulpice, Switzerland, Oct 1993)* Globe ▲ GLO 5151 [DDD]
Schubert, Franz:Ländler, D.734 [pno from Benignus Seidner, Vienna, ca 1815/20] *(rec St. Sulpice, Switzerland, Oct 1993)* Globe ▲ GLO 5151 [DDD]
Schubert, Franz:Minuet Pno, D.277a [pno from Benignus Seidner, Vienna, ca 1815/20] *(rec St. Sulpice, Switzerland, Oct 1993)* Globe ▲ GLO 5151 [DDD]
Schubert, Franz:Minuet Pno, D.334 [pno from Benignus Seidner, Vienna, ca 1815/20] *(rec St. Sulpice, Switzerland, Oct 1993)* Globe ▲ GLO 5151 [DDD]
Schubert, Franz:Scherzos Pno, D.593 [pno from Benignus Seidner, Vienna, ca 1815/20] *(rec St. Sulpice, Switzerland, Oct 1993)* Globe ▲ GLO 5151 [DDD]
Schubert, Franz:Son Pno, D.537 *(rec 1985 & 1990)* Jecklin-Disco 2-▲ J 4424/5-2 [ADD]
Schubert, Franz:Son Pno, D.557 *(rec 1985 & 1990)* Jecklin-Disco 2-▲ J 4424/5-2 [ADD]
Schubert, Franz:Son Pno, D.566 *(rec 1985 & 1990)* Jecklin-Disco 2-▲ J 4424/5-2 [ADD]
Schubert, Franz:Son Pno, D.568 *(rec 1985 & 1990)* Jecklin-Disco 2-▲ J 4424/5-2 [ADD]
Schubert, Franz:Son Pno, D.575 *(rec 1985 & 1990)* Jecklin-Disco 2-▲ J 4424/5-2 [ADD]
Schubert, Franz:Son Pno, D.664 *(rec 1985)* Jecklin-Disco 2-▲ J 4422/3-2 [ADD]
Schubert, Franz:Son Pno, D.784 *(rec 1984)* Jecklin-Disco 2-▲ J 4420/1-2 [ADD]
Schubert, Franz:Son Pno, D.845 *(rec 1984)* Jecklin-Disco 2-▲ J 4420/1-2 [ADD]
Schubert, Franz:Son Pno, D.850 *(rec 1985)* Jecklin-Disco 2-▲ J 4422/3-2 [ADD]
Schubert, Franz:Son Pno, D.894 *(rec 1984)* Jecklin-Disco 2-▲ J 4420/1-2 [ADD]
Schubert, Franz:Son Pno, D.958 *(rec 1985)* Jecklin-Disco 2-▲ J 4422/3-2 [ADD]
Schubert, Franz:Son Pno, D.959 *(rec 1984)* Jecklin-Disco 2-▲ J 4420/1-2 [ADD]
Schubert, Franz:Son Pno, D.960 *(rec 1985)* Jecklin-Disco 2-▲ J 4422/3-2 [ADD]

Leonhardt, Trudelies (pno) (cont.)
Schubert, Franz:Waltzes, D.145 [pno from Benignus Seidner, Vienna, ca 1815/20] *(rec St. Sulpice, Switzerland, Oct 1993)* Globe ▲ GLO 5151 [DDD]
Leoni, Carmen (hpd)—see also ORCHESTRAS & ENSEMBLES Affetti Musicali members
Telemann, G.P.:Ovs—in g for Hpd *(rec The Netherlands, Jul 8–10, 1993)* Emergo ▲ EC 3952 2 [DDD]
Leonskaja, Elisabeth (pno)
Brahms, J.:Con 1 Pno, w. E. Inbal (cnd), Philharmonia Orch Teldec ("M Line" series) ▲ 97450–2
Brahms, J.:Con 2 Pno, w. K. Masur (cnd), Leipzig Gewandhaus Orch *(rec Gewandhaus, Leipzig, Jan. 1994)* Teldec ▲ 94544–2 [DDD]
Brahms, J.:Ernste Gesänge, w. B. Fassbaender (mez) Teldec ▲ 74872–2
Brahms, J.:Romanzen aus Tieck's *Magelone*, w. B. Fassbaender (mez) *(rec Berlin, March 1993)* Teldec ▲ 90854–2 [DDD]
Brahms, J.:Son 1 Pno Teldec ▲ 9031–73184–2 ZK [DDD]
Brahms, J.:Son 1 Pno Teldec 2–▲ 2292–46450–2 [DDD]
Brahms, J.:Son 2 Pno Teldec 2–▲ 2292–46450–2 [DDD]
Brahms, J.:Son 3 Pno Teldec 2–▲ 2292–46450–2 [DDD]
Brahms, J.:Son 3 Pno Teldec ▲ 9031–73184–2 ZK [DDD]
Brahms, J.:Songs, w. B. Fassbaender (mez) Teldec ▲ 74872–2
Brahms, J.:Vars on a Theme by Paganini Teldec 2–▲ 2292–46450–2 [DDD]
Chopin, F.:Nocturnes Teldec 2–▲ 9031–72297–2 ZA
Dvořák, A.:Polonaise Vc, w. H. Schiff (vc) Philips ▲ 412732–2 [DDD]
Liszt, F.:Années de pèlerinage 2—No. 7, "Dante Sonata" Teldec ▲ 2292–44948–2 ZK [DDD]
Liszt, F.:Son Pno Teldec ▲ 2292–44948–2 ZK [DDD]
Liszt, F.:Sonetti del Petrarca Pno—Nos. 104 & 123 Teldec ▲ 2292–44948–2 ZK [DDD]
Mussorgsky, M.:Pictures at an Exhibition Teldec ▲ 2292–43672–2
Rachmaninoff, S.:Son Vc, w. Heinrich Schiff (vc) Philips ▲ 412732–2 [DDD]
Schubert, Franz:Fant Pno, D.760, "Wandererfantasie" Teldec ▲ 2292–44189–2 ZK [DDD]
Schubert, Franz:Qnt Pno, D.667, w. G. Hörtnagel (db), Alban Berg String Quartet EMI Classics ▲ CDC 47448
Schubert, Franz:Son Pno, D.568 *(rec Berlin, Feb–Mar. 1994)* Teldec ▲ 90888–2 [DDD]
Schubert, Franz:Son Pno, D.850 *(rec Berlin, Feb.–Mar. 1994)* Teldec ▲ 90888–2 [DDD]
Schubert, Franz:Son Pno, D.894 Teldec ▲ 2292–44189–2 ZK [DDD]
Schumann, R.:Liederkreis, Op. 39, w. B. Fassbaender (mez) Teldec ▲ 74872–2
Shostakovich, D.:Con 1 Pno, w. H. Wolff (cnd), St. Paul CO Teldec ▲ 73282–2
Shostakovich, D.:Con 2 Pno, w. H. Wolff (cnd), St. Paul CO Teldec ▲ 73282–2
Shostakovich, D.:Son 2 Pno, w. H. Wolff (cnd), St. Paul CO Teldec ▲ 73282–2
Sibelius, J.:Malinconia, w. H. Schiff (vc) Philips ▲ 412732–2 [DDD]
Tchaikovsky, P.:Son Pno, Op. 37 Teldec ▲ 2292–43672–2
León-Tello, Luz Martín (castanets)—see ORCHESTRAS & ENSEMBLES Al Ayre Español
Leoson, Markus (mar)
Milhaud, D.:Con Mar, Royal Swedish Opera Orch Caprice ▲ CAP 21466
Leoson, Markus (perc)
Andersson, B.T.:Apollo Con, Royal Swedish Opera Orch Caprice ▲ CAP 21466
Fukushi, N.:Ground Caprice ▲ CAP 21466
Tanaka, T.:Movts Caprice ▲ CAP 21466
Xenakis, I.:Rebonds Perc Caprice ▲ CAP 21466
Leoson, Markus (vib)
Donatoni, F.:Omar Caprice ▲ CAP 21466
Lepkoff, Jesse (fl)
The Unicorn:Myth & Miracle in Medieval France (1200–1300), w. Anne Azema (sop), C. Ann Fulton (hps), Shira Kammen (rebec/vielle/hp) Erato ▲ 94380 [DDD]
Leppard, Raymond (hpd)
Handel, G.F.:Sons Ob, w. Malylin Zupniik (ob), Mark Shuman (vc)—in a, B♭, e, g & g ASV ▲ ASV 663 [DDD]
Telemann, G.P.:Sons Ob, w. M. Zupniik (ob), M. Shuman (vc)—4 Sonatas—Nos. 1 in c, 3 in F & 6 in g; & Sonata in B♭ ASV ▲ ASV 663 [DDD]
Vivaldi, A.:Music of, w. Wim Ten Have (va), Anthony Bailes (lt), Hans-Martin Linde (fl/rcr), Leppard, Linde (cnd), English CO, Prague CO, Danske Strings members—Concertino in D, RV.121; Cons. in f, RV.156; in G, RV.435 [Op. 10/4]; in D, RV.429; in F, RV.434 [Op. 10/5]; in D, RV.93; in d, RV.540; Son. in E♭, RV.130 [Al Santo Sepolcro] Classics for Pleasure ▲ CDCFP 4656 [ADD]
Lepri, Fernando (gtr)—see ORCHESTRAS & ENSEMBLES Trio Chitarristico
Lequien, Colette (va)
Debussy, C.:Son Fl, w. R. Bourdin (fl), A. Challan (hp) Philips ▲ 422839–2 [ADD]
Lerner, Bennett (pno)
Chambers, W.M.:Ten Grand, w. Ursula Oppens (pno), Walter Hilse (pno), Nurit Tiles (pno), Aleck Karis (pno), Edmund Niemann (pno), Joseph Kubera (pno), Martin Goldray (pno), Allen Shawn (pno), Elizabeth di Filice (pno), Geisel (cnd) Newport ▲ NPD 85553
Lerner, Rémi (cl)
Barraqué, J.:Con Cl, w. P. Méfano (cnd), Ensemble 2E2M Musique d'Abord ▲ HMA 1905199
Klein, G.:Divert Ob, w. Jean-Pierre Arnaud (ob), Jean-Marc Liet (ob), Christian Rocca (cl), Michel Tavernier (bn), Amaury Wallez (bn), Éric Karcher (hn), Philippe Queyraud (hn) Arion ▲ ARN 68272 [DDD]
Leroux, Robert (perc)
Lorrain, D.:The Other Shape Centrediscs ▲ CD 3288
Leroy, Bernard (pno)
Bernstein, L.:I Hate Music, w. Caryn Hartglass (sop) *(rec Châteaugay Church, France, June 1995)* Ligia Digital ▲ 0201033 [DDD]
Bernstein, L.:Mass (sels), w. Caryn Hartglass (sop), Myriam Cabaud-Chiaparin (fl)—A Simple Song; I Go On *(rec Châteaugay Church, France, June 1995)* Ligia Digital ▲ 0201033 [DDD]
Milhaud, D.:Chansons de Ronsard, w. Caryn Hartglass (sop) *(rec Châteaugay Church, France, June 1995)* Ligia Digital ▲ 0201033 [DDD]
Saint-Saëns, C.:La Libellule, w. Caryn Hartglass (sop) *(rec Châteaugay Church, France, June 1995)* Ligia Digital ▲ 0201033 [DDD]
Saint-Saëns, C.:Le Rossignol et la rose, w. Caryn Hartglass (sop) *(rec Châteaugay Church, France, June 1995)* Ligia Digital ▲ 0201033 [DDD]
Strauss, R.:Songs, Op. 68, w. Caryn Hartglass (sop) *(rec Châteaugay Church, France, June 1995)* Ligia Digital ▲ 0201033 [DDD]
Le Roy, R. (fl)
Mozart, W.A.:Con Fl Hp, w. L. Laskine (hp), T. Beecham (cnd), Royal PO *(rec 1947)* EMI Classics ("Great Recordings of the Century" series) ▲ CDH 63820
Le Sage, Eric (pno)
Chausson, E.:Andante et Allegro, w. P. Meyer (cl) Denon ▲ CO 79282 [DDD]
Debussy, C.:Son Vc, w. M. Coppey (vc) *(rec Feb. 2–6, 1993)* K617 ▲ 7031 [DDD]
Dutilleux, H.:Son Ob, w. François Meyer (ob) Sonpact ▲ SPT 94011 [DDD]
Emmanuel, M.:Son Vc, w. M. Coppey (vc) *(rec Feb. 2–6, 1993)* K617 ▲ 7031 [DDD]
Fauré, G.:Fant Fl, w. Emmanuel Pahud (fl) Skarbo ▲ SK 4965 [DDD]
Fauré, G.:Sicilienne, w. Emmanuel Pahud (fl) [trans for fl & pno] Skarbo ▲ SK 4965 [DDD]
Fauré, G.:Son 1 Vn, w. Emmanuel Pahud (fl) [trans for fl & pno] Skarbo ▲ SK 4965 [DDD]
Franck, C.:Son Vn, w. Emmanuel Pahud (fl) [trans for fl & pno] Skarbo ▲ SK 4965 [DDD]
Grieg, E.:Son Vc, w. Marc Coppey (vc) Harmonia Mundi France ▲ HMN 911550
Hindemith, P.:Son Ob, w. François Meyer (ob) Sonpact ▲ SPT 94011 [DDD]
Milhaud, D.:Caprice, w. P. Meyer (cl) Denon ▲ CO 79282 [DDD]
Milhaud, D.:Duo concertante Cl & Pno, w. P. Meyer (cl) Denon ▲ CO 79282 [DDD]
Milhaud, D.:Sonatina Cl, w. P. Meyer (cl) Denon ▲ CO 79282 [DDD]
Music at the Time of Beaumarchais, w. Montserrat Figueras (sop), Lawrence Monteyro (sop), Raphel Oleg (vn), Miguel da Silva (va), Christophe Coin (vc), Marc Coppey (vc), José Miguel Moreno (gtr), Paul Badura-Skoda (pno), Philippe Cassard (pno), Bob Van Asperen (hpd) Valois ▲ V 4767
Poulenc, F.:Son Ob, w. François Meyer (ob) Sonpact ▲ SPT 94011 [DDD]

Le Sage, Eric (pno) (cont.)
Saint-Saëns, C.:Son Ob, w. François Meyer (ob) Sonpact ▲ SPT 94011 [DDD]
Strauss, R.:Son Vc, w. Marc Coppey (vc) Harmonia Mundi France ▲ HMN 911550
Lesartre, Stacy (vn)—see ORCHESTRAS & ENSEMBLES Stratos
Leske, C. (pno)
Léon, T.:Ritual *(rec Oct. 21, 1992)* CRI ▲ CD 662 [DDD]
Leslie, Alayne (ob)—see ORCHESTRAS & ENSEMBLES L'Archibudelli
Lesser, Lawrence (vc)
Lazarof, H.:Con 1 Vc, w. G. Samuel (cnd), Oakland SO CRI ▲ CD 631
Lazarof, H.:Continuum, w. S. Plummer (vn), M. Thomas (va) *(rec 1970)* CRI ▲ CD 631
Spohr, L.:Double Qt 1, w. J. Heifetz (vn), I. Baker (vn), P. Amoyal (vn), P. Rosenthal (vn), M. Thomas (va), A. Harshman (va), G. Piatigorsky (vc) RCA Gold Seal ▲ 7870–2–RG (m/s) [ADD]
Lessing, Kolja (pno)
Goldschmidt, B.:Son Pno *(rec 1991)* Largo ▲ 5117 [DDD]
Markevitch, I.:L'Envol d'Icare, w. C. Lyndon-Gee (pno), J. Gagelmann (perc), R. Haeger (perc), F. Lang (perc) *(rec July 10–11, 1993)* Largo ▲ 5127 [DDD]
Markevitch, I.:Noces *(rec July 10–11, 1993)* Largo ▲ 5127 [DDD]
Lessing, Kolja (va)
Bohnke, E.:Son Va MD + G ▲ MDG 3250531 [DDD]
Lessing, Kolja (vn)—see also ORCHESTRAS & ENSEMBLES Alkan Trio
Bohnke, E.:Ciacona Vn MD + G ▲ MDG 3250531 [DDD]
Bohnke, E.:Son Vn MD + G ▲ MDG 3250531 [DDD]
Geiser, W.:Metamorphosen Grammont ▲ CTSP 21–2 [ADD]
Markevitch, I.:Serenade, w. W. Meyer (cl), D. Jensen (bn) *(rec Oct. 21–22, 1993)* Largo ▲ 5127 [DDD]
Lessing, Kolja (vn/pno)
J.S. Bach:Werk und Wirkung Ars Musici ▲ AM 0954 [DDD]
Lester, Harold (hpd)
Handel, G.F.:Royal Fireworks Music, w. Derek Wickens (ob), Alan Civil (hn), John Wilbraham (tpt), J. Somary (cnd), English CO *(rec Conway Hall, London, 1973)* Vanguard Classics ▲ SVC 47 [AAD]
Handel, G.F.:Water Music (comp), w. Derek Wickens (ob), Alan Civil (hn), John Wilbraham (tpt), J. Somary (cnd), English CO *(rec Conway Hall, London, 1973)* Vanguard Classics ▲ SVC 47 [AAD]
Lester, Harold (hpd/org)
Alfred Deller, w. Alfred Deller (ct), Robert Spencer (fl), Desmond Dupré (gtr) *(rec between 1965 & 1979)* Memoire Vive ▲ 262004 [ADD]
Lester, Harold (pno)
Martinů, B.:Double Con Pno & Timp, w. C. Mackerras (cnd), BBC SO IMP ("BBC Radio Classics" series) ▲ IMP 9135
Lester, N. (pno)—see ORCHESTRAS & ENSEMBLES Lester Roland Duo
Lester, Richard (vc)—see also ORCHESTRAS & ENSEMBLES Hausmusik, Florestan Trio
Boccherini, L.:Sons (5) Vc & Db, w. David Watkin (vc), Chi-Chi Nwanoku (db)—Sons. in c, A, E♭, C, & B♭ Hyperion ▲ CDA 66719
Rheinberger, J.:Suite Vn Vc, w. Paul Barritt (vn), Christopher Herrick (org) Hyperion ▲ CDA 66883
Lethiec, Michel (cl)
Bartók, B.:Contrasts, w. *(violinist unknown)*, Noël Lee (pno) Arion ▲ ARN 68327 [DDD]
Brahms, J.:Qnt Cl, w. Lindsay String Quartet Lyrinx ▲ LYX 123 [DDD]
Brahms, J.:Trio Cl, w. Katia Skavavi (vc), Truls Mork (pno) Lyrinx ▲ LYX 123 [DDD]
Bruch, M.:Pieces Cl, Op. 83/1–8, w. Vladimir Mendelssohn (va), Roberte Mamou (pno) *(rec Conservatoire de Tourcoing, Mar 1995)* Pavane ▲ ADW 7334 [DDD]
Hummel, J.N.:Qt Cl, w. Le Nouveau Trio Pasquier Talent ▲ 291037
Kreutzer, C.:Qt Cl, w. Le Nouveau Trio Pasquier Talent ▲ 291037
Pleyel, I.:Con in B♭ Cl, w. J.-P. Wallez (cnd), South Jutland SO *(rec Oct. 1992)* Talent ▲ DOM 2910 36 [DDD]
Schumann, R.:Märchenerzählungen, w. Vladimir Mendelssohn (va), Roberte Mamou (pno) *(rec Conservatoire de Tourcoing, Mar 1995)* Pavane ▲ ADW 7334 [DDD]
Vanhal, J.B.:Qt Cl, w. Le Nouveau Trio Pasquier Talent ▲ 291037
Lethiec, Saskia (vn)
Bach, J.S.:Con for 2 Vns, w. Gilles Colliard (vn), C. Meister (cnd), Brixi CO Prague *(rec Studio Martinek, Prague, Sept 5–8, 1994)* Doron ▲ DRC 5005 [DDD]
Letzbor, Gunar (vn)
Bach, J.S.:Cons Vn (comp), w. G. Letzbor (cnd), Ars Antiqua Austria Symphonia ▲ SYM 94134
Bach, J.S.:Con for 2 Vns, w. Daniel Sepec (vn), G. Letzbor (cnd), Ars Antiqua Austria Symphonia ▲ SYM 94134
Weichlein, R.:Encaenia musices, w. Daniel Sepec (vn), Herbert Lindsberger (va), Christoph Bitzinger (va), Michael Oman (vl), Gaetano Nasillo (vc), Roberto Sensi (vn), Andreas Lackner (nat tpt), Herbert Walser (nat tpt), Norbert Kirchner (hpd/org), G. Letzbor (cnd), Ars Antiqua Austria—Sons. Nos. I in C, II in g, III in a, IV in E, V in C & VI in F Symphonia ▲ SY 93S23
Leu, Christophe (gtr)
Duo de Guitares, w. Maya Obradovic (gtr) *(rec July 1987)* Gallo ▲ CD 533 [DDD]
Leuders, Kurt (org)
Romances et Méditations, w. Sheryl Staples (vn), John Novacek (pno) Arkay ▲ ARK 6097
Leuschner, M. (pno)
Clementi, M.:Sons Pno—in g, Op. 7/3; in D, Op. 40/3; in d, Op. 50/2 Brioso ▲ BR 102
Leuthold, Hansjürg (bas hn)
Mendelssohn, F.:Concert Pieces, w. H.R. Stalder (cl), J. von Vintschger (pno) *(rec 1981)* Jecklin-Disco ▲ JD 560–2 [ADD]
Mozart, W.A.:Diverts Bas Hns, K.Anh.229, w. H.R. Stalder (cl), H. Hofer (cl) [arr. for 3 basset horns]—No. 1 *(rec 1978)* Jecklin-Disco ▲ JD 549–2 [ADD]
Mozart, W.A.:Notturnos Sops, w. E. Speiser (sop), V. Gohl (cta), K. Widmer (bass), H.R. Stalder (cl), R. Kubli (bas hn) [I] *(rec 1968)* Jecklin-Disco ▲ JD 549–2 [ADD]
Mozart, W.A.:Più non si trovano, w. E. Speiser (sop), V. Gohl (cta), K. Widmer (bass), H.R. Stalder (cl), R. Kubli (bas hn) [I] *(rec 1968)* Jecklin-Disco ▲ JD 549–2 [ADD]
Lev, Wendi (fl)
O'Rourke, J.:Terminal Pharmacy, w. Tony Burr (cl), Jeff Cortazzo (b trbn), John McEntire (dr), Rob Prosser (acc), Isha Suftin (acc), Mike Dockter (vc), Hattie Franck (vc), Robert Keck (vc), Mary LaBreque (vc), Dan Loch (vc), Stan Saderk (vc), Lisa Hemmer (fl), Sue Oberg (fl), Jim Vanden (fl), Jim O'Rourke (gtr), Steve Braack (elec) Tzadik ▲ TZA 7011 [DDD]
Levant, Oscar (pno)
Gershwin, G.:Con Pno, w. A. Kostelanetz (cnd), New York PO *(rec 1942)* CBS ▲ MK 42514 (m) [ADD] ■ FMT 42514 (m)
Gershwin, G.:Con Pno, w. A. Kostelanetz (cnd), New York Philharmonic SO *(rec 1942)* Sony Masterworks ("Portrait" series) ▲ MPK 47681 [ADD]
Gershwin, G.:Con Pno, w. A. Toscanini (cnd), NBC SO *(rec Apr. 2, 1944)* Vintage Jazz Classics ▲ VJC 1034
Gershwin, G.:"I Got Rhythm" Vars, w. M. Gould (cnd), Morton Gould Orch *(rec 1949)* Sony Masterworks ("Portrait" series) ▲ MPK 47681 [ADD]
Gershwin, G.:"I Got Rhythm" Vars, w. M. Gould (cnd), Morton Gould Orch *(rec 1949)* CBS ▲ MK 42514 (m) [ADD] ■ FMT 42514 (m)
Gershwin, G.:Preludes (3) Pno *(rec 1941)* Sony Masterworks ("Portrait" series) ▲ MPK 47681 [ADD]
Gershwin, G.:Preludes (3) Pno CBS ▲ MLK 39454 ■ PMT 39454
Gershwin, G.:Preludes (3) Pno *(rec 1949)* CBS ▲ MK 42514 (m) [ADD] ■ FMT 42514 (m)
Gershwin, G.:Rhap in Blue, w. E. Ormandy (cnd), Philadelphia Orch *(rec 1945)* CBS ▲ MK 42514 (m) [ADD] ■ FMT 42514 (m)
Gershwin, G.:Rhap in Blue, w. E. Ormandy (cnd), Philadelphia Orch *(rec 1945)* Sony Masterworks ("Portrait" series) ▲ MPK 47681 [ADD]
Gershwin, G.:Second Rhap, w. M. Gould (cnd), Morton Gould Orch *(rec 1949)* Sony Masterworks ("Portrait" series) ▲ MPK 47681 [ADD]
Gershwin, G.:Second Rhap, w. M. Gould (cnd), Morton Gould Orch *(rec 1949)* CBS ▲ MK 42514 (m) [ADD] ■ FMT 42514 (m)

692 ▲ = CD ♦ = Enhanced CD Δ = MD ■ = Cassette Tape □ = DCC

Levay, Laura (fl)—see ORCHESTRAS & ENSEMBLES Tickmayer Formatio

Leveaux, Ursula (bn)
Davies, P.M.:Strathclyde Con 8, w. P. M. Davies (cnd), Scottish CO Collins Classics ▲ COL 1396 [DDD]

Levenson, Jeffrey (vc)—see ORCHESTRAS & ENSEMBLES Thouvenel String Quartet

Leventhal, Sharon (vn)—see also ORCHESTRAS & ENSEMBLES Marimolin
Aldridge, R.:Combo Platter, w. Albert Regni (s sax), Nancy Zeltsman (mar) Open Loop ▲ 034 [DDD]
Thomson, V.:Portraits, w. A. Tommasini (pno), J. Miller (vc), F.T. Cohen (ob), R. Haroutunian (bn)—Selected Portraits (13) for Pno (1935–42); Five Ladies for Vn & Pno (1930; 1940; 1983); A Portrait of 2, for Ob, Bn & Pno (1984); 3 Portraits for Pno (1940; arr Samuel Dushkin in 1947 for Vn & Pno); Etude for Vc & Pno:A Portrait of Frederic James (1966); Lili Hastings for Vc & Pno (1983) Northeastern ▲ NR 240–CD
Thomson, V.:Serenade, w. F. Smith (fl) Northeastern ▲ NR 240–CD
Thomson, V.:Son Vn, w. A. Tommasini (pno) Northeastern ▲ NR 240–CD

Levertov, Gad (vn)
Debussy, C.:Son Fl, w. E. Talmi (fl), A. Giles (hp) PWK Classics ▲ PWK 1141 [DDD]

Levin, Ida (vn)—see also ORCHESTRAS & ENSEMBLES Mendelssohn String Quartet
Vivaldi, A.:Music of, w. Salvatore Accardo (vn), Frederico Agostini (vn), Heinz Holliger (ob), Aurele Nicolet (fl), Massimo Paris (va d'amore), Angel Romero (gtr), Celedonio Romero (gtr), Celine Romero (gtr), Henryk Szeryng (vn), Pinchas Zukerman (vn), Academy of St. Martin in the Fields, English CO, I Musici, Naples Weekly International Soloists, St. Paul CO, Dresden Staatskapelle—The Four Seasons [Winter]; Con in D for Gtr [Largo]; Con in D for Fl, "Il gardellino" [Cantabile]; Con in C for Diverse Insts [Andante molto]; Con in g for Strs [Andante molto]; Con in D for 2 Vns & 2 Vcs [Largo]; Con in g for Ob, Vn, Ww & Strs [Larghetto]; Con in a for Gtr, "L'estro armonico" [Largo]; Con in F for 3 Vns [Andante]; Con in F for Fl [Largo]; Con in d for Va D'Amore [Largo]; Con in E for Vn & Strs, "Il riposo" [Allegro]; Con in G for Ob, Bn & Strs [Largo]; Con in B♭ for Vn & Strs [Largo]; Con in A for Gtr & Strs [Larghetto]; Con in E for Vn & Strs, "L'amoroso" [Allegro]; Con in G for Fl [Largo]; Con in A for Vn [Larghetto]; Con in c for Vn & Strs, "Il sospetto" [Andante]; Con in a for 2 Obs & Strs [Largo]; Con in g for Orch [Largo non molto]; Con in a for Vn [Largo]; Con in C for Ob [Adagio]; Con in g for Fl, "La notte" [Largo] Philips ▲ 454051–2 ■ 454 051–4

Levin, Michelle (pno)
Barber, S.:Son Vc, w. Y. Hanani (vc) *(rec May 1990)* Koch International Classics ▲ KIC 7070 [DDD]
Foss, L.:Capriccio, w. Y. Hanani (vc) *(rec May, 1990)* Koch International Classics ▲ KIC 7070 [DDD]
Ornstein, L.:Son Vc, w. Y. Hanani (vc) *(rec May 1990)* Koch International Classics ▲ KIC 7070 [DDD]
Rare Cello Music, w. Heled, Simca (vc), Daniel Edni (pno), Jonathan Feldman (pno), Alexander Peskanov (pno), Jonathan Zak (pno) *(rec 1976, 1982, 1983, 1985, 1)* Classico ▲ CLASSCD 153

Levin, Robert (pno)
Beethoven, L. van:Con 5 Pno, "Emperor", w. J. E. Gardiner (cnd), Orch Révolutionnaire et Romantique Archiv ▲ 447771–2
Beethoven, L. van:Fant Pno, Op. 80, "Choral Fant", w. J. E. Gardiner (cnd), Orch Révolutionnaire et Romantique, Monteverdi Choir London Archiv ▲ 447771–2
Britten, H.:Lachrymae, w. K. Kashkashian (va) ECM New Series ▲ 78118–21316–2 [ADD]
Carter, E.:Elegy Va, w. K. Kashkashian (va) ECM New Series ▲ 78118–21316–2 [ADD]
Glazunov, A.:Élégie Vc, w. K. Kashkashian (va) ECM New Series ▲ 78118–21316–2 [ADD]
Harbison, J.:Fant Duo, w. Rose Mary Harbison (vn) *(rec Kresge Auditorium, between 1988 & 1994)* Archetype ▲ 60104 [DDD]
Haydn, J.:Trios Pno, Vn & Vc, w. Vera Beths (vn), Anner Bylsma (vc)—No. 25 in C, H.XV:27; No. 26 in E, H.XV:28; No. 30 in E♭, H.XV:30 *(rec Sept. 2–5, 1992)* Sony Classical ▲ SK 53120 [DDD]
Hindemith, P.:Sons Va & Pno, w. K. Kashkashian (va)—Op. 11/4 (1919); Op. 25/4 (1922); Sonata (1939) ECM New Series 2–▲ 78118–21330–2 [DDD]
Kodály, Z.:Adagio Vn, w. K. Kashkashian (va) ECM New Series ▲ 78118–21316–2 [ADD]
Kurtág, G.:Hommage à R. Schumann, w. Eduard Brunner (cl), Kim Kashkashian (va) *(rec Beethovenhaus, Bonn, Aug. 1992 & May & Sept. 1)* ECM New Series ▲ 78118–21508–2 [DDD]
Liszt, F.:Romance oubliée, w. K. Kashkashian (va) ECM New Series ▲ 78118–21316–2 [ADD]
Mozart, W.A.:Con 9 Pno, w. C. Hogwood (cnd), Academy of Ancient Music *(rec Aug. 1993)* L'Oiseau-Lyre ▲ 443328–2 [DDD]
Mozart, W.A.:Con 11 Pno, w. C. Hogwood (cnd), Academy of Ancient Music L'oiseau-lyre ▲ 444571–2
Mozart, W.A.:Con 11 Pno, w. C. Hogwood (cnd), Academy of Ancient Music London ("Editions de l'oiseau-lyre" series) ▲ 444571–2
Mozart, W.A.:Con 12 Pno, w. C. Hogwood (cnd), Academy of Ancient Music *(rec Aug. 1993)* L'Oiseau-Lyre ▲ 443328–2 [DDD]
Mozart, W.A.:Con 13 Pno, w. C. Hogwood (cnd), Academy of Ancient Music L'oiseau-lyre ▲ 444571–2
Mozart, W.A.:Con 13 Pno, w. C. Hogwood (cnd), Academy of Ancient Music London ("Editions de l'oiseau-lyre" series) ▲ 444571–2
Mozart, W.A.:Con 18 Pno, w. C. Hogwood (cnd), Academy of Ancient Music London ▲ 452051–2
Mozart, W.A.:Con 19 Pno, w. C. Hogwood (cnd), Academy of Ancient Music London ▲ 452051–2
Mozart, W.A.:Pno Music 4-Hands, w. Malcolm Bilson (pno)—Fugue in c, K.426; Larghetto & Allegro in E♭ [compl. Levin] Elektra/Nonesuch ■ 78023–4
Mozart, W.A.:Rondo Pno Orch, K.386, w. C. Hogwood (cnd), Academy of Ancient Music London ▲ 444571–2
Mozart, W.A.:Son Pnos, K.448, w. M. Bilson (pno) Elektra/Nonesuch ■ 78023–4
Prokofiev, S.:Son Fl, w. E. Brunner (cl) [clarinet–piano trans. by Brunner] Tudor ▲ 727 [DDD]
Romances & Elegies for Viola & Piano, w. Kashkashian, Kim (va) ECM New Series ▲ 78118–21316–2 [ADD]
Schubert, Franz:Son Pno, D.537 Sony Classical ("Vivarte" series) ▲ SK 53981
Schubert, Franz:Son Pno, D.850 Sony Classical ("Vivarte" series) ▲ SK 53981
Schumann, R.:Fantasiestücke Cl, w. Eduard Brunner (cl) *(rec Beethovenhaus, Bonn, Aug. 1992 & May & Sept. 1)* ECM New Series ▲ 78118–21508–2 [DDD]
Schumann, R.:Märchenbilder, w. Kim Kashkashian (va) *(rec Beethovenhaus, Bonn, Aug. 1992 & May & Sept. 1)* ECM New Series ▲ 78118–21508–2 [DDD]
Schumann, R.:Märchenerzählungen, w. Eduard Brunner (cl), Kim Kashkashian (va) *(rec Beethovenhaus, Bonn, Aug. 1992 & May & Sept. 1)* ECM New Series ▲ 78118–21508–2 [DDD]
Shostakovich, D.:Son Va, w. K. Kashkashian (va) ECM New Series ▲ 78118–21425–2
Shostakovich, D.:Waltzes Fl, w. A. Adorján (fl), E. Brunner (cl) Tudor ▲ 727 [DDD]
Vieuxtemps, H.:Elégie, w. K. Kashkashian (va) ECM New Series ▲ 78118–21316–2 [ADD]

Levinas, Michaël (pno)
Beethoven, L. van:Bagatelles (24)—Op. 119 Adès ▲ ADE 141322 [DDD]
Beethoven, L. van:Sons Pno (comp)—No. 10, Op. 14/2; No. 19, Op. 49/1; No. 20, Op. 49/2; No. 28, Op. 101 Adès ▲ ADE 141392 [DDD]
Beethoven, L. van:Son 3 Pno Adès ▲ ADE 141322 [DDD]
Beethoven, L. van:Son 9 Pno Adès ▲ ADE 141372 [DDD]
Beethoven, L. van:Son 11 Pno Adès ▲ ADE 141372 [DDD]
Beethoven, L. van:Son 16 Pno Adès ▲ ADE 141382 [DDD]
Beethoven, L. van:Son 17 Pno, "Tempest" Adès ▲ ADE 141372 [DDD]
Beethoven, L. van:Son 18 Pno Adès ▲ ADE 141382 [DDD]
Beethoven, L. van:Son 26 Pno, "Les Adieux" Adès ▲ ADE 141382 [DDD]
Beethoven, L. van:Son 32 Pno Adès ▲ ADE 141322 [DDD]
Chopin, F.:Ballades Pno (comp) Adès ▲ ADE 140762 [DDD]
Chopin, F.:Berceuse Adès ▲ ADE 140762 [DDD]
Chopin, F.:Fant Adès ▲ ADE 140762 [DDD]
Schumann, R.:Fant Pno Adès ▲ ADE 140442 [AAD]
Schumann, R.:Kreisleriana Adès ▲ ADE 140442 [AAD]
Scriabin, A.:Etudes Pno (comp) Adès ▲ ADE 202432

Levine (gtr)
Rorem, N.:Romeo & Juliet, w. I. Dingfelder (fl) CRI ■ ACS 6007

Levine, Adrian (vn)—see also ORCHESTRAS & ENSEMBLES Ambache Chamber Ensemble, Ambache Chamber Ensemble members
Mozart, W.A.:Sons Vn Pno (misc), w. Diana Ambache (pno)—in G, K.301 Meridian ▲ MER 84329 [AAD]

Levine, Carin (a fl/b fl)
Platz, R.H.:Dunkles Haus, w. Maria Husmann (sop—Woman), Michael Busch (bar—Man), Udo Zickwolf (nar—Child/Bird/Man), R. Platz (cnd), Marstall Ensemble of the Bavarian State Opera *(rec 1991)* Thorofon ▲ CTH 2170

Levine, Caroline (va)
Brahms, J.:Sextet Strs, Op. 36, w. P. Carmirelli (vn), J. Toth (vn), P. Naegele (va), F. Arico (vc), D. Reichenberger (vc) Sony Classical ▲ SMK 46249 [ADD] ■ SMT 46249
Stahmer, K.H.:Ariadnes Faden, w. Stefan Eblenkamp (perc) Pro Viva ▲ ISPV 167 [DDD]

Levine, David (pno)
Reger, M.:Fant-Stücke CPO ▲ CPO 999074–2 [DDD]
Reger, M.:Humoresken CPO ▲ CPO 999074–2 [DDD]
Reger, M.:Improvs CPO ▲ CPO 999074–2 [DDD]
Reger, M.:Vars & Fugue on a Theme of J. S. Bach Koch Schwann ▲ CD 310008 [ADD]
Reger, M.:Vars & Fugue on a Theme of G. P. Telemann Koch Schwann ▲ CD 310008 [ADD]
Schubert, Franz:Son Pno, D.959 Virgin Classics ▲ CDZ 59694
Schubert, Franz:Son Pno, D.960 Virgin Classics ▲ CDZ 59694

Levine, James (pno)
Kathleen Battle in Concert, w. Kathleen Battle (sop) Deutsche Grammophon ("Masters" series) ▲ 445524–2 [DDD]
Poulenc, F.:Music of, w. Vienna Ensemble—Elegie; Sextet; 2 Sonatas; Trio Deutsche Grammophon ▲ 427639–2 [DDD]
Schubert, Franz:Fant Vn, D.934, w. J. Szigeti (vn) *(rec 1949)* Sony Masterworks ("Portrait" series) ▲ MPK 52538 (m) [ADD]
Schubert, Franz:Qt Fl, w. G. Hetzel (vn), W. Christ (va), G. Faust (vc), A. Posch (db) Deutsche Grammophon ▲ 431783–2
Schubert, Franz:Qnt Pno, D.667, w. G. Hetzel (vn), W. Christ (va), G. Faust (vc), A. Posch (db) Deutsche Grammophon ▲ 431783–2
Schubert, Franz:Son Arpeggione, w. L. Harrell (cello) RCA Gold Seal ("Papillon Collection" series) ▲ 6531–2–RG [ADD] ■ 6531–4–RG
Schubert, Franz:Songs (misc), w. K. Battle (sop) [G] Deutsche Grammophon ▲ 419237–2 [DDD]
Schubert, Franz:Winterreise, w. Christa Ludwig (mez) Deutsche Grammophon ("Masters" series) ▲ 445521–2
Scott Joplin:Greatest Hits, w. Dick Hyman (pno) RCA Victor ▲ 60842–2–RG ■ 60842–4–RG

Levine, Jesse (va)
American Flute, Vol. 1, w. Zizi Mueller (fl), Yuval Waldman (vn), S. Tahmiziàn (pno) Premier ▲ PRCD 1029 [DDD]

Levine, Joanna (vl/vc/vle)—see ORCHESTRAS & ENSEMBLES Palladian Ensemble

Levine, Julius (db)
Mozart, W.A.:Kleine Nachtmusik, w. Budapest String Quartet Sony Classical 3–▲ SM3K 46527
Schubert, Franz:Qnt Pno, D.667, w. M. Horszowski (pno), Budapest String Quartet members Sony Classical ("Essential Classics" series) ▲ SBK 46343 [ADD] ■ SBT 46343
Schubert, Franz:Qnt Pno, D.667, w. R. Serkin (pno), J. Laredo (vn), P. Naegele (va), L. Parnas (vc) *(rec 1967)* Sony Classical ▲ SMK 46252 [ADD]
Schubert, Franz:Qnt Pno, D.667, w. P. Serkin (pno), A. Schneider (vn), M. Tree (va), D. Soyer (vc) *(rec 1964)* Vanguard Classics ▲ OVC 8005 [ADD]
Stravinsky, I.:L'Histoire du soldat Suite Vn, w. G. Tarack (vn), C. Russo (cl), T. Weis (tpt), Loren Glickman (bn), J. Swallow (trbn), R. Desroches (perc), L. Stokowski (cnd) Vanguard Classics ▲ SVC 1 [AAD]

Levinson, Eugene (db)—see also ORCHESTRAS & ENSEMBLES Levinson Family Trio
Beethoven, L. van:Son 3 Vc, w. Gina Levinson (pno) Cala Records ("New York Legends" series) ▲ CAL CACD 507 [DDD]
Bruch, M.:Kol Nidrei, w. Gina Levinson (pno) Cala Records ("New York Legends" series) ▲ CAL CACD 507 [DDD]
Hindemith, P.:Son Db, w. Gina Levinson (pno) Cala Records ("New York Legends" series) ▲ CAL CACD 507 [DDD]
Koussevitsky, S.:Valse Caprice, w. Gina Levinson (pno) Cala Records ("New York Legends" series) ▲ CAL CACD 507 [DDD]
Ranjbaran, B.:Dance of Life, w. Gary Levinson (vn) Cala Records ("New York Legends" series) ▲ CAL CACD 507 [DDD]
Tchaikovsky, P.:Méditation, w. Gina Levinson (pno) Cala Records ("New York Legends" series) ▲ CAL CACD 507 [DDD]

Levinson, Gary (vn)—see also ORCHESTRAS & ENSEMBLES Levinson Family Trio
Ranjbaran, B.:Dance of Life, w. Eugene Levinson (db) Cala Records ("New York Legends" series) ▲ CAL CACD 507 [DDD]

Levinson, Gina (pno)—see also ORCHESTRAS & ENSEMBLES Levinson Family Trio
Beethoven, L. van:Son 3 Vc, w. Eugene Levinson (db) Cala Records ("New York Legends" series) ▲ CAL CACD 507 [DDD]
Bruch, M.:Kol Nidrei, w. Eugene Levinson (db) Cala Records ("New York Legends" series) ▲ CAL CACD 507 [DDD]
Hindemith, P.:Son Db, w. Eugene Levinson (db) Cala Records ("New York Legends" series) ▲ CAL CACD 507 [DDD]
Koussevitsky, S.:Valse Caprice, w. Eugene Levinson (db) Cala Records ("New York Legends" series) ▲ CAL CACD 507 [DDD]
Tchaikovsky, P.:Méditation, w. Eugene Levinson (db) Cala Records ("New York Legends" series) ▲ CAL CACD 507 [DDD]

Levinson, Josef (vc)—see ORCHESTRAS & ENSEMBLES Taneyev String Quartet

Levitch, Leon (pno)
Levitch, L.:Ricordo di Mario Pno, w. Greg Donovetsky (ob) [trans. for ob & Pno] Cambria ▲ CD 1059 [ADD]

Levitin, Susan (fl)
La Flûte Lumineuse, w. Gerald Rizzer (pno), Chicago Ensemble *(rec WFMT Studios, Chicago)* Mark ▲ MCD 1939

Levitzki, Mischa (pno)
Mischa Levitzki:1898–1941 Pearl ▲ PEA 9962 (m) [AAD]
Schumann, R.:Son 2 Pno *(rec 1933)* Pearl ▲ PEA 9962 (m) [AAD]

Levy, Al (kbd/elec/cmpt)
LFO Pops Orchestra LFO ▲ CD 1

Levy, Ammon (vn)
McLennan, J.S.:Qnt Vn, Va, Vc, Cl & Pno, w. B. Fine (va), A. Diaz (vc), P. Hancock (cl), R. Hodgkinson (pno) CRI ▲ CD 594 [DDD]

Levy, Daniel (pno)
Schumann, R.:Album für die Jugend Nimbus ▲ NI 5219 [DDD]
Schumann, R.:Arabeske Pno Nimbus ▲ NI 5256 [DDD]
Schumann, R.:Carnaval Pno Nimbus ▲ NI 5256 [DDD]
Schumann, R.:Davidsbündlertänze Nimbus ▲ NI 5215 [DDD]
Schumann, R.:Fantasiestücke Pno, Op. 12 Nimbus ▲ NI 5238 [DDD]
Schumann, R.:Faschingsschwank aus Wien Nimbus ▲ NI 5256 [DDD]
Schumann, R.:Gesänge der Frühe Nimbus ▲ NI 5250 [DDD]
Schumann, R.:Kinderszenen Nimbus ▲ NI 5215 [DDD]
Schumann, R.:Klavierstücke, Op. 32 Nimbus ▲ NI 5238 [DDD]
Schumann, R.:Nachtstücke Nimbus ▲ NI 5250 [DDD]
Schumann, R.:Pno Music (comp)—Album für die Jugend, Op. 68 Nimbus ▲ 5219–2 [DDD]
Schumann, R.:Pno Music (comp)—Arabeske, Op. 18; Carnaval, Op. 9; Faschingsschwank aus Wien, Op. 26 Nimbus ▲ 5256–2 [DDD]

Levy, Daniel (pno) (cont.)
Schumann, R.:Pno Music (comp)—Fantasiestücke, Op. 12; Klavierstücke, Op. 32; Sonata in g, Op. 22 — Nimbus ▲ 5238-2 [DDD]
Schumann, R.:Pno Music (comp)—Gesänge der Frühe, Op. 133; Waldscenen, Op. 82; Nachtstücke, Op. 23 — Nimbus ▲ 5250-2 [DDD]
Schumann, R.:Pno Music (comp)—Davidsbündlertanze, Op. 6; Kinderscenen, Op. 15 — Nimbus ▲ NI 5215 [DDD]
Schumann, R.:Waldscenen — Nimbus ▲ NI 5250 [DDD]
Levy, M. (t sax)—see ORCHESTRAS & ENSEMBLES Prism Saxophone Quartet
Levy, Mark (vl)—see also ORCHESTRAS & ENSEMBLES Cambridge Musick, Les Éléments
Telemann, G.P.:Con in a for Rcr, Vl, w. P. Pickett (rcr), P. Pickett (cnd), New London Consort — L'Oiseau-Lyre ▲ 433043-2 [DDD]
Levy, P. (vn)—see ORCHESTRAS & ENSEMBLES Apple Hill Chamber Players
Levy, Ron (pno)—see also ORCHESTRAS & ENSEMBLES Manchester Chamber Players
Brahms, J.:Son 1 Vc, w. S. Brubaker (vc) [trans S. Brubaker for hn & pno] — Koch International Classics ▲ KIC 7034-2 [DDD]
Brahms, J.:Son 2 Cl, w. S. Brubaker (hn) [trans S. Brubaker for hn & pno] — Koch International Classics ▲ KIC 7034-2 [DDD]
Cello Charms, w. Michael Rudiakov (vc) *(rec Marlboro, VT, May 1993)* — Centaur ▲ CRC 2192 [DDD]
Levy, T. (fl)—see ORCHESTRAS & ENSEMBLES Aspen Wind Quintet
Lew, P. Van (hn)
Koechlin, C.:Poème, w. E. Appia (cnd), RTF Orch *(rec 1957)* — Skarbo ▲ SKR 3924
Lewenthal, Raymond (pno)
Alkan, C.-V.:Etudes (12) in minor keys—Nos. 4-7 & 12 *(rec 1965-66)* — Élan ▲ CD 82276 [ADD]
Alkan, C.-V.:Grande son [Les quatre âges] *(rec 1965-66)* — Élan ▲ CD 82276 [ADD]
Alkan, C.-V.:Troisième recueil de chants—No. 6 (barcarolle) *(rec 1965-66)* — Élan ▲ CD 82276 [ADD]
Gershwin, G.:Con Pno, w. O. Danon (cnd), RCA Victor SO *(rec 1962)* — Chesky ▲ CD56 [ADD]
Gershwin, G.:Rhap in Blue, w. O. Danon (cnd), Metropolitan Orch *(rec 1962)* — Chesky ▲ CD56 [ADD]
Liszt, F.:Hexaméron *(rec 1965-66)* — Élan ▲ CD 82276 [ADD]
Lewertoff, Gad (va)
Martin, F.:Sonnets à Cassandre, w. U. Mayer-Reinach (mez), A. Sella (fl), N. Enoch (vc) — Gallo ▲ CD 633 [DDD]
Lewin, Giles (h-g/rebec/gittern/shm/pipe/tabor)—see ORCHESTRAS & ENSEMBLES Dufay Collective
Lewin, Michael (lt)
Music of the "Chapels Royal" of England, w. Marilyn Sansom (vc), Alastair Ross (org) — Erato ▲ 45987-2
Lewin, Michael (pno)
Balakirev, M.:Islamey *(rec June 1991)* — Centaur ▲ CRC 2134 [DDD]
Balakirev, M.:Paraphrase Pno *(rec June 1991)* — Centaur ▲ CRC 2134 [DDD]
Balakirev, M.:Toccata *(rec June 1991)* — Centaur ▲ CRC 2134 [DDD]
Glazunov, A.:Theme & Vars *(rec June 1991)* — Centaur ▲ CRC 2134 [DDD]
Liszt, F.:Études d'exécution transcendante, S.139—No. 10 — Centaur ▲ CRC 2066 [DDD]
Liszt, F.:Fant on Themes from Bellini's *La Sonnambula* — Centaur ▲ CRC 2066 [DDD]
Liszt, F.:Hungarian Rhaps—No. 8 — Centaur ▲ CRC 2066 [DDD]
Liszt, F.:Song Transcriptions—Chopin—Spring; Mendelssohn—Auf Flügeln des Gesanges; Schubert—Ave Maria; Schumann—Widmung — Centaur ▲ CRC 2066 [DDD]
Liszt, F.:Vars on "Weinen, Klagen, Sorgen, Zagen", S.179 — Centaur ▲ CRC 2066 [DDD]
Scriabin, A.:Pno Music (misc)—Etudes, Op. 2/1, Op. 8/5, Op. 42/4 & 5; Nocturne, Op. 9/2; Prelude, Op. 9/1 *(rec June 1991)* — Centaur ▲ CRC 2134 [DDD]
Scriabin, A.:Son 2 Pno *(rec June 1991)* — Centaur ▲ CRC 2134 [DDD]
Lewis, A. (hn)
Telemann, G.P.:Suite for 4 Hns, w. I. James (hn), T. Abramovici (hn), R. Teutsch (hn), V. Czarnecki (cnd), Southwest German CO Pforzheim — ebs ▲ ebs 6092 [DDD]
Lewis, Andrew (perc)—see ORCHESTRAS & ENSEMBLES Earplay
Lewis, Anthony (vc)—see ORCHESTRAS & ENSEMBLES Medici String Quartet
Lewis, Carol (vl)
Musiche Veneziene per Voce e Strumenti, w. Teresa Berganza (mez), Yasunori Imamura (lt/thb/gtr), Pere Ros (vl), Lynn Dickinson (vl), Silvie Mocquet (vl), Jörg Ewald Dähler (pno), Jörg Ewald Dähler (cnd) *(rec Kirche Saanen, Feb 1982)* — Claves ▲ CD 508206 [DDD]
Lewis, Cary (pno)—see also ORCHESTRAS & ENSEMBLES Lanier Trio, Lanier Trio members
Adler, S.:Double Portrait, w. W. Steck (vn) — Gasparo ▲ GS 297
Adler, S.:Little Suite, w. W. Steck (vn) — Gasparo ▲ GS 297
Adler, S.:Music of, w. W. Steck (vn), G. Peachey (pno), Y. Caruthers (vc)—Sons. 2-4; Etudes (4), "Meadowmountetudes"; Double Portrait; Little Suite; Close Encounters — Gasparo ▲ GS 297 [DDD/ADD]
Adler, S.:Trio 1 Pno, w. William Steck (vn), Dorothy Lewis (vc) — Gasparo ▲ GS 298 [DDD/DAD]
Boury, R.:Ballade, w. D. Lewis (vc) — Gasparo ▲ GS 274 ■ GS 274C
Bryant, C.:Son Vc, w. D. Lewis (vc) — Gasparo ▲ GS 274 ■ GS 274C
Gerschefski, E.:Vc & Pno Music, w. D. Lewis (vc)—Moderato, Op. 63/2; Nocturne, Op. 42/2; Vivace, Op. 63/1b — Gasparo ▲ GS 274 ■ GS 247C
Giannini, V.:Songs, w. J. Price (sop)—Songs on poems by Karl Flaster—Be Still My Heart; Far Above the Purple Hills; Heart Cry; I Did Not Know; I Only Know; I Shall Think of You; If I Had Known; It is a Spring Night; Little Girl in Blue; Longing; Love; Moonlight; My Love for You Has Grown; Parting; Sing to My Heart a Son; The Sun Had Set; Tell Me, Oh Blue, Blue Sky; There Were 2 Swans; 3 Oriental Chants; 3 Poems of the Sea [E] *(rec June 1991)* — ACA Digital Recording ▲ CM 20011
Gottschalk, L.M.:Music of, w. Trinidad Paniagua (sop), José Alberto Esteves (ten), Pablo Garcia (bar), Eugene List (pno), Brady Millican (pno), Adler, Buketoff (cnd), Berlin SO, Vienna State Opera Orch—Grande Tarantelle for Piano & Orchestra, Op. 67; Symphony No. 1, "La nuit des tropiques"; Symphony No. 2, "A Montevideo"; The Union (concert paraphrase on American national airs) for Piano & Orchestra, Op. 48; Variations on the Portuguese National Hymn for Piano & Orchestra, Op. 91; Grande fantaisie triomphale sur l'hymne national brésilien for Piano & Orchestra, Op. 69; Marche solennelle for Orchestra; Marcha triunfal y final de opera for Orchestra; Escenas campestres (opera in one act); Five Pieces for Piano Duet [Radieuse, Op. 72; Ses yeux, Op. 66; La Gallina, Op. 53; Ojos criollos, Op. 37; Pasquinade, Op. 59] — Vox Box 2-▲ CDX 5009 [ADD]
Gottschalk, L.M.:The Union, w. E. List (pno) [2-piano arr. by List] *(rec 1976)* — Vanguard Classics ▲ OVC 4051 [ADD]
Knox, C.:Prelude & Fugue Vc, w. D. Lewis (vc) — Gasparo ▲ GS 274 ■ GS 274C
Music by Southern Composers for Cello & Piano, w. Dorothy Lewis (vc) — Gasparo ▲ GSCD 274 ■ GS 274C
Newman, Anthony:Largo & Rondo, w. A. Newman (cnd), New York Arts Orch — Newport Classic ▲ NCD 60140 [DDD]
Presser, W.:Fant on Kedron Vc, w. D. Lewis (vc) — Gasparo ▲ GS 274 ■ GS 274C
Romances, w. Dorothy Lewis (vc) — ACA Digital ▲ CM 20013
Lewis, Dorothy (vc)—see also ORCHESTRAS & ENSEMBLES Lanier Trio members, Lanier Trio
Adler, S.:Trio 1 Pno, w. Cary Lewis (pno), William Steck (vn) — Gasparo ▲ GS 298 [DDD/DAD]
Boury, R.:Ballade, w. C. Lewis (pno) — Gasparo ▲ GS 274 ■ GS 274C
Bryant, C.:Son Vc, w. C. Lewis (pno) — Gasparo ▲ GS 274 ■ GS 274C
Gerschefski, E.:Vc & Pno Music, w. C. Lewis (pno)—Moderato, Op. 63/2; Nocturne, Op. 42/2; Vivace, Op. 63/1b — Gasparo ▲ GS 274 ■ GS 247C
Knox, C.:Prelude & Fugue Vc, w. C. Lewis (pno) — Gasparo ▲ GS 274 ■ GS 274C
Music by Southern Composers for Cello & Piano, w. C. Lewis (pno) — Gasparo ▲ GSCD 274 ■ GS 274C
Presser, W.:Fant on Kedron Vc, w. C. Lewis (pno) — Gasparo ▲ GS 274 ■ GS 274C
Romances, w. C. Lewis (pno) — ACA Digital ▲ CM 20013
Lewis, Eric (vn)—see ORCHESTRAS & ENSEMBLES Manhattan String Quartet
Lewis, George (trbn)
Rolnick, N.B.:Wondrous Love — O.O. Discs ▲ OO 8 [ADD]
Teitelbaum, R.:Con Grosso, w. Anthony Braxton (ww), Richard Teitelbaum (kbd/elec) *(rec Klaviere & Computer Festival, Cologne, May 3, 1985)* — Hat Hut ▲ hat ART CD 6004 [AAD]
Lewis, Harmon (org)
We Wish You a Merry Christmas, w. Gary Karr (db) — VQR Digital ▲ VQR 2036 [DDD]
Lewis, Harmon (pno)
The Spirit of Koussevitzky, w. Gary Karr (db) — VQR Digital ▲ VQR 2031 [DDD]
Lewis, Marianne (hpd)
Scarlatti, D.:Sons Kbd—K.24, 119, 120, 132, 133, 208, 209, 238, 239, 441, 442, 544, 545 — Connoisseur Society ▲ CD 4180 [DDD]
Lewis, Oliver (vn)
Elgar, E.:Son Vn, w. Jeremy Filsell (pno) *(rec Hillesden Church, Buckinghamshire, England)* — Guild ▲ GMCD 7124 [DDD]
Ferguson, H.:Son 2 Vn, w. Jeremy Filsell (pno) — Guild ▲ GMCD 7120 [DDD]
Goossens, E.:Lyric Poem, w. Jeremy Filsell (pno) *(rec Hillesden Church, Buckinghamshire, England)* — Guild ▲ GMCD 7124 [DDD]
Goossens, E.:Old Chinese Folksong, w. Jeremy Filsell (pno) *(rec Hillesden Church, Buckinghamshire, England)* — Guild ▲ GMCD 7124 [DDD]
Goossens, E.:Romance, w. Jeremy Filsell (pno) *(rec Hillesden Church, Buckinghamshire, England)* — Guild ▲ GMCD 7124 [DDD]
Goossens, E.:Son 1 Vn, w. Jeremy Filsell (pno) — Guild ▲ GMCD 7120 [DDD]
Goossens, E.:Son 2 Vn, w. Jeremy Filsell (pno) *(rec Hillesden Church, Buckinghamshire, England)* — Guild ▲ GMCD 7124 [DDD]
Ireland, J.:Son 2 Vn, w. Jeremy Filsell (pno) — Guild ▲ GMCD 7120 [DDD]
Lewis, Roy (vn)—see ORCHESTRAS & ENSEMBLES Manhattan String Quartet, Stratos
Lexutt, Walter (hn)
Haydn, J.:Con for 2 Hns, w. Erich Penzel (hn), H. Müller-Brühl (cnd), Cologne CO — Koch Schwann ▲ CD 316 026 [ADD]
Leyetchkiss, Vladimir (pno)
Beethoven, L. van:Vars on a waltz by Diabelli, Op. 120 *(rec in recital at Merkin Hall, New York, 1/16/84)* — Orion ■ OCD 8904
Tchaikovsky, P.:Pno Music—Chanson Triste, Op. 40/2; Valses, Op. 40/8 & 9; Mazurka, Op. 40/5; Valse de salon, Op. 51/1; Polka peu dansante, Op. 51/2; Minuetto Scherzoso, Op. 51/3; Natha-valse, Op. 51/4; Romance, Op. 51/5; Valse sentimentale, Op. 51/6; Tendres reproches, Op. 72/3; Scherzo fantasie, Op. 72/10; Un poco di Chopin, Op. 72/15; Polacca de concert, Op. 72/7; Scherzo from Symphony No. 6/74, "Pathétique" — Centaur ▲ CRC 2161 [DDD]
Leygraf, Hans (pno)
Schubert, Franz:Pno Music (misc)—Allegretto in c, D.915; Son. in A, D.664; 17 Ländler, D.366; Son. in c, D.958; Piano Piece in A, D.604; Minuet in c#, D.600; Trio in E, D.610; Son. in a, D.537; 12 German Dances, D.420; Son. in A, D.959; 2 Scherzos, D.593; Son. in a, D.784; 12 Ländler, D.790; Son. in B♭ — Caprice 3-▲ CAP 21444
Li, Honggang (va)—see ORCHESTRAS & ENSEMBLES Shanghai String Quartet
Li, Weigang (vn)—see ORCHESTRAS & ENSEMBLES Shanghai String Quartet
Liberman, Viktor (vn)
Crusell, B.H.:Qts (3) Cl, w. R. Hogerheijde (cl), G. Oldeman (va), Dora Mintcheva (vc) — Erasmus ▲ WVH 103
Kox, H.:Con 2 Vn, w. R. Dufallo (cnd), Rotterdam PO *(rec 1983)* — Attacca ▲ Babel 9262-1 [ADD/DDD]
Libouban, J. (fl)—see ORCHESTRAS & ENSEMBLES Stanislas Ensemble
Libove, C. (vn)
Rieti, V.:Partita Hpd, w. S. Marlowe (hpd), S. Baron (fl), R. Roseman (ob), A. Ajemian (vn), H. Zaratzian (va), C. McCraken (vc) — CRI ▲ CD 601 [ADD]
Licad, Cécile (pno)
Brahms, J.:Son 1 Vn, w. N. Salerno-Sonnenberg (vn) — EMI Classics ▲ CDC 54800
Brahms, J.:Son 2 Vn, w. N. Salerno-Sonnenberg (vn) — EMI Classics ▲ CDC 49410 [DDD]
Brahms, J.:Son 3 Vn, w. N. Salerno-Sonnenberg (vn) — EMI Classics ▲ CDC 54800
Brahms, J.:Trio Hn, w. J. Cerminaro (hn), N. Salerno-Sonnenberg (vn) — EMI Classics ▲ CDC 54800
Chopin, F.:Pno Music (misc)—Ballade in g, Op. 23; Etudes, Op. 10/1-12; Nocturne in f, Op. 15/1; Scherzo in b♭, Op. 31 — MusicMasters ▲ 01612-67124-2
Tchaikovsky, P.:Trio Pno, w. N. Salerno-Sonnenberg (vn), A. Meneses (vc) — EMI Classics ▲ CDC 54800
Licaret, Nicolae (hpd)
5 Centuries of German Music in Transylvania, w. H. Andreescu (cnd), Bucharest Virtuosi, Georgeta Stoleriu (sop), Adrian Petrescu (ob), René Cristian Popescu (vn), Gabriel Bala (va), Stefan Thomasz (db) — Electrecord ▲ ELC EDC 168 [DDD]
Lichten, Julia (vc)
Schubert, Franz:Qnt Strs, D.956, w. P. Frank (vn), F. Galimir (vn), S. Tenenbom (va), P. Wiley (vc) — Sony Classical ▲ SMK 45901 [ADD/DDD] ■ SMT 45901
Lichtenwalter, Jason (ob)
Brooke, N.:Obomobile, w. Brandon Adrien, Jennifer Baker, Karen Birch, Daniel Cate, Judy Christy, Richard Cochran, Jessica Cooper, Leslie Dominguez, Erin Hannigan, Dorothy Knight, Jay Moore, Hwa-Ling Russell, Toyin Spellman, Sarah Weiner, Jay Weinland — Opus One ▲ CD 160
Lichtmann, Theodor (pno)
Hindemith, P.:Concert Music Pno, Brass & Hps, w. M. Walter (hp), P.L. Jenks (hp), Summit Brass — Summit 2-▲ DCD 115 [DDD] 2-■ DCD 115
Hindemith, P.:Son Hn, w. G. Williams (hn) — Summit 2-▲ DCD 115 [DDD] 2-■ DCD 115
Hindemith, P.:Son Alto Hn, w. L. Strieby (hn) — Summit 2-▲ DCD 115 [DDD] 2-■ DCD 115
Hindemith, P.:Son Trbn, w. M. Lawrence (trbn) — Summit 2-▲ DCD 115 [DDD] 2-■ DCD 115
Hindemith, P.:Son Tpt, w. R. Mase (tpt) — Summit 2-▲ DCD 115 [DDD] 2-■ DCD 115
Hindemith, P.:Son Bass Tuba, w. G. Pokorny (tuba) — Summit 2-▲ DCD 115 [DDD] 2-■ DCD 115
Solo Pro:Contest Music for Horn, w. M. Morrow (hn) — Summit ■ DCD 104
Solo Pro:Contest Music for Tuba, w. Ronald Davis (tuba) — Summit ■ DCD 106
Lichtmann, Jay (tpt)—see ORCHESTRAS & ENSEMBLES Brass Ring
Licther, B. (vc)
Boulez, P.:Messagesquisse, w. A. Loudos (vc), B. Feigenwinter (vc), M. Keller (vc), F. Schiltknecht (vc), P. Toso (vc), J. Wyttenbach (cnd) *(rec Switzerland, June 1993)* — ECM New Series 2-▲ 78118-21520-2 [DDD]
Liddell, Nona (vn)
Butterworth, G.:Songs (6) from *A Shropshire Lad*, w. John Shirley-Quirk (bar), Ivor McMahon (vn), Ambrose Gauntlett (vl), Martin Isepp (hpd/pno) — Saga Classics ▲ EC 3336
Haydn, J.:Qts Fl, w. Clive Conway (fl), Paul Silverthorne (va), Charles Tunnell (vc) — Meridian ▲ CDE 84118
Humfrey, P.:Anthems, w. John Shirley-Quirk (bar), Ivor McMahon (vn), Ambrose Gauntlett (vl), Martin Isepp (hpd/pno)—A Hymne to God the Father — Saga Classics ▲ EC 3336
Matthews, C.:Suns Dance, w. Sebastian Bell (pic), Gareth Hulse (ob), Michael Collins (b cl), John Orford (ctbn), Michael Thompson (hn), Joan Atherton (vn), Paul Silverthorne (va), Christopher van Kampen (vc), Robin McGee (db) *(rec All Saint's Church, Petersham, Oct 1992)* — Deutsche Grammophon ▲ 447067-2 [DDD]
Moeran, E.J.:Songs, w. John Shirley-Quirk (bar), Martin Isepp (hpd/pno), Ivor McMahon (vn), Ambrose Gauntlett (vl)—When Smoke Stood Up from Ludlow; Say, Lad, Have You Things to Do?; Farewell to Barn & Stack & Trees [all from Ludlow Town] — Saga Classics ▲ EC 3336
Purcell, H.:Songs, w. John Shirley-Quirk (bar), Martin Isepp (hpd/pno), Ivor McMahon (vn), Ambrose Gauntlett (vl)—Man Is for the Woman Made; Music for a While; Twas within a Furlong of Edinborough Town; When Night her Purple Veil — Saga Classics ▲ EC 3336
Liddle, David (org)
Harwood, B.:Org Music—Sonata No. 1 in c# for Organ, Op. 5 — Direct-to-Tape Recording ▲ DTR 8706 [DDD]
Hollins, A.:Org Music — Priory ▲ PRI 398 [DDD]
Liddle, D.:Ballades Org — Direct-to-Tape Recording ▲ DTR 8706 [DDD]
Liddle, E. (vl)—see ORCHESTRAS & ENSEMBLES Spectre de la Rose
Lidsky, Mikhail (pno)
Chopin, F.:Nocturnes—Opp. 48/2, 55/2 & 62/1 — Denon ▲ DEN 78842 [DDD]
Chopin, F.:Prelude, Op. 45 — Denon ▲ DEN 78842 [DDD]

▲ = CD ♦ = Enhanced CD Δ = MD ■ = Cassette Tape □ = DCC

Lidsky, Mikhail (pno) (cont.)
Liszt, F.:Pno Music (misc)—4 Mephisto Waltzes; 3 Valses oubliées; Mephisto Polka; Romance oubliée; Trauervorspiel *(rec Stadsgehoorzaal, Leiden, Jan 23-26, 1995)* Denon ▲ CO 78802 [DDD]
Medtner, N.:Son Pno, Op. 25/2 Denon ▲ DEN 78842 [DDD]

Lidström, Mats (vc)
Boëllmann, L.:Morceaux Vc, OP. 31, w. Bengt Forsberg (pno) Hyperion ▲ CDA 66888
Boëllmann, L.:Son Vc, w. Bengt Forsberg (pno) Hyperion ▲ CDA 66888
Godard, B.:Aubade et scherzo, w. Bengt Forsberg (pno) Hyperion ▲ CDA 66888
Godard, B.:Son Vc, w. Bengt Forsberg (pno) Hyperion ▲ CDA 66888
Kabalevsky, D.:Con 2 Vc, w. V. Ashkenazy (cnd), Gothenburg SO *(rec Gothenburg Concert Hall, Sweden, 1995)* BIS ▲ CD 719 [DDD]
Khachaturian, A.:Con Vc, w. V. Ashkenazy (cnd), Gothenburg SO *(rec Gothenburg Concert Hall, Sweden, 1995)* BIS ▲ CD 719 [DDD]
Rachmaninoff, S.:Vocalise, w. Vladimir Ashkenazy (pno) *(rec Gothenburg Concert Hall, Sweden, 1995)* BIS ▲ CD 719 [DDD]

Lieber, Edvard (pno)
Lieber, E.:Bacchus Concord Concerto ▲ CCD 42027 [ADD]
Lieber, E.:de Kooning Preludes Concord Concerto ▲ CCD 42027 [ADD]
Lieber, E.:Homage to Franz Kline Concord Concerto ▲ CCD 42027 [ADD]
Lieber, E.:Prelude to Jackson Pollock's 'Autumn Rhythm' Concord Concerto ▲ CCD 42027 [ADD]
Lieber, E.:Sea Wall Concord Concerto ▲ CCD 42027 [ADD]
Lieber, E.:Small Decoy Concord Concerto ▲ CCD 42027 [ADD]
Lieber, E.:Tomb of Hasegawa, w. Shoko Tanaka (nar) Concord Concerto ▲ CCD 42027 [ADD]

Lieberknecht, Andrea (fl)
Wagner, S.:Concertino Fl, w. W. A. Albert (cnd), Rhineland-Palatinate State PO *(rec Apr 1996)* CPO ▲ 999427-2 [DDD]

Lieberman, Carol (vn)
Carter, E.:Riconoscenza (per Goffredo Petrassi) Neuma ▲ 450-81
Dohnányi, E. von:Qnt 2 Pno, w. A. Wolf (pno), R. Lefkowitz (vn), M. Thompson (va), D. Finch (vc) AFKA ▲ SK 503
Dohnányi, E. von:Son Vn, w. L. Shapiro (pno) AFKA ▲ SK 503
Kovách, A.:Trio 2, w. R. Feldman (vc), L. Shapiro (pno) AFKA ▲ SK 503

Liebermann, Anatole (vc)—see ORCHESTRAS & ENSEMBLES Tchaikovsky Piano Trio

Liebich, Gustav (vn)
Mozart, W.A.:Rè pastore (sels), w. Maria Gerhart (sop), Victor Boschetti (pno) *(rec 1905 - 1944)* Minerva ▲ MN A14 [ADD]

Liebscher, Wolfgang (bn)
Strauss, R.:Duet-Concertino, w. M. Weise (cl), R. Kempe (cnd), Dresden Staatskapelle EMI Classics 3-▲ CDZC 64342

Liechti, M. (vc)
Vogel, W.:Sonances, w. H. Peter-Indermühle (fl), H. Elhorst (ob), K. Weber (cl), I. Backer (bn), K. Hanke (hn), U. Lehmann (vn), L. Dober (vn), H. Forster (va), R. Tschupp (cnd) Grammont ▲ CTSP 14-2 [ADD]

Liegeois, Frank (b vl)—see ORCHESTRAS & ENSEMBLES Romanesque

Liepa, Yolanda (pno)
Rosner, A.:Son Hn, w. Heidi Garson (hn) *(rec SUNY, Stony Brook)* Albany ▲ TROY 163 [DDD]

Lier, Kjell Axel (hp)
Schnittke, A.:Con Ob, w. H. Jahren (ob), L. Markiz (cnd), New Stockholm CO BIS ▲ CD 377 [DDD]

Liet, Jean-Marc (ob)
Klein, G.:Divert Ob, w. Jean-Pierre Arnaud (ob), Rémi Lerner (cl), Christian Rocca (cl), Michel Tavernier (bn), Amaury Wallez (bn), Eric Karcher (hn), Philippe Queyraud (hn) Arion ▲ ARN 68272 [DDD]

Lievens, Dirk (vn)
Berkeley, M.:For the Savage Messiah, w. Kristof van Gryspeere (pno), Kaat De Cock (va), Stefaan Craeynest (vc), Jan Verheye (db) *(rec Steurbaut Sound Recording Ctr)* René Gailly ▲ CD87 118 [DDD]

Lifchitz, Max (pno)
American Debuts:Piano Music by American Composers North/South Recordings ▲ NS 1002 [DDD]
Bazelon, I.:Sonatina Vienna Modern Masters ▲ CD 2002 [DDD]
Bell, E.:Night Music Vienna Modern Masters ▲ CD 2002 [DDD]
Blank, A.:Toccata Pno North/South Recordings ▲ N/S R 1002 [DDD]
Contemporary Romantics:American Piano Music North/South Recordings ▲ NS 1001 [DDD]
Diemer, E.L.:Encore Vienna Modern Masters ▲ CD 2002 [DDD]
Franco, J.H.G.:Pno Music—Theme & Variations (1944); Redemption Triptych (1960); Trio [middle section of Erik Satie's second piece from *Trois morceaux en forme de poire* for piano 4-hands, arranged by Franco for solo piano] North/South Recordings ▲ N/S R 1002 [DDD]
Greenberg, L.:Cycles Vienna Modern Masters ▲ CD 2002 [DDD]
Lifchitz, M.:Canto de paz, w. L. Vardaman (sop), L. Weiss (fl), G. Kitzis (vn), N. Ives (vc) Opus One ▲ 149
Lifchitz, M.:Elegia North/South Recordings ▲ N/S R 1001 [DDD]
Lifchitz, M.:Yellow Ribbons, w. L. Weiss (fl), M. Lifchitz (cnd), North/South Consonance Ensemble—Nos. 1 (1981) & 21 (1984) Opus One ▲ 149
Mason, C.N.:Blazing Macaw North/South Recordings ▲ N/S R 1002 [DDD]
Maves, D.:Sons (4) Pno *(rec SUNY Recital Hall, Stony Brook & Univ of Albany Recital Hall)* North/South ▲ N/S 1008 [DDD/AAD]
Max Lifchitz Plays American Piano Music Vienna Modern Masters ▲ VMM 2002 [DDD]
Mazurek, R.:The Voice Within North/South Recordings ▲ N/S R 1001 [DDD]
Ovens, D.:Moving Image North/South Recordings ▲ N/S R 1002 [DDD]
Pizer, E.:Pno Music—Expressions Intimes; Strains and Restraints North/South Recordings ▲ N/S R 1001 [DDD]
Pleskow, R.:Quatrains Pno *(rec Recital Hall of the Univ at Albany, May 25-26, 1995)* North/South ▲ N/S R 1007 [DDD]
Quilling, H.:Son 2 Pno North/South Recordings ▲ N/S R 1001 [DDD]
Quilling, H.:Son 3 Pno Vienna Modern Masters ▲ CD 2002 [DDD]
Quilling, H.:Son 4 Pno *(rec Recital Hall of the Univ at Albany, May 25-26, 1995)* North/South ▲ N/S R 1007 [DDD]
Rovics, H.:Son Pno *(rec Recital Hall of the Univ at Albany, May 25-26, 1995)* North/South ▲ N/S R 1007 [DDD]
Schiffman, H.:Bagatelles Pno North/South Recordings ▲ N/S R 1001 [DDD]
Schiffman, H.:Pieces Pno North/South Recordings ▲ N/S R 1001 [DDD]
Shaffer, S.:Lines from Shelley Vienna Modern Masters ▲ CD 2002 [DDD]
Stewart, R.:Vars Pno North/South Recordings ▲ N/S R 1002 [DDD]
Strunk, S.:Prisms Vienna Modern Masters ▲ CD 2002 [DDD]
Toutant, W.:Small Suite *(rec Recital Hall of the Univ at Albany, May 25-26, 1995)* North/South ▲ N/S R 1007 [DDD]
Van Appledorn, M.J.:A Liszt Fant North/South Recordings ▲ N/S R 1001 [DDD]
Van Appledorn, M.J.:Set of 5 *(rec Recital Hall of the Univ at Albany, May 25-26, 1995)* North/South ▲ N/S R 1007 [DDD]
Vega, A. de la:Homenagem Vienna Modern Masters ▲ CD 2002 [DDD]
Ziffrin, M.:Suite Pno North/South Recordings ▲ N/S R 1002 [DDD]

Lifschitz, Konstantin (pno)
Bach, J.S.:Partita Hpd, BWV 831, "Ov nach französischer Art" *(rec Moscow Conservatory, May-June 1990)* Denon/PCM Digital ▲ DEN 78907 [DDD]
Brahms, J.:Vars on a Hungarian Song *(rec live, Wigmore Hall, London)* Denon ▲ DEN 78773
Brahms, J.:Vars on an Original Theme *(rec live, Wigmore Hall, London)* Denon ▲ DEN 78773
Chopin, F.:Nocturnes—in g, Op. 37/1; in G, Op. 37/2 Denon ▲ CO 78908 [DDD]
Chopin, F.:Polonaises—in f#, Op. 44 Denon ▲ CO 78908 [DDD]
Couperin, F.:Pièces de clavecin (sels)—Huitième Ordre [from Book 2] *(rec live, Wigmore Hall, London)* Denon ▲ DEN 78773
Konstantin Lifshits Piano Recital Multisonic ("Russian Stars on Classics" series) ▲ MUL 310063 [DDD]

Lifschitz, Konstantin (pno) (cont.)
Medtner, N.:Fairy Tales, Op. 26—No. 4 in f# *(rec Moscow Conservatory, May & June 1990)* Denon/PCM Digital ▲ DEN 78907 [DDD]
Medtner, N.:Fairy Tales, Op. 34—No. 3 in a *(rec Moscow Conservatory, May & June 1990)* Denon/PCM Digital ▲ DEN 78907 [DDD]
Medtner, N.:Morceaux, Op. 31—Fairy Tale *(rec Moscow Conservatory, May & June 1990)* Denon/PCM Digital ▲ DEN 78907 [DDD]
Mozart, W.A.:Rondo Pno, K.511 Denon ▲ CO 78908 [DDD]
Rachmaninoff, S.:Preludes Pno—Nos 1, 2, 5, 6, 7 & 13 [all from Op. 32] *(rec live, Wigmore Hall, London)* Denon ▲ DEN 78773
Ravel, M.:Gaspard de la nuit Denon ▲ CO 78908 [DDD]
Schumann, R.:Papillons *(rec Moscow Conservatory, May & June 1990)* Denon/PCM Digital ▲ DEN 78907 [DDD]
Scriabin, A.:Mazurkas Pno, Op. 3—Nos. 6, 7 & 9 *(rec Moscow Conservatory, May & June 1990)* Denon/PCM Digital ▲ DEN 78907 [DDD]

Lifsitz, F. (vn)—see ORCHESTRAS & ENSEMBLES Alexander String Quartet

Ligeti, Péter (va)—see ORCHESTRAS & ENSEMBLES Festetics String Quartet

Li-Jian (pno)
Brahms, J.:Son 2 Vc, w. William De Rosa (vc) Audiofon ▲ CD 72045
Schumann, R.:Adagio & Allegro Hn, w. William De Rosa (vc) Audiofon ▲ CD 72045
Strauss, R.:Son Vc, w. William De Rosa (vc) Audiofon ▲ CD 72045

Likin, Jurij (ob)—see also ORCHESTRAS & ENSEMBLES Prague Wind Quintet
Martinů, B.:Madrigals Ob, w. Vlastimil Mareš (cl), Lumír Vanek (bn) *(rec Studio Martínek, Prague, Mar 3, 1995)* Panton ("Protokol XX" series) ▲ 811348-2 [DDD]
Martinů, B.:Les Rondes, w. Vlastimil Mareš (cl), Lumír Vanek (bn), Vladislav Kozderka (tpt), Jana Herojnová (vn), Pavel Kutman (vn), Ivan Klánský (pno) *(rec Studio Martínek, Prague, Mar 3, 1995)* Panton ("Protokol XX" series) ▲ 811348-2 [DDD]
Martinů, B.:Sxt Fl, Ob, Cl, 2 Bns & Pno, w. Jan Riedlbauch (fl), Vlastimil Mareš (cl), Lumír Vanek (bn), Svatopluk Čech (bn), Ivan Klánský (pno) *(rec Studio Martínek, Prague, Mar 3, 1995)* Panton ("Protokol XX" series) ▲ 811348-2 [DDD]

Liljequist, Björn (perc)
Bäck, S.-E.:Favola, w. Thore Janson (cl), Stig Arntorp (perc), Bengt Arsenius (perc), Roland Johansson (perc) Caprice ▲ CAP 21490
Nilsson, B.:Bass, w. Michael Lind (tuba) Caprice ▲ CAP 21493

Lill, John (pno)
Beethoven, L. van:Allegretto, WoO 56 Chandos 3-▲ CHAN 9084/86 [DDD]
Beethoven, L. van:Bagatelles (24), w. J. Lill (pno) Chandos 3-▲ CHAN 9084/86 [DDD]
Beethoven, L. van:Bagatelles (24) Chandos ▲ CHAN 9201 [DDD]
Beethoven, L. van:Cons Pno (comp), w. W. Weller (cnd), City of Birmingham SO Chandos 3-▲ CHAN 9084/86 [DDD]
Beethoven, L. van:Con 5 Pno, "Emperor", w. W. Weller (cnd), City of Birmingham SO Chandos ▲ CHAN 7028
Beethoven, L. van:Presto Chandos 3-▲ CHAN 9084/86 [DDD]
Beethoven, L. van:Sons Pno (comp)—Sons. 5, 6 & 7 ASV Quicksilva ▲ QS 6057 [ADD]
Beethoven, L. van:Sons Pno (comp)—Sons. 24, 25, 26 & 28 ASV Quicksilva ▲ QS 6062 [ADD]
Beethoven, L. van:Sons Pno (comp)—Nos. 21, 22 & 23 ASV Quicksilva ▲ QS 6061 [ADD]
Beethoven, L. van:Sons Pno (comp)—Sons. 11, 12 & 15 ASV Quicksilva ▲ QS 6059 [ADD]
Beethoven, L. van:Sons Pno (comp)—Nos. 27 & 29 ASV Quicksilva ▲ QS 6063 [ADD]
Beethoven, L. van:Sons Pno (comp)—Sons. 3, 4 & 8 ASV Quicksilva ▲ QS 6056 [ADD]
Beethoven, L. van:Sons Pno (comp)—Nos. 1, 2, 19 & 20 ASV Quicksilva ▲ QS 6055 [ADD]
Beethoven, L. van:Son 16 Pno ASV Quicksilva ▲ ASQ 6060 [ADD]
Beethoven, L. van:Son 17 Pno, "Tempest" ASV Quicksilva ▲ ASQ 6060 [ADD]
Beethoven, L. van:Son 18 Pno ASV Quicksilva ▲ ASQ 6060 [ADD]
Beethoven, L. van:Son 30 Pno ASV Quicksilva ▲ ASQ 6064 [ADD]
Beethoven, L. van:Son 31 Pno ASV Quicksilva ▲ ASQ 6064 [ADD]
Beethoven, L. van:Son 32 Pno ASV Quicksilva ▲ ASQ 6064 [ADD]
Brahms, J.:Con 1 Pno, w. J. Loughran (cnd), Hallé Orch ASV Quicksilva ▲ ASQ 6083 [DDD]
Brahms, J.:Con 2 Pno, w. J. Loughran (cnd), Hallé Orch ASV Quicksilva ▲ ASQ 6088 [DDD]
Brahms, J.:Qnt Pno, w. Medici String Quartet Medici Quartet ▲ MQT 8001 [DDD]
The Heart of the Piano Concerto, w. Cristina Ortiz (pno), J. L. Prats (pno), London SO [cnd:J. Judd, W. Morris], Royal PO [cnd:L. Foster, E. Bátiz] Pickwick ("The Orchid" series) ▲ PICORCD 11012
Lloyd Webber, W.S.:Air varié, w. J. Lloyd Webber (vc) ASV ▲ ASV 584 [DDD]
Lloyd Webber, W.S.:In the Half-Light, w. J. Lloyd Webber (vc) ASV ▲ ASV 584 [DDD]
Lloyd Webber, W.S.:Pno Music—6 early works:Badinage de Noël; Song without Words; Scherzo in g; Arabesque; Presto for Perseus; Romantic Evening ASV ▲ ASV 584 [DDD]
Lloyd Webber, W.S.:Pno Music—7 Pieces ASV ▲ ASV 961
Rachmaninoff, S.:Con 3 Pno, w. T. Otaka (cnd), BBC Welsh National Orch Nimbus ▲ NI 5348 [DDD]
Rachmaninoff, S.:Études-tableaux, Opp. 33 & 39 *(rec Concert Hall of the Nimbus Foundation, Jan. 25-26, 1995)* Nimbus ▲ NI 5439 [DDD]
Rachmaninoff, S.:Son 2 Pno Nimbus ▲ NI 5348 [DDD]
Tchaikovsky, P.:Con 1 Pno, w. J. Judd (cnd), London SO IMP ("Concert Classics" series) ▲ IMP PCD 1102
Tchaikovsky, P.:Con 1 Pno, w. J. Judd (cnd), London SO IMP Classics ("LSO Classic Masterpieces" series) ▲ IMPPCD 893 [DDD]

Lim, Elizabeth (vn)
Telemann, G.P.:Con in C for 2 Vns, w. P. Peabody (vn), R. Kapp (cnd), Philharmonia Virtuosi—4 Concerti—in D, a, E & D ESS.A.Y ▲ CD 1016
Vivaldi, A.:Con Lt, w. P. Press (gtr), P. Peabody (vn), J. Haffner (va), T. Mook (vc), E. Brewer (hpd) ESS.A.Y ▲ CD 1004 [DDD] ■ C 1004 (D)

Lim, S. A. (vn)—see ORCHESTRAS & ENSEMBLES Cassatt String Quartet

Lima, A. Moreira (pno)
Chopin, F.:Andante Spianato & Grande Polonaise, w. D. Manolov (cnd), Philharmonia Bulgarica Vivace 2-▲ G 218 [DDD]
Chopin, F.:Con 2 Pno, w. D. Manolov (cnd), Philharmonia Bulgarica Vivace 3-▲ E 322 [DDD]
Chopin, F.:Con 2 Pno, w. D. Manolov (cnd), Philharmonia Bulgarica Vivace 2-▲ G 107/108 [DDD/ADD]
Chopin, F.:Con 2 Pno, w. D. Manolov (cnd), Philharmonia Bulgarica Vivace 2-▲ G 218 [DDD]
Chopin, F.:Grand Fant on Polish Airs, w. D. Manolov (cnd), Philharmonia Bulgarica Vivace 2-▲ G 218 [DDD]
Chopin, F.:Krakowiak, w. D. Manolov (cnd), Philharmonia Bulgarica Vivace 2-▲ G 218 [DDD]
Chopin, F.:Vars on Mozart's *La ci darem la mano*, w. D. Manolov (cnd), Philharmonia Bulgarica Vivace 2-▲ G 218 [DDD]

Lima, Arthur (pno)
Chopin, F.:Polonaises BOMR 2-▲ 51-7617 [DDD]
Nazareth, E.:Pno Music—16 tangos Pro Arte ▲ CDD 512 [DDD]

Limbrick, Simon (perc)
New Music for Multi-Tracked Clarinets, w. Heaton, Roger (cl/a cl/b cl/ctb cl), D. Smith (pno) Clarinet Classics ▲ CC 0009

Limón, Roberto (gtr)
Kupferman, M.:Con Gtr, w. E. G. Barrios (cnd), Baja California Orch Soundspells ▲ CD 113 [DDD]
Kupferman, M.:Hexagon Skies, w. E. G. Barrios (cnd), Baja California Orch Soundspells ▲ CD 114 [DDD]
Kupferman, M.:Hexagon Skies, w. E. G. Barrios (cnd), Baja California Orch Soundspells ▲ CD 114 [DDD]

Lin, Cho-Liang (vn)
Arensky, A.:Trio 1 Pno, w. Y. Bronfman (pno), G. Hoffman (vc) *(rec Aug 25-27, 1992)* Sony Classical ▲ SK 53269 [DDD]
Boccherini, L.:Qnts Strs, w. Issac Stern (vn), Jaime Laredo (va), Yo-Yo Ma (vc), Sharon Robinson (vc)—Qnt in E for Strs, Op. 13/5 Sony Classical ▲ SK 53983

INSTRUMENT.

Lin, Cho-Liang (vn) (cont.)
Boccherini, L.:Qnt Strs, G.275, w. Isaac Stern (vn), Jaime Laredo (va), Yo-Yo Ma (vc), Sharon Robinson (vc) Sony Classical ▲ SK 53983
Brahms, J.:Sextet Strs, Op. 18, w. I. Stern (vn), J. Laredo (va), M. Tree (va), Yo-Yo Ma (vc), S. Robinson (vc) Sony Classical 2-▲ S2K 45820
Brahms, J.:Sextet Strs, Op. 36, w. I. Stern (vn), J. Laredo (va), M. Tree (va), Yo-Yo Ma (vc), S. Robinson (vc) Sony Classical 2-▲ S2K 45820
Bravural, w. Sandra Rivers (pno) CBS ▲ MK 39133 [DDD]
Bruch, M.:Con 1 Vn, w. L. Slatkin (cnd), Chicago SO CBS ▲ MK 42315 [DDD]
Bruch, M.:Con 1 Vn, w. L. Slatkin (cnd), Chicago SO CBS ▲ MDK 44902 [DDD] ■ MDT 44902 (D)
Bruch, M.:Scottish Fant Vn, w. L. Slatkin (cnd), Chicago SO CBS ▲ MK 42315 [DDD]
Debussy, C.:Music of, w. Paul Crossley (pno)—works for vn & pno; sels unknown Sony Classical ▲ SK 66839
Haydn, J.:Con 1 Vn, w. N. Marriner (cnd), Minnesota Orch CBS ▲ MK 37796 [DDD]
Haydn, J.:Con 1 Vn, w. N. Marriner (cnd), Minnesota Orch CBS ▲ MK 39310 ■ MT 39310
Ince, K.:Cross Scintillations, w. S. Wang (pno) *(rec Milwaukee, Sept. 1992 & Oct. 1993)* Northeastern ("Contemporary" series) ▲ NR 254
Kreisler, F.:Vn Pieces, w. S. Rivers (pno)—Liebesfreud CBS ▲ MDK 44902 [DDD] ■ MDT 44902 (D)
Mendelssohn, F.:Con in e Vn & Orch, Op. 64, w. P. Thomas (cnd), Philharmonia Orch CBS ▲ MDK 44902 [DDD] ■ MDT 44902 (D)
Mendelssohn, F.:Con in e Vn & Orch, Op. 64, w. P. Thomas (cnd), Philharmonia Orch CBS ▲ MK 39007 [DDD]
Mozart, W.A.:Adagio Vn, K.261, w. R. Leppard (cnd), English CO CBS ▲ MK 42364 [DDD]
Mozart, W.A.:Con 1 Vn, w. R. Leppard (cnd), English CO CBS ▲ MK 44503 [DDD]
Mozart, W.A.:Con 2 Vn, w. R. Leppard (cnd), English CO Sony Classical ▲ SK 44913 [DDD]
Mozart, W.A.:Con 3 Vn, w. R. Leppard (cnd), English CO CBS ▲ MK 42364 [DDD]
Mozart, W.A.:Con 4 Vn, w. R. Leppard (cnd), English CO CBS ▲ MK 44503 [DDD]
Mozart, W.A.:Con 5 Vn, w. R. Leppard (cnd), English CO CBS ▲ MK 42364 [DDD]
Mozart, W.A.:Con 7 Vn, w. R. Leppard (cnd), English CO Sony Classical ▲ SK 44913 [DDD]
Mozart, W.A.:Concertone Vns, w. J. Laredo (vn), R. Leppard (cnd), English CO Sony Classical ▲ SK 47693
Mozart, W.A.:Rondo Vn, K.269, w. R. Leppard (cnd), English CO CBS ▲ MK 44503 [DDD]
Mozart, W.A.:Rondo Vn, K.373, w. R. Leppard (cnd), English CO Sony Classical ▲ SK 44913 [DDD]
Mozart, W.A.:Sinf concertante Vn, K.364, w. J. Laredo (va), R. Leppard (cnd), English CO Sony Classical ▲ SK 47693
Nielsen, C.:Con Vn, w. E.-P. Salonen (cnd), Swedish RSO CBS ▲ MK 44548 [DDD]
Poulenc, F.:Music of, w. Paul Crossley (pno)—works for vn & pno; sels unknown Sony Classical ▲ SK 66839
Prokofiev, S.:Cons Vn (comp), w. E.-P. Salonen (cnd), Los Angeles PO *(rec Los Angeles, Nov. 9–10, 1992)* Sony Classical ▲ SK 53969 [DDD]
Ravel, M.:Music of, w. Paul Crossley (pno)—works for vn & pno; sels unknown Sony Classical ▲ SK 66839
Saint-Saëns, C.:Con 3 Vn, w. M. Tilson Thomas (cnd), Philharmonia Orch CBS ▲ MK 39007 [DDD]
Sarasate, P. de:Intro & Tarantella, w. S. Rivers (pno) CBS ▲ MDK 44902 [DDD] ■ MDT 44902 (D)
Schubert, Franz:Qnt Strs, D.956, w. Issac Stern (vn), Jaime Laredo (va), Yo-Yo Ma (vc), Sharon Robinson (vc) Sony Classical ▲ SK 53983
Schubert, Franz:Qnt Strs, D.956, w. Isaac Stern (vn), Jaime Laredo (va), Yo-Yo Ma (vc), Sharon Robinson (vc) Sony Classical ▲ SK 53983
Sibelius, J.:Con Vn, w. E.-P. Salonen (cnd), Swedish RSO CBS ▲ MK 44548 [DDD]
Stravinsky, I.:Con Vn, w. E.-P. Salonen (cnd), Los Angeles PO *(rec Los Angeles, Feb. 24, 1992)* Sony Classical ▲ SK 53969 [DDD]
Stravinsky, I.:Divert Vn, w. A.-M.Schub (pno) CBS ▲ MK 42101 [DDD]
Stravinsky, I.:Duo Concertant, w. A.-M.Schub (pno) CBS ▲ MK 42101 [DDD]
Stravinsky, I.:Suite italienne Vc, w. A.-M.Schub (pno) [vn-pno arr. Dushkin] CBS ▲ MK 42101 [DDD]
Tchaikovsky, P.:Trio Pno, w. Y. Bronfman (pno), G. Hoffman (vc) *(rec Aug. 25–27, 1992)* Sony Classical ▲ SK 53269 [DDD]
Vieuxtemps, H.:Con 5 Vn, w. N. Marriner (cnd), Minnesota Orch CBS ▲ MK 37796 [DDD]

Lin, Gillian (pno)
Britten, H.:Con Pno, w. J. Hopkins (cnd), Melbourne SO *(rec 1978)* Chandos ("Collect" series) ▲ CHAN 6580 [ADD]
Copland, A.:Con Pno, w. J. Hopkins (cnd), Melbourne SO *(rec 1978)* Chandos ("Collect" series) ▲ CHAN 6580 [ADD]

Lin, Maria (vn)
Thofanidis, C.:Qt 1 Strs, w. Adrian Justus (vn), Timothy Lees (va), James Holland (vc) Albany ▲ TROY 158 [DDD]

Lin, Sunghae Anna (vn)
Wigglesworth, F.:Trillium, w. Tara Helen O'Connor (fl) CRI ▲ C 733 [DDD]

Linale, Charles-André (vn)—see ORCHESTRAS & ENSEMBLES Orpheus String Quartet

Lincer, William (va)
Mozart, W.A.:Sinf Concertante, w. John Corigliano (vn), B. Walter (cnd), New York PO Enterprise ("The Radio Years" series) ▲ ENT RY 69

Linck, Carsten (gtr)—see ORCHESTRAS & ENSEMBLES Folkwang Guitar Duo

Lind, L. (fl)
Russo, J.:Son 1 Fl, w. L. W. Ignacio (pno) CRS ▲ CD 9257

Lind, Leif (hn)—see ORCHESTRAS & ENSEMBLES Copenhagen Wind Quintet

Lind, Michael (tuba)
Hindemith, P.:Son Bass Tuba, w. S. Harlos (pno) *(rec Nacka, Sweden, Aug. 12, 1977)* BIS ▲ CD 159 [AAD]
Jacobsen, J.:Tuba Buffo, w. G. Stern (cnd), Malmö SO Caprice ▲ CAP 21493
Lundquist, T.I.:Landscape, w. Andraes Röhn (vn), S. Westerberg (cnd), Swedish RSO Caprice ▲ CAP 21493
Nilsson, B.:Bass, w. Björn Liljequist (perc) Caprice ▲ CAP 21493
Vaughan Williams, R.:Con Bass Tuba, w. L. Segerstam (cnd), Royal Stockholm PO Caprice ▲ CAP 21493

Lindal, Maria (vn)
Biber, H. von:Harmonia artificiosa-ariosa, w. B. Sargent (vn), M. van der Velden (viol), E. Siebens (db), M. Spányi (hpd)—Partitas 3 & 5 *(rec Feb. 4–6, 1993)* BIS ▲ CD 608 [DDD]
Biber, H. von:Mystery (or Rosary) Sons, w. M. van der Velden (viol), E. Siebens (db), M. Spányi (hpd)—No. 10 *(rec Feb. 4–6, 1993)* BIS ▲ CD 608 [DDD]
Biber, H. von:Passacaglia Vn *(rec Feb. 4–6, 1993)* BIS ▲ CD 608 [DDD]
Biber, H. von:Sons Vn & Continuo, w. L. Swarts (vc), E. Siebens (db), M. Spányi (hpd) *(rec Feb. 4–6, 1993)* BIS ▲ CD 608 [DDD]
Biber, H. von:Son violino solo representativa, w. L. Swarts (vc), E. Siebens (db), M. Spányi (hpd) *(rec Feb. 4–6, 1993)* BIS ▲ CD 608 [DDD]
Mozart, W.A.:Church Sons, w. Yasuko Uyama-Bouvard (org), Manfred Kramer (vn), Lucia Swarts (vc), Richard Myron (db)—K.67, 144, 145, 241, 244, 245, 274, 328 & 336 Adda ▲ ADD 581274 [DDD]

Lindberg, Christian (trbn)
Aho, K.:Sym 9, w. O. Vänskä (cnd), Lahti SO *(rec Ristinkirkko, Lahti, Finland, Jan. 9, 1995)* BIS ▲ CD 706 [DDD]
Berio, L.:Sequenza V BIS ▲ CD 258 [DDD]
Berio, L.:Sequenza V BIS ▲ CD 388 [DDD]
Bloch, E.:Sym Trbn, w. L. Segerstam (cnd), Swedish RSO BIS ▲ CD 538 [DDD]
Bourgeois, D.:Con Trbn, w. G. Brand (cnd), London Winds Albany ▲ TROY 093 [DDD]
The Burlesque Trombone & Romantic Trombone Concertos, w. Roland Pöntinen (pno), Bamberg SO [cnd:Leif Segerstam] BIS ("BIS Twins" series) 2-▲ 318/378
Cage, J.:Solo Trbn BIS ▲ CD 388 [DDD]
Chávez, C.:Con Trbn, w. G. Llewellyn (cnd), BBC Welsh National SO *(rec Brangwyn Hall, Swansea, Wales, Dec 14–15, 1995)* BIS ▲ CD 788 [DDD]

Lindberg, Christian (trbn) (cont.)
Creston, P.:Fant Trbn, w. J. DePreist (cnd), Malmö SO *(rec 1993)* BIS ▲ CD 628 [DDD]
The Criminal Trombone, w. Roland Pöntinen (pno) BIS ▲ CD 328
David, Ferdinand:Concertino Trbn, w. L. Segerstam (cnd), Bamberg SO BIS ▲ CD 378 [DDD]
Eliasson, A.:Disegno Trbn BIS ▲ CD 388 [DDD]
Frumerie, G. de:Con Trbn, w. L. Segerstam (cnd), Bamberg SO BIS ▲ CD 378 [DDD]
Grondahl, L.:Con Trbn, w. L. Segerstam (cnd), Bamberg SO BIS ▲ CD 378 [DDD]
Guilmant, A.:Morceau symphonique, w. L. Segerstam (cnd), Bamberg SO BIS ▲ CD 378 [DDD]
Hindemith, P.:Son Trbn, w. R. Pöntinen (pno) BIS ▲ CD 258 [DDD]
Hindemith, P.:Son Trbn, w. R. Pöntinen (pno) *(rec Nacka, Sweden, Nov. 12, 1983)* BIS ▲ CD 159 [DDD]
Hovhaness, A.:Sym 29, w. K. Brion (cnd), Ohio State Univ Concert Band *(rec Ohio State Univ., Nov. 21–23, 1993 & Jan. 1)* Delos ▲ DE 3158 [DDD]
Larsson, L.-E.:Concertino Trbn, w. O. Kamu (cnd), New Stockholm CO BIS ▲ CD 348 [DDD]
Martin, F.:Ballade Trbn (or T Sax), w. Roland Pöntinen (pno) *(rec Nacka Aula, Nacka, Sweden, Nov 11, 1983)* BIS ▲ CD 71 [DDD]
Milhaud, D.:Concertino d'hiver, w. O. Kamu (cnd), New Stockholm CO BIS ▲ CD 348 [DDD]
Pöntinen, R.:Blue Winter, w. O. Kamu (cnd), New Stockholm CO BIS ▲ CD 348 [DDD]
Rabe, F.:Con Trbn, w. O. Vänskä (cnd), Tapiola Sinfonietta BIS ▲ CD 568 [DDD]
Rimsky-Korsakov, N.:Con Trbn, w. O. Vänskä (cnd), Tapiola Sinfonietta BIS ▲ CD 568 [DDD]
The Romantic Trombone, w. Roland Pöntinen (pno) BIS ▲ CD 298
Rota, N.:Con Trbn, w. O. Vänskä (cnd), Tapiola Sinfonietta BIS ▲ CD 568 [DDD]
Rouse, C.:Con Trbn, w. G. Llewellyn (cnd), BBC Welsh National SO *(rec Brangwyn Hall, Swansea, Wales, Dec 14–15, 1995)* BIS ▲ CD 788 [DDD]
The Russian Trombone, w. Roland Pöntinen (pno) BIS ▲ CD 478 [DDD]
The Sacred Trombone, w. Gunnar Idenstam (org) BIS ▲ CD 488 [DDD]
Sandström, J.:Con Trbn, w. L. Segerstam (cnd), Swedish RSO BIS ▲ CD 538 [DDD]
Schnittke, A.:Dialogue Vc, w. O. Vänskä (cnd), Tapiola Sinfonietta BIS ▲ CD 568 [DDD]
Schuller, G.:Eine kleine Posaunenmusik, w. J. DePreist (cnd), Malmö SO *(rec 1993)* BIS ▲ CD 628 [DDD]
Serocki, K.:Con Trbn, w. L. Segerstam (cnd), Swedish RSO BIS ▲ CD 538 [DDD]
The Solitary Trombone BIS ▲ CD 388 [DDD]
Stockhausen, K.:In Freundschaft BIS ▲ CD 388 [DDD]
Takemitsu, T.:Gémeaux, w. Masashi Honma (ob), Numajiri, Wakasugi (cnd), Tokyo Metropolitan SO *(rec Tokyo Metropolitan Art Space, July 25–29, 1994)* Denon ▲ CO 78944 [DDD]
Telemann, G.P.:Con Trbn, w. O. Kamu (cnd), New Stockholm CO BIS ▲ CD 348 [DDD]
10 Year Jubilee *(rec 1983, 1985–88, 1990–93)* BIS ▲ CD 638 [DDD]
Thomas, A.R.:Meditation, w. G. Llewellyn (cnd), BBC Welsh National SO *(rec Brangwyn Hall, Swansea, Wales, Dec 14–15, 1995)* BIS ▲ CD 788 [DDD]
Tomasi, H.:Con Trbn, w. O. Vänskä (cnd), Tapiola Sinfonietta BIS ▲ CD 568 [DDD]
Trombone & Voice in the Hapsburg Empire, w. Monica Groop (mez) *(rec 1992)* BIS ▲ CD 548 [DDD]
Trombone Odyssey:20th Century Landmarks for Trombone & Orchestra, w. Swedish RSO [cnd:Leif Segerstam] BIS ▲ CD 538 [DDD]
The Virtuoso Trombone, w. Roland Pöntinen (pno) BIS ▲ CD 258
Vivaldi, A.:Cons Vn, Op. 8/1–4, "The Four Seasons", w. O. Kamu (cnd), New Stockholm CO [trans. for solo trombone & strings]—Winter BIS ▲ CD 348 [DDD]
Walker, G.:Con Trbn, w. J. DePreist (cnd), Malmö SO *(rec 1993)* BIS ▲ CD 628 [DDD]
The Winter Trombone BIS ▲ CD 348 [DDD]
Xenakis, I.:Keren BIS ▲ CD 388 [DDD]
Zwilich, E.T.:Con Trbn, w. J. DePreist (cnd), Malmö SO *(rec 1993)* BIS ▲ CD 628 [DDD]

Lindborn, J. (fl)
Holborne, A.:Instrumental Consort Music, w. Dowland Consort—34 "Galliards, Almains & Other Short Airs" BIS ▲ CD 469 [DDD]

Lindberg, Jakob (gtr)
Baroque Music for Lute & Guitar BIS ▲ CD 327
Boccherini, L.:Qnts Gtr & Strs, w. Drottningholm Baroque Ensemble—in d, G.445; in E, G.446; in B♭, G.447 [all rec. Apr. 20–22, 1992]; in D, G.448 [rec. Dec. 13, 1992]; in D, G.449; in G, G.450 [both rec. Nov. 10–11, 1992] BIS 2-▲ CD 597/98 [DDD]
English Lute Duets, w. Paul O'Dette (gtr) BIS ▲ CD 267
English Lute Music BIS ▲ CD 211
Scottish Lute Music BIS ▲ CD 201
La Serenissima I (Lute Music in Venice, 1500–1550) BIS ▲ CD 399 [DDD]
Songs for the Guitar, w. Christina Högman (sop) BIS ▲ CD 293

Lindberg, Jakob (lt)
Bach, J.S.:Lt Music—BWV 995, 996, 997, 998, 999, 1000 & 1006a *(rec 1992)* BIS 2-▲ CD 587/88 [DDD]
Campion, T.:Songs, w. C. Högman (sop)—5 songs BIS ▲ CD 257 [DDD]
Dowland, J.:Lt Music—complete *(rec Djursholms Kapell, Sweden, Oct.-Dec. 1994)* BIS 4-▲ CD 722-24 [DDD]
Faire, Sweet & Cruell, w. Christina Högman (sop) BIS ▲ CD 257 [DDD]
Haydn, J.:Music for Lt & Strs, w. Drottningholm Baroque Ensemble BIS ▲ CD 360
La Serenissima II:Lute Music in Venice, 1550–1600 *(rec Nov. 4–10, 1991)* BIS ▲ CD 599 [DDD]
17th Century Italian & English Music for Recorder & Lute, w. Clas Pehrsson (rcr) BIS ▲ CD 266
Vivaldi, A.:Con Va d'amore Lt, w. M. Huggett (vn), Drottningholm Baroque Ensemble BIS ▲ CD 290 [DDD]
Vivaldi, A.:Trio Sons Vn Lt, w. N.-E. Sparf (vn), K. Ottesen (vc), M. Wieslander (hpd) BIS ▲ CD 290 [DDD]

Lindberg, Per-Ola (va)
Larsson, L.-E.:Concertinos, w. Jan Stigmer (vn), Bjøorg Vaernes (vc), Ingalill Hillerud (db), Joakim Kallhed (pno), Camerata Romana—Nos. 8–12 Intim Musik ▲ INT 31

Linde, Celia (gtr)
Latin American Guitar Music Bluebell ▲ BLU 048 [DDD]

Linde, Hans-Martin (fl)
Bach, J.S.:Brandenburg Con 2, w. N. Marriner (vn), I. Kipnis (hpd), N. Marriner (cnd), London Strings CBS ■ MGT 39802
Bach, J.S.:Brandenburg Con 5, w. N. Marriner (vn), I. Kipnis (hpd), N. Marriner (cnd), London Strings CBS ■ MGT 39802
Hans Martin Linde & Konrad Ragossnig, w. Konrad Ragossnig (gtr) Jecklin ▲ JEC 4402-2 [ADD]
Mozart, W.A.:Cons Fl, w. H.-M. Linde (cnd), Linde Consort [period instrs] Virgin Classics ("Veritas Edition" series) ▲ CDM 61176
Mozart, W.A.:Cons Fl, w. H. Stadlmair (cnd), Munich CO Deutsche Grammophon ("Resonance" series) ▲ 427211-2 [ADD]
Musik für Flöte und Gitarre, w. Konrad Ragossnig (gtr) Jecklin ▲ JEC 660-2 [DDD]
Romantic Baroque Klavier ▲ KCD 11005 [ADD]
Telemann, G.P.:Kleine Kammermusik, w. Ferdinand Conrad (rcr), Helmut Winschermann (ob), Susanne Lautenbacher (vn), Johannes Koch (vl), Hugo Ruf (hpd) *(rec Südwest-Tonstudio H. Jansen, Stuttgart, Jan. 1966)* Musicaphon ▲ 51539 [ADD]

Linde, Hans-Martin (fl/rcr)
Vivaldi, A.:Music of, w. Wim Ten Have (va), Anthony Bailes (lt), Raymond Leppard (hpd), Leppard, Linde (cnd), English CO, Prague CO, Danske Strings members—Concertino in D, RV.121; Cons. in f, RV.156; in G, RV.435 [Op. 10/4]; in D, RV.429; in F, RV.434 [Op. 10/5]; in D, RV.93; in d, RV.540; Son. in E♭, RV.130 [Al Santo Sepolcro] Classics for Pleasure ▲ CDCFP 4656 [ADD]

Linde, Hans-Martin (rcr)
Telemann, G.P.:Rcr Music (misc), w. M. Jappe (vl), E. Müller (hpd)—Fant. for Flute in A; Partita 5 in e; Son. in B♭; Son. in d Klavier ■ KC 511
Vivaldi, A.:Rcr Music (misc), w. M. Jappe (vl), E. Müller (hpd)—Son. 2 in C; Son. in d for Flute & Continuo; Son. in F Klavier ■ KC 511

▲ = CD ♦ = Enhanced CD Δ = MD ■ = Cassette Tape □ = DCC

Lindeblad, Mark (pno)
Doran, M.:Movts (4) Db, w. Susan Nigro (ctbn) *(rec AirWave Recording Studios, Chicago)* Crystal ▲ CD 346
Draganski, D.:Heart's Desire, w. Susan Nigro (ctbn) *(rec AirWave Recording Studios, Chicago)* Crystal ▲ CD 346
Muradian, V.:Con Ctbn, w. Susan Nigro (ctbn) *(rec AirWave Recording Studios, Chicago)* Crystal ▲ CD 346
Nicholson, R.:Miniature Suite, w. Susan Nigro (ctbn) *(rec AirWave Recording Studios, Chicago)* Crystal ▲ CD 346
Palider, A.:The Narwhal, w. Susan Nigro (ctbn) *(rec AirWave Recording Studios, Chicago)* Crystal ▲ CD 346
Warren, F.:Music for Ctbn, w. Susan Nigro (ctbn) *(rec AirWave Recording Studios, Chicago)* Crystal ▲ CD 346

Lindeke, Per-Olev (tpt)
Telemann, G.P.:Con Tpt 2 Obs, w. Taka Kitazato (ob), Marcel Ponseele (ob), Fred Jacobs (thb), Richte Van Der Meer (vc), Pierre Hantaï (hpd) *(rec St. Stefanus, Melsen, Belgium, June 1995)* Accent ▲ 95110 [DDD]
Telemann, G.P.:Essercizii musici (sels), w. Taka Kitazato (ob), Marcel Ponseele (ob), Pierre Hantaï (hpd), Fred Jacobs (thb), Richte Van Der Meer (vc)—Trio Son in E♭ for Ob, Hpd & Continuo *(rec St. Stefanus, Melsen, Belgium, June 1995)* Accent ▲ 95110 [DDD]
Telemann, G.P.:Der Getreue Music-Meister (sels), w. Taka Kitazato (ob), Marcel Ponseele (ob), Fred Jacobs (thb), Richte Van Der Meer (vc), Pierre Hantaï (hpd)—Son in a *(rec St. Stefanus, Melsen, Belgium, June 1995)* Accent ▲ 95110 [DDD]
Telemann, G.P.:Kleine Kammermusik, w. Taka Kitazato (ob), Marcel Ponseele (ob), Fred Jacobs (thb), Richte Van Der Meer (vc), Pierre Hantaï (hpd)—Partita IV in g *(rec St. Stefanus, Melsen, Belgium, June 1995)* Accent ▲ 95110 [DDD]
Telemann, G.P.:Musique de Table, w. Taka Kitazato (ob), Marcel Ponseele (ob), Fred Jacobs (thb), Richte Van Der Meer (vc), Pierre Hantaï (hpd)—Son in g *(rec St. Stefanus, Melsen, Belgium, June 1995)* Accent ▲ 95110 [DDD]
Telemann, G.P.:Son 2 Ob, w. Taka Kitazato (ob), Marcel Ponseele (ob), Fred Jacobs (thb), Richte Van Der Meer (vc), Pierre Hantaï (hpd) *(rec St. Stefanus, Melsen, Belgium, June 1995)* Accent ▲ 95110 [DDD]
Torelli, G.:Tpt Music, w. D. Staff (tpt), E. Tarr (tpt), G. Cassone (tpt), S. Vartolo (cnd), San Petronio Cappella Musicale Orch—Sinfs., G.1, 2, 8, 10, 11, 26, 29, 30, 31, 33; Sons. G.3–6, 13, 15–25; Con. G.27 Bongiovanni 3–▲ GB 5523/25

Lindemann, Jens (tpt/figl)—see ORCHESTRAS & ENSEMBLES Canadian Brass

Linden, Jaap ter (b vl)—see also ORCHESTRAS & ENSEMBLES Scaramouche
Geminiani, F.:Sons Vc & Continuo, Op. 5, w. H. Schiff (vc), T. Koopman (hpd)—Sonata No. 6 in a Philips ▲ 434124–2 [DDD]
Vivaldi, A.:Sons Vc, w. H. Schiff (vc), T. Koopman (hpd)—(4) in e, RV.40; in a, RV.43; in B♭, RV.45; in B♭, RV.46 Philips ▲ 434124–2 [DDD]

Linden, Jaap ter (vc)
Bach, J.S.:A Musical Offering, w. D. Moroney (hpd), J. See (fl), J. Holloway (vn), M. Cook (hpd) Harmonia Mundi France ▲ HMC 901260 [DDD]
Couperin, F.:Motets, w. J. Feldman (sop), I. Poulenard (sop), G. Reinhart (bass), D. Moroney (hpd)—[L] Musique d'Abord ▲ HMA 1901150
Handel, G.F.:Sons Rcr, w. Marion Verbruggen (rec/fl), Ton Koopman (hpd/chest org)—No. 1 in B♭; No. 2 in g, Op. 1/2; No. 4 in a, Op. 1/4; No. 7 in C, Op. 1/7; No. 9 in d, Op. 1/9; No. 11 in F, Op. 1/11 *(rec Waalse Kerk, Amsterdam, Apr 27–29, 1994)* Harmonia Mundi France ▲ HMU 907151
Haydn, J.:Trios Pno, Vn & Vc, w. Tini Mathot (hpd), Andrew Manze (vn)—in A, H.XV/9; in E♭, H.XV/10; in E♭, H.XV/11; in e, H.XV/12; in G, H.XV/25 *(rec Oud Katholieke Kerk, Utrecht, Nov. 1992)* Erato ▲ 4509-91728-2 [DDD]

Linden, Jaap Ter (vl)—see also ORCHESTRAS & ENSEMBLES Smithsonian Chamber Players
Buxtehude, D.:Sons Vn, Vl & Continuo, w. John Holloway (vn), Ursula Weiss (vn), Mogens Rasmussen (vl), Lars Ulrik Mortensen (hpd/org)—BuxWV 266, 267, 269 & 271–273 *(rec Radio House, Studio 2, Sept 25–28, 1994)* Marco Polo ("dacapo" series) ▲ 8.224005 [DDD]
Buxtehude, D.:Sons for 2 Vns, Op. 1, w. John Holloway (vn), Lars Ulrik Mortensen (hpd) *(rec Kastelskirken, Copenhagen, June 29–July 1, 1994)* Marco Polo ▲ 8.224003 [DDD]
Buxtehude, D.:Sons for 2 Vns, Op. 2, w. John Holloway (vn), Lars Ulrik Mortensen (hpd) *(rec Kastelskirken, Copenhagen)* Marco Polo ("dacapo" series) ▲ 8.224004 [DDD]
Hotteterre, J.:Music of, w. Wilbert Hazelzet (trns fl), Konrad Junghänel (thb), Jacques Ogg (hpd)—5 Airs; Passacaille; 8 Preludes in b, c, C, D, g, g, G, G; 3 Suites in c, g, G *(rec San Miguel Church, Cuenca, Spain, May 1996)* Glossa ▲ GCD 920801 [DDD]

Linden, Johan van der (s sax)—see ORCHESTRAS & ENSEMBLES Aurelia Saxophone Quartet

Linder, Albert (hn)—see also ORCHESTRAS & ENSEMBLES Gothenburg Wind Quintet
Atterberg, K.:Con Hn, w. G. Oskamp (cnd), Gothenburg SO Caprice ▲ CAP 21364 [DDD]
Beethoven, L. van:Qnt Pno, Ob, Cl, Hn & Bn, w. E. Knardahl (pno), E. Andersson (cl), E. Schleiffer (bn) BIS ▲ CD 44 [AAD]
Borwald, F.:Qt Pno, Cl, Hn & Bn, w. E. Knardahl (pno), E. Andersson (cl), E. Schleiffer (bn) BIS ▲ CD 44 [AAD]
Rimsky-Korsakov, N.:Qnt Fl, w. E. Andersson (cl), E. Schleiffer (bn), E. Knardahl (pno) BIS ▲ CD 44 [AAD]
Schubert, Franz:Songs (misc), w. Märta Schéle (sop), Ingemar Bergfelt (pno)—Auf dem Strome, Op. 119 *(rec Gothenburg Concert Hall, Sweden, May 8, 1976)* BIS ▲ CD 34 [AAD]

Linder, Jacques (pno)
Delio, T.:Music of, w. John Fonville (fl), Steven Shick (perc), Aleck Karis (pno), Sandra Sprecher (pno)—anti-paysage for Fl, Perc, Pno & Tape; Of for Tape; Though for solo Pno; so again for Tape; on again for Tape; of again for Tape *(rec Univ of CA, San Diego, Univ of Maryland, Catonsville & Washington D.C.)* Neuma ▲ 45090 [DDD]
Electro Acoustic Music III, w. Camilla Hoitenga (fl), William Buonocore (gtr), Maria Tegzes (sop), Robert McCormick (perc) Neuma ▲ 450-87 [DDD]

Lindgård, Jonal (va)
Lindblad, A.F.:Qnt Strs, w. Peter Olofsson (vn), Patrik Swedrup (vn), Tony Bauer (va), Lars Frykholm (vc) Musica Sveciae ▲ MSV 522 [DDD]
Randel, A.:Qt Strs, w. Peter Olofsson (vn), Patrik Swedrup (vn), Tony Bauer (va), Lars Frykholm (vc) Musica Sveciae ▲ MSV 522 [DDD]

Lindgård, Jonas (vn)—see ORCHESTRAS & ENSEMBLES Ferro String Quartet

Lindgård, Kristina (vc)—see ORCHESTRAS & ENSEMBLES Ferro String Quartet

Lindgren, Ingrid (pno)
Crumb, G.:Music For A Summer Evening (Makrokosmos III), w. B. Dahlman (pno), S. Asikainen (perc), R. Kuisma (perc) *(rec analog)* BIS ▲ CD 261
Crumb, G.:Pieces (5) Pno *(rec Studio BIS, Djursholm, Sweden, 1984)* BIS ▲ CD 52 [AAD]
Sjögren, E.:Impromptus Bluebell ▲ BLU 064 [DDD]
Sjögren, E.:Lyric Poems Bluebell ▲ BLU 064 [DDD]
Sjögren, E.:Pictures & Sketches Bluebell ▲ BLU 064 [DDD]
Sjögren, E.:Son Pno Bluebell ▲ BLU 064 [DDD]

Lindgren, Stefan (pno)
Andersson, R.:Son Pno Opus 3 ▲ OP 19303
Berwald, F.:Qnt Pno, w. Berwald String Quartet Musica Sveciae ▲ MSCD 521 [DDD]
Chopin, F.:Son Pno, Op. 58 Opus 3 ▲ OP 9202
Hägg, J.A.:Pno Music—Son Opus 3 ▲ OP 19303
Lindegren, J.:Stor sonat Opus 3 ▲ OP 19303
Liszt, F.:Mephisto Waltz 1 Pno Opus 3 ▲ OP 9202
Rachmaninoff, S.:Prelude Pno, Op. 3/2 Opus 3 ▲ OP 9202
Schumann, R.:Arabeske Pno Opus 3 ▲ OP 9202

Lindgren, W. (ob)—see ORCHESTRAS & ENSEMBLES Gothenburg Wind Quintet

Lindhout, Hendrik Jan (tpt)
Verbey, T.:Duet Tpts, w. Peter Masseurs (tpt) Donemus ▲ CV 31

Lindley, Simon (org)
Boëllmann, L.:Suite gothique Naxos ▲ 8.550581 [DDD]
Famous Organ Works *(rec Leeds Parish Church, 1991)* Naxos 4–▲ 8.504014 [DDD]
French Organ Music *(rec 1991)* Naxos ▲ 8.550581 [DDD]
Langlais, J.:Méditations Naxos ▲ 8.550581 [DDD]
A Song of Yorkshire, w. Honley Male Voice Choir, Leeds Parish Church Choir Boys' Voices, Sellers Engineering Band [cnd:P. McCann] Chandos Brass ▲ CHAN 4515 [DDD]
Widor, C.M.:Sym 5 Org—5th movement, Toccata Naxos ▲ 8.550581 [DDD]
The World's Most Beautiful Melodies, Vol. 3:The Golden Cornet of Phillip McCann, w. Philip McCann (cnt), Sellers Engineering Band Chandos Brass ▲ CHAN 4503 [DDD]
The World's Most Beautiful Melodies, Vol. 5, w. Phillip McCann (cnt), Sellers Engineering Band, Huddersfield Choral Society Youth Choir Chandos ▲ CHAN 4532 [DDD]

Lindo, Sharon (vns/rcr)
Old English Nursery Rhymes, w. Vivien Ellis (sop), Tim Laycock (sgr), Broadside Band [Jeremy Barlow (rcrs/perc), George Weigand (lt/mandore/cittern/gtr), Rosemary Thorndycraft (b vl/h-g), Ben Sansom (vn), Marilyn Sansom (vc)] *(rec Valley Recordings, Littleton-on-Severn, Feb 1996)* Saydisc ▲ CDSDL 419

Lindorff, Joyce (hpd)
Poglietti, A.:Rossignolo Titanic ▲ TIC 233 [DDD]

Lindroth, Scott (kbd)
Lindroth, S.:Syntax Centaur ▲ CRC 2039 [DDD]

Lindsberger, Herbert (va)
Weichlein, R.:Encaenia musices, w. Gunar Letzbor (vn), Daniel Sepec (vn), Christoph Bitzinger (va), Michael Oman (vl), Gaetano Nasillo (vc), Roberto Sensi (vn), Andreas Lackner (nat tpt), Herbert Walser (nat tpt), Norbert Kirchner (hpd/org), G. Letzbor (cnd), Ars Antiqua Austria—Sons. Nos. I in C, II in g, III in a, IV in E, V in C & VI in F Symphonia ▲ SY 93S23

Lindström, Mats (vc)
Chausson, E.:Chanson perpétuelle, w. Anne Sofie von Otter (mez), Nils-Erik Sparf (vn), Ulf Forsberg (vn), Matti Hirvikangas (va), Bengt Forsberg (pno) *(rec Stockholm, Nov 1994)* Deutsche Grammophon ▲ 447 752–2 [DDD]
Delage, M.:Poèmes hindous, w. Anne Sofie von Otter (mez), Andreas Alin (fl), Peter Rydström (fl/pic), Ulf Bjurenhed (cl/E hn), Lars Paulsson (cl), Per Billman (cl/b cl), Nils-Erik Sparf (vn), Ulf Forsberg (vn), Matti Hirvikangas (va), Mats Lindström (vc), Lisa Viguier (hp) *(rec Stockholm, Nov 1994)* Deutsche Grammophon ▲ 447 752–2 [DDD]
Fauré, G.:La bonne chanson, w. Anne Sofie von Otter (mez), Nils-Erik Sparf (vn), Ulf Forsberg (vn), Matti Hirvikangas (va), Tomas Gertonsson (db), Bengt Forsberg (pno) *(rec Stockhom, Nov 1994)* Deutsche Grammophon ▲ 447 752–2 [DDD]
Poulenc, F.:Rapsodie nègre, w. Anne Sofie von Otter (mez), Andreas Alin (fl), Lars Paulsson (cl), Nils-Erik Sparf (vn), Ulf Forsberg (vn), Matti Hirvikangas (va), Bengt Forsberg (pno) *(rec Stockhom, Nov 1994)* Deutsche Grammophon ▲ 447 752–2 [DDD]
Ravel, M.:Trois poèmes de Stéphane Mallarmé, w. Anne Sofie von Otter (mez), Peter Rydström (fl/pic), Andreas Alin (fl), Lars Paulsson (cl), Per Billman (cl/b cl), Nils-Erik Sparf (vn), Ulf Forsberg (vn), Matti Hirvikangas (va), Bengt Forsberg (pno) *(rec Stockholm, Nov 1994)* Deutsche Grammophon ▲ 447 752–2 [DDD]

Lindström, Sixten (bn)—see ORCHESTRAS & ENSEMBLES Sundsvall Wind Quartet

Line, Ildiko (vn)
Bach, Joh. Christian:Sinf concertante, T.284/6, w. Violetta Eckhardt (vn), Marianna Kruzse (ob), H. Gmür (cnd), Budapest Camerata *(rec Festetich Castle, Budapest, Mar 1994)* Naxos ▲ 8.553085 [DDD]

Linetzky, Vladislav (vn)
Dvořák, A.:Romance Vn, w. D. Bostock (cnd), Carlsbad SO *(rec Lazne III, Karlovy Vary, Czech Republic, Jan 13–15, 1996)* Classico ▲ CLASSCD 150

Linhares, Dagoberto (gtr)—see also ORCHESTRAS & ENSEMBLES Linhares Guitar Quartet
Dagoberto Linhares Gallo ▲ CD 507 [AAD]
Giuliani, M.:Con 1 Gtr, w. J. Wildner (cnd), Camerata Cassovia Naxos ▲ 8.550483 [DDD]
Moreno Torroba, F.:Sonatina Gtr Orch, w. J. Wildner (cnd), Camerata Cassovia Naxos ▲ 8.550483 [DDD]
Villa-Lobos & Popular Brazilian Music Gallo ▲ CD 738 [DDD]
Villa-Lobos, H.:Etudes Gtr Gallo ▲ CD 572 [AAD]
Villa-Lobos, H.:Preludes Gtr Gallo ▲ CD 572 [AAD]
Vivaldi, A.:Cons Gtr, w. J. Wildner (cnd), Camerata Cassovia—Concerti RV.82, 93 & 540 transcribed for guitar & orchestra Naxos ▲ 8.550483 [DDD]

Link, Oliver (cl)
Schacht, T. von:Cons Cl, w. D. Kloecker (cl), S. Wandel (cl), H. Stadlmair (cnd), Bamberg SO—in D & B for 1 Clarinet; in B for 2 Clarinets; in B for 3 Clarinets *(rec May 11–15, 1992)* Orfeo ▲ 290931 [DDD]

Link, Robbie (gtr)
Kouneva, P.:Aeon, w. Terry Rhodes (sop), Ellen Williams (mez), Penka Kouneva (pno), Lynn Glasscock (perc) Albany ▲ TROY 172 [DDD]

Linker, Tom (pno/syn)—see ORCHESTRAS & ENSEMBLES Zeitgeist

Linkola, Osmo (bas hn)
Mendelssohn, F.:Concert Pieces, w. Kari Kriikku (cl), Arto Satukangas (pno) Ondine ▲ ODE 820 [DDD]

Linsenberg, Judith (rcr)—see ORCHESTRAS & ENSEMBLES Musica Pacifica

Lintermans, Yvo (vn)—see ORCHESTRAS & ENSEMBLES Arriaga String Quartet

Lipatti, Dinu (hpd)
Bach, J.S.:Con 1 Hpd, w. E. van Beinum (cnd), Royal Concertgebouw Orch *(rec live Oct 2, 1947)* Jecklin-Disco ▲ JD 541–2

Lipatti, Dinu (pno)
Bach, J.S.:Chorale Preludes Org—3 EMI Classics ▲ CDH 69800
Bach, J.S.:Partitas Hpd, BWV 825–830—No. 1 EMI Classics ▲ CDH 69800
Brahms, J.:Waltzes Pno, Op. 39—7 Waltzes EMI Classics ▲ CDH 63038
Chopin, F.:Barcarolle Pno EMI Classics ▲ CDH 69802
Chopin, F.:Con 1 Pno, w. O. Ackermann (cnd), Zurich Tonhalle Orch *(rec live, 1950)* EMI Classics ▲ CDH 63497 (m) [ADD]
Chopin, F.:Con 1 Pno, w. O. Ackermann (cnd), Zurich Tonhalle Orch *(rec live Feb. 7, 1950)* Jecklin-Disco ▲ JD 541–2 [ADD]
Chopin, F.:Études (24)—Op. 25/5 & 10/5 *(rec live Feb. 7, 1950)* Jecklin-Disco ▲ JD 541–2 [ADD]
Chopin, F.:Mazurkas—Op. 50/3 EMI Classics ▲ CDH 69802
Chopin, F.:Nocturnes *(rec live Feb. 7, 1950)* Jecklin-Disco ▲ JD 541–2 [ADD]
Chopin, F.:Nocturnes—Op. 27/2 EMI Classics ▲ CDH 69802
Chopin, F.:Son Pno, Op. 58 EMI Classics ▲ CDH 63038
Chopin, F.:Waltzes—(14) Odyssey ■ YT 60058
Chopin, F.:Waltzes—(14) EMI Classics ▲ CDH 69802
Enescu, G.:Son Pno, Op. 24/3 EMI Classics ▲ CDH 63038
Grieg, E.:Con Pno, Op. 16, w. A. Galliera (cnd), Philharmonia Orch *(rec 1947)* EMI Classics ▲ CDH 63497 (m) [ADD]
Grieg, E.:Con Pno, Op. 16, w. A. Galliera (cnd), Philharmonia Orch Odyssey ■ YT 60141 (m)
Liszt, F.:Sonetti del Petrarca Pno—No. 104 EMI Classics ▲ CDH 63038
Mozart, W.A.:Son 8 Pno EMI Classics ▲ CDH 69800
Ravel, M.:Alborada del gracioso EMI Classics ▲ CDH 63038
Scarlatti, D.:Sons Kbd—(2) EMI Classics ▲ CDH 69800
Schubert, Franz:Impromptus Pno (comp)—(2) EMI Classics ▲ CDH 69800

Lipkin, Seymour (pno)
Beethoven, L. van:Son 6 Pno Audiofon ▲ CD 72034
Beethoven, L. van:Son 29 Pno, "Hammerklavier" Audiofon ▲ CD 72034
Beethoven, L. van:Son 30 Pno Audiofon ▲ CD 72034
Chausson, E.:Con Vn, Pno & Str Qt, w. Aaron Rosand (vn), Miami String Quartet Audiofon ▲ CD 72039

Lipkin, Seymour (pno) (cont.)
Franck, C.:Son Vn, w. Aaron Rosand (vn) Audiofon ▲ CD 72039
Grieg, E.:Sons Vn, Opp. 8, 13 & 45, w. A. Rosand (vn)—Op. 45 Audiofon ▲ CD 72026
Saint-Saëns, C.:Son 1 Vn, w. A. Rosand (vn) Audiofon ▲ CD 72026
Strauss, R.:Son Vn, w. A. Rosand (vn) Audiofon ▲ CD 72026
Stravinsky, I.:Con Pno Ww, w. L. Bernstein (cnd), New York PO *(rec Oct. 26, 1959)* Sony Classical ▲ SMK 47628 [ADD]

Lipman, Samuel (pno)
Gideon, M.:Questions on Nature, w. J. DeGaetani (mez), West (ob), Jekofsky (perc) CRI ■ C 343
Saint-Saëns, C.:Carnival of the Animals, w. Leo Litwin (pno), Martin Hoherman (vc), Hugh Downs (nar), A. Fiedler (cnd), Boston Pops Orch [verses rec. June 12, 1963] *(rec Symphony Hall, Boston, June 14, 1961)* RCA Living Stereo ▲ 09026-68131-2 [ADD]; ■ 09026-68131-4
Shostakovich, D.:From Jewish Folk Poetry, w. Benita Valente (sop), Jan de Gaetani (mez), Jon Humphrey (ten) *(rec live, Aspen Music Festival, 1980)* Bridge ▲ BCD 9048 [ADD]
Wild Classics:A Celebration of Animals & Nature, w. James Galway (fl), Ofra Harnoy (vc), Martin Hoherman (vc), Emily Mitchell (hp), Michael Dussek (pno), Leo Litwin (pno), Gerhard Oppitz (pno), Isao Tomita (synths), Boston Pops Orch [cnd:Arthur Fiedler], Chicago SO [cnd:Fritz Reiner] RCA Red Seal ▲ 09026-68483-2 ■ 09026-68483-4

Lipnik, Lawrence (t vl)—see ORCHESTRAS & ENSEMBLES New York Consort of Viols
Lippens, D. (vn)—see ORCHESTRAS & ENSEMBLES Hans Memling Trio

Lippi, Isabella (vn)
Rózsa, M.:Duo Vn, w. John Novacek (pno) Koch International Classics ▲ KIC 7256 [DDD]
Rózsa, M.:North Hungarian Peasant Songs & Dances, w. John Novacek (pno) Koch International Classics ▲ KIC 7256 [DDD]
Rózsa, M.:Son Vn Koch International Classics ▲ KIC 7256 [DDD]
Rózsa, M.:Vars on Hungarian Peasant Song, w. John Novacek (pno) Koch International Classics ▲ KIC 7256 [DDD]

Lippincott, Joan (org)
Alain, J.:Danses (3) [the organ in Cadet Chapel, U.S. Military Academy at West Point] Gothic ▲ G 49046 [DDD]
Duruflé, M.:Prélude, Adagio et Choral varié sur le thème du *Veni Creator* [at Princeton Univ. Chapel's Mander organ] Gothic ▲ G 49061 [DDD]
Howells, H.:Rhap in c# Org [Princeton Univ. Chapel's Mander organ] Gothic ▲ G 49061 [DDD]
Joan Lippincott & Philadelphia Brass, w. Philadelphia Brass [Brian Kuszyk (tpt), Lawrence Wright (tpt), Martin Webster (hn), John Ilika (trbn), Grant Moore II (tuba)] Gothic ▲ GOT 49072 [DDD]
Liszt, F.:Fant & Fugue on "Ad nos, ad salutarem undam" Org Gothic ▲ G 49039
Mendelssohn, F.:Sons Org [Princeton Univ. Chapel's Mander organ]—Sonata No. 3 Gothic ▲ G 49061 [DDD]
Mozart, W.A.:Org Music—Adagio, K.356; Adagio & Rondo, K.617; Andante, K.616; Andante & Allegro, K.594; Fant., K.608; Fugue, K.401; Gigue, K.574; Suite, K.399 Gothic ▲ G 49051
Pinkham, D.:Org Music—Epiphanes; Man's Days are Like the Grass; Revelations Gothic ▲ G 49039
Widor, C.M.:Sym 5 Org [Cadet Chapel, U.S. Military Academy at West Point] Gothic ▲ G 49046 [DDD]
Widor, C.M.:Sym 6 Org [Princeton Univ. Chapel's Mander organ]—Sonata No. 3 Gothic ▲ G 49061 [DDD]

Lippman, Bob (gtr)
Exquisite Corpses from P.S. 122, w. Watson, David (shears/stick vn/gtr/tpt), Judy Dunaway (gtr/balloons), Anthony Coleman (sampler), Raissa St. Pierre (drums), Guy Yarden (vn/pno), Leslie Ross (bn), Linda Austin (gtr), Bruce Kaplan (gtr), Doug Henderson (peckhorn/bass/toy pno), Sue Ann Harkey (gtr), Cinnie Cole (sampler), et al. ¿What Next? ▲ WN 0002 [ADD]

Lips, Friedrich (bayan)
Gubaidulina, S.:Silenzio, w. Gidon Kremer (vn), Vladimir Tonkha (vc) *(rec Lockenhaus Festival, Austria, 1995)* BIS ▲ CD 810 [DDD]

Lipsey, Michael (cloud-chamber bowls)
Partch, H.:Daphne of the Dunes, w. Frank Cassara (boo/spoils of war/kithara 2), Dominic Donato (b mar/surrogate kithara/boo), Dean Drummond (harmonic canons/kithara 2/spoils of war/kithara), Nina Kellman (kithara 2/harmonic canon/surrogate kithara), Ted Mook (vc/gourd tree/cone gongs), James Pugliese (diamond mar), Elizabeth Rodgers (chromelodeon/harmonic canon) *(rec Queens, NY, Mar. 12, 1991)* Mode ▲ MODE 33

Lipsey, Michael (instr)—see ORCHESTRAS & ENSEMBLES New Music Consort

Lipsky, Helmut (vn)
Fauré, G.:Trio, w. L. Snider (vc), M. Koslovsky (pno) Analekta ▲ ATM 29704
Granados, E.:Trio Pno, w. L. Snider (vc), M. Koslovsky (pno) Analekta ▲ ATM 29704

Lipson-Gruzen, Berenice (pno)
Debussy, C.:Pour le piano Infinity Digital ▲ QK 62386 [DDD]

Lipstein, Leopoldo (pno)
Chopin, F.:Barcarolle Pno FSM ▲ FSM 97710 [DDD]
Chopin, F.:Impromptus FSM ▲ FSM 97710 [DDD]
Chopin, F.:Nocturnes—Op. 9 FSM ▲ FSM 97710 [DDD]
Chopin, F.:Polonaises—Polonaise héroïque, Op. 53 FSM ▲ FSM 97710 [DDD]
Ginastera, A.:Son 1 Pno FSM-Fono ▲ 97724 [DDD]
Liszt, F.:Années de pèlerinage 2—No. 10, "Au lac de Wallenstadt" FSM-Fono ▲ 97724 [DDD]
Liszt, F.:Études d'exécution transcendante, S.139—No. 3 FSM-Fono ▲ 97724 [DDD]
Liszt, F.:Paraphrase on Verdi's Quartet FSM-Fono ▲ 97724 [DDD]
Ravel, M.:Sonatine Pno FSM-Fono ▲ FCD 97724 [DDD]

Liptak, David (pno)
Baker, C.:Omaggi e Fant Db, w. M. Cameron (db) Gasparo ▲ GS 286

Lisitsa, Valentina (pno)
Beethoven, L. van:Contredanses, WoO 14 [trans. for pno] Audiofon ▲ CD 72056
Bolcom, W.:Recuerdos, w. Alexei Kuznetsoff (pno) Audiofon ▲ CD 72054
Chopin, F.:Berceuse Audiofon ▲ CD 72056
Chopin, F.:Rondo for 2 Pnos, w. Alexei Kuznetsoff (pno) *(rec Miami, FL, Aug 1995)* Audiofon ▲ CD 72053
Debussy, C.:En blanc et noir, w. Alexei Kuznetsoff (pno) Audiofon ▲ CD 72054
Ginzburg, G.:Pno Transcriptions—Paraphrase on Figaro's Aria from Il Barbiere di Siviglia Audiofon ▲ CD 72055
Godowsky, L.:Transcriptions & Paraphrases, w. Alexei Kuznetsoff (pno)—Weber's "Invitation to the Dance" Audiofon ▲ CD 72054
Godowsky, L.:Transcriptions & Paraphrases—Paraphrase on Themes from Joh. Strauss' "Die Fledermaus" Audiofon ▲ CD 72055
Liszt, F.:Ballade 2 Pno Audiofon ▲ CD 72055
Liszt, F.:Études d'exécution transcendante d'après Paganini, S.140—No. 3, "La campanella" Audiofon ▲ CD 72055
Liszt, F.:Études d'exécution transcendante, S.139—No. 12 Audiofon ▲ CD 72070
Liszt, F.:Hungarian Rhaps—No. 2 Audiofon ▲ CD 72055
Liszt, F.:Hungarian Rhaps—No. 12 Audiofon ▲ CD 72070
Liszt, F.:Réminiscences de Don Juan, w. Alexei Kuznetsoff (pno) *(rec Miami, FL, Aug 1995)* Audiofon ▲ CD 72053
Liszt, F.:Rhap espagnole Audiofon ▲ CD 72055
Liszt, F.:Son Pno Audiofon ▲ CD 72070
Liszt, F.:Song Transcriptions—4 Schubert transcriptions—Die Stadt; Gute Nacht; Erstarrung; Erlkonig Audiofon ▲ CD 72055
Liszt, F.:Song Transcriptions—2 Schubert trans.—Gute Nacht; Erlkonig Audiofon ▲ CD 72056
Mozart, W.A.:Son 12 Pno Audiofon ▲ CD 72056
Prokofiev, S.:Son 7 Pno Audiofon ▲ CD 72056
Rachmaninoff, S.:Études-tableaux, Opp. 33 & 39—Op. 39/6 Audiofon ▲ CD 72070
Rachmaninoff, S.:Moments musicaux Audiofon ▲ CD 72070
Rachmaninoff, S.:Preludes Pno, Opp 23 & 32—3 preludes Audiofon ▲ CD 72056
Rachmaninoff, S.:Suite 1 for 2 Pnos, w. Alexei Kuznetsoff (pno) Audiofon ▲ CD 72053

Lisitsa, Valentina (pno) (cont.)
Schnittke, A.:Gogol Suite, w. Alexei Kuznetsoff (pno) Audiofon ▲ CD 72054
Schubert, Franz:Songs (misc)—Doppelganger; Auftenhalt [arr Liszt for solo pno] Audiofon ▲ CD 72070
Shostakovich, D.:Con 1 Pno, w. Viatcheslav Chtchennikov (tpt), S. Caldwell (cnd), Ekaterinburg PO Audiofon ▲ CD 72060
Shostakovich, D.:Con 1 Pno, w. S. Caldwell (cnd), Ekaterinburg PO Audiofon ▲ CD 72060
Shostakovich, D.:Suite for 2 Pnos, w. Alexei Kuznetsoff (pno) Audiofon ▲ CD 72053
Weber, C.M. von:Rondo brillante Audiofon ▲ CD 72056

Lislevand, Rolf (lt)
Vivaldi, A.:Lt Music—Trio in g for Vn, Lt & Cont, R.85; Con in d for Vl, Lt, Cont & Orch, R.540; Trio in C for Vn, Lt & Cont, R.82; Con in D for 2 Vns, Lt & Cont, R.93; plus others Astrée ▲ E 8587

Lislevand, Rolf (thb)—see also ORCHESTRAS & ENSEMBLES Rare Fruits Council
de Machy, S.:Suite in d, w. P. Pierlot (vl), S. Watillon (vl) Ricercar ▲ RIC 118100 [DDD]
de Machy, S.:Suite in G, w. P. Pierlot (vl), S. Watillon (vl) Ricercar ▲ RIC 118100 [DDD]
du Buisson:Suite Vls, w. P. Pierlot (vl), S. Watillon (vl) Ricercar ▲ RIC 118100 [DDD]
Marais, M.:Tombeau pour Monsieur de Ste Colombe, w. P. Pierlot (vl), S. Watillon (vl) Ricercar ▲ RIC 118100 [DDD]
Merula, T.:Arias & Capriccios, w. M. Figueras (sop), J.-P. Canihac (cnt), T. Koopman (hpd), J. Savall (vl), A. Laurence-King (hp), L. Duftschmid (vn) Astrée ▲ E 8503
Monteverdi, C.:Arie e Lamenti, w. M. Figueras (sop), T. Koopman (hpd/org), A. Lawrence-King (hp) Astrée ▲ E 8710

Lislevand, Rolf (thb/baroque gtr)
Forqueray, A.:Suites (5) Va da Gamba, w. Guido Balestracci (vl), Paolo Pandolfo (vl), Eduardo Eguez (thb/baroque gtr), Guido Morini (clvd) Glossa 2-▲ 920401

Lislevand, Rolf (thb/lt)
Vivaldi, A.:Sons Vn, w. F. Biondi (vn), R. Alessandrini (hpd), M. Naddeo (vc), P. Pandolfo (db)—Manchester Sons. 1, 2, 3, 6, 8 & 10 Arcana ▲ ACA 4 [DDD]
Vivaldi, A.:Sons Vn, w. F. Biondi (vn), R. Alessandrini (hpd), M. Naddeo (vc), P. Pandolfo (db)—Manchester Sons. 4, 5, 7, 9, 11 & 12 Arcana ▲ ACA 5 [DDD]

Lislevand, Rolf (vih)
Ortiz, D.:Trattado de Glosas, w. J. Savall (vl), T. Koopman (hpd/org), L. Duftschmid (vn), P. Pandolfo (b vl), A. Lawrence-King (hp) Astrée ▲ E 8717 [DDD]

Lisney, James (pno)
Schubert, Franz:Fant Vn, D.934, w. Elizabeth Layton (vn) IMP ("Classics" series) ▲ IMP 6700932
Schubert, Franz:Pno Music (misc)—Andante in C, D.29; Minuet in a, D.277a; Minuet in A, D.334; Hüttenbrenner Vars, D.576; Andante in A, D.604; Grazer Fant, D.605a; 3 Klavierstücke, D.946 Olympia ▲ OLY 479 [DDD]
Schubert, Franz:Rondo Vn, D.895, w. Elizabeth Layton (vn) IMP ("Classics" series) ▲ IMP 6700932
Schubert, Franz:Son Pno, D.157 Olympia ▲ OLY 560 [DDD]
Schubert, Franz:Son Pno, D.960 Olympia ▲ OLY 560 [DDD]
Schubert, Franz:Son Vn, D.574, w. Elizabeth Layton (vn) IMP ("Classics" series) ▲ IMP 6700932
Schubert, Franz:Vars Pno, D.156 Olympia ▲ OLY 560 [DDD]
Tchaikovsky, P.:Pno Music—Dumka (Russian Rustic Scene), Op. 59; Romance, Op. 5; Waltz-Scherzo, Op. 7 IMP Classics ▲ PCD 976 [DDD]
Tchaikovsky, P.:Les Saisons IMP Classics ▲ PCD 976 [DDD]

List, Eugene (pno)
Gershwin, G.:Con Pno, w. H. Hanson (cnd), Eastman-Rochester Orch Mercury Living Presence ▲ 434341-2
Gershwin, G.:Con Pno, w. S. Adler (cnd), Berlin SO *(rec 1971)* Vox Box 2-▲ CDX 5069 [ADD]
Gershwin, G.:Rhap in Blue, w. H. Hanson (cnd), Eastman-Rochester Orch Mercury Living Presence ▲ 434341-2
Gershwin, G.:Rhap in Blue, w. E. Kunzel (cnd), Cincinnati SO Telarc ▲ CD 80058 [DDD]
Gottschalk, L.M.:Music of, w. Trinidad Paniagua (sop), José Alberto Esteves (ten), Pablo Garcia (bar), Cary Lewis (pno), Brady Millican (pno), Adler, Buketoff (cnd), Berlin SO, Vienna State Opera Orch—Grande Tarantelle for Piano & Orchestra, Op. 67; Symphony No. 1, "La nuit des tropiques"; Symphony No. 2, "A Montevideo"; The Union (concert paraphrase on American national airs) for Piano & Orchestra, Op. 48; Variations on the Portuguese National Hymn for Piano & Orchestra, Op. 91; Grande fantaisie triomphale sur l'hymne national brésilien for Piano & Orchestra, Op. 69; Marche solennelle for Orchestra; Marcha triunfal y final de opera for Orchestra; Escenas campestres (opera in one act); Five Pieces for Piano Duet [Radieuse, Op. 72; Ses yeux, Op. 66; La Gallina, Op. 53; Ojos criollos, Op. 37; Pasquinade, Op. 59] Vox Box 2-▲ CDX 5009 [ADD]
Gottschalk, L.M.:Pno Music—The Banjo (fantaisie grotesque), Op. 15; Bamboula (danse de nègres), Op. 2; The maiden's blush (grande valse de concert); The last hope (méditation religieuse), Op. 16; Pasquinade (caprice), Op. 59; Le bananier (chanson nègre); The Dying Poet (méditation); Ojos criollos (danse cubaine); La savane (ballade creole); Souvenir de Porto Rico (marche des gibaros); Suis moi (caprice); Tournament galop *(rec 1956)* Vanguard Classics ▲ OVC 4050 [ADD]
Gottschalk, L.M.:Pno Music, w. assisting pianists Cary Lewis, Joseph Werner—La jota aragonesa; Souvenirs d'Andalousie; La gallina; Orfa; Marche de nuit; Printemps d'amour; Radieuse; Réponds-moi; Tremolo; L'Etincelle; Ses yeux *(rec 1976)* Vanguard Classics ▲ OVC 4051 [ADD]
Gottschalk, L.M.:The Union, w. C. Lewis (pno) [2-piano arr. by List] *(rec 1976)* Vanguard Classics ▲ OVC 4051 [ADD]
Grieg, E.:Con Pno, Op. 16, w. M. Kuntzsch (cnd), Stuttgart PO *(rec Südwest Tonstudio, Stuttgart, 1976)* Vox Legends 3-▲ CDX3 3504
Hanson, H.:Con Pno, w. D. Epstein (cnd), MIT SO Vox Box 2-▲ CDX 5091 [ADD]
Hummel, J.N.:Con Pno, Vn & Orch, Op. 17, w. C. Glenn (vn), E. Märzendorfer (cnd), Vienna CO Monitor ■ 55002
Hummel, J.N.:Septet Pno, w. Vermont Festival Players [variant arr. by Hummel for piano & string quartet] Monitor ■ 55002
Liszt, F.:Con 1 Pno, w. M. Kuntzsch (cnd), Stuttgart PO *(rec Südwest Tonstudio, Stuttgart, 1976)* Vox Legends 3-▲ CDX3 3504
Liszt, F.:Fant on Hungarian Folk Tunes, w. Z. Topolski (cnd), Vienna Tonkunstler Orch *(rec Südwest Tonstudio, Stuttgart, 1976)* Vox Legends 3-▲ CDX3 3504
Liszt, F.:Hexaméron, w. S. Landau (cnd), Westphalia SO *(rec Tonstudio Englesmann, Germany, 1973)* Vox Legends 3-▲ CDX3 3504
Macdowell, E.:Con 2 Pno, w. S. Landau (cnd), Westphalia SO *(rec 1972)* Vox Box 2-▲ CDX 5069 [ADD]
Mozart, W.A.:Con 20 Pno, w. Z. Topolski (cnd), Vienna CO *(rec Baumgartner Casino, Vienna, 1966)* Vox Legends 3-▲ CDX3 3504
Mozart, W.A.:Con 26 Pno, w. Z. Topolski (cnd), Vienna CO *(rec Baumgartner Casino, Vienna, 1966)* Vox Legends 3-▲ CDX3 3504
Rachmaninoff, S.:Con 2 Pno, w. M. Kuntzsch (cnd), Stuttgart PO Vox Legends 3-▲ CDX3 3504
Schubert, Franz:Qnt Pno, D.667, w. Rochester Chamber Players Vox Box 2-▲ CDX 5033 [ADD]
Tchaikovsky, P.:Con 1 Pno, w. Z. Topolski (cnd), Vienna Tonkunstler Orch *(rec Südwest Tonstudio, Stuttgart, 1976)* Vox Legends 3-▲ CDX3 3504

Lister, Jane (hp)
Essentially Christmas, w. East London Chorus, A. Doyle (sop), S. Liley (ten), P. Ayres (org), M. Kibbelwhite (cnd), Locke Brass Consort Koch International Classics ▲ KIC 7202 [DDD]

Lister-Sink, Barbara (pno)
Debussy, C.:Songs, w. B. Banovetz (ob)—Apparition; Claire de lune; Pantomime; Pierrot [trans. for oboe & piano] Well-Tempered Productions ▲ WPT 5163 [DDD]
Dvořák, A.:Love Songs, Op. 83, w. B. Banovetz (ob)—Never Will Love Lead Us to That Glad Goal; Nature Lies Peaceful in Slumber and Dreaming; In Deepest Forest Glade I Stand; I Know That on My Love to Thee; When Thy Sweet Glances on Me Fall; Thou Only Dear One, but for Thee [trans. for oboe & piano] Well-Tempered Productions ▲ WPT 5163 [DDD]
Falla, M. de:Canciones populares españolas (7), w. B. Banovetz (ob)—Apparition; Claire de lune; Pantomime; Pierrot [trans. for oboe & piano] Well-Tempered Productions ▲ WPT 5163 [DDD]
Fauré, G.:Songs, w. B. Banovetz (ob)—Nell; Ici-bas!; Après un rêve; Le papillon et la fluer; Prison; Fleur jetée [trans. for oboe & piano] Well-Tempered Productions ▲ WPT 5163 [DDD]

▲ = CD ♦ = Enhanced CD Δ = MD ■ = Cassette Tape □ = DCC

Lister-Sink, Barbara (pno) (cont.)
Sarasate, P. de:Vn & Pno Music, w. Charles Castleman (vn), Charles Tauber (pno)—Faust Fant.; Carmen; Zigeunerweisen; Les Adieux; Zapateado; Malaguena; Romance; others Music & Arts ▲ CD 855 [DDD]
Strauss, R.:Songs, w. B. Banovetz (ob) [trans. for oboe & piano]—Allerseelen; Ich schwebe; Nacht; Ständchen; Freundliche Vision; Kling! Well-Tempered Productions ▲ WPT 5163 [DDD]
Listokin, Robert (cl)—see ORCHESTRAS & ENSEMBLES New York Woodwind Soloists
Litaize, Gaston (org)
All'Organo di Carasso Gallo ▲ CD 536 [AAD]
Franck, C.:Prélude, fugue et var *(rec 1963)* Koch Schwann ▲ 3-1044-2 [ADD]
Litaize, G.:Org Music—Epiphanie; Improvisation sur Victimae paschali laudes Gallo ▲ CD 536
Messiaen, O.:La Nativité du Seigneur—Les anges Gallo ▲ CD 536
Satie, E.:Messe des pauvres, w. René DuClos Chorus Virgin Classics 2-▲ CDZB 62877
Vierne, L.:Org Music—Aubade, Op. 55; Impromptu, Op. 54 Gallo ▲ CD 536
Little, Margaret (vl)—see also ORCHESTRAS & ENSEMBLES Da Sonar Ensemble
Couperin, F.:Vl Music, w. Susie Napper (vl)—Concerts Nos. 12 & 13 for 2 Vls *(rec Saint-Joseph-de-Rivière-des-prairies Church, Montreal, Nov. 29-30, 1993)* CBC ("Musica Viva" series) ▲ MVV 1082 [DDD]
Marais, M.:Suite 2 for 2 Vls, w. Susie Napper (vl) *(rec Saint-Joseph-de-Rivière-des-prairies Church, Montreal, Nov. 29-30, 1993)* CBC ("Musica Viva" series) ▲ MVV 1082 [DDD]
Sainte-Colombe, M. de:Concerts for 2 B Vls, w. Susie Napper (vl)—Nos. 41 & 44 *(rec Saint-Joseph-de-Rivière-des-prairies Church, Montreal, Nov. 29-30, 1993)* CBC ("Musica Viva" series) ▲ MVV 1082 [DDD]
Little, Tasmin (vn)
Bruch, M.:Con 1 Vn, w. V. Handley (cnd), Royal Liverpool PO Classics for Pleasure ▲ CDCFP 4566 [DDD]
Delius, F.:Con Vn, w. C. Mackerras (cnd), Welsh National Opera Orch Argo ▲ 433704-2 [DDD]
Delius, F.:Double Con, w. Raphael Wallfisch (vc), C. Mackerras (cnd), Royal Liverpool PO Classics for Pleasure ("Eminence" series) ▲ CDEMX 2185 [DDD]
Dvořák, A.:Con Vn, w. V. Handley (cnd), Royal Liverpool PO Classics for Pleasure ▲ CDCFP 4566 [ADD]
Lloyd, G.:Lament, Air & Dance, w. M. Roscoe (pno) Albany ▲ TROY 029-2 [DDD] ■ TROY 029-4 (D)
Lloyd, G.:Son Vn, w. M. Roscoe (pno) Albany ▲ TROY 029-2 [DDD] ■ TROY 029-4 (D)
Rubbra, E.:Con Vn, w. V. Handley (cnd), Royal PO *(rec All Saints' Church, Petersham, Surrey, Dec. 10-11, 1993)* Conifer Classics ▲ 75605-51225-2 [DDD]
Saxton, R.:Con Vn, w. M. Bamert (cnd), BBC SO Collins Classics ▲ 12832
Vaughan Williams, R.:The Lark Ascending, w. A. Davis (cnd), BBC SO Teldec (British Line) ▲ 9031-73127-2 [DDD] ■ 9031-73127-4
Walton, W.:Con Vn, w. A. Litton (cnd), Bournemouth SO *(rec Guildhall, Southampton, Mar 1994)* London ▲ 444114-2 [DDD]
Litton, Andrew (pno)
Gershwin, G.:Con Pno, w. A. Litton (cnd), Bournemouth SO Virgin Classics ▲ CDZ 59693
Gershwin, G.:Con Pno, w. A. Litton (cnd), Royal PO RPO 2-▲ CDRPD 9002 [DDD]
Gershwin, G.:The George Gershwin Songbook—Swanee; Nobody but you; Do it again; Clap yo' hands RPO 2-▲ CDRPD 9002 [DDD]
Gershwin, G.:Porgy & Bess (sels), w. Cynthia Clarey (sop—Serena), Cynthia Haymon (sop—Bess), Damon Evans (ten—Sportin' Life), Gordon Hawkins (bar—Porgy), A. Litton (cnd), Dallas SO, Dallas Sym Chorus—Intro/Jasbo Brown; Summertime; A Woman Is a Sometime Thing; Gone, Gone, Gone; My Man's Gone Now; Leavin' for the Promise' Lan'; Oh I Got Plenty O' Nuttin'; Bess, You Is My Woman Now; Oh, I Can't Sit Down; I Ain't Got No Shame; It Ain't Necessarily So; Shame on All You Sinners; I Loves You, Porgy; Hurricane; There's a Boat Dat's Leavin' Soon for New York; Act 3, Scene 3 Orchestral Intro; Good Mornin', Sistuh; Oh Lawd, I'm on My Way! [concert suite arr A. Litton] *(rec Eugene McDermott Hall, Dallas, May 1995)* Dorian ▲ DOR 90223 [DDD]
Gershwin, G.:Rhap in Blue, w. B. Griffiths (vn), P. Whittaker (cl), R. Simmons (tpt), D. James (trbn), H. Fisher (dr), A. Litton (cnd), Royal PO [original big band orchestration] RPO ▲ RPO 5011 [DDD]
Gershwin, G.:Rhap in Blue, w. A. Litton (cnd), Royal PO RPO 2-▲ CDRPD 9002 [DDD]
Litvinenko, Alla (hpd)
Schnittke, A.:Suite in the Old Style, w. Igor Boguslavsky (va), Viktor Grishin (vib), Viktor Gabinsky (mar), Vadim Vasilykov (bells) [arr. unknown] *(rec 1989)* Consonance ▲ 81-0009 [DDD]
Litwin, Leo (pno)
Saint-Saëns, C.:Carnival of the Animals, w. Samuel Lipman (pno), Martin Hoherman (vc), Hugh Downs (nar), A. Fiedler (cnd), Boston Pops Orch [verses rec. June 12, 1963] *(rec Symphony Hall, Boston, June 14, 1961)* RCA Living Stereo ▲ 09026-68131-2 [ADD]; ■ 09026-68131-4
Wild Classics:A Celebration of Animals & Nature, w. James Galway (fl), Ofra Harnoy (vc), Martin Hoherman (vc), Emily Mitchell (hp), Michael Dussek (pno), Samuel Lipman (pno), Gerhard Oppitz (pno), Isao Tomita (synths), Boston Pops Orch [cnd:Arthur Fiedler], Chicago SO [cnd:Fritz Reiner] RCA Red Seal ▲ 09026-68483-2 ■ 09026-68483-4
Litwin, Stefan (pno)
Schoenberg, A.:Phantasy Vn Montaigne ▲ MO 782025
Webern, A.:Qnt Pno, w. LaSalle String Quartet Deutsche Grammophon ("20th Century Classics" series) ▲ 437036-2 [DDD]
Liu (va)
Reynolds, R.:Whispers out of Time, w. J. Négyesy (vn), P. Farrell (vc), B. Turetzky (db), H. Sollberger (cnd), San Diego SO Ensemble New World ▲ NW 80401-2 [DDD]
Liu, Han-An (hp)
Mercadante, S.:La Serenata, w. Andras Adorjan (fl) or Aurèle Nicolet (fl), Dieter Savelwski (Eng hn), Julius Berger (vc) Tudor ▲ TUD 763 [DDD]
Liu, Hui-Ying (pno)
Sibelius, J.:Malinconia, w. R. Sariola (vc) Finlandia ▲ 4509-95854-2 [DDD]
Sibelius, J.:Music for Vc Pno, w. R. Sariola (vc)—Malinconia, Op. 20; Elegie, Op. 27/1; Romance in C, Op. 42; Valse triste, Op. 44/3; Canzonetta, Op. 62a; Valse romantique, Op. 62b; Cantique & Devotion, Op. 77, Nos. 1 & 2; Impromptu, Romance, Religioso & Rigaudon, Op. 78, Nos. 1-4; Rondino, Op. 81/2 Finlandia ▲ 4509-95854-2 [DDD]
Liuzzi, Don (perc)
Maggio, R.:Barcarole, w. Scott St. John (vn), John Koen (vc), Hugh Sung (pno), J. Higdon (cnd) *(rec Settlement Music School, Germantown, PA, June 17, 1995)* CRI ▲ CD 720 [DDD]
Liuzzi, Don (vib)
Davidson, T.:Fire on the Mountain, w. Anthony Orlando (mar), Charles Abramovic (pno) CRI ▲ CD 681 [DDD]
Liuzzi, M. (clvd)—see ORCHESTRAS & ENSEMBLES Venice New Quintet
Lively, David (pno)
Balakirev, M.:Islamey Discover International ▲ DICD 920118 [DDD]
Busoni, F.:Con Pno, Op. 39, w. Freiburg Vocal Ensemble, M. Gielen (cnd), Southwest German RSO Baden-Baden Koch Schwann ▲ CD 311 160 [DDD]
Furtwängler, W.:Con Pno, w. A. Walter (cnd), Czech-Slovak State SO Marco Polo ▲ 8.223333
Honegger, A.:Son Vc, w. François Guye (vc) Gallo ▲ CD 468 [DDD]
Honegger, A.:Sonatina Cl, w. François Guye (vc) Gallo ▲ CD 468 [DDD]
Rachmaninoff, S.:Con 2 Pno, w. A. Rahbari (cnd), Brussels Belgian Radio-TV PO *(rec Concert Hall of the Belgian Radio & Television, Brussels, May 19-21, 1994)* Discover International ▲ DI 920221 [DDD]
Rachmaninoff, S.:Con 3 Pno, w. A. Rahbari (cnd), Brussels Belgian Radio-TV PO *(rec Concert Hall of the Belgian Radio & Television, Brussels, May 19-21, 1994)* Discover International ▲ DI 920221 [DDD]
Strauss, R.:Son Vc, w. F. Guye (vc) Gallo ▲ CD 468 [DDD]
Tchaikovsky, P.:Con 1 Pno, w. A. Rahbari (cnd), Slovak Radio New PO Discover International ▲ DICD 920118 [DDD]
Tchaikovsky, P.:Dumka:Russian Rustic Scene Discover International ▲ DICD 920118 [DDD]

Liviabella, Hans (vn)
Tosti, P.F.:Songs, w. E. Palacio (ten), M. Rapattoni (pno), G. Scabbia (fl), B. Giuffredi (gtr), C. Passerini (hp), M. Decimo (vc) [arr. Massimo de Bernart for instrumental accompaniment]—La serenata; Sogno; 'A vucchella; Segreto; Ideale; 2ème Aubade; Anima mia; Donna, vorrei morir; Aprile; Ancora!; Mattinata; L'ultima canzone; Malia; Non t'amo più; Il pescatore canta!; Tristezza; O falce di luna calante; L'abla separa dalla luce l'ombra; Mi guitarra dice "Te amo!"; Ricordati di me; Vuol note o banconote? Arkadia-Akademia ▲ 125 [DDD]
Livingston, Doug (gtr)
Matson, S.:Steel Chords, w. P. Kent (vn), M. Newman (vn), J. Derouin (vn), C. Moussas (vn), R. Tischer (va), E. Duke-Kirkpatrick (vc), B. Morgenthaler (db), S. Matson (cnd) *(rec Aug. 29-30, 1992)* Audioquest ▲ AQCD 1013
Livingston, Doug (gtr/mand)
Matson, S.:Range, w. Catherine Robbin (mez), Susan Greenberg (fl), Joseph Stone (fl), Glen Garrett (cl), Suren Karapetyan (hn), Peter Kent (vn), Kazi Pitelka (va), Sebastian Toettcher (vc), Don Ferrone (db), John Schneider (gtr), Amy Shulman (hp), Terry Schoenig (perc), S. Matson (cnd) *(rec Schnee Studio, Universal City, CA, Mar 12, 1995)* New Albion ▲ NA 091
Ljung, Michael (gtr)—see ORCHESTRAS & ENSEMBLES Duodecima
Ljungstrom, Carl (gtr)
Brouwer, L.:Gtr Music, w. Robert Beer (gtr), John Draper (gtr), Steven Patterson (gtr)—Musica Incidental Campesina; Vier Mikropiezas; Cuban Landscape with Rain; Preludios Epigrammaticos; El Decameron Negro; other works Koch Schwann ▲ SCH 311742 [DDD]
Llambias, Rodolfo (pno)
Brahms, J.:Sym 3, w. T. Lønskov (pno) [original 2-pianos vers.] *(rec Sept. 1992)* Kontrapunkt ▲ 32148 [DDD]
Brahms, J.:Vars on a Theme by Haydn, w. T. Lønskov (pno) *(rec Sept. 1992)* Kontrapunkt ▲ 32148 [DDD]
Debussy, C.:En blanc et noir, w. T. Lonskov (pno) Kontrapunkt 2-▲ KPT 32107 [DDD]
Debussy, C.:Epigraphes antiques, w. T. Lonskov (pno) Kontrapunkt 2-▲ KPT 32107 [DDD]
Debussy, C.:Lindaraja, w. T. Lonskov (pno) Kontrapunkt 2-▲ KPT 32107 [DDD]
Debussy, C.:La Mer, w. T. Lonskov (pno) Kontrapunkt 2-▲ KPT 32107 [DDD]
Debussy, C.:Nocturnes, w. T. Lonskov (pno) Kontrapunkt 2-▲ KPT 32107 [DDD]
Debussy, C.:Petite suite, w. T. Lonskov (pno) Kontrapunkt 2-▲ KPT 32107 [DDD]
Debussy, C.:Prélude à l'après-midi d'un faune, w. T. Lonskov (pno) Kontrapunkt 2-▲ KPT 32107 [DDD]
Messiaen, O.:Visions de l'Amen, w. T. Lonskov (pno) Kontrapunkt ▲ 32031 [DDD]
Schubert, Franz:Allegro Pno 4-Hands, D.947, w. Tove Lonskov (pno) Kontrapunkt ▲ KPT 32192 [DDD]
Schubert, Franz:Grandes marches Pno, w. Tove Lonskov (pno) Kontrapunkt ▲ KPT 32192 [DDD]
Schubert, Franz:Pno Music (4-hands), w. T. Lonskov (pno)—Fantasie, D.940; Ov. in D, D.592, "Im italienischen Stil"; Trois marches militaires, D.733; Variationen über ein französisches Lied, D.624 Kontrapunkt ▲ KPT 32183 [DDD]
Stolarczyk, W.:Earth Air Fire Water, w. Amalie Malling (pno), John Damgaard (pno), Anne Øland (pno), Teddy Teirup (pno), Friedrich Gürtler (pno), Rosalind Bevan (pno), Poul Rosenbaum (pno), Bella Horn-Ribera (pno), Anders Riber (pno), Elisabeth Sigurdsson (pno), Thomas Tronheim (pno), Elsebeth Broderson (pno), Erik Kaltoft (pno), Jørgen Hald Nielsen (pno), Aino Gilemann (pno), Birgit Kjær (pno), Jørgen Thomsen (pno), Gunhild Donslund (pno), Henrik Bo Hansen (pno), Lone Karlsson (pno), Erik Fessel (pno), Lasse Nilsson (pno), Janos Ferenczi (pno), Erik Bach (pno), Axel Momme (pno), Arne de Cros Dich (pno), Sven Micha Slot (pno), Hanne Bramsen Buhl (pno), Lili Olesen (pno), Susannah Carlsson (pno), Ulla Erml (pno), Vagn Sørensen (pno), Leif Greibe (pno), Bodil Krogh (pno), Kirsten Ottosen (pno), Inger Bergenholz (pno), Karsten Gylendorf (pno), Bjønr Elkjær (pno), Jacob Bjørn Jensen (pno), Jørgen Kaad (pno), Anne Marie Hjelm (pno), Carl Ulrik Munk Andersen (pno), Poul Lumbye (pno), Oluf Hildebrandt Nielsen (pno), Joachim Olsson (pno), Peter Pade Rasmsøe Jacobsen (pno), Astrid Pollmann (pno), Jette Borsch (pno), Kirsten Karlshøj (pno), Maria Teresa Assing (pno), Allan Dahl Hansen (pno), Johan Hugossen (pno), Tine Fenger Pederson (pno), Arne Jørgen Fæø (pno), Anja Høgsted (pno), Anne Sophie Parbo (pno), Inga Lindmark (pno), Teresa Drabik Stathakis (pno), Anne Ruth Ferenczi (pno), Irene Hasager (pno), Yuka Ichikawa (pno), Birgitte Baur (pno), Malene Thastum (pno), Jens E. Rasmussen (pno), Birgitte Zielke (pno), Claus Zielke (pno), Stefan Kasch (pno), Bin Qiao (pno), Inger Johanne Teirup (pno), Lindy Rosborg (pno), Liisa Heininen (pno), David Højer (pno), Ellen Refstrup (pno), Thomas K. Søorensen (pno), Erik Kure (pno), Michael Rauff (pno), Jan beck Eriksson (pno), Tanja Zapolski (pno), Vibeke Skagbo (pno), Pål Eide Lindtner (pno), Ha-Young Sul (pno), Benedicte Palko (pno), Inke Kesseler (pno), Anne Marie Meineche (pno), Sverre Larsen (pno), Kasper Peter Bach (pno), Elisabetta Eliseo (pno), Olga Magieres (pno), Carl Erik Kühl (pno), Thorkild Borup Nielsen (pno), Valeria Zanini (pno), Lars Stenhoft (perc), Dennis Boel (perc), Winnie Dahlgren (perc), Susanne Vind (perc), Claus Byrith (elec), Anne Marie Storm (elec), J. Ribera (cnd) *(rec live, Koldinghaus Castle, Denmark, May 2, 1996)* Danica ▲ DCD 1996
Tchaikovsky, P.:Festival Ov, w. Tove Løonskov (pno) Kontrapunkt ▲ KPT 32204
Tchaikovsky, P.:Sym 6, w. Tove Løonskov (pno) [orig arr for Pno 4-Hands, 1893] Kontrapunkt ▲ KPT 32204
Llewelyn-Jones, Iwan (pno)
Liszt, F.:Pno Music (misc)—Au bord d'une source; Consolation No. 3; Etude de concert No. 2; Legends; Liebestraum No. 3; Sonetto 104 del Petrarca; Sposalizio; Vallée d'Obermann IMP Masters ▲ MCD 39 [DDD]
Lloyd, F. (pno)—see ORCHESTRAS & ENSEMBLES Nash Ensemble
Lloyd, Frank (hn)
Mendelssohn, F.:Songs (4) (1830), w. J. Baker (mez), R. Masters (hp), R. Hickox (cnd), City of London Sinfonia, London Sym Chorus Virgin Classics ▲ CDC 59589
Mozart, W.A.:Cons Hn, w. R. Hickox (cnd), Northern Sinfonia of England Chandos ▲ CHAN 9150 [DDD]
Mozart, W.A.:Rondo Hn, K.371, w. R. Hickox (cnd), Northern Sinfonia of England Chandos ▲ CHAN 9150 [DDD]
Scelsi, G.:Khoom, w. Michiko Hirayama (sop), Maurizio Ben Omar (perc), A. Brizzi (cnd), Arditti String Quartet Salabert ▲ SCD 8904-5
Lloyd, Peter (fl)
Ferroud, P.-O.:Pièces (3) Fl IMP Classics ▲ PCD 991 [DDD]
French Flute Music, w. Rebecca Holt (pno) IMP Classics ▲ PCD 991 [DDD]
Gaubert, P.:Son 1 Fl IMP Classics ▲ PCD 991 [DDD]
Poulenc, F.:Son Fl IMP Classics ▲ PCD 991 [DDD]
Siegmeister, E.:Con Fl, w. E. Siegmeister (pno), London SO *(rec 1973)* Premier ("Composer" series) ▲ PRCD 1010 [ADD]
Williams, John:Con Fl, w. L. Slatkin (cnd), London SO Varèse Sarabande ▲ VSD 5345
Lloyd Webber, Julian (vc)
Arnold, M.:Fant Vc ASV ▲ ASV CD 592
Britten, H.:Suite 3 Vc ASV ▲ ASV CD 592
Britten, H.:Tema "Sacher" ASV ▲ ASV CD 592
Bridge, F.:Elégie Vc, w. J. McCabe (pno) ASV ▲ ASV 807
Bridge, F.:Scherzetto Vc, w. J. McCabe (pno) ASV ▲ ASV 807
Cello Song, w. J. Lenehan (pno) Philips ▲ 434917-2
Debussy, C.:Son Vc, w. Y. Seow (pno) ASV Quicksilva ▲ QS 6072 [ADD]
Delius, F.:Caprice & Elegy, w. E. Fenby (cnd), Royal PO Unicorn-Kanchana ▲ UK 2076
Delius, F.:Son Vc & Pno, w. Eric Fenby (pno) Unicorn-Kanchana ("Souvenir" series) ▲ UK 2074
Elgar, E.:Salut d'amour, w. Y. Seow (pno) ASV Quicksilva ▲ QS 6051 [ADD/DDD]
English Idyll, w. Academy of St. Martin in the Fields [cnd:Neville Marriner] Philips ▲ 442530-2
Ireland, J.:The Holy Boy, w. John McCabe (pno) [arr vc & pno] ASV ▲ ASV CD 592
Ireland, J.:Son Vc, w. J. McCabe (pno) ASV ▲ ASV 807
Lloyd Webber, A.:Music of, w. B. Wordsworth (cnd), Royal PO—highlights from Aspects of Love, Cats, Phantom of the Opera, Starlight Express, Jesus Christ Superstar, Evita, Requiem, Song and Dance, Joseph and His Amazing Technicolor Dreamcoat Philips ▲ 426484-2 [DDD]
Lloyd Webber, W.S.:Air varié, w. J. Lill (pno) ASV ▲ ASV 584 [DDD]

INSTRUMENT.

Lloyd Webber, Julian (vc) (cont.)
Lloyd Webber, W.S.:In the Half-Light, w. J. Lill (pno) ASV ▲ ASV 584 [DDD]
Lloyd Webber, W.S.:Nocturne Vc ASV ▲ ASV 961
Miaskovsky, N.:Con Vc, w. M. Shostakovich (pno), London SO Philips ▲ 434106-2 [DDD]
Rachmaninoff, S.:Pieces Vc, w. Y. Seow (pno) ASV Quicksilva ▲ QS 6072 [ADD]
Rachmaninoff, S.:Son Vc, w. Y. Seow (pno) ASV Quicksilva ▲ QS 6072 [ADD]
Rawsthorne, A.:Son Vc, w. John McCabe (pno) ASV ▲ ASV CD 592
Romantic Cello, w. Yitkin Seow (pno) ASV ("Quicksilva" series) ▲ ASV 6014 [ADD]
Stanford, C.V.:Son 2 Vc, w. J. McCabe (pno) ASV ▲ ASV 807
Sullivan, A.:Con Vc, w. C. Mackerras (cnd), London SO EMI Classics ▲ CDM 64726
Tchaikovsky, P.:Vars on a Rococo Theme, w. M. Shostakovich (cnd), London SO Philips ▲ 434106-2 [DDD]
Walton, W.:Passacaglia for Vc ASV ▲ ASV CD 592

Lluna, Joan Enric (bas hn)
Mozart, W.A.:Con Cl, w. A. Pay (cnd), English CO Cala ▲ CAL 88010 [DDD]
Mozart, W.A.:Qnt Cl, K.581, w. A. Pay (cnd), Brodsky String Quartet Cala ▲ CAL 88010 [DDD]

Lobanov, Vassili (pno)
Beethoven, L. van:Son 3 Vn, w. Oleg Kagan (vn) *(rec Ettlingen Palace, Stuttgart, Mar 8, 1988)* Live Classics ▲ LCL 144 [ADD]
Beethoven, L. van:Son 8 Vn, w. Oleg Kagan (vn) *(rec Chamber Music Festival Kuhmo, Finland, July 22, 1985)* Live Classics ▲ LCL 144 [DDD]
Beethoven, L. van:Son 10 Vn, w. Oleg Kagan (vn) *(rec Chamber Music Festival Kuhmo, Finland, July 22, 1985)* Live Classics ▲ LCL 144 [DDD]
Brahms, J.:Qt 1 Pno, w. Oleg Kagan (vn), Diemuth Poppen (va), Natalia Gutman (vc) *(rec Chamber Music Festival Kuhmo, Finland, July, 19, 1989)* Live Classics ▲ LCL 124 [DDD]
Dvořák, A.:Romantic Pieces, Op. 75, w. Oleg Kagan (vn) *(rec Chamber Music Festival Kuhmo, Finland, July, 15, 1983)* Live Classics ▲ LCL 124 [ADD]
Lobanow, W.:Son Cl, w. E. Brunner (cl) Tudor ▲ 727 [DDD]
Lobanow, W.:Son Fl, w. A. Adorján (fl) Tudor ▲ 727 [DDD]
Schnittke, A.:Son 1 Pno *(rec 1989)* Consonance ▲ 81-0009 [DDD]
Tchaikovsky, P.:Sérénade mélancolique, w. O. Kagan (vn) Ondine ▲ ODE 733-2 [DDD]
Tchaikovsky, P.:Souvenir d'un lieu cher, w. O. Kagan (vn) Ondine ▲ ODE 733-2 [DDD]
Tchaikovsky, P.:Valse-Scherzo Vn, w. O. Kagan (vn) Ondine ▲ ODE 733-2 [DDD]

Lobet, Dominique (va)—see ORCHESTRAS & ENSEMBLES Paris String Quartet

Loch, Dan (vc)
O'Rourke, J.:Terminal Pharmacy, w. Tony Burr (cl), Jeff Cortazzo (b trbn), John McEntire (dr), Rob Prosser (acc), Isha Suftin (acc), Mike Dockter (vc), Hattie Franck (vc), Robert Keck (vc), Mary LaBreque (vc), Stan Saderk (vc), Lisa Hemmer (fl), Sue Oberg (fl), Wendi Lev (fl), Jim Vanden (fl), Jim O'Rourke (gtr), Steve Braack (elec) Tzadik ▲ TZA 7011 [DDD]

Locher, Paul (vn)
Holliger, H.:Alb-Chehr, w. Oswald Brumann (bass), Sabine Gertschen (dlc), Edmund Volken (dlc), Elmar Schmid (cl), Klaus Schmid (cl), Markus Tenisch (Swiss org), Marcel Volken (Swiss org), Franziskus Abgottspon (nar) ECM New Series ▲ 78118-21540-2 [DDD]

Lochner, Gretchen (vc)
Hazzan Rishon, Legendary Cantorial Recitativi, Opuses 1 & 2, w. David Montefiore (cant), C. Vineburg (pno), V. Zeltser (vn), A. Bacelar (vc), C. Morrison (va) Behar/Berg 2-▲ 001494

Löchner, H.-D. (cl)
Mozart, W.A.:Qnt Cl, K.581, w. Krauss Quartet LaserLight ▲ 15 878 [DDD]

Lockhart, Derek (tpt)—see ORCHESTRAS & ENSEMBLES New World Brass

Lockhart, James (pno)
Brahms, J.:Songs, w. M. Price (sop)—19 songs [G] Orfeo ▲ 058831
Liszt, F.:Songs, w. Margaret Price (sop), Jack Brymer (cl)—O lieb', so lang du lieben kannst!; Die Lorelei; Die stille Wasserrose; Es muss ein Wunderbares sein; Kling leise, mein Lied Classics for Pleasure ▲ CFP 4669
Schubert, Franz:Songs (misc), w. Margaret Price (sop), Jack Brymer (cl)—Auf der Riesenkoppe, D.611; Der Hirt auf dem Felsen [The Shepherd on the Rock], D.965 Classics for Pleasure ▲ CFP 4669
Schumann, R.:Frauenliebe und -leben, w. Margaret Price (sop) Classics for Pleasure ▲ CFP 4669
Schumann, R.:Frauenliebe und -leben, w. M. Price (sop) [G] Orfeo ▲ 031821 [DDD]
Schumann, R.:Songs, w. M. Price (sop) [G] Orfeo ▲ 031821 [DDD]
Tchaikovsky, P.:Songs, w. Margaret Price (sop), Jack Brymer (cl)—None but the Weary Heart, Op. 6/6; Do Not Believe, My Friend, Op. 6/1; At the Ball, Op. 38/3 Classics for Pleasure ▲ CFP 4669

Lockwood, Arthur (tpt)
Shostakovich, D.:Con 1 Pno, w. Eileen Joyce (pno), L. Heward (cnd), Hallé Orch *(rec Houldsworth Hall, Manchester, Oct. 24, 1941)* Dutton Laboratories ▲ CDAX 8010 [ADD]

Lockwood, Peter (pno)
Saint-Saëns, C.:Caprice arabe, w. Julian Reynolds (pno) *(rec Utrecht, Apr 1996)* Globe ▲ GLO 5152 [DDD]
Saint-Saëns, C.:Carnival of the Animals, w. Julian Reynolds (pno), J. Reynolds (cnd), Concentus Bestiales *(rec Utrecht, Apr 1996)* Globe ▲ GLO 5152 [DDD]
Saint-Saëns, C.:Danse macabre, w. Julian Reynolds (pno) [trans Saint-Saëns for 2 pnos] *(rec Utrecht, Apr 1996)* Globe ▲ GLO 5152 [DDD]
Saint-Saëns, C.:Polonaise for 2 Pnos, w. Julian Reynolds (pno) *(rec Utrecht, Apr 1996)* Globe ▲ GLO 5152 [DDD]
Saint-Saëns, C.:Scherzo, w. Julian Reynolds (pno) *(rec Utrecht, Apr 1996)* Globe ▲ GLO 5152 [DDD]
Saint-Saëns, C.:Variations on a Theme of Beethoven, w. Julian Reynolds (pno) *(rec Utrecht, Apr 1996)* Globe ▲ GLO 5152 [DDD]

Lodéon, Frederic (vc)
Fauré, G.:Qts Pno, Opp. 15 & 45, w. J.P. Collard (pno), A. Dumay (vn), B. Pasquier (va) EMI Classics 2-▲ ZDMB 62548
Fauré, G.:Son 1 Vc, w. J.P. Collard (pno) EMI Classics 2-▲ CDC 62545
Fauré, G.:Son 2 Vc, w. J.P. Collard (pno) EMI Classics 2-▲ CDC 62545
Fauré, G.:Trio, w. A. Dumay (vn), J.P. Collard (pno) EMI Classics 2-▲ CDC 62545
Tchaikovsky, P.:Trio Pno, w. P. Rogé (pno), P. Amoyal (vn) Erato ▲ 45972-2
Ysaÿe, E.:Poème nocturne, w. Gerard Jarry (vn), Georges Pludermarcher (pno) [arr. for piano trio] Koch Schwann ▲ SCH 317212 [DDD]
Ysaÿe, E.:Son Vc Koch Schwann ▲ SCH 317212 [DDD]

Loeb, David (shinobue)
Loeb, D.:Unkei, w. S. Kawalla (cnd), Slovak RSO Bratislava Vienna Modern Masters ▲ VMM 3006 [DDD]

Loebner, Wolfgang (fl)
Bach, J.S.:Trio Son for 2 Fls, BWV 1039, w. E. Haupt (fl), S. Pank (vl) *(rec June 1989 & Jan 1990)* Berlin Classics 2-▲ BER 1007 [DDD]

Loesser, Arthur (pno)
Brahms, J.:Son 1 Vn, w. T. Seidel (vn) *(rec 1931)* Biddulph ▲ LAB 013 [ADD]
Brahms, J.:Son 2 Vn, w. T. Seidel (vn) *(rec 1926)* Biddulph ▲ LAB 013 [ADD]
Grieg, E.:Sons Vn, Opp. 8, 13 & 45, w. T. Seidel (vn)—No. 3 in c, Op. 45 *(rec 1929)* Biddulph ▲ LAB 013 [ADD]

Loey, P. van (rcr)—see ORCHESTRAS & ENSEMBLES Paul Rans Ensemble, Flanders Recorder Quartet

Loft, Abram (vn)—see ORCHESTRAS & ENSEMBLES Fine Arts String Quartet

Logan, Lisa Emenheiser (pno)
Debussy, C.:Prélude à l'après-midi d'un faune, w. J. Baker (fl) [flute & piano trans. J. Jaubert] *(rec live, 1982)* VAI Audio ▲ VAIA 1022 [ADD]
Fauré, G.:Après un rêve, w. J. Baker (mez) [flute & piano trans. Julius Baker] *(rec 1982)* VAI Audio ▲ VAIA 1022 [ADD]
Franck, C.:Son Vn, w. J. Baker (fl) *(rec live 1982)* VAI Audio ▲ VAIA 1022 [ADD]
Muczynski, R.:Son Fl, w. J. Baker (fl) *(rec live 1982)* VAI Audio ▲ VAIA 1022 [ADD]
Poulenc, F.:Son Fl, w. J. Baker (fl) *(rec live 1982)* VAI Audio ▲ VAIA 1022 [ADD]

Loger, Alain (vn)
Eccles, H.:Son Db, w. B. Cazauran (db), J. M. Denis (vn), N. Carles (va), E. Petit (vc) *(rec Aug. 29-30, 1992)* Gallo ▲ CD 753 [ADD]

Loguin, Anders (perc)
Nilsson, T.:Music of, w. Ingmari Landin (alt), Lars Sjögren (ten), Lage Wedin (bass), Jerker Halldén (fl), Nils-Erik Sparf (vn), Hans-Ola Ericsson (org), Torsten Nilsson (cnd), Gustaf Sjökvist (cnd), Swedish Radio Chorus—Ordinarium Missae; Balthasar/Daniel; Drei Gedichte Phono Suecia ▲ PHN 40 [AAD]

Loguin, Anders (tubular bells)
Schnittke, A.:Hymns Vc, w. Torleff Thedéen (vc), Entcho Rdoukanov (db), Christian Davidsson (bn), Ingegerd Fredlund (hp), M. Kamata (hpd), Anders Holdar (tubular bells/timp) BIS ("BIS Twins" series) 2-▲ CD 437/507
Schnittke, A.:Hymns Vc, w. T. Thedéen (vc), E. Radoukanov (db), C. Davidsson (bn), I. Fredlund (hp), M. Kamata (hpd), A. Holdar (tubular bells / timp) BIS ▲ CD 507 [DDD]

Lohff, Carsten (hpd/org)—see ORCHESTRAS & ENSEMBLES Cantus Cologne

Lohmann, Jens (vn)
Fritz, G.:Con Vn, w. H. Griffiths (cnd), English CO Novalis ▲ 150099 [DDD]

Lohr, Bernward (hpd)—see also ORCHESTRAS & ENSEMBLES Affetti Musicali
Bach, J.S.:Con for 4 Hpds, w. Gregor Hollmann (hpd), Rudolf Innig (hpd), Ludger Rémy (hpd), Musica Alta Ripa MD + G ▲ MDG CD 3090681

Lohrer, Klaus (double bn)—see ORCHESTRAS & ENSEMBLES Sabine Meyer Wind Ensemble

Lohse, Peter (gtr)—see ORCHESTRAS & ENSEMBLES Rotenbeck Trio

Lohuis, Ardyth (org)—see ORCHESTRAS & ENSEMBLES Murray/Lohuis Duo

Lom, Thomas (db)
Abert, J.J.:Columbus, w. W. Stiefel (cnd), Bohuslav Martinů PO Bayer ▲ BR 100160 [DDD]
Abert, J.J.:Con Db, w. W. Stiefel (cnd), Bohuslav Martinů PO Bayer ▲ BR 100160 [DDD]

Loman, Judy (hp)
Adeste Fideles, w. Louis Quilico (bar), Gino Quilico (bar), Toronto SO members [cnd:Jean Ashworth Bartle], Toronto Children's Chorus CBC Records ("SM 5000" series) ▲ SMCD 5119 [DDD]
Bach, J.S.:Sons Vl, BWV 1027-1029, w. Rivka Golani (va)—BWV 1028 [trans. for viola & harp] *(rec St. Timothy's Church, Toronto)* Marquis Classics ▲ MAR 131 [DDD]
Bax, A.:Fant Son, w. Rivka Golani (va) *(rec St. Timothy's Church, Toronto)* Marquis Classics ▲ MAR 131 [DDD]
Britten, H.:Suite Hp Marquis ▲ MAR 165
Buhr, G.:Tanzmusik Marquis ▲ MAR 165
Folksongs of the British Isles, w. Lois Marshall (sop) *(rec 1976)* Marquis Classics ▲ MARD 102 [AAD]
Hindemith, P.:Son Hp Marquis ▲ MAR 165
Houdy, P.:Qnt Hp, w. Orford String Quartet Centrediscs 2-▲ CMCCD 41/4292 [DDD]
Luedeke, R.:The Moon in the Labyrinth, w. Orford String Quartet Centrediscs 2-▲ CMCCD 41/4292 [DDD]
Meditations, w. Daniel Domb (vc) Pro Arte ▲ CDD 3414
Morawetz, O.:Son Va, w. Rivka Golani (va) *(rec St. Timothy's Church, Toronto)* Marquis Classics ▲ MAR 131 [DDD]
Mozart, W.A.:Con Fl Hp, w. N. Shulman (fl), M. Bernardi (cnd), CBC Vancouver SO CBC ("SM 5000" series) ▲ SMCD 5133 [DDD]
Rutter, J.:Dancing Day, w. Toronto Children's Chorus Marquis ▲ ERAD 135 [DDD]
Salzedo, C.:Hp Music—9 original works:Flight; Idyllic poem; Inquietude; Quietude; Iridescence; Whirlwind; Prelude intimes; I wonder as I wander; Jeux d'eau; trans. for harp of works by Corelli *(Giga)*, Handel *(The Harmonious Blacksmith)*, Haydn *(Theme & Variations)*, Pescetti *(Sonata in c)* Marquis ▲ ERAD 117 [DDD]
Salzedo, C.:Vars on a Theme in the Olden Style Marquis ▲ MAR 165
Schafer, R.M.:Con Hp, w. A. Davis (cnd), Toronto SO CBC ("SM 5000" series) ▲ SMCD 5114 [DDD]
Schafer, R.M.:The Crown of Ariadne, w. Orford String Quartet Centrediscs 2-▲ CMCCD 41/4292 [DDD]
Schafer, R.M.:Theseus, w. Orford String Quartet Centrediscs 2-▲ CMCCD 41/4292 [DDD]
Tailleferre, G.:Son Hp Marquis ▲ MAR 165
Tournier, M.:Sonatine Hp Marquis ▲ MAR 165
Weinzweig, J.:Pieces Hp *(rec live, Walter Hall, Univ. of Toronto, Mar. 11, 1993)* Centrediscs ▲ CMC 5295 [DDD]

Loman, Lars Olof (ob)
Rangström, T.:Vauxhall, w. Bengt Christiansson (fl), Lars Almgren (cl), Sven Aarflot (bn), Rolf Bengtsson (hn), Rune Bodin (trbn), Rozalina Skytt (hp), O. Vänskä (cnd), Stockholm PO *(rec Stockholm Concert Hall, Jan. 16 & 18, 1985)* Caprice ▲ CAP 21195 [DDD]

Lombard, François (org)
Duruflé, M.:Org Music (comp)—Scherzo, Op. 2; Suite, Op. 5 Motette ▲ CD 50241 [DDD]
Guilmant, A.:Org Music—Morceau de concert; Marche nuptiale; Fugue in D; Canzone in a; Lamentatio in d; Tempo di minuetto in C; Légende et Final Symphonique in d; Prière et Berceuse in Ab; Pastorale in A; Morceau Symphonique in a Motette ▲ CD 11561 [DDD]

Lombardi, Daniele (pno)
Antheil, G.:Preludes (45) Pno—20 Preludes [after Max Ernst] Nuova Era ▲ NUO 7240 [DDD]
Antheil, G.:Sonatina Pno, "Death of the Machines" Nuova Era ▲ NUO 7240 [DDD]
Lombardi, D.:Faustimmung, w. Daniele Lombardi (pno—Faust), Sheila Concari (sgr—Fela), Margherita (vc—Margherita) *(rec Emmequattro, Rome, Oct 4, 1987)* Musicaimmagine ▲ MR 10013
Lourié, A.:Formes en l'air Nuova Era ▲ NUO 7240 [DDD]
Lourié, A.:Synthesis Nuova Era ▲ NUO 7240 [DDD]
Ornstein, L.:A la chinoise Nuova Era ▲ NUO 7240 [DDD]
Ornstein, L.:Moods Nuova Era ▲ NUO 7240 [DDD]
Ornstein, L.:Suicide in an Airplane Nuova Era ▲ NUO 7240 [DDD]

Lonardi, Massimo (archlt)—see ORCHESTRAS & ENSEMBLES Conserto Vago

Lonardi, Massimo (lt)—see also ORCHESTRAS & ENSEMBLES Il Desiderio
Borrono, P.P.:Lt Music—Pavane; Saltarelli; Toccata-Fant.-Pescatore che va cantando; Toccata da sonare nel fine del ballo Stradivarius ▲ STR 33314 [DDD]
Francesco Canova di Milano:Fants—Nos. 28, 30, 32, 33, 40, 41, 67 & 81 Stradivarius ▲ STR 33314 [DDD]
Francesco Canova di Milano:Ricercares—Nos. 2, 4, 7, 11, 16, 51, 52, 64, 70, 84 & 85 Stradivarius ▲ STR 33314 [DDD]
Francesco Canova di Milano:Tochata Stradivarius ▲ STR 33314 [DDD]

Lonberg-Holm, Fred (travicello)
Exquisite Corpses from P.S. 122, w. Watson, David (shears/stick vn/gtr/tpt), Judy Dunaway (gtr/balloons), Anthony Coleman (sampler), Raissa St. Pierre (drums), Guy Yarden (vn/pno), Leslie Ross (bn), Linda Austin (gtr), Bruce Kaplan (gtr), Doug Henderson (peckhorn/bass/toy pno), Sue Ann Harkey (gtr), Cinnie Cole (sampler), et al. ¿What Next? ▲ WN 0002 [ADD]

Londeix, J.-M. (sax)
Debussy, C.:Rapsodie, w. L. de Froment (cnd), Luxembourg RSO *(rec 1972)* Vox Box 2-▲ CDX 5053 [ADD]
Debussy, C.:Rapsodie, w. J. Martinon (cnd), French National RSO EMI Classics ▲ CDM 69668

London, Frank (tpt)
Lebaron, A.:The E. & O. Line (sels), w. Louise Cloutier (mez—Eurydice/Vendors), Hugh Panero (ten—Hermes), Lawrence Hamilton (bar—Orpheus/Men), Marcus Rojas (tuba), Myra Melford (pno/kbd), Davey Williams (gtr), Fred Hopkins (elec bass), Thurman Barker (dr), A. LeBaron (cnd)—Juke Joint Jam Session; Eurydice Meets Hermes; Eurydice's Death [Funeral Band]; Eurydice's River Journey; Orpheus Laments [Looked Away] *(rec Coolidge Auditorium, Library of Congress, 1987)* Mode ▲ Mode 42
Zorn, J.:Kristallnacht, w. David Krakauer (cl/b cl), Mark Feldman (vn), Marc Ribot (gtr), Mark Dresser (electric bass), Anthony Coleman (kbd), William Winant (perc) Tzadik ▲ TZA 7301 [ADD]

Long, Marguerite (pno)
Beethoven, L. van:Con 3 Pno, w. F. von Weingartner (cnd), Paris Conservatory Societé des Concerts Orch *(rec 1939)* Koch Legacy ▲ 3-7128-2 H1
Debussy, C.:Pno Music (misc)—Deux Arabesques; La plus que lente; Estampes No. 3, "Jardins sous la pluie" *(rec 1930 French Columbia reco)* Pearl ▲ PEA 9927 (m) [AAD]

▲ = CD ♦ = Enhanced CD Δ = MD ■ = Cassette Tape □ = DCC

Long, Marguerite (pno) (cont.)
Fauré, G.:Ballade Pno, w. P. Gaubert (cnd), *(orch unknown) (rec ca. 1931 French Columbia)* Pearl ▲ PEA 9927 (m) [AAD]
Fauré, G.:Pno Music—Impromptus No. 2 in f, Op. 31 & No. 5 in f#, Op. 102; Nocturne No. 4 in Eb, Op. 36 *(rec 1935 & 1938)* Pearl ▲ PEA 9927 (m) [AAD]
Fauré, G.:Qt 2 Pno, w. Jacques Thibaud (vn), Maurice Vieux (va), Pierre Fournier (vc) *(rec June 10, 1940)* Enterprise ("Strings" series) ▲ ENT QT 99302
Fauré, G.:Qt 2 Pno, w. Jacques Thibaud (vn), Maurice Vieux (va), Pierre Fournier (vc) *(rec June 10, 1940)* Iron Needle 2–▲ IN 1342/43 (m) [ADD]
Mozart, W.A.:Sons Vn Pno (misc), w. Jacques Thibaud (vn) Biddulph ▲ LAB 114
Ravel, M.:Con in G Pno, w. M. Ravel (cnd), Lamoureux Orch *(rec 1932 for Columbia)* Pearl ▲ PEA 9927 (m) [AAD]

Long, Marsha Heather (org)
Dupré, M.:Resurrection Koch International Classics ▲ KIC 7008–2 [DDD] ■ 3–7008–4 (D)
Dupré, M.:Vars sur un vieux Noël Koch International Classics ▲ KIC 7008–2 [DDD] ■ 3–7008–4 (D)
Jongen, J.:Toccata Org Koch International Classics ▲ KIC 7008–2 [DDD] ■ 3–7008–4 (D)
Karg-Elert, S.:Impressions—Nos. 1 & 2 only Koch International Classics ▲ KIC 7008–2 [DDD] ■ 3–7008–4 (D)
Reger, M.:Pieces Org, Op. 59—Toccata & Fuge in d Koch International Classics ▲ KIC 7008–2 [DDD] ■ 3–7008–4 (D)
Romantic French & German Organ Music, w. Long, Marsha Heather (org) Koch International Classics ▲ KIC 7008 [DDD]
Vierne, L.:Carillon de Westminster Koch International Classics ▲ KIC 7008–2 [DDD] ■ 3–7008–4 (D)
Vierne, L.:Méditation Koch International Classics ▲ KIC 7008–2 [DDD] ■ 3–7008–4 (D)
Vierne, L.:Naiades Koch International Classics ▲ KIC 7008–2 [DDD] ■ 3–7008–4 (D)
Vierne, L.:Stèle pour un enfant défunt Koch International Classics ▲ KIC 7008–2 [DDD] ■ 3–7008–4 (D)

Long, Michael (gtr)
Hovhaness, A.:Sym 39, w. V. Jordania (cnd), KBS SO—also includes a Korean folk song "Milyang Arirang" arr. Kim Hee Jo Koch International Classics ▲ KIC 7208 [DDD]

Longhurst, John (org)
Alain, J.:Org Music (misc) [Great Organ of the Mormon Tabernacle, Salt Lake City]—Litanies; Le Jardin suspendu Klavier ▲ KCD 11069 [DDD]
Boëllmann, L.:Rondo français [Great Organ of the Mormon Tabernacle, Salt Lake City] [trans. Gaston Choisnel for Org] Klavier ▲ KCD 11069 [DDD]
Boëllmann, L.:Suite 2 Org [Great Organ of the Mormon Tabernacle, Salt Lake City]—Andantino Klavier ▲ KCD 11069 [DDD]
Dupré, M.:Cortège et litanie [Great Organ of the Mormon Tabernacle, Salt Lake City]—No. 2 Klavier ▲ KCD 11069 [DDD]
Franck, C.:Fant Org [Great Organ of the Mormon Tabernacle, Salt Lake City] Klavier ▲ KCD 11069 [DDD]
Mormon Tabernacle Organ Philips ▲ 412217–2 PH [DDD]
Simple Gifts, w. Frederica von Stade (mez), Mormon Tabernacle Choir, Utah SO [cnd:Joseph Silverstein] London ▲ 436284–2 LH [DDD]
A Tabernacle Organ Duo Extravaganza, w. Robert Cundick (org) Argo ▲ 430426–2 ZH [DDD]
Vierne, L.:Maestoso [Great Organ of the Mormon Tabernacle, Salt Lake City] Klavier ▲ KCD 11069 [DDD]
Vierne, L.:Pièces de fant [Great Organ of the Mormon Tabernacle, Salt Lake City]—Clair de lune [from Suite 2, Op. 53]; Les cloches de Hinckley [from Suite 4, Op. 55] Klavier ▲ KCD 11069 [DDD]
Widor, C.M.:Sym 1 Org [Great Organ of the Mormon Tabernacle, Salt Lake City]—Intermezzo Klavier ▲ KCD 11069 [DDD]
Widor, C.M.:Sym 4 Org [Great Organ of the Mormon Tabernacle, Salt Lake City]—Andante cantabile Klavier ▲ KCD 11069 [DDD]
Widor, C.M.:Sym 5 Org [Great Organ of the Mormon Tabernacle, Salt Lake City]—Toccata Klavier ▲ KCD 11069 [DDD]

Longoni, Maurizio (cl)—see ORCHESTRAS & ENSEMBLES Arnold Quintet

Longworth, Peter (pno)
Berg, O.:Var Set Centaur ▲ CRC 2167 [DDD]

Lønskov, Tove (pno)
Brahms, J.:Sym 3, w. R. Llambias (pno) [original 2–pianos vers.] *(rec Sept. 1992)* Kontrapunkt ▲ 32148 [DDD]
Brahms, J.:Vars on a Theme by Haydn, w. R. Llambias (pno) *(rec Sept. 1992)* Kontrapunkt ▲ 32148 [DDD]
Debussy, C.:En blanc et noir, w. R. Llambias (pno) Kontrapunkt 2–▲ KPT 32107 [DDD]
Debussy, C.:Epigraphes antiques, w. R. Llambias (pno) Kontrapunkt 2–▲ KPT 32107 [DDD]
Debussy, C.:Lindaraja, w. R. Llambias (pno) Kontrapunkt 2–▲ KPT 32107 [DDD]
Debussy, C.:La Mer, w. R. Llambias (pno) Kontrapunkt 2–▲ KPT 32107 [DDD]
Debussy, C.:Nocturnes, w. R. Llambias (pno) Kontrapunkt 2–▲ KPT 32107 [DDD]
Debussy, C.:Petite suite, w. R. Llambias (pno) Kontrapunkt 2–▲ KPT 32107 [DDD]
Debussy, C.:Prélude à l'après-midi d'un faune, w. R. Llambias (pno) Kontrapunkt 2–▲ KPT 32107 [DDD]
Heise, P.:Dyveke's Songs, w. M. Bjerno (sop) Kontrapunkt ▲ KPT 32170 [DDD]
Lady Plays the Bass, w. Mette Hanskov (db), N. E. Aggesea (orgn) *(rec Apr. 1991)* Danacord ▲ DACOCD 378 [DDD]
Messiaen, O.:Visions de l'Amen, w. R. Llambias (pno) Kontrapunkt ▲ 32031 [DDD]
Nielsen, C.:Songs, w. Lars Thodberg Bertelsen (bar)—Bjarke's Lay [When Odin Waves...]; You Are Setting Out on Life's Journey; If Luck Should Abandon You... [Comfort in Adversity]; I Praise Our World a Thousandfold; The Rose Now Blooms in Dana's Garden [Denmark, My Joy]; Out of the Mist Emerges My Native Soil [Jutland] [all from 20 Danish Songs]; Old Anders the Cowherd's Song [There Stands a Stunted Tree]; Are You Coming Soon, You Cottagers! [The Shout Rises...] [both from the play Son of Wolf]; The Merchant's Song; Hymn to Denmark [Denmark for a Thousand Years] [both from the Cant for the Merchant Society's Centenary]; Gone Are the Days of Old; On the Ground...; That Tiny Lark on the Moors; The Noble Nature-Lover; A Fisherman Sat So Pensive; I Only Looked Back; Like the Deepest Well...; Freedom is the Purest Gold; The Barques Meet...; Heavy, Sombre Clouds of Night [all from 20 Popular Melodies]; O Danish Man [Patriotic Song]; Halloge's Song [My Helmet is Too Shiny & Heavy for Me; from the play Hagbarth & Signe]; The Bard's Lay [The Days Inscribe the Runes of Fortune; from the play The Liar]; Now Shall It Be Revealed; The Song Casts Light; Christmas Song [all from 4 Popular Melodies]; Heaven Darkens, Great & Silent; In Praise of Bjørnson [We Mention a Name]; Breezy Morning [The Wind Is With Us]; King David [I Was a Lad Keeping Watch O'er the Sheep]; Sign of Light [We Gaze Out Where Ever We Are]; Do You Notice, It is Brightening...; There Is a Lovely Land Rondo Grammofon ▲ RCD 8325
Nielsen, C.:Songs, w. Eva Hess Thaysen (sop), Mette Ejsing (alt), John Laursen (ten), Lars Thodberg Bertelsen (bar), Frode Stengaard (org)—Little Helle; Sir Oluf's Song; Dance–Song; Dawn [all from the play Sir Oluf He Rides]; The Storm Wages over the Dark Waters; My Girl Is as Fair as Amber; The Day the Eagle was Ready to Fly; A Mother was Told at the Feast; The Thistle Crop Looks Promising; Once When Death was Awaited; So Bitter was My Heart; Like a Venturous Fleet at Anchor [all from the play The Mother]; The Sign & the Word of the Cross; Of All the Flowers that Grow on Earth; As the Golden Sun Breaks Through; There is a Path; It Is No Great Struggle; Daffodil, Why Are You Here? [all from Hymns & Sacred Songs]; The Sun Springs Out Like a Rose [from the play Cosmus]; The Great Master Comes; See My Fragile Web; Our Eyes May Rejoice; When Summer's Song is Sung; Earth in Whose Embrace [all from 20 Popular Melodies]; Of What are You Singing? [The Lark]; Teach Me, O Stars of Night [both from 4 Popular Melodies]; Italian Shepherd's Song; We Love You, Our Lofty North!; Vocalise; The Power that Gave Me My Little Song [all from Amor & the Poet]; May Song [Merrily, with Joyful Song!] Rondo Grammofon ▲ RCD 8329
Rachmaninoff, S.:Son Vc, w. N. Sylvest (vc) Canzone ▲ KPTCAN 33009 [DDD]
Schoenberg, A.:Book of the Hanging Gardens, w. S. Lange (mez) [G] Kontrapunkt 3–▲ 32028/30 [DDD]

Lønskov, Tove (pno) (cont.)
Schoenberg, A.:Songs, w. S. Lange (mez), L. Thodberg Bertelsen (bar)—Seven Early Songs; Two Songs, Op. 1; Four Songs, Op. 2; Six Songs, Op. 3; Gruss in die Ferne; Eight Songs, Op. 6; Two Ballads, Op. 12; Two Songs, Op. 14; The Book of the Hanging Gardens, Op. 15; Two Songs (Gedenken; Am Strande); Four Deutsche Volkslieder; Three Songs, Op. 48 [G] Kontrapunkt 3–▲ 32028/30 [DDD]
Schubert, Franz:Allegro Pno 4–Hands, D.947, w. Rodolfo Llambias (pno) Kontrapunkt ▲ KPT 32192 [DDD]
Schubert, Franz:Grandes marches Pno, w. Rodolfo Llambias (pno) Kontrapunkt ▲ KPT 32192 [DDD]
Schubert, Franz:Pno Music (4–hands), w. R. Llambias (pno)—Fantasie, D.940; Ov. in D, D.592, "Im italienischen Stil"; Trois marches militaires, D.733; Variationen über ein französisches Lied, D.624 Kontrapunkt ▲ KPT 32183 [DDD]
Strauss, R.:Ariadne auf Naxos, w. N. Sylvest (vc) [arr. for cello] Canzone ▲ KPTCAN 33009 [DDD]
Strauss, R.:Son Vc, w. N. Sylvest (vc) Canzone ▲ KPTCAN 33009 [DDD]
Tchaikovsky, P.:Festival Ov, w. Rodolfo Llambias (pno) Kontrapunkt ▲ KPT 32204
Tchaikovsky, P.:Sym 6, w. Rodolfo Llambias (pno) [orig arr for Pno 4–Hands, 1893] Kontrapunkt ▲ KPT 32204

Loosemore, Penny (fl)
Bach, J.S.:Sons Fl, BWV 1030–35—BWV 1031 [transc. by Alkan] Symposium ▲ 1062

Lopez, E. (vc)
Tchaikovsky, P.:Vars on a Rococo Theme, w. E. de Carvalho (cnd), Paraiba SO Delos ▲ DE 1018 [DDD]

Lopez, Felipe (org)
Cabezón, A. de:Vocal Music, w. Luis Lozano Virumbrales (cnd), Alfonso X El Sabio Group—Libro de Canto Nuevo RNE/Spanish National Radio ▲ AME 004
Martin Y Coll, A.:Vocal Music, w. Luis Lozano Virumbrales (cnd), Alfonso X El Sabio Group—Flores de Musica RNE/Spanish National Radio ▲ AME 004

Lorango, Thomas (pno)
Schumann, R.:Con Pno, w. A. Newman (cnd), New Brandenburg Collegium [period instruments; period Viennese piano built by Johann Baptist Streicher] Newport Classic ▲ NPD 60034 [DDD]
Schumann, R.:Pno Music (misc) [period Viennese piano built by Johann Baptist Streicher]—5 selections from Kinderscenen, Op. 15; Romance in F#, Op. 28, No. 2; Warum?, from Fantasiestücke, Op. 12; Gesänge der Frühe, Op. 133, No. 1 Newport Classic ▲ NPD 60034 [DDD]

Lord, Kathy (ob)
Rorem, N.:Studies for 11, w. E. Ostling (fl), G. Raden (cl), J. Sutte (tpt), S. Copes (vn), C.–J. Chang (va), J. Lastrapes (vc), K. Englichova (hp), R. Uchida (pno), A. LaFargue (perc), R. Laveille (perc), R. Milanov (cnd) New World ▲ 80445–2

Lord, Melody (pno)
Beethoven, L. van:Romances Vn, w. Donald Peck (fl) [arr fl & pno] *(rec DePaul Concert Hall, Chicago, June 30, 1996)* Boston Records ▲ BR 1014 CD [DDD]
Debussy, C.:Chansons de Bilitis (recitation), w. Lola Rand (nar), Donald Peck (fl) [arr Peck] *(rec DePaul Concert Hall, Chicago, June 30, 1996)* Boston Records ▲ BR 1014 CD [DDD]
Donald Peck:Flute, w. Donald Peck (fl) *(rec DePaul Concert Hall, Chicago, IL, live, July 14, 1993 & Aug)* Boston Records ▲ BR 1010
Ferris, W.:Son Fl, w. Donald Peck (fl) *(rec DePaul Concert Hall, Chicago, June 30, 1996)* Boston Records ▲ BR 1014 CD [DDD]
Franck, C.:Son Vn, w. Donald Peck (fl) [arr for fl & pno] *(rec DePaul Concert Hall, Chicago, June 30, 1996)* Boston Records ▲ BR 1014 CD [DDD]

Loreggian, Roberto (hpd)
Fernini, G.B.:Hpd Music—23 sels:Tastata per clavicembalo; Ballos di Mantova; Arias di Fiorenza; Spagnolettas; Balletos; Galiardas; Toccatas, etc. *(rec Feb 1996)* Tactus ▲ 600601 [DDD]

Lorentz, Robin (vn)—see also ORCHESTRAS & ENSEMBLES California EAR Unit
Lyons, R.:Electronique, w. Erika Duke Kirkpatrick (vc), Amy Knoles (perc) Cambria ▲ CD 1088
Lyons, R.:Gigue Vn Cambria ▲ CD 1088
Lyons, R.:Ice Cream Truck from Hell, w. Erika Duke Kirkpatrick (vc), Amy Knoles (perc) Cambria ▲ CD 1088
Smith, W.L.:Music of, w. Erika Duke (vc), Dorothy Stone (fl/pic), Martin Walker (cl), Wadada Leo Smith (tpt/flgl/fls/bells), Vicki Ray (pno/cel), Mika Noda (vib/bells/timp), David Philipson (perc/bells)—Another Wave More Waves; Double Thunderbolt; Tao-Njia; and others Tzadik ("Composer" series) ▲ TZA 7017 [DDD]

Lorentz, Robin (vn/perc)
Adams, J.L.:Earth & the Great Weather, w. R. Lawrence (va), M. Finckel (vc), R. Black (db/perc), A. Knoles (perc), J. L. Adams (perc), J. Nageak (Iñupiat Eskimo performer), D. Simmonds (Iñupiat Eskimo performer), L. Tritt (Gwich'in Indian performer), A. P. Raboff (Gwich'in Indian performer), D. Hunsaker (Latin voice), J.L. Adams (cnd) *(rec Fairbanks, Mar. 8-11, 1993)* New World ▲ 80459–2

Lorenz, A. (vn)
Mageau, M.J.:Triple Con, w. G. Williams (vc), W. Lorenz (pno), Petronsky (cnd), Slovak RSO Bratislava Vienna Modern Masters ▲ VMM 3001 [DDD]

Lorenz, Andreas (ob)
Mozart, W.A.:Sinf concertante Ob, K.Anh.9, w. Sebastian Weiglo (hn), Eckart Konigstedt (bn), Klaus Kirbach (hpd), H. Haenchen (cnd), C.P.E. Bach CO Berlin Classics ▲ BER 2004

Lorenz, Matthias (vc)
Ruzicka, P.:Chamber Music, w. Carol Tainton (pno), Hamburg String Quartet MD + G ▲ MDG 6250549

Lorenz, W. (pno)
Mageau, M.J.:Furies, w. L. Williams (cnd), Queensland SO Vienna Modern Masters ▲ VMM 3036 [DDD]
Mageau, M.J.:Triple Con, w. A. Lorenz (vn), G. Williams (vc), Petronsky (cnd), Slovak RSO Bratislava Vienna Modern Masters ▲ VMM 3001 [DDD]

Lorenzetti, Stefano (hpd)
Cimarosa, D.:Con Hpd, w. R. Cirri (cnd), Ars Cantus *(rec Sept 7-10, 1995)* Bongiovanni ▲ GB 2184 [DDD]

Lorenzetti, Stefano (hpd/org)—see ORCHESTRAS & ENSEMBLES Consort Fontegara

Lorho, Eric (bas hn)—see ORCHESTRAS & ENSEMBLES Trio di Bassetto

Loriaut, V. (org)
Rameau, J.P.:Dardanus (sels) [St. Laurent d'Aubenas church organ]—Ov.; Marche pour les différentes nations; Menuet en rondeau; Tambourins I & II; Entrée pour les guerriers; Air vif; Rigaudons I & II Ritournelle vive; Air grave; Air vif; Entr Gallo ▲ CD 768 [DDD]

Loriod, J. (ondes Martenot)
Landowski, M.:Music of, w. A. Marion (fl), F. Clidat (pno), M. Becquet (trbn), J. Houtmann (cnd), Lorraine PO—Concerto for Ondes Martenot & Orchestra; Concerto for Flute & Strings; Concerto for Piano & Orchestra; Concertino for Trombone & Strings Koch Schwann ▲ CD 311175 [DDD]
Messiaen, O.:Petites liturgies (3) de la Présence Divine, w. Y. Loriod (pno), B. Kulínský (cnd), Prague SO, Kühn Women's Chorus *(rec Dec. 5-6, 1987)* Supraphon ▲ 11 0404–2 [DDD]
Messiaen, O.:Turangalîla–sym, w. Y. Loriod (pno), L. de Froment (cnd), Luxembourg RSO Forlane 2–▲ FOR 16504/05 [AAD/DDD]
Messiaen, O.:Turangalîla–sym, w. Y. Loriod (pno), M.–W. Chung (cnd), Bastille Orch Deutsche Grammophon ▲ 431781–2 [DDD]

Loriod, Yvonne (pno)
Falla, M. de:Noches en los jardines de España, w. M. Rosenthal (cnd), Paris Opera Orch—9 sels Adès ▲ ADE 202502 [AAD]
Falla, M. de:El sombrero de tres picos, w. M. Rosenthal (cnd), Paris Opera Orch Adès ▲ ADE 202502 [AAD]
Messiaen, O.:Cantéyodjayâ, w. Olivier Messiaen (pno) Adès ▲ ADE 203142
Messiaen, O.:Concert à Quatre, w. Catherine Cantin (fl), Heinz Holliger (ob), Mstislav Rostropovich (vc), M.–W. Chung (cnd), Bastille Opera Orch Deutsche Grammophon ("4D Audio" series) ▲ 445947–2
Messiaen, O.:Couleurs de la cité céleste, w. P. Boulez (cnd), Domaine Musical Orch, Strasbourg Instrumental Percussion Group Sony Classical ("Pierre Boulez Edition" series) ▲ SMK 68332
Messiaen, O.:Couleurs de la cité céleste, w. P. Boulez (cnd), Ensemble InterContemporain Montaigne ▲ MO 781111

Loriod, Yvonne (pno) (cont.)
Messiaen, O.:Haïkaï, w. P. Boulez (cnd), Ensemble InterContemporain — Montaigne ▲ MO 781111
Messiaen, O.:Oiseaux exotiques, w. P. Boulez (cnd), Ensemble InterContemporain — Montaigne ▲ MO 781111
Messiaen, O.:Petites liturgies (3) de la Présence Divine, w. J. Loriod (ondes Martenot), B. Kulínsky (cnd), Prague SO, Kühn Women's Chorus *(rec Dec. 5–6, 1987)* — Supraphon ▲ 11 0404–2 [DDD]
Messiaen, O.:Quatuor pour la fin du temps, w. Wolfgang Meyer (cl), Christoph Poppen (vn), M. Fischer-Dieskau (vc) — EMI Classics ▲ CDC 54395
Messiaen, O.:Regards sur l'Enfant Jésus — Adès 2–▲ ADE 203752 [AAD]
Messiaen, O.:La Transfiguration de Notre Seigneur Jésus-Christ, w. Ludwig van Gijsegem (ten), R. de Leeuw (cnd), Hilversum RSO, BRT Choir — Montaigne 2–▲ MO 782040
Messiaen, O.:Turangalîla-sym, w. J. Loriod (ondes Martenot), M.-W. Chung (cnd), Bastille Orch — Deutsche Grammophon ▲ 431781–2 [DDD]
Messiaen, O.:Turangalîla-sym, w. J. Loriod (ondes Martenot), L. de Froment (cnd), Luxembourg RSO — Forlane 2–▲ FOR 16504/05 [AAD/DDD]
Messiaen, O.:Visions de l'Amen, w. Olivier Messiaen (pno) — Adès ▲ ADE 203142 [AAD]
Messiaen, O.:Un Vitrail et des oiseaux, w. P. Boulez (cnd), Ensemble InterContemporain — Montaigne ▲ MO 781111

Lorkovic, Fran (timp)
Hauser, F.:Die Welle, w. Martin André Grütter (cym/tamtam), Roli Fischer (cym), Barbara Frey (cym), Cyril Lützelschwab (cym), Lukas Rohner (cym), Severin Steinhauser (cym), Hans Ulrich (cym), Ruud Wiener (cym), Michael Erni (timp), F. Hauser (cnd) *(rec Studio DRS, Basel, Switzerland, Nov. 6, 1988)* — Hat Hut ▲ hat ART CD 6017 [ADD]

Lortie, Louis (pno)
Beethoven, L van:Son 1 Pno — Chandos ▲ CHAN 9212 [DDD]
Beethoven, L van:Son 2 Pno — Chandos ▲ CHAN 9212 [DDD]
Beethoven, L van:Son 3 Pno — Chandos ▲ CHAN 9212 [DDD]
Beethoven, L van:Son 4 Pno — Chandos ▲ CHAN 9347 [DDD]
Beethoven, L van:Son 5 Pno — Chandos ▲ CHAN 9101 [DDD]
Beethoven, L van:Son 6 Pno — Chandos ▲ CHAN 9101 [DDD]
Beethoven, L van:Son 7 Pno — Chandos ▲ CHAN 9101 [DDD]
Beethoven, L van:Son 8 Pno, "Pathétique" — Chandos ▲ CHAN 9024 [DDD]
Beethoven, L van:Son 9 Pno — Chandos ▲ CHAN 9347 [DDD]
Beethoven, L van:Son 10 Pno — Chandos ▲ CHAN 9347 [DDD]
Beethoven, L van:Son 21 Pno, "Waldstein" — Chandos ▲ CHAN 9024 [DDD]
Beethoven, L van:Son 26 Pno, "Les Adieux" — Chandos ▲ CHAN 9024 [DDD]
Beethoven, L van:Son 28 Pno — Chandos ▲ CHAN 9435
Beethoven, L van:Son 29 Pno, "Hammerklavier" — Chandos ▲ CHAN 9435
Beethoven, L van:Son Pno 4-Hands, w. Hélène Mercier (pno) — Chandos ▲ CHAN 9347 [DDD]
Brahms, J.:Vars on a Theme of Robert Schumann, Op. 9 — Chandos ▲ CHAN 9289 [DDD]
Chopin, F.:Con 2 Pno, w. N. Järvi (cnd), Philharmonia Orch — Chandos ▲ CHAN 9061 [DDD]
Chopin, F.:Études (24) — Chandos ▲ CHAN 8482 [DDD]
Chopin, F.:Nouvelles études — Chandos ▲ CHAN 8482 [DDD]
Fauré, G.:Ballade Pno, w. R. Frühbeck de Burgos (cnd), London SO — Chandos ▲ CHAN 8773 [DDD]
Gershwin, G.:Rhap in Blue, w. R. Dufallo (cnd), Netherlands Wind Ensemble — Chandos ("New Direction" series) ▲ CHAN 9210 [DDD]
Gershwin, G.:Rhap in Blue [Gershwin's solo piano arr.] — Chandos ▲ CHAN 8733 [DDD]
Liszt, F.:Années de pèlerinage 2 — Chandos ▲ CHAN 8900 [DDD]
Liszt, F.:Études de concert (3) Pno — Chandos ▲ CHAN 8548 [DDD]
Liszt, F.:Son Pno — Chandos ▲ CHAN 8548 [DDD]
Mozart, W.A.:Andante & Vars Pno 4-Hands, w. H. Mercier (pno) — Chandos ▲ CHAN 9162 [DDD]
Mozart, W.A.:Con 12 Pno, w. Y. Turovsky (cnd), Montreal Musici — Chandos ▲ CHAN 8455 [DDD]
Mozart, W.A.:Con 14 Pno, w. Y. Turovsky (cnd), Montreal Musici — Chandos ▲ CHAN 8455 [DDD]
Mozart, W.A.:Son Pnos, K.448, w. H. Mercier (pno) — Chandos ▲ CHAN 9162 [DDD]
Prokofiev, S.:Romeo & Juliet Pno—Nos. 4,6 & 10 only—"Juliet's Girlhood," "Montagues and Capulets" & "Romeo and Juliet at Parting" — Chandos ▲ CHAN 8733 [DDD]
Ravel, M.:A la manière de Borodine & de Chabrie — Chandos ▲ CHAN 8647 [DDD]
Ravel, M.:Boléro, w. H. Mercier (pno) [Ravel's 1930 two-piano arr.] — Chandos ▲ CHAN 8905 [DDD]
Ravel, M.:Con Pno (left hand), w. R. Frühbeck de Burgos (cnd), London SO — Chandos ▲ CHAN 8773 [DDD]
Ravel, M.:Con in G Pno, w. R. Frühbeck de Burgos (cnd), London SO — Chandos ▲ CHAN 8773 [DDD]
Ravel, M.:Gaspard de la nuit — Chandos ▲ CHAN 8647 [DDD]
Ravel, M.:Intro & Allegro, w. H. Mercier (pno) [Ravel's two-piano arr.] — Chandos ▲ CHAN 8905 [DDD]
Ravel, M.:Jeux d'eau — Chandos ▲ CHAN 8620 [DDD]
Ravel, M.:Ma mère l'oye Pno, w. H. Mercier (pno) — Chandos ▲ CHAN 8905 [DDD]
Ravel, M.:Menuet sur le nom d'Haydn — Chandos ▲ CHAN 8647 [DDD]
Ravel, M.:Miroirs — Chandos ▲ CHAN 8647 [DDD]
Ravel, M.:Pno Music—Pavane pour une infante défunte; Le Tombeau de Couperin; Sérénade grotesque; Jeux d'eau; Valse nobles et sentimentales; La Valse; Gaspard de la nuit; Menuet antique; Menuet sur le nom de Haydn; A la manière de Borodine; A la manière de Chabrier; Prélude; Miroirs; Sonatine — Chandos 2–▲ CHAN 7004/05 [DDD]
Ravel, M.:Prélude Pno — Chandos ▲ CHAN 8647 [DDD]
Ravel, M.:Rapsodie espagnole, w. H. Mercier (pno) [Ravel's piano duet arr.] — Chandos ▲ CHAN 8905 [DDD]
Ravel, M.:Sonatine Pno — Chandos ▲ CHAN 8647 [DDD]
Ravel, M.:Le Tombeau de Couperin — Chandos ▲ CHAN 8620 [DDD]
Ravel, M.:La Valse [Ravel's solo piano arr.] — Chandos ▲ CHAN 8733 [DDD]
Ravel, M.:La Valse, w. H. Mercier (pno) [Ravel's 1921 two-piano arr.] — Chandos ▲ CHAN 8905 [DDD]
Ravel, M.:La Valse — Chandos ▲ CHAN 8620 [DDD]
Schubert, Franz:Fant Pno, D.940, w. H. Mercier (pno) — Chandos ▲ CHAN 9162 [DDD]
Schumann, R.:Blumenstück — Chandos ▲ CHAN 9289 [DDD]
Schumann, R.:Bunte Blätter — Chandos ▲ CHAN 9289 [DDD]
Schumann, R.:Con Pno, w. N. Järvi (cnd), Philharmonia Orch — Chandos ▲ CHAN 9061 [DDD]
Stravinsky, I.:Pétrouchka (3 Scenes) — Chandos ▲ CHAN 8733 [DDD]
20th Century Original Piano Transcriptions — Chandos ▲ CHAN 8733 [DDD]

Lortz, Mark (perc)
Mahin, B.:Rituals, w. Kujit Rehney (perc) — Capstone ▲ CPS 8611
Mahin, B.:Rituals, w. K. Rehney (perc) — Capstone ▲ CPS 8061

Losakiewicz, Pawel (vn)—see ORCHESTRAS & ENSEMBLES Wilanów String Quartet

Lösch, G. (vc)—see also ORCHESTRAS & ENSEMBLES Berlin German Opera Orch Soloists
Martinů, B.:La Revue de Cuisine (sels), w. T. Tomaszewski (vn), R. Schönemann (cl), V. Knappe (bn), A. Lange (tpt), S. Schubert-Weber (pno)—Suite for Violin, Cello, Clarinet, Bassoon, Trumpet & Piano — FSM-Adagio ▲ FCD 97 219

Lotoro, Francesco (pno)
Haas, P.:Suite Pno — Arion ▲ ARN 68339
Karel, R.:Theme & Vars Pno — Arion ▲ ARN 68339
Klein, G.:Son Pno — Arion ▲ ARN 68339
Ullmann, V.:Sons Pno—No. 6, Op. 44 — Arion ▲ ARN 68339

Lotto, Albert (pno)
Davison, J.:Son 1 Vn, w. Carol Stein Amado (vn) — Albany ▲ TROY 199 [DDD]
Liszt, F.:Années de pèlerinage 1—No. 6, "Vallée d'Obermann" — Protone ■ CSPR 160
Liszt, F.:Études d'exécution transcendante, S.139—Nos. 9 & 10 only — Protone ■ CSPR 160
Liszt, F.:Hungarian Rhaps—No. 8 — Protone ■ CSPR 160
Liszt, F.:Paraphrase on Verdi's Quartet — Protone ■ CSPR 160

Loubry, Luc (bn)
Bréval, J.B.:Sym concertante, w. Berten D'Hollander (fl), F. Heyerick (cnd), Collegium Instrumentale Brugense — Arcobaleno ▲ AAOC 9324
The Golden Age of the Harp & French Bassoon — Arcobaleno ▲ SBCD 1511

Loubry, Luc (bn) (cont.)
Mozart, W.A.:Con Bn, w. F. Heyerick (cnd), Collegium Instrumentale Brugense — Arcobaleno ▲ AAOC 9324
Vivaldi, A.:Con Fl Bn, w. Berten D'Hollander (fl), F. Heyerick (cnd), Collegium Instrumentale Brugense — Arcobaleno ▲ AAOC 9324

Louchart, Jean-Michel (pno)
Koechlin, C.:Pieces Ob & Pno, w. Jacques Vandeville (ob/ob d'amore/E hn) — Arion ▲ ARN 68286 [DDD]
Koechlin, C.:Son Ob, w. Jacques Vandeville (ob) — Arion ▲ ARN 68286 [DDD]
Koechlin, C.:Symphonic Pieces, w. Jacques Vandeville (E hn)—Au loin [arr for E hn & Pno] — Arion ▲ ARN 68286 [DDD]

Loudos, A. (vc)
Boulez, P.:Messagesquisse, w. B. Licther (vc), B. Feigenwinter (vc), M. Keller (vc), F. Schiltknecht (vc), P. Toso (vc), J. Wyttenbach (cnd) *(rec Switzerland, June 1993)* — ECM New Series 2–▲ 78118–21520–2 [DDD]

Louhivuori, Heikki (vn)
Segerstam, L.:Divert Vns, w. J. Rahkonen (vn), E. Kamu (va), V. Höylä (vc), L. Segerstam (cnd), Helsinki CO — BIS ▲ CD 84 [AAD]

Louie, Gary (sax)
Ibert, J.:Concertino da camera, w. R.A. Clark (cnd), Manhattan CO — Newport Classic ("Manhattan CO" series) ▲ NPD 85598 [DDD]

Louwenaar (hpd)
Penn, W.:Essays Tuba, w. J. Stevens (tuba) — CRI ■ C 367

Loveday, Alan (vn)
Vivaldi, A.:Cons Vn, Op. 4, "La stravaganza", w. N. Marriner (cnd), Academy of St. Martin in the Fields—RV.249 — London ■ 417100–4
Vivaldi, A.:Cons Vn, Op. 8/1–4, "The Four Seasons", w. N. Marriner (cnd), Academy of St. Martin in the Fields — Argo ▲ 414486–2 [ADD]

Lovenstein, Jonathan (pno)
Lovenstein, J.:Music of, w. Mary Brockenbrough (sop), Laura Sanders (sop), Barton Green (ten), Rockland Osgood (ten), David Murray (bar), Benjamin Sears (bar), Heather O'Donnell (pno), James Silvers (pno), Rocy Reider (fl), Jason Horowitz (vn), Adrianna Hulscher (vn), James Johnston (vn), Mimi Ragson (vn), Peter Landeen (vc), Reinmar Seidler (vc)—Blake Songs; other works — Titanic ▲ Ti 221 [DDD]

Low (cel)
Pinkham, D.:Con Cel, w. D. Pinkham (hpd) — CRI ■ C 109

Lowbury, Pauline (vn)
Simpson, R.:Qt Hn, w. R. Watkins (hn), C. Dearnley (vc), C. Green Armytage (pno) — Hyperion ▲ CDA 66695
Simpson, R.:Son Vn, w. Christopher Green Armytage (pno) — Hyperion ▲ CDA 66737
Simpson, R.:Trio Hn, w. R. Watkins (hn), C. Green Armytage (pno) — Hyperion ▲ CDA 66695

Lowe, Laurence (hn)—see ORCHESTRAS & ENSEMBLES Missouri Quintet

Lowe, Mundell (gtr)
Kiri Sidetracks, w. Kiri Te Kanawa (sop), André Previn (pno), Ray Brown (db) — Philips ▲ 434092–2 PH [DDD] ■ 434092–4 PH (D)

Lowe, Rona (pno)
Quilter, R.:The Arnold Book of Old Songs, w. J. Benton (bar) — Symposium ▲ 1159
Quilter, R.:Shakespeare Songs (misc), w. Jeffrey Benton (bar), Graham Kirkland (pno)—Orpheus with His Lute, Op. 32/1; When Icicles Hang by the Wall, Op. 32/2; Come away, Death, Op. 6/1; Oh Mistress Mine, Op. 6/2; Blow, Blow, Thou Winter Wind, Op. 6/3; Who Is Sylvia?, Op. 30/1; When Daffodils Begin to Peer, Op. 30/2; How Should I Your True Love Know?, Op. 30/3; Sigh No More, Ladies, Op. 30/4; Fear No More the Heat of the Sun, Op. 23/1; Under the Greenwood Tree, Op. 23/2; It Was a Lover & His Lass, Op. 23/3; Take, O Take Those Lips away, Op. 23/4; Hey, Ho, the Wind & the Rain, Op. 23/5 — Symposium ▲ SYM 1184
Quilter, R.:Songs, w. J. Benton (bar)—Fairy Lullaby; songs set to the poems of Heywood *(Morning Song)*, Ben Jonson *(Drink to me only with thine eyes)*, Percy *(Over the Mountains)*, John Irvine *(My Lady Greensleeves; Wind from the South)*, Thomas Moore *(Believe me, if all those endearing young charms...; Oh, tis sweet to think)*, Burns *(Ye Banks and Braes; Ca the yowes to the knowes)*, Rodney Bennett *(The man behind the plow...; The ash grove)*, Tennyson *(Now sleeps the Crimson petal)*, Mary Coleridge *(The valley and the hill...)*, William Blake *(Dream Valley)*, Edmund Waler *(Go lovely rose)*, Thomas Dekker *(O, the month of May)*, Shelley *(Love's Philosophy)*; a Manx ballad *(The Fuchsia tree)* — Symposium ▲ 1159
Quilter, R.:Songs, w. Jeffrey Benton (bar), Graham Kirkland (pno)—To Julia [Prelude/The Bracelet/The Maiden Blush/To Daisies/The Night Piece/Julia's Hair/Cherry Ripe; poems by Herrick], Op. 8; Weep You No More; My Life's Delight [Campion]; Damask Roses; The Faithless Shepherdess [Byrd]; Browen Is My Love; By a Fountainside [Ben Johnson]; Fair House of Joy — Symposium ▲ SYM 1184
Schubert, Franz:Winterreise, w. J. Benton (bar) [E] — Symposium ▲ SYM 1118

Lowenstern, Michael (b cl)
Sharp, E.:JAG, w. Quintet of the Americas *(rec Vassar College, June 25–29, 1995)* — CRI ▲ CD 722 [DDD]
Spasm, w. Heather Barringer (voc), Mark Gibbons (voc), Jay Johnson (voc), Jerome Kitzke (voc), Matt Lambiase (voc), Tom Linker (voc), Ed Lowenstern (voc), Michael Lowenstern (voc) *(rec Creation Audio, Minneapolis, NYU Studios, New York City & Studio A, Stony Brook, Aug 1994–July 1996)* — New World ▲ 80468–2
Xenakis, I.:Échange, w. C. Z. Bornstein (cnd), ST-X Ensemble — Mode ▲ MODE 56

Lowenthal, Jerome (pno)
Lazarof, H.:Duo Vc & Pno, w. J. Solow (vc) — Laurel ▲ LR 845CD [AAD]
Lazarof, H.:Trio Pno, Vn & Vc, w. Y. Matsudo (vn), J. Solow (vc) — Laurel ▲ LR 845CD [AAD]
Liszt, F.:Con Pno, Op. posth., w. S. Comissiona (cnd), Vancouver SO — Music & Arts ▲ CD 803 [DDD]
Liszt, F.:Con 1 Pno, w. S. Comissiona (cnd), Vancouver SO — Music & Arts ▲ CD 803 [DDD]
Liszt, F.:Malédiction, w. S. Comissiona (cnd), Vancouver SO [2 versions] — Music & Arts ▲ CD 803 [DDD]
Liszt, F.:Totentanz, w. S. Comissiona (cnd), Vancouver SO — Music & Arts ▲ CD 803 [DDD]
Rorem, N.:Con 3 Pno, w. J. Mester (cnd), Louisville Orch — Albany ▲ TROY 047 [AAD]
Sinding, C.:Pno Music—Sonata in b, Op. 91; Con fuoco; Melodie; Marche grotesque; Serenade; Irrlicht; Capriccio; Alla marcia; Pomposo; Rustles of Spring — Arabesque ▲ Z 6578 [DDD]
Taneyev, S.:Qnt Pno Strs, w. P. Rosenthal (vn), Y. Kamei (vn), M. Thompson (va), S. Kates (vc) — Arabesque ▲ Z 6539 [DDD]
Tchaikovsky, P.:Concert Fant, w. S. Comissiona (cnd), London SO [original version] — Arabesque ▲ Z 6611
Tchaikovsky, P.:Con 1 Pno, w. S. Comissiona (cnd), London SO [original version] — Arabesque ▲ Z 6611
Tchaikovsky, P.:Con 2 Pno, w. S. Comissiona (cnd), London SO — Arabesque ▲ Z 6583
Tchaikovsky, P.:Con 3 Pno, w. S. Comissiona (cnd), London SO — Arabesque ▲ Z 6583

Lower, Janna (vn)
Harrison, L.:Con Vn, w. David Colson (perc), R. Brown (cnd), Continuum Percussion Quartet — New World ▲ NW 382–2 [AAD]
White, J.:Music for Vn, w. Kevin Sharpe (pno) — Opus One ▲ CD 167 [DDD]

Lowry, Ronald (vc)
Kraft, William:Con Perc, w. Dean Anderson (perc), Renee Krimsier (fl), Diane Heffner (cl), Nancy Cirillo (vn/va), Hugh Hinton (pno) — Albany ▲ TROY 218 [DDD]
Kraft, William:Gallery 4–5, w. Diane Heffner (cl), Nancy Cirillo (vn), Ronald Copes (va), Hugh Hinton (pno) — Albany ▲ TROY 218 [DDD]
Kraft, William:Settings from Pierrot Lunaire, w. Jane Manning (sop), Renee Krimsier (fl), Diane Heffner (cl), Nancy Cirillo (vn/va), Dean Anderson (perc), Hugh Hinton (pno) — Albany ▲ TROY 218 [DDD]

Loy, Christopher Morgan (pno)
Fairlie-Kennedy, M.:Windrider/Final Ascent, w. Laura Campbell (fl) *(rec MasterView SoundCrafts Recording Studios)* — Capstone ▲ CPS 8631

Lozier, F. Joseph (pno)
Schoenberg, A.:Pierrot lunaire, w. Leslie Boucher (nar), Julie Stone (fl/pic), Tod Kerstetter (cl/b cl), Andrew Carlson (vn), Philip Singleton (va), Juanita Karpf (vc) *(rec Roswell United Methodist Church, Roswell, GA, July 20, Aug. 2 & Sept. 1)* ACA Digital ▲ CM 20027
Zwilich, E.T.:Passages, w. Leslie Boucher (sop), Julie Stone (fl/pic), Tod Kerstetter (cl/b cl), Andrew Carlson (vn), Philip Singleton (va), Juanita Karpf (vc), Joanna Parks (perc), Shannon O'Kelley (perc) *(rec Roswell United Methodist Church, Roswell, GA, July 20, Aug. 2 & Sept. 1)* ACA Digital ▲ CM 20027

Lüannerholm, S. (hp)
Crumb, G.:Madrigals (4 books), w. A.–M. Mühle (sop), A.–M. Bergström (fl), S. Röjder (db), S. Asikainen (perc)—[Sp] *(rec digital)* BIS ▲ CD 261

Lubambo, Romero (gtr)
Chesky, D.:Music of *(rec 1992)* Chesky ▲ JD–72 [DDD]
Chesky, D.:Music of Chesky ▲ JD39 [DDD]
So Many Stars, w. Kathleen Battle (sop), Antonio Hart (sax), Grover Washington Jr (sax), Tom Harrell (flgl), James Carter (b cl), Cyrus Chestnut (pno), Jon Herrington (gtr), Ira Coleman (elec bass), Christian McBride (elec bass), Cyro Baptista (perc), Steven Berrios (perc) *(rec Hit Factory, Clinton Recording Studios, R.P.M. Sound Studios, Unique Recording Studios, Power Station)* Sony Classical ▲ SK 68473 [DDD]

Lubik, Hédi (hp)
Liszt, F.:Music of, w. A. Kiss (n), Z. Tóth (va), E. Banda (vc), M. Perényi (vc), I. Lantos (pno/org), S. Margittay (harm)—Angelus; La lugubre gondola; Epithalam; Am Grabe Richard Wagners; Romance oubliée; Elégies 1 & 2; Offertorium; Benedictus Hungaroton ▲ HCD 11798 [DDD]
Silent Night, w. Imre Kovacs (fl), Ferenc Gergely (org), Frigyes Hidas (org), Gabor Lehotka (org), Hungarian State Orch CO, Csanyi (cnd), Szekeres (cnd), Budapest Children's Choir Madrigal Choir Hungaroton ▲ HCD 16598

Lubimov, Alexei (clvd)
Bortnyansky, D.:Son 1 Pno Russian Compact Disc ▲ RCD 19101 [ADD]
Bortnyansky, D.:Son 2 Pno Russian Compact Disc ▲ RCD 19101 [ADD]
Karaulov, V.:Russian Songs with Vars—Lots of Gnats in Our Forest; You, My Little Nowhere Child; Sick as I Am Russian Compact Disc ▲ RCD 19101 [ADD]
Pratch, I.:Rondo Russian Compact Disc ▲ RCD 19101 [ADD]
Pratch, I.:Son Pno Russian Compact Disc ▲ RCD 19101 [ADD]
Trutovsky, V.:Vars on Russian Folksongs Russian Compact Disc ▲ RCD 19101 [ADD]

Lubimov, Alexei (hpd)
Anglebert, J.–H. d':Pièces de clavecin—Suite 2 in g *(rec 1985)* Russian Compact Disc ▲ RCD 19102 [ADD]
Couperin, L.:Suites Hpd—Suites in g & d *(rec 1985)* Russian Compact Disc ▲ RCD 19102 [ADD]

Lubimov, Alexei (pno)
Beethoven, L. van:Son 8 Pno, "Pathétique" Erato ▲ 94356–2
Beethoven, L. van:Son 14 Pno, "Moonlight Son" Erato ▲ 94356–2
Beethoven, L. van:Son 21 Pno, "Waldstein" Erato ▲ 94356–2
Brahms, J.:Ballades, Op. 10 *(rec Eglise Notre-Dame du Liban, Paris, June 8–10, 1994)* Erato ▲ 98474–2 [DDD]
Brahms, J.:Rhaps Pno, Op. 79 Erato ▲ 98474–2 [DDD]
Brahms, J.:Vars & Fugue on a Theme by Handel Erato ▲ 98474–2 [DDD]
Chopin, F.:Ballades Pno (comp) Erato ▲ 2292–45990–2
Chopin, F.:Barcarolle Pno Erato ▲ 2292–45990–2
Chopin, F.:Berceuse Erato ▲ 2292–45990–2
Chopin, F.:Fant Erato ▲ 2292–45990–2
Mozart, W.A.:Allegro & Andante & Rondo Erato ▲ 2292–45510–2 [DDD]
Mozart, W.A.:Allegro in Son form Erato ▲ 2292–45622–2 [DDD]
Mozart, W.A.:Fant Pno, K.475 Erato ▲ 2292–45622–2 [DDD]
Mozart, W.A.:Sons Pno—Nos. 7–9, K.309–311 Erato ▲ 2292–45590–2 [DDD]
Mozart, W.A.:Sons Pno—Nos. 1–3, K.279–281 Erato ▲ 2292–45615–2 [DDD]
Mozart, W.A.:Sons Pno—Nos. 15–17, K.545, 570 & 576 Erato ▲ 2292–45510–2 [DDD]
Mozart, W.A.:Sons Pno—Nos. 13 & 14, K.333 & K.457 Erato ▲ 2292–45622–2 [DDD]
Schubert, Franz:Impromptus Pno (comp) Erato ▲ 2292–45630–2 ZK
Silvestrov, V.:Postludium, w. D. Robertson (cnd), Berlin SO *(rec Jesus-Christus-Kirche, Berlin, Jan 25–30, 1995)* Sony Classical ▲ SK 66825 [DDD]

Lubin, Robert (pno)
Stravinsky, I.:Easy Pieces Pno 4–Hands (5), w. A. Karis (pno) *(rec Mar. 12–14, 1993)* Bridge ▲ BCD 9051 [DDD]
Stravinsky, I.:Son Pnos, w. A. Karis (pno) *(rec Mar. 12–14, 1993)* Bridge ▲ BCD 9051 [DDD]

Lubin, Steven (pno)—see also ORCHESTRAS & ENSEMBLES Mozartean Players
Beethoven, L. van:Cons Pno (comp), w. C. Hogwood (cnd), Academy of Ancient Music L'Oiseau-Lyre 3–▲ 421408–2 [DDD]
Beethoven, L. van:Son Hn, w. L. Greer (nat hn) Harmonia Mundi USA ▲ HMU 907037
Beethoven, L. van:Son 8 Pno, "Pathétique" L'Oiseau-Lyre ▲ 425836–2 [DDD]
Beethoven, L. van:Son 14 Pno, "Moonlight Son" L'Oiseau-Lyre ▲ 425836–2 [DDD]
Beethoven, L. van:Son 23 Pno, "Appassionata" L'Oiseau-Lyre ▲ 425836–2 [DDD]
Brahms, J.:Trio Hn, w. L. Greer (nat hn), S. Chase (vn) Harmonia Mundi USA ▲ HMU 907037
Krufft, N. von:Son Hn & Pno, w. L. Greer (hn) Harmonia Mundi USA ▲ HMU 907037
Mozart, W.A.:Con 12 Pno, w. S. Lubin (cnd), Mozartean Players Arabesque ▲ Z 6552 [DDD]
Mozart, W.A.:Con 15 Pno, w. S. Lubin (cnd), Mozartean Players Arabesque ▲ Z 6552 [DDD]
Mozart, W.A.:Con 20 Pno, w. S. Lubin (cnd), Mozartean Players Arabesque ▲ Z 6530
Mozart, W.A.:Con 23 Pno, w. S. Lubin (cnd), Mozartean Players Arabesque ▲ Z 6530
Schubert, Franz:Qnt Pno, D.667, w. Academy of Ancient Music Chamber Ensemble L'Oiseau-Lyre ▲ 433848–2 [DDD]

Lübke, B. (vc)—see ORCHESTRAS & ENSEMBLES Pro Arte String Quartet

Lubotsky, Mark (vn)
Beethoven, L. van:Con Vn, Op. 61, w. A. Volmer (cnd), Estonian State SO [1st movt cadenza by A. Schnittke] *(rec Tallinn, Estonia, Mar 1996)* Globe ▲ GLO 5155 [DDD]
Beethoven, L. van:Romances Vn, w. A. Volmer (cnd), Estonian State SO *(rec Tallinn, Estonia, Mar 1996)* Globe ▲ GLO 5155 [DDD]
Mahler, G.:Qt Pno [comp Schnittke], w. Ralf Gothoni (pno), Matti Hirvikangas (va), Martti Rousi (vc) Ondine ▲ ODE 840 [DDD]
Prokofiev, S.:Mélodies, w. B. Berman (pno) Ottavo ▲ OTT 79136 [DDD]
Prokofiev, S.:Son Vn, Op. 94bis, w. B. Berman (pno) Ottavo ▲ OTT 79136 [DDD]
Prokofiev, S.:Son 1 Vn, w. B. Berman (pno) Ottavo ▲ OTT 79136 [DDD]
Roslavets, N.:Dances, w. Julia Bochkovskaya (pno) Olympia ▲ OLY 559 [DDD]
Roslavets, N.:Nocturne, w. Julia Bochkovskaya (pno) Olympia ▲ OLY 559 [DDD]
Roslavets, N.:Poema, w. Julia Bochkovskaya (pno) Olympia ▲ OLY 559 [DDD]
Roslavets, N.:Preludes in All the Keys, w. Julia Bochkovskaya (pno) Olympia ▲ OLY 559 [DDD]
Roslavets, N.:Son 1 Vn, w. Julia Bochkovskaya (pno) Olympia ▲ OLY 558 [DDD]
Roslavets, N.:Son 2 Vn, w. Julia Bochkovskaya (pno) Olympia ▲ OLY 558 [DDD]
Roslavets, N.:Son 4 Vn, w. Julia Bochkovskaya (pno) Olympia ▲ OLY 558 [DDD]
Roslavets, N.:Son 6 Vn, w. Julia Bochkovskaya (pno) Olympia ▲ OLY 558 [DDD]
Schnittke, A.:Canon Vn, w. E. Lampson (cnd), Hamburg Academy Orch *(rec June 11–12, 1991)* Sony Classical ▲ SK 53357 [DDD]
Schnittke, A.:Con 1 Vn, w. E. Klas (cnd), Malmö SO BIS ▲ CD 487 [DDD]
Schnittke, A.:Con 2 Vn, w. E. Klas (cnd), Malmö SO BIS ▲ CD 487 [DDD]
Schnittke, A.:Gratulationsrondo, w. I. Schnittke (pno) *(rec June 11–12, 1991)* Sony Classical ▲ SK 53357 [DDD]
Schnittke, A.:Quasi una son, w. M. Rostropovich (cnd), English CO *(rec Aug. 12–15, 1992)* Sony Classical ▲ SK 53271 [DDD]
Schnittke, A.:Suite in the Old Style, w. R. Gothoni (pno) Ondine ▲ ODE 800 [DDD]

Lubotsky, Mark (vn) (cont.)
Schnittke, A.:Trio Pno, w. I. Schnittke (pno), Mstislav Rostropovich (vc) *(rec Aug. 12–15, 1992)* Sony Classical ▲ SK 53271 [DDD]
Strauss, R.:Qt Pno, w. Ralf Gothoni (pno), Matti Hirvikangas (va), Martti Rousi (vc) Ondine ▲ ODE 840 [DDD]
Tubin, E.:Con 1 Vn, w. N. Järvi (cnd), Gothenburg SO BIS ▲ CD 286 [DDD]
Tubin, E.:Estonian Dance Suite, w. N. Järvi (cnd), Gothenburg SO BIS ▲ CD 286 [DDD]

Luca, Sergiu (vn)
Bach, J.S.:Sons & Partitas Vn, BWV 1001–1006 Elektra/Nonesuch 2–▲ 73030–2–FD 3–■ 73030–4
Bach, J.S.:Sons Vn, w. A. Fuller (hpd)—BWV 1019 Facet ▲ FCD 8005 [AAD]
Bolcom, W.:Con Vn, w. D. R. Davies (cnd), American Composers Orch Argo ▲ 433077–2 [DDD]
Busoni, F.:Son 2 Vn, w. L. Golub (pno) Facet ▲ FCD 8005 [AAD]
Dvořák, A.:Romantic Pieces, Op. 75, w. P. Schoenfield (pno) Elektra/Nonesuch ■ 71350–4
Janácek, L.:Son Vn, w. P. Schoenfield (pno) Elektra/Nonesuch ■ 71350–4
Kodály, Z.:Duo Vn & Vc, w. Roel Dieltiens (vc) Harmonia Mundi France ▲ HMC 901560
Mozart, W.A.:Sons Vn Pno (misc), w. M. Bilson (pno)—K.454, 481, 526 & 547 Elektra/Nonesuch 2–▲ 79112–2 [DDD]
Schubert, Franz:Fant Vn, D.934, w. J. Kalichstein (pno) Elektra/Nonesuch ■ 71370–4
Schubert, Franz:Rondo Vn, D.895, w. J. Kalichstein (pno) Elektra/Nonesuch ■ 71370–4
Schubert, Franz:Sonatina Vn, D.384, w. J. Kalichstein (pno) Elektra/Nonesuch ■ 71370–4
Smetana, B.:From the Homeland, w. P. Schoenfield (pno) Elektra/Nonesuch ■ 71350–4
Veress, S.:Son Vn Harmonia Mundi France ▲ HMC 901560

Lucarelli, Humbert (ob)
Baksa, R.:Qnt Ob & Strs, w. N. Tanaka (vn), M. Yanagita (vn), S. Winterbottom (va), T. Hoyle (vc) Capstone ▲ CPS 8610
Barber, S.:Canzonetta, w. D. Spieth (cnd), Lehigh Valley CO Koch International Classics ▲ KIC 7023–2 [DDD] ■ 3–7023–4 (D)
Barlow, W.:The Winter's Past, w. M. Barrett (cnd), Brooklyn PO Koch International Classics ▲ KIC 7187 [DDD]
Bloom, Robert:Narrative, w. M. Barrett (cnd), Brooklyn PO Koch International Classics ▲ KIC 7187 [DDD]
Bloom, Robert:Requiem, w. M. Barrett (cnd), Brooklyn PO Koch International Classics ▲ KIC 7187 [DDD]
Corigliano, J.:Aria Ob & Str, w. M. Barrett (cnd), Brooklyn PO Koch International Classics ▲ KIC 7187 [DDD]
Corigliano, J.:Con Ob, w. K. Akiyama (cnd), American SO RCA Gold Seal ▲ 60395–2–RG [ADD]
Corigliano, J.:Poem in October, w. R. White (ten), T. Nyfenger (fl), J. Rabbai (cl), Maurice Press (hpd), M. Press (cnd), American String Quartet RCA Gold Seal ▲ 60395–2–RG [ADD]
Ibert, J.:Symphonie concertante, w. R.A. Clark (cnd), Manhattan CO Newport Classic ("Manhattan CO" series) ▲ NPD 85598 [DDD]
The Sensual Sound of the Soulful Oboe, w. Friends Special Music ▲ SCD 4527 [DDD]
The Sounds of Remembered Dreams, w. Susan Jolles (hp), Frank Morelli (bn) Vox ("Classics" series) ▲ VOX 7504 [DDD]
Strauss, R.:Con Ob, w. D. Spieth (cnd), Lehigh Valley CO Koch International Classics ▲ KIC 7023–2 [DDD] ■ 3–7023–4 (D)
Telemann, G.P.:Kleine Kammermusik, w. A. Brown (bn), G. Ranck (hpd) Well-Tempered Productions ▲ WPT 5169 [ADD]
Vaughan Williams, R.:Con Ob, w. D. Spieth (cnd), Lehigh Valley CO Koch International Classics ▲ KIC 7023–2 [DDD] ■ 3–7023–4 (D)
Wilder, A.:Con Ob, w. M. Barrett (cnd), Brooklyn PO Koch International Classics ▲ KIC 7187 [DDD]
Wilder, A.:Piece Ob, w. M. Barrett (cnd), Brooklyn PO Koch International Classics ▲ KIC 7187 [DDD]
Wolf-Ferrari, E.:Idillio-Concertino, w. D. Spieth (cnd), Lehigh Valley CO Koch International Classics ▲ KIC 7023–2 [DDD] ■ 3–7023–4 (D)

Lucas, Andrew (org)
The English Anthem, w. [cnd:John Scott], St. Paul's Cathedral Choir Hyperion ▲ CDA 66519 [DDD]
The English Anthem, Vol. 4, w. [cnd:John Scott], St. Paul's Cathedral Choir Hyperion ▲ CDA 66678 [DDD]
The English Anthem, Vol. 5, w. [cnd:John Scott], St. Paul's Cathedral Choir Hyperion ▲ CDA 66758
Famous Organ Works *(rec St. Paul's Cathedral, London, Jan 3,4,6, 1994)* Naxos 4–▲ 8.504014 [DDD]
Goss, J.:O Saviour of the World, w. Maldwyn Davies (ten), David Wilson-Johnson (bar), John Scott (cnd), St. Paul's Cathedral Choir, St. Paul's Cathedral Special Choir Conifer Classics ▲ 75605–51193–2 [DDD]
Organ Showpieces from St. Paul's Cathedral *(rec Jan. 2, 4 & 6, 1994)* Naxos ▲ 8.550955 [DDD]
Psalms from St. Paul's, Vol. 2, w. St. Paul's Cathedral Choir [cnd:John Scott] Hyperion ▲ CDP 11002
Psalms from St. Paul's, Vol. 5, w. St. Paul's Cathedral Choir [cnd:John Scott] Hyperion ▲ 11005
St. Paul's Cathedral Organ Mirabilis ▲ MRCD 905 [DDD]
Stainor, J.:The Crucifixion, w. Maldwyn Davies (ten), David Wilson-Johnson (bar), John Scott (cnd), St. Paul's Cathedral Choir, St. Paul's Cathedral Special Choir Conifer Classics ▲ 75605–51193–2 [DDD]

Lucas, Brenda (pno)
Arensky, A.:Suite 1 for 2 Pnos, w. John Ogdon (pno) EMI Classics 2–▲ CDFB 69386
Bizet, G.:Jeux d'enfants, w. John Ogdon (pno) EMI Classics 2–▲ CDFB 69386
Debussy, C.:Petite Suite, w. John Ogdon (pno) EMI Classics 2–▲ CDFB 69386
Khachaturian, A.:Gayane (sels), w. John Ogdon (pno)—Sabre Dance [arr. 2 Pnos] EMI Classics 2–▲ CDFB 69386
Ogdon, J.:Pno Music—5 Preludes (early 1960s); Sonatina (1965); Sonata No. 4 ("An American Sonata"—1984); 25 Preludes (1985) Gamut Classics ▲ GAM 528 [DDD]
Rachmaninoff, S.:Duets Pno 4–Hands, w. John Ogdon (pno) EMI Classics 2–▲ CDFB 69386
Rachmaninoff, S.:Suite 1 for 2 Pnos, w. John Ogdon (pno) EMI Classics 2–▲ CDFB 69386
Rachmaninoff, S.:Suite 2 for 2 Pnos, w. John Ogdon (pno) EMI Classics 2–▲ CDFB 69386
Rawsthorne, A.:Con Pnos, w. John Ogdon (pno), J. Pritchard (cnd), London PO IMP ("BBC Radio Classics" series) ▲ IMP 5691762
Saint-Saëns, C.:Carnival of the Animals, w. J. Ogdon (pno), L. Frémaux (cnd), City of Birmingham SO Klavier ▲ KCD 11011 [ADD]
Saint-Saëns, C.:Carnival of the Animals, w. J. Ogdon (pno), L. Frémaux (cnd), City of Birmingham SO Klavier ■ KC 527
Shostakovich, D.:Concertino for 2 Pnos, w. John Ogdon (pno) EMI Classics 2–▲ CDFB 69386

Lucas, Hélène (pno)
Gouvy, T.:Songs, w. Cyrille Gerstenhaber (sop)—sels from 40 poèmes of Ronsard & 18 sonnets & chansons of Desportes *(rec l'Auditorium Tibor Varga à Sion, July 27 – Aug 1, 1995)* K617 ▲ 7054 [DDD]

Lucas, Scott (org)
1812 Priory ▲ PRCD 238 [DDD]

Lucas, Wendy Horner (hp)—see ORCHESTRAS & ENSEMBLES Glorian Duo

Lucche, A. dalle (s sax)—see ORCHESTRAS & ENSEMBLES Seicentonovecento Ensemble

Lucchetti, Alessandro (pno)
Busoni, F.:Fant contrappuntistica Pno 4–Hands, w. P. Giarmana (pno) Nuova Era ▲ NUO 7161 [DDD]
Busoni, F.:Finnländische Volksweisen, w. P. Giarmana (pno) Nuova Era ▲ NUO 7161 [DDD]
Busoni, F.:Improvisation on Bach's *Wie wohl ist mir*, w. P. Giarmana (pno) Nuova Era ▲ NUO 7161 [DDD]
Chabrier, E.:Pno Music 4–Hands, w. P. Giarmanà (pno)—España; 3 Valses romantiques [both for 2 Pnos]; Cortège burlesque; Bourrée fantasque; Prélude et marche française; Souvenirs de Munich [Quadrille sur les themes favoris de Tristan et Isolde] [all for Pno 4–Hands] *(rec RSI studio Auditorio, Lugano, 1994)* Gallo ▲ CD 818 [DDD]
Liszt, F.:Pno Music (misc), w. P. Giarmanà (pno)—Rhap Hongroise No. 2; Gaudeamus Igitur; Fest Polonaise; Weihnachtsbaum Gallo ▲ CD 817

INSTRUMENT.

Luccini, V. (cembalo)
Vivaldi, A.:Sons Vn, Op. 5, w. F. Fantini (vn), M. Ferarris (vn), A. Ephrikaim (vn), A. Pocaterra (vc), G. Ghetti (vc), I. De Carli (cembalo) Rivoalto ▲ CRA 9005 [ADD]

Lucia, Paco de (gtr)
Albéniz, I.:Iberia Suite, w. J. Bandera (gtr), J. Cañizares (gtr) [trans Paco de Lucia for 3 gtrs] Verve ▲ 314-510301-2
Pavarotti & Friends for War Child, w. Luciano Pavarotti (ten), Eric Clapton (sgr), Sheryl Crow (sgr), Elton John (sgr), Liza Minelli (sgr), Joan Osborne (sgr), Jon Secada (sgr), Eric Clapton (gtr), John McLaughlin (gtr), Marco Armiliato, Edoardo Bennato, José Molina, Al DiMeola, Kelly Family, Ligabue, Litfiba, P *(rec Modena, Italy, 1996)* London ▲ 452900-2 ■ 452900-4
Rodrigo, J.:Concierto de Aranjuez, w. E. Colomer (cnd), Orch de Cadaques Verve ▲ 314-510301-2

Lücke, Markus (cl)
Austin, E.:Gathering Threads Capstone ▲ CPS 8625
Austin, E.:Music of, w. Jeananne Albee (pno), Jerome Reed (pno), Mary Lou Rylands (vc), Ursula Trede–Boettcher (hpd), Sibylle Dotzauer (pno), Constitution Brass, Gerald Kegelmann (cnd), Heidelberg State Music School Chamber Choir—To Begin for Brass Qnt; Klavier Double for Pno & Tape; Circling for Vc & Pno; Lighthouse I for solo Hpd; Gathering Threads for solo Cl; Zodiac Suite for Pno; An Die Nachgeborenen [To Those Born Later] Capstone ▲ CPS 8625

Luckhardt, Hilmar (fl)
Partch, H.:Settings (2) from "Finnegan's Wake", w. Lola Harding (sop), Dorothy Holden (fl), Harry Partch (kithara) *(rec 1945)* Innova 4-▲ 401

Luckhardt, Hilmar (tin whistle)
Partch, H.:Yankee Doodle Fant, w. Lola Harding (sop), Don Thompson (tin whistle/ob), Lee Hoiby (flex-a-tones), Harry Partch (chromelodeon) *(rec 1945)* Innova 4-▲ 401

Lucktenberg, George (hpd)
Couperin, L.:Chaconnes & Passacailles—Passacaille in C ACA Digital Recording ■ CM 20016
Forqueray, A.:Pièces de viole [trans. by composer's son, Jean Baptiste for harpsichord]—La Couperin; La Leclair; La Sylva; La Mandoline ACA Digital Recording ■ CM 20016
Froberger, J.J.:Hpd Music—Tombeau fait à Paris sur la mort de M. Blancrocher ACA Digital Recording ■ CM 20016
Hakim, N.:Suite Hpd, "Shasta" ACA Digital Recording ■ CM 20016
Jacquet De La Guerre, E.:Le Raccomondement comique de Pierrot et de Nicole—in a ACA Digital Recording ■ CM 20016

Ludewig-Verdehr, Elsa (cl)—see ORCHESTRAS & ENSEMBLES Verdehr Trio

Ludwig, Günter (pno)
Baur, J.:Moments musicaux, w. I. Ozim (vn) *(rec Sept. 30, 1977)* Koch Schwann ▲ SCH 311982 [ADD/DDD]

Ludwig, Mark (va)—see also ORCHESTRAS & ENSEMBLES Hawthorne String Quartet
Schulhoff, E.:Concertino Fl, w. F. Smith (fl), E. Barker (db)—Andante con moto moderato; Furiant; Andante; Rondino *(rec May 1992)* Northeastern ▲ NR 248-CD

Ludwig, Michael (vn)
Coleridge-Taylor, S.:Ballade, w. V. Eskin (pno) *(rec 9/90)* Koch International Classics ▲ KIC 7056-2 [DDD]

Ludwig, William (bn)
Brahms, J.:Son 1 Cl, w. A. Epperson (pno) [trans for bn & pno] Centaur ▲ CRC 2130
Hayden, P.:Hambidge Quavers, w. M. Ostoich (ob) Opus One ▲ CD 154
Prokofiev, S.:Son Fl, w. A. Epperson (pno) [bassoon & piano trans.] Centaur ▲ CRC 2130
Schumann, R.:Fantasiestücke Cl, w. A. Epperson (pno) [bassoon & piano trans.] Centaur ▲ CRC 2130

Lueders, Kurt (org)
Romantic Rarities AFKA ▲ SK 514 [DDD] ■ SKL 325

Luft, Carlo van (car)
The Carillon of the St. Rombouts Cathedral at Malines, w. Geert D'hollander (car), Jos D'hollander (car), Eddy Marien (car) René Gailly ▲ CD 88903 [DDD]

Lugli, Lorenzo (va)—see ORCHESTRAS & ENSEMBLES Paganini String Quartet

Lugossy, Melinda (pno)
Truscott, H.:Son Vc, w. Judit Kiss Domonkos (vc) *(rec Alpha-Line Studio, Festetich Castle, Budapest, 1994)* Marco Polo ▲ 8.223727 [DDD]
Truscott, H.:Son 1 Cl, w. István Varga (cl) *(rec Alpha-Line Studio, Festetich Castle, Budapest, 1994)* Marco Polo ▲ 8.223727 [DDD]

Luisada, Jean-Marc (pno)
Chopin, F.:Pno Music (misc), w. Martha Argerich (pno), Vladimir Ashkenazy (pno), Stanislav Bunin (pno), Halina Czerny-Stefanska (pno), Jan Ekier (pno), Yuval Fichman (pno), Kemal Gekic (pno), Adam Harasiewicz (pno), Krzysztof Jablonski (pno), Louis Kentner (pno), Garrick Ohlsson (pno), Ivo Pogorelich (pno), Maurizio Pollini (pno), Dang Thai Son (pno)—includes Ballade (Nos. 1 & 2); Barcarolle, Op. 60; Concerto Nos. 1 & 2; Études (Op. 10, Nos. 1, 5, 8, 10 & 12 & Op. 25, No. 10, 18 & 25); Grand valse brillante; Impromptus (Nos. 3 & 4); Mazurkas (Op. 24, Nos. 1–4; Op. 30, Nos. 1–4; Op. 50, No. 32; Op. 59, Nos. 1–3); Nocturnes (Op. 9, No. 3; Op. 37, No. 12; Op. 48, No. 13; Op. 55, No. 16)Polonaise (Op. 40, Nos. 3 & 4; Op. 44, No. 5; Op. 53, No. 6; Op. 61, No. 7); Preludes (Op. 28 Nos. 13–18, 21–24 & Op. 45, No. 25); Scherzos (Nos. 1–3); Sonatas (Nos. 2 & 3); Waltzes (No. 1 & 6) LaserLight 5-▲ 15 961 [ADD/DDD]

Luisi, D. (baroque vn)—see ORCHESTRAS & ENSEMBLES Il Parnaso Musicale

Luit, Peter (db)—see ORCHESTRAS & ENSEMBLES Ives Ensemble members

Lujyendijk, Leo (va)
Klatzow, P.:Qt Strs, w. Petri Salonen (vn), Jürgen Schwietering (vn), Eric Martens (vc) Claremont ▲ GSE 1524

Lukács, Peter (va)
Erkel, F.:Intro & Verbunkos, w. I. Kassai (pno) Marco Polo ▲ 8.223317
Schubert, Franz:Qt Fl, w. Z. Jeney (fl), Szendrey-Karper (gtr), Banda (vc) White Label ▲ HRC 146 [ADD]

Lukas, Kathryn (fl)
Tavener, J.:To a Child Dancing in the Wind, w. P. Rozario (sop), S. Tees (va), H. Tunstall (hp) Collins Classics ▲ COL 1428 [DDD]

Lukavsky, Radovan (tpt)
Eben, Petr:Vox clamantis, w. V. Neumann (cnd), Czech PO Panton ▲ 81 1141-2911

Luke, Jeffrey (tpt)—see ORCHESTRAS & ENSEMBLES Atlantic Brass Quintet

Lukin, Valentin (vn)
Ustvolskaya, G.:Octet Obs, w. Nicolay Neretin (ob), Piotr Tosenko (ob), Alexander Stang (vn), Olga Ribaltchenko (vn), Nikolay Tkachenko (vn), Valerii Znamenskii (timp), Oleg Malov (pno), O. Malov (cnd) *(rec St. Petersburg Radio House, Oct. & Nov. 1994)* Megadisc ▲ 7865

Lukowicz, Elzbieta Stefanska (hpd)
Cimarosa, D.:Con Hpd, w. R. Schumacher (cnd), Masterplayers Fonit Cetra ("Italia" series) ▲ FCT CDC 98
Cimarosa, D.:Sinfs Hpd, w. R. Schumacher (cnd), Masterplayers—in B♭ [L'Italiana in londra]; in D [Caio Mario]; in D [I Due Supposti Conti] Fonit Cetra ("Italia" series) ▲ FCT CDC 98

Lukowicz, Jerzy (pno)—see ORCHESTRAS & ENSEMBLES Wawelskie Trio

Lukowski, Guy (gtr)
Guitar Festival Pavane ▲ ADW 7263 [DDD]

Lumsden, Andrew (org)
Bliss, A.:Choral Music, w. P. Spicer (cnd), Finzi Wind Ensemble, Finzi Singers—Shield of Faith for Chorus & Organ (1975); The world is charged with the grandeur of God for Chorus, Winds & Brass (1969); [a cappella works]—Birthday Song for a Royal Child (1959); River Music (1967); Mar Portugues (1973) [E] Chandos ▲ CHAN 8980 [DDD]
Howells, H.:Choral Music, w. Paul Spicer (cnd), Finzi Singers—Te Deum; Thee Will I Love; Haec dies; Blessed Are the Dead; Behold O God Our Defender; Inheritance; Here Is the Little Door; A Spotless Rose; Sing Lullaby; Even Such Is Time; God Is Gone Up; The Scribe Chandos ▲ CHAN 9458
Psalms Vol. 1, Psalms from the first half of the Psalter, w. Westminster Abbey Choristers [cnd:M. Neary] Virgin Classics ▲ CDC 59632

Lumsden, Andrew (org) (cont.)
Walton, W.:Choral Music, w. Finzi Singers—Coronation Te Deum; Set Me as a Seal upon Thy Heart; Jubilate Deo; 4 Christmas Carols; The Twelve; Magnificat and Nunc Dimittis; A Litany; Missa Brevis; Cantico del Sole; Where Does the Uttered Music Go; Antiphon Chandos ▲ CHAN 9222 [DDD]

Lund, Odd (goat's hn)
Habbestad, K.:Moster Suite, w. Kristin Kjølberg (sop), Njål Sparbo (bar), T. Mikkelsen (cnd), Lithuanian National SO, Oslo Phil Women's Chamber Choir Norway Music ▲ 2912
Habbestad, K.:Song-Dance, w. Ashild Watne (Medieval lyre), T. Mikkelsen (cnd), Scapoli, Oslo Phil Women's Chamber Choir Norway Music ▲ 2912

Lundén, Elisif (pno)
Debussy, C.:Chansons de Bilitis, w. Märta Schéle (sop) *(rec Nacka Aula, Nacka, Sweden, Aug. 14, 1975)* BIS ▲ CD 28 [AAD]
Debussy, C.:Chansons de Bilitis, w. Märta Schéle (sop) *(rec Nacka Aula, Nacka, Sweden, Aug 13 & 14, 1975)* BIS ▲ CD 34 [AAD]
Gefors, H.:Songs of Trusting (4), w. *(vocalist unknown)* BIS ▲ CD 38
Hallnäs, H.:Songs, w. Marta Schele (sop), Birgit Finnila (cta), Rolf Leanderson (bar)—3 sels BIS ▲ CD 38
Lidholm, I.:Songs, w. *(vocalist unknown)*—6 sels BIS ▲ CD 38
Milhaud, D.:Catalogue de fleurs, w. Märta Schéle (sop) *(rec Nacka Aula, Nacka, Sweden, Aug 13 & 14, 1975)* BIS ▲ CD 34 [AAD]
Nystroem, G.:Songs, w. Marta Schele (sop), Birgit Finnila (cta), Rolf Leanderson (bar)—3 sels BIS ▲ CD 38
Nystroem, G.:Songs at the Sea, w. Marta Schele (sop), Birgit Finnila (cta), Rolf Leanderson (bar) BIS ▲ CD 38
Ravel, M.:Mélodies populaires grecques, w. Märta Schéle (sop) *(rec Nacka Aula, Nacka, Sweden, Aug 13 & 14, 1975)* BIS ▲ CD 34 [AAD]
Rosenberg, H.:Chinese Songs, w. Marta Schele (sop), Birgit Finnila (cta), Rolf Leanderson (bar) BIS ▲ CD 38
Werle, L.J.:Night Hunt, w. Marta Schele (sop), Birgit Finnila (cta), Rolf Leanderson (bar) BIS ▲ CD 38

Lundkvist, Erik (org)
Rangström, T.:Sym 4, w. Y. Ahronovitch (cnd), Stockholm PO *(rec Stockholm Concert Hall, Jan. 16 & 18, 1985)* Caprice ▲ CAP 21195 [DDD]
Thybo, L.:Aus dem Stundenbuch, w. S. Lange (mez) *(rec Vangede Church, Mar. 13, Apr. 11, 12 & 25)* Marco Polo/Dacapo ▲ 8.224009 [DDD]
Thybo, L.:Mvt symphonique, w. J. Petersen (trbn) *(rec Vangede Church, Mar. 13, Apr. 11, 12 & 25)* Marco Polo/Dacapo ▲ 8.224009 [DDD]

Lung, Daian (hn)
Haydn, J.:Con for 2 Hns, w. Vasile Oprea (hn), C. Mandeal (cnd), Cluj-Napoca PO Electrecord ▲ ELCD 107 [AAD]
Schumann, R.:Konzertstück Hns, w. V. Oprea (hn), A. Marc (hn), T. Tulbure (hn), C. Mandeal (cnd), Cluj-Napoca PO Electrecord ▲ ELCD 107 [AAD]

Lunn, Doug (fretless bass)
Passage, 138 B.C.-A.D. 1611, w. Empire Brass Quintet, Laurie Monahan (sgr), M. Collver (sgr), Pete Maunu (acoustic/elec/12string gtr), D. Goldblatt (syn), K. Wortman (elec/acoustic perc) *(rec Lenox, MA & Los Angeles, CA May 27-29 & June 28-July)* Telarc ▲ CD 80355 [DDD]

Lunt, Sam (bongos)
Allen, J.:Di Me, Lluvia, w. Carol Redman (fl/whistle), Toni Austin-Allen (pno/claves), Tom Maguire (perc) *(rec Santuario de Guadalupe, Sante Fe, NM, Sept 29-30, 1995)* Wild Iris ▲ WI 001

Lunt, Sam (mar)
Allen, J.:In Memory of a Once New World, w. Ron Grinage (pno), Tom Maguire (perc) *(rec Santuario de Guadalupe, Sante Fe, NM, Sept 29-30, 1995)* Wild Iris ▲ WI 001

Lunt, Sam (perc)
Allen, J.:Brazilian Son, w. Ron Grinage (pno), Shana Norton (hp), Carol Redman (fl), Charly Drobeck (fl/alt fl/pic), Tom Maguire (perc) *(rec Santuario de Guadalupe, Sante Fe, NM, Sept 29-30, 1995)* Wild Iris ▲ WI 001

Luolajan-Mikkola, Mikko-Ville (vn)
Braxton, A.:Composition 144, w. Anthony Braxton (fl/s sax/a sax), Seppo Baron Paakkunainen (fl/t sax/br sax), Pentti Lahti (fl/s sax/a sax), Pepa Päivinen (fl/t sax/sop sax/b cl), Mircea Stan (trbn), Teppo Hauta-aho (db/vc), Jukka Wasama (dr) *(rec Järvenpää House, Järvenpää, Finland, Nov 7, 1988)* Leo ▲ LR 233
Braxton, A.:Composition 145, w. Anthony Braxton (fl/s sax/a sax), Seppo Baron Paakkunainen (fl/t sax/br sax), Pentti Lahti (fl/s sax/a sax), Pepa Päivinen (fl/t sax/sop sax/b cl), Mircea Stan (trbn), Teppo Hauta-aho (db/vc), Jukka Wasama (dr) *(rec Järvenpää House, Järvenpää, Finland, Nov 7, 1988)* Leo ▲ LR 233

Lupo, B. (pno)
Rota, N.:Con-soirée, w. M. de Bernart (cnd), Sicilian SO Nuova Era ▲ 7063 [DDD]

Lupsa, Marius (cl)
Hollós, M.:Dúli-dúli, w. Zoltán Rémann (cl), Marian Ghisa (cl) *(rec Academy of Music G. Dima in Cluj)* Hungaroton ("Classic" series) ▲ HCD 31572 [DDD]

Luptáčik, Jozef (cl)
Hummel, J.N.:Qt Cl, w. Bratislava String Trio *(rec Moyzes Hall of the Slovak Philharmonic, Bratislava, June 1995)* Slovart ▲ SR 0011-2-131 [DDD]
Mozart, W.A.:Con Cl, w. R. Edlinger (cnd), Mozart Academy *(rec Concert Hall of the Slovak PO, Bratislava, July 1987)* Lydian ▲ 18058 [DDD]

Lupták, Jozef (vc)—see also ORCHESTRAS & ENSEMBLES Albrecht String Quartet
Godár, V.:Déploration sur la mort de Witold Lutoslawski, w. Eleonóra Škutová-Slaničková (pno), Peter Biely (vn), Ivana Pristašová (vn), Peter Šesták (va)*(rec Residence of Slovak Composers, Apr 1996)* Slovart ▲ SR 0018-2-131 [DDD]
Godár, V.:Ricercar, w. Eleonóra Škutová-Slaničková (pno), Ivana Pristašová (vn), Peter Šesták (va)*(rec Residence of Slovak Composers, Apr 1996)* Slovart ▲ SR 0018-2-131 [DDD]
Godár, V.:Talisman, w. Eleonóra Škutová-Slaničková (pno), Peter Krajniak (vn)*(rec Residence of Slovak Composers, Apr 1996)* Slovart ▲ SR 0018-2-131 [DDD]

Lupu, Radu (pno)
Beethoven, L. van:Son 8 Pno, "Pathétique" London ("Weekend Classics" series) ▲ 421031-2 [AAD] ■ 421031-4
Beethoven, L. van:Son 14 Pno, "Moonlight Son" London ("Weekend Classics" series) ▲ 421031-2 [AAD] ■ 421031-4
Beethoven, L. van:Son 21 Pno, "Waldstein" London ("Weekend Classics" series) ▲ 421031-2 [AAD] ■ 421031-4
Brahms, J.:Intermezzos Pno, Op. 117 London ▲ 417599-2 [ADD]
Brahms, J.:Pieces Pno, Op. 118 London ▲ 417599-2 [ADD]
Brahms, J.:Pieces Pno, Op. 119 London ▲ 417599-2 [ADD]
Brahms, J.:Rhaps Pno, Op. 79 London ▲ 417599-2 [ADD]
Busoni, F.:Fant mechanical Org, w. M. Perahia (pno) Sony Classical ▲ SK 44915
Debussy, C.:Son Vn, w. H.-Y. Chung (hp) London ▲ 421154-2 [ADD]
Franck, C.:Son Vn, w. K. W. Chung (vn) London ▲ 421154-2 [ADD]
Mozart, W.A.:Andante & Vars Pno 4-Hands, w. M. Perahia (pno) Sony Classical ▲ SK 44915
Mozart, W.A.:Con 7 Pnos, w. M. Perahia (pno), English CO [arr. Mozart for 2 pianos & orch.] Sony Classical ▲ SK 44915
Mozart, W.A.:Con 10 Pnos, w. M. Perahia (pno), English CO Sony Classical ▲ SK 44915
Mozart, W.A.:Con 10 Pnos, w. A. Previn (pno), A. Previn (cnd), London SO EMI Classics ▲ CDM 65180
Mozart, W.A.:Son Pnos, K.448, w. M. Perahia (pno) CBS ▲ MK 39511 [DDD]
Schubert, Franz:Fant Pno, D.940, w. M. Perahia (pno) CBS ▲ MK 39511 [DDD]
Schubert, Franz:Son Pno, D.157 London ("Jubilee" series) ▲ 425033-2 [ADD]
Schubert, Franz:Son Pno, D.664 London ▲ 440295-2 [DDD]
Schubert, Franz:Son Pno, D.784 London ("Jubilee" series) ▲ 425033-2 [ADD]
Schubert, Franz:Son Pno, D.845 London ▲ 417640-2 [ADD]
Schubert, Franz:Son Pno, D.894 London ▲ 417640-2 [ADD]
Schubert, Franz:Son Pno, D.959 London ("Jubilee" series) ▲ 425033-2 [ADD]

Lupu, Radu (pno) (cont.)
Schubert, Franz:Son Pno, D.960 London ▲ 440295-2 [DDD]
Schubert, Franz:Songs (comp), w. B. Hendricks (sop), S. Meyer (cl), B. Schneider (hn)—Der Hirt auf dem Felsen; Lachen und weinen; Ständchen; Die Männer sind méchant, Auf dem Strom; Sehnsucht; Liebesbotschaft; Versunken; An den Mond; Du liebst mich nicht; Die Liebe hat gelogen; Die junge Nonne; Klaglied; Ellens Gesang III; Delphine; Heidenröslein [G] EMI Classics ▲ CDC 54239
Schumann, R.:Humoreske Pno *(rec Salle de Châtonneyre, Corseaux, Switzerland, Jan 1993)* London ▲ 440496-2 [DDD]
Schumann, R.:Kinderszenen *(rec Salle de Châtonneyre, Corseaux, Switzerland, Jan 1993)* London ▲ 440496-2 [DDD]
Schumann, R.:Kreisleriana *(rec Salle de Châtonneyre, Corseaux, Switzerland, Jan 1993)* London ▲ 440496-2 [DDD]

Lupu, Sherban (vn)
Ernst, H.W.:Adagio sentimentale, w. Peter Pettinger (pno) Continuum ▲ CON 1017 [DDD]
Ernst, H.W.:Airs hongrois variés, w. Peter Pettinger (pno) Continuum ▲ CON 1017 [DDD]
Ernst, H.W.:Polonaise Vn, w. Peter Pettinger (pno) Continuum ▲ CON 1017 [DDD]
Ernst, H.W.:Rondo Papageno, w. Peter Pettinger (pno) Continuum ▲ CON 1017 [DDD]
Wieniawski, H.:Adagio élégiaque, w. Peter Pettinger (pno) Continuum ▲ CON 1017 [DDD]
Wieniawski, H.:Le Carnaval russe, w. Peter Pettinger (pno) Continuum ▲ CON 1017 [DDD]
Wieniawski, H.:Fant orientale, w. Peter Pettinger (pno) Continuum ▲ CON 1017 [DDD]
Wieniawski, H.:Grand caprice fantastique, w. Peter Pettinger (pno) Continuum ▲ CON 1017 [DDD]

Luria, M. Knoll (pno)
Mozart, W.A.:Con 26 Pno, w. P. Freeman (cnd), London SO Centaur ▲ CRC 2093 [DDD]
Mozart, W.A.:Son 9 Pno Centaur ▲ CRC 2093 [DDD]
Mozart, W.A.:Son 12 Pno Centaur ▲ CRC 2093 [DDD]

Lurie, Mitchell (cl)
Brahms, J.:Qnt Cl, w. Muir String Quartet EcoClassics ▲ ECO CD 001
Mozart, W.A.:Qnt Cl, K.581, w. Muir String Quartet *(rec Jan. 2–5, 1992)* EcoClassics ▲ ECO CD 001
Ravel, M.:Intro & Allegro, w. Ann Mason Stockton (hp), Arthur Gleghorn (fl), Hollywood String Quartet Testament ▲ TESSBT 1053 (m) [ADD]

Lush, Ernest (pno)
Jacqueline Du Pré:Her Early BBC Recordings, Vol. 2, w. Jacqueline Du Pré (vc), William Pleeth (vc) EMI Classics ▲ CDM 63166
A Recital of Russian & Polish Songs, w. Alfred Orda (bar), Josephine Lee (pno) Symposium ▲ SYM 1067

Lushtak, Faina (pno)
Rachmaninoff, S.:Morceaux de fant *(rec Recital Hall, Univ of New Orleans, Apr & May 1995)* Centaur ▲ CRC 2287 [DDD]
Rachmaninoff, S.:Preludes Pno, Opp 23 & 32—Opp. 23/6 & 32/5, 8 & 12 *(rec Recital Hall, Univ of New Orleans, Apr & May 1995)* Centaur ▲ CRC 2287 [DDD]
Scriabin, A.:Son 2 Pno *(rec Recital Hall, Univ of New Orleans, Apr & May 1995)* Centaur ▲ CRC 2287 [DDD]
Scriabin, A.:Son 3 Pno *(rec Recital Hall, Univ of New Orleans, Apr & May 1995)* Centaur ▲ CRC 2287 [DDD]

Lustman, Julie (pno)
Regondi, G.:Serenade, w. D. Rogers (conc) Bridge ▲ BCD 9039 [DDD]
Regondi, G.:Songs, w. D'Anna Fortunato (mez)—As Slowly Part the Shades of Night; L'Avviso; Tell Me Heart! Why So Desponding?; Absence *(rec Feb. & May, 1994)* Bridge ▲ BCD 9055 [DDD]

Lüthi, Marianne (rcr)
Blavet, M.:Recueil de pièces, w. Manfred Harras (rcr), Brian Franklin (vl), Rudolf Scheidegger (hpd)—Prélude de Mr. Blavet; Pourquoi doux Rossignols; Entrée de chasse *(rec Reformierte Kirche, Arlesheim, Schweiz, May 18–19, 1987)* Musicaphon ▲ 56802 [DDD]
Boismortier, J.B. de:Chamber Music, w. Manfred Harras (rcr), Richard Gwilt (baroque vn), Arno Jochem (vl), Brian Franklin (vl), Sally Fortino (hps)—Con. in C, "Zampogna"; Son. in F, Op. 91/1; Son. in A, Op. 10/2; Trio Son. in D, Op. 37/3; Son. in e, Op. 34/3; Con. in A, Op. 38/4; Suite No. 1, Op. 59; Balet de village en trio, Op. 52/4 *(rec Reformed Church, Bubendorf, Switzerland, Feb. 9–11, 1989)* Musicaphon ▲ 56812 [DDD]
Dornel, L.-A.:Concert 1, w. Manfred Harras (rcr), Brian Franklin (vl), Rudolf Scheidegger (hpd) *(rec Reformierte Kirche, Arlesheim, Schweiz, May 18–19, 1987)* Musicaphon ▲ 56802 [DDD]
Philidor, P.:Music of, w. Manfred Harras (rcr), Brian Franklin (vl), Rudolf Scheidegger (hpd)—Première suite in C; Deuxième suite in B; Septième suite in b *(rec Reformierte Kirche, Arlesheim, Schweiz, May 18–19, 1987)* Musicaphon ▲ 56802 [DDD]

Lüthy, Johannes (va)
Krommer, F.:Qt Bn, Op. 46/1, w. Eckart Hbner (bn), Steuart Eaton (va), Reinhard Latzko (vc) *(rec Hans-Rosbaud Studio, Oct 10–11, 1994)* CPO ▲ CPO 999297-2 [DDD]
Krommer, F.:Qt Bn, Op. 46/2, w. Eckart Hbner (bn), Steuart Eaton (va), Reinhard Latzko (vc) *(rec Hans-Rosbaud Studio, Oct 10–11, 1994)* CPO ▲ CPO 999297-2 [DDD]

Lütschg, Andrej (vn)
Ave Maria, w. [cnd:Alphons von Aarburg], Zurich Boys' Choir, Daniel Perret (trb), Frieder Lang (ten), Alain Clément (bass), Praxedis Rütti (hp), Daniel Winiger (org) Tudor ▲ TUD 7029 [DDD]

Lutszke, M. (vc)
Bach, J.S.:Cons Vn (comp), w. J. Schröder (vn), S. Ritchie, N. TeBrake, R. Brown, J. Griffin, M. Willems, A. Fuller *(rec June 6–8, 1986)* Reference ▲ RR 23 CD [DDD]
Vivaldi, A.:Cons for 2 Vns, w. J. Schröder (vn), S. Ritchie (vn), N. TeBrake (vn), R. Brown (vn), J. Griffin (va), M. Willems (db), A. Fuller (hpd) *(rec June 6–8, 1986)* Reference ▲ RR 23 CD [DDD]
Vivaldi, A.:Sinf, RV.116, w. J. Schröder (vn), S. Ritchie (vn), J. Griffin (va), M. Willems (db), A. Fuller (hpd) *(rec June 6–8, 1986)* Reference ▲ RR 23 CD [DDD]
Vivaldi, A.:Trio Sons 2 Vns & Bc, w. J. Schröder (vn), S. Ritchie (vn), A. Fuller (hpd)—RV.73 *(rec June 6–8, 1986)* Reference ▲ RR 23 CD [DDD]

Luttinger, Laurance (perc)
Caltabiano, R.:Torched Liberty, w. N. Pilgrim (sop), V. Pritsker (vn), G. Macero (vc), L. Greene (pic/fl/alt fl), K. Schempf (E♭/A/B♭ cl), G. Coble (tpt), S. Heyman (pno), R. Caltabiano (cnd) Opus One ▲ CD 168 [DDD]
Willey, J.:Society Music, w. L. Greene (fl), G. Coble (tpt), W. Harris (trbn), D. Resue (hn), S. Heyman (pno), E. Gustafson (via), G. Macero (vc), E. Castilano (db), E. Murray (cnd) Opus One ▲ CD 168 [DDD]

Lutz, David (pno)
Mahler, G.:Lieder eines fahrenden Gesellen, w. T. Hampson (bar) Teldec ▲ 74002
Schubert, Franz:Die Schöne Müllerin, w. R. Holl (bar) [G] Preiser ▲ 93400
Schubert, Franz:Schwanengesang, w. Robert Hall (bar) Preiser ▲ PRE 93402 [DDD]
Schubert, Franz:Songs (misc), w. Robert Hall (bar)—selected Mayrhofer Lieder [Am Strome; Auf der Donau; Heliopolis I & II; Nach einem Gewitter; Liane; others] Pearl ▲ PEA 9155 [ADD]
Warren, E.R.:The Sleeping Beauty, w. Maria Venuti (mez—Princess), Thomas Hampson (bar—Prince), Gerd Nienstedt (b-bar—King), B. Ferden (cnd), Cracow RSO, Cracow Radio Chorus *(rec Church of the Bernardines, Cracow, Poland, June 21–24, 1993)* Cambria ▲ CD 1095 [DDD]

Lutz, Rudolf (pno)
Salut d'Amour, w. Kowalski, Andrzej (vn) *(rec Rosslyn Hill Unitarian Chapel, Hampstead, London)* Guild ▲ GMCD 7125 [DDD]

Lützelschwab, Cyril (cym)
Hauser, F.:Die Welle, w. Martin André Grütter (cym/tamtam), Roli Fischer (cym), Barbara Frey (cym), Lukas Rohner (cym), Severin Steinhauser (cym), Hans Ulrich (cym), Ruud Wiener (cym), Michael Erni (timp), Fran Lorkovic (timp), F. Hauser (cnd) *(rec Studio DRS, Basel, Switzerland, Nov. 6, 1988)* Hat Hut ▲ hat ART CD 6017 [ADD]

Lutzke, Myron (vc)—see also ORCHESTRAS & ENSEMBLES Mozartean Players, St. Luke's Chamber Ensemble, Old Fairfield Academy Orch members
A Baroque Christmas from the Metropolitan Museum of Art Concerts, w. Julianne Baird (sop), Aulos Ensemble [Anne Briggs (trns fl), Marc Schachman (baroque ob), Linda Quan (baroque vn), Arthur Haas (hpd/org)] MusicMasters ▲ 01612-67119-2 ■ 01612-67119-4

Lutzke, Myron (vc) (cont.)
In Concert, w. Kathleen Battle (sop), Jean-Pierre Rampal (fl), Anthony Newman (hpd), Margo Garrett (pno), John Steel Ritter (pno) *(rec Feb. 24, 1991)* Sony Classical ▲ SK 53106 [ADD] ■ ST 53106
Songs of Love & War:Italian Dramatic Songs of the 17th & 18th Centuries, w. Julianne Baird (sop), Colin Tilney (hpd) Dorian ▲ DOR 90104 [DDD]

Lutzky, Grigory (vn)—see ORCHESTRAS & ENSEMBLES Taneyev String Quartet

Luvisi, Lee (pno)
Bartók, B.:Son for 2 Pnos, w. G. Kalish (pno), R. Fitz (perc), Gottlieb (perc) *(rec Feb. 1, 1993)* Delos ▲ DE 3151 [DDD]
Brahms, J.:Gypsy Songs (8), w. J. DeGaetani (mez) *(rec , Aspen Music Festival 7/7/83)* Bridge ▲ BCD 9025 [ADD]
Brahms, J.:Songs, w. J. DeGaetani (mez), L. Dutton (va)—O kühler Wald, Op. 72/3; Verzagen, Op. 72/4; Geistliches Wiegenlied, Op. 91/2 [G] *(rec Aspen Music Festival 7/7/83)* Bridge ▲ BCD 9025 [ADD]
Fauré, G.:La Chanson d'Eve, w. J. DeGaetani (mez) [F] *(rec Aspen Music Festival 7/20/81)* Bridge ▲ BCD 9023 [ADD]
Hindemith, P.:Con Pno, w. L. Leighton Smith (cnd), Louisville Orch *(rec 1987)* Louisville ▲ LCD 002 [AAD]
Schumann, R.:Frauenliebe und -leben, w. J. DeGaetani (mez) [G] *(rec Aspen Music Festival, 7/7/83)* Bridge ▲ BCD 9025 [ADD]

Luy, André (org)
Martin, F.:Requiem, w. E. Speiser (sop), R. Bollen (cta), E. Tappy (ten), P. Lagger (bass), F. Martin (cnd), Swiss-Italian Orch, Union Chorale, Choir of Our Lady of Lausanne, Ars Laeta Vocal Group *(rec live, May 4, 1973)* Jecklin-Disco ▲ JD 631-2 [ADD]

Luzanov, Fedor (vc)
Rachmaninoff, S.:Trio élégiaque 2, w. Evgeni Svetlanov (pno), Leonid Kogan (vn) Russian Disc ▲ RUS 10046 [AAD]

Lydecker, Martin (trbn)
Scelsi, G.:Anahit, w. Paul Zukofsky (vn), Julie Bogorad (fl), Peggy Russell (fl), Courtney Westcott (fl), Lawrence McDonald (cl), Joan Waryha (cl), Jean Hansen (b cl), Bill Suite (e hn), Nita VanPelt (sax), Bob Zobal (tpt), John Carter (trbn), Stan Cortman (hn), Robert Ward (hn), William Curry (va), Jody Rowitsch (va), Irene Wade (va), Anne Fagerburg (vc), John Gockel (vc), Sue Manz (bass), Steven Stearman (bass) *(rec Oberlin Conservatory of Music, Oct 8, 1973)* CP² ▲ CP2 108 [AAD]

Lydolph, Mogens (vn)—see ORCHESTRAS & ENSEMBLES Copenhagen String Quartet

Lyjak, Wiktor (org)
Lewandowksi, L.L.:Org Music—5 Festive Preludes, Op. 37; Consolations, Op. 44; 5 Pieces for Harmonuim, Op. 46, Synogogen Melodien, Op. 47 Olympia ▲ OLY 399 [DDD]

Lyman, Kent (pno)
Thomson, V.:Synthetic Waltzes, w. L. Skelton (pno) *(rec Oct. 10 & 11, 1992 & Jan.)* Centaur ▲ CRC 2180 [DDD]

Lympany, Moura (pno)
Best Loved Piano Classics
Favorite Piano, w. Daniel Adni (pno), A. Brownridge (pno), J. Février (pno), J. Ogdon (pno), G. Tacchino (pno) Classics for Pleasure ▲ CDCFP 4622 [ADD/DDD]
Liszt, F.:Con 1 Pno, w. A. Fiedler (cnd), BBC Concert Orch IMP ("BBC Radio Classics" series) ▲ IMP 5691652
Prokofiev, S.:Con 3 Pno, w. A. Collins (cnd), London New SO Olympia ▲ OLY 191 [AAD]
Rachmaninoff, S.:Con 3 Pno, w. A. Collins (cnd), London New SO Olympia ▲ OLY 191 [AAD]

Lynch, Charles (pno)
Bax, A.:Son 3 Vn & Pno, w. May Harrison (vn) *(rec live 2/3/36)* Symposium ▲ 1075
Warlock, P.:Songs Bar, w. S. Austin (bar), M. Harrison (vn), H. Gaskell (ob)—(2) Ha'Nacker Mill; Away to Twiver *(rec live 2/3/36)* Symposium ▲ 1075

Lynch, Peter (gtr)
Fauré, G.:Pavane Orch, w. P. Davis (fl), J. Crellin (ob) [flute-oboe-guitar arr. Peter Lynch] Move ▲ MD 3090 [DDD]
Ponce, M.:Son 3 Gtr Move ▲ MD 3090 [DDD]
Ravel, M.:Pavane pour une infante défunte, w. P. Davis (fl), J. Crellin (ob) [flute-oboe-guitar arr. by Peter Lynch] Move ▲ MD 3090 [DDD]

Lyndon-Gee, Christopher (pno)
Markevitch, I.:L'Envol d'Icare, w. K. Lessing (pno), J. Gagelmann (perc), R. Haeger (perc), F. Lang (perc) *(rec July 10–11, 1993)* Largo ▲ 5127 [DDD]

Lyons, William (fl/rcr/bgps/shm/pipe/tabor/long-necked lt/perc)—see ORCHESTRAS & ENSEMBLES Dufay Collective

Lyons, William (fls/rcr)—see ORCHESTRAS & ENSEMBLES Kithara

Lysell, B. (vc)
Mozart, W.A.:Trio Pno, K.502, w. I. Wikström (pno), O. Karlsson (vc) Proprius ▲ PRCD 9054

Lysell, Bernt (vn)
Berwald, F.:Trios, w. L. Negro (pno), O. Karlsson (vc)—No. 3 Musica Sveciae ▲ MSCD 521 [DDD]
Mozart, W.A.:Sinf concertante Vn, K.364, w. N. Sparf (vn), J.-O. Wodin (cnd), Stockholm Sinfonietta BIS ▲ CD 205
Mozart, W.A.:Trio Pno, K.542, w. I. Wikström (pno), O. Karlsson (vc) Proprius ▲ PRCD 9054
Stenhammar, W.:Sentimental Romances, w. Borodin String Quartet Swedish Society ▲ SCD 1032

Lysy, Alberto (vn)
Bach, J.S.:Cons Vn (comp), w. Y. Menuhin (cnd), Camerata Lysy Discover International ▲ DICD 920138 [DDD]
Bach, J.S.:Con 2 Vn, w. Y. Menuhin (cnd), Camerata Lysy Gstaad Discover International ▲ DICD 92140 [DDD]
Bach, J.S.:Con Vn, BWV 1058, w. Y. Menuhin (cnd), Camerata Lysy Gstaad Discover International ▲ DICD 920138 [DDD]
Bach, J.S.:Sons Vn—in g, BWV 1001 Discover International ▲ DICD 920138 [DDD]
Haydn, J.:Con 1 Vn, w. A. Lysy (cnd), Camerata Lysy Gstaad *(rec Kirche Saanen-Gstaad, Nov 1979 & Feb 1983)* Claves ▲ CD 508303 [DDD]
Haydn, J.:Con 3 Vn, w. A. Lysy (cnd), Camerata Lysy Gstaad *(rec Kirche Saanen-Gstaad, Nov 1979 & Feb 1983)* Claves ▲ CD 508303 [DDD]
Haydn, J.:Con 4 Vn, w. A. Lysy (cnd), Camerata Lysy Gstaad *(rec Kirche Saanen-Gstaad, Nov 1979 & Feb 1983)* Claves ▲ CD 508303 [DDD]
International Menuhin Music Academy, w. International Menuhin Music Academy, Nora Chastain (vn), Paul Coletti (vn), Hu-Kun (vn), Mi-Kyung Lee (vn) Arcobaleno ▲ SBCD 4700 [DDD]
Purcell, H.:Chamber Music, w. Robert Masters (vn), Yehudi Menuhin (vn), Cecil Arnowitz (va), Walter Gerhard (va), Derek Simpson (vc), Ambrose Gauntlett (vl), Roy Jesson (hpd/org)—Trio Sons Nos. 2 in C, 6 in G & 8 in G; Fants Nos. 4 in g, 7 in c, 8 in d & 13 in F, "Upon One Note" EMI Classics ("Baroque" series) ▲ CDK 65734
Purcell, H.:Fants, w. Robert Masters (vn), Yehudi Menuhin (vn), Cecil Aronowitz (va), Walter Gerhard (va), Derek Simpson (vc), Ambrose Gauntlett (vl), Roy Jesson (hpd/org)—Nos. 4 in g, 7 in c, 8 in d, 13 in F EMI Classics ▲ CDK 65734
Purcell, H.:Sons (22) Vns, w. Robert Masters (vn), Yehudi Menuhin (vn), Cecil Aronowitz (va), Walter Gerhard (va), Derek Simpson (vc), Ambrose Gauntlett (vl), Roy Jesson (hpd/org)—Nos. 2, 6, & 8 EMI Classics ▲ CDK 65734
Ravel, M.:Berceuse sur le nom de Gabriel Fauré, w. A. Delle-Vigne (pno) Arcobaleno ▲ SBCD 6400 [DDD]
Ravel, M.:Son Vn Pno, w. A. Delle-Vigne (pno) Arcobaleno ▲ SBCD 6400 [DDD]
Ravel, M.:Sonate posthume, w. A. Delle-Vigne (pno) Arcobaleno ▲ SBCD 6400 [DDD]
Ravel, M.:Tzigane, w. A. Delle-Vigne (pno) Arcobaleno ▲ SBCD 6400 [DDD]
Telemann, G.P.:Cons Vn, w. Y. Menuhin (cnd), Camerata Lysy Discover International ▲ DICD 92140 [DDD]

Lysy, Oskar (va)
Reger, M.:Serenades Fl, Opp. 77a & 141a, w. A. Adorján (fl), A. Chumachenco (vn) Tudor ▲ TUD 755 [DDD]

Ma, Yo-Yo (alto vn)
Bartók, B.:Con Va, w. D. Zinman (cnd), Baltimore SO *(rec Joseph Meyerhoff Hall, Baltimore, MD, Mar. 6-7, 1993)* Sony Classical ▲ SK 57961 [DDD]; ■ ST 57961
Ma, Yo-Yo (vc)
Albert, S.:Con Vc, w. D. Zinman (cnd), Baltimore SO *(rec Joseph Meyerhoff Hall, Baltimore, MD, Mar 6-7, 1993)* Sony Classical ▲ SK 57961 [DDD]; ■ ST 57961
Anything Goes, w. Stéphane Grappelli (vn) CBS ▲ MK 45574 [DDD]
Bach, Joh. Christian:Sinf concertante, T.284/4, w. P. Zukerman (vn), P. Zukerman (cnd), St. Paul CO CBS ▲ MK 39964
Bach, J.S.:Sons Vl, BWV 1027-1029, w. K. Cooper (hpd) CBS ▲ MK 37794 [DDD] ■ IMT 37794 (D)
Bach, J.S.:Suites Vc, BWV 1007-1012—Nos. 5 & 6 CBS ■ IMT 39509 (D)
Bach, J.S.:Suites Vc, BWV 1007-1012 CBS 2-▲ M2K 37867
Barber, S.:Con Vc, w. Yo-Yo Ma, D. Zinman (cnd), Baltimore SO CBS ▲ MK 44900 [DDD]
Beethoven, L. van:Con Vn, Vc & Pno, "Triple Con", w. A. S. Mutter (vn), M. Zeltser (pno), H. von Karajan (cnd), Berlin PO Deutsche Grammophon ▲ 415276-2 [ADD]
Beethoven, L. van:Con Vn, Vc & Pno, "Triple Con", w. Itzhak Perlman (vn), Daniel Barenboim (pno), Berlin PO EMI Classics ▲ CDC 55516
Beethoven, L. van:Qt Pno, Op. 16, w. E. Ax (pno), I. Stern (vn), J. Laredo (va) *(rec Mar. 9-12, 1992)* Sony Classical ▲ SK 53339 [DDD]
Beethoven, L. van:Sons Vc (comp), w. E. Ax (pno) CBS 2-▲ M2K 42446 [DDD]
Beethoven, L. van:Son 1 Vc, w. E. Ax (pno) CBS ▲ MK 37251 [DDD] ■ IMT 37251 (D)
Beethoven, L. van:Son 2 Vc, w. E. Ax (pno) CBS ▲ MK 37251 [DDD] ■ IMT 37251 (D)
Beethoven, L. van:Son 3 Vc, w. E. Ax (pno) CBS ▲ MK 39024 [DDD] ■ IMT 39024 (D)
Beethoven, L. van:Son 4 Vc, w. E. Ax (pno) CBS ▲ MK 42121 [DDD]
Beethoven, L. van:Son 5 Vc, w. E. Ax (pno) CBS ▲ MK 39024 [DDD] ■ IMT 39024 (D)
Beethoven, L. van:Vars on "Ein Mädchen oder Weibchen" from Mozart's *Die Zauberflöte*, w. E. Ax (pno) CBS 2-▲ M2K 42446 [DDD]
Beethoven, L. van:Vars on "Ein Mädchen oder Weibchen" from Mozart's *Die Zauberflöte*, w. E. Ax (pno) CBS ▲ MK 42121 [DDD]
Beethoven, L. van:Vars on "See, the Conquering Hero Comes" from Handel's *Judas Maccabaeus*, w. E. Ax (pno) CBS ▲ MK 42121 [DDD]
Beethoven, L. van:Vars on "Bei Männern" from Mozart's *Die Zauberflöte*, w. E. Ax (pno) CBS 2-▲ M2K 42446 [DDD]
Beethoven, L. van:Vars on "Bei Männern" from Mozart's *Die Zauberflöte*, w. E. Ax (pno) CBS ▲ MK 42121 [DDD]
Bernstein, L.:Son Cl, w. J. Kahane (pno) [trans Ma for vc & pno] *(rec June 15-19, 1992)* Sony Classical ▲ SK 53126 [DDD] Δ SM 53126 [DDD]
Bloch, E.:Schelomo, w. D. Zinman (cnd), Baltimore SO *(rec Joseph Meyerhoff Hall, Baltimore, MD, Mar. 6-7, 1993)* Sony Classical ▲ SK 57961 [DDD]; ■ ST 57961
Boccherini, L.:Con Vc, G.482, w. P. Zukerman (cnd), St. Paul CO CBS ▲ MK 39964
Boccherini, L.:Qnts Strs, w. Issac Stern (vn), Cho-Liang Lin (vn), Jaime Laredo (va), Sharon Robinson (vc)—Qnt in E for Strs, Op. 13/5 Sony Classical ▲ SK 53983
Boccherini, L.:Qnt Strs, G.275, w. Cho-Liang Lin (vn), Isaac Stern (vn), Jaime Laredo (va), Sharon Robinson (vc) Sony Classical ▲ SK 53983
Bolling, C.:Suite Vc, w. Claude Bolling Trio CBS ▲ MK 39059 ■ FMT 39059
Brahms, J.:Con Vn & Vc, "Double Con", w. I. Stern (vn), C. Abbado (cnd), Chicago SO CBS ▲ MK 42387 [DDD]
Brahms, J.:Qts Pno (comp), w. E. Ax (pno), I. Stern (vn), J. Laredo (va) Sony Classical 2-▲ S2K 45846 [DDD] 2-■ S2T 45846 (D)
Brahms, J.:Qts Pno (comp), w. Emanuel Ax (pno), Isaac Stern (vn), Jalme Laredo (va) Sony Classical ("Isaac Stern:A Life in Music" series) 3-▲ SM3K 64520
Brahms, J.:Qt 3 Pno, w. E. Ax (pno), I. Stern (vn), J. Laredo (va) CBS ▲ MK 42387 [DDD]
Brahms, J.:Sextet Strs, Op. 18, w. I. Stern (vn), C.-L. Lin (vn), J. Laredo (va), M. Tree (va), S. Robinson (vc) Sony Classical 2-▲ S2K 45820
Brahms, J.:Sextet Strs, Op. 36, w. I. Stern (vn), Cho-Liang Lin (vn), J. Laredo (va), M. Tree (va), S. Robinson (vc) Sony Classical 2-▲ S2K 45820
Brahms, J.:Sons Vc (comp), w. E. Ax (pno) Sony Classical Δ SM 48191 [DDD]
Brahms, J.:Sons Vc (comp), w. E. Ax (pno) Sony Classical ▲ SK 48191 [DDD]
Brahms, J.:Sons Vc (comp), w. E. Ax (pno) RCA Gold Seal ▲ 09026-61355-2 ■ 09026-61355-4
Brahms, J.:Son 3 Vn, w. E. Ax (pno) [trans. for cello & piano] Sony Classical ▲ SK 48191 [DDD]
Britten, H.:Son Vc, w. E. Ax (pno) CBS ▲ MK 44980 [DDD]
Britten, H.:Sym Vc, w. D. Zinman (cnd), Baltimore SO CBS ▲ MK 44900 [DDD]
Chopin, F.:Son Vc, w. Emanuel Ax (pno) *(rec Jordan Hall, New England Conservatory, Boston, MA, June 8-10, 1992)* Sony Classical ▲ SK 53112 [DDD]
Chopin, F.:Trio Pno, w. Emanuel Ax (pno), Pamela Frank (vn) *(rec Jordan Hall, New England Conservatory, Boston, MA, June 8-10, 1992)* Sony Classical ▲ SK 53112 [DDD]
Danielpour, R.:Con Vc, w. D. Zinman (cnd), Philadelphia Orch Sony Classical ▲ SK 66299
Danielpour, R.:Con Vc, w. D. Zinman (cnd), Philadelphia Orch Sony Classical ▲ SK 66299
Dvořák, A.:Con Vc, w. K. Masur (cnd), New York PO *(rec Avery Fisher Hall, Lincoln Center for the Performing Arts, Jan 27 & 30, 1995)* Sony Classical ▲ SK 67173 [DDD]
Dvořák, A.:Con Vc, w. L. Maazel (cnd), Berlin PO CBS ▲ MK 42206 [DDD] ■ IMT 42206 (D) □ NM 42206
Dvořák, A.:Con Vc, w. L. Maazel (cnd), Berlin PO CBS 2-▲ M2K 44562 [ADD/DDD] 2-■ M2T 44562 (D)
Dvořák, A.:Music of, w. Frederica von Stade (mez), Itzhak Perlman (vn), Rudolf Firkusny (pno), S. Ozawa (cnd), Boston SO, Czech Phil Chorus—Carnival Ov., Op. 92; Romance in f for Vn & Orch, Op. 11; Klid [Silent Woods] for Vc & Orch, Op. 68/5; Humoresque in Gb, Op. 101/1 & 7; Mesícku na nebi hlubokém [from Rusalka, Op. 114]; Psalm 149 for Chorus & Orch, Op. 79; Gypsy Songs for Voice & Piano, Op. 55/4 & 5; Allegro [from Trio for Vn, Vc & Pno, Op. 90]; Slavonic Dances, Op. 72/2 & 7 *(rec Smetana Hall, Prague, Dec. 16, 1993)* Sony Classical ("Front Line" series) ▲ SK 46687 [DDD]; ■ ST 46687
Dvořák, A.:Rondo, w. L. Maazel (cnd), Berlin PO CBS ▲ MK 42206 [DDD] ■ IMT 42206 (D) □ NM 42206
Dvořák, A.:Silent Woods, w. L. Maazel (cnd), Berlin PO CBS ▲ MK 42206 [DDD] ■ IMT 42206 (D) □ NM 42206
Dvořák, A.:Trio 3 Pno, w. Y. U. Kim (vn), E. Ax (pno) CBS ▲ MK 44527 [DDD]
Dvořák, A.:Trio 4 Pno, "Dumky", w. Y. U. Kim (vn), E. Ax (pno) CBS ▲ MK 44527 [DDD]
Elgar, E.:Con Vc, w. A. Previn (cnd), London SO CBS 2-▲ M2K 44562 [ADD/DDD] 2-■ M2T 44562 (D)
Elgar, E.:Con Vc, w. A. Previn (cnd), London SO CBS ▲ MK 39541 [DDD]
Fauré, G.:Qt 1 Pno, w. E. Ax (pno), J. Laredo (vn), I. Stern (vn) Sony Classical ▲ SK 48066 [DDD]
Fauré, G.:Qt 2 Pno, w. E. Ax (pno), J. Laredo (vn), I. Stern (vn) Sony Classical ▲ SK 48066 [DDD]
Gershwin, G.:Preludes (3) Pno [trans. J. Heifetz] *(rec June 15-19, 1992)* Sony Classical ▲ SK 53126 [DDD] Δ SM 53126 [DDD]
Gubaidulina, S.:Rejoice, w. G. Kremer (vn) CBS ▲ MK 44924 [DDD]
Haydn, J.:Con 1 Vc, w. J.-L. Garcia (cnd), English CO CBS ▲ MK 36674 ■ MT 36674
Haydn, J.:Con 2 Vc, w. J.-L. Garcia (cnd), English CO CBS ▲ MK 36674 ■ MT 36674
Haydn, J.:Con 2 Vc, w. J.-L. Garcia (cnd), English CO CBS ▲ MK 39310 ■ MT 39310
Haydn, J.:Con 2 Vc, w. J.-L. Garcia (cnd), English CO CBS 2-▲ M2K 44562 [ADD/DDD] 2-■ M2T 44562 (D)
Herbert, V.:Con 2 Vc, w. K. Masur (cnd), New York PO *(rec Avery Fisher Hall, Lincoln Center for the Performing Arts, Jan 27 & 30, 1995)* Sony Classical ▲ SK 67173 [DDD]
Hush, w. Bobby McFerrin (sgr) Sony Classical ▲ SK 48177 Δ SM 48177 ■ ST 48177
Ives, C.:Trio Pno, w. G. Kalish (pno), R. Lefkowitz (vn) *(rec June 15-19, 1992)* Sony Classical ▲ SK 53126 [DDD]
Japanese Melodies, w. P. Zander (hpd), M. Mamiya, Pro Musica Nipponia CBS ▲ MK 39703 ■ FMT 39703
Kabalevsky, D.:Con 1 Vc, w. E. Ormandy (cnd), Philadelphia Orch CBS ▲ MK 37840 [DDD]

Ma, Yo-Yo (vc) (cont.)
Kirchner, L.:Con Vc, w. D. Zinman (cnd), Philadelphia Orch Sony Classical ▲ SK 66299
Kirchner, L.:Music for Vc & Orch, w. D. Zinman (cnd), Philadelphia Orch Sony Classical ▲ SK 66299
Kirchner, L.:Triptych, w. L. Chang (vn) *(rec May 7-8, 1991)* Sony Classical ▲ SK 53126 [DDD]
Kreisler, F.:Vn Pieces [cello arrs. by Ma] CBS ▲ MK 37280 [DDD]
Lalo, E.:Con Vc, w. L. Maazel (cnd), Orch National CBS ▲ MK 35848 [DDD]
Lieberson, P.:King Gesar, w. Emanuel Ax (pno), Peter Serkin (pno), Omar Ebrahim (nar), Andras Adorjan (fl), Deborah Marshall (cl), William Purvis (hn), David Taylor (trbn), Stefan Huge (perc) Sony Classical ▲ SK 57971
Meyer, E.:Chamber Music, w. Mark O'Connor (vn), Edgar Meyer (bass)—Mama; First Impressions; Etienne et Petunia; Pickles; Schizoozy *(rec Sound Emporium, Nashville, Aug 17-20, 1995)* Sony Classical ▲ SK 68460 [DDD] Δ SM 68460 ■ ST 68460
Meyer, E.:Chamber Music, w. Mark O'Connor (vn), Edgar Meyer (bass)—Druid Fluid *(rec Sound Emporium, Nashville, Aug 17-20, 1995)* Sony Classical ▲ SK 68460 [DDD] Δ SM 68460 ■ ST 68460
Mozart, W.A.:Adagio & Fugue Strs, w. Gidon Kremer (vn), Jean-Marc Phillips (vn), Kim Kashkashian (va) CBS ▲ MK 42134 [DDD]
Mozart, W.A.:Duo Bn Vc, w. A. Heller (bn) Sony Classical ▲ SMK 46248 [ADD]
Mozart, W.A.:Trio Vn, K.563, w. G. Kremer (vn), K. Kashkashian (va) CBS ▲ MK 39561 [DDD]
O'Connor, M.:Chamber Music, w. Mark O'Connor (vn), Edgar Meyer (bass)—Appalachia Waltz; Butterfly's Day Out; F.C.'s Jig; Old Country Fairytale; Fair Dancer Reel *(rec Sound Emporium, Nashville, Aug 17-20, 1995)* Sony Classical ▲ SK 68460 [DDD] Δ SM 68460 ■ ST 68460
Paganini, N.:Caprices Vn—Nos. 9,13,14,17 & 24 CBS ▲ MK 37280 [DDD]
Paganini, N.:Intro & Vars on "Dal tuo stellato soglio", w. P. Zander (pno) [arr. Silva] CBS ▲ MK 37280 [DDD]
Portrait of Yo-Yo Ma CBS ▲ MK 44796 [DDD/ADD] ■ MT 44796
Prokofiev, S.:Son Vc, w. E. Ax (pno) Sony Classical ▲ SK 46486 ■ ST 46486
Prokofiev, S.:Sym-Con Vc, w. L. Maazel (cnd), Pittsburgh SO Sony Classical ▲ SK 48382 [DDD]
Rachmaninoff, S.:Son Vc, w. E. Ax (pno) Sony Classical ▲ SK 46486 ■ ST 46486
Rouse, C.:Con Vc, w. D. Zinman (cnd), Philadelphia Orch Sony Classical ▲ SK 66299
Rouse, C.:Con Vc, w. D. Zinman (cnd), Philadelphia Orch Sony Classical ▲ SK 66299
Saint-Saëns, C.:Con 1 Vc, w. L. Maazel (cnd), French National Orch CBS 2-▲ M2K 44562 [ADD/DDD] 2-■ M2T 44562 (D)
Saint-Saëns, C.:Con 1 Vc, w. L. Maazel (cnd), French National Orch CBS ▲ MK 35848 [DDD]
Schoenberg, A.:Con Vc, w. S. Ozawa (cnd), Boston SO CBS ▲ MK 39863 [DDD]
Schoenberg, A.:Verklärte Nacht, w. W. Trampler (va), Juilliard String Quartet [arr. for string sextet] Sony Classical ▲ SK 47690 [DDD]
Schubert, Franz:Qt 15 Strs, w. G. Kremer (vn), D. Phillips (vn), K. Kashkashian (va) CBS ▲ MK 42134 [DDD]
Schubert, Franz:Qnt Strs, D.956, w. Cleveland String Quartet CBS ▲ MK 39134 [DDD] ■ IMT 39134
Schubert, Franz:Qnt Strs, D.956, w. Issac Stern (vn), Cho-Liang Lin (vn), Jaime Laredo (va), Sharon Robinson (vc) Sony Classical ▲ SK 53983
Schubert, Franz:Qnt Strs, D.956, w. Cho-Liang Lin (vn), Isaac Stern (vn), Jaime Laredo (va), Sharon Robinson (vc) Sony Classical ▲ SK 53983
Schumann, R.:Adagio & Allegro Hn, w. E. Ax (pno) CBS ▲ MK 42663 [DDD]
Schumann, R.:Con Vc, w. C. Davis (cnd), Bavarian RSO CBS 2-▲ M2K 44562 [ADD/DDD] 2-■ M2T 44562 (D)
Schumann, R.:Con Vc, w. C. Davis (cnd), Bavarian RSO CBS ▲ MK 42663 [DDD]
Schumann, R.:Fantasiestücke Cl, w. Emanuel Ax (pno) CBS ▲ MK 42663 [DDD]
Schumann, R.:Qt Pno, Op. 47, w. E. Ax (pno), I. Stern (vn), J. Laredo (va) *(rec Mar. 9-12, 1992)* Sony Classical ▲ SK 53339 [DDD]
Schumann, R.:Stücke im Volkston, w. E. Ax (pno) CBS ▲ MK 42663 [DDD]
Shostakovich, D.:Con 1 Vc, w. E. Ormandy (cnd), Philadelphia Orch CBS ▲ MDK 44903 [DDD] ■ MDT 44903 (D)
Shostakovich, D.:Con 1 Vc, w. E. Ormandy (cnd), Philadelphia Orch CBS ▲ MK 37840
Shostakovich, D.:Qt 15 Strs, w. G. Kremer (vn), D. Phillips (vn), K. Kashkashian (va) CBS ▲ MK 44924 [DDD]
Shostakovich, D.:Son Vc, w. E. Ax (pno) CBS ▲ MK 44664 [DDD]
Shostakovich, D.:Trio 2 Pno, w. I. Stern (vn), E. Ax (pno) CBS ▲ MK 44664 [DDD]
Strauss, R.:Don Quixote, w. S. Ozawa (cnd), Boston SO CBS ▲ MK 39863 [DDD]
Strauss, R.:Son Vc, w. E. Ax (pno) CBS ▲ MK 44980 [DDD]
Tchaikovsky, P.:Music of, w. I. Perlman (vn), J. Norman (sop), Y. Temirkanov (cnd), Leningrad PO, Leningrad Military Orch—Waltz & Polonaise from Eugene Onegin; Sérénade mélancolique, Op. 26; Valse scherzo, Op. 34; Variations on a Rococo Theme, Op. 33; Overture 1812, Op. 49; Symphony No. 6 (3rd movt.); 3 Chansons française from Op. 65, for Voice & Piano; Aria (Adieu, forêts) from The Maid of Orleans *(rec live, Leningrad)* RCA Red Seal ▲ 60739-2-RC [DDD] ■ 09026-60739-4-RC (CrO2) □ 09026-60739-5
Tchaikovsky, P.:Vars on a Rococo Theme, w. L. Maazel (cnd), Pittsburgh SO Sony Classical ▲ SK 48382 [DDD]
Walton, W.:Con Vc, w. A. Previn (cnd), London SO CBS ▲ MK 39541 [DDD]
Maas, Robert (vc)—see ORCHESTRAS & ENSEMBLES Pro Arte String Quartet
Maatz, G. (fl)—see ORCHESTRAS & ENSEMBLES Freiburg Baroque Soloists
Maatz, Jörn (ob)
Boccherini, L.:Syms, w. S. Prunnbauer (gtr), Jürgen Hollerbuhl (ob), B. Vestre (ob), H. Maile (vn), H. Ganz (vn), R. Forest (vc), J. Stárek (cnd), Berlin RIAS Sinfonietta—in C, G.495 (Op. 21/3) *(rec Dec. 1979)* Koch Treasure ▲ 31612-2 [ADD]
Maazel, Lorin (glock)
Strauss, Josef:Music of, w. Lorin Maazel (vn), L. Maazel (cnd), Vienna PO—The Girl from Nasswald, Op. 267; The Dancing Muse, Op. 266; Jockey Polka, Op. 278 *(rec live, Vienna, Jan 1, 1996)* RCA Red Seal 2-▲ 09026-68421-2
Maazel, Lorin (vn)
Chausson, E.:Con Vn, Pno & Str Qt, w. I. Margalit (pno), Cleveland Orch String Quartet *(rec 1979)* Telarc ▲ CD 80046 [DDD]
Mozart, W.A.:Cassation, K.99/63a, w. L. Maazel (cnd), English CO Klavier ▲ KCD 11046
Mozart, W.A.:Con 3 Vn, w. L. Maazel (cnd), English CO Klavier ▲ KCD 11046
Mozart, W.A.:Con 5 Vn, w. L. Maazel (cnd), English CO Klavier ▲ KCD 11046 [ADD]
Strauss, Josef:Music of, w. Lorin Maazel (glock), L. Maazel (cnd), Vienna PO—The Girl from Nasswald, Op. 267; The Dancing Muse, Op. 266; Jockey Polka, Op. 278 *(rec live, Vienna, Jan 1, 1996)* RCA Red Seal 2-▲ 09026-68421-2
Vivaldi, A.:Cons Vn, Op. 8/1-4, "The Four Seasons", w. L. Maazel (cnd), Orch National CBS ▲ MK 39008 [DDD]
McAllister, Timothy (sax)—see ORCHESTRAS & ENSEMBLES Duo Nuova
McAlpine, John (pno)
Cage, J.:Four Walls, w. Beth Griffith (sop) *(rec DeutschlandRadio Cologne Recording House, Apr 29-30, 1994)* Largo ▲ 5132 [DDD]
Macaluso, Vincenzo (gtr)
10 String Guitar Interprets French Classics Klavier ■ KC 523
The 10 String Guitar Intreprets Classics Klavier ■ KC 508
10 String Guitar Spectacular Klavier ▲ KCD 11003 [ADD]
McArthur, David (pno)
Arnold, M.:Sonatina Cl, w. Nicholas Carpenter (cl) Herald ▲ HAVPCD 152
Dunhill, T.:Phantasy Suite, w. Nicholas Carpenter (cl) Herald ▲ HAVPCD 152
Finzi, G.:Bagatelles, Op. 23, w. Nicholas Carpenter (cl) Herald ▲ HAVPCD 152
Henry, M.:Jazz Song, w. Nicholas Carpenter (cl) Herald ▲ HAVPCD 152
Ireland, J.:Fant-Son Cl & Pno, w. Nicholas Carpenter (cl) Herald ▲ HAVPCD 152
McCabe, J.:Pieces Cl, w. Nicholas Carpenter (cl) Herald ▲ HAVPCD 152
McArthur, Edwin (pno)
In Copenhagen, w. Kirsten Flagstad (sop) Danacord ▲ DACOCD 325 (m)

▲ = CD ♦ = Enhanced CD Δ = MD ■ = Cassette Tape □ = DCC

MacArthur, Frederick (org)
The Old Brass Organ & Timpani, w. Old South Brass [cnd:Roger Voisin] Pro Organo ▲ POCD 7051 [DDD]

McAslan, Lorraine (vn)
Beethoven, L. van:Son 5 Vn, "Spring", w. J. Blakely (pno) IMP ▲ PCD 833 [DDD]
Beethoven, L. van:Son 9 Vn, "Kreutzer", w. J. Blakely (pno) IMP ▲ PCD 833 [DDD]
Britten, H.:Con Vn, w. S. Bedford (cnd), English CO *(rec 10/89)* Collins Classics ▲ 13012 [DDD]
Britten, H.:Reveille Vn, w. J. Blakely (pno) Continuum ▲ CCD 1022 [DDD]
Britten, H.:Suite Vn, w. J. Blakely (pno) Continuum ▲ CCD 1022 [DDD]
Bridge, F.:Cradle Song Vn, w. J. Blakely (pno) Continuum ▲ CCD 1022 [DDD]
Bridge, F.:Heart's Ease, w. J. Blakely (pno) Continuum ▲ CCD 1022 [DDD]
Bridge, F.:Norse Legend, w. J. Blakely (pno) Continuum ▲ CCD 1022 [DDD]
Bridge, F.:Serenade Vn, w. J. Blakely (pno) Continuum ▲ CCD 1022 [DDD]
Bridge, F.:Son Vn, w. J. Blakely (pno) Continuum ▲ CCD 1022 [DDD]
Bridge, F.:Vn & Pno Music, w. J. Blakely (pno)—Romanze Continuum ▲ CCD 1022 [DDD]
Elgar, E.:Son Vn, w. John Blakely (pno) ASV/Quicksilva ▲ ASQ CD 6191
Holst, G.:Orchestral Works, w. A. Baillie (vc), D. Atherton (cnd), London PO, London SO—A Winter Idyll; Elegy in Memoriam William Morris; Indra, Symphonic Poem for Orchestra, Op. 13; A Song of the Night, Op. 19/1; Sita:Interlude from Act III, Op. 23; Invocation, Op. 19/2; The Lure; Dances from the Morning of the Year, Op. 45/2 Lyrita ▲ SRCD 209
Mozart, W.A.:Sinf concertante Vn, K.364, w. Yuko Inoue (va), R. Pople (cnd), London Festival Orch ASV ("Quicksilva" series) ▲ ASQ 6139 [DDD]
20th Century Recital, w. Nigel Clayton (pno) Collins Classics ▲ COL 1173 [DDD]
Walton, W.:Son Vn & Pno, w. John Blakely (pno) ASV/Quicksilva ▲ ASQ CD 6191

McBride, Christian (elec bass)
So Many Stars, w. Kathleen Battle (sop), Antonio Hart (sax), Grover Washington Jr (sax), Tom Harrell (flgl), James Carter (b cl), Cyrus Chestnut (pno), Jon Herrington (gtr), Romero Lubambo (gtr), Ira Coleman (elec bass), Cyro Baptista (perc), Steven Berrios (perc) *(rec Hit Factory, Clinton Recording Studios, R.P.M. Sound Studios, Unique Recording Studios, Power Station)* Sony Classical ▲ SK 68473 [DDD]

McCabe, John (pno)
Adams, J.:Phrygian Gates *(rec 1990)* Continuum 2-▲ CCD 1028/1029
Bax, A.:Qt Pno Strs, w. English String Quartet members Chandos ▲ CHAN 8391 [DDD]
Bax, A.:Son 1 Vn & Pno, w. E. Gruenberg (vn) [1945 version] Chandos ▲ CHAN 8845 [DDD]
Bax, A.:Son 2 Vn & Pno, w. E. Gruenberg (vn) Chandos ▲ CHAN 8845 [DDD]
Bennett, Richard Rodney:Noctuary Continuum 2-▲ CCD 1028/1029
Brahms, J.:Sons Cl (comp), w. M. Khouri (cl) Continuum ▲ CCD 1027
Bridge, F.:Elégie Vc, w. J. Lloyd Webber (vc) ASV ▲ ASV 807
Bridge, F.:Scherzetto Vc, w. J. Lloyd Webber (vc) ASV ▲ ASV 807
Carter, E.:Son Pno Continuum 2-▲ CCD 1028/1029
Gal, H.:Son Cl, w. M. Khouri (cl) Continuum ▲ CCD 1027
Hindemith, P.:Ludus Tonalis Hyperion ▲ CDA 66824
Hindemith, P.:Suite "1922" Hyperion ▲ CDA 66824
Howells, H.:Pno Music—Finizi's Rest; Berkeley's Hunt; Walton's Toye; Ralph's Pavane; and others Hyperion ▲ CDA 66689
Ireland, J.:The Holy Boy, w. Julian Lloyd Webber (vc) [arr vc & pno] ASV ▲ ASV CD 592
Ireland, J.:Son Vc, w. J. Lloyd Webber (vc) ASV ▲ ASV 807
Previn, A.:The Invisible Drummer Continuum 2-▲ CCD 1028/1029
Rawsthorne, A.:Son Vc, w. Julian Lloyd Webber (vc) ASV ▲ ASV CD 592
Rochberg, G.:Carnival Music Continuum 2-▲ CCD 1028/1029
Satie, E.:Pno Music (misc)—3 Gymnopedies; 5 Gnossiennes; 3 Pièces froides; Sports et divertissements; 6 Pièces; Sontine bureaucratique; Veritable preludes flasques; Vieux sequins et vieilles; Sarabandes Nos. 1 & 3 Emergo ("Corneille" series) ▲ EC 3970
Stanford, C.V.:Son 2 Vc, w. J. Lloyd Webber (vc) ASV ▲ ASV 807

McCabe, Robin (pno)
Bartók, B.:Allegro barbaro BIS ▲ CD 182 [ADD]
Bartók, B.:Burleskes, Op. 8c BIS ▲ CD 182 [ADD]
Bartók, B.:Dance Suite BIS ▲ CD 182 [ADD]
Bartók, B.:Romanian Dances BIS ▲ CD 182 [ADD]
Bartók, B.:Romanian Folk Dances Pno BIS ▲ CD 182 [ADD]
French Flute Music, w. Aitken, Robert (fl) BIS ▲ CD 184 [AAD]
Liszt, F.:Études de concert (2) Pno *(rec Djursholm, Sweden, June-July 1981)* BIS ▲ CD 185 [AAD]
Liszt, F.:Harmonies poétiques et religieuses—"Funérailles" only *(rec Djursholm, Sweden, June-July 1981)* BIS ▲ CD 185 [AAD]
Liszt, F.:Hungarian Rhaps—No. 12 One-Eleven ▲ URS 91060 [ADD]
Liszt, F.:Paraphrase on Verdi's Quartet *(rec Djursholm, Sweden, June-July 1981)* BIS ▲ CD 185 [AAD]
Liszt, F.:Sonetti del Petrarca Pno—No. 104 *(rec Djursholm, Sweden, June-July 1981)* BIS ▲ CD 185 [AAD]
Liszt, F.:Song Transcriptions—4 transcriptions—Schubert:Das Wandern & Ständchen von Shakespeare; Chopin:Mädchens Wunsch; Meine Freuden *(rec Djursholm, Sweden, June-July 1981)* BIS ▲ CD 185 [AAD]
Mozart, F.X.W.:Rondo Fl, w. R. Aitken (fl) *(rec Nacka Aula, Nacka, Sweden, Sept. 14-16, 1980)* BIS ▲ CD 183 [AAD]
Reinecke, C.:Son Fl, w. R. Aitken (fl) *(rec. Studio BIS, Djursholm, Sweden, May 31 & June 2, 1981)* BIS ▲ CD 183 [AAD]
Schubert, Franz:Intro & Vars Fl on "Tröckne Blumen", w. R. Aitken (fl) *(rec Studio BIS, Djursholm, Sweden, May 31 & June 2, 1981)* BIS ▲ CD 183 [AAD]
Walton, W.:Qt Pno, w. English String Quartet Meridian ▲ CDE 84139

McCall (vc)
Babbitt, M.:Composition for 4 Instrs, w. Wummer (fl), Drucker (cl), March (vn) CRI ■ C 138

McCallum, Stephanie (pno)—see also ORCHESTRAS & ENSEMBLES australYSIS members
Alkan, C.-V.:Etudes (12) in major keys *(rec Newcastle Conservatorium Hall, Dec 1992)* Tall Poppies ▲ TP 055 [DDD]
Notations *(rec ABC Studio 200, ABC Ultimo Centre, Sydney, 1993)* Tall Poppies ▲ TP 37 [DDD]

McCandless, Paul (instr)
Mozart, W.A.:Music of, w. Philip Aaberg, Todd Boekelheide, Chris Botti, Henry Adam Curtis, Steve Erquiaga, Béla Fleck, Eugene Friesen, Tim Story, Richard Schönherz, Tracy Scott Silverman, Thea Suits-Silverman, ValGardena, Modern Mandolin Quartet Imaginary Road ▲ 314534065-2 ■ 314534065-4

McCann, Phillip (cnt)
All of the World's Most Beautiful Melodiesl, w. Gordon Langford (cnd), Roy Newsome (cnd), Peter Parkes (cnd), Black Dyke Mills Band, Sellers Engineering Band, Academy of St. Martin in the Fields Chamber Ensemble, Huddersfield Choral Society, Leeds Parish Church Boys Choir Chandos ("Brass" series) 5-▲ CHN 4536(5)
More of the World's Most Beautiful Melodies, w. Black Dyke Mills Band Chandos Brass ▲ CHAN 4502 [DDD]
The World's Most Beautiful Melodies, w. Black Dyke Mills Band Chandos Brass ▲ CHAN 4501 [DDD]
The World's Most Beautiful Melodies, Vol. 3:The Golden Cornet of Phillip McCann, w. Sellers Engineering Band, Simon Lindley (org) Chandos Brass ▲ CHAN 4503 [DDD]
The World's Most Beautiful Melodies, Vol. 5, w. Sellers Engineering Band, Huddersfield Choral Society Youth Choir, S. Lindley (org) Chandos ▲ CHAN 4532 [DDD]

Maccari, U. (cl)—see ORCHESTRAS & ENSEMBLES Seicentonovecento Ensemble

McCarthy, J. (rcr)—see ORCHESTRAS & ENSEMBLES Gavin Bryars Ensemble

McCartney, Stanley (cl)
McDougall, I.:Con Cl, w. M. Bernardi (cnd), CBC Vancouver SO CBC ("SM 5000" series) ▲ SMCD 5094 [DDD]

McCartney, Stanley (cl) (cont.)
Ravel, M.:Intro & Allegro, w. E. Goodman (hp), S. Shulman (fl), Amadeus Ensemble members CBC ("Musica Viva" series) ▲ MVCD 1054 [DDD]

McCarty, Evelyn (ob)
Doran, M.:Sonatina Ob, w. Imelda Delgado (pno) *(rec Chorus Room of Symphony Hall, Boston, MA, Feb 26-27, 1994)* Boston Records ▲ BR 1012
Gems for Oboe & Piano, w. Imelda Delgado (pno) *(rec Chorus Room of Symphony Hall, Boston, MA, Feb 26-27, 1994)* Boston Records ▲ BR 1012
Madden, J.:Songes of Sadness & Pitie, w. Imelda Delgado (pno) *(rec Chorus Room of Symphony Hall, Boston, MA, Feb 26-27, 1994)* Boston Records ▲ BR 1012
Rubbra, E.:Son Ob, w. Imelda Delgado (pno) *(rec Chorus Room of Symphony Hall, Boston, MA, Feb 26-27, 1994)* Boston Records ▲ BR 1012
Schelling, E.:Impressions from an Artist's Life, w. Imelda Delgado (pno)—Nocturne for Ob & Pno [Var No. 7] *(rec Chorus Room of Symphony Hall, Boston, MA, Feb 26-27, 1994)* Boston Records ▲ BR 1012
Sinigaglia, L.:Variations (12) on a theme of Schubert, w. Imelda Delgado (pno) *(rec Chorus Room of Symphony Hall, Boston, MA, Feb 26-27, 1994)* Boston Records ▲ BR 1012
Widerkehr, J.:Duo Ob, w. Imelda Delgado (pno) *(rec Chorus Room of Symphony Hall, Boston, MA, Feb 26-27, 1994)* Boston Records ▲ BR 1012

McCarty, Patricia (va)
Clarke, R.:Passacaglia on an Old English Tune, w. V. Eskin (pno) Northeastern ("Classical Arts" series) ▲ NR 212-CD
Clarke, R.:Pieces (2) Va, w. M. M. Babcock (vc) Northeastern ("Classical Arts" series) ▲ NR 212-CD
Clarke, R.:Prelude, Allegro & Pastorale, w. P. Hadcock (cl) Northeastern ("Classical Arts" series) ▲ NR 212-CD
Clarke, R.:Son Va, w. V. Eskin (pno) Northeastern ("Classical Arts" series) ▲ NR 212-CD

McCausland-Dieppa, Roberto (pno)
Chopin, F.:Waltzes—in D♭, Op. 64/1 *(rec Beachwood Studios, Cleveland, OH)* Fine Arts ▲ 67122 [DDD]
Clementi, M.:Sons Pno—in C, Op. 36/1 *(rec Beachwood Studios, Cleveland, OH)* Fine Arts ▲ 67122 [DDD]
Debussy, C.:La Fille aux cheveaux de lin Pno *(rec Beachwood Studios, Cleveland, OH)* Fine Arts ▲ 67122 [DDD]
Liszt, F.:Années de pèlerinage 3—Les jeux d'eaux à la Villa d'Este *(rec Cleveland, OH)* E D Arte ▲ 67124 [DDD]
Liszt, F.:Liebesträume—No. 3 *(rec Cleveland, OH)* E D Arte ▲ 67124 [DDD]
Liszt, F.:La Lugubre gondola Pno *(rec Cleveland, OH)* E D Arte ▲ 67124 [DDD]
Liszt, F.:Mephisto Waltz 1 Orch *(rec Cleveland, OH)* E D Arte ▲ 67124 [DDD]
Liszt, F.:Son Pno *(rec Beachwood Studios, Cleveland, OH)* Fine Arts ▲ 67122 [DDD]
Ravel, M.:Le Tombeau de Couperin *(rec Cleveland, OH)* E D Arte ▲ 67124 [DDD]

McChesney, David (tpt)
Fox, F.:Time Messages, w. David Dzubay (tpt), Michael Galbraith (hn), Andrew Glendenning (trbn), Andrew Oppenheim (tuba) *(rec Musical Arts Ctr, Bloomington, IN, Nov 30, 1989)* Indiana Univ School of Music ▲ 0-253-32433-5

McChesney, J. (pno)
Beethoven, L. van:Vars on a Theme by Count Waldstein, WoO 67, w. C. Rae-Gerrard (pno) Koch Schwann ▲ CD 310133 [DDD]
Mozart, W.A.:Son Pno 4-Hands, K.381, w. C. Rae-Gerrard (pno) Koch Schwann ▲ CD 310133 [DDD]
Schubert, Franz:Fant Pno, D.940, w. C. Rae-Gerrard (pno) Koch Schwann ▲ CD 310133 [DDD]
Schubert, Franz:Marche militaire, D.733/1, w. C. Rae-Gerrard (pno) Koch Schwann ▲ CD 310133 [DDD]

Macchia, Salvatore (db)
Macchia, S.:En trouvant les tombeaux, w. Lynn Klock (sax), Laura Klock (hn) *(rec Eastman Theater, Eastman School of Music)* Open Loop ▲ OL 021
Trombly, P.:Trio in 3 Mvts, w. R. Rudich (fl), K. Grossman (perc) CRI ▲ CD 568 [DDD]

Macchia-Kadlubkiewicz, Veronica (vn)
Bolle, J.:Duo Vn & Db, w. Robert Black (db) Gasparo ▲ GSCD 317 [DDD]
Sowerby, L.:Songs, w. D'Anna Fortunato (mez), Tessa van Buskirk (vn), Virginia Christensen (va), Michael Curry (vc)—Premonition; Kisses; Midnight; Reassurance; Adventure [all text L. E. Thomas] Gasparo ▲ GSCD 315 [DDD]
Sowerby, L.:Songs of Resignation, w. D'Anna Fortunato (mez), Steven Jackson (cl), Anthony de Mare (pno) Gasparo ▲ GSCD 315 [DDD]

McChrystal, Gerard (sax)
Debussy, C.:Rapsodie, w. Y.P. Tortelier (cnd), Ulster Orch *(rec June 3-4, 1992)* Chandos ▲ CHAN 9129 [DDD]
Heath, David:The Celtic, w. M. Stephenson (cnd), London Musici Silva Classics ▲ SIL 6010
McGlynn, M.:From Nowhere to Nowhere, w. M. Stephenson (cnd), London Musici Silva Classics ▲ SIL 6010
Nyman, M.:Where the Dee Dances, w. M. Stephenson (cnd), London Musici Silva Classics ▲ SIL 6010
Torke, M.:Con Sax, w. M. Stephenson (cnd), London Musici Silva Classics ▲ SIL 6010
Wilson, I.:I Sleep at Waking, w. M. Stephenson (cnd), London Musici Silva Classics ▲ SIL 6010

McColl, William (bas hn)—see ORCHESTRAS & ENSEMBLES New World Basset Horn Trio

McConnell, Pamela (va)
Debussy, C.:Son Fl, w. C. Nield (fl), M. Klinko (hp) Audiofon ▲ CD 72036

McCormack, Gina (vn)—see ORCHESTRAS & ENSEMBLES Sorrel String Quartet

McCormack, Jack (db)
Haydn, J.:Die Schöpfung, w. Helena Döse (sop—Eva), Lucia Popp (sop—Gabriel), Werner Hollweg (ten—Uriel), Benjamin Luxon (bar—Adam), Kurt Moll (bass—Raphael), David Strange (vc), Antal Dorati (hpd), A. Dorati (cnd), Royal PO, Brighton Festival Chorus *(rec Kingsway Hall, London, Dec 1976)* London 2-▲ 443027-2 [ADD]

McCormick, Kim (fl)—see ORCHESTRAS & ENSEMBLES McCormick Duo

McCormick, Robert (perc)—see also ORCHESTRAS & ENSEMBLES McCormick Duo
Electro Accoustic Music III, w. Camilla Hoitenga (fl), William Buonocore (gtr), Maria Tegzes (sop), Jacques Linder (pno) Neuma ▲ 450-87 [DDD]

McCormick, Tom (sax)
Colgrass, M.:Urban Requiem, w. David Fernandez (sax), Stephen Welsh (sax), George Weremchuk (sax), G. Green (cnd), Univ of Miami Wind Ensemble *(rec Miami Beach, Feb 1996)* Albany ▲ TROY 212 [DDD]

MacCourt, Donald (bn)—see also ORCHESTRAS & ENSEMBLES Contemporary Chamber Players
Wuorinen, C.:Variations Bn, w. Susan Jolles (hp), Gordon Gottlieb (timp) New World ▲ 80517-2

MacCourt, Ronald (bn)
Albinoni, T.:Con in C Tpt, w. Gerard Schwarz (tpt), Ronald Roseman (ob), Susan Weiner (ob), Virginia Brewer (ob), William Scribner (bn), Edward Brewer (hpd) Vox Box 2-▲ CDX 5124 [ADD]
Hertel, J.W.:Con à cinque, w. Gerard Schwarz (tpt), Ronald Roseman (ob), Susan Weiner (ob), Virginia Brewer (ob), William Scribner (bn), Edward Brewer (hpd) Vox Box 2-▲ CDX 5124 [ADD]
Telemann, G.P.:Cons Tpt, w. Gerard Schwarz (tpt), Ronald Roseman (ob), Susan Weiner (ob), Virginia Brewer (ob), William Scribner (bn), Edward Brewer (hpd) Vox Box 2-▲ CDX 5124 [ADD]

McCoy, Robert (pno)
Con Amores:Spanish & Portuguese Songs, w. Carmen Balthrop (sgr) Elan ▲ CD 2208 [DDD]

McCracken, H. Jac (pno)
Dankner, S.:Songs of Bygone Days, w. E. Frohnmayer (sop), P. Frohnmayer (bar) Albany ▲ TROY 067 [DDD]

McCracken, Melanie Wilsden (ob)
Johnson, H.:Trio Fl, Ob & Pno, w. R. Troxler (fl), E. A. Holding (pno) Albany ▲ TROY 061 [DDD]

McCraken, C. (vc)
Rieti, V.:Partita Hpd, w. S. Marlowe (hpd), S. Baron (fl), R. Roseman (ob), C. Libove (vn), A. Ajemian (vn), H. Zaratzian (va) CRI ▲ CD 601 [ADD]

McCraw, Michael (bn)
Telemann, G.P.:Con in F Rcr Bn, w. C. Pehrsson (rcr), Drottningholm Baroque Ensemble *(rec May 27–28, 1984)* BIS ▲ CD 617 [DDD]
Telemann, G.P.:Con in F Rcr Bn, w. C. Pehrsson (rcr), Drottningholm Baroque Ensemble BIS ▲ CD 271 [DDD]
Vivaldi, A.:Cons Bn, w. Drottningholm Baroque Ensemble—RV.485 BIS ▲ CD 271 [DDD]
McCready, Ivan (vc)—see ORCHESTRAS & ENSEMBLES Duke String Quartet
McCroskey, Lenora (org)
Historic Organs of New Orleans, w. George Bozeman (org), James S. Darling (org), Jesse E. Eschbach (org), Gerald D. Frank (org), John Gearhart (org), James Hammann (org), Frederick Hohman (org), Mary Gifford Matthys (org), Lorenz Maycher (org), Donald Messer (org) *(rec June 1989)* Organ Historical Society 2–▲ OHS 89
McCune, A. Bromeley (pno)
Liszt, F.:Totentanz, w. P. Freeman (cnd), Yugoslavia RSO Pro Arte ▲ 575
McCutcheon, Peter (gtr)
Diferencias *(rec Salle Claude-Champagne, Montréal, Dec. 1994)* Ummus ▲ UMM 305
McDermott, Kerry (vn)
Corigliano, J.:Soliloquy, w. Stanley Drucker (cl), Lisa Kim (vn), Rebecca Young (va), Gerald Appleman (vc) Cala Records ("New York Legends" series) ▲ CAL CACD 509 [DDD]
McDermott, Maureen (vc)—see ORCHESTRAS & ENSEMBLES CELLO
McDonald (pno)
Freund, D.W.:Silverling, w. S. Friedman (tpt) Ode/New Zealand ▲ ODE 1327 [DDD]
McDonald, Anna (vn)
Bach, Joh. Christian:Sinf concertante, T.284/1, w. Graham Cracknell (vn), Angela East (vc), A. Halstead (cnd), Hanover Band *(rec Rosslyn Hill Chapel, London, Dec 1995)* CPO ▲ CPO 999348–2 [DDD]
Bach, Joh. Christian:Sinf concertante, T.284/6, w. Graham Cracknell (vn), Anthony Robson (ob), A. Halstead (cnd), Hanover Band *(rec Rosslyn Hill Chapel, London, Dec 1995)* CPO ▲ CPO 999348–2 [DDD]
Bach, Joh. Christian:Sinf concertante, T.288/4, w. Graham Cracknell (vn), Angela East (vc), A. Halstead (cnd), Hanover Band *(rec Rosslyn Hill Chapel, London, Dec 1995)* CPO ▲ CPO 999348–2 [DDD]
McDonald, Boyd (pno)
Beethoven, L. van:Sons Vc (comp), w. Paul Pulford (vc) ebs 2–▲ 6030 [DDD]
Beethoven, L. van:Vars on "Ein Mädchen oder Weibchen" from Mozart's *Die Zauberflöte*, w. Paul Pulford (vc) ebs 2–▲ 6030 [DDD]
Beethoven, L. van:Vars on "See, the Conquering Hero Comes" from Handel's *Judas Maccabaeus*, w. Paul Pulford (vc) ebs 2–▲ 6030 [DDD]
Beethoven, L. van:Vars on "Bei Männern" from Mozart's *Die Zauberflöte*, w. Paul Pulford (vc) ebs 2–▲ 6030 [DDD]
MacDonald, David (org)
Bach, J.S.:Org Music (misc)—Chorale Preludes (5), BWV 659, 667, 683a, 731, 734; Fugue in g, BWV 578; Pastorale in F, BWV 590; Prelude & Fugue in a, BWV 543; Trio Sonata No. 5 in C, BWV 529; *[CD-only bonus track]* CBC ("Musica Viva" series) ▲ MVCD 1030 [DDD]
MacDonald, George (cl)
Jeux d'Enfants, w. Christopher Hyde-Smith (fl/pic), Emma Johnson (cl), Gordon Back (pno), Academy of St. Martin in the Fields [cnd:Neville Marriner], Mexico City PO, Mexico State SO, Royal PO [cnd:Enrique Bátiz], Northern Sinfonia of England [cnd ASV Quicksilva ▲ ASQ 6182
McDonald, Hector (hn)
Förster, C.:Con Hn, w. B. Kelly (cnd), Melbourne Academy Tall Poppies ▲ TP 42 [DDD]
Haydn, J.:Con 1 Hn, w. B. Kelly (cnd), Melbourne Academy Tall Poppies ▲ TP 42 [DDD]
Telemann, G.P.:Con Hn, w. B. Kelly (cnd), Melbourne Academy Tall Poppies ▲ TP 42 [DDD]
Teyber, A.:Con Hn, w. B. Kelly (cnd), Melbourne Academy Tall Poppies ▲ TP 42 [DDD]
Weber, C.M. von:Concertino Hn, w. M. Haselböck (cnd), Vienna Academy Novalis ▲ 150113 [DDD]
McDonald, Hector (nat hn)
Puccini, M.:Concertone Fl, w. Christian Gurtner (fl), Lisa Klevit-Ziegler (cl), Reinhold Friedrich (tpt), M. Haselböck (cnd), Vienna Academy *(rec Sofiensäle, Vienna, Oct 17–20, 1994)* Capriccio ▲ 10 598 [DDD]
McDonald, Judith (pno)
Harbison, J.:Simple Daylight, w. Karol Bennett (sop) *(rec Kresge Auditorium, between 1988 & 1994)* Archetype ▲ 60104 [DDD]
The Lyric Trumpet, w. Stanley Friedman (tpt), Bruce Greenfield (pno), Elizabeth Biggs (sop), et al. Ode/New Zealand ▲ ODE 1327 [DDD]
McDonald, Lawrence (cl)
Miller, E.J.:Going Home, w. P. Takacs (pno) Opus One ▲ 138
Miller, E.J.:Seven Sides of a Crystal, w. P. Takacs (pno) Opus One ▲ 138
Mozart, W.A.:Qnt Cl, K.581, w. Smithson String Quartet [period instrs] Smithsonian Collection 5–▲ ND 031
Mozart, W.A.:Trio Cl, K.498, w. J. Griffin (va), J. Weaver (pno) [period instrs] Smithsonian Collection 5–▲ ND 031
Scelsi, G.:Anahit, w. Paul Zukofsky (vn), Julie Bogorad (fl), Peggy Russell (fl), Courtney Westcott (fl), Joan Waryha (cl), Jean Hansen (b cl), Bill Suite (e hn), Nita VanPelt (sax), Bob Zobal (tpt), John Carter (trbn), Martin Lydecker (trbn), Stan Cortman (hn), Robert Ward (hn), William Curry (va), Jody Rowitsch (va), Irene Wade (va), Anne Fagerburg (vc), John Gockel (vc), Sue Manz (bass), Steven Stearman (bass) *(rec Oberlin Conservatory of Music, Oct 8, 1973)* CP² ▲ CP2 108 [AAD]
McDonald, Marilyn (va)
Mozart, W.A.:Sinf concertante Vn, K.364, w. J. Schroeder (vn), J. Schröder (cnd), Smithsonian CO [period instrs] Smithsonian Collection 5–▲ ND 031
McDonald, Marilyn (vn)—see also ORCHESTRAS & ENSEMBLES Smithsonian Chamber Players
Reger, M.:Serenade, Op. 141a, w. R. Willoughby (fl), J. Tattaglia (va) Gasparo Gallante ▲ GG 1003 [AAD]
McDonald, Robert (pno)
Avshalomov, A.:Songs, w. Daniel Avshalomov (va)—Nocturne/Kwei Fei's Lamnet; Lantern Dance [arr J. Avshalomov] Albany ▲ TROY 216 [DDD]
Avshalomov, D.:Torn Curtain, w. Daniel Avshalomov (va) Albany ▲ TROY 216 [DDD]
Avshalomov, J.:Evocations, w. Daniel Avshalomov (va) Albany ▲ TROY 216 [DDD]
Avshalomov, J.:Sonatine, w. Daniel Avshalomov (va) Albany ▲ TROY 216 [DDD]
Bruch, M.:Romanze Va, w. K. Dreyfus (va) Bridge ▲ BCD 9016 [DDD]
Debussy, C.:Beau soir, w. K. Dreyfus (va)—trans. Karen Dreyfus for viola & piano Bridge ▲ BCD 9016 [DDD]
Elmar Oliveira, w. Oliveira, Elmar (vn) Vox Box 2–▲ CDX 5086 [DDD]
Encore!, w. Midori (vn) Sony Classical ▲ SK 52568 ▲ SM 52568 ■ ST 52568
Falla, M. de:Suite populaire espagnole, w. K. Dreyfus (va) [trans Paul Kochanski for vn & pno] Bridge ▲ BCD 9016 [DDD]
Hindemith, P.:Son Va & Pno, Op. 11/4, w. K. Dreyfus (va) Bridge ▲ BCD 9016 [DDD]
Live at Carnegie Hall, w. Midori (vn) Sony Classical ▲ SK 46742 [DDD] ■ ST 46742 (D)
Schumann, R.:Märchenbilder, w. K. Dreyfus (va) Bridge ▲ BCD 9016 [DDD]
McDonald, Ruth Ann (pno)
Moss, L.:Miracles, w. James McDonald (ten), Edward Walters (cl) *(rec Peabody Conservatory of Music, Baltimore, MD)* Capstone ▲ CPS 8619
Moss, L.:Portals, w. James McDonald (ten) Capstone ▲ CPS 8619
McDonald, Susan (hp)
Badings, H.:Ballade Fl & Hp, w. L. di Tullio (fl) Klavier ▲ KCD 11019 [ADD]
Badings, H.:Cavatina A Fl & Hp, w. L. di Tullio (a fl) Klavier ▲ KCD 11019 [ADD]
Dussek, J.L.:Sons Hp, Op. 34 *(rec Pasadena, CA, 1971)* Orion ▲ 7815–2 [AAD]
Dussek, J.L.:Son Pno, Fl & Vc [arr solo harp] *(rec Pasadena, CA, 1971)* Orion ▲ 7815–2 [AAD]
Dussek, J.L.:Son with The Lass of Richmond Hill *(rec Pasadena, CA, 1971)* Orion ▲ 7815–2 [AAD]
Harp Spectacular Klavier ▲ KCD 11004 [ADD]
Lauber, J.:Medieval Dances, w. L. di Tullio (fl) Klavier ▲ KCD 11019 [ADD]
Masters of Flute & Harp, w. Louise di Tullio(fl) Klavier ▲ KCD 11019 [ADD]

McDonald, Susan (hp) (cont.)
Masters of Flute & Harp, Vol. 1, w. Louise di Tullio (fl) Klavier ■ KC 556
Masters of Flute & Harp, Vol. 2, w. Louise di Tullio (fl) Klavier ■ KC 560
Persichetti, V.:Serenade 10 Fl, w. L. di Tullio (fl) Klavier ▲ KCD 11019 [ADD]
Renié, H.:Légende Klavier ▲ KCD 11019 [ADD]
The Romantic Harp Klavier ■ KC 525
Rosetti, F.A.:Sons Hp—in F, E♭, B♭, G, B♭ & C *(rec Pasadena, CA, 1971)* Orion ▲ 7815–2 [AAD]
Sonatas for Flute & Harp, w. Louise di Tullio (fl) Klavier ▲ KCD 11015 [ADD]
Spohr, L.:Son 5 Vn, w. Louis Kaufman (vn) Music & Arts ▲ CD 905 [ADD]
Twentieth Century Harp Klavier ■ KC 508
The Virtuoso Harp Klavier ■ KC 543
The World of the Harp Delos ▲ DCD 3005 [DDD]
McDowall, Ruth (cl)
Ravel, M.:Intro & Allegro, w. M. Golden (hp), M. Meisenbach (fl), R. Neal (vn), D. Pettys (vn), D. Hermann (va), G. Manasjan (vc) Centaur ▲ CRC 2114 [DDD]
Vivaldi, A.:Cons Diverse Instrs, w. Joanna Graham (bn), David Rix (ct), Deborah Davis (fl), Duke Dobing (fl), Tim Caister (hn), Stephen Stirling (hn), Christopher Hooker (ob), Helen McQueen (ob), Michael Meekes (tpt), Crispian Steele-Perkins (tpt), Nicholas Kraemer (hpd), N. Kraemer (cnd), London Sinfonietta—Cons. in F, RV.539; in C, RV.533; in D, RV.122; in C, RV.537; in C, RV.560; in F, RV.538; in G, RV.545 *(rec All Saints Church, East Finchley, Oct. 1994 & Jan. 1995)* Naxos ("Vivaldi Collection" series) ▲ 8.553204 [DDD]
McDuffie, Robert (vn)
Diamond, D.:Sons (2) Vn, w. William Black (pno) *(rec RCA Studio A, New York City)* New World ▲ 80508–2
Diamond, D.:Sons (2) Vn, w. William Black (pno) Grenadilla ■ GSC 1064
Kreisler, F.:Vn Pieces, w. E. Kunzel (cnd), Cincinnati Pops Orch—Midnight Bells; Poupée Valsante; Tambourin Chinois; Liebesleid; Caprice Viennois; Schön Rosmarin; La Chasse; Liebesfreud; Serenade from 'Frasquita', Viennese Melody; Rondino *(rec Music Hall, Cincinatti, OH, Nov 11 & 13, 1995)* Telarc ▲ CD 80402 [DDD]
Lehár, F.:Music of, w. E. Kunzel (cnd), Cincinnati Pops Orch—Con Vn; Magyar Ábránd; Vergissmennicht *(rec Music Hall, Cincinatti, OH, Nov 11 & 13, 1995)* Telarc ▲ CD 80402 [DDD]
Sieczynski, R.:Wien Wien nur du Allein, w. E. Kunzel (cnd), Cincinnati Pops Orch *(rec Music Hall, Cincinatti, OH, Nov 11 & 13, 1995)* Telarc ▲ CD 80402 [DDD]
Strauss (II), Joh.:Hochzeitspräludium, w. E. Kunzel (cnd), Cincinnati Pops Orch [arr Erich Kunzel for Orch] *(rec Music Hall, Cincinatti, Ohio, Nov 11 & 13, 1995)* Telarc ▲ CD 80402 [DDD]
McEntire, John (dr)
O'Rourke, J.:Terminal Pharmacy, w. Tony Burr (cl), Jeff Cortazzo (b trbn), Rob Prosser (acc), Isha Suftin (acc), Mike Dockter (vc), Hattie Franck (vc), Robert Keck (vc), Mary LaBreque (vc), Dan Loch (vc), Stan Saderk (vc), Lisa Hemmer (fl), Sue Oberg (fl), Wendi Lev (fl), Jim Vanden (fl), Jim O'Rourke (gtr), Steve Braack (elec) Tzadik ▲ TZA 7011 [DDD]
Macero, George (vc)
Caltabiano, R.:Torched Liberty, w. N. Pilgrim (sop), V. Pritsker (vn), L. Greene (pic/fl/alt fl), K. Schempf (E♭/A/B♭ cl), G. Coble (tpt), S. Heyman (pno), L. Luttinger (perc), R. Caltabiano (cnd) Opus One ▲ CD 168 [DDD]
Lindenfeld, H.:From the Grotte des Combarelles, w. V. Pritsker (vn), S. Heyman (pno) Opus One ▲ CD 168 [DDD]
Willey, J.:Society Music, w. L. Greene (fl), G. Coble (tpt), W. Harris (trbn), D. Resue (hn), S. Heyman (pno), E. Gustafson (vla), E. Castilano (db), L. Luttinger (perc), E. Murray (cnd) Opus One ▲ CD 168 [DDD]
Macerollo, Joseph (acc)
Buczynski, W.:Fant on Themes of the Past, w. G. Kulesha (cnd), Composers Orch *(rec Glenn Gould Studio, CBC Toronto, Mar 17, 1994 & Mar 13 & 2)* CBC ▲ MVCD 1096 [DDD]
Camilleri, C.:Con Acc, w. G. Kulesha (cnd), Composers Orch *(rec Glenn Gould Studio, CBC Toronto, Mar 17, 1994 & Mar 13 & 2)* CBC ▲ MVCD 1096 [DDD]
Louie, A.:Earth Cycles *(rec Glenn Gould Studio, CBC Toronto, Mar 17, 1994 & Mar 13 & 2)* CBC ▲ MVCD 1096 [DDD]
Louie, A.:Refuge, w. Erica Goodman (hp), Beverley Johnston (perc) *(rec Glenn Gould Studio, CBC Toronto, Mar 17, 1994 & Mar 13 & 2)* CBC ▲ MVCD 1096 [DDD]
Lundquist, T.I.:Duell, w. Beverley Johnston (perc) *(rec Glenn Gould Studio, CBC Toronto, Mar 17, 1994 & Mar 13 & 2)* CBC ▲ MVCD 1096 [DDD]
Symonds, N.:Persuasion, w. Robert W. Stevenson (b cl) *(rec Glenn Gould Studio, CBC Toronto, Mar 17, 1994 & Mar 13 & 2)* CBC ▲ MVCD 1096 [DDD]
McEwan, Robert (perc)
Xenakis, I.:Rebonds "b" & "a" Perc *(rec live, Thread Waxing Space, New York, June 21, 1995)* Mode ▲ mode 53
McFadden, Jeffery (gtr)
Sor, F.:Gtr Music—Intro & Vars on "Que ne suis-je la fougère", Op. 26; Intro & Vars on "Gentil Hausard", Op. 27; Intro & Vars on "Malbroug", Op. 28; Etudes, Op. 29; Fant & Vars Brillantes, Op. 30 *(rec Newmarket, Canada, June 1995)* Naxos ▲ 8.553451 [DDD]
McFarland, Patrick (E hn)
Diversions for English Horn Arundax ▲ 80140 [DDD]
Ferlendis, G.:Con 2 Ob, w. J. Flint (cnd), *(orch unknown)* [arr Marcia Kraus for E hn] Arundax ▲ 21339
Mozart, W.A.:Adagio E Hn, w. David Braitberg (vn), Beth Newdome (vn), Paul Murphy (va), Dona Klein (vc) [trans Renate Rosenbaltt] Arundax ▲ 21339
Rachmaninoff, S.:Vocalise, w. David Braitberg (vn), Beth Newdome (vn), Paul Murphy (va), Dona Klein (vc), Larry LeMaster (vc), Gloria Jones (db) [trans John Wildermuth] Arundax ▲ 21339
Ravel, M.:Pièce en forme de Habanera, w. Beverly Gilbert (pno) Arundax ▲ 21339
Tchaikovsky, P.:Les Saisons, w. Beverly Gilbert (pno) [trans Renate Rosenblatt] Arundax ▲ 21339
McFarlane, Ronn (lt)—see also ORCHESTRAS & ENSEMBLES Baltimore Consort members
Dowland, J.:Lt Music—Sir John Smith's Almain; Captain Digorie Piper's Galliard; My Lord Willoughby's welcome home; Melancholy galliard; My Lady Hunsdon's Puffe; Piper's Pavan; The Earl of Essex Galliard; Fantaisie No. 1; Fortune my foe; Lady Laiton's Almain; Lachrimae; Queen Elizabeth's Galliard; Tarleton's Resurrection; Mrs Winter's Jump; Preludium; Dowland's Galliard; Go from my window; Round battle galliard; What if a day; The shoemaker's wife; A Fancy No. 5; Mr Dowland's Midnight; Dr Case's Pavan; Orlando sleepeth; Lady Clifton's Spirit; Semper Dowland, Semper Dolens; The Frog Galliard; Mrs White's Nothing Dorian ▲ DOR 90148 [DDD]
The English Lute Song, w. Julianne Baird (sop) Dorian ▲ DOR 90109 [DDD]
Greensleeves:A Collection of English Lute Songs, w. Julianne Baird (sop) Dorian ▲ DOR 90126 [DDD]
The Italian Lute Song, w. Julianne Baird (sop) *(rec Troy Savings Bank Music Hall, Troy, NY, Oct 1995 & Feb 1996)* Dorian ▲ DOR 90236 [DDD]
O Mistress Mine:A Collection of English Lute Songs, w. Frederick Urrey (ten) Dorian ▲ DOR 90136 [DDD]
The Renaissance Lute *(rec Apr. & June, 1993)* Dorian ▲ DOR 90186 [DDD]
The Scottish Lute Dorian ▲ DOR 90129 [DDD]
McFaul, Rebecca (vn)—see ORCHESTRAS & ENSEMBLES Meaux String Quartet
McGee, Robin (db)
Matthews, C.:Suns Dance, w. Sebastian Bell (pic), Gareth Hulse (ob), Michael Collins (b cl), John Orford (ctbn), Michael Thompson (hn), Nona Liddell (vn), Joan Atherton (vn), Paul Silverthorne (va), Christopher van Kampen (vc) *(rec All Saint's Church, Petersham, Oct 1992)* Deutsche Grammophon ▲ 447067–2 [DDD]
McGegan, Nicholas (hpd)
Matteis, N.:Suites & Sonatas from *Ayres for the Violin*, w. N. McGegan (cnd), Arcadian Academy—Sonata in c (Book I, Nos. 46–49); Suite in g (Book II, Nos. 10–18); Suite in A (Book IV, Nos. 1–11); Sonata in C (Book IV, from Nos. 12–20); Suite in e (Book IV, from Nos. 21–29); Suite in d (Book IV, Nos. 33–36) Harmonia Mundi USA ▲ HMU 907067

McGegan, Nicholas (hpd/clvd)
Bach, J.S.:Anna Magdalena Bach Notebook, w. L. Hunt (sop), D. Bowles (baroque vc)—French Suite No. 1, BWV 812; French Suite No. 2, BWV 813—first 3 sections; various minuets & other short pieces; 5 solo clavichord sels.; 4 Polonaises, in d,F,G & g; Prelude No. 1 from the Well-tempered Clavier Book 1; 5 Arias & Recitatives for Soprano & Continuo instruments *(Arias—Bist du bei mir, BWV 508; Willst du mein Herz mir schenken, BWV 518; Gedenke doch, mein Geist; Schlummert, ein; Recitative—Ich habe genug)* Harmonia Mundi USA ▲ HMU 907042

McGill, David (bn)
Orchestral Excerpts for Bassoon *(rec Plymouth Church Chapel, Shaker Heights, OH)* Summit ▲ DCD 162 [DDD]

McGillvray, Katherine (va)
Biber, H. von:Sonatae tam aris quam aulis servientes, w. Mark Bennett (tpt), Michael Laird (tpt), Jane Rogers (va), Tim Cronin (va), Purcell Quartet Chandos ▲ CHAN 0591

McGowan, Monica (handbells)
Vees, J.:Stigmata non Grata, w. Dorian Ringers (handbells), Cammi Carteng (handbells), Jan Dudiet (handbells), JoAnn Kerns (handbells), B. Mathis (cnd) CRI ("Emergency Music" series) ▲ CD 730 [DDD]

MacGregor, Joanna (pno)
American Piano Classics Collins Classics ▲ COL 1299 [DDD]
Bach, J.S.:The Art of the Fugue Collins Classics 2-▲ COL 7043
Bartók, B.:Dances (6) Pno Collins Classics ▲ COL 1404 [DDD]
Birtwistle, H.:Antiphonies, w. M. Gielen (cnd), Royal PO Collins Classics ▲ COL 1414
Britten, H.:Con Pno, w. S. Bedford (cnd), English CO—[standard 1945 revised version, plus the original 3rd movement] Collins Classics ▲ 11022 [DDD]
Britten, H.:Con Pno, w. S. Bedford (cnd), English CO *(rec 10/89)* Collins Classics ▲ 13012 [DDD]
Copland, A.:Vars Pno Collins Classics ▲ 12992 [DDD]
Debussy, C.:Etudes—6 Etudes Collins Classics ▲ COL 1404 [DDD]
Gershwin, G.:Con Pno, w. C. Davis (cnd), London SO Collins Classics ▲ COL 1362 [DDD]
Gershwin, G.:Con Pno, w. C. Davis (cnd), London SO Collins Classics ▲ 11392 [DDD]
Gershwin, G.:The George Gershwin Songbook—16 sels. from *The George Gershwin Songbook,* plus 8 pop standards in avant-garde classical solo piano arangements by Django Bates *(Harold Arlen—It's only a paper moon; Richard Rodgers—June is bustin' out all over),* Gary Carpenter *(Cole Porter—Love for sale; My heart belongs to daddy; Night & day),* Michael Finnissy *(Jerome Kern—Can't help lovin' dat man),* & Alasdair Nicolson *(Sammy Fain—I'll be seeing you; Harry Warren—42nd Street)* Collins Classics ▲ 11372 [DDD]
Gershwin, G.:The George Gershwin Songbook Collins Classics ▲ COL 1362 [DDD]
Gershwin, G.:Rhap in Blue, w. C. Davis (cnd), London SO Collins Classics ▲ COL 1362 [DDD]
Ives, C.:Pno Music Collins Classics ▲ 12992 [DDD]
Ives, C.:Three-Page Son Collins Classics ▲ 12992 [DDD]
Krauze, Z.:Quatuor pour la naissance, w. D. Campbell (cl), M. Mitchell (vn), C. van Kampen (vc) Collins Classics ▲ COL 1393 [DDD]
Messiaen, O.:Quatuor pour la fin du temps, w. D. Campbell (cl), M. Mitchell (vn), C. van Campen (vc) Collins Classics ▲ COL 1393 [DDD]
Nancarrow, C.:Canons for Ursula—3 sels Collins Classics 2-▲ COL 7043
Nancarrow, C.:Studies—Nos. 3C, 6 & 11 Collins Classics 2-▲ COL 7043
Ravel, M.:Alborada del gracioso [arr. piano] Collins Classics ▲ COL 1404 [DDD]
Ravel, M.:Pavane pour une infante défunte Collins Classics ▲ COL 1404 [DDD]
Ravel, M.:Valses nobles et sentimentales [arr. piano] Collins Classics ▲ COL 1404 [DDD]
Satie, E.:Pno Music (misc)—Sports et divertissements; Gnossiennes Nos. 1,3,4 & 5; Pièces froides (Airs à faire fuir); Embryons desséchés; Trois Gymnopédies; Véritables préludes flasques (pour un chien); Les trois valses distinguées du précieüx dégôuté; Avant-dernières Pensées; Vieux sequins et vieilles cuirasses; Prélude de la Porte Héroïque du Ciel; Heures séculaires et instantanées; Je te veux; Ragtime-Parade *(rec 8/89)* Collins Classics ▲ 10532 [DDD]

McGross, J. (vn)—see ORCHESTRAS & ENSEMBLES Aviv String Quartet

McGuire, Marshall (hp)
Conyngham, B.:Awakening *(rec Studio 200, ABC Ultimo Centre, Sydney, 1994)* Tall Poppies ▲ TP 071 [DDD]
Conyngham, B.:Streams, w. Geoffrey Collins (fl), Patricia Pollett (va) *(rec Studio 200, ABC Ultimo Centre, Sydney, 1994)* Tall Poppies ▲ TP 071 [DDD]
Fowler, J.:Threaded Stars *(rec Studio 200, ABC Ultimo Centre, Sydney, 1994)* Tall Poppies ▲ TP 071 [DDD]
Gifford, H.:Fable *(rec Studio 200, ABC Ultimo Centre, Sydney, 1994)* Tall Poppies ▲ TP 071 [DDD]
Glanville-Hicks, P.:Son Hp *(rec Studio 200, ABC Ultimo Centre, Sydney, 1994)* Tall Poppies ▲ TP 071 [DDD]
Koehne, G.:To His Servant Bach God Grants a Final Glimpse:The Morning Star [trans McGuire] *(rec Studio 200, ABC Ultimo Centre, Sydney, 1994)* Tall Poppies ▲ TP 071 [DDD]
Sculthorpe, P.:From Kakadu [trans McGuire] *(rec Studio 200, ABC Ultimo Centre, Sydney, 1994)* Tall Poppies ▲ TP 071 [DDD]
Sculthorpe, P.:Into the Dreaming [trans McGuire] *(rec Studio 200, ABC Ultimo Centre, Sydney, 1994)* Tall Poppies ▲ TP 071 [DDD]
Sculthorpe, P.:Night Pieces *(rec Studio 200, ABC Ultimo Centre, Sydney, 1994)* Tall Poppies ▲ TP 071 [DDD]
Whiticker, M.:After the Fire Vox Australis ▲ VAST 0192

McGushin, Michael (pno)
Bowles, P.:Nocturne for 2 Pnos, w. Irene Herrmann (pno) Koch International Classics ▲ KIC 7343 [DDD]
Tailleferre, G.:Galliarde, w. Karen Baccaro (tpt) *(rec UC, Santa Cruz, May 1992)* Helicon Classics ▲ HE 1008
Tailleferre, G.:Waltzes, w. Irene Herrmann (pno) *(rec UC, Santa Cruz, May 1992)* Helicon Classics ▲ HE 1008

Mach, Vít (vle)—see ORCHESTRAS & ENSEMBLES Pro Arte Antiqua Prague

Machado, Regina (perc)
Chevalier, C.:Music of, w. Teca Calazans (sgr), Ze-Luis (sgr), Regina Machado (sgr), Nigel Scragg (fl/a sax), Rosihna de Valenca (gtr), Jean-Yves Candela (pno), Wilson das Neves (perc), Silvano Michelino (perc)—Comme d'habitude; Couleur café; Une histoire d'amour; Les feuilles mortes; Les moulins de mon coeur; Syracuse; Je t'aimerai; Ces petits rien; La valse des lilas; L'absent; Que reste-il de nos amours; Un homme et une femme *(rec Studio Bastille)* Iris ▲ 010 [DDD]

Machamer, Steven (vib)
Bach, J.S.:Chorale Preludes (Schübler), w. Ranck (hpd)—BWV 650 [performer trans for vib & pno] Ashlar ▲ 1009
Bach, J.S.:Italian Con, w. Ranck (hpd) [trans. vibraphone & piano Machamer & Ranck] Ashlar ▲ 1009
Bach, J.S.:Sons Vn, w. Ranck (hpd)—in E, BWV 1016 [trans. Machamer for vibraphone & piano] Ashlar ▲ 1009
Handel, G.F.:Trio Sons, w. Eric Wyrick (vn), Gerald Ranck (hpd/pno) [performer trans. for vibraphone, violin & piano]—Op. 2, No. 3 for 2 Violins & Keyboard Ashlar ▲ 1009
Leclair, J.-M.:Son 3 for 2 Vns, w. E. Wyrick (vn) [performer trans. for vibraphone & violin] Ashlar ▲ 1009
Vibrant Baroque, w. Gerald Ranck (pno), Eric Wyrick (vn) Ashlar Records ▲ 1009

McInnes, Donald (va)
Berlioz, H.:Harold in Italy, w. L. Bernstein (cnd), French National Orch EMI Classics ▲ CDM 64745
Schoenberg, A.:Verklärte Nacht, w. J. Pegis (vc), LaSalle String Quartet Deutsche Grammophon ▲ 423250-2 [ADD]

McIntosh, Carolyn (vc)—see ORCHESTRAS & ENSEMBLES Porter String Quartet

McIntosh, Kathleen (hpd)
Bach, J.S.:Inventions (30) Hpd *(rec Ponytracks Farm, May 1992)* Gasparo ▲ GS 304 [DDD]
Bach, J.S.:Preludes Hpd, BWV 933-38, "Little Preludes" *(rec Ponytracks Farm, May 1992)* Gasparo ▲ GS 304 [DDD]

McIntosh, Kathleen (hpd) (cont.)
Boismortier, J.B. de:Hpd Music—Sons Nos. 1-4; 5 Pieces *(rec Weckesser Hall, College of Sante Fe, Sante Fe, NM)* Gasparo ▲ GSCD 309 [DDD]

McIntosh, Thomas (hpd)
Chilcot, T.:Con Hpd, w. T. McIntosh (cnd), City of London CO *(rec 1980)* Allegretto ▲ ACD 8165 [DDD] ■ ACS 8165

McIntosh, Thomas (org)
Arne, T.:Con 2 Org, w. T. McIntosh (cnd), City of London CO *(rec 1980)* Allegretto ▲ ACD 8165 [DDD] ■ ACS 8165
Stanley, J.:Con in c Org, w. T. McIntosh (cnd), City of London CO *(rec 1980)* Allegretto ▲ ACD 8165 [DDD] ■ ACS 8165

Maciocchi, Françoise (pno)
Rossini, G.:Petite messe solennelle, w. E. Schmitt (sop), S. Gregoire (cta), R. Garin (ten), A. Golven (bass), F. Maciocchi (pno) J.-F. Hatton (harm), Paris Opéra-Comique Chorus IMP Masters ▲ IMP MCD61

Mack, Ellen (pno)
Lewis, R.H.:Combinazioni IV, w. Stephen Kates (vc) *(rec Peabody Institute Concert Hall, Baltimore, MD, Oct 26, 1978)* Albany ▲ TROY 166 [ADD/DDD]

Mack, John (ob)—see also ORCHESTRAS & ENSEMBLES Plymouth Trio
Britten, H.:Metamorphoses Ob Crystal ■ C 325
Britten, H.:Metamorphoses Ob Crystal ▲ CD323
Hindemith, P.:Son Ob, w. E. Podis (pno) Crystal ▲ CD324
Hindemith, P.:Son Ob, w. E. Podis (pno) Crystal ■ C 324
John Mack:Oboe, w. Eunice Podis (pno) Crystal ▲ CD324
Loeffler, C.M.:Rhaps, w. A. Skernick (va), E. Podis (pno) Crystal ■ C 323
Loeffler, C.M.:Rhaps, w. A. Skernick (va), E. Podis (pno) Crystal ▲ CD323
Mozart, W.A.:Qt Ob, K.370, w. D. Majeske (vn), A. Skernick (va), S. Geber (vc) Crystal ▲ CD323 ■ C 323
Orchestral Excerpts for Oboe Summit ▲ DCD 160 [DDD]
Paladilhe, E.:Solo de concert Ob Crystal ■ C 325
Paladilhe, E.:Solo de concert Ob Crystal ▲ CD323
Poulenc, F.:Son Ob, w. E. Podis (pno) Crystal ■ C 324
Poulenc, F.:Son Ob, w. E. Podis (pno) Crystal ▲ CD324
Saint-Saëns, C.:Son Ob, w. E. Podis (pno) Crystal ■ C 325
Saint-Saëns, C.:Son Ob, w. E. Podis (pno) Crystal ▲ CD324
Schumann, R.:Romances Ob, w. E. Podis (pno) Crystal ■ C 325
Schumann, R.:Romances Ob, w. E. Podis (pno) Crystal ▲ CD324
Sonatas for Oboe, w. Eunice Podis (pno) Crystal ■ C 324
Zwilich, E.T.:Con Ob, w. J. Sedares (cnd), Louisville Orch Koch International Classics ▲ KIC 7278 [DDD]

McKay, James (bn)
Françaix, J.:Heure du berger Orch, w. Suzanne Shulman (fl), James Mason (ob), James Campbell (cl), James Sommerville (hn), André Laplante (pno) *(rec Glenn Gould Studio, CBC Toronto, Mar. 26-27, 1994)* CBC ("Musica Viva" series) ▲ MVV 1089 [DDD]
Martinů, B.:La Revue de Cuisine, w. James Campbell (cl), Guy Few (tpt), Moshe Hammer (vn), Tsuyoshi Tsutsumi (vc), André Laplante (pno) *(rec Glenn Gould Studio, CBC Toronto, Mar. 26-27, 1994)* CBC ("Musica Viva" series) ▲ MVV 1089 [DDD]
Nielsen, C.:Serenata in vano, w. James Campbell (cl), James Sommerville (hn), Tsuyoshi Tsutsumi (vc), Joel Quarrington (db) *(rec Glenn Gould Studio, CBC Toronto, Mar. 26-27, 1994)* CBC ("Musica Viva" series) ▲ MVV 1089 [DDD]
Strauss, R.:Till Eulenspiegels lustige Streiche, w. James Campbell (cl), James Sommerville (hn), Martin Beaver (vn), Joel Quarrington (db)—[arr. Franz Hasenöhrl as Einmal Anders! (frolic for 5 instruments; 1954)] *(rec Glenn Gould Studio, CBC Toronto, Mar. 26-27, 1994)* CBC ("Musica Viva" series) ▲ MVV 1089 [DDD]
Vivaldi, A.:Con Vc, RV.409, w. O. Harnoy (vc), P. Robinson (cnd), Toronto CO RCA Red Seal ▲ 7774-2-RC [DDD] ■ 7774-4-RC (CrO2)

McKean, Randy (sax)
Ziporyn, E.:Kekembangan, w. Chris Jonas (sax), Dan Plonsey (sax), Evan Ziporyn (sax), Sekar Jaya Gamelan Orch New World ▲ 804302

McKeand, Vanessa (hp)
Ravel, M.:Intro & Allegro, w. C. Wincenc (fl), D. Campbell (cl), Allegri String Quartet Virgin Classics ▲ CDZ 59695
Ravel, M.:Le Tombeau de Couperin, w. C. Wincenc (fl), D. Campbell (cl), Allegri String Quartet Virgin Classics ▲ CDZ 59695

McKenzie, Julie (fl)
Lewis, P.S.:Little Trio, w. L. Granger (vc), M. Shapiro (pno) New Albion ▲ NA 060 [DDD]

Mackenzie, Norman (pno)
Badings, H.:Chansons bretonnes, w. Robert Shaw (cnd), Robert Shaw Festival Singers *(rec Church of St. Pierre, Gramat, France, July 26-28, 1994)* Telarc ▲ CD 80408 [DDD]
Brahms, J.:Liebeslieder Waltzes SATB, w. J. Wustman (pno), Robert Shaw Festival Singers [G] *(rec Aug. 6-7, 1992)* Telarc ▲ CD 80326 [DDD]
Brahms, J.:Neue Liebeslieder Waltzes, w. J. Wustman (pno), Robert Shaw Festival Singers [G] *(rec Aug. 6-7, 1992)* Telarc ▲ CD 80326 [DDD]
Brahms, J.:Songs, w. J. Wustman (pno), Robert Shaw Festival Singers—7 Abendlieder [G] *(rec Aug. 6-7, 1992)* Telarc ▲ CD 80326 [DDD]
Schubert, Franz:Choral Music, w. M. Ackerman (gtr), R. Shaw (cnd), Robert Shaw Chamber Singers—Die Nacht; Der Nachtigall [w. K. Dent (tenor)]; Wehmuth; Der Gondelfahrer; Mondenschein [w. Dent]; Nachthelle [w. Dent]; Das Dörfchen [w. Dent]; Die Einsiedelei; Sehnsucht; Grab und Mond; Frühlingsgesang [w. Dent & R. Clement (tenor)]; Liebe; Widerspruch; An den Frühling; La pastorella; Ständchen [w. M. Hart (mezzo-soprano)]; Der Entfernten *(rec Oct. 17-18, 1992)* Telarc ▲ CD 80340 [DDD]

Mackerras, Charles (pno)
Janácek, L.:Conte, w. Gary Hoffman (vc) EMI Classics ▲ CDC 55585
Janácek, L.:Son Vn, w. Pierre Amoyal (vn) EMI Classics ▲ CDC 55585

Mackey, Steven (gtr)
Lansky, P.:Not So Heavy Metal New Albion ▲ NA 030 [DDD]

Mackintosh, Catherine (vl)
Vivaldi, A.:Cons Va d'amore, w. C. Mackintosh (cnd), Orch of the Age of Enlightenment [period instr]—in D, RV.392; in d, RV.395; in d, RV.393; in a, RV.397; in d, RV.394; in A, RV.396 Hyperion ▲ CDA 66795

Mackintosh, Catherine (vn)—see also ORCHESTRAS & ENSEMBLES Purcell Quartet
Purcell, H.:Music of, w. Catherine Bott (sop), Emma Kirkby (sop), James Bowman (alt), Anthony Rooley (lt), Monica Huggett (vn), Christophe Coin (vc), Paula Chateauneuf (gtr), Hill, Hogwood (cnd), Brandenburg Consort, Academy of Ancient Music, Anthony Lewis (cnd), David Hill (cnd), St. Anthony Singers, Taverner Choir, Winchester Cathedral Choir—The Double Dealer; Come Ye Sons of Art; The Old Bachelor; Birthday Song for Queen Mary; Oedipus; King Arthur; Bonduca; The Fairy Queen; Son. No. 9 in F; Dido & Aeneas; Abdelazer; Bess of Bedlam; The Married Beau; Hear My Prayer, O Lord; Rejoice in the Lord Always L'Oiseau-Lyre ▲ 444620-2
Purcell, H.:Music of, w. Catherine Bott (sop), Emma Kirkby (sop), James Bowman (alt), Anthony Rooley (lt), Paula Chateauneuf (gtr), Monica Huggett (vn), Christophe Coin (vc), Hill, Hogwood (cnd), Academy of Ancient Music, Brandenburg Consort, David Hill (cnd), Anthony Lewis (cnd), St. Anthony Singers, Taverner Choir, Winchester Cathedral Choir—The Double Dealer; Come Ye Sons of Art; The Old Bachelor; Birthday Song for Queen Mary; Oedipus; King Arthur; Bonduca; The Fairy Queen; Son. No. 9 in F; Dido & Aeneas; Abdelazer; Bess of Bedlam; The Married Beau; Hear My Prayer, O Lord; Rejoice in the Lord Always London ("Editions de l'oiseau-lyre" series) ▲ 444620-2
Purcell, H.:Sons (10) Vns, Z.802-811, w. M. Huggett (vn), C. Coin (b vl), C. Hogwood (chamber org/spinet) L'Oiseau-Lyre ▲ 433190-2 [ADD]
Vivaldi, A.:Sons Vn, w. Purcell Quartet Chandos ("Chaconne" series) ▲ CHAN 0502 [DDD]

INSTRUMENT.

Mackintosh, Catherine (vn/pic)
Bach, J.S.:Brandenburg Cons, w. C. Mackintosh (cnd), Orch of the Age of Enlightenment Virgin Classics 2-▲ CDCB 59152

McLachlan, Murray (pno)
Camilleri, C.:Pno Music—Sonatina Folklpristica; Sonatina Modale; Sonatina Serena; Sonatina No. 1; Sonatina Semplice; African Dreams; Etudes [Books 1 & 2]; Times of Day Olympia ▲ OLY 478 [DDD]
Center, R.:Bagatelles, Op. 3 Olympia ▲ OCD 264 [DDD]
Center, R.:Children at Play Olympia ▲ OCD 264 [DDD]
Center, R.:Son Pno Olympia ▲ OCD 264 [DDD]
Kabalevsky, D.:Preludes & Fugues Pno *(rec London, 1992)* Olympia ▲ OCD 294 [DDD]
Miaskovsky, N.:Prelude Olympia ▲ OCD 217 [DDD]
Miaskovsky, N.:Reminiscences Olympia ▲ OCD 252 [DDD]
Miaskovsky, N.:Rondo-Son Olympia ▲ OCD 252 [DDD]
Miaskovsky, N.:Scherzo Olympia ▲ OCD 252 [DDD]
Miaskovsky, N.:Sons Pno—No. 7 in C, Op. 82; No. 8 in d, Op. 83; No. 9 in F, Op. 84 Olympia ▲ OCD 252 [DDD]
Miaskovsky, N.:Sons Pno—No. 1 in d, Op. 6; No. 2 in f#, Op. 13; No. 3 in c, Op. 19; No. 6 in Ab, Op. 64/2 Olympia ▲ OCD 214 [DDD]
Miaskovsky, N.:Sons Pno—No. 4 in c, Op. 27 & No. 5 in B, Op. 64/1 Olympia ▲ OCD 217 [DDD]
Miaskovsky, N.:Sonatine Pno Olympia ▲ OCD 217 [DDD]
Miaskovsky, N.:Yellowed Leaves Olympia ▲ OCD 252 [DDD]
Piano Music from Malta Olympia ▲ OLY 489 [DDD]
Prokofiev, S.:Pieces Pno, Op. 4 Olympia ▲ OCD 257 [DDD]
Prokofiev, S.:Sons Pno (comp)—Sonata Nos. 2,7 & 8 Olympia ▲ OCD 256 [DDD]
Prokofiev, S.:Sons Pno (comp)—Sonata Nos. 1,4,5,9 & 10 Olympia ▲ OCD 255 [DDD]
Prokofiev, S.:Sons Pno (comp)—Sonata Nos. 3, 5 [1923 version] & 6 Olympia ▲ OCD 257 [DDD]
Prokofiev, S.:Sonatinas Pno—No. 1 Olympia ▲ OCD 257 [DDD]
Scott, F.G.:Songs Pno Olympia ▲ OCD 264 [DDD]
Shchedrin, R.:Polyphonic Book Olympia 2-▲ OLY 438 [DDD]
Shchedrin, R.:Preludes & Fugues Pno Olympia 2-▲ OLY 438 [DDD]
Stevenson, R.:Con 1 Pno, w. J. Clayton (cnd), Chetham's SO Olympia ▲ OLY 429 [DDD]
Stevenson, R.:Con 2 Pno, w. J. Clayton (cnd), Chetham's SO Olympia ▲ OLY 429 [DDD]
Stevenson, R.:Pno Music—Beltane Bonfire; Two Scottish Ballads Olympia ▲ OCD 264 [DDD]
Tcherepnin, A.:Con 1 Pno, w. J. Clayton (cnd), Chetham's SO Olympia ▲ OLY 440 [DDD]
Tcherepnin, A.:Con 2 Pno, w. J. Clayton (cnd), Chetham's SO Olympia ▲ OLY 439 [DDD]
Tcherepnin, A.:Con 3 Pno, w. J. Clayton (cnd), Chetham's SO Olympia ▲ OLY 439 [DDD]
Tcherepnin, A.:Con 4 Pno, w. J. Clayton (cnd), Chetham's SO Olympia ▲ OLY 440 [DDD]
Tcherepnin, A.:Con 5 Pno, w. J. Clayton (cnd), Chetham's SO Olympia ▲ OLY 440 [DDD]
Tcherepnin, A.:Con 6 Pno, w. J. Clayton (cnd), Chetham's SO Olympia ▲ OLY 439 [DDD]

McLaren, Neil (fl)
Benda, F.:Con in G Fl & Strs, w. J.H. Jones (cnd), Cambridge Baroque Camerata [period instrs] Amon Ra ▲ CD-SAR 52 [DDD]
Naudot, J.-C.:Cons Fl, w. J.H. Jones (cnd), Cambridge Baroque Camerata—No. 1 [period instrs] Amon Ra ▲ CD-SAR 52 [DDD]
Quantz, J.J.:Con in e Fl & Strs, w. J.H. Jones (cnd), Cambridge Baroque Camerata [period instrs] Amon Ra ▲ CD-SAR 52 [DDD]
Tartini, G.:Con in G Fl, w. J.H. Jones (cnd), Cambridge Baroque Camerata [period instrs] Amon Ra ▲ CD-SAR 52 [DDD]

McLaughlin, John (gtr)
McLaughlin, J.:Con Gtr, w. M. Tilson Thomas (cnd), London SO CBS ▲ MK 45578 [DDD]
McLaughlin, J.:Duos, w. K. Labèque (pno) CBS ▲ MK 45578 [DDD]
Pavarotti & Friends for War Child, w. Pavarotti, Luciano (ten), Eric Clapton (sgr), Sheryl Crow (sgr), Elton John (sgr), Liza Minelli (sgr), Joan Osborne (sgr), Jon Secada (sgr), Eric Clapton (gtr), Marco Armiliato, Edoardo Bennato, José Molina, Al DiMeola, Kelly Family, Ligabue, Litfiba, P *(rec Modena, Italy, 1996)* London ▲ 452900-2 ■ 452900-4

MacLean, Alan (pno)
Berners:Fant espagnole, w. Peter Lawson (pno) Albany ▲ TROY 142 [DDD]
Berners:Morceaux (3), w. Peter Lawson (pno) Albany ▲ TROY 142 [DDD]
Berners:Valses bourgeoises, w. Peter Lawson (pno) Albany ▲ TROY 142 [DDD]
Lambert, C.:Ov Pno 4-Hands, w. Peter Lawson (pno) Albany ▲ TROY 142 [DDD]
Lambert, C.:Pièces nègres pour les touches blanches, w. Peter Lawson (pno) Albany ▲ TROY 142 [DDD]
Lane, P.:Badinages, w. Peter Lawson (pno) Albany ▲ TROY 142 [DDD]
Rawsthorne, A.:The Creel, w. Peter Lawson (pno) Albany ▲ TROY 142 [DDD]
Walton, W.:Duets for Children, w. Peter Lawson (pno) Albany ▲ TROY 142 [DDD]

McLean, Barton (kbd/clariflute/syn/elec)
McLean, B.:Earth Music, w. Priscilla McLean (sgr/perc/ocarinas/elec) Capstone ▲ CPS 8622

McLean, Barton (perc)
McLean, P.:Wilderness, w. Priscilla McLean (sgr) [w. animal, bird, insect, & surreal instrumental sounds on stereo tape] Capstone ▲ CPS 8622

McLean, Barton (rcr/clariflute)
McLean, B.:Rainforest Images, w. Panaiotis (sgr), I. Troselj (sgr), K. Ryan (sgr), P. McLean (sgr/rcr/vn), B. Dickie (didgeridoo) Capstone ▲ CPS 8617n

McLean, Hugh (org)
Handel, G.F.:Con Hp, w. M. Bernardi (cnd), CBC Vancouver SO [arr org & orch] CBC ▲ 5163 [DDD]

McLean, Joyhn (instrs)
Judeo-Spanish Songs, w. Bessis, Sandra (sgr) ARB ▲ 1413

McLin, Katherine (vn)—see ORCHESTRAS & ENSEMBLES Alorian String Quartet

McMahon, Don (pno)
Beach, A.M.C.:Songs, w. L. Kolb (sop)—Nachts; Fairy Lullaby Far awa'i; Extase; Take, O Take Those Lips away; The Western Wind; Forgotten; Wir Drei Albany ▲ TROY 109
Poldowski:Songs, w. L. Kolb (sop)—Colombine; Bruxelles; Spleen; Dimanche d'Avril; Cythère; L'attente; Créspuscule du soir mystique; Dansons la Gigue, Op. 23 Albany ▲ TROY 109
Schumann, C.:Songs, w. L. Kolb (sop)—Ich stand in dunklen Träumen; Sie liebten sich Beide; Liebesgarten; Der Mond kommt still gegangen; Ich hab' in deinem Auge; Die stille Lotosblume Albany ▲ TROY 109

McMahon, Ivor (vn)
Butterworth, G.:Songs (6) from *A Shropshire Lad*, w. John Shirley-Quirk (bar), Nona Liddell (vn), Ambrose Gauntlett (vl), Martin Isepp (hpd/pno) Saga Classics ▲ EC 3336
Humfrey, P.:Anthems, w. John Shirley-Quirk (bar), Nona Liddell (vn), Ambrose Gauntlett (vl), Martin Isepp (hpd/pno)—A Hymne to God the Father Saga Classics ▲ EC 3336
Moeran, E.J.:Songs, w. John Shirley-Quirk (bar), Martin Isepp (hpd/pno), Nona Liddell (vn), Ambrose Gauntlett (vl)—When Smoke Stood Up from Ludlow; Say, Lad, Have You Things to Do?; Farewell to Barn & Stack & Trees [all from Ludlow Town] Saga Classics ▲ EC 3336
Purcell, H.:Songs, w. John Shirley-Quirk (bar), Martin Isepp (hpd/pno), Nona Liddell (vn), Ambrose Gauntlett (vl)—Man Is for the Woman Made; Music for a While; Twas within a Furlong of Edinborough Town; When Night her Purple Veil Saga Classics ▲ EC 3336

McMahon, Michael (pno)
Brahms, J.:Songs, w. C. Robbin (mez)—Blinde Kuh; Die Mainacht; Sonntag; Von ewiger Liebe [G] Marquis ▲ ERAD113
Brahms, J.:Songs, w. K. McMillan (bar)—Es schauen die Blumen; Meerfahrt; Der Tod, das ist die kühle Nacht [G] CBC ("Musica Viva" series) ▲ MVCD 1052 [DDD]
Catherine Robbin, w. Catherine Robbin (mez) *(rec 1985)* Marquis Classics ▲ ERAD113
Honegger, A.:Songs, w. C. Robbin (mez)—Saluste du Bartas [F] Marquis ▲ ERAD113
Lieder on Poems of Heinrich Heine, w. Kevin McMillan (bar) CBC Records ("Musica Viva" series) ▲ MVCD 1052 [DDD]

McMahon, Michael (pno) (cont.)
Liszt, F.:Songs, w. K. McMillan (bar)—Du bist wie eine Blume; Ein Fichtenbaum steht einsam; Im Rhein, im schönen Strome; Vergiftet sind meine Lieder [G] CBC ("Musica Viva" series) ▲ MVCD 1052 [DDD]
Mendelssohn, F.:Songs, w. K. McMillan (bar)—Allnächtlich im Traume seh' ich dich; Auf Flügeln des Gesanges; Gruss; Neue Liebe [G] CBC ("Musica Viva" series) ▲ MVCD 1052 [DDD]
Schubert, Franz:Songs (misc), w. K. McMillan (bar)—Der Atlas; Der Doppelgänger [G] CBC ("Musica Viva" series) ▲ MVCD 1052 [DDD]
Schubert, Franz:Songs (misc), w. C. Robbin (mez)—Der Fischer; Der König; Suleika [G] Marquis ▲ ERAD113
Schumann, R.:Frauenliebe und -leben, w. C. Robbin (mez) [G] CBC ("Musica Viva" series) ▲ MVCD 1050 [DDD]
Schumann, R.:Liederkreis, Op. 24, w. C. Robbin (mez) [G] CBC ("Musica Viva" series) ▲ MVCD 1050 [DDD]
Schumann, R.:Songs, w. C. Robbin (mez)—5 Maria Stuart Songs, Op. 135 [G] CBC ("Musica Viva" series) ▲ MVCD 1050 [DDD]

McMahon, Richard (pno)
Benjamin, A.:Music of, w. M. Jones (pno)—Jamaican Rumba, 2 Jamaican Street Songs, Caribbean Dance, From San Domingo, Jamaicalypso Pianissimo ▲ PP 11192 [DDD]
Chabrier, E.:Pno Music (misc)—Impromptu in C; Bourrée Fantasque Pianissimo ▲ PP 10792 [DDD]
Chabrier, E.:Pièces pittoresques Pianissimo ▲ PP 10792 [DDD]
Grainger, P.:Fant on Gershwin's *Porgy & Bess*, w. M. Jones (pno) Pianissimo ▲ PP 11192 [DDD]
Grainger, P.:Lincolnshire Posy, w. M. Jones (pno) Pianissimo ▲ PP 11192 [DDD]

Macmillan, Andrew (org)
A Sound Came From Heaven, w. [cnd:Philip Walsh], Wellington Cathedral Choir Herald ▲ HAPVCD 191 [DDD]

MacMillan, B. (vl/baroque vc)—see ORCHESTRAS & ENSEMBLES Arion Ensemble

MacMillan, E. (org)
Bach, J.S.:Preludes & Fugues, BWV 531-552—in Eb, BWV 552, "St. Anne" *(rec Sept 24, 1950)* Analekta ▲ AN 2 7804

MacMillan, E. (pno)
Grieg, E.:Son 2 Vn, w. K. Parlow (vn) *(rec Oct. 13, 1941)* Analekta ▲ AN 2 7804

McMullen, William (ob)—see also ORCHESTRAS & ENSEMBLES Moran Woodwind Quintet
Pinkham, D.:Songs, w. Margaret Kennedy (sop), Paul Barnes (pno)—Carols & Cries; Music, Thou Soul of Heaven; Slow, Slow, Fresh Fount; The Hour Glass; Heaven-Haven/World Welter; The Moon Was But a Chin of Gold; To Make a Prairie; A Partridge in a Pear Tree; 3 Canticles from Luke; For Echo is the Soul of the Voice; When Love Was Gone; 3 Alleluias Arkay ▲ ARK 6153 [DDD]
Snyder, R.:Qnt 3 Fl, w. John Bailey (fl), Eric Ginsberg (cl), Allen French (hn), Gary Echols (bn) Coronet ▲ COR 400-9

McMunn, Brent (pno)
Bartók, B.:Rhaps (2) Vn & Orch, w. M. Lefkowitz (vn)—No. 1 Cambria ▲ 1029 [DDD]
Bloch, E.:Baal Shem, "3 Pictures of Chassidic Life", w. M. Lefkowitz (vn) Cambria ▲ 1029 [DDD]
Cage, J.:Melodies (6) Vn & Kbd, w. M. Makarski (vn) New World ▲ 80391-2 [DDD]
Debussy, C.:Son Vn, w. M. Lefkowitz (vn) Cambria ▲ 1029 [DDD]
Virtuoso Violin Classics, w. Lefkowitz, Mischa (vn) *(rec 1/87)* Cambria ▲ CD 1029 [DDD]
Wyner, Y.:Concert Duo Vn, w. M. Makarski (vn) New World ▲ 80391-2 [DDD]
Ysaÿe, E.:Caprice after Saint-Saëns' "Etude en forme de valse", w. M. Lefkowitz (vn) Cambria ▲ 1029 [DDD]

MacNamara, Hilary (pno)
Rachmaninoff, S.:Suite 1 for 2 Pnos, w. H. Shelley (pno) Hyperion ▲ CDA 66375 [DDD]
Rachmaninoff, S.:Suite 2 for 2 Pnos, w. H. Shelley (pno) Hyperion ▲ CDA 66375 [DDD]
Rachmaninoff, S.:Symphonic Dances, w. H. Shelley (pno) Hyperion ▲ CDA 66375 [DDD]

MacNamara, Mandy (db)
Vivaldi, A.:Cons Rcr, w. Piers Adams (rcr), Ray Goodman (vn), Miles Golding (vn), Jane Compton (va), Jane Coe (vc), David Miller (archlt), Robert King (hpd/org)—in F for Treble Rcr, Op. 10/1; in a for Sopranino Rcr, RV.440; in c for Treble Rcr, RV.441; in D for Sopranino Rcr, Op. 10/3; in g for Treble Rcr, Op. 10/2; in C for Sopranino Rcr, RV.443 *(rec Radley College, Abingdon, Oxon)* United ▲ CAL 88015 [DDD]

McNaught, Graeme (pno)
Copland, A.:Old American Songs, w. W. White (bass) [E] Chandos ▲ CHAN 8960 [DDD]
Sarasate, P. de:Vn & Pno Music, w. R. Ricci (vn)—Fantaisie on Themes from Gounod's Faust; Jota de S. Fermin; Romanian Melody; Jota Aragonesa, Op. 27; Serenata Andalusa, Op. 28; The Song of the Nightingale, Op. 29; Pateneras, Op. 35; Adios montanas mias, Op. 37; Zortzico d'Iparaguirre, Op. 39; Miramar (Zortzico), Op. 42; Chansons Russes, Op. 49; Jota de Pablo, Op. 52 Dynamic ▲ CD 94 [DDD]
10 American Spirituals, w. Willard White (bass) Chandos ▲ CHAN 8960 [DDD]

McNeely, John (pno)
Bernstein, L.:Waltz for Mippy III, w. Warren Deck (tuba) Cala Records ("New York Legends" series) ▲ CAL CACD 508 [DDD]
Ewazen, E.:Son Hn, w. Joseph Alessi (trbn) Cala Records ("New York Legends" series) ▲ CAL CACD 508 [DDD]
Peaslee, R.:Arrows of Time, w. Joseph Alessi (trbn) Cala Records ("New York Legends" series) ▲ CAL CACD 508 [DDD]
Ropartz, J.G.:Concert Piece, w. Joseph Alessi (trbn) Cala Records ("New York Legends" series) ▲ CAL CACD 508 [DDD]
Rush, S.:Rebellion, w. Joseph Alessi (trbn), Christopher Lamb (perc) Cala Records ("New York Legends" series) ▲ CAL CACD 508 [DDD]

McNicol (fl)
Debussy, C.:Son Fl, w. R. Best (va), Kelly (hp) Chandos ▲ CHAN 8385 [ADD]
Debussy, C.:Syrinx Chandos ▲ CHAN 8385 [ADD]

Macomber, Curtis (vn)
Adolphe, B.:Soliloquy Koch International Classics ▲ KIC 7145-2 [DDD]
Beach, A.M.C.:Invocation, w. Diane Walsh (pno) Koch International Classics ▲ KIC 7223 [DDD]
Beach, A.M.C.:Romance, w. Diane Walsh (pno) Koch International Classics ▲ KIC 7223 [DDD]
Beach, A.M.C.:Son Vn, w. Diane Walsh (pno) Koch International Classics ▲ KIC 7223 [DDD]
Bland, W.:Qt Fl, Cl, Vn & Pno, w. H. Starreveld (fl), C. Neidich (cl), R. Eckhardt (pno) Bridge ▲ BCD 9013 [DDD]
Carter, E.:Riconoscenza (per Goffredo Petrassi) *(rec Recital Hall, Music Division, SUNY, Purchase, New York, May 10, 1991 & Feb 5, 199)* CRI ▲ CD 706 [DDD]
Corigliano, J.:Son Vn & Pno, w. Diane Walsh (pno) Koch International Classics ▲ KIC 7223 [DDD]
Davidovsky, M.:Synchronism 9 *(rec Recital Hall, Music Division, SUNY, Purchase, New York, May 10, 1991 & Feb 5, 199)* CRI ▲ CD 706 [DDD]
Gerber, S.:Fant Vn *(rec Recital Hall, Music Division, SUNY, Purchase, New York, May 10, 1991 & Feb 5, 199)* CRI ▲ CD 706 [DDD]
Gerber, S.:Songs without Words (3) *(rec Recital Hall, Music Division, SUNY, Purchase, New York, May 10, 1991 & Feb 5, 199)* CRI ▲ CD 706 [DDD]
Harbison, J.:Songs of Solitude (4) *(rec Recital Hall, Music Division, SUNY, Purchase, New York, May 10, 1991 & Feb 5, 199)* CRI ▲ CD 706 [DDD]
Hoffman, J.:Partenze Koch International Classics ▲ KIC 7145-2 [DDD]
Ibert, J.:Chamber Music, w. Sue Ann Kahn (fl), Eleanor Lawrence (fl), Peggy Schecter (fl), Rie Schmidt (fl), David Krakauer (cl), Lauren Goldstein (bn), Susan Jolles (hp), Frederic Hand (gtr), Andrew Willis (pno)—2 Mouvements; Aria; Histoires; Pastoral; Aria; Entr'acte Albany ▲ TROY 145 [DDD]
Ibert, J.:Interludes, w. Sue Ann Kahn (fl), Susan Jolles (hp) Albany ▲ TROY 145 [DDD]
Ibert, J.:Music of, w. C. Schadeberg (sop), Sue Ann Kahn (fl), E. Lawrence (fl), P. Schechter (fl), R. Schmidt (fl), David Krakauer (cl), L. Goldstein (bn), Susan Jolles (hp), Frederick Hand (gtr), Arthur Willis (pno)—Entr'acte; Jeux; Sonatine; 2 Movements; 2 Interludes; Aria; Pièce for solo Fl; Histoires; 2 Stèles orientées; Pastoral; Aria; Entr'acte Albany ▲ TROY 145
Parris, R.:Son Vn *(rec Recital Hall, Music Division, SUNY, Purchase, New York, May 10, 1991 & Feb 5, 199)* CRI ▲ CD 706 [DDD]

▲ = CD ♦ = Enhanced CD Δ = MD ■ = Cassette Tape □ = DCC

Macomber, Curtis (vn) (cont.)
- Ran, S.:Inscriptions *(rec Recital Hall, Music Division, SUNY, Purchase, New York, May 10, 1991 & Feb 5, 199)* CRI ▲ CD 706 [DDD]
- Sessions, R.:Duo Vn & Vc, w. J. Krosnick (vc) Koch International Classics ▲ KIC 7153–2 [DDD]
- Sessions, R.:Duo Vn & Pno, w. B. D. Salwen (pno) Koch International Classics ▲ KIC 7153–2 [DDD]
- Sessions, R.:Pieces Vc Koch International Classics ▲ KIC 7153–2 [DDD]
- Sessions, R.:Son Vn Koch International Classics ▲ KIC 7153–2 [DDD]
- Sessions, R.:Son Vn Koch International Classics ▲ KIC 7145–2 [DDD]
- Wuorinen, C.:Album Leaf, w. F. Sherry (vc) Koch International Classics ▲ KIC 7242–2 [DDD]
- Wuorinen, C.:Fortune, w. A. R. Kay (cl), F. Sherry (vc), J. Winn (pno) Koch International Classics ▲ KIC 7242–2 [DDD]
- Wuorinen, C.:Tashi, w. J. Kopperud (cl), F. Sherry (vc), J. Winn (pno) Koch International Classics ▲ KIC 7242–2 [DDD]

Macomber, Douglas (org)
- Alain, J.:Litanies Arkay ▲ ARK 6152 [DDD]
- Dupré, M.:Vars sur un vieux Noël Arkay ▲ ARK 6152 [DDD]
- Duruflé, M.:Org Music (sels)—Sicilienne; Prelude & Fugue; Toccata Arkay ▲ ARK 6152 [DDD]
- Roger-Ducasse, J.:Pastoral Org Arkay ▲ ARK 6152 [DDD]
- Vierne, L.:Carillon de Westminster Arkay ▲ ARK 6152 [DDD]
- Widor, C.M.:Andante sostenuto Arkay ▲ ARK 6152 [DDD]

McPhee, Colin (pno)
- McPhee, C.:Balinese Ceremonial Music, w. Benjamin Britten (pno) Pearl ▲ PEA 9177 [ADD]

McQueen, Helen (E hn)
- American Music Sampler, w. Gomez, Jill (sop), Crispian Steele (tpt), Wayne Marshall (pno), City of London Sinfonia [cnd:R. Hickox] Virgin Classics 2–▲ CDC 59089
- Copland, A.:Quiet City, w. C. Steele-Perkins (tpt), R. Hickox (cnd), City of London Sinfonia Virgin Classics ▲ 59520 [DDD]

McQueen, Helen (ob)
- Vivaldi, A.:Cons Diverse Instrs, w. Joanna Graham (bn), Ruth McDowall (cl), David Rix (ct), Deborah Davis (fl), Duke Dobing (fl), Tim Caister (hn), Stephen Stirling (hn), Christopher Hooker (ob), Michael Meekes (tpt), Crispian Steele-Perkins (tpt), Nicholas Kraemer (hpd), N. Kraemer (cnd), London Sinfonietta—Cons. in F, RV.539; in C, RV.533; in D, RV.122; in C, RV.537; in C, RV.560; in F, RV.538; in G, RV.545 *(rec All Saints Church, East Finchley, Oct. 1994 & Jan. 1995)* Naxos ("Vivaldi Collection" series) ▲ 8.553204 [DDD]

McSkimming, David (pno)
- Duparc, H.:Songs, w. Rosamund Illing (sop)—Chanson triste; Extase; Sérénade Florentine; Le manoir de Rosemonde; La vague et la cloche; Testament; Soupir; Elégie; Lamento; Au pays où se fait la guerre; Phidylé; L'invitation au voyage; La vie antérieure Chandos ▲ CHAN 9427
- Poulenc, F.:Songs, w. Rosamund Illing (sop) Chandos ▲ CHAN 9427

McTier, Duncan (db)
- Davies, P.M.:Strathclyde Con 7, w. P. M. Davies (cnd), Scottish CO Collins Classics ▲ COL 1396 [DDD]
- Dvořák, A.:Notturno, w. Chilingirian String Quartet Chandos ▲ CHAN 9046 [DDD]
- Dvořák, A.:Qnt Strs, Op. 77, w. Chilingirian String Quartet Chandos ▲ CHAN 9046 [DDD]

McVeigh, Don (va)
- Bononcini, A.:Stabat Mater, w. Felicity Palmer (sop), Paul Esswood (ct), Philip Langridge (ten), Christopher Keyte (bass), John Scott (org), John Willison (vn), Chris Wellington (va), G. Guest (cnd), Philomusica Antiqua of London, St. John's College Choir Cambridge *(rec 1977)* London 2–▲ 443868–2 [ADD]
- Caldara, A.:Crucifixus, w. Felicity Palmer (sop), Paul Esswood (ct), Philip Langridge (ten), Christopher Keyte (bass), John Scott (org), John Willison (vn), Chris Wellington (va), G. Guest (cnd), Philomusica Antiqua of London, St. John's College Choir Cambridge *(rec 1977)* London 2–▲ 443868–2 [ADD]
- Lotti, A.:Crucifixus, w. Felicity Palmer (sop), Paul Esswood (ct), Philip Langridge (ten), Christopher Keyte (bass), John Scott (org), John Willison (vn), Chris Wellington (va), G. Guest (cnd), Philomusica Antiqua of London, St. John's College Choir Cambridge *(rec 1977)* London 2–▲ 443868–2 [ADD]

McWilliam, Fergus (hn)—see ORCHESTRAS & ENSEMBLES Berlin Philharmonic Wind Quintet

Madar, Christine-Gabrielle (lt/mand)—see ORCHESTRAS & ENSEMBLES Isabella D'Este

Madar, Christine-Gabrielle (thb)—see ORCHESTRAS & ENSEMBLES Isabella D'Este

Madge, Geoffrey Douglas (pno)
- Gershwin, G.:An American in Paris, w. I. Stupel (cnd), Artur Rubinstein PO *(rec Apr. 1992)* Danacord ▲ DACOCD 412 [DDD]
- Gershwin, G.:Con Pno, w. I. Stupel (cnd), Artur Rubinstein PO *(rec Apr. 1992)* Danacord ▲ DACOCD 412 [DDD]
- Gershwin, G.:Rhap in Blue, w. I. Stupel (cnd), Artur Rubinstein PO *(rec Apr. 1992)* Danacord ▲ DACOCD 412 [DDD]
- Krenek, E.:Pno Music—Toccata & Chaconne, Op. 13 (1922); A Little Suite, Op. 13a (1922); Twelve Variations in Three Movements, Op. 79 (1937; rev. 1940 & 1957); George Washington Variations, Op. 120 (1950); Echoes from Austria, Op. 166 (1958) CPO ▲ CPO 999099–2 [DDD]
- Krenek, E.:Sons Pno—No. 1, Op. 2 (1919); No. 3, Op. 92/4 (1943; rev. 1960); No. 5, Op. 121 (1950) Koch Schwann ▲ CD 310047 [DDD]
- Krenek, E.:Sons Pno—No. 2, Op. 59 (1928); No. 4, Op. 114 (1948); No. 6, Op. 128 (1951); No. 7, Op. 240 (1988) Koch Schwann ▲ CD 310048 [DDD]
- Medtner, N.:Con 1 Pno, w. I. Stupel (cnd), Artur Rubinstein PO *(rec Oct. 1991)* Danacord ▲ DACOCD 401 [DDD]
- Medtner, N.:Con 2 Pno, w. I. Stupel (cnd), Artur Rubinstein PO *(rec Oct. 1991)* Danacord ▲ DACOCD 402 [DDD]
- Medtner, N.:Con 3 Pno, w. I. Stupel (cnd), Artur Rubinstein PO *(rec Oct. 1991)* Danacord ▲ DACOCD 403 [DDD]
- Medtner, N.:Forgotten Melodies 1—No. 1 *(rec Oct. 1991)* Danacord ▲ DACOCD 403 [DDD]
- Medtner, N.:Forgotten Melodies 2—No. 5 *(rec Oct. 1991)* Danacord ▲ DACOCD 402 [DDD]
- Medtner, N.:Son Pno, Op. 22 *(rec Oct. 1991)* Danacord ▲ DACOCD 401 [DDD]
- Wolpe, S.:Battle Piece CPO ▲ CPO 999055 [DDD]
- Wolpe, S.:Passacaglia CPO ▲ CPO 999055 [DDD]
- Wolpe, S.:Pno Music (misc)—Gesang, weil ich etwas Teures verlassen mich (1920); Stehende Musik (1925); Tango (1927); Rag-Caprice (1927); Marche caractéristique, Op. 10/1 (1928); Dance in Form of a Chaconne (1938); Displaced Spaces (1946); Form IV:Broken Sequences for Piano (1969) CPO ▲ CPO 999055 [DDD]
- Wolpe, S.:Toccata in 3 Parts Pno *(rec 1969)* CPO ▲ CPO 999055 [DDD]

Madojan, Nikolai (vn)
- Prokofiev, S.:Mélodies, w. E. Westenholz (pno) Kontrapunkt ▲ KPT 32185 [DDD]
- Prokofiev, S.:Son Vn, Op. 94bis, w. E. Westenholz (pno) Kontrapunkt ▲ KPT 32185 [DDD]
- Prokofiev, S.:Son 1 Vn, w. E. Westenholz (pno) Kontrapunkt ▲ KPT 32185 [DDD]

Madriguera, Enric (gtr)
- Old World, New World *(rec Resurrection Lutheran Church Chapel, Plano, TX, July, Sept. & Oct. 1994)* EPR ▲ EPR 9406 [DDD]

Madsen, Jesper Helmuth (cl)—see also ORCHESTRAS & ENSEMBLES Danish Wind Octet, Scandinavian Wind Quintet
- Jersild, J.:Fant e canto affetuoso, w. Lena Bust Nielsen (fl), Hege Waldeland (vc), Sonja Gislinge (hp) Paula ▲ PACD 75 [DAD]
- Maegaard, J.:Musica Riservata II, w. Klas Sjöblom (ob/E hn), Jørgen Bove (sax), Peter Andersen (bn) *(rec Copenhagen, 1995–96)* Marco Polo/Dacapo ▲ 8.224050 [DDD]

Madsen, Karsten Dalsgaard (vn)
- Saeverud, H.:Small Duets, w. T. Saeverud (vn) Simax ▲ PSC 1087 [DDD]

Madsen, Per Lund (vn)
- Gade, N.W.:Octet, w. Anne Egendal (vn), Sune Ranmo (va), Hans Nygaard (vc), Kontra String Quartet *(rec Torpen Kapel, Humlebaek, Denmark, May, 5–8, 1992)* BIS ▲ CD 545 [DDD]

Madsen, Søren Bødker (gtr)—see also ORCHESTRAS & ENSEMBLES Danish Guitar Duo
- The Danish Guitar Duo, w. Morten Skott (gtr) Point ▲ PCD 5107

Madzar, Aleksandar (pno)
- Schulhoff, E.:Con Pno, w. A. Delfs (cnd), German CO *(rec Freie Waldorfschule, Bremen, Oct 1994)* London ▲ 444819–2 [DDD]
- Schulhoff, E.:Double Con Fl, w. Bettina Wild (fl), A. Delfs (cnd), German CO *(rec Freie Waldorfschule, Bremen, Oct 1994)* London ▲ 444819–2 [DDD]

Maebe, J. (instr)—see ORCHESTRAS & ENSEMBLES Quintessens

Maeder, Thierry (org)—see ORCHESTRAS & ENSEMBLES Les Cyclopes

Maertens, Falk (tpt)
- Shostakovich, D.:Con 1 Pno, w. Veronika Reznikovskaja (pno), J.-P. Weigle (cnd), German Music School Orch Ars Musici ▲ 1128

Maestri, Gigino (vn)
- Danzi, F.:Qts Bn, Op. 40, w. M. Monguzzi (bn), A. Anjos (va), A. Riccardi (vc) Bongiovanni ▲ GB 5520 [DDD]
- Krommer, F.:Qt Bn, Op. 46/1, w. M. Monguzzi (cl), A. Anjos (va), A. Riccardi (vc) Bongiovanni ▲ GB 5520 [DDD]

Maeyer, Jan de (ob)
- Brod, H.:Nocturne Ob, w. Godelieve Verstraelen (pno) Arcobaleno ▲ AAOC 9328
- Dallier, H.:Fant Caprice, w. Godelieve Verstraelen (pno) Arcobaleno ▲ AAOC 9328
- Demersseman, J.A.:Fant Suisse, w. Godelieve Verstraelen (pno) Arcobaleno ▲ AAOC 9328
- Godard, B.:Scènes écossaise, w. Godelieve Verstraelen (pno) Arcobaleno ▲ AAOC 9328
- Lalliet, T.:Carnival de Venise, w. Godelieve Verstraelen (pno) Arcobaleno ▲ AAOC 9328
- Saint-Saëns, C.:Son Ob, w. G. Verstraelen (pno) Arcobaleno ▲ AAOC 9328

Maffei, Alessandro (pno)
- Alfano, F.:Son Vn, w. Marco Rizzi (vn) Sarx ▲ SRX 14 [DDD]
- Respighi, O.:Pieces Vn, w. Marco Rizzi (vn)—5 sels Sarx ▲ SRX 14 [DDD]
- Respighi, O.:Son Vn, w. Marco Rizzi (vn) Sarx ▲ SRX 14 [DDD]

Magad, Samuel (vn)
- Rimsky-Korsakov, N.:Scheherazade, w. D. Barenboim (cnd), Chicago SO Erato ▲ 91717–2 [DDD]
- Rimsky-Korsakov, N.:The Tale of Tsar Saltan Orch, Op. 57, w. D. Barenboim (cnd), Chicago SO Erato ▲ 91717–2

Magaloff, Nikita (pno)
- Brahms, J.:Son 3 Pno *(rec 1986)* Fonè ▲ 87F07–19 [DDD]
- Chopin, F.:Etudes (24) *(rec live 1967)* Fonè 2–▲ 91F 06 [ADD]
- Chopin, F.:Music of, w. Claudio Arrau (pno), Rotterdam PO [cnd:David Zinman], E. Inbal (cnd), London PO—Con. No. 2 in f for Pno, Op. 21 [Larghetto]; Berceuse in D♭, Op. 57; Nocturnes No. 1 in b♭, Op. 9/1; No. 2 in E♭, Op. 9/2; No. 5 in F#, Op. 15/2; No. 8 in D♭, Op. 27/2; No. 20 in c#, Op. posth.; No. 21 in c, Op. posth.; Prelude No. 7 in A, Op. 28; Andante spianato; Prelude No. 4 in e, Op. 28; Waltz No. 9 in A♭, Op. 69/1; Con. No. 1 in e for Pno, Op. 11 [Romance] Philips ▲ 446629–2 ■ 446629–4
- Chopin, F.:Pno Music (misc)—Nocturne, Op. posth.; Polonaise, Op. 53; Waltz, Op. 64/2 *(rec live 1967)* Fonè 2–▲ 91F 06 [ADD]
- Chopin, F.:Polonaises—Op. 74, Nos. 1–6 *(rec 1986)* Fonè ▲ 87F07–19 [DDD]
- Chopin, F.:Preludes, Op. 28 Denon ▲ CO 79158 [DDD]
- Chopin, F.:Son Pno, Op. 4 *(rec live 1967)* Fonè 2–▲ 91F 06 [ADD]
- Chopin, F.:Son Pno, Op. 58 Denon ▲ CO 79158 [DDD]
- Chopin, F.:Son Pno, Op. 58 *(rec 1957, 1960 & 1966)* Praga ▲ PR 250 042
- Chopin, F.:Songs Sop (comp), w. L. Gencer (sop) [Pol] Arkadia-Akademia ▲ 101 [ADD]
- Debussy, C.:Children's Corner Adès ▲ ADE 202952
- Fasch, J.F.:Con Tpt, 2 Obs & Strs, w. N.-E. Sparf (cnd), Drottningholm Baroque Ensemble [period instrs] *(rec Petruskyrkan, Stockholm, Sweden, Aug 8–11, 1995)* Naxos ▲ 8.553531 [DDD]
- Fauré, G.:Impromptus Pno, Opp. 25, 31, 34, 91 & 102—Opp. 31 & 34 Adès ▲ ADE 202952
- Handel, G.F.:Sons Vn, w. Joseph Szigeti (vn)—No. 4 in d, HWV 364 Grammofono 2000 ▲ GRM 78630
- Handel, G.F.:Sons Vn, w. Joseph Szigeti (vn)—in d Iron Needle ▲ 1321 [ADD]
- Handel, G.F.:Suite Tpt & Org, w. N.-E. Sparf (cnd), Drottningholm Baroque Ensemble *(rec Petruskyrkan, Stockholm, Sweden, Aug 8–11, 1995)* Naxos ▲ 8.553531 [DDD]
- Haydn, J.:Con Org & Strs, H.XVIII/2, w. A. Orizio (cnd), Brescia & Bergamo Festival CO Fonè ▲ 86F 06–12 [ADD]
- I Bis di Nikita Magaloff Fonè ▲ 87 F 06–18 CD [DDD]
- Liszt, F.:Années de pèlerinage 2—Sonetti del Petrarca Nos. 47, 104 & 123 *(rec 1986)* Fonè ▲ 87F07–19 [DDD]
- Liszt, F.:Song Transcriptions—Chopin—6 songs from Op. 74 Arkadia-Akademia ▲ 101 [ADD]
- Mendelssohn, F.:Trio 1 Pno, w. A. Grumiaux (pno), P. Fournier (vn) Arkadia ▲ 606
- Mendelssohn, F.:Trio 2 Pno, w. A. Grumiaux (vn), P. Fournier (vc) Arkadia ▲ 606
- Mozart, W.A.:Sons Vn Pno (misc), w. Joseph Szigeti (vn)—No. 21 in e, K.304 Grammofono 2000 ▲ GRM 78630
- Mozart, W.A.:Sons Vn Pno (misc), w. Joseph Szigeti (vn)—in e, K.304 Iron Needle ▲ 1321 [ADD]
- Mozart, W.A.:Sons Vn Pno (misc), w. J. Szigeti (vn)—Son. No. 21 *(rec 1928–1937)* Music & Arts 2–▲ CD 813 [AAD]
- Nikita Magaloff, w. Magaloff, Nikita (pno) *(rec Apr. 27, 1991)* Ermitage ▲ ERM 415 [DDD]
- Purcell, H.:Son Tpt, w. N.-E. Sparf (cnd), Drottningholm Baroque Ensemble *(rec Petruskyrkan, Stockholm, Sweden, Aug 8–11, 1995)* Naxos ▲ 8.553531 [DDD]
- Ravel, M.:Le Tombeau de Couperin Adès ▲ ADE 202952
- Ravel, M.:Valses nobles et sentimentales Adès ▲ ADE 202952
- Schubert, Franz:Impromptus Pno, D.899—No. 2 in E♭ Fonè ▲ 87 F 08–20 [DDD]
- Schubert, Franz:Rondo Vn, D.895, w. J. Szigeti (vn) *(rec 1928–1937)* Music & Arts 2–▲ CD 813 [AAD]
- Schubert, Franz:Son Pno, D.960 Fonè ▲ 87 F 08–20 [DDD]
- Schubert, Franz:Trio 2 Pno, w. A. Grumiaux (vn), P. Fournier (vc) Arkadia ▲ 598
- Schumann, R.:Carnaval Pno FNAC Music ("Via Classics" series) ▲ 642331
- Schumann, R.:Etudes after Paganini's Caprices, Op. 3 Fonè ▲ 85F 01 [ADD]
- Schumann, R.:Fant Pno Fonè ▲ 85F 01 [ADD]
- Schumann, R.:Sym Etudes FNAC Music ("Via Classics" series) ▲ 642331
- Scriabin, A.:Etudes Pno (comp) Valois ▲ V 4714
- La Valse Adès ▲ ADE 141792 [DDD]
- The Waltz Adès ▲ ADE 204142 [DDD]
- Weber, C.M. von:Invitation to the Dance Pno [solo piano trans. by Carl Tausig] Denon ▲ CO 77346 [DDD]

Magani, Giuseppe (vn)
- Ferré, L.:Music of, w. L. Ferré (cnd), Liège SO, Milan SO—Le chant du hibou; Muss es sein es muss sein; Le superlatif EPM ▲ EPM 982372 [AAD]

Magen, S. (vc)
- Avni, T.:Love under a Different Sun, w. E. Berendsen (sgr), M. Meltzer (fl), E. Zaltsman (vn) Symposium ▲ 1110
- Avni, T.:A Monk Observes a Skull, w. A. Reich (sgr) Symposium ▲ 1110

Magendanz, Donna (vc)
- Paisiello, G.:Qts Fl, w. Luigi Palmisano (fl), Franco Mezzena (vn), Arturo Mazza (va) *(rec Trento, Italy, Nov 1979)* Dynamic ▲ CDS 12 [ADD]

Magg, Fritz (vc)
- Eaton, J.:Fant Romance, w. Kari Miller (pno) *(rec Musical Arts Ctr, Bloomington, IN, Nov 3, 1989)* Indiana Univ School of Music ▲ 0–253–31842–4
- Orrego-Salas, J.:Serenata, w. Kyril Magg (fl) *(rec Musical Arts Ctr, Bloomington, IN, Mar 12, 1989)* Indiana Univ School of Music ▲ IUSM 02

Magg, Kyril (fl)
- Orrego-Salas, J.:Serenata, w. Fritz Magg (vc) *(rec Musical Arts Ctr, Bloomington, IN, Mar 12, 1989)* Indiana Univ School of Music ▲ IUSM 02

Magiera, Leone (pno)
Live in Concert, w. Piero Cappuccilli (bar) *(rec aria & song recital, 5/15/84)*
Bongiovanni ▲ GB 2501-2 [ADD]

Magill, Sam (vc)
Haydn, J.:Diverts Fl, Vn & Vc, w. Laurel Zucker (fl), Shirien Taylor (vn)—in D, H.IV/6; in G, H.IV/7; H.IV/8 *(rec Concordia College)* Cantilena ▲ 66013-2 [DDD]
Haydn, J.:Trios Fls & Vc, "London Trios", w. Renée Siebert (fl), Laurel Zucker (fl) *(rec Concordia College)* Cantilena ▲ 66013-2 [DDD]
Mozart, W.A.:Qts Fl, w. Laurel Zucker (fl), Shirien Taylor (vn), Mary Hammann (va)—K.285, 285b & 298 *(rec Academy of Arts & Letters, New York City, June 11, 1994)* Cantilena ▲ C 660072 [DDD]
Still, W.G.:Folk Suites, w. Leonard Garrison (fl), Robert Umiker (cl), Arthur Tollefson (pno) Cambria ▲ CD 1060 [ADD]

Magin, Milosz (pno)
Magin, M.:Music of, w. W. Czepiel (cnd), Lódz PO—Stabat Mater; Musique des morts; Con No. 3 for Pno; Polish Miniatures; Sonatina; Polish Triptych; Polka *(rec 1991)* Polskie Nagrania ▲ PNCD 129 [DDD]

Magistrelli, Luigi (bas hn)
Neumann, H.:Serenade Bas Hn, w. Massimo Laura (gtr) Bayer ▲ 100280 [DDD]
Neumann, H.:Serenade Bas Hn, w. Massimo Laura (gtr), Rossella Perrone (gtr) Bayer ▲ 100280 [DDD]

Magistrelli, Luigi (cl)
Neumann, H.:Schweizer Serenade, w. Massimo Laura (gtr) Bayer ▲ 100280 [DDD]
Neumann, H.:Serenade Cl, w. Massimo Laura (gtr) Bayer ▲ 100280 [DDD]
Neumann, H.:Theme & Vars Paisiello, w. Massimo Laura (gtr) Bayer ▲ 100280 [DDD]
Neumann, H.:Theme & Vars Schubert, w. Massimo Laura (gtr) Bayer ▲ 100280 [DDD]

Magnes, Frances (vn)
Wolpe, S.:Son Vn, w. David Tudor (pno) *(rec Esoteric Studios, NY, 1954)* Hat Hut ▲ CD 6182 [AAD]

Magnin, Alexandre (fl)
Bach, J.S.:Sons Fl, BWV 1030-35, w. R. Hairgrove (pno)—BWV 1030-1032 Gallo ▲ CD 566 [DDD]
Bach, J.S.:Sons Vn, w. R. Hairgrove (pno)—BWV 1020 [doubtful; trans. for flute & continuo] Gallo ▲ CD 566 [DDD]
Gaudibert, E.:Syzygy, w. E. Gaudibert (pno) *(rec Jan. 20, 1971)* Grammont ▲ CTSP 8-2 [ADD]
Mozart, W.A.:Andante Fl, K.315/285a, w. A. Jordan (cnd), Lausanne CO Gallo ▲ CD 368
Mozart, W.A.:Cons Fl, w. A. Jordan (cnd), Lausanne CO Gallo ▲ CD 368
Quantz, J.J.:Con in G Fl & Strs, w. Baroque Strings Gallo ▲ CD 372
Vivaldi, A.:Cons Fl, Op. 10, w. Baroque Strings—Nos. 2 & 3 Gallo ▲ CD 372

Magnúsdóttir, A. (hpd)
Tómasson, H.:Eco del passato, w. Á. Haraldsdóttir (fl) Music from Iceland ▲ ITM 707

Magnusson, Inge (cl)—see ORCHESTRAS & ENSEMBLES Sundsvall Wind Quartet

Magnússon, Örn (pno)
Isólfsson, P.:Pieces (3) Pno Music from Iceland ▲ ITM 802 [DDD]
Leifs, J.:Pno Music—Vökudraumur (1913); Torrek—Intermezzo, Op. 1/2 (1919); Pieces (4) for Piano, Op. 2 (1921); Icelandic Folk-Songs (1925); Icelandic Dances, Op. 11 (1928); New Icelandic Dances, Op. 14b (1931); Boy's Song, Op. 49 (1960) *(rec Malmö Concert Hall, Sweden, Aug. 13-15, 1994)* BIS ▲ CD 692 [DDD]
Leifs, J.:Pieces Pno, Op. 2 Music from Iceland ▲ ITM 802 [DDD]
Music for Flute by Icelandic Composers, w. Martial Nardeau (fl) Music from Iceland ▲ ITM 806
Sigurbjörnsson, H.:Var Pno Music from Iceland ▲ ITM 802 [DDD]
Sigurbjörnsson, T.:Hans Vars Music from Iceland ▲ ITM 802 [DDD]
Sveinbjörnsson, S.:Pno Music—Idylle; Dance Music from Iceland ▲ ITM 802 [DDD]
Thórdarson, H.:Oh, Yellow Wonderworld Music from Iceland ▲ ITM 802 [DDD]
Thorkelsdóttir, M.:Greetings Music from Iceland ▲ ITM 802 [DDD]

Magome, Isamu (bn)
Nishimura, A.:Tapas, w. M. Enkoji (cnd), Sendai PO Camerata ▲ 32CM 175
Yoshimatsu, T.:Unicorn Circuit, w. M. Enkoji (cnd), Sendai PO Camerata ▲ 32CM 175

Magowan, Leslie (bn)—see ORCHESTRAS & ENSEMBLES Essex Winds Woodwind Quintet

Maguire, Hugh (vn)
Debussy, C.:Son Vn, w. I. Brown (pno) Chandos ▲ CHAN 8385 [ADD]
Strauss, R.:Ein Heldenleben, w. L. Ludwig (cnd), London SO *(rec Walthamstow Assembly Hall, London)* Everest ▲ EVC 9033 [AAD]

Maguire, Tom (perc)
Allen, J.:Brazilian Son, w. Ron Grinage (pno), Shana Norton (hp), Carol Redman (fl), Charly Drobeck (fl/alt fl/pic), Sam Lunt (perc) *(rec Santuario de Guadalupe, Sante Fe, NM, Sept 29-30, 1995)* Wild Iris ▲ WI 001
Allen, J.:Di Me, Lluvia, w. Carol Redman (fl/whistle), Toni Austin-Allen (pno/claves), Sam Lunt (bongos) *(rec Santuario de Guadalupe, Sante Fe, NM, Sept 29-30, 1995)* Wild Iris ▲ WI 001
Allen, J.:In Memory of a Once New World, w. Ron Grinage (pno), Sam Lunt (mar) *(rec Santuario de Guadalupe, Sante Fe, NM, Sept 29-30, 1995)* Wild Iris ▲ WI 001

Magyar, František (va)
Bella, J.L.:Qnt Strs, w. Moyzes String Quartet *(rec Moyzes Hall, Slovak Philharmonic, Bratislava, Dec. 6, 1993)* Marco Polo ▲ 8.223658 [DDD]

Magyar, Gábor (vc)—see ORCHESTRAS & ENSEMBLES Haydn String Quartet Budapest, New Haydn String Quartet

Magyari, Imre (hn)
Atterberg, K.:Son Vc, w. I. Prunyi (pno) [arr. hn & pno] Marco Polo ▲ 8.223405 [DDD]

Mahin, Bruce (elec wind inst)
Mahin, B.:Flautus Aeterna *(rec Presbyterian Church of Radford, Oct 1994)* Capstone ♦ CPS 8624 [DDD]
Mahin, B.:For Every Season *(rec Presbyterian Church of Radford, Oct 1994)* Capstone ♦ CPS 8624 [DDD]
Mahin, B.:Synapse *(rec Presbyterian Church of Radford, Oct 1994)* Capstone ♦ CPS 8624 [DDD]
Mahin, B.:Time Chants I. Los Angeles, April-May 1992 *(rec Presbyterian Church of Radford, Oct 1994)* Capstone ♦ CPS 8624 [DDD]

Mahler, Gustav (pno)
Mahler, G.:Pno Music—Ging heut morgens übers Feld; Ich ging mit Lust durch einen grünen Wald; 4th movt [arr from Sym 4]; 1st movt [arr from Sym 5] [piano rolls] Conifer Classics 2-▲ 75605-51277-2 [DDD]
Mahler, G.:Songs, w. Y. Kenny (sop), C. Carlson (mez) [from 4 rolls for automatic piano Mahler created from his own music in 1905]—Ging heut' morgen übers Feld; Ich ging mit Lust durch einen grünen Wald IMP Classics ▲ IMPGLRS 101 [DDD]
Mahler, G.:Sym 4 [from 4 rolls for automatic piano Mahler created from his own music in 1905]—last movt. IMP Classics ▲ IMPGLRS 101 [DDD]
Mahler, G.:Sym 5 [from 4 rolls for automatic piano Mahler created from his own music in 1905]—first movt. IMP Classics ▲ IMPGLRS 101 [DDD]

Mahonske, Adam (pno)
Mahin, B.:Impressions:Fear Capstone ▲ CPS 8611
Mahin, B.:Impressions:Fear Capstone ▲ CPS 8061

Maiben, Dana (va)
Holzbauer, I.:Qnt Fl, w. Zephyrus *(rec Faith Lutheran Church, Bloomington, July 5-7, 1994)* Focus ▲ FOCUS 945 [DDD]

Maidre, Ines (org)
Tobias, R.:Des Jonah Sendung, w. Pille Lill (sop), Urve Tauts (mez), Peter Svensson (ten), Raimo Laukka (bar), Mati Palm (bass), N. Järvi (cnd), Estonian State SO, Oratorio Choir, Estonian Phil Chamber Choir, Tallinn Boys' Choir *(rec Estonia Concert Hall, Tallinn, Estonia, June 23-29, 1995)* BIS 2-▲ CD 731/732 [DDD]

Maier, Franzjosef (vn)
Beethoven, L. van:Con Vn, Vc & Pno, "Triple Con", w. A. Bylsma (vc), P. Badura-Skoda (pno), Collegium Aureum Editio Classica ▲ 77063-2-RG [ADD]

Maier, Franzjosef (vn) (cont.)
Beethoven, L. van:Songs, w. James Griffett (ten), Rudolf Mandalka (vc), Bradford Tracey (pno)—To the Aeolian Harp; Sally in Our Alley; The Soldier; Sympathy; The Farewell Song; Come, Darby Dear, Easy; The Shepherd's Song; The British Light Dragoons Ars Musici ▲ 1142 [ADD]
Haydn, J.:Songs, w. James Griffett (ten), Rudolf Mandalka (vc), Bradford Tracey (pno)—Will Ye Got to Flanders; The Glancing of Her Apron; Jockie & Sandy; O Can Ye Sew Cushions; Margret's Ghost; Up in the Morning Early; Barbara Allen; Green Grow the Rashes; Lizae Baillie; Blue Bonnets Ars Musici ▲ 1142 [ADD]

Maile, Hans (vn)—see also ORCHESTRAS & ENSEMBLES Göbel Trio Berlin
Boccherini, L.:Syms, w. S. Prunnbauer (gtr), Jürgen Hollerbuhl (ob), B. Vestre (ob), Jörn Maatz (ob), H. Ganz (vn), R. Forest (vc), J. Stárek (cnd), Berlin RIAS Sinfonietta—in C, G.495 (Op. 21/3) *(rec Dec. 1979)* Koch Treasure ▲ 31612-2 [ADD]
Copland, A.:Son Vn & Pno, w. H. Göbel (pno) Thorofon ▲ CTH 2012 [DDD]
Dietrich, A.:Con Vn, w. J. López-Cobos (cnd), Berlin RSO Koch Schwann ▲ CD 311070 [DDD]
Egk, W.:Geigenmusik, w. A. Sander (cnd), Berlin RSO Koch Schwann ▲ SCH 310752 [DDD]
Hartmann, K.A.:Con funèbre, w. A. Sander (cnd), Berlin RSO Koch Schwann ▲ SCH 310752 [DDD]
Joachim, J.:Nocturne Vn, w. J. López-Cobos (cnd), Berlin RSO Koch Schwann ▲ CD 311070 [DDD]
Reger, M.:Romances Vn, w. U. Lajovic (cnd), Berlin RSO Koch Schwann ▲ CD 311 076 [ADD]
Reger, M.:Suite Vn Pno, w. U. Lajovic (cnd), Berlin RSO *(rec 1981)* Koch Schwann ▲ CD 311 122 [ADD]
Rheinberger, J.:Sons Vn, w. H. Göbel (pno) Thorofon 6-▲ BCTH 2161/6
Zimmermann, B.A.:Con Vn, w. A. Sander (cnd), Berlin RSO Koch Schwann ▲ SCH 310752 [DDD]

Maillard, R. (vc)
Mendelssohn, Fanny:Trio Pno, w. E. Popa (vn), F. Tillard (pno) *(rec June 16-19, 1992)* Opus 111 ▲ OPS 30-71

Mainardi, Enrico (vc)
Beethoven, L. van:Trio 4 Pno, "Ghost", w. Edwin Fischer (pno), W. Schneiderhan (vn) *(rec 1954)* Arkadia 2-▲ 568 (m) [ADD]
Beethoven, L. van:Trio 4 Pno, "Ghost", w. Edwin Fischer (pno), Wolfgang Schneiderhan (vn) *(rec Salzburg, 1952-53)* Music & Arts 2-▲ CD 840 [AAD]
Beethoven, L. van:Trio 6 Pno, "Archduke", w. Edwin Fischer (pno), Wolfgang Schneiderhan (vn) *(rec Salzburg, 1952-53)* Music & Arts 2-▲ CD 840 [AAD]
Brahms, J.:Con Vn & Vc, "Double Con", w. W. Schneiderhan (vn), K. Böhm (cnd), Vienna PO Datum 2-▲ DAT 12305 [ADD]
Brahms, J.:Trios (3) Pno, w. E. Fischer (pno), W. Schneiderhan (vn) *(rec 1954)* Arkadia 2-▲ 568 (m) [ADD]
Brahms, J.:Trio 1 Pno, w. E. Fischer (pno), W. Schneiderhan (vn) *(rec 1953)* Music & Arts ▲ CD 739 (m)
Brahms, J.:Trio 2 Pno, w. E. Fischer (pno), W. Schneiderhan (vn) *(rec 1951)* Music & Arts ▲ CD 739 (m)
Mozart, W.A.:Trio Pno, K.548, w. Edwin Fischer (pno), Wolfgang Schneiderhan (vn) *(rec Salzburg, 1952-53)* Music & Arts 2-▲ CD 840 [AAD]
Schumann, R.:Trio 1 Pno, w. Edwin Fischer (pno), Wolfgang Schneiderhan (vn) *(rec 1954)* Arkadia 2-▲ 568 (m) [ADD]
Schumann, R.:Trio 1 Pno, w. Edwin Fischer (pno), Wolfgang Schneiderhan (vn) *(rec Salzburg, 1952-53)* Music & Arts 2-▲ CD 840 [AAD]

Maine, Wayne du (tpt)—see ORCHESTRAS & ENSEMBLES Meridian Arts Ensemble

Mainetti, Pablo (band)
Piazzolla, A.:Con Band, w. J. Pons (cnd), Teatre Lliure CO Harmonia Mundi France ▲ HMC 901595

Maioli, Renato (pno)
Donatoni, F.:Cloches III, w. A. Orvieto (pno), G. Facchin (cnd), Támmittam Percussion Ensemble Dynamic ▲ CD 97 [DDD]
The Flute from '700 to '900, w. Enzo Caroli (fl), Daniela Colonna Romano (hp) Stradavarius ▲ SIP 25
Maderna, B.:Music of, w. A. Orvieto (pno), G. Facchin (cnd), Támmittam Percussion Ensemble—Concerto for Two Pianos & Instruments (1948); Serenata per un satellite (1969) Dynamic ▲ CD 97 [DDD]
Tailleferre, G.:Music of, w. A. Orvieto (pno), G. Facchin (cnd), Támmittam Percussion Ensemble—Hommage a Rameau (1964); Suite burlesque for Piano 4-Hands; Première prouesses for Piano 4-Hands Dynamic ▲ CD 97 [DDD]

Maione, Orazio (pno)
Bach, J.S.:Con 1 Hpd, w. E. Aadland (cnd), European Community CO *(rec Oct 1990)* IMP Classics ▲ PCD 964 [DDD]

Mair, Marilynn (mand)—see ORCHESTRAS & ENSEMBLES Mair-Davis Duo

Maisenberg, Oleg (pno)
Bartók, B.:Sons (2) Vn & Pno, w. D. Oistrakh (vn), G. Kremer (vn), F. Bauer (pno) *(rec 1969, 1972 & 1978)* Praga ▲ PR 250 038
Berg, A.:Chamber Con, w. T. Zehetmair (vn), H. Holliger (cnd), CO of Europe Teldec ▲ 2292-46019-2 [DDD]
Franck, C.:Son Vn, w. G. Kremer (vn) *(rec 1978?)* Praga ▲ PR 250 024
Milhaud, D.:Son Cl, w. E. Brunner (cl) Orfeo ▲ 060831
Milhaud, D.:Son Fl, Cl, Ob & Pno, w. A. Nicolet (fl), E. Brunner (cl), H. Holliger (ob) Orfeo ▲ 060831
Milhaud, D.:Sonatina Fl, w. A. Nicolet (fl) Orfeo ▲ 060831
Milhaud, D.:Sonatina Ob, w. H. Holliger (ob) Orfeo ▲ 060831
Rachmaninoff, S.:Duets Pno 4-Hands, w. B. Engerer (pno) Harmonia Mundi France 2-▲ HMC 901301/02
Rachmaninoff, S.:Pno Music (2 pnos & pno 4- & 6-hands), w. B. Engerer (pno)—Polka italienne; Romance in G; *(4 hands)*; Valse; Romance *(6-hands, w. 3rd pianist Elena Bachkirova)* Harmonia Mundi France 2-▲ HMC 901301/02
Rachmaninoff, S.:Russian Rhap, w. B. Engerer (pno) Harmonia Mundi France 2-▲ HMC 901301/02
Rachmaninoff, S.:Suite 1 for 2 Pnos, w. B. Engerer (pno) Harmonia Mundi France 2-▲ HMC 901301/02
Rachmaninoff, S.:Suite 2 for 2 Pnos, w. B. Engerer (pno) Harmonia Mundi France 2-▲ HMC 901301/02
Rachmaninoff, S.:Symphonic Dances, w. B. Engerer (pno) Harmonia Mundi France 2-▲ HMC 901301/02
Schubert, Franz:Allegretto Pno, D.900 Orfeo ▲ 043831 [DDD]
Schubert, Franz:Andantino Pno, D.348 Orfeo ▲ 043831 [DDD]
Schubert, Franz:Fant Pno, D.760, "Wandererfantasie" Orfeo ▲ 043831
Schubert, Franz:Son Pno, D.784 Orfeo ▲ 043831 [DDD]
Schubert, Franz:Sonatinas Vn, w. G. Kremer (vn) Deutsche Grammophon ▲ 437092-2

Maisky, Mischa (vc)
Adagio, w. Orch de Paris [cnd:S. Bychkov] Deutsche Grammophon ▲ 435781-2 GH [DDD]
Bach, J.S.:Goldberg Vars, w. Sitkovetsky (vn), Caussé (va) [string Trio version arr. Dmitri Sitkovetsky] Orfeo ▲ 138851 ■ 138851
Bach, J.S.:Sons Vl, BWV 1027-1029, w. M. Argerich (pno) Deutsche Grammophon ▲ 415471-2 [DDD]
Bach, J.S.:Suites Vc, BWV 1007-1012 Deutsche Grammophon ▲ 445373-2 [DDD]
Beethoven, L. van:Son 1 Vc, w. M. Argerich (pno) Deutsche Grammophon ▲ 431801-2 [DDD]
Beethoven, L. van:Son 2 Vc, w. M. Argerich (pno) Deutsche Grammophon ▲ 431801-2 [DDD]
Beethoven, L. van:Son 3 Vc, w. M. Argerich (pno) Deutsche Grammophon ▲ 437514-2 [DDD]
Beethoven, L. van:Son 4 Vc, w. M. Argerich (pno) Deutsche Grammophon ▲ 437514-2 [DDD]
Beethoven, L. van:Son 5 Vc, w. M. Argerich (pno) Deutsche Grammophon ▲ 437514-2 [DDD]
Beethoven, L. van:Vars on "Ein Mädchen oder Weibchen" from Mozart's *Die Zauberflöte*, w. M. Argerich (pno) Deutsche Grammophon ▲ 431801-2 [DDD]
Beethoven, L. van:Vars on "See, the Conquering Hero Comes" from Handel's *Judas Maccabaeus*, w. M. Argerich (pno) Deutsche Grammophon ▲ 437514-2
Beethoven, L. van:Vars on "Bei Männern" from Mozart's *Die Zauberflöte*, w. M. Argerich (pno) Deutsche Grammophon ▲ 431801-2 [DDD]
Bloch, E.:Schelomo, w. L. Bernstein (cnd), Israel PO Deutsche Grammophon ▲ 427347-2 [DDD]

712 ▲ = CD ♦ = Enhanced CD Δ = MD ■ = Cassette Tape □ = DCC

Maisky, Mischa (vc) (cont.)
Boccherini, L.:Con Vc, G.479, Orpheus CO Deutsche Grammophon ▲ 447022-2
Boccherini, L.:Con Vc, G.480, Orpheus CO Deutsche Grammophon ▲ 447022-2
Boccherini, L.:Minuetto, Orpheus CO Deutsche Grammophon ▲ 447022-2
Brahms, J.:Con Vn & Vc, "Double Con", w. G. Kremer (vn), L. Bernstein (cnd), Vienna PO Deutsche Grammophon ▲ 431031-2 [DDD]
Cellissimo, w. D. Hovora (pno) Deutsche Grammophon ▲ 439863-2
Dvořák, A.:Con Vc, w. L. Bernstein (cnd), Israel PO Deutsche Grammophon ▲ 427347-2 [DDD]
Elgar, E.:Con Vc, w. G. Sinopoli (cnd), Philharmonia Orch Deutsche Grammophon ▲ 431685-2 [DDD]
Haydn, J.:Con 1 Vc, w. M. Maisky (cnd), CO of Europe Deutsche Grammophon ▲ 419786-2 [DDD]
Haydn, J.:Con 2 Vc, w. M. Maisky (cnd), CO of Europe Deutsche Grammophon ▲ 419786-2 [DDD]
Haydn, J.:Con 4 Vn, w. M. Maisky (cnd), CO of Europe [arr. for cello & orch.] Deutsche Grammophon ▲ 419786-2 [DDD]
Miaskovsky, N.:Con Vc, w. M. Pletnev (cnd), Russian National Orch Deutsche Grammophon ▲ 449 821-2
Prokofiev, S.:Sinf Concertante, w. M. Pletnev (cnd), Russian National Orch Deutsche Grammophon ▲ 449 821-2
Saint-Saëns, C.:Carnival of the Animals, w. M. Argerich (pno), N. Freire (pno), G. Kremer (vn), I. van Keulen (vn), T. Zimmermann (va), et al. Philips ("Digital Classics" series) ▲ 416841-2 [DDD]
Schubert, Franz:Son Arpeggione, w. M. Argerich (pno) Philips ▲ 412230-2 [DDD]
Schubert, Franz:Son Arpeggione, w. Daria Hovora (pno) *(rec Rittersaal, Rapperswil Palace, Jan 1996)* Deutsche Grammophon ▲ 449817-2 [DDD]
Schubert, Franz:Songs (misc), w. Daria Hovora (pno)—Der Neugierige, D.795/6; Der Müller & der Bach, D.795/19 [both from Die schöne Müllerin]; Lied der Mignon, D.877/4 [from Gesänge aus Wilhelm Meister]; Täuschung, D.911/19; Der Leiermann, D.911/24 [both from Winterreise]; Nacht & Träume, D.827; Am Meer, D.957/12; Ständchen, D.957/4 [both from Schwanengesang]; An die Musik, D.547; Die Forelle, D.550; Der Einsame, D.800; Heidenröslein, D.257; Litanei auf das Fest Allerseelen, D.343; Du bist die Ruh, D.776 *(rec Rittersaal, Rapperswil Palace, Jan 1996)* Deutsche Grammophon ▲ 449817-2 [DDD]
Schumann, R.:Fantasiestücke Cl, w. M. Argerich (pno) Philips ▲ 412230-2 [DDD]
Schumann, R.:Stücke im Volkston, w. M. Argerich (pno) Philips ▲ 412230-2 [DDD]
Tchaikovsky, P.:Vars on a Rococo Theme, w. G. Sinopoli (cnd), Philharmonia Orch Deutsche Grammophon ▲ 431685-2 [DDD]
Vivaldi, A.:Cons Vc, Orpheus CO—Cons RV. 401, 418, 422 [Largo] & 424 Deutsche Grammophon ▲ 447022-2

Majek, Robert (pno)
Schumann, R.:Andante & Vars Hn, w. Mario Venzago (pno), Käthi Gohl (vc), Rama Jucker (vc), Francesco Raselli (hn) Accord ▲ ACD 201572 [AAD]

Majeske, Daniel (vn)—see also ORCHESTRAS & ENSEMBLES Cleveland Orch String Quartet
Mozart, W.A.:Qt Ob, K.370, w. J. Mack (ob), A. Skernick (va), S. Geber (vc) Crystal ▲ CD323 ■ C 323

Majewski, Virginia (va)
Brahms, J.:Sextet Strs, Op. 36, w. J. Heifetz (vn), I. Baker (vn), W. Primrose (va), G. Piatigorsky (vc), G. Rejto (vc) RCA Gold Seal ▲ 7965-2-RG [ADD]
Mozart, W.A.:Qnt Strs, K.516, w. J. Heifetz (vn), I. Baker (vn), W. Primrose (va), G. Piatigorsky (vc) RCA Gold Seal ▲ 7869-2 (m/s) [ADD] ■ 7869-4 (m/s)

Major, Douglas (org)
Bach, J.S.:Music of, w. Empire Brass Quintet EMI Classics ▲ CDC 47395-2 [DDD] ■ 4DS 37353
Festival Music Gothic ▲ GOT 118316
The Great Organ of Washington National Cathedral Gothic ▲ GOT 49058 [DDD]
Marches Gothic ▲ GOT 18828 [DDD]
Noël:Traditional Christmas Carols & Masterworks of the 20th Century, w National Cathedral Choir [cnd:Richard W. Dirksen] VQR Digital ▲ VQR 2006 [DDD]

Major, M. (va)—see ORCHESTRAS & ENSEMBLES Aeolian String Quartet

Makara, P. (vn)
O'Brien, E.:Taking Measures, w. R. Spano (cnd), Bowling Green State Univ New Music Festival Ensemble Capstone ▲ CPS 8603

Makarenko, Micha (balalaika)
Classical Balalaika & Piano Duo, w. Anne Perchat (pno) Arcobaleno ▲ SBCD 9500

Makarov, Arsenii (bn)
Ustvolskaya, G.:Composition 3, w. Natalia Danilina (fl), Maria Osipova (fl), Inna Rodina (fl), Michail Tokarev (fl), Kirill Sokolov (bn), Dmitrii Krasnik (bn), Konstantin Shevchuk (bn), Galina Sandovskaya (pno), O. Malov (cnd) *(rec St. Petersburg Radio House, Jan. 1994)* Megadisc ▲ 7867

Makarski, Michelle (vn)
Cage, J.:Melodies (6) Vn & Kbd, w. B. McMunn (pno) New World ▲ 80391-2 [DDD]
Harbison, J.:Songs of Solitude (4) New World ▲ 80391-2 [DDD]
Hartke, S.:Oh Them Rats Is Mean in My Kitchen, w. Ronald Copes (pno) New World ▲ 80391-2 [DDD]
Wyner, Y.:Concert Duo Vn, w. B. McMunn (pno) New World ▲ 80391-2 [DDD]

Makell, Robert (hn)
Debussy, C.:Chamber Music, w. William Bennett (fl), David Campbell (cl), James Campbell (cl), Nicholas Daniel (ob), Richard Watkins (hn), Robin Kennard (bn), Rachel Gough (bn), Simon Haram (sax), Ieuan Jones (hp), Clifford Benson (pno), Julius Drake (pno), John York (pno), Roger Tapping (va)—Rapsodie for Eng hn; Syrinx; Première rapsodie; Son for Fl, Va & Hp; Le petit nègre; Petite pièce; Rapsodie for Sax *(rec All Saints' Church, East Finchley, London, Jan 12-20, 1994)* Cala 2-▲ CACD 1017 [DDD]
Saint-Saëns, C.:Chamber Music, w. W. Bennett (fl), D. Campbell (cl), J. Campbell (cl), N. Daniel (ob), R. Watkins (hn), R. Kennard (bn), R. Gough (bn), S. Haram (sax), I. Jones (hp), C. Benson (pno), J. Drake (pno), J. York (pno), R. Tapping (va)—Odelette, Op. 162; Son for Cl, Op. 167; Feuillet d'album, Op. 81; Son for Bn, Op. 168; Caprice on Danish & Russian Airs, Op. 79; Son for Ob, Op. 166; Romance in D♭, Op. 37; Tarantelle, Op. 6 *(rec All Saints' Church, East Finchley, London, Jan 12-20, 1994)* Cala 2-▲ CACD 1017 [DDD]

Maki, Paul-Martin (org)
Bourgeois, D.:Serenade Org [Aeolian-Skinner/G. Donald Harrison Org] *(rec Jacksonville, IL, July 9-11, 1990)* Titanic ▲ TI 226 [DDD]
Elgar, E.:Son Org [Aeolian-Skinner/G. Donald Harrison Org] *(rec Jacksonville, IL, July 9-11, 1990)* Titanic ▲ TI 226 [DDD]
Reger, M.:Trios Org [Aeolian-Skinner/G. Donald Harrison Org] *(rec Jacksonville, IL, July 9-11, 1990)* Titanic ▲ TI 226 [DDD]
Roger-Ducasse, J.:Pastoral Org [Aeolian-Skinner/G. Donald Harrison Org] *(rec Jacksonville, IL, July 9-11, 1990)* Titanic ▲ TI 226 [DDD]
Whitlock, P.:Fant Choral 2 [Aeolian-Skinner/G. Donald Harrison Org] *(rec Jacksonville, IL, July 9-11, 1990)* Titanic ▲ TI 226 [DDD]

Makowska, Krystyna (pno)
Chopin, F.:Intro, Theme & Vars, w. Anna Wesotowska (pno)—Vars *(rec Warsaw, 1987)* Selene ▲ CD 9404.20 [DDD]
Chopin, F.:Rondo for 2 Pnos, w. Anna Wesotowska (pno) *(rec Warsaw, 1987)* Selene ▲ CD 9404.20 [DDD]

Malan, Roy (vn)—see also ORCHESTRAS & ENSEMBLES San Francisco Contemporary Music Players, Porter String Quartet
Curran, A.:Why Is This Night Different Than All Other Nights?, w. Donald Haas (acc), Peter Wahrhaftig (tuba), Alvin Curran (pno), William Winant (perc) Tzadik ("The Composers" series) ▲ TZA 7001 [DDD]

Malanotte, Edmondo (vn)
Vivaldi, A.:Cons Vn (misc), w. R. Fasano (cnd), Rome Virtuosi—in g, Op. 8/5, "La tempesta di mare" *(rec Opéra de Rome, Oct. 1959)* EMI Classics ▲ CDK 65338 [ADD]
Vivaldi, A.:Cons for 4 Vns, w. Luigi Ferro (vn), Franco Gulli (vn), Angelo Stefanato (vn), R. Fasano (cnd), Rome Virtuosi—in b, Op. 3/10 *(rec Opéra de Rome, July & August, 1959)* EMI Classics ▲ CDK 65338 [ADD]

Malazzo, John (tpt)
Inwood, M.:Son Tpt, w. Robert Lanaghan (pno) Capstone ▲ CPS 8616 [DDD]

Malcolm, George (hpd)
Bach, C.P.E.:Con Hpd & Strs, H.427, w. Y. Menuhin (cnd), Bach Festival Orch EMI Classics ("Baroque" series) ▲ CDK 65733
Bach, J.S.:Con 7 Hpd, w. H. Winschermann (cnd), German Bach Soloists *(rec 1967)* Musicaphon ▲ 51356 [AAD]
Bach, J.S.:Sons Fl, BWV 1030-35, w. W. Bennett (fl) ASV Quicksilva ▲ 6108 [DDD]
Corelli, A.:Sons Vn, Op. 5, w. Yehudi Menuhin (vn), Robert Donnington (vl)—Nos. 1 in D, 5 in g & 12 in d EMI Classics ("Baroque" series) ▲ CDK 65731
18th Century Italian Recorder Sonatas, w. Michala Petri (rcr) Philips ▲ 412632-2
Handel, G.F.:Messiah, w. Kenneth McKellar (ten), Ralph Downes (org), A. Boult (cnd), London SO, London Sym Chorus—And the glory of the Lord; And He shall purify; For unto us a Child is born; Glory to God in the highest; His yoke is easy; Behold the Lamb of God; Surely He hath borne our griefs; And with His stripes we are healed; All we like sheep have gone astray; All they that see Him...He trusted in God; Lift up your heads; The Lord gave the word; Their sound has gone out; Let us break the bonds asunder; Hallelujah; Since by man came death; Worthy is the Lamb...Amen London ▲ 436569-2
Handel, G.F.:Water Music (comp) ASV ("Quiksilva" series) ▲ ASQ 6152 [DDD]
Highlights from the Julian Bream Edition, w. Bream, Julian (gtr), John Eliot Gardiner (cnd), Monteverdi Orch, Julian Bream Consort RCA Gold Seal ▲ 09026-61848-2
Purcell, H.:Music of, w. April Cantelo (sop), Alfred Deller (ct), Maurice Bevan (bar), Neville Marriner (vn), Peter Gibbs (vn), Granville Jones (vn), Desmond Dupré (vl), Walter Bergmann (hpd)—15 Songs & Airs; Fantasia upon a Ground in d for 3 Violins & Continuo, Z.731; Fantasia upon One Note in F for 5 Viols, Z.745; Hornpipe in e (from The Old Bachelor); Music Lessons 1-12 from Musick's Hand-Maid, Part II; A New Irish Tune, "Lilliburlero," Z.646; Pavan in g for 3 Violins & Bass Viol, Z.752; Sonata in g for Violin & Continuo, Z.780; Sonata No. 9 in F, "Golden Sonata," Z.810 (from Ten Sonatas in Four Parts); Suite in D for Harpsichord, Z.667 Vanguard Classics ("The Bach Guild" series) 2-▲ OVC 2002/03 [ADD]
Purcell, H.:Musick's Hand-maid 2 *(rec 1958)* Vanguard Classics ▲ OVC 4044 [ADD]
Purcell, H.:Suite 6 Hpd *(rec 1958)* Vanguard Classics ▲ OVC 4044 [ADD]

Malcolm, George (pno)
Mozart, W.A.:Andante & Vars Pno 4-Hands, w. A. Schiff (pno) London ▲ 440474-2
Mozart, W.A.:Fant Mechanical Org, w. A. Schiff (pno) London ▲ 440474-2
Mozart, W.A.:Org Music, w. A. Schiff (pno)—A piece for an Organ in A Clock, K.594 London ▲ 440474-2
Mozart, W.A.:Son Pno 4-Hands, K.497, w. A. Schiff (pno) London ▲ 440474-2
Mozart, W.A.:Son Pno 4-Hands, K.521, w. A. Schiff (pno) London ▲ 440474-2

Malcuzynski, Witold (pno)
Chopin, F.:Con 2 Pno, w. W. Susskind (cnd), London SO *(rec Kingsway Hall, London, Aug. 1959)* EMI Classics 2-▲ ZDMB 68226 [ADD]
Chopin, F.:Mazurkas—Nos. 5, 7, 15, 17, 20-23, 25, 27, 32, 41, 45, 47 & 49 *(rec Salle Wagram, Paris, Oct. 1961)* EMI Classics 2-▲ ZDMB 68226 [ADD]
Chopin, F.:Polonaises—Op. 26/1 & 2; Op. 40/1 & 2; Op. 44; Op. 53 *(rec National Philharmonic, Warsaw & Zelazowa Wola, Jan-Apr 1975 & May-June 1)* Polskie Nagrania ▲ PNCD 013
Chopin, F.:Son Pno, Op. 58 *(rec Salle Wagram, Paris, June 1961)* EMI Classics 2-▲ ZDMB 68226 [ADD]
Chopin, F.:Waltzes—Nos. 1-14 *(rec Salle Wagram, Paris, May 1959)* EMI Classics 2-▲ ZDMB 68226 [ADD]
Szymanowski, K.:Etude Pno *(rec Warsaw, 1959)* Polskie Nagrania ▲ PLN 066 [ADD]

Malferrari, Stefano (pno)
Ravel, M.:Shéhérazade Mez, w. Carlo Mazzoli (pno) [arr. Ravel for Pno 4-Hands] Nuova Era ▲ NUO 7205 [DDD]
Rimsky-Korsakov, N.:Scheherazade, w. Carlo Mazzoli (pno) [arr. Rimsky-Korsakov for Pno 4-Hands] Nuova Era ▲ NUO 7205 [DDD]

Malfeyt, Philippe (lt/chit/perc)—see ORCHESTRAS & ENSEMBLES Romanesque

Malfeyt, Philippe (thb)—see ORCHESTRAS & ENSEMBLES Ricercar Consort, Paul Rans Ensemble

Malgoire, Florence (vn)—see also ORCHESTRAS & ENSEMBLES Les Nièces de Rameau
Mondonville, J.-J.C. de:Sons Hpd, w. C. Rousset (hpd) Pierre Verany ▲ PV.790093 [DDD]

Malicki, Waldemar (pno)
Chopin, F.:Intro, Theme & Vars, w. Tamara Granat (pno)—Vars *(rec Warsaw Philharmonic Hall, June 27-30, 1994)* Canyon Classics ▲ CD 248
Paderewski, I.J.:Con Pno, w. W. Michniewski (cnd), Gdansk SO Accord ▲ ACD 201732 [DDD]
Paderewski, I.J.:Fant polonaise, w. W. Michniewski (cnd), Gdansk SO Accord ▲ ACD 201732 [DDD]
Paderewski, I.J.:Miscellanea Adda ▲ ADD 581186 [DDD]
Paderewski, I.J.:Pno Music (comp)—Son, Op. 21; Miscellanea Accord ▲ ACD 242852 [DDD]
Paderewski, I.J.:Son Pno Adda ▲ ADD 581186 [DDD]
Penderecki, K.:Chamber Music, w. A. Romanski (cl), Silesian String Quartet—Qts. Nos. 1 & 2 for Strings; Trio for Strings; Der unterbrochene Gedanke; Son. for Violin & Piano; Miniature, Op. 15; 3 Miniatures for Clarinet & Piano; Cadenza for Viola; Per Slava; Capriccio for Siegfried Palm; Proludo in B♭ for solo Clarinet Wergo ▲ WER 6258-2
Zarebski, J.:Qnt Pno, w. Varsovia String Quartet Pavane ▲ ADW 7218 [DDD]

Malikova, Anna (pno)
Chopin, F.:Con 1 Pno, w. J. Kovatchev (cnd), Turin PO RS Prestige ▲ 951-0019 [DDD]
Chopin, F.:Con 2 Pno, w. J. Kovatchev (cnd), Turin PO RS Prestige ▲ 951-0019 [DDD]

Malina, János (rcr)—see ORCHESTRAS & ENSEMBLES Affetti Musicali

Malina, Natalia (org)
Tournemire, C.:Sym 3, w. A. de Almeida (cnd), Moscow SO *(rec Mosfilm Studios, May 1994)* Marco Polo ▲ 8.223808 [DDD]

Malinin, Vladimir (vn)
The Spirit of Russia, w. Gidon Kremer (vn), Mark Pekarsky (cymbals), Leonid Bobylev (pno), Alexander Melnikov (vn) Vox Box 2-▲ CDX 5115 [ADD]

Malinova, Margarita (pno)—see ORCHESTRAS & ENSEMBLES Malinova Sisters

Malinova, Olga (pno)—see ORCHESTRAS & ENSEMBLES Malinova Sisters

Malinquist, Björn (db)
Blak, K.:Con Db, w. P. Helasvuo (cnd), Finnish-Estonian Baroque Orch *(rec Nordic House, Tórshavn, June 1994)* Tutl ▲ FKT 8

Malinyin, Evgeny (pno)
Mussorgsky, M.:Pictures at an Exhibition Multisonic ▲ MUL 310271

Maliska, Bohumil (hn)
Saeverud, H.:Peer Gynt Suites, w. Sveinung Sand (vn), Anna Dolezych (va), Kjersti Dahle (ob/E hn), Gyrid Erlandsen (cl), A. Dmitriev (cnd), Stavanger SO *(rec Stavanger Konserthus, Stavanger, Norway, Nov 13-17, 1995)* BIS ▲ CD 762 [DDD]

Malvicino, Horacio (elec gtr)
Piazzolla, A.:Music of, w. F.S. Paz (vn), Hector Console (db), A. Piazolla (band), Pablo Ziegler (pno)—Verando porteño; Lunfardo; Milonga del angel; Muerte del angel; Astor's Speech; La camorra; Mumuki; Adios Nonino; Contra bajissmo; Michelangelo; Concierto para quinteto *(rec Sept. 6, 1987)* Chesky ▲ JD 107 [DDD]

Mallette, Mercelle (vn)—see ORCHESTRAS & ENSEMBLES Montreal Chamber Group

Malling, Amalie (pno)
Debussy, C.:En blanc et noir, w. H. Pålsson (pno) *(rec May 11, 1975)* BIS ▲ CD 58 [AAD]
Gade, N.W.:Sym 5, w. M. Schønwandt (cnd), Collegium Musicum *(rec March 18-20, 1988)* Marco Polo ▲ DCCD 9004
Glass, L.:Romance Vc, w. Morten Zeuthen (vc) *(rec Copenhagen, Mar & June 1996)* Marco Polo/Dacapo ▲ 8.224052 [DDD]
Glass, L.:Son Vc, w. Morten Zeuthen (vc) *(rec Copenhagen, Mar & June 1996)* Marco Polo/Dacapo ▲ 8.224052 [DDD]
Grainger, P.:La Scandinavie, w. Morten Zeuthen (vc) *(rec Copenhagen, Mar & June 1996)* Marco Polo/Dacapo ▲ 8.224052 [DDD]

INSTRUMENT.

Malling, Amalie (pno) (cont.)
Hamerik, A.:Concert-Romanze, w. Morten Zeuthen (vc) [arr for vc & pno] *(rec Copenhagen, Mar & June 1996)* Marco Polo/Dacapo ▲ 8.224052 [DDD]
Heise, P.:Chamber Music, w. M. Zeuthen (vc), Kontra String Quartet—Quintet in F for Piano & Strings (1869); Cello Sonata in a (1867); 2 Fantasy Pieces for Cello & Piano Marco Polo/Dacapo ▲ DCCD 9113 [DDD]
Mozart, W.A.:Son Pnos, K.448, w. H. Půlsson (pno) *(rec May 29–30, 1976)* BIS ▲ CD 58 [AAD]
Nielsen, T.:Character Pieces Point ▲ PCD 5089
Schoenberg, A.:Con Pno, w. M. Schønwandt (cnd), Danish National RSO Chandos ▲ CHAN 9375 [DDD]
Schumann, R.:Con Pno, w. M. Schønwandt (cnd), Danish National RSO Chandos ▲ CHAN 9375 [DDD]
Schumann, R.:Davidsbündlertänze *(rec 1994)* Kontrapunkt ▲ KPT 32201
Schumann, R.:Humoreske Pno *(rec 1994)* Kontrapunkt ▲ KPT 32201
Sehested, H.:Fant Pieces, w. Morten Zeuthen (vc) *(rec Copenhagen, Mar & June 1996)* Marco Polo/Dacapo ▲ 8.224052 [DDD]
Stolarczyk, W.:Earth Air Fire Water, w. John Damgaard (pno), Anne Øland (pno), Teddy Teirup (pno), Friedrich Gürtler (pno), Rosalind Bevan (pno), Poul Rosenbaum (pno), Rodolfo Llambias (pno), Bella Horn–Ribera (pno), Anders Riber (pno), Elisabeth Sigurdsson (pno), Thomas Tronheim (pno), Elsebeth Broderson (pno), Erik Kaltoft (pno), Jørgen Hald Nielsen (pno), Aino Gilemann (pno), Birgit Kjær (pno), Jørgen Thomsen (pno), Gunhild Donslund (pno), Henrik Bo Hansen (pno), Lone Karlsson (pno), Erik Fessel (pno), Lasse Nilsson (pno), Janos Ferenczi (pno), Erik Bach (pno), Axel Momme (pno), Arne de Cros Dich (pno), Sven Micha Slot (pno), Hanne Bramsen Buhl (pno), Lili Olesen (pno), Susannah Carlsson (pno), Ulla Erml (pno), Vagn Sørensen (pno), Leif Greibe (pno), Bodil Krogh (pno), Kirsten Ottosen (pno), Inger Bergenholz (pno), Karsten Gylendorf (pno), Bjønr Elkjær (pno), Jacob Bjørn Jensen (pno), Jørgen Kaad (pno), Anne Marie Hjelm (pno), Carl Ulrik Munk Andersen (pno), Poul Lumbye (pno), Oluf Hildebrandt Nielsen (pno), Joachim Olsson (pno), Peter Pade Ramsøe Jacobsen (pno), Astrid Pollmann (pno), Jette Borsch (pno), Kirsten Karlshøj (pno), Maria Teresa Assing (pno), Allan Dahl Hansen (pno), Johan Hugossen (pno), Tine Fenger Pederson (pno), Arne Jørgen Fæø (pno), Anja Høgsted (pno), Anne Sophie Parbo (pno), Inga Lindmark (pno), Teresa Drabik Stathakis (pno), Anne Ruth Ferenczi (pno), Irene Hasager (pno), Yuka Ichikawa (pno), Birgitte Baur (pno), Malene Thastum (pno), Jens E. Rasmussen (pno), Birgitte Zielke (pno), Claus Zielke (pno), Stefan Kasch (pno), Bin Qiao (pno), Inger Johanne Teirup (pno), Lindy Rosborg (pno), Liisa Heininen (pno), David Højer (pno), Ellen Refstrup (pno), Thomas K. Søorensen (pno), Erik Kure (pno), Michael Rauff (pno), Jan beck Eriksson (pno), Tanja Zapolski (pno), Vibeke Skagbo (pno), Pål Eide Lindtner (pno), Ha–Young Sul (pno), Benedicte Palko (pno), Inke Kesseler (pno), Anne Marie Meineche (pno), Sverre Larsen (pno), Kasper Peter Bach (pno), Elisabetta Eliseo (pno), Olga Magieres (pno), Carl Erik Kühl (pno), Thorkild Borup Nielsen (pno), Valeria Zanini (pno), Lars Stenhoft (perc), Dennis Boel (perc), Winnie Dahlgren (perc), Susanne Vind (perc), Claus Byrith (elec), Anne Marie Storm (elec), J. Ribera (cnd) *(rec live, Koldinghaus Castle, Denmark, May 2, 1996)* Danica ▲ DCD 1996
Stravinsky, I.:Con Pnos, w. H. Pålsson (pno) *(rec May 29–30, 1976)* BIS ▲ CD 58 [AAD]

Mallon, Kevin (vn)
Campra, A.:Motets, w. Véronique Gens (sop), Anne Gotkovski (sop), Jean–Paul Fouchécourt (alt), Douglas Nasrawi (ten), Peter Harvey (bar), Marcos Loureiro de Så (bar), H. Niquet (cnd), Concert Spirituel Orch, Concert Spirituel Vocal Ensemble—Te Deum; Notus in Judea Deus; Deus in Nomine Tuo Adda ▲ ADD 241942 [DDD]

Mallory, Matt (fl)
Cage, J.:Roaratorio:An Irish Circus on Finnegans Wake, w. J. Cage (voice), J. Heaney (sgr), P. Glackin (fid), M. Mercier (bodrhan), P. Mercier (bodrhan), S. Ellis (uillean pipes) Wergo ▲ WER 6303–2
Cage, J.:Roaratorio:An Irish Circus on Finnegans Wake, w. J. Cage (voice), J. Heaney (sgr), P. Glackin (fid), M. Mercier (bodrhan), P. Mercier (bodrhan), S. Ellis (uillean pipes) Mode 2–▲ mode 28/29

Malone, E. (hp)
Hanson, H.:Con Org, w. David Craighead (org), D. Fetler (cnd), Rochester CO Albany ▲ TROY 129 [ADD]

Maloney, T. (cl)
Wagner, R.:Siegfried Idyll, w. T. Holowach (vn), M. Skazinetsky (vn), L. Toman (va), R. Laurie (vc), C. Elliott (db), S. Shulman (fl), J. Valdepenas (cl), J. Fetherston (cl), S. Mosher (bn), S. Wilson (hn), R. Cohen (hn), J. Cowell (tpt), G. Gould (cnd) *(rec July 27–29 & Sept. 8, 198)* Sony Classical ▲ SMK 52650 [ADD]

Malov, Oleg (pno)
Bach, J.S.:Con 1 Hpd, w. A. Titov (cnd), St. Petersburg Classical Music Studio Orch Infinity Digital ▲ QK 57720 [DDD]
Bach, J.S.:Con 3 Hpd, w. A. Titov (cnd), St. Petersburg Classical Music Studio Orch Infinity Digital ▲ QK 57720 [DDD]
Bach, J.S.:Con 5 Hpd, w. A. Titov (cnd), St. Petersburg Classical Music Studio Orch Infinity Digital ▲ QK 57720 [DDD]
Bach, J.S.:Con 1 for 2 Hpds, w. A. Kustariova (pno), A. Titov (cnd), St. Petersburg Classical Music Studio Orch Infinity Digital ▲ QK 57720 [DDD]
Knaifel, A.:O Heavenly King:Prayer to the Holy Spirit [trans for pno] *(rec St. Petersburg Radio House, Russia)* Megadisc ▲ MDC 7855
Knaifel, A.:Passacaglia [trans for pno] *(rec St. Petersburg Radio House, Russia)* Megadisc ▲ MDC 7855
Knaifel, A.:Postludia [trans for pno] *(rec St. Petersburg Radio House, Russia)* Megadisc ▲ MDC 7855
Knaifel, A.:Scarry March [trans for pno] *(rec St. Petersburg Radio House, Russia)* Megadisc ▲ MDC 7855
Ustvolskaya, G.:Composition 1, w. Michail Tokarev (pic), Alexei Arbuszov (tuba) *(rec St. Petersburg Radio House, Jan. 1994)* Megadisc ▲ 7867
Ustvolskaya, G.:Duet Vn, w. Alexander Shustin (vn) *(rec St. Petersburg Radio House, Oct. & Nov. 1994)* Megadisc ▲ 7863
Ustvolskaya, G.:Grand Duet Vc, w. Alexei Vassiliev (vc) *(rec St. Petersburg Radio House, Oct. & Nov. 1994)* Megadisc ▲ 7863
Ustvolskaya, G.:Octet Obs, w. Nicolay Neretin (ob), Piotr Tosenko (ob), Alexander Stang (vn), Olga Ribaltchenko (vn), Valentin Lukin (vn), Nikolay Tkachenko (vn), Valerii Znamenskii (timp), O. Malov (cnd) *(rec St. Petersburg Radio House, Oct. & Nov. 1994)* Megadisc ▲ 7865
Ustvolskaya, G.:Preludes Pno *(rec St. Petersburg Radio House, Jan. 1994)* Megadisc ▲ 7867
Ustvolskaya, G.:Sons Pno *(rec St. Petersburg Radio House, Aug.–Sept. 1993)* Megadisc ▲ 7876
Ustvolskaya, G.:Son Vn, w. Alexander Shustin (vn) *(rec St. Petersburg Radio House, Oct. & Nov. 1994)* Megadisc ▲ 7865
Ustvolskaya, G.:Trio Cl, w. Adil Feodorov (cl), Alexander Shustin (vn) *(rec St. Petersburg Radio House, Oct. & Nov. 1994)* Megadisc ▲ 7865

Malraux, Madeleine (pno)
Madeleine Malraux K617 ▲ 7019 [DDD]

Malsbury, Angela (cl)
Mozart, W.A.:Con Cl, w. J. Glover (cnd), London Mozart Players ASV ▲ ASV 795 [DDD]
Prokofiev, S.:Ov on Hebrew Themes, w. D. Petit (pno), Coull String Quartet Hyperion ▲ CDA 66573

Malvern, G. (tpt)
Pepping, E.:Suite Tpt, w. C. Leaman (sax), D. Hamilton (trbn) CRS ▲ 9051

Malvicino, Horacio (gtr)—see ORCHESTRAS & ENSEMBLES New Tango Sex–tet

Maly, František (pno)—see also ORCHESTRAS & ENSEMBLES Antonín Dvořák Trio
Martinů, B.:Ariette, w. Mikael Ericsson (vc) *(rec Martínek Studio, Prague, Nov. 29–30 & Dec. 1, 1993)* Panton ("Protokol XX" series) ▲ PAN 811269 [DDD]
Martinů, B.:Etudes & Polkas *(rec Martinek Studio, Prague, June 29–July 1, 1995)* Panton ("Czech 20th–Century Music" series) ▲ PAN 811426 [AAD]
Martinů, B.:Fant & Toccata *(rec Martinek Studio, Prague, June 29–July 1, 1995)* Panton ("Czech 20th–Century Music" series) ▲ PAN 811426 [AAD]
Martinů, B.:Nocturnes Vc, w. Mikael Ericsson (vc) *(rec Martínek Studio, Prague, Nov. 29–30 & Dec. 1, 1993)* Panton ("Protokol XX" series) ▲ PAN 811269 [DDD]
Martinů, B.:Pastorales, w. Mikael Ericsson (vc) *(rec Martínek Studio, Prague, Nov. 29–30 & Dec. 1, 1993)* Panton ("Protokol XX" series) ▲ PAN 811269 [DDD]

Malý, František (pno) (cont.)
Martinů, B.:Son Pno *(rec Czechoslovak Radio Studio No. 1, Prague, Mar 25, 1979)* Panton ("Czech 20th–Century Music" series) ▲ PAN 811426 [AAD]
Martinů, B.:Vars on a Theme by Rossini, w. Mikael Ericsson (vc) *(rec Martínek Studio, Prague, Nov. 29–30 & Dec. 1, 1993)* Panton ("Protokol XX" series) ▲ PAN 811269 [DDD]
Martinů, B.:Vars on a Slovak folksong, w. Mikael Ericsson (vc) *(rec Martínek Studio, Prague, Nov. 29–30 & Dec. 1, 1993)* Panton ("Protokol XX" series) ▲ PAN 811269 [DDD]

Malý, Lubomir (va)
Berlioz, H.:Harold in Italy, w. F. Jílek (cnd), Czech PO *(rec 1981)* Supraphon ▲ SUP CD 3095
Dittersdorf, K.D. von:Concertino Va, w. F. Pasta (db), F. Vajnar (cnd), Dvořák CO Supraphon ▲ CD 110951 [DDD]
Dittersdorf, K.D. von:Con Va, w. F. Vajnar (cnd), Dvořák CO Supraphon ▲ CD 110951 [DDD]
Dvořák, A.:Qnt Strs, Op. 97, w. Suk String Quartet Praga ▲ PR 250078
Forsyth, C.:Con Va, w. M. Konvalinka (cnd), Prague SO *(rec Smetana Hall, Prague, Dec. 15 & 21–22, 1987)* Panton ("Panorama" series) ▲ PAN 811306
Martinů, B.:Rhap–Con Va, w. Z. Košler (cnd), Prague RSO Panton ▲ PAN 811204
Vaughan Williams, R.:Flos Campi, w. M. Konvalinka (cnd), Prague SO, Prague Radio Chorus *(rec Smetana Hall, Prague, Dec. 15 & 21–22, 1987)* Panton ("Panorama" series) ▲ PAN 811306
Vivaldi, A.:Con Va d'amore Lt, w. L. Brabec (gtr), O. Vlček (cnd), Prague CO Supraphon ▲ 10 4126–2 [DDD]

Mamou, Roberte (pno)
Bruch, M.:Pieces Cl, Op. 83/1–8, w. Michel Lethiec (cl), Vladimir Mendelssohn (va) *(rec Conservatoire de Tourcoing, Mar 1995)* Pavane ▲ ADW 7334 [DDD]
Dvořák, A.:Qnt Pno, Op. 81, w. Ami Flammer (vn), Silvia Marcovici (vn), Gerard Causse (va), Robert Cohen (vc) *(rec Mozart Festival, Lille, France, 1994)* Verdi Classics ▲ AU 32 250
Dvořák, A.:Romantic Pieces, Op. 75, w. Silvia Marcovici (vn) *(rec Mozart Festival, Lille, France, 1994)* Verdi Classics ▲ AU 32 250
Dvořák, A.:Rondo, w. Robert Cohen (vc) [arr for vc & pno] *(rec Mozart Festival, Lille, France, 1994)* Verdi Classics ▲ AU 32 250
Field, J.:Nocturnes Pno (comp) Pavane ▲ ADW 7110 [DDD]
Haydn, J.:Son Pno, H.XVII/6, "Andante with Vars"—Vars. only Pavane ▲ ADW 7202 [DDD]
Haydn, J.:Trios Pno, Fl & Vc, w. Shigenori Kudo (fl), Dominique de Williencourt (vc) Pavane ▲ ADW 7202 [DDD]
Mozart, W.A.:Con 20 Pno, w. G. Oskamp (cnd), Berlin SO Verdi Classics ▲ AU 32 147
Mozart, W.A.:Con 24 Pno, w. G. Oskamp (cnd), Berlin SO Verdi Classics ▲ AU 32 147
Schumann, R.:Märchenerzählungen, w. Michel Lethiec (cl), Vladimir Mendelssohn (va) *(rec Conservatoire de Tourcoing, Mar 1995)* Pavane ▲ ADW 7334 [DDD]

Man, Annelie de (hpd)
Bruynèl, T.:Le jardin, w. Karin van der Poel (voc), Harrie Starreveld (fl) Donemus ▲ NEAR 01 [DDD]
Denisov, E.:Chamber Music Va, w. N. Imai (va), L. Markiz (cnd), Amsterdam New Sinfonietta *(rec 6/91)* BIS ▲ CD 518 [DDD]
Denisov, E.:Con for 2 Vas, w. N. Imai (va), P. Vahle (va), L. Markiz (cnd), Amsterdam New Sinfonietta *(rec 6/91)* BIS ▲ CD 518 [DDD]
A Lady Shaves Her Legs, w. R. Westerheide (gtr) Erasmus ▲ WVH 072 [DDD]

Man, Wu (pipa)
Shea, D.:Hsi–Yu Chi, w. Sim Cain (perc), Hideki Kato (bass instrument), Zeena Parkins (hp/pno/acc), Jim Pugliese (perc), Mark Ribot (gtr/banjo), David Shea (sampler/pno/turntables), Alex Tobias (celtic dr/misc.), Rebecca Wilson (screaming), John Zorn (a sax) Tzadik ("The Composers" series) ▲ TZA 7005 [DDD]

Manasjan, G. (vc)
Ravel, M.:Intro & Allegro, w. M. Golden (hp), M. Meisenbach (fl), R. McDowall (cl), R. Neal (vn), D. Pettys (vn), D. Hermann (va) Centaur ▲ CRC 2114 [DDD]

Manasse, Jon (cl)
Cohn, J.:Con Cl, XLNT Sinfonietta *(rec Oct. 1993)* XLNT ▲ CD 18009 [DDD]
Cohn, J.:Music of, w. M. Piccinini (fl), M. Dine (ob), M. Finn (bn), J. Tarpley (hn), N. Akamatsu (db), S. Alderking (pno)—Wind Quintet, Op. 36b (1981); Goldfinch Variations for Wind Trio, Op. 61 (1984); Little Overture for Wind Quartet, Op. 59 (1982); Suite Champêtre for Wind Quintet (after Rameau), Op. 47 (1968) XLNT ■ C 2
Cohn, J.:Music of, w. M. Piccinini (fl), M. Dine (ob), M. Finn (bn), J. Tarpley (hn), N. Akamatsu (db), S. Alderking (pno)—Wind Quintet, Op. 36b (1981); Little Overture for Wind Quintet, Op. 59 (1982); Sonatina for Clarinet & Piano, Op. 56 (1981); Sonata Romantica for Double Bass & Piano, Op. 18 (1952); Sonata Robusta for Bassoon & Piano, Op. 55 (1980); Sonata for Flute & Piano, Op. 52 (1974); Goldfinch Variations for Three Treble Instruments, Op. 61 (1984) *(rec 1985)* XLNT ▲ CD 18006 [ADD]
Gershwin, G.:Preludes (3) Pno, XLNT Sinfonietta [arr. for clarinet & strings James Cohn] *(rec Oct. 1993)* XLNT ▲ CD 18009 [DDD]
Mozart, W.A.:Qnt Cl, K.581, w. Shanghai String Quartet *(rec Oct. 1993)* XLNT ▲ CD 18009 [DDD]
Spohr, L.:Fant & Vars on a Theme of Danzi, w. Shanghai String Quartet *(rec Oct. 1993)* XLNT ▲ CD 18009 [DDD]
Weber, C.M. von:Andante & Rondo ungarese Bn, w. L. Foss (cnd), Brooklyn PO [newly arranged by James Cohn for clarinet & orchestra] XLNT ▲ CD 18005 [DDD]
Weber, C.M. von:Concertino Cl, w. L. Foss (cnd), Brooklyn PO XLNT ▲ CD 18005 [DDD]
Weber, C.M. von:Con 1 Cl, w. L. Foss (cnd), Brooklyn PO XLNT ▲ CD 18005 [DDD]
Weber, C.M. von:Con 2 Cl, w. L. Foss (cnd), Brooklyn PO XLNT ▲ CD 18005 [DDD]
Weber, C.M. von:Grand duo concertant Cl, w. S. Sanders (pno) XLNT ▲ CD 18004 [DDD]
Weber, C.M. von:Intro, Theme & Vars Cl, w. Manhattan String Quartet XLNT ▲ CD 18004 [DDD]
Weber, C.M. von:Qnt Cl, w. Manhattan String Quartet XLNT ▲ CD 18004 [DDD]
Weber, C.M. von:Vars on a Theme from *Silvana* Cl, w. S. Sanders (pno) XLNT ▲ CD 18004 [DDD]

Manceau, Régis (fl)
Telemann, G.P.:Con Rcr, Fl, w. Jean–Marc Labylle (rcr), P. Kuentz (cnd), Paul Kuentz Orch Pierre Verany ▲ PVY 730046

Mancini, David (perc)—see ORCHESTRAS & ENSEMBLES Eastman Percussion Ensemble members

Mancini, Stefano (fl)
Respighi, O.:Gli uccelli, w. Alberto Cesaraccio (ob), Antonio Puglia (cl), Paloma Tironi (hp), Stefano Melis (cel), R. Tigani (cnd), Sassari SO *(rec Rome, Oct 11–14, 1994)* Bongiovanni ▲ GB 2166 [DDD]

Mandalka, Rudolf (vc)
Beethoven, L. van:Songs, w. James Griffett (ten), Franzjosef Maier (vn), Bradford Tracey (pno)—To the Aeolian Harp; Sally in Our Alley; The Soldier; Sympathy; The Farewell Song; Come, Darby Dear, Easy; The Shepherd's Song; The British Light Dragoons Ars Musici ▲ 1142 [ADD]
Haydn, J.:Songs, w. James Griffett (ten), Franzjosef Maier (vn), Bradford Tracey (pno)—Will Ye Got to Flanders; The Glancing of Her Apron; Jockie & Sandy; O Can Ye Sew Cushions; Margret's Ghost; Up in the Morning Early; Barbara Allen; Green Grow the Rashes; Lizae Baillie; Blue Bonnets Ars Musici ▲ 1142 [ADD]

Mandat, Eric (cl)—see ORCHESTRAS & ENSEMBLES Tone Road Ramblers, Ciosoni Trio

Mandel, Alan (pno)
American Piano, Vol. 1 Premier ▲ PRCD 1013 [DDD]
American Piano, Vol. 3:Rags And Other Riches Premier ▲ PRCD 1021 [DDD]
Beach, A.M.C.:Songs, w. Jerome Barry (bar)—The Year's at the Spring; Villanelle *(rec Harmony Hall, Hyattsville, MD, Nov 17–20, 1994)* Premier ▲ PRCD 1047 [DDD]
Carpenter, J.A.:Songs, w. Jerome Barry (bar)—In Spring; May, the Maiden; Sicilian Lullaby; To 1 Unknown *(rec Harmony Hall, Hyattsville, MD, Nov 17–20, 1994)* Premier ▲ PRCD 1047 [DDD]
Chadwick, G.W.:Songs, w. Jerome Barry (bar)—In Bygone Days; Sweet Wind; Sweetheart, Thy Lips Are Touched with Flame; Before the Dawn; The Bobolink; The Northern Days; O Love & Joy *(rec Harmony Hall, Hyattsville, MD, Nov 17–20, 1994)* Premier ▲ PRCD 1047 [DDD]
Duke, V.:Souvenir de Venise Premier ▲ PRCD 1013 [DDD]

714
▲ = CD ♦ = Enhanced CD Δ = MD ■ = Cassette Tape ▯ = DCC

Mandel, Alan (pno) (cont.)
Foote, A.:Songs, w. Jerome Barry (bar)—The Wanderer to His Heart's Desire; A Song of 4 Seasons; The Nightingale Has a Lyre of Gold; The Rose & the Gardener; If Love Were What the Rose Is; Before Sunrise; Constancy; The Hawthorne Wins the Damask Rose; Love Me, If I Live!; A Song of Summer; Love in Her Cold Grave Lies *(rec Harmony Hall, Hyattsville, MD, Nov 17–20, 1994)* Premier ▲ PRCD 1047 [DDD]
Gottschalk, L.M.:Pno Music—[CD 1] Battle Cry of Freedom:Grand caprice de concert, Op. 55; Grand Scherzo, Op. 57; Bamboula:Danse des nègres, Op. 2; Pasquinade, Op. 59; Le Bananier, chanson nègre, Op. 55; Souvenirs d'Andalousie, Op. 22; The Last Hope, Op. 16; La Jota Aragonesa, Op. 14; The Maiden's Blush, Op. 106; La Galina, Op. 53; Impromptu, Op. 54; The Dying Poet, Op. 110; L'Union, Op. 48 [CD 2] Jeunesse:Mazurka brillante, Op. 70; Love and Chivalry:Caprice élégant en forme de schottische, Op. 97; Danza, Op. 33; O! Ma Charmante, Espargnez Moil; Sixth Ballade, Op. 85; Suis-moi caprice, Op. 45; Pensée poétique, Op. 62; America, Op. 41; Ricordati, Op. 26; Tournament Galop; Berceuse, Op. 47; Redieuse, Op. 116; Brazilian National Anthem, Op. 69 [CD 3] Souvenir de la Havane, Op. 39; Chant du soldat, Op. 23; The Banjo, Op. 15; La Scintilla, Op. 20; Souvenir de Porto Rico, marche des Gibaros, Op. 31; Ojos Criollos, danse cubaine, caprice brillant, Op. 37; Two Mazurkas:Colliers d'Or, Op. 6; Marche de nuit, Op. 17; Manchega, étude de concert, Op. 38; Ossian:Deux Ballades, Op. 4; Minuit à Seville, Op. 30; El Cocoyé, Op. 80; Forget Me Not, mazurka caprice Vox Box 3-▲ CD3X 3033 [ADD]
Gould, M.:Prelude & Toccata Premier ▲ PRCD 1013 [DDD]
Ives, C.:Pno Music—Three-Page Sonata; Song Without (Good) Words; Studies Nos. 2, 5–9, 15, 18, & 20–22; Rough & Ready; Scene Episode; Waltz-Rondo; March in G & D "Here's To Good Old Yale"; The Celestial Railroad, a Phantasie for Piano Solo; The Seen and Unseen; Anthem-Processional; Bad Resolutions and Good; Storm and Distress; Allegretto (Invention); Baseball Take-Off; Varied Air and Variations Vox Box 3-▲ CD3X 3034 [ADD]
Ives, C.:Son 1 Pno Vox Box 3-▲ CD3X 3034 [ADD]
Ives, C.:Son 2 Pno Vox Box 3-▲ CD3X 3034 [ADD]
Loewe, C.:Grand Duo, w. Elisabeth Small (vn) *(rec Belmont Univ., Studio A, Dec. 15–18, 1994)* Premier ▲ PRCD 1037 [DDD]
North, A.:Streetcar Named Desire (pno sequences) Premier ▲ PRCD 1013 [DDD]
Paine, J.K.:Songs, w. Jerome Barry (bar)—A Bird Upon a Rosy Bough; Matin Song; I Wore Your Roses Yesterday *(rec Harmony Hall, Hyattsville, MD, Nov 17–20, 1994)* Premier ▲ PRCD 1047 [DDD]
Parker, H.:Songs, w. Jerome Barry (bar)—The Complacent Lover; Pack, Clouds Away!; Come, O Come My Life's Delight; Slumber Song; Once I Loved a Maiden Fair *(rec Harmony Hall, Hyattsville, MD, Nov 17–20, 1994)* Premier ▲ PRCD 1047 [DDD]
Rochberg, G.:Carnival Music Grenadilla ■ GSC 1069
Röntgen, J.:Son Vn, w. Elisabeth Small (vn) *(rec Belmont Univ., Studio A, Dec. 15–18, 1994)* Premier ▲ PRCD 1037 [DDD]
Siegmeister, E.:Sunday in Brooklyn Premier ▲ PRCD 1013 [DDD]
Sousa, J.P.:Pno Music—The Presidential Polonaise (1889); Moonlight on the Potomac Waltzes, Op. 3 (1901) Premier ▲ PRCD 1021 [DDD]
Whiting, A.B.:Songs, w. Jerome Barry (bar)—O Love, Stay By & Sing *(rec Harmony Hall, Hyattsville, MD, Nov 17–20, 1994)* Premier ▲ PRCD 1047 [DDD]

Mandrin, Emmanuel (harm)
Rossini, G.:Petite messe solennelle, w. Françoise Pollet (sop), Jacqueline Mayeur (mez), Jean-Luc Viala (ten), Michel Piquemal (bar), Raymond Alessandrini (pno), Michel Piquemal (cnd), Michel Piquemal Vocal Ensemble Accord 2-▲ ACD 203562 [DDD]

Mandrin, Emmanuel (org)
Charpentier, M.-A.:Music of, w. Emmanuel Mandrin (cnd), Les Demoiselles de Saint-Cyr—Ave Regina cælorum; Sicut spina rosam; Gaude felix Anna; Magnificat; Quam pulchra es; Omni die dic Mariæ; Alma redemptoris mater; In nativitate; Regina cæli; Alma Dei creatoris; Ego mater agnitionis; Salve Regina; Sub tuum; Litanies de la Vierge; Inviolata integra *(rec Paris, Feb 1995)* FNAC Music ▲ 592036 [DDD]

Manelis, Dmitrij (pno)
Ischchenko, Y.:Ukrainian Rhap, w. J. Pantelyat 9vc) *(rec Sept. 1993)* Dorian Discovery ▲ DIS 80122 [DDD]
Kossenko, V.:Son Vc, w. J. Pantelyat (vc) *(rec Sept. 1993)* Dorian Discovery ▲ DIS 80122 [DDD]
Lisogub, I.:Son Vc, w. J. Pantelyat (vc) *(rec Sept. 1993)* Dorian Discovery ▲ DIS 80122 [DDD]
Shtogarenko, A.:Ballad Vc, w. J. Pantelyat (vc) *(rec Sept. 1993)* Dorian Discovery ▲ DIS 80122 [DDD]

Mangiavacchi, Orietta (perc)
Amendola, F.:Ricercari, w. D. Patumi (db), A. Frederico (elecs/pno), A. Flore (voc), G. Lanzini (cl), L. Ciolfi (vn), C. Cavalieri (vn), C. Sanzo (vc), Donizetti Ensemble Bongiovanni ▲ GB 5519 [DDD]

Mangiocavallo, Luigi (vn)—see also ORCHESTRAS & ENSEMBLES L'Astrée Ensemble, Clemencic Consort
Bonporti, F.A.:Concertini e Serenate, Op. 12, w. M. Mencoboni (hpd), C. Ronco (vc)—Concertini Nos. 3 in G & 7 in E♭; Serenatas Nos. 2 in F, 4 in g & 6 in G Nuova Era ("Ancient Music" series) ▲ 6939 [DDD]
Veracini, F.M.:Sons Vn, Op. 1, w. C. Ronco (vc), M. Mencoboni (hpd)—Sonata No. 12 in F Nuova Era ("Ancient Music" series) ▲ 6900 [DDD]
Veracini, F.M.:Sonate accademiche, w. C. Ronco (vc), M. Mencoboni (hpd)—Sonatas No. 5 in g & No. 6 in A Nuova Era ("Ancient Music" series) ▲ 6900 [DDD]

Mangor, Viggo (baroque lt)
Weiss, S.L.:Lt Music—Partita Grande in c; Sonata in D Paula (Denmark) ▲ CD 43
Weiss, S.L.:Lt Music—Sons in A, d & F [Le fameux corsaire]; Tombeau *(rec Torslunde Church, 1994)* Kontrapunkt ▲ KPT 32222 [DDD]

Mangos, Georgia (pno)
Liszt, F.:Symphonic Poems, w. L. Mangos (pno) [trans. by the composer for piano duo]—Nos. 1, 2, 3 & 4 *(rec Jan. 22–23, 1993)* Cedille ▲ CDR 90000 014 [DDD]
Liszt, F.:Symphonic Poems, w. Louise Mangos (pno)—Prometheus; Mazeppa; Festklänge; Hèroïde funèbre [all trans Liszt for Pno duo] *(rec Mandel Hall, Univ of Chicago, June 12, 14 & 16, 1995)* Cedille ▲ CDR 90000 024 [DDD]

Mangos, Louise (pno)
Liszt, F.:Symphonic Poems, w. G. Mangos (pno) [trans. by the composer for piano duo]—Nos. 1, 2, 3 & 4 *(rec Jan. 22–23, 1993)* Cedille ▲ CDR 90000 014 [DDD]
Liszt, F.:Symphonic Poems, w. Georgia Mangos (pno)—Prometheus; Mazeppa; Festklänge; Hèroïde funèbre [all trans Liszt for Pno duo] *(rec Mandel Hall, Univ of Chicago, June 12, 14 & 16, 1995)* Cedille ▲ CDR 90000 024 [DDD]

Manker, Brain (vc)—see ORCHESTRAS & ENSEMBLES Arman Ensemble

Manley, T. (perc)
Harrison, L.:Fugue Perc, w. William Winant (perc), Dan Kennedy (perc), D. Rosenthal (perc) New Albion ▲ NA 055
Harrison, L.:Song of Quetzalcoatl, w. William Winant (perc), Dan Kennedy (perc), D. Rosenthal (perc) New Albion ▲ NA 055

Mann, Elizabeth (fl)
Poulenc, F.:Sxt Pno, w. André Previn (pno), Steve Taylor (ob), David Shifrin (cl), Dennis Godburn (bn), Richard Todd (hn) *(rec Manhattan Center Studios, New York City, Apr. 7–8, 1993)* RCA Red Seal ▲ 09026-68181-2 [DDD]

Mann, Nicholas (vn)—see ORCHESTRAS & ENSEMBLES Mendelssohn String Quartet

Mann, Robert (vn)—see also ORCHESTRAS & ENSEMBLES Juilliard String Quartet
Brahms, J.:Sons Vn (comp), w. Stephen Hough (pno) *(rec Rectial Hall, Music Division, SUNY, Purchase, NY, June 22–23, 1993)* Music Masters Classics ▲ 01612-67165-2

Mannberg, Karl-Ove (vn)
Pettersson, G.A.:Sons for 2 Vns, w. Josef Grünfarb (vn) Caprice ▲ CAP 21401 [AAD]

Manne, Shelly (dr)
A Different Kind of Blues, w. Itzhak Perlman (vn), Andre Previn (pno), Jim Hall (gtr), Red Mitchell (bass) Angel ▲ CDM 64319 [DDD]
It's a Breeze, w. Itzhak Perlman (vn), Andre Previn (pno), Jim Hall (gtr), Red Mitchell (bass) Angel ▲ CDM 64318 [DDD]
Joplin, S.:Music of, w. J.-P. Rampal (fl), J. S. Ritter (pno/hpds), Johnson (tubas) CBS ▲ MK 37818

Manne, Shelly (dr) (cont.)
Saxophone Quartet, w. Harvey Pittel (sax), Monty Budwig (bass) Crystal ■ C 155

Manne, Shelly (perc)
Bolling, C.:California Suite, w. H. Laws (fl), C. Bolling (pno), C. Damonico (db) CBS ▲ MK 36691
Dring, M.:Pastel Panche, w. Bud Shank (fl), Bill Perkins (sax/fl), Ray Brown (bass), Leigh Kaplan (pno)—Teal for Two; Muave Mood; Lime Clash Cambria ▲ CD 1084 [ADD]
Dring, M.:Shades of Dring, w. Bud Shank (fl), Bill Perkins (sax/fl), Ray Brown (bass), Leigh Kaplan (pno)—In the Pink; Hallelujah Red; Brown and Out; Hello Yellow; Saxy Blue Cambria ▲ CD 1084 [ADD]

Mannes, Leopold (pno)
Schumann, R.:Stücke im Volkston, w. P. Casals (vc) *(rec Prades, France, May 28–29, 1953)* Sony Classical ("The Casals Edition" series) ▲ SMK 58993 [ADD]

Mannheimer, Irène (pno)
Liljefors, R.:Con Pno, w. M. Liljefors (cnd), Gävelborg SO *(rec Concert Hall of the Royal Swedish Academy of Music, Stockholm, May 15 & June 6, 1995)* Sterling ▲ 1017 [DDD]
Stenhammar, W.:Late Summer Nights Sterling ▲ CDS 1004

Manning, Dwight (ob)—see ORCHESTRAS & ENSEMBLES Georgia Woodwind Quintet

Manning, J. (tuba)—see ORCHESTRAS & ENSEMBLES Atlantic Brass Quintet

Manning, John (tuba)—see also ORCHESTRAS & ENSEMBLES Atlantic Brass Quintet
Lutyens, E.:Music of, w. R. Montgomery (cnd), Jane's Minstrels—Chamber Concerto No. 1; The Valley of Hatsu-se; 6 Tempi for 10 Instruments; Lament of Isis on the Death of Osiris; Triolet 1; Requiescat; Triolet 2 NM Classics ▲ NMCD 011 [DDD]

Manning, P. (vn)—see ORCHESTRAS & ENSEMBLES Britten String Quartet

Manno, Marco Di (fl)—see ORCHESTRAS & ENSEMBLES Consort Fontegara

Manno, R. (cl)
Hindemith, P.:Duets Cl & Vn, w. *(vn unknown)* CPO ▲ CPO 999302
Hindemith, P.:Qt Cl, Vn, Vc & Pno, w. *(vn unknown)* CPO ▲ CPO 999302
Hindemith, P.:Son Cl, w. *(pno unknown)* CPO ▲ CPO 999302

Mann-Polk, S. (pno)
Bach, J.S.:Partitas Hpd, BWV 825–830 Cappella 2-▲ CR 100 [ADD]

Manoogian, Vartan (vn)—see also ORCHESTRAS & ENSEMBLES Roscoe Mitchell New Chamber Ensemble
Mitchell, R.:Duet, w. R. Mitchell (sax) Lovely Music ▲ LCD 2021 [AAD]
Ward, R.:Son 1 Vn, w. Anne Epperson (pno) Albany ▲ TROY 204 [DDD]

Manríquez, Luz (pno)
It's Peaceful Here:Little Gems for the Violin, w. Andrés Cárdenes (vn) Arabesque ▲ ARA 6655 [DDD]
Made in the U.S.A., w. Andrés Cárdenes (vn) *(rec Carnegie Library of Homestead, Munhall, PA, Oct 21–23, 1996)* Ocean ▲ OR 103

Manshardt, Thomas (pno)
Chopin, F.:Son Pno, Op. 58 APR ▲ APR 5550 [DDD]
Liszt, F.:Consolations—No. 3 in D APR ▲ APR 5550 [DDD]
Liszt, F.:Légendes APR ▲ APR 5550 [DDD]
Manshardt, T.:Hommage à Debussy APR ▲ APR 5550 [DDD]
Manshardt, T.:Hommage à Liapunov APR ▲ APR 5550 [DDD]
Manshardt, T.:Hommage à Mendelssohn APR ▲ APR 5550 [DDD]
Mozart, W.A.:Son 5 Pno APR ▲ APR 5550 [DDD]

Manson, Jonathan (vc)
Bach, J.S.:Brandenburg Con 5, w. Steven Preston (fl), Jane Rogers (va), Purcell Quartet Chandos ("Chaconne" series) ▲ CHAN 0595
Bach, J.S.:Con 3 Hpd, w. Jane Rogers (va), Purcell Quartet Chandos ("Chaconne" series) ▲ CHAN 0595
Bach, J.S.:Con 5 Hpd, w. Jane Rogers (va), Purcell Quartet Chandos ("Chaconne" series) ▲ CHAN 0595
Bach, J.S.:Con 3 for 2 Hpds, w. Jane Rogers (va), Paul Nicholson (hpd), Purcell Quartet Chandos ("Chaconne" series) ▲ CHAN 0595

Mantcheva, Iskra (pno)
Christoff, D.:Chaconne *(rec Salle Bulgaria, Sofia, Bulgaria, Jan 1996)* Concord Concerto ▲ CCD 42037 [DDD]
Christoff, D.:Son 1 Pno *(rec Salle Bulgaria, Sofia, Bulgaria, Jan 1996)* Concord Concerto ▲ CCD 42037 [DDD]
Christoff, D.:Son 2 Pno *(rec Salle Bulgaria, Sofia, Bulgaria, Jan 1996)* Concord Concerto ▲ CCD 42037 [DDD]
Christoff, D.:Son 3 Pno *(rec Salle Bulgaria, Sofia, Bulgaria, Jan 1996)* Concord Concerto ▲ CCD 42037 [DDD]
Christoff, D.:Son 4 Pno *(rec Salle Bulgaria, Sofia, Bulgaria, Jan 1996)* Concord Concerto ▲ CCD 42037 [DDD]
Christoff, D.:Son 5 Pno *(rec Salle Bulgaria, Sofia, Bulgaria, Jan 1996)* Concord Concerto ▲ CCD 42037 [DDD]

Mantoux, Christophe (org)
Guilain, J.-A.:Pièces d'orgue pour le Magnificat Adda ▲ ADD 581151 [DDD]
Marchand, L.:Pieces Org—Suite du cinquième ton Adda ▲ ADD 581151 [DDD]

Manuguerra, Michele (gtr)
Segoviana:Duets for Violin & Guitar, w. Anna Alessandra Gelmini (vn) Kicco Classic ▲ 295

Manz, Petra (vl)
Love Songs & Dances:Consort Music for Lute & Voices from "Pratum Musicum", w. Lutz Kirchhof (lt), Marie-Claude Vallin (sop), Claudio Cavina (altus), Max van Egmond (bar), Sabine Dreier (trns fl) *(rec Evangelische Kirche, St Osdag, Mandelsloh, Germany, Nov 21–24, 1994)* Sony Classical ("Vivarte" series) ▲ SK 66263 [DDD]

Manz, Wolfgang (pno)—see also ORCHESTRAS & ENSEMBLES Duo Reine Elisabeth
Beethoven, L. van:Con Vn, Vc & Pno, "Triple Con", w. Frank Peter Zimmermann (vn), Robert Cohen (vc), J.-P. Saraste (cnd), English CO Classics for Pleasure ("Silver Doubles" series) 2-▲ CFP CDCFP 4775 [ADD/DDD]
Dohnányi, E. von:Qnt 1 Pno, w. Gabrieli String Quartet Chandos ▲ CHAN 8718 [DDD]

Manzanilla, Ivan (perc)—see ORCHESTRAS & ENSEMBLES Tambuco Camerata

Manze, Andrew (baroque vn)—see also ORCHESTRAS & ENSEMBLES Romanesca
Biber, H. von:Passacaglia Vn *(rec East Woodhay, UK, Sept. 15–18, 1993 & Jan.)* Harmonia Mundi USA 2-▲ HMU 907134/35
Biber, H. von:Sons Vn & Continuo, w. Romanesca—8 Sons. *(rec East Woodhay, UK, Sept. 15–18, 1993 & Jan.)* Harmonia Mundi USA 2-▲ HMU 907134/35
Biber, H. von:Son violino solo representativa, w. Romanesca *(rec East Woodhay, UK, Sept. 15–18, 1993 & Jan.)* Harmonia Mundi USA 2-▲ HMU 907134/35
Schmelzer, J.H.:Sons Instrs, w. Romanesca Harmonia Mundi ▲ HMU 907143
Vivaldi, A.:Sons Vn, Op. 2, w. Romanesca Harmonia Mundi USA 2-▲ HMU 907089/90

Manze, Andrew (vn)—see also ORCHESTRAS & ENSEMBLES Scaramouche, Cambridge Musick
Corbett, W.:Le Bizzarie universali, w. R. Goodman (vn), R. Goodman (cnd), European Community Baroque Orch—9 concerti Channel Classics ▲ CCS 1391 [DDD]
Haydn, J.:Trios Pno, Vn & Vc, w. Tini Mathot (hpd), Jaap ter Linden (vc)—in A, H.XV/9; in E♭, H.XV/10; in E♭, H.XV/11; in e, H.XV/12; in G, H.XV/25 *(rec Oud Katholieke Kerk, Utrecht, Nov. 1992)* Erato ▲ 4509-91728-2 [DDD]
Hellendaal, P.:Concerti grossi, w. Roy Goodman (vn), R. Goodman (cnd), European Community Baroque Orch—complete Channel Classics ▲ CCS 3492 [DDD]
Telemann, G.P.:Fants Vn Harmonia Mundi France ▲ HMU 907137
Telemann, G.P.:Suite for 2 Vns, w. Caroline Balding (vn) Harmonia Mundi France ▲ HMU 907137
Three Parts upon a Ground, w. John Hollowy (vn), Stanley Ritchie (vn), Mary Springfels (vl), Nigel North (lt), John Toll (hpd/org) Harmonia Mundi USA ▲ HMU 907091
Vivaldi, A.:Cons Vn, Op. 4, "La stravaganza", La Stravaganza Cologne—Nos. 1–4 Denon/PCM Digital ▲ DEN 75598 [DDD]

INSTRUMENT.

Manzini, Laura (pno)
Paganini's Violin:Salvatore Accardo Plays Paganini's Guarneri del Gesù 1742, w. Salvatore Accardo (vn) *(rec Dynamic's, Genova, Mar 13–14, 1995)* Dynamic ▲ CDS 175 [DDD]

Manzone, Jacques Francis (vn)
Vivaldi, A.:Con Vn Vcs, w. P. Tortelier (vc), M. Tortelier (vc), P. Ledger (cnd), London Mozart Players *(rec 11/79)* EMI ("Studio" series) ▲ CDM 769835-2 [ADD]

Mao, Ruotao (vn)
Roussakis, N.:Pas de deux, w. Xun Pan (pno) *(rec American Academy of Arts & Letters Auditorium, New York, Sept 19, 1994)* CRI ▲ CD 709 [DDD]

Maovsessian, C. (cl)
Fleischer, T.:In the Mountains of Armenia, w. V. Lepejian (nar), Armenian Church School Girls' Choir
Old Jerusalem Opus One ▲ Cd 158 [DDD]

Marangella, Joel (ob)
Martinů, B.:Qt Ob, w. Kathryn Selby (pno), Charmian Gadd (vn), Alexander Ivashkin (vc) *(rec Australian Festival of Chamber Music, July 1994)* Naxos ▲ 8.553916 [DDD]

Marc, Alexandru (hn)
Schumann, R.:Konzertstück Hns, w. V. Oprea (hn), D. Lung (hn), T. Tulbure (hn), C. Mandeal (cnd), Cluj-Napoca PO Electrecord ▲ ELCD 107 [AAD]

Marc, Sébastien (rcr)
Maskes & Fantazies, w. Le Concert Français [cnd:P. Hantaï] *(rec 1992)* Astrée ▲ E 8504 [DDD]

Marcante, Emanuela (hpd)—see ORCHESTRAS & ENSEMBLES II Ruggiero
Marcante, Emanuela (hpd/org)—see ORCHESTRAS & ENSEMBLES II Ruggiero
Marcante, Emanuela (org)—see ORCHESTRAS & ENSEMBLES I Filarmonici

Marcellus, Robert (cl)
Mozart, W.A.:Con Cl, w. G. Szell (cnd), Cleveland Orch *(rec 1961)* CBS ▲ MYK 37810 [AAD] ■ MYT 37810
Mozart, W.A.:Con Cl, w. G. Szell (cnd), Cleveland Orch *(rec Cleveland, OH, Oct 21, 1961)* Sony Classical ("Essential Classics" series) ▲ SBK 62424 [ADD] ■ SBT 62424

March (vn)
Babbitt, M.:Composition for 4 Instrs, w. Wummer (fl), Drucker (cl), McCall (vc) CRI ■ C 138

Marchal, André (org)
Bach, J.S.:Org Music (misc)—Nun komm der Heiden Heiland; Gott durch deine Güte; Christ, der ein'ge Gottes Sohn; Puer natus in Bethlehem; Gelobet sei'st du, Jesu Christ; Der Tag, der ist so freudenreich; Von Himmel hoch, da komm ich her; Vom Himmel kam der Engel Schar; Lobt Gott, ihr Christen allzugleich; In Dulci Jubilo; Jesu, meine Freude; Christum wir sollen loben schon; Wir Christenleut'; Das alte Jahr vergangen ist; In dir ist Freude [all from Das Orgelbüchlein]; Prélude & Fugue in C, BWV 547; Prélude & Fugue in a, BWV 543; Fant in G, BWV 572; Prélude & Fugue in b, BWV 544; Schmücke dich, o liebe Seele, BWV 654 Adès ▲ ADE 132792 [AAD]

Marchand, Isabelle (bowed h-g)—see ORCHESTRAS & ENSEMBLES La Nef
Marchand, Jérôme (vn)—see ORCHESTRAS & ENSEMBLES Phillips String Quartet
Marchello, Danilo (hn)—see ORCHESTRAS & ENSEMBLES Italiano Octet, Rossini Wind Quartet

Marchese, Catherine (bn)
Bassoon Recital, w. Emile Naoumoff (pno) Gega ▲ GD 162 [DDD]
Naoumoff, E.:In Memoriam Lili Boulanger, w. E. Naoumoff (pno) *(rec June 14–17, 1993)* Marco Polo ▲ 8.223636 [DDD]

Marchi, Alessandro de (hpd)
Pasquini, B.:Sons for 2 Hpds, w. A. Cremonesi (hpd) Symphonia ▲ SYM 91S26 [DDD]
Vivaldi, A.:Sons Fl, w. Jean-Christophe Frisch (trns fl), Christine Plubeau (vl), Pascale Boquet (archlt), Claude Wassmer (bn)—in F, d, e, g, c, D & g Adda ▲ ADD 241882

Marchio, Uliano (gtr)
Klatzow, P.:Chamber Con, w. Beat Wenger (fl), Jimmy Reinders (cl), Robert Grishkoff (hn), Lamar Crowson (pno), Barry Jordan (elec org), Peter Hamblin (perc), P. Klatzow (cnd) Claremont ▲ GSE 1524

Marchwinski, Jerzy (pno)
Ptaszynska, M.:Songs of Despair & Lonliness, w. Ewa Podles (mez) *(rec Polish Radio Studio S2, Oct. 9–11)* Polskie Nagrania ▲ PLN 075 [ADD]

Marciano, R. (pno)
Tailleferre, G.:Ballade, w. L. de Froment (cnd), Luxembourg RSO Allegretto ▲ ACD 8157 [ADD] ■ ACS 8157

Marciano, Sergio (org)
Marciano, S.:Org Music Bongiovanni 7-▲ 5590/96

Marcinkowska, Barbara (vc)
Bernstein, C.H.:Les Trois Jonas Arcobaleno 2-▲ AAOC 93922

Marcke, L. van (hn)—see also ORCHESTRAS & ENSEMBLES Algae Trio
Beethoven, L. van:Son Hn, w. D. Blumenthal (pno) *(rec Apr. 1993)* Pavane ▲ ADW 7295 [DDD]

Marcon, Andrea (org)
Festal Music for 3 Organs & for Organ 4-Hands, w. Annerös Hulliger (org), Philip Swanton (org) Koch Schwann ▲ SCH 310472 [DDD]

Marcone, Donald (perc)
Davidovsky, M.:Synchronism 5, w. R. DesRoches (perc), R. Fitz (perc), Heldrich (perc), van Hyning (perc), H. Sollberger (cnd) CRI ▲ CD 611 [ADD]
Harrison, L.:Con in slendro, w. Daniel Kobialka (vn), Machiko Kobialka (pno), James Barbagallo (pno), Patricia Jennerjohn (cel), J. Neff (perc), R. Hughes (cnd) *(rec 1972)* CRI ▲ CD 613 [ADD]

Marcotulli, Claudio (gtr)
Guilini, M.:Rossiniana Opra Tres ▲ 1007 [DDD]
Mertz, K.J.:Gtr Music—Opera Transcriptions:Verdi's La Trovatore, Op. 8/27; Bellini's Norma, Op. 8/17; Rossini's Il barbieri di Siviglia, Op. 8/23 Opra Tres ▲ 1007 [DDD]
Sor, F.:Vars on a Theme of Mozart Opra Tres ▲ 1007 [DDD]
Tárrega, F.:Gtr Music—Fant. on Motifs from Verdi's La Traviata Opra Tres ▲ 1007 [DDD]

Marcovecchio, Elisabetta de (fid)—see ORCHESTRAS & ENSEMBLES Sequentia

Marcovici, Silvia (vn)
Dvořák, A.:Qnt Pno, Op. 81, w. Roberte Mamou (pno), Ami Flammer (vn), Gerard Causse (va), Robert Cohen (vc) *(rec Mozart Festival, Lille, France, 1994)* Verdi Classics ▲ AU 32 250
Dvořák, A.:Romantic Pieces, Op. 75, w. Roberte Mamou (pno) *(rec Mozart Festival, Lille, France, 1994)* Verdi Classics ▲ AU 32 250
Dvořák, A.:Terzetto, w. Ami Flammer (vn), Gerard Causse (va) *(rec Mozart Festival, Lille, France, 1994)* Verdi Classics ▲ AU 32 250
Glazunov, A.:Con Vn, w. L. Stokowski (cnd), London SO *(rec live, Royal Festival Hall, London, 6/14/72)* Intaglio ▲ INCD 7221 [ADD]
Sibelius, J.:Con Vn, w. S. Marcovici (vn), N. Järvi (cnd), Gothenburg SO BIS ▲ CD 372 [DDD]

Marcus, Marshall (vn)
Rossini, G.:Sons Str Qt, w. E. Wallfisch (vn), R. Tunnicliffe (vc), C.-C. Nwanoku (db) Hyperion ▲ CDA 66595

Marcusson, Göran (fl)
Alfvén, H.:Bergakungen, w. T. Svedlund (cnd), Gothenburg SO—Shepherd-girl's dance Intim Musik ▲ INT 18 [DDD]
Atterberg, K.:Music of, w. T. Svedlund (cnd), Gothenburg SO—Adagio amoros Intim Musik ▲ INT 18 [DDD]
Biscardi, C.:Son Fl & Pno, w. Joakim Kallhed (pno) Intim Musik ▲ INT 34
Burton, E.:Sonatina Fl, w. Joakim Kallhed (pno) Intim Musik ▲ INT 34
Copland, A.:Duo Fl, w. Joakim Kallhed (pno) Intim Musik ▲ INT 34
Doppler, A.F.:Rigoletto-fant, w. Joakim Kallhed (pno) Intim ▲ INT 40
Frumerie, G. de:Pastoral Suite, w. T. Svedlund (cnd), Gothenburg SO Intim Musik ▲ INT 18 [DDD]
Gaubert, P.:Madrigal, w. Joakim Kallhed (pno) Intim ▲ INT 40
Grieg, E.:Music of, Camerata Romana—Bröllopsdag på Troldhaugen; Våren; Jeg elsker Dig Intim Musik ▲ INT 23 [DDD]
Jolivet, A.:Chant de Linos, w. Joakim Kallhed (pno) Intim ▲ INT 40
Larsson, L.-E.:Concertinos, Camerata Romana—for Fl Intim Musik ▲ INT 23 [DDD]

Marcusson, Göran (fl) (cont.)
Liebermann, L.:Son Fl, w. Joakim Kallhed (pno) Intim Musik ▲ INT 34
Lindberg, O.:Music of, Camerata Romana—Gammal fäbodpsalm Intim Musik ▲ INT 23 [DDD]
Martinů, B.:Son 1 Fl, w. Joakim Kallhed (pno) Intim ▲ INT 40
Nystroem, G.:Partita Fl, w. T. Svedlund (cnd), Gothenburg SO Intim Musik ▲ INT 18 [DDD]
Peterson-Berger, W.:Music of, w. T. Svedlund (cnd), Gothenburg SO—Sommarsång; Till Rosorna; Gratulation; Lawn Tennis; Frösö kyrka; Rentrée Intim Musik ▲ INT 18 [DDD]
Piston, W.:Son Fl, w. Joakim Kallhed (pno) Intim Musik ▲ INT 34
Prokofiev, S.:Son Fl, w. Joakim Kallhed (pno) Intim ▲ INT 40
Roman, J.H.:Con Fl, w. T. Svedlund (cnd), Camerata Romana Intim Musik ▲ INT 32
Roman, J.H.:Con Fl, Camerata Romana Intim Musik ▲ INT 23 [DDD]

Marder, Marc (db)
Schoenberg, A.:Trans Chamber Ensemble, w. Hakon Ausbö (harm), Michel Béroff (perc), Isabelle Berteletti (perc), Louise Bessette (pno), Paul Meyer (cl), Michel Moraguès (fl), Arditti String Quartet—Busoni:Berceuse élégiaque (1920); Mahler:Songs of a Wayfarer (1920) [w. Jean-Luc Chaignaud (baritone)]; Joh. Strauss:Kaiserwalzer (1925); Roses from the South (1921) Montaigne ▲ MO 789011 [DDD]

Mardirosian, Haig (org)
Langlais, J.:Characteristic Pieces Centaur ▲ CRC 2042 [DDD]
Langlais, J.:Suite brève Centaur ▲ CRC 2042 [DDD]

Mare, Anthony de (pno)
Becker, J.J.:Con arabesque, w. J. Bolle (cnd), Monadnock Music Festival Orch Koch International Classics ▲ KIC 7207 [DDD]
Becker, J.J.:Sound Piece 1, w. J. Bolle (cnd), Monadnock Music Festival Orch Koch International Classics ▲ KIC 7207 [DDD]
Becker, J.J.:Sound Piece 5 Koch International Classics ▲ KIC 7207 [DDD]
Biscardi, C.:Companion Piece *(rec SUNY Purchase Recital Hall, Feb. 12, 1993)* CRI ▲ CD 686 [DDD]
Biscardi, C.:Incitation to Desire *(rec SUNY Purchase Recital Hall, Feb. 12, 1993)* CRI ▲ CD 686 [DDD]
Biscardi, C.:Mestiere CRI ▲ CD 565 [DDD]
Biscardi, C.:Son Pno CRI ▲ CD 565 [DDD]
Childs, M.E.:The Capacity of Calm Endurance XI Compact Discs ▲ XI 114
Childs, M.E.:Kilter, w. Kathy Supové (pno) XI Compact Discs ▲ XI 114
Rzewski, F.:De Profundis O.O. Discs ▲ OO 16 [DDD]
Rzewski, F.:Piece 4 Pno O.O. Discs ▲ OO 16 [DDD]
Rzewski, F.:Son Pno O.O. Discs ▲ OO 16 [DDD]
Rzewski, F.:Winnsboro Cotton Mill Blues O.O. Discs ▲ OO 16 [DDD]
Sowerby, L.:Songs of Resignation, w. D'Anna Fortunato (mez), Veronica Macchia-Kadlubkiewicz (vn), Steven Jackson (cl) Gasparo ▲ GSCD 315 [DDD]
Speach, B.:Music of, w. J. Schanzer, L. Krech (trbn), J. Williams (gtr), Michael Pugliese (perc), T. Davis (speaker), et al., B. Speach (cnd), Bowery Ensemble—Moto for Trombone, Percussion & Piano (1982); Pensées for Guitar (1983); Trajet for Trombone & Percussion (1983); Sonata for Piano (1986); Shattered Glass for Percussion (1987); Telepathy (Poetry/Music Suite) for Speaker, Contrabas Mode ▲ 16

Mare, Anthony de (pno/prepared pno)
Cage, J.:Pno Music—Two Pieces (1935, rev. 1974); Primitive (1942); A Room (1943); Tossed as it is Untroubled (1943); Root of an Unfocus (1944); Ophelia (1946); In a Landscape (1948); ASLSP (1985) Koch International Classics ▲ KIC 7104-2 [DDD]

Mare, Anthony de (pno/sgr)
Cage, J.:Songs—The Wonderful Widow of Eighteen Springs (1942); Nowth Upon Nacht (1984) Koch International Classics ▲ KIC 7104-2 [DDD]
Monk, M.:Songs—Paris (1972); The Tale (1973); Travel Song (1981); Gamemaster's Song (1983); Memory Song (1983); Double Fiesta (1986) Koch International Classics ▲ KIC 7104-2 [DDD]

Maréchal, Maurice (vc)
The Art of Maurice Maréchal, Book 1 (1929–1937), w. various pianists *(rec 1929–37)* Enterprise ("Strings" series) ▲ ENT QT 99301
Debussy, C.:Son Vc, w. R. Casadesus (pno) *(rec 1930 for French Columbia)* Pearl ▲ PEA 9348 (m) [AAD]
Debussy, C.:Son Vc, w. Robert Casadesus (pno) *(rec 1929 – 1943)* Iron Needle ▲ IN 1324 [ADD]
Honegger, A.:Con Vc, w. A. Honegger (cnd), Paris Conservatory Societé des Concerts Orch *(rec 1929 – 1943)* Iron Needle ▲ IN 1324 [ADD]
Honegger, A.:Con Vc, w. A. Honegger (cnd), Paris Conservatory Societé des Concerts Orch EMI Classics ▲ CDC 55036
Honegger, A.:Pastorale d'été, w. A. Honegger (cnd), Paris Conservatory Societé des Concerts Orch EMI Classics ▲ CDC 55036
Lalo, E.:Con Vc, w. P. Gaubert (cnd), Paris SO *(rec 1929 – 1943)* Iron Needle ▲ IN 1324 [ADD]
Vivaldi, A.:Cons Vn, Op. 3/1–12, "L'estro armonico", w. Maurice Faure (pno)—No. 9 in D *(rec 1929 – 1943)* Iron Needle ▲ IN 1324 [ADD]

Marek, Jan (va)
Reicha, A.:Qts Fl, w. Jiri Válek (fl), Jan Buble (vn), Ladislav Pospfsil (vc) Panton ▲ PAN 811003
Marek, Jan (vn)—see ORCHESTRAS & ENSEMBLES Prague Chamber Ensemble

Mareš, P. (vn)
Handel, G.F.:Con for 2 Vns & 2 Hns, w. J. Opsitos (vn), B. Tylšar (F hn), Z. Tylšar (F hn), L. Pešek (cnd), Dvořák CO Supraphon ▲ 103907-2 [DDD]

Mareš, Vlastimil (cl)—see also ORCHESTRAS & ENSEMBLES Prague Wind Quintet
Krommer, F.:Con Cl, w. L. Pešek (cnd), Prague CO Supraphon ▲ SUP 111596 [DDD]
Krommer, F.:Cons for 2 Cls, w. *(2nd clarinetist unknown)*, L. Pešek (cnd), Prague CO Supraphon ▲ SUP 111596 [DDD]
Krommer, F.:Qnt Cl, w. Stamic String Quartet Supraphon ▲ SUP 0017 [DDD]
Martinů, B.:Madrigals Ob, w. Jurij Likin (ob), Lumír Vanek (bn) *(rec Studio Martínek, Prague, Mar 3, 1995)* Panton ("Protokol XX" series) ▲ 811348-2 [DDD]
Martinů, B.:Qt Cl, Hn, Vc & Side Drum, w. Czech Nonet *(rec Nov 1995–Jan 1996)* Praga ▲ PR 250097
Martinů, B.:Qt Cl, Hn, Vc & Side Drum, w. Vladimíra Klánská (hn), Petr Holub (side dr), Jitka Vlašánková (vc) *(rec Studio Martínek, Prague, Mar 3, 1995)* Panton ("Protokol XX" series) ▲ 811348-2 [DDD]
Martinů, B.:Les Rondes, w. Jurij Likin (ob), Lumír Vanek (bn), Vladislav Kozderka (tpt), Jana Herojnová (vn), Pavel Kutman (vn), Ivan Klánsky (pno) *(rec Studio Martínek, Prague, Mar 3, 1995)* Panton ("Protokol XX" series) ▲ 811348-2 [DDD]
Martinů, B.:Sxt Fl, Ob, Cl, 2 Bns & Pno, w. Jan Riedlbauch (fl), Jurij Likin (ob), Lumír Vanek (bn), Svatopluk Čech (bn), Ivan Klánský (pno) *(rec Studio Martínek, Prague, Mar 3, 1995)* Panton ("Protokol XX" series) ▲ 811348-2 [DDD]
Mozart, W.A.:Con Cl, w. L. Pešek (cnd), Prague RSO Supraphon Collection ▲ 11 0621-2 [ADD]
Mozart, W.A.:Qnt Cl, K.581, w. Stamic String Quartet Supraphon ▲ SUP 0017 [DDD]
Reicha, A.:Qnt Cl, Op. 89, w. Stamic String Quartet Supraphon ▲ SUP 0051
Reicha, A.:Qnt Ob, w. Stamic String Quartet Supraphon ▲ SUP 0051

Maretsky, Nikolai (mand)
Hummel, J.N.:Con Mand & Strs, w. V. Kruglov (mand), Northern Crown Soloists Ensemble MK ▲ MKA 417114
Vivaldi, A.:Con Lt, w. V. Kruglov (mand), Northern Crown Soloists Ensemble MK ▲ MKA 417114
Vivaldi, A.:Con Mand, RV.425, w. V. Kruglov (mand), Northern Crown Soloists Ensemble MK ▲ MKA 417114
Vivaldi, A.:Con for 2 Mands, w. V. Kruglov (mand), Northern Crown Soloists Ensemble MK ▲ MKA 417114
Vivaldi, A.:Trio Son Vn Lt, RV. 82, w. V. Kruglov (mand), Northern Crown Soloists Ensemble MK ▲ MKA 417114

Margalit, Israela (pno)
Barber, S.:Canzone Fl & Pno, w. Jeanne Baxtresser (fl) EMI Classics ("Anglo-American Chamber Music" series) ▲ CDC 55400

▲ = CD ♦ = Enhanced CD Δ = MD ■ = Cassette Tape ◻ = DCC

Margalit, Israela (pno) (cont.)
Barber, S.:Pno Music—Excursions; Nocturne; Pas de deux; 2-Step EMI Classics ("Anglo-American Chamber Music" series) ▲ CDC 55400
Barber, S.:Son Vc, w. Alan Stepansky (vc) EMI Classics ("Anglo-American Chamber Music" series) ▲ CDC 55400
Beethoven, L. van:Son 1 Pno Chandos ▲ CHAN 8582 [DDD]
Beethoven, L. van:Son 14 Pno, "Moonlight Son" Chandos ▲ CHAN 8582 [DDD]
Beethoven, L. van:Son 23 Pno, "Appassionata" Chandos ▲ CHAN 8582 [DDD]
Brahms, J.:Con 1 Pno, w. B. Thomson (cnd), London SO Chandos ▲ CHAN 8724 [DDD]
Chausson, E.:Con Vn, Pno & Str Qt, w. L. Maazel (vn), Cleveland Orch String Quartet *(rec 1979)* Telarc ▲ CD 80046 [DDD]
Copland, A.:Duo Fl, w. Jeanne Baxtresser (fl) EMI Classics ("Anglo-American Chamber Music" series) ▲ CDC 55405
Copland, A.:Qt Pno, w. Glenn Dicterow (vn), Rebecca Young (va), Alan Stepansky (vc) EMI Classics ("Anglo-American Chamber Music" series) ▲ CDC 55405
Copland, A.:Rodeo Pno EMI Classics ("Anglo-American Chamber Music" series) ▲ CDC 55405
Copland, A.:Son Vn & Pno, w. Charles Rex (vn) EMI Classics ("Anglo-American Chamber Music" series) ▲ CDC 55405
Delius, F.:Son Vc & Pno, w. Moray Welsh (vc) EMI Classics ("Anglo-American Chamber Music" series) ▲ CDC 55399
Delius, F.:Son 1 Vn & Pno, w. Janice Graham (vn) EMI Classics ("Anglo-American Chamber Music" series) ▲ CDC 55399
Delius, F.:Son 2 Vn & Pno, w. Janice Graham (vn) EMI Classics ("Anglo-American Chamber Music" series) ▲ CDC 55399
Delius, F.:Son 3 Vn & Pno, w. Alexander Barantschik (vn) EMI Classics ("Anglo-American Chamber Music" series) ▲ CDC 55399
Elgar, E.:Qnt Pno Strs, w. Alexander Barantschick (vn), Janice Graham (vn), Paul Silverthorne (va), Moray Welsh (vc) EMI Classics ("Anglo-American Chamber Music" series) ▲ CDC 55403
Ives, C.:Largo, w. Glenn Dicterow (vn), Stanley Drucker (cl) EMI Classics ("Anglo-American Chamber Music" series) ▲ CDC 55406
Ives, C.:Son 2 Vn, w. Glenn Dicterow (vn) EMI Classics ("Anglo-American Chamber Music" series) ▲ CDC 55406
Ives, C.:Son 4 Vn, w. Glenn Dicterow (vn) EMI Classics ("Anglo-American Chamber Music" series) ▲ CDC 55406
Korngold, E.W.:Son Vn, w. Glenn Dicterow (vn) EMI Classics ("Anglo-American Chamber Music" series) ▲ CDC 55401
Korngold, E.W.:Trio Pno, w. Glenn Dicterow (vn), Alan Stepansky (vc) EMI Classics ("Anglo-American Chamber Music" series) ▲ CDC 55401
Mendelssohn, F.:Capriccio brillante, w. B. Thomson (cnd), London SO Chandos ▲ CHAN 8724 [DDD]
Mozart, W.A.:Con 24 Pno, w. L. Maazel (cnd), Rome RAI SO Diamante ▲ ARCD 2043 [ADD]
Saint-Saëns, C.:Con 2 Pno, w. B. Thomson (cnd), London PO Chandos ▲ CHAN 8546 [DDD]
Schnittke, A.:Con Pno, w. D. Barra (cnd), Moscow PO *(rec Sept. 1992)* Koch International Classics ▲ KIC 7159 [DDD]
Schumann, R.:Con Pno, w. B. Thomson (cnd), London PO Chandos ▲ CHAN 8546 [DDD]
Shostakovich, D.:Con 1 Pno, w. M. Khanin (tpt), D. Barra (cnd), Moscow PO *(rec Sept. 1992)* Koch International Classics ▲ KIC 7159 [DDD]
Shostakovich, D.:Dances of the Dolls *(rec Sept. 1992)* Koch International Classics ▲ KIC 7159 [DDD]
Shostakovich, D.:Fantastic Dances, w. D. Barra (cnd), Moscow PO *(rec Sept. 1992)* Koch International Classics ▲ KIC 7159 [DDD]

Margittay, Sandor (harm)
Liszt, F.:Music of, w. A. Kiss (n), Z. Tóth (va), E. Banda (vc), M. Perényi (vc), H. Lubik (hp), I. Lantos (pno/org)—Angelus; La lugubre gondola; Epithalam; Am Grabe Richard Wagners; Romance oubliée; Elégies 1 & 2; Offertorium; Benedictus Hungaroton ▲ HCD 11798 [DDD]

Margot, François (org)
Gounod, C.:Mass 2, w. A. Charlet (cnd), Brassus Chorale *(rec 1992 & 1993)* Claves ▲ CD 9326 [DDD]
Gounod, C.:Requiem, w. M. Veillon (db), C. Fleischmann (hp), A. Charlet (cnd), Romande Chamber Choir *(rec 1992 & 1993)* Claves ▲ CD 9326 [DDD]

Mariage, Sylvie (vc)
Villette, P.:Qts Strs, w. L. Bobesco (vn), J.-M. Defalque (vn), D. Huybrechts (va)—Nos. 1-6 in A, C, F, B♭, E♭ & E Talent ▲ DOM 2910 46 [DDD]

Mariani, Angela (hp)—see ORCHESTRAS & ENSEMBLES Altramar Medieval Music Ensemble

Mariano, J. (fl)
Griffes, C.T.:Poem Fl, w. H. Hanson (cnd), Eastman-Rochester Orch Mercury Living Presence ▲ 434307-2 [ADD]

Marie, Jean-Bernard (pno)
Lentz, G.:Caeli enarrant...V Tall Poppies ▲ TP 35

Marien, Edy (car)
The Carillon of the St. Rombouts Cathedral at Malines, w. Geert D'hollander (car), Jos D'hollander (car), Carlo van Luft (car) René Gailly ▲ CD 88903 [DDD]

Marin, A. (sgr/va)—see ORCHESTRAS & ENSEMBLES Rossmann

Marincola, Federico (lt)
Holborne, A.:Lt Music—Almaine No. 4; Fant No. 2; Piece without Title; Pavan No. 2; Galliard No. 2; As It Fell on a Holy Eve; Pavan No. 1 [Last Will & Testament]; Galliard No. 5 [The New Year's Gift]; Pavan No. 17 [Patienca]; Almaine No. 3 [The Night Watch]; Galliard No. 11 [Passion]; Pavan No. 3 [Sedet Sola]; Galliard No. 3 [The Fairy Round]; Fant No. 1; Pavan No. 1; Lute Galliard No. 1; Playfellow No. 1; Playfellow No. 2 [Wanton]; Pavan No. 15 [Countess of Pembrook's Paradise]; Galliard No. 14 [Muy Linda]; Fant No. 3; Vars Pierre Verany ▲ PVY 795112

Marincola, Federico (lt/gtr)
Morlaye, G.:Lt & Gtr Music—Fant.; Ta privaulte; Gaillarde piemontoise; Paduane "Au ioly bois"; Conte clare; Qui souhetes; Pavane des dieux; Gaillarde des dieux; Si son esperit; Gaillarde; Sans liberte; Praelude romanesque; Pavane de romanesque; Romaine; Bransle; Tin que tin tin; Bransle "Scaramella"; others *(rec Oct. 26-28, 1993)* Pierre Verany ▲ PV794052 [DDD]

Marincola, Federico (tiorba)—see ORCHESTRAS & ENSEMBLES L'Arte dell'Arco

Marineau, M. (pno)
Danzi, F.:Son Vc & Pno, w. K. Puddy (vc) Clarinet Classics ▲ CC 0004

Marinelli, R. (vn)
Mozart, W.A.:Con 3 Vn, w. A. Lizzio (cnd), Mozart Festival Orch Vivace ▲ 594 [DDD]
Mozart, W.A.:Con 3 Vn, w. A. Lizzio (cnd), Mozart Festival Orch Vivace 3-▲ E 325 [ADD/DDD]
Mozart, W.A.:Con 4 Vn, w. A. Lizzio (cnd), Mozart Festival Orch Vivace ▲ 594 [DDD]
Mozart, W.A.:Con 4 Vn, w. A. Lizzio (cnd), Mozart Festival Orch Vivace 3-▲ E 325 [ADD/DDD]

Marinissen, Arnold (perc)—see ORCHESTRAS & ENSEMBLES Ives Ensemble members

Marinkovic, Mateja (vn)
Medtner, N.:Son 1 Vn, w. Linn Hendry (pno) ASV ▲ ASV CD 951
Medtner, N.:Son 3 Vn, w. Linn Hendry (pno) ASV ▲ ASV CD 951
Schnittke, A.:Chamber Music, w. Linn Hendry (pno), et al.—Suite in the Old Style; À Paganini; Gratulations Rondo; Madrigal in Memoriam Oleg Kagan; Mozart; Praeludium in Memoriam Shostakovich; Stille Musik; Stille Nacht ASV ▲ ASV 877 [DDD]
Schnittke, A.:Trio Strs, w. P. Silverthorne (va), T. Hugh (vc) ASV ▲ ASV 868 [DDD]
Ysaÿe, E.:Sons Vn Collins Classics ▲ COL 1376 [DDD]

Mariño, Nibya (pno)
Schumann, R.:Kinderszenen Mastersound ▲ MST 34 [DDD]
Schumann, R.:Papillons Mastersound ▲ MST 34 [DDD]
Schumann, R.:Sym Etudes Mastersound ▲ MST 34 [DDD]

Marinos, Dimitris (mand)
First, C.P.:Tantrum Capstone ▲ SCI 6

Marion, A. (pno)
Beethoven, L. van:Trio for 3 Fls, w. J.-P. Rampal (fl), C. Larde (bn) Vox Box 2-▲ CDX 5000 [ADD]
Roussel, A.:Joueurs de flûte, w. P. Rogé (pno) Denon ▲ CO 1476 [DDD]

Marion, Alain (fl)
Bach, C.P.E.:Sons Fl, w. D. Roi (bc)—in d, H.505 (W.83); in B♭,D & G, H.552-554 (W.125-127); in D & B♭, H.556 & H.560 (W.129-130); in G, H.564 (W.133) Fonè ▲ 89 F 02-26 [DDD]
Bach, C.P.E.:Trio Sons (misc), w. M. Conti (fl), D. Roi (hpd)—in B♭ & in d Fonè ▲ 89F04-28 [DDD]
Beethoven, L. van:Allegro & Minuet, w. J.-P. Rampal (fl) Vox Box 2-▲ CDX 5000 [ADD]
Cambini, G.M.:Son 2 Fl & Hpd, w. D. Roi (hpd) Fonè ▲ 89 F 01-25 [DDD]
Cambini, G.M.:Trio 1 for 2 Fls & Hpd, w. M. Conti (fl), D. Roi (hpd) Fonè ▲ 89 F 03-27 [DDD]
Clementi, M.:Son 1 Vn, w. D. Roi (hpd) Fonè ▲ 89 F 01-25 [DDD]
Devienne, F.:Con 7 Fl, w. M. Valdes (cnd), Nice PO Denon ▲ 7923 [DDD]
Doppler, A.F.:Music of, w. J.-L. Beaumadier (fl), E. Exerjean (pno)—Souvenir, Op. 24; Sommnambula, Op. 42; Chanson d'amour, Op. 20; L'oiseau des bois; Casilda fant. [w. F. Pierre (harp)]; Duettino americain, Op. 37; Duettino hongrois, Op. 36 *(rec 1993)* Calliope ▲ CAL 9224 [DDD]
Fauré, G.:Fant Fl, w. P. Rogé (pno) Denon ▲ CO 1476 [DDD]
Honegger, A.:Chamber Music (comp), w. D.-S. Kang (vn), P.-H. Xuereb (va), R. Wallfisch (vc), M. Arrignon (cl), A. Haraldsdottir (fl), C. Moreaux (ob), T. Caens (tpt), M. Becquet (trbn), P. Zanlonghi (hp), P. Devoyon (pno), F. Kondo (mez), Ludwig String Quartet—Sonatine for Clarinet & Piano (1921-22); Rapsodie for 2 Flutes, Clarinet & Piano (1917); Danse de la Chèvre for Solo Flute (1921); Romance for Flute & Piano (1953); Petite Suite for 2 Flutes & Piano (1934); Trois Contrepoints for Piccolo, Oboe, Violin & Cello (1922); Intrada for Trumpet & Piano (1947); Hommage du trombone exprimant la tristesse de l'auteur absent for Trombone & Piano (1925); J'avais un fidèle amant for String Quartet (1929); Chanson de Ronsard & 3 Chansons de la petite Sirène for Mezzo, Flute & String Quartet (1924); Introduction et Danse for Flute, Harp & String Trio [undated]; Colloque for Flute, Celesta, Violin & Viola [undated] Timpani ▲ IC1010 [DDD]
Honegger, A.:Rapsodie for 2 Fl, w. et al. Timpani ▲ IC1010 [DDD]
Ibert, J.:Con Fl, w. M. Valdes (cnd), Nice PO Denon ▲ 7923 [DDD]
Landowski, M.:Music of, w. J. Loriod (ondes Martenot), F. Clidat (pno), M. Becquet (trbn), J. Houtmann (cnd), Lorraine PO—Concerto for Ondes Martenot & Orchestra; Concerto for Flute & Strings; Concerto for Piano & Orchestra; Concertino for Trombone & Strings Koch Schwann ▲ CD 311175 [DDD]
Locatelli, P.:Son 10 Fl & Hpd, w. D. Roi (hpd) Fonè ▲ 89 F 01-25 [DDD]
Martinů, B.:Music of, w. Marc-André Hamelin (pno) *(violinist unknown)*—Son for Fl, Vn & Pno; Promenades for Fl, Vn & Hpd; Son for Fl & Pno; 5 Madrigal Stanzas for Fl, Vn & Pno; Scherzo for Fl & Pno; Madrigal Son for Fl, Vn & Pno Analekta ▲ AN 28709
Molique, W.B.:Con Fl, w. M. Valdes (cnd), Nice PO Denon ▲ 7923 [DDD]
Mozart, W.A.:Music of, w. Angèle Dubeau (vn)—sels from Die Zauberflöte, Die Entführung aus dem Serail, Don Giovanni, Le Nozze di Figaro [trans for fl & vn] Analekta Fleur de Lys ▲ FL 23076 [DDD]
Nardini, P.:Son Fl, w. D. Roi (hpd) Fonè ▲ 89 F 01-25 [DDD]
Nardini, P.:Son Terza, w. M. Conti (fl), D. Roi (hpd) Fonè ▲ 89 F 03-27 [DDD]
Platti, G.B.:Sons Fl, w. D. Roi (hpd)—No. 2 Fonè ▲ 89 F 01-25 [DDD]
Platti, G.B.:Trio Fls, w. M. Conti (fl), D. Roi (hpd) Fonè ▲ 89 F 03-27 [DDD]
Poulenc, F.:Son Fl, w. P. Rogé (pno) Denon ▲ CO 1476 [DDD]
Saint-Saëns, C.:Romance Fl, w. P. Rogé (pno) Denon ▲ CO 1476 [DDD]
Sammartini, G.B.:Son terza Fls, w. M. Conti (fl), D. Roi (hpd) Fonè ▲ 89 F 03-27 [DDD]
Vivaldi, A.:Cons Fl, Op. 10, Franz Liszt CO Denon ▲ CO 1406 [DDD]
Widor, C.M.:Suite Fl, w. P. Rogé (pno) Denon ▲ CO 1476 [DDD]

Mariotti, D. (vc)
Bach, J.S.:Suites Vc, BWV 1007-1012, w. D. Mariotti (vc) [arr. for guitar by John W. Duarte]—No. 3 *(rec 1984)* Jecklin ▲ JS 240-2 [ADD]

Mariotti, Deborah (gtr)
Gitarrenmusik aus Spanien und Südamerika, w. Mariotti, Deborah (gtr) Jecklin ▲ JEC 263-2 [ADD]
Giuliani, M.:Grand Ov *(rec 1984)* Jecklin ▲ JS 240-2 [ADD]
Giuliani, M.:Rossiniana—No. 1; "Gitarrenmusik von Bach und Giuliani" *(rec 1984)* Jecklin ▲ JS 240-2 [ADD]
Mertz, K.J.:Concertino *(rec 1991)* Jecklin ▲ JS 293-2 [DDD]
Mertz, K.J.:Elegie *(rec 1991)* Jecklin ▲ JS 293-2 [DDD]
Mertz, K.J.:Morceaux *(rec 1991)* Jecklin ▲ JS 293-2 [DDD]
Regondi, G.:Fête Villageoise *(rec 1991)* Jecklin ▲ JS 293-2 [DDD]
Regondi, G.:Intro et caprice *(rec 1991)* Jecklin ▲ JS 293-2 [DDD]
Regondi, G.:Nocturne *(rec 1991)* Jecklin ▲ JS 293-2 [DDD]

Mariozzi, Vincenzo (cl)
Bottesini, G.:Gran Duo Cl, w. M. Giorgi (db), V. Antonellini (cnd), I Solisti Aquilani Nuova Era ▲ 6810 [DDD]
Brahms, J.:Sons Cl (comp), w. S. de Palma (pno) Giulia ▲ GIU 201031 [DDD]
Mercadante, S.:Con in B♭ Cl, Op. 101, w. V. Antonellini (cnd), I Solisti Aquilani Nuova Era ▲ 6910 [DDD]
Rossini, G.:Intro, Theme & Vars Cl, w. V. Antonellini (cnd), I Solisti Aquilani Nuova Era ▲ 6910 [DDD]

Maris, Di (mar)
Klatzow, P.:Mass, w. Rob Grishkoff (hn), Barry Smith (cnd), St. Georges Singers Claremont ▲ GSE 1524

Marisaldi, Patrizia (hpd)
Bach, J.S.:Sons Vl, BWV 1027-1029, w. A. Rasi (vl) *(rec Mar 1992)* Bongiovanni ▲ GB 5535 [DDD]
Bach, J.S.:Toccatas Hpd, BWV 910-16—BWV 916 *(rec Mar 1992)* Bongiovanni ▲ GB 5535 [DDD]

Marjanovic, Gordana (pno)
Maric, L.:From the Darkness Chanting, w. Aleksandra Ivanovic (mez) Emergo ▲ EC 3951 [DDD]
Maric, L.:Ostinato super thema octoicha, w. Inge Frimout-hei (hp), Camerata Academica Novi Sad Emergo ▲ EC 3951 [DDD]
Maric, L.:Preludes Emergo ▲ EC 3951 [DDD]
Maric, L.:Son Vn & Pno, w. Maja Jokanovic (vn) Emergo ▲ EC 3951 [DDD]
Slavenski, J.:Slavenska son, w. Maja Jokanovic (vn), Camerata Academica Novi Sad Emergo ▲ EC 3950 [DDD]

Marjoram, Keith (db)
John Williams & Friends, w. J. Williams (gtr), Carlos Bonell (gtr), Brian Gascoigne (mar/vib), Morris Pert (mar/vib) CBS ▲ MK 35108 [AAD]

Mark, Andrew (vc)—see also ORCHESTRAS & ENSEMBLES Griffin Music Ensemble, Core Ensemble
The Cantorial Voice of the Cello, w. Coenraad Bloemendal (vc), Valerie Tryon (pno), Andrés Díaz (vc) *(rec Troy Savings Bank Music Hall, Troy, NY, May 1994)* Dorian ▲ DOR 90208 [DDD]
Kirchner, L.:Qt 1 Strs, w. M. Beaulieu (vn), C. Hoener (vn), S. Woolweaver (va) Albany ▲ TROY 137 [DDD]
Kirchner, L.:Qt 2 Strs, w. M. Beaulieu (vn), C. Hoener (vn), S. Woolweaver (va) Albany ▲ TROY 137 [DDD]
Kirchner, L.:Qt 3 Strs, w. M. Beaulieu (vn), C. Hoener (vn), S. Woolweaver (va) Albany ▲ TROY 137 [DDD]
Martino, D.:Canzone e Tarantella, w. Ian Greitzner (cl) *(rec Jordan Hall, New England Conservatory of Music, Boston, MA, June 1996)* New World ▲ 80518-2
Martino, D.:Parisonatina *(rec Houghton Chapel, Wellesley College, MA, June 1995)* New World ▲ 80518-2

Märker, Hermann (hn)
Schumann, R.:Konzertstück Hns, w. P. Damm (hn), W. Pilz (hn), G. Böhner (hn), F. Konwitschny (cnd), Leipzig Gewandhaus Orch *(rec 1960-61)* Berlin Classics ("Eterna" series) 3-▲ BER 2016 [ADD]

Markevitch, Dimitry (vc)
Bach, J.S.:Suites Vc, BWV 1007-1012—Nos. 2, 4 & 6 Gallo ▲ CD 671 [ADD]
Bach, J.S.:Suites Vc, BWV 1007-1012—Nos. 1, 3 & 5 Gallo ▲ CD 670 [ADD]
Beethoven, L. van:Son 1 Vc, w. D. Spiegelberg (pno) *(rec 2/91)* Gallo ▲ CD 673 [ADD]
Beethoven, L. van:Son 2 Vc, w. D. Spiegelberg (pno) Gallo ▲ CD 673 [ADD]
Beethoven, L. van:Son 3 Vc, w. D. Spiegelberg (pno) *(rec 2/91)* Gallo ▲ CD 672 [ADD]
Beethoven, L. van:Son 5 Vc, w. D. Spiegelberg (pno) Gallo ▲ CD 673 [ADD]
Beethoven, L. van:Son Hn, w. D. Spiegelberg (pno) *(rec 2/91)* Gallo ▲ CD 673 [ADD]
Beethoven, L. van:Trio Strs, Op. 3, w. D. Spiegelberg (pno) *(rec 2/91)* Gallo ▲ CD 672 [ADD]

INSTRUMENT.

Markham, Mark (pno)
Carter, E.:Poems (3) of Robert Frost, w. Phyllis Bryn–Julson (sop) [arr for sop & pno] Music & Arts ▲ CD 900 [DDD]
Carter, E.:Songs, w. Phyllis Bryn–Julson (sop)—Voyage; Warble for Lilac Time Music & Arts ▲ CD 900 [DDD]
Dallapiccola, L.:Songs, w. Phyllis Bryn–Julson (sop) Music & Arts ▲ CD 912
Messiaen, O.:Poèmes pour Mi, w. Phyllis Bryn–Julson (sop) Music & Arts ▲ CD 912
Schuller, G.:Early Songs, w. Phyllis Bryn–Julson (sop) Music & Arts ▲ CD 900 [DDD]
Wuorinen, C.:Songs, w. Phyllis Bryn–Julson (sop) Music & Arts ▲ CD 912
Wuorinen, C.:A Winter's Tale, w. Phyllis Bryn–Julson (sop) Music & Arts ▲ CD 900 [DDD]

Markham, Richard (pno)
Arnold, M.:Con for 2 Pnos, w. David Nettle (pno), V. Handley (cnd), Royal PO Conifer Classics ▲ 75605–51240–2 [DDD]
Holst, G.:The Planets, w. D. Nettle (pno) [2 piano version] Saga Classics ▲ 3346 [AAD]
Nettle & Markham in England, w. David Nettle (pno) IMP ("Classics" series) ▲ IMP 6700172
Nettle & Markham in France, w. David Nettle (pno) IMP ("Masters" series) ▲ IMP 6600142
Saint–Saëns, C.:Carnival of the Animals, w. P. Schickele (nar), K. Broadway (pno), Y. Levi (cnd), Atlanta SO [poems by Schickele] *(rec Mar. 20 & June 16, 1993)* Telarc ▲ CD 80350 [DDD] ■ CS 30350
Vaughan Williams, R.:Con Pno, w. K. Broadway (pno), Y. Menuhin (cnd), Royal PO Virgo ▲ CDZ 61105
Vaughan Williams, R.:Sym 5, w. K. Broadway (pno), Y. Menuhin (cnd), Royal PO Virgo ▲ CDZ 61105

Marki, Robert (org)
Ducommun, S.:Concertino Tpt, w. P.A. Monot (tpt) Gallo ▲ CD 654 [DDD]
Ducommun, S.:Org Music, w. S. Ducommun (org), J. Molnar (hn), P.–A. Monot (tpt), P. Lehmann (tpt)—10 Invocations for Organ; Sonata da Chiesa for Horn & Organ; Sonata da Chiesa for 2 Trumpets & Organ; Variations on a Theme by François Nadler for Organ *(rec 1959, 1985 & 1991)* Gallo ▲ CD655
Ducommun, S.:Toccata et Dialogue, w. Quatror de cuivres Novus Gallo ▲ CD 654 [DDD]

Markl, Markus (hpd)
Deutsche Barocklieder, w. Andreas Scholl (ct), Alix Verzier (vc), Karl Ernst Schroder (lt), Friederike Heumann (va), Juan Manuel Quintana (va), Stephanie Pfister (vn), Pable Valetti (vn) Harmonia Mundi France ▲ HMC 901505

Markov, Alexander (vn)
Encores, w. Dmitriy Cogan (pno) Erato ▲ 98481–2
Markov, A.:Con Vn, w. S.–C. Lü (cnd), New Russia Orch Sunrise ▲ 8532
Markov, A.:Formosa Suite, w. S.–C. Lü (cnd), New Russia Orch Sunrise ▲ 8532
Markov, A.:Porgy Rhap, w. S.–C. Lü (cnd), New Russia Orch Sunrise ▲ 8532
Paganini, N.:Caprices Vn Erato ▲ 2292–45502–2 [DDD]
Paganini, N.:Con 1 Vn, w. M. Viotti (cnd), Saarbrück RSO Erato ▲ 2292–45788–2
Paganini, N.:Con 2 Vn, w. M. Viotti (cnd), Saarbrück RSO Erato ▲ 2292–45788–2

Markovich, Alexander (pno)
Beethoven, L. van:Son 9 Vn, "Kreutzer", w. M. Vengerov (vn) Teldec ▲ 9031–74001–2 ZK
Brahms, J.:Son 2 Vn, w. M. Vengerov (vn) Teldec ▲ 9031–74001–2 ZK
Carmen Fantasy, w. Sergei Nakariakov (tpt) *(rec Teldec Studio, Berlin, Apr. 1994)* Teldec ▲ 94554–2 [DDD]

Marks, Alan (pno)
Copland, A.:Blues Nimbus ▲ NI 5267 [DDD]
Copland, A.:Old American Songs, solo piano arrangement by Alan Marks Nimbus ▲ NI 5267 [DDD]
Copland, A.:Rodeo—performing Copland's 1962 solo piano arr. Nimbus ▲ NI 5267 [DDD]
Copland, A.:Vars Pno Nimbus ▲ NI 5267 [DDD]
Goldschmidt, B.:Letzte Kapitel, w. P. Schwarz (cnd), Berlin Ars Nova Ensemble *(rec June 1990)* Largo ▲ 5115 [DDD]
Gomezanda, A.:Danzas Mexicanas (6), w. J. Velazco (cnd), Berlin SO Koch Schwann ▲ SCH 310232
Gomezanda, A.:Fant Mexicana, w. J. Velazco (cnd), Berlin SO Koch Schwann ▲ SCH 310232
Gomezanda, A.:Logos, w. Wolfgang Boettcher (vc), J. Velazco (cnd), Berlin SO Koch Schwann ▲ SCH 310232
Gottschalk, L.M.:Pno Music—Souvenirs d'Andalousie; Le Banjo; Grand Scherzo; Pasquinade Caprice; Berceuse; Tournament Galop; Mazurk; Union; The Last Hope; Scherzo romantique; Le Mancenillier; The Dying Poet Nimbus ▲ NI 5014 [DDD]
Gottschalk, L.M.:Pno Music, w. N. Barrett (pno)—Réponds moi (danse cubaine), Op. 50; Printemps d'amour, Op. 40; Marche de Nuit, Op. 17; Ses Yeux, Op. 66; La Jota Argonesa, Op. 14; La Bananier, Op. 5; Ojos Criollos, Op. 37; Orfa (grande polka), Op. 71; La Scintilla, Op. 21; Marche funèbre, Op. 64; La Gallina, Op. 53; Radieuse, Op. 72; Grande Tarantelle, Op. 67 Nimbus ▲ NI 5324 [DDD]
Gottschalk, L.M.:The Union Nimbus ▲ NI 5014 [DDD]
Liszt, F.:Années de pèlerinage 2 Nimbus ▲ NI 5226 [DDD]
Liszt, F.:Operatic Paraphrases & Transcriptions—Gounod's Faust:Waltz; Handel's Almira:Sarabande & Chaconne; Mozart:Paraphrase on Le nozze di Figaro; Tchaikovsky's Eugen Onegin:–Polonaise; Verdi's Trovatore:Miserere; Wagner's Parsifal:Solemn March; Tristan und Isolde:Isoldes Liebestod Nimbus ▲ NI 5115 [DDD]
Schumann, R.:Fant Pno Nimbus ▲ NI 5181 [DDD]
Schumann, R.:Son Pno, Op. 14 Nimbus ▲ NI 5181 [DDD]

Marks, Christoph (vc)—see ORCHESTRAS & ENSEMBLES Kontraste Ensemble

Markus, Waldemar (hn)
Brahms, J.:Choral Music, w. Gunther Opitz (hn), Margarethe Kluvetasch (hp), Horst Neumann (cnd), Leipzig Radio Chorus—Opp. 17, 42, 62 & 104 Berlin Classics ▲ BER CD 9276

Marlow, R. (org)
Bach, J.S.:Org Music (misc) [Metzler organ, Trinity College, Cambridge]—Orgelbüchlein, sels. unknown Mirabilis ▲ MRCD 904

Marlowe, Sylvia (hpd)
Rieti, V.:Con Hpd, w. S. Baron (fl), chamber orch CRI ▲ CD 601 [ADD]
Rieti, V.:Partita Hpd, w. S. Baron (fl), R. Roseman (ob), C. Libove (vn), A. Ajemian (vn), H. Zaratzian (va), C. McCraken (vc) CRI ▲ CD 601 [ADD]

Maron, Lisa (pic)
Kraft, L.:Cloud Studies, w. Margaret Swinchoski (pic), Tanya Dusevic (fl), Adrienne Flynn (fl), Christina Jennings (fl), Zara Lawler (fl), Joseph Piscitelli (fl), Michelle Ryang (fl), Dominique Soucy (fl), Diane Taublieb (fl), Laurel Ann Maurer (alt fl), Richard Wyton (alt fl), J. Solum (cnd) *(rec Skinner Recital Hall, Vassar College, Poughkeepsie, NY, Mar 24–26, 1994)* CRI ▲ CD 712 [DDD]

Maros, Éva (hp)
Classical Gems on Trumpet & Harp, w. G. Geiger (tpt) Hungaroton ▲ HCD 31542 [DDD]
Fauré, G.:Requiem, w. D. Karasszon (org), J. Dobra (cnd), Hungarian Virtuosi CO, Budapest SO Winds, Tomkins Vocal Ensemble Hungaroton ▲ HCD 31424 [DDD]
Ravel, M.:Intro & Allegro, w. Z. Gyöngyössy (fl), B. Kovács (cl), Kodály String Quartet *(rec Dec. 6–8, 1988)* Naxos ▲ 8.550249 [DDD]

Marq, Sébastien (rcr)
Telemann, G.P.:Music of, w. P. Hantaï (cnd), Le Concert Français—Trio in A for Rcr, Hpd & Bc; Con in F for Rcr, Hn & Bc; Fant in A for Rcr; Trio Son in F for Rcr, Vl & Bc; Trio Son in a for Rcr, Vn & Bc; Trio Son in B♭ for Rcr, Hpd & Bc; Son in C for Rcr & Bc; Fant in F [originally C] for Rcr; Trio Son in a for Rcr, Ob & Bc Astrée ▲ E 8554

Marquez, Sal (tpt)
Symphonic Boleros, w. V. Lewis (cnd), Royal PO, Ettore Stratta (cnd), Ernie Watts (sax), Clare Fischer (pno), Jorge Callandrelli (pno), Brian Monroney (gtr) Teldec ▲ 91180–2 ■ 91180–4

Marriner, Andrew (cl)
Mozart, W.A.:Con Cl, w. J. Glover (cnd), London Mozart Players Classics for Pleasure ▲ CDCFP 4484 [DDD]
Mozart, W.A.:Qnt Cl, K.581, w. Chilingirian String Quartet Classics for Pleasure ▲ CDCFP 4377 [ADD]
Ravel, M.:Intro & Allegro, w. S. Kanga (hp), W. Bennett (fl), Academy of St. Martin in the Fields Chamber Ensemble Chandos ▲ CHAN 8621 [DDD]
Tavener, J.:The Repentant Thief, w. M. Tilson Thomas (cnd), London SO Collins Classics ▲ 20052 [DDD]

Marriner, Andrew (cl) (cont.)
Weber, C.M. von:Concertino Cl, w. N. Marriner (cnd), Academy of St. Martin in the Fields Philips ▲ 432146–2 [DDD]
Weber, C.M. von:Con 1 Cl, w. N. Marriner (cnd), Academy of St. Martin in the Fields Philips ▲ 432146–2 [DDD]
Weber, C.M. von:Con 2 Cl, w. N. Marriner (cnd), Academy of St. Martin in the Fields Philips ▲ 432146–2 [DDD]

Marriner, Neville (vn)—see also ORCHESTRAS & ENSEMBLES London Chamber Players
Bach, J.S.:Brandenburg Con 2, w. H.–M. Linde (fl), I. Kipnis (hpd), N. Marriner (cnd), London Strings CBS ■ MGT 39802
Bach, J.S.:Brandenburg Con 5, w. H.–M. Linde (fl), I. Kipnis (hpd), N. Marriner (cnd), London Strings CBS ■ MGT 39802
Purcell, H.:Music of, w. April Cantelo (sop), Alfred Deller (ct), Maurice Bevan (bar), Peter Gibbs (vn), Granville Jones (vn), Desmond Dupré (vl), George Malcolm (hpd), Walter Bergmann (hpd)—15 Songs & Airs; Fantasia upon a Ground in d for 3 Violins & Continuo, Z.731; Fantasia upon One Note in F for 5 Viols, Z.745; Hornpipe in e (from The Old Bachelor); Music Lessons 1–12 from Musick's Hand–Maid, Part II; A New Irish Tune, "Lilliburlero," Z.646; Pavan in g for 3 Violins & Bass Viol, Z.752; Sonata in g for Violin & Continuo, Z.780; Sonata No. 9 in F, "Golden Sonata," Z.810 (from Ten Sonatas in Four Parts); Suite in D for Harpsichord, Z.667 Vanguard Classics ("The Bach Guild" series) 2–▲ OVC 2002/03 [ADD]

Marriott, Dave (trbn)
Dempster, S.:Music of, w. Stuart Dempster (trbn/didjeridu/conch), Jay Bulen (trbn), Jeff Domoto (trbn), Moc Escobedo (trbn/didjeridu/conch), Scott Higbee (trbn), Gretchen Hopper (trbn), Nathaniel Irby–Oxford (trbn), Chad Kirby (trbn/conch), Greg Powers (trbn), Debra Sykes (cym)—Conch Calling; Morning Light; Didjerilayover; Secret Currents; Melodic Communion; Shell Shock; Cloud Landings *(rec Fort Worden, Port Townsend, WA, June 18, 1994)* New Albion ▲ NA 076

Marrs, Dale (tpt)—see ORCHESTRAS & ENSEMBLES Pfeiffer Trumpet Consort

Mars, Marin (vn)
Britten, H.:Phantasy Qt, w. P. Oosternrijk (ob), S. van Els (va), J. Insinger (vc) Channel Classics ▲ CCS 9326 [DDD]

Marsalis, Branford (s sax)
Romances for Saxophone, w. English CO [cnd:Andrew Litton] CBS ▲ MK 42122 ■ PMT 42122

Marsalis, Branford (sax)
Debussy, C.:Arabesques (2), w. A. Litton (cnd), English CO—No. 1, orchd. Michel Colombier CBS ▲ MK 42122
Debussy, C.:L'Isle joyeuse, w. A. Litton (cnd), English CO [orchd. Michel Colombier] CBS ▲ MK 42122
Fauré, G.:Pavane Orch, w. A. Litton (cnd), English CO CBS ▲ MK 42122
Fauré, G.:Sicilienne, w. A. Litton (cnd), English CO CBS ▲ MK 42122
Rachmaninoff, S.:Vocalise, w. A. Litton (cnd), English CO CBS ▲ MK 42122
Ravel, M.:Pièce en forme de Habanera, w. A. Litton (cnd), English CO CBS ▲ MK 42122
Satie, E.:Gymnopédies, w. A. Litton (cnd), English CO—No. 3 CBS ▲ MK 42122
Villa–Lobos, H.:Bachiana brasileira 5, w. A. Litton (cnd), English CO [arr. by Michel Colombier] CBS ▲ MK 42122

Marsalis, Wynton (tpt)
Baroque Duet, w. Kathleen Battle (sop), Anthony Newman (hpd/org), Orch of St. Luke [cnd:John Nelson] Sony Classical ▲ SK 46672 Δ SM 46672 ■ ST 46672
Biber, H. von:Son in A Tpts, w. R. Leppard (cnd), English CO CBS ▲ MK 42478 [DDD] ■ MT 42478
Copland, A.:Quiet City, w. P. Koch (E hn), D. Hunsberger (cnd), Eastman Wind Ensemble CBS ▲ MK 44916 [DDD] ■ MT 44916 (D)
Fasch, J.F.:Con Tpt & 2 Obs, w. R. Leppard (cnd), English CO CBS ▲ MK 39061 [DDD] ■ IMT 39061 (D)
Fasch, J.F.:Con Tpt & 2 Obs, w. R. Leppard (cnd), English CO *(rec St. Giles Church, Cripplegate, London, England, Feb. 17 & 19–23, 1993)* Sony Classical ▲ SK 57497 [DDD]; ■ ST 57497
Handel, G.F.:Arias, w. E. Gruberova (sop), R. Leppard (cnd), English CO, "Eternal Source of Light Divine," from *Birthday Ode for Queen Anne* & "Let the Bright Seraphim," from *Samson* [E] CBS ▲ MK 39061 [DDD]; ■ IMT 39061 (D)
Haydn, J.:Con Tpt, w. R. Leppard (cnd), National PO London CBS ▲ MK 37846 [DDD] ■ IMT 37846 (D)
Haydn, J.:Con Tpt, w. R. Leppard (cnd), English CO *(rec St. Giles Church, London, Feb. 17–23, 1993)* Sony Classical ("Front Line" series) ▲ SK 57497 [DDD]; ■ ST 57497
Haydn, J.:Con Tpt, w. R. Leppard (cnd), National PO London CBS ▲ MK 39310 ■ MT 39310
Haydn, M.:Con Tpt, Hns & Strs, w. R. Leppard (cnd), English CO CBS ▲ MK 42478 [DDD] ■ MT 42478
Hummel, J.N.:Con in E♭ Tpt, S.49, w. R. Leppard (cnd), National PO London CBS ▲ MK 37846 [DDD] ■ IMT 37846 (D)
Hummel, J.N.:Con in E♭ Tpt, S.49, w. R. Leppard (cnd), English CO *(rec St. Giles Church, London, Feb. 17–23, 1993)* Sony Classical ("Front Line" series) ▲ SK 57497 [DDD]; ■ ST 57497
In Gabriel's Garden, w. English CO [cnd:Anthony Newman] *(rec St. Giles Church, Cripplegate, London, June 19–23 & 25, 1995)* Sony Classical ▲ SK 66244 [DDD]
Jolivet, A.:Concertino Tpt, w. C. Sheppard (pno), E.–P. Salonen (cnd), Philharmonia Orch CBS ▲ MK 42096 [DDD]
Jolivet, A.:Con 2 Tpt, w. E.–P. Salonen (cnd), Philharmonia Orch CBS ▲ MK 42096 [DDD]
Kathleen Battle & Wynton Marsalis:Baroque Duet Sony Classical ▲ SK 46672 ■ ST 46672
Molter, J.M.:Con 2 Tpt, w. R. Leppard (cnd), English CO CBS ▲ MK 39061 [DDD] ■ IMT 39061 (D)
Mozart, L.:Con Tpt, w. R. Leppard (cnd), English CO *(rec St. Giles Church, Cripplegate, London, England, Feb. 17 & 19–23, 1993)* Sony Classical ▲ SK 57497 [DDD]; ■ ST 57497
Mozart, L.:Con Tpt, w. R. Leppard (cnd), National PO London CBS ▲ MK 37846 [DDD] ■ IMT 37846 (D)
On the 20th Century, w. Judith Lynn Stillman (pno) *(rec Jan. 20–24, 1992)* Sony Classical ▲ SK 47193 [DDD] Δ SM 47193–2 [DDD]; ■ ST 47193–4
Pachelbel, J.:Canon, w. R. Leppard (cnd), English CO [arranged by R. Leppard for 3 Trumpets & Strings] CBS ▲ MK 42478 [DDD] ■ MT 42478
Purcell, H.:Music of, w. E. Gruberova (sop), R. Leppard (cnd), English CO—sels. from *The Indian Queen, King Arthur* & *Come Ye Sons of Art* CBS ▲ MK 39061 [DDD] ■ IMT 39061 (D)
Telemann, G.P.:Con for 3 Tpts, w. R. Leppard (cnd), English CO CBS ▲ MK 42478 [DDD] ■ MT 42478 (D)
Tomasi, H.:Con Tpt, w. E.–P. Salonen (cnd), Philharmonia Orch CBS ▲ MK 42096 [DDD]
Torelli, G.:Sons à 5 Tpts, w. R. Leppard (cnd), English CO—2 sons for Tpt & Strs CBS ▲ MK 39061 [DDD] ■ IMT 39061 (D)
Vivaldi, A.:Con for 2 Tpts, w. R. Leppard (cnd), English CO CBS ▲ MK 42478 [DDD] ■ MT 42478 (D)

Marsden, Marina (vn)
Grieg, E.:Son 1 Vn, w. Robert Chamberlain (pno) *(rec Iwaki Auditorium, ABC, Melbourne, Sept 1994)* Tall Poppies ▲ TP 67 [DDD]
Heim, C.:Transformation, w. Robert Chamberlain (pno) *(rec Iwaki Auditorium, ABC, Melbourne, Sept 1994)* Tall Poppies ▲ TP 67 [DDD]
Kreisler, F.:Caprice viennois *(rec Iwaki Auditorium, ABC, Melbourne, Sept 1994)* Tall Poppies ▲ TP 67 [DDD]
Nielsen, C.:Son 1 Vn, w. Robert Chamberlain (pno) *(rec Iwaki Auditorium, ABC, Melbourne, Sept 1994)* Tall Poppies ▲ TP 67 [DDD]
Sculthorpe, P.:Irkanda I *(rec Iwaki Auditorium, ABC, Melbourne, Sept 1994)* Tall Poppies ▲ TP 67 [DDD]

Marsh, George (vn)
Riley, T.:In C, w. Bruce Ackley, Steve Adams, Don R. Baker, Chris Brown, George Brooks, Steve Coughlin, Blake Derby, Bill Douglass, Mihr'un'Nisa Douglass, Hank Dutt, David Harrington, Don Howe, Joan Jeanrenaud, Alden Jenks, Warner Jepson, Henry Kaiser, Jaron Lanier, Bill Maginnis, Shabda Owens, Jon Raskin, Gyan Riley, Terry Riley, Gino Robair, John Sackett, Ramón Sender, John Sherba, Toyji Tomita, Danny Tunick, William Winant, Evan Ziporyn *(rec Jan. 14, 1990)* New Albion ▲ NA 071
Vainberg, M.:Trio Pno, w. Joseph Holt (pno), Steven Honigberg (vc) Albany ▲ TROY 157 [DDD]

▲ = CD ♦ = Enhanced CD Δ = MD ■ = Cassette Tape □ = DCC

Marsh, Peter (vn)

Lazarof, H.:Oct Strs, w. Yukiko Kamei (vn), Yoko Matsuda (vn), Miwako Watanabe (vn), Paul Silverthorne (va), Milton Thomas (va), Godfried Hoogeveen (vc), David Speltz (vc), H. Lazarof (cnd) Laurel ▲ LR 843 [DDD]

Marshall, Deborah (cl)

Lieberson, P.:King Gesar, w. Yo-Yo Ma (vc), Emanuel Ax (pno), Peter Serkin (pno), Omar Ebrahim (nar), Andras Adorjan (fl), William Purvis (hn), David Taylor (trbn), Stefan Huge (perc) Sony Classical ▲ SK 57971

Milhaud, D.:Cataloque de fleurs, w. Ulrike Sonntag (sop), Irmela Nolte (fl), Michael Weigel (bn), Renate Eggebrecht (vn), Stefan Berg (va), Friedemann Kupsa (vc), Arpat György (db) *(rec Ludwigsburg, Germany, Jan. 1995)* Troubadisc ▲ TROCD 01410 [DDD]

Milhaud, D.:Machines agricoles, w. Ulrike Sonntag (sop), Irmela Nolte (fl), Michael Weigel (bn), Renate Eggebrecht (vn), Stefan Berg (va), Friedemann Kupsa (vc), Arpat György (db) *(rec Ludwigsburg, Germany, Jan. 1995)* Troubadisc ▲ TROCD 01410 [DDD]

Tailleferre, G.:Arabesque, w. A. Gassenhuber (pno) *(rec Dec. 1992)* Troubadisc ▲ TRO 01406 [DDD]

Tailleferre, G.:Image, w. U. Siebler (fl), H. Stralendorf (cel), A. Gassenhuber (pno), Fanny Mendelssohn String Quartet *(rec Dec. 1992)* Troubadisc ▲ TRO 01406 [DDD]

Tailleferre, G.:Son Cl *(rec Dec. 1992)* Troubadisc ▲ TRO 01406 [DDD]

Marshall, Frank (pno)

Falla, M. de:Canciones populares españolas (7), w. C. Supervia (mez) *(rec , Paris 1930)* Nimbus (Prima Voce) 2-▲ NI 7836/7 [ADD]

Marshall, Kimberly (org)

European Organ Tour, w. Graham Barber (org), Marc Rochester (org), John Scott Whiteley (org) *(rec 1983–88)* Priory ▲ PRCD 903

15th–20th Century Organ Music Gamut Classics ▲ GAM 539 [DDD]

Franck, C.:Org Music (misc)—Chorale No. 2; Fantaisie in C, Op. 16 IMP Classics ▲ PCD 1005 [DDD]

A Little French Music IMP Classics ▲ PCD 1005 [DDD]

Marchand, L.:Pièces choisies IMP Classics ▲ PCD 1005 [DDD]

Marshall, Mike (mand)—see ORCHESTRAS & ENSEMBLES Modern Mandolin Quartet

Marshall, Wayne (chamber org)

A Banquet of Voices:Music for Mulitple Choirs, w. [cnd:John Rutter], Cambridge Singers, H. Gough (baroque vc), W. Hunt (violone) *(rec London, Feb. 1993)* Collegium ▲ COLCD 123

Marshall, Wayne (org)

Saint-Saëns, C.:Sym 3, w. M. Jansons (cnd), Oslo PO EMI Classics ▲ CDC 55184

Marshall, Wayne (pno)

American Music Sampler, w. Jill Gomez (sop), Crispian Steele (tpt), Helen McQueen (E hn), City of London Sinfonia [cnd:R. Hickox] Virgin Classics 2-▲ CDC 59089

Gershwin, G.:"I Got Rhythm" Vars, w. W. Marshall (cnd), Aalborg SO Virgin Classics ▲ CDM 61247

Gershwin, G.:Rhap in Blue, w. R. Hickox (cnd), City of London Sinfonia [original Paul Whiteman Orchestra arr.] Virgin Classics ▲ 59520 [DDD]

Gershwin, G.:Rhap in Blue, w. W. Marshall (cnd), Aalborg SO Virgin Classics ▲ CDM 61247

Gershwin, G.:Rhap in Blue, w. R. Hickox (cnd), City of London Sinfonia Virgin Classics ▲ CDZ 59693

Marshev, Oleg (pno)

Rubinstein, A.:Con 3 Pno, w. I. Stupel (cnd), Artur Rubinstein PO Danacord ▲ DACOCD 411 [DDD]

Rubinstein, A.:Con 4 Pno, w. I. Stupel (cnd), Artur Rubinstein PO Danacord ▲ DACOCD 411 [DDD]

Martel, François (cl)

Vivier, C.:Kopernikus, "A Ritual Opera of Death", w. Y. Parent (sop), P. Vaillancourt (sop), M.-D. Parent (sop), J. Fleury (cta), D. Doane (ten), M. Ducharme (bar), Y. Saint-Amant (bass), M. Bélanger (vn), L. Bouchard (tpt), L. Vaillancourt (cnd), *(orch unknown)* *(rec Feb. 1991)* CBC ("Musica Viva" series) ▲ MVCD 1047 [DDD]

Martell, Helen (a sax)—see ORCHESTRAS & ENSEMBLES Resounding Winds Saxophone Quartet

Martenot, Ginette (ondes martenot)

Jolivet, A.:Con for Ondes Martenot, w. A. Jolivet (cnd), Paris Opera Orch Adès ▲ ADE 203492 [ADD]

Martens, Eric (vc)

Klatzow, P.:Qt Strs, w. Petri Salonen (vn), Jürgen Schwietering (vn), Leo Lujyendijk (va) Claremont ▲ GSE 1524

Marthinsen, J. O. (hn)—see ORCHESTRAS & ENSEMBLES Oslo Wind Ensemble

Martignoni, Jean-Philippe (vc)—see ORCHESTRAS & ENSEMBLES Paris String Quartet

Martignoni, Sofia (vl)—see ORCHESTRAS & ENSEMBLES Consort Fontegara

Martin, Andreas (lt)

English Folksongs & Lute Songs, w. Andreas Scholl (ct) Harmonia Mundi France ▲ HMC 901603

Martin, Andrew (perc)—see ORCHESTRAS & ENSEMBLES Ensemble Bash

Martin, Bryan (lt)—see ORCHESTRAS & ENSEMBLES Sine Nomine Ensemble

Martin, Frank (pno)

Brahms, J.:Songs, w. H. Rehfuss (bar)—Feldeinsamkeit; Vergebliches Ständchen; Mein Mädel hat einen Rosenmund Claves ▲ CD 9327 [ADD]

Brahms, J.:Songs, w. H. Rehfuss (bar)—3 songs *(rec 1964)* FNAC Music ▲ 642313

Martin, F.:Chants de Noël, w. E. Ameling (sop), P. Odé (fl) [F] Jecklin-Disco ▲ JD 563-2 [ADD]

Martin, F.:Monologe (6) aus "Jedermann", w. H. Rehfuss (bar) Jecklin-Disco ▲ JD 563-2 [ADD]

Martin, F.:Preludes Jecklin-Disco ▲ JD 563-2 [ADD]

Martin, F.:Songs, w. E. Ameling (sop), P. Odé (fl)—Drey Minnelieder:Ach Herzeliep; Es stuont ein frouwe alleine; Under der linden [G] Jecklin-Disco ▲ JD 563-2 [ADD]

Martin, F.:Le Vin herbé, w. B. Retchitzka (sop), H. Morath (cta), O. de Nyzankowskyi (ten), H. Rehfuss (bar), D. Olsen (bass), V. Desarzens (cnd), Winterthur State Orch members Jecklin-Disco 2-▲ JD 581/2-2 [ADD]

Schubert, Franz:Songs (misc), w. H. Rehfuss (bar)—Frühlingsglaube; Der Lindenbaum; Der Wanderer; Der Wanderer an den Mond; An die Laute; Der Doppelgänger Claves ▲ CD 9327 [ADD]

Schumann, R.:Songs, w. H. Rehfuss (bar)—Widmung; Du bist wie eine Blume; Die Lotosblume; Die beiden Grendadiere Claves ▲ CD 9327 [ADD]

Wolf, H.:Songs (misc), w. H. Rehfuss (bar)—Der Tambour; Der Rattenfänger Claves ▲ CD 9327 [ADD]

Martin, Frédéric (vn)

Rebel, J.-F.:Sons 2 or 3 Parts, w. Odile Edouard (vn), Christine Plumbeau (vl), Eric Bellocq (thb), Noëlle Spieth (hpd)—Nos. 1-7 [L'immortelle; L'apollon; Tombeau de monsieur de Lully; La venus; La flore; La pallas; La junon] Adda ▲ ADD 581265 [DDD]

Martin, Jean (hn)—see ORCHESTRAS & ENSEMBLES Georgia Woodwind Quintet

Martin, Jean (pno)

Brahms, J.:Fants Pno, Op. 116 Arion ▲ ARN 68282 [AAD]

Brahms, J.:Intermezzos Pno, Op. 117 Arion ▲ ARN 68282 [AAD]

Brahms, J.:Scherzo Pno, Op. 4 Arion ▲ ARN 68282 [AAD]

Brahms, J.:Vars on a Theme of Robert Schumann, Op. 9 Arion ▲ ARN 68282 [AAD]

Fauré, G.:Nocturnes (13) Pno—Opp. 33/1-3, 36, 37 & 63 *(rec July & Nov. 1993)* Naxos ▲ 8.550794 [DDD]

Fauré, G.:Nocturnes (13) Pno—Opp. 74, 84/8, 97, 99, 194/1, 107, 119 *(rec July & Nov. 1993)* Naxos ▲ 8.550795 [DDD]

Fauré, G.:Préludes, Op. 103 *(rec July & Nov. 1993)* Naxos ▲ 8.550795 [DDD]

Fauré, G.:Romances sans paroles, Op. 17 *(rec July & Nov. 1993)* Naxos ▲ 8.550795 [DDD]

Fauré, G.:Theme & Vars Pno *(rec July & Nov. 1993)* Naxos ▲ 8.550794 [DDD]

Heller, S.:Blumen-, Frucht- und Dornenstücke Marco Polo ▲ 8.223435 [DDD]

Heller, S.:Preludes Pno, Op. 81 *(rec 1991)* Marco Polo ▲ 8.223434 [DDD]

Heller, S.:Preludes Pno, Op. 150 *(rec 1991)* Marco Polo ▲ 8.223434 [DDD]

Reger, M.:Blätter und Blüten *(rec Clara Wieck Auditorium, May 25–27, 1994)* Naxos ▲ 8.550932 [DDD]

Reger, M.:Morceaux *(rec Clara Wieck Auditorium, May 25–27, 1994)* Naxos ▲ 8.550932 [DDD]

Reger, M.:Silhouetten *(rec Clara Wieck Auditorium, May 25–27, 1994)* Naxos ▲ 8.550932 [DDD]

Schumann, R.:Etudes after Paganini's Caprices (comp), Opp. 3 & 10 Arion ▲ ARN 68226 [DDD]

Schumann, R.:Nachtstücke Arion ▲ ARN 68226 [DDD]

Martin, Laurent (org)

Alkan, C.-V.:Org Music—4 impromptus; 2eme recueil d'impromptus; Salut, cendre du pauvre!; Alleluia; Rondeau chromatique; Vars on a theme from Steibelt:Orage; Super flumina Babylonis Marco Polo ▲ 8.223657 [DDD]

Martin, Laurent (pno)

Alkan, C.-V.:Motifs, "Esquisses" *(rec Dec 1990)* Marco Polo ▲ 8.223352 [DDD]

Alkan, C.-V.:Preludes Pno, Op. 31 Marco Polo ▲ 8.223284

Berlioz, H.:Les Nuits d'été, w. Isabelle Vernet (sop) Ligia Digital ▲ 0201032

Berlioz, H.:Songs, w. Isabelle Vernet (sop)—La Belle Isabeau; Le Chasseur danois; Le Dépit de la bergère; Le Jeune patre Bréton; La Mort d'Ophélie; Petit oiseau; Zaide Ligia Digital ▲ 0201032

Gounod, C.:Songs, w. I. Vernet (sop)—Venise; Le lever; Le chant de Eurydice; Départ; Déesse ou femme; Chanson de printemps; Aubade; Repentir; O ma belle rebelle; Medjé; Marguerite; A toi mon coeur; L'absent; Tombez mes ailes; Le calme; Si la mort est le but; Noël; Ave Maria Ligia Digital ▲ 0201010 [DDD]

Mompou, F.:Pno Music (misc)—Scènes d'enfants; Impression intimes; Chants Magiques; Musica Callada; Fêtes lointaines; Trois Vars. *(rec May 1993)* Ligia Digital ▲ 0103009 [DDD]

Scriabin, A.:Etudes Pno, Op. 8—Nos. 2 & 10-12 Ligia Digital ▲ 0103034

Scriabin, A.:Etudes Pno, Op. 42 Ligia Digital ▲ 0103034

Scriabin, A.:Pieces Pno Op. 49—No. 1 Ligia Digital ▲ 0103034

Scriabin, A.:Pieces Pno Op. 56—No. 4 Ligia Digital ▲ 0103034

Scriabin, A.:Preludes Pno, Op. 11—Nos. 1, 2 & 11 Ligia Digital ▲ 0103034

Scriabin, A.:Son 10 Pno Ligia Digital ▲ 0103034

Scriabin, A.:Vers la flamme Ligia Digital ▲ 0103034

Martin, Lois (va)—see also ORCHESTRAS & ENSEMBLES Group for Contemporary Music String Quartet, Atlantic Sinfonietta members, Fidelio

Bourland, R.:Dark Paintings (3), w. Al Regni (sax), Beverly Lauridsen (vc) Open Loop ▲ 034 [DDD]

Bourland, R.:Sax Qnt, w. Al Regni (s sax), Laura Seton (vn), Mark Feldman (vn), Beverly Davidson (vc) Open Loop ▲ 034 [DDD]

Bourland, R.:Stone Qt, w. Al Regni (sax), Beverly Lauridsen (vc), T. O. Sterrett (pno) Open Loop ▲ 034 [DDD]

Fine, I.:Fant Str Trio, w. L. Quan (vn), C. Finckel (vc) CRI ▲ CD 574 [ADD]

Silver, S.:Dance Converging, w. William Purvis (hn), Lisa Moore (pno), Thad Wheeler (perc) *(rec Recital Hall, Music Division, SUNY, Purchase, New York, Apr 12, 1995)* CRI ▲ CD 708 [DDD]

Starer, R.:Episodes Va, w. Harry Clark (vc), Sanda Schuldmann (pno) Albany ▲ TROY 152 [DDD]

Wuorinen, C.:Qt 3 Strs, w. B. Hudson (vn), C. Zeavin (vn), F. Sherry (vc) New World ▲ NW 385-2 [DDD]

Zaimont, J.L.:Sky Curtains, w. Kathleen Nester (fl), Daniel Gilbert (cl), Bob Wagner (bn), Christopher Finkel (vc) *(rec SUNY Purchase, Theatre C, Jan 8–10 & Feb 20, 1995)* Arabesque ▲ ARA 6667 [DDD]

Martin, Marya (fl)

Rorem, N.:Bright Music, w. A.-M. Schub (pno), A. Kavafian (vn), I. Kavafian (vn), F. Sherry (vc) New World ▲ 80416-2 [DDD]

Martin, Philip (pno)

Addinsell, R.:Music of, w. Roderick Elms (pno), K. Alwyn (cnd), BBC Concert Orch—Theme from Goodbye Mr. Chips; Invitation Waltz [from Ring Round the Moon]; The Smokey Mountains (con.); The Isle of Apples; The Prince & the Showgirl (sel.); Tom Brown's Schooldays [Ov.]; Festival; Journey to Romance; Fire Over England (suite); Theme from A Tale of Two Cities *(rec Golders Green Hippodrome, London, Apr. 20 & 21, 1994)* Marco Polo ("British Light Music" series) ▲ 8.223732 [DDD]

Gottschalk, L.M.:Pno Music—Bamboula; Suis-moi; Miserere from Il trovatore; Pasquinade; La Savane; Ballade No. 8; Souvenir de Lima; Marche de nuit; Caprice polka; Grand fantaisie; Triomphale; Scherzo romantique; Polka in B♭; Polka, 1859; Ballade, 1853; Ynes; La Hyperion ▲ CDA 66697

Grainger, P.:Folk Song Settings, w. M. Welsh (vc), K. Montgomery (cnd), Bournemouth Sinfonietta—Blithe bells; Country gardens; Green bushes; Handel in the Strand; Mock morris; Molly on the shore; My Robin is to the greenwood gone; Shepherd's hey; Spoon River; Walking tune; Youthful rapture; Youthful Suite *(rec ca. 1979)* Chandos ("Collect" series) ▲ CHAN 6542 [ADD]

Martin, P.:Elegies, w. Ruxandra Colan (vn) Altarus ▲ CD 9011

Martin, P.:Light Music, w. Penelope Price Jones (sop) Altarus ▲ CD 9011

Martin, P.:The Rainbow Comes & Goes Altarus ▲ CD 9011

Martin, P.:Songs, w. P. Price Jones (sop) Altarus ▲ CD 9009

Reizenstein, F.:Pno Music—Legend, Op. 27 (1949); Scherzo in A, Op. 21 (1946); Sonata No. 2 in A♭, Op. 40 (1964); Suite, Op. 6 (1936); Variations on "The Lambeth Walk" (1938) Continuum ▲ CCD 1007

Martin, Robert (vc)—see ORCHESTRAS & ENSEMBLES Sequoia String Quartet

Martin, Thomas (db)

Bottesini, G.:Duetto Cl & Db, w. E. Johnson (cl) ASV ▲ ASV 563 [DDD]

Bottesini, G.:Gran Con Db, w. A. Litton (cnd), English CO ASV ▲ ASV 563 [DDD]

Bottesini, G.:Gran Duo Concertant, w. J. L. Garcia (vn) ASV ▲ ASV 563 [DDD]

Bottesini, G.:Music for Db, w. A. Halstead (pno)—Capriccio di Bravura; Elegia; Fant. on Beatrice di Tenda; Fant. on Lucia di Lammermoor; Grand Allegro di Concerto; Romanza drammatica [w. J. Fugelle (soprano)]; Intro. & Bolero ASV ▲ ASV 626 [DDD]

Martin, Victor (vn)

Turina, J.L.:Con Vn, w. V. P. Pérez (cnd), Tenerife SO Discobi ▲ DIS 2010 [DDD]

Martineau, Malcolm (pno)

An American Recital, w. Jennifer Stinton (fl) Collins Classics ▲ COL 1385 [DDD]

Beethoven, L. van:Son 5 Vn, "Spring", w. J. Stinton (fl) Collins Classics ▲ COL 1347

Brahms, J.:Intermezzos Pno, Op. 117 IMP Allegro ▲ ALG PCD 994 [DDD]

Brahms, J.:Sons Cl (comp), w. K. Puddy (B♭ cl) *(rec 1990, Meiningen)* IMP Allegro ▲ ALG PCD 994 [DDD]

Debussy, C.:Proses lyriques, w. D. Jones (mez) Chandos ▲ CHAN 9147 [DDD]

Duparc, H.:Songs, w. D. Jones (mez)—L'Invitation au voyage; Extase; La vie anterieure [F] Chandos ▲ CHAN 9147 [DDD]

The Early Clarinet Family, w. Keith Puddy (cl), Gary Brodie (cl/bass chalumeaux), P. Price (bass chalumeaux), Susan Dent (baroque hn), Alastair Mitchell (8-keyed bn) Clarinet Classics ▲ CC 0004

Fauré, G.:Songs, w. S. Walker (mez)—Le Jardin clos (cycle of 8 songs), Op. 106 (1914); plus 20 individual songs composed ca. 1861-1904—Mai, Op. 1/2; Chant d'automne, Op. 5/1; Rêve d'amour, Op. 5/2; Dans les ruines d'un abbaye (1867); L'aurore (ca. 1871); Après un rêve (ca. 1878); Tristesse, Op. 6/2; Nell, Op. 18/1; Automne, Op. 18/3; Les Berceaux, Op. 23/1; Notre amour, Op. 23/2; Le Secret, Op. 23/3; Noël, Op. 43/1; Les Présents, Op. 46/1; La Rose, Op. 51/4; En Prière (1890); La parfum impérissable, Op. 76/1; Soir, Op. 83/2; Dans la forêt de septembre, Op. 85/1; Le Ramier, Op. 87/2 CRD ▲ 3476 [DDD]

Fauré, G.:Songs, w. S. Walker (mez)—Le Papillon et la fleur, Op. 1/1; Ici-bas!, Op. 8/3; Sérénade Toscane, Op. 3/2; Nocturne, Op. 43/2; Au bord de l'eau, Op. 8/1; Seule!, Op. 3/1; Larmes, Op. 51/1; Aurore, Op. 39/1; Fleur jetée, Op. 39/2; Le Pays des rêves, Op. 39/3; Les Roses d'Ispahan, Op. 39/4; Chanson, Op. 94; C'est la paix, Op. 114; La fée aux chansons, Op. 27/2; L'absent, Op. 5/3; Arpège, Op. 76/2; Le plus doux chemin, Op. 87/1; Accompagnement, Op. 85/3; Au Cimitière, Op. 51/2; Le Don silencieux, Op. 92; Chanson de Mélisande (1898); Clair de lune, Op. 46/2; Vocalise (1907); Puisqu'ici bas toute âme, Op. 10/1; Tarantelle, Op. 10/2 [F] *(rec 1991)* CRD ▲ 3477 [DDD]

Finzi, G.:Bagatelles, Op. 23, w. E. Johnson (cl) ASV ▲ ASV 787 [DDD]

Pastoral:Emma Johnson Plays British Clarinet Music, w. Emma Johnson (cl), J. Howarth (sop) ASV ▲ ASV 891 [DDD]

Poulenc, F.:Songs, w. D. Jones (mez)—3 songs—Banalities; La bestaire; La souris les Chemines de l'amour [F] Chandos ▲ CHAN 9147 [DDD]

Quilter, R.:Songs, w. John Mark Ainsley (ten)—Now Sleeps the Crimson Petal; Go, Lovely Rose; plus others Hyperion ▲ CDA 66878

Satie, E.:Songs, w. D. Jones (mez)—Trois melodies; La diva de l'empire; Ludions [F] Chandos ▲ CHAN 9147 [DDD]

Schubert, Franz:Intro & Vars Fl on "Tröckne Blumen", w. J. Stinton (fl) Collins Classics ▲ COL 1347

Martineau, Malcolm (pno) (cont.)
Schubert, Franz:Son Arpeggione, w. J. Stinton (fl) Collins Classics ▲ COL 1347
Schubert, Franz:Songs (misc), w. Simon Keenlyside (bar)—The Solitary; Serenade [from Cymbeline]; To Sylvia [from The 2 Gentlemen of Verona]; The Youth by the Spring; Sailor's Song to the Dioscuri; Group from Hades; The Gods of Greece; In the Forest; The Wanderer's Address to the Moon; Voluntary Oblivion; Intimations of Heaven; Prometheus; The Gondolier; The Stars; At Bruck; Wild Rose; In the Wood; Dame's Violets; With You Alone; You Are Repose Classics for Pleasure ("Eminence" series) ▲ CDEMX 2224 [DDD]
Spanish Songs, w. Della Jones (mez) Chandos ▲ CHAN 9277 [DDD]
Stanford, C.V.:Intermezzi, w. E. Johnson (cl) ASV ▲ ASV 787 [DDD]

Martini, Alberto (vn)—see ORCHESTRAS & ENSEMBLES I Filarmonici

Martini, Carlo de (vn)—see ORCHESTRAS & ENSEMBLES Ricordanze String Quartet

Martinotti, Bruno (fl)
The Flute of Bruno Martinotti Suite ▲ STE 8001

Martinova, Olga (vn)
Bach, J.S.:Con for 2 Vns, w. Mikhail Gantvarg (vn), M. Gantvarg (cnd), St. Petersburg Soloists Audiophile Classics ▲ 101.021

Martins, João Carlos (pno)
Bach, J.S.:Brandenberg Con 5, w. Lydia Oshavkova (fl), Liudmil Nenchev (vn), P. Djurov (cnd), Sofia Soloists CO *(rec Salle Bulgaria, Sofia, Bulgaria, 1996)* Concord Concerto ▲ CCD 42042 [DDD]
Bach, J.S.:Con 2 Hpd, w. P. Djurov (cnd), Sofia Soloists CO *(rec Salle Bulgaria, Sofia, Bulgaria, 1996)* Concord Concerto ▲ CCD 42042 [DDD]
Bach, J.S.:Con 4 Hpd, w. P. Djurov (cnd), Sofia Soloists CO *(rec Salle Bulgaria, Sofia, Bulgaria, 1996)* Concord Concerto ▲ CCD 42042 [DDD]
Bach, J.S.:English Suites—Nos. 4 & 5 *(rec Salle Bulgaria, Sophia, Bulgaria, Mar 1995)* Concord Concerto ▲ CCD 42035 [DDD]
Bach, J.S.:Fant Org, BWV 562 *(rec Salle Bulgaria, Sophia, Bulgaria, Mar 1995)* Concord Concerto ▲ CCD 42035 [DDD]
Bach, J.S.:Toccatas Hpd, BWV 910–16—in c *(rec Salle Bulgaria, Sophia, Bulgaria, Mar 1995)* Concord Concerto ▲ CCD 42035 [DDD]

Martinson, J. (org)
Rutter, J.:Church Music, w. T. Seelig (cnd), Dallas Women's Chorus, Turtle Creek Chorale—Praise Ye the Lord; The Lord Is My Light & My Salvation; All Things Bright & Beautiful; Lord, Make Me an Instrument of Thy Peace *(rec July 28–29, 1993)* Reference ▲ RR 57 CD [DDD]
Rutter, J.:Requiem, w. N. Keith (sop), T. Seelig (cnd), Dallas Women's Chorus, Turtle Creek Chorale *(rec July 28–29, 1993)* Reference ▲ RR 57 CD [DDD]

Martirano, Dorothy (vn)
Martirano, S.:Sampler—Everything Goes When The Whistle Blows Centaur ▲ CRC 2045 [DDD]

Martirano, Dorothy (zeta vn)
Martirano, S.:Elec & Cmpt Music, w. Salvatore Martirano (cmpt/kbd)—SATBehind Demo; Look at the Back of My Head for Awhile; 4 Not 2; Electronic Dance No. 1 Centaur ▲ CRC 2266 [DDD]

Marton, D. (va)—see ORCHESTRAS & ENSEMBLES Parrenin String Quartet

Maruko, Hiroko (pno)
Burgmüller, N.:Son Pno MD + G ▲ L 3224 [DDD]
Kirchner, T.:Neue Davidsbündlertanze MD + G ("Gold" series) ▲ MDG 3130389 [DDD]
Schumann, R.:Davidsbündlertänze MD + G ("Gold" series) ▲ MDG 3130389 [DDD]
Schumann, R.:Son 1 Pno MD + G ▲ L 3224 [DDD]

Maruzsa, Tibor (hn)—see ORCHESTRAS & ENSEMBLES Budapest Festival Horn Quartet

Marval, Marie-Louise de (pno)
Gerber, R.:Concertino Pno, w. T. Loosli (cnd), Bern Chamber Ensemble Gallo ▲ CD 549 [AAD]

Marville, Yovanka (hpd)
Queens of the Night, w. Luca Antoniotti (org), Raoul Esmerode (perc) Gallo ▲ CD 658 [ADD]

Marvin, Frederick (pno)
Berger, L.:Son-Pathétique *(rec Crouse Auditorium, Syracuse, Univ, NY, Nov 27, 1974)* Genesis ▲ GCD 109 [ADD]
Dussek, J.L.:Sons Pno—in C, Op. 4/3; in g, Op. 10/2; in c, Op. 35/3 *(rec Syracuse Univ. between 1975 & 1979)* Dorian Discovery ▲ DIS 80125 [ADD]
Dussek, J.L.:Son Pno, Op. 18/2 Dorian Discovery (Discovery) ▲ DIS 80110 [ADD]
Dussek, J.L.:Son Pno, Op. 61, "Elégie harmonique sur la mort du Prince Louis Ferdinand de Prusse" *(rec Syracuse Univ. between 1975 & 1979* Dorian Discovery ▲ DIS 80125 [ADD]
Dussek, J.L.:Son Pno, Op. 69/3 Dorian Discovery (Discovery) ▲ DIS 80110 [ADD]
Dussek, J.L.:Son Pno, Op. 77, "L'invocation" Dorian Discovery (Discovery) ▲ DIS 80110 [ADD]
Liszt, F.:Grosses Konzertsolo *(rec Crouse Auditorium, Syracuse, Univ, NY, Oct 29, 1972)* Genesis ▲ GCD 109 [ADD]
Moscheles, I.:Son caractéristique *(rec Crouse Auditorium, Syracuse, Univ, NY, Nov 30, 1974)* Genesis ▲ GCD 109 [ADD]

Marwood, Anthony (vc)
Fauré, G.:Qnts Pno & Strs, Opp. 89 & 115, w. Domus String Quartet Hyperion ▲ CDA 66766

Marwood, Anthony (vn)—see ORCHESTRAS & ENSEMBLES Florestan Trio

Marwood, Catherine (vc)—see also ORCHESTRAS & ENSEMBLES Vanbrugh String Quartet
Davies, P.M.:Strathclyde Con 5, w. J. Clark (vn), P. M. Davies (cnd), Scottish CO Collins Classics ▲ COL 1303 [DDD]

Maryška, Lubomír (tuba)
Purcell, H.:Son Tpt, w. Jaroslav Halíř (tpt), Marek Vajo (tpt), Radek Nemec (tpt), Jan Vobořil (hn), Jiří Nauš (trbn), Pavel Černy (org), Oldřich Šatava (timp) [trans. F. Antonín Vaigl] *(rec Mirror Chapel of the Prague Klementinum, Mar 26, 1995)* Panton ▲ 811368-2 [DDD]

März, C.-H. (pno)
Liszt, F.:Son Pno *(rec 5/89)* FSM ▲ FCD 97727 [DDD]
Schumann, R.:Son 1 Pno *(rec 5/89)* FSM ▲ FCD 97727 [DDD]

Masala, Mauro (pno)
Satie, E.:Pno Music (misc)—Sports et divertissements; 3 gymnopédies; Heures séculaires et instantanées; 4 Préludes; 3 Valses du précieux dégoûté; 3 Sarabandes; 4 Préludes flasques Nuova Era ▲ NUO 7202 [DDD]

Masan, Alicja (pno)
Holmès, A.:Songs, w. Eva Csapó (sop)—Sérénade d'hiver; Berceuse; Souvenir; Rondel; Chanson du chamelier; Le chemin du ciel; Journée fleurie; L'opprimée; Sérénade de toujours; Sérénade printanière; Sérénade d'été; Sérénade d'automne; Le brick l'espérance; Fleur de neige; Tireli; En chemin; Chanson catalane; Le château de rêve; Le chevalier au lion Accord ▲ ACD 201252 [DDD]

Maschkowski, Z. (vc)—see ORCHESTRAS & ENSEMBLES Daniel String Quartet, Ophir Trio

Masciadri, Milton (db)
Songs with a Touch of Bass, w. David Stoffel (b-bar), Ivan Frazier (pno) *(rec Central Presbyterian Church, Athens, GA 1995)* ACA Digital Recording ▲ CM 20030

Mase, Raymond (tpt)—see also ORCHESTRAS & ENSEMBLES American Brass Quintet, Speculum Musicae
Baroque Trumpetissimo, w. David Bilger (tpt), Stephen Burns (tpt), Edward Carroll (tpt), Alex Holton (tpt), Timothy Morrison (tpt), Lee Soper (tpt), Atsuko Sato (bn), Ben Harms (timp), Edward Brewer (org/hpd), Philharmonia Virtuosi [cnd:Richard Kapp] ESS.A.Y ▲ ESS 1035 [DDD]
Hindemith, P.:Son Tpt, w. T. Lichtman (pno) Summit 2-▲ DCD 115 [DDD] 2-■ DCD 115
Stravinsky, I.:Octet, w. M. Parloff (fl), D. Schiffrin (cl), F. Morelli (bn), S. Heinneman (bn), C. Gekker (tpt), R. Borror (trbn), D. Taylor (trbn), G. Schuller (cnd) *(rec Sep. 1991)* GM ▲ GM 2030
Trumpet in Our Time Summit ▲ DCD 148 [DDD]

Mase, Raymond (tpt/flgl)—see ORCHESTRAS & ENSEMBLES American Brass Quintet

Mäser, Rolf (pno)
Moeschinger, A.:Son in modo disinvolto, w. R. Jucker (vc) Grammont ▲ CTSP 1-2 [ADD]

Mashev, O. (pno)
Prokofiev, S.:Pno Music (misc)—Dumka; Sons., Opp. 82 & 83; Visions Fugitives, Op. 22 Danacord ▲ DACOCD 391
Prokofiev, S.:Pno Music (misc)—Four Pieces, Op. 3; Old Grandmother's Tales, Op. 31; Sons., Opp. 1 & 84; Three Pieces, Op. 3 Danacord ▲ DACOCD 392

Masi, Pier Narciso (pno)—see also ORCHESTRAS & ENSEMBLES Bartholdy Piano Quartet
Kreisler, F.:Vn Pieces, w. L. A. Bianchi (vn)—Tambourin Chinois; Schön Rosmarin; Liebesleid; Liebesfreud; Caprice Viennoise; Gypsy Caprice; La Gitana; Syncopation; Londonderry Air; Dancing Doll; Polichinelle Serenade; Rondino; Toy Soldiers March; Old Refrain; Marche Miniature Viennoise; Viennese Rapsodic Fantasietta; Recitativo und Scherzo *(rec 6/91)* Dynamic ▲ CD 88 [DDD]
Molique, W.B.:Intro, Andante & Polonaise, w. M. Ancillotti (fl) Dynamic ▲ CD 104
Reinecke, C.:Son Fl, w. M. Ancillotti (fl) Dynamic ▲ CD 104
Rietz, J.:Son Fl, w. M. Ancillotti (fl) Dynamic ▲ CD 104

Masó, Jordi (pno)
Gerhard, R.:Pno Music (comp)—Dos apunts; Soirées de Barcelona; Dances from Don quixote; Impromptus (3) *(rec Waldenburg, Switzerland, Sept 18–22, 1993)* Marco Polo ▲ 8.223867 [DDD]
Homs, J.:Son 2 Pno *(rec Waldenburg, Switzerland, Sept 18–22, 1993)* Marco Polo ▲ 8.223867 [DDD]

Mason, Barry (baroque gtr)
Masters of the Baroque Guitar Amon Ra ▲ CDSAR 45 [DDD]

Mason, Barry (lt/baroque gtr/chit)
Now What Is Love?, w. Glenda Simpson (mez) Amon Ra ▲ CDSAR 50 [DDD]

Mason, James (ob)
Françaix, J.:Heure du berger Orch, w. Suzanne Shulman (fl), James Campbell (cl), James Sommerville (hn), James McKay (bn), André Laplante (pno) *(rec Glenn Gould Studio, CBC Toronto, Mar. 26–27, 1994)* CBC ("Musica Viva" series) ▲ MVV 1089 [DDD]
Reinecke, C.:Trio Ob, w. James Sommerville (hn), Rena Sharon (pno) Marquis Classics ▲ MAR 157 [DDD]

Mason, Kevin (thb/lt)
Musick for Severall Friends, w. M. Springfels (cnd), Newberry Consort, Drew Minter (ct), David Douglass (vn) Harmonia Mundi France ("Musique d'abord" series) ▲ HMA 1907013

Mason, Molly (gtr)
Gohl, M.:The West, w. Nana Vasconcelos (sgr), Seamus Eagan (sgr), Jay Ungar (vn), *(other artists unknown)*, M. Gohl (cnd), Black Elk Voices Sony Classical ▲ SK 62727 ■ ST 62727

Mason, Timothy (vc)—see also ORCHESTRAS & ENSEMBLES Capricorn, London Fortepiano Trio, Capricorn members
Vivaldi, A.:Con Vn Vc, RV.546, w. M. Huggett (vn), N. Kraemer (cnd), Raglan Baroque Players Veritas 2-▲ VCD 7 90803-2 [DDD] 2-■ VCD 7 90803-4 (D)

Mason, Will (saz-lt/chitarra/vih/ham dlc/perc)
Sonus Chanterai:Music of Medieval France, w. James Carrier (shm/rcrs/oud/hp/gemshn), Hazel Ketchum (sgr/saz-lt/perc), J. Holenko (oud/chitarra/psaltery/saz-lt/perc) *(rec St. John's Episcopal Church, Columbia, MD, Sept. 1993)* Dorian Discovery ▲ DIS 80123 [DDD]

Masseli, Josef (cl)
Lutoslawski, W.:Dance Preludes Cl, Hp, Pno, Perc & Strs, w. A. Grüber (cnd), Berlin SO Vox Box 2-▲ CDX 5133

Masselos, William (pno)
Helps, R.:Recollections CRI ("American Masters" series) ▲ CD 717 [ADD]
Mayer, William:Octagon, w. K. Schermerhorn (cnd), Milwaukee SO CRI ▲ CD 584 [ADD]
Mayer, William:Son 1 Pno CRI ▲ CD 584 [ADD]
Rudhyar, D.:Pno Music—Paeans (1927); Stars (1926); Granites (1929) CRI ▲ CD 584 [ADD]

Masseurs, Peter (tpt)
Shostakovich, D.:Con 1 Pno, w. R. Brautigam (pno), R. Chailly (cnd), Royal Concertgebouw Orch London ▲ 433702-2 [DDD]
Verbey, T.:Duet Tpts, w. Hendrik Jan Lindhout (tpt) Donemus ▲ CV 31

Mastalini, A. (vn)—see ORCHESTRAS & ENSEMBLES Stauffer String Quartet

Mastero, Nicole (hp)
Arpeggio *(rec Sept. 1990)* Erasmus ▲ WVH 073 [DDD]
Busser, H.:Ballade Hp *(rec 1988)* FSM-Adagio ▲ FCD 97722 [DDD]
Fauré, G.:Impromptu Hp *(rec 1988)* FSM-Adagio ▲ FCD 97722 [DDD]
Saint-Saëns, C.:Fant Hp *(rec 1988)* FSM-Adagio ▲ FCD 97722 [DDD]
Saint-Saëns, C.:Fant Vn, w. E.-J. David (hp) *(rec 1988)* FSM-Adagio ▲ FCD 97722 [DDD]
Tournier, M.:Fresque Marine FSM-Adagio ▲ FCD 97722 [DDD]

Masters, Rachel (hp)
Alwyn, W.:Lyra Angelica, w. R. Hickox (cnd), City of London Sinfonia Chandos ▲ CHAN 9065 [DDD]
Debussy, C.:Danses sacrée et profane, w. Y.P. Tortelier (cnd), Ulster Orch Chandos ▲ CHAN 8972 [DDD]
Ginastera, A.:Con Hp, w. R. Hickox (cnd), City of London Sinfonia Chandos ▲ CHAN 9094 [DDD]
Glière, R.:Con Hp, w. R. Hickox (cnd), City of London Sinfonia Chandos ▲ CHAN 9094 [DDD]
Mendelssohn, F.:Songs (4) (1830), w. J. Baker (mez), F. Lloyd (hn), R. Hickox (cnd), City of London Sinfonia, London Sym Chorus Virgin Classics ▲ CDC 59589
Mozart, W.A.:Con Fl Hp, w. Philippa Davies (fl), R. Hickox (cnd), City of London Sinfonia IMP ▲ IMP 2011
Ravel, M.:Intro & Allegro, w. Y.P. Tortelier (cnd), Ulster Orch Chandos ▲ CHAN 8972 [DDD]

Masters, Robert (vn)
Purcell, H.:Chamber Music, w. Alberto Lysy (vn), Yehudi Menuhin (vn), Cecil Arnowitz (va), Walter Gerhard (va), Derek Simpson (vc), Ambrose Gauntlett (vl), Roy Jesson (hpd/org)—Trio Sons Nos. 2 in C, 6 in G & 8 in G; Fants Nos. 4 in g, 7 in c, 8 in d & 13 in F, "Upon One Note" EMI Classics ("Baroque" series) ▲ CDK 65734
Purcell, H.:Fants, w. Alberto Lysy (vn), Yehudi Menuhin (vn), Cecil Aronowitz (va), Walter Gerhard (va), Derek Simpson (vc), Ambrose Gauntlett (vl), Roy Jesson (hpd/org)—Nos. 4 in g, 7 in c, 8 in d, 13 in F EMI Classics ▲ CDK 65734
Purcell, H.:Sons (22) Vns, w. Alberto Lysy (vn), Yehudi Menuhin (vn), Cecil Aronowitz (va), Walter Gerhard (va), Derek Simpson (vc), Ambrose Gauntlett (vl), Roy Jesson (hpd/org)—Nos. 2, 6, & 8 EMI Classics ▲ CDK 65734

Mastini, Andrea (cnt)
Mercadante, S.:Sinf concertante 1, w. Luca Truffelli (fl), Roberto Saltini (cl), Giovanni Sora (cl), C.F. Sedazzari (cnd), Camerata Schubert Bongiovanni ▲ GB 2199 [DDD]
Mercadante, S.:Sinf concertante 2, w. Luca Truffelli (fl), Roberto Saltini (cl), C.F. Sedazzari (cnd), Camerata Schubert Bongiovanni ▲ GB 2199 [DDD]
Mercadante, S.:Sinf concertante 3, w. Luca Truffelli (fl), Roberto Saltini (cl), Giovanni Sora (cl), C.F. Sedazzari (cnd), Camerata Schubert Bongiovanni ▲ GB 2199 [DDD]

Mastro, Sergio del (cl)
Rossini, G.:Chamber Music, w. Sergio Lamberto (vn), Guido Corti (hn), Ricardo Caramella (pno) Nuova Era ▲ NUO 7245

Mastrogiovanni-Kraxner, Waltraut (shofar)
Hiller, W.:Schulamit, w. Regina Klepper (sop), Edeltraud Knabel (alt), Michael Schopper (bass), Elisabeth Woska (nar), H.R. Zöbeley (cnd), Munich Residenz Orch, Munich Percussion Ensemble, Calw Aurelius Boys' Choir Soloists, Munich Motet Choir Wergo ▲ WER 6280-2

Matarazzo, Lucio (gtr)
Duo Guitarists, w. Mario Fragnito (gtr) Ducale ▲ DUC 9 [DDD]

Matarazzo, Lucio (pno)
Carcassi, M.:Capricci, Op. 26 Agorá ▲ 025 [DDD]
Carcassi, M.:Etudes Gtr, Op. 60 Agorá ▲ 025 [DDD]

Máté, Balázs (vc)—see also ORCHESTRAS & ENSEMBLES Trio Cristofori
Handel, G.F.:Sons Fl, w. Christian Gurtner (fl), Martin Haselböck (hpd/org)—Op. 1, Nos. 1, 4 & 5 *(rec Lutheran City Church, Vienna, Oct 1995)* Novalis ▲ 150120 [DDD]
Handel, G.F.:Sons Fl, "Halle Sons", w. Christian Gurtner (fl), Martin Haselböck (hpd/org) *(rec Lutheran City Church, Vienna, Oct 1995)* Novalis ▲ 150120 [DDD]
Handel, G.F.:Son Fl, HWV 378, w. Christian Gurtner (fl), Martin Haselböck (hpd/org) *(rec Lutheran City Church, Vienna, Oct 1995)* Novalis ▲ 150120 [DDD]
Handel, G.F.:Son Fl, HWV 379, w. Christian Gurtner (fl), Martin Haselböck (hpd/org)—excerpt *(rec Lutheran City Church, Vienna, Oct 1995)* Novalis ▲ 150120 [DDD]

▲ = CD ♦ = Enhanced CD Δ = MD ■ = Cassette Tape □ = DCC

Máté, Balázs (vc) (cont.)
Monteverdi, C.:Music of, w. M. Spányi (org), S. Benyus (db), I. Szabó (thb), Monteverdi Chamber Choir—Laudate pueri, Lauda Ierusalem, Nisi Dominus Hungaroton ▲ HCD 31273 [DDD]

Maté, Janos (vn)
Rossini, G.:Tancredi, w. Veronica Cangemi (sop—Roggiero), Eva Mei (sop—Amenaide), Vasselina Kasarova (mez—Tancredi), Melinda Paulsen (cta—Isaura), Ramón Vargas (ten—Argirio), Harry Peeters (bass—Orbazzano), Gottfried Greiner (vc), Ingo Nawra (db), David Syrus (hpd), R. Abbado (cnd), Munich RSO, Bavarian Radio Chorus *(rec Studio 1, Munich, July 17–30, 1995)* RCA Red Seal 3-▲ 09026-68349-2 [DDD]

Matejcek, Peter (a sax)
Hölszky, A.:Flux-Reflux Koch Schwann ▲ 3-1062-2 [DDD]

Mathé, Christiane (pno)
Castérède, J.:Diagrammes Koch Schwann ▲ SCH 315262 [DDD]
Castérède, J.:Études (4) Pno Koch Schwann ▲ SCH 315262 [DDD]
Castérède, J.:Hommage à Thelonious Monk Koch Schwann ▲ SCH 315262 [DDD]
Castérède, J.:Impromptu Koch Schwann ▲ SCH 315262 [DDD]
Castérède, J.:Son Pno Koch Schwann ▲ SCH 315262 [DDD]
Castérède, J.:Vars Pno Koch Schwann ▲ SCH 315262 [DDD]
Jolivet, A.:Pno Music—5 danses rituèlles; Mana; Cosmogonie; Son.; Etude sur des Modes antiques Koch Schwann ▲ SCH 311322 [DDD]
Martin, F.:Pno Music—Préludes; Guitare (4 Short Pieces); Claire de Lune; Esquisse; Etude rhythmique; Fant. on Flamenco Rhythms Koch Schwann ▲ SCH 312212 [DDD]

Máthé, Győző (va)
Beethoven, L. van:Septet Strs, w. Ildikó Hegyi (vn), Péter Szabó (vc), István Tóth (db), József Balogh (cl), Jenő Keveházi (hn), József Vajda (bn) *(rec Scottish Church, Budapest, Apr. 21–23 & May 29–31, 1)* Naxos ▲ 8.553090 [DDD]
Beethoven, L. van:Sxt Hns, Op. 81b, w. Jenő Keveházi (hn), János Keveházi (hn), Ildikó Hegyi (vn), Péter Popa (vn), Péter Szabó (vc) *(rec Scottish Church, Budapest, Apr. 21–23 & May 29–31, 1)* Naxos ▲ 8.553090 [DDD]

Mathé, Ulrike-Anima (vn)
Korngold, E.W.:Con Vn, w. A. Litton (cnd), Dallas SO *(rec Eugene McDermott Hall, Morton H. Meyerson Sym Center, Dallas, TX, Nov. 1994)* Dorian ▲ DOR 90216 [DDD]
Kreisler, F.:Vn Pieces, w. Samuel Sanders (pno)—Schön Rosmarin; Tambourin Chinois; Caprice Viennois; Liebesleid; Marche Miniature Viennoise; Viennese Rhapsodic Fantasietta; Sicilienne & Rigaudon; Midnight Bells; Danse Espagnole; Lotusland; Syncopation; Tango; Scherzo; Cavatina; Slavonic Dances; 2 Mazurkas; Gypsy Song *(rec Sept 1995)* Dorian ▲ DOR 90231 [DDD]
Reger, M.:Sons Vn, Op. 91—Nos. 1, 3, 5 & 6 *(rec Troy Savings Bank Music Hall, Troy, NY, Sept. 1994)* Dorian ▲ DOR 90212 [DDD]
Reger, M.:Sons Vn, Op. 91—Nos. 2, 4 & 7 Dorian ▲ DOR 90175 [DDD]

Mathern, Bernard (vn)
Bach, J.S.:Con 1 for 2 Hpds, w. Daniel Arrignon (ob), J.-P. Berlingen (cnd), Normandy Orchestral Ensemble [reconstructed for ob & vn in d] *(rec Kusatsu Concert Hall, Nov 2–3, 1991)* Camerata ▲ 32CM284 [DDD]

Mathews, Shirley (hpd)
Frescobaldi, G.:Toccate e partite d'intavolatura Gasparo ▲ GS 241 [ADD]
Froberger, J.J.:Hpd Music—Suite VI in C; Toccata II in d; Suite II in d; Lamentation in F; Suite XVII in F; Tombeau fait à Paris; Suite XIX in c; Suite XXIX in E♭; Toccata XIX in d; Suite XIII in d Gasparo ▲ GS 299 [DDD]
Haydn, J.:Sons Pno—5 Sonatas—H.XVI/Nos. 20, 23, 26, 28, 32 Gasparo ▲ GS 284 [DDD]

Mathieu, Bruno (org)
Dupré, M.:Sym 2 Adda ▲ ADD 581278 [DDD]
Dupré, M.:Sym-Passion, "The World Awaiting the Saviour" Adda ▲ ADD 581278 [DDD]
Vierne, L.:Sym 3 Org [Dalstein-Haerpfer Org, Eglise Saint-Sébastien de Nancy] *(rec Eglise Saint-Sébastien, Nancy, France, June 4 & 5, 1995)* Naxos ("The Organ Encyclopedia" series) ▲ 8.553524 [DDD]
Vierne, L.:Sym 6 Org [Dalstein-Haerpfer Org, Eglise Saint-Sébastien de Nancy] *(rec Eglise Saint-Sébastien, Nancy, France, June 4 & 5, 1995)* Naxos ("The Organ Encyclopedia" series) ▲ 8.553524 [DDD]

Mathieu, Chantal (hp)
Amon, J.A.:Son Fl & Hp, w. M.U. Senn (fl) *(rec 1979)* Jecklin-Disco ▲ JD 548-2 [ADD]
Martin, F.:Petite sym concertante, w. C. Rütti (hpd), V. Graf (pno), E. de Stoutz (cnd), Zurich CO Gallo ▲ CD 713 [ADD]
Spohr, L.:Son 1 Vn, w. M. U. Senn (fl) *(rec 1979)* Jecklin-Disco ▲ JD 548-2 [ADD]
Spohr, L.:Son 5 Vn, w. M. U. Senn (fl) *(rec 1979)* Jecklin-Disco ▲ JD 548-2 [ADD]

Mathieu, Ilse (vn)
Marti, H.:Correspondance (...à la sourdine), w. O. Seger (pno) Grammont ▲ CTS P 22-2 [ADD]

Mathijs, M. (pno)
Gershwin, G.:Rhap in Blue, w. N. Nozy (cnd), Belgian Guides Symphonic Band René Gailly ▲ CD 87076 [DDD]

Mathis, I. (org)
Bach, J.S.:Fugue on "Meine Seele erhebet den Herren" [at the Disentis Monastery Church Choral Organ] Ars Musici ▲ 1101 [DDD]
Bach, J.S.:Partite diverse sopra *Sei gegrüsset, Jesu gütig* [at the Disentis Monastery Church Choir Organ] Ars Musici ▲ 1101 [DDD]
Bach, J.S.:Preludes & Fugues, BWV 531–552 [at the Disentis Monastery Church Choir Organ]—in C, BWV 547 Ars Musici ▲ 1101 [DDD]
Brahms, J.:Chorale Preludes, Op. 122 [at the Monastery Church Main Organ]—Herzlich tut mich erfreuen; Schmücke dich, o liebe Seele; O wie selig seid ihr doch, ihr Frommen; O Gott, du frommer Gott Ars Musici ▲ 1101 [DDD]
Flury, P.T.:Chorale with Vars, "Maria durch ein Dornwald ging" [at the Marienkirche Organ] Ars Musici ▲ 1101 [DDD]
Gigout, E.:Toccata Org [Monastery Church Main Organ] Ars Musici ▲ 1101 [DDD]
Mendelssohn, F.:Sons Org [Monastery Church Main Organ]—Son. 3 in A Ars Musici ▲ 1101 [DDD]

Mathis-Blöchliger, Imelda (org)
Cloister Organs Disentis Ars Musici ▲ AM 1101

Mathot, Tini (hpd)
Bach, J.S.:The Art of the Fugue, w. T. Koopman (hpd)—2 harpsichord version *(rec Amsterdam, Nov 1993)* Erato ▲ 96387-2 [DDD]
Haydn, J.:Trios Pno, Vn & Vc, w. Andrew Manze (vn), Jaap ter Linden (vc)—in A, H.XV/9; in E♭, H.XV/10; in E♭, H.XV/11; in e, H.XV/12; in G, H.XV/25 *(rec Oud Katholieke Kerk, Utrecht, Nov. 1992)* Erato ▲ 4509-91728-2 [DDD]

Matiffa, Elisabeth (b vl)
Clérambault, L.N.:Cants, w. Noémi Rime (sop), Jean-Paul Fouchécourt (ten), Nicolas Rivenq (bass), Hiro Kurosaki (vn), Ryo Terakado (vn), Marc Hantaï (fl), Eric Bellocq (thb), Bruno Croscet (basse de vn), W. Christie (cnd), Les Arts Florissants—Pyrame et Tisbé, La Muse de l'opéra ou les Caractères Lyriques, La Mort d'Hercule, Orphée Musique d'Abord ▲ HMA 1901329

Matison, Yvietta (va)
Marc Grauwels & Friends, w. Marc Grauwels (fl), Marie-Noelle de Callataÿ (sop), Hiroko Masaki (sop), Dennis James (glass hmc), Ingrid Procureur (hp), Yves Storms (gtr), Mark Drobinsky (vc), Alain De Rijckere (bn), Daniel Blumenthal (pno), Frank Michiels (perc), Belgian RSO, W Syrinx 2-▲ 96101 [DDD]
Schubert, Franz:Qt Fl, w. M. Grauwels (fl), Y. Storms (gtr), M. Drobinsky (vc) Syrinx ▲ 93105 [DDD]

Mätlik, Heiki (gtr)—see ORCHESTRAS & ENSEMBLES Camerata Tallinn

Matousek, Bohuslav (vn)—see ORCHESTRAS & ENSEMBLES Stamitz String Quartet

Matoušek, Bohuslav (vn)
Haydn, J.:Con 1 Vn, w. L. Hlaváček (cnd), Prague CO Supraphonet ▲ 11 1119-2 [AAD]
Haydn, J.:Con 2 Vn, w. L. Hlaváček (cnd), Prague CO Supraphonet ▲ 11 1119-2 [AAD]
Haydn, J.:Con 4 Vn, w. L. Hlaváček (cnd), Prague CO *(rec 1971)* Supraphonet ▲ 11 1119-2 [AAD]

Matsuda, Yoko (vn)—see also ORCHESTRAS & ENSEMBLES Sequoia String Quartet
Lazarof, H.:Oct Strs, w. Yukiko Kamei (vn), Peter Marsh (vn), Miwako Watanabe (vn), Paul Silverthorne (va), Milton Thomas (va), Godfried Hoogeveen (vc), David Speltz (vc), H. Lazarof (cnd) Laurel ▲ LR 843 [DDD]
Lazarof, H.:Trio Pno, Vn & Vc, w. J. Lowenthal (pno), J. Solow (vc) Laurel ▲ LR 845CD [AAD]
Wilson, R.:Music Vn, w. F. Sherry (vc) CRI ▲ CD 602 [ADD]

Matsui, Naomi (org)
Ikebe, S.-I.:Dimorphism, w. K. Sato (cnd), Tokyo Metropolitan SO Camerata ▲ 30CM 374 [DDD]

Matsukura, Toshiyuki (uchimono)
Fujieda, M.:Music of, w. Mamoru Fujieda (cmpt), Makiko Sakurai (shomyo/Buddhist chant), Mineko Grimmer (audible sculptures), Kodo Uesugi (fukimono), Kazuko Takada (hikimono), Satoshi Sakai (uchimono), Koshin Ebihara (jumon)—The Night Chant III; Wind Chant; Cocoon Chant; Duct Chant; Falling Chant; The Night Chant I Tzadik ("The Composers" series) ▲ TZA 7003 [DDD]

Matsunaga, Kayako (pno)
Kalimullin, R.:Son 2 Pno *(rec live, Suntory Hall, Tokyo, Sept 30, 1991)* Vienna Modern Masters ▲ VMM 2013 [DDD]
Kayako Matsunaga:Pianist Vienna Modern Masters ▲ VMM 2014 [DDD]
Matsunaga, M.:Constellations, w. K. Akiyama (cnd), Tokyo SO Vienna Modern Masters ▲ VMM 3034 [DDD]

Matsuzawa, Yuki (pno)
Scriabin, A.:Etudes Pno, Op. 8 *(rec St. Martin's Church, East Woodhay, Dec. 6–7, 1993)* Pianissimo ▲ PP 10394 [DDD]
Scriabin, A.:Son 3 Pno *(rec St. Martin's Church, East Woodhay, Dec. 6–7, 1993)* Pianissimo ▲ PP 10394 [DDD]
Scriabin, A.:Son 4 Pno *(rec St. Martin's Church, East Woodhay, Dec. 6–7, 1993)* Pianissimo ▲ PP 10394 [DDD]
Scriabin, A.:Son 5 Pno *(rec St. Martin's Church, East Woodhay, Dec. 6–7, 1993)* Pianissimo ▲ PP 10394 [DDD]

Mattax, Charlotte (hpd)
Bach, J.S.:Arias, w. David Gordon (ten), Emily Newbold (fl), Loretta O'Sullivan (vc), G. Funfgeld (cnd), Bethlehem Bach Festival Orch—Ermunter dich [from Cant.180]; Der Ewigkeit [from Cant. 198]; Ach, schlage doch [from Cant. 95]; Benedictus [from Mass in b, BWV 232]; Woferne du [from Cant. 41]; O Seelenparadies [from Cant. 172]; Frohe Hirten [from Christmas Oratorio, BWV 248] *(rec St. Michael's Church, New York City, June 1994)* Newport Classic ▲ NPD 85582 [DDD]
Bach, J.S.:Partitas Hpd, BWV 825–830—BWV 828 Koch International Classics ▲ KIC 7046-2 [DDD]
Bach, J.S.:Sons (5) Kbd—in d, BWV 964 [arrangement of the solo Violin Sonata, BWV 1003] Koch International Classics ▲ KIC 7046-2 [DDD]
Bach, J.S.:Toccatas Hpd, BWV 910–16—BWV 910 & 912 Koch International Classics ▲ KIC 7046-2 [DDD]

Matteoli, Giorgio (fl)
Sammartini, G.:Sons 2 Fls, w. Tommaso Rossi (fl), Fête Rustique *(rec Jungle Studios, Milan, June 25–26, 1995)* Agora Musica ▲ AG 020 [DDD]

Mattes, Gunhard (ob)
Gerber, R.:Chamber Music, w. Fränzi Badertscher-Jaquiéry (fl), Dimitri Ashkenazy (cl), Claude Delley (cl), Pierre-Yves Dubois (cl), Anne de Dadelsen (pno)—Pièce lente; Habanera; Berceuse [all for Cl & Pno]; Trio for Fl, Ob & Pno; Son for Fl & Pno; Ballet for Fl & Pno; Sonatine for 3 Cl; Pavane for Fl & Pno; Suite for Fl & Pno; Prélude et fugue sur le nom de Bach for Cl Gallo ▲ CD 788 [DAD]

Matthe, J. (vc)—see ORCHESTRAS & ENSEMBLES Arte del Suono String Quartet

Matthes, Michaël (org)
Messiaen, O.:L'Ascension Org Deutsche Grammophon ▲ 435854-2
Michael Matthes at the Historic Klais Organ Prezioso ▲ 800.017
Saint-Saëns, C.:Sym 3, w. M.-W. Chung (cnd), Bastille Opera Orch Deutsche Grammophon ▲ 435854-2
Saint-Saëns, C.:Sym 3, w. E. Krivine (cnd), Lyon National Orch Denon ▲ CO 75024 [DDD]

Matthew, Charles (pno)
Bax, A.:Fant Son, w. Richard Crabtree (va) Olympia ▲ OLY 454 [DDD]
Bax, A.:Legend Va, w. Richard Crabtree (va) Olympia ▲ OLY 454 [DDD]
Bax, A.:Pno Music—What the Minstrel Told Us; In a Vodka Shop; 2 Russian Tone Pictures; Lullaby Olympia ▲ OLY 454 [DDD]

Matthews, David (vn)—see ORCHESTRAS & ENSEMBLES Medici String Quartet

Matthews, Denis (pno)
Beethoven, L. van:Bagatelles (24) *(rec Mozart Hall, Vienna, Nov. 12 & 13, 1958)* Vanguard Classics ▲ OVC 8073 [ADD]
Beethoven, L. van:Vars on an Original Theme, Op. 34 *(rec Mozart Hall, Vienna, Nov. 11, 1958)* Vanguard Classics ▲ OVC 8074 [ADD]
Beethoven, L. van:Vars & Fugue Pno, Op. 35, "Eroica" *(rec Mozart Hall, Vienna, Nov. 11, 1958)* Vanguard Classics ▲ OVC 8074 [ADD]
Beethoven, L. van:Vars Pno, WoO 80 *(rec Mozart Hall, Vienna, Nov. 11, 1958)* Vanguard Classics ▲ OVC 8074 [ADD]

Matthews, Graham (org)
Bach, J.S.:Clavier-Übung III Herald ▲ HAVPCD 130

Matthews, Ingrid (baroque vn)
In Stil Moderno, w. Byron Schenkman (hpd) *(rec Shrine to Music Museum, Vermillion, SD, Jan 1995)* Wildboar ▲ WLBR 9512 [DDD]

Matthews, Ingrid (vn)—see also ORCHESTRAS & ENSEMBLES Zephyrus, Zephyrus members
Jacquet De La Guerre, E.:Sons Vn, w. Byron Schenkman (hpd), Margriet Tindemans (vl) Wildboar ▲ WLBR 9601 [DDD]
Jacquet De La Guerre, E.:Suites Hpd, w. Byron Schenkman (hpd), Margriet Tindemans (vl)—Prélude in a; Toccata; Chaconne "L'Inconstante" Wildboar ▲ WLBR 9601 [DDD]

Matthews, S. (hpd)
Frescobaldi, G.:Hpd Music Gasparo ▲ GS 241 ■ GS 241C

Matthews, William (gtr)
Music for Lute, Guitar & Mandolin, w. Konrad Ragossnig (gtr), Anton Stingl (lt), Michael Schäffer (lt), Karl Scheit (gtr), Leo Witoszinskyj (gtr), Paul Grund (mand), Artur Rumetsch (mand), Edith Bauer-Slais (mand), Elfriede Kunschak (mand) Vox Box 3-▲ CD3X 3022

Matthies, Silke-Thora (pno)
Dvořák, A.:From the Bohemian Forest, w. Christian Köhn (pno) *(rec Sandhausen, Apr 1995)* Naxos ▲ 8.553137 [DDD]
Dvořák, A.:Legends, Op. 59, w. Christian Köhn (pno) *(rec Sandhausen, Apr 1995)* Naxos ▲ 8.553137 [DDD]
Dvořák, A.:Slavonic Dances (comp), w. Christian Köhn (pno) *(rec Sandhausen, Apr 1995)* Naxos ▲ 8.553138 [DDD]
Dvořák, A.:Slavonic Dances (comp), w. Christian Köhn (pno) *(rec Sandhausen, Apr 1995)* Naxos ▲ 8.553138 [DDD]
Klebe, G.:Feuersturz *(rec Cologne, Jan. 23–25, 1995)* Marco Polo ("WDR" series) ▲ 8.223712 [DDD]
Klebe, G.:Glockentürme, w. Christian Köhn (pno) *(rec Cologne, Jan. 23–25, 1995)* Marco Polo ("WDR" series) ▲ 8.223712 [DDD]
Klebe, G.:Music of, w. Christian Köhn (pno), J. Jacobs (acc), Cologne Chamber Choir—Warum hat die sonne einen Aschenrand; Der Schrei; Glockentürme Academy ▲ ACA 8509
Klebe, G.:Nachklang for 2 Pnos, w. Christian Köhn (pno) *(rec Cologne, Jan. 23–25, 1995)* Marco Polo ("WDR" series) ▲ 8.223712 [DDD]
Klebe, G.:Son for 2 Pnos, w. Christian Köhn (pno) *(rec Cologne, Jan. 23–25, 1995)* Marco Polo ("WDR" series) ▲ 8.223712 [DDD]

INSTRUMENT.

Matthys, Mary Gifford (org)
Historic Organs of New Orleans, w. George Bozeman (org), James S. Darling (org), Jesse E. Eschbach (org), Gerald D. Frank (org), John Gearhart (org), James Hammann (org), Frederick Hohman (org), Lenora McCroskey (org), Lorenz Maycher (org), Donald Messer (org) *(rec June 1989)* Organ Historical Society 2-▲ OHS 89

Mattila, Anssi (hpd)
Bach, J.S.:Partita Fl, BWV 1013, w. Petri Alanko (fl) *(rec Järvenpää, Dec 1995)* Naxos ▲ 8.553754 [DDD]
Bach, J.S.:Sons Fl, BWV 1030–35, w. Petri Alanko (fl)—BWV 1031, 1032 & 1034 [w. Jukka Rautasalo (vc)] *(rec Järvenpää, Dec 1995)* Naxos ▲ 8.553754 [DDD]
Bach, J.S.:Sons Fl, BWV 1030–35, w. Petri Alanko (fl)—BWV 1031, 1032 & 1034 [w. Jukka Rautasalo (vc)] *(rec Järvenpää Hall, Dec 1995)* Naxos ▲ 8.553754 [DDD]

Mattis, K. (vn)
Mozart, W.A.:Qnt Hn, K.407, w. R. Pandolfi (hn), J. Korman (vn), J. Korman (va), J. Sant'Ambrogio (vc) *(rec 1975–79)* Vox Box 3-▲ CD3X 3014 [ADD]

Matus, J. (elec gtr)
Shields, A.:Apocalypse, w. A. Shields (voc/kbd/syn—The Woman, the Seaweed & Chorus), M. Willson (Shiva) CRI ▲ CD 647 [DDD]

Matuz, István (fl)
Pierné, G.:Son Vn, w. N. Szelecsenyi (pno) Marco Polo ▲ 8.223189

Mätzener, H. (cl)
Milhaud, D.:Caprice, w. R. Hairgrove (pno) Koch Schwann ▲ 3-1310-2 [DDD]
Milhaud, D.:Duo concertante Cl & Pno, w. R. Hairgrove (pno) Koch Schwann ▲ 3-1310-2 [DDD]
Milhaud, D.:Petit Concert, w. R. Hairgrove (pno) Koch Schwann ▲ 3-1310-2 [DDD]
Milhaud, D.:Sonatina Cl, w. R. Hairgrove (pno) Koch Schwann ▲ 3-1310-2 [DDD]

Mauersberger, Rudolf (pno/cnd)
From Boy Alto of the Dresden Kreuzchor to Lyric Tenor, w. Peter Schreier (alt/ten), Walter Olbertz (pno), Norman Shetler (pno), various orchs *(rec ca. 1950)* Berlin Classics 4-▲ BER 9041 [ADD]

Mauk, Steven (a sax)
Distances within Me:Contemporary Classics for Alto Saxophone, w. Steven Mauk (s sax), Mary Ann Covert (pno) Open Loop ▲ OL 012

Mauk, Steven (s sax)
Bach, J.S.:Music of, w. Mary Ann Covert (pno)— Suite 2, BWV 1067 [Bandinerie; arr Mauk/Covert]; Pastorale in F, BWV 590 [Aria; arr M. Brown]; Son in g, BWV 1020 [arr J. Harle]; Suite 3, BWV 1068 [Air; arr N. Ramsay]; Cant 147, Jesu, Joy of Man's Desiring [arr Mauk/Covert]; Son in C, BWV 1033 [arr C. F. Peters] Cant 156 [Sinf; arr H. Voxman]; Prelude in C [Ave maria; arr Mauk/Covert]; Partita Fl in A, BWV 1013 [arr P. G. Buffardin] *(rec Ithaca, NY, May 1994)* Open Loop ▲ 029
Classical Bouquet:Music for Soprano Saxophone & Piano, w. Mary Ann Covert (pno) Open Loop ▲ OL 008
Distances within Me:Contemporary Classics for Alto Saxophone, w. S. Mauk (a sax), Mary Ann Covert (pno) Open Loop ▲ OL 012

Mauk, Steven (sax)
Kupferman, M.:Sound Phantoms 7, w. G. Stout (perc) Soundspells ▲ SP 103

Mauk, Steven (t sax)
Tenor Excursions, w. Mary Ann Covert (pno) *(rec Walter Ford Hall Auditorium, Ithaca College, Ithaca, New York, June 1–3, 1993)* Open Loop ▲ OL 019 [DDD]

Maule, Carolyn (pno)
Le Souvenir, w. Sally Dibblee (sop), Russell Braun (bar) Centrediscs ("Lacalée" series) ▲ CMC CD 5696 [DDD]

Maund, P. (perc)
Jewels of the Sephardim, Vol. 1:Songs from Medieval Spain, w. L. Pomerantz (vocs/period dlc), K. Higginson (rcr) Songbird ▲ AEACD 1401
Jewels of the Sephardim, Vol. 2:Wings of Time—The Sephardic Legacy of Multi-Cultural Medieval Spain, w. L. Pomerantz (vocs/period dlc), K. Higginson (rcr), S. Kammen (vielle/rebec) Songbird ▲ AEACD 1405

Maunu, Pete (acoustic/elec/12string gtr)
Passage, 138 B.C.–A.D. 1611, w. Empire Brass Quintet, Laurie Monahan (sgr), M. Collver (sgr), Doug Lunn (fretless bass), D. Goldblatt (syn), K. Wortman (elec/acoustic perc) *(rec Lenox, MA & Los Angeles, CA May 27–29 & June 28–July)* Telarc ▲ CD 80355 [DDD]

Maur, Mauro (tpt)
Dashow, J.:Morfologie *(rec Wonderland Studio, Rome)* Neuma ▲ 45090 [DDD]

Maurer, Laurel Ann (alt fl)
Kraft, L.:Cloud Studies, w. Lisa Maron (pic), Margaret Swinchoski (pic), Tanya Dusevic (fl), Adrienne Flynn (fl), Christina Jennings (fl), Zara Lawler (fl), Joseph Piscitelli (fl), Michelle Ryang (fl), Dominique Soucy (fl), Diane Taublieb (fl), Richard Wyton (alt fl), J. Solum (cnd) *(rec Skinner Recital Hall, Vassar College, Poughkeepsie, NY, Mar 24–26, 1994)* CRI ▲ CD 712 [DDD]

Maurer, Laurel Ann (fl)
Barber, S.:Canzone Fl & Pno, w. Joanne Martin Pearce (pno) Albany ▲ TROY 167 [DDD]
Copland, A.:Duo Fl, w. Joanne Martin Pearce (pno) Albany ▲ TROY 167 [DDD]
Kraft, L.:Fant Fl & Pno, w. Joanne Martin Pearce (pno) Albany ▲ TROY 167 [DDD]
Kupferman, M.:Chaconne Son, w. Joanne Martin Pearce (pno) Albany ▲ TROY 167 [DDD]
Muczynski, R.:Son Fl, w. Joanne Martin Pearce (pno) Albany ▲ TROY 167 [DDD]
Tower, J.:Hexachords Albany ▲ TROY 167 [DDD]

Maurer, M. (cl)
Wyttenbach, J.:Lamentoroso, w. L. Akerlund (sop), H. Bissegger (cl), N. Calame (cl), E. Molinari (cl), M. Weber (cl), H. Zwahlen (cl) *(rec May 19–20, 1990)* Grammont ▲ CTSP 37-2 [ADD]

Maurer, Peter (pno)—see ORCHESTRAS & ENSEMBLES Rondo Piano

Maurette, Ariane (vl)
Couperin, F.:Pièces de violes avec la bass chifrée, w. J. Savall (vl), T. Koopman (hpd) Astrée ▲ E 7744 [AAD]

Maurette, Ariane (vl/rcr)—see ORCHESTRAS & ENSEMBLES Isabella D'Este

Maury, C. (hn)—see ORCHESTRAS & ENSEMBLES Biedermeier Quintet, Biedermeier Quintet members

Maury, Lowndes (pno)
Copland, A.:Son Vn & Pno, w. M. Sandler (vn)—originally released 1970 Crystal ■ C631
Ives, C.:Sons Vn, w. M. Sandler (vn)—No. 2 Crystal ■ C631
Maury, L.:Son in Memory of the Korean War, w. M. Sandler (vn) Crystal ■ C631

Maus, Frank (pno)
Kahn, E.I.:Chansons Populaires, w. C. Gayer (sop) CRI ▲ CD 563 [DDD]
Kahn, E.I.:Pieces on Medieval German Poems, w. C. Gayer (sop) [G,F] CRI ▲ CD 563 [DDD]

Mauser, Shawn (bn)
Sierra, R.:Con Tres, w. William Helmers (cl), Stefanie Jacob (pno) CRI ▲ CD 724 [DDD]

Mauser, Siegfried (pno)
Hartmann, K.A.:Jazz-Toccata & Fugue Virgin Classics ▲ CDC 59017
Hartmann, K.A.:Kleine Suiten (2) Virgin Classics ▲ CDC 59017
Hartmann, K.A.:Son:27 April 1945 Virgin Classics ▲ CDC 59017
Hindemith, P.:Con Pno, w. W.A. Albert (cnd), Frankfurt RSO CPO ▲ CPO 999078-2 [DDD]
Hindemith, P.:The Four Temperaments, w. W.A. Albert (cnd), Frankfurt RSO CPO ▲ CPO 999078-2 [DDD]
Hindemith, P.:Kammermusik 2, w. W.A. Albert (cnd), Frankfurt RSO CPO ▲ CPO 999138 [DDD]
Hindemith, P.:Klaviermusik Book 1—Nos. 1 & 2 Wergo ▲ WER 6271-2
Hindemith, P.:Ludus Tonalis Wergo ▲ WER 6250-2
Hindemith, P.:Tanzstücke Wergo ▲ WER 6271-2
Killmayer, W.:Brahms-Bildnis, w. C. Altenburger (vn), J. Berger (vc) CPO ▲ CPO 999020-2 [DDD]
Killmayer, W.:Qt Pno, w. C. Altenburger (vn), B. Westphal (va), J. Berger (vc) CPO ▲ CPO 999020-2 [DDD]
Killmayer, W.:Romances, w. C. Altenburger (vn) CPO ▲ CPO 999020-2 [DDD]

Mautz, Jennifer (timp)
Rutter, J.:Requiem, w. Karyn List (sop), Kathy Farmer (fl), Barbara Cook (ob), Julie Albertson (hp), Mary Alice Swope (vc), Tom Alderman (org), Mike Del Campo (perc), Michael O'Neal (cnd), Michael O'Neal Singers *(rec Roswell United Methodist Church, Atlanta, GA, Mar 27, 1995)* ACA Digital Recording ▲ CM 20048 [DDD]

Max, Randy (timp)
Hovhaness, A.:Tzaikerk, w. Paul Edmund-Davies (fl), Arnold Kobyliansky (vn), R. Werthen (cnd), I Fiamminghi CO *(rec Basilica of Bonne Espérance, Vellereille-les-Brayeux, Belgium, Aug. 18–20, 1994)* Telarc ▲ CD 80392 [DDD]

Maxián, František (pno)
Dvořák, A.:Qnt Pno, Op. 81, w. Ondriček String Quartet Praga ▲ PR 250078
Fišer, L.:Con for 2 Pnos, w. Garrick Ohlsson (pno), L. Pešek (cnd), Czech PO Supraphon ▲ SUP 0035 [DDD]
Franck, C.:Les Djinns, w. J. Fournet (cnd), Czech PO Supraphon ("Collection" series) ▲ 11 0613-2 [ADD]
Kabeláč, M.:Fated Dramas of Man, w. M. Kejmar (tpt), Prague Percussion Ensemble *(rec 1993)* Panton ▲ PAN 811143
Prokofiev, S.:Con 3 Pno, w. A. Klima (cnd), Prague RSO Sound ▲ 3437 [AAD]

Maximilien, Wanda (pno)
Bazelon, I.:Imprints...On Ivory & Strs CRI ■ CAS 532
Bazelon, I.:Pieces (5) Pno CRI ■ CAS 532
Bazelon, I.:Trajectories, w. H. Farberman (cnd), London SO Albany ▲ TROY 054 [DDD]

Maxin, Jack (pno)
Wolpe, S.:Qt Tpt, w. Bob Nagel (tpt), Al Cohn (t sax), Al Howard (perc), S. Baron (cnd) *(rec Esoteric Studios, NY, 1954)* Hat Hut ▲ CD 6182 [AAD]

Maxin, Nicolae (fl)
Enescu, G.:Dectet Ww, w. Virgil Francu (fl), Valeriu Barbuceanu (cl), Leontin Boanta (cl), Adrian Petrescu (ob), Viorica Feher (bn), Goedri Orban (bn), Florin Ionoaia (Eng hn), Dan Cinca (hn), Simon Jebeleanu (hn), H. Andreescu (cnd) Olympia ▲ OLY 445 [DDD]

Maxwell, Melinda (ob)
Gough, O.:Late, w. Roger Heaton (cl), Orlando Gough (kbd), Smith String Quartet *(rec London, 1995)* Catalyst ▲ 0902-668332-2 [DDD]

May, Angelica (vc)
Bach, J.S.:Anna Magdalena Bach Notebook, w. E. Ameling (sop), H.-M. Linde (bar), G. Leonhardt (hpd), J. Koch (va)—sels. Editio Classica ▲ 77150-2-RG [DDD]
Dvořák, A.:Con Vc, w. V. Neumann (cnd), Czech PO Supraphon ▲ SUP 11 1544 [DDD]
Dvořák, A.:Rondo, w. V. Neumann (cnd), Czech PO Supraphon ▲ SUP 11 1544 [DDD]
Dvořák, A.:Silent Woods, w. V. Neumann (cnd), Czech PO Supraphon ▲ SUP 11 1544 [DDD]

May, E. (fl)—see ORCHESTRAS & ENSEMBLES Vienna Flautists

Mayama-Livesay, Y. (pno)
Waschka (II), R.:Last Night, w. P. Barham (sax) Centaur ▲ CRC 2133 [DDD]

Maycher, Lorenz (org)
Historic Organs of New Orleans, w. George Bozeman (org), James S. Darling (org), Jesse E. Eschbach (org), Gerald D. Frank (org), John Gearhart (org), James Hammann (org), Frederick Hohman (org), Lenora McCroskey (org), Mary Gifford Matthys (org), Donald Messer (org) *(rec June 1989)* Organ Historical Society 2-▲ OHS 89
Sowerby, L.:Dialogue, w. James Culp (pno) [1949 Aeolian-Skinner Org, 1st Presbyterian Church, Kilgore, TX] *(rec Oct. 21, 1994)* Raven ▲ OAR 310 [DDD]
Sowerby, L.:Org Music [1949 Aeolian-Skinner Org, 1st Presbyterian Church, Kilgore, TX]—Comes Autumn Time; Requiescat in pace; Air w. Vars; Arioso; Whimsical Vars; Sonatina; Carillon [William Watkins (org); rec. 1951] *(rec Oct. 21, 1994)* Raven ▲ OAR 310 [DDD]

Mayer, Albrecht (ob)—see ORCHESTRAS & ENSEMBLES Sabine Meyer Wind Ensemble

Mayer, Lajos (mand)
Beethoven, L. van:Adagio, WoO 43/2 & Andante & Vars, WoO 44/2, w. Rohmann (pno) Hungaroton ▲ HCD 12303
Beethoven, L. van:Sonatina Mand, WoO 43, w. I. Rohmann (pno) Hungaroton ▲ HCD 12303
Beethoven, L. van:Sonatina Mand, WoO 44, w. I. Rohmann (pno) Hungaroton ▲ HCD 12303
Vivaldi, A.:Cons Diverse Instrs, w. B. Glaetzner (ob), Güttler (tpt), Sandau (tpt), Botvay, Pommer (cnd), New Bach Collegium Musicum, Budapest Strings LaserLight ▲ 15518 [DDD]

Mayer, Steven (pno)
Liszt, F.:Divertissement sur la cavatine "I tuoi frequenti palpiti" ASV ▲ ASV 783 [DDD]
Liszt, F.:Harmonies poétiques et religieuses ASV ▲ ASV 783 [DDD]
Liszt, F.:Pno Music (misc)—Bénédiction de Dieu dans le solitude (from Harmonies poétiques et religieuses); Divertissement sur la cavatine "I tuoi frequenti palpiti" from Pacini's Niobe, S.419; Solo piano transcription of Weber's Konzertstück in f, Op. 79 ASV ▲ ASV 783 [DDD]
Liszt, F.:Transcriptions & Paraphrases—Weber:Konzertstück in f, Op. 79 ASV ▲ ASV 783 [DDD]
Thalberg, S.:Fants & Vars on Opera Themes—Fants. on themes from Rossini's Mosè ASV ▲ ASV 783 [DDD]
Thalberg, S.:Fant on "God Save the Queen" ASV ▲ ASV 783 [DDD]

Mayer, Xaver (org)
Schubert, Franz:Mass 1, w. Laurence Dutoit (sop), Rose Bahl (alt), Kurt Equiluz (ten), Kunikazu Ohashi (bass), G. Barati (cnd), Vienna State Opera Orch, Vienna Academy Chamber Choir *(rec 1960)* Tuxedo ▲ TUXCD 1040 [ADD]
Schubert, Franz:Mass 4, w. Laurence Dutoit (sop), Rose Bahl (alt), Kurt Equiluz (ten), Kunikazu Ohashi (bass), G. Barati (cnd), Vienna State Opera Orch, Vienna Academy Chamber Choir *(rec 1960)* Tuxedo ▲ TUXCD 1040 [ADD]

Mayerl, Billy (pno)
Mayerl, W.J.:Music of, w. Raie Da Costa (pno), R. Noble (cnd), New Mayfair Orch, Fred Hartley Quintet—Marigold; Pianolettes (6); Pno Exaggerations (4); 4 aces Suite; plus others Happy Days Nostalgia ▲ CDHD 205

Mayforth, R. (vn)—see ORCHESTRAS & ENSEMBLES Lark String Quartet

Maynard, J. D. (org)
Van Appledorn, M.J.:Missa Brevis, w. B. Hagemeier (sop) CRS ▲ CD 9052

Mayorga, Lincoln (pno)
Beach, A.M.C.:Compositions, w. Arnold Steinhardt (vn) Sheffield Lab ▲ SLS 10063
A Bouquet of Familiar Classics Town Hall ▲ THCD 40
Brahms, J.:Pieces Pno, Op. 119 Sheffield Lab ("Salon" series) ▲ SLS 505
Chopin, F.:Prelude in A♭ Sheffield Lab ("Salon" series) ▲ SLS 505
Chopin, F.:Prelude, Op. 45 Sheffield Lab ("Salon" series) ▲ SLS 505
Dvořák, A.:Romantic Pieces, Op. 75, w. A. Steinhardt (vn) Sheffield Lab ("Audiophile Reference" series) ▲ 10039-2
Dvořák, A.:Romantic Pieces, Op. 75, w. Arnold Steinhardt (vn) Sheffield Lab ▲ SLS 10039
Dvořák, A.:Sonatina Vn, w. A. Steinhardt (vn) Sheffield Lab ("Audiophile Reference" series) ▲ 10039-2
Dvořák, A.:Sonatina Vn, w. Arnold Steinhardt (vn) Sheffield Lab ▲ SLS 10039
Dvořák, A.:Sonatina Vn, w. A. Steinhardt (vn) *(rec Culver City, CA, Nov 30– Dec 1, 1985)* Sheffield Lab ("Salon" series) ▲ SLS 501
Fiddle-de-Bop:American Music for Violin & Piano, w. Linda Rosenthal (vn) *(rec East Chatham, New York, Jan 1995)* Town Hall ▲ THCD 45
Gershwin, G.:"I Got Rhythm" Vars, w. D. Kitayenko (cnd), Moscow PO Sheffield Lab ▲ CD 28
Gershwin, G.:Music of, w. D. Kitayenko (cnd), Moscow PO—I Got Rhythms Vars for Pno & Orch; Rhap in Blue; Promenade [Walking the Dog]; 3 Preludes; 2 Waltzes in C; Rialto Ripples Rag; Impromptu in 2 Keys; Lullaby for Str Qt; Summertime [Impromptu Jam] Sheffield Lab ▲ SLS 10044
Gershwin, G.:Preludes (3) Pno Sheffield Lab ▲ CD 28
Gershwin, G.:Rhap in Blue, w. D. Kitayenko (cnd), Moscow PO Sheffield Lab ▲ CD 28
Gershwin, G.:Songs, w. M. Nixon (sop) Reference ▲ RR 19CD [DDD]
Grieg, E.:Son 3 Vn, w. Arnold Steinhardt (vn) Sheffield Lab ▲ SLS 10063
Grieg, E.:Son 3 Vn, w. A. Steinhardt (vn) *(rec Culver City, CA, Nov 30– Dec 1, 1985)* Sheffield Lab ("Salon" series) ▲ SLS 501

▲ = CD ♦ = Enhanced CD △ = MD ■ = Cassette Tape □ = DCC

Mayorga, Lincoln (pno) (cont.)
Herbert, V.:A la Valse, w. Arnold Steinhardt (vn) Sheffield Lab ▲ SLS 10063
Herbert, V.:A la Valse, w. A. Steinhardt (vn) *(rec Culver City, CA, Nov 30- Dec 1, 1985)* Sheffield Lab ("Salon" series) ▲ SLS 501
Kern, J.:Songs, w. M. Nixon (sop) Reference ▲ RR 28CD [DDD]
Kreisler, F.:Apple Blossoms (sels), w. Arnold Steinhardt (vn)—Who Can Tell?; Miniature Viennese March; Syncopation; Cavatina; Hungarian Dance Sheffield Lab ▲ SLS 10063
Kreisler, F.:Vn Pieces, w. A. Steinhardt (vn)—Miniature Viennese March; Syncopation; Who can tell? [all from the operetta Apple Blossoms]; Cavatina; Hungarian Dance in f *(rec Culver City, CA, Nov 30- Dec 1, 1985)* Sheffield Lab ("Salon" series) ▲ SLS 501
Prokofiev, S.:Pieces Pno, Op. 96 Sheffield Lab ("Salon" series) ▲ SLS 505
Strauss, R.:Son Vn, w. A. Steinhardt (vn) Sheffield Lab ("Audiophile Reference" series) ▲ 10039-2
Strauss, R.:Son Vn, w. Arnold Steinhardt (vn) Sheffield Lab ▲ SLS 10039

Mayorov, Alexander (vn)
Mozart, W.A.:Serenata Notturna, w. Irina Belskaya (vn), Ilya Shpiegelman (va), Sergey Kirichenko (db), A. Rudin (cnd), Musica Viva CO *(rec Moscow Conservatory Great Hall, 1996)* Russian Compact Disc ▲ RCD 30201 [DDD]

Mayr, Fritz (jew's hp)
Albrechtsberger, J.G.:Cons Jew's Hp, w. D. Kirsch (mandora), H. Stadlmair (cnd), Munich CO Orfeo ▲ 035821 [DDD]

Mazur, M. (dr)—see ORCHESTRAS & ENSEMBLES Antifonale Chamber Ensemble

Mazurkevich, Yuri (vn)—see ORCHESTRAS & ENSEMBLES Leontóvych String Quartet

Mazza, Arturo (va)
Paisiello, G.:Qts Fl, w. Luigi Palmisano (fl), Franco Mezzena (vn), Donna Magendanz (vc) *(rec Trento, Italy, Nov 1979)* Dynamic ▲ CDS 12 [ADD]

Mazza, Luigi (vn)—see ORCHESTRAS & ENSEMBLES Giovane Quartetto Italiano

Mazza, Matteo (dr)
Bolling, C.:Con Gtr, w. Franco Trentin (gtr), Ivo Antognini (pno), Rino Rossi (db) Gallo ▲ CD 820 [DDD]

Mazza, Roberto (ob)
Battiato, F.:Haiku, w. Franco Battiato (voc), Pouran Ghaffarpour (voc), Antonio Ballista (pno), Marco Boni (vc), Guido Corti (cnt), Filippo Destrieri (kbd/computer), John Giblin (bass), Gavin Harrison (dr/perc), Jakko Jakszyk (gtr), Fabrizio Merlini (va), Angelo Privitera (kbd/computer), Mino Bordignon (cnd), Milan Chamber Music Choir Hemisphere ▲ 837234-2
Battiato, F.:Ricerca sul Terzo, w. Franco Battiato (voc), Alessio Alba (tamboura), Antonio Ballista (pno), Marco Boni (vc), Debendra Kanti Chakraborty (tabla), Guido Corti (cnt), Filippo Destrieri (kbd/computer), John Giblin (bass), Buddhadeu Das Gupta (sarod), Gavin Harrison (dr/perc), Jakko Jakszyk (gtr), Fabrizio Merlini (va), Angelo Privitera (kbd/computer), Mino Bordignon (cnd), Milan Chamber Music Choir Hemisphere ▲ 837234-2

Mazzanti, Allesandra (org)
Liszt, F.:Via Crucis, w. Elisa Savani Zamballi (sop), Simone Alberghini (bar), Bonifacio Manduchi (cnd), Fabio de Bologne Polyphonic Chorus [orig version] Studio SM 2-▲ 2515 [DDD]

Mazzanti, Livia (org)
Hindemith, P.:Sons Org Fonè ▲ 92 F 03 [DDD]
Messiaen, O.:L'Ascension Org Fonè ▲ 92 F 03 [DDD]
Scelsi, G.:In nomine lucis Fonè ▲ 92 F 03 [DDD]
Schoenberg, A.:Vars on a Recitative Org Fonè ▲ 92 F 03 [DDD]

Mazzola, Patrizio (pno)
Schumann, C.:Romances Pno Pan Classics ▲ CD 510091 [DDD]
Schumann, R.:Impromptus on a Theme by Clara Wieck Pno, Op. 5 Pan Classics ▲ CD 510091 [DDD]
Schumann, R.:Romances Pno Pan Classics ▲ CD 510091 [DDD]
Schumann, R.:Son Pno, Op. 14 Pan Classics ▲ CD 510091 [DDD]

Mazzoleni, N. (vn)—see ORCHESTRAS & ENSEMBLES Concerto Rococo

Mazzoli, Carlo (pno)
Ravel, M.:Shéhérazade Mez, w. Stefano Malferrari (pno) [arr. Ravel for Pno 4-Hands] Nuova Era ▲ NUO 7205 [DDD]
Rimsky-Korsakov, N.:Scheherazade, w. Stefano Malferrari (pno) [arr. Rimsky-Korsakov for Pno 4-Hands] Nuova Era ▲ NUO 7205 [DDD]

Mealy, R. (h-g)—see ORCHESTRAS & ENSEMBLES Project Ars Nova Ensemble

Meanwell, George (vc/gtr/mand)—see ORCHESTRAS & ENSEMBLES Gelato Quartet

Mechler, Thierry (org)
Bach, J.S.:Org Music (misc)—Chorale, Schmücke dich, O liebe Seele; Chorale, Nun komm der heiden Heiland, BWV 659; Fantasia & Fugue in g, BWV 542; Preludes & Fugues, BWV 541 & 548; Toccata & Fugue in F, BWV 540; Trio Sonata in C REM ▲ 311144 XCD [DDD]
Liszt, F.:Fant & Fugue on "Ad nos, ad salutarem undam" Org [Fischer & Krämer organ at the Notre-Dame Basilica at Thierenbach] REM ▲ REM 311203 [DDD]
Liszt, F.:Orpheus [Fischer & Krämer organ at the Notre-Dame Basilica at Thierenbach] REM ▲ REM 311203 [DDD]
Noëls (13 Noëls for organ) Motette ▲ CD 11351 [DDD]
Reubke, J.:Son Org [Fischer & Krämer organ at the Notre-Dame Basilica at Thierenbach] REM ▲ REM 311203 [DDD]
Schumann, R.:Org Music (comp)—6 Fugues on B-A-C-H, Op. 60; 6 Studies in Canon Form for Pedal-Piano, Op. 56; 4 Skizzen for Pedal Piano, Op. 58 Motette ▲ CD 11041 [DDD]

Meckier, M. (hpd)
Fleischer, T.:Girl-Butterfly-Girl, w. G. Abrahamson (sop), N. Rogel (rcr) Opus One ▲ Cd 158 [DDD]

Medeiros, Xisto (db)—see ORCHESTRAS & ENSEMBLES Paraíba Quintet

Medlam, Charles (vc)—see also ORCHESTRAS & ENSEMBLES London Baroque
Muffat, G.:Son Vn, w. London Baroque Musique d'Abord ▲ HMA 1901220

Mednikoff, Nikolai (pno)
The Victor Recordings (1926-1928), w. Pablo Casals (vc) Biddulph ▲ LAB 017 [ADD]

Medveczky, A. (hn)
Haydn, J.:Diverts for 2 Obs, Hns & Bns, H.II/7, 15, D18, 23 & deest, w. P Pongrácz (ob), B. Hock (ob), D. Mesterházy (hn), T. Fülemile (bn), A. Nagy (bn) White Label ▲ HRC 155 [ADD]

Medvedeva, Irina (vn)
Prokofiev, S.:Mélodies, w. Boris Petrov (pno) Musidisc ▲ MUS 291462 [DDD]
Prokofiev, S.:Son 1 Vn, w. Boris Petrov (pno) Musidisc ▲ MUS 291462 [DDD]
Prokofiev, S.:Son 2 Vn, w. Boris Petrov (pno) Musidisc ▲ MUS 291462 [DDD]

Meecham, Nicola (pno)
Schwertsik, K.:Nocturnes Pno *(rec May 1994)* Largo ▲ 5125 [DDD]

Meekes, Michael (tpt)
Vivaldi, A.:Cons Diverse Instrs, w. Joanna Graham (bn), Ruth McDowall (cl), David Rix (ct), Deborah Davis (fl), Duke Dobing (fl), Tim Caister (hn), Stephen Stirling (hn), Christopher Hooker (ob), Helen McQueen (ob), Crispian Steele-Perkins (tpt), Nicholas Kraemer (hpd), N. Kraemer (cnd), London Sinfonietta—Cons. in F, RV.539; in C, RV.533; in D, RV.122; in C, RV.537; in C, RV.560; in F, RV.538; in G, RV.545 *(rec All Saints Church, East Finchley, Oct. 1994 & Jan. 1995)* Naxos ("Vivaldi Collection" series) ▲ 8.553204 [DDD]
Vivaldi, A.:Con for 2 Tpts, w. C. Steele-Perkins (tpt), N. Ward (vn), A. Watkinson (vn), A. Watkinson (cnd), City of London Sinfonia Virgin Classics ▲ CDZ 59651

Meer, Janneke van der (db)
Hollander, H.:Sacred Music, w. S. van Grootel (sop), K. van der Poel (mez), J. Boswinkel (bass), P. Rikkers (vn), T. van Eijk (org), Cappella Breda—Cantabant sancti; Domine Jesu Christe; Domine Deus; Ecce vicit leo; O nomen Jesu; Recipe me; Quem vidistis pastores; Sanctus Jacobus; Quid est hoc; O vos omnes; Ecce clamo; Ave Maria; O Beatum Virum; O bone Jesu; Te gloriosus Erasmus ▲ WVH 047 [DDD]

Meer, Richte van der (vc)—see also ORCHESTRAS & ENSEMBLES Al Ayre Español
Boismortier, J.B. de:Sons, Op. 40, w. D. Bond (bn)—No. 1 Accent ▲ 58331 [DDD]
Boismortier, J.B. de:Sons, Op. 26, w. D. Bond (bn), R. Kohnen (hpd)—Nos. 1, 2 & 3 Accent ▲ 58331 [DDD]
Corrette, M.:Sons, w. D. Bond (bn), R. Kohnen (hpd)—Sons. 1, 3 & 5 Accent ▲ 58331 [DDD]

Meer, Richte van der (vc) (cont.)
de Fesch, W.:Son Voice, w. R. Kanji (fl), J. Ogg (hpd)—No. 1 *(rec Apr. 1993)* Globe ▲ GLO 5101 [DDD]
Devienne, F.:Sons Bn, Op. 24, w. D. Bond (bn), R. Kohnen (hpd) *(rec Dec. 1992)* Accent ▲ 9290
Geminiani, F.:Sons Vc & Continuo, Op. 5, w. R. Dieltiens (vc), R. Kohnen (hpd)—Sonata in d; Sonata No. 3 in C; Sonata No. 6 in a Accent ▲ 9181 [DDD]
Ruloffs, B.:Sons Hpd, w. T. Mothot (hpd), M. Huggett (vn)—No. 1 in G Erasmus ▲ WVH 010 [ADD]
Schenck, J.:Fant 1 Voc, w. R. Kanji (rcr), J. Ogg (hpd) *(rec Apr. 1993)* Globe ▲ GLO 5101 [DDD]
Telemann, G.P.:Con Tpt 2 Obs, w. Per-Olev Lindeke (tpt), Taka Kitazato (ob), Marcel Ponseele (ob), Fred Jacobs (thb), Pierre Hantaï (hpd) *(rec St. Stefanus, Melsen, Belgium, June 1995)* Accent ▲ 95110 [DDD]
Telemann, G.P.:Essercizii musici (sels), w. Taka Kitazato (ob), Marcel Ponseele (ob), Pierre Hantaï (hpd), Per-Olev Lindeke (tpt), Fred Jacobs (thb)—Trio Son in E♭ for Ob, Hpd & Continuo *(rec St. Stefanus, Melsen, Belgium, June 1995)* Accent ▲ 95110 [DDD]
Telemann, G.P.:Der Getreue Music-Meister (sels), w. Taka Kitazato (ob), Marcel Ponseele (ob), Per-Olev Lindeke (tpt), Fred Jacobs (thb), Pierre Hantaï (hpd)—Son in a *(rec St. Stefanus, Melsen, Belgium, June 1995)* Accent ▲ 95110 [DDD]
Telemann, G.P.:Kleine Kammermusik, w. Taka Kitazato (ob), Marcel Ponseele (ob), Per-Olev Lindeke (tpt), Fred Jacobs (thb), Pierre Hantaï (hpd)—Partita IV in g *(rec St. Stefanus, Melsen, Belgium, June 1995)* Accent ▲ 95110 [DDD]
Telemann, G.P.:Musique de Table, w. Taka Kitazato (ob), Marcel Ponseele (ob), Per-Olev Lindeke (tpt), Fred Jacobs (thb), Pierre Hantaï (hpd)—Son in g *(rec St. Stefanus, Melsen, Belgium, June 1995)* Accent ▲ 95110 [DDD]
Telemann, G.P.:Son 2 Ob, w. Taka Kitazato (ob), Marcel Ponseele (ob), Per-Olev Lindeke (tpt), Fred Jacobs (thb), Pierre Hantaï (hpd) *(rec St. Stefanus, Melsen, Belgium, June 1995)* Accent ▲ 95110 [DDD]
Van Wassenaer, U.:Sons Rcr, w. R. Kanji (rcr), J. Ogg (hpd)—Primata in F; Seconda in g; Terza in g *(rec Apr. 1993)* Globe ▲ GLO 5101 [DDD]

Méfano, Jacqueline (pno)
Klein, G.:Son Pno Arion ▲ ARN 68272 [DDD]
Klein, G.:Songs, w. Sharon Cooper (sop) Arion ▲ ARN 68272 [DDD]
Yun, I.:Garak, w. Pierre-Yves Artaud (fl) Adda ▲ ADD 581166 [DDD]
Yun, I.:Garak, w. Pierre-Yves Artaud (fl) Adda ▲ ADD 243422 [DDD]

Megévand, Denise (celtic hp)
Chaynes, C.:Oginoha, "Lights from Japanese Poetry", w. Y. Nara (sop), P.-Y. Artaud (fl), C. Giot (perc) REM ▲ REM 311194 [DDD]

Meggido, Marc (db)—see ORCHESTRAS & ENSEMBLES australYSIS members

Meglio, Rosario di (vn)
Sui Palchi Delle Stelle:Sacred Music in the Neapolitan Conservatories at the Time of Francesco Provenzale, w. [cnd:Antonio Florio], Cappella Pietà de Turchini, Antonella Ippolito (sop), Jane Haughton (sop), Daniela del Monaco (alt), Sebastiano Cassarà (vn), Antonella Bologna (va), Paolo Dionisio (vl), Antonio Florio (vc), Pierluigi Ciappareli (thb), Enrico Baiano (org/hpd) Symphonia ▲ SY 93S20 [DDD]

Mehl, Arnold (baroque tpt)
Bach Trumpet Gala, Vol. 1, w. Peter Epp (baroque tpt), Rudolf Ulrich (baroque tpt), Munich Bach Trumpet Ensemble, Franz Lehrndorfer (org) Ars Musici ▲ 0869

Mehne, R. (vn)
Vanhal, J.B.:Divert Strs, w. C. Solothurski (va), G. Dzwiza (db), K. Stoll (db) Signum ▲ X 45-00

Meiarini, Tomaso (org)
150 Years of Italian Music, w. Rinaldo Alessandrini (cnd) Opus 111 ▲ OPS 30-119

Meienberg, Werner (cl)
Burkhard, W.:Serenade Fl, Op. 77, w. S. Gärtner (fl), J. Stavicek (bn), M. Gugel (hn), M. Paccagnella (hp), H. Schneeberger (vn), C. Schiller (va), B. Wyganth (db) *(rec between 1985 & 1989)* Jecklin-Disco ▲ JD 647-2 [ADD]

Meier, Bruno (fl)
Krommer, F.:Qnts Fl, w. Stamitz String Quartet—Op. 55 in e;Op. 58 in C;Op. 109 in G Koch Schwann ▲ 3-1049-2 [DDD]
Krommer, F.:Qnts Fl, w. Stamitz String Quartet—Opp. 49, 63 & 101 Koch Schwann ▲ SCH 310972 [DDD]
Mysliveček, J.:Con Fl, Prague CO Koch Schwann ▲ CD 311104 [DDD] ■ 211104 (D)
Vanhal, J.B.:Con Fl, Prague CO Koch Schwann ▲ CD 311104 [DDD] ■ 211104 (D)
Witt, F.:Con Fl, Prague CO Koch Schwann ▲ CD 311104 [DDD] ■ 211104 (D)

Meier, Kurt (ob)
Eichner, E.:Con 3 Ob, w. H. Griffiths (cnd), Northern Sinfonia of England Pan Classics ▲ 510088 [DDD]
Holzbauer, I.:Con Ob, w. H. Griffiths (cnd), Northern Sinfonia of England Pan Classics ▲ 510088 [DDD]
Lebrun, L.A.:Con Ob, w. H. Griffiths (cnd), Northern Sinfonia of England Pan Classics ▲ 510088 [DDD]
Winter, P. von:Con 2 Ob, w. H. Griffiths (cnd), Northern Sinfonia of England Pan Classics ▲ 510088 [DDD]

Meillier, Bruno (sax)
Exquisite Corpses from P.S. 122, w. Watson, David (shears/stick vn/gtr/tpt), Judy Dunaway (gtr/balloons), Anthony Coleman (sampler), Raissa St. Pierre (drums), Guy Yarden (vn/pno), Leslie Ross (bn), Linda Austin (gtr), Bruce Kaplan (gtr), Doug Henderson (peckhorn/bass/toy pno), Sue Ann Harkey (gtr), Cinnie Cole (sampler), et al. ¿What Next? ▲ WN 0002 [ADD]

Meinders, Fréderic (pno)
Chausson, E.:Con Vn, Pno & Str Qt, w. R. Kussmaul (vn), Schoenberg String Quartet Koch Schwann ▲ SCH 312312 [DDD]
Debussy, C.:Son Vn, w. R. Kussmaul (vn) Koch Schwann ▲ SCH 312312 [DDD]

Meininger, Christiane (fl)—see also ORCHESTRAS & ENSEMBLES Meininger Trio
Bon Di Venezia, A.:Sons Fl, Op. 1, w. T. Kloft (hpd) Bayer ▲ BR 100 057CD [DDD]
Boulanger, L.:D'un matin de printemps Fl & Pno, w. Christopher Arpin (pno) Bayer ▲ BR 100 266 [DDD]
Boulanger, L.:Nocturne, w. Christopher Arpin (pno) Bayer ▲ BR 100 266 [DDD]
Gubaidulina, S.:Allegro rustico, w. Christopher Arpin (pno) Bayer ▲ BR 100 266 [DDD]

Meinis (vl)
Bach, J.S.:Anna Magdalena Bach Notebook, w. Blegen (sop), Luxon (bar), Kipnis (hpd/clvd) [G] Elektra/Nonesuch 2-▲ 79020-2 [DDD]

Meints, Catharina (vc)
Roussel, A.:Trio Fl, w. R. Willoughby (fl), K. Plummer (va) Gasparo Gallante ▲ GG 1003 [AAD]

Meints, Catharina (vl)
Bach, J.S.:Sons Vl, BWV 1027-1029, w. D. Ornstein (hpd) Gasparo Gallante ▲ GG 1001 [AAD]
Pierné, G.:Son da camera Fl, w. R. Willoughby (fl), W. Price (pno) Gasparo Gallante ▲ GG 1003 [AAD]

Meirelles, Maria (pno)
Bréval, J.B.:Son Vc, w. I. Babini (vc) Centaur ▲ CRC 2058 [DDD]
Kabalevsky, D.:Son Vc, w. I. Babini (vc) Centaur ▲ CRC 2058 [DDD]
Schumann, R.:Fantasiestücke Cl, w. I. Babini (vc) [cello & piano trans.] Centaur ▲ CRC 2058 [DDD]
Tchaikovsky, P.:Nocturne Vc, w. I. Babini (vc) Centaur ▲ CRC 2058 [DDD]
Weber, C.M. von:Rondo Vc, w. I. Babini (vc) Centaur ▲ CRC 2058 [DDD]

Meisen, Paul (fl)
Bach, J.S.:Lt Music, w. Hedwig Bilgram (hpd)—Partita in c, BWV 997 [arr for Fl & Hpd] *(rec Augustinian Monastery Mens' Choir, Polling, West Germany, Sept 21-24, 1977)* Camerata ▲ 32CM 281 [AAD]
Bach, J.S.:Partita Fl, BWV 1013 *(rec Augustinian Monastery Mens' Choir, Polling, West Germany, Sept 21-24, 1977)* Camerata ▲ 32CM 281 [AAD]
Bach, J.S.:Sons Fl, BWV 1030-35, w. Hedwig Bilgram (hpd)—in b, BWV 1030; in A, BWV 1032 *(rec Augustinian Monastery Mens' Choir, Polling, West Germany, Sept 21-24, 1977)* Camerata ▲ 32CM 281 [AAD]

Meisen, Paul (fl) (cont.)
Bach, J.S.:Sons Vn, w. Hedwig Bilgram (hpd)—in g, BWV 1020 [arr for Fl & Hpd] *(rec Augustinian Monastery Mens' Choir, Polling, West Germany, Sept 21-24, 1977)* Camerata ▲ 32CM 281 [AAD]
Prokofiev, S.:Son Fl, w. G. Rosenberg (pno) MD + G ▲ L 3255 [DDD]
Reger, M.:Son Vn Pno, Op. 84, w. G. Rosenberg (pno) [arr fl & pno] MD + G ▲ L 3255 [DDD]
Reinecke, C.:Son Fl, w. G. Rosenberg (pno) MD + G ▲ L 3255 [DDD]

Meisenbach, Megan (fl)
Bax, A.:Elegiac Trio, w. B. Williams (va), M. Golden (hp) *(rec 6 & 8/91)* Centaur ▲ CRC 2114 [DDD]
Debussy, C.:Chansons de Bilitis (recitation), w. L. Jeffrey (fl), W. Dudley (hp), M. Golden (hp), K. Tamagawa (cel)—no speaker *(rec 6 & 8/91)* Centaur ▲ CRC 2114 [DDD]
Debussy, C.:Music of, w. M. Golden (hp) [arr. for flute & harp of En Bateau; Clair de Lune; Golliwogg's Cakewalk; Rêverie *(rec 6 & 8/91)* Centaur ▲ CRC 2114 [DDD]
Debussy, C.:Prélude à l'après-midi d'un faune, w. W. Dudley (hp), M. Golden (hp) [arr. flute & 2 harps Whit Dudley] *(rec 6 & 8/91)* Centaur ▲ CRC 2114 [DDD]
Ravel, M.:Intro & Allegro, w. M. Golden (hp), R. McDowall (cl), R. Neal (vn), D. Pettys (vn), D. Hermann (va), G. Manasjan (vc) Centaur ▲ CRC 2114 [DDD]

Meisner, Andreas (org)
Eben, Petr:Moto ostinato Motette ▲ CD 40151 [DDD]
Peeters, F.:Choral Preludes Motette ▲ MOT CD 40161 [DDD]
Peeters, F.:Toccata Org Motette ▲ MOT CD 40161 [DDD]

Meissl, Johannes (vn)—see also ORCHESTRAS & ENSEMBLES Artis String Quartet
Magnard, A.:Qt Strs, Op. 16, w. Peter Schuhmayer (vn), Herbert Kefer (va), Othmar Müller (vc) Accord ▲ ACD 201982 [DDD]

Meister, Barbara (pno)
Haydn, J.:Sons Pno—5 Sonatas—Nos. 32, 34, 40, 48 & 50 Centaur ▲ CRC 2118
Nielsen, C.:Chaconne *(rec LSU Recital Hall, Baton Rouge, LA, Jan 8-9 & Dec 19-20, 1994)* Centaur ▲ CRC 2254 [DDD]
Nielsen, C.:Humoreske-Bagateller *(rec LSU Recital Hall, Baton Rouge, LA, Jan 8-9 & Dec 19-20, 1994)* Centaur ▲ CRC 2254 [DDD]
Nielsen, C.:Pieces Pno, Op. 3 *(rec LSU Recital Hall, Baton Rouge, LA, Jan 8-9 & Dec 19-20, 1994)* Centaur ▲ CRC 2254 [DDD]
Nielsen, C.:Pieces Pno, Op. 59 *(rec LSU Recital Hall, Baton Rouge, LA, Jan 8-9 & Dec 19-20, 1994)* Centaur ▲ CRC 2254 [DDD]
Nielsen, C.:Pno Music for Young & Old *(rec LSU Recital Hall, Baton Rouge, LA, Jan 8-9 & Dec 19-20, 1994)* Centaur ▲ CRC 2254 [DDD]
Nielsen, C.:Theme & Vars *(rec LSU Recital Hall, Baton Rouge, LA, Jan 8-9 & Dec 19-20, 1994)* Centaur ▲ CRC 2254 [DDD]

Meister, Rudolf (pno)
Ernst, S.:Quattro mani dentro e fuori, w. Siegrid Ernst (pno) Vienna Modern Masters ▲ VMM 2018 [DDD]

Méjean, Véronique (vn)
Schobert, J.:Music of, w. L. Sgrizzi (pno), C. Ganchini (vn), Philipp Bosbach (vc)—Qts. in f, Op. 7/2 & in E♭, Op. 14/1; Sons. in d & A, Op. 14/4 & 5; Trios in D & B♭, Op. 16/1 & 4 Musique d'Abord ▲ HMA 1901294

Melbourne, John (perc)
A Secret Place, w. Rebello, Simone (perc), Andrew Scott (a sax), Liz Gilliver (mar), Kalengo Percussion Ensemble, Eryl Roberts (perc), Chris Bastock (perc), Richard Dyson (perc) *(rec Zion Institute, Manchester, 1995)* Doyen ▲ CD 040 [DDD]

Melcher, Wilhelm (vn)—see ORCHESTRAS & ENSEMBLES Melos String Quartet

Melchersson, Ingemar (org)
Duello a Due Organi, Vol. 1, w. Melchersson, Ingemar (org), Rupert Gottfried Frieberger (org) Christophorus ▲ 77141 [DDD]
Missa et Officium de Beata Maria Virgine, w. [cnd:Rupert Gottfried Frieberger], Salzburg Univ Choral Group Entrée ▲ 0056

Meldau, Ulrich (org)
Dupré, M.:Esquisses, Op. 41 Motette ▲ CD 40111 [DDD]
Dupré, M.:Org Music—Fileuse (from Suite Bretonne), Op. 21/2; Iste confessor (from Le tombeau de Titelouze), Op. 38/12 Motette ▲ CD 40111 [DDD]

Meldau, Ulrich (pno)
Dupré, M.:Sym-Passion, "The World Awaiting the Saviour" Motette ▲ CD 40111 [DDD]
Dupré, M.:Sym, Op. 25, w. D. Schweizer (cnd), Zurich SO Motette ▲ CD 40111 [DDD]

Meldorf, Myra (pno)
Cage, J.:Pno Music, w. Joshua Pierce (pno), Borah Bergman (pno), Dorothy Jones (pno), Joseph Kubera (pno), Fumiko Miyanoo (pno)—Music Walk; Jazz Study; Experiences I & II; plus others Wergo ▲ WER 61592

Mele, Andrea de (vn)
Albanese, G.:Songs, w. Luana Gentile (sop), Antonella Trovarelli (sop), Marina Gentile (mez), Stefano Consolini (ten), Paolo Speca (bar), Sirio Benedetto (sax), Roberto Rupo (pno)—Aria di Natale; Duettino e coro muto (w. Carlo Moreno) [both w. Giorgina Dell'Immagine, Tito Petralia (cnd), EIAR Orch & Chorus]; Passione (M. Gentile); Serenata (Speca); Alzati, o bella... (Trovarelli); Mattinata (Speca); Il sogno d'una suora (Trovarelli); Ninna Nanna (M. Gentile); Barcarola (Rupo); Madrigale (L. Gentile); Ninna nanna...900 (L. Gentile); Variazioni (L. Gentile); Non so qual io mi voglia... (L. Gentile); Io sono un augellin... (L. Gentile); Bravo, bene, bis...(va bene) (Consolini & Di Benedetto); Che caviale (Consolini); Ma non sapete chi sono io? (Consolini & L. & M. Gentile); Grappoli di stelle (Consolini); Notte di Capri (Consolini & Di Mele); Una rosa di ferro battuto (Consolini, Speca & L. & M. Gentile) *(rec Ortona, Teatro Zambra, Feb 21, 22, 23 & Mar 1 &)* Bongiovanni ▲ GB 5054-2 [DDD]

Melford, Myra (pno)
Jenkins, L.:Monkey on the Dragon, w. Leroy Jenkins (vn), Henry Threadgill (fl), Don Byron (cl), Marth Ehrlich (b cl), Janet Frice (bn), Vincent Chancey (hn), Frank Gordon (tpt), Jeff Hoyer (trbn), David Soldier (vn), Jane Henry (vn) Ron Lawrence (va), Mary Wooton (vc), Lindsey Horner (db), Thurman Barker (traps), T. Léon (cnd) *(rec live, Merkin Concert Hall, New York City, Apr. 9, 1992)* CRI ("eXchange" series) ▲ CD 663 [DDD]

Melford, Myra (pno/kbd)
Lebaron, A.:The E. & O. Line (sels), w. Louise Cloutier (mez—Eurydice/Vendors), Hugh Panero (ten—Hermes), Lawrence Hamilton (bar—Orpheus/Men), Frank London (tpt), Marcus Rojas (tuba), Davey Williams (gtr), Fred Hopkins (elec bass), Thurman Barker (dr), A. LeBaron (cnd)—Juke Joint Jam Session; Eurydice Meets Hermes; Eurydice's Death [Funeral Band]; Eurydice's River Journey; Orpheus Laments [Looked Away] *(rec Coolidge Auditorium, Library of Congress, 1987)* Mode ▲ Mode 42

Melis, Stefano (cel)
Respighi, O.:Gli uccelli, w. Stefano Mancini (fl), Alberto Cesaraccio (ob), Antonio Puglia (cl), Paloma Tironi (hp), R. Tigani (cnd), Sassari SO *(rec Rome, Oct 11-14, 1994)* Bongiovanni ▲ GB 2166 [DDD]

Melkus, Eduard (vl)—see ORCHESTRAS & ENSEMBLES Deller Consort

Mellis, Carol (fl)
A Baby's Prayer, w. Adrienne Bridgewater (hp) PHD ▲ PHD 570016

Melnikov, Alexander (pno)
Prokofiev, S.:Son Vc, w. Leonid Gorokhov (vc) *(rec 1995)* Supraphon ▲ SUP 3243
Shostakovich, D.:Son Vc, w. Leonid Gorokhov (vc) *(rec 1995)* Supraphon ▲ SUP 3243
Stravinsky, I.:Suite italienne Vc, w. Leonid Gorokhov (vc) *(rec 1995)* Supraphon ▲ SUP 3243

Melnikov, Alexander (vn)—see also ORCHESTRAS & ENSEMBLES Moscow Contemporary Music Ensemble
The Spirit of Russia, w. Gidon Kremer (vn), Vladimir Malinin (vn), Mark Pekarsky (cymbals), Leonid Bobylev (pno) Vox Box 2-▲ CDX 5115 [ADD]

Melnitzky, M.-K. (hp)—see ORCHESTRAS & ENSEMBLES Estampie

Meloni, Massimo (bn)—see ORCHESTRAS & ENSEMBLES Rara Ensemble

Melsted, Linda (vn)
Out of the Orient Crystall Skyes, w. Nancy Zylstra (sop), Margriet Tindemans (vl), Jillion Stopples Dupree (hpd/org), Michael Sand (baroque vn/vl), Olga Hauptmann (baroque va), Ellen Siebert (vl), Russell Paige (vl) Wildboar ▲ WLBR 8901 [DDD]

Meltzer, M. (fl)
Avni, T.:Love under a Different Sun, w. E. Berendsen (sgr), E. Zaltsman (vn), S. Magen (vc) Symposium ▲ 1110

Memelsdorff, Pedro (rcr)
Delight in Disorder, w. Andreas Staier (hpd) Deutsche Harmonia Mundi ▲ 05472-77318-2 [DDD]

Mencarelli (fl)
Puccini, M.:Concertone Fl, w. di Girolamo (cl), G. Bodanza (tpt), Caproni (hn), G. Cosmi (cnd), Lucca Teatro Comunale del Giglio Orch Bongiovanni ▲ GB 2048 [DDD]

Mencoboni, Marco (hpd)
Bonporti, F.A.:Concertini e Serenate, Op. 12, w. L. Mangiocavallo (vn), C. Ronco (vc)—Concertini Nos. 3 in G & 7 in E♭; Serenatas Nos. 2 in F, 4 in g & 6 in G Nuova Era ("Ancient Music" series) ▲ 6939 [DDD]
Veracini, F.M.:Sons Vn, Op. 1, w. L. Mangiocavallo (vn), C. Ronco (vc)—Sonata No. 12 in F Nuova Era ("Ancient Music" series) ▲ 6900 [DDD]
Veracini, F.M.:Sonate accademiche, w. L. Mangiocavallo (vn), C. Ronco (vc)—Sonatas No. 5 in g & No. 6 in A Nuova Era ("Ancient Music" series) ▲ 6900 [DDD]

Mendelsohn, Jack (vc)—see also ORCHESTRAS & ENSEMBLES Catherine Wilson Trio
Catherine Wilson & Friends:Classical Potpourri, w. Catherine Wilson (pno), Mark Skazinetsky (vn), Norman Hathaway (va), Joel Quarrington (db) Doremi ▲ DHR 71111

Mendelssohn, Vladimir (va)—see also ORCHESTRAS & ENSEMBLES Garingas Baryton Trio, Mozart String Trio
Berens, H.:Trio Strs, w. J.-J. Kantarow (vn), H.-J. Stegenga (vc) Erasmus ▲ WVH 017 [DDD]
Brahms, J.:Qnt Cl, w. W. Boeykens (cl), J.-J. Kantarow (vn), A. Czifra (vn), H.-J. Stegenga (vc) Erasmus ▲ WVH 017 [DDD]
Bruch, M.:Pieces Cl, Op. 83/1-8, w. Michel Lethiec (cl), Roberte Mamou (pno) *(rec Conservatoire de Tourcoing, Mar 1995)* Pavane ▲ ADW 7334 [DDD]
Schumann, R.:Märchenerzählungen, w. Michel Lethiec (cl), Roberte Mamou (pno) *(rec Conservatoire de Tourcoing, Mar 1995)* Pavane ▲ ADW 7334 [DDD]
Shostakovich, D.:Son Va, w. L. Markiz (cnd), Amsterdam New Sinfonietta [arr. V. Mendelssohn for orch.] *(rec Oct & Dec. 1992)* Globe ▲ GLO 5093 [DDD]

Mendenhall, J. (fl)
Hanson, H.:Serenade Fl, w. Susan Jolles (hp), G. Schwarz (cnd), Seattle SO Delos ▲ DE 3105 [DDD]
Hanson, H.:Serenade Fl, w. Susan Jolles (hp), G. Schwarz (cnd), Seattle SO Delos 4-▲ DE 3150 [DDD]

Mendez, Eke (pno)
Schubert, Franz:Winterreise, w. Jakob Stämpfli (bass) Accord ▲ ACD 221142 [DDD]

Méndez, Rafael (tpt)
The Legendary Trumpet Virtuosity of Rafael Méndez, Vol. 1 Summit ▲ SMT 177 [ADD]

Mendieta, Anna Maria (hp)
Enchanted Christmas Sugo ▲ SUG 9311 [DDD] ■ SUG 9311

Mendl, Stefan (pno)—see ORCHESTRAS & ENSEMBLES Vienna Piano Trio

Mendoza, Francisca (vn)
Debussy, C.:Son Vn, w. Xavier Borràs (pno) *(rec Barcelona, July 8, 9, 22 & 23, 1994)* Edicions Albert Moraleda ▲ 1294-18 [DDD]
Prokofiev, S.:Son Vn, Op. 94bis, w. Xavier Borràs (pno) *(rec Barcelona, July 8, 9, 22 & 23, 1994)* Edicions Albert Moraleda ▲ 1294-18 [DDD]

Mendoze, Christian (rcr)
Bach, J.S.:Sons Fl, BWV 1030-35, w. J. Barbolini (hpd), B. Re (vl)—BWV 1035 Pierre Verany ▲ PV 787023 [DDD]
Corelli, A.:Sons Vn, Op. 5, w. G. Barbolini (hpd), B. Re (vl)—No. 9 Pierre Verany ▲ PV 787023 [DDD]
Handel, G.F.:Sons Fl, w. Bruno Re (vl), Giorgio Barbolini (hpd)—Op. 1, Nos. 4 & 7 Pierre Verany ▲ PV 787023 [DDD]
Praetorius, M.:Terpsichore, w. C. Mendoze (cnd), Musica Antiqua Ensemble—Branles de la Royne No. 7; Courante No. 4; Branles Double No. 3; Suite de Gavottes; Philou No. 6; Pavane de Spaigne No. 8; Spagnoletta No. 9; La Canarie No. 10; La bourrée; Courante No. 16; Branles de Montirande Nos. 1 & 11; Suite de Branles de Villages; Suite de Courantes; Suite de Ballets; Ballet des Bacchanales No. 19; Ballet des Matelotz No. 21; Ballet des Feus; Ballet des Cocos; Suite de Voltes Pierre Verany ▲ PVY 730067 [DDD]
Six Venetian Concerti, w. Cologne CO Pierre Verany ▲ 787093 [DDD]
Sonatas for Recorder & Basso Continuo Pierre Verany ▲ 787023 [DDD]
Telemann, G.P.:Son Rcr in F, w. G. Barbolini (hpd), B. Re (vl) Pierre Verany ▲ PV 787023 [DDD]
Vivaldi, A.:Cons Fl (misc), w. W. Ehrhardt (cnd), Concerto Cologne—RV.433, 439, 434 Pierre Verany ▲ PV 787093 [DDD]
Vivaldi, A.:Il pastor fido, w. G. Barbolini (hpd), B. Re (viol)—No. 6 Pierre Verany ▲ PV 787023 [DDD]

Meneses, Antonio (vc)
Ghedini, G.F.:Con for 2 Vcs, w. W. Thomas-Mifune (vc), G. Schmöhe (cnd), Bamberg SO *(rec 1/90)* Koch Schwann ▲ 311106 H1 [DDD]
Graziani, C.:Sons Vc, Op. 3, w. Rosana Lanzelotte (hpd), Gustavo Tavares (vc) Sanctus 2-▲ 002/003 [DDD]
Popper, D.:Music of, w. R. Zollman (cnd), Basel SO—Con for Vc & Orch, Op. 24; Suite for Vc & Orch, Op. 50; Papillon, Op. 3/4; Tarantelle, Op. 33; Hungarian Rhap for Vc & Orch, Op. 86; Elfentanz, Op. 39 Pan Classics ▲ 510075 [DDD]
Romberg, B.:Con Vcs, w. W. Thomas-Mifune (vc), G. Schmöhe (cnd), Bamberg SO Koch Schwann ▲ 311106 H1 [DDD]
Strauss, R.:Don Quixote, w. H. von Karajan (cnd), Berlin PO Deutsche Grammophon ("Karajan Gold" series) ▲ 439027-2 [DDD]
Tchaikovsky, P.:Trio Pno, w. C. Licad (pno), N. Salerno-Sonnenberg (vn) EMI Classics ▲ CDC 54800

Menger, R. (org)
Walther (I), Joh.:Org Music [Gottfried Silbermann Organ at Dittersbach]—not advised of selections FSM ▲ FSM 97717 [DDD]

Menges, I. (gtr)
Beethoven, L. van:Son 9 Vn, "Kreutzer", w. A. de Greef (pno) *(rec 1925)* Biddulph ▲ BID LAB 076
Brahms, J.:Son 2 Vn, w. H. Samuel (pno) *(rec 1929)* Biddulph ▲ BID LAB 076
Brahms, J.:Son 3 Vn, w. H. Samuel (pno) *(rec 1929)* Biddulph ▲ BID LAB 076

Menges, Isolde (vn)
Bach, J.S.:Sons Vn, w. H. Samuel (hpd)—in E, BWV 1016 *(1928 HMV recording)* Koch Legacy 2-▲ 3-7137-2

Menissier, Francois (org)
The Organ in Lorraine:Works by Composers of the Region from 1537 to the Present—, w. Anne-Catherine Bucher (org), Michel Chapuis (org), Norbert Petry (org) K617 2-▲ 7055

Mensah, S. (perc)
Kinney, M.:You Are So Stingingly Demure, w. T. Cora (vc), M. Kinney (vc), M. Anderson (perc) Innova ▲ MN 107

Mense, Lucia (fl)—see ORCHESTRAS & ENSEMBLES Cologne Flautando

Menual, R. (hn)
Karg-Elert, S.:Jugend, w. D. Worthen (fl), R. Shaughnessy (cl), J. Weber (pno) Leonarda ▲ LE 335 [DDD]

Menuhin, Hepzibah (pno)
Bach, J.S.:Sons Vn Hpd, BWV 1014-1019, w. Yehudi Menuhin (vn)—BWV 1016 *(rec 1936-40)* Biddulph 2-▲ LAB 124-25
Beethoven, L. van:Rondo Vn, WoO 41, w. Yehudi Menuhin (vn) *(rec 1936-40)* Biddulph 2-▲ LAB 124-25
Beethoven, L. van:Son 7 Vn, w. Yehudi Menuhin (vn) *(rec 1936-40)* Biddulph 2-▲ LAB 124-25
Beethoven, L. van:Son 8 Vn, w. Yehudi Menuhin (vn) *(rec 1936-40)* Biddulph 2-▲ LAB 124-25

Menuhin, Hepzibah (pno) (cont.)
Beethoven, L. van:Son 9 Vn, "Kreutzer", w. Yehudi Menuhin (vn) *(rec 1936–40)* Biddulph 2-▲ LAB 124–25
Beethoven, L. van:Son 10 Vn, w. Yehudi Menuhin (vn) *(rec 1936–40)* Biddulph 2-▲ LAB 124–25
Beethoven, L. van:Trio 3 Pno, w. Y. Menuhin (vn), P. Casals (vc) *(rec live July 18, 1959)* Music & Arts 4-▲ CD 688 (m) [AAD]
Beethoven, L. van:Trio 4 Pno, "Ghost", w. Yehudi Menuhin (vn), Maurice Eisenberg (vc) *(rec 1936)* Biddulph ▲ LAB 127
Brahms, J.:Son 1 Vn, w. Yehudi Menuhin (vn) *(rec 1936–40)* Biddulph 2-▲ LAB 124–25
Brahms, J.:Son 3 Vn, w. Yehudi Menuhin (vn) *(rec 1936–40)* Biddulph 2-▲ LAB 124–25
The Complete Solo Columbia Recordings, w. Georges Enescu (vn), Edward C. Harris (pno), Yehudi Menuhin (pno), Sanford Schlüssel (pno) *(rec 1924 & 1929)* Biddulph ▲ LAB 066 [ADD]
Enescu, G.:Son 3 Vn, w. Y. Menuhin (vn) *(rec 1936)* Biddulph ▲ LAB 066 [ADD]
Franck, C.:Son Vn, w. Y. Menuhin (vn) *(rec 1936)* Biddulph ▲ LAB 058 [ADD]
Lekeu, G.:Son Vn, w. Yehudi Menuhin (vn) *(rec 1938)* Biddulph ▲ LAB 058 [ADD]
Mozart, W.A.:Con 13 Pno, w. G. Cleve (cnd), Midsummer Mozart Festival Orch *(rec live, Berkeley, CA)* Bainbridge ▲ BCD 6273 [DDD]
Pizzetti, I.:Son 1 Vn, w. Y. Menuhin (vn) *(rec 1938, from HMV DB 3579/82)* Biddulph ▲ LAB 067 [ADD]
Schubert, Franz:Rondo Vn, D.895, w. Y. Menuhin (vn) *(rec 1938, from HMV DB 3583/84)* Biddulph ▲ LAB 067 [ADD]
Schumann, R.:Son 2 Vn, w. Y. Menuhin (vn) *(rec 1934)* Biddulph ▲ LAB 067 [ADD]
Tchaikovsky, P.:Trio Pno, w. Yehudi Menuhin (vn), Maurice Eisenberg (vc) *(rec 1936)* Biddulph ▲ LAB 127

Menuhin, Jeremy (pno)
Dvořák, A.:Qnt Pno, Op. 81, w. Chilingirian String Quartet Chandos ▲ CHAN 9173 [DDD]

Menuhin, Yehudi (vn)
Bach, J.S.:Con 1 Vn, *(orch unknown)* Memories ("Golden" series) 2-▲ MEM 3007
Bach, J.S.:Sons & Partitas Vn, BWV 1001–1006—Son. 3 Biddulph ▲ LAB 032 [ADD]
Bach, J.S.:Sons Vn, w. G. Gould (hpd)—BWV 1017 *(rec Oct 25–26, 1965)* Sony Classical ▲ SMK 52688 [ADD]
Bach, J.S.:Sons Vn Hpd, BWV 1014–1019, w. Hephzibah Menuhin (pno)—BWV 1016 *(rec 1936–40)* Biddulph 2-▲ LAB 124–25
Bartók, B.:Con 1 Vn, w. A. Dorati (cnd), Dallas SO RCA Gold Seal ▲ 09026-61395-2
Bartók, B.:Con 2 Vn, w. A. Dorati (cnd), Minneapolis SO *(rec Carnegie Hall, New York City, Feb. 17, 1957)* Mercury Living Presence ▲ 434350-2
Bartók, B.:Con 2 Vn, w. W. Furtwängler (cnd), Philharmonia Orch *(rec 1953)* EMI Classics ▲ CDH 69804 (m) [ADD]
Bartók, B.:Son Vn *(rec late 1940s)* EMI Classics ▲ CDH 69804 (m) [ADD]
Beethoven, L. van:Con Vn, Op. 61, w. W. Furtwängler (cnd), Berlin PO *(rec live Sept 30, 1947)* Music & Arts ▲ CD 708-1 [AAD]
Beethoven, L. van:Con Vn, Op. 61, w. W. Furtwängler (cnd), Philharmonia Orch EMI Classics (Great Recordings of the Century) ▲ CDH 69799 (m) [ADD]
Beethoven, L. van:Con Vn, Op. 61, w. O. Klemperer (cnd), Philharmonia Orch EMI Classics ▲ CDM 64324
Beethoven, L. van:Romances Vn, w. J. Pritchard (cnd), New Philharmonia Orch EMI Classics ▲ CDM 64324
Beethoven, L. van:Rondo Vn, WoO 41, w. Hephzibah Menuhin (pno) *(rec 1936–40)* Biddulph 2-▲ LAB 124–25
Beethoven, L. van:Sons Vn (comp), w. W. Kempff (pno) Deutsche Grammophon 4-▲ 415874-2 [ADD]
Beethoven, L. van:Son 1 Vn, w. H. Giesen (pno) *(rec 1929)* Biddulph ▲ LAB 032 [ADD]
Beethoven, L. van:Son 5 Vn, "Spring", w. W. Kempff (pno) Deutsche Grammophon ("Galleria" series) ▲ 427251-2 [ADD]
Beethoven, L. van:Son 7 Vn, w. Hephzibah Menuhin (pno) *(rec 1936–40)* Biddulph 2-▲ LAB 124–25
Beethoven, L. van:Son 8 Vn, w. Hephzibah Menuhin (pno) *(rec 1936–40)* Biddulph 2-▲ LAB 124–25
Beethoven, L. van:Son 9 Vn, "Kreutzer", w. Hephzibah Menuhin (pno) *(rec 1936–40)* Biddulph 2-▲ LAB 124–25
Beethoven, L. van:Son 9 Vn, "Kreutzer", w. W. Kempff (pno) Deutsche Grammophon ("Galleria" series) ▲ 427251-2 [ADD]
Beethoven, L. van:Son 10 Vn, w. G. Gould (pno) *(rec Oct. 25–26, 1965)* Sony Classical ▲ SMK 52688 [ADD]
Beethoven, L. van:Son 10 Vn, w. Hephzibah Menuhin (pno) *(rec 1936–40)* Biddulph 2-▲ LAB 124–25
Beethoven, L. van:Trio 3 Pno, w. H. Menuhin (pno), P. Casals (vc) *(rec live July 18, 1959)* Music & Arts 4-▲ CD 688 (m) [AAD]
Beethoven, L. van:Trio 4 Pno, "Ghost", w. Hepzibah Menuhin (pno), Maurice Eisenberg (vc) *(rec 1936)* Biddulph ▲ LAB 127
Ben-Haim, P.:Son Vn [He] Gallo ▲ CD 530 [AAD]
Brahms, J.:Con Vn, w. R. Kempe (cnd), Royal PO EMI Classics ▲ CDE 67766
Brahms, J.:Son 1 Vn, w. Hephzibah Menuhin (pno) *(rec 1936–40)* Biddulph 2-▲ LAB 124–25
Brahms, J.:Son 3 Vn, w. Hephzibah Menuhin (pno) *(rec 1936–40)* Biddulph 2-▲ LAB 124–25
Brahms, J.:Trio 1 Pno, w. Eugene Istomin (pno), Pablo Casals (vc) Stradivarius ▲ STV 10020 [ADD]
Brahms, J.:Trio 1 Pno, w. E. Istomin (pno), P. Casals (vc) *(rec live July 13, 1955)* Music & Arts 4-▲ CD 689 (m) [AAD]
Brahms, J.:Trio 2 Pno, w. E. Istomin (pno), P. Casals (vc) *(rec live July 13, 1955)* Music & Arts 4-▲ CD 689 (m) [AAD]
Brahms, J.:Trio 3 Pno, w. Eugene Istomin (pno), Pablo Casals (vc) Stradivarius ▲ STV 10020 [ADD]
Brahms, J.:Trio 3 Pno, w. E. Istomin (pno), P. Casals (vc) *(rec live July 13, 1955)* Music & Arts 4-▲ CD 688 (m) [AAD]
Bruch, M.:Con 1 Vn, w. W. Susskind (cnd), Philharmonia Orch EMI Classics ("Laser" series) 3-▲
Bruch, M.:Con 1 Vn, w. L. Ronald (cnd), London SO *(rec 1931)* Biddulph ▲ LAB 031 [ADD]
Chausson, E.:Poème Vn, w. G. Enescu (cnd), Paris SO *(rec 1933)* Biddulph ▲ LAB 058 [ADD]
The Complete Solo Columbia Recordings, w. Georges Enescu (vn), Edward C. Harris (pno), Hepzibah Menuhin (pno), Sanford Schlüssel (pno) *(rec 1924 & 1929)* Biddulph ▲ LAB 066 [ADD]
Corelli, A.:Sons Vn, Op. 5, w. Robert Donnington (vl), George Malcolm (hpd)—Nos. 1 in D, 5 in g & 12 in d EMI Classics ("Baroque" series) ▲ CDK 65731
Debussy, C.:Preludes Pno (sels), w. P. Monteux (cnd), San Francisco SO—sels. from Book 1:No. 8, "La Fille aux cheveux de lin" RCA Gold Seal ▲ 09026-61395-2
Delius, F.:Con Vn, w. M. Davies (cnd), Royal PO EMI Classics ▲ CDM 64725
Elgar, E.:Con Vn, w. A. Boult (cnd), New Philharmonia Orch EMI Classics ▲ CDM 64725
Enescu, G.:Son 3 Vn, w. H. Menuhin (pno) *(rec 1936)* Biddulph ▲ LAB 066 [ADD]
Foss, L.:Orpheus & Euridice, w. E. Michell (vn), L. Foss (cnd), Brooklyn PO New World ▲ NW 375-2 [DDD]
Franck, C.:Son Vn, w. H. Menuhin (pno) *(rec 1936)* Biddulph ▲ LAB 058 [ADD]
Lalo, E.:Sym espagnole, w. G. Enescu (cnd), Paris Conservatory Societé des Concerts Orch *(rec 1933 HMV recording)* Biddulph ▲ LAB 046 [ADD]
Lalo, E.:Sym espagnole, w. P. Monteux (cnd), San Francisco SO RCA Gold Seal ▲ 09026-61395-2
Lekeu, G.:Son Vn, w. Hepzibah Menuhin (pno) *(rec 1938)* Biddulph ▲ LAB 058 [ADD]
Mendelssohn, F.:Con in e Vn & Orch, Op. 64, w. A. Boult (cnd), London SO EMI Classics ▲ CDE 67767
Mendelssohn, F.:Con in e Vn & Orch, Op. 64, w. W. Furtwängler (cnd), Berlin PO EMI Classics ("Great Recordings of the Century" series) ▲ CDH 69799 (m) [ADD]
Menuhin & Grappelli Play, w. Stephane Grappelli (vn/pno) EMI Classics ▲ CDM 69219
Menuhin & Grappelli Play Jalousie & Other Great Standards, w. Stephane Grappelli (vn/pno) EMI Classics ▲ CDM 69220
Mozart, W.A.:Con 1 Vn, w. Y. Menuhin (cnd), Bath Festival Orch EMI Classics ▲ CDE 67779
Mozart, W.A.:Con 3 Vn, w. G. Enescu (cnd), Paris SO *(rec 1935 for HMV)* Biddulph ▲ LAB 004 [ADD]
Mozart, W.A.:Con 3 Vn, w. Y. Menuhin (cnd), Bath Festival Orch EMI Classics ▲ CDE 67779

Menuhin, Yehudi (vn) (cont.)
Mozart, W.A.:Con 5 Vn, w. Y. Menuhin (cnd), Bath Festival Orch EMI Classics ▲ CDE 67779
Mozart, W.A.:Con 7 Vn, w. P. Monteux (cnd), Paris SO *(rec 1932 HMV recording)* Biddulph ▲ LAB 004 [ADD]
Mozart, W.A.:Con Vn, K.Anh.294a, w. P. Monteux (cnd), Paris SO *(rec 1934 HMV recording)* Biddulph ▲ LAB 004 [ADD]
Mozart, W.A.:Qt Pno, K.493, w. M. Horszowski (pno), W. Wallfisch (va), P. Casals (vc) *(rec live, Prades Festival, July 7, 1956)* Music & Arts 4-▲ CD 688 (m) [AAD]
Paganini, N.:Con 1 Vn, w. A. Erede (cnd), Royal PO EMI Classics ▲ CDC 47088
Paganini, N.:Con 2 Vn, w. A. Erede (cnd), Royal PO EMI Classics ▲ CDC 47088
Pizzetti, I.:Son 1 Vn, w. H. Menuhin (pno) *(rec 1938, from HMV DB 3579/82)* Biddulph ▲ LAB 067 [ADD]
Purcell, H.:Chamber Music, w. Alberto Lysy (vn), Robert Masters (vn), Cecil Arnowitz (va), Walter Gerhard (va), Derek Simpson (vc), Ambrose Gauntlett (vl), Roy Jesson (hpd/org)—Trio Sons Nos. 2 in C, 6 in G & 8 in G; Fants Nos. 4 in g, 7 in c, 8 in d & 13 in F, "Upon One Note" EMI Classics ("Baroque" series) ▲ CDK 65734
Purcell, H.:The Fairy Queen (sels), w. Joan Carlyle (sop), Y. Menuhin (cnd), Bath Festival Orch—Entry of Phoebus; Syms. [Acts 4 & 5]; Dance for the Haymakers; 1st Music; Dance for the Fairies; Prelude; 2nd Music; 1st Act Tune *(rec Abbey Road Studio 1, London, July 1965)* EMI Classics ▲ CDK 65341 [ADD]
Purcell, H.:Fants, w. Alberto Lysy (vn), Robert Masters (vn), Cecil Aronowitz (va), Walter Gerhard (va), Derek Simpson (vc), Ambrose Gauntlett (vl), Roy Jesson (hpd/org)—Nos. 4 in g, 7 in c, 8 in d, 13 in F EMI Classics ▲ CDK 65734
Purcell, H.:The Indian Queen (sels), w. Joan Carlyle (sop), Y. Menuhin (cnd), Bath Festival Orch—Tpt Tune; 4th Act Tune; I Attempt from Love's Sickness to Fly in Vain; Syms. [Acts 2 & 3]; 1st Music; Air *(rec Abbey Road Studio 1, London, July 1965)* EMI Classics ▲ CDK 65341 [ADD]
Purcell, H.:King Arthur (sels), w. Joan Carlyle (sop), Y. Menuhin (cnd), Bath Festival Orch—Tpt Tune; 2nd Music; Sym.; Passacaglia; Aria of Venus; 2nd Act Tune *(rec Abbey Road Studio 1, London, July 1965)* EMI Classics ▲ CDK 65341 [ADD]
Purcell, H.:Music for the Theater, w. Joan Carlyle (sop), Y. Menuhin (cnd), Bath Festival Orch—Bonduca [ov.]; The Old Bachelor [ov.]; Abdelazar [rondeau]; Bonduca [air]; Pausanias [air of Pandora:Sweeter than Roses or Cool Evening Breeze]; The Married Beau [jig]; Distressed Innocence [air]; Amphitryon [sarabande]; The Double Dealer [air] *(rec Abbey Road Studio 1, London, July 1965)* EMI Classics ▲ CDK 65341 [ADD]
Purcell, H.:Sons (22) Vns, w. Alberto Lysy (vn), Robert Masters (vn), Cecil Aronowitz (va), Walter Gerhard (va), Derek Simpson (vc), Ambrose Gauntlett (vl), Roy Jesson (hpd/org)—Nos. 2, 6, & 8 EMI Classics ▲ CDK 65734
Schoenberg, A.:Phantasy Vn, w. G. Gould (pno) *(rec Oct. 25–26, 1965)* Sony Classical ▲ SMK 52688 [ADD]
Schubert, Franz:Rondo Vn, D.895, w. H. Menuhin (pno) *(rec 1938, from HMV DB 3583/84)* Biddulph ▲ LAB 067 [ADD]
Schumann, R.:Son 2 Vn, w. H. Menuhin (pno) *(rec 1934)* Biddulph ▲ LAB 067 [ADD]
Schumann, R.:Trio 2 Pno, w. M. Horszowski (pno), P. Casals (vc) *(rec live 1950s)* Music & Arts 4-▲ CD 689 (m) [AAD]
Sir Yehudi Menuhin 75th Birthday Edition, w. Pierre Boulez (cnd), Adrian Boult (cnd), Antal Dorati (cnd), Paul Kletzki (cnd), Mogens Wöldike (cnd), et al. EMI Classics ("Studio" series) 5-▲ CDME 63984
Tartini, G.:Son Vn "Devil's Trill", w. A. Balsam (pno) *(rec 1932)* Biddulph ▲ LAB 046 [ADD]
Tchaikovsky, P.:Trio Pno, w. Hepzibah Menuhin (pno), Maurice Eisenberg (vc) *(rec 1936)* Biddulph ▲ LAB 127
Vivaldi, A.:Cons Vn, Op. 8/1–4, "The Four Seasons", *(orch unknown)* EMI Classics ▲ CDE 67792
The Young Yehudi Menuhin:The 1932 HMV Recordings, w. Artur Balsam (pno) Biddulph ▲ LAB 046 [ADD]
The Young Yehudi Menuhin:The 1928–29 HMV Recordings, w. Louis Persinger (pno) Biddulph ▲ LAB 031 [ADD]
The Young Yehudi Menuhin:The 1929–30 HMV Recordings, w. Hubert Giesen (pno) Biddulph ▲ LAB 032 [ADD]

Menzler, Helmut (vc)—see ORCHESTRAS & ENSEMBLES Pellegrini String Quartet
Meo, Sandro (vc)—see ORCHESTRAS & ENSEMBLES Italian Piano Quartet
Mercelli, L. (pno)
Haydn, J.:Trios Pno, Vn & Vc, w. M. Mercelli (vn), C. Casadei (vc)—HXV No. 30 in F—piano-flute-cello Bongiovanni ▲ GB 5508 [DDD]

Mercelli, Massimo (fl)
Bach, Joh. Christian:Trio for 2 Fls, Op. 2, w. M. Larrieu (fl), L. Bavaj (hpd)—in G Bongiovanni ▲ GB 5529 [DDD]
Bach, W.F.:Duets Fls, F.54–59, w. M. Larrieu—Nos. 3 & 6 Bongiovanni ▲ GB 5529 [DDD]
Bach, W.F.:Trios Fls, F.47–49, w. M. Larrieu, L. Bavaj (harpsichord)—Nos. 1–3 Bongiovanni ▲ GB 5529 [DDD]
Bellafronte, R.:Le Jardin au fond de la mer *(rec Villa Torano, Imola, Dec 1994)* Bongiovanni ▲ GB 5049-2 [DDD]
Haydn, J.:Trios Fls & Vc, "London Trios", w. Maxence Larrieu (fl), C. Casadei (vc) Bongiovanni ▲ GB 5508 [DDD]
Haydn, J.:Trios Pno, Vn & Vc, w. L. Mercelli (pno), C. Casadei (vc)—HXV No. 30 in F—piano-flute-cello Bongiovanni ▲ GB 5508 [DDD]
Martini, G.B.:Cons (2) Fl Strs, w. L. Ferrara (cnd), Benedetto Marcello CO Bongiovanni ▲ GB 5517 [DDD]
Martini, G.B.:Music for Fls, w. N. Guidetti (fl), G. Perrucci (fl), M. Vangi (fl)—(2 works for 2 Flutes) Sonata in C; Sonata in D; (3 works for 2 Flutes & Continuo) Allegro in C; Allegro & Rondo in C; Pastorale in C Bongiovanni ▲ GB 5517 [DDD]

Mercier, Éric (shawm/bgp)—see ORCHESTRAS & ENSEMBLES La Nef
Mercier, Hélène (pno)
Beethoven, L. van:Son Pno 4-Hands, w. Louis Lortie (pno), Hélène Mercier (pno) Chandos ▲ CHAN 9347 [DDD]
Mozart, W.A.:Andante & Vars Pno 4-Hands, w. L. Lortie (pno) Chandos ▲ CHAN 9162 [DDD]
Mozart, W.A.:Son Pnos, K.448, w. L. Lortie (pno) Chandos ▲ CHAN 9162 [DDD]
Ravel, M.:Boléro, w. L. Lortie (pno) [Ravel's 1930 two-piano arr.] Chandos ▲ CHAN 8905 [DDD]
Ravel, M.:Intro & Allegro, w. L. Lortie (pno) [Ravel's two-piano arr.] Chandos ▲ CHAN 8905 [DDD]
Ravel, M.:Ma mère l'oye Pno, w. L. Lortie (pno) Chandos ▲ CHAN 8905 [DDD]
Ravel, M.:Rapsodie espagnole, w. L. Lortie (pno) [Ravel's piano duet arr.] Chandos ▲ CHAN 8905 [DDD]
Ravel, M.:La Valse, w. L. Lortie (pno) [Ravel's 1921 two-piano arr.] Chandos ▲ CHAN 8905 [DDD]
Schubert, Franz:Fant Pno, D.940, w. L. Lortie (pno) Chandos ▲ CHAN 9162 [DDD]

Mercier, Mel (bodhran)
Cage, J.:Roaratorio:An Irish Circus on Finnegans Wake, w. J. Cage (voice), J. Heaney (sgr), P. Glackin (fid), P. Mercier (bodhran), M. Mallory (fl), S. Ellis (uillean pipes) Wergo ▲ WER 6303-2
Cage, J.:Roaratorio:An Irish Circus on Finnegans Wake, w. J. Cage (voice), J. Heaney (sgr), P. Glackin (fid), P. Mercier (bodhran), M. Mallory (fl), S. Ellis (uillean pipes) Mode 2-▲ mode 28/29

Mercier, Peadher (bodhran)
Cage, J.:Roaratorio:An Irish Circus on Finnegans Wake, w. J. Cage (voice), J. Heaney (sgr), P. Glackin (fid), M. Mercier (bodhran), M. Mallory (fl), S. Ellis (uillean pipes) Mode 2-▲ mode 28/29
Cage, J.:Roaratorio:An Irish Circus on Finnegans Wake, w. J. Cage (voice), J. Heaney (sgr), P. Glackin (fid), M. Mercier (bodhran), M. Mallory (fl), S. Ellis (uillean pipes) Wergo ▲ WER 6303-2

Mercuri, Stefania (ob)—see ORCHESTRAS & ENSEMBLES Rara Ensemble
Mercz, Nóra (hp)
The Romance Collection, w. János Bálint (fl) *(rec Rottenbiller Street Studio, Budapest, Dec 14–18, 1992)* Naxos 4-▲ 8.504005 [DDD]
Romantic Music for Flute & Harp, w. János Bálint (fl) *(rec Dec. 1992)* Naxos ▲ 8.550741 [DDD]

Merfeld, R. (pno)—see ORCHESTRAS & ENSEMBLES Apple Hill Chamber Players

Merkoulova, T. (pno)
Dvořák, A.:Zigeunermelodien, Op. 55, w. Igor Politkovsky (vn)—Gypsy Song in c [trans F. Kreisler for vn & pno] *(rec 1961)* Russian Compact Disc ("Talents of Russia" series) ▲ RCD 16279 [ADD]
Tchaikovsky, P.:Mélodie, w. Igor Politkovsky (vn) [trans for vn & pno] *(rec 1961)* Russian Compact Disc ("Talents of Russia" series) ▲ RCD 16279 [ADD]

Merlet, Dominique (pno)
Brahms, J.:Rhaps Pno, Op. 79 Accord ▲ ACD 201802
Brahms, J.:Son 3 Pno Accord ▲ ACD 201802
Satie, E.:Aperçus désagréables, w. Jean–Pierre Armengaud (pno) Mandala ▲ MAN 4882
Satie, E.:La belle excentrique, w. Jean–Pierre Armengaud (pno) Mandala ▲ MAN 4882
Satie, E.:En habit de cheval, w. Jean–Pierre Armengaud (pno) Mandala ▲ MAN 4882
Satie, E.:Morceaux en forme de poire, w. Jean–Pierre Armengaud (pno) Mandala ▲ MAN 4882
Satie, E.:Parade, w. Jean–Pierre Armengaud (pno) [arr for pno 4–hands] Mandala ▲ MAN 4882
Satie, E.:Petites pièces montées, w. Jean–Pierre Armengaud (pno) Mandala ▲ MAN 4882
Schumann, R.:Arabeske Pno Accord ▲ ACD 202612 [AAD]
Schumann, R.:Davidsbündlertänze Accord ▲ ACD 202612 [AAD]
Schumann, R.:Sym Etudes Accord ▲ ACD 202612 [AAD]
Weber, C.M. von:Son 2 Pno Accord ▲ ACD 202782 [AAD]

Merlini, Fabrizio (va)
Battiato, F.:Haiku, w. Franco Battiato (voc), Pouran Ghaffarpour (voc), Antonio Ballista (pno), Marco Boni (vc), Guido Corti (cnt), Filippo Destrieri (kbd/computer), John Giblin (bass), Gavin Harrison (dr/perc), Jakko Jakszyk (gtr), Roberto Mazza (ob), Angelo Privitera (kbd/computer), Mino Bordignon (cnd), Milan Chamber Music Choir Hemisphere ▲ 837234–2
Battiato, F.:Ricerca sul Terzo, w. Franco Battiato (voc), Alessio Alba (tamboura), Antonio Ballista (pno), Marco Boni (vc), Debendra Kanti Chakraborty (tabla), Guido Corti (cnt), Filippo Destrieri (kbd/computer), John Giblin (bass), Buddhadeu Das Gupta (sarod), Gavin Harrison (dr/perc), Jakko Jakszyk (gtr), Roberto Mazza (ob), Angelo Privitera (kbd/computer), Mino Bordignon (cnd), Milan Chamber Music Choir Hemisphere ▲ 837234–2

Mermoud, Philippe (vc)
Bach, C.P.E.:Trio Sons (misc), w. C. Delafontaine (fl), F. Sarnau (vn), M. Jordan (hpd)—in b, a, d, B♭ & D *(rec Jan 4, 5 & 6, 1988)* Gallo ▲ CD 541
Bach, J.S.:Sons Vn, w. A. Grumiaux (vn), C. Jaccottet (hpd)—BWV 1014–1019, 1021 & 1023; BWV 1020 & 1022 [doubtful] Philips 2–▲ 426452–2 [ADD]
Bach, J.S.:Sons Vn, w. Arthur Grumiaux (vn), Christiane Jaccottet (hpd)—BWV 1014–1023 Philips 2–▲ 454011–2

Mernier, Benoit (org)
Mernier on 3 Organs at the Abbey de Muri Suisse Studio SM ▲ 12 22 47

Merrill, K. (pno)
Pleskow, R.:From Holy Week in Genoa, w. J. Cable (sop) CRS ▲ CD 9153
Pleskow, R.:Songs (2) on Latin Fragments, w. J. Cable (sop) CRS ▲ CD 9153

Merrill, William (pno)
Sullivan, A.:Songs, w. Richard Conrad (bar)—Guinevere; O Mistress Mine; A Life That Lives for You; If Dought Deeds; Arabian Love Song; I Would I Were a King; others Pearl ▲ PEA 9636 [DDD]

Merscher, Kristin (pno)
Brahms, J.:Sons Vc (comp), w. M. Kliegel (vc) *(rec Nov. 1992)* Naxos ▲ 8.550655 [DDD]
Brahms, J.:Son in D Vc, w. M. Kliegel (vc) *(rec Nov. 1992)* Naxos ▲ 8.550655 [DDD]
Schubert, Franz:Son Arpeggione, w. M. Kliegel (vc) *(rec Dec. 14–15, 1991)* Naxos ▲ 8.550654 [DDD]
Schumann, R.:Adagio & Allegro Hn, w. M. Kliegel (vc) *(rec Dec. 14–15, 1991)* Naxos ▲ 8.550654 [DDD]
Schumann, R.:Fantasiestücke Cl, w. M. Kliegel (vc) [arr. for cello & piano] *(rec Dec. 14–15, 1991)* Naxos ▲ 8.550654 [DDD]
Schumann, R.:Stücke im Volkston, w. M. Kliegel (vc) *(rec Dec. 14–15, 1991)* Naxos ▲ 8.550654 [DDD]

Mersson, Boris (pno)
Mozart, W.A.:Con 12 Pno, w. B. Mersson (cnd), Montreux SO Doron ▲ DRC 3013
Mozart, W.A.:Con 26 Pno, w. B. Mersson (cnd), Montreux SO Doron ▲ DRC 3013

Mertens, Theo (instr)—see ORCHESTRAS & ENSEMBLES Chamber Opera Quintet

Merwijk, Willem van (bar sax)—see ORCHESTRAS & ENSEMBLES Aurelia Saxophone Quartet

Merzhanov, Victor (pno)
Brahms, J.:Vars on a Theme by Paganini *(rec 1951)* Rondo Grammofon ▲ RCD 16209 (m) [AAD]
Liszt, F.:Études d'exécution transcendante d'après Paganini, S.140 *(rec 1955)* Rondo Grammofon ▲ RCD 16209 (m) [AAD]
Prokofiev, S.:Tales of an Old Grandmother MCA Classics/Melodiya ▲ MLD 32111 ■ MLC 32122
Rachmaninoff, S.:Con 3 Pno, w. K. Ivanov (cnd), Russian State SO Multisonic ▲ MUL 310352

Meshulam, Benita (pno)
Albéniz, I.:Iberia Suite—Books I & II (complete); Book III (El Albaicín); Book IV (Málaga) *(rec Sept 1989)* Classic Masters ▲ CMCD 1033 [DDD]
Granados, E.:Goyescas—No. 4 *(rec Sept. 1989)* Classic Masters ▲ CMCD 1033 [DDD]

Messens, Rigo (vc)—see ORCHESTRAS & ENSEMBLES Gaggini String Quartet

Messer, Donald (org)
Historic Organs of New Orleans, w. George Bozeman (org), James S. Darling (org), Jesse E. Eschbach (org), Gerald D. Frank (org), John Gearhart (org), James Hammann (org), Frederick Hohman (org), Lenora McCroskey (org), Mary Gifford Matthys (org), Lorenz Maycher (org) *(rec June 1989)* Organ Historical Society 2–▲ OHS 89

Messiaen, Olivier (org)
Messiaen, O.:Le Banquet céleste EMI Classics ▲ CDC 55037

Messiaen, Olivier (pno)
Messiaen, O.:Cantéyodjayâ, w. Yvonne Loriod (pno) Adès ▲ ADE 203142
Messiaen, O.:Visions de l'Amen, w. Yvonne Loriod (pno) Adès ▲ ADE 203142 [AAD]

Messiereur, Petr (vn)—see also ORCHESTRAS & ENSEMBLES Talich String Quartet
Beethoven, L. van:Sons Vn (comp), w. Stanislav Bogunia (pno) Calliope 3–▲ CAL 9251.3 [DDD]
Beethoven, L. van:Son 5 Vn, "Spring", w. Stanislav Bogunia (pno) Calliope ▲ CAL 9252
Beethoven, L. van:Son 6 Vn, w. Stanislav Bogunia (pno) Calliope ▲ CAL 9252
Beethoven, L. van:Son 7 Vn, w. Stanislav Bogunia (pno) Calliope ▲ CAL 9252
Martinů, B.:Primrose, w. S. Bogunia (pno), P. Kühn (cnd), Kühn Women's Chorus Supraphon 2–▲ 11 0752–2 [DDD]
Mozart, W.A.:Sons Vn Pno (misc), w. Stanislav Bogunia (pno)—K.376, K.481 *(rec 1980–85)* Calliope ▲ CAL 6628 [ADD]
Mozart, W.A.:Sons Vn Pno (misc), w. S. Bogunia (pno)—K.296 Calliope ▲ CAL 9244
Paganini, N.:Grand Son Vn, w. M. Zelenka (gtr) *(rec 1983)* Supraphon ▲ 10 3647–2 [AAD]
Paganini, N.:Son concertata, w. M. Zelenka (gtr) *(rec 1983)* Supraphon ▲ 10 3647–2 [AAD]
Paganini, N.:Terzetto Vn, w. E. Rattay (vc), M. Zelenka (gtr) *(rec 1983)* Supraphon ▲ 10 3647–2 [AAD]
Smetana, B.:From the Homeland, w. Václav Snítil (vn), Josef Hála (pno) or Jarmila Kozderková (pno) Panton ▲ PAN 811202
Suk, J.:Ballade Vn, w. Václav Snítil (vn), Josef Hála (pno), Jarmila Kozderková (pno) Panton ▲ PAN 811202

Messina, Joseph (db)
Macchia, S.:Chamber Con 3, w. J. Tanner (fl/alt fl), M. Sussman (cl), F. Cohen (ob/E hn), D. Fedora (bn), L. Klock (hn), V. Kadlubkiewicz (vn), P. Tanner (perc) *(rec July 1992)* Gasparo ▲ GS 226 [DDD]

Messineo, David J. (org)
Love Is Come Again, w. Cathedral of the Sacred Heart Choir Newark *(rec 1992)* Pro Organo ▲ POCD 7041 [DDD]

Messiter, Christine (fl)
Hovhaness, A.:Elibris, w. D. Amos (cnd), Philharmonia Orch Crystal ▲ CD 810 [DDD] ■ C 810 (D)

Messiter, Malcolm (ob)
Albinoni, T.:Cons Obs, w. Guildhall String Ensemble RCA Red Seal ▲ 60224–2–RC [DDD] ■ 60224–4–RC (CrO2)
Albinoni, T.:Cons à 5 Obs, Op. 9, w. Guildhall String Ensemble—No. 2 RCA Red Seal ▲ 60224–2 [DDD] ■ 60224–4 (CrO2)
Bach, J.S.:Con Ob, BWV 1056, w. Guildhall String Ensemble RCA Red Seal ▲ 60224–2–RC [DDD] ■ 60224–4–RC (CrO2)
Handel, G.F.:Cons (3) Ob, w. Guildhall String Ensemble—No. 3 in g RCA Red Seal ▲ 60224–2–RC [DDD]; ■ 60224–4–RC (CrO2)
Marcello, A.:Con Ob & Strs, w. Guildhall String Ensemble RCA Red Seal ▲ 60224–2–RC [DDD] ■ 60224–4–RC (CrO2)
Vivaldi, A.:Cons Ob, w. Guildhall String Ensemble—in C, R.447 & in d, R.454 RCA Red Seal ▲ 60224–2–RC [DDD] ■ 60224–4–RC (CrO2)

Messler, Guy (tpt)
Molter, J.M.:Cons Tpt, w. G. Touvron (tpt), J. Faerber (cnd), Württemberg CO RCA Red Seal ▲ 09026–61200–2

Messlinger, Dieter (vc)
Bach, J.S.:Cant 203, w. Claus Ocker (bass), Martin Galling (hpd), R. Ewerhart (cnd) *(rec 1966)* Vox Box 3–▲ CD3X 3039

Mesterházy, Dezsó (hn)
Haydn, J.:Diverts for 2 Obs, Hns & Bns, H.II/7, 15, D18, 23 & deest, w. P Pongrácz (ob), B. Hock (ob), A. Medveczky (hn), T. Fülemile (bn), A. Nagy (bn) White Label ▲ HRC 155 [ADD]

Metcalfe, John (va)—see ORCHESTRAS & ENSEMBLES Duke String Quartet

Metheny, Pat (gtr)
Reich, S.:Electric Counterpoint Elektra/Nonesuch ▲ 79176–2 ■ 79176–4

Metson, Marian Ruhl (org)
Bacon, E.:Spirits & Places Raven ▲ OAR 210 [DDD]
Bacon, E.:Tpt Tune Raven ▲ OAR 210 [DDD]
Buck, D.:Concert Vars on The Star–spangled Banner Raven ▲ OAR 190 CD [DDD]
Cook, J.:Org Music [1935 Aeolian Skinner Organ, Church of the Advent, Boston, Mass.]—The Carols [A Babe is Born; Gabriel's Message; God is Ascended]; Fanfare; Five Studies in Form of a Sonata; Improvisation on Veni Creator Spiritus; Invocation & Allegro Giojoso; Paean on Divinum Mysterium; Passacharlia Raven ▲ OAR 150 CD [DDD]
Cook, J.:Org Music—Fantasy on a Scottish Hymn Tune (Martyrs); Improvisation on Veni Creator Spiritus; Variations on Alles ist an Gottes Segen Raven ▲ OAR 210 [DDD]
Ives, C.:Vars on *America* Raven ▲ OAR 190 CD [DDD]
Yankee:Come Home! (A Pickle for the Knowing Ones) Raven ▲ OAR 190 [DDD]

Metz, Edward (perc)
Brass on Broadway, w. Canadian Brass, Luther Henderson (kbd), Star of Indiana Drummers Philips ▲ 442133–2

Metz, Henrik (pno)
Mozart, W.A.:Songs, w. H. Hinz (sop)—Abendempfindung; An Chloë; Das Kinderspiel; Schlafe, mein Prinzchen; Trennungslied; Die Verschweigung; Warnung Kontrapunkt ▲ 32052 [DDD]
Nielsen, C.:Songs, w. K. Westi (ten)—Den Danske sang er en ung blond pige; Der dukker af disen min faedrende jord; Farvel min velsignede fødeby; Grøn er varens haek; Hvem sidder der bag skaermen; Hvor sødt i sommeraftenstunden; I skyggen vi vanke; Jeg baerer med smil min byrde; Jeg laegger mig sa trygt til ro; Jeg ved en laerkerede; Min pige er lys som rav; Nu er dagen fuld af sang; Nu er da varen kommen; De refsnaes drenge, de samsø piger; Saenk kun dit hoved, du blomst; Se dig ud en sommerdag; Skal blomsterne da visne?; Solen er sa rød, mor; Den spillemand spiller pa strenge; Ud gar du nu pa livets vej; Underlige aftenlufte; Vender sig lykken fra dig [Da] Kontrapunkt ▲ 32047 [DDD]
Schubert, Franz:Songs (misc), w. H. Hinz (sop)—An die Musik; An die Nachtigall; An Sylvia; Fischerweise; Die Forelle; Fruhlingslaube; Ganymed; Im Frühling; Heidenröslein; Lachen und Weinen; Wiegenlied Kontrapunkt ▲ 32052 [DDD]

Metz, John (hpd)
Jacquet De La Guerre, E.:Suites Hpd—No. 1 in D & No. 4 in F from Book One (1687); No. 1 in d from Book Two (1707) Summit ▲ SMT 136 [DDD]

Metz, S. (vc)—see ORCHESTRAS & ENSEMBLES Orlando String Quartet

Metzger, Jörg (vc)
Neubauer, F.C.:Con Vc, w. V. Lukas (cnd), Lukas Consort Campion ▲ 1329 [DDD]

Metzger, Nancy (hpd)
Bach, J.S.:Das wohltemperierte Klavier—Book 1/6 & 8; Book 2/5 Arkay ▲ ARK 6132 [DDD]
Froberger, J.J.:Hpd Music—Suite 3 in g; Tombeau fait a Paris sur la mort de Monsieur Blancrocher Arkay ▲ ARK 6132 [DDD]

Metzger, Nancy (org)
Stanley, J.:Voluntaries Org—Full Organ Voluntary; Trumpet Voluntary Arkay ▲ ARK 6132 [DDD]

Metzger, Roland (va)—see also ORCHESTRAS & ENSEMBLES Sinnhoffer String Quartet members
Brahms, J.:Songs, Op. 91, w. C. Wulkopf (alt), K. Schilde (pno) [G] Ars Produktion ▲ FCD 368305

Metzmacher, R. (vc)
Beethoven, L. van:Sons Vc (comp), w. E. Steen–Nökleberg (pno) Brioso 2–▲ BR 100
Beethoven, L. van:Vars on "Ein Mädchen oder Weibchen" from Mozart's *Die Zauberflöte*, w. E. Steen–Nökleberg (pno)—No. 3 Brioso 2–▲ BR 100
Beethoven, L. van:Vars on "See, the Conquering Hero Comes" from Handel's *Judas Maccabaeus*, w. E. Steen–Nökleberg (pno)—No. 1 Brioso 2–▲ BR 100
Beethoven, L. van:Vars on "Bei Männern" from Mozart's *Die Zauberflöte*, w. E. Steen–Nökleberg (pno)—No. 2 Brioso 2–▲ BR 100
Brahms, J.:Sons Vc (comp), w. E. Steen–Nörkleberg (pno) Brioso ▲ BR 101

Meunier, Alain (vc)
Bach, J.S.:Suites Vc, BWV 1007–1012—BWV 1007, 1008 & 1009 Harmonic ▲ H 9243
Bayer, F.:Music of, w. Donatienne Michel–Dansac (sop), Jean–Louis Haguenauer (pno), Renaud Francois, Francesca Paderni, Tetra Ensemble Pierre Verany ▲ PVY 796093
Beethoven, L. van:Trio 7 Pno, w. R. Serkin (pno), R. Stolzman (cl) Sony Classical ▲ SMK 47296 [ADD]
Hindemith, P.:Son Vc & Pno (1948), w. Christian Ivaldi (pno) Arion ▲ ARN 68319
Norman, L.:Qt Pno, Op. 10, w. Christian Ivaldi (pno), Sylvie Gazeau (vn), Gérard Caussé (vn) Musica Sveciae ▲ MSV 518 [DDD]
Offenbach, J.:Duos for 2 Vcs, w. P. Muller (vc)—Opp. 52/3 & 53/1–3 Arion ▲ ARN 68234 [AAD]
Ohana, M.:Anneau du Tamarit, w. M. Andreae (cnd), French National Orch *(rec 1990)* Erato ("Musifrance" series) ▲ 2292–45503–2 [ADD/DDD]

Meves, C. (fl)
Foss, L.:Thirteen Ways of Looking at a Blackbird, w. E. LaBruce (mez), A. Brovan (pno), M. Shadd (perc) [E] *(rec 1989–90)* Koss Classics ▲ KC 1006 [DDD]

Meyer, Allan (perc)—see ORCHESTRAS & ENSEMBLES Nova Ensemble

Meyer, Brigitte (pno)
Mendelssohn, F.:Charakteristische Stücke *(rec May 1991)* Jecklin ▲ JD 661–2 [DDD]
Mendelssohn, F.:Lieder ohne Worte Pno *(rec July 1993 & Apr 1994)* Jecklin 2–▲ JD 693/4
Mendelssohn, F.:Son Pno, Op. 6 *(rec May 1991)* Jecklin ▲ JD 661–2 [DDD]
Mendelssohn, F.:Son Pno, Op. 106 *(rec May 1991)* Jecklin ▲ JD 661–2 [DDD]
Mozart, W.A.:Con 9 Pno, w. I. Brown (cnd), Norwegian CO Omega ▲ OCD 1003 [DDD]
Mozart, W.A.:Con 23 Pno, w. I. Brown (cnd), Norwegian CO Omega ▲ OCD 1003 [DDD]
Poulenc, F.:Con for 2 Pnos, w. Alexandre Rabinovitch (pno), P. Crispini (cnd), European Concerts Orch Doron ▲ DRC 3022 [DDD]

Meyer, D. (mand)
Vivaldi, A.:Cons Mand, w. C. Schneider (mand), K. Redel (cnd), Grenoble Instrumental Ensemble—Concerti in C & D for Mandolin & Strings; Concerto in G for 2 Mandolins & Strings; Concerto in C for 2 Mandolins & Orchestra Forlane ▲ FOR 16548 [AAD]

Meyer, Edgar (db)
O'Connor, M.:Qt Vn, w. Mark O'Connor (vn), Daniel Phillips (va), Carter Brey (vc) *(rec Blair Recital Hall, Vanderbilt Univ., Nashville, TN, Dec. 1990)* Warner Bros. ▲ 45846–2

▲ = CD ♦ = Enhanced CD Δ = MD ■ = Cassette Tape ▯ = DCC

Meyer, Edgar (db) (cont.)
Prokofiev, S.:Qnt Ob, w. A. Vogel (ob), D. Shifrin (cl), P. Frank (vn), S. Tenebom (va) *(rec July 1–4, 1992)* Delos ▲ DE 3136 [DDD]

Meyer, François (ob)
Britten, H.:Metamorphoses Ob Sonpact ▲ SPT 94011 [DDD]
Dutilleux, H.:Son Ob, w. Eric Le Sage (pno) Sonpact ▲ SPT 94011 [DDD]
Hindemith, P.:Son Ob, w. Eric Le Sage (pno) Sonpact ▲ SPT 94011 [DDD]
Poulenc, F.:Son Ob, w. Eric Le Sage (pno) Sonpact ▲ SPT 94011 [DDD]
Saint-Saëns, C.:Son Ob, w. Eric Le Sage (pno) Sonpact ▲ SPT 94011 [DDD]

Meyer, Gerhard (pno)
Romantic Russian Music for Paino Duo, w. Siegfried Schuber-Weber (pno) FSM ▲ 91007 [ADD]

Meyer, Hannes (org)
Corrette, M.:Cons Org, Op. 26, w. Noda (db), Sonare String Quartet—concerto in A Claves ▲ CD 8511 [DDD]
Durante, F.:Con Org, w. Noda (db), Sonare String Quartet Claves ▲ CD 8511 [DDD]
Meyer, H.:Suite paysanne, w. Noda (db), Sonare String Quartet Claves ▲ CD 8511 [DDD]
Paradies, P.D.:Con Org, w. I. Noda (db), Sonare String Quartet Claves ▲ CD 8511 [DDD]
Spiel Orgel spiel [Play Organ Play] *(rec 1977 & 1981)* Claves ("Favor Collection" series) ▲ CLF 8102 [ADD]
Stanley, J.:Con in c Org, w. Noda (db), Sonare String Quartet Claves ▲ CD 8511 [DDD]

Meyer, Krzysztof (pno)
Meyer, K.:Preludes Pro Viva ▲ ISPV 174
Meyer, K.:Qnt Pno, w. Wilanów String Quartet *(rec SFB Studio Kleiner Sendesaal, Berlin, June 1992)* Pro Viva ▲ ISPV 171 [DDD]

Meyer, Leif (hpd)
Blavet, M.:Sons Trns Fl, w. Dan Laurin (rcr), Mogens Rasmussen (vl)—Son Terza; Son Seconda *(rec Furuby Church, Sweden, May 8–11, 1995)* BIS ▲ CD 745 [DDD]
Braun, J.D.:Son Terza, w. Dan Laurin (rcr), Mogens Rasmussen (vl) or Leif Meyer (hpd) *(rec Furuby Church, Sweden, May 8–11, 1995)* BIS ▲ CD 745 [DDD]
Dornel, L.-A.:Sons Vn & Suites Fl, Op. 2, w. Dan Laurin (rcr), Mogens Rasmussen (vl)—Suite II[5] *(rec Furuby Church, Sweden, May 8–11, 1995)* BIS ▲ CD 745 [DDD]
Leclair, J.-M.:Sons Vn (Books 1–4), w. Dan Laurin (rcr), Mogens Rasmussen (vl)—Son II *(rec Furuby Church, Sweden, May 8–11, 1995)* BIS ▲ CD 745 [DDD]

Meyer, Marcelle (pno)
Milhaud, D.:Scaramouche for 2 Pnos, w. D. Milhaud (pno) EMI Classics ▲ CDC 54604

Meyer, Paul (bn)
Mozart, W.A.:Adagio Bas Hns, K.410/440d, w. H.R. Stalder (bas hn), E. Schmid (bas hn) *(rec 1978)* Jecklin-Disco ▲ JD 549-2 [ADD]

Meyer, Paul (cl)
Brahms, J.:Sons Cl (comp), w. François-René Duchable (pno)—Allegro gracioso; Vivace [both from Son 1]; Allegro amabile [from Son 2] *(rec Chateau de Châtonneyre, Corseaux, Switzerland, Oct. 1989)* Erato ▲ 94679-2
Bruch, M.:Con Cl & Va, w. G. Caussé (va), K. Nagano (cnd), Lyon Opera Orch Erato ▲ 2292-45483-2 ZK [DDD]
Bruch, M.:Pieces Cl, Op. 83/1–8, w. Gérard Caussé (va), François-René Duchable (pno)—No. 8 [Moderato in e♭] *(rec Studio 106, Radio France, Feb. 1989)* Erato ▲ 94679-2
Bruch, M.:Trios Cl, Va & Pno, Op. 83, w. G. Caussé (va), F.-R. Duchable (pno) Erato ▲ 2292-45483-2 ZK [DDD]
Busoni, F.:Concertino Cl, w. D. Zinman (cnd), English CO *(rec Mar. 27–29, 1992)* Denon ▲ CO 75289 [DDD]
Chausson, E.:Andante et Allegro, w. E. Le Sage (pno) Denon ▲ CO 79282 [DDD]
Copland, A.:Con Cl, w. D. Zinman (cnd), English CO *(rec Mar. 27–29, 1992)* Denon ▲ CO 75289 [DDD]
Danzi, F.:Concertante Fl, w. Jean-Pierre Rampal (fl), J.-P. Rampal (cnd), Franz Liszt CO *(rec Italian Institute, Budapest, Jan. 4–7, 1993)* Denon ▲ CO 78911 [DDD]
Fuchs, R.:Qnt Cl, w. Carmina String Quartet *(rec Landgasthof Riehen, Switzerland, Apr 2, 3 18 & 19, 1995)* Denon ▲ CO 78801 [DDD]
Milhaud, D.:Caprice, w. E. Le Sage (pno) Denon ▲ CO 79282 [DDD]
Milhaud, D.:Duo concertante Cl & Pno, w. E. Le Sage (pno) Denon ▲ CO 79282 [DDD]
Milhaud, D.:Sonatina Cl, w. E. Le Sage (pno) Denon ▲ CO 79282 [DDD]
Mozart, W.A.:Con Cl, w. D. Zinman (cnd), English CO *(rec Mar. 27–29, 1992)* Denon ▲ CO 75289 [DDD]
Pleyel, I.:Con in B♭ Cl, w. J.-P. Rampal (cnd), Franz Liszt CO *(rec Italian Institute, Budapest, Jan. 4–7, 1993)* Denon ▲ CO 78911 [DDD]
Pleyel, I.:Con in C Cl, w. J.-P. Rampal (cnd), Franz Liszt CO *(rec Italian Institute, Budapest, Jan. 4–7, 1993)* Denon ▲ CO 78911 [DDD]
Pleyel, I.:Sinf concertante 5, w. D. Becker (fl), Schottstädt (bn), Schneider (hn), J. Faerber (cnd), Württemberg CO MD + G ▲ L 3396 [DDD]
Schoenberg, A.:Trans Chamber Ensemble, w. Hakon Ausbö (harm), Michel Béroff (perc), Isabelle Berteletti (perc), Louise Bessette (pno), Marc Marder (db), Michel Moraguès (fl), Arditti String Quartet—Busoni:Berceuse élégiaque (1920); Mahler:Songs of a Wayfarer (1920) [w. Jean-Luc Chaignaud (baritone)]; Joh. Strauss:Kaiserwalzer (1925); Roses from the South (1921) Montaigne ▲ MO 789011 [DDD]
Strauss, R.:Duet-Concertino, w. K. Sonstevold (bn), E.-P. Salonen (cnd), New Stockholm CO CBS ▲ MK 44702 [DDD]
20th Century Music for Unaccompanied Clarinet *(rec Zurich, Oct. 28–31, 1993)* Denon ▲ CO 78917 [DDD]
Weber, C.M. von:Grand duo concertant Cl, w. François-René Duchable (pno)—Andante con moto *(rec Chateau de Châtonneyre, Corseaux, Switzerland, Oct. 1989)* Erato ▲ 94679-2
Weber, C.M. von:Qnt Cl, w. Carmina String Quartet *(rec Landgasthof Riehen, Switzerland, Apr 2, 3 18 & 19, 1995)* Denon ▲ CO 78801 [DDD]

Meyer, R. (cl)
Berio, L.:Opus Number Zoo, w. B. Demottaz (ob), B. Schenkel (fl), G. Cass (hn), R. Birnstingl (bn) *(rec June 1987)* Gallo ▲ CD 527
Bizet, G.:Jeux d'enfants, w. B. Demottaz (ob), B. Schenkel (fl), G. Cass (hn), R. Birnstingl (bn) *(rec June 1987)* Gallo ▲ CD 527
Saint-Saëns, C.:Carnival of the Animals, w. B. Demottaz (ob), B. Schenkel (inst), G. Cass (horn), R. Birnstingl (bn) *(rec June 1987)* Gallo ▲ CD 527

Meyer, Sabine (cl)—see also ORCHESTRAS & ENSEMBLES Trio di Clarone, Sabine Meyer Wind Ensemble
Danzi, F.:Concertante Fl, w. J. Galway (fl), J. Faerber (cnd), Württemberg CO RCA Red Seal ▲ 09026-61976-2; ■ 09026-61976-4
Danzi, F.:Phantasie on "La ci darem la mano" from Mozart's *Don Giovanni*, w. J. Faerber (cnd), Württemberg CO RCA Red Seal ▲ 09026-61976-2; ■ 09026-61976-4
Küffner, J.:Intro, Theme & Vars, w. Berlin Philharmonia String Quartet Denon/PCM Digital ▲ DEN 8098 [DDD]
Lachner, F.P.:Octet, w. N. Frisch (hn), J. Steinbrecher (bn), Chalumeau Quintet Ambitus ▲ 97825 [DDD]
Mozart, W.A.:Music of, w. Alban Berg Quartet, F. P. Zimmermann (vn), A. Dumay (vn), A. S. Mutter (vn), R. Vlatkovi (hn), C. Zacharias (pno), *(sels unknown)* EMI Classics ▲ CDC 54165
Mozart, W.A.:Qnt Cl, K.581, w. Berlin Philharmonia String Quartet Denon ▲ CO 8003 [DDD]
Mozart, W.A.:Qnt Cl, K.581, w. Berlin Philharmonia String Quartet Denon/PCM Digital ▲ DEN 8098 [DDD]
Opera Themes & Variations for Clarinet & Orchestra, w. Zurich Opera Orch [cnd:Franz Welser-Möst] EMI Classics ▲ CDC 56137
Schubert, Franz:Songs (comp), w. B. Hendricks (sop), R. Lupu (pno), B. Schneider (hn)—Der Hirt auf dem Felsen; Lachen und weinen; Ständchen; Die Männer sind méchant, Auf dem Strom; Sehnsucht; Liebesbotschaft; Versunken; An den Mond; Du liebst mich nicht; Die Liebe hat gelogen; Die junge Nonne; Klaglied; Ellens Gesang III; Delphine; Heidenröslein [G] EMI Classics ▲ CDC 54239

Meyer, Sabine (cl) (cont.)
Stamitz, C.:Cons Cl, w. I. Brown (cnd), Academy of St. Martin in the Fields—No. 3 in B♭; No. 10 in B; No. 11 in E♭ EMI Classics ▲ CDC 54842 [DDD]
Stamitz, C.:Con Cl, w. I. Brown (cnd), Academy of St. Martin in the Fields—No. 3 in B♭; No. 10 in B; No. 11 in E♭ EMI Classics ▲ CDC 54842 [DDD]

Meyer, Vera (glass armonica)
The Maestros Tea Party:Mr. Einstein Visits the Queen, w. Mary Jane Rupert (pno), Diana Salomon (vn), Patricia Wenzel (vn), Ella Lou Weiler (va), Fern Meyers (vc), Gerhard Finkenbeiner (glass armonica) *(rec Euphoria Sound Studio, Revere, MA)* Cultured Kids ▲ unknown ■ 120012FM-4

Meyer, W. (tpt)
Molter, J.M.:Cons Cl, w. V. Czarnecki (cnd), Southwest German CO Pforzheim Amati ▲ 9009 [DDD]

Meyer, W. (vn)
Beethoven, L. van:Trio 7 Pno, w. P. Cohen (pno), C. Coin (vc) Harmonia Mundi France ▲ HMC 901475

Meyer, Wolfgang (cl)—see also ORCHESTRAS & ENSEMBLES Trio di Clarone
Danzi, F.:Concertante Fl, w. D. Becker (fl), J. Faerber (cnd), Württemberg CO *(rec 1/91)* MD + G ▲ L 3396 [DDD]
Markevitch, I.:Serenade, w. K. Lessing (vn), D. Jensen (bn) *(rec Oct. 21–22, 1993)* Largo ▲ 5127 [DDD]
Messiaen, O.:Quatuor pour la fin du temps, w. Christoph Poppen (vn), M. Fischer-Dieskau (vc), Y. Loriod (pno) EMI Classics ▲ CDC 54395
Mozart, W.A.:Qnt Cl, K.581, w. A. Mitterer (vn), Mosaïques Ensemble Astrée ▲ E 8736
Mozart, W.A.:Trio Cl, K.498, w. A. Mitterer (va), P. Cohen (pno) Astrée ▲ E 8736

Meyer-Moortgat, H.-D. (pno)
Karg-Elert, S.:Fl & Pno Music, w. H.-M. Zill (fl)—Sinfonische Kanzone, Op. 114; Sonata in B, Op. 121; Impression exotiques, Op. 134; Suite pointillistique, Op. 135; Sonata appassionata, Op. 140 Ambitus ▲ 97833 [DDD]

Meyerriecks, Jeffrey (gtr)
Gibson, R.:Sketches (3), w. George Hummel (fl) Capstone ▲ CPS 8621

Meyers, Anne Akiko (vn)
Baker, D.:Blues Vn, w. André-Michel Schub (pno) [adaptation from Deliver My Soul of Psalm 22] *(rec Am. Acad. of Arts & Letters, NYC, Aug 30–31 & Sept 1–2, 199)* RCA Red Seal ▲ 09026-68114-2 [DDD]
Barber, S.:Con Vn, w. C. Seaman (cnd), Royal PO *(rec Sept. 18–20, 1988)* Canyon Classics ▲ 3699 [DDD]
Barber, S.:Con Vn, w. C. Seaman (cnd), Royal PO RPO Records Impact ▲ RPO 5002 [DDD]
Bruch, M.:Con 1 Vn, w. C. Seaman (cnd), Royal PO RPO Records Impact ▲ RPO 5002 [DDD]
Bruch, M.:Con 1 Vn, w. C. Seaman (cnd), Royal PO *(rec Sept. 18–20, 1988)* Canyon Classics ▲ 3699 [DDD]
Bruch, M.:Scottish Fant Vn, w. J. López-Cobos (cnd), Royal PO RCA Red Seal ▲ 09026-60942-2 ■ 09026-60942-4
Copland, A.:Nocturne, w. André-Michel Schub (pno) *(rec Am. Acad. of Arts & Letters, NYC, Aug 30–31 & Sept 1–2, 199)* RCA Red Seal ▲ 09026-68114-2 [DDD]
Copland, A.:Son Vn & Pno, w. André-Michel Schub (pno) *(rec Am. Acad. of Arts & Letters, NYC, Aug 30–31 & Sept 1–2, 199)* RCA Red Seal ▲ 09026-68114-2 [DDD]
Fauré, G.:Son 1 Vn, w. S. Rivers (pno) *(rec May 26 & 27, 1989)* Canyon Classics ▲ 3658 [DDD]
Franck, C.:Son Vn, w. R. de Silva (pno) RCA Red Seal ▲ 09026-61283-2
The Heart of the Violin Concerto, w. Kovacic, Ernst (vn), Jaime Laredo (vn), Elmar Oliveire (vn), Hideko Udagawa (vn) Pickwick ("The Orchid" series) ▲ PICORCD 11013
Ives, C.:Son 4 Vn, w. André-Michel Schub (pno) [arr for vn & pno] *(rec Am. Acad. of Arts & Letters, NYC, Aug 30–31 & Sept 1–2, 199)* RCA Red Seal ▲ 09026-68114-2 [DDD]
Lalo, E.:Sym espagnole, w. J. López-Cobos (cnd), Royal PO RCA Red Seal ▲ 09026-60942-2 ■ 09026-60942-4
Piston, W.:Sonatina Vn, w. André-Michel Schub (pno) *(rec Am. Acad. of Arts & Letters, NYC, Aug 30–31 & Sept 1–2, 199)* RCA Red Seal ▲ 09026-68114-2 [DDD]
Saint-Saëns, C.:Son 1 Vn, w. S. Rivers (pno) *(rec May 26 & 27, 1989)* Canyon Classics ▲ 3658 [DDD]
Salut d'Amour RCA Red Seal ▲ 09026-62546-2
Strauss, R.:Son Vn, w. R. De Silva (pno) RCA Red Seal ▲ 09026-61283-2

Meyers, Fern (vc)
The Maestros Tea Party:Mr. Einstein Visits the Queen, w. Mary Jane Rupert (pno), Diana Salomon (vn), Patricia Wenzel (vn), Ella Lou Weiler (va), Gerhard Finkenbeiner (glass armonica), Vera Meyer (glass armonica) *(rec Euphoria Sound Studio, Revere, MA)* Cultured Kids ▲ unknown ■ 120012FM-4

Meyerson, Mitzi (hpd)
Bach, J.S.:Sons Fl, BWV 1030–35, w. M. Verbruggen (rcr)—BWV 1031 [trans. Verbruggen] Harmonia Mundi USA ▲ HMU 907119
Bach, J.S.:Trio Sons Org, BWV 525–530, w. M. Verbruggen (rcr)—BWV 525, 527, 529 & 530 [trans. Verbruggen] Harmonia Mundi USA ▲ HMU 907119
Forqueray, A.:Pièces de clavecin (5 suites) Broadway Angel ▲ CDC 59310
Leclair, J.-M.:Sons Vn (Books 1–4), w. Christoph Huntgeburth (fl), Hildegard Perl (vl)—Op. 2/1, 3 & 11; Op. 9/2 & 7 ASV ("Gaudeamus" series) ▲ ASV CD 158

Meyerson, Mitzi (hpd/org)
Purcell, H.:Songs, w. D. Minter (ct), P. O'Dette (archlt), M. Springfels (vl)—Be Welcome Then, Great Sir; Celia Has a Thousand Charmes; Crown the Altar; The Fatal Hour Comes On Apace; From Silent Shades; Hark! How All Things; Hark! the Echoing Air; Here the Dieties Approve; I Attempt From Love's Sickness to Fly; If Musick be the Food of Love; Lord, What is Man; Musick For A While; Not All My Torments; Now That the Sun Hath Veil's His Light; O Solitude; Sleep, Adam, Sleep; Sweeter Than Roses; Thrice Happy Lovers; 'Tis Nature's Voice [E] Harmonia Mundi USA ▲ HMU 907035

Meylan, R. (fl)
Reichel, B.:Pièce concertante, w. M. Cichirdan (cnd), Craiova PO Gallo ▲ CD 619 [ADD]

Meyr, Christine (hpd)
Sarti, G.:Sons Fl, w. Claudio Ferrarini (fl), Sokol Koka (vc) Stradivarius ▲ STV 33368 [DDD]

Mezei, János (org)
Werner, G.J.:Vesperae de Confessoris, w. Éva Bodrogi (sop), Regina Fülöp (cta), Kornél Pechan (ten), Péter Cser (bass), J. Mezei (cnd), Vienna-Szász CO, Budapest Schola Cantorum *(rec St. Columba's Presbyterian Church, Budapest, June 12–15, 1995)* Hungaroton ▲ HCD 31646 [DDD]

Mezger, M. (rcr)—see ORCHESTRAS & ENSEMBLES Trio Basiliensis

Mező, L. (vc)—see ORCHESTRAS & ENSEMBLES Bartók String Quartet

Mezo, Laszio (vc)
Goldmark, K.:Qnt Strs, Op. 9, w. Lajtha String Quartet Hungaroton ▲ HCD 31556
Goldmark, K.:Qnt Strs, Op. 30, w. Lajtha String Quartet Hungaroton ▲ HCD 31556

Mezzena, Bruno (pno)—see also ORCHESTRAS & ENSEMBLES Mezzena-Bonucci Trio
Pizzetti, I.:Son 1 Vn, w. Franco Mezzena (vn) Arcobaleno ▲ AAOC 9362
Respighi, O.:Son Vn, w. Franco Mezzena (vn) Arcobaleno ▲ AAOC 9362

Mezzena, Franco (vn)—see also ORCHESTRAS & ENSEMBLES Mezzena-Bonucci Trio
Paganini, N.:Cantabile, w. A. Sebastiani (gtr) Dynamic ▲ CD 62 [DDD]
Paganini, N.:Cantabile & Waltz, w. A. Sebastiani (gtr) Dynamic ▲ CD 62 [DDD]
Paganini, N.:Duetto amoroso Vn, w. A. Sebastiani (gtr) Dynamic ▲ CD 62 [DDD]
Paganini, N.:Inno patriottico con variazioni, w. A. Sebastiani (gtr) Dynamic ▲ CD 03 [AAD]
Paganini, N.:Moto perpetuo Vn & Gtr, w. A. Sebastiani (gtr) Dynamic ▲ CD 03 [AAD]
Paganini, N.:Sons Vn & Gtr, Op. 2, w. A. Sebastiani (gtr) Dynamic ▲ CD 62 [DDD]
Paganini, N.:Sons Vn & Gtr, Op. 3, w. A. Sebastiani (gtr) Dynamic ▲ CD 62 [DDD]
Paganini, N.:Tarantella Vn, w. A. Plotino (cnd), Genoa CO Dynamic ▲ CD 27 [ADD]
Paganini, N.:Theme & Vars Vn, w. A. Sebastiani (gtr) Dynamic ▲ CD 03 [AAD]
Paganini, N.:Vars on "La Carmagnole", w. A. Sebastiani (gtr) Dynamic ▲ CD 03 [AAD]
Paganini, N.:Vars on "O mamma, mamma cara", w. A. Sebastiani (gtr) Dynamic ▲ CD 03 [AAD]
Paisiello, G.:Qts Fl, w. Luigi Palmisano (fl), Arturo Mazza (va), Donna Magendanz (vc) *(rec Trento, Italy, Nov 1979)* Dynamic ▲ CDS 12 [ADD]
Pizzetti, I.:Son 1 Vn, w. Bruno Mezzena (pno) Arcobaleno ▲ AAOC 9362

Mezzena, Franco (vn) (cont.)
Respighi, O.:Son Vn, w. Bruno Mezzena (pno) Arcobaleno ▲ AAOC 9362
Viotti, G.B.:Cons Vn, w. L. Borin (cnd), Viotti CO—No. 8 in D, No. 11 in A, & No. 12 in B♭ Dynamic ▲ CD 63 [DDD]
Viotti, G.B.:Cons Vn, w. L. Borin (cnd), Viotti CO—No. 1 in C, No. 2 in E, & No. 19 in g Dynamic ▲ CD 86 [DDD]

Micault, Jean (pno)
Chopin, F.:Songs Sop (comp), w. C. Verhaeghe (sop) [Pol] Arcobaleno ▲ SBCD 8100
Liszt, F.:Transcriptions & Paraphrases—Chopin:5 songs [Pol] Arcobaleno ▲ SBCD 8100
Mendelssohn, Fanny:Songs, w. Claudie Verhaeghe (sop)—Opp. 1 & 7 Arcobaleno ▲ AAOC 9329
Schumann, C.:Songs, w. Claudie Verhaeghe (sop)—Opp. 12 & 13 Arcobaleno ▲ AAOC 9329
Werfel, A.M.:Songs, w. Claudie Verhaeghe (sop)—7 sels Arcobaleno ▲ AAOC 9329

Micay, Harold (gtr)
La Rosa:A Passion for Guitar Fleur de son ▲ FDS 57919 [DDD]

Micconi, Roberto (org)
Venetian Organ Music Motette ▲ MOD 10561 [DDD]

Michael, Sigurd (ob)—see also also ORCHESTRAS & ENSEMBLES Stuttgart Wind Quintet
Haas, P.:Suite Ob, w. Dennis Russell Davies (pno) [rev František Suchy] Orfeo ("Musica Rediviva" series) ▲ 386961 [DDD]

Michaels, Jost (cl)
Mozart, W.A.:Con Cl, w. H. Reichert (cnd), Westphalia SO Allegretto ▲ ACD 8013 [ADD] ■ ACS 8013
Mozart, W.A.:Con Cl, w. H. Reichert (cnd), Westphalia SO—Allegro Special Music Co. ("Classics of the Heart" series) ▲ SCD 5196
Mozart, W.A.:Con Cl, w. H. Reichert (cnd), Westphalia SO—Allegro Special Music Co. ▲ SCD 5200
Mozart, W.A.:Qnt Cl, K.581, w. Endres String Quartet Allegretto ▲ ACD 8013 [ADD] ■ ACS 8013
Mozart, W.A.:Qnt Cl, K.581, w. Endres String Quartet Vivace 3–▲ E 319 [DDD]

Michaels, Jost (pno)
Berger, W.:Qnt Pno, w. Verdi String Quartet *(rec Leipzig, Jan.–Mar. 1964)* MD + G ("Gold" series) ▲ MDG 3080506 [DDD]

Michal, Luis (vn)—see also also ORCHESTRAS & ENSEMBLES Munich Violin Duo
Viotti, G.B.:Con 2 Vn, w. M. Carfi (vn), L. Michal (cnd), Bavarian CO Calig ▲ CAL 50917 [DDD]
Viotti, G.B.:Sym Concertante 1, w. M. Carfi (vn), L. Michal (cnd), Bavarian CO Calig ▲ CAL 50917 [DDD]
Viotti, G.B.:Sym Concertante 2, w. M. Carfi (vn), L. Michal (cnd), Bavarian CO Calig ▲ CAL 50917 [DDD]

Michal, Metelka (vn)
Flury, R.:Die alte Truhe, w. U. J. Flury (cnd), Prague Czech SO Gallo ▲ CD 860 [DDD]
Flury, R.:Pieces (6) Orch, w. U. J. Flury (cnd), Prague Czech SO Gallo ▲ CD 860 [DDD]

Michalak, Dan (pno)
Banfield, W.:Wagussyduke Innova ▲ 510 [DDD]

Michalakakos, M. (va)
Rossé, F.:Music of, w. Y. Haym (ob), P. Ruby (gtr), C. Roy (vc), I. Assayag (hpd)—Zembrocordal; Digitales; Lance du Souvenant; Impromptu 0990; For a Little Hot Quaint Time Quantum ▲ QM 6949

Michalica, Peter (vn)
Tchaikovsky, P.:Con Vn, w. R. Zimmer (cnd), Philharmonia Cassovia *(rec Moyzes Hall of the Slovak PO, Bratislava, Mar. 1988)* Lydian ▲ 18084 [DDD]

Michaut, Jean (rainsticks)
Cage, J.:Four³, w. Ami Flammer (vn/rainsticks), Dominique Alchourroun (pno/rainsticks), Martine Joste (pno/rainsticks) *(rec Radio France, Paris, Jan. 18–4, 1994)* Mode ▲ mode 44

Michaux, David (tpt)
Zwilich, E.T.:Clarino Qt, w. David Flello (tpt), Christopher Lane (tpt), Louis Ranger (tpt) *(rec Univ of Victoria, May 1994)* Crystal ▲ CD 669

Michejew, Alexander (vc)
Boccherini, L.:Con in D Vc, w. W. Boughton (cnd), English String Orch Nimbus ▲ NI 5035
Bridge, F.:Son Vc, w. M. Jones (pno) Nimbus ▲ NI 5275 [ADD]
Dvořák, A.:Con Vc, w. W. Boughton (cnd), London SO Nimbus ▲ NI 5127 [DDD]
Haydn, J.:Con 1 Vc, w. W. Boughton (cnd), English String Orch Nimbus ▲ NI 5035
Haydn, J.:Con 2 Vc, w. W. Boughton (cnd), English String Orch Nimbus ▲ NI 5035
Kodály, Z.:Son Vc, Op. 8 Nimbus ▲ NI 5275 [ADD]
Saint-Saëns, C.:Con 1 Vc, w. W. Boughton (cnd), London SO Nimbus ▲ NI 5127 [DDD]

Michel, Catherine (hp)
Chopin, F.:Vars on Rossini's *Non più mesta*, w. M. Grauwels (fl) Marco Polo ▲ 8.220441 [DDD]
Cras, J.:Qnt, w. T. Prevost (fl), M.–C. Milliere (vn), J.–F. Benatar (va), P. Bary (vc) Quantum ▲ QM 6897 [DDD] ■ QM 1992 (D)
Donizetti, G.:Larghetto & Allegro, w. Grauwels (fl) Marco Polo ▲ 8.220441 [DDD]
Drouet, L.:Intro & Vars on an English Theme, w. M. Grauwels (fl) Marco Polo ▲ 8.220441 [DDD]
Françaix, J.:Con 2 Hps, w. Susanna Mildonian (hp), A. Moglia (cnd), Toulouse National CO *(rec Apr 1995)* Pavane ▲ ADW 7337 [DDD]
Gossec, F.-J.:Symphonie concertante for 2 Hps, w. Susanna Mildonian (hp), A. Moglia (cnd), Toulouse National CO *(rec Apr 1995)* Pavane ▲ ADW 7337 [DDD]
Legrand, M.:Film Music, w. Michel Legrand (hpd), M. Legrand (cnd), Large SO—Suite for Hp & Orch [from The Umbrellas of Cherbourg]; Concertino for Hp & Orch [from The Summer of '42]; Suite for Hp, Hpd & Orch [from Le Messager]; Suite for Hp, Hpd & Orch [from Yentl] Travelling ("Movies & Music" series) ▲ K 1020
Malecki, M.:Concertino dans un style ancien, w. Susanna Mildonian (hp), A. Moglia (cnd), Toulouse National CO *(rec Apr 1995)* Pavane ▲ ADW 7337 [DDD]
Mozart, W.A.:Con Fl Hp, w. R. Siebert (fl), J. Faerber (cnd), Württemberg CO Vox Box 3–▲ CD3X 3003 [ADD]
Rodrigo, J.:Concert-Serenade, w. A. de Almeida (cnd), Monte Carlo Opera Orch Philips ("Solo" series) ▲ 442392-2
Rossini, G.:Andante con variazioni Hp, w. M. Grauwels (fl) Marco Polo ▲ 8.220441 [DDD]
Spohr, L.:Son 1 Vn, w. M. Grauwels (fl) [arr for fl & hp] Marco Polo ▲ 8.220441 [DDD]

Michel, P. (ob)—see ORCHESTRAS & ENSEMBLES SONOR Ensemble of Univ of California San Diego members

Michelangeli, Arturo Benedetti (pno)
Arturo Benedetti Michelangeli EMI Classics ▲ CDH 64490
Bach, J.S.:Italian Con Enterprise ("Sirio" series) ▲ ENT SO 53003
Bach, J.S.:Italian Con *(rec Jan. 22, 1943)* Teldec ("Historic" series) ▲ 93671-2 [ADD]
Beethoven, L. van:Con 4 Pno, w. Z. Zdravkovich (cnd), Belgrade PO Exclusive ▲ EXL 17 [ADD]
Beethoven, L. van:Con 4 Pno, w. Z. Zdravkovich (cnd), Belgrade PO Legend ▲ LGD 100 [ADD]
Beethoven, L. van:Con 5 Pno, "Emperor", w. M. Freccia (cnd), Rome RAI SO *(rec May 14, 1960)* Emozioni ▲ CDAR 2006 [ADD]
Beethoven, L. van:Con 5 Pno, "Emperor", w. W. Steinberg (cnd), New York PO *(rec live, New York 1/8/66)* Memories 2–▲ HR 4368/69 (m) [ADD]
Beethoven, L. van:Con 5 Pno, "Emperor", w. S. Celibidache (cnd), Swedish RSO *(rec live, Helsinki 5/20/69)* Arkadia ▲ 592 [ADD]
Beethoven, L. van:Con 5 Pno, "Emperor", w. S. Celibidache (cnd), Swedish RSO *(rec 1969)* Legend ▲ LGD 115 [ADD]
Beethoven, L. van:Con 5 Pno, "Emperor", w. M. Freccia (cnd), *(orch unknown)* Cetra Classic 3–▲ 02 [ADD]
Beethoven, L. van:Son 3 Pno *(rec 1966)* Legend ▲ LGD 120 [ADD]
Beethoven, L. van:Son 3 Pno Ermitage ▲ ERM 123
Beethoven, L. van:Son 3 Pno EMI Classics ▲ CDH 64490
Beethoven, L. van:Son 3 Pno *(rec live 2/12/52)* Arkadia ▲ 903 [ADD]
Beethoven, L. van:Son 3 Pno *(rec live, Warsaw 1955)* Melodram 2–▲ CD 28019 (m)
Beethoven, L. van:Son 11 Pno *(rec 1978–83)* Exclusive ▲ EXL 14 [ADD]
Beethoven, L. van:Son 12 Pno, "Funeral March" *(rec 1978–83)* Exclusive ▲ EXL 14 [ADD]
Beethoven, L. van:Son 32 Pno *(rec 1961)* Legend ▲ LGD 120 [ADD]

Michelangeli, Arturo Benedetti (pno) (cont.)
Beethoven, L. van:Son 32 Pno *(rec live, London 10/1/61)* Memories 2–▲ HR 4368/69 (m) [ADD]
Brahms, J.:Ballades, Op. 10 *(rec 1960–73)* Music & Arts 2–▲ CD 817 [AAD]
Brahms, J.:Vars on a Theme by Paganini *(rec live, 2/12/52)* Arkadia ▲ 903 [ADD]
Brahms, J.:Vars on a Theme by Paganini EMI Classics ▲ CDH 64490
Brahms, J.:Vars on a Theme by Paganini *(rec live 1955, Warsaw)* Melodram 2–▲ CD 28019 (m)
Brahms, J.:Vars on a Theme by Paganini *(rec 1960–73)* Music & Arts 2–▲ CD 817 [AAD]
Busoni, F.:Chaconne Pno *(rec live, Warsaw, 1955)* Melodram 2–▲ CD 28019 (m)
Busoni, F.:Chaconne Pno *(rec 1960–73)* Music & Arts 2–▲ CD 817 [AAD]
Chopin, F.:Ballades Pno (comp)—Op. 23 (1836) *(rec 1957, 1960 & 1966)* Praga ▲ PR 250 042
Chopin, F.:Ballade Pno, Op. 23 Cetra Classic 3–▲ 01 [ADD]
Chopin, F.:Ballade Pno, Op. 23 *(rec Royal Albert Hall, London, 1957)* Testament 2–▲ SBT 2088
Chopin, F.:Berceuse Enterprise ("Sirio" series) ▲ ENT SO 53003
Chopin, F.:Berceuse *(rec 1942)* Enterprise ("The Piano Library" series) ▲ ENT 183
Chopin, F.:Berceuse *(rec Sept. 9, 1942)* Teldec ("Historic" series) ▲ 93671-2 [ADD]
Chopin, F.:Fant Cetra Classic 3–▲ 01 [ADD]
Chopin, F.:Fant Ermitage ▲ ERM 123
Chopin, F.:Fant *(rec 1960–73)* Music & Arts 2–▲ CD 817 [AAD]
Chopin, F.:Fant *(rec Royal Albert Hall, London, 1957)* Testament 2–▲ SBT 2088
Chopin, F.:Mazurkas—Opp. 30/3, 33/4 & 68/2 Cetra Classic 3–▲ 01 [ADD]
Chopin, F.:Mazurkas—Op. 33/4 *(rec 1942)* Enterprise ("The Piano Library" series) ▲ ENT 183
Chopin, F.:Mazurkas—in b, Op. 33/4 *(rec Sept. 9, 1942)* Teldec ("Historic" series) ▲ 93671-2 [ADD]
Chopin, F.:Mazurkas—Op. 33/4 Enterprise ("Sirio" series) ▲ ENT SO 53003
Chopin, F.:Pno Music (misc)—Andante spianato e grande polacca brillante, Op. 22; Ballade, Op. 23; Scherzo, Op. 31; Mazurkas, Opp. 30/3, 33/4, 68/2; Berceuse, Op. 57; Waltzes, Opp. 34/1, 69/1 & Op.Post. in B♭ Ermitage ▲ ERM 122
Chopin, F.:Pno Music (misc)—Andante Spinato & Grand Polonaise, Op. 22; Ballade No. 1, Op. 23; Scherzo No. 1 in B♭, Op. 31; Mazurkas Nos. 2–4, Opp. 68, 30 & 33; Berceuse in D♭, Op. 57; Waltzes, Opps. 34, 69 & Psth; Fant in F, Op. 49 *(rec Turin, 1962)* Music & Arts ▲ CD 924
Chopin, F.:Pno Music (misc)—Ballade No. 1 in g, Op. 23; 6 Mazurkas; Grande Polonaise brillante in E♭, Op. 22 *(rec live, Teatro Grande in Brescia, Italy June 1967)* Fonè ▲ 90F 32 [ADD]
Chopin, F.:Scherzos—Op. 31 Cetra Classic 3–▲ 01 [ADD]
Chopin, F.:Son Pno, Op. 35 *(rec live, 2/12/52)* Arkadia ▲ 903 [ADD]
Chopin, F.:Son Pno, Op. 35 *(rec Oct. 29, 1983)* Exclusive ▲ EXL 14 [ADD]
Chopin, F.:Son Pno, Op. 35 *(rec live, Teatro Grande in Brescia, Italy June 1967)* Fonè ▲ 90F 32 [ADD]
Chopin, F.:Son Pno, Op. 35 *(rec 1957, 1960 & 1966)* Praga ▲ PR 250 042
Chopin, F.:Son Pno, Op. 35, w. Z. Zdravkovich (cnd), Belgrade PO Legend ▲ LGD 100 [ADD]
Chopin, F.:Waltzes—in E♭, Op. posth. *(rec Royal Albert Hall, London, 1957)* Testament 2–▲ SBT 2088
Chopin, F.:Waltzes—Waltz, Op. 69; Waltz brillante, Op. 34, No. 1; Waltz opera postuma Cetra Classic 3–▲ 01 [ADD]
Chopin, F.:Waltzes *(rec 1960–73)* Music & Arts 2–▲ CD 817 [AAD]
Debussy, C.:Children's Corner *(rec live, Lugano, 1968)* Memories 2–▲ HR 4368/69 (m) [ADD]
Debussy, C.:Children's Corner Deutsche Grammophon ▲ 415372-2 [AAD]
Debussy, C.:Children's Corner Cetra Classic 3–▲ 02 [ADD]
Debussy, C.:Images (6) Pno Ermitage ▲ ERM 123
Debussy, C.:Images (6) Pno *(rec Royal Albert Hall, London, 1957)* Testament 2–▲ SBT 2088
Debussy, C.:Images (6) Pno Deutsche Grammophon ▲ 415372-2 [AAD]
Debussy, C.:Images (6) Pno Cetra Classic 3–▲ 02 [ADD]
Debussy, C.:Images (6) Pno *(rec live, Warsaw 1955)* Melodram 2–▲ CD 28019 (m)
Debussy, C.:Preludes Pno—Book 1 Deutsche Grammophon ▲ 413450-2 [AAD]
Debussy, C.:Preludes Pno—Book 2 Deutsche Grammophon ▲ 427391-2 [DDD]
Debussy, C.:Preludes Pno (sels)—Canope; Bruyères Cetra Classic 3–▲ 02 [ADD]
First Performances of the Young Arturo Benedetti Michelangeli, w. Swiss Romande Orch [cnd:Ernest Ansermet] Arkadia ▲ 624
Galuppi, B.:Sons (12) Hpd—Sonata in D *(rec live 8/13/62)* Arkadia ▲ 904 [ADD]
Grieg, E.:Con Pno, Op. 16, w. A. Galliera (cnd), La Scala Orch *(rec 1941)* Enterprise ("The Piano Library" series) ▲ ENT 183
Grieg, E.:Con Pno, Op. 16, *(cnd & orch unknown)* Memories 2–▲ MEM CD 3009
Grieg, E.:Erotik Enterprise ("Piano Library" series) ▲ ENT PL 211
Grieg, E.:Lyric Pieces—Lyriske smaastykker, Op. 43/5 *(rec Sept. 6, 1942)* Teldec ("Historic" series) ▲ 93671-2 [ADD]
Haydn, J.:Con Hpd, Obs, Hns & Strs, H.XVIII/11, w. M. Rossi (cnd), *(orch unknown)* Cetra Classic 3–▲ 02 [ADD]
Haydn, J.:Con Hpd, Obs, Hns & Strs, H.XVIII/11, w. M. Rossi (cnd), Turin RAI SO *(rec Dec. 18, 1959)* Emozioni ▲ CDAR 2006 [ADD]
Liszt, F.:Con 1 Pno, w. R. Kubelik (cnd), *(orch unknown)* Cetra Classic 3–▲ 01 [ADD]
Liszt, F.:Con 1 Pno, w. R. Kubelik (cnd), Turin RAI SO *(rec Apr. 28, 1961)* Emozioni ▲ CDAR 2003 [ADD]
Liszt, F.:Con 1 Pno, w. M. Rossi (cnd), Rome Radio-TV SO Arkadia ▲ 507 [AAD]
Liszt, F.:Totentanz, w. M. Rossi (cnd), Rome Radio-TV SO Arkadia ▲ 507 [AAD]
Michelangeli:The First Recordings/Zecchi:Great Recordings, w. Benedetti, Arturo Michelangeli (pno) *(rec 1941–42)* Pearl 2–▲ PEA 9086 [ADD]
Mompou, F.:Cancons—Cancon from No. 6 *(rec Royal Albert Hall, London, 1957)* Testament 2–▲ SBT 2088
Mozart, W.A.:Con 13 Pno, w. F. Caracciolo (cnd), Naples Alessandro Scarlatti RAI Orch EMI Classics ("Great Recordings of the Century" series) ▲ CDH 63819
Mozart, W.A.:Con 13 Pno, w. C.M. Giulini (cnd), *(orch unknown)* Cetra Classic 3–▲ 01 [ADD]
Mozart, W.A.:Con 13 Pno, w. C. M. Giulini (cnd), Rome RAI SO *(rec Dec. 15, 1951)* Emozioni ▲ CDAR 2001 [ADD]
Mozart, W.A.:Con 15 Pno, w. H. Scherchen (cnd), Swiss-Italian RSO Andromeda ▲ ANR 2503 [ADD]
Mozart, W.A.:Con 15 Pno, w. H. Scherchen (cnd), RTSI Orch *(rec live, Lugano, 1956)* As Disc ▲ ASD 2601 (m)
Mozart, W.A.:Con 15 Pno, w. M. Rossi (cnd), Turin RAI SO *(rec Dec. 23, 1955)* Emozioni ▲ CDAR 2004
Mozart, W.A.:Con 15 Pno, w. M. Rossi (cnd), *(orch unknown)* Cetra Classic 3–▲ 02 [ADD]
Mozart, W.A.:Con 15 Pno, w. E. Gracis (cnd), Milan Pomeriggi Musicali Chamber SO EMI Classics ("Great Recordings of the Century" series) ▲ CDH 63819
Mozart, W.A.:Con 20 Pno, w. C.M. Giulini (cnd), *(orch unknown)* Cetra Classic 3–▲ 01 [ADD]
Mozart, W.A.:Con 20 Pno, w. C. M. Giulini (cnd), Rome RAI SO *(rec Dec. 15, 1951)* Emozioni ▲ CDAR 2001 [ADD]
Mozart, W.A.:Con 20 Pno, w. D. Mitropoulos (cnd), Florence Maggio Musicale Orch *(rec live, June 17, 1953)* Arkadia 3–▲ 552 (m) [ADD]
Mozart, W.A.:Con 23 Pno, w. F. Caracciolo (cnd), Naples Alessandro Scarlatti RAI Orch EMI Classics ("Great Recordings of the Century" series) ▲ CDH 63819
Mozart, W.A.:Con 23 Pno, w. C.M. Giulini (cnd), *(orch unknown)* Cetra Classic 3–▲ 02 [ADD]
Mozart, W.A.:Con 23 Pno, w. C. M. Giulini (cnd), Rome RAI SO *(rec Dec. 15, 1951)* Emozioni ▲ CDAR 2004
Ravel, M.:Con in G Pno, w. S. Celibidache (cnd), London SO *(rec 1979–82)* Exclusive 2–▲ EXL 61 [ADD]
Ravel, M.:Con in G Pno, w. N. Sanzogno (cnd), Turin RAI SO *(rec 2/1/52)* Arkadia ▲ 904 [ADD]
Ravel, M.:Gaspard de la nuit *(rec live, 1969)* Arkadia ▲ 904 [ADD]
Ravel, M.:Gaspard de la nuit *(rec live, 1957)* Multisonic ("Prague Spring Collection" series) ▲ 31 0193 [ADD]
Ravel, M.:Gaspard de la nuit *(rec 1960–73)* Music & Arts 2–▲ CD 817 [AAD]
Ravel, M.:Gaspard de la nuit *(rec live, Turin, 1962)* Memories 2–▲ HR 4368/69 (m) [ADD]
Ravel, M.:Valses nobles et sentimentales *(rec live, Feb. 12, 1952)* Arkadia ▲ 904 [ADD]
Scarlatti, D.:Sons Kbd—K.27 & 96 Enterprise ("Sirio" series) ▲ ENT SO 53003

▲ = CD ♦ = Enhanced CD Δ = MD ■ = Cassette Tape □ = DCC

Michelangeli, Arturo Benedetti (pno) (cont.)
Scarlatti, D.:Sons Kbd—4 sonatas *(rec live in Warsaw, 1955)* Melodram 2-▲ MEL 28019 (m)
Scarlatti, D.:Sons Kbd—L.449 & 465 *(rec 1942)* Enterprise ("The Piano Library" series) ▲ ENT 183
Scarlatti, D.:Sons Kbd—in b, K.27; in D, K.96 *(rec Jan. 20, 1943)* Teldec ("Historic" series) ▲ 93671-2 [ADD]
Schumann, R.:Carnaval Pno *(rec 1960-73)* Music & Arts 2-▲ CD 817 [AAD]
Schumann, R.:Carnaval Pno *(rec live 1957)* Multisonic ("Prague Spring Collection" series) ▲ 31 0193 [ADD]
Schumann, R.:Carnaval Pno *(rec Royal Albert Hall, London, 1957)* Testament 2-▲ SBT 2088
Schumann, R.:Con Pno, w. G. Gavazzeni (cnd), *(orch unknown)* Cetra Classic 3-▲ 01 [ADD]
Schumann, R.:Con Pno, w. S. Celibidache (cnd), Swedish RSO *(rec live, Stockholm, 11/19/67)* Arkadia ▲ 592 [ADD]
Schumann, R.:Con Pno, w. G. Gavazzeni (cnd), Rome RAI SO *(rec Apr. 28, 1962)* Emozioni ▲ CDAR 2003 [ADD]
Schumann, R.:Con Pno, w. A. Pedrotti (cnd), La Scala Orch Enterprise ("Piano Library" series) ▲ ENT PL 211
Schumann, R.:Con Pno, w. W. Rowicki (cnd), Warsaw PO *(rec live, Warsaw, 1955)* Melodram 2-▲ CD 28019 (m)
Schumann, R.:Con Pno, *(orch unknown)* Memories ("Golden" series) 2-▲ MEM 3005
Schumann, R.:Con Pno, w. H. Scherchen (cnd), RTSI Orch *(rec live, Lugano, 1956)* As Disc ▲ ASD 2601 (m)
Schumann, R.:Con Pno, w. H. Scherchen (cnd), Swiss-Italian RSO Andromeda ▲ ANR 2503 [ADD]
Schumann, R.:Faschingsschwank aus Wien *(rec live, Warsaw, 1955)* Melodram 2-▲ MEL 28019 (m)
Schumann, R.:Faschingsschwank aus Wien *(rec Royal Albert Hall, London, 1957)* Testament 2-▲ SBT 2088
Tomeoni, P.:Allegro *(rec Jan. 22, 1943)* Teldec ("Historic" series) ▲ 93671-2 [ADD]
Tomeoni, P.:Allegro Enterprise ("Piano Library" series) ▲ ENT PL 211

Michelini, L. (pno)
Rota, N.:Film Music, w. S. Gazzelloni (fl) [trans. L. Michelini]—La Strada; La dolce vita; Rocco e I suoi fratelli; Amarcord; Il Padrino II; Il Gattopardo; Il Padrino; G. Degli Spiriti; Romeo e Giulietta; Otto e Mezzo CAM ▲ CVS 006 [AAD]

Michelino, Silvano (perc)
Chevalier, C.:Music of, w. Teca Calazans (sgr), Ze-Luis (sgr), Regina Machado (sgr), Nigel Scragg (fl/a sax), Rosihna de Valenca (gtr), Jean-Yves Candela (pno), Wilson das Neves (perc), Regina Machado (perc)—Comme d'habitude; Couleur café; Une histoire d'amour; Les feuilles mortes; Les moulins de mon coeur; Syracuse; Je t'aimerai; Ces petits rien; La valse des lilas; L'absent; Que reste-il de nos amours; Un homme et une femme *(rec Studio Bastille)* Iris ▲ 010 [DDD]

Michell, Edna (vn)
Foss, L.:Orpheus & Euridice, w. Y. Menuhin (vn), L. Foss (cnd), Brooklyn PO New World ▲ NW 375-2 [DDD]

Michelucci, Roberto (vn)
Bach, J.S.:Sons & Partitas Vn, BWV 1001-1006 Fonè 3-▲ 90F 27 [DDD]
Bach, J.S.:Sons & Partitas Vn, BWV 1001-1006—Sonata 1 & Partita 1, BWV 1001, 1002 Fonè ▲ 88 F 01-21 [DDD]
Vivaldi, A.:Cons Vn (misc), I Musici—RV.362 Philips ▲ 420356-2 [ADD]
Vivaldi, A.:Cons Vn, Op. 3/1-12, "L'estro armonico", I Musici Philips ("Duo" series) 2-▲ 446169-2
Vivaldi, A.:Cons Vn, Op. 8/1-4, "The Four Seasons", I Musici Philips ▲ 420356-2 [ADD]

Michiels, Frank (perc)
Marc Grauwels & Friends, w. Grauwels, Marc (fl), Marie-Noelle de Callataÿ (sop), Hiroko Masaki (sop), Dennis James (glass hmc), Ingrid Procureur (hp), Yves Storms (gtr), Yvietta Matison (va), Mark Drobinsky (vc), Alain De Rijckere (bn), Daniel Blumenthal (pno), Belgian RSO, et al. Syrinx 2-▲ 96101 [DDD]

Mickisch, S. (pno)
Bach, J.S.:Jesu bleibet meine Freude *(rec July 9-10 & Sept 26-27, 1)* Calig ▲ CAL 50904 [DDD]
Bach, J.S.:Preludium & Fugue Hpd, BWV 849 *(rec July 9-10 & Sept 26-27, 1)* Calig ▲ CAL 50904 [DDD]
Franck, C.:Prélude, choral et fugue *(rec July 9-10 & Sept 26-27, 1)* Calig ▲ CAL 50904 [DDD]
Mickisch, S.:Improv & Fugue *(rec July 9-10 & Sept 26-27, 1)* Calig ▲ CAL 50904 [DDD]
Reger, M.:Vars & Fugue on a Theme of J. S. Bach *(rec July 9-10 & Sept 26-27, 1)* Calig ▲ CAL 50904 [DDD]

Middelbeek, Annette (pno)
Honegger, A.:Pno Music—Toccata et Variations (1916); Trois pièces (1919); Sept pièces breves (1919-20); Sarabande (1920); La Cahier Romand (1921-22); Hommage à Albert Roussel (1928); Prélude, Arioso & Fughette sur le nom de Bach (1932); Deux Esquisses (1944); Souvenir de Chopin (1947) Koch Schwann ▲ 3-1220-2 [DDD]

Middleton (fl)
Peck, R.:Automobile, w. Ragains (sop), Calvetti (db), Johnson (perc) CRI ■ C 367

Midena, Sylvie (pno)
Moscheles, I.:Grande Son Pno 4-Hands, w. Danielle Torchon d'Avat (pno) *(rec Festetich Castle, Budapest, June 1994)* Pyramid ▲ 13513 [DDD]
Moscheles, I.:Grande sonate symphonique 2, w. Danielle Torchon d'Avat (pno) *(rec Festetich Castle, Budapest, June 1994)* Pyramid ▲ 13513 [DDD]
Moscheles, I.:Hommage à Händel, w. Danielle Torchon d'Avat (pno) *(rec Festetich Castle, Budapest, June 1994)* Pyramid ▲ 13513 [DDD]

Midori (vn)
Bach, J.S.:Con for 2 Vns, w. P. Zukerman (vn), P. Zukerman (cnd), St. Paul CO Philips ▲ 416389-2 [DDD]
Bartók, B.:Con 1 Vn, w. Z. Mehta (cnd), Berlin PO Sony Classical ▲ SK 45941 [DDD]
Bartók, B.:Con 2 Vn, w. Z. Mehta (cnd), Berlin PO Sony Classical ▲ SK 45941 [DDD]
Bruch, M.:Scottish Fant Vn, w. Z. Mehta (cnd), Israel PO *(rec F. Mann Auditorium, Tel Aviv, Israel, July 26-30, 1993)* Sony Classical ▲ SK 58967 [DDD]; ■ ST 58967
Dvořák, A.:Con Vn, w. Z. Mehta (cnd), New York PO CBS ▲ MK 44923 [DDD] ■ MT 44923 (D) □ NM 44923
Dvořák, A.:Romance Vn, w. Z. Mehta (cnd), New York PO CBS ▲ MK 44923 [DDD] ■ MT 44923 (D) □ NM 44923
Encorel, w. Robert McDonald (pno) Sony Classical ▲ SK 52568 ▲ SM 52568 ■ ST 52568
Live at Carnegie Hall, w. Robert McDonald (pno) Sony Classical ▲ SK 46742 [DDD] ■ ST 46742 (D)
Paganini, N.:Caprices Vn CBS ▲ MK 44944 [DDD] ■ MT 44944 (D)
Paganini, N.:Con 1 Vn, w. L. Slatkin (cnd), London SO Philips ▲ 420943-2 [DDD]
Sibelius, J.:Con Vn, w. Z. Mehta (cnd), Israel PO *(rec F. Mann Auditorium, Tel Aviv, Israel, July 26-30, 1993)* Sony Classical ▲ SK 58967 [DDD]; ■ ST 58967
Tchaikovsky, P.:Sérénade mélancolique, w. L. Slatkin (cnd), London SO Philips ▲ 420943-2 [DDD]
Tchaikovsky, P.:Valse-Scherzo Vn, w. L. Slatkin (cnd), London SO Philips ▲ 420943-2 [DDD]

Mielke, Detlef (vc)
Besozzi, A.:Trio Sons (6), w. Claudio Ferrarini (fl), Lavard Skou Larsen (vn) Stradivarius ▲ STV 33317 [ADD]

Miersch, Holger (cel)
Berlinski, H.:Das Gebet Bonhoeffers, w. Nancy Gibson (sop), Matthias Weichert (bass), Olaf Georgi (fl), Bernhard Hentrich (vc), Herman Berlinski (org), Martin Homann (perc), Hans-Christoph Rademann (cnd), Dresden Chamber Choir Vienna Modern Masters ▲ VMM 3027 [DDD]

Migdal, Marian (pno)
Grieg, E.:Ballade Pno Swedish Society ▲ SCD 1054
Grieg, E.:Holberg Suite Swedish Society ▲ SCD 1054
Grieg, E.:Son Pno Swedish Society ▲ SCD 1054
Mozart, W.A.:Con 12 Pno, w. U. Björlin (cnd), Cappella Coloniensis LaserLight ▲ 15 870 [DDD]
Mozart, W.A.:Con 25 Pno, w. U. Björlin (cnd), Cappella Coloniensis LaserLight ▲ 15 870 [DDD]

Migliorini, Carlo Mascilli (gtr)
Geminiani, F.:The Art of Playing the Gtr or Citra, w. Anna Clemente (cembalo) Koch Schwann ▲ SCH 313592

Migliorini, Carlo Mascilli (gtr) (cont.)
Gragnani, F.:Gtr Music, w. M. Annunziati (gtr), R. Bini (gtr), M. Fornaciari (vn)—3 Sonatas for Violin & Guitar; 3 Duets for 2 Guitars Fonè ▲ FON 93F 18 [DDD]
Marella, G.:Compositions, w. Anna Clemente (cembalo) Koch Schwann ▲ SCH 313592
Merchi, J.B.:Ariettes et vaudevilles nouveaux, w. Donatella Debolini (sop), Maria Smuraglia (gtr) Entrée ▲ 0073
Merchi, J.B.:Duets Gtrs, w. Maria Smuraglia (gtr) Entrée ▲ 0073

Migy, Raymond (gtr)—see ORCHESTRAS & ENSEMBLES Linhares Guitar Quartet

Mihailovich, Zora (pno)
Chopin, F.:Polonaises—in f#, Op. 44 *(rec Little Bridges Hall, Pomona College, Claremont, CA, May 17-18, 1995)* Centaur ▲ CRC 2270 [DDD]
Chopin, F.:Son Pno, Op. 35 *(rec Little Bridges Hall, Pomona College, Claremont, CA, May 17-18, 1995)* Centaur ▲ CRC 2270 [DDD]
Chopin, F.:Son Pno, Op. 58 *(rec Little Bridges Hall, Pomona College, Claremont, CA, May 17-18, 1995)* Centaur ▲ CRC 2270 [DDD]
Rubinstein, A.:Pno Music—Kamennoi-Ostrow, Op. 10/22; Polka-Bohème, Op. 82/7; Melody in F, Op. 3/1; Turkish March [from The Ruins of Athens]; Barcarolles, No. 1, Op. 30/1; No. 2, Op. 45; No. 3, Op. 50/5; No. 4; No. 5, Op. 90/4; No. 6, Op. 104/4; Romance, Op. 44; Valse Caprice *(rec David L. Abell Digital Studio, Los Angeles, CA, Oct. 1994)* Centaur ▲ CRC 2235 [DDD]

Mihule, Jiří (ob)
Beethoven, L. van:Qnt Ob, 3 Hns & Bn, w. Z. Tylšar (hn), B. Tylšar (hn), R. Beránek (hn), F. Herman (bn) Supraphon ▲ 11 1445-2 [DDD]
Mozart, W.A.:Con Ob, K.314, w. V. Neumann (cnd), Czech PO Supraphon Collection ▲ 11 0636-2 [ADD]

Mijnders, Wouter (vc)
Mendelssohn, F.:Assai tranquillo, w. P. Beijersbergen van Henegouwen (pno) Partridge ▲ 1137-2 [DDD]
Mendelssohn, F.:Lied ohne Worte Vc, w. P. Beijersbergen van Henegouwen (pno) Partridge ▲ 1137-2 [DDD]
Mendelssohn, F.:Son 1 Vc, w. P. Beijersbergen van Henegouwen (pno) Partridge ▲ 1137-2 [DDD]
Mendelssohn, F.:Son 2 Vc, w. P. Beijersbergen van Henegouwen (pno) Partridge ▲ 1137-2 [DDD]
Mendelssohn, F.:Vars concertantes, w. P. Beijersbergen van Henegouwen (pno) Partridge ▲ 1137-2 [DDD]
Pijper, W.:Son 1 Vc, w. Peter Beijersbergen van Henegouwen (pno) Donemus ▲ CV 15
Pijper, W.:Trio 2 Pno, w. Peter Beijersbergen van Henegouwen (pno), Ronald Hoogeveen (vn) Donemus ▲ CV 15

Mikaelian, Kevork (vn)
Nikolov, L.:Qt 3 Strs, w. A. Ilchev (vn), V. Gerov (va), G. Dean (vc) Gega ▲ GD 149 [DDD]

Mikhashoff, Yvar (pno)
Cage, J.:Europera 5, w. M. Herr (sop), G. Burgess (ten), J. Wiliams (victrola [78 rpm]), D. Metz (tape) *(rec Apr. 12, 1991)* Mode ▲ MOD 36 [DDD]
Curran, A.:For Cornelius [Cardew] Mode ("Edition Yvar Mikhashoff" series) ▲ mode 49 [ADD]
Curran, A.:The Last Acts of Julian Beck Mode ("Edition Yvar Mikhashoff" series) ▲ mode 49 [ADD]
Curran, A.:Schtetl Vars Mode ("Edition Yvar Mikhashoff" series) ▲ mode 49 [ADD]
Thomson, V.:Portraits, w. M. Herr (sop), J. Boudler (perc), D. Kuehn (tpt)—30 sels composed from 1926-1982 New Albion ▲ NA 034 [ADD]

Miki, Mie (accordion)
Yun, I.:Concertino Acc, w. Nomos String Quartet CPO ▲ CPO 999075-2 [DDD]

Mikkelborg, Palle (perc)
Nørgård, P.:Music for Perc, w. Gert Sørensen (perc/kbd/cmpt), Per Nørgård (kbd/vocals)—Waves; Isternia; I Ching; Energy Fields Forever; Nemo Dynamo; Bulan; Circus City Marco Polo ("dacapo" series) ▲ 8.224024-25 [DDD]

Mikkelsen, Kelly (vc)—see ORCHESTRAS & ENSEMBLES Sierra Winds

Mikkelsen, Sven-Ingvart (org)
Böhm, G.:Org Music—Praeludium & Fuga in C; Aus Tiefer not; Allein Gott in der Höh; Christum wir sollen loben; Schon; Gelobet seist du, Jesu Christ; Vom Himmel hoch; Herr, Jesu Christ; Nun bitten wir den heiligen Geist; Christ lag in todesbanden; Praeludium in d; Auf meinen lieben Gott; Vater unser; Christe, der du bist; Praeludium & Fuga in a Kontrapunkt ▲ KPT 32213
Bruhns, N.:Org Music—Praeludia in G & 2 in e; Praeludium & Fuga; Nun komm, der Heiden Heiland *(rec Eckernförde & Husum, Germany)* Kontrapunkt ▲ KPT 32198
Flor, C.:Org Music—Werde Munter; Mein Gemüte; Auf meinen Lieben Bott; Jesu, meine Freude; Wie schön leuchtet der Morgenstern; Ein feste Burg ist unser Gott; Treuer Gott, ich muss Ihr Klagen; Helft mir Gottes Güte Preisen; Fuga in d Kontrapunkt ▲ KPT 32198
Scheidemann, H.:Org Music—Christ lag in Todesbanden; Praeambulum in d; Praeambulum in F Kontrapunkt ▲ KPT 32198

Miklós, A. (vn)—see ORCHESTRAS & ENSEMBLES Danubius Quartet

Mikulak, Marcia (pno)
Rudhyar, D.:Transmutation CRI ▲ CD 604 [AAD]

Mikulka, Vladimir (gtr)
Dusek, F.X.:Sons Kbd—in G & C [arr for Gtr] *(rec Mont St. Guibert Church, May 1994)* GHA ▲ 126.032
Ibero-American Guitar Music BIS ▲ CD 340
Jelinek, I.:Suite Lt *(rec Mont St. Guibert Church, May 1994)* GHA ▲ 126.032
Koshkin, N.:The Prince's Toys BIS ▲ CD 240 [DDD]
Kozeluch, Joh. A.:Music of—Andantino; Pastorale [both from La ritrovata figlia di Ottone II; arr for gtr] *(rec Mont St. Guibert Church, May 1994)* GHA ▲ 126.032
Losy, J.A.:Gtr Music—Suite in a; Sarabande *(rec Mont St. Guibert Church, May 1994)* GHA ▲ 126.032
Rak, S.:Music for Gtr—Farewell Finland; Romance; Temptation of the Renaissance BIS ▲ CD 240 [DDD]
Rak, S.:Music for Gtr—Voces de profundis GHA ▲ 126.034
Rak, S.:Music for Gtr—Voces de profundis (after Hitchcock's Psycho); Toccata; Andante; The Last Disco; The Tom Thumb's Laugh; Variations on a Theme by Jaromira Klempíre; Little Nocturne (on a Finnish folk song); Homenage a Tarrega GHA ▲ CD 126.003
Vanhal, J.B.:Music of—Cantabile; Minuetto *(rec Mont St. Guibert Church, May 1994)* GHA ▲ 126.032

Milà, Leonora (pno)
Beethoven, L. van:Con Vn, Vc & Pno, "Triple Con", w. P. León (vn), P. Corostola (vc), H. Zongjie (cnd), Chinese Central PO Regis Tro ▲ RTAC 003 [DDD]
Falla, M. de:El amor brujo (ritual fire dance) Regis Tro ▲ 009 [DDD]
Falla, M. de:Canciones populares españolas (7) Regis Tro ▲ 009 [DDD]
Falla, M. de:Noches en los jardines de España, w. M. A. G. Martínez (cnd), Spanish National Radio-TV SO Regis Tro ▲ RTAC 002 [DDD]
Granados, E.:Danzas españolas (10)—Nos. 2 & 5 Regis Tro ▲ 009 [DDD]
Granados, E.:Escenas romanticas (6) Regis Tro ▲ 009 [DDD]
Granados, E.:Pno Music (misc)—La Maya y El Ruiseñor Regis Tro ▲ 009 [DDD]
Milà, L.:Con 2 Pno, w. M. A. G. Martínez (cnd), Spanish National Radio-TV SO Regis Tro ▲ RTAC 002 [DDD]
Milà, L.:Pno Music—Havaneres Nos. 1-10, Opp. 48, 52, 53, 54, 55, 57, 58, 59 & 60; Llunyania, Op. 56; 4 Etudes, Op. 54; Nocturne, Op. 23; Equitant, Op. 42 Regis Tro ▲ RTAC 006 [DDD]

Milan, Susan (fl)
Beethoven, L. van:Duo 1 Fl & Bn, w. S. Azzolini (bn) Chandos ▲ CHAN 9108 [DDD]
Beethoven, L. van:Serenade Fl, Op. 25, w. L. Chilingirian (vn), L. Williams (va) Chandos ▲ CHAN 9108 [DDD]
Beethoven, L. van:Trio Fl, WoO 37, w. S. Azzolini (bn), I. Brown (pno) Chandos ▲ CHAN 9108 [DDD]
Chaminade, C.:Concertino Fl, w. R. Hickox (cnd), City of London Sinfonia Chandos ▲ CHAN 8840 [DDD]
La Flûte enchantée, w. City of London Sinfonia [cnd:Richard Hickox] Chandos ▲ CHAN 8840 [DDD]
Flute Fantaisie:Virtuoso French Flute Repertoire, w. Ian Brown (pno) Chandos ▲ CHAN 8609 [DDD]

INSTRUMENT.

Milan, Susan (fl) (cont.)
Gaubert, P.:Fl & Pno Music, w. I. Brown (pno)—Romance (1905); Nocturne et Allegro scherzando (1906); Berceuse (1907); Madrigal (1908); Sur l'eau (1910); Fantaisie (1912); Deux esquisses (1914); Sicilienne (1914); Sonata No. 1 (1917); Suite (1921); Sonata No. 2 (1924); Ballade (1927); Sonata No. 3 (1933); Sonatina (1937) Chandos 2–▲ CHAN 8981/82 [DDD]
Godard, B.:Suite de trois morceaux, w. R. Hickox (cnd), City of London Sinfonia Chandos ▲ CHAN 8840 [DDD]
Martin, F.:Ballade Fl, w. M. Dussek (pno), R. Hickox (cnd), City of London Sinfonia Chandos ▲ CHAN 8840 [DDD]
Martinů, B.:Son Fl & Pno, w. I. Brown (pno) Chandos ▲ CHAN 8823 [DDD]
Mozart, W.A.:Andante Fl, K.315/285a, w. R. Leppard (cnd), English CO Chandos ▲ CHAN 8613 [DDD]
Mozart, W.A.:Cons Fl, w. R. Leppard (cnd), English CO Chandos ▲ CHAN 8613 [DDD]
Mozart, W.A.:Con Fl Hp, w. S. Kanga (hp), R. Hickox (cnd), City of London Sinfonia Chandos ▲ CHAN 9051 [DDD]
Mozart, W.A.:Qts Fl, w. Chilingirian String Quartet members Chandos ▲ CHAN 8872 [DDD]
Mozart, W.A.:Rondo Vn, K.373, w. R. Leppard (cnd), English CO Chandos ▲ CHAN 8613 [DDD]
Reinecke, C.:Son Fl, w. I. Brown (pno) Chandos ▲ CHAN 8823 [DDD]
Saint-Saëns, C.:Airs de ballet d' *Ascanio*, w. R. Hickox (cnd), City of London Sinfonia Chandos ▲ CHAN 8840 [DDD]
Salieri, A.:Con Fl, w. D. Theodore (ob), R. Hickox (cnd), City of London Sinfonia Chandos ▲ CHAN 9051 [DDD]
Schmidt, O.:Con Fl, w. O. Schmidt (cnd), Royal Northern College of Music CO *(rec Mariot, France, 1994–95)* Marco Polo/Dacapo ▲ 8.224035 [DDD]
Schubert, Franz:Intro & Vars Fl on "Tröckne Blumen", w. I. Brown (pno) Chandos ▲ CHAN 8823 [DDD]
Telemann, G.P.:Con Fl, Vn, Vc, w. L. Friedman (cnd), St. Andrew Camerata Omega ▲ OCD 1006 [DDD]
Telemann, G.P.:Suite in a Fl, w. L. Friedman (cnd), St. Andrew Camerata Omega ▲ OCD 1006 [DDD]

Milani, Luca (cl)—see ORCHESTRAS & ENSEMBLES Italiano Octet

Milani, Luigi (db)—see ORCHESTRAS & ENSEMBLES Italiano Octet

Milanova, Dora (pno)
Brahms, J.:Son 1 Vn, w. S. Milanova (vn) Monitor ■ 55005
Brahms, J.:Son 2 Vn, w. S. Milanova (vn) Monitor ■ 55006
Brahms, J.:Son 3 Vn, w. S. Milanova (vn) Monitor ■ 55006
Brahms, J.:Trio Hn, w. S. Grigorov (hn) Monitor 2–■ 55005/06

Milanova, Stoika (vn)
Brahms, J.:Son 1 Vn, w. D. Milanova (pno) Monitor ■ 55005
Brahms, J.:Son 2 Vn, w. D. Milanova (pno) Monitor ■ 55006
Brahms, J.:Son 3 Vn, w. D. Milanova (pno) Monitor ■ 55006
Bruch, M.:Con 1 Vn, w. V. Stefanov (cnd), Philharmonia Bulgarica Vivace 3–▲ E 324 [ADD/DDD]
Glazunov, A.:Con Vn, w. V. Stefanov (cnd), Philharmonia Bulgarica Vivace 3–▲ E 324 [ADD/DDD]
Prokofiev, S.:Cons Vn (comp), w. Stefanov (cnd), *(orch unknown)* Monitor ■ 55007

Milanova, Vanya (vn)
Tchaikovsky, P.:Con Vn, w. J. Kovatchev (cnd), Sofia Festival Orch RS Prestige ▲ 951–0066 [DDD]
Tchaikovsky, P.:Sérénade mélancolique, w. J. Kovatchev (cnd), Sofia Festival Orch RS Prestige ▲ 951–0066 [DDD]

Milanovich, Donna (fl)—see ORCHESTRAS & ENSEMBLES Glorian Duo

Milarsky, Jeffery (glock)
Kernis, A.J.:Nocturne, w. Nancy Allen Lundy (sop), John Dent (tpt), Benjamin Herman (glock), Leslie Stifelman (pno), Lisa Moore (pno), M. Barrett (cnd) *(rec Manhattan Center Studios, New York, May 31–June 3, 1995)* New Albion ♦ NA 083CD

Milarsky, Jeffery (timp)
Handel, G.F.:Royal Fireworks Music, w. Mary Jane Newman (org), Collegium Brass [arr Newman for org, 3 tpt & timp] *(rec Presbyterian Church, Mt. Kisco, NY, Aug 26–27, 1995)* Helicon ▲ HE 1006 [DDD]

Milarsky, Jeffrey (perc)
Kernis, A.J.:America(n) (Day) Dreams, w. Kim Barber (mez), Mary Rowell (vn), Leslie Tomkins (va), Tonya Tomkins (vc), Robert Black (db), Kathleen Nester (fl), Larry Guy (cl/b cl), John Dent (tpt), Anthony Cecere (hn), Leslie Stifelman (pno), Susan Jolles (hp), Jeffrey Milarsky (perc), M. Barrett (cnd)—A Navajo Blanket; Wednesday at the Waldorf; The Pregnant Dream; The Blue Bottle; "So Long" to the Moon from the Men of Apollo; Epilogue:The Pure Suit of Happiness *(rec Manhattan Center Studios, New York, May 31–June 3, 1995)* New Albion ♦ NA 083CD

Mildonian, Susanna (hp)
Debussy, C.:Chansons de Bilitis (recitation), w. A. Lochner (nar), A. Adorjan (fl), M. Larrieu (fl), Y. Nagae (hp), E. Sun (cel) [F] Quantum ▲ QM 6912 [DDD]
Debussy, C.:Danses sacrée et profane, w. A. Moglia (cnd), Toulouse National CO *(rec Apr 1995)* Pavane ▲ ADW 7337 [DDD]
Duo Recital, w. Maxence Larrieu (fl) Denon ▲ CO 7301 [DDD]
Françaix, J.:Con 2 Hps, w. Catherine Michel (hp), A. Moglia (cnd), Toulouse National CO *(rec Apr 1995)* Pavane ▲ ADW 7337 [DDD]
Gossec, F.-J.:Symphonie concertante for 2 Hps, w. Catherine Michel (hp), A. Moglia (cnd), Toulouse National CO *(rec Apr 1995)* Pavane ▲ ADW 7337 [DDD]
Harp Recital Pavane ▲ ADW 7215 [DDD]
Malecki, M.:Concertino dans un style ancien, w. Catherine Michel (hp), A. Moglia (cnd), Toulouse National CO *(rec Apr 1995)* Pavane ▲ ADW 7337 [DDD]
Mozart, W.A.:Con Fl Hp, w. András Adorján (fl), H. Stadlmair (cnd), Munich CO Denon ▲ 7804 [DDD]
Ravel, M.:Intro & Allegro, w. A. Moglia (cnd), Toulouse National CO *(rec Apr 1995)* Pavane ▲ ADW 7337 [DDD]

Milenkovich, Stefan (vn)
Paganini, N.:Divertimenti carnevaleschi, w. Pier Domenico Sommati (vn), Riccardo Agosti (vc) *(rec Dynamic's, Genova, Feb 22–24, 1995)* Dynamic ▲ CD 105 [DDD]
Paganini, N.:Duetti Vn, w. Riccardo Agosti (vc) *(rec Dynamic's, Genova, Feb 22–24, 1995)* Dynamic ▲ CD 105 [DDD]
Paganini, N.:In cuor più non mi sento, w. Pier Domenico Sommati (vn), Riccardo Agosti (vc) *(rec Dynamic's, Genova, Feb 22–24, 1995)* Dynamic ▲ CD 105 [DDD]

Milesi, Piero (kbd)
Milesi, P.:Arte degli Ambienti—Pantelleria Cuneiform ▲ Rune 7

Milewski, Piotr (vn)
Baer, W.:Con Vn, w. G. Nowak (cnd), Bieler SO Gallo ▲ CD 582 [DDD]
Martin, F.:Con Vn, w. G. Nowak (cnd), Bieler SO Gallo ▲ CD 582 [DDD]
Meier, J.:Trames I–IV, w. G. Nowak (cnd), Bieler SO Gallo ▲ CD 582 [DDD]

Milford, Julian (pno)
Vaughan Williams, R.:Fant on Greensleeves, w. Lydia Mordkovitch (vn) IMP ("Masters" series) ▲ IMP 6600132
Vaughan Williams, R.:The Lark Ascending, w. Lydia Mordkovitch (vn) IMP ("Masters" series) ▲ IMP 6600132
Vaughan Williams, R.:Pieces Vn & Pno, w. Lydia Mordkovitch (vn) IMP ("Masters" series) ▲ IMP 6600132
Vaughan Williams, R.:Son Vn, w. Lydia Mordkovitch (vn) IMP ("Masters" series) ▲ IMP 6600132
Vaughan Williams, R.:Studies in English Folk-Song, w. Lydia Mordkovitch (vn) IMP ("Masters" series) ▲ IMP 6600132

Milhaud, Darius (pno)
Milhaud, D.:Scaramouche for 2 Pnos, w. M. Meyer (pno) EMI Classics ▲ CDC 54604

Miliaeva, Olga (va)
Vivaldi, A.:Cons Vn, Op. 8/1–4, "The Four Seasons", w. Jerome Franke (vn), Karine Garibova (vn), Pasquale Laurino (vn), Roza Borisova (vc), Mika Hennessy (db), Melanie Panush (ham dlc), Stanislav Venglevski (bayan), Mike Kashou (arabic tabla), Daryl Stuermer (gtr), Ed Paloucek (celtic fid), Gary Bottoni (highland pipe), Dubuffet String Quartet *(rec July–Sept 1995)* EarthBeat! ▲ 35270–2 [DDD]

Milian, A. (vn)
Wissmer, P.:Con 3 Vn, w. D. Fanal (cnd), Olsztyn State PO Quantum ▲ QM 6935 [DDD]

Militello, Bobby (sax)—see ORCHESTRAS & ENSEMBLES Dave Brubeck Quartet

Millard, Christopher (bn)
Mélange:French Music for Bassoon, w. Kenneth Broadway (pno), Camille Churchfield (fl) Summit ▲ DCD 128 [DDD] ■ DCD 128

Miller (bn)
Mozart, W.A.:Con Bn, w. N. Marriner (cnd), St. Mary's Chamber Players Pro Arte ▲ CDD 195 [DDD]

Miller (pno)
Perle, G.:Toccata Pno CRI ■ ACS 6015

Miller, C. (bn)
Vanhal, J.B.:Con Bn, w. N. Marriner (cnd), St. Mary's Chamber Players Pro Arte ▲ CDD 195 [DDD]

Miller, David (archlt)
Vivaldi, A.:Cons Rcr, w. Piers Adams (rcr), Ray Goodman (vn), Miles Golding (vn), Jane Compton (va), Jane Coe (vc), Mandy MacNamara (db), Robert King (hpd/org)—in F for Treble Rcr, Op. 10/1; in a for Sopranino Rcr, RV.440; in c for Treble Rcr, RV.441; in D for Sopranino Rcr, Op. 10/3; in g for Treble Rcr, Op. 10/2; in C for Sopranino Rcr, RV.443 *(rec Radley College, Abingdon, Oxon)* United ▲ CAL 88015 [DDD]

Miller, David (archlt/gtr/thb)
Vivaldi, A.:Sons Vc, w. Helen Ghough (vc), Robert King (hpd/org), David Watkin (vc)—Sonatas in E♭, RV.39; e, RV.40; F, RV.41; g, RV.42; a, RV.43; a, RV.44; B♭, RV.45; B♭, RV.46; B♭, RV.47 Hyperion 2–▲ CDA 66881/82

Miller, David (archlt/thb/baroque gtr)
Purcell, H.:Songs, w. B. Bonney (sop), S. Gritton (sop), J. Bowman (ct), R. Covey-Crump (ten), C. Daniels (ten), M. George (bass), M. Caudle (b vl), R. King (chamber org)—Draw near, you lovers; While Thyrsis, wrapt in downy sleep; Love, thou canst hear, I lov'd fair Celia; What hope for us remains now he is gone; Pastora's beauties, when unblown; A thousand sev'ral ways I tried; Urge me no more; Farewell all joys; If music be the food of love [1st setting]; Amidst the shades and cool refreshing streams; They say you're angry; Let each gallant heart; This poet sings the Trojan wars; Ah, how pleasant 'tis to love; My heart whenever you appear; On the brow of Richard Hill; Rashly I swore I would disown; Since the pox or the plague; Beneath a dark and melancholy grove; Musing on cares of human fate; Whilst Cynthia sung, all angry winds lay still Hyperion ▲ CDA 66710
Purcell, H.:Songs, w. B. Bonney (sop), S. Gritton (sop), J. Bowman (ct), R. Covey-Crump (ten), C. Daniels (ten), M. George (bass), M. Caudle (b vl), R. King (org/hpd), King's Consort—Incassum Lesbia; Gentle Shepherds, you that know the charms; I love and I must; Through mournful shades and solitary groves; The Knotting Song Hyperion ▲ CDA 66720 [DDD]

Miller, David (kbd)
Wesley-Smith, M.:Nonsense, Truth & Lewis Carroll, w. Michael Askill (perc), John Grundy (cnd), Sydney Philharmonia Motet Choir Vox Australis 2–▲ VAST 010–2

Miller, David (lt)
Danyel, J.:Songs, w. Nigel Short (ct)—Coy Daphne fled; Thou pretty bird; He whose desires are still abroad; Like as the lute delights; Dost thou withdraw thy grace?; Stay, cruel, stay!; The Passymeasures Galliard; Time, cruel, time; Grief keep within; Drop not, mine eyes; Let not Chloris think; Can doeful notes?; No, let chromatic tunes; Uncertain turns of thought; Eyes, look no more; Rosamund; If I could shut the gate; I die whenas I do not see; What delight they can enjoy; Now the earth, the skies, the air; Mistress Anne Grene Hyperion ▲ CDA 66714

Miller, David (lt/gtr)
Consort Songs, w. Amsterdam Loeki Stardust Quartet, Connor Burrowes (trb) Channel Classics ▲ CCS 9196

Miller, David (pno)
Bremner, A.:In the Shrubbery, w. Judy Glen (nar), Gerard Willems (pno), Philip South (perc), Roland Peelman (cnd), Song Company *(rec Studio 200, ABC Ultimo Centre, Apr 1993)* Tall Poppies ▲ TP 064 [DDD]
Broadstock, B.:Eheu Fugaces, w. Marilyn Richardson (sop), Christine Draeger (fl), Roslyn Dunlop (cl), Fiona Ziegler (vn), Susan Blake (vc), Daryl Pratt (perc) Vox Australis ▲ VAST018–2 [DDD]
Humble, K.:Son Fl, w. Geoffrey Collins (fl) *(rec Studios 200 & 227, ABC Ultimo Centre, Jan–Feb 1995)* Tall Poppies ▲ TP 069 [DDD]
Lemmoné, J.:Fl Music, w. Paul Curtis (fl)—Graceful Dance; Fant on Scottish Melodies; Wind Amongst the Trees; Dainty Dance; Serenade; Valse de Concert; A Fant; Danse Romantique; The Elves; La Danseuse; Minuet; Fant Caprice; Aria *(rec Newcastle Conservatorium of Music Concert Hall, Nov 1994–Feb 1995)* Tall Poppies ▲ TP 68 [DDD]
Messiaen, O.:Harawi, w. Jane Manning (sop) Unicorn-Kanchana ("Souvenir" series) ▲ UKCD 2084
Negro Spirituals, w. Jeanette Thompson (sop), Ieper Chamber Choir Pavane ▲ ADW 7267 [DDD]
Sculthorpe, P.:The Stars Turn, w. Marilyn Richardson (sop), Susan Blake (vc) Vox Australis ▲ VAST018–2 [DDD]
Sitsky, L.:Deep in My Hidden Country, w. Marilyn Richardson (sop), Christine Draeger (fl), Susan Blake (vc), Daryl Pratt (perc) Vox Australis ▲ VAST018–2 [DDD]
Vine, C.:Son Fl, w. Geoffrey Collins (fl) *(rec Studios 200 & 227, ABC Ultimo Centre, Jan–Feb 1995)* Tall Poppies ▲ TP 069 [DDD]

Miller, David (thb/baroque gtr)—see ORCHESTRAS & ENSEMBLES Spectre de la Rose

Miller, David (thb/lt)—see ORCHESTRAS & ENSEMBLES Kithara

Miller, David (va)—see ORCHESTRAS & ENSEMBLES Haydn Baryton Trio, Old Fairfield Academy Orch members

Miller, Earl L. (org)
First Congregational Church, Great Barrington, Mass., Oct 14, 1983 Organ Historical Society ■ OHSC 4
Kimball organ at Worcester Memorial Auditorium *(rec Organ Historical Society National Convention 1983)* Organ Historical Society ■ OHSC 3
The Kotzschmar Memorial Organ, Portland City Hall Auditorium, Portland, Maine AFKA ■ SKL 324
Music for a Grand Organ AFKA ■ SKL 314
Music for a Turn-of-the-Century Residence Organ AFKA ■ SKL 326

Miller, Frank (vc)
Brahms, J.:Con Vn & Vc, "Double Con", w. M. Mischakoff (vn), A. Toscanini (cnd), NBC SO RCA Gold Seal ▲ 60259–2–RG [ADD] ■ 60259–4–RG (CrO2)
Brahms, J.:Con Vn & Vc, "Double Con", w. M. Mischakoff (vn), A. Toscanini (cnd), NBC SO RCA Gold Seal 4–▲ 60325–2–RG (m) [ADD] 4–■ 60325–4–RG (CrO2)
Strauss, R.:Don Quixote, w. A. Toscanini (cnd), NBC SO RCA Gold Seal ▲ 60295–2–RG (m) [ADD] ■ 60295–4–RG (CrO2)

Miller, Gregory (hn)—see ORCHESTRAS & ENSEMBLES New World Brass

Miller, John (bn)
Vivaldi, A.:Cons Bn, w. N. Marriner (cnd), St. Mary's Chamber Players—RV.477,483,484,504 *(rec 1/86)* Pro Arte ▲ CDD 273 [DDD]

Miller, Jonathan (vc)
Thomson, V.:Portraits, w. A. Tommasini (pno), S. Leventhal (vn), F.T. Cohen (ob), R. Haroutunian (bn)—Selected Portraits (13) for Pno (1935–42); Five Ladies for Vn & Pno (1930; 1940; 1983); A Portrait of 2, for Ob, Bn & Pno (1984); 3 Portraits for Pno (1940; arr Samuel Dushkin in 1947 for Vn & Pno); Etude for Vc & Pno:A Portrait of Frederic James (1966); Lili Hastings for Vc & Pno (1983) Northeastern ▲ NR 240–CD

Miller, Kari (pno)
Eaton, J.:Fant Romance, w. Fritz Magg (vc) *(rec Musical Arts Ctr, Bloomington, IN, Nov 3, 1989)* Indiana Univ School of Music ▲ 0–253–31842–4

Miller, Leta (baroque fl)
Bach, C.P.E.:Sons Fl, w. L. Burman-Hall (hpd), R. Hutchinson (vl)—in G, H.548 (W.134); in G, H.550 (W.123); in e, H.551 (W.124); in B♭, H.552 (W.125); in D, H.553 (W.126); in G, H.554 (W.127) Centaur ▲ CRC 2087 [DDD]

Miller, Leta (fl)
Tailleferre, G.:Forlane, w. Irene Herrmann (pno) *(rec UC, Santa Cruz, May 1992)* Helicon Classics ▲ HE 1008

Miller, Leta (ocarina)
Harrison, L.:Ariadne, w. William Winant (perc) MusicMasters ▲ 7051-2-C [DDD]
Harrison, L.:Canticle 3, w. R. Strizich (gtr), William Winant, et al. (perc), D.R. Davies (cnd) MusicMasters ▲ 7051-2-C [DDD]

Miller, Malcolm (pno)
Delius, F.:Fennimore & Gerda (sels), w. Louise Jones (vn)—2 interludes Meridian ▲ MER 84298 [DDD]
Delius, F.:Hassan, w. Louise Jones (vn)—serenade; lullaby Meridian ▲ MER 84298 [DDD]
Delius, F.:Légende, w. Louise Jones (vn) Meridian ▲ MER 84298 [DDD]
Delius, F.:Son Vn, w. Louise Jones (vn) Meridian ▲ MER 84298 [DDD]
Delius, F.:Son 1 Vn & Pno, w. Louise Jones (vn) Meridian ▲ MER 84298 [DDD]
Delius, F.:Son 2 Vn & Pno, w. Louise Jones (vn) Meridian ▲ MER 84298 [DDD]
Delius, F.:Son 3 Vn & Pno, w. Louise Jones (vn) Meridian ▲ MER 84298 [DDD]

Miller, Mark (elec bass)
Sato, M.:Improvs, w. Michihiro Sato (tsugaru shamisen), Bill Frisell (elec gtr), Fred Frith (elec gtr), Tenko (sgr), Nicolas Collins (elec), Christian Marclay (turntables), Steve Colemann (sax), Tom Cora (vc), Joey Baron (perc), Mark Dresser (elec bass), Gerry Hemingway (perc), Toh Ban Djan [Ikue Mori (perc), Luli Shioi (elec bass/sgr)], Semantics [Elliott Sharp (electric gtr/bass), Samm Bennett (perc), Ned Rothenberg (sax)]—23 improvisations with various accompaniment combinations *(rec Baby Monster Studio, NY, Apr. 11-16, 1988)* Hat Hut ▲ hat ART CD 6015 [ADD]

Miller, Michael (ob)
Cage, J.:Ryoanji for 4 Soloists, w. Anthony D'Amico (db), Fenwick Smith (fl), Petur Eiriksson (b trbn), S. Drury (cnd), New England Conservatory Avant-Garde Ensemble *(rec New England Conservatory of Music, Boston, MA, Mar. 4 & 6, 1991)* Mode ▲ MODE 41

Miller, Robert (pno)
Babbitt, M.:Post-Partitions *(rec Colombia Studios, NYC)* New World ▲ 80466-2
Babbitt, M.:Reflections *(rec Colombia Studios, NYC)* New World ▲ 80466-2
Berger, A.:Pieces (5) Pno *(rec Rutgers Presbyterian Church, New York City)* New World ▲ 80308-2
Cage, J.:Sons & Interludes—Sons. Nos. 1, 5, 10 & 12; Interlude No. 2 New World ▲ 80203-2
Cowell, H.:Pno Music—The Banshee; Aeolian Harp; Piano Piece New World ▲ 80203-2
Johnston, B.:Son for Microtonal Pno New World ▲ 80203-2
Nancarrow, C.:Studies—Nos. 1, 27 & 36 New World ▲ 80203-2
Wuorinen, C.:Son 1 Pno Music & Arts ▲ CD 932
Wyner, Y.:Short Fants CRI ("American Masters" series) ▲ CD 701 [ADD]

Miller, Robin (ob)
Bach, J.S.:Con Vn & Ob, w. O. Shumsky (vn), Scottish CO Nimbus ▲ NI 5325 [DDD]
Handel, G.F.:Cons (3) Ob, w. A. Gibson (cnd), Scottish CO ASV/Quicksilva ▲ ASQCD 6188

Miller, T. (bar sax)—see ORCHESTRAS & ENSEMBLES Prism Saxophone Quartet

Miller, Tess (ob)
Bach, J.S.:Con 1 for 2 Hpds, w. Carmel Kaine (vn), Christopher Hogwood (bc), Nicholas Kraemer (bc), N. Marriner (cnd), Academy of St. Martin in the Fields [trans for vn & ob] *(rec St. John's, Smith Square, London, Aug 1974 & Feb 1975)* Boston Skyline ▲ BSD 127 [ADD]

Milleret, Lisette (vl)—see ORCHESTRAS & ENSEMBLES Isabella D'Este

Millet, Florence (pno)
Pesson, G.:Music of, w. Donatienne Michel-Dansac (sop), Sandra Roulx (mez), Stuart Patterson (ten), Paul-Alexandre Dubois (bar), Pascal Sausy (bar), D. My (cnd), Fa Ensemble, Paris String Quartet—Le gel, par jeu for Fl, Cl, Hn, Bass Mar, Vn & Vc; Qt for Strs; Non Sapremo Mai di Questo Mi for Fl, Vn & Pno; 5 Poèmes de Sandro Penna for Bar, B Cl, Hn, Vn & Vc; La lumière n'a pas de bras pour nous porter for Amplified Pno; La vita è come l'albero di natale for Vn & Pno; Nocturnes en quatuor for Cl, Pno, Vn & Vc; Les chants faëz for Pno & 10 Instrs; Sur-le-champ for 4 Voices & 9 Instrs [from a text by Pierre Alferi] Accord ▲ ACD 204682 [DDD]

Millet, Gilles (vn)—see ORCHESTRAS & ENSEMBLES Danel String Quartet

Millican, Brady (pno)
Gottschalk, L.M.:Music of, w. Trinidad Paniagua (sop), José Alberto Esteves (ten), Pablo Garcia (bar), Eugene List (pno), Cary Lewis (pno), Adler, Buketoff (cnd), Berlin SO, Vienna State Opera Orch—Grande Tarantelle for Piano & Orchestra, Op. 67; Symphony No. 1, "La nuit des tropiques"; Symphony No. 2, "A Montevideo"; The Union (concert paraphrase on American national airs) for Piano & Orchestra, Op. 48; Variations on the Portuguese National Hymn for Piano & Orchestra, Op. 91; Grande fantaisie triomphale sur l'hymne national brésilien for Piano & Orchestra, Op. 69; Marche solennelle for Orchestra; Marcha triunfal y final de opera for Orchestra; Escenas campestres (opera in one act); Five Pieces for Piano Duet [Radieuse, Op. 72; Ses yeux, Op. 66; La Gallina, Op. 53; Ojos criollos, Op. 37; Pasquinade, Op. 59] Vox Box 2-▲ CDX 5009 [ADD]

Millière, Gérard (tpt)
Hummel, J.N.:Con in E♭ Tpt, S.49, w. L. de Froment (cnd), Luxembourg Radio-TV SO Forlane ▲ FRL 42 [ADD]

Millière, Marie-Christine (vn)
Cras, J.:La Flûte de Pan, w. D. Henry (bar), T. Prevost (fl), J.-F. Benatar (va), P. Bary (vc)—[F] Quantum ▲ QM 6897 [DDD] ■ QM 1992 (D)
Cras, J.:Qnt, w. C. Michel (hp), T. Prevost (fl), J.-F. Benatar (va), P. Bary (vc) Quantum ▲ QM 6897 [DDD] ■ QM 1992 (D)
Cras, J.:Trio, w. J.-F. Benatar (va), P. Bary (vc) Quantum ▲ QM 6897 [DDD] ■ QM 1992 (D)
Martinů, B.:Duo Vn & Vc, w. P. Bary (vc) Quantum ▲ QM 6910 [DDD] ■ QM 2004 (D)
Martinů, B.:Madrigals Vn, w. J. Benatar (va) Quantum ▲ QM 6910 [DDD] ■ QM 2004 (D)

Mills, Frederic (tpt)—see ORCHESTRAS & ENSEMBLES Canadian Brass

Mills, Jonathan (org)
Veni, Veni, Emmanuel, w. [cnd:Timothy Prosser], Emmanuel College Chapel Choir Cambridge ASV ▲ ASV CD 2104

Mills, Margaret (pno)
Gideon, M.:Of Shadows Numberless Newport Classic ▲ NCD 60048 [DDD] ■ NCC 60048 (D)
Lauer, E.:Sonatina Pno Newport Classic ▲ NCD 60048 [DDD] ■ NCC 60048 (D)
Newman, Anthony:Chamber Music, w. P.J. Bacchus (fl), Y. Waldman (vn), D. Wan, Flute Force, Laurentian String Quartet—Qnt for Piano & Strings, "Easter"; Qt for 4 Flutes; Introduction & Toccata for Flute & Piano; Vars & Toccata for Violin Newport Classic ▲ NCD 60032 [DDD]
Newman, Anthony:Var & Fugue Newport Classic ▲ NCD 60048 [DDD] ■ NCC 60048 (D)
Wilson, R.:Intercalations Newport Classic ▲ NCD 60048 [DDD] ■ NCC 60048 (D)

Milman, Misha (vc)
Schubert, Franz:Qnt Strs, D.956, w. Borodin String Quartet *(rec Teldec Studio, Berlin, July 1994)* Teldec ▲ 94564-2 [DDD]
Vivaldi, A.:Con for 2 Vns Vc, R.565, w. V. Spivakov (vn), A. Fouter (vn), V. Spivakov (cnd), Moscow Virtuosi RCA Red Seal ▲ 60240-2-RC [DDD]

Milne, Hamish (pno)
Medtner, N.:Pno Music (misc) CRD ▲ 3338 [ADD]
Medtner, N.:Pno Music (misc)—Sonata Triad, Op. 11; Sonata in e, "The Night Wind," Op. 25/2 CRD ▲ 3339 [ADD]
Medtner, N.:Pno Music (misc)—Two Skazki, Op. 8; Three Novelles, Op. 17; Sonata in g, Op. 22; Romantic Sketches for the Young, Op. 54 CRD ▲ 3460 [DDD]
Medtner, N.:Pno Music (misc)—Sonata in f, Op. 5; Second Improvisation (in variation form), Op. 47 CRD ▲ 3461 [DDD]
Walton, W.:Qt Pno, w. K. Sillito (vn), R. Smissen (va), S. Orton (vc) Chandos ▲ CHAN 8999 [DDD]
Walton, W.:Son Vn & Pno, w. K. Sillito (vn) Chandos ▲ CHAN 8999 [DDD]
Weber, C.M. von:Invitation to the Dance Pno CRD ▲ 3485 [DDD]
Weber, C.M. von:Polacca brillante CRD ▲ 3486 [DDD]
Weber, C.M. von:Rondo brillante CRD ▲ 3485 [DDD]
Weber, C.M. von:Sons Pno—Nos. 3 & 4 CRD ▲ 3486 [DDD]
Weber, C.M. von:Sons Pno—Nos. 1 & 2 CRD ▲ 3485 [DDD]

Milosi, Rodrigue (vn)
Constant, M.:Cent-trois regards dans l'eau, w. C. Bardon (cnd), Caen Orch *(rec Feb. 25-27, 1994)* Chamade ▲ 5606 [DDD]
Tanguy, É.:Con Vn, w. C. Bardon (cnd), Caen Orch *(rec Feb. 25-27, 1994)* Chamade ▲ 5606 [DDD]

Milozzi, Dante (fl)—see ORCHESTRAS & ENSEMBLES Briccialdi Wind Quintet

Milstein, Nathan (vn)
The Art of Nathan Milstein *(rec 1955-66)* EMI Classics 6-▲ ZDMF 64830
Bach, J.S.:Sons & Partitas Vn, BWV 1001-1006—Part in d, BWV 1004 Bridge ▲ BRI 9066
Bach, J.S.:Sons & Partitas Vn, BWV 1001-1006 Deutsche Grammophon 2-▲ 423294-2 [ADD]
Bach, J.S.:Sons & Partitas Vn, BWV 1001-1006—Partita 2 in d, BWV 1004 One-Eleven ▲ URS 50140 [ADD]
Bach, J.S.:Sons & Partitas Vn, BWV 1001-1006 EMI Classics 2-▲ ZDMB 64793
Bach, J.S.:Sons & Partitas Vn, BWV 1001-1006—Son in g, BWV 1001; Partita in d, BWV 1004; Son in C, BWV 1005; Tempo di Borea [from Son in b, BWV 1002]; Präludium [from Son in E, BWV 1006] *(rec Aug 4, 1957)* Orfeo d'or ("Festspiel Dokumente" series) ▲ 400951
Bach, J.S.:Sons & Partitas Vn, BWV 1001-1006, w. Josef Blatt (pno)—Son in g, BWV 1001 *(rec Coolidge Auditorium, Library of Congress, Oct 7, 1946)* Bridge ▲ BCD 9064
Baroque Masterpieces, w. Leopold Mittman (pno) Biddulph ▲ LAB 055 [ADD]
Beethoven, L. van:Son 5 Vn, "Spring", w. Artur Balsam (pno) Bridge ▲ BRI 9066
Beethoven, L. van:Son 8 Vn, w. A. Balsam (pno) *(rec 1939)* Biddulph ▲ LAB 063 [ADD]
Brahms, J.:Con Vn, w. V. de Sabata (cnd), New York PO *(rec live, Carnegie Hall 1950)* Melodram ▲ MEL 18008
Brahms, J.:Con Vn & Vc, "Double Con", w. G. Piatigorsky (vc), F. Reiner (cnd), Robin Hood Dell Orch Philadelphia RCA Gold Seal ▲ 09026-61485-2
Brahms, J.:Son 3 Vn, w. Artur Balsam (pno) *(rec Library of Congress, Mar 13, 1953)* Bridge ▲ 9066
Brahms, J.:Son 3 Vn, w. V. Horowitz (pno) RCA Gold Seal ▲ 60461-2-RG (m) [ADD] ■ 60461-4-RG (CrO2)
Bruch, M.:Con 1 Vn, *(cnd & orch unknown)* Memories 2-▲ MEM CD 3011
Bruch, M.:Con 1 Vn, w. L. Barzin (cnd), Philharmonia Orch Classics for Pleasure ▲ CDCFP 4374 [ADD]
Chopin, F.:Nocturnes, w. Josef Blatt (pno)—No. 20 in c# [arr Milstein for vn & pno] *(rec Coolidge Auditorium, Library of Congress, Oct 7, 1946)* Bridge ▲ BCD 9064
Goldmark, K.:Con 1 Vn, w. B. Walter (cnd), New York PO One-Eleven ▲ URS 50140
Goldmark, K.:Con 1 Vn, w. H. Bleech (cnd), Philharmonia Orch Testament ▲ TES SBT 1047
Great Musicians In Copenhagen, w. Vladimir Horowitz (pno), Rudolf Serkin (pno), Wanda Landowska (hpd), Gregor Piatigorsky (vc), Fritz Busch (cnd), Nicolai Malko (cnd) Danacord ▲ DACOCD 303
Lalo, E.:Sym espagnole, w. V. Golschmann (cnd), St. Louis SO Testament ▲ TES SBT 1047
Lalo, E.:Sym espagnole, *(cnd & orch unknown)* Memories 2-▲ MEM CD 3011
The Last Recital, w. Georges Pludermacher (pno) *(rec Berwaldhallen, Stockholm, June 1986)* Teldec ▲ 95998-2 [DDD]
Mendelssohn, F.:Con in d Vn & Strs, *(orch unknown)* Memories ("Golden" series) 2-▲ MEM 3007
Mendelssohn, F.:Con in e Vn & Orch, Op. 64, w. L. Barzin (cnd), Philharmonia Orch Classics for Pleasure ▲ CDCFP 4374 [ADD]
Mendelssohn, F.:Con in e Vn & Orch, Op. 64, w. Josef Blatt (pno) *(rec Coolidge Auditorium, Library of Congress, Oct 7, 1946)* Bridge ▲ BCD 9064
Milstein, N.:Paganiniana, w. Josef Blatt (pno) *(rec Coolidge Auditorium, Library of Congress, Oct 7, 1946)* Bridge ▲ BCD 9064
Mozart, W.A.:Sons Vn Pno (misc), w. A. Balsam (pno)—K.296 *(rec 1939)* Biddulph ▲ LAB 063 [ADD]
Nathan Milstein, w. Leopold Mittman (pno) Pearl ▲ PEA 9401 (m) [AAD]
Paganini, N.:Caprices Vn—in a *(rec Aug 4, 1957)* Orfeo d'or ("Festspiel Dokumente" series) ▲ 400951
Plays Bach, w. Vladimir Horowitz (pno) RCA Gold Seal ▲ 60461-2-RG (m) [ADD]
Saint-Saëns, C.:Music of, w. G. Prêtre, Dervaux, Menuhin—Carnival of the Animals, Danse macabre, Phaéton, Rouet d'Omphale, Bacchanale; Introduction & Rondo capriccioso, Havanaise EMI Classics ("Studio" series) ▲ CDM 69112
Stamitz, C.:Con Vn, w. A. Balsam (pno) [arr. for violin & piano]—Adagio & Rondo movts. *(rec 1940)* Biddulph ▲ LAB 063 [ADD]
Suk, J.:Burleska, w. A. Balsam (pno) *(rec 1940)* Biddulph ▲ LAB 063 [ADD]
Tartini, G.:Son Vn "Devil's Trill", w. L. Mittman (pno) Biddulph ▲ LAB 055 [ADD]
Tchaikovsky, P.:Con Vn, *(cnd & orch unknown)* Memories 2-▲ MEM CD 3011
Tchaikovsky, P.:Con Vn, w. F. Stock (cnd), Chicago SO *(rec 1940)* Biddulph ▲ LAB 063 [ADD]
A Tribute to Nathan Milstein, w. Artur Balsam (pno) One-Eleven ▲ URS 50020 [ADD]
Vitali, T.A.:Chaconne Vn Pno, w. Josef Blatt (pno) *(rec Coolidge Auditorium, Library of Congress, Oct 7, 1946)* Bridge ▲ BCD 9064
Wieniawski, H.:Vn & Pno Music, w. Josef Blatt (pno)—Scherzo-Tarantelle *(rec Coolidge Auditorium, Library of Congress, Oct 7, 1946)* Bridge ▲ BCD 9064

Milstein, Sergueï (pno)
Shostakovich, D.:Son Va, w. A. Kholodenko (va) REM ▲ REM 311210 [DDD]
Shostakovich, D.:Son Vn, w. A. Kholodenko (vn) REM ▲ REM 311210 [DDD]

Miltenberger, James (pno)
Aguila, M. del:Son 2 Pno ACA Digital Recording ▲ CM 20021
Gershwin, G.:Songs [aleatoric improvisations]—Nice Work If You Can Get It; Embraceable You; The Man I Love; But Not for Me; Our Love Is Here to Stay; Fascinating Rhythm ACA Digital Recording ▲ CM 20021
Ginastera, A.:Son 1 Pno ACA Digital Recording ▲ CM 20021
Green, S.:Onata-say Too ACA Digital Recording ▲ CM 20021
Morillo, R.G.:Son 4 Pno ACA Digital Recording ▲ CM 20021

Mimura, Kazuko (pno)
Dvořák, A.:Qnt Pno, Op. 81, w. Talich String Quartet *(rec 1993)* Calliope ▲ CAL 9229 [DDD]

Minchev, Mincho (vn)
Brahms, J.:Con Vn, w. V. Stefanov (cnd), Philharmonia Bulgarica Vivace ▲ 586 [ADD]
Brahms, J.:Con Vn, w. V. Stefanov (cnd), Philharmonia Bulgarica Vivace 3-▲ E 325 [ADD/DDD]
Mozart, W.A.:Sinf concertante Vn, K.364, w. C. Paskalev (va), E. Tabakov (cnd), Sofia Soloists CO Vivace 3-▲ E 316 [DDD]
Mozart, W.A.:Sinf concertante Vn, K.364, w. C. Paskalev (va), E. Tabakov (cnd), Sofia Soloists CO Vivace ▲ E 576 [ADD]
Paganini, N.:Con 5 Vn, w. D. Petkov (cnd), Plovdiv PO Vivace ▲ E 534 [ADD]
Paganini, N.:Terzetto Vn, w. L. Gerogiev (vc), M. Sao Marcos (gtr) Vivace ▲ E 534 [ADD]
Stamitz, C.:Sinf Concertante, w. C. Paskalev (va), E. Tabakov (cnd), Sofia Solisti Vivace ▲ E 576 [ADD]

Minderaa, Frank (ob)
Van Baaren, K.:Septet Vn, w. J. Walta (vn), J. de Wit (fl), et al. Olympia ▲ OCD 505 [AAD]

Minella, Silvano (vn)—see ORCHESTRAS & ENSEMBLES Fauré Trio

Minen, Carla (gtr)—see ORCHESTRAS & ENSEMBLES Linhares Guitar Quartet

Ming, L. Pui (pno)
Pui Ming, L.:Music for Pno—Shepherdess; What's Up; C'est Bon!; The Yan-Min Suite; Xun Song; Strange Beauty; The Swing; Piano Percussion; For "Ma" *(rec New York, Apr. 1994)* Dorian ▲ DOR 90206 [DDD]

Ming, Liu Xiao (pno)
Czerny, C.:Con Pno 4-Hnds, w. Horst Göbel (pno), N. Athinãos (cnd), Frankfurt on the Oder State Orch *(rec Frankfurt, June 24-28, 1996)* Signum ▲ X 78-00 [DDD]

Mings, D. (baroque bn)—see ORCHESTRAS & ENSEMBLES La Dada

Mings, D. (bn)—see ORCHESTRAS & ENSEMBLES Senario Ensemble

Minkoff, U. (pno)—see ORCHESTRAS & ENSEMBLES Linea Ensemble

Minkowski, Marc (bn)—see also also ORCHESTRAS & ENSEMBLES Ricercar Consort
Telemann, G.P.:Con in F Rcr Bn, w. F. de Roos (rcr), Ricercar Consort Ricercar ▲ RIC 44021 [DDD]

Minola, Ottavio (pno)—see ORCHESTRAS & ENSEMBLES Fauré Trio

Mintcheva, Dora (vc)
Crusell, B.H.:Qts (3) Cl, w. R. Hogerheijde (cl), V. Liberman (vn), G. Oldeman (va) Erasmus ▲ WVH 103

Mintz, Shlomo (va)
Mozart, W.A.:Sinf concertante Vn, K.364, w. V. Spivakov (vn), Moscow Virtuosi RCA Red Seal ▲ 09026-60467-2

Mintz, Shlomo (vn)
Dvořák, A.:Con Vn, w. J. Levine (cnd), Berlin PO Deutsche Grammophon ▲ 419618-2 [DDD]

Mintz, Shlomo (vn) (cont.)
Paganini, N.:Caprices Vn — Deutsche Grammophon ▲ 415043-2 [DDD]
Prokofiev, S.:Cons Vn (comp), w. C. Abbado (cnd), Chicago SO — Deutsche Grammophon ▲ 410524-2 [DDD]
Prokofiev, S.:Cons Vn (comp), w. C. Abbado (cnd), Chicago SO — Deutsche Grammophon 3-▲ 435151-2 [ADD]
Sibelius, J.:Con Vn, w. J. Levine (cnd), Berlin PO — Deutsche Grammophon ▲ 419618-2 [DDD]
Vivaldi, A.:Cons Vn (misc), Israel CO—in A, RV.763, "L'Ottavina"; in F, RV.286; in E♭, RV.261; in B♭, RV.366; in E♭, RV.260; in b, RV.387 — MusicMasters ▲ 01612-67155-2
Vivaldi, A.:Cons Vn (misc), w. S. Mintz (cnd), Israel CO—RV.189, 197, 215, 241, 321 & 329 *(rec Eglise du Liban, Aug 1992)* — MusicMasters ("Vivaldi Collection" series) ▲ 01612-67168-2
Vivaldi, A.:Cons Vn (misc), w. S. Mintz (cnd), Israel CO—Op. 6/1–6; Coucou, RV 335 *(rec Paris, Aug 1992 & Mar 1993)* — MusicMasters ("Classics" series) ▲ 671792
Vivaldi, A.:Cons Vn (misc), w. S. Mintz (cnd), Israel CO—12 concerti—RV.171, 186, 199, 208, 230, 232, 249, 254, 265, 271, 310, 356 — MusicMasters 2-▲ 01612-67085-2
Vivaldi, A.:Cons Vn (misc), w. S. Mintz (cnd), Israel CO—"Anna Maria" Concertos, RV.223, 349, 248, 229, 343 & 267 — MusicMasters ▲ 1612-67120-2

Miolin, Anders (alt gtr)
Satie, E.:Pno Music (misc) [arr. Miolin]—Trois Sarabandes; Trois Gymnopédies; Gnossiennes; Musique rosicrucienne; Le fils des étoiles; Prélude d'Eginhard; A l'occation d'une grande peine; Caresse; Piè froides; Airs à faire fuir 1–3; Nostalgie *(rec July 1992)* — BIS ▲ CD 586 [DDD]

Miquelle, Georges (vc)
Bloch, E.:Schelomo, w. H. Hanson (cnd), Eastman-Rochester Orch — Mercury Living Presence ▲ 432718-2 [ADD]
Herbert, V.:Con 2 Vc, w. H. Hanson (cnd), Eastman-Rochester Orch — Mercury Living Presence ▲ 434355-2

Mirani, Micheline (hpd)
Albicastro, H.:Son Vn, Op. 5/3, w. R. Elmiger (vn) — Gallo ▲ CD 625 [ADD]
Burkhard, W.:Sonatine Vn, w. R. Elmiger (vn) — Gallo ▲ CD 625 [ADD]
Burkhard, W.:Suite en miniature Vn, w. R. Elmiger (vn) — Gallo ▲ CD 625 [ADD]
Segond, P.:Petite sérénade, w. R. Elmiger (vn) — Gallo ▲ CD 625 [ADD]

Mirani, Micheline (pno)
Fritz, G.:Son Vn, Op. 2/4, w. R. Elmiger (vn) — Gallo ▲ CD 625 [AAD]

Miravalle, Augusto (pno)
Clementi, M.:Pno Music (comp), w. Aldo Antognazzi (pno), Yi Fang Huang (vn)—Sons (3) for Pno & Vn, Op. 3, Nos. 5 & 6; Sons (6) for Pno & Vn, Op. 4 — Aura Classics ▲ AU 32288

Mirkin, K. (va)
Swack, I.:Duets Vn, w. O. Ravina (vn) — Opus One ▲ 149

Mironovich, Eugenia (pno)
Denisov, E.:Son Fl, w. Leonid Mironovich (fl) *(rec Tsai Performance Center, Boston, MA)* — Sonora ▲ SO 22567 [DDD]
Gubaidulina, S.:Allegro rustico, w. Leonid Mironovich (fl) *(rec Tsai Performance Center, Boston, MA)* — Sonora ▲ SO 22567 [DDD]
Nagovitzin, V.:Son Fl & Pno, w. Leonid Mironovich (fl) *(rec Tsai Performance Center, Boston, MA)* — Sonora ▲ SO 22567 [DDD]
Sinisalo, H.-R.:Miniatures, w. Leonid Mironovich (fl) *(rec Tsai Performance Center, Boston, MA)* — Sonora ▲ SO 22567 [DDD]
Taktakishvili, O.:Son Fl, w. Leonid Mironovich (fl) *(rec Tsai Performance Center, Boston, MA)* — Sonora ▲ SO 22567 [DDD]
Vasilenko, S.:The Spring Suite, w. Leonid Mironovich (fl) *(rec Tsai Performance Center, Boston, MA)* — Sonora ▲ SO 22567 [DDD]

Mironovich, Leonid (fl)
Denisov, E.:Son Fl, w. Eugenia Mironovich (pno) *(rec Tsai Performance Center, Boston, MA)* — Sonora ▲ SO 22567 [DDD]
Gubaidulina, S.:Allegro rustico, w. Eugenia Mironovich (pno) *(rec Tsai Performance Center, Boston, MA)* — Sonora ▲ SO 22567 [DDD]
Nagovitzin, V.:Son Fl & Pno, w. Eugenia Mironovich (pno) *(rec Tsai Performance Center, Boston, MA)* — Sonora ▲ SO 22567 [DDD]
Sinisalo, H.-R.:Miniatures, w. Eugenia Mironovich (pno) *(rec Tsai Performance Center, Boston, MA)* — Sonora ▲ SO 22567 [DDD]
Taktakishvili, O.:Son Fl, w. Eugenia Mironovich (pno) *(rec Tsai Performance Center, Boston, MA)* — Sonora ▲ SO 22567 [DDD]
Vasilenko, S.:The Spring Suite, w. Eugenia Mironovich (pno) *(rec Tsai Performance Center, Boston, MA)* — Sonora ▲ SO 22567 [DDD]

Mirring, Peter (vn)
Bach, J.S.:Trio Son Fl, Vn & Hpd, w. E. Haupt (fl), C. Schornsheim (hpd) *(rec June 1989 & 1990)* — Berlin Classics 2-▲ BER 1007 [DDD]
Mozart, W.A.:Qt Fl, K.285, w. E. Haupt (fl), P. Schikora (va), G. Pluskwik (vc) — LaserLight ▲ 15 878 [DDD]

Mirschel, A. (ob)
Gluck, C.W.:Ovs, w. J. Felmlee (fl), P. R. Klecka (hpd), J. Corazolla (cnd), Rhenish CO—Euristeo; Iphigénie en Aulide; Orfeo ed Euridice; Don Juan — Entrée ▲ 0064

Mirynski, Janusz (vn)
Van De Vate, N.:Distant Worlds, w. S. Kawalla (cnd), Polish Radio-TV SO — Vienna Modern Masters ▲ VMM 3008 [ADD]
Van De Vate, N.:Trio Vn, w. Z. Lapinski (vc), M. Mitelski (pno) — Vienna Modern Masters ▲ VMM CD 2001 [ADD]

Mischakoff, Mischa (vn)
Brahms, J.:Con Vn & Vc, "Double Con", w. F. Miller (vc), A. Toscanini (cnd), NBC SO — RCA Gold Seal ▲ 60259-2-RG [ADD] ■ 60259-4-RG (CrO2)
Brahms, J.:Con Vn & Vc, "Double Con", w. F. Miller (vc), A. Toscanini (cnd), NBC SO — RCA Gold Seal 4-▲ 60325-2-RG (m) [ADD] 4-■ 60325-4-RG (CrO2)

Mischuk, Vladimir (pno)
Rachmaninoff, S.:Con 1 Pno, w. A. Tchernushenko (cnd), St. Petersburg State Academic Cappella SO — Audiophile Classics ▲ 101.037

Mišejka, Peter (vc)
Domazlicky, F.:Czech Folk Songs, w. Z. Jiroušek (vn), J. Mráček (vn), O. Smola (va), J. Karas (cnd), Disman Radio Children's Ensemble *(rec June 1992)* — Channel Classics ▲ CCS 5193 [DDD]

Mishory, Gilead (pno)
Janácek, L.:Pno Music, w. András Adorján (pic), Saschko Gawriloff (vn), Wen-Sinn Yang (vc)—Son. for Vn & Pno; Allegro for Vn & Pno; Romance for Vn & Pno; Dumka for Vn & Pno; Tema Con Vars. for Pno; Fairy Tale for Vc & Pno; Presto for Vc & Pno; March of the Bluebreasts for Pic & Pno; Music for Excercises w. Clubs for Pno; In Memoriam for Pno; Reminiscence for Pno — Tudor ▲ TUD 7003 [DDD]

Mistry, Jagdish (vn)
Antheil, G.:Music of, w. Martyn Hill (ten), Hermann Kretzschmar (pno), H. K. Gruber (cnd), Ensemble Modern—Printemps I; Ballet mécanique; Fighting the Waves; A Jazz Symphony; Lithuanian Night; Jazz Sonata; Concerto for CO; Son 1 Vn; Printemps II *(rec Frankfurt, Germany, June 27–30 & Dec 20–23, 1)* — RCA Red Seal ▲ 09026-68066-2 [DDD]

Mitchell, Alastair (8-keyed bn)
The Early Clarinet Family, w. Keith Puddy (cl), Gary Brodie (cl/bass chalumeaux), P. Price (bass chalumeaux), Susan Dent (baroque hn), Malcolm Martineau (pno) — Clarinet Classics ▲ CC 0004

Mitchell, Alastair (bn)
Beethoven, L. van:Duos, WoO 27, w. K. Puddy (cl) [Puddy uses 5-keyed B♭ cl] — Clarinet Classics ▲ CC 0004

Mitchell, Danlee (bass mar)
Partch, H.:The Mock Turtle Song & Jabberwocky, w. Harry Partch (voc/harmonic canon)—O Frabjous Day! *(rec Mill Valley Outdoor Club's Young People's Concert Series, Feb 13, 1954)* — Innova 4-▲ 401

Mitchell, Danlee (kithara/harmonic canon)
Partch, H.:Bless This Home, w. Harry Partch (voc/adapted va), Vincenzo Prockelo (ob), Joseph Varhula (mazda mar), J. Garvey (cnd) *(rec Univ of Illinois, 1961)* — Innova 4-▲ 401

Mitchell, Emily (hp)
Carol of the Drum, w. Chieftains, Richard Stoltzman (cl), Michala Petri (rcr), James Galway (fl), Hampton String Quartet, Royal PO, Boys' Choir of Harlem — RCA Victor ▲ 09026-61839-2 ■ 09026-61839-4
Flying Dreams:A Lullaby Album, w. James Galway (fl) — RCA Victor ▲ 09026-61188-2 [DDD] ■ 09026-61188-4
O Holy Night:Christmas Favorites, w. James Galway (fl), Richard Stoltzman (cl), Michala Petri (rcr), Canadian Brass, Boston Pops Orch [cnd:Arthur Fiedler] — RCA Victor ▲ 09026-61836-2 ■ 09026-61836-4
Wild Classics:A Celebration of Animals & Nature, w. James Galway (fl), Ofra Harnoy (vc), Martin Hoherman (vc), Michael Dussek (pno), Samuel Lipman (pno), Leo Litwin (pno), Gerhard Oppitz (pno), Isao Tomita (synths), Boston Pops Orch [cnd:Arthur Fiedler], Chicago SO [cnd:Fritz Reiner] — RCA Red Seal ▲ 09026-68483-2 ■ 09026-68483-4

Mitchell, Ian (cl)
Lumsdaine, D.:What Shall I Sing?, w. M. Wiegold (sop), E. Pillinger (cl) — NM Classics ▲ NMCD 007 [DDD]

Mitchell, Madeline (vn)
Krauze, Z.:Quatuor pour la naissance, w. D. Campbell (cl), C. van Kampen (vc), J. MacGregor (pno) — Collins Classics ▲ COL 1393 [DDD]
Messiaen, O.:Quatuor pour la fin du temps, w. D. Campbell (cl), C. van Campen (vc), J. MacGregor (pno) — Collins Classics ▲ COL 1393 [DDD]

Mitchell, Marjorie (pno)
Bloch, E.:Con symphonique, w. V. Golschmann (cnd), Vienna State Opera Orch *(rec 1961)* — Vanguard Classics ▲ OVC 4052 [ADD]
Carpenter, J.A.:Concertino Pno Orch, w. W. Strickland (cnd), Göteborg SO *(rec 1963)* — Citadel ▲ CTD 88118 [ADD]
Litolff, H.C.:Con Symphonique 4, w. V. Golschmann (cnd), Vienna State Opera Orch—Scherzo *(rec 1961)* — Vanguard Classics ▲ OVC 4052 [ADD]
Piston, W.:Concertino Pno, w. W. Strickland (cnd), Göteborg SO — CRI ■ C 180
Ross, W.:Mosaics, Slovak RSO Bratislava — Master Musicians Collective ▲ MMC 2020
Ross, W.:Mosaics, w. L. Muti (cnd), St. Stephen's CO — Albany ▲ TROY 111 [DDD]

Mitchell, Michael (baroque va)—see ORCHESTRAS & ENSEMBLES In Nomine Players

Mitchell, P. Gustaf (trbn)
Liszt, F.:Ave Maria von Arcadelt, w. Donald Sutherland (org) [at St. Patrick's Church Org, Washington, DC] — Gothic ▲ G 49080 [DDD]
Liszt, F.:Evocation à la Chapelle Sixtine, w. Donald Sutherland (org) [at St. Patrick's Church Org, Washington, DC] — Gothic ▲ G 49080 [DDD]
Liszt, F.:Fant & Fugue on "Ad nos, ad salutarem undam" Org, w. Donald Sutherland (org) [at St. Patrick's Church Org, Washington, DC] — Gothic ▲ G 49080 [DDD]
Liszt, F.:Transcriptions & Paraphrases, w. Donald Sutherland (org)—Cujus animam [from Stabat mater; at St. Patrick's Church Org, Washington, DC] — Gothic ▲ G 49080 [DDD]
Liszt, F.:Vars on "Weinen, Klagen, Sorgen, Zagen", S.179, w. Donald Sutherland (org) [at St. Patrick's Church Org, Washington, DC] — Gothic ▲ G 49080 [DDD]

Mitchell, Red (db)
A Different Kind of Blues, w. Itzhak Perlman (vn), Andre Previn (pno), Shelly Manne (drums), Jim Hall (gtr) — Angel ▲ CDM 64319 [DDD]
It's a Breeze, w. Itzhak Perlman (vn), Andre Previn (pno), Shelly Manne (drums), Jim Hall (gtr) — Angel ▲ CDM 64318 [DDD]

Mitchell, Roscoe (a sax)
Hamilton, T.:Off-Hour Wait State, w. Thomas Buckner (voc), Ralph Samuelson (shak), Peter Zummo (trbn), Tom Hamilton (syn/elec), Jonathan Haas (perc) — O.O. Discs ▲ OO 26 [DDD]

Mitchell, Roscoe (sax)
Mitchell, R.:Duet, w. V. Manoogian (vn) — Lovely Music ▲ LCD 2021 [AAD]

Mitchell, Roscoe (sax/ww/perc)—see ORCHESTRAS & ENSEMBLES Roscoe Mitchell New Chamber Ensemble

Mitchell, Scott (pno)
Carpenter, J.A.:Concertino Pno Orch, w. W. Strickland (cnd), Göteborg SO — CRI ■ C 180

Mitelski, M. (pno)
Van De Vate, N.:Trio Vn, w. J. Mirynski (vn), Z. Lapinski (vc) — Vienna Modern Masters ▲ VMM CD 2001 [ADD]

Mitrani, Micheline (hpd)
Bach, J.S.:Sons Vn, w. R. Elmiger (vn)—BWV 1021, 1023 & 1024 — Gallo ▲ CD 694 [ADD]
Bonporti, F.A.:Invenzioni (10) de camera, w. R. Elmiger (vn)—Nos. 2, 5, 6, & 7 — Gallo ▲ CD 694 [ADD]
Bonporti, F.A.:Invenzioni (10) de camera, w. R. Elmiger (vn)—Nos. 1, 3, 4, 8, 9, & 10 — Gallo ▲ CD 693 [ADD]
Milhaud, D.:Sailor Song, w. R. Elmiger (vn) — Gallo ▲ CD 585 [AAD]
Milhaud, D.:Son Vn & Hpd, Op. 144, w. R. Elmiger (vn) — Gallo ▲ CD 585 [AAD]
Milhaud, D.:Son Vn & Hpd, Op. 257, w. R. Elmiger (vn) — Gallo ▲ CD 585 [AAD]
Rieti, V.:Son breve, w. R. Elmiger (vn) — Gallo ▲ CD 585 [AAD]
Vivaldi, A.:Sons Vn, w. R. Elmiger (vn)—(6) RV.2, 3, 12, 28, 29 & 34 — Gallo ▲ CD 602 [AAD]
Vivaldi, A.:Sons Vn, w. R. Elmiger (vn)—RV.5, 10, 14, 15, 17a, 21, 26, & 35 *(rec July 1987)* — Gallo ▲ CD 526

Mitsuhashi, Kifu (hsiao)
Shui-Lung, M.:The Peacock Flies Southeast, w. H. Sung-jen (cnd), Yomiuri Nippon SO — Sunrise ▲ 8501

Mitsuhashi, Kifu (shak)
Miki, M.:Music of, w. N. Yoshimura (koto), Y. Tanaka (shamisen), Masur (cnd), Tokyo Metropolitan SO, Tokyo PO, Leipzig Gewandhaus Orch—Jo No Kyoju; Prelude for Shakuhachi, Koto & Strings; Ha No Kyoku; Con. for Koto & Orch.; Kyu no Kyoku; Sym. for Two Worlds — Camerata 2-▲ 30CM 223/24
Minami, S.:Coloration-Project III, w. N. Yoshimura (koto) *(rec Iruma City Auditorium, Dec. 14, 1990)* — Camerata ▲ 32CM 189 [DDD]
Nishimura, A.:Nanae, w. N. Yoshimura (koto) *(rec Iruma City Auditorium, Dec. 14, 1990)* — Camerata ▲ 32CM 189 [DDD]
Satoh, S.:Kamu-Ogi-Guoto, w. N. Yoshimura (koto) *(rec Iruma City Auditorium, Dec. 14, 1990)* — Camerata ▲ 32CM 189 [DDD]
Satoh, S.:Tamaogi-Koto, w. Teiko Kikuchi (17-string koto) *(rec Saitama Arts Theater Concert Hall, Apr 27–28, 1995)* — Camerata ▲ 30CM 267 [DDD]
Shinohara, M.:Cooperation, w. A. Nishigata (shamisen), K. Mitsuhashi (shakuhachi), M. Akao (fue), S. Yaotani (hichiriki), K. Ishikawa (sho), C. Fukunaga (koto), J. Ueda (biwa), M. Yoshizawa (kokyu), I. Tsuji (oboe), T. Takahashi (cl), G. Kitamura (tpt), A. Murata (trbn), S. Eiso (perc), S. Ueki (vn), S. Katsuta (vc), Y. Shibuya (pno), K. Komatsu (cnd) *(rec live Casals Hall, Tokyo, Mar. 5, 1994)* — Camerata ▲ 30CM 375 [DDD]
Shinohara, M.:Kyudo B, w. M. Kimura (vn) *(rec live Casals Hall, Tokyo, Mar. 5, 1994)* — Camerata ▲ 30CM 375 [DDD]
Yoshimatsu, T.:Moyura, w. N. Yoshimura (koto) *(rec Iruma City Auditorium, Dec. 14, 1990)* — Camerata ▲ 32CM 189 [DDD]
Yuasa, J.:Cosmos Haptic 3, w. N. Yoshimura (koto) *(rec Iruma City Auditorium, Dec. 14, 1990)* — Camerata ▲ 32CM 189 [DDD]

Mitsui, Y. (hpd)
Mozart, W.A.:Con Pno, K.107, w. M. Cichirdan (cnd), Craiova PO — Gallo ▲ CD 662 [ADD‡DDD]
Mozart, W.A.:Vars Pno, K.265, w. M. Cichirdan (cnd), Craiova PO — Gallo ▲ CD 662 [ADD‡DDD]

Mitsui, Y. (pno)
Mozart, W.A.:Son 8 Pno — Gallo ▲ CD 663 [DDD]
Mozart, W.A.:Son 10 Pno — Gallo ▲ CD 663 [DDD]
Mozart, W.A.:Son 11 Pno — Gallo ▲ CD 663 [DDD]
Mozart, W.A.:Son 12 Pno — Gallo ▲ CD 663 [DDD]

▲ = CD ♦ = Enhanced CD Δ = MD ■ = Cassette Tape □ = DCC

Mitsui, Y. (pno) (cont.)
Mozart, W.A.:Son 13 Pno Gallo ▲ CD 663 [DDD]
Mittelbach, W. (wind instr)
Kelterborn, R.:Songs for 4 Winds & Chorus, w. T. Jones (trbn), M. Hoffmann (wind instr), G. Pettinger (wind instr), G. Kember (cnd), Bavarian Radio Chorus *(rec May 13, 1983)* Grammont ▲ CTSP 35-2 [ADD]
Mitterer, Anita (va)—see also also ORCHESTRAS & ENSEMBLES Mosaïques String Quartet
Mozart, W.A.:Trio Cl, K.498, w. W. Meyer (cl), P. Cohen (pno) Astrée ▲ E 8736
Mitterer, Anita (vn)
Mozart, W.A.:Qnt Cl, K.581, w. W. Meyer (cl), Mosaïques Ensemble Astrée ▲ E 8736
Mittman, Leopold (pno)
Baroque Masterpieces, w. Nathan Milstein (vn) Biddulph ▲ LAB 055 [ADD]
Grieg, E.:Albumblade, Op. 28, w. M. Elman (vn) [trans. for violin & piano]—No. 3 in A *(rec 1947)* RCA Red Seal ▲ 09026-61826-2
Nathan Milstein, w. Nathan Milstein (vn) Pearl ▲ PEA 9401 (m) [AAD]
Tartini, G.:Son Vn "Devil's Trill", w. Nathan Milstein (vn) Biddulph ▲ LAB 055 [ADD]
Mitts, J. Thomas (org)
Historic Organs of New Orleans, w. George Bozeman (org), James S. Darling (org), Jesse E. Eschbach (org), Gerald D. Frank (org), John Gearhart (org), James Hammann (org), Frederick Hohman (org), Lenora McCroskey (org), Mary Gifford Matthys (org), Lorenz Maycher (org), Donald Messer (org) *(rec June 1989)* Organ Historical Society 2-▲ OHS 89
Miura, Yoichi (pno)
In Recital, 1965, w. Ettore Bastianini (bar) *(rec Tokyo, June 9, 1965)* Legendary ▲ CD 1002
Miyamoto (ob)
Mozart, W.A.:Qt Ob, K.370, w. Mannheim String Quartet Novalis ▲ 150006 [DDD]
Miyanoo, Fumiko (pno)
Cage, J.:Pno Music, w. Joshua Pierce (pno), Borah Bergman (pno), Dorothy Jones (pno), Joseph Kubera (pno), Myra Meldorf (pno)—Music Walk; Jazz Study; Experiences I & II; plus others Wergo ▲ WER 61592
Miyashita, S. (koto)
Satoh, S.:Kougetsu, w. A. Nakamura (shakuhachi fl) *(rec Aug. 18, 1993)* New Albion ▲ NA 069
Satoh, S.:Sanyou, w. A. Nakamura (shakuhachi fl) *(rec Aug. 18, 1993)* New Albion ▲ NA 069
Miyata, Mayumi (shô)
Cage, J.:Two⁴, w. Josje ter Haar (vn) *(rec Theater Romein, Leeuwarden, the Netherlands, Jan 14-17, 1996)* Hat Art ("Hat NOW." series) 2-▲ 6192 [DDD]
Hosokawa, T.:Landscape V, w. Arditti String Quartet Montaigne ▲ MO 782078
Mizraki, Raphael (lts/rebec/perc)—see ORCHESTRAS & ENSEMBLES Dufay Collective
Mizushima, Kazue (perc)
Peebles, S.:Aqua Babble, w. Yakashi Harada (ondes martenot), Sarah Peebles (shô/elec/perc) *(rec live, Studio Kinshicho, Japan, June 11, 1993)* Innova ▲ 506
Mincak-Spychala, Malgorzata (vn)—see ORCHESTRAS & ENSEMBLES Tutti e solo
Mocquet, Silvie (vl)
Musiche Veneziene per Voce e Strumenti, w. Teresa Berganza (mez), Yasunori Imamura (lt/thb/gtr), Pere Ros (vl), Lynn Dickinson (vl), Carol Lewis (vl), Jörg Ewald Dähler (pno), Jörg Ewald Dähler (cnd) *(rec Kirche Saanen, Feb 1982)* Claves ▲ CD 508206 [DDD]
Modrian, Joszef (vn)
Berwald, F.:Trio Fragments, w. K. Drafi (pno), G. Kertész (vc) *(rec June 7-16, 1991)* Marco Polo ▲ 8.223430 [DDD]
Berwald, F.:Trios, w. K. Drafi (pno), G. Kertész (vc)—in C (1845); No. 4 *(rec June 7-16, 1991)* Marco Polo ▲ 8.223430 [DDD]
Modugno, Giuseppe (pno)
Mendelssohn, F.:Allegro brillant, w. Alberto Spinelli (pno) Nuova Era ▲ NUO 7204 [DDD]
Mendelssohn, F.:Duo concertant, w. Alberto Spinelli (pno) Nuova Era ▲ NUO 7204 [DDD]
Mendelssohn, F.:Fant Pno Duet, w. Alberto Spinelli (pno) Nuova Era ▲ NUO 7204 [DDD]
Mendelssohn, F.:Vars Pno 4-Hands, w. Alberto Spinelli (pno) Nuova Era ▲ NUO 7204 [DDD]
Moe, Eric (pno/hpd/org)
Cage, J.:Harmonies Vn & Kbd, w. Roger Zahab (vn)—also includes condensed version Koch International Classics ▲ KIC 7130 [DDD]
Zahab, R.:Verging Lightfall, w. Roger Zahab (vn) Koch International Classics ▲ KIC 7130 [DDD]
Moe, Lawrence (org)
Bach, J.S.:Canonic Vars on "Von Himmel hoch..." *(rec 1967)* Somerset ▲ SCD 10000
Bach, J.S.:Preludes & Fugues, BWV 531-552—BWV 536 *(rec 1967)* Somerset ▲ SCD 10000
Felciano, R.:In Celebration of Golden Rain, w. R. Felciano (cnd), Scripps Javanese Gamelan of Univ of California Opus One ▲ 155 CD
Frescobaldi, G.:Org Music—Capriccio on Fra Jacopino & Toccata No. 1 [from Toccate e Partite, Book 1 (1635)]; Toccata for the Elevation [from Fiori musicali (1635)] *(rec 1967)* Somerset ▲ SCD 10000
Sweelinck, J.P.:Org Music—Toccata No. 23; Vars on "Mein junges Leben hat ein End" *(rec 1967)* Somerset ▲ SCD 10000
Moe, Sharon (hn)—see ORCHESTRAS & ENSEMBLES Bronx Arts Ensemble
Moerlen, M. (org)
Franck, C.:Cantabile Quantum ▲ QM 6911 [DDD]; ■ QM 2006 (D)
Franck, C.:Chorals Org, M.38-40 Quantum ▲ QM 6911 [DDD]; ■ QM 2006 (D)
Franck, C.:Fant Org Quantum ▲ QM 6911 [DDD]; ■ QM 2006 (D)
Franck, C.:Prélude, fugue et var Quantum ▲ QM 6911 [DDD]; ■ QM 2006 (D)
Moersch, William (mar/dlc)
Rzewski, F.:Moonrise with Memories, w. David Taylor (b trbn), David Carp (kazoo), Bill Blount (cl), Allan Dean (tpt), Louise Schulman (vn), Robert Wolinsky (gtr) *(rec RCA Studios, NYC, June 4, 1981)* New World ▲ 80494-2
Moerschel, Joel (vc)—see also also ORCHESTRAS & ENSEMBLES Collage New Music Ensemble
Bazelon, I.:Legends & Love Letters, w. J. Heller (sop), F. Epstein (perc), C. Oldfather (pno), R. Annis (cl), J. Scolnik (fl), C. Fussell (cnd), Collage New Music Ensemble Albany ▲ TROY 054 [DDD]
Chardon, Y.:Son Tpt, w. Charles Schlueter (tpt) *(rec Symphony Hall, Boston, MA, Sept. 1994)* Vox Classics ▲ VOX 7513 [DDD]
Mogensen, Morten (pno)—see also also ORCHESTRAS & ENSEMBLES Copenhagen Trio
Brahms, J.:Scherzo Vn, w. S. Elbæk (vn) Kontrapunkt ▲ KPT 32177 [DDD]
Brahms, J.:Sons Vn (comp), w. S. Elbæk (vn) Kontrapunkt ▲ KPT 32177 [DDD]
Lange-Müller, P.E.:An Autumn Fantasia Kontrapunkt ▲ KPT 32228
Lange-Müller, P.E.:Fant Pieces, w. S. Elbaek (vn) *(rec 1991)* Kontrapunkt ▲ KPT 32208
Lange-Müller, P.E.:Forest Pieces Kontrapunkt ▲ KPT 32228
Lange-Müller, P.E.:In Memoriam Kontrapunkt ▲ KPT 32228
Lange-Müller, P.E.:Romance, w. Søoren Elbaek (vn) Kontrapunkt ▲ KPT 32208
Lange-Müller, P.E.:Soft Melodies Kontrapunkt ▲ KPT 32228
Roussel, A.:Chamber Music, w. Majken Bjerno (sop), Toke Lund Christiansen (fl), Bjørn Carl Nielsen (ob), Niels Thomsen (cl), Per Jacobsen (hn), Asger Svendsen (bn), Ketil Christensen (tpt), Anne Søe Hansen (vn), Zwi Carmelli (va), Piotr Zelazny (va), Niels Ullner (vc), Michael Dabelsteen (db), Tine Rehling (hp), Per Salo (pno), Per Jensen (perc)—Divertissement, Op. 6; Trio, Op. 40; Joueurs de Flute, Op. 27; Serenade, Op. 30; Le marchand de sable qui passe, Op. 13; Andante et scherzo, Op. 13; 2 poèmes de ronsard, Op. 26; Aria; Elpenor, Op. 59; Pipe Kontrapunkt 2-▲ KPT 32218 [DDD]
Mogilevskaya, Lia (pno)
Mussorgsky, M.:Sunless, w. G. Vishnevskaya (sop), M. Rostropovich (pno/vc), O. Kagan (vn) *(rec Jan. 17, 1973)* Russian Disc ▲ RUS 11003 [AAD]
Shostakovich, D.:Songs Sop, Op. 127, w. G. Vsichnevskaya (sop), M. Rostropovich (pno/vc), O. Kagan (vn) *(rec Jan. 17, 1973)* Russian Disc ▲ RUS 11003 [AAD]
Stravinsky, I.:Songs, w. G. Vsichnevskaya (sop), M. Rostropovich (pno/vc), O. Kagan (vn)—2 songs *(rec Jan. 17, 1973)* Russian Disc ▲ RUS 11003 [AAD]
Mogilevsky, Eugene (pno)
Chopin, F.:Pno Music (misc)—Polonaise-Fantaisie, Op. 61; Scherzo No. 3, Op. 39; 2 Mazurkas, Opp. 17/4 & 68/2; Berceuse, Op. 52 Pavane ▲ ADW 7264 [DDD]
Chopin, F.:Polonaise-fant Pavane ▲ ADW 7264 [DDD]
Mogilevsky, Eugene (pno) (cont.)
Chopin, F.:Preludes, Op. 28 Pavane ▲ ADW 7264 [DDD]
Prokofiev, S.:Son 7 Pno *(rec 1974)* MK ▲ 418021 [AAD]
Schumann, R.:Kreisleriana *(rec 1974)* MK ▲ 418021 [AAD]
Moglia, Alain (vn)
Bach, J.S.:Con for 2 Vns, w. M.-A. Nicholas (vn), J.-C. Malgoire (cnd), National CO Valois ▲ V 4697
Glazunov, A.:Suite Strs, w. A. Moglia (cnd), Toulouse National CO Pierre Verany ▲ PVY 730069
Mozart, L.:Con Hn, w. Thierry Caens (tpt), A. Moglia (cnd), Toulouse National CO, Les Cuivres Francais Pierre Verany ▲ PVY 730070
Mozart, L.:Serenade Tpt, w. Thierry Caens (tpt), A. Moglia (cnd), Toulouse National CO, Les Cuivres Francais Pierre Verany ▲ PVY 730070
Tchaikovsky, P.:Serenade Strs, w. A. Moglia (cnd), Toulouse National CO Pierre Verany ▲ PVY 730069
Vivaldi, A.:Cons Vn, Op. 8/1-4, "The Four Seasons", w. A. Moglia (cnd), Toulouse National CO Pierre Verany ▲ PVY 730038
Moguillansy, Alejandro (rcr)—see ORCHESTRAS & ENSEMBLES Affetti Musicali members
Mohnsen, Rosalind (org)
Historic Organs of New Orleans, w. George Bozeman (org), James S. Darling (org), Jesse E. Eschbach (org), Gerald D. Frank (org), John Gearhart (org), James Hammann (org), Frederick Hohman (org), Lenora McCroskey (org), Mary Gifford Matthys (org), Lorenz Maycher (org), Donald Messer (org) *(rec June 1989)* Organ Historical Society 2-▲ OHS 89
Mohr, E. (vc)—see ORCHESTRAS & ENSEMBLES Aequalis
Möhring, Hans-Jürgen (fl)
Mozart, W.A.:Missa, K.427, w. S. Meinardus (sop), G. Passin (ob), F. Essmann (bn), H. Müller-Brühl (cnd), Cologne CO—Et incarnatus est [L] *(rec May 1968)* Koch Treasure ▲ 316182 [ADD]
Moinár, Zsolt (vc)
Franck, C.:Messe solennelle, w. Attila Wendler (ten), Dezső Karasszon (org), Andrea Kocsis (hp), Ferenc Nagy (db), Salomon Kamp (cnd), Debrecen Kodaly Choir Hungaroton ▲ HCD 31579 [DDD]
Moinet, Philippe (cl)—see ORCHESTRAS & ENSEMBLES Stanislas Ensemble
Moinian, Christoph (hn)—see ORCHESTRAS & ENSEMBLES Acht Ensemble, L'Archibudelli
Moiseiwitsch, Benno (pno)
Beethoven, L. van:Andante, WoO 57, "Andante favori" Pearl 2-▲ PEA 9192
Benno Moiseiwitsch, Vol. 1 Pearl ▲ PEA 9135 [ADD]
A Centenary Celebration *(rec 1928)* Koch Legacy ▲ 3-7035-2
Chopin, F.:Etudes (24) Pearl 2-▲ PEA 9192
Chopin, F.:Fant-Impromptu Pearl 2-▲ PEA 9192
Chopin, F.:Son Pno, Op. 58 Pearl 2-▲ PEA 9192
Mussorgsky, M.:Pictures at an Exhibition Pearl 2-▲ PEA 9192
Palmgren, S.:West Finnish Dance Pearl 2-▲ PEA 9192
Rachmaninoff, S.:Con 2 Pno, w. W. Goehr (cnd), London PO *(rec Nov. 24 & Dec. 13, 1937)* APR ▲ APR 5505 [ADD]
Rachmaninoff, S.:Con 2 Pno, w. H. Rignold (cnd), Philharmonia Orch Royal Classics ▲ ROY 6451
Rachmaninoff, S.:Moments musicaux—No. 4 in e *(rec Oct. 20, 1943)* APR ▲ APR 5505 [ADD]
Rachmaninoff, S.:Pno Transcriptions—Scherzo from Mendelssohn's Midsummer Night's Dream *(rec Mar. 17, 1939)* APR ▲ APR 5505 [ADD]
Rachmaninoff, S.:Prelude Pno, Op. 3/2 *(rec Aug. 2, 1940)* APR ▲ APR 5505 [ADD]
Rachmaninoff, S.:Preludes Pno, Opp 23 & 32—No. 6 in g , Op. 23/5; No. 16 in G, Op. 32/5; No. 21 in b, lOp./ 32/10; No. 23 in g#, Op. 32/12 *(rec Aug. 2, 1940, Oct. 3, 194)* APR ▲ APR 5505 [ADD]
Rachmaninoff, S.:Rhapsody on a Theme of Paganini, w. H. Rignold (cnd), Philharmonia Orch Royal Classics ▲ ROY 6451
Rachmaninoff, S.:Rhapsody on a Theme of Paganini, w. B. Cameron (cnd), London PO *(rec Dec. 5, 1938)* APR ▲ APR 5505 [ADD]
Schumann, R.:Carnaval Pno Pearl 2-▲ PEA 9192
Schumann, R.:Kreisleriana Pearl 2-▲ PEA 9192
Schumann, R.:Sym Etudes Pearl 2-▲ PEA 9192
Solo Piano Recordings, 1938-50, w. Moiseiwitsch, Benno (pno) APR ▲ APR 7005 [AAD]
Tchaikovsky, P.:Con 1 Pno, w. G. Weldon (cnd), Philharmonia Orch *(rec 1944)* APR ▲ APR 5518 [ADD]
Tchaikovsky, P.:Con 2 Pno, w. G. Weldon (cnd), Liverpool PO *(rec 1944)* APR ▲ APR 5518 [ADD]
Tchaikovsky, P.:Morceaux, Op. 40—No.2, "Chanson triste" *(rec 1945)* APR ▲ APR 5518 [ADD]
Mok, Gwendolyn (pno)
Ravel, M.:Con in G Pno, w. G. Simon (cnd), Philharmonia Orch *(rec St. Jude-on-the-HIll, Hampstead, London, Feb 8-12, 1991)* Cala ▲ CACD 1005 [DDD]
Mokrosch, Viola (pno)
Clarke, R.:Son Vc, w. E. Stahl (vc) Bayer ▲ BR 100 200CD [DDD]
Firsova, E.:Son Vc, w. E. Stahl (vc) Bayer ▲ BR 100 200CD [DDD]
Fromm-Michaels, I.:Vars on One's Own Theme Bayer ▲ BR 100 200CD [DDD]
Janácek, L.:Fairy Tale, w. D. Panke (vc) Vengo ▲ 354.404
Mol, Jan Van (hpd)
Boccherini, L.:Qts Strs, G.195-200, w. P. van Parys (hpd) [anon. late 18th cent. trans. for 2 Harpsichords] Pavane ▲ ADW 7282 [DDD]
Grétry, A.-E.-M.:Sons (2) for 2 Hpds, w. P. van Parys (hpd) Pavane ▲ ADW 7282 [DDD]
Mol, Jan Van (org)
Oley, J.C.:Org Music—Meine Hoffnung stehet feste; O Gott, du frommer Gott; Dir, dir, Jehova, will ich singen; Verzage nicht, o frommer Christ; Lasset uns den Herren preisen; J. meine Zuversicht; Ach was soll ich Sünder machen; Du, o schönes Welt-Gebäude; Wie schön leuchtet der Morgenstern; Jesu meine Freude; Sey Lob und Ehr dem höchsten Gut; Der Tag ist hin, mein Jesu Christ; Nun danket alle Gott; Wir Christen-Leut; Warum sollt ich mich denn grämen; Kommt her zu mir, spricht Gottes Sohn; Werde munter mein Gemühte; Treuer Gott, ich muss dir klagen; Freu dich, sehr, o meine Seele; Nun bitten wir den heiligen Geist; Brunquell aller Güter; Nun lob mein Seel den Herren; Herr Jesu Christ du höchstes Gut; Herr Gott, dich loben alle wir; Warum betrübst du dich, mein Herz; Die Seele Christi heil'ge mich; Es ist vollbracht [Steinfeld Basilica Organ] *(rec Feb. 1994)* Pavane ▲ ADW 7314 [DDD]
Møldrup, Erling (gtr)
Gefors, H.:La Boîte chinoise *(rec Concert Hall at the Royal Academy of Music, Århus, Denmark, 1988-93)* Marco Polo ("dacapo" series) ▲ DC 9316 [DDD]
Gudmunsen-Holmgreen, P.:Solo for Gtr *(rec Concert Hall at the Royal Academy of Music, Århus, Denmark, 1988-93)* Marco Polo ("dacapo" series) ▲ DC 9316 [DDD]
Nielsen, T.:Frosty Silence *(rec Concert Hall at the Royal Academy of Music, Århus, Denmark, 1988-93)* Marco Polo ("dacapo" series) ▲ DC 9316 [DDD]
Nørgård, P.:Tales from a Hand—No. 3 [Clubs among Jokers] *(rec Concert Hall at the Royal Academy of Music, Århus, Denmark, 1988-93)* Marco Polo ("dacapo" series) ▲ DC 9316 [DDD]
Nørholm, I.:Son Gtr *(rec Concert Hall at the Royal Academy of Music, Århus, Denmark, 1988-93)* Marco Polo ("dacapo" series) ▲ DC 9316 [DDD]
Olsen, P.R.:Nostalgie *(rec Concert Hall at the Royal Academy of Music, Århus, Denmark, 1988-93)* Marco Polo ("dacapo" series) ▲ DC 9316 [DDD]
Moleux, Georges (db)
Schubert, Franz:Qnt Pno, D.667, w. George Szell (pno), Budapest String Quartet members *(rec Coolidge Auditorium, Library of Congress, May 16, 1946)* Bridge ▲ BCD 9062
Molinari, Ernesto (cl)
Carter, E.:Esprit rude/esprit doux, w. P. Racine (fl) ECM New Series ▲ 78118-21391-2 [DDD]
Carter, E.:Triple Duo, w. P. Racine (fl), H. Schneeberger (vn), P. Cleeman (va), T. Demenga (vc), G. Huber (perc) ECM New Series ▲ 78118-21391-2 [DDD]
Wyttenbach, J.:Lamentoroso, w. L. Akerlund (sop), H. Bissegger (cl), N. Calame (cl), M. Maurer (cl), M. Weber (cl), H. Zwahlen (cl) *(rec May 19-20, 1990)* Grammont ▲ CTSP 37-2 [ADD]
Wyttenbach, J.:Serenade in Luftschlössern, w. P. Racine (fl) *(rec May 19-20, 1990)* Grammont ▲ CTSP 37-2 [ADD]

Molinari, Paola (hpd)
Righini, V.:Alcide al Bivio, w. L. Serra (sop), S. Browne (cta), W. McKinney (ten), R. El Hage (bass), M. Barta (ob), T. Gotti (cnd), Swiss-Italian RSO, Swiss-Italian Radio Chorus *(rec 1979)* Bongiovanni 2-▲ GB 2157/58 [ADD]

Molinari, Paola (pno)
Tosti, P.F.:Songs, w. W. Matteuzzi (ten)—Chi sei tu; Van gli effluvi; O falce di luna calante; Ninna Nanna; That Day; Speak!; Pierrot's Lament; I Am Not Fair; Summer; Starlight; Lasciami; L'alba separa dalla luce l'ombra; In van preghi; Che dici Dynamic ▲ CD 109 [DDD]
Vincenzo La Scola, w. Vincenzo La Scola(ten) *(rec Apr 15, 1996)* Bongiovanni ▲ GB 2520 [DDD]

Molinelli, Roberto (va)
Reinecke, C.:Fantasiestücke Va, w. R. Bartoli (pno) *(rec June 19–22, 1993)* Bongiovanni ▲ GB 5537 [DDD]

Moll, Philip (hpd)
Bach, J.S.:A Musical Offering, w. J. Galway (fl), Kyung-Wha Chung (vn)—Trio Sonata Section RCA Red Seal ("Papillon Collection" series) ▲ 6517-2-RG [ADD] ■ 6517-4-RG
Bach, J.S.:Sons Fl, BWV 1030–35, w. James Galway (fl), Sarah Cunningham (vl)—BWV 1032 RCA Red Seal ▲ 0902-668182-2 [DDD]
Bach, J.S.:Son Fl, BWV 1079, w. J. Galway (fl), K.-W. Chung (vn), M. Welsh (vc) RCA Gold Seal ("Papillon Collection" series) ▲ 6517-2-RG [ADD] ■ 6517-4-RG
Bach, J.S.:Son Fl, BWV 1079, w. James Galway (fl), Monica Huggett (vn), Sarah Cunningham (vl) RCA Red Seal ▲ 0902-668182-2 [DDD]
Bach, J.S.:Trio Son, BWV 1038, w. James Galway (fl), Monica Huggett (vn), Sarah Cunningham (vl) RCA Red Seal ▲ 0902-668182-2 [DDD]
Bach, J.S.:Trio Son for 2 Fls, BWV 1039, w. J. Galway (fl), K.-W. Chung (vn), M. Welsh (vc) RCA Gold Seal ("Papillon Collection" series) ▲ 6517-2-RG [ADD] ■ 6517-4-RG
Bach, J.S.:Trio Son for 2 Fls, BWV 1039, w. James Galway (fl), Jeanne Galway (fl), Sarah Cunningham (vl) RCA Red Seal ▲ 0902-668182-2 [DDD]

Moll, Philip (pno)
Beethoven, L. van:Son Fl, w. J. Galway (vc) RCA Red Seal ▲ 7756-2-RC [DDD] ■ 7756-4-RC
Brahms, J.:Zigeunerlieder, w. U. Gronostay (cnd), Berlin RIAS Chamber Choir [G] *(rec March 1984)* Koch Treasure ▲ 31616-2 [ADD]
Fantasie, w. Bacon, Thomas (hn) Crystal ■ C 379
Lutoslawski, W.:Partita Vn, Orch & Obbligato Pno, w. Anne-Sophie Mutter (vn), W. Lutoslawski (cnd), BBC SO Deutsche Grammophon ▲ 423696-2 [DDD]
Milhaud, D.:Le Bal martiniquais, w. J. Alder (pno) Classic Studio Berlin ▲ CS 11108 [DDD]
Milhaud, D.:Scaramouche for 2 Pnos, w. J. Alder (pno) Classic Studio Berlin ▲ CS 11108 [DDD]
Nielsen, C.:Fants Ob, w. James Galway (fl) *(rec CBS Studios, London, Feb 25, 1986)* RCA Red Seal ▲ 07863-56359-2 [ADD]
Poulenc, F.:Capriccio Pnos, w. J. Alder (pno) *(rec 1985)* Classic Studio Berlin ▲ CS 11108 [DDD]
Poulenc, F.:Élégie Pnos, w. J. Alder (pno) Classic Studio Berlin ▲ CS 11108 [DDD]
Poulenc, F.:L'Embarquement pour Cythère, w. J. Alder (pno) Classic Studio Berlin ▲ CS 11108 [DDD]
Poulenc, F.:Son for 2 Pnos, w. J. Alder (pno) *(rec 1985)* Classic Studio Berlin ▲ CS 11108 [DDD]
Recital, w. Takezawa, Kyoko (vn) RCA Red Seal ▲ 09026-60704-2
Ruzicka, P.:Etym, w. P. Ruzicka (cnd), Berlin RSO *(rec Mar 1975)* Thorofon ▲ CTH 2220
Wilder, A.:Easy Pieces Hn, w. Thomas Bacon (hn) *(rec Arizona State Univ., May 16–18, 1994)* Summit ▲ DCD 170 [DDD]
Wilder, A.:Son 1 Hn, w. Thomas Bacon (hn) *(rec Arizona State Univ., May 16–18, 1994)* Summit ▲ DCD 170 [DDD]
Wilder, A.:Son 2 Hn, w. Thomas Bacon (hn) *(rec Arizona State Univ., May 16–18, 1994)* Summit ▲ DCD 170 [DDD]
Wilder, A.:Son 3 Hn, w. Thomas Bacon (hn) *(rec Arizona State Univ., May 16–18, 1994)* Summit ▲ DCD 170 [DDD]
Wilder, A.:Suite Hn, w. Thomas Bacon (hn) *(rec Arizona State Univ., May 16–18, 1994)* Summit ▲ DCD 170 [DDD]

Möller, Günther (perc)—see ORCHESTRAS & ENSEMBLES Karl Peinkofer Percussion Ensemble

Möller, Stephan (pno)
Wagner, R.:Pno Music—Fantasia in f#, Op. 3 (1831); Polonaise (1832); Polonaise for Piano 4-Hands (1832); Albumblatt für E.B. Kietz (1840); Polka (1853); Züricher Vielliebchen-Walzer (1854); Notenbrief für Mathilde Wesendonck (1857); Elegie in A♭ (1859; rev. 1882); In das Album der Fürstin Metternich (1861); Ankunft bei den schwarzen Schwänen (1861); Albumblatt für Frau Betty Schott (1875) Koch Schwann ▲ 3-1362-2 [DDD]
Wagner, R.:Pno Music—Sonata in B♭, Op. 1 (1831); Sonata in A, Op. 4 (1832); Eine Sonate in das Album von Frau Mathilde Wesendonck (1853) Koch Schwann ▲ 3-1361-2 [DDD]

Möller, Wouter (vc)—see also also ORCHESTRAS & ENSEMBLES La Real Camera
Bach, J.S.:Partita Fl, BWV 1013, w. W. van Hauwe (rcr), T. Satoh (lt), G. Wilson (hpd)—in c *(rec 1988)* Channel Classics ▲ CCS 4492 [DDD]
Telemann, G.P.:Der Getreue Music-Meister (sels), w. W. Van Hauwe (rcr), B. Van Asperen (hpd)—Sonata in f for recorder & continuo Globe ▲ GLO 5016 [ADD]
Telemann, G.P.:Rcr Music (misc), w. W. van Hauwe (ob), T. Satoh (lt), G. Wilson (hpd)—Fantasies Nos. 1 & 8; Partita No. 5 in e; Son. d; Son. D; Trio Son. in B♭ *(rec 1988)* Channel Classics ▲ CCS 4492 [DDD]
Telemann, G.P.:Sonate metodiche, w. W. Van Hauwe (fl), B. Van Asperen (hpd)—Son No. 10 in B♭ for voice flute & continuo Globe ▲ GLO 5016 [ADD]

Molnár, H. (pic)
Daetwyler, J.:Capriccio, Andante et Humoresque, w. J. Molnar (alphn), P. Falentin (tpt), A. Ramirez (perc), Bern Chamber Ensemble Gallo ▲ CD 548 [AAD]

Molnár, Jozsef (alphn)
Daetwyler, J.:Capriccio, Andante et Humoresque, w. H. Molnar (pic), P. Falentin (tpt), A. Ramirez (perc), Bern Chamber Ensemble Gallo ▲ CD 548 [AAD]
Daetwyler, J.:Con Alphn, w. U. Schneider (cnd), Slovak PO Marco Polo ▲ 8.223101 [DDD]
Daetwyler, J.:Dialog mit der Natur, w. U. Schneider (cnd), Capella Istropolitana Marco Polo ▲ 8.223101 [DDD]
Farkas, F.:Concertino rustico, w. U. Schneider (cnd), Capella Istropolitana Marco Polo ▲ 8.223101 [DDD]
Mozart, L.:Sym in G, "Sinf pastorella", w. U. Schneider (cnd), Capella Istropolitana Marco Polo ▲ 8.223101 [DDD]

Molnár, Jozsef (hn)
Ducommun, S.:Org Music, w. S. Ducommun (org), R. Märki (org), P.-A. Monot (tpt), P. Lehmann (tpt)—10 Invocations for Organ; Sonata da Chiesa for Horn & Organ; Sonata da Chiesa for 2 Trumpets & Organ; Variations on a Theme by François Nadler for Organ *(rec 1959, 1985 & 1991)* Gallo ▲ CD655

Moltisanti, S. (pno)
Cimarosa, D.:Sons (50) Kbd Zuma Records ▲ ZMA 101
Crumb, G.:A Little Suite for Christmas:A.D. 1979 Zuma Records ▲ ZMA 101
Crumb, G.:Vox balaenae, w. J. Schlefer (fl), L. Zoernig (vc) Zuma Records ▲ ZMA 102
Messiaen, O.:Regards sur l'Enfant Jésus Zuma Records ▲ ZMA 101
Napoli, J.:Arias, w. Donatella (sop)—Per la tomba; Figlio dormi, dormi Figlio; Filastrocca; Deisperata; Vucca vasata nun perdi vintura; Jesce, Jesce, sole Zuma Records ▲ ZMA 102
Scriabin, A.:Son 7 Pno Zuma Records 0 ▲ ZMA 101

Molvaer, Nils Petter (tpt)
Schulkowsky, R.:Hastening Westward at Sundown to Obtain a Better View, w. Robyn Schulkowsky (perc) [rev for tpt & perc] *(rec Rainbow Studio, Oslo, Jan 1995)* ECM New Series ▲ ECM 1564 [DDD]
Schulkowsky, R.:Pier & Ocean, w. Robyn Schulkowsky (perc) *(rec Rainbow Studio, Oslo, Jan 1995)* ECM New Series ▲ ECM 1564 [DDD]

Momme, Axel (pno)
Stolarczyk, W.:Earth Air Fire Water, w. Amalie Malling (pno), John Damgaard (pno), Anne Øland (pno), Teddy Teirup (pno), Friedrich Gürtler (pno), Rosalind Bevan (pno), Poul Rosenbaum (pno), Rodolfo Llambias (pno), Bella Horn-Ribera (pno), Anders Riber (pno), Elisabeth Sigurdsson (pno), Thomas Tronheim (pno), Elsebeth Broderson (pno), Erik Kaltoft (pno), Jørgen Hald Nielsen (pno), Aino Gilemann (pno), Birgit Kjær (pno), Jørgen Thomsen (pno), Gunhild Donslund (pno), Henrik Bo Hansen (pno), Lone Karlsson (pno), Erik Fessel (pno), Lasse Nilsson (pno), Janos Ferenczi (pno), Erik Bach (pno), Arne de Cros Dich (pno), Sven Micha Slot (pno), Hanne Bramsen Buhl (pno), Lili Olesen (pno), Susannah Carlsson (pno), Ulla Erml (pno), Vagn Sørensen (pno), Leif Greibe (pno), Bodil Krogh (pno), Kirsten Ottosen (pno), Inger Bergenholz (pno), Karsten Gylendorf (pno), Bjønr Elkjær (pno), Jacob Bjørn Jensen (pno), Jørgen Kaad (pno), Anne Marie Hjelm (pno), Carl Ulrik Munk Andersen (pno), Poul Lumbye (pno), Oluf Hildebrandt Nielsen (pno), Joachim Olsson (pno), Peter Pade Ramsøe Jacobsen (pno), Astrid Pollmann (pno), Jette Borsch (pno), Kirsten Karlshøj (pno), Maria Teresa Assing (pno), Allan Dahl Hansen (pno), Johan Hugossen (pno), Tine Fenger Pederson (pno), Arne Jørgen Fæø (pno), Anja Høgsted (pno), Anne Sophie Parbo (pno), Inga Lindmark (pno), Teresa Drabik Stathakis (pno), Anne Ruth Ferenczi (pno), Irene Hasager (pno), Yuka Ichikawa (pno), Birgitte Baur (pno), Malene Thastum (pno), Jens E. Rasmussen (pno), Birgitte Zielke (pno), Claus Zielke (pno), Stefan Kasch (pno), Bin Qiao (pno), Inger Johanne Teirup (pno), Lindy Rosborg (pno), Liisa Heininen (pno), David Højer (pno), Ellen Refstrup (pno), Thomas K. Søorensen (pno), Erik Kure (pno), Michael Rauff (pno), Jan beck Eriksson (pno), Tanja Zapolski (pno), Vibeke Skagbo (pno), Pål Eide Lindtner (pno), Ha-Young Sul (pno), Benedicte Palko (pno), Inke Kesseler (pno), Anne Marie Meineche (pno), Sverre Larsen (pno), Kasper Peter Bach (pno), Elisabetta Eliseo (pno), Olga Magieres (pno), Carl Erik Kühl (pno), Thorkild Borup Nielsen (pno), Valeria Zanini (pno), Lars Stenhoft (perc), Dennis Boel (perc), Winnie Dahlgren (perc), Susanne Vind (perc), Claus Byrith (elec), Anne Marie Storm (elec), J. Ribera (cnd) *(rec live, Koldinghaus Castle, Denmark, May 2, 1996)* Danica ▲ DCD 1996

Monaco, Anne Marie (hn)—see ORCHESTRAS & ENSEMBLES Essex Winds Woodwind Quintet

Monahan, Gordon (pno)
Monahan, G.:Pno Mechanics CBC ("Musica Viva" series) ▲ MVCD 1055 [DDD]

Mönch, Georg (vn)
Berecuse Lullaby Wiegenlied, w. Jeanne Marie Bima (sop), Massimiliano Damerini (pno) *(rec Roma, Italy, Feb 1987)* Arts ▲ 447282-2 [DDD]
Franck, C.:Son Vn, w. Massimiliano Damerini (pno) *(rec Rome, Italy, May 21–25, 1989)* Arts Music ▲ 447106-2 [DDD]

Mondavio, Sergio (cl)—see ORCHESTRAS & ENSEMBLES Rara Ensemble

Mondelci, Federico (sax)
Mondelci, F.:Pan Intermezzo Media ("900 Musica" series) ▲ MDI 25171 [DDD]
Pisati, M.:S Intermezzo Media ("900 Musica" series) ▲ MDI 25171 [DDD]
Rossi Re, F. de:Vampyr Intermezzo Media ("900 Musica" series) ▲ MDI 25171 [DDD]
Samori, A.:Ensemble invisibile Intermezzo Media ("900 Musica" series) ▲ MDI 25171 [DDD]
Sbordoni, A.:Xohon Intermezzo Media ("900 Musica" series) ▲ MDI 25171 [DDD]
Scelsi, G.:Music of, w. Michiko Hirayama (sop), Maurizio Ben Omar (gtr/perc), A. Brizzi (cnd), Gruppo Musica Insieme, Nuovo Ensemble Italiano—Pranam I for Voice, 12 Instrs & Band; Ko-Tha [3 danses de Shiva] for Gtr; I presagi for 11 Instruments; Riti [I funerali di Alessandro Magno]; Trio for 3 Percussionists; Manto per quattro for Voice, Fl, Trbn & Vc; Kya for Sax & 7 Instruments; Entretiens avec Giacento Scelsi Memoire Vive ▲ CD 262009 [ADD/DDD]
Scogni, F.E.:Duplum Intermezzo Media ("900 Musica" series) ▲ MDI 25171 [DDD]

Monden, Godelieve (gtr)
Guitar Duos, w. Narciso Yepes (gtr) RCA Red Seal ▲ 09026-60764-2

Mondini, Alberto (pno)
Mercadante, S.:Arias, w. Francesca Rotondo (sop)—La rosa; La sposa de lo marenaro; La palomma; Lo zucchero d'amore; Il zeffiro; La primavera; Il Pastore svizzero; Il bolero; Il desiato ritorno; Il fiore e la lagrima; La prece Dell'Orfana; T'amo l'abbandonata; Salve Maria Stradivarius ▲ STV 1003 [DDD]

Monetti, Mariaclara (pno)
Mozart, W.A.:Con 20 Pno, w. I. Bolton (cnd), Royal PO Royal Philharmonic Collection ▲ TRP 45 [DDD]
Mozart, W.A.:Con 27 Pno, w. I. Bolton (cnd), Royal PO Royal Philharmonic Collection ▲ TRP 45 [DDD]
Paisiello, G.:Cons Hpd, English CO—Nos. 2, 3, 4 & 6 ASV ▲ ASV 872 [DDD]
Paisiello, G.:Cons Hpd, English CO—Nos. 1, 5, 7 & 8 ASV ▲ ASV 873 [DDD]
Paisiello, G.:Cons Hpd, w. S. Gonley (cnd), English CO—8 Cons (complete) ASV 2-▲ ASV 229

Monguzzi, Mauro (bn)
Danzi, F.:Qts Bn, Op. 40, w. G. Maestri (vn), A. Anjos (va), A. Riccardi (vc) Bongiovanni ▲ GB 5520 [DDD]
Krommer, F.:Qt Bn, Op. 46/1, w. G. Maestri (vn), A. Anjos (va), A. Riccardi (vc) Bongiovanni ▲ GB 5520 [DDD]

Monighetti, Ivan (vc)
Fröhlich, F.T.:Son Vc, w. *(pno unknown)* Musiques Suisses ▲ 6116
Ivan Monighetti, w. Monighetti, Ivan (vc), Erika Kilcher (pno) Calliope ▲ CAL 9673 [ADD]
Penderecki, K.:Con 2 Vc, w. A. Wit (cnd), Polish National RSO Katowice Polskie Nagrania ▲ PLN 20 [AAD]
Prokofiev, S.:Sym-Con Vc, w. I. Shpiller (cnd), USSR Radio-TV Large SO Audiophile Classics ("Legacy Collection" series) ▲ 101.506

Monk, Meredith (elec org/jews hp/sgr)
Monk, M.:Key, w. Daniel Sverdlik (sgr), Dick Higgins (sgr), Collin Walcott (sgr/mrdingam), Mark Berger (nar), Lanny Harrison (nar) *(rec live, Gary Weis' loft, Santa Monica, CA, Ace Gallery, Los Angeles, CA, The House, New York City, The Farm, Los Angeles, CA, July 1970–Jan 1971)* Lovely Music ▲ LCD 1051 [ADD]

Monk, Meredith (org/pno/pitchpipes/voc)
Monk, M.:Boat Song, w. Robert Een (voc) ECM New Series ▲ 78118-21482-2 [DDD]
Monk, M.:Facing North, w. Robert Een (voc) ECM New Series ▲ 78118-21482-2 [DDD]
Monk, M.:Vessel, w. Robert Een (sgr) ECM New Series ▲ 78118-21482-2 [DDD]

Monosoff (vn)
Vivaldi, A.:Cons Vn, Op. 8/1–4, "The Four Seasons", w. A. Bronne (vn), Kwalwasser (va), G. Koutzen (vc), M. Goberman (cnd), New York Sinfonietta Odyssey ■ YT 60132

Monot, P.-A. (tpt)—see also also ORCHESTRAS & ENSEMBLES Quatror de cuivres Novus
Ducommun, S.:Concertino Tpt, w. R. Märki (org) Gallo ▲ CD 654 [DDD]
Ducommun, S.:Org Music, w. S. Ducommun (org), R. Märki (org), J. Molnar (hn), P. Lehmann (tpt)—10 Invocations for Organ; Sonata da Chiesa for Horn & Organ; Sonata da Chiesa for 2 Trumpets & Organ; Variations on a Theme by François Nadler for Organ *(rec 1959, 1985 & 1991)* Gallo ▲ CD655

Monrad, Søren (perc)
Cascade, w. Royal Danish Brass, Per Jensen (perc) *(rec 1996)* Rondo ▲ RCD 8352
Koppel, H.D.:Variazioni Libère, w. John Kruse (cl), Rene Højlund (cl), Kenneth Larsen (b cl) *(rec Det Fynske Musikkonservatorium, 1993)* Paula ▲ PACD 78 [DAD]

Monroney, Brian (gtr)
Symphonic Boleros, w. V. Lewis (cnd), Royal PO, Ettore Stratta (cnd), Ernie Watts (sax), Sal Marquez (tpt), Clare Fischer (pno), Jorge Callandrelli (pno) Teldec ▲ 91180-2 ■ 91180-4

Montafia, C. (fl)—see ORCHESTRAS & ENSEMBLES Venice New Quintet

Montanari, Marco (org)
Omaggio a Magda Olivero, w. Magda Olivero (sop), Carmelina Gandolfo (pno) Great Opera Performances 2-▲ GOP 795

Monteilhet, Pascal (lt)
Couperin, F.:Leçons de ténèbres (for Good Friday), w. M. Van Der Sluis (sop), G. Laurens (mez), M. Muller (vl), L. Boulay (hpd/org)—[L] Erato (Musifrance) ▲ 2292-45012-2 [DDD]
Couperin, F.:Magnificat, w. M. Van Der Sluis (sop), G. Laurens (mez), M. Muller (vl), L. Boulay (hpd/org)—[L] Erato (Musifrance) ▲ 2292-45012-2 [DDD]
Dufault, F.:Lt Music—Suites (6) in b, C, g, c, D & g; Pavane in e *(rec Jan. 11–14, 1993)* FNAC Music ▲ 592267 [DDD]
Gallot, J.:Lt Music—Suite in f#; Suite in a; Suite in C; Suite in c; Suite in f FNAC Music ▲ 592053 [DDD]

734

▲ = CD ♦ = Enhanced CD Δ = MD ■ = Cassette Tape ▯ = DCC

Monteilhet, Pascal (thb)
Handel, G.F.:Sons Rcr, w. Jérôme Hantaï (vl), Pierre Hantaï (hpd/org), H. Reyne (cnd)—HWV 358, 360, 362, 365, 367, 369, 377 (complete) Harmonia Mundi France ▲ HMC 905211
Leclair, J.-M.:Premier livres de sonates, w. F. Biondi (vn), M. Naddeo (vc), R. Alessandrini (org)—Sons. III, VII, VIII, XI Arcana ▲ ACA 39 [DDD]
Tartini, G.:Sons Vn & Continuo, w. F. Biondi (vn), M. Naddeo (vc), R. Alessandrini (hpd)—5 Sonatas—in g (B g11); in B♭ (B b3); in g (B g10); in A (B A15); in G (B G17) Opus 111 ▲ OPS 59-9205 [DDD]
Veracini, F.M.:Sonate accademiche, w. Fabio Biondi (vn), Maurizio Naddeo (vc), Rinaldo Alessandrini (hpd)—Nos. 7 in d, 8 in e, 9 in A, 12 in d; Capriccio in g Opus 111 ▲ OPS 30-138

Monteilhet, Pascal (va)
Festa Italiana, w. Barbara Schlick (sop), Fabio Biondi (vn), Maurizio Naddeo (vc), Rinaldo Alessandrini (hpd), Concerto Italiano, Europa Galante Opus 111 5-▲ 2001

Montgomery, David (pno)
Great Ragtime Classics, w. Paul Hersh (pno) Victrola ■ ALK1-9543

Montgomery, Glen (pno)
Brahms, J.:Sons Vc (comp), w. Denis Brott (vc) *(rec St Augustin de Mirabel Church, Québec, Nov 1994)* Analekta Fleur de Lys ▲ FL 2 3009 [DDD]
Brahms, J.:Son in D Vc, w. Denis Brott (vc) *(rec St Augustin de Mirabel Church, Québec, Nov 1994)* Analekta ▲ AN 29901 [DDD]

Monti, A. (gtr)—see ORCHESTRAS & ENSEMBLES Seicentonovecento Ensemble
Montiel, Javier (va)—see ORCHESTRAS & ENSEMBLES Latin American String Quartet
Montin, P. (cl)—see ORCHESTRAS & ENSEMBLES Seicentonovecento Ensemble

Montoya, Alison (va)
Debussy, C.:Son Fl, w. Conchi Vacas (fl), Zoraida Avila (hp) *(rec Madrid, Oct 1-3 1990)* RNE/Spanish National Radio ▲ M3/06 [DDD]
Falla, M. de:Psyché, w. Elena Montaña (sop), Conchi Vacas (fl), Zoraida Avila (hp), Wen-Yu Ku (vn), Gloria Cuerda (vc) *(rec Madrid, Oct 1-3 1990)* RNE/Spanish National Radio ▲ M3/06 [DDD]
Guibert, A.:The Bath Tub, w. Elena Montaña (sop), Conchi Vacas (fl), Wen-Yu Ku (vn), Gloria Cuerda (vc), Zoraida Avila (hp) *(rec Madrid, Oct 1-3 1990)* RNE/Spanish National Radio ▲ M3/06 [DDD]
Roussel, A.:Sérénade, w. Conchi Vacas (fl), Wen-Yu Ku (vn), Gloria Cuerda (vc), Zoraida Avila (hp) *(rec Madrid, Oct 1-3 1990)* RNE/Spanish National Radio ▲ M3/06 [DDD]

Montoya, Carlos (gtr)
Carlos Montoya:Guitarist *(rec 1990)* Allegretto ▲ ACD 8063 [ADD] ■ ACS 8063

Moody, Howard (pno)
Beethoven, L. van:Son 2 Vc, w. David Watkin (vc) Chandos ("Chaconne" series) ▲ CHAN 0561
Beethoven, L. van:Son 3 Vc, w. David Watkin (vc) Chandos ("Chaconne" series) ▲ CHAN 0561
Beethoven, L. van:Son 5 Vc, w. David Watkin (vc) Chandos ("Chaconne" series) ▲ CHAN 0561

Moody, James (pno)
Thanks for the Memory, w. Tommy Reilly (hmc) Chandos ▲ CHAN 8645 [AAD]

Moog, Johannes (cl)
Beethoven, L. van:Qnt Pno, Ob, Cl, Hn & Bn, w. C. Eschenbach (pno), A. Leek (ob), S. Scott (hn), U. Freund (bn) Signum ▲ X 06-00
Mozart, W.A.:Qnt Pno, K.452, w. C. Eschenbach (pno), A. Leek (ob), S. Scott (hn), U. Freund (bn) Signum ▲ X 06-00
Villa-Lobos, H.:Qt Fl, w. Joachim Schmitz (fl), Petra Fluhr (ob), Ulrich Freund (bn) Bayer ▲ BR 100117 [DDD]
Villa-Lobos, H.:Trio Ob, w. Petra Fluhr (ob), Ulrich Freund (bn) Bayer ▲ BR 100117 [DDD]

Moog, Rainer (va)
Britten, H.:Lachrymae, w. D. Atherton (cnd), RIAS Sinfonietta Koch Treasure ▲ 31610-2 [ADD]
Bruch, M.:Romanze Va, w. W. Balzer (cnd), Rhenish PO ebs ▲ ebs 6071 [DDD]
Martinů, B.:Qt 1 Pno, w. Daniel Adni (pno), Isabelle van Keulen (vn), Young-Chang Cho (vc) *(rec Australian Festival of Chamber Music, July 1994)* Naxos ▲ 8.553916 [DDD]
Martinů, B.:Qnt Strs, w. Charmian Gadd (vn), Solomia Soroka (vn), Theodore Kuchar (va), Young-Chang Cho (vc) *(rec Australian Festival of Chamber Music, July 1994)* Naxos ▲ 8.553916 [DDD]
Martinů, B.:Son 1 Va, w. Daniel Adni (pno) *(rec Australian Festival of Chamber Music, July 1994)* Naxos ▲ 8.553916 [DDD]
Reger, M.:Serenades Fl Vn Va, w. Peter-Lukas Graf (fl), Sandor Vegh (vn) *(rec Kirche Reutigen, Dec 1980)* Claves ▲ CD 508104 [ADD]

Mook, Ted (ten vn)
Partch, H.:17 Lyrics by Li Po, w. Stephen Kalm (voc) Tzadik ▲ TZA 7012 [DDD]

Mook, Ted (vc)—see also also ORCHESTRAS & ENSEMBLES Musicians' Accord members, Musicians' Accord
Monk, T.:Round Midnight, w. Dean Drummond (zmz), Dominic Donato (zmz), Frank Cassara (zmz) [arr. Drummond for cello & 3 zoomoozophones] *(rec The Magic Shop, New York City, Jan. 31, 1993)* Mode ▲ MODE 33
Rosenblum, M.:Circadian Rhythms, w. James Pugliese (perc), Elizabeth Rodgers (kbd/pno) *(rec Floral Park, NY, Mar. 19, 1990)* Mode ▲ MODE 33
Vivaldi, A.:Con Lt, w. P. Press (gtr), P. Peabody (vn), E. Lim (vn), J. Haffner (va), E. Brewer (hpd) ESS.A.Y ▲ CD 1004 [DDD] ■ C 1004 (D)
Zaimont, J.L.:Dance/Inner Dance, w. Kathleen Nester (fl), Rheta Smith (ob) *(rec SUNY Purchase, Theatre C, Jan 8-10 & Feb 20, 1995)* Arabesque ▲ ARA 6667 [DDD]

Mook, Ted (vc/gourd tree/cone gongs)
Partch, H.:Daphne of the Dunes, w. Frank Cassara (boo/spoils of war/kithara 2), Dominic Donato (b mar/surrogate kithara/boo), Dean Drummond (harmonic canons/kithara 2/spoils of war/kithara), Nina Kellman (kithara 2/harmonic canon/surrogate kithara), Michael Lipsey (cloud-chamber bowls), James Pugliese (diamond mar), Elizabeth Rodgers (chromelodeon/harmonic canon) *(rec Queens, NY, Mar. 12, 1991)* Mode ▲ MODE 33

Mooke, Martha (va)—see ORCHESTRAS & ENSEMBLES Musicians' Accord members

Moolman, Jeanne-Louise (va)
Grové, S.:Son Va, w. Piet Moolman (pno) Claremont ▲ GSE 1546 [DDD]

Moolman, Piet (pno)
Grové, S.:Son Va, w. Jeanne-Louise Moolman (va) Claremont ▲ GSE 1546 [DDD]

Moore, David (vc)
Fennelly, B.:Scintilla Prisca, w. Brian Fennelly (pno) Capstone ▲ CPS 8631
Schubel, M.:Christmas Treat, w. Andrew Thomas (hpd) Opus One ▲ CD 151

Moore, David (vn)
Telemann, G.P.:Con in a for Rcr, Ob, w. L. Cavasanti (rcr), P. Faldi (ob), C. Boersma (vc), S. Ciomei (hpd) *(rec July 23-26, 1991)* Nuova Era ("Ancient Music" series) ▲ NUO 7067 [DDD]
Telemann, G.P.:Quartet in G for Recorder, Oboe, Violin & Continuo, w. L. Cavasanti (rcr), P. Faldi (ob), S. Ciomei (hpd) *(rec July 23-26, 1991)* Nuova Era ("Ancient Music" series) ▲ NUO 7067 [DDD]

Moore, Deborah (perc)
Tower, J.:Black Topaz, w. Stephen Gosling (pno), Patricia Spencer (fl), Laura Flax (cl), Chris Gekker (tpt), Mike Powell (trbn), Jonathan Haas (perc) *(rec American Academy of Arts & Letters, New York City, Sept. 26-28, 1994)* New World ▲ 80470-2

Moore, Gerald (pno)
Arias & Songs, w. Irmgard Seefried (sop), Hermann von Nordberg (pno), Wilhelm Schmidt (pno), London Mozart Players [cnd:Harry Blech] Testament ▲ SBT 1026 [ADD]
The Art of Kathleen Ferrier, w. Kathleen Ferrier (cta), Isobel Baillie (sop), Netherlands Opera Orch [cnd:Charles Bruck] EMI Classics ("Great Recordings of the Century" series) ▲ CDH 61003 (m)
Brahms, J.:Ernste Gesänge, w. A. Kipnis (bass) *(rec 1936)* Music & Arts 2-▲ CD 661 (m) [AAD]
Brahms, J.:Ernste Gesänge, w. A. Kipnis (bass) *(rec 1936)* Preiser 2-▲ 89204 (m) [AAD]
Brahms, J.:Son 1 Vc, w. Beatrice Harrison (vc) *(rec 1926 & 27)* Symposium ▲ SYM 1140
Brahms, J.:Son 2 Cl, w. W. Primrose (cl) *(rec 1937)* Biddulph ▲ LAB 011 [ADD]
Brahms, J.:Songs, w. Elisabeth Grümmer (sop)—Regenlied; Das Mädchen; Geheimnis; Mädchenlied; Wiegenlied Testament ▲ 1086
Brahms, J.:Sym 1, w. W. Primrose (va)—2nd movt. *(rec 1937)* Pearl ▲ PEA 9045 [AAD]
The Columbia Recordings, Vol. 2, w. Jacqueline Du Pré (vc), Michael Taube (pno), Theo van der Pas (pno), Wolfgang Rebner (pno) *(rec 1930-1939)* Pearl ▲ PEA 9443 (m) [AAD]

Moore, Gerald (pno) (cont.)
The Columbia Recordings, Vol. 3, w. Jacqueline Du Pré (vc), Myra Hess (pno), Paul Hindemith (va/cnd), Szymon Goldberg (cnd) *(rec 1930-1939)* Pearl ▲ PEA 9446 (m) [AAD]
The Early Recordings, 1942-1953, w. Victoria de los Angeles (sop), Ivor Newton (pno), Agrupación de Cámara Barcelona, Ars Musicae Barcelona Testament ▲ SBT 1087
Encores, w. Elisabeth Schwarzkopf (sop), Geoffrey Parsons (pno) EMI Classics ▲ CDM 63654
Falla, M. de:Canciones populares españolas (7), w. V. de los Angeles (sop) [Sp] *(rec 9/12/51)* EMI Classics ▲ CDH 64028-2 (m) [ADD]
Great Voices of the Century, w. Povla Frijsh (sop), Elena Gerhardt (sop), Lotte Lehmann (sop) *(rec 1929-1939)* Sanctus ▲ 001 [ADD]
Grieg, E.:Peer Gynt (sels), w. Elisabeth Grümmer (sop)—Der Winter mag scheiden Testament ▲ 1086
Grieg, E.:Songs, w. Elisabeth Grümmer (sop)—Schlaf, du teuerster Knabe mein! Testament ▲ 1086
Les introuvables de Dietrich Fischer-Dieskau, w. Dietrich Fischer-Dieskau (bar), Kark Engel (pno), Hertha Klust (pno), Aribert Reimann (pno), Robert Veyron-Lacroix (hpd) EMI Classics 6-▲ CDZF 68509
Lieder Recital, w. Elisabeth Schwarzkopf (sop) *(rec Aug 7, 1956)* EMI Classics ▲ CDM 66084
Mussorgsky, M.:Songs (comp), w. B. Christoff (bass), Alexandre Labinsky (pno), Gerald Moore (pno), French National Radio Orch EMI Classics ("Great Recordings of the Century" series) 3-▲ CHS 63025 (m) [ADD]
Schubert, Franz:Die Schöne Müllerin, w. D. Fischer-Dieskau (bar) [G] Deutsche Grammophon ▲ 415186-2 [ADD]
Schubert, Franz:Die Schöne Müllerin, w. Aksel Schiotz (ten) *(rec London, Nov 1945)* Preiser ▲ PRE 90293
Schubert, Franz:Die Schöne Müllerin, w. D. Fischer-Dieskau (bar) [G] *(rec 1951)* EMI Classics ("Studio" series) 3-▲ CDMC 63559 (m) [ADD]
Schubert, Franz:Schwanengesang, w. D. Fischer-Dieskau (bar) [G] *(rec 1951-58)* EMI Classics ("Studio" series) 3-▲ CDMC 63559 (m) [ADD]
Schubert, Franz:Schwanengesang, w. D. Fischer-Dieskau (bar) [G] Deutsche Grammophon ▲ 415188-2 [ADD]
Schubert, Franz:Son Arpeggione, w. E. Feuermann (vc) *(rec 6/30/37)* EMI Classics ▲ CDH 64250-2 (m) [ADD]
Schubert, Franz:Son Arpeggione, w. E. Feuermann (vc) *(rec 1937)* Pearl ▲ PEA 9442 (m) [AAD]
Schubert, Franz:Songs (comp), w. D. Fischer-Dieskau (bar)—171 songs [G] Deutsche Grammophon 9-▲ 437225-2
Schubert, Franz:Songs (misc), w. Elisabeth Schumann (sop) Gerald Moore (pno), Leo Rosenek (pno), Elizabeth Coleman (pno)—An die Nachtigall, D.497; Die Forelle, D.550; Ave Maria (Ellens Gesang III), D.839; An die Musik, D.547; Auf dem Wasser zu singen, D.774; Des Fischers Liebesglück, D.933; Der Musensohn, D.764; Fischerweise, D.881; Gretchen am Spinrade, D.118; Liebesbotschaft ("Schwanegesang" No. 1), D.957; Nacht und Träume, D.827; Seligkeit, D.433; Nähe des Geliebten, D.162; Lachen und Weinen, D.777; Frühlingstraum ("Winterreise" No. 11), D.911; Der Einsame, D.800; Nachtviolen, D.752; An die Geliebte, D.303; Wiegenlied (Schlafe, Schlafe), D.498; Der Schmetterling, D.633; Des Baches Wiegenlied (Die Schöne Müllerin" No. 20), D.957; Der Jüngling und der Tod, D.545; Das Heimweh, D.456; Dass sie hier gewesen, D.775; Der Vollmond strahlt ("Rosamunde" Romanze), D.797; Der Junge Nonne, D.828 *(rec 1933-1945)* Minerva ▲ MN-A22 [ADD]
Schubert, Franz:Songs (misc), w. E. Schwarzkopf (sop), G. Parsons (pno) EMI Classics ▲ CDM 63656
Schubert, Franz:Songs (misc), w. Elisabeth Grümmer (sop)—Suleikas Gesang II; Auf dem Wasser zu singen; Wiegenlied; Rastlose Liebe; Vor meiner Wiege; Die Forelle; Fischerweise Testament ▲ 1086
Schubert, Franz:Songs (misc), w. D. Fischer-Dieskau (bar), K. Engel (pno)—37 songs *(rec 1958-65)* EMI Classics ("Studio" series) 2-▲ CDMB 63566 [ADD]
Schubert, Franz:Songs (misc), w. D. Fischer-Dieskau (bar)—D.257, 300, 314, 328, 343, 456, 531, 536, 545, 550, 565, 649, 741, 765, 774, 785, 871, 889, 917, 938 [G] EMI Classics ("Studio" series) ▲ CDM 69503 [ADD]
Schubert, Franz:Songs (misc), w. D. Fischer-Dieskau (bar)—234 songs [G] Deutsche Grammophon 9-▲ 437215-2 [ADD]
Schubert, Franz:Winterreise, w. H. Hotter (b-bar) [G] EMI Classics ("Great Recordings of the Century" series) ▲ CDH 61002 (m)
Schubert, Franz:Winterreise, w. D. Fischer-Dieskau (bar) [G] *(rec 1955)* EMI Classics ("Studio" series) 3-▲ CDMC 63559 (m) [ADD]
Schubert, Franz:Winterreise, w. D. Fischer-Dieskau (bar) [G] Deutsche Grammophon ▲ 415187-2 [ADD]
Schwarzkopf & Seefried, Duets, w. Elisabeth Schwarzkopf (sop), Irmgard Seefried (sop), Philharmonia Orch [cnd:H. von Karajan] EMI Classics ▲ CDH 69793
Sings Select Lieder, w. Helge Rosvaenge (ten), Bruno Seidler-Winkler (pno), Michael Raucheisen (pno) *(rec 1936-44)* Preiser ▲ PRE CD 89992
Strauss, R.:Songs, w. Fischer-Dieskau (bar)—contains "all Strauss lieder suited to the baritone voice" [G] EMI Classics 6-▲ CDMF 63995
Verdi, G.:Otello (sels), w. Elisabeth Grümmer (sop)—Nun in der Nächt'gen Stille [Love Duet, Act I] Testament ▲ 1086
Verdi, G.:Songs, w. Elisabeth Grümmer (sop) Ave Maria; Lied von der Weide (Willow Song) Testament ▲ 1086
Wagner, R.:Wesendonck Songs, w. Kirsten Flagstad (sop) [G] *(rec 5/25-26/48)* EMI Classics ("Great Recordings of the Century" series) ▲ CDH 63030 (m) [ADD]
Weigl, V.:New England Suite, w. S. Drucker (cl), Sass (vc) CRI ■ C 326
Wolf, H.:Italienische Liederbücher (sels), w. E. Schwarzkopf (sop), D. Fischer-Dieskau (bar) EMI Classics ▲ CDM 63732
Wolf, H.:Songs (misc), w. E. Schwarzkopf (sop) *(rec live 1958)* EMI Classics ▲ CDC 64905
Wolf, H.:Songs (misc), w. E. Schwarzkopf (sop), G. Parsons (pno)—Lieder EMI Classics ▲ CDM 63653
Wolf, H.:Songs (misc), w. A. Kipnis (bass), Coenraad V. Bos (pno), Ernst Victor Wolff (pno)—Grenzen der Menschheit; Um Mitternacht; Sterb' ich, so hüllt in Blumen meine Glieder; Michelangelo-Lieder I-III *[w. Bos, rec. 1933-4]*; Cophtisches Lied I; Der Musikant; Der Soldat I; Der Schreckenberger *[w. Moore, rec. 1935]*; Wie glänzt der helle Mond; Nun lasst uns Frieden schliessen; Wir haben beide lange Zeit geschwiegen; Geselle, woll'n wir uns in Kutten hüllen; Heb' auf dein blondes Haupt; Wie viele Zeit verlor ich; Was für ein Lied soll dir gesungen werden *[w. Wolff, rec. 1934]* *(rec 1933-35)* Preiser 2-▲ 89204 (m) [AAD]
Wolf, H.:Songs (misc), w. A. Kipnis (bass), Coenraad V. Bos (pno), Ernst Victor Wolff (pno)—Grenzen der Menschheit; Um Mitternacht; Sterb' ich, so hüllt in Blumen meine Glieder; Michelangelo-Lieder I-III *[w. Bos, rec. 1933-4]*; Cophtisches Lied I; Der Musikant; Der Soldat I; Der Schreckenberger *[w. Moore, rec. 1935]*; Wie glänzt der helle Mond; Nun lasst uns Frieden schliessen; Wir haben beide lange Zeit geschwiegen; Geselle, woll'n wir uns in Kutten hüllen; Heb' auf dein blondes Haupt; Wie viele Zeit verlor ich; Was für ein Lied soll dir gesungen werden *[w. Wolff, rec. 1934]* *(rec "Hugo Wolf Society," 1933-35)* Music & Arts 2-▲ CD 661 (m) [AAD]

Moore II, Grant (tuba)—see ORCHESTRAS & ENSEMBLES Philadelphia Brass

Moore, Ian (acc)
The Classic Buskers, w. Michael Copley (ww) Newport Classic ▲ NPD 85559 [DDD]

Moore, K. (vc)
Walton, W.:Façade, w. J. Bookspan (nar), S. Baron (fl), C. Russon (cl), H. Estrin (sax), M. Broiles (tpt), H. Harris (perc), D. Epstein (cnd) Allegretto ▲ ACD 8153 [ADD] ■ ACD 8153

Moore, Lisa (Fender Rhodes)
Andriessen, L.:Hoketus, w. Katherine Pendry (panpipes), James Poke (panpipes), Evan Ziporyn (a sax), Richard Craig (a sax), Steven Schick (congas), Amy Knoles (congas), Lisa Moore (Fender Rhodes), Damian LeGassick (Fender Rhodes), Cees van Zeeland (pno), Gerard Bouwhuis (pno), Robert Black (bass gtr), Mark Stewart (bass gtr) *(rec Air Recording Studios, Lyndhurst Hall, Hampstead, London, June 29-July 3, 1994)* Sony Classical ▲ SK 66483 [DDD]

Moore, Lisa (kbd)—see ORCHESTRAS & ENSEMBLES Bang on a Can members

Moore, Lisa (pno)—see also also ORCHESTRAS & ENSEMBLES Bang on a Can
Andriessen, L.:Hout, w. Evan Ziporyn (t sax), Mark Stewart (elec gtr), Steven Schick (perc) *(rec Air Recording Studios, Lyndhurst Hall, Hampstead, London, June 29-July 3, 1994)* Sony Classical ▲ SK 66483 [DDD]

INSTRUMENT.

Moore, Lisa (pno) (cont.)
Carter, E.:Son Vc, w. David Pereira (vc) *(rec Eugene Goossens Hall, ABC, Jan 1993)* Tall Poppies ▲ TP 32 [DDD]
Edwards, R.:Etymalong *(rec Studio 200 ABC, Aug 1993)* Tall Poppies ▲ TP 51 [DDD]
Jewels of the Classics, w. R. Kapp (cnd), Philharmonia Virtuosi *(rec Apr. 7-9, 1993)* RCA Victor ▲ 09026-61935-2 ■ 09026-61935-4
Kernis, A.J.:Nocturne, w. Nancy Allen Lundy (sop), John Dent (tpt), Jeff Milarsky (glock), Benjamin Herman (glock), Leslie Stifelman (pno), M. Barrett (cnd) *(rec Manhattan Center Studios, New York, May 31-June 3, 1995)* New Albion ♦ NA 083CD
Prokofiev, S.:Son Vc, w. David Pereira (vc) *(rec Concert Hall, Newcastle Conservaorium of Music, Dec 1991)* Tall Poppies ▲ TP 32 [DDD]
Rzewski, F.:Piece 4 Pno *(rec The Hit Factory, New York, Oct 4-8, 1995)* Sony Classical ▲ SK 62254 [DDD]
Schnittke, A.:Son Vc, w. D. Pereira (vc) *(rec July 1992)* Tall Poppies ▲ TP 018 [DDD]
Shostakovich, D.:Son Vc, w. D. Pereira (vc) *(rec July 1992)* Tall Poppies ▲ TP 018 [DDD]
Silver, S.:Dance Converging, w. Lois Martin (va), William Purvis (hn), Thad Wheeler (perc) *(rec Recital Hall, Music Division, SUNY, Purchase, New York, Apr 12, 1995)* CRI ▲ CD 708 [DDD]
Stroke, w. Moore, Lisa (pno) Tall Poppies ▲ TP 40 [DDD]
Wolfe, J.:Lick, w. Evan Ziporyn (s sax), Mark Stewart (elec gtr), Steven Schick (perc), Maya Beiser (vc), Robert Black (db) *(rec Air Recording Studios, Lyndhurst Hall, Hampstead, London, June 29-July 3, 1994)* Sony Classical ▲ SK 66483 [DDD]

Moore, M. (pno)
Avshalomov, A.:Con Pno, w. M. Moore, J. Avshalomov (cnd), Portland Youth PO CRI ▲ CD 667 [ADD]

Moore, Thomas (pno)
Gibson, R.:A Sound Within Capstone ▲ CPS 8621
Smith, S.S.:Family Portraits O.O. Discs ▲ OO 11 [DDD]

Moore, Tom (fl)
Telemann, G.P.:Sons for 2 Fls, w. Kimberly Reighley (fl) *(rec Crosswicks Friends Meeting, Crosswicks, New Jersey, Apr 24-26 & May 4-5, 1995)* Lyrichord ("Early Music" series) ▲ LYR 8019 [DDD]

Moorse, Peter (org)
Maunder, J.H.:From Olivet to Calvary, w. J. Mitchinson (ten), F. Harvey (bar), Guildford Cathedral Choir [E] Classics for Pleasure ▲ CDCFP 4619 [ADD]

Moosdorf, Matthias (vc)—see ORCHESTRAS & ENSEMBLES Leipzig String Quartet

Moosmann, Christoph Maria (org)
Cage, J.:Souvenir Org *(rec St. Martin Cathedral, Rottenburg, Apr. 12-14, 1994)* New Albion ▲ NA 074
Pärt, A.:Annum per annum *(rec St. Martin Cathedral, Rottenburg, Apr. 12-14, 1994)* New Albion ▲ NA 074
Pärt, A.:Mein Weg hat Gipfel und Wellentäler *(rec St. Martin Cathedral, Rottenburg, Apr. 12-14, 1994)* New Albion ▲ NA 074
Pärt, A.:Pari intervallo *(rec St. Martin Cathedral, Rottenburg, Apr. 12-14, 1994)* New Albion ▲ NA 074
Pärt, A.:Trivium *(rec St. Martin Cathedral, Rottenburg, Apr. 12-14, 1994)* New Albion ▲ NA 074
Scelsi, G.:In nomine lucis *(rec Collégiale St. Hippolyte, June 10, 1992)* New Albion ▲ NA 074

Moquet, Sylvie (b vl)
Sainte-Colombe, M. de:Concerts for 2 B Vls, w. Anne Marie Lasla (b vl) *(rec Jan. 1993)* Alphée ▲ 9308002 [DDD]

Moquet, Sylvie (va/vc)—see ORCHESTRAS & ENSEMBLES Concerto Soave

Moquet, Sylvie (vl)—see ORCHESTRAS & ENSEMBLES Orlando Gibbons Viol Ensemble

Moraguès, Michel (fl)
Schoenberg, A.:Trans Chamber Ensemble, w. Hakon Ausbö (harm), Michel Béroff (perc), Isabelle Berteletti (perc), Louise Bessette (pno), Marc Marder (db), Paul Meyer (cl), Arditti String Quartet—Busoni:Berceuse élégiaque (1920); Mahler:Songs of a Wayfarer (1920) [w. Jean-Luc Chaignaud (baritone)]; Joh. Strauss:Kaiserwalzer (1925); Roses from the South (1921) Montaigne ▲ MO 789011 [DDD]

Moraguès, Pascal (cl)
Brahms, J.:Qnt Cl, w. Talich String Quartet Pyramid ▲ PYR 13489
Fauré, G.:Trio, w. Patrick Cohen (pno), Christophe Coin (vc) Adès ▲ ADE 203952 [DDD]
Indy, V. d':Trio Cl, w. Christophe Coin (vc), Patrick Cohen (pno) Adès ▲ ADE 203952 [DDD]

Morais, M. J. (pno)
Chopin, F.:Impromptus Arcobaleno ▲ SBCD 9100
Chopin, F.:Son Pno, Op. 35 Arcobaleno ▲ SBCD 9100
Scarlatti, D.:Sons Kbd—in C, D & E Arcobaleno ▲ SBCD 9100

Morales, Angelica (pno)
Beethoven, L. van:Con Vn, Vc & Pno, "Triple Con", w. R. Odnoposoff (vn), S. Auber (vc), F. von Weingartner (cnd), Vienna PO *(rec 10/20-21/37)* Pearl ▲ PEA 9358 (m) [AAD]

Morales, Leonel (pno)
Montsalvatge, X.:Concierto breve, w. A. Ros-Marbá (cnd), Madrid SO *(rec live, National Music Auditorium, Madrid, Nov. 23, 1993)* Marco Polo ▲ 8.223753 [DDD]

Morassutti, Luca (va)—see ORCHESTRAS & ENSEMBLES Venice String Quartet

Moratz, Karen (fl)
Zaimont, J.L.:Hidden Heritage, w. David Krakauer (cl/b cl/t sax), David Finkel (vc), Clinton Adams (pno), Barry Dove (perc), D. Kosloff (cnd) *(rec SUNY Purchase, Theatre C, Jan 8-10 & Feb 20, 1995)* Arabesque ▲ ARA 6667 [DDD]

Moravec, Ivan (pno)
Beethoven, L. van:Bagatelles (24)—in A, Op. 33/4 *(rec 1970)* VAI Audio ▲ VAIA 1096
Beethoven, L. van:Bagatelle, WoO 59, "Für Elise" *(rec 1969)* VAI Audio ▲ VAIA 1096
Beethoven, L. van:Con 3 Pno, w. V. Neumann (cnd), Czech PO Supraphon ("Tribute to Václav Neumann" Collection) ▲ 11 0719-2 [ADD/DDD]
Beethoven, L. van:Con 4 Pno, w. M. Turnovsky (cnd), Vienna Musikverein Orch *(rec Oct. 6-7, 1963)* VAI Audio ▲ VAIA 1021 [ADD]
Beethoven, L. van:Son 8 Pno, "Pathétique" VAI Audio ▲ VAIA 1069 (m) [ADD]
Beethoven, L. van:Son 14 Pno, "Moonlight Son" VAI Audio ▲ VAIA 1069 (m) [ADD]
Beethoven, L. van:Son 23 Pno, "Appassionata" VAI Audio ▲ VAIA 1069 (m) [ADD]
Beethoven, L. van:Son 26 Pno, "Les Adieux", w. I. Moravec VAI Audio ▲ VAIA 1069 (m) [ADD]
Beethoven, L. van:Son 27 Pno *(rec 1966)* VAI Audio ▲ VAIA 1021 [ADD]
Beethoven, L. van:Vars Pno, WoO 80 *(rec 1966)* VAI Audio ▲ VAIA 1021 [ADD]
Brahms, J.:Con 1 Pno, w. E. Mata (cnd), Dallas SO Dorian ▲ DOR 90172
Brahms, J.:Con 1 Pno, w. J. Belohlávek (cnd), Czech PO Supraphon ▲ SUP 111993
Brahms, J.:Con 2 Pno, w. J. Belohlávek (cnd), Czech PO Supraphon ▲ SUP 111993
Brahms, J.:Intermezzos Pno, Op. 117—No. 2 *(rec 1970)* VAI Audio ▲ VAIA 1096
Brahms, J.:Pno Music (misc)—7 Fants., Op. 116; 3 Intermezzos, Op. 117; 18 Pieces, Opp. 76, 118 & 119 Elektra/Nonesuch ■ 79063-4 (D)
Brahms, J.:Pieces Pno, Op. 118—No. 2 [Intermezzo in A] *(rec 1970)* VAI Audio ▲ VAIA 1096
Chopin, F.:Ballades Pno (comp)—Op. 52 *(rec 1963)* Supraphon Collection ▲ 11 0630-2 [ADD]
Chopin, F.:Ballades Pno (comp) *(rec 1966-67)* VAI Audio ▲ VAIA 1092
Chopin, F.:Barcarolle Pno *(rec 1969)* Vai Audio ▲ VAIA 1039
Chopin, F.:Études (24)—Op. 25, Nos. 1 & 7 Dorian ▲ DOR 90140 [DDD]
Chopin, F.:Études (24)—Op. 25/7 *(rec 1969)* Vai Audio ▲ VAIA 1039
Chopin, F.:Mazurkas *(rec 1969)* VAI Audio ▲ VAIA 1092
Chopin, F.:Mazurkas—in f Op. 63/2, in a Op. 68/2, in B♭ Op. 7/1, in c# Op.30/4, in b Op. 33/4 Vox Box 2-▲ CDX 5103 [DDD]
Chopin, F.:Mazurkas—Opp. 7/5, 41/1, 56/2 & 68/4 Dorian ▲ DOR 90140 [DDD]
Chopin, F.:Nocturnes Elektra/Nonesuch 2-▲ 79233-2
Chopin, F.:Polonaises—in c#, Op. 26/1 Vox Box 2-▲ CDX 5103 [DDD]
Chopin, F.:Polonaise-fant Vox Box 2-▲ CDX 5103 [DDD]
Chopin, F.:Preludes, Op. 28 *(rec 1976)* Supraphon Collection ▲ 11 0630-2 [ADD]
Chopin, F.:Preludes, Op. 28 *(rec 1965)* Vai Audio ▲ VAIA 1039
Chopin, F.:Scherzos—Op. 20 *(rec 1969)* Vai Audio ▲ VAIA 1039

Moravec, Ivan (pno) (cont.)
Chopin, F.:Scherzos Dorian ▲ DOR 90140 [DDD]
Chopin, F.:Waltzes—in a Op. 34/2, in c# Op. 64/2, in e Op. posth. Vox Box 2-▲ CDX 5103 [DDD]
Debussy, C.:Estampes Vox Box 2-▲ CDX 5103 [DDD]
Debussy, C.:Images (6) Pno Vox Box 2-▲ CDX 5103 [DDD]
Debussy, C.:Pno Music (misc)—Claire de Lune, Children's Corner Suite, Five Preludes, Jardins sous la pluie, La puerta del vino, Ondine, Feuilles mortes, Pour le piano—suite *(rec 1963-69)* VAI Audio 2-▲ VAIA 1043-2 [ADD]
Debussy, C.:Preludes Pno (sels)—Book 1/6 Vox Box 2-▲ CDX 5103 [DDD]
Dvořák, A.:Biblical Songs, Op. 99, w. Vera Soukupova (alt) Supraphon ▲ SUP 0206 [AAD]
Dvořák, A.:Con Pno, w. J. Belohlávek (cnd), Czech PO *(rec June 26-29, 1982)* Supraphon ("Collection" series) ▲ 11 0675-2 [ADD]
Franck, C.:Prélude, choral et fugue *(rec 1963-69)* VAI Audio 2-▲ VAIA 1043-2 [ADD]
Janácek, L.:In the Mists Elektra/Nonesuch ■ 79041-4 (D)
Janácek, L.:Pno Music Elektra/Nonesuch ■ 79041-4 (D)
Korte, O.:Son Pno *(rec House of Artists, Prague, Dec. 18-19, 1984)* Panton ▲ PAN 811257 [DDD]
Mozart, W.A.:Con 14 Pno, w. J. Vlach (cnd), *(orch unknown)* Supraphon ▲ SUP 3076
Mozart, W.A.:Con 23 Pno, w. J. Vlach (cnd), *(orch unknown)* Supraphon ▲ SUP 3076
Mozart, W.A.:Con 23 Pno, w. J. Vlach (cnd), Czech PO *(rec 1974)* Supraphon ("Great Artists" series) ▲ 11 0271-2 [AAD]
Mozart, W.A.:Con 25 Pno, w. J. Vlach (cnd), Czech PO *(rec 1973)* Supraphon ("Great Artists" series) ▲ 11 0271-2 [AAD]
Mozart, W.A.:Con 25 Pno, w. J. Vlach (cnd), *(orch unknown)* Supraphon ▲ SUP 3076
Mozart, W.A.:Fant Pno, K.475 *(rec 1967)* VAI Audio ▲ VAIA 1096
Mozart, W.A.:Son 14 Pno *(rec 1967)* VAI Audio ▲ VAIA 1096
Mozart, W.A.:Son 16 Pno VAI Audio ▲ VAIA 1096
Prokofiev, S.:Con 1 Pno, w. K. Ančerl (cnd), Czech PO Praga ▲ PR 254004
Ravel, M.:Sonatine Pno *(rec 1963-69)* VAI Audio 2-▲ VAIA 1043-2 [ADD]
Schumann, R.:Con Pno, w. E. Mata (cnd), Dallas SO Dorian ▲ DOR 90172
Schumann, R.:Kinderszenen Elektra/Nonesuch ■ 79063-4 (D)

Moravec, P. (pno)
Schumann, R.:Arabeske Pno Elektra/Nonesuch ■ 79063-4 (D)

Moravec, P. (syn)
Moravec, P.:Devices & Desires Centaur ▲ CRC 2052 [DDD]

Mordini, Piero (vn)
Paganini, N.:Con 4 Vn, w. R. Ricci (vn), T. Hlasek (cnd), Hungarian Philharmonia One-Eleven ▲ URS 91030 [ADD]

Mordkovitch, Elena (pno)
Grieg, E.:Sons Vn, Opp. 8, 13 & 45, w. L. Mordkovich (vn) Chandos ▲ CHAN 9184 [DDD]

Mordkovitch, Lydia (vn)
Alwyn, W.:Con Vn, w. R. Hickox (cnd), London SO Chandos ▲ CHAN 9187 [DDD]
Bach, J.S.:Sons & Partitas Vn, BWV 1001-1006 Chandos 2-▲ CHAN 8835/36 [DDD]
Bartók, B.:Duos (44) IMP ("Masters" series) ▲ IMP 6600042
Brahms, J.:Con Vn & Vc, "Double Con", w. R. Wallfisch (vc), N. Järvi (cnd), London SO Chandos ▲ CHAN 8667 [DDD]
Bruch, M.:Con 1 Vn, w. N. Järvi (cnd), London SO Chandos ▲ CHAN 8667 [DDD]
Busoni, F.:Son 1 Vn, w. V. Postnikova (pno) Chandos ▲ CHAN 8868 [DDD]
Busoni, F.:Son 2 Vn, w. V. Postnikova (pno) Chandos ▲ CHAN 8868 [DDD]
Dyson, G.:Con Vn, w. R. Hickox (cnd), City of London Sinfonia Chandos ▲ CHAN 9369 [DDD]
Fauré, G.:Son 1 Vn, w. G. Oppitz (pno) Chandos ▲ CHAN 8417 [DDD]
Ferguson, H.:Discovery, w. Clifford Benson (pno) Chandos ▲ CHAN 9316 [DDD]
Ferguson, H.:Irish Folksongs, Op. 17, w. Clifford Benson (pno) Chandos ▲ CHAN 9316 [DDD]
Ferguson, H.:Mediaeval Carols (3), w. Clifford Benson (pno) Chandos ▲ CHAN 9316 [DDD]
Ferguson, H.:Son 1 Vn, w. Clifford Benson (pno) Chandos ▲ CHAN 9316 [DDD]
Ferguson, H.:Son 2 Vn, w. Clifford Benson (pno) Chandos ▲ CHAN 9316 [DDD]
Franck, C.:Son Vn, w. M. Gusak-Grin (pno) Chandos ▲ CHAN 9109 [DDD]
Glazunov, A.:Grand Waltz, w. M. Gusak-Grin (pno) Chandos ▲ CHAN 8500 [DDD]
Grieg, E.:Sons Vn, Opp. 8, 13 & 45, w. E. Mordkovich (pno) Chandos ▲ CHAN 9184 [DDD]
Ireland, J.:Phantasie Trio, w. Ian Brown (pno), Karine Georgian (vc) Chandos ▲ CHAN 9377/8 [DDD]
Ireland, J.:Son 1 Vn, w. Ian Brown (pno) Chandos ▲ CHAN 9377/8 [DDD]
Ireland, J.:Son 2 Vn, w. Ian Brown (pno) Chandos ▲ CHAN 9377/8 [DDD]
Ireland, J.:Trio 2 Pno, w. Ian Brown (pno), Karine Georgian (vc) Chandos ▲ CHAN 9377/8 [DDD]
Ireland, J.:Trio 3 Pno, w. Ian Brown (pno), Karine Georgian (vc) Chandos ▲ CHAN 9377/8 [DDD]
Kabalevsky, D.:Con Vn, w. N. Järvi (cnd), Scottish National Orch Chandos ▲ CHAN 8918 [DDD]
Khachaturian, A.:Con Vn, w. N. Järvi (cnd), Scottish National Orch Chandos ▲ CHAN 8918 [DDD]
Medtner, N.:Son 1 Vn, w. G. Tozer (pno) Chandos ▲ CHAN 9293 [DDD]
Medtner, N.:Son 2 Vn, w. G. Tozer (pno) Chandos ▲ CHAN 9293 [DDD]
Messiaen, O.:Thème et vars, w. M. Gusak-Grin (pno) Chandos ▲ CHAN 9109 [DDD]
Moeran, E.J.:Con Vn, w. V. Handley (cnd), Ulster Orch Chandos ▲ CHAN 8807 [DDD]
Nielsen, C.:Son 1 Vn, w. C. Benson (pno) Chandos ▲ CHAN 8598 [DDD]
Nielsen, C.:Son 2 Vn, w. C. Benson (pno) Chandos ▲ CHAN 8598 [DDD]
Poème:Lyrical Encore Pieces for Violin & Piano, w. Marina Gusak-Grin (pno) Chandos ▲ CHAN 8748 [DDD]
Prokofiev, S.:Cons Vn (comp), w. N. Järvi (cnd), Scottish National Orch Chandos ▲ CHAN 8709 [DDD]
Prokofiev, S.:Mélodies, w. M. Gusak-Grin (pno) Chandos ▲ CHAN 8500 [DDD]
Prokofiev, S.:Son solo Vn, Op. 115 Chandos ▲ CHAN 8988 [DDD]
Prokofiev, S.:Son for 2 Vns, w. E. Young (vn) Chandos ▲ CHAN 8988 [DDD]
Rachmaninoff, S.:Romance Vn, w. Marina Gusak-Grin (pno) Chandos ▲ CHAN 8500 [DDD]
Ravel, M.:Son Vn Pno, w. Clifford Benson (pno) Chandos ▲ CHAN 9351 [DDD]
Ravel, M.:Sonate posthume, w. Clifford Benson (pno) Chandos ▲ CHAN 9351 [DDD]
Respighi, O.:Ballad of the Gnomes, w. E. Downes (cnd), BBC PO Chandos ▲ CHAN 9232 [DDD]
Respighi, O.:Con gregoriano, w. E. Downes (cnd), BBC PO Chandos ▲ CHAN 9232 [DDD]
Respighi, O.:Poema autunnale, w. E. Downes (cnd), BBC PO Chandos ▲ CHAN 9232 [DDD]
Respighi, O.:Son Vn, w. Clifford Benson (pno) Chandos ▲ CHAN 9351 [DDD]
Russian Music for Violin & Piano, w. Marina Gusak-Grin (pno) Chandos ▲ CHAN 8500 [DDD]
Saint-Saëns, C.:Son 1 Vn, w. M. Gusak-Grin (pno) Chandos ▲ CHAN 9109 [DDD]
Scharwenka, X.:Serenade Vn, w. Seta Tanyel (pno) Collins Classics ▲ COL 1448 [DDD]
Scharwenka, X.:Son Vn, w. Seta Tanyel (pno) Collins Classics ▲ COL 1448 [DDD]
Scharwenka, X.:Trio 1 Pno, w. Seta Tanyel (pno), Colin Carr (vc) Collins Classics ▲ COL 1448 [DDD]
Schnittke, A.:Praeludium in memoriam Dmitri Shostakovich, w. E. Young (vn) Chandos ▲ CHAN 8988 [DDD]
Schubert, Franz:Fant Vn, D.934, w. G. Oppitz (pno) Chandos ▲ CHAN 8544 [DDD]
Schubert, Franz:Son Vn, D.574, w. G. Oppitz (pno) Chandos ▲ CHAN 8544 [DDD]
Shostakovich, D.:Con 1 Vn, w. N. Järvi (cnd), Scottish National Orch Chandos ▲ CHAN 8820 [DDD]
Shostakovich, D.:Con 2 Vn, w. N. Järvi (cnd), Scottish National Orch Chandos ▲ CHAN 8820 [DDD]
Shostakovich, D.:Son Vn, w. C. Benson (pno) Chandos ▲ CHAN 8988 [DDD]
Stanford, C.V.:Irish Rhaps, w. R. Wallfisch (vc), V. Handley (cnd), Ulster Orch Chandos 2-▲ CHAN 7002/03 [DDD]
Stanford, C.V.:Irish Rhap 6, w. V. Handley (cnd), Ulster Orch Chandos ▲ CHAN 8884 [DDD]
Strauss, R.:Son Vn, w. G. Oppitz (pno) Chandos ▲ CHAN 8417 [DDD]
Stravinsky, I.:Con Vn, w. N. Järvi (cnd), Swiss Romande Orch Chandos ▲ CHAN 9236 [DDD]
Stravinsky, I.:Parasha's Song, w. M. Gusak-Grin (pno) Chandos ▲ CHAN 8500 [DDD]
Szymanowski, K.:Myths, w. M. Gusak-Grin (pno) Chandos ▲ CHAN 8747 [DDD]
Szymanowski, K.:Notturno e Tarantella, w. M. Gusak-Grin (pno) Chandos ▲ CHAN 8747 [DDD]
Szymanowski, K.:Son Vn, w. M. Gusak-Grin (pno) Chandos ▲ CHAN 8747 [DDD]
Tchaikovsky, P.:Sérénade mélancolique, w. M. Gusak-Grin (pno) Chandos ▲ CHAN 8500 [DDD]
Tchaikovsky, P.:Souvenir d'un lieu cher, w. M. Gusak-Grin (pno) Chandos ▲ CHAN 8500 [DDD]
Tchaikovsky, P.:Valse-Scherzo Vn, w. M. Gusak-Grin (pno) Chandos ▲ CHAN 8500 [DDD]

Mordkovitch, Lydia (vn) (cont.)
Vaughan Williams, R.:Fant on Greensleeves, w. Julian Milford (pno) IMP ("Masters" series) ▲ IMP 6600132
Vaughan Williams, R.:The Lark Ascending, w. Julian Milford (pno) IMP ("Masters" series) ▲ IMP 6600132
Vaughan Williams, R.:Pieces Vn & Pno, w. Julian Milford (pno) IMP ("Masters" series) ▲ IMP 6600132
Vaughan Williams, R.:Son Vn, w. Julian Milford (pno) IMP ("Masters" series) ▲ IMP 6600132
Vaughan Williams, R.:Studies in English Folk-Song, w. Julian Milford (pno) IMP ("Masters" series) ▲ IMP 6600132
Walton, W.:Con Vn, w. J. Latham-König (cnd), London PO Chandos ▲ CHAN 9073 [DDD]
Walton, W.:Pieces Vn, w. J. Latham-König (cnd), London PO Chandos ▲ CHAN 9073 [DDD]
Walton, W.:Son Vn & Orch, w. J. Latham-König (cnd), London PO Chandos ▲ CHAN 9073 [DDD]
Ysaÿe, E.:Sons Vn Chandos ▲ CHAN 8599 [DDD]

Moreau, Félix (org)
French Organ Music of the 17th & 18th Centuries Forlane ▲ FRL 16716 [DDD]

Moreaux, Christine (ob)
Honegger, A.:Chamber Music (comp), w. D.-S. Kang (vn), P.-H. Xuereb (va), R. Wallfisch (vc), M. Arrignon (cl), A. Marion (fl), A. Haraldsdottir (fl), T. Caens (tpt), M. Becquet (trbn), P. Zanlonghi (hp), P. Devoyon (pno), F. Kondo (mez), Ludwig String Quartet—Sonatine for Clarinet & Piano (1921–22); Rapsodie for 2 Flutes, Clarinet & Piano (1917); Danse de la Chèvre for Solo Flute (1921); Romance for Flute & Piano (1953); Petite Suite for 2 Flutes & Piano (1934); Trois Contrepoints for Piccolo, Oboe, Violin & Cello (1922); Intrada for Trumpet & Piano (1947); Hommage du trombone exprimant la tristesse de l'auteur absent for Trombone & Piano (1925); J'avais un fidèle amant for String Quartet (1929); Chanson de Ronsard & 3 Chansons de la petite Sirène for Mezzo, Flute & String Quartet (1924); Introduction et Danse for Flute, Harp & String Trio [undated]; Colloque for Flute, Celesta, Violin & Viola [undated] Timpani ▲ IC1010 [DDD]

Morehen, John (org)
Britten, H.:Choral Music, w. D. Lumsden (cnd), New College Choir Oxford—Te Deum in C; Jubilate Deo in C; Antiphon; Hymn to St. Peter Saga Classics ▲ EC 3385
Purcell, H.:Sacred Choral & Vocal Music, w. D. Lumsden (cnd), New College Choir Oxford—Magnificat and Nunc Dimittis in g; O Lord God of Hosts; Praise the Lord, O Jerusalem Saga Classics ▲ EC 3385

Moreira-Lima, Arthur (pno)
Chopin, F.:Con 1 Pno, w. D. Manolov (cnd), Philharmonia Bulgarica Vivace 3-▲ E 322 [DDD]
Chopin, F.:Con 1 Pno, w. D. Manolov (cnd), Philharmonia Bulgarica Vivace 2-▲ G 218 [DDD]
Chopin, F.:Con 1 Pno, w. D. Manolov (cnd), Philharmonia Bulgarica Sound 2-▲ E 220 [DDD]
Chopin, F.:Con 2 Pno, w. D. Manolov (cnd), Philharmonia Bulgarica Sound 2-▲ E 220 [DDD]

Morel, Dominique (pno)
Debussy, C.:Prélude à l'après-midi d'un faune, w. D. Nemish (pno) Analekta ▲ AN 29251
Ravel, M.:La Valse, w. D. Nemish (pno) Analekta Fleur de Lys ▲ FL 2 3046
Stravinsky, I.:Pétrouchka, w. D. Nemish (pno) Analekta Fleur de Lys ▲ FL 2 3046

Morelli, Frank (bn)
Mozart, W.A.:Con Bn, Orpheus CO Deutsche Grammophon ▲ 423623-2 [DDD]
Mozart, W.A.:Con Bn, Orpheus CO Deutsche Grammophon 3-▲ 431665-2 [DDD]
Rorem, N.:Winter Pages, w. T. Palmer (cl), I. Kavafian (vn), F. Sherry (vc), C. Wadsworth (pno) New World ▲ 80416-2 [DDD]
The Sounds of Remembered Dreams, w. Humbert Lucarelli (ob), Susan Jolles (hp) Vox ("Classics" series) ▲ VOX 7504 [DDD]
Stravinsky, I.:Octet, w. M. Parloff (fl), D. Schiffrin (cl), S. Heinneman (bn), R. Mase (tpt), C. Gekker (tpt), R. Borror (trbn), D. Taylor (trbn), G. Schuller (cnd) *(rec Sep. 1991)* GM ▲ GM 2030

Moreno, Alfonso (gtr)
Bizet, G.:Jeux d'enfants, w. E. Bátiz (cnd), Mexico City PO Pickwick ▲ PIC IMG 1604 [DDD]
Castelnuovo-Tedesco, M.:Con 1 Gtr, w. E. Bátiz (cnd), Mexico City PO Pickwick ▲ PIC IMG 1604 [DDD]
Fauré, G.:Dolly, w. E. Bátiz (cnd), Mexico City PO Pickwick ▲ PIC IMG 1604 [DDD]
Ponce, M.:Concierto del sur, w. E. Bátiz (cnd), Mexican State SO ASV ▲ ASV 952
Ponce, M.:Concierto del sur, w. F. Lozano (cnd), Carlos Chávez SO Forlane ▲ FRL 16733 [DDD]
Ponce, M.:Concierto del sur, w. E. Bátiz (cnd), *(orch unknown)* ASV ▲ ASV 871 [DDD]
Ponce, M.:Concierto del sur, w. F. Lozano (cnd), Carlos Chávez SO Forlane ▲ FRL 16757
Rodrigo, J.:Concierto de Aranjuez, w. F. Lozano (cnd), Carlos Chávez SO Forlane ▲ FOR 16736 [DDD]
Rodrigo, J.:Concierto de Aranjuez, w. E. Bátiz (cnd), Mexican State SO ASV ▲ ASV 887 [DDD]
Rodrigo, J.:Concierto para una fiesta, w. E. Bátiz (cnd), Mexican State SO ASV ▲ ASV 887 [DDD]
Rodrigo, J.:Fant para un gentilhombre, w. E. Bátiz (cnd), Mexican State SO ASV ▲ ASV 887 [DDD]
Villa-Lobos, H.:Con Gtr, w. E. Bátiz (cnd), Mexico City PO Pickwick ▲ PIC IMG 1604 [DDD]

Moreno, Emilio (vl)—see ORCHESTRAS & ENSEMBLES Ensemble 415

Moreno, Emilio (vn)—see ORCHESTRAS & ENSEMBLES L'Academia d'Harmonia, La Real Camera

Moreno, Emilio (va)
Boccherini, L.:Qnt Pno, G.407–412, w. L. Alvini (pno), E. Gatti (vn), O. Edouard (vn), R. Gini (vc)—Nos. 1, 5 & 6 Tactus ▲ TC 740203

Moreno, Hector (pno)
Brahms, J.:Academic Festival Ov, w. Norberto Capelli (pno) [arr pno 4-hands] *(rec Accademia Bartolomeo Cristofori, Florence, Italy, Aug 1993)* Arts ▲ 4471362 [DDD]
Brahms, J.:Hungarian Dances Pno 4-Hands, w. Norberto Capelli (pno) *(rec Accademia Bartolomeo Cristofori, Florence, Italy, Aug 1993)* Arts ▲ 4471362 [DDD]

Moreno, Israel (perc)
Chávez, C.:Tambuco, w. Rodrigo Alvarado (perc), Tambuco Camerata *(rec Sala Nezahualcóyotl, Mexican National Independent Univ., Oct. 1994)* Dorian ▲ DOR 90215 [DDD]
Chávez, C.:Toccata for 6 Perc, w. Rodrigo Alvarado (perc), Tambuco Camerata *(rec Sala Nezahualcóyotl, Mexican National Independent Univ., Oct. 1994)* Dorian ▲ DOR 90215 [DDD]
Chávez, C.:Xochipilli, w. Rodrigo Alvarado (perc), E. Mata (cnd), Tambuco Camerata *(rec Sala Nezahualcóyotl, Mexican National Independent Univ., Oct. 1994)* Dorian ▲ DOR 90215 [DDD]

Moreno, José Miguel (gtr)
Canto del Cavallero *(rec 1992)* Glossa ▲ GCD 920101 [DDD]
Carulli, F.:Andante affettuoso, w. Marta Almajano (sop) Glossa ▲ GCD 920202
Giuliani, M.:Songs, w. Marta Almajano (sop)—3 Ariettas; 3 Cavatinas Glossa ▲ GCD 920202
La Guitarra Española (1526–1836) *(rec Mar. 1994)* Glossa ▲ 920103 [DDD]
Mertz, K.J.:Song without Words, w. Marta Almajano (sop) Glossa ▲ GCD 920202
Music at the Time of Beaumarchais, w. Montserrat Figueras (sop), Lawrence Monteyro (sop), Raphel Oleg (vn), Miguel da Silva (va), Christophe Coin (vc), Marc Coppey (vc), Paul Badura-Skoda (pno), Philippe Cassard (pno), Éric Le Sage (pno), Bob Van Asperen (h Valois ▲ V 4767
Soler, P.A.:Songs, w. Marta Almajano (sop)—4 Canzonettas Glossa ▲ GCD 920202
Sor, F.:Songs, w. Marta Almajano (sop)—Mouvement prière religieuse; 4 Ariettas; Nel cor piu mi sento; 5 Seguidillas Glossa ▲ GCD 920202
Weiss, S.L.:Lt Music—Ciaconne; Suonata in re major; Prélude; Menuet; Fant.; Ciacona; Suonata in re menor *(rec June 1993)* Glossa ▲ GCD 920102 [DDD]

Moreno, José Miguel (thb)
Visée, R. de:Pieces Thb—Pieces in G; Entrée des Espagnols de M. Lully; Logistille de M. Lully; Chaconne des Harlequins de M. Lully; Pieces in C; Les Sylvains de M. Couperin; Les Bergeries de M. Couperin *(rec San Lorenzo de El Escorial, Spain, Nov 1995)* Glossa ▲ 920104 [DDD]

Moretti, Fabrice (sax)
Arma, P.:Music of, w. Josette Morata (nar), Régis Poulain (bn), Jean-Marie Cottet (pno), Alain Béghin (perc), Francis Petit (perc), J.-L. Petit (cnd), Avray Atelier Musique—Phases contre phases for S Sax & Pno; Celui qui dort et dort for Nar, Bn, Xyl & Perc [after poems by Max Jacob]; 5 esquisses for Pno [from a Hungarian Theme]; Divertissement 1600 for Fls [w. Jean-Noël Catrice (fl), Béatrice Delpierre (fl), Pascale Haarscher (fl), Marie-Aude Menou (fl)]; 3 Regards for solo Ob [w. Jacques Vandeville (ob)]; Divert No. 6 for Cl & Pno [w. Dominique Vidal (cl)]; Parlando for solo Fl [w. Patrice Bocquillon (fl)] REM ▲ REM 311266 [DDD]
Chen, Q.:Feu d'Ombres, w. J.-L. Petit (cnd), Ville d'Avray Instrumental Ensemble REM ▲ REM 311223 [DDD]

Moretti, Isabelle (hp)
Pierné, G.:Concertstück Hp, w. K. Arp (cnd), Southwest German RSO Baden-Baden Koch Schwann ▲ SCH 313392 [ADD/DDD]
Saint-Saëns, C.:Fant Vn, w. C. Henkel (vc) Valois ("Musique Française" series) ▲ V 4657

Morf, Antony (cl)
Debussy, C.:Première rapsodie, w. A. Jordan (cnd), Monte Carlo Opera Orch Erato ▲ 94679-2
Mozart, W.A.:Trio Cl, K.498, w. C. Veress (va), I. von Alpenheim (pno) BIS 2-▲ CD 513/14 [DDD]
Müller-Zurich, P.:Petite Sonate, w. J. Eichenberger (pno) Grammont ▲ CTSP 20-2
Ponchielli, A.:Paolo et Virginia, w. Thomas Füri (vn), Gérard Wyss (pno) Accord ▲ ACD 220682 [AAD]
Ponchielli, A.:Qt Fl, w. Heinrich Keller (fl), Omar Zoboli (ob), Bruno Furlanetto (E♭ cl), Gérard Wyss (pno) Accord ▲ ACD 220682 [AAD]

Morgan, Ann Marie (vc)—see ORCHESTRAS & ENSEMBLES Tempesta di Mare

Morgan, Ann Marie (vl)
Man with the Wooden Flute, w. Chris Norman (fl), Robin Bullock (gtr/cittern/fid), Pete Sutherland (fid) Dorian ▲ DOR 90166 [DDD]

Morgan, Carole (fl)
Eaton, J.:Ars Poetica, w. Nelda Nelson (sop), Daniel Rothmuller (vc), Beverly Wesner-Hoehn (hp), C. Colnot (cnd) *(rec Dec 18, 1986)* Indiana Univ School of Music ▲ 0-253-31842-4
Eaton, J.:From the Cave of the Sybil:Sonority Movt, w. C. Colnot (cnd), Indiana Univ Harp Ensemble *(rec Musical Arts Ctr, Bloomington, IN, Nov 20, 1986)* Indiana Univ School of Music ▲ 0-253-31842-4
Eaton, J.:A Greek Vision, w. Elsa Charlston (sop) *(rec Musical Arts Ctr, Bloomington, IN, Aug 28, 1986)* Indiana Univ School of Music ▲ 0-253-31842-4

Morgan, Geoffrey (org)
Crucifixus, w. [cnd:Andrew Millington], Guildford Cathedral Choir *(rec Guilford Cathedral, July 1993)* Herald ▲ HAVPCD 166 [DDD]

Morgan, L. (cl)—see ORCHESTRAS & ENSEMBLES Danish Wind Octet

Morgan, Melissa (hp)
Redolfi, M.:Underwater Music, w. Lanie Goodman (fl), Michel Redolfi (syn), Ricercar Ensemble—Effractions (1988); Sunny Afternoon at Bird Rock Beach (1983); Full Scale Ocean (1989) *(rec Pacific Ocean, CA & Nice, France, 1983 & 1989)* Hat Hut ("NOW." series) ▲ hat ART CD 6026 [ADD]

Morgan, Paul (org)
Wesley, S.S.:Air w. Vars Org, "Holsworthy Church Bells" [orgs of Exeter Cathedral & Killerton House, Devon] Priory ("Celebration" series) ▲ PRI 3 [ADD]
Wesley, S.S.:Pieces Chamber Org [orgs of Exeter Cathedral & Killerton House, Devon] Priory ("Celebration" series) ▲ PRI 3 [ADD]

Morgan, Richard (ob)
Doyle, P.:Sense & Sensibility, w. Jane Eaglen (sop), Jonathan Snowdon (fl), Robert Hill (cl), Tony Hymas (pno), R. Ziegler (cnd), *(orch unknown)* *(rec Air Studios, Lyndhurst Hall)* Sony Classical ▲ SK 62258 [DDD]

Morgensen, Morten (pno)
Hartmann, J.P.E.:Son 1 Vn, w. Søren Elbaek (vn) *(rec Mar 1995)* Kontrapunkt 2-▲ KPT 32206
Hartmann, J.P.E.:Son 2 Vn, w. Søren Elbaek (vn) *(rec Mar 1995)* Kontrapunkt ▲ KPT 32206
Hartmann, J.P.E.:Son 3 Vn, w. Søren Elbaek (vn) *(rec Mar 1995)* Kontrapunkt ▲ KPT 32206
Nielsen, C.:Son 1 Vn, w. Søren Elbaek (vn) *(rec 1994)* Kontrapunkt ▲ KPT 32200
Nielsen, C.:Son 2 Vn, w. Søren Elbaek (vn) *(rec 1994)* Kontrapunkt ▲ KPT 32200
Ravel, M.:Son Vn Pno, w. S. Elbæk (vn) Kontrapunkt ▲ KPT 32174 [DDD]
Ravel, M.:Sonate posthume, w. S. Elbæk (vn) Kontrapunkt ▲ KPT 32174 [DDD]
Ravel, M.:Tzigane, w. S. Elbæk (vn) Kontrapunkt ▲ KPT 32174 [DDD]

Morgenstern, Gil (vn)—see ORCHESTRAS & ENSEMBLES Broyhill Chamber Ensemble

Morgenthaler, B. (db)
Matson, S.:i-5, w. A. Shulmann (hp), P. Kent (vn), M. Newman (vn), R. Tischer (va), E. Duke-Kirkpatrick (vc) *(rec Aug. 29–30, 1992)* Audioquest ▲ AQCD 1013
Matson, S.:Steel Chords, w. D. Livingston (gtr), P. Kent (vn), M. Newman (vn), J. Derouin (vn), C. Moussas (vn), R. Tischer (va), E. Duke-Kirkpatrick (vc), S. Matson (cnd) *(rec Aug. 29–30, 1992)* Audioquest ▲ AQCD 1013

Mori, Chieko (koto)
Noda, T.:Mutation, w. Katsuya Yokoyama (shak), Toshi Fujita (koto), Mikiko Haga (koto), T. Otaka (cnd), Tokyo Metropolitan SO *(rec live, Tokyo Bunka-Kaikan, Large Hall, May 24, 1980)* Camerata ▲ 32CM-292 [AAD]

Mori, Ikue (perc)
Exquisite Corpses from P.S. 122, w. David Watson (shears/stick vn/gtr/tpt), Judy Dunaway (gtr/balloons), Anthony Coleman (sampler), Raissa St. Pierre (drums), Guy Yarden (vn/pno), Leslie Ross (bn), Linda Austin (gtr), Bruce Kaplan (gtr), Doug Henderson (peckhorn/bass/toy pno), Sue Ann Harkey (gtr), Cinnie Cole (sampler), et al. ¿What Next? ▲ WN 0002 [ADD]
Sato, M.:Improvs, w. Michihiro Sato (tsugaru shamisen), Bill Frisell (elec gtr), Fred Frith (elec gtr), Tenko (sgr), Mark Miller (elec bass), Nicolas Collins (elec), Christian Marclay (turntables), Steve Coleman (sax), Tom Cora (vc), Joey Baron (perc), Mark Dresser (elec bass), Gerry Hemingway (perc), Toh Ban Djan, Semantics—23 Improvisations with various accompaniment combinations *(rec Baby Monster Studio, NY, Apr. 11–16, 1988)* Hat Hut ▲ hat ART CD 6015 [ADD]

Mori, Mika (pno)
Dvořák, A.:Sonatina Vn, w. Barbara Gisler-Haase (fl) *(rec Studio Baumgarten, Vienna, Feb. 2 & 3, 1994)* Camerata ▲ 30CM 393 [DDD]
Hindemith, P.:Son Fl, w. Barbara Gisler-Haase (fl) *(rec Studio Baumgarten, Vienna, Feb. 2 & 3, 1994)* Camerata ▲ 30CM 393 [DDD]
Hindemith, P.:Son Fl, w. Barbara Gisler-Haase (fl) Camerata ▲ 30CM 358 [DDD]
Hummel, J.N.:Son Vn & Pno, Op. 50, w. Barbara Gisler-Haase (fl) *(rec Studio Baumgarten, Vienna, Feb. 2 & 3, 1994)* Camerata ▲ 30CM 393 [DDD]
Martinů, B.:Son Fl & Pno, w. Barbara Gisler-Haase (fl) *(rec Studio Baumgarten, Vienna, Feb. 2 & 3, 1994)* Camerata ▲ 30CM 393 [DDD]

Moriarty, D. (pno)
Lennon, J.A.:Distances Within Me, w. J. Forger (sax) CRI ▲ CD 599 [ADD/DDD]

Morice, Daniel (va)
Weber, C.M. von:Qnt Cl, w. L. Fuchs (cl), M. Solms (vn), O. Sipahi (vn), P. Caldwell (vc) Gallo ▲ CD 570 [DDD]

Morini, Erica (vn)
Mozart, W.A.:Con 5 Vn, w. P. Casals (cnd), Perpignan Festival Orch *(rec Perpignan, France, July 13, 1951)* Sony Classical ("The Casals Edition" series) ▲ SMK 58983 [ADD]
Mozart, W.A.:Con 5 Vn, w. G. Szell (cnd), RTF National Orch Sony Classical ("Festspiel Dokumente:Salzburger Festspiele" series) ▲ SMK 68446

Morini, Guido (clvd)
Forqueray, A.:Suites (5) Va da Gamba, w. Guido Balestracci (vl), Paolo Pandolfo (vl), Eduardo Eguez (thb/baroque gtr), Rolf Lislevand (thb/baroque gtr) Glossa 2-▲ 920401

Morini, Guido (hpd)
Bononcini, G.:Italian Cants, w. C. Miatello (sop), A. Fossà (vc)—Ah, non avesse, no, permesso il fato; Che tirannia di stelle; Cieco nume, tiranno spietato; Vidi in cimento due vaghi amori [I] Tactus ▲ TC 660002
Scarlatti, A.:Cants, w. C. Miatello (sop), A. Fossà (vc)—Andante, o miei sospiri; Per un momento solo; Lascia più di tormentarmi; Lontan dalla sua Clori [I] Tactus ▲ TC 660002
Veracini, F.M.:Sons Vn, Op. 1, w. Enrico Gatti (vn), Alain Gervreau (vc)—Nos. 1 & 8 Arcana ▲ ACA 27
Veracini, F.M.:Sonate accademiche, w. Enrico Gatti (vn), Alain Gervreau (vc)—Nos. 6 & 12 Arcana ▲ ACA 27

Morini, Guido (org/hpd)—see ORCHESTRAS & ENSEMBLES Aurora Ensemble

Morisset-Balier, Marie-André (org)
Vierne, L.:Messe basse pour les défunts Motette ▲ CD 10411
Widor, C.M.:Sym 9 Org Motette ▲ CD 10411

Mork, Truls (pno)
Brahms, J.:Trio Cl, w. Michel Lethiec (cl), Katia Skavavi (vc) Lyrinx ▲ LYX 123 [DDD]
Mørk, Truls Otterbach (vc)
Britten, H.:Sym Vc, w. N. Järvi (cnd), Bergen PO BIS ▲ CD 420 [DDD]
Dvořák, A.:Con Vc, w. M. Jansons (cnd), Oslo PO Virgin Classics ▲ CDC 59325
Grieg, E.:Intermezzo, w. J.–Y. Thibaudet (pno) Virgin Classics ▲ CDC 45034
Grieg, E.:Son Vc, w. J.–Y. Thibaudet (pno) Virgin Classics ▲ CDC 45034
Haydn, J.:Con 1 Vc, w. I. Brown (cnd), Norwegian CO Virgin Classics ▲ CDC 45014
Haydn, J.:Con 2 Vc, w. I. Brown (cnd), Norwegian CO Virgin Classics ▲ CDC 45014
Miaskovsky, N.:Con Vc, w. Jean–Yves Thibaudet (pno) [arr vc & pno] Virgin Classics ▲ CDC 45119
Rachmaninoff, S.:Pieces Vc, w. Jean–Yves Thibaudet (pno) Virgin Classics ▲ CDC 45119
Rachmaninoff, S.:Son Vc, w. Jean–Yves Thibaudet (pno) Virgin Classics ▲ CDC 45119
Rachmaninoff, S.:Vocalise, w. Jean–Yves Thibaudet (pno) [arr vc & pno] Virgin Classics ▲ CDC 45119
Shostakovich, D.:Con 1 Vc, w. M. Jansons (cnd), London PO Virgin Classics ▲ CDC 45145
Shostakovich, D.:Con 2 Vc, w. M. Jansons (cnd), London PO Virgin Classics ▲ CDC 45145
Sibelius, J.:Malinconia, w. J.–Y. Thibaudet (pno) Virgin Classics ▲ CDC 45034
Sibelius, J.:Pieces Vn, w. J.–Y. Thibaudet (pno) Virgin Classics ▲ CDC 45034
Tchaikovsky, P.:Vars on a Rococo Theme, w. M. Jansons (cnd), Oslo PO Virgin Classics ▲ CDC 59325
Thommessen, O.A.:Through a Prism, w. Kåre Nordstoga (org), K. Andersen (cnd), Oslo PO
Caprice ▲ CAP 21403
Morley, Matthew (org)
Bruckner, A.:motets, w. Richard Cheetham (trbn), Adrian Lane (trbn), Steven Saunders (trbn), Simon Wills (trbn), Robert James (cnd), James St. Bride's Church Choir—Os justi; Locus iste; Libera me [in f, 1854]; Ave maria; Ecce sacerdos; Vexilla regis; Salvum fac populum tuum [1884]; Afferentur regi; Pange lingua; Tota pulchra es [Daniel Norman (tenor)]; Virga Jesse; Inveni David; Iam lucis orto sidere [Hymnus, 1868]; Tantum ergo [in D, 1988]; Christus factus est *(rec St. Bride's Church, Fleet Street, London, Jan. 27–29, 1994)* Naxos ▲ 8.550956 [DDD]
Child of Light, w. [cnd:Matthew Greenall], Elysian Singers London, Hugh Webb (hp)
Continuum ▲ CON 1043 [DDD]
Music for Christmas, w. [cnd:Matthew Greenall], Elysian Singers London, Hugh Webb (hp)
Continuum ▲ CCD 1043
Morley, Rosamund (trb vl/t vl)—see ORCHESTRAS & ENSEMBLES New York Consort of Viols
Morley, Simon (org)
Great Cathedral Anthems, Volume 5, w. [cnd:David Briggs], Truro Cathedral Choir
Priory ▲ PRI 429 [DDD]
Moroney, Davitt (chamber org/hpd)
Biber, H. von:Mystery (or Rosary) Sons, w. J. Holloway (vn), Tragicomedia
Virgin Classics ("Veritas" series) 2–▲ 59551 [DDD]
Moroney, Davitt (hpd)
Bach, J.S.:The Art of the Fugue Harmonia Mundi France 2–▲ HMC 901169/70
Bach, J.S.:Cons for 3 Hpds (comp), w. C. Tilney (hpd), C. Rousset (hpd), C. Hogwood (cnd), Academy of Ancient Music L'Oiseau–Lyre ▲ 433053–2 [DDD]
Bach, J.S.:Con for 4 Hpds, w. C. Tilney (hpd), C. Rousset (hpd), C. Hogwood (hpd), C. Hogwood (cnd), Academy of Ancient Music L'Oiseau–Lyre ▲ 433053–2 [DDD]
Bach, J.S.:French Suites Virgin Classics ("Veritas" series) 2–▲ ZDCB 59011–2 [DDD]
Bach, J.S.:Italian Con Virgin Classics ▲ CDC 59272
Bach, J.S.:A Musical Offering, w. J. See (fl), J. Holloway (vn), J. ter Linden (vc), M. Cook (hpd)
Harmonia Mundi France ▲ HMC 901260 [DDD]
Bach, J.S.:Preludium, Fugue & Allegro Hpd, BWV 998 Virgin Classics ▲ CDC 59272
Bach, J.S.:Sons Fl, BWV 1030–35, w. J. See (baroque fl), M. Springfels (vl)—includes alternate manuscript solo flute version of BWV 1033 Harmonia Mundi USA 2–▲ HMU 907024/25 2–
Bach, J.S.:Sons Vn, w. J. See (baroque fl), M. Springfels (vl)—BWV 1020 [doubtful; trans. for flute & continuo] Harmonia Mundi USA 2–▲ HMU 907024/25 2–
Bach, J.S.:Das wohltemperierte Klavier Musique D'Abord 4–▲ HMA 1901285.88
Bach, J.S.:Das wohltemperierte Klavier Harmonia Mundi Plus ▲ HMP 3901285
Couperin, F.:Motets, w. J. Feldman (sop), I. Poulenard (sop), G. Reinhart (bass), J. ter Linden (bass vl)—[L] Musique d'Abord ▲ HMA 1901150
Couperin, F.:Pièces de clavecin (sels), w. Olivier Baumont (hpd)—13th–19th books
Erato 2–▲ ERA 92859 [DDD]
Moroney, Davitt (kbd)
Bach, J.S.:Suites Kbd, BWV 818a & 819a Virgin Classics ("Veritas" series) 2–▲ ZDCB 59011–2 [DDD]
Moroney, Davitt (virs/hpd)
Purcell, H.:Hpd Music (comp) Virgin Classics ▲ CDC 45166
Morosco, Victor (a sax)
An American Collage Vol. II, w. Constance Keene (pno), Ayke Agus (pno), Anita Swearingen (pno), Michael Lang (pno), Diane Lang Bryan (cl), James Smith (gtr), Sherry Kloss (vn), Laila Padorr (fl)
Protone ▲ PRCD 1114 [DDD]
Morosco, Victor (sax)
Morosco, V.:Blue Caprice Protone ▮ CSPR 153
Roccisano, J.:Sonorities, w. F. Seykora (vc), J. Porcaro (perc) Protone ▮ CSPR 153
Woods, P.:Son Sax, w. Lang (pno) Protone ▮ CSPR 153
Moroz, Sergey (vc)—see ORCHESTRAS & ENSEMBLES Baroque Chamber Ensemble
Morozova, Irina (va)—see ORCHESTRAS & ENSEMBLES Australia Ensemble
Morrell, Andrew (perc)
Moran, R.:Rocky Road, w. Joseph Goodrich (kbd), Kevin Hanson (gtr), Erik Johnson (perc) *(rec Chapel of Girard College, Philadelphia & Henry Wood Hall, London, Mar 17, 1994 & Dec 13, 19)*
Argo ▲ 444540–2 [DDD]
Morris, Andy (perc)
Peebles, S.:Phoenix Calling, w. Ikuo Kakehashi (shô), Sarah Peebles (shô), Bugaku Percussion Ensemble *(rec live, Shukôji Temple, Kawasaki)* Innova ▲ 506
Morris, Geoffery (gtr)
Dench, C.:Severance Vox Australis ▲ VAST 0192
Morris, R. (fl)
Vivaldi, A.:Cons Diverse Instrs, w. G. Vicari (mand), C. de Filippis (mand), J. Wummer (fl), W. Vacchiano (tpt), N. Prager (tpt), E. Brenner (b ob), C. Stavrache (hp), A. Wurtzler (hp), J. Gorigliano (vn), L. Varga (vc), L. Bernstein (cnd), New York PO—in C, RV.558 *(rec Dec. 15, 1958)*
Sony Classical ("Leonard Bernstein:The Royal Edition" series) ▲ SMK 47642 [ADD]
Morris, R. (org)
Buck, D.:Grand Son Org New World ▲ 80280–2
Paine, J.K.:Fantaisie on *Ein feste Burg ist unser Gott* Org, Op. 13 New World ▲ 80280–2
Parker, H.:Compositions Org—No. 3, Fugue in c New World ▲ 80280–2
Thayer, E.:Vars on Russian National Hymn New World ▲ 80280–2
Whiting, G.:Postlude Org New World ▲ 80280–2
Morris, Victor (pno)
Elgar, E.:Songs, w. J. Brecknock (ten), D. Temple (cnd), London Phil Chamber Choir—20 songs—O Happy Eyes; Love; To Her Beneath Whose Stedfast Star; Is She Not Passing Fair?; Sheperd's Song; Weary Wind of the West; Evening Scene; Windlass Song; Poet's Life; Song of Autumn; Death on the Hills; Serenade; Credo in e; Was it Some Golden Star?; Speak, Music; Lo! Christ the Lord is Risen; O Mightiest of the Mighty; The River; How Calmly the Evening; Good Morrow [E]
Meridian ▲ CDE 84173
Rita Hunter in Concert, w. Rita Hunter (sop) Tall Poppies ▲ TP 21
Morriset-Balier, M.–A. (org)
Vierne, L.:Messe basse pour les défunts Motette ▲ CD 11231 [DDD]
Widor, C.M.:Sym 2 Org Motette ▲ CD 11231 [DDD]
Morrison, Alan (org)
Alan Morrison *(rec 1987)* ACA Digital ▲ CM 20015
Demessieux, J.:Te Deum [Aeolian–Skinner Org] *(rec St. Philip's Cathedral, Atlanta, GA)*
Gothic ▲ G 49083 [DDD]

Morrison, Alan (org) (cont.)
Dupré, M.:Préludes & Fugues, Op. 7—in g, Op. 7/3 [Aeolian–Skinner Org] *(rec St. Philip's Cathedral, Atlanta, GA)* Gothic ▲ G 49083 [DDD]
Dupré, M.:Vars sur un vieux Noël [Aeolian–Skinner Org] *(rec St. Philip's Cathedral, Atlanta, GA)*
Gothic ▲ G 49083 [DDD]
Duruflé, M.:Prélude et fugue sur le nom d'Alain ACA Digital Recording ▲ CM 20015
Duruflé, M.:Suite Org [at the organ of Roswell United Methodist Church, Roswell, GA]
ACA Digital ▮ CM 20019–19
Duruflé, M.:Suite Org [Aeolian–Skinner Org] *(rec St. Philip's Cathedral, Atlanta, GA)*
Gothic ▲ G 49083 [DDD]
Franck, C.:Chorals Org, M.38–40—No. 3 in a [Aeolian–Skinner org] *(rec St. Philip's Cathedral, Atlanta, GA)* Gothic ▲ G 49083 [DDD]
Krape, W.E.:Choral Triptych ACA Digital Recording ▲ CM 20015
Langlais, J.:Hommage à Frescobaldi ACA Digital Recording ▲ CM 20015
Live from Spivey Hall *(rec Spivey Hall, Morrow, GA, Mar. 5, 1993)*
ACA Digital ▲ CM 20022 ▮ CM 20022
Locklair, D.:Voyage ACA Digital ▲ CM 20022 ▮ CM 20022
Reubke, J.:Son Org [at the organ of Roswell United Methodist Church, Roswell, GA]
ACA Digital ▮ CM 20019–19
Weaver, J.:Passacaglia on a Theme by Dunstable ACA Digital Recording ▲ CM 20015
Morrison, Catherine (va)
Hazzan Rishon, Legendary Cantorial Recitativi, Opuses 1 & 2, w. David Montefiore (cant), C. Vineburg (pno), V. Zeltser (vn), A. Bacelar (vc), G. Lochner (vc) Behar/Berg 2–▲ 001494
Morrison, Jeannine (pno)
A Virtuoso Duo–Piano Showcase, w. Jeannine Morrison (pno), Joanne Rogers (pno) *(rec Spivey Hall, Morrow, GA, June 8 & 9, 1993)* ACA Digital ▲ CM 20023 ▮ CM 20023
Morrison, P. (vc)
Lentz, G.:Caeli enarrant...IV, w. Georges Lentz (vn), J. Booth (vn), D. Wicks (va) Tall Poppies ▲ TP 35
Morrison, Timothy (tpt)
Baroque Trumpetissimo, w. David Bilger (tpt), Stephen Burns (tpt), Edward Carroll (tpt), Alex Holton (tpt), Raymond Mase (tpt), Lee Soper (tpt), Atsuko Sato (bn), Ben Harms (timp), Edward Brewer (org/hpd), Philharmonia Virtuosi [cnd:Richard Kapp] ESS.A.Y ▲ ESS 1035 [DDD]
Morrow, M. (hn)
Solo Pro:Contest Music for Horn, w.T. Lichtmann (pno) Summit ▮ DCD 104
Mortensen, Gert (perc)
Gudmunsen–Holmgreen, P.:Triptykon, w. J. Panula (cnd), Danish National RSO
BIS ▲ CD 256 [AAD/DDD]
Nørgård, P.:I Ching BIS ▲ CD 256 [AAD/DDD]
Sallinen, A.:Sym 2, w. O. Kamu (cnd), Malmö SO BIS ▲ CD 511 [DDD]
Xenakis, I.:Psappha BIS ▲ CD 256 [AAD/DDD]
Xenakis, I.:Psappha BIS ▲ CD 482 [AAD/DDD]
Mortensen, Gert (timp)
Carter, E.:Pieces (8) Timp—Nos. 1, 4, 6 & 8 *(rec Studio 2, Danmarks Radio, Copenhagen, Denmark, Jan 14, 1982)* BIS ▲ CD 52 [AAD]
Mortensen, Jan (b trbn)—see ORCHESTRAS & ENSEMBLES Royal Danish Brass
Mortensen, Kristian Buhl (lt)
Ulrik Cold, w. Ulrik Cold (bass) Danacord ▲ DACOCD 376 [DDD]
Mortensen, Lars Ulrik (hpd)—see also ORCHESTRAS & ENSEMBLES Veracini Trio, London Baroque
Bach, J.S.:Chromatic Fant & Fugue Kontrapunkt ▲ 32012 [DDD]
Bach, J.S.:French Suites Kontrapunkt 2–▲ KPT 32103 [DDD]
Bach, J.S.:Toccatas Hpd, BWV 910–16—BWV 912–914 & 916 Kontrapunkt ▲ 32012 [DDD]
Buxtehude, D.:Hpd Music—Aria:La Capricciosa; Aria:Rofilis; Preludium in g; Suites in A, C, e, & g
Kontrapunkt ▲ 32069 [DDD]
Buxtehude, D.:Sons for 2 Vns, Op. 1, w. John Holloway (vn), Jaap ter Linden (vl) *(rec Kastelskirken, Copenhagen, June 29–July 1, 1994)* Marco Polo ▲ 8.224003 [DDD]
Buxtehude, D.:Sons for 2 Vns, Op. 2, w. John Holloway (vn), Jaap ter Linden (vl) *(rec Kastelskirken, Copenhagen)* Marco Polo ("dacapo" series) ▲ 8.224004 [DDD]
Castello, D.:Sons (3) Rcr, w. V. Boeckman (rcr), F. Hansen (vl) *(rec 9/90)*
Kontrapunkt ▲ 32059 [DDD]
Cima, G.P.:Sons 1 & 2 Rcr, w. V. Boeckman (rcr), F. Hansen (db) *(rec 9/90)*
Kontrapunkt ▲ 32059 [DDD]
Duphly, J.:La du Buq Chandos ("Chaconne" series) ▲ CHAN 0531 [DDD]
Duphly, J.:La de Redemond Chandos ("Chaconne" series) ▲ CHAN 0531 [DDD]
Fontana, G.B.:Sons 2, 3 & 4 Rcr, w. V. Boeckman (rcr), F. Hansen (vl) *(rec 9/90)*
Kontrapunkt ▲ 32059 [DDD]
Forqueray, J.–B.:La Morangis ou la plissay Chandos ("Chaconne" series) ▲ CHAN 0531 [DDD]
Frescobaldi, G.:Canzona detta la Bernadinia, w. V. Boeckman (rcr), F. Hansen (db) *(rec 9/90)*
Kontrapunkt ▲ 32059 [DDD]
Frescobaldi, G.:Canzona quatra, w. V. Boeckman (rcr), F. Hansen (db) *(rec 9/90)*
Kontrapunkt ▲ 32059 [DDD]
Froberger, J.J.:Hpd Music—Six Suites—Nos. 6 in D, 11 in D, 12 in C, 18 in g, 19 in c & 20 in D; Toccatas I & II (1649); Tombeau Kontrapunkt ▲ 32040 [DDD]
Greene, M.:Songs, w. Emma Kirkby (sop), A. Rooley (cnd), Consort of Musicke
Musica Oscura ("The Handel Circle" series) ▲ MOS 70978
Guillemain, L.–G.:Son Vn, w. S. Standage (vn) Chandos ("Chaconne" series) ▲ CHAN 0531 [DDD]
Haydn, J.:Sons Pno—H.XVI/20,24,31,32,37 Kontrapunkt ▲ 32004 [DDD]
Leclair, J.–M.:Sons Vn (Books 1–4), w. S. Standage (vn)—Sonata in a, Op. 5/7; Sonata in A, Op. 9/4
Chandos ("Chaconne" series) ▲ CHAN 0531 [DDD]
Merula, T.:Music for Rcr, w. V. Boeckman (rcr), F. Hansen (vl)—La Merula; L'Arisia; La Dada; & La Pighetta *(rec 9/90)* Kontrapunkt ▲ 32059 [DDD]
Mondonville, J.–J.C. de:Son Hpd, Op. 3/5, w. S. Standage (vn)
Chandos ("Chaconne" series) ▲ CHAN 0531 [DDD]
Tallis, T.:Church Music, w. B. Holten (cnd), Ars Nova—Videte miraculum; Felix namque (I & II); Salvator mundi (I); O Nata lux [L] Kontrapunkt ▲ 32003 [DDD]
Telemann, G.P.:Sons (6) Rcr, w. V. Boeckman (rcr), F. Hansen (vl) *(rec 9/88)*
Kontrapunkt ▲ 32014 [DDD]
Mortensen, Lars Ulrik (hpd/org)
Buxtehude, D.:Sons Vn, Vl & Continuo, w. John Holloway (vn), Ursula Weiss (vn), Jaap ter Linden (vl), Mogens Rasmussen (vl)—BuxWV 266, 267, 269 & 271–273 *(rec Radio House, Studio 2, Sept 25–28, 1994)* Marco Polo ("dacapo" series) ▲ 8.224005 [DDD]
Morton, Greg (bn)—see ORCHESTRAS & ENSEMBLES Wizards!
Morton, Jonathan (vn)
Debussy, C.:Son Vn, w. C. Presland (pno) *(rec Oct. 1992)* Pavane ▲ ADW 7280 [DDD]
Lekeu, G.:Son Vn, w. C. Presland (pno) *(rec Oct. 1992)* Pavane ▲ ADW 7280 [DDD]
Suk, J.:Ballade Vn, w. C. Presland (pno) *(rec Oct., 1992)* Pavane ▲ ADW 7280 [DDD]
Szymanowski, K.:Myths, w. C. Presland (pno) *(rec Oct. 1992)* Pavane ▲ ADW 7280 [DDD]
Mosca, Antonio (vc)
The Piemontese School of the 18th Century, w. Enrico Gatti (vn), Giorgio Tabacco (hpd)
Symphonia ▲ SYM 92S13 [DDD]
Mosca, Marco (vc)
Platti, G.B.:Sons Vc, w. Marco Decimo (vc)—in D, G, A, c, B♭ & F *(rec Santuario dell'Addolorata, Ceceglio, Turin, Oct 28–30, 1995)* Agora Musica ▲ AG 016.1 [DDD]
Mosca, Paola (vc)—see ORCHESTRAS & ENSEMBLES Paganini String Quartet
Moscari, Karoly (pno)
Liszt, F.:Son Pno, w. J. Komives (cnd), Ensemble Opus 95—orig version for pno & version for 15 instruments REM ▲ REM 311265 [DDD]
Moseiwitsch, Benno (pno)
Beethoven, L. van:Con 5 Pno, "Emperor", w. G. Szell (cnd), London PO *(rec 1938)*
Koch Legacy ▲ 3-7035-2

Moseiwitsch, Benno (pno) (cont.)
Godowsky, L.:Transcriptions & Paraphrases—Paraphrase on Joh. Strauss's "Die Fledermaus" for Piano *(rec 1928)* Koch Legacy ▲ 3-7035-2
Liszt, F.:Fant on Hungarian Folk Tunes, w. C. Lambert (cnd), London PO *(rec 1939)* Koch Legacy ▲ 3-7035-2

Moser, Jürg (gtr)
Albéniz, I.:Suite española (sels), w. Fredy Rahm (gtr)—Nos. 1 & 3 [tran Tarrago for 2 gtrs] Gallo ▲ CD 881 [DDD]
Albéniz, I.:Tango Español, w. Fredy Rahm (gtr) [trans Tarrago for 2 gtrs] Gallo ▲ CD 881 [DDD]
Cabezón, A. de:Differencias, w. Fredy Rahm (gtr)—Differencias sobre el canto del caballero; Differencias sobre la gallarda milanesa [trans Tarrago for 2 gtrs] Gallo ▲ CD 881 [DDD]
Froelicher, A.:Muleta, w. Fredy Rahm (gtr) Gallo ▲ CD 881 [DDD]
Granados, E.:Danzas españolas (10), w. Fredy Rahm (gtr)—No. 2 [trans Hopman for 2 gtrs] Gallo ▲ CD 881 [DDD]
Granados, E.:Goyescas (intermezzo), w. Fredy Rahm (gtr) [trans Pujol for 2 gtrs] Gallo ▲ CD 881 [DDD]
Sor, F.:Fants Gtr, w. Fredy Rahm (gtr)—Op. 54bis Gallo ▲ CD 881 [DDD]
Sor, F.:Waltzes, w. Fredy Rahm (gtr) Gallo ▲ CD 881 [DDD]

Moser, K. (vc)—see ORCHESTRAS & ENSEMBLES Röhn Trio

Mosher, Stephen (bn)
Wagner, R.:Siegfried Idyll, w. T. Holowach (vn), M. Skazinetsky (vn), L. Toman (va), R. Laurie (vc), C. Elliott (db), S. Shulman (fl), T. Maloney (cl), J. Valdepenas (cl), J. Fetherston (cl), S. Mosher (bn), S. Wilson (hn), R. Cohen (hn), J. Cowell (tpt), G. Gould (cnd) *(rec July 27-29 & Sept. 8, 198)* Sony Classical ▲ SMK 52650 [ADD]

Moshevelov, Y. (hn)—see ORCHESTRAS & ENSEMBLES Collegium dell'Arte

Moskovitz, Marc (vc)
Popper, D.:Vc & Pno Music, w. Michael Boyd (pno)—Romanze, Op. 5; Im Walde, Op. 50; Nocturne, Op. 42; Polonaise de Concert, Op. 14; Suite for 2 Vc, Op. 16 [w. Steven Shumway (vc)]; Requiem for 3 Vc & Pno [w. Steven Shumway (vc), Freya Samuels (vc)] *(rec Collingwood Arts Center Theater, Toledo, OH, Apr. 25-26 & May 11, 1994)* VAI Audio ▲ VAIA 1109

Moss, Jed (pno)
Babin, V.:Hillandale Waltzes, w. Kathy Pope (cl) Pope ▲ CD 001
Bach, J.S.:Chromatic Fant & Fugue, w. Kathy Pope (cl) [arr G. Langenus for cl & pno] Pope ▲ CD 001
Bach, J.S.:Sons Fl, BWV 1030-35, w. Kathy Pope (cl) [arr Ulmar Gateau for cl & pno] Pope ▲ CD 001
Giampieri, A.:Il Carnevale di Venezia, w. Kathy Pope (cl) [trans for cl & pno] Pope ▲ CD 001
Harvey, P.:Suite on Themes of Gershwin, w. Kathy Pope (cl) Pope ▲ CD 001
Trumpet, w. Bret Jackson (tpt) Summit ▲ DCD 153 [DDD]

Moss, Linda (va)
Diamond, D.:Qnt Cl, w. Lawrence Sobol (cl), Louise Schulman (va), Timothy Eddy (vc), Fred Sherry (vc) *(rec RCA Studio A, New York City)* New World ▲ 80508-2

Moss, Phyllis (pno)
Chopin, F.:Preludes, Op. 28 Centaur ▲ CRC 2072 [DDD]
Chopin, F.:Son Pno, Op. 58 Centaur ▲ CRC 2072 [DDD]
Liszt, F.:Transcriptions & Paraphrases—Paganini:6 Grand Etudes; Schubert:Songs from Die Schöne Muüllerin; Soirees De Vienne; Verdi:Concert Paraphrase on Rigoletto; Bach:Organ Fant & Fugue in g Centaur ▲ CRC 2240
Schumann, R.:Faschingsschwank aus Wien Centaur ▲ CRC 2106 [DDD]

Mossop, Sue (mand)
Music for Mandolin, w. Alison Stephens (mand), Poppy Holden (sop), Richard Burnett (pno) Amon Ra ▲ CDSAR 53 [DDD]

Mossyrsch, Gabriela (hp)
Brahms, J.:Choral Music, w. A. Korondi (sop), J. Keiding (hn), J. Widihofer (hn), E. Ortner (cnd), Arnold Schoenberg Choir—Lieder und Romanzen, Op. 93a; 3 Gesänge, Op. 42; 7 Lieder, Op. 62; 5 Gesänge, Op. 104; 4 Gesänge, Op. 17 Teldec ▲ 4509-92058-2 [DDD]
del Aguila, M.:Herbsttag, w. M. Bayer St. Mary (fl), J. Farmer (bn), H. Earle (cnd), American Music Ensemble Vienna Albany ▲ TROY 066 [DDD]

Moszynski, Kazimierz (fl)
Arnaud, L.:In Memoriam, w. M. Mitsumoto (cnd), Cracow RSO *(rec Krakow, Poland, Sept. 20-22, 1993)* Cambria ▲ CMB 1074 [DDD]

Mothot, T. (hpd)
Ruloffs, B.:Sons Hpd, w. M. Huggett (vn), R. van der Meer (vc)—No. 1 in G Erasmus ▲ WVH 010 [ADD]
Ruppe, C.F.:Duets Vn, w. M. Huggett (vn)—No. 2 in G Erasmus ▲ WVH 010 [ADD]

Motohashi, Aya (perc)—see ORCHESTRAS & ENSEMBLES Bugaku Percussion Ensemble

Motoi, Mijuki (hpd)
Vivaldi, A.:Cons Pic, w. H. W. Dünshede (fl), W. Güttler (db), Berlin Philharmonia String Quartet—RV.441, 443, 444, 445 Denon ▲ 7076 [DDD]

Mott, David (sax)
Mott, D.:Regarding Starlight CBC ("Musica Viva" series) ▲ MVCD 1055 [DDD]
Mott, D.:Tiger running CBC ("Musica Viva" series) ▲ MVCD 1055 [DDD]
Siddall, J.:Jakarta Sleep, w. Arraymusic Ensemble CBC ("Musica Viva" series) ▲ MVCD 1057 [DDD]

Mott, Martha (vn)—see ORCHESTRAS & ENSEMBLES Bronx Arts Ensemble

Moukhariyamov, Yuri (fl)—see ORCHESTRAS & ENSEMBLES Baroque Chamber Ensemble

Mourao, Isabel (pno)
Grieg, E.:Pno Music (comp)—Lyric Pieces (complete); Humoresques, Op. 6; Scenes for Peasant Life, Op. 19 Vox Box 3-▲ CD3X 3023 [ADD]
Grieg, E.:Pno Music (comp)—Ballade in g, Op. 24; sels. from 4 Pieces, Op. 1; Poetic Tone Pictures, Op. 3; Norwegian Dances & Folksongs, Op. 17; Norwegian Peasant Dances, Op. 72; Album Leaves; Improvisations on 2 Norwegian Folksongs, Op. 29 Moods, Op. 73; sels. from Holberg's Time, Op. 40; sels. from 19 Norwegian Folk Melodies, Op. 66 Vox Box 2-▲ CDX 5097 [ADD]

Mourtazine-Chapochnikova, Marina (pno)
Amirov, F.:Pieces (6) Fl, w. Christian Delafontaine (fl) Gallo ▲ CD 894 [DDD]
Glière, R.:Pieces Fl & Pno, Op. 35, w. Christian Delafontaine (fl)—Melody; Waltz Gallo ▲ CD 894 [DDD]
Liadov, A.:Prelude Fl & Pno, w. Christian Delafontaine (fl) Gallo ▲ CD 894 [DDD]
Rachmaninoff, S.:Vocalise, w. Christian Delafontaine (fl) [trans fl & pno] Gallo ▲ CD 894 [DDD]
Taktakishvili, O.:Son Fl, w. Christian Delafontaine (fl) Gallo ▲ CD 894 [DDD]

Moussas, C. (vn)
Matson, S.:Steel Chords, w. D. Livingston (gtr), P. Kent (vn), M. Newman (vn), J. Derouin (vn), R. Tischer (va), E. Duke-Kirkpatrick (vc), B. Morgenthaler (db), S. Matson (cnd) *(rec Aug. 29-30, 1992)* Audioquest ▲ AQCD 1013

Moutin, François (bass gtr)
Constant, M.:Choruses & Interludes, w. Jean-Jacques Justafre (hn), Pierre-Marie Bonafosse (sax), Pierre Guignon (dr), Andy Emler (pno), J. Kaltenbach (cnd), Nancy SO *(rec Salle Poirel, Nancy, Apr. 4, 1990)* Erato ▲ 94815-2 [DDD]

Mouzalas, Elena (pno)
Antoniou, T.:Pno Music—Prélude; Toccata Adda ▲ ADD 581199 [ADD]
Constantinidis, Y.:Dances (8) from the Greek Adda ▲ ADD 581199 [ADD]
Hadjidakis, M.:For a Little White Seashell Adda ▲ ADD 581199 [ADD]
Haydn, J.:Con Hpd & Strs, H.XVIII/3, w. A. Duczmal (cnd), Amadeus CO Adda ▲ ADD 581228 [DDD]
Haydn, J.:Con Hpd & Strs, H.XVIII/4, w. A. Duczmal (cnd), Amadeus CO Adda ▲ ADD 581228 [DDD]
Haydn, J.:Con Hpd, Obs, Hns & Strs, H.XVIII/11, w. A. Duczmal (cnd), Amadeus CO Adda ▲ ADD 581228 [DDD]
Kalomiris, M.:Rhap 1 Pno Adda ▲ ADD 581199 [ADD]
Skalkottas, N.:Etude 3 Pno Adda ▲ ADD 581199 [ADD]
Theodorakis, M.:Préludes Pno—5 sels Adda ▲ ADD 581199 [ADD]

Mowrey, Gaylord (pno)
Feldman, Morton:Why Patterns, w. D. Stone (fl), A. Jarvinen (perc) *(rec 10/90)* New Albion ▲ NA 039 [DDD]

Mowrey, Gaylord (pno) (cont.)
Mosko, S.L.:for Morton Feldman, w. Dorothy Stone (fl), Erika Duke-Kirkpatrick (vc) New World ▲ 80456-2

Moye, E. (vc)
Bolcom, W.:Fant Concertante, w. J. Lyman Hill (va), D. R. Davies (cnd), American Composers Orch Argo ▲ 433077-2 [DDD]

Moyer, Frederick (pno)
Bach, J.S.:Das Orgelbüchlein—BWV 601 [trans. David Moyer for piano] Jupiter ■ J101
Bach, J.S.:Preludes & Fugues, BWV 531-552 [trans. Ferruccio Busoni for piano]—BWV 532 Jupiter ■ J101
Bach, J.S.:Sons & Partitas Vn, BWV 1001-1006— Partita No. 3 in E for Violin, BWV 1006 [3 movts; arr. Rachmaninoff for piano] Jupiter ▲ J106 ■ J106
Beethoven, L. van:Son 12 Pno, "Funeral March" Jupiter ■ J103
Beethoven, L. van:Son 14 Pno, "Moonlight Son" Jupiter ■ J103
Beethoven, L. van:Vars on a Russian Dance from P. Wranitzky's ballet "Das Waldmachen", WoO 71 Jupiter ■ J101
Britten, H.:Son Vc, w. N. Green (vc) Jupiter ■ J102
Debussy, C.:Son Vc, w. N. Green (vc) Jupiter ■ J102
Franck, C.:Prélude, fugue et var [trans. Harold Bauer for piano] Jupiter ■ J101
Liszt, F.:Etudes d'exécution transcendante d'après Paganini, S.140 [arr. Busoni]—Nos. 3,4 & 5 GM ▲ 2016CD [DDD] ■ 2016T (D)
Mendelssohn, F.:Pno Music (misc) [recorded live on the Bösendorfer 290 SE Computer-Based Reproducing Piano]—"Seven pieces in the form of a suite":Prelude, Op. 35/6; Etude, Op. 104/2; Barcarole, Op. 102/7; Lieder ohne Worte, Op. 67/5 & Op. 19/1; Albumblatt, Op. 117; fugue, Op. 35/1 GM ▲ 2024CD [DDD] ■ 2024T (D)
Mendelssohn, F.:Son 2 Vc, w. N. Green (vc) Jupiter ■ J102
Mussorgsky, M.:Pictures at an Exhibition [rec.'live' on the Bösendorfer 290 SE Computer-Based Reproducing Piano] GM ▲ 2024CD [DDD]
Rachmaninoff, S.:Etudes-tableaux, Opp. 33 & 39—Op. 33, No. 3 & Op. 39, Nos. 6 & 9 Jupiter ▲ 106 ■ J106
Rachmaninoff, S.:Preludes Pno, Opp 23 & 32—Op. 23, Nos. 2, 4 & 5 Jupiter ■ J101
Rachmaninoff, S.:Preludes Pno, Opp 23 & 32—Op. 23 Jupiter ▲ 106 ■ J106
Ravel, M.:Valses nobles et sentimentales GM ▲ 2016CD [DDD] ■ 2016T (D)
Reger, M.:Studies for the Left Hand GM ▲ 2016CD [DDD] ■ 2016T (D)
Rhapsody in Blue, etc. *(rec Roseholm Studios, New York)* Jupiter ▲ J 107
Schumann, R.:Fantasiestücke Cl, w. N. Green (vc) [arr. cello & piano] Jupiter ■ J102
Walker, G.:Son 4 Pno GM ▲ 2016CD [DDD] ■ 2016T (D)

Moyer, Karl (org)
As the Dew from Heaven Distilling Raven ▲ OAR 290 [DDD]

Moyse, Marcel (fl)—see also ORCHESTRAS & ENSEMBLES Adolf Busch Chamber Players
Beethoven, L. van:Octet, Op. 103, w. Marlboro Festival Ensemble members *(rec Marlboro, VT, Aug 30, 1957)* Sony Classical ("Essential Classics" series) ▲ SBK 62412 [ADD] ■ SBT 62412
Debussy, C.:Son Fl, w. E. Ginot (va), L. Laskine (hp) *(rec ca. 1927)* Pearl ▲ PEA 9348 (m) [AAD]
Mozart, W.A.:Cons Fl, w. E. Bigot (cnd), *(orch unknown)* *(rec 1930-36)* Pearl ▲ PEA 9118 [ADD]
Mozart, W.A.:Con Fl Hp, w. L. Laskine (hp), E. Bigot (cnd), *(orch unknown)* *(rec 1930-36)* Pearl ▲ PEA 9118 [ADD]

Mozes, Robert (vn)
Caplet, A.:Conte fantastique, w. A. Giles (hp), R. Kaminkovsky (vn), Y. Kaminkovsky (va), Y. Alperin (vc) PWK Classics ▲ PWK 1141 [DDD]
Ravel, M.:Intro & Allegro, w. A. Giles (hp), E. Talmi (fl), A. Arnheim (cl), R. Kaminkovsky (vn), Y. Kaminkovsky (va), Y. Alperin (vc) PWK Classics ▲ PWK 1141 [DDD]

Mozzato, Guido (vn)
Vivaldi, A.:Cons Vn, Op. 8/1-4, "The Four Seasons", w. Luigi Ferro (vn), R. Fasano (cnd), Rome Virtuosi *(rec Abbey Road Studios, London, Mar. 1959)* EMI Classics ▲ CDK 65338 [ADD]

Mráček, Jan (vn)
Domazlicky, F.:Czech Folk Songs, w. Z. Jiroušek (vn), O. Smola (va), P. Mišejka (vc), J. Karas (cnd), Disman Radio Children's Ensemble *(rec June 1992)* Channel Classics ▲ CCS 5193 [DDD]

Mrhal, Jiří (gtr)—see ORCHESTRAS & ENSEMBLES Prague Guitar Quartet

Mrongovius, Begonia-Uriarte (harm)
Strauss, R.:Hochzeitspräludium, w. Karl-Hermann Mrongovius (harm) *(rec Kleiner Konzertsaal, Gasteig, Munich, June 18, 1986)* Arts Music ▲ 447260-2 [DDD]

Mrongovius, Begonia-Uriarte (pno)
Strauss, R.:Aus italien, w. Karl-Hermann Mrongovius (pno) [arr for pno 4-hands] *(rec Kleine Konzertsall, Gasteig, Germany, Mar 22-23, 1988)* Arts ▲ 47262-2 [DDD]
Strauss, R.:Enoch Arden, w. Elisabeth Woska (nar) *(rec Kleiner Konzertsaal, Gasteig, Munich, June 18, 1986)* Arts Music ▲ 447260-2 [DDD]
Strauss, R.:Serenade Ww, w. Karl Hermann Mrongovius (pno) [arr for Pno 4-hands] Arts ▲ 47266-2 [DDD]
Strauss, R.:Suite Wws, w. Karl-Hermann Mrongovius (pno) [arr for pno 4-hands] *(rec Kleine Konzertsall, Gasteig, Germany, Mar 22-23, 1988)* Arts ▲ 47262-2 [DDD]
Strauss, R.:Sym in f, w. Karl Hermann Mrongovius (pno) [arr for Pno 4-hands] Arts ▲ 47266-2 [DDD]

Mrongovius, Karl-Hermann (harm)
Strauss, R.:Hochzeitspräludium, w. Begonia-Uriarte Mrongovius (harm) *(rec Kleiner Konzertsaal, Gasteig, Munich, June 18, 1986)* Arts Music ▲ 447260-2 [DDD]

Mrongovius, Karl-Hermann (pno)—see also ORCHESTRAS & ENSEMBLES Uriarte-Mrongovius Duo
Ogermann, C.:Music for 2 Pnofortes, w. B. Uriarte (pno) Mobile Fidelity ▲ MFCD 786 [DDD]
Schubert, Franz:Allegro Moderato & Andante Pno 4-Hands, w. Begoña Uriarte (pno) Calig ▲ CAL 50950 [DDD]
Schubert, Franz:Andantino Varie, w. Begoña Uriarte (pno) Calig ▲ CAL 50950 [DDD]
Schubert, Franz:Fant Pno, D.940, w. Begoña Uriarte (pno) Calig ▲ CAL 50950 [DDD]
Schubert, Franz:Ländler Pno, D.814, w. Begoña Uriarte (pno) Calig ▲ CAL 50950 [DDD]
Schubert, Franz:Marches militaires, D.733, w. Begoña Uriarte (pno) Calig ▲ CAL 50950 [DDD]
Schubert, Franz:Vars on an Original Theme Pno 4-Hands, w. Begoña Uriarte (pno) Calig ▲ CAL 50950 [DDD]
Strauss, R.:Aus italien, w. Begonia-Uriarte Mrongovius (pno) [arr for pno 4-hands] *(rec Kleine Konzertsall, Gasteig, Germany, Mar 22-23, 1988)* Arts ▲ 47262-2 [DDD]
Strauss, R.:Das Schloss am Meere, w. Elisabeth Woska (nar) *(rec Kleiner Konzertsaal, Gasteig, Munich, June 18, 1986)* Arts Music ▲ 447260-2 [DDD]
Strauss, R.:Serenade Ww, w. Begonia-Uriarte Mrongovius (pno) [arr for Pno 4-hands] Arts ▲ 47266-2 [DDD]
Strauss, R.:Suite Wws, w. Begonia-Uriarte Mrongovius (pno) [arr for pno 4-hands] *(rec Kleine Konzertsall, Gasteig, Germany, Mar 22-23, 1988)* Arts ▲ 47262-2 [DDD]
Strauss, R.:Sym in f, w. Begonia-Uriarte Mrongovius (pno) [arr for Pno 4-hands] Arts ▲ 47266-2 [DDD]

Mucha, Barbara (hpd)—see ORCHESTRAS & ENSEMBLES Tutti e solo

Mucha, Stanislav (vn)—see also ORCHESTRAS & ENSEMBLES Moyzes String Quartet
Schmidt, F.:Qnt Cl, w. A. Jánoska (cl), A. Lakatos (va), J. Slávik (vc), D. Ruso (pno) Marco Polo ▲ 8.223414

Muck, Conrad (vn)—see also ORCHESTRAS & ENSEMBLES Petersen String Quartet
Schulhoff, E.:Son Vn *(rec Berlin, June 6-8 & Nov 7-8, 1994)* Capriccio ▲ 10 539 [DDD]

Mueller, Zizi (fl)
American Flute, Vol. 1, w. Yuval Waldman (vn), Jesse Levine (va), S. Tahmizián (pno) Premier ▲ PRCD 1029 [DDD]
Crumb, G.:An Idyll for the Misbegotten, w. G. Gottlieb (timp), B. Herman (perc), S. Paysen (perc) New World ▲ NW 357-2
Crumb, G.:Vox balaenae, w. F. Sherry (vc), J. Gemmell (pno) New World ▲ NW 357-2

Muetter, Bertl (trbn/voc)
Trio L.T.D.:Vexations, w. Bertl Muetter (trbn/voc), LTD Trio *(rec Bremen Radio Studio, Bremen & Neckarsound Studio, Tubingen, May 11, 1993 & June 5, 19)* Leo ▲ LR 234

Muggerdige, Dorothy (vc)—see ORCHESTRAS & ENSEMBLES Valley String Quartet
Mugnolo, G. (fl)
19th Century Music for Flute & Harp, w. G. Mugnolo (fl), Ilde Bonelli (hp) Bongiovanni ▲ GB 5039 [DDD]
Mühlberg, Volker (vn)—see ORCHESTRAS & ENSEMBLES Affetti Musicali
Muhr, Roland (org)
Knecht, J.H.:Die Auferstehung Jesu Calig ▲ CAL 50 889 [DDD]
Knecht, J.H.:Die durch ein Donnerwetter unterbrochne Hirtenwonne Calig ▲ CAL 50 889 [DDD]
Knecht, J.H.:Org Music [Fux Organ in the Fürstenfeld Monastery Church]—Die Auferstehung Jesu [Prelude, The Resurrection of Jesus]; Die durch ein Donnerwetter unterbrochne Hirtenwonne [The Shepherd's Bliss Interrupted by a Thunderstorm] *(rec Apr. 14–15, 21, 1989)* Calig ▲ CAL 50889 [DDD]
Mozart, L.:Morgen und Abend *(rec Apr. 14–15, 21, 1989)* Calig ▲ CAL 50889 [DDD]
Trumpet & Organ, w. Gerd Zapf (tpt) *(rec Oct. 14–15 & 21–22, 1983)* Calig ▲ CAL 50832 [DDD]
Mukaiyama, Tomoko (elec pno)
Andriessen, L.:Contra tempus, w. Gerard Bouwhuis (pno), Sepp Grotenhuis (pno), Nico de Rooij (elec pno) *(rec Amsterdam Music Theater, Oct 3–6, 1994)* Donemus ▲ CV 54 [DDD]
Mukherji, Katherine Flanders (fl/pic)—see ORCHESTRAS & ENSEMBLES Musicians' Accord members
Mulbury, David (org)
Liszt, F.:Consolations [Great Org, Methuen Memorial Music Hall, Methuen, MA]—No. 1 in E; No. 4 in D♭ Afka ▲ SK 535
Liszt, F.:Fant & Fugue on "Ad nos, ad salutarem undam" Org [Great Org, Methuen Memorial Music Hall, Methuen, MA] Afka ▲ SK 535
Liszt, F.:Prelude & Fugue on the name B-A-C-H [Great Org, Methuen Memorial Music Hall, Methuen, MA] Afka ▲ SK 535
Liszt, F.:Vars on "Weinen, Klagen, Sorgen, Zagen", S.179 [Great Org, Methuen Memorial Music Hall, Methuen, MA] Afka ▲ SK 535
Sowerby, L.:Con Org, w. J. Welsh (cnd), Fairfield Orch *(rec St. Bartholomew's Church, New York City, May 3–5, 1994)* Marco Polo ▲ 8.223725 [DDD]
Sowerby, L.:Festival Musick, w. Carl Albach (tpt), Susan Radcliff (tpt), Jeffrey Caswell (trbn), Tom Hutchinson (trbn), Dan Haskins (timp), J. Welsh (cnd), Fairfield Orch *(rec St. Bartholomew's Church, New York City, May 5, 1994)* Marco Polo ▲ 8.223725 [DDD]
Mule, Marcel (sax)
"Le Patron" of the Saxophone, w. Guy Chauvet (ten), G. Charon (sgr), F. l'Homme (sgr), P. Romby (sgr), Eugène Bozza (cnd), Francis Çebron (cnd), Phillipe Gaubert (cnd), *(orchs unknown)*, Joseph Benvenutti (pno), Marcel Gaveau (pno), Marthe Pellas-Lenom (pno), François Combelle (sax) *(rec 1930–1940)* Clarinet Classics ▲ CC 0013 [AAD]
Mullan, Brian (vc)—see ORCHESTRAS & ENSEMBLES Sterling String Quartet
Muller, Dana (pno)
Muller & Steigerwalt, w. Gary Steigerwalt (pno) *(rec Aug.–Sept. 1991)* Centaur ▲ CRC 2127 [DDD]
Müller, Dario (pno)
American Indian Music:ca. 1900 Nuova Era ▲ NUO 6821 [DDD]
The American Indianists *(rec Lugano, Switzerland, Apr. & Aug. 1993)* Marco Polo ▲ 8.223715 [DDD]
The American Indianists, Vol 2 Marco Polo ▲ 8.223738 [DDD]
Müller, Eduard (hpd)
Bach, J.S.:Con for 4 Hpds, w. G. Leonhardt (hpd), J. van Wering (hpd), A. Uittenbosch (hpd), G. Leonhardt (cnd), Leonhardt Consort Teldec 3-▲ 2292-42726-2 [ADD]
Telemann, G.P.:Rcr Music (misc), w. H. Linde (rcr), M. Jappe (vl)—Fant. for Flute in A; Partita 5 in e; Son. in B♭; Son. in d Klavier ■ KC 511
Vivaldi, A.:Rcr Music (misc), w. H. Linde (rcr), M. Jappe (vl)—Son. 2 in C; Son. in d for Flute & Continuo; Son. in F Klavier ■ KC 511
Müller, Hannelore (vl)—see ORCHESTRAS & ENSEMBLES August Wenzinger Ensemble
Müller, Hanns Udo (pno)
Beethoven, L. van:An die ferne Geliebte, w. G. Hüsch (bar) [G] *(rec Berlin 1936 for HMV)* Preiser ("Lebendige Vergangenheit" series) 2-▲ 89202 (m) [AAD]
Haydn, M.:Requiem in c, w. Siglinde Damisch (sop), Gabriele Schreckenbach (mez), Chris Merritt (ten), Gerhard Walterskirchen (org), E. Hinreiner (cnd), Salzburg RSO, Mozart Choir *(rec June 1981)* Koch Treasure ▲ 31608-2 [ADD]
Schubert, Franz:Die Schöne Müllerin, w. G. Hüsch (bar) [G] *(rec Berlin, 1935 for HMV)* Pearl ▲ PEA 9479 (m) [AAD]
Schubert, Franz:Die Schöne Müllerin, w. G. Hüsch (bar) Preiser ("Lebendige Vergangenheit" series) 2-▲ 89202 (m) [AAD]
Schubert, Franz:Schwanengesang, w. G. Hüsch (bar) [G]—6 selections—Nos. 4,7,10,12,13 & 14 *(rec 1937–39 HMV recordings, s)* Preiser ("Lebendige Vergangenheit" series) ▲ 89017 (m) [AAD]
Schubert, Franz:Songs (misc), w. G. Hüsch (bar)—5 songs—Der Wanderer; Widerschein; Lied eines Schiffers an die Dioskuren, D.360; Der Musensohn, D.764; Ständchen, D.957/4 [G] *(rec 1933–39 for HMV)* Pearl ▲ PEA 9479 (m) [AAD]
Schubert, Franz:Songs (misc), w. G. Hüsch (bar), et al.—11 songs—D.328, 360, 479–481, 547, 698, 764, 775, 949 [G] *(rec 1934–39)* Preiser ("Lebendige Vergangenheit" series) ▲ 89017 (m) [AAD]
Schubert, Franz:Winterreise, w. G. Hüsch (bar) [G] *(rec 1933 for HMV)* Pearl ▲ PEA 9469 (m) [AAD]
Schubert, Franz:Winterreise, w. G. Hüsch (b-bar) [G] *(rec 1933 for HMV)* Preiser ("Lebendige Vergangenheit" series) 2-▲ 89202 (m) [AAD]
Schumann, R.:Dichterliebe, w. Gerhard Hüsch (bar) *(rec 1936)* Pearl ▲ PEA 9119 [ADD]
Müller, M. (pno)
Ibert, J.:Escales—Palerme; Tunis Nefta; & Valence Gallo ▲ CD 680 [DDD]
Milhaud, D.:Suite Pno Gallo ▲ CD 680 [DDD]
Turina, J.:Danzas gitanes Gallo ▲ CD 680 [DDD]
Muller, Marianne (vl)—see also ORCHESTRAS & ENSEMBLES Les Nièces de Rameau
Boësset, A.:Music of, w. Marcel Bozonnet (nar), Véronique Dietschy (sop), Alain Zaepffel (ct), Christophe Le Paludier (ten), Jacques Bone (bass), Claire Antonini (lt)—Madame de la fayette; Airs de cour; La princesse de cleves (sels) Adès ▲ ADE 204722
Couperin, F.:Leçons de ténèbres (for Good Friday), w. M. Van Der Sluis (sop), G. Laurens (mez), P. Monteilhet (lt), L. Boulay (hpd/org)—[L] Erato (Musifrance) ▲ 2292-45012-2 [DDD]
Couperin, F.:Magnificat, w. M. Van Der Sluis (sop), G. Laurens (mez), P. Monteilhet (lt), L. Boulay (hpd/org)—[L] Erato (Musifrance) ▲ 2292-45012-2 [DDD]
Marais, M.:Pièces de viole (misc), w. *(other instrumentalists unknown)*—Suite in d [from Book 1]; Tombeau pour Monsieur de Lulli in b [from Book 2]; Suite in G [from Book 3]; Caprice & Son [from Book 4]; Caprice in a [from Book 5] Adès ▲ ADE 202352 [DDD]
Scarlatti, A.:Cants & Duets, w. Véronique Dietschy (sop), Alain Zaepffel (ct), Macha Yanuchevskaia (vc), Aline Zylberajch (hpd/org), Yasunori Imamura (thb)—Il Sonno; Clori e Mirtillo; Marcantonio e Cleopatra; Doralbo e Niso Adès ▲ ADE 202172 [DDD]
Müller, Mathias (timp)
Festive Trumpet Concerti, w. Pfeiffer Trumpet Consort, Peter Schumann (org) *(rec St Juliana Parish Church, Malsch, July 4–6, 1995)* Cantate ▲ C 58001 [DDD]
Müller, Othmar (vc)—see also ORCHESTRAS & ENSEMBLES Artis String Quartet
Magnard, A.:Qt Strs, Op. 16, w. Johannes Meissl (vn), Peter Schuhmayer (vn), Herbert Kefer (va) Accord ▲ ACD 201982 [DDD]
Muller, Philippe (vc)
Alain, J.:Music of, w. Delphine Collot (sop), Bruno Boterf (ten), Jacques Bona (bar), Françoise Gyps (fl), Laurent Decker (ob), Bruno Pazqueir (va), Georges Guillard (org), Ludwig String Quartet, Georges Guillard (cnd), St. Louis Camerata Vocal Ensemble—2 Melodies for Sop & Pno; Nuptial Song for Bar, Bass, Vc & Org; Post-Scriptum for 3 Female Voices & Pno; Canticle in Phrygian Mode for 4 Mixed-Voice, Sop & Strs; Invention for Fl, Ob & Cl; Monody for solo Fl; Prelude for Str Qnt; Adagio for Str Qnt; Funerals for Str Qnt; March of the Horiaces & the Curiaces for 2 Bugles, Drum & Org Arion ▲ ARN 68321
Debussy, C.:Trio Pno, w. J. Rouvier (pno), J. J. Kantorow (vn) Denon ▲ CO 72508 [DDD]

Muller, Philippe (vc) (cont.)
Offenbach, J.:Duos for 2 Vcs, w. A. Meunier (vc)—Opp. 52/3 & 53/1–3 Arion ▲ ARN 68234 [AAD]
Ravel, M.:Trio Pno, w. J. Rouvier (pno), J. J. Kantorow (vn) Denon ▲ CO 72508 [DDD]
Muller, Roland (vn)
Legrand, H.:Concertino Vn, w. E. Berchot (pno), J.-J. Werner (cnd), Youth Orch Arcobaleno ▲ SBCD 7300
Virtuoso Showpieces for Violin, w. Philippe Reymond (pno) Sonpact ▲ SPT 95016 [DDD]
Müller, Viktor (hpd)—see ORCHESTRAS & ENSEMBLES Zurich New Music Ensemble
Müller, Viktor (pno)—see ORCHESTRAS & ENSEMBLES Zurich New Music Ensemble
Muller, Wim Statius (pno)
Falla, M. de:Fant bética René Gailly ▲ 87097 [DDD]
Kabalevsky, D.:Son 3 Pno René Gailly ▲ 87097 [DDD]
Ravel, M.:Valses nobles et sentimentales René Gailly ▲ 87097 [DDD]
Statius Muller, W.:Antillean Dances René Gailly ▲ CD 87018 [DDD]
Wagenaar, B.:Son Pno René Gailly ▲ 87097 [DDD]
Müller-Brincken, Jochen (ob)
Albinoni, T.:Cons à 5 Obs, Op. 7, w. I. Gortizki (ob), J. E. Dähler (hpd), H. L. Hirsch (cnd), Accademia Instrumentalis Claudio Monteverdi—Nos. 1,2 & 4 Claves ■ C 601
Müller-Nishio, Wolfgang (vn)
Furtwängler, W.:Son 2 Vn, w. Rudolf Dennemarck (pno) Bayer ▲ 100268 [ADD]
Müllerová, Hana (hp)
Benda, F.:Sons (2) Fl, w. Vítezslav Drápal (fl) Panton ▲ PAN 811004
Copland, A.:Con Cl, w. Jiří Hlaváč (cl), Ivan Klánský (pno), S. Bogunia (cnd), Suk CO *(rec ZK Motorlet Prague Studio, Sept 4–6 & 14–15, 1986)* Panton ▲ PAN 810884
Krumpholtz, J.-B.:Sons (3) Fl & Hp, w. Vítezslav Drápal (fl) Panton ▲ PAN 811004
Krumpholtz, J.-B.:Sons (6) Hp Supraphon ▲ 11 1573-2 [DDD]
Mozart, W.A.:Con Fl Hp, w. J. Válek (fl), R. Edlinger (cnd), Capella Istropolitana *(rec 1988)* Naxos ▲ 8.550159 [DDD]
Vanhal, J.B.:Son 1 Fl, w. Vítezslav Drápal (fl) Panton ▲ PAN 811004
Müllerová-Jouzová, Hana (hp)
Mozart, W.A.:Con Fl Hp, w. Jiří Válek (fl), V. Válek (cnd), Czech Phil CO *(rec House of Artists, Prague, Feb 1–3, 1996)* Canyon Classics 2-▲ 336
Müller-Pering, Thomas (gtr)
Granados, E.:Danzas españolas (10), w. M. Barrueco (gtr) EMI Classics ▲ CDC 54456
Mullova, Viktoria (vn)
Bach, J.S.:Sons & Partitas Vn, BWV 1001–1006 Philips ("Digital Classics" series) ▲ 420948-2 [DDD]
Bach, J.S.:Sons & Partitas Vn, BWV 1001–1006—Partitas 1, BWV 1002, 2, BWV 1004 & 3, BWV 1006 Philips ▲ 434075-2
Bach, J.S.:Sons Vn, w. B. Canino (pno)—1014, 1015 & 1019; BWV 1024 [spurious] Philips ▲ 434084-2
Bartók, B.:Son Vn Philips ("Digital Classics" series) ▲ 420948-2 [DDD]
Beethoven, L. van:Trio 6 Pno, "Archduke", w. André Previn (pno), Heinrich Schiff (vc) Philips ▲ 442123-2
Brahms, J.:Con Vn, w. C. Abbado (cnd), Berlin PO Philips ▲ 438998-2
Brahms, J.:Trio 1 Pno, w. André Previn (pno), Heinrich Schiff (vc) Philips ▲ 442123-2
Debussy, C.:Son Vn, w. Piotr Anderszewski (pno) Philips ▲ 446091-2
Janácek, L.:Son Vn, w. Piotr Anderszewski (pno) Philips ▲ 446091-2
Mendelssohn, F.:Con in d Vn & Strs, w. N. Marriner (cnd), Academy of St. Martin in the Fields Philips ▲ 432077-2 [DDD]
Mendelssohn, F.:Con in e Vn & Orch, Op. 64, w. N. Marriner (cnd), Academy of St. Martin in the Fields Philips ▲ 432077-2
Paganini, N.:Con 1 Vn, w. N. Marriner (cnd), Academy of St. Martin in the Fields Philips ▲ 422332-2 [DDD]
Paganini, N.:Intro & Vars on "Nel cor più" Philips ("Digital Classics" series) ▲ 420948-2
Prokofiev, S.:Con 2 Vn, w. A. Previn (cnd), Royal PO Philips ▲ 422364-2 [DDD]
Prokofiev, S.:Son 1 Vn, w. Piotr Anderszewski (pno) Philips ▲ 446091-2
Shostakovich, D.:Con 1 Vn, w. A. Previn (cnd), Royal PO Philips ▲ 422364-2 [DDD]
Sibelius, J.:Con Vn, w. S. Ozawa (cnd), Boston SO Philips ▲ 416821-2 [DDD] ◻ 416821-5
Tchaikovsky, P.:Con Vn, w. S. Ozawa (cnd), Boston SO Philips ▲ 416821-2 [DDD] ◻ 416821-5
Vieuxtemps, H.:Con 5 Vn, w. N. Marriner (cnd), Academy of St. Martin in the Fields Philips ▲ 422332-2 [DDD]
Vivaldi, A.:Cons Diverse Instrs, w. C. Abbado (cnd), CO of Europe Philips ▲ 420216-2 [DDD]
Vivaldi, A.:Cons Vn, Op. 8/1–4, "The Four Seasons", w. C. Abbado (cnd), CO of Europe Philips ▲ 420216-2 [DDD]
Mumelter, Martin (vn)
Bartók, B.:Duos (44), w. P. Lefor (vn) Koch Schwann ▲ CD 310 054 [ADD]
Dünser, R.:Tage- und Nachtbucher, w. Martin Schelling (cl), Walter Nothas (vc), Alfons Kontarsky (pno) Koch Schwann ▲ SCH 311882
Messiaen, O.:Quatuor pour la fin du temps, w. Martin Schelling (cl), Walter Nothas (vc), Alfons Kontarsky (pno) Koch Schwann ▲ SCH 311882
Mumma, Gordon (hn)
Tailleferre, G.:Chansons populaires françaises, w. Patrice Maginnis (sop), John Fairweather (vn), David Ryther (vn), Jill Cohen (va), Karen Andrie (vc), Elizabeth Bodine (ob), Andy Connell (cl), June Orzel (bn), N. Paiement (cnd) *(rec UC, Santa Cruz, May 1992)* Helicon Classics ▲ HE 1008
Tailleferre, G.:Image, w. John Fairweather (vn), David Ryther (vn), Jill Cohen (va), Karen Andrie (vc), Elizabeth Bodine (ob), Andy Connell (cl), June Orzel (bn), N. Paiement (cnd) *(rec UC, Santa Cruz, May 1992)* Helicon Classics ▲ HE 1008
Munar, A. (pno)
Lecuona, E.:Pno Music—Andalucía; Aquella Tarde; Canto Indio; Como el Arrullo de Palmas; La Comparsa; Dame de tus Rosas; Danza Lucumi; Malagueña; Noche Azul; Potpurrí Cubano; Siboney; Siempre en mi Corazón Montilla ▲ MNT 2094
Münch, Roland (org)
Bach, C.P.E.:Cons Org, H.444, w. H. Haenchen (cnd), C.P.E. Bach CO Capriccio ▲ 10135
Bach, C.P.E.:Fant & Fugue Org, H.103 Capriccio ▲ 10135
Bach, C.P.E.:Prelude Org, H.107 Capriccio ▲ 10135
Munday, Kenneth (bn)
Beethoven, L. van:Qnt Pno, Ob, Cl, Hn & Bn, w. C. Rosenberger (pno), A. Vogel (ob), D. Shifrin (cl), R. Graham (hn) Delos ▲ DCD 3024 [DDD]
Mozart, W.A.:Qnt Pno, K.452, w. C. Rosenberger (pno), A. Vogel (ob), D. Shifrin (cl), R. Graham (hn) Delos ▲ DCD 3024 [DDD]
Muñiz, Dagmar (pno)
Grieg, E.:Son 3 Vn, w. Eva León (vn) *(rec Estudis Albert Moraleda de Barcelona, Mar 1995)* Edicions Albert Moraleda ▲ CD 049523 [DDD]
Sarasate, P. de:Aires bohemios, w. Eva León (vn) *(rec Estudis Albert Moraleda de Barcelona, Mar 1995)* Edicions Albert Moraleda ▲ CD 049523 [DDD]
Toldrá, E.:Sonnets Vn, w. Eva León (vn) *(rec Estudis Albert Moraleda de Barcelona, Mar 1995)* Edicions Albert Moraleda ▲ CD 049523 [DDD]
Muniz, S. (pno)
Villa-Lobos, H.:Chôro 8, w. E. Sawyer (pno), E. de Carvalho (cnd), Paraiba SO Delos ▲ DE 1017 [DDD]
Munn, Zoe (vc/perc/voc)
Powell, Morgan:Faces *(rec live 1981)* Opus One ▲ CD 164
Munro, Ian (pno)
Arensky, A.:Suite 1 for 2 Pnos, w. Stephen Coombs (pno) Hyperion ▲ CDA 66755
Arensky, A.:Suite 2 for 2 Pnos, "Silhouettes", w. Stephen Coombs (pno) Hyperion ▲ CDA 66755
Arensky, A.:Suite 3 for 2 Pnos, "Vars", w. Stephen Coombs (pno) Hyperion ▲ CDA 66755
Arensky, A.:Suite 4 for 2 Pnos, w. Stephen Coombs (pno) Hyperion ▲ CDA 66755
Mendelssohn, F.:Cons (2) for 2 Pnos, w. S. Coombs (pno), J. Maksymiuk (cnd), BBC Scottish SO Hyperion ▲ CDA 66567 [DDD]

▲ = CD ◆ = Enhanced CD Δ = MD ■ = Cassette Tape ◻ = DCC

Munro, Ian (pno) (cont.)
A Patchwork of Shadows *(rec Llewellyn Hall, Canberra School of Music, Dec. 1992)* Tall Poppies ▲ TP 58 [DDD]

Munroe, Lorne (vc)
Falla, M. de:Con Hpd, w. I. Kipnis (hpd), P. Brook (fl), H. Gomberg (ob), S. Drucker (cl), E. Chapo (vn), P. Boulez (cnd), New York PO *(rec Mar. 2, 1975)* Sony Classical ▲ SBK 53264 ■ SBT 53264
Haydn, J.:Sinf concertante, w. John DeLancie (ob), Bernard Garfield (bn), Jacob Krachmalnick (vn), E. Ormandy (cnd), Philadelphia Orch Sony Classical ("Essential Classics" series) ▲ SBK 62649 ■ SBT 62649
Strauss, R.:Don Quixote, w. E. Ormandy (cnd), Philadelphia Orch Sony Classical ("Essential Classics" series) ▲ SBK 47656 ■ SBT 47656
Strauss, R.:Don Quixote, w. L. Bernstein (cnd), New York PO *(rec Oct. 24, 1968)* Sony Classical ▲ SMK 47625 [ADD]

Münten, Adolf (cl)
Baur, J.:Ostinato senza fine, "Pour rien", w. H. Fischer (cl), C. Crespo (hn), *(not advised of 2nd hn)*, F. Effmann (bn), S. Fasang (bn) *(rec May 13, 1981)* Koch Schwann ▲ SCH 311982 [ADD/DDD]

Muntian, Mikhail (pno)
Bruch, M.:Kol Nidrei, w. Y. Bashmet (vc) [arr. viola-piano] RCA Red Seal ▲ 60112-2-RC [DDD]
Enescu, G.:Concertpiece Va, w. Y. Bashmet (va) RCA Red Seal ▲ 60112-2-RC [DDD]
Glinka, M.:Son Va, w. Y. Bashmet (va) RCA Red Seal ▲ 09026-61273-2
Roslavets, N.:Son Va, w. Y. Bashmet (va)—not advised of which sonata is played here RCA Red Seal ▲ 09026-61273-2
Schumann, R.:Adagio & Allegro Hn, w. Y. Bashmet (vn) RCA Red Seal ▲ 60112-2-RC [DDD]
Schumann, R.:Märchenbilder, w. Y. Bashmet (vn) RCA Red Seal ▲ 60112-2-RC [DDD]
Shostakovich, D.:Son Va, w. Y. Bashmet (va) RCA Red Seal ▲ 09026-61273-2

Muntoni, Giampaolo (pno)
Schubert, Franz:Waltzes Pno—Erste Walzer (36), D.365; Valses sentimentales (34), D.779; Grazer Walzer (12), D.924; Valses nobles (12), D.969; Deuche Tänze (5), D.973 & 974 *(rec May 8 & 9, 1995)* Arts ▲ 47362-2 [DDD]

Muntyan, Mikhail (pno)
Rubinstein, A.:Son 1 Vc, w. Alla Vasilieva (vc) *(rec State House for Radio Broadcasting, May 1994)* Russian Disc ▲ RD CD 10038 [AAD]

Muraco, Thomas (pno)
Bergsma, W.:Fantastic Vars on a Theme from Tristan, w. J. Graham (va) CRI ■ ACS 6018 (CrO2)
Shapey, R.:Evocation 3 Va, w. J. Graham (va) CRI ■ ACS 6016 (CrO2)
Shostakovich, D.:Son Va, w. J. Graham (va) CRI ■ ACS 6018 (CrO2)

Murai, N. (pno)
Beethoven, L. van:Son 2 Vn, w. J. van Weijenberg (vn) *(rec Jan. 1989)* Eufoda ▲ 1130 [DDD]
Beethoven, L. van:Son 5 Vn, "Spring", w. J. van Weijenberg (vn) *(rec Jan. 1989)* Eufoda ▲ 1130 [DDD]
Beethoven, L. van:Son 10 Vn, w. J. van Weijenberg (vn) Eufoda ▲ 1130 [DDD]
Brahms, J.:Sons Vn (comp), w. J. van Weijenberg (vn) Eufoda ▲ 1156 [DDD]
Mozart, W.A.:Sons Vn Pno (misc), w. J. van Weijenberg (vn)—in G, K.301; in e, K.304; in G, K.379; in B, K.454 Eufoda ▲ EUF 1182 [DDD]

Murai, Yuji (cl)
Mozart, W.A.:Qnt Pno, K.452, w. Keiko Toyama (pno), Günther Passin (ob), Gottfried Langenstein (hn), Koji Okazaki (bn) *(rec Shibukawa Shimin Kaikan, Sept 1, 1981)* Camerata ▲ 32CM 180 [DDD]

Muraro, Roger (pno)
Messiaen, O.:Catalogue d'oiseaux—No. 7 [La rousserolle effarvatte] Accord ▲ ACD 201822 [DDD]
Messiaen, O.:Preludes Pno Accord ▲ ACD 201822 [DDD]
Rachmaninoff, S.:Moments musicaux Accord ▲ ACD 205412 [DDD]
Rachmaninoff, S.:Son 2 Pno Accord ▲ ACD 205412 [DDD]
Rachmaninoff, S.:Variations on a Theme by Corelli Accord ▲ ACD 205412 [DDD]

Murata, A. (trbn)
Shinohara, M.:Cooperation, w. A. Nishigata (shamisen), K. Mitsuhashi (shakuhachi), M. Akao (fue), S. Yaotani (hichiriki), K. Ishikawa (sho), C. Fukunaga (koto), J. Ueda (biwa), M. Yoshizawa (kokyu), I. Tsuji (oboe), T. Takahashi (cl), G. Kitamura (tpt), S. Eiso (perc), S. Ueki (vn), S. Katsuta (vc), Y. Shibuya (pno), K. Komatsu (cnd) *(rec live Casals Hall, Tokyo, Mar. 5, 1994)* Camerata ▲ 30CM 375 [DDD]
Shinohara, M.:Tabiyuki, w. A. Ogawa (mez), M. Kakagawa (fl), I. Tsuji (ob), T. Takahashi (cl), K. Okazaki (fagotto), G. Kitamura (tpt), S. Eiso (perc), S. Ueki (vn), A. Nakakoji (va), S. Katsuta (vc), M. Komuro (contrabass), K. Komatsu (cnd) *(rec live Casals Hall, Tokyo, Mar. 5, 1994)* Camerata ▲ 30CM 375 [DDD]

Murawski, Marcin (va)
Jarzebski, A.:Music of, w. Tutti e solo—Berlinesa; Cantate Domino; Tamburetta; Con Primo *(rec Grand Ballroom, Rydzyna Castle, Poland, Sept 1994)* Dorian Discovery ▲ DIS 80136 [DDD]

Murdoch, Jane (vn)
Bach, J.S.:Con 2 Vn, w. J. Rees (cnd), Scottish Ensemble Virgin Classics ▲ CDZ 59641
Bach, J.S.:Con for 2 Vns, w. C. Dale (vn), J. Rees (cnd), Scottish Ensemble Virgin Classics ▲ CDZ 59641
Virgo Collections, w. C. Dale (vn), S. Heath (vc), Scottish Ensemble [cnd:J. Rees (vn)] Virgin Classics ▲ CDZ 59652

Murdoch, William (pno)
Elgar, E.:Son Vn, w. A. Sammons (vn) *(rec 1935 for Columbia Records)* Pearl ▲ PEA 9496 (m) [AAD]
Mendelssohn, F.:Trio 2 Pno, w. A. Sammons (vn), L. Tertis (vc) [violin-viola-piano arr.] *(rec 12/9/25 for Columbia Reco)* Biddulph ▲ LAB 023 [ADD]

Murdock, K. (va)
Copland, A.:Threnodies I & II, w. F. Smith (fl), S. Chase (vn), R. Thomas (vc) Northeastern ("Classical Arts" series) ▲ NR 227-CD
Foote, A.:Nocturne, w. F. Smith (fl), L. Chang (vn), V. Uritzky (vn), B. Coppock (vc) Northeastern ("Classical Arts" series) ▲ NR 227-CD

Murdock, Katherina (va)—see ORCHESTRAS & ENSEMBLES Mendelssohn String Quartet

Murgier, Michel (vc)—see ORCHESTRAS & ENSEMBLES Capriccio Stravagante

Murina, Ekaterina (pno)
Beethoven, L. van:Music of, w. Nodar Gabunia (pno), A. Titov (cnd), New Classical Orch—Allegro con brio [from Sym No. 5]; Adagio sostenuto [from Son No. 14 for Pno]; Scherzo; Allegro vivace [both from Sym No. 3]; Adagio cantabile [from Son No. 8 for Pno]; Egmont Ov; Allegro ma non troppo [from Son No. 23 for Pno]; Adagio un poco moto; Rondo; Allegro [all from Con No. 5 for Pno]; Leonore Ov No. 3 Infinity Digital ▲ QK 61975 [DDD]
Beethoven, L. van:Son 2 Pno Infinity Digital ▲ QK 57229 [DDD]
Beethoven, L. van:Son 8 Pno, "Pathétique" Infinity Digital ▲ QK 57229 [DDD]
Beethoven, L. van:Son 23 Pno, "Appassionata" Infinity Digital ▲ QK 57229 [DDD]

Murphy, Maurice (tpt)
Bazelon, I.:Spires, w. H. Faberman (cnd), London SO Albany ▲ TROY 054 [DDD]
Pinkham, D.:Serenades Tpt, w. J. Sedares (cnd), London SO Koch International Classics ▲ KIC 7179 [DDD]
Shostakovich, D.:Con 1 Pno, w. G. Ohlsson (pno), G. Levine (cnd), Cracow PO Arabesque ▲ Z 6610

Murphy, Paul (va)—see also ORCHESTRAS & ENSEMBLES Atlanta Chamber Players
Mozart, W.A.:Adagio E Hn, w. Patrick McFarland (E hn), David Braitberg (vn), Beth Newdome (vn), Dona Klein (vc) [trans Renate Rosenbaltt] Arundax ▲ 21339
Rachmaninoff, S.:Vocalise, w. Patrick McFarland (E hn), David Braitberg (vn), Beth Newdome (vn), Dona Klein (vc), Larry LeMaster (vc), Gloria Jones (db) [trans John Wildermuth] Arundax ▲ 21339

Murray, B. (pno)
Goosen, F.:Pno Music—Sonata; Piano Music Tenebrae Opus One ▲ CD 159 [DDD]
Goosen, F.:Pno Music—Suite; Fant., Aria & Fugue; Labyrinth; Serenade Opus One ▲ CD 163

Murray, Gordon (org)
Bach, J.S.:Music of, w. R. Jacobs (ct), La Chapelle Royale Orch, Ensemble 415, Collegium Vocale—selections from Cantatas 35, 78 & 82, St. John Passion, St. Matthew Passion, & the Well-tempered Clavier; Chorale Prelude, BWV 622; Flute Sonata, BWV 1034; Toccata & Fugue in d *(rec 1969–88)* Harmonia Mundi Plus ▲ HMP 390801

Murray, Martial (zither)
Christmas Cithare, w. Bernard Bigo (gtr) Studio SM ▲ 1222.49 [AAD]

Murray, Michael (org)
An American Masterpiece AFKA ▲ SK 507
At the Cathedral of St. John the Divine [New York City] Telarc ▲ CD 80169 [DDD]
Bach, J.S.:Chorale Preludes Org—BWV 671, 680 Telarc ▲ CD 80097 [DDD]
Bach, J.S.:Chorale Preludes Org—Liebster Jesu, wir sind hier, BWV 731 Telarc ▲ CD 80127 [DDD]
Bach, J.S.:Chorale Preludes Org—Christ Lag in Todesbanden, BWV 625 (1st & 2nd versions); O Mensch, Bewein dein Sünde Gross, BWV 622; Ach, Gott und Herr, BWV 714 Telarc ▲ CD 80286 [DDD]
Bach, J.S.:Chorale Settings, BWV 651–668—BWV 658 Telarc ▲ CD 80097 [DDD]
Bach, J.S.:Cons Org, BWV 592–597—BWV 593 Telarc ▲ CD 80088 [DDD]
Bach, J.S.:Org Music (misc) Telarc ▲ CD 80049 [DDD]
Bach, J.S.:Org Music (misc) Telarc ▲ CD 80179 [DDD]
Bach, J.S.:Org Music (misc)—Toccata & Fugue in d, BWV 565; Fant & Fugue in g, BWV 542; Preludes in C, BWV 531; in c, BWV 546; in C, BWV 547; Sinf [from Cant No. 29]; Prelude & Fugue in G, BWV 541; Fugues in g, BWV 578; in d, BWV 680; Con No. 2 in a, BWV 593 Telarc ▲ CD 80316 [DDD]
Bach, J.S.:Org Music (misc) [at the Great Schnitger Organ, St. Michael's, Zwolle]—Fantasia, BWV 735; Herzlich tut, BWV 727; Nun komm, BWV 659; Prelude & Fugue, BWV 532; Prelude & Fugue, BWV 534; Prelude & Fugue, BWV 548; Vor deinen Thron, BWV 668 *(rec St. Michael's, Zwolle; St. Nicholas Church, Kampen))* Telarc ▲ CD 80385 [DDD]
Bach, J.S.:Das Orgelbüchlein—BWV 604, 605, 615, 639 Telarc ▲ CD 80097 [DDD]
Bach, J.S.:Das Orgelbüchlein—BWV 601, 619, 630 Telarc ▲ CD 80127 [DDD]
Bach, J.S.:Preludes & Fugues, BWV 531–552—BWV 545 Telarc ▲ CD 80097 [DDD]
Bach, J.S.:Preludes & Fugues, BWV 531–552—BWV 533 Telarc ▲ CD 80169 [DDD]
Bach, J.S.:Preludes & Fugues, BWV 531–552—BWV 541, 543 & 546 Telarc ▲ CD 80127 [DDD]
Bach, J.S.:Preludes & Fugues, BWV 531–552—BWV 537, 547 & 552 Telarc ▲ CD 80286 [DDD]
Bach, J.S.:Preludes & Fugues, BWV 531–552—BWV 532, 544 Telarc ▲ CD 80088 [DDD]
Bach, J.S.:Toccata, Adagio & Fugue Org, BWV 564 Telarc ▲ CD 80127 [DDD]
Bach, J.S.:Toccata & Fugue Org, BWV 538, "Dorian" Telarc ▲ CD 80088 [DDD]
Bach, J.S.:Toccata & Fugue Org, BWV 538, "Dorian"—BWV 537, 547 & 552 Telarc ▲ CD 80286 [DDD]
Bach, J.S.:Toccata & Fugue Org, BWV 565 Telarc ▲ CD 80088 [DDD]
Ceremonial Music for Trumpet & Symphonic Organ, w. Rolf Smedvig (tpt) Telarc ▲ CD 80341 [DDD]
Dupré, M.:Org Music—Cortège et Litanie, Op. 42/2; 7 Pieces, Op. 27—Final Telarc ▲ CD 80169 [DDD]
Dupré, M.:Préludes & Fugues, Op. 7—No. 3 Telarc ▲ CD 80097 [DDD]
Dupré, M.:Sym, Op. 25, w. J. Ling (cnd), Royal PO *(rec 1986)* Telarc ▲ CD 80136 [DDD]
Encores à la française Telarc ▲ CD 80104 [DDD]
Franck, C.:Chorals Org, M.38–40—No. 2 Telarc ▲ CD 80169 [DDD]
Franck, C.:Fant Org Telarc ▲ CD 80096 [DDD]
Franck, C.:Final Telarc ▲ CD 80097 [DDD]
Franck, C.:Org Music (comp) [Cavaillé-Coll Organ at Saint Sernin Basilica, Toulouse] [Disc 1]—Fantaisie in A; Cantabile; Pièce héroïque; Fantaisie in C; Prélude, Fugue et Variation; Prière; Final in B♭; [Disc 2]—Pastorale; Grande pièce symphonique; Trois Chorals *(rec 7/18–21/89)* Telarc 2-▲ CD 80234 [DDD]
Franck, C.:Pastorale Telarc ▲ CD 80096 [DDD]
The French Collection AFKA ▲ SK 512 [DDD]
Jongen, J.:Symphonie Concertante, w. E. de Waart (cnd), San Francisco SO Telarc ▲ CD 80096 [DDD]
The Longwood Gardens Organ, Vol. 1 Direct-to-Tape Recording ▲ DTR 8305CD ■ DTR 8305
Messiaen, O.:La Nativité du Seigneur—No. 9, "Dieu parmi nous" Telarc ▲ CD 80097 [DDD]
Michael Murray
Music for Organ, Brass & Percussion, w. Empire Brass Telarc ▲ CD 80218 [DDD] ■ CS-30218 (D)
An Organ Blaster Sampler Telarc ▲ CD 80277 [DDD]
Poulenc, F.:Con Org, w. R. Shaw (cnd), Atlanta SO Telarc ▲ CD 80104 [DDD]
Rheinberger, J.:Con 1 Org, w. J. Ling (cnd), Royal PO Telarc ▲ CD 80136 [DDD]
Saint-Saëns, C.:Sym 3, w. C. Badea (cnd), Royal PO Telarc ▲ CD 80274 [DDD]
Vierne, L.:Meditation & Prelude Telarc ▲ CD 80169 [DDD]
Vierne, L.:Sym 1 Org *(rec July 29–30, 1992)* Telarc ▲ CD 80329 [DDD]
Vierne, L.:Sym 3 Org *(rec July 29–30, 1992)* Telarc ▲ CD 80329 [DDD]
Widor, C.M.:Sym 6 Org AFKA ▲ SK 512 [DDD]
Widor, C.M.:Sym 6 Org—Adagio movt Telarc ▲ CD 80097 [DDD]
Widor, C.M.:Sym 6 Org—finale Telarc ▲ CD 80169 [DDD]
The Willis Organ at Salisbury Cathedral [England] Telarc ▲ CD 80255 [DDD]

Murray, Michael (vc)—see ORCHESTRAS & ENSEMBLES Hawthorne Trio

Murray, Robert (vn)—see also ORCHESTRAS & ENSEMBLES Murray/Lohuis Duo
Sowerby, L.:American Pieces, w. Gail Quillman (pno) *(rec Virginia Commonwealth Univ, Richmond, VA, Aug & Oct, 1994)* Premier ▲ PRCD 1049 [DDD]
Sowerby, L.:Folksong Arrs, w. Gail Quillman (pno) Premier ▲ PRCD 1049
Sowerby, L.:Son Vn (1922), w. Gail Quillman (pno) *(rec Virginia Commonwealth Univ, Richmond, VA, Aug & Oct, 1994)* Premier ▲ PRCD 1049 [DDD]
Sowerby, L.:Son Vn (1944), w. Gail Quillman (pno) Premier ▲ PRCD 1049
Sowerby, L.:Son Vn (1959), w. Gail Quillman (pno) *(rec Virginia Commonwealth Univ, Richmond, VA, Aug & Oct, 1994)* Premier ▲ PRCD 1049 [DDD]

Murray, Sandra (pno)—see ORCHESTRAS & ENSEMBLES Ouellet/Murray Duo

Murray, Thomas (org)
Bach, J.S.:Preludes & Fugues, BWV 531–552—BWV 552 AFKA ▲ SK 507
Elgar, E.:The Black Knight [Newberry Memorial Organ, Yale Univ]—Solemn March Gothic ▲ GOT 49076 [DDD]
Elgar, E.:Carillon [Newberry Memorial Organ, Yale Univ] Gothic ▲ GOT 49076 [DDD]
Elgar, E.:Chanson de matin [Newberry Memorial Organ, Yale Univ] Gothic ▲ GOT 49076 [DDD]
Elgar, E.:Chanson de nuit [Newberry Memorial Organ, Yale Univ] Gothic ▲ GOT 49076 [DDD]
Elgar, E.:Imperial March [Newberry Memorial Organ, Yale Univ] Gothic ▲ GOT 49076 [DDD]
Elgar, E.:Son Org [Newberry Memorial Organ, Yale Univ] Gothic ▲ GOT 49076 [DDD]
Elgar, E.:Son Org AFKA ▲ SK 507
Elgar, E.:Vesper Voluntaries [Newberry Memorial Organ, Yale Univ] Gothic ▲ GOT 49076 [DDD]
Gade, N.W.:Tone Pieces Org, Op. 22 AFKA ▲ SK 507
Lemare, E.H.:Org Music—Toccata di Concerto, Op. 59; Rondo capriccio (a study in accents), Op. 64; Summer Sketches, Op. 73; Carillon (a study in legato pedalling), Op. 74; Concert-Piece in the form of a Polonaise, Op. 80; Toccata & Fugue in d, Op. 98; Minuet nuptiale, Op. 103; Fantaisie serène, Op. 160 AFKA ▲ SK 515
Mulet, H.:Org Music (misc) [at the Austin Organ of the National Shrine of Our Lady of Czestochowa, Doylestown, PA]—Byzantine Sketches; other works Arkay ■ ARK 4111
Mulet, H.:Org Music (misc)—Byzantine Sketches; Campanile; Carillon Sortie; Chant funèbre; In Paradisum; Méditation Religieuse; Noël; Procession; Tu es petra Arkay ▲ AR 6111 [DDD]
Rameau, J.P.:Le Temple de la gloire (gavotte) AFKA ▲ SK 515
Rheinberger, J.:Sons Org—No. 5 in f#, Op. 111 AFKA ▲ SK 507
Saint-Saëns, C.:Danse macabre AFKA ▲ SK 515
Saint-Saëns, C.:Sym 3, w. E. Ormandy (cnd), Philadelphia Orch Telarc ▲ CD 80051 [DDD]

Musafia, Julien (pno)
Enescu, G.:Romanian Rhap 1 Ebs ▲ 6043 [DDD]

Musakodzhaeva, Aiman (vn)
Rakhmadiev, E.:Con Vn, w. P. Kogan (cnd), Moscow SO *(rec 1990)* Consonance ▲ 81-0003 [DDD]

Mushabec, R. (vc)
Reynolds, R.:The Ivanov Suite, w. P. Larson (bar), J. Fonville (pic), E. Harkins (tpt), J. Ngyesy (vn), S. Schick (perc) New World ▲ 80431-2

INSTRUMENT.

Mushabec, R. (vc) (cont.)
Reynolds, R.:Versions/Stages, w. P. Larson (bar), J. Fonville (pic), E. Harkins (tpt), J. Ngyesy (vn), S. Schick (perc) New World ▲ 80431-2
Mussumeli, Bettina (vn)—see ORCHESTRAS & ENSEMBLES Il Ruggiero
Muster, Thilo (org)
Beauvarlet-Charpentier, J.-J.:Org Music—Magnificat du 7 Ton avec un Carillon des Morts au Gloria Patri du Magnificat Gallo ▲ CD 863/864 [ADD]
Beauverlet-Charpentier, J.-M.:Magnificats, Op. 7—Magnificat du 7e Ton avec un Carillon des Morts au Gloria Patri du Magnificat *(rec Souvigny, Dec 26-28, 1994)* Gallo 2-▲ CD 863/64 [ADD]
Bovet, G.:Suite pour Souvigny *(rec Souvigny, Dec 26-28, 1994)* Gallo 2-▲ CD 863/64 [ADD]
Guilain, J.-A.:Org Music—Suite du Quatrieme Ton Gallo 2-▲ CD 863/864 [ADD]
Guilain, J.-A.:Suite du quatrième ton *(rec Souvigny, Dec 26-28, 1994)* Gallo 2-▲ CD 863/64 [ADD]
Marais, M.:Pièces de viole [Book 2] (sels) [trans. Thilo Muster] *(rec Souvigny, Dec 26-28, 1994)* Gallo 2-▲ CD 863/64 [ADD]
Marais, M.:Tombeau pour Lully Gallo ▲ CD 863/864 [ADD]
Rameau, J.P.:Les Boréades (suite) [sels trans. Thilo Muster] *(rec Souvigny, Dec 26-28, 1994)* Gallo 2-▲ CD 863/64 [ADD]
Rameau, J.P.:Org Music—Extraits des Boreades Gallo ▲ CD 863/864 [ADD]
Rebel, J.-F.:Les Élémens [trans. Thilo Muster] *(rec Souvigny, Dec 26-28, 1994)* Gallo 2-▲ CD 863/64 [ADD]
Rebel, J.-F.:Org Music—Extraits des Elemens Gallo ▲ CD 863/864 [ADD]
Mustonen, Olli (pno)
Alkan, C.-V.:Preludes Pno, Op. 31 London ▲ 433055-2 [DDD]
Bach, J.S.:Con 3 Hpd, w. J.-P. Saraste (cnd), German Chamber PO London ▲ 443118-2
Balakirev, M.:Islamey London ▲ 436255-2 [DDD]
Beethoven, L. van:Con 6 Pno, w. J.-P. Saraste (cnd), German Chamber PO London ▲ 443118-2
Beethoven, L. van:Pno Music (misc)—Vars & Bagatelle London ▲ 452206-2
Beethoven, L. van:Vars Pno—9 on Quant'e piu bello by Paisello, WoO 69; 6 on an original theme in F, Op. 34; 5 on Rule Britannia, WoO 79; 7 on God Save the King, WoO 78; 32 in c, WoO 80; 6 on Nel cor piu non mi sento by Paisello, WoO 70; 15 with Fugue in E♭, "Eroica," Op. 35; 12 on the Russian Dance from Wranitsky's Ballet Das Waldmachen, WoO 71 *(rec June 14-15, 1992)* London ▲ 436834-2 [DDD]
Chopin, F.:Con 1 Pno, w. H. Blomstedt (cnd), San Francisco SO *(rec Davies Symphony Hall, San Francisco, May 16 & 17, 1994)* London ▲ 444518-2 [DDD]
Hindemith, P.:Ludus Tonalis London ▲ 444803-2
Janácek, L.:Fairy Tale, w. Steven Isserlis (vc)—2 versions *(rec Great Hall, Blackheath Concert Halls, London, May 1995)* RCA Red Seal ▲ 09026-68437-2 [DDD]
Mussorgsky, M.:Pictures at an Exhibition London ▲ 436255-2 [DDD]
Mustonen, O.:Ballade *(rec June 5, 1989, Aug. 8-9, 1)* Finlandia ▲ 4509-95860-2 [DDD]
Mustonen, O.:Fant, w. J. Kangas (cnd), Ostrobothnian CO *(rec June 5, 1989, Aug. 8-9, 1)* Finlandia ▲ 4509-95860-2 [DDD]
Mustonen, O.:Music of—Six Bagatelles; Three Preludes; Gavotte; Two Meditations; On all Fours for Piano Four Hands [w. R. Kerppo (piano)]; Three Simple Pieces for Cello & Piano [w. M. Rousi (cello)] *(rec June 5, 1989, Aug. 8-9, 1)* Finlandia ▲ 4509-95860-2 [DDD]
Mustonen, O.:Toccata, w. E. Laine (db), Orion String Quartet *(rec June 5, 1989, Aug. 8-9, 1)* Finlandia ▲ 4509-95860-2 [DDD]
Prokofiev, S.:Mélodies, w. Joshua Bell (vn) London ▲ 440926-2 [DDD]
Prokofiev, S.:Son Vc, w. Steven Isserlis (vc) *(rec Great Hall, Blackheath Concert Halls, London, May 1995)* RCA Red Seal ▲ 09026-68437-2 [DDD]
Prokofiev, S.:Son Vn, Op. 94bis, w. Joshua Bell (vn) London ▲ 440926-2 [DDD]
Prokofiev, S.:Son 1 Vn, w. Joshua Bell (vn) London ▲ 440926-2 [DDD]
Prokofiev, S.:Visions fugitives London ▲ 444803-2
Shostakovich, D.:Preludes Pno, Op. 34 London ▲ 433055-2 [DDD]
Shostakovich, D.:Son Vc, w. Steven Isserlis (vc) *(rec Great Hall, Blackheath Concert Halls, London, May 1995)* RCA Red Seal ▲ 09026-68437-2 [DDD]
Stravinsky, I.:Capriccio, w. V. Ashkenazy (cnd), Berlin German SO *(rec Aug.-Sept. 1992)* London ▲ 440229-2 [DDD]
Stravinsky, I.:Con Pno Ww, w. V. Ashkenazy (cnd), Berlin German SO *(rec Aug.-Sept. 1992)* London ▲ 440229-2 [DDD]
Stravinsky, I.:Movts Pno, w. V. Ashkenazy (cnd), Berlin German SO *(rec Aug.-Sept. 1992)* London ▲ 440229-2 [DDD]
Tchaikovsky, P.:Album pour enfants London ▲ 436255-2 [DDD]
Muto, S. (vn)
Yashiro, A.:Qt Strs, w. C. Tanaka (vn), T. Uzuka (va), K. Yasuda (vc) Camerata ▲ 30CM 51
Mutter, Anne-Sophie (vn)
Anne-Sophie Mutter, w. Chicago SO [cnd:J. Levine] Deutsche Grammophon ▲ 437093-2 GH
Bach, J.S.:Cons Vn (comp), w. S. Accardo (cnd), English CO EMI Classics ▲ CDC 47005-2 [DDD]
Bach, J.S.:Con 2 Vn, w. R. Muti (cnd), Philharmonia Orch EMI Classics 3-▲ CDMC 69878
Bach, J.S.:Con for 2 Vns, w. S. Accardo (vn), S. Accardo (cnd), English CO EMI Classics ▲ CDC 47005-2 [DDD]
Bach, J.S.:Con for 2 Vns, w. S. Accardo (vn), S. Ozawa (cnd), French National Orch EMI Classics 3-▲ CDMC 69878
Bartók, B.:Con 2 Vn, w. S. Ozawa (cnd), Boston SO Deutsche Grammophon ▲ 431626-2 [DDD] □ 431626-5
Beethoven, L. van:Con Vn, Op. 61, w. H. von Karajan (cnd), Berlin PO Deutsche Grammophon ▲ 413818-2 [ADD]
Beethoven, L. van:Con Vn, Op. 61, w. H. von Karajan (cnd), Berlin PO Deutsche Grammophon 4-▲ 415565-2 [ADD]
Beethoven, L. van:Con Vn, Vc & Pno, "Triple Con", w. Yo-Yo Ma (vc), M. Zeltser (pno), H. von Karajan (cnd), Berlin PO Deutsche Grammophon ▲ 415276-2 [ADD]
Beethoven, L. van:Serenade Strs, Op. 8, w. B. Giuranna (vn), M. Rostropovich (vc) Deutsche Grammophon 2-▲ 427687-2 [DDD]
Beethoven, L. van:Trio Strs, Op. 3, w. B. Giuranna (va), M. Rostropovich (vc) Deutsche Grammophon 2-▲ 427687-2 [DDD]
Beethoven, L. van:Trios Strs, Op. 9, w. B. Giuranna (va), M. Rostropovich (vc) Deutsche Grammophon 2-▲ 427687-2 [DDD]
Berg, A.:Con Vn, w. J. Levine (cnd), Chicago SO Deutsche Grammophon ▲ 437093-2
Brahms, J.:Con Vn, w. H. von Karajan (cnd), Berlin PO Deutsche Grammophon 4-▲ 415565-2 [ADD/DDD]
Brahms, J.:Hungarian Dances Pno 4-Hands, w. Lambert Orkis (pno)—Nos. 2 & 5 [arr vn & pno] Deutsche Grammophon ▲ 445 826-2
Brahms, J.:Scherzo Vn, w. Lambert Orkis (pno) Deutsche Grammophon ▲ 445 826-2
Bruch, M.:Con 1 Vn, w. A.-S, H. von Karajan (cnd), Berlin PO Deutsche Grammophon 4-▲ 415565-2 [ADD/DDD]
Carmen Fantasy, w. Vienna PO [cnd:J. Levine] Deutsche Grammophon ▲ 437544-2 ■ 437544-4
Debussy, C.:Beau soir, w. Lambert Orkis (pno) [arr vn & pno] Deutsche Grammophon ▲ 445 826-2
Debussy, C.:Son Vn, w. Lambert Orkis (pno) Deutsche Grammophon ▲ 445 826-2
Franck, C.:Son Vn, w. Lambert Orkis (pno) Deutsche Grammophon ▲ 445 826-2
Lalo, E.:Sym espagnole, w. S. Ozawa (cnd), French National Orch EMI Classics 3-▲ CDMC 69878
Lalo, E.:Sym espagnole, w. S. Ozawa (cnd), French National Orch EMI Classics ▲ CDC 47318 [DDD]
Lutoslawski, W.:Chain 2, w. W. Lutoslawski (cnd), BBC SO Deutsche Grammophon ▲ 423696-2 [DDD]
Lutoslawski, W.:Partita Vn, Orch & Obbligato Pno, w. Phillip Moll (pno), W. Lutoslawski (cnd), BBC SO Deutsche Grammophon ▲ 423696-2 [DDD]
Mendelssohn, F.:Con in e Vn & Orch, Op. 64, w. H. von Karajan (cnd), Berlin PO Deutsche Grammophon 4-▲ 415565-2 [ADD/DDD]
Moret, N.:En rêve, w. S. Ozawa (cnd), Boston SO Deutsche Grammophon ▲ 431626-2 [DDD] □ 431626-5
Mozart, W.A.:Con 1 Vn, w. N. Marriner (cnd), Academy of St. Martin in the Fields EMI Classics ▲ CDC 54302

Mutter, Anne-Sophie (vn) (cont.)
Mozart, W.A.:Con 2 Vn, w. S. Accardo (cnd), English CO EMI Classics 3-▲ CDMC 69878
Mozart, W.A.:Con 2 Vn, w. R. Muti (cnd), Philharmonia Orch EMI Classics ▲ CDC 47011 [DDD]
Mozart, W.A.:Con 3 Vn, w. S. Accardo (cnd), English CO EMI Classics 3-▲ CDMC 69878
Mozart, W.A.:Con 3 Vn, w. H. von Karajan (cnd), Berlin PO Deutsche Grammophon ▲ 429814-2 [ADD]
Mozart, W.A.:Con 4 Vn, w. R. Muti (cnd), Philharmonia Orch EMI Classics ▲ CDC 47011 [DDD]
Mozart, W.A.:Con 5 Vn, w. H. von Karajan (cnd), Berlin PO Deutsche Grammophon ▲ 429814-2 [ADD]
Mozart, W.A.:Music of, w. Alban Berg Quartet, F. P. Zimmermann (vn), A. Dumay (vn), S. Meyer (cl), R. Vlatkovi (hn), C. Zacharias (pno), *(sels unknown)* EMI Classics ▲ CDC 54165
Mozart, W.A.:Sinf concertante Vn, K.364, w. B. Giuranna (va), N. Marriner (cnd), Academy of St. Martin in the Fields EMI Classics ▲ CDC 54302
Mozart, W.A.:Sons Vn Pno (misc), w. Lambert Orkis (pno)—in e, K.304 Deutsche Grammophon ▲ 445 826-2
Mutter Modern, w. Mutter, Anne-Sophie (vn) Deutsche Grammophon 3-▲ 445487-2
Prokofiev, S.:Con 2 Vn, w. M. Rostropovich (cnd), National SO Washington D.C. Erato ▲ 45708-2
Rihm, W.:Gesungene Zeit, w. J. Levine (cnd), Chicago SO Deutsche Grammophon ▲ 437093-2
Romance, w. Mutter, Anne-Sophie (vn) Deutsche Grammophon ▲ 447070-2
Sarasate, P. de:Zigeunerweisen, w. S. Ozawa (cnd), French National Orch EMI Classics ▲ CDC 47318 [DDD]
Sarasate, P. de:Zigeunerweisen, w. S. Ozawa (cnd), French National Orch, English CO EMI Classics 3-▲ CDMC 69878
Stravinsky, I.:Con Vn, w. P. Sacher (cnd), Philharmonia Orch Deutsche Grammophon ▲ 423696-2 [DDD]
Tchaikovsky, P.:Con Vn, w. H. von Karajan (cnd), Vienna PO *(rec live, Salzburg 1988)* Deutsche Grammophon ▲ 419241-2 [DDD]
Vivaldi, A.:Cons Vn, Op. 8/1-4, "The Four Seasons", w. H. von Karajan (cnd), Vienna PO EMI Classics ▲ CDC 47043
Muzquiz, Ernest (perc)—see ORCHESTRAS & ENSEMBLES Eastman Percussion Ensemble members
Myers, Herbert (curtal fl/rcr/va/shm)—see ORCHESTRAS & ENSEMBLES The Whole Noyse
Myers, Philip (hn)
Barber, S.:Summer Music, w. Jeanne Baxtresser (fl), Joseph Robinson (ob), Stanley Drucker (cl), Judith LeClair (bn) EMI Classics ("Anglo-American Chamber Music" series) ▲ CDC 55400
Schuman, W.:Colloquies Hn, w. Z. Mehta (cnd), New York PO New World ▲ NW 326-2 [DDD]
Myerscough, Nadia (vn)—see ORCHESTRAS & ENSEMBLES Rogeri Trio
Mylnik, Naum Walter (pno)
Khachaturian, A.:Gayane (sels), w. Leonid Kogan (vn)—Sabre Dance [trans. for violin & piano] Russian Disc ▲ RUS 11063 [AAD]
Khachaturian, A.:Song-Poem, w. Leonid Kogan (vn) Russian Disc ▲ RUS 11063 [AAD]
Myong, Seon-Hee (pno)
In Memoriam Pablo Casals, w. Lluís Claret (vc), Barcelona Cello Ensemble Valois ▲ V 4733
Myron, Richard (db)—see also ORCHESTRAS & ENSEMBLES Al Ayre Español, Schönbrunn Ensemble Amsterdam
Mozart, W.A.:Kleine Nachtmusik, w. Smithson String Quartet [period instrs] Smithsonian Collection 5-▲ ND 031
Mozart, W.A.:Kleine Nachtmusik, w. Smithson String Quartet [period instrs] Smithsonian Collection ▲ ND 039
Mysliviček, M. (gtr)
Vivaldi, A.:Con for 2 Mands, w. L. Brabec (gtr), O. Vlček (cnd), Prague CO Supraphon ▲ 10 4126-2 [DDD]
Mytnik, Andrei (pno)
Brahms, J.:Sons Vn (comp), w. Leonid Kogan (vn) Arlecchino ▲ ARL11
Brahms, J.:Son 1 Vn, w. Leonid Kogan (vn) *(rec 1953-63)* Arlecchino ARL
Brahms, J.:Son 2 Vn, w. Leonid Kogan (vn) *(rec 1953-63)* Arlecchino ARL
Strauss, R.:Son Vn, w. Leonid Kogan (vn) *(rec 1953-63)* Arlecchino ARL
Myung-Sok, Yang (piri)
Kim, J.H.:Piri Qt, w. Chung Jae-Guk (piri), Park Jong-Sol (piri), Joseph Celli (ob/E hn) O. O. Discs ▲ 0024
Nabeshima, Motoko (hpd)
Bach, J.S.:Preludium, Fugue & Allegro Hpd, BWV 998 *(rec EMS Studios, Brussels, 1991)* Discover International ▲ DI 920283 [DDD]
Böhm, G.:Hpd Music—Suite in D *(rec EMS Studios, Brussels, 1991)* Discover International ▲ DI 920283 [DDD]
Froberger, J.J.:Hpd Music—Suite in g; Toccata in F *(rec EMS Studios, Brussels, 1991)* Discover International ▲ DI 920283 [DDD]
Kerll, J.C.:Kbd Music—Passacaglia in d *(rec EMS Studios, Brussels, 1991)* Discover International ▲ DI 920283 [DDD]
Kuhnau, J.:Musicalische Vorstellung einiger biblischer Historien—No. 4 in c *(rec EMS Studios, Brussels, 1991)* Discover International ▲ DI 920283 [DDD]
Scheidemann, H.:Hpd Music—Galliarda in D *(rec EMS Studios, Brussels, 1991)* Discover International ▲ DI 920283 [DDD]
Schildt, M.:Kbd Music—Paduana Lachrymae Nach J. Dowland *(rec EMS Studios, Brussels, 1991)* Discover International ▲ DI 920283 [DDD]
Naboré, William (pno)
Cage, J.:Music for Marcel Duchamp *(rec Jan. 1993)* Doron ▲ DRC 3002 [DDD]
Cage, J.:The Perilous Night *(rec Jan. 1993)* Doron ▲ DRC 3002 [DDD]
Hahn, R.:Portraits de peintres Accord ▲ ACD 200592 [DDD]
Ives, C.:Three-Page Son *(rec Jan. 1993)* Doron ▲ DRC 3002 [DDD]
Poulenc, F.:L'Histoire de Babar, w. Caroline Gautier (nar) Accord ▲ ACD 200592 [DDD]
Saint-Saëns, C.:Le Cygne, w. Raphaël Pidoux (vc) Accord ▲ ACD 200592 [DDD]
Satie, E.:Sports et divertissements Accord ▲ ACD 200592 [DDD]
Sessions, R.:Son 3 Pno *(rec Jan. 1993)* Doron ▲ DRC 3002 [DDD]
Naboré, William (prepared pno)
Cage, J.:Bacchanale *(rec Jan. 1993)* Doron ▲ DRC 3002 [DDD]
Nadal, Philippe (vc)
Juon, P.:Chamber Music, w. Claire Vergnory-Mion (cl), Jean-François Benatar (va), Pierre Lenert (va), Hélène Calef (pno)—Trio Miniatures for Cl, Vc & Pno; Son in D for Va & Pno, Op. 15; Divert for Cl & 2 Vas, Op. 34; Trio for Cl, Vc & Pno, Op. 17 REM ▲ REM 311267 [DDD]
Naddeo, Maurizio (vc)—see also ORCHESTRAS & ENSEMBLES Europa Galante
Festa Italiana, w. Barbara Schlick (sop), Fabio Biondi (vn), Pascal Monteilhet (va), Rinaldo Alessandrini (hpd), Concerto Italiano, Europa Galante Opus 111 5-▲ 2001
Leclair, J.-M.:Premier livres de sonates, w. F. Biondi (vn), P. Montelheit (thb), R. Alessandrini (org)—Sons. III, VII, VIII, XI Arcana ▲ ACA 39 [DDD]
Tartini, G.:Sons Vn & Continuo, w. F. Biondi (vn), R. Alessandrini (hpd), P. Montheillet (thb)—5 Sonatas—in g (B g11); in B♭ (B b3); in g (B g10); in A (B A15); in G (B G17) Opus 111 ▲ OPS 59-9205 [DDD]
Veracini, F.M.:Sonate accademiche, w. Fabio Biondi (vn), Rinaldo Alessandrini (hpd), Pascal Monteilhet (tiorba)—Nos. 7 in d, 8 in e, 9 in A, 12 in d; Capriccio in g Opus 111 ▲ OPS 30-138
Vivaldi, A.:Cons Vc, w. F. Biondi (cnd), Europa Galante—RV.407 *(rec Apr. 1993)* Opus 111 ▲ OPS 3086 [DDD]
Vivaldi, A.:Con for 2 Vcs, w. A. Fantinuoli (vc), F. Biondi (cnd), Europa Galante *(rec Apr. 1993)* Opus 111 ▲ OPS 3086 [DDD]
Vivaldi, A.:Sons Vn, w. F. Biondi (vn), R. Alessandrini (hpd), P. Pandolfo (db), R. Lislevand (thb/lt)—Manchester Sons. 1, 2, 3, 6, 8 & 10 Arcana ▲ ACA 4 [DDD]

Naddeo, Maurizio (vc) (cont.)
Vivaldi, A.:Sons Vn, w. F. Biondi (vn), R. Alessandrini (hpd), P. Pandolfo (db), R. Lislevand (thb/lt)—Manchester Sons. 4, 5, 7, 9, 11 & 12 Arcana ▲ ACA 5 [DDD]

Nadelmann, Leo (pno)
Albéniz, I.:Rumores de la caleta APR 2-▲ APR 7025 [AAD]
Beethoven, L. van:Son 10 Pno APR ▲ APR 7026 [AAD]
Chopin, F.:Pno Music (misc)—Polonaise No. 4; Anadante spianato & grande polonaise, Op. 22; Nocturnes Nos. 8, 13 & 19; Mazurkas Nos. 7, 13 & 25; Introduction & Vars. on a German Air; Waltzes Nos. 7, 8 & 13; Ballade No. 3 APR 2-▲ APR 7025 [AAD]
Debussy, C.:Pno Music (misc)—Arabesques Nos. 1 & 2; Minstrels; La cathédrale engloutie; Feux d'artifice; Feuilles mortes; Children's Corner; Estampes APR 2-▲ APR 7025 [AAD]
Haydn, J.:Sons Pno—in E♭, H.XVI/49 APR ▲ APR 7026 [AAD]
Haydn, J.:Son Pno, H.XVII/6, "Andante with Vars" APR ▲ APR 7026 [AAD]
Haydn, J.:Vars Pno, "Six Easy Vars" APR ▲ APR 7026 [AAD]
Mozart, W.A.:Fant Pno, K.396 APR ▲ APR 7026 [AAD]
Mozart, W.A.:Son 10 Pno APR ▲ APR 7026 [AAD]
Ravel, M.:Jeux d'eau APR 2-▲ APR 7025 [AAD]
Ravel, M.:Pavane pour une infante défunte APR 2-▲ APR 7025 [AAD]
Schubert, Franz:Impromptus Pno, D.935 APR ▲ APR 7026 [AAD]
Schubert, Franz:Son Pno, D.960 APR ▲ APR 7026 [AAD]

Naegele, Philipp (va)
Brahms, J.:Sextet Strs, Op. 36, w. P. Carmirelli (vn), J. Toth (vn), C. Levine (va), F. Arico (vc), D. Reichenberger (vc) Sony Classical ▲ SMK 46249 [ADD] ■ SMT 46249
Nielsen, C.:Qnt Strs, w. Kontra String Quartet BIS 2-▲ CD 503/04 [DDD]
Schubert, Franz:Qnt Pno, D.667, w. R. Serkin (pno), J. Laredo (vn), L. Parnas (vc), J. Levine (db) *(rec 1967)* Sony Classical ▲ SMK 46252 [ADD]

Naegele, Philipp (vn)
Spohr, L.:Son Vn Hp, Op. 113, w. Giselle Herbert (hp) Bayer ▲ 100264 [DDD]
Spohr, L.:Son Vn Hp, Op. 115, w. Giselle Herbert (hp) Bayer ▲ 100264 [DDD]

Nagae, Yoko (hp)
Debussy, C.:Chansons de Bilitis (recitation), w. A. Lochner (nar), A. Adorjan (fl), M. Larrieu (fl), S. Mildonian (hp), E. Sun (cel) [F] Quantum ▲ QM 6912 [DDD]

Nagai, Yukie (pno)
Beethoven, L. van:Son 14 Pno, "Moonlight Son" BIS ▲ CD 281 [DDD]
Beethoven, L. van:Son 27 Pno BIS ▲ CD 281 [DDD]
Beethoven, L. van:Son 30 Pno BIS ▲ CD 281 [DDD]
Debussy, C.:Images (6) Pno—Set 2 BIS ▲ CD 405 [DDD]
Debussy, C.:Images (6) Pno—Set 1 BIS ▲ CD 371 [DDD]
Debussy, C.:Lindaraja, w. D. Achatz (pno) BIS ▲ CD 526 [DDD]
Debussy, C.:La Mer, w. D. Achatz (pno) [2-piano arr. André Caplet] BIS ▲ CD 526 [DDD]
Debussy, C.:Nocturnes, w. D. Achatz (pno) [2-piano trans. Maurice Ravel] BIS ▲ CD 526 [DDD]
Debussy, C.:Petite suite, w. D. Achatz (pno) BIS ▲ CD 526 [DDD]
Debussy, C.:Preludes Pno—Book 1 BIS ▲ CD 371 [DDD]
Debussy, C.:Preludes Pno—Book 2 BIS ▲ CD 405 [DDD]
Ichiyanagi, T.:Cloud Atlas *(rec Studio 2, Swedish Broadcasting Corporation, Stockholm, Dec 1–3, 1995)* BIS ▲ CD 766 [DDD]
Kako, T.:Poésie *(rec Studio 2, Swedish Broadcasting Corporation, Stockholm, Dec 1–3, 1995)* BIS ▲ CD 766 [DDD]
Miyoshi, A.:Diary—Arabesque of Waves; The Keyboard Sunken; Good Night, Sunset; Waves & the Evening Moon *(rec Studio 2, Swedish Broadcasting Corporation, Stockholm, Dec 1–3, 1995)* BIS ▲ CD 766 [DDD]
Rachmaninoff, S.:Pno Transcriptions, w. Dag Achatz (pno)—Glazunov:Sym No. 6 *(rec Växjö Concert Hall, Sweden, Aug 6–8, 1995)* BIS ▲ CD 746 [DDD]
Rachmaninoff, S.:The Rock, w. Dag Achatz (pno) [trans Rachmaninoff for Pno Duo] *(rec Växjö Concert Hall, Sweden, Aug 6–8, 1995)* BIS ▲ CD 746 [DDD]
Ravel, M.:Boléro, w. D. Achatz (pno) [piano duet version] BIS ▲ CD 489 [DDD]
Ravel, M.:Con Pno (left hand), w. J. Hirokami (cnd), Malmö SO *(rec Malmö Concert Hall, Sweden, Jan. 28, 1994)* BIS ▲ CD 666 [DDD]
Ravel, M.:Con in G Pno, w. J. Hirokami (cnd), Malmö SO *(rec Malmö Concert Hall, Sweden, Jan. 11, 1991)* BIS ▲ CD 666 [DDD]
Ravel, M.:Daphnis et Chloé (suite 2), w. D. Achatz (pno) [2-piano trans. by Lucien Garbon & Dag Achatz] BIS ▲ CD 489 [DDD]
Ravel, M.:Gaspard de la nuit *(rec Järvenpää Hall, Finland, Oct. 24–25, 1994)* BIS ▲ CD 666 [DDD]
Ravel, M.:Ma mère l'oye Pno, w. D. Achatz (pno) BIS ▲ CD 489 [DDD]
Ravel, M.:Miroirs BIS ▲ CD 246 [DDD]
Ravel, M.:Pavane pour une infante défunte *(rec Järvenpää Hall, Finland, Oct. 24–25, 1994)* BIS ▲ CD 666 [DDD]
Ravel, M.:Rapsodie espagnole, w. D. Achatz (pno) [Ravel's two-piano arr.] BIS ▲ CD 489 [DDD]
Scriabin, A.:Sym 4, w. Dag Achatz (pno) [trans Leon Conus for Pno Duo] *(rec Växjö Concert Hall, Sweden, Aug 6–8, 1995)* BIS ▲ CD 746 [DDD]
Takahashi, Y.:Kwanju, May 1980 *(rec Studio 2, Swedish Broadcasting Corporation, Stockholm, Dec 1–3, 1995)* BIS ▲ CD 766 [DDD]
Takemitsu, T.:For Away *(rec Studio 2, Swedish Broadcasting Corporation, Stockholm, Dec 1–3, 1995)* BIS ▲ CD 766 [DDD]
Takemitsu, T.:Rain Tree Sketch *(rec Studio 2, Swedish Broadcasting Corporation, Stockholm, Dec 1–3, 1995)* BIS ▲ CD 766 [DDD]
Tchaikovsky, P.:Sleeping Beauty (sels), w. D. Achatz (pno) [arr. Rachmaninoff for 2 pianos] *(rec Oct. 9–12, 1993)* BIS ▲ CD 627 [DDD]
Tchaikovsky, P.:Swan Lake (sels), w. D. Achatz (pno) [arr. for 2 pianos Debussy] *(rec Oct. 9–12, 1993)* BIS ▲ CD 627 [DDD]
Tchaikovsky, P.:Sym 5, w. D. Achatz (pno) [arr. Taneyev for 2 pianos] *(rec Oct. 9–12, 1993)* BIS ▲ CD 627 [DDD]
Yashiro, A.:Son Pno *(rec Studio 2, Swedish Broadcasting Corporation, Stockholm, Dec 1–3, 1995)* BIS ▲ CD 766 [DDD]

Nagai-Irizuki, (pno)
Ravel, M.:Le Tombeau de Couperin BIS ▲ CD 246

Naganuma, Yuriko (vn)
Pergolesi, G.B.:Con Vn, w. J.-W. Audoli (cnd), Audoli Instrumental Ensemble Arion ▲ ARN 68026 [DDD]

Nagaoka, Sumiko (pno)
Beethoven, L. van:Son 8 Pno, "Pathétique" *(rec July 28–29, 1992)* Canal Grande ▲ CG 9219 [DDD]
Beethoven, L. van:Son 21 Pno, "Waldstein" *(rec July 28–29, 1992)* Canal Grande ▲ CG 9219 [DDD]
Beethoven, L. van:Son 31 Pno *(rec July 28–29, 1992)* Canal Grande ▲ CG 9219 [DDD]

Nagasako, Mari (hp)
Takemitsu, T.:Music of, w. Y. Nagano Tashi (mez), H. Ibe (gtr), K. Abe (vib), Y. Takahashi (pno), R. Noguchi (fl), M. Hamada (lt), T. Koizumi (picc), S. Ueki (vn), Y. Hattori (vc), R. Stoltzman (cl), P. Serkin (pno), Ozawa, Wakasugi (cnd), Boston SO—Quatrain; Stanza I; Sacrifice; Ring; Valeria; A Flock Descends into the Pentagonal Garden Deutsche Grammophon ("20th Century Classics" series) ▲ 423253-2 [ADD]

Nagasawa, Masumi (hp)
Debussy, C.:Children's Corner, w. Ernestine Stoop (hp) [trans. for 2 hps by Shigeaki Saegusa] *(rec Amsterdam & Utrecht)* Globe ▲ GLO 5144 [DDD]

Nagata, Kuniko (vn)
Tchaikovsky, P.:Music of, w. E. Guilels (pno)—Méditation; Scherzo; Mélody; Sérénade Méloncolique; Valse-Scherzo; Romance; Feuillet d'Album; Chant sans paroles; Valse sentimentale; Chanson d'automne; Andante cantabile; Barcarolle; Chanson Triste Talent ▲ DOM 2910 25 [DDD]

Nagel, Bob (tpt)
Wolpe, S.:Qt Tpt, w. Al Cohn (t sax), Al Howard (perc), Jack Maxin (pno), S. Baron (cnd) *(rec Esoteric Studios, NY, 1954)* Hat Hut ▲ CD 6182 [AAD]

Nagel, Karsten (bn)—see also ORCHESTRAS & ENSEMBLES Roseau Wind Quintet
Strauss, R.:Beauty & the Beast, w. M. Spangenberg (cl) Amati ▲ 9205
Strauss, R.:Duet-Concertino, w. M. Spangenberg (cl), Polish Chamber PO Amati ▲ 9205

Nagel, N. (cl)—see ORCHESTRAS & ENSEMBLES Roseau Wind Quintet

Nagy, András (bn)
Haydn, J.:Diverts for 2 Obs, Hns & Bns, H.II/7, 15, D18, 23 & deest, w. P Pongrácz (ob), B. Hock (ob), A. Medveczky (hn), D. Mesterházy (hn), T. Fülemile (bn) White Label ▲ HRC 155 [ADD]

Nagy, Béla (vn)
Janácek, L.:Concertino Pno, w. Thomas Hlawatsch (pno), Vilmos Oláh (vn), Csaba Babácsi (va), Géza Bánhegyi (cl), Károly Ambrus (hn), István Hartenstein (bn) *(rec Budapest, May 1995)* Naxos ▲ 8.553587 [DDD]
Truscott, H.:Trio Fl, w. Imre Kovács (fl), László Bársony (va) *(rec Alpha-Line Studio, Festetich Castle, Budapest, 1994)* Marco Polo ▲ 8.223727 [DDD]

Nagy, Ferenc (db)
Franck, C.:Messe solennelle, w. Attila Wendler (ten), Dezső Karasszon (org), Andrea Kocsis (hp), Zsolt Moinár (vc), Salomon Kamp (cnd), Debrecen Kodaly Choir Hungaroton ▲ HCD 31579 [DDD]

Nagy, Miklós (hn)—see ORCHESTRAS & ENSEMBLES Budapest Festival Horn Quartet

Nagy, Péter (pno)
Leonidas Kavakos, w. Leonidas Kavakos (vn) Delos ▲ DE 3116 [DDD]
Mendelssohn, F.:Lieder ohne Worte Pno *(rec Jan. 10, 16–17, 1990)* Naxos ▲ 8.550453 [DDD]
Romantic Piano Favorites, w. Nagy, Péter (pno) *(rec Apr. 25–May 6, 1988)* Naxos ▲ 8.550216 [DDD]
Romantic Piano Favorites, Vol. 2 *(rec Sept. 17–21, 1987)* Naxos ▲ 8.550053 [DDD]
Vol. 4 *(rec Dec. 1987 & Jan. 1988)* Naxos ▲ 8.550141 [DDD]
Vol. 8 *(rec Sept. 24–27, 1988)* Naxos ▲ 8.550217 [DDD]
Vol. 10 *(rec Mar. 18–26, 1988)* Naxos ▲ 8.550219 [DDD]

Nagy, Robert (vc)—see ORCHESTRAS & ENSEMBLES Vienna Phil Trio

Najnar, Jiří (va)—see also ORCHESTRAS & ENSEMBLES Kocian String Quartet
Dvořák, A.:Sextet, w. V. Bernasek (vc), Talich String Quartet Calliope ▲ CAL 9217 [DDD]

Najoom, Dennis (tpt)
Sierra, R.:Piezas Características, w. William Helmers (b cl), Catherine Schubilske (vn), Scott Tisdel (vc), Stefanie Jacob (pno), Thomas Wetzel (perc), N. Gittleman (cnd) CRI ▲ CD 724 [DDD]

Nakagawa, Masami (fl)
Hachimura, Y.:Maniera *(rec Hadano City Auditorium July 16, 1982)* Camerata ▲ 32CM 118 [DDD]
Hayashi, H.:Pieces Sop & Fl, w. Yumi Aikawa (sop) *(rec Niiza City Auditorium, May 1, 1985)* Camerata ▲ 32CM 118 [DDD]
Nakagawa, I.:Lied, w. Michiko Takita (koto) *(rec Iruma City Auditorium, Sept. 9, 1987)* Camerata ▲ 32CM 118 [DDD]
Noda, T.:Ecologue, w. S. Yoshihara (perc) Camerata ▲ 32CM 58
Sato, M.:Bleusy Fragments *(rec Niiza City Auditorium, May 1, 1985)* Camerata ▲ 32CM 118 [DDD]

Nakakoji, A. (va)
Shinohara, M.:Tabiyuki, w. A. Ogawa (mez), M. Kakagawa (fl), I. Tsuji (ob), T. Takahashi (cl), K. Okazaki (fagotto), G. Kitamura (tpt), A. Murata (trbn), S. Eiso (perc), S. Ueki (vn), S. Katsuta (vc), M. Komuro (contrabass), K. Komatsu (cnd) *(rec live Casals Hall, Tokyo, Mar. 5, 1994)* Camerata ▲ 30CM 375 [DDD]

Nakamura, A. (shak)
Satoh, S.:Kazeno Kyoku *(rec Aug. 18, 1993)* New Albion ▲ NA 069
Satoh, S.:Kougetsu, w. S. Miyashita (koto) *(rec Aug. 18, 1993)* New Albion ▲ NA 069
Satoh, S.:Sanyou, w. S. Miyashita (koto) *(rec Aug. 18, 1993)* New Albion ▲ NA 069

Nakamura, Hiroko (pno)
Dvořák, A.:Qnt Pno, Op. 81, w. Tokyo String Quartet CBS ▲ MK 44920 [DDD]

Nakamura, Isao (perc)
Lehmann, H.U.:Kammermusik, w. K. Graf (sop), A.-K. Graf (fl), E. Schmid (cl), W. Grimmer (vc) Jecklin ▲ JD 689

Nakanishi, Yoshiyuki (bn)
Hummel, J.N.:Con Bn, w. N. Cleobury (cnd), London Mozart Players ASV ("Quicksilva" series) ▲ ASQ 6159
Mozart, W.A.:Con Bn, w. J. Glover (cnd), London Mozart Players Classics for Pleasure ▲ CDCFP 4484 [DDD]
Stamitz, C.:Con Bn, w. N. Cleobury (cnd), London Mozart Players ASV ("Quicksilva" series) ▲ ASQ 6159
Weber, C.M. von:Andante & Rondo ungarese Bn, w. N. Cleobury (cnd), London Mozart Players ASV ("Quicksilva" series) ▲ ASQ 6159
Weber, C.M. von:Con Bn, w. N. Cleobury (cnd), London Mozart Players ASV ("Quicksilva" series) ▲ ASQ 6159

Nakano, Tetsuya (vl)
18th Century "New Generation" German Flute Music, w. Masahiro Arita (trns fl), Chiyoko Arita (hpd) *(rec Nov. 11–12, 1991 & Feb. 2)* Denon ▲ CO 75025 [DDD]

Nakao, Yoshinori (cl)
Gieseking, W.:Qnt Hn, w. J. Cox (hn), F. Korman (ob), B. Fillmore (bn), K. George (pno) *(rec 8/91)* Centaur ▲ CRC 2122 [DDD]

Nakariakov, Sergei (tpt)
Carmen Fantasy, w. Sergei Nakariakov (tpt), Alexander Markovich (pno) *(rec Teldec Studio, Berlin, Apr. 1994)* Teldec ▲ 94554-2 [DDD]

Nakayama, Hiroshi (va)—see ORCHESTRAS & ENSEMBLES Akiko Tatsumi String Quartet

Nakayama, Kaoru (hp)
Hosokawa, T.:Landscape II, w. Arditti String Quartet Montaigne ▲ MO 782078

Nale, David (pno)
Kurtz, E.:Logo I, w. R. Nunemaker (cl), Continuum Percussion Quartet New World ▲ NW 382-2 [AAD]

Nalin, Giuseppe (ob)—see ORCHESTRAS & ENSEMBLES Ensemble Barocco Padua Sans Souci

Nancarrow, Conlon (pno)
Nancarrow, C.:Studies—Nos. 42, 45a, 45b, 45c, 48a, 48b, 48c, 49a, 49b, 49c *(rec Mexico City, Jan 10 & 12, 1988)* Wergo ▲ WER 60165-50 [DDD]
Nancarrow, C.:Studies—[CD 1] Nos. 1, 2a, 2b, 7, 8, 10, 15, 21, 23, 24, 25, 33, 43, 50; [CD 2] Nos. 9, 11, 12, 13, 16, 17, 18, 19, 27, 28, 29, 34, 36, 46, 47 *(rec Mexico City, Jan 10 & 12, 1988)* Wergo 2-▲ WER 60166/67-50 [DDD]

Nanes, Richard (pno)
Nanes, R.:Con 2 Pno Delfon ▲ CDR 2030 [DDD] ■ KST 2030
Nanes, R.:Grand Etude Delfon ▲ CDR 3040 [DDD] ■ DRS 3040C (D)
Nanes, R.:Nocturnes Delfon ▲ CDR 1015 [DDD] ■ DRS 1015C (D)
Nanes, R.:Prelude & Rhap 5 Delfon ▲ CDR 2030 [DDD] ■ KST 2030
Nanes, R.:Rhap & Fugato Delfon ▲ CDR 3040
Nanes, R.:Sonnets Delfon ▲ CDR 6070 [DDD] ■ KST 6070 (D)

Naoumoff, Emile (pno)
Bassoon Recital, w. Catherine Marchese (bn) Gega ▲ GD 162 [DDD]
Boulanger, N.:Pieces (2) Vc & Pno, w. R. Pidoux (vc) *(rec June 14–17, 1993)* Marco Polo ▲ 8.223636 [DDD]
Boulanger, N.:Songs, w. I. Sabrié (sop), S. Robert (sop), D. Reinhardt (mez)—Lux aeterna [w. O. Charlier (violin) & R. Pidoux (cello)]; Le Couteau *(rec June 14–17, 1993)* Marco Polo ▲ 8.223636 [DDD]
Boulanger, N.:Vers la vie nouvelle *(rec June 14–17, 1993)* Marco Polo ▲ 8.223636 [DDD]
Françaix, J.:Con Hpd, w. J. Françaix (cnd), Saarbrück RSO *(rec 9/88)* Wergo ▲ WER 6198-2 [AAD]
Mozart, W.A.:Con 20 Pno, w. A. Lombard (cnd), Bordeaux-Aquitaine National Orch Forlane ▲ FRL 16626 [DDD]
Mozart, W.A.:Con 24 Pno, w. A. Lombard (cnd), Bordeaux-Aquitaine National Orch Forlane ▲ FRL 16626 [DDD]
Naoumoff, E.:In Memoriam Lili Boulanger, w. C. Marchese (bn) *(rec June 14–17, 1993)* Marco Polo ▲ 8.223636 [DDD]
Rachmaninoff, S.:Pno Music (misc)—Etude-tableaux, Op. 39/4; Polichinelle, Op. 3/4; Preludes in c#, Op. 3/2 & in g, Op. 32/12; Vocalise, Op. 34/14 Thésis ▲ THC 82018

Napper, Susie (vc)—see also ORCHESTRAS & ENSEMBLES Da Sonar Ensemble
Geminiani, F.:The Enchanted Forest, w. Elizabeth Wilcock (vn), Stanley Ritchie (vn), Janet See (fl), Barbara Kallaur (fl), Patrick Wedd (hpd), J.E. Gardiner (cnd), CBC Vancouver SO CBC ▲ 5163 [DDD]

Napper, Susie (vl)
Couperin, F.:Vl Music, w. Margaret Little (vl)—Concerts Nos. 12 & 13 for 2 Vls *(rec Saint-Joseph-de-Rivière-des-prairies Church, Montreal, Nov. 29–30, 1993)* CBC ("Musica Viva" series) ▲ MVV 1082 [DDD]
Marais, M.:Suite 2 for 2 Vls, w. Margaret Little (vl) *(rec Saint-Joseph-de-Rivière-des-prairies Church, Montreal, Nov. 29–30, 1993)* CBC ("Musica Viva" series) ▲ MVV 1082 [DDD]
Sainte-Colombe, M. de:Concerts for 2 B Vls, w. Margaret Little (vl)—Nos. 41 & 44 *(rec Saint-Joseph-de-Rivière-des-prairies Church, Montreal, Nov. 29–30, 1993)* CBC ("Musica Viva" series) ▲ MVV 1082 [DDD]

Nappi, Christopher (perc)
Cage, J.:Music for 4 for Perc, w. K. Grossman (perc), M. Pugliese (perc), W. Trigg (perc) *(rec in concert at Merkin Concert Hall, New York City, 4/4/89)* Mode ▲ 25

Nardeau, Martial (fl)
Music for Flute by Icelandic Composers, w. O. Magnusson (pno) Music from Iceland ▲ ITM 806

Nardo, Angela (vn)—see ORCHESTRAS & ENSEMBLES Ensemble Barocco Padua Sans Souci

Narell, Andy (perc)
Giteck, J.:Callin' Home Coyote, w. John Duykers (ten), Deborah Deloria (db) [E] Mode ▲ 14 ■ 14CS (CrO2)

Näsbom, Pär (vn)—see ORCHESTRAS & ENSEMBLES Winterthur String Quartet

Nasedkin, Alexis (pno)
Glazunov, A.:Con 1 Pno, w. A. Zhuraitis (cnd), USSR Radio-TV Orch Russian Disc ▲ RUS 11 024 [ADD]
Rubinstein, A.:Qnt Pno, w. V. Zverov (fl), V. Sokolov (cl), A. Demim (hn), S. Krasavin (bn) Russian Disc ("The A. Rubinstein Edition" series) ▲ RUS 11 061 [ADD]

Nashman, Laura (fl)
French Connection, w. John Arpin (pno) Pro Arte ▲ CDD 585 [DDD]

Nasillo, Gaetano (vc)
Weichlein, R.:Encaenia musices, w. Gunar Letzbor (vn), Daniel Sepec (vn), Herbert Lindsberger (va), Christoph Bitzinger (va), Michael Oman (vl), Roberto Sensi (vn), Andreas Lackner (nat tpt), Herbert Walser (nat tpt), Norbert Kirchner (hpd/org), G. Letzbor (cnd), Ars Antiqua Austria—Sons. Nos. I in C, II in g, III in a, IV in E, V in C & VI in F Symphonia ▲ SY 93S23

Nasillo, Gaetano (vl)—see ORCHESTRAS & ENSEMBLES Il Parnaso Musicale, Il Desiderio

Nasveld, Robert (pno)
Bruynèl, T.:Brouillard Donemus ▲ NEAR 01 [DDD]
Crumb, G.:Celestial Mechanics (Makrokosmos IV), w. J. Bogaart (pno) Attacca ▲ CD 8740
Crumb, G.:A Little Suite for Christmas:A.D. 1979 Attacca ▲ CD 8740
Crumb, G.:Processional Attacca ▲ CD 8740

Nat, Yves (pno)
Schumann, R.:Con Pno, w. E. Bigot (cnd), *(orch unknown)* Enterprise ("The Piano Library" series) ▲ ENT 181
Schumann, R.:Fantasiestücke Pno, Op. 12 Enterprise ("The Piano Library" series) ▲ ENT 181
Schumann, R.:Faschingsschwank aus Wien Enterprise ("The Piano Library" series) ▲ ENT 181
Schumann, R.:Kinderszenen Enterprise ("The Piano Library" series) ▲ ENT 181

Natochenny, Lev (pno)
Brahms, J.:Qnt Pno, w. Penderecki String Quartet Marquis Classics ▲ MAR 187
Schnittke, A.:Qnt Pno, w. Penderecki String Quartet Marquis Classics ▲ MAR 183
Schubert, Franz:Schwanengesang, w. K. McMillan (bar) Marquis ▲ MAR 151
Schubert, Franz:Son Pno, D.959 Marquis Classics ▲ MAR 187
Schubert, Franz:Songs (misc), w. K. McMillan (bar) Marquis ▲ MAR 151
Shostakovich, D.:Qnt Pno, w. Penderecki String Quartet Marquis Classics ▲ MAR 183

Nátola-Ginastera, Aurora (vc)
Ginastera, A.:Son Vc, w. A. Porugheis (pno) ASV ▲ ASV 865

Nauš, Jiří (trbn)
Purcell, H.:Son Tpt, w. Jaroslav Halíř (tpt), Marek Vajo (tpt), Radek Nemec (tpt), Jan Vobořil (hn), Lubomír Maryška (tuba), Pavel Černy (org), Oldřich Šatava (timp) [trans. F. Antonín Vaigl] *(rec Mirror Chapel of the Prague Klementinum, Mar 26, 1995)* Panton ▲ 811368-2 [DDD]

Navarra, A. (pno)
Saint-Saëns, C.:Le Cygne, w. A. d' Arco (cnd) Calliope ▲ CAL 9854 [ADD]

Navarra, André (vc)
Bloch, E.:Schelomo, w. K. Ančerl (cnd), Czech PO *(rec Feb. 7–9, 1964)* Supraphon ("Collection" series) ▲ 11 0674-2 [ADD]
Bloch, E.:Schelomo, w. K. Ančerl (cnd), Czech PO *(rec 1964)* Supraphon ("Great Artists" series) ▲ 11 1002-2 [AAD]
Bloch, E.:Schelomo, w. K. Ančerl (cnd), Czech PO Supraphon ▲ SUP 111940 [AAD]
Boccherini, L.:Sons (34) Vc, w. Erika Kilcher (pno)—2 sels in A & G *(rec 1981)* Approche ▲ CAL 6673 [ADD]
Boëllmann, L.:Son Vc, w. A. d'Arco (pno) Calliope ▲ CAL 9854 [ADD]
Chopin, F.:Son Vc, w. A. d'Arco (pno) Calliope ▲ CAL 9854 [ADD]
Dvořák, A.:Con Vc, w. F. Stupka (cnd), Prague RSO *(rec ca. 1951)* Multisonic (Prague Spring Collection) ▲ 31 0039-2 [ADD]
Eight Japanese Melodies, w. André Navarra (vc), Annie d'Arco (pno) Calliope ▲ CAL 9818 [ADD]
Elgar, E.:Con Vc, w. J. Barbirolli (cnd), Hallé Orch EMI Classics (Phoenixa) ▲ CDM 63955
Falla, M. de:Suite populaire espagnole vc, w. Erika Kilcher (pno) *(rec 1981)* Approche ▲ CAL 6673 [ADD]
Fauré, G.:Après un rêve, w. A. d'Arco (pno) [cello-piano arr.] Calliope ▲ CAL 9854 [ADD]
Fauré, G.:Elégie, w. A. d'Arco (pno) Calliope ▲ CAL 9854 [ADD]
Fauré, G.:Papillon, w. A. d'Arco (pno) Calliope ▲ CAL 9854 [ADD]
Fauré, G.:Romance Vc, w. A. d'Arco (pno) Calliope ▲ CAL 9854 [ADD]
Fauré, G.:Sérénade, w. A. d'Arco (pno) Calliope ▲ CAL 9854 [ADD]
Granados, E.:Goyescas (intermezzo), w. Erika Kilcher (pno) [trans G. Cassado] *(rec 1981)* Approche ▲ CAL 6673 [ADD]
Kodály, Z.:Adagio Vn, w. Josef Suk (vn), Pierre Fournier (vc), Tatjana Sadovskaja (pno) Praga ▲ PR 250065
Kodály, Z.:Duo Vn & Vc, w. Josef Suk (vn), Pierre Fournier (vc) Praga ▲ PR 250065
Kodály, Z.:Son Vc, Op. 8, w. Pierre Fournier (vc) Praga ▲ PR 250065
Kodály, Z.:Sonatina Vc & Pno, w. Pierre Fournier (vc), Tatjana Sadovskaja (pno) Praga ▲ PR 250065
Locatelli, P.:Son Vc, w. Erika Kilcher (pno) *(rec 1981)* Approche ▲ CAL 6673 [ADD]
Nin, J.:Chants d' Espagne, w. Erika Kilcher (pno) *(rec 1981)* Approche ▲ CAL 6673 [ADD]
Prokofiev, S.:Sym-Con Vc, w. K. Ančerl (cnd), Czech PO Supraphon ("Czech Philharmonic Series") ▲ SUP 111950 [ADD]
Respighi, O.:Adagio con variazioni Vc Orch, w. K. Ančerl (cnd), Czech PO *(rec 1965)* Supraphon ("Great Artists" series) ▲ 11 1002-2 [AAD]
Respighi, O.:Adagio con variazioni Vc Orch, w. K. Ančerl (cnd), Czech PO Supraphon ▲ SUP 111940 [AAD]
Saint-Saëns, C.:Allegro appassionato, w. A. d'Arco (pno) Calliope ▲ CAL 9854 [ADD]
Saint-Saëns, C.:Son 1 Vc, w. A. d'Arco (pno) Calliope ▲ CAL 9818 [ADD]
Saint-Saëns, C.:Son 2 Vc, w. A. d'Arco (pno) Calliope ▲ CAL 9818 [ADD]
Schumann, R.:Con Vc, w. K. Ančerl (cnd), Czech PO *(rec 1964)* Supraphon ("Great Artists" series) ▲ 11 1002-2 [AAD]
Schumann, R.:Con Vc, w. K. Ančerl (cnd), Czech PO ASV ▲ SUP 111940 [AAD]
Schumann, R.:Con Vc, w. K. Ančerl (cnd), Czech PO Supraphon ▲ SUP 111940 [AAD]
Valentini, G.:Son Vc, w. Erika Kilcher (pno) *(rec 1981)* Approche ▲ CAL 6673 [ADD]

Navarre, Randy (sax)
Moss, L.:Saxpressivo Capstone ▲ CPS 8619

Navarro, Manuel Guillén (vn)
Sarasate, P. de:Navarra, w. Gabriel Croitoru (vn), J. Bodmer (cnd), Málaga City Orch [orchd] Regis Tro ▲ RTAC 010/2 [DDD]

Navez, Hugues (gtr)
Vivaldi, A.:Con Gtr, RV.93, w. A. Moglia (cnd), Toulouse National CO Pierre Verany ▲ PVY 730038
Vivaldi, A.:Con Mand, RV.425, w. A. Moglia (cnd), Toulouse National CO Pierre Verany ▲ PVY 730038

Návrat, Václav (s vl)—see ORCHESTRAS & ENSEMBLES Pro Arte Antiqua Prague

Nawra, Ingo (db)
Rossini, G.:Tancredi, w. Veronica Cangemi (sop—Roggiero), Eva Mei (sop—Amenaide), Vasselina Kasarova (mez—Tancredi), Melinda Paulsen (cta—Isaura), Ramón Vargas (ten—Argirio), Harry Peeters (bass—Orbazzano), Janos Maté (vn), Gottfried Greiner (vc), David Syrus (hpd), R. Abbado (cnd), Munich RSO, Bavarian Radio Chorus *(rec Studio 1, Munich, July 17–30, 1995)* RCA Red Seal 3-▲ 09026-68349-2 [DDD]

Neal, Ronald (vn)
Ravel, M.:Intro & Allegro, w. M. Golden (hp), M. Meisenbach (fl), R. McDowall (cl), D. Pettys (vn), D. Hermann (va), G. Manasjan (vc) Centaur ▲ CRC 2114 [DDD]

Neary, Alice (vc)
Tavener, J.:Innocence, w. Patricia Rozario (sop), Leigh Nixon (ten), Graham Titus (bass), Charles Fullbrook (bells), Martin Baker (org), Martin Neary (cnd), Westminster Abbey Choir *(rec Westminster Abbey, May 1–5, 1995)* Sony Classical ▲ SK 66613 [DDD]

Nebois, Joseph (org)
Bach, J.S.:Christmas Oratorio, w. E. Roon (sop), D.H. Braun (mez), E. Majkut (ten), W. Berry (bass), L. Dutoit (echo), B. Seidlhofer (hpd), F. Grossmann (cnd), Vienna SO, Akademie Chamber Choir Vox Box 2-▲ CDX 5096 [ADD]
Bach, J.S.:St. Luke Passion, w. Christiane Sorell (sop), Maura Moreira (alt), Kurt Equiluz (ten), Franz Wimer (bass), G. Barati (cnd), Vienna State Opera Orch, Akademie Chamber Choir Soloists Sarx 2-▲ SRX 2026 [ADD]

Nebolsin, Eldar (pno)
Chopin, F.:Pno Music (misc)—Valse in D♭, Op. 70/3; Grande Valse in A♭, Op. 42 *(rec May 31–June 1, 1993)* London ▲ 440935-2 [DDD]
Chopin, F.:Son Pno, Op. 58 *(rec May 31–June 1, 1993)* London ▲ 440935-2 [DDD]
Liszt, F.:Hungarian Rhaps *(rec May 31–June 1, 1993)* London ▲ 440935-2 [DDD]
Liszt, F.:Pno Music (misc)—Apres une lecture du Dante:Fant. quasi Son. *(rec May 31–June 1, 1993)* London ▲ 440935-2 [DDD]

Nedeltchev, Boris (pno)
Duparc, H.:Son Vc, w. R. Clavreul (vc) Gega ▲ GD 151 [DDD]
Poulenc, F.:Son Vc, w. R. Clavreul (vc) Gega ▲ GD 151 [DDD]
Stoyanov, V.:Con 1 Pno, w. V. Kazandjiev (cnd), Bulgarian SO Gega ▲ GD 107 [DDD]
Vladigerov, P.:Con 3 Pno, w. V. Kazandjiev (cnd), Bulgarian SO Gega ▲ GD 107 [DDD]

Neeley, Marilyn (pno)
Lewis, R.H.:Duetto da Camera, w. Robert Gerle (vn) Albany ▲ TROY 166 [ADD/DDD]

Neely, David (vn)—see ORCHESTRAS & ENSEMBLES Rawlins Piano Trio

Nefedov, Vladimir (db)
Ustvolskaya, G.:Composition 2, w. Igo Propischin (db), Leonid Kolosov (db), Vitalii Goryachev (db), Vladimir Vulih (db), Vyacheslav Kovalenko (db), Alexei Peresipkin (db), Dmitrii Sokolov (db), Valerii Javnertchik (perc), Galina Sandovskaya (pno), O. Malov (cnd) *(rec St. Petersburg Radio House, Jan. 1994)* Megadisc ▲ 7867

Neff, J. (perc)
Harrison, L.:Con in slendro, w. Daniel Kobialka (vn), Machiko Kobialka (pno), James Barbagallo (pno), Patricia Jennerjohn (cel), Don Marconi (perc), R. Hughes (cnd) *(rec 1972)* CRI ▲ CD 613 [ADD]

Negri, R. (pno)
Leoncavallo, R.:Arias, w. F. Tenzi (tenor)—19 unpublished arias Nuova Era ▲ NUO 7178 [DDD]

Negro, Lucia (pno)
Berwald, F.:Trios, w. B. Lysell (vn), O. Karlsson (vc)—No. 3 Musica Sveciae ▲ MSCD 521 [DDD]
Brahms, J.:Duets, Op. 28, w. Edith Thallaug (alt), Erland Hagegard (bar) *(rec Nacka Aula, Nacka, Sweden, 1976)* BIS ▲ CD 77 [AAD]
Brahms, J.:Duets, Op. 28, w. E. Thallaug (alt), E. Hagegård (ten) *(rec Nacka Aula, Nacka Sweden, Dec. 20–22, 1976)* BIS ▲ CD 70 [AAD]
Brahms, J.:Vars on an Original Theme *(rec Nacka Aula, Nacka Sweden, Dec. 20–22, 1976)* BIS ▲ CD 70 [AAD]
Dorothy Dorow, w. Dorothy Dorow (sop), Gunilla von Bahr (fl) BIS ▲ CD 45 [AAD]
Martin, F.:Étude de lecture *(rec Nacka Aula, Nacka, Sweden, Oct 10, 1976)* BIS ▲ CD 71 [AAD]
Martin, F.:Preludes *(rec Nacka Aula, Nacka, Sweden, Oct 10, 1976)* BIS ▲ CD 71 [AAD]
Mendelssohn, F.:Vars sérieuses *(rec Nacka Aula, Nacka, Sweden, 1976)* BIS ▲ CD 71 [AAD]
Schumann, R.:Fant Pno MAP ▲ MAPCD 9130
Schumann, R.:Faschingsschwank aus Wien MAP ▲ MAPCD 9130
Schumann, R.:Kinderszenen MAP ▲ MAPCD 9130
Schumann, R.:Songs, w. Erland Hagegard (bar)—Der Contrabandiste *(rec Nacka Aula, Nacka, Sweden, 1976)* BIS ▲ CD 77 [AAD]
Schumann, R.:Spanisches Liederspiel, w. Märta Schéle (sop), Edith Thallaug (alt), Gösta Winbergh (ten), Erland Hagegard (bar) *(rec Nacka Aula, Nacka, Sweden, 1976)* BIS ▲ CD 77 [AAD]
Shostakovich, D.:Songs Sop, Op. 127, w. J. Delman (sop), E. Dekov (vn), A. Olofsson (vc) [R] BIS ▲ CD 26 [AAD]
Stenhammar, W.:Pno Music (comp solo)—Three Fantasies, Op. 11; Intermezzo; Three Small Piano Pieces; Impromptu; Impromptu-Vals; Allegro con moto ed appassionato; Sensommarnätter (Late Summer Nights), Op. 33 BIS ▲ CD 554 [DDD]

Négyesy, János (elec vn)
Loy, G.:Blood From a Stone *(rec 1992)* Centaur ▲ CRC 2133 [DDD]

Négyesy, János (vn)—see also ORCHESTRAS & ENSEMBLES SONOR Ensemble of Univ of California San Diego members
Bartók, B.:Duos (44), w. P. Nykter (vn) Neuma ▲ 45082 [DDD]
Reynolds, R.:The Ivanov Suite, w. P. Larson (bar), J. Fonville (pic), E. Harkins (tpt), R. Mushabec (vc), S. Schick (perc) New World ▲ 80431-2
Reynolds, R.:Personae, w. R. Steiger (cnd), SONOR Ensemble of Univ of California San Diego Neuma ▲ 450-78 [DDD]
Reynolds, R.:Versions/Stages, w. P. Larson (bar), J. Fonville (pic), E. Harkins (tpt), R. Mushabec (vc), S. Schick (perc) New World ▲ 80431-2
Reynolds, R.:Whispers out of Time, w. Liu (va), P. Farrell (vc), B. Turetzky (db), H. Sollberger (cnd), San Diego SO Ensemble New World ▲ NW 80401-2 [DDD]

Négyesy, János (vn/va)—see ORCHESTRAS & ENSEMBLES SONOR Ensemble of Univ of California San Diego members

Neidenbach-Rahbari, Sohre (sax)
Milhaud, D.:Scaramouche Sax, w. A. Rahbari (cnd), Brussels BRT PO Marco Polo ▲ 8.223374

Neidich, Charles (cl)—see also ORCHESTRAS & ENSEMBLES Mozzafiato, Old Fairfield Academy Orch members
Bland, W.:Qt Fl, Cl, Vn & Pno, w. H. Starreveld (fl), C. Macomber (vn), R. Eckhardt (pno) Bridge ▲ BCD 9013 [DDD]
Brahms, J.:Qnt Cl, w. Juilliard String Quartet Sony Classical 2-▲ S2K 66285
I Carry Your Heart, w. Ruth Ann Swenson (sop), Warren Jones (pno) EMI Classics ▲ CDC 56158
Hummel, J.N.:Qt Cl, w. L'Archibudelli *(rec Schloss Grafenegg, Reitschule, Austria, Sept. 19–22, 1993)* Sony Classical ▲ SK 57968 [DDD]
Mozart, W.A.:Con Cl, Orpheus CO Deutsche Grammophon ▲ 423377-2 [DDD] □ 423377-5
Mozart, W.A.:Con Cl, Orpheus CO Deutsche Grammophon 3-▲ 431665-2 [DDD]
Mozart, W.A.:Qts Cl, w. V. Beths (vn), J. Kussmaul (va), A. Bylsma (vc)—in B♭ after K.378 Sony Classical ("Vivarte" series) ▲ SK 53366 [DDD]
Mozart, W.A.:Qnt Cl, K.581, w. V. Beths (vn), J. Kussmaul (va), A. Bylsma (vc) Sony Classical ("Vivarte" series) ▲ SK 53366 [DDD]

▲ = CD ♦ = Enhanced CD Δ = MD ■ = Cassette Tape □ = DCC

Neidich, Charles (cl) (cont.)
Reicha, A.:Qnt Cl, Op. 89, w. L'Archibudelli *(rec Schloss Grafenegg, Reitschule, Austria, Sept. 19–22, 1993)* Sony Classical ▲ SK 57968 [DDD]
Rossini, G.:Intro, Theme & Vars Cl, Orpheus CO Deutsche Grammophon ▲ 435875–2
Rossini, G.:Intro, Theme & Vars Cl, Orpheus CO Deutsche Grammophon ("Masters" series) ▲ 445569–2
Weber, C.M. von:Concertino Cl, Orpheus CO Deutsche Grammophon ▲ 435875–2
Weber, C.M. von:Con 1 Cl, Orpheus CO Deutsche Grammophon ▲ 435875–2
Weber, C.M. von:Con 2 Cl, Orpheus CO Deutsche Grammophon ▲ 435875–2
Weber, C.M. von:Qnt Cl, w. L'Archibudelli *(rec Schloss Grafenegg, Reitschule, Austria, Sept. 19–22, 1993)* Sony Classical ▲ SK 57968 [DDD]

Neidich, Charles (vn)
Mozart, W.A.:Trio Cl, K.498, w. V. Beths (vn), J. Kussmaul (va), A. Bylsma (vc) Sony Classical ("Vivarte" series) ▲ SK 53366 [DDD]

Neikrug, George (vc)
Mozart, W.A.:Qts Fl, w. R. Siebert (fl), R. Friend (vn), W. Trampler (va) Vox Box 3–▲ CD3X 3003 [ADD]

Neikrug, Marc (pno)
Beethoven, L. van:Sons Vn (comp), w. P. Zukerman (vn) RCA Red Seal 4–▲ 09026–60991–2
Beethoven, L. van:Son 5 Vn, "Spring", w. P. Zukerman (vn) RCA Red Seal ▲ 09026–61561–2
Beethoven, L. van:Son 9 Vn, "Kreutzer", w. P. Zuckerman (vn) RCA Red Seal ▲ 09026–61561–2
Beethoven, L. van:Son 10 Vn, w. P. Zukerman (vn) RCA Red Seal ▲ 09026–61219–2 ■ 09026–61219–4 □ 09026–61219–5
Brahms, J.:Scherzo Vn, w. Pinchas Zukerman (vn) *(rec Manhattan Center Studios, New York, Mar 8, 1993)* RCA Red Seal ▲ 09026–61697–2 [DDD]
Brahms, J.:Sons Cl (comp), w. P. Zukerman (va) RCA Red Seal ▲ 09026–61276–2
Brahms, J.:Sons Vn (comp), w. Pinchas Zukerman (vn) *(rec Manhattan Center Studios, New York, Apr 30 & Aug 14–15, 1992)* RCA Red Seal ▲ 09026–61697–2 [DDD]
Brahms, J.:Songs, Op. 91, w. M. Horne (mez), P. Zukerman (va) [G] RCA Red Seal ▲ 09026–61276–2
Debussy, C.:Son Vn, w. Pinchas Zukerman (vn) RCA Red Seal ▲ 09026–62697–2
Fauré, G.:Son 1 Vn, w. Pinchas Zukerman (vn) RCA Red Seal ▲ 09026–62697–2
Franck, C.:Son Vn, w. Pinchas Zukerman (vn) RCA Red Seal ▲ 09026–62697–2
Mozart, W.A.:Sons Vn Pno (comp), w. P. Zukerman (vn)—K.9, 26, 31, 196 & 547 RCA Red Seal ▲ 09026–60744–2
Mozart, W.A.:Sons Vn Pno (misc), w. P. Zukerman (vn)—K.28, 30, 304 & 526 RCA Red Seal ▲ 09026–60742–2
Mozart, W.A.:Sons Vn Pno (misc), w. P. Zukerman (vn)—K.301, 306 & 378 RCA Red Seal ▲ 09026–60743–2 [DDD]
Mozart, W.A.:Sons Vn Pno (misc), w. P. Zukerman (vn)—K.8, 377, 379 RCA Red Seal ▲ 60447–2 [DDD] ■ 60447–4 (CrO2)
Mozart, W.A.:Sons Vn Pno (misc), w. P. Zukerman (vn)—K.27, 303 & 454 RCA Red Seal ▲ 60740–2 [DDD]
Mozart, W.A.:Vars Vn Pno, K.359, w. P. Zukerman (vn) RCA Red Seal ▲ 60740–2 [DDD]
Mozart, W.A.:Vars Vn Pno, K.360, w. P. Zukerman (vn) RCA Red Seal ▲ 60447–2 [DDD] ■ 60447–4 (CrO2)
Schumann, R.:Fantasiestücke Cl, w. Pinchas Zukerman (vn) RCA Red Seal 2–▲ 09026–68052–2
Schumann, R.:Märchenbilder, w. Pinchas Zukerman (va) RCA Red Seal 2–▲ 09026–68052–2
Schumann, R.:Romances Ob, w. Pinchas Zukerman (vn) RCA Red Seal 2–▲ 09026–68052–2
Schumann, R.:Son 1 Vn, w. Pinchas Zukerman (vn) RCA Red Seal 2–▲ 09026–68052–2
Schumann, R.:Son 2 Vn, w. Pinchas Zukerman (vn) RCA Red Seal 2–▲ 09026–68052–2

Neill, (hp)
Sings Classic Irish Songs, w. Judith Pearce (sgr) Protone ■ CSPR 162

Neill, B. (tpt)
Behrman, D.:Music of, w. T. Kosugi (vn), R. Chatham (tpt), C. Mondshine (sound effects), Jakino (keyboard improvisation)—Interspecies Small Talk (1984); Leapday Night (1983–86); A Traveller's Dream Journal (1988–90) Lovely Music ▲ LCD 1042 [ADD]

Neimann, Edward (pno)
Dresher, P.:This Same Temple, w. Nurit Tiles (pno) Lovely Music ▲ LCD 2011 [ADD]

Neiweem, Ralph (pno)
Brahms, J.:Con 1 Pno, w. Claire Aebersold (pno) [arr. Brahms for Piano 4–Hands] *(rec WFMT Radio, Chicago, IL)* Summit ▲ SMT 184 [DDD]
Brahms, J.:Waltzes Pno, Op. 39, w. Claire Aebersold (pno) *(rec WFMT Radio, Chicago, IL)* Summit ▲ SMT 184 [DDD]

Nejtek, Pavel (db)
Dvořák, A.:Qnt Strs, Op. 77, w. J. Panocha (vn), P. Zejfart (vn), M. Sehnoutka (va), J. Kulhan (vc) Supraphon ▲ SUP 11 1461 [DDD]

Nel, Anton (pno)
Bach & Noodles, w. Harvey Pittel (sax), Gabor Rejto (vc), Levering Rothfuss (pno) Crystal ▲ CD 654
Handel, D.:The Poems of Our Climate, w. Sheryl Woods (sop), Pamela Watson (fl), Brian Delay (gtr), Val Griffen (vc), Jack Brennan (perc), James Culley (perc), Allen Otte (perc), G. Samuel (cnd) Vienna Modern Masters ▲ VMM 2019 [DDD]
Haydn, J.:Sons Pno—Nos. 31 in E, 32 in b, 46 in A♭ & 52 in E♭ MusicMasters ▲ 7023–2–C [DDD]
Jaffe, S.:Double Son for 2 Pnos, w. B. Snyder (pno) *(rec Nov. 22 & 23, 1991)* Bridge ▲ BCD 9047 [DDD]
Liptak, D.:Illusions, w. D. Harman (cl) Gasparo ▲ GS 286
Liptak, D.:Songs Bar & Pno, w. W. Sharp (bar) Gasparo ▲ GS 286
Rodrigo, J.:Pno Music (comp), w. G. Allen (pno)—Suite for Piano (1923); Berceuse d'automne (1923); Cinco piezas infantiles (1924); Preludio al Gallo mañanero, Zarabanda lejana, Pastorale & Bagatela (1926); Berceuse de printemps (1928); Air de Ballet (1930); Serenata española (1931); Sonada de Adios (1935); Cuatra Piezas (1936–38); Tres Danzas de España & Gran Marcha de los Subsecretarios (1941); A l'ombre de Torre Bermeja (1945); Cuatra Estampas Andaluzas (1946–52); El Album de Cecilia (1948); Cinco Sonatas de Castilla (1950–51); Danza de la Amapola (1972); Artadecer (1975); Sonatina para dos Muñecas (1977); Tres Evocaciones (1980–81); Preludio de Añoranza (1987) Bridge 2–▲ BCD 9027 [DAD]
Saint-Saëns, C.:Carnival of the Animals, w. K. Snell (pno), R. Stamp (cnd), Academy of London Orch Virgin Classics ▲ 59533 [DDD]
Saint-Saëns, C.:Pno Music—Allegro appassionata; Bagatelles in E♭ & F; Bourée & Elegie for the Left Hand alone; Caprice sur les Airs de Ballet de Alceste; Etude en forme de Valse; Gavotte in c; Mazurka No. 2; Rhapsodie d'Auvergne; Toccata MusicMasters ▲ 01612–67083–2 [DDD]
Tea Time:A Collection of Favorites for Violin & Piano, w. Mela Tenenbaum (vn) *(rec Purchase College, Recital Hall, Sept 1994)* ESS.A.Y. ▲ 1042 [DDD]

Nel, Rudolf (va)
Brahms, J.:Qt 1 Pno, w. E. Fischer (pno), V. Brero (vn), T. Schürgers (vc) *(rec Berlin, ca. 1939/41, Electrola DB)* Koch Historic ▲ 7701–2 [AAD]

Nell, William (org)
Purcell, H.:Trumpet Tune & Ayre, w. Edward Carroll (tpt) Sony Classical ▲ MLK 62369 [ADD/DDD]

Nelson, Gary Lee (MIDI hn)
Nelson, G.L.:Refractions Opus One ▲ CD 160

Nelson, Jon (tpt)—see ORCHESTRAS & ENSEMBLES Meridian Arts Ensemble

Nelson, M. (pno)
Cummings, B.:Fant Breve, w. S. Parker (pno) *(rec 12/90–1/91)* Crystal ▲ CD 691
Diemer, E.L.:Vars Pno 4–Hands, w. W. Nelson (pno) CRS ▲ CD 8949

Nelson, Mark (tuba)
Calabro, L.:Son–Fant Tuba, w. S. Parker (pno) *(rec 12/90–1/91)* Crystal ▲ CD 691
New England Reveries, w. Mark Nelson (tuba), Sylvia Parker (pno) Crystal ▲ CD 691
Persichetti, V.:Parable 22 Crystal ▲ CD 691
Ross, W.:Escher's Sketches Crystal ▲ CD 691

Nelson, Roger (pno)—see ORCHESTRAS & ENSEMBLES New Performance Group of the Cornish Institute

Nelson, Timothy C. (fl)
Songs around Konrad von Würzburg, w. Andrea von Ramm, Sterling Jones (hp), Christian Schmid–Cadalbert (recitation) Christophorus ▲ CD 74542 [DDD]

Nelson, W. (pno)
Diemer, E.L.:Vars Pno 4–Hands CRS ▲ CD 8949

Nelsova, Zara (vc)
Bloch, E.:Schelomo, w. M. Abravanel (cnd), Utah SO *(rec 1967)* Vanguard Classics ▲ OVC 4047 [ADD]
Dvořák, A.:Con Vc, w. W. Susskind (cnd), St. Louis SO Vox Box 2–▲ CDX 5015 [ADD]
Dvořák, A.:Rondo, w. W. Susskind (cnd), St. Louis SO Vox Box 2–▲ CDX 5015 [ADD]
Dvořák, A.:Silent Woods, w. W. Susskind (cnd), St. Louis SO Vox Box 2–▲ CDX 5015 [ADD]

Nemec, Radek (tpt)
Purcell, H.:Son Tpt, w. Jaroslav Halíř (tpt), Marek Vajo (tpt), Jan Vobořil (hn), Jiří Nauš (trbn), Lubomír Maryška (tuba), Pavel Černy (org), Oldřich Šatava (timp) [trans. F. Antonín Vaigl] *(rec Mirror Chapel of the Prague Klementinum, Mar 26, 1995)* Panton ▲ 811368–2 [DDD]

Nemes, Katalin (pno)
Mendelssohn, F.:Lieder ohne Worte Pno—Opp. 38/2 & 5; 53/3; 62/1 & 6; 85/2 White Label ▲ HRC 149 [ADD]

Németh, Géza (va)—see also ORCHESTRAS & ENSEMBLES Bartók String Quartet
Bartók, B.:Con Va, w. A. Kóródi (cnd), Budapest PO Hungaroton ▲ HCD 31050
Brahms, J.:Qt 1 Pno, w. C. Szabó (pno), P. Kolmós (vn), K. Botvay (vc) *(rec 1972–74)* Hungaroton 2–▲ HCD 11597/98 [ADD]
Brahms, J.:Qt 2 Pno, w. I. Lantos (pno), P. Kolmós (vn), K. Botvay (vc) *(rec 1972–74)* Hungaroton 2–▲ HCD 11597/98 [ADD]
Brahms, J.:Qt 3 Pno, w. S. Falvai (pno), P. Kolmós (vn), K. Botvay (vc) *(rec 1972–74)* Hungaroton 2–▲ HCD 11597/98 [ADD]
Mozart, W.A.:Trio Cl, K.498, w. B. Kovács (cl), F. Rados (pno) White Label ▲ HRC 128 [ADD]

Németh, Zsuzsanna (vn)
Bach, Joh. Christian:Sinf concertante, T.284/6, w. Béla Bánfalvi (vn), Lajos Lencsés (ob), Budapest Strings Capriccio ▲ 10509 [DDD]
Vivaldi, A.:Cons for 2 Vns, w. Béla Bánfalvi (vn), Budapest Strings—in G, RV.516 *(rec Unitarian Church, Budapest, Nov. 1991)* Naxos ▲ 8.553028 [DDD]

Nemirovsky, F. (vc)
Klein, G.:Fant & Fugue, w. M. Kugel (vn), C. Leiman (vn), O. Shiran (vn) Koch International Classics ▲ KIC 7230–2 [DDD]
Klein, G.:Trio Vn, w. O. Shiran (vn), M. Kugel (va) Koch International Classics ▲ KIC 7230–2 [DDD]

Nemish, Douglas (pno)
Debussy, C.:Prélude à l'après-midi d'un faune, w. D. Morel (pno) Analekta ▲ AN 29251
Ravel, M.:La Valse, w. D. Morel (pno) Analekta Fleur de Lys ▲ FL 2 3046
Stravinsky, I.:Pétrouchka, w. D. Morel (pno) Analekta Fleur de Lys ▲ FL 2 3046

Némuth, Pál (fl)
Naudot, J.–C.:Cons Fl, Capella Savaria Hungaroton ▲ HCD 31600 [DDD]

Nenchev, Liudmil (vn)
Bach, J.S.:Brandenberg Con 5, w. João Carlos Martins (pno), Lydia Oshavkova (fl), P. Djurov (cnd), Sofia Soloists CO *(rec Salle Bulgaria, Sofia, Bulgaria, 1996)* Concord Concerto ▲ CCD 42042 [DDD]

Nenoiu, Miltiade (bn)
Vivaldi, A.:Cons Bn, w. Ionescu–Galati Brancusi (cnd), Iasi Moldova Phil CO—Concerti in d, C, a, e; Concerti RV.472 & 501 Electrecord ▲ ELCD 128 [AAD]

Nepalov, Evgeni (ob)
Telemann, G.P.:Cons Ob, w. Pierre Pierlot (ob), Piotr Dubrov (ob), Andrei Abramenkov (vn), Rudolf Barshai (vn), Leonid Poleess (vn), R. Barshaï (cnd), Moscow CO—in B♭ for 3 Obs, 3 Vns & Bc *(rec Salle Wagram, Paris, June 1964)* EMI Classics ▲ CDK 65340 [ADD]

Nerat, Harald (hn)
Mozart, W.A.:Cassation, K.63, w. G. Hölscher (ob), S. Winiarczyk (ob), R. Schnepps (hn), Salzburg CO *(rec March 28–30, 1992)* Naxos ▲ 8.550609 [DDD]
Mozart, W.A.:Cassation, K.99/63a, w. G. Hölscher (ob), S. Winiarczyk (ob), R. Schnepps (hn), Salzburg CO *(rec March 28–30, 1992)* Naxos ▲ 8.550609 [DDD]
Mozart, W.A.:Cassation, K.100/62a, w. G. Hölscher (ob), S. Winiarczyk (ob), R. Schnepps (hn), Salzburg CO *(rec March 28–30, 1992)* Naxos ▲ 8.550609 [DDD]

Neretin, Nicolay (ob)
Ustvolskaya, G.:Octet Obs, w. Piotr Tosenko (ob), Alexander Stang (vn), Olga Ribaltchenko (vn), Valentin Lukin (vn), Nikolay Tkachenko (vn), Valerii Znamenskii (timp), Oleg Malov (pno), O. Malov (cnd) *(rec St. Petersburg Radio House, Oct. & Nov. 1994)* Megadisc ▲ 7865

Neriki, Shigeo (pno)
Brahms, J.:Son in D Vc, w. J. Starker (vc) RCA Red Seal ▲ 09026–60598–2 [DDD]
Popper, D.:Vc & Pno Music, w. J. Starker (vc)—Papillon; Gnomentanz; Wiegenlied; Elfentanz; Spinning Song; Tarantelle; & 14 others Delos ▲ DCD 3065 [DDD]
Rachmaninoff, S.:Son Vc, w. J. Starker (vc) RCA Red Seal ▲ 09026–60598–2 [DDD]
Schumann, R.:Fantasiestücke Cl, w. J. Starker (vc) [cello–piano trans.] RCA Red Seal ▲ 09026–60598–2 [DDD]

Nero, Peter (pno)
Classic Connections, w. Rochester PO [cnd:Peter Nero] Pro Arte ▲ CDS 576 [DDD]
Rodgers, R.:Music of, w. S. Bass (sgr), J. Andrews (sgr), P. Como (sgr), D. Reese (sgr), J. Jones (sgr), N. Luboff (sgr), M. Gold (sgr), N. Walker (sgr), H. Bowen (sgr), V. Damone (sgr), J. P. Morgan (sgr), E. Fisher (sgr), B. Goodman (cl), Ann–Margaret (sgr), Shorty Rogers (sgr), D. Shore (sgr), T. Martin (sgr), M. King (sgr), A. Newley (sgr) RCA ▲ 8590–2 R ■ 8590–4 R

Nesbitt, Dennis (vl)—see also ORCHESTRAS & ENSEMBLES In Nomine Players
Corelli, A.:Sons Vn, Op. 5, w. R. Ricci (vn), I. Keyes (hpd)—Sons. 8, 9, 10, 11 & 12 One–Eleven 2–▲ URS 92030 [ADD]

Nesleny, J. (pno)
Poulenc, F.:Con for 2 Pnos, w. J. R. Crossan (pno), M. Perriere (cnd), Festival SO Janus ■ JAN 1104 (CrO2)

Nester, Kathleen (fl)
Kernis, A.J.:America(n) (Day) Dreams, w. Kim Barber (mez), Mary Rowell (vn), Leslie Tomkins (va), Tonya Tomkins (vc), Robert Black (db), Larry Guy (cl/b cl), John Dent (tpt), Anthony Cecere (hn), Leslie Stifelman (pno), Susan Jolles (hp), Jeffrey Milarsky (perc), M. Barrett (cnd)—A Navajo Blanket; Wednesday at the Waldorf; The Pregnant Dream; The Blue Bottle; "So Long" to the Moon from the Men of Apollo; Epilogue:The Pure Suit of Happiness *(rec Manhattan Center Studios, New York, May 31–June 3, 1995)* New Albion ◆ NA 083CD
Maggio, R.:Qts for 2 Fls & 2 Vcs, w. Bart Feller (fl), Fred Sherry (vc), Jonathan Spitz (vc), B. Lubman (cnd) *(rec St. Peter's Church, Chelsea, New York, May 22, 1995)* CRI ▲ CD 720 [DDD]
Zaimont, J.L.:Dance/Inner Dance, w. Rheta Smith (ob), Theodore Mook (vc) *(rec SUNY Purchase, Theatre C, Jan 8–10 & Feb 20, 1995)* Arabesque ▲ ARA 6667 [DDD]
Zaimont, J.L.:Sky Curtains, w. Daniel Gilbert (cl), Bob Wagner (bn), Lois Martin (va), Christopher Finkel (vc) *(rec SUNY Purchase, Theatre C, Jan 8–10 & Feb 20, 1995)* Arabesque ▲ ARA 6667 [DDD]

Nestor, Gregg (gtr)
Boccherini, L.:Fandango, w. B. Janofsky (hpd) [arr. for guitar & harpsichord] Cambria ▲ CD 1049 [DDD]
Cantares, w. Bartos, Anna (sop) *(rec The Place, NYC)* Town Hall ▲ THCD 44
Castelnuovo–Tedesco, M.:Qnt Gtr & Str Cambria ▲ CD 1049 [DDD]
Debussy, C.:Petite suite, w. *(ensemble unknown)* Cambria ▲ CD 1049 [DDD]
Falla, M. de:Homenaje 'Le tombeau de Debussy' Cambria ▲ CD 1049 [DDD]
Gold, E.:Music of, w. H. Dilworth (sop), F. Benedetti (gtr), R. Gianattosio (pno), Holmby String Quartet—Sonata for Piano (1980); Songs of Love & Parting (1963); Quartet No. 1 for Strings (1948) *(rec 1983 & 1990)* Cambria ▲ CD 1062 [DDD/ADD]
Levitch, L.:Ricordo di Mario (gtr) Cambria ▲ CD 1049 [DDD]
Ravel, M.:Le Tombeau de Couperin, w. *(ensemble unknown)* Cambria ▲ CD 1049 [DDD]

Nestor, Toomas (vn)—see ORCHESTRAS & ENSEMBLES Tallinn String Quartet

Neswick, Bruce (org)
Bruce Neswick Raven ▲ OAR 240 [DDD]
Netanel, Deborah (vc)
Handel, D.:The Tyger, w. Mary Henderson (sop), Sara Lambert Bloom (ob), Gabrielle Robinson (vn), Jina Lee (vn), Rebecca Boughton (va), Mark Butler (pno), C. Zimmerman (cnd) Vienna Modern Masters ▲ VMM 2019 [DDD]
Nettle, David (pno)
Arnold, M.:Con for 2 Pnos, w. Richard Markham (pno), V. Handley (cnd), Royal PO Conifer Classics ▲ 75605-51240-2 [DDD]
Holst, G.:The Planets, w. R. Markham (pno) [2 piano version] Saga Classics ▲ 3346 [AAD]
Nettle & Markham in England, w. Richard Markham (pno) IMP ("Classics" series) ▲ IMP 6700172
Nettle & Markham in France, w. Richard Markham (pno) IMP ("Masters" series) ▲ IMP 6600142
Neubauer, Paul (va)—see also ORCHESTRAS & ENSEMBLES Lincoln Center Chamber Music Society members
Beethoven, L. van:Serenade Fl, Op. 25, w. J. Galway (fl), J. Swensen (vn) RCA Red Seal ▲ 7756-2-RC [DDD] ■ 7756-4-RC
Diamond, D.:Qnt Cl, w. D. Schifrin (cl), W. Trampler (va), H. Cheifetz (vc), W. Lash (vc) *(rec 6 & 7/90)* Delos ▲ 3088 [DDD]
Dohnányi, E. von:Serenade, w. J. Silverstein (vn), G. Hoffman (vc) *(rec Apr. 14, 1993)* Delos ▲ DE 3151 [DDD]
Kernis, A.J.:Still Movement with Hymn, w. Pamela Frank (vn), Carter Brey (vc), Christopher O'Riley (pno) *(rec Florence Gould Auditorium, Seiji Ozawa Hall, Tanglewood, June 19 & 20, 1995)* Argo ▲ 448174-2 [DDD]
Kodály, Z.:Serenade for 2 Vns & Va, w. A. Kavafian (vn), J. Silverstein (vn) *(rec Feb. 22, 1993)* Delos ▲ DE 3151 [DDD]
Loeffler, C.M.:Rhaps, w. A. Vogel (ob), I. Vallecillo (pno) *(rec July 1-4, 1992)* Delos ▲ DE 3136 [DDD]
Porter, Q.:Qnt Cl, w. D. Schifrin (cl), T. Arm (vn), E. Sato (vn), W. Lash (vc) *(rec 6 & 7/90)* Delos ▲ 3088 [DDD]
Schubert, Franz:Qt 12 Strs, w. I. Kavafian (vn), A. Kavafian (vn), F. Sherry (vc) Omega ▲ OCD 1015 [DDD]
Schubert, Franz:Qnt Strs, D.956, w. A. Kavafian (vn), I. Kavafian (vn), L. Parnas (vc), F. Sherry (vc) Omega ▲ OCD 1015 [DDD]
Neuburger, Hans (va)—see ORCHESTRAS & ENSEMBLES Gaudeamus String Quartet
Neufeld, Sharon (va)—see ORCHESTRAS & ENSEMBLES Meaux String Quartet
Neuhaus, Heinrich (pno)
Bach, J.S.:Das wohltemperierte Klavier—Book 1 [Preludes & Fugues Nos. 13-18] *(rec 1951)* Russian Compact Disc ("Talents of Russia" series) ▲ RCD 16244 [ADD]
Beethoven, L. van:Son 14 Pno, "Moonlight Son" *(rec 1950)* Russian Compact Disc ▲ RCD 16245 [ADD]
Beethoven, L. van:Son 17 Pno, "Tempest" *(rec 1946)* Russian Compact Disc ▲ RCD 16245 [ADD]
Beethoven, L. van:Son 24 Pno *(rec 1952)* Russian Compact Disc ("Talents of Russia" series) ▲ RCD 16244 [ADD]
Beethoven, L. van:Son 30 Pno *(rec 1950)* Russian Compact Disc ▲ RCD 16245 [ADD]
Beethoven, L. van:Son 31 Pno *(rec 1947)* Russian Compact Disc ▲ RCD 16245 [ADD]
Chopin, F.:Barcarolle Pno Russian Disc ▲ RUS 15007 [AAD]
Chopin, F.:Con 1 Pno, w. A. Gauk (cnd), All-Union RSO Russian Disc ▲ RUS 15007 [AAD]
Chopin, F.:Impromptus Russian Disc ▲ RUS 15007 [AAD]
Chopin, F.:Nocturnes Russian Disc ▲ RUS 15007 [AAD]
Chopin, F.:Polonaise-fant Russian Disc ▲ RUS 15007 [AAD]
Debussy, C.:Pno Music (misc)—8 Preludes Melodiya ("Russian Piano School" series) ▲ 74321-25174-2
Mozart, W.A.:Rondo Pno, K.511 *(rec 1950)* Russian Compact Disc ("Talents of Russia" series) ▲ RCD 16244 [ADD]
Mozart, W.A.:Son Pnos, w. Stanislav Neuhaus (pno) Melodiya ("Russian Piano School" series) ▲ 74321-25174-2
Mozart, W.A.:Son Pnos, w. S. Neuhaus (pno) *(rec 1950)* Russian Compact Disc ("Talents of Russia" series) ▲ RCD 16244 [ADD]
Prokofiev, S.:Visions fugitives Melodiya ("Russian Piano School" series) ▲ 74321-25174-2
Scriabin, A.:Con Pno, w. N. Golovanov (cnd), All-Union RSO Russian Disc ▲ RUS 15 004 [AAD]
Scriabin, A.:Con Pno, w. N. Golovanov (cnd), Moscow RSO *(rec 1950)* Multisonic ("Russian Treasures" series) ▲ 31 0254
Scriabin, A.:Fant Pno Russian Disc ▲ RUS 15 004 [AAD]
Scriabin, A.:Poèmes Pno (sels) Russian Disc ▲ RUS 15 004 [AAD]
Scriabin, A.:Preludes Pno (misc) Russian Disc ▲ RUS 15 004 [AAD]
Neuhaus, Stanislav (pno)
Mozart, W.A.:Son Pnos, w. Heinrich Neuhaus (pno) Melodiya ("Russian Piano School" series) ▲ 74321-25174-2
Mozart, W.A.:Son Pnos, w. Heinrich Neuhaus (pno) *(rec 1950)* Russian Compact Disc ("Talents of Russia" series) ▲ RCD 16244 [ADD]
Neuhaus, Werner (vn)
Fauré, G.:Qnts Pno & Strs, Opp. 89 & 115, w. J. Eymar (pno), G. Kehr (vn), E. Sichermann (va), B. Braunholz (vc) *(rec 1970)* Vox Box 2-▲ CDX 5073 [ADD]
Neukirchner, Manfred (hn)
Forgotten Romantic Songs, Vol. 1, w. Cornelia Wulkopf (cta), Klaus Schilde (pno) Ars Produktion ▲ FCD 368315 [DDD]
Sacred Horn Music, w. Allgäuer Horn Ensemble, U. Köbl (hn), C. Wulkopf (cta), J. Skudlik (org) Ars Produktion ▲ FCD 368304
Neuman, Maxine (vc)
Fine, V.:Missa Brevis, w. Jan DeGaetani (mez), Eric Barlett (vc), David Finckel (vc), Michael Finckel (vc) CRI ▲ CD 692 [ADD]
Rosner, A.:Son 1 Vc, w. Joan Stein (pno) *(rec SUNY, Stony Brook)* Albany ▲ TROY 163 [DDD]
Shawn, A.:Trio Cl, w. D. Krakauer (cl), A. Shawn (pno) Opus One ▲ CD 157
Neumann, Peter (org)
Brahms, J.:Fugue Org MD + G ▲ MDG 3320598 [DDD]
Brahms, J.:Kyrie, w. Cologne Chamber Choir MD + G ▲ MDG 3320598 [DDD]
Brahms, J.:Missa Canonica, w. Cologne Chamber Choir MD + G ▲ MDG 3320598 [DDD]
Schumann, R.:Mass, w. Cologne Chamber Choir MD + G ▲ MDG 3320598 [DDD]
Neunecker, Marie-Luise (hn)
Mozart, W.A.:Qnt Hn, K.407, w. Mannheim String Quartet Novalis ▲ 150006 [DDD]
Neve, Guido de (vn)
Boeck, A. de:Con Vn, w. F. Devreese (cnd), Royal Flanders PO *(rec Elisabeth Hall, Antwerp, July 1994)* Marco Polo ("Anthology of Flemish Music" series) ▲ 8.223740 [DDD]
Devreese, G.:Con 1 Vn, w. F. Devreese (cnd), Brussels Belgian Radio-TV PO *(rec Brussels, 1993)* Marco Polo ▲ 8.223680 [DDD]
Neve, Leo de (va)
Maes, J.:Con Va, w. G. Oskamp (cnd), Royal Flanders PO *(rec Elisabeth Hall, Antwerp, July 1994)* Marco Polo ("Anthology of Flemish Music" series) ▲ 8.223741 [DDD]
Neves, Wilson das (perc)
Chevalier, C.:Music of, w. Teca Calazans (sgr), Ze-Luis (sgr), Regina Machado (sgr), Nigel Scragg (fl/a sax), Rosihna de Valenca (gtr), Jean-Yves Candela (pno), Regina Machado (perc), Silvano Michelino (perc)—Comme d'habitude; Couleur café; Une histoire d'amour; Les feuilles mortes; Les moulins de mon coeur; Syracuse; Je t'aimerai; Ces petits rien; La valse des lilas; L'absent; Que reste-il de nos amours; Un homme et une femme *(rec Studio Bastille)* Iris ▲ 010 [DDD]
Neveu, Ginette (vn)
Beethoven, L. van:Con Vn, Op. 61, w. H. Rosbaud (cnd), South German RSO *(rec Baden-Baden, Sept. 1949)* Music & Arts 2-▲ CD 837 [AAD]

Neveu, Ginette (vn) (cont.)
Beethoven, L. van:Con Vn, Op. 61, w. H. Rosbaud (cnd), Southwest German RSO Baden-Baden *(rec live, 1949)* Music & Arts ▲ CD 550 (m) [AAD]
Brahms, J.:Con Vn, w. A. Dorati (cnd), Residentie Orch The Hague *(rec The Hague, June 10, 1949)* Music & Arts 2-▲ CD 837 [AAD]
Brahms, J.:Con Vn, w. H. Schmidt-Isserstedt (cnd), North German RSO Acanta ▲ CD 43314 [DDD]
Chausson, E.:Poème Vn, w. C. Munch (cnd), *(orch unknown)* Music & Arts 2-▲ CD 837 [AAD]
Debussy, C.:Son Vn, w. Jean Neveu (pno) Polskie Nagrania Edition ▲ ECD 055
Dinicu, G.:Hora staccato, w. Jean Neveu (pno) Polskie Nagrania Edition ▲ ECD 055
Falla, M. de:La vida breve (interlude & dance 1), w. Jean Neveu (pno)—Dance Polskie Nagrania Edition ▲ ECD 055
Ravel, M.:Pièce en forme de Habanera, w. Jean Neveu (pno) Polskie Nagrania Edition ▲ ECD 055
Ravel, M.:Tzigane, w. C. Munch (cnd), *(orch unknown)* Music & Arts 2-▲ CD 837 [AAD]
Ravel, M.:Tzigane, w. Jean Neveu (pno) Polskie Nagrania Edition ▲ ECD 055
Scarlatesco, I.:Bagatelle, w. Jean Neveu (pno) Polskie Nagrania Edition ▲ ECD 055
Sibelius, J.:Con Vn, w. *(cnd & orch unknown)* Memories 2-▲ MEM CD 3011
Suk, J.:Pieces Vn Pno, w. Jean Neveu (pno) Polskie Nagrania Edition ▲ ECD 055
Neveu, Jean (pno)
Debussy, C.:Son Vn, w. Ginette Neveu (vn) Polskie Nagrania Edition ▲ ECD 055
Dinicu, G.:Hora staccato, w. Ginette Neveu (vn) Polskie Nagrania Edition ▲ ECD 055
Falla, M. de:La vida breve (interlude & dance 1), w. Ginette Neveu (vn)—Dance Polskie Nagrania Edition ▲ ECD 055
Ravel, M.:Pièce en forme de Habanera, w. Ginette Neveu (vn) Polskie Nagrania Edition ▲ ECD 055
Ravel, M.:Tzigane, w. Ginette Neveu (vn) Polskie Nagrania Edition ▲ ECD 055
Scarlatesco, I.:Bagatelle, w. Ginette Neveu (vn) Polskie Nagrania Edition ▲ ECD 055
Suk, J.:Pieces Vn Pno, w. Ginette Neveu (vn) Polskie Nagrania Edition ▲ ECD 055
Neveux, Alain (pno)
Berg, A.:Son Pno Accord ▲ ACD 200852 [DDD]
Schoenberg, A.:Little Pieces Pno Accord ▲ ACD 200852 [DDD]
Schoenberg, A.:Pieces Pno, Op. 11 Accord ▲ ACD 200852 [DDD]
Schoenberg, A.:Pieces Pno, Op. 23 Accord ▲ ACD 200852 [DDD]
Schoenberg, A.:Suite Pno, Op. 25 Accord ▲ ACD 200852 [DDD]
Webern, A.:Vars Pno Accord ▲ ACD 200852 [DDD]
Neville, Peter (mar)
Hames, R.D.:Djurunga, w. Carl Rosman (b cl) Vox Australis ▲ VAST 0192
Newberry, Alfred (vc)
Stainer, J.:The Crucifixion, w. J. Griffett (ten), M. George (bass), S. Vann (cnd), Peterborough Cathedral Choir ASV Quicksilva ▲ ASQ 6100 [ADD]
Newbold, Claire (tpt)—see ORCHESTRAS & ENSEMBLES Brass Ring
Newbold, Emily (fl)
Bach, J.S.:Arias, w. David Gordon (ten), Loretta O'Sullivan (vc), Charlotte Mattax (hpd), G. Funfgeld (cnd), Bethlehem Bach Festival Orch—Ermunter dich [from Cant.180]; Der Ewigkeit [from Cant. 198]; Ach, schlage doch [from Cant. 95]; Benedictus [from Mass in b, BWV 232]; Woferne du [from Cant. 41]; O Seelenparadies [from Cant. 172]; Frohe Hirten [from Christmas Oratorio, BWV 248] *(rec St. Michael's Church, New York City, June 1994)* Newport Classic ▲ NPD 85582 [DDD]
Frederick II:Cons (4) Fl, w. R.A. Clark (cnd), Manhattan CO—No. 4 in D *(rec St. Jean Baptiste Church, New York, Jan 1996)* Helicon Classics ▲ HE 1003
Newdome, Beth (vn)
Mozart, W.A.:Adagio E Hn, w. Patrick McFarland (E hn), David Braitberg (vn), Paul Murphy (va), Dona Klein (vc) [trans Renate Rosenbaltt] Arundax ▲ 21339
Rachmaninoff, S.:Vocalise, w. Patrick McFarland (E hn), David Braitberg (vn), Paul Murphy (va), Dona Klein (vc), Larry LeMaster (vc), Gloria Jones (db) [trans John Wildermuth] Arundax ▲ 21339
Newell, Laura (hp)
Debussy, C.:Son Fl, w. John Wummer (fl), Milton Katims (va) Ambassador ▲ ARC 1013
Newman, Anthony (hpd)
Bach, C.P.E.:Qts (3) Fl, w. E. Zukerman (fl), P. Zukerman (va)—H.538 [fl, vi & fortepno version] BOMR 2-▲ 617505 [DDD] 2-■ 517504 (D)
Bach, J.S.:Brandenburg Con 5, w. E. Zukerman (fl), P. Zukerman (vn), Howard (vc) BOMR 3-▲ 617505 [DDD] 2-■ 517504 (D)
Bach, J.S.:Con Fl, Vn & Hpd, w. E. Zukerman (fl), P. Zukerman (vn), Howard (vc) BOMR 3-▲ 617505 [DDD] 2-■ 517504 (D)
Bach, J.S.:Goldberg Vars Infinity Digital ▲ QK 62582 [DDD]
Bach, J.S.:Jesu bleibet meine Freude Infinity Digital ▲ QK 62385 [DDD]
Bach, J.S.:Sons Vn, w. P. Zukerman (vn)—BWV 1023 BOMR 2-▲ 617505 [DDD] 2-■ 517504 (D)
Bach, J.S.:Suites Orch, BWV 1066-1069, w. A. Newman (cnd), Madeira Festival Orch *(rec Elite Recordings, NYC, 1981)* Allegretto ▲ ACD 8194
Bach, J.S.:Toccata & Fugue Org, BWV 565 Infinity Digital ▲ QK 62385 [DDD]
Falla, M. de:Con Hpd, w. A. Birney (cnd), Pennsylvania Sinfonia Orch members Newport Classic ▲ NC 60017 [DDD] ■ NC 60017 (D)
In Concert, w. Kathleen Battle (sop), Jean-Pierre Rampal (fl), Myron Lutzke (vc), Margo Garrett (pno), John Steel Ritter (pno) *(rec Feb. 24, 1991)* Sony Classical ▲ SK 53106 [ADD] ■ ST 53106
Martin, F.:Petite sym concertante, w. V. Drake (hp), R. Hoca (pno), R. Kapp (cnd), Philharmonia Virtuosi ESS.A.Y ▲ CD 1014 [DDD]
Mozart, W.A.:Kleine Nachtmusik, w. Shanghai String Quartet *(rec Church of the Ascension, New York, Oct 19-22, 1994)* Delos ▲ DE 3173 [DDD]
Scarlatti, D.:Sons Kbd Sony Classical ("Essential Classics" series) ▲ SBK 62654 ■ SBT 62654
Telemann, G.P.:Suite in a Fl, w. A. Newman (cnd), Madeira Festival Orch *(rec Elite Recordings, NYC, 1981)* Allegretto ▲ ACD 8194
Newman, Anthony (hpd/org)
Baroque Duet, w. Kathleen Battle (sop), Wynton Marsalis (tpt), Orch of St. Luke [cnd:John Nelson] Sony Classical ▲ SK 46672 Δ SM 46672 ■ ST 46672
Newman, Anthony (kbd)
Beethoven, L. van:Music of, w. Eileen Farrell (sop), *(other artists unknown)*, Giulini (cnd), *(orchs unknown)*—sels from Syms 5, 7 & 9; Son No. 8 for Pno; sels from Fidelio; plus others Sony Classical ("Greatest Hits" series) ▲ MLK 62681 ■ MLT 62681
Newman, Anthony (org)
Bach, J.S.:Fant & Fugue Org, BWV 542 Helicon Classics ▲ HE 1010
Bach, J.S.:Org Music (misc)—Chorale Preludes (9), BWV 609, 610, 626, 691, 699, 704, 706, 724, 734; Preludes & Fugues (9), BWV 533, 534, 539, 542, 543, 544, 545, 547, 552; Toccata, Adagio & Fugue in C, BWV 564; Toccata & Fugue in F, BWV 540; Toccata & Fugue in d, BWV 565 Vox Box 2-▲ CDX 5013 [ADD]
Bach, J.S.:Org Music (misc)—Passacaglia & Fugue in c, BWV 582; Wer nur den lieben Gott lässt walten, BWV 690; Preludes & Fugues in D, BWV 532, in e, BWV 548, in G, BWV 550, in A, BWV 536, in c, BWV 546, in c, BWV 549, in g, BWV 535, in C, BWV 531, in G, BWV 541; Nun komm' der Heiden Heiland, BWV 599; Was fürcht'st du, Feind Herodes, sehr, BWV 696; Fughetta:Gottes Sohn ist kommen, BWV 703; Christe, du Lamm Gottes, BWV 619; Der Tag, der ist so freudenreich, BWV 605; Toccata & Fugue in d, BWV 538; Ach Gott und Herr, BWV 714; Da Jesus an dem Kreuze stund', BWV 621; Das alte Jahr vergangen ist, BWV 614; Jesus, meine Zuversicht, BWV 728, Fant. & Fugue in c, BWV 537; O Lamm Gottes, unschuldig Vox Box 2-▲ CDX 5100 [ADD]
Bach, J.S.:Passacaglia & Fugue Org Helicon Classics ▲ HE 1010
Bach, J.S.:Preludes & Fugues, BWV 531-552—BWV 531, 532, 535, 539, 541, 543, 548 Helicon Classics ▲ HE 1010
Bach, J.S.:Preludes & Fugues, BWV 531-552—BWV 537, 541 Delos ▲ DCD 3028 [DDD]
Bach, J.S.:Toccata, Adagio & Fugue Org, BWV 564 Helicon Classics ▲ HE 1010

▲ = CD ♦ = Enhanced CD Δ = MD ■ = Cassette Tape □ = DCC

Newman, Anthony (org) (cont.)
Handel, G.F.:Music of, w. Edward Carroll (tpt), New York Trumpet Ensemble—Ov; Bourrée; La Paix; La Rejouissance; Minuets I & II [all from Royal Fireworks Music]; Grand Fugues Nos. 2, 3 & 6 in G, B♭ & c [from Fugues faciles]; Martial Sym [from Belshazzar]; Tpt Ov [from Atalanta]; 2 Marches [from Floridante]; Grand March [from Rinaldo]; March in D [from Hercules]; Chorus & March [from Judas Maccabaeus]; Con in B♭ [from Select Harmony]; Suite in D [from Water Music] *(rec Rye Presbyterian Church, Rye, NY, Sept 1985)* Allegretto ▲ ACD 8205
The Joy of Christmas, w. Chestnut Brass Company [cnd:William Noll], Choral Guild of Atlanta, Choral Guild of Atlanta Brass & Percussion, Benjamin Harms (timp), Walter Huff (org) Sony Classical ▲ SFK 62698 ■ SFT 62698
Poulenc, F.:Con Org, w. A. Birney (cnd), Pennsylvania Sinfonia Orch Newport Classic ▲ NC 60017 [DDD] ■ NC 60017 (D) (CrO2)
Saint-Saëns, C.:Sym 3, w. L. Maazel (cnd), Pittsburgh SO Sony Classical ▲ SK 53979

Newman, Anthony (pno)
Bach, J.C.F:Son Fl, HW.VIII/1-2, w. E. Zukerman(fl)—in D BOMR 3–▲ 617505 [DDD] 2–■ 517504 (D)
Bach, J.S.:A Musical Offering, w. E. Zukerman (fl), P. Zukerman (vn), Howard (vc) BOMR 3–▲ 617505 [DDD] 2–■ 517504 (D)
Jane's Hand:The Jane Austen Songbooks, w. Julianne Baird (sop), Elizabeth Henreckson-Farnum (sop), Lorie Gratis (mez), Daniel Pincus (ten), Philip Anderson (ten), Martil Dillon (ten), Nancy Wilson (bar vn), Peter Segal (bar gtr), Mary Jane Newman (pno/hpd) Vox Classics ▲ VOX 7537 [DDD]
Newman, Anthony:Concertino Pno, w. A. Birney (cnd), Pennsylvania Sinfonia Orch Newport Classic ▲ NC 60017 [DDD] ■ NC 60017 (D)

Newman, Lesley (fl)
Amirov, F.:Pieces (6) Fl, w. Amanda Hurton (pno) Cala ▲ CAL CACD 88026 [DDD]
Feld, J.:Son Fl, w. Amanda Hurton (pno) Cala ▲ CAL CACD 88026 [DDD]
Gubaidulina, S.:Allegro rustico, w. Amanda Hurton (pno) Cala ▲ CAL CACD 88026 [DDD]
Gubaidulina, S.:Sounds of the Forest, w. Amanda Hurton (pno) Cala ▲ CAL CACD 88026 [DDD]
Martinů, B.:Son Fl & Pno, w. Amanda Hurton (pno) Cala ▲ CAL CACD 88026 [DDD]
Taktakishvili, O.:Son Fl, w. Amanda Hurton (pno) Cala ▲ CAL CACD 88026 [DDD]

Newman, Maria (va)
Rózsa, M.:Con Va, w. R. Kaufman (cnd), Nuremberg SO Varèse Sarabande ▲ VSD 5329 [DDD]
Rózsa, M.:Intro & Allegro *(rec Adequate Sound, 1990)* Raptoria Caam ▲ RCD 1005

Newman, Maria (vn)—see also ORCHESTRAS & ENSEMBLES Amelite Consortium, Viklarbo Chamber Ensemble
Matson, S.:i-5, w. A. Shulmann (hp), P. Kent (vn), R. Tischer (va), E. Duke-Kirkpatrick (vc), B. Morgenthaler (db) *(rec Aug. 29–30, 1992)* Audioquest ▲ AQCD 1013
Matson, S.:Steel Chords, w. D. Livingston (gtr), P. Kent (vn), J. Derouin (vn), C. Moussas (vn), R. Tischer (va), E. Duke-Kirkpatrick (vc), B. Morgenthaler (db), S. Matson (cnd) *(rec Aug. 29–30, 1992)* Audioquest ▲ AQCD 1013
Newman, M.:Music of, w. Randy Newman (nar)—The Selfish Giant for Vn & Nar; The Nightingale & the Rose for Vn & Nar Raptoria Caam ▲ RCD 1003

Newman, Mary Jane (org)
Bach, J.S.:Air on the G String, w. Lisa Rautenberg (vn) *(rec Presbyterian Church, Mt. Kisco, NY, Aug 26–27, 1995)* Helicon ▲ HE 1006 [DDD]
Bach, J.S.:Arioso Ob, w. Melanie Feld (ob) [arr ob & org] *(rec Presbyterian Church, Mt. Kisco, NY, Aug 26–27, 1995)* Helicon ▲ HE 1006 [DDD]
Bach, J.S.:Chorale Preludes Org, w. Collegium Brass—BWV 79, Now Thank We All Our God *(rec Presbyterian Church, Mt. Kisco, NY, Aug 26–27, 1995)* Helicon ▲ HE 1006 [DDD]
Bach, J.S.:Fant Org, BWV 572 *(rec Presbyterian Church, Mt. Kisco, NY, Aug 26–27, 1995)* Helicon ▲ HE 1006 [DDD]
Bach, J.S.:Jesu bleibet meine Freude, w. Rich Kelley (tpt) *(rec Presbyterian Church, Mt. Kisco, NY, Aug 26–27, 1995)* Helicon ▲ HE 1006 [DDD]
Bach, J.S.:Sons Vn Hpd, BWV 1014-1019, w. Lisa Rautenberg (vn)—No. 3 in E, BWV 1016:Adagio only [arr vn & org] *(rec Presbyterian Church, Mt. Kisco, NY, Aug 26–27, 1995)* Helicon ▲ HE 1006 [DDD]
Clarke, J.:Tpt Voluntary, w. Ruch Kelley (tpt) *(rec Presbyterian Church, Mt. Kisco, NY, Aug 26–27, 1995)* Helicon ▲ HE 1006 [DDD]
Handel, G.F.:Cons (16) Org, w. M. J. Newman (cnd), New York Musica Antiqua—Op. 4/2 *(rec Presbyterian Church, Mt. Kisco, NY, Aug 26–27, 1995)* Helicon ▲ HE 1006 [DDD]
Handel, G.F.:Royal Fireworks Music, w. Jeffery Milarsky (timp), Collegium Brass [arr Newman for org, 3 tpt & timp] *(rec Presbyterian Church, Mt. Kisco, NY, Aug 26–27, 1995)* Helicon ▲ HE 1006 [DDD]
Handel, G.F.:Serse (sels), w. Rich Kelley (tpt)—Largo *(rec Presbyterian Church, Mt. Kisco, NY, Aug 26–27, 1995)* Helicon ▲ HE 1006 [DDD]
Purcell, H.:Tpt Tune, Z.t678, w. Ruch Kelley (tpt) *(rec Presbyterian Church, Mt. Kisco, NY, Aug 26–27, 1995)* Helicon ▲ HE 1006 [DDD]

Newman, Mary Jane (org/cnd)
Splendor of the High Holydays, w. Stacey Lowe (sop), Russell Ashley (bar), Lisa Rautenberg (vn) *(rec SUNY, Purchase, 1995)* Vox Classics ▲ VOX 7510 [DDD]

Newman, Mary Jane (pno/hpd)
Jane's Hand:The Jane Austen Songbooks, w. Julianne Baird (sop), Elizabeth Henreckson-Farnum (sop), Lorie Gratis (mez), Daniel Pincus (ten), Philip Anderson (ten), Martil Dillon (ten), Nancy Wilson (bar vn), Peter Segal (bar gtr), Anthony Newman (pno) Vox Classics ▲ VOX 7537 [DDD]

Newman, Michael (gtr)—see also ORCHESTRAS & ENSEMBLES Newman/Oltman Guitar Duo
Albéniz, I.:Torre bermeja [trans Tárrega & Llobet] Sheffield Lab ("Salon" series) ▲ SLS 504 [A-D]
Bach, J.S.:Sons & Partitas Vn, BWV 1001-1006 [trans Newman] Sheffield Lab ("Salon" series) ▲ SLS 504 [A-D]
Carulli, F.:Petit Duos, Op. 90, w. Laura Oltman (pno) Sheffield Lab ("Salon" series) ▲ SLS 504 [A-D]
Giuliani, M.:Intro, Theme, Vars & Polonaise, w. Sequoia String Quartet Sheffield Lab ("Salon" series) ▲ SLS 504 [ADD]
Laments & Dances:Music from the Folk Traditions, w. Laura Oltman (gtr) *(rec Feb 7, 13 & 24, 1994)* MusicMasters ▲ 01612-67145-2 [DDD]
Legnani, L.:Intro, Theme, Vars & Finale Sheffield Lab ("Salon" series) ▲ SLS 504 [A D]
Piazzolla, A.:Tango Suite, w. L. Oltman (gtr) MusicMasters ▲ 7071-2 [DDD]
Sainz de la Maza, E.:Campanas del Alba Sheffield Lab ("Salon" series) ▲ SLS 504 [A-D]
Turina, J.:Fandanguillo Sheffield Lab ("Salon" series) ▲ SLS 504 [A-D]

Newnham, H. (ct/perc)
Codax, M.:Cantigas d'amigo (7), w. R. Wilkinson (vielle/rcr), R. Bandt (rcr/fl/psalter/perc), J. Griffiths (lt/gtr morisca) Vox Australis ▲ VAST 005-2
Codax, M.:Music of, w. R. Wilkinson (vielle/rcr), R. Bandt (rcr/fl/psalter/perc), J. Griffiths (lt/gtr morisca)—L'Autrier Jost' una Sebissa; Istanpitta Gaetta; Bel m'es Quant Son Li Fruit Madur; Slatarello Vox Australis ▲ VAST 005-2

Newton, Ivor (pno)
The Early Recordings, 1942-1953, w. Victoria de los Angeles (sop), Gerald Moore (pno), Agrupación de Cámara Barcelona, Ars Musicae Barcelona Testament ▲ SBT 1087
The Farewell Recitals, w. Maria Callas (sop), Giusepe Di Stefano (ten) *(rec Philadelphia & Miami & Cincinnati)* Ornamenti 2–▲ FE 124
Weber, C.M. von:Sons Vn, w. G. Piatigorsky (vc) [arr. by Piatigorsky for cello & piano]—No. 5 in A, J.103 *(rec 1934)* Pearl ▲ PEA 9447 (m) [AAD]

Newton, James (fl)
Red Square Blue Russian Composers, w. Fred Hersch (pno), Toots Thielemans (hmc), Phil Woods (a sax), Erik Friedlander (vc), Steve La Spina (bass), Jeff Hirshfield (drums) Angel ▲ CDC 54743

Newton, Molly (pno)
Cameos, w. Charles Stier (cl) Elan ▲ CD 2246 [DDD]
Winter, w. Molly Newton (pno) Halcyon ▲ HP 30106 [DDD]
Winter, w. Molly Newton (pno) *(rec 1995)* Halcyon ▲ HP 30106 [DDD]

Ney, Elly (pno)
Beethoven, L. van:Con 5 Pno, "Emperor", w. K. Böhm (cnd), Vienna PO Datum 2–▲ DAT 12305 [ADD]

Ney, Elly (pno) (cont.)
Beethoven, L. van:Son 23 Pno, "Appassionata" *(rec live, Berlin 10/28/52)* Melodram ▲ MEL 18015 (m) [AAD]
Beethoven, L. van:Vars on Paisiello's duet "Nel cor più non mi sento", WoO 70 *(rec 1937–41)* Pearl ▲ PEA 9170 [ADD]
Brahms, J.:Con 2 Pno, w. F. Konwitschny (cnd), Leipzig Gewandhaus Orch *(rec live 3/3/55)* Melodram ▲ MEL 18015 (m) [AAD]
Brahms, J.:Con 2 Pno, w. M. Fiedler (cnd), Berlin PO *(rec 1937–41)* Pearl ▲ PEA 9170 [ADD]
Schubert, Franz:Fant Pno, D.760, "Wandererfantasie" *(rec 1937–41)* Pearl ▲ PEA 9170 [ADD]

Ngoc, Stéphane Tran (vn)
Schumann, R.:Son 1 Vn, w. B. Ganz (pno) REM ▲ REM 311218 [DDD]
Schumann, R.:Son 2 Vn, w. B. Ganz (pno) REM ▲ REM 311218 [DDD]

Ngwenyama, Nokuthula (va)—see ORCHESTRAS & ENSEMBLES Delius String Quartet

Nibley, Reid (pno)
Gershwin, G.:Con Pno, w. M. Abravanel (cnd), Utah SO MCA Classics 2–▲ MCAD2-9800
Gottschalk, L.M.:Grande Tarantelle, w. M. Abravanel (cnd), Utah SO *(rec 1962)* Vanguard Classics ▲ OVC 4051 [ADD]
Gottschalk, L.M.:Grande Tarantelle, w. M. Abravanel (cnd), Utah SO *(rec Univ. of Utah, Salt Lake City, Dec. 1962)* Vanguard Classics ▲ SVC 9 [AAD]

Nicholas, M.-A. (vn)
Bach, J.S.:Cons Vn (comp), w. J.-C. Malgoire (cnd), National CO Valois ▲ V 4697
Bach, J.S.:Con for 2 Vns, w. A. Moglia (vn), J.-C. Malgoire (cnd), National CO Valois ▲ V 4697

Nicholls, Chris (vn)
Liszt, F.:Music of, w. Jonathan Ayerst (pno)—Grand Duo con.; Duo [Son.]; Epithalam; Valse Caprice after Schubert [arr. Oistrakh]; Consolation No. 3 [arr. Milstein]; Hungarian Rhap. No. 12 [arr. Joachim]; Mephisto Waltz No. 1 [arr. Milstein]; Valse oubliée [arr. Hubay] Hyperion ▲ CDA 66743

Nicholls, Simon (pno)
Boehm, T.:Compositions Fl, w. Rachel Brown (fl)—Grande Polonaise, Op. 16; First Potpourri of Waltzes on Franz Schubert's & other Favourite Melodies, Op. 18; Fant. on a Schubert Air, Op. 21 Chandos ("Chaconne" series) ▲ CHAN 0565 [DDD]
Schubert, Franz:Intro & Vars Fl on "Tröckne Blumen", w. Rachel Brown (fl) Chandos ("Chaconne" series) ▲ CHAN 0565 [DDD]
Schubert, Franz:Schwanengesang, w. Rachel Brown (fl)—Am Meer [arr. Theobald Boehm for fl & pno] Chandos ("Chaconne" series) ▲ CHAN 0565 [DDD]
Schubert, Franz:Winterreise, w. Rachel Brown (fl)—Gute Nacht; Der Lindenbaum [both arr. Leopold Jansa for fl & pno] Chandos ("Chaconne" series) ▲ CHAN 0565 [DDD]

Nicholson, David (fl)
Davies, P.M.:Strathclyde Con 6, w. P. M. Davies (cnd), Scottish CO Collins Classics ▲ COL 1303 [DDD]

Nicholson, Graham (baroque tpt)
Trumpet Concerti of the Italian Baroque, w. Friedemann Immer (baroque tpt), Werner Ehrhard (vn), Cologne Concerto MD + G ▲ L 3271 [DDD]

Nicholson, Linda (pno)—see also ORCHESTRAS & ENSEMBLES London Fortepiano Trio
Mozart, W.A.:Con 9 Pno, w. N. Kraemer (cnd), Capella Coloniensis Capriccio ▲ 10 621 [DDD]
Mozart, W.A.:Con 12 Pno, w. N. Kraemer (cnd), Cappella Coloniensis Capriccio ▲ 10 622 [DDD]
Mozart, W.A.:Con 13 Pno, w. N. Kraemer (cnd), Cappella Coloniensis LaserLight ▲ 15 871 [DDD]
Mozart, W.A.:Con 13 Pno, w. N. Kraemer (cnd), Cappella Coloniensis Capriccio ▲ 10 623 [DDD]
Mozart, W.A.:Con 18 Pno, w. N. Kraemer (cnd), Cappella Coloniensis Capriccio ▲ 10 622 [DDD]
Mozart, W.A.:Con 21 Pno, w. N. Kraemer (cnd), Capella Coloniensis Capriccio ▲ 10 621 [DDD]
Mozart, W.A.:Con 23 Pno, w. N. Kraemer (cnd), Cappella Coloniensis LaserLight ▲ 15 871 [DDD]
Mozart, W.A.:Con 23 Pno, w. N. Kraemer (cnd), Cappella Coloniensis Capriccio ▲ 10 623 [DDD]

Nicholson, Paul (hpd)—see also ORCHESTRAS & ENSEMBLES Locatelli Trio
Arne, T.:Sons or Lessons (8)—No. 1 Amon Ra ▲ CD-SAR 42 [DDD]
Bach, J.S.:Con Fl, Vn & Hpd, w. Lisa Beznosiuk (fl), Elizabeth Wallfisch (vn), E. Wallfisch (cnd), Orch of the Age of Enlightenment Virgin Classics ▲ CD 45190
Bach, J.S.:Con 3 for 2 Hpds, w. Jane Rogers (va), Jonathan Manson (vc), Purcell Quartet Chandos ("Chaconne" series) ▲ CHAN 0595
Bach, J.S.:Sons Fl, BWV 1030-35, w. R. Canter (ob)—BWV 1030 & 1031 *(rec May 1992)* Amon Ra ▲ CD-SAR 60 [DDD]
Bach, J.S.:Sons Vl, BWV 1027-1029, w. R. Canter (ob)—BWV 1027 *(rec May 1992)* Amon Ra ▲ CD-SAR 60 [DDD]
Bach, J.S.:Sons Vn, w. R. Canter (ob)—BWV 1020 *(rec May 1992)* Amon Ra ▲ CD-SAR 60 [DDD]
Handel, G.F.:Hpd Music—8 Suites for Hpd; 6 Fugues or Voluntaries; Fugues in E & F Hyperion 2–▲ CDA 66931/32

Nicholson, Paul (hpd/virginal)
Philips, P.:Kbd Music—Alamande; Galliard; Aria del Gran Duca; Veni sancte spiritus; Pavana "The first one Philips made"; Pavana Pagget; Gilliarda Pagget; Pavana Dolorosa; Galliarda Dolorosa; Passamezzo Pavana, G. Passamezzo; Fantasia in f; Madrigal Settings:Tirsi [by Marenzio]; Fece da voi [Cavaletta]; Chi fara al cielo [by Striggio]; Amarilli [by Caccini]; Bon jour mon cuer [by Lassus] Hyperion ▲ CDA 66734

Nicholson, Paul (kbd)—see also ORCHESTRAS & ENSEMBLES Locatelli Trio
Arne, T.:Favourite Cons (6)—No. 1 [solo harpsichord version] Amon Ra ▲ CD-SAR 42 [DDD]
Arne, T.:Favourite Cons (6), w. P. Nicholson (cnd), Parley of Instruments—each on organ, harpsichord & piano Hyperion ▲ CDA 66509
Music for Viols, w. Fretwork, C. Wilson (lt), M. Chance (alt) Virgin Classics ▲ CDZ 59691

Nicholson, Paul (org)
Gibbons, O.:The Cryes of London, w. Fretwork, Red Byrd—Cries & Fancies; Fantasias, In Nomines Virgin Classics ▲ CDC 59191
Lawes, W.:Consort Setts, w. Fretwork—Consort Setss à 5—in c & F; Consort Setts à 6—in c & F; Divisions for two bass viols & organ in g; Airs for three lyra viols Virgin Classics ▲ 59021 [DDD]

Nicklin, Celia (ob)
Cowell, H.:Hymn & Fuguing Tune 10, w. N. Marriner (cnd), Academy of St. Martin in the Fields Argo ▲ 417818-2 [ADD]
Mozart, W.A.:Con Ob, K.314, w. J. Glover (cnd), London Mozart Players ASV ▲ ASV 795 [DDD]
Vivaldi, A.:Con Ob Bn, w. G. Sheen (bn), N. Marriner (cnd), Academy of St. Martin in the Fields Philips ▲ 412892-2 [DDD]
Vivaldi, A.:Cons for 2 Obs, w. B. Davis (ob), N. Marriner (cnd), Academy of St. Martin in the Fields—RV.536 Philips ▲ 412892-2 [DDD]

Nickol, Christopher (org)
Bridge, F.:Org Music—6 Pieces; 3 Pieces (1905); Lento [from A Little Organ Book]; 3 Pieces (1935) Priory ▲ PRI 537
Vaughan Williams, R.:Org Music—Prelude & Fugue in c; 2 Org Preludes Founded on Welsh Folk Songs; 2nd Movt [from Sym No. 2]; 3 Pieces Founded on Welsh Hymn Tunes Priory ▲ PRI 537

Nickrenz, Erika (vc)—see ORCHESTRAS & ENSEMBLES Eroica Trio

Nickrenz, Scott (va)—see also ORCHESTRAS & ENSEMBLES Claremont String Quartet
Lerdahl, F.:Waltzes, w. R. Schulte (vn), F. Sherry (vc), D. Palme (db) CRI ▲ CD 580 [ADD/DDD]

Nicolai, Helmut (va)
Bloch, E.:Concertino, w. M. M. Kofler (fl), A. Duczmal (cnd), Amadeus CO *(rec 1990)* CPO ▲ CPO 999096-2 [DDD]

Nicolas, Jean-Pierre (rec)—see ORCHESTRAS & ENSEMBLES Fitzwilliam Ensemble

Nicolas, Marie-Annick (vn)
Brahms, J.:Sons Vn (comp), w. A. Bonatta (pno) Valois ▲ V 4709 [DDD]
Cras, J.:Pieces (4) Vn & Pno, w. Jean-Pierre Ferey (pno) *(rec 1993)* Skarbo ▲ SK 4941 [DDD]
Cras, J.:Suite en Duo, w. Jean-Pierre Ferey (pno) *(rec 1993)* Skarbo ▲ SK 4941 [DDD]
Lemeland, A.:Con funèbre, w. E. Plasson (cnd), Toulouse National CO Skarbo ▲ SKR 3922 [DDD]
Lemeland, A.:Con Vn, w. E. Plasson (cnd), Toulouse National CO Skarbo ▲ SKR 3922 [DDD]
Lemeland, A.:Con 2 Vn, w. E. Plasson (cnd), Toulouse National CO Skarbo ▲ SKR 3922 [DDD]

Nicolet, Aurèle (fl)
Bach, C.P.E.:Cons Fl, w. Leppard, Zinman (cnd), Netherlands CO, English CO—in a, W.166; in B♭, W.167; in A, W.168; in G, W.169 Philips ("Classics" series) 2–▲ 442592-2

INSTRUMENTALISTS 747

Nicolet, Aurèle (fl) (cont.)
Bach, J.S.:Cant 203, w. Dietrich Fischer-Dieskau (bar), Helmut Keller (vn), Irmgard Poppen (vc), Edith Picht-Axenfeld (hpd) EMI Classics ("Baroque" series) ▲ CDK 65729
Bach, J.S.:Partita Fl, BWV 1013 Denon ▲ 7331 [DDD]
Bach, J.S.:Sons Fl, BWV 1030–35, w. C. Jaccottet (hpd), M. Fuijiwara (vc)—BWV 1030, 1032, 1034, 1035 Denon ▲ 7331 [DDD]
Bach, J.S.:Trio Sons Org, BWV 525–530, w. et al.—BWV 530 Denon ▲ 7953 [DDD]
Bach, J.S.:Trio Son for 2 Vns, w. et al. Denon ▲ 7953 [DDD]
Berio, L.:Sequenza I *(rec 1967)* Wergo ▲ WER 6021-2 [AAD]
Boccherini, L.:Qnts Fl, G.419–424, w. Athenaeum Enesco String Quartet—Nos. 1, 5 & 6 Novalis ▲ 150082 [DDD]
Boccherini, L.:Qnts Fl, G.425–430, w. Athenaeum Enesco String Quartet—Nos. 2 & 4 Novalis ▲ 150082 [DDD]
Boehm, T.:Compositions Fl, w. A. Adorján (fl), W. Bennett (fl), U. Burkhard (fl), M. Debost (fl), I. Grafenauer (fl), B. Weber (pno)—works for Flute & Piano *(Andante pastorale, from Souvenir des Alpes; Elegie in A♭, Op. 47; Fantaisie sur un air allemand, Op. 22; Fantaisie in A♭ on a Theme by Schubert; Grande Polonaise in D, Op. 16; Variations on Nel cor più non mi sento)*; works for Flute Ensemble *(Duettino in D, Pièce facile in C & Romanza in F [Nos. 66–68]; plus a six-flute ensemble performance of the 2nd movt. from Boismortier's Flute Concerto No. 1 in G)* *(rec live, Cuvilliés Theater, Munich 11/27/81)* Orfeo ▲ 018821 [DDD]
Danzi, F.:Concertante Fl, w. E. Brunner (cl), J. Faerber (cnd), Württemberg CO Tudor ▲ 702 [ADD]
Franck, C.:Son Vn, w. B. Berman (pno) Titanic ▲ Ti 164 [DDD]
Franck, C.:Son Vn, w. B. Berman (pno) [flute-piano arr.] Tudor ▲ 721 [ADD]
Gossec, F.-J.:Qts Fl, Op. 14, w. Le Nouveau Trio Pasquier *(rec DRS Studio, May 18–19, 1984)* Talent ▲ DOM 291050 [DDD]
Holliger, H.:Scardanelli-Zyklus, w. H. Holliger (cnd), Ensemble Modern, London Voices ECM New Series 2-▲ 78118-21472-2 [DDD]
Honegger, A.:Antigone, w. Heinz Holliger (E hn), John Constable (pno)—sels. [arr. for flute, English horn & piano] *(rec St. John's, London, Oct. 8–11, 1991)* Philips ▲ 434105-2
Honegger, A.:Con da camera, w. Heinz Holliger (E hn), N. Marriner (cnd), Academy of St. Martin in the Fields *(rec St. John's, London, Oct. 8–11, 1991)* Philips ▲ 434105-2
Honegger, A.:Petite Suites, w. Heinz Holliger (E hn), John Constable (pno) *(rec St. John's, London, Oct. 8–11, 1991)* Philips ▲ 434105-2
Kraus, J.M.:Qnt Fl, w. Athenaeum Enesco String Quartet Novalis ▲ 150082 [DDD]
Martin, F.:Pièce brève Fl, w. Heinz Holliger (ob), Ursula Holliger (hp) *(rec St. John's, London, Oct. 8–11, 1991)* Philips ▲ 434105-2
Mercadante, S.:Duetto Concertante, w. Andras Adorjan (fl) Tudor ▲ TUD 763 [DDD]
Mercadante, S.:Fant Fl, w. Andras Adorjan (fl) Aurèle Nicolet (fl) Tudor ▲ TUD 763 [DDD]
Mercadante, S.:La Serenata, w. Andras Adorjan (fl) Aurèle Nicolet (fl), Han-An Liu (hp), Dieter Savelwski (Eng hn), Julius Berger (vc) Tudor ▲ TUD 763 [DDD]
Mercadante, S.:Serenate for 3 Fls, w. Andras Adorjan (fl), Marianne Hendel (fl) Tudor ▲ TUD 763 [DDD]
Mercadante, S.:Trio for 2 Fls, w. Andras Adorjan (fl) Tudor ▲ TUD 763 [DDD]
Milhaud, D.:Son Fl, Cl, Ob & Pno, w. O. Maisenberg (pno), E. Brunner (cl), H. Holliger (ob) Orfeo ▲ 060831
Milhaud, D.:Sonatina Fl, w. O. Maisenberg (pno) Orfeo ▲ 060831
Paporisz, Y.:Florianata Gallo ▲ CD 530 [AAD]
Salieri, A.:Con Fl, w. P. Maag (cnd), Bamberg SO Deutsche Grammophon ("Resonance" series) ▲ 427211-2 [ADD]
Stamitz, A.:Con Fls, w. C. Nicolet (fl), J. Faerber (cnd), Württemberg CO Tudor ▲ 702 [ADD]
Telemann, G.P.:Cants, w. Dietrich Fischer-Dieskau (bar), Helmut Keller (vn), Irmgard Poppen (vc), Edith Picht-Axenfeld (hpd)—Die Hoffnung ist mein Leben EMI Classics ("Baroque" series) ▲ CDK 65729
Vivaldi, A.:Music of, w. Salvatore Accardo (vn), Frederico Agostini (vn), Heinz Holliger (ob), Ida Levin (vn), Massimo Paris (va d'amore), Angel Romero (gtr), Celedonio Romero (gtr), Celine Romero (gtr), Henryk Szeryng (vn), Pinchas Zukerman (vn), Academy of St. Martin in the Fields, English CO, I Musici, Naples Weekly International Soloists, St. Paul CO, Dresden Staatskapelle—The Four Seasons [Winter]; Con in D for Gtr [Largo]; Con in D for Fl, "Il gardellino" [Cantabile]; Con in C for Diverse Insts [Andante molto]; Con in g for Strs [Andante molto]; Con in D for 2 Vns & 2 Vcs [Largo]; Con in g for Ob, Vn, Ww & Strs [Larghetto]; Con in a for Gtr, "L'estro armonico" [Largo]; Con in F for 3 Vns [Andante]; Con in F for Fl [Largo]; Con in d for Va D'Amore [Largo]; Con in E for Vn & Strs, "Il riposo" [Allegro]; Con in G for Ob, Bn & Strs [Largo]; Con in B♭ for Vn & Strs [Largo]; Con in A for Gtr & Strs [Larghetto]; Con in E for Vn & Strs, "L'amoroso" [Allegro]; Con in G for Fl [Largo]; Con in A for Vn [Larghetto]; Con in c for Vn & Strs, "Il sospetto" [Andante]; Con in a for 2 Obs & Strs [Largo]; Con in g for Orch [Largo non molto]; Con in a for Vn [Largo]; Con in C for Ob [Adagio]; Con in g for Fl, "La notte" [Largo] Philips ▲ 454051-2 ■ 454 051-4
Weber, C.M. von:Sons Pno, w. B. Berman (pno) [19th cent. flute-piano arr.]—Son. No. 2 Tudor ▲ 721 [ADD]
Weber, C.M. von:Sons Vn, w. B. Canino (pno) Novalis ▲ 150065 [DDD]
Weber, C.M. von:Trio Fl, w. R. Filippini (vc), B. Canino (pno) Novalis ▲ 150065 [DDD]

Nicolet, Christine (fl)
Bach, J.S.:A Musical Offering, w. et al.—trio sonata section only Denon ▲ 7953 [DDD]
Stamitz, A.:Con Fls, w. A. Nicolet (fl), J. Faerber (cnd), Württemberg CO Tudor ▲ 702 [ADD]

Nicoletti, S. (s sax)—see ORCHESTRAS & ENSEMBLES Il Cortegiano

Nicolosi, Francesco (pno)
Bellini, V.:Pno Music—Capriccio Nuova Era ▲ 6880 [DDD]
Cilea, F.:Son Vc, w. L. Signorini (vc) Nuova Era ▲ NUO 7191 [DDD]
Liszt, F.:Réminiscences de Norma Nuova Era ▲ 6880 [DDD]
Mozart, W.A.:Vars Pno (complete)—K.264, 265, 352, 353 & 398 *(rec Dec. 16–22, 1991)* Naxos ▲ 8.550612 [DDD]
Mozart, W.A.:Vars Pno (complete)—6 Vars. in F, K.54; 8 Vars. in G on the Dutch Song "Laat ons juichen, Batavieren!" by Christian Ernst Graaf, K.24; 7 Vars. in D on the Dutch Song "Willem van Nassau," K.25; 6 Vars. in G on "Mio caro Adone" from Salieri's opera "La fiera di Venezia," K.180; 12 Vars. in C on a Minuet by Johann Christian Fischer, K.179; 12 Vars. in E♭ on the Romance "Je suis Lindor" from Antoine-Laurent Baudron's comedy "Le barbier de Séville," K.354 *(rec Dec. 16–22, 1991)* Naxos ▲ 8.550611 [DDD]
Mozart, W.A.:Vars Pno (complete)—K.455, 460, 500, 573 & 613 *(rec Dec. 16–22, 1991)* Naxos ▲ 8.550613 [DDD]
Rachmaninoff, S.:Variations on a Theme by Chopin Nuova Era ("Ancient Music" series) ▲ NUO 7174 [DDD]
Rachmaninoff, S.:Variations on a Theme by Chopin Nuova Era ▲ NUO 7168 [DDD]
Rachmaninoff, S.:Variations on a Theme by Corelli Nuova Era ▲ NUO 7168 [DDD]
Rachmaninoff, S.:Variations on a Theme by Corelli Nuova Era ("Ancient Music" series) ▲ NUO 7174 [DDD]
Respighi, O.:Adagio con variazioni Vc Pno, w. L. Signorini (vc) Nuova Era ▲ NUO 7191 [DDD]
Thalberg, S.:Fants & Vars on Opera Themes—on La traviata, Op. 78; on Il trovatore, Op. 77; Souvenir de Un ballo in maschera, Op. 81; Souvenir de Rigoletto, Op. 82; Impromptu on Le sieège de Corinthe, Op. 3; on Norma, Op. 12 *(rec Budapest, Nov. 10–14, 1993)* Marco Polo ▲ 8.223367 [DDD]
Thalberg, S.:Fants & Vars on Opera Themes—Fants. on Bellini's La Straniera, Op. 9; I Capuletti, Op. 10; Norma, Op. 12; La Sonnambula, Op. 46; Beatrice di Tenda, Op. 49 Marco Polo ▲ 8.223355 [DDD]
Thalberg, S.:Fants & Vars on Opera Themes—Fants. on Rossini's Semiramide, Op. 51; La Donna del lago, Op. 40; Il Barbiere di Siviglia, Op. 63; Moise, Op. 33 Marco Polo ▲ 8.223366
Thalberg, S.:Fants & Vars on Opera Themes—Fants. on Donizetti's La fille du régiment, Op. 68; Don Pasquale, Op. 67; Lucrezia Borgia, Op. 50; Andante Final on Lucia di Lammermoor, Op. 44; Introduction & Var. on Elisir d'amore, Op. 66 Marco Polo ▲ 8.223365
Thalberg, S.:Fant on Hexameron from Bellini's *La Sonnambula* Nuova Era ▲ 6880 [DDD]

Nicolson, J. (dbl vir/org)
Byrd, W.:Org Music *(rec Emmaus-Kapelle, Hatzfeld/Eder; Community Center, Stonington, CT, Oct. 1991 & 1992)* Titanic ▲ TI 225

Nicolson, J. (dbl vir/org) (cont.)
Byrd, W.:Vir Music *(rec Emmaus-Kapelle, Hatzfeld/Eder; Community Center, Stonington, CT, Oct. 1991 & 1992)* Titanic ▲ TI 225

Nied, Johannes (db)
Holliger, H.:Beiseit, w. David James (ct), Teodoro Anzellotti (acc), Elmar Schmid (cl), H. Holliger (cnd) ECM New Series ▲ 78118-21540-2 [ADD]

Niederhammer, Josef (db)
Mišek, A.:Son 1 Db, w. Marialena Fernandes (pno) Ambitus ▲ 97890 [DDD]
Mišek, A.:Son 2 Db, w. Marialena Fernandes (pno) Ambitus ▲ 97890 [DDD]
Mišek, A.:Son 3 Db, w. Marialena Fernandes (pno) Ambitus ▲ 97890 [DDD]

Niederle, Jan (vn)—see ORCHESTRAS & ENSEMBLES Kubín String Quartet

Niehusmann, Volker (gtr)—see ORCHESTRAS & ENSEMBLES Folkwang Guitar Duo

Nield-Capote, Christine (fl)
Debussy, C.:Son Fl, w. P. McConnell (va), M. Klinko (hp) Audiofon ▲ CD 72036
Ravel, M.:Intro & Allegro, w. M. Klinko (hp), R. Hancock (cl), Miami String Quartet Audiofon ▲ CD 72036
Surinach, C.:Double Con Fl, w. Lucas Drew (db), T.M. Sleeper (cnd), Univ of Miami SO *(rec Maurice Gusman Concert Hall, The University of Miami, Florida, Oct 1993 & Nov 1994)* Centaur ▲ CRC 2256 [DDD]
Surinach, C.:Sinf chica, w. Lucas Drew (db), T.M. Sleeper (cnd), Univ of Miami SO *(rec Maurice Gusman Concert Hall, The University of Miami, Florida, Oct 1993 & Nov 1994)* Centaur ▲ CRC 2256 [DDD]
Surinach, C.:Symphonic Melismas, w. Lucas Drew (db), T.M. Sleeper (cnd), Univ of Miami SO *(rec Maurice Gusman Concert Hall, The University of Miami, Florida, Oct 1993 & Nov 1994)* Centaur ▲ CRC 2256 [DDD]

Nielsen, Bjarne (tpt)
Hansen, T.:Qnt Brass, w. Ketil Christensen (tpt), Mogens Andresen (eup), Keld Jørgensen (trbn), Henning Hansen (Fr hn) *(rec Anneberg Mansion, Denmark, 1983)* Rondo Grammofon ▲ RCD 8350
Jørgensen, A.:Qnt Brass, w. Ketil Christensen (tpt), Mogens Andresen (eup), Keld Jørgensen (trbn), Henning Hansen (Fr hn) *(rec Anneberg Mansion, Denmark, 1983)* Rondo Grammofon ▲ RCD 8350
Langgaard, R.:Ribe Early Morning, w. Ketil Christensen (tpt), Mogens Andresen (eup), Keld Jørgensen (trbn), Henning Hansen (Fr hn) *(rec Anneberg Mansion, Denmark, 1986)* Rondo Grammofon ▲ RCD 8350

Nielsen, Björn Carl (ob)
Nielsen, C.:Qnt Ww, w. James Galway (fl), Niels Thomsen (cl), Jens Tofte-Hansen (bn), Björn Fosdal (hn) *(rec Vangede Church, Copenhagen, Mar 16, 1985)* RCA Red Seal ▲ 07863-56359-2 [ADD]
Roussel, A.:Chamber Music, w. Majken Bjerno (sop), Toke Lund Christiansen (fl), Niels Thomsen (cl), Per Jacobsen (hn), Asger Svendsen (bn), Ketil Christensen (tpt), Anne Søe Hansen (vn), Zwi Carmelli (va), Piotr Zelazny (va), Niels Ullner (vc), Michael Dabelsteen (db), Tine Rehling (hp), Morten Mogensen (pno), Per Salo (pno), Per Jensen (perc)—Divertissement, Op. 6; Trio, Op. 40; Joueurs de Flute, Op. 27; Serenade, Op. 30; Le marchand de sable qui passe, Op. 13; Andante et scherzo, Op. 13; 2 poèmes de ronsard, Op. 26; Aria; Elpenor, Op. 59; Pipe Kontrapunkt 2-▲ KPT 32218 [DDD]
Strauss, R.:Con Ob, w. M. Schønwandt (cnd), Collegium Musicum Kontrapunkt ▲ 32039 [DDD]
Vesth, T.:Music of, w. Jan Sommer (gtr), Nils Sylvest Jeppesen (vc), Per Friman (vn), Gert-Inge Andersson (va), Berit Spaelling (hp), Bent Larsen (fl), Svend Rasmussen (cl), Henrik Simonsen (db)—Cuddling Rain; Waltz the Blue Sea; Kaspers Lullaby; Autumn Sunshine; Red Fox Hunting Tea Party; Off White Eternity; Tartan Fl Danica ▲ DCD 8142

Nielsen, J. (va)—see ORCHESTRAS & ENSEMBLES Vestjysk Chamber Ensemble

Nielsen, Jørgen Hald (pno)
Cello Favorites, Vol. 3, w. Anders Gron (vc) Danica ▲ DCD 8158
Stolarczyk, W.:Earth Air Fire Water, w. Amalie Malling (pno), John Damgaard (pno), Anne Øland (pno), Teddy Teirup (pno), Friedrich Gürtler (pno), Rosalind Bevan (pno), Poul Rosenbaum (pno), Rodolfo Llambias (pno), Bella Horn-Ribera (pno), Anders Riber (pno), Elisabeth Sigurdsson (pno), Thomas Tronheim (pno), Elsebeth Broderson (pno), Erik Kaltoft (pno), Aino Gilemann (pno), Birgit Kjær (pno), Jørgen Thomsen (pno), Gunhild Donslund (pno), Henrik Bo Hansen (pno), Lone Karlsson (pno), Erik Fessel (pno), Lasse Nilsson (pno), Janos Ferenczi (pno), Erik Bach (pno), Axel Momme (pno), Arne de Cros Dich (pno), Sven Micha Slot (pno), Hanne Bramsen Buhl (pno), Lili Olesen (pno), Susannah Carlsson (pno), Ulla Erml (pno), Vagn Sørensen (pno), Leif Greibe (pno), Bodil Krogh (pno), Kirsten Ottosen (pno), Inger Bergenholz (pno), Karsten Gylendorf (pno), Bjønr Elkjær (pno), Jacob Bjørn Jensen (pno), Jørgen Kaad (pno), Anne Marie Hjelm (pno), Carl Ulrik Munk Andersen (pno), Poul Lumbye (pno), Oluf Hildebrandt Nielsen (pno), Joachim Olsson (pno), Peter Pade Ramsøe Jacobsen (pno), Astrid Pollmann (pno), Jette Borsch (pno), Kirsten Karlshøj (pno), Maria Teresa Assing (pno), Allan Dahl Hansen (pno), Johan Hugossen (pno), Tine Fenger Pederson (pno), Arne Jørgen Fæø (pno), Anja Høgsted (pno), Anne Sophie Parbo (pno), Inga Lindmark (pno), Teresa Drabik Stathakis (pno), Anne Ruth Ferenczi (pno), Irene Hasager (pno), Yuka Ichikawa (pno), Birgitte Baur (pno), Malene Thastum (pno), Jens E. Rasmussen (pno), Birgitte Zielke (pno), Claus Zielke (pno), Stefan Kasch (pno), Bin Qiao (pno), Inger Johanne Teirup (pno), Lindy Rosborg (pno), Liisa Heininen (pno), David Højer (pno), Ellen Refstrup (pno), Thomas K. Søorensen (pno), Erik Kure (pno), Michael Rauff (pno), Jan beck Eriksson (pno), Tanja Zapolski (pno), Vibeke Skagbo (pno), Pål Eide Lindtner (pno), Ha-Young Sul (pno), Benedicte Palko (pno), Inke Kesseler (pno), Anne Marie Meineche (pno), Sverre Larsen (pno), Kasper Peter Bach (pno), Elisabetta Eliseo (pno), Olga Magieres (pno), Carl Erik Kühl (pno), Thorkild Borup Nielsen (pno), Valeria Zanini (pno), Lars Stenhoft (perc), Dennis Boel (perc), Winnie Dahlgren (perc), Susanne Vind (perc), Claus Byrith (elec), Anne Marie Storm (elec), J. Ribera (cnd) *(rec live, Koldinghaus Castle, Denmark, May 2, 1996)* Danica ▲ DCD 1996

Nielsen, Lena Bust (fl)—see also ORCHESTRAS & ENSEMBLES Copenhagen Wind Quintet
Jersild, J.:Fant e canto affetuoso, w. Jesper Helmuth Madsen (cl), Hege Waldeland (vc), Sonja Gislinge (hp) Paula ▲ PACD 75 [DAD]

Nielsen, Niels Henrik (org)
Brahms, J.:Choral Music, w. E. Munk (cnd), St. Annae Girls' Choir—Es ist ein Ros' entsprungen; O Welt, ich muss dich lassen; O Welt, ich muss dich lassen [2nd version]; Herzlich tut mich verlangen; Fest- und Gedenksprüche, Op. 109 Canzone ▲ CAN 33007 [DDD]
Lange-Müller, P.E.:Tre Madonnasange, w. E. Munk (cnd), St. Annae Girls' Choir *(rec 1991)* Canzone ▲ CAN 33007 [DDD]
Liszt, F.:Missa choralis, w. Irene Graaner (sop), Else Paaske (alt), Kai Hansen (ten), Michael Hansen (bar), Hans Christian Andersen (bass), Tamás Vetö (cnd), Copenhagen Univ Choir Point ▲ PCD 5075 [ADD]
Tchaikovsky, P.:Sacred Pieces, w. E. Munk (cnd), St. Annae Girls' Choir—3 Pieces *(rec 1991)* Canzone ▲ CAN 33007 [DDD]

Nielsen, Per (tpt)
Albinoni, T.:Con Tpt, Op. 7/2, w. South Jutland SO members Danica ▲ DCD 8095
Haydn, M.:Con Tpt, Hns & Strs, w. South Jutland SO members Danica ▲ DCD 8095
Mozart, L.:Con Tpt, w. South Jutland SO members Danica ▲ DCD 8095
Telemann, G.P.:Cons Tpt, w. South Jutland SO members—in D Danica ▲ DCD 8095
Tessarini, C.:Music of, w. South Jutland SO members—Son in D Danica ▲ DCD 8095
Torelli, G.:Sinf Tpt, w. South Jutland SO members Danica ▲ DCD 8095

Nielsen, Torill (hp)
Jersild, J.:For Sensitive Players, w. Benedikte Johansen (hp) Paula ▲ PACD 75 [DAD]

Niemann, Edmund (pno)—see also ORCHESTRAS & ENSEMBLES Double Edge
Biscardi, C.:Traverso, w. Tara Helen O'Connor (fl) *(rec SUNY Purchase Recital Hall, Feb. 12, 1993)* CRI ▲ CD 686 [DDD]
Chambers, W.M.:Ten Grand, w. Ursula Oppens (pno), Walter Hilse (pno), Bennett Lerner (pno), Nurit Tiles (pno), Aleck Karis (pno), Edmund Niemann (pno), Joseph Kubera (pno), Martin Goldray (pno), Allen Shawn (pno), Elizabeth di Filice (pno), Geisel (cnd) Newport ▲ NPD 85553
Imbrie, A.W.:Three Piece Suite, w. Barbara Allen (hp) *(rec Mar. 14, 1994)* New World ▲ 80441-2
Imbrie, A.W.:To a Traveler, w. Alan R. Kay (cl), Cyrus Stevens (vn) *(rec Sept. 24, 1993)* New World ▲ 80441-2
Kolb, B.:Solitaire, w. J. Haas (vib) New World ▲ 80422-2 [DDD]

748 ▲ = CD ♦ = Enhanced CD Δ = MD ■ = Cassette Tape □ = DCC

Niemann, Edmund (pno) (cont.)
Lang, D.:Music of, w. J. Rozen (elec tuba), D. Lang (nar), N. Tilles (pno), R. Schulte (vn), U. Oppens (pno), L. Vaillancourt (cnd), Le Nouvel Ensemble Moderne—Are You Experienced?; Orpheus Over & Under; Spud; Illumination Rounds CRI ▲ CD 625 [DDD]
Nienstedt, Dörte (rcr)
Ernst, S.:Concertantes Duo, w. Masakazu Nishimine (perc) Vienna Modern Masters ▲ VMM 2018 [DDD]
Niesemann, Michael (ob)
Mozart, W.A.:Con Ob, K.314, Concerto Cologne Capriccio Δ 70375
Niessen, Josef (vn)—see ORCHESTRAS & ENSEMBLES Capella Clementina
Niessen, Michiel (bass lt)
Scarlatti, D.:Sons Kbd, w. T. Satoh (archlt)—Sonatas, K.30, 208, 322, 380, 440, 476 & 481 *(rec 1/90)* Channel Classics ▲ CCS 2291 [DDD]
Niethamer, D. (cl)
Ornstein, L.:Nocturne Cl, w. J. Rinehart (pno) Opus One ▲ 146
Nieuwkoop, Hans van (org)
Breuker, W.:Lost Ground—4 movts NM Classics ▲ NM 92034
Mozart, W.A.:Kleine Nachtmusik, w. J. van Oortmerssen (org) [trans. performers for organ duet] BIS ▲ CD 418 [DDD]
Mozart, W.A.:Sym 40, w. J. van Oortmerssen (org) [trans. Carl Czerny as organ duet] BIS ▲ CD 418 [DDD]
Mozart, W.A.:Vars (from flute quartet), w. J. van Oortmerssen (org) [trans. performers for organ duet] BIS ▲ CD 418 [DDD]
Nigro, Susan (ctbn)
Doran, M.:Movts (4) Db, w. Mark Lindeblad (pno) *(rec AirWave Recording Studios, Chicago)* Crystal ▲ CD 346
Draganski, D.:Heart's Desire, w. Mark Lindeblad (pno) *(rec AirWave Recording Studios, Chicago)* Crystal ▲ CD 346
Muradian, V.:Con Ctbn, w. Mark Lindeblad (pno) *(rec AirWave Recording Studios, Chicago)* Crystal ▲ CD 346
Nicholson, R.:Miniature Suite, w. Mark Lindeblad (pno) *(rec AirWave Recording Studios, Chicago)* Crystal ▲ CD 346
Palider, A.:The Narwhal, w. Mark Lindeblad (pno) *(rec AirWave Recording Studios, Chicago)* Crystal ▲ CD 346
Warren, F.:Music for Ctbn, w. Mark Lindeblad (pno) *(rec AirWave Recording Studios, Chicago)* Crystal ▲ CD 346
Nika, Lelo (acc)
Werner, S.E.:Tango Studies, w. Majken Bell (acc), Heidi Hansen (acc), Carsten Holbek (acc), Hans Jorgen Holbek (acc), Morten Rossen (acc), Anders Vesterdahl (acc) *(rec Danish Accordian Academy, Oct. 1994)* Marco Polo ("dacapo" series) ▲ 8.224006 [DDD]
Nikkanen, Kurt (vn)
Bartók, B.:Romanian Folk Dances Pno, w. R. de Silva (pno) [arr. for violin & piano Zoltán Szekely] *(rec 9/90)* Collins Classics ▲ 12032 [DDD]
Nikolayev, A. (perc)
Babadjanyan, A.:Music of, w. A. Arutiunyan (pno), Arno Babadjanyan (pno), B. Chekmenyov (gtr), A. Tarasov (gtr), Silantiev, Mavisakhalyan (cnd), All-Union Radio-TV Sym Variety Orch, Armenian Radio-TV Orch—Nocturne; Prelude & Vagarshapat Dance; Capriccio; Polyphonic Son; Exprompt; Armenian Rhap; Elegy in Commemoration of A. Khachaturyan; 6 Pictures; Melody & Humoresque; Fant on Give Me My Music Back; Fant on Dum spiro spero; Fant on Winer Love; Fant on Call Me; Piece for the Pno & Orch [Dreams] *(rec 1953–83)* Russian Compact Disc ("Talents of Russia" series) ▲ RCD 16251 [ADD]
Nikolayeva, Tatiana (hpd)
Bach, J.S.:Goldberg Vars *(rec 1970)* Relief ▲ CR 861006 [ADD]
Nikolayeva, Tatiana (pno)
Bach, J.S.:The Art of the Fugue Hyperion 2-▲ CDA 66631/32
Bach, J.S.:Capriccio Departure MK ▲ MKA 418013 [DDD]
Bach, J.S.:Chromatic Fant & Fugue MK ▲ MKA 418013 [DDD]
Bach, J.S.:Duets Hpd, BWV 802–805 MK ▲ MKA 418013 [DDD]
Bach, J.S.:Fants Hpd—BWV 906 MK ▲ MKA 418013 [DDD]
Bach, J.S.:Goldberg Vars Hyperion ▲ CDA 66589
Bach, J.S.:Inventions (30) Hpd—2 Part, BWV 722–786) *(rec Apr 1977)* MK ▲ 418023
Bach, J.S.:Italian Con MK ▲ MKA 418013 [DDD]
Bach, J.S.:Music of—Toccata & Fugue in d, BWV 565; Cantata No. 147 (sels.); Chorale Preludes, BWV 639, 645 & 659; Fugue in g, BWV 578; Chaccone in d, BWV 1004–5; Sonata for Flute, BWV 1031 (sels.) *(rec Apr 1982)* MK ▲ MK 418024 [AAD]
Bach, J.S.:Sinfs—BWV 787–801 *(rec Apr 1977)* MK ▲ 418023
Bach, J.S.:Das wohltemperierte Klavier—Book 1 *(rec May 1984)* MK ▲ 418042
Beethoven, L. van:Sons Pno (comp)—No. 7 in D, Op. 10/3; No. 8 in c, Op. 13, "Pathétique"; No. 9 in E, Op. 14/1; No. 10 in G, Op. 14/2 *(rec live, 1983)* Olympia ▲ OLY 563 [ADD]
Beethoven, L. van:Sons Pno (comp)—Nos. 4–6 Olympia ▲ OLY 562 [ADD]
Beethoven, L. van:Sons Pno (comp)—No. 11 in B♭, Op. 22; No. 12 in A♭, Op. 26; No. 13 in E♭, Op. 27/1; No. 14 in c#, Op. 27/2, "Moonlight" *(rec live, 1983)* Olympia ▲ OLY 564 [ADD]
Beethoven, L. van:Sons Pno (comp)—Nos. 23–27 *(rec live, 1983)* Olympia ▲ OLY 567 [ADD]
Beethoven, L. van:Sons Pno (comp)—Nos. 28 & 29 *(rec live, 1983)* Olympia ▲ OLY 568 [ADD]
Beethoven, L. van:Sons Pno (comp)—Nos. 1–3 Olympia ▲ OLY 561 [ADD]
Beethoven, L. van:Sons Pno (comp)—Nos. 1–17 Olympia 5-▲ OLY 5010 [ADD]
Beethoven, L. van:Sons Pno (comp)—Nos. 30–32 Olympia ▲ OLY 569 [ADD]
Beethoven, L. van:Son 21 Pno, "Waldstein" Novalis ▲ 150101 [DDD]
Beethoven, L. van:Son 23 Pno, "Appassionata" Novalis ▲ 150101 [DDD]
Beethoven, L. van:Vars & Fugue Pno, Op. 35, "Eroica" Olympia ▲ OLY 570 [ADD]
Beethoven, L. van:Vars on a waltz by Diabelli, Op. 120 Olympia ▲ OLY 570 [ADD]
Beethoven, L. van:Vars Pno, WoO 80 Olympia ▲ OLY 569 [ADD]
Borodin, A.:In the Steppes of Central Asia *(rec May 10 & 11, 1991)* Relief ▲ CR 911026 [DDD]
Borodin, A.:Scherzo Pno *(rec May 10 & 11, 1991)* Relief ▲ CR 911026 [DDD]
Liadov, A.:Barcarolle Pno *(rec May 10 & 11, 1991)* Relief ▲ CR 911026 [DDD]
Liadov, A.:Vars on a Polish Folk Theme *(rec May 10 & 11, 1991)* Relief ▲ CR 911026 [DDD]
Prokofiev, S.:The Love for 3 Oranges (march) *(rec May 10 & 11, 1991)* Relief ▲ CR 911026 [DDD]
Prokofiev, S.:Prelude Pno—No. 7 in C, Op. 12 *(rec May 10 & 11, 1991)* Relief ▲ CR 911026 [DDD]
Schumann, R.:Pno Music (misc)—Intermezzi, Op. 4; Kinderszenen, Op. 15; Arabeske in C, Op. 18, Aus Drei Romanzen, Op. 28/2; Aus Faschingsschwank aus Wien, Op. 26; Frühlingsnacht aus dem Liederkreis, Op. 39/12 Relief ▲ CR 911027
Shostakovich, D.:Pno Music—3 Fantastic Dances, Op. 5 Hyperion ▲ CDA 66620
Shostakovich, D.:Preludes Pno, Op. 34 Hyperion ▲ CDA 66620
Shostakovich, D.:Son 2 Pno Hyperion ▲ CDA 66620
Tchaikovsky, P.:Concert Fant, w. K. Kondrashin (cnd), Russian State SO *(rec 1950)* Multisonic ("Russian Treasures" series) ▲ 31 0238
Tchaikovsky, P.:Con 1 Pno, w. K. Masur (cnd), Leipzig Gewandhaus Orch Berlin Classics ("Dokumente" series) ▲ BER 2134 [ADD]
Tchaikovsky, P.:Son Pno, Op. 37 Relief ▲ CR 911028
Tchaikovsky, P.:Waltzes—in A♭, Op. 40/8; Valse à 5 Temps, Op. 72/16 Relief ▲ CR 911028
Nikolitch, Gordan (vn)
de Fesch, W.:Music of, w. A. van Beek (cnd), Auvergne CO—Cons Grossi, Op. 2/6, Op. 3/3 & 4, Op. 5/2 & Op. 10/4 & 5; Cons for Vn, Op. 2/2 & 5, Op. 3/6 & Op. 5/5 Olympia ▲ OLY 450 [DDD]
Nikonovich, Igor (pno)
Medtner, N.:Pno Music (misc)—Stimmungsbilder, Op. 9 [excerpts]; 9 Skazhi [Fairy-tales]; 3 Noveletten, Op. 17; March Funebre, Op. 31/2; Idyll, Op. 7/1; Son. in a, Op. 30 Russian Disc ▲ RUS 10014 [AAD]

Nikonovich, Igor (pno) (cont.)
Scriabin, A.:Pno Music (misc)—Fugue in e; Son-Fant in g#; 2 Nocturnes, Op. 5; 2 Impromptus, Op. 10; 10 Preludes, Opp. 15 & 16; 4 Preludes, Op. 39; Poème in D♭, Op. 41; 8 Études, Op. 42; 6 Pieces, Opp. 45 & 49; Feuille d'album in F#; Scherzo in C, Op. 46 Olympia ▲ OLY 550 [DDD]
Nilsson, Alf (cl)
Rimsky-Korsakov, N.:Concertstück Cl, w. G. Rozhdestvensky (cnd), Stockholm Concert Band Chandos ▲ CHAN 9444
Nilsson, Alf (ob)
Söderlundh, L.B.:Concertino Ob, w. E.-P. Salonen (cnd), Stockholm Sinfonietta BIS ▲ CD 285 [DDD]
Strauss, R.:Con Ob, w. N. Järvi (cnd), Stockholm Sinfonietta BIS ▲ CD 470 [DDD]
Nilsson, Arne (bn)
Vanhal, J.B.:Con Bns, w. Annika Wallin (bn), J.-P. Saraste (cnd), Umeå Sinfonietta BIS ▲ CD 288 [DDD]
Nilsson, Bo (tpt)
Britten, H.:Fanfare for St. Edmundsbury, w. J. Hjelm (tpt), R. Tilly (tpt) BIS ▲ CD 31 [AAD]
Guyonnet, J.:La Cantate interrompue, w. F. Rochaix (nar), S. Stenhammar (sop), S. Seban (pno), G. Calame (pno), E. Séjourne (perc), P. Geiss, E. Tarr (tpt), H. Ries (trbn), H. Rückert (trbn), J.-M. Collet, J. Guyonnet (cnd), Geneva Collegium Academicum [F] *(rec Nov. 15, 1986)* Grammont ▲ CTSP 30-2
Nilsson, Helena (vc)—see also ORCHESTRAS & ENSEMBLES Tale String Quartet
Jolivet, A.:Fl Music (comp), w. Manuela Wiesler (fl), Erica Goodman (hp), Patrik Swedrup (vn), Håkan Olsson (va), Christian Davidsson (bn), Roland Pöntinen (pno), P. Järvi (cnd), Tapiola Sinfonietta, Kroumata Percussion Ensemble—Alla rustica for Fl & Hp; Chant de Linos for Fl, Hp & Str Trio; Pastorales de Noël for Fl, Bn & Hp; Con for Fl & Strs; Suite en concert for Fl & 4 Perc Players; Fant-Caprice for Fl & Pno; Cabrioles for Fl & Pno *(rec Danderyd Grammar School, Sweden, Tapiola Hall, Tapiola, Finland, Gothenburg Concert Hall, Sweden & Studio 2, Radiohuset, Stockholm, Sweden)* BIS ▲ CD 739 [DDD]
Penderecki, K.:Qt Cl, w. M. Fröst (cl), P. Swedrup (vn), I. Kierkegaard (va) *(rec Feb. 18–20, 1994)* BIS ▲ CD 652 [DDD]
Penderecki, K.:Trio Strs, w. T. Olsson (vn), I. Kierkegaard (va) *(rec Feb. 18–20, 1994)* BIS ▲ CD 652 [DDD]
Nilsson, Lasse (pno)
Stolarczyk, W.:Earth Air Fire Water, w. Amalie Malling (pno), John Damgaard (pno), Anne Øland (pno), Teddy Teirup (pno), Friedrich Gürtler (pno), Rosalind Bevan (pno), Poul Rosenbaum (pno), Rodolfo Llambias (pno), Bella Horn-Ribera (pno), Anders Riber (pno), Elisabeth Sigurdsson (pno), Thomas Tronheim (pno), Elsebeth Broderson (pno), Erik Kaltoft (pno), Jørgen Hald Nielsen (pno), Aino Gilemann (pno), Birgit Kjær (pno), Jørgen Thomsen (pno), Gunhild Donslund (pno), Henrik Bo Hansen (pno), Lone Karlsson (pno), Erik Fessel (pno), Janos Ferenczi (pno), Erik Bach (pno), Axel Momme (pno), Arne de Cros Dich (pno), Sven Micha Slot (pno), Hanne Bramsen Buhl (pno), Lili Olesen (pno), Susannah Carlsson (pno), Ulla Erml (pno), Vagn Sørensen (pno), Leif Greibe (pno), Bodil Krogh (pno), Kirsten Ottosen (pno), Inger Bergenholz (pno), Karsten Gylendorf (pno), Bjønr Elkjær (pno), Jacob Bjørn Jensen (pno), Jørgen Kaad (pno), Anne Marie Hjelm (pno), Carl Ulrik Munk Andersen (pno), Poul Lumbye (pno), Oluf Hildebrandt Nielsen (pno), Joachim Olsson (pno), Peter Pade Ramsøe Jacobsen (pno), Astrid Pollmann (pno), Jette Borsch (pno), Kirsten Karlshøj (pno), Maria Teresa Assing (pno), Allan Dahl Hansen (pno), Johan Hugossen (pno), Tine Fenger Pederson (pno), Arne Jørgen Fæø (pno), Anja Høgsted (pno), Anne Sophie Parbo (pno), Inga Lindmark (pno), Teresa Drabik Stathakis (pno), Anne Ruth Ferenczi (pno), Irene Hasager (pno), Yuka Ichikawa (pno), Birgitte Baur (pno), Malene Thastum (pno), Jens E. Rasmussen (pno), Birgitte Zielke (pno), Claus Zielke (pno), Stefan Kasch (pno), Bin Qiao (pno), Inger Johanne Teirup (pno), Lindy Rosborg (pno), Liisa Heininen (pno), David Højer (pno), Ellen Refstrup (pno), Thomas K. Søorensen (pno), Erik Kure (pno), Michael Rauff (pno), Jan beck Eriksson (pno), Tanja Zapolski (pno), Vibeke Skagbo (pno), Pål Eide Lindtner (pno), Ha-Young Sul (pno), Benedicte Palko (pno), Inke Kesseler (pno), Anne Marie Meineche (pno), Sverre Larsen (pno), Kasper Peter Bach (pno), Elisabetta Eliseo (pno), Olga Magieres (pno), Carl Erik Kühl (pno), Thorkild Borup Nielsen (pno), Valeria Zanini (pno), Lars Stenhoft (perc), Dennis Boel (perc), Winnie Dahlgren (perc), Susanne Vind (perc), Claus Byrith (elec), Anne Marie Storm (elec), J. Ribera (cnd) *(rec live, Koldinghaus Castle, Denmark, May 2, 1996)* Danica ▲ DCD 1996
Nilsson, Mats (pno)
A Swedish Bouquet, w. Andersson, Anders (ten), Folke Alin (pno), Uppsala Univ Choir [cnd:Cecilia Rydinger-Alin] BIS ▲ CD 591 [DDD]
Nilsson, Ola (hn)—see ORCHESTRAS & ENSEMBLES Royal Danish Brass, Scandinavian Wind Quintet
Nilsson, Stig (vn)
Thoresen, L.:Yr Norway Music ▲ ACD 4968
Nimmo, Naomi Chaitkin (hpd)
Bach, J.S.:Sons Fl, BWV 1030–35, w. Floyd Cooley (tuba)—in E♭, BWV 1031 [trans. Cooley] Crystal ▲ CD 120
Nimmo, Naomi Chaitkin (pno)
Brahms, J.:Ernste Gesänge, w. Floyd Cooley (tuba) [trans. John Elwood Williams] Crystal ▲ CD 120
Nin, Joaquin (pno)
Nin, J.:Songs, w. Ninon Vallin (sop)—Tonada de la niña perdida; Canto andaluz; Granadina; Montañesa; El jilguerillo con pico de oro; Malagueña; Polo *(rec 1931)* VAI Audio ▲ VAIA 1127 [ADD]
Nippes, Ernst (va)
Mozart, W.A.:Adagio & Rondo Glass Armonica, w. B. Hoffmann (glass armonica), K.H. Ulrich (fl), H. Hucke (ob), H. Plumacher (vc) Allegretto ▲ ACD 8174 [ADD] ■ ACS 8174
Naumann, J.G.:Qt Glass Hmc, w. B. Hoffmann (glass hmc), K.H. Ulrich (fl), H. Plumacher (vc) Allegretto ▲ ACD 8174 [ADD] ■ ACS 8174
Reichardt, J.F.:Rondeau, w. B. Hoffmann (glass hmc), H. Anrath (vn), W. Albers (vn), H. Plumacher (vc), G. Nose (db) Allegretto ▲ ACD 8174 [ADD] ■ ACS 8174
Röllig, K.L.:Qnt Glass Hmc, w. B. Hoffmann (glass hmc), W. Albers (vn), H. Anrath (vn), H. Plumacher (vc) Allegretto ▲ ACD 8174 [ADD] ■ ACS 8174
Nirsalapova, R. (vn)—see ORCHESTRAS & ENSEMBLES Northern Crown Soloists Ensemble
Nisbet, Allen (vc)
Dankner, S.:Sextet, w. L. Skelton (pno), V. Poullette (vn), E. Tanner (vn), M. Gyurik (va), R. Kassinger (db) Albany ▲ TROY 067
Dankner, S.:Trio Cl, w. Steven Cohen (cl), Peter Collins (pno) Albany ▲ TROY 144 [DDD]
Nishida, N. (fl)
Haydn, J.:Trios Pno, Fl & Vc, w. Josef Pálaníček (pno), W. Boettcher (vc)—in D Camerata ▲ 30CM 376
Nishigata, A. (shamisen)
Shinohara, M.:Cooperation, w. K. Mitsuhashi (shakuhachi), M. Akao (fue), S. Yaotani (hichiriki), K. Ishikawa (sho), C. Fukunaga (koto), J. Ueda (biwa), M. Yoshizawa (kokyu), I. Tsuji (oboe), T. Takahashi (cl), G. Kitamura (tpt), A. Murata (trbn), S. Eiso (perc), S. Ueki (vn), S. Katsuta (vc), Y. Shibuya (pno), K. Komatsu (cnd) *(rec live Casals Hall, Tokyo, Mar. 5, 1994)* Camerata ▲ 30CM 375 [DDD]
Shinohara, M.:Nagare *(rec live Casals Hall, Tokyo, Mar. 5, 1994)* Camerata ▲ 30CM 375 [DDD]
Nishimine, Masakazu (perc)
Ernst, S.:Concertantes Duo, w. Dörte Nienstedt (rcr) Vienna Modern Masters ▲ VMM 2018 [DDD]
Nishizaki, Takako (vn)
Bach, J.S.:Cons Vn (comp), w. O. Dohnányi (cnd), Capella Istropolitana *(rec 1989)* Naxos ▲ 8.550194 [DDD]
Bach, J.S.:Con for 2 Vns, w. A. Jablokov (vn), O. Dohnányi (cnd), Capella Istropolitana *(rec 1989)* Naxos ▲ 8.550194 [DDD]
Beethoven, L. van:Con Vn, Op. 61, w. K. Jean (cnd), Slovak PO Naxos ▲ 8.550149 [DDD]
Beethoven, L. van:Romances Vn, w. K. Jean (cnd), Slovak PO Naxos ▲ 8.550149 [DDD]
Beethoven, L. van:Son 1 Vn, w. J. Jandó (pno) Naxos ▲ 8.550284 [DDD]
Beethoven, L. van:Son 2 Vn, w. J. Jandó (pno) Naxos ▲ 8.550284 [DDD]
Beethoven, L. van:Son 3 Vn, w. J. Jandó (pno) Naxos ▲ 8.550284 [DDD]
Beethoven, L. van:Son 4 Vn, w. J. Jandó (pno) *(rec Feb. & Sept. 1992)* Naxos ▲ 8.550285 [DDD]
Beethoven, L. van:Son 5 Vn, "Spring", w. J. Jandó (pno) *(rec 4/89)* Naxos ▲ 8.550283 [DDD]
Beethoven, L. van:Son 6 Vn, w. J. Jandó (pno) *(rec 10/89)* Naxos ▲ 8.550286 [DDD]
Beethoven, L. van:Son 7 Vn, w. J. Jandó (pno) *(rec 10/89)* Naxos ▲ 8.550286 [DDD]
Beethoven, L. van:Son 8 Vn, w. J. Jandó (pno) *(rec 10/89)* Naxos ▲ 8.550286 [DDD]
Beethoven, L. van:Son 9 Vn, "Kreutzer", w. J. Jandó (pno) *(rec 4/89)* Naxos ▲ 8.550283 [DDD]

Nishizaki, Takako (vn) (cont.)
Beethoven, L. van:Son 10 Vn, w. J. Jandó (pno) *(rec Feb. & Sept. 1992)* Naxos ▲ 8.550285 [DDD]
Beethoven, L. van:Trio 4 Pno, "Ghost", w. C. Onczay (vc), J. Jandó (pno) *(rec May 27–30, 1991)* Naxos ▲ 8.550442 [DDD]
Beethoven, L. van:Trio 6 Pno, "Archduke", w. J. Jandó (pno), C. Onczay (vc) *(rec May 27–30, 1991)* Naxos ▲ 8.550442 [DDD]
Beethoven, L. van:Vars on Mozart's, "Se vuol ballare," WoO 40, w. J. Jandó (pno) *(rec Feb. & Sept. 1992)* Naxos ▲ 8.550285 [DDD]
Bériot, C.–A. de:Con 1 Vn, "Military", w. A. Walter (cnd), Brussels RTBF SO Marco Polo ▲ 8.220440 [DAD]
Bériot, C.–A. de:Con 8 Vn, w. A. Walter (cnd), Brussels RTBF SO Marco Polo ▲ 8.220440 [DAD]
Bériot, C.–A. de:Con 9 Vn, w. A. Walter (cnd), Brussels RTBF SO Marco Polo ▲ 8.220440 [DAD]
Brahms, J.:Con Vn, w. S. Gunzenhauser (cnd), Slovak PO *(rec 5/89)* Naxos ▲ 8.550195 [DDD]
Bruch, M.:Con 1 Vn, w. S. Gunzenhauser (cnd), Slovak PO *(rec 5/89)* Naxos ▲ 8.550195 [DDD]
Butterfly Lovers, w. Czech–Slovak RSO [cnd:K. Jean] Marco Polo ▲ 8.223350
Chen, G.:Songs, w. S. Gunzenhauser (cnd), Capella Istropolitana [arr. for solo violin & orchestra]—Bells from the Temple; Flowing Water and Floating Clouds; The Hungry Horse Rattles His Bridle *(rec Shatin Town Hall, Hong Kong, June 23, 1987)* Marco Polo ("Chinese Composers" series) ▲ 8.223908 [DDD]
Chen, G.:Wang Zhaojun Con, w. Lam Fung (pipa), Y.W. Sie (cnd), Hong Kong PO *(rec Shatin Town Hall, Hong Kong, June 23, 1987)* Marco Polo ("Chinese Composers" series) ▲ 8.223908 [DDD]
Cui, C.:Suite concertante, w. K. Schermerhorn (cnd), Hong Kong PO Marco Polo ▲ 8.220308 [DDD]
Du, M.:Xinjiang Dances (10), w. C. Hoey (cnd), Singapore SO *(rec Victoria Memorial Hall, Singapore, June 3–7, 1985)* Marco Polo ("Chinese Composers" series) ▲ 8.223903 [DDD]
Franck, C.:Son Vn, w. J. Jandó (pno) *(rec 2/90)* Naxos ▲ 8.550417 [DDD]
Grieg, E.:Lyric Pieces, w. J. Jandó (pno) [arr. Vladimir Godar for vn & pno] *(rec 2/90)* Naxos ▲ 8.550417 [DDD]
Grieg, E.:Sons Vn, Opp. 8, 13 & 45, w. J. Jandó (pno)—No. 3 *(rec 2/90)* Naxos ▲ 8.550417 [DDD]
Joachim, J.:Con 3 Vn, w. M. Minsky (cnd), Stuttgart RSO Marco Polo ▲ 8.223373
Mozart, W.A.:Adagio Vn, K.261, w. S. Gunzenhauser (cnd), Capella Istropolitana Naxos ▲ 8.550418 [DDD]
Mozart, W.A.:Con 1 Vn, w. J. Wildner (cnd), Capella Istropolitana Naxos ▲ 8.550414 [DDD]
Mozart, W.A.:Con 2 Vn, w. J. Wildner (cnd), Capella Istropolitana *(rec April 3–9, 1990)* Naxos ▲ 8.550414 [DDD]
Mozart, W.A.:Con 3 Vn, w. S. Gunzenhauser (cnd), Capella Istropolitana Naxos ▲ 8.550418 [DDD]
Mozart, W.A.:Con 4 Vn, w. S. Gunzenhauser (cnd), Capella Istropolitana *(rec Nov. 1989)* Naxos ▲ 8.550332 [DDD]
Mozart, W.A.:Con 5 Vn, w. S. Gunzenhauser (cnd), Capella Istropolitana Naxos ▲ 8.550418 [DDD]
Mozart, W.A.:Rondo Vn, K.269, w. J. Wildner (cnd), Capella Istropolitana Naxos ▲ 8.550414 [DDD]
Mozart, W.A.:Rondo Vn, K.373, w. S. Gunzenhauser (cnd), Capella Istropolitana Naxos ▲ 8.550418 [DDD]
Mozart, W.A.:Serenade Vn, K.250, w. J. Wildner (cnd), Capella Istropolitana *(rec Apr. 1990)* Naxos ▲ 8.550333 [DDD]
Mozart, W.A.:Sinf concertante Vn, K.364, w. L. Kyselak (va), S. Gunzenhauser (cnd), Capella Istropolitana *(rec Nov. 1989)* Naxos ▲ 8.550332 [DDD]
Respighi, O.:Bach Transcriptions, w. O. Dohnányi (cnd), Capella Istropolitana—Son. for Violin & Basso Continuo, BWV.1023 trans. for violin & strings *(rec 1989)* Naxos ▲ 8.550194 [DDD]
Respighi, O.:Poema autunnale, w. C. Hoey (cnd), Singapore SO Marco Polo ▲ 8.220152 [DDD]
The Romance Collection, w. Wolf Harden (pno) *(rec Festeburgkirche, Frankfurt, 1982–84)* Naxos 4–▲ 8.504005 [DDD]
Romantic Violin Favorites, w. Wolf Harden (pno) Naxos ▲ 8.550125 [DDD]
Rubinstein, A.:Con Vn, w. M. Halász (cnd), Slovak PO Marco Polo ▲ 8.220359 [DDD]
Saint–Saëns, C.:Andante Vn, w. J. Wildner (cnd), Capella Istropolitana Naxos ▲ 8.550414 [DDD]
Spohr, L.:Con 7 Vn, w. L. Pešek (cnd), Bratislava Philharmonic CO Marco Polo ▲ 8.220406 [DDD]
Spohr, L.:Con 12 Vn, w. L. Pešek (cnd), Bratislava Philharmonic CO Marco Polo ▲ 8.220406 [DDD]
Violin Miniatures, w. Jenő Jandó (pno) *(rec May 21 & 27, 1989)* Naxos ▲ 8.550306 [DDD]
Vivaldi, A.:Cons Vn, Op. 8/1–4, "The Four Seasons", w. S. Gunzenhauser (cnd), Capella Istropolitana Naxos ▲ 8.550056 [DDD] Δ 7.550056 [DDD]
Zi, H.:Three Wishes for a Rose, w. H. Shek (cnd), Gunma SO [arr Akira Nishimura] Camerata ("After Hours Classics" series) ▲ 20 CM 423 [DDD]

Nisse, Anneliese (pno)
Bartók, B.:Son 1 Vn & Pno, w. Denes Zsigmondy (vn) Klavier ▲ KCD 11056 [ADD]
Bartók, B.:Son 2 Vn & Pno, w. Denes Zsigmondy (vn) Klavier ▲ KCD 11056 [ADD]
The Romantic Violin, w. Denes Zsigmondy (vn), Vienna Kohonaden Orch [cnd:Hans Hagen] Klavier ▲ KCD 11037 [ADD]

Nitto, Franco di (pno)
Schubert, Franz:Pno Music (misc)—Erste Walzer, D.365; Kupelwieser–Walzer, D.Anh.1/14; 16 German Dances & 2 Sketches, D.783; Galop & Sketch, D.735; Cotillon, D.976; 2 Ländlern, D.366; 17 Valses sentimentales, D.779; 12 Valses nobles, D.969 René Gailly ▲ CD 87031 [DDD]

Nitz, M. (hpd)—see ORCHESTRAS & ENSEMBLES Sancoussi Ensemble Hamburg

Niwa, Gail (pno)
Boutry, R.:Interferences, w. Bruce Grainger (bn) *(rec DePaul Univ. Concert Hall, Chicago, Sept 1992)* Centaur ▲ CRC 2244 [DDD]
Cascarino, R.:Son Bn, w. Bruce Grainger (bn) *(rec DePaul Univ. Concert Hall, Chicago, Sept 1992)* Centaur ▲ CRC 2244 [DDD]
Elgar, E.:Romance Bn, w. Bruce Grainger (bn), Gary Stucka (vc) *(rec DePaul Univ. Concert Hall, Chicago, Sept 1992)* Centaur ▲ CRC 2244 [DDD]
Etler, A.:Son Bn, w. Bruce Grainger (bn) *(rec DePaul Univ. Concert Hall, Chicago, Sept 1992)* Centaur ▲ CRC 2244 [DDD]
Hindemith, P.:Son Bn, w. Bruce Grainger (bn) *(rec DePaul Univ. Concert Hall, Chicago, Sept 1992)* Centaur ▲ CRC 2244 [DDD]
Saint–Saëns, C.:Son Bn, w. B. Grainger (bn) *(rec DePaul Univ. Concert Hall, Chicago, Sept 1992)* Centaur ▲ CRC 2244 [DDD]

Nixon, Darryl (hpd)
Boismortier, J.B. de:Sons, Op. 26, w. Kim Walker (bn), Cléna Stein (db)—Sonata No. 4 Gallo ▲ CD 367 [ADD]
Boismortier, J.B. de:Sons, Op. 50, w. Kim Walker (bn), Cléna Stein (db)—Sonata Nos. 1,2,4 & 5 Gallo ▲ CD 367 [ADD]

Nixon, June (org)
Grand Music for Great Occasions Walsingham Classics ▲ WAL 8002 [DDD]

Noakes, Anna (fl)
Damase, J.–M.:Qnt Fl, Hp & Strs, w. Gillian Tingay (hp), Richard Friedman (vn), Jane Atkins (vl), Ferenc Szucs (vc) ASV ▲ ASV 898 [DDD]
Damase, J.–M.:Son Fl & Hp, w. Gillian Tingay (hrp) ASV ▲ ASV 898 [DDD]
Damase, J.–M.:Trio Fl, w. Gillian Tingay (hp), Ferenc Szucs (vc) ASV ▲ ASV 898 [DDD]
Damase, J.–M.:Vars on *Early Morning*, w. Gillian Tingay (hp) ASV ▲ ASV 898 [DDD]
Fantaisie for Flute & Harp, w. Gillian Tingay (hp) ASV ▲ ASV 2101
Jolivet, A.:Alla rustica, w. Gillian Tingay (hp) ASV ("French Chamber Music" series) ▲ ASV 948
Jolivet, A.:Fantaise–Caprice, w. Kathron Sturrock (pno) ASV ("French Chamber Music" series) ▲ ASV 948
Jolivet, A.:Petite suite, w. Jonathan Barritt (va), Gillian Tingay (hp) ASV ("French Chamber Music" series) ▲ ASV 948
Jolivet, A.:Son Fl, w. Kathron Sturrock (pno) ASV ("French Chamber Music" series) ▲ ASV 948
Jolivet, A.:Sonatine Fl, w. Leslie Craven (cl) ASV ("French Chamber Music" series) ▲ ASV 948
Jolivet, A.:Suite en concert, w. Graham Cole (perc), Kate Eyre (perc), Rachel Gledhill (perc), Gary Kettel (perc) ASV ("French Chamber Music" series) ▲ ASV 948
Reger, M.:Serenades Fl, Opp. 77a & 141a, w. B. Wilde (vn), G. Robertson (va) ASV ▲ ASV 875 [DDD]

Nobel, Felix de (pno)
In Recital (1957 & 1962), w. Elisabeth Schwarzkopf (sop) Verona ▲ 27021 (m) [AAD]

Nobel, Felix de (pno) (cont.)
Mozart, W.A.:Songs, w. E. Schwarzkopf (sop)—Als Louise die Briefe; Un moto di gioia [G,I] *(rec in recital, 1957)* Verona ▲ 27021 (m) [AAD]
Schubert, Franz:Songs (misc), w. E. Schwarzkopf (sop)—5 songs—An Sylvia; Der Einsame; Romanze aus Rosamunde; Die Vögel; Gretchen am Spinnrade [G] *(rec in recital, 1957)* Verona ▲ 27021 (m) [AAD]
Strauss, R.:Songs, w. E. Schwarzkopf (sop)—3 songs—Ruhe meine Seele; Schlechtes Wetter; Hat gesagt:bleibt nicht dabei [G] *(rec in recital, 1957)* Verona ▲ 27021 (m) [AAD]
Wolf, H.:Songs (misc), w. E. Schwarzkopf (sop)—13 songs [G] *(rec in recital, 1962)* Verona ▲ 27021 (m) [AAD]

Noble, Anthony (hpd)
Handel, G.F.:Hpd Music [Kirckman hpd of 1769]—Ov [from Radamisto]; Ciacone in G; Suites in e & B♭ *(rec Apr 1995)* Herald ▲ HAVPCD 181 [DDD]
Haydn, J.:Sons Pno [Kirckman hpd of 1769]—in E, Hob. XVI/13; in D, Hob. XVI/4; in D, Hob. XVII/D1 *(rec Apr 1995)* Herald ▲ HAVPCD 181 [DDD]

Nockles, Bruce (tpt)
Gough, O.:Currulao, w. Beverly Davison (vn), Roger Heaton (cl), John Pigneguy (hn), David Stewart (trbn), Tracey Goldsmith (acc), Orlando Gough (kbd), Paul Clarvis (perc) *(rec London, 1995)* Catalyst ▲ 0902–668332–2 [DDD]
Gough, O.:Saeta, w. Pepe de la Matrona (voc), Michael Thompson (hn), John Pigneguy (hn), David Purser (trbn), Orlando Gough (kbd) *(rec London, 1995)* Catalyst ▲ 0902–668332–2 [DDD]

Noda, Ichiro (db)
Corrette, M.:Cons Org, Op. 26, w. H. Meyer (org), Sonare String Quartet—concerto in A Claves ▲ CD 8511 [DDD]
Durante, F.:Con Org, w. H. Meyer (org), Sonare String Quartet Claves ▲ CD 8511 [DDD]
Meyer, H.:Suite paysanne, w. H. Meyer (org), Sonare String Quartet Claves ▲ CD 8511 [DDD]
Paradies, P.D.:Con Org, w. H. Meyer (org), Sonare String Quartet Claves ▲ CD 8511 [DDD]
Stanley, J.:Con in c Org, w. H. Meyer (org), Sonare String Quartet Claves ▲ CD 8511 [DDD]

Noda, Mika (vib/bells/timp)
Smith, W.L.:Music of, w. Robin Lorentz (vn), Erika Duke (vc), Dorothy Stone (fl/pic), Martin Walker (cl), Wadada Leo Smith (tpt/flgl/fls/bells), Vicki Ray (pno/cel), David Philipson (perc/bells)—Another Wave More Waves; Double Thunderbolt; Tao–Njia; and others Tzadik ("Composer" series) ▲ TZA 7017 [DDD]

Noda, Yumiko (va)
Rheinberger, J.:Qnt Pno, w. Horst Göbel (pno), Sonare String Quartet *(rec 1989)* Thorofon 6–▲ BCTH 2161/6
Rheinberger, J.:Qnt Strings, w. Sonare String Quartet Thorofon ▲ CTH 2060 [DDD]
Rheinberger, J.:Qnt Strings, w. Sonare String Quartet *(rec 1989)* Thorofon 6–▲ BCTH 2161/6

Nodaira, Icharo (pno)
Hosokawa, T.:Vertical Time Study III, w. Irvine Arditti (vn) Montaigne ▲ MO 782078

Noehren, Robert (org)
Alain, J.:Vars sur un thème de Jannequin Delos ▲ DCD 3045 [DDD]
Bach, J.S.:Chorale Preludes Org—BWV 721, 767 Delos ▲ DCD 3028 [DDD]
Bach, J.S.:Org Music (misc)—Prelude & Fugue in a; Chorale Prelude Delos ▲ DCD 3045 [DDD]
Bach, J.S.:Das Orgelbüchlein—BWV 625 Delos ▲ DCD 3028 [DDD]
Bach, J.S.:Toccata & Fugue Org, BWV 565 Delos ▲ DCD 3028 [DDD]
Bach, J.S.:Trio Sons Org, BWV 525–530—BWV 529 Delos ▲ DCD 3028 [DDD]
Brahms, J.:Chorale Preludes, Op. 122—Nos. 6 & 9 Delos ▲ DCD 3045 [DDD]
Buxtehude, D.:Org Music (misc)—Chorale Fantasia, "Wie schön leuchtet der Morgenstern"; Chorale Preludes, "Ach Herr, mich armen Sünder" & "Ich ruf zu Dir, Herr Jesu Christ"; Fugue in C; Prelude & Fugue in a; Prelude & Fugue in e; Prelude & Fugue in f#; Prelude & Fugue in F; Prelude & Fugue in g; Prelude, Fugue & Chaconne in C Delos ▲ DCD 3023 [DDD]
Couperin, F.:Pièces d'orgue consistantes en deux Messes—No. 1 Delos ▲ DCD 3046 [DDD]
Dupré, M.:Org Music—Cortège et Litanie, Op. 19; Carillon; Fileuse; In Dulci Jubilo Facet ▲ FCD 8001 [AAD]
Dupré, M.:Préludes & Fugues, Op. 7 Facet ▲ FCD 8001 [AAD]
Hindemith, P.:Sons Org—No. 1 Delos ▲ DCD 3045 [DDD]
Karg–Elert, S.:Fugue, Canzone und Epilog Delos ▲ DCD 3045 [DDD]
Messiaen, O.:La Nativité du Seigneur—No. 9, "Dieu parmi nous" Delos ▲ DCD 3045 [DDD]
A Temple of Tone Pro Organo ▲ POCD 7019 [DDD]
Widor, C.M.:Sym 6 Org—Allegro movt. Delos ▲ DCD 3045 [DDD]

Noël, Hervé (tpt)
Organ & Trumpet Recital, w. Helga Schauerte–Maubouet (org) Quantum ▲ QM 6951

Noferini, Andrea (vc)
Offenbach, J.:Chants du soir, w. Steven Roach (pno) Bongiovanni ▲ GB 5569 [DDD]
Offenbach, J.:Harmonie du soir, w. Steven Roach (pno) Bongiovanni ▲ GB 5569 [DDD]
Offenbach, J.:Les Larmes de Jacqueline, w. Steven Roach (pno) Bongiovanni ▲ GB 5569 [DDD]
Offenbach, J.:Rêveries, w. Steven Roach (pno) Bongiovanni ▲ GB 5569 [DDD]
Paganini, N.:Serenata Va, w. A. Farulli (va), A. Sebastiani (gtr) Dynamic ▲ CD 76 [DDD]
Paganini, N.:Terzetto concertante Va, w. A. Farulli (va), A. Sebastiani (gtr) Dynamic ▲ CD 76 [DDD]
Paganini, N.:Terzetto Vn, w. D. Bratchkova (vn), A. Sebastiani (gtr) Dynamic ▲ CD 76 [DDD]

Noguchi, Ryu (fl)
Takemitsu, T.:Music of, w. Y. Nagano Tashi (mez), H. Ibe (gtr), M. Nagasako (hp), K. Abe (vib), Y. Takahashi (pno), R. Noguchi (fl), M. Hamada (lt), T. Koizumi (picc), S. Ueki (vn), Y. Hattori (vc), R. Stoltzman (cl), P. Serkin (pno), Ozawa, Wakasugi (cnd), Boston SO—Quatrain; Stanza I; Sacrifice; Ring; Valeria; A Flock Descends into the Pentagonal Garden Deutsche Grammophon ("20th Century Classics" series) ▲ 423253–2 [ADD]
Yashiro, A.:Son Fls, w. S. Koide (fl), F. Inoue (pno) Camerata ▲ 30CM 50

Nohara, Midori (pno)
Damase, J.–M.:Intro & Allegro *(rec Nov. 27, 1992)* REM ▲ REM 311187 [DDD]
Liszt, F.:Son Pno *(rec Nov. 27, 1992)* REM ▲ REM 311187 [DDD]

Noiri, Shizuko (fl)—see ORCHESTRAS & ENSEMBLES Isabella D'Este

Nojima, Minoru (pno)
Liszt, F.:Pno Music (misc)—Mephisto–Waltz; 3 Études (La campanella, Feux follets, Harmonies du soir) Reference ▲ RR 25CD [DDD]
Liszt, F.:Son Pno Reference ▲ RR 25CD [DDD]
Matsumura, T.:Con 2 Pno, w. H. Iwaki (cnd), Tokyo Metropolitan SO *(rec Jan 30, 1992)* Camerata ▲ 30 CM 261 [DDD]
Ravel, M.:Gaspard de la nuit Reference ▲ RR 35CD [DDD]
Ravel, M.:Miroirs Reference ▲ RR 35CD [DDD]

Nolan, David (vn)
Vivaldi, A.:Cons Vn, Op. 8/1–4, "The Four Seasons", w. D. Nolan (cnd), London PO Collins Quest ▲ 30182 [DDD]

Nolan, Julia (sax)
Maurice, P.:Tableaux de Provence, w. M. Bernardi (cnd), CBC Vancouver SO CBC ("SM 5000" series) ▲ SMCD 5135 [DDD]

Nolf, Bram (ob)
Berkeley, M.:Moods (3) *(rec Steurbaut Sound Recording Ctr)* René Gailly ▲ CD87 118 [DDD]

Nolte, Irmela (fl)
Jirásek, J.:Labyrinth, w. Jan Jirásek (voice/syn), Pavel Skála (perc) *(rec Audiostudio of Czech Radio, Prague)* Arta ▲ 0054 [DDD]
Milhaud, D.:Cataloque de fleurs, w. Ulrike Sonntag (sop), Deborah Marshall (cl), Michael Weigel (bn), Renate Eggebrecht (vn), Stefan Berg (va), Friedemann Kupsa (vc), Arpat György (db) *(rec Ludwigsburg, Germany, Jan. 1995)* Troubadisc ▲ TROCD 01410 [DDD]
Milhaud, D.:Machines agricoles, w. Ulrike Sonntag (sop), Deborah Marshall (cl), Michael Weigel (bn), Renate Eggebrecht (vn), Stefan Berg (va), Friedemann Kupsa (vc), Arpat György (db) *(rec Ludwigsburg, Germany, Jan. 1995)* Troubadisc ▲ TROCD 01410 [DDD]

Noras, Arto (vc)—see also ORCHESTRAS & ENSEMBLES Sibelius Academy String Quartet
Agopov, V.:Con Vc, "Tres Viae", w. J.–P. Saraste (cnd), Finnish RSO *(rec May 1988)* Finlandia ▲ 4509-95866-2 [DDD]
Bartók, B.:Rhap 1 Vc, w. J.–P. Saraste (cnd), Finnish RSO *(rec May 25–27, 1992)* Finlandia ▲ 4509-95872-2 [DDD]
Dutilleux, H.:Con Vc, "Tout un Monde Lointain", w. J.–P. Saraste (cnd), Finnish RSO *(rec Aug. 1991)* Finlandia ▲ 4509-95866-2 [DDD]
Masterpieces for Cello, w. Tapani Valsta (pno/org) Finlandia ▲ 4509-95883-2 [AAD]
Saint-Saëns, C.:Con 1 Vc, w. J.–P. Saraste (cnd), Finnish RSO *(rec Feb. 28–March 1, 1990)* Finlandia ▲ 4509-95872-2 [DDD]
Sibelius, J.:Pieces Vn, w. J.–P. Saraste (cnd), Finnish RSO *(rec May 25–27, 1992)* Finlandia ▲ 4509-95872-2 [DDD]
Tchaikovsky, P.:Vars on a Rococo Theme, w. J.–P. Saraste (cnd), Finnish RSO *(rec May 25–27, 1992)* Finlandia ▲ 4509-95872-2 [DDD]

Nordberg, Hermann von (pno)
Arias & Songs, w. Irmgard Seefried (sop), Gerald Moore (pno), Wilhelm Schmidt (pno), London Mozart Players [cnd:Harry Blech] Testament ▲ SBT 1026 [ADD]

Norde, Christian (vl)
Bach, C.P.E.:Sons Fl, w. W. Hazelzet (fl), J. Ogg (pno)—W. 124, 128, 130, 131 & 134 *(rec Oct 1992)* Globe ▲ GLO 5091 [DDD]

Nordenfelt, Eva (hpd)
Agrell, J.:Sons (6) Hpd Prophone ▲ PCD 004
Bach, J.S.:Goldberg Vars Proprius ▲ PRCD 9999
Roman, J.H.:Sons Fl, w. P. Evison (fl), C. Huntgeburth (fl), K. Ottesen (vc), O. Larsson (vc)—Nos. 1, 2, 5, 6, 7 & 9 Proprius ▲ PRCD 9020
Roman, J.H.:Sons Fl, w. P. Evison (fl), O. Larsson (vc)—Nos. 3, 4, 8, 10, 11 & 12 Proprius ▲ PRCD 9019
Roman, J.H.:Sons Hpd *(rec Aug. 16–20, 1993)* Swedish Society 2–▲ SCD 1060/61

Nordenfelt, Eva (hpd/org)
Roman, J.H.:Sacred Music, w. G. Ryhming (sop), M. Spaeter (thb), K. Ottesen (vc)—Psalms 4, 5, 81, 103, 124 & 125; Mon coeur tressaille de joie; Oiseaux, animaux sauvages; Mes prères, hâtez–vous; Dieu, Dieu de to Gallo ▲ CD 764 [DDD]

Nordin, Mona (vn)
Bashmakov, L.:Con da camera, w. Gunilla von Bahr (pic/fl), Paavo Pohjola (vn), Zahari Tchavdarov (va), Elemér Lavotha (vc) *(rec Grünewald Hall, Stockholm, Sweden, May 11, 1974)* BIS ▲ CD 11 [AAD]

Nordmann, Marielle (hp)
Duets for Harp, w. Lily Laskine (hp) Erato ▲ 92862-2
Hoffmann, E.T.A.:Qnt Hp, w. French String Trio Koch Schwann ▲ SCH 313392 [ADD/DDD]
Music for Flute & Harp, w. Jean–Pierre Rampal (fl) Sony Classical ▲ SK 44552 [DDD]
Parish Alvars, E.:Concertino Hp, w. T. Guschlbauer (pno) *(rec June 22 & 30, 1992)* FNAC Music ▲ 592266 [DDD]
Parish Alvars, E.:Con Hp, w. F.–R. Duchable (cnd), Strasbourg SO *(rec June 22 & 30, 1992)* FNAC Music ▲ 592266 [DDD]
Parish Alvars, E.:Fant Hp, w. T. Guschlbauer (pno) *(rec June 22 & 30, 1992)* FNAC Music ▲ 592266 [DDD]

Nordstoga, Kåre (org)
Thommessen, O.A.:Through a Prism, w. Truls Mörk (vc), K. Andersen (cnd), Oslo PO Caprice ▲ CAP 21403

Nordwall, Eva (hpd)
Ligeti, G.:Continuum BIS ▲ CD 53

Norell, J. (hpd)
Mozart, W.A.:Sons Fl Hpd (comp), w. R. Siebert (fl) Vox Box 3–▲ CD3X 3003 [ADD]

Nørgård, Per (kbd/voc)
Nørgård, P.:Music for Perc, w. Palle Mikkelborg (perc), Gert Sørensen (perc/kbd/cmpt)—Waves; Isternia; I Ching; Energy Fields Forever; Nemo Dynamo; Bulan; Circus City Marco Polo ("dacapo" series) ▲ 8.224024–25 [DDD]

Norman, Chris (fl)
Man with the Wooden Flute, w. Robin Bullock (gtr/cittern/fid), Ann Marie Morgan (vl), Pete Sutherland (fid) Dorian ▲ DOR 90166 [DDD]

Norman, Edward (pno)
English Tuba, w. Eugene Dowling (tuba), London SO [cnd:Paul Freeman] Pro Arte ▲ CDD 595 [DDD]
Jacob, G.:Suite Tuba, w. E. Dowling (tuba) Pro Arte/Fanfare ▲ CDD 595 [DDD]

Normann, Jürgen (db)
Bach, C.P.E.:Duo Cl, w. D. Klöcker (cl), K.–O. Hartmann (bn) MD + G ▲ L 3365 [DDD]
Mozart, W.A.:Don Giovanni, w. Gernot Schmalfub (ob), Christian Hartmann (ob), Dieter Klöcker (cl), Waldemar Wandel (cl), Sara Willis (hn), Christian Auer (hn), Karl–Otto Hartmann (bn), Eberhard Buschmann (bn), Consortium Classicum Bayer ▲ BR 100 135 [DDD]
Tausch, F.W.:Duo, w. D. Klöcker (cl), K.–O. Hartmann (bn) MD + G ▲ L 3366 [DDD]

Nørregaard, Alice (pno)
Schested, H.:Suite Cnt, w. Ketil Christensen (tpt) [arr. Christensen & Nørregaard] *(rec Anneberg Mansion, Denmark, 1995)* Rondo Grammofon ▲ RCD 8350

Norris, David Owen (pno)
Bax, A.:Qnt Pno & Strs, w. Mistry String Quartet Chandos ▲ CHAN 8795 [DDD]
Saint–Saëns, C.:Carnival of the Animals, w. Y. Turovsky (cnd), Montreal Musici Chandos ▲ CHAN 9246 [DDD]
Saint–Saëns, C.:Wedding Cake, w. Y. Turovsky (cnd), Montreal Musici Chandos ▲ CHAN 9246 [DDD]

Norris, Leslie Stratton (hp)
Read, G.:Chamber Music, w. Janet Packer (vn), Gerald Berthiaume (cel), Barbara Harbach (hpd), Joseph Holt (pno), Howard Karp (pno), Boston Composers String Quartet—5 Aphorisms, Op. 150; Son. da Chiesa, Op. 61; Sonoric Fant. No. 1, Op. 102; Qt. 1 Strings, Op. 100 Northeastern ▲ NOR 253 [DDD]
Read, G.:Sonoric Fantasia 1, w. Gerald Berthiaume (cel), Barbara Harbach (hpd) *(rec KWSU–TV Studios, Pullman, WA, Nov. 1993)* Northeastern ("Classical Arts, Contemporary" series) ▲ NR 253

Norris, M. (pno)
Finney, R.L.:Chamber Music (36 songs), w. J. Lombard (sop) Master Musicians Collective ▲ MMC 2012

North, Nigel (archlt/cittern/thb/gtr)
Corelli, A.:Sons Vn, Op. 5, w. Sonnerie Trio—comp. Virgin Classics 2–▲ ZDCB 59554
Corelli, A.:Sons Vn, Op. 5, w. Sonnerie Trio—comp. Veritas 2–▲ VCD 7 90840–2 [DDD] 2–■ VC 7 90840–4 (D)
Guitar Collection, w. Maggie Cole (virs/pno) Amon Ra ▲ CDSAR 18 [DDD]
Lawes, W.:Royall Consort Suites, w. Paul O'Dette (thb), Purcell Quartet Chandos ("Early Music" series) 2–▲ CHAN 0584/5 [DDD]
Music of the Renaissance Virtuosi, w. James Tyler (lt/baroque gtr/mand), Douglas Wootton (lt/bandora), Jane Ryan (b vl) Saga Classics ▲ 3350 [ADD]
Telemann, G.P.:Sons Ob, w. Paul Goodwin (ob), John Toll (hpd), Susan Sheppard (vc) Harmonia Mundi ▲ HMU 907152
Vivaldi, A.:Sons Ob, w. P. Goodwin (ob), G. Hennessey (ob), J. Holloway (vn), C. Lawson (cl), S. Sheppard (vc), F. Eustace (bn), J. Toll (hpd/org)—RV.53, 58, 81 & 779 Harmonia Mundi USA ▲ HMU 907104

North, Nigel (lt)
Bach, J.S.:Lt Music—BWV 995, 999, 1000, 1006a Amon Ra ▲ CD–SAR 23 [DDD]
Bach, J.S.:Suites Vc, BWV 1007–1012—BWV 1007, 1008 & 1010 [trans North] *(rec St. Martins' Church, East Woodhay, Oct 2–5, 1995)* Linn ▲ HON 5049
Biber, H. von:Passacaglia Lt *(rec East Woodhay, UK, Sept. 15–18, 1993 & Jan.)* Harmonia Mundi USA 2–▲ HMU 907134/35
Concord of Sweet Sounds, w. Lisa Beznosiuk (fls) Amon Ra ▲ CDSAR 33 [DDD]
Purcell, H.:Ayres & Songs, w. Jill Feldman (sop), Sarah Cunningham (b vl) Arcana ▲ ACA 2 [DDD]

North, Nigel (lt) (cont.)
Three Parts upon a Ground, w. John Hollowy (vn), Stanley Ritchie (vn), Andrew Manze (vn), Mary Springfels (vl), John Toll (hpd/org) Harmonia Mundi USA ▲ HMU 907091

North, Nigel (lt/thb)—see ORCHESTRAS & ENSEMBLES Romanesca

Northcutt, Barbara (E hn)
Howard, J.N.:Primal Fear, w. Terence Blanchard (hn), A. Kane (cnd), *(orch unknown) (rec Paramount Pictures, Scoring Stage M, Los Angeles)* Milan ▲ 73138-35716-2 [DDD]

Norton, Leslie (hn)—see ORCHESTRAS & ENSEMBLES Blair Woodwind Quintet

Norton, Nick (tpt)
The Colors of the Baroque, w. Anthony Plog (tpt), chamber ensembles Summit ▲ DCD 108 [DDD] ■ MCD 108 (D)

Norton, Shana (hp)
Allen, J.:Brazilian Son, w. Ron Grinage (pno), Carol Redman (fl), Charly Drobeck (fl/alt fl/pic), Sam Lunt (perc), Tom Maguire (perc) *(rec Santuario de Guadalupe, Sante Fe, NM, Sept 29–30, 1995)* Wild Iris ▲ WI 001

Nosaka, Keiko (koto)
Ifukube, A.:Mono Yu Mai Camerata ▲ 32CM 290
Miki, M.:Music of, w. T. Tamura (cnd), Pro Musica Nipponia—Con Requiem for 20–string Koto & Japanese Instruments; Hanayagi; Autumn Fant; Sao–no–Kyoku; Tatsuta–no–Kyoku Camerata ▲ 32CM 55

Nose, Gert (db)
Reichardt, J.F.:Rondeau, w. B. Hoffmann (glass hmc), H. Anrath (vn), W. Albers (vn), E. Nippes (va), H. Plumacher (vc) Allegretto ▲ ACD 8174 [ADD] ■ ACS 8174

Nosowska, Maria (pno)
Polish Piano Music, w. Teresa Rutkowska (pno), Marian Brokowski (pno), Baroara Halska (pno) Olympia ▲ OLY 394 [AAD]

Nothas, Walter (vc)
Dünser, R.:Tage– und Nachtbucher, w. Martin Schelling (cl), Martin Mumelter (vn), Alfons Kontarsky (pno) Koch Schwann ▲ SCH 311882
Messiaen, O.:Quatuor pour la fin du temps, w. Martin Schelling (cl), Martin Mumelter (vn), Alfons Kontarsky (pno) Koch Schwann ▲ SCH 311882
Nishimura, A.:Con Vc, w. C. Escher (cnd), Linz Bruckner Orch Camerata ▲ 32CM 199
Nishimura, A.:Into the Lights, w. C. Escher (cnd), Linz Bruckner Orch Camerata ▲ 32CM 199

Novacek, John (pno)
Albéniz, I.:Pno Music—Asturias; Sevilla; Tango *(rec St. John Vianney Church, Juanita, WA, Aug. 16–18, 1994)* Ambassador ▲ ARC 1014 [DDD]
Flute Music by French Composers, w. Mary Palchak (fl) *(rec Santa Ana High School Auditorium, Santa Ana, CA, June 1995)* Ambassador ▲ ARC 1016 [DDD]
Ginastera, A.:Danzas argentinas *(rec St. John Vianney Church, Juanita, WA, Aug. 16–18, 1994)* Ambassador ▲ ARC 1014 [DDD]
Granados, E.:Goyescas—No. 4 [Quejas o la maja y el ruiseñor] *(rec St. John Vianney Church, Juanita, WA, Aug. 16–18, 1994)* Ambassador ▲ ARC 1014 [DDD]
Liszt, F.:Rhap espagnole *(rec St. John Vianney Church, Juanita, WA, Aug. 16–18, 1994)* Ambassador ▲ ARC 1014 [DDD]
Ponce, M.:Pno Music—Estrellita [improv. by Novacek] *(rec St. John Vianney Church, Juanita, WA, Aug. 16–18, 1994)* Ambassador ▲ ARC 1014 [DDD]
Ravel, M.:Alborada del gracioso *(rec St. John Vianney Church, Juanita, WA, Aug. 16–18, 1994)* Ambassador ▲ ARC 1014 [DDD]
Romances et Méditations, w. Kurt Leuders (org), Sheryl Staples (vn) Arkay ▲ ARK 6097
Rózsa, M.:Duo Vn, w. Isabella Lippi (vn) Koch International Classics ▲ KIC 7256 [DDD]
Rózsa, M.:North Hungarian Peasant Songs & Dances, w. Isabella Lippi (vn) Koch International Classics ▲ KIC 7256 [DDD]
Rózsa, M.:Vars on Hungarian Peasant Song, w. Isabella Lippi (vn) Koch International Classics ▲ KIC 7256 [DDD]
Soler, P.A.:Fandango *(rec St. John Vianney Church, Juanita, WA, Aug. 16–18, 1994)* Ambassador ▲ ARC 1014 [DDD]

Novacek, Steven (gtr)
Castelnuovo–Tedesco, M.:Romancero gitano, w. Joan Catoni Conlon (cnd), Pacific Northwest Chamber Chorus Ambassador ▲ ARC 1015
Guitar Music of the Americas, w. Steven Novacek (gtr) Ambassador ▲ ARC 1007 [DDD] ■ ARC 1007
The Gypsy Influence, w. Steven Novacek (gtr), Gary Bissiri (gtr) Ambassador ▲ ARC 1005 [ADD] ■ ARC 1005
Rodrigo, J.:Tonadilla, w. G. Bissiri (gtr) Ambassador ▲ ARC 1005 [ADD] ■ ARC 1005
Sor, F.:Salon Pieces, Op. 33 *(rec St. John's Chrysostom Church, Newmarket, Canada, Jan 22–26, 1995)* Naxos ▲ 8.553341 [DDD]
Sor, F.:Studies, Op. 35 *(rec St. John's Chrysostom Church, Newmarket, Canada, Jan 22–26, 1995)* Naxos ▲ 8.553341 [DDD]

Novaes, Guiomar (pno)
Beethoven, L van:Con 4 Pno, w. O. Klemperer (cnd), Vienna SO Vox Box ("Legends" series) 2–▲ CDX2 5501 [ADD]
Beethoven, L van:Con 5 Pno, "Emperor", w. J. Perlea (cnd), Bamberg SO Allegretto ▲ ACD 8026 [ADD] ■ ACS 8026
Beethoven, L van:Con 5 Pno, "Emperor", w. J. Perlea (cnd), Bamberg SO *(rec 1950s)* Vox Box ("Legends" series) 2–▲ CDX2 5512 [ADD]
Beethoven, L van:Life & Music of, w. J. Perlea (cnd), Bamberg SO—narration with selected excerpts from Syms. Nos. 3 & 5–9; Minuet, WoO 10/2; German Dances, WoO 8/1 & 2; Sonatina, Anh. 5/2; Sons. Nos. 14 & 23 for Piano, Opp. 27 & 57; Ovs., Opp. 43, 62 & 72; Con. for Violin, Op. 61; Con. No. 5 for Piano, Op. 73, plus a complete version of Con. No. 5 for Piano in E♭, Op. 73, "Emperor" Vox ("Music Masters" series) ▲ MMD 8507 [ADD] ■ MMC 8507
Beethoven, L van:Son 14 Pno, "Moonlight Son" Vanguard Classics ▲ OVC 8072 [ADD]
Beethoven, L van:Son 17 Pno, "Tempest" Allegretto ▲ ACD 8152 [ADD] ■ ACS 8152
Beethoven, L van:Son 21 Pno, "Waldstein" Allegretto ▲ ACD 8152 [ADD] ■ ACS 8152
Beethoven, L van:Son 32 Pno Vanguard Classics ▲ OVC 8072 [ADD]
Chopin, F.:Berceuse *(rec 1950s)* Vox Box ("Legends" series) 2–▲ CDX2 5513 [ADD]
Chopin, F.:Con 1 Pno, w. J. Perlea (cnd), Bamberg SO *(rec 1950s)* Vox Box ("Legends" series) 2–▲ CDX2 5513 [ADD]
Chopin, F.:Con 1 Pno, w. J. Perlea (cnd), Bamberg SO Allegretto ▲ ACD 8006 [ADD] ■ ACS 8006
Chopin, F.:Con 2 Pno, w. O. Klemperer (cnd), Vienna SO Vox Box ("Legends" series) 2–▲ CDX2 5501 [ADD]
Chopin, F.:Études (24) *(rec 1950s)* Vox Box ("Legends" series) 3–▲ CDX3 3501 [ADD]
Chopin, F.:Impromptus—in F♯, Op. 36 *(rec 1950s)* Vox Box ("Legends" series) 2–▲ CDX2 5513 [ADD]
Chopin, F.:Nocturnes *(rec 1950s)* Vox Box ("Legends" series) 3–▲ CDX3 3501 [ADD]
Chopin, F.:Pno Music (misc)—Ballade No. 3 in A♭, Op. 47; Polonaise in A♭, Op. 53; Berceuse, Op. 57; Étude in G♭, Op. 25/9; Étude in G♭, Op. 10/5; Ballade No. 4 in f, Op. 52; Polonaise in f♯, Op. 44; 3 Ecossaises, Op. 72 Vanguard Classics ▲ OVC 8071
Chopin, F.:Scherzos—in b, Op. 20 *(rec 1950s)* Vox Box ("Legends" series) 2–▲ CDX2 5513 [ADD]
Chopin, F.:Son Pno, Op. 35 *(rec 1950s)* Vox Box ("Legends" series) 3–▲ CDX3 3501 [ADD]
Chopin, F.:Son Pno, Op. 58 *(rec 1950s)* Vox Box ("Legends" series) 2–▲ CDX2 5513 [ADD]
Falla, M. de:Noches en los jardines de España, w. H. Swarowsky (cnd), Vienna SO *(rec 1950s)* Vox Box ("Legends" series) 2–▲ CDX2 5513 [ADD]
Grieg, E.:Con Pno, Op. 16, w. H. Swarowsky (cnd), Vienna SO *(rec 1950s)* Vox Box ("Legends" series) 2–▲ CDX2 5513 [ADD]
Guiomar Novaes, w. Guiomar Novaes (pno), Vienna SO [cnd:Otto Klemperer] *(rec 1950s & early 1960s)* Vox Box 2–▲ CDX2 5501 [ADD]
Mozart, W.A.:Con 9 Pno, w. H. Swarowsky (cnd), Vienna SO *(rec 1950s)* Vox Box ("Legends" series) 2–▲ CDX2 5512 [ADD]
Mozart, W.A.:Con 20 Pno, w. H. Swarowsky (cnd), Vienna SO *(rec 1950s)* Vox Box ("Legends" series) 2–▲ CDX2 5512 [ADD]

Novaes, Guiomar (pno) (cont.)
Mozart, W.A.:Son 5 Pno *(rec 1950s)* Vox Box ("Legends" series) 2-▲ CDX2 5512 [ADD]
Mozart, W.A.:Son 11 Pno *(rec 1950s)* Vox Box ("Legends" series) 2-▲ CDX2 5512 [ADD]
Mozart, W.A.:Son 15 Pno *(rec 1950s)* Vox Box ("Legends" series) 2-▲ CDX2 5512 [ADD]
Schumann, R.:Con Pno, w. O. Klemperer (cnd), Vienna SO
Vox Box ("Legends" series) 2-▲ CDX2 5501 [ADD]

Novák, Antonín (vn)—see also ORCHESTRAS & ENSEMBLES Suk String Quartet
Eben, Petr:Old Testament Frescoes (3), w. Jaroslav Šaroun (pno)*(rec Martínek Studio in Prague)*
Panton ▲ 81 1398-2 [DDD]

Novak, Jiri (vn)
Mozart, W.A.:Con 4 Vn, w. V. Talich (cnd), Czech PO *(rec 1954–55)*
Supraphon ▲ SUP 11 1906 [AAD]

Novak, Thomas (bn)—see ORCHESTRAS & ENSEMBLES Quintet of the Americas

Novakova, Clara (fl)
Burgan, P.:Music of, w. Liliane Mazeron (sop), Michel Arrignon (cl), Alain Jacquon (pno), Henry Trio—Jeux de femmes [6 Erotic Poems of Verlaine]; Rondes Nocturnes; Bavardage; Berceuse
Maguelone ▲ 350.529

Novenko, Michael (org)
Frescobaldi, G.:Fiori musicali Supraphon ▲ SUP 11 1862 [DDD]

Novotná, Kveta (pno)
Schumann, R.:Davidsbündlertänze Panton ▲ PAN 810891
Schumann, R.:Papillons Panton ▲ PAN 810891
Schumann, R.:Toccata Pno Panton ▲ PAN 810891
Schumann, R.:Vars on A–B–E–G–G Panton ▲ PAN 810891

Novotny, B. (vn)
Bach, J.S.:Sons & Partitas Vn, BWV 1001–1006 *(rec 1972)* Supraphon 2-▲ SUP 111806 [DDD]

Novotny, Frantisek (vn)
Dvořák, A.:Con Vn, w. J. Belohlávek (cnd), Prague Chamber PO Studio Matous ▲ MAT 31 [DDD]
Dvořák, A.:Mazurek, w. J. Belohlávek (cnd), Prague Chamber PO Studio Matous ▲ MAT 31 [DDD]
Dvořák, A.:Romance Vn, w. J. Belohlávek (cnd), Prague Chamber PO Studio Matous ▲ MAT 31 [DDD]

Novotny, J. (fl)
Stravinsky, I.:L'Histoire du soldat Suite Ensemble, w. K. Zlatníková, K. Krautgartner (cl), L. Pešek (cnd), Prague Chamber Harmony *(rec May 18–22, 1964)*
Supraphon ("Collection" series) ▲ 11 0672-2 [ADD]
Vivaldi, A.:Cons Fl (misc), w. J. Válek (fl), J. Stivín (flautino), *(orch unknown)*—Flute Concerti, RV.108, 533, & in F; Flautino Concerti, RV.443, 444 & 445 Naxos ▲ 8.550385 [DDD]

Novotny, Jan (pno)
Smetana, B.:Czech Dances—2nd series (Nos. 5–14) Supraphon ▲ SUP CD 3070
Smetana, B.:Morceaux caractéristiques Supraphon ▲ SUP CD 3070
Stravinsky, I.:Pno–Rag–Music *(rec Dec. 27, 1967)*
Supraphon ("Collection" series) ▲ 11 0672-2 [ADD]

Novotný, Jiří (ten tuba)
Janáček, L.:Capriccio, w. Daniel Wiesner (pno), Jan Riedlbauch (fl/pic), Vladislav Kozderka (tpt), Jan Fišer (tpt), Václav Ferebauer (trbn), Jan Hynčica (trbn), Antonín Keller (trbn), L. Svárovský (cnd) *(rec Martínek Studio in Prague)* Panton ▲ 81 1393-2 [DDD]

Novovic, P. (va)
Bach, C.P.E.:Trio Son in F, w. C. Pehrsson (bass rcr), A. Petersén (bass vl), A. Östman (hpd) [period instrs] BIS ▲ CD 220 [DDD]

Novovic, P. (vn)
Quantz, J.J.:Trio Sons, w. C. Pehrsson (rcr), A. Petersén (b vl), A. Östman (hpd) [period instrs]—in C
BIS ▲ CD 220 [DDD]
Vivaldi, A.:Trio Sons (misc), w. C. Pehrsson (rcr), A. Petersén (b vl), A. Östman (hpd) [period instrs]—in g BIS ▲ CD 220 [DDD]

Novšak, Primoz (vn)
Boccherini, L.:Duets (6) for 2 Vns, w. I. Ozim (vn) ebs ▲ ebs 6009 [DDD]
Mieg, P.:Septet, w. Peter Solomon (hpd), Günter Rumpel (fl), Simon Fuchs (ob), Marius Ungureanu (va), Carolyn Hopkins Marti (vc), Ronald Dangel (db) *(rec 1993)* Jecklin ▲ JS 314-2 [DDD]

Nowak, Lionel (pno)
Fine, V.:Momenti Pno CRI ▲ CD 692 [ADD]

Nowels-Stenholm, Nanette (pno)
Carissimi, G.:Ferma lascia ch'io parli, w. Lena Nordin (sop), Maria Wieslander (org), Sven Åberg (chit), Chrichan Larsson (vc), M. Guidarini (cnd), *(orch unknown)* Swedish Society ▲ SCD 1076
Donizetti, G.:Maria Stuarda (sels), w. Lena Nordin (sop), Carina Morling (mez), Ingus Peterssons (ten), Anders Bergström (bar), Tord Wallström (bar), Maria Wieslander (org), Sven Åberg (chit), Chrichan Larsson (vc), M. Guidarini (cnd), *(orch unknown)* Swedish Society ▲ SCD 1076
Schumann, R.:Gedichte, Op. 135, w. Lena Nordin (sop) Swedish Society ▲ SCD 1076

Nowicki, Bogumil (pno)—see ORCHESTRAS & ENSEMBLES Chopin Trio

Nowicki, Susan (pno)
Davison, J.:Son Tpt, w. Terry Everson (tpt) Albany ▲ TROY 199 [DDD]
Krzywicki, J.:Snow Night, w. Anthony Orlando (mar) Capstone ▲ CPS 8631

Nugent, B. (fl)—see ORCHESTRAS & ENSEMBLES Aspen Wind Quintet

Nulens, Gerrit (perc)—see ORCHESTRAS & ENSEMBLES Percussive Rotterdam

Numata, Sonoko (vn)
Ikenouchi, T.:Sonatine Vn *(rec Saitama Geijyutsu gekijo Music Hall, Apr 26, 1995)*
Camerata ▲ 30CM 409 [DDD]
Miyoshi, A.:Son Vn *(rec Saitama Geijyutsu Gekijo Music Hall, Apr 26, 1995)*
Camerata ▲ 30CM 409 [DDD]
Noda, T.:In the Garden, w. Akemi Tadenuma (pno) Camerata ▲ 30CM 344
Noda, T.:In the Garden, w. Akemi Tadenuma (pno) *(rec Saitama Geijyutsu Gekijo Music Hall, Apr 26, 1995)* Camerata ▲ 30CM 409 [DDD]
Takemitsu, T.:Hika, w. Akemi Tadenuma (pno) *(rec Saitama Geijyutsu Gekijo Music Hall, Apr 26, 1995)*
Camerata ▲ 30CM 409 [DDD]
Yamada, K.:Music of, w. Akemi Tadenuma (pno)—Lullaby [from the Chugoku Area]; Red Dragonfly *(rec Saitama Geijyutsu Gekijo Music Hall, Apr 26, 1995)* Camerata ▲ 30CM 409 [DDD]

Nunemaker, Richard (cl)
English, P.:The Sax, w. *(not advised of narrator)* Master Musicians Collective ▲ MMC 2005 [DDD]
Kurtz, E.:Logo I, w. D. Nale (pno), Continuum Percussion Quartet New World ▲ NW 382-2 [AAD]
McKinley, W.T.:Golden Petals Master Musicians Collective ▲ MMC 2005 [DDD]
Misurell-Mitchell, J.:Alone Together Master Musicians Collective ▲ MMC 2005 [DDD]
Shaw, A.:Con Cl, w. *(orch unknown)* [arr. N. Wayland]
Master Musicians Collective ▲ MMC 2005 [DDD]
Stravinsky, I.:Ebony Con, w. *(orch unknown)* Master Musicians Collective ▲ MMC 2005 [DDD]

Nuñez, Antonio (vn)
Villa-Lobos, H.:Trio 2 Vn, w. J. Humeston (vc), M. Duphil (pno) Marco Polo ▲ 8.223164

Nussbaumer, Madeline (pno)—see ORCHESTRAS & ENSEMBLES Kammermusik Ensemble Chamäleon

Nwanoku, Chi-chi (db)
Boccherini, L.:Sons (5) Vc & Db, w. Richard Lester (vc), David Watkin (vc)—Sons. in c, A, E♭, C, & B♭
Hyperion ▲ CDA 66719
Chamber Music Sampler, w. Domus, et al. Virgin Classics 2-▲ CDC 59092
Rossini, G.:Sons Str Qt, w. E. Wallfisch (vn), M. Marcus (vn), R. Tunnicliffe (vc) Hyperion ▲ CDA 66595

Nyfenger, Thomas (fl)
Corigliano, J.:Poem in October, w. R. White (ten), B. Lucarelli (ob), J. Rabbai (cl), Maurice Press (hpd), M. Press (cnd), American String Quartet RCA Gold Seal ▲ 60395-2-RG [ADD]

Nyffenegger, Esther (vc)
Bach, J.S.:Sons Vl, BWV 1027–1029, w. G. Wyss (pno) Divox ▲ CDX 25206 [ADD]
Brahms, J.:Sons Vc (comp), w. G. Wyss (pno) Divox ▲ CDX 25202 [ADD]
Chopin, F.:Son Vc, w. G. Wyss (pno) Divox ▲ CDX 25204 [ADD]
Franck, C.:Son Vn, w. G. Wyss (pno) [trans. for cello & piano] Divox ▲ CDX 25204 [ADD]
Francoeur, F.:Sons (22) Vn & Continuo, w. G. Wyss (pno)—in E Divox ▲ CDX 25206 [ADD]

Nyffenegger, Esther (vc) (cont.)
Grieg, E.:Son Vc, w. G. Wyss (pno) Divox ▲ CDX 25204 [ADD]
Janácek, L.:Fairy Tale, w. G. Wyss (pno) Divox ▲ CDX 25205 [ADD]
Locatelli, P.:Son Vc, w. G. Wyss (pno) Divox ▲ CDX 25206 [ADD]
Lully, J.-B.:Passacaglia Vc & Pno, w. G. Wyss (pno) Divox ▲ CDX 25206 [ADD]
Mendelssohn, F.:Son 1 Vc, w. G. Wyss (pno) Divox ▲ CDX 25203 [ADD]
Mendelssohn, F.:Son 2 Vc, w. G. Wyss (pno) Divox ▲ CDX 25203 [ADD]
Pfitzner, H.:Son Vc, w. G. Wyss (pno) Divox ▲ CDX 25205 [ADD]
Schubert, Franz:Son Arpeggione, w. G. Wyss (pno) Divox ▲ CDX 25202 [ADD]
Schumann, R.:Stücke im Volkston, w. G. Wyss (pno) Divox ▲ CDX 25203 [ADD]
Strauss, R.:Son Vc, w. G. Wyss (pno) Divox ▲ CDX 25205 [ADD]

Nygaard, Hans (vc)
Gade, N.W.:Andante & Allegro molto, w. Kontra String Quartet *(rec Torpen Kapel, Humlebaek, Denmark, May, 5–8, 1992)* BIS ▲ CD 545 [DDD]
Gade, N.W.:Octet, w. Anne Egendal (vn), Per Lund Madsen (vn), Sune Ranmo (va), Kontra String Quartet *(rec Torpen Kapel, Humlebaek, Denmark, May, 5–8, 1992)* BIS ▲ CD 545 [DDD]

Nyikos, Markus (vc)
Auric, G.:Imaginées II, w. J. Smykal (pno) Koch Schwann ▲ CD 310059 [DDD]
Cirri, G.B.:Con Vc & Str, w. H. Maile (cnd), Berlin RSO Koch Schwann ▲ CD 311063 [DDD]
Honegger, A.:Son Vc, w. J. Smykal (pno) Koch Schwann ▲ CD 310 059 [DDD]
Honegger, A.:Sonatina Cl, w. J. Smykal (pno) Koch Schwann ▲ CD 310 059 [DDD]
Milhaud, D.:Elégie, w. J. Smykal (pno) Koch Schwann ▲ CD 310 059 [DDD]
Milhaud, D.:Son Vc, w. J. Smykal (pno) Koch Schwann ▲ CD 310 059 [DDD]
Poulenc, F.:Son Vc, w. J. Smykal (pno) Koch Schwann ▲ CD 310 059 [DDD]
Vivaldi, A.:Cons Vc, w. H. Maile (cnd), Berlin RSO—2 concerti—RV.407, 410
Koch Schwann ▲ CD 311063 [DDD]

Nyiregyházi, Ervin (pno)
At the Opera, w. Ervin Nyiregyházi (pno) *(rec 1978)* VAI Audio ▲ VAIA/IPA 1003 (m) [ADD]
Nyiregyhazi, E.:Piano Music—paraphrases on operas by Leoncavallo *(Pagliacci)*, Tchaikovsky *(Eugene Onegin)*, Verdi *(Un ballo in maschera; Otello; Il trovatore)*, Wagner *(Rienzi; Lohengrin)* *(rec San Francisco, Mar. 1978)* VAI Audio ▲ VAIA/IPA 1003

Nykter, P. (vn)
Bartók, B.:Duos (44), w. J. Négyesy (vn) Neuma ▲ 45082 [DDD]

Nylén, G. (db)—see ORCHESTRAS & ENSEMBLES Musica Holmiae

Nyobe, Tom (conga)
Nørgård, P.:Twilight, w. J. Latham-König (cnd), Danish National RSO *(rec Danish Radio Concert Hall, 1982)* Marco Polo/Dacapo ▲ 8.224041 [AAD]

Nyquist, Kristian (hpd)
Bach, J.S.:Preludes & Fugues Hpd—in a, BWV 894 *(rec Mannheim, Germany)*
Pavane ▲ ADW 7367 [DDD]
Bull, J.:Kbd Music—Pavana of My Lord Lumley [Fitzwilliam Virginal Book No. 41]; Galliarda to My Lord Lumley's Paven [Fitzwilliam Virginal Book No. 11] *(rec Mannheim, Germany)*
Pavane ▲ ADW 7367 [DDD]
Marchand, L.:Pièces de clavecin (sels)—Suite in d *(rec Mannheim, Germany)*
Pavane ▲ ADW 7367 [DDD]
Scarlatti, D.:Sons Kbd—in C, K.132; in a, K.175; in g, K.426; in G, K.427 *(rec Mannheim, Germany)*
Pavane ▲ ADW 7367 [DDD]
Vogt, H.:Ostinato-Studie *(rec Mannheim, Germany)* Pavane ▲ ADW 7367 [DDD]

Oakes, Rodney (MIDI trbn)
Oakes, R.:Blues Danube Cambria ▲ CD 1088

Oakland, Ronald (vn)
Colgrass, M.:Concert Masters, w. Robert Rudie (vn), Masako Yanagita (vn), K. Akiyama (cnd), American SO *(rec 1977)* Vox Box ("The American Composers" series) 2-▲ CDX 5158

Obdrzálek, Mrek (vn)—see ORCHESTRAS & ENSEMBLES Bohuslav Martinů Philharmonic String Quartet

Oberacker, Betty (pno)
Biggs, J.:Vars on a Theme of Shostakovich, w. S. Kawalla (cnd), Polish Radio–TV SO Cracow
Vienna Modern Masters ▲ VMM 3002 [DDD]

Oberdorfer, H. (vn)—see ORCHESTRAS & ENSEMBLES Orlando String Quartet

Oberg, Sue (fl)
O'Rourke, J.:Terminal Pharmacy, w. Tony Burr (cl), Jeff Cortazzo (b trbn), John McEntire (dr), Rob Prosser (acc), Isha Suftin (acc), Mike Dockter (vc), Hattie Franck (vc), Robert Keck (vc), Mary LaBreque (vc), Dan Loch (vc), Stan Saderk (vc), Lisa Hemmer (fl), Wendi Lev (fl), Jim Vanden (fl), Jim O'Rourke (gtr), Steve Braack (elec) Tzadik ▲ TZA 7011 [DDD]

Oberson, René (org)
Noëls romantiques et modernes, w. Oberson, René (org) Gallo ▲ CD700 [DDD]

Obetz, John (org)
Casavant Organ Inaugural Recital, w. Obetz, John (org) RBW ▲ RBW 006 [DDD]
Festival of Organ & Brass, w. Missouri Brass Quintet, Jon Donald (perc) *(rec RLDS Peace Temple, Independence, MO)* RBW ▲ RBWCD 008

Oborin, Lev (pno)
Beethoven, L. van:Con Vn, Vc & Pno, "Triple Con", w. D. Oistrakh (vn), S. Knushevitsky (vc), R. Kubelik (cnd), Prague SO Multisonic ("Prague Spring" Collection) ▲ 31 0104 [ADD]
Beethoven, L. van:Con Vn, Vc & Pno, "Triple Con", w. David Oistrakh (vn), Sviatoslav Knushevitzy (vc), M. Sargent (cnd), Philharmonia Orch EMI Classics 2-▲ CDFB 69331
Beethoven, L. van:Sons Vn (comp), w. D. Oistrakh (vn) Philips 4-▲ 412570-2 [ADD]
Beethoven, L. van:Son 5 Vn, "Spring", w. D. Oistrakh (vn) Philips ▲ 412255-2 [ADD]
Beethoven, L. van:Son 9 Vn, "Kreutzer", w. D. Oistrakh (vn) Philips ▲ 412255-2 [ADD]
David Oistrakh, w. David Oistrakh (vn), Vladimir Yampolsky (pno)
Vanguard Classics 3-▲ OVC 4080/02 [ADD]
Grieg, E.:Sons Vn, Opp. 8, 13 & 45, w. D. Oistrakh (vn)—No. 2, Op. 13 Praga ▲ PR 250 048
Haydn, J.:Trios Pno, Vn & Vc, w. David Oistrakh (vn), Sviatoslav Knushevitsky (vc)—H.XV/27 *(rec live, 1961)* Multisonic ("Prague Spring Collection" series) ▲ 31 0105-2 [ADD]
Khachaturian, A.:Con Pno, w. E. Mravinsky (cnd), Czech PO Praga ▲ 250017
Schubert, Franz:Son Vn, D.574, w. D. Oistrakh (vn) *(rec 1958)* MK ▲ MKA 417111 [AAD]
Schubert, Franz:Trio 1 Pno, w. D. Oistrakh (vn), S. Knushevitsky (vc) *(rec live 1961)*
Multisonic ("Prague Spring Collection" series) ▲ 31 0105-2 [ADD]
Shostakovich, D.:Trio 2 Pno, w. D. Oistrakh (vn), S. Knushevitsky (vc) *(rec live 1961)*
Multisonic ("Prague Spring Collection" series) ▲ 31 0105-2 [ADD]
Tchaikovsky, P.:Son Pno, Op. 37 Multisonic ▲ MUL 310265

Obradovic, Maya (gtr)
Duo de Guitares, w. Christophe Leu (gtr) *(rec July 1987)* Gallo ▲ CD 533 [DDD]

O'Brien, Vincent (pno)
Leider Singer, w. John McCormack (ten), E. Schneider (sgr), Grace Moore (sop), F. Kreisler (vn), L. Bori (sop), L. Kennedy (vc) Symposium ▲ 1164

O'Byrne, Patrick (pno)
Granados, E.:Goyescas—Nos. 1–6 & El Pelele Bayer ▲ 100286 [DDD]

Ochi, Sylvia (mand)
Vivaldi, A.:Cons Diverse Instrs, w. Takashi Ochi (man), Jean-Marc Labylle (pic), Monique Frasca-Colombier (vn), Laurence Paugam (vn), P. Kuentz (cnd), Paul Kuentz Orch—in G for 2 Man; in C for Rcr; in B♭ for Bn [La notte]; in d for Vl; in a for Bn; in A for Vn & other Vns in echo
Pierre Verany ▲ PVY 730052 [DDD]
Vivaldi, A.:Con Mand, RV.425, w. T. Ochi (mand), R. Kuentz (cnd), Kuentz CO
Deutsche Grammophon ("Resonance" series) ▲ 429528-2 [ADD] ■ 429528-4
Vivaldi, A.:Con for 2 Mands, w. T. Ochi (mand), P. Kuentz (cnd), Kuentz CO
Deutsche Grammophon ("Resonance" series) ▲ 429528-2 [ADD] ■ 429528-4

▲ = CD ♦ = Enhanced CD Δ = MD ■ = Cassette Tape □ = DCC

Ochi, Takashi (mand)
Vivaldi, A.:Cons Diverse Instrs, w. Sylvia Ochi (man), Jean-Marc Labylle (pic), Monique Frasca-Colombier (vn), Laurence Paugam (vn), P. Kuentz (cnd), Paul Kuentz Orch—in G for 2 Man; in C for Rcr; in B♭ for Bn [La notte]; in d for Vl; in a for Bn; in A for Vn & other Vns in echo Pierre Verany ▲ PVY 730052 [DDD]
Vivaldi, A.:Con Mand, RV.425, w. S. Ochi (mand), R. Kuentz (cnd), Kuentz CO Deutsche Grammophon ("Resonance" series) ▲ 429528-2 [ADD] ■ 429528-4
Vivaldi, A.:Con for 2 Mands, w. S. Ochi (mand), P. Kuentz (cnd), Kuentz CO Deutsche Grammophon ("Resonance" series) ▲ 429528-2 [ADD] ■ 429528-4
Ochsenhofer, Hans Peter (va)—see ORCHESTRAS & ENSEMBLES Vienna String Quintet
Ockers, G. (hp)
Yun, I.:Novelette Fl, w. J. Kracht (vn), D. Esser (vc) Attacca ▲ BABEL 9056-3 [DDD]
Ockert, Christian (db)
Schubert, Franz:Minuets & Trios, D.89, w. Leipzig String Quartet MD + G ▲ MDG CD 3070604
Ockwell, Frederick (pno)
Songs, Dances & Fantasy, w. Jerry Fuller (db), Kenneth Dorsch (hpd), William Ferris (pno), Steve Hartman (hp), Thomas Potter (bar), John Vorrasi (ten), Anne Waller (gtr) Musical Arts Society ▲ CD 41589 [AAD] ■ CS 41589
O'Connor, Mark (vn)
Meyer, E.:Chamber Music, w. Yo-Yo Ma (vc), Edgar Meyer (bass)—Druid Fluid *(rec Sound Emporium, Nashville, Aug 17–20, 1995)* Sony Classical ▲ SK 68460 [DDD] △ SM 68460 ■ ST 68460
Meyer, E.:Chamber Music, w. Yo-Yo Ma (vc), Edgar Meyer (bass)—Mama; First Impressions; Étienne et Petunia; Pickles; Schizoozy *(rec Sound Emporium, Nashville, Aug 17–20, 1995)* Sony Classical ▲ SK 68460 [DDD] △ SM 68460 ■ ST 68460
O'Connor, M.:Chamber Music, w. Yo-Yo Ma (vc), Edgar Meyer (bass)—Appalachia Waltz; Butterfly's Day Out; F.C.'s Jig; Old Country Fairytale; Fair Dancer Reel *(rec Sound Emporium, Nashville, Aug 17–20, 1995)* Sony Classical ▲ SK 68460 [DDD] △ SM 68460 ■ ST 68460
O'Connor, M.:Con Fid, w. M. Alsop (cnd), Concordia Orch *(rec John Harms Center for the Arts, Englewood, NJ, Oct. 1994)* Warner Bros. ▲ 45846-2
O'Connor, M.:Qt Vn, w. Daniel Phillips (va), Carter Brey (vc), Edgar Meyer (db) *(rec Blair Recital Hall, Vanderbilt Univ., Nashville, TN, Dec. 1990)* Warner Bros. ▲ 45846-2
O'Connor, Tara Helen (fl)
Biscardi, C.:Traverso, w. Edmund Niemann (pno) *(rec SUNY Purchase Recital Hall, Feb. 12, 1993)* CRI ▲ CD 686 [DDD]
Wigglesworth, F.:Trillium, w. Sunghae Anna Lin (vn) CRI ▲ C 733 [DDD]
Yun, I.:Etudes Fl Arcadia ▲ ARC 1997-2 [DDD]
O'Conor, John (pno)
Autumn Songs:Popular Works for Solo Piano *(rec Mechanics Hall, Worcester, MA, Feb. 21–23, 1995)* Telarc ▲ CD 80391 [DDD]
Beethoven, L. van:Bagatelles (24) *(rec Mechanics Hall, Worcester, MA, Feb 21–23, 1995)* Telarc ▲ CD 80423 [DDD]
Beethoven, L. van:Music of, w. R. Serkin (pno), Shaw (cnd), Cleveland Orch, Atlanta SO—sels. from Syms. 5,6,7 & 9, Moonlight Son., Pno Con. 5, etc. Telarc ▲ CD 80240 [DDD] ■ CS 30240 (D)
Beethoven, L. van:Presto *(rec Mechanics Hall, Worcester, MA, Feb 21–23, 1995)* Telarc ▲ CD 80423 [DDD]
Beethoven, L. van:Sons Pno (comp)—Nos. 5, 6, 7 & 12 Telarc ▲ CD 80237 [DDD]
Beethoven, L. van:Sons Pno (comp)—Nos. 30–32 Telarc ▲ CD 80261 [DDD]
Beethoven, L. van:Sons Pno (comp)—Nos. 1, 2 & 3 Telarc ▲ CD 80214 [DDD]
Beethoven, L. van:Sons Pno (comp)—Sons. 9, 10, 19, 20, 22, 24 & 25 Telarc ▲ CD 80293 [DDD]
Beethoven, L. van:Sons Pno (comp)—Nos. 15, 16 & 18 Telarc ▲ CD 80185 [DDD]
Beethoven, L. van:Sons Pno (comp)—Nos. 17, 21 & 26 Telarc ▲ CD 80160 [DDD]
Beethoven, L. van:Sons Pno (comp)—Sons. 8, 14 & 23 Telarc ▲ CD 80118 [DDD]
Beethoven, L. van:Son 4 Pno *(rec Jan. 7–9, 1993)* Telarc ▲ CD 80363 [DDD]
Beethoven, L. van:Son 11 Pno *(rec Jan. 7–9, 1993)* Telarc ▲ CD 80363 [DDD]
Beethoven, L. van:Son 13 Pno *(rec Jan. 7–9, 1993)* Telarc ▲ CD 80363 [DDD]
Beethoven, L. van:Son 14 Pno, "Moonlight Son" Telarc ▲ CD 80118 [DDD]
Beethoven, L. van:Son 15 Pno, "Pastoral" Telarc ▲ CD 80185 [DDD]
Beethoven, L. van:Son 16 Pno Telarc ▲ CD 80185 [DDD]
Beethoven, L. van:Son 18 Pno Telarc ▲ CD 80185 [DDD]
Beethoven, L. van:Son 21 Pno, "Waldstein" Telarc ▲ CD 80160 [DDD]
Beethoven, L. van:Son 23 Pno, "Appassionata" Telarc ▲ CD 80118 [DDD]
Beethoven, L. van:Son 27 Pno *(rec Aug. 12–13, 1992)* Telarc ▲ CD 80335 [DDD]
Beethoven, L. van:Son 28 Pno *(rec Aug. 12–13, 1992)* Telarc ▲ CD 80335 [DDD]
Beethoven, L. van:Son 29 Pno, "Hammerklavier" *(rec Aug. 12–13, 1992)* Telarc ▲ CD 80335 [DDD]
Field, J.:Cons Pno (comp), w. J. Fürst (cnd), New Irish CO—Nos. 1–7 Onyx 3-▲ 101/103 [AAD]
Field, J.:Cons Pno (comp), w. J. Fürst (cnd), New Irish CO—Nos. 6 & 7 Sound ▲ 3414
Field, J.:Con 2 Pno, w. C. Mackerras (cnd), Scottish CO *(rec Feb. 27–28 & Mar. 1, 1993)* Telarc ▲ CD 80370 [DDD]
Field, J.:Con 3 Pno, w. C. Mackerras (cnd), Scottish CO *(rec Feb. 27–28 & Mar. 1, 1993)* Telarc ▲ CD 80370 [DDD]
Field, J.:Nocturnes Pno (misc)—15 nocturnes—Nos. 1, 2, 4–6, 8–16 & 18, as numbered in the Peters Edition Telarc ▲ CD 80199 [DDD]
Field, J.:Nocturnes Pno (misc)—3 Nocturnes—No. 3 in A♭, No. 7 in C & No. 17 in E Telarc ▲ CD 80290 [DDD]
Field, J.:Sons Pno (comp) Telarc ▲ CD 80290 [DDD]
Mozart, W.A.:Con 17 Pno, w. C. Mackerras (cnd), Scottish CO Telarc ▲ CD 80306 [DDD]
Mozart, W.A.:Con 18 Pno, w. C. Mackerras (cnd), Scottish CO Telarc ▲ CD 80285 [DDD]
Mozart, W.A.:Con 19 Pno, w. C. Mackerras (cnd), Scottish CO Telarc ▲ CD 8028 [DDD]
Mozart, W.A.:Con 20 Pno, w. C. Mackerras (cnd), Scottish CO *(rec Oct. 30–31, 1991)* Telarc ▲ CD 80308 [DDD]
Mozart, W.A.:Con 21 Pno, w. C. Mackerras (cnd), Scottish CO Telarc ▲ CD 80219 [DDD]
Mozart, W.A.:Con 22 Pno, w. C. Mackerras (cnd), Scottish CO *(rec Oct. 30–31, 1991)* Telarc ▲ CD 80308 [DDD]
Mozart, W.A.:Con 23 Pno, w. C. Mackerras (cnd), Scottish CO Telarc ▲ CD 80285 [DDD]
Mozart, W.A.:Con 24 Pno, w. C. Mackerras (cnd), Scottish CO Telarc ▲ CD 80306 [DDD]
Mozart, W.A.:Con 27 Pno, w. C. Mackerras (cnd), Scottish CO Telarc ▲ CD 80219 [DDD]
Mozart, W.A.:Rondo Pno Orch, K.386, w. C. Mackerras (cnd), Scottish CO Telarc ▲ CD 80285 [DDD]
Popular Works for Solo Piano Telarc ▲ CD 80313 [AAD]
Schubert, Franz:Impromptus Pno (comp) *(rec Jan. 10–11, 1993)* Telarc ▲ CD 80337 [DDD]
Schubert, Franz:Moments musicaux *(rec Mechanics Hall, Worcester, MA, Jan. 10–11, 1993)* Telarc ▲ CD 80369 [DDD]
Schubert, Franz:Qnt Pno, D.667, w. J. VanDemark (db), Cleveland String Quartet members Telarc ▲ CD 80225 [DDD]
Schubert, Franz:Son Pno, D.959 *(rec Mechanics Hall, Worcester, MA, Jan. 10–11, 1993)* Telarc ▲ CD 80369 [DDD]
Schubert, Franz:Waltzes Pno—(12) D.145 *(rec Jan. 10–11, 1993)* Telarc ▲ CD 80337 [DDD]
Octors, Georges-Elie (pno)
Mozart, W.A.:Con 7 Pnos, w. O. Ouziel (pno), D. Ouziel (pno), G. Octors (cnd), Walloon & French Community of Belgium CO [arr. for 2 Pianos by Mozart] *(rec Jan. 1991)* Pavane ▲ ADW 7257 [DDD]
Odé, Pieter (fl)
Martin, F.:Chants de Noël, w. E. Ameling (sop), F. Martin (pno) [F] Jecklin-Disco ▲ JD 563-2 [ADD]
Martin, F.:Songs, w. E. Ameling (sop), F. Martin (pno)—Drey Minnelieder:Ach Herzeliep; Es stuont ein frouwe alleine; Under der linden [G] Jecklin-Disco ▲ JD 563-2 [ADD]
O'Dette, Paul (archlt)
Purcell, H.:Songs, w. D. Minter (ct), M. Springfels (vl), M. Meyerson (hpd/org)—Be Welcome Then, Great Sir; Celia Has a Thousand Charmes; Crown the Altar; The Fatal Hour Comes On Apace; From Silent Shades; Hark! How All Things; Hark! the Echoing Air; Here the Dieties Approve; I Attempt From Love's Sickness to Fly; If Musick be the Food of Love; Lord, What is Man; Musick For A While; Not All My Torments; Now That the Sun Hath Veil's His Light; O Solitude; Sleep, Adam, Sleep; Sweeter Than Roses; Thrice Happy Lovers; 'Tis Nature's Voice [E] Harmonia Mundi USA ▲ HMU 907035
O'Dette, Paul (gtr)
English Lute Duets, w. Jakob Lindberg (gtr) BIS ▲ CD 267
O'Dette, Paul (lt)
Borrono, P.P.:Lt Music—Pavana chiamata la Desperata; Saltarello; Tocha tocha la Canella; Fantasia; Pavana la Gombertina; Saltarello; Saltarello chiamato el Mazolo Harmonia Mundi USA ▲ HMU 907043
Canzonetta:16th Century Canzoni & Instrumental Dances, w. D. Douglass (cnd), King's Noyse, Ellen Hargis (sop) Harmonia Mundi USA ▲ HMU 907127
Dowland, J.:Lachrimae, or Seaven Teares, w. P. Holman (cnd), Parley of Instruments—[period instrs] Hyperion ▲ CDA 66637
Dowland, J.:Lt Music Harmonia Mundi ▲ HMU 907162
Dowland, J.:Lt Music Harmonia Mundi ("Production USA" series) ▲ HMU 907163
Dowland, J.:Lt Music Harmonia Mundi France ▲ HMU 907161
Francesco Canova di Milano:Fants—Fant. (Castelfranco MS); Fant. No. 83; Pourquoy allez-vous seullette; Fant. No. 26; Fant. No. 39; Fant. No. 8; Fant. dolcissima et amorosa; Fant. No. 56 Harmonia Mundi USA ▲ HMU 907043
Francesco Canova di Milano:Ricercares—Ricercar No. 13 Harmonia Mundi USA ▲ HMU 907043
The Golden Dream:17th Century Music from the Low Countries, w. M. Springfels (cnd), Newberry Consort, Marion Verbruggen (rcr) *(rec Troy Savings Bank Music Hall, Nov 1–3, 1993)* Harmonia Mundi France ▲ HMU 907123
Lord Herbert of Cherbury's Lute Book Harmonia Mundi ▲ HMU 907068
Marco da L'Aquila:Lt Music—Ricercar; Il est bel et bon; Ricercar Lautre jour No. 101; Nous bergiers; La traditora No. 3; Ricercar No. 16; La traditora No. 2; La battaglia; Ricercar No. 33 Harmonia Mundi USA ▲ HMU 907043
Ripa, A. da:Lt Music—Fant. No. 22; L'eccho; Fant. No. 8 Harmonia Mundi USA ▲ HMU 907043
O'Dette, Paul (lt/chit)
Kapsberger, G.G.:Music for Lt—25 Toccatas, Gagliarde, etc. Harmonia Mundi USA ▲ HMU 907020
O'Dette, Paul (lt/orpharion)
Dowland, J.:Lt Music Harmonia Mundi France ▲ HMU 907160
O'Dette, Paul (thb)
Lawes, W.:Royall Consort Suites, w. Nigel North (thb), Purcell Quartet Chandos ("Early Music" series) 2-▲ CHAN 0584/5 [DDD]
Rosenmüller, J.:Music of, w. Ellen Hargis (sop), Mary Springfels (va), D. Douglass (cnd), King's Noyse—Suite in C [from Studentenmusik]; Jubilent aethera; Son X à 5; Son VII à 4; In te, Domine, speravi; Son XI à 5; Son IV à 3; Ach Herr, strafe mich nicht in deinem Zorn; Son III à 2; Leiber Herre Gott, Wecke uns auf Harmonia Mundi ▲ HMU 907179
O'Dette, Paul (thb/cittern/lt)
Purcell, H.:Musick's Hand-maid, w. Ellen Hargis (sop), Ian Honeyman (ten), Rodrigo del Pozo (ten), Harry van der Kamp (bass), Andrew Lawrence-King (hps/org/hpd), A. Lawrence-King (cnd), Harp Consort Astrée ▲ E 8564
Odiaga, Lola (pno)
Haydn, J.:Pno Music—Capriccio in G, H.XVI/1 (1765); Variations on the song "Gott erhalte Franz den Kaiser" Titanic ▲ Ti 156
Haydn, J.:Sons Pno—in G, E♭, F, A, E, H.VXI/27-31; in C, H.XVI/4 Albany ▲ TROY 094 [DDD]
Haydn, J.:Sons Pno—H.XVI/24, 25, 26, 35, 49 & 51 Albany ▲ TROY 062 [DDD]
Haydn, J.:Sons Pno—in D, H.XVI/14; in B♭, H.XVI/18; in E♭, H.XVI/49; in b, H.XVI/32; in e, H.XVI/34; in D, H.XVI/37 Albany ▲ TROY 147 [DDD]
Haydn, J.:Sons Pno—H.XVI/19,39,48 & 50 Titanic ▲ Ti 156
Haydn, J.:Sons Pno—5 Sonatas—in C, H.XVI/21; in E, H.XVI/22; in F, H.XVI/23; in D, H.XVI/33; in A♭, H.XVI/43 Albany ▲ TROY 045-2 [DDD]
Haydn, J.:Sons Pno—H.XVI/20,44,45 & 46 Titanic ▲ Ti 166 [DDD]
Haydn, J.:Vars Pno, "Six Easy Vars" Titanic ▲ Ti 166 [DDD]
Odnoposoff, Richard (vn)
Beethoven, L. van:Con Vn, Vc & Pno, "Triple Con", w. S. Auber (vc), A. Morales (pno), F. von Weingartner (cnd), Vienna PO *(rec 10/20–21/37)* Pearl ▲ PEA 9358 (m) [AAD]
Chausson, E.:Poème Vn, w. G. Rivoli (cnd), Geneva RSO *(rec Mar. 10, 1960)* Doron ▲ DRC 4004 [ADD]
Dvořák, A.:Con Vn, w. W. Goehr (cnd), Concerts de Paris SO *(rec June 5–6, 1957)* Doron ▲ DRC 4002 [ADD]
Encores II Bayer ▲ 200008 [ADD]
Glazunov, A.:Con Vn, w. W. Goehr (cnd), Concerts de Paris SO *(rec June 5–6, 1957)* Doron ▲ DRC 4002 [ADD]
Joachim, J.:Vars Vn, w. J. Stárek (cnd), Stuttgart RSO *(rec June 7, 1974)* Doron ▲ DRC 4004 [ADD]
Saint-Saëns, C.:Introduction & Rondo capriccioso, w. G. Rivoli (cnd), Geneva RSO *(rec Mar. 10, 1960)* Doron ▲ DRC 4004 [ADD]
Sarasate, P. de:Zigeunerweisen, w. G. Rivoli (cnd), Geneva RSO *(rec Mar. 10, 1960)* Doron ▲ DRC 4004 [ADD]
O'Donnell, Heather (pno)
Lovenstein, J.:Music of, w. Mary Brockenbrough (sop), Laura Sanders (sop), Barton Green (ten), Rockland Osgood (ten), David Murray (bar), Benjamin Sears (bar), Jonathan Lovenstein (pno), James Silvers (pno), Rocy Reider (fl), Jason Horowitz (vn), Adrianna Hulscher (vn), James Johnston (vn), Mimi Ragson (vn), Peter Landeen (vc), Reinmar Seidler (vc)—Blake Songs; other works Titanic ▲ Ti 221 [DDD]
O'Donnell, James (org)
Erbach, C.:Sacred Music, w. J. West (cnd), His Majesties Sagbutts & Cornetts, Westminster Cathedral Choir—Sacredotes Dei; Canzona decundi toni; Alleluia, Hic est sacredos; Fantasia sub elevatione; Toccata octavi toni [frag.]; Post-communion; Posuisti Domine; La Paglia Hyperion ▲ CDA 66688
Hassler, H.L.:Sacred Music, w. J. West (cnd), His Majesties Sagbutts & Cornetts, Westminster Cathedral Choir—Canzon duodecimi toni; Cantate Dominio canticum novum; Toccata in G; Canzon noni toni; O sacrum convivium; Domine Dominus noster Hyperion ▲ CDA 66688
Morales, C. de:Sacred Music, w. Westminster Cathedral Choir—Missa Quaeramus cum pastoribus; Andreas Christi famulus; Clamabat autem mulier Chananea; O sacrum convivium; Regina caeli; Sancta Maria, succurre miseris; O magnum mysterium; Lamentebatur Jacob Hyperion ▲ CDA 66635 [DDD]
Victoria, T.L. de:Masses, w. Westminster Cathedral Choir—Dum complerentur Hyperion ▲ CDA 66886
Victoria, T.L. de:Sacred Choral Music, w. Westminster Cathedral Choir—Popule meus & 5 other hymns Hyperion ▲ CDA 66886
O'Donnell, Mildred (va)—see ORCHESTRAS & ENSEMBLES Valley String Quartet
O'Donovan, Michael (bn)—see ORCHESTRAS & ENSEMBLES Mozzafiato
Odori, Orio (cl)—see ORCHESTRAS & ENSEMBLES Harmonia Ensemble
Odriozola, Jane (vc)
Christensen, M.:Reflets de cristal, w. Ricardo Odriozola (vn) *(rec Jetsmark Kirke, Denmark, June 1993 & Dec. 1994)* Point ▲ PCD 5116
Odriozola, R.:Dances, w. Ricardo Odriozola (vn) *(rec Jetsmark Kirke, Denmark, June 1993 & Dec. 1994)* Point ▲ PCD 5116
Odriozola, R.:Danish Miniatures, w. Ricardo Odriozola (vn) *(rec Jetsmark Kirke, Denmark, June 1993 & Dec. 1994)* Point ▲ PCD 5116
Odriozola, R.:Psalms *(rec Jetsmark Kirke, Denmark, June 1993 & Dec. 1994)* Point ▲ PCD 5116
Odriozola, Ricardo (vn)
Christensen, M.:Dreamless Fragments *(rec Jetsmark Kirke, Denmark, June 1993 & Dec. 1994)* Point ▲ PCD 5116

INSTRUMENT.

Odriozola, Ricardo (vn) (cont.)
Christensen, M.:Reflets de cristal, w. Jane Odriozola (vc) *(rec Jetsmark Kirke, Denmark, June 1993 & Dec. 1994)* Point ▲ PCD 5116
Christensen, M.:Winter Light, w. Helle Kristensen (rcr) *(rec Jetsmark Kirke, Denmark, June 1993 & Dec. 1994)* Point ▲ PCD 5116
Odriozola, R.:Dances, w. Jane Odriozola (vc) *(rec Jetsmark Kirke, Denmark, June 1993 & Dec. 1994)* Point ▲ PCD 5116
Odriozola, R.:Danish Miniatures, w. Jane Odriozola (vc) *(rec Jetsmark Kirke, Denmark, June 1993 & Dec. 1994)* Point ▲ PCD 5116
Odstčil, J. (vn)—see ORCHESTRAS & ENSEMBLES Kocian String Quartet
O'Dwyer, Timothy (sax)
O'Dwyer, T.:Bar-do'i-thos-grol—3rd chakra Vox Australis ▲ VAST 0192
Oehmichen, Isabelle (pno)
Chopin, F.:Pno Music (misc)—Polonaise in c#, Op. 20/1; Étude in E, Op. 10/3; Ballade in g, Op. 23; Mazurka in f *(rec Studio S2, Polish Radio, Warsaw, May 16–18, 1990)* Polskie Nagrania ▲ PNCD 069 [DDD]
Magin, M.:Son 2 Pno *(rec Studio S2, Polish Radio, Warsaw, May 16–18, 1990)* Polskie Nagrania ▲ PNCD 069 [DDD]
Oei, David (pno)—see also ORCHESTRAS & ENSEMBLES Chamber Music Northwest members
Grieg, E.:Son Vc, w. Sonia Wieder Atherton (vc) Adda ▲ ADD 581128 [DDD]
Husa, K.:Son Vn, w. Elmar Oliveira (vn) *(rec Right Track Recordings, NYC)* New World ▲ 80493-2
Husa, K.:Son Vn, w. Elmar Oliveira (vn) Grenadilla ■ GSC 1032
Piston, W.:Son Vn, w. E. Sato (vn) Grenadilla ■ GSC 1073
Schumann, R.:Adagio & Allegro Hn, w. Sonia Wieder Atherton (vc) Adda ▲ ADD 581128 [DDD]
Schumann, R.:Fantasiestücke Cl, w. Sonia Wieder Atherton (vc) Adda ▲ ADD 581128 [DDD]
Schumann, R.:Stücke im Volkston, w. Sonia Wieder Atherton (vc) Adda ▲ ADD 581128 [DDD]
Wilder, A.:Son 1 Hn, w. David Jolley (hn) *(rec SUNY Purchase Recital Hall)* Arabesque ▲ ARA 6665 [DDD]
Wilder, A.:Son 2 Hn, w. David Jolley (hn) *(rec SUNY Purchase Recital Hall)* Arabesque ▲ ARA 6665 [DDD]
Wilder, A.:Son 3 Hn, w. David Jolley (hn) *(rec SUNY Purchase Recital Hall)* Arabesque ▲ ARA 6665 [DDD]
Wilder, A.:Suite Cl, w. Alan Kay (cl), David Jolley (hn) *(rec SUNY Purchase Recital Hall)* Arabesque ▲ ARA 6665 [DDD]
Wilder, A.:Suite 1 Hn, w. David Jolley (hn), Sam Pilafian (tuba) *(rec SUNY Purchase Recital Hall)* Arabesque ▲ ARA 6665 [DDD]
Oelbaum, Michael (pno)
Beethoven, L. van:Vars on a waltz by Diabelli, Op. 120 Bridge ▲ BCD 9010 [ADD]
Offermans, W. (fl/b fl)
Offermans, W.:How to Survive in Paradise II, w. J. Ueda (voc/satsuma-biwa) Gallo ▲ CD 732 [DDD]
Offermans, W.:Voice & Noise, w. J. Ueda (voc/satsuma-biwa) Gallo ▲ CD 732 [DDD]
Offord, Colin (mountain earth hp)
Offord, C.:Music of—Three Sisters; Earthharp; West Wind Drift; Heartland; Last of the Night; Pacifica Suite; Riding on the Rim Vox Australis ▲ VAST 002-2 [DDD]
Ogano, Kumi (pno)
Mendelssohn, F.:Pno Music (misc)—Phantasie, Op. 28; Rondo, Op. 14; Sieben Charakterstücke, Op. 7; Trois caprices, Op. 33 Arcobaleno ▲ SBCD 5700
Ogawa, Noriko (pno)
Takemitsu, T.:Pno Music—Litany (1950/1989); Pause interrompue (1952–59); Piano Distance (1961); For Away (1973); Les Yeux clos (1979); Les Yeux clos II (1988); Rain Tree Sketch (1982); Rain Tree Sketch II (1992) *(rec Danderyd Grammar School, Sweden, July 11–12, 1996)* BIS ▲ CD 805 [DDD]
Ogden, Craig (gtr)
Bennett, Richard Rodney:Impromptus (5) *(rec Nimbus Foundation Concert Hall, Wyastone Leys, Monmouth)* Nimbus ▲ NI 5390 [DDD]
Berkeley, L.:Sonatina Gtr *(rec Nimbus Foundation Concert Hall, Wyastone Leys, Monmouth)* Nimbus ▲ NI 5390 [DDD]
Tippett, M.:The Blue Gtr *(rec Nimbus Foundation Concert Hall, Wyastone Leys, Monmouth)* Nimbus ▲ NI 5390 [DDD]
Walton, W.:Bagatelles Gtr *(rec Nimbus Foundation Concert Hall, Wyastone Leys, Monmouth)* Nimbus ▲ NI 5390 [DDD]
Yoshimatsu, T.:Con Gtr, "Pegasus Effect", w. S. Fujioka (cnd), BBC PO Chandos ▲ CHAN 9438
Ogden, John (pno)
Bach, J.S.:Preludium & Fugue Hpd, BWV 849 Altarus ▲ CD 9072
Beethoven, L. van:Son 30 Pno Altarus ▲ CD 9072
Chopin, F.:Ballades Pno (comp)—Op. 23 Altarus ▲ CD 9072
Chopin, F.:Etudes (24)—Op. 25/1 Altarus ▲ CD 9072
Liszt, F.:Pno Music (misc)—Son après une lecture de Dante Altarus ▲ CD 9072
Lloyd, G.:The Road Through Samarkand Altarus ▲ CD 9072
Ogdon, John (pno)
Alwyn, W.:Preludes (12) Pno Chandos ▲ CHAN 8399 [DDD]
Arensky, A.:Suite 1 for 2 Pnos, w. Brenda Lucas (pno) EMI Classics 2-▲ CDFB 69386
Beethoven, L. van:Son 8 Pno, "Pathétique" IMP ("Classic" series) ▲ IMP 2032
Beethoven, L. van:Son 14 Pno, "Moonlight Son" IMP ("Classic" series) ▲ IMP 2032
Beethoven, L. van:Son 23 Pno, "Appassionata" IMP ("Classic" series) ▲ IMP 2032
Bizet, G.:Jeux d'enfants, w. Brenda Lucas (pno) EMI Classics 2-▲ CDFB 69386
Busoni, F.:Con Pno, Op. 39, w. male chorus, D. Revenaugh (cnd), Royal PO EMI Classics ▲ CDH 69850
Busoni, F.:Elegies (7) Pno—All'Italia Altarus 2-▲ AIR-CD 9063
Busoni, F.:Fant nach J. S. Bach Pno Altarus 2-▲ AIR-CD 9063
Chopin, F.:Barcarolle Pno IMP ▲ IMP 2008
Chopin, F.:Berceuse IMP ▲ IMP 2008
Chopin, F.:Fant IMP ▲ IMP 2008
Chopin, F.:Nocturnes—in F, Op. 15/1 IMP ▲ IMP 2008
Chopin, F.:Polonaises—in c, Op. 40/2 IMP ▲ IMP 2008
Chopin, F.:Son Pno, Op. 58 IMP ▲ IMP 2008
Debussy, C.:Petite Suite, w. Brenda Lucas (pno) EMI Classics 2-▲ CDFB 69386
Fauré, G.:Ballade Pno, w. L. Frémaux (cnd), City of Birmingham SO Klavier ▲ KCD 11011 [ADD]
Favorite Piano, w. Daniel Adni (pno), A. Brownridge (pno), J. Février (pno), M. Lympany (pno), G. Tacchino (pno) Classics for Pleasure ▲ CDCFP 4622 [ADD/DDD]
Grieg, E.:Con Pno, Op. 16, w. P. Berglund (cnd), New Philharmonia Orch EMI Classics ▲ CDE 67772
John Ogdon, w. Ogdon, John (pno) IMP ("Classics" series) ▲ IMP 6701202
Khachaturian, A.:Gayane (sels), w. Brenda Lucas (pno)—Sabre Dance [arr. 2 Pnos] EMI Classics 2-▲ CDFB 69386
Litolff, H.C.:Con Symphonique 4, w. L. Frémaux (cnd), City of Birmingham SO Klavier ■ KC 527
Litolff, H.C.:Con Symphonique 4, w. L. Frémaux (cnd), City of Birmingham SO—Scherzo Klavier ▲ KCD 11011 [ADD]
Mendelssohn, F.:Con 1 Pno, w. A. Ceccato (cnd), London SO Klavier ▲ KCD 11029 [ADD]
Mendelssohn, F.:Con 1 Pno, w. A. Ceccato (cnd), London SO Klavier ■ KC 531
Mendelssohn, F.:Con 2 Pno, w. A. Ceccato (cnd), London SO Klavier ■ KC 531
Mendelssohn, F.:Con 2 Pno, w. A. Ceccato (cnd), London SO Klavier ▲ KCD 11029 [ADD]
Mendelssohn, F.:Rondo brilliant, w. A. Ceccato (cnd), London SO Klavier ■ KC 531
Mendelssohn, F.:Rondo brilliant, w. A. Ceccato (cnd), London SO Klavier ▲ KCD 11011 [ADD]
Nocturnal Classics, w. B. Wilde (cnd), Serenata of London, Cristina Ortiz (pno), F. Lott (sop) Pickwick ("The Orchid" series) ▲ PICORCD 11007
Ogdon, J.:Dance Suite Altarus 2-▲ AIR-CD 9063
Rachmaninoff, S.:Duets Pno 4-Hands, w. Brenda Lucas (pno) EMI Classics 2-▲ CDFB 69386
Rachmaninoff, S.:Suite 1 for 2 Pnos, w. Brenda Lucas (pno) EMI Classics 2-▲ CDFB 69386
Rachmaninoff, S.:Suite 2 for 2 Pnos, w. Brenda Lucas (pno) EMI Classics 2-▲ CDFB 69386

Ogdon, John (pno) (cont.)
Rawsthorne, A.:Con 2 Pno, w. J. Pritchard (cnd), BBC SO IMP ("BBC Radio Classics" series) ▲ IMP 5691762
Rawsthorne, A.:Con Pnos, w. Brenda Lucas (pno), J. Pritchard (cnd), London PO IMP ("BBC Radio Classics" series) ▲ IMP 5691762
Saint-Saëns, C.:Carnival of the Animals, w. B. Lucas (pno), L. Frémaux (cnd), City of Birmingham SO Klavier ■ KC 527
Saint-Saëns, C.:Carnival of the Animals, w. B. Lucas (pno), L. Frémaux (cnd), City of Birmingham SO Klavier ▲ KCD 11011 [ADD]
Shostakovich, D.:Concertino for 2 Pnos, w. Brenda Lucas (pno) EMI Classics 2-▲ CDFB 69386
Simpson, R.:Con Pno, w. C. Silvestri (cnd), Bournemouth SO IMP ("BBC Radio Classics" series) ▲ IMP 5691762
Sorabji, K.S.:Opus clavicembalisticum Altarus ▲ CD 9075
Stevenson, R.:Sonatina 1 Pno Altarus 2-▲ AIR-CD 9063
Tippett, M.:Con Pno, w. C. Davis (cnd), Philharmonia Orch EMI Classics 2-▲ ZDMB 63522
Tippett, M.:Sons Pno (comp)—Nos. 1 & 2 EMI Classics 2-▲ ZDMB 63522
Ogg, Jacques (hpd)—see also ORCHESTRAS & ENSEMBLES Senario Ensemble
Bach, C.P.E.:Trio Son Fl, H.367, w. Wilbert Hazelzet (fl), Alda Stuurop (vn), Richte van der Meer (vc) *(rec Utrecht, Sept 1993)* Globe ▲ GLO 5110 [DDD]
Bach, C.P.E.:Trio Son Fl, H.371, w. Wilbert Hazelzet (fl), Alda Stuurop (vn), Richte van der Meer (vc) *(rec Utrecht, Sept 1993)* Globe ▲ GLO 5110 [DDD]
Bach, C.P.E.:Trio Son Fl, H.570, w. Wilbert Hazelzet (fl), Alda Stuurop (vn), Richte van der Meer (vc) *(rec Utrecht, Sept 1993)* Globe ▲ GLO 5110 [DDD]
Bach, C.P.E.:Trio Son Fl, H.574, w. Wilbert Hazelzet (fl), Alda Stuurop (vn), Richte van der Meer (vc) *(rec Utrecht, Sept 1993)* Globe ▲ GLO 5110 [DDD]
Bach, C.P.E.:Trio Son for 2 Fls, H.580, w. Kate Clarke (fl), Wilbert Hazelzet (fl), Alda Stuurop (vn), Richte van der Meer (vc) *(rec Utrecht, Sept 1993)* Globe ▲ GLO 5110 [DDD]
Bach, Joh. Christian:Cons Hpd, T.298/1, w. A. Stuurop (cnd), Les Éléments—Nos. 2 & 5 *(rec Utrecht, 1995)* Globe ▲ GLO 5139 [DDD]
Bach, Joh. Christian:Con Hpd, T.301/4, w. A. Stuurop (cnd), Les Éléments *(rec Utrecht, 1995)* Globe ▲ GLO 5139 [DDD]
Bach, J.S.:Goldberg Vars *(rec Utrecht, Oct 1994)* Globe 2-▲ GLO 5129 [DDD]
Bustijn, P.:Suite 6 Hpd *(rec Apr. 1993)* Globe ▲ GLO 5101 [DDD]
de Fesch, W.:Son Voice, w. R. van der Meer (cello), R. Kanji (fl)—No. 1 *(rec Apr. 1993)* Globe ▲ GLO 5101 [DDD]
Forqueray, A.:Pièces de clavecin (5 suites) *(rec Utrecht, June & Dec. 1994)* Globe 2-▲ GLO 6027 [DDD]
Hotteterre, J.:Music of, w. Wilbert Hazelzet (trns fl), Jaap ter Linden (vl), Konrad Junghänel (thb)—5 Airs; Passacaille; 8 Preludes in b, c, C, D, g, g, G, G; 3 Suites in c, g, G *(rec San Miguel Church, Cuenca, Spain, May 1996)* Glossa ▲ GCD 920801 [DDD]
Philidor, P.:Music of, w. W. Hazelet (trns fl), K. Clark (trns fl), M. Fentross (lt/thb), T. Zwart (vl)—Trios 1 & 2 in G & e for 2 Flutes & Continuo; Suite No. 3 in D for 2 Flutes; Suites Nos. 5, 6 & 12 in e, b & D for Flute & Continuo *(rec June 1993)* Globe ▲ GLO 5107 [DDD]
Schenck, J.:Fant 1 Voc, w. R. Kanji (rcr), R. van der Meer (vc) *(rec Apr. 1993)* Globe ▲ GLO 5101 [DDD]
Telemann, G.P.:Cons (misc), w. Les Éléments—Con. a 9 in E for Piccolo, Flute, Oboe d'amore, Strings & Continuo *(rec June 1993)* Globe ▲ GLO 5104 [DDD]
Telemann, G.P.:Cons for 2 Fls, w. Les Éléments—(1) in D *(rec June 1993)* Globe ▲ GLO 5104 [DDD]
Telemann, G.P.:Con in F Rcr Bn, w. Les Éléments *(rec June 1993)* Globe ▲ GLO 5104 [DDD]
Van Blanckenburg, Q.:Fuga obligata *(rec Apr. 1993)* Globe ▲ GLO 5101 [DDD]
Van Wassenaer, U.:Sons Rcr, w. R. Kanji (rcr), R. van der Meer (vc)—Primata in F; Seconda in g; Terza in g *(rec Apr. 1993)* Globe ▲ GLO 5101 [DDD]
Ogg, Jacques (pno)
Bach, C.P.E.:Fl & Pno Music, w. W. Hazelzet (fl)—Duettos in C, W.73 (H.504) & in E, W.84 (H.506); (Trio) Sonata in B♭, W.161/2 Channel Classics ▲ CCS 0790 [DDD]
Bach, C.P.E.:Kbd Music—La Stahl, H.94 (W.117/25); Les langueurs tendres, H.110 (W.117/30 Channel Classics ▲ CCS 0790 [DDD]
Bach, C.P.E.:Sons Fl, w. W. Hazelzet (fl)—in D, H.505 (W.83) Channel Classics ▲ CCS 0790 [DDD]
Bach, C.P.E.:Sons Fl, w. W. Hazelzet (fl), Christian Norde (vl)—W. 124, 128, 130, 131 & 134 *(rec Oct 1992)* Globe ▲ GLO 5091 [DDD]
Benda, G.A.:Sons Pno—No. 1 in B♭; No. 5 in g; No. 7 in c; No. 9 in a; No. 13 in E♭; No. 16 in C *(rec Oct. 1992)* Globe ▲ GLO 5092 [DDD]
Benda, G.A.:Sonatinas Pno—No. 3 in a; No. 6 in d; No. 13 in c; No. 21 in F; No. 23 in g; No. 34 in D *(rec Oct. 1992)* Globe ▲ GLO 5092 [DDD]
Haydn, J.:Sons Pno—Sons. 43–47, H.XVI:28–32 *(rec May 1993)* Globe ▲ GLO 5103 [DDD]
Ledesma, M.R.:Divert Marcial, w. Jorge Caryevschi (fl) *(rec Madrid, Feb 6–10, 1989)* RNE/Spanish National Radio ▲ AME 006 [DDD]
Ribas, J.M. del C.:Music for Fl Pno, w. Jorge Caryevschi (fl)—El Sereni; La Cachucha; Fant Octava *(rec Madrid, Feb 6–10, 1989)* RNE/Spanish National Radio ▲ AME 006 [DDD]
Ognibene, Joseph (hn)—see ORCHESTRAS & ENSEMBLES Reykjavik Wind Quintet
Ogranovitch, Olga (vc)
Funk, E.:Con Vc, "Homage to Jaqueline DuPré", w. V. Válek (cnd), Czech RSO *(rec 1994)* MMC ▲ MMC 2033 [DDD]
Ohanian, David (hn)—see ORCHESTRAS & ENSEMBLES Canadian Brass
O'Hara, Mary (hp)
The Instrumental Collection:16 Beautiful Melodies for Harp, w. O'Hara, Mary (hp) Valentine ▲ VALD 8059 [DDD]
Ohlsson, Garrick (pno)
Beethoven, L. van:Son 2 Pno Arabesque ▲ ARA 6638 [DDD]
Beethoven, L. van:Son 8 Pno, "Pathétique" *(rec SUNY Purchase Performing Arts Center, June 27–29, 1995)* Arabesque ▲ Z-6677 [DDD]
Beethoven, L. van:Son 14 Pno, "Moonlight Son" *(rec SUNY Purchase Performing Arts Center, June 27–29, 1995)* Arabesque ▲ Z-6677 [DDD]
Beethoven, L. van:Son 23 Pno, "Appassionata" Arabesque ▲ ARA 6638 [DDD]
Beethoven, L. van:Son 23 Pno, "Appassionata" *(rec SUNY Purchase Performing Arts Center, June 27–29, 1995)* Arabesque ▲ Z-6677 [DDD]
Beethoven, L. van:Son 30 Pno Arabesque ▲ ARA 6638 [DDD]
Busoni, F.:Con Pno, Op. 39, w. Cleveland Chorus, C. von Dohnányi (cnd), Cleveland Orch [G] Telarc ▲ CD 80207 [DDD]
Chopin, F.:Ballades Pno (comp) Arabesque ▲ 6630 [DDD]
Chopin, F.:Impromptus *(rec SUNY/Purchase Performing Arts Center Theatre C)* Arabesque 2-▲ Z 6642-2
Chopin, F.:Impromptus Arabesque 2-▲ ARA 6642 [DDD]
Chopin, F.:Nocturnes *(rec SUNY, Purchase Performing Arts Center, Theatre C)* Arabesque 2-▲ ARA 6653-2 [DDD]
Chopin, F.:Nocturnes—14 Nocturnes Royal Classics ▲ ROY 6408
Chopin, F.:Pno Music (comp)—24 Preludes, Op. 28; Prelude in A♭, Op. posth.; Rondo in C, Op. 1; Rondo in c, Op. 5 Arabesque ▲ 6629 [DDD]
Chopin, F.:Pno Music (comp)—The Four Ballades; Rondo in E♭, Op. 16; Rondo in C, Op. 73 Arabesque ▲ 6630 [DDD]
Chopin, F.:Pno Music (comp)—Scherzi Arabesque ▲ ARA 6633 [DDD]
Chopin, F.:Pno Music (comp)—19 Waltzes *(rec SUNY, Puchase Performing Arts Center, Theater C, Sept & Nov 1995)* Arabesque ▲ Z 6669 [DDD]
Chopin, F.:Pno Music (comp)—Sonatas Nos. 1, 2 & 3 Arabesque ▲ 6618 [DDD]

754 ▲ = CD ♦ = Enhanced CD Δ = MD ■ = Cassette Tape □ = DCC

Ohlsson, Garrick (pno) (cont.)

Chopin, F.:Pno Music (misc), w. Martha Argerich (pno), Vladimir Ashkenazy (pno), Stanislav Bunin (pno), Halina Czerny–Stefanska (pno), Jan Ekier (pno), Yuval Fichman (pno), Kemal Gekic (pno), Adam Harasiewicz (pno), Krzysztof Jablonski (pno), Louis Kentner (pno), Jean–Marc Luisada (pno), Garrick Ohlsson (pno), Ivo Pogorelich (pno), Maurizio Pollini (pno), Dang Thai Son (pno)—includes Ballade (Nos. 1 & 2); Barcarolle, Op. 60; Concerto Nos. 1 & 2; Études (Op. 10, Nos. 1, 5, 8, 10 & 12 & Op. 25, No. 10, 18 & 25); Grand valse brillante; Impromptus (Nos. 3 & 4); Mazurkas (Op. 24, Nos. 1–4; Op. 30, Nos. 1–4; Op. 50, No. 32; Op. 59, Nos. 1–3); Nocturnes (Op. 9, No. 3; Op. 37, No. 12; Op. 48, No. 13; Op. 55, No. 16)Polonaise (Op. 40, Nos. 3 & 4; Op. 44, No. 5; Op. 53, No. 6; Op. 61, No. 7); Preludes (Op. 28 Nos. 13–18, 21–24 & Op. 45, No. 25); Scherzos (Nos. 1–3); Sonatas (Nos. 2 & 3); Waltzes (No. 1 & 6) LaserLight 5–▲ 15 961 [ADD/DDD]
Chopin, F.:Polonaises—in g, Op. posth.; B♭, Op. posth.; A♭, Op. posth.; g#, Op. posth.; b♭, Op. posth.; G♭, Op. posth.; d, Op. 71/1; B♭, Op. 71/2; f, Op. 71/3; c#, Op. 26/1; e♭, Op. 26/2 "Siberian"; A, Op. 40/1 "Military"; c, Op. 40/2 Arabesque 2–▲ Z 6642–2
Chopin, F.:Polonaises Arabesque ▲ ARA 6642 [DDD]
Chopin, F.:Polonaises—8 polonaises Royal Classics ▲ ROY 6407
Chopin, F.:Polonaise–fant *(rec SUNY/Purchase Performing Arts Center Theatre C)* Arabesque 2–▲ Z 6642–2
Chopin, F.:Preludes, Op. 28 Arabesque ▲ 6629 [DDD]
Chopin, F.:Son Pno, Op. 4 Arabesque ▲ 6628 [DDD]
Chopin, F.:Son Pno, Op. 35 Arabesque ▲ 6628 [DDD]
Chopin, F.:Son Pno, Op. 58 Arabesque ▲ 6628 [DDD]
Copland, A.:Con Pno, w. M. Tilson Thomas (cnd), San Francisco SO *(rec Davies Symphony Hall, San Francisco, June 25, 1996)* RCA Red Seal ▲ 09026–68541–2 [DDD]
Debussy, C.:Etudes Arabesque ▲ Z 6601
Debussy, C.:Suite bergamasque Arabesque ▲ Z 6601
Fišer, L.:Con for 2 Pnos, w. Frantisek Maxian (pno), L. Pešek (cnd), Czech PO Supraphon ▲ SUP 0035 [DDD]
Gershwin, G.:Rhap in Blue, w. E. de Waart (cnd), Minnesota Orch Virgin Classics ▲ 59619 [DDD]
Gershwin, G.:Rhap in Blue, w. E. de Waart (cnd), Minnesota Orch Virgin Classics ("Ultraviolet" series) ▲ CUV 61194
Haydn, J.:Sons Pno—H.XVI/50, 51 & 52 Arabesque ▲ ARA 6625 [DDD]
Haydn, J.:Son Pno, H.XVII/6, "Andante with Vars"—Vars. only Arabesque ▲ ARA 6625 [DDD]
Liszt, F.:Cons Pno, w. M. Atzmon (cnd), New PO Royal Classics ▲ ROY 6445
Liszt, F.:Les Préludes, w. C. Silvestri (cnd), Philharmonia Orch Royal Classics ▲ ROY 6445
Scriabin, A.:Con Pno, w. L. Pešek (cnd), Czech PO *(rec Dvořák Hall, 1986)* Supraphon ▲ SUP 104149
• Shostakovich, D.:Con 1 Pno, w. M. Murphy (tpt), G. Levine (cnd), Cracow PO Arabesque ▲ Z 6610
Weber, C.M. von:Invitation to the Dance Pno Arabesque 2–▲ Z 6584–2
Weber, C.M. von:Momento capriccioso Arabesque 2–▲ Z 6584–2
Weber, C.M. von:Rondo brillante Arabesque 2–▲ Z 6584–2
Weber, C.M. von:Sons Pno Arabesque 2–▲ Z 6584–2
Wolpe, S.:Son Vn, w. J. Fleezanis (vn) *(rec Nov. 9–10, 1991)* Koch ▲ KIC 7112 [DDD]
Wuorinen, C.:The Blue Bamboula Bridge ▲ BCD 9008 [DDD]
Wuorinen, C.:Con 3 Pno, w. H. Blomstedt (cnd), San Francisco SO Elektra/Nonesuch ▲ 79185–2 [DDD]
Wuorinen, C.:Fant Vn, w. B. Hudson (vn) Bridge ▲ BCD 9008 [DDD]
Wuorinen, C.:The Golden Dance, w. H. Blomstedt (cnd), San Francisco SO Elektra/Nonesuch ▲ 79185–2 [DDD]
Wuorinen, C.:Pieces Vn, w. B. Hudson (vn) Bridge ▲ BCD 9008 [DDD]
Wuorinen, C.:Son Vn, w. B. Hudson (vn) New World ▲ NW 385–2 [DDD]

O'Hora, Ronan (pno)

Britten, H.:Holiday Diary, w. S. Hough (pno) Virgin Classics ▲ CDC 59027
Grieg, E.:Con Pno, Op. 16, w. J. Judd (cnd), Royal PO Royal Philharmonic Collection ▲ TRP 24 [DDD]
Grieg, E.:Lyric Pieces Royal Philharmonic Collection ▲ TRP 24 [DDD]
Mozart, W.A.:Con 21 Pno, w. J. Carney (cnd), Royal PO Royal Philharmonic Collection ▲ TRP 43 [DDD]
Mozart, W.A.:Con 23 Pno, w. J. Carney (cnd), Royal PO Royal Philharmonic Collection ▲ TRP 43 [DDD]
Schubert, Franz:Qnt Pno, D.667, w. J. Carney (cnd), Royal Phil Chamber Ensemble Tring ("Royal Philharmonic Collection" series) ▲ TRP 16 [DDD]
Tchaikovsky, P.:Con 1 Pno, w. J. Judd (cnd), Royal PO Royal Philharmonic Collection ▲ TRP 23 [DDD]
Tchaikovsky, P.:Les Saisons—8 sels Royal Philharmonic Collection ▲ TRP 23 [DDD]

Öhrwall, Anders (hpd)—see ORCHESTRAS & ENSEMBLES Musica Holmiae

Ohtaki, Katsuhisa (bn)—see ORCHESTRAS & ENSEMBLES Orphée Piano & Wind Quintet

Ohyama, Heiichiro (va)

Mozart, W.A.:Qts Pno, w. A. Previn (pno), Y. U. Kim (vn), G. Hoffman (vc) RCA Red Seal ▲ 09026–60713–2
Rorem, N.:The Santa Fe Songs, w. Kurt Ollman (bar), Sheryl Staples (vn), Peter Rejto (vc), Lydia Artymiw (pno) *(rec live, Tucson Chamber Music Festival, Mar 12, 1995)* Arizona Friends of Chamber Music ▲ 1995 [DDD]
Schumann, R.:Qt Pno in c, w. A. Previn (pno), Young Uck Kim (vn), G. Hoffman (vc) RCA Red Seal ▲ 09026–61384–2
Schumann, R.:Qt Pno, Op. 47, w. A. Previn (pno), Young Uck Kim (vn), G. Hoffman (vc) RCA Red Seal ▲ 09026–61384–2

Øien, Ingegärd (hn)

Alfvén, H.:Notturno elegiaco, w. Geir Henning Braaten (pno) *(rec Sweden, 1980 & 1982)* BIS ▲ CD 171 [AAD]
Jeppesen, K.:Little Trio Fl, Hn & Pno, w. Per Øien (fl), Geir Henning Braaten (pno) *(rec Sweden, 1980 & 1982)* BIS ▲ CD 171 [AAD]
Kvandal, J.:Intro & Allegro, w. Geir Henning Braaten (pno) *(rec Sweden, 1980 & 1982)* BIS ▲ CD 171 [AAD]
Nielsen, C.:Canto serioso, w. Geir Henning Braaten (pno) *(rec Sweden, 1980 & 1982)* BIS ▲ CD 171 [AAD]
Olsen, S.:Aubade, w. Per Øien (fl) *(rec Sweden, 1980 & 1982)* BIS ▲ CD 171 [AAD]

Øien, Per (fl)

Blavet, M.:Con Fl, w. T. Tønnesen (cnd), Norwegian CO *(rec Sept. 2–3, 1978)* BIS ▲ CD 118 [AAD]
Doppler, A.F.:Fant pastorale hongroise, w. Robert Aikten (fl), Geir Henning Braaten (pno), Elisabeth Westenholz (pno) BIS ▲ CD 166
Doppler, A.F.:Music Fl & Pno, w. R. Aitken (fl), Gier Hanning Braaten (pno) BIS 2–▲ CD 145/46
Jeppesen, K.:Little Trio Fl, Hn & Pno, w. Ingegärd Øien (hn), Geir Henning Braaten (pno) *(rec Sweden, 1980 & 1982)* BIS ▲ CD 171 [AAD]
Luening, O.:Lyric Scene, w. J. Serebrier (cnd), Oslo PO Phoenix ▲ PHCD 101 [AAD]
The Norwegian Flute, w. G. H. Braaten (pno), Norwegian CO *(rec 1978 & 1980)* BIS ▲ CD 103 [AAD]
Olsen, S.:Aubade, w. Ingegärd Øien (hn) *(rec Sweden, 1980 & 1982)* BIS ▲ CD 171 [AAD]
Quantz, J.J.:Con in G Fl & Strs, w. T. Tønnesen (cnd), Norwegian CO *(rec Sept. 2–3, 1978)* BIS ▲ CD 118 [AAD]
Taffanel, P.:Fant on Freischütz, w. Robert Aikten (fl), Elisabeth Westenholz (pno), Geir Henning Braaten (pno) BIS ▲ CD 166
Tartini, G.:Con in G Fl, w. T. Tønnesen (cnd), Norwegian CO *(rec Sept. 2–3, 1978)* BIS ▲ CD 118 [AAD]
Vivaldi, A.:Cons Fl (misc), w. T. Tønnesen (cnd), Norwegian CO *(rec Sept. 2–3, 1978)* BIS ▲ CD 118 [AAD]

Oistrakh, David (va)

Mozart, W.A.:Sinf concertante Vn, K.364, w. I. Oistrakh (vn), D. Oistrakh (cnd), Berlin PO EMI Classics ▲ CDM 64632

Oistrakh, David (vn)

Bach, J.S.:Cons Vn (comp), w. D. Oistrach (cnd), Vienna SO Deutsche Grammophon ("The Originals" series) 2–▲ 447427–2
Bartók, B.:Con 1 Vn, w. G. Rozhdestvensky (cnd), Moscow RSO *(rec 1962)* Forlane ▲ FRL 16589 [AAD]
Bartók, B.:Sons (2) Vn & Pno, w. G. Kremer(vn), F. Bauer (pno), O. Maisenberg (pno) *(rec 1969, 1972 & 1978)* Praga ▲ PR 250 038
Beethoven, L. van:Con Vn, Op. 61, w. H. Abendroth (cnd), Berlin RSO *(rec live, Berlin 3/31/50)* Melodram ▲ MEL 18020 (m) [AAD]
Beethoven, L. van:Con Vn, Op. 61, w. H. Albert (cnd), Naples Alessandro Scarlatti RAI Orch *(rec live 4/15/65)* Melodram 2–▲ CDM 28034 [AAD]
Beethoven, L. van:Con Vn, Vc & Pno, "Triple Con", w. Sviatoslav Knushevitzy (vc), Lev Oborin (pno), M. Sargent (cnd), Philharmonia Orch EMI Classics 2–▲ CDFB 69331
Beethoven, L. van:Con Vn, Vc & Pno, "Triple Con", w. S. Knushevitsky (vc), L. Oborin (pno), R. Kubelik (cnd), Prague SO Multisonic ("Prague Spring" Collection) ▲ 31 0104 [ADD]
Beethoven, L. van:Con Vn, Vc & Pno, "Triple Con", w. M. Rostropovich (vc), S. Richter (pno), H. von Karajan (cnd), Berlin PO EMI Classics ▲ CDM 64744
Beethoven, L. van:Romances Vn, w. H. Abendroth (cnd), Berlin RSO—Op. 40 *(rec live, Berlin 3/31/50)* Melodram ▲ MEL 18020 (m) [AAD]
Beethoven, L. van:Romances Vn, w. E. Goossens (cnd), Royal PO Deutsche Grammophon ("The Originals" series) 2–▲ 447427–2
Beethoven, L. van:Romances Vn, w. K. Ančerl (cnd), Czech PO Supraphon ▲ SUP 3005
Beethoven, L. van:Sons Vn (comp), w. L. Oborin (pno) Philips 4–▲ 412570–2 [ADD]
Beethoven, L. van:Son 5 Vn, "Spring", w. L. Oborin (pno) Philips ▲ 412255–2 [ADD]
Beethoven, L. van:Son 5 Vn, "Spring", w. Frida Bauer (pno) *(rec live Smetana Hall, Prague, May 19, 1969)* Praga ▲ PR 250 058
Beethoven, L. van:Son 9 Vn, "Kreutzer", w. L. Oborin (pno) Philips ▲ 412255–2 [ADD]
Brahms, J.:Con Vn, w. O. Klemperer (cnd), French National RSO EMI Classics ▲ CDM 64632
Brahms, J.:Con Vn, w. C. Bruck (cnd), ORTF PO *(rec May 30, 1967)* Memoire Vive ▲ 262007 [ADD]
Brahms, J.:Con Vn, w. A. Pedrotti (cnd), Czech PO *(rec ca. 1961)* Multisonic ("Prague Spring Collection" series) 2–▲ 31 0020–2 [ADD]
Brahms, J.:Con Vn, w. F. Rieger (cnd), Munich PO *(rec live 1973)* Topazio ▲ TOP 26048
Brahms, J.:Con Vn, w. F. Konwitschny (cnd), Dresden Staatskapelle Deutsche Grammophon ("The Originals" series) 2–▲ 447427–2
Brahms, J.:Con Vn & Vc, "Double Con", w. Pierre Fournier (vc), A. Galliera (cnd), Philharmonia Orch EMI Classics 2–▲ CDFB 69331
Brahms, J.:Con Vn & Vc, "Double Con", w. M. Rostropovich (vc), G. Szell (cnd), Cleveland Orch EMI Classics ▲ CDM 64744
Brahms, J.:Son 1 Vn, w. Frida Bauer (pno) *(rec live Smetana Hall, Prague, July 17, 1994)* Praga ▲ PR 250 058
Brahms, J.:Son 3 Vn, w. F. Bauer (pno) *(rec live Prague Spring Festival, 1966)* Multisonic (Prague Spring Collection) ▲ 31 0109–2 [ADD]
Brahms, J.:Son 3 Vn, w. Frida Bauer (pno) *(rec live in Prague, Smetana Hall, May 18, 1966)* Praga ▲ PR 250 058
Chausson, E.:Poème Vn, w. F. Rieger (cnd), Munich PO *(rec live, 1971)* Topazio ▲ TOP 26048
David Oistrakh, w. Lev Oborin (pno), Vladimir Yampolsky (pno) Vanguard Classics 3–▲ OVC 4080/02 [ADD]
Dvořák, A.:Con Vn, w. K. Ančerl (cnd), Prague RSO *(rec May 1950)* Praga ▲ PR 254 006
Franck, C.:Son Vn, w. S. Richter (pno) Vox Box 2–▲ CDX 5120
Grieg, E.:Sons Vn, Opp. 8, 13 & 45, w. L. Oborin (pno)—No. 2, Op. 13 Praga ▲ PR 250 048
Haydn, J.:Trios Pno, Vn & Vc, w. Lev Oborin (pno), Sviatoslav Knushevitsky (vc)—H.XV/27 *(rec live, 1961)* Multisonic ("Prague Spring Collection" series) ▲ 31 0105–2 [ADD]
Hindemith, P.:Con Vn, w. G. Rozhdestvensky (cnd), USSR State SO *(rec 1962)* Forlane ▲ FRL 16589 [AAD]
Hindemith, P.:Con Vn, w. P. Hindemith (cnd), London SO London ("Enterprise" series) ▲ 433081–2 [ADD]
Khachaturian, A.:Con Vn, w. A. Khachaturian (cnd), USSR Radio–TV Orch *(rec 1965)* Russian Disc ▲ RUS 11 012
Khachaturian, A.:Con Vn, w. A. Khachaturian (cnd), Moscow Radio Grand SO Vox Box 2–▲ CDX 5120
Khachaturian, A.:Con Vn, w. A. Khachaturian (cnd), Philharmonia Orch EMI Classics ▲ CDC 55035
Khachaturian, A.:Con Vn, w. R. Kubelik (cnd), Prague SO *(rec ca. 1947)* Multisonic ("Prague Spring Collection" series) ▲ 31 0038–2 [ADD]
Khachaturian, A.:Con Vn, w. R. Kubelik (cnd), Prague RSO Praga ▲ 250017
Mozart, W.A.:Adagio Vn, K.261, w. D. Oistrakh (cnd), Berlin PO EMI Classics ▲ CDM 64868
Mozart, W.A.:Con 3 Vn, w. K. Ančerl (cnd), Czech PO Supraphon ("Czech Philharmonic" series) ▲ SUP 111936 [AAD]
Mozart, W.A.:Con 3 Vn, w. M. Sargent (cnd), Philharmonia Orch EMI Classics 2–▲ CDFB 69331
Mozart, W.A.:Con 4 Vn, w. D. Oistrakh (cnd), Berlin PO EMI Classics ▲ CDM 64868
Mozart, W.A.:Con 4 Vn, w. D. Oistrakh (cnd), Berlin PO EMI Classics ("Studio" series) ▲ CDM 69064
Mozart, W.A.:Con 5 Vn, w. F. Konwitschny (cnd), Leipzig Gewandhaus Orch Berlin Classics ("Dokumente" series) ▲ BER 2131 [ADD]
Mozart, W.A.:Con 5 Vn, w. D. Oistrakh (cnd), Berlin PO EMI Classics ▲ CDM 64868
Mozart, W.A.:Con 5 Vn, w. D. Mitropoulos (cnd), New York PO One–Eleven ▲ URS 50140 [ADD]
Mozart, W.A.:Con 5 Vn, w. D. Oistrakh (cnd), Berlin PO EMI Classics ("Studio" series) ▲ CDM 69064
Mozart, W.A.:Con 5 Vn, w. K. Kondrashin (cnd), USSR State Orch *(rec 1958–59)* Tuxedo ▲ TUXCD 1052
Mozart, W.A.:Rondo Vn, K.269, w. D. Oistrakh (cnd), Berlin PO EMI Classics ▲ CDM 64868
Mozart, W.A.:Rondo Vn, K.373, w. D. Oistrakh (cnd), Berlin PO EMI Classics ▲ CDM 64868
Prokofiev, S.:Con 1 Vn, w. R. Kubelik (cnd), Prague SO *(rec ca. 1947)* Multisonic ("Prague Spring Collection" series) ▲ 31 0038–2 [ADD]
Prokofiev, S.:Con 1 Vn, w. Y. Temirkanov (cnd), Moscow PO *(rec 1966, 1969 & 1970)* Praga ▲ PR 250 041
Prokofiev, S.:Con 2 Vn, w. M. Sargent (cnd), Philharmonia Orch EMI Classics 2–▲ CDFB 69331
Prokofiev, S.:Mélodies, w. F. Bauer (pno) *(rec live, Czechoslovak Radio Prague, 1966)* Multisonic ("Prague Spring Collection" series) ▲ 31 0109–2 [ADD]
Prokofiev, S.:Mélodies, w. F. Bauer (pno) *(rec 1966, 1969 & 1970)* Praga ▲ PR 250 041
Prokofiev, S.:Son 1 Vn, w. F. Bauer (pno) *(rec 1966, 1969 & 1970)* Praga ▲ PR 250 041
Ravel, M.:Son Vn Pno, w. F. Bauer (pno) *(rec live, Czechoslovak Radio Prague, 1966)* Multisonic ("Prague Spring Collection" series) ▲ 31 0109–2 [ADD]
Rimsky–Korsakov, N.:Capriccio espagnol, w. N. Anosov (cnd), Bolshoi Theater Orch, Moscow RSO *(rec 1960)* Multisonic ("Russian Treasures" series) ▲ 31 0186
Saint–Saëns, C.:Introduction & Rondo capriccioso, w. C. Munch (cnd), Boston SO RCA Gold Seal ▲ 09026–60683–2
Schubert, Franz:Son Vn, D.574, w. F. Bauer (pno) *(rec live, Czechoslovak Radio Prague, 1966)* Multisonic ("Prague Spring Collection" series) ▲ 31 0109–2 [ADD]
Schubert, Franz:Son Vn, D.574, w. L. Oborin (pno) *(rec 1958)* MK ▲ MKA 417111 [AAD]
Schubert, Franz:Trio 1 Pno, w. L. Oborin (pno), S. Knushevitsky (vc) *(rec live 1961)* Multisonic ("Prague Spring Collection" series) ▲ 31 0105–2 [ADD]
Shostakovich, D.:Con 1 Vn, w. G. Rozhdestvensky (cnd), Philharmonia Orch IMP ("BBC Radio Classics" series) ▲ IMP 5691702
Shostakovich, D.:Con 1 Vn, w. M. Shostakovich (cnd), New Philharmonia Orch [original Op. 77 version] *(rec live, Royal Festival Hall, London 11/20/72)* Intaglio ▲ INCD 7241 [ADD]
Shostakovich, D.:Con 1 Vn, w. E. Mravinsky (cnd), Czech PO Praga ▲ PR 250052
Shostakovich, D.:Con 2 Vn, w. K. Kondrashin (cnd), Moscow PO *(rec 1968)* Russian Disc ▲ RUS 11025 [AAD]
Shostakovich, D.:Con 2 Vn, w. E. Svetlanov (cnd), USSR State SO *(rec live, Royal Albert Hall, London, August 1968)* Intaglio ▲ INCD 7241 [ADD]
Shostakovich, D.:Son Vn, w. S. Richter (pno) Vox Box 2–▲ CDX 5120

Oistrakh, David (vn) (cont.)
Shostakovich, D.:Trio 2 Pno, w. L. Oborin (pno), S. Knushevitsky (vc) *(rec live 1961)* Multisonic ("Prague Spring Collection" series) ▲ 31 0105-2 [ADD]
Sibelius, J.:Con Vn, w. N.-E. Fougstedt (cnd), Finnish RSO *(rec live 1954)* Ondine ▲ ODE 809 [ADD]
Sibelius, J.:Con Vn, w. E. Ormandy (cnd), Philadelphia Orch *(rec 1959)* Sony Classical ("Essential Classics" series) ▲ SBK 47659 ■ SBT 47659
Sibelius, J.:Con Vn, w. G. Rozhdestvensky (cnd), Moscow RSO Vox Box 2-▲ CDX 5120
Szymanowski, K.:Con 1 Vn, w. K. Sanderling (cnd), Leningrad PO *(rec 1959)* Forlane ▲ FRL 16589 [AAD]
Taneyev, S.:Suite de Concert, w. N. Malko (cnd), Philharmonia Orch EMI Classics ▲ CDM 65419
Tchaikovsky, P.:Con Vn, w. E. Ormandy (cnd), Philadelphia Orch Sony Classical ("Essential Classics" series) ▲ SBK 46339 [ADD] ■ SBT 46339
Tchaikovsky, P.:Con Vn, w. A. Gauk (cnd), All-Union RSO *(rec 1939)* Russian Disc ▲ RUS 15002 [AAD]
Tchaikovsky, P.:Con Vn, w. S. Samosud (cnd), Bolshoi Theater Orch *(rec 1958-59)* Tuxedo ▲ TUXCD 1052
Tchaikovsky, P.:Con Vn, w. F. Konwitschny (cnd), Dresden Staatskapelle Deutsche Grammophon ("The Originals" series) 2-▲ 447427-2
Vivaldi, A.:Cons for 2 Vns, w. I. Stern (vn), E. Ormandy (cnd), Philadelphia Orch *(rec 1955-6)* CBS 4-▲ M4K 42003 (m/s) [ADD]

Oistrakh, Igor (vn)—see also ORCHESTRAS & ENSEMBLES Igor Oistrakh Trio
Bartók, B.:Con 2 Vn, w. G. Rozhdestvensky (cnd), Moscow State SO Audiophile Classics ▲ APL 101519
Chausson, E.:Poème Vn, w. USSR Radio-TV Large SO Audiophile Classics ▲ APL 101.514 [ADD]
Mendelssohn, F.:Con in e Vn & Orch, Op. 64, w. F. Konwitschny (cnd), Leipzig Gewandhaus Orch Berlin Classics ▲ BER 2076 [ADD]
Mozart, W.A.:Duos Vn & Va, w. Rudolf Barshay (va)—K.424 Multisonic ▲ MUL 310355
Mozart, W.A.:Sinf concertante Vn, K.364, w. D. Oistrakh (va), D. Oistrakh (cnd), Berlin PO EMI Classics ▲ CDM 64632
Mozart, W.A.:Sons Vn Pno (misc), w. N. Zertsalova (pno)—in C, K.296; in G, K.301; in D♭, K.302; in C, K.303; in e, K.304; in A, K.305; in D, K.306; in F, K.376; in F, K.377 Vox Box 2-▲ CDX 5128 [DDD]
Prokofiev, S.:Con 1 Vn, w. G. Rozhdestvensky (cnd), USSR Radio-TV Large SO Audiophile Classics ("Legacy" series) ▲ 101.505 [ADD]
Prokofiev, S.:Con 1 Vn, w. G. Rozhdestvensky (cnd), USSR Radio-TV Large SO Allegretto ▲ ACD 8184 [ADD] ■ ACS 8184
Prokofiev, S.:Mélodies, w. N. Zertsalova (pno) Allegretto ▲ ACD 8188 [DDD] ■ ACS 8188
Prokofiev, S.:Son for 2 Vns, w. V. Oistrakh (vn) Art & Electronics ▲ AED 68022 [DDD]
Ravel, M.:Son Vn Pno, w. N. Zertsalova (pno) Allegretto ▲ ACD 8188 [DDD] ■ ACS 8188
Schubert, Franz:Fant Vn, D.934, w. N. Zertsalova (pno) Allegretto ▲ ACD 8188 [DDD] ■ ACS 8188
Svetlanov, E.:Poem, w. E. Svetlanov (cnd), Russian State SO *(rec 1978)* Russian Disc ▲ RUS 11042 [AAD]
Vivaldi, A.:Con Vn Vc, RV.547, w. Ofra Harnoy (vc), P. Robinson (cnd), Toronto CO, *(Toronto, Feb 1992)* RCA Victor Red Seal ▲ 09026-68228-2 [DDD]
Wieniawski, H.:Con 2 Vn, w. F. Konwitschny (cnd), Leipzig Gewandhaus Orch Berlin Classics ("Dokumente" series) ▲ BER 2131 [ADD]

Oistrakh, Valen (vn)—see also ORCHESTRAS & ENSEMBLES Igor Oistrakh Trio
Prokofiev, S.:Son for 2 Vns, w. I. Oistrakh (vn) Art & Electronics ▲ AED 68022 [DDD]

Okada, M. (perc)
Fukushi, N.:Chromosphere, w. J. Arase (perc), S. Sato (perc), H. Yamazaki (perc), S. Yoshihara (perc), T. Otaka (cnd), Tokyo PO *(rec live Tokyo Bunka-Kaikan, Large Hall, May 30, 1981)* Camerata ▲ 32CM 293 [AAD]

Okada, Yoshiko (pno)
Debussy, C.:Children's Corner *(rec New Hope Methodist Church, Methuen, MA, Aug 12-13, 1995)* Ongaku ▲ 024-106 [DDD]
Fauré, G.:Nocturnes (13) Pno—No. 6 in D♭, Op. 63 *(rec New Hope Methodist Church, Methuen, MA, Aug 12-13, 1995)* Ongaku ▲ 024-106 [DDD]
Mozart, W.A.:Con 20 Pno, w. M. Sewen (cnd), Warsaw CO Emergo ("Corneille" series) ▲ EC 3971
Mozart, W.A.:Con 27 Pno, w. M. Sewen (cnd), Warsaw CO Emergo ("Corneille" series) ▲ EC 3971
Ravel, M.:Gaspard de la nuit *(rec New Hope Methodist Church, Methuen, MA, Aug 12-13, 1995)* Ongaku ▲ 024-106 [DDD]
Satie, E.:Gnossiennes Pno *(rec New Hope Methodist Church, Methuen, MA, Aug 12-13, 1995)* Ongaku ▲ 024-106 [DDD]
Satie, E.:Gymnopédies *(rec New Hope Methodist Church, Methuen, MA, Aug 12-13, 1995)* Ongaku ▲ 024-106 [DDD]

Okashiro, Chitose (pno)
Brahms, J.:Fants Pno, Op. 116—No. 6 Pro Piano ▲ PPR 224501
Chopin, F.:Etudes (24)—in c, Op. 10/12 Pro Piano ▲ PPR 224501
Debussy, C.:Images (3) Pno—Set 1 *(rec New York, June 16 & 17, 1994)* Pro Piano ▲ PPR 224502 [DDD]
Debussy, C.:Preludes Pno (sels)—Des pas sur la neige; Ce qu'a vu le vent d'Ouest; La fille aux cheveux de lin [from Book 1]; Brouillards; La Puerta del Vino; Feux d'artifice [from Book 2] *(rec New York, June 16 & 17, 1994)* Pro Piano ▲ PPR 224502 [DDD]
Franck, C.:Son Vn, w. Yukiko Kamei (vn) *(rec SUNY Purchase Studio C, Aug. 15 & 16, 1994)* ProPiano ▲ PPR 224505 [DDD]
Mozart, W.A.:Son 16 Pno Pro Piano ▲ PPR 224501
Okashiro, I.:Moon *(rec New York, June 16 & 17, 1994)* Pro Piano ▲ PPR 224502 [DDD]
Scarlatti, D.:Sons Kbd—in C, K.420 Pro Piano ▲ PPR 224501
Schumann Symphonic Etudes *(rec Academy of Arts & Letters, New York, Sept. 23 & 24, 1993)* Pro Piano ▲ PPR 224501 [DDD]
Schumann, R.:Arabeske Pno Pro Piano ▲ PPR 224501
Schumann, R.:Sym Etudes Pro Piano ▲ PPR 224501
Scriabin, A.:Etudes Pno (comp) *(rec Academy of Arts & Letters, New York, Nov 10-11, 1995)* Pro Piano ("Pianist's Perspective Recording" series) ▲ PPR 224510
Scriabin, A.:Etudes Pno, Op. 42—No. 5 Pro Piano ▲ PPR 224501
Scriabin, A.:Son 5 Pno *(rec New York, June 16 & 17, 1994)* Pro Piano ▲ PPR 224502 [DDD]
Takemitsu, T.:Rain Tree Sketch *(rec New York, June 16 & 17, 1994)* Pro Piano ▲ PPR 224502 [DDD]
Walton, W.:Son Vn & Pno, w. Yukiko Kamei (vn) *(rec SUNY Purchase Studio C, Aug. 15 & 16, 1994)* ProPiano ▲ PPR 224505 [DDD]
Walton, W.:Vars Vn, w. Y. Kamei (vn) *(rec Purchase, NY, Aug. 15 & 16, 1994)* Pro Piano ▲ PPR 224505 [DDD]

Okazaki, Koji (bn)
Mozart, W.A.:Qnt Pno, K.452, w. Keiko Toyama (pno), Günther Passin (ob), Yuji Murai (cl), Gottfried Langenstein (hn) *(rec Shibukawa Shimin Kaikan, Sept 1, 1981)* Camerata ▲ 32CM 180 [DDD]
Shinohara, M.:Tabiyuki, w. A. Ogawa (mez), M. Kakagawa (fl), I. Tsuji (ob), T. Takahashi (cl), G. Kitamura (tpt), A. Murata (trbn), S. Eiso (perc), S. Ueki (vn), A. Nakakoji (va), S. Katsuta (vc), M. Komuro (contrabass), K. Komatsu (cnd) *(rec live Casals Hall, Tokyo, Mar. 5, 1994)* Camerata ▲ 30CM 375 [DDD]

O'Kelley, Shannon (perc)
Zwilich, E.T.:Passages, w. Leslie Boucher (sop), Julie Stone (fl/pic), Tod Kerstetter (cl/b cl), Andrew Carlson (vn), Philip Singleton (va), Juanita Karpf (vc), F. Joseph Lozier (pno), Joanna Parks (perc) *(rec Roswell United Methodist Church, Roswell, GA)* ACA Digital ▲ CM 20027

Økermark, L. (bn)—see ORCHESTRAS & ENSEMBLES Frösunda Wind Quintet

Okubo, Izumi (vn/va)
Schoenberg, A.:The Cabaret Songs, w. Yumi Nara (sop), Machiko Takahashi (fl/pic), Vincent Jacquemin (cl/b cl), François Deppe (vc), Brigitte Foccroulle (pno), J.-P. Peuvion (cnd), Liège New Music Ensemble [arr Patrick Davin for Salon Orch] Adda ▲ ADD 581273 [DDD]

Okubo, Izumi (vn/va) (cont.)
Schoenberg, A.:Pierrot lunaire, w. Yumi Nara (sop), Machiko Takahashi (fl/pic), Vincent Jacquemin (cl/b cl), François Deppe (vc), Brigitte Foccroulle (pno), J.-P. Peuvion (cnd), Liège New Music Ensemble Adda ▲ ADD 581273 [DDD]

Oláh, Vilmos (vn)
Janácek, L.:Concertino Pno, w. Thomas Hlawatsch (pno), Béla Nagy (vn), Csaba Babácsi (va), Géza Bánhegyi (cl), Károly Ambrus (hn), István Hartenstein (bn) *(rec Budapest, May 1995)* Naxos ▲ 8.553587 [DDD]

Øland, Anne (pno)
Holmboe, V.:Chamber Con 1, w. H. Koivula (cnd), Danish Radio Concert Orch *(rec Danish Radio Studio 2, June & Sept 1996)* Marco Polo/Dacapo ▲ 8.224038 [DDD]
Kuhlau, F.:Duos brillants, w. Henrik Wenzel Andreasen (fl)—No. 1 *(rec College of Music, Malmö, Sweden, Aug 8-9, 1994)* Naxos ▲ 8.553333 [DDD]
Nielsen, C.:Pno Music (complete)—Suite, Op. 45; 3 Klaverstykker; Klavermusik for små og store, Op. 53 *(rec Dec 1992)* Paula ▲ PACD 80 [DAD]
Nielsen, C.:Pno Music (complete)—5 Pno Pieces; Symphonic Suite, Op. 8; Humoresque Bagatelles; Festival Prelude; Dream of "Silent Night"; Chaconne, Op. 32; Theme with Vars, Op. 40 *(rec Dec 1992)* Paula ▲ PACD 79 [DAD]
Nørholm, I.:Chamber Music, w. T. L. Christiansen (fl), B. Rørbech (vn), M. Vitek (vn), H. Olsen (va), I. Olsen (gtr), N. Ullner (vc)—Essai Prismatique; Medusa's Shadow; Mosaic; Prelude to My Wintermorning; Sonata Quasi Variazioni *(rec 2/89)* Kontrapunkt ▲ 32019 [DDD]
Schierbeck, P.:The Night, w. M. Schønwandt (cnd), South Jutland SO Point ▲ PCD 5085 [ADD]
Stolarczyk, W.:Earth Air Fire Water, w. Amalie Malling (pno), John Damgaard (pno), Teddy Teirup (pno), Friedrich Gürtler (pno), Rosalind Bevan (pno), Poul Rosenbaum (pno), Rodolfo Llambias (pno), Bella Horn-Ribera (pno), Anders Riber (pno), Elisabeth Sigurdsson (pno), Thomas Tronheim (pno), Elsebeth Broderson (pno), Erik Kaltoft (pno), Jørgen Hald Nielsen (pno), Aino Gilemann (pno), Birgit Kjær (pno), Jørgen Thomsen (pno), Gunhild Donslund (pno), Henrik Bo Hansen (pno), Lone Karlsson (pno), Erik Fessel (pno), Lasse Nilsson (pno), Janos Ferenczi (pno), Erik Bach (pno), Axel Momme (pno), Arne de Cros Dich (pno), Sven Micha Slot (pno), Hanne Bramsen Buhl (pno), Lili Olesen (pno), Susannah Carlsson (pno), Ulla Erml (pno), Vagn Sørensen (pno), Leif Greibe (pno), Bodil Krogh (pno), Kirsten Ottosen (pno), Inger Bergenholz (pno), Karsten Gylendorf (pno), Bjønr Elkjær (pno), Jacob Bjørn Jensen (pno), Jørgen Kaad (pno), Anne Marie Hjelm (pno), Carl Ulrik Munk Andersen (pno), Poul Lumbye (pno), Oluf Hildebrandt Nielsen (pno), Joachim Olsson (pno), Peter Pade Ramsøe Jacobsen (pno), Astrid Pollmann (pno), Jette Borsch (pno), Kirsten Karlshøj (pno), Maria Teresa Assing (pno), Allan Dahl Hansen (pno), Johan Hugossen (pno), Tine Fenger Pederson (pno), Arne Jørgen Fæø (pno), Anja Høgsted (pno), Anne Sophie Parbo (pno), Inga Lindmark (pno), Teresa Drabik Stathakis (pno), Anne Ruth Ferenczi (pno), Irene Hasager (pno), Yuka Ichikawa (pno), Birgitte Baur (pno), Malene Thastum (pno), Jens E. Rasmussen (pno), Birgitte Zielke (pno), Claus Zielke (pno), Stefan Kasch (pno), Bin Qiao (pno), Inger Johanne Teirup (pno), Lindy Rosborg (pno), Liisa Heininen (pno), David Højer (pno), Ellen Refstrup (pno), Thomas K. Søorensen (pno), Erik Kure (pno), Michael Rauff (pno), Jan beck Eriksson (pno), Tanja Zapolski (pno), Vibeke Skagbo (pno), Pål Eide Lindtner (pno), Ha-Young Sul (pno), Benedicte Palko (pno), Inke Kesseler (pno), Anne Marie Meineche (pno), Sverre Larsen (pno), Kasper Peter Bach (pno), Elisabetta Eliseo (pno), Olga Magieres (pno), Carl Erik Kühl (pno), Thorkild Borup Nielsen (pno), Valeria Zanini (pno), Lars Stenhoft (perc), Dennis Boel (perc), Winnie Dahlgren (perc), Susanne Vind (perc), Claus Byrith (elec), Anne Marie Storm (elec), J. Ribera (cnd) *(rec live, Koldinghaus Castle, Denmark, May 2, 1996)* Danica ▲ DCD 1996
Weyse, C.E.F.:Rondeau Fl, w. Henrik Wenzel Andreasen (fl) *(rec College of Music, Malmö, Sweden, Aug. 8-9, 1994)* Naxos ▲ 8.553333 [DDD]

Olavson, Bridget (pno)
Dankner, S.:Dance Suite Albany ▲ TROY 144 [DDD]
Dankner, S.:Son Pno *(rec Loyola Univ.)* Centaur ▲ CRC 2247

Olbertz, Walter (pno)
Beethoven, L. van:Songs, w. P. Schreier (ten)—Liebeslieder Berlin Classics ▲ BER 2083 [ADD]
Beethoven, L. van:Songs, w. A. Stolte (sop), P. Schreier (ten)—Scherlieder; Ariettas (4) & duet, Op. 82; Ernste Lieder Berlin Classics ▲ BER 2084 [DDD]
Beethoven, L. van:Songs, w. P. Schreier (ten)—An die ferne Geliebte, Op. 98; Sechs Lieder, Op. 48; Lieder nach Goethe Berlin Classics ▲ BER 2082 [ADD]
Haydn, J.:Sons Pno *(rec 1968-72)* Berlin Classics 3-▲ BER 9237
Haydn, J.:Sons Pno—Nos. 25-40 Berlin Classics 3-▲ BER 9238
Peter Screier:From Boy Alto of the Dresden Kreuzchor to Lyric Tenor, w. Peter Schreier (alt/ten), Rudolf Mauersberger (pno/cnd), Norman Shetler (pno), various orchs *(rec ca. 1950)* Berlin Classics 4-▲ BER 9041 [ADD]
Schubert, Franz:Songs (misc), w. Arleen Augér (sop)—songs after Goethe Berlin Classics ▲ BER 2185 [ADD]
Schumann, R.:Songs, w. Arleen Augér (sop) Berlin Classics ▲ BER 2186 [ADD]

Oldeman, Gerrit (va)
Crusell, B.H.:Qts (3) Cl, w. R. Hogerheijde (cl), V. Liberman (vn), Dora Mintcheva (vc) Erasmus ▲ WVH 103

Oldenburg, Fred (pno)
Holt, S. ten:Horizon, w. Yoko Abe (pno), Polo de Haas (pno), Margaret Krill (pno) Donemus 2-▲ CV 5/6

Oldfather, Christopher (pno)—see also ORCHESTRAS & ENSEMBLES Collage New Music Ensemble, New Music Consort, Speculum Musicae
Bazelon, I.:Legends & Love Letters, w. J. Heller (sop), F. Epstein (perc), R. Annis (cl), J. Scolnik (fl), J. Moerchel (vc), C. Fussell (cnd), Collage New Music Ensemble Albany ▲ TROY 054 [DDD]
Berger, A.:Duos, w. J. Smirnoff (vn), J. Krosnick (vc), G. Kalish (pno), P. Lanini (ob), D. Stewart (cl)—Duo No. 1 for Violin & Piano (1948); Duo for Cello & Piano (1951); Duo for Oboe & Clarinet (1952) New World ▲ NW 360-2 [DDD]
Carter, E.:Duo Vn & Pno, w. *(violinist unknown)* Sony Classical 2-▲ S2K 47229
Cory, E.:Hemispheres, w. Chris Finckel (vc) Soundspells ▲ CD 116 [DDD]
Gruenberg, L.:Jazz Epigrams, Op. 30b GM ▲ GM 2015CD
Gruenberg, L.:Rhap Vn, w. J. Smirnoff (vn) GM ▲ GM 2015CD
Gruenberg, L.:White Lilacs, w. J. Smirnoff (vn) GM ▲ GM 2015CD
McPhee, C.:Tabuh-Tabuhan, w. Peter Basquin (pno), D. R. Davies (cnd), American Composers Orch *(rec Manhattan Center, New York, May 1994)* Argo ▲ 444560-2 [DDD]
Ustvolskaya, G.:Grand Duet Vc, w. Maya Beiser (vc) Koch International Classics ▲ KIC 7258 [DDD]

Oldham, Barbara (hn)—see ORCHESTRAS & ENSEMBLES Quintet of the Americas

Oldham, Denver (pno)
Dett, R.N.:Bible Vignettes New World ▲ NW 367-2 [DDD]
Dett, R.N.:In the Bottoms New World ▲ NW 367-2 [DDD]
Dett, R.N.:Magnolia New World ▲ NW 367-2 [DDD]
Dett, R.N.:Pno Music—After the Cake Walk; Cave of the Winds; Inspiration Waltzes; Enchantment [romantic suite] Altarus ▲ AIR 9013
Paine, J.K.:Pno Music—Christmas Gift; Characteristic Pieces (4); Romance, Op. 12; Piano Pieces (3); Valse Caprice; Scetches (10):In the Country; Character Pieces (4); Funeral March in Memory of President Lincoln; Romance, Op. 39; Son Pno, Op. 1; Nocturne *(rec 1992)* New World 2-▲ 804242
Still, W.G.:Pno Music—Dark Horseman [3 Visions, No. 1]; Radiant Pinnacle [3 Visions, No. 3]; Marionette; Dance [from Costaso]; Rising Tide; Quit dat Fool'nish; Entrance of the Porteuses [from La Giuablesse]; A Deserted Plantation Altarus ▲ AIR 9013
Still, W.G.:Pno Music—Bells; 7 Traceries; Blues from "Lenox Avenue"; Swanee River; 5 Preludes; Summerland from "3 Visions"; Africa Koch International Classics ▲ KIC 7084-2 [DDD]

Oldham, Kevin (pno)
Carpenter, J.A.:Diversions New World ▲ NW 328/29-2 [DDD]
Carpenter, J.A.:Pno Music (comp)—Sonata in g; Diversions; Nocturne; Polonaise américaine; Impromptu; Tango américaine; Minuet; Little Dancer; Little Indian; Twilight Reverie; Danza New World ▲ NW 328/29-2 [DDD]
Carpenter, J.A.:Son Pno New World ▲ NW 328/29-2 [DDD]

▲ = CD ♦ = Enhanced CD Δ = MD ■ = Cassette Tape □ = DCC

Oldham, Kevin (pno) (cont.)
Liszt, F.:Fant & Fugue on "Ad nos, ad salutarem undam" Org [trans. Ferruccio Busoni & Ernest Nichols for pno] VAI Audio ▲ VAIA 1104
Schubert, Franz:Pno Music (misc)—Frühlingsglaube [Die linden Lüfte sind erwacht; trans. Liszt for pno] VAI Audio ▲ VAIA 1104
Schulz-Evler, A.:Arabesque on Themes from Johann Strauss' *The Beautiful Blue Danube* VAI Audio ▲ VAIA 1104

Olding, Dene (vn)—see also ORCHESTRAS & ENSEMBLES Australia Ensemble
Kos, B.:Con Vn, w. J. Hopkins (cnd), Queensland SO *(rec live)* Vox Australis ▲ VAST 015-2 [DDD]

Olechovsky, Joseph (pno)
Ponce, M.:Music of, w. Idelfonso Cedillo (vc)—Son for Vc & Pno; Preludes; Granada; Estrellita Spartacus ▲ SPR 21008 [DDD]

Olefsky, P. (vc)
Boccherini, L.:Con Vc, G.482, w. P. Olefsky (cnd), English CO Amatius Classics ▲ ACCD 1001 [DDD]
Tchaikovsky, P.:Nocturne Vc, w. P. Olefsky (cnd), Amatius Orch of New York Amatius Classics ▲ ACCD 1002 [DDD]
Tchaikovsky, P.:Pezzo capriccioso, w. P. Olefsky (cnd), Amatius Orch of New York Amatius Classics ▲ ACCD 1002 [DDD]
Vivaldi, A.:Cons Vc, w. P. Olefsky (cnd), English CO—3 Concerti—in a, c (RV.401) & D Amatius Classics ▲ ACCD 1001 [DDD]
Vivaldi, A.:Con for 2 Vcs, w. H. Zheng (vc), P. Olefsky (cnd), English CO Amatius Classics ▲ ACCD 1001 [DDD]

Oleg, Raphael (va)
Schubert, Franz:Son Arpeggione, w. G. Wyss (pno) Denon/PCM Digital ▲ DEN 75636 [DDD]

Oleg, Raphael (vn)
Beethoven, L. van:Qts Pno, WoO 36, w. Philippe Cassard (pno), Miguel da Siva (va), Marc Copey (vc) Valois 2-▲ V 4715
Beethoven, L. van:Qt Pno, Op. 16, w. Philippe Cassard (pno), Miguel da Siva (va), Marc Copey (vc) Valois 2-▲ V 4715
Brahms, J.:Con Vn, w. L. Pešek (cnd), Royal Liverpool PO Denon ▲ CO 79944 [DDD]
Brahms, J.:Sextet Strs, Op. 18, w. Régis Pasquier (vn), Bruno Pasquier (va), Jean Dupouy (va), Roland Pidoux (vc), Etienne Péclard (vc)—No. 1 Harmonia Mundi France ("Musique d'abord" series) ▲ HMA 1901073
Bruch, M.:Con 1 Vn, w. L. Pešek (cnd), Royal Liverpool PO Denon ▲ CO 79944 [DDD]
Kodály, Z.:Duo Vn & Vc, w. Sonia Wieder-Atherton (vc) Valois ▲ V 4716
Martinů, B.:Duo Vn & Vc, w. Sonia Wieder-Atherton (vc) Valois ▲ V 4716
Music at the Time of Beaumarchais, w. Montserrat Figueras (sop), Lawrence Monteyro (sop), Raphel Oleg (vn), Miguel da Silva (va), Christophe Coin (vc), Marc Coppey (vc), José Miguel Moreno (gtr), Paul Badura-Skoda (pno), Philippe Cassard (pno), Éric Le Sage (pno), Bob Van Asperen (hpd). et al. Valois ▲ V 4767
Schubert, Franz:Fant Vn, D.934, w. G. Wyss (pno) Denon/PCM Digital ▲ DEN 75636 [DDD]
Schubert, Franz:Rondo Vn, D.895, w. G. Wyss (pno) Denon/PCM Digital ▲ DEN 75636 [DDD]

Olejniczak, Janusz (pno)
Chopin, F.:Con 2 Pno, w. C. Coin (cnd), Mosaïques Ensemble—Larghetto *(rec May-June 1990)* Opus 111 ▲ OPS 43-9107 [DDD]
Chopin, F.:Grand Fant on Polish Airs, w. K. Kord (cnd), Warsaw PO *(rec Warsaw Philharmonic Hall, June 27-30, 1994)* Canyon Classics ▲ CD 248
Chopin, F.:Mazurkas—Opp. 17/2 & 4, 24/4, 41/2 Opus 111 ▲ OPS 43-9107 [DDD]
Chopin, F.:Pno Music (misc)—Polonaise in A, Op. 40/1; Berceuse in D♭, Op. 57; Scherzo No. 2 in b♭, Op. 31; Mazurkas, Op. 17/1-4; Barcarolle in F#, Op. 60; Nocturne in c, Op. 48/1; Ballade No. 2 in F, Op. 38; Nocturne in e, Op. posth.; Waltzes, Op. 34/2, Op. posth. & Op. 64/1 & 2 *(rec Warsaw, 1987)* Selene ▲ CD 9102 [ADD]
Chopin, F.:Pno Music (misc)—Sherzo, Op. 20; Nocturne, Op. 62/1; 3 Préludes, Op. 28; Nocturne, Op. posth.; Waltz, Op. 69/1; Marche funèbre; Son No. 2, Op. 35 *(rec Rzeszow, Dec 10-11, 1994)* Selene ▲ CD 9501.24 [DDD]
Chopin, F.:Pno Music (misc)—Ballade No. 1; Etude "Revolutionary"; Mazurka, Op. 17/4; Nocturne, Op. posth; Polonaise "Heroic"; Scherzo No. 1; Waltz, Op. 64/2 *(rec Warsaw Concert Hall, Feb – Mar 1978)* Camerata ▲ 32 CM 159 [ADD]
Chopin, F.:Pno Music (misc)—Etude, Op. 10/12; Marche funebre, Op. 35; Nocturne, Op. 48; Polonaise, Op. 44; Prelude, Op. 28/4 & 7; Waltz, Op. 64/1 *(rec May-June 1990)* Opus 111 ▲ OPS 43-9107 [DDD]
Chopin, F.:Polonaises—Opp. 22, 26/1, 40/1 & 2, 44, 53; Op. posthumous in g, B♭, & A♭ *(rec Jan. 1992)* Opus 111 ▲ OPS 38-9102 [DDD]
Chopin, F.:Songs Sop (comp), w. Stefania Toczyska (mez)—Op. 74/6, 9, 16 & 17 *(rec Rzeszow, May 15-17, 1995)* Selene ▲ CD 9503.26 [DDD]
Karlowicz, M.:Songs, w. Stefania Toczyska (mez)—Op. 1/1-3, 5 & 6; Op. 3/1-5 & 7; Pod jaworem; Po szerokim; O, nie wiesz!; Z nowa wiosna *(rec Rzeszow, May 15-17, 1995)* Selene ▲ CD 9503.26 [DDD]
Moniuszko, S.:Songs, w. Stefania Toczyska (mez)—Piesn wieczorna; Zlota rybka; Kozak; Ojcze z niebios *(rec Rzeszow, May 15-17, 1995)* Selene ▲ CD 9503.26 [DDD]

Olesen, Kristian (org)
Kayser, L.:Fant & Hymn Point ▲ PCD 5097
Kayser, L.:Hymn to St Canute, Duke & Martyr Point ▲ PCD 5097
Kayser, L.:Paraphrase over Gergorian Motifs Point ▲ PCD 5097
Kayser, L.:Psalms Bar & Org, w. Jorgen Ole Borch (bar) Point ▲ PCD 5097
Kayser, L.:Sonatina Org Point ▲ PCD 5097

Olesen, Lili (pno)
Stolarczyk, W.:Earth Air Fire Water, w. Amalie Malling (pno), John Damgaard (pno), Anne Øland (pno), Teddy Teirup (pno), Friedrich Gürtler (pno), Rosalind Bevan (pno), Poul Rosenbaum (pno), Rodolfo Llambias (pno), Bella Horn-Ribera (pno), Anders Riber (pno), Elisabeth Sigurdsson (pno), Thomas Tronheim (pno), Elsebeth Broderson (pno), Erik Kaltoft (pno), Jørgen Hald Nielsen (pno), Aino Gilemann (pno), Birgit Kjær (pno), Jørgen Thomsen (pno), Gunhild Donslund (pno), Henrik Bo Hansen (pno), Lone Karlsson (pno), Erik Fessel (pno), Lasse Nilsson (pno), Janos Ferenczi (pno), Erik Bach (pno), Axel Momme (pno), Arne de Cros Dich (pno), Sven Micha Slot (pno), Hanne Bramsen Buhl (pno), Susannah Carlsson (pno), Ulla Erml (pno), Vagn Sørensen (pno), Leif Greibe (pno), Bodil Krogh (pno), Kirsten Ottosen (pno), Inger Bergenholz (pno), Karsten Gylendorf (pno), Bjønr Elkjær (pno), Jacob Bjørn Jensen (pno), Jørgen Kaad (pno), Anne Marie Hjelm (pno), Carl Ulrik Munk Andersen (pno), Poul Lumbye (pno), Oluf Hildebrandt Nielsen (pno), Joachim Olsson (pno), Peter Pade Ramsøe Jacobsen (pno), Astrid Pollmann (pno), Jette Borsch (pno), Kirsten Karlshøj (pno), Maria Teresa Assing (pno), Allan Dahl Hansen (pno), Johan Hugossen (pno), Tine Fenger Pederson (pno), Arne Jørgen Fæø (pno), Anja Høgsted (pno), Anne Sophie Parbo (pno), Inga Lindmark (pno), Teresa Drabik Stathakis (pno), Anne Ruth Ferenczi (pno), Irene Hasager (pno), Yuka Ichikawa (pno), Birgitte Baur (pno), Malene Thastum (pno), Jens E. Rasmussen (pno), Birgitte Zielke (pno), Claus Zielke (pno), Stefan Kasch (pno), Bin Qiao (pno), Inger Johanne Teirup (pno), Lindy Rosborg (pno), Liisa Heininen (pno), David Højer (pno), Ellen Refstrup (pno), Thomas K. Søorensen (pno), Erik Kure (pno), Michael Rauff (pno), Jan beck Eriksson (pno), Tanja Zapolski (pno), Vibeke Skagbo (pno), Pål Eide Lindtner (pno), Ha-Young Sul (pno), Benedicte Palko (pno), Inke Kesseler (pno), Anne Marie Meineche (pno), Sverre Larsen (pno), Kasper Peter Bach (pno), Elisabetta Eliseo (pno), Olga Magieres (pno), Carl Erik Kühl (pno), Thorkild Borup Nielsen (pno), Valeria Zanini (pno), Lars Stenhoft (perc), Dennis Boel (perc), Winnie Dahlgren (perc), Susanne Vind (perc), Claus Byrith (elec), Anne Marie Storm (elec), J. Ribera (cnd) *(rec live, Koldinghaus Castle, Denmark, May 2, 1996)* Danica ▲ DCD 1996

Olevsky, Estela (pno)
Piano Solos of Latin America *(rec Univ. of Mass., Amherst, July & Aug., 1993)* Centaur ▲ CRC 2202 [DDD]

Oliveira, Elmar (vn)
Bach, J.S.:Sons & Partitas Vn, BWV 1001-1006—Son. 1, BWV 1001 & Partita No. 2, BWV 1004 Élan ▲ CD 2212 [DDD]
Barber, S.:Con Vn, w. L. Slatkin (cnd), St. Louis SO EMI Classics ▲ CDC 47850 [DDD]

Oliveira, Elmar (vn) (cont.)
Barber, S.:Con Vn, w. L. Slatkin (cnd), St. Louis SO EMI Classics ("American Composer" series) ▲ CDM 64305
Elmar Oliveira, w. Robert McDonald (pno) Vox Box 2-▲ CDX 5086 [DDD]
The Heart of the Violin Concerto, w. Ernst Kovacic (vn), Jaime Laredo (vn), Anne Akiko Meyers (vn), Hideko Udagawa (vn) Pickwick ("The Orchid" series) ▲ PICORCD 11013
Husa, K.:Son Vn, w. David Oei (pno) *(rec Right Track Recordings, NYC)* New World ▲ 80493-2
Husa, K.:Son Vn, w. David Oei (pno) Grenadilla ■ GSC 1032
Laderman, E.:Con Vn, w. L. Leighton Smith (cnd), Louisville Orch Louisville ▲ LCD 004 [AAD]
Layman, P.:Gravitation I Grenadilla ■ GSC 1032
Martinů, B.:Madrigals Vn, w. S. Robbins (va) Élan ▲ CD 2212 [DDD]
Vivaldi, A.:Cons Vn, Op. 8/1-4, "The Four Seasons", w. G. Schwarz (cnd), Los Angeles CO Delos ▲ DCD 3007 [DDD]

Oliver, Barry (pno)
Encore, w. [cnd:Duain Wolfe], Colorado Children's Chorale, Rick Chinski (gtr), Robert Davine (acc), Laurie Kahler (pno), Samuel Lancaster (pno), Marylin Preston (fl), Karen Yonovitz (fl), Peter Cooper (ob), Andy Stevens (cl), Lionel Young (vn), Basil Vendreys (va), Wayne Templeman (vc), Charle *(rec Denver Center Media)* Colorado Children's Chorale ▲ 001

Olivera, Hector (org)
Saint-Saëns, C.:Sym 3, w. J. Mester (cnd), Pasadena SO Auracle ▲ NCAU 1001

Oliveros, Pauline (acc)
Oliveros, P.:Crone Music Lovely Music ▲ LCD 1903 [DDD]

Oliveros, Pauline (acc/elec)
Deep Listening Band:Music of Deep Listening Band, w. Stuart Dempster (trbn/didjeridu/garden hose), David Gamper (org/fl/elec)—Invocation; Processional [both w. Julie Lyon Balliet (sgr)]; Hi Bali, Hi; Sanctuary; Non-Stop Flight [w. Thomas Buckner (sgr), Julie Lyon Balliet (sgr), Joe McPhee (b cl/tpt), Margarit Shenker (acc/sgr), Nego Gato (perc), Carol Chappell (perc), Jason Finkleman (perc), Women Who Drum (perc)] *(rec Trinity United Methodist Church Sanctuary, 1993-94)* Mode ▲ mode 46
Oliveros, P.:The Roots of the Moment, w. Peter Ward (elecs) *(rec Studio Lussi, Allschwil, Switzerland, Nov. 10, 1987)* Hat Hut ("NOW." series) ▲ hat ART CD 6009 [ADD]

Oliveros, Pauline (acc/voc/whistles)
Deep Listening Band:Troglodyte's Delight, w. Stuart Dempster (trbn), Panaiotis (voc), Julie Lyon Balliett (voc), Fritz Hauser (perc) *(rec Tarpaper Cave, Rosendale, NY, June 1989)* ¿What Next? ▲ WN 003 ■ WN 0003

Olkiewicz, Grzegorz (fl)
Bach, C.P.E.:Cons Hpd & Strs, w. A. Duczmal (cnd), Poznan Polish Radio-TV CO—Con in d, H.425 (W.22) [arr fl & strs] *(rec Assembly Hall of Poznan Univ, May 18-22, 1988)* Polskie Nagrania Edition ▲ ECD 029 [DDD]
Bach, J.S.:Suite 2 Orch, w. A. Duczmal (cnd), Poznan Polish Radio-TV CO *(rec Assembly Hall of Poznan Univ, May 18-22, 1988)* Polskie Nagrania Edition ▲ ECD 029 [DDD]
Chopin, F.:Vars on a Theme from *La Cenerentola*, w. Edward Wolanin (pno) *(rec Warsaw Philharmony Hall, May 15, 1994)* Canyon Classics ▲ 238
Debussy, C.:Syrinx *(rec Assembly Hall of Poznan Univ, May 18-22, 1988)* Polskie Nagrania Edition ▲ ECD 029 [DDD]
Mercadante, S.:Cons (6) Fl (1819), w. A. Duczmal (cnd), Poznan Polish Radio-TV CO—in e *(rec Assembly Hall of Poznan Univ, May 18-22, 1988)* Polskie Nagrania Edition ▲ ECD 029 [DDD]

Øllegaard, Niels (vn)
Lauridsen, L.:Trio Vn, Va & Pno, w. Henrik Krarup (va), Teddy Telrup (pno) Rondo Grammofon ▲ RCD 8316

Øllgard, N. C. (vn)—see ORCHESTRAS & ENSEMBLES Vestjysk Chamber Ensemble

Ollivo, Yann (pno)
Escaich, T.:Scènes d'enfants, w. Christel Rayneau (fl), Philippe Pennanguer (vc) Chamade ▲ CHCD 5638 [DDD]

Olof, T. (vn)
Badings, H.:Con Vns, w. H. Krebbers (vn), W. van Otterloo (cnd), The Hague PO Donemus ▲ CV 26

Olofsson, Ake (vc)
Shostakovich, D.:Songs Sop, Op. 127, w. J. Delman (sop), E. Dekov (vn), L. Negro (pno) [R] BIS ▲ CD 26 [AAD]

Olofsson, Peter (vn)
Lindblad, A.F.:Qnt Strs, w. Patrik Swedrup (vn), Tony Bauer (va), Jonal Lindgård (va), Lars Frykholm (vc) Musica Sveciae ▲ MSV 522 [DDD]
Randel, A.:Qt Strs, w. Patrik Swedrup (vn), Tony Bauer (va), Jonal Lindgård (va), Lars Frykholm (vc) Musica Sveciae ▲ MSV 522 [DDD]

Olsen, Henrik (va)
Bach, Joh. Christian:Qts (4) for 2 Fls, w. B. Larsen (fl), B. Pedersen (fl), P. Elbaek (vn), B. Holst Christensen (vc) Kontrapunkt ▲ 32048 [DDD]
Bach, Joh. Christian:Trios for 2 Fls & Strs, w. B. Larsen (fl), B. Pedersen (fl), P. Elbaek (vn), B. Holst Christensen (vc) Kontrapunkt ▲ 32048 [DDD]
Beethoven, L. van:Qnt Fl, Vn, 2 Vas & Vc, w. T. L. Christiansen (fl), J. Søe Hansen (vn), M. Dolgin (va), T.S. Hermansen (vc) Kontrapunkt 2-▲ 32160/61 [DDD]
Kuhlau, F.:Qnts Fl, w. T.L. Christiansen (fl), J. Søe Hansen (vn), M. Dolgin (va), T.S. Hermansen (vc) Kontrapunkt 2-▲ 32160/61 [DDD]
Nørholm, I.:Chamber Music, w. T. L. Christiansen (fl), B. Rørbech (vn), M. Vitek (vn), I. Olsen (gtr), N. Ullner (vc), A. Øland (pno)—Essai Prismatique; Medusa's Shadow; Mosaic; Prelude to My Wintermorning; Sonata Quasi Variazioni *(rec 2/89)* Kontrapunkt ▲ 32019 [DDD]
Schubert, Franz:Qt Fl, w. T. L. Christiansen (fl), I. Olsen (gtr), N. Ullner (vc) Kontrapunkt ▲ 32024 [DDD]

Olsen, Ingolf (gtr)
Erling Blöndal Bengtsson, w. Erling Blöndal Bengtsson (vc) *(rec Sept. 22-25, 1986)* Danacord ▲ DACOCD 335
Nørholm, I.:Chamber Music, w. T. L. Christiansen (fl), B. Rørbech (vn), M. Vitek (vn), H. Olsen (va), N. Ullner (vc), A. Øland (pno)—Essai Prismatique; Medusa's Shadow; Mosaic; Prelude to My Wintermorning; Sonata Quasi Variazioni *(rec 2/89)* Kontrapunkt ▲ 32019 [DDD]
Schubert, Franz:Qt Fl, w. T. L. Christiansen (fl), H. Olsen (va), N. Ullner (vc) Kontrapunkt ▲ 32024 [DDD]

Olsen, Ivar (hn)
Crusell, B.H.:Con 2 Cl, w. K.-I. Stevensson (cl), K. Sönstevold (bn), O. Kamu (cnd), Swedish RSO Musica Sveciae ▲ MSV 527 [DDD]
Crusell, B.H.:Intro, Theme & Vars on a Swedish Air, w. K.-I. Stevensson (cl), K. Sönstevold (bn), O. Kamu (cnd), Swedish RSO Musica Sveciae ▲ MSV 527 [DDD]
Crusell, B.H.:Sinf concertante, w. K.-I. Stevensson (cl), K. Sönstevold (bn), O. Kamu (cnd), Swedish RSO Musica Sveciae ▲ MSV 527 [DDD]

Olshansky, (pno)
Beethoven, L. van:Son 30 Pno Monitor ■ 55013
Beethoven, L. van:Son 31 Pno Monitor ■ 55013
Chopin, F.:Ballades Pno (comp) Monitor ■ 55003
Chopin, F.:Pno Music (misc) Monitor ■ 55003

Olson, Lesley (fl)—see ORCHESTRAS & ENSEMBLES Illinois Performers' Workshop Ensemble

Olsson, Håkan (va)
Jolivet, A.:Fl Music (comp), w. Manuela Wiesler (fl), Erica Goodman (hp), Patrik Swedrup (vn), Helena Nilsson (vc), Christian Davidsson (bn), Roland Pöntinen (pno), P. Järvi (cnd), Tapiola Sinfonietta, Kroumata Percussion Ensemble—Alla rustica for Fl & Hp; Chant de Linos for Fl, Hp & Str Trio; Pastorales de Noël for Fl, Bn & Hp; Con for Fl & Strs; Suite en concert for Fl & 4 Perc Players; Fant-Caprice for Fl & Pno; Cabrioles for Fl & Pno *(rec Danderyd Grammar School, Sweden, Tapiola Hall, Tapiola, Finland, Gothenburg Concert Hall, Sweden & Studio 2, Radiohuset, Stockholm, Sweden)* BIS ▲ CD 739 [DDD]

Olsson, Tale (vn)—see also ORCHESTRAS & ENSEMBLES Tale String Quartet
Penderecki, K.:Trio Strs, w. I. Kierkegaard (va), H. Nilsson (vc) *(rec Feb. 18-20, 1994)* BIS ▲ CD 652 [DDD]

Olsson, Tale (vn) (cont.)
Schnittke, A.:Con grosso 3, w. P. Swedrup (vn), L. Markiz (cnd), Stockholm CO BIS ▲ CD 537 [DDD]
Oltman, Laura (gtr)—see also ORCHESTRAS & ENSEMBLES Newman/Oltman Guitar Duo
Laments & Dances:Music from the Folk Traditions, w. Michael Newman (gtr) *(rec Feb 7, 13 & 24, 1994)* MusicMasters ▲ 01612-67145-2 [DDD]
Piazzolla, A.:Tango Suite, w. M. Newman (gtr) MusicMasters ▲ 7071-2 [DDD]
Oltman, Laura (pno)
Carulli, F.:Petit Duos, Op. 90, w. M. Newman (gtr) Sheffield Lab ("Salon" series) ▲ SLS 504 [A–D]
Olzenak, C. (cl)
Sowash, R.:Anecdotes & Reflections, w. Mirecourt Trio Gasparo ▲ GS 285
Sowash, R.:Daweswood Suite, w. Mirecourt Trio Gasparo ▲ GS 285
Sowash, R.:Street Suite, w. K. Goldsmith (vn) Gasparo ▲ GS 285
Oman, Michael (vl)
Weichlein, R.:Encaenia musices, w. Gunar Letzbor (vn), Daniel Sepec (vn), Herbert Lindsberger (va), Christoph Bitzinger (va), Gaetano Nasillo (vc), Roberto Sensi (vn), Andreas Lackner (nat tpt), Herbert Walser (nat tpt), Norbert Kirchner (hpd/org), G. Letzbor (cnd), Ars Antiqua Austria—Sons. Nos. I in C, II in g, III in a, IV in E, V in C & VI in F Symphonia ▲ SY 93S23
O'Meara, William (org)
Bach, J.S.:Music of, w. Wendy Humphreys (sop), Daniel Lichti (b–bar), Stuart Laughton (tpt/nat tpt/Renaissance cnt), David Campion (timp/perc)—Prelude & Fugue in G; Grosser Herr [from Christmas Oratorio]; Mein gläubiges Herz [from Cant 68]; 3 Chorale Preludes; Prelude & Fugue in A Doremi ▲ DHR 9303 [DDD]
Baroque Banquet, w. Wendy Humphreys (sop), Daniel Lichti (b–bar), Stuart Laughton (tpt/nat tpt/cnt), David Campion (timp/perc) Doremi ▲ 9303
Clarke, J.:The Prince of Denmark's March Doremi ▲ DHR 9303 [DDD]
Franceschini, P.:Son à 7, w. Stuart Laughton (tpt), David Campion (timp/perc) Doremi ▲ DHR 9303 [DDD]
Handel, G.F.:Samson (sels), w. Wendy Humphreys (sop), Daniel Lichti (b–bar), Stuart Laughton (tpt/nat tpt/Renaissance cnt), David Campion (timp/perc)—Let the Bright Seraphim Doremi ▲ DHR 9303 [DDD]
Handel, G.F.:Suite Tpt & Org, w. Stuart Laughton (tpt) Doremi ▲ DHR 9303 [DDD]
Opening Day, w. Wendy Humphreys (sop), Stuart Laughton (tpt), Wendy Humphreys (Celtic hp), Peter Tiefenbach (org/pno) Doremi ▲ 9301 [DDD]
Scarlatti, A.:Endimione e Cintia, w. Wendy Humphreys (sop), Daniel Lichti (b–bar), Stuart Laughton (tpt/nat tpt/Renaissance cnt), David Campion (timp/perc)—Vaga Cintia Doremi ▲ DHR 9303 [DDD]
Susato, T.:Music of, w. Stuart Laughton (tpt), David Campion (timp/perc)—Renaissance Dance Suite Doremi ▲ DHR 9303 [DDD]
Telemann, G.P.:Musique héroïque, w. Stuart Laughton (tpt), David Campion (timp/perc) Doremi ▲ DHR 9303 [DDD]
Omoumi, Hossein (ney)
Persian Classical Music, w. Madjid Khaladj (tombak/daf) *(rec 1992)* Nimbus ▲ NI 5359 [DDD]
Onay, Gulsin (pno)
Piano Variations Ars Musici ▲ 1114
Saygun, A.A.:Con 1 Pno, w. G. Aykal (cnd), North German RSO Koch Schwann ▲ SCH 313502 [DDD]
Saygun, A.A.:Con 2 Pno, w. G. Aykal (cnd), North German RSO Koch Schwann ▲ SCH 313502 [DDD]
Onczay, Csaba (vc)
Bach, J.S.:Suites Vc, BWV 1007–1012—BWV 1007, 1008 & 1009 *(rec Oct 1992)* Naxos ▲ 8.550677 [DDD]
Beethoven, L. van:Son 1 Vc, w. J. Jandó (pno) *(rec June 25–27, 1991)* Naxos ▲ 8.550479
Beethoven, L. van:Son 2 Vc, w. J. Jandó (pno) Naxos ▲ 8.550479
Beethoven, L. van:Son 3 Vc, w. J. Jandó (pno) *(rec 12/90)* Naxos ▲ 8.550478 [DDD]
Beethoven, L. van:Son 4 Vc, w. J. Jandó (pno) Naxos ▲ 8.550478 [DDD]
Beethoven, L. van:Son 5 Vc, w. J. Jandó (pno) Naxos ▲ 8.550478 [DDD]
Beethoven, L. van:Trio 4 Pno, "Ghost", w. T. Nishizaki (vn), J. Jandó (pno) *(rec May 27–30, 1991)* Naxos ▲ 8.550442 [DDD]
Beethoven, L. van:Trio 6 Pno, "Archduke", w. J. Jandó (pno), T. Nishizaki (vn) *(rec May 27–30, 1991)* Naxos ▲ 8.550442 [DDD]
Beethoven, L. van:Vars on "Ein Mädchen oder Weibchen" from Mozart's *Die Zauberflöte*, w. J. Jandó (pno) *(rec June 25–27, 1991)* Naxos ▲ 8.550479
Beethoven, L. van:Vars on "See, the Conquering Hero Comes" from Handel's *Judas Maccabaeus*, w. J. Jandó (pno) *(rec June 25–27, 1991)* Naxos ▲ 8.550479
Beethoven, L. van:Vars on "Bei Männern" from Mozart's *Die Zauberflöte*, w. J. Jandó (pno) *(rec June 25–27, 1991)* Naxos ▲ 8.550479
Berwald, F.:Trios, w. I. Prunyi (pno), A. Kiss (vn)—Nos. 1–3 Marco Polo ▲ 8.223170
Brahms, J.:Qnt Cl, w. J. Balogh (cl), Danubius Quartet *(rec Oct. 16–18, 1991)* Naxos ▲ 8.550391 [DDD]
Brahms, J.:Trio Cl, w. J. Balogh (cl), J. Jandó (pno) *(rec Oct. 16–18, 1991)* Naxos ▲ 8.550391 [DDD]
Ondrozeck, Dennis (pno)—see ORCHESTRAS & ENSEMBLES Rawlins Piano Trio
Onnou, Alphonse (vn)—see ORCHESTRAS & ENSEMBLES Pro Arte String Quartet
Oomen, Antoine (pno)
Brahms, J.:Sons Vn (comp), w. R. Koelman (vn) Ars Produktion ▲ ARS 368320 [DDD]
Oortmerssen, Jacques van (org)
Bach, C.P.E.:Prelude Org, H.107 BIS ▲ CD 569 [DDD]
Bach, C.P.E.:Sons Org, H.84–87 BIS ▲ CD 569 [DDD]
Brahms, J.:Chorale Preludes, Op. 122 BIS ▲ CD 479 [DDD]
Brahms, J.:Org Musc (comp) BIS ▲ CD 479 [DDD]
Mozart, W.A.:Kleine Nachtmusik, w. H. van Nieuwkoop (org) [trans. performers for organ duet] BIS ▲ CD 418 [DDD]
Mozart, W.A.:Sym 40, w. H. van Nieuwkoop (org) [trans. Carl Czerny as organ duet] BIS ▲ CD 418 [DDD]
Mozart, W.A.:Vars (from flute quartet), w. H. van Nieuwkoop (org) [trans. performers for organ duet] BIS ▲ CD 418 [DDD]
Old Spanish & French Organ Music, w. Oortmerssen, Jacques van (org) *(rec St. Lambertus Church, Holland)* BIS ▲ CD 316
Oost, Gert (org)
Dutch Royal Organs (Music from the Dutch Royal House Archives) NM Classics ▲ NM 92031
Oostendorp, Tjeerd (tuba)
Wagemans, P.J.:Alla marcia, w. H. Vonk (cnd), The Hague PO Donemus ▲ CV 56 [DDD]
Oostenrijk, Pauline (ob)
Armando, G.:Con Ob, w. Sonora Hungarica *(rec Amsterdam, Feb 1993)* Verdi Classics ▲ AU 32 251 [DDD]
Britten, H.:Insect Pieces (2), w. I. Janssen (pno) Channel Classics ▲ CCS 9326 [DDD]
Britten, H.:Metamorphoses Ob Channel Classics ▲ CCS 9326 [DDD]
Britten, H.:Phantasy Qt, w. M. Mars (vn), S. van Els (va), J. Insinger (vc) Channel Classics ▲ CCS 9326 [DDD]
Britten, H.:Temporal Vars Ob, w. I. Janssen (pno) Channel Classics ▲ CCS 9326 [DDD]
Castelnuovo-Tedesco, M.:Con da Camera, w. Sonora Hungarica *(rec Amsterdam, Feb 1993)* Verdi Classics ▲ AU 32 251 [DDD]
Cimarosa, D.:Con in C Ob, w. Sonora Hungarica *(rec Amsterdam, Feb 1993)* Verdi Classics ▲ AU 32 251 [DDD]
Gibilaro, A.:Fant on British Airs, w. Sonora Hungarica *(rec Amsterdam, Feb 1993)* Verdi Classics ▲ AU 32 251 [DDD]
Vaughan Williams, R.:Blake Songs, w. N. Oosternrijk (sgr) Channel Classics ▲ CCS 9326 [DDD]
White, J.:Poem, w. S. van Els (va), D. Kuyken (pno) Channel Classics ▲ CCS 9326 [DDD]
Oostrem, L. van (b sax)
Torstensson, K.:Solo B Sax Donemus ▲ CV 13

Opitz, Günther (hn)
Brahms, J.:Choral Music, w. Waldemar Markus (hn), Margarethe Kluvetasch (hp), Horst Neumann (cnd), Leipzig Radio Chorus—Opp. 17, 42, 62 & 104 Berlin Classics ▲ BER CD 9276
Britten, H.:Serenade, Op. 31, w. Peter Schreier (ten), H. Kegel (cnd), Leipzig RSO Berlin Classics ▲ BER 9035 [ADD]
Opland, Bradley (db)
Gould, M.:Benny's Gig, w. Larry Combs (cl) *(rec Bennett Hall, Highland Park, IL, Jan. 18, 24 & 25, 1994)* Summit ▲ DCD 172 [DDD]
Oppenheim, Andrew (tuba)
Fox, F.:Time Messages, w. David Dzubay (tpt), David McChesney (tpt), Michael Galbraith (hn), Andrew Glendenning (trbn) *(rec Musical Arts Ctr, Bloomington, IN, Nov 30, 1989)* Indiana Univ School of Music ▲ 0-253-32433-5
Oppenheim, David (cl)
Brahms, J.:Qnt Cl, w. Budapest String Quartet *(rec 1959)* Sony Masterworks ("Portrait" series) ▲ MPK 45553 [ADD]
Brahms, J.:Trio Cl, w. P. Casals (vc), E. Istomin (pno) *(rec live July 3, 1955)* Music & Arts 4-▲ CD 689 (m) [AAD]
Mozart, W.A.:Qnt Cl, K.581, w. Budapest String Quartet Sony Classical 3-▲ SM3K 46527
Oppens, Ursula (pno)
American Piano Music of Our Time, Vol. 2 Music & Arts ▲ MUA 699 [DDD]
Beethoven, L. van:Fant Pno, Op. 77 Music & Arts ▲ CD 734-1 [DDD]
Beethoven, L. van:Son 11 Pno Music & Arts ▲ CD 734-1 [DDD]
Beethoven, L. van:Son 29 Pno, "Hammerklavier" Music & Arts ▲ CD 734-1 [DDD]
Brahms, J.:Scherzo Vn, w. B. Westphal (va) [trans Westphal for va & pno] Bridge ▲ BCD 9021 [DDD]
Brahms, J.:Sons Cl (comp), w. B. Westphal (va) Bridge ▲ BCD 9021 [DDD]
Carter, E.:Con Pno, w. M. Gielen (cnd), Cincinnati SO *(rec live, 10/5–6/84)* New World ▲ NW 347-2 [DDD/ADD] ■ NW 347-4
Chambers, W.M.:Ten Grand, w. Walter Hilse (pno), Bennett Lerner (pno), Nurit Tiles (pno), Aleck Karis (pno), Edmund Niemann (pno), Joseph Kubera (pno), Martin Goldray (pno), Allen Shawn (pno), Elizabeth di Filice (pno), Geisel (cnd) Newport ▲ NPD 85553
Davis, A.:Middle Passage Music & Arts ▲ CD 699-1 [DDD]
Feldman, Morton:Spring of Chosroes, w. P. Zukofsky (vn) CP2 Recordings ▲ CP2 102 [ADD]
Harbison, J.:Son 1 Pno, "Roger Sessions In Memoriam" Music & Arts ▲ CD 699-1 [DDD]
Hudson, J.:Sonare, w. Rolf Schulte (vn), Paul Dunkel (fl), Laura Flax (cl), Joseph Passaro (perc) CRI ■ C 382
Lang, D.:Music of, w. J. Rozen (elec tuba), D. Lang (nar), E. Niemann (pno), N. Tilles (pno), R. Schulte (vn), L. Vaillancourt (cnd), Le Nouvel Ensemble Moderne—Are You Experienced?; Orpheus Over & Under; Spud; Illumination Rounds CRI ▲ CD 625 [DDD]
Luening, O.:Son Pno CRI ■ ACS 6011
Luening, O.:Son Pno CRI ("American Masters" series) ▲ CD 716 [ADD]
Nancarrow, C.:Canons Music & Arts ▲ CD 699-1 [DDD]
Picker, T.:Old & Lost Rivers Music & Arts ▲ CD 699-1 [DDD]
Picker, T.:When Soft Voices Die *(rec 1979)* CRI ▲ CD 589 [ADD]
Rzewski, F.:Mayn Yingele Music & Arts ▲ CD 699-1 [DDD]
Rzewski, F.:The People United Will Never Be Defeated *(rec Apr. 1978)* Vanguard Classics ▲ OVC 8056 [ADD]
Schnabel, A.:Son Vn Pno, w. P. Zukovsky (vn) CP2 Recordings ▲ CP2 102
Schoenberg, A.:Book of the Hanging Gardens, w. P. Bryn-Julson (sop) [G] Music & Arts ▲ CD 650 [DDD]
Schoenberg, A.:The Cabaret Songs, w. P. Bryn-Julson (sop) [G] Music & Arts ▲ CD 650 [DDD]
Schoenberg, A.:Songs, Op. 2, w. P. Bryn-Julson (sop) [G] Music & Arts ▲ CD 650 [DDD]
Thorne, F.:Con 3 Pno, w. P.L. Dunkel (cnd), Westchester PO *(rec Jan. 18, 1993)* New World ▲ 80443-2
Wilson, R.:Concert Piece, w. R. Schulte (vn) CRI ▲ CD 602 [ADD]
Oppitz, G. (vn)
Saint-Saëns, C.:Son 1 Vn, w. G. Shaham (pno) Deutsche Grammophon ▲ 429729-2 [DDD]
Oppitz, Gerhard (pno)
Bach, J.S.:Con 1 for 3 Hpds, w. J. Frantz (pno), C. Eschenbach (pno), C. Eschenbach (cnd), Hamburg PO Deutsche Grammophon ▲ 415655-2 [DDD]
Bach, J.S.:Con for 4 Hpds, w. J. Frantz (pno), C. Eschenbach (pno), H. Schmidt (pno), C. Eschenbach (cnd), Hamburg PO Deutsche Grammophon ▲ 415655-2 [DDD]
Beethoven, L. van:Con 1 Pno, w. M. Janowski (cnd), Leipzig Opera Orch *(rec Grand Hall of the Leipzig Opera House, Jan 26–Feb 4, 1995)* RCA Red Seal ▲ 09026-68226-2 [DDD]
Beethoven, L. van:Con 3 Pno, w. M. Janowski (cnd), Leipzig Opera Orch *(rec Grand Hall of the Leipzig Opera House, Jan 26–Feb 4, 1995)* RCA Red Seal ▲ 09026-68226-2 [DDD]
Beethoven, L. van:Con 4 Pno, w. M. Janowski (cnd), Leipzig Gewandhaus Orch *(rec 1995–96)* RCA Red Seal ▲ 0902-668417-2 [DDD]
Beethoven, L. van:Con 5 Pno, "Emperor", w. M. Janowski (cnd), Leipzig Gewandhaus Orch *(rec 1995–96)* RCA Red Seal ▲ 0902-668417-2 [DDD]
Beethoven, L. van:Son 15 Pno, "Pastoral" RCA Red Seal ▲ 09026-61969-2
Beethoven, L. van:Son 17 Pno, "Tempest" RCA Red Seal ▲ 09026-61969-2
Beethoven, L. van:Son 26 Pno, "Les Adieux" RCA Red Seal ▲ 09026-61969-2
Beethoven, L. van:Trio 6 Pno, "Archduke", w. D. Sitkovetsky (vn), D. Geringas (vc) Novalis ▲ 150008 [DDD]
Beethoven, L. van:Trio 9 Pno, "Kakadu", w. D. Sitkovetsky (vn), D. Geringas (vc) Novalis ▲ 150008 [DDD]
Brahms, J.:Ballades, Op. 10 RCA Red Seal ▲ 09026-61618-2
Brahms, J.:Con 1 Pno, w. C. Davis (cnd), Bavarian RSO RCA Red Seal ▲ 09026-61618-2
Brahms, J.:Con 2 Pno, w. C. Davis (cnd), Bavarian RSO RCA Red Seal ▲ 09026-61619-2
Brahms, J.:Pno Music (misc) Eurodisc 5-▲ 69245-2-RG [DDD]
Brahms, J.:Pieces Pno, Op. 76 RCA Red Seal ▲ 09026-61619-2
Brahms, J.:Pieces Pno, Op. 119 Orfeo ▲ 020821 [ADD]
Brahms, J.:Rhaps Pno, Op. 79—No. 1 RCA Red Seal ▲ 09026-61811-2
Brahms, J.:Sons Cl (comp), w. K. Leister (cl) Orfeo ▲ 086841 ■ 086841
Brahms, J.:Son 3 Pno Orfeo ▲ 020821 [ADD]
Brahms, J.:Vars & Fugue on a Theme by Handel RCA Red Seal ▲ 09026-61811-2
Brahms, J.:Vars on a Theme by Paganini RCA Red Seal ▲ 09026-61811-2
Fauré, G.:Son 1 Vn, w. L. Mordkovitch (vn) Chandos ▲ CHAN 8417 [DDD]
Franck, C.:Son Vn, w. G. Shaham (vn) Deutsche Grammophon ▲ 429729-2 [DDD]
Grieg, E.:Pno Music (comp)—Lyric Pieces RCA Red Seal 3-▲ 09026-61568-2
Grieg, E.:Pno Music (comp) RCA Red Seal 4-▲ 09026-61569-2
Liszt, F.:Ballades Pno—No. 2 RCA Red Seal ▲ 09026-60954-2
Liszt, F.:Cons Pno, w. R. Abbado (cnd), Bamberg SO RCA Red Seal ▲ 09026-60953-2
Liszt, F.:Consolations RCA Red Seal ▲ 09026-60954-2
Liszt, F.:Fant on Hungarian Folk Tunes, w. R. Abbado (cnd), Bamberg SO RCA Red Seal ▲ 09026-60953-2
Liszt, F.:Légendes RCA Red Seal ▲ 09026-60954-2
Liszt, F.:Pno Music (misc)—R.W.–Venice; At the Grave of Richard Wagner; Solemn March to the Holy Grail [from Parsifal]; Love–death; Final Scene [both from Tristan und Isolde] *(rec Villa Wahnfried, Wagner-Museum, Bayreuth, Mar 30–Apr 3, 1993)* BMG ▲ 61843-2
Liszt, F.:Vars on "Weinen, Klagen, Sorgen, Zagen", S.179 RCA Red Seal ▲ 09026-60954-2
Nocturne *(rec Reitstadel, Neumarkt, Germany, July 24–26, 1993)* RCA Red Seal ▲ 09026-61968-2 [DDD]
Ravel, M.:Tzigane, w. G. Shaham (vn) Deutsche Grammophon ▲ 429729-2 [DDD]
Reger, M.:Albumblatt & Tarantella, w. E. Brunner (cl) Tudor ▲ 724 [DDD]
Reger, M.:Con Pno, w. H. Stein (cnd), Bamberg SO Koch Schwann ▲ CD 311058 [DDD]
Reger, M.:Son Cl, Op. 107, w. E. Brunner (cl) Tudor ▲ 724 [DDD]

▲ = CD ♦ = Enhanced CD Δ = MD ■ = Cassette Tape □ = DCC

Oppitz, Gerhard (pno) (cont.)
Schoenberg, A.:Chamber Sym 1, w. A. Andorjan (fl), E. Brunner (cl), D. Sitkovetzky (vn), D. Geringas (vc) [Webern's 1923 arr. for Flute, Clarinet, Violin, Cello & Piano] Tudor ▲ 717 [DDD]
Schubert, Franz:Fant Vn, D.934, w. L. Mordkovitch (vn) Chandos ▲ CHAN 8544 [DDD]
Schubert, Franz:Son Vn, D.574, w. L. Mordkovitch (vn) Chandos ▲ CHAN 8544 [DDD]
Schubert, Franz:Trio 1 Pno, w. D. Sitkovetsky (vn), D. Geringas (vc) Novalis ▲ 150002
Schubert, Franz:Trio 2 Pno, w. D. Sitkovetsky (vn), D. Geringas (vc) Novalis ▲ 150003
Schumann, R.:Carnaval Pno RCA Red Seal ▲ 09026-60977-2
Schumann, R.:Fant Pno RCA Red Seal ▲ 09026-60856-2
Schumann, R.:Kinderszenen RCA Red Seal ▲ 09026-60856-2
Schumann, R.:Nachtstücke RCA Red Seal ▲ 09026-60977-2
Schumann, R.:Papillons RCA Red Seal ▲ 09026-60856-2
Schumann, R.:Waldscenen RCA Red Seal ▲ 09026-60977-2
Strauss, R.:Son Vn, w. L. Mordkovitch (vn) Chandos ▲ CHAN 8417 [DDD]
Wagner, R.:Pno Music—A Sonata for the Album of Frau M.W.; Albumleaf for Frau Betty Schott; Arrival of the Black Swans *(rec Villa Wahnfried, Wagner-Museum, Bayreuth, Mar 30–Apr 3, 1993)* BMG ▲ 61843-2
Wagner, R.:Songs, w. N. Stutzmann (cta)—Mignonne; Waiting [from 3 Melodies]; All Things Are but Fleeting Images; 2 Grenadiers; In the Greenhouse [study for Tristan und Isolde] *(rec Villa Wahnfried, Wagner-Museum, Bayreuth, Mar 30–Apr 3, 1993)* BMG ▲ 61843-2
Weber, C.M. von:Grand duo concertant Cl, w. E. Brunner (cl) Orfeo ▲ 187891
Weber, C.M. von:Trio Fl, w. A. Adorjan (fl), B. Pergamenschikow (vc) Orfeo ▲ 187891
Weber, C.M. von:Vars on a Theme from *Silvana* Cl, w. E. Brunner (cl) Orfeo ▲ 187891
Wild Classics:A Celebration of Animals & Nature, w. James Galway (fl), Ofra Harnoy (vc), Martin Hoherman (vc), Emily Mitchell (hp), Michael Dussek (pno), Samuel Lipman (pno), Leo Litwin (pno), Isao Tomita (synths), Boston Pops Orch [cnd:Arthur Fiedler], Chicago SO [cnd:Fritz Reiner] RCA Red Seal ▲ 09026-68483-2 ■ 09026-68483-4
Zemlinsky, A. von:Trio Cl, w. E. Brunner (cl), D. Geringas (vc) Tudor ▲ 717 [DDD]

Oprea, Vasile (hn)
Haydn, J.:Con for 2 Hns, w. Daian Lung (hn), C. Mandeal (cnd), Cluj-Napoca PO Electrecord ▲ ELCD 107 [AAD]
Schumann, R.:Konzertstück Hns, w. D. Lung (hn), A. Marc (hn), T. Tulbure (hn), C. Mandeal (cnd), Cluj-Napoca PO Electrecord ▲ ELCD 107 [AAD]

Oprean, Adelina (vn)
Enescu, G.:Son 2 Vn, w. J. Oprean (pno) Hyperion ▲ CDA 66484
Enescu, G.:Son 3 Vn, w. J. Oprean (pno) Hyperion ▲ CDA 66484
Enescu, G.:Torso, w. J. Oprean (pno) Hyperion ▲ CDA 66484
Magnard, A.:Trio Pno, w. Christoph Keller (pno), Thomas Demenga (vc) Accord ▲ ACD 200102 [DDD]

Oprean, Justin (pno)
Enescu, G.:Son 2 Vn, w. A. Oprean (vn) Hyperion ▲ CDA 66484
Enescu, G.:Son 3 Vn, w. A. Oprean (vn) Hyperion ▲ CDA 66484
Enescu, G.:Torso, w. A. Oprean (vn) Hyperion ▲ CDA 66484

Opsitos, J. (vn)
Handel, G.F.:Con for 2 Vns & 2 Hns, w. P. Mareš (vn), B. Tylšar (F hn), Z. Tylšar (F hn), L. Pešek (cnd), Dvořák CO Supraphon ▲ 103907-2 [DDD]

Oramo, Sakari (vn)
Kurtág, G.:Kafka Fragments, w. Anu Komsi (sop) Ondine ▲ ODE CD 868

Oravecz, György (pno)
Bretón, T.:Trio Pno, w. New Budapest String Quartet members *(rec Rottenbiller Street Studio, Budapest, Jan. 29–30, 1992)* Marco Polo ▲ 8.223745 [DDD]
Liszt, F.:Fant on Hungarian Folk Tunes, w. B. Kocsár (cnd), Budapest SO *(rec Italian Cultural Institute, Budapest, June 26–27, 1992)* Hungaroton ▲ HCD 31461 [DDD]
Liszt, F.:Totentanz, w. B. Kocsár (cnd), Budapest SO—also solo pno version *(rec Italian Cultural Institute, Budapest, Apr. 21–22, 1992)* Hungaroton ▲ HCD 31461 [DDD]

Orban, Goedri (bn)
Enescu, G.:Dectet Ww, w. Virgil Francu (fl), Nicolae Maxin (fl), Valeriu Barbuceanu (cl), Leontin Boanta (cl), Adrian Petrescu (ob), Viorica Feher (bn), Florin Ionoaia (Eng hn), Dan Cinca (hn), Simon Jebeleanu (hn), H. Andreescu (cnd) Olympia ▲ OLY 445 [DDD]

Orbelian, Constantine (pno)
Khachaturian, A.:Con Pno, w. N. Järvi (cnd), Scottish National Orch Chandos ▲ CHAN 8542 [DDD]
Schnittke, A.:Qnt Pno, w. Moscow String Quartet Russian Disc ▲ RUS 10 031 [DDD]
Shostakovich, D.:Qnt Pno, w. Moscow String Quartet Russian Disc ▲ RUS 10 031 [DDD]
Tchaikovsky, P.:Con 1 Pno, w. N. Järvi (cnd), Philharmonia Orch Chandos ▲ CHAN 8777 [DDD]

Orchard, Jennifer (vn)—see ORCHESTRAS & ENSEMBLES Lark String Quartet

Ordman, Ava (trbn)
Erb, D.:Con Trbn, w. C. Comet (cnd), Grand Rapids SO *(rec DeVos Hall, Grand Rapids, MI, May 22, 1994)* Koss Classics ▲ KC 3002 [DDD]

O'Reilly, C. (pno)
Adams, J.:China Gates Albany ▲ TROY 038 [DDD]
Adams, J.:Phrygian Gates Albany ▲ TROY 038 [DDD]
Brief, T.:Nightsong Albany ▲ TROY 038 [DDD]
Helps, R.:Hommages Albany ▲ TROY 038-2 [DDD]
Ravel, M.:Gaspard de la nuit Albany ▲ TROY 052
Ravel, M.:Miroirs Albany ▲ TROY 052
Sessions, R.:Son 1 Pno Albany ▲ TROY 038 [DDD]

Orenstein, Janet (vn)—see ORCHESTRAS & ENSEMBLES Guild Piano Trio

Orford, John (bn)
Music for Trumpet & Organ, w. Graham Ashton (tpt), Leslie Pearson (org), Gordon Hunt (ob), Denis Vigay (vc) IMP Classics ▲ PCD 986 [DDD]
Trumpet & Organ:Sonatas & Suites, w. Graham Ashton (tpt), Leslie Pearson (org), Gordon Hunt (ob), Denis Vigay (vc) IMP ("Classics" series) ▲ IMP 6700922

Orford, John (ctbn)
Matthews, C.:Suns Dance, w. Sebastian Bell (pic), Gareth Hulse (ob), Michael Collins (b cl), Michael Thompson (hn), Nona Liddell (vn), Joan Atherton (vn), Paul Silverthorne (va), Christopher van Kampen (vc), Robin McGee (db) *(rec All Saint's Church, Petersham, Oct 1992)* Deutsche Grammophon ▲ 447067-2 [DDD]

O'Riley, Christopher (pno)
Beach, A.M.C.:Songs—Give Me Not Love, Op. 61 [w. Lauren Flanigan (sop), Paul Groves (ten)]; In the Twilight, Op. 85 [w. Charlotte Hellekant (mez)]; O Mistress Mine, Op. 37/1 [w. Paul Groves (ten)]; Dark is the Night, Op. 11/1 [w. Lauren Flanigan (sop)]; Jeune fille et jeune fleur, Op. 1/3 [w. Thomas Paul (bass)] *(rec St. Peter's Episcopal Church, New York City, May 15, 1995)* Delos ▲ DE 3170 [DDD]
Busoni, F.:Chaconne Pno Centaur ▲ CRC 2036 [DDD]
Busoni, F.:Fant contrappuntistica Pno Centaur ▲ CRC 2036 [DDD]
Busoni, F.:Mephisto-Waltz Centaur ▲ CRC 2036 [DDD]
Danielpour, R.:The Enchanted Garden Koch International Classics ▲ KIC 7100-2 [DDD]
Danielpour, R.:Psalms Koch International Classics ▲ KIC 7100-2 [DDD]
Danielpour, R.:Qnt Pno & Strs, Lincoln Center Chamber Music Society Koch International Classics ▲ KIC 7100-2 [DDD]
Debussy, C.:La Fille aux cheveaux de lin Voice, w. James Galway (fl) [trans Galway for flute & piano] *(rec Meggen, Switzerland, Dec 6 & 7, 1994)* RCA Red Label ▲ 09026-68351-2 [DDD] ■ 09026-68351-4
Debussy, C.:Petite suite, w. James Galway (fl)—En bateau [trans Galway for flute & piano] *(rec Meggen, Switzerland, Dec 6 & 7, 1994)* RCA Red Label ▲ 09026-68351-2 [DDD] ■ 09026-68351-4
Debussy, C.:La Plus que lente, w. James Galway (fl) [trans Galway for flute & piano] *(rec Meggen, Switzerland, Dec 6 & 7, 1994)* RCA Red Label ▲ 09026-68351-2 [DDD] ■ 09026-68351-4
Debussy, C.:Prélude à l'après-midi d'un faune, w. James Galway (fl) [trans Galway for flute & piano] *(rec Meggen, Switzerland, Dec 6 & 7, 1994)* RCA Red Label ▲ 09026-68351-2 [DDD] ■ 09026-68351-4

O'Riley, Christopher (pno) (cont.)
Fauré, G.:Son 1 Vn, w. James Galway (fl) [trans Galway for flute & piano] *(rec Meggen, Switzerland, Dec 6 & 7, 1994)* RCA Red Label ▲ 09026-68351-2 [DDD] ■ 09026-68351-4
Flute Flavors, w. Paul Fried (fl), Ronald Feldman (vc), David Sussman (gtr) Golden Tone ▲ GTCD 002
Kernis, A.J.:Still Movement with Hymn, w. Pamela Frank (vn), Paul Neubauer (va), Carter Brey (vc) *(rec Florence Gould Auditorium, Seiji Ozawa Hall, Tanglewood, June 19 & 20, 1995)* Argo ▲ 448174-2 [DDD]
Kernis, A.J.:Superstar Etude 1 *(rec Manhattan Center Studios, New York, May 31–June 3, 1995)* New Albion ♦ NA 083CD
Schickele, P.:The Short-Tempered Clavier *(rec Mechanics Hall, Worcester, MA, Feb. 22, 1995)* Telarc ▲ CD 80390 [DDD]
Schumann, R.:Adagio & Allegro Hn, w. R. Schulte (vn) Centaur ▲ CRC 2097 [DAD]
Schumann, R.:Fantasiestücke Cl, w. R. Schulte (vn) [violin & piano arrs.] Centaur ▲ CRC 2097 [DAD]
Schumann, R.:Märchenbilder, w. R. Schulte (vn) Centaur ▲ CRC 2097 [DAD]
Schumann, R.:Romances Ob, w. R. Schulte (vn) [violin & piano arrs.] Centaur ▲ CRC 2097 [DAD]
Stravinsky, I.:Apollon musagète (reduction) Elektra/Nonesuch ▲ 79343-2
Stravinsky, I.:L'Histoire du soldat (pno) Elektra/Nonesuch ▲ 79343-2
Stravinsky, I.:Scenes Pno—3 movts. Elektra/Nonesuch ▲ 79343-2
Widor, C.M.:Suite Fl, w. James Galway (fl) *(rec Meggen, Switzerland, Dec 6 & 7, 1994)* RCA Red Label ▲ 09026-68351-2 [DDD] ■ 09026-68351-4

Orion, Stephen (vc)
Panufnik, A.:Sxt Strs, w. Roger Chase (va), Chilingirian String Quartet Conifer Classics ▲ 74321-16190-2

Orkis, Lambert (pno)—see also ORCHESTRAS & ENSEMBLES American Chamber Players, Penn Contemporary Players
Brahms, J.:Hungarian Dances Pno 4-Hands, w. Anne-Sophie Mutter (vn)—Nos. 2 & 5 [arr vn & pno] Deutsche Grammophon ▲ 445 826-2
Brahms, J.:Scherzo Vn, w. Anne-Sophie Mutter (vn) Deutsche Grammophon ▲ 445 826-2
Brahms, J.:Sons Vc (comp), w. Anner Bylsma (vc) Sony Classical ("Vivarte" series) ▲ SK 68249
Corigliano, J.:Sym 1, w. David Hardy (vc), Glenn Garlick (vc), L. Slatkin (cnd), National SO Washington D.C. *(rec J. F. K. Center for the Performing Arts, Washington, D. C.)* RCA Red Seal ▲ 09026-68450-2 [DDD]
Crumb, G.:A Little Suite for Christmas:A.D. 1979 Bridge ▲ BCD 9003 ■ BCS 7003
Crumb, G.:A Little Suite for Christmas:A.D. 1979 *(rec 8/82)* Bridge ▲ BCD 9028 [ADD]
Debussy, C.:Beau soir, w. Anne-Sophie Mutter (vn) [arr vn & pno] Deutsche Grammophon ▲ 445 826-2
Debussy, C.:Son Vn, w. Anne-Sophie Mutter (vn) Deutsche Grammophon ▲ 445 826-2
Franck, C.:Son Vn, w. Anne-Sophie Mutter (vn) Deutsche Grammophon ▲ 445 826-2
Gottschalk, L.M.:Pno Music—Second Banjo, Op. 82; Solitude, Op. 65; La brise (valse de concert); Souvenir de la Havane (grand caprice de concert), Op. 39; Le Chant du martyr (grand caprice religieux); Manchega (étude de concert), Op. 38; La Savane (ballade créole), Op. 3; The Union, Op. 48 [1865 Chickering concert grand] Smithsonian Collection ▲ ND 033 [AAD]
Gottschalk, L.M.:The Union Smithsonian Collection ▲ ND 033 [AAD]
Mozart, W.A.:Sons Vn Pno (misc), w. Anne-Sophie Mutter (vn)—in e, K.304 Deutsche Grammophon ▲ 445 826-2
Schubert, Franz:Impromptus Pno (comp) [1826 Graf fortepiano] Virgin Classics ▲ 59600 [DDD]
Schubert, Franz:Impromptus Pno, D.899—No. 1 in c Virgin Classics ▲ CDC 59288
Schubert, Franz:Moments musicaux Virgin Classics ▲ CDC 59288
Schubert, Franz:Pieces Pno, D.459—3 sels. Virgin Classics ▲ CDC 59288
Schubert, Franz:Pieces Pno, D.946 Virgin Classics ▲ CDC 59288
Schubert, Franz:Songs (misc), w. A. Augér (sop)—23 songs [G] Virgin Classics ▲ 59630 [DDD]
Schumann, R.:Stücke im Volkston, w. Anner Bylsma (vc) Sony Classical ("Vivarte" series) ▲ SK 68249
Weber, C.M. von:Sons Vn, w. William Steck (vn) *(rec Glendale Baptist Church, Nashville, TN)* Gasparo ▲ GAS 263 [DDD]
Weber, C.M. von:Vars on a Norwegian Air Vn, w. William Steck (vn) *(rec Glendale Baptist Church, Nashville, TN)* Gasparo ▲ GAS 263 [DDD]
Wernick, R.:Son Pno, "Reflections of a Dark Light" Bridge ▲ BCD 9003 ■ BCS 7003

Orland, B. Herr (ob)
La Barbara, J.:L'Albero della foglie azzure Centaur ▲ CRC 2166

Orlandi, Ugo (mand)
Italian Mandolin Concertos, w. Aquilani Solisti [cnd:Vittorio Antonellini] Koch Schwann ▲ SCH 311171 [DDD]

Orlandini, Luis (gtr)
Giuliani, M.:Rossiniana CPO 2-▲ CPO 999103 [DDD]
Sor, F.:Fants Gtr—Opp. 4, 7, 10, 12, 16, 21, 30, 40, 46, 52, 56, 58 & 59 CPO 3-▲ CPO 999199 [DDD]

Orlando, Anthony (mar)
Davidson, T.:Fire on the Mountain, w. Don Liuzzi (vib), Charles Abramovic (pno) CRI ▲ CD 681 [DDD]
Krzywicki, J.:Snow Night, w. Susan Nowicki (pno) Capstone ▲ CPS 8631

Orleans, J. (db)—see ORCHESTRAS & ENSEMBLES Griffin Music Ensemble

Orlovetsky, Alexei (pno)
Rachmaninoff, S.:Con 3 Pno, w. A. Titov (cnd), St. Petersburg New Classical Orch Infinity Digital ▲ QK 57260 [DDD]

Orlovsky, Harold (vn)
Reger, M.:Con in Olden Style, w. H. Stein (cnd), Bamberg SO Koch Schwann ▲ CD 313542 [DDD]
Reger, M.:Sinfonietta, w. H. Stein (cnd), Bamberg SO Koch Schwann ▲ CD 313542 [DDD]

Ormand, Fred (cl)
Banfield, W.:4 Persons, w. Harry Sargous (ob), Lynette Diers Cohen (bn), Ellen Weckler (pno) Innova ▲ 510 [DDD]

Ormandy, Martin (vc)
Sondheim, S.:Songs, w. Marc Heller (ten), Alfred Heller (pno)—The Hills of Tomorrow; Take Me to the World; Another 100 People; Not While I'm Around; You Must Meet My Wife; Send in the Clowns; Comedy Tonight; Love I Hear; Later; Anyone Can Whistle; Pretty Women; Losing My Mind; Johanna; Good Thing Going; Silly People; Ev'rybody Says Don't; Loving You; Green Finch & Linnet Bird; Being Alive; One More Kiss; Sunday Etcetera ▲ KTC 1185

Orner, Ellen (vn)
Lees, B.:Invenzione Albany ▲ TROY 138 [DDD]
Lees, B.:Son 1 Vn, w. J. Wizansky (pno) Albany ▲ TROY 138 [DDD]
Lees, B.:Son 2 Vn, w. J. Wizansky (pno) Albany ▲ TROY 138 [DDD]
Lees, B.:Son 3 Vn, w. J. Wizansky (pno) Albany ▲ TROY 138 [DDD]

Ornstein, Doris (hpd)—see also ORCHESTRAS & ENSEMBLES Oberlin Baroque Ensemble
Bach, J.S.:Sons Vl, BWV 1027–1029, w. C. Meints (vl) Gasparo Gallante ▲ GG 1001 [AAD]

Ornung, Kaare (pno)
Reizenstein, F.:Sonatina Ob, w. Brynjar Hoff (ob) Norway Music ▲ LCD 1004
Schumann, R.:Romances Ob, w. Brynjar Hoff (ob) Norway Music ▲ LCD 1004

O'Rourke, Jim (gtr)
O'Rourke, J.:Terminal Pharmacy, w. Tony Burr (cl), Jeff Cortazzo (b trbn), John McEntire (dr), Rob Prosser (acc), Isha Suftin (acc), Mike Dockter (vc), Hattie Franck (vc), Robert Keck (vc), Mary LaBreque (vc), Dan Loch (vc), Stan Saderk (vc), Lisa Hemmer (fl), Sue Oberg (fl), Wendi Lev (fl), Jim Vanden (fl), Jim O'Rourke (gtr), Steve Braack (elec) Tzadik ▲ TZA 7011 [DDD]

O'Rourke, Micaél (pno)
Chopin, F.:Andante Spianato & Grande Polonaise Chandos ▲ CHAN 9353 [DDD]
Chopin, F.:Ballades Pno (comp) Chandos ▲ CHAN 9353 [DDD]
Chopin, F.:Polonaise-fant Chandos ▲ CHAN 9353 [DDD]
Debussy, C.:Estampes Chandos ▲ CHAN 9078 [DDD]
Debussy, C.:Preludes Pno (sels)—Book 1 Chandos ▲ CHAN 9078 [DDD]
Field, J.:Con 1 Pno, w. M. Bamert (cnd), London Mozart Players Chandos ▲ CHAN 9368 [DDD]
Field, J.:Con 2 Pno, w. M. Bamert (cnd), London Mozart Players Chandos ▲ CHAN 9368 [DDD]
Field, J.:Con 3 Pno, w. M. Bamert (cnd), London Mozart Players Chandos ▲ CHAN 9495

INSTRUMENT.

O'Rourke, Micaél (pno) (cont.)
Field, J.:Con 4 Pno, w. M. Bamert (cnd), London Mozart Players Chandos ▲ CHAN 9442
Field, J.:Con 5 Pno, "L'Incendie par l'orage", w. M. Bamert (cnd), London Mozart Players Chandos ▲ CHAN 9495
Field, J.:Con 6 Pno, w. M. Bamert (cnd), London Mozart Players Chandos ▲ CHAN 9442
Field, J.:Nocturnes Pno (comp) Chandos 2-▲ CHAN 8719/20 [DDD]
Field, J.:Pno Music—Air du bon Roi H. IV; Irish Dance; Sehnsuchtswalzer; Fantaisie sur l'air de Martini; Rondeau écossois; Andante inédit in E♭; Chanson russe variée; Kamarinskaya—Air russe varié; Marche triompale; Nouvelle fantaisie in G; Nocturne in B♭; Polonaise en rondeau; Fantaisie sur un air russe; 2 Album Leaves in c; Rondo in A♭ Chandos ▲ CHAN 9315 [DDD]
Field, J.:Sons Pno (comp) Chandos ▲ CHAN 8787 [DDD]
Schumann, R.:Carnaval Pno Chandos ▲ CHAN 9388 [DDD]
Schumann, R.:Kreisleriana Chandos ▲ CHAN 9388 [DDD]

Orozco, Rafael (pno)
Falla, M. de:Noches en los jardines de España, w. E. Colomer (cnd), Spanish National Youth Orch—4 Spanish Pieces; Nights in the Gardens of Spain; Fant. Baetica; Homage to Debussy; Homage to Paul Dukas Valois ▲ V 4724
Rachmaninoff, S.:Con 2 Pno, w. E. de Waart (cnd), Royal PO Philips 2-▲ 438383-2
Rachmaninoff, S.:Music of, w. E. de Waart (cnd), Royal PO Philips 2-▲ 438326-2
Rachmaninoff, S.:Rhapsody on a Theme of Paganini, w. E. de Waart (cnd), Royal PO Philips 2-▲ 438383-2
Rachmaninoff, S.:Vocalise, w. E. de Waart (cnd), Royal PO Philips 2-▲ 438383-2
Schubert, Franz:Fant Pno, D.760, "Wandererfantasie" Valois ▲ V 4683
Schubert, Franz:Son Pno, D.960 Valois ▲ V 4683
Schumann, R.:Fant Pno Philips ("Solo" series) ▲ 442653-2
Schumann, R.:Kreisleriana Philips ("Solo" series) ▲ 442653-2

Orsin, B. (baroque vn)—see ORCHESTRAS & ENSEMBLES Musica Holmiae

Ortenberg, Edgar (vn)—see ORCHESTRAS & ENSEMBLES Budapest String Quartet

Ortiz, Cristina (pno)
Addinsell, R.:Warsaw Con, w. M. Atzmon (cnd), Royal PO London ▲ 414348-2 [DDD]
Beethoven, L. van:Con 1 Pno, w. R. Hickox (cnd), City of London Sinfonia IMP Masters ▲ PCD 854 [DDD]
Beethoven, L. van:Con 2 Pno, w. R. Hickox (cnd), City of London Sinfonia IMP Masters ▲ PCD 854 [DDD]
Beethoven, L. van:Con 3 Pno, w. R. Hickox (cnd), City of London Sinfonia IMP Classics ▲ PCD 879 [DDD]
Beethoven, L. van:Con 4 Pno, w. R. Hickox (cnd), City of London Sinfonia IMP Classics ▲ PCD 879 [DDD]
Beethoven, L. van:Con 5 Pno, "Emperor", w. R. Hickox (cnd), City of London Sinfonia IMP ("Classic" series) ▲ IMP 2038
Beethoven, L. van:Son 8 Pno, "Pathétique" Royal Philharmonic Collection ▲ TRP 27 [DDD]
Beethoven, L. van:Son 14 Pno, "Moonlight Son" Royal Philharmonic Collection ▲ TRP 27 [DDD]
Beethoven, L. van:Son 17 Pno, "Tempest" Royal Philharmonic Collection ▲ TRP 27 [DDD]
Beethoven, L. van:Son 21 Pno, "Waldstein" IMP ("Classic" series) ▲ IMP 2038
Chabrier, E.:Pno Music (misc)—No. 7, "Danse villageoise" IMP Classics ▲ PCD 846 [DDD]
Chopin, F.:Pno Music (misc)—Andante Spianato; Ballade No. 4; Études, Op. 10, No. 12 & Op. 25, No. 11; Fantasie Impromptu, Op. 66; Impromptu, Op. 29, No. 1; Mazurkas, Op. 24, No. 4 & Op. 67, No. 3; Nocturnes, Op. 15, No. 1 & Op. 48, No. 1; Scherzo, Op. 39; Waltzes, Op. 64, Nos. 1 & 2 & Op. 69, No. 1 IMP Classics ▲ PCD 872 [DDD]
French Impressionist Piano IMP Classics ▲ PCD 846 [DDD]
The Heart of the Piano Concerto, w. Lill, John (pno), J. L. Prats (pno), London SO [cnd:J. Judd, W. Morris], Royal PO [cnd:L. Foster, E. Bátiz] Pickwick ("The Orchid" series) ▲ PICORCD 11012
Milhaud, D.:Saudades do Brasil—No. 4, "Copacabana" IMP Classics ▲ PCD 846 [DDD]
Nocturnal Classics, w. B. Wilde (cnd), Serenata of London, J. Ogdon (pno), F. Lott (sop) Pickwick ("The Orchid" series) ▲ PICORCD 11007
Poulenc, F.:Mélancolie Pno IMP Classics ▲ PCD 846 [DDD]
Rachmaninoff, S.:Con 2 Pno, w. M. Atzmon (cnd), Royal PO London ▲ 414348-2 [DDD]
Ravel, M.:Alborada del gracioso IMP Classics ▲ PCD 846 [DDD]
Saint-Saëns, C.:Carnival of the Animals, w. P. Rogé (pno), C. Dutoit (cnd), London Sinfonietta London ▲ 414460-2 [ADD] ■ 414460-4
Saint-Saëns, C.:Carnival of the Animals, w. P. Rogé (pno), C, C. Dutoit (cnd), London Sinfonietta London ▲ 430720-2 [DDD]
Satie, E.:Gymnopédies—No. 1 IMP Classics ▲ PCD 846 [DDD]
Schumann, R.:Carnaval Pno IMP Classics ▲ PCD 899 [DDD]
Schumann, R.:Con Pno, w. L. Foster (cnd), Royal PO RPO Records Impact ▲ RPO 5004 [DDD]
Schumann, R.:Kinderszenen IMP Classics ▲ PCD 899 [DDD]
Schumann, R.:Papillons IMP Classics ▲ PCD 899 [DDD]
Shostakovich, D.:Con 2 Pno, w. V. Ashkenazy (cnd), Royal PO London ▲ 425793-2 [DDD]
Stenhammar, W.:Con 2 Pno, w. N. Järvi (cnd), Gothenburg SO BIS ▲ CD 476 [DDD]
Villa-Lobos, H.:Cons Pno (comp), w. M. A. Gómez Martínez (cnd), Royal PO London 2-▲ 430628-2 [DDD]

Orton, Stephen (vc)—see also ORCHESTRAS & ENSEMBLES Academy of St. Martin in the Fields Chamber Ensemble
Debussy, C.:Son Vc, w. I. Brown (pno) Chandos ▲ CHAN 8385 [ADD]
Mozart, W.A.:Duo Bn Vc, w. K. Thunemann (bn) Philips ▲ 422390-2 [DDD]
Walton, W.:Qt Pno, w. H. Milne (pno), K. Sillito (vn), R. Smissen (va) Chandos ▲ CHAN 8999 [DDD]

Orvieto, Aldo (pno)
Dietrich, A.:Trio 1 Pno, w. Dora Bratchkova (vn), Michel Dispa (vc) *(rec Dynamic's, Genova, May 17–19, 1994)* Dynamic ▲ CD 121 [DDD]
Dietrich, A.:Trio 2 Pno, w. Dora Bratchkova (vn), Michel Dispa (vc) *(rec Dynamic's, Genova, May 17–19, 1994)* Dynamic ▲ CD 121 [DDD]
Donatoni, F.:Cloches III, w. R. Maioli (pno), G. Facchin (cnd), Tâmmittam Percussion Ensemble Dynamic ▲ CD 97 [DDD]
Maderna, B.:Music of, w. R. Maioli (pno), G. Facchin (cnd), Tâmmittam Percussion Ensemble—Concerto for Two Pianos & Instruments (1948); Serenata per un satellite (1969) Dynamic ▲ CD 97 [DDD]
Martucci, G.:Qnt Pno, w. Ex Novo Ensemble *(rec Dec. 1992)* Dynamic ▲ CD 99 [DDD]
Respighi, O.:Qnt Pno, w. Ex Novo Ensemble *(rec Dec. 1992)* Dynamic ▲ CD 99 [DDD]
Tailleferre, G.:Music of, w. R. Maioli (pno), G. Facchin (cnd), Tâmmittam Percussion Ensemble—Hommage a Rameau (1964); Suite burlesque for Piano 4-Hands; Première prouesses for Piano 4-Hands Dynamic ▲ CD 97 [DDD]

Orzel, June (bn)
Tailleferre, G.:Chansons populaires françaises, w. Patrice Maginnis (sop), John Fairweather (vn), David Ryther (vn), Jill Cohen (va), Karen Andrie (vc), Elizabeth Bodine (ob), Andy Connell (cl), Gordon Mumma (hn), N. Paiement (cnd) *(rec UC, Santa Cruz, May 1992)* Helicon Classics ▲ HE 1008
Tailleferre, G.:Image, w. John Fairweather (vn), David Ryther (vn), Jill Cohen (va), Karen Andrie (vc), Elizabeth Bodine (ob), Andy Connell (cl), Gordon Mumma (hn), N. Paiement (cnd) *(rec UC, Santa Cruz, May 1992)* Helicon Classics ▲ HE 1008

Osetinskaya, P. (pno)
Mozart, W.A.:Con 24 Pno, w. S. Litkov (cnd), St. Petersburg Festival Orch Infinity Digital ▲ QK 64333 [DDD]

Oshavkova, Lydia (fl)
Albinoni, T.:Cons Obs, w. I. Kozhouharov (cnd), Sofia Camerata Classica—in G Divertimento ▲ DIV 41001 [DDD]
Bach, J.S.:Brandenberg Con 5, w. João Carlos Martins (pno), Liudmil Nenchev (vn), P. Djurov (cnd), Sofia Soloists CO *(rec Salle Bulgaria, Sofia, Bulgaria, 1996)* Concord Concerto ▲ CCD 42042 [DDD]
Benda, F.:Con in e Fl & Orch, w. I. Kozhouharov (cnd), Sofia Camerata Classica Divertimento ▲ DIV 41001 [DDD]

Oshavkova, Lydia (fl) (cont.)
Boccherini, L.:Con in D Fl [attrib], w. I. Kozhouharov (cnd), Sofia Camerata Classica Divertimento ▲ DIV 41001 [DDD]
Mercadante, S.:Cons (6) Fl (1819), w. I. Kozhouharov (cnd), Sofia Camerata Classica—in e Divertimento ▲ DIV 41001 [DDD]
Mozart, W.A.:Adagio & Rondo Glass Armonica, w. A. Atanasov (org), C. T. Kasmetski (ob), Ognian Stantchev (va), N. Bespalov (vc) Divertimento ▲ DIV 31020 [DDD]
Mozart, W.A.:Con Fl Hp, w. C. Antonelli (hp), I. Kozhouharov (cnd), Sofia New Chamber Ensemble Divertimento ▲ DIV 31020 [DDD]
Mozart, W.A.:Qnt Pno, K.452, w. V. Tchutchov (pno), C. T. Kasmetski (ob), P. Radev (cl), S. Kunchev (hn) Divertimento ▲ DIV 31020 [DDD]

Oshima, Ayako (cl)—see ORCHESTRAS & ENSEMBLES Mozzafiato

Oshima, M. (va)—see ORCHESTRAS & ENSEMBLES Cassatt String Quartet

Oshinakaev, Chanyafi (ob)
Vivaldi, A.:Cons Ob Vn, w. A. Stang (vn), L. Korkhin (cnd), Renaissance CO—in B♭, RV.548 Infinity Digital ▲ QK 57244 [DDD]
Vivaldi, A.:Cons for 2 Obs, w. P. Tosenko (ob), L. Korkhin (cnd), Renaissance CO—in a, RV.536 Infinity Digital ▲ QK 57244 [DDD]

Osinchuk, Juliana (pno)
Tchaikovsky, P.:Pno Music—Un Poco di Chopin; Valse a Cinq; Vars. in F; Valse de Salon; Polka peu dansante; Valse sentimentale; Natha-Valse; Romance in F; Concert Paraphrase [from Eugen Onegin]; Danse Russe; Romance in f; Humoresque; Nocturne *(rec Performing Arts Center, SUNY, Purchase, June 3–5, 1991)* Chaconne ▲ CHA 94001 [DDD]

Osinska, Eva (pno)
Chopin, F.:Intro & Polonaise, "Polonaise brilliante"—for piano solo *(rec Henry Wood Hall, London, Oct. 17–19, 1989)* Sony Classical ▲ SK 53112 [DDD]
Mozart, W.A.:Con 6 Pno, w. J. Maksymiuk (cnd), Polish CO *(rec Studio S II, Polish Radio, Warsaw, Oct 8–10, 1985)* Polskie Nagrania ▲ PNCD 316
Mozart, W.A.:Con 16 Pno, w. J. Maksymiuk (cnd), Polish CO *(rec Studio S II, Polish Radio, Warsaw, Oct 8–10, 1985)* Polskie Nagrania ▲ PNCD 316
Mozart, W.A.:Con 21 Pno, w. J. Maksymiuk (cnd), Polish CO *(rec Studio S II, Polish Radio, Warsaw, May 19–20, 1980)* Polskie Nagrania ▲ PNCD 316
Twentieth Century Piano Music From Poland, w. Andrzej Dutkiewicz (pno) Olympia ▲ OCD 316 [AAD]

Osipova, Maria (fl)
Ustvolskaya, G.:Composition 3, w. Natalia Danilina (fl), Inna Rodina (fl), Michail Tokarev (fl), Kirill Sokolov (bn), Dmitrii Krasnik (bn), Arsenii Makarov (bn), Konstantin Shevchuk (bn), Galina Sandovskaya (pno), O. Malov (cnd) *(rec St. Petersburg Radio House, Jan. 1994)* Megadisc ▲ 7867

Osorio, Jorge Federico (pno)
Beethoven, L. van:Con 4 Pno, w. E. Bátiz (cnd), Royal PO ASV Quicksilva ▲ ASQ 6129 [DDD]
Beethoven, L. van:Con 4 Pno, w. E. Bátiz (cnd), Royal PO Alfa ▲ 1003 [DDD]
Beethoven, L. van:Con 5 Pno, "Emperor", w. E. Bátiz (cnd), Royal PO ASV Quicksilva ▲ ASQ 6129 [ADD]
Beethoven, L. van:Con 5 Pno, "Emperor", w. E. Bátiz (cnd), Royal PO Alfa ▲ 1003 [DDD]
Beethoven, L. van:Son 14 Pno, "Moonlight Son" IMP Classics ▲ IMPPCD 1095 [DDD]
Beethoven, L. van:Son 21 Pno, "Waldstein" IMP Classics ▲ IMPPCD 1095 [DDD]
Beethoven, L. van:Son 23 Pno, "Appassionata" IMP Classics ▲ IMPPCD 1095 [DDD]
Beethoven, L. van:Son 26 Pno, "Les Adieux" IMP Classics ▲ IMPPCD 1095 [DDD]
Brahms, J.:Ballades, Op. 10 ASV ("Quicksilva" series) ▲ ASQ 6161 [DDD]
Brahms, J.:Vars & Fugue on a Theme by Handel ASV ("Quicksilva" series) ▲ ASQ 6161 [DDD]
Brahms, J.:Vars on a Theme of Robert Schumann, Op. 9 ASV ("Quicksilva" series) ▲ ASQ 6161 [DDD]
Falla, M. de:Noches en los jardines de España, w. H. de la Fuente (cnd), Xalapa SO IMP Classics ▲ IMPPCD 1074 [DDD]
Fauré, G.:Andante Vn, w. Mayumi Fujikawa (vn) ASV ("Quicksilva" series) ▲ ASQ 6170
Fauré, G.:Berceuse Vn, w. Mayumi Fujikawa (vn) ASV ("Quicksilva" series) ▲ ASQ 6170
Franck, C.:Symphonic Vars, w. E. Bátiz (cnd), Royal PO ASV Quicksilva ▲ ASQ 6092 [DDD]
Mozart, W.A.:Con 18 Pno, w. E. Bátiz (cnd), Royal PO ASV Quicksilva ▲ QS 6015 [DDD]
Mozart, W.A.:Con 19 Pno, w. E. Bátiz (cnd), Royal PO ASV Quicksilva ▲ QS 6015 [DDD]
Mozart, W.A.:Con 24 Pno, w. E. Bátiz (cnd), Royal PO ASV Quicksilva ▲ QS 6015 [DDD]
Ponce, M.:Balada mexicana Pno, w. E. Bátiz (cnd), Mexican State SO ASV ▲ ASV 926 [DDD]
Ponce, M.:Con Pno, w. E. Bátiz (cnd), Mexican State SO ASV ▲ ASV 926 [DDD]
Ponce, M.:Con Pno, w. E. Bátiz (cnd), Mexican State SO ASV ▲ ASV 952
Ponce, M.:Pno Music—Balada Mexicana; Arrulladora; Tema Mexicano Variado; Romanza de Amor; Prelude & Fugue on a Theme of Handel; & Mazurkas; Scherzino Mexicano; Gavota; Intermezzo No. 1; Rapsodia Cubana No. 1 ASV ▲ ASV 874 [DDD]
Rachmaninoff, S.:Rhapsody on a Theme of Paganini *(orch unknown)* IMP Classics ▲ IMPPCD 1074 [DDD]
Ravel, M.:Con Pno (left hand), w. E. Bátiz (cnd), Royal PO ASV Quicksilva ▲ ASQ 6092 [DDD]
Saint-Saëns, C.:Wedding Cake, w. E. Bátiz (cnd), Royal PO ASV ▲ ASV 665 [DDD]
Saint-Saëns, C.:Wedding Cake, w. E. Bátiz (cnd), Royal PO ASV Quicksilva ▲ ASQ 6092 [DDD]
Saint-Saëns, C.:Wedding Cake, w. E. Bátiz (cnd), Royal PO ASV Quicksilva ▲ QS 6026 [DDD]
Schumann, R.:Con Pno, w. E. Bátiz (cnd), Royal PO ASV Quicksilva ▲ ASQ 6092 [DDD]
Tchaikovsky, P.:Con 1 Pno, w. H. de la Fuente (cnd), Xalapa SO IMP Classics ▲ IMPPCD 1074 [DDD]

Osostowicz, Krysia (vn)
Brahms, J.:Sons Vn (comp), w. S. Tomes (pno) Hyperion ▲ CDA 66465
Fauré, G.:Son 1 Vn, w. S. Tomes (pno) Hyperion ▲ CDA 66277
Fauré, G.:Son 2 Vn, w. S. Tomes (pno) Hyperion ▲ CDA 66277
Martinů, B.:Sonatina for 2 Vns, w. E. Kovacic (vn), S. Tomes (pno) Hyperion ▲ CDA 66473 [DDD]
Milhaud, D.:Duo for 2 Vns, w. E. Kovacic (vn) Hyperion ▲ CDA 66473 [DDD]
Milhaud, D.:Son for 2 Vns, w. E. Kovacic (vn), S. Tomes (pno) Hyperion ▲ CDA 66473 [DDD]
Prokofiev, S.:Son for 2 Vns, w. E. Kovacic (vn) Hyperion ▲ CDA 66473 [DDD]

Østergaard, Eva (fl)
Holmboe, V.:Chamber Con 2, w. Mikkel Futtrup (vn), H. Koivula (cnd), Danish Radio Concert Orch *(rec Danish Radio Studio 2, June & Sept 1996)* Marco Polo/Dacapo ▲ 8.224038 [DDD]

Ostertag, Martin (vc)
Auber, D.-F.:Rondo Vc, w. R. Paternostro (cnd), Berlin RSO Koch Schwann ▲ 311039 [DDD] ■ 211039 (D)
Bottesini, G.:Duo Concertant on Themes from Bellini's *I Puritani*, w. W. Güttler (db), M. Bamert (cnd), Berlin RSO Koch Schwann ▲ CD 311042 [DDD]
Glière, R.:Duets Vn, Op. 39, w. Ernő Sebestyen (vn) Koch Schwann ▲ SCH 317272
Kodály, Z.:Duo Vn & Vc, w. Ernő Sebestyen (vn) Koch Schwann ▲ SCH 317272
Massenet, J.:Fant Vc, w. R. Paternostro (cnd), Berlin RSO Koch Schwann ▲ 311039 [DDD] ■ 211039 (D)
Popper, D.:Con Vc, Op. 24, w. R. Paternostro (cnd), Berlin RSO Koch Schwann ▲ 311039 [DDD] ■ 211039 (D)
Ravel, M.:Son Vn Vc, w. Ernő Sebestyen (vn) Koch Schwann ▲ SCH 317272
Rheinberger, J.:Suite Org, w. A. Juffinger (org), E. Sebestyén (vn), H. Haenchen (cnd), Berlin RSO Capriccio ▲ CD 10 337 [DDD]
Spohr, L.:Con Str Qt, w. E. Sebestyen (vn), H. Ganz (vn), H. Beyerle (va), G. Albrecht (cnd), Berlin RSO Koch Schwann ▲ CD 311088 [DDD] ■ MC 211088 (D)
Spohr, L.:Var, Op. 6, w. E. Sebestyen (vn), H. Ganz (vn), H. Beyerle (va) Koch Schwann ▲ CD 311088 [DDD] ■ MC 211088 (D)

Ostling, Elizabeth (fl)
Rorem, N.:Studies for 11, w. K. Lord (ob), G. Raden (cl), J. Sutte (tpt), S. Copes (vn), C.-J. Chang (va), J. Lastrapes (vc), K. Englichova (hp), R. Uchida (pno), A. LaFargue (perc), R. Laveille (perc), R. Milanov (cnd) New World ▲ 80445-2

Östman, Arnold (hpd)
Bach, C.P.E.:Trio Son in F, w. C. Pehrsson (bass rcr), P. Novovic (va), A. Petersén (bass vl) [period instrs] BIS ▲ CD 220 [DDD]

▲ = CD ♦ = Enhanced CD Δ = MD ■ = Cassette Tape □ = DCC

Östman, Arnold (hpd) (cont.)
Quantz, J.J.:Trio Sons, w. C. Pehrsson (rcr), P. Novovic (vn), A. Petersén (b vl) [period instrs]—in C BIS ▲ CD 220 [DDD]
Telemann, G.P.:Sons Rcr, w. C. Pehrsson (rcr), A. Petersén (bass vl) [played on period instruments] BIS ▲ CD 220 [DDD]
Vivaldi, A.:Trio Sons (misc), w. C. Pehrsson (rcr), P. Novovic (vn), A. Petersén (b vl) [period instrs]—in g BIS ▲ CD 220 [DDD]
Östman, Arnold (pno)
Pettersson, G.A.:Barefoot Songs, w. M. Rödin (mez) Swedish Society ▲ SCD 1033
Pettersson, G.A.:Songs, w. E. Saedén (bar) Swedish Society ▲ SCD 1033
Ostoich, M. (ob)
Hayden, P.:Hambidge Quavers, w. W. Ludwig (bn) Opus One ▲ CD 154
Ostrack, J. (cl)
Mozart, W.A.:Con Cl, w. A. Lizzio (cnd), Mozart Festival Orch Vivace 3–▲ E 315 [DDD]
Ostrowski, Matthew (syn)
Exquisite Corpses from P.S. 122, w. Watson, David (shears/stick vn/gtr/tpt), Judy Dunaway (gtr/balloons), Anthony Coleman (sampler), Raissa St. Pierre (drums), Guy Yarden (vn/pno), Leslie Ross (bn), Linda Austin (gtr), Bruce Kaplan (gtr), Doug Henderson (peckhorn/bass/toy pno), Sue Ann Harkey (gtr), Cinnie Cole (sampler), Mike Sap ¿What Next? ▲ WN 0002 [ADD]
Ostryniec, James (ob)
Crawford, R.:Diaphonic Suites (4)—1 Suite CRI ▲ CD 658 [ADD]
Crawford, R.:Songs (3), w. P. Berlin (mez), D.C. Armstrong (perc), P. Hoffman (pno) CRI ▲ CD 658 [ADD]
Luening, O.:Legend, w. D. Rossi (va), Alard String Quartet CRI ■ ACS 6011
Rochberg, G.:La Bocca della verità, w. C. Wuorinen (pno) CRI ■ ACS 6013
O'Sullivan, Loretta (vc)—see also ORCHESTRAS & ENSEMBLES Haydn Baryton Trio, Four Nations Ensemble
Bach, J.S.:Arias, w. David Gordon (ten), Emily Newbold (fl), Charlotte Mattax (hpd), G. Funfgeld (cnd), Bethlehem Bach Festival Orch—Ermunter dich [from Cant.180]; Der Ewigkeit [from Cant. 198]; Ach, schlage doch [from Cant. 95]; Benedictus [from Mass in b, BWV 232]; Woferne du [from Cant. 41]; O Seelenparadies [from Cant. 172]; Frohe Hirten [from Christmas Oratorio, BWV 248] *(rec St. Michael's Church, New York City, June 1994)* Newport Classic ▲ NPD 85582 [DDD]
Oswald, John (kbd/a sax/elec)
Oswald, J.:Parade, w. Paul Plimley (kbd), Alex Varty (gtr), Cora Risdall (baby) ReR ▲ CMCD [DDD]
Oswald, Tamara B. (hp)
Beside Thy Cradle, w. [cnd:Ralph B. Woodward], Salt Lake Children's Choir, Janet Peterson (hp), Kaily Parkinson (vn), Victoria Ferris (vn), Hadley Ferris (va), Ellen Bridger (vc) *(rec Maurice Abravanel Hall, Salt Lake City)* Cherbourne ▲ CH 121
Otaki, Michiko (pno)
Kabalevsky, D.:Preludes & Fugues Pno ACA Digital Recording ▲ CM 20004
Kabalevsky, D.:Preludes Pno, Op. 38 ACA Digital Recording ▲ CM 20004
Poulenc, F.:Sxt Pno, w. Warsaw Wind Quintet Koch Schwann ▲ SCH 313942 [DDD]
Tansman, A.:Danse de la sorcière, w. Warsaw Wind Quintet Koch Schwann ▲ SCH 313942 [DDD]
Thuille, L.:Sxt Pno, w. Warsaw Wind Quintet Koch Schwann ▲ SCH 313942 [DDD]
Otani, M. (vn)—see ORCHESTRAS & ENSEMBLES Cassatt String Quartet
Otis, Cynthia (hp)
Flowering of Vocal Music in America, 1767-1823, w. Susan Belling (sop), Cynthia Clarey (sop), Barbara Wallace (sop), Debra Vanderlinde (sop), D'Anna Fortunato (mez), Evelyn Petros (mez), Charles Bressler (ten), Richard Anderson (bar), James Tyeska (bar), Joseph McKee (bass), Cynthia Otis (hp), Leonard Rav New World ▲ 80467-2
Ott, Olaf (trbn)—see ORCHESTRAS & ENSEMBLES Triton Trombone Quartet
Otte, Allen (perc)
Handel, D.:Barge Music, w. Bradley Garner (a fl), Rodney Studky (gtr), Jon Pascolini (db), Russell Burge (perc) Vienna Modern Masters ▲ VMM 2019 [DDD]
Handel, D.:The Poems of Our Climate, w. Sheryl Woods (sop), Pamela Watson (fl), Brian Delay (gtr), Val Griffen (vc), Anton Nel (pno), Jack Brennan (perc), James Culley (perc), G. Samuel (cnd) Vienna Modern Masters ▲ VMM 2019 [DDD]
Otte, Hans (pno)
Otte, H.:Das Buch der Klänge Kuckuck ▲ 11069-2 2-■ 12069-4
Ottensamer, Ernst (cl)
Mozart, W.A.:Con Cl, w. J. Wildner (cnd), Vienna Mozart Academy *(rec Oct. 1989)* Naxos ▲ 8.550345 [DDD]
Schmidt, F.:Qnt Cl, w. R. Keuschnig (pno), J. Hell (vn), P. Wächter (vn), P. Pecha (va), R. Wallfisch (vc) *(rec Jan. 7, 1991)* Orfeo ▲ 287921 [DDD]
Spohr, L.:Con 1 Cl, w. J. Wildner (cnd), Slovak State PO Košice *(rec House of Arts, Košice, Sept., 16–19, 1991 & Feb.)* Naxos ▲ 8.550688 [DDD]
Spohr, L.:Con 2 Cl, w. J. Wildner (cnd), Slovak RSO Bratislava *(rec Concert Hall of the Slovak Radio, Bratislava, Jan. 31– Feb. 4, 1994)* Naxos ▲ 8.550689 [DDD]
Spohr, L.:Con 3 Cl, w. J. Wildner (cnd), Slovak State PO Košice *(rec House of Arts, Košice, Sept., 16–19, 1991 & Feb.)* Naxos ▲ 8.550688 [DDD]
Spohr, L.:Con 4 Cl, w. J. Wildner (cnd), Slovak RSO Bratislava *(rec Concert Hall of the Slovak Radio, Bratislava, Jan. 31– Feb. 4, 1994)* Naxos ▲ 8.550689 [DDD]
Spohr, L.:Fant & Vars on a Theme of Danzi, w. J. Wildner (cnd), Slovak RSO Bratislava *(rec Concert Hall of the Slovak Radio, Bratislava, Feb. 20, 1994)* Naxos ▲ 8.550689 [DDD]
Spohr, L.:Potpourri, w. J. Wildner (cnd), Slovak RSO Bratislava *(rec House of Arts, Košice, Sept., 16–19, 1991 & Feb.)* Naxos ▲ 8.550688 [DDD]
Weber, C.M. von:Con 1 Cl, w. J. Wildner (cnd), Czech–Slovak State PO *(rec 2/90)* Naxos ▲ 8.550378 [DDD]
Weber, C.M. von:Con 2 Cl, w. J. Wildner (cnd), Czech–Slovak State PO *(rec 2/90)* Naxos ▲ 8.550378 [DDD]
Ottesen, Kari (vc)
Roman, J.H.:Sacred Music, w. G. Ryhming (sop), M. Spaeter (thb), E. Nordenfelt (hpd/org)—Psalms 4, 5, 81, 103, 124 & 125; Mon coeur tressaille de joie; Oiseaux, animaux sauvages; Mes prères, hâtez-vous; Dieu, Dieu de to Gallo ▲ CD 764 [DDD]
Roman, J.H.:Sons Fl, w. P. Evison (fl), C. Huntgeburth (fl), O. Larsson (vc), E. Nordenfeldt (hpd)—Nos. 1, 2, 5, 6, 7 & 9 Proprius ▲ PRCD 9020
Roman, J.H.:Songs, w. S. Rydén (sop), N. E. Sparf (vn), S. Überg (thb/lt/gtr), B. Gäfvert (org/hpd)—Thet är en kostelig ting; 4 Songs from *Vårbetraktelser* [text by Jacob Freese]:Mit hierta rörs af frögd/I foglar, vilde djur/Min andagt/Gud, alla härars Gud; Ihr Augen worzu nutzt ihr mir [w. E. Nordenfelt (harpsichord)]; Sein eigen Hertze fressen [w. Nordenfelt]; Kom tysta enslighet; La Ragion gli affetti ascolta; The Happy Man; For the Few Hours; Herren lofver af Himlen hög [Ps. 148]; 5 Songs by Olof von Dalin:Åta litet, dricka vatten/At ju mången har idag/Födas, gråta dij och lindas/År det hela tidsfördrifvet/Den är lycklig född til Verlden; Herre når jag tig hafver; Jag förtröstar på Herran; Gud, jag will sjunga om din makt *(rec May 9–11 & July 10, 1994)* Swedish Society ▲ SCD 1066
Vivaldi, A.:Trio Sons Vn Lt, w. N.-E. Sparf (vn), J. Lindberg (lt), M. Wieslander (hpd) BIS ▲ CD 290 [DDD]
Ottesen, Mark (va)
Rosner, A.:Duet Va, w. Diedre Buckley (va) Albany ▲ TROY 210 [DDD]
Otto, Hans (org)
Bach, J.S.:Org Music (misc), w. J. E. Hansen (org), H. Rilling (org), K. Vad (org)—Toccata & Fugue in d, BWV 565; Fugue in g, BWV 578; Passacaglia & Fugue in c, BWV 582; Fantasia & Fugue in g, BWV 542; Chorales, BWV 147, 583, 608, 622, 645 Denon ▲ CO 8009 [DDD]
Bach, J.S.:Org Music (misc)—Prelude & Fugue in d, BWV 565; Schubler Chorales, BWV 645/50; Prelude & Fugue in g, BWV 535; Trio in c, BWV 585; Fantasia in C, BWV 570; Trio in G, BWV 586; Prelude & Fugue in C, BWV 545; Fugue in g, BWV 578 Denon ▲ 7004 [DDD]

Otto, Hans (org) (cont.)
Schütz, H.:Psalmen Davids, w. E.–L. Hammer (vl), W. Jaroslawski (vl), R. Mauersberger (cnd), Dresden Church Choir—Singet dem Herrn ein neues Lied, denn er tut Wunder, Psalm 98; Wohl dem, der nicht wandelt im Rat der Gottlosen, Psalm 1; Warum toben die Heiden, Psalm 2; Jauchzet dem Herrn, alle Welt, dienet dem Herren mit Freuden, Psalm 100; Der Herr ist mein Hirt, mir wird nichts mangeln, Psalm 23; Wie lieblich sind deine Wohnungen, Herr Zebaoth, Psalm 84; Aus der Tiefe ruf' ich, Herr, zu dir, Psalm 130; Ach Herr, Straf mich nicht in deinem Zorn, Psalm 6; Ich hebe meine Augen auf zu den Bergen, Psalm 121; Nun lob, mein Seel, den Herren, SWV 41; Ich danke dem Herrn von ganzem Herzen, Psalm 111 [w. Dresden State Orch. members] *(rec Oct. 1965)* Berlin Classics ▲ BER 2070–2 [ADD]
Ottosen, Kirsten (pno)
Stolarczyk, W.:Earth Air Fire Water, w. Amalie Malling (pno), John Damgaard (pno), Anne Øland (pno), Teddy Teirup (pno), Friedrich Gürtler (pno), Rosalind Bevan (pno), Poul Rosenbaum (pno), Rodolfo Llambias (pno), Bella Horn–Ribera (pno), Anders Riber (pno), Elisabeth Sigurdsson (pno), Thomas Tronheim (pno), Elsebeth Broderson (pno), Erik Kaltoft (pno), Jørgen Hald Nielsen (pno), Aino Gilemann (pno), Birgit Kjær (pno), Jørgen Thomsen (pno), Gunhild Donslund (pno), Henrik Bo Hansen (pno), Lone Karlsson (pno), Erik Fessel (pno), Lasse Nilsson (pno), Janos Ferenczi (pno), Erik Bach (pno), Axel Momme (pno), Arne de Cros Dich (pno), Sven Micha Slot (pno), Hanne Bramsen Buhl (pno), Lili Olesen (pno), Susannah Carlsson (pno), Ulla Erml (pno), Vagn Sørensen (pno), Leif Greibe (pno), Bodil Krogh (pno), Kirsten Ottosen (pno), Inger Bergenholz (pno), Karsten Gylendorf (pno), Bjørr Elkjær (pno), Jacob Bjørn Jensen (pno), Jørgen Kaad (pno), Anne Marie Hjelm (pno), Carl Ulrik Munk Andersen (pno), Poul Lumbye (pno), Oluf Hildebrandt Nielsen (pno), Joachim Olsson (pno), Peter Pade Ramsøe Jacobsen (pno), Astrid Pollmann (pno), Jette Borsch (pno), Kirsten Karlshøj (pno), Maria Teresa Assing (pno), Allan Dahl Hansen (pno), Johan Hugossen (pno), Tine Fenger Pederson (pno), Arne Jørgen Fæø (pno), Anja Høgsted (pno), Anne Sophie Parbo (pno), Inga Lindmark (pno), Teresa Drabik Stathakis (pno), Anne Ruth Ferenczi (pno), Irene Hasager (pno), Yuka Ichikawa (pno), Birgitte Baur (pno), Malene Thastum (pno), Jens E. Rasmussen (pno), Birgitte Zielke (pno), Claus Zielke (pno), Stefan Kasch (pno), Bin Qiao (pno), Inger Johanne Teirup (pno), Lindy Rosborg (pno), Liisa Heininen (pno), David Højer (pno), Ellen Refstrup (pno), Thomas K. Søørensen (pno), Erik Kure (pno), Michael Rauff (pno), Jan beck Eriksson (pno), Tanja Zapolski (pno), Vibeke Skagbo (pno), Pål Eide Lindtner (pno), Ha–Young Sul (pno), Benedicte Palko (pno), Inke Kesseler (pno), Anne Marie Meineche (pno), Sverre Larsen (pno), Kasper Peter Bach (pno), Elisabetta Eliseo (pno), Olga Magieres (pno), Carl Erik Kühl (pno), Thorkild Borup Nielsen (pno), Valeria Zanini (pno), Lars Stenhoft (perc), Dennis Boel (perc), Winnie Dahlgren (perc), Susanne Vind (perc), Claus Byrith (elec), Anne Marie Storm (elec), J. Ribera (cnd) *(rec live, Koldinghaus Castle, Denmark, May 2, 1996)* Danica ▲ DCD 1996
Oudenaarden, H. (vn)
Saint-Saëns, C.:Carnival of the Animals, w. D. Wayenberg (vn), J. Hagen (fl), H. de Fraaf (cl), H. Krul (db), W. Vos (xyl), M. Dekkers (acc), Daniel String Quartet *(rec Rotterdam, May 28, 1985)* Erasmus ▲ WHV 001 [DDD]
Oudenaarden, Hans (pno)
Gershwin, G.:Rhap in Blue, w. Louis van Dijk (pno) or Marinus Flipse (pno) or Hans Oudenaarden (pno) or Daniel Wayenberg (pno)—version for 2 pnos Erasmus ▲ WVH 117
Poulenc, F.:Con for 2 Pnos, w. D. Wayenberg (pno), G. Oskamp (cnd), Limburg SO *(rec Nov. 1992 & May 1993)* Erasmus ▲ WVH 099 [DDD]
Saint-Saëns, C.:Carnival of the Animals, w. D. Wayenberg (pno), G. Oskamp (cnd), Limburg SO *(rec Nov. 1992 & May 1993)* Erasmus ▲ WVH 099 [DDD]
Tchaikovsky, P.:Pno Music—Romeo & Juliet; Waltz [from *Serenade for Strings*]; Andante Cantabile [from *Sym. No. 5*]; Marche slave; Andante Cantabile [from *Qt. No. 1 for Strings, Op. 11*]; Waltz [from *Sleeping Beauty*]; sels. from Nutcracker Suite; [trans. Tchaikovsky] Erasmus ▲ WVH 077 [DDD]
Ouellet, Claire (pno)—see ORCHESTRAS & ENSEMBLES Ouellet/Murray Duo
Ouellet, F. (hn)—see ORCHESTRAS & ENSEMBLES Pentaèdre Ensemble
Oun, Jaan (fl/dir)—see ORCHESTRAS & ENSEMBLES Camerata Tallinn
Oundjian, P. (pno)
Champagne, C.:Danse villageoise, w. W. Tritt (pno) CBC ("Musica Viva" series) ▲ MVCD 1060 [DDD]
Oundjian, Peter (vn)—see also ORCHESTRAS & ENSEMBLES Tokyo String Quartet
Debussy, C.:Son Vn, w. W. Tritt (pno) CBC ("Musica Viva" series) ▲ MVCD 1060 [DDD]
Dela, M.:Sonatine, w. W. Tritt (pno) CBC ("Musica Viva" series) ▲ MVCD 1060 [DDD]
Messiaen, O.:Thème et vars, w. W. Tritt (pno) CBC ("Musica Viva" series) ▲ MVCD 1060 [DDD]
Ravel, M.:Son Vn Pno, w. W. Tritt (pno) CBC ("Musica Viva" series) ▲ MVCD 1060 [DDD]
Ouspenskaya, Anna (pno)
Shchedrin, R.:Polyphonic Book Altarus ▲ CD 9006
Shchedrin, R.:Polyphonic Pieces Altarus ▲ CD 9006
Ousset, Cécile (pno)
Brahms, J.:Con 2 Pno, w. K. Masur (cnd), Leipzig Gewandhaus Orch Berlin Classics ▲ BER 2161 [ADD]
Brahms, J.:Con 2 Pno, w. K. Masur (cnd), Leipzig Opera Orch Accord ▲ ACD 201152 [AAD]
Brahms, J.:Vars on a Theme by Paganini Accord ▲ ACD 201152 [AAD]
Debussy, C.:Pno Music (misc)—Pour le piano; Poisson d'or [from Image pour Piano]; L'isle joyeuse; 4 Preludes; 2 Études; Jardins sous la pluie [from Estampes] Berlin Classics ("Eterna" series) ▲ BER 2171 [ADD]
Rachmaninoff, S.:Con 2 Pno, w. S. Rattle (cnd), City of Birmingham SO EMI ▲ CDC 47223
Rachmaninoff, S.:Rhapsody on a Theme of Paganini, w. S. Rattle (cnd), City of Birmingham SO EMI ▲ CDC 47223
Ravel, M.:Con Pno (left hand), w. S. Rattle (cnd), City of Birmingham SO EMI Classics ▲ CDC 54158
Ravel, M.:Con in G Pno, w. S. Rattle (cnd), City of Birmingham SO EMI Classics ▲ CDC 54158
Outram, Martin (va)—see ORCHESTRAS & ENSEMBLES Maggini String Quartet
Ouziel, Dalia (pno)
Beethoven, L. van:Vars on a march by Dressler, WoO 63 *(rec EMS Studios, Brussels, Nov. 1994)* Discover International ▲ DI 920261 [DDD]
Beethoven, L. van:Vars on a Swiss Song, WoO 64 *(rec EMS Studios, Brussels, Nov. 1994)* Discover International ▲ DI 920261 [DDD]
Beethoven, L. van:Vars on Righini's Arietta "Venni amore", WoO 65 *(rec EMS Studios, Brussels, Nov. 1994)* Discover International ▲ DI 920261 [DDD]
Beethoven, L. van:Vars on Ditterdorff's arietta "Es war einmal ein alter Mann", WoO 66 *(rec EMS Studios, Brussels, Nov. 1994)* Discover International ▲ DI 920261 [DDD]
Beethoven, L. van:Vars on Haibel's "Menuet à la Viganò", WoO 68 *(rec EMS Studios, Brussels, Nov. 1994)* Discover International ▲ DI 920261 [DDD]
Kreisler, F.:Vn Pieces, w. J. Rubenstein (vn)—8 original works for violin & piano *(La gitana; Liebesfreud; Liebesleid; Caprice viennois; Schön Rosmarin' Tambourin chinois; Polichinelle; Syncopation)*; 6 works composed in the styles of Boccherini *(Allegretto)*, Couperin *(Chanson Louis XIII; la Précieuse)*, Martini *(Andantino; Tempo di Minuetto)* & Paganini *(Praeludium et allegro)*; 7 arrs. of works by Albéniz *(Tango)*, Dvořák *(Slavonic Dances No. 1 in g & No. 2 in e)*, Falla *(Danse espagnole from La vida breve)*, Granados *(Danse espagnole)* & Tartini *(Fugue in A; Variations on a Theme by Corelli)* Pavane ▲ ADW 7222 [DDD]
Mozart, W.A.:Con 7 Pnos, w. O. Ouziel (pno), G. Octors (pno), G. Octors (cnd), Walloon & French Community of Belgium CO [arr. for 2 Pianos by Mozart] *(rec Jan. 1991)* Pavane ▲ ADW 7257 [DDD]
Mozart, W.A.:Con 10 Pnos, w. O. Ouziel (pno), G. Octors (cnd), Walloon & French Community of Belgium CO *(rec Jan. 1991)* Pavane ▲ ADW 7257 [DDD]
Ouziel, Orit (pno)
Mozart, W.A.:Con 7 Pnos, w. D. Ouziel (pno), G. Octors (pno), G. Octors (cnd), Walloon & French Community of Belgium CO [arr. for 2 Pianos by Mozart] *(rec Jan. 1991)* Pavane ▲ ADW 7257 [DDD]
Mozart, W.A.:Con 10 Pnos, w. D. Ouziel (pno), G. Octors (cnd), Walloon & French Community of Belgium CO *(rec Jan. 1991)* Pavane ▲ ADW 7257 [DDD]
Ouzounian, Michael (va)
Strauss, R.:Don Quixote, w. Jerry Grossman (vc), Raymond Gniewek (vn), J. Levine (cnd), Metropolitan Opera Orch *(rec Manhattan Ctr, NY, May 1995)* Deutsche Grammophon ▲ 447762–2 [DDD]
Ouzounoff, Alexandre (bn)
Poulenc, F.:Son Cl Bn, w. Lucien Aubert (cl) Accord ▲ ACD 205192 [DDD]

INSTRUMENT.

INSTRUMENTALISTS 761

Ouzounoff, Alexandre (bn) (cont.)
Poulenc, F.:Trio Ob, w. Claude Bassoon (ob), Kun Woo Paik (pno) Accord ▲ ACD 205192 [DDD]
Ovcharek, Vladimir (vn)—see ORCHESTRAS & ENSEMBLES Taneyev String Quartet
Ovchinikov, Vladimir (pno)
Rachmaninoff, S.:Études-tableaux, Opp. 33 & 39 EMI Classics ▲ CDC 54077 [DDD]
Overduin, Jan (org)
Bach, J.S.:Suite 3 Orch, w. E. Schultz (tpt) ebs ▲ ebs 6041 [DDD]
Bellini, V.:Con Tpt & Org, w. E. Schultz (tpt) ebs ▲ ebs 6041 [DDD]
Christmas Music for Trumpet & Organ, w. Schultz, Erik (tpt) ebs ▲ ebs 6004 [DDD]
Handel, G.F.:Suite Tpt & Org, w. Erik Schultz (tpt) ebs ▲ ebs 6041 [DDD]
Music for Trumpet & Organ, Vol. 3, w. Schultz, Erik (tpt) ebs ▲ ebs 6003 [DDD]
Telemann, G.P.:Suite in g Tpt, w. E. Schultz (tpt) ebs ▲ ebs 6041 [DDD]
Viviani, B.:Son 1 Tpt, w. E. Schultz (tpt) ebs ▲ ebs 6041 [DDD]
Viviani, B.:Son 2 Tpt, w. E. Schultz (tpt) ebs ▲ ebs 6041 [DDD]
Ovigny, André (vn)
Hérold, F.:Le Pré aux clercs, w. Benedetti (cnd), Radio-Lyrique Orch, *(unknown radio chorus)* Musidisc 2-▲ MUS 202012 [AAD]
Owen, Charles (pno)
Goldmark, K.:Son Vc, w. Christoph Stradner (vc)—Andante *(rec Chapel of Palais Liechtenstein, Vienna, July 1995)* Dorian ▲ DOR 80145 [DDD]
Strauss, R.:Son Vc, w. Christoph Stradner (vc) *(rec Chapel of Palais Liechtenstein, Vienna, July 1995)* Dorian ▲ DOR 80145 [DDD]
Suk, J.:Ballade & Serenade, w. Christoph Stradner (vc) *(rec Chapel of Palais Liechtenstein, Vienna, July 1995)* Dorian ▲ DOR 80145 [DDD]
Webern, A.:Little Pieces Vc, w. Christoph Stradner (vc) *(rec Chapel of Palais Liechtenstein, Vienna, July 1995)* Dorian ▲ DOR 80145 [DDD]
Webern, A.:Pieces Vc, w. Christoph Stradner (vc) *(rec Chapel of Palais Liechtenstein, Vienna, July 1995)* Dorian ▲ DOR 80145 [DDD]
Webern, A.:Son Vc, w. Christoph Stradner (vc) *(rec Chapel of Palais Liechtenstein, Vienna, July 1995)* Dorian ▲ DOR 80145 [DDD]
Owen, K. (hn)—see ORCHESTRAS & ENSEMBLES Atlantic Brass Quintet
Owen, Sally (spinet/vl)—see ORCHESTRAS & ENSEMBLES Extempore String Ensemble
Oxenfort, Christiane (fl)—see ORCHESTRAS & ENSEMBLES VIF Flute Quartet
Oxenvad, Aage (cl)
Nielsen, C.:Qnt Ww, w. H.G. Jespersen (fl), S.C. Felumb (ob), H. Sorensen (hn), K. Larsson (bn) *(rec Jan. 24 & 25, 1936)* Clarinet Classics ▲ CC 0002
Nielsen, C.:Serenata in vano, w. K. Larsson (bn), H. Sorensen (hn), L. Jensen (vc), L. Hegner (db) *(rec Feb. 2, 1937)* Clarinet Classics ▲ CC 0002
Oyens, Tera de Marez (pno)
Marez Oyens, T. de:Charon's Gift Donemus ▲ CV 8702 [AAD]
Oyens, T. de M.:Hymns, w. Madelon Michael (sop) Capstone ▲ CPS 8632
Ozeki, Hiroaki (vn)
Haydn, J.:Trios Cl, Vn & Vc, H.IV/Es1, Es2 & B1, w. Eduard Brunner (cl), Mineo Hayashi (vc) *(rec Maebashi Shimin Bunka Kaikan, Aug 31-Sept 2, 1984)* Camerata ▲ 25CM 356 [DDD]
Özer, Ihsan Mehmet (psaltery)—see ORCHESTRAS & ENSEMBLES Ensemble Saraband
Ozim, Igor (vn)
Baur, J.:Moments musicaux, w. Günter Ludwig (pno) *(rec Sept. 30, 1977)* Koch Schwann ▲ SCH 311982 [ADD/DDD]
Boccherini, L.:Duets (6) for 2 Vns, w. P. Novšak (vn) ebs ▲ ebs 6009 [DDD]
Schubert, Franz:Fant Vn, D.934, w. I. von Alpenheim (pno) BIS 4-▲ CD 521/24 [DDD]
Schubert, Franz:Rondo Vn, D.895, w. I. von Alpenheim (pno) BIS 4-▲ CD 521/24 [DDD]
Schubert, Franz:Son Vn, D.574, w. I. von Alpenheim (pno) BIS 4-▲ CD 521/24 [DDD]
Schubert, Franz:Sonatinas Vn, w. I. von Alpenheim (pno) BIS 4-▲ CD 521/24 [DDD]
Ozolins, Arthur (pno)
Dohnányi, E. von:Vars on a Nursery Song, w. M. Bernardi (cnd), Toronto SO CBC ("SM 5000" series) ▲ SMCD 5052 [DDD]
Litolff, H.C.:Con Symphonique 3, w. M. Bernardi (cnd), Toronto SO—Scherzo CBC ("SM 5000" series) ▲ SMCD 5052 [DDD]
Rachmaninoff, S.:Con 1 Pno, w. M. Bernardi (cnd), Toronto SO CBC ("SM 5000" series) ▲ SMCD 5052 [DDD]
Rachmaninoff, S.:Con 2 Pno, w. M. Bernardi (cnd), Toronto SO CBC ("SM 5000" series) ▲ SMCD 5108 [DDD] ■ SMC 5108 (D)
Strauss, R.:Burleske, w. M. Bernardi (cnd), Toronto SO CBC ("SM 5000" series) ▲ SMCD 5128 [DDD]
Willan, H.:Con Pno, w. M. Bernardi (cnd), Toronto SO CBC ("SM 5000" series) ▲ SMCD 5108 [DDD] ■ SMC 5108 (D)
Paakkunainen, Seppo Baron (fl/t sax/br sax)
Braxton, A.:Composition 144, w. Anthony Braxton (fl/s sax/a sax), Pentti Lahti (fl/s sax/a sax), Pepa Päivinen (fl/t sax/sop sax/b cl), Mircea Stan (trbn), Mikko-Ville Luolajan-Mikkola (vn), Teppo Hauta-aho (db/vc), Jukka Wasama (dr) *(rec Järvenpää House, Järvenpää, Finland, Nov 7, 1988)* Leo ▲ LR 233
Braxton, A.:Composition 145, w. Anthony Braxton (fl/s sax/a sax), Pentti Lahti (fl/s sax/a sax), Pepa Päivinen (fl/t sax/sop sax/b cl), Mircea Stan (trbn), Mikko-Ville Luolajan-Mikkola (vn), Teppo Hauta-aho (db/vc), Jukka Wasama (dr) *(rec Järvenpää House, Järvenpää, Finland, Nov 7, 1988)* Leo ▲ LR 233
Paccagnella, Luca (vc)
Dashow, J.:Disclosures Neuma ▲ 450-75 [DDD]
Dashow, J.:Mappings, w. James Dashow (elec) *(rec Studio Lead, Rome, May 1991)* Pro Viva ▲ ISPV 177 CD [DDD]
Paccagnella, Marina (hp)
Burkhard, W.:Serenade Fl, Op. 77, w. S. Gärtner (fl), W. Meienberg (cl), J. Stavicek (bn), M. Gugel (hn), H. Schneeberger (vn), C. Schiller (va), B. Wyganth (db) *(rec between 1985 & 1989)* Jecklin-Disco ▲ JD 647-2 [ADD]
Pacey, Prunella (va)
Bruckner, A.:Intermezzo Str Qnt, w. Raphael String Quartet Globe ▲ GLO 5078 [DDD]
Bruckner, A.:Qnt Strs, w. Raphael String Quartet Globe ▲ GLO 5078 [DDD]
Debussy, C.:Son Fl, w. Eleonore Pameijer (fl), Ernestine Stoop (hp) *(rec Amsterdam & Utrecht, Sept & Nov 1993)* Globe ▲ GLO 5144 [DDD]
Pache, Nicolas (va)—see also ORCHESTRAS & ENSEMBLES Sine Nomine String Quartet
Balissat, J.:Vars (7), w. P. Genet, F. Gottraux (vn), M. Jaermann (vc), R. Birnstigl (db), F. Rapin (cl), F. Schmocker (bn), M. Veillon (hn), J. Balissat (cnd) Grammont ▲ CTSP 17-2 [ADD]
Pacht, Nurit (vn)—see ORCHESTRAS & ENSEMBLES Delius String Quartet
Paciorkiewicz, Artur (va)—see ORCHESTRAS & ENSEMBLES Wilanów String Quartet
Pacitti, Daniel (cl)
Backofen, J.G.:Con for 2 Cls, w. Nicola Bulfone (cl), W. Themel (cnd), Udine CO *(rec Oct 14-15, 1995)* Agora Musica ▲ 039 [DDD]
Bernstein, L.:Son Cl, w. Massimo Palumbo (pno) *(rec Arona, Italy, July 1994)* Agorá ▲ 027 [DDD]
Castelnuovo-Tedesco, M.:Son Cl & Pno, w. Massimo Palumbo (pno) *(rec Arona, Italy, July 1994)* Agorá ▲ 027 [DDD]
Copland, A.:Con Cl, w. Carlo Balzaretti (pno), D. Pacitti (cnd), Moldavian Radio-TV SO Agorá ▲ 026 [DDD]
Devienne, F.:Sinf concertante Cls, w. Nicola Bulfone (cl), W. Themel (cnd), Udine CO *(rec Oct 14-15, 1995)* Agora Musica ▲ 039 [DDD]
Guastavino, C.:Son Cl, w. Carlo Balzaretti (pno) Agorá ▲ 026 [DDD]
Hoffmeister, F.A.:Con for 2 Cls, w. Nicola Bulfone (cl), W. Themel (cnd), Udine CO *(rec Auditorium di Remanzacco, Oct 12-13, 1995)* Agora Musica ▲ AG 033.1 [DDD]
Krommer, F.:Cons for 2 Cls, w. Nicola Bulfone (cl), W. Themel (cnd), Udine CO *(rec Auditorium di Remanzacco, Oct 12-13, 1995)* Agora Musica ▲ AG 023.1 [DDD]
Mendelssohn, F.:Concert Pieces, w. Nicola Bulfone (cl), W. Themel (cnd), Udine CO *(rec Auditorium di Remanzacco, Oct 12-13, 1995)* Agora Musica ▲ AG 023.1 [DDD]

Pacitti, Daniel (cl) (cont.)
Piazzolla, A.:Contemplación y danza, w. D. Pacitti (cnd), Moldavian Radio-TV SO Agorá ▲ 026 [DDD]
Rota, N.:Son Va, w. Massimo Palumbo (pno) [arr. for cl & pno] *(rec Arona, Italy, July 1994)* Agorá ▲ 027 [DDD]
Stamitz, C.:Con for 2 Cls, w. Nicola Bulfone (cl), W. Themel (cnd), Udine CO *(rec Oct 14-15, 1995)* Agora Musica ▲ 039 [DDD]
Stravinsky, I.:Pieces Cl Agorá ▲ 026 [DDD]
Tausch, F.W.:Concertante 2, w. Nicola Bulfone (cl), W. Themel (cnd), Udine CO *(rec Auditorium di Remanzacco, Oct 12-13, 1995)* Agora Musica ▲ AG 033.1 [DDD]
Telemann, G.P.:Con 2 Chl, w. Nicola Bulfone (cl), W. Themel (cnd), Udine CO *(rec Auditorium di Remanzacco, Oct 12-13, 1995)* Agora Musica ▲ AG 033.1 [DDD]
Packer, Janet (vn)
Read, G.:Chamber Music, w. Gerald Berthiaume (cel), Leslie Stratton Norris (hp), Barbara Harbach (hpd), Joseph Holt (pno), Howard Karp (pno), Boston Composers String Quartet—5 Aphorisms, Op. 150; Son. da Chiesa, Op. 61; Sonoric Fant. No. 1, Op. 102; Qt. 1 Strings, Op. 100 Northeastern ▲ NOR 253 [DDD]
Read, G.:5 Aphorisms, w. Howard Karp (pno) *(rec Tsai Performance Center, Boston Univ., May 1993)* Northeastern ("Classical Arts, Contemporary" series) ▲ NR 253
Rieti, V.:Serenata Vn, w. M. Strauss (cnd), Longy Artists Ensemble *(rec 1990)* CRI ▲ CD 601 [DDD]
Paderewski, Ignace Jan (pno)
The Art of Paderewski, Vol. 1 Pearl ▲ PEA 9499 (m) [AAD]
The Art of Paderewski, Vol. 2 Pearl ▲ PEA 9943 (m) [AAD]
The Art of Paderewski, Vol. 3 *(rec 1911-1930)* Pearl ▲ PEA 9109 [ADD]
Brahms, J.:Hungarian Dances Pno—Nos. 6 & 7 *(rec 1911-37)* Enterprise ("The Piano Library" series) ▲ ENT 182
Chopin, F.:Ballades Pno (comp)—Opp. 23 & 47 Klavier ▲ KCD 11014 [ADD]
Chopin, F.:Études (24)—Op. 10/12; Op. 25/1, 2 & 11 *(rec 1911-37)* Enterprise ("The Piano Library" series) ▲ ENT 182
Chopin, F.:Mazurkas—Op. 24/4 Klavier ▲ KCD 11014 [ADD]
Chopin, F.:Nocturnes—Op. 15/1 *(rec 1911-37)* Enterprise ("The Piano Library" series) ▲ ENT 182
Chopin, F.:Nocturnes—Op. 37/2 Klavier ▲ KCD 11014 [ADD]
Chopin, F.:Pno Music (misc)—"Marcia Funebre" [from Son 2, Op. 35]; Etudes, Op. 10/3-5, 25/6, 7 & 9; Waltzes, Opp. 18, 34/1, 42; Preludes, Op. 28/15 & 17; Mazurkas, Opp. 17/4, 33/2, 59/2 & 3, 63/3; Berceuse, Op. 57; Nocturnes, Opp. 9/2, 15/1 & 2, 62/1 *(rec 1911-38)* Enterprise ("Piano Library" series) ▲ ENT PL 217
Chopin, F.:Pno Music (misc)—Polonaise, Op. 40/1; Ballades, Opp. 23/1 & 47/3; Mazurka, Op. 24/4; Valse brillante, Op. 34/1; Scherzo, Op.39/3 Klavier ▲ KCD 11014 [ADD]
Chopin, F.:Pno Music (misc)—Ballade in f, Op. 52; 5 Études (Op. 10, Nos. 3,5 & 7 & Op. 25, Nos. 6 & 9); 2 Mazurkas (Op. 17/4 in a & Op. 63/3 in c#); 3 Nocturnes (Op. 9, No. 2 & Op. 62, Nos. 1 & 2); Polonaise in A, Op. 40/1; Sonata No. 2 in b♭, Op. 35 (3rd movt. only); 2 Songs, arr. Liszt (Maiden's wish; My joys); Waltz in A♭, Op. 34/1 *(rec 1911-1938)* Pearl ▲ PEA 9397 (m) [AAD]
Chopin, F.:Polonaises—Op. 53 *(rec 1911-37)* Enterprise ("The Piano Library" series) ▲ ENT 182
Chopin, F.:Polonaises—Op. 40/1 Klavier ▲ KCD 11014 [ADD]
Chopin, F.:Scherzos—Op. 39/3 Klavier ▲ KCD 11014 [ADD]
Chopin, F.:Waltzes—Op. 64/2 *(rec 1911-37)* Enterprise ("The Piano Library" series) ▲ ENT 182
Chopin, F.:Waltzes—Valse brillante, Op. 34/1 Klavier ▲ KCD 11014 [ADD]
Chopin, F.:Waltzes—Op. 42 in A♭ *(rec 1900-10)* Adès ▲ ADE 203932 [AAD]
Ignace Paderewski Plays Beethoven, Liszt, Schubert, Debussy, Vol. 1 Klavier ▲ KCD 11018 [ADD]
Liszt, F.:Soirées de Vienne *(rec 1900-10)* Adès ▲ ADE 203932 [AAD]
Mendelssohn, F.:Lieder ohne Worte Pno—La Fileuse (No. 4) *(rec 1900-10)* Adès ▲ ADE 203932 [AAD]
Mendelssohn, F.:Lieder ohne Worte Pno—Op. 19/3 [Jägerlied]; Op. 53/4; Op. 67/4 [Spinnelied] *(rec 1911-37)* Enterprise ("The Piano Library" series) ▲ ENT 182
Paderewski, w. Paderewski, Ignace Jan (pno) RCA Gold Seal ("Legendary Performers" series) ▲ 09026-60923-2
Rubinstein, A.:Valse-Caprice *(rec 1911-37)* Enterprise ("The Piano Library" series) ▲ ENT 182
Schubert, Franz:Impromptus Pno, D.935—No. 2 in A♭ Klavier ▲ KCD 11014 [ADD]
Schumann, R.:Fantasiestücke Pno, Op. 12—Nos. 1-3 *(rec 1911-37)* Enterprise ("The Piano Library" series) ▲ ENT 182
Schumann, R.:Nachtstücke—No. 4 *(rec 1911-37)* Enterprise ("The Piano Library" series) ▲ ENT 182
Paderewski, Maciej (pno)
Lutoslawski, W.:Grave, w. Marian Wasiolka (vc) Accord ▲ ACD 201142 [DDD]
Lutoslawski, W.:Partita Vn & Pno, w. Tadeusz Gadzina (vn) Accord ▲ ACD 201142 [DDD]
Szymanowski, K.:Myths, w. T. Gadzina (vn) Koch Schwann ▲ 311552 [DDD]
Szymanowski, K.:Notturno e Tarantella, w. T. Gadzina (vn) Koch Schwann ▲ 311552 [DDD]
Wieniawski, H.:Vn & Pno Music, w. S. Stalanowski (vn)—Souvenir de Poznan & Mazurka in a, Op. 3/1 & 2; Polonaise de Concert in D, Op. 4; Souvenir de Moscou, Op. 6; Romance sans parole et Rondo élégant, Op. 9; La Champêtre & Chanson polonaise, Op. 12/1 & 2; Scherzo tarantelle in g, Op. 16; Légende, Op. 17; Obertas & La ménétrier, Op. 19/1 & 2; Polonaise brillante in A, Op. 21 Pavane ▲ ADW 7213 [DDD]
Padilla, Annamaría (gtr)
Albéniz, I.:Gtr Music—Granada; Leyenda *(rec Meyant Enterprises 1994)* Música Mundial ▲ MMP 1
Pachelbel, J.:Canon *(rec Meyant Enterprises 1994)* Música Mundial ▲ MMP 1
Sanlucar, M. de:Mantillas de feria *(rec Meyant Enterprises 1994)* Música Mundial ▲ MMP 1
Schubert, Franz:Ave Maria! Jungfrau mild! *(rec Meyant Enterprises 1994)* Música Mundial ▲ MMP 1
Sor, F.:Estudio 13 Gtr *(rec Meyant Enterprises 1994)* Música Mundial ▲ MMP 1
Sor, F.:Estudio 15 Gtr *(rec Meyant Enterprises 1994)* Música Mundial ▲ MMP 1
Tárrega, F.:Gtr Music—Adelita; Lagrima; Mazurka; Recuerdos de Alhambra *(rec Meyant Enterprises 1994)* Música Mundial ▲ MMP 1
Padorr, Laila (fl)
An American Collage Vol. II, w. Constance Keene (pno), Ayke Agus (pno), Anita Swearingen (pno), Michael Lang (pno), Diane Lang Bryan (cl), James Smith (gtr), Sherry Kloss (vn), Victor Morosco (a sax) Protone ▲ PRCD 1114 [DDD]
Copland, A.:Duo Fl, w. Swearengin (pno) Protone ■ CSPR 114
Copland, A.:Vocalise, w. Swearengin (pno) Protone ■ CSPR 114
Dello Joio, N.:The Developing Flutist, w. Swearengin (pno) Protone ■ CSPR 114
Muczynski, R.:Preludes Fl Protone ■ CSPR 114
Piston, W.:Son Fl, w. Swearengin (pno) Protone ■ CSPR 114
Paer, Lewis (db)
Brandt, H.:Ghost Nets, w. J. Stephens (cnd), American Camerata for New Music AmCam ▲ ACR 10303
Pagani, M. (vn)
Milesi, P.:Modi 2, w. L. M. Pickova (sop), Françoise Goddard (alt), M. Ferradini (ten), B. Andersen (bass), D. Cassamagnaghi (fl), S. Scanziani (ob), A. Bianchi (cl/b cl), E. Crisafulli (bn), C. Gazzola (hn), F. Gualandris (tuba), A. Girardi (celtic hp), R. Anedda (vn), E. Groppo (vn), M. Pagani (vn), M. Ravasio (va), S. Righini (vc), P. Rizzi (db), J. Scully (perc), P. Milesi (cnd) Cuneiform ▲ RUNE 63
Pagano, Caio (pno)
Beethoven, L. van:Bagatelle, WoO 59, "Für Elise" Summit ▲ SMT 111 [DDD]
Beethoven, L. van:Son 7 Pno Summit ▲ SMT 111 [DDD]
Beethoven, L. van:Son 21 Pno, "Waldstein" Summit ▲ SMT 111 [DDD]
Debussy, C.:Clair de lune Summit ▲ DCD 110 [DDD]
Debussy, C.:Images (6) Pno—Set 1 Summit ▲ DCD 110 [DDD]
Debussy, C.:Preludes Pno (sels)—Book 2, No. 7, "Terrasses des audiences au clair de lune" & No. 8, "Ondine" Summit ▲ DCD 110 [DDD]
Franck, C.:Prélude, choral et fugue Summit ▲ DCD 110 [DDD]
Paganotti, Bernard (bass gtr)
D.W.W., w. Richard Pinhas (syns/gtr), J. Philippe Goude (syn programming/drums/gtr), Patrick Gauthier (syns/pno/drums), Alain Bellaich (synthesized gtr) Cuneiform ▲ Rune 40

▲ = CD ♦ = Enhanced CD Δ = MD ■ = Cassette Tape □ = DCC

Pagliani, Stefano (vn)—see also ORCHESTRAS & ENSEMBLES La Scala String Trio
Rota, N.:Film Music, w. Giuseppe Bodanza (tpt), R. Muti (cnd), La Scala Orch—Ballet Suite [from La Strada]; Dances [from Il Gattopardo] *(rec Abanella Theatre, Milan, Italy, Apr. 9–14, 1994)* Sony Classical ▲ SK 66279 [DDD]

Pagliarin, V. (vn)
Blanchard, P.:Music of, w. P. Blanchard (vn), C. Mouton (bass), C. Terranova (kbd), L. Robin (dr), M. Garay (perc)—Isidora; Koid'9; Perdoname; Folklores; Train de sables; Lithops; Marquesas Keys; Bodas de sangue *(rec Nov. 1992)* OMD ▲ CD 1538 [DDD]

Pagnini, Francesca (fl)
Dussek, J.L.:Trio Son Pno, Op. 65, w. Paolo Bidoli (pno), Mauro Valli (vc) Enterprise ("Tiziano" series) ▲ ENT TZ 96002 [DDD]
Kalkbrenner, F.:Son Fl, w. Paolo Bidoli (pno), Mauro Valli (vc) Enterprise ("Tiziano" series) ▲ ENT TZ 96002 [DDD]
Kreutzer, C.:Son Fl, Vc & Pno, w. Mauro Valli (vc), Paolo Bidoli (pno) Enterprise ("Tiziano" series) ▲ ENT TZ 96002 [DDD]

Pagny, Patricia (pno)
Glass, Paul:Pieces (5) Pno *(rec Mar 4, 1991)* Grammont ▲ CTSP 43 [AAD]
Schubert, Franz:Pno Music (misc)—Adagio in G, D.178; Hungarian Melody in b, D.817; Kupelwieser Waltz in G♭; Pno Piece in A, D.604; Son in a, Op. 42, D.845; 10 Vars on an Original Theme in F, D.156; 13 Vars on a Theme by Hüttenbrenner in a, D.576 Novalis ▲ CD 150123 [DDD]

Pahud, Emmanuel (fl)
Fauré, G.:Fant Fl, w. Eric LeSage (pno) Skarbo ▲ SK 4965 [DDD]
Fauré, G.:Sicilienne, w. Eric LeSage (pno) [trans for fl & pno] Skarbo ▲ SK 4965 [DDD]
Fauré, G.:Son 1 Vn, w. Eric LeSage (pno) [trans for fl & pno] Skarbo ▲ SK 4965 [DDD]
Franck, C.:Son Vn, w. Eric LeSage (pno) [trans for fl & pno] Skarbo ▲ SK 4965 [DDD]

Paige, Russell (vl)
Out of the Orient Crystall Skyes, w. Nancy Zylstra (sop), Margriet Tindemans (vl), Jillion Stopples Dupree (hpd/org), Michael Sand (baroque vn/vl), Linda Melsted (baroque vn), Olga Hauptmann (baroque va), Ellen Siebert (vl) Wildboar ▲ WLBR 8901 [DDD]

Paik, HaeSun (pno)
Tchaikovsky, P.:Con 1 Pno, w. B. Zander (cnd), New England Conservatory Youth PO *(rec Teatro Colon, Buenos Aires, 1995)* CPI ▲ CPI 329405 [DDD]

Paik, Kun Woo (pno)
Debussy, C.:Suite bergamasque Virgin Classics ▲ CDZ 59653
Liszt, F.:Am Grabe Richard Wagners—Bk. 1, No. 2a Le lac de Wallenstadt & 2b Au bord d'une source Virgin Classics ▲ CDC 59646
Liszt, F.:Harmonies poétiques et religieuses Virgin Classics ▲ CDC 59646
Liszt, F.:Hungarian Rhaps—No. 12 Virgin Classics ▲ CDC 59646
Liszt, F.:Liebesträume—No. 3 Virgin Classics ▲ CDC 59646
Liszt, F.:Mephisto Waltz 3 Pno—No. 1 Virgin Classics ▲ CDC 59646
Liszt, F.:Pno Music (misc)—Jeux d'eau à la Villa d'Este Virgin Classics ▲ CDC 59646
Liszt, F.:Vars on a Theme of Bach, S.180 Virgin Classics ▲ CDC 59646
Poulenc, F.:Intermezzo in A♭ Virgin Classics ▲ CDZ 59653
Poulenc, F.:Movts perpétuels Virgin Classics ▲ CDZ 59653
Poulenc, F.:Nocturnes Pno—Nos. 1, 2 & 6 Virgin Classics ▲ CDZ 59653
Poulenc, F.:Pno Music (misc)—Improvisations Nos. 10, 12 & 15 Virgin Classics ▲ CDZ 59653
Poulenc, F.:Presto Pno Virgin Classics ▲ CDZ 59653
Poulenc, F.:Son Cl Pno, w. Jacques di Donato (cl) Accord ▲ ACD 205192 [DDD]
Poulenc, F.:Son Ob, w. Claude Villevieille (ob) Accord ▲ ACD 205192 [DDD]
Poulenc, F.:Trio Ob, w. Claude Bassoon (ob), Alexandre Ouzounoff (bn) Accord ▲ ACD 205192 [DDD]
Prokofiev, S.:Con 1 Pno, w. A. Wit (cnd), Polish National RSO Katowice *(rec May 13–18, 1991)* Naxos ▲ 8.550566 [DDD]
Prokofiev, S.:Con 2 Pno, w. A. Wit (cnd), Polish National RSO Katowice *(rec May 13–18, 1991)* Naxos ▲ 8.550565 [DDD]
Prokofiev, S.:Con 3 Pno, w. A. Wit (cnd), Polish National RSO Katowice *(rec May 13–18, 1991)* Naxos ▲ 8.550566 [DDD]
Prokofiev, S.:Con 4 Pno, w. A. Wit (cnd), Polish National RSO Katowice *(rec May 13–18, 1991)* Naxos ▲ 8.550566 [DDD]
Prokofiev, S.:Con 5 Pno, w. A. Wit (cnd), Polish National RSO Katowice *(rec May 13–18, 1991)* Naxos ▲ 8.550565 [DDD]
Ravel, M.:Con Pno (left hand), w. G. Bertini (cnd), Stuttgart RSO Orfeo ▲ 013821 [DDD]
Ravel, M.:Con in G Pno, w. G. Bertini (cnd), Stuttgart RSO Orfeo ▲ 013821 [DDD]
Satie, E.:Embryons desséchés Virgin Classics ▲ CDZ 59653
Satie, E.:Gnossiennes Pno—Nos. 4 & 5 Virgin Classics ▲ CDZ 59653
Satie, E.:Gymnopédies Virgin Classics ▲ CDZ 59653
Satie, E.:Ogives Pno—Nos. 1 & 2 Virgin Classics ▲ CDZ 59653
Satie, E.:Pno Music (misc)—Casque; Celle qui parle trop; Espagnagna; Vaisseaux Virgin Classics ▲ CDZ 59653

Paik, W. (pno)
Hahn, R.:Pno Music, w. H. Sermet (pno)—Ruban dénoué (a cycle of 12 waltzes), Preludes, Caprices, Berceuses, etc. Valois ("Musique Française" series) ▲ V 4658

Paisner, Caryl (vc)—see ORCHESTRAS & ENSEMBLES CELLO

Päivinen, Pepa (fl/t sax/s sax/b cl)
Braxton, A.:Composition 144, w. Anthony Braxton (fl/s sax/a sax), Seppo Baron Paakkunainen (fl/t sax/br sax), Pentti Lahti (fl/s sax/a sax), Mircea Stan (trbn), Mikko-Ville Luolajan-Mikkola (vn), Teppo Hauta-aho (db/vc), Jukka Wasama (dr) *(rec Järvenpää House, Järvenpää, Finland, Nov 7, 1988)* Leo ▲ LR 233
Braxton, A.:Composition 145, w. Anthony Braxton (fl/s sax/a sax), Seppo Baron Paakkunainen (fl/t sax/br sax), Pentti Lahti (fl/s sax/a sax), Mircea Stan (trbn), Mikko-Ville Luolajan-Mikkola (vn), Teppo Hauta-aho (db/vc), Jukka Wasama (dr) *(rec Järvenpää House, Järvenpää, Finland, Nov 7, 1988)* Leo ▲ LR 233

Pala, Samuele (pno)
Donaudy, S.:Airs de style ancien, w. Ernesto Palacio (ten) *(rec Jungle Studios, Milan, July 26–28, 1995)* Agorá ▲ 028 [DDD]
Zingarelli, N.A.:Dante:Inferno, w. Ernesto Palacio (ten) *(rec S. Martino Church, Tirano, June 30, 1995)* Agorá ▲ 018 [DDD]

Paladin, Mario (va)—see ORCHESTRAS & ENSEMBLES L'Arte dell'Arco

Páleníček, Josef (pno)
Haydn, J.:Trios Pno, Fl & Vc, w. N. Nishida (fl), W. Boettcher (vc)—in D Camerata ▲ 30CM 376
Janácek, L.:In the Mists Supraphon ▲ 10 1481-2 [AAD]
Janácek, L.:On an Overgrown Path Supraphon ▲ 10 1481-2 [AAD]
Janácek, L.:Son October 1, 1905 Supraphon ▲ 10 1481-2 [AAD]

Palanker, Edward (cl)
Myers, T.:Cadenza & Lament, w. D. Rothlisberger (cnd), Towson State Univ Sym Band Vienna Modern Masters ▲ VMM 3034 [DDD]

Palchak, Mary (fl)
Flute Music by French Composers, w. John Novacek (pno) *(rec Santa Ana High School Auditorium, Santa Ana, CA, June 1995)* Ambassador ▲ ARC 1016 [DDD]

Paleczny, Piotr (pno)
Chopin, F.:Ballades Pno (comp) *(rec Apr. 10–13, 1990)* Canyon ▲ EC 3646-2 [DDD]
Chopin, F.:Con 1 Pno, w. K. Kord (cnd), Warsaw PO *(rec Apr. 22–26, 1991)* Canyon Classics ▲ 3650 [DDD]
Chopin, F.:Con 2 Pno, w. K. Kord (cnd), Warsaw PO *(rec Apr. 22–26, 1991)* Canyon Classics ▲ 3650 [DDD]
Chopin, F.:Impromptus *(rec Apr. 10–13, 1990)* Canyon ▲ EC 3646-2 [DDD]
Chopin, F.:Krakowiak, w. K. Kord (cnd), Warsaw PO *(rec Warsaw Philharmonic Hall, June 27–30, 1994)* Canyon Classics ▲ CD 248
Chopin, F.:Scherzos *(rec Apr. 10–13, 1990)* Canyon Classics ▲ 3637 [DDD]

Paleczny, Piotr (pno) (cont.)
Lutoslawski, W.:Con Pno, w. A. Wit (cnd), Polish National RSO Katowice *(rec Katowice, Poland, 1994–95)* Naxos ▲ 8.553169 [DDD]
Mussorgsky, M.:Pictures, w. W. Rowicki (cnd), Warsaw PO [both versions] Polskie Nagrania Edition ▲ ECD 026
Paderewski, I.J.:Con Pno, w. J. Maksymiuk (cnd), Polish National SO Sound ▲ CD 3446
Paderewski, I.J.:Con Pno, w. T. Strugala (cnd), Polish National RSO Katowice Olympia ▲ OLY 398 [DDD]

Paleníček, Josef (pno)
Janácek, L.:The Diary of One Who Disappeared, w. Véra Soukupová (mez), Stepanka Stepanova (mez), Beno Blachut (ten), Nicolai Gedda (ten), Prague Radio Women's Chorus, Czech Chamber Singers Female Chorus—contains 2 complete performances *(rec 1984 & 1956)* Supraphon ▲ SUP 0022 [DDD/ADD]
Martinů, B.:Con 3 Pno, w. K. Ančerl (cnd), Czech PO Supraphon ("Czech Philharmonic" series) ▲ SUP 111929 [AAD]

Paley, Alexander (pno)
Balakirev, M.:Pno Music—[CD 1] transcriptions of works by Glinka (Kamarinskaya; Ne govori; Jota Aragonesca), Chopin (Romance from Con. No. 1 in e, Op. 11), Beethoven (Cavatina from Qt. No. 13 in B♭, Op. 130; Allegretto from Qt. No. 8 in e, Op. 59/2), Zapolsky (Rêverie), Balakirev (Pustinya; Impromptu on the Themes of 2 Preludes by Chopin), Berlioz (Introd. to La Fuite en Egypte); [CD 2] Valse di bravura No. 1 in G; Valse mélancholique No. 2 in f; Valse-Impromptu No. 3 in D; Waltzes Nos. 4 in B♭, 5 in D♭, 6 in f# & 7 in g#; Polka; Tarantella; Valses-Caprices Nos. 1 in A♭ & 2 in D♭ *(rec SUNY Purchase, NY, Oct. 5, 6, 19 & 20, 1992)* ESS.A.Y 2-▲ CD 1030/31 [DDD]
Balakirev, M.:Pno Music—Islamey, Oriental Fant.; Fant. on Themes from Glinka's *A Life for the Tsar*, Fantasiestück; Nocturne No. 1 in b♭; Nocturne No. 2 in b; Nocturne No. 3 in d; Capriccio; Son. No. 1 in b♭, Op. 5; Sonatina; Son. in b♭ ESS.A.Y 2-▲ CD 1028/29 [DDD]
Balakirev, M.:Pno Music—Mazurkas; Scherzos; Dumka; Au jardin; Gondolllied; Berceuse; The Lark; Spanish Serenade; Spanish Melody; La fileuse; Tyrolienne; Chant du pêcheur; Humoresque; Rêverie; Novellett; Toccata ESS.A.Y 2-▲ CD 1032/33 [DDD]
Rubinstein, A.:Con 2 Pno, w. I. Golovshin (cnd), Moscow State SO Russian Disc ▲ RUS 11 360 [DDD]
Rubinstein, A.:Con 4 Pno, w. I. Golovshin (cnd), Moscow State SO Russian Disc ▲ RUS 11 360 [DDD]
Weber, C.M. von:Les Adieux *(rec Fisher Hall, Santa Rosa, CA, Jan. 10–15, 1994)* Naxos ▲ 8.553006 [DDD]
Weber, C.M. von:Grand polonaise *(rec Fisher Hall, Santa Rosa, CA, Jan. 10–15, 1994)* Naxos ▲ 8.550989 [DDD]
Weber, C.M. von:Invitation to the Dance Pno *(rec Fisher Hall, Santa Rosa, CA, Jan. 10–15, 1994)* Naxos ▲ 8.550988 [DDD]
Weber, C.M. von:Momento capriccioso *(rec Fisher Hall, Santa Rosa, CA, Jan. 10–15, 1994)* Naxos ▲ 8.550990 [DDD]
Weber, C.M. von:Polacca brillante *(rec Fisher Hall, Santa Rosa, CA, Jan. 10–15, 1994)* Naxos ▲ 8.553006 [DDD]
Weber, C.M. von:Rondo brillante *(rec Fisher Hall, Santa Rosa, CA, Jan. 10–15, 1994)* Naxos ▲ 8.553006 [DDD]
Weber, C.M. von:Son 1 Pno—No. 1 *(rec Fisher Hall, Santa Rosa, CA, Jan. 10–15, 1994)* Naxos ▲ 8.550988 [DDD]
Weber, C.M. von:Son 2 Pno—No. 2 *(rec Fisher Hall, Santa Rosa, CA, Jan. 10–15, 1994)* Naxos ▲ 8.550989 [DDD]
Weber, C.M. von:Son 3 Pno—No. 3 *(rec Fisher Hall, Santa Rosa, CA, Jan. 10–15, 1994)* Naxos ▲ 8.550990 [DDD]
Weber, C.M. von:Son 4 Pno—No. 4 *(rec Fisher Hall, Santa Rosa, CA, Jan. 10–15, 1994)* Naxos ▲ 8.553006 [DDD]
Weber, C.M. von:Vars on the Air de ballet from Vogler's *Castor et Pollux* Pno, J.40 *(rec Fisher Hall, Santa Rosa, CA, Jan. 10–15, 1994)* Naxos ▲ 8.550990 [DDD]
Weber, C.M. von:Vars on an Original Theme Pno, J.7 *(rec Fisher Hall, Santa Rosa, CA, Jan. 10–15, 1994)* Naxos ▲ 8.550988 [DDD]
Weber, C.M. von:Vars on an Original Theme Pno, J.55 *(rec Fisher Hall, Santa Rosa, CA, Jan. 10–15, 1994)* Naxos ▲ 8.550990 [DDD]
Weber, C.M. von:Vars on *Woher mag dies wohl kommen?* Pno, J.43 *(rec Fisher Hall, Santa Rosa, CA, Jan. 10–15, 1994)* Naxos ▲ 8.550989 [DDD]
Weber, C.M. von:Vars on *Vien quà, Dorina bella* Pno, J.53 *(rec Fisher Hall, Santa Rosa, CA, Jan. 10–15, 1994)* Naxos ▲ 8.550990 [DDD]
Weber, C.M. von:Vars on *A peine au sortir de l'enfance* Pno, J.141 *(rec Fisher Hall, Santa Rosa, CA, Jan. 10–15, 1994)* Naxos ▲ 8.553006 [DDD]
Weber, C.M. von:Vars on *Schöne Minka* Pno, J.179 *(rec Fisher Hall, Santa Rosa, CA, Jan. 10–15, 1994)* Naxos ▲ 8.550988 [DDD]
Weber, C.M. von:Vars on a Gypsy Song Pno, J.219 *(rec Fisher Hall, Santa Rosa, CA, Jan. 10–15, 1994)* Naxos ▲ 8.550989 [DDD]

Palitsky, E. (vc)—see ORCHESTRAS & ENSEMBLES Northern Crown Soloists Ensemble

Pallieri, Annabella (hp)—see ORCHESTRAS & ENSEMBLES Bilitis Ensemble

Pälli, Ilkka (vc)—see ORCHESTRAS & ENSEMBLES Sinfonia Lahti Chamber Ensemble members
Gubaidulina, S.:Detto 2 Vc, w. O. Vänskä (cnd), Lahti Chamber Ensemble *(rec Aug. 16–19, 1993)* BIS ▲ CD 636 [DDD]

Palm, Siegfried (vc)
Casella, A.:Con Vc, w. G. Garbarino (cnd), Villa Marigola Festival Orch Nuova Era 2-▲ 7143/44 [DDD]
Daus, A.:The Twelfth Sonnet Gallo ▲ CD 530 [AAD]
Kagel, M.:An Tasten, w. Bruno Canino (pno), Saschko Gawriloff (vn) Montaigne ▲ MO 782043
Kagel, M.:Klangwölfe, w. Bruno Canino (pno), Saschko Gawriloff (vn) Montaigne ▲ MO 782043
Kagel, M.:Trio Pno, w. Saschko Gawriloff (vn), Bruno Canino (pno) Montaigne ▲ MO 782043
Kagel, M.:Unguis incarnatus est, w. Bruno Canino (pno), Saschko Gawriloff (vn) Montaigne ▲ MO 782043
Kaufmann, D.:Der Tod des Trompeters Kirilenko, w. Erich Auer (speaker), I. Karabtchevsky (cnd), Lower Austria Tonkünst Orch Vienna Modern Masters ▲ VMM 3020 [AAD]
Kelemen, M.:Changeant, w. E. Bour (cnd), Southwest German RSO Baden-Baden *(rec Nov 1972)* BIS ▲ CD 742 [AAD]
Kelemen, M.:Drammatico, w. A. Tamayo (cnd), Bavarian RSO *(rec Munich, Germany, Feb 22, 1991)* BIS ▲ CD 742 [DDD]
Malipiero, G.F.:Con Vc, w. G. Garbarino (cnd), Villa Marigola Festival Orch Nuova Era ▲ 6998 [DDD]
Messiaen, O.:Quatuor pour la fin du temps, w. Hans Deinzer (cl), Saschko Gawrilov (vn), Alfons Kontarsky (pno) EMI Classics 2-▲ CDZ 47463 [DDD]
Wildberger, J.:Die Stimme, die alte, schwächer werdende Stimme, w. K. Graf (sop), L. Zagrosek (cnd), Southwest German RSO Baden-Baden [G] *(rec May 30, 1980)* Grammont ▲ CTSP 25-2 [ADD]
Yun, I.:Con Vc, w. H. Zender (cnd), Berlin RSO *(rec March 25, 1976)* Camerata ▲ 30CM 22

Palm, Thomas (pno)
Bassi, L.:Fant di concerto on Verdi's *Rigoletto*, w. N. Friedrich (cl) Bayer ▲ 100131
Bassi, L.:Melodies from *I Puritani*, w. N. Friedrich (cl) Bayer ▲ 100131
Cavallini, E.:Fant on Motifs from Bellini's *I somnambula*, w. N. Friedrich (cl) Bayer ▲ 100131
Labanchi, G.:Fant on Verdi's *Aida*, w. N. Friedrich (cl) Bayer ▲ 100131
Lovreglio, D.:Fant da concerto on Motifs of Verdi's *La traviata*, w. N. Friedrich (cl) Bayer ▲ 100131
Pfitzner, H.:Heine-lieder, w. B. Possemeyer (ten) Ars Produktion ▲ ARS 368326 [DDD]
Schubert, Franz:Schwanengesang, w. B. Possemeyer (ten) Ars Produktion ▲ ARS 368326 [DDD]
Schumann, R.:Dichterliebe, w. B. Possemeyer (ten) Ars Produktion ▲ ARS 368326 [DDD]
Wolf, H.:Goethe-Lieder (sels), w. W. Hlazmair (bar) Collins Classics ▲ COL 1402 [DDD]

Palma, Donald (db)
Wuorinen, C.:Spinoff, w. B. Hudson (vn), J. Passaro (perc) Bridge ▲ BCD 9008 [DDD]
Wuorinen, C.:Trio Bass Trbn, w. D. Taylor (trbn), D. Braynard (tuba) *(rec Sept. 11–13, 1991)* Koch International Classics ▲ KIC 7123-2 [DDD]

Palma, Susan (pno)
Brahms, J.:Sons Cl (comp), w. V. Mariozzi (cl) Giulia ▲ GIU 201031 [DDD]

INSTRUMENT.

Palma, Susan (fl)—see also ORCHESTRAS & ENSEMBLES Contemporary Chamber Ensemble
Biscardi, C.:At the Still Point, w. Jeanne Ingraham (vn), Gilbert Kalish (pno), P. Dunkel (cnd), American Composers Orch *(rec Whitman Auditorium, Brooklyn College, NY, Feb. 1982)* CRI ▲ CD 686 [ADD]
Mozart, W.A.:Andante Fl, K.315/285a, Orpheus CO Deutsche Grammophon ▲ 427677-2 [DDD]
Mozart, W.A.:Cons Fl, Orpheus CO Deutsche Grammophon ▲ 427677-2 [DDD]
Mozart, W.A.:Cons Fl, Orpheus CO Deutsche Grammophon 3-▲ 431665-2 [DDD]
Mozart, W.A.:Con Fl Hp, w. N. Allen (hp), Orpheus CO Deutsche Grammophon 3-▲ 431665-2 [DDD]
Mozart, W.A.:Con Fl Hp, w. N. Allen (hp), Orpheus CO Deutsche Grammophon ▲ 427677-2 [DDD]
Rosenzweig, M.:Diptych, w. A. Blustine (cl), B. Hudson (vn), C. Finckel (vc), E. Garth (pno), M. Rosenzweig Centaur ▲ CRC 2103 [DDD]
Roxbury, R.:Songs of Walt Whitman, w. P. Mason (bar), D. Starobin (gtr) [E] Bridge ▲ BCD 9022 [DDD]
Searle, H.:2 Practical Cats, w. P. Mason (bar), D. Starobin (gtr), T. Eddy (vc) [E] Bridge ▲ BCD 9022 [DDD]

Palma, Susan (pic)
Kurtág, G.:The Little Predicament, w. D. Starobin (gtr), S. Taylor (trbn) Bridge ▲ BCD 9004 ■ BC5-7004

Palmboom, Manken (kbd)
Country Morning, w. Anastasi Mavrides (arr/syn) Real Music ▲ 65555-2 [DDD]

Palme, Donald (db)
Lerdahl, F.:Waltzes, w. R. Schulte (vn), S. Nickrenz (va), F. Sherry (vc) CRI ▲ CD 580 [ADD/DDD]

Palmer, Caroline (pno)
Fuchs, R.:Fantasiestücke Vc, Op. 78, w. N. Green (vc) Biddulph ▲ LAW 005 [DDD]
Fuchs, R.:Son 1 Vc & Pno, w. N. Green (vc) Biddulph ▲ LAW 005 [DDD]
Fuchs, R.:Son 2 Vc & Pno, w. N. Green (vc) Biddulph ▲ LAW 005 [DDD]

Palmer, Larry (hpd)
Bach, J.S.:Kbd Music (misc)—Toccata in D, BWV 912; Prelude & Fugue in f, BWV 881; Con., BWV 971 [nach italienischem Gusto]; Ov., BWV 831 [nach französischer Art] *(rec Resurrection Lutheran Church Chapel, Plano, TX, June 30–July 2, 1994)* EPR ("Gold" series) ▲ EPR 9405 [DDD]

Palmer, Larry (org)
Dedication Recital:Fisk Organ, Op. 101, w. Palmer, Larry (org) *(rec Caruth Auditorium, Southern Methodist Univ., Dallas, TX, Sept. 18, 1993)* EPR ▲ EPR 9303 [DDD]

Palmer, Rudolph (pno)
Dvořák, A.:Songs, w. C. Ciesinski (mez), G. Hirst (ten), J. Ostendorf (bass-bar)—Serbian Songs, Op. 6; Folk Tunes, Op. 73; 4 Lieder, Op. 82; Love Songs, Op. 83; Russian Folk Duets Erasmus ▲ WVH 084
Teasin':Turn of the Century Parlor Songs & Rags, w. Julianne Baird (sop), Magic Circle Ensemble *(rec Mallory Room, Rutger's University, Camden, NJ, June 1995)* Helicon ▲ HE 1001

Palmer, Todd (cl)
Hermit Songs, w. Carol Archer (pno) Koch International Classics ▲ KIC 7148 [DDD]
Rorem, N.:Winter Pages, w. F. Morelli (bn), I. Kavafian (vn), F. Sherry (vc), C. Wadsworth (pno) New World ▲ 80416-2 [DDD]

Palmier, Nadine (pno)
Mozart, W.A.:Adagio & Fugue Strs, w. J. Rigal (pno)—Adagio Arion ▲ ARN 68028 [DDD]
Mozart, W.A.:Fugue Pnos, K.426, w. J. Rigal (pno) Arion ▲ ARN 68028 [DDD]
Mozart, W.A.:Pno Music, w. J. Rigal (pno)—2 son. movts. in B♭, Allegro in c & Fugue in G, K.Anh.42–45; Larghetto & Allegro in E♭ [arr. P. Badura-Skoda for 2 pianos, 1781] Arion ▲ ARN 68028 [DDD]
Mozart, W.A.:Son Pno 4-Hands, K.19d, w. J. Rigal (pno) Arion ▲ ARN 68028 [DDD]
Mozart, W.A.:Son Pnos, K.448, w. J. Rigal (pno) Arion ▲ ARN 68028 [DDD]

Palmieri, L. (pno)
Schumann, R.:Son 1 Vn, w. M. Fornaciari (vn) Fonè ▲ 86 F 02-8 [ADD]
Schumann, R.:Son 2 Vn, w. M. Fornaciari (vn) Fonè ▲ 86 F 02-8 [ADD]

Palmisano, Luigi (fl)
Paisiello, G.:Qts Fl, w. Franco Mezzena (vn), Arturo Mazza (va), Donna Magendanz (vc) *(rec Trento, Italy, Nov 1979)* Dynamic ▲ CDS 12 [ADD]

Palomares, Joaquín (vn)
Granados, E.:Son Vn, w. M. Wagemans (pno) PROdigital ▲ PRO 1229 [DDD]
Grieg, E.:Sons Vn, Opp. 8, 13 & 45, w. Michel Wagemans (pno) *(rec Elder Forest Studios, Elder Forest, CA)* PROdigital ▲ PRO 1314 [DDD]
Turina, J.:El poema de una sanluqueña, w. M. Wagemans (pno) PROdigital ▲ PRO 1229 [DDD]
Turina, J.:Son 1 Vn, w. M. Wagemans (pno) PROdigital ▲ PRO 1229 [DDD]
Turina, J.:Son 2 Vn, w. M. Wagemans (pno) PROdigital ▲ PRO 1229 [DDD]

Paloucek, Ed (celtic fid)
Vivaldi, A.:Cons Vn, Op. 8/1–4, "The Four Seasons", w. Jerome Franke (vn), Karine Garibova (vn), Pasquale Laurino (vn), Olga Miliaeva (va), Roza Borisova (vc), Mika Hennessy (db), Melanie Panush (ham dlc), Stanislav Venglevski (bayan), Mike Kashou (arabic tabla), Daryl Stuermer (gtr), Gary Bottoni (highland pipe), Dubuffet String Quartet *(rec July–Sept 1995)* EarthBeat! ▲ 35270-2 [DDD]

Palovič, Ivan (pno)
Hummel, J.N.:Con Pno, Op. 85, w. L. Slovák (cnd), Slovak PO Koch Schwann ▲ CD 311120

Pålsson, Hans (pno)
Beethoven, L. van:Son 22 Pno *(rec Apr. 11, 1976)* BIS ▲ CD 36 [DDD]
Blomdahl, K.-B.:Pno Music—3 Polyphonic Pieces (1945); 3 Short Pieces (1945); Little Theme & Vars. (1948) BIS ▲ CD 579 [DDD]
Börtz, D.:Pno Music—Monologhi 6 & 11 (1977 & 1983–84) BIS ▲ CD 579 [DDD]
Brahms, J.:Ernste Gesänge, w. E. Saedén (bar) *(rec Nacka Aula, Nacka Sweden, July 26–27, 1976)* BIS ▲ CD 70 [AAD]
Debussy, C.:Ballades (3) de François Villon, w. Erik Saeden (bar) *(rec Nacka Aula, Nacka, Sweden, June 14, 1975)* BIS ▲ CD 28 [AAD]
Debussy, C.:Son Vc, w. Frans Helmerson (vc) *(rec Nacka Aula, Nacka, Sweden, July 22, 1975)* BIS ▲ CD 28 [AAD]
Debussy, C.:Son Vn, w. Arve Tellefsen (vn) *(rec Nacka Aula, Nacka, Sweden, Apr. 28, 1975)* BIS ▲ CD 28 [AAD]
Fauré, G.:Trio, w. A. Tellefsen (vn), F. Helmerson (vc) *(rec Apr. 26–27, 1975)* BIS ▲ CD 35 [AAD]
Franck, C.:Son Vn, w. A. Tellefsen (vn) *(rec Oct. 24, 1975)* BIS ▲ CD 35 [AAD]
Haydn, J.:Sons Pno—No. 12 in A, H.XVI/12 *(rec Apr. 11, 1976)* BIS ▲ CD 36 [DDD]
Jersild, J.:Duo Concertante, w. Jørgen Jersild (pno) *(rec 1990–91)* Paula ▲ PACD 61 [DAD]
Jersild, J.:Fant Pno *(rec 1990–91)* Paula ▲ PACD 61 [DAD]
Jersild, J.:Jeu polyrythmique *(rec 1990–91)* Paula ▲ PACD 61 [DAD]
Jersild, J.:Pièces en Concert *(rec 1990–91)* Paula ▲ PACD 61 [DAD]
Jersild, J.:Pieces for Julie *(rec 1990–91)* Paula ▲ PACD 61 [DAD]
Lidholm, I.:Pno Music—På konungens slott [At the King's Castle] (1943); Son for Piano (1947); Sonatinas Nos 1 & 2 (1947 & 1950); 7 Pieces from 10 Miniatures (1948); Klavierstück (1949); Stamp Music (1971) BIS ▲ CD 579 [DDD]
Mozart, W.A.:Fant Pno, K.396 *(rec Apr. 11, 1976)* BIS ▲ CD 36 [DDD]
Mozart, W.A.:Son Pnos, K.448, w. A. Malling (pno) *(rec May 29–30, 1976)* BIS ▲ CD 58 [AAD]
Mussorgsky, M.:Pictures at an Exhibition BIS ▲ CD 16 [AAD]
Mussorgsky, M.:Songs & Dances, w. E. Saedén (bar) BIS ▲ CD 16 [AAD]
Nilsson, T.:Con 1 Pno, w. V. Handley (cnd), Malmö SO Caprice ▲ CAP 21417 [DDD]
Nilsson, T.:Con 2 Pno, w. J. Panula (cnd), Stockholm PO Caprice ▲ CAP 21417 [DDD]
Nilsson, T.:Grand Suite Caprice ▲ CAP 21417 [DDD]
Prokofiev, S.:Son Vc, w. A. Tellefsen (vn), F. Helmerson (vc) *(rec June 13, 1975)* BIS ▲ CD 35 [AAD]
Shostakovich, D.:Trio 2 Pno, w. A. Tellefsen (vn), F. Helmerson (vc) BIS ▲ CD 26 [AAD]
Stravinsky, I.:Con Pnos, w. A. Malling (pno) *(rec May 29–30, 1976)* BIS ▲ CD 58 [AAD]

Paludi, Marcela (pno)
Clementi, M.:Pno Music (comp), w. Federico Aldao (pno), Aldo Antognazzi (pno), Ana Chavez (pno), Lorena Di Florio (pno), Ricardo Zanon (pno)—Sons (6) for Pno, Op. 1, Nos. 4–6; Sons (6) for Pno, Op. 2, Nos. 2, 4 & 6 Aura Classics ▲ AU 32072

Palumbo, Massimo (pno)
Bach, J.S.:Partitas Hpd, BWV 825–830—BWV 825, 826 & 830 Nuova Era ▲ NUO 7219
Bernstein, L.:Son Cl, w. Daniel Pacitti (cl) *(rec Arona, Italy, July 1994)* Agorá ▲ 027 [DDD]
Carulli, F.:Duo in C Gtr & Pno, w. L. Saracino (gtr) Nuova Era ("Ancient Music" series) ▲ NUO 7167 [DDD]
Carulli, F.:Duo in D Gtr & Pno, w. L. Saracino (gtr) Nuova Era ("Ancient Music" series) ▲ NUO 7174 [DDD]
Carulli, F.:Grand Duo, Op. 45, w. L. Saracino (gtr) Nuova Era ("Ancient Music" series) ▲ NUO 7167 [DDD]
Carulli, F.:Grand Duo, Op. 70, w. L. Saracino (gtr) Nuova Era ("Ancient Music" series) ▲ NUO 7169 [ADD]
Carulli, F.:Grand Duo, Op. 86, w. L. Saracino (gtr) Nuova Era ("Ancient Music" series) ▲ NUO 7169 [ADD]
Carulli, F.:Gtr Music, w. L. Saracino (gtr)—Opp. 134, 135, 150, 151 & 233 Nuova Era ("Ancient Music" series) ▲ NUO 7175 [DDD]
Carulli, F.:Gtr Music, w. L. Saracino (gtr)—12 Ovs. by Rossini:Cenerentola; Bianca e Falliero; L'Italiana in Algeri; Tancredi; Otello; L'Inganno felice; Il barbiere di Siviglia; La Gazza Ladra; Semiramide; Torvaldo e Dorliska; Eduardo e Cristina; Armida Nuova Era ("Ancient Music" series) 2-▲ NUO 7188 [DDD]
Carulli, F.:Gtr Music, w. Leopoldo Saracino (gtr) Nuova Era ("Ancient Music" series) ▲ NUO 7190 [DDD]
Carulli, F.:Nocturnes Gtr, "Mélange su temi di Rossini", w. L. Saracino (gtr) Nuova Era ("Ancient Music" series) ▲ NUO 7174 [DDD]
Carulli, F.:Nocturne Gtr, Op. 127, w. L. Saracino (gtr) Nuova Era ("Ancient Music" series) ▲ NUO 7167 [DDD]
Carulli, F.:Petits Duos, Op. 92, w. L. Saracino (gtr) Nuova Era ("Ancient Music" series) ▲ NUO 7169 [ADD]
Carulli, F.:Sonatines (3) Gtr & Pno, w. L. Saracino (gtr) Nuova Era ("Ancient Music" series) ▲ NUO 7174 [DDD]
Carulli, F.:Valses, Op. 32, w. L. Saracino (gtr) Nuova Era ("Ancient Music" series) ▲ NUO 7169 [ADD]
Carulli, F.:Vars on Theme by Beethoven, w. L. Saracino (gtr) Nuova Era ("Ancient Music" series) ▲ NUO 7167 [DDD]
Castelnuovo-Tedesco, M.:Son Cl & Pno, w. Daniel Pacitti (cl) *(rec Arona, Italy, July 1994)* Agorá ▲ 027 [DDD]
Diabelli, A.:Divert molto facili, w. Leopoldo Saracino (gtr) Nuova Era ▲ NUO 7203 [DDD]
Diabelli, A.:Easy Pieces (11), w. Leopoldo Saracino (gtr) Nuova Era ▲ NUO 7203 [DDD]
Diabelli, A.:Grande Son Brillante, w. Leopoldo Saracino (gtr) Nuova Era ▲ NUO 7203 [DDD]
Diabelli, A.:Vars on a Theme by Rode, w. Leopoldo Saracino (gtr) Nuova Era ▲ NUO 7203 [DDD]
Haydn, J.:Sons Pno—Nos. 2 in B♭, 4 in D, 9 in F, 10 in C, 13 in E, 20 in c, 24 in D & 26 in A Enterprise ("Tiziano" series) ▲ ENT TZ 96005 [DDD]
Haydn, J.:Sons Vn & Pno, w. Roberto Baraldi (vn)—Nos. 1, 3, 4 & 6 Nuova Era ▲ NUO 7229
Respighi, E.O.S.:Songs, w. Tiziana Cisternino (sop)—3 Spanish Songs; 4 Rubaiyat Songs; 2 Songs Nuova Era ("Icarus" series) ▲ NUO 7182 [DDD]
Respighi, O.:Ancient Airs & Dances, w. A. Bassi (pno) Bongiovanni ▲ GB 5528 [DDD]
Respighi, O.:Gösdemlan, w. A. Bassi (pno) Bongiovanni ▲ GB 5528 [DDD]
Respighi, O.:Little Pieces Pno, w. A. Bassi (pno) Bongiovanni ▲ GB 5528 [DDD]
Respighi, O.:Pno Music—Sonata in a; Suite in G; Andante in F; Andante in D; Sonata in f; Prlude in b♭; Allegro da Concerto; Prelude in d; Prelude in b♭ Nuova Era ▲ NUO 7156 [DDD]
Respighi, O.:Pieces Vn, w. Nuovo Quartetto Modigliani members *(rec July 1992)* Nuova Era ▲ NUO 7159 [DDD]
Respighi, O.:Qnt Pno, w. Nuovo Quartetto Modigliani *(rec July 1992)* Nuova Era ▲ NUO 7159 [DDD]
Respighi, O.:Son Vn, w. Nuovo Quartetto Modigliani members *(rec July 1992)* Nuova Era ▲ NUO 7159 [DDD]
Respighi, O.:Songs, w. Tiziana Cisternino (sop)—5 unpublished songs; Miranda, Ballata alla luna; Voici Noel; Il pleut, gentil berger; Canzone sarda, La funtanelle Nuova Era ("Icarus" series) ▲ NUO 7182 [DDD]
Respighi, O.:Waltz Pno, w. A. Bassi (pno) Bongiovanni ▲ GB 5528 [DDD]
Rota, N.:Son Va, w. Daniel Pacitti (cl) [arr. for cl & pno] *(rec Arona, Italy, July 1994)* Agorá ▲ 027 [DDD]
Schubert, Franz:Son Vn, D.574, w. Renata Spotti (vn) Enterprise ("Tiziano" series) ▲ ENT TZ 96009 [DDD]
Schubert, Franz:Sonatinas Vn, w. Renata Spotti (vn) Enterprise ("Tiziano" series) ▲ ENT TZ 96009 [DDD]

Palviainen, Eero (lt)
Takemitsu, T.:Music of, w. Mikael Helasvuo (fl), Jukka Savijoki (gtr), Timothy Ferchen (vib/crotales)—Sacrifice; Voice; All in Twilight; Ring; Folios; Itinerant; Toward the Sea Ondine ▲ ODE 839 [DDD]

Pameijer, Eleonore (fl)
Debussy, C.:Son Fl, w. Prunella Pacey (va), Ernestine Stoop (hp) *(rec Amsterdam & Utrecht, Sept & Nov 1993 & Oct 199)* Globe ▲ GLO 5144 [DDD]
Flute & Organ, w. Leo van Doeselaar (org) Vivace ▲ E 539 [ADD]
Janssen, G.:Zoek, w. Guuse Janssen (hpd), L. Markiz (cnd), Amsterdam New Sinfonietta NM Classics ▲ NM 92041
Verbey, T.:Hommage Donemus ▲ CV 31

Pameijer, L. (fl)
Berio, L.:Tempi Concertati, w. J. E. van Regteren Altena (vn), D. Porcelijn (cnd), Asko Ensemble *(rec live, Amsterdam 3/6/90)* Attacca ▲ Babel 9057-4 [DDD]

Pan, Xun (pno)
Roussakis, N.:MI e FA *(rec American Academy of Arts & Letters Auditorium, New York, Sept 19, 1994)* CRI ▲ CD 709 [DDD]
Roussakis, N.:Pas de deux, w. Ruotao Mao (vn) *(rec American Academy of Arts & Letters Auditorium, New York, Sept 19, 1994)* CRI ▲ CD 709 [DDD]

Pandolfi, Roland (bn)
Beethoven, L. van:Qnt Ob, 3 Hns & Bn, w. A. Simon (ob), R. Woodhams (hn), G. Stilfies (hn), G. Berry (hn) *(rec 1975–79)* Vox Box 3-▲ CD3X 3014 [ADD]

Pandolfi, Roland (hn)
Mozart, W.A.:Qnt Hn, K.407, w. J. Korman (vn), K. Mattis (vn), J. Korman (va), J. Sant'Ambrogio (vc) *(rec 1975–79)* Vox Box 3-▲ CD3X 3014 [ADD]
Mozart, W.A.:Qnt Pno, K.452, w. W. Klien (pno), P. Bowman (ob), G. Silfies (cl), G. Berry (bn) *(rec 1975–79)* Vox Box 3-▲ CD3X 3014 [ADD]

Pandolfo, Paolo (b vl)
Ortiz, D.:Trattado de Glosas, w. J. Savall (vl), T. Koopman (hpd/org), L. Duftschmid (vn), R. Lislevand (vih), A. Lawrence-King (hp) Astrée ▲ E 8717 [DDD]

Pandolfo, Paolo (db)
Scarlatti, A.:Cants & Duets, w. C. Miatello (sop), C. Cavina (alt), G. Fagotto (ten), L. Scoppola (sgr), R. Sensi (sgr), R. Alessandrini (cnd)—Clori mia, Clori bella (cant for sop, fl & bc); Dimmi crudele, e quando (duet for sop, alt & bc); Son pur care le catene (duet for sop, alt & bc); Sovente Amor mi chiama (cant for alt & bc); Ammore, brutto figlio de pottana (cant for ten & bc) [I] Tactus ▲ TC 661901
Vivaldi, A.:Sons Vn, w. F. Biondi (vn), R. Alessandrini (hpd), M. Naddeo (vc), R. Lislevand (thb/lt)—Manchester Sons. 1, 2, 3, 6, 8 & 10 Arcana ▲ ACA 4 [DDD]
Vivaldi, A.:Sons Vn, w. F. Biondi (vn), R. Alessandrini (hpd), M. Naddeo (vc), R. Lislevand (thb/lt)—Manchester Sons. 4, 5, 7, 9, 11 & 12 Arcana ▲ ACA 5 [DDD]

Pandolfo, Paolo (vl)—see also ORCHESTRAS & ENSEMBLES Labyrinto
Bach, C.P.E.:Sons Vl, w. R. Alessandrini (bc)—in g (w. obbligato keyboard), H.510 (W.88); in C & D, H.558–559 (W.136–137) Tactus ▲ TC 710201 [DDD]

▲ = CD ♦ = Enhanced CD Δ = MD ■ = Cassette Tape □ = DCC

Pandolfo, Paolo (vl) (cont.)
Bach, J.S.:Sons Vl, BWV 1027–1029, w. Rinaldo Alessandrini (hpd) Harmonia Mundi France ("Documenta" series) ▲ HMC 905218
Bach, J.S.:Suites Vc, BWV 1007–1012—in d Harmonia Mundi France ("Documenta" series) ▲ HMC 905218
Forqueray, A.:Suites (5) Va da Gamba, w. Guido Balestracci (vl), Eduardo Eguez (thb/baroque gtr), Rolf Lislevand (thb/baroque gtr), Guido Morini (clvd) Glossa 2–▲ 920401

Paneblanco, S. (hn)—see ORCHESTRAS & ENSEMBLES Arnold Quintet

Panenka, Jan (pno)—see also ORCHESTRAS & ENSEMBLES Suk Trio
Beethoven, L. van:Con 2 Pno, w. V. Smetáček (cnd), Prague SO *(rec Sept. 27–28, 1968)* Supraphon ("Collection" series) ▲ 11 0678–2 [ADD]
Beethoven, L. van:Con 3 Pno, w. V. Smetáček (cnd), Prague SO Vivace ▲ E 574 [ADD]
Beethoven, L. van:Con 4 Pno, w. V. Smetáček (cnd), Prague SO *(rec 6/71)* Supraphon ▲ 110652–2 [ADD]
Dvořák, A.:Qnt Pno, Op. 5, w. Panocha String Quartet Supraphon ▲ SUP 11 1465 [DDD]
Dvořák, A.:Qnt Pno, Op. 5, w. Smetana String Quartet Supraphon ▲ 10 4115–2 [DDD]
Dvořák, A.:Qnt Pno, Op. 81, w. Smetana String Quartet Supraphon ▲ 10 4115–2 [DDD]
Dvořák, A.:Qnt Pno, Op. 81, w. Panocha String Quartet Supraphon ▲ SUP 11 1465 [DDD]
Dvořák, A.:Sonatina Vn, w. Josef Suk (vn) Supraphon ▲ SUP 110270 [AAD]
Janáček, L.:Son Vn, w. Josef Suk (vn) Supraphon ▲ SUP 110270 [AAD]
Martinů, B.:Divertimento for Pno Left Hand & Orch, w. B. Gregor (cnd), Prague CO Supraphon ("Great Artists" series) ▲ 11 0273–2 [DDD]
Martinů, B.:Sinfonietta giocosa Pno, w. B. Gregor (cnd), Prague CO Supraphon ("Great Artists" series) ▲ 11 0273–2 [DDD]
Smetana, B.:From the Homeland, w. Josef Suk (vn) Supraphon ▲ SUP 110270 [AAD]
Suk, J.:Pieces Vn Pno, w. Josef Suk (vn) Supraphon ▲ SUP 110270 [AAD]
Suk, J.:Qt Pno, w. J. Suk (vn), J. Talich (va), M. Fukačová (vc) Supraphon ▲ SUP 111532 [DDD]

Pank, Siegfried (va)
Zelenka, J.D.:Trio Sons Obs, w. Burkhard Glaetzer (ob), Ingo Goritzki (ob), Knut Sønstevold (bn), Achim Beyer (vn), Walter-Heinz Bernstein (hpd) Berlin Classics 4–▲ BER 1150 [DDD]

Pank, Siegfried (vc)
Devienne, F.:Sons Ob, Op. 70, w. B. Glaetzner (ob), C. Shornsheim (hpd) Berlin Classics ▲ BER 1017 [DDD]
Devienne, F.:Sons Ob, Op. 71, w. B. Glaetzner (ob), C. Shornsheim (hpd) Berlin Classics ▲ BER 1017 [DDD]

Pank, Siegfried (vl)
Bach, C.P.E.:Sons Fl, w. Haupt (fl), Thalheim (hpd)—in e, H.551 (W.124); in G, H.554 (W.127); in a, H.555 (W.128); in D, H.556 (W.129); in G, H.564 (W.133); in G, H.548 (W.134) Capriccio ▲ 10101
Bach, C.P.E.:Sons Vl, w. Jaccottet (pno)—in g (w. obbligato keyboard), H.510 (W.88); in C & D, H.558–559 (W.136–137) Capriccio ▲ 10102
Bach, J.S.:Sons Fl, BWV 1030–35, w. E. Haupt (fl), C. Schornsheim (hpd)—BWV 1030–1035 & 1033 [reconstruction after Marshall] *(rec June 1989 & Jan 1990)* Berlin Classics 2–▲ BER 1007 [DDD]
Bach, J.S.:Sons Vl, BWV 1027–1029, w. I. Ahlgrimm (hpd) Capriccio ▲ CDC 10043 [DDD]
Bach, J.S.:Trio Son for 2 Fls, BWV 1039, w. E. Haupt (fl), W. Loebner (fl) *(rec June 1989 & Jan 1990)* Berlin Classics 2–▲ BER 1007 [DDD]
Fasch, J.F.:Trio Sons, w. B. Glaetzner (ob), I. Goritzki (ob), T. Reinhardt (bn), A. Beyer (vle), C. Schornsheim (hpd) Berlin Classics ▲ BER 1069 [DDD]
Vivaldi, A.:Sons Ob, w. B. Glaetzner (ob), I. Goritzki (ob), K. Suske (vn), A. Bayer (vn), T. Reinhardt (bn), C. Schornsheim (org/hpd)—RV.28, 34, 53, 81 & 779 Capriccio ▲ CD 10143 [DDD] ■ CAS 27153 (CrO2)
Zelenka, J.D.:Trio Sons Obs, w. B. Glaetzner (ob), I. Goritzki (ob), K. Sønstevold (bn), A. Beyer (vn), W. H. Bernstein (hpd) Berlin Classics 2–▲ BER 1070 [DDD]

Panke, Dietrich (vc)
Janáček, L.:Fairy Tale, w. V. Mokrosch (pno) Vengo ▲ 354.404

Panneton, Hélène (org)
Fantasia REM ▲ 311085 [DDD]

Panocha, Jiří (vn)—see also ORCHESTRAS & ENSEMBLES Panocha String Quartet, Musiktage Mondsee Ensemble
Dvořák, A.:Qnt Strs, Op. 77, w. P. Zejfart (vn), M. Sehnoutka (va), J. Kulhan (vc), P. Nejtek (db) Supraphon ▲ SUP 11 1461 [DDD]

Panteleyev, Vladimir (vc)—see ORCHESTRAS & ENSEMBLES Leontóvych String Quartet

Panteleyat, Julia (vc)
Ishchenko, Y.:Ukrainian Rhap, w. D. Manelis (pno) *(rec Sept. 1993)* Dorian Discovery ▲ DIS 80122 [DDD]
Kossenko, V.:Son Vc, w. D. Manelis (pno) *(rec Sept. 1993)* Dorian Discovery ▲ DIS 80122 [DDD]
Lisogub, I.:Son Vc, w. D. Manelis (pno) *(rec Sept. 1993)* Dorian Discovery ▲ DIS 80122 [DDD]
Shtogarenko, A.:Ballad Vc, w. D. Manelis (pno) *(rec Sept. 1993)* Dorian Discovery ▲ DIS 80122 [DDD]

Panteyeva, L. (pno)
Rubinstein, A.:Son Va, w. F. Druzhnin (va) Russian Disc ("The A. Rubinstein Edition" series) ▲ RUS 11 061 [ADD]

Pantillon, Christoph (vc)—see ORCHESTRAS & ENSEMBLES Pantillon Trio

Pantillon, Louis (vn)—see also ORCHESTRAS & ENSEMBLES Pantillon Trio
Franck, C.:Son Vn, w. S. Huter (pno) Gallo ▲ CD 632 [AAD]
Lekeu, G.:Son Vn, w. S. Huter (pno) Gallo ▲ CD 632 [AAD]

Pantillon, Marc (pno)—see also ORCHESTRAS & ENSEMBLES Pantillon Trio
Bach, J.S.:Partitas Hpd, BWV 825–830—BWV 826 Gallo ▲ CD 608 [AAD]
Beethoven, L. van:Son 8 Pno, "Pathétique" Gallo ▲ CD 608 [AAD]
Mozart, W.A.:Fant Pno, K.475 Gallo ▲ CD 608 [AAD]
Mozart, W.A.:Son 14 Pno Gallo ▲ CD 608 [AAD]

Panush, Melanie (ham dlc)
Vivaldi, A.:Cons Vn, Op. 8/1–4, "The Four Seasons", w. Jerome Franke (vn), Karine Garibova (vn), Pasquale Laurino (vn), Olga Miliaeva (va), Roza Borisova (vc), Mika Hennessy (db), Stanislav Venglevski (bayan), Mike Kashou (arabic tabla), Daryl Stuermer (gtr), Ed Paloucek (celtic fid), Gary Bottoni (highland pipe), Dubuffet String Quartet *(rec July–Sept 1995)* EarthBeat! ▲ 35270–2 [DDD]

Panzera-Baillot, Madeleine (pno)
Fauré, G.:La bonne chanson, w. C. Panzéra (bar) [F] *(rec 1936 for HMV)* Pearl ▲ PEA 9919 (m) [AAD]
Fauré, G.:Songs, w. C. Panzéra (bar)—Les berceaux; La chanson du pêcheur [F] Pearl ▲ PEA 9919 (m) [AAD]

Panzieri, Mauro (ob)—see ORCHESTRAS & ENSEMBLES Rara Ensemble

Paolini, Adriano (pno)
Bellafronte, R.:Bankiwa, w. Marco Laganà (pno) *(rec Villa Torano, Imola, Dec 1994)* Bongiovanni ▲ GB 5049–2 [DDD]
Bellafronte, R.:Bulerìas *(rec Villa Torano, Imola, Dec 1994)* Bongiovanni ▲ GB 5049–2 [DDD]
Bellafronte, R.:La Danza del serpente *(rec Villa Torano, Imola, Dec 1994)* Bongiovanni ▲ GB 5049–2 [DDD]
Bellafronte, R.:Era estate del '64, w. Gabriella Munari (sop) *(rec Villa Torano, Imola, Dec 1994)* Bongiovanni ▲ GB 5049–2 [DDD]

Papadakos, Dorothy (org)
Gubaidulina, S.:In Croce, w. Maya Beiser (vc) Koch International Classics ▲ KIC 7258 [DDD]

Papaioannou, John (pno)
Bizet, G.:Songs, w. Ursula Mayer-Reinach (mez)—Adieux de l'Hotesse Arabe; Ouvre ton Coeur Gallo ▲ CD 605
David, Felicien:Songs, w. Ursula Mayer-Reinach (mez)—Le Tchibouk; Tristesse de l'Odalisque; Reverie Gallo ▲ CD 605
Garcia Lorca, F.:Canciones, w. Ursula Mayer-Reinach (mez)—La Morillas de Jaen; Nana de Sevilla Gallo ▲ CD 605

Papaioannou, John (pno) (cont.)
Hadjidakis, M.:Songs, w. Ursula Mayer-Reinach (mez)—Pera sto tholo potami; Kelomai se gongyla; Tassa alla Venise Gallo ▲ CD 605
Meyerbeer, G.:Songs, w. Ursula Mayer-Reinach (mez)—Sie und Uch; Scirocco Gallo ▲ CD 605
Offenbach, J.:Songs, w. Ursula Mayer-Reinach (mez)—Chanson Tzigane Gallo ▲ CD 605

Paperno, Dmitri (pno)
Beethoven, L. van:Son 7 Pno Cedille ▲ CDR 90000 002 [DDD]
Brahms, J.:Fants Pno, Op. 116 Cedille ▲ CDR 90000 002 [DDD]
Busoni, F.:Chaconne Pno Cedille ▲ CDR 90000 002 [DDD]
Chopin, F.:Pno Music (misc)—Scherzo No. 1 in b, Op. 20; Impromptu No. 2 in f#, Op. 38; Ballade No. 4 in f, Op. 52; Nocturne in c#, Op. 27/1; Fant in f, Op. 49; Prelude in c#, Op. 45; Etudes in a, Op. 10/2 & in F, Op. 10/8; Con in f, Op. 21 [2nd movt]; Mazurkas in f#, Op. 59/3 & in Ab, Op. 41/4; Scherzo No. 4 in E, Op. 54 Cedille ▲ CDR 90000026 [DDD]
Liadov, A.:Vars on a Polish Folk Theme Cedille ▲ CDR 90000 001 [DDD]
Medtner, N.:Forgotten Melodies 1—Nos. 6–8, "Canzona serenata, Danza silvestra & alla Reminiscenza" Cedille ▲ CDR 90000 001 [DDD]
Rachmaninoff, S.:Preludes Pno, Opp 23 & 32—Op. 23, Nos. 7 & 10; Op 32, Nos. 5,10,11 & 12 Cedille ▲ CDR 90000 001 [DDD]
Schubert, Franz:Son Pno, D.894—"Fantasy" movt. Cedille ▲ CDR 90000 002 [DDD]
Scriabin, A.:Son 2 Pno Cedille ▲ CDR 90000 001 [DDD]
Tchaikovsky, P.:Pno Music—Meditation, Op. 72/5; 4 selections from The Seasons (Op. 37b, Nos. 8–11) Cedille ▲ CDR 90000 001 [DDD]
Uncommon Encores Cedille ▲ CDR 90000 007 [DDD]

Papp, D. (tpt)
Gregson, E.:Celebration, w. M. Kane (tpt), J. Burgess (tpt), E. Corporon (cnd), Cincinnati College Conservatory of Music Wind Sym Klavier ▲ KCD 11047 [DDD]

Papp, Sándor (va)—see also ORCHESTRAS & ENSEMBLES Éder String Quartet
Spohr, L.:Qnts Strs (comp), w. Haydn String Quartet Budapest—No. 5, Op. 106 & No. 6, Op. 129 *(rec Unitarian Church, Budapest, Sept. 6–10, 1993)* Marco Polo ▲ 8.223598 [DDD]
Spohr, L.:Qnts Strs (comp), w. New Haydn String Quartet—No. 3 in b, Op. 69 & No. 4 in a, Op 91 *(rec Unitarian Church, Budapest, Apr 17–20, 1994)* Marco Polo ▲ 8.223599 [DDD]
Spohr, L.:Qnts Strs, Op. 33, w. Danubius Quartet *(rec Budapest)* Marco Polo ▲ 8.223597 [DDD]

Pappano, Antonio (pno)
Rossini, G.:Songs, w. Rockwell Blake (ten)—La promessa; La gita in gondola; L'orgia; Il rimprovero; La danza; La partenza; Le dodo des enfants; Romeó; Le sylvain; Le Lazzarone; Ariette à l'ancienne; Au chevet d'un mourant; La dichiarazione; Il fanciullo smarito; La lontanza; L'esule; Nizza; Mi lagnero tacendo (9 versions); La duo des chats [w Gérard Lesne (ct)] EMI Classics ▲ CDC 55614

Pappas, Iakovos (hpd)
Bach, J.S.:Cons solo Hpd, BWV 972–987—BWV 972 & 978 Arkadia-Akademia 2–▲ 120
Le Roux, G.:Kbd Music, w. P. Baylac (hpd)—Suites 1–7 Arkadia-Akademia ▲ 127 [DDD]
Platti, G.B.:Sons Hpd Arkadia-Akademia ▲ 132 [DDD]
Vivaldi, A.:Sons for 2 Vns, Op. 1 [trans. Pappas for harpsichord] Arkadia-Akademia 2–▲ 120

Parakilas, James (pno)—see ORCHESTRAS & ENSEMBLES Penumbra

Paraskivesco, Théodore (pno)
Ravel, M.:Chansons madécasses, w. J. Herbillon (bar), C. Lardé (fl), P. Degenne (vc) [F] Calliope ▲ CAL 9893 [ADD]

Paratore, Anthony (pno)
Beethoven, L. van:Vars on "Ich denke dein", WoO 74, w. J. Paratore (pno) Koch Schwann ▲ CD 310 088 [ADD]
Classics to Broadway, w. Joseph Paratore (pno) Koch Schwann ▲ SCH 310115 [DDD]
Downey, J.:Adagio Lyrico, w. J. Paratore (pno) Gasparo ▲ GS 276
Gottschalk, L.M.:Sym 1, "La nuit des tropiques", w. J. Paratore (pno) [arr. in 1948 for 2 pianos] New World ▲ 80208–2
Grainger, P.:Fant on Gershwin's *Porgy & Bess*, w. J. Paratore (pno) Koch Schwann ▲ CD 310 115 [DDD] ■ MC 210 115 (D)
Lutoslawski, W.:Vars on a Theme of Paganini for 2 Pnos, w. J. Paratore (pno) Koch Schwann ▲ CD 310 088 [ADD]
Mendelssohn, F.:Cons (2) for 2 Pnos, w. J. Paratore (pno), U. Lajovic (cnd), Berlin Radio Sinfonietta Koch Schwann ▲ CD 311 051 [ADD]
Mendelssohn, F.:Cons (2) for 2 Pnos, w. J. Paratore (pno), U. Lajovic (cnd), Berlin Radio Sinfonietta CBS ▲ MK 42523 [DDD]
Mendelssohn, F.:Sym 1, w. J. Paratore (pno) [Busoni's 1890 two-piano trans.] Koch Schwann ▲ CD 310113 [ADD]
Mendelssohn, F.:Vars Pno 4-Hands, w. J. Paratore (pno) Koch Schwann ▲ CD 310 088 [ADD]
Mussorgsky, M.:Pictures at an Exhibition, w. J. Paratore (pno) [trans Reginald Haché for 2 pianos] Koch Schwann ▲ CD 310113 [ADD]
Saint-Saëns, C.:Variations on a Theme of Beethoven, w. J. Paratore (pno) Koch Schwann ▲ CD 310 088 [ADD]
Schoenberg, A.:Chamber Sym 1, w. J. Paratore (pno) [Berg's 1915 arr. for piano duet] Koch Schwann ▲ CD 311 034 [ADD]
Schumann, R.:Andante & Vars Pnos, w. J. Paratore (pno) Koch Schwann ▲ CD 310 088 [ADD]
Schumann, R.:Andante & Vars Pnos, w. J. Paratore (pno) *(rec mid/late 1970s)* Koch Treasure ▲ 31627–2 [ADD]
Stravinsky, I.:Con Pnos, w. Joseph Paratore (pno) Koch Schwann ▲ SCH 314382 [DDD]
Stravinsky, I.:Le Sacre du printemps Pno, w. Joseph Paratore (pno) Koch Schwann ▲ SCH 314382 [DDD]
Variations for 4-Hands, w. Paratore, Anthony (pno), Joseph Paratore (pno) Koch Schwann ▲ SCH 310088 [ADD]

Paratore, Joseph (pno)
Beethoven, L. van:Vars on "Ich denke dein", WoO 74, w. A. Paratore (pno) Koch Schwann ▲ CD 310 088 [ADD]
Classics to Broadway, w. Anthony Paratore (pno) Koch Schwann ▲ SCH 310115 [DDD]
Downey, J.:Adagio Lyrico, w. A. Paratore (pno) Gasparo ▲ GS 276
Gottschalk, L.M.:Sym 1, "La nuit des tropiques", w. A. Paratore (pno) [arr. in 1948 for 2 pianos] New World ▲ 80208–2
Grainger, P.:Fant on Gershwin's *Porgy & Bess*, w. A. Paratore (pno) Koch Schwann ▲ CD 310 115 [DDD] ■ MC 210 115 (D)
Lutoslawski, W.:Vars on a Theme of Paganini for 2 Pnos, w. A. Paratore (pno) Koch Schwann ▲ CD 310 088 [ADD]
Mendelssohn, F.:Cons (2) for 2 Pnos, w. A. Paratore (pno), U. Lajovic (cnd), Berlin Radio Sinfonietta CBS ▲ MK 42523 [DDD]
Mendelssohn, F.:Cons (2) for 2 Pnos, w. A. Paratore (pno), U. Lajovic (cnd), Berlin Radio Sinfonietta Koch Schwann ▲ CD 311 051 [ADD]
Mendelssohn, F.:Sym 1, w. A. Paratore (pno) [Busoni's 1890 two-piano trans.] Koch Schwann ▲ CD 310113 [ADD]
Mendelssohn, F.:Vars Pno 4-Hands, w. A. Paratore (pno) Koch Schwann ▲ CD 310 088 [ADD]
Mussorgsky, M.:Pictures at an Exhibition, w. A. Paratore (pno) [trans Reginald Haché for 2 pianos] Koch Schwann ▲ CD 310113 [ADD]
Saint-Saëns, C.:Variations on a Theme of Beethoven, w. A. Paratore (pno) Koch Schwann ▲ CD 310 088 [ADD]
Schoenberg, A.:Chamber Sym 1, w. A. Paratore (pno) [Berg's 1915 arr. for piano duet] Koch Schwann ▲ CD 311 034 [ADD]
Schumann, R.:Andante & Vars Pnos, w. A. Paratore (pno) Koch Schwann ▲ CD 310 088 [ADD]
Schumann, R.:Andante & Vars Pnos, w. A. Paratore (pno) *(rec mid/late 1970s)* Koch Treasure ▲ 31627–2 [ADD]
Stravinsky, I.:Con Pnos, w. Anthony Paratore (pno) Koch Schwann ▲ SCH 314382 [DDD]
Stravinsky, I.:Le Sacre du printemps Pno, w. Anthony Paratore (pno) Koch Schwann ▲ SCH 314382 [DDD]
Variations for 4-Hands, w. Anthony Paratore (pno) Koch Schwann ▲ SCH 310088 [ADD]

INSTRUMENT.

Parchman, Thomas (cl)—see ORCHESTRAS & ENSEMBLES Penumbra
Parejo, Alvarez (pno)
Braga, E.:Songs, w. T. Berganza (mez)—6 songs [Port] Claves ▲ CD 8401 [DDD]
Guastavino, C.:Songs, w. T. Berganza (mez)—9 songs [Sp] Claves ▲ CD 8401 [DDD]
Villa-Lobos, H.:Songs, w. T. Berganza (sop)—6 songs [Port] Claves ▲ CD 8401 [DDD]
Parham, Lucy (pno)
Fauré, G.:Ballade Pno, w. J.-C. Casadesus (cnd), Royal PO RPO ▲ RPO 7023 [DDD]
Franck, C.:Les Djinns, w. J.-C. Casadesus (cnd), Royal PO RPO ▲ RPO 7023 [DDD]
Franck, C.:Symphonic Vars, w. J.-C. Casadesus (cnd), Royal PO RPO ▲ RPO 7023 [DDD]
Ravel, M.:Con in G Pno, w. J.-C. Casadesus (cnd), Royal PO RPO ▲ RPO 7023 [DDD]
Showcase:The Classics, w. B. Wordsworth (cnd), BBC Concert Orch IMP ("Classics" series) ▲ IMP 6700662
Parikian, Manoug (vn)
Vivaldi, A.:Cons Vn, Op. 8/1-4, "The Four Seasons", w. Jose-Luis Garcia (vn), Maurice Hasson (vn), Daniel Phillips (vn), Y. Menuhin (cnd), English CO [each movt. w. different vn soloist] Start Classics ▲ SCD 13
Paris, Massimo (vl)
Vivaldi, A.:Music of, w. Salvatore Accardo (vn), Frederico Agostini (vn), Heinz Holliger (ob), Ida Levin (vn), Aurele Nicolet (fl), Angel Romero (gtr), Celedonio Romero (gtr), Celine Romero (gtr), Henryk Szeryng (vn), Pinchas Zukerman (vn), Academy of St. Martin in the Fields, English CO, I Musici, Naples Weekly International Soloists, St. Paul CO, Dresden Staatskapelle—The Four Seasons [Winter]; Con in D for Gtr [Largo]; Con in D for Fl, "Il gardellino" [Cantabile]; Con in C for Diverse Insts [Andante molto]; Con in g for Strs [Andante molto]; Con in D for 2 Vns & 2 Vcs [Largo]; Con in g for Ob, Vn, Ww & Strs [Larghetto]; Con in a for Gtr, "L'estro armonico" [Largo]; Con in F for 3 Vns [Andante]; Con in F for Fl [Largo]; Con in d for Va D'Amore [Largo]; Con in E for Vn & Strs, "Il riposo" [Allegro]; Con in G for Ob, Bn & Strs [Largo]; Con in B♭ for Vn & Strs [Largo]; Con in A for Gtr & Strs [Larghetto]; Con in E for Vn & Strs, "L'amoroso" [Allegro]; Con in G for Fl [Largo]; Con in A for Vn [Larghetto]; Con in c for Vn & Strs, "Il sospetto" [Andante]; Con in a for 2 Obs & Strs [Largo]; Con in g for Orch [Largo non molto]; Con in a for Vn [Largo]; Con in C for Ob [Adagio]; Con in g for Fl, "La notte" [Largo] Philips ▲ 454051-2 ■ 454 051-4
Parisi, Osvaldo (lt)
Eschenbach, W. von:Titurel, w. Reinhold Wiedenmann (voc)—2 fragments Koch Schwann ▲ SCH 318322 [DDD]
Parisot, (vc)
Vivaldi, A.:Con for 2 Vcs, w. J. Starker (vc), E. de Carvalho (cnd), Paraiba SO—Finale Delos ▲ DE 1018 [DDD]
Park, Jong-Sol (piri)
Kim, J.H.:Piri Qt, w. Chung Jae-Guk (piri), Yang Myung-Sok (piri), Joseph Celli (ob/E hn) O. O. Discs ▲ OO24
Park, S.-W. (kayagum/ajang/sgr)—see ORCHESTRAS & ENSEMBLES Far East Side Band
Párkányi, Tibor (vc)
David, Felicien:Trio 2 Pno, w. I. Prunyi (pno), E. Pérény (vn) Marco Polo ▲ 8.223492
David, Felicien:Trio 3 Pno, w. I. Prunyi (pno), E. Pérény (vn) Marco Polo ▲ 8.223492
Parkening, Christopher (gtr)
Angels' Glory, w. Kathleen Battle (sop) Sony Classical ▲ SK 62723 ■ ST 62723
The Artistry of Christopher Parkening EMI Classics ▲ CDC 54853 ■ 4DS 54853
Bach, J.S.:Jesu bleibet meine Freude EMI Classics ■ 4DS 37343-4 (D)
Bach, J.S.:Music of EMI Classics ▲ CDC 47191-2
Bach, J.S.:Music of, w. Los Angeles CO EMI Classics ▲ CDC 47195-2
Bach, J.S.:Sheep May Safely Graze EMI Classics ■ 4DS 37343-4 (D)
The Great Recordings EMI Classics 2-▲ ZDCB 54905 2-■ 4D2S 54905
In the Spanish Style EMI Classics ▲ CDC 47194 ■ 4XS 36020
Music of Bach, Handel, Visée, Weiss, F. Couperin, A. Scarlatti EMI Classics ▲ CDC 47191
Pleasures of Their Company, w. Kathleen Battle (sop) EMI Classics ▲ CDC 47196 [DDD] ■ 4DS 37351 (D)
Ponce, M.:Preludes Gtr EMI Classics ■ 4XS 36020
Rodrigo, J.:Concierto de Aranjuez, w. A. Litton (cnd), Royal PO EMI Classics ▲ CDC 54665 ■ 4DS 54665
Rodrigo, J.:Fant para un gentilhombre, w. A. Litton (cnd), Royal PO EMI Classics ▲ CDC 54665 ■ 4DS 54665
Simple Gifts Angel ▲ CDC 47525
A Tribute to Segovia EMI Classics ▲ CDC 49404 [DDD] ■ 4DS 49404 (D)
Virtuoso Duets, w. David Brandon (gtr) EMI Classics ▲ CDC 49406
Walton, W.:Bagatelles Gtr, w. A. Litton (cnd), Royal PO EMI Classics ▲ CDC 54665 ■ 4DS 54665
Parker, Andrew (va)—see ORCHESTRAS & ENSEMBLES Balanescu String Quartet
Parker, Glenn (pno)
Brahms, J.:Liebeslieder Waltzes SATB, w. Nancianne Parrella (pno), Joseph Flummerfeldt (cnd), Westminster Choir—Nos. 8-16 *(rec Bristol Chapel, Westminster Choir College of Rider Univ., Princeton, NJ, May 14-16, 1995)* Delos ▲ DE 3193 [DDD]
Brahms, J.:Neue Liebeslieder Waltzes, w. Nancianne Parrella (pno), Joseph Flummerfeldt (cnd), Westminster Choir—No. 15 *(rec Bristol Chapel, Westminster Choir College of Rider Univ., Princeton, NJ, May 14-16, 1995)* Delos ▲ DE 3193
Brahms, J.:Qts SATB, Op. 64, w. Nancianne Parrella (pno), Joseph Flummerfeldt (cnd), Westminster Choir—Nos. 1 & 2 *(rec Bristol Chapel, Westminster Choir College of Rider Univ., Princeton, NJ, May 14-16, 1995)* Delos ▲ DE 3193 [DDD]
Brahms, J.:Qts SATB, Op. 92, w. Nancianne Parrella (pno), Joseph Flummerfeldt (cnd), Westminster Choir—Nos. 2 & 3 *(rec Bristol Chapel, Westminster Choir College of Rider Univ., Princeton, NJ, May 14-16, 1995)* Delos ▲ DE 3193 [DDD]
Brahms, J.:Zigeunerlieder, w. Nancianne Parrella (pno), Joseph Flummerfeldt (cnd), Westminster Choir—Nos 5-9 *(rec Bristol Chapel, Westminster Choir College of Rider Univ., Princeton, NJ, May 14-16, 1995)* Delos ▲ DE 3193 [DDD]
Parker, Jamie (pno)—see ORCHESTRAS & ENSEMBLES Montreal Chamber Group, Gryphon Piano Trio
Parker, John Kimura (pno)
Chopin, F.:Pno Music (misc)—Ballade in A♭, Op. 47; 2 Études, Op. 10/3 & 12; 2 Nocturnes, Op. 9/2 & Op. 27/2; Polonaise in A, Op. 40/1; Scherzo in b♭, Op. 31; 2 Waltzes, Op. 64/1 & 2 Telarc ▲ CD 80147 [DDD]
Chopin, F.:Pno Music (misc)—Scherzo in B♭, Op. 31; Ballade in A♭, Op. 47; Sonata No. 2 in b♭, Op. 35; 2 Études, Op. 10; Polonaise in A, Op. 40/1; 2 Waltzes, Op. 64; 2 Nocturnes, Op. 9/2 & Op. 27/2 Telarc ▲ CD 82003
Chopin, F.:Son Pno, Op. 35 Telarc ▲ CD 80147 [DDD]
Prokofiev, S.:Con 3 Pno, w. A. Previn (cnd), Royal PO Telarc ▲ CD 80124 [DDD]
Parker, Sylvia (pno)
Calabro, L.:Son-Fant Tuba, w. M. Nelson (tuba) *(rec 12/90-1/91)* Crystal ▲ CD 691
Cummings, B.:Fant Breve, w. M. Nelson (pno) *(rec 12/90-1/91)* Crystal ▲ CD 691
New England Reveries, w. Mark Nelson (tuba) Crystal ▲ CD 691
Tchaikovsky, P.:Con 1 Pno, w. A. Previn (cnd), Royal PO Telarc ▲ CD 80124 [DDD]
Parker-Smith, Jane (org)
Janácek, L.:Slavonic Mass, w. F. Palmer (sop), A. Gunson (mez), M. King (mez), J. Mitchinson (ten), S. Rattle (cnd), City of Birmingham SO, City of Birmingham Sym Chorus EMI ▲ CDC 47504
Popular French Romantics ASV ▲ ASV 539
Widor, C.M.:Sym 5 Org ASV ▲ ASV 958 [DDD]
Widor, C.M.:Sym 7 Org ASV ▲ ASV 958 [DDD]
Parkhouse, David (pno)
Elgar, E.:Son Vn, w. H. Bean (vn) Classics for Pleasure ▲ CDCFP 4632 [ADD]
Gershwin, G.:"I Got Rhythm" Vars, w. B. Herrmann (cnd), London Festival Recording Ensemble *(rec DECCA Studio No. 3, West Hampstead, London, Nov 1971)* London ("Phase 4 Stereo" series) ▲ 444785-2 [ADD]
Parkin, Eric (pno)
American Piano Works, Vol. 1, w. Parkin, Eric (pno) Preamble ▲ PAM 1776 [DDD]
Antheil, G.:Son 4 Pno Preamble ▲ PRCD 1776 [DDD]
Barber, S.:Ballade Chandos ▲ CHAN 9177 [DDD]
Barber, S.:Excursions Preamble ▲ PRCD 1776 [DDD]
Barber, S.:Excursions Chandos ▲ CHAN 9177 [DDD]
Barber, S.:Nocturne, "Homage to John Field" Chandos ▲ CHAN 9177 [DDD]
Barber, S.:Son Pno Chandos ▲ CHAN 9177 [DDD]
Barber, S.:Souvenirs [arr. for solo piano] Chandos ▲ CHAN 9177 [DDD]
Bax, A.:Pno Music—Country-Tune (1920); Lullaby (1920); Winter Waters (1915) Chandos ▲ CHAN 8496 [DDD]
Bax, A.:Pno Music—A Hill Tune (1920); In a Vodka Shop (1915); Water Music (1920) Chandos ▲ CHAN 8497 [DDD]
Bax, A.:Son 1 Pno Chandos ▲ CHAN 8496 [DDD]
Bax, A.:Son 2 Pno Chandos ▲ CHAN 8496 [DDD]
Bax, A.:Son 3 Pno Chandos ▲ CHAN 8497 [DDD]
Bax, A.:Son 4 Pno Chandos ▲ CHAN 8497 [DDD]
Chaminade, C.:Pno Music (misc)—Minuetto, Op. 23; Sérénade, Op. 29; Air de ballet, Op. 30; Guitare, Op. 32; Autumne (No. 2 from Six études de concert, Op. 35); Pas des écharpes, Op. 37; Toccata, Op. 39; Pierrette, Op. 41; La Lisonjera, Op. 50; Lolita (caprice espagnol), Op. 54; Three Romances sans paroles (Nos. 1,3 & 6 from Six Romances sans paroles, Op. 76); Autrefois (No. 4 from Six pièces humoristiques, Op. 87); Danse créole, Op. 94; Valse arabesque (No. 4 from Feuillets d'Album, Op. 98); Sous le masque, Op. 116; Contes bleus No. 2, Op. 122; Air à danser, Op. 164; Pas des sylphes [Intermezzo] (1908) Chandos ▲ CHAN 8888 [DDD]
Copland, A.:Midday Thoughts Preamble ▲ PRCD 1776 [DDD]
Copland, A.:Our Town Pno Preamble ▲ PRCD 1776 [DDD]
Copland, A.:Pno Music—The Cat & the Mouse; Midsummer Nocturne; plus others Silva America ▲ SSD 1009 ■ SSC 1009
Copland, A.:Proclamation Preamble ▲ PRCD 1776 [DDD]
Dyson, G.:Con Leggiero, w. R. Hickox (cnd), City of London Sinfonia Chandos ▲ CHAN 9076 [DDD]
Gershwin, G.:Preludes (3) Pno Preamble ▲ PRCD 1776 [DDD]
Granados, E.:Goyescas Chandos ▲ CHAN 9412 [DDD]
Ireland, J.:Con Pno, w. B. Thomson (cnd), London PO Chandos ▲ CHAN 8461 [DDD]
Ireland, J.:Legend, w. B. Thomson (cnd), London PO Chandos ▲ CHAN 8461 [DDD]
Ireland, J.:Pno Music—Piano Sonata in e (1918-20); Four Preludes (1913-15); Decorations (suite for piano—1912); Rhapsody (1915); Summer Evening (1919); The Almond Tree (1913); The Towing-Path; Merry Andrew Chandos ▲ CHAN 9056 [DDD]
Ireland, J.:Pno Music—In Those Days; London Pieces (1917-20); Leaves from a Child's Sketchbook; The Darkened Valley; 2 Pieces; Equinox; Sonatina (1927-27); Prelude in E♭; Ballade (1929); Greenways Chandos ▲ CHAN 9140 [DDD]
Ireland, J.:Pno Music—A Sea Idyll; On a Birthday Morning; Soliloquy; April; Bergomask; Spring Will Not Wait; February's Child; Aubade; Ballade of London Nights; Month's Mind; A Grecian Lad; The Boy Bishop; Puck's Birthday; Columbine; Sarnia Chandos ▲ CHAN 9250 [DDD]
Mayerl, W.J.:Pno Music—Ace of Hearts, Ace of Diamonds & The Joker (from the *Four Aces* Suite); Prelude, Merlin the Wizard, Lady of the Lake & The Passing of Arthur (from *The Legends of King Arthur*); Railroad rhythm; Marigold; Almond blossom; April's fool; The harp of the winds; From a Spanish lattice; Song of the fir tree; Nimble fingered gentleman; Shallow waters; Evening primrose Chandos ▲ CHAN 8560 [DDD]
Mayerl, W.J.:Pno Music—Aquarium Suite; Ace of Clubs and Ace of Spades (from the Four Aces Suite); Three Dances in Syncopation, Op. 73; Autumn crocus; Hollyhock; Mistletoe; White heather; Bats in the belfry; Green tulips; Sweet William; Parade of the sandwich-board man; Kop-o'-my-thumb; Jill all alone Chandos ▲ CHAN 8848 [DDD]
Mayerl, W.J.:Pno Music—Filigree; 3 Miniatures in Syncopation; Siberian Lament; In My Garden:Summertime; from 3 Japanese Pictures; Beguine Impromptu; The Big Top; Legends of King A.; Honky-Tonk; In My Garden; Autumntime; Romanesque; Insect Oddities; Leprechaun's Leap Chandos ▲ CHAN 9141 [DDD]
Poulenc, F.:Pno Music (misc)—Adagietto (from *Les biches*); Badinage; Intermezzo No. 3 in A♭; Mouvements perpétuels; Napoli (suite); Les Soirées de Nazelles; Suite for Piano; Trois pièces; Valse-Improvisation sur le nom de Bach Chandos ▲ CHAN 8637 [DDD]
Poulenc, F.:Pno Music (misc)—Suite Française; Villageoises; 15 Improvisations; Thème varié; 3 Novelettes; 2 Intermezzi; Humoresque; Mélancolie; Presto in B♭ Chandos ▲ CHAN 8847 [DDD]
Roussel, A.:Pno Music—Rustiques, Op. 5; Suite in f♯, Op. 14; Sonatine, Op. 16; Segovia, Op. 29; Prélude et Fugue, Op. 46; Trois pièces, Op. 49; Doute (1919) Chandos ▲ CHAN 8887 [DDD]
Rózsa, M.:Bagatellen Cambria ▲ CD 1081 [ADD]
Rózsa, M.:Son Pno Cambria ▲ CD 1081 [ADD]
Rózsa, M.:Vars Pno Cambria ▲ CD 1081 [ADD]
Rózsa, M.:The Vintner's Daughter Cambria ▲ CD 1081 [ADD]
Stevens, H.:Intrada Preamble ▲ PRCD 1776 [DDD]
Stevens, H.:Inventions Preamble ▲ PRCD 1776 [DDD]
Walton, W.:Sinf Concertante, w. J. Latham-König (cnd), London PO Chandos ▲ CHAN 9148 [DDD]
Waxman, F.:The Charm Bracelet Pno Preamble ▲ PRCD 1776 [DDD]
Parkins, Maggie (vc/sgr)—see ORCHESTRAS & ENSEMBLES Gangster Band
Parkins, Margaret (vc)—see ORCHESTRAS & ENSEMBLES Bantam Orch
Parkins, Robert (org)
Brahms, J.:Org Musc (comp) [at the Flentrop Organ, Chapel of Duke Univeristy, Durham, NC] *(rec Jan. 4-5, 1994)* Naxos ▲ 8.550824 [DDD]
Early Iberian Organ Music, w. *(rec Apr. 1992)* Naxos ▲ 8.550705 [DDD]
Parkins, Sara (vn)—see ORCHESTRAS & ENSEMBLES Bantam Orch, Gangster Band
Parkins, Zeena (elec hp/sampler/pno)—see ORCHESTRAS & ENSEMBLES Gangster Band
Parkins, Zeena (hp/pno/acc)
Shea, D.:Hsi-Yu Chi, w. Sim Cain (perc), Hideki Kato (bass instrument), Wu Man (pipa), Jim Pugliese (perc), Mark Ribot (gtr/banjo), David Shea (sampler/pno/turntables), Alex Tobias (celtic dr/misc.), Rebecca Wilson (screaming), John Zorn (a sax) Tzadik ("The Composers" series) ▲ TZA 7005 [DDD]
Parkins, Zeena (kbd)
Exquisite Corpses from P.S. 122, w. David Watson (shears/stick vn/gtr/tpt), Judy Dunaway (gtr/balloons), Anthony Coleman (sampler), Raissa St. Pierre (drums), Guy Yarden (vn/pno), Leslie Ross (bn), Linda Austin (gtr), Bruce Kaplan (gtr), Doug Henderson (peckhorn/bass/toy pno), Sue Ann Harkey (gtr), Cinnie Cole (sampler), et. al. ¿What Next? ▲ WN 0002 [ADD]
Parkins, Zeena (org/syn)
Sharp, E.:20 Below, w. Anthony Coleman (toy pno/org), Wayne Horvitz (syn), Joseph Paul Taylor (elec/syn), Gwen Toth (reed org), David Weinstein (org/syn) Newport Classics ▲ NPD 85504
Parkinson, Kelly (vn)
Beside Thy Cradle, w. [cnd:Ralph B. Woodward], Salt Lake Children's Choir, Tamara B. Oswald (hp), Janet Peterson (hp), Victoria Ferris (vn), Hadley Ferris (va), Ellen Bridger (vc) *(rec Maurice Abravanel Hall, Salt Lake City)* Cherbourne ▲ CH 121
Parkinson, Rebecca (org)
Gawthrop, D.:This Child, This King, w. Tamara Bischoff-Oswald (hp), Dennis Griffin (timp), Will Kesling (cnd), Utah State Univ Chamber Singers *(rec Kent Concert Hall, USU Chase Fine Arts Center, Logan, UT, Feb. 4-5, 1995)* Integra Classic ▲ IMCD 951 [DDD]
Parkinson, Zaidee (pno)
Debussy, C.:Preludes Pno (sels)—Book 1 Connoisseur Society ▲ CD 4198
Janácek, L.:In the Mists Connoisseur Society ▲ CD 4198
Parks, Joanna (perc)
Zwilich, E.T.:Passages, w. Leslie Boucher (sop), Julie Stone (fl/pic), Tod Kerstetter (cl/b cl), Andrew Carlson (vn), Philip Singleton (va), Juanita Karpf (vc), F. Joseph Lozier (pno), Shannon O'Kelley (perc) *(rec Roswell United Methodist Church, Roswell, GA)* ACA Digital ▲ CM 20027
Parloff, Michael (fl)
Michael Parloff, w. Gerald Ranck (hpd), Warren Jones (pno) ESS.A.Y ▲ ESS 1027

▲ = CD ♦ = Enhanced CD Δ = MD ■ = Cassette Tape □ = DCC

Parloff, Michael (fl) (cont.)
Stravinsky, I.:Octet, w. D. Schiffrin (cl), F. Morelli (bn), S. Heinneman (bn), R. Mase (tpt), C. Gekker (tpt), R. Borror (trbn), D. Taylor (trbn), G. Schuller (cnd) *(rec Sep. 1991)* GM ▲ GM 2030

Parlow, Kathleen (vn)
Grieg, E.:Son 2 Vn, w. E. MacMillan (pno) *(rec Oct. 13, 1941)* Analekta ▲ AN 2 7804

Parmentier, Edward (hpd)—see also ORCHESTRAS & ENSEMBLES Musica Pacifica
Anglebert, J.-H. d':Pièces de clavecin—Prelude in g; Passacaglia d'Armide; Tombeau de Monsieur Chambonnières Wildboar ▲ WLBR 8502 [DDD]
Bach, J.S.:Partitas Hpd, BWV 825–830 *(rec Bethel United Church of Christ, Manchester, MI, June 1991)* Wildboar 2-▲ WLBR 9101 [DDD]
Chambonnières, J.C. de:Hpd Music—Pièces de clavecin in F [Rondeau, Chaconne, Brusque] Wildboar ▲ WLBR 8502 [DDD]
Couperin, L.:Suites Hpd—Suite in D Wildboar ▲ WLBR 8502 [DDD]
Froberger, J.J.:Hpd Music—Tocatta IV; Canzon VI; Suite in c; Tombeau de Monsieur de Blanrocher Wildboar ▲ WLBR 8502 [DDD]
Marais, M.:Dances, w. Y. Schotten (va) Crystal ▲ CD 635
Musick as befitts a Quene:English Virginal Music 1570–1650 *(rec June 1992)* Wildboar ▲ WLBR 9102 [DDD]
Scarlatti, D.:Sons Kbd—Fugue in D, K.417; Sons, K.24, 27, 87, 140, 213, 214, 219, 224, 263 & 264 *(rec First United Church, Manchester, MI, 1981 & 1985)* Wildboar ▲ WLBR 8501 [DDD]

Parnas, Leslie (vc)
Bach, J.S.:A Musical Offering, w. J.-P. Rampal (fl), I. Stern (vn), J. Ritter (hpd)—trio, section 8 CBS ▲ MK 37813 [DDD]
Dohnányi, E. von:Son Vc, w. W. Kim (pno) *(rec 1992)* Arcadia ▲ ARC 1998-2 [DDD]
Hindemith, P.:Son Vc, Op. 25/3 Arcadia ▲ ARC 1992-2 [DDD]
Kabalevsky, D.:Son Vc, w. M. Frager (pno) Arcadia ▲ ARC 1992-2 [DDD]
Porpora, N.A.:Son Vc, w. W. Kim (pno) *(rec 1992)* Arcadia ▲ ARC 1998-2 [DDD]
Reger, M.:Son Vc, Op. 5, w. W. Kim (pno) *(rec 1992)* Arcadia ▲ ARC 1998-2 [DDD]
Schubert, Franz:Qnt Pno, D.667, w. R. Serkin (pno), J. Laredo (vn), P. Naegele (va), J. Levine (db) *(rec 1967)* Sony Classical ▲ SMK 46252 [ADD]
Schubert, Franz:Qnt Strs, D.956, w. A. Kavafian (vn), I. Kavafian (vn), P. Neubauer (va), F. Sherry (vc) Omega ▲ OCD 1015 [DDD]
Shostakovich, D.:Son Vc, w. M. Frager (pno) Arcadia ▲ ARC 1992-2 [DDD]
Yun, I.:Nore Vc, w. W. Kim (pno) *(rec 1992)* Arcadia ▲ ARC 1998-2 [DDD]

Parodi, Giancarlo (org)
Valeri, G.:Sons Org—15 sels *(rec Morcote, Switzerland, 1979)* Dynamic ▲ CDS 09 [ADD]

Parola, Michael (mar)
Martino, D.:Set for Mar *(rec Houghton Chapel, Wellesley College, MA, June 1995)* New World ▲ 80518-2

Parola, Michael (perc)—see ORCHESTRAS & ENSEMBLES Aequalis, Core Ensemble

Parr, Patricia (pno)—see also ORCHESTRAS & ENSEMBLES Amici Quartet
Bernstein, L.:Son Cl, w. J. Valdepeñas (cl) CBC ("Musica Viva" series) ▲ MVCD 1016 [DDD]
Debussy, C.:Petite pièce, w. J. Valdepeñas (cl) CBC ("Musica Viva" series) ▲ MVCD 1016 [DDD]
Lutoslawski, W.:Dance Preludes Cl, Hp, Pno, Perc & Strs, w. J. Valdepeñas (cl) CBC ("Musica Viva" series) ▲ MVCD 1016 [DDD]
Morawetz, O.:Son Cl, w. J. Valdepeñas (cl) CBC ("Musica Viva" series) ▲ MVCD 1016 [DDD]
Morawetz, O.:Weaver, w. M. DuBois (ten), J. Valdepeñas (cl) Centrediscs ▲ CDCCD 3589 [DDD]
Penderecki, K.:Miniatures Cl, w. J. Valdepeñas (cl) CBC ("Musica Viva" series) ▲ MVCD 1016 [DDD]
Weber, C.M. von:Grand duo concertant Cl, w. J. Valdepeñas (cl) CBC ("Musica Viva" series) ▲ MVCD 1016 [DDD]

Parra, Gustavo Delgado (org)
Autour du livre d'orgue de Mexico, w. Ofelia Castellanos (org) K617 ▲ 7059

Parran, J.D. (cl)
Lockwood, A.:Thousand Year Dreaming, w. Art Baron (conch shell/trbn/didjerido), Liby Van Cleve (ob/E hn), Jon Gibson (didjeridu), Michael Publiese (perc), Scott Robinson (conch shell/perc), John Snyder (didjeridu/waterphone), Charles Wood (tam-tam, stones), Peter Zummo (trbn/didjeridu) ¿What Next? ▲ WN 0010

Parrella, Nancienne (pno)
Brahms, J.:Liebeslieder Waltzes SATB, w. Glenn Parker (pno), Joseph Flummerfeldt (cnd), Westminster Choir—Nos. 8–16 *(rec Bristol Chapel, Westminster Choir College of Rider Univ., Princeton, NJ, May 14-16, 1995)* Delos ▲ DE 3193 [DDD]
Brahms, J.:Neue Liebeslieder Waltzes, w. Glenn Parker (pno), Joseph Flummerfeldt (cnd), Westminster Choir—No. 15 *(rec Bristol Chapel, Westminster Choir College of Rider Univ., Princeton, NJ, May 14-16, 1995)* Delos ▲ DE 3193
Brahms, J.:Qts SATB, Op. 64, w. Glenn Parker (pno), Joseph Flummerfeldt (cnd), Westminster Choir—Nos. 1 & 2 *(rec Bristol Chapel, Westminster Choir College of Rider Univ., Princeton, NJ, May 14-16, 1995)* Delos ▲ DE 3193 [DDD]
Brahms, J.:Qts SATB, Op. 92, w. Glenn Parker (pno), Joseph Flummerfeldt (cnd), Westminster Choir—Nos. 2 & 3 *(rec Bristol Chapel, Westminster Choir College of Rider Univ., Princeton, NJ, May 14-16, 1995)* Delos ▲ DE 3193 [DDD]
Brahms, J.:Zigeunerlieder, w. Glenn Parker (pno), Joseph Flummerfeldt (cnd), Westminster Choir—Nos 5–9 *(rec Bristol Chapel, Westminster Choir College of Rider Univ., Princeton, NJ, May 14-16, 1995)* Delos ▲ DE 3193 [DDD]

Parrenin, Jacques (vn)—see ORCHESTRAS & ENSEMBLES Parrenin String Quartet

Parris, R. (org)
Sowerby, L.:Org Music [1927 E.M. Skinner Organ, St. Paul's Episcopal Church, Rochester, NY]—Picardy; Bright, Blithe & Brisk; Jubilee; Carillon; Comes Autumn Time; Pageant of Autumn; Fant. for Flute Stops Premier ▲ PRCD 1039

Parrot, Reynald (ob)
Telemann, G.P.:Sons Ob, w. Maurice Allard (bn)—Son in a *(rec Lutheran Church of la Villette, Sept 13 & 17, 1983)* Studio SM ▲ 2527
Telemann, G.P.:Suite Ob, w. Maurice Allard (bn), Richard Siegel (hpd) *(rec Lutheran Church of la Villette, Sept 13 & 17, 1983)* Studio SM ▲ 2527

Parsons, Geoffrey (pno)
Amazing Grace, w. Jessye Norman (sop), Dalton Baldwin (pno), Christopher Bowers-Broadbent (org), Alexander Gibson (cnd), Willis Patterson (cnd), Royal PO, Ambrosian Singers Philips ▲ 432546-2 PH [DDD] ■ 432546-4 PH
Beethoven, L. van:An die ferne Geliebte, w. Thomas Hampson (bar) *(rec live, Usher Hall, Edinburgh, Aug. 20-21, 1993)* EMI Classics ▲ CDC 55147 [DDD]
Beethoven, L. van:Songs, w. O. Bär (bar) EMI Classics ▲ CDC 54879
Brahms, J.:Songs, w. L. Popp (sop)—12 songs [G] Acanta ▲ 43510 [DDD]
Brahms, J.:Songs, w. J. Norman (sop) [G] Philips ▲ 416439-2 [ADD]
Britten, H.:Folksong Arrs, w. S. Brightman (sop)—Early One Morning; Come You Not from Newcastle?; Sweet Polly Oliver; The Trees They Grow So High; The Ash Grove; O Waly, Waly; How Sweet the Answer; The Plough Boy; Voici le printemps; The Last Rose of Summer; La belle est au jardin d'amour; Fileuse; Dear Harp of My Country; Little Sir William; O Can Ye Sew Cushions?; Oft in the Silly Night; Quand j'etais chez mon père; There's None to Soothe; Oliver Cromwell Classics for Pleasure ▲ CDCFP 4636 [DDD]
Butterworth, G.:Bredon Hill & Other Songs, w. T. Allen (bar) [E] Virgin Classics ▲ 59581 [DDD]
Butterworth, G.:Songs (6) from *A Shropshire Lad*, w. T. Allen (bar) [E] Virgin Classics ▲ 59581 [DDD]
Elgar, E.:Sea Pictures, w. Birgit Finnilä (cta) *(rec Nacka Aula, Nacka, Sweden, Sept 21, 1975)* BIS ▲ CD 127 [AAD]
Encores, w. Elisabeth Schwarzkopf (sop), Gerald Moore (pno) EMI Classics ▲ CDM 63654
An Evening with Victoria de Los Angeles, w. Victoria de los Angeles (sop) *(rec Wigmore Hall Recital, 5/3/90)* Collins Classics ▲ COL 1247 [DDD]
Franz, R.:Songs, w. Thomas Hampson (bar)—Nun holt mir eine Kanne Wein; Ihr Auge; Die süsse Dirn' von Inverness *(rec live, Usher Hall, Edinburgh, Aug. 20-21, 1993)* EMI Classics ▲ CDC 55147 [DDD]
French Songs & Song Cycles, w. Hugues Cuénod (ten) Nimbus ▲ NI 5027

Parsons, Geoffrey (pno) (cont.)
Grieg, E.:Lieder, Op. 48, w. Thomas Hampson (bar) *(rec live, Usher Hall, Edinburgh, Aug. 20-21, 1993)* EMI Classics ▲ CDC 55147 [DDD]
In Recital, w. Jessye Norman (sop) *(rec live at Hohenems, June 1987)* Philips ▲ 422048-2 PH [DDD]
Lieder, w. Olaf Bär (bar) EMI Classics ▲ ZDHB 64292 [DDD]
Lieder aus "Des Knaben Wunderhorn", w. Thomas Hampson (bar) Teldec ▲ 2292-44923-2 [DDD]
Loewe, C.:Ballads, w. Roland Hermann (bar)—includes Kaiser Karl V Historial Ballads (4), Op. 99; Gregor auf dem Stein, Legend in 5 Parts, Op. 38 Claves ▲ 50-8106
Loewe, C.:Songs, w. Thomas Hampson (bar)—Findlay *(rec live, Usher Hall, Edinburgh, Aug. 20-21, 1993)* EMI Classics ▲ CDC 55147 [DDD]
Mahler, G.:Des Knaben Wunderhorn, w. T. Hampson (bar) Teldec ▲ 74726-2
Mahler, G.:Lieder eines fahrenden Gesellen, w. J. Baker (mez) [G] Hyperion ▲ CDA 66100
Mahler, G.:Lieder und Gesänge aus der Jugendzeit, w. Roland Hermann (bar) Claves ▲ 50-9011
Mahler, G.:Lieder und Gesänge aus der Jugendzeit, w. A. Reynolds (mez) IMP Classics ▲ IMPCD 1053 [DDD]
Mahler, G.:Songs, w. J. Baker (mez)—Im Lenz; Winterlied [G] Hyperion ▲ CDA 66100
Mahler, G.:Songs, w. L. Popp (sop)—9 songs [G] Acanta ▲ 43510 [DDD]
Le Maître de la Melodie, w. Hugues Cuénod (ten) *(rec ca. 1978)* Nimbus ▲ NI 5337 [ADD]
Mendelssohn, F.:Songs, w. B. Bonney (sop) Teldec ▲ 2292-44946-2 ZK
Mozart, W.A.:Songs, w. B. Bonney (sop) Teldec ▲ 2292-46334-2
Peel, G.:In Summertime on Bredon, w. T. Allen (bar) [E] Virgin Classics ▲ 59581 [DDD]
Quilter, R.:Elizabethan Lyrics, w. T. Allen (bar) [E] Virgin Classics ▲ 59581 [DDD]
Quilter, R.:Now Sleeps the Crimson Petal, w. T. Allen (bar) [E] Virgin Classics ▲ 59581 [DDD]
Recital, w. Elisabeth Schwarzkopf (sop) (rec. live, from a Swiss-Italian Radio 2 broadcast 10/6/67) Ermitage ▲ ERM 109 [ADD]
Schubert, Franz:Songs (misc), w. Barbara Bonney (sop)—Gretchen am Spinnrade; Gretchens Bitte; Heidenröslein; Auf dem Wasser zu Singen; Horch, horch die Lerch im Atherblau; Nähe des Geliebten; Ganymed; Die Forelle; Du bist die Ruth; Mignon Lieder [Kennst du das Land; Heiss mich nicht reden; So lasst mich scheinen; Nur wer die Sehnsucht kennt]; Liebhaber in allen Gestalten; Im Abenrot; Ave Maria; Der Hirt auf dem Felsen [w. Sharon Kam (clarinet)]; Liebe Schwärmt auf allen Wegen; An die Nachtigall *(rec Belin, Apr. 1994)* Teldec ▲ 90873-2 [DDD]
Schubert, Franz:Songs (misc), w. M. Lipovsek (sop)—15 songs [G] Orfeo ▲ 159871 [DDD]
Schubert, Franz:Songs (misc), w. J. Norman (sop) [G] Philips ▲ 422048-2 [DDD]
Schubert, Franz:Songs (misc), w. E. Schwarzkopf (sop), G. Moore (pno) EMI Classics ▲ CDM 63656
Schumann, R.:Dichterliebe, w. Thomas Hampson (bar) *(rec live, Usher Hall, Edinburgh, Aug. 20-21, 1993)* EMI Classics ▲ CDC 55147 [DDD]
Schumann, R.:Frauenliebe und -leben, w. C. Ludwig (mez) *(rec 1966)* Praga ▲ PR 254052 (m)
Schumann, R.:Songs, w. J. Norman (sop) [G] Philips ▲ 422048-2 [DDD]
Schumann, R.:Songs, w. Hampson (bar)—5 early Kerner-Lieder (1828); 12 Kerner-Lieder, Op. 35; Fünf Lieder, Op. 40 [G] Teldec ▲ 2292-44935-2 [DDD]
Schumann, R.:Songs, w. Thomas Hampson (bar)—Niemand; Dem roten Röslein gleicht mein Lieb *(rec live, Usher Hall, Edinburgh, Aug. 20-21, 1993)* EMI Classics ▲ CDC 55147 [DDD]
Strauss, R.:Songs, w. J. Norman (sop)—20 songs [G] Philips ▲ 416298-2 [DDD]
Traditional Catalan Songs, w. Victoria de los Angeles (sop) Collins Classics ▲ COL 1318 [DDD]
Vaughan Williams, R.:The House of Life, w. T. Allen (bar) [E] Virgin Classics ▲ 59581 [DDD]
Vaughan Williams, R.:Songs, w. T. Allen (bar)—Linden Lea, a Dorset Song (1902) [E] Virgin Classics ▲ 59581 [DDD]
Wolf, H.:Goethe-Lieder (sels), w. F. Lott (sop)—9 songs [G] Chandos ▲ CHAN 8726 [DDD]
Wolf, H.:Italienische Liederbücher (comp), w. B. Bonney (sop), H. Hagegård (bar) Teldec ▲ 72301
Wolf, H.:Mörike-Lieder (sels), w. F. Lott (sop)—10 songs [G] Chandos ▲ CHAN 8726 [DDD]
Wolf, H.:Songs (misc), w. T. Allen (bar) [G] Virgin Classics ▲ CDC 59221
Wolf, H.:Songs (misc), w. E. Schwarzkopf (sop), G. Moore (pno)—Lieder EMI Classics ▲ CDM 63653
Wolf, H.:Spanisches Liederbuch, w. Anne Sofie von Otter (mez), Olaf Bar (bar) EMI Classics ▲ CDC 55325

Parsons, Paul (org)
St. Mary, Finedon Organ, w. Parsons, Paul (org) *(rec May-June 1993)* Mirabilis ▲ MMSCD 1 [DDD]

Parsons, William (perc)—see ORCHESTRAS & ENSEMBLES Univ of Illinois Contemporary Chamber Players

Partch, Harry (adapted gtr/voc)
Partch, H.:Barstow, w. William Wendlant (voc), Christine Charnstrom (chromelodeon), Lee Hoiby (kitara) *(rec 1945)* Innova 4-▲ 401
Partch, H.:US Highball, w. William Wendlandt (bar), Christine Charnstrom (chromelodeon), Lee Hoiby (kitara), Fralia Hancock (db canon) *(rec 1946)* Innova 4-▲ 401

Partch, Harry (adapted va)
Partch, H.:By the Rivers of Babylon, w. William Wendlandt (bar), Christine Charnstrom (chromelodeon), Lee Hoiby (kithara) *(rec 1945)* Innova 4-▲ 401
Partch, H.:Dark Brother, w. William Wendlandt (bar), Christine Charnstrom (chromelodeon), Lee Hoiby (kithara), Fralia Hancock (Indian dr) *(rec 1945)* Innova 4-▲ 401
Partch, H.:17 Lyrics by Li Po, w. William Wendlant (spkr)—10 Lyrics [A Dream; An Encounter in the Field; On Hearing the Flute; The Intruder; I am a Peach Tree; With a Man of Leisure; A Midnight Farewell; Before the Cask of Wine; On the Ship of Spicewood; By the Great Wall] *(rec 1947)* Innova 4-▲ 401

Partch, Harry (adapted va/ voc)
Partch, H.:San Francisco, w. Christine Charnstrom (chromelodeon), Lee Hoiby (kitara) *(rec 1945)* Innova 4-▲ 401

Partch, Harry (chromelodeon)
Partch, H.:Yankee Doodle Fant, w. Lola Harding (sop), Hilmar Luckhardt (tin whistle), Don Thompson (tin whistle/ob), Lee Hoiby (flex-a-tones) *(rec 1945)* Innova 4-▲ 401

Partch, Harry (kithara)
Partch, H.:Settings (2) from "Finnegan's Wake", w. Lola Harding (sop), Dorothy Holden (fl), Hilmar Luckhardt (fl) *(rec 1945)* Innova 4-▲ 401

Partington, Adrian (org)
Harwood, B.:Org Music—Sonata No. 1 in c# for Organ, Op. 5 Priory ▲ PRI 384 [DDD]
Howells-Britten-Gibbons, w. [cnd:Donald Hunt], Worcester Cathedral Choir IMP ("Classics" series) ▲ IMP 6700422
Merkel, G.A.:Org Music—Fant & Fugue in C, Op. 5; Son No. 6 in e, Op. 137 [Chorale-Son]; Allegretto & Allegro, Op. 117; Pastorale, Op. 49 [No. 1 in G]; Vars on a Theme of Beethoven, Op. 45; Son No. 2 in g, Op. 42 Priory ▲ PRI 501 [DDD]
Saint-Saëns, C.:Preludes & Fugues, Op. 99 Priory ▲ PRI 384 [DDD]
Saint-Saëns, C.:Preludes & Fugues, Op. 109 Priory ▲ PRI 384 [DDD]
Wesley, S.S.:Anthems, w. D. Hunt (cnd), Worcester Cathedral Choir—selections include The face of the Lord; I will exalt Thee; Man that is born of a woman; O Give thanks unto the Lord; O Lord, my God; O Lord, thou art my God; Praise the Lord, o my soul; Wash me thoroughly from my wickedness Hyperion ▲ CDA 66449
Wesley, S.S.:Anthems, w. D. Hunt (cnd), Worcester Cathedral Choir—selections include Ascribe unto the Lord; Blessed be the God and Father; Cast me not away; Let us lift up our heart with our hands; Thou wilt keep him in perfect peace; The Wilderness Hyperion ▲ CDA 66446

Partridge, Jennifer (pno)
Schubert, Franz:Die Schöne Müllerin, w. Ian Partridge (ten) Classics for Pleasure ▲ CDCFP 4672
Schubert, Franz:Songs (misc), w. Ian Partridge (ten)—An Silvia; Auflösung; Der Wanderer an den Mond; Wanderers Nachtlied II; Die Forelle; An die Laute; Der Einsame; Der Schiffer; An die Musik ASV Quicksilva ▲ ASQ 6171

Parys, Paule van (hpd)
Boccherini, L.:Qts Strs, G.195–200, w. J. Van Mol (hpd) [anon. late 18th cent. trans. for 2 Harpsichords] Pavane ▲ ADW 7282 [DDD]
Bon Di Venezia, A.:Sons (6) Hpd Pavane ▲ ADW 7338
Grétry, A.-E.-M.:Sons (2) for 2 Hpds, w. J. Van Mol (hpd) Pavane ▲ ADW 7282 [DDD]

Pascal, A. (vn)
Saint-Saëns, C.:Son 1 Vn, w. I. Philipp (pno) *(rec 1935)* Pearl ▲ PEA 9174 [ADD]
Pascal, Denis (pno)
Glière, R.:Pieces, Op. 35, w. Hervé Joulain (hn)—Intermezzo for Hn & Pno [No. 11] Arion ▲ ARN 68311 [DDD]
Sinigaglia, L.:Pezzi Hn & Pno, w. Hervé Joulain (hn)—No. 1 Arion ▲ ARN 68311 [DDD]
Strauss, R.:Das Alphorn, w. Delphine Collot (sop), Hervé Joulain (hn) Arion ▲ ARN 68311 [DDD]
Pascher, Hartmut (va)—see ORCHESTRAS & ENSEMBLES Franz Schubert String Quartet
Pascoe, K. (vn)—see ORCHESTRAS & ENSEMBLES Britten String Quartet
Pascolini, Jon (db)
Handel, D.:Barge Music, w. Bradley Garner (a fl), Rodney Studky (gtr), Russell Burge (perc), Allen Otte (perc) Vienna Modern Masters ▲ VMM 2019 [DDD]
Pasero, Stevan (gtr)
Christmas Classics for Guitar Sugo ▲ SUG 8602 [DDD] ■ SUG 8602
Tchaikovsky, P.:Nutcracker Suite [trans. for guitar] Sugo ▲ SUG 8501 [DDD] ■ SUG 8501
Pashinskaya, Irina (hp)
Schnittke, A.:Hymns Vc, w. A. Ivashkin (vc), Y. Rudometkin (bn), V. Barsalkin (db), V. Chasovennaya (hpd), V. Grishin, N. Grishin (perc/bells)—No. 1 for Cello, Harp & Timpani [Quasi andante]; No. 2 for Cello & Double *(rec National Radio House, Moscow, 1987)* Vox Box 2–▲ CDX 5121 [ADD]
Paskalev, C. (va)
Mozart, W.A.:Sinf concertante Vn, K.364, w. M. Minchev (vn), E. Tabakov (cnd), Sofia Soloists CO Vivace 3–▲ E 316 [DDD]
Mozart, W.A.:Sinf concertante Vn, K.364, w. M. Minchev (vn), E. Tabakov (cnd), Sofia Soloists CO Vivace ▲ E 576 [ADD]
Stamitz, C.:Sinf Concertante, w. M. Minchev (vn), E. Tabakov (cnd), Sofia Solisti Vivace ▲ E 576 [ADD]
Pasmanick, Kenneth (bn)
Amram, D.:Con Bn, w. R.A. Clark (cnd), Manhattan CO *(rec SUNY, Oct 1993)* Newport Classics ▲ NPD 85601 [DDD]
Schuller, G.:Con Bn, w. G. Schuller (cnd), Saarbrück RSO GM ▲ GM 2044
Pasquale, Joseph de (va)
Berlioz, H.:La Damnation de Faust, w. Suzanne Danco (sop), David Poleri (ten), Martial Singher (bar), Donald Gramm (bass), McHenry Boatwright (bass), Louis Speyer (hn), C. Munch (cnd), Boston SO, Harvard Glee Club, Radcliffe Choral Society *(rec Feb 1954)* RCA Victor Gold Seal 8–▲ 0902–668444–2 [ADD]
Berlioz, H.:Harold in Italy, w. E. Ormandy (cnd), Philadelphia Orch *(rec Jan. 21, 1965)* Sony Classical ▲ SBK 53255 ■ SBT 53255
Dvořák, A.:Qnt Pno, Op. 81, w. J. Lateiner (pno), M. Baker (va), J. Heifetz (vn), G. Piatigorsky (vc) RCA Gold Seal ▲ 7965–2–RG [ADD]
Françaix, J.:Trio Vn, Va & Vc, w. J. Heifetz (vn), G. Piatigorsky (vc) RCA Gold Seal ▲ 7872–2–RG (m/s) [ADD]
Pasquier, B. (pno)
Berlioz, H.:Harold in Italy, w. J.–F. Heisser (va) [Liszt's va–pno trans] Musique d'Abord ▲ HMA 1901246
Schmitt, F.:Hasards, w. E. Herbin (pno), A. Galpérine (pno), M. Drobinsky (pno) Gallo ▲ CD 711 [ADD]
Pasquier, Bruno (va)—see also ORCHESTRAS & ENSEMBLES Le Nouveau Trio Pasquier
Brahms, J.:Qt 1 Pno, w. Jean–Claude Pennetier (pno), Régis Pasquier (vn), Roland Pidoux (vc) Harmonia Mundi ▲ HMT 7901062
Brahms, J.:Sextet Strs, Op. 18, w. Régis Pasquier (vn), Raphaël Oleg (vn), Jean Dupouy (va), Roland Pidoux (vc), Etienne Péclard (vc)—No. 1 Harmonia Mundi France ("Musique d'abord" series) ▲ HMA 1901073
Brahms, J.:Sons Cl (comp), w. J.–C. Pennetier (pno) Musique d'Abord ▲ HMA 1901092 [ADD]
Chausson, E.:Con Vn, Pno & Str Qt, w. R. Daugareil (vn), R. Pasquier (vn), G. Simonot (vn), R. Pidoux (vc), J.–C. Pennetier (pno) Harmonia Mundi Plus ▲ HMP 3901135
Constant, M.:Chamber Music, w. Radu Blidar (vn), Francis Pierre (hp), Elizabeth Chojnacka (hpd) Salabert ▲ SCD 9401
Fauré, G.:Qts Pno, Opp. 15 & 45, w. J.P. Collard (pno), A. Dumay (vn), F. Lodeon (vc) EMI Classics 2–▲ ZDMB 62548
Herbin, R.:Qt Pno, w. E. Herbin (pno), Alexis Galpérine (vn), Mark Drobinsky (vc) Gallo ▲ CD 711 [ADD]
Mozart, W.A.:Duos Vn, w. R. Pasquier (vn) Musique d'Abord ▲ HMA 1901052 [DDD]
Onslow, G.:Qnt Strs, Op. 78/1, w. Y. Caracilly (vn), French String Trio *(rec 1978)* Koch Treasure ▲ 316232 [ADD]
Schubert, Franz:Trio Strs, D.471, w. R. Pasquier (vn), R. Pidoux (vc) Harmonia Mundi France ▲ HMC 901035
Schubert, Franz:Trio Strs, D.581, w. R. Pasquier (vn), R. Pidoux (vc) Harmonia Mundi France ▲ HMC 901035
Schumann, R.:Märchenbilder, w. J.–F. Heisser (pno) Musique d'Abord ▲ HMA 1901246
Pasquier, Bruno (vn)
Boccherini, L.:Qnts Fl, G.437–442, w. Jean–Pierre Rampal (fl), Régis Pasquier (vn), Roland Pidoux (vc concertante), Mathilde Sternat (vc)—1–3, 5 & 6 Sony Classical ▲ SK 62679
Pasquier, Régis (vn)—see also ORCHESTRAS & ENSEMBLES Le Nouveau Trio Pasquier
The Art of the Violin, w. Patrice Fontanarosa (vn), Jean–Jacques Kantorow (vn), Gérard Poulet (vn) Arion ▲ ARN 60262
Bach, J.S.:Con for 2 Vns, w. Z. Francescatti (vn), R. Baumgartner (cnd), Lucerne Festival Strings Deutsche Grammophon ("Musikfest" series) ▲ 429151–2 [ADD]
Bartók, B.:Duos (44), w. Gérard Poulet (vn) Arion ▲ ARN 68327 [DDD]
Boccherini, L.:Qnts Fl, G.437–442, w. Jean–Pierre Rampal (fl), Bruno Pasquier (vn), Roland Pidoux (vc concertante), Mathilde Sternat (vc)—1–3, 5 & 6 Sony Classical ▲ SK 62679
Brahms, J.:Qt 1 Pno, w. Jean–Claude Pennetier (pno), Bruno Pasquier (va), Roland Pidoux (vc) Harmonia Mundi ▲ HMT 7901062
Brahms, J.:Sextet Strs, Op. 18, w. Raphaël Oleg (vn), Bruno Pasquier (va), Jean Dupouy (va), Roland Pidoux (vc), Etienne Péclard (vc)—No. 1 Harmonia Mundi France ("Musique d'abord" series) ▲ HMA 1901073
Brahms, J.:Son 3 Vn, w. Jean–Claude Pennetier (pno) Harmonia Mundi ▲ HMT 7901062
Chausson, E.:Con Vn, Pno & Str Qt, w. R. Daugareil (vn), G. Simonot (vn), B. Pasquier (va), R. Pidoux (vc), J.–C. Pennetier (pno) Harmonia Mundi Plus ▲ HMP 3901135
Colonel Chabert, w. Lluis Claret (vc), Philippe Cassard (pno), Pierre Hantaï (hpd) Travelling ▲ K 1013
Mozart, W.A.:Duos Vn, w. B. Pasquier (va) Musique d'Abord ▲ HMA 1901052 [DDD]
Ravel, M.:Berceuse sur le nom de Gabriel Fauré, w. B. Engerer (pno) Harmonia Mundi France ▲ HMC 901364
Ravel, M.:Kaddisch, w. B. Engerer (pno) Harmonia Mundi France ▲ HMC 901364
Ravel, M.:Pièce en forme de Habanera, w. B. Engerer (pno) [Fritz Kreisler trans. for violin & piano] Harmonia Mundi France ▲ HMC 901364
Ravel, M.:Son Vn Pno, w. B. Engerer (pno) Harmonia Mundi France ▲ HMC 901364
Ravel, M.:Sonate posthume, w. B. Engerer (pno) Harmonia Mundi France ▲ HMC 901364
Ravel, M.:Tzigane, w. B. Engerer (pno) Harmonia Mundi France ▲ HMC 901364
Schubert, Franz:Trio 1 Pno, w. Jean–Claude Pennetier (pno), Roland Pidoux (vc) Harmonia Mundi ("Suite" series) ▲ HMT 7901048
Schubert, Franz:Trio Strs, D.471, w. B. Pasquier (va), R. Pidoux (vc) Harmonia Mundi France ▲ HMC 901035
Schubert, Franz:Trio Strs, D.581, w. B. Pasquier (va), R. Pidoux (vc) Harmonia Mundi France ▲ HMC 901035
Sibelius, J.:Con Vn, w. P. Bartholomée (cnd), Liège PO Valois ▲ V 4746
Passaggio, Stefano (va)
Stephan, R.:Music for 7 Stringed Instrs, w. B. Hartog (vn), I. Schliephake (vn), G. Donderer (vc), A. Akahoshi (db), C. Tainton (pno), M. Schmidt (hp) *(rec 1983)* Koch Schwann ▲ CD 311 122 [ADD]
Passaro, Joseph (perc)—see also ORCHESTRAS & ENSEMBLES Jazzantiqua, Contemporary Chamber Ensemble
Hudson, J.:Sonare, w. Rolf Schulte (vn), Paul Dunkel (fl), Laura Flax (cl), Ursula Oppens (pno) CRI ■ C 382
Léon, T.:Batéy, w. D. Ponce (conga), E. Charlston (perc), T. Léon (cnd), Western Wind CRI ▲ CD 662 [DDD]
Wuorinen, C.:Spinoff, w. B. Hudson (vn), D. Palma (db) Bridge ▲ BCD 9008 [DDD]
Passerini, Cristiana (hp)
Tosti, P.F.:Songs, w. E. Palacio (ten), M. Rapattoni (pno), H. Liviabella (vn), G. Scabbia (fl), B. Giuffredi (gtr), M. Decimo (vc) [arr. Massimo de Bernart for instrumental accompaniment]—La serenata; Sogno; 'A vucchella; Segreto; Ideale; 2ème Aubade; Anima mia; Donna, vorrei morir; Aprile; Ancoral; Mattinata; L'ultima canzone; Malìa; Non t'amo più; Il pescatore cantal; Tristezza; O falce di luna calante; L'abla separa dalla luce l'ombra; Mi guitarra dice "Te amo!"; Ricordati di me; Vuol note o banconote? Arkadia–Akademia ▲ 125 [DDD]
Passin, Günther (ob)
Mozart, W.A.:Missa, K.427, w. S. Meinardus (sop), H.–J. Möhring (fl), F. Essmann (bn), H. Müller–Brühl (cnd), Cologne CO—Et incarnatus est [L] *(rec May 1968)* Koch Treasure ▲ 316182 [ADD]
Mozart, W.A.:Qnt Pno, K.452, w. Keiko Toyama (pno), Yuji Murai (cl), Gottfried Langenstein (hn), Koji Okazaki (bn) *(rec Shibukawa Shimin Kaikan, Sept 1, 1981)* Camerata ▲ 32CM 180 [DDD]
Passin, Günther (ob/ob d'amore)
Donizetti, G.:Concertinos (4) solo Winds, w. J. Fadle (cl), K.–B. Sebon (fl), J. Starek (cnd), Berlin RIAS Sinfonietta *(rec 1979)* Koch Schwann ▲ CD 311 121 [ADD/DDD]
Pasta, Frantisek (db)
Dittersdorf, K.D. von:Concertino Va, w. L. Maly (va), F. Vajnar (cnd), Dvořák CO Supraphon ▲ CD 110951 [DDD]
Dittersdorf, K.D. von:Con Db, w. F. Vajnar (cnd), Dvořák CO Supraphon ▲ CD 110951 [DDD]
Pasternack, Benjamin (pno)
Paine, J.K.:Son Vn, Op. 24, w. R. Druian (vn) GM ▲ GM 2021CD
Schuller, G.:Duologue, w. R. Druian (vn) GM ▲ GM 2021CD
Pastor, J. (vn)—see ORCHESTRAS & ENSEMBLES Berlin String Quintet
Pastukhoff, Vsevolod (pno)
Rachmaninoff, S.:Songs, w. Maria Kurenko (sop), Laurence Rosenthal (pno)—Melody; On the Death of a Linnet; Night Is Mournful; I Ask Mercy; Vocalise; Arion; I Remember That Day; Music; At Night in My Garden; To Her; Daisies; The Rat–Catcher; A Dream; A–ou; The Fountain; Yesterday We Met; The Changing Wind; Fragment from Alfred de Musset; It Is Pleasant Here; 2 Partings:A Dialogue (w. Vadim Gontzoff); What Happiness; Everything Is Taken from Me; The Ring; I Am Alone Again; We Will Rest; The Muse; Dissonance VAI Audio ▲ VAIA 1094 [ADD]
Pasveer, Kathinka (fl)
Stockhausen, K.:Tierkreis, w. S. Stephens (cl), M. Stockhausen (tpt/pno) Acanta ▲ CD 43201 [DDD]
Pásztory–Bartók, Ditta (pno)
Bartók, B.:Pno Music, w. B. Bartók (pno), V. Medgyaszay (sop), M. Basilides (cta), F. Székelyhidy (ten), J. Szigeti (vn), B. Goodman (cl), H. J. Baker, E. J. Rubsam (perc)—studio, broadcast & piano roll recordings of music by Bartók, Kodály, Beethoven, Debussy, Liszt & Scarlatti, chronologically arranged from ca. 1920 through 1945—Sonatina; 6 Romanian Folk Dances; Evening in Transylvania; 8 sels. from 15 Hungarian Peasant Songs; Suite, Op. 14 (both the issued & test recordings); Allegro barbaro; 5 sels. from 2 Romanian Dances, 3 Burlesques, 10 Easy Pieces & 14 Bagatelles; & 4 Sons. by D. Scarlatti (test recordings); 8 sels. from 15 Hungarian Peasant Songs; 4 sels. from 9 Little Piano Pieces, Petite Suite & 3 Rondos on Folk Melodies; & "Sursum corda" from Liszt's Années de pèlerinage; 20 Hungarian Folk Songs; 5 Hungarian Folk Tunes; 8 Hungarian Folksongs; Hungarian Folk Tunes; 6 Romanian Folk Dances; Rhap. 1 Violin & Piano; Contrasts for Clarinet, Violin & Piano; 2 sels. from Mikrokosmos; 32 sels. from Mikrokosmos; Rhap. 1; Son. No. 2; Beethoven's "Kreutzer" Son.; Debussy's Son. 3; Son. 2 Pianos & Percussion; Petite Suite; 3 Hungarian Folk Tunes; 11 sels. from Improvs. on Hungarian Peasant Songs; Mikrokosmos; 3 Rondos on Folk Melodies; 9 Little Piano Pieces; 14 Bagatelles; 15 sels. from For Children & 2 sels. from 10 Easy Pieces Hungaroton 6–▲ HCD 12326/31 (m) [ADD]
Paternoster, Vito (vc)
Bellafronte, R.:Suite 1 Vc, w. Marco Salcito (chitarra) *(rec Auditorium del Conservatorio, Bari, Nov 1994)* Bongiovanni ▲ GB 5049–2 [DDD]
Clementi, M.:Sons Pno, Fl & Vc, Op. 21, w. A. Coen (hpd), E. Casularo (fl) Bongiovanni ▲ GB 10007 [DDD]
Clementi, M.:Sons Pno, Fl & Vc, Op. 22, w. A. Coen (hpd), E. Casularo (fl) Bongiovanni ▲ GB 10007 [DDD]
Geminiani, F.:Sons Vc & Continuo, Op. 5, w. A. Coen (vc), P. Bosna (hpd)—No. 3 Bongiovanni ▲ GB 10015 [DDD]
Marcello, B.:Son Vc, Op. 2/4, w. A. Coen (vc), P. Bosna (hpd) Bongiovanni ▲ GB 10015 [DDD]
Martino, F.:Son Vc, w. A. Coen (vc), P. Bosna (hpd) Bongiovanni ▲ GB 10015 [DDD]
Paternoster, V.:Inzaffirio:Prayers (6) to the Virgin Mary, w. P. Pace (sop), F. Colusso (cnd), Seicentonovecento Ensemble Musicaimmagine ▲ MR 10006
Pergolesi, G.B.:Sinf Vc, w. A. Coen (vc), P. Bosna (hpd) Bongiovanni ▲ GB 10015 [DDD]
Scipriani, F.P.:Sinf Vc, w. A. Coen (cv), P. Bosna (hpd) Bongiovanni ▲ GB 10015 [DDD]
Paterson, Alan (hn)
Mozart, W.A.:Qnt Pno, K.452, w. Landon Bilyeu (pno), Philip Teachey (ob), Charles West (cl), Bruce Hammel (bn) Klavier ▲ KCD 11072 [DDD]
Paterson, Douglas (va)—see ORCHESTRAS & ENSEMBLES Schubert Ensemble of London
Paterson, Robin (pno)
Dring, M.:Pno Duo Tour, w. Leigh Kaplan (pno), Susan Pits (pno)—Carribean Dance; Danza Gaya [w Susan Pits (pno)]; Tarantelle; Italian Dance [w Robin Paterson (pno)] Cambria ▲ CD 1084 [ADD]
Patipatanakoon, Annalee (vn)—see ORCHESTRAS & ENSEMBLES Gryphon Piano Trio
Patregnani, Amanda (fl)—see ORCHESTRAS & ENSEMBLES Bilitis Ensemble
Patterson, Rebecca (vc)
Shewan, S.:The Widow's Lament in Springtime, w. Jill Richardson (sop), Amy Anderson (ob), Stephen Shewan (pno) Albany ▲ TROY 149 [DDD]
Patterson, Ronald (vn)—see also ORCHESTRAS & ENSEMBLES Shepherd String Quartet, Patterson Duo
Cooper, P.:Con 2 Vn, w. L. Foster (cnd), Monte Carlo PO CRI ▲ CD 579 [ADD]
Patterson, Roxanna (va)—see ORCHESTRAS & ENSEMBLES Patterson Duo
Patterson, S. (pno)—see ORCHESTRAS & ENSEMBLES Scott Chamber Players
Patterson, Steven (gtr)
Brouwer, L.:Gtr Music, w. Robert Beer (gtr), John Draper (gtr), Carl Ljungstrom (gtr)—Musica Incidental Campesina; Vier Mikropiezas; Cuban Landscape with Rain; Preludios Epigrammaticos; El Decameron Negro; other works Koch Schwann ▲ SCH 311742 [DDD]
Patterson, W. (vn)—see ORCHESTRAS & ENSEMBLES New World String Quartet
Patumi, Daniele (db)
Amendola, F.:Ricercari, w. A. Frederico (elecs/pno), A. Flore (voc), G. Lanzini (cl), L. Ciolfi (vn), C. Cavalieri (vn), C. Sanzo (vc), O. Mangiavacchi (perc), Donizetti Ensemble Bongiovanni ▲ GB 5519 [DDD]
Patumi, D.:Improvvisi Bongiovanni ▲ GB 5519 [DDD]
Patykula, John (gtr)
The Classical Banjo, w. John Bullard (banjo), Steve Bennett (hp gtr), William Comita (vc), Greg Giannascoli (vib) *(rec Big Audio, Richmond, VA, May–July 1992, Oct. 1994)* Dargason Music ▲ DM 115 [DDD]; ■ DM 115
Pau, Maria de la (pno)
Saint-Saëns, C.:Wedding Cake, w. L. Frémaux (cnd), City of Birmingham SO Klavier ▲ KCD 11011 [ADD]
Paugam, Laurence (vn)
Vivaldi, A.:Cons Diverse Instrs, w. Sylvia Ochi (man), Takashi Ochi (man), Jean–Marc Labylle (pic), Monique Frasca–Colombier (vn), P. Kuentz (cnd), Paul Kuentz Orch—in G for 2 Man; in C for Rcr; in B♭ for Bn [La notte]; in d for Vl; in a for Bn; in A for Vn & other Vns in echo Pierre Verany ▲ PVY 730052 [DDD]

768

▲ = CD ♦ = Enhanced CD Δ = MD ■ = Cassette Tape □ = DCC

Pauk, György (va)
Mozart, W.A.:Qnt Strs, K.515, w. Takács String Quartet London ▲ 430772-2 [DDD]

Pauk, György (vn)
Bartók, B.:Andante, w. Jenő Jandó (pno) *(rec Unitarian Church, Budapest, June 27–28, 1993)* Naxos ▲ 8.550886 [DDD]
Bartók, B.:Rhaps Vn & Pno, Sz.86 & 89, w. Jenő Jandó (pno) *(rec Unitarian Church, Budapest, June 27–28, 1993)* Naxos ▲ 8.550886 [DDD]
Brahms, J.:Sons Vn (comp), w. R. Vignoles (pno) *(rec 7/90)* Ottavo ▲ OTR C79030 [DDD]
Handel, G.F.:Sons Vn & Kbd, w. Frank (vc), Sebestyén (pno)—Op. 1, Nos. 1b, 3, 6, 10, 12, 13, 14 Hungaroton ▲ HCD 12657 [DDD]
Mozart, W.A.:Adagio Vn, K.261, w. J. Rolla (cnd), Franz Liszt CO Hungaroton 3-▲ HCD 31030/32 [DDD]
Mozart, W.A.:Cons Vn, w. J. Rolla (cnd), Franz Liszt CO—Nos. 1–5 Hungaroton 3-▲ HCD 31030/32 [DDD]
Mozart, W.A.:Con 4 Vn, w. J. Faerber (cnd), Württemberg CO Allegretto ▲ ACD 8141 [ADD] ■ ACS 8141
Mozart, W.A.:Con 5 Vn, w. J. Faerber (cnd), Württemberg CO Allegretto ▲ ACD 8141 [ADD] ■ ACS 8141
Mozart, W.A.:Concertone Vns, w. J. Rolla (vn), J. Rolla (cnd), Franz Liszt CO Hungaroton 3-▲ HCD 31030/32 [DDD]
Mozart, W.A.:Rondo Vn, K.269, w. J. Rolla (cnd), Franz Liszt CO Hungaroton 3-▲ HCD 31030/32 [DDD]
Mozart, W.A.:Rondo Vn, K.373, w. J. Rolla (cnd), Franz Liszt CO Hungaroton 3-▲ HCD 31030/32 [DDD]
Mozart, W.A.:Sinf concertante Vn, K.364, w. J. Rolla (va), J. Rolla (cnd), Franz Liszt CO Hungaroton 3-▲ HCD 31030/32 [DDD]

Paul, Jennifer (hpd)
Couperin, A.-L.:Pièces de clavecin—La victoire;Allemande; Courantes la de croissy; Le cacqueteuses; la grégoire; l'Intrépide; 1st & 2nd Menuets; l'Arlequine ou la Adam; La blanchet; La de boisgelou; La foucquet; La semillante, ou la joly; La turpin; 1st & 2nd Gavottes; 1st & 2nd Menuets; La du breüil; La chéron; l'Affligée; l'Enjouée; Le tendres sentimens; Rondeau gracieux Klavier ▲ KCD 11041 [DDD]

Paul, Pamela Mia (pno)
Beaser, R.:Con Pno, w. D. R. Davies (cnd), American Composers Orch Argo ▲ 440337-2 [DDD]
Mozart, W.A.:Trio Cl, K.498, w. G. Silfies (cl), T. Dumm (va) *(rec 1975–79)* Vox Box 3-▲ CD3X 3014 [ADD]

Paul, Reginald (pno)
Burleigh, H.T.:Songs, w. Margaret Harrison (vn)—Southland Sketches Symposium ▲ SYM 1140

Paulechava, Zuzana (pno)
Chopin, F.:Con 1 Pno, w. O. Trhlík (cnd), Philharmonia Cassovia *(rec House of Arts, Kosice, Jan. 31, 1990)* Lydian ▲ 18102 [DDD]

Paulicka, Ivan (bn)
Respighi, O.:Liriche su parole di poeti armeni, w. Denisa Šlepkovská (mez), Vladimír Havran (fl), Michal Sintál (ob), Gabriel Koncer (cl), Ivan Viskup (b cl), Frantisek Kovács (trbn), Katarína Vavreková (hp), M. Adriano (cnd) [arr. for chamber group by Adriano] *(rec Slovak Radio Concert Hall, Bratislava)* Marco Polo ▲ 8.223595 [DDD]

Paull, Jennifer (ob)
Caix D'Hervelois, L. de:La Gracieuse, w. Stefano Canuti (bn), Christine Sartoretti (hpd) *(rec English Church, Villars, Switzerland, Apr 21–22, 1995)* Doron ▲ DRC 5006 [DDD]
Caix D'Hervelois, L. de:Les Vendangeuses, w. Stefano Canuti (bn), Christine Sartoretti (hpd) *(rec English Church, Villars, Switzerland, Apr 21–22, 1995)* Doron ▲ DRC 5006 [DDD]
Marais, M.:Vars on *Folies d'Espagne*, w. Stefano Canuti (bn), Christine Sartoretti (hpd) *(rec English Church, Villars, Switzerland, Apr 21–22, 1995)* Doron ▲ DRC 5006 [DDD]

Paulsson, Anders (s sax)
Morales, C. de:Sacred Music, w. Erik Westberg (cnd), Erik Westberg Vocal Ensemble—Parce mihi domine Opus 3 ▲ 19506 [AAD]
Paulsson, A.:Lullaby Opus 3 ▲ 19506 [AAD]

Paulsson, Lars (cl)
Delage, M.:Poèmes hindous, w. Anne Sofie von Otter (mez), Andreas Alin (fl), Peter Rydström (fl/pic), Ulf Bjurenhed (ob/E hn), Per Billman (cl/b cl), Nils-Erik Sparf (vn), Ulf Forsberg (vn), Matti Hirvikangas (va), Mats Lindström (vc), Lisa Viguier (hp) *(rec Stockholm, Nov 1994)* Deutsche Grammophon ▲ 447 752-2 [DDD]
Poulenc, F.:Rapsodie nègre, w. Anne Sofie von Otter (mez), Andreas Alin (fl), Nils-Erik Sparf (vn), Ulf Forsberg (vn), Matti Hirvikangas (va), Mats Lindström (vc), Bengt Forsberg (pno) *(rec Stockhom, Nov 1994)* Deutsche Grammophon ▲ 447 752-2 [DDD]
Ravel, M.:Trois poèmes de Stéphane Mallarmé, w. Anne Sofie von Otter (mez), Peter Rydström (fl/pic), Andreas Alin (fl), Per Billman (cl/b cl), Nils-Erik Sparf (vn), Ulf Forsberg (vn), Matti Hirvikangas (va), Mats Lindström (vc), Bengt Forsberg (pno) *(rec Stockholm, Nov 1994)* Deutsche Grammophon ▲ 447 752-2 [DDD]

Paulus, Janet (hp)—see ORCHESTRAS & ENSEMBLES Gioccarpa
Pavan, Franco (archlt)—see ORCHESTRAS & ENSEMBLES Basso Generale
Pavan, Giancarlo (db)—see ORCHESTRAS & ENSEMBLES L'Astrée Ensemble

Pavlas, Bohuslav (vc)
Eben, Petr:Suita balladica, w. H. Dvořáková (pno) *(rec 11/90)* Multisonic ▲ 31 0065-2 [DDD]
Janácek, L.:Fairy Tale, w. H. Dvořáková (pno) *(rec 11/90)* Multisonic ▲ 31 0065-2 [DDD]
Martinů, B.:Son 3 Vc, w. H. Dvořáková (pno) *(rec 11/90)* Multisonic ▲ 31 0065-2 [DDD]

Pavlík, Cenek (vn)—see also ORCHESTRAS & ENSEMBLES Guarneri Trio Prague, Guarneri Trio Prague members
Mozart, W.A.:Con 3 Vn, w. J. Belohlávek (cnd), Czech PO Panton ▲ PAN 811207
Mozart, W.A.:Con 3 Vn, w. J. Belohlávek (cnd), Czech PO—Adagio Special Music Co. ("Classics of the Heart" series) ▲ SCD 5197
Mozart, W.A.:Con 5 Vn, w. J. Belohlávek (cnd), Czech PO Panton ▲ PAN 811207

Pavlinek, Ferdo (mand)
Vivaldi, A.:Con for 2 Mands, w. A. Ganoci (mand), A. Janigro (cnd), Zagreb Solisti *(rec 1964)* Vanguard Classics ("The Bach Guild" series) ▲ OVC 2006 [ADD]

Pavlorek, Ales (cl)
Armanini, M.:Nocturne Cl, w. J. Zoltek (cnd), Bohuslav Martinů PO Chroma ▲ CHR CD 10001 [DDD]

Pavlovitch, T. (pno/org)
Nightingales, w. [cnd:Irina Stiglich], Vassil Arnaudov Sofia Chamber Choir Gega ▲ GD 195

Pavlutskaya, Matalia (vc)—see ORCHESTRAS & ENSEMBLES Canterbury Cellists
Pavolini, C. (va)—see ORCHESTRAS & ENSEMBLES Stauffer String Quartet

Pavri, Fali (pno)
Britten, H.:Son Vc, w. Timothy Gill (vc) Guild ▲ GMCD 7114 [DDD]
Mayer, J.:Calcutta-Nagar Guild ▲ GMCD 7114 [DDD]
Mayer, J.:Prabhanda, w. Timothy Gill (vc) Guild ▲ GMCD 7114 [DDD]
Rubbra, E.:Son Vc, w. Timothy Gill (vc) [arr vc & pno] Guild ▲ GMCD 7114 [DDD]

Pawlica, Gerhard (vc)
Pfiffner, E.:Monologue on Peace & War, w. F. Reinmann (bar), J. Allen (vn), A. Rosenfeld (vn), C. Anderes (va) *(rec May 1992)* Pro Viva ▲ ISPV 170 [DDD]
Wehrli, W.:Son Vc, w. Anne de Dadelsen (pno) *(rec 1989)* Jecklin ▲ JS 301-2 [ADD]

Pawluk, Anna (pno)
Moniuszko, S.:Songs & Arias, w. Hanna Rumowska-Machnikowska (sop), Wicherek (cnd), Polish Radio-TV SO, Polish RSO, Warsaw Theatr Wielk Orch—Do Faona; Przasniczka; Mogila; Nad Rzeka; Powiedzcie Mi; Czy Powroci; Gdyby Kto Mnie Kochal Szczerze; Przepioreczka; Nawrócona; Hola Ptaszki; O, Sama Nie Wiem; Oj, Polece Ja Daleko; Jako Od Wichru Krzew Polamany; Ol Jakzebym Kleczec Juz Chciala Gdyby Rannym Slonkiem; Ha! Dzieciatko Nam Umiera O Mój Malenki Polskie Nagrania ("Polskie Radio" series) ▲ PNCD 322

Pawquier, (db)
Dvořák, A.:Qnt Strs, Op. 77, w. Sine Nomine String Quartet Cascavelle ▲ CVL 1018 [DDD]

Pay, Anthony (cl)
Birtwistle, H.:Melencolia I, w. *(not advised of hp)*, O. Knussen (cnd), London Sinfonietta NM Classics ▲ NMCD 009 [DDD]
Krommer, F.:Con for 2 Cls, Op. 35, w. T. Friedli (cl), A. Pay (cnd), English CO Claves ▲ CD 8602 [DDD]
Mozart, W.A.:Con Cl, w. C. Hogwood (cnd), Academy of Ancient Music L'Oiseau-Lyre ▲ 414339-2 [DDD]
Vivaldi, A.:Cons Obs Cls, w. S. Hammer (ob), F. de Bruine (ob), E. Hoeprich (cl), C. Hogwood (cnd), Academy of Ancient Music—RV.559 London ▲ 433674-2
Weber, C.M. von:Concertino Cl, Orch of the Age of Enlightenment Virgin Classics ▲ 59002 [DDD]
Weber, C.M. von:Con 1 Cl, Orch of the Age of Enlightenment Virgin Classics ▲ 59002 [DDD]
Weber, C.M. von:Con 2 Cl, Orch of the Age of Enlightenment Virgin Classics ▲ 59002 [DDD]

Pay, Anthony (cl/b cl)
Schoenberg, A.:Pierrot lunaire, w. Y. Minton (speaker), P. Zukerman (vn/va), L. Harrell (vc), D. Barenboim (pno), M. Debost (fl/pic), P. Boulez (cnd) *(rec June 20–21, 1977)* Sony Classical ▲ SMK 48466 [ADD]

Payeur, Ève (perc)
Messe de Sainte-Cécile, w. Stéphane Caillet Vocal Ensemble ARB ▲ 1417

Payne, Carol Wallace (pno)
Gershwin, G.:Music of, w. P. Huybregts (pno)—Fant. "An Afternoon with Gershwin" Love Is Here to Stay, Mine & A Foggy Day; Nice Work If You Can Get It; They Can't Take That away from Me; Oh, Lady Be Good; Somebody Loves Me; Love Walked in; Strike up the Band; 'S Wonderful; I Got Rhythm; Soon Let's Call the Whole Thing Off; Fant. "An Evening with Gershwin" Of Thee I Sing; Who Cares; Embraceable You; Fascinating Rhythm [all arr. Huybregts] *(rec Nov. 1992)* Centaur ▲ CRC 2178 [DDD]
Gershwin, G.:Pno Music, w. P. Huybregts (pno)—The Man I Love, 2-piano arr. by Huybregts Centaur ▲ CRC 2117 [DDD]
Grainger, P.:Fant on Gershwin's *Porgy & Bess*, w. P. Huybregts (pno) Centaur ▲ CRC 2117 [DDD]
Poulenc, F.:Élégie Pnos, w. P. Huybregts (pno) Centaur ▲ CRC 2117 [DDD]
Poulenc, F.:L'Embarquement pour Cythère, w. P. Huybregts (pno) Centaur ▲ CRC 2117 [DDD]
Poulenc, F.:Son Pno 4-Hands, w. P. Huybregts (pno) Centaur ▲ CRC 2117 [DDD]
Poulenc, F.:Son for 2 Pnos, w. P. Huybregts (pno) Centaur ▲ CRC 2117
Rodgers, R.:Music of, w. Pierre Huybregts (pno)—Oklahoma Suite; My Funny Valentine; The Lady Is a Tramp; Bewitched; Where or When; Blue Moon; The Sweetest Sounds; You Are Too Beautiful; Falling in Love with Love; With a Song in My Heart; If I Loved You; Lover [all arr Huybregts for Pno Duo] *(rec Recital Hall, Pensacola, FL, Feb 1994)* Centaur ▲ CRC 2264 [DDD]

Payne, Joseph (hpd)
Bach, J.S.:French Suites BIS 2-▲ CD 589/90 [DDD]
Bach, J.S.:Goldberg Vars BIS ▲ CD 519 [DDD]
Bach, J.S.:Inventions (30) Hpd—2 Part, BWV 772–786 BIS 2-▲ CD 589/90 [DDD]
Bach, J.S.:Preludes Hpd, BWV 933–38, "Little Preludes" BIS 2-▲ CD 589/90 [DDD]
Bull, J.:Music of—Chromatic Pavan & Galliard [for Queen Elizabeth]; Fantastic Pavan & Galliard; Pavan & Galliards [St. Thomas Wake]; Spanish Pavan; Trumpet Pavan; Prince's Galliard; Italian Galliard; Melancholy Pavan; Quadran Pavan & Galliard [II & III] *(rec Forde Estate, Boston, MA, July 6–14, 1994)* BIS ▲ CD 729 [DDD]
Couperin, F.:Pièces de clavecin (sels)—23 selections from Ordres 2, 5, 6, 7, 10, 13, 14, 15, 17, 21 & 24 BIS ▲ CD 559 [DDD]
de Albero, S.:Sons Hpd—in C, K.143; in f#, K.142; in G, K.144; Nos. 1–14 *(rec May 20, 21 & 27, 1993)* BIS ▲ CD 629 [DDD]
Pachelbel, J.:Keyboard Suites—in A, C, d, e, e, F, g, g, G [from a collection of 21 suites attr Pachelbel 1693] *(rec Forde Estate, Boston, Oct 11–12, 1995)* BIS ▲ CD 809 [DDD]
Roman, J.H.:Sons Hpd *(rec Boston, MA)* BIS 2-▲ CD 669/70 [DDD]
Scarlatti, D.:Sons Kbd—Sons. K.1–30 BIS ▲ CD 499 [DDD]

Payne, Joseph (org)
Compère, L.:Org Music—Ave Maria gratia plena; Paranimphus salutat virginem *(rec Univ. of Vermont, Burlington, Mar. 1994)* Naxos ▲ 8.553214 [DDD]
Corrette, G.:Messe du huitième ton à l'usage des dames réligieuses *(rec Univ. of Vermont, Burlington, Mar. 1994)* Naxos ▲ 8.553214 [DDD]
Early English Organ Music, Vol. 1 *(rec Nov. 12 & 13, 1989)* Naxos ▲ 8.550718 [DDD]
Early English Organ Music, Vol. 2 *(rec Feb. 3, 1987)* Naxos ▲ 8.550719 [DDD]
Early French Organ Music, Vol. 2 *(rec St. Mark's Church, Grand Rapids, MI, Sept. 1994)* Naxos ▲ 8.553215 [DDD]
Famous Organ Works *(rec St. Paul's Church, MA (tracks 1–16) & Annisquam Village Church, MA (tracks 17–34), Nov 12–13, 1989)* Naxos 4-▲ 8.504014 [DDD]
German Organ Music, Vol. 1 *(rec July & Oct. 1993)* Naxos ▲ 8.550964 [DDD]
German Organ Music, Vol. 2 *(rec July & Oct. 1993)* Naxos ▲ 8.550965 [DDD]
Grigny, N. de:Org Music—Ave maris stella (hymn); A solis ortus [Crudelis Herodes] (hymn); Fugue à 5 *(rec Univ. of Vermont, Burlington, Mar. 1994)* Naxos ▲ 8.553214 [DDD]
Japart, J.:Fortuna d'un gran tempo *(rec Univ. of Vermont, Burlington, Mar. 1994)* Naxos ▲ 8.553214 [DDD]
Marchand, L.:Pieces Org—Book 2 *(rec Univ. of Vermont, Burlington, Mar. 1994)* Naxos ▲ 8.553214 [DDD]
Paumann, C.:Org Music—Incipit Fundamentum M.C.P.C.; In idem Redeunter; Bonus Tactus *(rec Southern College, TN, May 1995)* Naxos ▲ 8.553468 [DDD]
Stanford, C.V.:Sons Org (misc)—Nos. 2 in g, Op. 151, "Eroica"; 3 in d, Op. 152, "Britannica"; 4 in c, Op. 153, "Celtica" *(rec St. Stephen Presbyterian Church, Fort Worth, TX, June 9, 1994)* Marco Polo ▲ 8.223754 [DDD]

Payne, Joseph (vir)
The Fitzwilliam Virginal Book Vox Box 2-▲ CDX 5085 [ADD]
The Queenes Command:Masterpieces of Elizabethan Keyboard Music BIS ▲ CD 539 [DDD]

Payne, Maggi (fl)
Behrman, D.:On the Other Ocean, w. David Behrman (elec), Arthur Stidfole (bn), Kim-1 (computer) *(rec Mills College, Oakland, CA, Sep 18, 1977)* Lovely Music ▲ LCD 1041 [ADD]

Payne, Maggi (fl/elec)
Payne, M.:Music of—Crystal for Moog synthesizer (1982); Scirocco for Flute & Tape Delay (1983); Solar Wind [electronic score] (1983); White Night [synthesized speech] (1984); Subterranean Network [electronic score] (1985); Ahh-Ahh (ver. 2.1) [acoustic-electronic work] (1987); Phase Transitions for Synthesizer (1989) Lovely Music ▲ LCD 2061 [DDD]

Paysen, Stephen (perc)
Crumb, G.:An Idyll for the Misbegotten, w. Z. Mueller (fl), G. Gottlieb (timp), B. Herman (perc) New World ▲ NW 357-2

Paysen, Steven (vib)
Roussakis, N.:Trigono, w. Ronald Borror (tbn), Gregory Charnon (perc) CRI ▲ CD 709 [DDD]

Paz, F. S. (vn)
Piazzolla, A.:Music of, w. Horacio Malivicino (elec gtr), Hector Console (db), A. Piazolla (band), Pablo Ziegler (pno)—Verando porteño; Lunfardo; Milonga del angel; Muerte del angel; Astor's Speech; La camorra; Mumuki; Adios Nonino; Contra bajissmo; Michelangelo; Concierto para quinteto *(rec Sept. 6, 1987)* Chesky ▲ JD 107 [DDD]

Pazqueir, Bruno (va)
Alain, J.:Music of, w. Delphine Collot (sop), Bruno Boterf (ten), Jacques Bona (bar), Françoise Gyps (fl), Laurent Decker (ob), Philippe Muller (vc), Georges Guillard (org), Ludwig String Quartet, Georges Guillard (cnd), St. Louis Camerata Vocal Ensemble—2 Melodies for Sop & Pno; Nuptial Song for Bar, Bass, Vc & Org; Post-Scriptum for 3 Female Voices & Pno; Canticle in Phrygian Mode for 4 Mixed-Voice, Sop & Strs; Invention for Fl, Ob & Cl; Monody for solo Fl; Prelude for Str Qnt; Adagio for Str Qnt; Funerals for Str Qnt; March of the Horiaces & the Curiaces for 2 Bugles, Drum & Org Arion ▲ ARN 68321

INSTRUMENT.

Peabody, Paul (vn)
Bach, J.S.:Cons Vn (comp), w. R. Kapp (cnd), Philharmonia Virtuosi ESS.A.Y ▲ CD 1002 [DDD] ■ C 1002 (D)
Bach, J.S.:Con Vn & Ob, w. S. Taylor (ob), R. Kapp (cnd), Philharmonia Virtuosi ESS.A.Y ▲ CD 1002 [DDD] ■ C 1002 (D)
Bach, J.S.:Con for 3 Vns, w. R. Rood (vn), E. Sato (vn), R. Kapp (cnd), Philharmonia Virtuosi ESS.A.Y ▲ CD 1002 [DDD] ■ C 1002 (D)
Telemann, G.P.:Con Va, w. R. Kapp (cnd), Philharmonia Virtuosi ESS.A.Y ▲ CD 1016
Telemann, G.P.:Cons Vn, w. R. Kapp (cnd), Philharmonia Virtuosi—4 Concerti—in D, a, E & D ESS.A.Y ▲ CD 1016
Telemann, G.P.:Con in C for 2 Vns, w. E. Lim (vn), R. Kapp (cnd), Philharmonia Virtuosi—4 Concerti—in D, a, E & D ESS.A.Y ▲ CD 1016
Vivaldi, A.:Con Lt, w. P. Press (gtr), E. Lim (vn), J. Haffner (va), T. Mook (vc), E. Brewer (hpd) ESS.A.Y ▲ CD 1004 [DDD] ■ C 1004 (D)
Vivaldi, A.:Cons Vn (misc), w. R. Kapp (cnd), Philharmonia Virtuosi—in A, in D, in c, in g & in G ESS.A.Y ▲ CD 1024 [DDD]
Vivaldi, A.:Cons Vn, Op. 8/1–4, "The Four Seasons", w. R. Kapp (cnd), Philharmonia Virtuosi ESS.A.Y ▲ CD 1001 [DDD] ■ C 1001 (D)
Vivaldi, A.:Cons for 2 Vns, w. Richard Rood (vn), R. Kapp (cnd), Philharmonia Virtuosi—RV.522 ESS.A.Y ▲ CD 1001 [DDD] ■ C 1001 (D)
Vivaldi, A.:Trio Sons Gtr Vn, w. P. Press (gtr), R. Shell (vc), E. Brewer (hpd)—(2) in C, RV.82 & in g, RV.85 ESS.A.Y ▲ CD 1004 [DDD] ■ C 1004 (D)
Vivaldi, A.:Trio Sons Vn Lt, w. Peter Press (gtr), Roger Shell (vc), Edward Brewer (hpd) ESS.A.Y ▲ ESS 1004 [DDD]

Peace, Paula (pno/cnd)—see ORCHESTRAS & ENSEMBLES Atlanta Chamber Players

Peachey, George (pno)
Adler, S.:Music of, w. W. Steck (vn), C. Lewis (pno), Y. Caruthers (vc)—Sons. 2–4; Etudes (4), "Meadowmountetudes"; Double Portrait; Little Suite; Close Encounters Gasparo ▲ GS 297 [DDD/ADD]
Adler, S.:Sons Vn, w. W. Steck (vn)—Son. No. 2; Sons. Nos. 3 & 4 [w. C. Lewis] Gasparo ▲ GS 297

Pearce, Joanne Martin (pno)
Barber, S.:Canzone Fl & Pno, w. Laurel Ann Maurer (fl) Albany ▲ TROY 167 [DDD]
Copland, A.:Duo Fl, w. Laurel Ann Maurer (fl) Albany ▲ TROY 167 [DDD]
Kraft, L.:Fant Fl & Pno, w. Laurel Ann Maurer (fl) Albany ▲ TROY 167 [DDD]
Kupferman, M.:Chaconne Son, w. Laurel Ann Maurer (fl) Albany ▲ TROY 167 [DDD]
Muczynski, R.:Son Fl, w. Laurel Ann Maurer (fl) Albany ▲ TROY 167 [DDD]

Pearce, Judith (fl/va)—see also ORCHESTRAS & ENSEMBLES New Music Consort
Maw, N.:Qt Fl, w. Monticello Trio members ASV ▲ ASV 920 [DDD]

Pearce, Richard (org)
Stairway to Heaven, w. [cnd:Richard Marlow], Trinity College Choir Cambridge, Philip Rushforth (org), Silas Standage (org) *(rec Trinity College Chapel, Cambridge)* Conifer Classics ▲ 75605-51521-2 [DDD]

Pearl, Ronald (gtr)—see also ORCHESTRAS & ENSEMBLES Classical Guitar Duo
Homages & Evocations, w. Julian Gray (gtr) *(rec Troy Savings Bank Music Hall, Troy, NY, Sept 1995)* Dorian ▲ DOR 90230 [DDD]
The Magic Circle:Music for 2 Guitars, w. Julian Gray (gtr) Dorian Discovery ▲ DIS 80111

Pearson, Leslie (hpd/org continuo)
A Portrait of John Williams, w. John Williams (gtr) CBS ▲ MK 37791

Pearson, Leslie (org)
Clarke, J.:Suite Tpt, w. G. Ashton (tpt) IMP Classics ▲ PCD 986 [DDD]
Music for Trumpet & Organ, w. Graham Ashton (tpt), John Orford (bn), Gordon Hunt (ob), Denis Vigay (vc) IMP Classics ▲ PCD 986 [DDD]
Respighi, O.:Suite Org, w. G. Simon (cnd), Philharmonia Orch *(rec Goldsmith's College, London, Dec 19–22, 1990)* Cala ▲ CACD 1007 [DDD]
Trumpet & Organ:Sonatas & Suites, w. Graham Ashton (tpt), Gordon Hunt (ob), John Orford (bn), Denis Vigay (vc) IMP ("Classics" series) ▲ IMP 6700922

Pearson, Leslie (pno)
Ketèlbey, A.W.:Music of, w. J. Temperley (mez), V. Mdegley (ten), J. Lanchbery (cnd), Philharmonia Orch, Ambrosian Singers—In a Persian Market; In a Monastery Garden; Chal Romano; In the Mystic Land of Egypt; The Clock and the Dresden Figures; Bells across the Meadows; In a Chinese Temple; In the Moonlight; Sanctuary of the Heart Classics for Pleasure ▲ CDCFP 4637 [ADD]

Pearson, M. (vn)—see ORCHESTRAS & ENSEMBLES Apple Hill Chamber Players

Pearson, Peggy (ob)—see also ORCHESTRAS & ENSEMBLES Quintet of the Americas
Child, P.:Sonatina Ob CRI ▲ CD 605 [DDD]
Tcherepnin, I.:Flores musicales, w. Wilma Smith (vn), Ivan Tcherepnin (psaltery/org/elecs) *(rec Harvard Univ. Electronic Music Studio, Oct. & Dec. 1981)* CRI ▲ CD 684 [ADD]

Peasgood, Siu (fl)
Telemann, G.P.:Cons for 2 Fls, w. R. Brown (fl), S. Standage (vn), J. Coe (vc), S. Standage (cnd), Collegium Musicum 90—(1) in D Chandos ("Chaconne" series) ▲ CHAN 0512 [DDD]

Pech, Thorsten (org)
Trumpet & Organ Music from the Altenberg Cathedral, w. Uwe Komischke (tpt) Koch Schwann ▲ SCH 313902 [DDD]

Pecha, Pamela (ob)
Bliss, A.:Qnt Ob, w. Audubon String Quartet IMP ("Classics" series) ▲ IMP 6701032
Britten, H.:Phantasy Qt, w. Audubon String Quartet IMP ("Classics" series) ▲ IMP 6701032

Pecha, Peter (va)
Schmidt, F.:Qnt Cl, w. E. Ottensamer (cl), R. Keuschnig (pno), J. Hell (vn), P. Wächter (vn), R. Wallfisch (vc) *(rec Jan. 7, 1991)* Orfeo ▲ 287921 [DDD]
Schmidt, F.:Qnt Pno, w. R. Keuschnig (pno), J. Hell (vn), P. Wächter (vn), G. Iberer (vc) *(rec Jan. 7, 1991)* Orfeo ▲ 287921 [DDD]

Peck, David (cl)
Mozart, W.A.:Con Cl, w. C. Eschenbach (cnd), Houston SO *(rec Stude Concert Hall, Shephard School of Music, Rice Univ, July 12–16, 1993)* IMP ("Masters" series) ▲ IMP MCD 91

Peck, Donald (fl)
Beethoven, L. van:Romances Vn, w. Melody Lord (pno) [arr fl & pno] *(rec DePaul Concert Hall, Chicago, June 30, 1996)* Boston Records ▲ BR 1014 CD [DDD]
Debussy, C.:Chansons de Bilitis (recitation), w. Lola Rand (nar), Melody Lord (pno) [arr Peck] *(rec DePaul Concert Hall, Chicago, June 30, 1996)* Boston Records ▲ BR 1014 CD [DDD]
Debussy, C.:Syrinx *(rec DePaul Concert Hall, Chicago, June 30, 1996)* Boston Records ▲ BR 1014 CD [DDD]
Donald Peck:Flute, w. Melody Lord (pno) *(rec DePaul Concert Hall, Chicago, IL, live, July 14, 1993 & Aug)* Boston Records ▲ BR 1010
Ferris, W.:Son Fl, w. Melody Lord (pno) *(rec DePaul Concert Hall, Chicago, June 30, 1996)* Boston Records ▲ BR 1014 CD [DDD]
Franck, C.:Son Vn, w. Melody Lord (pno) [arr for fl & pno] *(rec DePaul Concert Hall, Chicago, June 30, 1996)* Boston Records ▲ BR 1014 CD [DDD]

Peck, Richard (a sax/s sax/ten sax)—see ORCHESTRAS & ENSEMBLES Philip Glass Ensemble

Peckham, Merry (vc)
Erb, D.:Qt 2 Strs, w. A. Fullard (vn), S. Waterbury (vn), E. Eckert (va) Albany ▲ TROY 092 [DDD]

Péclard, Etienne (vc)
Bloch, E.:Schelomo, w. A. Lombard (cnd), Bordeaux-Aquitaine National Orch Forlane ▲ FRL 16680 [DDD]
Brahms, J.:Sextet Strs, Op. 18, w. Régis Pasquier (vn), Raphaël Oleg (vn), Bruno Pasquier (va), Jean Dupouy (va), Roland Pidoux (vc)—No. 1 Harmonia Mundi France ("Musique d'abord" series) ▲ HMA 1901073
Offenbach, J.:Grand duos concertants, w. R. Pidoux (vc) Musique d'Abord ▲ HMA 1901043
Prokofiev, S.:Sym-Con Vc, w. A. Lombard (cnd), Bordeaux-Aquitaine National Orch Forlane ▲ FRL 16680 [DDD]

Péclard, Etienne (vc) (cont.)
Telemann, G.P.:Son in a Vc, w. Richard Siegel (hpd) *(rec Lutheran Church of la Villette, Sept 13 & 17, 1983)* Studio SM ▲ 2527

Pecola, Andrea (vn)
Gragnani, F.:Gtr Music, w. Marco Riboni (gtr), Leopoldo Saracino (gtr), Emilio Vapi (fl), Anna Maria Giaquinta (cl), Andrea Bellato (vc)—Qt in A for Vn, Cl & 2 Gtrs, Op. 8; Duet No. 1 in A for Vn & Gtr; Trio in D for Fl, Vn & Gtr, Op. 13; Duet No. 2 in A for Vn & Gtr; Sxt in A for Fl, Cl, Vn, 2 Gtrs & Vc, Op. 9 Stradivarius ▲ STV 33385 [DDD]

Pedersen, Birger (fl)
Bach, Joh. Christian:Qts (4) for 2 Fls, w. B. Larsen (fl), P. Elbaek (vn), H. Olsen (va), B. Holst Christensen (vc) Kontrapunkt ▲ 32048 [DDD]
Bach, Joh. Christian:Trios for 2 Fls & Strs, w. B. Larsen (fl), P. Elbaek (vn), H. Olsen (va), B. Holst Christensen (vc) Kontrapunkt ▲ 32048 [DDD]

Pedersen, Erling (org)
Danish Chirsmas Carols, w. St. Annae Girls' Choir, Ketil Christensen (tpt), Flemming Dreisig (org) Danica ▲ DCD 8103

Pedersen, Georg (vc)—see ORCHESTRAS & ENSEMBLES Mozartrois, australYSIS members

Peebles, Anthony (pno)
Liszt, F.:Transcriptions & Paraphrases—Donizetti:Reminiscences de Lucrezia [2 versions]; Bellini:La Sonnambula; Meyerbeer:Illustrations du Prophète; Beethoven:Fant on Motives from Ruins of Athens; Berlioz:March to the Scaffold [from Symphonie Fantastique] Meridian ▲ MER 84278 [DDD]

Peebles, Sarah (kbd/elec/perc/shô)
Peebles, S.:Tomoé, w. Hiromi Yoshida (shô/û), Ikuo Kakehashi (perc/kbd) *(rec live, Shukôji Temple, Kawasaki, Sept 25, 1993)* Innova ▲ 506

Peebles, Sarah (shô)
Peebles, S.:Phoenix Calling, w. Ikuo Kakehashi (shô), Andy Morris (perc), Bugaku Percussion Ensemble *(rec live, Shukôji Temple, Kawasaki)* Innova ▲ 506

Peebles, Sarah (shô/elec/perc)
Peebles, S.:Aqua Babble, w. Yakashi Harada (ondes martenot), Kazue Mizushima (perc) *(rec live, Studio Kinshicho, Japan, June 11, 1993)* Innova ▲ 506

Pegis, Christopher (vc)—see also ORCHESTRAS & ENSEMBLES Florida String Quartet
Stravinsky, S.S.:Son Vc, w. E. Gilgore (pno) *(rec May 1992)* Centaur ▲ CRC 2141 [DDD]

Pegis, Jonathan (vc)
Schoenberg, A.:Verklärte Nacht, w. D. McInnes (va), LaSalle String Quartet Deutsche Grammophon ▲ 423250-2 [ADD]

Pegreffi, Elisa (vn)—see ORCHESTRAS & ENSEMBLES Quartetto Italiano

Pehrsson, Claas (a rcr)
Scarlatti, A.:Son Fl, w. Drottningholm Baroque Ensemble BIS ▲ CD 8

Pehrsson, Claas (bass rcr)
Bach, C.P.E.:Trio Son in F, w. P. Novovic (va), A. Petersén (bass vl), A. Östman (hpd) [period instrs] BIS ▲ CD 220 [DDD]

Pehrsson, Claas (rcr)
Burkhart, F.:Adventslieder (3), w. Solvieg Faringer (sop), Jörgen Rörby (gtr) *(rec Castle Wik, Sweden, Jan 19, 20 & 26, 1974)* BIS ▲ CD 202 [AAD]
Clas Pehrsson *(rec 1976, 1982)* BIS ▲ CD 48 [AAD]
Handel, G.F.:Sons Rcr, w. Bengt Ericson (vc), Thomas Schuback (hpd) BIS ▲ CD 208
Hovland, E.:Cantus II, w. Thomas Schuback (pno) *(rec Studio BIS, Djursholm, Sweden, May 11–13, 1981)* BIS ▲ CD 202 [AAD]
Kukuck, F.:Die Brücke, w. Solvieg Faringer (sop), Jörgen Rörby (gtr) *(rec Castle Wik, Sweden, Jan 19, 20 & 26, 1974)* BIS ▲ CD 202 [AAD]
Linde, H.-M.:Amarilli, mia bella *(rec Tyresö Church, Sweden, Feb 29, 1976)* BIS ▲ CD 202 [AAD]
Lundén, L.:Little Toe & Nine More, w. Solvieg Faringer (sop), Jörgen Rörby (gtr) *(rec Castle Wik, Sweden, Jan 19, 20 & 26, 1974)* BIS ▲ CD 202 [AAD]
Örhängen, w. Elisabeth Söderström (sop), Hakan Sund (pno) *(rec June 15–18, 1981)* BIS ▲ CD 187 [AAD]
Quantz, J.J.:Trio Sons, w. P. Novovic (vn), A. Petersén (b vl), A. Östman (hpd) [period instrs]—in C BIS ▲ CD 220 [DDD]
Sammartini, G.:Cons Rcr, w. Drottningholm Baroque Ensemble—in F BIS ▲ CD 210
17th Century Italian & English Music for Recorder & Lute, w. Jakob Lindberg (lt) BIS ▲ CD 266
Shinohara, M.:Fragmente *(rec Tyresö Church, Sweden, Feb 29, 1976)* BIS ▲ CD 202 [AAD]
Staeps, H.U.:Son Trb Rcr, w. Thomas Schuback (pno) *(rec Studio BIS, Djursholm, Sweden, May 11–13, 1981)* BIS ▲ CD 202 [AAD]
Telemann, G.P.:Con in F Rcr Bn, w. M. McCraw (bn), Drottningholm Baroque Ensemble BIS ▲ CD 271 [DDD]
Telemann, G.P.:Con in F Rcr Bn, w. M. McCraw (bn), Drottningholm Baroque Ensemble *(rec May 27–28, 1984)* BIS ▲ CD 617 [DDD]
Telemann, G.P.:Con Rcr, Fl, w. P. Evison (fl), Drottningholm Baroque Ensemble BIS ▲ CD 249 [DDD]
Telemann, G.P.:Con Rcr, Fl, w. P. Evison (fl), Drottningholm Baroque Ensemble *(rec Apr. 8–9, 1983)* BIS ▲ CD 617 [DDD]
Telemann, G.P.:Con in C Rcr, w. Drottningholm Baroque Ensemble BIS ▲ CD 271 [DDD]
Telemann, G.P.:Con in F Rcr, w. Drottningholm Baroque Ensemble BIS ▲ CD 8
Telemann, G.P.:Con in a for Rcr, Vl, w. O. Larsson (vc), Drottningholm Baroque Ensemble *(rec Apr. 13, 1993)* BIS ▲ CD 617 [DDD]
Telemann, G.P.:Con in a for 2 Rcrs, w. D. Laurin (rcr), Drottningholm Baroque Ensemble *(rec May 31, 1993)* BIS ▲ CD 617 [DDD]
Telemann, G.P.:Con in B♭ for 2 Rcrs, w. A.-Per Johsson (rcr), Drottningholm Baroque Ensemble BIS ▲ CD 220 [AAD]
Telemann, G.P.:Con in B♭ for 2 Rcrs, w. D. Laurin (rcr), Drottningholm Baroque Ensemble *(rec May 31, 1993)* BIS ▲ CD 617 [DDD]
Telemann, G.P.:Con in B♭ for 2 Rcrs, w. A.-Per Johsson (rcr), Drottningholm Baroque Ensemble BIS ▲ CD 8
Telemann, G.P.:Sons Rcr, w. A. Petersén (bass vl), A. Östman (hpd) [played on period instruments] BIS ▲ CD 220 [DDD]
Telemann, G.P.:Suite in a Fl, w. Drottningholm Baroque Ensemble BIS ▲ CD 210
Vivaldi, A.:Cons Rcr, w. Drottningholm Baroque Ensemble—R. 428 BIS ▲ CD 210
Vivaldi, A.:Trio Sons (misc), w. P. Novovic (vn), A. Petersén (b vl), A. Östman (hpd) [period instrs]—in g BIS ▲ CD 220 [DDD]

Peinemann, Edith (vn)
Kraus, J.M.:Con Vn, w. M. Sieghart (cnd), Stuttgart CO *(rec 3/91)* Orfeo ▲ 254921 [DDD]

Peinkofer, Karl (perc)—see also ORCHESTRAS & ENSEMBLES Karl Peinkofer Percussion Ensemble
Orff, C.:Schulwerk (complete), w. Godela Orff (nar), Carolin Widmann (vn), Sonja Korkeala (vn), Markus Zahnhausen (rcr), Andreas Schumacher (perc), Wilfried Hiller (perc/mar), Martin Ruhland (mar), Munich Hochschule Madrigal Choir—Wessobrun Prayer for a capella Choir; 2 Pieces for a capella Choir; 8 Pieces for 2 Vns; Mater et filia for women's a capella Choir; Devotional Yodel for male a capella Choir; 5 Pieces for Sop, Rcr & Perc; Death for Nar., Wood Bells, Bass Xyl & Tam-Tam; Omnia tempus habent for mixed Choir, Timp & Little Dr; Rubato, molto allegro, rubato; Abenlied for Nar, Bass Metallophon, Bass Xyl, Large Dr & Wine Glass; 5 Pieces for Fl & Perc; Devotional Yodel for male Choir [version 2]; 7 Pieces for 2 Xyl *(rec Munich, 1994–95)* Celestial Harmonies ▲ 13105-2

Peiretti, Rita (hpd)
Albinoni, T.:Fl Music, w. Enrico di Felice (German fl), R. Peiretti (cnd), Accademia dei Solinghi—Sons. in a, Nos. 3 in E, 5 in D & 6 in b; Cons. Nos. 1 in G & 2 in G Stradivarius ▲ STV 33377 [DDD]

Peisteiner, Klaus (va)—see also ORCHESTRAS & ENSEMBLES Vienna String Quartet
Mozart, W.A.:Trio Cl, K.498, w. Peter Schmidl (cl), Keiko Toyama (pno) *(rec Tsukuba Nova Hall, Oct 12, 1990)* Camerata ▲ 32CM 180 [DDD]

Pekarsky, Mark (cymbals)
The Spirit of Russia, w. Gidon Kremer (vn), Vladimir Malinin (vn), Leonid Bobylev (pno), Alexander Melnikov (vn) Vox Box 2-▲ CDX 5115 [ADD]

Pekinel, Güher (pno)
Encores for 2 Pianos, w. Süher Pekinel (pno) Berlin Classics ▲ BER 1118 [DDD]

770 ▲ = CD ♦ = Enhanced CD Δ = MD ■ = Cassette Tape □ = DCC

Pekinel, Güher (pno) (cont.)
Granados, E.:Goyescas, w. S. Pekinel (pno) [arr. for two pianos]—No. 4, "Quejas o la maja y el ruiseñor" Teldec ▲ 2292-44931-2 [DDD]
Infante, M.:Danzas andaluzas, w. S. Pekinel (pno) Teldec ▲ 2292-44931-2 [DDD]
Poulenc, F.:Con for 2 Pnos, w. S. Pekinel (pno), M. Janowski (cnd), Radio France PO Teldec ▲ 2292-46155-2 [DDD]
Poulenc, F.:Con for 2 Pnos, w. Süher Pekinel (pno), M. Janowski (cnd), ORTF SO Teldec ("M Line" series) ▲ 97445-2
Ravel, M.:Rapsodie espagnole, w. S. Pekinel (pno) [Ravel's two-piano arr.] Teldec ▲ 2292-44931-2 [DDD]
Ravel, M.:La Valse, w. S. Pekinel (pno) [Ravel's two-piano arr.] Teldec ▲ 2292-44931-2 [DDD]
Saint-Saëns, C.:Carnival of the Animals, w. S. Pekinel (pno), M. Janowski (cnd), ORTF SO Teldec ("M Line" series) ▲ 97445-2
Saint-Saëns, C.:Carnival of the Animals, w. S. Pekinel (pno), M. Janowski (cnd), French Radio PO Teldec ▲ 2292-46155-2 [DDD]

Pekinel, Süher (pno)
Encores for 2 Pianos, w. Güher Pekinel (pno) Berlin Classics ▲ BER 1118 [DDD]
Granados, E.:Goyescas, w. G. Pekinel (pno) [arr. for two pianos]—No. 4, "Quejas o la maja y el ruiseñor" Teldec ▲ 2292-44931-2 [DDD]
Infante, M.:Danzas andaluzas, w. G. Pekinel (pno) Teldec ▲ 2292-44931-2 [DDD]
Poulenc, F.:Con for 2 Pnos, w. G. Pekinel (pno), M. Janowski (cnd), Radio France PO Teldec ▲ 2292-46155-2 [DDD]
Poulenc, F.:Con for 2 Pnos, w. Güher Pekinel (pno), M. Janowski (cnd), ORTF SO Teldec ("M Line" series) ▲ 97445-2
Ravel, M.:Rapsodie espagnole, w. G. Pekinel (pno) [Ravel's two-piano arr.] Teldec ▲ 2292-44931-2 [DDD]
Ravel, M.:La Valse, w. G. Pekinel (pno) [Ravel's two-piano arr.] Teldec ▲ 2292-44931-2 [DDD]
Saint-Saëns, C.:Carnival of the Animals, w. G. Pekinel (pno), M. Janowski (cnd), ORTF SO Teldec ("M Line" series) ▲ 97445-2
Saint-Saëns, C.:Carnival of the Animals, w. G. Pekinel (pno), M. Janowski (cnd), French Radio PO Teldec ▲ 2292-46155-2 [DDD]

Pekkala, Lea (vc)
Suilamo, H.:BIAS, w. Marjut Tynkkynen (acc) Finlandia ▲ FIN 12179 [DDD]
Suilamo, H.:...half-moon of his nails..., w. Jouko Laivuori (pno) Finlandia ▲ FIN 12179 [DDD]

Pelliccione, Carlo (db)
Brennan, J.W.:Atanos, w. Andrea Formenti (a sax), Tomas Dratva (pno) *(rec Sept. 1993 & Jan. 1994)* Jecklin ▲ JS 301-2

Pelikan, Tina (va)
Rosenhaus, S.:Kol Nidre Prelude, w. Dawn Buckholz (vc) *(rec Tom Tom Studios, NYC)* Capstone ▲ CPS 8616 [ADD]

Pelissier, Alain (va)—see ORCHESTRAS & ENSEMBLES Manfred String Quartet

Pell, J. (gtr)
Sowash, R.:Fant on "Shenandoah", w. Shelburne String Quartet Gasparo ▲ GS 236

Pell, Susanna (Renaissance b vl)—see ORCHESTRAS & ENSEMBLES Kithara

Pell, Susanna (vielle/perc)—see ORCHESTRAS & ENSEMBLES Dufay Collective

Pell, Susanna (vl)—see ORCHESTRAS & ENSEMBLES Spectre de la Rose

Pellas-Lenom, Marthe (pno)
"Le Patron" of the Saxophone, w. Marcel Mule (sax), Guy Chauvet (ten), G. Charon (sgr), F. l'Homme (sgr), P. Romby (sgr), Eugène Bozza (cnd), Francis Çebron (cnd), Phillipe Gaubert (cnd), *(orchs unknown)*, Joseph Benvenutti (pno), Marcel Gaveau (pno), François Combelle (sax) *(rec 1930-1940)* Clarinet Classics ▲ CC 0013 [AAD]

Pellegrini, Antonio (vn)—see ORCHESTRAS & ENSEMBLES Pellegrini String Quartet

Pellerin, Louise (ob)
Keller, A.:Der enthüllte Stern, w. D. Fueter (sop), K. Graf (sop), A. K. Graf (fl), E. Schmid (cl), U. Walker (vn), C. Schiller (va), P. Demenga (vc), P. Hug-Rutti (hp), F. Eberle (dr) [G] Grammont ▲ CTSP 19-2 [ADD]

Pellerin, Myriam (vn)—see ORCHESTRAS & ENSEMBLES Montreal Musica Camerata, Montreal Musica Camerata members

Pellerite, James (fl)—see also ORCHESTRAS & ENSEMBLES Baroque Chamber Players, Musica Sonora
Barati, G.:Chant to Pele *(rec Indiana Univ, 1984)* Centaur ▲ CRC 2286 [DDD]

Pelletier, G. (fl)—see ORCHESTRAS & ENSEMBLES Pentaèdre Ensemble

Pelletier, Louis-Philippe (pno)
Beethoven, L. van:Son 30 Pno ISBA ▲ ISB 5014
Beethoven, L. van:Son 31 Pno ISBA ▲ ISB 5014
Beethoven, L. van:Son 32 Pno ISBA ▲ ISB 5014
Vivier, C.:Shiraz *(rec Ottawa, 1983 & 1984)* Centredisques ▲ CMC 5194 [DDD]

Peltzer, Dwight (pno)
Schoenberg, A.:Pierrot lunaire, w. Maureen McNalley (nar), Eric Rosenblith (vn/va), Chris Finckel (vc), Sue Ann Kahn (fl), Anand Devendra (cl/b cl), J. Thome (cnd), Orch of Our Time Vox Box 2-▲ CDX 5144

Peña, Adela (pno)—see ORCHESTRAS & ENSEMBLES Eroica Trio

Peña, Paco (gtr)
The Art of Paco Peña Nimbus ▲ NI 7011 [DDD]
Fragments of a Dream, w. John Williams (gtr), Inti-Illimani (flamenco gtr) CBS ▲ MK 44574 [ADD] ■ FMT 44574

Pénassou, Pierre (vc)—see also ORCHESTRAS & ENSEMBLES Parrenin String Quartet
Jolivet, A.:Nocturne, w. Jacqueline Robin (pno) Arion ▲ ARN 68299 [AAD]

Pendlebury, Jane (vc)
The Flute Album, w. Karen Jones (fl), Aline Brewer (hp), Catherine Edwards (pno) Conifer Classics 2-▲ 75605-51905-2 [DDD]

Pendlebury, Nic (va)—see ORCHESTRAS & ENSEMBLES Smith String Quartet

Pendry, Katherine (panpipes)
Andriessen, L.:Hoketus, w. James Poke (panpipes), Evan Ziporyn (a sax), Richard Craig (a sax), Steven Schick (congas), Amy Knoles (congas), Lisa Moore (Fender Rhodes), Damian LeGassick (Fender Rhodes), Cees van Zeeland (pno), Gerard Bouwhuis (pno), Robert Black (bass gtr), Mark Stewart (bass gtr) *(rec Air Recording Studios, Lyndhurst Hall, Hampstead, London, June 29-July 3, 1994)* Sony Classical ▲ SK 66483 [DDD]

Peneva, Bogdana (vc)
Gallagher, J.:Persistence of Memory, w. T. Delibozov (cnd), Ruse PO Vienna Modern Masters ▲ VMM 3036 [DDD]

Pennanguer, Philippe (vc)
Escaich, T.:Scènes d'enfants, w. Christel Rayneau (fl), Yann Ollivo (pno) Chamade ▲ CHCD 5638 [DDD]
Kaufmann, S.:Cantabile, w. B. Calmel (cnd), Bernard Calmel Orch *(rec Feb 1996)* Pavane ▲ ADW 7362 [DDD]
Kaufmann, S.:Un Matin à varsovie, w. Béatrice Barbary (sop), Serge Kaufmann (nar), B. Calmel (cnd), Bernard Calmel Orch *(rec Feb 1996)* Pavane ▲ ADW 7362 [DDD]

Pennario, Leonard (pno)
Debussy, C.:Music of, w. Alexis Weissenberg (pno)— also Munch, Boston SO; Reiner, Chicago SO; Morton Gould & His Orch. RCA ■ ALK1-4981
Gershwin, G.:Pno Music—Ballet from "Primrose"; Merry-Andrew; Promenade from "Shall We Dance"; Rialto Ripples; Three Preludes; Three-Quarter Blues; 2 Waltzes in C EMI Classics ▲ CDM 64668-2 [ADD/DDD]; ■ EG 64668-4
Gershwin, G.:Preludes (3) Pno Classics for Pleasure ("Eminence" series) ▲ CDEMX 2175
Gershwin, G.:Rhap in Blue, w. F. Slatkin (cnd), Hollywood Bowl SO Classics for Pleasure ("Eminence" series) ▲ CDEMX 2175
Gottschalk, L.M.:Pno Music EMI Classics ▲ CDM 64667-2 ■ EG 64667-4
Gottschalk, L.M.:Pno Music—Ballade; Columbia-Caprice American; La Gallina; Marguerite-Grand Valse Brillante; O, Ma Charmante, Epargnez-Moi, Caprice; Suis-Moil-Follow Mel-Caprice EMI Classics ▲ CDM 64668-2 [ADD/DDD]; ■ EG 64668-4

Pennario, Leonard (pno) (cont.)
Rachmaninoff, S.:Con 2 Pno, w. E. Leinsdorf (cnd), Los Angeles PO EMI Classics ■ 4XG 60237
Rachmaninoff, S.:Music of, w. Anna Moffo (sop), Alexander Brailowsky (pno), Alexis Weissenberg (pno), *(orch unknown)* RCA ■ 5697-4-RV
Rachmaninoff, S.:Prelude Pno, Op. 3/2, w. E. Leinsdorf (cnd), Los Angeles PO EMI Classics ■ 4XG 60237
Rachmaninoff, S.:Preludes Pno, Opp 23 & 32, w. E. Leinsdorf (cnd), Los Angeles PO—in g EMI Classics ■ 4XG 60237

Pennetier, Jean-Claude (pno)
Brahms, J.:Qt 1 Pno, w. Régis Pasquier (vn), Bruno Pasquier (va), Roland Pidoux (vc) Harmonia Mundi ▲ HMT 7901062
Brahms, J.:Sons Cl (comp), w. B. Pasquier (va) Musique d'Abord ▲ HMA 1901092 [ADD]
Brahms, J.:Son 3 Vn, w. Régis Pasquier (vn) Harmonia Mundi ▲ HMT 7901062
Chausson, E.:Con Vn, Pno & Str Qt, w. R. Daugareil (vn), R. Pasquier (vn), G. Simonot (vn), B. Pasquier (va), R. Pidoux (vc) Harmonia Mundi Plus ▲ HMP 3901135
Chausson, E.:Pièce Vc & Pno, w. R. Pidoux (vc) Harmonia Mundi Plus ▲ HMP 3901135
Ohana, M.:Caprices Pno *(rec 1989)* Arion ▲ ARN 68091 [DDD]
Ohana, M.:Préludes Pno Arion ▲ ARN 68091 [AAD]
Rossini, G.:Sacred Music, w. Evelyne Razimowsky (sop), Michel Piquemal (bar), Myriam Richardot (org), Michel Piquemal (cnd), Michel Piquemal Vocal Ensemble—La passegiata; Ave Marie; Inno Alla Pace; Ave Maria; Toast pour le nouvel an; Duetto Buffo di Due Batti; La fede; La speranza; La carita; Cantemus Domino; La notte del Santo Natalie; Preghiera; I Gondolieri Adès ▲ ADE 204192 [AAD]
Schubert, Franz:Son Arpeggione, w. Pidoux (vc) Harmonia Mundi France ▲ HMC 901035
Schubert, Franz:Son Pno, D.664 Harmonia Mundi ("Suite" series) ▲ HMT 7901048
Schubert, Franz:Trio 1 Pno, w. Régis Pasquier (vn), Roland Pidoux (vc) Harmonia Mundi ("Suite" series) ▲ HMT 7901048

Penneys, Rebecca (pno)
Gershwin, G.:Rhap in Blue [solo pno] *(rec Sept. 26, 1992)* Centaur ▲ CRC 2159 [DDD]
Mendelssohn, F.:Lieder ohne Worte Pno—3 sels Centaur ▲ CRC 2159
Mozart, W.A.:Son 15 Pno *(rec Sept. 26, 1992)* Centaur ▲ CRC 2159 [DDD]
Portrait of an Artist, Vol. 4, w. Ruggiero Ricci (vn), Helmut Barth, Univ of Michigan CO One-Eleven ▲ URS 93040 [ADD]
Schubert, Franz:Impromptus Pno, D.899 *(rec Sept. 26, 1992)* Centaur ▲ CRC 2159 [DDD]

Pennies, R. (pno)
Arnold, M.:Pieces (6) Vn, w. R. Ricci (vn) One-Eleven ▲ URS 91060 [ADD]
Beethoven, L. van:Son 3 Vn, w. R. Ricci (vn) One-Eleven ▲ URS 91060 [ADD]
Bull, O.:Music of, w. R. Ricci (vn) One-Eleven ▲ URS 91060 [ADD]
Franck, C.:Son Vn, w. R. Ricci (vn) One-Eleven ▲ URS 91060 [ADD]

Penson, Guy (hpd/org)—see ORCHESTRAS & ENSEMBLES Ricercar Consort

Penson, Guy (hpd)
Bach, W.F.:Con in F for 2 Hpds, w. Florian Heyerick (hpd) Ricercar 2-▲ 089125/26
Bach, W.F.:Trios Fls, F.47-49, w. Patrick Beukels (trns fl), Daniele Etienne (trns fl) *(rec 1992)* Ricercar 2-▲ 089125/26
Boccherini, L.:Sons (34) Vc, w. H. Suzuki (vc), R. Zipperling (vc)—Son. duets in B♭, G.8, in E♭, G.10, in A, G.13, in C G.17 & in B♭, G.565 Ricercar ▲ RIC 122107
Haydn, J.:Adagio in G Pno, H.XV/22 Eufoda ▲ EUF 1185 [DDD]
Haydn, J.:Trios Pno, Fl & Vc, w. Jan de Winne (fl), Roel Dieltiens (vc) Eufoda ▲ EUF 1185 [DDD]

Penson, Guy (org)
Mozart, W.A.:Music of, w. Philip Defrancq (ten), Reginaldo Pinheiro (ten), Jan Van Der Crabben (bar), Jan Vermeulen (pno), P. Peire (cnd), Collegium Instrumentale Brugense, Capella Brugensis—Zerfliesset heut', geliebte Brüder [song]; Dir Seele des Weltalls [cant]; O heiliges Band der Freundschaft [song]; Die ihr einem Neuen Grade [Maurer-Geselienlied]; Die Maurerfreude [cant]; Maurerische Trauermusik; Die ihr der unermesslichen Weltalls Schöpfer ehrt [Kleine deutsche Kantate]; Laut verkünde unsre Freude [Eine kleine Freimaurerkantate]; Lasst uns mit geschlugnen Händen [hymn]; Ihr unsre neuen Leiter [song] *(rec Studio Steurbaut, Gent, Dec 1992)* René Gailly ▲ 92013 [DDD]

Penson, Guy (pno)
Musiques De Salon, w. Sylvia Bernier (pno) Ricercar ▲ RIC 147135 [ADD]

Penzel, Erich (hn)
Haydn, J.:Con for 2 Hns, w. Walter Lexutt (hn), H. Müller-Brühl (cnd), Cologne CO Koch Schwann ▲ CD 316 026 [ADD]
Reicha, A.:Trios Hns, Op. 82, w. et al.—4 trios, not identified on disc or in notes Koch Schwann ▲ CD 316026 [ADD]

Pepicelli, Angelo (pno)—see ORCHESTRAS & ENSEMBLES Pepicelli Duo

Pepicelli, Francesco (vc)—see ORCHESTRAS & ENSEMBLES Pepicelli Duo

Peplowski, Ken (cl/ten sax)—see ORCHESTRAS & ENSEMBLES Ken Peplowski Jazz Quartet

Perahia, Murray (pno)
The Aldeburgh Recital Sony Classical ▲ SK 46437 [DDD]
Bartók, B.:Son for 2 Pnos, w. G. Solti (pno), D. Corkhill (perc), E. Glennie (perc) CBS ▲ MK 42625 [DDD]
Beethoven, L. van:Cons Pno (comp), w. B. Haitink (cnd), Royal Concertgebouw Orch CBS 3-▲ M3K 44575 [DDD]
Beethoven, L. van:Con 1 Pno, w. B. Haitink (cnd), Royal Concertgebouw Orch [w. newly discovered cadenza] CBS ▲ MK 42177 [DDD]
Beethoven, L. van:Con 2 Pno, w. B. Haitink (cnd), Royal Concertgebouw Orch CBS ▲ MK 42177 [DDD]
Beethoven, L. van:Con 3 Pno, w. B. Haitink (cnd), Royal Concertgebouw Orch CBS ▲ MK 39814 [DDD]
Beethoven, L. van:Con 4 Pno, w. S. Celibidache (cnd), South German RSO *(rec 1985)* Originals ▲ ORISH 811 [ADD]
Beethoven, L. van:Con 4 Pno, w. B. Haitink (cnd), Royal Concertgebouw Orch CBS ▲ MK 39814 [DDD]
Beethoven, L. van:Con 5 Pno, "Emperor", w. B. Haitink (cnd), Royal Concertgebouw Orch CBS ▲ MK 42330 [DDD] ■ MT 42330 (D)
Beethoven, L. van:Qnt Pno, Ob, Cl, Hn & Bn, w. English CO Wind Ensemble CBS ▲ MK 42099 [DDD]
Beethoven, L. van:Son 1 Pno Sony Classical ▲ SK 64397
Beethoven, L. van:Son 2 Pno Sony Classical ▲ SK 64397
Beethoven, L. van:Son 3 Pno Sony Classical ▲ SK 64397
Beethoven, L. van:Son 7 Pno CBS ▲ MK 39344 [DDD]
Beethoven, L. van:Son 17 Pno, "Tempest" CBS ▲ MK 42319 [DDD]
Beethoven, L. van:Son 18 Pno CBS ▲ MK 42319 [DDD]
Beethoven, L. van:Son 23 Pno, "Appassionata" CBS ▲ MK 42448 [AAD/DDD]
Beethoven, L. van:Son 23 Pno, "Appassionata" CBS ▲ MK 39344 [DDD]
Beethoven, L. van:Son 26 Pno, "Les Adieux" CBS ▲ MK 42319 [DDD]
Beethoven, L. van:Vars Pno, WoO 80 Sony Classical ▲ SK 46437 [DDD]
Brahms, J.:Pieces Pno, Op. 76—No. 2, Capriccio Sony Classical ▲ SK 47181
Brahms, J.:Pieces Pno, Op. 118—No. 6 Sony Classical ▲ SK 47181
Brahms, J.:Pieces Pno, Op. 119—No. 4 Sony Classical ▲ SK 47181
Brahms, J.:Qt 1 Pno, w. Amadeus String Quartet members CBS ▲ MK 42361 [DDD]
Brahms, J.:Rhaps Pno, Op. 79—No. 2, Capriccio Sony Classical ▲ SK 47181
Brahms, J.:Son 3 Pno Sony Classical ▲ SK 47181
Brahms, J.:Vars on a Theme by Haydn, w. G. Solti (pno)— Op. 56b [2-piano vers.] CBS ▲ MK 42625 [DDD]
Busoni, F.:Fant mechanical Org, w. R. Lupu (pno) Sony Classical ▲ SK 44915
Chopin, F.:Barcarolle Pno CBS ▲ MK 42400 [DDD/AAD]
Chopin, F.:Barcarolle Pno CBS ▲ MK 39708 [DDD]
Chopin, F.:Berceuse CBS ▲ MK 39708 [DDD]
Chopin, F.:Berceuse CBS ▲ MK 42400 [DDD/AAD]
Chopin, F.:Con 1 Pno, w. Z. Mehta (cnd), Israel PO Sony Classical ▲ SK 44922 [DDD] ■ ST 44922 (CrO2)

INSTRUMENT.

Perahia, Murray (pno) (cont.)
Chopin, F.:Con 1 Pno, w. Z. Mehta (cnd), New York PO CBS ▲ MK 42400 [AAD/DDD]
Chopin, F.:Con 2 Pno, w. Z. Mehta (cnd), Israel PO Sony Classical ▲ SK 44922 [DDD] ■ ST 44922 (CrO2)
Chopin, F.:Fant CBS ▲ MK 42400 [DDD/AAD]
Chopin, F.:Fant CBS ▲ MK 39708 [DDD]
Chopin, F.:Impromptus CBS ▲ MK 39708 [DDD]
Chopin, F.:Impromptus—No. 4 CBS ▲ MK 42448 [AAD/DDD]
Chopin, F.:Preludes, Op. 28—Nos. 6,7 & 15 CBS ▲ MK 42448 [AAD/DDD]
Chopin, F.:Son Pno, Op. 35 CBS ▲ MK 32780 [ADD]
Chopin, F.:Son Pno, Op. 58 CBS ▲ MK 32780 [ADD]
Franck, C.:Prélude, choral et fugue Sony Classical ▲ SK 47180
Grieg, E.:Con Pno, Op. 16, w. C. Davis (cnd), Bavarian RSO CBS ▲ MK 44899 [DDD]
Liszt, F.:Pno Music (misc)—Consolation No. 3 in D♭; Hungarian Rhapsody No. 12 Sony Classical ▲ SK 46437 [DDD]
Liszt, F.:Pno Music (misc)—Au bord d'une source; Études de concert (Waldesrauschen & Gnomenreigen); Mephisto Waltz No. 1; Rhapsodie espagnole; Sonetto 104 del Petrarca Sony Classical ▲ SK 47180
Mendelssohn, F.:Con 1 Pno, w. N. Marriner (cnd), Academy of St. Martin in the Fields CBS ▲ MK 42401 [AAD]
Mendelssohn, F.:Con 2 Pno, w. N. Marriner (cnd), Academy of St. Martin in the Fields CBS ▲ MK 42401 [AAD]
Mendelssohn, F.:Preludes & Fugues Pno, Op. 35—No. 1 CBS ▲ MK 37838 [DDD]
Mendelssohn, F.:Preludes & Fugues Pno, Op. 35—No. 1 CBS ▲ MK 42401 [DDD]
Mendelssohn, F.:Rondo capriccioso CBS ▲ MK 37838 [DDD]
Mendelssohn, F.:Rondo capriccioso CBS ▲ MK 42448 [AAD/DDD]
Mendelssohn, F.:Rondo capriccioso CBS ▲ MK 42401 [DDD]
Mendelssohn, F.:Son Pno, Op. 6 CBS ▲ MK 37838 [DDD]
Mendelssohn, F.:Vars sérieuses CBS ▲ MK 37838 [DDD]
Mendelssohn, F.:Vars sérieuses CBS ▲ MK 42401 [DDD]
Mozart, W.A.:Allegro & Andante & Rondo Sony Classical ▲ SK 48233 [DDD]
Mozart, W.A.:Andante & Vars Pno 4–Hands, w. R. Lupu (pno) Sony Classical ▲ SK 44915
Mozart, W.A.:Con Pno, K.107, w. M. Perahia (cnd), English CO CBS ▲ MK 39222 [DDD]
Mozart, W.A.:Cons Pno, w. M. Perahia (cnd), English CO—Nos. 1-6, 8, 9 & 11-27 Sony Classical 12–▲ SX12K 46441
Mozart, W.A.:Cons 1–4 Pno, w. M. Perahia (cnd), English CO CBS ▲ MK 39225 [DDD]
Mozart, W.A.:Con 5 Pno, w. M. Perahia (cnd), English CO CBS ▲ MK 37267 [DDD]
Mozart, W.A.:Con 6 Pno, w. M. Perahia (cnd), English CO CBS ▲ MK 39223
Mozart, W.A.:Con 7 Pnos, w. R. Lupu (pno), English CO [arr. Mozart for 2 pianos & orch.] Sony Classical ▲ SK 44915
Mozart, W.A.:Con 9 Pno, w. M. Perahia (cnd), English CO CBS ▲ MK 34562 [AAD]
Mozart, W.A.:Con 10 Pnos, w. R. Lupu (pno), English CO Sony Classical ▲ SK 44915
Mozart, W.A.:Con 10 Pnos, w. M. Perahia (cnd), English CO CBS ▲ MK 42243 [AAD]
Mozart, W.A.:Con 12 Pno, w. M. Perahia (cnd), English CO CBS ▲ MK 42243 [AAD]
Mozart, W.A.:Con 13 Pno, w. M. Perahia (cnd), English CO CBS ▲ MK 39223
Mozart, W.A.:Con 14 Pno, w. M. Perahia (cnd), English CO CBS ▲ MK 42243 [AAD]
Mozart, W.A.:Con 15 Pno, w. M. Perahia (cnd), English CO CBS ▲ MK 37824 [DDD]
Mozart, W.A.:Con 16 Pno, w. M. Perahia (cnd), English CO CBS ▲ MK 37824 [DDD]
Mozart, W.A.:Con 17 Pno, w. M. Perahia (cnd), English CO CBS ▲ MK 36686 [DDD]
Mozart, W.A.:Con 18 Pno, w. M. Perahia (cnd), English CO CBS ▲ MK 36686 [DDD]
Mozart, W.A.:Con 18 Pno, w. M. Perahia (cnd), English CO CBS ▲ MK 39064 [DDD]
Mozart, W.A.:Con 19 Pno, w. M. Perahia (cnd), English CO CBS ▲ MK 39064 [DDD]
Mozart, W.A.:Con 20 Pno, w. M. Perahia (cnd), English CO CBS ▲ MK 42241 [AAD]
Mozart, W.A.:Con 21 Pno, w. M. Perahia (cnd), English CO CBS ▲ MK 34562 [AAD]
Mozart, W.A.:Con 22 Pno, w. M. Perahia (cnd), English CO CBS ▲ MK 42242 [AAD]
Mozart, W.A.:Con 23 Pno, w. M. Perahia (cnd), English CO CBS ▲ MK 39064 [DDD]
Mozart, W.A.:Con 24 Pno, w. M. Perahia (cnd), English CO CBS ▲ MK 42242 [AAD]
Mozart, W.A.:Con 25 Pno, w. M. Perahia (cnd), English CO CBS ▲ MK 37267 [DDD]
Mozart, W.A.:Con 26 Pno, w. M. Perahia (cnd), English CO CBS ▲ MK 39224 [DDD]
Mozart, W.A.:Con 27 Pno, w. M. Perahia (cnd), English CO CBS ▲ MK 42241 [AAD]
Mozart, W.A.:Qnt Pno, K.452, w. English CO Wind Ensemble CBS ▲ MK 42099 [DDD]
Mozart, W.A.:Rondo Pno Orch, K.382, w. M. Perahia (cnd), English CO CBS ▲ MK 42448 [AAD/DDD]
Mozart, W.A.:Rondo Pno Orch, K.382, w. M. Perahia (cnd), English CO Sony Classical 12–▲ SX12K 46441
Mozart, W.A.:Rondo Pno Orch, K.382, w. M. Perahia (cnd), English CO CBS ▲ MK 39224 [DDD]
Mozart, W.A.:Rondo Pno Orch, K.386, English CO CBS ▲ MK 39224 [DDD]
Mozart, W.A.:Rondo Pno Orch, K.386, English CO Sony Classical 12–▲ SX12K 46441
Mozart, W.A.:Son 8 Pno Sony Classical ▲ SK 48233 [DDD] Δ SM 48233 [DDD]
Mozart, W.A.:Son 11 Pno Sony Classical ▲ SK 48233 [DDD] Δ SM 48233 [DDD]
Mozart, W.A.:Son Pnos, K.448, w. R. Lupu (pno) CBS ▲ MK 39511 [DDD]
A Portrait of Murray Perahia *(rec 1975–1983)* CBS ▲ MK 42448 [AAD/DDD]
Rachmaninoff, S.:Études-tableaux, Opp. 33 & 39—Op. 33, No. 2 & Op. 39, Nos. 5,6 & 9 Sony Classical ▲ SK 46437 [DDD]
Schubert, Franz:Fant Pno, D.940, w. R. Lupu (pno) CBS ▲ MK 39511 [DDD]
Schubert, Franz:Impromptus Pno (comp) CBS ▲ MK 37291 [DDD]
Schubert, Franz:Son Pno, D.959 CBS ▲ MK 44569 [DDD]
Schubert, Franz:Wandererfantasie CBS ▲ MK 42124 [DDD]
Schubert, Franz:Winterreise, w. D. Fischer-Dieskau (bar) Sony Classical ▲ SK 48237 [DDD]
Schumann, R.:Con Pno, w. C. Davis (cnd), Bavarian RSO CBS ▲ MK 44899 [DDD]
Schumann, R.:Davidsbündlertänze CBS ▲ MK 32299 [ADD]
Schumann, R.:Fant Pno CBS ▲ MK 42124 [DDD]
Schumann, R.:Fantasiestücke Pno, Op. 12 CBS ▲ MK 32299 [ADD]
Schumann, R.:Faschingsschwank aus Wien Sony Classical ▲ SK 46437 [DDD]
Schumann, R.:Papillons CBS ▲ MK 42448 [AAD/DDD]
Schumann, R.:Papillons CBS ▲ MK 34539 [ADD]
Schumann, R.:Son 2 Pno CBS ▲ MK 44569 [DDD]
Schumann, R.:Sym Etudes—& 5 Posthumous Etudes CBS ▲ MK 34539 [ADD]

Perantoni, Daniel (tuba)
Daniel in the Lion's Den Summit ▲ DCD 163 [DDD]
Powell, Morgan:Transitions, w. E. London (cnd), Univ of Illinois Contemporary Chamber Players *(rec Univ of Illinois, 1976)* New World ▲ 80499-2
Ung, C.:Spiral II, w. Judy May Sellheim (mez), Robert Hamilton (pno), A. Weisberg (cnd) *(rec Kerr Center, Tempe, AZ, Jan 29, 1991)* CRI ▲ CRI 710 [DDD/ADD]

Perchat, Anne (pno)
Classical Balalaika & Piano Duo, w. Micha Makarenko (balalaika) Arcobaleno ▲ SBCD 9500

Perconti, Bill (sax)
Duo I point 5 Crystal ▲ CD 653

Pereira, David (vc)
Bach, J.S.:Suites Vc, BWV 1007-1012—No. 5 *(rec Dec 1991)* Tall Poppies ▲ TP017 [DDD]
Brahms, J.:Sngs, w. David Bollard (pno)—Feldeinsamkeit; Wie Melodien zieht es mir; Sapphische Ode; Wiegenlied; Liebstreu; Minnelied [all arr Norbert Salter for vc & pno] Tall Poppies ▲ TP 078 [DDD]
Butterly, N.:The Wind Stirs Gently, w. Geoffrey Collins (fl) *(rec Studios 200 & 227, ABC Ultimo Centre, Jan–Feb 1995)* Tall Poppies ▲ TP 069 [DDD]
Carter, E.:Son Vc, w. Lisa Moore (pno) *(rec Eugene Goossens Hall, ABC, Jan 1993)* Tall Poppies ▲ TP 32 [DDD]
Evocations:The Poet, w. Pereira, David (vc), David Bollard (cl) Tall Poppies ▲ TP 10 [DDD]
Falla, M. de:Suite populaire espagnole, w. David Bollard (pno) Tall Poppies ▲ TP 078 [DDD]
Ginastera, A.:Pampeana 2, w. David Bollard (pno) Tall Poppies ▲ TP 078 [DDD]
Kodály, Z.:Son Vc, Op. 8 *(rec Dec. 1991)* Tall Poppies ▲ TP 017 [DDD]

Pereira, David (vc) (cont.)
Nin, J.:songs, w. David Bollard (pno)—Montañesa; Tonada murciana; Saeta; Granadina [all arr Kochanski for vn & pno & tran for vc] Tall Poppies ▲ TP 078 [DDD]
Prokofiev, S.:Son Vc, w. Lisa Moore (pno) *(rec Concert Hall, Newcastle Conservaorium of Music, Dec 1991)* Tall Poppies ▲ TP 32 [DDD]
Schnittke, A.:Son Vc, w. L. Moore (pno) *(rec July 1992)* Tall Poppies ▲ TP 018 [DDD]
Schubert, Franz:Qnt Strs, D.956, w. Australia Ensemble *(rec July 1991)* Tall Poppies ▲ TP 011 [DDD]
Schumann, R.:Stücke im Volkston, w. David Bollard (pno) Tall Poppies ▲ TP 078 [DDD]
Sculthorpe, P.:Threnody Vc *(rec July 1992)* Tall Poppies ▲ TP 017 [DDD]
Shostakovich, D.:Ballet Suite 2, w. David Bollard (pno) [arr vc & pno] Tall Poppies ▲ TP 078 [DDD]
Shostakovich, D.:Son Vc, w. L. Moore (pno) *(rec July 1992)* Tall Poppies ▲ TP 018 [DDD]

Pereira, Joe (perc)
Argento, D.:I Hate & I Love, w. Timothy Sivils (perc), Robert Shaw (cnd), Robert Shaw Festival Singers *(rec Church of St. Pierre, Gramat, France, July 26–28, 1994)* Telarc ▲ CD 80408 [DDD]

Perényi, Eszter (vn)
Atterberg, K.:Chamber Music, w. A. Kiss (vn), I. Prunyi (pno), S. Falvay (pno), G. Kertész (vc), D. Spikay (hp)—Son. in b for Violin, Op. 27; Höstballader, Op. 15; Valse monotone in C; Rondeau Rétrospectif, Op. 26; Trio Concertante in g, Op. 57 Marco Polo ▲ 8.223404
David, Felicien:Trio 2 Pno, w. I. Prunyi (pno), T. Párkányi (vc) Marco Polo ▲ 8.223492
David, Felicien:Trio 3 Pno, w. I. Prunyi (pno), T. Párkányi (vc) Marco Polo ▲ 8.223492

Perényi, Miklós (vc)
Bach, C.P.E.:Cons Vc, H.432, 436 & 439, w. J. Rolla (cnd), Franz Liszt CO Musique d'Abord Δ HMA 1903026
Bartók, B.:Rhap 1 Vc, w. Z. Kocsis (pno) Hungaroton ▲ HCD 31140 [DDD]
Beethoven, L. van:Sons Vc (comp), w. D. Ránki (pno) Hungaroton 2–▲ HCD 11928/29
Debussy, C.:Petite suite, w. Z. Kocsis (pno)—performers' arrangement for cello & piano Hungaroton ▲ HCD 31140 [DDD]
Debussy, C.:Son Vc, w. Z. Kocsis (pno) Hungaroton ▲ HCD 31140 [DDD]
Fauré, G.:Elégie, w. Z. Kocsis (pno) Hungaroton ▲ HCD 31140 [DDD]
Haydn, J.:Con 1 Vc, w. J. Rolla (cnd), Franz Liszt CO LaserLight ▲ 14 009 [DDD]
Haydn, J.:Con 2 Vc, w. J. Rolla (cnd), Franz Liszt CO LaserLight ▲ 14 009 [DDD]
Kodály, Z.:Chorale Preludes, w. Z. Kocsis (pno) Hungaroton ▲ HCD 31140 [DDD]
Kodály, Z.:Son Vc, Op. 8 Hungaroton ▲ HCD 31046
Kodály, Z.:Son Vc & Pno, Op. 4, w. J. Jandó (pno) Hungaroton ▲ HCD 31046
Kodály, Z.:Sonatina Vc & Pno, w. Z. Kocsis (pno) Hungaroton ▲ HCD 31140 [DDD]
Kurtág, G.:Ligatura—Message to Frances-Marie (version 1), w. György Kurtág (cel), Keller String Quartet members *(rec Casino Zögernitz, Vienna, Nov 1995)* ECM New Series ▲ 78118-21598-2 [DDD]
Kurtág, G.:Ligatura—Message to Frances-Marie (version 2), w. György Kurtág (cel), Keller String Quartet members *(rec Casino Zögernitz, Vienna, Nov 1995)* ECM New Series ▲ 78118-21598-2 [DDD]
Ligeti, G.:Con Vc, w. P. Eötvös (cnd), Ensemble Modern *(rec Aug. 2–3, 1990)* Sony Classical ▲ SK 58945 [DDD]
Liszt, F.:Music of, w. A. Kiss (n), Z. Tóth (va), E. Banda (vc), H. Lubik (hp), I. Lantos (pno/org), S. Margittay (harm)—Angelus; La lugubre gondola; Epithalam; Am Grabe Richard Wagners; Romance oubliée; Elégies 1 & 2; Offertorium; Benedictus Hungaroton ▲ HCD 11798 [DDD]
Mozart, W.A.:Trio Pno, K.502, w. András Schiff (pno), Yuuko Shiokawa (vn) Teldec ▲ TEL 99205 [DDD]
Mozart, W.A.:Trio Pno, K.542, w. András Schiff (pno), Yuuko Shiokawa (vn) Teldec ▲ TEL 99205 [DDD]
Tchaikovsky, P.:Souvenir de Florence, w. K. Kashkashian (va), Keller String Quartet Erato ▲ 94819

Pérès, Marcel (org)
Campra, A.:Mass for Christmas Day, w. M. Pérès (cnd), Organum Ensemble, Versailles Boys' Choir Harmonia Mundi France ▲ HMC 901480

Peresipkin, Alexei (db)
Ustvolskaya, G.:Composition 2, w. Igo Propischin (db), Leonid Kolosov (db), Vitalii Goryachev (db), Vladimir Vulih (db), Vyacheslav Kovalenko (db), Dmitrii Sokolov (db), Vladimir Nefedov (db), Valerii Javnertchik (perc), Galina Sandovskaya (pno), O. Malov (cnd) *(rec St. Petersburg Radio House, Jan. 1994)* Megadisc ▲ 7867

Pérez, Maria Teresa (pno)
Bartók, B.:Hungarian Folksongs Vn, w. Antonia Rodriguez (fl)—Suite campesina hungara *(rec Madrid, Sept 4–7, 1990)* RNE/Spanish National Radio ▲ M3/04 [DDD]
Borne, F.:Fant brillante sur Carmen, w. Antonia Rodriguez (fl) *(rec Madrid, Sept 4–7, 1990)* RNE/Spanish National Radio ▲ M3/04 [DDD]
Chaminade, C.:Concertino Fl, w. Antonia Rodriguez (fl) *(rec Madrid, Sept 4–7, 1990)* RNE/Spanish National Radio ▲ M3/04 [DDD]
Franck, C.:Son Vn, w. Antonia Rodriguez (fl) *(rec Madrid, Sept 4–7, 1990)* RNE/Spanish National Radio ▲ M3/04 [DDD]
Galway, J.:Fl Music, w. Antonia Rodriguez (fl)—Popular Love Song *(rec Madrid, Sept 4–7, 1990)* RNE/Spanish National Radio ▲ M3/04 [DDD]
Martin, F.:Ballade Fl, w. Antonia Rodriguez (fl) *(rec Madrid, Sept 4–7, 1990)* RNE/Spanish National Radio ▲ M3/04 [DDD]

Perez, Terry (vc)
Crossover Cello *(rec Purchase Univ, White Plains, NY, Sept 21–22, 1995)* Golden String ▲ GSCD 025A [DDD]

Perfetti, Anthony (tpt)
Schubel, M.:Divert Tpt, w. Barry David Salwen (pno), J. E. Suben (cnd), Polish National RSO Katowice Opus One ▲ CD 171 [DDD]

Pergamenschikov, Boris (vc)
Debussy, C.:Music of, w. Pavel Gililov (pno)—Golliwogg's Cake-Walk; Beau soir; Menuet; Minstrels *(rec Walchstadt, Studio Kraus, Mar 1–3, 1994)* Orfeo ▲ 349951 [DDD]
Fauré, G.:Music for Vc & Pno, w. Pavel Gililov (pno)—Elegie; Romance; Serenade; Papillon; Après un rêve; Sicilienne; Berceuse *(rec Walchstadt, Studio Kraus, Mar 1–3, 1994)* Orfeo ▲ 349951 [DDD]
Glazunov, A.:Con ballata, w. D. Shallon (cnd), Bavarian RSO Koch Schwann ▲ CD 311 119 [DDD]
Glazunov, A.:Serenade espagnole, w. D. Shallon (cnd), Bavarian RSO Koch Schwann ▲ CD 311 119 [DDD]
Hummel, J.N.:Adagio, Vars & Rondo on "Schöne Minka", w. P. Gililov (pno), A. Adorján (fl) *(rec Apr. 23–25, 1991)* Orfeo ▲ 252931 [DDD]
Hummel, J.N.:Son Vc, w. P. Gililov (pno) *(rec Apr. 23–25, 1991)* Orfeo ▲ 252931 [DDD]
Ibert, J.:Music of, w. Pavel Gililov (pno)—La meneuse de tortues d'or; La cage de cristal; Le vieux mendiant; Le petit âne blanc *(rec Walchstadt, Studio Kraus, Mar 1–3, 1994)* Orfeo ▲ 349951 [DDD]
Janácek, L.:Fairy Tale, w. A. Schiff (pno) *(rec July 21–30, 1992)* London ▲ 440312-2 [DDD]
Janácek, L.:Presto, w. Andrs Schiff (pno) *(rec July 21–30, 1992)* London ▲ 440312-2 [DDD]
Penderecki, K.:Con 2 Vc, w. K. Penderecki (cnd), Bamberg SO Orfeo ▲ 285931 [DDD]
Penderecki, K.:Qt Cl, w. Sharon Kam (cl), Christoph Poppen (vn), Kim Kashkashian (va) *(rec National Philharmonic Hall, Warsaw, Poland, Nov. 23, 1993)* Sony Classical ▲ SK 66284 [DDD]
Prokofiev, S.:Adagio Vc, w. P. Gililov (pno) Orfeo ▲ 249921 [DDD]
Prokofiev, S.:Ballade Vc, w. P. Gililov (pno) Orfeo ▲ 249921 [DDD]
Prokofiev, S.:Son Vc, w. P. Gililov (pno) Orfeo ▲ 249921 [DDD]
Ravel, M.:Pièce en forme de Habanera, w. Pavel Gililov (pno) *(rec Walchstadt, Studio Kraus, Mar 1–3, 1994)* Orfeo ▲ 349951 [DDD]
Roslavets, N.:Chamber Music, w. P. Gililov (pno)—Méditation for Cello & Piano (1921); Sonata for Cello & Piano (1921) Orfeo ▲ 249921 [DDD]
Saint-Saëns, C.:Allegro appassionato, w. P. Gililov (pno) *(rec Walchstadt, Studio Kraus, Mar 1–3, 1994)* Orfeo ▲ 349951 [DDD]
Saint-Saëns, C.:Le Cygne, w. P. Gililov (pno) *(rec Walchstadt, Studio Kraus, Mar 1–3, 1994)* Orfeo ▲ 349951 [DDD]

Pergamenschikov, Boris (vc) (cont.)
Shostakovich, D.:Qt 13 Strs, w. G. Kremer (vn), T. Zehetmair (vn), N. Imai (va) *(rec Lockenhaus Festival, 1985)* ECM New Series 2-▲ 78118-21347-2 [DDD]
Tishchenko, B.:Con Vc, w. D. Shallon (cnd), Bavarian RSO Koch Schwann ▲ CD 311 119 [DDD]
Weber, C.M. von:Trio Fl, w. A. Adorjan (fl), G. Oppitz (pno) Orfeo ▲ 187891

Pergoraro, Cristiana (pno)
Liszt, F.:Song Transcriptions—Schumann:Widmung; Frühlingsnacht Nuova Era ▲ NUO 7236 [DDD]
Schumann, R.:Son 1 Pno Nuova Era ▲ NUO 7236 [DDD]
Schumann, R.:Son 2 Pno Nuova Era ▲ NUO 7236 [DDD]

Perina, Pavel (va)
Schulhoff, E.:Concertino Fl, w. Pavel Foltyn (fl), Emanuel Kumpera (db) Supraphon ▲ SUP 112170 [DDD]

Périnelli, René (tpt)
Jolivet, A.:Arioso barocco, w. Daniel Roth (org) Arion ▲ ARN 68299 [AAD]

Perkins, Bill (sax/fl)
Dring, M.:Pastel Panche, w. Bud Shank (fl), Ray Brown (bass), Leigh Kaplan (pno), Shelley Manne (perc), Shank Perkins Brown—Teal for Two; Muave Mood; Lime Clash Cambria ▲ CD 1084 [ADD]
Dring, M.:Shades of Dring, w. Bud Shank (fl), Ray Brown (bass), Leigh Kaplan (pno), Shelley Manne (perc)—In the Pink; Hallelujah Red; Brown and Out; Hello Yellow; Saxy Blue Cambria ▲ CD 1084 [ADD]

Perkins, C. (tpt)
Steel, C.:Pieces Tpt Priory ▲ PRCD 189 [DDD]

Perkins, K. (pno)
Gershwin, G.:Rhap in Blue, w. M. Brown (cnd), American SO Allegretto ▲ ACD 8034 [ADD] ■ ACS 8034

Perkins, K. (vn)—see ORCHESTRAS & ENSEMBLES Orford String Quartet

Perkins, Laurence (bn)
Serenade for Susan:A Musical Tribute, w. Manchester Camerata Orch *(rec Sept. 8, 11 & 12, 1989)* IMP Classics ▲ PCD 1031 [DDD]

Perl, Hildegard (vl)
Leclair, J.-M.:Sons Vn (Books 1-4), w. Christoph Huntgeburth (fl), Mitzi Meyerson (hpd)—Op. 2/1, 3 & 11; Op. 9/2 & 7 ASV ("Gaudeamus" series) ▲ ASV CD 158

Perle, (pno)
Perle, G.:Rilke Songs, w. B. Beardslee (sop) [E] CRI ■ ACS 6015

Perlemuter, Vlado (pno)
Bach, J.S.:Italian Con Nimbus ▲ NI 5080 [DDD]
Beethoven, L. van:Qnt Pno, Ob, Cl, Hn & Bn, w. Albion Wind Ensemble Nimbus ▲ NI 5157 [DDD]
Beethoven, L. van:Son 21 Pno, "Waldstein" Nimbus ▲ NI 5340 [DDD]
Beethoven, L. van:Son 23 Pno, "Appassionata" Nimbus ▲ NI 5133 [DDD]
Beethoven, L. van:Vars & Fugue Pno, Op. 35, "Eroica" Nimbus ▲ NI 5133 [DDD]
Chopin, F.:Ballades Pno (comp) Nimbus ▲ NI 5209 [ADD]
Chopin, F.:Barcarolle Pno Nimbus ▲ NI 5038 [AAD]
Chopin, F.:Berceuse Nimbus ▲ NI 5064 [AAD]
Chopin, F.:Études (24) Nimbus ▲ NI 5095 [DDD]
Chopin, F.:Fant Nimbus ▲ NI 5064 [AAD]
Chopin, F.:Mazurkas—3—Opp. 17/4, 30/4, 50/3 Nimbus ▲ NI 5080 [DDD]
Chopin, F.:Nocturnes—Opp. 9/3, 15/1-3, 27/1-2, 48/1-2, 55/2, 62/1 Nimbus ▲ NI 5012
Chopin, F.:Nouvelles études Nimbus ▲ NI 5095 [DDD]
Chopin, F.:Pno Music (misc)—Berceuse, Op. 57; selected Études & Nocturnes Nimbus ▲ NI 1409 [DDD]
Chopin, F.:Pno Music (misc)—Ballades; Nocturnes; Études; Preludes; Mazurkas; Polonaises; Sonatas Nos. 2 & 3; Scherzo No. 3; Tarantelle in A♭ Nimbus 6-▲ NI 1787
Chopin, F.:Polonaises—Op. 44 in f# Nimbus ▲ NI 5209 [ADD]
Chopin, F.:Polonaise-fant Nimbus ▲ NI 5209 [ADD]
Chopin, F.:Preludes, Op. 28 Nimbus ▲ NI 5064 [AAD]
Chopin, F.:Prelude, Op. 45 Nimbus ▲ NI 5064 [AAD]
Chopin, F.:Scherzos—No. 3 Nimbus ▲ NI 5340 [DDD]
Chopin, F.:Son Pno, Op. 35 Nimbus ▲ NI 5038 [AAD]
Chopin, F.:Tarantelle Nimbus ▲ NI 5080 [DDD]
Debussy, C.:Images (3) Pno—No. 1 Nimbus ▲ NI 5080 [DDD]
Debussy, C.:L'Isle joyeuse Nimbus ▲ NI 5080 [DDD]
Debussy, C.:Pour le piano Nimbus ▲ NI 5080 [DDD]
Fauré, G.:Barcarolles (13)—No. 5 Nimbus ▲ NI 5165 [DDD]
Fauré, G.:Impromptus Pno, Opp. 25, 31, 34, 91 & 102—No. 2 Nimbus ▲ NI 5165 [DDD]
Fauré, G.:Nocturnes (13) Pno—Nos. 1,6,7,12 & 13 Nimbus ▲ NI 5165 [DDD]
Fauré, G.:Qnts Pno & Strs, Opp. 89 & 115, w. Parrenin String Quartet *(rec May 31, 1966)* Memoire Vive ▲ 262003 [ADD]
Fauré, G.:Theme & Vars Pno Nimbus ▲ NI 5165 [DDD]
Franck, C.:Qnt Pno, w. Parrenin String Quartet *(rec June 2, 1967)* Memoire Vive ▲ 262003 [ADD]
Liszt, F.:Son Pno Nimbus ▲ NI 5299 [ADD]
Mendelssohn, F.:Vars sérieuses Nimbus ▲ NI 5340 [DDD]
Mozart, W.A.:Qnt Pno, K.452, w. Albion Wind Ensemble Nimbus ▲ NI 5157 [DDD]
Ravel, M.:À la manière de Borodine & de Chabrie Nimbus ▲ NI 5011
Ravel, M.:Con Pno (left hand), w. J. Horenstein (cnd), Colonne Concert Orch Accord ▲ ACD 201052 [AAD]
Ravel, M.:Con Pno (left hand), w. J. Horenstein (cnd), Paris Concerts Colonne Orch *(rec 1955)* Vox Box ("Legends" series) 2-▲ CDX2 5507 [ADD]
Ravel, M.:Con in G Pno, w. J. Horenstein (cnd), Colonne Concert Orch Accord ▲ ACD 201052 [AAD]
Ravel, M.:Con in G Pno, w. J. Horenstein (cnd), Paris Concerts Colonne Orch *(rec 1955)* Vox Box ("Legends" series) 2-▲ CDX2 5507 [ADD]
Ravel, M.:Gaspard de la nuit Nimbus ▲ NI 5005
Ravel, M.:Gaspard de la nuit, w. J. Horenstein (cnd), Paris Concerts Colonne Orch *(rec 1955)* Vox Box ("Legends" series) 2-▲ CDX2 5507 [ADD]
Ravel, M.:Jeux d'eau Nimbus ▲ NI 5005
Ravel, M.:Ma mère l'oye Pno, w. A. Farmer (pno) Nimbus ▲ NI 5340 [DDD]
Ravel, M.:Menuet antique Nimbus ▲ NI 5011
Ravel, M.:Menuet sur le nom d'Haydn Nimbus ▲ NI 5011
Ravel, M.:Miroirs *(rec 1955)* Vox Box ("Legends" series) 2-▲ CDX2 5507 [ADD]
Ravel, M.:Miroirs Nimbus ▲ NI 5005
Ravel, M.:Pavane pour une infante défunte Nimbus ▲ NI 5005
Ravel, M.:Pno Music—Jeux d'eau; Menuet antique; Menuet sur le nom de Haydn; Pavane pour une infante défunte; Prélude *(rec 1955)* Vox Box ("Legends" series) 2-▲ CDX2 5507 [ADD]
Ravel, M.:Prélude Pno Nimbus ▲ NI 5011
Ravel, M.:Sonatine Pno Nimbus ▲ NI 5011
Ravel, M.:Sonatine Pno *(rec 1955)* Vox Box ("Legends" series) 2-▲ CDX2 5507 [ADD]
Ravel, M.:Le Tombeau de Couperin *(rec 1955)* Vox Box ("Legends" series) 2-▲ CDX2 5507 [ADD]
Ravel, M.:Le Tombeau de Couperin Nimbus ▲ NI 5011
Ravel, M.:Valses nobles et sentimentales Nimbus ▲ NI 5011
Ravel, M.:Valses nobles et sentimentales *(rec 1955)* Vox Box ("Legends" series) 2-▲ CDX2 5507 [ADD]
Schumann, R.:Fant Pno Nimbus ▲ NI 5299 [ADD]
Schumann, R.:Kreisleriana Nimbus ▲ NI 5108 [DDD]
Schumann, R.:Sym Etudes Nimbus ▲ NI 5108 [DDD]

Perlman, Itzhak (vn)
The Art of Perlman EMI Classics 4-▲ ZDMD 64617
The Bach Album, w. Kathleen Battle (sop) Deutsche Grammophon ▲ 429737-2 GH [DDD] ■ 429737-4 GH (D) □ 429737-5
Bach, J.S.:Arias, w. K. Battle (sop) Deutsche Grammophon ▲ 429737-2 [DDD] □ 429737-5
Bach, J.S.:Cons Vn (comp), w. D. Barenboim (cnd), English CO EMI Classics ▲ CDC 47856-2

Perlman, Itzhak (vn) (cont.)
Bach, J.S.:Con Vn & Ob, w. R. Still (ob), Israel PO EMI Classics ▲ CDC 47073-2 [DDD]
Bach, J.S.:Con for 2 Vns, w. I. Stern (vn), Z. Mehta (cnd), New York PO CBS ■ MGT 39798
Bach, J.S.:Con for 2 Vns, w. I. Stern (vn), Z. Mehta (cnd), New York PO CBS ▲ MK 36692 [DDD]
Bach, J.S.:Con for 2 Vns, w. I. Stern (vn), Z. Mehta (cnd), New York PO CBS ▲ MYK 38487 ■ MYT 38487
Bach, J.S.:Con for 2 Vns, w. P. Zukerman (vn), D. Barenboim (cnd), English CO EMI Classics ▲ CDC 47856-2
Bach, J.S.:Con for 2 Vns, w. Isaac Stern (vn), Z. Mehta (cnd), New York PO Sony Classical ▲ SMK 66471
Bach, J.S.:Sons & Partitas Vn, BWV 1001-1006 EMI Classics 2-▲ ZDCB 49483-2 [DDD]
Barber, S.:Con Vn, w. S. Ozawa (cnd), Boston SO EMI Classics ▲ CDC 55360
Basic 100, Vol. 70, w. André Previn (cnd), Erich Leinsdorf (cnd) RCA Victor ▲ 09026-68338-2 ■ 09026-68338-4
Beethoven, L. van:Con Vn, Op. 61, w. C. M. Giulini (cnd), Philharmonia Orch EMI Classics ▲ CDC 47002 [DDD]
Beethoven, L. van:Con Vn, Op. 61, w. D. Barenboim (cnd), Berlin PO EMI Classics ▲ CDC 49567 [DDD]
Beethoven, L. van:Con Vn, Vc & Pno, "Triple Con", w. Yo-Yo Ma (vc), Daniel Barenboim (pno), Berlin PO EMI Classics ▲ CDC 55516
Beethoven, L. van:Romances Vn, w. D. Barenboim (cnd), Berlin PO EMI Classics ▲ CDC 49567 [DDD]
Beethoven, L. van:Serenade Strs, Op. 8, w. P. Zukerman (va), L. Harrell (vc) EMI Classics 2-▲ ZDCB 54198
Beethoven, L. van:Sons Vn (comp), w. V. Ashkenazy (pno) London ("Jubilee" series) 4-▲ 421453-2 [ADD]
Beethoven, L. van:Son 5 Vn, "Spring", w. V. Ashkenazy (pno) London ▲ 410554-2 [ADD]
Beethoven, L. van:Son 7 Vn, w. V. Ashkenazy (pno) London ▲ 411948-2 [ADD]
Beethoven, L. van:Son 9 Vn, "Kreutzer", w. V. Ashkenazy (pno) London ▲ 410554-2 [ADD]
Beethoven, L. van:Son 10 Vn, w. V. Ashkenazy (pno) London ▲ 411948-2
Beethoven, L. van:Trio 6 Pno, "Archduke", w. V. Ashkenazy (pno), L. Harrell (vc) EMI Classics ▲ CDC 47010 [DDD]
Beethoven, L. van:Trio Strs, Op. 3, w. P. Zukerman (va), L. Harrell (vc) EMI Classics 2-▲ ZDCB 54198
Beethoven, L. van:Trios Strs, Op. 9, w. P. Zukerman (va), L. Harrell (vc) EMI Classics 2-▲ ZDCB 54198
Ben-Haim, P.:Con Vn EMI Classics ▲ CDC 54296
Berg, A.:Con Vn, w. S. Ozawa (cnd), Boston SO *(rec Symphony Hall, Boston, Feb & Nov 1978)* Deutsche Grammophon ("The Originals" series) ▲ 447445-2 [ADD]
Berlioz, H.:Rêverie et caprice, w. D. Barenboim (cnd), Orch de Paris Deutsche Grammophon ("Digital Midprice" series) ▲ 445549-2
Bernstein, L.:Serenade, w. S. Ozawa (cnd), Boston SO EMI Classics ▲ CDC 55360
Bits & Pieces, w. S. Sanders (pno) EMI Classics ▲ CDC 54882
Brahms, J.:Con Vn, w. C.M. Giulini (cnd), Chicago SO EMI Classics ▲ CDC 47166
Brahms, J.:Con Vn, w. D. Barenboim (cnd), Berlin PO EMI Classics ▲ CDC 54580
Brahms, J.:Sons Vn (comp), w. V. Ashkenazy (pno) EMI Classics ▲ CDC 47403 [DDD]
Brahms, J.:Sons Vn (comp), w. D. Barenboim (pno) Sony Classical ▲ SK 45819 [DDD]
Brahms, J.:Trio Hn, w. B. Tuckwell (hn), V. Ashkenazy (pno) London ▲ 414128-2 [ADD]
Brahms, J.:Trios (3) Pno, w. V. Ashkenazy (pno), L. Harrell (vc) EMI Classics ▲ CDCB 54725
Brahms, J.:Trio in A Pno (posth), w. V. Ashkenazy (pno), L. Harrell (vc) EMI Classics ▲ CDCB 54725
Bruch, M.:Con 1 Vn, w. B. Haitink (cnd), Royal Concertgebouw Orch EMI Classics ▲ CDC 47074 [DDD]
Bruch, M.:Con 2 Vn, w. Z. Mehta (cnd), Israel PO EMI Classics ▲ CDC 49071
Bruch, M.:Scottish Fant Vn, w. Z. Mehta (cnd), Israel PO EMI Classics ▲ CDC 49071
Castelnuovo-Tedesco, M.:Con 2 Vn, "The Prophets" EMI Classics ▲ CDC 54296
Chausson, E.:Con Vn, Pno & Str Qt, w. J. Bolet (pno), Juilliard String Quartet CBS ▲ MK 37814 [DDD]
Chausson, E.:Poème Vn, w. Z. Mehta (cnd), New York PO Deutsche Grammophon ("Masters" series) ▲ 445564-2
Chausson, E.:Poème Vn, w. Z. Mehta (cnd), New York PO Deutsche Grammophon ▲ 423063-2 [DDD]
Chausson, E.:Poème Vn, w. J. Martinon (cnd), Orch de Paris EMI Classics ▲ CDC 47725
Debussy, C.:Son Vn, w. Vladimir Ashkenazy (pno) *(rec Henry Wood Hall, London, May 1994)* London ▲ 444318-2 [DDD]
A Different Kind of Blues, w. Andre Previn (pno), Shelly Manne (drums), Jim Hall (gtr), Red Mitchell (bass gtr) Angel ▲ CDM 64319 [DDD]
Duets for Voice & Violin, w. Plácido Domingo (ten) EMI Classics ▲ CDQ 54266 ■ 4DQ 54266
Dvořák, A.:Con Vn, w. D. Barenboim (cnd), London PO EMI Classics 3-▲ ZDMC 69881
Dvořák, A.:Con Vn, w. D. Barenboim (cnd), London PO EMI Classics ▲ CDC 47168 [ADD]
Dvořák, A.:Music of, w. Frederica von Stade (mez), Yo-Yo Ma (vc), Rudolf Firkusny (pno), S. Ozawa (cnd), Boston SO, Czech Phil Chorus—Carnival Ov., Op. 92; Romance in f for Vn & Orch, Op. 11; Klid [Silent Woods] for Vc & Orch, Op. 68/5; Humoresque in G♭, Op. 101/1 & 7; Mesícku na nebi hlubokém [from Rusalka, Op. 114]; Psalm 149 for Chorus & Orch, Op. 79; Gypsy Songs for Voice & Piano, Op. 55/4 & 5; Allegro [from Trio for Vn, Vc & Pno, Op. 90]; Slavonic Dances, Op. 72/2 & 7 *(rec Smetana Hall, Prague, Dec. 16, 1993)* Sony Classical ("Front Line" series) ▲ SK 46687 [DDD]; ■ ST 46687
Dvořák, A.:Qt 5 Strs, w. D. Barenboim (cnd), London PO EMI Classics 3-▲ ZDMC 69881
Dvořák, A.:Romance Vn, w. D. Barenboim (cnd), London PO EMI Classics ▲ CDC 47168 [ADD]
Dvořák, A.:Romantic Pieces, Op. 75, w. S. Sanders (pno) EMI Classics ▲ CDC 47399 [DDD]
Dvořák, A.:Sonatina Vn, w. S. Sanders (pno) EMI Classics ▲ CDC 47399 [DDD]
Elgar, E.:Con Vn, w. D. Barenboim (cnd), Chicago SO Deutsche Grammophon ("Masters" series) ▲ 445564-2
Encores, w. Janet Goodman Guggenheim (pno) EMI Classics ▲ CDC 54108 ■ 4DS 54108
Encores, w. Samuel Sanders (pno) EMI Classics ▲ CDC 49514
Falla, M. de:Suite populaire espagnole, w. S. Sanders (pno) [trans Paul Kochanski for vn & pno] EMI Classics ▲ CDM 63533
Foss, L.:American Pieces (3), w. S. Ozawa (cnd), Boston SO EMI Classics ▲ CDC 55360
Franck, C.:Son Vn, w. V. Ashkenazy (pno) London ▲ 414128-2 [ADD]
Giuliani, M.:Son Vn, w. J. Williams (gtr) CBS ▲ MK 34508 [AAD] ■ MT 34508
Glazunov, A.:Con Vn, w. Z. Mehta (cnd), Israel PO EMI Classics ▲ CDC 49814
Great Romantic Concertos EMI Classics 3-▲ ZDMC 64922
It's a Breeze, w. Andre Previn (pno), Shelly Manne (drums), Jim Hall (gtr), Red Mitchell (bass gtr) Angel ▲ CDM 64318 [DDD]
The Itzhak Perlman Collection EMI Classics 20-▲ ZDMT 83177
Itzhak Perlman Greatest Hits, w. New York PO [cnd:Zubin Mehta], Orch de Paris [cnd:Daniel Barenboim] Deutsche Grammophon ▲ 437737-2 GH
Joplin, S.:Music of, w. A. Previn (pno) EMI Classics ▲ CDC 47170 ■ 4XS 37113
Khachaturian, A.:Con Vn, w. Z. Mehta (cnd), Israel PO EMI Classics ▲ CDC 47087 [DDD]
Korngold, E.W.:Con Vn, w. A. Previn (cnd), Pittsburgh SO EMI Classics ▲ CDC 47846
Kreisler, F.:Vn Pieces, w. Samuel Sanders (pno)—short pieces & transcriptions EMI Classics ▲ CDC 47467
Lalo, E.:Sym espagnole, w. D. Barenboim (cnd), Orch de Paris Deutsche Grammophon ("3D Classics" series) ▲ 429977-2 [DDD]
Lalo, E.:Sym espagnole, w. D. Barenboim (cnd), Orch de Paris Deutsche Grammophon ("Digital Midprice" series) ▲ 445549-2
Lalo, E.:Sym espagnole, w. E. Leinsdorf (cnd), Boston SO RCA Victor ▲ 09026-68338-2 ■ 09026-68338-4
Lalo, E.:Sym espagnole, w. A. Previn (cnd), London SO *(rec ca. 1966/68)* RCA Gold Seal ▲ 07863-56520-2 ■ 07863-56520-4
Leclair, J.-M.:Sons for 2 Vns, Op. 3, w. P. Zukerman (vn)—No. 4 in F RCA Red Seal ▲ 60735-2-RC [DDD] ■ 60735-4-RC (CrO2)
Mendelssohn, F.:Con in e Vn & Orch, Op. 64, w. D. Barenboim (cnd), Chicago SO Erato ▲ 91732-2
Mendelssohn, F.:Con in e Vn & Orch, Op. 64, w. B. Haitink (cnd), Royal Concertgebouw Orch EMI Classics ▲ CDC 47074 [DDD]

INSTRUMENT.

Perlman, Itzhak (vn) (cont.)
Mendelssohn, F.:Con in e Vn & Orch, Op. 64, w. L. Foster (cnd), Royal PO
EMI Classics 3-▲ ZDMC 69881
Mozart, W.A.:Adagio Vn, K.261, w. J. Levine (cnd), Vienna PO
Deutsche Grammophon ("Digital Midprice" series) 2-▲ 445535-2 [DDD]
Mozart, W.A.:Cons Vn, w. J. Levine (cnd), Vienna PO—Nos. 1-5
Deutsche Grammophon ("Digital Midprice" series) 2-▲ 445535-2 [DDD]
Mozart, W.A.:Con 1 Vn, w. J. Levine (cnd), Vienna PO Deutsche Grammophon ▲ 415958-2 [DDD]
Mozart, W.A.:Con 2 Vn, w. J. Levine (cnd), Vienna PO Deutsche Grammophon ▲ 415975-2 [DDD]
Mozart, W.A.:Con 3 Vn, w. J. Levine (cnd), Vienna PO Deutsche Grammophon ▲ 410020-2 [DDD]
Mozart, W.A.:Con 3 Vn, w. J. Levine (cnd), Vienna PO
Deutsche Grammophon ("3D Classics" series) ▲ 431282-2 [DDD]
Mozart, W.A.:Con 4 Vn, w. J. Levine (cnd), Vienna PO
Deutsche Grammophon ("3D Classics" series) ▲ 431282-2 [DDD]
Mozart, W.A.:Con 4 Vn, w. J. Levine (cnd), Vienna PO Deutsche Grammophon ▲ 415975-2 [DDD]
Mozart, W.A.:Con 5 Vn, w. J. Levine (cnd), Vienna PO Deutsche Grammophon ▲ 410020-2 [DDD]
Mozart, W.A.:Concertone Vns, w. P. Zukerman (vn), Z. Mehta (cnd), Israel PO
Deutsche Grammophon ▲ 415486-2 [DDD]
Mozart, W.A.:Duos Vn, w. P. Zukerman (va) RCA Red Seal ▲ 60735-2 [DDD] ■ 60735-4 (CrO2)
Mozart, W.A.:Rondo Vn, K.269, w. J. Levine (cnd), Vienna PO
Deutsche Grammophon ▲ 415958-2 [DDD]
Mozart, W.A.:Rondo Vn, K.269, w. J. Levine (cnd), Vienna PO
Deutsche Grammophon ("3D Classics" series) ▲ 431282-2 [DDD]
Mozart, W.A.:Rondo Vn, K.373, w. J. Levine (cnd), Vienna PO
Deutsche Grammophon ▲ 415958-2 [DDD]
Mozart, W.A.:Rondo Vn, K.373, w. J. Levine (cnd), Vienna PO
Deutsche Grammophon ("Digital Midprice" series) 2-▲ 445535-2 [DDD]
Mozart, W.A.:Sinf concertante Vn, K.364, w. P. Zukerman (va), Z. Mehta (cnd), Israel PO
Deutsche Grammophon ▲ 415486-2 [DDD]
Mozart, W.A.:Sons Vn Pno (misc), w. D. Barenboim (pno)—(16) K.296, 301-306, 376-380, 454, 481, 526 & 547 Deutsche Grammophon 4-▲ 431784-2 [DDD]
Mozart, W.A.:Sons Vn Pno (misc), w. D. Barenboim (pno)—K.526 & 547
Deutsche Grammophon ▲ 431687-2 [DDD]
Mozart, W.A.:Sons Vn Pno (misc), w. D. Barenboim (pno)—K.454 & 481
Deutsche Grammophon ▲ 431673-2 [DDD]
Mozart, W.A.:Sons Vn Pno (misc), w. D. Barenboim (pno)—K.378, 379 & 380
Deutsche Grammophon ▲ 423229-2 [DDD]
Paganini, N.:Cantabile, w. J. Williams (gtr) CBS ▲ MK 34508 [AAD] ■ MT 34508
Paganini, N.:Caprices Vn EMI Classics ▲ CDC 47171
Paganini, N.:Con 1 Vn, w. L. Foster (cnd), Royal PO EMI Classics ▲ CDC 47101
Paganini, N.:Con 6 Vn, w. D. Barenboim (cnd), London SO, London PO, Royal PO
EMI Classics 3-▲ ZDMC 69881
Paganini, N.:Son concertata, w. J. Williams (gtr) CBS ▲ MK 34508 [AAD] ■ MT 34508
Paganini, N.:Sons Vn & Gtr, w. J. Williams (gtr)—Op. 64/1 CBS ▲ MK 34508 [AAD] ■ MT 34508
Paganini, N.:Sons Vn & Gtr, Op. 3, w. J. Williams (gtr)—No. 6 CBS ▲ MK 34508 [AAD] ■ MT 34508
Prokofiev, S.:Cons Vn (comp), w. G. Rozhdestvensky (cnd), BBC SO EMI Classics ▲ CDC 47025 [DDD]
Prokofiev, S.:Con 2 Vn, w. E. Leinsdorf (cnd), Boston SO RCA Gold Seal ▲ 09026-61454-2
Prokofiev, S.:Son Vn, Op. 94bis, w. V. Ashkenazy (pno) RCA Gold Seal ▲ 09026-61454-2
Prokofiev, S.:Son 1 Vn, w. V. Ashkenazy (pno) RCA Gold Seal ▲ 09026-61454-2
Ravel, M.:Orchestral Music, w. A. Previn (cnd), London SO—Bolero; Rapsodie Espagnole:Prélude à la nuit; Malaguiena, Habanera, Feria; Pavane pour une infante défunte; La valse; Alborada del gracioso; Tzigane RCA Victor ▲ 09026-61712-2; ■ 09026-61712-4
Ravel, M.:Trio Pno, w. Vladimir Ashkenazy (pno), Lynn Harrell (vc) *(rec Henry Wood Hall, London, May 1994)* London ▲ 444318-2 [DDD]
Ravel, M.:Tzigane, w. J. Martinon (cnd), Orch de Paris EMI Classics ▲ CDC 47725
Ravel, M.:Tzigane, w. Z. Mehta (cnd), New York PO Deutsche Grammophon ▲ 423063-2 [DDD]
Ravel, M.:Tzigane, w. A. Previn (cnd), London SO *(rec ca. 1966/68)*
RCA Gold Seal ▲ 07863-56520-2 [ADD] ■ 07863-56520-4
Ravel, M.:Tzigane, w. Z. Mehta (cnd), New York PO *(rec Manhattan Ctr, NY, Sept 1986)*
Deutsche Grammophon ("The Originals" series) ▲ 447445-2 [DDD]
Saint-Saëns, C.:Con 3 Vn, w. D. Barenboim (cnd), Orch de Paris
Deutsche Grammophon ("3-D Classics" series) ▲ 429977-2 [DDD]
Saint-Saëns, C.:Con 3 Vn, w. D. Barenboim (cnd), Orch de Paris
Deutsche Grammophon ("Digital Midprice" series) ▲ 445549-2
Saint-Saëns, C.:Con 3 Vn, w. D. Barenboim (cnd), Orch de Paris
Deutsche Grammophon ▲ 410526-2 [DDD]
Saint-Saëns, C.:Havanaise Vn, w. Z. Mehta (cnd), New York PO
Deutsche Grammophon ▲ 423063-2 [DDD]
Saint-Saëns, C.:Havanaise Vn, w. J. Martinon (cnd), Orch de Paris EMI Classics ▲ CDC 47725
Saint-Saëns, C.:Introduction & Rondo capriccioso, w. J. Martinon (cnd), Orch de Paris
EMI Classics ▲ CDC 47725
Saint-Saëns, C.:Introduction & Rondo capriccioso, w. Z. Mehta (cnd), New York PO
Deutsche Grammophon ▲ 423063-2 [DDD]
Sarasate, P. de:Carmen Fant, w. Z. Mehta (cnd), New York PO
Deutsche Grammophon ▲ 423063-2 [DDD]
Sarasate, P. de:Carmen Fant, w. L. Foster (cnd), Royal PO EMI Classics ▲ CDC 47101
Sarasate, P. de:Carmen Fant, w. L. Foster (cnd), Royal PO EMI Classics 3-▲ ZDMC 69881
Sarasate, P. de:Zigeunerweisen, w. A. Previn (cnd), Pittsburgh SO EMI Classics ▲ CDM 63533
Shostakovich, D.:Con 1 Vn, w. Z. Mehta (cnd), Israel PO EMI Classics ▲ CDC 49814
Sibelius, J.:Con Vn, w. E. Leinsdorf (cnd), Boston SO *(rec ca. 1966/68)*
RCA Gold Seal ▲ 07863-56520-2 [ADD] ■ 07863-56520-4
Sibelius, J.:Con Vn, w. A. Previn (cnd), London SO
RCA Victor ▲ 09026-68338-2 ■ 09026-68338-4
Smetana, B.:From the Homeland, w. S. Sanders (pno) EMI Classics ▲ CDC 47399 [DDD]
Stravinsky, I.:Con Vn, w. S. Ozawa (cnd), Boston SO *(rec Symphony Hall, Boston, Feb & Nov 1978)*
Deutsche Grammophon ("The Originals" series) ▲ 447445-2 [ADD]
Tchaikovsky, P.:Con Vn, w. E. Ormandy (cnd), Philadelphia Orch EMI Classics ▲ CDC 47106
Tchaikovsky, P.:Con Vn, w. A. Wallenstein (cnd), London SO *(rec 1960s)* Chesky ▲ CD 12
Tchaikovsky, P.:Con Vn, w. E. Leinsdorf (cnd), Boston SO
RCA Gold Seal ("Papillon Collection" series) ▲ 6526-2-RG [ADD] ■ 6526-4-RG
Tchaikovsky, P.:Con Vn, w. Z. Mehta (cnd), Israel PO EMI Classics ▲ CDC 54108 ■ 4DS 54108
Tchaikovsky, P.:Méditation, w. Z. Mehta (cnd), Israel PO EMI Classics ▲ CDC 47087 [DDD]
Tchaikovsky, P.:Music of, w. J. Norman (sop), Yo-Yo Ma (vc), Y. Temirkanov (cnd), Leningrad PO, Leningrad Military Orch—Waltz & Polonaise from Eugene Onegin; Sérénade mélancolique, Op. 26; Valse scherzo, Op. 34; Variations on a Rococo Theme, Op. 33; Overture 1812, Op. 49; Symphony No. 6 (3rd movt.); 3 Chansons française from Op. 65, for Voice & Piano; Aria (Adieu, forêts) from The Maid of Orleans *(rec live, Leningrad)*
RCA Red Seal ▲ 60739-2-RC [DDD] ■ 09026-60739-4-RC (CrO2) □ 09026-60739-5
Tchaikovsky, P.:Sérénade mélancolique, w. E. Ormandy (cnd), Philadelphia Orch
EMI Classics ▲ CDC 47106
Tchaikovsky, P.:Trio Pno, w. V. Ashkenazy (pno), L. Harrell (vc) EMI Classics ▲ CDC 47988 [ADD]
Tradition:Popular Jewish Melodies, w. Dov Seltzer (cnd) EMI Classics ▲ CDC 47904 [DDD]
Tribute to Jascha Heifetz, w. Samuel Sanders (pno) EMI Classics ▲ CDC 49604
Vivaldi, A.:Cons Vn (misc), w. I. Perlman (cnd), Israel PO—RV.199, 317, 347, 356
EMI Classics ▲ CDC 47076 [DDD]
Vivaldi, A.:Cons Vn, Op. 8/1-4, "The Four Seasons", w. Z. Mehta (cnd), Israel PO
Deutsche Grammophon ▲ 419214-2 [DDD] ■ 419214-4
Vivaldi, A.:Cons Vn, Op. 8/1-4, "The Four Seasons", w. I. Perlman (cnd), Israel PO
EMI Classics ▲ CDM 64333

Perlman, Itzhak (vn) (cont.)
Vivaldi, A.:Cons Vn, Op. 8/1-4, "The Four Seasons", w. I. Perlman (cnd), Israel PO
EMI Classics ▲ CDC 47319 [DDD] ■ 4DS 38123 (D)
Vivaldi, A.:Con for 3 Vns, w. P. Zukerman (vn), I. Stern (vn), Z. Mehta (cnd), New York PO
CBS ▲ MK 36692 [DDD]
Wieniawski, H.:Con 2 Vn, w. D. Barenboim (cnd), Orch de Paris
Deutsche Grammophon ▲ 410526-2 [DDD]

Perlot, P. (ob)
Mozart, W.A.:Adagio & Rondo Glass Armonica, w. J. Rampal (fl), Pasquier Trio
Sony Classical ▲ SK 47230

Pernel, A. (vn)
Mozart, W.A.:Qt Ob, K.370, w. M. Tabuteau (ob), K. Tuttle (va), P. Tortelier (vc) *(rec live June 1953)*
Music & Arts 4-▲ CD 689 (m) [AAD]

Pernot, Louis (lt)
Dufault, F.:Lt Music—Suites in c, a, F, d & g Accord ▲ ACD 200262 [DDD]
Gaultier, D.:La Rhétorique des dieux Accord 2-▲ ACD 200702 [DDD]

Perotin, Gerard (perc)
Bartók, B.:Son for 2 Pnos, w. J.-F. Heisser (pno), G. Pludermacher (pno), G.-J. Cipriana (perc)
Erato ▲ 2292-45861-2

Perpich, Alessandro (vn)
Grieg, E.:Sons Vn, Opp. 8, 13 & 45, w. Fabio Bidini (pno) *(rec Mesquite Performing Arts Center, TX, Apr 1996)* EPR ▲ EPR 9613 [DDD]

Perrett, Danielle (hp)
Dussek, J.L.:Hp Music, w. James Ellis (vn), Helen Verney (vc), Warwick Cole (pno), Gillian Jones (hand-hn)—A Favorite Duet for Hp & Pno, Op. 11; Son in E♭ for Hp, Op. 34/1; Favorite Son for Hp, Vn & Vc, Op. 37; Son in B♭ for Hp, Op. 34/2; Duo for Hp, Pno & Hand-Horn, Op. 38
Meridian ▲ MER 84244 [DDD]

Perretti, C. (pno)
Wissmer, P.:Con 2 Pno, w. P. Wissmer (cnd), Swiss Romande Orch *(rec 1969)* Quantum ▲ QM 6918

Perrier, Eric (cl)
Sauguet, H.:Suite Cl, w. Isabelle Henrich (pno) Sonpact ▲ SPT 96017 [DDD]

Perrier-Layec, Chantal (hpd)
The Harpsichord in Europe *(rec 1995)* Pierre Verany ▲ PVY 730065

Perrin, Catherine (hpd)
Shchedrin, R.:Stalin Cocktail, w. Y. Turovsky (cnd), Montreal Musici Chandos ▲ CHAN 9288 [DDD]

Perrin, Françoise (vn)
Beethoven, L. van:Trio Pno, Op.38, w. Thierry Ravassard (pno), Pierre Feyler (db) Gallo ▲ CD 761
Chausson, E.:Poème Vn, w. Thierry Ravassard (pno), Pierre Feyler (db) [arr Antoine Duhamel for trio] *(rec 1994)* Gallo ▲ CD 801 [DDD]
Kreisler, F.:Music of, w. Pierre Feyler (db), Thierry Ravassard (pno)—Liebesleid Gallo ▲ CD 761
Massenet, J.:Méditation from *Thaïs*, w. Thierry Ravassard (pno), Pierre Feyler (db) [arr for Pno, Vn & Db]
Gallo ▲ CD 761
Monti, A.:Czardas, w. Thierry Ravassard (pno), Pierre Feyler (db) Gallo ▲ CD 761
Ravel, M.:Tzigane, w. Pierre Feyler (db), Thierry Ravassard (pno) [arr Antoine Duhamel for trio] *(rec 1994)* Gallo ▲ CD 801 [DDD]

Perrin, J. (pno)
Perrin, J.:Con grosso, w. C. Dutoit (cnd), Beromünster Orch *(rec Radio Zürich, Mar 5, 1962)*
Grammont ▲ CTSP 45 [AAD]

Perrin, Raymond (org)
Fauré, G.:Requiem, w. D. Rocheleau (sop), M. L. de Rozel (cnd), Radio Canada Orch, Petits Chanteurs du Mont-Royal, Cap-de-la-Madeleine Choir, Petits Chanteurs de Trois-Rivières [L] *(rec 6/88)*
REM ▲ 311096 XCD [DDD]

Perrone, Rossella (gtr)
Neumann, H.:Serenade Bas Hn, w. Luigi Magistrelli (bas hn), Massimo Laura (gtr)
Bayer ▲ 100280 [DDD]

Perrucci, G. (fl)
Martini, G.B.:Music for Fls, w. M. Mercelli (fl), N. Guidetti (fl), M. Vangi (fl)—(2 works for 2 Flutes) Sonata in C; Sonata in D; (3 works for 2 Flutes & Continuo) Allegro in C; Allegro & Rondo in C; Pastorale in C Bongiovanni ▲ GB 5517 [DDD]

Perry, Douglas (va)
Hatzis, C.:Nadir, w. Peter Hannan (rcr) CBC ("Musica Viva" series) ▲ MVCD 1055 [DDD]
Mozart, W.A.:Adagio & Rondo Glass Armonica, w. J. Petric (acc), M. Hammer (fl), M. Berard (ob), D. Hetherington (vc) [trans. for accordion & string quartet] *(rec June 12-13, 1991)*
CBC ("Musica Viva" series) ▲ MVCD 1056 [DDD]

Perry, Robert (vc)
The Plymouth Trio, w. Plymouth Trio *(rec 1992)* Crystal ▲ 641
The Plymouth Trio, w. Plymouth Trio Crystal ▲ CD 640

Perry, William (pno)
Perry, W.:Film Music—The Silent Years Theme; The Gold Rush; The General; The Mark of Zorro; The Beloved Rouge; Orphans of the Storm; Blood & Sand; The Silent Years Closing Theme
Premier ▲ PRCD 1034 [ADD]

Perry-Camp, Jane (pno)
Schiffman, H.:Spectrum, My Layde Jane's Booke *(rec Andres Editions Studios, Tallahassee, FL, June 27-29, 1995)* North/South Recordings ▲ N/S R 1009 [DDD]

Perschtman, D. (vc)
Miaskovsky, N.:Son 2 Vc, w. M. Baslawskaya (pno) Globe ▲ GLO 5041 [DDD]
Schnittke, A.:Son Vc, w. M. Baslawskaya (pno) Globe ▲ GLO 5041 [DDD]
Shostakovich, D.:Son Vc, w. M. Baslawskaya (pno) Globe ▲ GLO 5041 [DDD]

Persichelli, Angelo (fl)—see ORCHESTRAS & ENSEMBLES Italiano Octet

Persinger, Louis (pno)
Paganini, N.:Intro & Vars on "Dal tuo stellato soglio", w. R. Ricci (vn) [arr vn & pno]
One-Eleven ▲ URS 50060 [ADD]
Paganini, N.:Le Streghe, w. R. Ricci (vn) One-Eleven ▲ URS 50060 [ADD]
The Young Yehudi Menuhin:The 1928-29 HMV Recordings, w. Menuhin, Yehudi (vn)
Biddulph ▲ LAB 031 [ADD]

Persson, Mats (pno)
Cage, J.:Winter Music, w. Steffen Schleiermacher (pno), Kristine Scholz (pno), Nils Vigeland (pno), Eberhard Blum (pic/fl/alt fl)—for 4 pianos; for 4 pianos with flute parts from Atlas Eclipticalis *(rec Sender Freies Berlin & Hessen Radio, Frankfurt, Feb. 10-11, 1992)*
Hat Hut ("NOW." series) ▲ hat ART CD 6141 [DDD]
The Virtuoso Clarinet, w. Kjell Fagéus (cl), Kjell-Inge Stevensson (cl), Eva Knardahl (pno) *(rec Nacka Aula, Nacka, Sweden, June 10-12, 1976)* BIS ▲ CD 62 [AAD]

Pert, Morris (mar/vib)
John Williams & Friends, w. John Williams (gtr), J. Williams (gtr), Carlos Bonell (gtr), Brian Gascoigne (mar/vib), Keith Marjoram (db) CBS ▲ MK 35108 [AAD]

Pert, Morris (pno)
Lutyens, E.:This Green Tide, w. Georgina Dobrée (bas hn) Clarinet Classics ▲ CC 0012 [AAD]
Lutyens, E.:Valediction, w. Georgina Dobrée (cl) Clarinet Classics ▲ CC 0012 [AAD]

Perticaroli, Sergio (pno)
Khachaturian, A.:Con Pno, w. A. Khachaturian (cnd), Turin RAI SO Diamante ▲ ARCD 2042 [ADD]
Rimsky-Korsakov, N.:Con Pno, w. M. Pradella (cnd), Turin RAI SO Diamante ▲ ARCD 2042 [ADD]

Pertis, P. (pno)
Liszt, F.:Années de pèlerinage 1—No. 6, "Vallée d'Obermann" Centaur ▲ CRC 2063 [DDD]
Liszt, F.:Années de pèlerinage 2—No. 7, "Dante Sonata" Centaur ▲ CRC 2063 [DDD]
Liszt, F.:Harmonies poétiques et religieuses—Funérailles Centaur ▲ CRC 2063 [DDD]
Liszt, F.:Hungarian Rhaps—No. 8 Centaur ▲ CRC 2063 [DDD]

Pertis, Zsuzsa (clvd)
Handel, G.F.:Sons Rcr, w. Zsolt Harsányi (rcr)—Op. 1, Nos. 2 in g, 4 in a, 7 in C, 11 in F; H.367a in d *(rec May 4-7, 1992)* Naxos ▲ 8.550700 [DDD]

▲ = CD ♦ = Enhanced CD Δ = MD ■ = Cassette Tape □ = DCC

Pertis, Zsuzsa (clvd) (cont.)
Handel, G.F.:Trio Sons, w. László Czidra (rcr), Zsolt Harsányi (rcr/bn), Pál Kelemen (vc)—in F, H.405 *(rec May 4–7, 1992)* Naxos ▲ 8.550700 [DDD]
Pertis, Zsuzsa (hpd)
Kocsár, M.:Movts Cl, w. B. Kovács (vn), M. Kocsár (cnd), Franz Liszt CO Hungaroton ▲ HCD 31188 [DDD]
Vivaldi, A.:Trio Sons Vn Lt, w. J. Rolla (va), D. Benkö (lt) Hungaroton ▲ HCD 11978
Pertorini, Reszö (vc)—see ORCHESTRAS & ENSEMBLES Festetics String Quartet
Perugi, Andrea (hpd)—see ORCHESTRAS & ENSEMBLES L'Homme Armé
Perulli, Raphaël (vl)
Couperin, F.:Leçons de ténèbres (for Good Friday), w. A. Deller (ct), P. Todd (ten), M. Chapuis (org) [L] Musique d'Abord ▲ HMA 190210
Peruška, Jan (va)—see also ORCHESTRAS & ENSEMBLES Stamitz String Quartet
Halvorsen, J.:Passacaglia & Sarabande con variazioni, w. Bohumil Kotmel (vn) Supraphon ▲ SUP 0049 [DDD]
Martinů, B.:The Prophecy of Isaiah, w. N. Romanová (sop), D. Drobková (alto), R. Novák (bass), V. Kozderka (tpt), I. Kiezlich (timp), S. Bogunia (pno), P. Kühn (cnd), Prague Radio Men's Chorus, Kühn Chorus [Cz] *(rec 2–3/88)* Supraphon ▲ 11 0751–2 [DDD]
Mozart, W.A.:Duos Vn, w. Bohumil Kotmel (vn) Supraphon ▲ SUP 0049 [DDD]
Rolla, A.:Duo 2 Vn, w. Bohumil Kotmel (vn) Supraphon ▲ SUP 0049 [DDD]
Spohr, L.:Duo Vn, w. Bohumil Kotmel (vn) Supraphon ▲ SUP 0049 [DDD]
Stamitz, A.:Con Va, w. J. Belohlávek (cnd), Prague Chamber PO *(rec Studio Martínek, Prague)* Panton ▲ PAN 811422 [DDD]
Stamitz, C.:Con Va, w. J. Belohlávek (cnd), Prague Chamber PO *(rec Studio Martínek, Prague)* Panton ▲ PAN 811422 [DDD]
Stamitz, J.W.A.:Con Va, w. J. Belohlávek (cnd), Prague Chamber PO *(rec Studio Martínek, Prague)* Panton ▲ PAN 811422 [DDD]
Stamitz, C.:Duos Vn Va, w. Bohumil Kotmel (vn) Supraphon ▲ SUP 0049 [DDD]
Peschko, Sebastian (pno)
Strauss, R.:Songs, w. Lisa Della Casa (sop)—Morgen!, Op. 27/4; Einerlei, Op. 69/3; Waldseligkeit, Op. 49/1; Hat gesagt...bleibt's nicht dabei, Op. 36/3; Seitdem dein Aug' in meines schaute, Op. 17/1; Schlechtes Wetter, Op. 69/5; Begreit, Op. 39/4 Testament ▲ SBT 1036 [ADD]
Peskanov, Alexander (pno)
Peskanov, A.:Dances Pno *(rec Baldwin Pianos, New York)* TW Classics ▲ TW 1001
Peskanov, A.:Lyrical Pieces *(rec Baldwin Pianos, New York)* TW Classics ▲ TW 1001
Peskanov, A.:Pno Music—Toccata; Temptations; Ghost Story; Carmen Fant; Perpetual Motion *(rec Baldwin Pianos, New York)* TW Classics ▲ TW 1001
Peskanov, A.:Poems of Nature *(rec Baldwin Pianos, New York)* TW Classics ▲ TW 1001
Rare Cello Music, w. Simca Heled (vc), Daniel Edni (pno), Jonathan Feldman (pno), Michael Levin (pno), Jonathan Zak (pno) *(rec 1976, 1982, 1983, 1985)* Classico ▲ CLASSCD 153
Peskanov, Mark (vn)
Ludwig, T.:Con Vn, w. T.M. Sleeper (cnd), Univ of Miami SO *(rec Maurice Gusman Concert Hall, Miami, Oct 23, 1994)* Albany ▲ TROY 195 [DDD]
Williams, John:Con Vn, w. L. Slatkin (cnd), London SO Varèse Sarabande ▲ VSD 5345
Peskey, John (va)—see ORCHESTRAS & ENSEMBLES Sierra Winds
Petash, Valeri (pno)
Chopin, F.:Nocturnes—Opp. 27/2 & 62/1 MK ▲ MKA 417110
Debussy, C.:Preludes Pno (sels)—Book 2:Feux d'artifice MK ▲ MKA 417110
Petash, V.:Pno Music—When the Cranes Fly away; Gone through the Fingers; Farewell; Blues; About Traveling & Sailing; Song for Pan Flute MK ▲ MKA 417110
Ravel, M.:Jeux d'eau MK ▲ MKA 417110
Ravel, M.:Pavane pour une infante défunte MK ▲ MKA 417110
Scriabin, A.:Etude Pno, Op. 2/1 MK ▲ MKA 417110
Scriabin, A.:Mazurkas Pno, Op. 25—No. 3 in e MK ▲ MKA 417110
Petchersky, Alma (pno)
Albéniz, I.:Suite española ASV Quicksilva ▲ QS 6079 [ADD]
Falla, M. de:Fant bética ASV Quicksilva ▲ QS 6079 [ADD]
Granados, E.:Allegro di Concierto ASV Quicksilva ▲ QS 6079 [ADD]
Scriabin, A.:Poèmes Pno, Op. 32 ASV ("Quicksilva" series) ▲ ASQ 6153 [DDD]
Scriabin, A.:Son 3 Pno ASV ("Quicksilva" series) ▲ ASQ 6153 [DDD]
Tchaikovsky, P.:Son Pno, Op. 37 ASV ("Quicksilva" series) ▲ ASQ 6153 [DDD]
Villa-Lobos, H.:Bachiana brasileira 4 ASV ▲ ASV 607 [DDD]
Villa-Lobos, H.:Chôro 5 ASV ▲ ASV 607 [DDD]
Villa-Lobos, H.:Ciclo brasiliero ASV ▲ ASV 607 [DDD]
Villa-Lobos, H.:Cirandas Pno ASV ▲ ASV 959
Villa-Lobos, H.:Rudepoema ASV ▲ ASV 959
Villa-Lobos, H.:Valsa da dor ASV ▲ ASV 607 [DDD]
Petcu, Adrian (vn)—see ORCHESTRAS & ENSEMBLES Crawford Trio
Petech, Diana (hpd)
Duphly, J.:Pièces de clavecin (4 books)—sels. from books 1–3 *(rec 4/91)* Giulia ▲ GS 201011 [DDD]
Lanzetti, S.:Sons Vc, w. C. Ronco (vc), S. Veggetti (vc), J. Held (bc)—Nos. 5–9, 11 & 12 *(rec 5/91)* Nuova Era ("Ancient Music" series) ▲ 7048 [DDD]
Peter, Hans (pno)
Brahms, J.:Hungarian Dances Pno 4-Hands, w. Volker Stenzl (pno)—Nos. 1–6 *(rec live)* Ars Musici ▲ AM 1130 [DDD]
Brahms, J.:Serenade 1 Orch, w. Volker Stenzl (pno) [arr J. Brahms for pno 4–hands] *(rec live)* Ars Musici ▲ AM 1130 [DDD]
Brahms, J.:Vars on a Theme of Robert Schumann, Op. 23, w. Volker Stenzl (pno) *(rec live)* Ars Musici ▲ AM 1130 [DDD]
Brahms, J.:Waltzes Pno, Op. 39, w. Volker Stenzl (pno)—No. 15 *(rec live)* Ars Musici ▲ AM 1130 [DDD]
Britten, H.:Introduction & Rondo alla burlesca & Mazurka elegiaca, w. Volker Stenzl (pno)—No. 1 *(rec Düsseldorf, Jan. 29 & Feb. 1, 1990)* Ars Musici ▲ AM 1088–2 [DDD]
Lutoslawski, W.:Vars on a Theme of Paganini for 2 Pnos, w. Volker Stenzl (pno) *(rec Düsseldorf, Jan. 29 & Feb. 1, 1990)* Ars Musici ▲ AM 1088–2 [DDD]
Ravel, M.:La Valse, w. Volker Stenzl (pno) *(rec Düsseldorf, Jan. 29 & Feb. 1, 1990)* Ars Musici ▲ AM 1088–2 [DDD]
Schubert, Franz:Fant Pno, D.940, w. V. Stenzl (pno) Ars Musici ▲ AM 1087–2
Schubert, Franz:Son Pno 4–Hands, D.812, w. V. Stenzl (pno) Ars Musici ▲ AM 1087–2
Stravinsky, I.:Con Pnos, w. Volker Stenzl (pno) *(rec Düsseldorf, Jan. 29 & Feb. 1, 1990)* Ars Musici ▲ AM 1088–2 [DDD]
Peter-Indermühle, H. (fl)
Vogel, W.:Sonances, w. H. Elhorst (ob), K. Weber (cl), I. Backer (bn), K. Hanke (hn), U. Lehmann (vn), L. Dober (vn), H. Forster (va), M. Liechti (vc), R. Tschupp (cnd) Grammont ▲ CTSP 14–2 [ADD]
Peterková, Ludmila (cl)
Bruch, M.:Trios Cl, Va & Pno, Op. 83, w. Josef Suk (va), Josef Hála (pno) Supraphon ▲ SUP 3014
Mozart, W.A.:Trio Cl, K.498, w. Josef Suk (va), Josef Hála (pno) Supraphon ▲ SUP 3014
Pokorny, P.:Summer Evening in the Mountains, w. Kamil Dolezal (cl) *(rec Martínek Studio, Prague)* Panton ▲ 811397–2 [DDD]
Petermandl, Hans (pno)
Hindemith, P.:Pno Music—Ludus Tonalis; Kleine Klaviermusik, Op. 45/4 Marco Polo ▲ 8.223338
Hindemith, P.:Pno Music—Suite "1922," Op. 26; In einer Nacht, Op. 15; Tanzstücke, Op. 19; Berceuse; Lied; Kleines Klavierstück Marco Polo ▲ 8.223335
Hindemith, P.:Pno Music—Klaviermusik & Reihe Kleiner Stücke, Op. 37/1 & 2; Übung in drei Stücken, Op. 31/1; Sonata, Op. 17; Zwei kleine Klavierstücke Marco Polo ▲ 8.223336
Hindemith, P.:Pno Music—3 Sonatas [1936]; Variations Marco Polo ▲ 8.223337
Peters, Christian (sax)
Blacher, B.:Songs, w. Katharina Richter (sop), Cornelia Wosnitza (sop), Markus Köhler (bar), Horst Göbel (pno), Chatschatur Kanajan (vn), Piotr Prysiasnik (vn), Fred Günther (va), Ithay Khen (vc), Christian Peters (sax), Markus Weidmann (bn)—3 Chansons; Ungereimtes; 4 Lieder; Nebel; 13 Ways of Looking at a Blackbird; 5 Sinnsprüche Omars des Zeltmachers; 3 Psalmen; Aprèslude; Francesca da Rimini; Jazz–Koloraturen Signum ▲ SIG X73–00 [DDD]
Peters, J. (bn)—see ORCHESTRAS & ENSEMBLES Munich Residenz Quintet members
Peters, Josef (bn)
Hovhaness, A.:Tzaikerk, w. G. Shanley (fl), E. Shapiro (vn) Crystal ■ C 800
Peters, Mark (vc)
Vivaldi, A.:Con for 2 Vcs, w. P. Sigl (vc), M. Haselböck (cnd), Vienna Academy [period instrs] Novalis ▲ 150074 [DDD]
Peters, Mitchell (perc)
Chou Wen-Chung:Soliloquy of a Bhiksuni, w. T. Stevens (tpt), Los Angeles Brass Society Crystal ▲ CD 667
Peters, Steve (sax)
Exquisite Corpses from P.S. 122, w. David Watson (shears/stick vn/gtr/tpt), Judy Dunaway (gtr/balloons), Anthony Coleman (sampler), Raissa St. Pierre (drums), Guy Yarden (vn/pno), Leslie Ross (bn), Linda Austin (gtr), Bruce Kaplan (gtr), Doug Henderson (peckhorn/bass/toy pno), Sue Ann Harkey (gtr), Cinnie Cole (sampler), et. al. ¿What Next? ▲ WN 0002 [ADD]
Petersén, A. (bass vl)
Bach, C.P.E.:Trio Son in F, w. C. Pehrsson (bass rcr), P. Novovic (va), A. Östman (hpd) [period instrs] BIS ▲ CD 220 [DDD]
Quantz, J.J.:Trio Sons, w. C. Pehrsson (rcr), P. Novovic (vn), A. Östman (hpd) [period instrs]—in C BIS ▲ CD 220 [DDD]
Telemann, G.P.:Sons Rcr, w. C. Pehrsson (rcr), A. Östman (hpd) [played on period instruments] BIS ▲ CD 220 [DDD]
Vivaldi, A.:Trio Sons (misc), w. C. Pehrsson (rcr), P. Novovic (vn), A. Östman (hpd) [period instrs]—in g BIS ▲ CD 220 [DDD]
Petersen, Erling Helmer (pno)
Enescu, G.:Suite Pno, Op. 10 *(rec 1994)* Danica ▲ DCD 8165
Liszt, F.:Consolations *(rec 1994)* Danica ▲ DCD 8165
Liszt, F.:Schlaflos, Frage und Antwort *(rec 1994)* Danica ▲ DCD 8165
Sibelius, J.:Finlandia [adapted by Petersen from Sibelius' Pno version] *(rec 1994)* Danica ▲ DCD 8165
Petersen, John (trbn)
Thybo, L.:Mvt symphonique, w. E. Lundkvist (org) *(rec Vangede Church)* Marco Polo/Dacapo ▲ 8.224009 [DDD]
Petersen, Ulrike (vn)
Spohr, L.:Duets Vns, Op. 67, w. Heinz Schunk (vn) CPO ▲ CPO 999343 [DDD]
Peterson, Barbara (fl)—see ORCHESTRAS & ENSEMBLES Trio Bariano
Peterson, Janet (hp)
Beside Thy Cradle, w. [cnd:Ralph B. Woodward], Salt Lake Children's Choir, Tamara B. Oswald (hp), Kelly Parkinson (vn), Victoria Ferris (vn), Hadley Ferris (va), Ellen Bridger (vc) *(rec Maurice Abravanel Hall, Salt Lake City)* Cherbourne ▲ CH 121
Peterson, Leslie (hn)
Porter, T.:Pieces Ww Qnt, w. Linda Schmidt (fl), Deirdre Fay (ob), Loran Eckroth (cl), Holly Holm (bn) Meyer ▲ MC 0108
Peterson, O. (pno)
Gershwin, G.:Porgy & Bess (sels) Verve ▲ 314 519807–2
Petit, D. (pno)
Prokofiev, S.:Ov on Hebrew Themes, w. A. Malsbury (cl), Coull String Quartet Hyperion ▲ CDA 66573
Petit, Emmanuel (vc)
Eccles, H.:Son Db, w. B. Cazauran (db), J. M. Denis (vn), A. Loger (vn), N. Carles (va) *(rec Aug. 29–30, 1992)* Gallo ▲ CD 753 [ADD]
Petit, Francis (perc)
Arma, P.:Music of, w. Josette Morata (nar), Fabrice Moretti (sax), Régis Poulain (bn), Jean–Marie Cottet (pno), Alain Béghin (perc), J.–L. Petit (cnd), Avray Atelier Musique—Phases contre phases for S Sax & Pno; Celui qui dort et dort for Nar, Bn, Xyl & Perc [after poems by Max Jacob]; 5 esquisses for Pno [from a Hungarian Theme]; Divertissement 1600 for Fls [w. Jean–Noël Catrice (fl), Béatrice Delpierre (fl), Pascale Haarscher (fl), Marie–Aude Menou (fl)]; 3 Regards for solo Ob [w. Jacques Vandeville (ob)]; Divert No. 6 for Cl & Pno [w. Dominique Vidal (cl)]; Parlando for solo Fl [w. Patrice Bocquillon (fl)] REM ▲ REM 311266 [DDD]
Brass & Organ at the Church of the Madeleine, w. François–Henri Houbart (org), Concert Arban Brass Quintet Pierre Verany ▲ 785096 [DDD]
Petit, Marie-Ange (baroque perc)
Lully, J.–B.:Le Bourgeois gentilhomme (sels), w. P. Goodwin (cnd), London Oboe Band—wedding music Harmonia Mundi ▲ HMU 907122
Lully, J.–B.:Cadmus et Hermione (sels), w. P. Goodwin (cnd), London Oboe Band—wedding music Harmonia Mundi ▲ HMU 907122
Lully, J.–B.:Les Noces de village (sels), w. P. Goodwin (cnd), London Oboe Band—wedding music Harmonia Mundi ▲ HMU 907122
Philidor, A.D.:Le Mariage de la couture avec la grosse Cathos (sels), w. P. Goodwin (cnd), London Oboe Band—wedding music Harmonia Mundi ▲ HMU 907122
Petit, Marie-Madeleine (pno)
Koechlin, C.:Son Va, w. A. Foucheux (va) *(rec 1976)* Skarbo ▲ SKR 3924
Messiaen, O.:Chants de Terre et de Ciel, w. M. Command (sop) [F] *(rec 1977)* EMI Classics 2–▲ CMS 64092–2 [ADD]
Messiaen, O.:Harawi, w. M. Command (sop) [F] *(rec 1977)* EMI Classics 2–▲ CMS 64092–2 [ADD]
Messiaen, O.:Mélodies, w. M. Command (sop) [F] *(rec 1977)* EMI Classics 2–▲ CMS 64092–2 [ADD]
Messiaen, O.:Poèmes pour Mi, w. M. Command (sop) [F] *(rec 1977)* EMI Classics 2–▲ CMS 64092–2 [ADD]
Petöfi, Erika (vn)—see ORCHESTRAS & ENSEMBLES Affetti Musicali, Festetics String Quartet
Petra, Hans (cl)—see ORCHESTRAS & ENSEMBLES Ives Ensemble members
Petracchi, Francesco (db)
Bottesini, G.:Gran Duo Concertant, w. R. Ricci (vn), P. Bellugi (cnd), Royal PO Sony Classical ("Essential Classics" series) ▲ SBK 47661 ■ SBT 47661
Schubert, Franz:Qnt Pno, D.667, w. P. Farulli (vla), Fiesole Trio Fonè ▲ 90F21 [DDD]
Petrescu, Adrian (ob)
Enescu, G.:Dectet Ww, w. Virgil Francu (fl), Nicolae Maxin (fl), Valeriu Barbuceanu (cl), Leontin Boanta (cl), Viorica Feher (bn), Goedri Orban (bn), Florin Ionoaia (Eng hn), Dan Cinca (hn), Simon Jebeleanu (hn), H. Andreescu (cnd) Olympia ▲ OLY 445 [DDD]
5 Centuries of German Music in Transylvania, w. H. Andreescu (cnd), Bucharest Virtuosi, Georgeta Stoleriu (sop), René Cristian Popescu (vn), Gabriel Bala (va), Stefan Thomasz (db), Nicolae Licaret (hpd) Electrecord ▲ ELC EDC 168 [DDD]
Petrescu, Sorin (pno)
Gerber, R.:Con for 2 Pnos, w. M. Ungereanu (pno), M. Cichirdan (cnd), Craiova PO Gallo ▲ CD 580 [AAD]
Petri, Egon (pno)
Alkan, C.–V.:Etudes (12) in minor keys—4 sels *(rec live, ca. 1952/3)* Pearl ▲ PEA 9966 (m) [AAD]
Alkan, C.–V.:Etudes (12) in minor keys—Symphony Symposium ▲ SYM 1145
Beethoven, L. van:Son 14 Pno, "Moonlight Son" APR ▲ APR 7024 [AAD]
Beethoven, L. van:Son 24 Pno *(rec 1936)* Pearl ▲ PEA 9916 (m) [AAD]
Beethoven, L. van:Son 24 Pno APR 2–▲ APR 7024 [AAD]
Beethoven, L. van:Son 27 Pno APR 2–▲ APR 7024 [AAD]
Beethoven, L. van:Son 32 Pno APR 2–▲ APR 7024 [AAD]
Brahms, J.:Pieces Pno, Op. 119—No. 4 in E♭ APR 2–▲ APR 7024 [AAD]
Brahms, J.:Rhaps Pno, Op. 79 APR 2–▲ APR 7024 [AAD]

INSTRUMENT.

Petri, Egon (pno) (cont.)
Brahms, J.:Son 3 Vn, w. Joseph Szigeti (vn) Grammofono 2000 ▲ GRM 78630
Brahms, J.:Son 3 Vn, w. Joseph Szigeti (vn) Iron Needle ▲ 1321 [ADD]
Brahms, J.:Son 3 Vn, w. J. Szigeti (vn) *(rec 1928–1937)* Music & Arts 2–▲ CD 813 [AAD]
Brahms, J.:Vars & Fugue on a Theme by Handel APR 2–▲ APR 7024 [AAD]
Brahms, J.:Vars on a Theme by Paganini APR 2–▲ APR 7024 [AAD]
Brahms, J.:Vars on a Theme by Paganini *(rec 1937)* Pearl ▲ PEA 9916 (m) [AAD]
Busoni, F.:Bach Transcriptions—Nun komm, der Heiden Heiland; Wachet auf, ruft uns die Stimme; Prelude, Fugue & Allegro in E♭, BWV 998 *(rec 1942 & 1948)* Pearl ▲ PEA 9966 (m) [AAD]
Busoni, F.:Pno Music—Sonatina No. 6 ("Carmen Fantasy"); Red Indian Diary, Book 1; Fantasia after music by Bach; "All'Italia" (Elegy No. 2); Sonatina (No. 3) ad usum infantis; Serenade from Mozart's Don Giovanni *(rec 1936–38)* Pearl ▲ PEA 9347 (m) [AAD]
Busoni, F.:Spanish Rhap Pno, w. D. Mitropoulos (cnd), Minneapolis SO *(rec 1938)* Pearl ▲ PEA 9347 (m) [AAD]
Chopin, F.:Ballades Pno (comp)—Op. 47 only *(rec 1936–1951)* Pearl ▲ CD 9078 [AAD]
Chopin, F.:Nocturnes *(rec 1936–1951)* Pearl ▲ CD 9078 [AAD]
Egon Petri, Vol. 1 Pearl ▲ PEA 9916 (m) [AAD]
Egon Petri, Vol. 2 *(rec 1929–1953 for Columbia)* Pearl ▲ PEA 9966 (m) [AAD]
His Recordings 1929–1942, Vol. 3 APR 2–▲ CDAPR 7027 [ADD]
Liszt, F.:Pno Music (misc) *(rec 1929–1937)* Pearl ▲ PEA 9966 (m) [AAD]

Petri, Michala (rcr)
Albinoni, T.:Cons à 5 Obs, Op. 7, w. C. Scimone (cnd), Venice Solisti—Nos. 3,6,9 & 12 RCA Red Seal ▲ 60207–2 [DDD]
Albinoni, T.:Cons à 5 Obs, Op. 9, w. C. Scimone (cnd), Venice Solisti—Nos. 2,5,8 & 11 RCA Red Seal ▲ 60207–2 [DDD]
Arnold, M.:Con Rcr, w. O. Kamu (cnd), English CO *(rec Hit Factory, London, Sept. 21–23, 1992)* RCA Red Seal ▲ 09026–62543–2 [DDD]
Bach, J.S.:Sons Fl, BWV 1030–35, w. K. Jarrett (hpd) RCA Red Seal ▲ 09026–61274–2 ■ 09026–61274–4 □ 09026–61274–5
Carol of the Drum, w. Chieftains, Emily Mitchell (hp), Richard Stoltzman (cl), James Galway (fl), Hampton String Quartet, Royal PO, Boys' Choir of Harlem RCA Victor ▲ 09026–61839–2 ■ 09026–61839–4
Christiansen, A.L.:Dance Suite, w. O. Kamu (cnd), English CO *(rec Hit Factory, London, Sept. 21–23, 1992)* RCA Red Seal ▲ 09026–62543–2 [DDD]
18th Century Italian Recorder Sonatas, w. George Malcolm (hpd) Philips ▲ 412632–2
Handel, G.F.:Cons Rcr, w. I. Brown (cnd), Academy of St. Martin in the Fields—1—in F Philips ▲ 400075–2 [ADD]
Handel, G.F.:Sons Rcr, w. Academy of St. Martin in the Fields Chamber Ensemble Philips ("Digital Classics" series) ▲ 412602–2 [DDD]
Handel, G.F.:Sons Rcr, w. Kieth Jarrett (hpd) RCA Red Seal ▲ 60441–2–RC [DDD]; ■ 60441–4–RC (CrO2) □ 09026–60441–5
Heberle, A.:Con Rcr, w. P. Zukerman (cnd), St. Paul CO Philips ("Digital Classics" series) ▲ 420243–2
Holmboe, V.:Con Rcr, w. O. Kamu (cnd), English CO *(rec Hit Factory, London, Sept. 21–23, 1992)* RCA Red Seal ▲ 09026–62543–2 [DDD]
Koppel, T.:Moonchild's Dream, w. O. Kamu (cnd), English CO *(rec Hit Factory, London, Sept. 21–23, 1992)* RCA Red Seal ▲ 09026–62543–2 [DDD]
Kulesha, G.:Con Rcr, w. O. Kamu (cnd), English CO *(rec Hit Factory, London, Sept. 21–23, 1992)* RCA Red Seal ▲ 09026–62543–2 [DDD]
Noël! Noël! Noël!:Christmas with Michala Petri, w. orch & chorus RCA Victor ▲ 60060–2–RC [DDD] ■ 60060–4–RC
O Holy Night:Christmas Favorites, w. James Galway (fl), Richard Stoltzman (cl), Emily Mitchell (hp), Canadian Brass, Boston Pops Orch [cnd:Arthur Fiedler] RCA Victor ▲ 09026–61836–2 ■ 09026–61836–4
Sammartini, G.:Cons Rcr, w. I. Brown (cnd), Academy of St. Martin in the Fields—in F Philips ▲ 400075–2 [ADD]
Sammartini, G.:Cons Rcr, w. V. Spivakov (cnd), Moscow Virtuosi—Con in F *(rec Gijon Laboral Univ Theater, Spain, June 1995)* RCA Red Seal ▲ 0902–668543–2 [DDD]
Souvenir, w. L. Hannibal (gtr) RCA Red Seal ▲ 09026–62530–2
Telemann, G.P.:Con in F Rcr Bn, w. K. Thunemann (bn), I. Brown (cnd), Academy of St. Martin in the Fields Philips ▲ 410041–2 [DDD]
Telemann, G.P.:Con Rcr, Fl, w. K. Bennett (fl), I. Brown (cnd), Academy of St. Martin in the Fields Philips ▲ 410041–2 [DDD]
Telemann, G.P.:Con in C Rcr, w. I. Brown (cnd), Academy of St. Martin in the Fields Philips ▲ 400075–2 [ADD]
Telemann, G.P.:Con in a for Rcr, Vl, w. P. Zukerman (va), P. Zukerman (cnd), St. Paul CO Philips ("Digital Classics" series) ▲ 420243–2 [DDD]
Telemann, G.P.:Duet Rcr & Vn, w. P. Zukerman (vn), P. Zukerman (cnd), St. Paul CO Philips ("Digital Classics" series) ▲ 420243–2 [DDD]
Telemann, G.P.:Sons Vn, Op. 2, w. E. Selin (rcr) RCA Red Seal ▲ 7903–2–RC [DDD]
Telemann, G.P.:Suite in a Fl, w. I. Brown (cnd), Academy of St. Martin in the Fields Philips ▲ 410041–2 [DDD]
Vivaldi, A.:Cons Rcr, w. V. Spivakov (cnd), Moscow Virtuosi—Cons Op. 10, RV 433, 439, 428, 435, 434 & 437 *(rec Gijon Laboral Univ Theater, Spain, June 1995)* RCA Red Seal ▲ 0902–668543–2 [DDD]
Vivaldi, A.:Cons Rcr, w. I. Brown (cnd), Academy of St. Martin in the Fields—RV.443 Philips ▲ 400075–2
Vivaldi, A.:Cons Rcr, w. C. Scimone (cnd), Venice Solisti—RV.108 & RV.441–445 RCA Red Seal ▲ 7885–2–RC [DDD]

Petric, Joseph (acc)
Huggett, A.:Suite Acc, w. G. Few (pno) *(rec June 12–13, 1991)* CBC ("Musica Viva" series) ▲ MVCD 1056 [DDD]
Jaeger, D.:Shadow Box Centrediscs ▲ CD 3288
Molique, W.B.:Son Concertina, w. G. Few (pno) *(rec June 12–13, 1991)* CBC ("Musica Viva" series) ▲ MVCD 1056 [DDD]
Molique, W.B.:Songs without Words, w. E. Goodman (hp) *(rec June 12–13, 1991)* CBC ("Musica Viva" series) ▲ MVCD 1056 [DDD]
Mozart, W.A.:Adagio & Rondo Glass Armonica, w. M. Hammer (fl), M. Berard (ob), D. Perry (va), D. Hetherington (vc) [trans. for accordion & string quartet] *(rec June 12–13, 1991)* CBC ("Musica Viva" series) ▲ MVCD 1056 [DDD]
Mozetich, M.:Dance, w. Amadeus Ensemble CBC ("Musica Viva" series) ▲ MVCD 1038 [DDD]
Scarlatti, D.:Sons Kbd—K.159 & 406 *(rec June 12–13, 1991)* CBC ("Musica Viva" series) ▲ MVCD 1056 [DDD]
Soler, P.A.:Sons Hpd [trans. for accordion by Petric]—Sonata No. 62 in B♭ *(rec June 12–13, 1991)* CBC ("Musica Viva" series) ▲ MVCD 1056 [DDD]

Petrie, Thomas (vn)
Kreisler, F.:Qt Strs, w. F. Kreisler (vn), W. Primrose (va), L. Kennedy (vc) Biddulph 3–▲ LAB 001–3 (m) [ADD]
Kreisler, F.:Scherzo 'in the style of Dittersdorf', w. F. Kreisler (vn), W. Primrose (va), L. Kennedy (vc) Biddulph 3–▲ LAB 001–3 (m) [ADD]

Petrov, Boris (pno)
Prokofiev, S.:Mélodies, w. Irina Medvedeva (vn) Musidisc ▲ MUS 291462 [DDD]
Prokofiev, S.:Son 1 Vn, w. Irina Medvedeva (vn) Musidisc ▲ MUS 291462 [DDD]
Prokofiev, S.:Son 2 Vn, w. Irina Medvedeva (vn) Musidisc ▲ MUS 291462 [DDD]

Petrov, Nikolai (pno)
Berlioz, H.:Sym fantastique [trans. Petrov based on Liszt] Russian Compact Disc ▲ RCD 13002 [DDD]
Brahms, J.:Vars & Fugue on a Theme by Handel Olympia ▲ OLY 276 [DDD]
Kapustin, N.:Sons Pno—No. 2 Olympia ▲ OCD 280 [DDD]
Khachaturian, A.:Con Pno, w. A. Khachaturian (cnd), USSR Radio–TV Orch *(rec 1977)* Russian Disc ▲ RUS 11 012

Petrov, Nikolai (pno) (cont.)
Khachaturian, A.:Con–Rhap Pno, w. A. Khachaturian (cnd), USSR Radio–TV Large SO Russian Disc ▲ RUS 11 014 [AAD]
Prokofiev, S.:Son 6 Pno *(rec 4/22/91)* Olympia ▲ OCD 280 [DDD]
Saint-Saëns, C.:Con 2 Pno [arr. Bizet for solo piano] Olympia ▲ OLY 276 [DDD]
Saint-Saëns, C.:Le Cygne [arr Godowsky for solo pno] Olympia ▲ OLY 276 [DDD]
Schubert, Franz:Fant Pno, D.760, "Wandererfantasie" Olympia ▲ OLY 275 [AAD]
Schubert, Franz:Son Pno, D.960 Olympia ▲ OLY 275 [AAD]
Schulhoff, E.:Son 3 Pno Olympia ▲ OCD 280 [DDD]
Schumann, R.:Etudes in the Form of Free Variations on a Theme by Beethoven Olympia ▲ OLY 276 [DDD]
Shchedrin, R.:Con 2 Pno, w. E. Svetlanov (cnd), USSR SO Russian Disc ▲ RUS 11129 [AAD]
Stravinsky, I.:Con Pno Ww, w. S. Ehrling (cnd), Stockholm Symphonic Wind Orch *(rec Berwald Hall, Mar. 1991)* Caprice ▲ CAP 21384 [DDD]
Stravinsky, I.:Son Pno Olympia ▲ OCD 280 [DDD]

Petrowska, Christina (pno)
Buhr, G.:Con Pno, w. B. Tovey (cnd), Winnipeg SO *(rec Winnipeg, Manitoba, Mar. 16 & 18, 1993)* CBC ("SM 5000" series) ▲ SMCD 5141 [DDD]

Petrucci, Gian-Luca (fl d'amore)
Mercadante, S.:Fant concertante on Themes from Orazi e Curiazi, w. Luca Truffelli (fl), C.F. Sedazzari (cnd), Camerata Schubert Bongiovanni ▲ GB 2199 [DDD]

Petrucci, Gian-Luca (fl)
Angrisani, G.:Con Fl, w. C.F. Sedazzari (cnd), Schubert Camerata *(rec live, Rome, July 27, 1995)* Bongiovanni ▲ GB 5553 [ADD]
Handel, G.F.:Duets for 2 Fls, Op. 2, w. W. Bennett (fl) Bongiovanni ▲ GB 5516 [DDD]
Mercadante, S.:Duets for 2 Fls, w. Severino Gazzelloni (fl) Bongiovanni ▲ GB 5543 [DDD]
Papa, F.:Con Fl, w. C.F. Sedazzari (cnd), Schubert Camerata *(rec live, Rome, July 27, 1995)* Bongiovanni ▲ GB 5553 [ADD]
Prota, T.:Con Fl, w. C.F. Sedazzari (cnd), Schubert Camerata *(rec live, Rome, July 27, 1995)* Bongiovanni ▲ GB 5553 [ADD]
Sciroli, G.:Con Fl, w. C.F. Sedazzari (cnd), Schubert Camerata *(rec live, Rome, July 27, 1995)* Bongiovanni ▲ GB 5553 [ADD]
Servillo, M.:Con 1 Fl, w. C.F. Sedazzari (cnd), Schubert Camerata *(rec live, Rome, July 27, 1995)* Bongiovanni ▲ GB 5553 [ADD]
Viotti, G.B.:Qts Fl, Op. 22, w. Kodály String Quartet members Tudor ▲ TUD 7021 [DDD]

Petrushansky, Boris (pno)
Brahms, J.:Sextet Strs, Op. 18 Symposium ▲ 1092
Brahms, J.:Vars & Fugue on a Theme by Handel Symposium ▲ 1092
Brahms, J.:Vars on a Theme by Paganini Symposium ▲ 1092
Levina, Z.:Con 2 Pno, w. V. Dudarova (cnd), Moscow SO Russian Disc ▲ RUS 11 382 [DDD]
Shostakovich, D.:Preludes & Fugues Pno *(rec Moscow, Jan. 1992)* Dynamic 3–▲ CD 117/1–3

Petry, Norbert (org)
The Organ in Lorraine:Works by Composers of the Region from 1537 to the Present, w. Anne-Catherine Bucher (org), Michel Chapuis (org), Francois Menissier (org) K617 2–▲ 7055

Pettersson, S. (cl)—see ORCHESTRAS & ENSEMBLES Gothenburg Wind Quintet

Petteys, Leslie (pno)
Hoover, K.:Qnt Pno & Strs, "Da pacem", w. Montclaire String Quartet Koch International Classics ▲ KIC 7147 [DDD]
Stevens, H.:Qnt Fl, w. Wendell Dobbs (fl), Montclaire String Quartet Koch International Classics ▲ KIC 7147 [DDD]

Pettinger, G. (wind instr)
Kelterborn, R.:Songs for 4 Winds & Chorus, w. T. Jones (trbn), M. Hoffmann (wind instr), W. Mittelbach (wind instr), G. Kember (cnd), Bavarian Radio Chorus *(rec May 13, 1983)* Grammont ▲ CTSP 35–2 [ADD]

Pettinger, Peter (pno)
Arnold, M.:Sonatina Cl, w. M. Khouri (cl) *(rec June 1991)* Continuum ▲ CCD 1038
Bax, A.:Son Cl & Pno, w. M. Khouri (cl) *(rec 6/91)* Continuum ▲ CCD 1038
Elgar, E.:Chanson de matin, w. N. Kennedy (vn) Chandos ▲ CHAN 8380 [DDD]
Elgar, E.:Chanson de nuit, w. N. Kennedy (vn) Chandos ▲ CHAN 8380 [DDD]
Elgar, E.:Pno Music—Chantant (ca. 1872); Pastourelle (air de ballet) (1881); Rosemary (1882); Griffenesque (1884); Sonatina (original version, 1889); Presto (1889); Minuet, Op. 21 (1897); May Song (1901); Dream Children, Op. 43 (1902); Skizze (1903); In Smyrna (1905); Concert Allegro (1901–06); Carissima (1913); Sonatina (published version, 1931); Serrenade (1932); Adieu (1932) Chandos ▲ CHAN 8438 [DDD]
Elgar, E.:Salut d'amour, w. S. Isserlis (vc) Chandos ▲ CHAN 8380 [DDD]
Elgar, E.:Son Vn, w. N. Kennedy (vn) Chandos ▲ CHAN 8380 [DDD]
Elgar, E.:Sospiri, w. N. Kennedy (vn) Chandos ▲ CHAN 8380 [DDD]
Elgar, E.:Vn & Pno Music, w. N. Kennedy (vn)—Mot d'amour, Op. 13; Canto popolare (In the moonlight, from *In the South*); 6 Very Easy Pieces in the First Position, Op. 22 Chandos ▲ CHAN 8380 [DDD]
Ernst, H.W.:Adagio sentimentale, w. Sherban Lupu (vn) Continuum ▲ CON 1017 [DDD]
Ernst, H.W.:Airs hongrois variés, w. Sherban Lupu (vn) Continuum ▲ CON 1017 [DDD]
Ernst, H.W.:Polonaise Vn, w. Sherban Lupu (vn) Continuum ▲ CON 1017 [DDD]
Ernst, H.W.:Rondo Papageno, w. Sherban Lupu (vn) Continuum ▲ CON 1017 [DDD]
Finzi, G.:Bagatelles, Op. 23, w. M. Khouri (cl) *(rec 6/91)* Continuum ▲ CCD 1038
Glazunov, A.:Chant du ménéstrel, w. Y. Turovsky (vc) Chandos ▲ CHAN 8555 [DDD]
Glazunov, A.:Elégie Vc, w. Y. Turovsky (vc) Chandos ▲ CHAN 8555 [DDD]
Glazunov, A.:Serenade espagnole, w. Y. Turovsky (vc) Chandos ▲ CHAN 8555 [DDD]
Horovitz, J.:Sonatina Cl, w. M. Khouri (cl) *(rec 6/91)* Continuum ▲ CCD 1038
Ireland, J.:Fant–Son Cl & Pno, w. M. Khouri (cl) *(rec 6/91)* Continuum ▲ CCD 1038
Nigel Kennedy Plays Jazz, w. Nigel Kennedy (vn) Chandos ("Collect" series) ▲ CHAN 6513 [DDD]
Prokofiev, S.:Chout (suite), w. Y. Turovsky (vc) [cello & piano arr.] Chandos ▲ CHAN 8555 [DDD]
Prokofiev, S.:Music of, w. Y. Turovsky (vc)—Adagio from *Cinderella*; Dance from *Romeo & Juliet*; Waltz from *(Tale of the Stone Flowers)* Chandos ▲ CHAN 8555 [DDD]
Shostakovich, D.:Preludes Pno, Op. 34, w. E. Turovsky (vn) [arr. for violin & piano]— 19 preludes, omitting Nos. 4,7,9,14 & 23 Chandos ▲ CHAN 8555 [DDD]
Wieniawski, H.:Adagio élégiaque, w. Sherban Lupu (vn) Continuum ▲ CON 1017 [DDD]
Wieniawski, H.:Le Carnaval russe, w. Sherban Lupu (vn) Continuum ▲ CON 1017 [DDD]
Wieniawski, H.:Fant orientale, w. Sherban Lupu (vn) Continuum ▲ CON 1017 [DDD]
Wieniawski, H.:Grand caprice fantastique, w. Sherban Lupu (vn) Continuum ▲ CON 1017 [DDD]

Petty, Oscar (ob)
Hanson, H.:Pastorale Ob, w. U. Barnea (cnd), Billings SO Innova ▲ MN 501
Haydn, J.:Con Ob, w. U. Barnea (cnd), Billings SO Innova ▲ MN 501
Kay, U.:Brief Elegy, w. U. Barnea (cnd), Billings SO Innova ▲ MN 501
Lombardo:Con Ob, w. U. Barnea (cnd), Billings SO Innova ▲ MN 501

Pettys, Delmar (vn)
Beethoven, L. van:Serenade Strs, Op. 8, w. C. Brubaker (va), D. Hopman (vc) [violin–viola–guitar arr.] Gajo ▲ GR 1002 [DAD]
Ravel, M.:Intro & Allegro, w. M. Golden (hp), M. Meisenbach (fl), R. McDowall (cl), R. Neal (vn), D. Hermann (va), G. Manasjan (vc) Centaur ▲ CRC 2114 [DDD]

Pettys, Valerie (fl)
Beaser, R.:Mountain Songs, w. D. Hopman (gtr) Gajo ▲ GR 1002 [DAD]

Petukhov, Mikhail (pno)
Petukhov, M.:Élégie romantique, w. Sergei Girshenko (vn), Sergei Kalyanov (vc) *(rec Great Hall of Moscow Conservatory, July 25 & Aug 10, 1995)* Pavane ▲ ADW 7365 [DDD]
Petukhov, M.:Son Pno *(rec Great Hall of Moscow Conservatory, July 25 & Aug 10, 1995)* Pavane ▲ ADW 7365 [DDD]
Petukhov, M.:Souvenir de Bruges *(rec Great Hall of Moscow Conservatory, July 25 & Aug 10, 1995)* Pavane ▲ ADW 7365 [DDD]

Petukhov, Mikhail (pno) (cont.)
Shostakovich, D.:Con 1 Pno, w. V. Kozhukar (cnd), USSR SO String Group *(rec 1989)*
Consonance ▲ 81-0009 [DDD]

Peyer, Gervase de (cl)
Beethoven, L. van:Trio 7 Pno, w. D. Barenboim (pno), J. Du Pré (vc) *(rec live, Brighton Festival 1970)*
Arkadia 2-▲ 589 [ADD]
Brahms, J.:Sons Cl (comp), w. G. Pryor (pno) — Chandos ▲ CHAN 8563 [DDD]
Cave, M.:Son Cl & Pno, w. M. Cave (pno) — MCM ■ 0086.1
Chopin, F.:Nocturnes—Op. 27/2 in D♭ [arr. for solo clarinet] — MCM ■ 0086.1
Debussy, C.:Première rapsodie, w. G. Pryor (pno) — Chandos ▲ CHAN 8526 [DDD]
English Music for Clarinet & Piano, w. Gwenneth Pryor (pno) — Chandos ▲ CHAN 8549 [DDD]
French Music for Clarinet & Piano — Chandos ▲ CHAN 8526 [DDD]
Gervase De Peyer, w. Michael Cave (pno) — MCM ■ 0086.1
Ireland, J.:Fant-Son Cl & Pno, w. Gwenneth Pryor (pno) — Chandos ▲ CHAN 9377/8 [DDD]
Mathias, W.:Con Cl, w. D. Atherton (cnd), London SO — Lyrita ▲ SRCD 325
Messiaen, O.:Quatuor pour la fin du temps—excerpt-solo clarinet section, "Abime des oiseaux" — MCM ■ 0086.1
Mozart, W.A.:Qnt Cl, K.581, w. Amadeus String Quartet
Deutsche Grammophon 2-▲ 437137-2 [ADD]
Mozart, W.A.:Qnt Cl, K.581, w. Melos Ensemble — EMI Classics ▲ CDM 63116
Mozart, W.A.:Qnt Cl, K.581, w. Amadeus String Quartet
Deutsche Grammophon ▲ 429819-2 [ADD]
Poulenc, F.:Son Cl Pno, w. G. Pryor (pno) — Chandos ▲ CHAN 8526 [DDD]
Saint-Saëns, C.:Son Cl, w. G. Pryor (pno) — Chandos ▲ CHAN 8526 [DDD]
Schubert, Franz:Son Arpeggione, w. M. Cave (pno) — MCM ■ 0086.1
Schubert, Franz:Son Arpeggione, w. G. Pryor (pno) — Chandos ▲ CHAN 8506 [DDD]
Schumann, R.:Fantasiestücke Cl, w. G. Pryor (pno) — Chandos ▲ CHAN 8506 [DDD]
Schumann, R.:Romances Ob, w. M. Cave (pno) — MCM ■ 0086.1
Schumann, R.:Romances Ob, w. G. Pryor (pno) — Chandos ▲ CHAN 8506 [DDD]
Weber, C.M. von:Vars on a Theme from *Silvana*, w. M. Cave (pno) — MCM ■ 0086.1
Weber, C.M. von:Vars on a Theme from *Silvana*, w. G. Pryor (pno) — Chandos ▲ CHAN 8506 [DDD]

Peyser, Ruth (gtr)
Exquisite Corpses from P.S. 122, w. David Watson (shears/stick vn/gtr/tpt), Judy Dunaway (gtr/balloons), Anthony Coleman (sampler), Raissa St. Pierre (drums), Guy Yarden (vn/pno), Leslie Ross (bn), Linda Austin (gtr), Bruce Kaplan (gtr), Doug Henderson (peckhorn/bass/toy pno), Sue Ann Harkey (gtr), Cinnie Cole (sampler), et. al.
What Next? ▲ WN 0002 [ADD]

Pezzani, Luciano (vc)—see also ORCHESTRAS & ENSEMBLES Zurich Chamber Players
Moret, N.:Double Con, w. R. Pezzani (vn), P. Sacher (cnd), Zurich Collegium Musicum *(rec live Nov. 18, 1982)*
Grammont ▲ CTSP 23-2 [ADD]

Pezzani, R. (vn)
Moret, N.:Double Con, w. L. Pezzani (vc), P. Sacher (cnd), Zurich Collegium Musicum *(rec live Nov. 18, 1982)*
Grammont ▲ CTSP 23-2 [ADD]

Pezzimenti, Carlo (gtr)
Angulo, H.:Cantos Yoruba de Cuba—Asokere I; ya Mi Ille; Borotiti; Asokere II; Suayo; Asokere III *(rec The Guitar Room, Dallas, Texas)*
Troost Press ▲ no catalog number ■ no catalog number
Atheria — Elba ▲ no cat # [DDD]
Brouwer, L.:Prelude Gtr *(rec The Guitar Room, Dallas, Texas)*
Troost Press ▲ CD 1677 [DDD] ■ CS 1677
Castelnuovo-Tedesco, M.:Platero y yo *(rec The Guitar Room, Dallas, Texas)*
Troost Press ▲ no catalog number [DDD] ■ no catalog number
Falla, M. de:Pièces espagnoles (4)—Homage to Debussy; Recit Du Pecheur; Chanson Du Feu Follet *(rec The Guitar Room, Dallas, Texas)*
Troost Press ▲ CD 1677 [DDD] ■ CS 1677
Ginastera, A.:Songs–Triste; Danza Criolla *(rec The Guitar Room, Dallas, Texas)*
Troost Press ▲ no catalog number [DDD] ■ no catalog number
Mompou, F.:Suite compostelana *(rec The Guitar Room, Dallas, Texas)*
Troost Press ▲ CD 1677 [DDD] ■ CS 1677
Moreno Torroba, F.:Sonatina Gtr Orch *(rec The Guitar Room, Dallas, Texas)*
Troost Press ▲ CD 1677 [DDD] ■ CS 1677
Moreno Torroba, F.:Suite castellana *(rec The Guitar Room, Dallas, Texas)*
Troost Press ▲ CD 1677 [DDD] ■ CS 1677
Mosaic *(rec Resurrection Lutheran Church Chapel, Plano, TX, Aug. 16, 18 & 23, 1994)*
EPR ▲ EPR 9407 [DDD]
Phelps, J.:Story-Telling—I; II; III *(rec The Guitar Room, Dallas, Texas)*
Troost Press ▲ no catalog number [DDD] ■ no catalog number
Ponce, M.:Sonatina meridional Gtr *(rec The Guitar Room, Dallas, Texas)*
Troost Press ▲ no catalog number [DDD] ■ no catalog number
Sainz de la Maza, E.:Preludes Gtr–Habanera *(rec The Guitar Room, Dallas, Texas)*
Troost Press ▲ CD 1677 [DDD] ■ CS 1677

Pezzone, Brian (pno)
Cage, J.:Europera 3, w. Suzan Hanson (sop), Ruby Hinds (mez), Patricia McAfee (mez), Michael Lyon (ten), Richard Powell (ten), Kevin Bell (bass), Vicki Ray (pno), Hannes Geiger (record players), Joseph Giri (record players), William Houston (record players), Dren McDonald (record players), Ronda Rindone (record players), Clarice Ross (record players), Scott Fraser (tape), A. Culver (cnd), Long Beach Opera Orch *(rec Center Theater, Long Beach, CA, Nov. 13, 1993)*
Mode 2-▲ MODE 38/39
Cage, J.:Europera 4, w. Anne-Marie Ketchum (sop), Daisetta Kim (sop), Jerry Wheeler (victrola), Scott Fraser (tape), A. Culver (cnd), Long Beach Opera Orch *(rec Center Theater, Long Beach, CA, Nov. 13, 1993)*
Mode 2-▲ MODE 38/39
Powell, Mel:Setting, w. T. Dye (pno) — Harmonia Mundi USA ▲ HMU 907096

Pezzotti, Daniel (vc)
Ringger, R.U.:Memories 2, w. L. Akerlund (sop), M. Ziegler (fl), P. Zaugg (hp), U. Walker (vn), F. Mohr, R.U. Ringger [G]
Grammont ▲ CTSP 29-2 [ADD]
Ringger, R.U.:Memories of Tomorrow, w. L. Akerlund (sop), M. Ziegler (fl), P. Zaugg (hp), U. Walker (vn), F. Mohr, R.U. Ringger [G]
Grammont ▲ CTSP 29-2 [ADD]

Pfeiffer, Harald (tpt)—see ORCHESTRAS & ENSEMBLES Pfeiffer Trumpet Consort
Pfeiffer, Joachim (tpt)—see ORCHESTRAS & ENSEMBLES Pfeiffer Trumpet Consort
Pfeiffer, Martin (tpt)—see ORCHESTRAS & ENSEMBLES Pfeiffer Trumpet Consort
Pfenninger, Andreas (vn)—see ORCHESTRAS & ENSEMBLES Zurich Chamber Players

Pfister, Stephanie (vn)
Deutsche Barocklieder, w. Andreas Scholl (ct), Alix Verzier (vc), Markus Markl (hpd), Karl Ernst Schroder (lt), Friederike Heumann (va), Juan Manuel Quintana (va), Pable Valetti (vn)
Harmonia Mundi France ▲ HMC 901505

Pfitzner, Hans (pno)
Pfitzner, H.:Songs, w. G. Hüsch (bar)—Hast du von den Fischerkindern, Op. 7/1; Zum Abschiede meiner Tochter, Op. 10/3; Der Gärtner, Op. 9/1; Die Einsame, Op. 9/2; Abbitte, Op. 29/1; In Danzig, Op. 22/1; Nachts, Op. 26/2; Michaelskirchplatz, Op. 19/2; Hussens Kerker, Op. 32/1; Sœrspruch, Op. 32/2; Leuchtende Tage, Op. 40/1; Herbstgefühl, Op. 40/4 [G]
Preiser ▲ 90029 (m) [AAD]

Pflüger, Hans Georg (org)
Pflüger, H.G.:Harmagedon — Bayer ▲ 800910

Phelps, Cynthia (va)—see also ORCHESTRAS & ENSEMBLES Bargemusic
Brahms, J.:Sextet Strs, Op. 36, w. Benny Kim (vn), Ani Kavafian (vn), Randolph Kelly (va), Colin Carr (vc), Peter Rejto (vc) *(rec live, Tucson Chamber Music Festival, Mar 11, 1994)*
Arizona Friends of Chamber Music ▲ 1994 [DDD]
Mozart, W.A.:Qnt Strs, K.516, w. Ani Kavafian (vn), Benny Kim (vn), Randolph Kelley (va), Colin Carr (vc) *(rec Tuscon Winter Chamber Festival; Mar 11, 1994)*
Arizona Friends of Chamber Music ▲ 1994/5 [DDD]

Phelps, Melissa (vc)
Schubert, Franz:Qnt Strs, D.956, w. Medici String Quartet — Medici Quartet ▲ MQT 9002 [DDD]

Phelps-Beckstead, Melissa (vn)
Jacob, G.:Qnt Cl, w. Daniel Geeting (cl), David Stenske (vn), Richard Rintoul (va), Joyce Geeting (vc) *(rec Memorial Chapel, Univ. of Redlands, Redlands, CA)*
PROdigital ▲ PRO 9226 [DDD]

Phelps-Wetzel, Stacy (vn)
Barati, G.:Trio Cl, w. William Wohlmacher (cl), Lawrence Granger (vc) *(rec Emeryville Recording Company, Emeryville, CA, 1994)*
Centaur ▲ CRC 2286 [DDD]

Philipp, Günter (pno)
Denisov, E.:Con Pno, w. W.-D. Hauschild (cnd), Leipzig RSO — Berlin Classics ▲ BER 9260
Denisov, E.:Peinture, w. W.-D. Hauschild (cnd), Berlin RSO — Berlin Classics ▲ BER 9260

Philipp, I. (pno)
Saint-Saëns, C.:Son 1 Vc, w. P. Bazelaire (vc) — Pearl ▲ PEA 9174 [ADD]
Saint-Saëns, C.:Son 2 Vc, w. P. Bazelaire (vc) — Pearl ▲ PEA 9174 [ADD]
Saint-Saëns, C.:Son 1 Vn, w. A. Pascal (vn) *(rec 1935)* — Pearl ▲ PEA 9174 [ADD]

Philips, Margaret (org)
20th Century Christmas Collection, w. [cnd:Harry Christophers], The Sixteen
Collins Classics ▲ COL 1270 [DDD]

Phillipson, David (perc/bells)
Smith, W.L.:Music of, w. Robin Lorentz (vn), Erika Duke (vc), Dorothy Stone (fl/pic), Martin Walker (cl), Wadada Leo Smith (tpt/flgl/fls/bells), Vicki Ray (pno/cel), Mika Noda (vib/bells/timp)—Another Wave More Waves; Double Thunderbolt; Tao-Njia; and others
Tzadik ("Composer" series) ▲ TZA 7017 [DDD]

Phillebaum, Katja (pno)
Art Songs by American Composers, w. Yolanda Marcoulescou-Stern (sop) — Gasparo ▲ GSCD 287
French Art Songs, w. Yolanda Marcoulescou-Stern (sop) — Gasparo ▲ GSCD 293

Phillips, Craig (org)
Hymns through the Ages, w. [cnd:Thomas Foster], Beverly Hills All Saints' Episcopal Church Choir *(rec All Saints' Church, Beverly Hills)*
Gothic ▲ GOT 49074
Silence & Music, w. [cnd:Thomas Foster], Beverly Hills All Saints' Episcopal Church Choir *(rec May 30-June 3, 1993)*
Gothic ▲ GOT 49064

Phillips, Daniel (va)
O'Connor, M.:Qt Vn, w. Mark O'Connor (vn), Carter Brey (vc), Edgar Meyer (db) *(rec Blair Recital Hall, Vanderbilt Univ., Nashville, TN, Dec. 1990)*
Warner Bros. ▲ 45846-2

Phillips, Daniel (vn)
Bland, W.:Trio 2, "Elegy & Consolation", w. S. Doane (vc), A. Feinberg (pno)
Bridge ▲ BCD 9013 [DDD]
Brahms, J.:Trio Hn, w. W. Purvis (hn), R. Goode (pno) — Bridge ▲ BCD 9012 [DDD]
Kodály, Z.:Duo Vn & Vc, w. J. Grossman (vc) — Elektra/Nonesuch ▲ 79074-2
Schubert, Franz:Qt 15 Strs, w. G. Kremer (vn), K. Kashkashian (va), Yo Yo Ma (vc)
CBS ▲ MK 42134 [DDD]
Shostakovich, D.:Qt 15 Strs, w. G. Kremer (vn), K. Kashkashian (va), Yo Yo Ma (vc)
CBS ▲ MK 44924 [DDD]
Vivaldi, A.:Cons Vn, Op. 8/1-4, "The Four Seasons", w. Jose-Luis Garcia (vn), Maurice Hasson (vn), Manoug Parikian (vn), Y. Menuhin (cnd), English CO [each movt. w. different vn soloist]
Start Classics ▲ SCD 13

Phillips, Jean-Marc (vn)—see also ORCHESTRAS & ENSEMBLES Phillips String Quartet
Mozart, W.A.:Adagio & Fugue Strs, w. Gidon Kremer (vn), Kim Kashkashian (va), Yo-Yo Ma (vc)
CBS ▲ MK 42134 [DDD]

Phillips, Karen (va)
Bazelon, I.:Duo Va & Pno, w. G. Jacobson (pno) — CRI ▲ CD 623 [ADD]
Feldman, Morton:The Va in My Life, w. A. Ajemian (vn), M. Feldman (cnd) *(rec 12/7/70)*
CRI ▲ CD 620 [ADD]

Phillips, Margaret (org)
Duparc, H.:Benedicat vobis Dominus, w. John Poole (cnd), BBC Singers
IMP ("BBC Radio" series) ▲ IMP 5691482
18th Century English Organ Music — Gamut Classics ▲ GAM CD 514 [DDD]
Martin, F.:Mass, w. John Poole (cnd), BBC Singers
IMP ("BBC Radio" series) ▲ IMP 5691482
19th Century English Organ Music — Gamut Classics ▲ GAM CD 522 [DDD]
Purcell, H.:Songs, w. Jean Nibbs (sop), Geoffrey Mitchell (ct), Peter Hall (ten), David Thomas (bass), Michael Howard (cnd), Cantores in Ecclesia—Hear My Prayer, O Lord; Song of the 3 Children; Remember Not, Lord, Our Offences; Voluntary for Single Organ; Magnificat & Nunc Dimittis in g; Thy Work is a Lantern; Burial Sentences for Queen Mary [Man That is Born of a Woman]; In the Midst of Life We Are in Death; Thou Knowest, Lord, the Secrets of Our Hearts]; O God, Thou Art My God; Magnificat & Nunc Dimittis in B♭; Voluntary on the 100th Psalm Tune; Turn Thou Us, O Good Lord; O Give Thanks Unto the Lord [Psalm 106]
IMP ("BBC Radio Classics" series) ▲ IMP 9126
A Treasury of English Organ Music — Gamut Classics ▲ IMCD 702 [DDD]

Phillips, Odile (va)—see ORCHESTRAS & ENSEMBLES Phillips String Quartet
Phillips, Robert (lt)—see ORCHESTRAS & ENSEMBLES Rowallan Consort

Philliptsch, Frank
Helmschrott, R.:Cross & Freedom, w. Helmut Schatz, Nancy Gibson (sop), Frieder Aurich (ten), Matthias Weichert (bass), Manfred Ball (nar), Anett Baumann (vn), Linda Robbins, Gerhard Wolf, Martin Homann (perc), Robert M. Helmschrott (org), H.-C. Rademann (cnd), Munich Trombone Quartet, Dresden Chamber Choir
Vienna Modern Masters ▲ VMM 3027 [DDD]

Pianezzola, Giambettista (vn)—see also ORCHESTRAS & ENSEMBLES Quartotto Modì
Finzi, A.:Son Vn, w. Simonetta Heger (pno) — Nuova Era ▲ NUO 7249

Piastrelloni, Oscar (vc)
Respighi, O.:Seranata, w. R. Tigani (cnd), Sassari SO *(rec Rome, Oct 11-14, 1994)*
Bongiovanni ▲ GB 2166 [DDD]

Piastro, Mishel (vn)
Beethoven, L. van:Con Vn, Vc & Pno, "Triple Con", w. Joseph Schuster (vc), Ania Dorfman (pno), A. Toscanini (cnd), New York PO
Grammofono 2000 ▲ GRM 78636

Piatigorsky, Gregor (vc)
Beethoven, L. van:Serenade Strs, Op. 8, w. J. Heifetz (vn), W. Primrose (va)
RCA Gold Seal ▲ 7870-2-RG (m/s) [ADD]
Beethoven, L. van:Son 2 Vc, w. A. Schnabel (pno) *(rec 1934)* — Music & Arts ▲ CD 674 [AAD]
Beethoven, L. van:Son 2 Vc, w. A. Schnabel (pno) *(rec 12/6 & 16/34)* — Pearl ▲ PEA 9447 [m] [ADD]
Beethoven, L. van:Trios Strs, Op. 9, w. J. Heifetz (vn), W. Primrose (va)—No. 2
RCA Gold Seal ▲ 7873-2-RG [ADD] ■ 7873-4-RG
Brahms, J.:Con Vn & Vc, "Double Con", w. J. Heifetz (vn), A. Wallenstein (cnd), RCA Victor SO
RCA Red Seal ▲ 6778-2-RC [ADD]
Brahms, J.:Con Vn & Vc, "Double Con", w. N. Milstein (vn), F. Reiner (cnd), Robin Hood Dell Orch Philadelphia
RCA Gold Seal ▲ 09026-61485-2
Brahms, J.:Qt 3 Pno, w. J. Lateiner (pno), J. Heifetz (vn), S. Schonbach (va)
RCA Gold Seal ▲ 7873-2-RG [ADD] ■ 7873-4-RG
Brahms, J.:Sextet Strs, Op. 36, w. J. Heifetz (vn), I. Baker (vn), W. Primrose (va), V. Majewski (va), G. Rejto (vc)
RCA Gold Seal ▲ 7965-2-RG [ADD]
Brahms, J.:Sons Vc (comp), w. Artur Rubinstein (pno) *(rec American Legion Hall, Hollywood, Oct 11, 1966)*
RCA Gold Seal ▲ 09026-62592-2
Brahms, J.:Son 1 Vc, w. A. Rubinstein (pno) *(rec 1936 from HMV DB 2952-54)*
Pearl ▲ PEA 9447 [m] [AAD]
Brahms, J.:Son 1 Vc, w. A. Rubinstein (pno) *(rec 1936 from HMV DB 2952-54)*
Music & Arts ▲ CD 674 [AAD]
Dvořák, A.:Con Vc, w. C. Munch (cnd), Boston SO *(rec 1957 & 1960)*
RCA Gold Seal ▲ 09026-61498-2 ■ 09026-61498-4
Dvořák, A.:Qnt Pno, Op. 81, w. J. Lateiner (pno), M. Baker (va), J. Heifetz (vn), J. de Pasquale (va)
RCA Gold Seal ▲ 7965-2-RG [ADD]
Françaix, J.:Trio Vn, Va & Vc, w. J. Heifetz (vn), J. de Pasquale (va)
RCA Gold Seal ▲ 7872-2-RG (m/s) [ADD]
Great Musicians In Copenhagen, w. Vladimir Horowitz (pno), Rudolf Serkin (pno), Wanda Landowska (hpd), Nathan Milstein (vn), Fritz Busch (cnd), Nicolai Malko (cnd)
Danacord ▲ DACOCD 303
Gregor Piatigorsky — Biddulph ▲ LAB 117
Martinů, B.:Duo Vn & Vc, w. J. Heifetz (vn)
RCA Gold Seal ▲ 7871-2-RG (m/s) [ADD]

Piatigorsky, Gregor (vc) (cont.)
Mendelssohn, F.:Trio 1 Pno, w. A. Rubenstein (pno), J. Heifetz (vn) RCA Gold Seal ▲ 7768-2-RG (m) [ADD]
Mozart, W.A.:Qnt Strs, K.516, w. J. Heifetz (vn), I. Baker (vn), W. Primrose (va), V. Majewski (va) RCA Gold Seal ▲ 7869-2 (m/s) [ADD] ■ 7869-4 (m/s)
Ravel, M.:Trio Pno, w. A. Rubinstein (pno), J. Heifetz (vn) RCA Gold Seal ▲ 7871-2-RG (m/s) [ADD]
Rózsa, M.:Theme & Vars Vn, w. J. Heifetz (vn) RCA Gold Seal ▲ 7963-2-RG [ADD]
Schubert, Franz:Qnt Strs, D.956, w. J. Heifetz (vn), I. Baker (vn), W. Primrose (va), G. Rejto (vc) RCA Gold Seal ▲ 7964-2-RG [ADD] ■ 7964-4-RG (CrO2)
Schubert, Franz:Trio Strs, D.581, w. J. Heifetz (vn), W. Primrose (va) RCA Gold Seal ▲ 7964-2-RG [ADD] ■ 7964-4-RG (CrO2)
Schumann, R.:Con Vc, w. J. Barbirolli (cnd), London PO *(rec 1934)* Music & Arts ▲ CD 674 [AAD]
Schumann, R.:Con Vc, w. J. Barbirolli (cnd), London PO *(rec 1934)* Pearl ▲ PEA 9447 (m) [AAD]
Spohr, L.:Double Qt 1, w. J. Heifetz (vn), I. Baker (vn), P. Amoyal (vn), P. Rosenthal (vn), M. Thomas (va), A. Harshman (va), L. Lesser (vc) RCA Gold Seal ▲ 7870-2-RG (m/s) [ADD]
Strauss, R.:Don Quixote, w. C. Munch (cnd), Boston SO RCA Gold Seal ▲ 09026-61485-2
Tchaikovsky, P.:Trio Pno, w. A. Rubinstein (pno), J. Heifetz (vn) RCA Gold Seal ▲ 7768-2-RG (m) [ADD]
Walton, W.:Con Vc, w. C. Munch (cnd), Boston SO *(rec 1957 & 1960)* RCA Gold Seal ▲ 09026-61498-2 ■ 09026-61498-4
Weber, C.M. von:Sons Vn, w. I. Newton (pno) [arr. by Piatigorsky for cello & piano]—No. 5 in A, J.103 *(rec 1934)* Pearl ▲ PEA 9447 (m) [AAD]

Piazzini, Carmen (pno)
Brahms, J.:Qts SATB, Op. 64, w. Wolfgang Seeliger (cnd), Darmstadt Concert Choir Entrée ▲ 0080 [ADD]
Brahms, J.:Son 2 Vc, w. Werner Thomas-Mifune (vc) Koch Schwann ▲ SCH 318232
Brahms, J.:Son in D Vc, w. Werner Thomas-Mifune (vc) Koch Schwann ▲ SCH 318232
Fauré, G.:Son 1 Vc, w. W. Thomas (vc) Calig ▲ CAL 50881 [DDD]
Gretchaninoff, A.:Vc & Pno Music, w. W. Thomas (vc)—Fantasia; Nocturne, Op. 86; Sonata in E, Op. 113 Calig ▲ CAL 50881 [DDD]
Hummel, F.:Archipelagos Col legno ▲ AU 31802 [DDD]
Rachmaninoff, S.:Son Vc, w. W. Thomas (vc) *(rec Dec. 21-22, 1987)* Calig ▲ CAL 50871 [DDD]
Saint-Saëns, C.:Chant saphique, w. W. Thomas (vc) *(rec Dec. 22-23, 1986)* Calig ▲ CAL 50862 [DDD]
Saint-Saëns, C.:Son 1 Vc, w. W. Thomas (vc) *(rec Dec. 22-23, 1986)* Calig ▲ CAL 50862 [DDD]
Saint-Saëns, C.:Son 2 Vc, w. W. Thomas (vc) *(rec Dec. 22-23, 1986)* Calig ▲ CAL 50862 [DDD]
Schubert, Franz:Son Arpeggione, w. Werner Thomas-Mifune (vc) Calig ▲ CAL 50949 [DDD]
Schumann, R.:Adagio & Allegro Hn, w. Werner Thomas-Mifune (vc) Calig ▲ CAL 50949 [DDD]
Schumann, R.:Fantasiestücke Cl, w. Werner Thomas-Mifune (vc) Calig ▲ CAL 50949 [DDD]
Schumann, R.:Romances Ob, w. Werner Thomas-Mifune (vc) Calig ▲ CAL 50949 [DDD]
Strauss, R.:Son Vc, w. W. Thomas (vc) *(rec Dec. 21-22, 1987)* Calig ▲ CAL 50871 [DDD]
Wolf, H.:Im stillen Friedhof, w. Wolfgang Seeliger (cnd), Darmstadt Concert Choir Entrée ▲ 0080 [ADD]

Piazzolla, Astor (band)—see also ORCHESTRAS & ENSEMBLES New Tango Sex-tet
Piazzolla, A.:Adiós Nonino, w. M. Hadjidakis (cnd), Athens Colours Orch [arr for band, pno, hp & perc] *(rec Ancient Herod Odeon, Athens, Greece, July 3, 1990)* Milan ▲ 73138-35758-2
Piazzolla, A.:Con Band, w. M. Hadjidakis (cnd), Athens Colours Orch *(rec Ancient Herod Odeon, Athens, Greece, July 3, 1990)* Milan ▲ 73138-35758-2
Piazzolla, A.:Music of, w. F.S. Paz (vn), Horacio Malivicino (elec gtr), Hector Console (db), Pablo Ziegler (pno)—Verano porteño; Lunfardo; Milonga del angel; Muerte del angel; Astor's Speech; La camorra; Mumuki; Adios Nonino; Contra bajissmo; Michelangelo; Concierto para quinteto *(rec Sept. 6, 1987)* Chesky ▲ JD 107 [DDD]
Piazzolla, A.:Tangos Band, w. M. Hadjidakis (cnd), Athens Colours Orch *(rec Ancient Herod Odeon, Athens, Greece, July 3, 1990)* Milan ▲ 73138-35758-2

Picard, Carmen (pno)—see ORCHESTRAS & ENSEMBLES Montreal Chamber Group

Piccinini, Marina (fl)
Boulez, P.:Sonatine Fl & Pno, w. A. Haefliger (pno) Connoisseur Society ▲ CD 4183 [DDD]
Cohn, J.:Music of, w. M. Dine (ob), J. Manasse (cl), M. Finn (bn), J. Tarpley (hn), N. Akamatsu (db), S. Alderking (pno)—Wind Quintet, Op. 36b (1981); Goldfinch Variations for Wind Trio, Op. 61 (1984); Little Overture for Wind Quartet, Op. 59 (1982); Suite Champêtre for Wind Quintet (after Rameau), Op. 47 (1968) XLNT ■ C 2
Cohn, J.:Music of, w. M. Dine (ob), J. Manasse (cl), M. Finn (bn), J. Tarpley (hn), N. Akamatsu (db), S. Alderking (pno)—Wind Quintet, Op. 36b (1981); Little Overture for Wind Quintet, Op. 59 (1982); Sonatina for Clarinet & Piano, Op. 56 (1981); Sonata Romantica for Double Bass & Piano, Op. 18 (1952); Sonata Robusta for Bassoon & Piano, Op. 55 (1980); Sonata for Flute & Piano, Op. 52 (1974); Goldfinch Variations for Three Treble Instruments, Op. 61 (1984) *(rec 1985)* XLNT ▲ CD 18006 [ADD]
Jolivet, A.:Chant de Linos, w. A. Haefliger (pno) Connoisseur Society ▲ CD 4183 [DDD]
Prokofiev, S.:Son Fl, w. A. Haefliger (pno) Connoisseur Society ▲ CD 4183 [DDD]

Picht-Axenfeld, Edith (hpd)
Bach, J.S.:Cant 203, w. Dietrich Fischer-Dieskau (bar), Aurèle Nicolet (fl), Helmut Keller (vn), Irmgard Poppen (vc) EMI Classics ("Baroque" series) ▲ CDK 65729
Bach, J.S.:Sons Fl, BWV 1030-35, w. Chang Kook Kim (fl), in b, BWV 1030 *(rec Iruma Shimin Kaikan, Japan, May 1979)* Camerata ▲ 32CM 262
Bach, J.S.:Sons Vn, w. Chang Kook Kim (fl), BWV 1020 [doubtful] *(rec Iruma Shimin Kaikan, Japan, May 1979)* Camerata ▲ 32CM 262
Telemann, G.P.:Cants, w. Dietrich Fischer-Dieskau (bar), Aurèle Nicolet (fl), Helmut Keller (vn), Irmgard Poppen (vc)—Die Hoffnung ist mein Leben EMI Classics ("Baroque" series) ▲ CDK 65729

Picker, Tobias (pno)
Picker, T.:Keys to the City, w. L. Foss (cnd), Brooklyn PO CRI ▲ CD 554 [DDD]
Picker, T.:Rhap Vn, w. B. Hudson (vn) *(rec 1979)* CRI ▲ CD 589 [ADD]

Pickett, Philip (rcr)—see also ORCHESTRAS & ENSEMBLES L'École d'Orphée
Telemann, G.P.:Con in C Rcr, w. P. Pickett (cnd), New London Consort L'Oiseau-Lyre ▲ 433043-2 [DDD]
Telemann, G.P.:Con in a for Rcr, Vl, w. M. Levy (vl), P. Pickett (cnd), New London Consort L'Oiseau-Lyre ▲ 433043-2 [DDD]
Telemann, G.P.:Suite in a Fl, w. P. Pickett (cnd), New London Consort L'Oiseau-Lyre ▲ 433043-2 [DDD]

Pidoux, Roland (vc)—see also ORCHESTRAS & ENSEMBLES Le Nouveau Trio Pasquier
Boccherini, L.:Qnts Fl, G.437-442, w. Jean-Pierre Rampal (fl), Bruno Pasquier (vn), Régis Pasquier (vn), Mathilde Sternat (vc)—1-3, 5 & 6 Sony Classical ▲ SK 62679
Boulanger, N.:Pieces (2) Vc & Pno, w. E. Naoumoff (pno) *(rec June 14-17, 1993)* Marco Polo ▲ 8.223636 [DDD]
Brahms, J.:Qt 1 Pno, w. Jean-Claude Pennetier (pno), Régis Pasquier (vn), Bruno Pasquier (va) Harmonia Mundi ▲ HMT 7901062
Brahms, J.:Sextet Strs, Op. 18, w. Régis Pasquier (vn), Raphaël Oleg (vn), Bruno Pasquier (va), Jean Dupouy (va), Etienne Péclard (vc)—No. 1 Harmonia Mundi France ("Musique d'abord" series) ▲ HMA 1901073
Chausson, E.:Con Vn, Pno & Str Qt, w. R. Daugareil (vn), R. Pasquier (vn), G. Simonot (vn), B. Pasquier (va), J.-C. Pennetier (pno) Harmonia Mundi Plus ▲ HMP 3901135
Chausson, E.:Pièce Vc & Pno, w. J.-C. Pennetier (pno) Harmonia Mundi Plus ▲ HMP 3901135
Haydn, J.:Divert Hn, Vn & Vc, H.IV/5, w. Hervé Joulain (hn), Jean-Jacques Kantorow (vn) Arion ▲ ARN 68311 [DDD]
Offenbach, J.:Grand duos concertants, w. E. Péclard (vc) Musique d'Abord ▲ HMA 1901043
Saint-Saëns, C.:Le Cygne, w. William Nabore (pno) Accord ▲ ACD 200592 [DDD]
Saint-Saëns, C.:Suite Vc, w. H. Sermet (pno) Valois ("Musique Française" series) ▲ V 4657
Schubert, Franz:Qnt Strs, D.956, w. Bulgarian String Quartet Musique d'Abord ▲ HMA 190980
Schubert, Franz:Son Arpeggione, w. Pennetier (pno) Harmonia Mundi France ▲ HMC 901035

Pidoux, Roland (vc) (cont.)
Schubert, Franz:Trio 1 Pno, w. Jean-Claude Pennetier (pno), Régis Pasquier (vn) Harmonia Mundi ("Suite" series) ▲ HMT 7901048
Schubert, Franz:Trio Strs, D.471, w. R. Pasquier (vn), B. Pasquier (va) Harmonia Mundi France ▲ HMC 901035
Schubert, Franz:Trio Strs, D.581, w. R. Pasquier (vn), B. Pasquier (va) Harmonia Mundi France ▲ HMC 901035
Schumann, R.:Andante & Vars Hn, w. Marie-Josèphe Jude (pno), Laurent Cabasso (pno), Michel François (vc), Hervé Joulain (hn) Harmonia Mundi France ("Les Nouveaux Interprètes" series) ▲ HMN 911559
Schumann, R.:Songs, w. Marie-Josèphe Jude (pno), Laurent Cabasso (pno), Michel François (vc), Hervé Joulain (hn)—Abendlied, Op. 107/6 Harmonia Mundi France ("Les Nouveaux Interprètes" series) ▲ HMN 911559

Piedemonte, Yvonne (pno)
Enescu, G.:Qt 1 Pno, w. Voces Intimae String Quartet members *(rec 1981)* Olympia ▲ OCD 412 [AAD]
Enescu, G.:Qt 2 Pno, w. Voces Intimae String Quartet members *(rec 1981)* Olympia ▲ OCD 412 [AAD]

Piedicuta, Emilian (vn)—see ORCHESTRAS & ENSEMBLES Orpheus String Quartet

Piemonti, E. (pno)—see ORCHESTRAS & ENSEMBLES Matisse Trio

Pierce, Eluned (hp)
Eller, H.:Elegia, w. N. Järvi (cnd), Scottish National Orch Chandos ▲ CHAN 8525 [DDD]

Pierce, Joshua (pno)
Berezowsky, N.:Fant for 2 Pnos, w. D. Jonas (pno), D. Amos (cnd), Polish Radio-TV SO Albany ▲ TROY 112 [DDD]
Brahms, J.:Con 1 Pno, w. P. Freeman (cnd), Slovak PO *(rec Philharmonic Hall, Bratislava, Slovakia, June 24, 1993)* Pro Arte ▲ CDS 3488 [DDD]
Brisman, H.:Con Pno, w. R. Black (cnd), Slovak RSO Bratislava *(rec Slovak Radio & TV Studios, Slovak National Republic)* MMC ▲ MMC 2016 [DDD]
Britten, H.:Introduction & Rondo alla burlesca & Mazurka elegiaca, w. D. Jonas (pno) Koch International Classics ▲ KIC 7013- 2 [DDD] ■ 3-7013-4 (D)
Britten, H.:Scottish Ballad, w. Dorothy Jonas (pno), E. Stratta (cnd), Luxembourg RSO Phoenix ▲ PHCD 104 [DDD]
Cage, J.:A Book of Music, w. Maro Ajemian (pno) *(rec 1976-89)* Wergo ▲ WER 6158-2 [ADD]
Cage, J.:Four Walls, w. Robert White (ten) Albany ▲ TROY 197 [DDD]
Cage, J.:In the Name of the Holocaust Albany ▲ TROY 197 [DDD]
Cage, J.:Nocturne, w. F. Almond (vn) Wergo ▲ WER 60157-50
Cage, J.:Ophelia Albany ▲ TROY 197 [DDD]
Cage, J.:Our Spring Will Come Albany ▲ TROY 197 [DDD]
Cage, J.:Pno Music—Mysterious Adventure for prepared pno (1945); TV Koeln for pno (1958); Daughters of the Lonesome Isle for prepared pno (1945); Dream for pno (1948); The Perilous Night for prepared pno (1944); 3 Dances for 2 prepared pnos (1944-45) [w. D. Jonas (pno)] Wergo ▲ WER 60157-50
Cage, J.:Pno Music, w. Borah Bergman (pno), Dorothy Jones (pno), Joseph Kubera (pno), Myra Meldorf (pno), Fumiko Miyanoo (pno)—Music Walk; Jazz Study; Experiences I & II; plus others Wergo ▲ WER 61592
Cage, J.:Primitive (1944) Albany ▲ TROY 197 [DDD]
Cage, J.:Quest Albany ▲ TROY 197 [DDD]
Cage, J.:Sons & Interludes Wergo ▲ WER 60156-50
Casella, A.:Partita, w. A. Nanut (cnd), Slovenian Radio-TV Orch *(rec Apr. 10-11, 1991)* Phoenix ▲ PHCD 124 [DDD]
Classically Broadway, w. Dorothy Jonas (pno) Kem-Disc ▲ 1009 [DDD]
Copland, A.:Danzón Cubano, w. D. Jonas (pno) Koch International Classics ▲ KIC 7002-2 [DDD] ■ 3-7002-4 (D)
Copland, A.:Rodeo, w. D. Jonas (pno)—Hoedown; Saturday Night Waltz; arr. by Gold & Fizdale for two pianos Koch International Classics ▲ KIC 7002-2 [DDD] ■ 3-7002-4 (D)
Copland, A.:El salón México, w. D. Jonas (pno)—two-piano arrangement by Leonard Bernstein Koch International Classics ▲ KIC 7002-2 [DDD] ■ 3-7002-4 (D)
Creston, P.:Con for 2 Pnos, w. D. Jonas (pno), D. Amos (cnd), Polish Radio-TV SO Albany ▲ TROY 112 [DDD]
Flagello, N.:Pno Music, w. Paul Price Percussion Ensemble—Divert for Pno & Perc (1960); Electra for Pno solo, Cel, Hp & Perc (1966); Son for Pno (1962); Prelude, Ostinato & Fugue (1960); 2 Waltzes (1953); 3 Episodes (1957); Etude:Homage to Chopin (1941) Premier ("Composer" series) ▲ PRCD 1014 [ADD/DDD]
Gould, M.:Dance Vars, w. D. Jonas (pno), D. Amos (cnd), Royal PO Koch International Classics ▲ KIC 7002-2 [DDD] ■ 3-7002-4 (D)
Khachaturian, A.:Con Pno, w. P. Freeman (cnd), Berlin RSO Phoenix ▲ PHCD 117 [DDD]
Liszt, F.:Con 1 Pno, w. P. Freeman (cnd), Russian SO *(rec Moscow, Sept. 17, 1993)* Intersound ▲ CDS 3488
Liszt, F.:Con 1 Pno, w. P. Freeman (cnd), Slovak PO *(rec Great Hall of the Moscow Radio Union, Sept. 17, 1993)* Pro Arte ▲ CDS 3488 [DDD]
Liszt, F.:Totentanz, w. P. Freeman (cnd), RTV SO Mastersound ▲ MST 215 [DDD]
Lopatnikoff, N.:Con for 2 Pnos, w. Dorothy Jonas (pno), D. Amos (cnd), Slovak State PO Košice Centaur ▲ CRC 2269
Lutoslawski, W.:Vars on a Theme of Paganini for 2 Pnos, w. D. Jonas (pno) Koch International Classics ▲ KIC 7013- 2 [DDD] ■ 3-7013-4 (D)
Malipiero, G.F.:Dialogo 7, w. Dorothy Jonas (pno), D. Amos (cnd), Slovak State PO Košice Centaur ▲ CRC 2269
Martinů, B.:Con 2 Pnos, w. Dorothy Jonas (pno), E. Stratta (cnd), Luxembourg RSO Phoenix ▲ PHCD 104 [DDD]
Mendelssohn, F.:Cons 2 Pnos, w. Dorothy Jonas (pno), B. Rezucha (cnd), Slovak State PO Košice *(rec House of Art, Košice, Oct & Nov 1995)* Vox Classics ▲ VOX 7538 [DDD]
Mozart, W.A.:Pno Music Pnos, w. Dorothy Jonas (pno)—Con. in E♭, K.365; Son. in D, K.448; Adagio, K.546; Fugue, K.426; Larghetto & Allegro in E♭ *(rec Philharmonic Hall, Bratislava, Slovakia, June 26, 1993)* Pro Arte ▲ CDD 3475 [DDD]
Piston, W.:Con for 2 Pnos, w. D. Jonas (pno), D. Amos (cnd), Royal PO Koch International Classics ▲ KIC 7002-2 [DDD] ■ 3-7002-4 (D)
Poulenc, F.:Con for 2 Pnos, w. D. Jonas (pno), D. Amos (cnd), Polish Radio-TV SO Albany ▲ TROY 112 [DDD]
Rachmaninoff, S.:Rhapsody on a Theme of Paganini, w. A. Nanut (cnd), Slovenian Radio-TV Orch *(rec Apr. 10-11, 1991)* Phoenix ▲ PHCD 124 [DDD]
Rachmaninoff, S.:Russian Rhap, w. D. Jonas (pno) Koch International Classics ▲ KIC 7013- 2 [DDD] ■ 3-7013-4 (D)
Rachmaninoff, S.:Symphonic Dances, w. D. Jonas (pno) Koch International Classics ▲ KIC 7013- 2 [DDD] ■ 3-7013-4 (D)
Respighi, O.:Toccata Pno, w. A. Nanut (cnd), Slovenian Radio-TV Orch *(rec Apr. 10-11, 1991)* Phoenix ▲ PHCD 124 [DDD]
Saint-Saëns, C.:Danse macabre, w. D. Jonas (pno) Koch International Classics ▲ KIC 7013- 2 [DDD] ■ 3-7013-4 (D)
Tansman, A.:Suite 2 Pnos, w. Dorothy Jonas (pno), D. Amos (cnd), Slovak State PO Košice Centaur ▲ CRC 2269
Tchaikovsky, P.:Con 1 Pno, w. P. Freeman (cnd), RTV SO Mastersound ▲ MST 215 [DDD]
Tchaikovsky, P.:Con 3 Pno, w. P. Freeman (cnd), RTV SO Mastersound ▲ MST 215 [DDD]
20th Century Romantic Music for 2 Pianos, w. Dorothy Jonas (pno) Koch International Classics ▲ KIC 7013 [DDD]

Pierce, Joshua (toy pno)
Cage, J.:Music Amplified Toy Pnos, w. Marilyn Crispell (toy pno), Joe Kubera (toy pno) [3 toy pno version] *(rec 1976-89)* Wergo ▲ WER 6158-2 [ADD]

778
▲ = CD ♦ = Enhanced CD Δ = MD ■ = Cassette Tape □ = DCC

Pierce, Joshua (toy pno/pno)
Cage, J.:Suite Toy Pno, [toy pno version & pno version] *(rec 1976–89)* Wergo ▲ WER 6158–2 [ADD]

Pieri, Sergio de (org)
Organ Music from the Venetian School Rivo Alto ▲ RIV 9403 [DDD]
Organi della Città di Treviso Foné ▲ FON 93F01 [DDD]

Pierlot, Philippe (fl)
Bartók, B.:Hungarian Peasant Songs, w. Angeline Pondepeyre (pno)—Popular Sad Songs; Scherzo; Old Dances [trans Arma for Fl & Pno] *(rec Apr 1992)* Maguelone ▲ 350.501 [DDD]
Hindemith, P.:Son Fl, w. Angeline Pondepeyre (pno) *(rec Apr 1992)* Maguelone ▲ 350.501 [DDD]
Martinů, B.:Son Fl & Pno, w. Angeline Pondepeyre (pno) *(rec Apr 1992)* Maguelone ▲ 350.501 [DDD]
Prokofiev, S.:Son Fl, w. Angeline Pondepeyre (pno) *(rec Apr 1992)* Maguelone ▲ 350.501 [DDD]

Pierlot, Philippe (vl)—see also ORCHESTRAS & ENSEMBLES Ricercar Consort
Defense de la Basse Viole contre les Enterprises du Violon et les Pretentions du Violoncelle [Defense of the Bass Viol against the Enterprise of the Violin & the Pretension of the Cello], w. François Fernandez (vn), Hidemi Suzuki (vc), Ricercar Consort Ricercar 3–▲ RIC 93005
de Machy, S.:Suite in d, w. S. Watillon (vl), R. Lislevand (thb) Ricercar ▲ RIC 118100 [DDD]
de Machy, S.:Suite in G, w. S. Watillon (vl), R. Lislevand (thb) Ricercar ▲ RIC 118100 [DDD]
du Buisson:Suite Vls, w. S. Watillon (vl), R. Lislevand (thb) Ricercar ▲ RIC 118100 [DDD]
Marais, M.:Tombeau pour Monsieur de Ste Colombe, w. S. Watillon (vl), R. Lislevand (thb) Ricercar ▲ RIC 118100 [DDD]
Sainte-Colombe, M. de:Concerts for 2 B Vls, w. R. Zipperling (vc)—No. 44, "Tombeau Les Regrets" Ricercar ▲ RIC 118100 [DDD]
Sainte-Colombe, M. de:Fant en rondeau, w. R. Zipperling (vc) Ricercar ▲ RIC 118100 [DDD]
Sainte-Colombe, M. de:Tombeau, w. R. Zipperling (vc) Ricercar ▲ RIC 118100 [DDD]
Telemann, G.P.:Con in F Rcr, B Vl, w. F. de Roos (rcr), Ricercar Consort Ricercar ▲ RIC 44021 [DDD]

Pierlot, Pierre (ob)
Albinoni, T.:Cons à 5 Obs, Op. 7, w. J. Roussel (cnd), Antiqua Musica CO—No. 3 in B♭ *(rec Salle Wagram, Paris, Mar 1965)* EMI Classics ▲ CDK 65337 [ADD]
Fasch, J.F.:Con Tpt & 2 Obs, w. Maurice André (tpt), Jacques Chambon (ob), J.-F. Paillard (cnd), Jean-François Paillard CO *(rec 1968)* Erato ▲ 98475–2 [ADD]
Handel, G.F.:Cons (3) Ob, w. L. Auriacombe (cnd), Toulouse CO—in g *(rec Chapelle des Italiens, Toulouse, July 1963)* EMI Classics ▲ CDK 65335 [ADD]
Haydn, J.:Cons for 2 Lire organizzata, w. Jean-Pierre Rampal (fl), J. Rolla (cnd), Franz Liszt CO CBS 2–▲ M2K 39772 [DDD]
Haydn, J.:Con Ob, w. Franz Liszt CO Sony Classical ("Essential Classics" series) ▲ SBK 62649 ■ SBT 62649
Haydn, J.:Con Ob, w. J. Rolla (cnd), Franz Liszt CO CBS 2–▲ M2K 39772 [DDD]
Poulenc, F.:Trio Ob, w. Maurice Allard (bn), Francis Poulenc (pno) Adès ▲ ADE 202522 [AAD]
Telemann, G.P.:Cons Ob, w. Evgeni Nepalov (ob), Piotr Dubrov (ob), Andrei Abramenkov (vn), Rudolf Barshai (vn), Leonid Poleess (vn), R. Barshaï (cnd), Moscow CO—in B♭ for 3 Obs, 3 Vns & Bc *(rec Salle Wagram, Paris, June 1964)* EMI Classics ▲ CDK 65340 [ADD]

Pierot, Alice (vn)—see also ORCHESTRAS & ENSEMBLES Les Nièces de Rameau
Bach, J.S.:Sons Vn, w. Martin Gester (org)—BWV 1014–1019 Accord 2–▲ ACD 205322 [DDD]

Pierotti, Susan (vn)
Melchoirre, A.:Halos Vox Australis ▲ VAST 0192

Pierre, Fabrice (hp)
Berio, L.:Circles, w. C. Berberian (sop), J.-P. Drouet (perc), J.-C. Casadesus (perc) *(rec 1967)* Wergo ▲ WER 6021–2 [AAD]
Constant, M.:Chamber Music, w. Radu Blidar (vn), Bruno Pasquier (va), Elizabeth Chojnacka (hpd) Salabert ▲ SCD 9401

Pierre, Nadine (vc)—see also ORCHESTRAS & ENSEMBLES Kandinsky Quartet
Mozart, W.A.:Qnt Hn & Strs, w. Hervé Joulain (hn), Élisabeth Glab (vn), Françoise Gnéri (va), Pascal Robault (va) Arion ▲ ARN 68311 [DDD]

Pierre, Odile (org)
Guilmant, A.:Marche funèbre et chant séraphique Motette ▲ CD 11251 [DDD]
Vierne, L.:Arabesque Motette ▲ CD 11251 [DDD]
Widor, C.M.:Sym 8 Org Motette ▲ CD 11251 [DDD]

Pierri, Alvaro (gtr)
Falla, M. de:Canciones populares españolas (7), w. Angèle Dubeau (vn) Analekta ▲ AN 28706
Falla, M. de:Canciones populares españolas (7), w. A. Dubeau (vn)—El paño moruno, Nana, Cancion, Jota, Asturiana, Polo Analekta Fleur de Lys ▲ FL 2 3034
Paganini, N.:Centone di sonate, w. A. Dubeau (vn) Analekta Fleur de Lys ▲ FL 2 3034
Paganini, N.:Son concertata, w. A. Dubeau (vn) Analekta Fleur de Lys ▲ FL 2 3034
Piazzolla, A.:Pieces Gtr Analekta Fleur de Lys ▲ FL 2 3034
Villa-Lobos, H.:Chôro 1 Analekta Fleur de Lys ▲ FL 2 3051
Villa-Lobos, H.:Etudes Gtr Analekta Fleur de Lys ▲ FL 2 3051
Villa-Lobos, H.:Preludes Gtr Analekta Fleur de Lys ▲ FL 2 3051

Piesk, Günther (bn)
Mozart, W.A.:Con Bn, w. H. von Karajan (cnd), Berlin PO EMI Classics ▲ CDM 64355 [ADD]

Pieters, Peter (gtr)
Sor, F.:Duos, w. Micheline Dumortier (gtr)—Divertissement, Op. 38 *(rec Studio Steuerbaut, Gent, June 1995)* René Gailly ▲ VTP CD92027 [DDD]
Sor, F.:Fants Gtr, w. Micheline Dumortier (gtr)—Encouragement, Op. 34; 2 Amis, Op. 41; Fant, Op. 54bis; Souvenir de Russie, Op 63 *(rec Studio Steuerbaut, Gent, June 1995)* René Gailly ▲ VTP CD92027 [DDD]

Pieterson, George (cl)
Brahms, J.:Trio Cl, w. Guarneri Trio Prague members Ottavo ▲ OTT 29134 [DDD]
Debussy, C.:Orchestral Music, w. Vera Badings (hp), Beinum (cnd), Royal Concertgebouw Orch—Berceuse héroique; Danses for Harp & Orch.; Images; Jeux; Marche écossaise; La mer; Nocturnes; Prélude à l'après-midi d'un faune; Première rapsodie for Clarinet & Orch Philips 2–▲ 438742–2

Pietikäinen, Mauri (va)—see ORCHESTRAS & ENSEMBLES Voces Intimae String Quartet, Segerstam String Quartet

Pietiläinen, Pauli (org)
Aho, K.:Pergamon, w. L. Paasikivi (nar), E.-L. Saarinen (nar), T. Nyman (nar), M. Lehtinen (nar), O. Vänskä (cnd), Lahti SO *(rec Lahti, Finland, May 23–25, 1994)* BIS ▲ CD 646 [DDD]
Sibelius, J.:Everyman, w. Lilli Paasikivi (mez), Petri Lehto (ten), Sauli Tiilikainen (bar), Leena Saarenpää (pno), O. Vänskä (cnd), Lahti SO, Lahti Chamber Choir *(rec Church of the Cross, Lahti, Finland, Jan 11–13, 1995)* BIS ▲ CD-735 [DDD]
Sibelius, J.:Swanwhite (incidental), w. Sakari Tepponen (vn), O. Vänskä (cnd), Lahti SO *(rec Church of the Cross, Lahti, Finland, Jan 8–12, 1996)* BIS ▲ CD 815 [DDD]

Pietropaolo, R. (vn)
Stanley, J.:Cons Org, Op. 10, w. A Frigé (hpd), F. Cipriani (vn), A. Fantinuoli (db), *(w. accompaniments for 2 vn & db)* Nuova Era ("Ancient Music" series) ▲ 7152

Pietsch, T. (vn)—see also ORCHESTRAS & ENSEMBLES Sancoussi Ensemble Hamburg
Mozart, W.A.:Sons Vn Pno (misc), w. R. Fuller (pno)—K.301, 302, 303 & 304 Ambitus ▲ 97816 [DDD]

Piette, Henry (pno)
Bach, W.F.:Son for 2 Hpds, w. J. Reding (piano) Olympia ▲ OCD 271 [AAD]
Brahms, J.:Vars on a Theme by Haydn, w. J. Reding (pno) Olympia ▲ OCD 271 [AAD]
Poot, M.:Rhap Pnos, w. J. Reding (pno) Olympia ▲ OCD 271 [AAD]
Reding & Piette Play Works for 2 Pianos, w. Janine Reding (pno) Olympia ▲ OCD 271 [AAD]
Vol. 2, w. Janine Reding (pno) Olympia ▲ OLY 272 [AAD]
Tansman, A.:Fant on Strauss Waltzes, w. J. Reding (pno) Olympia ▲ OCD 271 [AAD]

Pignata, Bruno (vn)—see also ORCHESTRAS & ENSEMBLES Paganini String Quartet
Paganini, N.:Duetto amoroso Vn, w. Pino Briasco (gtr) *(rec Dynamic's Genoa, Dec 10–13, 1995)* Dynamic ▲ CD 152 [DDD]
Sivori, C.:Music for Pno Trio, w. R. Agosti (vc), F. Giacosa (pno)—Mira la bianca luna on Rossini's Soirées musicales; La Pesca e La Promessa on Rossini's Soirées musicales; Il coro delle sirene on Weber's Oberon *(rec Jan. 12–14, 1994)* Dynamic ▲ CDS 115 [DDD]
Sivori, C.:Music for Vn—Phantasia on *Un ballo in maschera*, Op. 19; Romances Nos. 1 & 2 in E♭ & A♭; Andante amaroso for Violin & Piano [w. F. Giacosa]; Phantasia on *Il trovatore*, Op. 20; Tarantella for Violin & Piano, Op. 20 [w. F. Giacosa] *(rec Jan. 12–14, 1994)* Dynamic ▲ CDS 115 [DDD]

Pignatelli, Stefano (hn)
Poulenc, F.:Élégie Hn, w. Andrea Dindo (pno) *(rec Sala Maffeiana dell'Accademia Filarmonica di Verona, May 7–9, 1995)* Agorá ▲ 021 [DDD]
Poulenc, F.:Sxt Pno, w. Andrea Dindo (pno), Gianpaolo Pretto (fl), Paolo Grazia (ob), Alessandro Carbonare (cl), Roberto Giaccaglia (bn) *(rec Sala Maffeiana dell'Accademia Filarmonica di Verona, May 7–9, 1995)* Agorá ▲ 021 [DDD]

Pigneguy, John (hn)
Gough, O.:Currulao, w. Beverly Davison (vn), Roger Heaton (cl), Bruce Nockles (tpt), David Stewart (trbn), Tracey Goldsmith (acc), Orlando Gough (kbd), Paul Clarvis (perc) *(rec London, 1995)* Catalyst ▲ 0902–668332–2 [DDD]
Gough, O.:Saeta, w. Pepe de la Matrona (voc), Bruce Nockles (tpt), Michael Thompson (hn), David Purser (trbn), Orlando Gough (kbd) *(rec London, 1995)* Catalyst ▲ 0902–668332–2 [DDD]

Pi-hsien, Chen (pno)
Bach, J.S.:Goldberg Vars *(rec Oct 1985)* Naxos ▲ 8.550078 [DDD]

Pilafian, Sam (tuba)—see also ORCHESTRAS & ENSEMBLES Empire Brass Quintet
Wilder, A.:Suite 1 Hn, w. David Jolley (hn), David Oei (pno) *(rec SUNY Purchase Recital Hall)* Arabesque ▲ ARA 6665 [DDD]

Pilat, Richard (prepared pno)
Cage, J.:Amores, w. Kroumata Percussion Ensemble BIS ▲ CD 272 [DDD]

Pilati, Stefano (perc/sgr)—see ORCHESTRAS & ENSEMBLES Aurora Ensemble

Pillinger, Edward (cl)
Lumsdaine, D.:What Shall I Sing?, w. M. Wiegold (sop), I. Mitchell (cl) NM Classics ▲ NMCD 007 [DDD]

Pilot, Ann Hobson (hp)
Ann Hobson Pilot Boston Records ▲ BR 1002
Contrasts:American Music for Flute & Harp, w. Leone Buyse (fl) *(rec Seiji Ozawa Hall, Tanglewood, Lenox, MA, July 18–19, 1994)* Boston Records ▲ BR 1011
Ginastera, A.:Con Hp, w. I. Jackson (cnd), English CO Koch International Classics ▲ KIC 7261 [DDD]
Hindemith, P.:Son Hp Boston Records ▲ BR 1002 ■ BR 1002 CT
In The Family, w. Ronald Barron (trbn), Marianne Gedigian (fl), Douglas Yeo (trbn), Edwin Barker (bass), Thomas Gauger (perc) *(rec Morse Auditorium, Boston Univ, Dec 1995)* Boston Brass ▲ BB 1004
Mathias, W.:Con Hp, w. I. Jackson (cnd), English CO Koch International Classics ▲ KIC 7261 [DDD]
Salzedo, C.:Ballade Hp Boston Records ▲ BR 1002 ■ BR 1002 CT

Pilz, János (vn)—see ORCHESTRAS & ENSEMBLES Keller String Quartet, Keller String Quartet members

Pilz, Werner (hn)
Schumann, R.:Konzertstück Hns, w. P. Damm (hn), H. Märker (hn), G. Böhner (hn), F. Konwitschny (cnd), Leipzig Gewandhaus Orch *(rec 1960–61)* Berlin Classics ("Eterna" series) 3–▲ BER 2016 [ADD]

Pineda, Kim (trns fl)
Bach, J.S.:Partita Fl, BWV 1013 Focus ▲ FOCUS 944 [DDD]
Bach, J.S.:Sons Fl, BWV 1030–35, w. Elisabeth Wright (hpd), Elisabeth Reed (vc)—Nos. 1 in b, 3 in A, 5 in e & 6 in E Focus ▲ FOCUS 944 [DDD]

Pinel, Anthony (org)
Brahms, J.:Motets (comp), w. M. Archer (cnd), Bristol Cathedral Choir—Op. 30 & Op. 110/2 [G] Meridian ▲ CDE 84188
Dvořák, A.:Mass, w. Coupe (trb), S. Taylor (ct), P. Cave (ten), S. Foulkes (bass), M. Archer (cnd), Bristol Cathedral Choir [L] Meridian ▲ CDE 84188
Elgar, E.:Choral Songs (sels), w. Malcolm Archer (cnd), Bristol Cathedral Special Choirs—Ave Verum Corpus; Benedictus in F; Give Unto the Lord, O Ye Mighty; Great is the Lord; Hear Thy Children, Gentle Jesus; Imperial March; Psalm 67; Spirit of the Lord; Te Deum in F [E,L] *(rec 8/88)* Meridian ▲ CDE 84168

Pinet, Jean-Pierre (fl)
Bach, J.S.:Sons Fl, BWV 1030–35, w. Geneviève Soly (hpd)—BWV 1030 & 1032 *(rec Oct 1995)* Analekta Fleur de Lys ▲ FL 23061 [DDD]

Pinhas, Richard (syns/gtr)—see also ORCHESTRAS & ENSEMBLES Heldon
Chronolyse, w. Didier Batard (bass), François Auger (perc) Cuneiform ▲ Rune 30
D.W.W., w. J. Philippe Goude (syn programming/drums/gtr), Patrick Gauthier (syns/pno/drums), Bernard Paganotti (bass gtr), Alain Bellaich (synthesized gtr) Cuneiform ▲ Rune 40
East/West, w. Norman Spinrad (voc), Dominique E. (voc), Patrick Gauthier (syn), G. Grunblatt (syn), François Auger (perc), Steve Shehan (perc), Didier Batard (bass gtr) Cuneiform ▲ Rune 31
L'Ethique, w. Gilles Deleuze (voc), J. P. Goude (syn/perc), G. Grunblatt (syn), Patrick Gauthier (syn/bass), Bernard Paganotti (bass), François Auger (drums), Clément Bailly (drums) Cuneiform ▲ Rune 36X
Iceland, w. Jean-Phillippe Goude (syn), François Auger (perc) Cuneiform ▲ Rune 44X
Rhizosphere/Live, Paris 1982, w. Patrick Gauthier (syns), Bernard Paganotti (bass), François Auger (perc), Clement Bailly (perc) Cuneiform ▲ Rune 61

Pini, Anthony (vc)
Beethoven, L. van:Trio 6 Pno, "Archduke", w. Solomon (pno), H. Holst (vn) APR ▲ APR 5503 [ADD]
Beethoven, L. van:Trio 7 Pno, w. Solomon (pno), Henry Holst (vn) *(rec Abbey Road, Studio No. 3)* Dutton Laboratories ▲ DUT 7015 [ADD]
Brahms, J.:Sextet Strs, Op. 36, w. Budapest Quartet, Alfred Hobday (va) Biddulph 2–▲ LAB 120–21
Elgar, E.:Con Vc, w. E. van Beinum (cnd), London PO Beulah ▲ 2PD15 (m) [ADD]

Pinkas, Sally (pno)
Debussy, C.:Estampes Centaur ▲ CRC 2169
Debussy, C.:Etudes Centaur ▲ CRC 2169
Ives, C.:Halloween, w. L. Hyla (dr), Lydian String Quartet Centaur ▲ CRC 2069 [DDD]
Schulhoff, E.:Son Fl, w. F. Smith (fl)—Allegro moderato; Scherzo; Allegro giocosco; Aria; Andante; Rondo-Finale; Allegro molto gajo *(rec June 1992)* Northeastern ▲ NR 248–CD
Wolff, C.:Bread & Roses Mode ▲ Mode 43 [DDD]
Wolff, C.:Hay una Mujer Desaparecida Mode ▲ Mode 43 [DDD]
Wolff, C.:Pno Song, "I Am a Dangerous Woman" Mode ▲ Mode 43 [DDD]
Wolff, C.:Preludes Pno Mode ▲ Mode 43 [DDD]

Pinkham, D. (hpd)
Bavicchi, J.:Short Son, w. Brink (vn) CRI ■ C 138
Cowell, H.:Prelude, w. Brink (vn) CRI ■ C 109
Hovhaness, A.:Duet Vn & Hpd, w. F. van den Brink (cl) CRI ■ C 109
Pinkham, D.:Cantilena & Capriccio, w. F. Brink (cl) CRI ■ C 109
Pinkham, D.:Con Cel, w. Low (cel) CRI ■ C 109

Pinnock, Trevor (hpd)
At the Victoria & Albert Museum CRD ▲ 3307 [ADD]
Bach, Joh. Christian:Sinfs, Op. 9, w. K. Montgomery (cnd), Bournemouth Sinfonietta—Sinf No. 2 in E♭ EMI Classics ("Baroque" series) ▲ CDK 65733
Bach, Joh. Christian:Sinfs, Op. 18, w. K. Montgomery (cnd), Bournemouth Sinfonietta—Sinf No. 4 in D EMI Classics ("Baroque" series) ▲ CDK 65733
Bach, J.S.:Con Fl, Vn & Hpd, w. L. Beznosiuk (fl), S. Standage (vn), T. Pinnock (cnd), English Concert Archiv ▲ 413731–2 [DDD]
Bach, J.S.:Goldberg Vars Archiv ▲ 415130–2 [ADD]
Bach, J.S.:Italian Con Archiv ▲ 413591–2 [DDD]
Bach, J.S.:Sons Fl, BWV 1030–35, w. S. Preston (baroque fl), J. Savall (vl) CRD 2–▲ 3314/15 [ADD]
Bach, J.S.:Sons Fl, BWV 1030–35, w. J.-P. Rampal CBS 2–▲ M2K 39746

Pinnock, Trevor (hpd) (cont.)
Bach, J.S.:Sons Vn, w. J.-P. Rampal (fl)—BWV 1020 [doubtful; trans. for flute & continuo] CBS 2-▲ M2K 39746
The Harmonious Blacksmith:Favorite Harpsichord Pieces Archiv ▲ 413591-2 [DDD]
Haydn, J.:Con Hpd, Obs, Hns & Strs, H.XVIII/11, w. T. Pinnock (cnd), English Concert Archiv ▲ 431678-2 [DDD]
Music of 16th Century England CRD ▲ 3350
Scarlatti, D.:Sons Kbd—K. 46, 87, 95, 99, 124, 201, 204a, 490, 491, 492, 513, 520, 521 CRD ▲ CD 3368
Scarlatti, D.:Sons Kbd—K.460, 461, 478, 479, 502, 516-519, 529, 544-547 Archiv ▲ 419632-2 [DDD]
Scarlatti, D.:Sons Kbd—K.124, 99, 201, 87, 46, 95, 204a, 490, 491, 520, 521, 523 CRD ▲ CRD 3368

Pinto, Yerko (vn)—see ORCHESTRAS & ENSEMBLES Paraíba Quintet

Piotrovski, Maciej (pno)
Chopin, F.:Rondos Pno & 4-Hands, w. B. Hesse-Bukovska (pno) *(rec Dec. 1991)* Canyon ▲ EC 3634-2 [DDD]

Piquet, (ob)
Mozart, W.A.:Con Ob, K.314, w. C. Hogwood (cnd), Academy of Ancient Music L'Oiseau-Lyre ▲ 414339-2 [DDD]

Pires, Maria João (pno)
Bach, J.S.:Con 1 Hpd, w. M. Corboz (cnd), Lisbon Gulbenkian Foundation CO Erato ▲ 92864-2
Bach, J.S.:Con 4 Hpd, w. M. Corboz (cnd), Lisbon Gulbenkian Foundation CO Erato ▲ 92864-2
Bach, J.S.:Con 5 Hpd, w. M. Corboz (cnd), Lisbon Gulbenkian Foundation CO Erato ▲ 92864-2
Bach, J.S.:English Suites—No. 3 Deutsche Grammophon ▲ 447894-2
Bach, J.S.:French Suites—No. 2 Deutsche Grammophon ▲ 447894-2
Bach, J.S.:Partitas Hpd, BWV 825-830—No. 1 Deutsche Grammophon ▲ 447894-2
Beethoven, L. van:Son 8 Pno, "Pathétique" Erato ("Bonsai" series) ▲ 2292-45924-2 ■ 2292-45924-4
Beethoven, L. van:Son 14 Pno, "Moonlight Son" Erato ("Bonsai" series) ▲ 2292-45924-2 ■ 2292-45924-4
Beethoven, L. van:Son 17 Pno, "Tempest" Erato ("Bonsai" series) ▲ 2292-45924-2 ■ 2292-45924-4
Beethoven, L. van:Son 23 Pno, "Appassionata" Erato ("Bonsai" series) ▲ 2292-45924-2 ■ 2292-45924-4
Brahms, J.:Sons Vn (comp), w. A. Dumay (vn) Deutsche Grammophon ▲ 435800-2
Chopin, F.:Con 2 Pno, w. A. Previn (cnd), Royal PO Deutsche Grammophon ▲ 437817-2
Chopin, F.:Nocturnes *(rec Munich & London, Jan 1995, Jan, Apr & June 1996)* Deutsche Grammophon 2-▲ 447 096-2 [DDD]
Chopin, F.:Preludes, Op. 28 Deutsche Grammophon ▲ 437817-2
Grieg, E.:Sons Vn, Opp. 8, 13 & 45, w. A. Dumay (vn) Deutsche Grammophon ▲ 437525-2 [DDD]
Mozart, W.A.:Allegro & Andante & Rondo Deutsche Grammophon 6-▲ 431760-2 [DDD]
Mozart, W.A.:Con 14 Pno, w. C. Abbado (cnd), Vienna PO Deutsche Grammophon ▲ 437529-2
Mozart, W.A.:Con 17 Pno, w. C. Abbado (cnd), CO of Europe *(rec Teatro Comunale, Ferrara, June 1993)* Deutsche Grammophon ▲ 439941-2 [DDD]
Mozart, W.A.:Con 21 Pno, w. C. Abbado (cnd), CO of Europe *(rec Teatro Comunale, Ferrara, June 1993)* Deutsche Grammophon ▲ 439941-2 [DDD]
Mozart, W.A.:Con 26 Pno, w. C. Abbado (cnd), Vienna PO Deutsche Grammophon ▲ 437529-2
Mozart, W.A.:Con 26 Pno, w. T. Guschlbauer (cnd), Lisbon Gulbenkian Foundation CO Erato ▲ 45934-2 [ADD] ■ 45934-4
Mozart, W.A.:Con 27 Pno, w. A. Jordan (cnd), Lausanne CO Erato ▲ 45934-2 [ADD] ■ 45934-4
Mozart, W.A.:Fant Pno, K.397 Deutsche Grammophon ▲ 429739-2 [DDD]
Mozart, W.A.:Fant Pno, K.475 Deutsche Grammophon ▲ 429739-2 [DDD]
Mozart, W.A.:Fant Pno, K.475 Deutsche Grammophon 6-▲ 431760-2 [DDD]
Mozart, W.A.:Rondo Pno Orch, K.382, w. A. Jordan (cnd), Lausanne CO Erato ▲ 45934-2 [ADD] ■ 45934-4
Mozart, W.A.:Sons Pno—K.284, 309, 310 & 485 Denon/PCM Digital ▲ DEN 8072
Mozart, W.A.:Sons Pno—K.279, 280, 281, 282 & 283 Denon/PCM Digital ▲ DEN 8071
Mozart, W.A.:Sons Pno—K.331, 310, 545, 570 Denon/PCM Digital ▲ DEN 8007
Mozart, W.A.:Sons Pno—K.311, 330, 331 & 511 Denon/PCM Digital ▲ DEN 8073
Mozart, W.A.:Sons Pno—K.332, 333 & 475 Denon/PCM Digital ▲ DEN 8074
Mozart, W.A.:Sons Pno—K.533, 545, 570, 576 & 397 Denon/PCM Digital ▲ DEN 8075
Mozart, W.A.:Sons Pno Deutsche Grammophon 6-▲ 431760-2 [DDD]
Mozart, W.A.:Son 8 Pno Denon ▲ CO 8007 [DDD]
Mozart, W.A.:Son 11 Pno Deutsche Grammophon ▲ 429739-2 [DDD]
Mozart, W.A.:Son 11 Pno Denon ▲ CO 8007 [DDD]
Mozart, W.A.:Son 14 Pno Deutsche Grammophon ▲ 429739-2 [DDD]
Mozart, W.A.:Son 15 Pno Denon ▲ CO 8007 [DDD]
Mozart, W.A.:Son 16 Pno Denon ▲ CO 8007 [DDD]
Schubert, Franz:Moments musicaux Deutsche Grammophon ▲ 427769-2 [DDD]
Schubert, Franz:Son Pno, D.784 Deutsche Grammophon ▲ 427769-2 [DDD]

Pirner, Gitti (pno)
Mendelssohn, F.:Fant Pno, "Sonate écossaise" *(rec Mar. 10-12, 1986)* Calig ▲ CAL 50854
Mendelssohn, F.:Preludes & Fugues Pno, Op. 35 *(rec Mar. 10-12, 1986)* Calig ▲ CAL 50854
Strauss, R.:Fugue *(rec Kleine Konzertsall, Gasteig, Germany, Mar 22-23, 1988)* Arts ▲ 47261-2 [DDD]
Strauss, R.:Marches Pno—Parade-Marsch des Regiments Königs-Jäger zu Pferde, AV 97; Parade-Marsch Cavallerie, AV 98; De brandenburgsche Marsch, AV 99; Königsmarsch, AV 100 Arts ▲ 47266-2 [DDD]
Strauss, R.:Pieces Pno *(rec Munich, May 1995)* Arts ▲ 47265-2 [DDD]
Strauss, R.:Son Pno *(rec Munich, May 1995)* Arts ▲ 47265-2 [DDD]
Strauss, R.:Stimmungsbilder *(rec Munich, May 1995)* Arts ▲ 47265-2 [DDD]

Piscitelli, Joseph (fl)
Kraft, L.:Cloud Studies, w. Lisa Maron (pic), Margaret Swinchoski (pic), Tanya Dusevic (fl), Adrienne Flynn (fl), Christina Jennings (fl), Zara Lawler (fl), Michelle Ryang (fl), Dominique Soucy (fl), Diane Taublieb (fl), Laurel Ann Maurer (alt fl), Richard Wyton (alt fl), J. Solum (cnd) *(rec Skinner Recital Hall, Vassar College, Poughkeepsie, NY, Mar 24-26, 1994)* CRI ▲ CD 712 [DDD]

Pishchugin, S. (vn)—see ORCHESTRAS & ENSEMBLES Shostakovich String Quartet

Piskounov, Andrei (ob)—see ORCHESTRAS & ENSEMBLES Baroque Chamber Ensemble

Pistorius, A. (pno)
Liszt, F.:Fant on Themes from Weber's *Freischütz* LaserLight ▲ 15631 [DDD]

Pitchon, J. (vn)
Granados, E.:Serenade for 2 Vns, w. R. Waterman (vn), D. Riva (pno) Centaur ▲ CRC 2043 [DDD]

Pitelka, Kazi (va)
Matson, S.:Range, w. Catherine Robbin (mez), Susan Greenberg (fl), Joseph Stone (fl), Glen Garrett (cl), Suren Karapetyan (hn), Peter Kent (vn), Sebastian Toettcher (vc), Don Ferrone (db), Doug Livingston (gtr/mand), John Schneider (gtr), Amy Shulman (hp), Terry Schoenig (perc), S. Matson (cnd) *(rec Schnee Studio, Universal City, CA, Mar 12, 1995)* New Albion ▲ NA 091

Pitone, Eduardo (va)
Ragazzi, A.:Con Grosso, w. Marco Rogliano (vn), Andrea Guerrini (vn), Aurelio Bertucci (vc), Antonella Cristiano (hpd), I. Caiazza (cnd), I Solisti Partenopei *(rec Mar 1996)* Kicco Classics ▲ 396 [DDD]

Pits, Susan (pno)
Dring, M.:Pno Duo Tour, w. Leigh Kaplan (pno), Robin Paterson (pno)—Danza Gaya Cambria ▲ CD 1084 [ADD]

Pittel, Harvey (sax)
Bach & Noodles, w. Gabor Rejto (vc), Levering Rothfuss (pno), Anton Nel (pno) Crystal ▲ CD 654
Rodby, J.:Con Sax, w. E. Howarth (cnd), London Sinfonietta Crystal ■ C500
Saxophone Quartet, w. Shelly Manne (drums), Monty Budwig (bass) Crystal ■ C 155
Trio, w. Julian Fifer (vc), Levering Rothfuss (pno) Crystal ■ C 157

Pittman, Caroline (fl)
Misurell-Mitchell, J.:On Thin Ice, w. Jeffrey Kust (gtr) Opus One ▲ CD 160
Misurell-Mitchell, J.:Sub-Music Opus One ▲ CD 160
Schwantner, J.:Consortium I, w. Boston Musica Viva Delos ▲ DCD 1011 [AAD]

Pituch, David (sax)
Bloch, A.:Notes *(rec Trixi Tonstudio, Munich)* Pro Viva ▲ ISPV 175 [ADD]
Fennelly, B.:Con Sax, w. W. Michniewski (cnd), Polish CO *(rec Apr 1986)* Pro Viva ▲ ISPV 175 [ADD]
Fennelly, B.:Tesserae VIII *(rec Trixi Tonstudio, Munich)* Pro Viva ▲ ISPV 175 [ADD]
Palester, R.:Concertino Sax, w. J. Maksymiuk (cnd), Polish CO *(rec Polish Radio, 1982)* Pro Viva ▲ ISPV 175 [ADD]
Yuasa, J.:Not I, But the Wind *(rec Trixi Tonstudio, Munich)* Pro Viva ▲ ISPV 175 [ADD]

Pivka, Marian (pno)
The Masterpiece Collection:Piano Unison ▲ V 80062
Schubert, Franz:Scherzo Pno, D.593/1 Critics Choice 2-▲ CCD 946 [DDD]
Tchaikovsky, P.:Les Saisons—February:Carnaval; October:Autumn Song Critics Choice 2-▲ CCD 945 [DDD]

Pivoda, Radomír (fl)
Nedbal, O.:Nightingale's Waltz, w. Bohumil Kotmel (vn), G. Albrecht (cnd), Czech PO *(rec House of Artists, Prague, Dec 31, 1995)* Canyon Classics 2-▲ 323
Stamitz, A.:Con Fls, w. J. Válek (fl), F. Vajnar (cnd), Prague CO Supraphon ▲ 11 1424-2 [DDD]

Piwowarski, Maciej (org)
Gloria Tibi Trinitas:Sacred Music of Slav Composers 18th-20th Centuries, w. [cnd:Andrzej Filaber], Warsaw Cathedral Choir, Jolanta Kaufman (sop), Anna Lubanska (alt), Ryszard Wróblewski (ten), Czeslaw Galka (bass) Polskie Nagrania Edition ▲ ECD 057 [DDD]

Pizarro, Artur (pno)
Kabalevsky, D.:Preludes Pno, Op. 5 Collins Classics ▲ COL 1418
Kabalevsky, D.:Recitative & Rondo Collins Classics ▲ COL 1418
Kabalevsky, D.:Son 1 Pno Collins Classics ▲ COL 1418
Kabalevsky, D.:Son 2 Pno Collins Classics ▲ COL 1418
Kabalevsky, D.:Son 3 Pno Collins Classics ▲ COL 1418
Liszt, F.:Légendes Collins Classics ▲ COL 1357
Liszt, F.:Son Pno Collins Classics ▲ COL 1357
Liszt, F.:Sonetti di Petrarca Voice & Pno Collins Classics ▲ COL 1357
Voříšek, J.V.:Fant Pno Collins Classics ▲ COL 1458 [DDD]
Voříšek, J.V.:Impromptus Pno, Op. 7 Collins Classics ▲ COL 1458 [DDD]
Voříšek, J.V.:Son Pno Collins Classics ▲ COL 1458 [DDD]
Voříšek, J.V.:Theme & Vars Collins Classics ▲ COL 1458 [DDD]

Pizzarelli, John (gtr)
Miller, G.:Music of, w. K. Lockhart (cnd), Boston Pops Orch, King's Singers—Runnin' Wild; A String of Pearls; Moonlight Serenade; Chattanooga Choo-Choo; The Nearness of You; My Blue Heaven; Song of the Volga Boatmen; Sunrise Serenade; Kalamazoo; Serenade in Blue; The Anvil Chorus; St. Louis Blues March; A Nightingale Sang in Berkeley Square; American Patrol; Little Brown Jug; In the Mood *(rec Symphony Hall, Boston, May 30-June 1, 1996)* RCA Victor ▲ 09026-68598-2 [DDD] ■ 09026-68598-4

Pizzaro, Artur (pno)
Rachmaninoff, S.:Suite 1 for 2 Pnos, w. Sequeira Costa (pno) RPO ▲ RPO 7024 [DDD]

Plagge, Rolf (pno)—see also ORCHESTRAS & ENSEMBLES Duo Reine Elisabeth, Pallas Trio
Spohr, L.:Adagio, w. Wolfram Geiss (vc) Musicaphon ▲ M 56822 [DDD]
Spohr, L.:Rondo brillant, w. Kathrin Rabus (vn) Musicaphon ▲ M 56822 [DDD]

Plagge, Wolfgang (pno)
Groven, E.:Con Pno, w. O.K. Ruud (cnd), Trondheim SO Simax ▲ PSC 3111
Groven, E.:Sym 2, w. O.K. Ruud (cnd), Trondheim SO Simax ▲ PSC 3111
Plagge, W.:Son 3 Hn, w. Frøydis Ree Wekre (hn) Crystal ▲ CD 678

Planès, Alain (pno)
Baker, D.:Son Vc, w. Janos Starker (vc) *(rec Indiana Univ Opera House, Bloomington, 1980)* Laurel ▲ LR 817
Chabrier, E.:Pno Music (misc)—Dix pièces pittoresques; Bourée fantastique; Impromptu; Habañera; Ballabile; Ronde champêtre; Feuillet d'album; Air de ballet Harmonia Mundi France ▲ HMC 901465
Chopin, F.:Son Vc, w. Lluís Claret (vc) Musique d'Abord ▲ HMA 1901370
Janácek, L.:In the Mists Harmonia Mundi France ▲ HMC 901508
Janácek, L.:On an Overgrown Path Harmonia Mundi France ▲ HMC 901508
Janácek, L.:Son October 1, 1905 Harmonia Mundi France ▲ HMC 901508
Janácek, L.:Souvenir Harmonia Mundi France ▲ HMC 901508
Martinů, B.:Double Con Pno, Tim, w. J.-F. Heisser (pno), J. Camosi (perc), J. Conlon (cnd), French National Orch Erato ▲ 2292-45499-2 ZK
Ravel, M.:À la manière de Borodine & de Chabrie—A la manière de Chabrier Harmonia Mundi France ▲ HMC 901465
Schubert, Franz:German Dances Pno, D.790 Harmonia Mundi France ▲ HMC 901564
Schubert, Franz:Impromptus Pno (comp)—Op. 90/1-4 Harmonia Mundi France ▲ HMC 901564
Schubert, Franz:Son Pno, D.958 Harmonia Mundi France ▲ HMC 901564
Strauss, R.:Son Vc, w. Lluís Claret (vc) Musique d'Abord ▲ HMA 1901370

Plant, Michael (trbn)
Pelosi, L.:Triptych, w. Roxanne Joyner (tpt), Stewart Sundholm (hn) Opus One ▲ CD 160

Plantard, Robert (pno)
Ladmirault, P.:Son Vc, w. Yvan Chiffoleau (vc) *(rec Radio-France, Paris, 1980)* Skarbo ▲ SK 4952 [ADD]
Ladmirault, P.:Son Cl, w. Jacques Lancelot (cl) *(rec Nantes National Conservatory Auditorium, 1980)* Skarbo ▲ SK 4952 [ADD]
Ladmirault, P.:Son Vn, w. Roland Daugareil (vn) *(rec Nantes National Conservatory Auditorium, 1980)* Skarbo ▲ SK 4952 [ADD]

Planté, Francis (pno)
Ricardo Viñes & Francis Planté, w. Ricardo Viñes (pno) *(rec between 1928 & 1936)* Pearl ▲ PEA 9857 [ADD]

Plante, G. (cl)—see ORCHESTRAS & ENSEMBLES Pentaèdre Ensemble

Planyavsky, Peter (org)
Bach, J.S.:Org Music (misc)—Toccata & Fugue, BWV 565; Prelude & Fugue, BWV 547; Fugue, BWV 578; Prelude & Fugue, BWV 552; Wer nur den lieben Gott lasst walten, BWV 642; Wachet auf, ruft uns die Stimme, BWV 645; An wasserflussen Babylon, BWV 653; Schmucke dich, o liebe seele, BWV 654; Herr Jesu Christ, dich zu uns wend, BWV 655; Nun komm' der Heiden Heiland, BWV 659; Jesus bliebet meine freude, BWV 147 *(rec Fukushima-shi Ongakudo, Nov 7-8, 1986)* Camerata ▲ 32CM 197 [DDD]

Plasson, E. (vn)
Lemeland, A.:Con 2 Vn, w. M. Tardue (cnd), Grenoble Instrumental Ensemble *(rec 9/90)* Quantum ▲ QM 6902 [DDD]

Platt, Julie (vc)—see ORCHESTRAS & ENSEMBLES Canterbury Cellists

Platt, Rosemary (pno)
Van De Vate, N.:Preludes Pno Vienna Modern Masters ▲ VMM CD 2001 [ADD]
Van De Vate, N.:Son Va, w. M. Davis (va) Vienna Modern Masters ▲ VMM CD 2001 [ADD]
Vercoe, E.:Herstory III, w. S. Mabry (mez) [E] Owl ▲ OWL 35 [DAD]

Plawutsky, Eugene (pno)
Guarnieri, C.M.:Coletanea, w. Martin Foster (vn) SNE ▲ SNE-593-CD
Miguez, L.:Son Vn, w. Martin Foster (vn) SNE ▲ SNE-593-CD
Nobre, M.:Desafio III, w. Martin Foster (vn) [arr. vn & pno] SNE ▲ SNE-593-CD
Villa-Lobos, H.:Son 2 Vn, w. Martin Foster (vn) SNE ▲ SNE-593-CD

Pleeth, Anthony (vc)
Battiato, F.:L'Ombra della Luce, w. Franco Battiato (voc), Antonio Ballista (pno), Roger Chase (va), Filippo Destrieri (kbd/computer), Gavin Wright (vn), G. Pio (cnd), London Astarte Orch Hemisphere ▲ 837234-2

▲ = CD ♦ = Enhanced CD Δ = MD ■ = Cassette Tape □ = DCC

Pleeth, Anthony (vc) (cont.)
Battiato, F.:Povera Patria, w. Franco Battiato (voc), Antonio Ballista (pno), Roger Chase (va), Filippo Destrieri (kbd/computer), Gavin Wright (vn), G. Pio (cnd), London Astarte Orch — Hemisphere ▲ 837234-2
Battiato, F.:Le Sacre Sinfonie del Tiempo, w. Franco Battiato (voc), Antonio Ballista (pno), Roger Chase (va), Filippo Destrieri (kbd/computer), Gavin Wright (vn), G. Pio (cnd), London Astarte Orch — Hemisphere ▲ 837234-2
Beethoven, L. van:Music of, w. Melvyn Tan (pno) — Hyperion 2-▲ CDD 22004
Brahms, J.:Sextet Strs, Op. 18, w. C. Aronowitz (va), Amadeus String Quartet — Deutsche Grammophon 3-▲ 419875-2 [ADD]
Brahms, J.:Sextet Strs, Op. 36, w. C. Aronowitz (va), Amadeus String Quartet — Deutsche Grammophon 3-▲ 419875-2 [ADD]
Oboe Collection, w. Robin Canter (ob), Melvyn Tan (hpd), Richard Burnett (pnos), James Wood (perc) — Amon Ra ▲ CDSAR 22 [DDD]

Pleeth, William (vc)
Jacqueline Du Pré:Her Early BBC Recordings, Vol. 2, w. Jacqueline Du Pré (vc), Ernest Lush (pno) — EMI Classics ▲ CDM 63166

Pleshakov, Vladimir (pno)
Dukas, P.:La plainte, au loin, du faune... *(rec Hillsborough, CA, 1972)* — Orion ▲ 7820-2 [AAD]
Dukas, P.:Vars, Interlude et Finale sur en thème de Rameau *(rec Hillsborough, CA, 1972)* — Orion ▲ 7820-2 [AAD]
Milhaud, D.:Le Bal martiniquais, w. E. Winther (pno) — Sonpact ▲ SPT 92004 [DDD]
Milhaud, D.:Concertino d'automne, w. E. Winther (pno), A. de Almeida (cnd), Ensemble — Sonpact ▲ SPT 92004 [DDD]
Milhaud, D.:Fant pastorale, w. E. Winther (pno) [two-piano arr.] — Sonpact ▲ SPT 92004 [DDD]
Milhaud, D.:Scaramouche for 2 Pnos, w. E. Winther (pno) — Sonpact ▲ SPT 92004 [DDD]
Milhaud, D.:Les Songes, Op. 237, w. E. Winther (pno) — Sonpact ▲ SPT 92004 [DDD]
Milhaud, D.:Suite for 2 Pnos, w. E. Winther (pno), A. de Almeida (cnd), Ensemble — Sonpact ▲ SPT 92004 [DDD]

Plesser, Z. (vc)—see ORCHESTRAS & ENSEMBLES Aviv String Quartet
Pletnev, Mikhail (pno)
Beethoven, L. van:Son 14 Pno, "Moonlight Son" — Virgin Classics ▲ 59142 [DDD]
Beethoven, L. van:Son 14 Pno, "Moonlight Son" — Virgin Classics ▲ CDC 45131
Beethoven, L. van:Son 21 Pno, "Waldstein" — Virgin Classics ▲ CDC 45131
Beethoven, L. van:Son 21 Pno, "Waldstein" — Virgin Classics ▲ 59142 [DDD]
Beethoven, L. van:Son 23 Pno, "Appassionata" — Virgin Classics ▲ 59142 [DDD]
Beethoven, L. van:Son 23 Pno, "Appassionata" — Virgin Classics ▲ CDC 45131
Chopin, F.:Barcarolle Pno — Virgin Classics ▲ CDC 45076
Chopin, F.:4 Nocturnes — Virgin Classics ▲ CDC 45076
Chopin, F.:Scherzos — Virgin Classics ▲ CDC 45076
Chopin, F.:Son Pno, Op. 35 — Virgin Classics ▲ CDC 45076
Haydn, J.:Sons Pno—Nos. 33, 60 & 62 — Virgin Classics ▲ CDC 45254
Haydn, J.:Son Pno, H.XVII/6, "Andante with Vars" — Virgin Classics ▲ CDC 45254
Mozart, W.A.:Con 9 Pno, w. M. Pletnev (cnd), German Chamber PO — Virgin Classics ▲ CDC 45130
Mozart, W.A.:Con 20 Pno, w. M. Pletnev (cnd), German Chamber PO — Virgin Classics ▲ CDC 45130
Mozart, W.A.:Con 23 Pno, w. M. Pletnev (cnd), German CO — Virgin Classics ▲ CDC 59280
Mozart, W.A.:Con 24 Pno, w. M. Pletnev (cnd), German CO — Virgin Classics ▲ CDC 59280
Mussorgsky, M.:Pictures at an Exhibition — Virgin Classics ▲ 59611 [DDD]
Piano Sampler — Virgin Classics 2-▲ CDC 59086
Rachmaninoff, S.:Con 1 Pno, w. L. Pešek (cnd), Philharmonia Orch — Virgin Classics ▲ 59506 [DDD]
Rachmaninoff, S.:Rhapsody on a Theme of Paganini, w. L. Pešek (cnd), Philharmonia Orch — Virgin Classics ▲ 59506 [DDD]
Scarlatti, D.:Sons Kbd — Virgin Classics ▲ ZDCB 45123
Tchaikovsky, P.:Concert Fant, w. V. Fedoseyev (cnd), Philharmonia Orch — Virgin Classics ▲ 59612 [DDD]
Tchaikovsky, P.:Con 1 Pno, w. V. Fedoseyev (cnd), Philharmonia Orch — Virgin Classics ▲ 59612 [DDD]
Tchaikovsky, P.:Con 2 Pno, w. V. Fedoseyev (cnd), Philharmonia Orch — Virgin Classics ▲ CDC 59631
Tchaikovsky, P.:Con 3 Pno, w. V. Fedoseyev (cnd), Philharmonia Orch — Virgin Classics ▲ CDC 59631
Tchaikovsky, P.:Morceaux, Op. 21 — Virgin Classics ▲ CDC 45042
Tchaikovsky, P.:Les Saisons — MK ▲ MKA 418008 [DDD]
Tchaikovsky, P.:Les Saisons — Virgin Classics ▲ CDC 45042
Tchaikovsky, P.:Sleeping Beauty (sels)—11 sels. [arr. for solo piano Pletnev] — Virgin Classics ▲ 59611 [DDD]

Plimley, Paul (kbd)
Oswald, J.:Parade, w. John Oswald (kbd/a sax/elec), Alex Varty (gtr), Cora Risdall (baby) — ReR ▲ CMCD [DDD]

Pliquett, Joachim (tpt)
Bach, J.S.:Cant 143, w. Arvid Gast (org) [excerpt for tpt & org] — Entrée ▲ 0071
Bach, J.S.:Cons Org, BWV 592-597, w. Arvid Gast (org)—in G, BWV 592 — Entrée ▲ 0071
Bach, J.S.:Toccata & Fugue Org, BWV 565, w. Arvid Gast (org) — Entrée ▲ 0071
Baldassare, P.:Son 1 Tpt, w. Arvid Gast (org) — Entrée ▲ 0071
400 Years of Music for Trumpet & Organ, w. Arvid Gast (org) — Classic Studio Berlin ▲ CS 11808 [DDD]
Krebs, J.L.:Org Music, w. Arvid Gast (org)—Fant in C for Org & Tpt — Entrée ▲ 0071
Loeillet, J.-B.:Son Tpt, w. Arvid Gast (org) — Entrée ▲ 0071
Purcell, H.:Org Music, w. Arvid Gast (org)—Son in D; Suite in C — Entrée ▲ 0071
Stanley, J.:Voluntaries Org, w. Arvid Gast (org)—Tpt Voluntary — Entrée ▲ 0071
Trumpet & Organ, w. Arno Lange (tpt), Ulrich Bremsteller (org), Arvid Gast (org) — Classic Studio Berlin ▲ CS 12 208 [DDD]

Plog, Anthony (tpt)
Campo, F.:Studies (2) Tpt, w. Sanders (gtr) — Crystal ▲ CD 663 [DDD]
The Colors of the Baroque, w. Nick Norton (tpt), chamber ensembles — Summit ▲ DCD 108 [DDD] ■ MCD 108 (D)
Erickson, R.:Kryl — Crystal ▲ CD 663 [DDD]
Petrassi, G.:Fanfare for 3 Tpts, w. G. B. Dillon (tpt), R. Karon (tpt) — Crystal ▲ CD 663 [DDD]
Plog, A.:Animal Ditties 2, w. Smith (spkr), Davis (pno) — Crystal ▲ CD 663 [DDD]
Stevens, H.:Son Tpt, w. Davis (pno) — Crystal ▲ CD 663 [DDD]
The Trumpet in Baroque Chamber Settings, w. various assisting artists — Centaur ▲ CRC 2068 [DDD]
Tull, F.:Profiles Tpt — Crystal ▲ CD 663 [DDD]
20th Century Music for Trumpet & Organ, w. Hans-Ola Ericsson (org) *(rec Mar. 1992)* — BIS ▲ CD 565 [DDD]

Plonsey, Dan (sax)
Ziporyn, E.:Kekembangan, w. Chris Jonas (sax), Randy McKean (sax), Evan Ziporyn (sax), Sekar Jaya Gamelan Orch — New World ▲ 804302
Plubeau, Christine (vl)
Vivaldi, A.:Sons Fl, w. Jean-Christophe Frisch (trns fl), Pascale Boquet (archlt), Claude Wassmer (bn), Alessandro de Marchi (hpd)—in F, d, e, g, c, D & g — Adda ▲ ADD 241882
Pludermacher, Georges (pno)
Bartók, B.:Son for 2 Pnos, w. J.-F. Heisser (pno), G.-J. Cipriana (perc), G. Perotin (perc) — Erato ▲ 2292-45861-2
Bartók, B.:Suite for 2 Pnos, w. J.-F. Heisser (pno) — Erato ▲ 2292-45861-2
Boucourechliev, A.:Les Archipels, w. Brigitte Sylvestre (hp), Elisabeth Chojnacka (hpd), Françoise Rieunier (org), Roland Auzet, Jean-Pierre Drouet (perc), Hakon Austbö (pno), Françoise-Frédéric Guy (pno), Claude Helffer (pno), Ysaÿe String Quartet, Les Pléiades Ensemble — Musique Francaise d'Aujourd'hui ("Collection MFA-Radio France" series) ▲ MFA 216001
Brahms, J.:Sons Cl (comp), w. M. Portal (cl) — Harmonia Mundi France ▲ HMC 90904
Debussy, C.:Children's Corner — Harmonia Mundi France ▲ HMC 901504
Debussy, C.:Épigraphes antiques — Harmonia Mundi France ▲ HMC 901504
Debussy, C.:Estampes — Harmonia Mundi France ▲ HMC 901503

Pludermacher, Georges (pno) (cont.)
Debussy, C.:Images Orch, w. J.-F. Heisser (pno) [2-piano trans. André Caplet] — Erato ▲ 2292-45698-2 ZK
Debussy, C.:Images (6) Pno — Harmonia Mundi France ▲ HMC 901503
Debussy, C.:Images (3) Pno — Harmonia Mundi France ▲ HMC 901503
Debussy, C.:La Mer, w. J.-F. Heisser (pno) [2-piano trans. André Caplet] — Erato ▲ 2292-45698-2 ZK
Debussy, C.:Nocturnes, w. J.-F. Heisser (pno) [2-piano trans. Mauruice Ravel]—Nuages & Fêtes — Erato ▲ 2292-45698-2 ZK
Debussy, C.:Pour le piano — Harmonia Mundi France ▲ HMC 901504
Debussy, C.:Suite bergamasque — Harmonia Mundi France ▲ HMC 901504
Debussy, C.:Transcriptions for 2 Pnos, w. J.-F. Heisser (pno)—Wagner:Der fliegende Holländer Ov.; Schumann:6 Studies in Canon Form, Op. 56; Saint-Saëns:Introduction & Rondo capriccioso; Gluck:Caprice on airs [from *Alceste*]; Tchaikovsky:3 Dances [from *Swan Lake*]; Debussy:Prélude à l'après-midi d'un faune — Erato ▲ 93209
Hindemith, P.:Son Vc & Pno, Op. 11/3, w. Christoph Henkel (vc) — Signum ▲ X64-00 [DDD]
The Last Recital, w. Nathan Milstein (vn) *(rec Berwaldhallen, Stockholm, June 1986)* — Teldec ▲ 95998-2 [DDD]
Pfitzner, H.:Son Vc, w. Christoph Henkel (vc) — Signum ▲ X64-00 [DDD]
Ravel, M.:Con Pno (left hand), w. J.-C. Casadesus (cnd), Lille National Orch — Harmonia Mundi ▲ HMT 7901434
Ravel, M.:Con in G Pno, w. J.-C. Casadesus (cnd), Lille National Orch — Harmonia Mundi ▲ HMT 7901434
Strauss, R.:Son Vc, w. Christoph Henkel (vc) — Signum ▲ X64-00 [DDD]
Ysaÿe, E.:Poème nocturne, w. Gerard Jarry (vn), Frederic Lodeon (vc) [arr. for piano trio] — Koch Schwann ▲ SCH 317212 [DDD]

Pluhar, Christina (hp/thb/gtr/tripla)—see ORCHESTRAS & ENSEMBLES Concerto Soave
Pluhar, Christina (thb)
Piccinini, A.:Music of, w. Matthias Spaeter (archlt)—Toccatas II, VI, XI, XIII, XVI & XX; Aria Francese & Corrente; Ricercar Primo; Chiaconne in partite varie; Saravanda alla Francesca; Aria di Feorenze; Toccata a dui Liuti; Aria III; Passacaglia; Baletto in Diverse partite a requisitione dell' illustrissimo conte Alessandro Bentivoglio; Aria di Sarabanda in varie partite; Chiacona Mariona — L'Empreinte Digitale ▲ ED 13057

Pluhar, Christina (triple hp)—see ORCHESTRAS & ENSEMBLES La Fenice Ensemble
Plumacher, Hans (vc)
Haydn, J.:Die Schöpfung, w. Jeannette van Dijck (sop), Peter Schreier (ten), Theo Adam (bass), Heinz Detering (db), Fritz Lehan (hpd), G. Wand (cnd), Cologne Gürzenich Orch, Cologne Gürzenich Chorus — Accord 2-▲ ACD 200422 [AAD]
Mozart, W.A.:Adagio & Rondo Glass Armonica, w. B. Hoffmann (glass armonica), K.H. Ulrich (fl), H. Hucke (ob), E. Nippes (va) — Allegretto ▲ ACD 8174 [ADD] ■ ACS 8174
Naumann, J.G.:Qt Glass Hmc, w. B. Hoffmann (glass hmc), K.H. Ulrich (fl), E. Nippes (va) — Allegretto ▲ ACD 8174 [ADD] ■ ACS 8174
Reichardt, J.F.:Rondeau, w. B. Hoffmann (glass hmc), H. Anrath (vn), W. Albers (vn), E. Nippes (va), G. Nose (db) — Allegretto ▲ ACD 8174 [ADD] ■ ACS 8174
Röllig, K.L.:Qnt Glass Hmc, w. B. Hoffmann (glass hmc), W. Albers (vn), H. Anrath (vn), E. Nippes (va) — Allegretto ▲ ACD 8174 [ADD] ■ ACS 8174

Plumbeau, Christine (vl)
Rebel, J.-F.:Sons 2 or 3 Parts, w. Frédéric Martin (vn), Odile Edouard (vn), Eric Bellocq (thb), Noëlle Spieth (hpd)—Nos. 1-7 [L'immortelle; L'apollon; Tombeau de monsieur de Lully; La venus; La flore; La pallas; La junon] — Adda ▲ ADD 581265 [DDD]
Plumeyer, Henning (trbn)—see ORCHESTRAS & ENSEMBLES Weser-Renaissance Ensemble
Plummer, Carolyn (vn)—see also ORCHESTRAS & ENSEMBLES Notre Dame String Trio
Haimo, E.:Rhap Vn, w. Barry David Salwen (pno) *(rec Annenberg Audit., Snite Museum of Art, Univ. of Notre Dame, May & June 1994)* — Centaur ▲ CRC 2253 [DDD]
Plummer, Kathryn (va)
Roussel, A.:Trio Fl, w. R. Willoughby (fl), C. Meints (vc) — Gasparo Gallante ▲ GG 1003 [AAD]
Plummer, S. (vn)
Lazarof, H.:Continuum, w. M. Thomas (va), L. Lesser (vc) *(rec 1970)* — CRI ▲ CD 631
Plumohira, Bruce (va)
Ashford, R.:Because, w. Mayumi Plumohira (vn), Catherine Bush (vn), Gregory Wood (vc) — Nigel Classics ▲ NC 10101
Ashford, R.:Summer's End, w. Mayumi Plumohira (vn), Catherine Bush (vn), Gregory Wood (vc) — Nigel Classics ▲ NC 10101

Plumohira, Mayumi (vn)
Ashford, R.:Because, w. Catherine Bush (vn), Bruce Plumohira (va), Gregory Wood (vc) — Nigel Classics ▲ NC 10101
Ashford, R.:Rise & Fall & Peaceful Rest, w. Mary Boyd (pno), Gregory Wood (vc) — Nigel Classics ▲ NC 10101
Ashford, R.:Short & Suite, w. Gregory Wood (vc) — Nigel Classics ▲ NC 10101
Ashford, R.:Summer's End, w. Catherine Bush (vn), Bruce Plumohira (va), Gregory Wood (vc) — Nigel Classics ▲ NC 10101
Ashford, R.:Vn & Vc Music, w. Gregory Wood (vc)—Young & Old Together; Far & Near Love Song; Young & Old Together — Nigel Classics ▲ NC 10101
Plunkett, Paul (baroque tpt)
Baroque Trumpet & Strings, w. string ensemble — Move ▲ MD 3127 [DDD]
Pluskwik, Gerhard (vc)
Mozart, W.A.:Qt Fl, K.285, w. E. Haupt (fl), P. Mirring (vn), P. Schikora (va) — LaserLight ▲ 15 878 [DDD]

Plutz, Eric (org)
Hovhaness, A.:Sacred Music, w. D. Pearson (cnd), St. John's Episcopal Cathedral Festival Orch, St. John's Episcopal Cathedral Boy & Girls' Choir, St. John's Episcopal Cathedral Choir—Magnificat, Op. 157; Psalm 23 [Cant from Sym No. 12, Op. 188]; A Rose Tree Blossoms, Op. 246/4; Jesus, Lover of My Soul, Op. 53b; Jesus Christ Is Risen Today, Op. 100/3b; The Lord's Prayer, Op. 35; Peace by Multiplied, Op. 259/1; O For a Shout of Sacred Joy, Op. 161; Out of the Depths, Op. 142/3; O God, Our Help in Ages Past, Op. 137 *(rec St. John's Episcopal Cathedral, Denver, Mar 6-8, 1995)* — Delos ▲ DE 3176 [DDD]
Sing We Merrily, w. [cnd:Donald Pearson], St. John's Episcopal Cathedral Choir Boy & Girls' Choir Denver — Delos ▲ DE 3125 [DDD]
Pluznick, Michael (perc)
Heat Beat, w. Derrick Jones (elec bass) — Well-Tempered Productions ("Well-Tempered World" series) ▲ WTP 5177 [DDD]
Postnikova, V. (pno)
Brahms, J.:Souvenir de la Russie, w. G. Rozhdestvensky (pno) — Allegretto ▲ ACD 8177 [DDD] ■ ACS 8177
Brahms, J.:Vars on a Theme of Robert Schumann, Op. 23, w. G. Rozhdestvensky (pno) — Allegretto ▲ ACD 8177 [DDD] ■ ACS 8177
Brahms, J.:Waltzes Pno, Op. 39, w. G. Rozhdestvensky (pno) [4-hands version] — Allegretto ▲ ACD 8177 [DDD] ■ ACS 8177

Poblocka, Ewa (pno)
Chopin, F.:Nocturnes—No. 1 in b♭, Op. 9/1; No. 2 in E♭, Op. 9/2; No. 3 in B, Op. 9/3; No. 4 in F, Op. 15/1; No. 5 in F#, Op. 15/2; No. 6 in g, Op. 15/3; No. 7 in c#, Op. 27/1; No. 8 in d♭, Op. 27/2; No. 9 in B, Op. 32/1; No. 10 in A♭, Op. 32 — Canyon Classics ▲ 3641 [DDD]
Chopin, F.:Nocturnes—No. 11 in g, Op. 37/1; No. 12 in G, Op. 37/2; No. 13 in c, Op. 48/2; No. 14 in f#, Op. 48/; No. 15 in f, Op. 55/1; No. 16 in E♭, Op. 55/2; No. 17 in B, Op. 62/1; No. 18 in E, Op. 62/2; No. 19 in e, Op. 72/1; No. 20 in c#; No. 21 in — Canyon Classics ▲ 3642 [DDD]
Chopin, F.:Son Pno, Op. 4 — Canyon Classics ▲ EC 3636
Chopin, F.:Son Pno, Op. 35 — Canyon Classics ▲ EC 3636
Chopin, F.:Son Pno, Op. 58 — Canyon Classics ▲ EC 3636
Grieg, E.:Con Pno, Op. 16, w. T. Wojciechowski (cnd), Polish National RSO Katowice — Conifer Classics 2-▲ 75605-51750-2 [DDD]

Poblocka, Ewa (pno) (cont.)
Mozart, W.A.:Con 20 Pno, w. J. Maksymiuk (cnd), Polish CO *(rec Concert Hall of the National Philharmonic, Warsaw, May 5–6, 1990)* Polskie Nagrania ▲ PNCD 077 [DDD]
Mozart, W.A.:Con 23 Pno, w. J. Maksymiuk (cnd), Polish CO *(rec Concert Hall of the National Philharmonic, Warsaw, May 5–6, 1990)* Polskie Nagrania ▲ PNCD 077 [DDD]
Pocaterra, Antonio (vc)—see also ORCHESTRAS & ENSEMBLES Milan Solisti
Marcello, B.:Sons Vc, w. B. Ferrari (vn), M.I. De Carli (cembalo) Rivoalto ▲ CRA 9008 [ADD]
Marcello, B.:Sons Vc, w. Benito Ferraris (vn), Maria Isabella de Carli (hpd) Rivoalto ▲ RIV 9008 [ADD]
Vivaldi, A.:Sons Vn, Op. 5, w. F. Fantini (vn), M. Ferarris (vn), A. Ephrikaim (vn), G. Ghetti (vc), I. De Carli (cembalo), V. Luccini (cembalo) Rivoalto ▲ CRA 9005 [ADD]
Pochtar, Y. (pno)
Liszt, F.:Pno Music (misc)—Impromptu; Elégies 1 & 2; Valse oubliée; Gondoles lugubres 1 & 2; Bagatelle sans tonalité; Czardas obstinée; Ave Maria; Nuages gris; Miserere d'après Palestrina; En rêve (nocturne); 4 Klavierstücke; Transcription of Wagner's Venezia *(rec Apr. 1993)* Opus 111 ▲ OPS 3093 [DDD]
Podger, Rachel (baroque vn)—see ORCHESTRAS & ENSEMBLES Les Éléments
Podger, Rachel (vn)—see also ORCHESTRAS & ENSEMBLES Palladian Ensemble
Haydn, J.:Songs, w. Mhairi Lawson (sop), Oleg Kogan (vc), Olga Tverskaya (pno) Opus 111 ▲ OPS 30-121
Purcell, H.:Sons (12) Vns, Z.790–801, w. Pavlo Beznosiuk (vn), Christophe Coin (b vl), Christopher Hogwood (org) *(rec Emmanuel College, Cambridge, Feb–Aug 1994)* L'Oiseau-Lyre ▲ 444449-2 [DDD]
Podis, Eunice (pno)
Hindemith, P.:Son Ob, w. J. Mack (ob) Crystal ▲ CD324
Hindemith, P.:Son Ob, w. J. Mack (ob) Crystal ■ C 324
John Mack:Oboe, w. John Mack (ob) Crystal ▲ CD324
Loeffler, C.M.:Rhaps, w. J. Mack (ob), A. Skernick (va) Crystal ■ C 323
Loeffler, C.M.:Rhaps, w. J. Mack (ob), A. Skernick (va) Crystal ▲ CD323
Poulenc, F.:Son Ob, w. J. Mack (ob) Crystal ■ C 324
Poulenc, F.:Son Ob, w. J. Mack (ob) Crystal ▲ CD324
Saint-Saëns, C.:Son Ob, w. J. Mack (ob) Crystal ■ C 325
Saint-Saëns, C.:Son Ob, w. J. Mack (ob) Crystal ▲ CD324
Schumann, R.:Romances Ob, w. J. Mack (ob) Crystal ■ C 325
Schumann, R.:Romances Ob, w. J. Mack (ob) Crystal ▲ CD324
Sonatas for Oboe, w. John Mack (ob) Crystal ■ C 324
Podlovski, David (vn)
Caudella, E.:Con 1 Vn, w. Baciu, Vintila (cnd), Iasi Moldava PO *(rec 1975 & 1983)* Electrecord ▲ ELCD 104 [AAD]
Pogorelich, Ivo (pno)
Beethoven, L. van:Son 32 Pno Deutsche Grammophon ▲ 410520-2 [DDD]
Brahms, J.:Intermezzos Pno, Op. 117 Deutsche Grammophon ▲ 437460-2 [DDD]
Brahms, J.:Pieces Pno, Op. 76—No. 1, Capriccio Deutsche Grammophon ▲ 437460-2 [DDD]
Brahms, J.:Pieces Pno, Op. 118—No. 2 Deutsche Grammophon ▲ 437460-2 [DDD]
Brahms, J.:Rhaps Pno, Op. 79 Deutsche Grammophon ▲ 437460-2 [DDD]
Chopin, F.:Ballades Pno (comp)—Op. 38 Capriccio ▲ CDC 10024 [AAD]
Chopin, F.:Études (24)—Op. 10, Nos. 8 & 10; Op. 25, No. 6 Capriccio ▲ CDC 10024 [AAD]
Chopin, F.:Mazurkas—Op. 59/1–3 Capriccio ▲ CDC 10024 [AAD]
Chopin, F.:Nocturnes—Op. 55/2 Capriccio ▲ CDC 10024 [AAD]
Chopin, F.:Pno Music (misc)—Ballade 2; Études, Op. 10, Nos. 8 & 10, & Op. 25, No. 6; Mazurkas, Op. 59, Nos. 1–3; Polonaise, Op. 44; Preludes, Nos. 21–25; Scherzo No. 3 Vivace 3-▲ E 330 [ADD/DDD]
Chopin, F.:Pno Music (misc) Deutsche Grammophon ▲ 415123-2 [ADD]
Chopin, F.:Pno Music (misc), w. Martha Argerich (pno), Vladimir Ashkenazy (pno), Stanislav Bunin (pno), Halina Czerny-Stefanska (pno), Jan Ekier (pno), Yuval Fichman (pno), Kemal Gekic (pno), Adam Harasiewicz (pno), Krzysztof Jablonski (pno), Louis Kentner (pno), Jean-Marc Luisada (pno), Garrick Ohlsson (pno), Maurizio Pollini (pno), Dang Thai Son (pno)—includes Ballade (Nos. 1 & 2); Barcarolle, Op. 60; Concerto Nos. 1 & 2; Études (Op. 10, Nos. 1, 5, 8, 10 & 12 & Op. 25, No. 10, 18 & 25); Grand valse brillante; Impromptus (Nos. 3 & 4); Mazurkas (Op. 24, Nos. 1–4; Op. 30, Nos. 1–4; Op. 50, No. 32; Op. 59, Nos. 1–3); Nocturnes (Op. 9, No. 3; Op. 37, No. 12; Op. 48, No. 13; Op. 55, No. 16)Polonaise (Op. 40, Nos. 3 & 4; Op. 44, No. 5; Op. 53, No. 6; Op. 61, No. 7); Preludes (Op. 28 Nos. 13–18, 21–24 & Op. 45, No. 25); Scherzos (Nos. 1–3); Sonatas (Nos. 2 & 3); Waltzes (No. 1 & 6) LaserLight 5-▲ 15 961 [ADD/DDD]
Chopin, F.:Pno Music (misc) *(rec live, Warsaw, 10/80)* Master Digital ▲ 23004 [ADD]
Chopin, F.:Polonaises—No. 5 in f#, Op. 44 Capriccio ▲ CDC 10024 [AAD]
Chopin, F.:Preludes, Op. 28 Deutsche Grammophon ▲ 429227-2 [DDD]
Chopin, F.:Preludes, Op. 28—Nos. 21–24 Capriccio ▲ CDC 10024 [AAD]
Chopin, F.:Prelude, Op. 45 Capriccio ▲ CDC 10024 [AAD]
Chopin, F.:Scherzos—No. 3 Capriccio ▲ CDC 10024 [AAD]
Chopin, F.:Son Pno, Op. 35 Deutsche Grammophon ▲ 415123-2 [AAD]
Haydn, J.:Sons Pno—2 Sonatas—No. 19 In A♭; No. 46 in D Deutsche Grammophon ▲ 435618-2 [DDD]
Liszt, F.:Son Pno Deutsche Grammophon ▲ 429391-2 [DDD]
Mozart, W.A.:Fant Pno, K.397 Deutsche Grammophon ▲ 437763-2 [DDD]
Mozart, W.A.:Son 5 Pno Deutsche Grammophon ▲ 437763-2 [DDD]
Mozart, W.A.:Son 11 Pno Deutsche Grammophon ▲ 437763-2 [DDD]
Mussorgsky, M.:Pictures Deutsche Grammophon ▲ 437 667-2
Prokofiev, S.:Son 6 Pno Deutsche Grammophon ▲ 413363-2 [DDD]
Ravel, M.:Gaspard de la nuit Deutsche Grammophon ▲ 413363-2 [DDD]
Ravel, M.:Valses nobles et sentimentales Deutsche Grammophon ▲ 437 667-2
Scarlatti, D.:Sons Kbd—15 selections Deutsche Grammophon ▲ 435855-2 [DDD]
Schumann, R.:Sym Etudes Deutsche Grammophon ▲ 410520-2 [DDD]
Scriabin, A.:Son 2 Pno Deutsche Grammophon ▲ 429391-2 [DDD]
Tchaikovsky, P.:Con 1 Pno, w. C. Abbado (cnd), London SO Deutsche Grammophon ▲ 415122-2 [DDD]
Pohjola, Liisa (pno)
Merikanto, A.:Preludio Vn, w. P. Pohjola (vn) BIS ▲ CD 56 [AAD]
Segerstam, L.:Poem Vn, w. P. Pohjola (vn) BIS ▲ CD 56 [AAD]
Pohjola, Paavo (vn)
Bashmakov, L.:Con da camera, w. Gunilla von Bahr (pic/fl), Mona Nordin (vn), Zahari Tchavdarov (va), Elemér Lavotha (vc) *(rec Grünewald Hall, Stockholm, Sweden, May 11, 1974)* BIS ▲ CD 11 [AAD]
Merikanto, A.:Preludio Vn, w. L. Pohjola (pno) BIS ▲ CD 56 [AAD]
Meriläinen, U.:Opusculum BIS ▲ CD 56 [AAD]
Pergament, M.:Pezzo, w. G. von Bahr (fls), Z. Zirchev (vn), Z. Tchavdarov (va), U. Vrethammar (vc) *(rec Jan. 25, 1973)* BIS ▲ CD 37 [AAD]
Sallinen, A.:Cadenze Vn BIS ▲ CD 41 [AAD]
Segerstam, L.:Poem Vn, w. L. Pohjola (pno) BIS ▲ CD 56 [AAD]
Pohl, Klaus-Georg (pno)
Wyshnegradsky, I.:Chant nocturne, w. Martin Gelland (vn), Ute Gareis (pno) *(rec Tonhallen, Sundsvall/Sweden & Holmsund Church, Aug 24–27 & Sept 8, 1995)* Vienna Modern Masters ▲ VMM 2017 [DDD]
Pohlreich, Ferdinand (pno)
Dvořák, A.:Evening Songs, Op. 3, w. Beno Blachut (ten) Supraphon ▲ SUP 0206 [AAD]
Pohran, Alexandra (ob)
The French Oboe, w. J. Hayes (pno) Mastersound ▲ MST 23 [DDD]
Poiget, Christophe (vn)
Damaré, E.:Music of, w. Jean-Louis Beaumadier (petite fl), Marc Giradot (ophicleide/tuba), Circe Wind Quintet, La Follia Instrumental Ensemble—La Capricieuse, Op. 270; Feux follets, Op. 378; Les Échos des bois, Op. 220; Le Merle blanc, Op. 161; Tarentelle, Op. 391; L'Oiseau et les roses, Op. 153; Le Tourbillon, Op. 212; L'Alouette, Op. 172; Pizzicato, Op. 426; La Danse des grillons, Op. 380 *(rec 1996)* Calliope ▲ CAL 9869 [DDD]
Poirier, Réjean (hpd)—see also ORCHESTRAS & ENSEMBLES Da Sonar Ensemble
Clavecins à Tempéraments *(rec June 11–13, 1990)* Ummus ▲ UMM 302
Poirier, Sylvie (org)
Organ Duets, w. Philip Crozier (org) REM ▲ 335603 [DDD]
Poke, James (panpipes)
Andriessen, L.:Hoketus, w. Katherine Pendry (panpipes), Evan Ziporyn (a sax), Richard Craig (a sax), Steven Schick (congas), Amy Knoles (congas), Lisa Moore (Fender Rhodes), Damian LeGassick (Fender Rhodes), Cees van Zeeland (pno), Gerard Bouwhuis (pno), Robert Black (bass gtr), Mark Stewart (bass gtr) *(rec Air Recording Studios, Lyndhurst Hall, Hampstead, London, June 29–July 3, 1994)* Sony Classical ▲ SK 66483 [DDD]
Pokorny, Gene (tuba)
Hindemith, P.:Son Bass Tuba, w. T. Lichtman (pno) Summit 2-▲ DCD 115 [DDD] 2-■ DCD 115
Tuba Tracks *(rec May 30–31, 1986)* Summit ▲ DCD 129 [DDD] ■ DCD 129
Pokrzywinski, Miroslaw (cl)
Krauze, Z.:Quatour pour la naissance, w. Krzysztof Bakowski (vn), Andrzej Bauer (vc), Zygmunt Krauze (pno) *(rec National Philharmonic, Warsaw, Mar. 1991)* Polskie Nagrania ▲ PLN 113 [DDD]
Pol, Wijnand Van de (org)
Organi Nacchini e Dacci di Muzzana del Turgnano e Marano Lagunare Bongiovanni ▲ GB 5038 [DDD]
Polách, Emil (bn)
Vivaldi, A.:Cons Bn, w. O. Vlček (cnd), Prague Virtuosi—Con. in B♭, RV.501 *(rec 1991)* Emergo ▲ EC 3981 [DDD]
Vivaldi, A.:Con Ob Bn, w. J. Kolár (ob), O. Vlček (cnd), Prague Virtuosi *(rec 1991)* Emergo ▲ EC 3981 [DDD]
Polad, Mike (pno)
Beiderbecke, B.:Piano Music—In a Mist; Candlelights; Flashes; In the Dark; Davenport Blues ("Piano Deco, Vol. 1:M. Polad Plays American Music of the 1920's") Polecat ▲ CD 101
Bloom, Rube:Pno Music—Sapphire; Silhouette Polecat ▲ CD 101
Lane, E.:Adirondack Sketches Polecat ▲ CD 101
Lane, E.:American Dances Polecat ▲ CD 101
Lane, E.:Pno Music—Persimmon Pucker; Sea Burial; Girl on Tiptoe Polecat ▲ CD 101
Polato, Pierluigi (thb)—see ORCHESTRAS & ENSEMBLES Ensemble Barocco Padua Sans Souci
Poleess, Leonid (vn)
Telemann, G.P.:Cons Ob, w. Pierre Pierlot (ob), Evgeni Nepalov (ob), Piotr Dubrov (ob), Andrei Abramenkov (vn), Rudolf Barshai (vn), R. Barshai (cnd), Moscow CO—in B♭ for 3 Obs, 3 Vns & Bc *(rec Salle Wagram, Paris, June 1964)* EMI Classics ▲ CDK 65340 [ADD]
Polezhaev, Alexander (pno)
Davïdov, K.Y.:Pieces Vc & Pno, Op. 17, w. Marina Tarasova (vc) Olympia ▲ OLY 571 [DDD]
Davïdov, K.Y.:Salonstücke, Op. 30, w. Marina Tarasova (vc) Olympia ▲ OLY 571 [DDD]
Kabalevsky, D.:In Memory of Sergei Prokofiev, w. Marina Tarasova (vc) *(rec Moscow, 1993)* Olympia ▲ OCD 294 [DDD]
Kabalevsky, D.:Pno Music—Scherzo, Op. 27/14; Novelette, Op. 27/25; Round-Dance, Op. 60/2; Étude, Op. 27/3 *(rec Moscow, 1993)* Olympia ▲ OCD 294 [DDD]
Kabalevsky, D.:Son Vc, w. Marina Tarasova (vc) *(rec Moscow, 1993)* Olympia ▲ OCD 294 [DDD]
Miaskovsky, N.:Son 1 Vc, w. Marina Tarasova (vc) Olympia ▲ OLY 530 [DDD]
Miaskovsky, N.:Son 2 Vc, w. Marina Tarasova (vc) Olympia ▲ OLY 530 [DDD]
Polidori, P. (gtr)
Giuliani, G.F.:Grand Son, w. P. Depetris (fl) *(rec July 1993)* Pavane ▲ ADW 7298 [DDD]
Gragnani, F.:Son Fl, w. P. Depetris (fl) *(rec July 1993)* Pavane ▲ ADW 7298 [DDD]
Legnani, L.:Duetto concertante, w. P. Depetris (fl) *(rec July 1993)* Pavane ▲ ADW 7298 [DDD]
Paganini, N.:Son concertata, w. P. Depetris (fl) [arr fl & gtr] *(rec July 1993)* Pavane ▲ ADW 7298 [DDD]
Politis, Dimitris (gtr)
Cornologia, w. Budapest Festival Horn Quartet, Zoltán Varga (timp/perc), Ferenc Gayer (db/bass gtr), János Weszely (dr), Sándor Balogh (pno) *(rec Hungaroton Classic Studio, Feb 15–16, 1996)* Hungaroton ▲ HCD 31652 [ADD/DDD]
Politkovsky, Igor (vn)
Balakirev, M.:Impromptu Vn, w. I. Kollegorskaya (pno) *(rec 1957)* Russian Compact Disc ("Talents of Russia" series) ▲ RCD 16279 [ADD]
Dvořák, A.:Slavonic Dances (sels), w. E. Epstein (pno)—Op. 46/2 [trans F. Kreisler for vn & pno] *(rec 1974)* Russian Compact Disc ("Talents of Russia" series) ▲ RCD 16279 [ADD]
Dvořák, A.:Zigeunermelodien, Op. 55, w. T. Merkoulova (pno)—Gypsy Song in c [trans F. Kreisler for vn & pno] *(rec 1961)* Russian Compact Disc ("Talents of Russia" series) ▲ RCD 16279 [ADD]
Rachmaninoff, S.:Romance Vn, w. I. Kollegorskaya (pno) *(rec 1957)* Russian Compact Disc ("Talents of Russia" series) ▲ RCD 16279 [ADD]
Rubinstein, A.:Son 1 Vn, w. E. Epstein (pno) *(rec 1981)* Russian Compact Disc ("Talents of Russia" series) ▲ RCD 16279 [ADD]
Taneyev, S.:Son Vn, w. E. Epstein (pno) *(rec 1982)* Russian Compact Disc ("Talents of Russia" series) ▲ RCD 16279 [ADD]
Tchaikovsky, P.:Mélodie, w. T. Merkoulova (pno) [trans for vn & pno] *(rec 1961)* Russian Compact Disc ("Talents of Russia" series) ▲ RCD 16279 [ADD]
Polivnick, Paul (va)
Levitch, L.:Qnt Fl, w. Sheridan Stokes (fl), Kathleen Lenski (vn), Miwako Watanabe (vn), Jeffrey Solow (vc) Cambria ▲ CD 1059 [ADD]
Polk, Joanne (pno)
Schumann, C.:Songs, w. K. Uecker (sop)—19 lieder—Am Strand; Volkslied; Er ist gekommen in Sturm und Regen; Liebst du um Schönheit; Warum willst du and're fragen; Ich stand in dunklen Träumen; Sie liebten sich beide; Liebeszauber; Der Mond kommt still gegangen; Ich hab' in deinem Auge; Die stille Lotosblume; Loreley; O weh des Scheidens; Beim Abscheid; Was weinst du, Blümlein; An einem lichten Morgen; Geheimes Flüstern hier und dort; Das ist ein Tag, der klingen mag; Das Veilchen [G] Arabesque ▲ Z 6624 [DDD]
Pollack, D. (pno)
Chopin, F.:Ballades Pno (comp)—Op. 52 Infinity Digital ▲ QK 64373 [DDD]
Chopin, F.:Nocturnes—in D♭, Op. 27/2 Infinity Digital ▲ QK 64373 [DDD]
Chopin, F.:Son Pno, Op. 35 Infinity Digital ▲ QK 64373 [DDD]
Chopin, F.:Son Pno, Op. 58 Infinity Digital ▲ QK 64373 [DDD]
Pollack, Stephen (t sax)—see ORCHESTRAS & ENSEMBLES New Century Saxophone Quartet
Pollastri, P. (ob)
Vivaldi, A.:Sons Ob, Vivaldi Consort—in c, RV.53; in g, RV.81; in B♭, RV.34; in g, RV.51; in C, RV.48; in C (unpubl.); in g, RV.28 Tactus ▲ TC 672203
Pollet, Francis (bn)
Devienne, F.:Qts Bn, Op. 73, w. Eugene Ysaÿe String Trio—No. 3 in g Syrinx ▲ 93103 [DDD]
Mozart, W.A.:Duo Bn Vc, w. Eugene Ysaÿe String Trio Syrinx ▲ 93103 [DDD]
Stamitz, C.:Qt Bn, w. Eugene Ysaÿe String Trio Syrinx ▲ 93103 [DDD]
Vogel, J.C.:Qts Bn, w. Eugene Ysaÿe String Trio—No. 1 in F Syrinx ▲ 93103 [DDD]
Pollet, L. (fl)
Brahms, J.:Son 1 Vn, w. B. Vogt (pno) [trans Paul Klengel in D for vc & pno; adapted for fl] Titanic ▲ TI 216
Debussy, C.:Épigraphes antiques, w. B. Vogt (pno) [trans Anthony Summers; adapted] Titanic ▲ TI 216
Handel, G.F.:Sons Vn & Kbd, Op. 1, w. B. Vogt (pno)—in g Titanic ▲ TI 216
Mozart, W.A.:Sons Vn Pno (misc), w. B. Vogt (pno)—in F, K.376 Titanic ▲ TI 216

▲ = CD ♦ = Enhanced CD Δ = MD ■ = Cassette Tape ▯ = DCC

Pollett, Patricia (va)—see also ORCHESTRAS & ENSEMBLES Perihelion, Perihelion Ensemble members
Conyngham, B.:Streams, w. Geoffrey Collins (fl), Marshall McGuire (hp) *(rec Studio 200, ABC Ultimo Centre, Sydney, 1994)* Tall Poppies ▲ TP 071 [DDD]
Edwards, R.:Ecstatic Dance Va, w. Gwyn Roberts (vc) *(rec Nickson Room, Univ of Queensland, Feb 1993)* Tall Poppies ▲ TP 51 [DDD]

Pollikoff, Max (vn)
Luening, O.:Son III Vn CRI ("American Masters" series) ▲ CD 716 [ADD]

Pollini, Maurizio (pno)
Bartók, B.:Con 1 Pno, w. C. Abbado (cnd), Chicago SO Deutsche Grammophon ▲ 415371-2 [ADD]
Bartók, B.:Con 2 Pno, w. C. Abbado (cnd), Chicago SO Deutsche Grammophon ▲ 415371-2 [ADD]
Beethoven, L. van:Cons Pno (comp), w. C. Abbado (cnd), Berlin PO Deutsche Grammophon 3-▲ 439770-2 [DDD]
Beethoven, L. van:Con 3 Pno, w. H. von Karajan (cnd), Berlin PO *(rec Dec. 28, 1980)* Exclusive ▲ EXL 41 [AAD]
Beethoven, L. van:Con 3 Pno, w. A. Janigro (cnd), Milan RAI SO Fonit Cetra ("Emozioni" series) ▲ FCT CDAR 2033
Beethoven, L. van:Con 4 Pno, w. K. Böhm (cnd), Vienna PO Deutsche Grammophon 10-▲ 435091-2
Beethoven, L. van:Con 4 Pno, w. M. Pradella (cnd), Naples Alessandro Scarlatti RAI Orch Fonit Cetra ("Emozioni" series) ▲ FCT CDAR 2033
Beethoven, L. van:Con 4 Pno, w. G. Caracciolo (cnd), Milan Italian Radio-TV Orch *(rec 1966)* Arkadia ▲ 533 [AAD]
Beethoven, L. van:Con 5 Pno, "Emperor", w. C. Abbado (cnd), Vienna PO Exclusive ▲ EXL 64 [ADD]
Beethoven, L. van:Con 6 Pno, w. F. Caracciolo (cnd), Milan Italian Radio-TV Orch *(rec 1966)* Arkadia ▲ 533 [AAD]
Beethoven, L. van:Fant Pno, Op. 80, "Choral Fant", w. C. Abbado (cnd), Vienna PO, Vienna State Opera Chorus [G] Deutsche Grammophon ▲ 419779-2 [DDD]
Beethoven, L. van:Son 13 Pno Deutsche Grammophon ▲ 427770-2 [DDD] □ 427770-5
Beethoven, L. van:Son 14 Pno, "Moonlight Son" Deutsche Grammophon ▲ 427770-2 [DDD] □ 427770-5
Beethoven, L. van:Son 15 Pno, "Pastoral" Deutsche Grammophon ▲ 427770-2 [DDD] □ 427770-5
Beethoven, L. van:Son 17 Pno, "Tempest" Deutsche Grammophon ▲ 427642-2 [DDD]
Beethoven, L. van:Son 21 Pno, "Waldstein" Deutsche Grammophon ▲ 427642-2 [DDD]
Beethoven, L. van:Son 25 Pno Deutsche Grammophon ▲ 427642-2 [DDD]
Beethoven, L. van:Sons 28-32 Pno, "The Late Sons" Deutsche Grammophon 2-▲ 419199-2 [AAD]
Beethoven, L. van:Son 28 Pno Deutsche Grammophon ▲ 429569-2 [AAD]
Beethoven, L. van:Son 29 Pno, "Hammerklavier" Deutsche Grammophon ▲ 429569-2 [AAD]
Beethoven, L. van:Son 29 Pno, "Hammerklavier" *(rec live, Milan 10/28/70)* Arkadia ▲ 917 [ADD]
Beethoven, L. van:Son 30 Pno Deutsche Grammophon ▲ 429570-2 [AAD]
Beethoven, L. van:Son 31 Pno *(rec live, Milan 10/28/70)* Arkadia ▲ 917 [ADD]
Beethoven, L. van:Son 31 Pno Deutsche Grammophon ▲ 429570-2 [AAD]
Beethoven, L. van:Son 32 Pno Deutsche Grammophon ▲ 429570-2 [AAD]
Berg, A.:Son Pno Deutsche Grammophon ▲ 423678-2
Boulez, P.:Son 2 Pno Deutsche Grammophon ▲ 419202-2 [AAD]
Boulez, P.:Son 2 Pno *(rec 1971 & 1967)* Deutsche Grammophon ("The Originals" series) ▲ 447431-2
Brahms, J.:Qnt Pno, w. Quartetto Italiano Deutsche Grammophon ▲ 419673-2 [AAD]
Chopin, F.:Ballades Pno (comp)—Op. 23 EMI Classics ▲ CDM 64354 [ADD]
Chopin, F.:Con 1 Pno, w. P. Kletzki (cnd), Philharmonia Orch EMI Classics ▲ CDM 64354 [ADD]
Chopin, F.:Con 2 Pno, w. M. Inoue (cnd), South German RSO Artists ▲ FED 56 [ADD]
Chopin, F.:Études (24)—Op. 25, No. 11 *(rec live, Milan 10/28/70)* Arkadia ▲ 917 [ADD]
Chopin, F.:Études (24) Deutsche Grammophon 3-▲ 431221-2 [ADD/AAD]
Chopin, F.:Nocturnes—Op. 15/1 & 2 EMI Classics ▲ CDM 64354 [ADD]
Chopin, F.:Pno Music (misc), w. Martha Argerich (pno), Vladimir Ashkenazy (pno), Stanislav Bunin (pno), Halina Czerny-Stefanska (pno), Jan Ekier (pno), Yuval Fichman (pno), Kemal Gekic (pno), Adam Harasiewicz (pno), Krzysztof Jablonski (pno), Louis Kentner (pno), Jean-Marc Luisada (pno), Garrick Ohlsson (pno), Ivo Pogorelich (pno), Dang Thai Son (pno)—includes Ballade (Nos. 1 & 2); Barcarolle, Op. 60; Concerto Nos. 1 & 2; Etudes (Op. 10, Nos. 1, 5, 8, 10 & 12 & Op. 25, No. 10, 18 & 25); Grand valse brillante; Impromptus (Nos. 3 & 4); Mazurkas (Op. 24, Nos. 1-4; Op. 30, Nos. 1-4; Op. 50, No. 32; Op. 59, Nos. 1-3); Nocturnes (Op. 9, No. 3; Op. 37, No. 12; Op. 48, No. 13; Op. 55, No. 16)Polonaise (Op. 40, Nos. 3 & 4; Op. 44, No. 5; Op. 53, No. 6; Op. 61, No. 7); Preludes (Op. 28 Nos. 13-18, 21-24 & Op. 45, No. 25); Scherzos (Nos. 1-3); Sonatas (Nos. 2 & 3); Waltzes (No. 1 & 6) LaserLight 5-▲ 15 961 [ADD/DDD]
Chopin, F.:Pno Music (misc)—études, mazurkas, preludes *(rec 1960)* Arkadia ▲ 506 [AAD]
Chopin, F.:Polonaises—Nos. 1-7 Deutsche Grammophon ▲ 413795-2 [ADD]
Chopin, F.:Polonaises—Nos. 1-7 Deutsche Grammophon 3-▲ 431221-2 [ADD/AAD]
Chopin, F.:Polonaises—Op. 53 EMI Classics ▲ CDM 64354 [ADD]
Chopin, F.:Polonaise-fant Exclusive ▲ EXL 22
Chopin, F.:Preludes, Op. 28 Deutsche Grammophon ▲ 413796-2 [AAD]
Chopin, F.:Preludes, Op. 28 Deutsche Grammophon 3-▲ 431221-2 [ADD/AAD]
Chopin, F.:Son Pno, Op. 35 *(rec 1960)* Arkadia ▲ 506 [AAD]
Chopin, F.:Son Pno, Op. 35 Deutsche Grammophon ▲ 415346-2 [DDD]
Chopin, F.:Son Pno, Op. 58 Deutsche Grammophon ▲ 415346-2 [DDD]
Debussy, C.:Etudes Deutsche Grammophon ▲ 423678-2
Liszt, F.:Pno Music (misc)—Nuage gris; Unsternl-Sinistre; R.W. Venezia; La lugubre gondola Deutsche Grammophon ▲ 427322-2 [DDD]
Liszt, F.:Son Pno Deutsche Grammophon ▲ 427322-2 [DDD]
Liszt, F.:Totentanz, w. C. Groves (cnd), BBC SO *(rec live 1974 & 1979)* Artists ▲ FED 30 [ADD]
Mozart, W.A.:Adagio Pno, K.540 Exclusive ▲ EXL 16 [ADD]
Mozart, W.A.:Con 12 Pno, Vienna PO Exclusive ▲ EXL 35 [AAD]
Mozart, W.A.:Con 14 Pno, w. M. Pollini (cnd), Vienna PO Exclusive ▲ EXL 35 [AAD]
Mozart, W.A.:Con 18 Pno, w. K. Böhm (cnd), Vienna PO Deutsche Grammophon ▲ 429812-2 [ADD]
Mozart, W.A.:Con 19 Pno, w. K. Böhm (cnd), Vienna PO Deutsche Grammophon ▲ 429812-2 [ADD]
Mozart, W.A.:Con 19 Pno, w. M. Pollini (cnd), English CO Exclusive ▲ EXL 35 [AAD]
Mozart, W.A.:Con 20 Pno, w. M. Pollini (cnd), Vienna PO Exclusive ▲ EXL 35 [AAD]
Mozart, W.A.:Con 23 Pno, w. K. Böhm (cnd), Vienna PO Deutsche Grammophon ▲ 429812-2 [ADD]
Mozart, W.A.:Con 23 Pno, w. H. von Karajan (cnd), Vienna PO *(rec 1974)* Enterprise ("Document" series) ▲ ENT LV 938 [ADD]
Mozart, W.A.:Con 23 Pno, w. C. Abbado (cnd), La Scala Orch Exclusive ▲ EXL 64 [ADD]
Mozart, W.A.:Con 24 Pno, w. M. Pollini (cnd), English CO Exclusive ▲ EXL 35 [AAD]
Mozart, W.A.:Fant Pno, K.475 Exclusive ▲ EXL 16 [ADD]
Mozart, W.A.:Sons Pno—No. 14 in c, K.457; No. 17 in D, K.576 Exclusive ▲ EXL 16
Prokofiev, S.:Son 7 Pno Deutsche Grammophon ▲ 419202-2 [AAD]
Prokofiev, S.:Son 7 Pno *(rec 1971 & 1967)* Deutsche Grammophon ("The Originals" series) ▲ 447431-2
Schoenberg, A.:Con Pno, w. C. Abbado (cnd), Berlin PO Deutsche Grammophon ▲ 427771-2 [DDD]
Schoenberg, A.:Pno Music—3 Pieces, Op. 11 (1908); 6 Pieces, Op. 19 (1911); 5 Pieces, Op. 23 (1920-23); Suite, Op. 25 (1923); 2 Pieces, Op. 33a & 33b (1928; 1931) Deutsche Grammophon ("20th Century Classics" series) ▲ 423249-2 [ADD]
Schubert, Franz:Allegretto Pno, D.915 Deutsche Grammophon ▲ 427326-2 [DDD]
Schubert, Franz:Fant Pno, D.760, "Wandererfantasie" Deutsche Grammophon ▲ 419672-2 [ADD]
Schubert, Franz:Fant Pno, D.760, "Wandererfantasie" *(rec RCA Studio A, Rome, Nov 1973)* Deutsche Grammophon ("The Originals" series) ▲ 447451-2 [ADD]
Schubert, Franz:Pieces Pno, D.946 Deutsche Grammophon ▲ 427326-2 [DDD]
Schubert, Franz:Son Pno, D.784 *(rec live 1974 & 1979)* Artists ▲ FED 30 [ADD]
Schubert, Franz:Son Pno, D.845 Deutsche Grammophon ▲ 419672-2 [AAD]
Schubert, Franz:Son Pno, D.958 Deutsche Grammophon ▲ 427327-2 [DDD]
Schubert, Franz:Son Pno, D.959 Artists ▲ FED 56 [ADD]
Schubert, Franz:Son Pno, D.959 Deutsche Grammophon ▲ 427327-2 [DDD]

Pollini, Maurizio (pno) (cont.)
Schubert, Franz:Son Pno, D.960 Deutsche Grammophon ▲ 427326-2 [DDD]
Schumann, R.:Arabeske Pno Deutsche Grammophon ("Digital Midprice" series) ▲ 445522-2
Schumann, R.:Con Pno, w. C. Abbado (cnd), Berlin PO Deutsche Grammophon ▲ 427771-2 [DDD]
Schumann, R.:Con Pno, w. C. Abbado (cnd), Berlin PO Deutsche Grammophon ("Digital Midprice" series) ▲ 445522-2
Schumann, R.:Con Pno, w. H. von Karajan (cnd), Vienna PO *(rec 1974)* Enterprise ("Document" series) ▲ ENT LV 938 [ADD]
Schumann, R.:Davidsbündlertänze *(rec Salzburg, 1982-84)* Exclusive ▲ EXL 31 [ADD]
Schumann, R.:Fant Pno *(rec Hercules Room, Residenz, Munich, Apr 1973)* Deutsche Grammophon ("The Originals" series) ▲ 447451-2 [ADD]
Schumann, R.:Fant Pno Deutsche Grammophon ▲ 423134-2 [ADD]
Schumann, R.:Fantasiestücke Pno, Op. 12—No. 2 *(rec live, Milan 10/28/70)* Arkadia ▲ 917 [ADD]
Schumann, R.:Gesänge der Frühe, w. C. Groves (cnd), BBC SO *(rec live 1974 & 1979)* Artists ▲ FED 30 [ADD]
Schumann, R.:Kreisleriana *(rec Salzburg, 1982-84)* Exclusive ▲ EXL 31 [ADD]
Schumann, R.:Sym Etudes Deutsche Grammophon ("Digital Midprice" series) ▲ 445522-2
Stravinsky, I.:Pétrouchka (3 Scenes) *(rec 1971 & 1967)* Deutsche Grammophon ("The Originals" series) ▲ 447431-2
Stravinsky, I.:Scenes Pno Deutsche Grammophon ▲ 419202-2 [AAD]
Webern, A.:Vars Pno Deutsche Grammophon ▲ 419202-2 [AAD]
Webern, A.:Vars Pno *(rec 1971 & 1967)* Deutsche Grammophon ("The Originals" series) ▲ 447431-2

Pollock, Michael (pno)
Donizetti, G.:Arias, w. Nuccia Focile (sop)—6 arias Unicorn-Kanchana ▲ DKPCD 9161
Donizetti, G.:Songs, w. Nuccia Focile (sop)—Canzone Napoletane Unicorn-Kanchana ▲ DKPCD 9161
Puccini, G.:Songs, w. Nuccia Focile (sop)—Storiella d'amore; Sole e amore; A l'uccellino; Casa mio; Morire; Canto d'anime Unicorn-Kanchana ▲ DKPCD 9161
Verdi, G.:Songs, w. Nuccia Focile (sop)—Brindisi I & II; Perduta ho la pace; Deh pietoso, ho Addolorata; Stornello; L'Abandonée; E la vita; La Zingara; Il Tramonto Unicorn-Kanchana ▲ DKPCD 9161

Polmear, Jeremy (ob)
Pasculli, A.:Concerto on Themes from Donizetti's *La Favorita*, w. D. Ambache (pno) Meridian ▲ CDE 84147
Pasculli, A.:Fantaisie on Themes from Donizetti's *Poliuto*, w. D. Ambache (pno) Meridian ▲ CDE 84147

Polmear, Jeremy (ob/hn)
Donizetti, G.:Instrumental Music, w. D. Ambache (pno)—Concertino in G for English Horn & Orchestra; Sonata in F for Oboe & Piano; Waltz in C for Piano; Il barcaiolo Meridian ▲ CDE 84147

Pols, A. (vl)—see ORCHESTRAS & ENSEMBLES Kuijken Consort

Polson, Arthur (elec vn)
Davies, V.:Pulsations, w. E. Kunzel (cnd), London SO Campion ▲ RRCD 1339 [DDD]

Polson, Arthur (vn)
Davies, V.:Qt 1 Strs, "Fun for 4", w. Mark Ferris (vn), Nancy DiNovo (va), Ian Hampton (vc) Campion ▲ RRCD 1339 [DDD]
Davies, V.:Trio 1 Pno, "Silhouettes", w. Melinda Coffey (pno), Ian Hampton (vc) Campion ▲ RRCD 1339 [DDD]

Pålsson, H. (pno)
Debussy, C.:En blanc et noir, w. A. Malling (pno) *(rec May 11, 1975)* BIS ▲ CD 58 [AAD]

Pomarico, Francesco (E hn)
Villa-Lobos, H.:Qnt en forme de chôros, w. Andrea Griminelli (fl), Pietro Borgonovo (ob), Michele Carulli (cl), Rino Vernizzi (bn) *(rec Chiesa della Misericordia, Torino, Italy, Feb 1987)* Arts Music ▲ 447200-2 [DDD]

Pomarico, Francesco (ob)—see also ORCHESTRAS & ENSEMBLES Arnold Quintet
Cambini, G.M.:Trios Fl, Ob & Bn, w. R. Rivolta (fl), L. Dosso (bn) Stradivarius ▲ STR 33310 [DDD]
Milesi, P.:Modi 1, w. D. Cassamagnaghi (fl), A. Bianchi (cl), L. Dosso (bn), G. Govi (vn), D. Tellini (vn), M. Ravasio (va), S. Righini (vc), P. Rizzi (db), C. Vignani (hpd), J. Scully (perc), P. Milesi (cnd) Cuneiform ▲ RUNE 63

Pommier, Jean-Bernard (pno)
Beethoven, L. van:Sons Pno (comp), Sons. 11-20 Erato 3-▲ 2292-45812-2
Beethoven, L. van:Sons Pno (comp)—Sons. 1-10 Erato 3-▲ 2292-45598-2 [DDD]
Beethoven, L. van:Sons Pno (comp)—Nos. 21-27 Erato 2-▲ 91727
Brahms, J.:Sons Vn (comp), w. J. Laredo (vn) Virgin Classics ▲ CDZ 59642
Chopin, F.:Andante Spianato & Grande Polonaise Erato ▲ 92887-2
Chopin, F.:Polonaise-fant Erato ▲ 92887-2
Chopin, F.:Son Pno, Op. 58 Erato ▲ 92887-2
Chopin, F.:Waltzes Erato ▲ 92887-2
Debussy, C.:Petite suite, w. J.-B. Pommier (cnd), Northern Sinfonia of England Virgin Classics ▲ CDZ 59654
Fauré, G.:Masques et bergamasques (suite), w. J.-B. Pommier (cnd), Northern Sinfonia of England Virgin Classics ▲ CDZ 59654
Mozart, W.A.:Con 21 Pno, w. J.-B. Pommier (cnd), Sinfonia Varsovia Virgin Classics ("Ultraviolet" series) ▲ CUV 61123
Mozart, W.A.:Con 23 Pno, w. J.-B. Pommier (cnd), Sinfonia Varsovia Virgin Classics ("Ultraviolet" series) ▲ CUV 61123
Mozart, W.A.:Con 25 Pno, w. J.-B. Pommier (cnd), Philharmonia Orch *(rec Aldeburgh, Grande Bretagne, Aug. 1992)* Erato ▲ 2292-45999-2
Mozart, W.A.:Con 26 Pno, w. J.-B. Pommier (cnd), Philharmonia Orch *(rec Aldeburgh, Grande Bretagne, Aug. 1992)* Erato ▲ 2292-45999-2
Mozart, W.A.:Fant Pno, K.475 Virgo ▲ CDZ 61101
Rachmaninoff, S.:Con 2 Pno, w. L. Foster (cnd), Hallé Orch Virgin Classics ▲ DCD 59297 [DDD]
Tchaikovsky, P.:Con 1 Pno, w. L. Foster (cnd), Hallé Orch Virgin Classics ▲ CDC 59297 [DDD]

Ponce, Alberto (gtr)
The Guitar in the 20th Century Arion ▲ ARN 68212 [AAD]

Ponce, D. (conga)
Léon, T.:Batéy, w. E. Charlston (perc), J. Passaro (perc), T. Léon (cnd), Western Wind CRI ▲ CD 662 [DDD]

Ponce, Daniel (perc)—see ORCHESTRAS & ENSEMBLES New Generation

Pondepeyre, Angeline (pno)
Bartók, B.:Hungarian Peasant Songs, w. Philippe Pierlot (fl)—Popular Sad Songs; Scherzo; Old Dances [trans Arma for Fl & Pno] *(rec Apr 1992)* Maguelone ▲ 350.501 [DDD]
Encores! Bis!:Works for Double Bass, w. Jean-Marc Rollez (db) Maguelone ▲ 350.507
Hindemith, P.:Son Fl, w. Philippe Pierlot (fl) *(rec Apr 1992)* Maguelone ▲ 350.501 [DDD]
Leguerney, J.:Songs, w. Didier Henry (bar)—7 poèmes de François Maynard; La nuit (3 songs); La solitude (3 songs); Le carnaval (3 songs) [all from St. Amand]; Je vous envoie; Genièvres hérissés; Bel Aubépin; Je me lamente; Au sommeil; Si mille oeillets; A la fontaine Bellerie; Chanson triste; Villanelle; Un voile obscur; Invocation; Comme un qui s'est perdu; Sérénade d'un Barbon; Le Paresseux; L'Insouciant *(rec July 1995)* Maguelone ("Mélodiste francais" series) ▲ MAG 519.232 [DDD]
Martinů, B.:Son Fl & Pno, w. Philippe Pierlot (fl) *(rec Apr 1992)* Maguelone ▲ 350.501 [DDD]
Massenet, J.:Songs, w. Didier Henry (bar), Duo de Paris—Madrigal; Le sentier perdu; Nuit d'Espagne; Narcisse à la fontaine; Un adieu; Si les fleurs avaient des yeux; Sérénade de Zanetto; Puisqu'elle a pris ma vie; Vous aimerez demain; Élégie; A mignonne; La lettre; A colombine; Beaux yeux que j'Aime; Gavotte de Puyjoli; Fleurs cueillies; L'improvisateur; Poème du Souvenir *(rec 1868-1907)* Maguelone ▲ MAG 519.202 [DDD]
Prokofiev, S.:Son Fl, w. Philippe Pierlot (fl) *(rec Apr 1992)* Maguelone ▲ 350.501 [DDD]
Saint-Saëns, C.:Trio 1 Pno, w. Jeanne-Marie Conquer (vn), Philippe Bary (vc) REM ▲ REM 311273 [DDD]
Saint-Saëns, C.:Trio 2 Pno, w. Jeanne-Marie Conquer (vn), Philippe Bary (vc) REM ▲ REM 311273 [DDD]

INSTRUMENT.

Ponder, Michael (va)
Coates, E.:First Meeting, w. Eugene Asti (pno) *(rec St. Silas, London, Jan 25–27, 1994)* Marco Polo ▲ 8.223806 [DDD]

Pongrácz, Péter (ob)
Haydn, J.:Diverts for 2 Obs, Hns & Bns, H.II/7, 15, D18, 23 & deest, w. B. Hock (ob), A. Medveczky (hn), D. Mesterházy (hn), T. Fülemile (bn), A. Nagy (bn) White Label ▲ HRC 155 [ADD]
Kocsár, M.:Episodi, w. M. Kocsár (cnd), Franz Liszt CO Hungaroton ▲ HCD 31188 [DDD]

Ponomarev, Viocheslav (vc)
Fauré, G.:Élégie, w. E. Bátiz (cnd), Mexico City PO ASV ▲ ASV 686

Ponseele, Marcel (ob)
Bach, J.S.:Cant 49, w. N. Argenta (sop), K. Mertens (bass), S. Kuijken (vn), H. Suzuki (vc), P. Hantaï (org), La Petite Bande Accent ▲ ACC 9395 D [DDD]
Bach, J.S.:Cant 58, w. N. Argenta (sop), K. Mertens (bass), S. Kuijken (vn), H. Suzuki (vc), P. Hantaï (org), La Petite Bande Accent ▲ ACC 9395 D [DDD]
Bach, J.S.:Cant 82, w. N. Argenta (sop), K. Mertens (bass), S. Kuijken (vn), H. Suzuki (vc), P. Hantaï (org), La Petite Bande Accent ▲ ACC 9395 D [DDD]
Telemann, G.P.:Con Tpt 2 Obs, w. Per-Olev Lindeke (tpt), Taka Kitazato (ob), Fred Jacobs (thb), Richte Van Der Meer (vc), Pierre Hantaï (hpd) *(rec St. Stefanus, Melsen, Belgium, June 1995)* Accent ▲ 95110 [DDD]
Telemann, G.P.:Essercizii musici (sels), w. Taka Kitazato (ob), Pierre Hantaï (hpd), Per-Olev Lindeke (tpt), Fred Jacobs (thb), Richte Van Der Meer (vc)—Trio Son in E♭ for Ob, Hpd & Continuo *(rec St. Stefanus, Melsen, Belgium, June 1995)* Accent ▲ 95110 [DDD]
Telemann, G.P.:Der Getreue Music-Meister (sels), w. Taka Kitazato (ob), Per-Olev Lindeke (tpt), Fred Jacobs (thb), Richte Van Der Meer (vc), Pierre Hantaï (hpd)—Son in a *(rec St. Stefanus, Melsen, Belgium, June 1995)* Accent ▲ 95110 [DDD]
Telemann, G.P.:Kleine Kammermusik, w. Taka Kitazato (ob), Per-Olev Lindeke (tpt), Fred Jacobs (thb), Richte Van Der Meer (vc), Pierre Hantaï (hpd)—Partita IV in g *(rec St. Stefanus, Melsen, Belgium, June 1995)* Accent ▲ 95110 [DDD]
Telemann, G.P.:Musique de Table, w. Taka Kitazato (ob), Per-Olev Lindeke (tpt), Fred Jacobs (thb), Richte Van Der Meer (vc), Pierre Hantaï (hpd)—Son in g *(rec St. Stefanus, Melsen, Belgium, June 1995)* Accent ▲ 95110 [DDD]
Telemann, G.P.:Son 2 Ob, w. Taka Kitazato (ob), Per-Olev Lindeke (tpt), Fred Jacobs (thb), Richte Van Der Meer (vc), Pierre Hantaï (hpd) *(rec St. Stefanus, Melsen, Belgium, June 1995)* Accent ▲ 95110 [DDD]

Ponti, Michael (pno)
Albert, E. d':Con 2 Pno, w. P. Cao (cnd), Luxembourg RSO *(rec 1973)* Vox Box 2-▲ CDX 5067 [ADD]
Balakirev, M.:Con 2 Pno, w. S. Landau (cnd), Westphalia SO Recklinghausen *(rec 1975)* Vox Box 2-▲ CDX 5068 [ADD]
Brassin, L.:Magic Fire Music from *Die Walküre* *(rec ca. 1973)* Vox Box 2-▲ CDX 5047 [ADD]
Bronsart von Schellendorf, H.:Con Pno, w. R. Kapp (cnd), Westphalia SO Recklinghausen *(rec 1972)* Vox Box 2-▲ CDX 5067 [ADD]
Chopin, F.:Allegro de concert, w. V. Schmidt-Gertenbach (cnd), Berlin SO *(rec 1978)* Vox Box 2-▲ CDX 5064 [ADD]
Goetz, H.:Con 2 Pno, w. P. Cao (cnd), Luxembourg RSO *(rec 1973)* Vox Box 2-▲ CDX 5068 [ADD]
Grainger, P.:Paraphrase on Tchaikovsky's "Waltz of the Flowers" *(rec ca. 1973)* Vox Box 2-▲ CDX 5047 [ADD]
Henselt, A. von:Con Pno, w. O. Maga (cnd), Philharmonia Hungarica *(rec 1968)* Vox Box 2-▲ CDX 5064 [ADD]
Liapunov, S.:Rhap on Ukranian Themes, w. S. Landau (cnd), Westphalia SO *(rec 1975)* Vox Box 2-▲ CDX 5068 [ADD]
Liszt, F.:Malédiction, w. P. Angerer (cnd), Southwest German CO Pforzheim *(rec 1978)* Vox Box 2-▲ CDX 5067 [ADD]
Liszt, F.:Operatic Paraphrases & Transcriptions—Mozart:Réminiscences de Don Juan from "Don Giovanni"; Tchaikovsky:Polonaise from "Eugen Onegin"; Verdi:Concert Paraphrase on the Quartet from "Rigoletto"; Wagner:Festspiel und Brautlied from "Lohengrin:" *(rec ca. 1973)* Vox Box 2-▲ CDX 5047 [ADD]
Litolff, H.C.:Con Symphonique 3, w. V. Schmidt-Gertenbach (cnd), Berlin SO *(rec 1978)* Vox Box 2-▲ CDX 5065 [ADD]
Medtner, N.:Con 3 Pno, w. P. Cao (cnd), Luxembourg RSO *(rec 1973)* Vox Box 2-▲ CDX 5068 [ADD]
Melcer, H.:Con 1 Pno, w. T. Strugala (cnd), Warsaw PO Olympia ▲ OLY 398 [DDD]
Mendelssohn, F.:Capriccio brillante, w. V. Schmidt-Gertenbach (cnd), Berlin SO *(rec 1978)* Vox Box 2-▲ CDX 5065 [ADD]
Moscheles, I.:Con 3 Pno, w. O. Maga (cnd), Philharmonia Hungarica *(rec 1968)* Vox Box 2-▲ CDX 5065 [ADD]
Moszkowski, M.:Con Pno, w. H. R. Stracke (cnd), Philharmonia Hungarica *(rec 1969)* Vox Box 2-▲ CDX 5066 [ADD]
Moszkowski, M.:Operatic Paraphrases & Trans—Bizet:Danse Bohème after "Carmen"; Offenbach:Barcarolle from "Tales of Hoffmann"; Wagner:Isolde's Death from "Tristan und Isolde," & Venusberg Bachanale, Paraphrase for Piano after Music of Wagner *(rec ca. 1973)* Vox Box 2-▲ CDX 5047 [ADD]
Operatic Piano, w. Ponti, Michael (pno) *(rec 1970–75)* Vox Box 2-▲ CDX 5047 [ADD]
Pabst, P.:Concert Paraphrase on Tchaikovsky's *Eugen Onegin* *(rec ca. 1973)* Vox Box 2-▲ CDX 5047 [ADD]
Rachmaninoff, S.:Suite 1 for 2 Pnos, w. R. Leonardi (pno) Allegretto ▲ ACD 8162 [ADD] ■ ACS 8162
Rachmaninoff, S.:Suite 2 for 2 Pnos, w. R. Leonardi (pno) Allegretto ▲ ACD 8162 [ADD] ■ ACS 8162
Raff, J.:Con Pno, w. R. Kapp (cnd), Hamburg SO *(rec 1973)* Vox Box 2-▲ CDX 5067 [ADD]
Reinecke, C.:Cons Pno, w. P. Cao (nd), Luxembourg RSO—No. 1 *(rec. 1973)* Vox Box 2-▲ CDX 5065 [ADD]
Rheinberger, J.:Con Pno, w. V. Schmidt-Gertenbach (cnd), Berlin SO *(rec 1978)* Vox Box 2-▲ CDX 5065 [ADD]
Rimsky-Korsakov, N.:Con Pno, w. R. Kapp (cnd), Hamburg SO Vox Box 2-▲ CDX 5082 [ADD]
Rubinstein, A.:Con 4 Pno, w. O. Maga (cnd), Philharmonia Hungarica *(rec 1968)* Vox Box 2-▲ CDX 5066 [ADD]
Scharwenka, X.:Con 2 Pno, w. O. Maga (cnd), Philharmonia Hungarica *(rec 1972)* Vox Box 2-▲ CDX 5066 [ADD]
Scriabin, A.:Con Pno, w. H. Drewanz (cnd), Hamburg SO Allegretto ▲ ACD 8170 [ADD] ■ ACS 8170
Tausig, C.:Fant on Themes of Moniuszko's "Halka" *(rec ca. 1973)* Vox Box 2-▲ CDX 5047 [ADD]
Tausig, C.:Trans & Arr—Ride of the Valkyries [Wagner] *(rec ca. 1973)* Vox Box 2-▲ CDX 5047 [ADD]
Tchaikovsky, P.:Album pour enfants Vox Box 2-▲ CDX 5087 [ADD]
Tchaikovsky, P.:Concert Fant, w. R. Kapp (cnd), Prague SO Vox Box 2-▲ CDX 5024 [ADD]
Tchaikovsky, P.:Con 1 Pno, w. R. Kapp (cnd), Prague SO Vox Box 2-▲ CDX 5024 [ADD]
Tchaikovsky, P.:Con 2 Pno, w. R. Kapp (cnd), Prague SO Vox Box 2-▲ CDX 5024 [ADD]
Tchaikovsky, P.:Con 3 Pno, w. L. de Froment (cnd), Luxembourg RSO Vox Box 2-▲ CDX 5024 [ADD]
Tchaikovsky, P.:Pno Music—Scherzo à la russe, Op. 1/1; Impromptu, Op. 1/2; Ruines d'un chateau, Op. 2/1; Scherzo, Op. 2/2; Song without Words, Op. 2/3; Valse caprice, Op. 4; Romanze, Op. 5; Capriccio, Op. 8; Rêverie, Op. 9/1; Polka de salon, Op. 9/2; Mazurka de salon, Op. 9/3; Nocturne, Op. 10/1; Humoresque, Op. 10/2; Dumka, Op. 59; 5 Pieces without Opus Nos.; Valse Scherzo, Op. 7; Rêverie du soir, Op. 19/1; Scherzo humoristique, Op. 19/2; Feuillet d'album, Op. 19/3; Nocturne, Op. 19/4; Capriccioso, Op. 19/5; Theme & Variations, Op. 19/6; 6 Pieces on 1 Theme, Op. 21; 12 Etudes, Op. 40 Vox Box 3-▲ CD3X 3025 [ADD]
Tchaikovsky, P.:Pno Music—6 Pieces, Op. 51; 18 Pieces, Op. 72 Vox Box 2-▲ CDX 5087 [ADD]
Tchaikovsky, P.:Les Saisons Vox Box 2-▲ CDX 5087 [ADD]
Tchaikovsky, P.:Son Pno, Op. 37 Vox Box 3-▲ CD3X 3025 [ADD]
Tchaikovsky, P.:Son Pno, Op. 80 Vox Box 2-▲ CDX 5087 [ADD]
Thalberg, S.:Con Pno, w. R. Kapp (cnd), Westphalia SO *(rec 1973)* Vox Box 2-▲ CDX 5066 [ADD]

Ponti, Michael (pno) (cont.)
Thalberg, S.:Fants & Vars on Opera Themes—on Meyerbeer's Les Huguenots, Op. 20 & Robert le Diable, Op. 6 Vox Box 2-▲ CDX 5047 [ADD]

Pöntinen, Roland (pno)
Amirov, F.:Pieces (6) Fl, w. M. Wiesler (fl) BIS ▲ CD 419 [DDD]
Arban, J.-B.:Vars on a Theme from Bellini's *Norma*, w. H. Hardenberger (cnt) BIS ▲ CD 287 [DDD]
Bäck, S.-E.:Pno Music—Expansive Preludes (1949); Impromptu (1959); The Professor's Unfinished (1972); Sonata alla ricercare (1950); Sonata in Two Movements & Epilogue (1984) BIS ▲ CD 354 [DDD]
Beethoven, L. van:Bagatelles (24)—Op. 126 BIS ▲ CD 353 [DDD]
Beethoven, L. van:Son 12 Pno, "Funeral March" BIS ▲ CD 353 [DDD]
Beethoven, L. van:Vars & Fugue Pno, Op. 35, "Eroica" BIS ▲ CD 353 [DDD]
The Burlesque Trombone & Romantic Trombone Concertos, w. Christian Lindberg (trbn), Bamberg SO [cnd:Leif Segerstam] BIS ("BIS Twins" series) 2-▲ 318/378
Chopin, F.:Ballades Pno (comp)—No. 2 in F, Op. 38 *(rec Musikaliska Akademien, Stockholm, Sweden, Apr 19–22, 1995)* BIS ▲ CD 673 [DDD]
Chopin, F.:Barcarolle Pno *(rec Musikaliska Akademien, Stockholm, Sweden, Apr 19–22, 1995)* BIS ▲ CD 673 [DDD]
Chopin, F.:Bolero *(rec Musikaliska Akademien, Stockholm, Sweden, Apr 19–22, 1995)* BIS ▲ CD 673 [DDD]
Chopin, F.:Mazurkas—Opp. 30/3, 33/4, 56/1-3 & Op. posth. 68/4 *(rec Musikaliska Akademien, Stockholm, Sweden, Apr 19–22, 1995)* BIS ▲ CD 673 [DDD]
Chopin, F.:Nocturnes—Op. 62/1 & 2 *(rec Musikaliska Akademien, Stockholm, Sweden, Apr 19–22, 1995)* BIS ▲ CD 673 [DDD]
Chopin, F.:Scherzos—No. 4 in E, Op. 54 *(rec Musikaliska Akademien, Stockholm, Sweden, Apr 19–22, 1995)* BIS ▲ CD 673 [DDD]
The Criminal Trombone, w. Christian Lindberg (trbn) BIS ▲ CD 328
Davies, P.M.:Son Tpt, w. H. Hardenberger (tpt) BIS ▲ CD 287 [DDD]
Denisov, E.:Pieces (4) Fl, w. M. Wiesler (fl) BIS ▲ CD 419 [DDD]
Denisov, E.:Son Fl, w. M. Wiesler (fl) BIS ▲ CD 419 [DDD]
Evocation:Legendary Encores Played by Roland Pöntinen, w. Pöntinen, Roland (pno) *(rec Gamla Musikaliska Akademi, Stockholm, Sweden, May 31 & June 1–3, 1994)* BIS ▲ CD 661 [DDD]
Françaix, J.:Sonatine Tpt & Pno, w. H. Hardenberger (tpt) BIS ▲ CD 287 [DDD]
Glinka, M.:Son Va, w. N. Imai (va) BIS ▲ CD 358
Grieg, E.:Con Pno, Op. 16, w. L. Segerstam (cnd), Bamberg SO BIS ▲ CD 375
Grieg, E.:Con Pno, Op. 16, w. L. Segerstam (cnd), Bamberg SO BIS ("BIS Twins" series) 2-▲ CD 375/381
Grieg, E.:Sons Vn, Opp. 8, 13 & 45, w. D.-S. Kang (vn) *(rec Sept. 14–16, 1993)* BIS ▲ CD 647 [DDD]
Hartmann, J.:Vars on Rule Britannia, w. Håkan Hardenberger (tpt) BIS ▲ CD 287 [DDD]
Hindemith, P.:Meditation, w. N. Imai (va) *(rec Oct. 7–9, 1993)* BIS ▲ CD 651 [DDD]
Hindemith, P.:Son Trbn, w. C. Lindberg (trbn) *(rec Nacka, Sweden, Nov. 12, 1983)* BIS ▲ CD 159 [DDD]
Hindemith, P.:Son Trbn, w. C. Lindberg (trbn) BIS ▲ CD 258 [DDD]
Hindemith, P.:Sons Va, w. N. Imai (va)—Op. 11/5 (1919); Op. 25/1 (1922); Op. 31/4 (1924); Sonata (1937) *(rec Oct. 7–9, 1993)* BIS ▲ CD 651 [DDD]
Hindemith, P.:Son in C Vn & Pno, w. Ulf Wallin (vn) *(rec Musikaliska Akademien, Stockholm, Sweden, Aug 22–25, 1995)* BIS ▲ CD 761 [DDD]
Hindemith, P.:Son in E Vn & Pno, w. Ulf Wallin (vn) *(rec Musikaliska Akademien, Stockholm, Sweden, Aug 22–25, 1995)* BIS ▲ CD 761 [DDD]
Hindemith, P.:Son Vn & Pno, Op. 11/1, w. Ulf Wallin (vn)—complete son & fragment of a finale *(rec Musikaliska Akademien, Stockholm, Sweden, Aug 22–25, 1995)* BIS ▲ CD 761 [DDD]
Hindemith, P.:Son Vn & Pno, Op. 11/2, w. Ulf Wallin (vn) *(rec Musikaliska Akademien, Stockholm, Sweden, Aug 22–25, 1995)* BIS ▲ CD 761 [DDD]
Honegger, A.:Intrada Tpt & Pno, w. H. Hardenberger (tpt) BIS ▲ CD 287 [DDD]
Janáček, L.:Pno Music—Son. in e♭; On an Overgrown Path; In the Mists; Tema con variazioni; 3 Moravian Dances; Reminiscence *(rec Dec. 6–8, 1993)* BIS 2-▲ CD 663/64 [DDD]
Jolivet, A.:Chant de Linos, w. M. Wiesler (fl) *(rec Mar. 1992)* BIS ▲ CD 549 [DDD]
Jolivet, A.:Fl Music (comp), w. Manuela Wiesler (fl), Erica Goodman (hp), Patrik Swedrup (vn), Håkan Olsson (va), Helena Nilsson (vc), Christian Davidsson (bn), P. Järvi (cnd), Tapiola Sinfonietta, Kroumata Percussion Ensemble—Alla rustica for Fl & Hp; Chant de Linos for Fl, Hp & Str Trio; Pastorales de Noël for Fl, Bn & Hp; Con for Fl & Strs; Suite en concert for Fl & 4 Perc Players; Fant-Caprice for Fl & Pno; Cabrioles for Fl & Pno *(rec Danderyd Grammar School, Sweden, Tapiola Hall, Tapiola, Finland, Gothenburg Concert Hall, Sweden & Studio 2, Radiohuset, Stockholm, Sweden, June 21–22, 1995)* BIS ▲ CD 739 [DDD]
Jolivet, A.:Son Fl, w. M. Wiesler (fl) *(rec Mar. 1992)* BIS ▲ CD 549 [DDD]
Larsson, M.:Clockworks, w. Love Derwinger (pno), Johan Silvmark (perc), Stockholm Chamber Brass *(rec Studio 2, Swedish Radio, Nov. 13, 1994)* BIS ▲ CD 699 [DDD]
Martin, F.:Ballade Trbn (or T Sax), w. Christian Lindberg (trbn) *(rec Nacka Aula, Nacka, Sweden, Nov 11, 1983)* BIS ▲ CD 71 [DDD]
Mendelssohn, Fanny:Songs, w. Christina Högman (sop)—Die frühen Gräber; Die Mainacht; Italien; Fichtenbaum und Palme; Verlust; Warum sind denn die Rosen so blass; Dämmrung senkte sich von oben; Nach Süden; Vorwurf; Bergeslust *(rec Musikaliska Akademien, Stockholm, Sweden, May 24–27, 1995)* BIS ▲ CD 738 [DDD]
Mendelssohn, F.:Cons (2) for 2 Pnos, w. Love Derwinger (pno), L. Markiz (cnd), Amsterdam New Sinfonietta *(rec Concertgebouw, Haarlem, Holland, Sept 20–22, 1994)* BIS ▲ CD 688 [DDD]
Mozart, W.A.:Andantino Vc, w. H. Ruijsenaars (vc) Canal Grande ▲ CCS 9325 [DDD]
Music for a Rainy Day BIS ▲ CD 300 [DDD]
Orff, C.:Carmina burana, w. Lena Nordin (sop), Hans Dornbusch (ten), Peter Mattei (bar), Love Derwinger (pno), Kroumata Percussion Ensemble, Cecilia Rydinger Alin (cnd), Allmänna Sången, Uppsala Choir School Children's Chorus [chamber version] *(rec Uppsala Univ Hall, Uppsala, Sweden, June 9–11, 1995)* BIS ▲ CD 734 [DDD]
Poulenc, F.:Capriccio Pnos, w. L. Derwinger (pno) *(rec Apr. 1–2, 1993)* BIS ▲ CD 593 [DDD]
Poulenc, F.:Con for 2 Pnos, w. L. Derwinger (pno), O. Vänskä (cnd), Malmö SO *(rec Nov. 6–7, 1992)* BIS ▲ CD 593 [DDD]
Poulenc, F.:Élégie Pnos, w. L. Derwinger (pno) *(rec Apr. 1–2, 1993)* BIS ▲ CD 593 [DDD]
Poulenc, F.:L'Embarquement pour Cythère, w. L. Derwinger (pno) *(rec Apr 1–2, 1993)* BIS ▲ CD 593 [DDD]
Poulenc, F.:Son Pno 4-Hands, w. L. Derwinger (pno) *(rec Apr. 1–2, 1993)* BIS ▲ CD 593 [DDD]
Poulenc, F.:Son for 2 Pnos, w. L. Derwinger (pno) *(rec Apr. 1–2, 1993)* BIS ▲ CD 593 [DDD]
Prokofiev, S.:Son Vc, w. T. Thedéen (vc) BIS ▲ CD 386 [DDD]
Prokofiev, S.:Son Fl, w. M. Wiesler (fl) BIS ▲ CD 419 [DDD]
Rachmaninoff, S.:Son Vc, w. T. Thedéen (vc) BIS ▲ CD 386 [DDD]
The Romantic Trombone, w. Lindberg, Christian (trbn) BIS ▲ CD 298
Rubinstein, A.:Nocturne, w. N. Imai (va) BIS ▲ CD 358
Russian Cello Music, w. Torleif Thedeen (vc) BIS ▲ CD 336
The Russian Trombone, w. Christian Lindberg (trbn) BIS ▲ CD 478 [DDD]
Satie, E.:Avant-dernières pensées BIS ▲ CD 317 [DDD]
Satie, E.:Embryons desséchés BIS ▲ CD 317 [DDD]
Satie, E.:Gnossiennes Pno—Nos. 1–6 BIS ▲ CD 317 [DDD]
Satie, E.:Gymnopédies BIS ▲ CD 317 [DDD]
Satie, E.:Pièces froides BIS ▲ CD 317 [DDD]
Satie, E.:Sarabandes Pno—No. 3 BIS ▲ CD 317 [DDD]
Satie, E.:Sonatine bureaucratique BIS ▲ CD 317 [DDD]
Satie, E.:Valses (3) du précieux dégoûté BIS ▲ CD 317 [DDD]
Satie, E.:Véritables préludes flasques BIS ▲ CD 317 [DDD]
Schnittke, A.:Con Pno, w. L. Markiz (cnd), New Stockholm CO BIS ▲ CD 377 [DDD]
Schnittke, A.:Gratulationsrondo, w. U. Wallin (vn) BIS ▲ CD 527 [DDD]
Schnittke, A.:Qt Pno, w. Tale String Quartet members BIS ▲ CD 547 [DDD]

▲ = CD ♦ = Enhanced CD Δ = MD ■ = Cassette Tape □ = DCC

Pöntinen, Roland (pno) (cont.)
Schnittke, A.:Qnt Pno, w. Tale String Quartet BIS ▲ CD 547 [DDD]
Schnittke, A.:Son 1 Vn, w. C. Bergqvist (vn) BIS ▲ CD 364 [DDD]
Schnittke, A.:Son 1 Vn, w. U. Wallin (vn) BIS ▲ CD 527 [DDD]
Schnittke, A.:Son 2 Vn, w. U. Wallin (vn) BIS ▲ CD 527 [DDD]
Schnittke, A.:Stille Nacht, w. U. Wallin (vn) BIS ▲ CD 527 [DDD]
Schnittke, A.:Suite in the Old Style, w. U. Wallin (vn) BIS ▲ CD 527 [DDD]
Schubert, Franz:Son Arpeggione, w. H. Ruijsenaars (vc) Canal Grande ▲ CCS 9325 [DDD]
Schumann, C.:Songs, w. Christina Högman (sop)—Am Strande; Sie liebten sich beide; Beim Abschied; Er ist gekommen in Sturm und Regen; Liebst du um Schönheit; Warum willst du and're fragen; Die gute Nacht, die ich dir sage; Lorelei; Geheimes Flüstern hier und dort; O Lust, o Lust *(rec Musikaliska Akademien, Stockholm, Sweden, May 24–27, 1995)* BIS ▲ CD 738 [DDD]
Schumann, R.:Adagio & Allegro Hn, w. H. Ruijsenaars (vc) Canal Grande ▲ CCS 9325 [DDD]
Schumann, R.:Fantasiestücke Cl, w. H. Ruijsenaars (vc) Canal Grande ▲ CCS 9325 [DDD]
Scriabin, A.:Con Pno, w. L. Segerstam (cnd), Stockholm PO BIS ▲ CD 475 [DDD]
Scriabin, A.:Pno Music (misc), w. Dag Achatz (pno)—Études, Opp. 2/1, 8/12 & 42/3; Mazurka, Op. 3/3; Préludes, Opp. 16/4, 27/2 & 48/4; Feuillet d'album, Op. 45/1; Danse languide, Op. 51/4; Nuances, Op. 56/3; Désir, Op. 57/1; Caresse dansée, Op. 57/2; Poèmes, Op. 69/1 & 2; Vers la flamme, Op. 72; Sons Nos. 5, 7, 9 & 10 *(rec Nacka Aula, Nacka, Sweden & Danderyd Grammer School, Sweden, Aug 14–15, 1978)* BIS ▲ CD 119 [AAD/DDD]
Scriabin, A.:Son 7 Pno BIS ▲ CD 276 [DDD]
Shostakovich, D.:Son Va, w. N. Imai (va) BIS ▲ CD 358
Shostakovich, D.:Son Vn, w. C. Bergqvist (vn) BIS ▲ CD 364 [DDD]
Stravinsky, I.:Duo Concertant, w. C. Bergqvist (vn)—"Dithyramb" section BIS ▲ CD 364 [DDD]
Stravinsky, I.:Scenes Pno BIS ▲ CD 188 [DDD]
Stravinsky, I.:Scenes Pno BIS ▲ CD 276 [DDD]
Taktakishvili, O.:Son Fl, w. M. Wiesler (fl) BIS ▲ CD 419 [DDD]
Tchaikovsky, P.:Con 1 Pno, w. L. Segerstam (cnd), Bamberg SO BIS ▲ CD 375
Tchaikovsky, P.:Con 1 Pno, w. L. Segerstam (cnd), Bamberg SO BIS ("BIS Twins" series) 2-▲ CD 375/381
Tisné, A.:Héraldiques, w. H. Hardenberger (tpt) BIS ▲ CD 287 [DDD]
Tubin, E.:Ballade in the form of a Chaconne on a theme of Mart Saar BIS ▲ CD 269 [AAD]
Tubin, E.:Concertino Pno, w. N. Järvi (cnd), Gothenburg SO BIS ▲ CD 401 [DDD]
Tubin, E.:Son A Sax, w. Pekka Savijoki (a sax) BIS ▲ CD 269 [AAD]
Tubin, E.:Son Vn, w. Nils-Erik Sparf (vn) BIS ▲ CD 269 [AAD]
Viola Bouquet, w. Nobuko Imai (va) Philips ▲ 446 103-2
The Virtuoso Trombone, w. Christian Lindberg (trbn) BIS ▲ CD 258
The Virtuoso Trumpet, w. Hakan Hardenberger (tpt) BIS ▲ CD 287 [DDD]
Werfel, A.M.:Songs, w. Christina Högman (sop)—Licht in der Nacht; Waldseligkeit; Ansturm; Erntelied; Laue Sommernacht; Ich wandle unter Blumen; Der Erkennende; Lobgesang *(rec Musikaliska Akademien, Stockholm, Sweden, May 24–27, 1995)* BIS ▲ CD 738 [DDD]

Pontremoli, Anita (pno)
Bacewicz, G.:Son 4 Vn & Pno, w. T. Pontremoli (vn) Centaur ▲ CRC 2119
Beach, A.M.C.:Son Vn, w. T. Pontremoli (vn) Centaur ▲ CRC 2119

Pontremoli, Terri (vn)
Bacewicz, G.:Son 4 Vn & Pno, w. A. Pontremoli (pno) Centaur ▲ CRC 2119
Beach, A.M.C.:Son Vn, w. A. Pontremoli (pno) Centaur ▲ CRC 2119

Popa, Aurelian Octav (cl)
Haydn, M.:Con Fl, P.54, w. A. O. Popa (cnd), Quodlibet Musicum CO Olympia ("Explorer" series) ▲ OCD 406 [AAD]
Mozart, W.A.:Con Cl, w. M. Cristescu (cnd), Bucharest George Enescu PO *(rec 1971)* Electrecord ▲ ELCD 108 [AAD]
Weber, C.M. von:Con 1 Cl, w. M. Cristescu (cnd), Bucharest George Enescu PO *(rec 1971)* Electrecord ▲ ELCD 108 [AAD]
Weber, C.M. von:Con 2 Cl, w. M. Cristescu (cnd), Bucharest George Enescu PO *(rec 1971)* Electrecord ▲ ELCD 108 [AAD]

Popa, Edouard (vn)
Mendelssohn, Fanny:Trio Pno, w. R. Maillard (vc), F. Tillard (pno) *(rec June 16–19, 1992)* Opus 111 ▲ OPS 30-71

Popa, Péter (vn)
Beethoven, L. van:Sxt Hns, Op. 81b, w. Jenő Keveházi (hn), János Keveházi (hn), Ildikó Hegyi (vn), Győző Máthé (va), Péter Szabó (vc) *(rec Scottish Church, Budapest)* Naxos ▲ 8.553090 [DDD]

Poparic, Ivana (vc)
Maric, L.:Archaia, w. Julija Hartig (vn), Hans Rijkmans (va) Emergo ▲ EC 3951 [DDD]

Pope, Kathy (cl)
Babin, V.:Hillandale Waltzes, w. Jed Moss (pno) Pope ▲ CD 001
Bach, J.S.:Chromatic Fant & Fugue, w. Jed Moss (pno) [arr G. Langenus for cl & pno] Pope ▲ CD 001
Bach, J.S.:Sons Fl, BWV 1030–35, w. Jed Moss (pno) [arr Ulmar Gateau for cl & pno] Pope ▲ CD 001
Giampieri, A.:Il Carnevale di Venezia, w. Jed Moss (pno) [trans for cl & pno] Pope ▲ CD 001
Harvey, P.:Suite on Themes of Gershwin, w. Jed Moss (pno) Pope ▲ CD 001
Osborne, W.:Rhap Bn Pope ▲ CD 001

Popejoy, James (perc)
Veeneman, C.:The Wiry Concord, w. Susan Werner (banjo), Forrest Covington (hammered dlc/cimbalom), Georganne Assat (hp), Donald Martin Jenni (hpd), Mark Johnson (hpd), Barbara Phillips Farley (pno), James Austin (pno), Marta Soderberg (va), James Knutson (perc), Patrick Doyle (perc), Steven Butters (perc), M. Geary (cnd) Capstone ▲ SCI 6

Popelka, Josef (org)
Bach, J.S.:A Musical Offering Panton ▲ PAN 810750

Popescu, René Cristian (vn)
5 Centuries of German Music in Transylvania, w. H. Andreescu (cnd), Bucharest Virtuosi, Georgeta Stoleriu (sop), Adrian Petrescu (ob), Gabriel Bala (va), Stefan Thomasz (db), Nicolae Licaret (hpd) Electrecord ▲ ELC EDC 168 [DDD]

Popkov, Igor (vn)—see ORCHESTRAS & ENSEMBLES Baroque Chamber Ensemble

Pople, Ross (vn)
Franck, C.:Son Vn, w. P. Rogé (pno) [cello & piano trans.] ASV ▲ ASV 769 [DDD]

Popov, Alexander (bn)
Mosolov, A.:Pieces Bn, w. Victor Yampolsky (pno) *(rec Mosfilm Studio, Jan 1995)* Triton ▲ 17004 [DDD]

Popov, Nicolai (pno)
Honegger, A.:Sonatina Cl, w. W. Grund (cl) Gallo ▲ CD 573 [DAD]
Milhaud, D.:Caprice, w. W. Grund (cl) Gallo ▲ CD 573 [DAD]
Milhaud, D.:Duo concertante Cl & Pno, w. W. Grund (cl) Gallo ▲ CD 573 [DAD]
Milhaud, D.:Sonatina Cl, w. W. Grund (cl) Gallo ▲ CD 573 [DAD]
Poulenc, F.:Son Cl Pno, w. W. Grund (cl) Gallo ▲ CD 573 [DAD]
Tailleferre, G.:Arabesque, w. W. Grund (cl) Gallo ▲ CD 573 [DAD]

Popov, Valeri (bn)—see also ORCHESTRAS & ENSEMBLES Moscow Contemporary Music Ensemble
Gagnidze, M.:Trio Bn, w. Moscow Contemporary Music Ensemble members Olympia ▲ OLY 297 [DDD]
Gubaidulina, S.:Quasi hoquetus, w. Moscow Contemporary Music Ensemble members Olympia ▲ OLY 297 [DDD]
Vustin, A.:The Weeping Olympia ▲ OCD 282 [DDD]

Popova, Evgenia-Maria (vn)
Ysaÿe, E.:Sons Vn *(rec 9/91)* Léman Classics ▲ LC 42901 [DDD]

Popp, M. (ud/fl/shawm/fid)—see ORCHESTRAS & ENSEMBLES Estampie

Poppen, Christoph (vn)
Messiaen, O.:Quatuor pour la fin du temps, w. Wolfgang Meyer (cl), M. Fischer-Dieskau (vc), Y. Loriod (pno) EMI Classics ▲ CDC 54395
Penderecki, K.:Qt Cl, w. Sharon Kam (cl), Kim Kashkashian (va), Boris Pergamenschikov (vc) *(rec National Philharmonic Hall, Warsaw, Poland, Nov. 23, 1993)* Sony Classical ▲ SK 66284 [DDD]

Poppen, Diemuth (va)
Brahms, J.:Qt 1 Pno, w. Vassily Lobanov (pno), Oleg Kagan (vn), Natalia Gutman (vc) *(rec Chamber Music Festival Kuhmo, Finland, July, 19, 1989)* Live Classics ▲ LCL 124 [DDD]

Poppen, Irmgard (vc)
Bach, J.S.:Cant 203, w. Dietrich Fischer-Dieskau (bar), Aurèle Nicolet (fl), Helmut Keller (vn), Edith Picht-Axenfeld (hpd) EMI Classics ("Baroque" series) ▲ CDK 65729
Telemann, G.P.:Cants, w. Dietrich Fischer-Dieskau (bar), Aurèle Nicolet (fl), Helmut Keller (vn), Edith Picht-Axenfeld (hpd)—Die Hoffnung ist mein Leben EMI Classics ("Baroque" series) ▲ CDK 65729

Porcaro, Joe (perc)
Kellaway, R.:Music of, w. Roger Kellaway (pno/perc), Fred Seykora (vc), Chuck Domanico (elec b), Emil Richards (mar/perc), Bob Zimmitti (perc)—Thinking of You; Un canto per la pace [A Song for Peace]; Love of my Life; Eleventide; In My Heart; Eve; Windows; Winter [Parts 1–3] *(rec Ocean Way Recording Studio, Los Angeles, CA, May 1–5, 1993)* EMI Classics ▲ CDC 54903 [DDD]
Kellaway, R.:Music of, w. Fred Seykora (vc), Chuck Domanico (electric bass), Roger Kellaway (pno/perc), Emil Richards (mar/perc), Bob Zimmitti (perc)—Thinking of You; Un canto per la pace [A Song for Peace]; Love of my Life; Eleventide; In My Heart; Eve; Windows; Winter [Parts 1–3] *(rec Ocean Way Recording Studio, Los Angeles, CA, May 1–5, 1993)* Angel ▲ CDC 54903 [DDD]
Roccisano, J.:Sonorities, w. V. Morosco (sax), F. Seykora (vc) Protone ■ CSPR 153

Porgy, Pascal (hn)
Bryars, G.:Three Viennese Dances, w. Charles Fullbrook (perc), Arditti String Quartet ECM New Series ▲ 78118-21323-2 [DDD]

Poroshina, Inna (pno)
Liadov, A.:Pno Music—Mazurkas, Opp. 11/3, 15/2, 31/1, 42 & 57/3; Bagatelles, Opp. 30 & 53/1–3; Preludes, Opp. 10/1, 11/1, 13/1, 27/2, 33/1 & 40/3 *(rec Kiev, Ukraine, Nov 1–4, 1994)* ESS.A.Y ▲ ESS 1045 [DDD]
Liadov, A.:Pieces Pno, Op. 64 *(rec Kiev, Ukraine, Nov 1–4, 1994)* ESS.A.Y ▲ ESS 1045 [DDD]
Liadov, A.:Preludes, Op. 46 *(rec Kiev, Ukraine, Nov 1–4, 1994)* ESS.A.Y ▲ ESS 1045 [DDD]
Liadov, A.:Spillikins *(rec Kiev, Ukraine, Nov 1–4, 1994)* ESS.A.Y ▲ ESS 1045 [DDD]

Porroni, R. (gtr)
Paganini, N.:Con 6 Vn, w. R. Ricci (vn) [original version]—Adagio [cadenza Ricci] One-Eleven ▲ URS 93020 [ADD]

Portal, Michel (cl)
Boulez, P.:Domaines (Parts 1 & 2), w. D. Masson (cnd), Musique Vivante Ensemble Musique d'Abord ▲ HMA 190930 [ADD]
Brahms, J.:Qnt Cl, w. Melos String Quartet Harmonia Mundi France ▲ HMC 901349
Brahms, J.:Sons Cl (comp), w. G. Pludermacher (pno) Harmonia Mundi France ▲ HMC 90904
Poulenc, F.:Sxt Pno, w. P. Rogé (pno), P. Gallois (fl), M. Bourgue (ob), A. Wallez (bn), A. Cazalet (hn) London ▲ 421581-2 [DDD]
Poulenc, F.:Son Cl Pno, w. P. Rogé (pno) London ▲ 421581-2 [DDD]

Porter, Amy (fl)—see ORCHESTRAS & ENSEMBLES Atlanta Chamber Players

Porter, Eliot (db)
Seasons Remembered 2, w. Judith Lynn Stillman (pno), Toby Appel (va), John Deak (db), Diaz Trio [David Kim (vn), Roberto Diaz (va), Andres Diaz (vc)], Lutz Rath (vc), Fenwick Smith (fl), Ruth Waterman (vn) North Star ▲ 9837-40052-2 ■ 9837-40052-4

Porter, Samuel (org)
American Masterpiece:The Noack Organ Arkay ▲ ARK 6129 [DDD]

Porto, Heriberto Cavalcante (fl)
Everts, A.:Agua con Gas, w. Pierre-Paul Rudolph (gtr) *(rec Studio MOGNO, Belgium, May & June 1995)* René Gailly ▲ CD 87128 [DDD]
Falú, E.:Chôro, w. Pierre-Paul Rudolph (gtr) *(rec Studio MOGNO, Belgium, May & June 1995)* René Gailly ▲ CD 87128 [DDD]
Machado, C.:Brazilian Folk Themes, w. Pierre-Paul Rudolph (gtr) *(rec Studio MOGNO, Belgium, May & June 1995)* René Gailly ▲ CD 87128 [DDD]
Piazzolla, A.:Études tanguistiques, w. Pierre-Paul Rudolph (gtr)—No. 4 *(rec Studio MOGNO, Belgium, May & June 1995)* René Gailly ▲ CD 87128 [DDD]
Piazzolla, A.:Histoire du Tango, w. Pierre-Paul Rudolph (gtr) *(rec Studio MOGNO, Belgium, May & June 1995)* René Gailly ▲ CD 87128 [DDD]
Riera, R.:Prélude Créole, w. Pierre-Paul Rudolph (gtr) *(rec Studio MOGNO, Belgium, May & June 1995)* René Gailly ▲ CD 87128 [DDD]
Sardinha, A.A.:Chôro triste, w. Pierre-Paul Rudolph (gtr) *(rec Studio MOGNO, Belgium, May & June 1995)* René Gailly ▲ CD 87128 [DDD]
Senanes, G.:Don Mondongo, w. Pierre-Paul Rudolph (gtr) *(rec Studio MOGNO, Belgium, May & June 1995)* René Gailly ▲ CD 87128 [DDD]

Portugheis, Alberto (pno)
Chopin, F.:Ballades Pno (comp) ASV Quicksilva ▲ ASQ 6095 [ADD]
Ginastera, A.:Pampeana 1, w. *(violinist unknown)* ASV ▲ ASV 902 [DDD]
Ginastera, A.:Pno Music—Malambo; Milonga; Sons. Nos. 2 & 3; 3 Piezas, Op. 6; Piezas infantiles; Rondo sobre temas infantiles Argentos; Suite de danzas criollas; Toccata ASV ▲ ASV 000 [DDD]
Ginastera, A.:Pno Music—includes 3 Danzas Argentinas; Pequena Danza; 12 American Preludes; Sonata No. 1 for Piano; Trist for Cello & Piano; Pampeana No. 2 ASV ▲ ASV 865
Ginastera, A.:Qnt Pno, w. Bingham String Quartet ASV ▲ ASV 902 [DDD]
Ginastera, A.:Son Vc, w. A. Natola-Ginastera (vc) ASV ▲ ASV 865
Ginastera, A.:Songs, w. O. Blackburn (sop)—2 canciones, Op. 3; 5 canciones, Op. 5; Las horas de una estancia, Op. 11 ASV ▲ ASV 902 [DDD]
Khachaturian, A.:Con Pno, w. L. Tjeknavorian (cnd), London SO ASV ▲ ASV 589 [DDD]
Khachaturian, A.:Sonatina Pno ASV ▲ ASV 589 [DDD]
Khachaturian, A.:Toccata Pno ASV ▲ ASV 589 [DDD]
Rossini, G.:Péchés de vieillesse (sels)—14 pieces ASV ▲ ASV 901 [DDD]

Porzsolt, György (va)—see ORCHESTRAS & ENSEMBLES New Haydn String Quartet

Posch, Alois (db)—see also ORCHESTRAS & ENSEMBLES Vienna Ring Ensemble
Gubaidulina, S.:Meditation on a Bach Chorale, w. Elisabeth Chojnacka (hpd), Hanna Weinmeister (vn), Elvira Bekova (vn), Marius Stravinsky (va), Alfia Bekova (vc) *(rec Lockenhaus Festival, Austria, 1995)* BIS ▲ CD 810 [DDD]
Ridout, A.:Little Sad Sound, w. E. Bashkirova (nar), G. Kremer (nar) Philips ("Digital Classics" series) ▲ 416841-2 [DDD]
Schubert, Franz:Qt Fl, w. J. Levine (pno), G. Hetzel (vn), W. Christ (va), G. Faust (vc) Deutsche Grammophon ▲ 431783-2
Schubert, Franz:Qnt Pno, D.667, w. J. Levine (pno), G. Hetzel (vn), W. Christ (va), G. Faust (vc) Deutsche Grammophon ▲ 431783-2
Schubert, Franz:Qnt Pno, D.667, w. A. Schiff (pno), Hagen String Quartet London ▲ 411975-2 [DDD]

Posnak, Paul (pno)
Bloch, E.:Qnt 1 Pno, w. Portland String Quartet Arabesque ▲ 6618 [DDD]

Posner, B. (pno)
Field, J.:Pno Music, w. D. Garvelmann (pno)—complete piano duets Koch International Classics ▲ KIC 7287 [DDD]
Osborne, G.A.:Duo Brilliant, w. D. Garvelmann (pno) Koch International Classics ▲ KIC 7287 [DDD]
Trimble, J.:Pno Music, w. D. Garvelmann (pno)—complete piano duets Koch International Classics ▲ KIC 7287 [DDD]

Pospíšil, Ladislav (vc)
Reicha, A.:Qts Fl, w. Jiri Válek (fl), Jan Buble (vn), Jan Marek (va) Panton ▲ PAN 811003

Pospíchal, J. (vn)—see ORCHESTRAS & ENSEMBLES Vienna String Trio

Posses, Mary (fl)
Alain, J.:Org Music (comp), w. James Higdon (org) *(rec 1988)* RBW ▲ RBWCD 005
Wyner, Y.:Memorial Music, w. Susan Davenny Wyner (sop), Jonathan Drexler (fl), Peter Standaart (fl) *(rec Dwight Chapel, Yale University, 1975)* CRI ("American Masters" series) ▲ CD 701 [ADD]

Post, Andrew (org)
Matins for Ascension Day, w. [cnd:Colin Walsh], Lincoln Cathedral Choir Priory ▲ PRI 478 [DDD]

Post, Carol Lei (pno)
Beethoven, L. van:Son Hn, w. K.P. Thelander (hn) *(rec Sept. 28–30, 1991)* Crystal ▲ CD 677
Dauprat, L.–F.:Son Hn & Pno, w. K. Pederson Thelander (hn) *(rec Sept. 28–30, 1991)* Crystal ▲ CD 677
Kruftt, N. von:Son in E Hn & Pno, w. K. P. Thelander (hn) *(rec Sept. 28–30, 1991)* Crystal ▲ CD 677
Kuhlau, F.:Andante & Polacca, w. K.P. Thelander (hn) *(rec Sept. 28–30, 1991)* Crystal ▲ CD 677
Oestreich, C.:Andante Hn, w. K. P. Thelander (nat hn) *(rec Sept. 28–30, 1991)* Crystal ▲ CD 677

Postinghel, M. (bn)
Lachner, F.P.:Nonet, w. A. Duisberg (fl), D. Wollenweber (ob), P. Prieditis (cl), P. Douglas (hn), I. Grünkorn (vn), M. Gieler (va), T. Ruge (vc), F. Heidenreich (db) *(rec June 10, 1991)* Thorofon ▲ CTH 2132 [DDD]

Postma, Willy (hp)
Haug, H.:Dialogue, w. Sidsel Walstad (hp) Victoria ▲ VCD 19049 [DDD]

Postnikova, Viktoria (pno)
Busoni, F.:Son 1 Vn, w. L. Mordkovitch (vn) Chandos ▲ CHAN 8868 [DDD]
Busoni, F.:Son 2 Vn, w. L. Mordkovitch (vn) Chandos ▲ CHAN 8868 [DDD]
Chopin, F.:Con 1 Pno, w. G. Rozhdestvensky (cnd), USSR Radio–TV Large SO Audiophile Classics ("Legacy Collection" series) ▲ 101.502
Prokofiev, S.:Con 5 Pno, w. G. Rozhdestvensky (cnd), USSR Radio–TV Large SO Audiophile Classics ("Legacy Collection" series) ▲ 101.502
Schnittke, A.:Con grosso 6, w. Sasha Rozhdestvensky (vn), G. Rozhdestvensky (cnd), Royal Stockholm PO Chandos ▲ CHAN 9359 [DDD]
Schnittke, A.:Son 1 Vn, w. S. Rozhdestvensky (vn) Chandos ▲ CHAN 9274 [DDD]
Strauss, R.:Son Vn, w. S. Rozhdestvensky (vn) Chandos ▲ CHAN 9274 [DDD]
Tchaikovsky, P.:Con 1 Pno, w. G. Rozhdestvensky (cnd), Vienna SO London ▲ 430725–2 [DDD]

Postolovskaya, Nina (pno)
Romantic Piano Sugo ▲ SUG 9310 [DDD]

Potash, Eli (vc)
Bach, J.S.:Trio Son Fl, Vn & Hpd, w. J. Solum (fl), J.–M. Schwarz (vn), I. Kipnis (hpd) [period instrs] Arabesque ▲ ARA 6640 [DDD]
Bach, J.S.:Trio Son for 2 Fls, BWV 1039, w. J. Solum (trns fl), R. Wyton (trns fl), I. Kipnis (hpd) [period instrs] Arabesque ▲ ARA 6640 [DDD]
Handel, G.F.:Trio Sons, w. John Solum (trns fl), J.–M. Schwarz (vn) [period instrs]—in G, Op. 2/1, HWV 389; in F, Op. 2/4, HWV 386b Arabesque ▲ ARA 6640 [DDD]

Potash, Eli (vl)
Telemann, G.P.:Musique de Table, w. J. Solum (fl), I. Kipnis (hpd) [played on period instrument] Arabesque ▲ ARA 6640 [DDD]

Potts, Leo (sax)
Two Sides, w. Jack Reidling (pno) *(rec North Hollywood, CA, Nov. 20–21, 1994)* Cambria ▲ CD 1075 [ADD]

Pouchet, Jean–Luc (vn)
Debussy, C.:Images (3) Pno, w. O. Garnier (pno)—Poisson d'or [arr. for violin & piano] Analekta ▲ ATM 29725 [DDD]
Franck, C.:Son Vn, w. O. Garnier (pno) Analekta ▲ ATM 29725 [DDD]
Kodály, Z.:Duo Vn & Vc, w. Bertrand Braillard (vc) Analekta ▲ ATM 29721
Lafond, R.:À l'Aube, w. O. Garnier (pno) Analekta ▲ ATM 29725 [DDD]
Massenet, J.:Méditation from *Thaïs*, w. O. Garnier (pno) Analekta ▲ ATM 29725 [DDD]
Ravel, M.:Oiseaux Tristes Vn, w. O. Garnier (pno) Analekta ▲ ATM 29725 [DDD]
Ravel, M.:Tzigane, w. O. Garnier (pno) Analekta ▲ ATM 29725 [DDD]

Pougnet, Jean (vn)
Delius, F.:Con Vn, w. T. Beecham (cnd), Royal PO *(rec 1946)* EMI Classics ▲ CDM 64054

Poulain, Loïc (fl)
Vranicky, P.:Qts Fl, Op. 28, w. Dolexal String Quartet members Adda ▲ ADD 581300 [DDD]

Poulain, Régis (bn)
Arma, P.:Music of, w. Josette Morata (nar), Fabrice Moretti (sax), Jean–Marie Cottet (pno), Alain Béghin (perc), Francis Petit (perc), J.–L. Petit (cnd), Avray Atelier Musique—Phases contre phases for S Sax & Pno; Celui qui dort et dort for Nar, Bn, Xyl & Perc [after poems by Max Jacob]; 5 esquisses for Pno [from a Hungarian Theme]; Divertissement 1600 for Fls [w. Jean–Noël Catrice (fl), Béatrice Delpierre (fl), Pascale Haarscher (fl), Marie–Aude Menou (fl)]; 3 Regards for solo Ob [w. Jacques Vandeville (ob)]; Divert No. 6 for Cl & Pno [w. Dominique Vidal (cl)]; Parlando for solo Fl [w. Patrice Bocquillon (fl)] REM ▲ REM 311266 [DDD]

Poulenc, Francis (pno)
Chabrier, E.:Songs, w. P. Bernac (bar)—L'île heureuse; Villanelle des petits canards [F] *(rec 1950)* Sony Masterworks (Portrait) ▲ MPK 47684 [ADD]
Debussy, C.:Songs, w. Bernard Kruysen (bar), Jean–Charles Richard (pno)—Le Son du cor; L'èchelonnement des haies; Trois chansons de France; Fêtes galantes; Fête galantes; Trois poèmes de Mallarmé; Le promenoir des deux amants; Trois poèmes de Mallarmé Trois ballades de Villon; Trois chansons de France *(rec 1962–65)* Mémoire Vive ▲ 262010 (m)
Poulenc, F.:Aubade Pno, w. W. Straram (cnd), Walther Straram Orch EMI Classics ▲ CDC 55036
Poulenc, F.:Le Bal masqué, w. Pierre Bernac (bar), L. Frémaux (cnd), Paris Opera Orch Soloists Adès ▲ ADE 202522 [AAD]
Poulenc, F.:Élégie Hn, w. Lucien Thevet (hn) Adès ▲ ADE 202522 [AAD]
Poulenc, F.:Movts perpétuels EMI Classics ▲ CDC 55036
Poulenc, F.:Pno Music (misc)—Nocturne No. 1 in C (1929); Suite française; Trois mouvements perpetuels *(rec 1950)* Sony Masterworks ("Portrait" series) ▲ MPK 47684 [ADD]
Poulenc, F.:Son Fl, w. Jean–Pierre Rampal (fl) Adès ▲ ADE 202522 [AAD]
Poulenc, F.:Songs, w. P. Bernac (bar)—Tel jour, telle nuit; Dans le jardin d'Anna; Reine des mouttes; C'est ainsi que tu es; Paganini; "C"; Ftes galantes; Montparnasse EMI Classics ▲ CDC 54605
Poulenc, F.:Trio Ob, w. Pierre Pierlot (ob), Maurice Allard (bn) Adès ▲ ADE 202522 [AAD]
Poulenc, F.:Trio Ob, w. *(other soloists unknown)* EMI Classics ▲ CDC 55036
Satie, E.:Pno Music (misc)—Avants–dernières pensées; Croquis et agaceries d'un gros bonhomme en bois; Descriptions automatiques; Gnossienne No. 3; Gymnopédie No. 1; Sarabande No. 2 *(rec 1950)* Sony Masterworks ("Portrait" series) ▲ MPK 47684 [ADD]

Poulet, Gérard (vn)—see also ORCHESTRAS & ENSEMBLES Arion Trio
The Art of the Violin, w. Patrice Fontanarosa (vn), Jean–Jacques Kantorow (vn), Régis Pasquier (vn) Arion ▲ ARN 60262
Bach, J.S.:Sons & Partitas Vn, BWV 1001–1006 Arion 2–▲ ARN 268296 [DDD]
Bartók, B.:Duos (44), w. Régis Pasquier (vn) Arion ▲ ARN 68327 [DDD]
Bartók, B.:Rhaps (2) Vn & Orch, w. L. Pfaff (cnd), Turin RAI Orch Arion ▲ ARN 68250 [DDD]
Debussy, C.:Son Vn, w. N. Lee (pno) Arion ▲ ARN 68228 [DDD]
Hindemith, P.:Son in E Vn & Pno, w. Christian Ivaldi (pno) Arion ▲ ARN 68319
Lalo, E.:Con russe, w. V. Válek (cnd), Prague RSO Praga ▲ PR 250062
Lalo, E.:Sym espagnole, w. V. Válek (cnd), Prague RSO Praga ▲ PR 250062
Mozart, W.A.:Sons Vn Pno (misc), w. B. Verlet (pno)—first 16 sons. Philips 2–▲ 438803–2
Pierné, G.:Son Vn, w. N. Lee (pno) Arion ▲ ARN 68228 [DDD]
Ravel, M.:Son Vn Pno, w. N. Lee (pno) Arion ▲ ARN 68228 [DDD]
Schubert, Franz:Rondo Vn, D.895, w. N. Lee (pno) Arion 2–▲ ARN 268006 [AAD]
Schubert, Franz:Son Vn, D.574, w. N. Lee (pno) Arion 2–▲ ARN 268006 [AAD]
Schubert, Franz:Sonatinas Vn, w. N. Lee (pno) Arion 2–▲ ARN 268006 [AAD]
Stravinsky, I.:Music of, w. N. Lee (pno) [music for vn & pno & trans. Stravinsky & others]—Danse Russe; Firebird (3 movements); Le rossignol (2 selections); Chanson Russe; Tango; Fairy's Kiss (2 selections); Pastoralle; Duo Concertant *(rec 9/88)* Arion ▲ ARN 68062 [DDD]

Poulet, J.–L. (vn)
Schubert, Franz:Fant Vn, D.934, w. N. Lee (pno) Arion 2–▲ ARN 268006 [AAD]

Poulet, M. (vc)—see ORCHESTRAS & ENSEMBLES Ysaÿe String Quartet

Poullette, Valerie (vn)
Dankner, S.:Sextet, w. L. Skelton (pno), E. Tanner (vn), M. Gyurik (va), A. Nisbet (vc), R. Kassinger (db) Albany ▲ TROY 067

Poulsen, Tore Othmar (cl)—see ORCHESTRAS & ENSEMBLES Copenhagen Wind Quintet

Pound, Megan (vn)—see ORCHESTRAS & ENSEMBLES Sterling String Quartet

Poutanen, R. (vc)—see ORCHESTRAS & ENSEMBLES Tapiola Trio

Powell, Margaret (vc)—see ORCHESTRAS & ENSEMBLES Dussek Piano Trio

Powell, Michael (trbn)—see also ORCHESTRAS & ENSEMBLES American Brass Quintet
Tower, J.:Black Topaz, w. Stephen Gosling (pno), Patricia Spencer (fl), Laura Flax (cl), Chris Gekker (tpt), Jonathan Haas (perc), Deborah Moore (perc) *(rec American Academy of Arts & Letters, New York City, Sept. 26–28, 1994)* New World ▲ 80470–2

Powell, Morgan (trbn)—see ORCHESTRAS & ENSEMBLES Tone Road Ramblers

Powell, Ross (cl)
Erb, D.:Woody New World ▲ 80457–2

Powell, William (cl)
Baley, V.:Sculptured Birds, w. Virko Baley (pno) *(rec California Institute of the Arts)* Cambria ▲ CMB 1077 [DDD]

Power Biggs, Edward (hpd)
Bach, J.S.:Anna Magdalena Bach Notebook—sels. CBS ▲ MK 30539 ■ MT 30539

Power Biggs, Edward (org)
Bach, J.S.:Chorale Preludes Org—BWV 645, 720, 734a CBS ▲ MK 42644 [ADD] ■ MT 42644
Bach, J.S.:Chorale Preludes Org—BWV 680, 753 CBS ▲ MK 42643 [ADD]
Bach, J.S.:Fant & Fugue Org, BWV 542 CBS ■ MT 31424
Bach, J.S.:Fant Org, BWV 572 CBS ▲ MK 42643 [ADD]
Bach, J.S.:Jesu bleibet meine Freude CBS ▲ MK 30539 ■ MT 30539
Bach, J.S.:Music of, w. E. Ormandy, P. Casals (vc), et. al. CBS ■ MGT 31261
Bach, J.S.:Org Music (misc)—selections from the Anna Magdalena Book; Chorales; etc. CBS ▲ MK 30539 [ADD]
Bach, J.S.:Org Music (misc)—Fugues in g, BWV 542, in G, BWV 577 & in g, BWV 578 CBS ▲ MK 42644 [ADD]
Bach, J.S.:Org Music (misc), w. Rozsnyai, Rotzsch (cnd), Columbia Chamber SO, Leipzig Gewandhaus Orch—9 Organ Chorales from Cantatas 79, 129, 140, 142, 147, 207, 248; 5 Sinfonias to Cantatas 29, 31, 35, 49; Five Concerted Chorales, BWV 19, 130, 137, 250, 303; Unto us a child is born (concerto), from Christmas Cantata, BWV 142; My spirit be joyful (duet), from Easter Cantata, BWV 146; March from Cantata 207; Instrumental Trio & Sheep may safely graze from Birthday Cantata, BWV 208; In dulci jubilo (chorale prelude), from BWV 740 CBS ▲ MK 42646 [ADD]
Bach, J.S.:Org Music (misc) CBS ■ MT 31840
Bach, J.S.:Org Music (misc)—Pastorale in F, BWV 590; Passacaglia & Fugue in c, BWV 582; Preludes & Fugues (various); Toccata & Fugue in d, BWV 565 Sony Classical ("Essential Classics" series) ▲ SBK 46551 [ADD] ■ SBT 46551
Bach, J.S.:Passacaglia & Fugue Org CBS ▲ MK 42644 [ADD]
Bach, J.S.:Preludes & Fugues, BWV 531–552—BWV 533, 539, 541, 544, 546, 547 CBS ▲ MK 42647 [ADD]
Bach, J.S.:Preludes & Fugues, BWV 531–552—BWV 532, 542, 543, 545, 549, 552 CBS ▲ MK 42648 [ADD]
Bach, J.S.:Sheep May Safely Graze CBS ▲ MK 30539 ■ MT 30539
Bach, J.S.:Toccata, Adagio & Fugue Org, BWV 564 *(rec 1973)* CBS ▲ MK 42643 [ADD]
Bach, J.S.:Toccata, Adagio & Fugue Org, BWV 564 *(rec 1960)* CBS ▲ MK 42644 [ADD]
Bach, J.S.:Toccata, Adagio & Fugue Org, BWV 564 CBS ■ MT 32933
Bach, J.S.:Toccata & Fugue Org, BWV 538, "Dorian" CBS ■ MT 32933
Bach, J.S.:Toccata & Fugue Org, BWV 538, "Dorian" CBS ▲ MK 42643 [ADD]
Bach, J.S.:Toccata & Fugue Org, BWV 540 CBS ▲ MK 42643 [ADD]
Bach, J.S.:Toccata & Fugue Org, BWV 540 CBS ■ MT 32933
Bach, J.S.:Toccata & Fugue Org, BWV 565 CBS ■ MT 31840
Bach, J.S.:Toccata & Fugue Org, BWV 565 *(rec 1973)* CBS ▲ MK 42643 [ADD]
Bach, J.S.:Toccata & Fugue Org, BWV 565 *(rec 1960)* CBS ▲ MK 42644 [ADD]
Copland, A.:Sym Org & Orch, w. L. Bernstein (cnd), New York PO *(rec 1967)* Sony Classical 2–▲ SM2K 47232 [ADD]
Frescobaldi, G.:Music of, w. R. Burgin (cnd), Boston Brass Ensemble—Toccatas in d & G; Canzoni Nos 1–5 in G, C, a, g & g *(rec Harvard Univ, Cambridge, MA, Mar 26, 27, 30 & 31, 1959)* Sony Classical ("Masterworks Heritage" series) ▲ MHK 62353 [ADD]
Gabrieli, G.:Choral Music, w. Gregg Smith Singers, Texas Boys' Choir—7 Intonazioni d'organo; 7 Motets; 3 Mass Movements; Sonata in the 9th tone for 8 parts *(rec St. Mark's Basilica, Venice 1967)* CBS ▲ MK 42645 [ADD]
Gabrieli, G.:Fant VI toni, w. Boston Brass Ensemble *(rec Harvard Univ, Cambridge, MA, 1959)* Sony Classical ("Masterworks Heritage" series) ▲ MHK 62353 [ADD]
Gabrieli, G.:Intonationi d'organo, w. Boston Brass Ensemble—Del primo tono, secondo tono, terzo e quarto tono, ottavo tono, nono tono, dècimo tono, undicècimo tono & duodècimo tono *(rec Harvard Univ, Cambridge, MA, 1959)* Sony Classical ("Masterworks Heritage" series) ▲ MHK 62353 [ADD]
Gabrieli, G.:Sacred Music, w. Edward Tarr Brass Ensemble, La Fenice Ensemble, Gregg Smith Singers, Texas Boys' Choir—Deus, in nomine tuo; Beata es, virgo Maria; Juilemus singuli; Deus, Deus meus, ad te de luce vigilo; O quam suavis est; Kyrie; Sanctus; Benedictus; Cantate Domino; Domine, exuadi orationem meam; Hodie completi sunt; Magnificat; Surrexit Christus; Nunc dimittis; Jubilate Deo; Intonatio *(rec San Marco, Venice, Sept 14–22, 1967)* Sony Classical ("Essential Classics" series) ▲ SBK 62426 [ADD] ■ SBT 62426
Handel, G.F.:Cons (16) Org, w. A. Boult (cnd), London PO Odyssey 3–▲ MB3K 45825
Pachelbel, w. Jean–Pierre Rampal (fl), Igor Kipnis (hpd), Raymond Leppard (cnd), John Williams (gtr), Canadian Brass, et al. Sony Classical ("Greatest Hits" series) ▲ MLK 62680 ■ MLT 62680
Saint–Saëns, C.:Marche militaire française, w. E. Ormandy (cnd), Philadelphia Orch Sony Classical ("Essential Classics" series) ▲ SBK 47655 ■ SBT 47655
Saint–Saëns, C.:Sym 3, w. E. Ormandy (cnd), Philadelphia Orch Odyssey ▲ MBK 38920 [ADD] ■ YT 38920
Saint–Saëns, C.:Sym 3, w. E. Ormandy (cnd), Philadelphia Orch Sony Classical ("Essential Classics" series) ▲ SBK 47655 ■ SBT 47655

Powers, Greg (trbn)
Dempster, S.:Music of, w. Stuart Dempster (trbn/didjeridu/conch), Jay Bulen (trbn), Jeff Domoto (trbn), Moc Escobedo (trbn/didjeridu/conch), Scott Higbee (trbn), Gretchen Hopper (trbn), Nathaniel Irby–Oxford (trbn), Chad Kirby (trbn/conch), Dave Marriott (trbn), Debra Sykes (cym)—Conch Calling; Morning Light; Didjerilayover; Secret Currents; Melodic Communion; Shell Shock; Cloud Landings *(rec Fort Worden, Port Townsend, WA, June 18, 1994)* New Albion ▲ NA 076

Poy, Nardo (va)—see also ORCHESTRAS & ENSEMBLES Broyhill Chamber Ensemble
Dvořák, A.:Terzetto, w. Richard Rood (vn), Katsuko Esaki (vn) Music & Arts ▲ MUA CD 926

Pozsgai, Zoltán (pno)—see ORCHESTRAS & ENSEMBLES Budapest Piano Duet

Prado, Gildas (ob)
Telemann, G.P.:Cons Ob d'amore, w. P. Kuentz (cnd), Paul Kuentz Orch—in A Pierre Verany ▲ PVY 730046

Praetorius, Lisedor (hpd)
Rosenmüller, J.:Lamentationes Jeremiae, w. Fritz Wünderlich (ten), Fred Buck (vc) *(rec Stuttgart, Mar 24, 1957)* Bella Voce ▲ 7003 [AAD]

Prager, N. (tpt)
Vivaldi, A.:Cons Diverse Instrs, w. G. Vicari (mand), C. de Filippis (mand), J. Wummer (fl), R. Morris (fl), W. Vacchiano (tpt), E. Brenner (b ob), C. Stavrache (hp), A. Wurtzler (hp), J. Gorigliano (vn), L. Varga (vc), L. Bernstein (cnd), New York PO—in C, RV.558 *(rec Dec. 15, 1958)* Sony Classical ("Leonard Bernstein:The Royal Edition" series) ▲ SMK 47642 [ADD]

Praprotnik, Stanko (tpt)
Arutiunian, A.:Con Tpt, w. A. Nanut (cnd), Slovenian SO Audiophile Classics ▲ 101.040 [DDD]

Prati, P. (vn)
Respighi, O.:Qnt Pno, w. Venice String Quartet *(rec Oct. 23–25, 1992)* Ermitage ▲ ERM 410 [DDD]

Prats, Jorge Luis (pno)
Dohnányi, E. von:Vars on a Nursery Song, w. E. Bátiz (cnd), Royal PO IMP ▲ IMP 2048
Grieg, E.:Con Pno, Op. 16, w. E. Bátiz (cnd), Royal PO IMP Classics ▲ IMPPCD 1063 [DDD]

▲ = CD ♦ = Enhanced CD Δ = MD ■ = Cassette Tape □ = DCC

Prats, Jorge Luis (pno) (cont.)
Grieg, E.:Con Pno, Op. 16, w. E. Bátiz (cnd), Royal PO IMP ▲ IMP 2048
The Heart of the Piano Concerto, w. John Lill (pno), Cristina Ortiz (pno), London SO [cnd:J. Judd, W. Morris], Royal PO [cnd:L. Foster, E. Bátiz] Pickwick ("The Orchid" series) ▲ PICORCD 11012
Litolff, H.C.:Con Symphonique 4, w. E. Bátiz (cnd), Royal PO—Scherzo IMP Classics ▲ IMPPCD 1063 [DDD]
Rachmaninoff, S.:Con 2 Pno, w. E. Bátiz (cnd), Mexico City PO ASV Quicksilva ▲ ASQ 6128 [DDD]
Rachmaninoff, S.:Con 3 Pno, w. E. Bátiz (cnd), Mexico City PO IMG/Pickwick ▲ PICIMG 1605
Rachmaninoff, S.:Prince Rostislav, w. E. Bátiz (cnd), Mexico City PO IMG/Pickwick ▲ PICIMG 1605
Rachmaninoff, S.:Rhapsody on a Theme of Paganini, w. E. Bátiz (cnd), Mexico City PO ASV Quicksilva ▲ ASQ 6128 [DDD]

Pratt, Awadagin (pno)
Brahms, J.:Ballades, Op. 10 EMI Classics ▲ CDC 55025
Busoni, F.:Chaconne Pno EMI Classics ▲ CDC 55025
Franck, C.:Prélude, choral et fugue EMI Classics ▲ CDC 55025
Liszt, F.:Harmonies poétiques et religieuses—No. 7, "Funérailles" EMI Classics ▲ CDC 55025

Pratt, Daryl (perc)
Broadstock, B.:Eheu Fugaces, w. Marilyn Richardson (sop), Christine Draeger (fl), Roslyn Dunlop (cl), Fiona Ziegler (vn), Susan Blake (vc), David Miller (pno) Vox Australis ▲ VAST018-2 [DDD]
Sitsky, L.:Deep in My Hidden Country, w. Marilyn Richardson (sop), Christine Draeger (fl), Susan Blake (vc), David Miller (pno) Vox Australis ▲ VAST018-2 [DDD]

Prayer, Luisa (pno)
Heifetz, J.:Transcriptions Vn, w. Vincenzo Bolognese (vn)—trans. of works by Rameau, Chopin, Saint-Saëns, Dvořák, Prokofiev, Mozart, Schumann, Debussy, Rachmaninoff, Gershwin, others Musikstrasse ▲ 2107

Precz, Bogdan (acc)
Fusion, w. Zygmunt Zgraja (hmc) Opera Tres ▲ 1001

Preda, Maurizio (gtr)
Paganini, N.:Cantabile, w. Luigi Alberto Bianchi (vn) *(rec Dynamic's, Genova, June 22–23, 1995)* Dynamic ▲ CD 148 [DDD]
Paganini, N.:Cantibile, w. Luigi Alberto Bianchi (vn) *(rec Dynamic Studio, Genoa, Italy, June 22–23, 1995)* Dynamic 3–▲ 1571 [DDD]
Paganini, N.:Centone di sonate, w. L. A. Bianchi (vn)—Nos. 7–12 Dynamic ▲ CD 84 [DDD]
Paganini, N.:Centone di sonate, w. L. A. Bianchi (vn)—Nos. 13–18 Dynamic ▲ CD 34 [DDD]
Paganini, N.:Centone di sonate, w. Luigi Alberto Bianchi (vn)—Nos. 1–6 *(rec Dynamic's, Genova, June 22–23, 1995)* Dynamic ▲ CD 148 [DDD]
Paganini, N.:Centone di sonate, w. Luigi Alberto Bianchi (vn) *(rec Dynamic Studio, Genoa, Italy, Jan 1991; Oct 1991; June)* Dynamic 3–▲ 1571 [DDD]
Paganini, N.:Sons Vn & Gtr, w. L. A. Bianchi (vn)—30 Sons Dynamic 2–▲ CD 43/1–2

Préfontaine, Yves-G. (org/hpd)
Bach, J.S.:Motets, BWV 225–30, w. M. Lacasse (cnd), Prefontaine Montreal Choeur Classique Analekta Fleur de Lys ▲ FL 2 3001 [DDD]

Preis, Manfred (b cl)
Hindemith, P.:Septet Winds & Tpt, w. Thomas Clamor (tpt), Berlin Philharmonic Wind Quintet *(rec Berlin-Spandau, Sept 11–14, 1995)* BIS ▲ CD 752 [DDD]

Preis, Manfred (sax)
Tomasi, H.:Printemps, w. Berlin Philharmonic Wind Quintet BIS ▲ CD 536 [DDD]

Prelle, Johannes (vn)
Kahn, E.I.:Adagio, w. T. Gunther (pno) CRI ▲ CD 563 [DDD]

Prénat, A. C. (org)
Bach, J.S.:Org Music (misc) [the Organ of Lutry]—Toccata & Fugue in d, BMV 565; Passacaglia & Fugue in c, BWV 582; Chorale Settings, BWV 656 & 659; Son. 5 in C, BWV 529; Prelude & Fugue in e, BWV 548 Gallo ▲ CD 628 [DDD]

Presland, Carole (pno)
Debussy, C.:Son Vn, w. J. Morton (vn) *(rec Oct. 1992)* Pavane ▲ ADW 7280 [DDD]
Lekeu, G.:Son Vn, w. J. Morton (vn) *(rec Oct. 1992)* Pavane ▲ ADW 7280 [DDD]
Suk, J.:Ballade Vn, w. J. Morton (vn) *(rec Oct., 1992)* Pavane ▲ ADW 7280 [DDD]
Szymanowski, K.:Myths, w. J. Morton (vn) *(rec Oct. 1992)* Pavane ▲ ADW 7280 [DDD]

Presle, Frédéric (cnt/bgl)
Polkas & Varied Airs, 1900, w. R. Boutry (cnd), Republican Guard Orch of Harmony *(rec Feb. 10, 11 & 13, 1992)* Chamade ▲ 5603 [DDD]

Presle, Frédéric (tpt)
Albinoni, T.:Cons Tpt, w. J. Amade (org) [at the Grand Organ of St. Martin's Church, Masevaux]—in D, a, F, B♭, f, B♭ & D *(rec Oct 4–6, 1993)* Chamade ▲ 5617 [DDD]
Recital for Trumpet & Organ, w. Jacques Amade (org) Chamade ▲ 5629
Telemann, G.P.:Cons Tpt & Org, w. J. Amade (org) [the Grand Organ of St. Martin's Church, Masevaux]—in D, E♭, g, A & B♭; Son. de concert *(rec Oct. 5–7, 1992)* Chamade ▲ 5605 [DDD]
Vivaldi, A.:Cons Tpt, w. C. Poiget (cnd), La Follia Ensemble—in a, RV.461; in d, RV.454; in D, RV.453; in C, RV.447; in a, RV.463; in C, RV.450 Chamade ▲ 5616 [DDD]

Press, Maurice (hpd)
Corigliano, J.:Poem in October, w. R. White (ten), T. Nyfenger (fl), B. Lucarelli (ob), J. Rabbai (cl), M. Press (cnd), American String Quartet RCA Gold Seal ▲ 60395-2-RG [ADD]

Press, Peter (gtr)
Vivaldi, A.:Con Gtr, RV.93, w. R. Kapp (cnd), Philharmonia Virtuosi ESS.A.Y ▲ ESS 1004 [DDD]
Vivaldi, A.:Con Gtr Vl, w. Louise Schulman (vl), R. Kapp (cnd), Philharmonia Virtuosi ESS.A.Y ▲ ESS 1004 [DDD]
Vivaldi, A.:Con Lt, w. P. Peabody (vn), E. Lim (vn), J. Haffner (va), T. Mook (vc), E. Brewer (hpd) ESS.A.Y ▲ CD 1004 [DDD] ■ C 1004 (D)
Vivaldi, A.:Con Mand, RV.425, w. R. Kapp (cnd), Philharmonia Virtuosi ESS.A.Y ▲ CD 1004 [DDD] ■ C 1004 (D)
Vivaldi, A.:Con for 2 Mands, w. S. Kuney (gtr), R. Kapp (cnd), Philharmonia Virtuosi ESS.A.Y ▲ CD 1004 [DDD] ■ C 1004 (D)
Vivaldi, A.:Con Va d'amore Lt, w. L. Schulman (va), R. Kapp (cnd), Philharmonia Virtuosi ESS.A.Y ▲ CD 1004 [DDD] ■ C 1004 (D)
Vivaldi, A.:Trio Sons Gtr Vn, w. P. Peabody (vn), R. Shell (vc), E. Brewer (hpd)—(2) in C, RV.82 & in g, RV.85 ESS.A.Y ▲ CD 1004 [DDD] ■ C 1004 (D)
Vivaldi, A.:Trio Sons Vn Lt, w. Paul Peabody (vn), Roger Shell (vc), Edward Brewer (hpd) ESS.A.Y ▲ ESS 1004 [DDD]

Press, Peter (mand)
Vivaldi, A.:Con Mand, RV.425, w. R. Kapp (cnd), Philharmonia Virtuosi ESS.A.Y ▲ ESS 1004 [DDD]
Vivaldi, A.:Con for 2 Mands, w. Scott Kuney (mand), R. Kapp (cnd), Philharmonia Virtuosi ESS.A.Y ▲ ESS 1004 [DDD]

Press, Roger (pno)
Debussy, C.:Pour le piano Meridian ▲ CDE 84160
Prokofiev, S.:Son 7 Pno Meridian ▲ CDE 84160
Rachmaninoff, S.:Variations on a Theme by Corelli Meridian ▲ CDE 84160

Pressler, Menahem (pno)—see also ORCHESTRAS & ENSEMBLES Beaux Arts Trio
Beethoven, L. van:Fant Pno, Op. 80, "Choral Fant", w. K. Masur (cnd), Leipzig Gewandhaus Orch, *(chorus unknown)* Philips ▲ 438005-2
Dvořák, A.:Qts Pno Strs, Opp. 23 & 87, w. Emerson String Quartet members—in E♭ Deutsche Grammophon ▲ 439868-2
Dvořák, A.:Qnt Pno, Op. 81, w. Emerson String Quartet Deutsche Grammophon ▲ 439868-2
Fauré, G.:Son 1 Vn, w. S. Rolston (vn) [cello-piano arr.] Summit ▲ DCD 109 [DDD]
Franck, C.:Son Vn, w. S. Rolston (vc) [cello-piano arr.] Summit ▲ DCD 109 [DDD]

Pressley, Richard (tpt)
Dresher, P.:Channels Passing, w. P. Taub (fl), B. Shapiro (ob), C. Sereque (cl), S. Dempster (trbn), E.M. Gray (vn), W. Gray (vc) *(rec 1983–84)* New Albion ▲ NA 053
Sapieyevski, J.:Arioso, w. Westwood Wind Quintet Crystal ▲ CD 751

Preston, (fl)
Weber, C.M. von:Sons Vn, w. R. Burnett (pno)—Nos. 1, 3, 4, 6 Amon Ra ▲ CD-SAR 21 [DDD]
Weber, C.M. von:Trio Fl, w. J. .W. Clarke (vc), R. Burnett (pno) Amon Ra ▲ CD-SAR 21 [DDD]

Preston, B. (vn)
Hanson, H.:Con da Camera, w. I. Swenson (vn), C. Wiersma (vn), M. Lambros (va), Elizabeth Anderson (vc) Albany ▲ TROY 129 [DDD]

Preston, Brian (pno)
Hanson, H.:Yuletide Pieces (2) Albany ▲ TROY 129 [DDD]

Preston, Mary (org)
Duruflé, M.:Prélude, Adagio et Choral varié sur le thème du *Veni Creator (rec Myerson Symphony Center, Dallas, TX)* Gothic ▲ G 49079 [DDD]
Duruflé, M.:Suite Org *(rec Myerson Symphony Center, Dallas, TX)* Gothic ▲ G 49079 [DDD]
Widor, C.M.:Sym 3 Org *(rec Myerson Symphony Center, Dallas, TX)* Gothic ▲ G 49079 [DDD]

Preston, Marylin (fl)
Encore, w. [cnd:Duain Wolfe], Colorado Children's Chorale, Rick Chinski (gtr), Robert Davine (acc), Laurie Kahler (pno), Samuel Lancaster (pno), Barry Oliver (pno), Karen Yonovitz (fl), Peter Cooper (ob), Andy Stevens (cl), Lionel Young (vn), Basil Vendreys (va), Wayne Templeman (vc), Charle *(rec Denver Center Media)* Colorado Children's Chorale ▲ 001

Preston, S. (fl)—see ORCHESTRAS & ENSEMBLES L'École d'Orphée

Preston, Simon (kbd)
Sir Cristemas, w. [cnd:Louis Halsey], Elizabethan Singers, Ian Partridge (ten), Susan Longfield (sop), Christopher Keyte (bass) Boston Skyline ▲ BSD 124 [ADD]

Preston, Simon (org)
Bach, J.S.:Chorale Preludes (Schübler) Deutsche Grammophon ▲ 435381-2 [DDD]
Bach, J.S.:Cons Org, BWV 592–597 Deutsche Grammophon □ 423087-5
Bach, J.S.:Fant & Fugue Org, BWV 542 Deutsche Grammophon ▲ 435381-2 [DDD]
Bach, J.S.:Fant Org, BWV 572 Archiv ▲ 427668-2 [DDD]
Bach, J.S.:Das Orgelbüchlein Deutsche Grammophon ▲ 431816-2 [DDD]
Bach, J.S.:Passacaglia & Fugue Org Deutsche Grammophon ▲ 435381-2 [DDD]
Bach, J.S.:Preludes & Fugues, BWV 532, 552 Archiv ▲ 427668-2 [DDD]
Bach, J.S.:Toccata, Adagio & Fugue Org, BWV 564 Deutsche Grammophon ▲ 435381-2 [DDD]
Bach, J.S.:Toccata & Fugue Org, BWV 540 Deutsche Grammophon ▲ 435381-2 [DDD]
Bach, J.S.:Toccata & Fugue Org, BWV 565 Archiv ▲ 427668-2 [DDD]
Copland, A.:Sym Org & Orch, w. L. Slatkin (cnd), St. Louis SO *(rec Christ Church Cathedral, St. Louis, Sept 21, 1993)* RCA Red Seal ▲ 09026-68292-2 [DDD]
Early English Organ Music Archiv ▲ 415675-2 AH [DDD]
Handel, G.F.:Cons (16) Org, w. T. Pinnock (cnd), English CO—Nos. 2, 9–11 & 13 Archiv ("3D Baroque" series) ▲ 431708-2 [DDD]
Handel, G.F.:Music of, w. Pauline Tinsley (sop), James Bowman (ct), Anthony Rolfe-Johnson (ten), David Wilson-Johnson (ten), R. Leppard (cnd), English CO, London Phil Chorus—Zadok the Priest; Eternal Source of Light Divine; Tamerlano Ov; Dead March [from Saul]; When the Ear Heard Her; She Delivered the Poor That Cried; Their Bodies Are Buried in Peace; Glory Be to the Father; As It Was in the Beginning; Con a Due Cori in B♭; Waft Her Angels to the Skies; Con in g for Org, Op. 7/5; Hallelujah Chorus [from The Messiah] IMP ("BBC Radio Classics" series) ▲ IMP 5691522
Poulenc, F.:Con Org, w. S. Ozawa (cnd), Boston SO Deutsche Grammophon ▲ 437827-2
Saint-Saëns, C.:Sym 3, w. J. Levine (cnd), Berlin PO Deutsche Grammophon ▲ 419617-2 [DDD] □ 419617-5

Preston, Stephen (fl)
Bach, J.S.:Brandenburg Con 5, w. Jane Rogers (va), Jonathan Manson (vc), Purcell Quartet Chandos ("Chaconne" series) ▲ CHAN 0595
Bach, J.S.:Partita Fl, BWV 1013 CRD 2–▲ 3314/15 [ADD]
Bach, J.S.:Sons Fl, BWV 1030–35, w. T. Pinnock (hpd), J. Savall (vl) CRD 2–▲ 3314/15 [ADD]
Flute Collection, w. Lucy Carolan (kbds) Amon Ra ▲ CDSAR 19 [DDD]

Presutti, F. (va)—see ORCHESTRAS & ENSEMBLES Modo Antiquo

Pretto, Gianpaolo (fl)
Mozart, W.A.:Andante Fl, K.315/285a, w. E. Aadland (cnd), European Community CO *(rec Rosslyn Hill Chapel, London, Apr 16–19, 1992)* IMP ("Classics" series) ▲ IMP PCD 1107
Mozart, W.A.:Cons Fl, w. E. Aadland (cnd), European Community CO *(rec Rosslyn Hill Chapel, London, Apr 16–19, 1992)* IMP ("Classics" series) ▲ IMP PCD 1107
Mozart, W.A.:Rondo Fl, K.Anh.184, w. E. Aadland (cnd), European Community CO *(rec Rosslyn Hill Chapel, London, Apr 16–19, 1992)* IMP ("Classics" series) ▲ IMP PCD 1107
Poulenc, F.:Sxt Pno, w. Andrea Dindo (pno), Paolo Grazia (ob), Alessandro Carbonare (cl), Roberto Giaccaglia (bn), Stefano Pignatelli (hn) *(rec Sala Maffeiana dell'Accademia Filarmonica di Verona, May 7–9, 1995)* Agorá ▲ 021 [DDD]
Poulenc, F.:Son Fl, w. Andrea Dindo (pno) *(rec Sala Maffeiana dell'Accademia Filarmonica di Verona, May 7–9, 1995)* Agorá ▲ 021 [DDD]

Preucil, William (va)—see ORCHESTRAS & ENSEMBLES Lanier Trio members

Preucil, William (vn)—see also ORCHESTRAS & ENSEMBLES Cleveland String Quartet, Lanier Trio
Höller, K.:Fant Vn & Org, w. Barbara Harbach (org) Gasparo ▲ GS 278 ■ GS 278C
Paulus, S.:Con Vn, w. R. Shaw (cnd), Atlanta SO New World ▲ NW 363-2 [DDD]

Preuss, Frank (vn)
Program 2, w. Arnold Dolmetsch (vir), Marguerite Dolmetsch (vl), Carl Dolmetsch (rec), Nigel Foster (hpd) IMP Allegro ▲ PCD 990 [DDD]

Previn, André (pno)—see also ORCHESTRAS & ENSEMBLES Roth Trio
Beethoven, L. van:Fant Pno, Op. 80, "Choral Fant", w. A. Previn (cnd), Royal PO, *(chorus unknown)* RCA Victor ▲ 09026-61714-2; ■ 09026-61714-4
Beethoven, L. van:Qnt Pno, Ob, Cl, Hn & Bn, w. Vienna Wind Soloists Telarc ▲ CD 80114 [DDD]
Beethoven, L. van:Trio 6 Pno, "Archduke", w. Viktoria Mullova (vn), Heinrich Schiff (vc) Philips ▲ 442123-2
Brahms, J.:Ernste Gesänge, w. Janet Baker (mez) EMI Classics ("Doublefforte" series) 2–▲ CDFB 68667
Brahms, J.:Songs, Op. 91, w. Janet Baker (mez), Cecil Aronowitz (va) EMI Classics ("Doublefforte" series) 2–▲ CDFB 68667
Brahms, J.:Trio 1 Pno, w. Viktoria Mullova (vn), Heinrich Schiff (vc) Philips ▲ 442123-2
Debussy, C.:Trio Pno, w. Julie Rosenfeld (vn), Gary Hoffman (vc) RCA Red Seal ▲ 09026-68062-2
A Different Kind of Blues, w. Itzhak Perlman (vn), Shelly Manne (drums), Jim Hall (gtr), Red Mitchell (bass gtr) Angel ▲ CDM 64319 [DDD]
Dvořák, A.:Slavonic Dances (sels), w. H. Schiff (vc)—in g, Op. 46/8 Philips ▲ 434914-2
Gershwin, G.:Con Pno, w. A. Previn (cnd), London SO EMI Classics ▲ CDC 47161 ■ 4AM 34760
Gershwin, G.:Con Pno, w. A. Previn (cnd), Pittsburgh SO Philips ▲ 412611-2 [DDD] □ 412611-5
Gershwin, G.:Con Pno, w. A. Kostelanetz (cnd), Kostelanetz Orch *(rec 1960)* Odyssey ▲ MBK 46270 [ADD] ■ YT 46270
Gershwin, G.:Rhap in Blue, w. A. Previn (cnd), Pittsburgh SO Philips ▲ 412611-2 [DDD] □ 412611-5
Gershwin, G.:Rhap in Blue, w. A. Kostelanetz (cnd), Kostelanetz Orch *(rec 1960)* Odyssey ▲ MBK 46270 [ADD] ■ YT 46270
Gershwin, G.:Rhap in Blue, w. A. Previn (cnd), London SO EMI Classics ▲ CDC 47161 ■ 4AM 34760
It's a Breeze, w. Perlman, Itzhak (vn), Shelly Manne (drums), Jim Hall (gtr), Red Mitchell (bass) Angel ▲ CDM 64318 [DDD]
Joplin, S.:Music of, w. I. Perlman (vn) EMI Classics ▲ CDC 47170 ■ 4XS 37113
Kern, J.:Songs, w. S. McNair (sop), D. Finck (db)—Land Where the Good Songs Go; I Won't Dance; Nobody Else but Me; The Folks Who Live on the Hill; A Fine Romance; Remind Me; You Couldn't Be Cuter; Why Was I Born?; I'm Old Fashioned; et. al. Philips ▲ 442129-2
Kiri Sidetracks, w. Te Kanawa, Kiri (sop), Mundell Lowe (gtr), Ray Brown (db) Philips ▲ 434092-2 PH [DDD] ■ 434092-4 PH (D)
Milhaud, D.:La Création du monde (suite), w. Ani Kavafian (vn), Julie Rosenfeld (vn), Toby Hoffman (va), Carter Brey (vc) *(rec Manhattan Center Studios, New York City, May 25–26, 1993)* RCA Red Seal ▲ 09026-68181-2 [DDD]
Mozart, W.A.:Con 10 Pnos, w. A. de Larrocha (pno), A. Previn (cnd), Orch of St. Luke's *(rec Manhattan Center Studios, New York City, July 26–27, 1993)* RCA Red Seal ▲ 68044-2

INSTRUMENT.

Previn, André (pno) (cont.)
Mozart, W.A.:Con 10 Pnos, w. R. Lupu (pno), A. Previn (cnd), London SO EMI Classics ▲ CDM 65180
Mozart, W.A.:Con 17 Pno, w. A. Boult (cnd), London SO Royal Classics ▲ ROY 6449
Mozart, W.A.:Con 20 Pno, w. A. Previn (cnd), London SO EMI Classics ▲ CDM 65180
Mozart, W.A.:Con 24 Pno, w. A. Boult (cnd), London SO Royal Classics ▲ ROY 6449
Mozart, W.A.:Qts Pno, w. Y. U. Kim (vn), H. Ohyama (va), G. Hoffman (vc) RCA Red Seal ▲ 09026-60713-2
Mozart, W.A.:Qnt Pno, K.452, w. Vienna Wind Soloists Telarc ▲ CD 80114 [DDD]
Mozart, W.A.:Son 2 Pnos, w. A. de Larrocha (pno) *(rec Manhattan Center Studios, New York City, July 12–13, 1993)* RCA Red Seal ▲ 68044-2
Mozart, W.A.:Vars Pno, K.265 CBS ▲ MLK 39436 ■ MT 39436
Poulenc, F.:Sxt Pno, w. Elizabeth Mann (fl), Steve Taylor (ob), David Shifrin (cl), Dennis Godburn (bn), Richard Todd (hn) *(rec Manhattan Center Studios, New York City, Apr. 7–8, 1993)* RCA Red Seal ▲ 09026-68181-2 [DDD]
Rachmaninoff, S.:Russian Rhap, w. Vladimir Ashkenazy (pno) *(rec Kingsway Hall, London, 1979)* London ("Double Decker" series) 2-▲ 444845-2 [ADD]
Rachmaninoff, S.:Suite 1 for 2 Pnos, w. Vladimir Ashkenazy (pno) *(rec All Saints' Church, Petersham, 1974)* London ("Double Decker" series) 2-▲ 444845-2 [ADD]
Rachmaninoff, S.:Suite 2 for 2 Pnos, w. Vladimir Ashkenazy (pno) *(rec All Saints' Church, Petersham, 1974)* London ("Double Decker" series) 2-▲ 444845-2 [ADD]
Rachmaninoff, S.:Symphonic Dances, w. Vladimir Ashkenazy (pno) *(rec Kingsway Hall, London, 1979)* London ("Double Decker" series) 2-▲ 444845-2 [ADD]
Ravel, M.:Trio Pno, w. Julie Rosenfeld (vn), Gary Hoffman (vc) RCA Red Seal ▲ 09026-68062-2
Right As the Rain, w. Leontyne Price (sop) RCA Victor ▲ 2983-2-RG [ADD]
Saint-Saëns, C.:Spt Tpt, w. Thomas Stevens (tpt), Julie Rosenfeld (vn), Ani Kavafian (vn), Toby Hoffman (va), Carter Brey (vc), Jack Kulowitsch (db) *(rec Manhattan Center Studios, New York City, May 25–26, 1993)* RCA Red Seal ▲ 09026-68181-2 [DDD]
Schumann, R.:Qt Pno in c, w. Young Uck Kim (vn), H. Ohyama (va), G. Hoffman (vc) RCA Red Seal ▲ 09026-61384-2
Schumann, R.:Qt Pno, Op. 47, w. Young Uck Kim (vn), H. Ohyama (va), G. Hoffman (vc) RCA Red Seal ▲ 09026-61384-2
Shostakovich, D.:Con 1 Pno, w. W. Vacchiano (tpt), L. Bernstein (cnd), New York PO *(rec Apr. 8, 1962)* Sony Classical ▲ SMK 47618 [ADD]

Prevost, Christian (vn)
Vivaldi, A.:Con for 2 Vns Vcs, w. L. Hall (vn), A. Aubut (vc), B. Hurtubise (vc), Y. Turovsky (cnd), Montreal Musici—RV.542 in F Chandos ▲ CHAN 8651 [DDD]

Prévost, Germain (va)—see ORCHESTRAS & ENSEMBLES Pro Arte String Quartet

Prévost, Thomas (fl)
Bax, A.:Elegiac Trio, w. J. Dupouy (va), M. Geliot (hp) Quantum ▲ QM 6898 ■ QM 1993
Cras, J.:La Flûte de Pan, w. D. Henry (bar), M.-C. Milliere (vn), J.-F. Benatar (va), P. Bary (vc)—[F] Quantum ▲ QM 6897 [DDD] ■ QM 1992 (D)
Cras, J.:Qnt, w. C. Michel (hp), M.-C. Milliere (vn), J.-F. Benatar (va), P. Bary (vc) Quantum ▲ QM 6897 [DDD] ■ QM 1992 (D)
Debussy, C.:Son Fl, w. J. Dupouy (va), M. Geliot (hp) Quantum ▲ QM 6898 ■ QM 1993
Hommage à Martine Geliot (1948–1988), w. Martine Geliot (hp), Jean Dupouy (va) Quantum ▲ QM 6898 ■ QM 1993
Leclair, J.-M.:Trio Sons, w. J. Dupouy (va), M. Geliot (hp) [trans. for flute, viola & harp] Quantum ▲ QM 6898 ■ QM 1993
Lemeland, A.:To Holst's Memory, w. J. Dupouy (va), M. Geliot (hp) Quantum ▲ QM 6898 ■ QM 1993

Pribyl, Jiri (trbn)
Vejvanovsky, P.J.:Sons & Serenades, w. Vaclav Jirovec (vc), Jan Hasenöhrl (tpt), Frantisek Xaver (hpd), Milan Hruby (brass), Oldrich Vlcek (vn), O. Vlček (cnd), Prague Virtuosi—Intrada; Harmonia romana; Serenada; Offertur ad duos chorus; Son à 4 be mollis; Son paschalis; Son tribus quadrantibus; Son campanarum; Serenada *(rec Lobochovice castle, July 26–28, 1992)* Discover International ▲ DI 920243 [DDD]

Price, David (org)
Amner, J.:Sacred Music, w. P. Trepte (cnd), Parley of Instruments, Ely Cathedral Choir—Te Deum; I Will Sing unto the Lord As Long As I Live; Blessed Be the Lord God; O Ye Little Flock; Magnificat; Nunc dimitis; Sing, O Heav'ns; Vars. on "O Lord in Thee"; Consider, All Ye Passers by; Hear, O Lord; O Sing unto the Lord Hyperion ▲ CDA 66768
Carols from Many Lands, w. [cnd:Paul Trepte], Ely Cathedral Choir *(rec Ely Cathedral, Apr 1995)* Herald ▲ HAVPCD 178 [DDD]
Evensong for St. Etheldreda, w. [cnd:Paul Trepte], Ely Cathedral Choir *(rec Ely Cathedral, Jan 1996)* Herald ▲ HAPVCD 193 [DDD]
The Psalms of David, Vol. 8:Praise the Lord O My Soul, w. [cnd:Paul Trepte], Ely Cathedral Choir, Paul Trepte (org) Priory ▲ PRI 460 [DDD]

Price, J. (vn/violectra/mand/Yamaha DX-7/TX81-Z)
Price, J.R.:Ballet Suite 1 Innova ▲ MN 107

Price, John (bn)—see also ORCHESTRAS & ENSEMBLES Michael Thompson Wind Quintet
Danzi, F.:Sextet Ob, w. Richard Berry (hn), Michael Thompson (hn), John Bradburg (cl), Robert Hill (cl), Philip Tarlton (bn)—version for Harmonie ensemble *(rec St. Paul's Church, Rusthall, Kent, England, June 1994)* Naxos ▲ 8.553076 [DDD]
Stravinsky, I.:Pastorale, w. Neville Taweel (vn), Derek Wickens (ob), Leonard Brain (E hn), Thomas Kelly (cl), L. Stokowski (cnd), Royal PO *(rec Kingsway Hall, London, England, June 16–17, 1969)* London ("Phase 4 Stereo" series) ▲ 443898-2 [ADD]

Price, Paul (bass chalumeaux)
The Early Clarinet Family, w. Keith Puddy (cl), Gary Brodie (cl/bass chalumeaux), Susan Dent (baroque hn), Alastair Mitchell (8-keyed bn), Malcolm Martineau (pno) Clarinet Classics ▲ CC 0004

Price, Wilbur (pno)
Pierné, G.:Son da camera Fl, w. R. Willoughby (fl), Catherina Meints (vl) Gasparo Gallante ▲ GG 1003 [AAD]
Reger, M.:Suite Vn Pno, w. R. Willoughby (fl) [arr. unknown] Gasparo Gallante ▲ GG 1003 [AAD]

Price, Wilbur (vc)
Pierné, G.:Canzonetta Fl, w. R. Willoughby (fl) Gasparo Gallante ▲ GG 1003 [AAD]

Pridonoff, Eugene (pno)
Handel, D.:Scherzo Pno Vienna Modern Masters ▲ VMM 2019 [DDD]

Priebst, A. (vc)
Mauersberger, R.:Qt Strs, w. R. Straumer (vn) *(rec June 1991)* Thorofon ▲ CTH 2112 [DDD]
Mauersberger, R.:Trio Pno, w. W. Apel (pno), R. Straumer (vn) *(rec June 1991)* Thorofon ▲ CTH 2112 [DDD]

Prieditis, P. (cl)
Lachner, F.P.:Nonet, w. A. Duisberg (fl), D. Wollenweber (ob), P. Douglas (hn), M. Postinghel (bn), I. Grünkorn (vn), M. Gieler (va), T. Ruge (vc), F. Heidenreich (db) *(rec June 10, 1991)* Thorofon ▲ CTH 2132 [DDD]

Prieto, Carlos (vc)
Saint-Saëns, C.:Con 1 Vc, w. Mineria SO IMP Classics ▲ IMPPCD 1084 [DDD]
Shostakovich, D.:Con 1 Vc, w. H. de la Fuente (cnd), Xalapa SO IMP Classics ▲ IMPPCD 1084 [DDD]
Shostakovich, D.:Son Vc, w. D. Stevenson (pno) IMP Classics ▲ IMPPCD 1084 [DDD]

Příhoda, Váša (vn)
Dvořák, A.:Con Vn, w. P.V. Kempen (cnd), Berlin State Opera Orch *(rec live, Berlin, 1943)* Arkadia ▲ 623 [ADD]
Dvořák, A.:Con Vn, w. J. Krombholc (cnd), Prague RSO *(rec ca. 1956)* Multisonic (Prague Spring Collection) ▲ 31 0039-2 [ADD]
Dvořák, A.:Con Vn, w. P. Van Kempen (cnd), Berlin State Orch *(rec live, Berlin 1937)* Melodram ▲ CDM 18037 [ADD]
The Great Violinists Series One-Eleven ▲ URS 50090 [ADD]
The Great Violinists Series One-Eleven ▲ URS 50100 [ADD]
Paganini, N.:Con 1 Vn, w. Charles Cerné (pno) [arr for Vn & Pno] Biddulph ▲ LAB 135
Paganini, N.:I palpiti, w. Charles Cerné (pno) Biddulph ▲ LAB 135

Příhoda, Váša (vn) (cont.)
Paganini, N.:Son 12 Vn, w. Charles Cerné (pno) Biddulph ▲ LAB 135
Paganini, N.:Le Streghe, w. Charles Cerné (pno) [arr Vn & Pno] Biddulph ▲ LAB 135
Vieuxtemps, H.:Con 4 Vn, Berlin State Opera Orch Biddulph ▲ LAB 135
Wieniawski, H.:Con 2 Vn, Berlin State Opera Orch Biddulph ▲ LAB 135

Primes, Theodora Carras (pno)
Jacob, G.:Concertino Cl & Pno, w. Daniel Geeting (cl) *(rec Memorial Chapel, Univ. of Redlands, Redlands, CA)* PROdigital ▲ PRO 9226 [DDD]

Primrose, W. (cl)
Brahms, J.:Son 2 Cl, w. G. Moore (pno) *(rec 1937)* Biddulph ▲ LAB 011 [ADD]

Primrose, William (va)
Bartók, B.:Con Va, w. O. Klemperer (cnd), Royal Concertgebouw Orch *(rec live, Jan. 10, 1951)* Archipon ▲ ARC 101 (m) [ADD]
Bartók, B.:Con Va, w. O. Klemperer (cnd), Royal Concertgebouw Orch *(rec live, Jan.10, 1951)* Music & Arts ▲ CD 752-1 (m) [AAD]
Bax, A.:Son Va & Pno, w. H. Cohen (pno) *(rec 1937)* Pearl ▲ PEA 9453 (m) [AAD]
Beethoven, L. van:Serenade Strs, Op. 8, w. J. Heifetz (vn), G. Piatigorsky (vc) RCA Gold Seal ▲ 7870-2-RG (m/s) [ADD]
Beethoven, L. van:Trios Strs, Op. 9, w. J. Heifetz (vn), G. Piatigorsky (vc)—No. 2 RCA Gold Seal ▲ 7873-2-RG [ADD] ■ 7873-4-RG
Berlioz, H.:Harold in Italy, w. C. Munch (cnd), Boston SO RCA Gold Seal ▲ 09026-62582-2
Berlioz, H.:Harold in Italy, w. C. Munch (cnd), Boston SO *(rec Nov 1954)* RCA Victor Gold Seal 8-▲ 0902-668444-2 [ADD]
Berlioz, H.:Harold in Italy, w. T. Beecham (cnd), Royal PO *(rec 1951)* Sony Masterworks ("Portrait" series) ▲ MPK 47679 [ADD]
Bloch, E.:Suite Va & Pno, w. F. Kitzinger (pno) *(rec 1939)* Pearl ▲ PEA 9453 (m) [AAD]
Brahms, J.:Sextet Strs, Op. 36, w. J. Heifetz (vn), I. Baker (vn), V. Majewski (va), G. Piatigorsky (vc), G. Rejto (vc) RCA Gold Seal ▲ 7965-2-RG [ADD]
Brahms, J.:Sons Cl (comp), w. Rudolf Firkušný (pno) *(rec New York City, 1958–59)* EMI Classics ▲ CDM 66065
Brahms, J.:Sym 1, w. G. Moore (pno)—2nd movt. *(rec 1937)* Pearl ▲ PEA 9045 [AAD]
Casadesus, H.G.:Con Va, "Handel", w. W. Goehr (cnd), *(orch unknown)* *(rec 1937)* Pearl ▲ PEA 9045 [AAD]
Dohnányi, E. von:Serenade, w. J. Heifetz (vn), E. Feuermann (vc) Biddulph ▲ LAB 074 [ADD]
Halvorsen, J.:Passacaglia & Sarabande con variazioni, w. J. Heifetz (vn) Biddulph ▲ LAB 074 [ADD]
Handel, G.F.:Suites Hpd, w. Jascha Heifetz (vn)—No. 7 in g [Passacaglia; trans Halvorsen for vn & va] *(rec RCA Studio 2, New York City, May 22, 1941)* RCA Gold Seal 2-▲ 09026-61740-2 (m) [ADD]
Kreisler, F.:Qt Strs, w. F. Kreisler (vn), T. Petrie (vn), L. Kennedy (vc) Biddulph 3-▲ LAB 001-3 (m) [ADD]
Kreisler, F.:Scherzo 'in the style of Dittersdorf', w. F. Kreisler (vn), T. Petrie (vn), L. Kennedy (vc) Biddulph 3-▲ LAB 001-3 (m) [ADD]
Mozart, W.A.:Duo Vn, K.424, w. J. Heifetz (vn) Biddulph ▲ LAB 074 [ADD]
Mozart, W.A.:Duo Vn, K.424, w. Jascha Heifetz (vn) *(rec RCA Studio 2, New York City & RCA Studios, Hollywood, May 22 & Aug 29, 1941)* RCA Gold Seal 2-▲ 09026-61740-2 (m) [ADD]
Mozart, W.A.:Qnts Strs, w. Griller String Quartet—K.516 & 593 *(rec 1959)* Vanguard Classics ▲ OVC 8024 [ADD]
Mozart, W.A.:Qnts Strs, w. Griller String Quartet—K.406, 515 & 614 *(rec 1959)* Vanguard Classics ▲ OVC 8025 [ADD]
Mozart, W.A.:Qnt Strs, K.516, w. J. Heifetz (vn), I. Baker (vn), V. Majewski (va), G. Piatigorsky (vc) RCA Gold Seal ▲ 7869-2 (m/s) [ADD] ■ 7869-4 (m/s)
Mozart, W.A.:Sinf concertante Vn, K.364, w. J. Heifetz (vn), I. Solomon (cnd), RCA Victor SO RCA Red Seal ▲ 6778-2 [ADD]
Mozart, W.A.:Sinf concertante Vn, K.364, w. A. Spalding (vn), F. Stiedry (cnd), New Friends of Music Orch *(rec May 28, 1941)* Pearl ▲ PEA 9045 [AAD]
Mozart, W.A.:Sinf concertante Vn, K.364, w. I. Stern (vn), P. Casals (cnd), Perpignan Festival Orch *(rec Perpignan, France, July 5–8, 1951)* Sony Classical ("The Casals Edition" series) ▲ SMK 58983 [ADD]
Mozart, W.A.:Trio Vn, K.563, w. J. Heifetz (vn), E. Feuermann (vc) Biddulph ▲ LAB 074 [ADD]
Mozart, W.A.:Trio Vn, K.563, w. Jascha Heifetz (vn), Emanuel Feuermann (vc) *(rec RCA Studios, Hollywood, Sept 9, 1941)* RCA Gold Seal 2-▲ 09026-61740-2 (m) [ADD]
Schubert, Franz:Qnt Strs, D.956, w. J. Heifetz (vn), I. Baker (vn), G. Piatigorsky (vc), G. Rejto (vc) RCA Gold Seal ▲ 7964-2-RG [ADD] ■ 7964-4-RG (CrO2)
Schubert, Franz:Trio Strs, D.581, w. J. Heifetz (vn), G. Piatigorsky (vc) RCA Gold Seal ▲ 7964-2-RG [ADD] ■ 7964-4-RG (CrO2)
William Primrose Biddulph 2-▲ LAB 131-32
William Primrose *(rec 1934–39 Columbia)* Pearl ▲ PEA 9453 (m) [AAD]

Prince, H. (trbn)
Bloch, E.:Sym Trbn, w. J. Avshalomov (cnd), Portland Youth PO *(rec 1976)* CRI ▲ CD 634 [ADD]

Prinz, Alfred (cl)
Mozart, W.A.:Con Cl, w. K. Böhm (cnd), Vienna PO Deutsche Grammophon ▲ 413552-2 [ADD]
Mozart, W.A.:Con Cl, w. K. Böhm (cnd), Vienna PO Deutsche Grammophon ▲ 429816-2 [ADD] ■ 429816-4
Schmidt, F.:Qnt Cl, w. J. Demus (pno), A. Kamper (vn), F. Stangler (va), W. Resel (vc) *(rec 1965)* Preiser ▲ 93383 [ADD]

Prior, Gwennieth (pno)
Gershwin, G.:Con Pno, w. R. Williams (cnd), London SO IMP ("London SO" series) ▲ IMP 7
Gershwin, G.:Rhap in Blue, w. R. Williams (cnd), London SO IMP ("London SO" series) ▲ IMP 7

Priore, Orietta (trbn)—see ORCHESTRAS & ENSEMBLES Academy of Ancient Music Instumental Ensemble

Pristašová, Ivana (vn)—see also ORCHESTRAS & ENSEMBLES Albrecht String Quartet
Godár, V.:Déploration sur la mort de Witold Lutoslawski, w. Eleonóra Škutová-Slaničková (pno), Peter Biely (vn), Peter Šesták (va), Jozef Lupták (vc) *(rec Residence of Slovak Composers, Apr 1996)* Slovart ▲ SR 0018-2-131 [DDD]
Godár, V.:Ricercar, w. Eleonóra Škutová-Slaničková (pno), Peter Šesták (va), Jozef Lupták (vc) *(rec Residence of Slovak Composers, Apr 1996)* Slovart ▲ SR 0018-2-131 [DDD]

Pritchard, Eric (vn)—see ORCHESTRAS & ENSEMBLES Arman Ensemble, Alexander String Quartet

Pritchard, Evan (perc)—see ORCHESTRAS & ENSEMBLES Nova Ensemble

Pritsker, Vladimar (vn)
Caltabiano, R.:Torched Liberty, w. N. Pilgrim (sop), G. Macero (vc), L. Greene (pic/fl/alt fl), K. Schempf (E♭/A/B♭ cl), G. Coble (tpt), S. Heyman (pno), L. Luttinger (perc), R. Caltabiano (cnd) Opus One ▲ CD 168 [DDD]
Lindenfeld, H.:From the Grotte des Combarelles, w. G. Macero (vc), S. Heyman (pno) Opus One ▲ CD 168 [DDD]

Privitera, Angelo (kbd/cmpt)
Battiato, F.:Haiku, w. Franco Battiato (voc), Pouran Ghaffarpour (voc), Antonio Ballista (pno), Marco Boni (vc), Guido Corti (cnt), Filippo Destrieri (kbd/computer), John Giblin (bass), Gavin Harrison (dr/perc), Jakko Jakszyk (gtr), Roberto Mazza (ob), Fabrizio Merlini (va), Mino Bordignon (cnd), Milan Chamber Music Choir Hemisphere ▲ 837234-2
Battiato, F.:Messa Arcaica, w. Akemi Sakamoto (mez), Franco Battiato (voc), Filippo Destrieri (kbd/cmpt), Carlo Guaitoli (pno), A. Ballista (cnd), Italian Virtuosi, Filippo Maria Bressan (cnd), Athestis Chorus Hemisphere ▲ 837234-2
Battiato, F.:Ricerca sul Terzo, w. Franco Battiato (voc), Alessio Alba (tamboura), Antonio Ballista (pno), Marco Boni (vc), Debendra Kanti Chakraborty (tabla), Guido Corti (cnt), Filippo Destrieri (kbd/computer), John Giblin (bass), Buddhadeu Das Gupta (sarod), Gavin Harrison (dr/perc), Jakko Jakszyk (gtr), Roberto Mazza (ob), Fabrizio Merlini (va), Mino Bordignon (cnd), Milan Chamber Music Choir Hemisphere ▲ 837234-2

Prober, Wendy (pno)—see also ORCHESTRAS & ENSEMBLES Viklarbo Chamber Ensemble
Newman, M.:Maskil *(rec The Tujunga Dog House)* Raptoria Caam ▲ RCD 1007

Probst, Esther (E hn)—see ORCHESTRAS & ENSEMBLES Ives Ensemble members

788

▲ = CD ♦ = Enhanced CD Δ = MD ■ = Cassette Tape □ = DCC

Prockelo, Vincenzo (ob)
Partch, H.:Bless This Home, w. Harry Partch (voc/adapted va), Danlee Mitchell (kithara/harmonic canon), Joseph Varhula (mazda mar), J. Garvey (cnd) *(rec Univ of Illinois, 1961)* Innova 4–▲ 401

Procureur, Ingrid (hp)
Marc Grauwels & Friends, w. Marc Grauwels (fl), Marie-Noelle de Callataÿ (sop), Hiroko Masaki (sop), Dennis James (glass hmc), Yves Storms (gtr), Yvietta Matison (va), Mark Drobinsky (vc), Alain De Rijckere (bn), Daniel Blumenthal (pno), Frank Michiels (perc), Belgian RSO, et. al. Syrinx 2–▲ 96101 [DDD]

Prokofiev, Sergei (pno)
Great Composers at the Keyboard, w. Alfredo Casella (pno), Georges Enescu (pno) Foné ▲ FON 90F15 [DDD]
Prokofiev Plays Prokofiev LaserLight ▲ 14 203
Prokofiev, S.:Con 3 Pno, w. P. Coppola (cnd), London SO InSync ■ C 4148
Prokofiev, S.:Con 3 Pno, w. P. Coppola (cnd), London SO *(rec 1932)* Pearl ▲ PEA 9470 (m) [ADD]
Prokofiev, S.:Pno Music (misc)—Toccata, Op. 11; March, Op.12/1; Rigaudon, Op. 12/3; Prelude, Op. 12/7; Scherzo, Op. 12/10; Tales of the Old Grandmother, Op. 31/3; Sarcasms, Op. 17/1 & 2; Gavotte, Op. 12/2; Scherzo from The Love For Three Oranges; March from The Love For Three Oranges Klavier ▲ KCD 11038 [ADD]
Prokofiev, S.:Pno Music (misc)—8 pieces *(rec 1935)* Pearl ▲ PEA 9470 (m) [ADD]
Prokofiev, S.:Visions fugitives—Nos. 3,5,6,9,10,11,16,17,18 *(rec 1935)* Pearl ▲ PEA 9470 (m) [ADD]

Propischin, Igo (db)
Ustvolskaya, G.:Composition 2, w. Leonid Kolosov (db), Vitalii Goryachev (db), Vladimir Vulih (db), Vyacheslav Kovalenko (db), Alexei Peresipkin (db), Dmitrii Sokolov (db), Vladimir Nefedov (db), Valerii Javnertchik (perc), Galina Sandovskaya (pno), O. Malov (cnd) *(rec St. Petersburg Radio House, Jan. 1994)* Megadisc ▲ 7867

Prosser, Pietro (chit)—see ORCHESTRAS & ENSEMBLES Basso Generale
Prosser, Pietro (lt)—see ORCHESTRAS & ENSEMBLES Academy of Ancient Music Instumental Ensemble

Prosser, Rob (acc)
O'Rourke, J.:Terminal Pharmacy, w. Tony Burr (cl), Jeff Cortazzo (b trbn), John McEntire (dr), Isha Suftin (acc), Mike Dockter (vc), Hattie Franck (vc), Robert Keck (vc), Mary LaBreque (vc), Dan Loch (vc), Stan Saderk (vc), Lisa Hemmer (fl), Sue Oberg (fl), Wendi Lev (fl), Jim Vanden (fl), Jim O'Rourke (gtr), Steve Braack (elec) Tzadik ▲ TZA 7011 [DDD]

Protich, S. (pno)
Mussorgsky, M.:Nursery, w. A. Milcheva (mez) Pyramid ▲ PYR 13494
Mussorgsky, M.:Songs (misc), w. A. Milcheva (mez) Pyramid ▲ PYR 13494

Protopapas, Petros (fl)
Karaindrou, E.:Film Music, w. Vangelis Skouras (Fr hn), Alekos Christidis (timp), Eleni Karaindrou (voc), Lefteis Chalkiadakis (cnd)—Elegy for Rosa; Rosa's Song (text:Christofis) [both from Rosa] ECM ▲ 78118–21429–2 [AAD]

Protopopescu, Dana (pno)
Weber, C.M. von:Con 1 Pno, w. A. Rahbari (cnd), Belgian Radio-TV PO *(rec Concert Hall of the Belgian Radio & TV, Brussels, May 16–18, 1994)* Discover International ▲ DI 920222 [DDD]
Weber, C.M. von:Con 2 Pno, w. A. Rahbari (cnd), Belgian Radio-TV PO *(rec Concert Hall of the Belgian Radio & TV, Brussels, May 16–18, 1994)* Discover International ▲ DI 920222 [DDD]
Weber, C.M. von:Konzertstück Pno, w. A. Rahbari (cnd), Belgian Radio-TV PO *(rec Concert Hall of the Belgian Radio & TV, Brussels, May 16–18, 1994)* Discover International ▲ DI 920222 [DDD]

Proud, Malcolm (hpd)
Handel, G.F.:Cants, w. J. Baird (sop), J. Dornenburg (vl)—Occhi miei, che faceste?; Quel fior che all'alba ride; Solitudini care, amata liberata; Udite il mil consiglio [I] *(rec 6/90)* Meridian ▲ CDE 84189
Handel, G.F.:Son Vl, w. John Dornenburg (vl) *(rec 6/90)* Meridian ▲ CDE 84189
Handel, G.F.:Suites Hpd *(rec 6/90)* Meridian ▲ CDE 84189
Hasse, J.A.:Arias, w. Erin Headley (vl)—Ah Dio, ritornate [from *La conversione di Sant'Agostino*] *(rec May 30–June 1, 1991)* CRD ▲ CRD 3488 [DDD]
Hasse, J.A.:Cants, w. Julianne Baird (sop), Erin Headley (vl)—Quel vago seno, O Fille; Fille dolce, mio bene *(rec May 30–June 1, 1991)* CRD ▲ CRD 3488 [DDD]
Hasse, J.A.:Sons (12) Fl, w. Nancy Hadden (fl)—No. 6 in b *(rec May 30–June 1, 1991)* CRD ▲ CRD 3488 [DDD]
Hasse, J.A.:Sons Hpd, Op. 7—No. 6 in c *(rec May 30–June 1, 1991)* CRD ▲ CRD 3488 [DDD]
Hasse, J.A.:Songs, Airs & Solfeggi, w. Julianne Baird (sop)—Grazie agli inganni tuoi; No ste' a condanarme; Cosa e' sta Cossa?; Si', la gondola avere', no crie' *(rec May 30–June 1, 1991)* CRD ▲ CRD 3488 [DDD]
Purcell, H.:Hpd Music (misc)—Groups 1 in c, 2 in G & 3 in d Meridian ▲ MER 84280 [DDD]
Purcell, H.:Suites Hpd Meridian ▲ MER 84280 [DDD]

Prunnbauer, Sonja (gtr)
Boccherini, L.:Syms, w. Jürgen Hollerbuhl (ob), B. Vestre (ob), Jörn Maatz (ob), H. Maile (vn), H. Ganz (vn), R. Forest (vc), J. Stárek (cnd), Berlin RIAS Sinfonietta—in C, G.495 (Op. 21/3) *(rec Dec. 1979)* Koch Treasure ▲ 31612–2 [ADD]
Carulli, F.:Grand Duo, Op. 70, w. Robert Hill (pno) MD + G ▲ MDG 6030616
Carulli, F.:Grand Duo, Op. 86, w. Robert Hill (pno) MD + G ▲ MDG 6030616
Carulli, F.:Music for Gtr, w. Robert Hill (pno)—Op. 134 MD + G ▲ MDG 6030616
Carulli, F.:Valses, Op. 32, w. Robert Hill (pno) MD + G ▲ MDG 6030616
Carulli, F.:Vars on Theme by Beethoven, w. Robert Hill (pno) MD + G ▲ MDG 6030616
Castelnuovo-Tedesco, M.:Platero y yo, w. Jo Schaarschmidt (nar) Ars Musici ▲ 1138
Gragnani, F.:Qt for 2 Gtrs, w. I. Turnagoel (gtr), D. Klöcker (cl), H. Ganz (va) *(rec Sept. 1984)* Koch Treasure ▲ 31612–2 [ADD]
Tansman, A.:Musique de Cour, w. J. Stárek (cnd), Berlin RIAS Sinfonietta *(rec Dec. 1979)* Koch Treasure ▲ 31612–2 [ADD]
Virtuoso Music for Clarinet & Guitar, w. Dieter Klöcker (cl) MD + G ▲ L 3319 [DDD]

Prunyi, Ilona (pno)
Arensky, A.:Qnt Pno, w. Lajtha String Quartet *(rec Rottenbiller Street Studio, Budapest, Jan. 16–22, 1994)* Marco Polo ▲ 8.223811 [DDD]
Atterberg, K.:Chamber Music, w. E. Pérényi (vn), A. Kiss (vn), S. Falvay (pno), G. Kertész (vc), D. Spikay (hp)—Son. in b for Violin, Op. 27; Höstballader, Op. 15; Valse monotone in C; Rondeau Rétrospectif, Op. 26; Trio Concertante in g, Op. 57 Marco Polo ▲ 8.223404
Atterberg, K.:Qnt Pno, w. New Budapest String Quartet Marco Polo ▲ 8.223405 [DDD]
Atterberg, K.:Son Vc, w. Imre Magyari (hn) [arr. hn & pno] Marco Polo ▲ 8.223405 [DDD]
Bartók, B.:Songs, w. J. Hamari (mez), J. Kovács (cnd), Hungarian State Orch—5 Songs, Op. 15 [Sz.61] [orchd. by Zoltán Kodály]; 5 Songs, Op. 16 [Sz.63]; 5 Songs [from 8 Hungarian Folksongs, Sz.64]; Songs for Voice & Orch.; 5 Songs for Voice & Orch., Sz.101 [Hun] Hungaroton ▲ HCD 31535 [DDD]
Bennett, W.S.:Pno Music—Son. in A♭, Op. 46, "The Maid of Orleans" (1873); Allegro Grazioso, Op.18 (1840); 4 Pieces; 3 Musical Sketches, Op. 10 (1836); Geneviéve (1839); Scherzo, Op. 27 (1845); Rondo Piacevole, Op. 25 (1843) *(rec 1992)* Marco Polo ▲ 8.223512
Berwald, F.:Trios, w. A. Kiss (vn), C. Onczay (vc)—Nos. 1–3 Marco Polo ▲ 8.223170
Boëllmann, L.:Qt Pno & Strs, w. B. Bánfalvi (vn), J. Fejévári (va), K. Botvay (vc) Marco Polo ▲ 8.223524
Boëllmann, L.:Trio Pno, w. B. Bánfalvi (vn), J. Fejévári (va), K. Botvay (vc) Marco Polo ▲ 8.223524
Borodin, A.:Qnt Pno & Strs, w. New Budapest String Quartet Marco Polo ▲ 8.223172 [DDD]
Borodin, A.:Son Vc, w. O. Kertész (vc) Marco Polo ▲ 8.223172 [DDD]
David, Felicien:Trio 2 Pno, w. E. Pérény (vn), T. Párkányi (vc) Marco Polo ▲ 8.223492
David, Felicien:Trio 3 Pno, w. E. Pérény (vn), T. Párkányi (vc) Marco Polo ▲ 8.223492
Godowsky, L.:Walzermasken Marco Polo ▲ 8.223312 [DDD]
Indy, V. d':Qnt Pno, w. New Budapest String Quartet *(rec Alpha-Line Studio, Festetich Castle, Budapest, Oct 5–6, 1993)* Marco Polo ▲ 8.223691 [DDD]
Indy, V. d':Trio 2 Pno, w. New Budapest String Quartet members *(rec Alpha-Line Studio, Festetich Castle, Budapest, Oct 5–6, 1993)* Marco Polo ▲ 8.223691 [DDD]
Kiel, F.:Qnt 1, w. New Budapest String Quartet Marco Polo ▲ 8.223171

Prunyi, Ilona (pno) (cont.)
Kiel, F.:Qnt 2, w. New Budapest String Quartet Marco Polo ▲ 8.223171
Korngold, E.W.:Fairy Pictures *(rec Aug. 31 & Sept. 4, 1990)* Marco Polo ▲ 8.223384 [DDD]
Korngold, E.W.:Much Ado About Nothing *(rec Aug. 31 & Sept. 4, 1990)* Marco Polo ▲ 8.223384 [DDD]
Korngold, E.W.:Qnt Pno, w. Danubius Quartet Marco Polo ▲ 8.223385
Korngold, E.W.:Son 2 Pno *(rec Aug. 31 & Sept. 4, 1990)* Marco Polo ▲ 8.223384 [DDD]
Korngold, E.W.:Son Vn, w. A. Kiss (vn), Danubius Quartet Marco Polo ▲ 8.223385
Kuhlau, F.:Qt 1 Pno, w. New Budapest String Quartet *(rec Dec. 20–22, 1991)* Marco Polo ▲ 8.223482 [DDD]
Kuhlau, F.:Qt 2 Pno, w. New Budapest String Quartet *(rec Dec. 20–22, 1991)* Marco Polo ▲ 8.223482 [DDD]
Liszt, F.:Via Crucis, w. D. Várjon (pno), J. Dobra (cnd), Tomkins Vocal Ensemble [L] *(rec 2/91)* Hungaroton ▲ HCD 31424 [DDD]
Rachmaninoff, S.:Rhapsody on a Theme of Paganini, w. H. Williams (cnd), Pécs SO Hungaroton ▲ HCD 31551 [DDD]
Rachmaninoff, S.:Symphonic Dances, w. H. Williams (cnd), Pécs SO Hungaroton ▲ HCD 31551 [DDD]
Schubert, Franz:Allegro Pno 4-Hands, D.947, w. J. Jandó (pno) *(rec Nov. 5–8, 1991)* Naxos ▲ 8.550555 [DDD]
Schubert, Franz:Divertissement à l'hongroise, D.818, w. J. Jandó (pno) *(rec Nov. 5–8, 1991)* Naxos ▲ 8.550555 [DDD]
Schubert, Franz:Marches caractéristiques, w. J. Jandó (pno) *(rec Nov. 5–8, 1991)* Naxos ▲ 8.550555 [DDD]
Sinding, C.:Trios Pno, w. A. Kiss (vn), T. Koó (vc)—No. 1 in D, Op. 23 (1893) & No. 2 in a, Op. 64a (1902) Marco Polo ▲ 8.223283
Sterndale-Bennett, W.:Pno Works—The Maid of New Orleans; Allegro Grazioso; 4 pieces; 3 Musical Sketches; Geneviéve; Scherzo; Rondo Piacevole Marco Polo ▲ 8.223512
Tchaikovsky, P.:Pno Music—Chanson triste in g; Songs without Words in a & in F; Nocturne in c# *(rec July 13–14, 1988)* Naxos ▲ 8.550233 [DDD]
Tchaikovsky, P.:Pno Music—Polka peu dansante in b, Op. 51/2; Romance in F, Op. 51/5; Dumka in c, Op. 59; L'espiègle in E, Op. 72/12; Rêverie in D, Op. 9/1; Humoresque in e, Op. 10/2; Dialogue in B, Op. 72/8; Romance in f, Op. 5; Danse russe in a, Op. 40/10; Nocturne in F, Op. 10/1; Scherzo in F, Op. 2/2; Rêverie du soir in g, Op. 19/1; Tendres reproches in c#, Op. 72/3; Mazurka in D, Op. 40/ 5; Capriccioso in B♭, Op. 19/5; Polacca de concert in E♭, Op. 72/7 *(rec Jan. 11 & 13, 1991)* Naxos ▲ 8.550504 [DDD]
Tchaikovsky, P.:Les Saisons *(rec July 13–14, 1988)* Naxos ▲ 8.550233 [DDD]

Prutsman, Stephen (pno)
Bach, J.S.:Cons for 3 Hpds (comp), w. F. Braley (pno), B. Ganz (pno), P. Peire (cnd), Collegium Instrumentale Brugense René Gailly ▲ CD 87065 [DDD]
Mozart, W.A.:Con 7 Pnos, w. F. Braley (pno), B. Ganz (pno), P. Peire (cnd), Collegium Instrumentale Brugense René Gailly ▲ CD 87065 [DDD]
Rachmaninoff, S.:Pno Music (pno 6–hands), w. Frank Braley (pno), Brian Ganz (pno)—Romance; Valse René Gailly ▲ CD 87065 [DDD]

Pryor, Arthur (trbn)
Trombone Solos, w. Sousa Band, Pryor Band *(rec 1897–1911)* Crystal ■ C 451

Pryor, Gwenneth (pno)
Brahms, J.:Sons Cl (comp), w. G. De Peyer (cl) Chandos ▲ CHAN 8563 [DDD]
Debussy, C.:Première rapsodie, w. G.. de Peyer (cl) Chandos ▲ CHAN 8526 [DDD]
English Music for Clarinet & Piano, w. Gervase De Peyer (cl) Chandos ▲ CHAN 8549 [DDD]
Gershwin, G.:An American in Paris, w. R. Williams (cnd), London SO IMP ("LSO" series) ▲ IMP 6900072
Gershwin, G.:Con Pno, w. R. Williams (cnd), London SO IMP ("LSO" series) ▲ IMP 6900072
Gershwin, G.:Rhap in Blue, w. R. Williams (cnd), London SO IMP ("LSO" series) ▲ IMP 6900072
Ireland, J.:Fant-Son Cl & Pno, w. Gervase de Peyer (cl) Chandos ▲ CHAN 9377/8 [DDD]
Poulenc, F.:Son Cl Pno, w. G. de Peyer (cl) Chandos ▲ CHAN 8526 [DDD]
Saint-Saëns, C.:Son Cl, w. G. De Peyer (cl) Chandos ▲ CHAN 8526 [DDD]
Schubert, Franz:Son Arpeggione, w. G. de Peyer (cl) Chandos ▲ CHAN 8506 [DDD]
Schumann, R.:Fantasiestücke Cl, w. G. De Peyer (cl) Chandos ▲ CHAN 8506 [DDD]
Schumann, R.:Romances Ob, w. G. De Peyer (cl) Chandos ▲ CHAN 8506 [DDD]
Weber, C.M. von:Vars on a Theme from *Silvana*, w. G. De Peyer (cl) Chandos ▲ CHAN 8506 [DDD]

Prysiasnik, Piotr (vn)
Blacher, B.:Songs, w. Katharina Richter (sop), Cornella Wosnitza (sop), Markus Köhler (bar), Horst Göbel (pno), Chatschatur Kanajan (vn), Fred Günther (va), Ithay Khen (vc), Christian Peters (sax), Markus Weidmann (bn)—3 Chansons; Ungereimtes; 4 Lieder; Nebel; 13 Ways of Looking at a Blackbird; 5 Sinnsprüche Omars des Zeitmachers; 3 Psalmen; Aprèslude; Francesca da Rimini; Jazz-Koloraturen Signum ▲ SIG X73–00 [DDD]

Pschenitschnikova, Natalia (a fl/b fl)
Kancheli, G.:Exil, w. Catrin Demenga (sop), Maacha Deubner (sop), Ruth Killius (va), Rebecca Firth (vc), Christian Suttor (db) *(rec Propstei St. Gerold, Basel, May 1994)* ECM New Series ▲ 78118–21535–2 [DDD]

Pschenitschnikova, Natalia (a fl)
Kancheli, G.:Morning Prayers, w. Vasiko Tevdorashvili (sgr), D. R. Davies (cnd), Stuttgart CO *(rec Apr. 1994)* ECM New Series ▲ 78118–21510–2 [DDD]

Publiese, Michael (perc)
Lockwood, A.:Thousand Year Dreaming, w. Art Baron (conch shell/trbn/didjerido), Liby Van Cleve (ob/E hn), Jon Gibson (didjeridu), J.D. Parran (cl), Scott Robinson (conch shell/perc), John Snyder (didjeridu/waterphone), Charles Wood (tam-tam, stones), Peter Zummo (trbn/didjerido) ¿What Next? ▲ WN 0010

Puchelt, Gerhard (pno)
Hindemith, P.:Das Marienleben, w. Gerda Lammers (sop)—new 1948 version *(rec Studio Thienhaus, Hamburg, Apr–June 1961)* Cantate ▲ C 57610 [ADD]

Puddy, K. (vc)
Danzi, F.:Son Vc & Pno, w. M. Marineau (pno) Clarinet Classics ▲ CC 0004

Puddy, Keith (B♭ cl)
Brahms, J.:Sons Cl (comp), w. M. Martineau (pno) *(rec 1990, Meiningen)* IMP Allegro ▲ ALG PCD 994 [DDD]

Puddy, Keith (cl)
Beethoven, L. van:Duos, WoO 27, w. A. Mitchell (bn) [Puddy uses 5–keyed B♭ cl] Clarinet Classics ▲ CC 0004
Brahms, J.:Qnt Cl, w. Delmé String Quartet IMP Classics ▲ PCD 883 [DDD]
The Early Clarinet Family, w. Gary Brodie (cl/bass chalumeaux), P. Price (bass chalumeaux), Susan Dent (baroque hn), Alastair Mitchell (8–keyed bn), Malcolm Martineau (pno) Clarinet Classics ▲ CC 0004
Mozart, W.A.:Qnt Cl, K.581, w. Gabrieli String Quartet IMP Classics ▲ PCD 810 [DDD]

Pueyo, Eduardo del (pno)
Beethoven, L. van:Son 8 Pno, "Pathétique" Pavane 2–▲ ADW 7071/72
Beethoven, L. van:Son 14 Pno, "Moonlight Son" Pavane 2–▲ ADW 7071/72
Beethoven, L. van:Son 22 Pno Pavane 2–▲ ADW 7071/72
Beethoven, L. van:Son 23 Pno, "Appassionata" Pavane 2–▲ ADW 7071/72
Beethoven, L. van:Son 29 Pno, "Hammerklavier" Pavane 2–▲ ADW 7071/72
Beethoven, L. van:Son 31 Pno Pavane 2–▲ ADW 7071/72

Puffler, Helmuth (vn)—see ORCHESTRAS & ENSEMBLES Biedermeier Ensemble

Pugh, James (trbn)
Previn, A.:Honey & Rue, w. Kathleen Battle (sop), Chris Gekker (tpt), Rufus Reid (bass), Grady Tate (dr), A. Previn (cnd), Orch of St. Luke's Deutsche Grammophon ▲ 437787–2 ■ 437 787–4

Puglia, Antonio (cl)
Respighi, O.:Gli uccelli, w. Stefano Mancini (fl), Alberto Cesaraccio (ob), Paloma Tironi (hp), Stefano Melis (cel), R. Tigani (cnd), Sassari SO *(rec Rome, Oct 11–14, 1994)* Bongiovanni ▲ GB 2166 [DDD]

Pugliese, (perc)
Satoh, S.:Music of, w. Almond (vn), Leng Tan (pno), Messier (sop)—Birds in Warped Time II for Vn & Pno (1980); The Heavenly Spheres are Illuminated by Lights for Sop, Pno & Perc (1979); Incarnation II for solo Pno with tape delay (1970); Litania for 2 Pnos with tape delay (1973); A Gate into the Stars for solo Pno (1962) New Albion ▲ NA 008 [ADD]

Pugliese, James (diamond mar)
Partch, H.:Daphne of the Dunes, w. Frank Cassara (boo/spoils of war/kithara 2), Dominic Donato (b mar/surrogate kithara/boo), Dean Drummond (harmonic canons/kithara 2/spoils of war/kithara), Nina Kellman (kithara 2/harmonic canon/surrogate kithara), Michael Lipsey (cloud-chamber bowls), Ted Mook (vc/gourd tree/cone gongs), Elizabeth Rodgers (chromelodeon/harmonic canon) *(rec Queens, NY, Mar. 12, 1991)* Mode ▲ MODE 33

Pugliese, James (perc)
Hyla, L.:The Dream of Innocent III, w. Rhonda Rider (va), Lee Hyla (pno) CRI ▲ CD 564 [DDD]
Rosenblum, M.:Circadian Rhythms, w. Ted Mook (vc), Elizabeth Rodgers (kbd/pno) *(rec Floral Park, NY, Mar. 19, 1990)* Mode ▲ MODE 33
Shea, D.:Hsi-Yu Chi, w. Sim Cain (perc), Hideki Kato (bass instrument), Wu Man (pipa), Zeena Parkins (hp/pno/acc), Jim Pugliese (perc), Mark Ribot (gtr/banjo), David Shea (sampler/pno/turntables), Alex Tobias (celtic dr/misc.), Rebecca Wilson (screaming), John Zorn (a sax) Tzadik ("The Composers" series) ▲ TZA 7005 [DDD]
Zorn, J.:Dark River Tzadik ▲ TZA 7008 [DDD]
Zorn, J.:Redbird, w. Carol Emanuel (hp), Jill Jaffee (va), Erik Friedlander (vc) Tzadik ▲ TZA 7008 [DDD]

Pugliese, James (perc/vib)—see ORCHESTRAS & ENSEMBLES Gangster Band

Pugliese, James (syn)
Pugliese, J.:Freeze, w. Stefani Starin (alt fl), Dean Drummond (zmz), Dominic Donato (zmz) *(rec New York City, May 29, 1992)* Mode ▲ MODE 33

Pugliese, Michael (perc)—see also ORCHESTRAS & ENSEMBLES Musicians' Accord members, Musicians' Accord
Cage, J.:Music for 4 for Perc, w. K. Grossman (perc), C. Nappi (perc), W. Trigg (perc) *(rec in concert at Merkin Concert Hall, New York City, 4/4/89)* Mode ▲ 25
Feldman, Morton:The King of Denmark *(rec live, Merkin Concert Hall, New York City, 4/4/89)* Mode ▲ 25
Lebaron, A.:Rite of the Black Sun, w. W.A. Trigg (perc), F. Cassara (zoomoozophone), P. Guerguerian (perc), C. Heldrich (cnd), New Music Consort Mode ▲ 30
Nørgård, P.:Waves *(rec in concert at Merkin Concert Hall, New York City, 4/4/89)* Mode ▲ 25
Speach, B.:Music of, w. J. Schanzer, L. Krech (trbn), J. Williams (gtr), A. de Mare (pno), T. Davis (speaker), et al., B. Speach (cnd), Bowery Ensemble—Moto for Trbn, Perc & Pno (1982); Pensées for Gtr (1983); Trajet for Trbn & Perc (1983); Son for Pno (1986); Shattered Glass for Perc (1987); Telepathy (Poetry/Music Suite) for Speaker, Ctb; et. al. Mode ▲ 16
Vigeland, N.:Progress, w. J. Williams (perc) *(rec in concert at Merkin Concert Hall, New York City, 4/4/89)* Mode ▲ 25
Xenakis, I.:Psappha, "Perkin' at Merkin" *(rec in concert at Merkin Concert Hall, New York City, 4/4/89)* Mode ▲ 25

Pugliese, Michael (perc/voc)—see ORCHESTRAS & ENSEMBLES Musicians' Accord members

Pugno, Raoul (pno)
His Complete Published Piano Solos (1903) Opal ▲ CD 9836 (m) [AAD]

Puig-Roget, Henriette (pno)
Jolivet, A.:Concertino Tpt, w. Pierre Thibaud (tpt), K. Toyoda (cnd), Gunma SO *(rec Tone-Numata Public Hall, Japan, Sept 8-9, 1981)* Camerata ▲ 32CM 168 [DDD]
Tournemire, C.:Poème mystique *(rec 1973)* Memoire Vive ▲ 262006 [ADD]
Tournemire, C.:Sagesse, w. Bernard Plantey (ten) Memoire Vive ▲ CD 262024
Tournemire, C.:Sagesse, w. B. Plantey (ten) *(rec 1973)* Memoire Vive ▲ 262006 [ADD]
Tournemire, C.:Sonate-poème, w. D. Erlih (vn) *(rec 1973)* Memoire Vive ▲ 262006 [ADD]
Yashiro, A.:Trio Pno, w. C. Tanaka (vn), K. Yasuda (vc) Camerata ▲ 30CM 51

Pulford, Paul (vc)
Beethoven, L. van:Sons Vc (comp), w. Boyd McDonald (pno) ebs 2-▲ 6030 [DDD]
Beethoven, L. van:Vars on "Ein Mädchen oder Weibchen" from Mozart's *Die Zauberflöte*, w. Boyd McDonald (pno) ebs 2-▲ 6030 [DDD]
Beethoven, L. van:Vars on "See, the Conquering Hero Comes" from Handel's *Judas Maccabaeus*, w. Boyd McDonald (pno) ebs 2-▲ 6030 [DDD]
Beethoven, L. van:Vars on "Bei Männern" from Mozart's *Die Zauberflöte*, w. Boyd McDonald (pno) ebs 2-▲ 6030 [DDD]

Pulgram, Christopher (vn)—see ORCHESTRAS & ENSEMBLES Atlanta Chamber Players
Puliti, Damiano (vc)—see ORCHESTRAS & ENSEMBLES Harmonia Ensemble
Purdue, Eugene (vn)—see ORCHESTRAS & ENSEMBLES Thouvenel String Quartet
Purse, L. (kbd)—see ORCHESTRAS & ENSEMBLES Mother Mallard

Purser, David (trbn)
Gough, O.:Saeta, w. Pepe de la Matrona (voc), Bruce Nockles (tpt), Michael Thompson (hn), John Pigneguy (hn), Orlando Gough (kbd) *(rec London, 1995)* Catalyst ▲ 0902-668332-2 [DDD]
Mason, B.:Double Con, w. M. Thompson (hn), D. Mason (cnd), London Sinfonietta Bridge ▲ BCD 9045 [DDD]

Purvis, Jennifer (pno)
Baroque Beauties, w. J. Laredo (cnd), Scottish CO, City of London Sinfonia [cnd:R. Hickox], E. Ritchie (sop), Bowman (ct) Pickwick ("The Orchid" series) ▲ PICORCD 11010
The Best of Classical Song, w. Elizabeth Ritchie (sop), Victoria Soames (cl) IMP Classics ▲ PCD 987 [DDD]
Paer, F.:Una voce al cor mi parta, w. E. Ritchie (sop), V. Soames (cl) Clarinet Classics ▲ CC 0006 [ADD]
Spohr, L.:Faust (sels), w. E. Ritchie (sop), V. Soames (cl)—Ich bin allein Clarinet Classics ▲ CC 0006 [ADD]
Spohr, L.:Songs (misc), w. E. Ritchie (sop), V. Soames (cl)—6 deutsche Lieder, Op. 103 Clarinet Classics ▲ CC 0006 [ADD]
Spohr, L.:Vars in B♭ on a Theme from *Alruna*, w. V. Soames (cl) Clarinet Classics ▲ CC 0006 [ADD]

Purvis, William (hn)—see also ORCHESTRAS & ENSEMBLES Mozzafiato, Speculum Musicae
Brahms, J.:Trio Hn, w. D. Phillips (vn), R. Goode (pno) Bridge ▲ BCD 9012 [DDD]
Davison, J.:Son Hn, w. Alan Feinberg (pno) Albany ▲ TROY 199 [DDD]
Lieberson, P.:King Gesar, w. Yo-Yo Ma (vc), Emanuel Ax (pno), Peter Serkin (pno), Omar Ebrahim (nar), Andras Adorjan (fl), Deborah Marshall (cl), David Taylor (trbn), Stefan Huge (perc) Sony Classical ▲ SK 57971
Ligeti, G.:Trio Hn, Vn & Pno, w. R. Schulte (vn), A. Feinberg (pno) Bridge ▲ BCD 9012 [DDD]
Mozart, W.A.:Con Hn, K.417, w. Orpheus CO Deutsche Grammophon ▲ 423623-2 [DDD]
Mozart, W.A.:Con Hn, K.447, w. Orpheus CO Deutsche Grammophon ▲ 423623-2 [DDD]
Rosenzweig, M.:Delta, the Perfect King, w. M. Rosenzweig (cnd), Speculum Musicae *(rec Recital Hall, SUNY, Purchase, New York, Oct 15, 1991)* CRI ▲ CD 705 [DDD]
Silver, S.:Dance Converging, w. Lois Martin (va), Lisa Moore (pno), Thad Wheeler (perc) *(rec Recital Hall, Music Division, SUNY, Purchase, New York, Apr 12, 1995)* CRI ▲ CD 708 [DDD]
Silver, S.:Dynamis *(rec American Academy of Arts & Letters, New York, Apr 20, 1995)* CRI ▲ CD 708 [DDD]
Wuorinen, C.:Double Solo, w. B. Hudson (vn), J. Winn (pno) *(rec Oct. 17, 1991)* Koch International Classics ▲ KIC 7123-2 [DDD]
Wuorinen, C.:Trio Hn, w. B. Hudson (vn), A. Feinberg (pno) *(rec Sept. 11-13, 1991)* Koch International Classics ▲ KIC 7123-2 [DDD]
Wuorinen, C.:Trio Hn Continued, w. B. Hudson (vn), J. Winn (pno) *(rec Sept. 11-13, 1991)* Koch International Classics ▲ KIC 7123-2 [DDD]

Pusch, Gretchen (fl)—see ORCHESTRAS & ENSEMBLES Flute Force

Puschnig, Wolfgang (bass cl)
Puschnig, W.:Vexations 2015, w. Woody Schabata (vib) *(rec Vienna, Sept. 22, 1983)* Hat Hut ("NOW." series) ▲ hat ART CD 6024 [ADD]

Puschnig, Wolfgang (fl/s sax)
Rüegg, M.:Music of, w. Lauren Newton (sgr), Harry Sokal (s sax), Roman Schwaller (t sax), Karl Fian (tpt), Christian Radovan (trbn), Woody Schabata (vib)—Reflections on Aubade; Reflections on Méditation; Reflections on Sévère Réprimande; Reflections on Idylle; Reflections on Gnossiennes Nos. 1 & 2; Satie ist mir im traum 3x nicht erschienen *(rec Vienna, Sept. 20-22, 1983)* Hat Hut ("NOW." series) ▲ hat ART CD 6024 [ADD]

Putnam, Charles (hn)—see ORCHESTRAS & ENSEMBLES American Horn Quartet
Pütz, Friedhelm (hn)—see also ORCHESTRAS & ENSEMBLES Stuttgart Wind Quintet
Haas, P.:The Chosen One, w. Jörg Dürmüller (ten), Willy Freivogel (fl), Monika Hölszky-Wiedemann (vn), Dennis Russell Davies (pno) Orfeo ("Musica Rediviva" series) ▲ 386961 [DDD]

Puyana, Rafael (hpd)
Bach, J.S.:Sons Fl, BWV 1030-35, w. Maxence Larrieu (fl), Wieland Kuijken (vl) Philips 2-▲ 438809-2
Bach, J.S.:Sons Vl, BWV 1027-1029, w. Marçal Cervera (vl) Philips 2-▲ 438809-2
Bach, J.S.:Sons Vn, w. Maxence Larrieu (fl)—BWV 120 [doubtful; arr. flute & continuo] Philips 2-▲ 438809-2
Falla, M. de:Con Hpd, w. E. Mata (cnd), Mexican Soloists *(rec Sala Nezahualcóyotl, Universidad Nacional Autónoma de Mexico, Mexico City, Oct. 1994)* Dorian ▲ DOR 90214 [DDD]
Falla, M. de:Con Hpd, w. D. Sandeman (fl), N. Black (ob), T. King (cl), R. Cohen (vn), T. Weill (vc), C. Mackerras (cnd) *(rec 1969)* Philips ("Spanish" series) ▲ 432829-2 [ADD]
Falla, M. de:El retablo de maese Pedro, w. Lourdes Ambriz (sop), Julianne Baird (sop), Miguel Cortez (ten), William Alvarado (bar), E. Mata (cnd), Mexican Soloists *(rec Sala Nezahualcóyotl, Universidad Nacional Autónoma de Mexico, Mexico City, Oct. 1994)* Dorian ▲ DOR 90214 [DDD]
Orbón, J.:Cantigas del rey, w. *(sop unknown)*, E. Mata (cnd), Mexican Soloists *(rec Sala Nezahualcóyotl, Universidad Nacional Autónoma de Mexico, Mexico City, Oct. 1994)* Dorian ▲ DOR 90214 [DDD]
Scarlatti, D.:Sons Kbd—in F, K.518; in f, K.519; in D, K.443; in D, K.444; in E, K.206; in E, K.207; in C, K.159; in G., K.240; in G, K.241; in F, K.205; in a, K.7; in C, K.513; in E, K.380; in E, K.381; in a, K.54 Harmonia Mundi Plus ▲ HMP 3901164

Pyatt, David (hn)
Strauss, R.:Con 1 Hn, w. N. Cleobury (cnd), Britten Sinfonia Classics for Pleasure ("Eminence" series) ▲ CFP 2238
Strauss, R.:Con 2 Hn, w. N. Cleobury (cnd), Britten Sinfonia Classics for Pleasure ("Eminence" series) ▲ CFP 2238

Pye, David (perc)—see ORCHESTRAS & ENSEMBLES Nova Ensemble

Quagliata, Humberto (pno)
Alonso, M.:Atmosferas Discobi ▲ DIS 2001
Aracil, A.:Calmo Discobi ▲ DIS 2001
Balboa, M.:Intermezzo Discobi ▲ DIS 2001
Barce, R.:Preludes en nivel Discobi ▲ DIS 2001
Cano, F.:Fant Pno Discobi ▲ DIS 2001
Marco, Tomas:Campana Rajada Discobi ▲ DIS 2001
Marco, Tomas:Pno Music—Feitches; Le Palais du facteur cheval; Campana rajada; Cuatro cartas; Solea; Son de vesperia Discobi ▲ DIS 2007
Stefani, D.:Macumba Discobi ▲ DIS 2001

Quan, Linda (baroque vn)
A Baroque Christmas from the Metropolitan Museum of Art Concerts, w. Julianne Baird (sop), Aulos Ensemble [Anne Briggs (trns fl), Marc Schachman (baroque ob), Myron Lutzke (baroque vc), Arthur Haas (hpd/org)] MusicMasters ▲ 01612-67119-2 ■ 01612-67119-4

Quan, Linda (vn)—see also ORCHESTRAS & ENSEMBLES Helicon, Old Fairfield Academy Orch members
Fine, I.:Fant Str Trio, w. L. Martin (va), C. Finckel (vc) CRI ▲ CD 574 [ADD]
Picker, T.:Romance Vn, w. A. Karis (pno) *(rec 1979)* CRI ▲ CD 589 [ADD]

Quan, Ninh Lê (perc)
Cage, J.:Ryoanji Db, w. Joëlle Léandre (db) Montaigne ▲ MO 782076

Quant, Abbie de (fl)
Ketting, O.:For Moonlight Nights, w. O. Ketting (cnd), Royal PO Donemus ▲ CV 21

Quaranta, Salvatore (vn)—see ORCHESTRAS & ENSEMBLES Milan Quartet

Quarrington, Joel (db)
Catherine Wilson & Friends:Classical Potpourri, w. Catherine Wilson (pno), Mark Skazinetsky (vn), Norman Hathaway (va), Jack Mendelsohn (vc) Doremi ▲ DHR 71111
Nielsen, C.:Serenata in vano, w. James Campbell (cl), James McKay (bn), James Sommerville (hn), Tsuyoshi Tsutsumi (vc) *(rec Glenn Gould Studio, CBC Toronto, Mar. 26-27, 1994)* CBC ("Musica Viva" series) ▲ MVV 1089 [DDD]
Strauss, R.:Till Eulenspiegels lustige Streiche, w. James Campbell (cl), James McKay (bn), James Sommerville (hn), Martin Beaver (vn)—[arr. Franz Hasenöhrl as Einmal Anders! (frolic for 5 instruments; 1954)] *(rec Glenn Gould Studio, CBC Toronto, Mar. 26-27, 1994)* CBC ("Musica Viva" series) ▲ MVV 1089 [DDD]
Weinzweig, J.:Refrains, w. Mary Kenedi (pno) *(rec live, Walter Hall, Univ. of Toronto, Mar. 11, 1993)* Centrediscs ▲ CMC 5295 [DDD]

Queffélec, Anne (pno)
Debussy, C.:Fant Pno, w. Y.P. Tortelier (cnd), Ulster Orch Chandos ▲ CHAN 8972 [DDD]
Debussy, C.:Son Vc, w. Dominique de Williencourt (vc) Forlane ▲ FRL 16585 [DDD]
Fauré, G.:Elégie, w. Dominique de Williencourt (vc) Forlane ▲ FRL 16585 [DDD]
Fauré, G.:Papillon, w. Dominique de Williencourt (vc) Forlane ▲ FRL 16585 [DDD]
Fauré, G.:Romance Vc, w. Dominique de Williencourt (vc) Forlane ▲ FRL 16585 [DDD]
Fauré, G.:Sérénade, w. Dominique de Williencourt (vc) Forlane ▲ FRL 16585 [DDD]
Fauré, G.:Sicilienne, w. Dominique de Williencourt (vc) Forlane ▲ FRL 16585 [DDD]
Franck, C.:Son Vn, w. Dominique de Williencourt (vc) [arr for Vc & Pno] Forlane ▲ FRL 16585 [DDD]
Mozart, W.A.:Pno Music 4-Hands, w. I. Cooper (pno)—Fant., K.608:Allegro & Andante; Son., K.521; Son., K.497; Adagio & Allegro in F, K.594 Ottavo ▲ OTT 129242 [DDD]
Ravel, M.:Gaspard de la nuit Virgin Classics ▲ CDC 59322
Ravel, M.:Jeux d'eau Virgin Classics ▲ CDC 59322
Ravel, M.:Menuet antique Virgin Classics ▲ CDC 59233
Ravel, M.:Miroirs Virgin Classics ▲ CDC 59233
Ravel, M.:Pavane pour une infante défunte Virgin Classics ▲ CDC 59233
Ravel, M.:Le Tombeau de Couperin Virgin Classics ▲ CDC 59233
Ravel, M.:Valses nobles et sentimentales Virgin Classics ▲ CDC 59322
Satie, E.:Pno Music (misc)—Croquis et agaceries d'un gros bonhomme en bois; Description automatiques; Les trois valses distinguees du precieux degoute; Petite ouverte a danser; Deux ouvres de jeunesse; Les pantins dansent; Pièces froides; Premiere de la porte heroique cu ciel; Pasacaille; Poudre d'or; Trois Morceaux en forme de poire (w. C. Collard); La belle excentrique (w. C. Collard) Virgin Classics ▲ CDC 59296
Satie, E.:Pno Music (misc)—Avant-dernières pensées; Chapitres tournés en tous sens; Embryons desséchés; Heures séculaires et instantanées; Je te veux; Le Piccadilly (march); Six Gnossiennes; Sonatine bureaucratique; Sports et divertissements; Trois Gymnopédies; Trois véritables préludes flasques (pour un chien); Vieux séquins et vieilles cuirasses Virgin Classics ▲ 59515 [DDD]

Quelle, Ernst-August (pno)
Wusthoff, K.:Orchestral Music, w. Renate Erxleben (hp), P. Falk (cnd), Berlin RSO—A Little Hp Serenade; Concertino for Pno & Orch; 3 Russian Fants for Pno & Orch Koch Schwann ▲ SCH 318062

Quervain, B. de (ob d'amore)—see ORCHESTRAS & ENSEMBLES Freiburg Baroque Soloists

Queyras, Jean-Guihen (vc)
Ligeti, G.:Con Vc, w. P. Boulez (cnd), Ensemble InterContemporain Deutsche Grammophon ▲ 439808-2
Weber, C.M. von:Trio Fl, w. Philippe Bernold (fl), Laurent Cabasso (pno) Harmonia Mundi France ("Les Nouveaux Interprètes" series) ▲ HMN 911535

Queyraud, Philippe (hn)
Klein, G.:Divert Ob, w. Jean-Pierre Arnaud (ob), Jean-Marc Liet (ob), Rémi Lerner (cl), Christian Rocca (cl), Michel Tavernier (bn), Amaury Wallez (bn), Eric Karcher (hn) Arion ▲ ARN 68272 [DDD]

Queyroux, Yves (fl)
Escaich, T.:Intermezzi (3), w. Jean-Pierre Baraglioli (sax), Sylvain Frydman (cl) Chamade ▲ CHCD 5638 [DDD]

Quillman, Gail (pno)
Sowerby, L.:American Pieces, w. Robert Murray (vn) *(rec Virginia Commonwealth Univ, Richmond, VA, Aug & Oct, 1994)* Premier ▲ PRCD 1049 [DDD]
Sowerby, L.:Folksong Arrs, w. Robert Murray (vn) Premier ▲ PRCD 1049 [DDD]
Sowerby, L.:Passacaglia New World ▲ NW 376-2 [AAD]
Sowerby, L.:Son Vn (1922), w. Robert Murray (vn) *(rec Virginia Commonwealth Univ, Richmond, VA, Aug & Oct, 1994)* Premier ▲ PRCD 1049 [DDD]
Sowerby, L.:Son Vn (1944), w. Robert Murray (vn) Premier ▲ PRCD 1049 [DDD]
Sowerby, L.:Son Vn (1959), w. Robert Murray (vn) *(rec Virginia Commonwealth Univ, Richmond, VA, Aug & Oct, 1994)* Premier ▲ PRCD 1049 [DDD]
Sowerby, L.:Suite Pno New World ▲ NW 376-2 [AAD]

Quinn, Iain (org)
Bach, J.S.:Preludes & Fugues, BWV 531-552—in G, BWV 541 [at the Methuen Memorial Music Hall Org] *(rec Mar 5-7, 1995)* Raven ▲ OAR 360 [DDD]
Franck, C.:Chorals Org, M.38-40—No. 3 in a [at the Methuen Memorial Music Hall Org] *(rec Mar 5-7, 1995)* Raven ▲ OAR 360 [DDD]
Howard, L.:Moto di Gioia [at the Methuen Memorial Music Hall Org] *(rec Mar 5-7, 1995)* Raven ▲ OAR 360 [DDD]
Josephs, W.:Son Org [at the Methuen Memorial Music Hall Org] *(rec Mar 5-7, 1995)* Raven ▲ OAR 360 [DDD]
Liszt, F.:Org Music—Gebet, S.265; Ora pro nobis, S.262; Resignazione, S.263 [at the Methuen Memorial Music Hall Org] *(rec Mar 5-7, 1995)* Raven ▲ OAR 360 [DDD]
Másson, A.:Meditation [at the Methuen Memorial Music Hall Org] *(rec Mar 5-7, 1995)* Raven ▲ OAR 360 [DDD]

Quintana, Juan Manuel (va)
Deutsche Barocklieder, w. Andreas Scholl (ct), Alix Verzier (vc), Markus Markl (hpd), Karl Ernst Schroder (lt), Friederike Heumann (va), Stephanie Pfister (vn), Pable Valetti (vn) Harmonia Mundi France ▲ HMC 901505

Quintana, Juan Manuel (vl)—see ORCHESTRAS & ENSEMBLES Labyrinto

Raas, Jan (org)
Van Der Horst, A.:Symphonic Vars on J. S. Bach's "Christ lag in Todesbanden" NM Classics ▲ NM 92034

Raas, Karl (org)
Bach, J.S.:Cant 29, w. M. Schwarz (cnd), St. Gallen Collegium Musicum—Sinf Musiques Suisses ▲ 6125 [DDD]
Derungs, G.A.:Con da chiesa, w. Stephan Thomas (org), Peter Schneider (vib), Adrian Schilling (timp), M. Schwarz (cnd), St. Gallen Collegium Musicum Musiques Suisses ▲ 6125 [DDD]
Handel, G.F.:Cons (16) Org, w. M. Schwarz (cnd), St. Gallen Collegium Musicum—Con No. 13 in F for Org Musiques Suisses ▲ 6125 [DDD]
Haydn, J.:Con Org, Obs & Strs, H.XVIII/1, w. M. Schwarz (cnd), St. Gallen Collegium Musicum Musiques Suisses ▲ 6125 [DDD]
Huber, P.:Con Org, w. M. Schwarz (cnd), St. Gallen Collegium Musicum Musiques Suisses ▲ 6125 [DDD]
Organ Music at the Hofkirche Gallo ▲ CD 754 [ADD]

Rabas, Bohumir (org)
Czech Organ Music of the 18th Century, w. Jiri Reinberger (org) Panton ▲ PAN 811020

Rabas, Vaclav (org)
Kabeláč, M.:Fants 1 & 2 *(rec 1971)* Praga ▲ PR 255 004
Kabeláč, M.:Preludes Org *(rec 1971)* Praga ▲ PR 255 004
Kabeláč, M.:Sym 8, w. J. Jonasova (sop), Strasbourg Theater Percussionists *(rec 1971)* Praga ▲ PR 255 004
Slavický, K.:Sinfonietta 4, w. Brigita Šulcová (sop), Rudolf Pellar (nar), J. Belohlávek (cnd), Prague SO *(rec Dvořák Hall of Rudolfinum, Prague, Sept. 6 & 8, 1986)* Panton ("Protokol XX" series) ▲ PAN 811142 [DDD]

Rabbai, Joseph (cl)
Corigliano, J.:Poem in October, w. R. White (ten), T. Nyfenger (fl), B. Lucarelli (ob), Maurice Press (hpd), M. Press (cnd), American String Quartet RCA Gold Seal ▲ 60395-2-RG [ADD]
Rorem, N.:Ariel, w. Phyllis Curtin (sop), Ryan Edwards (pno) Phoenix ▲ PHCD 126
Starer, R.:Con a 3, w. G. Schwarz (tpt), P. Brevig (trbn), A. Kaplan (cnd), Camerata String Orch *(rec 1972)* CRI ▲ CD 612 [ADD]

Rabin, Michael (vn)
The Complete EMI Recordings EMI Classics 6-▲ CDMF 64123
Paganini, N.:Caprices Vn EMI Classics ▲ CDM 64560
Paganini, N.:Caprices Vn *(rec 1958)* EMI Classics 6-▲ CDMF 64123

Rabinoff, S. (pno)
Sibelius, J.:Music for Vn Pno, w. R. Ricci (vn)—4 Pieces, Op. 78; 6 Pieces, Op. 79; 2 Pieces, Op. 2; 5 danses champêtres One-Eleven 2-▲ URS 90033 [ADD]
Sibelius, J.:Novelette, w. R. Ricci (vn) One-Eleven 2-▲ URS 90033 [ADD]
Sibelius, J.:Pieces Vn Pno, Op. 81, w. R. Ricci (vn) One-Eleven 2-▲ URS 90033 [ADD]
Sibelius, J.:Pieces Vn Pno, Op. 115, w. R. Ricci (vn) One-Eleven 2-▲ URS 90033 [ADD]
Sibelius, J.:Pieces Vn Pno, Op. 116, w. R. Ricci (vn) One-Eleven 2-▲ URS 90033 [ADD]

Rabinovitch, Alexandre (pno)
Beethoven, L van:Vars on an Original Theme, Op. 76 Teldec ▲ TEL 95572 [DDD]
Beethoven, L van:Vars on a waltz by Diabelli, Op. 120 Teldec ▲ TEL 95572 [DDD]
Brahms, J.:Son for 2 Pnos, w. M. Argerich (pno) *(rec Berlin, Apr. 1993)* Teldec ▲ 92257-2 [DDD]
Brahms, J.:Vars on a Theme by Haydn, w. M. Argerich (pno) *(rec Berlin, Apr. 1993)* Teldec ▲ 92257-2 [DDD]
Brahms, J.:Waltzes Pno, Op. 39, w. M. Argerich (pno) *(rec Berlin, Apr. 1993)* Teldec ▲ 92257-2 [DDD]
Magnard, A.:Music of, w. M. Drobinsky (vc)—Sans lenteur; Sans faiblir; Funèbre; Rondement *(rec 1980 & 1993)* Talent ▲ DOM 2910 14 [DDD]
Mozart, W.A.:Andante & Vars Pno 4-Hands, w. M. Argerich (pno) *(rec Berlin, Nov. 1992 & Dec. 1993)* Teldec ▲ 91378-2 [DDD]
Mozart, W.A.:Son Pno 4-Hands, K.381, w. M. Argerich (pno) *(rec Berlin, Nov. 1992 & Dec. 1993)* Teldec ▲ 91378-2 [DDD]
Mozart, W.A.:Son Pno 4-Hands, K.521, w. M. Argerich (pno) *(rec Berlin, Nov. 1992 & Dec. 1993)* Teldec ▲ 91378-2 [DDD]
Mozart, W.A.:Son Pnos, K.448, w. M. Argerich (pno) *(rec Berlin, Nov. 1992 & Dec. 1993)* Teldec ▲ 91378-2 [DDD]
Poulenc, F.:Con for 2 Pnos, w. Brigitte Meyer (pno), P. Crispini (cnd), European Concerts Orch Doron ▲ DRC 3022 [DDD]
Rabinovitch, A.:Music for Pnos, w. M. Argerich (pno), M. Adamovitch (pno), A. Ieriomine (pno), A. Batagov (pno)—Musique Populaire for 2 Pianos; La Belle Musique for 4 Pianos; Liebliches Lied for Piano 4-hands; Musique triste, parfois tragique *(rec 1990 & 1992)* Valois ▲ V 4694 [DDD]
Rachmaninoff, S.:Suite 1 for 2 Pnos, w. M. Argerich (pno) Teldec ▲ 9031-74717-2 ZK
Rachmaninoff, S.:Suite 2 for 2 Pnos, w. M. Argerich (pno) Teldec ▲ 9031-74717-2 ZK
Rachmaninoff, S.:Symphonic Dances, w. M. Argerich (pno) Teldec ▲ 9031-74717-2 ZK

Rabinovitsj, Max (vn)
Beethoven, L van:Serenade Fl, Op. 25, w. J. Berg (fl), D. Barnes (va) *(rec 1975-79)* Vox Box 3-▲ CD3X 3014 [ADD]

Rabol, Georges (pno)
Chabrier, E.:España, w. S. Dugas (pno) [trans. for 2 pianos] *(rec Boulogne, France, Jan. 12-14, 1994)* Naxos ▲ 8.553080 [DDD]

Rabol, Georges (pno) (cont.)
Chabrier, E.:Pno Music (comp)—Bourrée fantasque; Feuillet d' album; Ballabile; Caprice; Petite valse; Habanera; 10 Pièces pittoresques *(rec Studio Ned Music, Boulogne, France, Dec. 16 & 17, 1993)* Naxos ▲ 8.553009 [DDD]
Chabrier, E.:Pno Music (misc)—Marche des Cipayes; Julia, Op. 1; Impromptu in C; Aubade; Ronde champêtre; Capriccio; Souvenir de Brunehaut *(rec Boulogne, France, Jan. 1994)* Naxos ▲ 8.553010 [DDD]
Chabrier, E.:Quadrilles on themes from *Tristan und Isolde*, w. S. Dugas (pno)—Prélude et marche française; Cortège burlesque; Air de ballet; Suite de valses *(rec Boulogne, France, Jan. 12-14, 1994)* Naxos ▲ 8.553080 [DDD]
Chabrier, E.:Souvenirs de Munich, w. S. Dugas (pno) *(rec Boulogne, France, Jan. 12-14, 1994)* Naxos ▲ 8.553080 [DDD]
Chabrier, E.:Valses romantiques (3), w. S. Dugas (pno) *(rec Boulogne, France, Jan. 12-14, 1994)* Naxos ▲ 8.553080 [DDD]
Clásicos de las Américas, w. Margot Pares-Reyna (sop), Marcel Quillevéré (ten), Jesús Castro Balbi (gtr), Noël Lee (pno), Erwartung Ensemble [cnd:Bernard Desgraupes], Jazzogène Orch [cnd:Jean-Luc Fillon] Opus 111 6-▲ 2000
Gershwin, G.:Porgy & Bess (suite) Pno *(rec June 1992)* Opus 111 ▲ OPS 30-64 [DDD]
Gershwin, G.:Rhap in Blue, w. J.-L. Fillon (cnd), Jazzogène Big Band *(rec June 1992)* Opus 111 ▲ OPS 30-64 [DDD]
Gottschalk, L.M.:Pno Music—Apothéose; Berceuse; El Cocoye; Danse Ossianique; Le deuxième Banjo; La Gitanilla; Grand Scherzo; La Mancenillier; La Manchega; Mazurka; Minuit à Séville; O ma charmante, épargnez-moi!; Souvenir de la Havane; Suis-moi Opus 111 ▲ OPS 50-9114
Guastavino, C.:Songs, w. M. Pares-Reyna (sop)—Alegria de la soledad; Apegado a mi; Cantilena; Corderito; Cuando acaba de llover; Desde que te conocí; Dones sencillos; Deseo; Donde habite el olvido; En los surcos del amor; Encantamiento; Esta iglesia no tiene; Hallazgo; Jardin antiguo; Meciendo; Mi garganta; Pájaro muerto; La palomita; Piececitos; Prestame tu pañuelito; La primera pregunta; La puertas de la mañana; Riqueza; Rocio; Romance de José Cubas; La rosa e el sauce; El Sampedrino; Se equivocó la paloma; Severa Villafañe; Siesta; Violetas; Viniendo de Chilecito; Ya me voy a retirar [Sp] *(rec 5/90)* Opus 111 ▲ OPS 30-9002 [DDD]

Rabot, André (bn)
Chabrier, E.:Songs, w. Renée Doria (sop), Julien Giovannetti (bar), Guy Fouché (sgr), Tasso Janopoulo (pno)—Lied; Tes yeux bleus; Sommation irrespectueuse; Toutes les fleurs; Ruy blas [A quoi bon entendre...]; Credo d'amour; Romance de l'étoile; Villanelle des petits; Les cigales; Ballade des gros dindons; Pastorale des cochons roses; L'île heureuse; Chanson pour jeanne; Duo de l'ouvreuse de l'opéra-comique et de l'employé du bon-marché; L'invitation au voyage Accord ▲ ACD 201392 [AAD]

Rabus, Kathrin (vn)—see also ORCHESTRAS & ENSEMBLES Kontraste Ensemble, Pallas Trio
Spohr, L.:Rondo brillant, w. Rolf Plagge (pno) Musicaphon ▲ M 56822 [DDD]

Rachlin, Julian (vn)
Prokofiev, S.:Con 1 Vn, w. V. Fedoseyev (cnd), Moscow RSO Sony Classical ▲ SK 66567
Saint-Saëns, C.:Con 3 Vn, w. Z. Mehta (cnd), Israel PO Sony Classical ▲ SK 48373 [DDD]
Sibelius, J.:Con Vn, w. L. Maazel (cnd), Pittsburgh SO *(rec Sept. 26-27, 1992)* Sony Classical ▲ SK 53272 [DDD]
Sibelius, J.:Serenades Vn, w. L. Maazel (cnd), Pittsburgh SO—No. 2 in g *(rec Sept. 26-27, 1992)* Sony Classical ▲ SK 53272 [DDD]
Tchaikovsky, P.:Con Vn, w. V. Fedoseyev (cnd), Moscow RSO Sony Classical ▲ SK 66567
Wieniawski, H.:Con 2 Vn, w. Z. Mehta (cnd), Israel PO Sony Classical ▲ SK 48373 [DDD]

Rachmaninoff, Sergei (pno)
Beethoven, L van:Son 8 Vn, w. F. Kreisler (vn) *(rec March 1926 for HMV)* Biddulph 3-▲ LAB 001-3 (m) [ADD]
Chopin, F.:Ballades Pno (comp)—Op. 47 RCA Gold Seal ▲ 09026-62533-2
Chopin, F.:Nocturnes—Op. 9/2 RCA Gold Seal ▲ 09026-62533-2
Chopin, F.:Pno Music (misc)—Valse brillante, Op. 34/3; Maiden's Wish, Op. 74; Scherzo in b♭, Op. 31; Grand valse brillante in E♭, Op. 18 Klavier ■ KC 103
Chopin, F.:Son Pno, Op. 35 RCA Gold Seal ▲ 09026-62533-2
Chopin, F.:Waltzes RCA Gold Seal ▲ 09026-62533-2
The Complete Recordings RCA Gold Seal 10-▲ 09026-61265-2
Grieg, E.:Sons Vn, Opp. 8, 13 & 45, w. F. Kreisler (vn)—No. 3 *(rec 1926 for HMV)* Biddulph 3-▲ LAB 001-3 (m) [ADD]
Rachmaninoff, S.:Cons Pno (comp), w. Ormandy, Stokowski (cnds), Philadelphia Orch RCA Gold Seal 10-▲ 09026-61265-2
Rachmaninoff, S.:Cons Pno (comp), w. Ormandy, Stokowski (cnds), Philadelphia Orch RCA Gold Seal 2-▲ 61658-2
Rachmaninoff, S.:Con 1 Pno, w. E. Ormandy (cnd), Philadelphia Orch RCA Red Seal ▲ 6659-2-RC (m) [ADD]
Rachmaninoff, S.:Con 2 Pno, w. L. Stokowski (cnd), Philadelphia Orch IMP Classics ▲ IMPGLRS 104 [ADD]
Rachmaninoff, S.:Con 2 Pno, w. *(cnd & orch unknown)* Memories 2-▲ MEM CD 3009
Rachmaninoff, S.:Con 2 Pno, w. L. Stokowski (cnd), Philadelphia Orch *(rec 1929)* RCA Red Seal ▲ 5997-2-RC (m) [ADD]
Rachmaninoff, S.:Con 3 Pno, w. E. Ormandy (cnd), Philadelphia Orch *(rec 1940)* RCA Red Seal ▲ 5997-2-RC (m) [ADD]
Rachmaninoff, S.:Con 4 Pno, w. E. Ormandy (cnd), Philadelphia Orch RCA Red Seal ▲ 6659-2 RC (m) [ADD]
Rachmaninoff, S.:Pno Music (misc)—From the Ampico piano roll recordings:Barcarolle; Elégie; Humoresque; Prélude in c♯; etc. London ("Historic" series) ▲ 425964-2 [ADD]
Rachmaninoff, S.:Pno Music (misc)—16 sels. by Chopin *(Grand valse brillante, Op. 18; Valse brillante, Op. 34/3)*, Gluck-Sgambati *(Melodie)*, Kreisler-Rachmaninoff *(Liebesleid)*, Mendelssohn *(Spinning song)*, Paderewski *(Minuet in G)*, Rachmaninoff *(Elegie, Op. 3/1; Polichinelle, Op. 3/4; Polka de W.R.; Barcarolle; Humoresque)*, Rimsky-Korsakov *(Flight of the bumble bee)*, Rubinstein *(Barcarolle No. 2)*, Schubert-Liszt *(Das Wandern)*, Tchaikovsky *(Troika en traineau, Op. 37/11; Valse)* Klavier ▲ KCD 11027 [ADD]
Rachmaninoff, S.:Pno Music (misc) RCA Gold Seal 10-▲ 09026-61265-2
Rachmaninoff, S.:Pno Music (misc)—25 sels., solo works & transcriptions RCA Gold Seal ▲ 7766-2-RG (m) [ADD] ■ 7766-4-RG (m)
Rachmaninoff, S.:Rhapsody on a Theme of Paganini, w. L. Stokowski (cnd), Philadelphia Orch RCA Gold Seal 10-▲ 09026-61265-2
Rachmaninoff, S.:Rhapsody on a Theme of Paganini, w. L. Stokowski (cnd), Philadelphia Orch RCA Red Seal ▲ 6659-2-RC (m) [ADD]
Rachmaninoff, S.:Rhapsody on a Theme of Paganini, w. L. Stokowski (cnd), Philadelphia Orch RCA Gold Seal 2-▲ 61658-2
Rachmaninoff, S.:Rhapsody on a Theme of Paganini, w. L. Stokowski (cnd), Philadelphia Orch IMP Classics ▲ IMPGLRS 104 [ADD]
Schubert, Franz:Son Vn, D.574, w. F. Kreisler (vn) *(rec 1926 for HMV)* Biddulph 3-▲ LAB 001-3 (m) [ADD]
Sergei Rachmaninoff in Concert Klavier ▲ KCD 11008 [ADD]
Sergei Rachmaninoff in Concert II Klavier ■ KC 107

Racine, Philippe (fl)
Bach, J.S.:Con in E Fl, w. S. Preston (cnd), English CO Novalis ▲ 150088 [DDD]
Bach, J.S.:Con in g Fl, w. S. Preston (cnd), English CO Novalis ▲ 150088 [DDD]
Bach, J.S.:Con Ob d'amore, w. S. Preston (cnd), English CO Novalis ▲ 150088 [DDD]
Bach, J.S.:Suites Orch, BWV 1066-1069, w. S. Preston (cnd), English CO Novalis ▲ 150088 [DDD]
Carter, E.:Enchanted Preludes, w. T. Demenga (vc) ECM New Series ▲ 78118-21391-2 [DDD]
Carter, E.:Esprit rude/esprit doux, w. E. Molinari (cl) ECM New Series ▲ 78118-21391-2 [DDD]
Carter, E.:Triple Duo, w. E. Molinari (cl), H. Schneeberger (vn), P. Cleeman (va), T. Demenga (vc), G. Huber (perc) ECM New Series ▲ 78118-21391-2 [DDD]
Koechlin, C.:Premier album de Lilian, w. Kathrin Graf (sop), Daniel Cholette (pno), Christine Simonin (ondes martinot) Accord ▲ ACD 201232 [DDD]

INSTRUMENT.

Racine, Philippe (fl) (cont.)
Koechlin, C.:Second album de Lilian, w. Christine Simonin (ondes martinot), Daniel Cholette (pno) Accord ▲ ACD 201232 [DDD]
Koechlin, C.:Stèle funéraire Accord ▲ ACD 201232 [DDD]
Mozart, W.A.:Andante Fl, w. P. Fournillier (cnd), English CO Novalis ▲ 150131 [DDD]
Mozart, W.A.:Cons Fl, w. P. Fournillier (cnd), English CO—No. 1 Novalis ▲ 150131 [DDD]
Mozart, W.A.:Rondo Vn, K.373, w. P. Fournillier (cnd), English CO [arr for fl & orch] Novalis ▲ 150131 [DDD]
Stamitz, C.:Con Fl, Op. 29, w. P. Fournillier (cnd), English CO Novalis ▲ 150131 [DDD]
Stamitz, C.:Con Fl in D, w. P. Fournillier (cnd), English CO Novalis ▲ 150131 [DDD]
Wyttenbach, J.:Serenade in Luftschlössern, w. E. Molinari (cl) *(rec May 19–20, 1990)* Grammont ▲ CTSP 37-2 [ADD]

Rácz, Ottó (ob)
Beethoven, L. van:Qnt Ob, 3 Hns & Bn, w. Jenő Keveházi (hn), János Keveházi (hn), Sándor Berki (hn), József Vajda (bn) Naxos ▲ 8.553090 [DDD]

Rácz, Zoltán (perc)
Bartók, B.:Son for 2 Pnos, w. Kocsis (pno), Ránki (pno), Cser (perc) *(rec 9/11/81)* Hungaroton ▲ HCD 12400

Radcliff, Susan (tpt)
Sowerby, L.:Festival Musick, w. Carl Albach (tpt), Jeffrey Caswell (trbn), Tom Hutchinson (trbn), Dan Haskins (timp), David Mulbury (org), J. Welsh (cnd), Fairfield Orch *(rec St. Bartholomew's Church, New York City, May 5, 1994)* Marco Polo ▲ 8.223725 [DDD]

Radding, Reuben (bc)
Gisberg:Music of, w. Christine Bard (perc), Christina Sun (erhu), Jeff O'Malley (nar), Jacqueline Leclair (ob), Quentin Chiappetta (sampler/pno/cpsr), Gisburg (voice/fl/cpsr)—Opening; No Stranger Not At All; Imaginary Movielandscape 1; Portrait; "Jowohl"; Mein Herz hat nicht vergessen [tango]; Ritual; Dying Takes Its Time; Fruits; Mic' N Drums Tzadik ("The Composers" series) ▲ TZA 7007 [DDD]

Raden, Gregory (cl)
Rorem, N.:Studies for 11, w. E. Ostling (fl), K. Lord (ob), J. Sutte (tpt), S. Copes (vn), C.-J. Chang (va), J. Lastrapes (vc), K. Englichova (hp), R. Uchida (pno), A. LaFargue (perc), R. Laveille (perc), R. Milanov (cnd) New World ▲ 80445-2

Radermacher, Erika (pno)
Tenney, J.:Bridge, w. Manfred Werder (pno) Hat Hut ("Now" series) ▲ ART CD 6193 [DDD]

Radev, Petkov (cl)
Mozart, W.A.:Qnt Pno, K.452, w. V. Tchutchov (pno), L. Oshavkova (fl), C. T. Kasmetski (ob), S. Kunchev (hn) Divertimento ▲ DIV 31020 [DDD]

Radigue, Elaine (syn)
Radigue, E.:Mila's Journey Inspired By A Dream, w. Lama Kunga Rinpoche (sgr), Robert Ashley (sgr) Lovely Music ▲ LCD 2002 [AAD]

Rados, Ferenc (pno)
Mozart, W.A.:Trio Cl, K.498, w. B. Kovács (cl), G. Németh (va) White Label ▲ HRC 128 [ADD]
Tartini, G.:Sons Vn & Continuo, w. R. Ricci (vn)—Devil's Trill One-Eleven ▲ URS 93050 [ADD]

Radoukanov, Entcho (db)
Schnittke, A.:Hymns Vc, w. T. Thedéen (vc), C. Davidsson (bn), I. Fredlund (hp), M. Kamata (hpd), A. Holdar (tubular bells / timp), A. Loguin (tubular bells) BIS ▲ CD 507 [DDD]

Radovan, Christian (trbn)
Rüegg, M.:Music of, w. Lauren Newton (sgr), Wolfgang Puschnig (fl/s sax), Harry Sokal (s sax), Roman Schwaller (t sax), Karl Fian (tpt), Woody Schabata (vib)—Reflections on Aubade; Reflections on Méditation; Reflections on Sévère Réprimande; Reflections on Idylle; Reflections on Gnossiennes Nos. 1 & 2; Satie ist mir im traum 3x nicht erschienen *(rec Vienna, Sept. 20–22, 1983)* Hat Hut ("NOW." series) ▲ hat ART CD 6024 [ADD]

Radulescu, Michael (org)
Handel, G.F.:Sons Rcr, w. Hans Maria Kneihs (rcr)—Op. 1/2, 4, 7 &11 Camerata ▲ 32CM 117
Muffat, G.:Apparatus Ars Musici ▲ 1108

Radziwonowicz, Karol (pno)
Paderewski, I.J.:Con Pno, w. R. Bader (cnd), Cracow PO *(rec 1991)* Koch Schwann ▲ 3-1145-2 [DDD]
Paderewski, I.J.:Con Pno, w. A. Wit (cnd), Polish National RSO Katowice *(rec Centre of Culture, Katowice, Jan 2–6, 1991)* Polskie Nagrania ▲ PNCD 105 [DDD]
Paderewski, I.J.:Fant polonaise, w. A. Wit (cnd), Polish National RSO Katowice *(rec Centre of Culture, Katowice, Jan 2–6, 1991)* Polskie Nagrania ▲ PNCD 105 [DDD]
Paderewski, I.J.:Pno Music (comp)—Miscellanea, Op. 16; Vars et fugue, Op. 11; Album de Mai, Op. 10; Danses polonaises, Op. 9; Klavierstücke, Op. 1; Son, Op. 21 *(rec Warsaw, 1991)* Selene 2-▲ CD 9302.9/9306.13 [DDD]
Paderewski, I.J.:Pno Music (comp)—Humoresques de concert, Op. 14; Stara suita, Op. 3; Impromptu; Elégie, Op. 4; Intermezzi Nos. 1 & 2; Danses polonaises, Op. 5; Dwa kanony; Powódz; Canzona [Chant sans paroles]; Rekopis; Dans le désert [Toccata, Op. 15]; Tatra [Album, Op. 12]; 3 morceaux pour pno, Op. 2; Introduction et toccata, Op. 6; Chants du voyageur, Op. 8; Vars et fugue, Op. 23 *(rec Warsaw, 1991)* Selene 2-▲ CD 9201.3/9203.6 [DDD]
Zarebski, J.:Pno Music—Fant Polonaise, Op. 9; Ballade, Op. 18; Berceuse, Op. 22; Étrennes, Op. 27; Gavotte, Op. 29; Mazurka de Concert, Op. 8; Romance sans paroles; Grande Polonaise, Op. 6 *(rec Rzeszow, Feb 20–21, 1993)* Selene ▲ CD 9505.28 [DDD]

Rae-Gerrard, C. (pno)
Beethoven, L. van:Vars on a Theme by Count Waldstein, WoO 67, w. J. McChesney (pno) Koch Schwann ▲ CD 310133 [DDD]
Mozart, W.A.:Son Pno 4-Hands, K.381, w. J. McChesney (pno) Koch Schwann ▲ CD 310133 [DDD]
Schubert, Franz:Fant Pno, D.940, w. J. McChesney (pno) Koch Schwann ▲ CD 310133 [DDD]
Schubert, Franz:Marche militaire, D.733/1, w. J. McChesney (pno) Koch Schwann ▲ CD 310133 [DDD]

Raekallio, Matti (pno)
Bartók, B.:Son for 2 Pnos, w. J. Lagerspätz (pno), T. Ferchen (perc), L. Erkkilä (perc) Ondine ▲ ODE 806 [DDD]
Bergman, E.:Borealis, w. J. Lagerspätz (pno), T. Ferchen (perc), L. Erkkilä (perc) Ondine ▲ ODE 806 [DDD]
Brahms, J.:Vars on a Theme by Paganini Ondine ▲ ODE 777-2 [DDD]
Friedman, I.:Studies on a Theme by Paganini Ondine ▲ ODE 777-2 [DDD]
Liszt, F.:Études d'exécution transcendante d'après Paganini, S.140 *(rec 8/91)* Ondine ▲ ODE 777-2 [DDD]
Moszkowski, M.:Con Pno, w. L. Grin (cnd), Tampere PO Ondine ▲ ODE 818 [DDD]
A Night at the Opera:Matt Raekallio Plays Opera Transcriptions for Piano Ondine ▲ ODE 834 [DDD]
Palmgren, S.:Cons Pno (comp)—No. 3, w. J. Mercier (cnd), Turku PO Finlandia 2-▲ 4509-95852-2 [DDD]
Prokofiev, S.:Son 4 Pno Ondine ▲ ODE 761-2 [DDD]
Prokofiev, S.:Son 5 Pno [original version] Ondine ▲ ODE 761-2 [DDD]
Prokofiev, S.:Son 6 Pno Ondine ▲ ODE 761-2 [DDD]
Rubinstein, A.:Con 4 Pno, w. L. Grin (cnd), Tampere PO Ondine ▲ ODE 818 [DDD]
Stravinsky, I.:Son Pnos, w. J. Lagerspätz (pno) Ondine ▲ ODE 806 [DDD]

Rael, Anthya (pno)—see also ORCHESTRAS & ENSEMBLES Cohen Piano Trio, Cohen Piano Trio members
Beethoven, L. van:Sons Vn (comp), w. R. Cohen (vn) Duo 3-▲ 89019 [DDD]

Raffaelli, Rebecca (pno)
Rahbee, D.G.:Son 1 Pno *(rec The Music Room)* Seda ▲ 333 [DDD]

Raffeiner, Hedwig (vn)—see ORCHESTRAS & ENSEMBLES Il Ruggiero

Rafn, Eyrind (fl)
Kuhlau, F.:Qnts Fl, w. Kim Sjøgren (vn), Georg Svendsen Andersen (va), Bjarne Boye Rasmussen (va), Lars Holm Johansen (vc) *(rec Torpen Kapel, Humlebaek, Nordsjaelland, Denmark, Aug 1985)* Naxos ▲ 8.553303 [DDD]

Ragaz, Christine (vn)—see also ORCHESTRAS & ENSEMBLES Bern String Quartet
Reger, M.:Trio Vn Vc, w. R. Häusler (vc), J. Buttrick (pno) *(rec 1985)* Jecklin-Disco ▲ JD 604-2 [ADD]

Ragent, Lawrence (hn)—see ORCHESTRAS & ENSEMBLES San Francisco Contemporary Music Players

Ragnarsson, Hjálmar (pno)
Leifs, J.:Music of, w. Sigríður Ella Magnúsdóttir (mez), Ólafur Vignir Albertsson (pno), Sólveig Anna Jónsdóttir (pno), Edda Erlendsdóttir (pno), Marteinn Hunger Fridriksson (org), Hildigunnur Halldórsdóttir (vn), Gréta Gudnadóttir (vn), Gudmundur Kristmundsson (va), Sigurdur Halldórsson (vc), Richard Korn (db), Iceland SO, Icelandic Opera Chorus, Langholts Church Graduale Choir, Hamrahlid Choir—Icelandic Cant, Op. 13/4; Valse Lento, Op. 2/1; Icelandic Dance, Op. 11/2 [Tempo Giusto]; Requiem; Lullaby [After the Riots]; Fairy-Tale in the Wood [from Baldr, Op. 34]; Funeral March; Separation [from Elegy, Op. 53]; Galdra Loftur Ov, Op. 10; Funeral March, Op. 6; Reverie; Reunion [from Elegy, Op. 53]; Fine I, Op. 55; Andante [The Last Supper]; Preludia Organo, Op. 16/3 [In the Church]; The Tear of Stone [from Elegy, Op. 53] Music From Iceland ▲ ITM 605 [DDD]
Ragnarsson, H.:Music of, w. S. E. Magnúsdóttir (mez), H. Halldórsdóttir (vn), G. Gudnadóttir (vn), G. Kristmundsson (va), S. Halldórsson (vc), R. Korn (db), Ó. V. Albertsson (pno), S. A. Jónsdóttir (pno), E. Erlendsdóttir (pno), M. H. Fridriksson (org), Sakari, Wilkinson (cnd), Iceland SO, G. Cortes (cnd), J. Stefánsson (cnd), T. Ingólfsdóttir (cnd), Hamrahlíd Choir, Icelandic Opera Chorus, Langholts Church Graduale Choir—Meine kleine Freundin [In the Ballroom]; Lovers Duet; After the concert; Meine kleine Freundin [Annie listens to the Radio]; Lif's Theme [On the Beach]; Lif's Theme II [Night Prayer]; Composing Ov [Vars I, II & III] Music From Iceland ▲ ITM 605 [DDD]

Ragni, Stefano (pno)
Casella, A.:Pupazzetti, w. P. Barbareschi (pno) Nuova Era 2-▲ 7143/44 [DDD]

Ragossnig, Konrad (gtr)
Albéniz, I.:Gtr Music—Torre bermeja; Zambra granadina; Asturias (Leyenda) *(rec Kirche Seon/AG, 1978)* Claves ▲ CD 50806 [ADD]
Albéniz, I.:Suite española (sels), w. P. Angerer (cnd), Southwest German CO Pforzheim—No. 1, "Granada"; No. 3. "Sevilla" Allegretto ▲ ACD 8175 [ADD] ∎ ACS 8175
Burkhard, W.:Serenade Fl, Op. 71/3, w. P.-L. Graf (fl) Claves ▲ CD 408 [ADD]
Carulli, F.:Serenade Fl & Gtr, w. P.-L. Graf (fl) Claves ▲ CD 408 [ADD]
Falla, M. de:El sombrero de tres picos (sels), w. P. Angerer (cnd), Southwest German CO Pforzheim—Miller's Dance Allegretto ▲ ACD 8175 [ADD] ∎ ACS 8175
Fasch, J.F.:Con Gtr, w. P. Angerer (cnd), Southwest German CO Pforzheim Allegretto ▲ ACD 8175 [ADD] ∎ ACS 8175
Giuliani, M.:Grand Duo Concertant, Op. 25, w. P.-L. Graf (fl) Claves ▲ CD 408 [ADD]
Granados, E.:Danzas españolas (10)—No. 10 [arr for gtr] *(rec Kirche Seon/AG, 1978)* Claves ▲ CD 50806 [ADD]
Granados, E.:Gtr Music—La maja de Goya Allegretto ▲ ACD 8175 [ADD] ∎ ACS 8175
Hans Martin Linde & Konrad Ragossnig, w. Hans Martin Linde (fl) Jecklin ▲ JEC 4402-2 [ADD]
Ibert, J.:Entracte, w. P.-L. Graf (fl) Claves ▲ CD 408 [ADD]
Llobet, M.:Gtr Music—Canciones Catalanas (2):El testamen de n'Amelia; El noy de la Mare *(rec Kirche Seon/AG, 1978)* Claves ▲ CD 50806 [ADD]
Musik für Flöte und Gitarre, w. Hans Martin Linde (fl) Jecklin ▲ JEC 660-2 [DDD]
Ravel, M.:Pavane pour une infante défunte, w. P.-L. Graf (fl) Claves ▲ CD 408 [ADD]
Ravel, M.:Pièce en forme de Habanera, w. P.-L. Graf (fl) Claves ▲ CD 408 [ADD]
Tárrega, F.:Gtr Music—Adelita (mazurka); Danza mora; Marieta (mazurka); Capricho árabe; Mazurka in G *(rec Kirche Seon/AG, 1978)* Claves ▲ CD 50806 [ADD]
Torroba, F.M.:Gtr Music—Fandanguillo; Arada; Nocturno; Madroños *(rec Kirche Seon/AG, 1978)* Claves ▲ CD 50806 [ADD]
Turina, J.:Gtr Music—Fant., Op. 29; Son., Op. 61 [Andante]; Fandanguillo, Op. 36; Homenaje a Tárrega, Op. 69; Ráfaga, Op. 53 Allegretto ▲ ACD 8175 [ADD] ∎ ACS 8175

Ragossnig, Konrad (lt)
Music for Tenor & Lute, w. Peter Schreier (ten) Capriccio ▲ CDC 10047 [DDD]

Ragossnig, Konrad (lt/gtr)
Dance Music of the Renaissance, w. Ulsamer Collegium Archiv ▲ 415294-2 AH [ADD]

Ragossnig, Konrad (gtr)
Dances from Spain & Latin America, w. Walter Feybli (gtr) *(rec 1973)* Entrée ▲ 0022-2 [AAD]
Music for Lute, Guitar & Mandolin, w. Anton Stingl (lt), Michael Schäffer (lt), Karl Scheit (gtr), Leo Witoszinskyj (gtr), William Matthews (gtr), Paul Grund (mand), Artur Rumetsch (mand), Edith Bauer-Slais (mand), Elfriede Kunschak (mand) Vox Box 3-▲ CD3X 3022

Ragson, Mimi (vn)
Lovenstein, J.:Music of, w. Mary Brockenbrough (sop), Laura Sanders (sop), Barton Green (ten), Rockland Osgood (ten), David Murray (bar), Benjamin Sears (bar), Jonathan Lovenstein (pno), Heather O'Donnell (pno), James Silvers (pno), Rocy Reider (fl), Jason Horowitz (vn), Adrianna Hulscher (vn), James Johnston (vn), Peter Landeen (vc), Reinmar Seidler (vc)—Blake Songs; other works Titanic ▲ Ti 221 [DDD]

Rahbari, F. (fl)—see ORCHESTRAS & ENSEMBLES Vienna Flautists

Rahbari, Sohre (a sax)
Debussy, C.:Rapsodie, w. A. Rahbari (cnd), Brussels Belgian Radio-TV PO Marco Polo ▲ 8.223374
Glazunov, A.:Con Sax, w. A. Rahbari (cnd), Brussels Belgian Radio-TV PO Marco Polo ▲ 8.223374
Ibert, J.:Concertino da camera, w. A. Rahbari (cnd), Brussels BRT PO Marco Polo ▲ 8.223374
Saxophone & Orchestra, w. Rahbari, Sohre (a sax), Brussels BRT PO [cnd:Alexander Rahbari] Marco Polo ▲ 8.223374

Rahkonen, Jorma (vn)—see also ORCHESTRAS & ENSEMBLES Voces Intimae String Quartet
Segerstam, L.:Divert Vns, w. H. Louhivuori (vn), E. Kamu (va), V. Höylä (vc), L. Segerstam (cnd), Helsinki CO BIS ▲ CD 84 [AAD]

Rahkonen, Margit (pno)
Boutry, R.:Divert Sax & Pno, w. P. Savijoki (sax) BIS ▲ CD 209 [AAD]
Contrabbasso con bravura, w. Jorma Katrama (db) *(rec Mar. 1989)* Finlandia ▲ 4509-95864-2 [DDD]
Françaix, J.:Danses exotiques, w. P. Savijoki (sax) BIS ▲ CD 209 [AAD]
Milhaud, D.:Scaramouche (transcriptions), w. P. Savijoki (sax) [saxophone-piano transcription] BIS ▲ CD 209 [AAD]

Rahm, Fredy (gtr)
Albéniz, I.:Suite española (sels), w. Jürg Moser (gtr)—Nos. 1 & 3 [tran Tarrago for 2 gtrs] Gallo ▲ CD 881 [DDD]
Albéniz, I.:Tango Español, w. Jürg Moser (gtr) [trans Tarrago for 2 gtrs] Gallo ▲ CD 881 [DDD]
Cabezón, A. de:Differencias, w. Jürg Moser (gtr)—Differencias sobre el canto del caballero; Differencias sobre la gallarda milanesa [trans Tarrago for 2 gtrs] Gallo ▲ CD 881 [DDD]
Froelicher, A.:Muleta, w. Jürg Moser (gtr) Gallo ▲ CD 881 [DDD]
Granados, E.:Danzas españolas (10), w. Jürg Moser (gtr)—No. 2 [trans Hopman for 2 gtrs] Gallo ▲ CD 881 [DDD]
Granados, E.:Goyescas (intermezzo), w. Jürg Moser (gtr) [trans Pujol for 2 gtrs] Gallo ▲ CD 881 [DDD]
Sor, F.:Fants Gtr, w. Jürg Moser (gtr)—Op. 54bis Gallo ▲ CD 881 [DDD]
Sor, F.:Waltzes, w. Jürg Moser (gtr) Gallo ▲ CD 881 [DDD]

Rahman, Sophia (pno)
Clarke, R.:Son Va, w. P. Dukes (va) Gamut Classics ▲ GAM 537 [DDD]
Maconchy, E.:Sketches, w. P. Dukes (va) Gamut Classics ▲ GAM 537 [DDD]
Shostakovich, D.:Son Va, w. P. Dukes (va) Gamut Classics ▲ GAM 537 [DDD]

Raicheva, Valentina (hp)
Minkus, L.:Ballets, w. Anna Takova-Baynova (vn), B. Spassov (cnd), Sofia National Opera Orch—La bayadère (sels.) (1877); Paquita (complete) (1846) *(rec Studio I, Bulgarian National Radio, Sofia, Feb 1994)* Capriccio ▲ 10 544 [DDD]

Raimi, Frederic (vc)—see ORCHESTRAS & ENSEMBLES Ciompi String Quartet

Raimi, Fred (vc)—see also ORCHESTRAS & ENSEMBLES Arman Ensemble
Hoiby, L.:Bermudas, w. Terry Rhodes (sop), Ellen Williams (mez), Hsiao-mei Ku (vn), Jonathan Bagg (va), Thomas Warburton (pno) Albany ▲ TROY 172 [DDD]
Ward, R.:Serenade for Mallarmé, w. Anna Wilson (fl), Jonathan Bagg (va), Jane Hawkins (pno) Albany ▲ TROY 204 [DDD]

Raimondi, Matthew (vn)
Bavicchi, J.:Trio 4 Cl, w. D. Glazer (cl), Dell'Aquila (hp) CRI ∎ C 138

▲ = CD ♦ = Enhanced CD △ = MD ∎ = Cassette Tape □ = DCC

Raimondi, Matthew (vn) (cont.)
Feldman, Morton:False Relationships & the Extended Ending, w. S. Barab (vc), P. Jacobs (pno), Y. Takahashi (pno), M. Feldman (cnd) *(rec 6/8/70)* CRI ▲ CD 620 [ADD]
Wyner, Y.:Concert Duo Vn, w. Yehudi Wyner (pno) CRI ("American Masters" series) ▲ CD 701 [ADD]

Rainer, Ingomar (org)
Mozart, W.A.:Missa solemnis, K.337, w. R. Ziesak (sop), E. von Magnus (alt), H. Wildhaber (ten), G. Hornik (bar), H. Hüttler (cant), M. Jankowitsch (cant), P. Jelosits (cant), M. Haselböck (cnd), Vienna Academy, Vienna Hofburg Chapel Choir [L] *(rec Apr. 1992)* Novalis ▲ 150087 [DDD]

Rajna, Thomas (pno)
Stravinsky, I.:Pno Music—Etudes (4); Serenade in A; Piano-Rag-Music; Sonata [3 movmnts]; Tango; Circus Polka *(rec 1968)* Saga Classics ▲ EC 3391 [DDD]

Rak, Stephen (gtr)
Rak, S.:Dedications [solo guitar works inspired by & dedicated to Elvis Presley, Glenn Gould, Mikhail Gorbachev, et al.]—Six Early Dances; Romance Ontario; Spanish Suite; Balalaika; Era of Rock & Roll:Happy Birthday John; Auld Lang Syne Nimbus ▲ NI 5239-2 [DDD]
Rak, S.:Music for Gtr—Czech Fairy Tales; Elegy; Mongoliana; Sonata; Tango; Variations on a Theme by John W. Duarte; Voces de Profundis Nimbus ▲ NI 5177 [DDD]

Rakich, Christa (org)
Beach, A.M.C.:Prelude on an Old Folk Tune AFKA ▲ SK 527
Borroff, E.:Passacaglia Afka ▲ SK 527
Deferred Voices:Organ Music by Women AFKA ▲ AFK 527
Demessieux, J.:Chorale Preludes (12) on Gregorian Themes Afka ▲ SK 527
Diemer, E.L.:Fant Afka ▲ SK 527
Mendelssohn, Fanny:Prelude Org Afka ▲ SK 527
Smyth, E.:Short Choral Preludes Afka ▲ SK 527
Wieruszowski, L.:Chorale Preludes AFKA ▲ SK 527

Rákos, László (hn)—see ORCHESTRAS & ENSEMBLES Budapest Festival Horn Quartet

Rakowski, Maciej (vn)
Haydn, J.:Con Org, Vn & Strs, H.XVIII/6, w. Oliver Roberti (hpd), K. Redel (cnd), English CO Pierre Verany ▲ PVY 793111 [DDD]

Raldugin, Sergei (vc)
Vivaldi, A.:Con for 2 Vcs, w. Z. Zaliyailo (vc), L. Korkhin (cnd), Renaissance CO Infinity Digital ▲ QK 57244 [DDD]

Ralls, Stephen (pno)
Beethoven, L. van:Songs, w. M. Pedrotti (bar)—Adelaïde [G] CBC ("Musica Viva" series) ▲ MVCD 1051 [DDD]
Brahms, J.:Liebeslieder Waltzes SATB, w. Kathleen Brett (sop), Catherine Robbin (mez), Benjamin Butterfield (ten), Russell Braun (bar), Bruce Ubukata (pno) *(rec Glenn Gould Studio, CBC Toronto, Dec. 7-9, 1993)* CBC ("Musica Viva" series) ▲ MVCD 1077 [DDD]
Brahms, J.:Songs, w. M. Pedrotti (bar)—Alte Liebe; An die Nachtigall; Feldeinsamkeit; Immer leiser und wird mein Schlummer; Wie Melodien [G] CBC ("Musica Viva" series) ▲ MVCD 1051 [DDD]
Duparc, H.:Songs, w. M. Pedrotti (bar)—Chanson triste; L'invitation au voyage; Le manoir de Rosamonde; Phidylé [F] CBC ("Musica Viva" series) ▲ MVCD 1051 [DDD]
Greer, J.:All Around the Circle, w. Kathleen Brett (sop), Catherine Robbin (mez), Benjamin Butterfield (ten), Russell Braun (bar), Bruce Ubukata (pno) *(rec Glenn Gould Studio, CBC Toronto, Dec. 7-9, 1993)* CBC ("Musica Viva" series) ▲ MVCD 1077 [DDD]
Morawetz, O.:Psalm 22, w. M. Pedrotti (bar) Centrediscs ▲ CDCCD 3589 [DDD]
Morawetz, O.:Songs, w. M. Pedrotti (bar)—Chimney-Sweeper; Grenadier; Mad Song [E] CBC ("Musica Viva" series) ▲ MVCD 1051 [DDD]
Morawetz, O.:Souvenirs, w. M. Pedrotti (bar) Centrediscs ▲ CDCCD 3589 [DDD]
Schumann, R.:Spanische Liebeslieder, w. Kathleen Brett (sop), Catherine Robbin (mez), Benjamin Butterfield (ten), Russell Braun (bar), Bruce Ubukata (pno) CBC ("Musica Viva" series) ▲ MVCD 1077 [DDD]
Strauss, R.:Songs, w. M. Pedrotti (bar)—Befreit; Heimliche Aufforderung; Die Nacht; Nichts [G] CBC ("Musica Viva" series) ▲ MVCD 1051 [DDD]
Tchaikovsky, P.:Songs, w. M. Pedrotti (bar)—Blagoslavlyayu vas, lesa; Net, tol'ka tot, kto znal; Serenada Don Zhuana; Sleza drazhyt f tvajom rivnivom vzore [R] CBC ("Musica Viva" series) ▲ MVCD 1051 [DDD]

Ralske, Erik (hn)
Leclaire, D.:Qt Hns, w. T. Bacon (hn), G. Hustis (hn), W. Caballero (hn) Summit ▲ DCD 135 [DDD]

Ramirez, Alain (perc)
Daetwyler, J.:Capriccio, Andante et Humoresque, w. H. Molnar (pic), J. Molnar (alphn), P. Falentin (tpt), Bern Chamber Ensemble Gallo ▲ CD 548 [AAD]
Daetwyler, J.:Con Tpt, w. P. Falentin (tpt), Bern Chamber Ensemble Gallo ▲ CD 548 [AAD]
Daetwyler, J.:Danses (3), w. Bern Chamber Ensemble Gallo ▲ CD 548 [AAD]

Ramírez, Alexander-Sergei (gtr)
Albéniz, I.:Asturias *(rec Aug 7-9, 1991)* Denon ▲ CO 75357 [DDD]
Ginastera, A.:Son Gtr *(rec Stadthalle Meinerzhagen, Germany, Oct. 12-15, 1993)* Denon ▲ CO 78931 [DDD]
Moreno Torroba, F.:Castillos de España (sels)—Fandanguillo; Arada; Danza *(rec Aug. 7-9, 1991)* Denon ▲ CO 75357 [DDD]
Recuerdos de la Alhambra:5 Centuries of Spanish Guitar Classics *(rec 1992)* Denon ▲ CO 75715
Rodrigo, J.:Gtr Music—Romace de Durandarte; En los Trigales *(rec Aug. 7-9, 1991)* Denon ▲ CO 75357 [DDD]
Rodrigo, J.:Invocación y danza *(rec Aug. 7-9, 1991)* Denon ▲ CO 75357 [DDD]
Sor, F.:Fants Gtr—Fant élégiaque, Op 59; Fant, Op. posth *(rec Stadthalle Meinerzhagen, Germany, Oct 4-6, 1994)* Denon ▲ DEN 78975 [DDD]
Sor, F.:Grand Solo *(rec Stadthalle Meinerzhagen, Germany, Oct 4-6, 1994)* Denon ▲ DEN 78975 [DDD]
Sor, F.:Sons Gtr, Opp. 15 & 22—in C, Op. 15b *(rec Stadthalle Meinerzhagen, Germany, Oct 4-6, 1994)* Denon ▲ DEN 78975 [DDD]
Sor, F.:Vars Gtr—Opp. 26 & 28 *(rec Stadthalle Meinerzhagen, Germany, Oct 4-6, 1994)* Denon ▲ DEN 78975 [DDD]
Turina, J.:Gtr Music—Ráfaga; Sevillanas *(rec Aug. 7-9, 1991)* Denon ▲ CO 75357 [DDD]
Turina, J.:Son Gtr—Ráfaga; Sevillanas *(rec Aug. 7-9, 1991)* Denon ▲ CO 75357 [DDD]
Villa-Lobos, H.:Etudes Gtr *(rec Stadthalle Meinerzhagen, Germany, Oct. 12-15, 1993)* Denon ▲ CO 78931 [DDD]
Villa-Lobos, H.:Preludes Gtr *(rec Stadthalle Meinerzhagen, Germany, Oct. 12-15, 1993)* Denon ▲ CO 78931 [DDD]

Ramirez, Ariel (kbd)
Ramirez, A.:Misa Criolla, w. J. Carreras (ten), Laredo Instrumental Ensemble, J. L. Ocejo (cnd), Bilbao Choral Society, Laredo Choral Salvé Philips ("Digital Classics" series) ▲ 420955-2 [DDD] □ 420955-5
Ramirez, A.:Navidad en Verano, w. J. Carreras (ten), Laredo Instrumental Ensemble, J. L. Ocejo (cnd), Bilbao Choral Society, Laredo Choral Salvé Philips ("Digital Classics" series) ▲ 420955-2 [DDD] □ 420955-5
Ramirez, A.:Navidad nuestra, w. J. Carreras (ten), Laredo Instrumental Ensemble, J. L. Ocejo (cnd), Bilbao Choral Society, Laredo Choral Salvé Philips ("Digital Classics" series) ▲ 420955-2 [DDD] □ 420955-5

Ramirez, B. (perc)
Levinson, G.:Dreamlight, w. A. Emelianoff (vc), P. Basquin (pno), P. Hostetter (perc) CRI ▲ CD 642 [DDD]

Ramirez, Lourdes (pno)
Turina, J.:Danzas gitanas—set 1 Amati ▲ 9404 [DDD]
Turina, J.:La procesión del Rocio [arr pno] Amati ▲ 9404 [DDD]
Turina, J.:Sanlucar de Barrameda Amati ▲ 9404 [DDD]

Rampal, Jean-Pierre (fl)
Bach, C.P.E.:Trio Son Fl, H.586, w. I. Stern (vn), J. Ritter (hpd) CBS ▲ MK 37813 [DDD]

Rampal, Jean-Pierre (fl) (cont.)
Bach, Joh. Christian:Trio Fl, Vn & Vc, w. I. Stern (vn), M. Rostropovich (vc) Sony Classical ▲ SK 44568 [DDD]
Bach, J.C.F:Son Fl, HW.VIII/1-2, w. I. Stern (vn), J. Ritter (hpd)—in C CBS ▲ MK 37813 [DDD]
Bach, J.S.:Con in g Fl, w. K. Ristenpart (cnd), Saar CO Odyssey ■ YT 32890
Bach, J.S.:Con 1 Vn, w. K. Ristenpart (cnd), Saar CO Odyssey ■ YT 32890
Bach, J.S.:Music of—Brandenburg Concerto No. 4; Orchestral Suite No. 2 in b; Air from Orchestral Suite No. 3 *(early recordings by Rampal, most likely from the Disques français LPs with Karl Ristenpart & the Saar Chamber Orchestra)* Takoma ▲ D21S 72706 (m)
Bach, J.S.:A Musical Offering, w. I. Stern (vn), J. Ritter (hpd), L. Parnas (vc)—trio, section 8 CBS ▲ MK 37813 [DDD]
Bach, J.S.:Sons Fl, BWV 1030-35, w. T. Pinnock (hpd) CBS 2-▲ M2K 39746
Bach, J.S.:Sons Vn, w. T. Pinnock (hpd)—BWV 1020 [doubtful; trans. for flute & continuo] CBS 2-▲ M2K 39746
Bach, J.S.:Trio Son Fl, Vn & Hpd, w. I. Stern (vn), J. Ritter (hpd) CBS ▲ MK 37813 [DDD]
Bartók, B.:Hungarian Peasant Songs, w. R. Veyron-Lacroix (hpd) [arr. Arma for flute & keyboard] Odyssey ■ YT 33905
Beethoven, L. van:Allegro & Minuet, w. A. Marion (fl) Vox Box 2-▲ CDX 5000 [ADD]
Beethoven, L. van:National Airs with Vars, Op. 107, w. R. Veyron-Lacroix [pno-fl ver.] Vox Box 2-▲ CDX 5000 [ADD]
Beethoven, L. van:Serenade Fl, Op. 41, w. R. Veyron-Lacroix (pno) Vox Box 2-▲ CDX 5000 [ADD]
Beethoven, L. van:Son Fl, w. R. Veyron-Lacroix (pno) Vox Box 2-▲ CDX 5000 [ADD]
Beethoven, L. van:Trio Fl, WoO 37, w. P. Hongne (bn), R. Veyron-Lacroix (pno) Vox Box 2-▲ CDX 5000 [ADD]
Beethoven, L. van:Trio for 3 Fls, w. C. Larde (bn), A. Marion (pno) Vox Box 2-▲ CDX 5000 [ADD]
Benda, F.:Con in e Fl & Orch, w. M. Munclinger (cnd), Prague CO *(rec 1956)* Supraphon ▲ 111308-2 [AAD]
Benda, F.:Son Fl & Hpd, w. V. Švihlíková (hpd)*(rec 1955)* Supraphon ▲ 111308-2 [AAD]
The Best of Jean-Pierre Rampal, w. various orchs Erato ▲ 4509-93242-2
Boccherini, L.:Qnts Fl, G.437-442, w. Bruno Pasquier (vn), Régis Pasquier (vn), Roland Pidoux (vc concertante), Mathilde Sternat (vc)—1-3, 5 & 6 Sony Classical ▲ SK 62679
Bolling, C.:Music of, w. C. Bolling (pno), A. Lagoya (gtr), et al.—California Suite, Con for Classic Gtr & Jazz Pno, Fl & Jazz Pno Suites Nos. 1 & 2, Vn & Jazz Pno Suite, Picnic Suite, & Toot Suite CBS ▲ MK 44608 ■ FMT 44608
Bolling, C.:Picnic Suite, w. A. Lagoya (gtr), Claude Bolling Trio CBS ▲ MK 35864 ■ PMT 35864
Bolling, C.:Suite 1 Fl, w. Claude Bolling Trio Milan ▲ 73138-35645-2 ■ 73138-35645-4
Bolling, C.:Suite 2 Fl, w. C. Bolling (pno), C. Sorin (db), C. Cordelette (perc) CBS ▲ MK 42318 [DDD] ■ FMT 42318 (D)
Carulli, F.:Con Fl, w. A. Lagoya (gtr), J. Rolla (cnd), Franz Liszt CO CBS ▲ MK 42130 [DDD]
Carulli, F.:Duos Fl & Gtr, Op. 104/1 & 3, w. S. Lagoya (gtr) CBS ▲ MK 42130 [DDD]
Carulli, F.:Fantasy on Themes from Bellini's *Il pirata,* w. S. Lagoya (gtr) CBS ▲ MK 42130 [DDD]
Carulli, F.:Nocturne Fl, w. S. Lagoya (gtr) CBS ▲ MK 42130 [DDD]
Children's Songs, w. [cnd:François Rauber], St. Laurent Children's Choir, St. Laurent Instrumental Ensemble, Maurice André (tpt) CBS ▲ MK 39669
Cimarosa, D.:Con for 2 Fls, w. S. Kudo (fl), J.-P. Rampal (cnd), Salzburg Mozarteum Orch Sony Classical ▲ SK 45930 [DDD]
Cimarosa, D.:Con for 2 Fls, w. Clémentine Scimone (fl), C. Scimone (cnd), Venice Solisti *(rec 1972)* Erato ▲ 2292-45836-2 [ADD]
Danzi, F.:Concertante Fl, w. Paul Meyer (cl), J.-P. Rampal (cnd), Franz Liszt CO *(rec Italian Institute, Budapest, Jan. 4-7, 1993)* Denon ▲ CO 78911 [DDD]
Debussy, C.:Syrinx Odyssey ■ YT 33905
Devienne, F.:Sinf concertante for 2 Fls, w. R. Wilson (fl), C. Scimone (cnd), Venice Solisti *(rec 1976)* Erato ▲ 2292-45836-2 [ADD]
Doppler, A.F.:Con Fls, w. A. Adorjan (fl), C. Scimone (cnd), Monte Carlo Opera Orch *(rec 1977)* Erato ▲ 2292-45836-2 [ADD]
Flute & Harp, w. Lily Laskine (hp) *(rec 1968)* Erato ▲ 45837-2 [ADD] ■ 45837-4
French Baroque Flute Concertos, w. Jean-François Paillard CO [cnd:Jean-François Paillard] Erato ▲ 45834-2
German Baroque Flute Concertos, w. Jean-François Paillard CO [cnd:Jean-François Paillard], Scottish CO [cnd:R. Leppard] Erato ▲ 45835-2
Gershwin, G.:Music of—Fascinatin' Rhythm/I Got Rhythm; Someone to Watch Over Me; Nice Work if You Can Get It; The Man I Love; Bess, You is My Woman Now; My Man's Gone Now; Summertime; Liza; Preludes for Piano; A Foggy Day (in London Town); An American in Paris CBS ▲ MK 39700
Greatest Hits, Vol. 1 CBS ▲ MK 34561 ■ MT 34561
Greatest Hits, Vol. 2 CBS ▲ MK 35176 ■ MT 35176
Handel, G.F.:Sons Fl, w. Robert Veyron-Lacroix (hpd)—Op. 1 Odyssey ■ YT 32371
Haydn, J.:Con Fl & Orch, w. Franz Liszt CO Sony Classical ("Essential Classics" series) ▲ SBK 62649 ■ SBT 62649
Haydn, J.:Con Fl, H.VIIf/D1, w. J. Rolla (cnd), Franz Liszt CO CBS 2-▲ M2K 39772 [DDD]
Haydn, J.:Cons for 2 Lire organizzata, w. Pierre Pierlot (ob), J. Rolla (cnd), Franz Liszt CO CBS 2-▲ M2K 39772 [DDD]
Haydn, J.:Diverts Vn, Va & Vc, H.IV/6-11, w. Issac Stern (vn), Msitslav Rostropovich (vc)—Nos. 2 & 6 CBS ▲ MK 37786 [DDD]
Haydn, J.:Trios Fls & Vc, "London Trios", w. Issac Stern (vn), Mstislav Rostropovich (vc) CBS 4-▲ M4K 42003 (m/s) [ADD]
Haydn, J.:Trios Fls & Vc, "London Trios", w. Issac Stern (vn), Mstislav Rostropovich (vc) CBS ▲ MK 37786 [DDD]
Haydn, J.:Trios Fls & Vc, "London Trios", w. W. Schulz (fl), Gilbert Audin (bn) [trans. for 2 flutes & bassoon] Sony Classical ▲ SK 48061 [DDD]
In Concert, w. Kathleen Battle (sop), Anthony Newman (hpd), Myron Lutzke (vc), Margo Garrett (pno), John Steel Ritter (pno) *(rec Feb. 24, 1991)* Sony Classical ▲ SK 53106 [ADD] ■ ST 53106
In Concert, w. Kathleen Battle (sop) Sony Classical ▲ SK 53106 [ADD] ■ ST 53106
Italian Baroque Flute Concertos, w. Venice Soloists [cnd:Claudio Scimone] Sony Classical ▲ SK 47228
Italian Baroque Flute Concertos, w. Jean-François Paillard CO [cnd:Jean-François Paillard] Erato ▲ 45833-2
Japanese Folk Melodies, w. Ensemble Lunaire CBS ▲ MK 35862 [ADD] ■ MT 35862
Japanese Melodies for Flute & Harp, w. Lily Laskine (hp) Denon ("Repertoire" series) ▲ CO 8115 [DDD]
Jean-Pierre Rampal, w. Shigenori Kudo (fls), John Steele Ritter (hpd/pno) Sony Classical ▲ SK 46482 [ADD]
Joplin, S.:Music of, w. J. S. Ritter (pno/hpds), S. Manne (dr), Johnson (tubas) CBS ▲ MK 37818
Khachaturian, A.:Con Vn, w. J. Martinon (cnd), French National Orch CBS ▲ MK 44665 [ADD]
Kuhlau, F.:Qnts Fl, w. Juilliard String Quartet CBS ▲ MK 44517 [DDD] ■ MT 44517 (D)
The Magic Flute:A Night at the Opera, w. Royal PO [cnd:Placido Domingo] CBS ▲ MK 42100 [DDD]
Mozart, W.A.:Adagio & Rondo Glass Armonica, w. P. Perlot (ob), Pasquier Trio Sony Classical ▲ SK 47230
Mozart, W.A.:Andante Fl, K.315/285a, w. *(cnd & orch unknown)* CBS ▲ MK 34559
Mozart, W.A.:Andante Fl, K.315/285a, w. T. Guschlbauer (cnd), Vienna SO *(rec 1966)* Erato ▲ 45832-2 [ADD] ■ 45832-4
Mozart, W.A.:Andante Fl, K.315/285a, w. Z. Mehta (cnd), Israel PO CBS ▲ MK 44919 [DDD]
Mozart, W.A.:Andante Mechanical Org, K.616 Sony Classical ▲ SK 47230
Mozart, W.A.:Cons Fl, w. Z. Mehta (cnd), Israel PO CBS ▲ MK 44919 [DDD]
Mozart, W.A.:Con Fl, K.313, w. T. Guschlbauer (cnd), Vienna SO *(rec 1966)* Erato ▲ 45832-2 [ADD] ■ 45832-4
Mozart, W.A.:Con Fl Hp, w. L. Laskine (hp), J.-F. Paillard (cnd), Jean-François Paillard CO *(rec 1964)* Erato ▲ 45832-2 [ADD] ■ 45832-4
Mozart, W.A.:Con Fl Hp, w. L. Laskine (hp), J.-F. Paillard (cnd), Jean-François Paillard CO Erato ▲ 45978-2 ■ 45978-4

Rampal, Jean-Pierre (fl) (cont.)
Mozart, W.A.:Concertone Vns, w. S. Kudo (fl), J.-P. Rampal (cnd), Salzburg Mozarteum Orch Sony Classical ▲ SK 45930 [DDD]
Mozart, W.A.:Divert Hns Strs, K.334, w. Pasquier Trio Sony Classical ▲ SK 47230
Mozart, W.A.:Qts Fl, w. I. Stern (vn), S. Accardo (vn), M. Rostropovich (vc) CBS ▲ MK 42320 [DDD]
Mozart, W.A.:Qts Fl, w. I. Stern (vn), A. Schneider (vn), L. Rose (vc) Odyssey ▲ MBK 42601
Mozart, W.A.:Qnt Strs, K.Anh.177, w. Pasquier Trio Sony Classical ▲ SK 47230
Mozart, W.A.:Rondo Fl, K.Anh.184, w. Z. Mehta (cnd), Israel PO CBS ▲ MK 44919 [DDD]
Mozart, W.A.:Sons Fl Hpd (comp), w. Robert Veyron-Lacroix (hpd) Odyssey ■ YT 32970
Mozart, W.A.:Sons Vn Pno (misc), w. J. S. Ritter (pno)—K.301, 305 & 403 CBS ▲ MK 42142 [DDD]
Mozart, W.A.:Trios Fl, w. I. Stern (vn), M. Rostropovich (vc) Sony Classical ▲ SK 44568 [DDD]
Mozart, W.A.:Vars Vn Pno, K.359, w. J. S. Ritter (pno) CBS ▲ MK 42142 [DDD]
Mozart, W.A.:Vars Vn Pno, K.360, w. J. S. Ritter (pno) CBS ▲ MK 42142 [DDD]
Music for Flute & Harp, w. Marielle Nordmann (hp) Sony Classical ▲ SK 44552 [DDD]
Music for Flute & Harp, w. Lily Laskine (hp) Odyssey ■ YT 33520
Music, My Love CBS ▲ MK 45548 (m/s)
Nielsen, C.:Con Fl, w. J. Frandsen (cnd), Sjaellends SO CBS ▲ MK 44665 [ADD]
Pachelbel, w. Igor Kipnis (hpd), Raymond Leppard (cnd), John Williams (gtr), Canadian Brass, E. Power Biggs (org), et al. Sony Classical ("Greatest Hits" series) ▲ MLK 62680 ■ MLT 62680
Penderecki, K.:Con Fl, w. K. Penderecki (cnd), Sinfonia Varsovia *(rec National Philharmonic Hall, Warsaw, Poland, Nov. 23, 1993)* Sony Classical ▲ SK 66284 [DDD]
Pergolesi, G.B.:Con Fl, w. K. Münchinger (cnd), Stuttgart CO London ("Weekend Classics" series) ▲ 417873-2 [AAD] ■ 417873-4
Plays His Favorite Encores, w. Tokyo Concert Orch [cnd:Shigenobu Yamaoka] CBS ▲ MK 34559
Portrait of Rampal, w. various assisting instr & orchs CBS ▲ MK 42477 [ADD/DDD] ■ MT 42477
Poulenc, F.:Son Fl, w. Francis Poulenc (pno) Adès ▲ ADE 202522 [AAD]
Poulenc, F.:Son Fl, w. R. Veyron-Lacroix (pno) Odyssey ■ YT 33905
Prokofiev, S.:Son Fl, w. R. Veyron-Lacroix (pno) Odyssey ■ YT 33905
Rameau, J.P.:Pièces de clavecin en concert, w. J. S. Ritter (hpd), I. Stern (vn) Sony Classical ▲ SK 45868 [DDD]
Reicha, A.:Vars & Fant on Mozart's "Se vuol ballare", w. I. Stern (vn), M. Rostropovich (vc), M. Später (lt) Sony Classical ▲ SK 44568 [DDD]
Sakura:Japanese Melodies for Flute & Harp, w. Lily Laskine (hp) CBS ▲ MK 34568 ■ MT 34568
Shankar, R.:Morning Love, w. R. Shankar (sitar) EMI Classics ("Studio" series) ▲ CDM 69121
Stamitz, A.:Con Fls, w. S. Kudo (fl), J.-P. Rampal (cnd), Salzburg Mozarteum Orch Sony Classical ▲ SK 45930 [DDD]
Stamitz, C.:Con Fl, Op. 29, w. V. Neumann (cnd), Prague CO *(rec 1955)* Supraphon ▲ 111308-2 [AAD]
Telemann, G.P.:Cons Fl (misc), w. J. Rolla (cnd), Franz Liszt CO—3—in D,e,G CBS ▲ MK 42362 [DDD]
Telemann, G.P.:Cons Fl (misc), w. K. Ristenpart (cnd), Saar CO Odyssey ■ YT 32890
Telemann, G.P.:Fants Fl Denon ▲ CO 1790 [DDD]
Telemann, G.P.:Fants Fl Odyssey ■ YT 33200
Telemann, G.P.:Qt Fl, w. I. Stern (vn), M. Rostropovich (vc), M. Später (lt) Sony Classical ▲ SK 44568 [DDD]
Telemann, G.P.:Suite in e Fl, w. J. Rolla (cnd), Franz Liszt CO CBS ▲ MK 42362 [DDD]
20th Century Flute Masterpieces, w. R. Veyron-Lacroix (hpd), Lamoureux Orch [cnd:Jean Martinon] Erato 2-▲ 45839-2 [ADD]
Viotti, G.B.:Sym Concertante Fls, w. R. Wilson (fl), C. Scimone (cnd), Venice Solisti *(rec 1976)* Erato ▲ 45836-2 [ADD]
Vivaldi, A.:Cons Fl (misc), w. C. Scimone (cnd), Venice Solisti Odyssey 2-▲ MB2K 45623
Vivaldi, A.:Cons Fl (misc), w. C. Scimone (cnd), Venice Solisti—RV.427 & 414 Erato ▲ 2292-45828-2 [ADD]
Vivaldi, A.:Cons Fl (misc), Louis de Froment CO—RV.90 Allegretto ▲ ACD 8036 [ADD] ■ ACS 8036
Vivaldi, A.:Cons Fl (misc), Franz Liszt CO—in e, RV.430; in D, RV.783; in d, RV.541 *(rec May 10–13, 1992)* Sony Classical ▲ SK 53105 [DDD] Δ SM 53105 [DDD]
Vivaldi, A.:Cons Fl, Op. 10, w. C. Scimone (cnd), Venice Solisti Erato ▲ 2292-45828-2 [ADD]
Vivaldi, A.:Cons Fl, Op. 10, w. C. Scimone (cnd), Venice Solisti CBS ▲ MK 39062 [DDD]
Vivaldi, A.:Cons Fl Vn, w. I. Stern (vn), J. Rolla (cnd), Franz Liszt CO Sony Classical ▲ SK 45867 [DDD] ■ ST 45867 (D)
Vivaldi, A.:Con for 2 Fls, w. S. Kudo (fl), J.-P. Rampal (cnd), Salzburg Mozarteum Orch Sony Classical ▲ SK 45930 [DDD]
Vivaldi, A.:Cons Pic, w. J.-L. Beaumadier (fl), French National Orch—RV.443, 444, 445 Calliope ▲ CAL 9630
Vivaldi, A.:Cons Vn, Op. 8/1–4, "The Four Seasons", w. J.-P. Rampal (cnd), Franz Liszt CO *(rec May 10–13, 1992)* Sony Classical ▲ SK 53105 [DDD] Δ SM 53105 [DDD]
Vivaldi, A.:Cons for 2 Vns, w. I. Stern (vn), J.-P. Rampal (cnd), Jerusalem Music Center CO—RV.514 CBS ▲ MK 38982
Yamanakabushi CBS ▲ MK 37295

Ramsen, D. (hp)
Shifrin, L.:Continuum Label "X" ▲ LXCD 11 [AAD]

Ramsey, Gordon Clark (org)
Edwardian Music for Organ AFKA ■ SK 319

Ramsey, Rebecca (vn)—see ORCHESTRAS & ENSEMBLES Sierra Winds

Ranck, Gerald (hpd)
Bach, J.S.:Chorale Preludes (Schübler), w. S. Machamer (vn)—BWV 650 [performer trans for vib & pno] Ashlar ▲ 1009
Bach, J.S.:Italian Con, w. S. Machamer (vn) [trans. vibraphone & piano Machamer & Ranck] Ashlar ▲ 1009
Bach, J.S.:Sons Fl, BWV 1030–35, w. S. Baron (fl), T. Eddy (vc)—Sons. BWV 1030-1032, 1034 & 1035 Soundspells ▲ CD 106 [DDD]
Bach, J.S.:Sons Vn, w. S. Machamer (vn)—in E, BWV 1016 [trans. Machamer for vibraphone & piano] Ashlar ▲ 1009
Michael Parloff, w. Michael Parloff (fl), Warren Jones (pno) ESS.A.Y ▲ ESS 1027
Telemann, G.P.:Kleine Kammermusik, w. H. Lucarelli (ob), A. Brown (bn) Well-Tempered Productions ▲ WPT 5169 [ADD]

Ranck, Gerald (hpd/pno)
Handel, G.F.:Trio Sons, w. S. Machamer (vib), Eric Wyrick (vn) [performer trans. for vibraphone, violin & piano]—Op. 2, No. 3 for 2 Violins & Keyboard Ashlar ▲ 1009

Ranck, Gerald (pno)
Vibrant Baroque, w. Steven Machamer (vib), Eric Wyrick (vn) Ashlar Records ▲ 1009

Randalu, Kalle (pno)
Hindemith, P.:Son Cl, w. Ulf Rodenhäuser (cl) MD + G ▲ MDG CD 3040695
Hindemith, P.:Son E Hn, w. Thomas Indermühle (E hn) Camerata ▲ 30CM 358 [DDD]
Hindemith, P.:Son E Hn, w. Ingo Goritzki (E hn) MD + G ▲ MDG CD 3040695
Hindemith, P.:Son Fl, w. Jean-Claude Gérard (fl) MD + G ▲ MDG CD 3040695
Hindemith, P.:Son Ob, w. Ingo Goritzki (ob) MD + G ▲ MDG CD 3040695
Hindemith, P.:Son Ob, w. Thomas Indermühle (ob) Camerata ▲ 30CM 358 [DDD]
Mozart, W.A.:Sons Vn Pno (misc), w. Thomas Indermuhle (ob)—in G, K.379; in B♭, K.454; in A, K.526 [all arr for Ob & Pno] Camerata ▲ 30CM 334 [DDD]
Pärt, A.:Variationen zur Gesundung von Arinuschka *(rec White Hall of St. Mauritius Merchant Guild, Tallinn/Estonia, 1993)* Catalyst ▲ 09026-68331-2 [DDD/ADD]

Randolph, David (tuba)
Baker, C.:Omaggi e Fant Tuba, w. R. Zimdars (pno) ACA Digital Recording ▲ CM 20018
Contrasts in Contemporary Music, w. P. Randolph (pno), R. Zimdars (pno) *(rec July–Aug. 1991)* ACA Digital ▲ CM 20018
George, T.R.:Son Tuba, w. P. Randolph (pno) ACA Digital Recording ▲ CM 20018
Stevens, H.:Sonatina Tuba, w. P. Randolph (pno) ACA Digital Recording ▲ CM 20018
Takács, J.:Son Capricciosa, w. P. Randolph (pno) ACA Digital Recording ▲ CM 20018

Randolph, David (tuba) (cont.)
Tuba Suites...& Other Sweets, w. Peggy Randolph (pno) *(rec Roswell United Methodist Church, Roswell, GA, Apr. & Aug. 1993)* ACA Digital ▲ CM 20025

Randolph, Peggy (pno)
Contrasts in Contemporary Music, w. David Randolph (tuba), R. Zimdars (pno) *(rec July–Aug. 1991)* ACA Digital ▲ CM 20018
George, T.R.:Son Tuba, w. D. Randolph (tuba) ACA Digital Recording ▲ CM 20018
Stevens, H.:Sonatina Tuba, w. D. Randolph (tuba) ACA Digital Recording ▲ CM 20018
Takács, J.:Son Capricciosa, w. D. Randolph (tuba) ACA Digital Recording ▲ CM 20018
Tuba Suites...& Other Sweets, w. David Randolph (tuba) *(rec Roswell United Methodist Church, Roswell, GA, Apr. & Aug. 1993)* ACA Digital ▲ CM 20025

Raney, Thomas (perc)
Bernstein, C.H.:Dimensions, w. Kimaree Gilad (E hn) Arcobaleno 2-▲ AAOC 93922
Kraft, William:Soliloquy:Encounters I Crystal ▲ CD 124

Rangell, Andrew (pno)
Bach, J.S.:Goldberg Vars Dorian ▲ DOR 90138 [DDD]
Bach, J.S.:A Musical Offering—the two Ricercares Dorian ▲ DOR 90138 [DDD]
Bach, J.S.:Toccata Hpd, BWV 910 Dorian ▲ DOR 90138 [DDD]
Beethoven, L. van:Son 28 Pno Dorian ▲ DOR 90143 [DDD]
Beethoven, L. van:Son 29 Pno, "Hammerklavier" Dorian ▲ DOR 90143 [DDD]
Beethoven, L. van:Son 30 Pno *(rec 3/91)* Dorian ▲ DOR 90158 [DDD]
Beethoven, L. van:Son 31 Pno *(rec 3/91)* Dorian ▲ DOR 90158 [DDD]
Beethoven, L. van:Son 32 Pno *(rec 3/91)* Dorian ▲ DOR 90158 [DDD]
A Recital of Intimate Works *(rec Studio I, WGBH, Boston, Nov 1994 & Mar 1995)* Dorian ▲ 80147 [DDD]

Ranger, Louis (tpt)
Carter, E.:Canon for 3, "In memoriam Igor Stravinsky", w. Stanley Rosenzweig (tpt), Gerard Schwarz (tpt) [2 versions] Phoenix ▲ PHCD 115 [AAD]
Coulthard, J.:Fanfare Son, w. Bruce Vogt (pno) *(rec Univ of Victoria, May 1994)* Crystal ▲ CD 669
Kupferman, M.:Infinities, w. Bruce Vogt (pno)—No. 22 (1967) *(rec Univ of Victoria, May 1994)* Crystal ▲ CD 669
Peeters, F.:Son Tpt, w. Bruce Vogt (pno) *(rec Univ of Victoria, May 1994)* Crystal ▲ CD 669
Shapero, H.:Son Tpt *(rec Univ of Victoria, May 1994)* Crystal ▲ CD 669
Zwilich, E.T.:Clarino Qt, w. David Flello (tpt), Christopher Lane (tpt), David Michaux (tpt) *(rec Univ of Victoria, May 1994)* Crystal ▲ CD 669

Ránki, Dezsö (pno)
Bartók, B.:Allegro barbaro Hungaroton ▲ HCD 31036
Bartók, B.:Burleskes, Op. 8c Hungaroton ▲ HCD 31036
Bartók, B.:Con 3 Pno, w. J. Ferencsik (cnd), Hungarian State Orch Hungaroton ▲ HCD 31036
Bartók, B.:Mikrokosmos Teldec 3-▲ 9031-76139-2 GX
Bartók, B.:Pictures Orch, w. Z. Kocsis (pno) [arr. 2-piano Kocsis] *(rec 9/11/81)* Hungaroton ▲ HCD 12400
Bartók, B.:Pieces Orch, Sz.51, w. Z. Kocsis (pno) [2-piano arr. Kocsis]—Nos. 1 & 2, Prelude & Scherzo *(rec 9/11/81)* Hungaroton ▲ HCD 12400
Bartók, B.:Romanian Christmas Carols Hungaroton ▲ HCD 31036
Bartók, B.:Romanian Folk Dances Pno Hungaroton ▲ HCD 31036
Bartók, B.:Son for 2 Pnos, w. Kocsis (pno), Cser (perc), Rácz (perc) *(rec 9/11/81)* Hungaroton ▲ HCD 12400
Bartók, B.:Sonatina Pno Hungaroton ▲ HCD 31036
Bartók, B.:Suite Pno Hungaroton ▲ HCD 31036
Beethoven, L. van:Sons Vc (comp), w. M. Perényi (vc) Hungaroton 2-▲ HCD 11928/29
Brahms, J.:Ballades, Op. 10 Quintana ▲ QUI 903082 ■ QUI 403082
Brahms, J.:Ballades, Op. 10 Musique d'Abord ▲ HMA 1903082
Brahms, J.:Fants Pno, Op. 116—No. 6 Musique d'Abord ▲ HMA 1903082
Brahms, J.:Pieces Pno, Op. 118—Nos. 1, 2, 3 & 6 Musique d'Abord ▲ HMA 1903082
Brahms, J.:Pieces Pno, Op. 119—Nos. 3 & 4 Musique d'Abord ▲ HMA 1903082
Brahms, J.:Qnt Pno, w. Bartók String Quartet Hungaroton ▲ HCD 11596
Brahms, J.:Scherzo Pno, Op. 4 Musique d'Abord ▲ HMA 1903082
Brahms, J.:Vars on a Theme by Haydn, w. Z. Kocsis (pno)—Op. 56b Hungaroton ▲ HCD 11646
Liszt, F.:Pno Music (misc)—Unstern!; En rêve; Klavierstück in f#; La lugubre Gondola No. 2; Weigenlied; In festo transfigurationis Domini nostri Jesu Christi; Impromptu; Sancta Dorothea; Mephisto Waltz No. 4; Mephisto Polka; Csárdás No. 1; C Musique d'Abord ▲ HMA 1903024
Liszt, F.:Son Pno Musique d'Abord ▲ HMA 1903024
Mozart, W.A.:Sons Pno 4-Hands, w. Z. Kocsis (pno) Hungaroton 2-▲ HCD 11794/95
Mozart, W.A.:Son Pnos, K.448, w. Z. Kocsis (pno) Hungaroton ▲ HCD 11646
Ravel, M.:Ma mère l'oye Pno, w. Z. Kocsis (pno) Hungaroton ▲ HCD 11646

Rankin, Elizabeth (vn)—see ORCHESTRAS & ENSEMBLES Cincinnati Contemporary Music Ensemble

Rankovich, Tatjna (pno)
Flagello, N.:Symphonic Waltzes *(rec 1995)* Citadel ▲ CTD 88115 [ADD/DDD]

Ranmo, Sune (va)
Gade, N.W.:Octet, w. Anne Egendal (vn), Per Lund Madsen (vn), Hans Nygaard (vc), Kontra String Quartet *(rec Torpen Kapel, Humlebaek, Denmark, May, 5–8, 1992)* BIS ▲ CD 545 [DDD]

Ransom, W. (pno)
Strauss, R.:Enoch Arden, w. M. Morgan (bar) [E] *(rec June 1989)* ACA Digital Recording ▲ CM 20014

Ranta, Iimo (pno)—see also ORCHESTRAS & ENSEMBLES Tapiola Trio
Grieg, E.:Songs, w. Monica Groop (mez)—Romancer, Op. 15; Romancer, Op. 39; Romancer og Ballader af Andreas Munch, Op. 9; Digte af Vilhelm Krag, Op. 60; 4 Songs without Opus numbers *(rec Danderyd Grammar School, Sweden, Jan 11–14, 1996)* BIS ▲ CD 787 [DDD]
Sibelius, J.:Songs, w. Karita Mattila (sop)—Svarta rosor; Flickan komifran sin äsklings möte; Var det en dröm; The Flower Songs Ondine ▲ ODE 856

Ranta, Michael (perc)—see ORCHESTRAS & ENSEMBLES Univ of Illinois Contemporary Chamber Players

Rantamäki, Tuija (vc)
Heiniö, M.:In G Vc & Pno, w. Juhani Lagerspetz (pno) Ondine ▲ ODE 870

Rantanen, Matti (acc)
Bashmakov, L.:Inventions (4), w. Jukka Tiensuu (hpd) Finlandia ▲ FIN 54404 [DDD]
Jokinen, E.:Con Acc, w. O. Pohjola (cnd), Avanti! CO Finlandia ▲ FIN 54404 [DDD]
Lindberg, M.:Jeux d'anches Finlandia ▲ FIN 54404 [DDD]
Lindberg, M.:Metalwork, w. Tim Ferchen (perc) Finlandia ▲ FIN 54404 [DDD]
Nevanlinna, T.:Foto, w. Kari Krükku (cl) Finlandia ▲ FIN 54404 [DDD]
Tiensuu, J.:Aufschwung Finlandia ▲ FIN 54404 [DDD]

Raoult, Andre (ob)
Bach, J.C.:Sinfs, Op. 6, w. G. Rumpel (fl), R. Tschupp (cnd), Zurich Camerata *(rec 1969, 1981)* Jecklin ▲ J 4408 [ADD]
Krommer, F.:Concertino Fl, Op. 65, w. G. Rumpel (fl), R. Tschupp (cnd), Zurich Camerata *(rec 1969, 1981)* Jecklin ▲ J 4408 [ADD]
Vanhal, J.B.:Sym in g, w. G. Rumpel (fl), R. Tschupp (cnd), Zurich Camerata *(rec 1969, 1981)* Jecklin ▲ J 4408 [ADD]

Rapattoni, Marco (pno)
Tosti, P.F.:Songs, w. E. Palacio (ten), H. Liviabella (vn), G. Scabbia (fl), B. Giuffredi (gtr), C. Passerini (hp), M. Decimo (vc) [arr. Massimo de Bernart for instrumental accompaniment]—La serenata; Sogno; 'A vucchella; Segreto; Ideale; 2ème Aubade; Anima mia; Donna, vorrei morir; Aprile; Ancora!; Mattinata; L'ultima canzone; Malìa; Non t'amo più; Il pescatore cantal; Tristezza; O falce di luna calante; L'abla separa dalla luce l'ombra; Mi guitarra dice "Te amo!"; Ricordati di me; Vuol note o banconote? Arkadia-Akademia ▲ 125 [DDD]

▲ = CD ♦ = Enhanced CD Δ = MD ■ = Cassette Tape □ = DCC

Rapf, Kurt (pno/org)
Mozart, W.A.:Masonic Music, w. K. Equiluz (ten), P. Maag (cnd), Vienna Volksoper Orch, Vienna Volksoper Chorus—Adagios, K.410 & 411; Adagio & Fugue, K.546; Adagio & Rondo, K.617; Anhang zum Schluss der Freimaurerloge, K.623a; Cants, K.429, 471, 619 & 623; Graduale, K.273; Lieder, K.148, 468, 483 & 484; Maurerische; Motet, K.618; Psalm 129, K.93 *(rec 1966)* Vox Box 2-▲ CDX 5055 [ADD]

Raphael, J. (pno)
Liszt, F.:Années de pèlerinage 3—Dante Sonata (fantasia quasi un sonata) Protone ▲ NRPR 2204 [DDD]
Liszt, F.:Harmonies poétiques et religieuses—Bénédiction de Dieu dans la solitude Protone ▲ NRPR 2204 [DDD]
Respighi, O.:Ancient Airs & Dances—Siciliana & Gagliarda Protone ▲ NRPR 2204 [DDD]
Respighi, O.:Liriche dal Poema paradisiaco di Gabriele d'Annunzio Protone ▲ NRPR 2204 [DDD]

Rapier, Wayne (ob d'amore)
Bach, J.S.:Con Ob d'amore, w. T. Dimitriades, Diaz-Shames-Diaz Trio *(rec live in concert, Oct 1, 1989)* Boston Records ▲ BR 1001 ■ BR 1001 CT

Rapier, Wayne (ob)
Bach, J.S.:Cant 187, w. Kendra Colton (sop)—Gott versorget alles Leben Boston Records ▲ BR 1013
Bach, J.S.:Con Ob, BWV 1053, w. T. Dimitriades, Diaz-Shames-Diaz Trio *(rec live in concert, Oct 1, 1989)* Boston Records ▲ BR 1001 ■ BR 1001 CT
Bach, J.S.:Partita Fl, BWV 1013 Boston Records ▲ BR 1013
Finzi, G.:Bagatelles, Op. 23, w. T. Dimitriades (str), Diaz-Shames-Diaz Trio *(rec live 10/1/89)* Boston Records ▲ BR 1001 ■ BR 1001 CT
Finzi, G.:Interlude Ob & Strs, w. R. Diaz (va), A. Diaz (vc), T. Dimitriades (str), J. Shames (pno) *(rec live Oct. 1, 1989)* Boston Records ▲ BR 1001
Goossens, E.:Con Ob, w. *(accompianists unknown)* Boston Records ▲ BR 1013
Hollingsworth, S.:Son Ob, w. Martin Amlin (pno) Boston Records ▲ BR 1013
Mozart, W.A.:Qt Ob, K.370, w. Diaz-Shames-Diaz Trio *(rec live in concert, Oct. 1, 1989)* Boston Records ▲ BR 1001 ■ BR 1001 CT
Piston, W.:Suite Ob, w. Martin Amlin (pno) Boston Records ▲ BR 1013
Saint-Saëns, C.:Son Ob, w. M. Amlin (pno) Boston Records ▲ BR 1013
Vaughan Williams, R.:Blake Songs, w. Kendra Colton (sop) Boston Records ▲ BR 1013
Wayne Rapier:Oboe, w. Rapier, Wayne (ob), Diaz-Shames-Diaz Trio, Tatiana Dimitriades (strs) Boston Records ▲ BR1001CD ■ BR1001CT

Rapin, Frederic (cl)
Balissat, J.:Vars (7), w. P. Genet, F. Gottraux (vn), N. Pache (va), M. Jaermann (vc), R. Birnstigl (db), F. Schmocker (bn), M. Veillon (hn), J. Balissat (cnd) Grammont ▲ CTSP 17-2 [ADD]
Weber, C.M. von:Con 1 Cl, w. J.-F. Antonioli (cnd), Timisoara Banatul PO Timpani ▲ 1031
Weber, C.M. von:Con 2 Cl, w. J.-F. Antonioli (cnd), Timisoara Banatul PO Timpani ▲ 1031

Rapp, Siegfried (pno)
Ravel, M.:Con Pno (left hand), w. K. Masur (cnd), Dresden PO Berlin Classics ("Masur Edition" series) ▲ BER 9158

Raps, Gena (pno)
Dvořák, A.:Slavonic Dances (comp), w. A. Balsam (pno) Arabesque ▲ Z 6559
Dvořák, A.:Theme with Vars Arabesque ▲ Z 6532 [DDD]
Dvořák, A.:Waltzes Pno, Op. 54 Arabesque ▲ Z 6532 [DDD]
Mozart, W.A.:Andante & Vars Pno 4-Hands, w. Artur Balsam (pno) *(rec SUNY, Purchase Theatre C, June 15–18, 1992)* Arabesque ▲ ARA 6652 [DDD]
Mozart, W.A.:Fant Mechanical Org, w. Artur Balsam (pno) [arr. for pno 4-hands] *(rec SUNY, Purchase Theatre C, June 15–18, 1992)* Arabesque ▲ ARA 6652 [DDD]
Mozart, W.A.:Pno Music 4-Hands, w. A. Balsam (pno)—Son. in F, K.497; Fant. No. 1 in f, K.594; Son. in B♭, K.358 Arabesque ▲ ARA 6635 [DDD]
Mozart, W.A.:Son Pno 4-Hands, K.381, w. Artur Balsam (pno) *(rec SUNY, Purchase Theatre C, June 15–18, 1992)* Arabesque ▲ ARA 6652 [DDD]
Mozart, W.A.:Son Pno 4-Hands, K.521, w. Artur Balsam (pno) *(rec SUNY, Purchase Theatre C, June 15–18, 1992)* Arabesque ▲ ARA 6652 [DDD]

Rapson, John (cl)
Cardy, P.:Virelai, w. M. Bernardi (cnd), CBC Vancouver SO CBC ("SM 5000" series) ▲ SMCD 5094 [DDD]

Rapson, Penelope (hpd)
Vivaldi, A.:Arias, w. K. Eckersley (sop), P. Rapson (cnd), Fiori Musicali—from La fida Ninfa:Alma oppressa; La Griselda:Agitata da due venti [I] Meridian ▲ CDE 84195
Vivaldi, A.:Cons Vn, Op. 8/1–4, "The Four Seasons", w. E. Wallfisch (vn), P. Rapson (cnd), Fiori Musicali Meridian ▲ CDE 84195
Vivaldi, A.:L'incoronazione di Dario, w. P. Rapson (cnd), Fiori Musicali—Sinf. Meridian ▲ CDE 84195
Vivaldi, A.:Motets, w. K. Eckersley (sop), P. Rapson (cnd), Fiori Musicali—In furore [I] Meridian ▲ CDE 84195

Rascher, Carina (sax)—see ORCHESTRAS & ENSEMBLES Rascher Saxophone Quartet

Rascher, Sigurd (a sax)
Koch, E. von:Music of, w. Andreas Röhn (vn), Kerstin Hindart (pno), S. Westerberg (cnd), Munich PO, Swedish RSO—Nordiskt Capriccio; Skandinaviska Danser; Saxofonkonsert; Svensk Dansrapsodi; Karaktärer Föor Vn Och Pno Phono Suecia ▲ PHN 55 [ADD]

Raschietti, Massimiliano (org)
Giordani, G.:Lamentazioni e Miserere, w. Il Terzo Suono Vocal Ensemble Symphonia 2-▲ SYM 94D 31

Raselli, Francesco (hn)
Schumann, R.:Andante & Vars Hn, w. Robert Majek (pno), Mario Venzago (pno), Käthi Gohl (vc), Rama Jucker (vc) Accord ▲ ACD 201572 [AAD]

Rasi, Alberto (vl)
Bach, J.S.:Sons Vl, BWV 1027-1029, w. P. Marisaldi (hpd) *(rec Mar 1992)* Bongiovanni ▲ GB 5535 [DDD]

Raskin, Mario (hpd)
Duphly, J.:Pièces de clavecin (4 books) Pierre Verany ▲ PVY 793021 [DDD]
Forqueray, A.:Pièces de viole [trans. Jean-Baptiste Forqueray] Pierre Verany ▲ PVY 794051 [DDD]
Soler, P.A.:Fandango Pierre Verany ▲ PVY 796061 [DDD]
Soler, P.A.:Sons Hpd—R.20, 21, 39, 40, 77, 87, 88, 90, 104, 113 & 117 Pierre Verany ▲ PVY 796061 [DDD]
Soler, P.A.:Sons Hpd—R.15, 23, 25, 27, 31, 36, 37, 45, 48, 49, 52, 54, 83 & 84 Pierre Verany ▲ PVY 796062 [DDD]

Rasková, Vera (fl)
Respighi, O.:La Primavera, w. Henrietta Lednárová (sop—Prima fanciulla), Jana Valásková (sop—Sirvard), Beata Geriová (mez—Seconda fanciullá), Miroslav Dvorsky (ten—Il giovine), Richard Haan (bar—L'orante), Vladimír Kubovčik (bass—Il vecchio), M. Adriano (cnd), Slovak RSO Bratislava, Slovak Phil Chorus *(rec Slovak Radio Concert Hall, Bratislava)* Marco Polo ▲ 8.223595 [DDD]

Rasmussen, Bjarne Boye (va)
Kuhlau, F.:Qnts Fl, w. Eyvind Rafn (fl), Kim Sjøgren (vn), Georg Svendsen Andersen (va), Lars Holm Johansen (vc) *(rec Torpen Kapel, Humlebaek, Nordsjaelland, Denmark, Aug 1985)* Naxos ▲ 8.553303 [DDD]

Rasmussen, Kristian (pno)
Beck, Jeremy:Son 1 Pno CRS Master ▲ CRS 9664
Germani, F.:Immotus CRS Master ▲ CRS 9664
Hegaard, L.:Preludes Pno CRS Master ▲ CRS 9664
Lorentzen, B.:Abgrund CRS Master ▲ CRS 9664
Lorentzen, B.:Goldranken CRS Master ▲ CRS 9664
Lund, G.:Dialogues CRS Master ▲ CRS 9664
Russo, J.:Toccata 1 Pno CRS Master ▲ CRS 9664
Russo, J.:Toccata 2 Pno CRS Master ▲ CRS 9664
Van Appledorn, M.J.:Contrasts CRS Master ▲ CRS 9664

Rasmussen, Mogens (vl)
Blavet, M.:Sons Trns Fl, w. Dan Laurin (rcr), Leif Meyer (hpd)—Son Terza; Son Seconda *(rec Furuby Church, Sweden, May 8–11, 1995)* BIS ▲ CD 745 [DDD]
Buxtehude, D.:Sons Vn, Vl & Continuo, w. John Holloway (vn), Ursula Weiss (vn), Jaap ter Linden (vl), Lars Ulrik Mortensen (hpd/org)—BuxWV 266, 267, 269 & 271-273 *(rec Radio House, Studio 2, Sept 25–28, 1994)* Marco Polo ("dacapo" series) ▲ 8.224005 [DDD]
Dornel, L.-A.:Sons Vn & Suites Fl, Op. 2, w. Dan Laurin (rcr), Leif Meyer (hpd)—Suite II[5] *(rec Furuby Church, Sweden, May 8–11, 1995)* BIS ▲ CD 745 [DDD]
Hume, T.:The First Part of Ayres—Hark, Hark; A Soldiers Galliard; I am falling; A Soldiers Resolution *(rec Strandmarks Church, Copenhagen, Denmark, Sept 1994)* Rondo Gramophon ▲ RCD 8343 [DDD]
Leclair, J.-M.:Sons Vn (Books 1–4), w. Dan Laurin (rcr), Leif Meyer (hpd)—Son II *(rec Furuby Church, Sweden, May 8–11, 1995)* BIS ▲ CD 745 [DDD]
Marini, B.:Sons, Syms & Retornelli, w. Mogens Andresen (b trbn), Karen Englund (hpd)—Son *(rec Strandmarks Church, Copenhagen, Denmark, Sept 1994)* Rondo Gramophon ▲ RCD 8343 [DDD]

Rasmussen, R. (hn)—see ORCHESTRAS & ENSEMBLES Atlantic Brass Quintet

Rasmussen, S. (perc)
Blak, K.:Music of, w. K. Blak (pno)—8 (sels.) *(rec Dec. 1990)* Tutl ▲ HJF 24

Rasmussen, Svend (cl)
Vesth, T.:Music of, w. Jan Sommer (gtr), Nils Sylvest Jeppesen (vc), Per Friman (vn), Gert-Inge Andersson (va), Berit Spaelling (hp), Bent Larsen (fl), Bjorn Nielsen (ob), Henrik Simonsen (db)—Cuddling Rain; Waltz the Blue Sea; Kaspers Lullaby; Autumn Sunshine; Red Fox Hunting Tea Party; Off White Eternity; Tartan Fl Danica ▲ DCD 8142

Rásonyi, Leila (vn)
Pizzetti, I.:Canti Vn, w. Alpaslan Ertüngealp (pno) *(rec Hungaroton Studio, Rottenbiller St, Budapest, May 17–18 & June 2, 1994)* Marco Polo ▲ 8.223812 [DDD]
Pizzetti, I.:Son 1 Vn, w. Alpaslan Ertüngealp (pno) *(rec Hungaroton Studio, Rottenbiller St, Budapest, May 17–18 & June 2, 1994)* Marco Polo ▲ 8.223812 [DDD]
Pizzetti, I.:Trio Pno, w. Alpaslan Ertüngealp (pno), László Fenyö (vc) *(rec Hungaroton Studio, Rottenbiller St, Budapest, May 17–18 & June 2, 1994)* Marco Polo ▲ 8.223812 [DDD]

Raspanti, M. (pno)
Caprioli, A.:Frammenti (7) dal Diario *(rec 1987)* Pro Viva ▲ ISPV 148 CD [ADD]

Rassoudova, Natalia (pno)
Shostakovich, D.:4 Verses by Captain Lebyadkin, w. Piotr Glouboky (bass) Russian Season ▲ RUS 288089
Shostakovich, D.:Songs, Op. 46, w. Piotr Glouboky (bass) Russian Season ▲ RUS 288089
Shostakovich, D.:Songs, Op. 62, w. Piotr Glouboky (bass) Russian Season ▲ RUS 288089
Shostakovich, D.:Songs, Op. 121, w. Piotr Glouboky (bass) Russian Season ▲ RUS 288089

Rath, Dana (mand)—see ORCHESTRAS & ENSEMBLES Modern Mandolin Quartet

Rath, Lutz (vc)—see also ORCHESTRAS & ENSEMBLES Bronx Arts Ensemble
Dashow, J.:Trio 4/3, w. Mia Wu (vn), Sylvia Kahan (pno) *(rec Studio Wonderland, Rome, June 1993)* Pro Viva ▲ ISPV 177 CD [DDD]
Seasons Remembered 2, w. Stillman, Judith Lynn (pno), Toby Appel (va), John Deak (db), Eliot Porter (db), Diaz Trio [David Kim (vn), Roberto Diaz (va), Andres Diaz (vc)], Fenwick Smith (fl), Ruth Waterman (vn) North Star ▲ 9837-40052-2 ■ 9837-40052-4

Raths, O. Nicholas (gtr)—see ORCHESTRAS & ENSEMBLES Minneapolis Guitar Quartet

Rattay, Evzen (vc)—see also ORCHESTRAS & ENSEMBLES Talich String Quartet
Paganini, N.:Terzetto Vn, w. P. Messiereur (vn), M. Zelenka (gtr) *(rec 1983)* Supraphon ▲ 10 3647-2 [AAD]

Rauch, František (pno)
Smetana, B.:Czech Dances Supraphon ▲ SUP 0080 [ADD]
Smetana, B.:Macbeth & the Witches Supraphon ▲ SUP 0080 [ADD]
Smetana, B.:Morceaux caractéristiques Supraphon ▲ SUP 0080 [ADD]
Smetana, B.:Sketches Pno, Op. 4 Supraphon ▲ SUP 0080 [ADD]
Smetana, B.:Sketches Pno, Op. 5 Supraphon ▲ SUP 0080 [ADD]

Raucheisen, Michael (pno)
Archive Performances, w. Fritz Kreisler (vn) Biddulph 3-▲ LAB 001-3 (m) [ADD]
Beethoven, L. van:Songs, w. Peter Anders (ten)—Adelaide Berlin Classics ▲ BER 2167 [ADD]
Brahms, J.:Songs, w. Peter Anders (ten)—Sehnsucht Berlin Classics ▲ BER 2167 [ADD]
Hans Hotter Sings Carl Lowe, w. Hans Hotter (bar) *(rec 1943–45)* Preiser ▲ PRE CD 90301
Schubert, Franz:Die Schöne Müllerin, w. J. Patzak (ten) *(rec 1943)* Preiser ▲ 93128 (m) [AAD]
Schubert, Franz:Songs (misc), w. Peter Anders (ten) *(rec 1942–44)* Berlin Classics ▲ BER 2166 [ADD]
Schubert, Franz:Winterreise, w. H. Hotter (b-bar) Deutsche Grammophon ▲ 437351-2
Schumann, R.:Songs, w. Peter Anders (ten) Berlin Classics ▲ BER 2167 [ADD]
Sings Select Lieder, w. Helge Rosvaenge (ten), Gerald Moore (pno), Bruno Seidler-Winkler (pno) *(rec 1936–44)* Preiser ▲ PRE CD 89992
Strauss, R.:Songs, w. Peter Anders (ten)—Allerseelen Berlin Classics ▲ BER 2167 [ADD]
Wolf, H.:Songs (misc), w. Peter Anders (ten) Berlin Classics ▲ BER 2167 [ADD]

Rauchs, Beatrice (pno)
Mendelssohn, Fanny:Das Jahr Bayer ▲ BR 100 250 [DDD]
Mendelssohn, Fanny:Pieces Pno (1836) Bayer ▲ BR 100 250 [DDD]

Raudales, Henry (vn)
Devreese, G.:Con 2 Vn, w. D. Brosse (cnd), New Flemish SO René Gailly ▲ CD 87080 [DDD]
Glière, R.:Duets Vn, Op. 39, w. F. Van Goethem (va) *(rec Mar. 1993)* Pavane ▲ ADW 7308 [DDD]
Halvorsen, J.:Passacaglia & Sarabande con variazioni, w. F. Van Goethem (va) *(rec Mar. 1993)* Pavane ▲ ADW 7308 [DDD]
Rolla, A.:Duo 3 Vn, w. F. Van Goethem (va) *(rec Mar. 1993)* Pavane ▲ ADW 7308 [DDD]

Rausch, John (perc)—see ORCHESTRAS & ENSEMBLES Louisiana State Univ New Music Ensemble

Raush, John (perc)
Constantinides, D.:Vocal Music, w. Cynthia Dewey (nar), Angela DeVerger (sop), Evelyn Petros (sop), Susan Faust Straley (sop), Eugenia Epperson (fl), Richard Jernigan (cl), Kelly Smith Toney (vn), Hye-Yun Chung (hp), Stephen Brown (pno), D. Constantinides (cnd), Louisiana State Univ New Music Ensemble—Reflections IV for Sop, Fl, Hp & Pno; Intimations [1 Act Opera]; 4 Songs on Poems by Sappho; Mutability for Sop & Str Qt.; 4 Greek Songs Vestige ▲ 04

Rautenberg, Lisa (va)
Dotzauer, F.:Qt Strs, w. Vera Beths (vn), Jody Gatwood (vn), Anner Bylsma (vc) *(rec New York City, Jan. 19–22, 1994)* Sony Classical ▲ SK 66259 [DDD]
Dotzauer, F.:Qnt Strs, w. Vera Beths (vn), Jody Gatwood (vn), Anner Bylsma (vc), Kenneth Slowik (vc) *(rec New York City, Jan. 19–22, 1994)* Sony Classical ("Vivarte" series) ▲ SK 64307 [DDD]

Rautenberg, Lisa (vn)
Bach, J.S.:Air on the G String, w. Mary Jane Newman (org) *(rec Presbyterian Church, Mt. Kisco, NY, Aug 26–27, 1995)* Helicon ▲ HE 1006 [DDD]
Bach, J.S.:Sons Vn Hpd, BWV 1014–1019, w. Mary Jane Newman (org)—No. 3 in E, BWV 1016:Adagio only [arr vn & org] *(rec Presbyterian Church, Mt. Kisco, NY, Aug 26–27, 1995)* Helicon ▲ HE 1006 [DDD]
Dotzauer, F.:Canon for 2 Vns, w. Vera Beths (vn) *(rec New York City, Jan. 19–22, 1994)* Sony Classical ("Vivarte" series) ▲ SK 64307 [DDD]
Schubert, Franz:Qnt Strs, D.956, w. J. Gatwood (vn), S. Dann (va), A. Bylsma (vc), K. Slowick (vc) Sony Classical ("Vivarte" series) ▲ SK 46669
Splendor of the High Holy Days, w. Stacey Lowe (sop), Russell Ashley (bar), Mary Jane Newman (org/cnd) *(rec SUNY, Purchase, 1995)* Vox Classics ▲ VOX 7510 [DDD]

Rautio, Erkki (vc)
Finnish Miniatures for Cello, w. Izumi Tateno (pno) *(rec Jan. 3 & 7, 1991)* Finlandia ▲ 4509-95871-2 [DDD]
Grieg, E.:Son Vc, w. I. Tateno (pno) *(rec Aug. 27–30, 1991)* Finlandia ▲ 4509-95867-2 [DDD]

Rautio, Erkki (vc) (cont.)
Merikanto, O.:Music of, w. Eeva–Jiisa Saarinen (mez), Jorma Hynninen (bar), Sauli Tiilikainen (bar), Kaija Saaikettu (vn), Pertti Eerola (pno), Ralf Gothoni (pno), Raija Kerppo (pno), Izumi Tateno (pno), Tauno Satomaa (cnd), Candomino Choir—Summer Evening (waltz); Valse lente; Romance; On the Highest Tree–Top; Annina; Bye, Bye Lullabye; The Weeping Flute; At Sea; Hey My Heart; Where Rustling Birches Bend; Play Softly, the Tune of Mourning; Fairy Tale by the Fireside; Idyll; Scherzo, Op. 6/4; O Dost Thou Remember That Hymn; Lade Ladoga; Why Do I Sing; The Thunderbird; The Happy Ones; Summer Evening's Idyll Finlandia ▲ FIN 500432 [AAD/DDD]
Ravasio, M. (va)
Milesi, P.:Modi 1, w. D. Cassamagnaghi (fl), F. Pomarico (ob), A. Bianchi (cl), L. Dosso (bn), G. Govi (vn), D. Tellini (vn), S. Righini (vc), P. Rizzi (db), C. Vignani (hpd), J. Scully (perc), P. Milesi (cnd) Cuneiform ▲ RUNE 63
Milesi, P.:Modi 2, w. L. M. Pickova (sop), Françoise Goddard (alt), M. Ferradini (ten), B. Andersen (bass), D. Cassamagnaghi (fl), S. Scanziani (ob), A. Bianchi (cl/b cl), E. Crisafulli (bn), C. Gazzola (hn), F. Gualandris (tuba), A. Girardi (celtic hp), R. Anedda (vn), E. Groppo (vn), M. Pagani (vn), S. Righini (vc), P. Rizzi (db), J. Scully (perc), P. Milesi (cnd) Cuneiform ▲ RUNE 63
Ravassard, Thierry (pno)
Beethoven, L. van:Trio Pno, Op.38, w. Françoise Perrin (vn), Pierre Feyler (db) Gallo ▲ CD 761
Chausson, E.:Poème Vn, w. Françoise Perrin (vn), Pierre Feyler (db) [arr Antoine Duhamel for trio] *(rec 1994)* Gallo ▲ CD 801 [DDD]
Kreisler, F.:Music of, w. Françoise Perrin (vn), Pierre Feyler (db)—Liebesleid Gallo ▲ CD 761
Massenet, J.:Méditation from *Thaïs*, w. Françoise Perrin (vn), Pierre Feyler (db) [arr for Pno, Vn & Db] Gallo ▲ CD 761
Monti, A.:Czardas, w. Françoise Perrin (vn), Pierre Feyler (db) Gallo ▲ CD 761
Ravel, M.:Tzigane, w. Françoise Perrin (vn), Pierre Feyler (db) [arr Antoine Duhamel for trio] *(rec 1994)* Gallo ▲ CD 801 [DDD]
Ravel, Maurice (pno)
Great Composers at the Keyboard, w. Camille Saint–Saëns (pno), Enrique Granados (pno) Fonè ▲ FON 90F14 [DDD]
Ravel, M.:Boléro [trans. pno] LaserLight ▲ 14 201
Ravel, M.:Chants populaires, w. M. Grey (sop)—No. 4, Chanson hébraïque [He] *(rec 1932)* InSync ■ C 4143
Ravel, M.:Gaspard de la nuit—No. 2 [Le Gibet] LaserLight ▲ 14 201
Ravel, M.:Melodies hébraïques, w. M. Grey (sop) *(rec 1932)* InSync ■ C 4143
Ravel, M.:Oiseaux Tristes Pno LaserLight ▲ 14 201
Ravel, M.:Pavane pour une infante défunte LaserLight ▲ 14 201
Ravel, M.:Pno Music—Gaspard de la Nuit; Oiseaux tristes; Pavane; Toccata; Valley of the Bells Klavier ▲ KC 137
Ravel, M.:Le Tombeau de Couperin—Toccata LaserLight ▲ 14 201
Ravel, M.:La Vallée des cloches LaserLight ▲ 14 201
Ravenscroft, Timothy (pno)—see ORCHESTRAS & ENSEMBLES English Piano Trio
Raver, Leonard (org)
Flowering of Vocal Music in America, 1767–1823, w. Susan Belling (sop), Cynthia Clarey (sop), Barbara Wallace (sop), Debra Vanderlinde (sop), D'Anna Fortunato (mez), Evelyn Petros (mez), Charles Bressler (ten), Richard Anderson (bar), James Tyeska (bar), Joseph McKee (bass), Cynthia Otis (hp), et. al. New World ▲ 80467–2
Saint–Saëns, C.:Sym 3, w. L. Bernstein (cnd), New York PO CBS ▲ MYK 37255 [ADD] ■ MYT 37255
Saint–Saëns, C.:Sym 3, w. L. Bernstein (cnd), New York PO Sony Classical ▲ SMK 47608
Schwartz, E.:Cycles & Gongs, w. A. Dean (tpt), E. Schwartz (tape) CRI ▲ CD 598 [ADD]
Schwartz, E.:Souvenir, w. J. Bunke (cl) CRI ▲ CD 598 [ADD]
Ravina, O. (vn)
Swack, I.:Duets Vn, w. K. Mirkin (va) Opus One ▲ 149
Ravnan, A. (pno)
Snyder, R.:Impromptus Vc, w. K. Ravnan (vc) CRS ▲ CD 9153
Ravnan, K. (vc)
Snyder, R.:Impromptus Vc, w. A. Ravnan (pno) CRS ▲ CD 9153
Rawicz, Marian (pno)
Saint–Saëns, C.:Carnival of the Animals, w. W. Landauer (pno), J. Barbirolli (cnd), Hallé Orch Dutton Laboratories ▲ DUT CDSJB 1002 [ADD]
Rawsthorne, Noel (org)
Liszt, F.:Fant & Fugue on the name B–A–C–H Klavier ▲ KCD 11036 [DDD]
Pipe Organ Spectacular Klavier ▲ KCD 11036 [DDD]
Reubke, J.:Son Org Klavier ▲ KCD 11036 [DDD]
Saint–Saëns, C.:Sym 3, w. E. Bátiz (cnd), London PO ASV ▲ ASV 665 [DDD]
Ray, Mary Ruth (va)—see ORCHESTRAS & ENSEMBLES Lydian String Quartet
Ray, Vicki (pno)
Cage, J.:Europera 3, w. Suzan Hanson (sop), Ruby Hinds (mez), Patricia McAfee (mez), Michael Lyon (ten), Richard Powell (ten), Kevin Bell (bass), Brian Pezzone (pno), Hannes Geiger (record players), Joseph Giri (record players), William Houston (record players), Dren McDonald (record players), Ronda Rindone (record players), Clarice Ross (record players), Scott Fraser (tape), A. Culver (cnd), Long Beach Opera Orch *(rec Center Theater, Long Beach, CA, Nov. 13, 1993)* Mode 2–▲ MODE 38/39
Ray, Vicki (pno/cel)
Smith, W.L.:Music of, w. Robin Lorentz (vn), Erika Duke (vc), Dorothy Stone (fl/pic), Martin Walker (cl), Wadada Leo Smith (tpt/flgl/fls/bells), Mika Noda (vib/bells/timp), David Philipson (perc/bells)—Another Wave More Waves; Double Thunderbolt; Tao–Njia; and others Tzadik ("Composer" series) ▲ TZA 7017 [DDD]
Rayer, P. (gtr)—see ORCHESTRAS & ENSEMBLES Versailles Guitar Quartet
Rayer, P. (vn)
Wissmer, P.:Con 2 Vn, w. D. Fanal (cnd), Olsztyn State PO Quantum ▲ QM 6936 [DDD]
Raymond, Richard (pno)
Beethoven, L. van:Son 32 Pno *(rec Jan. & Apr. 1993)* CBC ("Musica Viva" series) ▲ MVCD 1066 [DDD]
Gougeon, D.:Thèmes–solaires (6)—No. 1, "Piano–Soleil *(rec Jan. & Apr. 1993)* CBC ("Musica Viva" series) ▲ MVCD 1066 [DDD]
Hétu, J.:Vars Pno *(rec Jan. & Apr. 1993)* CBC ("Musica Viva" series) ▲ MVCD 1066 [DDD]
Liszt, F.:Années de pèlerinage 2 *(rec Jan. & Apr. 1993)* CBC ("Musica Viva" series) ▲ MVCD 1066 [DDD]
Schumann, R.:Bunte Blätter CBC ("Musica Viva" series) ▲ MVCD 1066 [DDD]
Raynaud, André (pno)
Bach, Joh. Christian:Sons Kbd—Op. 5/2–4 & 6; Op. 17/2 & 5 *(rec Mar 1991)* Pierre Verany ▲ PV.791091 [DDD]
Raynaud, Jean Claude (org)
A Sacred Christmas, w. [cnd:Josef Schabasser], Vienna Hofburg Chapel Choir, W. Kraft (org) Vox 90s ■ V9–9904
Raynaut, Jacques (pno)
Busoni, F.:Divert Fl, w. Jean–Louis Beaumadier (fl) Calliope ▲ CAL 9227 [DDD]
Fouad, H.:Thâksim, w. Jean–Louis Beaumadier (fl) Calliope ▲ CAL 9227 [DDD]
Henze, H.–W.:Sonatine Fl & Pno, w. Jean–Louis Beaumadier (fl) Calliope ▲ CAL 9227 [DDD]
Lenot, J.:Dans la rue du Jeune Anacharsis, w. Jean–Louis Beaumadier (fl) Calliope ▲ CAL 9227 [DDD]
Petronio, A.:Structures mobiles, w. Jean–Louis Beaumadier (fl) Calliope ▲ CAL 9227 [DDD]
Stravinsky, I.:Les Noces, w. M. Quercia (sop), S. Cooper (mez), P. Capelle (ten), P. Marinov (bass), Vieuxtemps (pno), R. Conil (pno), Arzoumanian (pno), R. Hayrabedian (cnd), Strasbourg Percussion Ensemble, Contemporary Choir Pierre Verany ▲ PV 787032 [DDD]
Rayneau, Christel (fl)
Escaich, T.:Scènes d'enfants, w. Philippe Pennanguer (vc), Yann Ollivo (pno) Chamade ▲ CHCD 5638 [DDD]
Rayson, John (va)—see ORCHESTRAS & ENSEMBLES Sterling String Quartet
Razafimbadâ, Marie France (vn)—see ORCHESTRAS & ENSEMBLES Denis Clavier String Quartet
Razbaum, Albert (fl)
Bach, J.S.:Suite 2 Orch, w. S. Miassojedov (cnd), Moscow Bach Center Orch *(rec Moscow, June 1993)* Arts ▲ 447133–2 [DDD]
Rdoukanov, Entcho (db)
Schnittke, A.:Hymns Vc, w. Torleff Thedéen (vc), Christian Davidsson (bn), Ingegerd Fredlund (hp), M. Kamata (hpd), Anders Holdar (tubular bells/timp), Anders Loguin (tubular bells) BIS ("BIS Twins" series) 2–▲ CD 437/507
Re, Bruno (b vl)
Bass Viol Suites, w. Robert Khonen (hpd) Pierre Verany ▲ 788012 [DDD]
Re, Bruno (vl)
Bach, J.S.:Sons Fl, BWV 1030–35, w. C. Mendoze (rcr), J. Barbolini (hpd)—BWV 1035 Pierre Verany ▲ PV 787023 [DDD]
Boismortier, J.B. de:Suite VI & Hpd, w. R. Kohnen (hpd) *(rec 6/87)* Pierre Verany ▲ PV.788012 [DDD]
Corelli, A.:Sons Vn, Op. 5, w. C. Mendoze (rcr), G. Barbolini (hpd)—No. 9 Pierre Verany ▲ PV 787023 [DDD]
Couperin, F.:Suite VI, w. R. Kohnen (hpd) *(rec 6/87)* Pierre Verany ▲ PV.788012 [DDD]
Handel, G.F.:Sons Fl, w. Christian Mendoze (rcr), Giorgio Barbolini (hpd)—Op. 1, Nos. 4 & 7 Pierre Verany ▲ PV 787023 [DDD]
Marais, M.:Suites VI & Hpd, w. R. Kohnen (hpd) *(rec 6/87)* Pierre Verany ▲ PV.788012 [DDD]
Telemann, G.P.:Son Rcr in F, w. C. Mendoze (rcr), G. Barbolini (hpd) Pierre Verany ▲ PV 787023 [DDD]
Vivaldi, A.:Il pastor fido, w. C. Mendoze (rcr), G. Barbolini (hpd)—No. 6 Pierre Verany ▲ PV 787023 [DDD]
Réach, Pierre (pno)
Bach, J.S.:Goldberg Vars Arcobaleno ▲ AAOC 9397
Liszt, F.:Transcriptions & Paraphrases—Sym fantastique; L'idee fixe; Andante amoroso sur un theme de la Sym fantastique Arcobaleno ▲ AAOC 9322
Read, Hugo (a sax)
Ibert, J.:Concertino da camera, w. P. Degenhardt (pno) [arr. alto saxophone & piano] Ars Musici ▲ AM 1100–2 [DDD]
Milhaud, D.:Scaramouche (transcriptions), w. P. Degenhardt (pno) Ars Musici ▲ AM 1100–2 [DDD]
Schulhoff, E.:Hot Son Sax, w. P. Degenhardt (pno) Ars Musici ▲ AM 1100–2 [DDD]
Read, Jesse (bn)
Pastorales de Noël, w. Rita Costanzi (hp), V. Costanzi (vn), K. Rudolph (fl) Skylark ▲ 9400 [DDD]
Reade, Paul (pno)
Reade, P.G.:The Match Girl & the Flame ASV ("White Line" series) ▲ ASV 2084 [DDD]
Reagin, Brian (vn)—see also ORCHESTRAS & ENSEMBLES II Quattro
Kauffman, I.:D.S. al Fine, w. Joen Vasquez (vn), Irvin Kauffman (gtr) Alanna ▲ ALA 5552
Paganini, N.:Sons Vn & Gtr, w. Irvin Kauffman (gtr)—in C Alanna ▲ ALA 5552
Reale, Annalisa (vn)
Handel, G.F.:Con for 2 Vns & Vc, w. M. Domini (vn), N. Chirivi (vc), M. Peca (cnd), Rome Stradivari Ensemble Bongiovanni ▲ GB 2100 [DDD]
Rebaudengo, Annibale (pno)
Schumann, R.:Frauenliebe und –leben, w. Clara Wirz (mez) Accord ▲ ACD 201572 [AAD]
Rebello, Simone (perc)
Fascinating Rhythm, w. Edwards Jazz Quartet, Brittania Building Society Brass Band [cnd:Howard Snell], Stewart Death (pno) Doyen ▲ CD 024 [DDD]
A Secret Place, w. Andrew Scott (a sax), Liz Gilliver (mar), Kalengo Percussion Ensemble, Eryl Roberts (perc), John Melbourne (perc), Chris Bastock (perc), Richard Dyson (perc) *(rec Zion Institute, Manchester, 1995)* Doyen ▲ CD 040 [DDD]
Rebner, Wolfgang (pno)
The Columbia Recordings, Vol. 2, w. Jacqueline Du Pré (vc), Michael Taube (pno), Theo van der Pas (pno), Gerald Moore (pno) *(rec 1930–1939)* Pearl ▲ PEA 9443 (m) [AAD]
Reboulot, Antoine (pno)
Reboulot, A.:Préludes Pno *(rec Studio 12, Radio–Canada Building, Montreal)* CBC ("Musica Viva" series) ▲ MVV 1084 [DDD]
Vierne, L.:Préludes Pno *(rec Studio 12, Radio–Canada Building, Montreal)* CBC ("Musica Viva" series) ▲ MVV 1084 [DDD]
Recchiuti, Michael (pno)
Britten, H.:The Holy Sonnets of John Donne, w. Paul Austin Kelly (ten) GM ▲ GM 2022 CD [DDD]
Britten, H.:The Holy Sonnets of John Donne, w. Paul Austin Kelly (ten) GM Recordings ▲ GMR 2022
Britten, H.:On This Island, w. Paul Austin Kelly (ten) GM ▲ GM 2022 CD [DDD]
Britten, H.:On this Island, w. Paul Austin Kelly (ten) GM Recordings ▲ GMR 2022
Britten, H.:Songs, w. Paul Austin Kelley (ten)—Holy Sonnets of John Donne; On This Island; plus others GM ▲ GM 2022CD
Quilter, R.:Elizabethan Lyrics, w. Paul Austin Kelly (ten) GM ▲ GM 2022 CD [DDD]
Quilter, R.:Elizabethan Lyrics, w. Paul Austin Kelly (ten) GM Recordings ▲ GMR 2022
Quilter, R.:Songs, w. Paul Austin Kelley (ten)—7 Elizabethan Lyrics; To Julia; plus others GM ▲ GM 2022CD
Quilter, R.:To Julia, w. Paul Austin Kelly (ten) GM ▲ GM 2022 CD [DDD]
Quilter, R.:To Julia, w. Paul Austin Kelly (ten) GM Recordings ▲ GMR 2022
Rechsteiner, Yves (hpd)
Della Ciaia, A.B.:Sons Hpd, Op. 4—6 sons *(rec Nov 1995)* Gallo ▲ CD 868 [ADD]
Rechsteiner, Yves (org)
Alain, J.:Org Music (comp)—Première Fant; Deuxième Fant; Le Jardin Suspendu; 2 Danses à Agni Yavishta; Climat; Lamento; Fantasmagorie; Chant donné; Choral Cistercien; Vars sur Lucis Creator; Postlude pour l'office de Complies; Intermezzo; Suite *(rec Apr 16–18, 1995)* Gallo ▲ CD 850 [ADD]
Janácek, L.:Mass in E♭, w. C. Gesseney (cnd), Lausanne Euterpe Vocal Ensemble Gallo ▲ CD 784 [DDD]
The Lausanne Vocal Ensemble Euterpe in Concert, w. [cnd:Christophe Gesseney], Euterpe, Christine Sortoretti (hpd), C. Delafontaine (pic), Marianne Amrein (fl douce/perc) Gallo ▲ CD 766 [DDD]
Reckert, Sascha (glass hmc)
Beethoven, L. van:Leonore Prohaska, w. Sylvia McNair (sop), Karoline Eichhorn (narr), Marie–Pierre Langlamet (hp), C. Abbado (cnd), Berlin PO, Berlin Radio Chorus *(rec Great Hall, Philharmonie, Berlin, Sept 1993)* Deutsche Grammophon ▲ 447748–2 [DDD]
Redaelli, Stefania (pno)
Honegger, A.:Sons Vn, w. C. Feige (vn)—Sonatas 1 & 2 for Violin & Piano; Sonatine for 2 Violins; Sonata for Solo Violin Giulia ▲ GIU 201015 [DDD]
Redd, Chuck (dr)—see ORCHESTRAS & ENSEMBLES Ken Peplowski Jazz Quartet
Redel, Kurt (fl)
Flûte et Guitare, w. Christian de Chabot (gtr) Arion ▲ ARN 68213 [DDD]
France Music for Flute & Piano, w. Noël Lee (pno) Arion ▲ ARN 68238 [AAD]
Kuhlau, F.:Duos brillants, w. Noël Lee (pno) Etcetera ▲ KTC 1189
Kuhlau, F.:Intro & Rondo on "Ah! quand il gèle" from *Le Colporteur*, w. Noël Lee (pno) Etcetera ▲ KTC 1189
Redik, Wolfgang (vn)—see ORCHESTRAS & ENSEMBLES Vienna Piano Trio
Reding, Janine (pno)
Bach, W.F.:Son for 2 Hpds, w. H. Piette (piano) Olympia ▲ OCD 271 [AAD]
Brahms, J.:Vars on a Theme by Haydn, w. H. Piette (pno) Olympia ▲ OCD 271 [AAD]
Poot, M.:Rhap Pnos, w. H. Piette (pno) Olympia ▲ OCD 271 [AAD]
Reding & Piette Play Works for 2 Pianos, w. Henry Piette (pno) Olympia ▲ OCD 271 [AAD]
Vol. 2, w. Henry Piette (pno) Olympia ▲ OLY 272 [AAD]
Tansman, A.:Fant on Strauss Waltzes, w. H. Piette (pno) Olympia ▲ OCD 271 [AAD]

Redman, Carol (fl)
Allen, J.:Brazilian Son, w. Ron Grinage (pno), Shana Norton (hp), Charly Drobeck (fl/alt fl/pic), Sam Lunt (perc), Tom Maguire (perc) *(rec Santuario de Guadalupe, Sante Fe, NM, Sept 29–30, 1995)* Wild Iris ▲ WI 001
Allen, J.:Midnight Sun, w. Jamie Allen (wood fl) *(rec Santuario de Guadalupe, Sante Fe, NM, Sept 29–30, 1995)* Wild Iris ▲ WI 001

Redman, Carol (fl/whistle)
Allen, J.:Di Me, Lluvia, w. Toni Austin-Allen (pno/claves), Sam Lunt (bongos), Tom Maguire (perc) *(rec Santuario de Guadalupe, Sante Fe, NM, Sept 29–30, 1995)* Wild Iris ▲ WI 001

Redolfi, Michel (syn)
Redolfi, M.:Underwater Music, w. Lanie Goodman (fl), Melissa Morgan (hp), Ricercar Ensemble—Effractions (1988); Sunny Afternoon at Bird Rock Beach (1983); Full Scale Ocean (1989) *(rec Pacific Ocean, CA & Nice, France, 1983 & 1989)* Hat Hut ("NOW." series) ▲ hat ART CD 6026 [ADD]

Redondi, Franco (pno)
Cambini, G.M.:Cons Hpd, Op. 15/1 & 3, w. P. Vaglieri (cnd), Milan CO Nuova Era ▲ 7059 [DDD]

Redwig, P. (trbn)—see ORCHESTRAS & ENSEMBLES Stuttgart Philharmonia Ensemble

Reed, Douglas (org)
At Pullman United Methodist Church, Chicago Organ Historical Society ■ OHSC 6

Reed, Douglas (org/hpd)
Albright, W.:Org & Hpd Music—Four Fancies for Harpsichord, In Memoriam for Organ, Pneuma for Organ, Sweet Sixteenths, Symphony for Organ, That Sinking Feeling Arkay ▲ AR 6112 [DDD]

Reed, Elisabeth (vc)
Bach, J.S.:Sons Fl, BWV 1030–35, w. Kim Pineda (trns fl), Elisabeth Wright (hpd)—Nos. 1 in b, 3 in A, 5 in e & 6 in E Focus ▲ FOCUS 944 [DDD]

Reed, Jerome (pno)
Austin, E.:Klavier Double Capstone ▲ CPS 8625
Austin, E.:Music of, w. Jeananne Albee (pno), Mary Lou Rylands (vc), Ursula Trede-Boettcher (hpd), Markus Lücke (cl), Sibylle Dotzauer (pno), Constitution Brass, Gerald Kegelmann (cnd), Heidelberg State Music School Chamber Choir—To Begin for Brass Qnt; Klavier Double for Pno & Tape; Circling for Vc & Pno; Lighthouse I for solo Hpd; Gathering Threads for solo Cl; Zodiac Suite for Pno; An Die Nachgeborenen [To Those Born Later] Capstone ▲ CPS 8625
Austin, E.:Zodiac Suite Capstone ▲ CPS 8625

Reede, Rien de (fl)
Yun, I.:Qt Fls, w. T. Roorda (fl), H. Starreveld (fl), M. Takahashi (fl) Attacca ▲ BABEL 9056–3 [DDD]

Reeder, Deborah (vc)—see ORCHESTRAS & ENSEMBLES Philadelphia Trio

Rees, Jonathan (vn)
Vivaldi, A.:Cons for 2 Vns, w. Iona Brown (vn), Briony Shaw (vn), Ralph de Souza (vn), I. Brown (cnd), Academy of St. Martin in the Fields—Nos. 3 & 10 *(rec London, Sept 1995)* Hänssler Classic ▲ CD 98.017 [DDD]

Rees, R. (pno)
Carter, E.:Songs, w. G. Smith (cnd), Adirondack CO—Warble for Lilac-Time; Voyage; 3 Poems of Robert Frost CRI ▲ CD 648 [ADD]

Reese, Vance (db)
Purcell, H.:Come Ye Sons of Art, w. Laura Goetz (ob), Sarah Weiner (ob), Davis Brooks (vn), Lisa Brooks (vn), Jann Cosart (va), Mary Burke (vl), Thomas Gerber (hpd), Henry H. Leck (cnd), Indianapolis Children's Choir [arr. Maurice Blower] *(rec The Lodge, May & June 1995)* VAI Audio ▲ VAIA 1130 [DDD]
Purcell, H.:Fly, Bold Rebellion (sels), w. Laura Goetz (ob), Sarah Weiner (ob), Davis Brooks (vn), Lisa Brooks (vn), Jann Cosart (va), Mary Burke (vl), Thomas Gerber (hpd), Henry H. Leck (cnd), Indianapolis Children's Choir—Be Welcome Then, Great Sir [arr. Steven Rickards] *(rec The Lodge, May & June 1995)* VAI Audio ▲ VAIA 1130 [DDD]
Purcell, H.:King Arthur (sels), w. Laura Goetz (ob), Sarah Weiner (ob), Davis Brooks (vn), Lisa Brooks (vn), Jann Cosart (va), Mary Burke (vl), Thomas Gerber (hpd), Henry H. Leck (cnd), Indianapolis Children's Choir—Fairest Isle [arr. Steven Rickards] *(rec The Lodge, May & June 1995)* VAI Audio ▲ VAIA 1130 [DDD]

Reeve, Basil (ob)
Bolle, J.:Con Ob, w. J. Bolle (cnd), Monadnock Music Festival Orch Gasparo ▲ GSCD 317 [DDD]
Bolle, J.:Pieces (8), w. Jorja Fleezanis (vn) Gasparo ▲ GSCD 317 [DDD]

Reeves, George (pno)
Delius, F.:Son 2 Vn & Pno, w. L. Tertis (va) *(rec 1929)* Pearl ▲ PEA 9918 (m) [AAD]

Reffkin, Gene (perc)
Dresher, P.:Destiny, w. Paul Dresher (elec gtr/elec) Lovely Music ▲ LCD 2011 [ADD]
Dresher, P.:Slow Fire, w. R. Eckert (sgr), P. Dresher (gtr/kbd/elec) [E] Minmax ▲ CD 010

Regef, Dominique (rebec/israj/h-g)
Troubadour Songs of the 12th & 13th Centuries, Vol. 2, w. Gérard Zuchetto (sgr), Jacques Khoudir (perc) Gallo ▲ CD 684 [DDD]

Regis, Isabelle (gtr)
Hommage à Segovia-Oeuvres pour Guitare *(rec May 1993)* Ligia Digital ▲ LIDI 0105006–93 [DDD]

Regni, Albert (s sax)
Aldridge, R.:Combo Platter, w. Sharon Leventhal (vn), Nancy Zeltsman (mar) Open Loop ▲ 034 [DDD]
Aldridge, R.:Prisoner, w. T. O. Sterrett (pno) Open Loop ▲ 034 [DDD]
Aldridge, R.:Qt for an Outdoor Festival, w. Mark Feldman (vn), Beverly Lauridsen (vc), T. O. Sterrett (pno) Open Loop ▲ 034 [DDD]
Bourland, R.:Sax Qnt, w. Laura Seton (vn), Mark Feldman (vn), Lois Martin (va), Beverly Davidson (vc) Open Loop ▲ 034 [DDD]

Regni, Albert (sax)
Bourland, R.:Dark Paintings (3), w. Lois Martin (va), Beverly Lauridsen (vc) Open Loop ▲ 034 [DDD]
Bourland, R.:Stone Qt, w. Lois Martin (va), Beverly Lauridsen (vc), T. O. Sterrett (pno) Open Loop ▲ 034 [DDD]

Regteren, Jan Erik van (va)
Schulhoff, E.:Sxt Strs, w. T. Kooistra (vc), Schoenberg String Quartet Koch Schwann ▲ SCH 312332 [DDD]

Řehák, Karel (va)—see also ORCHESTRAS & ENSEMBLES Suk String Quartet
Mozart, W.A.:Qnt Cl, K.581, w. Bohuslav Zahradnik (cl), Talich String Quartet Calliope 3–▲ CAL 9231.3 [DDD]
Mozart, W.A.:Qnt Pno, K.452, w. Talich String Quartet Calliope ▲ CAL 9232 [DDD]
Mozart, W.A.:Qnts Strs, w. Talich String Quartet Calliope 3–▲ CAL 9231.3 [DDD]
Mozart, W.A.:Qnt Strs, K.406, w. Talich String Quartet Calliope ▲ CAL 9232 [DDD]
Mozart, W.A.:Qnt Strs, K.593, w. Talich String Quartet *(rec 1995)* Calliope ▲ CAL 9233 [DDD]
Mozart, W.A.:Qnt Strs, K.614, w. Talich String Quartet *(rec 1995)* Calliope ▲ CAL 9233 [DDD]

Reher, Sven (va)
Levitch, L.:Qt Fl, Va, Vc & Pno, w. Sheridan Stokes (fl), Jeffrey Solow (vc), Irma Vallecillo-Gray (pno) Cambria ▲ CD 1059 [ADD]

Rehfeldt, W. (org)
Rheinberger, J.:Con 1 Org, w. B. Ader (cnd), Tübingen Cantata Orch Bayer ▲ 100074 [DDD]
Rheinberger, J.:Con 2 Org, w. B. Ader (cnd), Tübingen Cantata Orch Bayer ▲ 100074 [DDD]

Rehling, Tine (hp)
Entr'acte, w. Debost, Michel (fl), Toke Lund Christiansen (fl) Kontrapunkt ▲ 32043 [DDD]
Jersild, J.:Fant Hp Paula ▲ PACD 75 [DAD]
Jersild, J.:Pezzo elegiaco Paula ▲ PACD 75 [DAD]
Roussel, A.:Chamber Music, w. Majken Bjerno (sop), Toke Lund Christiansen (fl), Bjørn Carl Nielsen (ob), Niels Thomsen (cl), Per Jacobsen (hn), Asger Svendsen (bn), Ketil Christensen (tpt), Anne Søe Hansen (vn), Zwi Carmelli (va), Piotr Zelazny (va), Niels Ullner (vc), Michael Dabelsteen (db), Morten Mogensen (pno), Per Salo (pno), Per Jensen (perc)—Divertissement, Op. 6; Trio, Op. 40; Joueurs de Flute, Op. 27; Serenade, Op. 30; Le marchand de sable qui passe, Op. 13; Andante et scherzo, Op. 13; 2 poèmes de ronsard, Op. 26; Aria; Elpenor, Op. 59; Pipe Kontrapunkt 2–▲ KPT 32218 [DDD]

Rehm, Wilfried (vc)—see also ORCHESTRAS & ENSEMBLES Vienna String Trio
Shostakovich, D.:Sym 14, w. Elena Prokina (sop), Sergei Aleksashkin (bass), E. Inbal (cnd), Vienna SO *(rec Konzerthaus, Vienna, Apr 26–29, 1993)* Denon ▲ CO 78821 [DDD]

Rehney, Kujit (perc)
Mahin, B.:Rituals, w. M. Lortz (perc) Capstone ▲ CPS 8061
Mahin, B.:Rituals, w. Mark Lortz (perc) Capstone ▲ CPS 8611

Řehoř, David (perc)—see ORCHESTRAS & ENSEMBLES Prague Percussion Project

Reich, Steve (perc)
Reich, S.:Drumming, w. S. Reich (perc), Ensemble Elektra/Nonesuch ▲ 79170–2 [DDD] ■ 79170–4 (D)
Reich, S.:Music for Mallet Instruments, Voices & Electric Organ, w. Ensemble Elektra/Nonesuch ▲ 79220–2 ■ 79220–4

Reich, Steve (pno)
Reich, S.:Music for 18 Musicians, w. S. Reich (cnd), Ensemble ECM New Series ▲ 78118–21129–2 [AAD]; ■ 78118–21129–4
Reich, S.:Music for Large Ensemble, w. S. Reich (cnd), Ensemble ECM New Series ▲ 78118–21168–2 [AAD]; ■ 78118–21168–4

Reichenberg, David (ob d'amore)
Bach, J.S.:Con Ob d'amore, w. T. Pinnock (cnd), English Concert Archiv ▲ 413731–2 [DDD]

Reichenberg, David (ob)
Bach, J.S.:Con Vn & Ob, w. S. Standage (vn), T. Pinnock (cnd), English Concert Archiv ▲ 413731–2 [DDD]
Vivaldi, A.:Cons Ob, w. T. Pinnock (cnd), English CO—RV.461 Archiv ▲ 415674–2 [DDD]
Vivaldi, A.:Cons Ob, w. S. Standage (vn), T. Pinnock (cnd), English CO—RV.548 Archiv ▲ 415674–2 [DDD]

Reichenberger, Dorothy (vc)
Brahms, J.:Sextet Strs, Op. 36, w. P. Carmirelli (vn), J. Toth (vn), P. Naegele (va), C. Levine (va), F. Arico (vc) Sony Classical ▲ SMK 46249 [ADD] ■ SMT 46249

Reid, Mathew (cl)
Klatzow, P.:Con Cl, w. P. Klatzow (cnd), Claremont CO Claremont ▲ GSE 1524

Reider, Rocy (fl)
Lovenstein, J.:Music of, w. Mary Brockenbrough (sop), Laura Sanders (sop), Barton Green (ten), Rockland Osgood (ten), David Murray (bar), Benjamin Sears (bar), Jonathan Lovenstein (pno), Heather O'Donnell (pno), James Silvers (pno), Jason Horowitz (vn), Adrianna Hulscher (vn), James Johnston (vn), Mimi Ragson (vn), Peter Landeen (vc), Reinmar Seidler (vc)—Blake Songs; other works Titanic ▲ Ti 221 [DDD]

Reidling, Jack (pno)
Two Sides, w. Leo Potts (sax) *(rec North Hollywood, CA, Nov. 20–21, 1994)* Cambria ▲ CD 1075 [ADD]

Reighley, Kimberly (fl)
Telemann, G.P.:Sons for 2 Fls, w. Tom Moore (fl) *(rec Crosswicks Friends Meeting, Crosswicks, New Jersey, Apr 24–26 & May 4–5, 1995)* Lyrichord ("Early Music" series) ▲ LYR 8019 [DDD]

Reil, (org)
Haydn, J.:Mass 1a, Missa 'Rorate coeli desuper', w. G. Öhlinger (sop), M. Bayer (alt), M. Klietmann (ten), A. Lebeda (bass), Collegium Musicum Pragense Christophorus ▲ CD 74541 [DDD]
Haydn, J.:Salve regina, H.XXIIIb/2, Collegium Musicum Pragense Christophorus ▲ CD 74541 [DDD]

Reilly, C. O. (pno)
Ravel, M.:Valses nobles et sentimentales Albany ▲ TROY 052

Reilly, Tommy (hmc)
Arnold, M.:Con Hmc, w. C. Dumont (cnd), Basel RSO Chandos ▲ CHAN 9248 [DDD]
Farnon, R.:Prelude & Dance, w. R. Farnon (cnd), Robert Farnon Orch Chandos ▲ CHAN 9248 [DDD]
Jacob, G.:Divert Hmc, w. Hindar String Quartet *(rec 1972)* Chandos ▲ CHAN 8802 [AAD]
Jacob, G.:Pieces Hmc, w. N. Marriner (cnd), Academy of St. Martin in the Fields Chandos ▲ CHAN 8617 [AAD]
Moody, J.:Little Suite, w. N. Marriner (cnd), Academy of St. Martin in the Fields Chandos ▲ CHAN 8617 [ADD]
Moody, J.:Qnt Hmc, w. Hindar String Quartet *(rec 1972)* Chandos ▲ CHAN 8802 [AAD]
Moody, J.:Suite, w. S. Kanga (hp) *(rec 1980)* Chandos ▲ CHAN 8802 [AAD]
Moody, J.:Toledo, w. R. Farnon (cnd), Munich RSO Chandos ▲ CHAN 9248 [DDD]
Play British Folk Songs, w. Skaila Kanga (hp) Chandos ▲ CHAN 8559 [DDD]
Serenade, w. Academy of St. Martin in the Fields Chamber Ensemble Chandos ▲ CHAN 8486 [DDD]
Spivakovsky, M.:Con Hmc, w. C. Gerhardt (cnd), Munich RSO Chandos ▲ CHAN 9248 [DDD]
Tausky, V.:Concertino Harm, w. N. Marriner (cnd), Academy of St. Martin in the Fields Chandos ▲ CHAN 8617 [ADD]
Thanks for the Memory, w. James Moody (pno) Chandos ▲ CHAN 8645 [AAD]
Vaughan Williams, R.:Romance Hmc, w. N. Marriner (cnd), Academy of St. Martin in the Fields Chandos ▲ CHAN 8617 [ADD]
Vaughan Williams, R.:Romance Hmc, w. N. Marriner (cnd), Academy of St. Martin in the Fields London ("British Collection" series) ▲ 421392–2 [ADD]
Villa-Lobos, H.:Con Hmc, w. E. Smola (cnd), Southwest German RSO Baden-Baden Chandos ▲ CHAN 9248 [DDD]

Reimann, Aribert (pno)
Dehmel Lieder, w. Dietrich Fischer-Dieskau (bar), Kolja Blacher (vn) Orfeo d'or ▲ 390951
Hindemith, P.:Songs, w. Dietrich Fischer-Dieskau (bar)—19 songs:Sonnenuntergang; The wild flower's song; The moon; Sing on there in the swamp; On hearing "The Last rose of Summer"; Ehemals und jetzt; Brautgesang; Singet leise; Das ganze, nicht das Einzelne; Des Morgens; Fragment; Der Tod; Ich will nicht klagen mehr; Hymne; Abendphantasie; O, nun heb du an, dort in deinem Moor (1919); Vor dir schein' ich aufgewacht (1920); Die Sonne sinkt; An die Parzen [E,G] Orfeo ▲ 156861 [DDD]
Les introuvables de Dietrich Fischer-Dieskau, w. Dietrich Fischer-Dieskau (bar), Karl Engel (pno), Hertha Klust (pno), Gerald Moore (pno), Robert Veyron-Lacroix (hpd) EMI Classics 6–▲ CDZF 68509
Reimann, A.:Shine & Dark, w. D. Fischer-Dieskau (bar) Orfeo ▲ 212901
Schubert, Franz:Schwanengesang, w. B. Fassbaender (mez) [G] Deutsche Grammophon ▲ 429766–2 [DDD]
Schubert, Franz:Songs (misc), w. B. Fassbaender (mez)—5 Lieder [G] Deutsche Grammophon ▲ 429766–2 [DDD]
Zelter, C.F.:Songs, w. D. Fischer-Dieskau (bar) [G] Orfeo ▲ 097841 [DDD]

Reinberger, Jiri (org)
Bach, J.S.:Canonic Vars on "Von Himmel hoch..." Supraphon Collection ▲ 11 0626–2 [ADD]
Bach, J.S.:Chorale Preludes Org—BWV 681, 683, 727 Supraphon Collection ▲ 11 0626–2 [ADD]
Bach, J.S.:Preludes & Fugues, BWV 531–552—BWV 546,548 & 549 Supraphon Collection ▲ 11 0626–2 [ADD]
Bach, J.S.:Toccata & Fugue Org, BWV 565 Supraphon Collection ▲ 11 0626–2 [ADD]
Czech Organ Music of the 18th Century, w. Bohumir Rabas (org) Panton ▲ PAN 811020

Reinders, Jimmy (cl)
Klatzow, P.:Chamber Con, w. Beat Wenger (fl), Robert Grishkoff (hn), Uliano Marchio (gtr), Lamar Crowson (pno), Barry Jordan (elec org), Peter Hamblin (perc), P. Klatzow (cnd) Claremont ▲ GSE 1524

Reinecke, Frank (db)
Bentzon, N.V.:Duo Concertante, w. H. Slaatto (vn) Ambitus ▲ 97845 [DDD]
Biber, H. von:Son violino solo representativa, w. H. Slaatto (vn) Ambitus ▲ 97845 [DDD]
Sanri, E.:Settings of Visual Poems & a Visual Phantasie, w. H. Slaatto (vn) Ambitus ▲ 97845 [DDD]
Vogt, H.:Sonatina Vn, w. H. Slaatto (vn) Ambitus ▲ 97845 [DDD]
Yun, I.:Together, w. H. Slaatto (vn) Ambitus ▲ 97845 [DDD]

Reinecke, Frank (vn)
Schoenberg, A.:Ode to Napoleon, w. Roland Hermann (nar), Rim Vogler (vn), Stefan Fehlandt (va), Michael Sanderling (vc), Frank-Immo Zichner (pno) *(rec Siemensvilla, Berlin-Lankwitz, Aug. 1994)* EDA ▲ EDA 008–2 [DDD]

INSTRUMENT.

Reiner, Charles (pno)
Gluck, C.W.:Melodie, w. Henryk Szeryng (vn) *(rec Feb. 13–14, 1963)* Mercury Living Presence ▲ 434351–2
Kreisler, F.:Vn Pieces, w. Henryk Szeryng (vn)—Caprice Viennois; Schön Rosmarin; Liebesleid; Liebesfreud; Recitativo & Scherzo; Tempo di Minuetto; Praeludium & Allegro; Chanson Louis XIII & Pavane; Tambourin Chinois; Menuet; The Old Refrain; Rondino [on a theme by Beethoven]; Allegretto [in the style of Boccherini] *(rec Jan. 22–23, 1963)* Mercury Living Presence ▲ 434351–2
Leclair, J.–M.:Sons Vn (Books 1–4), w. Henryk Szeryng (vn)—No. 3 in D *(rec Feb. 13–14, 1963)* Mercury Living Presence ▲ 434351–2
Locatelli, P.:The Labyrinth, w. Henryk Szeryng (vn) *(rec Feb. 13–14, 1963)* Mercury Living Presence ▲ 434351–2

Reinhardt, Rolf (pno)
Bartók, B.:Son for 2 Pnos, w. G. Sándor (pno), O. Schad (perc), R. Sohm (perc) *(rec 1965)* Vox Box ("Legends" series) 2–▲ CDX2 5506 [ADD]
Schubert, Franz:Qnt Pno, D.667, w. Endres String Quartet Allegretto ▲ ACD 8054 [ADD] ■ ACS 8054

Reinhardt, Thomas (bn)
Fasch, J.F.:Trio Sons, w. B. Glaetzner (ob), I. Goritzki (ob), S. Pank (vl), A. Beyer (vle), C. Schornsheim (hpd) Berlin Classics ▲ BER 1069 [DDD]
Vivaldi, A.:Sons Ob, w. B. Glaetzner (ob), I. Goritzki (ob), K. Suske (vn), A. Bayer (vn), S. Pank (vl), C. Schornsheim (org/hpd)—RV.28, 34, 53, 81 & 779 Capriccio ▲ CD 10143 [DDD] ■ CAS 27153 (CrO2)

Reinhold, Sheila (vn)—see ORCHESTRAS & ENSEMBLES Hudson River String Trio

Reisenberg, Nadia (pno)
Chopin, F.:Allegro de concert *(rec 1958/59)* InSync ■ C 4157 (m)
Chopin, F.:Barcarolle Pno *(rec 1958/59)* InSync ■ C 4157 (m)
Chopin, F.:Berceuse *(rec 1958/59)* InSync ■ C 4157 (m)
Chopin, F.:Mazurkas—Nos. 23–42 *(rec 1958/59)* InSync ■ C 4156 (m)
Chopin, F.:Nocturnes—Nos. 1–11 *(rec 1958/59)* InSync ■ C 4158 (m)

Reiss, Scott (rcr)
Babell, W.:Con Fl, w. Hesperus Golden Apple ▲ GACD 7550 [DDD] ■ GAC 7550
Gibson, R.:Matin Capstone ▲ CPS 8621
Graupner, C.:Con Rcr, w. Hesperus Golden Apple ▲ GACD 7550 [DDD] ■ GAC 7550
Naudot, J.–C.:Con Rcr, w. Hesperus—No. 2 in C Golden Apple ▲ GACD 7550 [DDD] ■ GAC 7550
Telemann, G.P.:Con in C Rcr, w. Hesperus Golden Apple ▲ GACD 7550 [DDD] ■ GAC 7550
Vivaldi, A.:Cons Rcr, w. Hesperus—RV.428, 444 Golden Apple ▲ GACD 7550 [DDD] ■ GAC 7550

Reissberger, Helmut (fl)
Varèse, E.:Density 21.5 *(rec Nov 1968–Mar 1969)* Vox Box 2–▲ CDX 5142

Reiter, J. (pno)
Gershwin, G.:Con Pno, w. B. Güller (cnd), South German Youth PO *(rec 1988)* Ambitus ▲ 97836 [DDD]

Reiter, Walter (vn)
Mondonville, J.–J.C. de:Pièces de clavecin, Op. 3, w. Kenneth Weiss (hpd) Meridian ▲ MER 84302 [DDD]
Mondonville, J.–J.C. de:Pièces de clavecin, Op. 5, w. Linda Perillo (sop), Kenneth Weiss (hpd) Meridian ▲ MER 84302 [DDD]

Reitmayer, Karl (hn)—see also ORCHESTRAS & ENSEMBLES Roseau Wind Quintet
Dauprat, L.–F.:Trios Hns, Op. 4/1–3, w. U. Köbl (F hn), E. Schmid (F hn) Calig ▲ CAL 50865 [DDD]
Reicha, A.:Trios Hns, Op. 82, w. E. Schmid (hn), U. Köbl (hn)—6 trios—Nos. 19–24 Calig ▲ CAL 50865 [DDD]

Rejto, Gabor (vc)
Bach & Noodles, w. Harvey Pittel (sax), Levering Rothfuss (pno), Anton Nel (pno) Crystal ▲ CD 654
Bloch, E.:Suite Va & Pno, w. Adolph Baller (pno) [arr. for vc & pno Baller & Rejto] *(rec Los Angeles & Columbus, 1969 & 1979)* Orion ▲ 7813–2 [AAD]
Brahms, J.:Sextet Strs, Op. 36, w. J. Heifetz (vn), I. Baker (vn), W. Primrose (va), V. Majewski (va), G. Piatigorsky (vc) RCA Gold Seal ▲ 7965–2–RG [ADD]
Schubert, Franz:Qnt Strs, D.956, w. J. Heifetz (vn), I. Baker (vn), W. Primrose (va), G. Piatigorsky (vc) RCA Gold Seal ▲ 7964–2–RG [ADD] ■ 7964–4–RG (CrO2)

Rejto, Peter (vc)
Barber, S.:Son Vc, w. E. Rowley (pno) *(rec 1991)* Summit ▲ DCD 137 [DDD]
Brahms, J.:Sextet Strs, Op. 36, w. Benny Kim (vn), Ani Kavafian (vn), Cynthia Phelps (va), Randolph Kelly (va), Colin Carr (vc) *(rec live, Tucson Chamber Music Festival, Mar 11, 1994)* Arizona Friends of Chamber Music ▲ 1994 [DDD]
Debussy, C.:Son Vc, w. Monique Duphill (pno) *(rec Tuscon Winter Chamber Festival; Mar 5, 1995)* Arizona Friends of Chamber Music ▲ AFCD 19951
Debussy, C.:Son Vc, w. Monique Duphill (pno) *(rec 1994–95)* Arizona Friends of Chamber Music ▲ 1994/5 [DDD]
Janácek, L.:Fairy Tale, w. E. Rowley (pno) *(rec 1991)* Summit ▲ DCD 137 [DDD]
Kodály, Z.:Son Vc & Pno, Op. 4, w. E. Rowley (pno) *(rec 1991)* Summit ▲ DCD 137 [DDD]
Martinů, B.:Son 2 Vc, w. E. Rowley (pno) *(rec 1991)* Summit ▲ DCD 137 [DDD]
Rorem, N.:The Santa Fe Songs, w. Kurt Ollman (bar), Sheryl Staples (vn), Heiichiro Ohyama (va), Lydia Artymiw (pno) *(rec live, Tucson Chamber Music Festival, Mar 12, 1995)* Arizona Friends of Chamber Music ▲ 1995 [DDD]
Rózsa, M.:Con Vc, w. H. Williams (cnd), Pécs SO *(rec Franz Liszt Hall, Pécs, Hungary, Sept 1995)* Silva Classics ▲ SILKD 6011 [DDD]
Schurmann, G.:The Gardens of Exile, w. H. Williams (cnd), Pécs SO *(rec Franz Liszt Hall, Pécs, Hungary, Sept 1995)* Silva Classics ▲ SILKD 6011 [DDD]

Rekeszus, Heiner (cl)—see ORCHESTRAS & ENSEMBLES Westphalia PO Chamber Ensemble

Rémann, Zoltán (cl)
Hollós, M.:Dúli–dúli, w. Marian Ghisa (cl), Marius Lupsa (cl) *(rec Academy of Music G. Dima in Cluj)* Hungaroton ("Classic" series) ▲ HCD 31572 [DDD]

Remes, V. (vn)—see ORCHESTRAS & ENSEMBLES Prazak String Quartet

Rémillard, Chantal (baroque vn)—see ORCHESTRAS & ENSEMBLES Arion Ensemble

Rémillard, Chantal (vn)—see also ORCHESTRAS & ENSEMBLES Da Sonar Ensemble, Arion Ensemble
Bach, J.S.:Sons Vn Hpd, BWV 1014–1019, w. Geneviève Soly (hpd)—BWV 1015 & 1018 *(rec Oct 1995)* Analekta Fleur de Lys ▲ FL 23061 [DDD]

Remmers, Janjob (org)
Bijster, J.:Vars on an Old Dutch Song NM Classics ▲ NM 92034

Rémy, Ludger (hpd)
Bach, C.P.E.:Cons Hpd & Strs, w. Les Amis de Philippe—W.30, 37 & 38 CPO ▲ CPO 999350
Bach, J.S.:Con for 4 Hpds, w. Gregor Hollmann (hpd), Rudolf Innig (hpd), Bernward Lohr (hpd), Musica Alta Ripa MD + G ▲ MDG CD 3090681

Renard, Michel (vc)
Weber, C.M. von:Trio Fl, w. Maxence Larrieu (fl), Martine Joste (pno) Accord ▲ ACD 202782 [AAD]

Renard, Rosita (pno)
Rosita Renard at Carnegie Hall *(rec live, Jan 19, 1949)* VAI Audio 2–▲ VAIA/IPA 1028 (m) [ADD]

Renardy, Ossy (vn)
Paganini, N.:Caprices Vn, w. W. Robert (pno) [arr. David for violin & piano] *(rec 1940 for Victor)* Biddulph 2–▲ LAB 061/62 [ADD]

Rence, Dorian (va)
Schumann, R.:Märchenerzählungen, w. Stanley Drucker (cl), Sandra Shapiro (pno) *(rec Performing Arts Ctr/Purchase College–State Univ of NY Recital Hall, May 8, 1995)* Elysium ▲ GRK 709 [DDD]

Rende, Jennifer (va)
Bach, J.S.:Cant 20, w. Yuval Waldman (vn), José Cueto (vn), Gail Kruvand (db), Maryland Bach Aria Group members—Wacht auf Crystal ▲ CD 705 [DDD]
Bach, J.S.:Cant 82, w. Yuval Waldman (vn), José Cueto (vn), Gail Kruvand (db), Maryland Bach Aria Group members *(rec St. Peter's Church, Hale, Cheshire, Mar 14, 1994)* Naxos ▲ 8.550763 [DDD]

Rende, Jennifer (va) (cont.)
Bach, J.S.:Cant 110, w. Yuval Waldman (vn), José Cueto (vn), Gail Kruvand (db), Maryland Bach Aria Group members—Wachtet auf Crystal ▲ CD 705 [DDD]
Stradella, A.:Sinf alla Serenata, w. Yuval Waldman (vn), José Cueto (vn), Gail Kruvand (db), Maryland Bach Aria Group members Crystal ▲ CD 705 [DDD]
Torelli, G.:Son Tpt, G.1, w. Yuval Waldman (vn), José Cueto (vn), Gail Kruvand (db), Maryland Bach Aria Group members Crystal ▲ CD 705 [DDD]
Vivaldi, A.:Cons Bn, w. Yuval Waldman (vn), José Cueto (vn), Gail Kruvand (db), Maryland Bach Aria Group members—in B♭, RV.501, "La notte" Crystal ▲ CD 705 [DDD]

Renes, Hendrik Jan (tuba)
Lang, D.:Are You Experienced?, w. David Lang (nar), S. Mosko (cnd), Netherlands Wind Ensemble Chandos ▲ CHAN 9363 [DDD]

Renggli, Felix (fl)
Harvey, J.:Lotuses, w. Arditti String Quartet members Montaigne ▲ MO 782034
Martinů, B.:Son Fl & Pno, w. C. Hedinger (pno) Koch Schwann ▲ 310 107 [DDD]
Martinů, B.:Trio Fl, w. M. Brady (vc), C. Hedinger (pno) Koch Schwann ▲ 310 107 [DDD]

Reniero, Nicola (hpd)—see ORCHESTRAS & ENSEMBLES L'Arte dell'Arco

Renzi, Mike (pno)
Clair de Lune & Sister Moon, w. Thomas Young (ten), Jay Leonhart (bass), Grady Tate (dr) *(rec Nola Recording Studio, NYC, Oct 21 & 23, 1996)* Ocean ▲ OR 104

Renzo, Dao di (pno)
Clementi, M.:Pno Music (comp), w. Aldo Antognazzi (pno), Christian Badian (pno), Eduardo Cazaban (pno), Cristina Da Souza (pno), Pablo Lavandera (pno), Yi Fang Huang (vn), Silvina Cardenas (fl), Nestor Herzbaum (fl)—Sons (6) for Pno, Op. 2, Nos. 1, 3 & 5 (w. flutes); Duets (3) for Piano 4–Hands, Op. 3, Nos. 2 & 3; Sons (3) for Pno & Vn, Op. 3, No. 4 Aura Classics ▲ AU 32287

Repin, Vladim (vn)
Prokofiev, S.:Con 2 Vn, w. K. Nagano (cnd), Hallé Orch *(rec Paris 1995)* Erato ▲ 10696–2 [DDD]
Shostakovich, D.:Con 1 Vn, w. K. Nagano (cnd), Hallé Orch *(rec Paris 1995)* Erato ▲ 10696–2 [DDD]

Requejo, Ricardo (pno)
Chopin, F.:Son Vc, w. C. Starck (vc) Claves ▲ CD 703
Falla, M. de:Pno Music—Noturno; Mazurka do menor; Serenata andaluza; Cancion; Vals capricho; Cortejo de gnomos; Serenata; Allegro de concierto; Cuatro Piezas Españolas; Fantasía baetica; Pour le tombeau de Claude Debussy; Canto de los remeros del Volga; Pour le tombeau de Paul Dukas *(rec Centro Cultural Manuel de Falla, Granada, Apr 1–4, 1996)* Claves ▲ CD 509615 [DDD]
Herzogenberg, H. von:Trio Pno, Ob & Hn, w. Ingo Goritzki (ob), Barry Tuckwell (hn) Claves ▲ CD 803
Mussorgsky, M.:Nursery, w. Teresa Berganza (mez) *(rec Kirche Seon, June 1982)* Claves ▲ CD 508204 [DDD]
Poulenc, F.:Son Ob, w. I. Goritzki (ob) Claves ▲ CD 9020 [DDD]
Poulenc, F.:Trio Ob, w. I. Goritzki (ob), K. Thunemann (bn) Claves ▲ CD 9020 [DDD]
Reinecke, C.:Trio Ob, w. I. Goritzki (ob), B. Tuckwell (hn) Claves ▲ CD 803
Saint–Saëns, C.:Son Bn, w. K. Thunemann (bn) Claves ▲ CD 9020 [DDD]
Saint–Saëns, C.:Son Ob, w. I. Goritzki (ob) Claves ▲ CD 9020 [DDD]
Schumann, R.:Fantasiestücke Cl, w. Thomas Friedli (cl) *(rec Gstaad, Mar 1981)* Claves ▲ CD 508201 [ADD]
Schumann, R.:Frauenliebe und –leben, w. Teresa Berganza (mez) *(rec Kirche Seon, June 1982)* Claves ▲ CD 508204 [DDD]
Schumann, R.:Märchenbilder, w. Hirofumi Fukai (va) *(rec Gstaad, Mar 1981)* Claves ▲ CD 508201 [ADD]
Schumann, R.:Märchenerzählungen, w. Thomas Friedli (cl), Hirofumi Fukai (va) *(rec Gstaad, Mar 1981)* Claves ▲ CD 508201 [ADD]
Schumann, R.:Romances Ob, w. Ingo Goritzki (ob) *(rec Gstaad, Mar 1981)* Claves ▲ CD 508201 [ADD]
Turina, J.:Las musas de Andalucía, w. M. Bayo (sop), Sine Nomine String Quartet *(rec Apr. 1992)* Claves ▲ CD 9320 [DDD]
Turina, J.:Qt Strs, w. M. Bayo (sop), Sine Nomine String Quartet *(rec Apr. 1992)* Claves ▲ CD 9320 [DDD]
Turina, J.:Rapsodia sinfónica, w. J. de Udaeta (cnd), Granada City Orch Claves ▲ CD 9215 [DDD]

Resa, Neithard (va)—see ORCHESTRAS & ENSEMBLES Philharmonia String Quartet, Berlin Philharmonia String Quartet

Resch, F. (trbn)—see ORCHESTRAS & ENSEMBLES Stuttgart Philharmonia Ensemble

Reschke, Gudrun (ob)
Cage, J.:Ryoanji, w. John Patrick Thomas (voc), Eberhard Blum (fl), Iven Hausmann (trbn), Robert Black (db), Jan Williams (perc) *(rec Akademie der Künste, Berlin, June 22, 1995)* Hat Hut ("Now" series) ▲ hat ART CD 6183 [DDD]

Resel, Werner (vc)
Schmidt, F.:Qnt Cl, w. A. Prinz (cl), J. Demus (pno), A. Kamper (vn), F. Stangler (va) *(rec 1965)* Preiser ▲ 93383 [ADD]
Schmidt, F.:Qnt Pno, w. J. Demus (pno), A. Kamper (vn), W. Hink (vn), F. Stangler (va) *(rec 1965)* Preiser ▲ 93383 [ADD]

Restani, Sirio (hpd)—see ORCHESTRAS & ENSEMBLES Collegium Pro Musica

Resue, Donna (hn)
Willey, J.:Society Music, w. L. Greene (fl), G. Coble (tpt), W. Harris (trbn), S. Heyman (pno), E. Gustafson (via), G. Macero (vc), E. Castilano (db), L. Luttinger (perc), E. Murray (cnd) Opus One ▲ CD 168 [DDD]

Reuter, Gerard (ob)—see also ORCHESTRAS & ENSEMBLES American Brass Quintet
Boziwick, G.:Beyond the Last Thought, w. C. Pelton (sop), C. Iverson (bn), K. Grossman (mar) Opus One ▲ CD 162
Talma, L.:Let's Touch the Sky, w. Rebecka Troxler (fl), Peter Simmons (bn), Gregg Smith (cnd), Gregg Smith Singers Vox Box ("The American Composers" series) 3–▲ CDX 3037

Reutter, Hermann (pno)
Schubert, Franz:Winterreise, w. D. Fischer–Dieskau (bar) [G] *(rec broadcast, 1952)* Verona ▲ 2702 (m) [AAD]

Rév, Lívia (pno)
Chopin, F.:Pno Music (misc)—Prelude in D♭, "Raindrop"; Études, Opp. 10/3–5 & 12, 25/1 & 7; Nocturne, Op. 9/2; Mazurkas, Opp. 6/2 & 7/3; Souvenir de Paganini; Fant.–Impromptu in c#; Scherzo No. 3 in c# Saga Classics ▲ EC 3390
Debussy, C.:Children's Corner *(rec 1980)* Saga Classics ▲ EC 3377
Debussy, C.:Images (6) Pno—Set 2 Hyperion ▲ CDA 66487
Debussy, C.:Images (6) Pno *(rec 1980)* Saga Classics ▲ EC 3376
Debussy, C.:Images (3) Pno *(rec 1980)* Saga Classics ▲ EC 3376
Debussy, C.:Masques Hyperion ▲ CDA 66487
Debussy, C.:Pno Music (complete solo)—Preludes Book 2 *(rec 1980)* Saga Classics ▲ 3347 [AAD]
Debussy, C.:Pno Music (complete solo)—12 Etudes; Berceuse héroïque; Morceau de concours; Suite bergamasque *(rec 1980)* Saga Classics ▲ 3383 [AAD]
Debussy, C.:Pno Music (misc)—Suite Bergamasque; Pour le Pno; Estampes; Children's Corner; Images, Sets 1 & 2; L'isle joyeuse; Preludes, Books 1 & 2; Masques Hyperion 3–▲ CDS 44061/63
Debussy, C.:Pno Music (misc)—Danse bohémienne; Première arabesque; Deuxième arabesque; Ballade; Nocturne; Mazurka *(rec 1980)* Saga Classics ▲ EC 3376
Debussy, C.:Pno Music (misc)—Tarentelle styrienne; Hommage à Haydn; Page d'album; Élégie *(rec 1980)* Saga Classics ▲ EC 3377
Debussy, C.:La Plus que lente *(rec 1980)* Saga Classics ▲ EC 3377
Debussy, C.:Pour le piano *(rec 1980)* Saga Classics ▲ EC 3376
Debussy, C.:Preludes Pno—Book 2 Hyperion ▲ CDA 66487
Debussy, C.:Preludes Pno (sels) *(rec 1980)* Saga Classics ▲ EC 3377
Mendelssohn, F.:Lieder ohne Worte Pno—plus "No. 49" in g, Op. posth. Hyperion 2–▲ CDA 66221/22 [DDD]

Révész, László (org)
Liszt, F.:Choral Music, w. András Molnár (ten), Gábor Ugrin (cnd), Hungarian State Chorus—Ave Maria I, S.20/1; Domine salvum fac regem, S.23; Te Deum laudamus, S.27; Ave maris stella, S.34/1; Inno a Maria Vergine, S.39; Rosario, S.56; In domum Domini ibimus, S.57; Chor der Engel, S.85 [G,I,L] Hungaroton ▲ HCD 31103 [DDD]

Révész, László (pno)
Doppler, A.F.:Music Fl & Pno, w. Bea Berényi (fl), Ákos Dratsay (fl)—for 2 fls & pno composed by A. Doppler:Andante et Rondeau, Op. 25; Fantasie sur des motifs hongrois, Op. 35; Duettino sur des motifs hongrois, Op. 36; Duettino sur motifs Americains, Op. 37; La Sonnambula, Op. 42; for 2 fls & pno composed by A. Doppler & K. Doppler:Souvenir de Prague, Op. 24; Valse di Bravura, Op. 33; Rigoletto-fantasie, Op. 38 *(rec Jan 22–24, 1996)* Hungaroton ▲ HCD 31648 [DDD]

Rex, C. (vc)
Boelter, K.:Music of, w. Thamyris—To Know the Dark; One, Two, Three...Out; Peterborough Son.; No Longer of That World ACA Digital Recording ▲ CM 20007 [DDD]

Rex, Charles (vn)
Copland, A.:Son Vn & Pno, w. Israela Margalit (pno) EMI Classics ("Anglo-American Chamber Music" series) ▲ CDC 55405

Reyes, A. (pno)
Liszt, F.:Operatic Paraphrases & Transcriptions—Aida:Danza sacra e duetto final; Don Carlos:Coro di festa e marcia funèbre; Ernani:Concert Paraphrase; I Lombardi:Salve Maria dé Jerusalem; Rigoletto:Concert Paraphrase; Simon Boccanegra:Réminiscences Connoisseur Society ▲ CD 4187 [DDD]

Reymond, Philippe (pno)
Virtuoso Showpieces for Violin, w. Muller, Roland (vn) Sonpact ▲ SPT 95016 [DDD]

Reymond, Stéphane (hpd)
Dünki, J.-J.:Tétraptéron O–IV, w. P. Clemann (pno), J.-J. Dünki (clvd), P. Sublet (cel) *(rec Sept. 18, 1992)* Jecklin ▲ JS 289-2 [ADD]

Reymond, Stéphane (pno)
Glaus, D.:Toccata per Girolamo *(rec May 27, 1992)* Jecklin ▲ JS 289-2 [ADD]

Reynolds, Julian (pno)
Saint-Saëns, C.:Caprice arabe, w. Peter Lockwood (pno) *(rec Utrecht, Apr 1996)* Globe ▲ GLO 5152 [DDD]
Saint-Saëns, C.:Carnival of the Animals, w. Peter Lockwood (pno), J. Reynolds (cnd), Concentus Bestiales *(rec Utrecht, Apr 1996)* Globe ▲ GLO 5152 [DDD]
Saint-Saëns, C.:Danse macabre, w. Peter Lockwood (pno) [trans Saint-Saëns for 2 pnos] *(rec Utrecht, Apr 1996)* Globe ▲ GLO 5152 [DDD]
Saint-Saëns, C.:Polonaise for 2 Pnos, w. Peter Lockwood (pno) *(rec Utrecht, Apr 1996)* Globe ▲ GLO 5152 [DDD]
Saint-Saëns, C.:Scherzo, w. Peter Lockwood (pno) *(rec Utrecht, Apr 1996)* Globe ▲ GLO 5152 [DDD]
Saint-Saëns, C.:Variations on a Theme of Beethoven, w. Peter Lockwood (pno) *(rec Utrecht, Apr 1996)* Globe ▲ GLO 5152 [DDD]
Schumann, R.:Sons Vn (comp), w. Johannes Leertouwer (vn) *(rec Utrecht, 1995)* Globe ▲ GLO 5140 [DDD]

Reynolds, Michael (vc)—see also ORCHESTRAS & ENSEMBLES Muir String Quartet
Tchaikovsky, P.:Souvenir de Florence, w. A. Delmoni (vn), L. Chang (vn), M. Thompson (va), S. Ansel (va), R. Thomas (vc) *(rec Weston, MA, Jan. 1993)* Northeastern ▲ NOR 249 [DDD]

Reznikovskaya, Veronika (pno)
Mozart, W.A.:Con 23 Pno, w. A. Titov (cnd), St. Petersburg Classical Music Studio Orch Infinity Digital ▲ QK 57259 [DDD]
Mozart, W.A.:Con 27 Pno, w. A. Titov (cnd), St. Petersburg Classical Music Studio Orch Infinity Digital ▲ QK 57259 [DDD]
Shostakovich, D.:Con 1 Pno, w. Falk Maertens (tpt), J.-P. Weigle (cnd), German Music School Orch Ars Musici ▲ 1128

Rezven, J. (pno)
The Art of Arleen Augér, w. Augér, Arleen (sop) Koch International Classics ▲ KIC 7248 [DDD]

Rhee, Heasook (pno)
Carter, E.:Son Vc, w. T. Wick (vc) MD + G ▲ L 3397 [DDD]
Miaskovsky, N.:Son 2 Vc, w. T. Wick (vc) MD + G ▲ L 3397 [DDD]
Poulenc, F.:Son Vc, w. T. Wick (vc) MD + G ▲ L 3397 [DDD]

Rhind, Alison (pno)
Birtwistle, H.:Linoi 1, w. Mark van de Wiel (b cl) Olympia ▲ OLY 484 [DDD]

Rhode, Ron (org)
Ron & Chuck Rhode at the Byrd Theatre, w. Rhode, Ron (org), Chuck Rhode (ten) Organ Historical Society ▲ VTOS 1001 [DDD]

Rhodes, Cherry (org)
Hampton, C.:Dances (5) Org Pro Organo ▲ CD 7009
Hampton, C.:Prelude & Vars on Old 100th Pro Organo ▲ CD 7009
Hampton, C.:Prelude & Vars on Old 100th Pro Organo ▲ CD 7009

Rhodes, Paul (pno)
British Flute Music, Vol. 1:Summer Music, w. Kenneth Smith (fl) ASV ▲ ASV 739 [DDD]
British Flute Music, Vol. 2:Folk & Fantasy, w. Kenneth Smith (fl) ASV ▲ ASV 768 [DDD]
British Flute Music, Vol. 3:The Reed of Pan, w. Kenneth Smith (fl) ASV ▲ ASV 862 [DDD]
Golden Flute, w. Kenneth Smith (fl) ASV ▲ ASV CD 2102
Walking in the Air:21 Favorites for Flute, w. Kenneth Smith (fl) ASV ("White Line" series) ▲ ASV 2072

Rhodes, Samuel (va)—see also ORCHESTRAS & ENSEMBLES Juilliard String Quartet
Schubert, Franz:Qnt Pno, D.667, w. Hörtnagel (db), Beaux Arts Trio Philips ▲ 420716-2 [ADD]
Schumann, R.:Qt Pno, Op. 47, w. Beaux Arts Trio Philips ▲ 420791-2 [ADD]
Schumann, R.:Qnt Pno, w. D. Bettelheim (vn), Beaux Arts Trio Philips ▲ 420791-2 [ADD]

Riabchikova, Tatyana (pno)
Liatoshinsky, B.:Preludes Pno (misc)—in b♭, Op. 38/1; in e♭, Op. 38/2; in b, Op. 44/2; in e♭, Op. 44/3; Mourning Prelude in e♭ *(rec Tsai Performance Center, Boston)* Sonora ▲ SO 22571 [DDD]
Ryabchikova, T.:Barcarolle *(rec Tsai Performance Center, Boston)* Sonora ▲ SO 22570 [DDD]
Ryabchikova, T.:Dedication to J. S. Bach *(rec Tsai Performance Center, Boston)* Sonora ▲ SO 22570 [DDD]
Ryabchikova, T.:Scenes from Nature *(rec Tsai Performance Center, Boston)* Sonora ▲ SO 22570 [DDD]
Ryabchikova, T.:Son Pno *(rec Tsai Performance Center, Boston)* Sonora ▲ SO 22570 [DDD]
Shamo, I.:Gutzul Watercolors *(rec Tsai Performance Center, Boston)* Sonora ▲ SO 22571 [DDD]
Shamo, I.:Humoresque Pno *(rec Tsai Performance Center, Boston)* Sonora ▲ SO 22571 [DDD]
Shamo, I.:Prelude Pno *(rec Tsai Performance Center, Boston)* Sonora ▲ SO 22571 [DDD]
Silvestrov, V.:Pieces Pno *(rec Tsai Performance Center, Boston)* Sonora ▲ SO 22571 [DDD]
Stepovoy, Y.:Cossack's Song *(rec Tsai Performance Center, Boston)* Sonora ▲ SO 22571 [DDD]
Stepovoy, Y.:Lullaby *(rec Tsai Performance Center, Boston)* Sonora ▲ SO 22571 [DDD]

Riabov, Sergei (vn)
Taneyev, S.:Trio Strs, Op. 21, w. Lidiya Chavaukina (vn), Andrei Kevorkov (va) Allegretto ▲ ACD 8178 [DDD] ■ ACS 8178

Ribaltchenko, Olga (vn)
Ustvolskaya, G.:Octet Obs, w. Nicolay Neretin (ob), Piotr Tosenko (ob), Alexander Stang (vn), Valentin Lukin (vn), Nikolay Tkachenko (vn), Valerii Znamenskii (timp), Oleg Malov (pno), O. Malov (cnd) *(rec St. Petersburg Radio House, Oct. & Nov. 1994)* Megadisc ▲ 7865

Ribeiro, Gerardo (vn)
Szymanowski, K.:Con 1 Vn, w. V. Yampolsky (cnd), Northwestern Univ SO, *(Evanston, IL, Apr 1993)* Northwestern Univ School of Music ▲ 6702

Riber, Anders (pno)
Stolarczyk, W.:Earth Air Fire Water, w. Amalie Malling (pno), John Damgaard (pno), Anne Øland (pno), Teddy Teirup (pno), Friedrich Gürtler (pno), Rosalind Bevan (pno), Poul Rosenbaum (pno), Rodolfo Llambias (pno), Bella Horn-Ribera (pno), Elisabeth Sigurdsson (pno), Thomas Tronheim (pno), Elsebeth Broderson (pno), Erik Kaltoft (pno), Jørgen Hald Nielsen (pno), Aino Gilemann (pno), Birgit Kjær (pno), Jørgen Thomsen (pno), Gunhild Donslund (pno), Henrik Bo Hansen (pno), Lone Karlsson (pno), Erik Fessel (pno), Lasse Nilsson (pno), Janos Ferenczi (pno), Erik Bach (pno), Axel Momme (pno), Arne de Cros Dich (pno), Sven Micha Slot (pno), Hanne Bramsen Buhl (pno), Lili Olesen (pno), Susannah Carlsson (pno), Ulla Erml (pno), Vagn Sørensen (pno), Leif Greibe (pno), Bodil Krogh (pno), Kirsten Ottosen (pno), Inger Bergenholz (pno), Karsten Gylendorf (pno), Bjønr Elkjær (pno), Jacob Bjørn Jensen (pno), Jørgen Kaad (pno), Anne Marie Hjelm (pno), Carl Ulrik Munk Andersen (pno), Poul Lumbye (pno), Oluf Hildebrandt Nielsen (pno), Joachim Olsson (pno), Peter Pade Ramsøe Jacobsen (pno), Astrid Pollmann (pno), Jette Borsch (pno), Kirsten Karlshøj (pno), Maria Teresa Assing (pno), Allan Dahl Hansen (pno), Johan Hugossen (pno), Tine Fenger Pederson (pno), Arne Jørgen Fæø (pno), Anja Høgsted (pno), Anne Sophie Parbo (pno), Inga Lindmark (pno), Teresa Drabik Stathakis (pno), Anne Ruth Ferenczi (pno), Irene Hasager (pno), Yuka Ichikawa (pno), Birgitte Baur (pno), Malene Thastum (pno), Jens E. Rasmussen (pno), Birgitte Zielke (pno), Claus Zielke (pno), Stefan Kasch (pno), Bin Qiao (pno), Inger Johanne Teirup (pno), Lindy Rosborg (pno), Liisa Heininen (pno), David Højer (pno), Ellen Refstrup (pno), Thomas K. Søorensen (pno), Erik Kure (pno), Michael Rauff (pno), Jan beck Eriksson (pno), Tanja Zapolski (pno), Vibeke Skagbo (pno), Pål Eide Lindtner (pno), Ha-Young Sul (pno), Benedicte Palko (pno), Inke Kesseler (pno), Anne Marie Meineche (pno), Sverre Larsen (pno), Kasper Peter Bach (pno), Elisabetta Eliseo (pno), Olga Magieres (pno), Carl Erik Kühl (pno), Thorkild Borup Nielsen (pno), Valeria Zanini (pno), Lars Stenhoft (perc), Dennis Boel (perc), Winnie Dahlgren (perc), Susanne Vind (perc), Claus Byrith (elec), Anne Marie Storm (elec), J. Ribera (cnd) *(rec live, Koldinghaus Castle, Denmark, May 2, 1996)* Danica ▲ DCD 1996

Ribera, José (pno)
Argento, D.:From the Diary of V. Woolf, w. M. Schèle (sop), G. Schaub (fl) Proprius ▲ PRCD 9982
Holewa, H.:Con 1 Pno, w. L. Segerstam (cnd), Swedish RSO Phono Suecia ▲ PHN 49 [ADD]
Werle, L.J.:Chants for Dark Hours, w. M. Schèle (sop), G. Schaub (fl) Proprius ▲ PRCD 9982

Ribke, Gunter (vc)
Granados, E.:Danzas españolas (10), w. B. Hebb (gtr) [arr vc & gtr] Ambitus ▲ 97880
Tchaikovsky, P.:Morceaux, Op. 51, w. B. Hebb (gtr) [trans. for string] Ambitus ▲ 97880

Ribli, I. (vc)—see ORCHESTRAS & ENSEMBLES Danubius Quartet

Riboni, Marco (gtr)
Gragnani, F.:Gtr Music, w. Leopoldo Saracino (gtr), Andrea Pecola (vn), Emilio Vapi (fl), Anna Maria Giaquinta (cl), Andrea Bellato (vc)—Qt in A for Vn, Cl & 2 Gtrs, Op. 8; Duet No. 1 in A for Vn & Gtr; Trio in D for Fl, Vn & Gtr, Op. 13; Duet No. 2 in A for Vn & Gtr; Sxt in A for Fl, Cl, Vn, 2 Gtrs & Vc, Op. 9 Stradivarius ▲ STV 33385 [DDD]

Ribot, Marc (gtr)
Casseus, F.:Haitian Suite Music of the World ■ C 202
Zorn, J.:The Book of Heads Tzadik ▲ TZA 7009 [DDD]
Zorn, J.:Kristallnacht, w. David Krakauer (cl/b cl), Frank London (tpt), Mark Feldman (vn), Mark Dresser (electric bass), Anthony Coleman (kbd), William Winant (perc) Tzadik ▲ TZA 7301 [ADD]

Ribot, Marc (gtr/banjo)
Shea, D.:Hsi-Yu Chi, w. Sim Cain (perc), Hideki Kato (bass instrument), Wu Man (pipa), Zeena Parkins (hp/pno/acc), Jim Pugliese (perc), David Shea (sampler/pno/turntables), Alex Tobias (celtic dr/misc.), Rebecca Wilson (screaming), John Zorn (a sax) Tzadik ("The Composers" series) ▲ TZA 7005 [DDD]

Riccardi, Alfredo (vc)
Danzi, F.:Qts Bn, Op. 40, w. M. Monguzzi (bn), G. Maestri (vn), A. Anjos (va) Bongiovanni ▲ GB 5520 [DDD]
Krommer, F.:Qt Bn, Op. 46/1, w. M. Monguzzi (cl), G. Maestri (vn), A. Anjos (va) Bongiovanni ▲ GB 5520 [DDD]

Ricci, Ruggiero (vn)
Arnold, M.:Pieces (6) Vn, w. R. Pennies (pno) One-Eleven ▲ URS 91060 [ADD]
Arnold, M.:Son 2 Vn One-Eleven ▲ URS 91060 [ADD]
Bach, J.S.:Con 2 Vn, w. E. Bigot (cnd), Lamoureux Orch One-Eleven ▲ URS 50050 [ADD]
Bach, J.S.:Sons & Partitas Vn, BWV 1001-1006—Partita 2 in d, BWV 1004 One-Eleven 2-▲ URS 92030 [ADD]
Bach, J.S.:Sons & Partitas Vn, BWV 1001-1006—Prelude from BWV 1006 One-Eleven ▲ URS 93020 [ADD]
Bach, J.S.:Sons & Partitas Vn, BWV 1001-1006 MCA Classics 2-▲ MCAD2-9841 [ADD]
Bach, J.S.:Sons & Partitas Vn, BWV 1001-1006—BWV 1001, 1003, 1004 & 1006 One-Eleven ▲ URS 50060 [ADD]
Bach, J.S.:Sons & Partitas Vn, BWV 1001-1006—Partita 2 in d, BWV 1004 & Son. 2 in a, BWV 1003 *(rec June 11, 1988)* One-Eleven ▲ URS 89013 [ADD]
Bach, J.S.:Sons & Partitas Vn, BWV 1001-1006—Son. 3, Op. 1005 One-Eleven 2-▲ URS 90033 [ADD]
Baker, D.:Jazz Suite Vn, w. M. Andrews (pno) Grenadilla ■ 1056
Barber, S.:Con Vn, w. K. Clark (cnd), Pacific SO Reference ▲ RR 45CD [DDD]
Bartók, B.:Con 2 Vn, w. T. Hlasek (cnd), Hungarian Philharmonia One-Eleven ▲ URS 91030 [ADD]
Bartók, B.:Son Vn One-Eleven ▲ URS 92020 [ADD]
Beethoven, L. van:Con Vn, Op. 61, w. S. Vassilov (cnd), Bulgarian State PO One-Eleven ▲ URS 91050 [ADD]
Beethoven, L. van:Son 1 Vn One-Eleven ▲ URS 92020 [ADD]
Beethoven, L. van:Son 3 Vn, w. R. Pennies (pno) One-Eleven ▲ URS 91060 [ADD]
Beethoven, L. van:Son 9 Vn, "Kreutzer", w. J. Gilliam (pno) One-Eleven ▲ URS 93050 [ADD]
Bottesini, G.:Gran Duo Concertant, w. F. Petracchi (db), P. Bellugi (cnd), Royal PO Sony Classical ("Essential Classics" series) ▲ SBK 47661 ■ SBT 47661
Bruch, M.:Con 1 Vn, w. M. Kuntzsch (cnd), Bochum SO Allegretto ▲ ACD 8169 [ADD] ■ ACS 8169
Bull, O.:Music of, w. R. Pennies (pno) One-Eleven ▲ URS 91060 [ADD]
The Complete Electrola Recordings Biddulph ▲ LAB 044 [ADD]
Corelli, A.:Sons Vn, Op. 5, w. D. Nesbitt (va de gamba), I. Keyes (hpd)—Sons. 8, 9, 10, 11 & 12 One-Eleven 2-▲ URS 92030 [ADD]
Dallapiccola, L.:Studi (2) Vn, w. Rosalyn Tureck (pno) *(rec NY, May 2, 1952)* VAI Audio ▲ VAIA 1124 [ADD]
Dvořák, A.:Con Vn, w. H. Müller-Kray (cnd), South German RSO One-Eleven ▲ URS 93030 [ADD]
Dvořák, A.:Con Vn, w. W. Susskind (cnd), St. Louis SO Vox Box 2-▲ CDX 5015 [ADD]
Dvořák, A.:Mazurek, w. W. Susskind (cnd), St. Louis SO Vox Box 2-▲ CDX 5015 [ADD]
Dvořák, A.:Romance Vn, w. W. Susskind (cnd), St. Louis SO Vox Box 2-▲ CDX 5015 [ADD]
Ernst, H.W.:Polyphonic Studies (6) *(rec 1983)* Dynamic ▲ CD 28 [AAD]
Flury, U.J.:Son Vn *(rec Radio Studio, Bern, Nov. 23–24, 1973)* Gallo ▲ CD 802 [ADD]
Franck, C.:Son Vn, w. R. Pennies (pno) One-Eleven ▲ URS 91060 [ADD]
Ginastera, A.:Con Vn, w. H. de la Fuente (cnd), Orch of the Americas One-Eleven ▲ URS 91020 [ADD]
Ginastera, A.:Con Vn, w. H. de la Fuente (cnd), Orch of the Americas One-Eleven ▲ EPR 94020
Goldmark, K.:Con 1 Vn, w. L. de Froment (cnd), Luxembourg RSO *(rec 1977)* Allegretto ▲ ACD 8173 [ADD] ■ ACS 8173
Goldmark, K.:Con 1 Vn, w. H. Müller-Kray (cnd), South German RSO One-Eleven ▲ URS 93030 [ADD]
The Great Violinists Series One-Eleven ▲ URS 50100 [ADD]
Hindemith, P.:Son Vn, Op. 31/1 One-Eleven ▲ URS 50060 [ADD]
Hindemith, P.:Son Vn, Op. 31/2 One-Eleven 2-▲ URS 90033 [ADD]
Kay, U.:Portraits, w. Andrews (pno) Grenadilla ■ 1056
Kreisler, F.:Cadenzas for Beethoven's Con Vn, w. I. Davidovac (cnd), Zagreb Youth Orch—Beethoven:Con., Op. 61 One-Eleven ▲ URS 91050 [ADD]
Kreisler, F.:Recitativo & Scherzo-caprice *(rec June 11, 1988)* One-Eleven ▲ URS 89013 [ADD]
Lalo, E.:Sym espagnole, w. J. Hoffman (cnd), RFO SO One-Eleven ▲ URS 91040 [ADD]
Lees, B.:Con Vn, w. K. Akiyama (cnd), American SO *(rec 1976)* Vox Box ("The American Composers" series) 2-▲ CDX 5158

INSTRUMENT.

Ricci, Ruggiero (vn) (cont.)
The Making of a Legend, Vol. 3 One–Eleven ▲ URS 50080 [ADD]
The Making of a Legend, Vol. 4 One–Eleven ▲ URS 50110 [ADD]
The Making of a Legend, Vol. 6 One–Eleven ▲ URS 93060 [ADD]
Menotti, G.C.:Con Vn, w. K. Clark (cnd), Pacific SO Reference ▲ RR 45CD [DDD]
Mozart, W.A.:Con 3 Vn, w. F. Stassevitch (cnd), Budapest Chamber Ensemble One–Eleven ▲ URS 91040 [ADD]
Mozart, W.A.:Con 3 Vn, w. F. Stassevitch (cnd), Budapest Chamber Ensemble One–Eleven ▲ URS 93010 [ADD]
Mozart, W.A.:Con 4 Vn, w. I. Davidovac (cnd), Zagreb Youth Orch One–Eleven ▲ URS 91050 [ADD]
Mozart, W.A.:Con 5 Vn, w. P. Bellugi (cnd), Toscana Regional Orch One–Eleven ▲ URS 93020 [ADD]
Paganini, N.:Caprice d'adieux Vox Box 3–▲ CD3X 3020 [ADD]
Paganini, N.:Caprices Vn [plays on Paganini's "Cannon del Gesù" vn of 1742] Biddulph ▲ LAW 016
Paganini, N.:Caprices Vn—Nos. 13–24 *(rec June 11, 1988)* One–Eleven 2–▲ URS 89013 [ADD]
Paganini, N.:Caprices Vn—Nos. 13–24 One–Eleven ▲ URS 92020 [ADD]
Paganini, N.:Caprices Vn One–Eleven ▲ EPR 94010
Paganini, N.:Caprices Vn—No. 5 One–Eleven ▲ URS 93020 [ADD]
Paganini, N.:Caprices Vn Vox Box 3–▲ CD3X 3020 [ADD]
Paganini, N.:Con 1 Vn, w. H. de la Fuente (cnd), Orch of the Americas One–Eleven ▲ URS 91020 [ADD]
Paganini, N.:Con 1 Vn, w. E. Bigot (cnd), Lamoureux Orch One–Eleven ▲ URS 50050 [ADD]
Paganini, N.:Con 1 Vn, w. H. de la Fuente (cnd), Orch of the Americas One–Eleven ▲ EPR 94020
Paganini, N.:Con 4 Vn, w. Piero Mordini (vn), T. Hlasek (cnd), Hungarian Philharmonia One–Eleven ▲ URS 91030 [ADD]
Paganini, N.:Con 6 Vn, w. R. Porroni (gtr) [original version]—Adagio [cadenza Ricci] One–Eleven ▲ URS 93020 [ADD]
Paganini, N.:Con 6 Vn, w. H. Zimmermann (cnd), Academic SO One–Eleven ▲ URS 91080 [ADD]
Paganini, N.:Duo merveille Vn One–Eleven 2–▲ URS 90033 [ADD]
Paganini, N.:Intro & Vars on "Dal tuo stellato soglio", w. L. Persinger (pno) [arr vn & pno] One–Eleven ▲ URS 50060 [ADD]
Paganini, N.:Intro & Vars on "Nel cor più", w. J. Seurre (cnd), Paris Harmonie Orch One–Eleven ▲ URS 91070 [ADD]
Paganini, N.:Moto perpetuo Vn & Orch, w. C. Furstner (pno) [arr. for Violin & Piano] One–Eleven ▲ EPR 94010
Paganini, N.:Music of, w. S. Cardi (pno)—Cantabile in D; Taratella; Nel cor piu non mi sento; Cantabile & Waltz, Centone Son. No. 1; Son., Op. 2/1 & 4; Son., Op. 3/1–4 & 6; Moses Fant.; Variazioni di bravura; Son. in A, Op. posth. One–Eleven ▲ URS 93070 [DDD]
Paganini, N.:Music of—Vars on "God Save the Queen" One–Eleven ▲ URS 89013
Paganini, N.:Qts (15) Vn, w. A. Vismara (va), L. Signorini (vc), S. Cardi (gtr)—No. 7 Bongiovanni ▲ GB 5507 [DDD]
Paganini, N.:Son concertata, w. S. Cardi (gtr) Bongiovanni ▲ GB 5507 [DDD]
Paganini, N.:Le Streghe, w. L. Persinger (pno) One–Eleven ▲ URS 50060 [ADD]
Paganini, N.:Le Streghe, w. P. Bellugi (cnd), Royal PO One–Eleven ▲ URS 93030 [ADD]
Paganini, N.:Terzetto Vn, w. L. Signorini (vc), S. Cardi (gtr) Bongiovanni ▲ GB 5507 [DDD]
Paganini, N.:Vars on "God Save the King" *(rec June 11, 1988)* One–Eleven 2–▲ URS 89013 [ADD]
Paganini, N.:Vars on "God Save the King" One–Eleven 2–▲ URS 90033 [ADD]
Portrait of an Artist, Vol. 4, w. Helmut Barth, Rebecca Penneys (pno), Univ of Michigan CO One–Eleven ▲ URS 93040 [ADD]
Prokofiev, S.:Cons Vn (comp), w. L. de Froment (cnd), Luxembourg RSO Vox Box 3–▲ CD3X 3000 [ADD]
Prokofiev, S.:Con 2 Vn, w. F. Stassevitch (cnd), Budapest Chamber Ensemble One–Eleven ▲ URS 93010 [ADD]
Ravel, M.:Tzigane, w. E. Bigot (cnd), Lamoureux Orch One–Eleven ▲ URS 50050 [ADD]
Respighi, O.:Con gregoriano, w. F. Stassevitch (cnd), Budapest Chamber Ensemble One–Eleven ▲ URS 93010 [ADD]
Respighi, O.:Poema autunnale, w. K. Clark (cnd), Pacific SO Reference ▲ RR 15CD [ADD]
Ruggiero Ricci One–Eleven 2–▲ URS 92033 [ADD/DDD]
Saint-Saëns, C.:Caprice andalous, w. L. de Froment (cnd), Luxembourg RSO Vox Box 2–▲ CDX 5084 [ADD]
Saint-Saëns, C.:Con 1 Vn, w. P. Cao (cnd), Luxembourg RSO Vox Box 2–▲ CDX 5084 [ADD]
Saint-Saëns, C.:Con 2 Vn, w. P. Cao (cnd), Luxembourg RSO Vox Box 2–▲ CDX 5084 [ADD]
Saint-Saëns, C.:Con 3 Vn, w. P. Cao (cnd), Luxembourg RSO Vox Box 2–▲ CDX 5084 [ADD]
Saint-Saëns, C.:Con 3 Vn, w. E. Bigot (cnd), Lamoureux Orch One–Eleven ▲ URS 50050 [ADD]
Saint-Saëns, C.:Havanaise Vn, w. P. Cao (cnd), Luxembourg RSO Vox Box 2–▲ CDX 5084 [ADD]
Saint-Saëns, C.:Introduction & Rondo capriccioso, w. P. Cao (cnd), Luxembourg RSO Vox Box 2–▲ CDX 5084 [ADD]
Saint-Saëns, C.:Morceau de concert Vn, w. L. de Froment (cnd), Luxembourg RSO Vox Box 2–▲ CDX 5084 [ADD]
Saint-Saëns, C.:Romance Vn, w. L. de Froment (cnd), Luxembourg RSO Vox Box 2–▲ CDX 5084 [ADD]
Sarasate, P. de:Intro & Tarantella, w. I. Markevitch (cnd), Russian Radio Orch One–Eleven ▲ URS 91070 [ADD]
Sarasate, P. de:Spanish Dances, w. T. Bugaj (cnd), Pamplona Pablo Sarasate Orch—Zapateada, Op. 23/2 One–Eleven ▲ EPR 94020
Sarasate, P. de:Vn & Pno Music, w. G. McNaught (pno)—Fantaisie on Themes from Gounod's Faust; Jota de S. Fermin; Romanian Melody; Jota Aragonesa, Op. 27; Serenata Andalusa, Op. 28; The Song of the Nightingale, Op. 29; Pateneras, Op. 35; Adios montanas mias, Op. 37; Zortzico d'Iparaguirre, Op. 39; Miramar (Zortzico), Op. 42; Chansons Russes, Op. 49; Jota de Pablo, Op. 52 Dynamic ▲ CD 94 [DDD]
Sarasate, P. de:Zigeunerweisen, w. J. Hoffman (cnd), Royal Festival Opera SO One–Eleven ▲ URS 93020 [ADD]
Schubert, Franz:Qnt Pno, D.667, w. E. Taussig (pno), M. Virizly (vc), E. Klemmstein (va), G. Karr (db) One–Eleven ▲ URS 92010
Shostakovich, D.:Trio 2 Pno, w. S. Rodriguez (pno), N. Rosen (vc) One–Eleven ▲ URS 92010
Sibelius, J.:Con Vn, w. J. Mikael (cnd), Helsinki Festival Orch One–Eleven ▲ URS 91070 [ADD]
Sibelius, J.:Music for Vn Pno, w. S. Rabinoff (pno)—4 Pieces, Op. 78; 6 Pieces, Op. 79; 2 Pieces, Op. 2; 5 danses champêtres One–Eleven 2–▲ URS 90033 [ADD]
Sibelius, J.:Novelette, w. S. Rabinoff (pno) One–Eleven 2–▲ URS 90033 [ADD]
Sibelius, J.:Pieces Vn Pno, Op. 81, w. S. Rabinoff (pno) One–Eleven 2–▲ URS 90033 [ADD]
Sibelius, J.:Pieces Vn Pno, Op. 115, w. S. Rabinoff (pno) One–Eleven 2–▲ URS 90033 [ADD]
Sibelius, J.:Pieces Vn Pno, Op. 116, w. S. Rabinoff (pno) One–Eleven 2–▲ URS 90033 [ADD]
Spohr, L.:Duets Vns, Op. 3, w. S. Humphreys (vn)—No. 2 in F One–Eleven ▲ URS 92010
Strauss, R.:Son Vn, w. J. Gilliam (pno) One–Eleven ▲ URS 93050 [ADD]
Tárrega, F.:Recuerdos de la Alhambra *(rec June 11, 1988)* One–Eleven ▲ URS 89013 [ADD]
Tartini, G.:Sons Vn & Continuo, w. F. Rados (pno)—Devil's Trill One–Eleven ▲ URS 93050 [ADD]
Tchaikovsky, P.:Con Vn, w. J. Seurre (cnd), Paris Harmonie Orch One–Eleven ▲ URS 91070 [ADD]
Veerhoff, C.:Con Vn, w. D. Speer (cnd), Contemporary Music Group One–Eleven ▲ URS 91080 [ADD]
Vieuxtemps, H.:Vn & Pno Music (sels), w. Marco Vincenzi (pno)—Fant appassionata; Ballade et Polonaise; Chant d'amour; Désespoir; Souvenir; Rondino; Tarantella; Rêverie; Romance; Hommage à Paganini; Innocence; Yankee Doodle *(rec Dynamic's, Genoa, Italy, May 3–5, 1995)* Dynamic ▲ CDS 112 [DDD]
Virtuoso Recital by Ruggiero Ricci One–Eleven ▲ URS 91010 [ADD/DDD]
Wieniawski, H.:Con 2 Vn, w. H. Müller-Kray (cnd), Southwest German RSO One–Eleven ▲ URS 93020 [ADD]
Wieniawski, H.:L'Ecole moderne *(rec 1983)* Dynamic ▲ CD 28 [AAD]
Wieniawski, H.:L'Ecole moderne—Le Staccato One–Eleven ▲ URS 89013
Wieniawski, H.:Etudes-caprices, w. S. Humphreys (vn)—No. 4 One–Eleven ▲ URS 92010

Ricci, Ruggiero (vn) (cont.)
Wieniawski, H.:Vn & Pno Music, w. J. Gruenberg (pno)—Kuyawiak; Légende; Obertass Mazurka; Polonaise in A; Polonaise in D; Scherzo Souvenir de Moscow; Tarantelle; Variations on an Original Theme Unicorn-Kanchana ▲ UKCD 2048 [DDD]
Ysaÿe, E.:Sons Vn—No. 3 in d One–Eleven 2–▲ URS 90033 [ADD]
Ysaÿe, E.:Sons Vn—No. 3 in d One–Eleven ▲ URS 93050 [ADD]
Ysaÿe, T.:Sons Vn—No. 3 in d One–Eleven ▲ URS 91050 [ADD]

Ricci, Stefano (cl)—see ORCHESTRAS & ENSEMBLES Briccialdi Wind Quintet

Rice, Victor (elec bass)
Wheeler, T.:The Dancing Bird, w. F. Vanasco (vc), T. Wheeler (perc) Albany ▲ TROY 114

Rich, Elizabeth (pno)
Schumann, C.:Con Pno, w. D. Burkh (cnd), Janáček PO *(rec Ostrava, Czech Republic, 1995)* Centaur ▲ 2283 [DDD]
Schumann, R.:Carnaval Pno Connoisseur Society ▲ CD 4188 [DDD]
Schumann, R.:Novelettes Connoisseur Society ▲ CD 4188 [DDD]
Weber, C.M. von:Con 1 Pno, w. D. Burkh (cnd), Janáček PO *(rec Ostrava, Czech Republic, 1995)* Centaur ▲ 2283 [DDD]
Weber, C.M. von:Con 2 Pno, w. D. Burkh (cnd), Janáček PO *(rec Ostrava, Czech Republic, 1995)* Centaur ▲ 2283 [DDD]

Richard, Jean-Charles (pno)
Debussy, C.:Songs, w. Bernard Kruysen (bar), Francis Poulenc (pno)—Le Son du cor; L'échelonnement des haies; Trois chansons de France; Fêtes galantes; Fête galantes; Trois poèmes de Mallarmé; Le promenoir des deux amants; Trois poèmes de Mallarmé Trois ballades de Villon; Trois chansons de France *(rec 1962–65)* Mémoire Vive ▲ 262010 (m)

Richardot, Myriam (org)
Rossini, G.:Sacred Music, w. Evelyne Razimowsky (sop), Michel Piquemal (bar), Jean-Claude Pennetier (pno), Michel Piquemal (cnd), Michel Piquemal Vocal Ensemble—La passegiata; Ave Marie; Inno Alla Pace; Ave Maria; Toast pour le nouvel an; Duetto Buffo di Due Batti; La fede; La speranza; La carita; Cantemus Domino; La notte del Santo Natalie; Preghiera; I Gondolieri Adès ▲ ADE 204192 [AAD]

Richards, Deborah (pno)
Koechlin, C.:Pno Music—L'ancienne maison de campagne, Op. 124 (1923–33); Nocturne chromatique, Op. 33 (1907); Paysages et marines, Op. 63 (1915–16) CPO ▲ CPO 999054-2 [DDD]
Satie, E.:Socrate, w. H. Helling (cta) [composer's version for voice & piano] Wergo ▲ WER 6186-2 [DDD]
Schumann, C.:Songs, w. I. Lippitz (sop)—25 lieder (composed 1834–53)—Walzer; Am Strand; Volkslied; Er ist gekommen; Liebst du um Schönheit; Warum willst du and're fragen; Die gute Nacht; Ich stand in dunklen Träumen; Sie liebten sich beide; Liebeszauber; Der Mond kommt still gegangen; Ich hab' in deinem Auge; Die stille Lotosblume; Loreley; O weh des Scheidens; Beim Abscheid; Mein Stern; Der Abendstern; Was weinst du, Blümlein; An einem lichten Morgen; Geheimes Flüstern; Auf einem grünen Hügel; Das ist ein Tag; O Lust, O Lust; Das Veilchen [G] Bayer ▲ 100206 [DDD]

Richards, E. Michael (cl)
Boulanger, N.:from Temporal Silence Neuma ▲ 450-73 [DDD]
Matsuo, M.:Hirai V, w. Kazuko Tanosaki (pno), M. Matsuo (cnd), Hamilton College Orch Opus One ▲ CD 156

Richards, Emil (mar/perc)
Kellaway, R.:Music of, w. Roger Kellaway (pno/perc), Fred Seykora (vc), Chuck Domanico (elec b), Joe Porcaro (perc), Bob Zimmitti (perc)—Thinking of You; Un canto per la pace [A Song for Peace]; Love of my Life; Eleventide; In My Heart; Eve; Windows; Winter [Parts 1–3] *(rec Ocean Way Recording Studio, Los Angeles, CA, May 1–5, 1993)* EMI Classics ▲ CDC 54903 [DDD]
Kellaway, R.:Music of, w. Fred Seykora (vc), Chuck Domanico (electric bass), Roger Kellaway (pno/perc), Joe Porcaro (perc), Bob Zimmitti (perc)—Thinking of You; Un canto per la pace [A Song for Peace]; Love of my Life; Eleventide; In My Heart; Eve; Windows; Winter [Parts 1–3] *(rec Ocean Way Recording Studio, Los Angeles, CA, May 1–5, 1993)* Angel ▲ CDC 54903 [DDD]

Richards, Steven (perc)—see ORCHESTRAS & ENSEMBLES Eastman Percussion Ensemble members

Richardson, Diane (pno)
Griffes, C.T.:Impressions, w. O. Stapp (mez) [F] New World ▲ NW 273-2 [ADD]

Richardson, W. (trbn)—see ORCHESTRAS & ENSEMBLES Wisconsin Brass Quintet

Richter, (pno)
Bach, J.S.:Con 1 Hpd, w. V. Talich (cnd), Czech PO *(rec live, Prague 1954)* Melodram ▲ MEL 18029 (m) [AAD]

Richter, Alfred (vc)
Music for Alphorn, Organ & Cello, w. Anton Wicky (alphn), H. Keller (org) Koch Schwann ▲ SCH 310812 [DDD]

Richter, Friederike (pno)—see ORCHESTRAS & ENSEMBLES Kontraste Ensemble

Richter, Karl (org)
Bach, J.S.:Chorale Preludes (Schübler)—BWV 645, 650 Deutsche Grammophon ("Musikfest" series) ▲ 415442-2 [ADD]
Bach, J.S.:Fant & Fugue Org, BWV 542 Deutsche Grammophon ("Musikfest" series) ▲ 415442-2 [ADD]
Bach, J.S.:Fant & Fugue Org, BWV 542 London ("Weekend Classics" series) ▲ 417679-2 [AAD]
Bach, J.S.:Passacaglia & Fugue Org London ("Weekend Classics" series) ▲ 417679-2 [AAD]
Bach, J.S.:Preludes & Fugues, BWV 531–552—BWV 552 Deutsche Grammophon ("Musikfest" series) ▲ 415442-2 [ADD]
Bach, J.S.:Preludes & Fugues, BWV 531–552—BWV 548 London ("Weekend Classics" series) ▲ 417679-2 [AAD]
Bach, J.S.:Toccata & Fugue Org, BWV 565 London ("Weekend Classics" series) ▲ 417679-2 [AAD]
Bach, J.S.:Toccata & Fugue Org, BWV 565 Deutsche Grammophon ("Musikfest" series) ▲ 415442-2 [ADD]

Richter, Konrad (pno)
Ullmann, V.:Con Pno, w. I. Yinon (cnd), Brno State PO Bayer ▲ 100228 [DDD]
Ullmann, V.:Sons Pno—Nos. 1–7, Opp. 10, 19, 26, 38, 45 & 49 Bayer 2–▲ 100113/114 [DDD]

Richter, M. S. (vn)
Rahbee, D.G.:Son breve, w. E. Jackendoff (pno) *(rec The Music Room)* Seda ▲ 333 [DDD]

Richter, Marga (pno)—see also ORCHESTRAS & ENSEMBLES Piano Circus
Richter, M.:Qhanri, w. D. Wells (vc) Leonarda ▲ LE 337
Richter, M.:Requiem Leonarda ▲ LE 337

Richter, S. (vn)
Saint-Saëns, C.:Con 1 Vn, w. C. Eschenbach (cnd), South German RSO Originals ▲ ORISH 810 [DDD]

Richter, Sigrun (lt)
Gautier, P.:Lt Suites—7 suites, Ballet, La Battaille & Chacone Ambitus ▲ 97828 [DDD]

Richter, Sviatoslav (pno)
Bach, J.S.:Capriccio Hpd *(rec Paterskirche Kempen, Niederrhein, Germany, Nov 2, 1991)* Live Classics ▲ LCL 421 [DDD]
Bach, J.S.:Capriccio Hpd Stradivarius ▲ STV 33323
Bach, J.S.:Con 8 Hpd, w. V. Talich (cnd), Czech PO *(rec 1954–55)* Supraphon ▲ SUP 11 1906 [AAD]
Bach, J.S.:Duets Hpd, BWV 802–805 *(rec Paterskirche Kempen, Niederrhein, Germany, Nov 2, 1991)* Live Classics ▲ LCL 421 [DDD]
Bach, J.S.:Duets Hpd, BWV 802–805 Stradivarius ▲ STV 33323
Bach, J.S.:English Suites—Nos. 4 & 6 Stradivarius ▲ STV 33334 [DDD]
Bach, J.S.:English Suites—Nos. 1 & 3 Stradivarius ▲ STV 33333 [DDD]
Bach, J.S.:Fants Hpd—BWV 906 *(rec Nov 14, 1991)* Stradivarius ▲ STR 33335 [DDD]
Bach, J.S.:Fants Hpd—in c, BWV 906 *(rec Paterskirche Kempen, Niederrhein, Germany, Nov 2, 1991)* Live Classics ▲ LCL 421 [DDD]
Bach, J.S.:French Suites—BWV 813 & 815 *(rec Nov 14, 1991)* Stradivarius ▲ STR 33335 [DDD]
Bach, J.S.:Italian Con *(rec Paterskirche Kempen, Niederrhein, Germany, Nov. 2, 1991)* Live Classics ▲ LCL 421 [DDD]
Bach, J.S.:Italian Con Stradivarius ▲ STV 33323

Richter, Sviatoslav (pno) (cont.)

Bach, J.S.:Sons (5) Kbd—No. 4 in D, BWV 963 *(rec Paterskirche Kempen, Niederrhein, Germany, Nov. 2, 1991)* Live Classics ▲ LCL 421 [DDD]

Bach, J.S.:Sons (5) Kbd—in D, BWV 963; in d, BWV 964; in C, BWV 966 Stradivarius ▲ STV 33323

Bach, J.S.:Toccatas Hpd, BWV 910–16—BWV 913 *(rec Nov 14, 1991)* Stradivarius ▲ STR 33335 [DDD]

Bach, J.S.:Toccatas Hpd, BWV 910–16—No. 1 in d, BWV 913 *(rec Paterskirche Kempen, Niederrhein, Germany, Nov. 2, 1991)* Live Classics ▲ LCL 421 [DDD]

Bartók, B.:Con 2 Pno, w. L. Maazel (cnd), Orch de Paris EMI Classics ("Doublefforte" series) 2–▲ CDFB 68637

Beethoven, L. van:Bagatelles (24)—Op. 126/1, 4 & 6 *(rec live, Czech Radio Broadcast, 1975)* Praga ▲ PR 254060

Beethoven, L. van:Con 1 Pno, w. K. Ančerl (cnd), Czech PO Prelude ▲ PRE 2157 [ADD]

Beethoven, L. van:Con 1 Pno, w. B. Bakala (cnd), Brno State PO *(rec 1956)* Praga ▲ PR 254024

Beethoven, L. van:Con 1 Pno, w. K. Kondrashin (cnd), Moscow PO Russian Disc ▲ CD 11041 [AAD]

Beethoven, L. van:Con 1 Pno, w. C. Eschenbach (cnd), Schleswig–Holstein Festival Orch RCA Red Seal ▲ 09026–61534–2 [DDD]

Beethoven, L. van:Con 1 Pno, w. C. Munch (cnd), Boston SO RCA Gold Seal ▲ 6804–2–RG [ADD]

Beethoven, L. van:Con 3 Pno, w. K. Ančerl (cnd), Czech PO Prelude ▲ PRE 2157 [ADD]

Beethoven, L. van:Con 3 Pno, w. B. Bakala (cnd), Brno State PO *(rec 1956)* Praga ▲ PR 254024

Beethoven, L. van:Con 3 Pno, w. K. Kondrashin (cnd), Moscow PO Russian Disc ▲ CD 11041 [AAD]

Beethoven, L. van:Con 3 Pno, w. R. Muti (cnd), Philharmonia Orch EMI Classics ▲ CDM 64750

Beethoven, L. van:Con Vn, Vc & Pno, "Triple Con", w. D. Oistrakh (vn), M. Rostropovich (vc), H. von Karajan (cnd), Berlin PO EMI Classics ▲ CDM 64744

Beethoven, L. van:Qnt Pno, Ob, Cl, Hn & Bn, w. *(wind players unknown)* Philips ("Richter:The Authorized Recordings" series) 2–▲ 438624–2

Beethoven, L. van:Rondos Pno, Op. 51 *(rec live, Czech Radio Broadcast, 1986)* Praga ▲ PR 254060

Beethoven, L. van:Sons Vc (comp), w. M. Rostropovich (vc) Philips ("Duo" series) 2–▲ 442565–2

Beethoven, L. van:Son 2 Vc, w. M. Rostropovich (vc) Philips ("Insignia" series) ▲ 434163–2 [ADD]

Beethoven, L. van:Sons Pno (comp)—Nos. 1, 7, 12, 27, 28, 29, 31 Music & Arts 2–▲ MUA CD 946

Beethoven, L. van:Son 3 Pno Music & Arts 2–▲ CD 910

Beethoven, L. van:Son 3 Pno Olympia ▲ OLY 336 [ADD]

Beethoven, L. van:Son 3 Pno Olympia 5–▲ OLY 5013 [DDD/ADD]

Beethoven, L. van:Son 3 Pno *(rec June 2, 1975)* Praga ▲ PR 254020 [ADD]

Beethoven, L. van:Son 4 Pno Music & Arts 2–▲ CD 910

Beethoven, L. van:Son 4 Pno Olympia ▲ OLY 336 [ADD]

Beethoven, L. van:Son 4 Pno Olympia 5–▲ OLY 5013 [DDD/ADD]

Beethoven, L. van:Son 6 Pno *(rec live, Salle Pleyel, Paris 11/7/80)* Pyramid 2–▲ PYR 13500/01 [ADD]

Beethoven, L. van:Son 7 Pno *(rec Nov. 1, 1975)* Praga ▲ PR 254020 [ADD]

Beethoven, L. van:Son 7 Pno *(rec live, Salle Pleyel, Paris, 11/7/80)* Pyramid 2–▲ PYR 13500/01 [ADD]

Beethoven, L. van:Son 9 Pno Philips ("Richter:The Authorized Recordings" series) 2–▲ 438617–2

Beethoven, L. van:Son 11 Pno *(rec 1968)* Historical Performers ▲ HPS 18 [ADD]

Beethoven, L. van:Son 12 Pno, "Funeral March" Philips ("Richter:The Authorized Recordings" series) 2–▲ 438617–2

Beethoven, L. van:Son 12 Pno, "Funeral March" *(rec Nov. 1, 1975)* Praga ▲ PR 254020 [ADD]

Beethoven, L. van:Son 12 Pno, "Funeral March" RCA Gold Seal ▲ 6804–2–RG [ADD]

Beethoven, L. van:Son 17 Pno, "Tempest" *(rec live, Carnegie Hall, New York 5/3/65)* Intaglio ▲ INCD 7111 [ADD]

Beethoven, L. van:Son 17 Pno, "Tempest" Music & Arts 2–▲ CD 910

Beethoven, L. van:Son 17 Pno, "Tempest" *(rec June 6, 1965)* Praga ▲ PR 254021 [ADD]

Beethoven, L. van:Son 17 Pno, "Tempest" *(rec live, Salle Pleyel, Paris 11/7/80)* Pyramid 2–▲ PYR 13500/01 [ADD]

Beethoven, L. van:Son 18 Pno *(rec live, Carnegie Hall, New York 5/3/65)* Intaglio ▲ INCD 7111 [ADD]

Beethoven, L. van:Son 18 Pno Music & Arts 2–▲ CD 910

Beethoven, L. van:Son 18 Pno *(rec June 6, 1965)* Praga ▲ PR 254021 [ADD]

Beethoven, L. van:Son 18 Pno *(rec live, Salle Pleyel, Paris 11/7/80)* Pyramid 2–▲ PYR 13500/01 [ADD]

Beethoven, L. van:Son 22 Pno *(rec Bauerntheater Terofal, Schliersee, July 10, 1992)* Live Classics ▲ 431

Beethoven, L. van:Son 22 Pno *(rec Schliersee, July 10, 1992)* Live Classics ▲ LCL 622 [DDD]

Beethoven, L. van:Son 22 Pno RCA Gold Seal ▲ 6804–2–RG [ADD]

Beethoven, L. van:Son 23 Pno, "Appassionata" *(rec Nov. 1, 1959)* Praga ▲ PR 254021 [ADD]

Beethoven, L. van:Son 23 Pno, "Appassionata" *(rec 1960)* RCA Gold Seal ▲ 07863–56518–2 [ADD] ■ 07863–56518–4

Beethoven, L. van:Son 23 Pno, "Appassionata" Music & Arts 2–▲ CD 910

Beethoven, L. van:Son 27 Pno *(rec live, Carnegie Hall, New York, 5/3/65)* Intaglio ▲ INCD 7161 [ADD]

Beethoven, L. van:Son 27 Pno Olympia ▲ OLY 336 [ADD]

Beethoven, L. van:Son 27 Pno Olympia 5–▲ OLY 5013 [DDD/ADD]

Beethoven, L. van:Son 27 Pno Olympia ▲ OLY 580 [ADD/DDD]

Beethoven, L. van:Son 27 Pno *(rec June 2, 1965)* Praga ▲ PR 254022 [ADD]

Beethoven, L. van:Son 28 Pno *(rec live, Carnegie Hall, New York 5/3/65)* Intaglio ▲ INCD 7161 [ADD]

Beethoven, L. van:Son 28 Pno Philips ("Richter:The Authorized Recordings" series) 2–▲ 438624–2

Beethoven, L. van:Son 28 Pno *(rec May 18, 1986)* Praga ▲ PR 254022 [ADD]

Beethoven, L. van:Son 29 Pno, "Hammerklavier" *(rec June 2, 1975)* Praga ▲ PR 254022 [ADD]

Beethoven, L. van:Son 29 Pno, "Hammerklavier" *(rec live, London)* Stradivarius ▲ STV 33313 [ADD]

Beethoven, L. van:Son 30 Pno *(rec live, Carnegie Hall, New York 5/3/65)* Intaglio ▲ INCD 7111 [ADD]

Beethoven, L. van:Son 30 Pno *(rec Kieler Schloss, Germany, Oct. 27, 1992)* Live Classics ▲ LCL 422 [DDD]

Beethoven, L. van:Son 31 Pno *(rec Kieler Schloss, Germany, Oct. 27, 1992)* Live Classics ▲ LCL 422 [DDD]

Beethoven, L. van:Son 31 Pno *(rec June 2, 1965)* Praga ▲ PR 254023 [ADD]

Beethoven, L. van:Son 32 Pno Music & Arts 2–▲ CD 910

Beethoven, L. van:Son 2 Vn, w. Oleg Kagan (vn) *(rec Large Room of the Conservatory, Moscow, Oct 27 & Nov 6, 1975)* Live Classics ▲ LCL 145 [ADD]

Beethoven, L. van:Son 4 Vn, w. Oleg Kagan (vn) *(rec Large Room of the Conservatory, Moscow, Oct 27 & Nov 6, 1975)* Live Classics ▲ LCL 145 [ADD]

Beethoven, L. van:Son 5 Vn, "Spring", w. Oleg Kagan (vn) *(rec Large Room of the Conservatory, Moscow, Oct 27 & Nov 6, 1975)* Live Classics ▲ LCL 145 [ADD]

Beethoven, L. van:Trio 6 Pno, "Archduke" Philips ("Richter:The Authorized Recordings" series) 2–▲ 438624–2

Beethoven, L. van:Vars on an Original Theme, Op. 34 *(rec live, Carnegie Hall, New York 4/5/70)* Intaglio ▲ INCD 7161 [ADD]

Beethoven, L. van:Vars on an Original Theme, Op. 34 *(rec 1970)* Olympia ▲ OLY 339 [ADD]

Beethoven, L. van:Vars on an Original Theme, Op. 34 Olympia 5–▲ OLY 5013 [DDD/ADD]

Beethoven, L. van:Vars & Fugue Pno, Op. 35, "Eroica" *(rec live, Festival Hall, London, 10/20/68)* AS Disc (Notes) ▲ ASD PGP 11004 [ADD]

Beethoven, L. van:Vars & Fugue Pno, Op. 35, "Eroica" *(rec live, Teatro La Venice, Venice, Italy 1/6/70)* Arkadia ▲ 919 [ADD]

Beethoven, L. van:Vars & Fugue Pno, Op. 35, "Eroica" *(rec live, Carnegie Hall, New York 4/5/70)* Intaglio ▲ INCD 7161 [ADD]

Beethoven, L. van:Vars & Fugue Pno, Op. 35, "Eroica" *(rec live, London 10/20/68)* Memories 2–▲ HR 4436/37 [ADD]

Richter, Sviatoslav (pno) (cont.)

Beethoven, L. van:Vars & Fugue Pno, Op. 35, "Eroica" *(rec June 1, 1970)* Music & Arts ▲ CD 879 [ADD]

Beethoven, L. van:Vars & Fugue Pno, Op. 35, "Eroica" *(rec 1970)* Olympia ▲ OLY 339 [ADD]

Beethoven, L. van:Vars & Fugue Pno, Op. 35, "Eroica" Olympia 5–▲ OLY 5013 [DDD/ADD]

Beethoven, L. van:Vars & Fugue Pno, Op. 35, "Eroica" *(rec 1968)* Historical Performers ▲ HPS 18 [ADD]

Beethoven, L. van:Vars on an Original Theme, Op. 76 *(rec live, Teatro La Venice, Venice, Italy 1/6/70)* Arkadia ▲ 919 [ADD]

Beethoven, L. van:Vars on an Original Theme, Op. 76 *(rec live, Carnegie Hall, New York 4/5/70)* Intaglio ▲ INCD 7161 [ADD]

Beethoven, L. van:Vars on an Original Theme, Op. 76 *(rec June 1, 1970)* Music & Arts ▲ CD 879 [ADD]

Beethoven, L. van:Vars on an Original Theme, Op. 76 *(rec 1970)* Olympia ▲ OLY 339 [ADD]

Beethoven, L. van:Vars on an Original Theme, Op. 76 Olympia 5–▲ OLY 5013 [DDD/ADD]

Beethoven, L. van:Vars on a waltz by Diabelli, Op. 120 *(rec live, Teatro La Venice, Venice, Italy 1/6/70)* Arkadia ▲ 919 [ADD]

Beethoven, L. van:Vars on a waltz by Diabelli, Op. 120 *(rec June 1, 1970)* Music & Arts ▲ CD 879 [ADD]

Beethoven, L. van:Vars on a waltz by Diabelli, Op. 120 *(rec May 18, 1986)* Praga ▲ PR 254023 [ADD]

Brahms, J.:Con 2 Pno, w. K. Kondrashin (cnd), Czech PO Multisonic ▲ 31 0335

Brahms, J.:Con 2 Pno, w. K. Kondrashin (cnd), Czech PO *(rec ca. 1950)* Multisonic ("Prague Spring Collection" series) 2–▲ 31 0020–2 [ADD]

Brahms, J.:Con 2 Pno, w. E. Mravinsky (cnd), Leningrad PO *(rec Dec. 27, 1961)* Russian Disc ▲ RUS 11 158 [AAD]

Brahms, J.:Con 2 Pno, w. E. Leinsdorf (cnd), Chicago SO *(rec 1960)* RCA Gold Seal ▲ 07863–56518–2 [ADD] ■ 07863–56518–4

Brahms, J.:Fants Pno, Op. 116—No. 5 *(rec live Locarno, 1966)* Ermitage ▲ ERM 113 [ADD]

Brahms, J.:Pieces Pno, Op. 76—No. 8 *(rec live Locarno, 1966)* Ermitage ▲ ERM 113 [ADD]

Brahms, J.:Pieces Pno, Op. 118—No. 3 *(rec live Locarno, 1966)* Ermitage ▲ ERM 113 [ADD]

Brahms, J.:Pieces Pno, Op. 119—No. 4 *(rec live Locarno, 1966)* Ermitage ▲ ERM 113 [ADD]

Brahms, J.:Romanzen aus Tieck's *Magelone*, w. D. Fischer–Dieskau (bar) *(rec 1965)* Historical Performers ▲ HPS 1 [ADD]

Brahms, J.:Romanzen aus Tieck's *Magelone*, w. Dietrich Fischer–Dieskau (bar) *(rec live, 1965)* As Disc ▲ ASD 2602

Brahms, J.:Son 1 Pno *(rec live in recital, ca. 1986/89)* London ▲ 436457–2 [DDD]

Brahms, J.:Son 1 Pno Philips ("Richter:The Authorized Recordings" series) 2–▲ 438477–2

Brahms, J.:Son 1 Pno Praga ▲ PR 254059

Brahms, J.:Son 1 Pno *(rec live, 1988)* RCA Red Seal ▲ 09026–60859–2

Brahms, J.:Son 2 Pno *(rec live, in recital, ca. 1986/89)* London ▲ 436457–2 [DDD]

Brahms, J.:Son 2 Pno Philips ("Richter:The Authorized Recordings" series) 2–▲ 438477–2

Brahms, J.:Son 2 Pno Praga ▲ PR 254059

Brahms, J.:Son 1 Vn, w. Oleg Kagan (vn) Olympia 5–▲ OLY 5013 [DDD/ADD]

Brahms, J.:Son 1 Vn, w. O. Kagan (vn) MK ▲ MKA 418014 [DDD]

Brahms, J.:Songs, w. D. Fischer–Dieskau (bar)—Op. 33 *(rec 1965)* Historical Performers ▲ HPS 1 [ADD]

Brahms, J.:Vars on a Theme by Paganini Philips ("Richter:The Authorized Recordings" series) 2–▲ 438477–2

Britten, H.:Introduction & Rondo alla burlesca & Mazurka elegiaca, w. B. Britten (pno)—No. 1 *(rec live, Aldeburgh 1967)* Music & Arts ▲ CD 709–1 [AAD]

Britten, H.:Lachrymae, w. Y. Bashmet (va) MK ▲ MKA 418015 [DDD]

Britten, H.:Son Vc, w. Natalia Gutman (vc) *(rec Kur- und Kongresszentrum, Rottach–Egern, July 12, 1992)* Live Classics ▲ LCL 641 [DDD]

Chopin, F.:Andante Spianato & Grande Polonaise, w. K. Kondrashin (cnd), London SO *(rec live, Royal Albert Hall 1961)* Intaglio ▲ INCD 707–1 [ADD]

Chopin, F.:Andante Spianato & Grande Polonaise, w. K. Kondrashin (cnd), London SO Historical Performers ▲ HP 13

Chopin, F.:Ballades Pno (comp)—Op. 23 Pyramid ▲ PYR 13507

Chopin, F.:Ballades Pno (comp) *(rec live, Czech Radio Broadcast, 1960)* Praga ▲ PR 254060

Chopin, F.:Ballades Pno (comp)—Op. 52 *(rec live, Budapest 2/8/58)* Memories 2–▲ HR 4436/37 [ADD]

Chopin, F.:Études (24)—Op. 10/1–3 & 12; Op. 25/5 & 6 *(rec live, Czech Radio Broadcast, 1960)* Praga ▲ PR 254060

Chopin, F.:Études (24) *(rec July, 1988)* Praga ▲ PR 254056

Chopin, F.:Études (24) RCA Red Seal ▲ 09026–61534–2 [DDD]

Chopin, F.:Nocturnes *(rec July, 1988)* Praga ▲ PR 254056

Chopin, F.:Pno Music (misc), w. K. Kondrashin (cnd), London SO—Scherzo in E, Op. 54; Polonaise Fant. No. 7, Op. 61; Waltzes No. 4, Op. 34; No. 13, Op. posth.; Etudes, Op. 25/7; Op. 10/1 & 12; Mazurkas, Op. 24/1–4 Historical Performers ▲ HP 13

Chopin, F.:Pno Music (misc)—Etude in c, Op. 10, No. 12; Prelude No. 15 in D♭ *(rec live, Salle Pleyel, Paris 11/7/80)* Pyramid 2–▲ PYR 13500/01 [ADD]

Chopin, F.:Polonaises—in c#, Op. 26/1; in A, Op. 40/1; in c, Op. 40/2 *(rec Konzerte St. Andreas, Seesen, 1992)* Live Classics ▲ 441

Chopin, F.:Polonaise–fant *(rec Bauerntheater Terofal, Schliersee, July 10, 1992)* Live Classics ▲ 431

Chopin, F.:Polonaise–fant *(rec July, 1988)* Praga ▲ PR 254056

Chopin, F.:Polonaise–fant *(rec Konzerte St. Andreas, Seesen, 1992)* Live Classics ▲ 441

Chopin, F.:Preludes, Op. 28—13 preludes *(rec live 2 & 3/79)* Olympia ▲ OCD 287 [DDD]

Chopin, F.:Rondos Pno & 4–Hands—Op. 5 Pyramid ▲ PYR 13507

Chopin, F.:Scherzos—No. 4, Op. 54 Olympia ▲ OLY 580 [ADD/DDD]

Chopin, F.:Scherzos Olympia 5–▲ OLY 5013 [DDD/ADD]

Chopin, F.:Scherzos *(rec July 1977)* Olympia ▲ OCD 338 [ADD]

Chopin, F.:Scherzos—No. 4 *(rec live, Prague, 1957)* Melodram ▲ MEL 18029 (m) [AAD]

Debussy, C.:En blanc et noir, w. B. Britten (pno) *(rec live, Aldeburgh 1967)* Music & Arts ▲ CD 709–1 [AAD]

Debussy, C.:L'Isle joyeuse *(rec Bauerntheater Terofal, Schliersee, July 10, 1992)* Live Classics ▲ 431

Debussy, C.:Preludes Pno (sels)—6 sels from Book 2 Stradivarius 2–▲ STV 33353 [DDD]

Debussy, C.:Preludes Pno (sels)—Book 1, Nos. 1–6,9 & 10 *(rec live, Budapest & London, 2/8/58 & 1968)* AS Disc ▲ AS[ADD

Debussy, C.:Preludes Pno (sels)—4 Preludes from Book 1 *(rec Oct 1961)* Vanguard Classics ▲ OVC 8076 [ADD]

Debussy, C.:Preludes Pno (sels)—Book 2 Pyramid ▲ PYR 13507

Dvořák, A.:Con Pno, w. V. Smetáček (cnd), Prague SO *(rec 1966)* Praga ▲ PR 250016

Dvořák, A.:Con Pno, w. V. Smetáček (cnd), Czech PO *(rec live, Prague 1964)* Melodram ▲ MEL 18029 (m) [AAD]

Dvořák, A.:Con Pno, w. K. Kondrashin (cnd), London SO *(rec 1961)* Intaglio ▲ ING 751 [ADD]

Dvořák, A.:Qnt Pno, Op. 5, w. Borodin String Quartet Philips ▲ 412429–2 [ADD]

Dvořák, A.:Qnt Pno, Op. 81, w. Borodin String Quartet Philips ▲ 412429–2 [ADD]

Franck, C.:Prélude, choral et fugue Monitor ▲ 72022–2

Franck, C.:Qnt Pno, w. Borodin String Quartet Philips ▲ 432142–2 [DDD]

Franck, C.:Son Vn, w. D. Oistrakh (vn) Vox Box 2–▲ CDX 5120

Gershwin, G.:Con Pno, w. C. Eschenbach (cnd), South German RSO Originals ▲ ORISH 810 [DDD]

Grieg, E.:Con Pno, Op. 16, w. K. Kondrashin (cnd), Moscow Philharmonic SO Praga ▲ PR 250 048

Grieg, E.:Con Pno, Op. 16, w. D. Oistrakh (cnd), Bergen SO *(rec 1968)* Intaglio ▲ ING 751 [ADD]

Grieg, E.:Lyric Pieces *(rec Bauerntheater Terofai, Schliersee, Germany, July 7, 1993)* Live Classics ▲ LCL 442 [DDD]

Grieg, E.:Lyric Pieces Stradivarius 2–▲ STV 33353 [DDD]

Handel, G.F.:Suites Hpd—Nos. 2, 3, 5 & 8 EMI Classics ("Doublefforte" series) 2–▲ CDFB 69337

INSTRUMENTALISTS 801

Richter, Sviatoslav (pno) (cont.)

Haydn, J.:Sons Pno—Nos. 24 & 52 Philips ("Richter:The Authorized Recordings" series) 2-▲ 438617-2
Haydn, J.:Sons Pno—Son. 39 in D, HXVI/24 *(rec Mar. 1985, Nov. 1966)* Praga ▲ PR 254025
Haydn, J.:Sons Pno—in c, H.XVI:20 *(rec Feb. 22, 1992)* Stradivarius ▲ STR 33343 [DDD]
Haydn, J.:Sons Pno—Son. in E♭, H.XVI/49 *(rec Oct 1961)* Vanguard Classics ▲ OVC 8076 [ADD]
Haydn, J.:Sons Pno—in A♭, H.XVI/46 *(rec Bauerntheater Terofal, Schliersee, July 10, 1992)* Live Classics ▲ 431
Haydn, J.:Sons Pno—No. 39 MK ▲ MKA 418014 [DDD]
Haydn, J.:Sons Pno—No. 39 in D, H.XVI/24 Olympia 5-▲ OLY 5013 [DDD/ADD]
Haydn, J.:Son Pno, H.XVII/6, "Andante with Vars" *(rec Feb. 22, 1992)* Stradivarius ▲ STR 33343 [DDD]
Hindemith, P.:Ludus Tonalis *(rec 1985)* Pyramid ▲ PYR 13497 [DDD]
Hindemith, P.:Sons Pno—No. 2 *(rec 1985)* Pyramid ▲ PYR 13497 [DDD]
Hindemith, P.:Sons Va & Pno, w. Yuri Bashmet (va)—Op. 11/4 (1919); Op. 25/4 (1922); Sonata (1939) MK ▲ MKA 418015 [DDD]
Hindemith, P.:Son in C Vn & Pno, w. Oleg Kagan (vn) *(rec Moscow, May 7, 1978)* Live Classics ▲ LCL 161 [ADD]
Hindemith, P.:Son in E Vn & Pno, w. Oleg Kagan (vn) *(rec Moscow, May 7, 1978)* Live Classics ▲ LCL 161 [ADD]
Hindemith, P.:Son Vn & Pno, Op. 11/1, w. Oleg Kagan (vn) *(rec Moscow, May 7, 1978)* Live Classics ▲ LCL 161 [ADD]
Hindemith, P.:Son Vn & Pno, Op. 11/2, w. Oleg Kagan (vn) *(rec Moscow, May 7, 1978)* Live Classics ▲ LCL 161 [ADD]
Liszt, F.:Cons Pno, w. K. Kondrashin (cnd), London SO Philips ("Insignia" series) ▲ 434163-2 [ADD]
Liszt, F.:Cons Pno, w. K. Kondrashin (cnd), London SO Fonit Cetra ("Fortissimo" series) ▲ FCT CDE 3012
Liszt, F.:Con 1 Pno, w. K. Kondrashin (cnd), London SO Philips ("Solo" series) ▲ 446200-2
Liszt, F.:Con 1 Pno, w. K. Ančerl (cnd), Czech PO Multisonic ▲ 31 0335
Liszt, F.:Con 1 Pno, w. K. Ančerl (cnd), Czech PO *(rec ca. 1954)* Multisonic ("Prague Spring Collection" series) ▲ 31 0038-2 [ADD]
Liszt, F.:Con 2 Pno, w. K. Kondrashin (cnd), London SO Philips ("Solo" series) ▲ 446200-2
Liszt, F.:Con 2 Pno, w. J. Ferencsik (cnd), Hungarian State Orch *(rec live, Hungarian Festival, 9/27/61)* Intaglio ▲ INCD 707-1 [ADD]
Liszt, F.:Con 2 Pno, w. J. Ferencsik (cnd), Hungarian State Orch *(rec 1961)* Music & Arts ▲ CD 760 [AAD]
Liszt, F.:Études d'exécution transcendante, S.139 *(rec Prague, 1956)* Praga ▲ PR 254057 (m)
Liszt, F.:Fant on Hungarian Folk Tunes, w. K. Kondrashin (cnd), London SO Fonit Cetra ("Fortissimo" series) ▲ FCT CDE 3012
Liszt, F.:Fant on Hungarian Folk Tunes, w. J. Ferencsik (cnd), Hungarian State Orch *(rec 1961)* Music & Arts ▲ CD 760 [AAD]
Liszt, F.:Pno Music (misc)—Consolation No. 6; Harmonies du soir; Hungarian Rhapsody No. 17; Scherzo & March *(rec live, Schleswig-Holstein Music Festival, 1988)* RCA Red Seal ▲ 09026-60859-2
Liszt, F.:Pno Music (misc)—Trancendental Etudes; Polonaise 2; Funerailles No. 7; Con 2 Pno; Hungarian Fant [both w. Hungarian State Orch] *(rec 1956-61)* Music & Arts ▲ MUA CD 945
Liszt, F.:Polonaises Pno—S.223/2 *(rec June 1956 & Sept. 1972)* Praga ▲ PR 254032
Liszt, F.:Son Pno, w. K. Kondrashin (cnd), London SO Philips ("Solo" series) ▲ 446200-2
Liszt, F.:Son Pno *(rec 1971)* Music & Arts ▲ CD 760 [AAD]
Liszt, F.:Son Pno *(rec live, Aldeburgh Festival, 1966)* Music & Arts ▲ CD 600 [AAD]
Liszt, F.:Son Pno *(rec live, 1966 & 1971)* Memories ▲ HR 4218 (m) [ADD]
Miaskovsky, N.:Sons Pno—No. 3 in c *(rec 1973)* Pyramid ▲ 13503 [ADD]
Mozart, W.A.:Allegro & Andante & Rondo Praga ▲ PR 254026
Mozart, W.A.:Allegro & Andante & Rondo Multisonic ▲ 31 0336
Mozart, W.A.:Allegro & Andante & Rondo *(rec live 1956)* Multisonic ("Prague Spring Collection" series) ▲ 31 0076-2 [ADD]
Mozart, W.A.:Con 9 Pno, w. L. Maazel (cnd), ORTF Orch *(rec 1965)* Historical Performers ▲ HPS 7 [ADD]
Mozart, W.A.:Con 17 Pno, w. E. Ormandy (cnd), Philadelphia Orch Stradivarius ▲ STV 33303
Mozart, W.A.:Con 17 Pno, w. E. Ormandy (cnd), Philadelphia Orch *(rec live, Philadelphia, Jan. 29, 1970)* Intaglio ▲ INCD 707-1 [ADD]
Mozart, W.A.:Con 22 Pno, w. B. Britten (cnd), English CO *(rec live, Aldeburgh, 1967)* Memories 2-▲ HR 4366/67 (m) [ADD]
Mozart, W.A.:Con 22 Pno, w. B. Britten (cnd), English CO *(rec 1967)* Music & Arts ▲ CD 761 [AAD]
Mozart, W.A.:Con 22 Pno, w. R. Muti (cnd), Philharmonia Orch EMI Classics ▲ CDM 64750
Mozart, W.A.:Con 24 Pno, w. R. Muti (cnd), Florence Maggio Musicale Orch Memories ▲ HR 4218 (m) [ADD]
Mozart, W.A.:Con 27 Pno, w. B. Britten (cnd), English CO *(rec 1965)* Historical Performers ▲ HPS 7 [ADD]
Mozart, W.A.:Con 27 Pno, w. B. Britten (cnd), English CO *(rec 1967)* Music & Arts ▲ CD 761 [AAD]
Mozart, W.A.:Fant Pno, K.475 *(rec Thürmer-Saal, Bochum, Germany, Oct. 21, 1992)* Live Classics ▲ LCL 422 [DDD]
Mozart, W.A.:Fant Pno, K.475 Philips ("Richter:The Authorized Recordings" series) 2-▲ 438480-2
Mozart, W.A.:Fant Pno, K.475 *(rec Oct. 2, 1991)* Stradivarius ▲ STR 33343 [DDD]
Mozart, W.A.:Son 2 Pno Philips ("Richter:The Authorized Recordings" series) 2-▲ 438480-2
Mozart, W.A.:Son 2 Pno *(rec Mar. 1985, Nov. 1966)* Praga ▲ PR 254025
Mozart, W.A.:Son 4 Pno Philips ("Digital Classics" series) ▲ 422583-2 [DDD]
Mozart, W.A.:Son 4 Pno *(rec Mar. 1985, Nov. 1966)* Praga ▲ PR 254025
Mozart, W.A.:Son 5 Pno *(rec live, Aldeburgh 1967)* Memories 2-▲ HR 4366/67 (m) [ADD]
Mozart, W.A.:Son 5 Pno *(rec in recital at the Aldeburgh Festival, 1966)* Music & Arts ▲ CD 600 [AAD]
Mozart, W.A.:Son 5 Pno Philips ("Richter:The Authorized Recordings" series) 2-▲ 438480-2
Mozart, W.A.:Son 7 Pno *(rec live, Prague 1968)* Memories 2-▲ HR 4366/67 (m) [ADD]
Mozart, W.A.:Son 8 Pno Philips ("Digital Classics" series) ▲ 422583-2 [DDD]
Mozart, W.A.:Son 8 Pno *(rec live 1956)* Multisonic ("Prague Spring Collection" series) ▲ 31 0076-2 [ADD]
Mozart, W.A.:Son 8 Pno Multisonic ▲ 31 0336
Mozart, W.A.:Son 8 Pno *(rec Mar. 1985, Nov. 1966)* Praga ▲ PR 254025
Mozart, W.A.:Son 13 Pno Praga ▲ PR 254026
Mozart, W.A.:Son 13 Pno Philips ("Richter:The Authorized Recordings" series) 2-▲ 438480-2
Mozart, W.A.:Son 14 Pno *(rec Thürmer-Saal, Bochum, Germany, Oct. 21, 1992)* Live Classics ▲ LCL 422 [DDD]
Mozart, W.A.:Son 14 Pno Stradivarius ▲ STV 33303
Mozart, W.A.:Son 14 Pno *(rec Oct. 2, 1991)* Stradivarius ▲ STR 33343 [DDD]
Mozart, W.A.:Son 14 Pno Philips ("Richter:The Authorized Recordings" series) 2-▲ 438480-2
Mozart, W.A.:Son 15 Pno *(rec live 1956)* Multisonic ("Prague Spring Collection" series) ▲ 31 0076-2 [ADD]
Mozart, W.A.:Son 15 Pno Multisonic ▲ 31 0336
Mozart, W.A.:Son 15 Pno Philips ("Digital Classics" series) ▲ 422583-2 [DDD]
Mozart, W.A.:Son 15 Pno Praga ▲ PR 254026
Mozart, W.A.:Son Pno 4-Hands, K.521, w. B. Britten (pno) *(rec live 1966)* Music & Arts ▲ CD 721-1 [AAD]
Mozart, W.A.:Son Pno 4-Hands, K.521, w. B. Britten (pno) *(rec live, Aldeburgh, 1967)* Memories 2-▲ HR 4366/67 (m) [ADD]
Mozart, W.A.:Son Pnos, K.448, w. B. Britten (pno) *(rec live, Aldeburgh, 1967)* Music & Arts ▲ CD 709-1 [AAD]
Mozart, W.A.:Sons Vn Pno (misc), w. Oleg Kagan (vn)—K.304-306 *(rec Small Room of the Conservatory, Moscow, May 16, 1975)* Live Classics ▲ LCL 122 [ADD]

Richter, Sviatoslav (pno) (cont.)

Mozart, W.A.:Sons Vn Pno (misc), w. Oleg Kagan (vn)—in B, K.372; in E♭, K.380; in C, K.403; in C, K.404; in B, K.454 *(rec Moscow, May 20, 1975)* Live Classics ("Kagan Edition" series) ▲ 123
Mozart, W.A.:Vars Pno, K.353 *(rec live, Prague 1968)* Memories 2-▲ HR 4366/67 (m) [ADD]
Mussorgsky, M.:Pictures at an Exhibition *(rec 1956)* Praga ▲ PR 254034
Mussorgsky, M.:Pictures at an Exhibition *(rec live, London, 11/68)* Memories 2-▲ HR 4436/37 [ADD]
Prokofiev, S.:Con 1 Pno, w. K. Ančerl (cnd), Prague SO *(rec 1954)* Supraphon ("Great Artists" series) ▲ 11 0268-2 (m) [AAD]
Prokofiev, S.:Con 5 Pno, w. W. Rowicki (cnd), Warsaw PO Deutsche Grammophon ▲ 415119-2 [ADD]
Prokofiev, S.:Con 5 Pno, w. L. Maazel (cnd), London SO EMI Classics ("Doublefforte" series) 2-▲ CDFB 68637
Prokofiev, S.:Pieces Pno, Op. 4—No. 4, "Suggestion diabolique" *(rec Oct 1961)* Vanguard Classics ▲ OVC 8076 [ADD]
Prokofiev, S.:Son Vc, w. Natalia Gutman (vc) *(rec Kur- und Kongresszentrum, Rottach-Egern, July 12, 1992)* Live Classics ▲ LCL 641 [DDD]
Prokofiev, S.:Son 2 Pno *(rec ca 1956-65)* Praga ▲ PR 250 015
Prokofiev, S.:Son 6 Pno *(rec live, Locarno 1966)* Ermitage ▲ ERM 113 [ADD]
Prokofiev, S.:Son 6 Pno Praga ▲ PR 250 015
Prokofiev, S.:Son 8 Pno *(rec 1973)* Pyramid ▲ 13503 [ADD]
Prokofiev, S.:Son 9 Pno Praga ▲ PR 250 015
Rachmaninoff, S.:Con 2 Pno, w. S. Wislocki (cnd), Warsaw PO Deutsche Grammophon ▲ 415119-2 [ADD]
Rachmaninoff, S.:Études-tableaux, Opp. 33 & 39 Olympia 5-▲ OLY 5013 [DDD/ADD]
Rachmaninoff, S.:Études-tableaux, Opp. 33 & 39 *(rec 1984)* Praga ▲ PR 254034
Rachmaninoff, S.:Preludes Pno, Opp 23 & 32—6 sels from Op. 23; 7 sels from Op. 32 Olympia 5-▲ OLY 5013 [DDD/ADD]
Rachmaninoff, S.:Preludes Pno, Opp 23 & 32—3 sels from Op. 23 Olympia ▲ OLY 580 [ADD/DDD]
Ravel, M.:Miroirs *(rec Prague, 1965)* Praga ▲ PR 254057 (m)
Ravel, M.:Valses nobles et sentimentales *(rec Prague, 1965)* Praga ▲ PR 254057 (m)
Saint-Saëns, C.:Son 1 Vc, w. N. Gutman (vc) *(rec Kur- und Kongresszentrum, Rottach-Egern, July 12, 1992)* Live Classics ▲ LCL 641 [DDD]
Schubert, Franz:Divertissement sur des motifs originaux français, D.823, w. B. Britten (pno)—Andantino varié [movt No. 2] *(rec live 1965)* Music & Arts ▲ CD 722-1
Schubert, Franz:Fant Pno, D.940, w. B. Britten (pno) *(rec live 1965)* Music & Arts ▲ CD 722-1
Schubert, Franz:Impromptus Pno (comp) Monitor ■ 55012
Schubert, Franz:Impromptus Pno, D.899—Nos. 2 & 4 in E♭ & A♭ Olympia ▲ OLY 288 [DDD]
Schubert, Franz:Impromptus Pno, D.899—No. 3 in G♭ *(rec June 1956 & Sept. 1972)* Praga ▲ PR 254032
Schubert, Franz:Moments musicaux—Nos. 1,3 & 6 *(rec live)* Olympia ▲ OLY 286 [DDD]
Schubert, Franz:Moments musicaux—3 sels. *(rec live 1965)* Music & Arts ▲ CD 722-1
Schubert, Franz:Pno Music (misc)—Son. in C Monitor ■ 55008
Schubert, Franz:Son Pno 4-Hands, D.812, w. B. Britten (pno) *(rec live 1965)* Music & Arts ▲ CD 721-1 [AAD]
Schubert, Franz:Son Pno, D.566 *(rec live, Aldeburgh Festival, 1964)* Music & Arts ▲ CD 642 (m/s) [ADD]
Schubert, Franz:Son Pno, D.566 *(rec 1964)* Historical Performers ▲ HPS 10 [ADD]
Schubert, Franz:Son Pno, D.575 *(rec live, Aldeburgh Festival, 1966)* Music & Arts ▲ CD 600 [AAD]
Schubert, Franz:Son Pno, D.575 *(rec live)* Olympia ▲ OLY 286 [DDD]
Schubert, Franz:Son Pno, D.625 *(rec live)* Olympia ▲ OLY 286 [DDD]
Schubert, Franz:Son Pno, D.625 Olympia ▲ OLY 580 [ADD/DDD]
Schubert, Franz:Son Pno, D.664 Olympia ▲ OLY 288 [DDD]
Schubert, Franz:Son Pno, D.784 Olympia ▲ OLY 288 [DDD]
Schubert, Franz:Son Pno, D.840 Monitor ■ 55008
Schubert, Franz:Son Pno, D.845 Monitor ■ 55012 (m)
Schubert, Franz:Son Pno, D.850 *(rec May 1954 & June 1956)* Praga ▲ PR 254031
Schubert, Franz:Son Pno, D.958 *(rec 1958)* Historical Performers ▲ HPS 10 [ADD]
Schubert, Franz:Son Pno, D.958 *(rec live, Budapest, 2/8/58)* Memories 2-▲ HR 4436/37 [ADD]
Schubert, Franz:Son Pno, D.958 *(rec 1972-73)* Olympia ▲ OLY 335 [ADD]
Schubert, Franz:Son Pno, D.960 *(rec 1972-73)* Olympia ▲ OLY 335 [ADD]
Schubert, Franz:Son Pno, D.960 *(rec June 1956 & Sept. 1972)* Praga ▲ PR 254032
Schubert, Franz:Son Pno, D.960 *(rec live, Aldeburgh Festival, 1964)* Music & Arts ▲ CD 642 (m/s) [ADD]
Schubert, Franz:Vars Pno, D.576 *(rec 1969)* Historical Performers ▲ HPS 10 [ADD]
Schubert, Franz:Vars on an Original Theme Pno 4-Hands, w. B. Britten (pno) *(rec live 1964)* Music & Arts ▲ CD 722-1
Schumann, R.:Bilder aus Osten, w. B. Britten (pno) *(rec live 1966, Aldeburgh)* Music & Arts ▲ CD 709-1 [AAD]
Schumann, R.:Bunte Blätter Olympia 5-▲ OLY 5013 [DDD/ADD]
Schumann, R.:Bunte Blätter *(rec Sept. 1977)* Olympia ▲ OLY 338 [ADD]
Schumann, R.:Con Pno, w. A. Gauk (cnd), Moscow RSO Multisonic ▲ MUL 310268
Schumann, R.:Con Pno, w. W. Rowicki (cnd), Warsaw PO *(rec National Philharmonic, Warsaw, Oct 1958)* Deutsche Grammophon ("The Originals" series) ▲ 447440-2 [ADD]
Schumann, R.:Fant Pno EMI Classics ▲ CDM 64625
Schumann, R.:Fant Pno *(rec live 1957)* Multisonic ("Prague Spring Collection" series) ▲ 31 0193 [ADD]
Schumann, R.:Fant Pno Philips ("Richter:The Authorized Recordings" series) 2-▲ 438477-2
Schumann, R.:Fant Pno Praga ▲ PR 254033
Schumann, R.:Fantasiestücke Pno, Op. 12—6 selections *(rec 1950s)* Deutsche Grammophon ("Dokumente" series) ▲ 435751-2 [ADD]
Schumann, R.:Fantasiestücke Pno, Op. 12 Monitor ▲ 72022-2
Schumann, R.:Fantasiestücke Pno, Op. 12 *(rec live 1979)* Olympia ▲ OCD 287 [DDD]
Schumann, R.:Faschingsschwank aus Wien EMI Classics ▲ CDM 64625
Schumann, R.:Humoreske Pno Monitor ▲ 72022-2
Schumann, R.:Intro & Allegro, Op. 134, w. S. Wislocki (cnd), Warsaw PO *(rec National Philharmonic, Warsaw, Apr 1959)* Deutsche Grammophon ("The Originals" series) ▲ 447440-2 [ADD]
Schumann, R.:Marches Pno—No. 2 *(rec 1950s)* Deutsche Grammophon ("Dokumente" series) ▲ 435751-2 [ADD]
Schumann, R.:Novelettes—No. 1 *(rec 1950s)* Deutsche Grammophon ("Dokumente" series) ▲ 435751-2 [ADD]
Schumann, R.:Novelettes—No. 1 only *(rec National Philharmonic, Warsaw, May 1959)* Deutsche Grammophon ("The Originals" series) ▲ 447440-2 [ADD]
Schumann, R.:Novelettes *(rec live 1979)* Olympia ▲ OCD 287 [DDD]
Schumann, R.:Novelettes Olympia ▲ OLY 580 [ADD/DDD]
Schumann, R.:Papillons EMI Classics ▲ CDM 64625
Schumann, R.:Sym Etudes *(rec 1971)* Olympia ▲ OLY 339 [ADD]
Schumann, R.:Sym Etudes Olympia 5-▲ OLY 5013 [DDD/ADD]
Schumann, R.:Sym Etudes *(rec live, London, 10/20/68)* Memories 2-▲ HR 4436/37 [ADD]
Schumann, R.:Sym Etudes Praga ▲ PR 254033
Schumann, R.:Toccata Pno *(rec National Philharmonic, Warsaw, Apr & May 1959)* Deutsche Grammophon ("The Originals" series) ▲ 447440-2 [ADD]
Schumann, R.:Waldscenen *(rec Rudolfinum, Main Room, Prague, Nov 1956)* Deutsche Grammophon ("The Originals" series) ▲ 447440-2 [ADD]
Scriabin, A.:Dances Pno *(rec Konzerte St. Andreas, Seesen, 1992)* Live Classics ▲ 441
Scriabin, A.:Etudes Pno, Op. 42—6 sels *(rec Oct 27, 1972)* Music & Arts ▲ CD 878 [ADD]
Scriabin, A.:Fant Pno *(rec Konzerte St. Andreas, Seesen, 1992)* Live Classics ▲ 441
Scriabin, A.:Mazurkas Pno, Op. 40 *(rec Bauerntheater Terofal, Schliersee, July 10, 1992)* Live Classics ▲ 431

▲ = CD ♦ = Enhanced CD Δ = MD ■ = Cassette Tape □ = DCC

Richter, Sviatoslav (pno) (cont.)
Scriabin, A.:Pno Music (misc)—24 Preludes (from Opp. 11, 13, 37, 39, 59, 74); 6 Etudes (Op. 42, Nos. 2–6 & 8); Poème in D, Op. 52/1 *(rec live, Warsaw, 10/27/72)* Arkadia ▲ 910 [ADD]
Scriabin, A.:Pieces Pno, Op. 52—No. 1 *(rec Oct 27, 1972)* Music & Arts ▲ CD 878 [ADD]
Scriabin, A.:Poème-nocturne Pno *(rec Konzerte St. Andreas, Seesen, 1992)* Live Classics ▲ 441
Scriabin, A.:Preludes Pno (misc)—24 preludes from Opp. 11, 13, 37, 39, 59 & 74 *(rec Oct 27, 1972)* Music & Arts ▲ CD 878 [ADD]
Scriabin, A.:Son 2 Pno *(rec live, Warsaw, 10/27/72)* Arkadia ▲ 910 [ADD]
Scriabin, A.:Son 2 Pno *(rec Oct 27, 1972)* Music & Arts ▲ CD 878 [ADD]
Scriabin, A.:Son 2 Pno *(rec Sep.–Oct., 1972)* Praga ▲ PR 254056
Scriabin, A.:Son 5 Pno *(rec live, Warsaw, 10/27/72)* Arkadia ▲ 910 [ADD]
Scriabin, A.:Son 5 Pno *(rec Oct 27, 1972)* Music & Arts ▲ CD 878 [ADD]
Scriabin, A.:Son 5 Pno *(rec Sep.–Oct., 1972)* Praga ▲ PR 254056
Scriabin, A.:Son 9 Pno *(rec live, Warsaw, 10/27/72)* Arkadia ▲ 910 [ADD]
Scriabin, A.:Son 9 Pno *(rec Oct 27, 1972)* Music & Arts ▲ CD 878 [ADD]
Scriabin, A.:Sym 5, w. E. Svetlanov (cnd), USSR SO *(rec live April 12, 1988)* Russian Disc ▲ RC CD 11 058 [AAD]
Scriabin, A.:Vers la flamme *(rec Konzerte St. Andreas, Seesen, 1992)* Live Classics ▲ 441
Shostakovich, D.:Preludes & Fugues Pno *(rec 1973)* Pyramid ▲ 13503 [ADD]
Shostakovich, D.:Qnt Pno, w. Borodin String Quartet *(rec July 17, 1966)* Intaglio ▲ ING 7561 [ADD]
Shostakovich, D.:Son Va, w. Y. Bashmet (va) MK ▲ MKA 418015 [DDD]
Shostakovich, D.:Son Vn, w. O. Kagan (vn) MK ▲ MKA 418014 [DDD]
Shostakovich, D.:Son Vn, w. Oleg Kagan (vn) Olympia 5–▲ OLY 5013 [DDD/ADD]
Shostakovich, D.:Son Vn, w. D. Oistrakh (vn) Vox Box 2–▲ CDX 5120
Tchaikovsky, P.:Con 1 Pno, w. K. Ançerl (cnd), Czech PO *(rec 1954)* Music & Arts ▲ CD 776 [AAD]
Tchaikovsky, P.:Con 1 Pno, w. K. Ancerl (cnd), Czech PO Supraphon 3–▲ SUP 0546 [AAD]
Tchaikovsky, P.:Con 1 Pno, w. K. Ancerl (cnd), Czech PO *(rec 1953)* Supraphon ("Great Artists" series) ▲ 11 0268–2 (m) [AAD]
Tchaikovsky, P.:Morceaux, Op. 51—No. 1 Olympia ▲ OLY 580 [ADD/DDD]
Tchaikovsky, P.:Pno Music—Nocturne in F, Op. 10/1; Waltz-Scherzo in a, Op. 7; Humoresque in F, Op. 10/2; Capriccioso in B♭, Op. 19/5; Chanson triste, Op. 40/8; Romance in f, Op. 5; Romance in F, Op. 51/5; Un poco di Chopin, Op. 77/15; L'espiegle, Op. 72/12; Reverie du soir, Op. 19/1; Menuetto scherzoso, Op. 51/3; Valse de salon, Op. 51/1; Meditation, Op. 72/5; from The Seasons, Op. 37 *(rec 1983)* Olympia ▲ OLY 334 [DDD]
Tchaikovsky, P.:Les Saisons—June Olympia ▲ OLY 580 [ADD/DDD]
Weber, C.M. von:Sons Pno—No. 3 *(rec live, Locarno, 1966)* Ermitage ▲ ERM 113 [ADD]
Weber, C.M. von:Sons Pno—No. 3 *(rec May 1954 & June 1956)* Praga ▲ PR 254031
Weber, C.M. von:Son 3 Pno Philips ("Richter:The Authorized Recordings" series) 2–▲ 438617–2
Wolf, H.:Mörike-Lieder (sels), w. Dietrich Fischer-Dieskau (bar)—26 sels Music & Arts ▲ CD 870

Richter-Haaser, Hans (pno)
Beethoven, L. van:Con 5 Pno, "Emperor", w. K. Sanderling (cnd), Danish National RSO *(rec live, October 1980)* Kontrapunkt 2–▲ 32020/21 [ADD]
Beethoven, L. van:Son 26 Pno, "Les Adieux" Royal Classics ▲ ROY 6437
Brahms, J.:Con 1 Pno, w. K. Sanderling (cnd), Danish National RSO *(rec live, March 1979)* Kontrapunkt 2–▲ 32020/21 [ADD]
Brahms, J.:Con 2 Pno, w. H. von Karajan (cnd), Berlin PO Royal Classics ▲ ROY 6437

Richtmeyer, Debra (a sax/s sax)
Melby, J.:Alto Rhap, w. Taimur Sullivan (sax), Paul Martin Zonn (cl), Wilma Zonn (ob) Zuma ▲ ZMA 105
Melby, J.:Con Cl & Tape, w. Paul Martin Zonn (cl), Taimur Sullivan (sax), Wilma Zonn (ob) Zuma ▲ ZMA 105
Zonn, P.M.:Cloning of Wilma Zonn Ww, w. Paul Martin Zonn (cl), Wilma Zonn (ob), Taimur Sullivan (sax) Zuma ▲ ZMA 105
Zonn, P.M.:Nimbus III Saxes Zuma ▲ ZMA 105 [DDD]
Zonn, P.M.:Nimbus III Ww, w. Paul Martin Zonn (cl), Wilma Zonn (ob), Taimur Sullivan (sax) Zuma ▲ ZMA 105
Zonn, P.M.:Shadow of the Condor Ww, w. Paul Martin Zonn (cl), Wilma Zonn (ob), Taimur Sullivan (sax) Zuma ▲ ZMA 105

Ricken, Johannes (org)
Silbermann's Organ at the Cathedral of Dresden *(rec May 15, 1992)* Motette ▲ MOD 11911 [DDD]

Riddell, Duncan (vn)
Martin, F.:Maria-Triptychon, w. Lynda Russell (sop), M. Bamert (cnd), London PO Chandos ▲ CHAN 9411 [DDD]

Riddle, Frederick (va)
Vaughan Williams, R.:Flos Campi, w. N. del Mar (cnd), Bournemouth Sinfonietta, Bournemouth Chorus Chandos ("Collect" series) ▲ CHAN 6545 [ADD]
Vaughan Williams, R.:Suite Va, w. N. del Mar (cnd), Bournemouth Sinfonietta Chandos ("Collect" series) ▲ CHAN 6545 [ADD]
Walton, W.:Con Va, w. W. Walton (cnd), London SO *(rec Dec. 6, 1937)* Dutton Laboratories ▲ CDAX 8003 [ADD]

Ridell, (fl)
Dreyfus, G.:Trio Fl, w. Swift (cl), G. Dreyfus (bn) Move ▲ MD 3071
Weiss, A.:Petite suite Fl, w. Swift (cl), G. Dreyfus (bn) Move ▲ MD 3071

Ridenour, T. (cl)
Lucier, A.:In Memoriam Jon Higgins Lovely Music ▲ LCD 1018 [ADD]

Rider, Rhonda (va)
Hyla, L.:The Dream of Innocent III, w. Lee Hyla (pno), James Pugliese (perc) CRI ▲ CD 564 [DDD]

Rider, Rhonda (vc)—see also ORCHESTRAS & ENSEMBLES Lydian String Quartet
Barber, S.:Son Vc, w. Lois Shapiro (pno) *(rec Campion Center, Weston, MA, Aug 3–4, 1993)* Centaur ▲ CRC 2267 [DDD]
Berger, A.:Duos, w. D. Kopp (pno)—Duo for Cello & Piano (1951) CRI ▲ CD 564 [DDD]
Carter, E.:Son Vc, w. Lois Shapiro (pno) *(rec Campion Center, Weston, MA, Aug 3–4, 1993)* Centaur ▲ CRC 2267 [DDD]
Mackey, S.:Rhondo Vars CRI ▲ CD 564 [DDD]
Martino, D.:Parisonatina al'dodecafonia CRI ▲ CD 564 [DDD]
Martino, D.:Suite of Vars on Medieval Melodies CRI ▲ CD 564 [DDD]
Shifrin, S.:Son Vc, w. Lois Shapiro (pno) *(rec Campion Center, Weston, MA, Aug 3–4, 1993)* Centaur ▲ CRC 2267 [DDD]
Webern, A.:Little Pieces Vc, w. R. Rider, D. Kopp CRI ▲ CD 564 [DDD]
Webern, A.:Pieces Vc, w. D. Kopp (pno) CRI ▲ CD 564 [DDD]
Webern, A.:Son Vc, w. R. Rider, D. Kopp CRI ▲ CD 564 [DDD]

Ridgway, Judith (pno)
Britten, H.:Canticles I–V, w. P. Esswood (ct), J. Griffett (ten), T. Walker (gtr)—Canticle II IMP Masters ▲ IMPMCD 57 [DDD]
Britten, H.:Folksong Arrs, w. P. Esswood (ct), J. Griffett (ten), T. Walker (gtr) IMP Masters ▲ IMPMCD 57 [DDD]

Rieber, Jean (va)
Fuchs, R.:Qt Pno, w. K. Schilde (pno), K. Heymann (vn), U. Bode (vc) MD + G ▲ L 3165
Mahler, G.:Qt Pno [1 movt], w. K. Schilde (pno), K. Heymann (vn), U. Bode (vc) MD + G ▲ L 3165

Riedlbauch, Jan (fl)—see also ORCHESTRAS & ENSEMBLES Prague Wind Quintet
Martinů, B.:Sxt Fl, Ob, Cl, 2 Bns & Pno, w. Jurij Likin (ob), Vlastimil Mareš (cl), Lumír Vanek (bn), Svatopluk Čech (bn), Ivan Klánský (pno) *(rec Studio Martínek, Prague, Mar 3, 1995)* Panton ("Protokol XX" series) ▲ 811348–2 [DDD]

Riedlbauch, Jan (fl/pic)
Janácek, L.:Capriccio, w. Daniel Wiesner (pno), Vladislav Kozderka (tpt), Jan Fišer (tpt), Václav Ferebauer (trbn), Jan Hynčica (trbn), Antonin Keller (trbn), Jiří Novotny (ten tuba), L. Svárovský (cnd) *(rec Martinek Studio in Prague)* Panton ▲ 811393–2 [DDD]

Riedo, Paul (org)
Music for Ceremony & Celebration, w. Richard Giangiulio (tpt), Dallas Sym Trumpets Crystal ▲ CD234

Riedo, Paul (org) (cont.)
Music for Festive Occasions, w. Richard Giangiulio (tpt) Crystal ▲ CD 232 [DDD] ■ C 232 (D)
Pistons & Pipes, w. Richard Giangiulio (tpt) Crystal ▲ CD 666
Pomp & Pipes, w. Paul Riedo (org), Dallas Wind Sym [cnd:F. Fennell] *(rec July 26–27, 1993)* Reference ▲ RR 58 [DDD]
Roman, J.H.:Drottningholmsmusiquen Suite, w. R. Giangiulio (tpt) Crystal ▲ CD234

Riefling, Robert (pno)
Grieg, E.:Ballade Pno NKF ▲ NKF 50029
Grieg, E.:Norwegian Peasant Dances, Op. 72 NKF ▲ NKF 50029
Grieg, E.:Son Pno NKF ▲ NKF 50029
Valen, F.:Pno Music—Legende, Op. 1 (1907); Sonata No. 1, Op. 2 (1910–12); Four Piano Pieces, Op. 22 (1934–5); Variations, Op. 23 (1935–6); Gavotte & Musette, Op. 24 (1936); Prelude & Fugue, Op. 28 (1937); Two Preludes, Op. 29 (1937); Intermezzo, Op. 36 (1939–40); Sonata No. 2, Op. 38 (1940) *(rec 1980)* BIS 2–▲ CD 173/74 [AAD]

Riegelbauer, Peter (db)
Mozart, W.A.:Qt Pno, K.478, w. Alfred Brendel (pno), Thomas Zehetmair (vn), Tabea Zimmermann (va), Richard Duven (vc) Philips ▲ 446001–2
Schubert, Franz:Qnt Pno, D.667, w. Alfred Brendel (pno), Thomas Zehetmair (vn), Tabea Zimmermann (va), Richard Duven (vc) Philips ▲ 446001–2

Rieger, Frederick (pno)—see also ORCHESTRAS & ENSEMBLES Menuhin Festival Piano Quartet
Bach, J.S.:Con for 4 Hpds, w. Rudolf Kempe (pno), Wolfgang Sawallisch (pno), Rafael Kubelík (pno), R. Kubelik (cnd), Bavarian RSO *(rec 1972)* Arkadia ▲ 494
Blumer, T.:The Animal Kingdom, w. C. Francesconi (fl) Ars Produktion ▲ FCD 368306 [DDD]
Blumer, T.:From Floral Realm, w. C. Francesconi (fl) Ars Produktion ▲ FCD 368306 [DDD]
Brahms, J.:Son 2 Cl, w. P. Coletti (va) Ars Produktion ▲ FCD 368308 [DDD]
Debussy, C.:Son Vn, w. N. Chastain (vn) Ars Produktion ▲ FCD 368311 [DDD]
Fauré, G.:Son 1 Vn, w. N. Chastain (vn) Ars Produktion ▲ FCD 368311 [DDD]
Guastavino, C.:Intro & Allegro, w. C. Francesconi (fl) Ars Produktion ▲ FCD 368306 [DDD]
Herzogenberg, H. von:Legenden, w. P. Coletti (va) Ars Produktion ▲ FCD 368308 [DDD]
Hindemith, P.:The Four Temperaments, w. R. Bohn (cnd), Sinfonietta Tübingen Ars Produktion ▲ ARS 368319 [DDD]
Honegger, A.:Sons Vn, w. N. Chastain (vn)—Sonata No. 1 for Violin & Piano (1916–18) Ars Produktion ▲ FCD 368311 [DDD]
Komma, K.M.:Lauda, w. C. Francesconi (fl) Ars Produktion ▲ FCD 368306 [DDD]
Komma, K.M.:Threnos, w. C. Francesconi (fl) Ars Produktion ▲ FCD 368306 [DDD]
Schumann, R.:Märchenbilder, w. P. Coletti (va) Ars Produktion ▲ FCD 368308 [DDD]
Turina, J.:Escena andaluza, w. P. Coletti (va), N. Chastain (vn), C. Busch (vn), A. B. Deutschler (va), F. Goutou (vc) *(rec May 25–28, 1993)* Claves ▲ CD 9403 [DDD]

Rieger, Wolfram (pno)
Schoeck, O.:Der Sänger, w. Kurt Streit (ten) *(rec Pere Casulleras, Christine Rosse, CH–Waldenburg, Apr, 1995)* Jecklin ▲ JD 679–2 [DDD]
Schoeck, O.:Songs (comp), w. J. Banse (sop), D. Henschel (ten)—Wandsbecker Liederbuch, Op. 52; Im Nebel, Op. 45; 6 Lieder, Op. 51; 3 Lieder, Op. 35 *(rec May 1991)* Jecklin ▲ JD 677–2 [DDD]
Schoeck, O.:Songs (comp), w. Christine Schäfer (sop)—Scheiden und Meiden; Auf den Tod eines Kindes [both from Op. 3]; An die Entfernte; Frühlingsblick [both from Op. 5]; In der Fremde; Erster Verlust [both from Op. 15]; Im Sommer; Gekommen ist der Maie; Erinnerung; Der frohe Wandersmann [all from Op. 17]; An einem heitern Morgen; Dichtersegen; Wein und Brot; Der Gärtner; Nachtlied [all from Op. 20]; 6 Lieder, Op. 6; 2 Lieder, Op. 12 *(rec Sept 1995)* Jecklin ▲ JD 671
Schoeck, O.:Songs (comp), w. Juliane Banse (sop), Dietrich Henschel (bar)—3 Songs, Op. 4; 4 Songs, Op. 8; Vorwurf, Op. 27; 3 Songs, Op. 10; 3 Songs, Op. 13; Lieder nach Gedichten von Goethe, Op. 19a; Lieder aus dem "Westöstlichen Divan" von Goethe, Op. 19b *(rec Feb 1994)* Jecklin ▲ JD 675

Rieker, Martin (org)
Bach, J.S.:Music of, w. Brassissimo Vienna—Brandenburg Con No. 2, BWV 1047; Bourreé [from English Suite No. 2, BWV 807]; Wie sich ein Vater erbarmet; Lobet den Herrn [both from Psalm 150, BWV 225]; Rondeau; Badinerie [both from Suite No. 1 for Orch, BWV 1067]; Ertöt uns durch dein Güte, BWV 22; Nun danket alle Gott, BWV 79; Was Gott tut, das ist wohlgetan, BWV 75; Air [from Suite No. 3 for Orch, BWV 1068]; Wie will ich mich freuen, BWV 146; Wachet auf, ruft uns die Stimme, BWV 645; Halleluja [from Lobet den Herrn, alle Heiden, BWV 230]; Italian Con No. 1, BWV 971; Contrapunctus I & IX [from Art of the Fugue, BWV 1080]; Grosser Herr und starker König; Kommst du nun, Jesu, vom Himmel herunter, BWV 650; Jesu bleibet meine Freude, BWV 147; Ov [from Nun komm der Heiden Heiland, BWV 61]; Ach, mein herzliebstes Jesulein; Nun seid ihr wohl gerochen *(rec Halle, Germany, Sept 1–4, 1994)* Brassissimo ▲ BVR 2572775 [DDD]

Riemann, A. (pno)
Tchaikovsky, P.:Songs, w. J. Varady (sop)—Songs, Opp. 65 & 73 Orfeo ▲ 053851

Ries, H. (trbn)
Guyonnet, J.:La Cantate interrompue, w. F. Rochaix (nar), S. Stenhammar (sop), S. Seban (pno), G. Calame (pno), E. Séjourne (perc), P. Geiss, E. Tarr (tpt), B. Nilsson (tpt), H. Rückert (trbn), J.–M. Collet, J. Guyonnet (cnd), Geneva Collogium Academicum [F] *(rec Nov. 15, 1986)* Grammont ▲ CTSP 30–2

Riesman, Michael (kbd)—see ORCHESTRAS & ENSEMBLES Philip Glass Ensemble

Riesman, Michael (org)
Glass, Philip:Dances (5), w. P. Glass (org), Philip Glass Ensemble CBS 2–▲ M2K 44765 [ADD]

Riessler, Michael (cl)
Curran, A.:Crystal Psalms, An Homage to Kristallnacht, w. F. Badaloni (cl), D. Keberlee (cl), A. Santoloci (cl), M. Capone (acc), L. Dublanchet (tuba), D. Rueff (tuba), A. Caggiano (perc), w. Ensemble Vocale Sesquialtera [cnd:E. Razzicchia], Radio France Chamber Choir [cnd:D. LaBorde]—[F] New Albion ▲ NA 067
Kagel, M.:Rrrrrrr... Cl, Vn & Pno, w. G. Wharton (vn), K. Becker (pno) Montaigne ▲ MO 782003 [DDD]

Riessler, Michael (cl/sax)
Kagel, M.:Blue's Blue:A Musico-Ethnological Reconstruction, w. M. Kagel (voice/glass tpt), T. Ross (gtr), G. Wharton (vn) Montaigne ▲ MO 782003 [DDD]

Riessler, Michael (sax)
Kagel, M.:Zwei Akte:Grand Duo, w. B. Sylvestre (hp) Montaigne ▲ MO 782003 [DDD]

Riet, Gaby van (fl)
Benoit, P.:Symphonic Poem Fl, w. S. van den Broeck (cnd), New Flemish SO René Gailly ▲ CD 87026 [DDD]
Benoit, P.:Symphonic Poem Fl, w. F. Devreese (cnd), Royal Flanders PO *(rec Elisabeth Hall, Antwerp, Belgium, Apr 1995)* Marco Polo ("Anthology of Flemish Music" series) ▲ 8.223827 [DDD]
Fétis, F.J.:Con Fl, w. S. van den Broeck (cnd), New Flemish SO René Gailly ▲ CD 87026 [DDD]
Honegger, A.:Con da camera, w. L. Lencsés (E hn), V. Czarnecki (cnd), Southwest German CO Pforzheim CPO ▲ CPO 999193–2 [ADD/DDD]
Waelput, H.:Con symphonique, w. S. van den Broeck (cnd), New Flemish SO René Gailly ▲ CD 87026 [DDD]

Rieu, André (vn)
The Vienna I Love, w. Johann Strauss Orch [cnd:André Rieu] Philips ▲ 314–528786–2 ■ 314–528786–4

Rieunier, Françoise (org)
Boucourechliev, A.:Les Archipels, w. Brigitte Sylvestre (hp), Elisabeth Chojnacka (hpd), Roland Auzet, Jean-Pierre Drouet (perc), Hakon Austbö (pno), Françoise-Frédéric Guy (pno), Claude Helffer (pno), Georges Pludermacher (pno), Ysaÿe String Quartet, Les Pléiades Ensemble Musique Francaise d'Aujourd'hui ("Collection MFA–Radio France" series) ▲ MFA 216001

Rifas, Helen (hp)
Harrison, L.:Music for Vn, w. William Bouton (vn), Richard Dee (cheng), William Colvig (sheng/fang-hsiang), Lou Harrison (piri) Phoenix ▲ PHCD 118 [AAD]

Riffault, P. (hn)—see ORCHESTRAS & ENSEMBLES Stanislas Ensemble

Rifkin, Joshua (pno)
Joplin, S.:Pno Music—The Easy Winners; The Entertainer; Magnetic Rag; Maple Leaf Rag; Paragon Rag; Pine Apple Rag EMI Classics ▲ CDM 64668–2 [ADD/DDD] ■ EG 64668–4

Rifkin, Joshua (pno) (cont.)
Joplin, S.:Pno Music—Maple Leaf Rag; The Entertainer; The Ragtime Dance; Gladiolus Rag; Fig Leaf Rag; Scott Joplin's New Rag; Euphonic Sounds; Elite Syncopations; Bethena; Paragon Rag; Solace; Pine Apple Rag; Weeping Willow; The Cascades; Country Club; Stoptime Rag; Magnetic Rag *(rec Sept. 1970, Jan. 1972)* Elektra/Nonesuch ▲ 979159-2 [AAD]

Rigacci, P. (pno)
Schumann, R.:Fantasiestücke Pno, Op. 12 Fonè ▲ 86F01-7 [ADD]
Schumann, R.:Faschingsschwank aus Wien Fonè ▲ 86F01-7 [ADD]

Rigai, Amiram (pno)
Gottschalk, L.M.:Pno Music—The Dying Poet; Tournament Galop; Bamboula, Op. 2; Ossian Ballade, Op. 4/1; Le bananier, Op. 5; Serenade, Op. 11; The Banjo, Op. 15; La scintilla (mazurka), Op. 20; Minuit à Seville, Op. 30; Souvenir de Puerto Rico, Op. 31; Danza, Op. 33; Ojos criollos, Op. 37; Berceuse, Op. 47; La gallina, Op. 53; Pasquinade, Op. 59; Morte, Op. 60; Marche funèbre, Op. 64 *(11 sels. originally issued in 1979 on Folkways 37485; 6 sels. newly recorded in 1991)* Smithsonian/Folkways ▲ SF 40803 [AAD]

Rigal, Joël (pno)
Mozart, W.A.:Adagio & Fugue Strs, w. N. Palmier (pno)—Adagio Arion ▲ ARN 68028 [DDD]
Mozart, W.A.:Fugue Pnos, K.426, w. N. Palmier (pno) Arion ▲ ARN 68028 [DDD]
Mozart, W.A.:Pno Music, w. N. Palmier (pno)—2 son. movts. in B♭, Allegro in c & Fugue in G, K.Anh.42–45; Larghetto & Allegro in E♭ [arr. P. Badura-Skoda for 2 pianos, 1781] Arion ▲ ARN 68028 [DDD]
Mozart, W.A.:Son Pno 4-Hands, K.19d, w. N. Palmier (pno) Arion ▲ ARN 68028 [DDD]
Mozart, W.A.:Son Pnos, K.448, w. N. Palmier (pno) Arion ▲ ARN 68028 [DDD]

Rigell, Nella (hp)
Adams, J.L.:Night Peace, w. C. Bray Lower (sop), M. Cebulski (perc) *(rec Sept. 1992)* New Albion ▲ NA 061
Tomorrow Shall Be My Dancing Day:Christmas at Emory University, w. [cnd:Alfred Calabrese], Emory Univ Concert Choir, Timothy Albrecht (org), Jane Flynn (org) *(rec Cathedral of St. Philip, Atlanta, GA, Apr. 30 & May 1, 1994)* ACA Digital ▲ CM 20035

Riggs, James (sax)
Whitacre, E.:Ghost Train Triptych, w. Pavel Wlosok (pno), E. Corporon (cnd), North Texas College of Music Wind Sym Klavier ▲ KCD 11077 [DDD]

Righarts, Huub (perc)
Górecki, H.-M.:Good Night, w. Elzbieta Szmytka (sop), Paul Edmund-Davies (a fl), Mireille Gleizes (pno) *(rec Abbey Bonne Espérance, Vellereille-les-Brayeux, Belgium; July 17–19, 1995)* Telarc ▲ CD-80417 [DDD]

Righini, M. (va)—see ORCHESTRAS & ENSEMBLES Quartetto Modì

Righini, Silvio (vc)
Mendelssohn, F.:Lied ohne Worte Vc, w. L. Alvini (pno) Giulia ▲ 201012 [DDD]
Mendelssohn, F.:Son 1 Vc, w. L. Alvini (pno) Giulia ▲ 201012 [DDD]
Mendelssohn, F.:Son 2 Vc, w. L. Alvini (pno) Giulia ▲ 201012 [DDD]
Mendelssohn, F.:Vars concertantes, w. L. Alvini (pno) Giulia ▲ 201012 [DDD]
Milesi, P.:Modi 1, w. D. Cassamagnaghi (fl), F. Pomarico (ob), A. Bianchi (cl), L. Dosso (bn), G. Govi (vn), D. Tellini (vn), M. Ravasio (va), P. Rizzi (db), C. Vignani (hpd), J. Scully (perc), P. Milesi (cnd) Cuneiform ▲ RUNE 63
Milesi, P.:Modi 2, w. L. M. Pickova (sop), Françoise Goddard (alt), M. Ferradini (ten), B. Andersen (bass), D. Cassamagnaghi (fl), S. Scanziani (ob), A. Bianchi (cl/b cl), E. Crisafulli (bn), C. Gazzola (hn), F. Gualandris (tuba), A. Girardi (celtic hp), R. Anedda (vn), E. Groppo (vn), M. Pagani (vn), M. Ravasio (va), P. Rizzi (db), J. Scully (perc), P. Milesi (cnd) Cuneiform ▲ RUNE 63

Rigon, Giovanni Battista (pno)—see ORCHESTRAS & ENSEMBLES Trio Italiano

Rigutto, Bruno (pno)
Chopin, F.:Berceuse *(rec Stadsgehoorzaal, Leiden, The Netherlands, Dec. 17–19, 1990)* Denon ▲ CO 78927 [DDD]
Chopin, F.:Con 1 Pno, w. E. Bergel (cnd), Budapest PO Denon ▲ CO 75637 [DDD]
Chopin, F.:Con 2 Pno, w. E. Bergel (cnd), Budapest PO Denon ▲ CO 75637 [DDD]
Chopin, F.:Impromptus—Op. 66 *(rec Stadsgehoorzaal, Leiden, The Netherlands, Dec. 17–19, 1990)* Denon ▲ CO 78927 [DDD]
Chopin, F.:Mazurkas—Nos. 13, Op. 14/4, 49, Op. 68/2 & 51, Op. 68/4 *(rec Stadsgehoorzaal, Leiden, The Netherlands, Dec. 17–19, 1990)* Denon ▲ CO 78927 [DDD]
Chopin, F.:Nocturnes—Nos. 7, 8, 13, 14 & 19 *(rec Stadsgehoorzaal, Leiden, The Netherlands, Dec. 17–19, 1990)* Denon ▲ CO 78927 [DDD]
Chopin, F.:Pno Music (comp)—Nocturnes, Op. 9; Fantaisie, Op. 49; Mazurkas, Opp. 30/4 & 33/4; Scherzo, Op. 31; Polonaises, Opp. 26/1 & 53 Denon ▲ CO 79556 [DDD]
Chopin, F.:Son Pno, Op. 35 *(rec Stadsgehoorzaal, Leiden, The Netherlands, Dec. 17–19, 1990)* Denon ▲ CO 78927 [DDD]
Koechlin, C.:Ballade Pno, w. A. Myrat (cnd), Monte Carlo PO EMI Classics ▲ CDM 64369

Riha, Vladimir (cl)
Mozart, W.A.:Con Cl, w. V. Talich (cnd), Czech PO *(rec 1954)* Supraphon ▲ SUP 11 1907 [AAD]

Riis, Peder (gtr)
Bach, J.S.:Lt Music—Suite No. 2 in c, BWV 997 *(rec June 1980–Sept 1982)* Opus 3 ▲ OP 8015 [AAD]
Turina, J.:Homenaje a Tárrega *(rec June 1980–Sept 1982)* Opus 3 ▲ OP 8015 [AAD]
Villa-Lobos, H.:Etudes Gtr—No. 8 *(rec June 1980–Sept 1982)* Opus 3 ▲ OP 8015 [AAD]
Villa-Lobos, H.:Preludes Gtr—No. 5 *(rec June 1980–Sept 1982)* Opus 3 ▲ OP 8015 [AAD]
Villa-Lobos, H.:Suite populaire brésilienne—Mazurka-Choro *(rec June 1980–Sept 1982)* Opus 3 ▲ OP 8015 [AAD]
Weiss, S.L.:Lt Music—Chaconne; Fant; Tombeau sur la Morte de M. Conte de Logy *(rec June 1980–Sept 1982)* Opus 3 ▲ OP 8015 [AAD]

Rijckere, Alain de (bn)
Bréval, J.B.:Sym concertante, w. M. Grauwels (fl), B. Labadie (cnd), Walloon CO Syrinx ▲ 92101 [DDD]
Marc Grauwels & Friends, w. Marc Grauwels (fl), Marie-Noelle de Callatay (sop), Hiroko Masaki (sop), Dennis James (glass hmc), Ingrid Procureur (hp), Yves Storms (gtr), Yvietta Matison (va), Mark Drobinsky (vc), Daniel Blumenthal (pno), Frank Michiels (perc), Belgian RSO, et. al. Syrinx 2-▲ 96101 [DDD]

Rijkmans, Hans (va)
Maric, L.:Archaia, w. Julija Hartig (vn), Ivana Poparic (vc) Emergo ▲ EC 3951 [DDD]

Rikkers, P. (vc)—see ORCHESTRAS & ENSEMBLES Senario Ensemble

Rikkers, P. (vn)
Hollander, H.:Sacred Music, w. S. van Grootel (sop), K. van der Poel (mez), J. Boswinkel (bass), J. van der Meer (db), T. van Eijk (org), Cappella Breda—Cantabant sancti; Domine Jesu Christe; Domine Deus; Ecce vicit leo; O nomen Jesu; Recipe me; Quem vidistis pastores; Sanctus Jacobus; Quid est hoc; O vos omnes; Ecce clamo; Ave Maria; O Beatum Virum; O bone Jesu; Te gloriosus Erasmus ▲ WVH 047 [DDD]

Riley, Terry (elec org/elec hpd)
Riley, T.:A Rainbow in Curved Air CBS ▲ MK 07315 [ADD]

Riley, Terry (pno)
Riley, T.:The Harp of New Albion *(rec Munich, 1/3-4/86)* Celestial Harmonies 2-▲ 14018/19 [DDD]
Riley, T.:Pno Music—Arica; Negro Hall; 15/16; Havana Man; Island of Never Anger; Peace Dance; Underworld Arising; Ecstacy; Lake; Mongolian Winds *(rec live, Teatro São Luis, Lisbon, Portugal, July 16, 1995)* New Albion ▲ NA 087 CD

Riley, Terry (syn)
Riley, T.:Songs for the 10 Voices of the 2 Prophets, w. T. Riley (voc) *(rec live, Munich, 5/10/82)* Kuckuck ■ 11067-4 (D)
Riley, T.:Songs for the 10 Voices of the 2 Prophets, w. T. Riley (voc) *(rec live, Munich, 5/10/82)* Kuckuck ▲ 12047-2

Rilling, Helmuth (hpd)
Bach, J.S.:Cant 152, w. A. Augér (sop), W. Schöne (bass), et al. [G] *(rec Mar–Apr 1976)* Hänssler Classic ▲ 98.826 [AAD]

Rilling, Helmuth (org)
Bach, J.S.:Chorale Preludes (Schübler)—BWV 645 & 648 Denon ▲ 7809 [DDD]
Bach, J.S.:Chorale Settings (misc)—BWV 655,659,661,667,686,688,701 & 729 Denon ▲ 7809 [DDD]
Bach, J.S.:Org Music (misc), w. J. E. Hansen (org), H. Otto (org), K. Vad (org)—Toccata & Fugue in d, BWV 565; Fugue in g, BWV 578; Passacaglia & Fugue in c, BWV 582; Fantasia & Fugue in g, BWV 542; Chorales, BWV 147, 583, 608, 622, 645 Denon ▲ CO 8009 [DDD]
Bach, J.S.:Das Orgelbüchlein—BWV 605,622,628,629 & 630 Denon ▲ 7809 [DDD]
Bach, J.S.:Das Orgelbüchlein, w. Helmuth Rilling (cnd), Stuttgart Gedächtnis Figural Choir—BWV 618–623, 625–630, 640, 641 *(rec Walcker, Ludwigsburg, 1957)* Cantate ▲ C 57608 [AAD]
Bach, J.S.:Das Orgelbüchlein, w. Helmuth Rilling (cnd), Stuttgart Gedächtnis Figural Choir—BWV 599–609, 611–615 *(rec Walcker, Ludwigsburg, 1957)* Cantate ▲ C 57607 [AAD]
Bach, J.S.:Das Orgelbüchlein, w. Helmuth Rilling (cnd), Stuttgart Gedächtnis Figural Choir—Komm, Gott Schöpfer, Heiliger Geist, BWV 631; Herr Jesu Christ, dich zu uns wend, BWV 632; Liebster Jesu, wir sind hier, BWV 633; Dies sind die heilgen zehn Gebot, BWV 635; Vater unser im Himmelreich, BWV 636; Durch Adams Fall ist ganz verderbt, BWV 637; Es ist das Heil uns kommen her, BWV 638; Ich ruf zu dir, Herr Jesu Christ, BWV 639; Hilf Gott, dass mirs gelinge, BWV 624; Jesu, meine Freude, BWV 610; Mit Fried und Freud ich fahr dahin, BWV 616; Herr Gott, n. schleuss d. Himmel auf BWV 617; Wer nur den lieben Gott läss walten, BWV 642; Alle Menschen müssen sterben, BWV 643; Ach wie flüchtig, ach wie nichtig, BWV 644 *(rec Southwest Sound Studio, Stuttgart, May 1963 & Mar 1965)* Cantate ▲ C 57609 [AAD]

Rimon, Meir (hn)
Dances Moods & Romances, w. David Amos (cnd), Israel PO members Crystal ▲ CD513
Glazunov, A.:Chant du ménéstrel, w. D. Amos (cnd), Israel PO Crystal ▲ CD 510 [DDD]
Hovhaness, A.:Artik, w. D. Amos (cnd), Israel PO Crystal ▲ CD 802
Meir Rimon, w. Israel PO [cnd:David Amos] Crystal ▲ CD 510 [DDD]
Tchaikovsky, P.:Les Saisons, w. D. Amos (cnd), Israel PO—No. 10, "Autumn Song" Crystal ▲ CD 510 [DDD]

Rinehart, J. (pno)
Ornstein, L.:Nocturne Cl, w. D. Niethamer (cl) Opus One ▲ 146

Ringborg, Tobias (vn)
Kreisler, F.:Vn Pieces, w. Anders Kilström (pno)—Romance, Op. 4; Recitativo & Scherzo-Caprice, Op. 6; Viennese Rhapsodic Fantasietta Caprice ▲ CAP 21455
Kreisleriana:The Lesser Known Works & Transcriptions of Fritz Kreisler, w. Anders Kilström (pno) Caprice ▲ CAP 21496
Poulenc, F.:Son Vn, w. Anders Kilström (pno) Caprice ▲ CAP 21455
Sjögren, E.:Son 2 Vn, w. Anders Kilström (pno) Caprice ▲ CAP 21455
Ysaÿe, E.:Sons Vn—No. 3 [Ballade] Caprice ▲ CAP 21455

Ringeissen, Bernard (pno)
Alkan, C.-V.:Etudes (12) in major keys Marco Polo ▲ 8.223351
Alkan, C.-V.:Etudes (12) in minor keys—(7) No. 1, "Comme le vent"; No. 2, "En rhythme molossique"; Nos. 4–7, "Symphonie"; No. 11, "Ouverture" Marco Polo ▲ 8.223285 [DDD]
Alkan, C.-V.:Etudes (12) in minor keys—No. 3 "Scherzo Diabolico"; No. 12 "Le Festin d'Esope" Marco Polo ▲ 8.223351
Alkan, C.-V.:Etudes (12) in minor keys—No. 3, "Scherzo diabilico" Musique d'Abord ▲ HMA 190927 [ADD]
Alkan, C.-V.:Pno Music—Barcarolle, Op. 67/6 (1876); Gigue, Op. 24 (1844); March No. 1 in a (1857); Nocturne No. 2 (1859); Saltarelle in e, Op. 23 (1844) Musique d'Abord ▲ HMA 190927 [ADD]
Alkan, C.-V.:Sonatina Pno Musique d'Abord ▲ HMA 190927 [ADD]
Balakirev, M.:Pno Music—Islamey; Berceuse; Dumka; 3 Esquisses; Valse No. 6 Adès 2-▲ ADE 141662 [AAD]
Borodin, A.:Petite Suite Adès 2-▲ ADE 141662 [AAD]
Cui, C.:Pno Music—12 Miniatures; Impromptu-Caprice; Waltz in e Adès 2-▲ ADE 141662 [AAD]
Debussy, C.:En blanc et noir, w. Noël Lee (pno) Astrée ▲ E 8568
Debussy, C.:Épigraphes antiques, w. Noël Lee (pno) Astrée ▲ E 8568
Debussy, C.:Lindaraja, w. Noël Lee (pno) Astrée ▲ E 8568
Debussy, C.:Petite suite, w. Noël Lee (pno) Astrée ▲ E 8568
Hahn, R.:Pno Music—1ère Etude; Portrait [Le rossignol éperdu No. 14]; Narghilé [Le rossignol éperdu No. 32]; Valse No. 9 [La Feuille]; Portrait [Juvenilia No. 1] Adès ▲ ADE 203432 [AAD]
Hahn, R.:Songs, w. Jean-Christophe Benoit (bar)—3 jours de vendange; Si mes vers avaient des ailes!; Les cygnes; Dans la nuit; Néère [Etudes latines No. 2]; Le printemps; Séraphine; Quand je fus pris au pavillon; Nocturne; Mai; L'heure exquise [Chansons grises No. 5]; Paysage; Sur l'eau; Tyndares [Etudes latines No. 7]; La nuit; Cantique sur le bonheur des justes et sur le malheur des réprouvés; Infidélité; A Chloris; D'une prison Adès ▲ ADE 203432 [AAD]
Kosma, J.:Songs, w. Jean-Christophe Benoit (bar)—Les Enfants qui s'aiment; Il Pleut; La Pêche a la aleine; La Dame pavot nouvelle épousée; Page d'écriture; La Belle jambe; Le Jardin; Les Feuilles mortes; Chanson de l'oiseleur; Le Chat qui ne ressemble a rien; Dans ma maison; La Petite chèvre; Paris at Night; Art poétique; Chansons pour les enfants l'Hiver; Barbara; Baptiste, suite d'orchestre Adès ▲ ADE 132922 [ADD]
Mussorgsky, M.:Pictures at an Exhibition Adès 2-▲ ADE 141662 [AAD]
Poulenc, F.:Con for 2 Pnos, w. G. Tacchino (pno), G. Prêtre (cnd), Monte Carlo PO EMI Classics ▲ CDM 64714
Rimsky-Korsakov, N.:Pieces Pno, Op. 11 Adès 2-▲ ADE 141662 [AAD]
Rimsky-Korsakov, N.:The Tale of Tsar Saltan (orch sels)—Flight of the Bumblebee Adès 2-▲ ADE 141662 [AAD]
Rimsky-Korsakov, N.:Vars on B-A-C-H Adès 2-▲ ADE 141662 [AAD]

Ringers, Dorian (handbells)
Vees, J.:Stigmata non Grata, w. Cammi Carteng (handbells), Jan Dudiet (handbells), JoAnn Kerns (handbells), Monica McGowan (handbells), B. Mathis (cnd) CRI ("Emergency Music" series) ▲ CD 730 [DDD]

Riniker, D. (hpd)—see ORCHESTRAS & ENSEMBLES Zurich New Music Ensemble

Riniker, David (vc)—see also ORCHESTRAS & ENSEMBLES Zurich New Music Ensemble, Universal Ensemble, Novanta Trio
Mieg, P.:Double Con Pno, Vc, w. K-A Kolly (pno), Southern Bohemian Chamber PO Budweis Jecklin ▲ JS 297-2 [ADD]
Mieg, P.:Son Vc, w. Karl-Andreas Kolly (pno) *(rec 1993)* Jecklin ▲ JS 314-2 [DDD]

Rintoul, Richard (va)
Jacob, G.:Qnt Cl, w. Daniel Geeting (cl), Melissa Phelps-Beckstead (vn), David Stenske (vn), Joyce Geeting (vc) *(rec Memorial Chapel, Univ. of Redlands, Redlands, CA)* PROdigital ▲ PRO 9226 [DDD]

Riona, D. (baroque vn)
Insalata, w. I Fagiolini, E. Kenny (theorbo), D. Burchell (hpd/org), Riona D.(baroque vn), T. Cronin (baroque vn), D. Clasen (bar) Metronome ▲ METCD 1004

Rios, O. (perc)—see ORCHESTRAS & ENSEMBLES New Generation

Ripoli, Pasquale (fl)
Vivaldi, A.:Cons Fl (misc), w. R. Fasano (cnd), Rome Virtuosi—in D, Op. 10/3, "Il gardellino" *(rec Opéra de Rome, July, 1962)* EMI Classics ▲ CDK 65338 [ADD]

Rische, Michael (pno)
Album des Six Koch Schwann ▲ SCH CD 317692
Ravel, M.:Miroirs Koch Schwann ▲ SCH 312152
Ravel, M.:Prélude Pno Koch Schwann ▲ SCH 312152
Saxophone & Piano, w. Detlef Bensmann (sax) Koch Schwann ▲ SCH 310071 [ADD]
Schulhoff, E.:Con Pno, w. G. Schuller (cnd), Cologne RSO Koch Schwann ▲ SCH 315972 [DDD]
Schulhoff, E.:Hot Son Sax, w. D. Bensmann (a sax) Koch Schwann ▲ SCH 313352 [DDD]

▲ = CD ♦ = Enhanced CD Δ = MD ■ = Cassette Tape ☐ = DCC

Rise, Harald (org)
Nielsen, L.:Org Music [Organ of Hadersley Cathedral]—Intrata Gotica, Op. 14; Fantasi i Koraltone, Op. 34; Vars on "Ingen vinner frem til den evige ro", Op. 2; Introduksjon og Fuge, Op. 6; Orgelmusikk i Pinsemessen, Op. 20a; Passacaglia on "Draumkvedet", Op. 23a; Fra "Orgelkoraler", Op. 5; Nidarosdomens klokker, Op. 37b — Victoria ▲ VCD 19107
Vierne, L.:Sym 2 Org *(rec Sept. 1993)* — Victoria ▲ VCD 19062
Vierne, L.:Sym 5 Org *(rec Sept. 1993)* — Victoria ▲ VCD 19062
Risler, Edouard Joseph (pno)
The Complete 1917 Pathé Recordings — Enterprise ("Piano Library" series) ▲ ENT PL 209
Risler, S. (pno)—see ORCHESTRAS & ENSEMBLES Linea Ensemble
Ritchie, George (org)
Bach, J.S.:Org Music (misc)—Toccata & Fugue in F, BWV 540; Sei gegrüsset, Jesu gütig, BWV 768; Canzona, BWV 588; Prelude & Fugue in D, BWV 532; Pastorella in F, BWV 590; Fant. & Fugue in g, BWV 542 — Raven ▲ OAR 250 [DDD]
Bach, J.S.:Org Music (misc) [Bedient Organ, Cornerstone, Lincoln, NE]—Chorale Preludes (4) Liebster Jesu, wir sind hier, BWV 633; Schmücke dich, o liebe Seele, BWV 654; Jesus Christus, unser Heiland, BWV 666; Vater unser im Himmelreich, BWV 682; Fugue in G, BWV 577, "Jig"; Fugue in g, BWV 578, "Little"; Preludes & Fugues (3) in A, BWV 536; in G, BWV 541; in e, BWV 548; Toccata & Fugue in d, BWV 565; Ricercar à 6 from Musical Offering, BWV 1079 — Titanic ▲ TI 158 [DDD]
Bach, J.S.:Preludes & Fugues, BWV 531–552—BWV 536, 541, 548 — Titanic ▲ TI 158 [DDD]
Bach, J.S.:Toccata & Fugue Org, BWV 565 — Titanic ▲ TI 158 [DDD]
Snyder, R.:Dances of Siva — Coronet ▲ COR 400–9
Ritchie, Stanley (vn)—see also ORCHESTRAS & ENSEMBLES Mozartean Players, Helicon
Bach, J.S.:Trio Son for 2 Vns, w. J. Schröder (vn), A. Fuller (hpd) *(rec June 6–8, 1986)* — Reference ▲ RR 23 CD [DDD]
Geminiani, F.:The Enchanted Forest, w. Elizabeth Wilcock (vn), Susie Napper (vc), Janet See (fl), Barbara Kallaur (fl), Patrick Wedd (hpd), J.E. Gardiner (cnd), CBC Vancouver SO — CBC ▲ 5163 [DDD]
Three Parts upon a Ground, w. John Hollowy (vn), Andrew Manze (vn), Mary Springfels (vl), Nigel North (lt), John Toll (hpd/org) — Harmonia Mundi USA ▲ HMU 907091
Vivaldi, A.:Cons Ob Vn, w. F. de Bruine (ob), C. Hogwood (cnd), Academy of Ancient Music—in g, RV.460 — L'Oiseau–Lyre ▲ 436172–2 [DDD]
Vivaldi, A.:Cons Vn (misc), w. C. Hogwood (cnd), Academy of Ancient Music—in D, RV.207; in e, RV.277; in A, RV.336; in G, RV.308; in c, RV.202 (Op. 11/1–5) — L'Oiseau–Lyre ▲ 436172–2 [ADD]
Vivaldi, A.:Cons for 2 Vns, w. J. Schröder (vn), N. TeBrake (vn), R. Brown (vn), J. Griffin (va), M. Lutszke (vc), M. Willems (db), A. Fuller (hpd) *(rec June 6–8, 1986)* — Reference ▲ RR 23 CD [DDD]
Vivaldi, A.:Sinf, RV.116, w. J. Schröder (vn), J. Griffin (va), M. Lutszke (vc), M. Willems (db), A. Fuller (hpd) *(rec June 6–8, 1986)* — Reference ▲ RR 23 CD [DDD]
Vivaldi, A.:Trio Sons 2 Vns & Bc, w. J. Schröder (vn), M. Lutszke (vc), A. Fuller (hpd)—RV.73 *(rec June 6–8, 1986)* — Reference ▲ RR 23 CD [DDD]
Ritis, Patrick de (bn)—see ORCHESTRAS & ENSEMBLES Briccialdi Wind Quintet
Ritt, Morey (pno)
Brings, A.:Duo Concertante Vc, w. P. Rosenfeld (vc) — Capstone ▲ CPS 8615
Perle, G.:Dickinson Songs, w. B. Beardslee (sop) [E] — CRI ■ ACS 6015
Ritter, John Steele (hpd)
Bach, C.P.E.:Trio Son Fl, H.586, w. J.–P. Rampal (fl), I. Stern (vn) — CBS ▲ MK 37813 [DDD]
Bach, J.C.F:Son Fl, HW.VIII/1–2, w. J.–P. Rampal (fl), I. Stern (vn)—in C — CBS ▲ MK 37813 [DDD]
Bach, J.S.:A Musical Offering, w. J.–P. Rampal (fl), I. Stern (vn), L. Parnas (vc)—trio, section 8 — CBS ▲ MK 37813 [DDD]
Bach, J.S.:Trio Son Fl, Vn & Hpd, w. J.–P. Rampal (fl), I. Stern (vn) — CBS ▲ MK 37813 [DDD]
Rameau, J.P.:Pièces de clavecin en concert, w. J.–P. Rampal (fl), I. Stern (vn) — Sony Classical ▲ SK 45868 [DDD]
Ritter, John Steele (hpd/pno)
Jean–Pierre Rampal, w. Jean–Pierre Rampal (fl), Shigenori Kudo (fls) — Sony Classical ▲ SK 46482 [ADD]
Joplin, S.:Music of, w. J.–P. Rampal (fl), S. Manne (dr), Johnson (tubas) — CBS ▲ MK 37818
Ritter, John Steele (keyboard)
Bach, W.F.:Trio Son in a Fl, w. Rampal, Stern — CBS ▲ MK 37813 [DDD]
Ritter, John Steele (pno)
In Concert, w. Kathleen Battle (sop), Jean–Pierre Rampal (fl), Anthony Newman (hpd), Myron Lutzke (vc), Margo Garrett (pno) *(rec Feb. 24, 1991)* — Sony Classical ▲ SK 53106 [ADD] ■ ST 53106
Mozart, W.A.:Sons Vn Pno (misc), w. J.–P. Rampal (fl)—K.301, 305 & 403 — CBS ▲ MK 42142 [DDD]
Mozart, W.A.:Vars Vn Pno, K.359, w. J.–P. Rampal (fl) — CBS ▲ MK 42142 [DDD]
Mozart, W.A.:Vars Vn Pno, K.360, w. J.–P. Rampal (fl) — CBS ▲ MK 42142 [DDD]
Ritzkowsky, Johannes (hn)
Strauss, R.:Andante Hn, w. Wolfgang Sawallisch (pno) *(rec Kleine Konzertsall, Gasteig, Germany, Mar 22–23, 1988)* — Arts ▲ 47261–2 [DDD]
Strauss, R.:Con 1 Hn, w. Wolfgang Sawallisch (pno) *(rec Kleine Konzertsall, Gasteig, Germany, Feb 28, 1985)* — Arts ▲ 47261–2 [DDD]
Strauss, R.:Con 2 Hn, w. Wolfgang Sawallisch (pno), Barton Weber (pno) *(rec Kleine Konzertsall, Gasteig, Germany, Mar 22–23, 1988)* — Arts ▲ 47261–2 [DDD]
Riva, Douglas (pno)
Granados, E.:Album, Paris—7 sels. — Centaur ▲ CRC 2043 [DDD]
Granados, E.:Azulejos — Centaur ▲ CRC 2043 [DDD]
Granados, E.:En la aldea, w. G. Kirchoff (pno) — Centaur ▲ CRC 2043 [DDD]
Granados, E.:Romanza, w. R. Waterman (vn) — Centaur ▲ CRC 2043 [DDD]
Granados, E.:Serenade for 2 Vns, w. R. Waterman (vn), J. Pitchon (vn) — Centaur ▲ CRC 2043 [DDD]
Rivard, Mike (elec bass)
Field, K.:Music of, w. Ken Field (sax/perc/syn/fl), Karen Aqua (perc), Ken Winokur (perc), John Fleagle (voice), Karen Gruber (perc)—A Space in a Place; Om on the Range; Takuskanskan; 5 Saxophones in Search of Meaning; Sanity; Perpetual Motion; Thoughts Unspoken; Berrendo; Sympathetic Magic; The Missing Soul; When I Fall in Love *(rec The Henge, Roswell, NM, Wellspring Sound, Concord, MA, The Chicken Loft, Cambridge, MA & The Basement, Cambridge, MA, 1988–1995)* — O.O. Discs ▲ OO 25
Rivera, Juan Carlos (gtr)
García, M.:Songs, w. Ernesto Palacio (ten), Juan Jose Chuquisengo (pno)—Yo que soy contrabandista; Y otras canciones; I Who Am a Bandit; others — Almaviva ▲ 0114
Rivera, Juan Carlos (thb/gtr)—see ORCHESTRAS & ENSEMBLES Al Ayre Español
Rivera, Juan Carlos (vih)
Narváez, L. de:Seys libros, w. Marta Almajano (sop)—sacred & secular works — Almaviva ▲ 116
Rivers, Sandra (pno)
Bravura!, w. Cho–Liang Lin (vn) — CBS ▲ MK 39133 [DDD]
Debut, w. Sarah Chang (vn) — EMI Classics ▲ CDC 54352 [DDD] ■ 4DS 54352
Fauré, G.:Son 1 Vn, w. A. A. Meyers (vn) *(rec May 26 & 27, 1989)* — Canyon Classics ▲ 3658 [DDD]
It Ain't Necessarily So, w. Nadja Salerno–Sonnenberg (vn) — EMI Classics ▲ CDC 54576 [DDD]
Kreisler, F.:Vn Pieces, w. Lin (vn)—Liebesfreud — CBS ▲ MDK 44902 [DDD] ■ MDT 44902 (D)
Saint–Saëns, C.:Son 1 Vn, w. A. A. Meyers (vn) *(rec May 26 & 27, 1989)* — Canyon Classics ▲ 3658 [DDD]
Sarasate, P. de:Carmen Fant, w. S. Chang (vn) — EMI Classics ▲ CDC 54352 [DDD] ■ 4DS 54352
Sarasate, P. de:Intro & Tarantella, w. Cho–Liang Lin (vn) — CBS ▲ MDK 44902 [DDD] ■ MDT 44902 (D)
Riviere, Pablo (va)—see ORCHESTRAS & ENSEMBLES Arlequin Trio
Rivolta, Renato (fl)—see also ORCHESTRAS & ENSEMBLES Arnold Quintet
Cambini, G.M.:Trios Fl, Ob & Bn, w. F. Pomarico (ob), L. Dosso (bn) — Stradivarius ▲ STR 33310 [DDD]
Maderna, B.:Musica su due dimensioni, w. B. Maderna (elec), M. Zuccheri (elec) — Stradivarius ▲ STR 33349
Rizeli, Ahmed Kadri (fid/perc)—see ORCHESTRAS & ENSEMBLES Ensemble Saraband
Rizner, F. (hn)
Mozart, W.A.:Con Hn, K.447, w. J.–L. Garcia (cnd), English CO — Summit ▲ DCD 131 [DDD]
Mozart, W.A.:Con Hn, K.495, w. J.–L. Garcia (cnd), English CO — Summit ▲ DCD 131 [DDD]

Rizzer, Gerald (pno)
La Flûte Lumineuse, w. Susan Levitin (fl), Chicago Ensemble *(rec WFMT Studios, Chicago)* — Mark ▲ MCD 1939
Rizzi, Marco (vn)
Alfano, F.:Son Vn, w. Alessandro Maffei (pno) — Sarx ▲ SRX 14 [DDD]
Locatelli, P.:Con Vn, w. A. Orizio (cnd), Brescia & Bergamo Festival CO — Fonè ▲ 91F07 [DDD]
Respighi, O.:Pieces Vn, w. Alessandro Maffei (pno)—5 sels — Sarx ▲ SRX 14 [DDD]
Respighi, O.:Son Vn, w. Alessandro Maffei (pno) — Sarx ▲ SRX 14 [DDD]
Rizzi, P. (db)
Milesi, P.:Modi 1, w. D. Cassamagnaghi (fl), F. Pomarico (ob), A. Bianchi (cl), L. Dosso (bn), G. Govi (vn), D. Tellini (vn), M. Ravasio (va), S. Righini (vc), C. Vignani (hpd), J. Scully (perc), P. Milesi (cnd) — Cuneiform ▲ RUNE 63
Milesi, P.:Modi 2, w. L. M. Pickova (sop), Françoise Goddard (alt), M. Ferradini (ten), B. Andersen (bass), D. Cassamagnaghi (fl), S. Scanziani (ob), A. Bianchi (cl/b cl), E. Crisafulli (bn), C. Gazzola (hn), F. Gualandris (tuba), A. Girardi (celtic hp), R. Anedda (vn), E. Groppo (vn), M. Pagani (vn), M. Ravasio (va), S. Righini (vc), J. Scully (perc), P. Milesi (cnd) — Cuneiform ▲ RUNE 63
Roach, David (sax)
Nyman, M.:Noises, w. Catherine Bott (sop), Hilary Summers (alt), Ian Bostridge (ten), Andrew Findon (sax), D. Debart (cnd), Basse Normandie Instrumental Ensemble *(rec Caen, June 1991 & Abbey Road Studios, London, June 1993)* — Argo ▲ 440842–2 [DDD]
Roach, Steven (pno)
Offenbach, J.:Chants du soir, w. Andrea Noferini (vc) — Bongiovanni ▲ GB 5569 [DDD]
Offenbach, J.:Harmonie du soir, w. Andrea Noferini (vc) — Bongiovanni ▲ GB 5569 [DDD]
Offenbach, J.:Les Larmes de Jacqueline, w. Andrea Noferini (vc) — Bongiovanni ▲ GB 5569 [DDD]
Offenbach, J.:Rêveries, w. Andrea Noferini (vc) — Bongiovanni ▲ GB 5569 [DDD]
Robault, Pascal (va)
Mozart, W.A.:Qnt Hn & Strs, w. Hervé Joulain (hn), Élisabeth Glab (vn), Françoise Gnéri (va), Nadine Pierre (vc) — Arion ▲ ARN 68311 [DDD]
Robbins, Alice (vc)
Hovhaness, A.:Sextet Rcr, w. J. Tyson (rcr), J. Starkman (vn), K. Shaw (vn), J. Cosart (va), F. Conover Fitch (hpd) — Titanic ▲ Ti 169 [DDD]
Something for Recorder & Strings, w. John Tyson (rcr), Frances Conover Fitch (hpd), Jane Starkman (vn), Katheryn Shaw (vn), Jann Cosart (va), Tom Coleman (db) — Titanic ▲ Ti 169 [DDD]
Robbins, D. (echo timp)
Albright, W.:Chasm, w. P. Decker (org) — Albany ▲ TROY 140 [DDD]
Robbins, Daniel (pno)
Rózsa, M.:Film Music—The Man in Half Moon Street; The Other Love; Fedora; Knight without Armor; The Macomber Affair; Kiss the Blood Off My Hands; A Woman's Vengeance & others — Intrada ▲ ITD CD 7057 [DDD]
Robbins, G. (pno)
Litolff, H.C.:Con Symphonique 4, w. E. van Remoortel (cnd), Monte Carlo Opera Orch — Genesis ▲ GCD 101 [ADD]
Reinecke, C.:Cons Pno, w. E. van Remoortel (cnd), Monte Carlo Opera Orch — Genesis ▲ GCD 102 [ADD]
Robbins, Sandra (va)—see also ORCHESTRAS & ENSEMBLES Bronx Arts Ensemble
Martinů, B.:Madrigals Vn, w. E. Oliveira (vn) — Élan ▲ CD 2212 [DDD]
Robert (cl)
Debussy, C.:Première rapsodie, w. Gugoltz (pno), E. Ansermet (cnd), Swiss Romande Orch *(rec 1964)* — London ▲ 433711–2 [ADD]
Robert, Anne (vn)—see also ORCHESTRAS & ENSEMBLES Montreal Chamber Group
Franck, C.:Son Vn, w. Sylvianne Deferne (pno) — REM ▲ REM 311260 [DDD]
Pierné, G.:Son Vn, w. Sylvianne Deferne (pno) — REM ▲ REM 311260 [DDD]
Tournemire, C.:Sonate–poème, w. Sylvianne Deferne (pno) — REM ▲ REM 311260 [DDD]
Robert, Guy (lt)
The Art of the Lute in the Middle Ages, w. Perceval Ensemble [cnd:Guy Robert] — Arion ▲ ARN 60264
Robert, Guy (medieval lt/oud/hp)
Tensons e partimens de Trobairitz, Vol. 3, w. Gérard Zuchetto (sgr), Katia Caré (sgr), Gisela Bellsolà (sgr), Patrice Brient (voc/h–g/rebeck) — Gallo ▲ CD 769 [DDD]
Robert, Jean Michel (lt/gtr)
Baroque Music for Lute, Guitar & Harpsichord, w. Brigitte Tramier (hpd) — Koch Schwann ▲ SCH 315442 [DDD]
Robert, Walter (pno)
Fauré, G.:Son 1 Vn, w. J. Gingold (vn) *(rec 1966)* — Music & Arts ▲ CD 286 [AAD]
Kreisler, F.:Short Pieces Vn, w. J. Gingold (vn) *(rec 1966)* — Music & Arts ▲ CD 286 [AAD]
Paganini, N.:Caprices Vn, w. O. Renardy (vn) [arr. David for violin & piano] *(rec 1940 for Victor)* — Biddulph 2–▲ LAB 061/62 [ADD]
Roberti, Oliver (hpd)
Haydn, J.:Con Hpd, Vns & Bass Instrument, H.XVIII/9, w. K. Redel (cnd), English CO — Pierre Verany ▲ PVY 793111 [DDD]
Haydn, J.:Con Org, Vns & Bass Instrument, H.XVIII/5, w. K. Redel (cnd), English CO — Pierre Verany ▲ PVY 793111 [DDD]
Haydn, J.:Con Org, Vn & Strs, H.XVIII/6, w. Maciej Rakowski (vn), K. Redel (cnd), English CO — Pierre Verany ▲ PVY 793111 [DDD]
Roberti, Oliver (pno)
Haydn, J.:Divert Kbd & Strs, H.XIV/8, w. K. Redel (cnd), English CO — Pierre Verany ▲ PVY 793111 [DDD]
Robertis, Mariolina de (pno)
Togni, C.:Gesang zur Nacht, w. Carla Henius (alt), Saschko Gawriloff (vn), Hans Damzel (cl), Werner Heider (pno) — Stradivarius ▲ STV DTM 90002 [ADD]
Robertroslot (pno)—see ORCHESTRAS & ENSEMBLES Walter Boeykens Ensemble
Roberts, Adelaide (pno)
Starer, R.:Night Thoughts, w. Theresa Santiago (sop), Jennifer Hines (mez), Anthony Griffey (ten), Neil Michaels (bar), Edgar Roberts (pno) — Albany ▲ TROY 151 [DDD]
Roberts, Bernard (pno)
Beethoven, L. van:Bagatelles (24)—Op. 126 — Nimbus ▲ Ni 5040
Beethoven, L. van:Polonaise Pno — Nimbus ▲ NI 5040
Beethoven, L. van:Sons Pno (comp) — Nimbus 11–▲ NI 1792 [DDD]
Beethoven, L. van:Son 1 Pno — Nimbus ▲ NI 5050 [DDD]
Beethoven, L. van:Son 2 Pno — Nimbus ▲ NI 5051 [DDD]
Beethoven, L. van:Son 3 Pno — Nimbus ▲ NI 5052 [DDD]
Beethoven, L. van:Son 4 Pno — Nimbus ▲ NI 5053 [DDD]
Beethoven, L. van:Son 5 Pno — Nimbus ▲ NI 5054 [DDD]
Beethoven, L. van:Son 6 Pno — Nimbus ▲ NI 5054 [DDD]
Beethoven, L. van:Son 8 Pno, "Pathétique" — Nimbus ▲ NI 5060 [DDD]
Beethoven, L. van:Son 8 Pno, "Pathétique" *(rec Wyastone Leys, Nov. 30, 1985)* — Nimbus ▲ NI 7707 [DDD]
Beethoven, L. van:Son 9 Pno — Nimbus ▲ NI 5058 [DDD]
Beethoven, L. van:Son 10 Pno — Nimbus ▲ NI 5053 [DDD]
Beethoven, L. van:Son 11 Pno — Nimbus ▲ NI 5055 [DDD]
Beethoven, L. van:Son 12 Pno, "Funeral March" — Nimbus ▲ NI 5059 [DDD]
Beethoven, L. van:Son 13 Pno — Nimbus ▲ NI 5057 [DDD]
Beethoven, L. van:Son 14 Pno, "Moonlight Son" — Nimbus ▲ NI 5059 [DDD]
Beethoven, L. van:Son 14 Pno, "Moonlight Son" *(rec Wyastone Leys, Apr. 25, 1982)* — Nimbus ▲ NI 7707 [DDD]
Beethoven, L. van:Son 15 Pno, "Pastoral" — Nimbus ▲ NI 5055 [DDD]
Beethoven, L. van:Son 16 Pno — Nimbus ▲ NI 5058 [DDD]
Beethoven, L. van:Son 17 Pno, "Tempest" — Nimbus ▲ NI 5056 [DDD]
Beethoven, L. van:Son 18 Pno — Nimbus ▲ NI 5056 [DDD]

Roberts, Bernard (pno) (cont.)
Beethoven, L. van:Son 19 Pno Nimbus ▲ NI 5052 [DDD]
Beethoven, L. van:Son 20 Pno Nimbus ▲ NI 5055 [DDD]
Beethoven, L. van:Son 21 Pno, "Waldstein" Nimbus ▲ NI 5052 [DDD]
Beethoven, L. van:Son 21 Pno, "Waldstein" *(rec Wyastone Leys, Aug. 21, 1984)* Nimbus ▲ NI 7707 [DDD]
Beethoven, L. van:Son 22 Pno Nimbus ▲ NI 5050 [DDD]
Beethoven, L. van:Son 23 Pno, "Appassionata" Nimbus ▲ NI 5050 [DDD]
Beethoven, L. van:Son 24 Pno Nimbus ▲ NI 5051 [DDD]
Beethoven, L. van:Son 25 Pno Nimbus ▲ NI 5056 [DDD]
Beethoven, L. van:Son 26 Pno, "Les Adieux" *(rec Wyastone Leys, Nov. 21, 1985)* Nimbus ▲ NI 7707 [DDD]
Beethoven, L. van:Son 27 Pno Nimbus ▲ NI 5060 [DDD]
Beethoven, L. van:Son 28 Pno Nimbus ▲ NI 5051 [DDD]
Beethoven, L. van:Son 29 Pno, "Hammerklavier" Nimbus ▲ NI 5057 [DDD]
Beethoven, L. van:Son 30 Pno Nimbus ▲ NI 5058 [DDD]
Beethoven, L. van:Son 30 Pno *(rec Nimbus Records, Wyastone Leys, June 17, 1988)* Nimbus ▲ NI 7709 [DDD]
Beethoven, L. van:Son 31 Pno *(rec Nimbus Records, Wyastone Leys, Sept. 10, 1985)* Nimbus ▲ NI 7709 [DDD]
Beethoven, L. van:Son 31 Pno Nimbus ▲ NI 5059 [DDD]
Beethoven, L. van:Son 32 Pno Nimbus ▲ NI 5060 [DDD]
Beethoven, L. van:Son 32 Pno *(rec Nimbus Records, Wyastone Leys, Nov. 21, 1985)* Nimbus ▲ NI 7709 [DDD]
Beethoven, L. van:Vars & Fugue Pno, Op. 35, "Eroica" Nimbus ▲ NI 5040
Beethoven, L. van:Vars & Fugue Pno, Op. 35, "Eroica" *(rec Nimbus Records, Wyastone Leys, Feb 17 & June 11–12, 1983)* Nimbus ▲ NI 7710 [DDD]
Beethoven, L. van:Vars on a waltz by Diabelli, Op. 120 *(rec Nimbus Records, Wyastone Leys, Feb 17 & June 11–12, 1983)* Nimbus ▲ NI 7710 [DDD]
Beethoven, L. van:Vars on a waltz by Diabelli, Op. 120 Nimbus ▲ NI 5193 [DDD]
Hindemith, P.:Ludus Tonalis *(rec Nimbus Foundation Concert Hall)* Nimbus 2-▲ NI 5459/60 [DDD]
Hindemith, P.:Sons Pno *(rec Nimbus Foundation Concert Hall)* Nimbus 2-▲ NI 5459/60 [DDD]
Hindemith, P.:Son Pno 4-Hands, w. David Strong (pno) *(rec Nimbus Foundation Concert Hall)* Nimbus 2-▲ NI 5459/60 [DDD]
Hindemith, P.:Son for 2 Pnos, w. David Strong (pno) *(rec Nimbus Foundation Concert Hall)* Nimbus 2-▲ NI 5459/60 [DDD]

Roberts, Dane (db)
Telemann, G.P.:Cons (misc), w. Masahiro Arita (trns fl/pic), Eric Hoeprich (chl), Hans Peter Westermann (ob), David Sinclair (db), La Stravaganza Cologne—in E for Trans Fl, Ob d'amore, Va d'amore, Strs & Continuo; in e for Trans Fl, Vn, Strs & Continuo; in D for Trans Fl, Strs & Continuo; in E♭ for Strs & Continuo; in G for Trans Fl, Chalumeau, Ob, 2 Db, Strs & Continuo *(rec Cologne, May 30–June 3, 1994)* Denon ("Aliare" series) ▲ CO 78933 [DDD]

Roberts, Edgar (pno)
Starer, R.:Night Thoughts, w. Theresa Santiago (sop), Jennifer Hines (mez), Anthony Griffey (ten), Neil Michaels (bar), Adelaide Roberts (pno) Albany ▲ TROY 151 [DDD]

Roberts, Eryl (perc)
A Secret Place, w. Simone Rebello (perc), Andrew Scott (a sax), Liz Gilliver (mar), Kalengo Percussion Ensemble, John Melbourne (perc), Chris Bastock (perc), Richard Dyson (perc) *(rec Zion Institute, Manchester, 1995)* Doyen ▲ CD 040 [DDD]

Roberts, Giles (kbd)—see ORCHESTRAS & ENSEMBLES Invocation

Roberts, Gwyn (rcr)
Veracini, F.M.:Sons Rcr, w. Tempesta di Mare—Sons I-VI PGM ▲ PGM 107

Roberts, Gwyn (vc)—see also ORCHESTRAS & ENSEMBLES Perihelion Ensemble members, Perihelion
Edwards, R.:Ecstatic Dance Va, w. Patricia Pollett (va) *(rec Nickson Room, Univ of Queensland, Feb 1993)* Tall Poppies ▲ TP 51 [DDD]

Roberts, Katherine (hpd)
Couperin, L.:Suites Hpd—Suites in C, g, D & a *(rec Jan. 4–5, 1992)* Koch International Classics ▲ KIC 7239 [DDD]

Roberts, Marcus (pno)
Gershwin, G.:"I Got Rhythm" Vars, w. R. Sadin (cnd), Lincoln Center Jazz Orch members, Orch of St. Luke members *(rec Masonic Grand Lodge, New York City, July 13, 1995)* Sony Classical ▲ SK 68488 [DDD]
Gershwin, G.:Rhap in Blue, w. R. Sadin (cnd), Lincoln Center Jazz Orch members, Orch of St. Luke members *(rec Masonic Grand Lodge, New York City, June 2, 6 & 7, 1995)* Sony Classical ▲ SK 68488 [DDD]
Johnson, J.P.:Pno Music, w. R. Sadin (cnd), Lincoln Center Jazz Orch members, Orch of St. Luke members—Yamekraw [orchd Still] *(rec Masonic Grand Lodge, New York City, June 2, 6 & 7, 1995)* Sony Classical ▲ SK 68488 [DDD]

Roberts, Mo (perc)
Smart Went Crazy, w. Meridian Arts Ensemble *(rec Mar. 1993)* Channel Crossings ▲ CCS 4192 [DDD]

Roberts, Paul (pno)
Debussy, C.:Estampes *(rec Hurstwood Farm, Kent, Nov 1994)* Classical Recording Co. ▲ CRC 501-2 [DDD]
Debussy, C.:Images (6) Pno—Set 2 *(rec Hurstwood Farm, Kent, Nov 1994)* Classical Recording Co. ▲ CRC 501-2 [DDD]
Debussy, C.:Preludes Pno—Book 1 *(rec Hurstwood Farm, Kent, Nov 1994)* Classical Recording Co. ▲ CRC 501-2 [DDD]

Roberts, Stephen (hn)—see ORCHESTRAS & ENSEMBLES Fine Arts Brass Ensemble
Roberts, Timothy (hpd)—see ORCHESTRAS & ENSEMBLES Spectre de la Rose
Roberts, Timothy (hpd/cnd)—see ORCHESTRAS & ENSEMBLES Invocation

Roberts, Timothy (hpd/org)
Tomkins, T.:Instr & Voc Music, w. John Bryan (hpd), Rose Consort of Viols, Red Byrd—Pavan in F; Almain in F; In Nomine; Above the stars; Fant. XIV; Fant. I; A Fancy, for 2 to play; Ut re mi; O Lord, let me know mine end; Fant. XII; In Nomine II; Pavan & galliard, Earl Strafford; Fant. for 6 Vls; Miserere; Voluntary; Pavan in a; Galliard; Thou art my King, O God *(rec Forde Abbey, Dorset)* Naxos ("Early Music" series) ▲ 8.550602 [DDD]

Roberts, Timothy (hpd/org/vir)
Gibbons, O.:Kbd Music—The Lord of Salisbury his Pavan & Galliard for Harpsichord; Preludium in G for Organ; A Mask:The Fairest Nymph for Virginals *(rec Forde Abbey, Dorset)* Naxos ▲ 8.550603 [DDD]

Roberts, Timothy (hpd/virs)
Byrd, W.:Kbd Music—John Come Kiss Me Now; Pavan in a; Qui passe *(rec Dorset, between Apr. & Nov. 1992)* Naxos ▲ 8.550604 [DDD]

Roberts, Timothy (pno)—see also ORCHESTRAS & ENSEMBLES Invocation
Benda, G.A.:Cephalus & Aurora, w. E. Kirby (sop), R. Müller (ten)—includes Du kleine Blondine; Belise starb; Mein Geliebter hat versprochen; Faulheit, itzo will ich dir; Philint ist still und fleiht die Schonen; Cephalus & Aurore; Ein trunkner Dichter; Wir Arem, denn des Fieberes Kraft; Philint stand vor Babes Thür; Du fehlest mir, wie einsam und wie stille; Das Andenken; Von nonan, O liebe, lass ich dein Reich; Mein Thrysis!; Ich liebe nur Ismene; Liebe Amor Hyperion ▲ CDA 66649

Roberts, Timothy (pno/hpd)
O Tuneful Voice:Songs & Duets from Late 18th Century England, w. Emma Kirkby (sop), Rufus Müller (ten), Frances Kelly (single-action hp) Hyperion ▲ CDA 66497 [DDD]

Roberts, Timothy (spinet/hpd/chamber org)
Blow, J.:Music for Kbd—Prelude in G; Minuet, "The Self-banish'd"; Morlake Ground; Suite No. 1 in d; Ground in g; Verse (voluntary) in g [anon., probably Blow]; Suite No. 3 in a; Ground in C *(rec Jan. 25–27, 1993)* Hyperion ▲ CDA 66646 [DDD]

Roberts, Timothy (spinet/hpd/chamber org) (cont.)
Blow, J.:Songs, w. J. M. Ainsley (ten), P. Chateauneuf (gtr/thb)—No More, the Dear, Lovely Nymph's No More; Lovely Selina, Innocent & Free; O Turn Not Those Fine Eyes away; Fairest Work of Happy Nature; Flavia Grown Old; Oh! That Mine Eyes Would Melt into a Flood; O Might God, Who Sit'st on High; Sabina Has a Thousand Charms; Of All the Torments, All the Cares; No, Lesbia, You Ask in Vain *(rec Jan. 25–27, 1993)* Hyperion ▲ CDA 66646 [DDD]

Roberts, Timothy (t sax)—see ORCHESTRAS & ENSEMBLES East Coast Saxophone Quartet

Robertson, George (va)
Reger, M.:Serenades Fl, Opp. 77a & 141a, w. A. Noakes (fl), B. Wilde (vn) ASV ▲ ASV 875 [DDD]
Reger, M.:Suites Va ASV ▲ ASV 875 [DDD]

Robertson, Martin (a sax)
Martin, F.:Ballade A Sax, w. M. Bamert (cnd), London PO Chandos ▲ CHAN 9380 [DDD]

Robertson, Martin (sax)—see ORCHESTRAS & ENSEMBLES Nash Ensemble

Robertson, Paul (vn)—see also ORCHESTRAS & ENSEMBLES Medici String Quartet
Elgar, E.:Son Vn, w. John Bingham (pno) Medici Quartet ▲ MQT 7001 [DDD]

Robilette, John (pno)
Chopin, F.:Impromptus *(rec 1993)* Pro Arte ▲ CDS 3491
Fauré, G.:Nocturnes (13) Pno—No. 3 in A♭, Op. 33/3 *(rec 1993)* Pro Arte ▲ CDS 3491
Franck, C.:Prélude, choral et fugue *(rec 1993)* Pro Arte ▲ CDS 3491
Franck, C.:Symphonic Vars, w. P. Freeman (cnd), St. Petersburg PO *(rec 1993)* Pro Arte ▲ CDS 3491
Poulenc, F.:Movts perpétuels *(rec 1993)* Pro Arte ▲ CDS 3491
Schumann, R.:Carnaval Pno Pro Arte ▲ CDS 3464
Schumann, R.:Con Pno, w. P. Freeman (cnd), St. Petersburg PO Pro Arte ▲ CDS 3464

Robilliard, Louis (org)
Arkadiev, M.:Missa brevis, w. L. Litsova (cnd), J. Berthelon (cnd), Saratov Phil Choir, Maîtrise de la Loire REM ▲ REM 311275 [DDD]
Bortnyansky, D.:Sacred Choral Music, w. L. Litsova (cnd), J. Berthelon (cnd), Saratov Phil Choir, Maîtrise de la Loire—Cons Nos. 34 & 35 REM ▲ REM 311275 [DDD]
Duruflé, M.:Motets on Gregorian Chants, Op. 10, w. L. Litsova (cnd), J. Berthelon (cnd), Saratov Phil Choir, Maîtrise de la Loire REM ▲ REM 311275 [DDD]
Mendelssohn, F.:Motets, Op. 39, w. L. Litsova (cnd), J. Berthelon (cnd), Saratov Phil Choir, Maîtrise de la Loire REM ▲ REM 311275 [DDD]
Poulenc, F.:Litanies à la vierge noire, w. L. Litsova (cnd), J. Berthelon (cnd), Saratov Phil Choir, Maîtrise de la Loire REM ▲ REM 311275 [DDD]
Tchesnokov, P.:Liturgie 6, w. L. Litsova (cnd), J. Berthelon (cnd), Saratov Phil Choir, Maîtrise de la Loire REM ▲ REM 311275 [DDD]

Robin, Jacqueline (pno)
Boëly, A.P.F.:Pno Music—Son., Op. 1/1; Caprices, Op. 2; Suite, Op. 16/2; Études, Opp. 6 & 13; Moderato Molto Legato, Op. 46/12; Pièce, Op. 48/11; Tempo Moderato, Op. 52/11 Arion ▲ ARN 68260 [AAD]
Jolivet, A.:Nocturne, w. Pierre Pénassou (vc) Arion ▲ ARN 68299 [AAD]

Robin, L. (dr)
Blanchard, P.:Music of, w. P. Blanchard (vn), V. Pagliarin (vn), C. Mouton (bass), C. Terranova (kbd), M. Garay (perc)—Isidora; Koid'9; Perdoname; Folklores; Train de sables; Lithops; Marquesas Keys; Bodas de sangue *(rec Nov. 1992)* OMD ▲ CD 1538 [DDD]

Robinson, Christopher (org)
Saint-Saëns, C.:Sym 3, w. L. Frémaux (cnd), City of Birmingham SO Royal Classics ▲ ROY 6440
Saint-Saëns, C.:Sym 3, w. L. Frémaux (cnd), City of Birmingham SO—Mvts. 1 & 2 Klavier ■ KC 526
Saint-Saëns, C.:Sym 3, w. L. Frémaux (cnd), City of Birmingham SO Klavier ▲ KCD 11010 [ADD]

Robinson, David (calliope)
Schickele, P.:Son da Circo, w. Peter Schickele (calliope) *(rec International Circus Hall of Fame, Peru, IN, May 30, 1995)* Telarc ▲ CD 80390 [DDD]

Robinson, Gabrielle (vn)
Handel, D.:The Tyger, w. Mary Henderson (sop), Sara Lambert Bloom (ob), Jina Lee (vn), Rebecca Boughton (va), Deborah Netanel (vc), Mark Butler (pno), C. Zimmerman (cnd) Vienna Modern Masters ▲ VMM 2019 [DDD]

Robinson, Joseph (ob)
Barber, S.:Summer Music, w. Jeanne Baxtresser (fl), Stanley Drucker (cl), Judith LeClair (bn), Philip Myers (hn) EMI Classics ("Anglo-American Chamber Music" series) ▲ CDC 55400
Rochberg, G.:Con Ob, w. Z. Mehta (cnd), New York PO New World ▲ NW 335-2 [DDD] ■ NW 335-4 (D)
Schumann, R.:Romances Ob, w. Thomas Hecht (pno) *(rec Performing Arts Ctr/Purchase College-State Univ of NY Recital Hall, May 8, 1995)* Elysium ▲ GRK 709 [DDD]

Robinson, S. (gtr)
Adler, S.:Son Gtr *(rec DeLand, FL, 1993)* Centaur ▲ CRC 2204 [DDD]
Blanchard, H.:Innocent Meandering *(rec DeLand, FL, 1993)* Centaur ▲ CRC 2204 [DDD]
Castelnuovo-Tedesco, M.:Son Cl & Pno Centaur ▲ CRC 2056 [DDD]
Hand, F.:Trilogy *(rec DeLand, FL, 1993)* Centaur ▲ CRC 2204 [DDD]
Moreno Torroba, F.:Castillos de España (sels)—5 selections Centaur ▲ CRC 2056 [DDD]
Ponce, M.:Son 3 Gtr Centaur ▲ CRC 2056 [DDD]
Rorem, N.:Suite Gtr *(rec DeLand, FL, 1993)* Centaur ▲ CRC 2204 [DDD]
Schiff, D.:Rhap Gtr *(rec DeLand, FL, 1993)* Centaur ▲ CRC 2204 [DDD]
Tansman, A.:Cavatina Centaur ▲ CRC 2056 [DDD]

Robinson, Scott (conch shell/perc)
Lockwood, A.:Thousand Year Dreaming, w. Art Baron (conch shell/trbn/didjerido), Liby Van Cleve (ob/E hn), Jon Gibson (didjeridu), J.D. Parran (cl), Michael Publiese (perc), John Snyder (didjeridu/waterphone), Charles Wood (tam-tam, stones), Peter Zummo (trbn/didjeridu) ¿What Next? ▲ WN 0010

Robinson, Sharon (vc)—see also ORCHESTRAS & ENSEMBLES Kalichstein-Laredo-Robinson Trio
Bland, W.:Rhap Vc & Pno, w. M. Garrett (pno) Bridge ▲ BCD 9013 [DDD]
Boccherini, L.:Qnts Strs, w. Issac Stern (vn), Cho-Liang Lin (vn), Jaime Laredo (va), Yo-Yo Ma (vc)—Qnt in E for Strs, Op. 13/5 Sony Classical ▲ SK 53983
Boccherini, L.:Qnt Strs, G.275, w. Cho-Liang Lin (vn), Isaac Stern (vn), Jaime Laredo (va), Yo-Yo Ma (vc) Sony Classical ▲ SK 53983
Brahms, J.:Sextet Strs, Op. 18, w. I. Stern (vn), C.-L. Lin (vn), J. Laredo (va), M. Tree (va), Yo-Yo Ma (vc) Sony Classical 2-▲ S2K 45820
Brahms, J.:Sextet Strs, Op. 36, w. I. Stern (vn), Cho-Liang Lin (vn), J. Laredo (va), M. Tree (va), Yo-Yo Ma (vc) Sony Classical 2-▲ S2K 45820
Brahms, J.:Trios (3) Pno, w. J. Kalichstein (pno), J. Laredo (vn) Vox Box 3-▲ CD3X 3029 [DDD]
Debussy, C.:Son Vc, w. M. Garrett (pno) Grenadilla ■ 1065
Dvořák, A.:Trio 4 Pno, "Dumky", w. J. Laredo (vn), J. Kalichstein (pno) Vox Box 3-▲ CD3X 3029 [DDD]
Fauré, G.:Elégie, w. M. Garrett (pno) Grenadilla ■ 1065
Mendelssohn, F.:Trio 1 Pno, w. J. Kalichstein (pno), J. Laredo (vn) Vox Box 3-▲ CD3X 3029 [DDD]
Mendelssohn, F.:Trio 2 Pno, w. J. Kalichstein (pno), J. Laredo (vn) Vox Box 3-▲ CD3X 3029 [DDD]
Rorem, N.:After Reading Shakespeare Grenadilla ■ 1065
Schubert, Franz:Qnt Strs, D.956, w. Cho-Liang Lin (vn), Isaac Stern (vn), Jaime Laredo (va), Yo-Yo Ma (vc) Sony Classical ▲ SK 53983
Zwilich, E.T.:Con Vn, w. Jaime Laredo (vn), Louisville Orch Louisville ▲ LCD 009 [ADD]

Robison, Paula (fl)
Andersen, J.:Fl & Pno Music, w. Samuel Sanders (pno)—Au Bord de la Mer, Op. 9; Babillard, Op. 24/6; Chant Pastorale, Op. 24/1; Alla Mazurka, Op. 24/3; Berceuse, Op. 28/1; Die Mühle, Op. 55/4; Reverie, Op. 24/2; Die Blumen, Op. 56/2; Impromptu, Op. 7; Scherzino, Op. 55/6; Melodie, Op. 52 *(rec SUNY, Purchase, Theatre C, Feb. 14–16, 1995)* Arabesque ▲ ARA 6668 [DDD]
Barber, S.:Canzone Fl & Pno, w. T. Hester (pno) MusicMasters ▲ 7019-2-C [DDD]
Barber, S.:Mélodies passagères, w. T. Hester (pno) MusicMasters ▲ 7019-2-C [DDD]
Beaser, R.:Mountain Songs, w. E. Fisk (gtr) MusicMasters ▲ 7038-2-C [DDD]
Beaser, R.:The Old Men Admiring Themselves In The Water, w. R. Beaser (pno) New World ▲ 80403-2 [DDD]

▲ = CD ♦ = Enhanced CD Δ = MD ■ = Cassette Tape □ = DCC

Robison, Paula (fl) (cont.)
Beaser, R.:Song of the Bells, w. A. Neale (cnd), Solisti New York CO New World ▲ 80403-2 [DDD]
Beaser, R.:Vars Fl, w. T. Hester (pno) MusicMasters ▲ 7019-2-C [DDD]
Boehm, T.:Compositions Fl, w. Samuel Sanders (pno)—Vars on "Nel cor più sento", Op. 4 *(rec New York City, 1974)* Vanguard Classics ▲ OVC 889 [ADD]
Borne, F.:Fant brillante sur Carmen, w. S. Sanders (pno) Vanguard Classics ▲ OVC 4058
Carmen Fantasy, w. Samuel Sanders (pno) Vanguard Classics ▲ OVC 4058
Copland, A.:Duo Fl, w. T. Hester (pno) MusicMasters ▲ 7019-2-C [DDD]
Dutilleux, H.:Sonatine Fl, w. S. Sanders (pno) Vanguard Classics ▲ OVC 4058
Flutes, w. Ransom Wilson (fl), Carol Wincenc (fl) New World ▲ 80403-2 [DDD]
French Masterpieces for Flute & Piano, w. Ruth Laredo (pno) MusicMasters ▲ 01612-67069-2
Gaubert, P.:Nocturne et Allegro scherzando, w. Samuel Sanders (pno) *(rec New York City, 1974)* Vanguard Classics ▲ OVC 889 [ADD]
Gaubert, P.:Son 1 Fl, w. S. Sanders (pno) Vanguard Classics ▲ OVC 4058
Genin, Paul A.:Vars on "Carnival of Venice", w. Samuel Sanders (pno) *(rec New York City, 1974)* Vanguard Classics ▲ OVC 889 [ADD]
Godard, B.:Suite de trois morceaux, w. Samuel Sanders (pno) [arr for fl & pno] *(rec New York City, 1974)* Vanguard Classics ▲ OVC 889 [ADD]
Grieg, E.:Songs, w. Samuel Sanders (pno)—Wedding Day at Troldhaugen, Op. 65/6; Love, Op. 67/5; 2 Brown Eyes, Op. 5/1; Solveig's Song [from Peer Gynt], Op. 23/19; I Love You!, Op. 5/3; A Swan, Op. 25/2; Spring, Op. 33/2; Thanks for Your Advice, Op. 21/4 *(rec SUNY, Purchase, Theatre C, Feb. 14-16, 1995)* Arabesque ▲ ARA 6668 [DDD]
Harris, R.:Lyric Study, w. Timothy Hester (pno) MusicMasters ▲ 7019-2-C [DDD]
Hummel, J.N.:Son Vn & Pno, Op. 50, w. Samuel Sanders (pno) *(rec New York City, 1974)* Vanguard Classics ▲ OVC 889 [ADD]
Mountain Songs:A Cycle of American Folk Music, w. Eliot Fisk (gtr) MusicMasters ▲ 7038-2-C [DDD]
Mozart, W.A.:Qts Fl, w. Tokyo String Quartet members Vanguard Classics ▲ OVC 4001 [ADD]
Taffanel, P.:Andante Pastorale et Scherzettino, w. S. Sanders (pno). Vanguard Classics ▲ OVC 4058

Robles, Marisa (hp)
Basic 100, Vol. 55, w. Richard Stoltzman (cl), James Galway (fl) RCA Victor ▲ 09026-68024-2 ■ 09026-68024-4
Debussy, C.:Son Fl, w. P. Davies (fl), R. Chase (va) Virgin Classics ▲ 59604 [DDD]
Harp Favourites London ("Weekend Classics" series) ▲ 436293-2 [ADD]
Marisa Robles, w. Academy of St. Martins in the Field [cnd:Iona Brown] London ("Serenata" series) ▲ 425723-2 [ADD]
Masterworks for the Harp, w. Robles, Marisa (hp) Boston Skyline ▲ BSD 119 [ADD]
Mozart, W.A.:Con Fl Hp, w. James Galway (fl), E. Mata (cnd), London SO RCA Gold Seal ▲ 09026-68113-2 [ADD]
Mozart, W.A.:Con Fl Hp, w. James Galway (fl), E. Mata (cnd), London SO RCA Gold Seal ▲ 6723-2 [ADD] ■ 6723-4 (CrO2)
Mozart, W.A.:Con Fl Hp, w. Jame Galway (fl), E. Mata (cnd), London SO RCA Victor ▲ 09026-68024-2; ■ 09026-68024-2
Mozart, W.A.:Con Fl Hp, w. James Galway (fl), J. Galway (cnd), CO of Europe RCA Red Seal 2-▲ 7861-2-RC [DDD]
Robertson, E.:The Namia Suite, w. C. Hyde-Smith (fl), Marisa Robles Harp Ensemble ASV ("White Line" series) ▲ WHL 2068 [DDD]

Robson, Anthony (ob d'amore)
Bach, J.S.:Con Ob, BWV 1053, w. E. Wallfisch (cnd), Orch of the Age of Enlightenment [arr Anthony Robson] Virgin Classics ▲ CD 45190
Bach, J.S.:Con Ob d'amore, w. E. Wallfisch (cnd), Orch of the Age of Enlightenment Virgin Classics ▲ CDC 45095

Robson, Anthony (ob)
Albinoni, T.:Cons à 5 Obs, Op. 7, w. S. Standage (cnd), Collegium Musicum 90—Nos. 3 in B♭, 6 in D, 9 in F & 12 in C Chandos ("Chaconne" series) ▲ CHAN 0579 [DDD]
Albinoni, T.:Cons à 5 Obs, Op. 9, w. S. Standage (cnd), Collegium Musicum 90—Nos. 2 in d, 5 in C, 8 in g & 11 in B♭ Chandos ("Chaconne" series) ▲ CHAN 0579 [DDD]
Bach, Joh. Christian:Con 2 Ob, w. A. Halstead (cnd), Hanover Band *(rec Rosslyn Hill Chapel, London, Mar-Apr 1995)* CPO ▲ CPO 999347-2 [DDD]
Bach, Joh. Christian:Sinf concertante, T.284/6, w. Graham Cracknell (vn), Anna McDonald (vn), A. Halstead (cnd), Hanover Band *(rec Rosslyn Hill Chapel, London, Dec 1995)* CPO ▲ CPO 999348-2 [DDD]
Bach, J.S.:Cant 82, w. Nathalie Stutzmann (cta), Roy Goodman (org), R. Goodman (cnd), Hanover Band *(rec Watford Town Hall, Hertfordshire, U.K, Jan 31-Feb 3, 1994)* RCA Red Seal ▲ 09026-62655-2 [DDD]
Bach, J.S.:Cant 170, w. Nathalie Stutzmann (cta), Roy Goodman (org), Alistair Ross (org), R. Goodman (cnd), Hanover Band *(rec Watford Town Hall, Hertfordshire, U.K, Jan 31-Feb 3, 1994)* RCA Red Seal ▲ 09026-62655-2 [DDD]
Bach, J.S.:Con Ob, BWV 1059, w. E. Wallfisch (cnd), Orch of the Age of Enlightenment [arr Anthony Robson] Virgin Classics ▲ CD 45190
Bach, J.S.:Con Vn & Ob, w. E. Wallfisch (vn), E. Wallfisch (cnd), Orch of the Age of Enlightenment Virgin Classics ▲ CDC 45095
Vivaldi, A.:Con Ob Vns, w. S. Standage (vn), M. Comberti (vn), S. Standage (cnd), Collegium Musicum 90 Chandos ("Chaconne" series) ▲ CHAN 0528 [DDD]
Vivaldi, A.:Cons for 2 Obs, w. C. Latham (ob), S. Standage (cnd), Collegium Musicum 90—RV.535 in d Chandos ("Chaconne" series) ▲ CHAN 0528 [DDD]

Robson, Anthony (sop rcr)
Arne, T.:Songs, w. John Mark Ainsley (ten), Miles Golding (vn), Roy Goodman (vn), Jane Coe (vc), Robert King (hpd/org)—Under the Greenwood Tree; Come Away Death; Where the Bee Sucks *(rec St Jude-on-the-Hill, London, Dec 20-21, 1968)* United ▲ CAL 88002 [DDD]

Robyn, Paul (va)—see ORCHESTRAS & ENSEMBLES Hollywood String Quartet

Rocca, Christian (cl)
Klein, G.:Divert Ob, w. Jean-Pierre Arnaud (ob), Jean-Marc Liet (ob), Rémi Lerner (cl), Michel Tavernier (bn), Amaury Wallez (bn), Eric Karcher (hn), Philippe Queyraud (hn) Arion ▲ ARN 68272 [DDD]

Rochberg, George (pno)
Rochberg, G.:Ricordanza, w. N. Fischer (vc) CRI ■ ACS 6013

Roche, Joseph (vn)
Boulanger, L.:Cortège, w. P. Freed (pno) Vox Box 2-▲ CDX 5029 [ADD]
Boulanger, L.:Nocturne, w. P. Freed (pno) Vox Box 2-▲ CDX 5029 [ADD]
Carreño, T.:Qt Strs, w. R. Zelnick (vn), T. Strasser (va), C. Heller (vc) Vox Box 2-▲ CDX 5029 [ADD]
Tailleferre, G.:Son 1 Vn, w. P. Freed (pno) Vox Box 2-▲ CDX 5029 [ADD]

Rochester, Marc (org)
European Organ Tour, w. Graham Barber (org), Kimberly Marshall (org), John Scott Whiteley (org) *(rec 1983-88)* Priory ▲ PRCD 903

Rodenhäuser, Ulf (cl)
Hindemith, P.:Son Cl, w. Kalle Randalu (pno) MD + G ▲ MDG CD 3040695

Rodes, Ignacio (gtr)
Bardwell, W.:Son Gtr Opra Tres ▲ 1010 [DDD]
Brouwer, L.:Son Gtr Opra Tres ▲ 1010 [DDD]
Esplá, O.:Tempo di Sonata Opra Tres ▲ 1010 [DDD]
Ginastera, A.:Son Gtr Opra Tres ▲ 1010 [DDD]

Rodgers, Elizabeth (chromelodeon/harmonic canon)
Partch, H.:Daphne of the Dunes, w. Frank Cassara (boo/spoils of war/kithara 2), Dominic Donato (b mar/surrogate kithara/boo), Dean Drummond (harmonic canons/kithara 2/spoils of war/kithara), Nina Kellman (kithara 2/harmonic canon/surrogate kithara), Michael Lipsey (cloud-chamber bowls), Ted Mook (vc/gourd tree/cone gongs), James Pugliese (diamond mar) *(rec Queens, NY, Mar. 12, 1991)* Mode ▲ MODE 33

Rodgers, Elizabeth (kbd/pno)
Rosenblum, M.:Circadian Rhythms, w. Ted Mook (vc), James Pugliese (perc) *(rec Floral Park, NY, Mar. 19, 1990)* Mode ▲ MODE 33

Rodgers, Elizabeth (pno)
American Journey:Poetry & Song in the 20th Century, w. New Amsterdam Singers Albany ▲ TROY 108 [DDD]
Hovhaness, A.:O Lady Moon, w. Barbara Martin (sop), Lawrence Sobol (cl) Grenadilla ■ GSC 1073
Husa, K.:Moravian Songs, w. Barbara Ann Martin (sop) Grenadilla ■ GSC 1073
Husa, K.:Moravian Songs, w. Barbara Ann Martin (sop) *(rec Sorcerer Sounds, NYC)* New World ▲ 80493-2

Rodin, Kirill (vc)
Tchaikovsky, P.:Trio Pno, w. L. Timofeyeva (pno), M. Fedotov (vn) MK ▲ 417001 [DDD]

Rodina, Inna (fl)
Ustvolskaya, G.:Composition 3, w. Natalia Danilina (fl), Maria Osipova (fl), Michail Tokarev (fl), Kirill Sokolov (bn), Dmitrii Krasnik (bn), Arsenii Makarov (bn), Konstantin Shevchuk (bn), Galina Sandovskaya (pno), O. Malov (cnd) *(rec St. Petersburg Radio House, Jan. 1994)* Megadisc ▲ 7867

Rodriguez, Antonia (fl)—see also ORCHESTRAS & ENSEMBLES Grupo Cosmos
Bartók, B.:Hungarian Folksongs Vn, w. Maria Teresa Pérez (pno)—Suite campesina hungara *(rec Madrid, Sept 4-7, 1990)* RNE/Spanish National Radio ▲ M3/04 [DDD]
Borne, F.:Fant brillante sur Carmen, w. Maria Teresa Pérez (pno) *(rec Madrid, Sept 4-7, 1990)* RNE/Spanish National Radio ▲ M3/04 [DDD]
Chaminade, C.:Concertino Fl, w. Maria Teresa Pérez (pno) *(rec Madrid, Sept 4-7, 1990)* RNE/Spanish National Radio ▲ M3/04 [DDD]
Franck, C.:Son Vn, w. Maria Teresa Pérez (pno) *(rec Madrid, Sept 4-7, 1990)* RNE/Spanish National Radio ▲ M3/04 [DDD]
Galway, J.:Fl Music, w. Maria Teresa Pérez (pno)—Popular Love Song *(rec Madrid, Sept 4-7, 1990)* RNE/Spanish National Radio ▲ M3/04 [DDD]
Martin, F.:Ballade Fl, w. Maria Teresa Pérez (pno) *(rec Madrid, Sept 4-7, 1990)* RNE/Spanish National Radio ▲ M3/04 [DDD]

Rodriguez, Clara (pno)
Moleiro, M.:Pno Music—Children's Suite; Concert Study; Joropo; Little Suite; Pictures of the Plains; Prelude & Fugue; Serenade; Sonatinas 1-5; Toccatas (3); Miniatures (2); Playera ASV ▲ ASV 890 [DDD]
Ruiz, F.:Pno Music—Triptico Tropical for Piano, plus others ASV ▲ ASV 962

Rodriguez, Santiago (pno)
Bach, J.S.:Brandenburg Con 3, w. P. Rösel (pno) Élan ▲ CD 2240 [DDD]
Bach, J.S.:Brandenburg Con 5, w. P. Rösel (pno) Élan ▲ CD 2240 [DDD]
Bach, J.S.:Chaconne Élan ▲ 2200 [DDD]
Brahms, J.:Studies (5) Piano—No. 5, Chaconne by J.S. Bach Élan ▲ 2200 [DDD]
Brahms, J.:Vars on a Theme by Paganini—24 vars. Élan ▲ 2200 [DDD]
Brahms, J.:Waltzes Pno, Op. 39 Élan ▲ 2200 [DDD]
Castelnuovo-Tedesco, M.:Con Pno, w. G. Manahan (cnd), Richmond Sinfonia Élan ▲ CD 2222 [DDD]
Chopin, F.:Son Pno, Op. 35 Élan ▲ CD 82262 [DDD]
Debussy, C.:Preludes Pno (sels)—Nos. 8, 10 & 11 [all from Book 2] Élan ▲ CD 82262 [DDD]
Ginastera, A.:Pno Music—Son No. 1, Op. 22; Son No. 2, Op. 53; Rondo on Argentine Children's Folk Tunes, Op. 19; 3Argentinian Dances, Op. 2; Danza criolla; Trieste [from American Preludes, Op. 12]; Tribute to Aaron Copland; Tribute to Juan Jose Castro; Tribute to Roberto Garcia Morillo; Pastorale; Milonga *(plus solo pno works by Albeniz, Falla, Granados & Ruvo)* Élan ▲ 2202 [DDD]
Grieg, E.:Con Pno, Op. 16, w. E. Tabakov (cnd), Sofia PO Élan ▲ CD 2228 [DDD]
Liszt, F.:Con 1 Pno, w. E. Tabakov (cnd), Sofia PO Élan ▲ CD 2228 [DDD]
Music for Piano Élan ▲ CD 2202 [DDD]
Prokofiev, S.:Con 3 Pno, w. E. Tabakov (cnd), Sofia PO Élan ▲ CD 2220 [DDD]
Rachmaninoff, S.:Con 3 Pno, w. P.A. McRae (cnd), Lake Forest SO Élan ▲ CD 82262 [DDD]
Rachmaninoff, S.:Con 3 Pno, w. E. Tabakov (cnd), Sofia PO Élan ▲ CD 2220 [DDD]
Rachmaninoff, S.:Morceaux de fant Élan ▲ CD 82248 [DDD]
Rachmaninoff, S.:Nocturnes Pno *(rec John Addison Concert Hall, Harmony Hall Regional Center, Fort Washington, Maryland, June 1994)* Élan ▲ CD 2250 [DDD]
Rachmaninoff, S.:Preludes Pno, Opp 23 & 32—10 Preludes, Op. 23 *(rec John Addison Concert Hall, Harmony Hall Regional Center, Fort Washington, Maryland, June 1994)* Élan ▲ CD 2250 [DDD]
Rachmaninoff, S.:Preludes Pno, Opp 23 & 32—13 Preludes, Op. 32 *(rec John Addison Concert Hall, Harmony Hall Regional Center, Fort Washington, Maryland, Apr. 1993)* Élan ▲ CD 2244 [DDD]
Rachmaninoff, S.:Son 1 Pno *(rec John Addison Concert Hall, Harmony Hall Regional Center, Fort Washington, Maryland, Jan., 1993)* Élan ▲ CD 2244 [DDD]
Rachmaninoff, S.:Son 2 Pno Élan ▲ CD 82248 [DDD]
Rachmaninoff, S.:Songs without Words *(rec John Addison Concert Hall, Harmony Hall Regional Center, Fort Washington, Maryland, June 1994)* Élan ▲ CD 2250 [DDD]
Rachmaninoff, S.:Variations on a Theme by Chopin Élan ▲ CD 82248 [DDD]
Rachmaninoff, S.:Variations on a Theme by Corelli *(rec John Addison Concert Hall, Harmony Hall Regional Center, Fort Washington, Maryland, June 1994)* Élan ▲ CD 2250 [DDD]
Reger, M.:Vars & Fugue on a Theme by Mozart, w. P. Rösel (pno) Élan ▲ CD 2240 [DDD]
Shostakovich, D.:Trio 2 Pno, w. R. Ricci (vn), N. Rosen (vc) One-Eleven ▲ URS 92010
A Spanish Album Élan ▲ CD 2206 [DDD]
Surinach, C.:Concertino Pno, w. G. Manahan (cnd), Richmond Sinfonia Élan ▲ CD 2222 [DDD]
Tchaikovsky, P.:Con 1 Pno, w. E. Tabakov (cnd), Sofia PO Élan ▲ CD 2228 [DDD]

Rodwell, Nicholas (cl)
Elgar, E.:Harmony Music I-V, w. Michael Cox (fl), Paul Edmund-Davies (fl), Roy Carter (ob), Martin Gatt (bn)—No. 4, "The Farmyard" EMI Classics ("Anglo-American Chamber Music" series) ▲ CDC 55403

Roehr, Gideon (va)
Atterberg, K.:Suite 3 Vn, w. M. Saulesco (vn), S. Westerberg (cnd), Swedish RSO Swedish Society ▲ SCD 1006

Roelofs, Laura (vn)
Bartók, B.:Contrasts, w. Charles West (cl), Landon Bilyeu (pno) Klavier ▲ KCD 11072 [DDD]

Roelofson, Hans (db)
Dvořák, A.:Qnt Strs, Op. 77, w. Prazak String Quartet Ottavo ▲ OTT 69237 [DDD]

Roerade, Hans (ob)
Roussel, A.:Chamber Music, w. Paul Verhey (fl), Herman Jeurissen (hn), Jean-Jacques Kantorow (vn), Herre-Jan Stengenga (vc), Jet Röling (pno) Olympia ▲ OLY 458 [DDD]
Roussel, A.:Chamber Music, w. Paul Verhey (fl/pic), Frank van den Brink (cl), Jos de Lange (bn), Herre-Jan Stegenga (vc), Jet Röling (pno), Schoenberg String Quartet—Trio for Fl, Va & Vc, Op. 40; Qt for Strs, Op. 45; Andante & Scherzo for Fl & Pno, Op. 51; Pipe for Pic & Pno; Trio for Strs, Op. 58; Music from Elpenor for Fl & Str Qt, Op. 59; Andante from an unfinished Ww Trio for Ob, Cl & Bn Olympia ▲ OLY 460 [DDD]

Rogé, Pascal (pno)
Debussy, C.:Arabesques (2) London ("Jubilee" series) ▲ 417792-2 [ADD]
Debussy, C.:Children's Corner London ("Jubilee" series) ▲ 417792-2 [ADD]
Debussy, C.:Images (6) Pno London ("Jubilee" series) ▲ 417792-2 [ADD]
Debussy, C.:Pno Music (misc) London ("Double Decker" series) 2-▲ 443021-2
Debussy, C.:Suite bergamasque London ("Jubilee" series) ▲ 417792-2 [ADD]
Fauré, G.:Barcarolles (13)—Nos. 1, 2 & 4 London ▲ 425606-2 [DDD]
Fauré, G.:Fant Fl, w. A. Marion (fl) Denon ▲ CO 1476 [DDD]
Fauré, G.:Impromptus Pno, Opp. 25, 31, 34, 91 & 102—Nos. 2 & 3 London ▲ 425606-2 [DDD]
Fauré, G.:Nocturnes (13) Pno—Nos. 1-5 London ▲ 425606-2 [DDD]
Fauré, G.:Romances sans paroles, Op. 17 London ▲ 425606-2 [DDD]
Fauré, G.:Valses-caprices (4)—one unspecified Valse London ▲ 425606-2 [DDD]
Franck, C.:Qnt Pno, w. London Festival Orch members ASV ▲ ASV 769 [DDD]
Franck, C.:Son Vn, w. R. Pople (vn) [cello & piano trans.] ASV ▲ ASV 769 [DDD]
Franck, C.:Symphonic Vars, w. R. Pople (cnd), London Festival Orch ASV ▲ ASV 769 [DDD]
French Chamber Music for Piano & Wind, w. Catherine Cantin (fl), M Bourgue (ob), et al. London ▲ 425861-2 [DDD]
Poulenc, F.:Con Pno, w. C. Dutoit (cnd), Philharmonia Orch *(rec Feb. 24-28, 1992)* London ▲ 436546-2

INSTRUMENT.

Rogé, Pascal (pno) (cont.)
Poulenc, F.:Con for 2 Pnos, w. Sylviane Deferne (pno), C. Dutoit (cnd), Philharmonia Orch *(rec Feb. 24-28, 1992)* London ▲ 436546-2
Poulenc, F.:Pno Music (misc)—Les soirées de Nazelles; 3 Mouvements perpétuels; 3 Novelettes; 9 Improvisations London ▲ 417438-2 [DDD]
Poulenc, F.:Pno Music (misc)—Eight Nocturnes; Suite in C; Thème varié; Improvisations 4,5,9 & 14; Two Intermezzi; Villageoises; Presto in B♭ London ▲ 425862-2 [DDD]
Poulenc, F.:Sxt Pno, w. P. Gallois (fl), M. Bourgue (ob), M. Portal (cl), A. Wallez (bn), A. Cazalet (hn) London ▲ 421581-2 [DDD]
Poulenc, F.:Son Cl Pno, w. M. Portal (cl) London ▲ 421581-2 [DDD]
Poulenc, F.:Son Fl, w. A. Marion (fl) Denon ▲ CO 1476 [DDD]
Poulenc, F.:Son Fl, w. P. Gallois (fl) London ▲ 421581-2 [DDD]
Poulenc, F.:Son Ob, w. M. Bourgue (ob) London ▲ 421581-2 [DDD]
Poulenc, F.:Trio Ob, w. M. Bourgue (ob), A. Wallez (bn) London ▲ 421581-2 [DDD]
Ravel, M.:Gaspard de la nuit London ("Double Decker" series) 2-▲ 440836-2
Ravel, M.:Jeux d'eau London ("Double Decker" series) 2-▲ 440836-2
Ravel, M.:Ma mère l'oye Pno, w. *(2nd pianist unknown)* London ("Double Decker" series) 2-▲ 440836-2
Ravel, M.:Pavane pour une infante défunte London ("Double Decker" series) 2-▲ 440836-2
Ravel, M.:Le Tombeau de Couperin London ("Double Decker" series) 2-▲ 440836-2
Roussel, A.:Joueurs de flûte, w. A. Marion (pno) Denon ▲ CO 1476 [DDD]
Saint-Saëns, C.:Carnival of the Animals, w. C. Ortiz (pno), C. Dutoit (cnd), London Sinfonietta London ▲ 414460-2 [ADD] ■ 414460-4
Saint-Saëns, C.:Carnival of the Animals, w. C, Ortiz (pno), C. Dutoit (cnd), London Sinfonietta London ▲ 430720-2 [DDD]
Saint-Saëns, C.:Cons Pno (comp), w. C. Dutoit (cnd), *(orch unknown)* London ("Double Decca" series) 2-▲ 443865-2
Saint-Saëns, C.:Cons Pno (comp), w. C. Dutoit (cnd), Royal PO London 2-▲ 417351-2 [ADD]
Saint-Saëns, C.:Romance Fl, w. A. Marion (fl) Denon ▲ CO 1476 [DDD]
Satie, E.:Gnossiennes Pno—Nos. 1-6 London ▲ 410220-2 ■ 410220-4 ▯ 410220-5
Satie, E.:Gymnopédies London ▲ 410220-2 [DDD] ■ 410220-4 ▯ 410220-5
Satie, E.:Pno Music (comp) London ▲ 410220-2 [DDD] ■ 410220-4 ▯ 410220-5
Satie, E.:Pno Music (comp)—17 pieces, incl. Pièces froides, 4 Nocturnes London ▲ 421713-2 [DDD]
Satie, E.:Pno Music (misc)—Gymnopedie Nos. 1-3; Gnossiennes (6) for Pno; Nocturnes (5) for Pno; Avant-dernieres pensées; 2 Pieces froides; Deux reveries nocturnes; Prélude de la porte heroïque du ciel; Idylle, à Debussy; Aubade, à Paul Dukas; Meditation, à Albert Roussel London ("Soft Sounds" series) ▲ 444958-2 ■ 444 958-4
Tchaikovsky, P.:Trio Pno, w. P. Amoyal (vn), F. Lodeon (vc) Erato ▲ 45972-2
Widor, C.M.:Suite Fl, w. A. Marion (fl) Denon ▲ CO 1476 [DDD]

Rogel, N. (rcr)
Fleischer, T.:Girl–Butterfly–Girl, w. G. Abrahamson (sop), M. Meckier (hpd) Opus One ▲ Cd 158 [DDD]

Rogelja, Bozo (ob)
Mozart, W.A.:Con Ob, K.314, w. K. Redel (cnd), Camerata Labacensis PMG ("Vienna Master" series) ▲ CD 160224 [DDD]
Mozart, W.A.:Con Ob, K.314, w. K. Redel (cnd), Camerata Labacensis Vivace ▲ 549 [DDD]
Mozart, W.A.:Con Ob, K.314, w. K. Redel (cnd), Camerata Labacensis Sound 2-▲ CDN 115/116 [DDD]

Rogers (pno)
Sessions, R.:From My Diary CRI ■ C 281

Rogers, Douglas (archlt)
Gianoncelli, B.:Il Liuto—Tastegiatas Nos. 1 & 2; Galliarda No. 1; Corrente No. 2; Baletti Primo-Quinto; Bergamasca Focus ▲ FOCUS 935 [DDD]
Kapsberger, G.G.:Libro I d'intavolatura di lauto—Toccatas Nos. 2, 3 & 5; Gagliardas Nos. 3, 10 & 12; Correntes Nos. 1, 9 & 12 Focus ▲ FOCUS 935 [DDD]

Rogers, Douglas (conc)
Regondi, G.:Conc Music—Leisure Moments 2, 3, 4, 5, 7 & 8 for Treble Concertina & Piano [w. Julie Lustman (piano)]; Remembrance for Baritone Concertina *(rec Feb. & May, 1994)* Bridge ▲ BCD 9055 [DDD]
Regondi, G.:Les Oiseaux, w. D. Starobin (gtr) Bridge ▲ BCD 9039 [DDD]
Regondi, G.:Serenade, w. J. Lustman (pno) Bridge ▲ BCD 9039 [DDD]

Rogers, Douglas (lt)
Zamboni, G.:Sons Lt—No. 10 Focus ▲ FOCUS 935 [DDD]

Rogers, Gregory (va)—see ORCHESTRAS & ENSEMBLES Vienna Lanner Ensemble

Rogers, Jane (va)
Bach, J.S.:Brandenburg Con 5, w. Steven Preston (fl), Jonathan Manson (vc), Purcell Quartet Chandos ("Chaconne" series) ▲ CHAN 0595
Bach, J.S.:Con 3 Hpd, w. Jonathan Manson (vc), Purcell Quartet Chandos ("Chaconne" series) ▲ CHAN 0595
Bach, J.S.:Con 5 Hpd, w. Jonathan Manson (vc), Purcell Quartet Chandos ("Chaconne" series) ▲ CHAN 0595
Bach, J.S.:Con 3 for 2 Hpds, w. Jonathan Manson (vc), Paul Nicholson (hpd), Purcell Quartet Chandos ("Chaconne" series) ▲ CHAN 0595
Biber, H. von:Sonatae tam aris quam aulis servientes, w. Mark Bennett (tpt), Michael Laird (tpt), Katherine McGillvray (va), Tim Cronin (va), Purcell Quartet Chandos ▲ CHAN 0591

Rogers, Joanne (pno)
Lybbert, D.:Son Brevis CRI ■ C 281
Talma, L.:Son 2 Pno CRI ■ C 281
A Virtuoso Duo-Piano Showcase, w. Jeannine Morrison (pno) *(rec Spivey Hall, Morrow, GA, June 8 & 9, 1993)* ACA Digital ▲ CM 20023 ■ CM 20023

Rogg, Lionel (org)
À l'Orgue de l'Eglise de l'Abbaye Benedictine d'Ottobeuren Gallo ▲ CD 544 [DDD]
Bach, J.S.:Org Music (comp) [at the Silbermann organ in Arlesheim, Switzerland]—CD 1 *(Preludes & Fugues)*, CD 2 *(Toccatas & Fugues)*, CD 3 *(Partitas, Canzone, Allabreve)* CDs 4 & 5 *(Das Orgelbüchlein)*, CD 6 *(Fantasies & Fugues)*, CDs 7 & 8 *(Leipzig Chorales)*, CD 9 *(Trio Sonatas)*, CDs 10 & 11 *(Deutsche Orgelmesse)*, CD 12 *(Preludes & Fugues) (rec early 1970s)* Harmonia Mundi 12-▲ HMX 290772/83
Handel, G.F.:Cons (16) Org, w. G. Armand (cnd), Toulouse CO—No. 11 [Op. 7/5] *(rec Eglise Abbatiale de Saint Michel de Gaillac, May 1974)* EMI Classics ▲ CDK 65335 [ADD]
Reger, M.:Fant & Fugue on B–A–C–H BIS ▲ CD 242 [DDD]
Reger, M.:Fant & Fugue Org BIS ▲ CD 242 [DDD]
Reger, M.:Pieces Org, Op. 59—Benedictus BIS ▲ CD 242 [DDD]
Reger, M.:Pieces Org, Op. 80—No. 5 "Ave Maria" BIS ▲ CD 242 [DDD]
Rogg, L.:Org Music, w. P. Rouet (org)—Recitativo for Organ 4-Hands (1989); Toccata ritmica for solo Organ Gallo ▲ CD 634 [ADD]
Rogg, L.:Org Music [organ of St. Hedwig, Stockholm]—Elegie, Etudes, Partitas, Variations BIS ▲ CD 346

Rogg, Lionel (syn)
Rogg, L.:Music of, w. J.-P. Goy—Pièce for Ob & Syn (991) BIS ▲ CD 546 [DDD]

Roggenkamp, Peter (pno)
Cage, J.:Music for Marcel Duchamp *(rec 1975)* Wergo ▲ WER 6074-2 [AAD]
Cage, J.:Sons & Interludes—No. 13 *(rec 1975)* Wergo ▲ WER 6074-2 [AAD]
Halaczinsky, R.:Con Pno, w. K. Bernbacher (cnd), Northwest German PO MD + G ▲ L 3451 [DDD]

Rogliano, Marco (vn)
Ragazzi, A.:Con Grosso, w. Andrea Guerrini (vn), Eduardo Pitone (va), Aurelio Bertucci (vc), Antonella Cristiano (hpd), I. Caiazza (cnd), I Solisti Partenopei *(rec Mar 1996)* Kicco Classics ▲ 396 [DDD]
Ragazzi, A.:Con Vn (1728), w. I. Caiazza (cnd), I Solisti Partenopei *(rec Mar 1996)* Kicco Classics ▲ 396 [DDD]
Ragazzi, A.:Con Vn (1729), w. I. Caiazza (cnd), I Solisti Partenopei *(rec Mar 1996)* Kicco Classics ▲ 396 [DDD]

Rognstad, Richard (vc)—see ORCHESTRAS & ENSEMBLES Rawlins Piano Trio

Rogossnig, Konrad (gtr)
Schubert, Franz:Die Schöne Müllerin, w. Peter Schreier (ten) Berlin Classics ▲ BER 1123 [ADD]

Rohde, Kurt (va)
Mozart, W.A.:Adagio Rondo, w. Carol Adee (fl), Noriko Kishi (vc), Roger Wiesmeyer (ob), J. Meredith (cnd), Sonos Handbell Ensemble Well-Tempered Productions ▲ WTP 5182 [DDD]

Rohde, P. Arne (pno)
Mendelssohn, F.:Lieder ohne Worte Pno Berlin Classics ("Eterna" series) ▲ BER 2022 [DDD]
Mendelssohn, F.:Rondo capriccioso Berlin Classics ("Eterna" series) ▲ BER 2022 [DDD]
Mendelssohn, F.:Vars sérieuses Berlin Classics ("Eterna" series) ▲ BER 2022 [DDD]

Rohmann, Imre (pno)
Bach, J.S.:Con for 4 Hpds, w. Z. Kocsis (pno), A. Schiff (pno), S. Falvai (pno), A. Simon (cnd), Franz Liszt Academy Orch Vivace ▲ E 563 [ADD]
Beethoven, L. van:Adagio, WoO 43/2 & Andante & Vars, WoO 44/2, w. L. Mayer (mand) Hungaroton ▲ HCD 12303
Beethoven, L. van:Sonatina Mand, WoO 43, w. L. Mayer (mand) Hungaroton ▲ HCD 12303
Beethoven, L. van:Sonatina Mand, WoO 44, w. L. Mayer (mand) Hungaroton ▲ HCD 12303

Röhn, Andreas (vn)—see also ORCHESTRAS & ENSEMBLES Röhn Trio
Koch, E. von:Music of, w. Sigurd Rascher (a sax), Kerstin Hindart (pno), S. Westerberg (cnd), Munich PO, Swedish RSO—Nordiskt Capriccio; Skandinaviska Danser; Saxofonkonsert; Svensk Dansrapsodi; Karaktärer Föor Vn Och Pno Phono Suecia ▲ PHN 55 [ADD]
Lundquist, T.I.:Landscape, w. Michael Lind (tuba), S. Westerberg (cnd), Swedish RSO Caprice ▲ CAP 21493

Röhn, Eric (vn)
Beethoven, L. van:Con Vn, Op. 61, w. W. Furtwängler (cnd), Berlin PO *(rec Jan 9, 1944)* Iron Needle ▲ IN 1340 (m) [ADD]
Beethoven, L. van:Con Vn, Op. 61, *(orch unknown)* Memories ("Golden" series) 2-▲ MEM 3007

Rohner, Lukas (cym)
Hauser, F.:Die Welle, w. Martin André Grütter (cym/tamtam), Roli Fischer (cym), Barbara Frey (cym), Cyril Lützelschwab (cym), Severin Steinhauser (cym), Hans Ulrich (cym), Ruud Wiener (cym), Michael Erni (timp), Fran Lorkovic (timp), F. Hauser (cnd) *(rec Studio DRS, Basel, Switzerland, Nov. 6, 1988)* Hat Hut ▲ hat ART CD 6017 [ADD]

Rohrig, James (cl)—see ORCHESTRAS & ENSEMBLES California EAR Unit

Rohrmann, Eva (vc)
Sarro, D.N.:Son Fl, w. U. Giani (fl), M. Tinarelli (db), G. Catalucci (hpd) *(rec Dec. 8, 1992)* Bongiovanni ▲ GB 2147 [DDD]

Roi, Daniele (hpd)
Bach, C.P.E.:Sons Fl, w. A. Marion (fl)—in d, H.505 (W.83); in B♭,D & G, H.552-554 (W.125-127); in D & B♭, H.556 & H.560 (W.129-130); in G, H.564 (W.133) Fonè ▲ 89 F 02-26 [DDD]
Bach, C.P.E.:Trio Sons (misc), w. A. Marion (fl), M. Conti (fl)—in B♭ & in d Fonè ▲ 89F04-28 [DDD]
Cambini, G.M.:Son 2 Fl & Hpd, w. A. Marion (fl) Fonè ▲ 89 F 01-25 [DDD]
Cambini, G.M.:Trio 1 for 2 Fls & Hpd, w. M. Conti (fl), A. Marion (fl) Fonè ▲ 89 F 03-27 [DDD]
Clementi, M.:Son 1 Vn, w. A. Marion (fl) Fonè ▲ 89 F 01-25 [DDD]
Locatelli, P.:Son 10 Fl & Hpd, w. A. Marion (fl) Fonè ▲ 89 F 01-25 [DDD]
Nardini, P.:Son Fl, w. A. Marion (fl) Fonè ▲ 89 F 01-25 [DDD]
Nardini, P.:Son Terza, w. A. Marion (fl), M. Conti (fl) Fonè ▲ 89 F 03-27 [DDD]
Platti, G.B.:Sons Fl, w. A. Marion (fl)—No. 2 Fonè ▲ 89 F 01-25 [DDD]
Platti, G.B.:Trio Fls, w. A. Marion (fl), M. Conti (fl) Fonè ▲ 89 F 03-27 [DDD]
Sammartini, G.B.:Son terza Fls, w. A. Marion (fl), M. Conti (fl) Fonè ▲ 89 F 03-27 [DDD]

Roi, Daniele (pno)
Bazzini, A.:Pieces (3) in the form of a Son, w. M. Fornaciari (vn) *(rec 5/88)* Fonè ▲ 88 F 02-22 [DDD]
Dashow, J.:Punti di Vista 1 *(rec Studio Lead, Rome, Dec 1991)* Pro Viva ▲ ISPV 177 CD [DDD]
Martucci, G.:Son Vn, w. M. Fornaciari (vn) *(rec 5/88)* Fonè ▲ 88 F 02-22 [DDD]
Respighi, O.:Son Vn, w. M. Fornaciari (vn) *(rec 5/88)* Fonè ▲ 88 F 02-22 [DDD]

Roig, Juan-Manuel (gtr)
Schulé, B.:Gtr Music—Promenade solitaire, Op. 153; Air et contredanse, Op. 101 *(rec 1990)* Jecklin-Disco ▲ JS 284-2 [DDD]
Schulé, B.:In Memoriam Dinu Lipatti, w. R. Cotutiu (fl) *(rec 1990)* Jecklin-Disco ▲ JS 284-2 [DDD]
Schulé, B.:Petit livre des formes musicales, w. R. Cotutiu (fl) *(rec 1990)* Jecklin-Disco ▲ JS 284-2 [DDD]
Schulé, B.:Triptyque, w. R. Cotutiu (fl) *(rec 1990)* Jecklin-Disco ▲ JS 284-2 [DDD]

Roisman, Josef (vn)—see also ORCHESTRAS & ENSEMBLES Budapest String Quartet members, Budapest String Quartet
Rachmaninoff, S.:Trio élégiaque 2, w. Artur Balsam (pno), Mischa Schneider (vc) *(rec Coolidge Auditorium, Library of Congress, Apr 4, 1952)* Bridge ▲ BRIDGE 9063

Rojak, John D. (bass trbn)—see ORCHESTRAS & ENSEMBLES American Brass Quintet

Rojas, Marcus (tuba)
Lebaron, A.:The E. & O. Line (sels), w. Louise Cloutier (mez—Eurydice/Vendors), Hugh Panero (ten—Hermes), Lawrence Hamilton (bar—Orpheus/Men), Frank London (tpt), Myra Melford (pno/kbd), Davey Williams (gtr), Fred Hopkins (elec bass), Thurman Barker (dr), A. LeBaron (cnd)—Juke Joint Jam Session; Eurydice Meets Hermes; Eurydice's Death [Funeral Band]; Eurydice's River Journey; Orpheus Laments [Looked Away] *(rec Coolidge Auditorium, Library of Congress, 1987)* Mode ▲ Mode 42

Röjder, S. (db)
Crumb, G.:Madrigals (4 books), w. A.-M. Mühle (sop), A.-M. Bergström (fl), S. Lüannerholm (hp), S. Asikainen (perc)—[Sp] *(rec digital)* BIS ▲ CD 261

Rojdestvenski, Alexandre (pno)
Bonis, M.:Son Vn, w. A. Constantin (vn) Thésis ▲ THC 82058
Debussy, C.:Son Vn, w. A. Constantin (vn) Thésis ▲ THC 82058
Franck, C.:Son Vn, w. A. Constantin (vn) Thésis ▲ THC 82058

Røkkum, O. (va)
Blak, K.:Svabo, w. A. E. Klett (cl), N. F. Jeppesen (hn), J. Koch (pno) Tutl ▲ FKT 6

Roknic, Rastko (va)
Bentzon, N.V.:Qt Cl, w. John Kruse (cl), Bjarbe Hansen (vn), Svend Winsløw (vc) *(rec Det Fynske Musikkonservatorium, 1993)* Paula ▲ PACD 78 [DAD]

Roldan, N. (pno)—see ORCHESTRAS & ENSEMBLES Lester Roland Duo

Röling, Jet (pno)
Fauré, G.:Barcarolles (13)—Nos. 9-13 *(rec 10/90)* Ottavo ▲ OTR CI09033 [DDD]
Fauré, G.:Impromptus Pno, Opp. 25, 31, 34, 91 & 102—No. 5 *(rec 10/90)* Ottavo ▲ OTR CI09033 [DDD]
Fauré, G.:Nocturnes (13) Pno—Nos. 10-13 *(rec 10/90)* Ottavo ▲ OTR CI09033 [DDD]
Fauré, G.:Pno Music—Nocturne No. 6 in D♭, Op. 63; Barcarolle No. 5 in f#, Op. 66; Barcarolle No. 6 in E♭, Op. 70; Theme & Vars in c#, Op. 73; Nocturne No. 7 in c#, Op. 74; 8 Short Pieces, Op. 84; Barcarolle No. 7 in d, Op. 90; Impromptu No. 4 in D♭, Op. 91; Barcarolle No. 8 in D♭, Op. 96 Ottavo ▲ OTT 49554 [DDD]
Fauré, G.:Préludes, Op. 103 *(rec 10/90)* Ottavo ▲ OTR CI09033 [DDD]
Grieg, E.:Andante con moto, w. R. Hoogeveen (vn), H. Lambooij (vc) Olympia ▲ OLY 432 [DDD]
Grieg, E.:Fugue, w. R. Hoogeveen (vn), H. Lambooij (vc) [arr for pno trio] Olympia ▲ OLY 432 [DDD]
Grieg, E.:Qt Strs (unfinished), w. R. Hoogeveen (vn), H. Lambooij (vc) [arr for pno trio] Olympia ▲ OLY 432 [DDD]
Grieg, E.:Qt Strs, Op. 27, w. R. Hoogeveen (vn), H. Lambooij (vc) Olympia ▲ OLY 432 [DDD]
Janácek, L.:Jealousy Ottavo ▲ OTR C38607 [DDD]
Janácek, L.:On an Overgrown Path Ottavo ▲ OTR C38607 [DDD]
Janácek, L.:Son October 1, 1905 Ottavo ▲ OTR C38607 [DDD]

▲ = CD ♦ = Enhanced CD Δ = MD ■ = Cassette Tape ▯ = DCC

Röling, Jet (pno) (cont.)
Roussel, A.:Chamber Music, w. Paul Verhey (fl/pic), Frank van den Brink (cl), Hans Roerade (ob), Jos de Lange (bn), Herre-Jan Stegenga (vc), Schoenberg String Quartet—Trio for Fl, Va & Vc, Op. 40; Qt for Strs, Op. 45; Andante & Scherzo for Fl & Pno, Op. 51; Pipe for Pic & Pno; Trio for Strs, Op. 58; Music from Elpenor for Fl & Str Qt, Op. 59; Andante from an unfinished Ww Trio for Ob, Cl & Bn Olympia ▲ OLY 460 [DDD]
Roussel, A.:Chamber Music, w. Paul Verhey (fl), Hans Roerade (ob), Herman Jeurissen (hn), Jean-Jacques Kantorow (vn), Herre-Jan Stengenga (vc) Olympia ▲ OLY 458 [DDD]

Rolla, János (va)
Mozart, W.A.:Sinf concertante Vn, K.364, w. G. Pauk (vn), J. Rolla (cnd), Franz Liszt CO Hungaroton 3-▲ HCD 31030/32 [DDD]
Vivaldi, A.:Trio Sons Vn Lt, w. D. Benkő (lt), Z. Pertis (hpd) Hungaroton ▲ HCD 11978

Rolla, János (vn)
Mozart, W.A.:Concertone Vns, w. G. Pauk (vn), J. Rolla (cnd), Franz Liszt CO Hungaroton 3-▲ HCD 31030/32 [DDD]

Rolland, Sophie (vc)
Lalo, E.:Con Vc, w. G. Varga (cnd), BBC PO ASV ▲ ASV 867 [DDD]
Massenet, J.:Fant Vc, w. G. Varga (cnd), BBC PO ASV ▲ ASV 867 [DDD]
Saint-Saëns, C.:Con 1 Vc, w. G. Varga (cnd), BBC PO ASV ▲ ASV 867 [DDD]
Strauss, R.:Son Vc, w. Marc-André Hamelin (pno) ASV ▲ ASV 913 [DDD]
Thuille, L.:Son Vc, w. Marc-André Hamelin (pno) ASV ▲ ASV 913 [DDD]

Rollez, Jean-Marc (db)
Encores! Bis!:Works for Double Bass, w. Angeline Pondepeyre (pno) Maguelone ▲ 350.507

Roloff, Elisabeth (org)
Elisabeth Roloff Plays Historical Organs in Jerusalem MD + G ▲ MDG 3190538 [DDD]

Rolston, Shauna (vc)
Duets:Ofra Harnoy & Friends, w. Ofra Harnoy (vc), Michael Dussek (pno), Orford String Quartet, Maureen Forrester (cta), Andrew Davis (pno), Jeanne Baxtresser (fl), Catherine Wilson (pno), Paul Brodie (sax), Armin Strings, Canadian Piano Trio, Adele Armin (vn) Mastersound ▲ MST 30 [DDD]
Elgar, E.:Con Vc, w. M. Bernardi (cnd), Calgary PO *(rec Calgary Centre for the Performing Arts, Mar 15-16, 1994)* CBC ("SM 5000" series) ▲ SM5 5153 [DDD]
Fauré, G.:Son 1 Vn, w. M. Pressler (pno) [cello-piano arr.] Summit ▲ DCD 109 [DDD]
Franck, C.:Son Vn, w. M. Pressler (pno) [cello-piano arr.] Summit ▲ DCD 109 [DDD]
Glazunov, A.:Chant du ménéstrel, w. M. Bernardi (cnd), Calgary PO *(rec Calgary Centre for the Performing Arts, Mar 15-16, 1994)* CBC ("SM 5000" series) ▲ SM5 5153 [DDD]
Popper, D.:Hungarian Rhap, w. M. Bernardi (cnd), Calgary PO *(rec Calgary Centre for the Performing Arts, Mar 15-16, 1994)* CBC ("SM 5000" series) ▲ SM5 5153 [DDD]
Saint-Saëns, C.:Con 1 Vc, w. M. Bernardi (cnd), Calgary PO *(rec Calgary Centre for the Performing Arts, Mar 15-16, 1994)* CBC ("SM 5000" series) ▲ SM5 5153 [DDD]
Tchaikovsky, P.:Andante cantabile, w. M. Bernardi (cnd), Calgary PO *(rec Calgary Centre for the Performing Arts, Mar 15-16, 1994)* CBC ("SM 5000" series) ▲ SM5 5153 [DDD]

Rolton, Julian (pno)—see ORCHESTRAS & ENSEMBLES Chagall Trio, Chagall Trio members

Romaner, Franziska (vc)—see ORCHESTRAS & ENSEMBLES Il Ruggiero

Romaní, Albert (hpd)—see ORCHESTRAS & ENSEMBLES L'Academia d'Harmonia

Romano, Daniela Colonna (hp)
The Flute from '700 to '900, w. Enzo Caroli (fl), Renato Maioli (pno) Stradavarius ▲ SIP 25

Romano, Francesco (gtr)
Giuliani, M.:Music for Gtr & Pno, w. Daniela Costa (pno)—Gran Duo Concertante; Due Rondo, Op. 68; Grandi Variazzioni Concertanti sul tema; Grand Pot-pourri National, Op. 93; Variazioni sul tema, Op. 104 Nuova Era ("Ancient Music" series) 2-▲ NUO 7227

Romanski, Aleksander (cl)
Penderecki, K.:Chamber Music, w. W. Malicki (pno), Silesian String Quartet—Qts. Nos. 1 & 2 for Strings; Trio for Strings; Der unterbrochene Gedanke; Son. for Violin & Piano; Miniature, Op. 15; 3 Miniatures for Clarinet & Piano; Cadenza for Viola; Per Slava; Capriccio for Siegfried Palm; Prelude in B♭ for solo Clarinet Wergo ▲ WER 6258-2

Romanul, M. (pno)—see ORCHESTRAS & ENSEMBLES Scarborough Chamber Players

Romanul, Myron (pno)
Becker, J.J.:At Dieppe, w. Susan Narucki (sop) Koch International Classics ▲ KIC 7207 [DDD]

Romanul, Victor (vn)
Mozart, W.A.:Qts Fl, w. P. Fried (fl), R. Barnes (va), R. Feldman (vc) Golden Tone ▲ GT 003

Romanyuk, Igor (vn)
Vivaldi, A.:Cons Vn, Op. 3/1-12, "L'estro armonico", w. V. Gluz (vn), A. Titov (cnd), St. Petersburg Classical Music Studio Orch—No. 8 in a, RV.522; No. 11 in d, RV.565 Infinity Digital ▲ QK 57243 [DDD]
Vivaldi, A.:Cons for 2 Vns, w. V. Gluz (vn), A. Titov (cnd), St. Petersburg Classical Music Studio Orch—in G, RV.516 Infinity Digital ▲ QK 57243 [DDD]
Vivaldi, A.:Cons for 2 Vns, w. Vladislav Gluz (vn), A. Titov (cnd), St. Petersburg New Classical Orch Infinity Digital ▲ QK 66725 [DDD]

Römer, B. (org)
Bach, J.S.:Chorale Preludes Org—(7) BWV 651, 653-655, 657-659 Hänssler Classic ▲ 98.967 [DDD]
Bach, J.S.:Passacaglia & Fugue Org Hänssler Classic ▲ 98.967 [DDD]
Bach, J.S.:Preludes & Fugues, BWV 531-552—BWV 541 Hänssler Classic ▲ 98.967 [DDD]

Romero, Angel (gtr)
Albéniz, I.:Gtr Music—Leyenda (Asturias) Telarc ▲ CD 80213 [DDD] CS 30213 (D)
Bach, J.S.:Chaconne *(rec Dec 10-15, 1990)* Telarc ▲ CD 80288 ■ CS 30288
Bach, J.S.:Jesu bleibet meine Freude *(rec Dec 10-15, 1990)* Telarc ▲ CD 80288 ■ CS 30288
Bach, J.S.:Suites Vc, BWV 1007-1012 [trans. for guitar]—Suite No. 1 *(rec Dec 10-15, 1990)* Telarc ▲ CD 80288 ■ CS 30288
Bach, J.S.:Das wohltemperierte Klavier—[Book 1] Prelude No. 1 *(rec Dec 10-15, 1990)* Telarc ▲ CD 80288 ■ CS 30288
Barrios, A.:Gtr Music—Choro de Saudade; Un Sueño en la Floresta; Aire de Zamba Telarc ▲ CD 80213 [DDD] ■ CS 30213 (D)
Bizet, G.:Carmen (suite 1), w. P. Romero (gtr) Philips ▲ 412609-2 [DDD]
Granados, E.:Danzas españolas (10), w. C. Romero (gtr) [trans. Angel Romero for two guitars] Telarc ▲ CD 80216 [DDD] ■ CS 30216 (D)
Noël, w. Canadian Brass, Canadian Brass Jazz All-Stars, *(children's choir unknown)*, Richard Stoltzman (cl), Harolyn Blackwell (sop), Jerry Hadley (ten), King's Singers, James Galway (fl) *(rec Apr. 17-20, 1994)* RCA Victor ▲ 09026-62683-2 ■ 09026-62683-4
Remembering the Future *(rec Soundtrack Studio, NYC, Dec 12-16, 1994)* RCA ▲ 09026-68268-2
Rodrigo, J.:Concierto Andaluz, w. P. Romero (gtr), N. Marriner (cnd), Academy of St. Martin in the Fields Philips ▲ 400024-2 [ADD]
Rodrigo, J.:Concierto de Aranjuez, w. A. Previn (cnd), London SO EMI Classics ▲ CDC 47693 [ADD]
Rodrigo, J.:Concierto madrigal, w. P. Romero (gtr), N. Marriner (cnd), Academy of St. Martin in the Fields Philips ▲ 400024-2
Rodrigo, J.:Concierto madrigal, w. P. Romero (gtr), N. Marriner (cnd), Academy of St. Martin in the Fields Philips ("Spanish" series) ▲ 432828-2 [ADD]
Rodrigo, J.:Elogio de la guitarra EMI Classics ▲ CDC 47693 [ADD]
Rodrigo, J.:Fant para un gentilhombre, w. A. Previn (cnd), London SO EMI Classics ▲ CDC 47693 [ADD]
Romero, C.:Suite Andaluza Telarc ▲ CD 80213 [DDD] ■ CS 30213 (D)
Sanz, G.:Suite Española Telarc ▲ CD 80213 [DDD] ■ CS 30213 (D)
A Touch of Class:Popular Classics Transcribed for Guitar Telarc ▲ CD 80134 [DDD] ■ CS 30134 (D)
A Touch of Romance Telarc ▲ CD 80213 [DDD] ■ CS 30213 (D)

Romero, Angel (gtr) (cont.)
Vivaldi, A.:Music of, w. Salvatore Accardo (vn), Frederico Agostini (vn), Heinz Holliger (ob), Ida Levin (vn), Aurele Nicolet (fl), Massimo Paris (va d'amore), Celedonio Romero (gtr), Celine Romero (gtr), Henryk Szeryng (vn), Pinchas Zukerman (vn), Academy of St. Martin in the Fields, English CO, I Musici, Naples Weekly International Soloists, St. Paul CO, Dresden Staatskapelle—The Four Seasons [Winter]; Con in D for Gtr [Largo]; Con in D for Fl, "Il gardellino" [Cantabile]; Con in C for Diverse Insts [Andante molto]; Con in g for Strs [Andante molto]; Con in D for 2 Vns & 2 Vcs [Largo]; Con in g for Ob, Vn, Ww & Strs [Larghetto]; Con in a for Gtr, "L'estro armonico" [Largo]; Con in F for 3 Vns [Andante]; Con in F for Fl [Largo]; Con in d for Va D'Amore [Largo]; Con in E for Vn & Strs, "Il riposo" [Allegro]; Con in G for Ob, Bn & Strs [Largo]; Con in B♭ for Vn & Strs [Largo]; Con in A for Gtr & Strs [Larghetto]; Con in E for Vn & Strs, "L'amoroso" [Allegro]; Con in G for Fl [Largo]; Con in A for Vn [Larghetto]; Con in c for Vn & Strs, "Il sospetto" [Andante]; Con in a for 2 Obs & Strs [Largo]; Con in g for Orch [Largo non molto]; Con in a for Vn [Largo]; Con in C for Ob [Adagio]; Con in g for Fl, "La notte" [Largo] Philips ▲ 454051-2 ■ 454 051-4

Romero, Celedonio (gtr)—see ORCHESTRAS & ENSEMBLES Los Romeros

Romero, Celin (gtr)—see also ORCHESTRAS & ENSEMBLES Los Romeros
Bach, J.S.:Sons & Partitas Vn, BWV 1001-1006—Partita No. 2, BWV 1004 [trans by Pepe Romero] Delos ▲ DE 1005 [AAD]
Bach, J.S.:Suites Vc, BWV 1007-1012 [trans gtr Pepe Romero]—No. 3 Delos ▲ DE 1005 [AAD]
Famous Spanish Dances, w. Pepe Romero (gtr) Philips ("Spanish" series) ▲ 432827-2 [ADD]
Giuliani, M.:Grand Ov Delos ▲ DCD 1004 [AAD]
Giuliani, M.:Vars on a Theme by Handel Delos ▲ DCD 1004 [AAD]
Granados, E.:Danzas españolas (10), w. A. Romero (gtr) [trans. Angel Romero for two guitars] Telarc ▲ CD 80216 [DDD] ■ CS 30216 (D)
Sanz, G.:Suite Española Delos ▲ DE 1005 [AAD]
Sor, F.:Sons Gtr, Opp. 15 & 22 Delos ▲ DCD 1004 [AAD]
Sor, F.:Vars on a Theme of Mozart Delos ▲ DCD 1004 [AAD]
Tárrega, F.:Gtr Music—Recuerdos de la Alhambra; 2 Sisters; Maria Tango Delos ▲ DCD 1004 [AAD]
Vivaldi, A.:Music of, w. Salvatore Accardo (vn), Frederico Agostini (vn), Heinz Holliger (ob), Ida Levin (vn), Aurele Nicolet (fl), Massimo Paris (va d'amore), Angel Romero (gtr), Celedonio Romero (gtr), Henryk Szeryng (vn), Pinchas Zukerman (vn), Academy of St. Martin in the Fields, English CO, I Musici, Naples Weekly International Soloists, St. Paul CO, Dresden Staatskapelle—The Four Seasons [Winter]; Con in D for Gtr [Largo]; Con in D for Fl, "Il gardellino" [Cantabile]; Con in C for Diverse Insts [Andante molto]; Con in g for Strs [Andante molto]; Con in D for 2 Vns & 2 Vcs [Largo]; Con in g for Ob, Vn, Ww & Strs [Larghetto]; Con in a for Gtr, "L'estro armonico" [Largo]; Con in F for 3 Vns [Andante]; Con in F for Fl [Largo]; Con in d for Va D'Amore [Largo]; Con in E for Vn & Strs, "Il riposo" [Allegro]; Con in G for Ob, Bn & Strs [Largo]; Con in B♭ for Vn & Strs [Largo]; Con in A for Gtr & Strs [Larghetto]; Con in E for Vn & Strs, "L'amoroso" [Allegro]; Con in G for Fl [Largo]; Con in A for Vn [Larghetto]; Con in c for Vn & Strs, "Il sospetto" [Andante]; Con in a for 2 Obs & Strs [Largo]; Con in g for Orch [Largo non molto]; Con in a for Vn [Largo]; Con in C for Ob [Adagio]; Con in g for Fl, "La notte" [Largo] Philips ▲ 454051-2 ■ 454 051-4

Romero, Celino (gtr)—see ORCHESTRAS & ENSEMBLES Los Romeros

Romero, Gustavo (pno)
Beethoven, L. van:Cons Pno (comp), w. J. Sedares (cnd), English CO Koch International Classics 3-▲ KIC 7317 [DDD]
Bowles, P.:Pno Music *(rec live, Paris, May 8, 1994)* Koch Schwann ▲ SCH 315742
Mompou, F.:Cançons i dansas Koch International Classics ▲ KIC 7185
Mompou, F.:Impresiones intimas Koch International Classics ▲ KIC 7185
Turina, J.:Rapsodia sinfónica, w. D. Barra (cnd), San Diego CO Koch International Classics ▲ KIC 7160-2 [DDD]

Romero, Hugo (gtr)—see ORCHESTRAS & ENSEMBLES Tango 7

Romero, Jorge (pno)
Falla, M. de:Songs, w. Yolanda Auyanet (sop)—7 songs Kicco Classic ▲ 1595
Granados, E.:Songs, w. Yolanda Auyanet (sop)—La Maja Dolorosa Kicco Classic ▲ 1595
Toldrá, E.:Songs, w. Yolanda Auyanet (sop)—Marinereo en Tierra Kicco Classic ▲ 1595
Turina, J.:Songs, w. Yolanda Auyanet (sop)—3 songs Kicco Classic ▲ 1595

Romero, Pepe (gtr)—see also ORCHESTRAS & ENSEMBLES Los Romeros
Arcas, J.:Gtr Music, w. Wilhelm Hellweg (pno)—Fant on Themes from Verdi's *La Traviata* Philips ▲ 446090-2
Bizet, G.:Carmen (suite 1), w. A. Romero (gtr) Philips ▲ 412609-2 [DDD]
Boccherini, L.:Qnts Gtr & Strs, w. Academy of St. Martin in the Fields Chamber Ensemble—Op. 50/4, 5, 6 Philips ▲ 420385-2 [ADD]
Boccherini, L.:Qnts Gtr & Strs, w. Academy of St. Martin in the Fields Chamber Ensemble—Op. 50/3 & 9 Philips ▲ 426092-2 [ADD]
Boccherini, L.:Qnts Gtr & Strs, w. Academy of St. Martin in the Fields Chamber Ensemble—includes La Ritirata de Madrid & Fandango Philips 2-▲ 438769-2
Castelnuovo-Tedesco, M.:Con 1 Gtr, w. N. Marriner (cnd), Academy of St. Martin in the Fields Philips ▲ 416357-2 [DDD]
Famous Spanish Dances, w. Celin Romero (gtr) Philips ("Spanish" series) ▲ 432827-2 [ADD]
Famous Spanish Guitar Music Philips ▲ 411033-2 [DDD]
Ferrer, J.:Gtr Music, w. Wilhelm Hellweg (pno)—Fant on Verdi's *Rigoletto* Philips ▲ 446090-2
Giuliani, M.:Con 1 Gtr, w. N. Marriner (cnd), Academy of St. Martin in the Fields Philips ▲ 420780-2 [ADD]
Giuliani, M.:Con 3 Gtr, w. N. Marriner (cnd), Academy of St. Martin in the Fields Philips ▲ 420780-2 [ADD]
Giuliani, M.:Gtr Music, w. N. Marriner (cnd), Academy of St. Martin in the Fields—includes Cons 1-3; Gran Son Eroica; Intro, Theme with Vars & Polonaise; Grande Overture; La Melanconia; Vars on a Theme by Handel; Variazioni Concertanti Philips ("Duo" series) 2-▲ 454 262-2
Giuliani, M.:Rossiniana Philips ▲ 446090-2
Gounod, C.:Waltzes, w. Wilhelm Hellweg (pno) [arr Hellweg] Philips ▲ 446090-2
Mertz, K.J.:Gtr Music, w. Wilhelm Hellweg (pno)—Fants on themes from Verdi's *Rigoletto* & *Trovatore* & Mozart's *Don Giovanni* Philips ▲ 446090-2
Noches de España:Romantic Guitar Classics Philips ▲ 442150-2
La Paloma:Spanish & Latin American Favorites Philips ▲ 432102-2 [DDD]
Rodrigo, J.:Concierto Andaluz, w. A. Romero (gtr), N. Marriner (cnd), Academy of St. Martin in the Fields Philips ▲ 400024-2 [ADD]
Rodrigo, J.:Concierto de Aranjuez, w. N. Marriner (cnd), Academy of St. Martin in the Fields Philips ▲ 411440-2 [ADD]
Rodrigo, J.:Concierto de Aranjuez, w. N. Marriner (cnd), Academy of St. Martin in the Fields Philips ("Spanish" series) ▲ 432828-2 [ADD]
Rodrigo, J.:Concierto de Aranjuez, w. N. Marriner (cnd), Academy of St. Martin in the Fields Philips ▲ 438016-2
Rodrigo, J.:Concierto madrigal, w. A. Romero (gtr), N. Marriner (cnd), Academy of St. Martin in the Fields Philips ▲ 400024-2
Rodrigo, J.:Concierto madrigal, w. A. Romero (gtr), N. Marriner (cnd), Academy of St. Martin in the Fields Philips ("Spanish" series) ▲ 432828-2 [ADD]
Rodrigo, J.:Concierto para una fiesta, w. N. Marriner (cnd), Academy of St. Martin in the Fields Philips ▲ 411133-2 [DDD]
Rodrigo, J.:Fant para un gentilhombre, w. N. Marriner (cnd), Academy of St. Martin in the Fields Philips ▲ 438016-2
Rodrigo, J.:Fant para un gentilhombre, w. N. Marriner (cnd), Academy of St. Martin in the Fields Philips ("Spanish" series) ▲ 432828-2 [ADD]
Rodrigo, J.:Invocación y danza Philips ▲ 438016-2
Rodrigo, J.:Piezas españolas Philips ▲ 438016-2
Romero, C.:Concierto de Málaga, w. N. Marriner (cnd), Academy of St. Martin in the Fields Philips ▲ 411133-2 [DDD]
Tárrega, F.:Gtr Music, w. Wilhelm Hellweg (pno)—Fant on themes from Arriete's *Marina* Philips ▲ 446090-2

Romero, Pepe (gtr) (cont.)
Villa-Lobos, H.:Con Gtr, w. N. Marriner (cnd), Academy of St. Martin in the Fields — Philips ▲ 416357-2 [DDD]
Villa-Lobos, H.:Etudes Gtr—No. 1 — Philips ▲ 420245-2 [DDD]
Villa-Lobos, H.:Preludes Gtr — Philips ▲ 420245-2 [DDD]
Villa-Lobos, H.:Suite populaire brésilienne — Philips ▲ 420245-2 [DDD]
Vivaldi, A.:Cons Gtr, I Musici — Philips ▲ 434082-2 [DDD]
Vivaldi, A.:Cons Mand, w. I. Brown (cnd), Academy of St. Martin in the Fields—3 concerti—RV.93, 425, 532 — Philips ▲ 412624-2 [DDD]
Vivaldi, A.:Con Mand, RV.425 [arr gtr Romero] — London ▲ 452485-2 ■ 452 485-4

Romm, Avis (pno)
Contrasts, w. Stanley Clark (trbn) — ebs ▲ ebs 6023 [DDD]

Romm, Ronald (tpt)—see ORCHESTRAS & ENSEMBLES Canadian Brass

Rommelspacher, S. (org)
Bruckner, A.:Motets, w. H. P. Blochwitz (ten), H. Skarba (trbn), H. Breika (trbn), H. Weimer (trbn), Freiburg Vocal Ensemble—Os justi; Afferentur regi; Christus factus est; Tota pulchra es Maria; Vexilla regis prodeunt; Ecce sacerdos magnus; Pange lingua; Locus iste; Ave Maria; Virga Jesse floruit — Entrée ▲ 0039 [ADD]

Rompré, Jean-François (fl)—see ORCHESTRAS & ENSEMBLES Essex Winds Woodwind Quintet

Ronald, Landon (pno)
Mozart, W.A.:Don Giovanni (sels), w. Emilia Corsi (sop), Adelina Patti (sop), John McCormack (ten), Mattia Battistini (bar), Ezio Pinza (bass), C. Sabajno (cnd)—Alfin Siam liberati...Là ci darem la mano; Finch'han del vino; Batti, batti, o bel Masetto; Il mio tesoro; L'amerò, sarò costante *(rec 1905 - 1944)* — Minerva ▲ MN A14 [ADD]

Ronchini, Maria (va)—see ORCHESTRAS & ENSEMBLES Milan Quartet

Ronchini, Matteo (vc)—see ORCHESTRAS & ENSEMBLES Milan Quartet

Ronco, Claudio (vc)—see also ORCHESTRAS & ENSEMBLES Clemencic Consort
Bonporti, F.A.:Concertini e Serenate, Op. 12, w. M. Mencoboni (hpd), L. Mangiocavallo (vn)—Concertini Nos. 3 in G & 7 in E♭; Serenatas Nos. 2 in F, 4 in g & 6 in G — Nuova Era ("Ancient Music" series) ▲ 6939 [DDD]
Lanzetti, S.:Sons Vc, w. S. Veggetti (vc), D. Petech (hpd), J. Held (bc)—Nos. 5-9, 11 & 12 *(rec 5/91)* — Nuova Era ("Ancient Music" series) ▲ 7048 [DDD]
Veracini, F.M.:Sons Vn, Op. 1, w. L. Mangiocavallo (vn), M. Mencoboni (hpd)—Sonata No. 12 in F — Nuova Era ("Ancient Music" series) ▲ 6900 [DDD]
Veracini, F.M.:Sonate accademiche, w. L. Mangiocavallo (vn), M. Mencoboni (hpd)—Sonatas No. 5 in g & No. 6 in A — Nuova Era ("Ancient Music" series) ▲ 6900 [DDD]

Rondin, Mats (vc)
Wiklander, K.:Music of, w. Kurt Wiklander (org), Eyvind Sand Kjeldsen (vn)—Toccata on the Easter Introitus for Org; 2 Chorales from Dalecarlia for Org; Fant. for Vc & Org; 4 Miniatures for Org; Meditation in Folk Style on B-A-C-H for Vn & Org; 3 Organ Chorales on Sacred Folk-Tunes in the Swedish Chorale; Fant. for Org on O Christ Who Art Light & Day; Scherzo Ostinato; Meditation for Org — BIS ▲ CD 659
Wirén, D.:Con Vc, w. P. Sakari (cnd), Swedish CO — Caprice ▲ CAP 21513

Rønnes, Robert (bn)
Bibalo, A.:Son Bn, w. E. Knardahl (pno) — Simax ▲ PSC 1077 [DDD]
Kvandal, J.:Légende, w. E. Knardahl (pno) — Simax ▲ PSC 1077 [DDD]
Lerstad, T.B.:Son 2 Bn, w. E. Knardahl (pno) — Simax ▲ PSC 1077 [DDD]
Plagge, W.:Son Bn, w. E. Knardahl (pno) — Simax ▲ PSC 1077 [DDD]
Saeverud, H.:Autumn, w. E. Knardahl (pno) — Simax ▲ PSC 1077 [DDD]
Sonstevold, G.:Sonatina Bn, w. E. Knardahl (pno) — Simax ▲ PSC 1077 [DDD]

Rood, Richard (vn)
Bach, J.S.:Con for 3 Vns, w. P. Peabody (vn), E. Sato (vn), R. Kapp (cnd), Philharmonia Virtuosi — ESS.A.Y ▲ CD 1002 [DDD] ■ C 1002 (D)
Dvořák, A.:Terzetto, w. Katsuko Esaki (vn), Nardo Poy (va) — Music & Arts ▲ MUA CD 926
Vivaldi, A.:Cons for 2 Vns, w. Paul Peabody (vn), R. Kapp (cnd), Philharmonia Virtuosi—RV.522 — ESS.A.Y ▲ CD 1001 [DDD] ■ C 1001 (D)

Rooij, Nico de (elec pno)
Andriessen, L.:Contra tempus, w. Gerard Bouwhuis (pno), Sepp Grotenhuis (pno), Tomoko Mukaiyama (elec pno) *(rec Amsterdam Music Theater, Oct 3-6, 1994)* — Donemus ▲ CV 54 [DDD]

Rooij, Nico de (pno)
Andriessen, L.:Anachrony 1, w. Sepp Grotenhuis (cel), Douceline Aleven (hp), Arthur Cune (vib), Nicolette Heerema (org), H. Williams (cnd), Netherlands Ballet Orch *(rec Amsterdam Music Theater, Oct 3-6, 1994)* — Donemus ▲ CV 54 [DDD]

Rooley, Anthony (chit)
Caccini, G.:Arias, w. David Thomas (bass) — Musica Oscura ("The Orpheus Circle" series) ▲ MOS 70974
India, S. d':Laments, w. E. Kirkby (sop)—Lamento d'Olimpia; & other laments [I] — Elektra/Nonesuch ▲ 79125-2
India, S. d':Laments, w. E. Kirkby (sop)—Lamento d'Olimpia; & other laments [I] — Hyperion ▲ CDA 66106
Monteverdi, C.:Lamento d'Olimpia, w. Kirkby (sop) [I] — Elektra/Nonesuch ▲ 79125-2
Monteverdi, C.:Lamento d'Olimpia, w. Kirkby (sop) [I] — Hyperion ▲ CDA 66106
Puliaschi, G.D.:Arias, w. David Thomas (bass) — Musica Oscura ("The Orpheus Circle" series) ▲ MOS 70974

Rooley, Anthony (gtr)
Renaissance Fantasias — Hyperion ▲ CDA 66089 [DDD]

Rooley, Anthony (lt)
Elizabethan Songs, w. Kirkby, Emma (sop) — L'Oiseau-Lyre ▲ 425892-2 OH [ADD]
Johnson, Robert:Music for Shakespeare's Plays, w. E. Kirkby (sop), D. Thomas (bass) — Virgin Classics ▲ CDC 59321
Jones, Robert:The Muses Gardin for Delights, or the Fifth Book of Ayres, w. E. Kirkby (sop) — Virgin Classics ▲ CDC 59633
Purcell, H.:Music of, w. Catherine Bott (sop), Emma Kirkby (sop), James Bowman (alt), Paula Chateauneuf (gtr), Monica Huggett (vn), Catherine Mackintosh (vn), Christophe Coin (vc), Hill, Hogwood (cnd), Academy of Ancient Music, Brandenburg Consort, David Hill (cnd), Anthony Lewis (cnd), St. Anthony Singers, Taverner Choir, Winchester Cathedral Choir—The Double Dealer; Come Ye Sons of Art; The Old Bachelor; Birthday Song for Queen Mary; Oedipus; King Arthur; Bonduca; The Fairy Queen; Son. No. 9 in F; Dido & Aeneas; Abdelazer; Bess of Bedlam; The Married Beau; Hear My Prayer, O Lord; Rejoice in the Lord Always — London ("Editions de l'oiseau-lyre" series) ▲ 444620-2
Purcell, H.:Songs, w. E. Kirkby (sop), D. Thomas (bass) — Hyperion ▲ CDA 66056 [DDD]
The Scyence of Lutynge — Musica Oscura ("The Orpheus Circle" series) ▲ MOS 70971

Rooley, Anthony (lt/orpharion)
Dowland, J.:Ayres, w. E. Kirkby (sop)—17 sels., from all books — Virgin Classics ▲ 59521 [DDD]
Dowland, J.:A Pilgrimes Solace, w. E. Kirkby (sop)—3 sels. — Virgin Classics ▲ 59521 [DDD]

Roorda, T. (fl)
Yun, I.:Qt Fls, w. R. de Reede (fl), H. Starreveld (fl), M. Takahashi (fl) — Attacca ▲ BABEL 9056-3 [DDD]

Roos, Frédéric de (rcr)—see also ORCHESTRAS & ENSEMBLES Ricercar Consort
Telemann, G.P.:Con in F Rcr, B Vl, w. P. Pierlot (vl), Ricercar Consort — Ricercar ▲ RIC 44021 [DDD]
Telemann, G.P.:Con in F Rcr Bn, w. M. Minkowski (bn), Ricercar Consort — Ricercar ▲ RIC 44021 [DDD]
Telemann, G.P.:Con in F Rcr Fl, w. P. Beuckels (fl), Ricercar Consort — Ricercar ▲ RIC 44021 [DDD]
Telemann, G.P.:Suite in a Fl, w. Ricercar Consort — Ricercar ▲ RIC 44021 [DDD]

Roos, Lars (pno)
Sjögren, E.:Son Pno — Swedish Society ▲ SCD 1028

Root, Martin (fl)—see also ORCHESTRAS & ENSEMBLES Biedermeier Quintet, Biedermeier Quintet members
Haydn, J.:Diverts Fl, Vn & Vc, w. Johannes Leertouwer (vn), Viola de Hoog (vc)—H.IV/6-11; Op. 11/2 & 5 *(rec Utrecht, Nov. 1994)* — Globe ▲ GLO 5131 [DDD]
Schubert, Franz:Intro & Vars Fl on "Tröckne Blumen", w. L. Van Doeselaar (pno) — Globe ▲ GLO 5040 [DDD]
Schubert, Franz:Qt Fl, w. S. Swierstra (va), F. Jacobs (gtr), V. De Hoog (vc) — Globe ▲ GLO 5040 [DDD]

Root, Martin (trns fl)—see also ORCHESTRAS & ENSEMBLES Schönbrunn Ensemble Amsterdam
Bach, J.S.:Partita Fl, BWV 1013 *(rec May 1993)* — Globe ▲ GLO 5102 [DDD]
Bach, J.S.:Sons Fl, BWV 1030-35, w. R. Egarr (hpd), V. de Hoog (vc)—1030, 1034 & 1035 *(rec May 1993)* — Globe ▲ GLO 5102 [DDD]

Røttingen, Einar (pno)
Saeverud, H.:Pno Music [comp works for pno] *(rec Norwegian State Academy, Oslo & Eidsvoll Church, 1994-95)* — Simax 3-▲ PSC 1116 [DDD]

Rørbeck, Bodil (vn)
Nørholm, I.:Chamber Music, w. T. L. Christiansen (fl), M. Vitek (vn), H. Olsen (va), I. Olsen (gtr), N. Ullner (vc), A. Øland (pno)—Essai Prismatique; Medusa's Shadow; Mosaic; Prelude to My Wintermorning; Sonata Quasi Variazioni *(rec 2/89)* — Kontrapunkt ▲ 32019 [DDD]
Nørholm, I.:Chamber Music, w. J. Christiansen (gtr), N. Ullner (vc), P. Salo (pno/hpd), G. Sørensen (perc), Kuhlau Flute Quartet—Before Silence, Op. 83; Contrast-Continuum, Op. 70; Guitar Sonata No. 2; The Orthodox Dream; So to Say, Op. 74; Turbulens-Laminar, Op. 93; Variants, Op. 19 *(rec 9/90)* — Kontrapunkt ▲ 32065 [DDD]

Rörby, Jörgen (gtr)
Burkhart, F.:Adventslieder (3), w. Solvieg Faringer (sop), Clas Pehrsson (rcr) *(rec Castle Wik, Sweden, Jan 19, 20 & 26, 1974)* — BIS ▲ CD 202 [AAD]
Kukuck, F.:Die Brücke, w. Solvieg Faringer (sop), Clas Pehrsson (rcr) *(rec Castle Wik, Sweden, Jan 19, 20 & 26, 1974)* — BIS ▲ CD 202 [AAD]
Lundén, L.:Little Toe & Nine More, w. Solvieg Faringer (sop), Clas Pehrsson (rcr) *(rec Castle Wik, Sweden, Jan 19, 20 & 26, 1974)* — BIS ▲ CD 202 [AAD]

Rorem, Ned (pno)
Rorem, N.:Dialogues, w. Anita Darian (sop), John Stewart (ten), Richard Cumming (pno) — Phoenix ▲ PHCD 116 [AAD]
Rorem, N.:Give All To Love, w. Gregg Smith (cnd), Gregg Smith Singers — Vox Box ("The American Composers" series) 3-▲ CDX 3037
Rorem, N.:Gloria, w. Phyllis Curtin (sop), Helen Vanni (mez) — Phoenix ▲ PHCD 126
Rorem, N.:Nantucket Songs, w. P. Bryn-Julson (sop) [E] *(rec Library of Congress, world premiere performance, 10/30/79)* — CRI ■ ACS 6007
Rorem, N.:Nantucket Songs, w. P. Bryn-Julson (sop) — CRI ▲ CD 657 [ADD]
Rorem, N.:Poems of Love & the Rain, w. Beverly Wolff (cta) — Phoenix ▲ PHCD 108 [AAD]
Rorem, N.:Some Trees, w. P. Curtin (sop), B. Wolff (cta), D. Gramm (bar) — CRI ▲ CD 657 [ADD]
Rorem, N.:Some Trees, w. P. Curtin (sop), B. Wolff (mez), D. Gramm (b-bar) [E] — CRI ■ C 238
Rorem, N.:Songs, w. R. Rees (sop)—Alleluia; 2 Poems of Edith Sitwell; 3 Poems of Tennyson; 2 Poems of Elizabeth Bishop; 7 Poems of Paul Goodman; 2 Medieval Lyrics; 2 Poems of Whitman; I am Rose; A Journey; Let's Take a Walk; See How They Love Me; Early in the Morning — Premier ▲ PRCD 1035 [ADD]
Rorem, N.:Women's Voices, w. K. Ciesinski (mez) — CRI ▲ CD 657 [ADD]

Rorive, Jean-Pierre (sax)
Famous Adagios:Saxophone & Organ, Vol. 4, w. André Lamproye (org) — Pavane ▲ 7333
Rêveries:Saxophone & Organ V, w. André Lamproye (org) *(rec 1996)* — Pavane ▲ ADW 7364 [DDD]
Saxophone & Organ, Vol. 3, w. J. Hermans (org) — Pavane ▲ ADW 7320 [DDD]

Ros, Carmen Maria (gtr)
Sor, F.:Gtr Music, w. Miguel Garcia Ferrer (gtr)—L'Encouragement, Op. 34; Divert, Op. 38; Seis valses, Op. 39; Los dos amigos, Op. 41; Seis valses, Op. 44 bis; Divert. Militar, Op. 49; Bolero a duo la premier pas vers moi, Op. 53; Fant., Op. 54 bis; Tres duos, Op. 55; Tres Pequeños divert., Op. 61; Divert., Op. 62; Souvenir de rusia, Op. 63 — Opra Tres 2-▲ 1008/09

Ros, Pere (vl)
Baroque Music for Recorder, w. Conrad Steinmann (rcr), Monica Huggett (baroque vn), Hopkinson Smith (lt/thb/gtr), Jordi Savall (vl), Claude Flagel (h-g), Johann Sonnleitner (hpd) — Claves ▲ CD 508103 [ADD]
Musiche Veneziene per Voce e Strumenti, w. Teresa Berganza (mez), Yasunori Imamura (lt/thb/gtr), Lynn Dickinson (vl), Carol Lewis (vl), Silvie Mocquet (vl), Jörg Ewald Dähler (pno), Jörg Ewald Dähler (cnd) *(rec Kirche Saanen, Feb 1982)* — Claves ▲ CD 508206 [DDD]

Rosa, Francesco di (ob)—see ORCHESTRAS & ENSEMBLES Briccialdi Wind Quintet

Rosa, William de (vc)
Brahms, J.:Son 2 Vc, w. Li-Jian (pno) — Audiofon ▲ CD 72045
Cellist's Holliday, w. Noreen Cassidy-Polera (pno) — Audiofon ▲ CD 72046
Schumann, R.:Adagio & Allegro Hn, w. Li-Jian (pno) — Audiofon ▲ CD 72045
Shostakovich, D.:Con 1 Vc, w. S. Caldwell (cnd), Ekaterinburg PO — Audiofon ▲ CD 72060
Strauss, R.:Son Vc, w. Li-Jian (pno) — Audiofon ▲ CD 72045

Rosado, Ana Maria (gtr)
We've Got (Poly)Rythm — Albany ▲ TROY 087 [DDD]

Rosa-Herseni, Hertha (vc)
Ernst, S.:Seven Miniatures on Japanese Haiku, w. Barbara Stein (alt), Susanne Geiger (pno) — Vienna Modern Masters ▲ VMM 2018 [DDD]

Rosand, Aaron (pno)
Aaron Rosand:Romances for Violin & Piano, w. Hugh Sung (pno) — Vox ("Classics" series) ▲ VOX 7505 [DDD]

Rosand, Aaron (vn)
Aaron Rosand, w. Luxembourg Radio Orch [cnd:Louis de Froment] *(rec 1971-73)* — Vox Box 2-▲ CDX 5102 [ADD]
Aaron Rosand Plays Sibelius, Tchaikovsky, Berlioz, Chausson, Ravel, Saint-Saëns, Lalo, w. Southwest German RSO [cnd:Rolf Reinhardt], Southwest German RSO Baden-Baden [cnd:Tibor Szöke] *(rec 1957-59)* — Vox Box 2-▲ CDX 5116
Achron, J.:Vn & Pno Music, w. J. Covelli (pno)—Hebrew Melody, Op. 33; Stimmungen, Op. 32/1; Hebrew Lullaby, Op. 35/2 — Audiofon ▲ CD 72033
Bach, J.S.:Sons & Partitas Vn, BWV 1001-1006—Son. 1, BWV 1001 & Partita No. 2, BWV 1004 — Audiofon ▲ CD 72012
Beethoven, L. van:Sons Vn (comp), w. Eileen Flissler (pno) *(rec 1961)* — Vox Box ("Legends" series) 3-▲ CDX3 3503 [ADD]
Beethoven, L. van:Son 5 Vn, "Spring", w. Flissler (pno) — Allegretto ▲ ACD 8082 [ADD] ■ ACS 8082
Beethoven, L. van:Son 9 Vn, "Kreutzer", w. Flissler (pno) — Allegretto ▲ ACD 8082 [ADD] ■ ACS 8082
Bloch, E.:Baal Shem, "3 Pictures of Chassidic Life", w. J. Covelli (pno) — Audiofon ▲ CD 72033
Bloch, E.:Son 1 Vn, w. J. Covelli (pno) — Audiofon ▲ CD 72033
Brahms, J.:Hungarian Dances Pno 4-Hands, w. H. Sung (pno) [Joseph Joachim's 1871 & 1880 arr.] — Biddulph ▲ LAW 003 [DDD]
Brahms, J.:Sons Vn (comp), w. Hugh Sung (pno) *(rec Philadelphia, Jan 1992)* — Vox Classics ▲ VOX 7535 [DDD]
Bruch, M.:Kol Nidrei, w. J. Covelli (pno) — Audiofon ▲ CD 72033
Chausson, E.:Con Vn, Pno & Str Qt, w. Seymour Lipkin (pno), Miami String Quartet — Audiofon ▲ CD 72039
Corelli, A.:Son Vn, Op. 5/12, "La Follia" — Biddulph ▲ LAW 006
Franck, C.:Son Vn, w. Seymour Lipkin (pno) — Audiofon ▲ CD 72039
Grieg, E.:Sons Vn, Opp. 8, 13 & 45, w. S. Lipkin (pno)—Op. 45 — Audiofon ▲ CD 72026
Handel, G.F.:Sons Vn & Kbd, w. Hugh Sung (pno)—includes Andante from Flute Sonata in B minor (Op. 1 No. 9) *(rec Jan. 9 & 10, 1992)* — Biddulph ▲ LAW 004 [DDD]
Hebraic Legacies — Audiofon ▲ CD 72033
Joachim, J.:Romance Vn, w. H. Sung (pno) — Biddulph ▲ LAW 003 [DDD]
Lalo, E.:Sym espagnole, w. T. Szöke (cnd), Southwest German RSO Baden-Baden — Allegretto ▲ ACD 8058 [ADD]
Mendelssohn, F.:Con in e Vn & Orch, Op. 64, w. L. de Froment (cnd), Luxembourg RSO *(rec 1973)* — Allegretto ▲ ACD 8207
Mendelssohn, F.:Con in e Vn & Orch, Op. 64, w. L. de Froment (cnd), Luxembourg RSO—Allegro molto appassionato — Special Music Co. ("Classics of the Heart" series) ▲ SCD 5197

▲ = CD ♦ = Enhanced CD Δ = MD ■ = Cassette Tape ◻ = DCC

Rosand, Aaron (vn) (cont.)
Mendelssohn, F.:Life & Music of, w. L. de Froment (cnd), Luxembourg RSO—narration with selected excerpts from Ov. [Midsummer Nights Dream], Op.21; Con. for 2 Pnos in Ab; Midsummer Night's Dream, Op. 61; Song Without Words 30, Op. 62/6; Octet, Op. 20; Hebrides Ov., Op. 26; Syms. Nos. 3 & 4; Ov [from Calm Sea & Prosperous Voyage], Op. 27; St. Paul, Op. 36; Con. No. 1 for Pno, Op. 25; Con for Vn, Op. 64; Song without Words 23, Op. 67/4; Ov. [from *Ruy Blas*], Op. 95; On Wings of Song, Op. 34/2, plus a complete version of Con in e for Vn & Orch, Op. 64 Vox Music Masters ("Music Masters" series) ▲ MMD 8503 [ADD] ■ MMC 8503
Pasquali, N.:Son Vn Biddulph ▲ LAW 006
Pergolesi, G.B.:Son Vn Biddulph ▲ LAW 006
Respighi, O.:Son Vn, w. J. Covelli (pno) Audiofon ▲ CD 72020
Saint-Saëns, C.:Con 3 Vn, w. T. Szöke (cnd), Southwest German RSO Baden-Baden Allegretto ▲ ACD 8058 [ADD]
Saint-Saëns, C.:Son 1 Vn, w. S. Lipkin (pno) Audiofon ▲ CD 72026
Sarasate, P. de:Caprice basque, w. E. Flissler (pno) Allegretto ▲ ACD 8160 [ADD] ■ ACS 8160
Sarasate, P. de:Carmen Fant, w. R. Reinhardt (cnd), Southwest German RSO Baden-Baden Allegretto ▲ ACD 8160 [ADD] ■ ACD 8160
Sarasate, P. de:Navarra, w. Eileen Flissler (pno) [Rosand plays both vn parts] Allegretto ▲ ACD 8160 [ADD] ■ ACS 8160
Sarasate, P. de:Spanish Dances, w. E. Flissler (pno) Allegretto ▲ ACD 8160 [ADD] ■ ACS 8160
Sarasate, P. de:Zigeunerweisen, w. R. Reinhardt (cnd), Southwest German RSO Baden-Baden Allegretto ▲ ACD 8160 [ADD] ■ ACS 8160
Sibelius, J.:Sonatina Vn, w. J. Covelli (pno) Audiofon ▲ CD 72020
Strauss, R.:Son Vn, w. S. Lipkin (pno) Audiofon ▲ CD 72026
Tartini, G.:Son Vn, Op. 1/10 Biddulph ▲ LAW 006
Tartini, G.:Son Vn "Devil's Trill" Biddulph ▲ LAW 006
Tchaikovsky, P.:Con Vn, w. L. de Froment (cnd), Luxembourg RSO *(rec 1973)* Allegretto ▲ ACD 8207
Tchaikovsky, P.:Con Vn, w. L. de Froment (cnd), Luxembourg RSO Vox Box 3-▲ CD3X 3025 [ADD]
Telemann, G.P.:Fants Vn—Nos. 4, 12 Audiofon ▲ CD 72012
The Violinist, w. Eileen Flissler (pno) Allegretto ▲ ACD 8149 [ADD] ■ ACS 8149
Vitali, T.A.:Chaconne Vn Biddulph ▲ LAW 006
Vivaldi, A.:Sons Vn, Op. 2—Nos. 2 & 11 Biddulph ▲ LAW 006
Walton, W.:Con Vn, w. J. Judd (cnd), Florida PO Harmonia Mundi USA ▲ HMU 907070
Walton, W.:Son Vn & Pno, w. J. Covelli (pno) Audiofon ▲ CD 72020
Ysaÿe, E.:Sons Vn—Nos. 2 & 6 Audiofon ▲ CD 72012

Rosbaud, Hans (pno)
Bartók, B.:Son for 2 Pnos, w. M. Bergmann (pno), W. Grabinger (perc), E. Seiler (perc) *(rec live, 1953)* Music & Arts ▲ CD 627 (m) [AAD]
Mozart, W.A.:Songs, w. T. Stich-Randall (mez)—(3) Abendempfindung (lied), K.523; Dans un bois solitaire (arietta), K.308; Oiseaux, si tous les ans (arietta), K.307 *(rec live, Aix-en-Provence July 31,1956)* Melodram 2-▲ CDM 26524 [ADD]
Recital, w. Elisabeth Schwarzkopf (sop), (rec. live, Aix-en-Provence 7/29/54) Melodram 2-▲ CDM 26524 [ADD]
Teresa Stich-Randall, w. Teresa Stich-Randall (sop) *(rec July 31, 1956)* Memoire Vive ▲ 262008 (m) [ADD]

Roscoe, Martin (pno)
Beach, A.M.C.:Qnt Pno, w. Endellion String Quartet ASV ▲ ASV 932 [DDD]
Clarke, R.:Son Va, w. *(other artist unknown)* ASV ▲ ASV 932 [DDD]
Clarke, R.:Trio Pno, w. Endellion String Quartet members ASV ▲ ASV 932 [DDD]
Dohnányi, E. von:Con 1 Pno, w. F. Glushchenko (cnd), BBC Scottish SO Hyperion ▲ CDA 66684 [DDD]
Dohnányi, E. von:Pno Music—Rhapsodies (4), Op. 11 (1902-03); Three Pieces [Ars, Valse Impromptu, Capriccio] (1912); Pastorale, Hungarian Christmas Song (1920); Four Pieces, Op. 2 [Scherzo in c#, Intermezzo in a, Intermezz in f, Capriccio in b] (1896-97) ASV ▲ ASV 863 [DDD]
Dohnányi, E. von:Qnt 1 Pno, w. Vanbrugh String Quartet ASV ▲ ASV 915 [DDD]
Dohnányi, E. von:Qnt 2 Pno, w. Vanbrugh String Quartet ASV ▲ ASV 915 [DDD]
Dohnányi, E. von:Suite im alten Stil ASV ▲ ASV 915 [DDD]
Fauré, G.:Pno Music, w. Kathryn Scott (pno)—[CD 1] Impromptu's; Theme and Vars.; Romances;[CD 2] Barcarolles;[CD 3] Nocturnes; Fugues; Fants.;[CD 4] Dolly Suite; Preludes; Mazurkas Hyperion 4-▲ CDA 66911/14
Lloyd, G.:Con 1 Pno, w. G. Lloyd (cnd), BBC PO Albany ▲ TROY 037-2 [DDD] ■ TROY 037-4
Lloyd, G.:Con 2 Pno, w. G. Lloyd (cnd), BBC PO Albany ▲ TROY 037-2 [DDD] ■ TROY 037-4
Lloyd, G.:Lament, Air & Dance, w. T. Little (vn) Albany ▲ TROY 029-2 [DDD] ■ TROY 029-4 (D)
Lloyd, G.:Pno Music—An African Shrine; The Aggressive Fishes; Intercom Baby; The Road Through Samarkand; St. Antony & the Bogside Beggar Albany ▲ AR 003-2 [DDD] ■ AR 003-4 (D)
Lloyd, G.:Son Vn, w. T. Little (vn) Albany ▲ TROY 029-2 [DDD] ■ TROY 029-4 (D)
Szymanowski, K.:Mazurkas—Nos. 1-4 *(rec St. Martin's Church, East Woodhay, Feb. 1994)* Naxos ▲ 8.553016 [DDD]
Szymanowski, K.:Metopes *(rec St. Martin's Church, East Woodhay, Feb. 1994)* Naxos ▲ 8.553016 [DDD]
Szymanowski, K.:Pno Music (comp)—Mazurkas, Op. 50/5-12; Vars on a Polish Theme, Op. 10; Masques, Op. 34; Fant in C, Op. 14 *(rec St. Martin's Church, Hampshire, Dec 1994)* Naxos ▲ 8.553300 [DDD]
Szymanowski, K.:Son 2 Pno *(rec St. Martin's Church, East Woodhay, Feb. 1994)* Naxos ▲ 8.553016 [DDD]
Szymanowski, K.:Studies Pno *(rec St. Martin's Church, East Woodhay, Feb. 1994)* Naxos ▲ 8.553016 [DDD]

Rosé, Alma (vn)
Bach, J.S.:Con for 2 Vns,w. *(orch unknown)* *(rec 1928)* Biddulph 2-▲ LAB 056/057 [ADD]
Bach, J.S.:Sons & Partitas Vn, BWV 1001-1006—Adagio from the Son. in g, BWV 1001 *(rec 1928)* Biddulph 2-▲ LAB 056/057 [ADD]

Rose, Barry (org)
Organ:The Magnificent, w. C. Dearnley (org), Francis Jackson (org) Pickwick ("The Orchid" series) ▲ PICORCD 11009

Rose, Bernard (pno)
Our Musical Past, Vol. 1:A Concert for Brass Band, Voice & Piano, w. Merja Sargon (sop) Library of Congress ▲ OMP 101/102 [ADD]

Rose, Jerome (pno)
Beethoven, L. van:Son 8 Pno, "Pathétique" *(rec 1978)* Allegretto ▲ ACD 8163 ■ ACS 8163
Beethoven, L. van:Son 14 Pno, "Moonlight Son" *(rec 1978)* Allegretto ▲ ACD 8163 ■ ACS 8163
Beethoven, L. van:Son 31 Pno *(rec 1978)* Allegretto ▲ ACD 8163 ■ ACS 8163
Chopin, F.:Sons Pno (comp) Infinity Digital ▲ QK 62388 [DDD]
Hill, A.:Konzertstück Pno, w. P. Cao (cnd), Luxembourg RSO *(rec 1973)* Vox Box 2-▲ CDX 5064 [ADD]
Liszt, F.:Années de pèlerinage (comp) *(rec 1973)* Vox Box 3-▲ CD3X 3004 [ADD]
Liszt, F.:Con 1 Pno, w. R. Saccani (cnd), Budapest PO Vox Box 2-▲ CDX 5106 [DDD]
Liszt, F.:Con 2 Pno, w. R. Saccani (cnd), Budapest PO Vox Box 2-▲ CDX 5106 [DDD]
Liszt, F.:Consolations *(rec 1974)* Vox Box 2-▲ CDX 5150
Liszt, F.:Études d'exécution transcendante, S.139 Vox Box 2-▲ CDX 5106 [DDD]
Liszt, F.:Grandes études de Paganini, S.141 Vox Box 3-▲ CD3X 3020 [ADD]
Liszt, F.:Harmonies poétiques et religieuses *(rec 1974)* Vox Box 2-▲ CDX 5150
Liszt, F.:Légendes *(rec 1974)* Vox Box 2-▲ CDX 5150
Liszt, F.:Totentanz, w. R. Saccani (cnd), Budapest PO Vox Box 2-▲ CDX 5106 [DDD]
Liszt, F.:Weihnachtsbaum *(rec 1974)* Vox Box 2-▲ CDX 5150
Mosonyi, M.:Con Pno, w. P. Cao (cnd), Luxembourg RSO *(rec 1973)* Vox Box 2-▲ CDX 5067 [ADD]
Schumann, R.:Davidsbündlertänze Vox Classics ▲ VOX 7515 [DDD]
Schumann, R.:Son 2 Pno Vox Classics ▲ VOX 7515 [DDD]

Rose, Leonard (vc)
Bach, J.S.:Sons Vl, BWV 1027-1029, w. G. Gould (pno) CBS 2-▲ M2K 42414 [AAD]
Beethoven, L. van:Con Vn, Vc & Pno, "Triple Con", w. John Corigliano (vn), Walter Hendl (pno), B. Walter (cnd), New York PO Sony Classical ("Bruno Walter:The Edition" series) ▲ SMK 64479
Beethoven, L. van:Con Vn, Vc & Pno, "Triple Con", w. Isaac Stern (vn), Eugene Istomin (pno), Ormandy (cnd), *(orch unknown)* Sony Classical 2-▲ SM2K 66941
Beethoven, L. van:Con Vn, Vc & Pno, "Triple Con", w. I. Stern (vn), E. Istomin (pno), E. Ormandy (cnd), Philadelphia Orch Sony Classical ("Essential Classics" series) 3-▲ SB3K 48397
Beethoven, L. van:Con Vn, Vc & Pno, "Triple Con", w. I. Stern (vn), E. Istomin (pno), E. Ormandy (cnd), Philadelphia Orch Sony Classical ("Essential Classics" series) ▲ SBK 46549 [ADD] ■ SBT 46549
Beethoven, L. van:Trio 1 Pno, w. Eugene Istomin (pno), Isaac Stern (vn) Sony Classical ("Isaac Stern:A Life in Music" series) 2-▲ SM2K 64510
Beethoven, L. van:Trio 2 Pno, w. Eugene Istomin (pno), Isaac Stern (vn) Sony Classical ("Isaac Stern:A Life in Music" series) 2-▲ SM2K 64510
Beethoven, L. van:Trio 3 Pno, w. Eugene Istomin (pno), Isaac Stern (vn) Sony Classical ("Isaac Stern:A Life in Music" series) 2-▲ SM2K 64510
Beethoven, L. van:Trio 4 Pno, "Ghost", w. Eugene Istomin (pno), Isaac Stern (vn) Sony Classical ("Isaac Stern:A Life in Music" series) 2-▲ SM2K 64513
Beethoven, L. van:Trio 4 Pno, "Ghost", w. E. Istomin (pno), I. Stern (vn) Sony Classical ("Essential Classics" series) ▲ SBK 53514 ■ SBT 53514
Beethoven, L. van:Trio 6 Pno, "Archduke", w. Eugene Istomin (pno), Isaac Stern (vn) Sony Classical ("Isaac Stern:A Life in Music" series) 2-▲ SM2K 64513
Beethoven, L. van:Trio 6 Pno, "Archduke", w. E. Istomin (pno), I. Stern (vn) Sony Classical ("Essential Classics" series) ▲ SBK 53514 ■ SBT 53514
Beethoven, L. van:Trio 8 Pno, w. Eugene Istomin (pno), Isaac Stern (vn) Sony Classical ("Isaac Stern:A Life in Music" series) 2-▲ SM2K 64510
Beethoven, L. van:Trio 9 Pno, "Kakadu", w. Eugene Istomin (pno), Isaac Stern (vn) Sony Classical ("Isaac Stern:A Life in Music" series) 2-▲ SM2K 64513
Beethoven, L. van:Trio Pno, Op. 44, w. Eugene Istomin (pno), Isaac Stern (vn) Sony Classical ("Isaac Stern:A Life in Music" series) 2-▲ SM2K 64510
Bloch, E.:Schelomo, w. E. Ormandy (cnd), Philadelphia Orch *(rec 1967)* Sony Classical ("Essential Classics" series) ▲ SBK 48278 [ADD] ■ SBT 48278
Brahms, J.:Con Vn & Vc, "Double Con", w. Isaac Stern (vn), Mehta, Barenboim (cnd), New York PO Sony Classical 2-▲ SM2K 66941
Brahms, J.:Con Vn & Vc, "Double Con", w. I. Stern (vn), E. Ormandy (cnd), Philadelphia Orch Sony Classical ("Essential Classics" series) ▲ SBK 46335 [ADD] ■ SBT 46335
Brahms, J.:Trios (3) Pno, w. Eugene Istomin (pno), Isaac Stern (vn) Sony Classical ("Isaac Stern:A Life in Music" series) 3-▲ SM3K 64520
Dvořák, A.:Con Vc, w. E. Ormandy (cnd), Philadelphia Orch Sony Classical (Essential Classics) ▲ SBK 46337 [ADD] ■ SBT 46337
Dvořák, A.:Con Vc, w. A. Rodzinski (cnd), New York PO *(rec 1945)* Legend ▲ LGD 141
Dvořák, A.:Con Vc, w. A. Rodzinski (cnd), New York PO *(rec New York, Jan 7, 1945)* Iron Needle ▲ IN 1338 (m) [ADD]
Fauré, G.:Elégie, w. E. Ormandy (cnd), Philadelphia Orch *(rec 1967)* Sony Classical (Essential Classics) ▲ SBK 48278 [ADD] ■ SBT 48278
Haydn, J.:Trios Pno, Vn & Vc, w. Eugene Istomin (pno), Issac Stern (vn)—H.XV/10 CBS 4-▲ M4K 42003 (m/s) [ADD]
Haydn, J.:Trios Pno, Vn & Vc, w. Eugene Istomin (pno), Isaac Stern (vn)—No. 20 Sony Classical ("Isaac Stern:A Life in Music" series) 2-▲ SM2K 64516
Lalo, E.:Con Vc, w. E. Ormandy (cnd), Philadelphia Orch *(rec 1967)* Sony Classical ("Essential Classics" series) ▲ SBK 48278 [ADD] ■ SBT 48278
Mendelssohn, F.:Trio 1 Pno, w. Eugene Istomin (pno), Isaac Stern (vn) Sony Classical ("Isaac Stern:A Life in Music" series) ▲ SMK 64519
Mendelssohn, F.:Trio 2 Pno, w. Eugene Istomin (pno), Isaac Stern (vn) Sony Classical ("Isaac Stern:A Life in Music" series) ▲ SMK 64519
Mozart, W.A.:Qts Fl, w. J.-P. Rampal (fl), I. Stern (vn), A. Schneider (vn) Odyssey ▲ MBK 42601
Mozart, W.A.:Qts Pno, w. Eugene Istomin (pno), Isaac Stern (vn), Milton Katims (va)—No. 2 Sony Classical ("Isaac Stern:A Life in Music" series) 2-▲ SM2K 64516
Saint-Saëns, C.:Con 1 Vc, w. E. Ormandy (cnd), Philadelphia Orch *(rec 1967)* Sony Classical ("Essential Classics" series) ▲ SBK 48276 [ADD] ■ SBT 48276
Schubert, Franz:Trio 1 Pno, w. Eugene Istomin (pno), Isaac Stern (vn) Sony Classical ("Isaac Stern:A Life in Music" series) 2-▲ SM2K 64516
Schubert, Franz:Trio 2 Pno, w. Eugene Istomin (pno), Isaac Stern (vn) Sony Classical ("Isaac Stern:A Life in Music" series) 2-▲ SM2K 64516
Schumann, R.:Con Vc, w. L. Bernstein (cnd), New York PO Sony Classical ▲ SMK 47609
Tchaikovsky, P.:Vars on a Rococo Theme, w. E. Ormandy (cnd), Philadelphia Orch *(rec 1962)* Sony Classical (Essential Classics) ▲ SBK 48278 [ADD] ■ SBT 48278

Rose, Maria (pno)
Clementi, M.:Sons Pno—in Bb, Op. 24/2; in f, Op. 13/6; in A, Op. 25/4; in b, Op. 40/2 Newport Classics ▲ NPT 85571

Rose, Stewart (hn)—see ORCHESTRAS & ENSEMBLES Mozzafiato

Rösel, Peter (pno)
Bach, J.S.:Brandenburg Con 3, w. S. Rodriguez (pno) Élan ▲ CD 2240 [DDD]
Bach, J.S.:Brandenburg Con 5, w. S. Rodriguez (pno) Élan ▲ CD 2240 [DDD]
Beethoven, L. van:Cons Pno (comp), w. C.P. Flor (cnd), Berlin SO Berlin Classics 3-▲ BER 2136 [DDD]
Beethoven, L. van:Con Vn, Vc & Pno, "Triple Con", w. C. Funke (vn), J. Timm (vc), H. Kegel (cnd), Dresden PO Capriccio ▲ 10150 [DDD]
Beethoven, L. van:Fant Pno, Op. 80, "Choral Fant", w. H. Kegel (cnd), Dresden PO, Leipzig Radio Chorus [G] Capriccio ▲ 10150 [DDD]
Beethoven, L. van:Rondo Pno, WoO 6, w. H. Bongartz (cnd), Leipzig Gewandhaus Orch Berlin Classics ▲ BER 2078 [DDD]
Beethoven, L. van:Rondo Pno, WoO 6, w. C.P. Flor (cnd), Berlin SO Berlin Classics 3-▲ BER 2136 [DDD]
Beethoven, L. van:Son 17 Pno, "Tempest" Berlin Classics 2-▲ BER CD 9279
Beethoven, L. van:Son 18 Pno Berlin Classics 2-▲ BER CD 9279
Beethoven, L. van:Son 24 Pno Berlin Classics 2-▲ BER CD 9279
Beethoven, L. van:Son 29 Pno, "Hammerklavier" Berlin Classics 2-▲ BER CD 9279
Brahms, J.:Ballades, Op. 10 Berlin Classics ▲ BER 9031 [ADD]
Brahms, J.:Fants Pno, Op. 116 Berlin Classics ▲ BER 9032 [ADD]
Brahms, J.:Intermezzos Pno, Op. 117 Berlin Classics ▲ BER 9031 [ADD]
Brahms, J.:Pieces Pno, Op. 76 Berlin Classics ▲ BER 9029 [ADD]
Brahms, J.:Pieces Pno, Op. 119 Berlin Classics ▲ BER 9030 [ADD]
Brahms, J.:Rhaps Pno, Op. 79 Berlin Classics ▲ BER 9032 [ADD]
Brahms, J.:Son 2 Pno Berlin Classics ▲ BER 9029 [ADD]
Brahms, J.:Son 3 Pno Berlin Classics ▲ BER 9030 [ADD]
Brahms, J.:Vars & Fugue on a Theme by Handel Berlin Classics ▲ BER 9031 [ADD]
Brahms, J.:Vars on an Original Theme Berlin Classics ▲ BER 9029 [ADD]
Brahms, J.:Vars on a Theme by Paganini Berlin Classics ▲ BER 9032 [ADD]
Brahms, J.:Vars on a Theme of Robert Schumann, Op. 9 Berlin Classics ▲ BER 9030 [ADD]
Busoni, F.:Bach Transcriptions—Prelude & Fugue in D, Op. 532; Toccata, Adagio & Fugue in C, Op. 564; Nun freut euch, lieben Christen; Nun komm der Heiden Heiland; In dir ist Freude; Wachet auf, ruft uns die Stimme Berlin Classics ▲ BER 1088 [DDD]
Busoni, F.:Chaconne Pno Berlin Classics ▲ BER 1088 [DDD]
Reger, M.:Vars & Fugue on a Theme by Mozart, w. S. Rodriguez (pno) Élan ▲ CD 2240 [DDD]
Schubert, Franz:Pno Music (misc)—Fant in C, "Graz"; Minuet & Trio in A; 2 Scherzi; 3 Pno Pieces; Adagio in E Berlin Classics ▲ BER 9272
Schumann, R.:Papillons Berlin Classics 2-▲ BER CD 9190
Schumann, R.:Romances Ob, w. Burkhard Glaetzner (ob) Berlin Classics ▲ BER 9189

Rösel, Peter (pno) (cont.)
Schumann, R.:Son 1 Pno Berlin Classics 2-▲ BER CD 9190
Schumann, R.:Son 2 Pno Berlin Classics 2-▲ BER CD 9190
Schumann, R.:Son 2 Vn, w. Christian Funke (vn) Berlin Classics ▲ BER 9189
Schumann, R.:Sym Etudes Berlin Classics 2-▲ BER CD 9190
Strauss, R.:Panathenäenzug, w. R. Kempe (cnd), Dresden Staatskapelle EMI Classics 3-▲ CDZC 64342
Strauss, R.:Parergon zur Symphonia domestica, w. R. Kempe (cnd), Dresden Staatskapelle EMI Classics 3-▲ CDZC 64342
Stravinsky, I.:Capriccio, w. H. Kegel (cnd), Dresden PO *(rec 1978 or 1981)* Berlin Classics ▲ BER 2044 [ADD]
Weber, C.M. von:Con 1 Pno, w. H. Blomstedt (cnd), Dresden Staatskapelle Berlin Classics ▲ BER 1058 [DDD]
Weber, C.M. von:Con 2 Pno, w. H. Blomstedt (cnd), Dresden Staatskapelle Berlin Classics ▲ BER 1058 [DDD]
Weber, C.M. von:Konzertstück Pno, w. H. Blomstedt (cnd), Dresden Staatskapelle Berlin Classics ▲ BER 1058 [DDD]

Roselli, Eros (gtr)
Giuliani, M.:Gtr Music, w. Urs Mächler Ensemble—Gran Qnt. for Gtr & Str Qt., Op. 65; 7 Pieces for Gtr & Vn, Op. 74; Intro. & Vars. for Gtr & Str Qt., Opp. 101-103 Nuova Era ▲ NUO 7194 [DDD]

Roseman, Ronald (ob)—see also ORCHESTRAS & ENSEMBLES New York Woodwind Soloists
Albinoni, T.:Con in C Tpt, w. Gerard Schwarz (tpt), Susan Weiner (ob), Virginia Brewer (ob), Ronald MacCourt (bn), William Scribner (bn), Edward Brewer (hpd) Vox Box 2-▲ CDX 5124 [ADD]
Hertel, J.W.:Con à cinque, w. Gerard Schwarz (tpt), Susan Weiner (ob), Virginia Brewer (ob), Ronald MacCourt (bn), William Scribner (bn), Edward Brewer (hpd) Vox Box 2-▲ CDX 5124 [ADD]
Kraft, L.:O Primavera, w. R. Stallman (fl), E. Gilmore (cl) *(rec 1989–1990)* Centaur ▲ CRC 2079 [ADD]
Kupferman, M.:Mask of Electra, w. Jan De Gaetani (mez), Joel Spiegelman (elec hpd) Soundspells ▲ SP 112 [ADD]
Rieti, V.:Partita Hpd, w. S. Marlowe (hpd), S. Baron (fl), C. Libove (vn), A. Ajemian (vn), H. Zaratzian (va), C. McCraken (vc) CRI ▲ CD 601 [ADD]
Telemann, G.P.:Cons Tpt, w. Gerard Schwarz (tpt), Susan Weiner (ob), Virginia Brewer (ob), Ronald MacCourt (bn), William Scribner (bn), Edward Brewer (hpd) Vox Box 2-▲ CDX 5124 [ADD]
Telemann, G.P.:Qt Bn, w. A. Weisberg (bn), S. Baron (fl), E. Brewer (hpd)—in d Elektra/Nonesuch ■ 71352-4

Rosen, Charles (pno)
Bach, J.S.:Goldberg Vars Sony Classical ("Essential Classics" series) ▲ SBK 48173 ■ SBT 48173
Beethoven, L. van:Con 2 Pno, w. W. Morris (cnd), London Symphonica IMP ("Classics" series) ▲ IMP 6700162
Beethoven, L. van:Con 4 Pno, w. W. Morris (cnd), London Symphonica IMP ("Classics" series) ▲ IMP 6700162
Beethoven, L. van:Vars on a waltz by Diabelli, Op. 120 IMP ("Classics" series) ▲ IMP 6700112
Chopin, F.:Ballades Pno (comp)—Op. 47 Music & Arts ▲ CD 609 [DDD]
Chopin, F.:Barcarolle Pno Music & Arts ▲ CD 609 [DDD]
Chopin, F.:Con 2 Pno, w. J. Pritchard (cnd), New Philharmonia Orch Odyssey ■ YT 31529
Chopin, F.:Nocturnes—Op. 27/2; Op. 62/1 *(rec American Academy of Arts & Letters, New York, June, July & Oct 1993)* MusicMasters ("Classics" series) ▲ 01612-67154-2 [DDD]
Chopin, F.:Pno Music (misc)—Die Loreley MusicMasters ▲ 01612-67154-2
Chopin, F.:Polonaise-fant Music & Arts ▲ CD 609 [DDD]
Chopin, F.:Son Pno, Op. 35 Music & Arts ▲ CD 609 [DDD]
Liszt, F.:Con 1 Pno, w. J. Pritchard (cnd), New Philharmonia Orch Odyssey ■ YT 31529
Liszt, F.:Con 1 Pno, w. J. Pritchard (cnd), New Philharmonia Orch CBS ▲ MYK 37804 [ADD] ■ MYT 37804
Liszt, F.:Pno Music (misc)—Die Loreley; Mes joies [arr from Chopin's Nocturne in D♭ for Piano, Op. 27/2] *(rec American Academy of Arts & Letters, New York, June, July & Oct 1993)* MusicMasters ("Classics" series) ▲ 01612-67154-2 [DDD]
Liszt, F.:Réminiscences de Don Juan *(rec American Academy of Arts & Letters, New York, June, July & Oct 1993)* MusicMasters ("Classics" series) ▲ 01612-67154-2 [DDD]
Mozart, W.A.:Son 11 Pno *(rec 1956)* Boston Skyline ▲ BSD 131 [AAD]
Mozart, W.A.:Son 13 Pno *(rec 1956)* Boston Skyline ▲ BSD 131 [AAD]
Scarlatti, D.:Sons Kbd—in F, K.44; in G, K.125; in E, K.134; in D, K.140; in C, K.242; in c♯, K.247 *(rec 1955)* Boston Skyline ▲ BSD 131 [AAD]
Schumann, R.:Davidsbündlertänze *(rec American Academy of Arts & Letters, New York, June, July & Oct 1993)* MusicMasters ("Classics" series) ▲ 01612-67154-2 [DDD]
Webern, A.:Pieces Vn, w. Isaac Stern (vn) Sony Classical ▲ SMK 64535 [ADD]

Rosen, Marcy (vc)—see ORCHESTRAS & ENSEMBLES Mendelssohn String Quartet

Rosen, Marvin (pno)
Hovhaness, A.:Music of, w. Alexa Still (fl), Jordania (cnd), Manhattan CO, New Zealand CO, KBS SO—The Prayer of St. Gregory; Elibris; Mystic Flute; Aria, Hymn & Fugue; Mountain Idylls; Gtr Sym; Adagio; Son; Fred the Cat; Aria [from Harotiun] Koch International Classics ▲ KIC 7311 [DDD]
Hovhaness, A.:Pno Music—Sonata, "Mt. Ossipee," Op. 299/2 (1977); Sonata, "Fred the Cat," Op. 301 (1977); Sonata, "Prospect Hill," Op. 346 (1980); Sonata, "Mt. Chocorua," Op. 335 (1980; rev. 1982); Dance Ghazal, Op. 37a (1931; rev. 1938); Slumber Song, Op. 52/2 (1938); Achtamar, Op. 64/1 (1948); Fantasy on an Ossetin Tune, Op. 85/6 (1951); Orbit No. 2, Op. 102/2 (1952); Macedonian Mountain Dance, Op. 144 (1938); Mountain Dance No. 2, Op. 144b (1941; rev. 1962) Koch International Classics ▲ KIC 7195-2 [DDD]
Hovhaness, A.:Pno Music—Toccata & Fugue No. 1, Op. 6; Prelude & Fugue, Op. 10/1; Do You Remember the Last Silence; Lousang Kisher; Fire Dance; Hymn IV [from Bare November Day]; Madras Son.; Son., Op. 145 Koch International Classics ▲ KIC 7288 [DDD]

Rosen, Nathaniel (vc)
Amram, D.:Honor Song for Sitting Bull, w. R.A. Clark (cnd), Manhattan CO *(rec SUNY, Oct 1993)* Newport Classics ▲ NPD 85601 [DDD]
Brahms, J.:Sons Vc (comp), w. D. Stevenson (pno) John Marks ▲ JMR 5 [DDD]
Ibert, J.:Con Vc, w. R.A. Clark (cnd), Manhattan CO Newport Classic ("Manhattan CO" series) ▲ NPD 85598 [DDD]
Mendelssohn, F.:Lied ohne Worte Vc, w. D. Stevenson (pno) John Marks ▲ JMR 5 [DDD]
Orientale:Romantic Music for Cello, w. Doris Stevenson (pno), Arturo Delmoni (vn) North Star ▲ NS 0027
Prokofiev, S.:Son Vc, w. P. Dokovska (pno) Élan ▲ CD 2226 [DDD]
Rachmaninoff, S.:Son Vc, w. P. Dokovska (pno) Élan ▲ CD 2226 [DDD]
Reverie:Romantic Music for Quiet Times, w. Kaaren Erickson (sop), Doris Stevenson (pno), Arturo Delmoni (vn) John Marks Records ▲ JMR 10
Schubert, Franz:Trio 2 Pno, w. E. Auer (pno), A. Delmoni (vn) *(rec Dec. 1993)* Clarity ▲ CCD 1007
Schumann, R.:Fantasiestücke Cl, w. D. Stevenson (pno) John Marks ▲ JMR 5 [DDD]
Shostakovich, D.:Con 1 Vc, w. E. Tabakov (cnd), Sofia PO John Marks ▲ JMR 3
Shostakovich, D.:Trio 2 Pno, w. S. Rodriguez (pno), R. Ricci (vn) One-Eleven ▲ URS 92010
Tchaikovsky, P.:Pezzo capriccioso, w. E. Tabakov (cnd), Sofia PO John Marks ▲ JMR 3
Tchaikovsky, P.:Vars on a Rococo Theme, w. E. Tabakov (cnd), Sofia PO John Marks ▲ JMR 3

Rosenak, Karen (pno)—see also ORCHESTRAS & ENSEMBLES Earplay members, Earplay
Feldman, Morton:Rothko Chapel, w. D. Dietrich (sop), D. Abel (vn), W. Winant (perc), Philip Brett (cnd), Univ of California at Berkeley Chamber Chorus *(rec 10/90)* New Albion ▲ NA 039 [DDD]
Kupferman, M.:Aristo Vars, w. L. Varga (vc) Soundspells ▲ CD 105
Kupferman, M.:Blue Son, w. L. Varga (vc) Soundspells ▲ CD 105
Kupferman, M.:Night Voices, w. L. Varga (vc), W. Anderson (gtr) Soundspells ▲ CD 105
Thow, J.:Remembering Music & Arts ▲ CD 915

Rosenbaum, Poul (pno)—see also ORCHESTRAS & ENSEMBLES Copenhagen Contemporary Players, Trio Con Brio
Dørumsgaard, A.:Dusk in the Enchanted Wood, w. Aage Haugland (bass) Point ▲ PCD 5088 [DDD]
Griffes, C.T.:Fant Pieces, Op. 6 Kontrapunkt ▲ KPT 32215 [DDD]
Griffes, C.T.:Preludes (3) Pno Kontrapunkt ▲ KPT 32215 [DDD]

Rosenbaum, Poul (pno) (cont.)
Griffes, C.T.:Roman Sketches, Op. 7 Kontrapunkt ▲ KPT 32215 [DDD]
Griffes, C.T.:Son Pno Kontrapunkt ▲ KPT 32215 [DDD]
Griffes, C.T.:Tone-Pictures, Op. 5 Kontrapunkt ▲ KPT 32215 [DDD]
Ibert, J.:Chansons de Don Quichotte, w. Aage Haugland (bass) Point ▲ PCD 5088 [DDD]
Medtner, N.:Son romantica *(rec July 1987)* Point ▲ PCD 5090 [DDD]
Mussorgsky, M.:Nursery, w. Aage Haugland (bass) Chandos 3-▲ CHAN 9336/38 [DDD]
Mussorgsky, M.:Nursery, w. Aage Haugland (bass) Point ▲ PCD 5098 [DAD]
Mussorgsky, M.:Songs (comp), w. Aage Haugland (bass) Chandos 3-▲ CHAN 9336/38 [DDD]
Mussorgsky, M.:Songs & Dances, w. Aage Haugland (bass) Point ▲ PCD 5088 [DDD]
Mussorgsky, M.:Songs & Dances, w. Aage Haugland (bass) Chandos 3-▲ CHAN 9336/38 [DDD]
Mussorgsky, M.:Songs & Dances, w. Aage Haugland (bass) Point ▲ PCD 5098 [DAD]
Mussorgsky, M.:Songs (misc), w. Aage Haugland (bass)—Master Haughty; The Classic; The Feast; Savishna; The Seminarist; The He-Goat; The Street-Urchin; Song of Mephistopheles; Evening Song Point ▲ PCD 5098 [DAD]
Mussorgsky, M.:Sunless, w. Aage Haugland (bass) Chandos 3-▲ CHAN 9336/38 [DDD]
Rachmaninoff, S.:Son 1 Pno *(rec Apr 1983)* Point ▲ PCD 5090 [DDD]
Ruders, P.:Dramaphonia, w. O. de la Martinez (cnd), Lontano *(rec Danish Radio Concert Hall, Copenhagen, Feb. 10, 1990)* Marco Polo ("dacapo" series) ▲ DC 9308 [DDD]
Stolarczyk, W.:Earth Air Fire Water, w. Amalie Malling (pno), John Damgaard (pno), Anne Øland (pno), Teddy Teirup (pno), Friedrich Gürtler (pno), Rosalind Bevan (pno), Rodolfo Llambias (pno), Bella Horn-Ribera (pno), Anders Riber (pno), Elisabeth Sigurdsson (pno), Thomas Tronheim (pno), Elsebeth Broderson (pno), Erik Kaltoft (pno), Jørgen Hald Nielsen (pno), Aino Gilemann (pno), Birgit Kjær (pno), Jørgen Thomsen (pno), Gunhild Donslund (pno), Henrik Bo Hansen (pno), Lone Karlsson (pno), Erik Fessel (pno), Lasse Nilsson (pno), Janos Ferenczi (pno), Erik Bach (pno), Axel Momme (pno), Arne de Cros Dich (pno), Sven Micha Slot (pno), Hanne Bramsen Buhl (pno), Lili Olesen (pno), Susannah Carlsson (pno), Ulla Erml (pno), Vagn Sørensen (pno), Leif Greibe (pno), Bodil Krogh (pno), Kirsten Ottosen (pno), Inger Bergenholz (pno), Karsten Gylendorf (pno), Bjønr Elkjær (pno), Jacob Bjørn Jensen (pno), Jørgen Kaad (pno), Anne Marie Hjelm (pno), Carl Ulrik Munk Andersen (pno), Poul Lumbye (pno), Oluf Hildebrandt Nielsen (pno), Joachim Olsson (pno), Peter Pade Ramsøe Jacobsen (pno), Astrid Pollmann (pno), Jette Borsch (pno), Kirsten Karlshøj (pno), Maria Teresa Assing (pno), Allan Dahl Hansen (pno), Johan Hugossen (pno), Tine Fenger Pederson (pno), Arne Jørgen Fæø (pno), Anja Høgsted (pno), Anne Sophie Parbo (pno), Inga Lindmark (pno), Teresa Drabik Stathakis (pno), Anne Ruth Ferenczi (pno), Irene Hasager (pno), Yuka Ichikawa (pno), Birgitte Baur (pno), Malene Thastum (pno), Jens E. Rasmussen (pno), Birgitte Zielke (pno), Claus Zielke (pno), Stefan Kasch (pno), Bin Qiao (pno), Inger Johanne Teirup (pno), Lindy Rosborg (pno), Liisa Heininen (pno), David Højer (pno), Ellen Refstrup (pno), Thomas K. Søorensen (pno), Erik Kure (pno), Michael Rauff (pno), Jan beck Eriksson (pno), Tanja Zapolski (pno), Vibeke Skagbo (pno), Pål Eide Lindtner (pno), Ha-Young Sul (pno), Benedicte Palko (pno), Inke Kesseler (pno), Anne Marie Meineche (pno), Sverre Larsen (pno), Kasper Peter Bach (pno), Elisabetta Eliseo (pno), Olga Magieres (pno), Carl Erik Kühl (pno), Thorkild Borup Nielsen (pno), Valeria Zanini (pno), Lars Stenhoft (perc), Dennis Boel (perc), Winnie Dahlgren (perc), Susanne Vind (perc), Claus Byrith (elec), Anne Marie Storm (elec), J. Ribera (cnd) *(rec live, Koldinghaus Castle, Denmark, May 2, 1996)* Danica ▲ DCD 1996

Rosenbaum, Sheldon (pno)
Handel, G.F.:Music of, w. Johanan Bickhardt (bar)—Arm, Arm Ye Brave; Father of Heaven; Dank Sei Dir Herr; See, the Raging Flames Arise [all are sels. from oratorios] *(rec StudioMedia, Evanston, IL)* ZC Music ■ 010893T
Mendelssohn, F.:Elijah (sels), w. Johanan Bickhardt (bar)—Draw Near All Ye People; Is Not His Word; What Have I to Do With Thee [w. Theresa Ludden (sop)] *(rec StudioMedia, Evanston, IL)* ZC Music ■ 010893T

Rosenbaum, Victor (pno)
Schubert, Franz:Moments musicaux Bridge ▲ 9070
Schubert, Franz:Son Pno, D.959 Bridge ▲ 9070

Rosenberg, G. (pno)
Cage, J.:Sons & Interludes VQR Digital ▲ VQR 2001 [DDD]
Prokofiev, S.:Son Fl, w. P. Meisen (fl) MD + G ▲ L 3255 [DDD]
Reger, M.:Son Vn Pno, Op. 84, w. P. Meisen (fl) [arr fl & pno] MD + G ▲ L 3255 [DDD]
Reinecke, C.:Son Fl, w. P. Meisen (fl) MD + G ▲ L 3255 [DDD]

Rosenberg, Tom (vc)—see also ORCHESTRAS & ENSEMBLES Chester String Quartet
Kernis, A.J.:Mozart en Route, w. Aaron Berofsky (vn), David Harding (va) *(rec Manhattan Center Studios, New York, May 31–June 3, 1995)* New Albion ♦ NA 083CD

Rosenberger, Carol (pno)
Barber, S.:Son Vc, w. J. Wang (vc) Delos ▲ DE 3097 [DDD]
Barber, S.:Songs, w. J. Wang (sgr) [trans. cello & piano Bejun Mehta]—With Rue My Heart is Laden, Op. 2/2 & Sure on this Shining Night, Op. 13/3 Delos ▲ DE 3097 [DDD]
Beethoven, L. van:Con 4 Pno, w. G. Schwarz (cnd), London SO Delos ▲ DCD 3027 [DDD]
Beethoven, L. van:Qnt Pno, Ob, Cl, Hn & Bn, w. A. Vogel (ob), D. Shifrin (cl), K. Munday (bn), R. Graham (hn) Delos ▲ DCD 3024 [DDD]
Beethoven, L. van:Son 23 Pno, "Appassionata" Delos ▲ DCD 3009 [DDD]
Beethoven, L. van:Son 32 Pno Delos ▲ DCD 3009 [DDD]
Bennett, Richard Rodney:Suite for Skip & Sadie, w. R. R. Bennett (pno) Delos ▲ DE 6002 [DDD] ■ CS 6002 (D)
Brahms, J.:Sons Cl (comp), w. D. Shifrin (cl) Delos ▲ DCD 3025 [DDD]
Chopin, F.:Intro & Polonaise, "Polonaise brilliante", w. J. Wang (vc) Delos ▲ DE 3097 [DDD]
Chopin, F.:Nocturnes—Opp. 27/2, 55/2 Delos ▲ DCD 3030 [DDD]
Chopin, F.:Son Vc, w. J. Wang (vc) Delos ▲ DE 3097 [DDD]
Debussy, C.:Pno Music (misc)—Jardins sous la pluie (from *Estampes*); Reflets dans l'eau & Poissons d'or (from *Images*); La Cathédrale engloutie & Ondine (from *Preludes*) Delos ▲ DCD 3006 [DDD]
Falla, M. de:Noches en los jardines de España, w. G. Schwarz (cnd), London SO Delos ▲ DCD 3060 [DDD]
Fauré, G.:Nocturnes (13) Pno—No. 6 Delos ▲ DCD 3030 [DDD]
Granados, E.:Goyescas (intermezzo)—No. 4, "The Maiden & the Nightingale" Delos ▲ DCD 3030 [DDD]
Griffes, C.T.:Notturno Delos ▲ DCD 3030 [DDD]
Griffes, C.T.:Roman Sketches, Op. 7—No. 2, "The Fountain of Acqua Paola" Delos ▲ DCD 3006 [DDD]
Hanson, H.:Con Pno, w. G. Schwarz (cnd), Seattle SO Delos ▲ DE 3130 [DDD]
Hanson, H.:Con Pno, w. G. Schwarz (cnd), Seattle SO Delos 4-▲ DE 3150 [DDD]
Hanson, H.:Fant Vars on a Theme of Youth, w. G. Schwarz (cnd), New York Chamber SO Delos 4-▲ DE 3150 [DDD]
Hanson, H.:Fant Vars on a Theme of Youth, w. G. Schwarz (cnd), New York Chamber SO Delos ▲ DE 3092 [DDD]
Haydn, J.:Con Org & Strs, H.XVIII/2, w. G. Schwarz (cnd), Scottish CO Delos ▲ DCD 3061
Haydn, J.:Con Org, Vns & Bass Instrument, H.XVIII/5, w. G. Schwarz (cnd), Scottish CO Delos ▲ DCD 3064 [DDD]
Hindemith, P.:The Four Temperaments, w. J. DePreist (cnd), Royal PO Delos ▲ DCD 1006 [AAD]
Liszt, F.:Années de pèlerinage 3—No. 4, "Les Jeux d'eaux à la Villa d'Este" Delos ▲ DCD 3006 [DDD]
Liszt, F.:Pno Music (misc)—Harmonies du soir No. 11 from *12 Transcendental Etudes*; Liebestraum Delos ▲ DCD 3030 [DDD]
Mozart, W.A.:Qnt Pno, K.452, w. A. Vogel (ob), D. Shifrin (cl), K. Munday (bn), R. Graham (hn) Delos ▲ DCD 3024 [DDD]
Night Moods Delos ▲ DCD 3030 [DDD]
Perchance to Dream:A Lullaby Album for Children & Adults Delos ▲ DE 3079 [DDD] ■ CS-3079 (D)
Presenting Jian Wang, w. Jian Wang (vc) Delos ▲ DE 3097 [DDD]
Prokofiev, S.:Music for Children, w. N. Makarova (nar)—includes the Russian fairy tale Prince Ivan & the Frog Princess [narr in E] Delos ▲ DE 6003 [DDD] ■ CS 6003 (D)
Ravel, M.:Jeux d'eau Delos ▲ DCD 3006 [DDD]
Reveries *(rec 1992)* Delos ▲ DE 3113 [DDD]
Schubert, Franz:Impromptus Pno, D.899 Delos ▲ DCD 3018 [DDD]
Schubert, Franz:Son Pno, D.960 Delos ▲ DCD 3018 [DDD]

▲ = CD ♦ = Enhanced CD Δ = MD ■ = Cassette Tape □ = DCC

Rosenberger, Carol (pno) (cont.)
Schumann, R.:Adagio & Allegro Hn, w. J. Wang (vc) Delos ▲ DE 3097 [DDD]
Schumann, R.:Fantasiestücke Cl, w. D. Shifrin (cl) Delos ▲ DCD 3025 [DDD]
Shostakovich, D.:Con 1 Pno, w. S. Burns (tpt), G. Schwarz (cnd), Los Angeles CO Delos ▲ DCD 3021 [DDD]
Singing on the Water:Piano Barcarolles *(rec 1st Congregational Church, Los Angeles, Dec 26–28, 1994)* Delos ▲ DE 3172 [DDD]
Songs & Arias, w. Mehta, Bejun (trb), David Shifrin (cl) Delos ▲ DCD 3019 [DDD]
Strauss, R.:Burleske, w. G. Schwarz (cnd), Seattle SO Delos ▲ DE 3109 [DDD]
Szymanowski, K.:Pno Music (sels)—Études, Op. 4 & Op. 33; Masques, Op. 34; Mazurkas, Op. 50, Nos. 1,2,3,7,11,15,18 & Op. 62 Delos ▲ DE 1002 [AAD]
Tchaikovsky, P.:The Snow Maiden, w. N. Makarova (nar) Delos ▲ DE 6004 [DDD] ■ CS 6004 (D)
Walton, W.:Duets for Children, w. R. R. Bennett (pno) Delos ▲ DE 6002 [DDD] ■ CS 6002 (D)
Water Music of the Impressionists Delos ▲ DCD 3006 [DDD]

Rosenblith, Eric (vn)
Pousseur, H.:Chants sacrés, w. Valarie Lamoree (sop), Jacob Glick (va), Michael Rudiakov (vc) Vox Box 2–▲ CDX 5144

Rosenblith, Eric (vn/va)
Schoenberg, A.:Pierrot lunaire, w. Maureen McNalley (nar), Dwight Peltzer (pno), Chris Finckel (vc), Sue Ann Kahn (fl), Anand Devendra (cl/b cl), J. Thome (cnd), Orch of Our Time Vox Box 2–▲ CDX 5144

Rosenblum, Ivan (kbd)
Weill, K.:Songs, w. Pamela Alexander (sop), Dale Wolford (sax/syn)—Complainte de la Seine; Le Roi d'Aquitaine; Youkali; Je ne t'aime pas; Le train du Ciel; Scène au Dancing; Es regnet; Der Abschiedsbrief; Pirate Jenny; Barbara Song; Die Muschel von Margate; Nanna's Lied; What Did She Get, That Soldier's Wife?; Surabaya Johnny *(rec Bay View Studios, Richmond, CA)* Laurel ▲ LR 855

Rosenblum, Ivan (pno)
More Than Sax:Baroque, Blues & Beyond, w. Dale Wolford (a sax/s sax), Stephanie Friedman (mez) *(rec Belmont, CA & Richmond, CA, Aug. 17–20, 1993* Gliddon ▲ GP 001 [DDD]

Rosenboom, David (pno)
Braxton, A.:Composition 107 (sels), w. A. Braxton (saxes), W. Winant (perc) Centaur ▲ CRC 2110 [DDD]

Rosenbusch, Thorsten (vn)
Mozart, W.A.:Concertone Vns, w. Erich Kruger (va), H. Haenchen (cnd), C.P.E. Bach CO Berlin Classics ▲ BER 2003
Mozart, W.A.:Sinf concertante Vn, K.364, w. Christian Trompler (va), H. Haenchen (cnd), C.P.E. Bach CO Berlin Classics ▲ BER 2003 [DDD]

Rosenek, Leo (pno)
Schubert, Franz:Songs (misc), w. Elisabeth Schumann (sop) Gerald Moore (pno), Elizabeth Coleman (pno)—An die Nachtigall, D.497; Die Forelle, D.550; Ave Maria (Ellens Gesang III), D.839; An die Musik, D.547; Auf dem Wasser zu singen, D.774; Des Fischers Liebesglück, D.933; Der Musensohn, D.764; Fischerweise, D.881; Gretchen am Spinrade, D.118; Liebesbotschaft ("Schwanegesang" No. 1), D.957; Nacht und Träume, D.827; Seligkeit, D.433; Nähe des Geliebten, D.162; Lachen und Weinen, D.777; Frühlingstraum ("Winterreise" No. 11), D.911; Der Einsame, D.800; Nachtviolen, D.752; An die Geliebte, D.303; Wiegenlied (Schlafe, Schlafe), D.498; Der Schmetterling, D.633; Des Baches Wiegenlied (Die Schöne Müllerin" No. 20), D.957; Der Jüngling und der Tod, D.545; Das Heimweh, D.456; Dass sie hier gewesen, D.775; Der Vollmond strahlt ("Rosamunde" Romanze), D.797; Der Junge Nonne, D.828 *(rec 1933–1945)* Minerva ▲ MN–A22 [ADD]

Rosenfeld, A. (vn)
Pfiffner, E.:Monologue on Peace & War, w. F. Reinmann (bar), J. Allen (vn), C. Anderes (va), G. Pawlica (vc) *(rec May 1992)* Pro Viva ▲ ISPV 170 [DDD]

Rosenfeld, Jayn (fl)—see also ORCHESTRAS & ENSEMBLES Continuum Chamber Ensemble, New York Camerata
Cory, E.:Pas de Quatre, w. Diane Bruce Sinclair (vn), Charles Forbes (vc), Meg Bachman Vas (pno), New York Camerata Soundspells ▲ CD 116 [DDD]
Lennon, J.A.:Echolilia CRI ▲ CD 599 [ADD/DDD]

Rosenfeld, Julie (vn)
Debussy, C.:Trio Pno, w. Andrè Previn (pno), Gary Hoffman (vc) RCA Red Seal ▲ 09026–68062–2
Milhaud, D.:La Création du monde (suite), w. André Previn (pno), Ani Kavafian (vn), Toby Hoffman (va), Carter Brey (vc) *(rec Manhattan Center Studios, New York City, May 25–26, 1993)* RCA Red Seal ▲ 09026–68181–2 [DDD]
Ravel, M.:Trio Pno, w. Andrè Previn (pno), Gary Hoffman (vc) RCA Red Seal ▲ 09026–68062–2
Saint-Saëns, C.:Spt Tpt, w. André Previn (pno), Thomas Stevens (tpt), Ani Kavafian (vn), Toby Hoffman (va), Carter Brey (vc), Jack Kulowitsch (db) *(rec Manhattan Center Studios, New York City, May 25–26, 1993)* RCA Red Seal ▲ 09026–68181–2 [DDD]

Rosenfeld, Peter (vc)
Brings, A.:Duo Concertante Vc, w. M. Ritt (pno) Capstone ▲ CPS 8615

Rosenfeld, Randall (vielle/gittern/fl/rcr)—see ORCHESTRAS & ENSEMBLES Sine Nomine Ensemble

Rosengren, Håkan (cl)
Nielsen, C.:Con Cl, w. E.–P. Salonen (cnd), Swedish RSO *(rec Sept. 10–18, 1991)* Sony Classical ▲ SK 53276 [DDD]

Rosenkranz, Helge (vn)—see ORCHESTRAS & ENSEMBLES Franz Schubert String Quartet

Rosenohl, Berta (pno)—see ORCHESTRAS & ENSEMBLES Montreal Musica Camerata members, Montreal Musica Camerata

Rosenthal, D. (perc)
Harrison, L.:Fugue Perc, w. William Winant (perc), Dan Kennedy (perc), T. Manley (perc) New Albion ▲ NA 055
Harrison, L.:Song of Quetzalcoatl, w. William Winant (perc), Dan Kennedy (perc), T. Manley (perc) New Albion ▲ NA 055

Rosenthal, Laurence (pno)
Rachmaninoff, S.:Songs, w. Maria Kurenko (sop), Vsevolod Pastukhoff (pno)—Melody; On the Death of a Linnet; Night Is Mournful; I Ask Mercy; Vocalise; Arion; I Remember That Day; Music; At Night in My Garden; To Her; Daisies; The Rat-Catcher; A Dream; A-ou; The Fountain; Yesterday We Met; The Changing Wind; Fragment from Alfred de Musset; It Is Pleasant Here; 2 Partings:A Dialogue (w. Vadim Gontzoff); What Happiness; Everything Is Taken from Me; The Ring; I Am Alone Again; We Will Rest; The Muse; Dissonance VAI Audio ▲ VAIA 1094 [ADD]

Rosenthal, Linda (vn)
Fiddle-de-Bop:American Music for Violin & Piano, w. Lincoln Mayorga (pno) *(rec East Chatham, New York, Jan 1995)* Town Hall ▲ THCD 45

Rosenthal, Martin (dr)
Rihm, W.:Lieder, w. R. Salter (bar), B. Wambach (pno), F. Lang (drum)—Vier Gedichte aus Atemwende [text by Paul Celan] for Voice & Piano (1973); Hölderlin–Fragmente for Voice & Piano (1976–7); Neue Alexanderlieder [5 poems by Ernst Herbeck] for Baritone & Piano 1979); Wölfli–Liederbuch for Baritone, Piano & 2 Drums (1980–81) [G] CPO ▲ CPO 999049–2 [ADD]

Rosenthal, Moritz (pno)
Moriz Rosenthal, Vol. 2 Pearl ▲ PEA 9963 [AAD]

Rosenthal, Paul (vn)
Spohr, L.:Double Qt 1, w. J. Heifetz (vn), I. Baker (vn), P. Amoyal (vn), M. Thomas (va), A. Harshman (va), G. Piatigorsky (vc), L. Lesser (vc) RCA Gold Seal ▲ 7870–2–RG (m/s) [ADD]
Taneyev, S.:Qnt Pno Strs, w. J. Lowenthal (pno), Y. Kamei (vn), M. Thompson (va), S. Kates (vc) Arabesque ▲ Z 6539 [DDD]
Vieuxtemps, H.:Con 1 Vn, w. C. Peacock (cnd), Heritage CO *(rec Salt Lake City, Nov. 13 & 14, 1992)* Biddulph ▲ LAW 011 [DDD]
Vieuxtemps, H.:Fant appassionata, w. C. Peacock (cnd), Heritage CO *(rec Salt Lake City, Nov. 13 & 14, 1992)* Biddulph ▲ LAW 011 [DDD]

Rosenwasser, Joel (pno)
Berg, A.:Son Pno Critics Choice ▲ CD 1111 [ADD] ■ CAS 1111
Borodin, A.:Petite Suite Critics Choice ▲ CD 1111 [ADD] ■ CAS 1111
Busoni, F.:Preludes Pno, Op. 37 Critics Choice ▲ CD 1111 [ADD] ■ CAS 1111

Rosenwasser, Joel (pno) (cont.)
Haydn, J.:Sons Pno—in D, H.XVII:D1; in G, H.XVI:8; in E♭; in D, H.XVI:4; in e, H.XVI:47; in B♭, H.XVI:2 *(rec Sadler Recording Studio)* Critics Choice ▲ CD 2111 [DDD]

Rosenzweig, Stanley (tpt)
Carter, E.:Canon for 3, "In memoriam Igor Stravinsky", w. Louis Ranger (tpt), Gerard Schwarz (tpt) [2 versions] Phoenix ▲ PHCD 115 [AAD]

Rosin, Armin (trbn)
Baroque Trombone & Brass, w. Franz Lehrendorfer (org), Stuttgart Phil Brass Hännsler Classic ▲ 98.985 [AAD]
Bloch, E.:Sym Trbn, w. U. Lajovic (cnd), Berlin RSO Koch Schwann ▲ CD 311 086
Martin, F.:Ballade Trbn (or T Sax), w. F. Martin (cnd), Lausanne CO [orchestrated] *(rec 1971)* Jecklin–Disco ▲ JD 529–2 [ADD]
The Trombone, w. Michel Becquet (trbn), Berlin Trombone Quintet, Berlin RIAS Sinfonietta [cnd:Ernő Sebestyen], Lorraine PO [cnd:Jacques Houtmann], Southwest German CO [cnd:Vladislav Czernedki] Koch Schwann ▲ SCH 313342 [DDD]
Trombone & Organ, w. Franz Lehrendorfer (org) Koch Schwann ▲ SCH 310992 [DDD]
Works for Trombone & Orchestra, w. Berlin RSO [cnd:Uros Lajovic] Koch Schwann ▲ SCH 311086

Roskao, Kamil (tpt)
Music for Trumpet & Organ, w. Vladimir Ruso (org) Lydian ▲ LYD 18104 [DDD]

Rosman, Carl (b cl)
Hames, R.D.:Djurunga, w. Peter Neville (mar) Vox Australis ▲ VAST 0192

Rosman, Carl (cl)
Hames, R.D.:Zurna Vox Australis ▲ VAST 0192

Ros-Marbá, Antonio (vn)
Mendelssohn, F.:Con in e Vn & Orch, Op. 64, w. J.–J. Kantorow (cnd), Netherlands CO Denon ▲ CO 8123 [DDD]

Rosoff, Elliot (elec)—see ORCHESTRAS & ENSEMBLES Postcards

Ross, A. (vc)
Carter, E.:Son Vc, w. E. Brancart (pno) Boston Records ▲ BR 1006
Rachmaninoff, S.:Son Vc, w. E. Brancart (pno) Boston Records ▲ BR 1006

Ross, A. (vn)
Harris, R.:Son Vn Albany ▲ TROY 105 [DDD]

Ross, Alistair (org)
Bach, J.S.:Cant 170, w. Nathalie Stutzmann (cta), Anthony Robson (ob), Roy Goodman (org), R. Goodman (cnd), Hanover Band *(rec Watford Town Hall, Hertfordshire, U.K, Jan 31–Feb 3, 1994)* RCA Red Seal ▲ 09026–62655–2 [DDD]
Music from 17th Century Germany, w. His Majesties Sagbutts & Cornetts, Richard Wistreich (bass) Meridian ▲ 84096
Music of the "Chapels Royal" of England, w. Michael Lewin (lt), Marilyn Sansom (vc) Erato ▲ 45987–2

Ross, Christopher (pno)
Proses Lyriques, w. Janet Howd (sop) Duo Records ▲ DUOCD 89005

Ross, G. (lt/sgr)—see ORCHESTRAS & ENSEMBLES Rossmarin

Ross, Leslie (bn)
Exquisite Corpses from P.S. 122, w. David Watson (shears/stick vn/gtr/tpt), Judy Dunaway (gtr/balloons), Anthony Coleman (sampler), Raissa St. Pierre (drums), Guy Yarden (vn/pno), Linda Austin (gtr), Bruce Kaplan (gtr), Doug Henderson (peckhorn/bass/toy pno), Sue Ann Harkey (gtr), Cinnie Cole (sampler), et. al. ¿What Next? ▲ WN 0002 [ADD]

Ross, Pamela (pno)
Bach, J.S.:English Suites—No. 2 in a, BWV 807 Connoisseur Society ▲ CD 4201 [DDD]
Bach, J.S.:French Suites—No. 6 in E, BWV 817 Connoisseur Society ▲ CD 4201 [DDD]
Bach, J.S.:Partitas Hpd, BWV 825–830—No. 3 in a, BWV 827 Connoisseur Society ▲ CD 4201 [DDD]
Bach, J.S.:Toccatas Hpd, BWV 910–16—in G, BWV 916 *(rec Music Hall, Tarrytown, NY, Feb. 22–24, 1994)* Connoisseur Society ▲ CD 4201 [DDD]
Schumann, R.:Faschingsschwank aus Wien *(rec 6/91)* Connoisseur Society ▲ CD 4185 [DDD]
Schumann, R.:Kreisleriana *(rec 6/91)* Connoisseur Society ▲ CD 4185 [DDD]

Ross, Paul (vc)—see ORCHESTRAS & ENSEMBLES Portland String Quartet

Ross, Scott (hpd)
Anglebert, J.–H. d':Kbd Music—The Four Suites—from *Pièces de clavecin (1689)*; *(Six) Pièces d'orgue* —Quatuor pour le Kyrie & 5 Fugues; *(Eight) Pièces diverses*—Prélude; Allemande du Vieux Gautier (La Vestemponade); Courantes du Vieux Gautier (La Superbe) Nos. 1–3; Sarabande/Mézangeot; Chaconne & Gigue du Vieux Gautier Erato (Musifrance) 2–▲ 2292–45007–2 ZA [DDD]
Bach, J.S.:Preludium, Fugue & Allegro Hpd, BWV 998 *(rec 1979 & 1983)* Memoire Vive ▲ 262021 [ADD]
Bach, J.S.:Toccatas Hpd, BWV 910–16—Toccata in E, BWV 912 *(rec 1979 & 1983)* Memoire Vive ▲ 262021 [ADD]
Duphly, J.:Pièces de clavecin (4 books)—Book 1 *(rec 1979 & 1983)* Memoire Vive ▲ 262021 [ADD]
Forqueray, A.:Pièces de clavecin (5 suites)—Suite No. 5 *(rec 1979 & 1983)* Memoire Vive ▲ 262021 [ADD]

Ross, Scott (hpd/org)
Scarlatti, D.:Sons Kbd (comp) Erato 34–▲ 2292–45309–2 [DDD]

Ross, Scott (hpd/vir)
The Art of Scott Ross CBC Records ("Perspective" series) ▲ PSCD 2006 [ADD]

Ross, Scott (org)
Scott Ross at the Organ *(rec 1974 & 1975)* Memoire Vive ▲ 262001 [ADD]

Ross, Theodor (gtr)
Kagel, M.:Blue's Blue:A Musico-Ethnological Reconstruction, w. M. Kagel (voice/glass tpt), M. Riessler (cl/sax), G. Wharton (vn) Montaigne ▲ MO 782003 [DDD]
Lachenmann, H.:Salut für Caldwell, w. W. Bruck (gtr) Col Legno ▲ AU 31804 [DDD]

Rossen, Morten (acc)
Werner, S.E.:Tango Studies, w. Majken Bell (acc), Heidi Hansen (acc), Carsten Holbek (acc), Hans Jorgen Holbek (acc), Lelo Nika (acc), Anders Vesterdahl (acc) *(rec Danish Accordian Academy, Oct. 1994)* Marco Polo ("dacapo" series) ▲ 8.224006 [DDD]

Rossi, Alberto (cnt)—see ORCHESTRAS & ENSEMBLES Academy of Ancient Music Instumental Ensemble

Rossi, Cristiano (vn)
Busoni, F.:Son in C Vn, w. M. Vincenzi (pno) Dynamic ▲ CD 87 [DDD]
Busoni, F.:Son 1 Vn, w. M. Vincenzi (pno) Dynamic ▲ CD 87 [DDD]
Busoni, F.:Son 2 Vn, w. M. Vincenzi (pno) Dynamic ▲ CD 87 [DDD]
Locatelli, P.:Sons Vn & Hpd, w. Bruno Canino (hpd) *(rec Dynamic's Studio, Genova, Italy, Mar. 2–3 & 7–8, 1994)* Dynamic ▲ CDS 105 [DDD]
Wolf–Ferrari, E.:Sons Vn, w. M. Vincenz (pno)—No. 1 in g, Op. 1 (1895); No. 2 in a, Op. 10 (1901); No. 3 in E, Op. 27 (1943) Dynamic ▲ CDS 68 [DDD]

Rossi, Danilo (va)—see also ORCHESTRAS & ENSEMBLES La Scala String Trio
Luening, O.:Legend, w. J. Ostryniec (ob), Alard String Quartet CRI ■ ACS 6011

Rossi, Franco (vc)—see ORCHESTRAS & ENSEMBLES Bartholdy Piano Quartet, Quartetto Italiano

Rossi, Jamal (sax)
Caprice:Solos for Saxophone, w. Rossi, Jamal (sax) *(rec Walter B. Ford Hall Auditorium, Ithaca College, NY)* Open Loop ▲ OL 016 [DDD]

Rossi, Jean (db)
Honegger, A.:Chamber Music (comp), w. D.–S. Kang (vn), J.–P. Audoli (vn), P.–H. Xuereb (va), R. Wallfisch (vc), P. Devoyon (pno)—Sonatine for 2 Violins (1920); Sonatine for Vn & Vc (1932); Son for Vc & Pno (1920); Son for Va & Pno (1920); Trio in f for Vn, Vc & Pno (1914); Paduana for Vc (1945); Prelude for Db & Pno (1932) Timpani ▲ IC1009 [DDD]

Rossi, L. (cl)
Alcalde Cordero, A.:Mon cher lit, w. D. Schneider (pno) *(rec Feb 1992)* Rossi ▲ NR 1104 [DDD]
Atehortúa, B.:Pieces (3) Cl *(rec Feb 1992)* Rossi ▲ NR 1104 [DDD]
Guastavino, C.:Son Cl, w. D. Schneider (pno) *(rec Feb. 1992)* Rossi ▲ NR 1104 [DDD]
Guastavino, C.:Tonada y Cueca, w. D. Schneider (pno) *(rec Feb. 1992)* Rossi ▲ NR 1104 [DDD]

Rossi, L. (cl) (cont.)
Lacerda, O.:Valsa–Choro, w. D. Schneider (pno) *(rec Feb. 1992)* Rossi ▲ NR 1104 [DDD]
Santoro, C.:Fant sul América *(rec Feb. 1992)* Rossi ▲ NR 1104 [DDD]
Rossi, Massimo (org)
The Neapolitan Organ School *(rec June 21–23, 1990)* Ummus ▲ UMM 303
Rossi, Philibert (mellotron)—see ORCHESTRAS & ENSEMBLES Heldon
Rossi, Rino (db)
Bolling, C.:Con Gtr, w. Franco Trentin (gtr), Ivo Antognini (pno), Matteo Mazza (dr) Gallo ▲ CD 820 [DDD]
Rossi, Tommaso (fl)
Sammartini, G.:Sons 2 Fls, w. Giorgio Matteoli (fl), Fête Rustique *(rec Jungle Studios, Milan, June 25–26, 1995)* Agora Musica ▲ AG 020 [DDD]
Rosslaud, Doris (pno)
Martin, F.:Petite sym concertante, w. E. Hunziker (hp), G. Vaucher–Clerc (hpd), F. Martin (cnd), Swiss–Italian Orch *(rec Sept. 3, 1970)* Jecklin–Disco ▲ JD 645-2 [ADD]
Rössler, Almut (org)
Messiaen, O.:Apparition de l'Eglise éternelle Koch Schwann ▲ SCH 310462 [DDD]
Messiaen, O.:L'Ascension Org *(rec 1965)* Koch Schwann ▲ CD 315 024 [ADD]
Messiaen, O.:Le Banquet céleste Koch Schwann ▲ SCH 310462 [DDD]
Messiaen, O.:Les Corps glorieux Koch Schwann ▲ CD 315 023 [ADD]
Messiaen, O.:Diptyque Koch Schwann ▲ SCH 310462 [DDD]
Messiaen, O.:Livre d'orgue *(rec 1965)* Koch Schwann ▲ CD 315 024 [ADD]
Messiaen, O.:Messe de la Pentecôte Koch Schwann ▲ CD 315 023 [ADD]
Messiaen, O.:La Nativité du Seigneur Koch Schwann ▲ SCH 310462 [DDD]
Messiaen, O.:Verset pour la fête de la dédicace *(rec 1965)* Koch Schwann ▲ CD 315 024 [ADD]
Rosso, Ubaldo (trns fl)—see ORCHESTRAS & ENSEMBLES L'Astrée Ensemble
Rost, Jürgen (gtr)
Albéniz, I.:Gtr Music, w. Monika Rost (gtr)—Castilla No. 7 Laserlight ▲ 15 602 [DDD]
Concierto de Aranjuez, w. Monika Zoltan Tokos (gtr), Budapest Strings [cnd:Bela Banfalvi] LaserLight ▲ 15602 [DDD]
Falla, M. de:Spanish Dance, w. Monika Rost (gtr) Laserlight ▲ 15 602 [DDD]
Sor, F.:Sons Gtr, Opp. 15 & 22, w. Monika Rost (gtr) Laserlight ▲ 15 602 [DDD]
Rost, Martin (org)
Guilmant, A.:Son 4 Org [Walcker–Orgel der St. Jakobuskirche, Ilmenau, Thüringen] *(rec St. Jakobus zu Ilmenau, June 1994)* Thorofon ▲ CTH 2247 [DDD]
Liszt, F.:Prelude & Fugue on the name B–A–C–H [Walcker–Orgel der St. Jakobuskirche, Ilmenau, Thüringen] *(rec St. Jakobus zu Ilmenau, June 1994)* Thorofon ▲ CTH 2247 [DDD]
Romantische Orgeln 3 [Romantic Organ 3], w. Rost, Martin (org) *(rec June 1993)* Thorofon ▲ CTH 2193 [DDD]
Widor, C.M.:Sym 4 Org [Walcker–Orgel der St. Jakobuskirche, Ilmenau, Thüringen] *(rec St. Jakobus zu Ilmenau, June 1994)* Thorofon ▲ CTH 2247 [DDD]
Rost, Monika (gtr)
Albéniz, I.:Gtr Music, w. J. Rost (gtr)—Castilla No. 7 Laserlight ▲ 15 602 [DDD]
Falla, M. de:Homenaje 'Le tombeau de Debussy' Laserlight ▲ 15 602 [DDD]
Falla, M. de:Spanish Dance, w. J. Rost (gtr) Laserlight ▲ 15 602 [DDD]
Granados, E.:Danzas españolas (10) Laserlight ▲ 15 602 [DDD]
Sor, F.:Sons Gtr, Opp. 15 & 22, w. J. Rost (gtr) Laserlight ▲ 15 602 [DDD]
Rostal, Max (vn)
Debussy, C.:Son Vn, w. C. Horsley (pno) *(rec 1957 EMI recording)* Symposium ▲ 1076
Schubert, Franz:Fant Vn, D.934, w. C. Horsley (pno) *(rec 1957 for EMI)* Symposium ▲ 1076
Schubert, Franz:Rondo Vn, D.895, w. C. Horsley (pno) *(rec 1957)* Symposium ▲ 1068
Schubert, Franz:Son Vn, D.574, w. C. Horsley (pno) *(rec 1957)* Symposium ▲ 1068
Schubert, Franz:Sonatinas Vn, w. C. Horsley (pno) *(rec 1957)* Symposium ▲ 1068
Schumann, R.:Son 1 Vn, w. C. Horsley (pno) *(rec 1957 for EMI)* Symposium ▲ 1076
Stravinsky, I.:Duo Concertant, w. C. Horsley (pno) *(rec 1957 EMI)* Symposium ▲ 1076
Tartini, G.:Cons Vn (misc), w. W. Goehr (cnd), Winterthur SO—in g Symposium ▲ 1079
Tartini, G.:Son Vn "Devil's Trill", w. K. Szreter (pno) Symposium ▲ 1079
Rostropovich, Mstislav (pno)
Dvořák, A.:Con Pno, w. V. Talich (cnd), Czech PO Supraphon ▲ SUP 111901 [AAD]
Rostropovich, Mstislav (pno/vc)
Mussorgsky, M.:Sunless, w. G. Vishnevskaya (sop), O. Kagan (vn), L. Mogilevskaya (pno) *(rec Jan. 17, 1973)* Russian Disc ▲ RUS 11003 [AAD]
Shostakovich, D.:Songs Sop, Op. 127, w. G. Vsichnevskaya (sop), O. Kagan (vn), L. Mogilevskaya (pno) *(rec Jan. 17, 1973)* Russian Disc ▲ RUS 11003 [AAD]
Stravinsky, I.:Songs, w. G. Vsichnevskaya (sop), O. Kagan (vn), L. Mogilevskaya (pno)—2 songs *(rec Jan. 17, 1973)* Russian Disc ▲ RUS 11003 [AAD]
Rostropovich, Mstislav (vc)
Bach, Joh. Christian:Trio Fl, Vn & Vc, w. J.–P. Rampal (fl), I. Stern (vn) Sony Classical ▲ SK 44568 [DDD]
Bach, J.S.:Suites Vc, BWV 1007–1012—BWV 1006, 1008 & 1011 *(rec ca 1956)* Vanguard Classics ▲ OVC 4083 [ADD]
Beethoven, L. van:Con Vn, Vc & Pno, "Triple Con", w. D. Oistrakh (vn), S. Richter (pno), H. von Karajan (cnd), Berlin PO EMI Classics ▲ CDM 64744
Beethoven, L. van:Serenade Strs, Op. 8, w. A.–S. Mutter (vn), B. Giuranna (vn) Deutsche Grammophon 2–▲ 427687–2 [DDD]
Beethoven, L. van:Sons Vc (comp), w. S. Richter (pno) Philips ("Duo" series) 2–▲ 442565–2
Beethoven, L. van:Son 2 Vc, w. S. Richter (pno) Philips ("Insignia" series) ▲ 434163–2 [ADD]
Beethoven, L. van:Trio 6 Pno, "Archduke", w. E. Gilels (pno), L. Kogan (vn) Monitor ■ 55010
Beethoven, L. van:Trio Strs, Op. 3, w. A.–S. Mutter (vn), B. Giuranna (va) Deutsche Grammophon 2–▲ 427687–2 [DDD]
Beethoven, L. van:Trios Strs, Op. 9, w. A.–S. Mutter (vn), B. Giuranna (va) Deutsche Grammophon 2–▲ 427687–2 [DDD]
Bernstein, L.:Music of, w. J. Norman (sop), K. Te Kanawa (sop), J. Anderson (sop), F. von Stade (mez), C. Ludwig (mez), T. Troyanos (mez), J. Carreras (ten), D. Garrison (ten), J. Hadley (ten), T. Hampson (bar), T. Daly (sgr), G. Kremer (vn), M.T. Thomas (va), L. Bernstein (cnd), *(orch unknown)*—various popular works Deutsche Grammophon ▲ 439251–2 ■ 439251–4
Bloch, E.:Schelomo, w. L. Bernstein (cnd), French National Orch EMI Classics ▲ CDC 49307 [ADD]
Brahms, J.:Con Vn & Vc, "Double Con", w. D. Oistrakh (vn), G. Szell (cnd), Cleveland Orch EMI Classics ▲ CDM 64744
Brahms, J.:Sons Vc (comp), w. R. Serkin (pno) Deutsche Grammophon ▲ 410510–2 [DDD]
Bridge, F.:Son Vc, w. Benjamin Britten (pno) London ("The Classic Sound" series) ▲ 443575–2
Britten, H.:Poet's Echo, w. G. Vishnevskaya (sop) London 2–▲ 433200–2
Britten, H.:Suite 1 Vc London ▲ 421859–2 [ADD]
Britten, H.:Suite 2 Vc London ▲ 421859–2 [ADD]
Les Chefs–d'Oeuvre du Violoncelle, w. Berlin PO [cnd:Herbert von Karajan], Israel PO [cnd:Leonard Bernstein] Deutsche Grammophon ("Double" series) 2–▲ 437952–2
Dvořák, A.:Con Vc, w. C.M. Giulini (cnd), London PO EMI Classics ▲ CDC 49306 [ADD]
Dvořák, A.:Con Vc, w. V. Talich (cnd), Czech PO Supraphon 3–▲ SUP 0546 [AAD]
Dvořák, A.:Con Vc, w. H. von Karajan (cnd), Berlin PO Deutsche Grammophon ▲ 413819–2 [ADD]
Dvořák, A.:Con Vc, w. V. Talich (cnd), Czech PO Supraphon ▲ SUP 111901 [AAD]
Dvořák, A.:Con Vc, w. H. von Karajan (cnd), Berlin PO Deutsche Grammophon ("The Originals" series) ▲ 447413–2
Haydn, J.:Con 1 Vc, w. B. Britten (cnd), English CO London ("Serenata" series) ▲ 430633–2 [ADD]
Haydn, J.:Con 1 Vc, w. I. Brown (cnd), Academy of St. Martin in the Fields EMI Classics ▲ CDC 49305
Haydn, J.:Con 2 Vc, w. I. Brown (cnd), Academy of St. Martin in the Fields EMI Classics ▲ CDC 49305
Haydn, J.:Diverts Vn, Va & Vc, H.IV/6–11, w. Jean–Pierre Rampal (fl), Issac Stern (vn)—Nos. 2 & 6 CBS ▲ MK 37786 [DDD]
Haydn, J.:Trios Fls & Vc, "London Trios", w. Jean–Pierre Rampal (fl), Issac Stern (vn) CBS 4–▲ M4K 42003 (m/s) [ADD]
Rostropovich, Mstislav (vc) (cont.)
Haydn, J.:Trios Fls & Vc, "London Trios", w. Jean–Pierre Rampal (fl), Issac Stern (vn) CBS ▲ MK 37786 [DDD]
Hoddinott, A.:Noctis Equi, w. K. Nagano (cnd), London SO Erato ▲ 2292–45489–2 [DDD]
Honegger, A.:Con Vc, w. K. Nagano (cnd), London SO Erato ▲ 2292–45489–2 [DDD]
Khachaturian, A.:Con–Rhap Vc, w. A. Khachaturian (cnd), USSR Radio–TV Large SO Russian Disc ▲ RUS 11 014 [AAD]
Knipper, L.K.:Con–Monologue, w. G. Rozhdestvensky (cnd), USSR SO Russian Disc ▲ RUS 11 111 [AAD]
Levitin, Y.A.:Concertino Vc, w. G. Rozhdestvensky (cnd), USSR SO Russian Disc ▲ RUS 11 111 [AAD]
Messiaen, O.:Concert à Quatre, w. Catherine Cantin (fl), Heinz Holliger (ob), Yvonne Loriod (pno), M.–W. Chung (cnd), Bastille Opera Orch Deutsche Grammophon ("4D Audio" series) ▲ 445947–2
Miaskovsky, N.:Con Vc, w. M. Sargent (cnd), Philharmonia Orch EMI Classics ▲ CDM 65419
Milhaud, D.:Con 1 Vc, w. K. Nagano (cnd), London SO Erato ▲ 2292–45489–2 [DDD]
Moret, N.:Con Vc, w. P. Sacher (cnd), Zurich Collegium Musicum Musiques Suisses ▲ CD 6103 [DDD]
Mozart, W.A.:Qts Fl, w. J–P. Rampal (fl), I. Stern (vn), S. Accardo (vn) CBS ▲ MK 42320 [DDD]
Mozart, W.A.:Trios Fl, w. J.–P. Rampal (fl), I. Stern (vn) Sony Classical ▲ SK 44568 [DDD]
Panufnik, A.:Con Vc, w. H. Wolff (cnd), London SO NMC ▲ NMC 10 [DDD]
Prokofiev, S.:Sym–Con Vc, w. S. Ozawa (cnd), London SO Erato ▲ 45708–2
Prokofiev, S.:Sym–Con Vc, w. K. Sanderling (cnd), Leningrad PO *(rec 1947)* Multisonic ("Russian Treasures" series) ▲ 31 0188
Reicha, A.:Vars & Fant on Mozart's "Se vuol ballare", w. J.–P. Rampal (fl), I. Stern (vn), M. Später (lt) Sony Classical ▲ SK 44568 [DDD]
Respighi, O.:Adagio con variazioni Vc Orch, w. G. Rozhdestvensky (cnd), London SO *(rec live at Carnegie Hall, 1967)* Intaglio ▲ ING 766 [ADD]
Saint–Saëns, C.:Con 1 Vc, w. C.M. Giulini (cnd), London PO EMI Classics ▲ CDC 49306 [ADD]
Schnittke, A.:Con 2 Vc, w. S. Ozawa (cnd), London SO Sony Classical ▲ SK 48241
Schnittke, A.:Con for 3, w. Gidon Kremer (vn), Yuri Bashmet (va), Y. Bashmet (cnd), Moscow Soloists EMI Classics ▲ CDC 55627
Schnittke, A.:In Memoriam, w.London SO Sony Classical ▲ SK 48241
Schnittke, A.:Menuet Vn, w. Gidon Kremer (vn), Yuri Bashmet (va) EMI Classics ▲ CDC 55627
Schnittke, A.:Trio Pno, w. I. Schnittke (pno), M. Lubotsky (vn) *(rec Aug. 12–15, 1992)* Sony Classical ▲ SK 53271 [DDD]
Schnittke, A.:Trio Strs, w. Gidon Kremer (vn), Yuri Bashmet (va) EMI Classics ▲ CDC 55627
Schubert, Franz:Qnt Strs, D.956, w. Emerson String Quartet Deutsche Grammophon ▲ 431792–2 [DDD] □ 431792–5
Schubert, Franz:Qnt Strs, D.956, w. Melos String Quartet Deutsche Grammophon ("Galleria" series) ▲ 415373–2 [ADD]
Schubert, Franz:Son Arpeggione, w. Benjamin Britten (pno) London ("The Classic Sound" series) ▲ 443575–2
Schumann, R.:Con Vc, w. L. Bernstein (cnd), French National Orch EMI Classics ▲ CDC 49307 [ADD]
Shostakovich, D.:Son Vc, w. D. Shostakovich (pno) *(rec 1959)* Multisonic ("Russian Treasures" series) ▲ 31 0179
Shostakovich, D.:Son Vc, w. D. Shostakovich (pno) *(rec 1958)* Russian Disc ▲ RUS 15 005 [AAD]
Strauss, R.:Don Quixote, w. K. Kondrashin (cnd), Moscow PO Russian Disc ▲ RUS 11 009 [ADD]
Tartini, G.:Con in A Vc, w. G. Rozhdestvensky (cnd), London SO *(rec live, Carnegie Hall, 1967)* Intaglio ▲ ING 766 [ADD]
Tchaikovsky, B.:Con Vc, w. K. Kondrashin (cnd), Moscow PO *(rec Mar. 13, 1964)* Russian Disc ▲ RUS 11 115 [AAD]
Tchaikovsky, P.:Vars on a Rococo Theme, w. H. von Karajan (cnd), Berlin PO Deutsche Grammophon ▲ 413819–2 [ADD]
Tchaikovsky, P.:Vars on a Rococo Theme, w. H. von Karajan (cnd), Berlin PO Deutsche Grammophon ("The Originals" series) ▲ 447413–2
Tchaikovsky, P.:Vars on a Rococo Theme, w. H. von Karajan (cnd), Berlin PO Deutsche Grammophon ▲ 431606–2 [ADD]
Telemann, G.P.:Qt Fl, w. J.–P. Rampal (fl), I. Stern (vn), M. Späier (lt) Sony Classical ▲ SK 44568 [DDD]
Vainberg, M.:Con Vc, w. G. Rozhdestvensky (cnd), USSR SO Russian Disc ▲ RUS 11 111 [AAD]
Villa–Lobos, H.:Bachiana brasileira 1, w. K. Kondrashin (cnd), Moscow PO Russian Disc ▲ RUS 11 009 [ADD]
Vivaldi, A.:Cons Vc, w. G. Rozhdestvensky (cnd), London SO—in C, G & g *(rec live, Carnegie Hall, 1967)* Intaglio ▲ ING 766 [ADD]
The Young Rostropovich:Rare Recordings from the 1950/1952 Years, w. A. Dedjuchin (pno) Enterprise ("Palladio" series) ▲ ENTPD 4157 [ADD]
Roth, Daniel (org)
Franck, C.:Org Music (comp)—Fantaisie in C; Grand pièce symphonique (*plus* several miscellaneous organ/harmonium works—Andantino in g [from L'Organiste, 1857], Andantino in A♭ & Offertoire in g [from Pièces posthumes, 1859], and Pièce in A [1854]) Motette ▲ CD 11381 [DDD]
Franck, C.:Org Music (comp)—Pastorale; Fantaisie in A; Final in B♭; Prière; Prélude, fugue et variation (*plus* organ/harmonium work—Offertoire sur un Noël breton [from L'Athénée musical, 1867] Motette ▲ CD 11391 [DDD]
Franck, C.:Org Music (comp)—Three Chorales; Pièce héroïque; Cantabile (*plus* several miscellaneous organ/harmonium works—Offertoire, etc.) Motette ▲ CD 11401 [DDD]
Jolivet, A.:Arioso barocco, w. René Périnelli (tpt) Arion ▲ ARN 68299 [AAD]
Jolivet, A.:Hymne à l'univers Arion ▲ ARN 68299 [AAD]
Jolivet, A.:Hymne à St. André, w. Dany Barraud (sop) Arion ▲ ARN 68299 [AAD]
Jolivet, A.:Mandala Arion ▲ ARN 68299 [AAD]
Widor, C.M.:Sym 3 Org Motette ▲ CD 11241 [DDD]
Widor, C.M.:Sym 7 Org Motette ▲ CD 11241 [DDD]
Roth, David (vn)—see ORCHESTRAS & ENSEMBLES Allegri String Quartet
Roth, Feri (vn)—see ORCHESTRAS & ENSEMBLES Roth Trio
Roth, I. (sax)
Moeschinger, A.:Con lyrique, w. R. Tschupp (cnd), Basel RSO Grammont ▲ CTSP 1–2 [ADD]
Moser, R.:Wal, w. B. Beaufreton (sax), M. Weiss (sax), J.–G. Koerper (sax), P. Egholm (sax), M. Venzago (cnd), Basel SO Grammont ▲ CTSP 12–2 [ADD]
Roth, Jerome (ob)—see ORCHESTRAS & ENSEMBLES New York Woodwind Quintet, New York Woodwind Quintet members
Rothbauer, Marek (bn)
Fučík, J.:Der alte Brummbär, w. D. Bostock (cnd), Carlsbad SO *(rec Lazne III, Karlovy Vary, Czech Republic, Jan 13–15, 1996)* Classico ▲ CLASSCD 150
Rothbrust, Dirk (perc)—see ORCHESTRAS & ENSEMBLES LTD Trio
Rothenberg, Ned (a sax/b cl/shak)
Namchylak, S.:Amulet, w. Sainkho Namchylak (voc) *(rec 1992–95)* Leo ▲ LC 5417
Rothenberg, Ned (sax)— see ORCHESTRAS & ENSEMBLES Semantics
Rothenberg, Sarah (pno)
Adagio & Allegro:German Romantic Works for Horn, w. David Jolley (hn) Arabesque ▲ ARA 6641 [DDD]
Lourié, A.:Poèmes Pno, Op. 10 *(rec June 1 & 2, 1991)* GM ▲ GM 2040 CD
Mendelssohn, Fanny:Das Jahr Arabesque ▲ ARA 6666
Mosolov, A.:Son 5 Pno *(rec June 1 & 2, 1991)* GM ▲ GM 2040 CD
Roslavets, N.:Compositions *(rec June 1 & 2, 1991)* GM ▲ GM 2040 CD
Roslavets, N.:Preludes Pno *(rec June 1 & 2, 1991)* GM ▲ GM 2040 CD
Roslavets, N.:Prélude Pno *(rec June 1 & 2, 1991)* GM ▲ GM 2040 CD
Roslavets, N.:Son 5 Pno *(rec June 1 & 2, 1991)* GM ▲ GM 2040 CD
Rothfuss, Levering (pno)
Bach & Noodles, w. Harvey Pittel (sax), Gabor Rejto (vc), Anton Nel (pno) Crystal ▲ CD 654
Trio, w. Harvey Pittel (sax), Julian Fifer (vc) Crystal ■ C 157

Rothfuss, Levering (pno) (cont.)
Vaughan Williams, R.:Songs, w. R. Golden (sop), T. Woodman (bar), N. Bean (vn)—From the House of Life; 4 Last Songs; Linden Lea; The Sky Above the Roof; Dreamland; Claribel; If I Were a Queen; 4 Poems by Fredegond Shove; Adieu; Think of Me; Along the Field *(rec Apr. 1992)* Koch International Classics ▲ KIC 7168 [DDD]
Wagner, R.:Arias & Scenes, w. Kenneth Lane (ten), Otto Herz (pno), Martin Kalmanoff (pno)—Rienzi's Prayer [from Rienzi]; In fernem Land, Mein Liebe Schwan [from Lohengrin]; Siegmund heiss' ich! [from Die Walküre]; Nothung! Nothung!, Schmiede mein Hammer! [from Siegfried]; O König!, Die alte Weise, O diese Sonne! [from Tristan und Isolde]; Prize Song [from Die Meistersinger]; Siegfried's Narration, Brünnhilde! Heilige Braut! [from Götterdämmerung]; Amfortas! Die Wunde!, Nur eine Waffe taugt [from Parsifal] Valhalla VRCD 1595 [ADD]
Warlock, P.:Songs Sop, w. R. Golden (sop)—(21) Late summer; I have a garden; My own country; Lullaby; Sweet content; Ha'nacker Mill; The night; To the memory of a great singer; The bords; Frostbound wood; The first mercy; Pretty ring time; Have you seen but a white lily grow; Cradle song; The cloths of heaven; Sleep; Lilygay [song cycle] Koch International Classics ▲ KIC 7118-2 [DDD]

Röthlisberger, Bernhard (cl)
Bassi, L.:Divert, w. Simon Andres (pno) Gallo ▲ CD 916 [DDD]
Cavallini, E.:Adagio sentimentale, "Una lagrima sulla tomba dell'immortale Rossini", w. Simon Andres (pno) Gallo ▲ CD 916 [DDD]
Cavallini, E.:Fant on Motifs from Bellini's *I somnambula* , w. Simon Andres (pno) Gallo ▲ CD 916 [DDD]
Labanchi, G.:Fant on Verdi's *Aida,* w. Simon Andres (pno) Gallo ▲ CD 916 [DDD]
Lovreglio, D.:Fant da concerto on Motifs of Verdi's *La traviata,* w. Simon Andres (pno) Gallo ▲ CD 916 [DDD]
Panizza, G.:Ballabile, w. Simon Andres (pno) Gallo ▲ CD 916 [DDD]
Spadina, A.:Duetto Concertante on Motifs from Bellini's *Norma,* w. Simon Andres (pno) Gallo ▲ CD 916 [DDD]

Rothmuller, Daniel (vc)
Eaton, J.:Ars Poetica, w. Nelda Nelson (sop), Carole Morgan (fl), Beverly Wesner–Hoehn (hp), C. Colnot (cnd) *(rec Dec 18, 1986)* Indiana Univ School of Music ▲ 0–253–31842–4

Rothwell, E. (ob)—see ORCHESTRAS & ENSEMBLES Adolf Busch Chamber Players

Rottersman, Sherri (gtr)
The Sensual Guitar Auric ▲ 8234462

Roubichou, C. (fl)
Lemeland, A.:Con grosso, w. M. Tardue (cnd), Grenoble Instrumental Ensemble Skarbo ▲ SKR 3913 [DDD]

Roudin, J. (va)
Bach, J.S.:Con for 2 Vas, w. P. Hadjaje (va), D. Rouits (cnd), Massy CO *(rec Mar 1990)* Quantum ▲ QM 6906 [DDD] ■ QM 2000
Vivaldi, A.:Cons for 2 Vas, w. P. Hadjaje (va), D. Rouits (cnd), Massy CO *(rec 3/90)* Quantum ▲ QM 6906 [DDD] ■ QM 2000

Rouet, Pascale (org)
Bach, J.S.:Org Music (misc)—Preludes & Fugues, BWV 553–560; Canzona in d, BWV 588; Fantasia in G, BWV 572; Pastorale, BWV 590; Some Canonical Vars. on the Carol "Von Himmel hoch da komm ich her", BWV 769 *(rec Sept 1–3, 1992)* Gallo ▲ CD 720 [DDD]
Chaynes, C.:A la recherche du sacré Gallo ▲ CD 634 [ADD]
Leguay, J.–P.:Préludes Org Gallo ▲ CD 637 [DDD]
Mather, B.:Studies Org Gallo ▲ CD 634 [ADD]
Rogg, L.:Org Music, w. L. Rogg (org)—Recitativo for Organ 4–Hands (1989); Toccata ritmica for solo Organ Gallo ▲ CD 634 [ADD]

Roumy, Cécile (rcr)—see ORCHESTRAS & ENSEMBLES Isabella D'Este

Rountree, Kathleen (pno)
Liebermann, L.:Son Fl, w. K. Kemler (fl) *(rec 1992)* Centaur ▲ CRC 2146 [DDD]
Reynolds, R.:Son Fl, w. K. Kemler (fl) *(rec 1992)* Centaur ▲ CRC 2146 [DDD]
Reynolds, V.:Son Fl, w. K. Kemler (fl) *(rec 1992)* Centaur ▲ CRC 2146 [DDD]

Rousi, Matti (vc)
Chopin, F.:Son Vc, w. J. Lagerspetz (pno) Ondine ▲ ODE 748–2 [DDD]
Mahler, G.:Qt Pno [comp Schnittke], w. Ralf Gothoni (pno), Mark Lubotsky (vn), Matti Hirvikangas (va) Ondine ▲ ODE 840 [DDD]
Rachmaninoff, S.:Son Vc, w. J. Lagerspetz (pno) Ondine ▲ ODE 748–2 [DDD]
Strauss, R.:Qt Pno, w. Ralf Gothoni (pno), Mark Lubotsky (vn), Matti Hirvikangas (va) Ondine ▲ ODE 840 [DDD]

Rousseau, Eugene (sax)
Bruch, M.:Kol Nidrei, w. F. Fennell (cnd), Indiana Winds [arr Makio Kimura] *(rec St. Mark's United Methodist Church, Bloomington, Indiana, Sept 12–14, 1994)* Delos ▲ DE 3188 [DDD]
Gershwin, G.:Porgy & Bess (sels), w. F. Fennell (cnd), Indiana Winds—Medley [arr. Ralph Hermann] *(rec St. Mark's United Methodist Church, Bloomington, Indiana, Sept 12–14, 1994)* Delos ▲ DE 3188 [DDD]
Heiden, B.:Diversion, w. F. Fennell (cnd), Indiana Winds *(rec St. Mark's United Methodist Church, Bloomington, Indiana, Sept 12–14, 1994)* Delos ▲ DE 3188 [DDD]
Heiden, B.:Fant Concertante, w. F. Fennell (cnd), Indiana Winds *(rec St. Mark's United Methodist Church, Bloomington, Indiana, Sept 12–14, 1994)* Delos ▲ DE 3188 [DDD]
Massenet, J.:Méditation from *Thaïs,* w. F. Fennell (cnd), Indiana Winds [arr James Curnow] *(rec St. Mark's United Methodist Church, Bloomington, Indiana, Sept 12–14, 1994)* Delos ▲ DE 3188 [DDD]
Muczynski, R.:Con A Sax, w. F. Fennell (cnd), Indiana Winds *(rec St. Mark's United Methodist Church, Bloomington, Indiana, Sept 12–14, 1994)* Delos ▲ DE 3188 [DDD]
Puccini, G.:Tosca (sels), w. F. Fennell (cnd), Indiana Winds—Tosca Fant [arr Ralph Hermann] *(rec St. Mark's United Methodist Church, Bloomington, Indiana, Sept 12–14, 1994)* Delos ▲ DE 3188 [DDD]
Saxophone Colors, w. Hans Graf (pno) Delos ▲ DE 1007 [AAD]

Roussel, Coco (perc)—see ORCHESTRAS & ENSEMBLES Heldon

Rousset, Christophe (hpd)
Bach, J.S.:Chromatic Fant & Fugue L'Oiseau–Lyre ▲ 433054–2 [DDD]
Bach, J.S.:Con 2 Hpd, w. C. Hogwood (cnd), Academy of Ancient Music *(rec Henry Wood Hall, London, Aug 12–14, 1994)* L'Oiseau–Lyre ▲ 443326–2 [DDD]
Bach, J.S.:Con 4 Hpd, w. C. Hogwood (cnd), Academy of Ancient Music *(rec EMI Studio No. 1, Abbey Road, London, Aug 5–8, 1993)* L'Oiseau–Lyre ▲ 443326–2 [DDD]
Bach, J.S.:Con 7 Hpd, w. C. Hogwood (cnd), Academy of Ancient Music *(rec EMI Studio No. 1, Abbey Road, London, Aug 5–8, 1993)* L'Oiseau–Lyre ▲ 443326–2 [DDD]
Bach, J.S.:Cons for 3 Hpds (comp), w. C. Tilney (hpd), D. Moroney (hpd), C. Hogwood (cnd), Academy of Ancient Music L'Oiseau–Lyre ▲ 433053–2 [DDD]
Bach, J.S.:Con for 4 Hpds, w. C. Tilney (hpd), D. Moroney (hpd), C. Hogwood (hpd), C. Hogwood (cnd), Academy of Ancient Music L'Oiseau–Lyre ▲ 433053–2 [DDD]
Bach, J.S.:Goldberg Vars *(rec St. Hippolyte, Castres, Sep 27–29, 1994)* L'Oiseau–Lyre ▲ 444866–2 [DDD]
Bach, J.S.:Italian Con L'Oiseau–Lyre ▲ 433054–2 [DDD]
Bach, J.S.:Partitas Hpd, BWV 825–830 L'Oiseau–Lyre ▲ 440217–2 [DDD]
Bach, J.S.:Partita Hpd, BWV 831, "Ov nach französischer Art" L'Oiseau–Lyre ▲ 433054–2 [DDD]
Bach, W.F.:Kbd Music—Sonata in a; Fantasy in c; Prelude; March in E♭; Suite in g; Fugues; Sonata in g Musique d'Abord ▲ HMA 1901305
Couperin, F.:L'Apothéose de Lully, w. William Christie (hpd) Harmonia Mundi 12–▲ 2901442.52
Couperin, F.:L'Apothéose de Lully, w. W. Christie (org)—2–harpsichord version Harmonia Mundi France ▲ HMC 901269 [DDD]
Couperin, F.:Hpd Music—Books 1–4 Harmonia Mundi 12–▲ 2901442.52
Couperin, F.:Music of, w. René Jacobs (alt), Gérard Lesne (alt), Kenneth Gilbert (hpd), W. Christie (cnd), Les Arts Florissants, Phillippe Herreweghe (cnd), Chapelle Royale Choir—Hpd pieces; Tenebeae Lessons [sels] Harmonia Mundi ("Great Baroque Composers" series) 3–▲ HMX 390870.72
Couperin, F.:Le Parnasse, L'apothéose de Corelli, w. W. Christie (org)—2–harpsichord version Harmonia Mundi France ▲ HMC 901269 [DDD]

Rousset, Christophe (hpd) (cont.)
Couperin, F.:Pièces de clavecin (comp)—Book 3 *(rec Nov. 1992)* Harmonia Mundi France 3–▲ HMC 901442/44
Couperin, F.:Pièces de clavecin (comp)—Book 1 Harmonia Mundi France 3–▲ HMC 901450/52
Handel, G.F.:Sons Vn, w. Ryo Terakado (baroque vn), H. Suzuki (baroque vc), Kaori Uemura (vl)—in d, HWV 359a; in A, HWV 361; in G, HWV 364a; in D, HWV 371; Violin movt in a, HWV 408; Violin movt (Allegro) in c, HWV 412 Denon/PCM Digital ▲ DEN 75858 [DDD]
Leclair, J.–M.:Sons Vn (Books 1–4), w. R. Terakado (baroque vn), K. Uemura (va da gamba), H. Suzuki (vc)—"Troisieme livre" (Book 3), Op. 5 *(rec Feb. 26–Mar. 9, 1993)* Denon/PCM Digital ▲ DEN 75720 [DDD]
Lully, J.–B.:Music of, w. René Jacobs (alt), Gérard Lesne (alt), Kenneth Gilbert (hpd), W. Christie (cnd), Les Arts Florissants, Phillippe Herreweghe (cnd), Chapelle Royale Choir—Hpd Pieces; 'Atys' excerpts; Dies Israe; Petits Motets Harmonia Mundi ("Great Baroque Composers" series) 3–▲ HMX 390870.72
Mondonville, J.–J.C. de:Sons Hpd, w. F. Malgoire (vn) Pierre Verany ▲ PV.790093 [DDD]
Rameau, J.P.:Music of, w. René Jacobs (alt), Gérard Lesne (alt), Kenneth Gilbert (hpd), W. Christie (cnd), Les Arts Florissants, Phillippe Herreweghe (cnd), Chapelle Royale Choir—Pieces; Les Indes Gallantes (sels) Harmonia Mundi ("Great Baroque Composers" series) 3–▲ HMX 390870.72
Rameau, J.P.:Nouvelles suites L'Oiseau–Lyre 2–▲ 425886–2 [DDD]
Rameau, J.P.:Pièces de clavecin avec une méthode sur la mécanique des doigts L'Oiseau–Lyre 2–▲ 425886–2 [DDD]
Rameau, J.P.:Pièces de clavecin en concert, w. Ryo Terakado (vn), Kaori Uemura (vl) Harmonia Mundi ▲ HMX 2901418
Rameau, J.P.:1e livre de pièces de clavecin L'Oiseau–Lyre 2–▲ 425886–2 [DDD]
Telemann, G.P.:Qts, Book 4, w. Masahiro Arita (trns fl), Ryo Terakado (baroque vn), Kaori Uemura (vl) Denon ▲ DEN 78844 [DDD]

Rousset, Christophe (kbd)
Bach, C.P.E.:Kleine Duetten (4), w. Christopher Hogwood (kbd) London ▲ 440649–2
Bach, Joh. Christian:Duet Kbd, Op. 15, w. Christopher Hogwood (kbd) London ▲ 440649–2
Bach, J.S.:The Art of the Fugue (sels), w. Christopher Hogwood (kbd)—Contrpuntus 13 London ▲ 440649–2
Bach, J.S.:Con 2 for 2 Hpds, w. Christopher Hogwood (kbd) London ▲ 440649–2
Bach, W.F.:Con for 2 Hpds, Op. 46, w. Christopher Hogwood (kbd) London ▲ 440649–2
Couperin, F.:Pièces de clavecin (sels)—Book 2 Harmonia Mundi France 3–▲ HMC 901447/49

Roussin, Annick (vn)
Szymanowski, K.:Lullaby, w. Pascal le Corre (pno) Accord ▲ ACD 201122 [DDD]
Szymanowski, K.:Myths, w. Pascal le Corre (pno) Accord ▲ ACD 201122 [DDD]
Szymanowski, K.:Romance, w. Pascal le Corre (pno) Accord ▲ ACD 201122 [DDD]
Szymanowski, K.:Son Vn, w. Pascal le Corre (pno) Accord ▲ ACD 201122 [DDD]

Routch, Robert (hn)—see ORCHESTRAS & ENSEMBLES Lincoln Center Chamber Music Society members

Rouva, Ada (hp)
Karaindrou, E.:The Suspended Step of the Stork, w. Vangelis Christopoulos (ob), Christos Sfetsas (vc), Nikos Spinoulas (hn), Andreas Tsekouras (acc), Dimitris Vraskos (vn), L. Chalkiadakis (cnd), *(orch unknown)* *(rec Sound, Athens, Apr & Aug 1991)* ECM ▲ 78118–21456–2 [AAD]

Rouvier, Jacques (pno)
Debussy, C.:Trio Pno, w. J. J. Kantorow (vn), P. Müller (vc) Denon ▲ CO 72508 [DDD]
Mendelssohn, F.:Son Vn (1820), w. Jean–Jacques Kantorow (vn) *(rec Stadsgehoorzaal, Leiden, the Netherlands, Jan. 28–30, 1992)* Denon ▲ DEN 78964 [DDD]
Mendelssohn, F.:Son Vn, Op. 4, w. Jean–Jacques Kantorow (vn) *(rec Stadsgehoorzaal, Leiden, the Netherlands, Jan. 28–30, 1992)* Denon ▲ DEN 78964 [DDD]
Mendelssohn, F.:Son Vn (1838), w. Jean–Jacques Kantorow (vn) *(rec Stadsgehoorzaal, Leiden, the Netherlands, Jan. 28–30, 1992)* Denon ▲ DEN 78964 [DDD]
Ravel, M.:Trio Pno, w. J. J. Kantorow (vn), Müller (vc) Denon ▲ CO 72508 [DDD]
Saint–Saëns, C.:Son 1 Vn, w. J.–J. Kantorow (vn) *(rec March 11–12, 1991)* Denon ▲ CO 79552 [DDD]
Saint–Saëns, C.:Son 2 Vn, w. J.–J. Kantorow (vn) *(rec March 11–12, 1991)* Denon ▲ CO 79552 [DDD]
Seduction of Violin Denon ▲ CO 77051 [DDD]

Roux, Daniel (fl)
Gluck, C.W.:Orfeo ed Euridice (sels), w. L. de Froment (cnd), Luxembourg Radio–TV SO Forlane ▲ FRL 46 [ADD]

Roux, V. (pno)
Martinů, B.:Qt 1 Pno, w. Millière String Trio Quantum ▲ QM 6910 [DDD] ■ QM 2004 (D)

Roveda, Egidio (vc)
Monteverdi, C.:Music of, w. Luciano Sgrizzi (hpd), E. Loehrer (cnd), Lugano Chamber Society Orch, Lugano Chamber Society Chorus—Altri Canti di Marte; Le Combat de Tancrede et Clorinde; Lamento Della Ninfa; Perche T'en Fuggi, O Fillide; Hor Ch'el Ciel e la Terra Accord ▲ ACD 220882

Rovinelli, M. (perc)—see ORCHESTRAS & ENSEMBLES Il Cortegiano

Rowan, Barbara (pno)
Moss, L.:Hommage, w. Constance Sablinsky (pno) Capstone ▲ CPS 8619

Rowe, Arthur (pno)
Enescu, G.:Légende, w. E. Schultz (tpt) ebs ▲ ebs 6022 [DDD]
Goedicke, A.:Concert Etude, w. E. Schultz (tpt) ebs ▲ ebs 6022 [DDD]
Hubeau, J.:Son for Chromatic Tpt, w. E. Schultz (tpt) ebs ▲ ebs 6022 [DDD]
Morawetz, O.:Son Tpt, w. E. Schultz (tpt) ebs ▲ ebs 6022 [DDD]
Stevens, H.:Son Tpt, w. E. Schultz (tpt) ebs ▲ ebs 6022 [DDD]

Rowell, Mary (vn)—see also ORCHESTRAS & ENSEMBLES Sirius String Quartet, New Music Consort
Davis, A.:Lost Moon Sisters, w. D. Ohrenstein (sop), P. Bush (pno), J. Cirker (mar/vib) *(rec Feb. & Apr. 1993)* CRI ▲ CD 654 [DDD]
Johnson, S.:Confetti on Flesh, w. D. Ohrenstein (sop), P. Bush (pno/syn), J. Cirker (mar/dr set) *(rec Feb. & Apr. 1993)* CRI ("Emergency Music" series) ▲ CD 654 [DDD]
Johnston, B.:Calamity Jane to Her Daughter, w. D. Ohrenstein (sop), P. Bush (pno), B. Ruyle (perc) *(rec Feb. & Apr. 1993)* CRI ("Emergency Music" series) ▲ CD 654 [DDD]
Kernis, A.J.:America(n) (Day) Dreams, w. Kim Barber (mez), Leslie Tomkins (va), Tonya Tomkins (vc), Robert Black (db), Kathleen Nester (fl), Larry Guy (cl/b cl), John Dent (tpt), Anthony Cecere (hn), Leslie Stifelman (pno), Susan Jolles (hp), Jeffrey Milarsky (perc), M. Barrett (cnd)—A Navajo Blanket; Wednesday at the Waldorf; The Pregnant Dream; The Blue Bottle; "So Long" to the Moon from the Men of Apollo; Epilogue:The Pure Suit of Happiness *(rec Manhattan Center Studios, New York, May 31–June 3, 1995)* New Albion ♦ NA 083CD
Lebaron, A.:Dish, w. D. Ohrenstein (sop), P. Bush (pno/syn), J. Thompson (elec bass), J. Cirker (dr), B. Ruyle (perc) *(rec Feb. & Apr. 1993)* CRI ("Emergency Music" series) ▲ CD 654 [DDD]

Rowell, Mary (vn/va)
Bouchard, L.:Black Burned Wood, w. D. Ohrenstein (sop), Phillip Bush (pno), J. Cirker (dr/perc), B. Ruyle (mar/xyl/perc) *(rec Feb. & Apr. 1993)* CRI ▲ CD 654 [DDD]

Rowitsch, Jody (va)
Scelsi, G.:Anahit, w. Paul Zukofsky (vn), Julie Bogorad (fl), Peggy Russell (fl), Courtney Westcott (fl), Lawrence McDonald (cl), Joan Waryha (cl), Jean Hansen (b cl), Bill Suite (e hn), Nita VanPelt (sax), Bob Zobal (tpt), John Carter (trbn), Martin Lydecker (trbn), Stan Cortman (hn), Robert Ward (hn), William Curry (va), Irene Wade (va), Anne Fagerburg (vc), John Gockel (vc), Sue Manz (bass), Steven Stearman (bass) *(rec Oberlin Conservatory of Music, Oct 8, 1973)* CP² ▲ CP2 108 [AAD]

Rowland, David (hpd/pno)—see ORCHESTRAS & ENSEMBLES Badinage

Rowland, Gilbert (hpd)
Rameau, J.P.:Hpd Music (comp solo)—Pièces de Clavecin (1706); Pièces de Clavecin (1724) *(rec Epsom College Concert Hall, Surrey, Apr. 11–13, 1994)* Naxos ▲ 8.553047 [DDD]
Soler, P.A.:Sons Hpd—Nos. 1, 15, 18, 19, 43, 54, 85, 90, 91, 101, 110 *(rec Epsom College Concert Hall, Surrey, England, July 3–5, 1995)* Naxos ▲ 8.553462 [DDD]
Soler, P.A.:Sons Hpd—15 Sonatas—R.4, 7, 10, 39, 47, 72, 73, 81, 84, 88, 103, 108, 113, 118, 119 Nimbus ▲ NI 5248 [ADD]

Rowland, Joan (pno)—see also ORCHESTRAS & ENSEMBLES Schnabel Piano Duo
Mozart, W.A.:Son Pno 4–Hands, K.497, w. K. Ulrich Schnabel (pno) Town Hall ▲ THCD 41
Schubert, Franz:Divertissement sur des motifs originaux français, D.823, w. K. U. Schnabel (pno) Town Hall ▲ THCD 41
Schubert, Franz:Vars Theme from Hérold's *Marie* Pno 4–Hands, w. K. U. Schnabel (pno)—No. 1 Town Hall ▲ THCD 41
Schumann, R.:Carnaval Pno *(rec Santa Monica, CA, Apr 27–29, 1993)* Town Hall ▲ THCD 43
Schumann, R.:Fant Pno *(rec Santa Monica, CA, Apr 27–29, 1993)* Town Hall ▲ THCD 43
Schumann, R.:Presto passionato *(rec Santa Monica, CA, Apr 27–29, 1993)* Town Hall ▲ THCD 43
Schumann, R.:Waldscenen—Abschied *(rec Santa Monica, CA, Apr 27–29, 1993)* Town Hall ▲ THCD 43

Rowland-Jones, Simon (va)—see also ORCHESTRAS & ENSEMBLES Chilingirian String Quartet
Bach, J.S.:Suites Vc, BWV 1007–1012—Nos. 1–3 [trans. Rowland-Jones] Meridian ▲ MER 84270 [DDD]
Tippett, M.:Triple Con, w. Levon Chilingirian (vn), Philip de Groote (vc), R. Hickox (cnd), Bournemouth SO Chandos ▲ CHAN 9384 [DDD]
Vaughan Williams, R.:Phantasy Qnt, w. Medici String Quartet Nimbus ▲ NI 5191 [DDD]

Rowley, Alec (pno)
Coleridge-Taylor, S.:Scenes from an Imaginary Ballet 3 *(rec 1926–35)* Pearl ▲ PEA 9965 (m) [AAD]

Rowley, Eugene (pno)
Barber, S.:Son Vc, w. P. Rejto (vc) *(rec 1991)* Summit ▲ DCD 137 [DDD]
Guion, D.:Pno Music—Mother Goose Suite, Nocturne in Blue, Valse Arabesque, Pastoral, Southern Nights, Two Country Jigs, The lonesome whistler; The harmonica player; Home on the Range; Turkey in the straw, Sheep & goat walkin' to pasture, The Arkansas traveler Premier ("Composer" series) ▲ PRCD 1024 [DDD]
Janácek, L.:Fairy Tale, w. P. Rejto (vc) *(rec 1991)* Summit ▲ DCD 137 [DDD]
Kodály, Z.:Son Vc & Pno, Op. 4, w. P. Rejto (vc) *(rec 1991)* Summit ▲ DCD 137 [DDD]
Martinů, B.:Son 2 Vc, w. P. Rejto (vc) *(rec 1991)* Summit ▲ DCD 137 [DDD]

Roy, C. (vc)
Rossé, F.:Music of, w. Y. Haym (ob), P. Ruby (gtr), M. Michalakakos (va), I. Assayag (hpd)—Zembrocordal; Digitales; Lance du Souvenant; Impromptu 0990; For a Little Hot Quaint Time Quantum ▲ QM 6949

Royannais, Damien (bar sax)
Gubaidulina, S.:Duo-Son, w. Claude Delangle (bar sax) *(rec Paris, July 1995)* BIS ▲ CD 765 [DDD]

Royen, Everard van (fl)—see ORCHESTRAS & ENSEMBLES Alma Musica Ensemble

Royen, Gusta van (hpd)—see ORCHESTRAS & ENSEMBLES Alma Musica Ensemble

Rozen, J. (elec tuba)
Lang, D.:Music of, w. D. Lang (nar), E. Niemann (pno), N. Tilles (pno), R. Schulte (vn), U. Oppens (pno), L. Vaillancourt (cnd), Le Nouvel Ensemble Moderne—Are You Experienced?; Orpheus Over & Under; Spud; Illumination Rounds CRI ▲ CD 625 [DDD]

Rozendaal, J. M. (vc)
Soler, P.A.:Qnt 1 Hpd, w. D. Schrader (hpd), C. Verrette (vn), M. Shelton (vn), P. Slowik (va) *(rec Oct. & Dec. 1992)* Cedille ▲ CDR 90000 013 [DDD]
Soler, P.A.:Qnt 2 Hpd, w. D. Schrader (hpd), C. Verrette (vn), M. Shelton (vn), P. Slowik (va) *(rec Oct. & Dec. 1992)* Cedille ▲ CDR 90000 013 [DDD]
Soler, P.A.:Qnt 3 Hpd, w. D. Schrader (hpd), C. Verrette (vn), M. Shelton (vn), P. Slowik (va) *(rec Oct. & Dec. 1992)* Cedille ▲ CDR 90000 013 [DDD]

Rozevics, Einars (va)—see ORCHESTRAS & ENSEMBLES Riga String Quartet

Rozhdestvensky, Gennadi (pno)
Brahms, J.:Souvenir de la Russie, w. V. Poatnikova (pno) Allegretto ▲ ACD 8177 [DDD] ■ ACS 8177
Brahms, J.:Vars on a Theme of Robert Schumann, Op. 23, w. V. Poatnikova (pno) Allegretto ▲ ACD 8177 [DDD] ■ ACS 8177
Brahms, J.:Waltzes Pno, Op. 39, w. V. Poatnikova (pno) [4-hands version] Allegretto ▲ ACD 8177 [DDD] ■ ACS 8177

Rozhdestvensky, Sasha (vn)
Schnittke, A.:Con grosso 6, w. Viktoria Postnikova (pno), G. Rozhdestvensky (cnd), Royal Stockholm PO Chandos ▲ CHAN 9359 [DDD]
Schnittke, A.:Son 1 Vn, w. V. Postnikova (pno) Chandos ▲ CHAN 9274 [DDD]
Strauss, R.:Son Vn, w. V. Postnikova (pno) Chandos ▲ CHAN 9274 [DDD]

Rozhkov, Michail (balalaika)
Michail Rozhkov *(rec 1961–90)* Russian Compact Disc ("Russian Performing School" series) ▲ RCD 16202

Rozova, Natalia (pno)
Brahms, J.:Sons Vn (comp), w. A. Shirinsky (vn) Olympia ▲ OLY 285 [DDD]
Fine Night, w. Alexander Shirinsky (vn) Mezhdunarodnaya Kniga ▲ MK 417030 [DDD]

Rozsa, Ernö (vn)
Schillings, M. von:Con Vn, w. A. Walter (cnd), Czech-Slovak State PO Marco Polo ▲ 8.223324 [DDD]

Rubenstein, Jerrold (vn)
Kreisler, F.:Vn Pieces, w. D. Ouziel (pno)—8 original works for violin & piano *(La gitana; Liebesfreud; Liebesleid; Caprice viennois; Schön Rosmarin; Tambourin chinois; Polichinelle; Syncopation)*; 6 works composed in the styles of Boccherini *(Allegretto)*, Couperin *(Chanson Louis XIII; la Précieuse)*, Martini *(Andantino; Tempo di Minuetto)* & Paganini *(Praeludium et allegro)*; 7 arrs. of works by Albéniz *(Tango)*, Dvořák *(Slavonic Dances No. 1 in g & No. 2 in e)*, Falla *(Danse espagnole from La vida breve)*, Granados *(Danse espagnole)* & Tartini *(Fugue in A; Variations on a Theme by Corelli)* Pavane ▲ ADW 7222 [DDD]
Pleyel, I.:Duets Vns, w. L. Bobesco (vn) Talent ▲ DOM 291016 [ADD]
Ysaÿe, E.:Andante Vn, w. M. Rodan (cnd), Belgian National Orch Koch Schwann ▲ CD 311099 [DDD]
Ysaÿe, E.:Chant d'hiver, w. M. Rodan, Belgian National Orch Koch Schwann ▲ CD 311099 [DDD]
Ysaÿe, E.:Exil, w. M. Rodan, Belgian National Orch Koch Schwann ▲ CD 311099 [DDD]
Ysaÿe, E.:Extase, w. M. Rodan, Belgian National Orch Koch Schwann ▲ CD 311099 [DDD]
Ysaÿe, E.:Poème élégiaque Vn & Orch, w. M. Rodan, Belgian National Orch Koch Schwann ▲ CD 311099 [DDD]
Ysaÿe, E.:Scène au rouet, w. M. Rodan, Belgian National Orch Koch Schwann ▲ CD 311099 [DDD]

Rubin, Amy (pno)
Rubin, A.:La Loba, w. Quintet of the Americas *(rec Vassar College, June 25–29, 1995)* CRI ▲ CD 722 [DDD]

Rubin, H. (vn)
Scott, K.L.:The Wind of Heaven, w. S. M. Wallace (org), K. Lee Scott (cnd), Lee Scott Singers VQR Digital ▲ QR 2051 [DDD]

Rubin, Jonathan (lt)—see also ORCHESTRAS & ENSEMBLES Geneva Baroque Duo
Concert de musique liturgique Juive à la synagogue de Lausanne, w. Lausanne Israeli Community Male Chorus, Alain Blum, Antoine D., André Stora, Gueorgui Popov, Jean Akiba, Oleg Kogan (hp), Christine Fleischmann (hp) Doron ▲ DRC 3003 [DDD]

Rubin, Justin (pno)
Xenakis, I.:Eonta, w. C. Z. Bornstein (cnd), ST-X Ensemble *(rec live, Thread Waxing Space, New York, June 21, 1995)* Mode ▲ mode 53

Rubin, Nathan (vn)
Rokeach, M.:Son Vn, w. E. Wasserman (pno) Capstone ▲ CPS 8615

Rubin, Sharyn (b vl)—see ORCHESTRAS & ENSEMBLES Geneva Baroque Duo

Rubino, J. (pno)
Dunner, L.B.:Motherless Child Songs, w. C. Sebron (mez), L.B. Dunner (cl)—Motherless Child; I Gave My Love a Cherry; Nobody Knows the Trouble I've Seen; Deep River Innova ▲ MN 108

Rubinstein, Artur (pno)
Artur Rubinstein *(rec 1928–33 HMV rec'gs)* Pearl ▲ PEA 9464 (m) [AAD]
Basic 100, Vol. 20 RCA Victor ▲ 09026-61717-2 ■ 09026-61717-4
Basic 100, Vol. 33, w. Anna Moffo (sop), Fritz Reiner (cnd), Leopold Stokowski (cnd) RCA Victor ▲ 09026-61851-2 ■ 09026-61851-4
Basic 100, Vol. 41 RCA Victor ▲ 09026-62561-2 ■ 09026-62561-4

Rubinstein, Artur (pno) (cont.)
Basic 100, Vol. 48, w. Alfred Wallenstein (cnd), Carlo Maria Giulini (cnd) RCA Victor ▲ 09026-62677-2 ■ 09026-62677-4
Basic 100, Vol. 58, w. Boston SO [cnd:Erich Leinsdorf] RCA Victor ▲ 09026-68083-2 ■ 09026-68083-4
Basic 100, Vol. 69, w. Alfred Wallenstein (cnd) RCA Victor ▲ 09026-68337-2 ■ 09026-68337-4
Basic 100, Vol. 77, w. Boston SO [cnd:Erich Leinsdorf] RCA Victor ▲ 09026-68454-2 ■ 09026-68454-4
Beethoven, L. van:Cons Pno (comp), w. J. Krips (cnd), Symphony of the Air RCA Gold Seal 3–▲ 09026-61260-2
Beethoven, L. van:Con 1 Pno, w. E. Leinsdorf (cnd), Boston SO RCA Victor ▲ 09026-68083-2; ■ 09026-68083-4
Beethoven, L. van:Con 1 Pno, w. E. Leinsdorf (cnd), Boston SO RCA Red Seal ▲ 5674-2-RC [ADD]
Beethoven, L. van:Con 2 Pno, w. E. Leinsdorf (cnd), Boston SO RCA Red Seal ▲ 5675-2-RC [ADD]
Beethoven, L. van:Con 3 Pno, w. E. Leinsdorf (cnd), Boston SO RCA Red Seal ▲ 5675-2-RC [ADD]
Beethoven, L. van:Con 3 Pno, w. A. Toscanini (cnd), NBC SO RCA Gold Seal ▲ 60261-2-RG (m) [ADD] ■ 60261-4-RG
Beethoven, L. van:Con 4 Pno, w. E. Leinsdorf (cnd), Boston SO RCA Red Seal ▲ 5676-2-RC [ADD]
Beethoven, L. van:Con 4 Pno, w. E. Leinsdorf (cnd), Boston SO RCA Victor ▲ 09026-68083-2; ■ 09026-68083-4
Beethoven, L. van:Con 4 Pno, w. D. Mitropoulos (cnd), New York PO *(rec 1951–54)* Legend ▲ LGD 102 [ADD]
Beethoven, L. van:Con 5 Pno, "Emperor", w. E. Leinsdorf (cnd), Boston SO RCA Red Seal ▲ 5676-2-RC [ADD]
Beethoven, L. van:Son 8 Pno, "Pathétique" RCA Victor ▲ 09026-62561-2 ■ 09026-62561-4
Beethoven, L. van:Son 8 Pno, "Pathétique" RCA ■ ARK1-4001
Beethoven, L. van:Son 8 Pno, "Pathétique" *(rec 1962 & 1963)* RCA Gold Seal ▲ 09026-61443-2
Beethoven, L. van:Son 14 Pno, "Moonlight Son" RCA ■ ARK1-4001
Beethoven, L. van:Son 14 Pno, "Moonlight Son" *(rec 1962 & 1963)* RCA Gold Seal ▲ 09026-61443-2
Beethoven, L. van:Son 14 Pno, "Moonlight Son" RCA Victor ▲ 09026-62561-2 ■ 09026-62561-4
Beethoven, L. van:Son 14 Pno, "Moonlight Son" RCA Red Seal ▲ 5674-2-RC [ADD]
Beethoven, L. van:Son 18 Pno RCA Gold Seal 3–▲ 09026-61260-2
Beethoven, L. van:Son 23 Pno, "Appassionata" RCA ■ ARK1-4001
Beethoven, L. van:Son 23 Pno, "Appassionata" *(rec 1962 & 1963)* RCA Gold Seal ▲ 09026-61443-2
Beethoven, L. van:Son 23 Pno, "Appassionata" *(rec live 1/15/75)* RCA Red Seal ▲ 09026-61160-2 ■ 09026-61160-4 □ 09026-61160-5
Beethoven, L. van:Son 23 Pno, "Appassionata" RCA Victor ▲ 09026-62561-2 ■ 09026-62561-4
Beethoven, L. van:Son 26 Pno, "Les Adieux" *(rec 1962 & 1963)* RCA Gold Seal ▲ 09026-61443-2
Beethoven, L. van:Son 26 Pno, "Les Adieux" RCA Victor ▲ 09026-62561-2 ■ 09026-62561-4
Beethoven, L. van:Son 5 Vn, "Spring", w. H. Szeryng (vn) RCA Gold Seal ▲ 09026-61861-2
Beethoven, L. van:Son 8 Vn, w. H. Szeryng (vn) RCA Gold Seal ▲ 6264-2-RG [ADD]
Beethoven, L. van:Son 8 Vn, w. H. Szeryng (vn) RCA Gold Seal ▲ 09026-61861-2
Beethoven, L. van:Son 9 Vn, "Kreutzer", w. H. Szeryng (vn) RCA Gold Seal ▲ 09026-61861-2
Beethoven, L. van:Trio 6 Pno, "Archduke", w. J. Heifetz (vn), E. Feuermann (vc) RCA Gold Seal ▲ 09026-60926-2 ■ 09026-60926-4
Brahms, J.:Ballades, Op. 10 RCA Red Seal ▲ 5672-2-RC [ADD]
Brahms, J.:Ballades, Op. 10 RCA Gold Seal ▲ 09026-61862-2
Brahms, J.:Con 1 Pno, w. F. Reiner (cnd), Chicago SO RCA Gold Seal ▲ 09026-61263-2 ■ 09026-61263-4
Brahms, J.:Con 2 Pno, w. A. Cluytens (cnd), Turin RAI SO *(rec Torino, May 1962)* Emozioni ▲ ARCD 2027
Brahms, J.:Con 2 Pno, w. J. Krips (cnd), RCA Victor SO *(rec 1958)* RCA Gold Seal ▲ 09026-61442-2
Brahms, J.:Fants Pno, Op. 116—No. 5 *(rec 1958)* RCA Gold Seal ▲ 09026-61442-2
Brahms, J.:Fants Pno, Op. 116—No. 6, Intermezzo RCA Gold Seal ▲ 09026-61862-2
Brahms, J.:Intermezzos Pno, Op. 117—No. 2 *(rec 1958)* RCA Gold Seal ▲ 09026-61442-2
Brahms, J.:Pno Music (misc)—Intermezzos in c#, Op. 117/3; in A, Op. 118/2; in E♭, Op. 118/6; in e, Op. 119/ 2; in C, Op. 119/3 *(rec RCA Studios, Hollywood, Aug 3, 5 & 7, 1953)* RCA Gold Seal ▲ 09026-62592-2
Brahms, J.:Pieces Pno, Op. 76—No. 2 RCA Gold Seal ▲ 09026-61263-2 ■ 09026-61263-4
Brahms, J.:Pieces Pno, Op. 118—No. 6 RCA Gold Seal ▲ 09026-61263-2 ■ 09026-61263-4
Brahms, J.:Pieces Pno, Op. 118—No. 6, Romance RCA Gold Seal ▲ 09026-61862-2
Brahms, J.:Pieces Pno, Op. 118—No. 5 RCA Red Seal ▲ 5672-2-RC [ADD]
Brahms, J.:Qt 1 Pno, w. Guarneri String Quartet members RCA Gold Seal ▲ 5677-2-RG [ADD] ■ 5677-4-RG (CrO2)
Brahms, J.:Qt 1 Pno, w. Pro Arte String Quartet members *(rec 1932)* Biddulph ▲ LAB 027 [ADD]
Brahms, J.:Qt 2 Pno, w. Busch String Quartet members *(rec 1932)* Biddulph ▲ LAB 027 [ADD]
Brahms, J.:Qt 3 Pno, w. Guarneri String Quartet members RCA Gold Seal ▲ 5677-2-RG [ADD] ■ 5677-4-RG (CrO2)
Brahms, J.:Rhaps Pno, Op. 79—No. 1 RCA Gold Seal ▲ 09026-61263-2 ■ 09026-61263-4
Brahms, J.:Rhaps Pno, Op. 79—No. 2 *(rec 1958)* RCA Gold Seal ▲ 09026-61442-2
Brahms, J.:Sons Vc (comp), w. Gregor Piatigorsky (vc) *(rec American Legion Hall, Hollywood, Oct 11, 1966)* RCA Gold Seal ▲ 09026-62592-2
Brahms, J.:Son 1 Vc, w. G. Piatigorsky (vc) *(rec 1936 from HMV DB 2952–54)* Music & Arts ▲ CD 674 [AAD]
Brahms, J.:Son 1 Vc, w. G. Piatigorsky (vc) *(rec 1936 from HMV DB 2952–54)* Pearl ▲ PEA 9447 (m) [AAD]
Brahms, J.:Son 3 Pno RCA Gold Seal ▲ 09026-61862-2
Brahms, J.:Son 3 Pno RCA Red Seal ▲ 5672-2-RC [ADD]
Brahms, J.:Son 1 Vn, w. H. Szeryng (vn) RCA Gold Seal ▲ 6264-2-RG [ADD]
Brahms, J.:Son 3 Vn, w. H. Szeryng (vn) RCA Gold Seal ▲ 6264-2-RG [ADD]
Brahms, J.:Trio 1 Pno, w. H. Szeryng (vn), P. Fournier (vc) *(rec 1972)* RCA Red Seal ▲ 6260-2-RC [ADD]
Brahms, J.:Trio 2 Pno, w. H. Szeryng (vn), P. Fournier (vc) *(rec 1972)* RCA Red Seal ▲ 6260-2-RC [ADD]
Busoni, F.:Chaconne Pno RCA Gold Seal ▲ 09026-62590-2
Carnegie Hall Highlights *(rec 1961)* RCA Gold Seal ▲ 09026-61445-2
Chabrier, E.:Pno Music (misc) *(rec 1963)* RCA Gold Seal ▲ 09026-61446-2
Chopin, F.:Andante Spianato & Grande Polonaise RCA Red Seal ▲ 5617-2-RC [ADD]
Chopin, F.:Andante Spianato & Grande Polonaise Enterprise ("The Piano Library" series) ▲ ENT 187
Chopin, F.:Andante Spianato & Grande Polonaise *(rec 1934–35)* Grammofono 2000 ▲ GRM 78501 [ADD]
Chopin, F.:Andante Spianato & Grande Polonaise, w. A. Wallenstein (cnd), London New SO RCA Gold Seal ▲ 60404-2-RG [ADD] ■ 60404-4-RG (CrO2)
Chopin, F.:Ballades Pno (comp) RCA Red Seal ▲ RCD1-7156
Chopin, F.:Barcarolle Pno RCA Gold Seal ▲ 60047-2-RG [ADD] ■ 60047-4-RG
Chopin, F.:Barcarolle Pno RCA Red Seal ▲ 5617-2 RC [ADD]
Chopin, F.:Barcarolle Pno Enterprise ("The Piano Library" series) ▲ ENT PL 201
Chopin, F.:Berceuse Enterprise ("The Piano Library" series) ▲ ENT PL 201
Chopin, F.:Berceuse RCA Gold Seal ▲ 60047-2-RG [ADD] ■ 60047-4-RG
Chopin, F.:Con 1 Pno, w. J. Krenz (cnd), Polish National RSO Katowice *(rec Warsaw, 1966)* Prelude ▲ PRE 2165 [ADD]
Chopin, F.:Con 1 Pno, w. B. Walter (cnd), New York SO *(rec 1947)* Historical Performers ▲ HPS 29
Chopin, F.:Con 1 Pno, w. S. Skrowaczewski (cnd), London New SO RCA Red Seal ▲ 5612-2-RC [ADD]
Chopin, F.:Con 1 Pno, w. B. Walter (cnd), New York PO *(rec live, 1948)* As Disc ▲ ASD 2401 (m)
Chopin, F.:Con 1 Pno, w. J. Barbirolli (cnd), London SO *(rec London, Apr 5, 1937)* Iron Needle ▲ IN 1345 (m) [ADD]

▲ = CD ♦ = Enhanced CD Δ = MD ■ = Cassette Tape □ = DCC

Rubinstein, Artur (pno) (cont.)

Chopin, F.:Con 1 Pno, w. J. Barbirolli (cnd), London SO *(rec London, 1931–37)* Grammofono 2000 ▲ GRM 78554
Chopin, F.:Con 1 Pno, w. J. Barbirolli (cnd), London SO *(rec 1937)* EMI Classics 2–▲ ZDHB 64491
Chopin, F.:Con 1 Pno, w. *(orch unknown)* Memories ("Golden" series) 2–▲ MEM 3005
Chopin, F.:Con 1 Pno EMI Classics 5–▲ CDHE 64933
Chopin, F.:Con 2 Pno, w. J. Barbirolli (cnd), London SO *(rec London, Jan 8–9, 1931)* Iron Needle ▲ IN 1345 (m) [ADD]
Chopin, F.:Con 2 Pno, w. A. Wallenstein (cnd), Symphony of the Air RCA Red Seal ▲ 5612–2–RC [ADD]
Chopin, F.:Con 2 Pno, w. E. Ormandy (cnd), Philadelphia Orch RCA Gold Seal ▲ 60404–2–RG [ADD] ■ 60404–4–RG (CrO2)
Chopin, F.:Con 2 Pno, w. J. Krenz (cnd), Polish National RSO Katowice *(rec Warsaw, 1966)* Prelude ▲ PRE 2165 [ADD]
Chopin, F.:Con 2 Pno, w. J. Barbirolli (cnd), London SO *(rec 1937)* EMI Classics 2–▲ ZDHB 64491
Chopin, F.:Con 2 Pno, w. *(orch unknown)* EMI Classics 5–▲ CDHE 64933
Chopin, F.:Con 2 Pno, w. J. Barbirolli (cnd), London SO *(rec London, 1931–37)* Grammofono 2000 ▲ GRM 78554
Chopin, F.:Fant RCA Red Seal ▲ 5616–2–RC [ADD]
Chopin, F.:Grand Fant on Polish Airs, w. E. Ormandy (cnd), Philadelphia Orch RCA Gold Seal ▲ 60404–2–RG [ADD] ■ 60404–4–RG (CrO2)
Chopin, F.:Impromptus RCA Red Seal ▲ 5617–2–RC [ADD]
Chopin, F.:Mazurkas EMI Classics 5–▲ CDHE 64933
Chopin, F.:Mazurkas RCA Red Seal 2–▲ 5614–2–RC [ADD]
Chopin, F.:Nocturnes RCA Red Seal 2–▲ 5613–2–RC [ADD]
Chopin, F.:Nocturnes—Nos. 1–19 RCA 2–■ CRK2–5018
Chopin, F.:Nocturnes—Nocturne No. 2, Op. 15 *(rec May 8, 1961)* Ermitage ▲ ERM 127
Chopin, F.:Nocturnes—Op. 55/1–4 *(rec London, 1931–37)* Grammofono 2000 ▲ GRM 78554
Chopin, F.:Nocturnes—Nos. 15 & 16, Op. 55/1 & 2 *(rec London, Oct 20 & May 28, 1936)* Iron Needle ▲ IN 1345 (m) [ADD]
Chopin, F.:Nocturnes *(rec 1936–37)* EMI Classics 2–▲ ZDHB 64491
Chopin, F.:Nocturnes EMI Classics 5–▲ CDHE 64933
Chopin, F.:Nouvelles études RCA Red Seal ▲ 5617–2–RC [ADD]
Chopin, F.:Pno Music (misc)—Mazurkas (complete); Scherzi (4); Polonaises (7); Barcarolle in F#, Op. 60; Berceuse in D♭, Op. 57; Valse in A♭, Op. 34/1; Andante Spianato & Grande Polonaise Brillante in E♭, Op. 22 *(rec 1928–1939)* EMI Classics 3–▲ ZDHC 64697
Chopin, F.:Pno Music (misc)—Fantasia in f, Op. 49; Preludes in f#, D♭, F, d, Op. 28/8, 15, 23 & 28; Ballade No. 3 in A♭, Op. 47; Berceuse in D♭, Op. 57; Waltz in c#, Op. 64/2; Etude in e, Op. 25/5 *(rec Nov. 7, 1970)* Ermitage ▲ ERM 127
Chopin, F.:Pno Music (misc)—Nocturnes Nos. 1–16; Polonaises No. 1–7; Andante spianato & Grand polonaise, Op. 22; Scherzos Nos. 1–4; Barcarolle, Op. 60; Berceuse, Op. 57; Valses, Op. 34/1 & Op. 64/2; Cons Nos. 1 & 2 for Pno [w. John Barbirolli (cnd), London SO] Grammofono 2000 4–▲ GRM 78654
Chopin, F.:Pno Music (misc) Pearl ▲ PEA 9464 (m) [AAD]
Chopin, F.:Pno Music (misc) RCA ■ RK 1172
Chopin, F.:Pno Music (misc)—Piano Cons. 1 & 2; Piano Sons. 2 & 3; Ballades; Impromptus; Scherzos; 52 Mazurkas; 19 Nocturnes; 7 Polonaises; Preludes (24), Op. 28 [rec. 1946]; 14 Waltzes; Andante Spianato & Grand Polonaise; Barcarolle; Berceuse; Bolero; Fantaisie in f; Tarantelle; Trois nouvelles etudes RCA Gold Seal 11–▲ 60822–2–RG
Chopin, F.:Pno Music (misc)—2 Études, Nocturne, Polonaise *(rec live 1/15/75)* RCA Red Seal ▲ 61160–2 ■ 61160–4 □ 09026–6116
Chopin, F.:Pno Music (misc) RCA Gold Seal ▲ 7725–2 RG [ADD] ■ 7725–4 RG6 (CrO2)
Chopin, F.:Pno Music (misc)—Bolero, Op. 19; Berceuse, Op. 57; Tarentelle, Op. 43 RCA Red Seal ▲ 5617–2–RC [ADD]
Chopin, F.:Pno Music (misc)—Polonaise "Military"; Nocturne, No. 2; Grand valse brillante; Waltz, No. 2; Minute Waltz; Polonaise heroique; Mazurka; Fantasia-Impromtu; Mazurka, No. 1; Nocturne, No. 1; Nocturne, No. 2; Nocturne, No. 2, Op. 27; Ballade; Scherzo, No. 2 RCA Victor ▲ 09026–61717–2; ■ 09026–61717–4
Chopin, F.:Pno Music (misc)—2 Ballades (Opp. 47 & 52); Berceuse; Etude, Op. 25/5; Fantaisie in f, Op. 49; 2 Mazurkas (Opp. 33/2 & 56/3); Polonaise, Op. 53; 3 Preludes (Op. 28, Nos. 8,15 & 24); Scherzo No. 2, Op. 31; Waltz, Op. 64/2 *(rec live, Milan 11/5/70)* Arkadia ▲ 918 [ADD]
Chopin, F.:Polonaises—Nos. 1–7 *(rec 1934–35)* Grammofono 2000 ▲ GRM 78501 [ADD]
Chopin, F.:Polonaises—7 RCA Red Seal ▲ 5615–2–RC [ADD]
Chopin, F.:Polonaises Enterprise ("The Piano Library" series) ▲ ENT 187
Chopin, F.:Preludes, Op. 28 RCA Gold Seal ▲ 60047–2–RG [ADD] ■ 60047–4–RG
Chopin, F.:Scherzos EMI Classics 5–▲ CDHE 64933
Chopin, F.:Scherzos *(rec 1933 for HMV)* Pearl ▲ PEA 9464 (m) [AAD]
Chopin, F.:Scherzos RCA Red Seal ▲ RCD1–7156
Chopin, F.:Son Pno, Op. 35 *(rec live, Lugano 5/8/61)* Ermitage ▲ ERM 108 [ADD]
Chopin, F.:Son Pno, Op. 35 RCA Gold Seal ▲ 60047–2–RG [ADD] ■ 60047–4–RG
Chopin, F.:Son Pno, Op. 35 RCA Red Seal ▲ 5616–2–RC [ADD]
Chopin, F.:Son Pno, Op. 58 RCA Red Seal ▲ 5616–2–RC [ADD]
Chopin, F.:Waltzes—Opp. 34/1 & 64/2 Enterprise ("The Piano Library" series) ▲ ENT PL 201
Chopin, F.:Waltzes—Op. 64/2 EMI Classics 2–▲ ZDHB 64491
Chopin, F.:Waltzes—14 waltzes RCA 2–■ CRK2–5018
Chopin, F.:Waltzes—14 waltzes RCA Red Seal ▲ RCD1–5492
Debussy, C.:Pno Music (misc)—La soirée dans Grenade; Jadins sous la pluie; Hommage à Rameau; Reflets dans l'eau; La plus que lente; Poisson d'or; Minstrels *(rec 1945 & 1952)* RCA Gold Seal ▲ 09026–61446–2
Debussy, C.:Pno Music (misc)—La plus que lente; Prelude in a *(rec live, 1/15/75)* RCA Red Seal ▲ 09026–61160–2 ■ 09026–61160–4 □ 09026–61160–5
Dvořák, A.:Qts Pno Strs, Opp. 23 & 87, w. Guarneri String Quartet members—Op. 87 RCA Red Seal ▲ 6256–2–RC [ADD]
Dvořák, A.:Qnt Pno, Op. 81, w. Guarneri String Quartet RCA Gold Seal ▲ 6263–2–RG [ADD] ■ 6263–4–RG (CrO2)
Falla, M. de:El amor brujo (ritual fire dance) RCA Gold Seal ▲ 09026–61863–2
Falla, M. de:Noches en los jardines de España, w. *(orch unknown)* RCA Gold Seal ▲ 09026–61863–2
Falla, M. de:Noches en los jardines de España, w. V. Golschmann (cnd), St. Louis SO RCA Gold Seal ▲ 09026–61261–2
Falla, M. de:Noches en los jardines de España, w. E. Jorda (cnd), San Francisco SO *(rec 1957)* RCA Gold Seal ▲ 60046–2–RG (m/s) [ADD]
Fauré, G.:Nocturnes (13) Pno—No. 3 *(rec 1963)* RCA Gold Seal ▲ 09026–61446–2
Fauré, G.:Qt 1 Pno, w. Guarneri String Quartet members RCA Red Seal ▲ 6256–2–RC [ADD]
Franck, C.:Prélude, choral et fugue RCA Red Seal ▲ 5673–2–RC [ADD]
Franck, C.:Prélude, choral et fugue RCA Gold Seal ▲ 09026–62590–2
Franck, C.:Son Vn, w. J. Heifetz (vn) Biddulph ▲ LAB 025 [ADD]
Franck, C.:Symphonic Vars, w. *(cond. & orch. unknown)* RCA Gold Seal ▲ 09026–61863–2
Franck, C.:Symphonic Vars, w. A. Wallenstein (cnd), Symphony of the Air *(rec 1956 & 1958)* RCA Gold Seal ▲ 09026–61496–2 ■ 09026–61496–4
Granados, E.:Goyescas, No. 4, "Quejas o la Maja y el Ruiseñor" *(rec live, Lugano, 5/8/61)* Ermitage ▲ ERM 108 [ADD]
Grieg, E.:Ballade Pno RCA Gold Seal ▲ 09026–60897–2; ■ 09026–60897–4 (CrO2)
Grieg, E.:Ballade Pno RCA Gold Seal ▲ 09026–61883–2
Grieg, E.:Con Pno, Op. 16, w. C. M. Giulini (cnd), Philharmonia Orch *(rec live Royal Festival Hall)* Intaglio ▲ INCD 7101 [ADD]
Grieg, E.:Con Pno, Op. 16, w. E. Ormandy (cnd), Philadelphia Orch RCA Gold Seal ▲ 09026–60897–2; ■ 09026–60897–4 (CrO2)

Rubinstein, Artur (pno) (cont.)

Grieg, E.:Con Pno, Op. 16, w. E. Ormandy (cnd), Philadelphia Orch *(rec 1942)* RCA Gold Seal ▲ 09026–61883–2
Grieg, E.:Con Pno, Op. 16, w. A. Wallenstein (cnd), RCA Victor SO RCA Gold Seal ▲ 09026–61262–2; ■ 09026–61262–4
Grieg, E.:Lyric Pieces—sels. RCA Gold Seal ▲ 09026–60897–2; ■ 09026–60897–4 (CrO2)
Grieg, E.:Lyric Pieces—11 Pieces *(rec 1953)* RCA Gold Seal ▲ 09026–61883–2
Haydn, J.:Son Pno, H.XVII/6, "Andante with Vars" RCA Gold Seal ▲ 7967–2–RG [ADD] ■ 7967–4–RG
Highlights from the Rubinstein Collection RCA Gold Seal ▲ 60211–2–RG [ADD] ■ 60211–4–RG
The Last Recital for Israel *(rec live, Ambassador College, California, 1/15/75)* RCA Red Seal ▲ 09026–61160–2 ■ 09026–61160–4 □ 09026–61160–5
Liszt, F.:Con 1 Pno, w. A. Wallenstein (cnd), RCA Victor SO RCA Red Seal ▲ 6255–2–RC [ADD]
Liszt, F.:Con 1 Pno, w. A. Dorati (cnd), Dallas SO *(rec 1952)* RCA Gold Seal ▲ 60046–2–RG (m/s) [ADD]
Liszt, F.:Con 1 Pno, w. A. Wallenstein (cnd), RCA Victor SO RCA Gold Seal ▲ 09026–61496–2 ■ 09026–61496–4
Liszt, F.:Mephisto Waltz 3 Pno *(rec live, Lugano, 5/8/61)* Ermitage ▲ ERM 108 [ADD]
Liszt, F.:Son Pno RCA Gold Seal ▲ 09026–62590–2
Liszt, F.:Son Pno RCA Red Seal ▲ 5673–2–RC [ADD]
Mendelssohn, F.:Trio 1 Pno, w. J. Heifetz (vn), G. Piatigorsky (vc) RCA Gold Seal ▲ 7768–2–RG (m) [ADD]
Mozart, W.A.:Con 17 Pno, w. *(cnd & orch unknown)* RCA Gold Seal ▲ 09026–61859–2
Mozart, W.A.:Con 20 Pno, w. A. Wallenstein (cnd), RCA Victor SO RCA Gold Seal ▲ 7967–2 [ADD] ■ 7967–4
Mozart, W.A.:Con 20 Pno, w. C. M. Giulini (cnd), Philharmonia Orch Intaglio ▲ INCD 7101 [ADD]
Mozart, W.A.:Con 20 Pno, w. A. Wallenstein (cnd), RCA Victor SO RCA Victor ▲ 09026–68337–2 ■ 09026–68337–4
Mozart, W.A.:Con 21 Pno, w. A. Wallenstein (cnd), RCA Victor SO RCA Gold Seal ▲ 7967–2 [ADD] ■ 7967–4
Mozart, W.A.:Con 21 Pno, w. J. Levine (cnd), Chicago SO RCA Victor ▲ 09026–61708–2; ■ 09026–61708–4
Mozart, W.A.:Con 23 Pno, w. A. Wallenstein (cnd), RCA Victor SO RCA Gold Seal ▲ 7968–2 [ADD]
Mozart, W.A.:Con 23 Pno, w. A. Wallenstein (cnd), RCA Victor SO RCA Victor ▲ 09026–68337–2 ■ 09026–68337–4
Mozart, W.A.:Con 23 Pno, w. *(cnd & orch unknown)* RCA Gold Seal ▲ 09026–61859–2
Mozart, W.A.:Con 23 Pno, w. *(cnd & orch unknown) (rec May 12, 1955)* Ermitage ▲ ERM 127
Mozart, W.A.:Con 24 Pno, w. J. Krips (cnd), RCA Victor SO RCA Gold Seal ▲ 7968–2 [ADD]
Mozart, W.A.:Qts Pno, w. Guarneri String Quartet members RCA Gold Seal ▲ 60406–2 [ADD] ■ 60406–4 (CrO2)
Mozart, W.A.:Rondo Pno, K.511 RCA Gold Seal ▲ 7968–2 [ADD] ■ 7968–4
Music of Spain RCA Gold Seal ▲ 09026–61261–2
Piano Greatest Hits, w. Boston SO, Chicago SO, RCA Victor SO RCA Victor ▲ 09026–62662–2 ■ 09026–62662–4
Poulenc, F.:Intermezzo in A♭ *(rec 1963)* RCA Gold Seal ▲ 09026–61446–2
Poulenc, F.:Movts perpétuels *(rec 1963)* RCA Gold Seal ▲ 09026–61446–2
Prokofiev, S.:The Love for 3 Oranges (march) *(rec live, Lugano, 5/8/61)* Ermitage ▲ ERM 108 [ADD]
Prokofiev, S.:March Pno RCA Gold Seal ▲ 09026–61863–2
Prokofiev, S.:Visions fugitives—12 sels *(rec live, Lugano, 5/8/61)* Ermitage ▲ ERM 108 [ADD]
Rachmaninoff, S.:Con 2 Pno, w. F. Reiner (cnd), Chicago SO RCA Red Seal ▲ RCD1–4934 ■ ARE1–4934
Rachmaninoff, S.:Rhapsody on a Theme of Paganini, w. F. Reiner (cnd), Chicago SO RCA Red Seal ▲ RCD1–4934 ■ ARE1–4934
Ravel, M.:Trio Pno, w. J. Heifetz (vn), G. Piatigorsky (vc) RCA Gold Seal ▲ 7871–2–RG (m/s) [ADD]
Ravel, M.:La Vallée des cloches *(rec 1963)* RCA Gold Seal ▲ 09026–61446–2
Ravel, M.:Valses nobles et sentimentales *(rec 1963)* RCA Gold Seal ▲ 09026–61446–2
Rubinstein:Melody in F Laserlight ▲ 15 603
Rubinstein, A.:Barcarolle 4 Pno RCA Gold Seal ▲ 09026–61860–2
Rubinstein, A.:Pieces Pno—No. 3 in E, "Mazurka" RCA Gold Seal ▲ 09026–61860–2
Rubinstein, A.:Valse-Caprice RCA Gold Seal ▲ 09026–61860–2
Saint-Saëns, C.:Con 2 Pno RCA Gold Seal ▲ 09026–61863–2
Saint-Saëns, C.:Con 2 Pno, w. A. Wallenstein (cnd), Symphony of the Air *(rec 1956 & 1958)* RCA Gold Seal ▲ 09026–61496–2 ■ 09026–61496–4
Schubert, Franz:Fant Pno, D.760, "Wandererfantasie" *(rec 1965)* RCA Red Seal ▲ 6257–2–RC [ADD]
Schubert, Franz:Impromptus Pno, D.899—Nos. 3 & 4 in G♭ & A♭ *(rec 1961)* RCA Red Seal ▲ 6257–2 RC [ADD]
Schubert, Franz:Son Pno, D.960 *(rec 1965)* RCA Red Seal ▲ 6257–2–RC [ADD]
Schubert, Franz:Trio 1 Pno, w. H. Szeryng (vn), E. Fournier (vc) RCA Gold Seal ▲ 6262–2–RG [ADD]
Schubert, Franz:Trio 1 Pno, w. J. Heifetz (vn), E. Feuermann (vc) RCA Gold Seal ▲ 09026–60926–2 ■ 09026–60926–4
Schumann, R.:Arabeske Pno *(rec 1969)* RCA Gold Seal ▲ 09026–61444–2
Schumann, R.:Carnaval Pno RCA Red Seal ▲ 5667–2–RC [ADD]
Schumann, R.:Con Pno, w. E. Leinsdorf (cnd), Boston SO RCA ("Basic 100" series) ▲ 09026–68454–2 ■ 09026–68454–4
Schumann, R.:Con Pno, w. J. Krips (cnd), RCA Victor SO *(rec 1958)* RCA Gold Seal ▲ 09026–61444–2
Schumann, R.:Con Pno, w. C.M. Giulini (cnd), Chicago SO RCA Red Seal ▲ 6255–2–RC [ADD]
Schumann, R.:Con Pno, w. F. Caracciolo (cnd), Naples RAI SO *(rec Naples, Apr. 1964)* Emozioni ▲ ARCD 2027
Schumann, R.:Fant Pno RCA Gold Seal ▲ 09026–61264–2
Schumann, R.:Fantasiestücke Pno, Op. 12 *(rec live 1/15/75)* RCA Red Seal ▲ 09026–61160–2 ■ 09026–61160–4 □ 09026–61160–5
Schumann, R.:Fantasiestücke Pno, Op. 12 RCA Red Seal ▲ 5667–2–RC [ADD]
Schumann, R.:Fantasiestücke Pno, Op. 12 *(rec live, Lugano, 5/8/61)* Ermitage ▲ ERM 108 [ADD]
Schumann, R.:Kreisleriana RCA Gold Seal ▲ 09026–61264–2
Schumann, R.:Novelettes—Nos. 1 & 2 RCA Red Seal ▲ 6255–2–RC [ADD]
Schumann, R.:Sym Etudes *(rec 1961)* RCA Gold Seal ▲ 09026–61444–2
Schumann, R.:Trio 1 Pno, w. I. Szerying (vn), P. Fournier (vc) RCA Gold Seal ▲ 6262–2–RG [ADD] ■ 6262–4–RG (CrO2)
Schumann, R.:Waldscenen—No. 7, "Vogel als Prophet" RCA Red Seal ▲ 5667–2–RC [ADD]
Szymanowski, K.:Sym 4, w. A. Wallenstein (cnd), Los Angeles PO *(rec 1947)* RCA Gold Seal ▲ 60046–2–RG (m/s) [ADD]
Tchaikovsky, P.:Con 1 Pno, w. E. Leinsdorf (cnd), Boston SO RCA ("Basic 100" series) ▲ 09026–68454–2 ■ 09026–68454–4
Tchaikovsky, P.:Con 1 Pno, w. E. Leinsdorf (cnd), Boston SO RCA Gold Seal ▲ 09026–61262–2 ■ 09026–61262–4
Tchaikovsky, P.:Trio Pno, w. J. Heifetz (vn), G. Piatigorsky (vc) RCA Gold Seal ▲ 7768–2–RG (m) [ADD]
The Very Young Arthur Rubinstein (1919–1925), Vols. 1 & 2 Klavier ■ KC 203
Villa-Lobos, H.:Prôle do bébé *(rec May 12, 1955)* Ermitage ▲ ERM 127

Rubio, Miguel (gtr)

Quatre Siecles de Musique Gallo ▲ CD 688 [AAD‡DAD]

Rub–Levi, Irit (pno)

Martinů, B.:Madrigal Son, w. Yossi Arnheim (fl), Elyakum Saltzman (vn) Kontrapunkt ▲ KPT 32205
Martinů, B.:Promenades, w. Yossi Arnheim (fl), Elyakum Saltzman (vn) Kontrapunkt ▲ KPT 32205
Martinů, B.:Son Fl & Pno, w. Yossi Arnheim (fl) Kontrapunkt ▲ KPT 32205
Martinů, B.:Son Fl, Vn & Pno, w. Yossi Arnheim (fl), Elyakum Saltman (vn) Kontrapunkt ▲ KPT 32205
Martinů, B.:Trio Fl, w. Yossi Arnheim (fl), Marcel Bergman (vc) Kontrapunkt ▲ KPT 32205

Rubsam, E. J. (perc)
Bartók, B.:Pno Music, w. B. Bartók (pno), V. Medgyaszay (sop), M. Basilides (cta), F. Székelyhidy (ten), J. Szigeti (vn), B. Goodman (cl), D. Bartók Pásztory (pno), H. J. Baker—studio, broadcast & piano roll recordings of music by Bartók, Kodály, Beethoven, Debussy, Liszt & Scarlatti, chronologically arranged from ca. 1920 through 1945—Sonatina; 6 Romanian Folk Dances; Evening in Transylvania; 8 sels. from 15 Hungarian Peasant Songs; Suite, Op. 14 (both the issued & test recordings); Allegro barbaro; 5 sels. from 2 Romanian Dances, 3 Burlesques, 10 Easy Pieces & 14 Bagatelles; & 4 Sons. by D. Scarlatti (test recordings); 8 sels. from 15 Hungarian Peasant Songs; 4 sels. from 9 Little Piano Pieces, Petite Suite & 3 Rondos on Folk Melodies; & "Sursum corda" from Liszt's Années de pèlerinage; 20 Hungarian Folk Songs; 5 Hungarian Folk Tunes; 8 Hungarian Folksongs; Hungarian Folk Tunes; 6 Romanian Folk Dances; Rhap. 1 Violin & Piano; Contrasts for Clarinet, Violin & Piano; 2 sels. from Mikrokosmos; 32 sels. from Mikrokosmos; Rhap. 1; Son. No. 2; Beethoven's "Kreutzer" Son.; Debussy's Son. 3; Son. 2 Pianos & Percussion; Petite Suite; 3 Hungarian Folk Tunes; 11 sels. from Improvs. on Hungarian Peasant Songs; Mikrokosmos; 3 Rondos on Folk Melodies; 9 Little Piano Pieces; 14 Bagatelles; 15 sels. from For Children & 2 sels. from 10 Easy Pieces — Hungaroton 6-▲ HCD 12326/31 (m) [ADD]

Rübsam, Wolfgang (org)
Alain, J.:Org Music (comp) — Bayer 2-▲ CD 100198/99 [DDD]
Bach, J.S.:Canonic Vars on "Von Himmel hoch..." [at the Taylor & Boody Organ, Holy Cross College, Worcester MA] *(rec June 21-22, 1993)* — Naxos ▲ 8.550927 [DDD]
Bach, J.S.:Chorale Preludes Org—BWV 537, 538, 545, 572 & 645-650 *(rec St. Michael's Church, Eutin, Germany, July 1988)* — Naxos ▲ 8.553150 [DDD]
Bach, J.S.:Chorale Settings, BWV 651-668 [at the Taylor & Boody Organ, Holy Cross College, Worcester MA] *(rec June 21-22, 1993)* — Naxos ▲ 8.550901 [DDD]
Bach, J.S.:Chorale Settings, BWV 651-668 [at the Taylor & Boody Organ, Holy Cross College, Worcester MA]—BWV 659-668 *(rec June 21-22, 1993)* — Naxos ▲ 8.550927 [DDD]
Bach, J.S.:Clavier-Übung III [at the Gottfried Silbermann Organ, Freiberg Cathedral, Germany]—BWV 552, 669-681 *(rec July 11-12, 1993)* — Naxos ▲ 8.550929 [DDD]
Bach, J.S.:Clavier-Übung III [at the Gottfried Silbermann Organ, Freiberg Cathedral, Germany]—BWV 552, 682-689 & 802-805 *(rec July 11-12, 1993)* — Naxos ▲ 8.550930 [DDD]
Bach, J.S.:Org Music (misc)—Toccata & Fugue in d, BWV 565; Fugue in g, BWV 578; Prelude & Fugue in E♭, BWV 552; Jesu bleibet meine Freude [w. Bertalan Hock (org)]; Toccata, Adagio & Fugue, BWV 564; Ich ruf' zu dir, Herr Jesu Christ; Passacaglia & Fugue, BWV 582 — Naxos ▲ 8.553859 [DDD]
Bach, J.S.:Partite diverse sopra *Sei gegrüsset, Jesu gütig* *(rec Apr 28-30 1992)* — Naxos ▲ 8.550704 [DDD]
Bach, J.S.:Passacaglia & Fugue Org *(rec Apr 28-30 1992)* — Naxos ▲ 8.550704 [DDD]
Bach, J.S.:Pastorale Org, BWV 590 — Naxos ▲ 8.550184 [DDD]
Bach, J.S.:Preludes & Fugues, BWV 531-552—in A, BWV 536; in G, BWV 541; in g, BWV 542; in a, BWV 544; in c, BWV 546 *(rec Nov 1989)* — Naxos ▲ 8.550652 [DDD]
Bach, J.S.:Preludes & Fugues, BWV 531-552—in a BWV 543 *(rec Nov 1989)* — Naxos ▲ 8.550651 [DDD]
Bach, J.S.:Preludes & Fugues, BWV 531-552—BWV 532, 548, 552 — Naxos ▲ 8.550184 [DDD]
Bach, J.S.:Preludes & Fugues, BWV 531-552—BWV 547 *(rec Nov 1989)* — Naxos ▲ 8.550653 [DDD]
Bach, J.S.:Toccata, Adagio & Fugue Org, BWV 564 [at the Taylor & Boody Organ, Holy Cross College, Worcester MA] *(rec June 21-22, 1993)* — Naxos ▲ 8.550901 [DDD]
Bach, J.S.:Toccata & Fugue Org, BWV 565 — Naxos ▲ 8.550184 [DDD]
Bach, J.S.:Trans Org [at the Flentrop Organ, St. Mark's Cathedral, Seattle WA]—Con. in C, BWV 594 [arr. from Vivaldi's Gross mogul Con. in D, R.208]; Con. in a, BWV 593 [arr. from Vivaldi's Con. in a, R.522]; Aria in F, BWV 587 [trans. from Couperin] — Naxos ▲ 8.550936 [DDD]
Bach, J.S.:Trio Sons Org, BWV 525-530—BWV 525-527 *(rec Nov 1989)* — Naxos ▲ 8.550651 [DDD]
Bach, J.S.:Trio Sons Org, BWV 525-530—BWV 528-530 *(rec Nov 1989)* — Naxos ▲ 8.550653 [DDD]
Famous Organ Works *(rec Warner Concert Hall, Oberlin College, Aug 1988)* — Naxos 4-▲ 8.504014 [DDD]

Rübsam, Wolfgang (pno)
Bach, J.S.:The Art of the Fugue (sels)—Contrapunctii 1-12, 14 & 15 *(rec Apr 28-30, 1992)* — Naxos ▲ 8.550703 [DDD]
Bach, J.S.:The Art of the Fugue (sels)—Contrapunctii 13, 17, 18 & 19 *(rec Apr 28-30, 1992)* — Naxos ▲ 8.550704 [DDD]
Bach, J.S.:Capriccio Departure *(rec May 1992)* — Naxos ▲ 8.550692
Bach, J.S.:Chromatic Fant & Fugue *(rec Clara Wieck Auditorium, Heidelberg, Nov 1991)* — Naxos ▲ 8.550709 [DDD]
Bach, J.S.:Clavier-Büchlein for W. F. Bach—Partia di Signore Steltzeln, BWV 929; Allemande, BWV 836; Menuets in G, BWV 841-843; (From 9 Little Preludes, BWV 924-930); Präludien, BWV 847-851 & BWV 853-857; Fuga à 3 in C, BWV 953; Suite in A, BWV 824 *(rec Orum Hall, Valparaiso, IN, Sept. & Oct. 1994)* — Naxos ▲ 8.553097 [DDD]
Bach, J.S.:Inventions (30) Hpd *(rec Orum Hall, Valparaiso, Indiana, Oct.-Nov. 1993)* — Naxos ▲ 8.550960 [DDD]
Bach, J.S.:Partitas Hpd, BWV 825-830—Nos. 1 & 2 *(rec May 1992)* — Naxos ▲ 8.550692
Bach, J.S.:Partitas Hpd, BWV 825-830—Nos. 3 & 4 *(rec May 1992)* — Naxos ▲ 8.550693
Bach, J.S.:Partitas Hpd, BWV 825-830—Nos. 5 & 6 *(rec May 1992)* — Naxos ▲ 8.550694
Bach, J.S.:Prelude & Fughetta Hpd—Nos. 1 & 2 *(rec May 1992)* — Naxos ▲ 8.550692
Bach, J.S.:Preludes Hpd, BWV 939-43, "Little Preludes" *(rec Orum Hall, Valparaiso, Indiana, U.S.A., Sep. & Oct. 1994)* — Naxos ▲ 8.553097 [DDD]
Bach, J.S.:Toccatas Hpd, BWV 910-16—BWV 910, 911, 912, 913, 914, 915, 916 *(rec Sept 1989)* — Naxos ▲ 8.550708 [DDD]

Ruby, P. (gtr)
Rossé, F.:Music of, w. Y. Haym (ob), M. Michalakakos (va), C. Roy (vc), I. Assayag (hpd)—Zembrocordal; Digitales; Lance du Souvenant; Impromptu 0990; For a Little Hot Quaint Time — Quantum ▲ QM 6949

Rückert, Hans (trbn)
Guyonnet, J.:La Cantate interrompue, w. F. Rochaix (nar), S. Stenhammar (sop), S. Seban (pno), G. Calame (pno), E. Séjourne (perc), P. Geiss, E. Tarr (tpt), B. Nilsson (tpt), H. Ries (trbn), J.-M. Collet, J. Guyonnet (cnd), Geneva Collegium Academicum [F] *(rec Nov. 15, 1986)* — Grammont ▲ CTSP 30-2

Rudd, Will (tpt/flgl)
Bernstein, L.:Dance Suite Chamber Ensemble, w. Bob Thompson (tpt/flgl), Alex Shuhan (hn/pno), Mark Kellogg (trbn/eup), Charles Villarrubia (tuba), David Gluck (dr/perc) *(rec Cliff Temple Baptist Church, Dallas, TX)* — D'Note Classics ▲ DND 1007 [DDD]
Corea, C.:Children's Songs, w. Bob Thompson (tpt/flgl), Alex Shuhan (hn/pno), Mark Kellogg (trbn/eup), Charles Villarrubia (tuba), David Gluck (dr/perc)—Nos 6 & 11 [arr Gluck/Shuhan] *(rec Cliff Temple Baptist Church, Dallas, TX)* — D'Note Classics ▲ DND 1007 [DDD]
Gershwin, G.:Porgy & Bess (sels), w. Bob Thompson (tpt/flgl), Alex Shuhan (hn/pno), Mark Kellogg (trbn/eup), Charles Villarrubia (tuba), David Gluck (dr/perc)—Summertime [arr Thompson] *(rec Cliff Temple Baptist Church, Dallas, TX)* — D'Note Classics ▲ DND 1007 [DDD]
Gluck, C.W.:Nicole, w. Bob Thompson (tpt/flgl), Alex Shuhan (hn/pno), Mark Kellogg (trbn/eup), Charles Villarrubia (tuba), David Gluck (dr/perc) *(rec Cliff Temple Baptist Church, Dallas, TX)* — D'Note Classics ▲ DND 1007 [DDD]
Khachaturian, A.:Gayane (suites), w. Bob Thompson (tpt/flgl), Alex Shuhan (hn/pno), Mark Kellogg (trbn/eup), Charles Villarrubia (tuba), David Gluck (dr/perc)—Sabre Dance [arr Gluck]; Lullaby; Dance of the Rose Maidens [both arr Villarrubia] *(rec Cliff Temple Baptist Church, Dallas, TX)* — D'Note Classics ▲ DND 1007 [DDD]
McCarthy, D.:American Dance Music, w. Bob Thompson (tpt/flgl), Alex Shuhan (hn/pno), Mark Kellogg (trbn/eup), Charles Villarrubia (tuba), David Gluck (dr/perc) *(rec Cliff Temple Baptist Church, Dallas, TX)* — D'Note Classics ▲ DND 1007 [DDD]

Rudd, Will (tpt/flgl) (cont.)
Scheidt, S.:Instr Music, w. Bob Thompson (tpt/flgl), Alex Shuhan (hn/pno), Mark Kellogg (trbn/eup), Charles Villarrubia (tuba), David Gluck (dr/perc)—Centone No. 5 [trans Verne Reynolds] *(rec Cliff Temple Baptist Church, Dallas, TX)* — D'Note Classics ▲ DND 1007 [DDD]

Ruddock, Gerald (tpt)
Vivaldi, A.:Con for 2 Tpts, w. G. Ashton (tpt), C. Warren-Green (cnd), London CO — Virgin Classics ▲ 59609 [DDD]

Rudel, Julius (pno/org)
Puccini, G.:Songs, w. P. Domingo (ten)—A te; Vexilla; Salve Regina Ad una morta; Mentia l'avviso; Storiella d'amore; Sole e amore; Avanti Urania; Inno a Diana; E l'uccellino; Terra e mare (performing both autograph & published versions); Canto d'anime; Casa mia, casa mia; Morire?; Inno a Roma [I] — CBS ▲ MK 44981 [DDD]
Songs of Inspiration, w. Kiri Te Kanawa (sop), Utah SO, Mormon Tabernacle Choir — London ▲ 425431-2 LH [DDD]

Rudiakov, Ariel (va)—see ORCHESTRAS & ENSEMBLES Manchester Chamber Players

Rudiakov, Michael (vc)—see ORCHESTRAS & ENSEMBLES Contemporary Chamber Players
Cello Charms, w. R. Levy (pno) *(rec Marlboro, VT, May 1993)* — Centaur ▲ CRC 2192 [DDD]
Pousseur, H.:Chants sacrés, w. Valarie Lamoree (sop), Eric Rosenblith (vn), Jacob Glick (va) — Vox Box 2-▲ CDX 5144

Rudiakov, Shoshana (pno)
Hindemith, P.:Son E Hn, w. Lajos Lencses (E hn) — CPO ▲ CPO 999332
Hindemith, P.:Son Ob, w. Lajos Lencses (ob) — CPO ▲ CPO 999332
Hindemith, P.:Trio Pno, w. Gunter Teuffel (va), Lajos Lencses (heckelphone) — CPO ▲ CPO 999332

Rudich, Rachel (fl)
Felder, D.:Music of, w. June in Buffalo CO, American Brass Quintet, Arditti String Quartet—Journal; Canzone XXXI; November Sky; 3rd Face; 3 Lines from 20 Poems — Bridge ▲ BCD 9049 [DDD]
Harrison, L.:Ariadne, w. K. Grossman (perc) — CRI ▲ CD 568 [DDD]
Harrison, L.:Con 1 Fl, w. K. Grossman (perc) — CRI ▲ CD 568 [DDD]
Melby, J.:Con 1 Fl & Tape — Centaur ▲ CRC 2110 [DDD]
Sollberger, H.:Double Triptych, w. K. Grossman (perc) — CRI ▲ CD 568 [DDD]
Sueyoshi, Y.:Correspondence V, w. K. Grossman (perc) — CRI ▲ CD 568 [DDD]
Trombly, P.:Duo Fl, w. K. Grossman (perc) — CRI ▲ CD 568 [DDD]
Trombly, P.:Trio in 3 Mvts, w. K. Grossman (perc), S. Macchia (db) — CRI ▲ CD 568 [DDD]

Rudie, Robert (vn)
Colgrass, M.:Concert Masters, w. Ronald Oakland (vn), Masako Yanagita (vn), K. Akiyama (cnd), American SO *(rec 1977)* — Vox Box ("The American Composers" series) 2-▲ CDX 5158

Rudin, Alexander (vc)
Haydn, J.:Con 1 Vc, w. S. Sondeckis (cnd), Lithuanian CO — Allegretto ▲ ACD 8186 [ADD] ■ ACS 8186
Haydn, J.:Con 2 Vc, w. S. Sondeckis (cnd), Lithuanian CO — Allegretto ▲ ACD 8186 [ADD] ■ ACS 8186
Tchaikovsky, P.:Nocturne Vc, w. N. Alexeiev (cnd), Musica Viva Ensemble — Russian Season ▲ LDC 2888082
Tchaikovsky, P.:Pezzo capriccioso, w. N. Alexeiev (cnd), Musica Viva Ensemble — Russian Season ▲ LDC 2888082
Tchaikovsky, P.:Serenade Strs, w. N. Alexeiev (cnd), Musica Viva Ensemble — Russian Season ▲ LDC 2888082
Tchaikovsky, P.:Vars on a Rococo Theme, w. N. Alexeiev (cnd), Musica Viva Ensemble — Russian Season ▲ LDC 2888082
Tcherepnin, A.:Rhap géorgienne, w. A. Rudin (cnd), Musica Viva CO — Olympia ▲ OLY 584 [DDD]

Rudner, Ola (vn)
Blomdahl, K.-B.:Con Vn, w. S. Westerberg (cnd), Helsingborg SO — MAP ▲ MAPCD 9024
Mendelssohn, F.:Con in d Vn, Pno & Strs, w. P. Entremont (pno), Vienna CO — Koch Schwann ▲ CD 311047 [DDD] ■ MC 211047 (D)
Viotti, G.B.:Con 3 Pno, w. P. Entremont (pno), Vienna CO — Koch Schwann ▲ CD 311047 [DDD] ■ MC 211047 (D)

Rudnytsky, Roman (pno)
Pianistic Portraits — Dana Recording Project ▲ DRP 3 [DDD]

Rudolf, Anfrás (va)—see ORCHESTRAS & ENSEMBLES Haydn String Quartet Budapest

Rudolph, Kathleen (fl)
Frumerie, G. de:Pastoral Suite, w. *(harpist unknown)*, M. Bernardi (cnd), CBC Vancouver SO *(rec Orpheum, Vancouver, British Columbia, Mar 1-2, 1992)* — CBC ▲ SMCD 5157 [DDD]
Pastorales de Noël, w. Rita Costanzi (hp), V. Costanzi (vn), Jesse Read (bn) — Skylark ▲ 9400 [DDD]
Silver Sounds for Flute, w. Kathleen Rudolph (fl), Rena Sharon (pno) — Musica Viva ▲ MVCD 1069 [DDD]

Rudolph, Pierre-Paul (gtr)
Everts, A.:Agua con Gas, w. Heriberto Cavalcante Porto (fl) *(rec Studio MOGNO, Belgium, May & June 1995)* — René Gailly ▲ CD 87128 [DDD]
Falú, E.:Chôro, w. Heriberto Cavalcante Porto (fl) *(rec Studio MOGNO, Belgium, May & June 1995)* — René Gailly ▲ CD 87128 [DDD]
Machado, C.:Brazilian Folk Themes, w. Heriberto Cavalcante Porto (fl) *(rec Studio MOGNO, Belgium, May & June 1995)* — René Gailly ▲ CD 87128 [DDD]
Piazzolla, A.:Études tanguistiques, w. Heriberto Cavalcante Porto (fl)—No. 4 *(rec Studio MOGNO, Belgium, May & June 1995)* — René Gailly ▲ CD 87128 [DDD]
Piazzolla, A.:Histoire du Tango, w. Heriberto Cavalcante Porto (fl) *(rec Studio MOGNO, Belgium, May & June 1995)* — René Gailly ▲ CD 87128 [DDD]
Riera, R.:Prélude Créole, w. Heriberto Cavalcante Porto (fl) *(rec Studio MOGNO, Belgium, May & June 1995)* — René Gailly ▲ CD 87128 [DDD]
Sardinha, A.A.:Chôro triste, w. Heriberto Cavalcante Porto (fl) *(rec Studio MOGNO, Belgium, May & June 1995)* — René Gailly ▲ CD 87128 [DDD]
Senanes, G.:Don Mondongo, w. Heriberto Cavalcante Porto (fl) *(rec Studio MOGNO, Belgium, May & June 1995)* — René Gailly ▲ CD 87128 [DDD]

Rudolph, Ralf (tuba)
Arnold, M.:Qnt Brass, w. Uwe Zaiser (tpt), Peter Leiner (tpt), Sjön Scott (hn), Jochen Scheerer (trbn) — Bayer ▲ BR 100251 [DDD]
Crespo, E.:Suite Americana 1, w. Uwe Zaiser (tpt), Peter Leiner (tpt), Sjön Scott (hn), Jochen Scheerer (trbn) — Bayer ▲ BR 100251 [DDD]
Ewald, V.:Qnt 1 Brass, w. Peter Leiner (tpt), Uwe Zaiser (tpt), Sjön Scott (hn), Jochen Scheerer (trbn) — Bayer ▲ BR 100251 [DDD]
Horovitz, J.:Music Hall Suite, w. Uwe Zaiser (tpt), Peter Leiner (tpt), Sjön Scott (hn), Jochen Scheerer (trbn) — Bayer ▲ BR 100251 [DDD]
Koetsier, J.:Qnt Brass, w. Peter Leiner (tpt), Uwe Zaiser (tpt), Sjön Scott (hn), Jochen Scheerer (posaune) — Bayer ▲ BR 100251 [DDD]

Rudometkin, Yuri (bn)
Schnittke, A.:Hymns Vc, w. A. Ivashkin (vc), I. Pashinskaya (hp), V. Barsalkin (db), V. Chasovennaya (hpd), V. Grishin, N. Grishin (perc/bells)—No. 1 for Cello, Harp & Timpani [Quasi andante]; No. 2 for Cello & Double *(rec National Radio House, Moscow, 1987)* — Vox Box 2-▲ CDX 5121 [ADD]

Rudy, Mikhail (pno)
Brahms, J.:Pieces Pno, Op. 76 — EMI Classics ▲ CDC 54233
Brahms, J.:Rhaps Pno, Op. 79 — EMI Classics ▲ CDC 54233
Brahms, J.:Scherzo Vn, w. V. Spivakov (vn) — RCA Red Seal ▲ 09026-61390-2 [DDD]
Brahms, J.:Sons Vn (comp), w. V. Spivakov (vn) — RCA Red Seal ▲ 09026-61390-2 [DDD]
Brahms, J.:Waltzes Pno, Op. 39 — EMI Classics ▲ CDC 54233
Janácek, L.:Cappriccio, w. C. Mackerras (cnd), Paris Opera Orch — EMI Classics ▲ CDC 55585
Janácek, L.:Concertino Pno, w. C. Mackerras (cnd), Paris Opera Orch — EMI Classics ▲ CDC 55585
Janácek, L.:Presto, w. Gary Hoffman (vc) — EMI Classics ▲ CDC 55585
Janácek, L.:Son October 1, 1905 Pno — EMI Classics ▲ CDC 54094 [DDD]
Rachmaninoff, S.:Con 1 Pno, w. M. Jansons (cnd), St. Petersburg PO — EMI Classics ▲ CDC 55188
Rachmaninoff, S.:Con 2 Pno, w. M. Jansons (cnd), Leningrad PO — EMI Classics ▲ CDC 54232
Rachmaninoff, S.:Con 3 Pno, w. M. Jansons (cnd), St. Petersburg PO — EMI Classics ▲ CDC 54880
Rachmaninoff, S.:Con 4 Pno, w. M. Jansons (cnd), St. Petersburg PO — EMI Classics ▲ CDC 55188

Rudy, Mikhail (pno) (cont.)
Rachmaninoff, S.:Rhapsody on a Theme of Paganini, w. M. Jansons (cnd), St. Petersburg PO
EMI Classics ▲ CDC 54880
Saint-Saëns, C.:Carnival of the Animals, w. T. Barto (pno), M. Plasson (cnd), Toulouse Capitole Orch
EMI Classics 2-▲ CDC 54465
Scriabin, A.:Dances Pno — Calliope ▲ CAL 9692 [ADD]
Scriabin, A.:Etudes Pno, Op. 65 — Calliope ▲ CAL 9692 [ADD]
Scriabin, A.:Poèmes Pno, Op. 69 — Calliope ▲ CAL 9692 [ADD]
Scriabin, A.:Poèmes Pno, Op. 71 — Calliope ▲ CAL 9692 [ADD]
Scriabin, A.:Preludes Pno, Op. 67 — Calliope ▲ CAL 9692 [ADD]
Scriabin, A.:Preludes Pno, Op. 74 — Calliope ▲ CAL 9692 [ADD]
Scriabin, A.:Son 8 Pno — Calliope ▲ CAL 9692 [ADD]
Scriabin, A.:Son 9 Pno — Calliope ▲ CAL 9692 [ADD]
Scriabin, A.:Son 10 Pno — Calliope ▲ CAL 9692 [ADD]
Scriabin, A.:Vers la flamme — Calliope ▲ CAL 9692 [ADD]
Shostakovich, D.:Con 1 Pno, w. Ole Edvard Antonsen (tpt), M. Jansons (cnd), Berlin PO
EMI Classics ▲ CDC 55361
Tchaikovsky, P.:Con 1 Pno, w. M. Jansons (cnd), Leningrad PO — EMI Classics ▲ CDC 54232

Ruede, C. (vc)
Franchomme, A.:Caprices, Op. 7 — Koch International Classics ▲ KIC 7226 [DDD]
Franchomme, A.:Études, Op. 35 — Koch International Classics ▲ KIC 7226 [DDD]

Rueff, David (tuba)
Curran, A.:Crystal Psalms, An Homage to Kristallnacht, w. F. Badaloni (cl), D. Keberlee (cl), M. Riesler (cl), A. Santoloci (cl), M. Capone (acc), L. Dublanchet (tuba), A. Caggiano (perc), w. Ensemble Vocale Sesquialtera [cnd:E. Razzicchia], Radio France Chamber Choir [cnd:D. LaBorde]—[F]
New Albion ▲ NA 067

Ruf, Hugo (hpd)
Telemann, G.P.:Kleine Kammermusik, w. Hans-Martin Linde (fl), Ferdinand Conrad (rcr), Helmut Winschermann (ob), Susanne Lautenbacher (vn), Johannes Koch (vl) *(rec Südwest-Tonstudio H. Jansen, Stuttgart, Jan. 1966)* — Musicaphon ▲ 51539 [ADD]

Ruge, T. (vc)
Lachner, F.P.:Nonet, w. A. Duisberg (fl), D. Wollenweber (ob), P. Prieditis (cl), P. Douglas (hn), M. Postinghel (bn), I. Grünkorn (vn), M. Gieler (va), F. Heidenreich (db) *(rec June 10, 1991)*
Thorofon ▲ CTH 2132 [DDD]
Rheinberger, J.:Son Vc, w. H. Göbel (pno) — Thorofon 6-▲ BCTH 2161/6
Rheinberger, J.:Son Vc, w. H. Göbel (pno) — Thorofon ▲ CTH 2108 [DDD]

Ruhland, Martin (mar)
Orff, C.:Schulwerk (complete), w. Godela Orff (nar), Carolin Widmann (vn), Sonja Korkeala (vn), Markus Zahnhausen (rcr), Karl Peinkofer (perc), Andreas Schumacher (perc), Wilfried Hiller (perc/mar), Munich Hochschule Madrigal Choir—Wessobrun Prayer for a capella Choir; 2 Pieces for a capella Choir; 8 Pieces for 2 Vns; Mater et filia for women's a capella Choir; Devotional Yodel for male a capella Choir; 5 Pieces for Sop, Rcr & Perc; Death for Nar., Wood Bells, Bass Xyl & Tam-Tam; Omnia tempus habent for mixed Choir, Timp & Little Dr; Rubato, molto allegro, rubato; Abenlied for Nar, Bass Metallophon, Bass Xyl, Large Dr & Wine Glass; 5 Pieces for Fl & Perc; Devotional Yodel for male Choir [version 2]; 7 Pieces for 2 Xyl *(rec Munich, 1994–95)* — Celestial Harmonies ▲ 13105-2

Ruhrseitz, Kurt (pno)
The Art of Joseph Szigeti, Vol. 1, w. Joseph Szigeti (vn) — Biddulph 2-▲ LAB 005-6 (m) [AAD]
Bloch, E.:Nigun, w. J. Szigeti (vn) *(rec 1928 for Columbia Records)* — Pearl ▲ PEA 9938 (m) [AAD]
Tartini, G.:Sons Vn & Continuo, w. Joseph Szigeti (vn)—in G — Iron Needle ▲ 1321 [AAD]
Tartini, G.:Sons Vn & Continuo, w. Joseph Szigeti (vn)—No. 12 in G, Op. 2
Grammofono 2000 ▲ GRM 78630

Ruijsenaars, Harro (vc)
Mozart, W.A.:Andantino Vc, w. R. Pöntinen (pno) — Canal Grande ▲ CCS 9325 [DDD]
Schubert, Franz:Son Arpeggione, w. R. Pöntinen (pno) — Canal Grande ▲ CCS 9325 [DDD]
Schumann, R.:Adagio & Allegro Hn, w. R. Pöntinen (pno) — Canal Grande ▲ CCS 9325 [DDD]
Schumann, R.:Fantasiestücke Cl, w. R. Pöntinen (pno) — Canal Grande ▲ CCS 9325 [DDD]

Ruiz, Adrian (pno)
Burgmüller, N.:Son Pno — Genesis ▲ GCD 108 [ADD]
Goetz, H.:Genrebilder — Genesis ▲ GCD 107 [ADD]
Goetz, H.:Lose Blätter — Genesis ▲ GCD 107 [ADD]
Goetz, H.:Sonatinas Pno, Op. 8 — Genesis ▲ GCD 107 [ADD]
Grieg, E.:Sons Vn, Opp. 8, 13 & 45, w. Arnold Belnick (vn) *(rec May 1993)*
Cambria ▲ CD 1076 [DDD]
Kirchner, T.:Pno Music—Aquarellen, Op. 21/3; Moderato, Op. 30/8; Allegro con passione, Op. 30/17; Moderato, Op. 71/100; Spring-Greeting, Op. 73/2; Days Gone By, Op. 73/4; Romanze, Op. 73/6; Nocturne, Op. 73/12; Elegy, Op. 73/16 — Genesis ▲ GCD 108 [ADD]
Rheinberger, J.:Con Pno, w. Z. Deáky (cnd), Nuremberg SO — Genesis ▲ GCD 106 [ADD]
Rubinstein, A.:Con 5 Pno, w. Z. Deáky (cnd), Nuremberg SO — Genesis ▲ GCD 103 [ADD]
Sgambati, G.:Con Pno, w. Z. Deáky (cnd), Nuremberg SO — Genesis ▲ GCD 106 [ADD]
Volkmann, R.:Fant Pno — Genesis ▲ GCD 108 [ADD]
Volkmann, R.:Son Pno — Genesis ▲ GCD 108 [ADD]

Ruiz, Gonzalo X. (ob)
Handel, G.F.:Sons Ob, w. Michael Eagan (archlt), Shelley Taylor (vc), Kathy Shao (hpd/org)—in B♭, after HWV 365; in g, HWV 364; in d, HWV 359a; in B♭, HWV 357; in a, after HWV 367b; in F, HWV 363a; in c, HWV 366 — Well-Tempered ▲ WTP 5174 [DDD]

Ruiz, Norman (gtr)
Albéniz, I.:Gtr Music—Cádiz; Mallorca; Oriental; Rumores de la Caleta (Malagueña); Zambra Granadina *(rec Audio Tech Center of Columbia College, Chicago, Apr & May 1995)* — Centaur ▲ 2279 [DDD]
Granados, E.:Danzas españolas (10)—No. 10 *(rec Audio Tech Center of Columbia College, Chicago, Apr & May 1995)* — Centaur ▲ 2279 [DDD]
Maláts, J.:Serenata Andaluza *(rec Audio Tech Center of Columbia College, Chicago, Apr & May 1995)*
Centaur ▲ 2279 [DDD]
Maláts, J.:Serenata Española *(rec Audio Tech Center of Columbia College, Chicago, Apr & May 1995)*
Centaur ▲ 2279 [DDD]
Moreno Torroba, F.:Gtr Music—Coplilla; Jerigonza; La llega el invierno; La Pastora; Seguidilla *(rec Audio Tech Center of Columbia College, Chicago, Apr & May 1995)* — Centaur ▲ 2279 [DDD]
Rodrigo, J.:En los trigales *(rec Audio Tech Center of Columbia College, Chicago, Apr & May 1995)*
Centaur ▲ 2279 [DDD]

Rukuda, Riko (pno)
Pinto, G.F.:Fant & Son Pno — Olympia ▲ OLY 494 [AAD]
Pinto, G.F.:A Grand Son Pno — Olympia ▲ OLY 494 [AAD]
Pinto, G.F.:Grand Sons Pno, Op. 3 — Olympia ▲ OLY 494 [AAD]

Rulon, C. B. (syn)—see ORCHESTRAS & ENSEMBLES First Avenue

Rumer, Walter (db)—see ORCHESTRAS & ENSEMBLES Innsbruck Salon Quintet

Rumessen, Vardo (pno)
Tubin, E.:Pno Music (comp) — BIS 3-▲ CD 414/16 [DDD]
Tubin, E.:Va & Pno Music, w. P. Vahle (va)—Sonata for Alto Saxophone & Piano [version for viola & piano] (1951); Sonata for Viola & Piano (1965) — BIS 2-▲ CD 541/42 [DDD]
Tubin, E.:Vn & Pno Music, w. A. Leibur (va)—Ballade (1939); Capriccio No. 1 (1937/1971); Capriccio No. 2 (1945); The Cock's Dance (1957–8); Meditation (1938); Prelude (1944); Sonata No. 1 (1934–36/1968–9); Sonata No. 2 (1949); Suite on Estonian Dances (1943); Three Pieces (1933)
BIS 2-▲ CD 541/42 [DDD]

Rumetsch, Artur (mand)
Music for Lute, Guitar & Mandolin, w. Konrad Ragossnig (gtr), Anton Stingl (lt), Michael Schäffer (lt), Karl Scheit (gtr), Leo Witoszinskyj (gtr), William Matthews (gtr), Paul Grund (mand), Edith Bauer-Slais (mand), Elfriede Kunschak (mand) — Vox Box 3-▲ CD3X 3022

Rumpel, Günter (fl)
Bach, J.C.:Sinfs, Op. 6, w. A. Raoult (ob), R. Tschupp (cnd), Zurich Camerata *(rec 1969, 1981)*
Jecklin ▲ J 4408 [ADD]

Rumpel, Günter (fl) (cont.)
Czerny, C.:Duo concertant, w. S. Andres (pno) *(rec 1977)* — Jecklin ▲ J 44102 [ADD]
Donizetti, G.:Son Fl & Pno, w. S. Andres (pno) *(rec 1977)* — Jecklin ▲ J 44102 [ADD]
Kreutzer, C.:Son Concertante, w. S. Andres (pno) *(rec 1977)* — Jecklin ▲ J 44102 [ADD]
Krommer, F.:Concertino Fl, Op. 65, w. A. Raoult (ob), R. Tschupp (cnd), Zurich Camerata *(rec 1969, 1981)* — Jecklin ▲ J 4408 [ADD]
Mieg, P.:Septet, w. Peter Solomon (hpd), Simon Fuchs (ob), Primroz Novsak (vn), Marius Ungareanu (va), Carolyn Hopkins Marti (vc), Ronald Dangel (db) *(rec 1993)* — Jecklin ▲ JS 314-2 [DDD]
Rossini, G.:Andante & Allegro Fl, w. S. Andres (pno) *(rec 1977)* — Jecklin ▲ J 44102 [ADD]
Rossini, G.:Fant Cl, w. S. Andres (pno) [arr flute] *(rec 1977)* — Jecklin ▲ J 44102 [ADD]
Vanhal, J.B.:Sym in g, w. A. Raoult (ob), R. Tschupp (cnd), Zurich Camerata *(rec 1969, 1981)*
Jecklin ▲ J 4408 [ADD]
Wehrli, W.:Sinfonietta Fl, w. S. Andres (pno), D. Schmid (cnd), Southern Bohemian Chamber PO Budweis *(rec 1993)* — Jecklin ▲ JS 297-2

Rundel, Peter (vn)
Zimmermann, B.A.:Présence, w. Hermann Kretzschmar (pno), Michael Stirling (vc) *(rec Frankfurt, May 1–4 & Oct 24–25, 1992)* — RCA Red Seal ▲ 09026-61181-2 [DDD]

Runge, Eckart (vc)
Brahms, J.:Songs, w. Peter Winhardt (pno)—Liebestreu [arr E. Runge for cello & piano]
Ars Musici ▲ AMP 5061-2 [DDD]
Debussy, C.:Son Vc, w. Peter Winhardt (pno) — Ars Musici ▲ AMP 5061-2 [DDD]
Dutilleux, H.:Strophes (3) sur le nom Sacher — Ars Musici ▲ AMP 5061-2 [DDD]
Fauré, G.:Papillon, w. Peter Winhardt (pno) — Ars Musici ▲ AMP 5061-2 [DDD]
Messiaen, O.:Quatour, w. Peter Winhardt (pno) [5th movt, "The Glorification of Jesus' Eternity"]
Ars Musici ▲ AMP 5061-2 [DDD]
Schumann, R.:Fantasiestücke Cl, w. Peter Winhardt (pno) — Ars Musici ▲ AMP 5061-2 [DDD]
Strauss, R.:Son Vc, w. Peter Winhardt (pno) — Ars Musici ▲ AMP 5061-2 [DDD]

Running, Arne (cl)—see ORCHESTRAS & ENSEMBLES Penn Contemporary Players

Rupert, Mary Jane (pno)
The Maestros Tea Party:Mr. Einstein Visits the Queen, w. Diana Salomon (vn), Patricia Wenzel (vn), Ella Lou Weiler (va), Fern Meyers (vc), Gerhard Finkenbeiner (glass armonica), Vera Meyer (glass armonica) *(rec Euphoria Sound Studio, Revere, MA)* — Cultured Kids ▲ unknown ■ 120012FM-4

Rupert, Sally (pno)—see ORCHESTRAS & ENSEMBLES Bowed Piano Ensemble

Rupo, Roberto (pno)
Albanese, G.:Songs, w. Luana Gentile (sop), Antonella Trovarelli (sop), Marina Gentile (mez), Stefano Consolini (ten), Paolo Speca (bar), Andrea De Mele (vn), Sirio Benedetto (sax)—Aria di Natale; Duettino e coro muto (w. Carlo Moreno) [both w. Giorgina Dell'Immagine, Tito Petralia (cnd), EIAR Orch & Chorus]; Passione (M. Gentile); Serenata (Speca); Alzati, o bella... (Trovarelli); Mattinata (Speca); Il sogno d'una suora (Trovarelli); Ninna Nanna (M. Gentile); Barcarola (Rupo); Madrigale (L. Gentile); Ninna nanna...900 (L. Gentile); Variazioni (L. Gentile); Non so qual io mi voglia... (L. Gentile); Io sono un augellin... (L. Gentile); Bravo, bene, bis...(va bene) (Consolini & Di Benedetto); Che caviale (Consolini); Ma non sapete chi sono io? (Consolini & L. & M. Gentile); Grappoli di stelle (Consolini); Notte di Capri (Consolini & Di Mele); Una rosa di ferro battuto (Consolini, Speca & L. & M. Gentile) *(rec Ortona, Teatro Zambra)* — Bongiovanni ▲ GB 5054-2 [DDD]

Rupp, Franz (pno)
Beethoven, L. van:Sons Vn (comp), w. F. Kreisler (vn)—Nos. 8 & 9 *(rec 1935 for HMV)*
Pearl ▲ PEA 9395 (m) [AAD]
Beethoven, L. van:Sons Vn (comp), w. F. Kreisler (vn)—Nos. 7 & 10 *(rec 1935 for HMV)*
Pearl ▲ PEA 9400 (m) [AAD]
Beethoven, L. van:Sons Vn (comp), w. F. Kreisler (vn)—Nos. 4–6 *(rec 1935 for HMV)*
Pearl ▲ PEA 9354 (m) [AAD]
Beethoven, L. van:Sons Vn (comp), w. F. Kreisler (vn)—Nos. 1–3 *(rec 1935 for HMV)*
Pearl ▲ PEA 9330 (m) [AAD]
The Voices of Living Stereo, Vol. 2, w. Eileen Farrell (sop), Birgit Nilsson (sop), Roberta Peters (sop), Leontyne Price (sop), Galina Vishnevskaya (sop), Rosalind Elias (mez), Shirley Verrett (mez), Marian Anderson (cta), Maureen Forrester (cta), Sergio Franchi (ten), Mario Lanza (ten), Richard Lewis (ten), Jan Pee, Alexander Dedyukhin (pno), Leo Taubman (pno), George Trovillo (pno), Charles Wadsworth (pno), Boston Pops Orch [cnd:Arthur Fiedler], Boston SO [cnd:Charles Munch], Chicago SO [cnd:Fritz Reiner], RCA Victor Orch, RCA Victor Chorus, et. al. *(rec Boston & Chicago & New York & Rome, 1957–1964)* — RCA Living Stereo ▲ 09026-68167-2 [ADD]

Rupp, Franz (pno/org)
Heinrich Sclusnus Liederalbum, w. Heinrich Schlusnus (bar), Hermann Weigert (cnd), Alois Melichar (cnd), Berlin State Opera Orch *(rec between 1930–34)* — Preiser 2-▲ PRE 89205 [ADD]

Rusche, Renate (b cl)
Celis, F.:Da uno a cinque — MD + G ▲ MDG 6240556
Erdmann, D.:Con B Cl — MD + G ▲ MDG 6240556
Genzmer, H.:Solo B Cl — MD + G ▲ MDG 6240556
Messiaen, O.:L'Abîme des oiseaux — MD + G ▲ MDG 6240556
Schoeck, O.:Sonata in the Late Romantic Spirit — MD + G ▲ MDG 6240556

Rushforth, Philip (org)
Stairway to Heaven, w. [cnd:Richard Marlow], Trinity College Choir Cambridge, Richard Pearce (org), Silas Standage (org) *(rec Trinity College Chapel, Cambridge)*
Conifer Classics ▲ 75605-51521-2 [DDD]

Ruske, Eric (hn)—see also ORCHESTRAS & ENSEMBLES Empire Brass Quintet
Mozart, W.A.:Cons Hn, w. C. Mackerras (cnd), Scottish CO *(rec Dec. 4–5, 1993)*
Telarc ▲ 80367 [DDD]

Ruskin, Abbott (pno)
Barber, S.:Con Pno, w. D. Epstein (cnd), MIT SO — Vox Box 2-▲ CDX 5091 [ADD]
Barber, S.:Con Pno, w. D. Epstein (cnd), MIT SO *(rec 1976)* — Vox Box 2-▲ CDX 5069 [ADD]

Rusó, Daniela (hpd)
Corelli, A.:Sons 2 Vns, Opp. 1–4 (sels), w. A. Hölbling (vn), O. Hölbling (vn), J. Slávik (vc)—Op. 1, No. 6; Op. 2, No. 4; Op. 4, No. 9 *(rec Oct. 21–23, 1990)* — Naxos ▲ 8.550619 [DDD]
Geminiani, F.:Sons (12) Vn, Vne & Hpd, w. A. Hölbling (vn), O. Hölbling (vn), J. Slávik (vc) *(rec Oct. 21–23, 1990)* — Naxos ▲ 8.550619 [DDD]
Zimmermann, A.:Sons Vn, w. B. Kucharsky (vn) — Trevak ▲ TRE 40003 [DDD]

Rusó, Daniela (pno)
Mendelssohn, F.:Lieder ohne Worte Pno — Lydian ▲ LYD 18112 [DDD]
Mendelssohn, F.:Lieder ohne Worte Pno — Lydian ▲ LYD 18113 [DDD]
Porpora, N.A.:Sinf da camera, w. A. Hölbling (vn), O. Hölbling (vn), J. Slávik (vc)—No. 6 only *(rec Oct. 21–23, 1990)* — Naxos ▲ 8.550619 [DDD]
Pugnani, G.:Trio Sons, Op. 1, w. A. Hölbling (vn), O. Hölbling (vn), J. Slávik (vc)—No. 3 *(rec Oct. 21–23, 1990)* — Naxos ▲ 8.550619 [DDD]
Schmidt, F.:Qnt Cl, w. A. Janoska (cl), F. Török (vn), A. Lakatos (va), J. Slávik (vc)
Marco Polo ▲ 8.223415
Schmidt, F.:Qnt Cl, w. A. Jánoska (cl), S. Mucha (vn), A. Lakatos (va), J. Slávik (vc)
Marco Polo ▲ 8.223414
Schmidt, F.:Romance Pno — Marco Polo ▲ 8.223415
Schmidt, F.:Toccata Pno Left-Hand — Marco Polo ▲ 8.223415

Rusó, Vladimir (hpd)
Mattheson, J.:Hpd Music — Trevak ▲ TRE 40001 [DDD]
Muffat, G.T.:Componimenti Musicali — Trevak ▲ TRE 40005 [DDD]

Rusó, Vladimir (org)
Music for Trumpet & Organ, w. Kamil Roskao (tpt) — Lydian ▲ LYD 18104 [DDD]
Vivaldi, A.:Son Vn Ob, RV.779, w. A. Hölbling (vn), O. Hölbling (vn) *(rec Oct. 21–23, 1990)*
Naxos ▲ 8.550619 [DDD]

Russell, David (gtr)
Bach, J.S.:Sons Fl, BWV 1030–35—BWV 1034 [trans. Russell] — GHA ▲ 126.034
David Russell — GHA ▲ CD 126.002

Russell, David (gtr) (cont.)
Giuliani, M.:Con 1 Gtr, w. W. Michniewski (cnd), Sinfonia Varsovia
Polskie Nagrania ▲ PNCD 103 [DDD]
Handel, G.F.:Suites Hpd [trans. for solo guitar]—Suite No. 7 GHA ▲ CD 126.006
Rodrigo, J.:Concierto de Aranjuez, w. Lidia Zabka (hn), W. Michniewski (cnd), Sinfonia Varsovia
Polskie Nagrania ▲ PNCD 103 [DDD]
Scarlatti, D.:Sons Kbd—K.177, 178, 202 & 232 GHA ▲ CD 126.006
Torroba, F.M.:Music of—Sonatina; Burgalesa; Suite Castellana; Madraños; Castillos de España; Nocturno; Aires de la Mancha *(rec Worcester, MA, Feb 11–13, 1996)* Telarc ▲ CD 80451 [DDD]

Russell, Helen (cl)
Samuel, G.:Nocturne on an Impossible Dream, w. Yehonatan Berick (vn), Alonzo Alexander (pno), G. Samuel (cnd), CCM Contemporary Music Ensemble *(rec Corbett Auditorium, Cincinnati Conservatory, OH)* Acoma ▲ GXD 5733 [DDD]

Russell, Linda (dlc/alt)
Foster, S.C.:Songs, w. J. Baird (sop), F. Urrey (ten), J. Van Buskirk (pno), R. Enslow (fid)—The Glendy Burke; Nelly Was a Lady; Melinda May; The Soirée Polka; The Moustache Song; O Willie, Is It You, Dear?; Mr. & Mr Albany ▲ TROY 119

Russell, Lucy (vn)
Schumann, R.:Son 1 Vn, w. R. Burnett (pno) Amon Ra ▲ CD-SAR 54 [DDD]

Russell, Peggy (fl)
Scelsi, G.:Anahit, w. Paul Zukofsky (vn), Julie Bogorad (fl), Courtney Westcott (fl), Lawrence McDonald (cl), Joan Waryha (cl), Jean Hansen (b cl), Bill Suite (e hn), Nita VanPelt (sax), Bob Zobal (tpt), John Carter (trbn), Martin Lydecker (trbn), Stan Cortman (hn), Robert Ward (hn), William Curry (va), Jody Rowitsch (va), Irene Wade (va), Anne Fagerburg (vc), John Gockel (vc), Sue Manz (bass), Steven Stearman (bass) *(rec Oberlin Conservatory of Music, Oct 8, 1973)* CP² ▲ CP2 108 [AAD]

Russo, Charles (cl)
Rossini, G.:Vars Cl, w. U. Barnea (cnd), Billings SO CRS ▲ CD 8840
Stravinsky, I.:L'Histoire du soldat Suite Vn, w. G. Tarack (vn), T. Weis (tpt), J. Levine (db), Loren Glickman (bn), J. Swallow (trbn), R. Desroches (perc), L. Stokowski (cnd)
Vanguard Classics ▲ SVC 1 [AAD]

Russo, Charles (cl/b cl)
Argento, D.:To Be Sung Upon The Water, w. John Stewart (ten), Donald Hassard (pno)
Phoenix ▲ PHCD 129

Russo, Eugenie (pno)
Copland, A.:Blues *(rec Neumarkt, Oberpfalz, Germany, Oct, 1995)* Campion ▲ 1336 [DDD]
Copland, A.:Rodeo [arr Aaron Copland] *(rec Neumarkt, Oberpfalz, Germany, Oct, 1995)*
Campion ▲ 1336 [DDD]
Copland, A.:El salón México [arr Leonard Bernstein] *(rec Neumarkt, Oberpfalz, Germany, Oct, 1995)*
Campion ▲ 1336 [DDD]
Copland, A.:Son Pno *(rec Neumarkt, Oberpfalz, Germany, Oct, 1995)* Campion ▲ 1336 [DDD]
Gershwin, G.:Pno Music—Rhap in Blue; 3 Preludes; The Man I Love; Swanee; Do It Again; Somebody Loves Me; Clap Yo' Hands; My One & Only; 's Wonderful; I Got Rhythm; Oh, Lady Be Good; Who Cares?; Liza; An American in Paris *(rec Great Hall, Glencairn, Bryn Athyn, Pennsylvania & Studio Weinberg, kefermarkt, Austria, Apr 1–2, 1994)* Campion ▲ 1337

Russo, G. (va)—see ORCHESTRAS & ENSEMBLES Seicentonovecento Ensemble

Russo, John (cl)
Alexander, W.:Cambridge Trio, w. C. Englert (ob), L. Walton Ignacio (pno) CRS ▲ CD 8949
Aubert, O.:Solo de Concours 1, w. L. Walton Ignacio (pno) CRS ▲ CD 8949
Bernstein, L.:Son Cl, w. L. Walton Ignacio (pno) CRS ▲ CD 8949
Bozza, E.:Caprice–Improvisation, w. L. W. Ignacio (pno) CRS ▲ CD 9257
Carter, E.:Pastoral E Hn, w. L. Walton Ignacio (pno) CRS ▲ 9255
Contemporary/Classic Masters, w. Lydia Walton Ignacio (pno), Mirjam Ingolfsson (vc), et al.
CRS ▲ 9255
Devienne, F.:Son 1 Cl, w. L. Walton Ignacio (pno) CRS ▲ 9255
Ewazen, E.:Ballade, w. E. Etters (hp), T. Crawford (cnd), New York Society Orch members
CRS ▲ CD 8840
Glazer, S.:Duo Cl, w. S. Dinion (perc) CRS ▲ CD 9153
Hindemith, P.:Son Cl, w. L. Walton Ignacio (pno) CRS ▲ 9051
Ibert, J.:Aria Cl & Pno, w. L. W. Ignacio (pno) CRS ▲ CD 9153
Masterworks for Clarinet & Piano, w. Lydia Walton Ignacio (pno) CRS Master ▲ CD 9561
Piston, W.:Con Cl, w. U. Barnea (cnd), Billings SO CRS ▲ CD 8840
Presser, W.:Partita Cl CRS ▲ CD 8840
Russo, J.:Largetto, w. S. Curtiss (va), L. Walton Ignacio (pno) CRS ▲ 9255
Russo, J.:Pieces Cl CRS ▲ CD 9257
Russo, J.:Son 1 Cl, w. L. Walton Ignacio (pno) CRS ▲ CD 9153
Russo, J.:Son 4 Cl, w. L. Walton Ignacio (pno) CRS ▲ 9255
Virtuoso Works for Clarinet & Orchestra CRS Master ▲ CD 9459

Russon, C. (cl)
Walton, W.:Façade, w. J. Bookspan (nar), S. Baron (fl), H. Estrin (sax), M. Broiles (tpt), K. Moore (vc), H. Harris (perc), D. Epstein (cnd) Allegretto ▲ ACD 8153 [ADD] ■ ACD 8153

Rust, R. (pno)
Noon, D.:Etudes Protone ▲ PRCD 1110 [ADD]
Prokofiev, S.:Son 6 Pno Protone ▲ PRCD 1110 [ADD]
Siegmeister, E.:Studies Pno Protone ▲ PRCD 1110 [ADD]
Starer, R.:Preludes Pno Protone ▲ PRCD 1110 [ADD]

Rust, Rebecca (vc)
Bridge, F.:Scherzetto Vc, w. David Apter (pno) *(rec Munich, Feb. 21–25, 1994)*
Marco Polo ▲ 8.223637 [DDD]
Bridge, F.:Son Vc, w. David Apter (pno) *(rec Munich, Feb. 21–25, 1994)*
Marco Polo ▲ 8.223637 [DDD]
Enescu, G.:Son Vc, w. D. Apter (pno) Marco Polo ▲ 8.223298
Tovey, D.F.:Elegiac Vars, w. David Apter (pno) *(rec Munich, Feb. 21–25, 1994)*
Marco Polo ▲ 8.223637 [DDD]
Tovey, D.F.:Son Vc, w. David Apter (pno) *(rec Munich, Feb. 21–25, 1994)*
Marco Polo ▲ 8.223637 [DDD]
Villa-Lobos, H.:Vc Pno Music, w. D. Apter (pno)—O canto do capodócio & O canto da nossa terra [prelude & aria from the Bachianas brasilieras]; Divigaçao (1946); Sonhar, Op. 14 (1915); O canto do Cisne Negro; Berceuse, Op. 50 (1915) Marco Polo ▲ 8.223298

Rusy, Magda (pno)
Wolf, H.:Goethe-Lieder (sels), w. Eduard Stocker (bass)—Grenzen der Menscheit; Genialisch treiben; Der Schäfer; Blumengruss; Gleich und gleich; Harfenspieler 1-11; Königlich gebet; Sankt Nepomuks vorabend; Der Rattenfänger; Frühling übers Jahr; Anakreons grab; Cophtisches Lied I & II; Phänomen
Accord ▲ ACD 202792 [AAD]

Ruth, Frans van (pno)
Schlegel, L.:Deutsche Liebeslieder, w. B. Pierik (sop), N. van der Meel (ten) [G]
Attacca ▲ 8951-4 [DDD]
Schlegel, L.:Songs Mez, w. A. van Wijk (mez) [G] Attacca ▲ 8951-4 [DDD]
Schlegel, L.:Songs Sop, w. T. Karlsen (sop) [G] Attacca ▲ 8951-4 [DDD]

Rutkowska, Teresa (pno)
Polish Piano Music, w. Marian Brokowski (pno), Maria Nosowska (pno), Baroara Halska (pno)
Olympia ▲ OLY 394 [AAD]

Rutledge, Christine (va)—see ORCHESTRAS & ENSEMBLES Notre Dame String Trio

Rutman, Neil (pno)
Mozart, W.A.:Con 12 Pno, w. R. Stamp (cnd), Academy of London Orch
ASV Quicksilva ▲ CD QS 6022 [DDD]
Mozart, W.A.:Con 22 Pno, w. R. Stamp (cnd), Academy of London Orch
ASV Quicksilva ▲ CD QS 6022 [DDD]

Rutscho, Michel (gtr)—see ORCHESTRAS & ENSEMBLES Alice Artzt Guitar Trio

Rutstein, Sedmara Zakarian (pno)
Nikolaev, A.:Cat's Hut Suite Albany ▲ TROY 096 [DDD]
Nikolaev, A.:Fairy Tale Albany ▲ TROY 096 [DDD]
Slonimsky, S.:Son Pno Albany ▲ TROY 135 [DDD]
Tishchenko, B.:Son 5 Pno Albany ▲ TROY 135 [DDD]
Tishchenko, B.:Son 7 Pno Albany ▲ TROY 096 [DDD]

Rütti, C. (hpd)
Martin, F.:Petite sym concertante, w. C. Mathieu (hp), V. Graf (pno), E. de Stoutz (cnd), Zurich CO
Gallo ▲ CD 713 [ADD]

Rütti, Praxedis (hp)
Ave Maria, w. [cnd:Alphons von Aarburg], Zurich Boys' Choir, Daniel Perret (trb), Frieder Lang (ten), Alain Clément (bass), Daniel Winiger (org), Andrej Lütschg (vn) Tudor ▲ TUD 7029 [DDD]

Rüttimann, Ursula (pno)
Vuataz, R.:Ballade, w. A. Vauquet (alt) *(rec Feb. 20, 1980)* Grammont ▲ CTSP 7-2 [ADD]

Ruyle, Bill (perc)
Bouchard, L.:Black Burned Wood, w. D. Ohrenstein (sop), M. Rowell (vn/va), Phillip Bush (pno), J. Cirker (dr/perc) *(rec Feb. & Apr. 1993)* CRI ▲ CD 654 [DDD]
Gibson, Jon:Running Commentary, w. T. Buckner (bar), J. Gibson (sax), J. Kubera (pno)
Lovely Music ▲ LCD 3022 [DDD]
Johnston, B.:Calamity Jane to Her Daughter, w. D. Ohrenstein (sop), M. Rowell (vn), P. Bush (pno) *(rec Feb. & Apr. 1993)* CRI ("Emergency Music" series) ▲ CD 654 [DDD]
Lebaron, A.:Dish, w. D. Ohrenstein (sop), M. Rowell (vn), P. Bush (pno/syn), J. Thompson (elec bass), J. Cirker (dr) *(rec Feb. & Apr. 1993)* CRI ("Emergency Music" series) ▲ CD 654 [DDD]
Weill, K.:Songs, w. A. Réaux (sop), R. Kapilow (pno), W. Schimmel (acc)—conceived & first performed by Angelina Réaux for the 1988 New York Shakespeare Festival, this one-woman show features 21 songs composed from 1928-1946 [E,F,G] Koch International Classics 2-▲ KIC 7087-2 [DDD]

Ruysenaars, Harro (vc)
Escher, R.:Sonate concertante, w. Ronald Brautigam (pno) *(rec Mar 7, 1984)*
Donemus ▲ CV 47 [ADD]

Ružičková, Zuzana (hpd)
Bach, J.S.:Chromatic Fant & Fugue Supraphon ▲ SUP 11 1489 [DDD]
Bach, J.S.:Cons solo Hpd, BWV 972-987—BWV.972, 973, 975, 976, 978, 980
Supraphon ▲ SUP 11 1518 [DDD]
Bach, J.S.:Con 1 Hpd, w. V. Neumann (cnd), Prague Chamber Soloists *(rec 1968)*
Supraphon Collection ▲ 11 0615-2 [ADD]
Bach, J.S.:Con 4 Hpd, w. V. Neumann (cnd), Prague Chamber Soloists *(rec 1966)*
Supraphon Collection ▲ 11 0615-2 [ADD]
Bach, J.S.:Con 6 Hpd, w. V. Neumann (cnd), Prague Chamber Soloists *(rec 1963)*
Supraphon Collection ▲ 11 0615-2 [ADD]
Bach, J.S.:English Suites—No. 3 Supraphon ▲ SUP 11 1489 [DDD]
Bach, J.S.:French Suites—No. 5 Supraphon ▲ SUP 11 1489 [DDD]
Bach, J.S.:Toccatas Hpd, BWV 910-16 Supraphon ▲ SUP 11 1489 [DDD]
English Virginal Music Orfeo ▲ CD 139861 [DDD] ■ MC 139861 (D)
Martinů, B.:Con Hpd, w. Z. Košler (cnd), Slovak Radio Sym CO Campion ▲ 1321 [DDD]
Scarlatti, D.:Sons Kbd—K.8, 12, 29, 84, 113, 159, 384, 388, 406, 420, 519
Orfeo ▲ 144851 [DDD]

Ryabov, Sergei (vn)—see ORCHESTRAS & ENSEMBLES Gosteleradio String Quartet

Ryan, Jane (b vl)
Music of the Renaissance Virtuosi, w. James Tyler (lt/baroque gtr/mand), Nigel North (lt/ thb/cittern), Douglas Wootton (lt/bandora) Saga Classics ▲ 3350 [ADD]

Ryan, Jane (b vl/baroque vc)
The Early Guitar, w. James Tyler (lt/baroque gtr/mand), Paul Elliott (ten), Monica Huggett (baroque vn), Robert Spencer (thb/baroque gtr) Saga Classics ▲ 3356 [ADD]

Ryan, Jane (vl)
Couperin, F.:Leçons de ténèbres (for Good Friday), w. E. Kirkby (sop), J. Nelson (mez), C. Hogwood (chamber org) L'Oiseau-Lyre ▲ 430283-2 [ADD]
Couperin, F.:Motets, w. E. Kirkby (sop), J. Nelson (mez), C. Hogwood (chamber org)
L'Oiseau-Lyre ▲ 430283-2 [ADD]
Purcell, H.:Songs, w. A. Deller (ct), R. Skeaping (vn), W. Kuijken (vl), W. Christie (hpd), R. Elliott (hpd)—An Evening Hymn; Fairest Isle; From Rosy Bow'rs; I Attempt From Love's Sickness; If Music Be the Food of Love; Not All My Torments; O Lead Me to Some Peaceful Gloom; O Solitude; The Plaint; Retired From My Dear Astrea's Sight; Sweeter Than Roses; Thrice Happy Lovers *(rec April 1979)*
Harmonia Mundi ▲ HML 590249

Ryang, Michelle (fl)
Kraft, L.:Cloud Studies, w. Lisa Maron (pic), Margaret Swinchoski (pic), Tanya Dusevic (fl), Adrienne Flynn (fl), Christina Jennings (fl), Zara Lawler (fl), Joseph Piscitelli (fl), Dominique Soucy (fl), Diane Taublieb (fl), Laurel Ann Maurer (alt fl), Richard Wyton (alt fl), J. Solum (cnd) *(rec Skinner Recital Hall, Vassar College, Poughkeepsie, NY, Mar 24–26, 1994)* CRI ▲ CD 712 [DDD]

Rybar, Peter (vn)
Beethoven, L. van:Con Vn, Op. 61, w. H. Moltkau (cnd), West Austrian SO Doron ▲ DRC 4001 [ADD]
Brahms, J.:Con Vn, w. H. Moltkau (cnd), West Austrian SO Doron ▲ DRC 4001 [ADD]
Brahms, J.:Qnt Pno, w. Clara Haskil (pno), Clemens Dahinden (vn), Heinz Wigand (va), Antonio Tusa (vc)
Doron 2-▲ DRC 4007/8 [ADD]
Brahms, J.:Sextet Strs, Op. 36, w. Clemens Dahinden (vn), Heinz Wigand (va), Oskar Kromer (va), Carl-Heinz Jucker (vc), Antonio Tusa (vc) Doron 2-▲ DRC 4007/8 [ADD]
Busoni, F.:Son 2 Vn, w. Clara Haskil (pno) Doron 2-▲ DRC 4007/8 [ADD]
Goldmark, K.:Con 1 Vn, w. H. Swoboda (cnd), Vienna SO *(rec 1950)* Doron ▲ DRC 4003 [ADD]
Mendelssohn, F.:Con in e Vn & Orch, Op. 64, w. V. Desarzens (cnd), Vienna Festival Orch
Doron ▲ DRC 4005
Mozart, W.A.:Son Vn Pno, K.454, w. Clara Haskil (pno) Doron 2-▲ DRC 4007/8 [ADD]
Schumann, R.:Con Vn, w. V. Desarzens (cnd), Lausanne SO *(rec Lausanne, 1951)*
Doron ("Legendary Artists" series) ▲ DRC 4009 [ADD]
Sibelius, J.:Con Vn, w. P. Burkhard (cnd), Zurich Beromünster Orch *(rec live, Zurich, 1952)*
Doron ("Legendary Artists" series) ▲ DRC 4009 [ADD]
Suk, J.:Fant Vn, w. M. Rodan (cnd), Kol Israël SO *(rec Oct. 26, 1966)* Doron ▲ DRC 4003 [ADD]
Tchaikovsky, P.:Con Vn, w. V. Desarzens (cnd), Vienna Festival Orch Doron ▲ DRC 4005

Rydström, Peter (fl/pic)
Delage, M.:Poèmes hindous, w. Anne Sofie von Otter (mez), Andreas Alin (fl), Ulf Bjurenhed (ob/E hn), Lars Paulsson (cl), Per Billman (cl/b cl), Nils-Erik Sparf (vn), Ulf Forsberg (vn), Matti Hirvikangas (va), Mats Lindström (vc), Lisa Viguier (hp) *(rec Stockholm, Nov 1994)*
Deutsche Grammophon ▲ 447 752-2 [DDD]
Ravel, M.:Trois poèmes de Stéphane Mallarmé, w. Anne Sofie von Otter (mez), Andreas Alin (fl), Lars Paulsson (cl), Per Billman (cl/b cl), Nils-Erik Sparf (vn), Ulf Forsberg (vn), Matti Hirvikangas (va), Mats Lindström (vc), Bengt Forsberg (pno) *(rec Stockholm, Nov 1994)*
Deutsche Grammophon ▲ 447 752-2 [DDD]

Rylands, Mary Lou (vc)
Austin, E.:Circling, w. Jeananne Albee (pno) Capstone ▲ CPS 8625
Austin, E.:Music of, w. Jeananne Albee (pno), Jerome Reed (pno), Ursula Trede-Boettcher (hpd), Markus Lücke (cl), Sibylle Dotzauer (pno), Constitution Brass, Gerald Kegelmann (cnd), Heidelberg State Music School Chamber Choir—To Begin for Brass Qnt; Klavier Double for Pno & Tape; Circling for Vc & Pno; Lighthouse I for solo Hpd; Gathering Threads for solo Cl; Zodiac Suite for Pno; An Die Nachgeborenen [To Those Born Later] Capstone ▲ CPS 8625
Vienna Nocturne:The Mair-Davis Duo & Friends Play Waltzes & Sonatas of the Golden Age, w. Mair-Davis Duo, Theodore Arm (vn), Susan Thomas (fl) North Star ▲ NS0034 [DDD]

Ryther, David (vn)
Tailleferre, G.:Chansons populaires françaises, w. Patrice Maginnis (sop), John Fairweather (vn), Jill Cohen (va), Karen Andrie (vc), Elizabeth Bodine (ob), Andy Connell (cl), Gordon Mumma (hn), June Orzel (bn), N. Paiement (cnd) *(rec UC, Santa Cruz, May 1992)* Helicon Classics ▲ HE 1008

Ryther, David (vn) (cont.)
Tailleferre, G.:Image, w. John Fairweather (vn), Jill Cohen (va), Karen Andrie (vc), Elizabeth Bodine (ob), Andy Connell (cl), Gordon Mumma (hn), June Orzel (bn), N. Paiement (cnd) *(rec UC, Santa Cruz, May 1992)* Helicon Classics ▲ HE 1008
Rzewski, Frederick (pno)
Beck, Julian:Songs, w. Irene Aebi (sgr), Steve Lacy (sax)—Theatre [w. lyrics by Julian Beck]; Joy; The Hour Is Late; 1st & Last Pain; Love & Politics; I Heard the Indian Sage; Do Not Judge Me Lightly; The True & the Contrary; The Melancholy Life of Woman; Do Not Judge Me Lightly No. 2 [all w. lyrics by Judith Malina] *(rec Studio Acousti, Paris, Mar 16–17, 1995)* New Albion ▲ NA 080
Rzhanov, E. (pno)
Liatoshinsky, B.:Slavonic Con, w. F. Glushchenko (cnd), Ukrainian State SO Russian Disc ▲ RUS 11 059
Saarenpää, Leena (pno)
Sibelius, J.:Everyman, w. Lilli Paasikivi (mez), Petri Lehto (ten), Sauli Tiilikainen (bar), Pauli Pietiläinen (org), O. Vänskä (cnd), Lahti SO, Lahti Chamber Choir *(rec Church of the Cross, Lahti, Finland, Jan 11–13, 1995)* BIS ▲ CD-735 [DDD]
Saarikettu, Kaija (vn)
Finnish Violin Miniatures, w. Raija Kerppo (pno) Finlandia ▲ 4509-95875-2 [DDD]
Merikanto, O.:Music of, w. Eeva-Jiisa Saarinen (mez), Jorma Hynninen (bar), Sauli Tiilikainen (bar), Erkki Rautio (vc), Pertti Eerola (pno), Ralf Gothoni (pno), Raija Kerppo (pno), Izumi Tateno (pno), Tauno Satomaa (cnd), Candomino Choir—Summer Evening (waltz); Valse lente; Romance; On the Highest Tree-Top; Annina; Bye, Bye Lullabye; The Weeping Flute; At Sea; Hey My Heart; Where Rustling Birches Bend; Play Softly, the Tune of Mourning; Fairy Tale by the Fireside; Idyll; Scherzo, Op. 6/4; O Dost Thou Remember That Hymn; Lade Ladoga; Why Do I Sing; The Thunderbird; The Happy Ones; Summer Evening's Idyll Finlandia ▲ FIN 500432 [AAD/DDD]
Saarinen, G. (pno)
Sallinen, A.:Kullervo, w. J. Silvasti (ten), J. Hynninen (bar), M. Salminen (bass), U. Söderblom (cnd), Finnish National Opera Orch, Finnish National Opera Chorus [Fin] Ondine 3-▲ ODE 780-3T [DDD], Chinook Trio
Saba, Emanuela (ob)
Respighi, O.:Di Sera, w. Alberto Cesaraccio (ob), R. Tigani (cnd), Sassari SO *(rec Rome, Oct 11–14, 1994)* Bongiovanni ▲ GB 2166 [DDD]
Saba, Geoffrey (pno)
Great Piano Transcriptions IMP ▲ PCD 858 [DDD]
Schubert, Franz:Impromptus Pno, D.899—Nos. 2 & 3 in E♭ & G♭ *(rec 2/90)* IMP Classics ▲ PCD 950 [DDD]
Schubert, Franz:Son Pno, D.625 *(rec 2/90)* IMP Classics ▲ PCD 950 [DDD]
Schubert, Franz:Son Pno, D.959 IMP Classics ▲ PCD 950 [DDD]
Sabajno, Carlo (pno)
Puccini, G.:Madama Butterfly (sels), w. Margaret Sheridan (sop), Ida Mannarini (mez), Lionello Cecil (ten), Vittorio Wenberg (sgr) *(rec La Scala, 1929–30)* Romophone ("Opera Magna" series) 2-▲ 89001-2
Sabin, David (pno)
Ashford, R.:Beauty, w. Linda Greene (fl) Nigel Classics ▲ NC 10101
Sabin, Nigel (cl)—see ORCHESTRAS & ENSEMBLES Perihelion Ensemble members, Perihelion
Sabinova, Natalia (vc)—see ORCHESTRAS & ENSEMBLES Moscow Contemporary Music Ensemble
Sablinsky, Constance (pno)
Moss, L.:Hommage, w. Barbara Rowan (pno) Capstone ▲ CPS 8619
Sacchetti, Arturo (org)
Bossi, M.E.:Con Org, w. S. Frontalini (cnd), Minsk PO Bongiovanni ▲ GB 5512 [DDD]
Bossi, M.E.:Siciliana & Gigue, w. S. Frontalini (cnd), Minsk PO Bongiovanni ▲ GB 5512 [DDD]
Bossi, M.E.:Symphonic Fant, w. S. Frontalini (cnd), Minsk PO Bongiovanni ▲ GB 5512 [DDD]
Composizioni da camera Arts ▲ 47153-2 [DDD]
Composizioni da chiesa Arts ▲ 47154-2 [DDD]
Organ Festival Arts ▲ 447209-2 [DDD]
Organ History:French Romanticism *(rec Aosta, Italy, Nov 3–6, 1985)* Arts ▲ 447113-2 [DDD]
Organ History:German Classicism *(rec Torino, Italy, Feb 20–24, 1985)* Arts ▲ 447111-2 [DDD]
Organ History:German Romanticism *(rec Bioglio, Italy, Feb 25–28, 1985)* Arts ▲ 447112-2 [DDD]
Organ History:Italian Operatic Transcription in the 19th Century *(rec Santhià, Vercelli, Italy, Feb–Mar 1985)* Arts ▲ 47163-2 [DDD]
Sachs, Joel (pno)—see also ORCHESTRAS & ENSEMBLES Continuum Chamber Ensemble
Lennon, J.A.:Translations, w. R. Rosales (sop), D. Krakauer (cl), M. Wu (vn) CRI ▲ CD 599 [ADD/DDD]
Moss, L.:Songs of the Earth, w. Nan Hughes (mez), Mark Steinberg (vn), David Krakauer (cl), Cheryl Seltzer (pno) Capstone ▲ CPS 8619
Saderk, Stan (vc)
O'Rourke, J.:Terminal Pharmacy, w. Tony Burr (cl), Jeff Cortazzo (b trbn), John McEntire (dr), Rob Prosser (acc), Isha Suftin (acc), Mike Dockter (vc), Hattie Franck (vc), Robert Keck (vc), Mary LaBreque (vc), Dan Loch (vc), Lisa Hemmer (fl), Sue Oberg (fl), Wendi Lev (fl), Jim Vanden (fl), Jim O'Rourke (gtr), Steve Braack (elec) Tzadik ▲ TZA 7011 [DDD]
Sadler, Ian (org)
British & Canadian Organ Works Musica Viva ▲ MVV 1068 [DDD]
Make We Joy!:Music for Christmas, w. [cnd:John Tuttle], Exultate Chamber Singers, Great Lakes Brass *(rec St. Thomas' Church, Toronto)* Exultate Chamber Singers ▲ ECS 02
The Organ of the St. James' Cathedral *(rec Feb. 25–26, 1992)* CBC Records ("Musica Viva" series) ▲ MVCD 1068 [DDD]
Sádlo, Miloš (vc)
Dvořák, A.:Con Vc, w. V. Neumann (cnd), Czech PO Supraphon Collection ▲ 11 0631-2 [ADD]
Dvořák, A.:Con Vc & Pno, w. V. Neumann (cnd), Czech PO Supraphon Collection ▲ 11 0631-2 [ADD]
Reicha, J.:Con Vc, w. M. Klemens (cnd), Prague Musici [rev & cadenza by Sádlo] *(rec House of Artists, Prague, Nov. 1972)* Panton ▲ PAN 811307 [AAD]
Shostakovich, D.:Con 1 Vc, w. K. Ančerl (cnd), Czech PO *(rec June 6–8, 1968)* Supraphon ("Collection" series) ▲ 11 0676-2 [ADD]
Shostakovich, D.:Sym 5, w. K. Ančerl (cnd), Czech PO *(rec Nov. 11–14, 1961)* Supraphon ("Collection" series) ▲ 11 0676-2 [ADD]
Vranicky, A.:Con Vc, w. M. Klemens (cnd), Prague Musici [rev & cadenza by Sádlo] *(rec House of Artists, Prague, Nov. 1972)* Panton ▲ PAN 811307 [AAD]
Sadlo, Peter (perc)
Classic Percussion Koch Schwann ▲ SCH 310141 [DDD]
Hummel, B.:Music of, w. F. Bach (perc), S. Gagelmann (perc), E. Guggeis (perc)—Tempo di valse, Op. 76c; 5 Szenen für 2 Schlagzeuger, Op. 58; Marimbana, Op. 95d; 5 Aspekte für Schlagzeuger, Op. 88d; Quattro pezzi für Schlagzeuger, Op. 92; Freken 70 für vier Schlagzeuger, Op. 38 *(rec Gasteig Munich, Dec. 1993)* Thorofon ▲ CTH 2233 [DDD]
Sadoff, Ronald (pno)
Gilbert, J.:If Time Remembers *(rec New York Univ.)* Capstone ▲ CPS 8616 [AAD]
Sadovskaja, Tatjana (pno)
Kodály, Z.:Adagio Vn, w. Josef Suk (vn), Pierre Fournier (vc), André Navarra (vc) Praga ▲ PR 250065
Kodály, Z.:Sonatina Vc & Pno, w. Pierre Fournier (vc), André Navarra (vc) Praga ▲ PR 250065
Saeverud, Trond (vn)
Saeverud, H.:Con Vn, w. K. Andersen (cnd), South Jutland SO Simax ▲ PSC 1087 [DDD]
Saeverud, H.:Elegie Vn Simax ▲ PSC 1087 [DDD]
Saeverud, H.:Romanza Vn, w. K. Andersen (cnd), South Jutland SO Simax ▲ PSC 1087 [DDD]
Saeverud, H.:Small Duets, w. K. Dalsgaard Madsen (vn) Simax ▲ PSC 1087 [DDD]
Safariants, Maria (vn)—see ORCHESTRAS & ENSEMBLES St. Petersburg Trio
Sagat, Milan (db)—see ORCHESTRAS & ENSEMBLES Biedermeier Ensemble
Saidenberg, Theodore (pno)
Bennett, Robert Russell:A Song Son, w. Louis Kaufman (vn) Cambria ("Historical" series) ▲ CD 1078 [ADD]
Milhaud, D.:Saudades do Brasil, w. Louis Kaufman (vn)—No. 5 [Ipanema] Cambria ("Historical" series) ▲ CD 1078 [ADD]

St. John, Scott (vn)
Dvořák, A.:Music of, w. Thomas Bagwell (pno)—2 Slavonic Dances; Humoresque; Mazurek; Capriccio; Romantic Pieces; Son. for Violin & Piano Marquis Classics ▲ MAR 159 [DDD]
Maggio, R.:Barcarole, w. John Koen (vc), Hugh Sung (pno), Don Liuzzi (perc), J. Higdon (cnd) *(rec Settlement Music School, Germantown, PA, June 17, 1995)* CRI ▲ CD 720 [DDD]
Paganini, N.:Cantabile, w. S. Wynberg (gtr) *(rec Mar. 1993)* Naxos ▲ 8.550690 [DDD]
Paganini, N.:Cantabile & Waltz, w. S. Wynberg (gtr) *(rec Mar. 1993)* Naxos ▲ 8.550759 [DDD]
Paganini, N.:Duetto amoroso Vn, w. S. Wynberg (gtr) *(rec Mar. 1993)* Naxos ▲ 8.550759 [DDD]
Paganini, N.:Son concertata, w. S. Wynberg (gtr) *(rec Mar. 1993)* Naxos ▲ 8.550690 [DDD]
Paganini, N.:Son large Va, w. S. Wynberg (gtr) [arr. for viola & guitar] *(rec Mar. 1993)* Naxos ▲ 8.550759 [DDD]
Paganini, N.:Sons Vn & Gtr, Op. 2, w. S. Wynberg (gtr) *(rec Mar. 1993)* Naxos ▲ 8.550759 [DDD]
Paganini, N.:Sons Vn & Gtr, Op. 3, w. S. Wynberg (gtr) *(rec Mar. 1993)* Naxos ▲ 8.550690 [DDD]
Paganini, N.:Vars on "Baracaba", w. S. Wynberg (gtr) *(rec Mar. 1993)* Naxos ▲ 8.550690 [DDD]
Paganini, N.:Vars di bravura, w. S. Wynberg (gtr) *(rec Mar. 1993)* Naxos ▲ 8.550759 [DDD]
St. Julien, Marcus G. (org)
Historic Organs of New Orleans, w. George Bozeman (org), James S. Darling (org), Jesse E. Eschbach (org), Gerald D. Frank (org), John Gearhart (org), James Hammann (org), Frederick Hohman (org), Lenora McCroskey (org), Mary Gifford Matthys (org), Lorenz Maycher (org), Donald Messer (org) *(rec June 1989)* Organ Historical Society 2-▲ OHS 89
St. Martin, C. (baroque fl)
Boismortier, J.B. de:Sons Fl & Continuo, w. C. Edelen (hpd)—(6) in D, g, G, e, A & c Focus ▲ FOCUS 936 [DDD]
St. Pierre, D. (pno)
Suchy, G.K.:Greek Maxims, w. L. Dougherty (sop) [E] Capstone ▲ CPS 8613
St. Pierre, Raissa (drums)
Exquisite Corpses from P.S. 122, w. Watson, David (shears/stick vn/gtr/tpt), Judy Dunaway (gtr/balloons), Anthony Coleman (sampler), Guy Yarden (vn/pno), Leslie Ross (bn), Linda Austin (gtr), Bruce Kaplan (gtr), Doug Henderson (peckhorn/bass/toy pno), Sue Ann Harkey (gtr), Cinnie Cole (sampler), Mike Sap ¿What Next? ▲ WN 0002 [ADD]
St. Sigurdardóttir, Gudridur (pno)
Eiríksdottir, Karolina:Land Possesed by Poems, w. Kristinn Sigmundsson (bar) Music from Iceland ▲ ITM 701 [ADD]
Eiríksdottir, Karolina:Rhap Pno Music from Iceland ▲ ITM 701 [ADD]
Saint-Denis, P. (fl)
Vivaldi, A.:Cons Vn, Op. 8/1–4, "The Four Seasons", w. I. Rechtman (cmpt) *(rec Oct. 1992)* Omega ▲ OCD 3020 [DDD]
Saint-Saëns, Camille (pno)
Great Composers at the Keyboard, w. Maurice Ravel (pno), Enrique Granados (pno) Foné ▲ FON 90F14 [DDD]
Sainz, Liliana (pno)
Deux Pianos:Mozart, Ravel, Milhaud, Bartók, Guastavino, Piazzolla, w. Jorge Bergaglio (pno) Gallo ▲ CD 800 [ADD]
Saitoh, Masahiro (pno)
Live in Tokyo, w. Ilona Tokody (sop) *(rec Apr. 20, 1991)* Live Notes ▲ WWCC 7220
Sajot, Jean-Louis (cl)
Françaix, J.:Octet, w. A. Wallez (bn), Carl Stamitz Ensemble Pierre Verany ▲ PVY 792102 [DDD]
Françaix, J.:Qnt Cl, w. Carl Stamitz Ensemble Pierre Verany ▲ PVY 792102 [DDD]
Weber, C.M. von:Intro, Theme & Vars Cl, w. Carl Stamitz Ensemble Pierre Verany ▲ PV.792021 [DDD]
Weber, C.M. von:Qnt Cl, w. Carl Stamitz Ensemble Pierre Verany ▲ PV.792021 [DDD]
Sakai, Satoshi (uchimono)
Fujieda, M.:Music of, w. Mamoru Fujueda (cmpt), Makiko Sakurai (shomyo/Buddhist chant), Mineko Grimmer (audible sculptures), Kodo Uesugi (fukimono), Kazuko Takada (hikimono), Toshiyuki Matsukura (uchimono), Koshin Ebihara (jumon)—The Night Chant III; Wind Chant; Cocoon Chant; Duct Chant; Falling Chant; The Night Chant I Tzadik ("The Composers" series) ▲ TZA 7003 [DDD]
Sakanov, Josef (vn)
In a Monastery Garden *(rec DECCA Studio No. 3, West Hampstead, London, Apr–Aug 1972)* London ("Phase 4 Stereo") ▲ 444 786-2 [ADD]
Sakharov, Vadim (pno)
Gubaidulina, S.:Dancer on a Tightrope, w. Gidon Kremer (vn) *(rec Lockenhaus Festival, Austria, 1995)* BIS ▲ CD 810 [DDD]
Sala, Antonio (vc)
Arensky, A.:Trio 1 Pno, w. E. Joyce (pno), H. Temianka (vn) *(rec 1938)* Biddulph 2-▲ LAB 059/60 [ADD]
Salaff, Peter (vn)—see ORCHESTRAS & ENSEMBLES Cleveland String Quartet
Salas, Osvalda (pno)
Aguirre, J.:Aires nacionales (sels)—5 Tristes [from Book I] Arcobaleno ▲ AAOC 9398
Ginastera, A.:Son 1 Pno Arcobaleno ▲ AAOC 9398
Mignone, F.:Preludes Arcobaleno ▲ AAOC 9398
Villa-Lobos, H.:Chôro 5 Arcobaleno ▲ AAOC 9398
Villa-Lobos, H.:A Lenda do Caboclo Arcobaleno ▲ AAOC 9398
Villa-Lobos, H.:Suite floral Arcobaleno ▲ AAOC 9398
Salas, Veronica (va)—see ORCHESTRAS & ENSEMBLES New Music Consort
Salcito, Marco (cht)
Bellafronte, R.:Suite 1 Vc, w. Vito Paternoster (vc) *(rec Auditorium del Conservatorio, Bari, Nov 1994)* Bongiovanni ▲ GB 5049-2 [DDD]
Salerno-Sonnenberg, Nadja (vn)
Barber, S.:Con Vn, w. M. Shostakovich (cnd), London SO EMI Classics ▲ CDC 54314-2 ■ 4DS 54314-4
Brahms, J.:Con Vn, w. E. de Waart (cnd), Minnesota Orch EMI Classics ▲ CDC 49429 [DDD]
Brahms, J.:Son 1 Vn, w. C. Licad (pno) EMI Classics ▲ CDC 54800
Brahms, J.:Son 2 Vn, w. C. Licad (pno) EMI Classics ▲ CDC 49410 [DDD]
Brahms, J.:Son 3 Vn, w. C. Licad (pno) EMI Classics ▲ CDC 54800
Brahms, J.:Trio Hn, w. J. Cerminaro (hn), C. Licad (pno) EMI Classics ▲ CDC 54800
Bruch, M.:Con 1 Vn, w. E. de Waart (cnd), Minnesota Orch EMI Classics ▲ CDC 49429 [DDD]
Chausson, E.:Poème Vn, w. M. Tilson Thomas (cnd), London SO EMI Classics ▲ CDC 54855
It Ain't Necessarily So, w. Sandra Rivers (pno) EMI Classics ▲ CDC 54576 [DDD]
Mendelssohn, F.:Con in e Vn & Orch, Op. 64, w. G. Schwarz (cnd), New York Chamber SO EMI Classics ▲ CDC 49276 [DDD] ■ 4DS 49276 (D)
Saint-Saëns, C.:Havanaise Vn, w. G. Schwarz (cnd), New York Chamber SO EMI Classics ▲ CDC 49276 [DDD] ■ 4DS 49276 (D)
Saint-Saëns, C.:Introduction & Rondo capriccioso, w. G. Schwarz (cnd), New York Chamber SO—& Massenet:Thaïs—Méditation EMI Classics ▲ CDC 49276 [DDD] ■ 4DS 49276 (D)
Shostakovich, D.:Con 1 Vn, w. M. Shostakovich (cnd), London SO EMI Classics ▲ CDC 54314 ■ 4DS 54314
Tchaikovsky, P.:Trio Pno, w. C. Licad (pno), A. Meneses (vc) EMI Classics ▲ CDC 54800
Vivaldi, A.:Cons Vn, Op. 8/1–4, "The Four Seasons", Orch of St. Luke EMI Classics ▲ CDC 49767 [DDD] ■ 4DS 49767 (D)
Salman, Mark (pno)
Alkan, C.-V.:Etudes (12) in minor keys—Symphonie *(rec Holy Trinity Church, NYC, Feb 26–28, 1993)* Titanic ▲ Ti 220
Beethoven, L. van:Son 31 Pno *(rec Holy Trinity Church, NYC, Feb 26–28, 1993)* Titanic ▲ Ti 220
Liszt, F.:Mephisto Waltz 2 Orch *(rec Holy Trinity Church, NYC, Feb 26–28, 1993)* Titanic ▲ Ti 220
Liszt, F.:Sarabande & Chaconne *(rec Holy Trinity Church, NYC, Feb 26–28, 1993)* Titanic ▲ Ti 220

Salmins, Ralph (dr)
Yoshioka, T.:Rhap Mar, w. Evelyn Glennie (mar), Edward Beckett (fl), Roy Howitt (cl), Chris Laurence (db) *(rec Whitfield Street Studios, London, Sept. 22–29, 1994)* Catalyst ▲ 09026-68193-2 [DDD]
Salmon, Jane (vc)—see ORCHESTRAS & ENSEMBLES Schubert Ensemble of London
Salmon, John (pno)
Brubeck, D.:Dave's Diary (sels)—Deck the House with Boughs of Pine; Christmas at the Ranch; Roundup Starts Tomorrow at Dawn; I'm Home *(rec Shirley Hall, Salem College, Winston-Salem, NC, Sept 1994 - Jan 1995)* Phoenix ▲ PHCD 130 [DDD]
Brubeck, D.:Glances *(rec Shirley Hall, Salem College, Winston-Salem, NC, Sept 1994 - Jan 1995)* Phoenix ▲ PHCD 130 [DDD]
Brubeck, D.:Points on Jazz [trans Howard Brubeck] *(rec Shirley Hall, Salem College, Winston-Salem, NC, Sept 1994 - Jan 1995)* Phoenix ▲ PHCD 130 [DDD]
Brubeck, D.:Reminiscences of the Cattle Country *(rec Shirley Hall, Salem College, Winston-Salem, NC, Sept 1994 - Jan 1995)* Phoenix ▲ PHCD 130 [DDD]
Brubeck, D.:They All Sang Yankee Doodle [trans Brubeck] *(rec Shirley Hall, Salem College, Winston-Salem, NC, Sept 1994 - Jan 1995)* Phoenix ▲ PHCD 130 [DDD]
Salness, David (vn)—see also ORCHESTRAS & ENSEMBLES Audubon String Quartet
Dohnányi, E. von:Serenade, w. Doris Lederer (va), Clyde Shaw (vc) *(rec LSU Recital Hall, Louisiana State Univ, Baton Rouge, July 23–25, 1995)* Centaur ▲ CRC 2309 [DDD]
Salo, Per (pno)
Andersen, J.:Fl & Pno Music, w. T. L. Christiansen (fl)—Valse Caprice, Op. 44; Impromptu, Op. 7; Morceaux pour la flûte, Op. 57; Fant on Bellini's *Norma;* Leichte Stücke, Op. 56; 8 Vortragsstücke, Op. 55 *(rec Mar 1991)* Kontrapunkt ▲ 32079 [DDD]
Bentzon, N.V.:Pno Music—Partita, Op. 38 (1945); Sonata No. 7, Op. 121 (1959); Sonata ("Hoffmann"), Op. 248 (1969); Woodcuts, Op. 65 (1951) *(rec 2/92)* Kontrapunkt ▲ 32111 [DDD]
Bentzon, N.V.:Son Cl, w. John Kruse (cl) *(rec Det Fynske Musikkonservatorium, 1993)* Paula ▲ PACD 78 [DAD]
Britten, H.:Son Vc, w. K. Bak Dinitzen (vc) Kontrapunkt 2–▲ KPT 32101 [DDD]
Ives, C.:Son 2 Pno, w. J. Jorgensen (va), T. L. Christiansen (fl) Kontrapunkt ▲ 32046 [DDD]
Koppel, H.D.:Vars Cl & Pno, w. John Kruse (cl) *(rec Det Fynske Musikkonservatorium, 1993)* Paula ▲ PACD 78 [DAD]
Nørgård, P.:Achilles Kontrapunkt ▲ KPT 32147 [DDD]
Nørgård, P.:Grooving Kontrapunkt ▲ KPT 32147 [DDD]
Nørgård, P.:Son 2 Pno Kontrapunkt ▲ KPT 32147 [DDD]
Nørgård, P.:Turn Kontrapunkt ▲ KPT 32147 [DDD]
Roussel, A.:Chamber Music, w. Majken Bjerno (sop), Toke Lund Christiansen (fl), Bjørn Carl Nielsen (ob), Niels Thomsen (cl), Per Jacobsen (hn), Asger Svendsen (bn), Ketil Christensen (tpt), Anne Søe Hansen (vn), Zwi Carmelli (va), Piotr Zelazny (va), Niels Ullner (vc), Michael Dabelsteen (db), Tine Rehling (hp), Morten Mogensen (pno), Per Jensen (perc)—Divertissement, Op. 6; Trio, Op. 40; Joueurs de Flute, Op. 27; Serenade, Op. 30; Le marchand de sable qui passe, Op. 13; Andante et scherzo, Op. 13; 2 poèmes de ronsard, Op. 26; Aria; Elpenor, Op. 59; Pipe Kontrapunkt 2–▲ KPT 32218 [DDD]
Ruders, P.:Throne, w. John Kruse (cl) *(rec Det Fynske Musikkonservatorium, 1993)* Paula ▲ PACD 78 [DAD]
Tarp, S.E.:Con Pno, w. M. Schønwandt (cnd), Danish National RSO *(rec Sept. 7, 1990)* Marco Polo ▲ DCCD 9005 [DDD]
Salo, Per (pno/hpd)
Nørholm, I.:Chamber Music, w. B. Rørbeck (vn), J. Christiansen (gtr), N. Ullner (vc), G. Sørensen (perc), Kuhlau Flute Quartet—Before Silence, Op. 83; Contrast–Continuum, Op. 70; Guitar Sonata No. 2; The Orthodox Dream; So to Say, Op. 74; Turbulens–Laminar, Op. 93; Variants, Op. 19 *(rec 9/90)* Kontrapunkt ▲ 32065 [DDD]
Salomon, Diana (vn)
The Maestros Tea Party:Mr. Einstein Visits the Queen, w. Mary Jane Rupert (pno), Patricia Wenzel (vn), Ella Lou Weiler (va), Fern Meyers (vc), Gerhard Finkenbeiner (glass armonica), Vera Meyer (glass armonica) *(rec Euphoria Sound Studio, Revere, MA)* Cultured Kids ▲ unknown ■ 120012FM-4
Salonen, Petri (vn)
Klatzow, P.:Qt Strs, w. Jürgen Schwietering (vn), Leo Lujyendijk (va), Eric Martens (vc) Claremont ▲ GSE 1524
Salquin, Hedy (pno)
Haller, H.:Nocturnes (3), w. A. von Tószeghi (alt) Grammont ▲ CTSP 10-2 [ADD]
Saltini, Roberto (cl)
Mercadante, S.:Sinf concertante 1, w. Luca Truffelli (fl), Giovanni Sora (cl), Andrea Mastini (cnt), C.F. Sedazzari (cnd), Camerata Schubert Bongiovanni ▲ GB 2199 [DDD]
Mercadante, S.:Sinf concertante 2, w. Luca Truffelli (fl), Andrea Mastini (cnt), C.F. Sedazzari (cnd), Camerata Schubert Bongiovanni ▲ GB 2199 [DDD]
Mercadante, S.:Sinf concertante 3, w. Luca Truffelli (fl), Giovanni Sora (cl), Andrea Mastini (cnt), C.F. Sedazzari (cnd), Camerata Schubert Bongiovanni ▲ GB 2199 [DDD]
Saltzman, Elyakum (vn)
Martinů, B.:Madrigal Son, w. Irit Rub-Levi (pno), Yossi Arnheim (fl) Kontrapunkt ▲ KPT 32205
Martinů, B.:Promenades, w. Yossi Arnheim (fl), Irit Rub-Levi (pno) Kontrapunkt ▲ KPT 32205
Martinů, B.:Son Fl, Vn & Pno, w. Yossi Arnheim (fl), Irit Rub-Levi (pno) Kontrapunkt ▲ KPT 32205
Salvador Sr, Guillermo (pno)
Saint-Saëns, C.:Carnival of the Animals, w. G. Salvador Jr (pno), E. Bátiz (cnd), Mexico City PO ASV ▲ ASV 665 [DDD]
Salvador Jr., Guillermo (pno)
Saint-Saëns, C.:Carnival of the Animals, w. G. Salvador Sr (pno), E. Bátiz (cnd), Mexico City PO ASV ▲ ASV 665 [DDD]
Salvatore, Antonio (vn)
Petrassi, G.:Duetto Vn Va, w. A. Vismara (va) Bongiovanni ▲ GB 5534 [DDD]
Salvatore, Ramon (pno)
American Piano, Vol. 2:Blue Voyage Premier ▲ PRCD 1019 [DDD]
Beach, A.M.C.:Improvs (5) Premier ▲ PRCD 1019 [DDD]
Bowles, P.:Carretera de Estepona Cedille ▲ CDR 90000 010 [DDD]
Bowles, P.:Latin American Pieces (6) Cedille ▲ CDR 90000 010 [DDD]
Carpenter, J.A.:Tango américain Premier ▲ PRCD 1019 [DDD]
Chadwick, G.W.:Pno Music—Prelude joyeux; Dans le canot; Le crepescule; Le reusseau (1905) Premier ▲ PRCD 1019 [DDD]
Copland, A.:Fant Pno *(rec WFMT, Chicago, Dec. 1994–Feb. 1995)* Cedille ▲ CDR 90000 021 [DDD]
Copland, A.:Pno Music—Sonnet II; 3 Moods; The Cat & the Mouse; Passacaglia; Down a Country Lane; Midsummer Nocturne; Proclamation; Midday Thoughts *(rec WFMT, Chicago, Dec. 1994–Feb. 1995)* Cedille ▲ CDR 90000 021 [DDD]
Copland, A.:Son in G Pno *(rec WFMT, Chicago, Dec. 1994–Feb. 1995)* Cedille ▲ CDR 90000 021 [DDD]
Farwell, A.:Navajo War Dance 2 Premier ▲ PRCD 1019 [DDD]
Farwell, A.:Pawnee Horses Premier ▲ PRCD 1019 [DDD]
Foote, A.:Poems Pno, Op. 41 Premier ▲ PRCD 1019 [DDD]
Foster, S.C.:Anadolia Premier ▲ PRCD 1019 [DDD]
Ganz, R.:Con Pno, w. P. Freeman (cnd), Chicago Sinfonietta *(rec Lund Auditorium, River Forest, IL, Feb 27, 1996)* Cedille ▲ CDR 90000 028 [DDD]
Johnson, H.:Son Pno Cedille ▲ CDR 90000 010 [DDD]
La Montaine, J.:Con 4 Pno, w. P. Freeman (cnd), Slovak RSO Bratislava *(rec Bratislava, Feb 26 & 27, 1995)* Cedille ▲ CDR 90000 028 [DDD]
La Montaine, J.:Son Pno Cedille ▲ CDR 90000 010 [DDD]
Paine, J.K.:Pno Music—Funeral March in Memory of President Lincoln (1865); Romance, Op. 39 (1883); Nocturne, Op. 45 (1889) Premier ▲ PRCD 1019 [DDD]
Palmer, R.:3rd Son Pno Cedille ▲ CDR 90000 010 [DDD]
Riegger, W.:Blue Voyage Premier ▲ PRCD 1019 [DDD]

Salvatore, Ramon (pno) (cont.)
Thomson, V.:2 Sentimental Tangos Premier ▲ PRCD 1019 [DDD]
Salwen, Barry David (pno)
Haimo, E.:Etudes (3) *(rec Annenberg Audit., Snite Museum of Art, Univ. of Notre Dame, May & June 1994 & Jan 199)* Centaur ▲ CRC 2253 [DDD]
Haimo, E.:Rhap Vn, w. Carolyn Plummer (vn) *(rec Annenberg Audit., Snite Museum of Art, Univ. of Notre Dame, May & June 1994 & Jan 199)* Centaur ▲ CRC 2253 [DDD]
Haimo, E.:Son Pno *(rec Annenberg Audit., Snite Museum of Art, Univ. of Notre Dame, May & June 1994 & Jan 199)* Centaur ▲ CRC 2253 [DDD]
Haimo, E.:Swenson Songs, w. Georgine Resick (sop) *(rec Annenberg Audit., Snite Museum of Art, Univ. of Notre Dame, May & June 1994 & Jan 199)* Centaur ▲ CRC 2253 [DDD]
Retzel, F.:Line Drawings & Earthen Clay Figures Opus One ▲ CD 165
Schubel, M.:Divert Tpt, w. Anthony Perfetti (tpt), J. E. Suben (cnd), Polish National RSO Katowice Opus One ▲ CD 171 [DDD]
Sessions, R.:Duo Vn & Pno, w. C. Macomber (vn) Koch International Classics ▲ KIC 7153-2 [DDD]
Sessions, R.:Pno Music—Sonata No. 1 (1927–30); From my Diary (1937–40); Sonata No. 2 (1946); Sonata No. 3 (1964–65); Five Pieces for Piano (1974–75); Waltz (1978) Koch International Classics ▲ KIC 7106-2 [DDD]
Wylie, R.S.:Mandala Opus One ▲ CD 165
Wylie, R.S.:Preludes Pno Opus One ▲ CD 165
Wylie, R.S.:Psychogram Opus One ▲ CD 165
Wylie, R.S.:Soliloquy Opus One ▲ CD 165
Wylie, R.S.:The White Raven Opus One ▲ CD 165
Samaltanos, Nikolaos (pno)
Segerstam, L.:Noem 1, w. Pia Segerstam (vc) *(rec Paris, Feb 28, 1996)* BIS ▲ CD 792 [DDD]
Segerstam, L.:Zweixly con ped...adagissimo con nostalgia!, w. Christophe Sirodeau (pno) *(rec Paris, Feb 28, 1996)* BIS ▲ CD 792 [DDD]
Samaroff, Olga (pno)
Olga Samaroff:An American Virtuoso on the World Stage Pearl ▲ PEA 9860
Samarotto, Bob (ww)—see ORCHESTRAS & ENSEMBLES Zeitgeist
Samman, Rafik (perc/oud)—see ORCHESTRAS & ENSEMBLES La Nef
Sammons, Albert (vn)
Elgar, E.:Con Vn, w. H. Wood (cnd), New Queen's Hall Orch *(rec 1929 for Columbia Records)* Pearl ▲ PEA 9496 (m) [AAD]
Elgar, E.:Son Vn, w. W. Murdoch (pno) *(rec 1935 for Columbia Records)* Pearl ▲ PEA 9496 (m) [AAD]
Halvorsen, J.:Passacaglia & Sarabande con variazioni, w. L. Tertis (va) *(rec 5/27/29 for Columbia Reco)* Biddulph ▲ LAB 023 [ADD]
Mendelssohn, F.:Trio 2 Pno, w. W. Murdoch (pno), L. Tertis (vc) [violin–viola–piano arr.] *(rec 12/9/25 for Columbia Reco)* Biddulph ▲ LAB 023 [ADD]
Mozart, W.A.:Sinf concertante Vn, K.364, w. L. Tertis (va), H. Harty (cnd), London PO *(rec Apr. 30, 1933 for Columbi)* Biddulph ▲ LAB 023 [ADD]
10,000 Voices, w. G. Jones (bar), D. O'Neill (ten), World Choir, Massed Guards Bands [cnd:O. Arwel Hughes] *(rec live May 23, 1992)* EMI Classics ▲ CDC 54628-2 [DDD]
Samoilenko, Victor (pno)
Stravinsky, I.:Songs, w. O. Romanko (sop), A. Golyshev (cnd), Bolshoi Theater Chamber Music Ensemble—The Cloud; 3 Songs; Cats' Lullabies; Lullaby; 2 Lyrics by K. Balmont; Pastorale; Pribautiki; 3 Stories for Children; 4 Russian Folk-Songs; Little Harmonic Ramuziana; In Memoriam Dylan T.; The Owl & the Pussy-cat; 3 Lyrics from Japanese Poetry; 3 Songs to Lyrics by Shakespeare; 2 Songs to Lyrics by S. Gorodestsky, Op. 6 MK ▲ MKA 417126 [DDD]
Samoliov, Vladislav (va)—see ORCHESTRAS & ENSEMBLES Northern Crown Soloists Ensemble
Sampedro, Angel (vn)—see ORCHESTRAS & ENSEMBLES L'Academia d'Harmonia
Sampen, John (a sax)
Albright, W.:Son A Sax, w. M. Shrude (pno) Capstone ▲ CPS 8603
Babbitt, M.:Images, w. M. Shrude (pno) Neuma ▲ 45080 [DDD]
Mays, W.:Con A Sax, w. W. Mays (cnd), Wichita State Univ Faculty Ensemble CRI ■ C 361
Shrude, M.:Renewing the Myth, w. M. Shrude (pno) Neuma ▲ 450-80 [DDD]
Subotnick, M.:In 2 Worlds, w. M. Shrude (pno) Neuma ▲ 450-80 [DDD]
Wuorinen, C.:Divert Sax, w. M. Shrude (pno) Neuma ▲ 450-80 [DDD]
Samsing, Boris (vn)—see ORCHESTRAS & ENSEMBLES Kontra String Quartet
Samuel, Brent (vc)—see ORCHESTRAS & ENSEMBLES Delius String Quartet
Samuel, Harold (hpd)
Bach, J.S.:Chromatic Fant & Fugue Koch Legacy 2–▲ 3-7137-2
Bach, J.S.:English Suites—No. 2 in a, BWV 807 *(rec 1926)* Koch Legacy 2–▲ 3-7137-2
Bach, J.S.:Partitas Hpd, BWV 825–830—Partita BWV 825–826 Koch Legacy 2–▲ 3-7137-2
Bach, J.S.:Sons Vn, w. I. Menges (vn)—in E, BWV 1016 *(1928 HMV recording)* Koch Legacy 2–▲ 3-7137-2
Samuel, Harold (pno)
The Art of Harold Samuel Koch Legacy 2–▲ 3-7137-2
Bach, J.S.:Brandenburg Con 5, w. F. Black (cnd), NBC SO *(rec radio broadcast Dec 11, 1935)* Koch Legacy 2–▲ 3-7137-2
Bach, J.S.:Fant Org, BWV 562 Koch International Classics ▲ KIC 7610
Bach, J.S.:French Suites—Allemande Courante & Sarabande from No. 6 Nimbus ("Grand Piano" series) ▲ NI 8808
Bach, J.S.:Music of, w. Harold Bauer (pno), Ignaz Friedman (pno), Percy Grainger (pno), Myra Hess (pno)—Toccata No. 3 in G; Toccata & Fugue in d for Org [trans Tausig]; Well-Tempered Clavier Book 1, Nos. 5 & 21; Chorale [from Cant 147; trans Bauer]; Chromatic Fant & Fugue [trans von Bülow]; 2-Part Inventions Nos. 1, 6 & 8; Fant & Fugue in g for Org [trans Liszt]; Toccata & Fugue in g; French Suite No. 6; Gigue [from Partita in B♭, Book 1, No. 1] [all pno rolls] Nimbus ("Grand Piano" series) ▲ NI 8808 [DDD]
Bach, J.S.:Partitas Hpd, BWV 825–830—Gigue from No. 1 in B♭ Nimbus ("Grand Piano" series) ▲ NI 8808
Bach, J.S.:Toccata & Fugue in g Nimbus ("Grand Piano" series) ▲ NI 8808
Bach, J.S.:Das wohltemperierte Klavier—Book 1, No. 21 in B♭ Nimbus ("Grand Piano" series) ▲ NI 8808
Bach, J.S.:Das wohltemperierte Klavier—[Books 1 & 2] 4 sels *(rec 1923–27)* Koch Legacy 2–▲ 3-7137-2
Brahms, J.:Son 2 Vn, w. I. Menges (gtr) *(rec 1929)* Biddulph ▲ BID LAB 076
Brahms, J.:Son 3 Vn, w. I. Menges (gtr) *(rec 1929)* Biddulph ▲ BID LAB 076
Samuels, (hpd)—see ORCHESTRAS & ENSEMBLES Cologne Divitia Ensemble
Samuels, Dave (perc)
Synergy with Samuels Tall Poppies ▲ TP 30 [DDD]
Samuels, Dave (vib)
Harkl, w. Richard Stoltzman (cl), Eddie Gomez (perc), Jeremy Wall (kbd), Bill Douglas (bn), Harlem Boys Choir RCA Victor ▲ 09026-61272-2 [DDD] ■ 09026-61272-4 (CrO2)
In a Classical Groove, w. John Whitney Trio *(rec Clinton Recording Studio, New York City, Sept 18–20, 1995)* Golden String ▲ GSCD 028A
Spirits, w. Richard Stoltzman (cl), Eddie Gomez (db), David Torn (gtr), Bill Douglas (bn), King's Singers RCA Victor ▲ 09026-68416-2 ■ 09026-68416-4
Samuelson, Ralph (shak)
Hamilton, T.:Off-Hour Wait State, w. Thomas Buckner (voc), Roscoe Mitchell (a sax), Peter Zummo (trbn), Tom Hamilton (syn/elec), Jonathan Haas (perc) O.O. Discs ▲ OO 26 [DDD]
Sand, Michael (baroque vn/vl)
Out of the Orient Crystall Skyes, w. Nancy Zylstra (sop), Margriet Tindemans (vl), Jillion Stopples Dupree (hpd/org), Linda Melsted (baroque vn), Olga Hauptmann (baroque va), Ellen Siebert (vl), Russell Paige (vl) Wildboar ▲ WLBR 8901 [DDD]
Sand, Michael (vn)
Vivaldi, A.:Cons Vn, Op. 3/1–12, "L'estro armonico", w. M. Sand (cnd), Arcangeli Baroque Strings—Nos. 1, 6–8, 10 & 11 Meridian ▲ MER 84225 [DDD]

▲ = CD ♦ = Enhanced CD Δ = MD ■ = Cassette Tape □ = DCC

Sand, Sveinung (vn)
Saeverud, H.:Peer Gynt Suites, w. Anna Dolezych (va), Kjersti Dahle (ob/E hn), Gyrid Erlandsen (cl), Bohumil Maliska (hn), A. Dmitriev (cnd), Stavanger SO *(rec Stavanger Konserthus, Stavanger, Norway, Nov 13-17, 1995)* BIS ▲ CD 762 [DDD]

Sandau, Kurt (tpt)
Vivaldi, A.:Cons Diverse Instrs, w. L. Mayer (mand), B. Glaetzner (ob), Güttler (tpt), Botvay, Pommer (cnd), New Bach Collegium Musicum, Budapest Strings LaserLight ▲ 15518 [DDD]
Vivaldi, A.:Con for 2 Tpts, w. L. Güttler (tpt), M. Pommer (cnd), New Bach Collegium Musicum Laserlight ▲ 15 518

Sandeman, David (fl)
Falla, M. de:Con Hpd, w. R. Puyana (hpd), N. Black (ob), T. King (cl), R. Cohen (vn), T. Weill (vc), C. Mackerras (cnd) *(rec 1969)* Philips ("Spanish" series) ▲ 432829-2 [ADD]

Sander, Martin (org)
Reubke, J.:Son Org MD + G ▲ MDG 3120344 [DDD]

Sanderling, Michael (vc)
Schoenberg, A.:Ode to Napoleon, w. Roland Hermann (nar), Rim Vogler (vn), Frank Reinecke (vn), Stefan Fehlandt (va), Frank-Immo Zichner (pno) *(rec Siemensvilla, Berlin-Lankwitz, Aug. 1994)* EDA ▲ EDA 008-2 [DDD]
Schubert, Franz:Qnt Strs, D.956, w. Leipzig String Quartet MD + G ▲ MDG 3070603
Schulhoff, E.:Sxt Strs, w. Rainer Johannes Kimstedt (va), Petersen String Quartet *(rec Berlin, June 6-8 & Nov 7-8, 1994)* Capriccio ▲ 10 539 [DDD]

Sanders, Jack (gtr)
Bartók, B.:Romanian Folk Dances Pno, w. C. Haslop (vn) [arr. for violin & guitar]—6 dances Centaur ▲ CRC 2061 [DDD]
Campo, F.:Studies (2) Tpt, w. A. Plog (tpt) Crystal ▲ CD 663 [DDD]
Giuliani, M.:Grand Son Fl, w. C. Haslop (vn) [arr. for violin-guitar] Centaur ▲ CRC 2061 [DDD]
Kohn, K.:Concords, w. C. Haslop (vn) Centaur ▲ CRC 2061 [DDD]
Leisner, D.:Dances in the Madhouse, w. C. Haslop (vc) Centaur ▲ CRC 2061 [DDD]
Sarasate, P. de:Carmen Fant, w. C. Haslop (vn) [violin-guitar arr.] Centaur ▲ CRC 2061 [DDD]
Sarasate, P. de:Spanish Dances, w. C. Haslop (vn) [arr. for violin & guitar]—Op. 22/1, "Romanza andaluza" Centaur ▲ CRC 2061 [DDD]

Sanders, Samuel (pno)
Andersen, J.:Fl & Pno Music, w. Paula Robison (fl)—Au Bord de la Mer, Op. 9; Babillard, Op. 24/6; Chant Pastorale, Op. 24/1; Alla Mazurka, Op. 24/3; Berceuse, Op. 28/1; Die Mühle, Op. 55/4; Reverie, Op. 24/2; Die Blumen, Op. 56/2; Impromptu, Op. 7; Scherzino, Op. 55/6; Melodie, Op. 52 *(rec SUNY, Purchase, Theatre C, Feb. 14-16, 1995)* Arabesque ▲ ARA 6668 [DDD]
Bits & Pieces, w. Itzhak Perlman (vn) EMI Classics ▲ CDC 54882
Boehm, T.:Compositions Fl, w. Paula Robison (fl)—Vars on "Nel cor piu sento", Op. 4 *(rec New York City, 1974)* Vanguard Classics ▲ OVC 889 [ADD]
Borne, F.:Fant brillante sur Carmen, w. P. Robison (fl) Vanguard Classics ▲ OVC 4058
Brahms, J.:Sons Vc (comp), w. A. Diaz (vc) *(rec 1991)* Dorian ▲ DOR 90165 [DDD]
Carmen Fantasy, w. Robison, Paula (fl) Vanguard Classics ▲ OVC 4058
Dutilleux, H.:Sonatine Fl, w. P. Robison (fl) Vanguard Classics ▲ OVC 4058
Dvořák, A.:Romantic Pieces, Op. 75, w. I. Perlman (vn) EMI Classics ▲ CDC 47399 [DDD]
Dvořák, A.:Silent Woods, w. A. Diaz (vc) [Brahms's version for cello & piano] *(rec 1991)* Dorian ▲ DOR 90165 [DDD]
Dvořák, A.:Sonatina Vn, w. I. Perlman (vn) EMI Classics ▲ CDC 47399 [DDD]
Encores, w. Itzhak Perlman (vn) EMI Classics ▲ CDC 49514
Falla, M. de:Suite populaire espagnole, w. I. Perlman (vn) [trans Paul Kochanski for vn & pno] EMI Classics ▲ CDM 63533
Gaubert, P.:Nocturne et Allegro scherzando, w. Paula Robison (fl) *(rec New York City, 1974)* Vanguard Classics ▲ OVC 889 [ADD]
Gaubert, P.:Son 1 Fl, w. P. Robison (fl) Vanguard Classics ▲ OVC 4058
Genin, Paul A.:Vars on "Carnival of Venice", w. Paula Robison (fl) *(rec New York City, 1974)* Vanguard Classics ▲ OVC 889 [ADD]
Godard, B.:Suite de trois morceaux, w. Paula Robison (fl) [arr for fl & pno] *(rec New York City, 1974)* Vanguard Classics ▲ OVC 889 [ADD]
Grieg, E.:Songs, w. Paula Robison (fl)—Wedding Day at Troldhaugen, Op. 65/6; Love, Op. 67/5; 2 Brown Eyes, Op. 5/1; Solveig's Song [from Peer Gynt], Op. 23/19; I Love You!, Op. 5/3; A Swan, Op. 25/2; Spring, Op. 33/2; Thanks for Your Advice, Op. 21/4 *(rec SUNY, Purchase, Theatre C, Feb. 14-16, 1995)* Arabesque ▲ ARA 6668 [DDD]
Hummel, J.N.:Son Vn & Pno, Op. 50, w. Paula Robison (fl) *(rec New York City, 1974)* Vanguard Classics ▲ OVC 889 [ADD]
Joshua Bell, w. Joshua Bell (vn) London ▲ 417891-2 LH [DDD]
Kreisler, F.:Vn Pieces, w. I. Perlman (vn)—short pieces & transcriptions EMI Classics ▲ CDC 47467
Kreisler, F.:Vn Pieces, w. Ulrike-Anima Mathé (vn)—Schön Rosmarin; Tambourin Chinois; Caprice Viennois; Liebesleid; Marche Miniature Viennoise; Viennese Rhapsodic Fantasietta; Sicilienne & Rigaudon; Midnight Bells; Danse Espagnole; Lotusland; Syncopation; Tango; Scherzo; Cavatina; Slavonic Dances; 2 Mazurkas; Gypsy Song *(rec Sept 1995)* Dorian ▲ DOR 90231 [DDD]
Palmer, G.M.:Chamber Music, w. Robert White (ten) Indiana Univ School of Music ▲ 0-253-35061-1
Russian Romantics for Cello & Piano, w. Andrés Díaz (vc) *(rec Apr. 1993)* Dorian ▲ DOR 90188 [DDD]
Sarasate, P. de:Carmen Fant, w. R. Barton (vn) [arr. violin & piano] Dorian ▲ DOR 90183 [DDD]
Sarasate, P. de:Intro & Tarantella, w. R. Barton (vn) [arr. violin & piano] Dorian ▲ DOR 90183 [DDD]
Sarasate, P. de:Spanish Dances, w. R. Barton (vn) Dorian ▲ DOR 90183 [DDD]
Sarasate, P. de:Vn & Pno Music, w. R. Barton (vn)—Muiñera; Miramar; Adios, montaños mias Dorian ▲ DOR 90183 [DDD]
Smetana, B.:From the Homeland, w. I. Perlman (vn) EMI Classics ▲ CDC 47399 [DDD]
Taffanel, P.:Andante Pastorale et Scherzettino, w. P. Robison (fl), S. Sanders (pno). Vanguard Classics ▲ OVC 4058
Tribute to Jascha Heifetz, w. Itzhak Perlman (vn) EMI Classics ▲ CDC 49604
Villanelle:French Masterworks for Horn, w. David Jolley (hn), Joyce Guyer (sop), Nancy Allen (hp) *(rec SUNY, Purchase Recital Hall, May 24-26, 1995)* Arabesque ▲ Z 6678 [DDD]
Weber, C.M. von:Grand duo concertant Cl, w. J. Manasse (cl) XLNT ▲ CD 18004 [DDD]
Weber, C.M. von:Vars on a Theme from *Silvana* Cl, w. J. Manasse (cl) XLNT ▲ CD 18004 [DDD]

Sanderse, Ruben (va)—see ORCHESTRAS & ENSEMBLES Ives Ensemble members

Sandhoff, Martin (fl)
Mozart, W.A.:Con Fl Hp, w. S. Kwast (hp), Concerto Cologne Capriccio ▲ 70375

Sandhoff, Martin (rcr)
Vivaldi, A.:Cons Rcr, w. Cordula Breuer (rcr), Concerto Cologne LaserLight ▲ 14036 [DDD]

Sandklef, Per (vn)—see ORCHESTRAS & ENSEMBLES Musica Holmiae

Sandland, Richard (tuba)—see ORCHESTRAS & ENSEMBLES Fine Arts Brass Ensemble

Sandler, Alexander (pno)
Beethoven, L. van:Con 5 Pno, "Emperor", w. A. Titov (cnd), St. Petersburg New Philharmony Orch Infinity Digital ▲ QK 57222 [DDD]

Sandler, Myron (vn)
Copland, A.:Son Vn & Pno, w. L. Maury (pno)—originally released 1970 Crystal ■ C631
Ives, C.:Sons Vn, w. L. Maury (pno)—No. 2 Crystal ■ C631
Maury, L.:Son in Memory of the Korean War, w. L. Maury (pno) Crystal ■ C631

Sandor, Arpad (pno)
Strauss, R.:Son Vn, w. J. Heifetz (vn) *(rec 2/6/34)* Biddulph ▲ LAB 018 [ADD]

Sandor, György (pno)
Bartók, B.:Con Orch [composer's 1944 solo piano version] CBS ▲ MK 44526 [DDD]
Bartók, B.:Cons Pno (comp), w. Hollreiser, Gielen (cnd), Bamberg SO, Vienna SO *(rec 1958-59)* Vox Box ("Legends" series) 2-▲ CDX2 5506 [ADD]
Bartók, B.:Con 1 Pno, w. A. Fischer (cnd), Hungarian State Orch Sony Classical ▲ SK 45835 [DDD]
Bartók, B.:Con 2 Pno, w. A. Fischer (cnd), Hungarian State Orch Sony Classical ▲ SK 45835 [DDD]

Sandor, György (pno) (cont.)
Bartók, B.:Con 2 Pno, w. M. Gielen (cnd), Vienna Pro Musica Orch *(rec 1959)* Tuxedo ▲ TUXCD 1014
Bartók, B.:Con 3 Pno, w. M. Gielen (cnd), Vienna Pro Musica Orch *(rec 1959)* Tuxedo ▲ TUXCD 1014
Bartók, B.:Con 3 Pno, w. A. Fischer (cnd), Hungarian State Orch Sony Classical ▲ SK 45835 [DDD]
Bartók, B.:Dance Suite CBS ▲ MK 44526 [DDD]
Bartók, B.:Mikrokosmos *(rec 1955)* Sony Masterworks ("Portrait" series) 2-▲ MP2K 52528 (m) [ADD]
Bartók, B.:Petite Suite CBS ▲ MK 44526 [DDD]
Bartók, B.:Rhap Pno, w. R. Reinhardt (cnd), Southwest German RSO Baden-Baden *(rec 1958-59)* Vox Box ("Legends" series) 2-▲ CDX2 5506 [ADD]
Bartók, B.:Scherzo (Burlesque), w. P. Cao (cnd), Luxembourg RSO *(rec 1974)* Vox Box ("Legends" series) 2-▲ CDX2 5506 [ADD]
Bartók, B.:Son for 2 Pnos, w. R. Reinhardt (pno), O. Schad (perc), R. Sohm (perc) *(rec 1965)* Vox Box ("Legends" series) 2-▲ CDX2 5506 [ADD]
Prokofiev, S.:Pno Music (comp)—Sons. 1-9; Sonatinas, Op. 54/1 & 2; Etudes, Op. 2; 4 Pieces, Op. 3; 4 Pieces, Op. 4 Vox Box ("Legends" series) 3-▲ CDX3 3500

Sandoval, Arturo (tpt)
Arutiunian, A.:Con Tpt, w. L. Haza (cnd), London SO [Cadenza by Timofey Dokschizer] *(rec May 27-29 & July 16, 1993)* RCA Red Seal ▲ 09026-62661-2 [DDD]
Hummel, J.N.:Con in E♭ Tpt, S.49, w. L. Haza (cnd), London SO [Cadenza by Sandoval] *(rec May 27-29 & July 16, 1993)* RCA Red Seal ▲ 09026-62661-2 [DDD]
Mozart, L.:Con Tpt, w. L. Haza (cnd), London SO [Cadenza by Sandoval] *(rec May 27-29 & July 16, 1993)* RCA Red Seal ▲ 09026-62661-2 [DDD]
Sandoval, A.:Con Tpt, w. L. Haza (cnd), London SO [Cadenza by Timofey Dokschizer] *(rec May 27-29 & July 16, 1993)* RCA Red Seal ▲ 09026-62661-2 [DDD]

Sandovskaya, Galina (pno)
Ustvolskaya, G.:Composition 2, w. Igo Propischin (db), Leonid Kolosov (db), Vitalii Goryachev (db), Vladimir Vulih (db), Vyacheslav Kovalenko (db), Alexei Peresipkin (db), Dmitrii Sokolov (db), Vladimir Nefedov (db), Valerii Javnertchik (perc), O. Malov (cnd) *(rec St. Petersburg Radio House, Jan. 1994)* Megadisc ▲ 7867
Ustvolskaya, G.:Composition 3, w. Natalia Danilina (fl), Maria Osipova (fl), Inna Rodina (fl), Michail Tokarev (fl), Kirill Sokolov (bn), Dmitrii Krasnik (bn), Arsenii Makarov (bn), Konstantin Shevchuk (bn), O. Malov (cnd) *(rec St. Petersburg Radio House, Jan. 1994)* Megadisc ▲ 7867

Sandresky, Eleanor (kbds)—see ORCHESTRAS & ENSEMBLES Philip Glass Ensemble

Sandrof, E. (syn)—see also ORCHESTRAS & ENSEMBLES World Casio Quartet
First, D.:Lens Pt 2, w. M. Bard (gtr), D. First (gtr), C. Henderson (gtr) *(rec Oct. 1987)* O.O. Discs ▲ OO 5 [DDD]

Sanger, David (org)
Bach, Joh. Christian:Duets Org, Op. 18/5 & 6, w. Fagius (org) BIS ▲ CD 273 [DDD]
Bach, J.S.:Org Music (misc)—Canonic Vars [Vom Himmel Hoch, da Komm' ich Her, BWV 769a]; Con in a, BWV 593; The Schübler Chorales, BWV 645-650; Pastorale in F, BWV 590; Passacaglia in c, BWV 582 Meridian ▲ MER 84326 [DDD]
Franck, C.:Org Music (comp) BIS 2-▲ CD 214/15
Hesse, A.F.:Fant Org 4-Hands, Op. 35, w. Hans Fagius (org) BIS ▲ CD 273 [DDD]
Kellner, J.C.:Quartetto Org 4-Hands, w. H. Fagius (org) BIS ▲ CD 273 [DDD]
Merkel, G.A.:Son Org 4-Hands, w. Hans Fagius (org) BIS ▲ CD 273 [DDD]
Vierne, L.:Sym 1 Org Meridian ▲ CDE 84192
Vierne, L.:Sym 2 Org Meridian ▲ CDE 84192
Vierne, L.:Sym 3 Org Meridian ▲ CDE 84176
Vierne, L.:Sym 4 Org Meridian ▲ CDE 84176
Wesley, S.:Grand Duett Org, w. H. Fagius (org) BIS ▲ CD 273 [DDD]

Sangiorgio, Victor (pno)
Stravinsky, I.:Pno Music—Circus Polka; Serenade in A; Tango; 4 Études; Scherzo; Sonata; Rag Music; Sonata in f# Collins Classics ▲ COL 1374 [DDD]

Sangregorio, Conchi (perc)
Ginastera, A.:Cantos del Tucumán, w. Elena Montaña (sop), Conchi Vacas (fl), Wen-Yu Ku (vn), Zoraida Avila (hp) *(rec Madrid, Oct 1-3 1990)* RNE/Spanish National Radio ▲ M3/06 [DDD]

Sanromá, Jesús-María (pno)
The 1922-23 HMV & 1924 Victor Recordings, w. Jacques Thibaud (vn), Harold Craxton (pno), Alfred Cortot (pno) Biddulph ▲ LAB 014 [ADD]
Schumann, R.:Qnt Pno, w. Primrose String Quartet *(rec 1940)* Biddulph 2-▲ LAB 052 [ADD]

Sansom, Ben (vn)
Old English Nursery Rhymes, w. Vivien Ellis (sop), Tim Laycock (sgr), Broadside Band [Jeremy Barlow (rcrs/perc), Sharon Lindo (vns/rcr), George Weigand (lt/mandore/cittern/gtr), Rosemary Thorndycraft (b vl/h-g), Marilyn Sansom (vc)] *(rec Valley Recordings, Littleton-on-Severn, Feb 1996)* Saydisc ▲ CDSDL 419

Sansom, Marilyn (vc)
Music of the "Chapels Royal" of England, w. Michael Lewin (lt), Alastair Ross (org) Erato ▲ 45987-2

Sansom, Marylin (vc)
Scarlatti, A.:Domine refugium factus, w. Keith Majoram (bass), Charles Spinks (org), R. Norrington (cnd), Schütz Choir London *(rec 1973)* London 2-▲ 443868-2 [ADD]
Scarlatti, A.:O magnum mysterium, w. Keith Majoram (bass), Charles Spinks (org), Roger Norrington (cnd), Schütz Choir London *(rec 1973)* London 2-▲ 443868-2 [ADD]
Scarlatti, D.:Stabat mater, w. Keith Majoram (bass), Charles Spinks (org), R. Norrington (cnd), Schütz Choir London *(rec 1973)* London 2-▲ 443868-2 [ADD]

Sansone, Donato (fl)—see ORCHESTRAS & ENSEMBLES Consort Fontegara

Sant'Ambrogio, John (vc)
Brahms, J.:Qnt Cl, w. G. Siflies (cl), J. Korman (vn), J. Beiler (vn), D. Barnes (va) *(rec 1975-79)* Vox Box 3-▲ CD3X 3014 [ADD]
Mozart, W.A.:Qnt Cl, K.581, w. G. Siflies (cl), J. Korman (vn), J. Lind Jones (vn), J. Korman (va) *(rec 1975-79)* Vox Box 3-▲ CD3X 3014 [ADD]
Mozart, W.A.:Qnt Hn, K.407, w. R. Pandolfi (hn), J. Korman (vn), K. Mattis (vn), J. Korman (va) *(rec 1975-79)* Vox Box 3-▲ CD3X 3014 [ADD]

Sant'Ambrogio, Sara (vc)
Bernstein, L.:Songs & Duets, w. Judy Kaye (sop), William Sharp (bar), M. Barrett (pno), S. Blier (pno)—sels. from On The Town, 1944 *(Some other time; Lonely town; Carried away; I can cook)*; Peter Pan, 1949 *(Dream with me)*; Wonderful Town, 1952 *(A little bit in love)*; Songfest, 1977 *(Storyette, H.M.; To what you said)* [E] Koch International Classics ▲ KIC 7000-2 [DDD] ■ 3-7000-4 (D)

Sant'Ambrogio, Sara (vn)—see ORCHESTRAS & ENSEMBLES Eroica Trio

Sant'Ambrogio, Stephanie (vn)
Heiden, B.:Serenade, w. David DeBolt (bn), Katherine DeBolt (va), Richard Aaron (vc) Crystal ▲ CD 347

Santi, A. (bn)—see ORCHESTRAS & ENSEMBLES Modo Antiquo

Santoloci, Alfredo (cl)
Curran, A.:Crystal Psalms, An Homage to Kristallnacht, w. F. Badaloni (cl), D. Keberlee (cl), M. Riesler (cl), M. Capone (acc), L. Dublanchet (tuba), D. Rueff (tuba), A. Caggiano (perc), w. Ensemble Vocale Sesquialtera [cnd:E. Razzicchia], Radio France Chamber Choir [cnd:D. LaBorde]—[F] New Albion ▲ NA 067

Santos, Betina Maag (vn)
Telemann, G.P.:Fants Vn Gallo ▲ CD 718 [ADD]

Santos, Luis-Otavio (vn)—see ORCHESTRAS & ENSEMBLES Ricercar Consort

Sanvoisin, M. (fl)
Vivaldi, A.:Cons Fl, Op. 10, w. L. Auriacombe (cnd), Toulouse CO *(rec ca. 1967-69)* EMI Classics 2-▲ CDZB 769143-2 [ADD]

Sanzo, Cristiana (vc)
Amendola, F.:Ricercari, w. D. Patumi (db), A. Frederico (elecs/pno), A. Flore (voc), G. Lanzini (cl), L. Ciolfi (vn), C. Cavalieri (vn), O. Mangiavacchi (perc), Donizetti Ensemble Bongiovanni ▲ GB 5519 [DDD]

São Marcos, M.-L. (gtr)
Paganini, N.:Terzetto Vn, w. M. Minchev (vn), L. Gerogiev (vc) Vivace ▲ E 534 [ADD]

Saorgin, René (org)
Buxtehude, D.:Org Music (comp) Harmonia Mundi 5-▲ HMX 2901484/88
Buxtehude, D.:Org Music (misc)—Herr Christ, der einig Gottes Sohn; In dulci jubilo; Lobt Gott, ihr Christen allzugleich; Prelude & Fugue in g; Prelude & Fugue in F; Gelobet seist du, Jesu Christ; Te Deum Musique d'Abord ▲ HMA 190700 [ADD]
Buxtehude, D.:Org Music (misc)—8 Chorales; Magnificat primi toni; 4 Preludes & Fugues Musique d'Abord ▲ HMA 190942
Corrette, M.:Cons Org, Op. 26, w. G. Bezzina (cnd), Nice Baroque Ensemble Musique d'Abord ▲ HMA 1905148 [ADD]
Grigny, N. de:Premier livre d'orgue, w. M. Carey (bar)—5 Hymns [L] REM ▲ 311077 XCD [DDD]
Musiques théâtrales et militaires, w. Saorgin, René (org) Harmonia Mundi ("Musique d'Abord" series) ▲ HMA 190947
L'Orgue historique du palais Princier de Monaco REM ▲ 311043 [DDD]

Sapell, S. (va)—see also ORCHESTRAS & ENSEMBLES Vanbrugh String Quartet

Sapellnikoff, Vassily (pno)
Vassily Sapellnikoff Pearl ▲ PEA 9163 [ADD]
The Vocalion Recordings, 1923-27 Enterprise ("Piano Library" series) ▲ ENT PL 212

Saperton, David (pno)
Chopin, F.:Etudes (24) *(rec 1952, 1957)* VAI Audio 2-▲ VAIA/IPS 1037-2
Chopin, F.:Nouvelles études *(rec 1952, 1957)* VAI Audio 2-▲ VAIA/IPS 1037-2
Godowsky, L.:Java Suite—Nos. 1, 4, 9 *(rec 1952, 1957)* VAI Audio 2-▲ VAIA/IPS 1037-2
Godowsky, L.:Studies (53) after Chopin's Etudes—Nos. 4, 13-15, 25-26, 33, 36, 45, 47-48 *(rec 1952, 1957)* VAI Audio 2-▲ VAIA/IPS 1037-2
Godowsky, L.:Transcriptions & Paraphrases—Transcription of Albéniz's Triana [from *Iberia*]; Paraphrases after Strauss:on Die Fledermaus & Artist's Life [waltz] *(rec 1952, 1957)* VAI Audio 2-▲ VAIA/IPS 1037-2
Godowsky, L.:Triakontameron—Nos. 8, 11, 14, 15, 21 *(rec 1952, 1957)* VAI Audio 2-▲ VAIA/IPS 1037-2

Sapin, Marc (perc)
Jarrell, M.:Assonance VII Jecklin ▲ JS 304-2 [DDD]

Sappol, Mike (elec bass/busy box/tapes)
Exquisite Corpses from P.S. 122, w. Watson, David (shears/stick vn/gtr/tpt), Judy Dunaway (gtr/balloons), Anthony Coleman (sampler), Raissa St. Pierre (drums), Guy Yarden (vn/pno), Leslie Ross (bn), Linda Austin (gtr), Bruce Kaplan (gtr), Doug Henderson (peckhorn/bass/toy pno), Sue Ann Harkey (gtr), Cinnie Cole (sampler), et. al. ¿What Next? ▲ WN 0002 [ADD]

Saracino, Leopoldo (gtr)
Carulli, F.:Duo in C Gtr & Pno, w. M. Palumbo (pno) Nuova Era ("Ancient Music" series) ▲ NUO 7167 [DDD]
Carulli, F.:Duo in D Gtr & Pno, w. M. Palumbo (pno) Nuova Era ("Ancient Music" series) ▲ NUO 7174 [DDD]
Carulli, F.:Grand Duo, Op. 45, w. M. Palumbo (pno) Nuova Era ("Ancient Music" series) ▲ NUO 7167 [DDD]
Carulli, F.:Grand Duo, Op. 70, w. M. Palumbo (pno) Nuova Era ("Ancient Music" series) ▲ NUO 7169 [ADD]
Carulli, F.:Grand Duo, Op. 86, w. M. Palumbo (pno) Nuova Era ("Ancient Music" series) ▲ NUO 7169 [ADD]
Carulli, F.:Gtr Music, w. M. Palumbo (pno)—Opp. 134, 135, 150, 151 & 233 Nuova Era ("Ancient Music" series) ▲ NUO 7175 [DDD]
Carulli, F.:Gtr Music, w. M. Palumbo (pno)—12 Ovs. by Rossini:Cenerentola; Bianca e Falliero; L'Italiana in Algeri; Tancredi; Otello; L'Inganno felice; Il barbiere di Siviglia; La Gazza Ladra; Semiramide; Torvaldo e Dorliska; Eduardo e Cristina; Armida Nuova Era ("Ancient Music" series) 2-▲ NUO 7188 [DDD]
Carulli, F.:Gtr Music, w. Massimo Palumbo (pno) Nuova Era ("Ancient Music" series) ▲ NUO 7190 [DDD]
Carulli, F.:Nocturnes Gtr, "Mélange su temi di Rossini", w. M. Palumbo (pno) Nuova Era ("Ancient Music" series) ▲ NUO 7174 [DDD]
Carulli, F.:Nocturne Gtr, Op. 127, w. M. Palumbo (pno) Nuova Era ("Ancient Music" series) ▲ NUO 7167 [DDD]
Carulli, F.:Petits Duos, Op. 92, w. M. Palumbo (pno) Nuova Era ("Ancient Music" series) ▲ NUO 7169 [ADD]
Carulli, F.:Sonatines (3) Gtr & Pno, w. M. Palumbo (pno) Nuova Era ("Ancient Music" series) ▲ NUO 7174 [DDD]
Carulli, F.:Valses, Op. 32, w. M. Palumbo (pno) Nuova Era ("Ancient Music" series) ▲ NUO 7169 [ADD]
Carulli, F.:Vars on Theme by Beethoven, w. M. Palumbo (pno) Nuova Era ("Ancient Music" series) ▲ NUO 7167 [DDD]
Diabelli, A.:Divert molto facili, w. Massimo Palumbo (pno) Nuova Era ▲ NUO 7203 [DDD]
Diabelli, A.:Easy Pieces (11), w. Massimo Palumbo (pno) Nuova Era ▲ NUO 7203 [DDD]
Diabelli, A.:Grande Son Brillante, w. Massimo Palumbo (pno) Nuova Era ▲ NUO 7203 [DDD]
Diabelli, A.:Vars on a Theme by Rode, w. Massimo Palumbo (pno) Nuova Era ▲ NUO 7203 [DDD]
Gragnani, F.:Gtr Music, w. Marco Riboni (gtr), Andrea Pecola (vn), Emilio Vapi (fl), Anna Maria Giaquinta (cl), Andrea Bellato (vc)—Qt in A for Vn, Cl & 2 Gtrs, Op. 8; Duet No. 1 in A for Vn & Gtr; Trio in D for Fl, Vn & Gtr, Op. 13; Duet No. 2 in A for Vn & Gtr; Sxt in A for Fl, Cl, Vn, 2 Gtrs & Vc, Op. 9 Stradivarius ▲ STV 33385 [DDD]
Legnani, L.:Capriccios Nuova Era ▲ NUO 7239 [DDD]

Saram, Rohan de (vc)—see also ORCHESTRAS & ENSEMBLES Arditti String Quartet
Feldman, Morton:Patterns in a Chromatic Field, w. Marianne Schroeder (pno) *(rec West German Radio, Cologne, Sept. 29-Oct. 1, 1993)* Hat Hut ("Now." series) 2-▲ ART CD 2-6145 [DDD]

Sarasate, Pablo de (vn)
Pablo de Sarasate:The Complete Recordings *(rec 1904)* Opal ▲ CD 9851 (m) [AAD]

Sarbu, Eugène (vn)
Sibelius, J.:Con Vn, *(cnd & orch unknown)* Classics for Pleasure ("Silver Doubles" series) 2-▲ CFP CDCFP 4763 [ADD]

Sarbu, Mihail (pno)
Britten, H.:Lachrymae, w. J. Creitz (va) Dynamic ▲ CD 61 [DDD]
Enescu, G.:Concertpiece Va, w. J. Creitz (va) Dynamic ▲ CD 61 [DDD]
Franck, C.:Andantino quietoso, w. M. Sirbu (vn) Dynamic 2-▲ CD 21/1-2 [DDD]
Franck, C.:Gran Duo, w. M. Sirbu (vn) Dynamic 2-▲ CD 21/1-2 [DDD]
Franck, C.:Son Vn, w. M. Sirbu (vn) Dynamic 2-▲ CD 21/1-2 [DDD]
Franck, C.:Trios concertants, w. Academica Quartet members Dynamic 2-▲ CD 21/1-2 [DDD]
Shostakovich, D.:Son Va, w. J. Creitz (va) Dynamic ▲ CD 61 [DDD]
20th Century Viola, w. James Creitz (va) Dynamic ▲ CD 61 [DDD]

Sardelli, Federico Maria (fl)—see also ORCHESTRAS & ENSEMBLES Modo Antiquo
Cimarosa, D.:Con for 2 Fls, w. Marcello Gatti (fl), R. Cirri (cnd), Ars Cantus *(rec Sept 7-10, 1995)* Bongiovanni ▲ GB 2184 [DDD]

Sardy, David (dr/elec bass)
Exquisite Corpses from P.S. 122, w. Watson, David (shears/stick vn/gtr/tpt), Judy Dunaway (gtr/balloons), Anthony Coleman (sampler), Raissa St. Pierre (drums), Guy Yarden (vn/pno), Leslie Ross (bn), Linda Austin (gtr), Bruce Kaplan (gtr), Doug Henderson (peckhorn/bass/toy pno), Sue Ann Harkey (gtr), Cinnie Cole (sampler), et. al. ¿What Next? ▲ WN 0002 [ADD]

Sarge, Daniel (pno)
Spohr, L.:Songs (misc), w. Marjorie Patterson (sop)—Lied des verlassenen Mädchens, WoO 90; Nachgefühl, WoO 91 *(rec Clara Wieck Auditorium, Sandhausen, July 24, 25 & 27, 1995)* Marco Polo ▲ 8.223869 [DDD]
Spohr, L.:Songs, Op. 25, w. Marjorie Patterson (sop) *(rec Clara Wieck Auditorium, Sandhausen, July 24, 25 & 27, 1995)* Marco Polo ▲ 8.223869 [DDD]

Sarge, Daniel (pno) (cont.)
Spohr, L.:Songs, Op. 37, w. Marjorie Patterson (sop)—Nos. 1-5 *(rec Clara Wieck Auditorium, Sandhausen, July 24, 25 & 27, 1995)* Marco Polo ▲ 8.223869 [DDD]
Spohr, L.:Songs, Op. 41, w. Marjorie Patterson (sop) *(rec Clara Wieck Auditorium, Sandhausen, July 24, 25 & 27, 1995)* Marco Polo ▲ 8.223869 [DDD]
Spohr, L.:Songs, Op. 72, w. Marjorie Patterson (sop) *(rec Clara Wieck Auditorium, Sandhausen, July 24, 25 & 27, 1995)* Marco Polo ▲ 8.223869 [DDD]

Sargent, Barry (vn)—see also ORCHESTRAS & ENSEMBLES Al Ayre Español
Biber, H. von:Harmonia artificiosa-ariosa, w. M. Lindal (vn), M. van der Velden (viol), E. Siebens (db), M. Spányi (hpd)—Partitas 3 & 5 *(rec Feb. 4-6, 1993)* BIS ▲ CD 608 [DDD]

Sargon, Simon (pno)—see also ORCHESTRAS & ENSEMBLES Dallas Chamber Players
Bach, W.F.:Zerbrecht, zerreist, Aria, w. N. Keith, G. Hustis [G] *(rec Mar-July 1991)* Crystal ▲ CD675
Berlioz, H.:Songs, w. N. Keith (sop), G. Hustis (hn)—Le jeune pâtre breton [F] *(rec 3-7/91)* Crystal ▲ CD675
"Huntsman, What Quarry?", w. Nancy Keith (sop), Gregory Hustis (hn) Crystal ▲ CD675
Nicolai, O.:Variazioni concertanti, w. N. Keith (sop), G. Hustis (hn) [I] Crystal ▲ CD675
Sargon, S.:Music of, w. Lila Deis (sop), Stephen Dubov (ten), Stephen Girko (cl), Christopher Adkins (vc), Vesselin Demirev (vn), Deborah Baron (fl)—Shemà [Hear] for Sop, Fl, Cl, Vc & Pno; Before the Ark for Vn & Pno; Wedding Dance for Vn & Pno; Klezmuzik for Cl & Pno; At Gradmother's Knee [5 Yiddish Folk Songs] for Ten & Pno; Meditation for Vc & Pno; At Grandfather's Knee [5 Judeo-Spanish Folk Songs] for Sop & Pno *(rec Caruth Auditorium, SMU, Dallas, TX, Jan 1996)* Gasparo ▲ GAS 318
Schubert, Franz:Songs (misc), w. N. Keith (sop), G. Hustis (hn)—Auf dem Strom, D.943 [G] Crystal ▲ CD675
Strauss, R.:Das Alphorn, w. N. Keith (sop), G. Hustis (hn) [G] Crystal ▲ CD675

Sargous, Harry (ob)
Bach, J.S.:Sons Fl, BWV 1030-35, w. L. Ward (pno)—BWV 1030 [in g for oboe] Crystal ▲ CD 327 [DDD]
Banfield, W.:4 Persons, w. Fred Ormand (cl), Lynette Diers Cohen (bn), Ellen Weckler (pno) Innova ▲ 510 [DDD]
Bassett, L.:Dialogues, w. R. Conway (pno) Crystal ▲ CD326 [DDD]
Bolcom, W.:Aubade, "For the Continuation of Life", w. W. Bolcom (pno) Crystal ▲ CD326 [DDD]
Bolcom, W.:A Spring Concertino, w. C. St. Clair (cnd), Toronto Sinfonietta Crystal ▲ CD326 [DDD]
Cowell, H.:Ostinati (3) with Chorales, w. R. Conway (pno) Crystal ▲ CD326 [DDD]
Mead, A.:Scena Crystal ▲ CD 327 [DDD]
Pasculli, A.:Grand Con Ob, w. L. Ward (pno) Crystal ▲ CD 327 [DDD]
Singer, L.:Sensazione II, w. C. St. Clair (cnd), Toronto Sinfonietta Crystal ▲ CD326 [DDD]
Wolpe, S.:Son Ob, w. L. Ward (pno) Crystal ▲ CD 327 [DDD]

Sariola, Raimo (vc)
Sibelius, J.:Malinconia, w. Hui-Ying Liu (pno) Finlandia ▲ 4509-95854-2 [DDD]
Sibelius, J.:Music for Vc Pno, w. Hui-Ying Liu (pno)—Malinconia, Op. 20; Elegie, Op. 27/1; Romance in C, Op. 42; Valse triste, Op. 44/3; Canzonetta, Op. 62a; Valse romantique, Op. 62b; Cantique & Devotion, Op. 77, Nos. 1 & 2; Impromptu, Romance, Religioso & Rigaudon, Op. 78, Nos. 1-4; Rondino, Op. 81/2 Finlandia ▲ 4509-95854-2 [DDD]

Sárközy, Gergely (lt)
Bach, J.S.:Lt Music—Fuge Lt, BWV 1000; Partita Lt, BWV 997 [performed on Hpd Lt]; Prelude, Allegro & Fugue Lt; Prelude Lt, BWV 998; Suites Lt, BWV 995 & 996 *(rec 1980, 1984 & 1991)* Hungaroton 2-▲ HCD 31616/17 [ADD/DDD]
Bach, J.S.:Preludium, Fugue & Allegro Hpd, BWV 998—& Prelude in c, BWV 999; Fugue in g, BWV 1000 Hungaroton ▲ HCD 12157
Bach, J.S.:Suite Lt, BWV 995 Hungaroton ▲ HCD 12157
Scarlatti, D.:Sons Kbd—twelve sonatas, performed on lute-harpsichord *(K.77, 96, 159, 202, 244)*, guitar *(K.8, 377, 450)*, lute *(K.133, 284)*, viola bastarda *(K.90)*, & organ *(K.87)* Hungaroton ▲ HCD 12954 [DDD]

Sárközy, Gergely (va bastarda)
Bach, J.S.:Sons Vl, BWV 1027-1029, w. István Dénes (org), Péter Ella (hpd/lt hpd) *(rec 1980, 1984 & 1991)* Hungaroton 2-▲ HCD 31616/17 [ADD/DDD]

Sárközy, Gergely (va bastarda/lt)
Bach, J.S.:Cant 147, w. István Dénes (org), Péter Ella (hpd/lt hpd)—chorale *(rec 1980, 1984 & 1991)* Hungaroton 2-▲ HCD 31616/17 [ADD/DDD]

Sarlo, Dorella (pno)
Barber, S.:Souvenirs—[arr. pno] Nuova Era ▲ NUO 7195 [DDD]
Bernstein, L.:Anniversaries (5) Pno Nuova Era ▲ NUO 7195 [DDD]
Bernstein, L.:Anniversaries (13) Pno Nuova Era ▲ NUO 7195 [DDD]
Copland, A.:Blues Nuova Era ▲ NUO 7195 [DDD]
Copland, A.:Night Thoughts Nuova Era ▲ NUO 7195 [DDD]

Sarnau, Freidmann (vn)
Bach, C.P.E.:Trio Sons (misc), w. C. Delafontaine (fl), P. Mermoud (vc), M. Jordan (hpd)—in b, a, d, B♭ & D *(rec Jan 4, 5 & 6, 1988)* Gallo ▲ CD 541
Gerber, R.:Son Vn, w. Dagmar Clottu (pno) Gallo ▲ CD 861 [ADD]
Telemann, G.P.:Fants Vn Gallo ▲ CD 687 [DDD]

Sarobin, D. (gtr/mand)
Kolb, B.:Spring River Flowers Moon Night, w. B. Kolb (cnd), Brooklyn College Percussion Ensemble CRI ■ C 361
Kolb, B.:Spring River Flowers Moon Night, w. B. Kolb (cnd), Brooklyn College Percussion Ensemble CRI ▲ CD 576 [ADD]

Saroglou, Dimitris (pno)
Gouvy, T.:Qnt Pno, w. Denis Clavier String Quartet *(rec l'Auditorium Tibor Varga à Sion, July 27 - Aug 1, 1995)* K617 ▲ 7054 [DDD]

Sárosi, Péter (vn)—see ORCHESTRAS & ENSEMBLES New Haydn String Quartet

Saroun, Jaroslav (pno)
Eben, Petr:Old Testament Frescoes (3), w. Antonín Novák (vn) *(rec Martínek Studio in Prague, Jan 23 & 26 & Feb 13 & 14)* Panton ▲ 811398-2 [DDD]
Suk, J.:Songs, Op. 15, w. B. di Praga, L. Čermáková (pno), B. Kulínský (cnd)—Zal; Tuzba; Společný hrob; Pastýři na jaro; Diviná voda; Vily; Pastýř a pastyřka; Zpominky; Choutka po vdaní; Kéz by Vedeli [Cz] Multisonic ▲ 31 0111-2 [DDD]

Sartoretti, Christine (hpd)
Bach, J.S.:Cons Hpd, BWV 1052-1058, w. C. Jaccottet (hpd), N. Hostettler (hpd), L. Klinckerfus (hpd), J. Faerber (cnd), Württemberg CO *(rec 1978)* Vox Box 3-▲ CD3X 3018 [ADD]
Bach, J.S.:Cons for 2 Hpds (comp), w. C. Jaccottet (hpd), N. Hostettler (hpd), L. Klinckerfus (hpd), J. Faerber (cnd), Württemberg CO *(rec 1978)* Vox Box 3-▲ CD3X 3018 [ADD]
Bach, J.S.:Cons for 3 Hpds (comp), w. C. Jaccottet (hpd), N. Hostettler (hpd), L. Klinckerfus (hpd), J. Faerber (cnd), Württemberg CO *(rec 1978)* Vox Box 3-▲ CD3X 3018 [ADD]
Caix D'Hervelois, L. de:La Gracieuse, w. Jennifer Paull (ob), Stefano Canuti (bn) *(rec English Church, Villars, Switzerland, Apr 21-22, 1995)* Doron ▲ DRC 5006 [DDD]
Caix D'Hervelois, L. de:Les Vendangeuses, w. Jennifer Paull (ob), Stefano Canuti (bn) *(rec English Church, Villars, Switzerland, Apr 21-22, 1995)* Doron ▲ DRC 5006 [DDD]
Marais, M.:Vars on *Folies d'Espagne*, w. Jennifer Paull (ob), Stefano Canuti (bn) *(rec English Church, Villars, Switzerland, Apr 21-22, 1995)* Doron ▲ DRC 5006 [DDD]

Sasaki, Jean Dayton (pno)
Powell, Morgan:Suite Changes, w. Ray Sasaki (tpt) *(rec Urbana, IL, Oct 17, 1995)* New World ▲ 80499-2

Sasaki, Ray (tpt)—see also ORCHESTRAS & ENSEMBLES Tone Road Ramblers
Powell, Morgan:Suite Changes, w. Jean Dayton Sasaki (pno) *(rec Urbana, IL, Oct 17, 1995)* New World ▲ 80499-2

Sasaki, Saiko (pno)—see also ORCHESTRAS & ENSEMBLES Ravinia Trio
Brahms, J.:Son 2 Vc, w. P. Hörr (vc) Divox ▲ CDX 29106 [DDD]
Reinecke, C.:Sons Vc, w. Claudius Herrmann (vc) CPO ▲ CPO 999342

Šašina, Radoslav (db)
Zimmermann, A.:Con Db, w. P. Zajíček (cnd), Bratislava Musica Aeterna Trevak ▲ TRE 40010 [DDD]

824 ▲ = CD ◆ = Enhanced CD Δ = MD ■ = Cassette Tape □ = DCC

Šašina, Radoslav (db) (cont.)
Zimmermann, A.:Con in D Db, w. P. Zajíček (cnd), Bratislava Musica Aeterna
Trevak ▲ TRE 40010 [DDD]

Sass, (vc)
Weigl, V.:New England Suite, w. S. Drucker (cl), G. Moore (pno) CRI ■ C 326

Šatava, Oldřich (timp)
Purcell, H.:Son Tpt, w. Jaroslav Halíř (tpt), Marek Vajo (tpt), Radek Nemec (tpt), Jan Vobořil (hn), Jiří Nauš (trbn), Lubomír Maryška (tuba), Pavel Černý (org) [trans. F. Antonín Vaigl] *(rec Mirror Chapel of the Prague Klementinum, Mar 26, 1995)* Panton ▲ 811368-2 [DDD]

Sato, Atsuko (bn)
Baroque Trumpetissimo, w. David Bilger (tpt), Stephen Burns (tpt), Edward Carroll (tpt), Alex Holton (tpt), Raymond Mase (tpt), Timothy Morrison (tpt), Lee Soper (tpt), Ben Harms (timp), Edward Brewer (org/hpd), Philharmonia Virtuosi [cnd:Richard Kapp] ESS.A.Y ▲ ESS 1035 [DDD]

Sato, Eriko (vn)—see also ORCHESTRAS & ENSEMBLES Chamber Music Northwest members
Bach, J.S.:Con for 3 Vns, w. P. Peabody (vn), R. Rood (vn), R. Kapp (cnd), Philharmonia Virtuosi
ESS.A.Y ▲ CD 1002 [DDD] ■ C 1002 (D)
Ives, C.:Largo, w. D. Schifrin (cl), I. Vallecillo (pno) *(rec 6 & 7/90)* Delos ▲ 3088 [DDD]
Piston, W.:Son Vn, w. D. Oei (pno) Grenadilla ■ GSC 1073
Porter, Q.:Qnt Cl, w. D. Schifrin (cl), T. Arm (vn), P. Neubauer (va), W. Lash (vc) *(rec 6 & 7/90)*
Delos ▲ 3088 [DDD]

Sato, Hiroko (pno)
Desolation & Despair:Italian Drawing Room Music of the Romantic Era (1800's), w. Patricia Adkins Chiti (mez) Kicco Classics ▲ 1195 [DDD]

Sato, Michihiro (tsugaru shamisen)
Sato, M.:Improvs, w. Bill Frisell (elec gtr), Fred Frith (elec gtr), Tenko (sgr), Mark Miller (elec bass), Nicolas Collins (elec), Christian Marclay (turntables), Steve Colemann (sax), Tom Cora (vc), Joey Baron (perc), Mark Dresser (elec bass), Gerry Hemingway (perc), Toh Ban Djan [Ikue Mori (perc), Luli Shioi (elec bass/sgr)], Semantics [Elliott Sharp (electric gtr/bass), Samm Bennett (perc), Ned Rothenberg (sax)]—23 improvisations with various accompaniment combinations *(rec Baby Monster Studio, NY, Apr. 11-16, 1988)* Hat Hut ▲ hat ART CD 6015 [ADD]

Sato, S. (perc)
Fukushi, N.:Chromosphere, w. J. Arase (perc), M. Okada (perc), H. Yamazaki (perc), S. Yoshihara (perc), T. Otaka (cnd), Tokyo PO *(rec live Tokyo Bunka-Kaikan, Large Hall, May 30, 1981)*
Camerata ▲ 32CM 293 [AAD]

Satoh, Toyohiko (archlt)
Scarlatti, D.:Sons Kbd, w. Michiel Niessen (bass lt)—Sonatas, K.30,208,322,380,440,476 & 481 *(rec 1/90)* Channel Classics ▲ CCS 2291 [DDD]

Satoh, Toyohiko (lt)—see also ORCHESTRAS & ENSEMBLES Little Consort
Bach, J.S.:Chaconne *(rec Feb 1990)* Channel Classics ▲ CCS 0490 [DDD]
Bach, J.S.:Partita Fl, BWV 1013, w. W. van Hauwe (rcr), W. Möller (vc), G. Wilson (hpd)—in c *(rec 1988)*
Channel Classics ▲ CCS 4492 [DDD]
Bach, J.S.:Sons & Partitas Vn, BWV 1001-1006—Andante from Sonata, BWV 1003; Chaconne from Partita, BWV 1004 Channel Classics ▲ CCS 0490 [DDD]
Blockflutes 3:The Early 17th Century, w. Walter Van Hauwe (rcr) Channel Classics ▲ CCS 3392 [DDD]
Dowland, J.:Lt Music—Mellancoly Galliard *(rec 1/91)* Channel Classics ▲ CCS 2891 [DDD]
Satoh, T.:Music of—Tombeau de Mr. D. Philips Channel Classics ▲ CCS 0490 [DDD]
Telemann, G.P.:Rcr Music (misc), w. W. van Hauwe (ob), W. Möller (vc), G. Wilson (hpd)—Fantasies Nos. 1 & 8; Partita No. 5 in e; Son. d; Son. D; Trio Son. in B♭ *(rec 1988)*
Channel Classics ▲ CCS 4492 [DDD]
Weiss, S.L.:Lt Music—L'Infidele *(rec 2/90)* Channel Classics ▲ CCS 0490 [DDD]
Zamboni, G.:Sons Lt—Sonatas IXa & XIa Channel Classics ▲ CCS 2291 [DDD]

Satoh, Toyohiko (lt/vih)
The Art of Spanish Variations, w. Ireen Thomas (vih) Channel Classics ▲ CCS 3091 [DDD]
Baroque Lute Recital Channel Classics ▲ CCS 0490 [DDD]
Chaconne *(rec 2/90)* Channel Classics ▲ CCS 0490 [DDD]
Classical Lute Klavier ▲ KCD 11026 [ADD]

Satukangas, Arto (pno)
Enescu, G.:Son 2 Vn, w. P. Csaba (vn) Ondine ▲ ODE 789-2 [DDD]
Enescu, G.:Son 3 Vn, w. P. Csaba (vn) Ondine ▲ ODE 789-2 [DDD]
Mendelssohn, F.:Concert Pieces, w. Kari Kriikku (cl), Osmo Linkola (bas hn) Ondine ▲ ODE 820 [DDD]
Weber, C.M. von:Grand duo concertant Cl, w. Kari Kriikku (cl) Ondine ▲ ODE 820 [DDD]

Sauer, Emil von (pno)
Liszt, F.:Cons Pno, w. F. von Weingartner (cnd), Paris Conservatory Societé des Concerts Orch *(rec Dec. 1928)* Pearl ▲ PEA 9403 (m) [AAD]
Liszt, F.:Pno Music (misc)—La Campanella; Gnomenreigen; Valse oubliée & Consolation in D♭; Ricordanza *(rec 1927-28 & 1938-39)* Pearl ▲ PEA 9403 (m) [AAD]
1920-1940 Recordings Pearl ▲ PEA 9993 (m) [AAD]

Sauer, Martin (gtr)—see ORCHESTRAS & ENSEMBLES Prague Guitar Quartet

Sauer, Ralph (trbn)
Orchestral Excerpts for Trombone *(rec Mar. 29-31, 1993)* Summit ▲ DCD 143 [DDD]
Poulenc, F.:Son Tpt, w. T. Stevens (tpt), J. Cerminaro (hn) Crystal ■ C 367
Ralph Sauer, Trombone, w. Zita Carno (pno) Crystal ▲ CD 380

Sauerbeck, Agnes (org)
Harrison, L.:La Koro Sutro, w. William Winant (gamelan cnd), Karen Gottlieb (hp), P. Brett (cnd), Univ of California at Berkeley Chamber Chorus [Esperanto] New Albion ▲ NA 015 [ADD];

Saulesco, Mircea (vn)
Atterberg, K.:Suite 3 Vn, w. G. Roehr (va), S. Westerberg (cnd), Swedish RSO
Swedish Society ▲ SCD 1006

Saunders, Steven (trbn)
Bruckner, A.:motets, w. Richard Cheetham (trbn), Adrian Lane (trbn), Simon Wills (trbn), Matthew Morley (org), Robert James (cnd), James St. Bride's Church Choir—Os justi; Locus iste; Libera me [in f, 1854]; Ave maria; Ecce sacerdos; Vexilla regis; Salvum fac populum tuum [1884]; Afferentur regi; Pange lingua; Tota pulchra es [Daniel Norman (tenor)]; Virga Jesse; Inveni David; Iam lucis orto sidere [Hymnus, 1868]; Tantum ergo [in D, 1988]; Christus factus est *(rec St. Bride's Church, Fleet Street, London, Jan. 27-29, 1994)* Naxos ▲ 8.550956 [DDD]

Saunders, Teddy (pno/syn)—see ORCHESTRAS & ENSEMBLES Jazzantiqua

Savage, Brian (fl)—see ORCHESTRAS & ENSEMBLES Rhythm & Bluefield Band

Savage, D. (bn)—see also ORCHESTRAS & ENSEMBLES SONOR Ensemble of Univ of California San Diego members
Smith, S.S.:Here & There, w. J. Fonville (fl), D. Yoken (pno) O.O. Discs ▲ OO 11 [DDD]

Savage, Stephen (pno)
Beethoven, L. van:Son 30 Pno *(rec Studio 200, ABC Ultimo, Jan & July 1995)*
Tall Poppies ▲ TP 076 [DDD]
Beethoven, L. van:Son 31 Pno *(rec Studio 200, ABC Ultimo, Jan & July 1995)*
Tall Poppies ▲ TP 076 [DDD]
Beethoven, L. van:Son 32 Pno *(rec Studio 200, ABC Ultimo, Jan & July 1995)*
Tall Poppies ▲ TP 076 [DDD]

Savall, Jordi (vl)
Bach, J.S.:Sons Fl, BWV 1030-35, w. S. Preston (baroque fl), T. Pinnock (hpd)—BWV 1030-1035
CRD 2-▲ 3314/15 [ADD]
Bach, J.S.:Sons Vl, BWV 1027-1029, w. Ton Koopman (hpd) Virgin Classics ▲ CDM 61291
Baroque Music for Recorder, w. Conrad Steinmann (rcr), Monica Huggett (baroque vn), Hopkinson Smith (lt/thb/gtr), Pere Ros (vl), Claude Flagel (h-g), Johann Sonnleitner (hpd)
Claves ▲ CD 508103 [ADD]
Caccini, G.:Le nuove musiche, w. Montserrat Figueras (sop), R. Clancy (baroque gtr), H. Smith (baroque gtr), X. Schindler (hp), Schola Cantorum Basiliensis Editio Classica ▲ 77164-2-RG [ADD]
Couperin, F.:Pièces de violes avec la basse chifrée, w. A. Maurette (vl), T. Koopman (hpd)
Astrée ▲ E 7744 [AAD]
Hume, T.:The First Part of Ayres (sels) Astrée ▲ E 7723 [AAD]

Savall, Jordi (vl) (cont.)
Marais, M.:Pièces de viole [Book 3] (sels), w. T. Koopman (hpd), H. Smith (thb) Astrée ▲ E 8761
Marais, M.:Pièces de viole [Book 4] (sels), w. T. Koopman (hpd), H. Smith (baroque gtr)—"Suitte d'un Gout Etranger:" comprising eleven pieces from Book 4 of Pièces de viole Astrée ▲ E 7727 [AAD]
Merula, T.:Arias & Capriccios, w. M. Figueras (sop), J.-P. Canihac (cnt), T. Koopman (hpd), R. Lislevand (thb), A. Laurence-King (hp), L. Duftschmid (vn) Astrée ▲ E 8503
Milán, L. de:Maestro (sels), w. Andrew Lawrence-King (hp/psaltery) Astrée ▲ E 8535
Ortiz, D.:Trattado de Glosas, w. T. Koopman (hpd/org), L. Duftschmid (vn), R. Lislevand (vih), P. Pandolfo (b vl), A. Lawrence-King (hp) Astrée ▲ E 8717 [DDD]
Sainte-Colombe, M. de:Concerts for 2 B Vls, w. W. Kuijken (b vl)—Concerts XXVII, "Bourrasque"; XLVIII, "Le raporté"; XLI, "Le retour"; XLIV, "Tombeau les regrets"; LIV, "[La] Dubois"
Astrée ▲ E 7729 [AAD]
Sainte-Colombe, M. de:Concerts for 2 B Vls, w. W. Kuijken (b vl)—Concerts Nos. 3, 8, 42, 47 & 51 *(rec April 1992)* Astrée ▲ E 8743 [DDD]
Savall, J.:Joan of Arc, w. M. Figueras (sop), Hespèrion XX, La Capella Reial de Catalunya
Harmonia Mundi ▲ K 1006-2 ■ K 51006-4

Savary, Yves (vc)
Tartini, G.:Sons Vn & Continuo, w. I. Turban (vn), U. Deutschler (hpd)—Sonata in A, "Pastorale" (B A16); Sonata in C (B C11); Sonata in E (B E6); Sonata in g, "Devil's Trill" (B G5); Sonata in g, "Didone abbandonata" (B G10) Claves ▲ CD 9110 [DDD]

Savelwski, Dieter (E hn)
Mercadante, S.:La Serenata, w. Andras Adorjan (fl) or Aurèle Nicolet (fl), Han-An Liu (hp), Julius Berger (vc) Tudor ▲ TUD 763 [DDD]

Saver, Benjamin (pno)
Beethoven, L. van:Andante, WoO 57, "Andante favori"
Walsingham Classics ("The Sydney International Piano Competition" series) ▲ WAL 8019 [DDD]

Savery, Uffe (perc)—see ORCHESTRAS & ENSEMBLES Safri Duo

Savijoki, Jukka (gtr)
Bergman, E.:Midnight *(rec Studio BIS, Djursholm, Sweden, May 3-4, 1982)*
BIS ▲ CD 207 [AAD/DDD]
Berkeley, L.:Sonatina Gtr Ondine ▲ ODE 779-2 [DDD]
Berkeley, L.:Songs of the Half-Light, w. I. Partridge (ten) [E] Ondine ▲ ODE 779-2 [DDD]
Berkeley, L.:Theme & Vars Gtr Ondine ▲ ODE 779-2 [DDD]
Britten, H.:Folksong Arrs, w. I. Partridge (ten)—The soldier and the sailor; The shooting of his dear; Bonny at morn; Master Kilby; I will give my love an apple; Sailor-boy [E] [arr. Tenor & Guitar]
Ondine ▲ ODE 779-2 [DDD]
Britten, H.:Nocturnal Gtr Ondine ▲ ODE 779-2 [DDD]
Britten, H.:Songs from the Chinese, w. I. Partridge (ten) Ondine ▲ ODE 779-2 [DDD]
Buxtehude, D.:Gtr Music—Suite in e for Guitar *(rec Aug 25-26, 1980)* BIS ▲ CD 176 [AAD]
Corbetta, F.:Gtr Music—Suite in a for Guitar *(rec Aug 25-26, 1980)* BIS ▲ CD 176 [AAD]
Giuliani, M.:Music for Fl & Gtr (comp), w. M. Helasvuo (fl)—Duettino facile, Op. 77; Duo (1810-11); Grand Duetto Concertant, Op. 52; Grand Duo Concertant, Op. 85; Twelve Ländler, Op. 75
BIS ▲ CD 411 [DDD]
Giuliani, M.:Music for Fl & Gtr (comp), w. M. Helasvuo (fl)—Divertimenti Notturni, Op. 86; Grande Sérénade, Op. 82; Serenade, Op. 127; Variations, Op. 84 BIS ▲ CD 412 [DDD]
Giuliani, M.:Music for Fl & Gtr (comp), w. M. Helasvuo (fl)—Gran Pot-Pourri, Op. 126; Grand Potpourri, Op. 53; Pièces faciles et agréables, Op. 74; Potpourri tiré de l'Opéra Tancredi, Op. 76; Six Variations, Op. 81 BIS ▲ CD 413 [DDD]
Heininen, P.:...touching... *(rec Studio BIS, Djursholm, Sweden, May 3-4, 1982)*
BIS ▲ CD 207 [AAD/DDD]
Nordgren, P.H.:Butterflies *(rec Studio BIS, Djursholm, Sweden, May 3-4, 1982)*
BIS ▲ CD 207 [AAD/DDD]
Piazzolla, A.:Histoire du tango, w. M. Helasvuo (fl) Ondine ▲ ODE 781-2 [DDD]
Piazzolla, A.:Pieces Gtr Ondine ▲ ODE 781-2 [DDD]
Rautavaara, E.:Serenades of the Unicorn *(rec May 3, 1982)* BIS ▲ CD 66 [AAD]
Takemitsu, T.:Music of, w. Mikael Helasvuo (fl), Eero Palviainen (lt), Timothy Ferchen (vib/crotales)—Sacrifice; Voice; All in Twilight; Ring; Foloios; Itinerant; Toward the Sea
Ondine ▲ ODE 839 [DDD]

Savijoki, Jukka (lt)
Bach, J.S.:Prelude, Fugue & Allegro Lt, BWV 998 *(rec Aug 25-26, 1980)* BIS ▲ CD 176 [AAD]
Weiss, S.L.:Lt Music—Suite for Lute *(rec Aug 25-26, 1980)* BIS ▲ CD 176 [AAD]

Savijoki, Pekka (a sax)
Creston, P.:Son Sax, w. Jussi Siirala (pno) *(rec Nacka Aula, Nacka, Sweden, May 2, 1980)*
BIS ▲ CD 52 [AAD]
Hindemith, P.:Son Alto Hn, w. Jussi Siirala (pno) *(rec Nacka, Sweden, May 3, 1980)*
BIS ▲ CD 159 [AAD]
Larsson, L.-E.:Con Sax, w. J. Panula (cnd), Stockholm New CO BIS ▲ CD 218 [DDD]
Tubin, E.:Son A Sax, w. Roland Pöntinen (pno) BIS ▲ CD 269 [AAD]

Savijoki, Pekka (sax)
Boutry, R.:Divort Sax & Pno, w. M. Rahkonen (pno) BIS ▲ CD 209 [AAD]
Françaix, J.:Danses exotiques, w. M. Rahkonen (pno) BIS ▲ CD 209 [AAD]
Glazunov, A.:Con Sax, w. J. Panula (cnd), Stockholm New CO BIS ▲ CD 218 [DDD]
Maurice, P.:Tableaux de Provence, w. J. Siirala (pno) BIS ▲ CD 209 [AAD]
Milhaud, D.:Scaramouche (transcriptions), w. M. Rahkonen (pno) [saxophone-piano transcription]
BIS ▲ CD 209 [AAD]
Panula, J.:Adagio & Allegro, w. J. Panula (cnd), Stockholm New CO BIS ▲ CD 218 [DDD]

Savino, Richard (gtr)
Boccherini, L.:Qnts Gtr & Strs, w. Artaria String Quartet—Quintets VII & VIII
Harmonia Mundi USA ▲ HMU 907069
Boccherini, L.:Qnts Gtr & Strs, w. Artaria String Quartet—Quintets I, II & III
Harmonia Mundi USA ▲ HUC 907039
Giuliani, M.:Duettino, w. Laurel Zucker (fl) Cantilena ▲ 66012-2 [DDD]
Giuliani, M.:Grand Duo Concertant, Op. 25, w. Monica Huggett (vn)
Harmonia Mundi France ▲ HMU 907116
Giuliani, M.:Grand Son Fl, w. Laurel Zucker (fl) Cantilena ▲ 66012-2 [DDD]
Giuliani, M.:Qual Mesto Gemito, w. Laurel Zucker (fl) Cantilena ▲ 66012-2 [DDD]
Giuliani, M.:Qnt Gtr, w. Artaria String Quartet Harmonia Mundi USA ▲ HMU 907069
Giuliani, M.:Serenade Fl, w. Laurel Zucker (fl) Cantilena ▲ 66012-2 [DDD]
Paganini, N.:Grand Son Vn, w. Monica Huggett (vn) Harmonia Mundi France ▲ HMU 907116
Paganini, N.:Son concertata, w. Monica Huggett (vn) Harmonia Mundi France ▲ HMU 907116

Savinova, Natalie (vc)
Hindemith, P.:Kammermusik 3, w. A. Vinogradov (cnd), Moscow Contemporary Music Ensemble
Triton ▲ 17010 [DDD]
Hindemith, P.:Qt Cl, Vn, Vc & Pno, w. Oleg Tantzov (cl), Mikhail Tzinman (vn), Victor Yampolsky (pno) *(rec Mosfilm Studio, Dec 1994)* Triton ▲ 17005 [DDD]

Savkins, Jurijs (vn)—see ORCHESTRAS & ENSEMBLES Riga String Quartet

Savoie, Gary John (org)
Historic Organs of New Orleans, w. George Bozeman (org), James S. Darling (org), Jesse E. Eschbach (org), Gerald D. Frank (org), John Gearhart (org), James Hammann (org), Frederick Hohman (org), Lenora McCroskey (org), Mary Gifford Matthys (org), Lorenz Maycher (org), Donald Messer (org) *(rec June 1989)* Organ Historical Society 2-▲ OHS 89

Sawa, Marian (org)
Ave Maria, w. Bozena Betley (sop), Wieslaw Ochman (ten), Leonard Mróz (bass)
Polskie Nagrania Edition ▲ ECD 049 [DDD]

Sawai, Kazue (koto)
Cage, J.:Dances (3) for 2 Prepared Pnos [arr for koto] O.O. Imports ▲ MY 1
Kako, T.:Con Koto, *(orch unknown)* O.O. Imports ▲ MY 1
Takahashi, Y.:Music of, Gossamer; Horseheads Were Toward Eternity—The Wind Is Calling Me Outside; While I Was Crossing the Bridge; Song: O.O. Imports ▲ ALCD 37

INSTRUMENT.

Sawai, Kazue (koto) (cont.)
Wolff, C.:Malvina O.O. Imports ▲ MY 1

Sawai, Tadao (koto)
Matsumura, T.:Fant Koto, w. Sawai Koto Ensemble Camerata ▲ 32CM 92
Nishimura, A.:A River of Time, w. Sawai Koto Ensemble Camerata ▲ 32CM 92
Nishimura, A.:Iris of Time, w. Sawai Koto Ensemble Camerata ▲ 32CM 92
Nishimura, A.:Stratums of Time, w. Sawai Koto Ensemble Camerata ▲ 32CM 92
Sawai, T.:Gosechi No Mai, w. Sawai Koto Ensemble Camerata ▲ 32CM 92
Yuasa, J.:Koto Uta Basho's 5 Haiku, w. Sawai Koto Ensemble Camerata ▲ 32CM 92

Sawallisch, Wolfgang (pno)
Bach, J.S.:Con for 4 Hpds, w. Rudolf Kempe (pno), Fritz Rieger (pno), Rafael Kubelík (pno), R. Kubelik (cnd), Bavarian RSO *(rec 1972)* Arkadia ▲ 494
Brahms, J.:Liebeslieder Waltzes SATB, w. E. Mathis (sop), B. Fassbaender (mez), P. Schreier (ten), D. Fischer-Dieskau (bar), K. Engel (pno) [G] Deutsche Grammophon ▲ 423133-2 [DDD]
Brahms, J.:Neue Liebeslieder Waltzes, w. E. Mathis (sop), B. Fassbaender (mez), P. Schreier (ten), D. Fischer-Dieskau (bar), K. Engel (pno) [G] Deutsche Grammophon ▲ 423133-2 [DDD]
Mozart, W.A.:Con 20 Pno, w. W. Sawallisch (cnd), Philharmonia Orch EMI Classics ▲ CDE 67764
Mozart, W.A.:Con 21 Pno, w. W. Sawallisch (cnd), Philharmonia Orch EMI Classics ▲ CDE 67778
Mozart, W.A.:Con 22 Pno, w. W. Sawallisch (cnd), Philharmonia Orch EMI Classics ▲ CDE 67778
Rimsky-Korsakov, N.:Qnt Fl, w. Munich Residenz Quintet members Calig ▲ CAL 50898 [DDD]
Rubinstein, A.:Qnt Pno, w. Munich Residenz Quintet members Calig ▲ CAL 50898 [DDD]
Schubert, Franz:Der Hirt auf dem Felsen, w. M. Price (sop), H. Schöneberger (cl) [G] Orfeo ▲ 001811 [DDD]
Schubert, Franz:Songs (misc), w. M. Price (sop)—11 songs [G] Orfeo ▲ 001811 [DDD]
Strauss, R.:Andante Hn, w. Johannes Ritzkowsky (hn) *(rec Kleine Konzertsall, Gasteig, Germany, Mar 22–23, 1988)* Arts ▲ 47261-2 [DDD]
Strauss, R.:Aus alter Zeit:eine kleine Gavotte *(rec Kleine Konzertsall, Gasteig, Germany, Mar 22–23, 1988)* Arts ▲ 47261-2 [DDD]
Strauss, R.:Con 1 Hn, w. Johannes Ritzkowsky (hn) *(rec Kleine Konzertsall, Gasteig, Germany, Feb 28, 1985)* Arts ▲ 47261-2 [DDD]
Strauss, R.:Con 2 Hn, w. Johannes Ritzkowsky (hn), Barton Weber (pno) *(rec Kleine Konzertsall, Gasteig, Germany, Mar 22–23, 1988)* Arts ▲ 47261-2 [DDD]
Strauss, R.:4 Last Songs, w. Barbara Hendricks (sop), W. Sawallisch (cnd), Philadelphia Orch EMI Classics ▲ CDC 55594
Strauss, R.:Music of, w. Sinnhoffer String Quartet members—4 Stücke *(rec Kleiner Konzertsaal, Gasteig, Munich, Oct 17, 1985)* Arts Music ▲ 447259-2 [DDD]
Strauss, R.:Qt Pno, w. Sinnhoffer String Quartet members *(rec Kleiner Konzertsaal, Gasteig, Munich, Oct 17, 1985)* Arts Music ▲ 447259-2 [DDD]
Strauss, R.:Serenade Ww [arr for pno] *(rec Kleine Konzertsall, Gasteig, Germany, Mar 22–23, 1988)* Arts ▲ 47261-2 [DDD]
Strauss, R.:Songs, w. Barbara Hendricks (sop), W. Sawallisch (cnd), Philadelphia Orch—Ich wollt' ein Sträusslein binden; Säusle, liebe Myrthe; Kornblumen; Mohnblumen; Epheu; Wasserrose; Die Georgine; Die Zeitlose; Allerseelen; Ruhe, meine Seele!; Cäcilie; Heimliche Aufforderung; Morgen!; Das Rosenband; Heimkehr EMI Classics ▲ CDC 55594

Sawatzky, Shirley (pno)
Nishimura, A.:Heterophony, w. Judith Kehler Siebert (pno), B. Tovey (cnd), Winnipeg SO *(rec Winnipeg, Manitoba, Mar. 16 & 18, 1993)* CBC ("SM 5000" series) ▲ SMCD 5141 [DDD]

Sawyer, E. (pno)
Villa-Lobos, H.:Chôro 8, w. S. Muniz (pno), E. de Carvalho (cnd), Paraiba SO Delos ▲ DE 1017 [DDD]

Sax, (vn)
Hovhaness, A.:Sym 24, w. Martyn Hill (ten), John Wilbraham (tpt), A. Hovhaness (cnd), National PO London, John Alldis Choir [E] *(rec 1974)* Crystal ▲ CD 803 [ADD]

Sax, Manfred (bn)
Handel, G.F.:Sons Fl, w. Peter-Lukas Graf (fl), Jörg Ewald Dähler (hpd)—4 Sons—Op. 1, Nos. 1a,1b,5 & 9 Claves ▲ CD 238 [ADD]
Handel, G.F.:Sons Fl, "Halle Sons", w. Peter-Lukas Graf (fl), J.E. Dähler (cnd) Claves ▲ CD 238 [ADD]

Saxby, Joseph (hpd)—see ORCHESTRAS & ENSEMBLES Dolmetsch-Schoenfeld Ensemble

Sayer, Roger (org)
Essentially English, w. [cnd:Michael Kibblewhite], East London Chorus Koch Schwann ▲ SCH 312662 [DDD]
Hear My Voice, O God:Psalms of David, Vol. 9, w. [cnd:Barry Ferguson], Rochester Choir Priory ▲ PRI 461 [DDD]

Sayre, R. (vc)
Imbrie, A.W.:Son Vc, w. R. Bogas (pno) *(rec Dec. 18, 1971; originally)* CRI ▲ CD 632 [ADD]

Sbaraglia, Daniela (pno)
Song Recital, w. Paolo Coni (bar) Nuova Era ▲ NUO 6827 [DDD]
Tosti, P.F.:Songs, w. P. Coni (bar) Nuova Era ▲ 6827 [DDD]

Sbarcea, Laurentiu (vc)—see ORCHESTRAS & ENSEMBLES Orpheus String Quartet

Scabbia, Gaia (fl)
Tosti, P.F.:Songs, w. E. Palacio (ten), M. Rapattoni (pno), H. Liviabella (vn), B. Giuffredi (gtr), C. Passerini (hp), M. Decimo (vc) [arr. Massimo de Bernart for instrumental accompaniment]—La serenata; Sogno; 'A vucchella; Segreto; Ideale; 2ème Aubade; Anima mia; Donna, vorrei morir; Aprile; Ancoral; Mattinata; L'ultima canzone; Malìa; Non t'amo più; Il pescatore cantal; Tristezza; O falce di luna calante; L'abla separa dalla luce l'ombra; Mi guitarra dice "Te amo!"; Ricordati di me; Vuol note o banconote? Arkadia-Akademia ▲ 125 [DDD]

Scalera, Vincenzo (pno)
In Concert, w. Carlo Bergonzi (ten) *(rec live, 3/30/84)* Bongiovanni ▲ GB 2502-2 [ADD]

Scanziani, S. (ob)
Milesi, P.:Modi 2, w. L. M. Pickova (sop), Françoise Goddard (alt), M. Ferradini (ten), B. Andersen (bass), D. Cassamagnaghi (fl), A. Bianchi (cl/b cl), E. Crisafulli (bn), C. Gazzola (hn), F. Gualandris (tuba), A. Girardi (celtic hp), R. Anedda (vn), E. Groppo (vn), M. Pagani (vn), M. Ravasio (va), S. Righini (vc), P. Rizzi (db), J. Scully (perc), P. Milesi (cnd) Cuneiform ▲ RUNE 63

Scappini, Mauro (fl)—see ORCHESTRAS & ENSEMBLES Flautarte Quartet

Scarpelli, M. (vc)—see ORCHESTRAS & ENSEMBLES Seicentonovecento Ensemble

Scarpini, Pietro (pno)
Beethoven, L. van:Con 4 Pno, w. W. Furtwängler (cnd), Rome RAI Orch *(rec 1952–54)* Historical Performers ▲ HPS 23 [ADD]

Scarponi, C. (pno)
Arrigo, G.:Serenata per Andromeda, w. V. de Vita (cl), A. Vismara (va), K. Martin (cnd), Musica d'Oggi Bongiovanni ▲ GB 5511 [DDD]

Scarponi, Ciro (cl)
Bottesini, P.:Andante e Tema con variazioni, w. Monica Berni (fl), Rome Solisti *(rec Rome, 1996)* musicaimmagine ▲ MR 10031
Petrassi, G.:Grand septuor Cl, w. F. Maestri (cnd), Musica d'Oggi Bongiovanni ▲ GB 5534 [DDD]
Salieri, G.:Adagio e Tema con variazioni, w. Rome Solisti *(rec Rome, 1996)* musicaimmagine ▲ MR 10031

Schaaf, Peter (pno)
Schubert, Franz:Winterreise, w. J. Vickers (ten) [G] *(rec live 10/2/83)* VAI Audio 2-▲ VAIA 1007-2 [ADD]

Schaap, Nanneke (vl)—see ORCHESTRAS & ENSEMBLES Consort Fontegara

Schaarschmidt, Helmut (ob)—see ORCHESTRAS & ENSEMBLES Duo Geminiani

Schabata, Woody (vib)
Newton, L.:Vexations 1611, w. Lauren Newton (sgr) *(rec Vienna, Sept. 22, 1983)* Hat Hut ("NOW." series) ▲ hat ART CD 6024 [ADD]
Puschnig, W.:Vexations 2015, w. Wolfgang Puschnig (bass cl) *(rec Vienna, Sept. 22, 1983)* Hat Hut ("NOW." series) ▲ hat ART CD 6024 [ADD]

Schabata, Woody (vib) (cont.)
Rüegg, M.:Music of, w. Lauren Newton (sgr), Wolfgang Puschnig (fl/s sax), Harry Sokal (s sax), Roman Schwaller (t sax), Karl Fian (tpt), Christian Radovan (trbn)—Reflections on Aubade; Reflections on Méditation; Reflections on Sévère Réprimande; Reflections on Idylle; Reflections on Gnossiennes Nos. 1 & 2; Satie ist mir im traum 3x nicht erschienen *(rec Vienna, Sept. 20–22, 1983 & Mar.)* Hat Hut ("NOW." series) ▲ hat ART CD 6024 [ADD]

Schachman, Marc (ob)
A Baroque Christmas from the Metropolitan Museum of Art Concerts, w. Julianne Baird (sop), Aulos Ensemble [Anne Briggs (trns fl), Linda Quan (baroque vn), Myron Lutzke (baroque vc), Arthur Haas (hpd/org)] MusicMasters ▲ 01612-67119-2 ■ 01612-67119-4
Mozart, W.A.:Con Ob, w. T. Crawford (cnd), Old Fairfield Academy Orch MusicMasters ▲ 01612-67157-2 [DDD]
Wilson, R.:Persuasions, w. A. Burton (sop), B. Uribe (pno), J. Solum (alt fl), G. Dejean (bn/ctbn) Albany ▲ TROY 074 [DDD]

Schad, Otto (perc)
Bartók, B.:Son for 2 Pnos, w. G. Sándor (pno), R. Reinhardt (pno), R. Sohm (perc) *(rec 1965)* Vox Box ("Legends" series) 2-▲ CDX2 5506 [ADD]

Schaefer, Rick (perc)
Snyder, R.:Enneagram Studies, w. Eric Ginsberg (cl), Stephen Krahn (pno), Chris Casart (perc), Kelly Scheef (perc), Jason Varga (perc), Scott Zimmerman (perc) Coronet ▲ COR 400-9

Schaeffer, Boguslaw (pno)
Schaeffer, B.:Con 3 Pno, w. Marek Choloniewski (cmpt), B. Oledzki (cnd), Polish National RSO Katowice Pro Viva ▲ ISPV 168 [ADD]

Schäfer, Guido (cl)—see ORCHESTRAS & ENSEMBLES Acht Ensemble

Schäfer, M. (pno)—see also ORCHESTRAS & ENSEMBLES Munich Piano Trio
Schubert, Franz:Trio 1 Pno, w. I. Then-Bergh (vn), C. Hellmann (vc) *(rec Studio 3 des BR, Mar. 28–31, 1994)* Calig ▲ CAL 50931 [DDD]
Schubert, Franz:Trio 2 Pno, w. I. Then-Bergh (vn), C. Hellmann (vc) *(rec Studio 3 des BR, Mar. 28–31, 1994)* Calig ▲ CAL 50931 [DDD]

Schäfer, Stefan (db)—see ORCHESTRAS & ENSEMBLES Acht Ensemble

Schäffer, Hermann (org)
Brahms, J.:Org Musc (comp) Motette ▲ MOT 10711 [DDD]

Schäffer, Michael (lt)
Music for Lute, Guitar & Mandolin, w. Konrad Ragossnig (gtr), Anton Stingl (lt), Karl Scheit (gtr), Leo Witoszinskyj (gtr), William Matthews (gtr), Paul Grund (mand), Artur Rumetsch (mand), Edith Bauer-Slais (mand), Elfriede Kunschak (mand) Vox Box 3-▲ CD3X 3022

Schaling, E. (vc)—see ORCHESTRAS & ENSEMBLES La Primavera String Ensemble

Schalker, Arnold (pno)
Liszt, F.:Pno Music (misc)—Second Ballade; Rêverie et Adieux; Bénédiction et Serment; Le Triomphe Funèbre du Tasse; Réminiscences de Don Juan Altarus ▲ CD 9055

Schaller, Irmgard (va)—see ORCHESTRAS & ENSEMBLES Ensemble 415

Schaller, Irmgard (vn/va)—see ORCHESTRAS & ENSEMBLES Schönbrunn Ensemble Amsterdam

Schantz, Jack (tpt)
Banfield, W.:Sym 6, "4 Songs for 5 American Voices", w. John English (tpt), A. Balter (cnd), Akron SO *(rec Masonic Auditorium, Cleveland, OH, Feb 22, 1994)* Telarc ▲ CD 80409 [DDD]

Schanzer, J. (gtr)
Schanzer, J.:Tracings Gtr Avant ▲ 02

Schappé, Stephan (pno)—see ORCHESTRAS & ENSEMBLES Rondo Piano

Scharapan, Gérard (fl)—see ORCHESTRAS & ENSEMBLES Pariser Quartet

Scharinger, Anton (db)
Barockmusik für Posaunen und Gesang, w. Datura Trombone Quartet, C. Weigel (baroque vc), T. Strauss (org), J. Gagelmann (perc), R. Haeger (perc) Ars Musici ▲ AM 1094 [DDD]

Scharrer, Irene (pno)
The Best of Sir H. J. Wood, w. H. Wood (cnd) *(rec between 1932 & 1937)* Dutton Laboratories 2-▲ DUT 2002 [ADD]
Chopin, F.:Pno Music (misc)—12 pieces *(rec 1909–1933)* Pearl ▲ PEA 9978 (m) [AAD]
Irene Scharrer (1888–1971) Pearl ▲ PEA 9978 (m) [AAD]
Litolff, H.C.:Con Symphonique 4, w. H. Wood (cnd), London SO *(rec 1933)* Pearl ▲ PEA 9978 (m) [AAD]

Schattenberg, Hildegard (fl)—see ORCHESTRAS & ENSEMBLES VIF Flute Quartet

Schatz, Tatiana (pno)
Pärt, A.:Spiegel im Spiegel, w. D. Geringas (vc) Koch Schwann ▲ CD 310091 [DDD]
Schnittke, A.:Son Vc, w. D. Geringas (vc) Koch Schwann ▲ CD 310091 [DDD]

Schatzberger, Lesley (bas hn)
Mendelssohn, F.:Concert Pieces, w. A. Hacker (cl), R. Burnett (pno) [period instrs] Amon Ra ▲ CD-SAR 38 [DDD]
Mozart, W.A.:Clemenza di Tito (sels), w. Anne Sofie von Otter (mez—Sesto), J. E. Gardiner (cnd), English Baroque Soloists—Parto, ma tu ben mio *(rec Queen Elizabeth Hall, South Bank Ctr, London, June 1990)* Archiv ▲ 449938-2 [DDD]
Mozart, W.A.:Qnts Cl Bas Hn, w. Alan Hacker (cl), Salomon String Quartet members Amon Ra ▲ CD-SAR 17 [DDD]

Schaub, Gérard (fl)
Argento, D.:From the Diary of V. Woolf, w. M. Schèle (sop), J. Ribera (pno) Proprius ▲ PRCD 9982
Werle, L.J.:Chants for Dark Hours, w. M. Schèle (sop), J. Ribera (pno) Proprius ▲ PRCD 9982

Schauerte, Helge (org)
Alain, J.:Org Music (comp)—Premier Prélude Profane, AWV 57; Deuxième Prélude Profane, AWV 58; Première Fantaisie, AWV 59; Deux Danses à Agni Yavishta, AWV 61; Le jardin suspendu, AWV 63; Animato-Andante, AWV 65b; Fantasmagorie, AWV 73; Fileuse, AWV 74b; Deuxième Fantaisie, AWV 91; Trois Danses, AWV 119; Aria, AWV 120 Motette ▲ CD 11301 [DDD]
Alain, J.:Org Music (comp)—Suite in Three Parts, AWV 86, & fifteen various shorter works (chorales, variations, etc.); plus Les Fêtes de l'Année Israelite, AWV 85, performed by the composer ca. 1938 Motette ▲ CD 11311 [DDD]
J. S. Bach & His Time FSM ▲ 97726 [DDD]

Schauerte-Maubouet, Helga (org)
Organ & Trumpet Recital, w. Hervé Noël (tpt) Quantum ▲ QM 6951

Schaupp, Karen (gtr)
Schultz, Andrew:Mephisto, w. Sonia Croucher (fl), Michele Walsh (vn), Belinda Kendall-Smith (bass), G. Roberts (cnd), Perihelion Ensemble members *(rec Nickson Room, Music Dept, Univ of Queensland, Australia, Dec 1994)* Tall Poppies ▲ TP 065 [DDD]

Schauwecker, Frederick (pno)
At Carnegie Hall, w. Jussi (ten) Björling *(rec Mar 2, 1958)* RCA Gold Seal ▲ 60520-2-RG [ADD] ■ 60520-4-RG
Jussi Björling in Concert, w. Jussi (ten) Björling (ten) *(rec Glenn Memorial Auditorium, Atlanta, Georgia, 4/13/59)* Myto ▲ MCD 912.39 [ADD]
O Paradiso:Great Opera Arias, w. Jussi Björling, RCA Victor Orch [cnd:Renato Cellini], Rome Opera Orch [cnd:Erich Leinsdorf, Jonel Perlea], Robert Shaw Chorale [cnd:Robert Shaw] *(rec 1951–1959)* RCA Gold Seal ▲ 09026-68429-2 [ADD]
Three Tenors of the Golden Age, w. Jussi Björling, Mario Lanza (ten), Jan Peerce (ten), John Corigliano (vn), Constantine Callinicos (pno), RCA Victor Orch [cnd:Renato Cellini, Constantine Callinicos, Erich Leinsdorf, Sylvan Levin, Maximilian Pilzer, Frieder Weissmann], Rome Opera Orch, Rome Opera Chorus [cnd:Eri RCA Gold Seal ▲ 09026-68531-2 [ADD] ■ 09026-68531-4

Schechter, D. E. (pno)
Liapunov, S.:Pno Music—Variations on a Georgian Theme; Chant d'automne; Sonata in f; Rêverie du Soir; Toccata & Fugue in C *(rec Jan. 9, 1990)* Marco Polo ▲ 8.223468 [DDD]

Schechter, Myriam (pno)
The Golden Age of the Saxophone, w. Paul Brodie (sax) Musica Viva ▲ MVCD 1005 [ADD]

826 ▲ = CD ♦ = Enhanced CD Δ = MD ■ = Cassette Tape □ = DCC

Schechter, Peggy (fl)
Ibert, J.:Music of, w. C. Schadeberg (sop), Sue Ann Kahn (fl), E. Lawrence (fl), R. Schmidt (fl), David Krakauer (cl), L. Goldstein (bn), Curtis Macomber (vn), Susan Jolles (hp), Frederick Hand (gtr), Arthur Willis (pno)—Entr'acte; Jeux; Sonatine; 2 Movements; 2 Interludes; Aria; Pièce for solo Fl; Histoires; 2 Stèles orientées; Pastoral; Aria; Entr'acte — Albany ▲ TROY 145

Scheef, Kelly (perc)
Snyder, R.:Enneagram Studies, w. Eric Ginsberg (cl), Stephen Krahn (pno), Chris Casart (perc), Rick Schaefer (perc), Jason Varga (perc), Scott Zimmerman (perc) — Coronet ▲ COR 400-9

Scheele, Dyann (fl)
Paccione, P.:...Like Spring, w. Jane Walker (fl) — Capstone ▲ SCI 6

Scheer, N. (vn)—see also ORCHESTRAS & ENSEMBLES Bonn Telemann Ensemble
Rosier, N.–C.:Son Vn, w. T. Habel–Thormé (rcr), B. Wicke (org) *(rec 1992)* — FSM ▲ FCD 97759 [DDD]

Scheerer, Jochen (trbn)
Arnold, M.:Qnt Brass, w. Uwe Zaiser (tpt), Peter Leiner (tpt), Sjön Scott (hn), Ralf Rudolph (tuba) — Bayer ▲ BR 100251 [DDD]
Crespo, E.:Suite Americana 1, w. Uwe Zaiser (tpt), Peter Leiner (tpt), Sjön Scott (hn), Ralf Rudolph (tuba) — Bayer ▲ BR 100251 [DDD]
Ewald, V.:Qnt 1 Brass, w. Peter Leiner (tpt), Uwe Zaiser (tpt), Sjön Scott (hn), Ralf Rudolph (tuba) — Bayer ▲ BR 100251 [DDD]
Horovitz, J.:Music Hall Suite, w. Uwe Zaiser (tpt), Peter Leiner (tpt), Sjön Scott (hn), Ralf Rudolph (tuba) — Bayer ▲ BR 100251 [DDD]
Koetsier, J.:Qnt Brass, w. Peter Leiner (tpt), Uwe Zaiser (tpt), Sjön Scott (hn), Ralf Rudolph (tuba) — Bayer ▲ BR 100251 [DDD]

Scheide, Kathleen (org)
Liszt, F.:Alleluja et Ave Maria d'Arcadelt—Ave Maria [at the Mission Church Org, Boston] — Raven ▲ OAR 350 [DDD]
Liszt, F.:Transcriptions & Paraphrases—Allegri & Mozart:A la Chapelle Sixtine, S.461 [at the Mission Church Org, Boston] — Raven ▲ OAR 350 [DDD]
Liszt, F.:Vars on "Weinen, Klagen, Sorgen, Zagen", S.179 [arr. organ; at the Mission Church Org, Boston] — Raven ▲ OAR 350 [DDD]
Scheide, K.:Gnostic Incantation [at the Mission Church Org, Boston] — Raven ▲ OAR 350 [DDD]
Scheide, K.:Set Org [at the Mission Church Org, Boston] — Raven ▲ OAR 350 [DDD]
Scheide, K.:Vars on Amazing Grace [at the Mission Church Org, Boston] — Raven ▲ OAR 350 [DDD]

Scheidegger, Rudolf (hpd)
Bach, C.P.E.:Sonatina for 2 Hpds, w. G. Fetz (hpd) — Koch Schwann ▲ CD 311081 [ADD]
Bach, C.P.E.:Sonatina for 2 Hpds, w. G. Fetz (hpd) — Koch Schwann ▲ SCH 313422 [ADD]
Blavet, M.:Recueil de pièces, w. Manfred Harras (rcr), Marianne Lüthi (rcr), Brian Franklin (vl)—Prélude de Mr. Blavet; Pourquoi doux Rossignols; Entrée de chasse *(rec Reformierte Kirche, Arlesheim, Schweiz, May 18–19, 1987)* — Musicaphon ▲ 56802 [DDD]
Dornel, L.–A.:Concert 1, w. Manfred Harras (rcr), Marianne Lüthi (rcr), Brian Franklin (vl) *(rec Reformierte Kirche, Arlesheim, Schweiz, May 18–19, 1987)* — Musicaphon ▲ 56802 [DDD]
Philidor, P.:Music of, w. Manfred Harras (rcr), Marianne Lüthi (rcr), Brian Franklin (vl)—Première suite in C; Deuxième suite in B; Septième suite in b *(rec Reformierte Kirche, Arlesheim, Schweiz, May 18–19, 1987)* — Musicaphon ▲ 56802 [DDD]

Scheidegger, Rudolf (org)
Bach, J.S.:Cons Org, BWV 592–597—BWV 593, 594 & 596 — Divox ▲ CDX 29208 [DDD]
Bach, J.S.:Fugue on a Theme by Legrenzi — Divox ▲ CDX 29208 [DDD]
Burkhard, W.:Choral Triptychon — Ars Musici ▲ 1146

Schein, Ann (pno)
Berg, A.:Jugenlieder, w. Jessye Norman (sop) — Sony Classical ▲ SK 66826
Pilss, K.:Pezzi (3) in forma de sonata, w. Peter Landgren (hn) *(rec John Addison Concert Hall, Harmony Hall Regional Center, Fort Washington, Maryland, Dec. 1993 & Mar. 1994)* — Elan ▲ CD 2260 [DDD]
Rheinberger, J.:Son Hn, w. Peter Landgren (hn) *(rec John Addison Concert Hall, Harmony Hall Regional Center, Fort Washington, Maryland, Dec. 1993 & Mar. 1994)* — Elan ▲ CD 2260 [DDD]
Rorem, N.:King Midas, w. Sandra Walker (mez), John Stewart (ten) — Phoenix ▲ PHCD 126
Rorem, N.:Night Music, w. E. Carlyss (vn) — Phoenix ▲ PHCD 123
Schumann, R.:Adagio & Allegro Hn, w. Peter Landgren (hn) *(rec John Addison Concert Hall, Harmony Hall Regional Center, Fort Washington, Maryland, Dec. 1993 & Mar. 1994)* — Elan ▲ CD 2260 [DDD]
Schumann, R.:Fantasiestücke Cl, w. Peter Landgren (hn) *(rec John Addison Concert Hall, Harmony Hall Regional Center, Fort Washington, Maryland, Dec. 1993 & Mar. 1994)* — Elan ▲ CD 2260 [DDD]
Strauss, F.:Nocturne, w. Peter Landgren (hn) *(rec John Addison Concert Hall, Harmony Hall Regional Center, Fort Washington, Maryland, Dec. 1993 & Mar. 1994)* — Elan ▲ CD 2260 [DDD]

Scheit, Karl (gtr)
Christmas Songs & Tales, w. Irmgard Seefried (sop) — Preiser ▲ PRE 90050
Music for Lute, Guitar & Mandolin, w. Konrad Ragossnig (gtr), Anton Stingl (lt), Michael Schäffer (lt), Leo Witoszinskyj (gtr), William Matthews (gtr), Paul Grund (mand), Artur Rumetsch (mand), Edith Bauer–Slais (mand), Elfriede Kunschak (mand) — Vox Box 3–▲ CD3X 3022
Torelli, G.:Music of, w. W. Boettcher (cnd), Vienna Festival CO—Con in A for Gtr, Vn & Orch — Special Music Co. ("Classics of the Heart" series) ▲ SCD 5198

Scheja, Staffan (pno)
Chopin, F.:Barcarolle Pno *(rec Oct. 31–Nov. 2, 1981)* — BIS ▲ CD 197 [AAD]
Mozart, W.A.:Con 21 Pno, w. J.–O. Wedin (cnd), Stockholm Sinfonietta — BIS ▲ CD 205
Prokofiev, S.:Sarcasms *(rec Nacka Aula, Nacka, Sweden, Jan. 18–20, 1980)* — BIS ▲ CD 155 [AAD]
Prokofiev, S.:Son 3 Pno *(rec Nacka Aula, Nacka, Sweden, Jan. 18–20, 1980)* — BIS ▲ CD 155 [AAD]
Prokofiev, S.:Son 6 Pno *(rec Nacka Aula, Nacka, Sweden, Jan. 18–20, 1980)* — BIS ▲ CD 155 [AAD]

Schellenberger, Hansjörg (E hn)
Hindemith, P.:Son E Hn, w. Ferenc Bognár (pno) — Sony Classical ▲ SK 64400

Schellenberger, Hansjörg (ob)—see also ORCHESTRAS & ENSEMBLES Berlin Philharmonic Wind Ensemble
Albinoni, T.:Cons à 5 Obs, Op. 7, w. Italian Solisti—No. 6 — Denon ▲ CO 2301 [DDD]
Albinoni, T.:Cons à 5 Obs, Op. 9, w. Italian Solisti—No. 8 — Denon ▲ CO 2301 [DDD]
Albinoni, T.:Cons à 5 Obs, Op. 9, w. Italian Solisti—No. 11 *(rec July 24–27, 1992)* — Denon ▲ CO 75338 [DDD]
Bach, W.F.:Duets Fls, F.54–59, w. W. Schulz (flute) *(rec June 28–30, 1993)* — Sony Classical ▲ SK 58965 [DDD]
Beethoven, L. van:Qnt Pno, Ob, Cl, Hn & Bn, w. D. Barenboim (pno), L. Combs (cl), D. Damiano (bn), D. Clevenger (hn) — Erato ▲ 96359-2
Hindemith, P.:Kleine Kammermusik, w. Wolfgang Schulz (fl), Karl Leister (cl), Günter Högner (hn), Milan Turkovic (bn) — Sony Classical ▲ SK 64400
Marcello, A.:Con Ob & Strs, w. Italian Solisti — Denon ▲ CO 2301 [DDD]
Mozart, W.A.:Qt Ob, K.370, w. Berlin Philharmonia String Quartet members — Denon/PCM Digital ▲ DC 8003 [DDD]
Mozart, W.A.:Qnt Pno, K.452, w. D. Barenboim (pno), L. Combs (cl), D. Damiano (bn), D. Clevenger (hn) — Erato ▲ 96359-2
Sammartini, G.:Con in E♭ Ob, w. Italian Solisti — Denon ▲ CO 2301 [DDD]
Scarlatti, D.:Sinfs Ob, w. Italian Solisti—in G, G & B♭ *(rec July 24–27, 1992)* — Denon ▲ CO 75338 [DDD]
Vivaldi, A.:Cons Ob, w. Italian Solisti—RV.453, 455 — Denon ▲ CO 2301 [DDD]
Vivaldi, A.:Cons Ob, w. Italian Solisti—RV.454 & 447 *(rec July 24–27, 1992)* — Denon ▲ CO 75338 [DDD]
Works for Oboe & Organ, w. Hedwig Bilgram (org) *(rec July 29–Aug. 1, 1991)* — Denon ▲ CO 75081 [DDD]

Schelling, Martin (cl)
Dünser, R.:Tage– und Nachtbucher, w. Martin Mumelter (vn), Walter Nothas (vc), Alfons Kontarsky (pno) — Koch Schwann ▲ SCH 311882

Schelling, Martin (cl) (cont.)
Messiaen, O.:Quatuor pour la fin du temps, w. Martin Mumelter (vn), Walter Nothas (vc), Alfons Kontarsky (pno) — Koch Schwann ▲ SCH 311882

Schembri, Simon (gtr)
Guitare *(rec July & Sept 1995)* — Gallo ▲ CD 848 [DDD]
Musique Espagnole — Quantum ▲ QM 6916 [DDD] ■ QM 2009

Schempf, K. (cl)
Caltabiano, R.:Torched Liberty, w. N. Pilgrim (sop), V. Pritsker (vn), G. Macero (vc), L. Greene (pic/fl/alt fl), G. Coble (tpt), S. Heyman (pno), L. Luttinger (perc), R. Caltabiano (cnd) — Opus One ▲ CD 168 [DDD]

Schenck, G. F. (pno)
Brahms, J.:Gavotte by C. W. Gluck *(rec Sept. 24–26, 1990)* — Koch Schwann ▲ SCH 311722 [DDD]
Brahms, J.:Pno Music (misc)—Presto after Bach (1st Version); Presto after Bach (2nd Version); Chaconne after Bach (for the left hand); Hungarian Dances; Impromtu after Schubert (for the left hand); Etude after Chopin; Rondo after Weber *(rec Sept. 24–26, 1990)* — Koch Schwann ▲ SCH 311722 [DDD]
Brahms, J.:Theme & Vars Pno *(rec Sept. 24–26, 1990)* — Koch Schwann ▲ SCH 311722 [DDD]
Hindemith, P.:Dance of the Wooden Dolls — Koch Schwann ▲ CD 310007 [DDD]
Hindemith, P.:Dance Pieces — Koch Schwann ▲ CD 310007 [DDD]
Hindemith, P.:Klaviermusik Book 1 — Koch Schwann ▲ CD 310007 [DDD]
Hindemith, P.:Suite "1922" — Koch Schwann ▲ CD 310007 [DDD]

Schene, Daniel (pno)
Willey, J.:Some Connections, w. E. Szekeley (vn) — CRI ▲ CD 562 [DDD]

Schenk, G. J. (vn)
Hush, D.:Qt 1 Strs, w. J. Ingolfsson (vn), C.–J. Chang (va), M. Ingolfsson (vc) — CRS ▲ CD 9257
Van Appledorn, M.J.:Ayre, w. J. Ingolfsson (vn), C.–J. Chang (va), D. Foster (va), M. Ingolfsson (vc), S. Shao (vc) — CRS ▲ CD 9257

Schenkel, Bernard (fl)
Berio, L.:Opus Number Zoo, w. B. Demottaz (ob), R. Meyer (cl), G. Cass (hn), R. Birnstingl (bn) *(rec June 1987)* — Gallo ▲ CD 527
Ibert, J.:Pièces brèves, w. R. Birnstingl (bn), G. Cass (hn), B. Demottaz, R. Meyer, B. Schenkel *(rec June 1987)* — Gallo ▲ CD 527

Schenkel, Bernard (ob)
Bizet, G.:Jeux d'enfants, w. B. Demottaz (fl), R. Meyer (cl), G. Cass (hn), R. Birnstingl (bn) *(rec June 1987)* — Gallo ▲ CD 527
Saint–Saëns, C.:Carnival of the Animals, w. B. Demottaz (ob), R. Meyer (cl), G. Cass (horn), R. Birnstingl (bn) *(rec June 1987)* — Gallo ▲ CD 527

Schenkman, Byron (hpd)
Boismortier, J.B. de:Sons Fl, Op. 91, w. Stephen Schultz (baroque fl) *(rec Music Hall, Ponytracks Ranch, Portola Valley, CA, May 3–5, 1995)* — Naxos ▲ 8.553414 [DDD]
In Stil Moderno, w. Ingrid Matthews (baroque vn) *(rec Shrine to Music Museum, Vermillion, SD, Jan 1995)* — Wildboar ▲ WLBR 9512 [DDD]
Jacquet De La Guerre, E.:Sons Vn, w. Ingrid Matthews (vn), Margriet Tindemans (vl) — Wildboar ▲ WLBR 9601 [DDD]
Jacquet De La Guerre, E.:Suites Hpd, w. Ingrid Matthews (vn), Margriet Tindemans (vl)—Prélude in a; Toccata; Chaconne "L"Inconstante" — Wildboar ▲ WLBR 9601 [DDD]
Kerll, J.C.:Kbd Music—Suite in F; Toccatas Nos. 1, 5 & 7; Passagaglia Variata; Suite in d; Canzonas Nos. 2 & 3; Suite in D; Capriccio sopra il cucu; Ciaconna variata; Suite in a — Focus ▲ FOCUS 914 [DDD]

Schenkman, Byron (hpd/pno)—see ORCHESTRAS & ENSEMBLES Zephyrus

Schepkin, Sergei (pno)
Bach, J.S.:Goldberg Vars *(rec Jordan Hall, New England Conservatory, Boston, MA, Jan 15, 1995)* — Ongaku ▲ 024–107 [DDD]
Bach, J.S.:Partitas Hpd, BWV 825–830—BWV 825–828 *(rec Jordan Hall, New England Conservatory, Boston, Mar 18 & 21, 1995)* — Ongaku ▲ 024–108 [DDD]

Scheps, Ilya (pno)
Mussorgsky, M.:Songs & Dances, w. S. Yakovenko (bar) — Russian Season ("Russian Season" series) ▲ LDC 288031 [DDD]
Mussorgsky, M.:Songs (misc), w. S. Yakovenko (bar)—13 songs — Russian Season ("Russian Season" series) ▲ LDC 288031 [DDD]
Mussorgsky, M.:Sunless, w. S. Yakovenko (bar) — Russian Season ("Russian Season" series) ▲ LDC 288031 [DDD]
Russian Musical Satire, w. Sergei Yakovenko (bar), State Sym Cappella Choir [cnd:V. Poliansky] — Russian Season ▲ LDC 288075

Scherbakov, Konstantin (pno)
Godowsky, L.:Pno Music—Poems (4); Toccata, Op. 13; Pieces (3), Op. 12; Airs of the 18th Century; Waltz Poems (2); Mélodie méditative; Miniatures (5); Polonaise *(rec St. Martin's Church, Hampshire, Feb 1996)* — Marco Polo ▲ 8.223793 [DDD]
Liapunov, S.:Études d'exécution transcendante *(rec July 6–7, 1992)* — Marco Polo ▲ 8.223491 [DDD]
Respighi, O.:Con Pno, w. H. Griffiths (cnd), Slovak RSO Bratislava *(rec Concert Hall of the Slovak Radio, Bratislava, Sept. 19–22, 1994)* — Naxos ▲ 8.553207 [DDD]
Respighi, O.:Fant slava, w. H. Griffiths (cnd), Slovak RSO Bratislava *(rec Concert Hall of the Slovak Radio, Bratislava, Sept. 19–22, 1994)* — Naxos ▲ 8.553207 [DDD]
Respighi, O.:Toccata Pno, w. Ivan Tvrdík (vc), H. Griffiths (cnd), Slovak RSO Bratislava *(rec Concert Hall of the Slovak Radio, Bratislava, Sept. 19–22, 1994)* — Naxos ▲ 8.553207 [DDD]

Scherbaum, A. (tpt)
Vivaldi, A.:Con for 2 Tpts, w. Rudolf Haubold (tpt), Hamburg Scherbaum Baroque Ensemble — Deutsche Grammophon ("Musikfest" series) ▲ 413256–2 ■ 413256–4

Scherzer, Ernst–Günther (pno)
Brahms, J.:Liebeslieder Waltzes SATB, w. E. Berger (sop), G. Pfitzinger (alt), W. Ludwig (ten), E. Wenk (bass), G. Falbe (pno) *(rec 1959)* — FNAC Music ▲ 642313
Brahms, J.:Neue Liebeslieder Waltzes, w. E. Berger (sop), G. Pfitzinger (alt), W. Ludwig (ten), E. Wenk (bass), G. Falbe (pno) *(rec 1959)* — FNAC Music ▲ 642313

Scherzer, Manfred (vn)
Reger, M.:Con Vn, w. H. Blomstedt (cnd), Dresden Staatskapelle — Berlin Classics ▲ BER 9124

Schessl, Frank (va)—see ORCHESTRAS & ENSEMBLES Koeckert String Quartet

Schetzbach, Michael (va)
Pettersson, G.A.:Fantasistycke — CPO ▲ CPO 999169 [DDD]

Scheuerer, Franz (vn)—see ORCHESTRAS & ENSEMBLES Scheuerer Quartet

Scheuerer, Gertraud (pno)—see ORCHESTRAS & ENSEMBLES Scheuerer Quartet

Scheuerer, Gundi (vc)—see ORCHESTRAS & ENSEMBLES Scheuerer Quartet

Scheuerer, Severin (va)—see ORCHESTRAS & ENSEMBLES Scheuerer Quartet

Schiaffini, Giancarlo (tuba)
Scelsi, G.:Music of, w. Joëlle Léandre (sgr/db), Nicolas Isherwood (bass), Fances–Marie Uitti (vc), Karin Schmeer (hp), Robyn Schulkowsky (tamtam)—Maknongan for Low–Registered Instrument (1976) [3 versions:bass, double bass, tuba]; Tre pezzi for Trombone (1956); Wo Ma for Bass (1960); C'est bien la nuit for Double Bass (1972); Le réveil profond for Double Bass (1977); Et Maintenant, c'est a vous a jouer for Cello & Double Bass (1974); Okanagon for Harp, Double Bass & Tamtam (1968); Mantram for Double Bass (1987) *(rec Sendesaal, Hessen Radio, Frankfurt, Feb. 8–9, May 18–21 & Aug)* — Hat Hut ("NOW." series) ▲ hat ART CD 6124 [DDD]

Schiager, Halgeir (org)
Eben, Petr:Choral Phantasies (2) [organ of Hedvig Eleonora Church, Stockholm] *(rec June 1993)* — Victoria ▲ VCD 19080
Eben, Petr:Hommage à Buxtehude [organ of Hedvig Eleonora Church, Stockholm] *(rec June 1993)* — Victoria ▲ VCD 19080
Eben, Petr:Job [organ of Hedvig Eleonora Church, Stockholm] *(rec June 1993)* — Victoria ▲ VCD 19080
Eben, Petr:Landscapes of Patmos [organ of Hedvig Eleonora Church, Stockholm] *(rec June 1993)* — Victoria ▲ VCD 19080

Schiager, Halgeir (org) (cont.)
Eben, Petr:Laudes [organ of Hedvig Eleonora Church, Stockholm] *(rec June 1993)* Victoria ▲ VCD 19080

Schiani, E. (cl)
Vivaldi, A.:Cons Obs Cls, w. A. Caroldi (ob), A. Alvarosi (ob), A. Gerbi (cl), P. Santi (cnd), Milan Virtuosi Allegretto ▲ ACD 8036 [ADD] ■ ACS 8036

Schick, Steven (dr)—see ORCHESTRAS & ENSEMBLES Bang on a Can

Schick, Steven (perc)—see also ORCHESTRAS & ENSEMBLES Bang on a Can members
Andriessen, L.:Hoketus, w. Katherine Pendry (panpipes), James Poke (panpipes), Evan Ziporyn (a sax), Richard Craig (a sax), Steven Schick (congas), Amy Knoles (congas), Lisa Moore (Fender Rhodes), Damian LeGassick (Fender Rhodes), Cees van Zeeland (pno), Gerard Bouwhuis (pno), Robert Black (bass gtr), Mark Stewart (bass gtr) *(rec Air Recording Studios, Lyndhurst Hall, Hampstead, London, June 29–July 3, 1994)* Sony Classical ▲ SK 66483 [DDD]
Andriessen, L.:Hout, w. Evan Ziporyn (t sax), Mark Stewart (elec gtr), Lisa Moore (pno) *(rec Air Recording Studios, Lyndhurst Hall, Hampstead, London, June 29–July 3, 1994)* Sony Classical ▲ SK 66483 [DDD]
Bartók, B.:Son for 2 Pnos, w. J. Simms (pno), J. Avery (pno), T. L. Davis (perc) Music & Arts ▲ CD 648 [AAD/ADD]
Gaburo, K.:Enough!—(not enough)—, w. Lynceus Concert Music & Arts ▲ CD 832 [DDD]
Godfrey, D.:Music for Mar *(rec Oct. 14 & 15, 1990)* GM ▲ GM 2041 CD
Lang, D.:The Anvil Chorus *(rec Air Recording Studios, Lyndhurst Hall, Hampstead, London, June 29–July 3, 1994)* Sony Classical ▲ SK 66483 [DDD]
Lewis, P.T.:Music of, w. J. Ferrell (vn), J. Avery (pno), Peter Tod Lewis (elec), Center for New Music Ensemble, Columbia String Quartet—Bricolage (1979); Gestes (1973); Manestar (1970); ...of bells...and time (1967); Signs & Circuits—String Quartet No. 2 (1969) *(rec 1978–82)* CRI ▲ CD 619 [ADD]
Reynolds, R.:Autumn Island Neuma 2–▲ 450-91 [DDD]
Reynolds, R.:The Ivanov Suite, w. P. Larson (bar), J. Fonville (pic), E. Harkins (tpt), J. Ngyesy (vn), R. Mushabec (vc) New World ▲ 80431-2
Reynolds, R.:Versions/Stages, w. P. Larson (bar), J. Fonville (pic), E. Harkins (tpt), J. Ngyesy (vn), R. Mushabec (vc) New World ▲ 80431-2
Steiger, R.:Double Con, w. A. Karis (pno), R. Steiger (cnd), SONOR Ensemble of Univ of California San Diego *(rec May 27–June 1, 1992)* CRI ▲ CD 652 [DDD]
Stockhausen, K.:Kontakte, w. J. Avery (pno/perc), J. Spek (elec) Music & Arts ▲ CD 648 [AAD/ADD]
Wolfe, J.:Lick, w. Evan Ziporyn (s sax), Mark Stewart (elec gtr), Lisa Moore (pno), Maya Beiser (vc), Robert Black (db) *(rec Air Recording Studios, Lyndhurst Hall, Hampstead, London, June 29–July 3, 1994)* Sony Classical ▲ SK 66483 [DDD]
Xenakis, I.:Aïs, w. P. Larson (bar), T. Nee (cnd), La Jolla SO Neuma ▲ 450-86 [DDD]

Schickele, Peter (calliope)
Schickele, P.:Son da Circo, w. David Robinson (calliope) *(rec International Circus Hall of Fame, Peru, IN, May 30, 1995)* Telarc ▲ CD 80390 [DDD]

Schickele, Peter (org)
Schickele, P.:Chorale-Based Piecelets *(rec King Congregational Church, Fayray, ND, May 1, 1995)* Telarc ▲ CD 80390 [DDD]

Schickhaus, Johannes (hpd)
Beretta, P.:Son Dlc & Hpd, w. K.–H. Schickhaus (dlc) Tudor ▲ 736 [DDD]
Chiesa, M.:Son Dulcimer & Hpd, w. K.–H. Schickhaus (dulcimer) Tudor ▲ 736 [DDD]
Conti, A.:Son Dulcimer, w. K.–H. Schickhaus (dulcimer) Tudor ▲ 736 [DDD]
Monza, C.:Son Dulcimer, w. K.–H. Schickhaus (dlc) Tudor ▲ 736 [DDD]

Schickhaus, Karl-Heinz (ham dlc)
Beretta, P.:Son Dlc & Hpd, w. J. Schickhaus (hpd) Tudor ▲ 736 [DDD]
Chiesa, M.:Son Dulcimer & Hpd, w. J. Schickhaus (hpd) Tudor ▲ 736 [DDD]
Conti, A.:Son Dulcimer, w. J. Schickhaus (hpd) Tudor ▲ 736 [DDD]
Jommelli, N.:Sinf Dulcimer, w. H. Stadlmair (cnd), Munich CO Tudor ▲ 712 [ADD]
Monza, C.:Son Dulcimer, w. J. Schickhaus (hpd) Tudor ▲ 736 [DDD]
Piezas de Salterio:Spanish Dulcimer Music Tudor ▲ 738 [DDD]
Salulini, P.:Con Dlc, w. H. Stadlmair (cnd), Munich CO Tudor ▲ 712 [ADD]

Schidlof, Peter (va)
Mozart, W.A.:Concertone Vns, w. Norbert Brainin (vn), A. Gibson (cnd), English CO Chandos ▲ CHAN 8315 [DDD]
Mozart, W.A.:Sinf concertante Vn, K.364, w. N. Brainin (vn), A. Gibson (cnd), English CO Chandos ▲ CHAN 8315 [DDD]
Walton, W.:Con Va, w. C. Davis (cnd), BBC SO IMP ("BBC Radio Classics" series) ▲ IMP 5691732

Schieferstein, Eva (hpd)
Bach, J.S.:Trio Son for 2 Fls, BWV 1039, w. Elisabeth Weinzierl (fl), Edmund Wächter (fl) Entrée ▲ 0081 [DDD]
Buffardin, P.G.:Trio Son Fl, w. Elisabeth Weinzierl (fl), Edmund Wächter (fl) [arr for 2 flutes & bc] Entrée ▲ 0081 [DDD]
Lotti, A.:Trio Son Fl, w. Elisabeth Weinzierl (fl), Ulrich Fuchs (vc) Entrée ▲ 0081 [DDD]

Schifes, L. (kbd)
Jacchini, G.M.:Sons Vc, w. A. Bylsma (vc), B. Van Asperen (org)—Op. 1/7 & 8; Op. 3/9 & 10 Deutsche Harmonia Mundi ▲ 7978-2-RC [DDD]

Schiff, András (pno)
Bach, J.S.:Chromatic Fant & Fugue Hungaroton ▲ HCD 11690 [ADD]
Bach, J.S.:Cons Hpd, BWV 1052–1058, CO of Europe London 2–▲ 425676-2 [DDD]
Bach, J.S.:Con 1 Hpd, w. G. Malcolm (cnd), English CO Denon ▲ 7236 [DDD]
Bach, J.S.:Con 4 Hpd, w. G. Malcolm (cnd), English CO Denon ▲ 7236 [DDD]
Bach, J.S.:Con 5 Hpd, w. G. Malcolm (cnd), English CO Denon ▲ 7236 [DDD]
Bach, J.S.:Cons for 3 Hpds (comp), w. Z. Kocsis (pno), S. Falvai (pno), A. Simon (cnd), Franz Liszt Academy Orch Vivace ▲ E 563 [ADD]
Bach, J.S.:Con for 4 Hpds, w. Z. Kocsis (pno), S. Falvai (pno), I. Rohmann (pno), A. Simon (cnd), Franz Liszt Academy Orch Vivace ▲ E 563 [ADD]
Bach, J.S.:English Suites London 2–▲ 421640-2 [DDD]
Bach, J.S.:English Suites—BWV 809 Hungaroton ▲ HCD 11690 [ADD]
Bach, J.S.:French Suites—BWV 816 Omega ▲ OCD 1014 [ADD]
Bach, J.S.:French Suites London 2–▲ 433313-2 [DDD]
Bach, J.S.:Goldberg Vars London ▲ 417116-2 [DDD]
Bach, J.S.:Inventions (30) Hpd London ▲ 411974-2 [DDD]
Bach, J.S.:Italian Con London 2–▲ 433313-2 [DDD]
Bach, J.S.:Italian Con Omega ▲ OCD 1014 [ADD]
Bach, J.S.:Ov Hpd, BWV 820 London 2–▲ 433313-2 [DDD]
Bach, J.S.:Partitas Hpd, BWV 825–830—BWV 829 Hungaroton ▲ HCD 11690 [ADD]
Bach, J.S.:Partita Hpd, BWV 831, "Ov nach französischer Art" Omega ▲ OCD 1014 [ADD]
Bach, J.S.:Toccatas Hpd, BWV 910–16—BWV 912 Hungaroton ▲ HCD 11690 [ADD]
Bach, J.S.:Das wohltemperierte Klavier—Book 1 London 2–▲ 414388-2 [DDD]
Bach, J.S.:Das wohltemperierte Klavier—Book 2 London 2–▲ 417236-2 [DDD]
Bartók, B.:Dance Suite Denon ▲ 7092 [DDD]
Bartók, B.:Hungarian Peasant Songs Denon ▲ 7092 [DDD]
Bartók, B.:Romanian Folk Dances Pno Denon ▲ 7092 [DDD]
Bartók, B.:Rondos (3) on Folk Tunes Denon ▲ 7092 [DDD]
Beethoven, L. van:Bagatelles (24)—Op. 119 & Op. 126 Hungaroton ▲ HCD 11885
Beethoven, L. van:Pno Music (misc)—Allegretto in b, Op. 61; Allegretto quasi andante in g, K.61a; Waltz in E♭, K.84; Waltz in D, K.85; Eccossaise in E♭, K.86; Polonaise in C, Op. 89 Hungaroton ▲ HCD 11885
Beethoven, L. van:Songs, w. C. Bartoli (mez)—Ecco quel fiero istantel, WoO 124; Che fa il mio bene?, Op. 82/3; Che fa il mio bene?, Op. 82/4; T'intendo, si, mio cor, Op.82/1; Dimmi, ben mio, Op. 82/1; In questa tomba oscura, WoO 133 *(rec Aug. 5–8, 1992)* London ▲ 440297-2 [DDD]
Brahms, J.:Con 1 Pno, w. G. Solti (cnd), Vienna PO London ▲ 425110-2 [DDD]

Schiff, András (pno) (cont.)
Brahms, J.:Vars on a Theme of Robert Schumann, Op. 23, w. G. Solti (pno) London ▲ 425110-2 [DDD]
Haydn, J.:Arianna a Naxos, w. Cecelia Bartoli (mez) *(rec Aug. 5–8, 1992)* London ▲ 440297-2 [DDD]
Janácek, L.:Capriccio, w. Musiktage Mondsee Ensemble *(rec July 21–30, 1992)* London ▲ 440312-2 [DDD]
Janácek, L.:Concertino Pno, w. Musiktage Mondsee Ensemble *(rec July 21–30, 1992)* London ▲ 440313-2 [DDD]
Janácek, L.:Fairy Tale, w. B. Pergamenschikow (vc) *(rec July 21–30, 1992)* London ▲ 440312-2 [DDD]
Janácek, L.:In the Mists *(rec July 21–30, 1992)* London ▲ 440312-2 [DDD]
Janácek, L.:On an Overgrown Path *(rec July 21–30, 1992)* London ▲ 440313-2 [DDD]
Janácek, L.:Presto, w. B. Pergamenschikow (vc) *(rec July 21–30, 1992)* London ▲ 440312-2 [DDD]
Janácek, L.:Son October 1, 1905 Pno *(rec July 21–30, 1992)* London ▲ 440312-2 [DDD]
Janácek, L.:Son Vn, w. Y. Shiokawa (vn) *(rec July 21–30, 1992)* London ▲ 440313-2 [DDD]
Largo I, w. Vladimir Ashkenazy (pno), Alfred Brendel (pno), Alicia de Larrocha (pno), Julius Katchen (pno), Iliana Vered (pno), et al. Celestial Harmonies ▲ 35509-2 2–■ 35509-4
Largo II, w. Vladimir Ashkenazy (pno), Alfred Brendel (pno), Alicia de Larrocha (pno), Julius Katchen (pno), Iliana Vered (pno), et al. Celestial Harmonies ▲ 19504-2 ■ 19504-4
Mendelssohn, F.:Lieder ohne Worte Pno—sels London ▲ 421119-2 [DDD]
Mozart, W.A.:Adagio Glass Armonica London ▲ 421369-2 [DDD]
Mozart, W.A.:Adagio Pno, K.540 London ▲ 421369-2 [DDD]
Mozart, W.A.:Andante & Vars Pno 4-Hands, w. G. Malcolm (pno) London ▲ 440474-2
Mozart, W.A.:Andante Mechanical Org, K.616 London ▲ 421369-2 [DDD]
Mozart, W.A.:Arias, w. C. Bartoli (mez, A. Fischer (cnd), Vienna CO—arias from Clemenza di Tito, Così fan tutte, Don Giovanni & Le nozze di Figaro; & three concert arias [I] London ▲ 430513-2 [DDD]
Mozart, W.A.:Con 7 Pnos, w. D. Barenboim (pno); G. Solti (pno), G. Solti (cnd), English CO London ▲ 430232-2 [DDD]
Mozart, W.A.:Con 9 Pno, w. S. Végh (cnd), Salzburg Camerata Academica London ▲ 425466-2 [DDD]
Mozart, W.A.:Con 13 Pno, w. S. Végh (cnd), Salzburg Camerata Academica London ▲ 425466-2 [DDD]
Mozart, W.A.:Con 18 Pno, w. S. Végh (cnd), Salzburg Mozarteum Camerata Academica London ▲ 421259-2 [DDD] □ 421259-5
Mozart, W.A.:Con 19 Pno, w. S. Végh (cnd), Salzburg Mozarteum Camerata Academica London ▲ 421259-2 [DDD] □ 421259-5
Mozart, W.A.:Con 20 Pno, w. S. Végh (cnd), Salzburg Mozarteum Camerata Academica London ▲ 430510-2 [DDD]
Mozart, W.A.:Con 21 Pno, w. S. Végh (cnd), Salzburg Mozarteum Camerata Academica London ▲ 430510-2 [DDD]
Mozart, W.A.:Con 22 Pno, w. S. Végh (cnd), Salzburg Mozarteum Camerata Academica London ▲ 425855-2 [DDD]
Mozart, W.A.:Con 23 Pno, w. S. Végh (cnd), Salzburg Mozarteum Camerata Academica London ▲ 425855-2 [DDD]
Mozart, W.A.:Con 24 Pno, w. S. Végh (cnd), Camerata Academica London ▲ 425791-2 [DDD]
Mozart, W.A.:Con 25 Pno, w. S. Végh (cnd), Camerata Academica London ▲ 425791-2 [DDD]
Mozart, W.A.:Con 27 Pno, w. S. Végh (cnd), Salzburg Mozarteum Camerata Academica London ▲ 421259-2 [DDD] □ 421259-5
Mozart, W.A.:Fant Mechanical Org, w. G. Malcolm (pno) London ▲ 440474-2
Mozart, W.A.:Org Music, w. G. Malcolm (pno)—A piece for an Organ in A Clock, K.594 London ▲ 440474-2
Mozart, W.A.:Rondo Pno, K.511 London ▲ 421369-2 [DDD]
Mozart, W.A.:Sons Pno London 5–▲ 430333-2 [ADD]
Mozart, W.A.:Son Pno 4-Hands, K.497, w. G. Malcolm (pno) London ▲ 440474-2
Mozart, W.A.:Son Pno 4-Hands, K.521, w. G. Malcolm (pno) London ▲ 440474-2
Mozart, W.A.:Songs, w. C. Bartoli (mez)—Ridente la calma, K.152 *(rec Aug. 5–8, 1992)* London ▲ 440297-2 [DDD]
Mozart, W.A.:Trio Cl, w. Elmar Schmid (cl), Erich Höbarth (va) Teldec ▲ TEL 99205 [DDD]
Mozart, W.A.:Trio Pno, K.502, w. Yuuko Shiokawa (vn), Miklos Perényi (vc) Teldec ▲ TEL 99205 [DDD]
Mozart, W.A.:Trio Pno, K.542, w. Yuuko Shiokawa (vn), Miklos Perényi (vc) Teldec ▲ TEL 99205 [DDD]
Mozart, W.A.:Vars Pno, K.265 London ▲ 421369-2 [DDD]
Mozart, W.A.:Vars Pno, K.455 London ▲ 421369-2 [DDD]
Scarlatti, D.:Sons Kbd—K.175, 513, 402, 403, 144, 115, 116, 474, 475, 449, 450, 544, 545, 516, 517 London ▲ 421422-2 [DDD]
Scarlatti, D.:Sons Kbd—K.17, 27, 96, 162, 208, 322, 394, 420, 427, 491, 518, 519 Hungaroton ▲ HCD 11806
Schubert, Franz:Allegretto Pno, D.915 London ▲ 425638-2 [DDD]
Schubert, Franz:German Dances Pno, D.820 London ▲ 430425-2 [DDD]
Schubert, Franz:Grazer Galopp London ▲ 430425-2 [DDD]
Schubert, Franz:Impromptus Pno (comp) *(rec Tokyo, 1978)* Seven Seas ▲ SVS 137
Schubert, Franz:Impromptus Pno, D.935 London ▲ 425638-2 [DDD]
Schubert, Franz:Moments musicaux London ▲ 430425-2 [DDD]
Schubert, Franz:Pieces Pno, D.459 *(rec Brahms-Saal, Musikverein, Vienna, Apr. 1993)* London ▲ 440311-2 [DDD]
Schubert, Franz:Pieces Pno, D.946 London ▲ 425638-2 [DDD]
Schubert, Franz:Qnt Pno, D.667, w. A. Posch (db), Hagen String Quartet London ▲ 411975-2 [DDD]
Schubert, Franz:Qnt Strs, D.956, w. Alban Berg String Quartet EMI Classics ▲ CDC 47018 □ 0777-7-47018-5-3
Schubert, Franz:Die Schöne Müllerin, w. P. Schreier (ten) [G] London ▲ 430414-2 [DDD]
Schubert, Franz:Sons Pno (comp)—D.566; D.784; D.850 London ▲ 440305-2 [DDD]
Schubert, Franz:Sons Pno (comp)—D.571; D.840; D.845 London ▲ 440306-2 [DDD]
Schubert, Franz:Son Pno, D.157 *(rec Brahms-Saal, Musikverein, Vienna, Nov. 1992)* London ▲ 440311-2 [DDD]
Schubert, Franz:Son Pno, D.279 London ▲ 440310-2
Schubert, Franz:Son Pno, D.537 London ▲ 440309-2 [DDD]
Schubert, Franz:Son Pno, D.557 London ▲ 440307-2 [DDD]
Schubert, Franz:Son Pno, D.568 London ▲ 440308-2
Schubert, Franz:Son Pno, D.575 London ▲ 440307-2 [DDD]
Schubert, Franz:Son Pno, D.625 London ▲ 440310-2
Schubert, Franz:Son Pno, D.664 *(rec Brahms-Saal, Musikverein, Vienna, Nov. 1992)* London ▲ 440311-2 [DDD]
Schubert, Franz:Son Pno, D.894 London ▲ 440307-2 [DDD]
Schubert, Franz:Son Pno, D.958 London ▲ 440308-2
Schubert, Franz:Son Pno, D.959 London ▲ 440309-2 [DDD]
Schubert, Franz:Son Pno, D.960 London ▲ 440310-2
Schubert, Franz:Songs (misc), w. C. Bartoli (mez)—Vedi quanto adoro, D.510; Se dall'Etra, D.738; Io vuo' cantar di Cadmo, D.737; La pastorella, D.528; Non t'accostar all'urna, D.688/1; Guarda, che bianca luna, D.688/2; Da quel sembiante appresi, D.688/3; Mio ben ricordati, D.688/4; Pensa, che questo istante, D.76; Mi batte 'l cor, D.767 *(rec Aug. 5–8, 1992)* London ▲ 440297-2 [DDD]
Schubert, Franz:Songs (misc), w. Cecilia Bartoli (mez)—La pastorella; Vedi quanto adoro ancora ingrato! *(rec 1991 & 1992)* London ▲ 448300-2 [DDD]; ■ 448300-4
Schubert, Franz:Valses sentimentales (sels) London ▲ 430425-2 [DDD]
Schubert, Franz:Winterreise, w. P. Schreier (ten) *(rec Aug. 10–12, 1991)* London ▲ 436122-2 [DDD]
Schumann, R.:Andante & Vars Hn, w. P. Frankl (pno), L. Varga (vc), O. Hegedüs (vc), A. Halstead (hn) Vox Box 3–▲ CD3X 3001 [ADD]
Schumann, R.:Arabeske Pno Denon ▲ 7573 [DDD]

▲ = CD ♦ = Enhanced CD Δ = MD ■ = Cassette Tape □ = DCC

Schiff, András (pno) (cont.)
Schumann, R.:Ballszenen, w. P. Frankl (pno) Vox Box 3–▲ CD3X 3001 [ADD]
Schumann, R.:Bilder aus Osten, w. P. Frankl (pno) Vox Box 3–▲ CD3X 3001 [ADD]
Schumann, R.:Humoreske Pno Denon ▲ 7573 [DDD]
Schumann, R.:Kinderball, w. P. Frankl (pno) Vox Box 3–▲ CD3X 3001 [ADD]
Schumann, R.:Klavierstücke, Op. 85, w. P. Frankl (pno) Vox Box 3–▲ CD3X 3001 [ADD]
Schumann, R.:Papillons Denon ▲ 7573 [DDD]
Schumann, R.:Polonaises Pno 4–Hands, w. P. Frankl (pno) Vox Box 3–▲ CD3X 3001 [ADD]

Schiff, Heinrich (vc)
Beethoven, L. van:Con Vn, Vc & Pno, "Triple Con", w. U. Hoelscher (vn), C. Zacharias (pno), K. Masur (cnd), Leipzig Gewandhaus Orch EMI Classics ▲ ZDMC 63937
Beethoven, L. van:Trio 6 Pno, "Archduke", w. André Previn (pno), Viktoria Mullova (vn) Philips ▲ 442123–2
Brahms, J.:Trio 1 Pno, w. André Previn (pno), Viktoria Mullova (vn) Philips ▲ 442123–2
Dvořák, A.:Con Vc, w. C. Davis (cnd), Royal Concertgebouw Orch Philips ("Solo" series) ▲ 442401–2
Dvořák, A.:Con Vc, w. A. Previn (cnd), Vienna PO Philips ▲ 434914–2
Dvořák, A.:Polonaise Vc, w. E. Leonskaja (pno) Philips ▲ 412732–2 [DDD]
Dvořák, A.:Rondo, w. A. Previn (cnd), Vienna PO Philips ▲ 434914–2
Dvořák, A.:Silent Woods, w. A. Previn (cnd), Vienna PO Philips ▲ 434914–2
Dvořák, A.:Slavonic Dances (sels), w. A. Previn (pno)—in g, Op. 46/8 Philips ▲ 434914–2
Geminiani, F.:Sons Vc & Continuo, Op. 5, w. J. ter Linden (b vl), T. Koopman (hpd)—Sonata No. 6 in a Philips ▲ 434124–2 [DDD]
Haydn, J.:Con 1 Vc, w. N. Marriner (cnd), Academy of St. Martin in the Fields Philips ▲ 420923–2 [DDD]
Haydn, J.:Con 2 Vc, w. N. Marriner (cnd), Academy of St. Martin in the Fields Philips ▲ 420923–2 [DDD]
Pijper, W.:Con Vc, w. E. Spanjaard (cnd), Netherlands Radio CO NM Classics ▲ NM 92040
Rachmaninoff, S.:Son Vc, w. Elisabeth Leonskaja (pno) Philips ▲ 412732–2 [DDD]
Schumann, R.:Adagio & Allegro Hn, w. B. Haitink (cnd), Berlin PO [trans. for cello & orchestra] Philips ▲ 422414–2
Schumann, R.:Con Vc, w. B. Haitink (cnd), Berlin PO Philips ▲ 422414–2
Schumann, R.:Fantasiestücke Cl, w. B. Haitink (cnd), Berlin PO [cello & orch. trans.] Philips ▲ 422414–2
Schumann, R.:Stücke im Volkston, w. B. Haitink (cnd), Berlin PO [cello & orch. trans.] Philips ▲ 422414–2
Shostakovich, D.:Con 1 Vc, w. M. Shostakovich (cnd), Bavarian RSO Philips ▲ 412526–2 [DDD]
Shostakovich, D.:Con 2 Vc, w. M. Shostakovich (cnd), Bavarian RSO Philips ▲ 412526–2 [DDD]
Sibelius, J.:Malinconia, w. E. Leonskaja (pno) Philips ▲ 412732–2 [DDD]
Vivaldi, A.:Cons Vc, w. I. Brown (cnd), Academy of St. Martin in the Fields—5 concerti—RV.401, 411–413, 418, 424 Philips ▲ 411126–2 [DDD]
Vivaldi, A.:Sons Vc, w. T. Koopman (hpd), J. ter Linden (b vl)—(4) in e, RV.40; in a, RV.43; in B♭, RV.45; in B♭, RV.46 Philips ▲ 434124–2 [DDD]

Schiff, Zina (vn)
King David's Lyre, w. Cameron Grant (pno) *(rec SUNY, Mar 7–8, 1995)* 4–Tay ▲ 4002

Schiffer, Erwin (va)—see ORCHESTRAS & ENSEMBLES Dekany String Quartet

Schiffer, George (vc)—see ORCHESTRAS & ENSEMBLES Dekany String Quartet

Schiffer, René (baroque vc)
17th & 18th Century Chamber Music, w. Pieter–Jan Belder (rcr), H. Stinders (hpd) *(rec Nov. 1991)* Erasmus ▲ WVH 058 [DDD]

Schifrin, D. (cl)
Diamond, D.:Qnt Cl, w. P. Neubauer (va), W. Trampler (va), H. Cheifetz (vc), W. Lash (vc) *(rec 6 & 7/90)* Delos ▲ 3088 [DDD]
Herrmann, B.:Souvenirs de Voyage, w. P. Frank (vn), T. Arm (vn), W. Trampler (va), W. Lash (vc) *(rec 6 & 7/90)* Delos ▲ 3088 [DDD]
Ives, C.:Largo, w. E. Sato (vn), I. Vallecillo (pno) *(rec 6 & 7/90)* Delos ▲ 3088 [DDD]
Porter, Q.:Qnt Cl, w. T. Arm (vn), E. Sato (vn), P. Neubauer (va), W. Lash (vc) *(rec 6 & 7/90)* Delos ▲ 3088 [DDD]
Stravinsky, I.:Octet, w. M. Parloff (fl), F. Morelli (bn), S. Heinneman (bn), R. Mase (tpt), C. Gekker (tpt), R. Borror (trbn), D. Taylor (trbn), G. Schuller (cnd) *(rec Sep. 1991)* GM ▲ GM 2030

Schikora, Peter (va)
Mozart, W.A.:Qt Fl, K.285, w. E. Haupt (fl), P. Mirring (vn), G. Pluskwik (vc) LaserLight ▲ 15 878 [DDD]

Schilde, Klaus (pno)
Boccherini, L.:Fandango, w. M. M. Krüger (gtr) *(rec Jan. 7–9 & 19, 1991)* Calig ▲ CAL 50912 [DDD]
Brahms, J.:Songs, w. C. Wulkopf (alt)—4 Ernste Gesänge, Op. 121 [G] Ars Produktion ▲ FCD 368305
Brahms, J.:Songs, Op. 91, w. C. Wulkopf (alt), R. Metzger (va) [G] Ars Produktion ▲ FCD 368305
Castelnuovo–Tedesco, M.:Fant Gtr & Pno, w. M.M. Krüger (gtr) *(rec Jan. 7–9 & 19, 1991)* Calig ▲ CAL 50912 [DDD]
Dvořák, A.:Biblical Songs, Op. 99, w. C. Wulkopf (alt) [G] Ars Produktion ▲ FCD 368305
Forgotten Romantic Songs, Vol. 1, w. Cornelia Wulkopf (cta), Manfred Neukirchner (hn) Ars Produktion ▲ FCD 368315 [DDD]
Fuchs, R.:Qt Pno, w. K. Heymann (vn), J. Rieber (va), U. Bode (vc) MD + G ▲ L 3165
Giuliani, M.:Grand Duo Concertant Gtr, w. M. M. Krüger (gtr) *(rec Jan. 7–9 & 19, 1991)* Calig ▲ CAL 50912 [DDD]
Mahler, G.:Qt Pno [1 movt], w. K. Heymann (vn), J. Rieber (va), U. Bode (vc) MD + G ▲ L 3165
Weber, C.M. von:Divert assai facile, w. M. M. Krüger (gtr) *(rec Jan. 7–9 & 19, 1991)* Calig ▲ CAL 50912 [DDD]

Schill, Olle (cl)
Nielsen, C.:Con Cl, w. M.–W. Chung (cnd), Gothenburg SO BIS ▲ CD 321 [DDD]
Nielsen, C.:Con Cl, w. M.–W. Chung (cnd), Gothenburg SO BIS ▲ CD 616 [DDD]

Schiller, Allan (pno)
Bloch, E.:Baal Shem, "3 Pictures of Chassidic Life", w. Leonard Friedman (vn) ASV ▲ ASV 714
Bloch, E.:Son 1 Vn, w. L. Friedman (vn) ASV ▲ ASV 714
Bloch, E.:Son 2 Vn, "Poème mystique", w. L. Friedman (vn) ASV ▲ ASV 714
Bridge, F.:Qnt Pno, w. Coull String Quartet ASV ▲ ASV 678 [DDD]
Chabrier, E.:Bourée fantasque ASV ("Quicksilva" series) ▲ ASQ 6166
Chabrier, E.:Pièces pittoresques ASV ("Quicksilva" series) ▲ ASQ 6166
Chabrier, E.:Pièces posthumes ASV ("Quicksilva" series) ▲ ASQ 6166
Chabrier, E.:Suite de valses ASV ("Quicksilva" series) ▲ ASQ 6166
Chopin, F.:Waltzes ASV ("Quicksilva" series) ▲ ASQ 6149 [DDD]
Elgar, E.:Qnt Pno Strs, w. Coull String Quartet ASV ▲ ASV 678 [DDD]
Für Elise ASV ("Quicksilva" series) ▲ ASV 6032 [ADD]
Romantic Piano Music Vivace ▲ E 603 [DDD]

Schiller, Christoph (va)—see also ORCHESTRAS & ENSEMBLES Aria String Quartet
Burkhard, W.:Con Va, w. M. Venzago (cnd), Swiss–Italian Radio–TV Orch *(rec 1985 & 1989)* Jecklin–Disco ▲ JD 647–2 [ADD]
Burkhard, W.:Kleine Serenade Vn & Va, w. H. Schneeberger (vn) *(rec 1985 & 1989)* Jecklin–Disco ▲ JD 647–2 [ADD]
Burkhard, W.:Serenade Fl, Op. 77, w. S. Gärtner (fl), W. Meienberg (cl), J. Stavicek (bn), M. Gugel (hn), M. Paccagnella (hp), H. Schneeberger (vn), B. Wyganth (db) *(rec between 1985 & 1989)* Jecklin–Disco ▲ JD 647–2 [ADD]
Burkhard, W.:Sonata Va *(rec 1985 & 1989)* Jecklin–Disco ▲ JD 647–2 [ADD]
Huber, K.:Ohne Grenze und Rand, w. J. Wyttenbach (cnd), Bale SO Accord ▲ ACD 204532 [DDD]
Keller, A.:Der enthüllte Stern, w. D. Fueter (sop), K. Graf (sop), A. K. Graf (fl), L. Pellerin (ob), E. Schmid (cl), U. Walker (vn), C. Schiller (va), P. Demenga (vc), P. Hug–Rutti (hp), F. Eberle (dr) [G] Grammont ▲ CTSP 19–2 [ADD]
Koechlin, C.:Paysages et marines, w. Kiyoshi Kasai (fl), Elmar Schmid (cl), Alexandru Gavrilovici (vn), Urs Walker (vn), Patrick Demenga (vc) Accord ▲ ACD 201092 [DDD]
Koechlin, C.:Son Va, w. Christoph Keller (pno) Accord ▲ ACD 201092 [DDD]

Schiller, Christoph (va) (cont.)
Missa in festo Pentecostes, w. [cnd:Roman Bannwart], Einsiedein & Lucerne Choralschola, K. Graf, E. Schmid, T. Käser *(rec 1987)* Jecklin ▲ JEC 617–2 [ADD]
Mozart, W.A.:Trio Cl, K.498, w. K. Leister (cl), C. Ivaldi (pno) Tudor ▲ TUD 798 [DDD]
Müller–Zurich, P.:Cons Va Pno, w. S.–C. Wu (pno) Grammont ▲ CTSP 20–2
Reinecke, C.:Trio Pno, Op. 264, w. C. Ivaldi (pno), K. Leister (cl) Tudor ▲ TUD 798 [DDD]
Scelsi, G.:Coelocanth Accord ▲ ACD 200622 [DDD]
Scelsi, G.:Elegia per Thy, w. Patrick Demenga (vc) Accord ▲ ACD 200622 [DDD]
Scelsi, G.:Trio Strs, w. Robert Zimanksy (vn), Patrick Demenga (vc) Accord ▲ ACD 200622 [DDD]
Vivaldi, A.:Sons Ob, w. B. Glaetzner (ob), I. Goritzki (ob), K. Suske (vn), A. Bayer (vn), T. Reinhardt (bn), S. Pank (vl)—RV.28, 34, 53, 81 & 779 Capriccio ▲ CD 10143 [DDD] ■ CAS 27153 (CrO2)
Wildberger, J.:Diaphanie *(rec April 1, 1987)* Grammont ▲ CTSP 25–2 [ADD]
Zimmermann, B.A.:Son Va *(rec Feb & July 1995)* ECM New Series ▲ ECM 1571 [DDD]

Schilli, Stefan (ob)—see also ORCHESTRAS & ENSEMBLES Avalon Wind Quintet
Vivaldi, A.:Cons Ob, w. D. Jonas (ob), G. Thomas (hpd), G. Kósa (hpd), J. Kis Domonkos (vc), Nagy, Morandi (cnd), Failoni CO—RV 450, 452, 453, 454, 534, 535 & 536 *(rec Dec. 1992)* Naxos ▲ 8.550859 [DDD]
Vivaldi, A.:Cons Ob, w. G. Kósa (hpd), J. Kis Domonkos (vc), Nagy, Morandi (cnd), Failoni CO—RV 447, 451, 455, 457, 461 & 463 *(rec Apr. 1993)* Naxos ▲ 8.550860 [DDD]

Schilling, Adrian (timp)
Derungs, G.A.:Con da chiesa, w. Karl Raas (org), Stephan Thomas (org), Peter Schneider (vib), M. Schwarz (cnd), St. Gallen Collegium Musicum Musiques Suisses ▲ 6125 [DDD]

Schilling, Richard (gtr)
Sérénade, w. Margaret O'Keefe (sop) Titanic ▲ Ti 212 [DDD]

Schiltknecht, F. (vc)
Boulez, P.:Messagesquisse, w. B. Licther (vc), A. Loudos (vc), B. Feigenwinter (vc), M. Keller (vc), P. Toso (vc), J. Wyttenbach (cnd) *(rec Switzerland, June 1993)* ECM New Series 2–▲ 78118–21520–2 [DDD]

Schimmel, B. (acc)
Foss, L.:Curriculum Vitae with Time Bomb, w. J. Williams (perc) *(rec 1989–90)* Koss Classics ▲ KC 1006 [DDD]

Schimmel, William (acc)
Weill, K.:Songs, w. A. Réaux (sop), R. Kapilow (pno), B. Ruyle (perc)—conceived & first performed by Angelina Réaux for the 1988 New York Shakespeare Festival, this one–woman show features 21 songs composed from 1928–1946 [E,F,G] Koch International Classics 2–▲ KIC 7087–2 [DDD]

Schindler, Gisela (org)
Weber, C.M. von:Missa sancta 1, w. Maria Taborsky (sop), Gerda Kink (cta), Hermann Pöllmann (ten), Hans Huber (bass), E. Ehret (cnd), St. Michael Orch Munich, St. Michael Chorus Munich Koch Schwann ▲ SCH CD 316372
Weber, C.M. von:Missa sancta 2, w. Maria Taborsky (sop), Gerda Kink (alt), Hermann Pöllmann (ten), Hans Huber (bass), E. Ehret (cnd), Munich St. Michael's Orch, Munich St. Michael Choir Studio SM ▲ D 2454 [ADD]

Schindler, Xenia (hp)—see also ORCHESTRAS & ENSEMBLES Zurich New Music Ensemble
Caccini, G.:Le nuove musiche, w. Montserrat Figueras (sop), J. Savall (vl), R. Clancy (baroque gtr), H. Smith (baroque gtr), Schola Cantorum Basiliensis Editio Classica ▲ 77164–2–RG [ADD]

Schlefer, J. (fl)
Crumb, G.:Vox balaenae, w. L. Zoernig (vc), S. Moltisanti (pno) Zuma Records ▲ ZMA 102

Schleiermacher, Steffen (pno)—see also ORCHESTRAS & ENSEMBLES Avantgarde Ensemble
Antheil, G.:Airplane Son *(rec Sender Freies Berlin, Nov 13–14, 1993)* Hat Hut ("NOW." series) ▲ hat ART CD 6144 [DDD]
Antheil, G.:Jazz Son *(rec Sender Freies Berlin, Nov 13–14, 1993)* Hat Hut ("NOW." series) ▲ hat ART CD 6144 [DDD]
Antheil, G.:Son Sauvage *(rec Sender Freies Berlin, Nov 13–14, 1993)* Hat Hut ("NOW." series) ▲ hat ART CD 6144 [DDD]
Cage, J.:Winter Music, w. Mats Persson (pno), Kristine Scholz (pno), Nils Vigeland (pno), Eberhard Blum (pic/fl/alt fl)—for 4 pianos; for 4 pianos with flute parts from Atlas Eclipticalis *(rec Sender Freies Berlin & Hessen Radio, Frankfurt, Feb. 10–11, 1992 & June 6)* Hat Hut ("NOW." series) ▲ hat ART CD 6141 [DDD]
Cowell, H.:Pno Music—3 Irish Legends; Aeolian Hp; Banshee; Anger Dance; Dynamic Motion; 5 Encores to Dynamic Motion; Tiger *(rec Sender Freies Berlin, Nov 13–14, 1993)* Hat Hut ("NOW." series) ▲ hat ART CD 6144 [DDD]
Feldman, Morton:Intersections II & III *(rec Hessen Radio, Frankfurt, Dec. 16–17, 1993)* Hat Hut ("NOW." series) ▲ hat ART CD 6146 [DDD]
Feldman, Morton:Pno Music—Intermission V; Piano Piece; 2 Intermissions; 4 Last Pieces; Intermission VI; 5 Pianos [w. I. Mundry, M. Persson, K. Scholz, N. Vigeland] *(rec Berlin, 1993)* Hat Hut ("Now." series) ▲ ART CD 6143
Fukushima, K.:Ekagura, w. Eberhard Blum (alt fl) *(rec Sender Freies Berlin, Mar. 23–24, 1992)* Hat Hut ("NOW." series) ▲ hat ART CD 6114 [DDD]
Fukushima, K.:Kadha Karuna, w. Eberhard Blum (fl) *(rec Sender Freies Berlin, Mar. 23–24, 1992)* Hat Hut ("NOW." series) ▲ hat ART CD 6114 [DDD]
Fukushima, K.:Pieces (3) from Chu–u, w. Eberhard Blum (fl) *(rec Sender Freies Berlin, Mar. 23–24, 1992)* Hat Hut ("NOW." series) ▲ hat ART CD 6114 [DDD]
Fukushima, K.:A Ring of the Wind *(rec Sender Freies Berlin, Mar. 23–24, 1992)* Hat Hut ("NOW." series) ▲ hat ART CD 6114 [DDD]
Fukushima, K.:Sui–en *(rec Sender Freies Berlin, Mar. 23–24, 1992)* Hat Hut ("NOW." series) ▲ hat ART CD 6114 [DDD]
Lourié, A.:Formes en l'air *(rec Berlin, May 30 & 31, 1994)* Hat Hut ("Now." series) ▲ ART CD 6157 [DDD]
Lourié, A.:Poèmes Pno, Op. 8 *(rec Berlin, May 30 & 31, 1994)* Hat Hut ("Now." series) ▲ ART CD 6157 [DDD]
Lourié, A.:Synthesis *(rec Berlin, May 30 & 31, 1994)* Hat Hut ("Now." series) ▲ ART CD 6157 [DDD]
Mosolov, A.:Nocturnes Pno *(rec Berlin, May 30 & 31, 1994)* Hat Hut ("Now." series) ▲ ART CD 6157 [DDD]
Mosolov, A.:Pieces & Dances *(rec Berlin, May 30 & 31, 1994)* Hat Hut ("Now." series) ▲ ART CD 6157 [DDD]
Ornstein, L.:Pno Music—Impressions de Notre–Dame, Op. 16/1–2 (ca. 1915); Suicide in an Airplane (ca. 1915); Wild Men's Dance, Op. 13/2 (ca. 1914) *(rec Sender Freies Berlin, Nov 13–14, 1993)* Hat Hut ("NOW." series) ▲ hat ART CD 6144 [DDD]
Protopopov, S.:Son 2 Pno *(rec Berlin, May 30 & 31, 1994)* Hat Hut ("Now." series) ▲ ART CD 6157 [DDD]
Roslavets, N.:Preludes Pno *(rec Berlin, May 30 & 31, 1994)* Hat Hut ("Now." series) ▲ ART CD 6157 [DDD]
Wolff, C.:Exercises, w. Eberhard Blum (fl), Roland Dahinden (trbn), Jan Williams (perc) *(rec Hessischer Radio, Frankfurt, Aug 6–7, 1994)* Hat Hut ("Now" series) ▲ CD 6167 [DDD]
Wolff, C.:Pairs, w. Eberhard Blum (fl)—Versions 1 & 2 *(rec Hessen Radio, Frankfurt, Dec. 16–17, 1993)* Hat Hut ("NOW." series) ▲ hat ART CD 6146 [DDD]

Schleiffer, Eric (bn)—see also ORCHESTRAS & ENSEMBLES Gothenburg Wind Quintet
Beethoven, L. van:Qnt Pno, Ob, Cl, Hn & Bn, w. E. Knardahl (pno), E. Andersson (cl), A. Linder (hn) BIS ▲ CD 44 [AAD]
Berwald, F.:Qt Pno, Cl, Hn & Bn, w. E. Knardahl (pno), E. Andersson (cl), A. Linder (hn) BIS ▲ CD 44 [AAD]
Rimsky–Korsakov, N.:Qnt Fl, w. E. Andersson (cl), A. Linder (hn), E. Knardahl (pno) BIS ▲ CD 44 [AAD]

Schlessinger, L. (vc)—see ORCHESTRAS & ENSEMBLES New Works Calgary Ensemble

Schliephake, Ingrid (vn)
Stephan, R.:Music for 7 Stringed Instrs, w. B. Hartog (vn), S. Passaggio (va), G. Donderer (vc), A. Akahoshi (db), C. Tainton (pno), M. Schmidt (hp) *(rec 1983)* Koch Schwann ▲ CD 311 122 [ADD]

Schlierf, T. (fid/shawm)—see ORCHESTRAS & ENSEMBLES Estampie

Schloifer, Eckart (va)
Brandmüller, T.:Konzert auf dem E–Zweig Pro Viva ▲ ISPV 163 [DDD]

Schloifer, Eckart (va) (cont.)
Han, A.:Zeitumwandlung Pro Viva ▲ ISPV 163 [DDD]
Kalitzke, J.:Flucht im Gewölbe Pro Viva ▲ ISPV 163 [DDD]
Leyendecker, U.:Etude Va Pro Viva ▲ ISPV 163 [DDD]
Meyer, K.:Trio Fl, w. Robert Aitken (fl), Reinbert Evers (gtr) *(rec Munich, 1995)* Pro Viva ▲ ISPV 176 CD [DDD]
Staude, C.:Nachbild Pro Viva ▲ ISPV 163 [DDD]
Zender, H.:Hölderlin Lesen II, w. Elisabeth Langner (nar) Pro Viva ▲ ISPV 163 [DDD]

Schloss, Andrew (radio-drum)
Jaffe, D.A.:Seven Wonders of the Ancient World— *Great Pyramid, Hanging Gardens of Babylon, Statue of Zeus, Colossus of Rhodes* w. Mark Davis (gtr), Audrey Andrist (hpd), Jan Urke (bd), Marianne le Mentec (hp), Susan Greenway (harm), Tim Rawlings (perc), Brent van Dusen (perc), Marilyn Mair (mand), Robert Aitken (cnd); *Temple of Artemis; Mausoleum at Halicarnassus; Pharos of Alexandria* w. Alexander Dunn (gtr), Grace Quaglio (hpd), Michel Taddi (db), Victoria Drake (hp), Stephen Clarke (harm), Nicholas Coulter (perc), Grahm Hargrove (perc), Terrance Pender (mand), David Jaffe (mand), Stephen Colvin (cnd) Well-Tempered Productions ▲ WTP 5181 [DDD]

Schloter, Elmar (org)
Bach, J.S.:Fant & Fugue Org, BWV 542 [the Organ in the Munich Philharmonic Hall] *(rec Jan 13 & 27, 1989)* Calig ▲ CAL 50891 [DDD]
Bach, J.S.:Fant Org, BWV 572 [the Organ in the Munich Philharmonic Hall] *(rec Jan 13 & 27, 1989)* Calig ▲ CAL 50891 [DDD]
Brahms, J.:Ein Deutsches Requiem, w. A. M. Blasi (sop), B. Terfel (b-bar), C. Davis (cnd), Bavarian RSO, Bavarian Radio Chorus [G] RCA Red Seal ▲ 09026-60868-2
de Fesch, W.:Sons Vn, Op. 8a, w. S. Haak (vn), H. Herrmann (tpt)—No. 10 *(rec Nov. 18-21, 1991)* Koch Schwann ▲ SCH 310252 [DDD]
Handel, G.F.:Cons (16) Org, *(orch unknown)*—Op. 7/10 [Organ in the Munich Philharmonic Hall] *(rec Jan. 13 & 27, 1989)* Calig ▲ CAL 50891 [DDD]
Liszt, F.:Prelude & Fugue on the name B-A-C-H [Organ in the Munich Philharmonic Hall] *(rec Jan. 13 & 27, 1989)* Calig ▲ CAL 50891 [DDD]
Mozart, W.A.:Andante Mechanical Org, K.616 [organ in the Munich Philharmonic Hall] *(rec Jan. 13 & 27, 1989)* Calig ▲ CAL 50891 [DDD]

Schlueter, Charles (tpt)
Chardon, Y.:Son Tpt, w. Joel Moerschel (vc) *(rec Symphony Hall, Boston, MA, Sept. 1994)* Vox Classics ▲ VOX 7513 [DDD]
Hindemith, P.:Son Tpt, w. Deborah Dewolf Emery (pno) *(rec Symphony Hall, Boston, MA, Sept. 1994)* Vox Classics ▲ VOX 7513 [DDD]
Ketting, O.:Intrada *(rec Symphony Hall, Boston, MA, Sept. 1994)* Vox Classics ▲ VOX 7513 [DDD]
Suderburg, R.:Chamber Music VII, w. Robert Suderburg (pno) *(rec Symphony Hall, Boston, MA, Sept. 1994)* Vox Classics ▲ VOX 7513 [DDD]
Suderburg, R.:Chamber Music VIII, w. Robert Suderburg (pno) *(rec Symphony Hall, Boston, MA, Sept. 1994)* Vox Classics ▲ VOX 7513 [DDD]

Schlüssel, Sanford (pno)
Chausson, E.:Poème Vn, w. G. Enescu (vn) *(rec 1929)* Biddulph ▲ LAB 066 [ADD]
Chausson, E.:Poème Vn, w. George Enesco (vn) [arr for vn & pno] *(rec ca 1928)* Symposium ▲ 1156
The Complete Solo Columbia Recordings, w. Georges Enescu (vn), Edward C. Harris (pno), Yehudi Menuhin (pno), Hepzibah Menuhin (pno) *(rec 1924 & 1929)* Biddulph ▲ LAB 066 [ADD]

Schlüter, Karl-Heinz (pno)
Brahms, J.:Sym 1, w. Michael Schlüter (pno) [arr. for Piano Duet] Koch Schwann ▲ SCH 317412 [DDD]

Schlüter, Michael (pno)
Brahms, J.:Sym 1, w. Karl-Heinz Schlüter (pno) [arr. for Piano Duet] Koch Schwann ▲ SCH 317412 [DDD]

Schmahl, Gustav (vn)
Shostakovich, D.:Con 1 Vn, w. K. Masur (cnd), Dresden PO Berlin Classics ▲ BER CD 9153

Schmalfuss, Gernot (ob)
Bach, J.S.:Sons Fl, BWV 1030-35, w. W. Döling (hpd)—BWV 1030 & 1031 MD + G ▲ L 3461 [DDD]
Bach, J.S.:Sons Vn, w. W. Döling (hpd)—BWV 1013 & 1020 [trans. for oboe & continuo; BWV 1020 doubtful] MD + G ▲ L 3461 [DDD]
Haydn, J.:Qts Ob, w. Consortium Classicum MD + G ▲ L 3314 [DDD]
Mozart, W.A.:Don Giovanni, w. Christian Hartmann (ob), Dieter Klöcker (cl), Waldemar Wandel (cl), Sara Willis (hn), Christian Auer (hn), Karl-Otto Hartmann (bn), Eberhard Buschmann (bn), Jürgen Normann (db), Consortium Classicum Bayer ▲ BR 100 135 [DDD]
Mozart, W.A.:Qt Ob, K.370, w. Consortium Classicum MD + G ▲ L 3314 [DDD]

Schmalfuss, Peter (pno)
Chopin, F.:Nocturnes—Nos. 1-10, Opp. 9,15,27 & 32 PMG (Vienna Master) ▲ CD 160223 [DDD]
Chopin, F.:Waltzes—Nos. 1-14 PMG (Vienna Master) ▲ CD 160230 [DDD]
Mozart, W.A.:Rondo Pno, K.511 Vivace 3-▲ E 319 [DDD]
Mozart, W.A.:Son 11 Pno Vivace 3-▲ E 319 [DDD]
Mozart, W.A.:Son 15 Pno Vivace 3-▲ E 319 [DDD]
Mozart, W.A.:Vars Pno, K.265 Vivace 3-▲ E 319 [DDD]

Schmeer, Karin (hp)
Scelsi, G.:Music of, w. Joëlle Léandre (sgr/db), Nicolas Isherwood (bass), Giancarlo Schiaffini (trbn/tuba), Fances-Marie Uitti (vc), Robyn Schulkowsky (tamtam)—Maknongan for Low-Registered Instrument (1976) [3 versions:bass, double bass, tuba]; Tre pezzi for Trombone (1956); Wo Ma for Bass (1960); C'est bien la nuit for Double Bass (1972); Le réveil profond for Double Bass (1977); Et Maintenant, c'est a vous a jouer for Cello & Double Bass (1974); Okanagon for Harp, Double Bass & Tamtam (1968); Mantram for Double Bass (1987) *(rec Sendesaal, Hessen Radio, Frankfurt, Feb. 8-9, May 18-21 & Aug)* Hat Hut ("NOW." series) ▲ hat ART CD 6124 [DDD]

Schmeiser, Hansgeorg (fl)—see ORCHESTRAS & ENSEMBLES Vienna Quintet

Schmeisser, A. M. (hp)
Mozart, W.A.:Con Fl Hp, w. E. Bodensohn (fl), H. Rosbaud (cnd), Southwest German RSO Baden-Baden *(rec 1962)* Datum 2-▲ DAT 12303 [ADD]

Schmid, Andreas (vc)
Backofen, J.G.:Concertante Hp, w. H. R. Stalder (hp), U. Holliger (bas hn) *(rec 1981)* Jecklin-Disco ▲ JD 560-2 [ADD]

Schmid, Benjamin (vn)
Paganini, N.:Caprices Vn, w. Lisa Smirnova (pno) [arr Robert Schumann for vn & pno] MD + G ▲ MDG 3330674

Schmid, Elmar (bas hn)
Mozart, W.A.:Adagio Bas Hns, K.410/440d, w. H.R. Stalder (bas hn), P. Meyer (bn) *(rec 1978)* Jecklin-Disco ▲ JD 549-2 [ADD]
Mozart, W.A.:Adagio Cls, K.411, w. K. Leister (cl), P. Geisler (cl), H.R. Stalder (bas hn), H. Hofer (bas hn) *(rec 1978)* Jecklin-Disco ▲ JD 549-2 [ADD]
Mozart, W.A.:Adagio E Hn, w. K. Leister (cl), H.R. Stalder (bas hn), H. Hofer (bas hn) [arr. Raymond Meylan for clarinet & basset horn] *(rec 1978)* Jecklin-Disco ▲ JD 549-2 [ADD]

Schmid, Elmar (cl)—see also ORCHESTRAS & ENSEMBLES Musiktage Mondsee Ensemble
Holliger, H.:Alb-Chehr, w. Oswald Brumann (bass), Sabine Gertschen (dlc), Edmund Volken (dlc), Klaus Schmid (cl), Markus Tenisch (Swiss org), Marcel Volken (Swiss org), Paul Locher (vn), Franziskus Abgottspon (nar) ECM New Series ▲ 78118-21540-2 [DDD]
Holliger, H.:Beiseit, w. David James (ct), Teodoro Anzellotti (acc), Johannes Nied (db), H. Holliger (cnd) ECM New Series ▲ 78118-21540-2 [DDD]
Keller, A.:Der enthüllte Stern, w. D. Fueter (sop), K. Graf (sop), A. K. Graf (fl), L. Pellerin (ob), U. Walker (vn), C. Schiller (va), P. Demenga (vc), P. Hug-Rutti (hp), F. Eberle (dr) [G] Grammont ▲ CTSP 19-2 [ADD]
Keller, A.:Ewiger Augenblick, w. D. Fueter (sop), K. Graf (sop), A. K. Graf (fl), D. Isler (cel), P. Hug-Rutti (hp), U. Walker (vn), P. Demenga (vc) [G] Grammont ▲ CTSP 19-2 [ADD]
Koechlin, C.:Paysages et marines, w. Kiyoshi Kasai (fl), Alexandru Gavrilovici (vn), Urs Walker (vn), Christoph Schiller (va), Patrick Demenga (vc) Accord ▲ ACD 201092 [DDD]

Schmid, Elmar (cl) (cont.)
Kreutzer, C.:Trio for 2 Cls & Va, w. H. R. Stalder (cl), D. Jappe (va) [period instrs] *(rec 1984)* Jecklin-Disco ▲ JD 587-2 [ADD]
Lehmann, H.U.:Kammermusik, w. K. Graf (sop), A.-K. Graf (fl), W. Grimmer (vc), I. Nakamura (perc) Jecklin ▲ JD 689
Magnard, A.:Qnt Pno, w. Christoph Keller (pno), Anna-Katharina Graf (fl), Roman Schmid (ob), Jiri Flieger (bn) Accord ▲ ACD 200102 [DDD]
Mozart, W.A.:Trio Cl, w. Erich Höbarth (va), András Schiff (pno) Teldec ▲ TEL 99205 [DDD]

Schmid, Engelbert (hn)
Dauprat, L.-F.:Trios Hns, Op. 4/1-3, w. U. Köbl (F hn), K. Reitmayer (F hn) Calig ▲ CAL 50865 [DDD]
Reicha, A.:Trios Hns, Op. 82, w. K. Reitmayer (hn), U. Köbl (hn)—6 trios—Nos. 19-24 Calig ▲ CAL 50865 [DDD]

Schmid, Georg (va)
Hindemith, P.:Concert Music Va & Large Chamber Orch, w. R. Heger (cnd), Bavarian RSO Koch Schwann ▲ CD 310 045
Hindemith, P.:Kammermusik 5, w. R. Heger (cnd), Bavarian RSO Koch Schwann ▲ SCH 313372 [ADD/DDD]
Hindemith, P.:Kammermusik 5, w. R. Kubelik (cnd), Bavarian RSO Koch Schwann ▲ CD 310 045
Hindemith, P.:Der Schwanendreher, w. R. Kubelik (cnd), Bavarian RSO *(rec 1978)* Originals ▲ ORISH 804 [ADD]

Schmid, Klaus (cl)
Holliger, H.:Alb-Chehr, w. Oswald Brumann (bass), Sabine Gertschen (dlc), Edmund Volken (dlc), Elmar Schmid (cl), Markus Tenisch (Swiss org), Marcel Volken (Swiss org), Paul Locher (vn), Franziskus Abgottspon (nar) ECM New Series ▲ 78118-21540-2 [DDD]

Schmid, Kurt-Franz (cl)
Danzi, F.:Sinf concertante, w. C. Slepicka (bn), J.-P Rouchon (cnd), Maurice Ravel CO Divertimento ▲ DIV 31008 [DDD]
Hoffmeister, F.A.:Con Cl, Bn & Orch, w. C. Slepicka (bn), J.-P Rouchon (cnd), Maurice Ravel CO Divertimento ▲ DIV 31008 [DDD]
Mozart, W.A.:Arias, w. A. Raunig (ct), M. Dostal (org), W. Kobera (cnd), Vienna Amadeus Ensemble, Vienna Landstrasse Church Choir—Il padre adorato [from Idomneo]; Cara, lontano ancora [from Ascanio in Alba]; Parto, ma tu ben mio [from La clemenza di Tito] Divertimento ▲ DIV 31013 [DDD]
Mozart, W.A.:Exsultate, w. A. Raunig (ct), M. Dostal (org), W. Kobera (cnd), Vienna Amadeus Ensemble, Vienna Landstrasse Church Choir Divertimento ▲ DIV 31013 [DDD]
Salieri, A.:Arias, w. A. Raunig (ct), M. Dostal (org), W. Kobera (cnd), Vienna Amadeus Ensemble, Vienna Landstrasse Church Choir—Perdermi? [from Axur, Re d'ormus]; Lungi da te [from Armida]; A fulminas m'invita [from Anibale] Divertimento ▲ DIV 31013 [DDD]
Salieri, A.:Songs, w. A. Raunig (ct), M. Dostal (org), W. Kobera (cnd), Vienna Amadeus Ensemble, Vienna Landstrasse Church Choir—Fremat Thyrannus (motet) Divertimento ▲ DIV 31013 [DDD]
Vogel, J.C.:Sinf concertante Cl, w. C. Slepicka (bn), J.-P. Rouchon (cnd), Maurice Ravel CO Divertimento ▲ DIV 31008 [DDD]

Schmid, Roman (ob)
Magnard, A.:Qnt Pno, w. Christoph Keller (pno), Anna-Katharina Graf (fl), Elmar Schmid (cl), Jiri Flieger (bn) Accord ▲ ACD 200102 [DDD]

Schmid, Siegfried (perc)
Bartók, B.:Son for 2 Pnos, w. Gerhard Huber (perc), Janka & Jürg Piano Duo Accord ▲ ACD 220372

Schmid, Willi (vc)—see ORCHESTRAS & ENSEMBLES Munich Baryton Trio

Schmidhäusler, F. (tpt)
Frischknecht, H.E.:Composition, w. R. Schmidhäusler (tpt), H. E. Frischknecht (org) *(rec July 2, 1990)* Pro Viva ▲ ISPV 161 CD [DDD]

Schmidhäusler, R. (tpt)
Frischknecht, H.E.:Composition, w. F. Schmidhäusler (tpt), H. E. Frischknecht (org) *(rec July 2, 1990)* Pro Viva ▲ ISPV 161 CD [DDD]

Schmidinger, Marcus (hn)—see ORCHESTRAS & ENSEMBLES Brassissimo Vienna

Schmidinger, Rudolf (perc)
Christmas with Brassissimo, w. Brassissimo Vienna, Manfred Kaufmann (perc) *(rec MG-SOUND Studios, Vienna)* Brassissimo ▲ BVR 5356400 [DDD]
Strauss (I), Joh.:Radetzky March, w. Ralf Kircher (perc), Kevan Teherani (perc), Brassissimo Vienna *(rec Pfarrkirche Staatz, Nov 29-Dec 2, 1993)* Brassissimo ▲ BVR 2328517 [DDD]
Strauss (II), Joh.:Music of, w. Ralf Kircher (perc), Kevan Teherani (perc), Brassissimo Vienna—Maskenball-Quadrille; Unter Donner und Blitz; Etwas Kleines; Kaiserwalzer; Annenpolka; Waldmeister-Ov; Leichtes Blut; Auf der Jagd; Pizzikato-Polka [composed w. Josef Strauss]; Elyen a Magyar; Perpetuum Mobile; Fledermaus-Ov *(rec Pfarrkirche Staatz, Nov 29-Dec 2, 1993)* Brassissimo ▲ BVR 2328517 [DDD]
Strauss, Josef:Music of, w. Ralf Kircher (perc), Kevan Teherani (perc), Brassissimo Vienna—Ohne Sorgen; Moulinet-Polka; Pizzikato-Polka [composed w. Johann Strauss II]; Feuerfest *(rec Pfarrkirche Staatz, Nov 29-Dec 2, 1993)* Brassissimo ▲ BVR 2328517 [DDD]

Schmidl, Peter (cl)—see also ORCHESTRAS & ENSEMBLES Vienna Ring Ensemble
Fahrbach, P.:Music of, w. Dieter Flury (fl), Vienna Biedermeier Soloists—Die Schwärmer, Op. 43; Talmi-Polka, Op. 304; Lerchenfelder-Polka, Op. 178; Vienna Polka, Op. 109; S'Schwarzblatl Aus'n Weanerwald, Op. 61; Wiener-Feuerwehr, Op. 280; Marien-Polka, Op. 164; Wiener Polka, Op. 109 *(rec Studio Baumgarten, Vienna, 1991-95)* Camerata ▲ 30CM 411 [DDD]
Fahrbach (Jr.), P.:Music of, w. Dieter Flury (fl), Vienna Biedermeier Soloists—Der Klapperstorch, Op. 149; Wiener Lebensbilder, Op. 213; Reissausl, Op. 121; Pester Offiziers Casino Polka, Op. 83; Landsturm-Galopp, Op. 250; Erinnerung An Josef Strauss, Op. 53; Im Kahlenbergerdörfel, Op. 340 *(rec Studio Baumgarten, Vienna, 1991-95)* Camerata ▲ 30CM 411 [DDD]
Mozart, W.A.:Con Cl, w. L. Bernstein (cnd), Vienna PO Deutsche Grammophon ▲ 429221-2 [DDD]
Mozart, W.A.:Trio Cl, K.498, w. Klaus Peisteiner (va), Keiko Toyama (pno) *(rec Tsukuba Nova Hall, Oct 12, 1990)* Camerata ▲ 32CM 180 [DDD]
Songs of Mendelssohn, Schubert & Brahms, w. Edita Gruberova (sop), Friedrich Haider (pno) Nightingale Classics ▲ NIG CD 70860

Schmidt, Annerose (pno)
Grieg, E.:Con Pno, Op. 16, w. K. Masur (cnd), Dresden PO Berlin Classics ▲ BER CD 9152
Mozart, W.A.:Con 12 Pno, w. K. Masur (cnd), Dresden PO *(rec 1970)* Berlin Classics ▲ BER CD 9154
Mozart, W.A.:Con 18 Pno, w. K. Masur (cnd), Dresden PO Berlin Classics 2-▲ BER 9251
Mozart, W.A.:Con 20 Pno, w. K. Masur (cnd), Dresden PO Berlin Classics 2-▲ BER 9251
Mozart, W.A.:Con 21 Pno, w. K. Masur (cnd), Dresden PO Berlin Classics 2-▲ BER 9251
Mozart, W.A.:Con 27 Pno, w. K. Masur (cnd), Dresden PO Berlin Classics 2-▲ BER 9251
Mozart, W.A.:Son 14 Pno LaserLight ▲ 15 877 [DDD]
Mozart, W.A.:Son 15 Pno LaserLight ▲ 15 877 [DDD]

Schmidt, Benjamin (vn)—see also ORCHESTRAS & ENSEMBLES Pro Arte String Quartet
Bach, J.S.:Sons Fl, BWV 1030-35, w. Lisa Smirnova (pno) [arr Robert Schumann for pno] MD + G ▲ MDG 3330614

Schmidt, Diane (acc)
Hovhaness, A.:Rubaiyat, w. Michael York (nar), G. Schwarz (cnd), Seattle SO *(rec Seattle Opera House, June 6-7, 1994)* Delos ▲ DE 3168 [DDD]

Schmidt, Felix (vc)
Boccherini, L.:Con Vc, G.480, w. E. Heath (cnd), English CO IMP ("Classics" series) ▲ IMP 6700912
Elgar, E.:Con Vc, w. R. Frühbeck de Burgos (cnd), London SO IMP Classics ▲ PCD 930 [DDD]
Invitation to the Dance, w. London SO, Richard Williams (cnd), Rafael Fruhbeck de Burgos (cnd) Pickwick ("The Orchid" series) ▲ PICORCD 11002

Schmidt, Helmut (pno)
Bach, J.S.:Con for 4 Hpds, w. J. Frantz (pno), C. Eschenbach (pno), G. Oppitz (pno), C. Eschenbach (cnd), Hamburg PO Deutsche Grammophon ▲ 415655-2 [DDD]

Schmidt, Kimberly (pno)
Women at an Exposition, w. Sunny Joy Langton (sop), Susanne Mentzer (mez), Elain Skorodin (vn) *(rec Nov. 1991)* Koch International Classics ▲ KIC 7240 [ADD]

▲ = CD ♦ = Enhanced CD △ = MD ■ = Cassette Tape ☐ = DCC

Schmidt, Lars Ole (tpt)
Trumpet Concertos, Vol. 2, w. Ketil Christensen (tpt), Ole Andersen (tpt), Boemia CO [cnd:Hynec Farkac] — Rondo Grammofon ▲ RCD 8339
Trumpet Concertos, Vol. 3, w. Ketil Christensen (tpt), Ole Andersen (tpt), Moravian-Silesian CO [cnd:Preben Norgaard Christensen, Pavel Vitek] — Rondo Grammofon ▲ RCD 8345

Schmidt, Linda (fl)
Porter, T.:Pieces Ww Qnt, w. Deirdre Fay (ob), Loran Eckroth (cl), Leslie Peterson (hn), Holly Holm (bn) — Meyer ▲ MC 0108

Schmidt, Liz (pno)
Partch, H.:While My Heart Keeps Beating Time, w. Philip Blackburn (voc) [orig published under alias Paul Pirate] *(rec 1995)* — Innova 4-▲ 401

Schmidt, M. (vc)
Pellegrini, E.:Divert a tre Bn, w. D. N. Joseph (bn), V. Barton (vc) — CRS ▲ CD 8949

Schmidt, Marianna (hp)
Stephan, R.:Music for 7 Stringed Instrs, w. B. Hartog (vn), I. Schliephake (vn), S. Passaggio (va), G. Donderer (vc), A. Akahoshi (db), C. Tainton (pno) *(rec 1983)* — Koch Schwann ▲ CD 311 122 [ADD]

Schmidt, R. (vn)—see ORCHESTRAS & ENSEMBLES Ravinia Trio

Schmidt, Rie (fl)—see also ORCHESTRAS & ENSEMBLES Flute Force
Ibert, J.:Music of, w. C. Schadeberg (sop), Sue Ann Kahn (fl), E. Lawrence (fl), P. Schechter (fl), David Krakauer (cl), L. Goldstein (bn), Curtis Macomber (vn), Susan Jolles (hp), Frederick Hand (gtr), Arthur Willis (pno)—Entr'acte; Jeux; Sonatine; 2 Movements; 2 Interludes; Aria; Pièce for solo Fl; Histoires; 2 Stèles orientées; Pastoral; Aria; Entr'acte — Albany ▲ TROY 145

Schmidt, Stephan (gtr)
Scarlatti, D.:Sons Kbd — Valois ▲ V 4750

Schmidt, Wilhelm (pno)
Arias & Songs, w. Irmgard Seefried (sop), Gerald Moore (pno), Hermann von Nordberg (pno), London Mozart Players [cnd:Harry Blech] — Testament ▲ SBT 1026 [ADD]

Schmidt-Laukamp, Ursula (rcr)
Caix D'Hervelois, L. de:Pièces Trns Fl, w. Harald Hoeren (hpd)—2nd Suite in F [from Premier livre] — Ars Produktion ▲ ARS 368337
Couperin, F.:Nouveaux Concerts, "Les Goûts-réunis", w. Harald Hoeren (hpd)—Nos. 7 & 8 — Ars Produktion ▲ ARS 368337
Marais, M.:Pièces en trio, w. Peter Wendland (vl), Harald Hoeren (hpd)—No. 3 in D — Ars Produktion ▲ ARS 368337

Schmid-Wyss, Hanni (pno)
Martin, F.:Qnt Pno, w. Zurich Chamber Players *(rec 1989/90)* — Jecklin-Disco ▲ JD 646-2 [ADD]
Martin, F.:Trio sur les mélodies populaires irlandaises, w. Zurich Chamber Players *(rec 1989/90)* — Jecklin-Disco ▲ JD 646-2 [ADD]

Schmiedel, Reinhard (pno)
Donizetti, G.:Music for Pno 4-Hands, w. L. Kondratyeva (pno) — CPO 2-▲ CPO 999163 [DDD]
Krenek, E.:Reisebuch aus den österreichischen Alpen, w. M. Köhler (bar) — CPO ▲ CPO 999203 [DDD]

Schmieder, Birgit (ob)
French Sonatas of the 18th Century, w. Johannes Tappert (gtr) — MD + G ▲ MDG 6170631

Schmit-Lobis, Deborah (pno)
A Colorado Kind of Christmas, w. [cnd:Duain Wolfe], Colorado Children's Chorale, Mike Fitzmaurice (db), Rod Garnet (fl), William Hill (perc), Brett Walace (vc), Mary Louise Burke (pno), Laurie Kahler (pno), Helen Hope (hp) *(rec Denver Center Media)* — Colorado Children's Chorale ▲ XMAS

Schmitt, Thomas (gtr)
Guerau, F.:Poema harmónico *(rec Apr & Sept 1993)* — Musicaphon ▲ M 56819 [DDD]
Murcia, S. de:Gtr Music—Salvidar Códice No. 4 (1714); Passacalles y Obras (1732) *(rec Apr & Sept 1993)* — Musicaphon ▲ M 56819 [DDD]
Santa Cruz, A. de:Libro donde se verán Pasacalles *(rec Apr & Sept 1993)* — Musicaphon ▲ M 56819 [DDD]
Sanz, G.:Instrucción de Música *(rec Apr & Sept 1993)* — Musicaphon ▲ M 56819 [DDD]

Schmitz, Joaquim (fl)
Villa-Lobos, H.:Bachiana brasileira 6, w. Ulrich Freund (bn) — Bayer ▲ BR 100117 [DDD]
Villa-Lobos, H.:Qt Fl, w. Petra Fluhr (ob), Johannes Moog (cl), Ulrich Freund (bn) — Bayer ▲ BR 100117 [DDD]

Schmocker, F. (bn)
Balissat, J.:Vars (7), w. P. Genet, F. Gottraux (vn), N. Pache (va), M. Jaermann (vc), R. Birnstigl (db), F. Rapin (cl), M. Veillon (hn), J. Balissat (cnd) — Grammont ▲ CTSP 17-2 [ADD]

Schmöller, A. (vc)
Abel, C.F.:Son Fl, Vc & Hpd, w. Claude Arimany (fl), M. Grüber (hpd) — Motette ▲ MOT CD 30141 [DDD]
Bach, C.P.E.:Trio Son Fl, H.586, w. C. Arimany (fl), M. Grüber (hpd) — Motette ▲ MOT CD 30141 [DDD]

Schnabel, Artur (pno)
Plays Bach & Brahms, Vol. 1 — Pearl ▲ PEA 9399 (m) [AAD]
Artur Schnabel Plays Bach & Brahms, Vol. 2 — Pearl ▲ PEA 9376 (m) [AAD]
Bach, J.S.:Con 2 for 2 Hpds, w. K.U. Schnabel (pno), A. Boult (cnd), London SO *(rec Oct 28, 1936)* — Pearl ▲ PEA 9399 (m) [AAD]
Bach, J.S.:Italian Con — Klavier ■ KC 134
Bach, J.S.:Toccatas Hpd, BWV 910-16—BWV 911 & 912 *(rec Nov 24, 1937)* — Pearl ▲ PEA 9376 (m) [AAD]
Beethoven, L. van:Bagatelles (24)—Op. 126/4 *(rec live 1944)* — Pearl 3-▲ PEA 9063 [AAD]
Beethoven, L. van:Bagatelles (24)—Op. 33 *(rec 1932-38)* — Pearl 2-▲ PEA 9123 [AAD]
Beethoven, L. van:Bagatelles (24) *(rec 1932-37)* — Pearl 3-▲ PEA 9142 [ADD]
Beethoven, L. van:Bagatelle, WoO 59, "Für Elise" *(rec 1932-35)* — Iron Needle ▲ 1319 (m) [ADD]
Beethoven, L. van:Bagatelle, WoO 59, "Für Elise" *(rec live 1944)* — Pearl 3-▲ PEA 9063 [AAD]
Beethoven, L. van:Bagatelle, WoO 59, "Für Elise" *(rec 1932-38)* — Pearl 2-▲ PEA 9139 [AAD]
Beethoven, L. van:Cons Pno (comp), w. M. Sargent (cnd), London SO, London PO *(rec 1932-35)* — Pearl 3-▲ PEA 9063 [AAD]
Beethoven, L. van:Con 4 Pno, w. I. Solomon (cnd), Columbus PO *(rec live 1947)* — Pearl 3-▲ PEA 9063 [AAD]
Beethoven, L. van:Con 4 Pno, w. F. Stock (cnd), Chicago SO — RCA Gold Seal ▲ 09026-61393-2
Beethoven, L. van:Con 5 Pno, "Emperor", w. F. Stock (cnd), Chicago SO — RCA Gold Seal ▲ 09026-61393-2
Beethoven, L. van:Con 6 Pno, w. C. F. Adler (cnd), Vienna Orch *(rec early 1950s)* — Somerset ▲ SCD 10001 (m)
Beethoven, L. van:Fant Pno, Op. 77 *(rec 1932-38)* — Pearl 2-▲ PEA 9139 [AAD]
Beethoven, L. van:Minuets Orch, WoO 10—No. 2 — Klavier ■ KC 134
Beethoven, L. van:Pno Music (comp)—Sons., Opp. 2/1-3, 7, 10/1 & 2, 49/1 & 2; Rondo, WoO 49; Rondo a capriccio, Op. 129 *(rec 1933-37)* — Pearl 2-▲ PEA 9083 [AAD]
Beethoven, L. van:Pno Music (misc)—Diabelli Vars, Op. 120; Eroica Vars, Op. 35; Vars, Op. 34; Bagatelles, Opp. 33 & 126; Bagatelle in a [Für Elise]; Fant, Op. 77 — Enterprise ("The Piano Library" series) 2-▲ ENT PL 199
Beethoven, L. van:Rondos Pno, Op. 51—No. 2 — Klavier ■ KC 134
Beethoven, L. van:Rondos Pno, Op. 51—No. 1 in C *(rec live 1944)* — Pearl 3-▲ PEA 9063 [AAD]
Beethoven, L. van:Son 2 Vc, w. G. Piatigorsky (vc) *(rec 1934)* — Music & Arts ▲ CD 674 [AAD]
Beethoven, L. van:Son 2 Vc, w. G. Piatigorsky (vc) *(rec 12/6 & 16/34)* — Pearl ▲ PEA 9447 (m) [AAD]
Beethoven, L. van:Sons Pno (comp)—Nos. 14-18 *(rec 1932-38)* — Pearl 2-▲ PEA 9123 [AAD]
Beethoven, L. van:Sons Pno (comp)—Nos. 30-32 — Enterprise ("Piano Library" series) ▲ ENT PL 216
Beethoven, L. van:Sons Pno (comp)—Nos. 7-13 *(rec 1932-38)* — Pearl 2-▲ PEA 9099 [AAD]
Beethoven, L. van:Sons Pno (comp)—Nos. 21-27 *(rec 1932-38)* — Pearl 2-▲ PEA 9139 [AAD]
Beethoven, L. van:Sons Pno (comp)—Nos. 28 & 29 — Enterprise ("Piano Library" series) ▲ ENT PL 205
Beethoven, L. van:Sons Pno (comp)—Nos. 1-32 *(rec 1932-35)* — EMI Classics ("Great Recordings of the Century" series) 8-▲ CDHH 63765 (m) [ADD]
Beethoven, L. van:Son 8 Pno, "Pathétique" — Grammofono 2000 2-▲ GRM 78598 (m)
Beethoven, L. van:Son 14 Pno, "Moonlight Son" — Enterprise ("Sirio" series) ▲ ENT SO 53008

Schnabel, Artur (pno) (cont.)
Beethoven, L. van:Son 14 Pno, "Moonlight Son" — Grammofono 2000 2-▲ GRM 78598 (m)
Beethoven, L. van:Son 15 Pno, "Pastoral" — Grammofono 2000 2-▲ GRM 78598 (m)
Beethoven, L. van:Son 17 Pno, "Tempest" — Grammofono 2000 2-▲ GRM 78598 (m)
Beethoven, L. van:Son 21 Pno, "Waldstein" *(rec between 1933 & 1939)* — Grammofono 2000 ▲ GRM 78503 [ADD]
Beethoven, L. van:Son 21 Pno, "Waldstein" — Enterprise ("Sirio" series) ▲ ENT SO 53008
Beethoven, L. van:Son 21 Pno, "Waldstein" — Grammofono 2000 2-▲ GRM 78598 (m)
Beethoven, L. van:Son 23 Pno, "Appassionata" — Enterprise ("Sirio" series) ▲ ENT SO 53008
Beethoven, L. van:Son 23 Pno, "Appassionata" — Grammofono 2000 2-▲ GRM 78598 (m)
Beethoven, L. van:Son 26 Pno, "Les Adieux" — Grammofono 2000 2-▲ GRM 78598 (m)
Beethoven, L. van:Son 26 Pno, "Les Adieux" — Enterprise ("Sirio" series) ▲ ENT SO 53008
Beethoven, L. van:Sons 28-32 Pno, "The Late Sons" *(rec 1932-37)* — Pearl 3-▲ PEA 9142 [ADD]
Beethoven, L. van:Sons 28-32 Pno, "The Late Sons" — Grammofono 2000 2-▲ GRM 78549 (m)
Beethoven, L. van:Son 5 Vn, "Spring", w. J. Szigeti (vn) *(rec live Apr. 1948)* — Pearl ▲ PEA 9026 [AAD]
Beethoven, L. van:Son 10 Vn, w. J. Szigeti (vn) *(rec live Apr. 1948)* — Pearl ▲ PEA 9026 [AAD]
Beethoven, L. van:Vars on an Original Theme, Op. 34 *(rec 1932-35)* — Iron Needle ▲ 1319 (m) [ADD]
Beethoven, L. van:Vars on an Original Theme, Op. 34 *(rec 1932-38)* — Pearl 2-▲ PEA 9123 [AAD]
Beethoven, L. van:Vars & Fugue Pno, Op. 35, "Eroica" *(rec 1932-38)* — Pearl 2-▲ PEA 9139 [AAD]
Beethoven, L. van:Vars on a waltz by Diabelli, Op. 120 *(rec 1932-35)* — Iron Needle ▲ 1319 (m) [ADD]
Beethoven, L. van:Vars on a waltz by Diabelli, Op. 120 *(rec 1932-37)* — Pearl 3-▲ PEA 9142 [ADD]
Beethoven, L. van:Vars on a waltz by Diabelli, Op. 120 *(rec 1937 for HMV)* — Pearl ▲ PEA 9378 (m) [AAD]
Brahms, J.:Con 1 Pno, w. G. Szell (cnd), London PO *(rec 1/9 & 12/18 1938)* — Pearl ▲ PEA 9376 (m) [AAD]
Brahms, J.:Con 2 Pno, w. A. Boult (cnd), BBC SO *(rec 1935 for EMI)* — Pearl ▲ PEA 9399 (m) [AAD]
Mozart, W.A.:Allegro & Andante & Rondo *(rec live in recital, New York, Nov. 14, 1953)* — Music & Arts ▲ CD 750-1 [AAD]
Mozart, W.A.:Con 17 Pno, w. F. Stiedry (cnd), New Friends of Music Orch—excerpt from the 2nd movt. *(rec live March 22, 1942)* — Music & Arts ▲ CD 750-1 [AAD]
Mozart, W.A.:Con 20 Pno, w. G. Szell (cnd), New York Philharmonic SO *(rec live Dec. 24, 1944)* — Music & Arts ▲ CD 750-1 [AAD]
Mozart, W.A.:Con 21 Pno, *(orch unknown)* — Memories ("Golden" series) 2-▲ MEM 3005
Mozart, W.A.:Con 21 Pno, w. M. Sargent (cnd), London SO — Enterprise ("Piano Library" series) ▲ ENT PL 210
Mozart, W.A.:Con 21 Pno, w. M. Sargent (cnd), London SO — Enterprise ("Sirio" series) ▲ ENT SO 53006
Mozart, W.A.:Con 22 Pno, w. B. Walter (cnd), New York PO — Enterprise ("The Radio Years" series) ▲ ENT RY 69
Mozart, W.A.:Con 23 Pno, w. A. Rodzinski (cnd), New York Philharmonic SO *(rec live, Mar. 3, 1946)* — Music & Arts ▲ CD 632 (m) [AAD]
Mozart, W.A.:Con 24 Pno, w. A. Wallenstein (cnd), Standard SO *(rec live in Los Angeles, Dec. 1, 1946)* — Music & Arts ▲ CD 632 (m) [AAD]
Mozart, W.A.:Con 27 Pno, w. J. Barbirolli (cnd), London SO — Enterprise ("Sirio" series) ▲ ENT SO 53006
Mozart, W.A.:Con 27 Pno, w. J. Barbirolli (cnd), London SO — Enterprise ("Piano Library" series) ▲ ENT PL 210
Mozart, W.A.:Qt Pno, K.478, w. Pro Arte String Quartet members *(rec 1934)* — Iron Needle 2-▲ IN 1342/43 (m) [ADD]
Mozart, W.A.:Son 8 Pno *(rec between 1933 & 1939)* — Grammofono 2000 ▲ GRM 78503 [ADD]
Mozart, W.A.:Sons Vn Pno (misc), w. J. Szigeti (vn)—K.481 *(rec live Apr. 1948)* — Pearl ▲ PEA 9026 [AAD]
Schubert, Franz:Moments musicaux *(rec Nov 1937)* — Enterprise ("The Piano Library" series) ▲ ENT 186
Schubert, Franz:Moments musicaux *(rec 1937-39)* — EMI Classics ("References" series) 2-▲ CDHB 64259
Schubert, Franz:Pno Music (misc), March, D.606 *(rec ca. 1937/39)* — EMI Classics ("References" series) 2-▲ CDHB 64259
Schubert, Franz:Qnt Pno, D.667, w. Pro Arte String Quartet — EMI Classics ▲ CDH 63031
Schubert, Franz:Scherzos Pno, D.593—No. 1 — Klavier ■ KC 134
Schubert, Franz:Son Pno, D.850 *(rec ca. 1937-39)* — EMI Classics ("References" series) 2-▲ CDHB 64259
Schubert, Franz:Son Pno, D.959 *(rec between 1933 & 1939)* — Grammofono 2000 ▲ GRM 78503 [ADD]
Schubert, Franz:Son Pno, D.959 *(rec ca. 1937-39)* — EMI Classics ("References" series) 2-▲ CDHB 64259
Schubert, Franz:Son Pno, D.960 *(rec ca. 1937-39)* — EMI Classics ("References" series) 2-▲ CDHB 64259
Schubert, Franz:Son Pno, D.960 *(rec Jan 1939)* — Enterprise ("The Piano Library" series) ▲ ENT 186
Weber, C.M. von:Invitation to the Dance Pno — Klavier ■ KC 134

Schnabel, Karl Ulrich (pno)—see also ORCHESTRAS & ENSEMBLES Schnabel Piano Duo
Bach, J.S.:Con 2 for 2 Hpds, w. A. Schnabel (pno), A. Boult (cnd), London SO *(rec Oct 28, 1936)* — Pearl ▲ PEA 9399 (m) [AAD]
Mozart, W.A.:Son Pno 4-Hands, K.497, w. J. Rowland (pno) — Town Hall ▲ THCD 41
Schubert, Franz:Divertissement sur des motifs originaux français, D.823, w. J. Rowland (pno) — Town Hall ▲ THCD 41
Schubert, Franz:Vars Theme from Hérold's *Marie* Pno 4-Hands, w. J. Rowland (pno)—No. 1 — Town Hall ▲ THCD 41

Schnaus, Andrea (pno)
Kaleidoscope, w. Katja Pieweck (sop), Hannover Girls' Choir *(rec 1982 & 1993)* — Thorofon ▲ CTH 2174 [ADD/DDD]

Schneeberger, Hansheinz (vn)
Bach, J.S.:A Musical Offering, w. Peter-Lukas Graf (fl), et al., J.E. Dähler (cnd) — Claves ▲ CD 198 [ADD]
Bach, J.S.:Sons & Partitas Vn, BWV 1001-1006 *(rec 1987)* — Jecklin-Disco 2-▲ JS 266/7-2 [ADD]
Bartók, B.:Son Vn — Accord ▲ ACD 220372
Burkhard, W.:Kleine Serenade Vn & Va, w. C. Schiller (va) *(rec 1985 & 1989)* — Jecklin-Disco ▲ JD 647-2 [ADD]
Burkhard, W.:Serenade Fl, Op. 77, w. S. Gärtner (fl), W. Meienberg (cl), J. Stavicek (bn), M. Gugel (hn), M. Paccagnella (hp), C. Schiller (va), B. Wyganth (db) *(rec between 1985 & 1989)* — Jecklin-Disco ▲ JD 647-2 [ADD]
Carter, E.:Riconoscenza (per Goffredo Petrassi) — ECM New Series ▲ 78118-21391-2 [DDD]
Carter, E.:Triple Duo, w. P. Racine (fl), E. Molinari (cl), P. Cleeman (va), T. Demenga (vc), G. Huber (perc) — ECM New Series ▲ 78118-21391-2 [DDD]
Haydn, J.:Con Org, Vn & Strs, H.XVIII/6, w. E. Hashimoto (hpd), K. Toyoda (cnd), Tchikashi Tanaka Ensemble — Camerata ▲ 30CM 376
Lehmann, H.U.:Son da chiesa, w. J. Lehmann (org) *(rec Aug. 12, 1978)* — Grammont ▲ CTS P 4-2
Reger, M.:Son Vn Pno, Op. 122, w. J. Dünki (pno) — Jecklin-Disco ▲ JD 649-2 [DDD]
Reger, M.:Son Vn Pno, Op. 139, w. J. Dünki (pno) — Jecklin-Disco ▲ JD 649-2 [DDD]
Schumann, R.:Con Vn, w. F. Merz (cnd), South Westphalian PO — ebs ▲ ebs 6090
Schumann, R.:Son 1 Vn, w. J.-J. Dünki (hammerflügel) *(rec Dec. 1991)* — Jecklin-Disco ▲ JD 664-2 [DDD]
Spohr, L.:Con 1 Vn Hp, w. Ursula Holliger (hp), P.-L. Graf (cnd), English CO *(rec EMI Studio London, 1970)* — Claves ▲ CD 50208 [ADD]
Veress, S.:Son Vn — ECM New Series ▲ 78118-21477-2 [DDD]
Veress, S.:Trio, w. T. Zimmermann (va), T. Demenga (vc) — ECM New Series ▲ 78118-21477-2 [DDD]

Schneemann, Bart (ob)
Escher, R.:Chamber Music, w. Jacques Zoon (fl), Herman De Boer (cl), Zoltan Benyacs (va), Dmitri Ferschtman (vc), Glen Wilson (hpd)—includes Le Tombeau de Ravel; Trio for Strings; Trio for Cl, Va & Pno — NM Classics ▲ NM 92026

Schneeweiss, Kurt (gtr)
Weiss, S.L.:Lt Music—Son No. 29 (Trumpet Sonata) [arr for guitar Kurt Schneeweiss] Koch Schwann ▲ SCH 317162 [DDD]
Weiss, S.L.:Lt Music [trans. Schneeweiss]—Son. No. 17 Koch Schwann ▲ SCH 314122 [DDD]

Schneider, (hn)
Pleyel, I.:Sinf concertante 5, w. D. Becker (fl), P. Meyer (cl), Schottstädt (bn), J. Faerber (cnd), Württemberg CO MD + G ▲ L 3396 [DDD]

Schneider, (pno)
Liszt, F.:Sonetti di Petrarca Voice & Pno, w. J. Carreras (ten) [I] Acanta ▲ CD 43578

Schneider, Alexander (vn)—see also ORCHESTRAS & ENSEMBLES Budapest String Quartet
Beethoven, L. van:Trio 2 Pno, w. E. Istomin (pno), P. Casals (vc) *(rec Perpignan, France, Aug. 1951)* Sony Classical ("The Casals Edition" series) ▲ SMK 58989 [ADD]
Beethoven, L. van:Trio 5 Pno, w. E. Istomin (pno), P. Casals (vc) *(rec Perpignan, France, Aug. 1951)* Sony Classical ("The Casals Edition" series) ▲ SMK 58991 [ADD]
Beethoven, L. van:Trio 6 Pno, "Archduke", w. E. Istomin (pno), P. Casals (vc) *(rec Perpignan, France, Aug. 1951)* Sony Classical ("The Casals Edition" series) ▲ SMK 58990 [ADD]
Beethoven, L. van:Trio 7 Pno, w. E. Istomin (pno), P. Casals (vc) *(rec Perpignan, France, Aug. 1951)* Sony Classical ("The Casals Edition" series) ▲ SMK 58990 [ADD]
Boccherini, L.:Qnts Gtr, G.445–453, w. A. Diaz (gtr), F. Galimir (vn), M. Tree (va), D. Soyer (vc)—in C, G.446 *(rec 1965)* Vanguard Classics ▲ OVC 8006 [ADD]
Boccherini, L.:Qnts Strs, w. F. Galimir (vn), M. Tree (va), D. Soyer (vc), L. Harrell (vc)—Op. 13, No. 5 *(rec 1965)* Vanguard Classics ▲ OVC 8006 [ADD]
Brahms, J.:Sextet Strs, Op. 18, w. I. Stern (vn), M. Katims (va), M. Thomas (va), P. Casals (vc), M. Foley (vc) *(rec Prades, France, June 23–July 3, 1952)* Sony Classical ("The Casals Edition" series) ▲ SMK 58994 [ADD]
Brahms, J.:Sextet Strs, Op. 18, w. I. Stern (vn), M. Katims (va), M. Thomas (va), P. Casals (vc), M. Foley (vc) *(rec 1952)* Sony Masterworks ("Portrait" series) ▲ MPK 44851 [ADD]
Dvořák, A.:Qnt Pno, Op. 81, w. P. Serkin (pno), F. Galimir (vn), M. Tree (va), D. Soyer (vc) *(rec 1965)* Vanguard Classics ▲ OVC 8003 [ADD]
Mendelssohn, F.:Trio 1 Pno, w. Mieczyslaw Horszowski (pno), Pablo Casals (vc) *(rec White House, Washington, D.C., Nov 13, 1961)* Sony Classical ▲ SMK 66571 [ADD]
Mozart, W.A.:Qts Fl, w. J.-P. Rampal (fl), I. Stern (vn), L. Rose (vc) Odyssey ▲ MBK 42601
Mozart, W.A.:Qts Pno, w. P. Serkin (pno), M. Tree (va), D. Soyer (vc) *(rec 1965)* Vanguard Classics ▲ OVC 8007 [ADD]
Schubert, Franz:Qnt Pno, D.667, w. P. Serkin (pno), M. Tree (va), D. Soyer (vc), J. Levine (db) *(rec 1964)* Vanguard Classics ▲ OVC 8005 [ADD]
Schubert, Franz:Qnt Strs, D.956, w. I. Stern (vn), M. Katims (va), P. Casals (vc), P. Tortelier (vc) *(rec 1952)* CBS 4-▲ M4K 42003 (m/s) [ADD]
Schubert, Franz:Qnt Strs, D.956, w. I. Stern (vn), M. Katims (va), P. Casals (vc), P. Tortelier (vc) *(rec Prades, France, July 1–2, 1952)* Sony Classical ("The Casals Edition" series) ▲ SMK 58992 [ADD]
Schubert, Franz:Son Vn, D.574, w. P. Serkin (pno) Vanguard Classics ▲ OVC 8005 [ADD]
Schubert, Franz:Trio 1 Pno, w. E. Istomin (pno), P. Casals (vc) *(rec Perpignan, France, Aug. 1951)* Sony Classical ("Casals Edition" series) ▲ SMK 58989 [ADD]
Schubert, Franz:Trio 2 Pno, w. M. Horszowski (pno), P. Casals (vc) *(rec Prades, France, July 5–6, 1952)* Sony Classical ("The Casals Edition" series) ▲ SMK 58988 [ADD]
Schumann, R.:Trio 1 Pno, w. M. Horszowski (pno), P. Casals (vc) *(rec Prades, France, July 4, 1952)* Sony Classical ("The Casals Edition" series) ▲ SMK 58993 [ADD]

Schneider, Ansgar (vc)
Hindemith, P.:Die Serenaden, w. Ruth Ziesak (sop), Lajos Lencses (ob), Gunter Teuffel (va) CPO ▲ CPO 999332

Schneider, Bruno (hn)—see also ORCHESTRAS & ENSEMBLES Sabine Meyer Wind Ensemble
Schubert, Franz:Songs (comp), w. B. Hendricks (sop), R. Lupu (pno), S. Meyer (cl)—Der Hirt auf dem Felsen; Lachen und weinen; Ständchen; Die Männer sind mechant, Auf dem Strom; Sehnsucht; Liebesbotschaft; Versunken; An den Mond; Du liebst mich nicht; Die Liebe hat gelogen; Die junge Nonne; Klaglied; Ellens Gesang III; Delphine; Heidenröslein [G] EMI Classics ▲ CDC 54239
Strauss, R.:Con 2 Hn, w. M. Aeschbacher (cnd), Lausanne CO Claves ▲ CD 9010 [DDD]

Schneider, Christian (mand)
Vivaldi, A.:Cons Mand, w. D. Meyer (mand), K. Redel (cnd), Grenoble Instrumental Ensemble—Concerti in C & D for Mandolin & Strings; Concerto in G for 2 Mandolins & Strings; Concerto in C for 2 Mandolins & Orchestra Forlane ▲ FOR 16548 [AAD]

Schneider, D. (pno)
Alcalde Cordero, A.:Mon cher lit, w. L. Rossi (cl) *(rec Feb 1992)* Rossi ▲ NR 1104 [DDD]
Guastavino, C.:Son Cl, w. L. Rossi (cl) *(rec Feb. 1992)* Rossi ▲ NR 1104 [DDD]
Guastavino, C.:Tonada y Cueca, w. L. Rossi (cl) *(rec Feb. 1992)* Rossi ▲ NR 1104 [DDD]
Lacerda, O.:Valsa-Choro, w. L. Rossi (cl) *(rec Feb. 1992)* Rossi ▲ NR 1104 [DDD]

Schneider, David (cl)—see also ORCHESTRAS & ENSEMBLES Albert Schweitzer Wind Quintet
Contemporary Swiss Music for Clarinet Solo, w. Daniel Schneider (cl) *(rec May 1994)* Jecklin ▲ JEC 308
Copland, A.:Con Cl, w. J. Yannatos (cnd), Harvard-Radcliffe Orch AFKA ▲ SK 509
Yun, I.:Rondell, w. C. Dimigen (ob), E. Hübner (bn) *(rec Dec. 1991)* CPO ▲ CPO 999184 [DDD]

Schneider, Edwin (pno)
Brahms, J.:Romanzen aus Tieck's *Magelone*, w. Hans Peter Blochwitz (ten), Cornelia Froboess (nar) Berlin Classics ▲ BER 1125 [DDD]
Legendary Three Tenors, w. Enrico Caruso (ten), Beniamino Gigli (ten), John McCormack (ten), Ruggiero Leoncavallo (pno), Metropolitan Opera Orch, Metropolitan Opera Chorus [cnd:Giulio Setti], Philharmonia Orch, Philharmonia Chorus [cnd:Stanford Robinson] *(rec 1904–1950)* RCA Gold Seal ▲ 09026-68534-2 [ADD] ■ 09026-68534-4

Schneider, Elisabeth Zeuthen (vn)—see also ORCHESTRAS & ENSEMBLES Tre Musici, Copenhagen Contemporary Players, Tre Musici members
Hartmann, J.P.E.:Fant-Allegro, w. Bohumila Jedličkóva (pno) [arr for vn & pno] *(rec Frederiksdal Castle, Lolland, Feb 6–9 & Sept 3–5, 1995)* Marco Polo/Dacapo 2-▲ 8.224021/22 [DDD]
Hartmann, J.P.E.:Sons Vn (comp), w. Bohumila Jedličkóva (pno) *(rec Frederiksdal Castle, Lolland, Feb 6–9 & Sept 3–5, 1995)* Marco Polo/Dacapo 2-▲ 8.224021/22 [DDD]
Hartmann, J.P.E.:Suite Vn, w. Bohumila Jedličkóva (pno) [arr for vn & pno] *(rec Frederiksdal Castle, Lolland, Feb 6–9 & Sept 3–5, 1995)* Marco Polo/Dacapo 2-▲ 8.224021/22 [DDD]

Schneider, Gertrud (pno)
Tenney, J.:Flocking, w. Tomas Bächli (pno) Hat Hut ("Now" series) ▲ ART CD 6193 [DDD]

Schneider, Gottfried (vn)
Caprioli, A.:Serenata per Francesca, w. V. Fuchsberger (sgr), S. Winiarczyk (ob), A. Aigmüller (dr), R. Crow (instr), R. Huber (instr), K. Ager (cnd), Austrian Ensemble for New Music *(rec 1987)* Pro Viva ▲ ISPV 148 CD [ADD]
Goetz, H.:Con Vn, w. W. A. Albert (cnd), North German RSO CPO ▲ CPO 999076 [DDD]
Stamitz, C.:Qts Cl, w. E. Brunner (cl), A. Baader (va), H. Veihelmann (vc) Koch Schwann ▲ CD 310003 [DDD]

Schneider, John (gtr)—see also ORCHESTRAS & ENSEMBLES Just Strings Ensemble
Matson, S.:Range, w. Catherine Robbin (mez), Susan Greenberg (fl), Joseph Stone (fl), Glen Garrett (cl), Suren Karapetyan (hn), Peter Kent (vn), Kazi Pitelka (va), Sebastian Toettcher (vc), Don Ferrone (db), Doug Livingston (gtr/mand), Amy Shulman (hp), Terry Schoenig (perc), S. Matson (cnd) *(rec Schnee Studio, Universal City, CA, Mar 12, 1995)* New Albion ▲ NA 091

Schneider, Michael (rcr)
Handel, G.F.:Sons Rcr, w. Sabine Bauer (rcr), Cologne Camerata—8 Sonatas—Op. 1, Nos. 2, 4, 7 & 11; Sonatas in B♭, d & G; Sonata in F for 2 Recorders Editio Classica ▲ 77104-2-RG [DDD]

Schneider, Mischa (vc)—see also ORCHESTRAS & ENSEMBLES Budapest String Quartet members, Budapest String Quartet
Rachmaninoff, S.:Trio élégiaque 2, w. Artur Balsam (pno), Joseph Roisman (vn) *(rec Coolidge Auditorium, Library of Congress, Apr 4, 1952)* Bridge ▲ BRIDGE 9063

Schneider, Peter (vib)
Derungs, G.A.:Con da chiesa, w. Karl Raas (org), Stephan Thomas (org), Adrian Schilling (timp), M. Schwarz (cnd), St. Gallen Collegium Musicum Musiques Suisses ▲ 6125 [DDD]

Schneider, Richard (hn)—see ORCHESTRAS & ENSEMBLES Sabine Meyer Wind Ensemble

Schneider, Ronald (pno)
Caccini, G.:Music of, w. Gabriela Beňačková (sop) *(rec live, Prague, Oct. 8, 1995)* Supraphon ▲ SUP 3027
Lieder Recital, w. José Carreras (ten) Acanta ▲ CD 43578
Mozart, W.A.:Music of, w. Gabriela Beňačková (sop) *(rec live, Prague, Oct 8, 1995)* Supraphon ▲ SUP 3027

Schneiderhan, Wolfgang (vn)
Beethoven, L. van:Con Vn, Op. 61, w. E. Jochum (cnd), Berlin PO *(rec 1962 & 1967)* Deutsche Grammophon ("The Originals" series) ▲ 447403-2
Beethoven, L. van:Trio 4 Pno, "Ghost", w. Edwin Fischer (pno), E. Mainardi (vc) *(rec 1954)* Arkadia 2-▲ 568 (m) [ADD]
Beethoven, L. van:Trio 4 Pno, "Ghost", w. Edwin Fischer (pno), Enrico Mainardi (vc) *(rec Salzburg, 1952–53)* Music & Arts 2-▲ CD 840 [AAD]
Beethoven, L. van:Trio 6 Pno, "Archduke", w. Edwin Fischer (pno), Enrico Mainardi (vc) *(rec Salzburg, 1952–53)* Music & Arts 2-▲ CD 840 [AAD]
Brahms, J.:Con Vn & Vc, "Double Con", w. E. Mainardi (vc), K. Böhm (cnd), Vienna PO Datum 2-▲ DAT 12305 [ADD]
Brahms, J.:Trios (3) Pno, w. E. Fischer (pno), E. Mainardi (vc) *(rec 1954)* Arkadia 2-▲ 568 (m) [ADD]
Brahms, J.:Trio 1 Pno, w. E. Fischer (pno), E. Mainardi (vc) *(rec 1953)* Music & Arts ▲ CD 739 (m)
Brahms, J.:Trio 2 Pno, w. E. Fischer (pno), E. Mainardi (vc) *(rec 1951)* Music & Arts ▲ CD 739 (m)
Martin, F.:Con Vn, w. F. Martin (cnd), Luxembourg RSO *(rec 1971)* Jecklin-Disco ▲ JD 632-2 [ADD]
Martin, F.:Maria-Triptychon, w. E. Mathis (sop), J. Fournet (cnd), Swiss Festival Orch *(rec 1984)* Koch Treasure ▲ 31619-2 [DDD]
Martin, F.:Maria-Triptychon, w. I. Seefried (sop), F. Martin (cnd), Swiss-Italian Orch [L] *(rec Sept. 3, 1970)* Jecklin-Disco ▲ JD 645-2 [ADD]
Mozart, W.A.:Con 5 Vn, w. K. Ančerl (cnd), Czech PO *(rec live 1966)* Multisonic ("Prague Spring Collection" series) ▲ 31 0079-2 [ADD]
Mozart, W.A.:Con 5 Vn, w. W. Schneiderhan (cnd), Berlin PO *(rec 1962 & 1967)* Deutsche Grammophon ("The Originals" series) ▲ 447403-2
Mozart, W.A.:Trio Pno, K.548, w. Edwin Fischer (pno), Enrico Mainardi (vc) *(rec Salzburg, 1952–53)* Music & Arts 2-▲ CD 840 [AAD]
Schumann, R.:Trio 1 Pno, w. Edwin Fischer (pno), Enrico Mainardi (vc) *(rec 1954)* Arkadia 2-▲ 568 (m) [ADD]
Schumann, R.:Trio 1 Pno, w. Edwin Fischer (pno), Enrico Mainardi (vc) *(rec Salzburg, 1952–53)* Music & Arts 2-▲ CD 840 [AAD]

Schneiderman, John (lt)—see also ORCHESTRAS & ENSEMBLES Trioalanterie, Trio Galanterie
Baron, E.G.:Son Lute, w. J. Schneiderman *(rec Apr. 1–3, 1991)* Audioquest ▲ AQCD 1005
18th Century Lute Music Titanic ▲ Ti 165 [DDD]

Schneiter, Arthur (sounding stones)
Gasser, U.:Von der unerbittlichen Zufälligkeit des Todes, w. P. Bauer (cnd), Joueurs de Flute *(rec live, Heilig Kreuz Münster, Aug 26, 1995)* Jecklin ▲ JS 312-2 [DDD]

Schnell, Willy (ob)
Bach, J.S.:Cant 202, "Wedding Cant", w. Ursula Buckel (sop), Werner Keltsch (vn), Peter Buck (vc), Martin Galling (hpd), R. Ewerhart (cnd), Württemberg CO *(rec 1965)* Vox Box 3-▲ CD3X 3039
Bach, J.S.:Cant 204, w. Elisabeth Speiser (sop), Helmuth Steinkraus (fl), Dietmar Keller (ob), Susanne Lautenbacher (vn), R. Ewerhart (cnd), Württemberg CO *(rec 1966)* Vox Box 3-▲ CD3X 3039
Lutoslawski, W.:Die Strohkette, w. Barbara Miller (sop), Oksana Sowiak (mez), Robert Dohn (fl), Martin Klose (cl), Hartmut Stute (cl), Karl Steinbrecher (bn), A. Grüber (cnd) Vox Box 2-▲ CDX 5133

Schnepps, R. (hn)
Mozart, W.A.:Cassation, K.63, w. G. Hölscher (ob), S. Winiarczyk (ob), H. Nerat (hn), Salzburg CO *(rec March 28–30, 1992)* Naxos ▲ 8.550609 [DDD]
Mozart, W.A.:Cassation, K.99/63a, w. G. Hölscher (ob), S. Winiarczyk (ob), H. Nerat (hn), Salzburg CO *(rec March 28–30, 1992)* Naxos ▲ 8.550609 [DDD]
Mozart, W.A.:Cassation, K.100/62a, w. G. Hölscher (ob), S. Winiarczyk (ob), H. Nerat (hn), Salzburg CO *(rec March 28–30, 1992)* Naxos ▲ 8.550609 [DDD]

Schnirring, T. (hn)
Telemann, G.P.:Con for 2 Hns in E♭, w. I. James (hn), V. Czarnecki (cnd), Southwest German CO Pforzheim ebs ▲ ebs 6092 [DDD]

Schnittke, Irina (pno)
Schnittke, A.:Gratulationsrondo, w. M. Lubotsky (vn) *(rec June 11–12, 1991)* Sony Classical ▲ SK 53357 [DDD]
Schnittke, A.:Son 2 Pno *(rec Aug. 12–15, 1992)* Sony Classical ▲ SK 53271 [DDD]
Schnittke, A.:Trio Pno, w. M. Lubotsky (vn), Mstislav Rostropovich (vc) *(rec Aug. 12–15, 1992)* Sony Classical ▲ SK 53271 [DDD]

Schnöller, Isabelle (fl)
Mercadante, S.:Con in e Fl, Op. 57, w. A. Apolin (cnd), Pilsen RSO *(rec Sept 1994)* Jecklin ▲ JEC 704 [DDD]
Mozart, W.A.:Con Fl, K.314, w. A. Apolin (cnd), Pilsen RSO *(rec Sept 1994)* Jecklin ▲ JEC 704 [DDD]
Reinecke, C.:Con Fl, w. A. Apolin (cnd), Pilsen RSO *(rec Sept 1994)* Jecklin ▲ JEC 704 [DDD]

Schnorhk, Roland (trbn)
Roland Schnorhk, w. Georges Athanasiades (org) Studio SM ("Resonance Collection" series) ▲ 2544 [ADD]

Schober, A. (vc)
Bortnyansky, D.:Sinf concertante, w. H. Kann (pno), *(bn unknown)*, I. Angerer (hp), H. Bondarenko (vn), W. Knieps (va) Entrée ▲ 0051 [ADD]

Schocker, Gary (fl)
Gary Schocker:Flutist, w. Dennis Helmrich (hpd), Ted Hoyle (vc), Marco Granados (fl) Chesky ▲ CD 46 [DDD]

Schodl, Johann (trbn)—see ORCHESTRAS & ENSEMBLES Brassissimo Vienna

Schoeck, Othmar (pno)
Schoeck, O.:Das holde Bescheiden, w. Hilde Schoeck (sop)—Besuch in Urach [No. 36] *(rec live, Apr 1943)* Jecklin ▲ JD 692

Schoenberg, A. (pno)
Brahms, J.:Qt 1 Pno, w. S. Rattle (cnd), City of Birmingham SO EMI Classics 2-▲ CDCB 47300

Schoenfeld, Alice (vn)—see ORCHESTRAS & ENSEMBLES Dolmetsch-Schoenfeld Ensemble

Schoenfeld, Eleonore (vc)—see ORCHESTRAS & ENSEMBLES Dolmetsch-Schoenfeld Ensemble

Schoenfeld, S. (va)
Van Appledorn, M.J.:Duos Va, w. A. Follows (vc) Opus One ▲ 147

Schoenfield, Paul (pno)
Dvořák, A.:Romantic Pieces, Op. 75, w. S. Luca (vn) Elektra/Nonesuch ■ 71350-4
Janácek, L.:Son Vn, w. S. Luca (vn) Elektra/Nonesuch ■ 71350-4
Paulus, S.:All My Pretty Ones, w. R. Jacobson (sop) [E] Albany ▲ TROY 036-2 [DDD]
Schoenfield, P.:Achat Sha'alti, w. C. Wincenc (fl) New World ▲ 80403-2 [DDD]
Schoenfield, P.:Cafe Music, w. Y. N. Kim (vn), P. Howard (vc) Innova ▲ MN 108
Schoenfield, P.:Country Fiddle Pieces, w. R. Davidovici (vn) New World ▲ NW 334-2 [DDD]
Schoenfield, P.:Ufaratsta, w. C. Wincenc (fl) New World ▲ 80403-2 [DDD]
Smetana, B.:From the Homeland, w. S. Luca (vn) Elektra/Nonesuch ■ 71350-4

Schoenig, Terry (perc)
Matson, S.:Range, w. Catherine Robbin (mez), Susan Greenberg (fl), Joseph Stone (fl), Glen Garrett (cl), Suren Karapetyan (hn), Peter Kent (vn), Kazi Pitelka (va), Sebastian Toettcher (vc), Don Ferrone (db), Doug Livingston (gtr/mand), John Schneider (gtr), Amy Shulman (hp), S. Matson (cnd) *(rec Schnee Studio, Universal City, CA, Mar 12, 1995)* New Albion ▲ NA 091

Scholes, Kim (vc)
Blackwood, E.:Son Vc, w. E. Blackwood (pno) Cedille ▲ CDR 90000 008 [DDD]
Bridge, F.:Son Vc, w. E. Blackwood (pno) Cedille ▲ CDR 90000 008 [DDD]
Chopin, F.:Etudes (24), w. D. Breitman (pno)—No. 9 [trans. K. Scholes for cello & piano] *(rec June 1990)* Titanic ▲ TI 197 [DDD]
Chopin, F.:Intro & Polonaise, "Polonaise brilliante", w. D. Breitman (pno) *(rec June 1990)* Titanic ▲ TI 197 [DDD]
Chopin, F.:Son Vc, w. D. Breitman (pno) *(rec June 1990)* Titanic ▲ TI 197 [DDD]
Chopin, F.:Waltzes, w. D. Breitman (pno)—Op. 34/2 *(rec June 1990)* Titanic ▲ TI 197 [DDD]

Schöller, A. (vc)
Kirnberger, J.P.:Son Fl, w. C. Arimany (fl), M. Grüber (hpd) Motette ▲ MOT CD 30141 [DDD]
Müthel, J.G.:Son Fl, w. C. Arimany (fl), M. Grüber (hpd) Motette ▲ MOT CD 30141 [DDD]

Scholten, N. von (fl)—see ORCHESTRAS & ENSEMBLES Boreas Wind Quintet

Scholz, Karin (gtr)—see ORCHESTRAS & ENSEMBLES Duo Bergerac

Scholz, Kristine (pno)
Cage, J.:Winter Music, w. Mats Persson (pno), Steffen Schleiermacher (pno), Nils Vigeland (pno), Eberhard Blum (pic/fl/alt fl)—for 4 pianos; for 4 pianos with flute parts from Atlas Eclipticalis *(rec Sender Freies Berlin & Hessen Radio, Frankfurt, Feb. 10–11, 1992 & June 6)* Hat Hut ("NOW." series) ▲ hat ART CD 6141 [DDD]

Scholz, M. (bn)—see ORCHESTRAS & ENSEMBLES Freiburg Baroque Soloists

Scholz, S. (baroque vn)—see ORCHESTRAS & ENSEMBLES Il Parnaso Musicale

Scholze, Hansjürgen (org)
Mozart, W.A.:Org Music, w. R. Kuppelwieser (org)—Fant. in f, K.608; Son. in C, K.328 LaserLight ▲ 15 884 [DDD]
Silbermann's Organ at the Cathedral of Dresden *(rec May 11–14, 1992)* Motette ▲ MOT 11731 [DDD]

Schön, Miklos (pno)
10 Pièces pour violin et piano, w. Christopher Boulier (vn) REM ▲ 311256

Schön, S. (fl)—see ORCHESTRAS & ENSEMBLES Gothenburg Wind Quintet

Schonbach, Sanford (va)
Brahms, J.:Qt 3 Pno, w. J. Lateiner (pno), J. Heifetz (vn), G. Piatigorsky (vc) RCA Gold Seal ▲ 7873-2-RG [ADD] ■ 7873-4-RG

Schöneberger, Hans (cl)—see also ORCHESTRAS & ENSEMBLES Munich Residenz Quintet members
Schubert, Franz:Der Hirt auf dem Felsen, w. M. Price (sop), W. Sawallisch (pno) [G] Orfeo ▲ 001811 [DDD]
Spohr, L.:German Songs , Op. 103, w. J. Varady (sop), H. Höll (pno) [G] Orfeo ▲ 103841 [DDD] ■ M 103841A

Schönemann, R. (cl)—see also ORCHESTRAS & ENSEMBLES Berlin German Opera Orch Soloists
Martinů, B.:La Revue de Cuisine (sels), w. T. Tomaszewski (vn), G. Lösch (vc), V. Knappe (bn), A. Lange (tpt), S. Schubert-Weber (pno)—Suite for Violin, Cello, Clarinet, Bassoon, Trumpet & Piano FSM-Adagio ▲ FCD 97 219

Schonhage, Andreas (pno)
Albert, E. d':Waltzes, Op. 6, w. Tamara Korockin (pno) CPO ▲ CPO 999330
Strauss, R.:Sym in f, w. Tamara Korockin (pno) [arr for pno duet] CPO ▲ CPO 999330

Schönstedt, Arno (org)
Distler, H.:Org Music (complete)—30 Spielstücke; Wie schön leuchtet der Morgenstern (prelude & movt); Das alte Jahr vergangen ist (prelude & movt); Mit Freuden zart (prelude & movt); Son for Org; Christ, der du bist der helle Tag (partita); Ach wie flüchtig, ach wie nichtig (prelude & movt); Jesus Christus, unser Heiland (partita); Wachet auf, ruft uns die Stimme (partita); Christe, du Lamm Gottes (partita); Nun komm, der Heiden Heiland (partita) *(rec Christuskirche Recklinghausen, alt-reformierte Kirche in Campen & Münster zu Herford, May & July 1978)* Cantate 2-▲ 57613 [AAD]

Schoonbroodt, Hubert (hpd)
Tapray, J.F.:Sym Hpd, Op. 12, *(orch unknown)* Koch Schwann ▲ SCH 313422 [ADD]

Schoonbroodt, Hubert (org)
Chaumont, L.:Pièces d'Orgue sur les 8 tons *(rec 1970)* Koch Schwann 2-▲ 3-1278-2 [ADD]
Jongen, J.:Symphonie Concertante, w. R. Defossez (cnd), Liège SO Koch Schwann ▲ CD 315012 [DDD]

Schornsheim, Christine (hpd)
Bach, J.S.:Sons Fl, BWV 1030–35, w. E. Haupt (fl), S. Pank (vl)—BWV 1030–1035 & 1033 [reconstruction after Marshall] *(rec June 1989 & Jan 1990)* Berlin Classics 2-▲ BER 1007 [DDD]
Bach, J.S.:Trio Son Fl, Vn & Hpd, w. E. Haupt (fl), P. Mirring (vn) *(rec June 1989 & 1990)* Berlin Classics 2-▲ BER 1007 [DDD]
Fasch, J.F.:Trio Sons, w. B. Glaetzner (ob), I. Goritzki (ob), T. Reinhardt (bn), S. Pank (vl), A. Beyer (vle) Berlin Classics ▲ BER 1069 [DDD]
Jochen Kowalski:Aria from Berlin's Operatic History, w. Jochen Kowalski (ct), R. Alpermann (hpd), H. Friedrich (vc), Markus Stauch (db), Berlin CO [cnd:M. Pommer] Berlin Classics ▲ BER 1050 [DDD]

Schornsheim, Christine (pno)
Mozart, W.A.:Con 17 Pno, w. B. Glaetzner (cnd), New Bach Collegium Musicum LaserLight ▲ 15 872 [DDD]
Mozart, W.A.:Con 18 Pno, w. B. Glaetzner (cnd), New Bach Collegium Musicum LaserLight ▲ 15 872 [DDD]
Mozart, W.A.:Con 19 Pno, w. B. Glaetzner (cnd), New Bach Collegium Musicum Laserlight ▲ 15 872 [DDD]

Schott, Karin (vn)—see ORCHESTRAS & ENSEMBLES Acht Ensemble

Schotten, Yizhak (va)
Bloch, E.:Suite Va & Pno, w. K. Collier (pno) Crystal ▲ CD 637
Britten, H.:Lachrymae, w. R. Rosenberg (cnd), Great Lakes CO Crystal ▲ CD 635
Clarke, R.:Son Va, w. K. Collier (pno) Crystal ▲ CD 637
Hindemith, P.:Son Va & Pno, Op. 11/4, w. K. Collier (pno) Crystal ▲ CD 637
Marais, M.:Dances, w. E. Parmentier (hpd) Crystal ▲ CD 635
Schubert, Franz:Son Arpeggione, w. K. Collier (pno) Crystal ▲ CD 635
Shulman, A.:Theme & Vars, w. R. Rosenberg (cnd), Great Lakes CO Crystal ▲ CD 635

Schottstädt (bn)
Pleyel, I.:Sinf concertante 5, w. D. Becker (fl), P. Meyer (cl), Schneider (hn), J. Faerber (cnd), Württemberg CO MD + G ▲ L 3396 [DDD]

Schou, Jens (cl)—see also ORCHESTRAS & ENSEMBLES LINensemble, Danish Trio
Holten, B.:Con Cl, w. H. Graf (cnd), Danish National RSO Chandos ▲ CHAN 9272 [DDD]
Olsen, P.R.:Concertino Cl, w. Peder Elbaek (vn), Verner Skovlund (va), Svend Winsløv (vc), Rosalind Bevan (pno) *(rec PAULA's Recording Hall, 1984)* Paula ▲ PACD 36 [AAD]

Schpiller, Taisiya (pno)
Brahms, J.:Hungarian Dances Pno 4-Hands, w. Marina Yashvili (vn)—Nos. 1, 7, 16 & 17 [arr J. Joachim for vn & pno] *(rec 1975)* Russian Compact Disc ("Talents of Russia" series) ▲ RCD 16252 [ADD]
Brahms, J.:Songs, w. Marina Yashvili (vn)—Contemplation in D♭ [arr J. Heifitz for vn & pno] *(rec 1991)* Russian Compact Disc ("Talents of Russia" series) ▲ RCD 16252 [ADD]

Schrade, Rorianne (pno)
Balakirev, M.:Berceuse *(rec Worthington, MA, July 27 & 28, 1994)* Centaur ▲ CRC 2236 [DDD]
Balakirev, M.:Islamey *(rec Worthington, MA, July 27 & 28, 1994)* Centaur ▲ CRC 2236 [DDD]
Balakirev, M.:Pno Music—Fant. on Themes from Glinka's *A Life for the Tsar*, Nocturne No. 3 in d; Romance *(rec Worthington, MA, July 27 & 28, 1994)* Centaur ▲ CRC 2236 [DDD]
Balakirev, M.:Son Pno *(rec Worthington, MA, July 27 & 28, 1994)* Centaur ▲ CRC 2236 [DDD]

Schrader, David (hpd)
Bach, J.S.:Chromatic Fant & Fugue Cedille ▲ CDR 90000 020
Bach, J.S.:English Suites—No. 1 Cedille ▲ CDR 90000 020
Bach, J.S.:Italian Con Cedille ▲ CDR 90000 020
Bach, J.S.:Ov Hpd, BWV 820 Cedille ▲ CDR 90000 020
Soler, P.A.:Fandango Cedille ▲ CDR 90000 004 [DDD]

Schrader, David (hpd) (cont.)
Soler, P.A.:Qnt 1 Hpd, w. C. Verrette (vn), M. Shelton (vn), P. Slowik (va), J. M. Rozendaal (vc) *(rec Oct. & Dec. 1992)* Cedille ▲ CDR 90000 013 [DDD]
Soler, P.A.:Qnt 2 Hpd, w. C. Verrette (vn), M. Shelton (vn), P. Slowik (va), J. M. Rozendaal (vc) *(rec Oct. & Dec. 1992)* Cedille ▲ CDR 90000 013 [DDD]
Soler, P.A.:Qnt 3 Hpd, w. C. Verrette (vn), M. Shelton (vn), P. Slowik (va), J. M. Rozendaal (vc) *(rec Oct. & Dec. 1992)* Cedille ▲ CDR 90000 013 [DDD]
Soler, P.A.:Sons Hpd—Nos. 4, 9, 16, 24, 25, 60, 63 Cedille ▲ CDR 90000 004 [DDD]
Soler, P.A.:Sons Hpd—Nos. 1, 2, 3, 8, 10, 62, 70, 74, 81 Cedille ▲ CDR 90000 009 [DDD]

Schrader, David (org)
Bach, J.S.:Org Music (misc)—Toccatas & Fugues in d, BWV 538; in F, BWV 540; in d, BWV 565; in E, BWV 566; Toccata, Adagio & Fugue in C, BWV 564; Prelude & Fugue in e, BWV 548 Cedille ▲ CDR 90000 006 [DDD]
Bach, J.S.:Org Music (misc)—Fantasies in c, BWV 562, in b, BWV 563, in C, BWV 570; Fantasies & Fugues in c, BWV 537, in g, BWV 542; Fugues in c, BWV 564, in c, BWV 575, in G, BWV 577, "Gigue", in g, BWV 578, in b, BWV 579; Pièce d'orgue Fantasy in G, BWV 572; Pastorale in F, BWV 590 Cedille ▲ CDR 90000 012 [DDD]
Dupré, M.:Vars sur un vieux Noël [the Jaeckel Organ at the Pilgrim Congregational Church, Duluth, MN] *(rec Mar. 10 & 11, 1993)* Cedille ▲ CDR 90000 015 [DDD]
Franck, C.:Cantabile [Jaeckel Organ at the Pilgrim Congregational Church, Duluth, MN] *(rec Mar. 10 & 11, 1993)* Cedille ▲ CDR 90000 015 [DDD]
Franck, C.:Fant Org [Jaeckel Organ at the Pilgrim Congregational Church, Duluth, MN] *(rec Mar. 10 & 11, 1993)* Cedille ▲ CDR 90000 015 [DDD]
Franck, C.:Final [Jaeckel Organ at the Pilgrim Congregational Church, Duluth, MN] *(rec Mar. 10 & 11, 1993)* Cedille ▲ CDR 90000 015 [DDD]
Franck, C.:Pastorale [Jaeckel Organ at the Pilgrim Congregational Church, Duluth, MN] *(rec Mar. 10 & 11, 1993)* Cedille ▲ CDR 90000 015 [DDD]
Franck, C.:Pièce héroïque [Jaeckel Organ at the Pilgrim Congregational Church, Duluth, MN] *(rec Mar. 10 & 11, 1993)* Cedille ▲ CDR 90000 015 [DDD]
Franck, C.:Prélude, fugue et var [organ at the Pilgrim Congregational Church, Duluth, MN] *(rec Mar. 10 & 11, 1993)* Cedille ▲ CDR 90000 015 [DDD]

Schrader, David (pno)
Bloch, E.:Con grosso 1, w. A. Heatherington (cnd), Chicago String Ensemble *(rec June 2 & 3, 1992)* Centaur ▲ CRC 2140 [DDD]
Bloch, E.:From Jewish Life, w. J. Zumsteg (vc)—Prayer *(rec June 2 & 3, 1992)* Centaur ▲ CRC 2140 [DDD]
Bloch, E.:Suite modale, w. L. Leifer (fl) *(rec June 2 & 3, 1992)* Centaur ▲ CRC 2140 [DDD]

Schrama, Godelieve (hp)
Britten, H.:Suite Hp Canal Grande ▲ CCS 9530
Caplet, A.:Divertissements (2) Hp Canal Grande ▲ CCS 9530
Fauré, G.:Impromptu Hp Canal Grande ▲ CCS 9530
Hindemith, P.:Son Hp Canal Grande ▲ CCS 9530
Tailleferre, G.:Son Hp Canal Grande ▲ CCS 9530

Schranz, Károly (vn)—see ORCHESTRAS & ENSEMBLES Takács String Quartet

Schrecker, Bruno (vc)—see also ORCHESTRAS & ENSEMBLES Allegri String Quartet
Schubert, Franz:Qnt Strs, D.956, w. Aeolian String Quartet Saga Classics ▲ 3368 [ADD]

Schreiner, Alexander (org)
The Great Thanksgiving:Hymns & Songs of Thanks & Brotherhood, w. Mormon Tabernacle Choir, Frank Asper (org) *(rec Salt Lake City, Utah)* Sony Classical ▲ SMK 61983 ■ SMT 61983

Schröder, Jaap (vn)—see also ORCHESTRAS & ENSEMBLES Smithsonian Chamber Players, Helicon, Amsterdam Quartet
Bach, J.S.:Cons Vn (comp), w. C. Hogwood (cnd), Academy of Ancient Music L'Oiseau-Lyre ▲ 400080-2 [DDD]
Bach, J.S.:Cons Vn (comp), w. S. Ritchie, N. TeBrake, R. Brown, J. Griffin, M. Lutszke, M. Willems, A. Fuller *(rec June 6–8, 1986)* Reference ▲ RR 23 CD [DDD]
Bach, J.S.:Con 1 Vn, w. C. Hogwood (cnd), Academy of Ancient Music *(rec Kingsway Hall, London, Sept 14, 1981)* L'Oiseau-Lyre ▲ 443326-2 [DDD]
Bach, J.S.:Con for 2 Vns, w. C. Hirons (vn), C. Hogwood (cnd), Academy of Ancient Music L'Oiseau-Lyre ▲ 400080-2 [DDD]
Bach, J.S.:Sons & Partitas Vn, BWV 1001–1006 Smithsonian Collection 5-▲ ND 0380 [DDD]
Bach, J.S.:Sons & Partitas Vn, BWV 1001–1006 Smithsonian Collection 2-▲ ND 0382 [DDD]
Bach, J.S.:Trio Son for 2 Vns, w. S. Ritchie (vn), A. Fuller (hpd) *(rec June 6–8, 1986)* Reference ▲ RR 23 CD [DDD]
Handel, G.F.:German Arias, H.202-210, w. Elisabeth Speiser (sop), Kathy Gohl (vn), Johann Sonnleitner (hpd) [G] *(rec 1984)* Jecklin-Disco ▲ JD 589-2 [ADD]
Leclair, J.-M.:Cons Vn, Opp. 7 & 10, w. N. Harnoncourt (cnd), Vienna Concentus Musicus—Op. 7/3 & 5; Op. 10/6 Teldec ▲ 92180
Mozart, W.A.:Qt Fl, K.285, w. Cristopher Krueger (fl), J. Griffin (va), K. Slowik (vc) [period instrs] Smithsonian Collection 5-▲ ND 031
Mozart, W.A.:Qts Pno, w. J. Weaver (pno), J. Griffin (va), K. Slowik (vc0 [period instrs] Smithsonian Collection 5-▲ ND 031
Mozart, W.A.:Qnt Hn, K.407, w. L. Greer (hn), J. Griffin (vn), M. Graybeal (va), K. Slowik (vc) [period instrs] Smithsonian Collection 5-▲ ND 031
Mozart, W.A.:Qnt Hn, K.407, w. L. Greer (hn), J. Griffin (vn), M. Graybeal (va), K. Slowik (vc) [period instrs] Smithsonian Collection ▲ ND 039
Mozart, W.A.:Serenade Vn, K.204, Smithsonian CO [period instrs] Smithsonian Collection 5-▲ ND 031
Mozart, W.A.:Sinf concertante Vn, K.364, w. M. McDonald (va), J. Schröder (cnd), Smithsonian CO [period instrs] Smithsonian Collection 5-▲ ND 031
Mozart, W.A.:Sons Vn Pno (misc), w. J. Van Immerseel (pno)—K.378, 379 & 380 RCA Victrola ▲ 77556-2 [ADD]
Naudot, J.-C.:Con Rcr, w. F. Brüggen (rcr), N. Harnoncourt (cnd), Concentus Musicus Soloists—No. 5 in G Teldec ▲ 92180
Roman, J.H.:Assaggi—in g; in c; in A *(rec Studio 2, Radiohuset, Stockholm, May 7 & 8, 1986)* Musica Sveciae ▲ MS 406 [DDD]
Roman, J.H.:Sinfs, w. J. Schröder (cnd), Drottningholm Baroque Ensemble—Nos. 3 in E, 9 in G, 10 in F, 11 in B♭, 15 in G, 22 in e, 24 in D & 30 in g Musica Sveciae ▲ MSCD 418 [DDD]
Roman, J.H.:Sons Fl, w. Johann Sonnleitner (hpd)—No. 12 in D *(rec Studio 2, Radiohuset, Stockholm, May 7 & 8, 1986)* Musica Sveciae ▲ MS 406 [DDD]
Vivaldi, A.:Cons for 2 Vns, w. S. Ritchie (vn), N. TeBrake (vn), R. Brown (vn), J. Griffin (va), M. Lutszke (vc), M. Willems (db), A. Fuller (hpd) *(rec June 6–8, 1986)* Reference ▲ RR 23 CD [DDD]
Vivaldi, A.:Sinf, RV.116, w. S. Ritchie (vn), J. Griffin (va), M. Lutszke (vc), M. Willems (db), A. Fuller (hpd) *(rec June 6–8, 1986)* Reference ▲ RR 23 CD [DDD]
Vivaldi, A.:Trio Sons 2 Vns & Bc, w. S. Ritchie (vn), M. Lutszke (vc), A. Fuller (hpd)—RV.73 *(rec June 6–8, 1986)* Reference ▲ RR 23 CD [DDD]

Schröder, Karl Ernst (lt)
Daser, L.:Sacred Music, w. Martin Zöbeley (cnd), Munich Group for Early Music—Et verbum caro factum est; Hodie Deus homo factus *(rec Church in Attel, May 27–31, 1995)* ARS Musici ▲ AM 1175-2 [DDD]
Deutsche Barocklieder, w. Andreas Scholl (ct), Alix Verzier (vc), Markus Markl (hpd), Friederike Heumann (va), Juan Manuel Quintana (va), Stephanie Pfister (vn), Pablo Valetti (vn) Harmonia Mundi France ▲ HMC 901505
Isaac, H.:Sacred Music, w. Martin Zöbeley (cnd), Munich Group for Early Music—Puer natus *(rec Church in Attel, May 27–31, 1995)* ARS Musici ▲ AM 1175-2 [DDD]
Lassus, O. de:Motets, w. Martin Zöbeley (cnd), Munich Group for Early Music—Resonet in laudibus; Jubilemus singuli; Verbum caro factum est *(rec Church in Attel, May 27–31, 1995)* ARS Musici ▲ AM 1175-2 [DDD]
Lassus, O. de:Songs, w. Martin Zöbeley (cnd), Munich Group for Early Music—Der Tag, der ist so frewdenreich; Maria voll Genad *(rec Church in Attel, May 27–31, 1995)* ARS Musici ▲ AM 1175-2 [DDD]

Schröder, Karl Ernst (lt) (cont.)
Rore, C. de:Sacred Music, w. Martin Zöbeley (cnd), Munich Group for Early Music—Illuxit nunc sacra dies; Hodie Christus natus est *(rec Church in Attel, May 27-31, 1995)* ARS Musici ▲ AM 1175-2 [DDD]
Senfl, L.:Sacred Music, w. Martin Zöbeley (cnd), Munich Group for Early Music—Verbum caro factum est; Puer natus est nobis *(rec Church in Attel, May 27-31, 1995)* ARS Musici ▲ AM 1175-2 [DDD]
Schrodl, U. (trbn)—see ORCHESTRAS & ENSEMBLES Datura Trombone Quartet
Schroeder, Marianne (pno)
Feldman, Morton:For John Cage, w. P. Zukofsky (vn) CP2 Recordings ▲ 101 [DDD]
Feldman, Morton:Intermission 5 *(rec Studio Stolberger Strasse, Cologne, Aug. 1-4, 1989)* Hat Hut ("NOW." series) ▲ hat ART CD 6035 [DDD]
Feldman, Morton:Palais de Mari *(rec Studio Stolberger Strasse, Cologne, Aug. 1-4, 1989)* Hat Hut ("NOW." series) ▲ hat ART CD 6035 [DDD]
Feldman, Morton:Patterns in a Chromatic Field, w. Rohan de Saram (vc) *(rec West German Radio, Cologne, Sept. 29-Oct. 1, 1993)* Hat Art ("Now" series) 2-▲ 2-6145 [DDD]
Feldman, Morton:Patterns in a Chromatic Field, w. Rohan de Saram (vc) *(rec West German Radio, Cologne, Sept. 29-Oct. 1, 1993)* Hat Hut ("Now." series) 2-▲ ART CD 2-6145 [DDD]
Feldman, Morton:Piece to Philip Guston *(rec Studio Stolberger Strasse, Cologne, Aug. 1-4, 1989)* Hat Hut ("NOW." series) ▲ hat ART CD 6035 [DDD]
Feldman, Morton:Vertical Thoughts IV *(rec Studio Stolberger Strasse, Cologne, Aug. 1-4, 1989)* Hat Hut ("NOW." series) ▲ hat ART CD 6035 [DDD]
Scelsi, G.:Un Adieu *(rec Sendesaal Radio Bremen, May 13-17, 1991)* Hat Hut ("NOW." series) ▲ hat ART CD 6092 [DDD]
Scelsi, G.:Son 2 Pno *(rec Sendesaal Radio Bremen, May 13-17, 1991)* Hat Hut ("NOW." series) ▲ hat ART CD 6092 [DDD]
Scelsi, G.:Son 3 Pno *(rec Sendesaal Radio Bremen, May 13-17, 1991)* Hat Hut ("NOW." series) ▲ hat ART CD 6092 [DDD]
Scelsi, G.:Suite 8 Pno *(rec Sendesaal Radio Bremen, May 13-17, 1991)* Hat Hut ("NOW." series) ▲ hat ART CD 6092 [DDD]
Scelsi, G.:Suite 9 Pno *(rec Studio DRS, Zrich, Switzerland, Sept. 15 & 16, 1987)* Hat Hut ("NOW." series) ▲ hat ART CD 6006 [DDD]
Scelsi, G.:Suite 10 Pno *(rec Studio DRS, Zrich, Switzerland, Sept. 15 & 16, 1987)* Hat Hut ("NOW." series) ▲ hat ART CD 6006 [DDD]
Schroeder, M.:Lasciando *(rec July 1991)* Jecklin-Disco ▲ JD 667-2 [ADD]
Stiebler, E.:Trio '89, w. Frances-Marie Uitti (vc), Robyn Schulkowsky (perc) *(rec Sender Freies Berlin, Feb 13, 1994)* Hat Hut ("Now" series) ▲ CD 6169 [DDD]
Ustvolskaya, G.:Sons Pno *(rec Blumenstein Church, Thun, Switzerland, Feb 28-Mar 3, 1994)* Hat Hut ("Now" series) ▲ CD 6170 [DDD]
Schub, André-Michel (pno)
Baker, D.:Blues Vn, w. Anne Akiko Meyers (vn) [adaptation from Deliver My Soul of Psalm 22] *(rec Am. Acad. of Arts & Letters, NYC, Aug 30-31 & Sept 1-2, 199)* RCA Red Seal ▲ 09026-68114-2 [DDD]
Copland, A.:Nocturne, w. Anne Akiko Meyers (vn) *(rec Am. Acad. of Arts & Letters, NYC, Aug 30-31 & Sept 1-2, 199)* RCA Red Seal ▲ 09026-68114-2 [DDD]
Copland, A.:Son Vn & Pno, w. Anne Akiko Meyers (vn) *(rec Am. Acad. of Arts & Letters, NYC, Aug 30-31 & Sept 1-2, 199)* RCA Red Seal ▲ 09026-68114-2 [DDD]
Ives, C.:Son 4 Vn, w. Anne Akiko Meyers (vn) [arr for vn & pno] *(rec Am. Acad. of Arts & Letters, NYC, Aug 30-31 & Sept 1-2, 199)* RCA Red Seal ▲ 09026-68114-2 [DDD]
Piston, W.:Sonatina Vn, w. Anne Akiko Meyers (vn) *(rec Am. Acad. of Arts & Letters, NYC, Aug 30-31 & Sept 1-2, 199)* RCA Red Seal ▲ 09026-68114-2 [DDD]
Rorem, N.:Bright Music, w. M. Martin (fl), A. Kavafian (vn), I. Kavafian (vn), F. Sherry (vc) New World ▲ 80416-2 [DDD]
Stravinsky, I.:Divert Vn, w. C.-L. Lin (vn) CBS ▲ MK 42101 [DDD]
Stravinsky, I.:Duo Concertant, w. C.-L. Lin (vn) CBS ▲ MK 42101 [DDD]
Stravinsky, I.:Suite italienne Vc, w. C.-L. Lin (vn) [vn-pno arr. Dushkin] CBS ▲ MK 42101 [DDD]
Schubeck, Thomas (hpd)
Handel, G.F.:Sons Rcr, w. Class Pehrsson (rcr), Bengt Ericson (vc) BIS ▲ CD 208
Schuback, Thomas (pno)
Geijer, E.G.:Songs, w. Catharina Olsson (mez), Per-Arne Walhgren (bar) Musica Sveciae ▲ MSV 519 [ADD]
Hovland, E.:Cantus II, w. Clas Pehrsson (rcr) *(rec Studio BIS, Djursholm, Sweden, May 11-13, 1981)* BIS ▲ CD 202 [AAD]
Lindblad, A.F.:Songs, w. MariAnne Häggander (sop), Mikael Samuelson (bar), sels. unknown Caprice ▲ CAP 21425 [DDD]
Rangström, T.:Songs, w. B. Svendén (sop), H. Hagegård (bar) Musica Sveciae ▲ MSV 629 [DDD]
Staeps, H.U.:Son Trb Rcr, w. Clas Pehrsson (rcr) *(rec Studio BIS, Djursholm, Sweden, May 11-13, 1981)* BIS ▲ CD 202 [AAD]
Stenhammar, W.:Songs, w. A. S. von Otter (mez), H. Hagegard (bar), B. Forsberg (pno) Musica Sveciae ▲ MSCD 623
Zueignung [Dedication], w. Hagegård, Håkan (bar) BIS ▲ CD 54 [AAD]
Schubert (gtr)
Dreyfus, G.:Old Melbourne, w. G. Dreyfus (bn) Move ▲ MD 3071
Dreyfus, G.:Rush, w. G. Dreyfus (bn) Move ▲ MD 3071
Schubert, Gert Rainer (vn)
Hindemith, P.:Son Vn, Op. 31/2 Vienna Modern Masters ▲ VMM 2013 [DDD]
Schubert, Jochen (pno)
Merlyn Quaife, w. Merlyn Quaife (sop) Move ▲ MD 3115
Schubert-Weber, Siegfried (pno)
Martinů, B.:La Revue de Cuisine (sels), w. T. Tomaszewski (vn), G. Lösch (vc), R. Schönemann (cl), V. Knappe (bn), A. Lange (tpt)—Suite for Violin, Cello, Clarinet, Bassoon, Trumpet & Piano FSM-Adagio ▲ FCD 97 219
Romantic Russian Music for Paino Duo, w. Gerhard Meyer (pno) FSM ▲ 91007 [ADD]
Schubilske, Catherine (vn)
Sierra, R.:Piezas Caracteristicas, w. William Helmers (b cl), Scott Tisdel (vc), Dennis Najoom (tpt), Stefanie Jacob (pno), Thomas Wetzel (perc), N. Gittleman (cnd) CRI ▲ CD 724 [DDD]
Schuchro, Josef (vc)
Dvořák, A.:Sextet, w. J. Suk (va), Smetana String Quartet Supraphon ▲ SUP 111469 [DDD]
Schuchter, Gilbert (pno)
Mozart, W.A.:Pno Music (comp)—Son No. 1, K.279; Son No. 4, K.282; Theme in E♭, K.236; Fant & Fugue, K.394 Tudor ▲ TUD 7011 [ADD]
Mozart, W.A.:Pno Music (comp)—Sons Nos. 2, 5 & 6; Theme in F w. 5 Vars; 6 Vars in G [on Mio caro adone] Tudor ▲ TUD 7012 [ADD]
Pfitzner, H.:Pno Music (comp)—Aus dem Notenbuch des Elfjährigen; Liebesmelodie, "Das Herz"; 5 Klavierstücke, Op. 47; Six Studies, Op. 51 *(rec 1971)* Tudor ▲ 705 [ADD]
Schubert, Franz:Pno Music (comp)—5 Sonatas, D.557, 566, 850, 894 & 960; Erste Walzer, D.365, Nos. 1 & 2; Galopp & 8 Ecossaisen, D.735; 12 Deutsche Tänze ("Ländler"), D.790; Cotillon, D.976; Scherzo in B♭, D.593, No. 1; Menuett in E♯ (from D.568); Allegretto in c, D.900; Rondo in E, D.506 Tudor 3-▲ 750/52 [ADD]
Schubert, Franz:Pno Music (comp)—5 Sonatas, D.279, 537, 567, 575 & 664; Impromptus, D.899 & 935; Diabelli Variations, D.718; 6 Valses sentimentales (from D.779); 11 Ecossaisen (from D.781); 2 Deutsche Tänze, D.974; Deutscher Tanz für Hüttenbrenner (from D.643); Allegretto in c, D.915; Fantasia in c, D.993; Klavierstück in A, D.604; March in E, D.606; Scherzo in D♭, D.593, No. 2 Tudor 3-▲ 744/46 [ADD]
Schubert, Franz:Pno Music (comp)—4 Sonatas, D.157, 784, 958 & 959; Wanderer Fantasie, D.760; Variations (10) in F, D.156; Piano Pieces (3), D.946; 2 Ecossaisen (from D.783) & Deutscher Tanz, D.722; Fantasie in C (fragment), D.605 & Andante in C, D.29; Adagio in E, D.612 Tudor 3-▲ 747/49 [ADD]

Schuchter, Gilbert (pno) (cont.)
Schubert, Franz:Pno Music (comp)—4 Sonatas, D.459, 625, 840 & 845; Sonata fragment & Scherzo, D.570/571; Moments Musicaux, D.780; 16 Deutsche Tänze (from D.783); 9 Ecossaisen & 10 Ländler (from D.145); Adagio in G, D.178; Menuett in c♯, D.600; Waltz in G, "Albumblatt," D.844; 12 Valses nobles, D.969; Hüttenbrenner Variations in a, D.576; Fantasie in C, "Grazer Fantasie," D.605a; Ungarische Melodie, D.817 Tudor 3-▲ 741/43 [ADD]
Schuhmayer, Peter (vn)—see also ORCHESTRAS & ENSEMBLES Artis String Quartet
Magnard, A.:Qt Strs, Op. 16, w. Johannes Meissl (vn), Herbert Kefer (va), Othmar Müller (vc) Accord ▲ ACD 201982 [DDD]
Schul, Kees (pno)
Brahms, J.:Vocal Qts, w. Maurice Broussard (cnd), Ottovoci Ensemble—Opp. 31, 64, 92, 112 [G] Partridge ▲ 1133-2 [DDD]
Brahms, J.:Zigeunerlieder, w. M. Broussard (cnd), Ottovoci Ensemble [G] Partridge ▲ 1133-2 [DDD]
Schuldmann, Sanda (pno)—see also ORCHESTRAS & ENSEMBLES Fidelio
Starer, R.:Episodes Va, w. Lois Martin (va), Harry Clark (vc) Albany ▲ TROY 152 [DDD]
Starer, R.:Remembering Felix, w. Robert J. Lurtsema (nar), Harry Clark (vc) Albany ▲ TROY 151 [DDD]
Schuler, David (org)
Retzel, F.:Horae Opus One ▲ 155 CD
Schulhof, Otto (pno)
Beethoven, L. van:Minuets Orch, WoO 7, w. P. Casals (vc)—No. 2 in D [cello-piano arr.] *(rec 1930 for HMV)* Pearl 2-▲ PEAS 9461 (m) [AAD]
Bow & Baton:Complete 1929-30 HMV Singles & 1928 London Symphony Recordings, w. Pablo Casals (vc), Blas-Net (pno) Pearl ▲ PEA 9128 [ADD]
Schulhoff, Erwin (pno)
Schulhoff, E.:Esquisses de Jazz—Nos. 4 & 5 *(rec Berlin, 1928)* London ▲ 444819-2 (m)
Schulhoff, E.:Jazz Etudes Pno—Nos. 2-4 *(rec Berlin, 1928)* London ▲ 444819-2 (m) [DDD]
Schulhoff, E.:Rag Music—Nos. 3, 4, 7 & 8 *(rec Berlin, 1928)* London ▲ 444819-2 (m)
Schulkowsky, Robyn (perc)
Bouchard, L.:Pourtinade, w. K. Kashkashian (va) ECM New Series ▲ 78118-21425-2 [DDD]
Chihara, P.:Redwood, w. K. Kashkashian (va) ECM New Series ▲ 78118-21425-2 [DDD]
Scelsi, G.:Music of, w. Joëlle Léandre (sgr/db), Nicolas Isherwood (bass), Giancarlo Schiaffini (trbn/tuba), Fances-Marie Uitti (vc), Karin Schmeer (hp)—Maknongan for Low-Registered Instrument (1976) [3 versions:bass, double bass, tuba]; Tre pezzi for Trombone (1956); Wo Ma for Bass (1960); C'est bien la nuit for Double Bass (1972); Le réveil profond for Double Bass (1977); Et Maintenant, c'est a vous a jouer for Cello & Double Bass (1974); Okanagon for Harp, Double Bass & Tamtam (1968); Mantram for Double Bass (1987) *(rec Sendesaal, Hessen Radio, Frankfurt, Feb. 8-9, May 18-21 & Aug)* Hat Hut ("NOW." series) ▲ hat ART CD 6124 [DDD]
Schulkowsky, R.:Hastening Westward at Sundown to Obtain a Better View, w. Nils Petter Molvaer (tpt) [rev for tpt & perc] *(rec Rainbow Studio, Oslo, Jan 1995)* ECM New Series ▲ ECM 1564 [DDD]
Schulkowsky, R.:Pier & Ocean, w. Nils Petter Molvaer (tpt) *(rec Rainbow Studio, Oslo, Jan 1995)* ECM New Series ▲ ECM 1564 [DDD]
Stiebler, E.:Trio '89, w. Frances-Marie Uitti (vc), Marianne Schroeder (pno) *(rec Sender Freies Berlin, Feb 13, 1994)* Hat Hut ("Now" series) ▲ CD 6169 [DDD]
Volans, K.:Mbira, w. Deborah James (hpd), Kevin Volans (hpd) *(rec West German Radio, Cologne, Apr 20, 1984)* United ▲ CAL 88034 [ADD]
Volans, K.:She Who Sleeps with a Small Blanket *(rec West German Radio, Cologne, Apr 20, 1984)* United ▲ CAL 88034 [ADD]
Volans, K.:White Man Sleeps Hpds, w. Robert Hill (hpd), Kevin Volans (hpd), Margriet Tindemans (vl) *(rec West German Radio, Cologne & Watershed Recording Studio, London, Apr 20, 1984 & July 27, 1)* United ▲ CAL 88034 [ADD]
Schulman, Andrew (gtr)
Lullabies, Reveilles (& Siesta!):"Lullabies" Centaur ▲ CRC 2049 [DDD]
Schulman, Basinia (pno)
Mozart, W.A.:Con 18 Pno, w. R. Freisitzer (cnd), Moscow Orch Russian Compact Disc ▲ RCD 30006
Mozart, W.A.:Fant Pno, K.396 Russian Compact Disc ▲ RCD 30006
Mozart, W.A.:Vars Pno, K.398 Russian Compact Disc ▲ RCD 30006
Ravel, M.:Con Pno in G, w. R. Freisitzer (cnd), Moscow Orch Russian Compact Disc ▲ RCD 30006
Schulman, Louise (va)—see also ORCHESTRAS & ENSEMBLES St. Luke's Chamber Ensemble
Diamond, D.:Qnt Cl, w. Lawrence Sobol (cl), Linda Moss (va), Timothy Eddy (vc), Fred Sherry (vc) *(rec RCA Studio A, New York City)* New World ▲ 80508-2
Diamond, D.:Vocalises, w. Lucy Shelton (sop) *(rec RCA Studio A, New York City)* New World ▲ 80508-2
Husa, K.:Evocations of Slovakia, w. L. Sobol (cl), T. Eddy (vc) Grenadilla ■ GSC 1008
Vivaldi, A.:Con Va d'amore Lt, w. P. Press (gtr), R. Kapp (cnd), Philharmonia Virtuosi ESS.A.Y ▲ CD 1004 [DDD] ■ C 1004 (D)
Wuorinen, C.:Archangel, w. D. Taylor (trbn), B. Hudson (vn), C. Zeavin (vn), F. Sherry (vc) *(rec March 31, 1981)* Koch International Classics ▲ KIC 7110-2 [DDD]
Schulman, Louise (vl)
Vivaldi, A.:Con Gtr Vl, w. Peter Press (gtr), R. Kapp (cnd), Philharmonia Virtuosi ESS.A.Y ▲ ESS 1004 [DDD]
Schulman, Louise (vn)
Christmas in the New World, w. Western Wind, Albert de Ruiter (bass), Wendy Gillespie (vl), Joseph Karpienia (gtr), Elaine Comparone (hpd) MusicMasters ▲ 01612-67176-2
Rzewski, F.:Moonrise with Memories, w. David Taylor (b trbn), David Carp (kazoo), Bill Blount (cl), Allan Dean (tpt), Robert Wolinsky (gtr), Bill Moersch (mar/dlc) *(rec RCA Studios, NYC, June 4, 1981)* New World ▲ 80494-2
Vivaldi, A.:Con Va d'amore Lt, w. E. Fisk (gtr), Orch of St. Luke *(rec July 27 & Aug. 4, 1992)* MusicMasters ▲ 01612-67097-2 [DDD]
Schulmeister, Jan (vn)—see ORCHESTRAS & ENSEMBLES Wilhan String Quartet
Schulrufer, Alexander (vn)
Bach, J.S.:Con 1 Vn, w. A. Steinlucht (cnd), Mozarteum Orch Infinity Digital ▲ QK 57217 [DDD]
Bach, J.S.:Con 2 Vn, w. A. Steinlucht (cnd), Mozarteum Orch Infinity Digital ▲ QK 57217 [DDD]
Bach, J.S.:Con for 2 Vns, w. V. Siorenko (vn), A. Steinlucht (cnd), Mozarteum Orch Infinity Digital ▲ QK 57217 [DDD]
Schulte, Rolf (vn)
Babbitt, M.:The Joy of More Sextets, w. A. Feinberg (pno) New World ▲ 80364-2 [DDD]
Babbitt, M.:Sxts Vn, w. A. Feinberg (pno) New World ▲ 80364-2 [DDD]
Barker, T.E.:Trikhýlo, w. F. Sherry (vc), M. Amory (va) *(rec Nov. 1992)* CRI ▲ CD 661 [DDD]
Dembski, S.:Trio, w. F. Sherry (vc), A. Feinberg (pno) CRI ▲ CD 570 [DDD]
Hudson, J.:Sonare, w. Paul Dunkel (fl), Laura Flax (cl), Ursula Oppens (pno), Joseph Passaro (perc) CRI ■ C 382
Lang, D.:Music of, w. J. Rozen (elec tuba), D. Lang (nar), E. Niemann (pno), N. Tilles (pno), U. Oppens (pno), L. Vaillancourt (cnd), Le Nouvel Ensemble Moderne—Are You Experienced?; Orpheus Over & Under; Spud; Illumination Rounds CRI ▲ CD 625 [DDD]
Lerdahl, F.:Waltzes, w. S. Nickrenz (va), F. Sherry (vc), D. Palme (db) CRI ▲ CD 580 [ADD/DDD]
Ligeti, G.:Trio Hn, Vn & Pno, w. W. Purvis (hn), A. Feinberg (pno) Bridge ▲ BCD 9012 [DDD]
Moravec, P.:Open Secret, w. E. Bartlett (vc), E. Garth (pno) CRI ▲ CD 641 [DDD]
Picker, T.:Con Vn, w. P. Dunkel (cnd), American Composers Orch *(rec 1982)* CRI ▲ CD 589 [ADD]
Ruders, P.:Con 1 Vn, w. G. Rothman (cnd), Riverside SO *(rec SUNY, Purchase, Theater C, Nov 9, 1994)* Bridge ▲ BCD 9057 [DDD]
Schumann, R.:Adagio & Allegro Hn, w. C. O'Riley (pno) Centaur ▲ CRC 2097 [DAD]
Schumann, R.:Fantasiestücke Cl, w. C. O'Riley (pno) [violin & piano arrs.] Centaur ▲ CRC 2097 [DAD]
Schumann, R.:Märchenbilder, w. C. O'Riley (pno) Centaur ▲ CRC 2097 [DAD]
Schumann, R.:Romances Ob, w. C. O'Riley (pno) [violin & piano arrs.] Centaur ▲ CRC 2097 [DAD]
Wilson, R.:Concert Piece, w. U. Oppens (pno) CRI ▲ CD 602 [ADD]
Wuorinen, C.:Trio Vn, w. F. Sherry (vc), J. Winn (pno) *(rec Sept. 11-13, 1991)* Koch International Classics ▲ KIC 7123-2 [DDD]

834 ▲ = CD ♦ = Enhanced CD Δ = MD ■ = Cassette Tape □ = DCC

Schultz, B. (org)
Poulenc, F.:Con Org, w. J. Primavera (cnd), Philadelphia Youth Orch
Direct-to-Tape Recording ▲ DTR 8804CD ■ DTR 8804
Schultz, Carmen (baroque mand)—see ORCHESTRAS & ENSEMBLES Gervasio Duo
Schultz, Edward A. (fl)
Persichetti, V.:Cant 2 Fl, w. J. E. Barnes (perc), T. Brooks (cnd), Mendelssohn Club Chorus Philadelphia
New World ▲ 80316-2
Schultz, Erik (tpt)
Bach, J.S.:Suite 3 Orch, w. J. Overduin (org) ebs ▲ ebs 6041 [DDD]
Baldassare, P.:Son 1 Tpt, w. V. Czarnecki (cnd), Southwest German CO Pforzheim
ebs ▲ ebs 6053 [DDD]
Bellini, V.:Con Tpt & Org, w. J. Overduin (org) ebs ▲ ebs 6041 [DDD]
Biscogli, F.:Con in D, w. I. Franklin (ob), D. Haward (bn), V. Czarnecki (cnd), Southwest German CO Pforzheim ebs ▲ ebs 6054 [DDD]
Christmas Music for Trumpet & Organ, w. Jan Overduin (org) ebs ▲ ebs 6004 [DDD]
Corelli, A.:Son Tpt, w. V. Czarnecki (cnd), Southwest German CO Pforzheim ebs ▲ ebs 6053 [DDD]
Enescu, G.:Légende, w. A. Rowe (pno) ebs ▲ ebs 6022 [DDD]
Goedicke, A.:Concert Etude, w. A. Rowe (pno) ebs ▲ ebs 6022 [DDD]
Handel, G.F.:Suite Tpt & Org, w. Jan Overduin (org) ebs ▲ ebs 6041 [DDD]
Haydn, M.:Con 2 Tpt, w. V. Czarnecki (cnd), Southwest German CO Pforzheim ebs ▲ ebs 6053 [DDD]
Hertel, J.W.:Con à 6, w. I. Franklin (ob), V. Czarnecki (cnd), Southwest German CO Pforzheim
ebs ▲ ebs 6054 [DDD]
Hubeau, J.:Son for Chromatic Tpt, w. A. Rowe (pno) ebs ▲ ebs 6022 [DDD]
Molter, J.M.:Con 1 Tpt, w. V. Czarnecki (cnd), Southwest German CO Pforzheim
ebs ▲ ebs 6053 [DDD]
Morawetz, O.:Son Tpt, w. A. Rowe (pno) ebs ▲ ebs 6022 [DDD]
Mozart, L.:Con Tpt, w. V. Czarnecki (cnd), Southwest German CO Pforzheim ebs ▲ ebs 6053 [DDD]
Music for Trumpet & Organ, Vol. 3, w. Schultz, Erik (tpt), Jan Overduin (org) ebs ▲ ebs 6003 [DDD]
Pezel, J.C.:Son Tpt, w. D. Haward (bn), V. Czarnecki (cnd), Southwest German CO Pforzheim
ebs ▲ ebs 6054 [DDD]
Stevens, H.:Son Tpt, w. A. Rowe (pno) ebs ▲ ebs 6022 [DDD]
Telemann, G.P.:Suite in g Tpt, w. J. Overduin (org) ebs ▲ ebs 6041 [DDD]
Viviani, B.:Son 1 Tpt, w. J. Overduin (org) ebs ▲ ebs 6041 [DDD]
Viviani, B.:Son 2 Tpt, w. J. Overduin (org) ebs ▲ ebs 6041 [DDD]
Schultz, Stephen (baroque fl)
Boismortier, J.B. de:Sons Fl, Op. 91, w. Byron Schenkman (hpd) *(rec Music Hall, Ponytracks Ranch, Portola Valley, CA, May 3–5, 1995)* Naxos ▲ 8.553414 [DDD]
Schultz, Stephen (baroque fl/cnd)—see ORCHESTRAS & ENSEMBLES American Baroque
Schultz, Stephen (fl)
Vivaldi, A.:Con for 2 Fls, w. J. See (fl), N. McGegan (cnd), Philharmonia Baroque Orch
Harmonia Mundi France ▲ HMC 905193 [DDD]
Schultze, Siegfried (pno)
Bruch, M.:Kol Nidrei, w. B. Huberman (vc) [arr. violin-piano] *(rec 1930)*
The Classical Collector ▲ FDC 2003 (m) [AAD]
Chopin, F.:Waltzes, w. B. Huberman (vn) [violin-piano arr. by Huberman of the Waltz in c#, Op. 64, No. 2 *(rec 1932 for Columbia Records)* The Classical Collector ▲ FDC 2003 (m) [AAD]
Mendelssohn, F.:Con in e Vn & Orch, Op. 64, w. B. Huberman (vn) [violin-piano arr.]—2nd & 3rd movts. *(rec 1923)* Pearl ▲ GEMMCD 9332 [AAD]
Sarasate, P. de:Carmen Fant, w. B. Huberman (vn) [violin-piano arr.] *(rec 1926 for Polydor)*
The Classical Collector ▲ FDC 2003 (m) [AAD]
Sarasate, P. de:Spanish Dances, w. B. Huberman (vn)—"Romanza andlauza," Op. 22, No. 1 *(rec 1926 for Polydor)* The Classical Collector ▲ FDC 2003 (m) [AAD]
Schulz, Walter (vc)—see also ORCHESTRAS & ENSEMBLES Duo Postiglione
Haydn, J.:Divert for 4 Vns & Bass Instruments, H.II/39, "Echo", w. J.-P. Rampal (cnd) [arr "Echo" for 2 fls] Sony Classical ▲ SK 48061 [DDD]
Haydn, J.:Qts Strs, Op. 76, "Erdödy Qts", w. J.-P. Rampal (cnd)—No 5 [arr Samuel Arnold as Duet No. 4 for 2 Fls] Sony Classical ▲ SK 48061 [DDD]
Tchaikovsky, P.:Souvenir de Florence, w. J. Flieder (va), Franz Schubert String Quartet *(rec Nov. 9–12, 1993)* Nimbus ▲ NI 5399 [DDD]
Schulz, Wolfgang (fl)—see also ORCHESTRAS & ENSEMBLES Vienna Ring Ensemble
Bach, W.F.:Duets Fls, F.54-59, w. H.-J. Schellenberger (oboe) *(rec June 28–30, 1993)*
Sony Classical ▲ SK 58965 [DDD]
Haydn, J.:Trios Fls & Vc, "London Trios", w. Jean-Pierre Rampal (fl), Gilbert Audin (bn) [trans. for 2 flutes & bassoon] Sony Classical ▲ SK 48061 [DDD]
Hindemith, P.:Kleine Kammermusik, w. Hansjörg Schellenberger (ob), Karl Leister (cl), Günter Högner (hn), Milan Turkovic (bn) Sony Classical ▲ SK 64400
Hindemith, P.:Son Fl, w. Ferenc Bognár (pno) Sony Classical ▲ SK 64400
Mozart, W.A.:Con Fl Hp, w. N. Zabaleta (hp), K. Böhm (cnd), Vienna PO
Deutsche Grammophon ▲ 429815-2 [ADD]
Mozart, W.A.:Con Fl Hp, w. N. Zabaleta (hp), K. Böhm (cnd), Vienna PO
Deutsche Grammophon ▲ 413552-2 [ADD]
Schulz, Wolfgang (vc)—see ORCHESTRAS & ENSEMBLES Duo Postiglione
Schumacher, Andreas (perc)—see also ORCHESTRAS & ENSEMBLES Karl Peinkofer Percussion Ensemble
Orff, C.:Schulwerk (complete), w. Godela Orff (nar), Carolin Widmann (vn), Sonja Korkeala (vn), Markus Zahnhausen (rcr), Karl Peinkofer (perc), Wilfried Hiller (perc/mar), Martin Ruhland (mar), Munich Hochschule Madrigal Choir—Wessobrun Prayer for a capella Choir; 2 Pieces for a capella Choir; 8 Pieces for 2 Vns; Mater et filia for women's a capella Choir; Devotional Yodel for male a capella Choir; 5 Pieces for Sop, Rcr & Perc; Death for Nar., Wood Bells, Bass Xyl & Tam-Tam; Omnia tempus habent for mixed Choir, Timp & Little Dr; Rubato, molto allegro, rubato; Abenlied for Nar, Bass Metallophon, Bass Xyl, Large Dr & Wine Glass; 5 Pieces for Fl & Perc; Devotional Yodel for male Choir [version 2]; 7 Pieces for 2 Xyl *(rec Munich, 1994–95)* Celestial Harmonies ▲ 13105-2
Schumacher, Götz (pno)
Stockhausen, K.:Mantra, w. Andreas Grau (pno) Wergo ▲ WER 6267-2
Schumacher, Rainer (cl)—see ORCHESTRAS & ENSEMBLES Stuttgart Wind Quintet
Schumacher, Thomas (pno)
Prokofiev, S.:Son 6 Pno Élan ▲ 82242 [DDD]
Prokofiev, S.:Son 9 Pno Élan ▲ 82242 [DDD]
Scriabin, A.:Son 5 Pno Élan ▲ 82242 [DDD]
Scriabin, A.:Son 9 Pno Élan ▲ 82242 [DDD]
Schuman, Henry (ob)—see ORCHESTRAS & ENSEMBLES New York Woodwind Soloists
Schumann, Peter (org)
Festive Trumpet Concerti, w. Pfeiffer Trumpet Consort, Mathias Müller (timp) *(rec St Juliana Parish Church, Malsch, July 4–6, 1995)* Cantate ▲ C 58001 [DDD]
Schunk, Heinz (vn)
Reger, M.:Con in Olden Style, w. Karl Suske (vn), O. Suitner (cnd), Berlin Staatskapelle
Berlin Classics ▲ BER 9123
Spohr, L.:Duets Vns, Op. 67, w. Ulrike Petersen (vn) CPO ▲ CPO 999343 [DDD]
Schurack, S. (hn)—see ORCHESTRAS & ENSEMBLES Albert Schweitzer Wind Quintet
Schürgers, Theo (vc)
Brahms, J.:Qt 1 Pno, w. E. Fischer (pno), V. Brero (vn), R. Nel (va) *(rec Berlin, ca. 1939/41, Electrola DB)*
Koch Historic ▲ 7701-2 [AAD]
Schuring, Martin (ob)
Funk, E.:Con Ob, w. V. Válek (cnd), Czech RSO *(rec 1994)* MMC ▲ MMC 2033 [DDD]
Schuster, Joseph (vc)—see also ORCHESTRAS & ENSEMBLES Roth Trio
Beethoven, L. van:Con Vn, Vc & Pno, "Triple Con", w. Mishel Piastro (vn), Ania Dorfman (pno), A. Toscanini (cnd), New York PO Grammofono 2000 ▲ GRM 78636

Schut, M. (ob/E hn)
Francesconi, L.:Plot in the Fiction, w. D. Porcelijn (cnd), Asko Ensemble *(rec live Groningen, 3/8/90)*
Attacca ▲ Babel 9057-4 [DDD]
Schvartz, Haydée (pno)
Haydée Schvartz Mode ▲ MOD 31 [DDD]
Schwab, Jacqueline (pno)—see ORCHESTRAS & ENSEMBLES Renaissonics
Schwab, Josef (vc)
Khachaturian, A.:Spartacus, w. S. Grützmann (pno), J. Tuggle (cnd), Brandenburg PO *(rec Jan. 1993)*
Divox ▲ CDX 39307 [DDD]
Schwalbé, Michel (vn)
Vivaldi, A.:Cons Vn, Op. 8/1-4, "The Four Seasons", w. H. von Karajan (cnd), Berlin PO
Deutsche Grammophon ▲ 415301-2 [ADD]
Schwalke, Dietmar (vc)
Beethoven, L. van:Trio 7 Pno, w. J. Adler (pno), S. Shinohe (cl)
Classic Studio Berlin ▲ CS 10 308 [DDD]
Brahms, J.:Sons Vc (comp), w. J. Alder (pno) Classic Studio Berlin ▲ CS 10108 [DDD]
Brahms, J.:Trio Cl, w. S. Shinohe (cl), J. Adler (pno) Classic Studio Berlin ▲ CS 10 308 [DDD]
Debussy, C.:Son Vc, w. J. Adler (pno) *(rec 1984)* Classic Studio Berlin ▲ CS 10708 [DDD]
Popper, D.:Elfentanz Vc, w. J. Adler (pno) *(rec 1984)* Classic Studio Berlin ▲ CS 10708 [DDD]
Schubert, Franz:Son Arpeggione, w. J. Alder (pno) Classic Studio Berlin ▲ CS 10108 [DDD]
Schumann, R.:Fantasiestücke Cl, w. J. Adler (pno) *(rec 1984)*
Classic Studio Berlin ▲ CS 10708 [DDD]
Strauss, R.:Son Vc, w. J. Adler (pno) *(rec 1984)* Classic Studio Berlin ▲ CS 10708 [DDD]
Schwaller, Roman (t sax)
Rüegg, M.:Music of, w. Lauren Newton (sgr), Wolfgang Puschnig (fl/s sax), Harry Sokal (s sax), Karl Fian (tpt), Christian Radovan (trbn), Woody Schabata (vib)—Reflections on Aubade; Reflections on Méditation; Reflections on Sévère Réprimande; Reflections on Idylle; Reflections on Gnossiennes Nos. 1 & 2; Satie ist mir im traum 3x nicht erschienen *(rec Vienna, Sept. 20–22, 1983 & Mar.)*
Hat Hut ("NOW." series) ▲ hat ART CD 6024 [ADD]
Schwaller, R.:Vexations 1801 *(rec Vienna, Sept. 22, 1983)*
Hat Hut ("NOW." series) ▲ hat ART CD 6024 [ADD]
Schwamberger, M. (vc)—see ORCHESTRAS & ENSEMBLES Freiburg Baroque Soloists
Schwanda, Elisabeth (rcr)—see ORCHESTRAS & ENSEMBLES Affetti Musicali
Schwarb, Egon (org)
Heron, H.:Voluntary Org *(rec Pere Casulleras, CH-Waldenburg 1992)* Jecklin ▲ JS 309-2 [DDD]
Krebs, J.L.:Org Music—Praeambulum supra Ach Gott, vom Himmel sieh darein; Trio in c; Ach Gott, vom Himmel sieh darein Cantus firmus in Alt; Choralsatz von J.S. Bach *(rec Pere Casulleras, CH-Waldenburg 1992)* Jecklin ▲ JS 309-2 [DDD]
Zachow, F.W.:Kbd Music, w. Oskar Birchmeier (org)—Vars on "Jesu, meine Freude" *(rec Pere Casulleras, CH-Waldenburg 1992)* Jecklin ▲ JS 309-2 [DDD]
Schwartz, Angela (vc)
Hartke, S.:Night Rubrics *(rec Tituskirche, Basel, Switzerland, Aug. 29, 1994)* New World ▲ 80461-2
Schwartz, Elliott (pno)
Schwartz, E.:Maine Haiku Capstone ▲ CPS 863300
Schwartz, E.:Sinf Juxta, w. S. Jones (tpt), B. Theurer (tpt), S. Barnhart (perc)
Capstone ▲ CPS 8612 CD [DDD]
Schwartz, Julie (pno)—see also ORCHESTRAS & ENSEMBLES Oberlin Trio
Hoffman, D.:Son Cl, w. Rhonda Gowen (cl) Meyer ▲ MC 0108
Hoffman, D.:Trio Cl, Vn & Pno, w. Rhonda Gowen (cl), Kathleen Clothier-Angeroth (vn)
Meyer ▲ MC 0108
Meisner, D.:He Who Dwells, w. Lois Swenson (sop), Deirdre Fay (ob) Meyer ▲ MC 0108
Ost, M.:The Ride Home, w. Teri Fay Storhaug (hn) Meyer ▲ MC 0108
Walth, G.:A Musical Feast, w. G. Walth (cnd), Bismarck Mandan Civic Chorus Meyer ▲ MC 0108
Schwartz, Nathan (pno)—see ORCHESTRAS & ENSEMBLES Hampton-Schwartz Duo, Francesco Trio
Schwartz, Sergiu (vn)
Grieg, E.:Son 3 Vn, w. Rachel Franklin (pno) *(rec Feb 1988)* Allegretto ▲ ACD 8199
Sibelius, J.:Con Vn, w. P. Freeman (cnd), London SO *(rec Feb 1988)* Allegretto ▲ ACD 8199
Spohr, L.:Son 3 Vn, w. Rachel Talitman (hp) Arcobaleno ▲ AAOC 93642
Spohr, L.:Son 4 Vn, w. Rachel Talitman (hp) Arcobaleno ▲ AAOC 93642
Spohr, L.:Son 5 Vn, w. Rachel Talitman (hp) Arcobaleno ▲ AAOC 93642
Svendsen, J.:Romance Vn, w. P. Freeman (cnd), London SO *(rec Feb 1988)* Allegretto ▲ ACD 8199
Schwarz, Bernhard (vc)—see also ORCHESTRAS & ENSEMBLES Alkan Trio
Bohnke, E.:Son Vc MD + G ▲ MDG 3250531 [DDD]
Schwarz, Gerard (tpt)—see also ORCHESTRAS & ENSEMBLES American Brass Quintet
Albinoni, T.:Con in C Tpt, w. Ronald Roseman (ob), Susan Weiner (ob), Virginia Brewer (ob), Ronald MacCourt (bn), William Scribner (bn), Edward Brewer (hpd) Vox Box 2-▲ CDX 5124 [ADD]
Altenburg, J.E.:Con in C Tpts, w. G. Schwarz (cnd), New York Trumpet Ensemble, 92nd St. Y Chamber SO members Delos ▲ DCD 3002 [DDD]
A Baroque Trumpet Recital Elektra/Nonesuch ■ 71274-4
Biber, H. von:Son in C for 8 Tpts & Timp, w. G. Schwarz (cnd), 92nd St. Y Chamber SO, New York Trumpet Ensemble Delos ▲ DCD 3002 [DDD]
Brandt, H.:Con Tpt, w. H. Brandt (cnd), *(ensemble unknown)* Phoenix ▲ PHCD 115 [AAD]
Carter, E.:Canon for 3, "In memoriam Igor Stravinsky", w. Louis Ranger (tpt), Stanley Rosenzweig (tpt) [2 versions] Phoenix ▲ PHCD 115 [AAD]
Cornet Favorites, w. William Bolcom (pno) Elektra/Nonesuch ▲ 79157-2
Fontana, G.B.:Sons, w. Julie Feves (bn), Helen Katz (hpd) Vox Box 2-▲ CDX 5124 [ADD]
Frescobaldi, G.:Canzonas, Caprici & Ricercari, w. Julie Feves (bn), Helen Katz (hpd)
Vox Box 2-▲ CDX 5124 [ADD]
Hertel, J.W.:Con à cinque, w. Ronald Roseman (ob), Susan Weiner (ob), Virginia Brewer (ob), Ronald MacCourt (bn), William Scribner (bn), Edward Brewer (hpd) Vox Box 2-▲ CDX 5124 [ADD]
Hummel, J.N.:Con in E♭ Tpt, S.49, w. G. Schwarz (cnd), New York Chamber SO
Delos ▲ DCD 3001 [DDD]
Moryl, R.:Salvos Phoenix ▲ PHCD 115 [AAD]
Starer, R.:Con a 3, w. J. Rabbai (cl), P. Brevig (trbn), A. Kaplan (cnd), Camerata String Orch *(rec 1972)*
CRI ▲ CD 612 [ADD]
Telemann, G.P.:Cons Tpt, w. Ronald Roseman (ob), Susan Weiner (ob), Virginia Brewer (ob), Ronald MacCourt (bn), William Scribner (bn), Edward Brewer (hpd) Vox Box 2-▲ CDX 5124 [ADD]
Telemann, G.P.:Con Tpt Strs in D, w. G. Schwarz (cnd), 92nd St. Y Chamber SO
Delos ▲ DCD 3002 [DDD]
Torelli, G.:Sons à 5 Tpts, w. G. Schwarz (cnd), New York Trumpet Ensemble—Son in G
Delos ▲ DCD 3002 [DDD]
Vivaldi, A.:Con for 2 Tpts, w. G. Schwarz (cnd), 92nd St. Y Chamber SO, New York Trumpet Ensemble
Delos ▲ DCD 3002 [DDD]
Whittenberg, C.:Polyphony Phoenix ▲ PHCD 115 [AAD]
Wolpe, S.:Solo Piece Tpt Phoenix ▲ PHCD 115 [AAD]
Schwarz, J.-M. (vn)
Bach, J.S.:Trio Son Fl, Vn & Hpd, w. J. Solum (fl), I. Kipnis (hpd), E. Potash (vc) [period instrs]
Arabesque ▲ ARA 6640 [DDD]
Handel, G.F.:Trio Sons, w. John Solum (trns fl), E. Potash (vc) [period instrs]—in G, Op. 2/1, HWV 389; in F, Op. 2/4, HWV 386b Arabesque ▲ ARA 6640 [DDD]
Vivaldi, A.:Cons Vn, Op. 8/1-4, "The Four Seasons", w. I. Kipnis (hpd), I. Kipnis (cnd), Connecticut Early Music Festival Ensemble [period instrs] Chesky ▲ CD 78 [DDD]
Schwarz, Julie (pno)
Walth, G.:Spring Songs, w. Kari Swenson (sop)—Spring Meyer ▲ MC 0108
Schwarz, Niklas (va)—see ORCHESTRAS & ENSEMBLES Mannheim String Quartet
Schwarz, Peter (hpd)
Mahler, G.:Bach Orchestral Works, w. M.-U. Senn (fl), P. Siegele (org), P. Ruzicka (cnd), Berlin RSO
Koch Schwann ▲ 3-1204-2 [ADD]

INSTRUMENT.

Schwarz, Peter (org)
Bloch, A.:Duet Vn & Org, w. Ulf Hoelscher (vn) Pro Viva ▲ ISPV 172
Bloch, A.:For the Light Is Come, w. M. Schweigmann (nar), North German RSO, North German Radio Chorus Pro Viva ▲ ISPV 169
Lazarof, H.:Intonazione e Variazioni Laurel ▲ LR 844

Schwarz, R. (pno)
Pfitzner, H.:Songs, w. L. Goetz (sop)—16 songs (Opp. 5, 11 & 33) [G] Ars Produktion ▲ ARS 368301 [AAD]

Schwarz, Tim (vn)—see ORCHESTRAS & ENSEMBLES Upper Valley Duo

Schwarzenbach, Regula (fl)
Mozart, W.A.:Sons Fl Hpd (comp), w. Conrad Zwicky (org) [arr for fl & org] *(rec Jan–Mar 1996)* Jecklin ▲ JD 7082 [DDD]

Schween, Astrid (vc)—see ORCHESTRAS & ENSEMBLES Lark String Quartet

Schweitzer, Albert (org)
Bach, J.S.:Chorale Settings (misc)—BWV 731; Chorale Preludes; Preludes & Fugues, BWV 546, 547 & 548 Pearl ▲ PEA 9992 [AAD]
Bach, J.S.:Org Music (misc)—Toccata & Fugue in d, BWV 5565; Prelude in C, BWV 545; Prelude & Fugue in e, BWV 548; Fugue in g, BWV 578; Tocata, Adagio & Fugue in C, BWV 564; Choral Preludes "Liebster Jesu, wir sind hier," BWV 731; "Jesus Christus unser Heiland," BWV 665; "Christum, wir sollen loben schon," BWV 611; "O lamm Gottes, unschuldig," BWV 656 *(rec 1935–52)* EMI Classics ▲ CDH 64703
Bach, J.S.:Das Orgelbüchlein—BWV 611, 616, 618, 620, 621, 622, 626, 629 Pearl ▲ PEA 9992 [AAD]
Bach, J.S.:Preludes & Fugues, BWV 531–552—BWV 546–548 Pearl ▲ PEA 9992 [AAD]
Bach, J.S.:Toccata & Fugue Org, BWV 538, "Dorian" EMI Classics ▲ CDH 64703

Schweitzer, Jacqueline (pno)
Debussy, C.:Pour le piano Entr'acte ▲ ESCD 6505 [ADD]
Pierné, G.:Étude de concert Entr'acte ▲ ESCD 6505 [ADD]
Poulenc, F.:Pno Music (misc)—Mouvements perpétuels (1918); Pastourelle (1927); Toccata, from Trois pièces (1928) Entr'acte ▲ ESCD 6505 [ADD]
Ravel, M.:Alborada del gracioso Entr'acte ▲ ESCD 6505 [ADD]
Sauguet, H.:Son Pno Entr'acte ▲ ESCD 6505 [ADD]

Schwejda, Don (pno)
Chopin, F.:Nocturnes—in b♭, Op. 9/1; in E♭, Op. 9/2; in A♭, Op. 48/2; in f, Op. 55/1; in E♭, Op. 55/2 API Classical ▲ CD 191718–A [DDD]
Chopin, F.:Waltzes—in e, Op. posth.; in A♭, Op. 34/1; in a, Op. 34/2; Minute Waltz in D♭, Op. 64/1 API Classical ▲ CD 191718–A [DDD]
Grieg, E.:Pno Music (sels)—Poetic Tone-Pictures, Op. 3/4 & 6; Elfentanz, Op. 12/4; Album Leaf, Op. 12/7; Papillon, Op. 43/1; Elegie, Op. 47/7 API Classical ▲ CD 191718–A [DDD]

Schwertsik, Kurt (pno)
Schwertsik, K.:Da uhu schaud me su draurech au.., w. C. Schwertsik (sgr) *(rec May 1994)* Largo ▲ 5125 [DDD]
Schwertsik, K.:Gedichte an Ljuba, w. C. Schwertsik (sgr) *(rec May 1994)* Largo ▲ 5125 [DDD]
Schwertsik, K.:Ich sein Blumenbein, w. C. Schwertsik (sgr) *(rec May 1994)* Largo ▲ 5125 [DDD]

Schwietering, Jürgen (vn)
Klatzow, P.:Qt Strs, w. Petri Salonen (vn), Leo Luijvendijk (va), Eric Martens (vc) Claremont ▲ GSE 1524

Schwindl, E. (portative/organistum/h-g/bells)—see ORCHESTRAS & ENSEMBLES Estampie

Scimone, Clémentine (fl)
Cimarosa, D.:Con for 2 Fls, w. J.–P. Rampal (fl), C. Scimone (cnd), Venice Solisti *(rec 1972)* Erato ▲ 2292–45836–2 [ADD]
Telemann, G.P.:Cons Fl (misc), *(orch unknown)*—Cons. in f & D *(rec Sept. 1985)* Analekta ▲ AN 28502 [DDD]

Scodanibbio, Stefano (db)
Estrada, J.:Chamber Music, w. Arditti String Quartet Montaigne ("Auvidis" series) ▲ MO 782056
Ferneyhough, B.:Trittico per G. S. Montaigne ▲ MO 782029
Nono, L.:guai ai gelidi mostri, w. Susanne Otto (cta), Helena Rasker (alt), Klaus Burger (tuba/pic tpt), A. Richard (cnd), Recherche Ensemble Montaigne ▲ MO 782047

Scolnik, J. (fl)
Bazelon, I.:Legends & Love Letters, w. J. Heller (sop), F. Epstein (perc), C. Oldfather (pno), R. Annis (cl), J. Moerchel (vc), C. Fussell (cnd), Collage New Music Ensemble Albany ▲ TROY 054 [DDD]

Scott, Andrew (a sax)
A Secret Place, w. Rebello, Simone (perc), Liz Gilliver (mar), Kalengo Percussion Ensemble, Eryl Roberts (perc), John Melbourne (perc), Chris Bastock (perc), Richard Dyson (perc) *(rec Zion Institute, Manchester, 1995)* Doyen ▲ CD 040 [DDD]

Scott, B. (va)—see ORCHESTRAS & ENSEMBLES Scott Chamber Players

Scott, Cyril (pno)
Ravel, M.:Entre cloches, w. S. Coombs (pno) Gamut Classics ▲ GAM CD 517 [DDD]
Ravel, M.:Frontispiece, w. S. Coombs (pno) Gamut Classics ▲ GAM CD 517 [DDD]
Ravel, M.:Intro & Allegro, w. S. Coombs (pno) [Ravel's two-piano arr.] Gamut Classics ▲ GAM CD 517 [DDD]
Ravel, M.:Rapsodie espagnole, w. S. Coombs (pno) [Ravel's two-piano arr.] Gamut Classics ▲ GAM CD 517 [DDD]
Ravel, M.:Shéhérazade Pno, w. S. Coombs (pno) Gamut Classics ▲ GAM CD 517 [DDD]
Ravel, M.:La Valse, w. S. Coombs (pno) [Ravel's 1921 two-piano arr.] Gamut Classics ▲ GAM CD 517 [DDD]

Scott, Daryl (pno)
Harris, R.:Madrigal, w. R. Shewan (cnd), Roberts Wesleyan College Chorale *(rec Parmenter Chapel, Roberts Wesleyan College, Rochester, NY)* Albany ▲ TROY 164 [DDD]

Scott, Graham (pno)
Scriabin, A.:Etude Pno, Op. 2/1 *(rec 8/90)* Gamut Classics ▲ GAM 520
Scriabin, A.:Preludes Pno (misc)—26 Preludes—Opp. 2/2, 9/1, 16, 22, 27, 31, 33, 74 *(rec 8/90)* Gamut Classics ▲ GAM 520
Scriabin, A.:Son 3 Pno *(rec 8/90)* Gamut Classics ▲ GAM 520
Scriabin, A.:Son 9 Pno *(rec 8/90)* Gamut Classics ▲ GAM 520

Scott, John (org)
Bononcini, A.:Stabat Mater, w. Felicity Palmer (sop), Paul Esswood (ct), Philip Langridge (ten), Christopher Keyte (bass), John Willison (vn), Chris Wellington (va), Don McVeigh (va), G. Guest (cnd), Philomusica Antiqua of London, St. John's College Choir Cambridge *(rec 1977)* London 2–▲ 443868–2 [ADD]
Caldara, A.:Crucifixus, w. Felicity Palmer (sop), Paul Esswood (ct), Philip Langridge (ten), Christopher Keyte (bass), John Willison (vn), Chris Wellington (va), Don McVeigh (va), G. Guest (cnd), Philomusica Antiqua of London, St. John's College Choir Cambridge *(rec 1977)* London 2–▲ 443868–2 [ADD]
Duruflé, M.:Org Music (comp) [St. Paul's Cathedral Organ]—Scherzo, Op. 2; Prélude, adagio et choral varié sur le "Veni Creator," Op. 4; Suite, Op. 5; Prélude et fugue sur le nom d'Alain, Op. 7; Prelude on the Introit of the Epiphany; Fugue on the Theme of the Carillon of Hours of the Cathedral of Soissons Hyperion ▲ CDA 66368
Elgar, E.:Son Org Priory ▲ PRI 401 [DDD]
Family Carols, w. [cnd:David Willcocks], Bach Choir, Fanfare Trumpeters of the Royal Military School of Music, Graham Ashton Brass Ensemble Chandos ▲ CHAN 8973 [DDD]
Fauré, G.:Ave Verum, w. Matthew Best (cnd), Corydon Singers Hyperion ▲ CDA 66292
Fauré, G.:Cantique de Jean Racine, w. Matthew Best (cnd), Corydon Singers Hyperion ▲ CDA 66292
Fauré, G.:Cantique de Jean Racine, w. J. Rutter (cnd), Cambridge Singers [F] Collegium ▲ COLCD 109 [DDD] ▮ COLC 109 (D)
Fauré, G.:Messe basse (in 3 movts), w. D. Deam (sop), J. Rutter (cnd), Cambridge Singers [L] Collegium ▲ COLCD 109 [DDD] ▮ COLC 109 (D)
Fauré, G.:Messe basse (in 3 movts), w. M. Seers (sop), Matthew Best (cnd), Corydon Singers Hyperion ▲ CDA 66292
Fauré, G.:Tantum ergo, w. Matthew Best (cnd), Corydon Singers Hyperion ▲ CDA 66292

Scott, John (org) (cont.)
Great European Organs, No. 40, w. Scott, John (org) Priory ▲ PRI 485 [DDD]
Great Postludes, w. Scott, John (org) Priory ▲ PRCD 345 [DDD]
Harris, J.:Son Org Priory ▲ PRI 401 [DDD]
Lotti, A.:Crucifixus, w. Felicity Palmer (sop), Paul Esswood (ct), Philip Langridge (ten), Christopher Keyte (bass), John Willison (vn), Chris Wellington (va), Don McVeigh (va), G. Guest (cnd), Philomusica Antiqua of London, St. John's College Choir Cambridge *(rec 1977)* London 2–▲ 443868–2 [ADD]
Mathias, W.:Org Music—Fanfare; Fantasy, Op. 78; Fenestra; Recessional, Op. 96/4; Processional (1964); Invocations, Op. 35; Berceuse, Op. 95/3; Jubilate, Op. 67/2; Atniphonies, Op. 88/2; Chorale (1966) Nimbus ▲ NI 5367
Mendelssohn, F.:Org Music (comp)—Preludes & Fugues, Op. 37; Sonatas, Op. 65; various Andantes, Allegros & Fugues Hyperion 2–▲ CDA 66491/92
Mendelssohn, F.:Preludes & Fugues Org, Op. 37 Hyperion 2–▲ CDA 66491/92
Mendelssohn, F.:Sons Org Hyperion 2–▲ CDA 66491/92
Psalms from St. Paul's, Vol. 3, w. [cnd:Andrew Lucas], St. Paul's Cathedral Choir Hyperion ▲ CDP 11003
Walton, W.:Coronation Te Deum, w. D. Willcocks (cnd), Philharmonia Orch, Bach Choir [L] Chandos ▲ CHAN 8760 [DDD]

Scott, Kathryn (pno)
Chopin, F.:Barcarolle Pno Unicorn–Kanchana 2–▲ DKP CD 9147/48
Chopin, F.:Impromptus—Fantaisie-Impromptu in c#, Op. 66 Unicorn–Kanchana 2–▲ DKP CD 9147/48
Chopin, F.:Nocturnes Unicorn–Kanchana 2–▲ DKP CD 9147/48
Fauré, G.:Pno Music, w. Martin Roscoe (pno)—[CD 1] Impromptu's; Theme and Vars.; Romances;[CD 2] Barcarolles;[CD 3] Nocturnes; Fugues; Fants.;[CD 4] Dolly Suite; Preludes; Mazurkas Hyperion 4–▲ CDA 66911/14

Scott, L. (vn)—see ORCHESTRAS & ENSEMBLES Scott Chamber Players

Scott, P. (vc)—see ORCHESTRAS & ENSEMBLES Scott Chamber Players

Scott, Sjön (hn)
Arnold, M.:Qnt Brass, w. Uwe Zaiser (tpt), Peter Leiner (tpt), Jochen Scheerer (posaune), Ralf Rudolph (tuba) Bayer ▲ BR 100251 [DDD]
Beethoven, L. van:Qnt Pno, Ob, Cl, Hn & Bn, w. C. Eschenbach (pno), A. Leek (ob), J. Moog (cl), U. Freund (bn) Signum ▲ X 06–00
Crespo, E.:Suite Americana 1, w. Uwe Zaiser (tpt), Peter Leiner (tpt), Jochen Scheerer (posaune), Ralf Rudolph (tuba) Bayer ▲ BR 100251 [DDD]
Ewald, V.:Qnt 1 Brass, w. Peter Leiner (tpt), Uwe Zaiser (tpt), Jochen Scheerer (trbn), Ralf Rudolph (tuba) Bayer ▲ BR 100251 [DDD]
Horovitz, J.:Music Hall Suite, w. Uwe Zaiser (tpt), Peter Leiner (tpt), Jochen Scheerer (posaune), Ralf Rudolph (tuba) Bayer ▲ BR 100251 [DDD]
Koetsier, J.:Qnt Brass, w. Peter Leiner (tpt), Uwe Zaiser (tpt), Jochen Scheerer (posaune), Ralf Rudolph (tuba) Bayer ▲ BR 100251 [DDD]
Mozart, W.A.:Qnt Pno, K.452, w. C. Eschenbach (pno), A. Leek (ob), J. Moog (cl), U. Freund (bn) Signum ▲ X 06–00

Scott, Stephen (pno)—see ORCHESTRAS & ENSEMBLES Bowed Piano Ensemble

Scotts, Donald (vn)
Moeran, E.J.:Son Vn, w. John Talbot (pno) Chandos ▲ CHAN 8465 [ADD]

Scragg, Nigel (fl/a sax)
Chevalier, C.:Music of, w. Teca Calazans (sgr), Ze–Luis (sgr), Regina Machado (sgr), Rosihna de Valenca (gtr), Jean–Yves Candela (pno), Wilson das Neves (perc), Regina Machado (perc), Silvano Michelino (perc)—Comme d'habitude; Couleur café; Une histoire d'amour; Les feuilles mortes; Les moulins de mon coeur; Syracuse; Je t'aimerai; Ces petits rien; La valse des lilas; L'absent; Que reste–il de nos amours; Un homme et une femme *(rec Studio Bastille)* Iris ▲ 010 [DDD]

Screpis, Gabriele (bn)—see ORCHESTRAS & ENSEMBLES Italiano Octet

Scribner, William (bn)—see also ORCHESTRAS & ENSEMBLES Bronx Arts Ensemble
Albinoni, T.:Con in C Tpt, w. Gerard Schwarz (tpt), Ronald Roseman (ob), Susan Weiner (ob), Virginia Brewer (ob), Ronald MacCourt (bn), Edward Brewer (hpd) Vox Box 2–▲ CDX 5124 [ADD]
Hertel, J.W.:Con à cinque, w. Gerard Schwarz (tpt), Ronald Roseman (ob), Susan Weiner (ob), Virginia Brewer (ob), Ronald MacCourt (bn), Edward Brewer (hpd) Vox Box 2–▲ CDX 5124 [ADD]
Kupferman, M.:Qnt Bn, w. Bronx Arts Ensemble Soundspells ▲ CD 108 [DDD]
Telemann, G.P.:Cons Tpt, w. Gerard Schwarz (tpt), Ronald Roseman (ob), Susan Weiner (ob), Virginia Brewer (ob), Ronald MacCourt (bn), Edward Brewer (hpd) Vox Box 2–▲ CDX 5124 [ADD]

Scully, J. (perc)
Milesi, P.:Modi 1, w. D. Cassamagnaghi (fl), F. Pomarico (ob), A. Bianchi (cl), L. Dosso (bn), G. Govi (vn), D. Tellini (vn), M. Ravasio (va), S. Righini (vc), P. Rizzi (db), C. Vignani (hpd), P. Milesi (cnd) Cuneiform ▲ RUNE 63
Milesi, P.:Modi 2, w. L. M. Pickova (sop), Françoise Goddard (alt), M. Ferradini (ten), B. Andersen (bass), D. Cassamagnaghi (fl), S. Scanziani (ob), A. Bianchi (cl/b cl), E. Crisafulli (bn), C. Gazzola (hn), F. Gualandris (tuba), A. Girardi (celtic hp), R. Anedda (vn), E. Groppo (vn), M. Pagani (vn), M. Ravasio (va), S. Righini (vc), P. Rizzi (db), P. Milesi (cnd) Cuneiform ▲ RUNE 63

Seal, Richard (org)
Anthems from Salisbury, w. [cnd:Richard Seal], Salisbury Cathedral Choir Meridian ▲ 84025
Bach, J.S.:Fant Org, BWV 572 Meridian ▲ CDE 84140
Franck, C.:Prélude, fugue et var Meridian ▲ CDE 84140
Liszt, F.:Prelude & Fugue on the name B–A–C–H Meridian ▲ CDE 84140
Salisbury Cathedral Choir, w. [cnd:Richard Seal], Salisbury Cathedral Choir, Benjamin Dean (trb) Metronome ▲ MET CD 1016
Stanford, C.V.:For Lo, I Raise Up, w. Salisbury Cathedral Choir [E] Meridian ▲ CDE 84140
Stanford, C.V.:A Song of Peace, w. Salisbury Cathedral Choir [E] Meridian ▲ CDE 84140
Walmisley, T.A.:Remember, O Lord, What Is Come upon Us, w. Salisbury Cathedral Choir [E] Meridian ▲ CDE 84140

Seaman, Nigel (tuba)
Schnittke, A.:Sym 7, w. David Buckland (ctbn), Michael Wright (db), T. Otaka (cnd), BBC Welsh National SO *(rec Brangwyn Hall, Swansea, Wales, July 26–27, 1995)* BIS ▲ CD 747 [DDD]

Sears, Ann (pno)
Burleigh, H.T.:songs, w. Oral Moses (b-bar)—Deep River; Lovely Dark & Lonely One; Dry Bones; Wade in de Water; Ethiopia Saluting the Colors; The Dove & the Lily; Exile; Stan' Still, Jordan; Little Mother of Mine; Don't You Weep When I'm Gone; The Spring, My Dear, Is No Longer Spring; Oh! Rock Me, Julie; The Soldier; Mammy's Li'l Baby; Hear de Lambs A-Cryin'; The Trees Have Grown So; Thy Heart; Hard Trials; Didn't My Lord Deliver Daniel? Northeastern ▲ NR 252 [DDD]

Seaton, L. (vn)
Soldier, D.:Apotheosis of John Brown, w. R. McCauley, R. A. Clark, M. L. Kortes, N. Davoy, J. White, G. High, et al. Newport Classic ▲ NPB 85549 [ADD]
Soldier, D.:Duo Son, w. E. Friedlander (vc) Newport Classic ▲ NPB 85549 [ADD]

Seaton, Laura (vn)—see ORCHESTRAS & ENSEMBLES Soldier String Quartet, Sirius String Quartet

Seban, S. (pno)
Guyonnet, J.:La Cantate interrompue, w. F. Rochaix (nar), S. Stenhammar (sop), G. Calame (pno), E. Séjourne (perc), P. Geiss, E. Tarr (tpt), B. Nilsson (tpt), H. Ries (trbn), H. Rückert (trbn), J.–M. Collet, J. Guyonnet (cnd), Geneva Collegium Academicum [F] *(rec Nov. 15, 1986)* Grammont ▲ CTSP 30–2

Sebastiani, Adriano (gtr)
Carulli, F.:Ariettes (3) et romances italiennes (3), w. Antonia E. Brown (sop)—Frena le belle lagrime; Amo te sola; Ombre amene; Ecco quel fiero istante; Parlami pur sincero; Solitario bosc'ombroso *(rec Florence, Sept 11–12, 1994)* Dynamic ▲ CDS 124 [DDD]
Carulli, F.:Ariettes italiennes (3), w. Antonia E. Brown (sop)—Che fa il mio bene; Deh con me non vi sdegnate; Tornate sereni begl'astri *(rec Florence, Sept 11–12, 1994)* Dynamic ▲ CDS 124 [DDD]
Carulli, F.:Ariettes italiennes (12) sur motifs de Rossini, w. Antonia E. Brown (sop)—Ecco quel fiero istante; Sognai mia fillide; O bella fillide; Tornate sereni begl'astri; Ha negli occhi; Se son lontana; Già la notte s'avvicina; Amene selve, amiche piante; Conservati fedele; Amo te sola; Son lungi; Già pronta là t'aspetta *(rec Florence, Sept 11–12, 1994)* Dynamic ▲ CDS 124 [DDD]

▲ = CD ♦ = Enhanced CD Δ = MD ▮ = Cassette Tape ☐ = DCC

Sebastiani, Adriano (gtr) (cont.)
Carulli, F.:Les Folies d'Espagne variées Gtr—Instrumental *(rec Florence, Sept 11–12, 1994)* Dynamic ▲ CDS 124 [DDD]
Carulli, F.:Grand air italien, w. Antonia E. Brown (sop)—Senti mio bene *(rec Florence, Sept 11–12, 1994)* Dynamic ▲ CDS 124 [DDD]
Carulli, F.:Nocturnes (6) for 2 Voices & Gtr, w. Antonia E. Brown (sop), Lucia Sciannimanico (mez)—Dal di ch'io vi mirai; Di me chi vide mai; Quel cor che mi prometti; Io rivedrò sovente; V'è com'è bello il mar; Selve ombrose *(rec Florence, Sept 11–12, 1994)* Dynamic ▲ CDS 124 [DDD]
Paganini, N.:Cantabile, w. F. Mezzena (vn) Dynamic ▲ CD 62 [DDD]
Paganini, N.:Cantabile & Waltz, w. F. Mezzena (vn) Dynamic ▲ CD 62 [DDD]
Paganini, N.:Duetto amoroso Vn, w. F. Mezzena (vn) Dynamic ▲ CD 62 [DDD]
Paganini, N.:Inno patriottico con variazioni, w. F. Mezzena (vn) Dynamic ▲ CD 03 [AAD]
Paganini, N.:Moto perpetuo Vn & Gtr, w. F. Mezzena (vn) Dynamic ▲ CD 03 [AAD]
Paganini, N.:Serenata Va, w. A. Farulli (va), A. Noferini (vc) Dynamic ▲ CD 76 [DDD]
Paganini, N.:Serenata Vns, w. D. Bratchkova (vn), G. Hartmann (vn) Dynamic ▲ CD 76 [DDD]
Paganini, N.:Sons Vn & Gtr, Op. 2, w. F. Mezzena (vn) Dynamic ▲ CD 62 [DDD]
Paganini, N.:Sons Vn & Gtr, Op. 3, w. F. Mezzena (vn) Dynamic ▲ CD 62 [DDD]
Paganini, N.:Terzetto concertante Va, w. A. Farulli (va), A. Noferini (vc) Dynamic ▲ CD 76 [DDD]
Paganini, N.:Terzetto Vn, w. D. Bratchkova (vn), A. Noferini (vc) Dynamic ▲ CD 76 [DDD]
Paganini, N.:Terzetto Vns, w. D. Bratchkova (vn), G. Hartmann (vn) Dynamic ▲ CD 76 [DDD]
Paganini, N.:Theme & Vars Vn, w. F. Mezzena (vn) Dynamic ▲ CD 03 [AAD]
Paganini, N.:Vars on "La Carmagnole", w. F. Mezzena (vn) Dynamic ▲ CD 03 [AAD]
Paganini, N.:Vars on "O mamma, mamma cara", w. F. Mezzena (vn) Dynamic ▲ CD 03 [AAD]

Sebestyen, Ernö (va)
Bottesini, G.:Gran Duetto 2 Db & Va, w. W. Güttler (db) Koch Schwann ▲ CD 311042 [DDD]

Sebestyen, Ernö (vn)
Bottesini, G.:Gran Duo Concertant, w. W. Güttler (db), M. Bamert (cnd), Berlin RSO Koch Schwann ▲ CD 311042 [DDD]
Glière, R.:Duets Vn, Op. 39, w. Martin Ostertag (vc) Koch Schwann ▲ SCH 317272
Kodály, Z.:Duo Vn & Vc, w. Martin Ostertag (vc) Koch Schwann ▲ SCH 317272
Mysliveček, J.:Cons in C, D & F Vn, Berlin RSO *(rec 1981)* Koch Treasure ▲ 31614–2 [ADD]
Ravel, M.:Son Vn Vc, w. Martin Ostertag (vc) Koch Schwann ▲ SCH 317272
Rheinberger, J.:Suite Org, w. A. Juffinger (org), M. Ostertag (vc), H. Haenchen (cnd), Berlin RSO Capriccio ▲ CD 10 337 [DDD]
Rheinberger, J.:Suite Vn, Op. 150, w. A. Juffinger (org) Capriccio ▲ CD 10 337 [DDD]
Rheinberger, J.:Suite Vn, Op. 166, w. A. Juffinger (org) Capriccio ▲ CD 10 336 [DDD]
Riotte, J.P.:Notturno, w. E. Witsenburg (hp) Koch Schwann ▲ SCH 313392 [ADD/DDD]
Spohr, L.:Con Str Qt, w. H. Ganz (vn), H. Beyerle (va), M. Ostertag (vc), G. Albrecht (cnd), Berlin RSO Koch Schwann ▲ CD 311088 [DDD] ■ MC 211088 (D)
Spohr, L.:Var, Op. 6, w. H. Ganz (vn), H. Beyerle (va), M. Ostertag (vc) Koch Schwann ▲ CD 311088 [DDD] ■ MC 211088 (D)

Sebestyén, János (hpd)
Bach, J.S.:Adagio Clvd *(rec Feb–Mar, 1972)* Classical Diamonds ▲ CLD 4021 [ADD]
Bach, J.S.:Fants Hpd—Fantasia & Fugue in a, BWV 904; Fantasia in c, BWV 906; Chromatic Fantasia & Fugue in d, BWV 903 *(rec June 21–22, 1991)* Naxos ▲ 8.550571 [DDD]
Bach, J.S.:Inventions (30) Hpd—BWV 779 *(rec June 21–22, 1991)* Naxos ▲ 8.550571 [DDD]
Bach, J.S.:Italian Con *(rec June 21–22, 1991)* Naxos ▲ 8.550571 [DDD]
Bach, J.S.:Preludes & Fugues Hpd—BWV 925–30, 939–42, 998–99 *(rec June 21–22, 1991)* Naxos ▲ 8.550571 [DDD]
Bach, J.S.:Sons (5) Kbd—in d, BWV 964; in a, BWV 965; in C, BWV 966 *(rec Feb–Mar, 1972)* Classical Diamonds ▲ CLD 4021 [ADD]
Bach, J.S.:Sons Vn Hpd, BWV 1014–1019—Allegro in e, BWV 1019 *(rec Feb–Mar, 1972)* Classical Diamonds ▲ CLD 4021 [ADD]

Sebestyén, János (org)
Grand Duett:Music for 2 Organs, w. Luigi Celeghin (org), István Ella (org) Hungaroton ▲ HCD 31464 [DDD]
Mozart, W.A.:Org Music—Adagio, K.540; Andante, K.616; Andante Cantabile, K.15; Andante & Fugue, K.402; Fants., K.396 & 397; Gigue, K.574; Molto Allegro, K.72a; Ov., K.399; Prelude, K.284a; Son. da Chiesa, K.336; Vars., K.265 *(rec May 1991)* Naxos ▲ 8.550514 [DDD]
Mozart, W.A.:Sons Org, w. *(cnd unknown)*, Erkel CO *(rec Feb. 15–18, 1991)* Naxos ▲ 8.550512 [DDD]
Walther, Joh. G.:Transcriptions Org—trans of works by Albinoni (Cons in B♭ & F), Manzia (Con in g), Taglietti (Cons in B♭), Torelli (Con in d) Gentili (Con in A), Gregori (Con in B♭) Koch Treasure ▲ SCH 316252 [ADD]

Sebestyén, János (pno)
Bach, J.S.:Anna Magdalena Bach Notebook—Minuet in G, BWV Anh. 114; Minuet in g, BWV Anh. 115; Minuet in G, BWV Anh. 116; Polonaise in g, BWV Anh. 119; March in D, BWV Anh. 122; Polonaise in g, BWV Anh. 125; Musette in D, BWV Anh. 126; Minuet in d, BWV Anh. 132 *(rec July 6–9, 1992)* Naxos ▲ 8.550679 [DDD]
Bach, J.S.:Inventions (30) Hpd *(rec July 6–9, 1992)* Naxos ▲ 8.550679 [DDD]
Handel, G.F.:Sons Vn & Kbd, w. György Pauk (vn), Frank (vc)—Op. 1, Nos. 1b, 3, 6, 10, 12, 13, 14 Hungaroton ▲ HCD 12657 [DDD]

Sebok, Gyorgy (hpd)
Bach, J.S.:Sons Vl, BWV 1027–1029, w. J. Starker (vc)—BWV 1027 & 1028 Mercury Living Presence 2–▲ 432756–2 [ADD]

Sebok, Gyorgy (pno)
Bartók, B.:Burleskes, Op. 8c Erato 4–▲ ERA SEL 98476 [ADD]
Bartók, B.:Dance Suite Erato 4–▲ ERA SEL 98476 [ADD]
Bartók, B.:Hungarian Peasant Songs Erato 4–▲ ERA SEL 98476 [ADD]
Bartók, B.:Rhap 1 Vc, w. János Starker (vc) Mercury Living Presence ▲ 434358–2
Brahms, J.:Pieces Pno, Op. 118 Erato 4–▲ ERA SEL 98476 [ADD]
Brahms, J.:Son 1 Vc, w. Janos Starker (vc) Mercury Living Presence ▲ 434377–2
Brahms, J.:Son 2 Vc, w. Janos Starker (vc) Mercury Living Presence ▲ 434377–2
Brahms, J.:Vars & Fugue on a Theme by Handel Erato 4–▲ ERA SEL 98476 [ADD]
Brahms, J.:Waltzes Pno, Op. 39 Erato 4–▲ ERA SEL 98476 [ADD]
Chopin, F.:Barcarolle Pno Erato 4–▲ ERA SEL 98476 [ADD]
Chopin, F.:Intro & Polonaise, "Polonaise brilliante", w. János Starker (vc) Mercury Living Presence ▲ 434358–2
Chopin, F.:Polonaises (misc)—Op. 40/1 [Military] Erato 4–▲ ERA SEL 98476 [ADD]
Chopin, F.:Son Vc, w. János Starker (vc) Mercury Living Presence ▲ 434358–2
Chopin, F.:Son Pno, Op. 35 Erato 4–▲ ERA SEL 98476 [ADD]
Chopin, F.:Son Pno, Op. 58 Erato 4–▲ ERA SEL 98476 [ADD]
Debussy, C.:Images (6) Pno—Set 1 Erato 4–▲ ERA SEL 98476 [ADD]
Debussy, C.:Son Vc, w. János Starker (vc) Mercury Living Presence ▲ 434358–2
Debussy, C.:Suite bergamasque Erato 4–▲ ERA SEL 98476 [ADD]
Janos Starker Plays, w. Janos Starker (vc) *(rec Apr. 16 & 17, 1963 – June)* Mercury Living Presence ▲ 434344–2
Liszt, F.:Pno Music (misc)—Son in b; Funérailles [Harmonie poétique et religieuse No. 7]; Csárdás macabre; Mephisto Waltz; Rhap espagnole Erato 4–▲ ERA SEL 98476 [ADD]
Martinů, B.:Vars on a Theme by Rossini, w. János Starker (vc) Mercury Living Presence ▲ 434358–2
Mendelssohn, F.:Son 2 Vc, w. Janos Starker (vc) Mercury Living Presence ▲ 434377–2
Mendelssohn, F.:Vars concertantes, w. János Starker (vc) Mercury Living Presence ▲ 434358–2
Weiner, L.:Hungarian Wedding Dance, w. János Starker (vc) Mercury Living Presence ▲ 434358–2

Sebon, Karl–Bernhard (fl)—see also ORCHESTRAS & ENSEMBLES Sebon Quartet
Bach, Joh. Christian:Con Fl, w. H. Müller–Brühl (cnd), Cologne CO Koch Schwann ▲ CD 311081 [ADD]
Casella, A.:Sicilienne et burlesque Pno Trio, w. U. Lajovic (cnd), Berlin RSO [arr flute & orchestra] *(rec 1981)* Koch Treasure ▲ 316132 [ADD]
Chaminade, C.:Concertino Fl, w. U. Lajovic (cnd), Berlin RSO Koch Treasure ▲ 316132 [ADD]

Sebon, Karl–Bernhard (fl) (cont.)
Donizetti, G.:Concertinos (4) solo Winds, w. J. Fadle (cl), G. Passin (ob/ob d'amore), J. Starek (cnd), Berlin RIAS Sinfonietta *(rec 1979)* Koch Schwann ▲ CD 311 121 [ADD/DDD]
Doppler, A.F.:Fant pastorale hongroise, w. U. Lajovic (cnd), Berlin RSO Koch Treasure ▲ 316132 [ADD]
Kelemen, M.:Passionato, w. Heinz Mende (cnd), Bavarian Radio Chorus *(rec Munich, Germany, May 18, 1979)* BIS ▲ CD 742 [AAD]
Popp, W.:Fant brillante, w. U. Lajovic (cnd), Berlin RSO Koch Treasure ▲ 316132 [ADD]
Saint–Saëns, C.:Tarantelle Fl, w. J. Fadle (cl), U. Lajovic (cnd), Berlin RSO [flute, clarinet & orchestra arr.] Koch Treasure ▲ 316132 [ADD]

Sebring, R. (hn)
Mozart, W.A.:Qnt Pno, K.452, w. P. Serkin (pno), A. Genovese (ob), H. Wright (cl), F. Svoboda (bn) *(rec Aug. 1992)* Boston Records ▲ BR 1004

Séché, M. (bn)—see also ORCHESTRAS & ENSEMBLES Bonn Telemann Ensemble
Telemann, G.P.:Son Bn, w. B. Wicke (org) *(rec 1992)* FSM ▲ FCD 97759 [DDD]

Secondi, Mario de (vc)—see ORCHESTRAS & ENSEMBLES Opus 8 Trio

Sedivy, Zdenek (tpt)
Albinoni, T.:Con Tpt, Strs & Continuo, w. P. Škvor (cnd), Philharmonic CO Panton ▲ PAN 811023
Fasch, J.F.:Con Tpt & 2 Obs, w. Frantisek Kimel (ob), Ivan Sequardt (ob), P. Škvor (cnd), Philharmonic CO Panton ▲ PAN 811023
Korte, O.:Con grosso, w. Miroslav Kejmar (tpt), Josef Hála (pno), J. Belohlávek (cnd), Czech PO *(rec House of Artists, Prague, Dec. 2–4, 1987)* Panton ▲ PAN 811257 [DDD]
Telemann, G.P.:Con Tpt 2 Obs, w. Frantisek Kimel (ob), Ivan Sequardt (ob), P. Škvor (cnd), Philharmonic CO Panton ▲ PAN 811023
Telemann, G.P.:Con Tpt Strs in D, w. P. Škvor (cnd), Philharmonic CO Panton ▲ PAN 811023
Torelli, G.:Sons à 5 Tpts, w. P. Škvor (cnd), Philharmonic CO—Nos. 1 & 7 Panton ▲ PAN 811023
Vejvanovsky, P.J.:Sons & Serenades, w. M. Kejmar (tpt), L. Pešek (cnd), Prague CO—Serenades in A & C; Sonata a 4; Sonata a 5; Sonata Secunda a 6; Sonata Venatoria in D; Sonata Vespertina a 8 Supraphon ▲ 10 3593 [DDD]
Veracini, F.M.:Con Tpt, w. P. Škvor (cnd), Philharmonic CO Panton ▲ PAN 811023

See, Janet (fl)
Bach, J.S.:A Musical Offering, w. D. Moroney (hpd), J. Holloway (vn), J. ter Linden (vc), M. Cook (hpd) Harmonia Mundi France ▲ HMC 901260 [DDD]
Bach, J.S.:Partita Fl, BWV 1013 Harmonia Mundi USA 2–▲ HMU 907024/25 2–
Bach, J.S.:Sons Fl, BWV 1030–35, w. D. Moroney (hpd), M. Springfels (vl)—includes alternate manuscript solo flute version of BWV 1033 Harmonia Mundi USA 2–▲ HMU 907024/25 2–
Bach, J.S.:Sons Vn, w. D. Moroney (hpd), M. Springfels (vl)—BWV 1020 [doubtful; trans. for flute & continuo] Harmonia Mundi USA 2–▲ HMU 907024/25 2–
Geminiani, F.:The Enchanted Forest, w. Elizabeth Wilcock (vn), Stanley Ritchie (vn), Susie Napper (vc), Barbara Kallaur (fl), Patrick Wedd (hpd), J.E. Gardiner (cnd), CBC Vancouver SO CBC ▲ 5163 [DDD]
Vivaldi, A.:Cons Fl (misc), w. N. McGegan (cnd), Philharmonia Baroque Orch—RV.427–429, 436, 438 & 440 Harmonia Mundi France ▲ HMC 905193 [DDD]
Vivaldi, A.:Cons Fl, Op. 10, w. N. McGegan (cnd), Philharmonia Baroque Orch Harmonia Mundi ▲ HMX 2905193
Vivaldi, A.:Con for 2 Fls, w. S. Schultz (fl), N. McGegan (cnd), Philharmonia Baroque Orch Harmonia Mundi France ▲ HMC 905193 [DDD]

Seebass, Stephan (pno)
Foss, L.:Pieces (3) Fl & Pno, w. Brooks de Wetter–Smith (fl) Crystal ▲ CD 318
Gaubert, P.:Son 1 Fl, w. Brooks de Wetter–Smith (fl) Crystal ▲ CD 318
Pierné, G.:Son Vn, w. Brooks de Wetter–Smith (fl) Crystal ▲ CD 318
Reynolds, V.:Son Fl, w. Brooks de Wetter–Smith (fl) Crystal ▲ CD 318

Seeman, Carl (pno)
Hindemith, P.:Klaviermusik Book 1 *(rec 1960 & 1963)* Koch Schwann ▲ SCH 315702
Hindemith, P.:Sons Pno—No. 3 *(rec 1960 & 1963)* Koch Schwann ▲ SCH 315702

Segal, Peter (gtr)
Jane's Hand:The Jane Austen Songbooks, w. Julianne Baird (sop), Elizabeth Henreckson–Farnum (sop), Lorie Gratis (mez), Daniel Pincus (ten), Philip Anderson (ten), Martil Dillon (ten), Nancy Wilson (bar vn), Mary Jane Newman (pno/hpd), Anthony Newman (pno) Vox Classics ▲ VOX 7537 [DDD]

Segall, Bernardo (pno)
Liszt, F.:Totentanz, w. O. Klemperer (cnd), Los Angeles PO Grammofono 2000 ▲ GRM 78643

Seger, Otto (pno)
Marti, H.:Correspondance (...à la sourdine), w. I. Mathieu (vn) Grammont ▲ CTS P 22–2 [ADD]

Segerstam, Hannele (vn)—see also ORCHESTRAS & ENSEMBLES Segerstam String Quartet
Bergman, E.:Con Vn, w. L. Segerstam (cnd), Finnish RSO BIS ▲ CD 326
Hämeenniemi, E.:Con Vn, w. J.–P. Saraste (cnd), Finnish RSO Ondine ▲ ODE 835 [DDD]
Nordgren, P.H.:Con 2 Vn, w. L. Segerstam (cnd), Finnish RSO BIS ▲ CD 326
Schmitt, F.:Habeyssée, w. L. Segerstam (cnd), Rhineland–Palatinate State PO *(rec Philharmonie Hall, Ludwigshafen, Germany, Sept. 14, 1988)* Marco Polo ▲ 8.223689 [DDD]
Segerstam, L.:Con 1 Vn, w. L. Segerstam (cnd), Finnish RSO BIS ▲ CD 326
Segerstam, L.:Con 1 Vn, w. L. Segerstam (cnd), Austrian RSO BIS ▲ CD 84 [AAD]
Segerstam, L.:Con–Fant Vn, w. R. Keuschnig (pno), L. Segerstam (cnd), ORF SO Kontrapunkt ▲ KPT 32184 [DDD]
Segerstam, L.:Epitaph 6, w. Pia Segerstam (vc), L. Segerstam (cnd), Malmö SO Ondine ▲ ODE CD 877
Segerstam, L.:Skizzen aus Pandora, w. L. Segerstam (cnd), Austrian RSO BIS ▲ CD 84 [AAD]
Segerstam, L.:3 Moments Parting, w. R. Gothóni (pno) BIS ▲ CD 84 [AAD]

Segerstam, Leif (pno)
Segerstam, L.:Rituals in La, w. Lasse Werner (pno) *(rec Swedish Broadcasting Co. Studio 4, Stockholm, Sweden, Oct 15, 1974)* BIS ▲ CD 20 [AAD]
Segerstam, L.:7 Questions to Infinity *(rec Paris, Feb 28, 1996)* BIS ▲ CD 792 [DDD]

Segerstam, Leif (vn)—see ORCHESTRAS & ENSEMBLES Segerstam String Quartet

Segerstam, Pia (vc)
Segerstam, L.:A"on m...på..m–poème"–now..., w. Christophe Sirodeau (pno) *(rec Paris, Feb 28, 1996)* BIS ▲ CD 792 [DDD]
Segerstam, L.:At the Border, w. Christophe Sirodeau (pno) *(rec Paris, Mar 1, 1996)* BIS ▲ CD 792 [DDD]
Segerstam, L.:Epitaph 6, w. Hannele Segerstam (vn), L. Segerstam (cnd), Malmö SO Ondine ▲ ODE CD 877
Segerstam, L.:Noem 1, w. Nikolaos Samaltanos (pno) *(rec Paris, Feb 28, 1996)* BIS ▲ CD 792 [DDD]
Segerstam, L.:Noem 11 *(rec Paris, June 17, 1995)* BIS ▲ CD 792 [DDD]

Segovia, Andrés (gtr)
Andrés Segovia, w. Andrés Segovia (gtr) Enterprise ("Sirio" series) ▲ ENT SO 53002
Bach, J.S.:Music of—Cello Suite No. 3, BWV 1009 (arr. Duarte); selections from Violin Partitas No. 1 (Sarabande, Bourrée, Double), No. 2 (Chaconne) & No. 3 (Gavotte en rondeau); 3 Pieces for Lute (Allemande, Sarabande, Gigue); Prelude for Lute; Siciliano (from Violin Sonata No. 1) *(rec 1952–1968)* MCA Classics ▲ MCAD 2068 [AAD] ■ MCAC 42068
Bach, J.S.:Sons & Partitas Vn, BWV 1001–1006—Gavotte en Rondeau [from Partita No. 3, BWV 1006; arr for gtr] *(rec May 2, 1927)* Iron Needle ▲ IN 1347 (m) [ADD]
Bach, J.S.:Suites Vc, BWV 1007–1012—Prélude [from Suite in G, BWV 1007; arr for gtr] *(rec Apr 2, 1935)* Iron Needle ▲ IN 1347 (m) [ADD]
Castelnuovo–Tedesco, M.:Son Cl & Pno MCA ■ MCAC 2523
The EMI Recordings, 1927–1939:Vol. 1 EMI Classics ("Great Recordings of the Century" series) ▲ CDH 61048 (m)
The EMI Recordings, 1927–1939:Vol. 2 EMI Classics ("Great Recordings of the Century" series) ▲ CDH 61049 (m)
Froberger, J.J.:Hpd Music—Gigue [arr for gtr] *(rec Jan 17, 1939)* Iron Needle ▲ IN 1347 (m) [ADD]
Guitar Recital Ermitage ▲ ERM 131 [ADD]
Guitar Recital *(rec live, Locarno, Italy, 10/3/68)lite□* Ermitage ▲ ERM 119 [ADD]
Malats, J.:Impresiones de España—Serenata [arr for gtr] *(rec Oct 6, 1930)* Iron Needle ▲ IN 1347 (m) [ADD]

Segovia, Andrés (gtr) (cont.)
Ponce, M.:Gtr Music—Suite in A; Folies d'Espagne; Son No. 3; Postlude; Mazurka; Petite Valse *(rec Oct 6–7, 1930 & Apr 9, 19)* Iron Needle ▲ IN 1347 (m) [ADD]
Ponce, M.:Son clásica Gtr MCA ■ MCAC 2532
Ponce, M.:Son 1 Gtr MCA ■ MCAC 2532
The Segovia Collection, Vol. 1
The Segovia Collection, Vol. 2 MCA Classics ▲ MCAD 42067 ■ MCAC 42067
The Segovia Collection, Vol. 3 MCA Classics ▲ MCAD 42069 ■ MCAC 42069
The Segovia Collection, Vol. 4:The Baroque Guitar *(rec 1952 & 1960–69)lite□*
MCA Classics ▲ MCAD 42070 (m/s) [ADD] ■ MCAC 42070 (m/s)
The Segovia Collection, Vol. 5:Spanish Guitar MCA Classics ▲ MCAD 42071 ■ MCAC 42071
The Segovia Collection, Vol. 6:Ponce Sonatas MCA Classics ▲ MCAD 42072 ■ MCAC 42072
The Segovia Collection, Vol. 7:Guitar Etudes MCA Classics ▲ MCAD 42073 ■ MCAC 42073
The Segovia Collection, Vol. 8:Castelnuovo-Tedesco MCA Classics ▲ MCAD 10056 ■ MCAC 10056
The Segovia Collection, Vol. 9:The Romantic Guitar *(rec 1952–1969)*
MCA Classics ▲ MCAD 10281 (m/s) [AAD]
Segovia Rarities Theorema ▲ TH 121223
Sor, F.:Gtr Music—3 pieces MCA ■ MCAC 2532
Strictly Virtuosity, w. John Williams (gtr) Takoma ▲ CDP 72899
Tárrega, F.:Gtr Music—Etude in A *(rec Apr 9, 1935)* Iron Needle ▲ IN 1347 (m) [ADD]

Segre, Emanuele (gtr)
Castelnuovo-Tedesco, M.:Con 1 Gtr, w. G. Noseda (cnd), Milan Giuseppe Verdi Large SO *(rec live, Sala Verdi del Conservatorio, Milan, Dec 1, 2 & 4, 1994)* Claves ▲ CD 9516 [DDD]
Françaix, J.:Con Gtr, w. H. Richter (cnd), Southwest German CO Pforzheim
Wergo ▲ WER 6198-2 [AAD]
Giuliani, M.:Gtr Music—Rossiniana, Op. 119, No. 1; Giulianate, Op. 148 Claves ▲ CD 9303 [DDD]
Paganini, N.:Gtr Music—Sonata, M.S. 87; Sonata 33, M.S. 84; Grand Sonata, M.S. 3
Claves ▲ CD 9303 [DDD]
Rodrigo, J.:Concierto de Aranjuez, w. G. Noseda (cnd), Milan Giuseppe Verdi Large SO *(rec live, Sala Verdi del Conservatorio, Milan, Dec 1, 2 & 4, 1994)* Claves ▲ CD 9516 [DDD]
Rossini, G.:Ovs [trans. by Mauro Giuliani]—Semiramide Claves ▲ CD 9303 [DDD]
Villa-Lobos, H.:Con Gtr, w. G. Noseda (cnd), Milan Giuseppe Verdi Large SO *(rec live, Sala Verdi del Conservatorio, Milan, Dec 1, 2 & 4, 1994)* Claves ▲ CD 9516 [DDD]

Sehnoutka, Miroslav (va)—see also ORCHESTRAS & ENSEMBLES Musiktage Mondsee Ensemble, Panocha String Quartet
Dvořák, A.:Qnt Strs, Op. 77, w. J. Panocha (vn), P. Zejfart (vn), J. Kulhan (vc), P. Nejtek (db)
Supraphon ▲ SUP 11 1461 [DDD]

Seidel, Andreas (vn)—see also ORCHESTRAS & ENSEMBLES Leipzig String Quartet
Brown, E.:Tracking Pierrot, w. Josef Christof (pno) *(rec Sender Freies Berlin, Jan 16–17, 1995)*
Hat Hut ("Now" series) ▲ CD 6177 [DDD]

Seidel, Doug (gtr/congas)
Exquisite Corpses from P.S. 122, w. Watson, David (shears/stick vn/gtr/tpt), Judy Dunaway (gtr/balloons), Anthony Coleman (sampler), Raissa St. Pierre (drums), Guy Yarden (vn/pno), Leslie Ross (bn), Linda Austin (gtr), Bruce Kaplan (gtr), Doug Henderson (peckhorn/bass/toy pno), Sue Ann Harkey (gtr), Cinnie Cole (sampler), et. al. ¿What Next? ▲ WN 0002 [ADD]

Seidel, Toscha (vn)
Brahms, J.:Son 1 Vn, w. A. Loesser (pno) *(rec 1931)* Biddulph ▲ LAB 013 [ADD]
Brahms, J.:Son 2 Vn, w. A. Loesser (pno) *(rec 1926)* Biddulph ▲ LAB 013 [ADD]
Grieg, E.:Sons Vn, Opp. 8, 13 & 45, w. A. Loesser (pno)—No. 3 in c, Op. 45 *(rec 1929)*
Biddulph ▲ LAB 013 [ADD]

Seidenberg, Danny (va)—see ORCHESTRAS & ENSEMBLES Turtle Island String Quartet

Seidler, Reinmar (vc)—see also ORCHESTRAS & ENSEMBLES Renaissonics
Lovenstein, J.:Music of, w. Mary Brockenbrough (sop), Laura Sanders (sop), Barton Green (ten), Rockland Osgood (ten), David Murray (bar), Benjamin Sears (bar), Jonathan Lovenstein (pno), Heather O'Donnell (pno), James Silvers (pno), Rocy Reider (fl), Jason Horowitz (vn), Adrianna Hulscher (vn), James Johnston (vn), Mimi Ragson (vn), Peter Landeen (vc)—Blake Songs; other works
Titanic ▲ Ti 221 [DDD]

Seidler-Winkler, Bruno (pno)
Sings Select Lieder, w. Helge Rosvaenge (ten), Gerald Moore (pno), Michael Raucheisen (pno) *(rec 1936–44)* Preiser ▲ PRE CD 89992

Seidlhofer, B. (hpd)
Bach, J.S.:Christmas Oratorio, w. E. Roon (sop), D.H. Braun (mez), E. Majkut (ten), W. Berry (bass), L. Dutoit (echo), J. Nebois (org), F. Grossmann (cnd), Vienna SO, Akademie Chamber Choir
Vox Box 2-▲ CDX 5096 [ADD]

Seifert, Eckhard (vn)—see ORCHESTRAS & ENSEMBLES Vienna Ring Ensemble

Seifert, Gerd (hn)—see also ORCHESTRAS & ENSEMBLES Berlin PO Horns
Mozart, W.A.:Qnt Hn, K.407, w. Amadeus String Quartet
Deutsche Grammophon 2-▲ 437137-2 [ADD]
Strauss, R.:Con 1 Hn, w. Z. Mehta (cnd), Berlin PO Sony Classical ▲ SK 45800 [DDD]

Seifert, Ingrid (vn)—see ORCHESTRAS & ENSEMBLES London Baroque

Seiger, Joseph (pno)
Hebrew & Russian Melodies, w. Mischa Elman (vn) *(rec 1959, 1962 & 1966)*
Vanguard Classics ▲ OVC 8030 [ADD]

Seiler, Erich (perc)
Bartók, B.:Son for 2 Pnos, w. M. Bergmann (pno), H. Rosbaud (pno), W. Grabinger (perc) *(rec live, 1953)*
Music & Arts ▲ CD 627 (m) [AAD]

Seiler, Mayumi (vn)—see also ORCHESTRAS & ENSEMBLES Schubert Ensemble of London
Beethoven, L. van:Con Vn, Op. 61, w. R. Hickox (cnd), City of London Sinfonia
Virgin Classics ("Ultraviolet" series) ▲ CUV 61117
Gisberg:Music of, w. Gisburg (sgr/fl), Jeff O'Malley (nar), Ron Lawrence (va), Guy Tyler (db), Anthony Coleman (pno), Christine Bard (perc)—Low-End; Since You Have Left; The Woman Is Perfected; Sharks; Night & Wind; Saturnspacemonsters Walking on a Sandy Surface; Old Moon in Winter; Never Saw the Stars So Bright; Habe Die Liebe Verschlafen; W.A.L.S.H. Tzadik ▲ TZA CD 7019 [DDD]

Séjourne, Emmanuel (perc)
Guyonnet, J.:La Cantate interrompue, w. F. Rochaix (nar), S. Stenhammar (sop), S. Seban (pno), G. Calame (pno), E. Séjourne (perc), P. Geiss, E. Tarr (tpt), B. Nilsson (tpt), H. Ries (trbn), H. Rückert (trbn), J.-M. Collet, J. Guyonnet (cnd), Geneva Collegium Academicum [F] *(rec Nov. 15, 1986)*
Grammont ▲ CTSP 30-2

Sekerkaran, Kâmil (fl)
Sinangil, A.D.:Mevlâna Oratorio (sels), w. Leyla Demiris (sop), Isin Güyer (mez), Mesut Iktu (bar), Mustafa Iktu (bass), A. D. Sinangil (cnd), Istanbul State Opera Orch, Istanbul State Opera Chorus—Récitatif I; Choral; Récitatif II; V^e partie Gallo ▲ CD 836 [ADD]

Sektberg, William (pno)
On Tour in Russia, w. Leonard Warren (bar) RCA Gold Seal ▲ 7807-2-RG (m) [ADD]

Selby, Kathryn (pno)
Gershwin, G.:Con Pno, w. R. Hayman (cnd), Czech-Slovak RSO *(rec 6/89)* Naxos ▲ 8.550295 [DDD]
Gershwin, G.:Rhap in Blue, w. R. Hayman (cnd), Czech-Slovak RSO *(rec 6/89)*
Naxos ▲ 8.550295 [DDD]
Martinů, B.:Qt Ob, w. Joel Marangella (ob), Charmian Gadd (vn), Alexander Ivashkin (vc) *(rec Australian Festival of Chamber Music, July 1994)* Naxos ▲ 8.553916 [DDD]

Self, Jim (tuba)
Changing Colors Summit ▲ DCD 132 [DDD]

Seligman, Susan (vc)
Starer, R.:Elegy for a Woman Who Died Too Young, w. Carole Cowan (vn) Albany ▲ TROY 152 [DDD]

Selig-Plaskurova, Elisabeth (vn)
Purcell, H.:Sons (12) Vns, Z.790–801, w. Viktor Simcisko (vn), Dusan Dockal (vc), Marica Dobiasova (hpd)—Nos. 1–3 *(rec Bratislava, 1994)* Discover International ▲ DI 920251 [DDD]
Purcell, H.:Sons (10) Vns, Z.802–811, w. Viktor Simcisko (vn), Dusan Dockal (vc), Marica Dobiasova (hpd)—Nos. 2, 3, 5, 6 & 9 *(rec Bratislava, 1994)* Discover International ▲ DI 920251 [DDD]

Selin, Elisabeth (rcr)
Telemann, G.P.:Sons Vn, Op. 2, w. M. Petri (rcr) RCA Red Seal ▲ 7903-2-RC [DDD]

Sella, Amir (fl)
Martin, F.:Sonnets à Cassandre, w. U. Mayer-Reinach (mez), G. Lewertoff (va), N. Enoch (vc)
Gallo ▲ CD 633 [DDD]

Sellheim, Eckart (pno)
Mendelssohn, F.:Vars concertantes, w. F.-J. Sellheim (vc)
Sony Classical ("Essential Classics" series) ▲ SBK 48171 ■ SBT 48171
Schubert, Franz:Son Arpeggione, w. F.-J. Sellheim (vc) *(rec 1978)*
Sony Classical ("Essential Classics" series) ▲ SBK 48171 ■ SBT 48171
Schumann, R.:Fantasiestücke Cl, w. F.-J. Sellheim (vc) [cello & piano] *(rec 1978)*
Sony Classical ("Essential Classics" series) ▲ SBK 48171 ■ SBT 48171
Schumann, R.:Stücke im Volkston, w. F.-J. Sellheim (vc) *(rec 1978)*
Sony Classical ("Essential Classics" series) ▲ SBK 48171 ■ SBT 48171
Tower, J.:Clarinet Con, w. R. Spring (cl) Summit ▲ DCD 124 [DDD]
Tower, J.:Fant Cl, w. R. Spring (cl) Summit ▲ DCD 124 [DDD]

Sellheim, Friedrich-Jürgen (vc)
Mendelssohn, F.:Vars concertantes, w. E. Sellheim (pno)
Sony Classical ("Essential Classics" series) ▲ SBK 48171 ■ SBT 48171
Schubert, Franz:Son Arpeggione, w. E. Sellheim (pno) *(rec 1978)*
Sony Classical ("Essential Classics" series) ▲ SBK 48171 ■ SBT 48171
Schumann, R.:Fantasiestücke Cl, w. E. Sellheim (pno) [cello & piano] *(rec 1978)*
Sony Classical ("Essential Classics" series) ▲ SBK 48171 ■ SBT 48171
Schumann, R.:Stücke im Volkston, w. E. Sellheim (pno) *(rec 1978)*
Sony Classical ("Essential Classics" series) ▲ SBK 48171 ■ SBT 48171

Sellick, Phyllis (pno)
Arnold, M.:Con for 2 Pnos, w. C. Smith (pno), M. Arnold (cnd), City of Birmingham SO
EMI Classics ▲ CDM 64044-2
Fauré, G.:Dolly, w. C. Smith (pno) Nimbus ▲ NI 5178 (m) [AAD]
Franck, C.:Prélude, choral et fugue, w. C. Smith (pno) [piano duet version]
Nimbus ▲ NI 5178 (m) [AAD]
Mendelssohn, F.:Allegro brillant, w. C. Smith (pno) Nimbus ▲ NI 5178 (m) [AAD]
Schubert, Franz:Fant Pno, D.940, w. C. Smith (pno) Nimbus ▲ NI 5178 (m) [AAD]
Schubert, Franz:Son Pno, D.617, w. C. Smith (pno) Nimbus ▲ NI 5178 (m) [AAD]

Selmeczi, János (vn)—see ORCHESTRAS & ENSEMBLES Éder String Quartet

Seltzer, Cheryl (pno)—see also ORCHESTRAS & ENSEMBLES Continuum Chamber Ensemble
Lennon, J.A.:Ballade Belliss', w. M. Wu (vn) CRI ▲ CD 599 [ADD/DDD]
Moss, L.:Songs of the Earth, w. Nan Hughes (mez), Mark Steinberg (vn), David Krakauer (cl), Joel Sachs (pno) Capstone ▲ CPS 8619

Sempé, Skip (hpd)
Couperin, F.:L'Art de toucher le clavecin—(6) in C, d, g, A, B♭ & F
Deutsche Harmonia Mundi ▲ 77219-2-RC [DDD]
Couperin, F.:Pièces de clavecin (sels)—Le Dodo ou L'amour au Berceau
Deutsche Harmonia Mundi ▲ 05472-77315-2 [DDD]
Couperin, F.:Pièces de clavecin (sels)—Book 1:La ténébreuse, allemande; Première courante; Seconde courante; La lugubre, sarabande; L'espagnolète; La favorite, chaconne; La dangereuse, sarabande; Les ondes; Book 2:Les baricades mistérieuses; La Raphaèle; Allemenade l'Ausoniène; Première courante; Seconde courante; Sarabande l'unique; Gavotte; Rondeau; Gigue; Passacaille; Book 3:Le dodo ou L'amour au berçeau; Book 4:L'arlequine; Les vieux seigneurs, sarabande grave
Deutsche Harmonia Mundi ▲ 77219-2-RC [DDD]
Purcell, H.:Music of, w. S. Sempé (cnd), Capriccio Stravagante
Deutsche Harmonia Mundi ▲ 05472-77252-2

Sempé, Skip (hpd/cem)—see ORCHESTRAS & ENSEMBLES Capriccio Stravagante

Sempé, Skip (org)
Italian Arias & Cantatas, w. James Bowman (ct), Jay Bernfeld (va da gamba) *(rec 10/87)*
Arion ▲ ARN 68046 [DDD]

Semper, J. (va)
Suter, R.:Musikalisches Tagesbuch 1, w. B. Geiser-Payer (alt), H. Haldemann (pic/fl), H. Holliger (ob), H. Bochet (bn), J. Joubert (vn), W. Eugster (vc), M. Dellanoy (db) *(rec 1962)*
Grammont ▲ CSTP 6-2 [AAD]

Semyannikov, Alexander (vn)—see ORCHESTRAS & ENSEMBLES Gosteleradio String Quartet

Senft, Enno (db)—see ORCHESTRAS & ENSEMBLES CO of Europe Soloists

Senn, Martin-Ulrich (fl)
Amon, J.A.:Son Fl & Hp, w. C. Mathieu (hp) *(rec 1979)* Jecklin-Disco ▲ JD 548-2 [ADD]
Copland, A.:Duo Fl, w. H. Göbel (pno) Thorofon ▲ CTH 2012 [DDD]
Mahler, G.:Bach Orchestral Works, w. P. Siegele (org), P. Schwarz (hpd), P. Ruzicka (cnd), Berlin RSO
Koch Schwann ▲ 3-1204-2 [ADD]
Spohr, L.:Son 1 Vn, w. C. Mathieu (hp) *(rec 1979)* Jecklin-Disco ▲ JD 548-2 [ADD]
Spohr, L.:Son 5 Vn, w. C. Mathieu (hp) *(rec 1979)* Jecklin-Disco ▲ JD 548-2 [ADD]

Sensi, Roberto (vn)
Weichlein, R.:Encaenia musices, w. Gunar Letzbor (vn), Daniel Sepec (vn), Herbert Lindsberger (va), Christoph Bitzinger (va), Michael Oman (vl), Gaetano Nasillo (vc), Andreas Lackner (nat tpt), Herbert Walser (nat tpt), Norbert Kirchner (hpd/org), G. Letzbor (cnd), Ars Antiqua Austria—Sons. Nos. I in C, II in g, III in a, IV in E, V in C & VI in F Symphonia ▲ SY 93S23

Seow, Yitkin (pno)
Debussy, C.:Son Vc, w. J. L. Webber (vc) ASV Quicksilva ▲ QS 6072 [ADD]
Elgar, E.:Salut d'amour, w. J. L. Webber (vc) ASV Quicksilva ▲ QS 6051 [ADD/DDD]
Rachmaninoff, S.:Pieces Vc, w. J. L. Webber (vc) ASV Quicksilva ▲ QS 6072 [ADD]
Rachmaninoff, S.:Son Vc, w. J. L. Webber (vc) ASV Quicksilva ▲ QS 6072 [ADD]
Romantic Cello, w. Julian Lloyd Webber (vc) ASV ("Quicksilva" series) ▲ ASV 6014 [ADD]

Sepec, Daniel (vn)
Bach, J.S.:Con for 2 Vns, w. Gunar Letzbor (vn), G. Letzbor (cnd), Ars Antiqua Austria
Symphonia ▲ SYM 94134
Weichlein, R.:Encaenia musices, w. Gunar Letzbor (vn), Herbert Lindsberger (va), Christoph Bitzinger (va), Michael Oman (vl), Gaetano Nasillo (vc), Roberto Sensi (vn), Andreas Lackner (nat tpt), Herbert Walser (nat tpt), Norbert Kirchner (hpd/org), G. Letzbor (cnd), Ars Antiqua Austria—Sons. Nos. I in C, II in g, III in a, IV in E, V in C & VI in F Symphonia ▲ SY 93S23

Sequardt, Ivan (ob)
Fasch, J.F.:Con Tpt & 2 Obs, w. Zdenek Sedivy (tpt), Frantisek Kimel (ob), P. Škvor (cnd), Philharmonic CO Panton ▲ PAN 811023
Telemann, G.P.:Con Tpt 2 Obs, w. Zdenek Sedivy (tpt), Frantisek Kimel (ob), P. Škvor (cnd), Philharmonic CO Panton ▲ PAN 811023

Serafini, F. (db)
Caprioli, A.:Dialogue, w. E. Rojatti (cnd), Haydn PO Soloists *(rec 1987)*
Pro Viva ▲ ISPV 148 CD [ADD]

Seraphinoff, Richard (hn)
Dauprat, L.-F.:Melodie Hns, w. Jeffery Snedeker (hn), Marilyn Willbanks (pno) *(rec Univ of MA, Amherst, July 31–Aug 4, 1995)* Snedeker ▲ 001

Serban-Loanid, Constantin (vn)
Berlioz, H.:Rêverie et caprice, w. M. Soustrot (cnd), Loire PO Forlane ▲ FRL 63 [DDD]

Serbescu, Liana (pno)
Mendelssohn, Fanny:Pno Music—Das Jahr (suite of 13 pieces) CPO ▲ CPO 999013-2 [DDD]
Mendelssohn, Fanny:Pno Music—Sonatas in C & G; Sonata movement in E♭; Songs for Piano, Op. 6, Nos. 3 & 4 CPO ▲ CPO 999015-2 [DDD]
Smyth, E.:Pno Music (comp)—4 4-part Dances; Sons 1–3 for Pno; 2 Canons; Invention in D; Suite in E; To Youth!; Piano Piece in E; Vars in D♭ on an Original Theme; 2 Preludes & Fugues
CPO ▲ CPO 999327 [DDD]

▲ = CD ♦ = Enhanced CD Δ = MD ■ = Cassette Tape □ = DCC

Serebryakov, Pavel (pno)
Liszt, F.:Rhap espagnole, w. A. Shereshevsky (cnd), USSR State SO [arr. Busoni for orch.] *(rec 1951)* Multisonic ("Russian Treasures" series) ▲ 31 0190
Liszt, F.:Totentanz, w. A. Shereshevsky (cnd), USSR State SO *(rec 1958)* Multisonic ("Russian Treasures" series) ▲ 31 0190
Rubinstein, A.:Con 4 Pno, w. A. Shereshevsky (cnd), USSR State SO *(rec 1958)* Multisonic ("Russian Treasures" series) ▲ 31 0190
Tchaikovsky, P.:Con 1 Pno, w. E. Mravinsky (cnd), Leningrad PO Multisonic ▲ MUL 310352

Sereque, Christopher (cl)
Dresher, P.:Channels Passing, w. P. Taub (fl), B. Shapiro (ob), R. Pressley (tpt), S. Dempster (trbn), E.M. Gray (vn), W. Gray (vc) *(rec 1983–84)* New Albion ▲ NA 053

Sergeyeva, Tatiana (kbd)
Ryabov, V.:Con da passacaglia, w. V. Igolinsky (vn), S. Kravchenko (vn), V. Zhuk (vn) MCA Classics/Melodiya ▲ MLD 32131 [AAD] ■ MLC 32131

Sergeyeva, Tatiana (pno)
Dmitriev, G.:Fant Vn & Pno, "Warsaw", w. Vladislav Igolinsky (vn) *(rec Large Hall, Moscow Conservatory, 1990)* Russian Compact Disc ▲ RD CD 10003 [AAD]

Serkin, Peter (pno)—see also ORCHESTRAS & ENSEMBLES Tashi
Bach, J.S.:Goldberg Vars *(rec Manhattan Center Studios, New York, June 1–3, 1994)* RCA Red Seal ▲ 09026–68188–2 [DDD]
Bach, J.S.:Goldberg Vars Pro Arte 2–▲ CDD 331
Bach, J.S.:Italian Con *(rec Manhattan Center Studios, New York, June 1–3, 1994)* RCA Red Seal ▲ 09026–68188–2 [DDD]
Beethoven, L. van:Son 29 Pno, "Hammerklavier" Pro Arte ▲ CDD 270 [DDD]
Beethoven, L. van:Son 30 Pno Pro Arte ▲ CDD 362
Beethoven, L. van:Son 31 Pno Pro Arte ▲ CDD 362
Beethoven, L. van:Son 32 Pno Pro Arte ▲ CDD 362
Berio, L.:Feuerklavier *(rec Manhattan Center Studios, New York, June 13–15, 1994)* RCA Red Seal ▲ 09026–68189–2 [DDD]
The Best of Chopin, w. Géza Anda (pno), John Browning (pno), Emanuel Ax (pno), et al. Victrola ("Victrola Best of" series) ▲ 60770–2–RV [ADD] ■ 60770–4–RV
Brahms, J.:Con 1 Pno, w. R. Shaw (cnd), Atlanta SO Pro Arte ▲ CDD 266
Brahms, J.:Con 2 Pno, w. R. Shaw (cnd), Atlanta SO Pro Arte ▲ CDD 336 [DDD]
Brahms, J.:Sons Cl (comp), w. H. Wright (cl) *(rec Aug. 1992)* Boston Records ▲ BR 1005
Chopin, F.:Ballades Pno (comp)—Op. 52 Pro Arte ▲ CDD 246 [DDD]
Chopin, F.:Fant Pro Arte ▲ CDD 246 [DDD]
Chopin, F.:Pno Music (misc)—3 Mazurkas, Op. 63; 3 Waltzes; Ballade in f; Nocturne in B; 4 Mazurkas, Op. 41; Fantasy, Op. 49 Pro Arte ▲ CDD 246 [DDD]
Dvořák, A.:Qnt Pno, Op. 81, w. F. Galimir (vn), A. Schneider (vn), M. Tree (va), D. Soyer (vc) *(rec 1965)* Vanguard Classics ▲ OVC 8003 [ADD]
Goehr, A.:Con Pno, w. O. Knussen (cnd), London Sinfonietta NMC ▲ NMC 23 [DDD]
Goehr, A.:...In Real Time I *(rec Manhattan Center Studios, New York, June 13–15, 1994)* RCA Red Seal ▲ 09026–68189–2 [DDD]
Henze, H.-W.:Pno Music—Piece for Peter *(rec Manhattan Center Studios, New York, June 13–15, 1994)* RCA Red Seal ▲ 09026–68189–2 [DDD]
Ibert, J.:Escales—No. 2 only Boston Records ▲ BR 1004
Kirchner, L.:Interlude Pno *(rec Manhattan Center Studios, New York, June 13–15, 1994)* RCA Red Seal ▲ 09026–68189–2 [DDD]
Knussen, O.:Sonya's Lullaby Virgin Classics ▲ CDC 59308
Knussen, O.:Vars Pno *(rec Manhattan Center Studios, New York, June 13–15, 1994)* RCA Red Seal ▲ 09026–68189–2 [DDD]
Knussen, O.:Vars Pno Virgin Classics ▲ CDC 59308
Knussen, O.:Whitman Settings Sop & Pno, Op. 25, w. L. Shelton (sop) Virgin Classics ▲ CDC 59308
Lieberson, P.:Bagatelles Pno New World ▲ NW 344–2 [DDD] ■ NW 344–4 (D)
Lieberson, P.:Bagatelles Pno *(rec Manhattan Center Studios, New York, May 31, 1995)* RCA Red Seal ▲ 09026–68189–2 [DDD]
Lieberson, P.:Con Pno, w. S. Ozawa (cnd), Boston SO New World ▲ NW 325–2 [DDD]
Lieberson, P.:Fants Pno *(rec Manhattan Center Studios, New York, June 13–15, 1994)* RCA Red Seal ▲ 09026–68189–2 [DDD]
Lieberson, P.:Garland *(rec Manhattan Center Studios, New York, June 13–15, 1994)* RCA Red Seal ▲ 09026–68189–2 [DDD]
Lieberson, P.:King Gesar, w. Yo-Yo Ma (vc), Emanuel Ax (pno), Omar Ebrahim (nar), Andras Adorjan (fl), Deborah Marshall (cl), William Purvis (hn), David Taylor (trbn), Stefan Huge (perc) Sony Classical ▲ SK 57971
Loeffler, C.M.:Rhaps, w. A. Genovese (ob), B. Fine (va) *(rec Aug. 1992)* Boston Records ▲ BR 1004
Mozart, W.A.:Con 10 Pnos, w. R. Serkin (pno), A. Schneider (cnd), Marlboro Festival Orch *(rec 1962)* Sony Classical ▲ SMK 46255 [ADD]
Mozart, W.A.:Con 10 Pnos, w. R. Serkin (pno), A. Schneider (cnd), Marlboro Festival Orch Sony Classical 3–▲ SM3K 47207
Mozart, W.A.:Con 18 Pno, w. A. Schneider (cnd), English CO RCA Silver Seal ▲ 60790–2 [ADD] ■ 60790–4
Mozart, W.A.:Con 21 Pno, w. C. Abbado (cnd), London SO Deutsche Grammophon ▲ 410068–2 [DDD]
Mozart, W.A.:Con 21 Pno, w. C. Abbado (cnd), London SO Deutsche Grammophon ("3D Classics" series) ▲ 431278–2 [DDD]
Mozart, W.A.:Con 23 Pno, w. C. Abbado (cnd), London SO Deutsche Grammophon ▲ 410068–2 [DDD]
Mozart, W.A.:Qts Pno, w. A. Schneider (vn), M. Tree (va), D. Soyer (vc) *(rec 1965)* Vanguard Classics ▲ OVC 8007 [ADD]
Mozart, W.A.:Qnt Pno, K.452, w. A. Genovese (ob), H. Wright (cl), R. Sebring (hn), F. Svoboda (bn) *(rec Aug. 1992)* Boston Records ▲ BR 1004
Out Classics, w. Ofra Harnoy (vc), Richard Stoltzman (cl), Leonard Slatkin (cnd), London PO, et al. RCA Red Seal ▲ 09026–68261–2 ■ 09026–68261–4
Poulenc, F.:Son Ob, w. A. Genovese (ob) *(rec Aug. 1992)* Boston Records ▲ BR 1004
Schubert, Franz:Qnt Pno, D.667, w. A. Schneider (vn), M. Tree (va), D. Soyer (vc), J. Levine (db) *(rec 1964)* Vanguard Classics ▲ OVC 8005 [ADD]
Schubert, Franz:Son Vn, D.574, w. A. Schneider (vn) Vanguard Classics ▲ OVC 8005 [ADD]
Schumann, R.:Fantasiestücke Cl, w. H. Wright (cl) *(rec Aug. 1992)* Boston Records ▲ BR 1005
Schumann, R.:Qnt Pno, w. Budapest String Quartet CBS ▲ MYK 37256 [ADD] ■ MYT 37256
Schumann, R.:Romances Ob, w. A. Genovese (ob) *(rec Aug. 1992)* Boston Records ▲ BR 1004
Stravinsky, I.:Serenade Pno New World ▲ NW 344–2 [DDD] ■ NW 344–4 (D)
Stravinsky, I.:Son Pno New World ▲ NW 344–2 [DDD] ■ NW 344–4 (D)
Takemitsu, T.:Music of, w. Tashi, Y. Nagano (mez), H. Ibe (gtr), M. Nagasako (hp), K. Abe (vib), Y. Takahashi (pno), R. Noguchi (fl), M. Hamada (lt), T. Koizumi (picc), S. Ueki (vn), Y. Hattori (vc), R. Stoltzman (cl), Ozawa, Wakasugi (cnd), Boston SO—Quatrain; Stanza I; Sacrifice; Ring; Valeria; A Flock Descends into the Pentagonal Garden Deutsche Grammophon ("20th Century Classics" series) ▲ 423253–2 [ADD]
Takemitsu, T.:Pno Music—Litany; Uninterrupted Rest; Pno Distance; For Away; Les Yeux clos; Rain Tree Sketch; Les Yeux clos II; Rain Tree Sketch II *(rec New York, 1978–1996)* RCA Red Seal ▲ 09026–68595–2 [DDD/ADD]
Takemitsu, T.:Pno Music—Les yeux clos II *(rec Manhattan Center Studios, New York, June 13–15, 1994)* RCA Red Seal ▲ 09026–68189–2 [DDD]
Wolpe, S.:Form IV:Broken Sequences New World ▲ NW 344–2 [DDD] ■ NW 344–4 (D)
Wolpe, S.:Passacaglia New World ▲ NW 344–2 [DDD] ■ NW 344–4 (D)
Wolpe, S.:Pastorale New World ▲ NW 344–2 [DDD] ■ NW 344–4 (D)

Serkin, Rudolf (pno)—see also ORCHESTRAS & ENSEMBLES Adolf Busch Chamber Players
Bach, J.S.:Goldberg Vars [WELTE-MIGNON piano rolls] *(rec ca 1928)* Archipon ▲ ARC 105 [DDD]

Serkin, Rudolf (pno) (cont.)
Bach, J.S.:Sons Vn, w. Adolf Busch (vn)—in g, BWV 1001; in E, BWV 1016 Music & Arts 3–▲ CD 877 [ADD]
Bach, J.S.:Sons Vn, w. A. Busch (vn)—BWV 1021 & 1929 Pearl ▲ PEA 9942 (m) [AAD]
Beethoven, L. van:Bagatelles (24)—Op. 119 *(rec 1966)* Sony Masterworks ("Portrait" series) ▲ MPK 44837 [ADD]
Beethoven, L. van:Cons Pno (comp), w. S. Ozawa (cnd), Boston SO Telarc 3–▲ CD 80061 [DDD]
Beethoven, L. van:Con 1 Pno, w. E. Ormandy (cnd), Philadelphia Orch CBS ▲ MYK 37807 [ADD]
Beethoven, L. van:Con 1 Pno, w. G. Cantelli (cnd), New York PO *(rec live 3/29/53)* Melodram ▲ MEL 18010
Beethoven, L. van:Con 1 Pno, w. R. Kubelik (cnd), Bavarian RSO *(rec live, 1968)* AS Disc ▲ ASD 2603
Beethoven, L. van:Con 1 Pno, w. R. Kubelik (cnd), Bavarian RSO *(rec live 1977)* Artists ▲ FED 67 [ADD]
Beethoven, L. van:Con 1 Pno, w. E. Ormandy (cnd), Philadelphia Orch CBS ▲ MK 42259
Beethoven, L. van:Con 2 Pno, w. S. Ozawa (cnd), Boston SO Telarc ▲ CD 80064 [DDD]
Beethoven, L. van:Con 2 Pno, w. R. Kubelik (cnd), Bavarian RSO *(rec live 1977)* Artists ▲ FED 67 [ADD]
Beethoven, L. van:Con 2 Pno, w. R. Kubelik (cnd), Bavarian RSO *(rec live, 1968)* AS Disc ▲ ASD 2603
Beethoven, L. van:Con 3 Pno, w. L. Bernstein (cnd), New York PO CBS ▲ MK 42259
Beethoven, L. van:Con 3 Pno, w. L. Bernstein (cnd), New York PO CBS ▲ MYK 38526 [ADD] ■ MYT 38526
Beethoven, L. van:Con 3 Pno, w. L. Bernstein (cnd), New York PO *(rec New York, 1964)* Sony Classical ("Bernstein:The Royal Edition" series) ▲ SMK 47520 [ADD] Δ SM 47520 [ADD]
Beethoven, L. van:Con 3 Pno, w. S. Ozawa (cnd), Boston SO Telarc ▲ CD 80063 [DDD]
Beethoven, L. van:Con 4 Pno, w. S. Ozawa (cnd), Boston SO Telarc ▲ CD 80064 [DDD]
Beethoven, L. van:Con 4 Pno, w. A. Toscanini (cnd), NBC SO RCA Gold Seal ▲ 60268–2–RG ■ 60268–4–RG
Beethoven, L. van:Con 4 Pno, w. B. Walter (cnd), New York PO *(rec 1941)* Historical Performers ▲ HPS 15 [ADD]
Beethoven, L. van:Con 5 Pno, "Emperor", w. L. Bernstein (cnd), New York PO CBS ▲ MYK 37223 ■ MYT 37223
Beethoven, L. van:Con 5 Pno, "Emperor", w. L. Bernstein (cnd), New York PO *(rec New York, May 1, 1962)* Sony Classical ("Bernstein:The Royal Edition" series) ▲ SMK 47520 [ADD] Δ SM 47520 [ADD]
Beethoven, L. van:Con 5 Pno, "Emperor", w. G. Cantelli (cnd), New York PO *(rec live 1954)* Melodram ▲ MEL 18010
Beethoven, L. van:Con 5 Pno, "Emperor", w. S. Ozawa (cnd), Boston SO Telarc ▲ CD 80065 [DDD]
Beethoven, L. van:Con 5 Pno, "Emperor", w. B. Walter (cnd), New York PO *(rec New York, Dec 22, 1941)* Sony Classical ("Bruno Walter:The Edition, Vol. 4" series) ▲ SMK 64489 [ADD]
Beethoven, L. van:Fant Pno, Op. 77 Sony Classical ("Essential Classics" series) ▲ SBK 47666 ■ SBT 47666
Beethoven, L. van:Fant Pno, Op. 80, "Choral Fant", w. L. Bernstein (cnd), New York PO, Westminster Choir [G] CBS ▲ MYK 38526 [ADD] ■ MYT 38526
Beethoven, L. van:Fant Pno, Op. 80, "Choral Fant", w. L. Bernstein (cnd), New York PO, Westminster Choir Sony Classical 2–▲ SM2K 47522 [ADD]
Beethoven, L. van:Fant Pno, Op. 80, "Choral Fant", w. L. Bernstein (cnd), New York PO, New York Phil Chorus Odyssey ■ YT 42485
Beethoven, L. van:Fant Pno, Op. 80, "Choral Fant", w. S. Ozawa (cnd), Boston SO Telarc ▲ CD 80063 [DDD]
Beethoven, L. van:Music of, w. J. O'Conor (pno), Shaw (cnd), Cleveland Orch, Atlanta SO—sels. from Syms. 5,6,7 & 9, Moonlight Son., Pno Con. 5, etc. Telarc ▲ CD 80240 [DDD] ■ CS 30240 (D)
Beethoven, L. van:Qnt Pno, Ob, Cl, Hn & Bn, w. et al. Sony Classical ▲ SMK 47296 [ADD]
Beethoven, L. van:Sons Vc (comp), w. P. Casals (vc) *(rec Perpignan, France; Prades, France)* Sony Classical ("The Casals Edition" series) 2–▲ SM2K 58985 [ADD]
Beethoven, L. van:Son 3 Vc, w. P. Casals (vc) *(rec 1953)* Sony Masterworks ("Portrait" series) ▲ MPK 45682 [ADD]
Beethoven, L. van:Son 4 Vc, w. P. Casals (vc) Sony Masterworks ("Portrait" series) ▲ MPK 45682 [ADD]
Beethoven, L. van:Son 5 Vc, w. P. Casals (vc) Sony Masterworks ("Portrait" series) ▲ MPK 45682 [ADD]
Beethoven, L. van:Son 1 Pno *(rec Oct. 7, 1970)* Sony Classical 3–▲ SM3K 64490 [ADD]
Beethoven, L. van:Son 6 Pno *(rec live 1971, London)* Arkadia ▲ 912 [ADD]
Beethoven, L. van:Son 6 Pno *(rec Oct. 7, 1970)* Sony Classical 3–▲ SM3K 64490 [ADD]
Beethoven, L. van:Son 8 Pno, "Pathétique" *(rec live 1971, London)* Arkadia ▲ 912 [ADD]
Beethoven, L. van:Son 8 Pno, "Pathétique" CBS ▲ MYK 37219 ■ MYT 37219
Beethoven, L. van:Son 8 Pno, "Pathétique" Sony Classical ("Essential Classics" series) ▲ SBK 47666 ■ SBT 47666
Beethoven, L. van:Son 12 Pno, "Funeral March" *(rec live, London 1971)* Arkadia ▲ 911 [ADD]
Beethoven, L. van:Son 12 Pno, "Funeral March" *(rec Dec. 8, 1970)* Sony Classical 3–▲ SM3K 64490 [ADD]
Beethoven, L. van:Son 13 Pno *(rec live 1971, London)* Arkadia ▲ 911 [ADD]
Beethoven, L. van:Son 13 Pno *(rec Dec. 7, 1980)* Sony Classical 3–▲ SM3K 64490 [ADD]
Beethoven, L. van:Son 14 Pno, "Moonlight Son" CBS ▲ MYK 37219 ■ MYT 37219
Beethoven, L. van:Son 16 Pno *(rec Dec. 8, 1970)* Sony Classical 3–▲ SM3K 64490 [ADD]
Beethoven, L. van:Son 16 Pno *(rec live 1971, London)* Arkadia ▲ 912 [ADD]
Beethoven, L. van:Son 21 Pno, "Waldstein" *(rec live, London 1971)* Arkadia ▲ 911 [ADD]
Beethoven, L. van:Son 21 Pno, "Waldstein" *(rec Sept. 24–26, 1975)* Sony Classical 3–▲ SM3K 64490 [ADD]
Beethoven, L. van:Son 23 Pno, "Appassionata" *(rec live, London 1971)* Arkadia ▲ 912 [ADD]
Beethoven, L. van:Son 23 Pno, "Appassionata" CBS ▲ MYK 37219 ■ MYT 37219
Beethoven, L. van:Son 23 Pno, "Appassionata" Enterprise ("The Piano Library" series) ▲ ENT 189
Beethoven, L. van:Son 26 Pno, "Les Adieux", w. R. Serkin *(rec live, London 1971)* Arkadia ▲ 911 [ADD]
Beethoven, L. van:Son 29 Pno, "Hammerklavier" Sony Classical ("Essential Classics" series) ▲ SBK 47666 ■ SBT 47666
Beethoven, L. van:Son 30 Pno Deutsche Grammophon ▲ 427498–2 [DDD]
Beethoven, L. van:Son 30 Pno *(rec June 8, 1976)* Sony Classical 3–▲ SM3K 64490 [ADD]
Beethoven, L. van:Son 31 Pno *(rec Aug. 26, 1960)* Sony Classical 3–▲ SM3K 64490 [ADD]
Beethoven, L. van:Son 31 Pno Deutsche Grammophon ▲ 427498–2 [DDD]
Beethoven, L. van:Son 32 Pno Deutsche Grammophon ▲ 427498–2 [DDD]
Beethoven, L. van:Son 32 Pno *(rec Mar. 15–16, 1967)* Sony Classical 3–▲ SM3K 64490 [ADD]
Beethoven, L. van:Son 3 Vn, w. Adolf Busch (vn) *(rec May 5, 1931)* APR ▲ APR 5541 [ADD]
Beethoven, L. van:Son 3 Vn, w. Adolf Busch (vn) Enterprise ("The Piano Library" series) ▲ ENT 189
Beethoven, L. van:Son 3 Vn, w. A. Busch (vn) *(rec 1930 for HMV)* Pearl ▲ PEA 9942 (m) [AAD]
Beethoven, L. van:Son 5 Vn, "Spring", w. Adolf Busch (vn) *(rec May 17, 1933)* APR ▲ APR 5541 [ADD]
Beethoven, L. van:Son 7 Vn, w. Adolf Busch (vn) *(rec Sept 23, 1932 & May 16, 1)* APR ▲ APR 5541 [ADD]
Beethoven, L. van:Son 8 Vn, w. Adolf Busch (vn) Music & Arts 3–▲ CD 877 [ADD]
Beethoven, L. van:Son 9 Vn, "Kreutzer", w. Adolf Busch (vn), B. Walter (cnd), New York Philharmonic SO Biddulph ▲ LHW 026
Beethoven, L. van:Trio 4 Pno, "Ghost", w. S. Goldberg (vn), P. Casals (vc) *(rec live June 18, 1954)* Music & Arts 4–▲ CD 688 (m) [AAD]
Beethoven, L. van:Trio 5 Pno, w. S. Goldberg (vn), P. Casals (vc) *(rec live, June 18, 1954)* Music & Arts 4–▲ CD 688 (m) [AAD]
Beethoven, L. van:Trio 7 Pno, w. R. Stolzman (cl), A. Meunier (vc) Sony Classical ▲ SMK 47296 [ADD]

Serkin, Rudolf (pno) (cont.)
Beethoven, L. van:Trio 9 Pno, "Kakadu", w. Y. Horigome (vn), P. Wiley (vc) Sony Classical ▲ SMK 47296 [ADD]
Beethoven, L. van:Trio 9 Pno, "Kakadu", w. S. Goldberg (vn), P. Casals (vc) Music & Arts 4–▲ CD 688 (m) [AAD]
Beethoven, L. van:Vars on "Ein Mädchen oder Weibchen" from Mozart's *Die Zauberflöte*, w. P. Casals (vc) *(rec Perpignan, France, July 31, 1951)* Sony Classical ("The Casals Edition" series) 2–▲ SM2K 58985 [ADD]
Beethoven, L. van:Vars on "See, the Conquering Hero Comes" from Handel's *Judas Maccabaeus*, w. P. Casals (vc) *(rec Perpignan, France, Aug. 1951)* Sony Classical ("The Casals Edition" series) ▲ SMK 58991 [ADD]
Beethoven, L. van:Vars on "Bei Männern" from Mozart's *Die Zauberflöte*, w. P. Casals (vc) *(rec Perpignan, & Prades, France)* Sony Classical ("The Casals Edition" series) 2–▲ SM2K 58985 [ADD]
Beethoven, L. van:Vars on a waltz by Diabelli, Op. 120 *(rec 1957)* Sony Masterworks ("Portrait" series) ▲ MPK 44837 [ADD]
Brahms, J.:Con 1 Pno, w. F. Reiner (cnd), Pittsburgh SO LYS ▲ LYS 127
Brahms, J.:Con 1 Pno, w. G. Szell (cnd), Cleveland Orch CBS ▲ MK 42261 [ADD]
Brahms, J.:Con 1 Pno, w. G. Szell (cnd), Cleveland Orch CBS ▲ MYK 37803 [ADD] ■ MYT 37803
Brahms, J.:Con 1 Pno, w. G. Szell (cnd), Cleveland Orch Sony Classical ("Essential Classics" series) ▲ SBK 48166 ■ SBT 48166
Brahms, J.:Con 2 Pno, w. E. Ormandy (cnd), Philadelphia Orch *(rec 1960)* Odyssey ▲ MBK 46273 [ADD] ■ YT 46273
Brahms, J.:Con 2 Pno, w. G. Szell (cnd), Cleveland Orch CBS ▲ MK 42262 [ADD]
Brahms, J.:Con 2 Pno, w. G. Szell (cnd), Cleveland Orch CBS ▲ MYK 37258 [ADD] ■ MYT 37258
Brahms, J.:Con 2 Pno, w. G. Szell (cnd), Cleveland Orch *(rec Jan. 21–22, 1966)* Sony Classical ▲ SBK 53262 ■ SBT 53262
Brahms, J.:Liebeslieder Waltzes SATB, w. B. Valente (sop), M. Kleinman (cta), W. Conner (ten), M. Singher (bar), L. Fleisher (pno) [G] Sony Classical ("Essential Classics" series) ▲ SBK 48176 ■ SBT 48176
Brahms, J.:Pieces Pno, Op. 119 CBS ▲ MK 42262 [AAD]
Brahms, J.:Qt 2 Pno, w. A. Busch (vn), Busch String Quartet *(rec 1938)* EMI Classics ▲ CDH 64702
Brahms, J.:Qnt Pno, w. Budapest String Quartet *(rec 1963)* Sony Masterworks ("Portrait" series) ▲ MPK 45686 [ADD]
Brahms, J.:Qnt Pno, w. A. Busch (vn), Busch String Quartet *(rec 1938)* EMI Classics ▲ CDH 64702
Brahms, J.:Sons Vc (comp), w. M. Rostropovich (vc) Deutsche Grammophon ▲ 410510–2 [DDD]
Brahms, J.:Son 1 Vn, w. A. Busch (vn) EMI Classics ▲ CDH 64495
Brahms, J.:Son 2 Vn, w. A. Busch (vn) EMI Classics ▲ CDH 64495
Brahms, J.:Son 2 Vn, w. A. Busch (vn) *(rec 1932 HMV recording)* Pearl ▲ PEA 9942 (m) [AAD]
Brahms, J.:Son 3 Vn, w. Adolf Busch (vn) Music & Arts 3–▲ CD 877 [ADD]
Brahms, J.:Trio Hn, w. M. Bloom (hn), M. Tree (vn) Sony Classical ▲ SMK 46249 [ADD] ■ SMT 46249
Brahms, J.:Trio Hn, w. Aubrey Brain (hn), Adolf Brusch (vn) *(rec 1933)* Enterprise ("Strings" series) ▲ ENT QT 99302
Brahms, J.:Trio Hn, w. A. Brain (hn), A. Busch (vn) EMI Classics ▲ CDH 64495
Brahms, J.:Trio Hn, w. Aubrey Brain (hn), Adolf Busch (vn) *(rec 1933)* Iron Needle 2–▲ IN 1342/43 (m) [ADD]
Busch, A.:Son Vn, w. Adolf Busch (vn) Music & Arts 3–▲ CD 877 [ADD]
Chopin, F.:Études (24)—Op. 10/1; Op.25/2 & 11 *(rec approx. 1928)* Archipon ▲ ARC 105 [DDD]
Great Musicians In Copenhagen, w. Vladimir Horowitz (pno), Wanda Landowska (hpd), Nathan Milstein (vn), Gregor Piatigorsky (vc), Fritz Busch (cnd), Nicolai Malko (cnd) Danacord ▲ DACOCD 303
Mendelssohn, F.:Capriccio brillante, w. E. Ormandy (cnd), Philadelphia Orch Sony Classical ("Essential Classics" series) ▲ SBK 48166 ■ SBT 48166
Mendelssohn, F.:Con 1 Pno, w. E. Ormandy (cnd), Philadelphia Orch Sony Classical ("Essential Classics" series) ▲ SBK 46542 [ADD] ■ SBT 46542
Mendelssohn, F.:Con 2 Pno, w. E. Ormandy (cnd), Columbia SO Sony Classical ("Essential Classics" series) ▲ SBK 46542 [ADD] ■ SBT 46542
Mozart, W.A.:Con 10 Pnos, w. P. Serkin (pno), A. Schneider (cnd), Marlboro Festival Orch Sony Classical 3–▲ SM3K 47207
Mozart, W.A.:Con 10 Pnos, w. P. Serkin (pno), A. Schneider (cnd), Marlboro Festival Orch *(rec 1962)* Sony Classical ▲ SMK 46255 [ADD]
Mozart, W.A.:Con 12 Pno, w. A. Schneider (cnd), Marlboro Festival Orch *(rec 1962)* Sony Classical ▲ SMK 46255 [ADD]
Mozart, W.A.:Con 14 Pno, w. A. Schneider (cnd), Columbia SO Sony Classical 3–▲ SM3K 47207
Mozart, W.A.:Con 17 Pno, w. A. Schneider (cnd), English CO RCA Silver Seal ▲ 60790–2 [ADD] ■ 60790–4
Mozart, W.A.:Con 17 Pno, w. A. Schneider (cnd), Columbia SO Sony Classical 3–▲ SM3K 47207
Mozart, W.A.:Con 18 Pno, w. G. Szell (cnd), Columbia SO Sony Classical 3–▲ SM3K 47207
Mozart, W.A.:Con 18 Pno, w. G. Szell (cnd), Columbia SO CBS ▲ MYK 37236 [ADD] ■ MYT 37236
Mozart, W.A.:Con 19 Pno, w. G. Szell (cnd), Columbia SO CBS ▲ MYK 37236 [ADD] ■ MYT 37236
Mozart, W.A.:Con 19 Pno, w. G. Szell (cnd), Columbia SO Sony Classical 3–▲ SM3K 47207
Mozart, W.A.:Con 20 Pno, w. G. Szell (cnd), Columbia SO CBS ▲ MYK 37236 [ADD] ■ MYT 37236
Mozart, W.A.:Con 20 Pno, w. G. Szell (cnd), Columbia SO Odyssey ▲ MBK 42533 ■ YT 42533
Mozart, W.A.:Con 20 Pno, w. G. Szell (cnd), Columbia SO Sony Classical 3–▲ SM3K 47207
Mozart, W.A.:Con 20 Pno, w. C. Abbado (cnd), London SO Deutsche Grammophon ("3D Classics" series) ▲ 431278–2 [DDD]
Mozart, W.A.:Con 21 Pno, w. C. Abbado (cnd), London SO Deutsche Grammophon ("Masters" series) ▲ 445516–2
Mozart, W.A.:Con 22 Pno, w. C. Abbado (cnd), London SO Deutsche Grammophon ("3–D Classics" series) ▲ 429978–2 [DDD]
Mozart, W.A.:Con 22 Pno, w. P. Casals (cnd), Perpignan Festival Orch *(rec July 26, 1951)* Sony Classical ▲ SMK 66570 [ADD]
Mozart, W.A.:Con 25 Pno, w. C. Abbado (cnd), London SO Deutsche Grammophon ("3–D Classics" series) ▲ 429978–2 [DDD]
Mozart, W.A.:Con 27 Pno, w. C. Abbado (cnd), London SO Deutsche Grammophon ("Masters" series) ▲ 445516–2
Mozart, W.A.:Con 27 Pno, w. E. Ormandy (cnd), Philadelphia Orch Odyssey ▲ MBK 42533 ■ YT 42533
Mozart, W.A.:Con 27 Pno, w. E. Ormandy (cnd), Philadelphia Orch Sony Classical 3–▲ SM3K 47207
Mozart, W.A.:Rondo Pno, K.511 Sony Classical 3–▲ SM3K 47207
Mozart, W.A.:Rondo Pno Orch, K.382, *(cnd & orch unknown)* Sony Classical 3–▲ SM3K 47207
Mozart, W.A.:Sons Vn Pno (misc), w. Adolf Busch (vn)—in E♭, K.380; in E♭, K.481 Music & Arts 3–▲ CD 877 [ADD]
Mozart, W.A.:Trio Pno, K.502, w. J. Laredo (vn), M. Foley (vc) *(rec 1968)* Sony Classical ▲ SMK 46255 [ADD]
Rudolf Serkin:The First Recordings EMI Classics 2–▲ CDC 54374
Schubert, Franz:Fant Vn, D.934, w. *(vn unknown) (rec 1931–38)* Pearl 2–▲ PEA 9141 [ADD]
Schubert, Franz:Der Hirt auf dem Felsen, w. B. Valente (sop), H. Wright (cl) [G] Sony Classical ("Essential Classics" series) ▲ SBK 48176 ■ SBT 48176
Schubert, Franz:Der Hirt auf dem Felsen, w. B. Valente (sop), H. Wright (cl) [G] *(rec 1960)* Sony Classical ▲ SMK 45901 [ADD/DDD] ■ SMT 45901
Schubert, Franz:Impromptus Pno, D.935 *(rec live, London, 1971)* Arkadia ▲ 913 [ADD]
Schubert, Franz:Qnt Pno, D.667, w. J. Laredo (vn), P. Naegele (va), L. Parnas (vc), J. Levine (db) *(rec 1967)* Sony Classical ▲ SMK 46252 [ADD]
Schubert, Franz:Rondo Vn, D.895, w. Adolf Busch (vn) Music & Arts 3–▲ CD 877 [ADD]
Schubert, Franz:Son Pno, D.958 [WELTE-MIGNON piano rolls] *(rec approx. 1928)* Archipon ▲ ARC 105 [DDD]
Schubert, Franz:Son Pno, D.960 *(rec live, London 1971)* Arkadia ▲ 913 [ADD]
Schubert, Franz:Trio 2 Pno, w. Busch String Quartet members *(rec 1931–38)* Pearl 2–▲ PEA 9141 [ADD]

Serkin, Rudolf (pno) (cont.)
Schumann, R.:Con Pno, w. E. Ormandy (cnd), Philadelphia Orch CBS ▲ MYK 37256 [ADD] ■ MYT 37256
Schumann, R.:Con Pno, w. E. Ormandy (cnd), Philadelphia Orch Sony Classical ("Essential Classics" series) ▲ SBK 46543 [ADD] ■ SBT 46543
Schumann, R.:Intro & Allegro appassionato, Op. 92, w. E. Ormandy (cnd), Philadelphia Orch Sony Classical ("Essential Classics" series) ▲ SBK 46543 [ADD] ■ SBT 46543
Schumann, R.:Intro & Allegro appassionato, Op. 92, w. E. Ormandy (cnd), Philadelphia Orch *(rec 1964)* Odyssey ▲ MBK 46273 [ADD] ■ YT 46273
Schumann, R.:Intro & Allegro, Op. 134, w. E. Ormandy (cnd), Philadelphia Orch *(rec 1968)* Sony Classical ("Essential Classics" series) ▲ SBK 48166 ■ SBT 48166
Schumann, R.:Son 1 Vn, w. Adolf Busch (vn) Enterprise ("The Piano Library" series) ▲ ENT 189
Schumann, R.:Son 1 Vn, w. Adolf Busch (vn) Music & Arts 3–▲ CD 877 [ADD]
Schumann, R.:Son 2 Vn, w. Adolf Busch (vn) Music & Arts 3–▲ CD 877 [ADD]
Schumann, R.:Trio 3 Pno, w. S. Vegh (vn), P. Casals (vc) *(rec live July 11, 1956)* Music & Arts 4–▲ CD 688 (m) [AAD]
Strauss, R.:Burleske, w. E. Ormandy (cnd), Philadelphia Orch CBS ▲ MK 42261 [ADD]
Strauss, R.:Burleske, w. E. Ormandy (cnd), Philadelphia Orch *(rec Feb. 3, 1966)* Sony Classical ▲ SBK 53262 ■ SBT 53262

Sermet, Huseyin (pno)
Hahn, R.:Pno Music, w. W. Paik (pno)—Ruban dénoué (a cycle of 12 waltzes), Preludes, Caprices, Berceuses, etc. Valois ("Musique Française" series) ▲ V 4658
Saint-Saëns, C.:Qt Pno Valois ("Musique Française" series) ▲ V 4657
Saint-Saëns, C.:Suite Vc, w. R. Pidoux (vc) Valois ("Musique Française" series) ▲ V 4657
Schmitt, F.:Soirs Pno Valois ▲ V 4687
Schmitt, F.:Symphonie concertante, w. D. Robertson (cnd), Monte Carlo PO Valois ▲ V 4687

Seroussi, Reuben (gtr)
Guitar Masterpieces of the 20th Century Nuova Era ▲ NUO CD 7255

Serov, Yury (pno)
Rimsky-Korsakov, N.:Songs, w. Anna Kovaleva (sop), Marianna Tarassova (mez), Konstantine Pluzhnikov (ten), Andrey Stavny (bar), Nikolai Okhotnikov (bass)—4 Romances, Op. 2; 4 Romances, Op. 3; 4 Romances, Op. 4; 4 Romances, Op. 7; 6 Romances, Op. 8; 2 Romances, Op. 25; 4 Romances, Op. 26; 4 Romances, Op. 27 *(rec St. Catherine's Lutheran Church, St. Petersburg, Sept–Dec 1993)* Russian Compact Disc ▲ RDCD 10051 [DDD]

Serovatov, Konstantin (pno)
Rachmaninoff, S.:Rhapsody on a Theme of Paganini, w. A. Anichanov (cnd), St. Petersburg State SO Audiophile Classics ▲ 101.038

Serrano, Agustin (pno)
Bartók, B.:Romanian Folk Dances Vn, w. Anabel Garcia del Castillo (vn) *(rec Madrid, Oct 1–3, 1990)* RNE/Spanish National Radio ▲ M3/10 [DDD]
Debussy, C.:Son Vn, w. Anabel Garcia del Castillo (vn) *(rec Madrid, Oct 1–3, 1990)* RNE/Spanish National Radio ▲ M3/10 [DDD]
Stravinsky, I.:Suite italienne Vc, w. Anabel Garcia del Castillo (vn) *(rec Madrid, Oct 1–3, 1990)* RNE/Spanish National Radio ▲ M3/10 [DDD]
Turina, J.:Son 1 Vn, w. Anabel Garcia del Castillo (vn) *(rec Madrid, Oct 1–3, 1990)* RNE/Spanish National Radio ▲ M3/10 [DDD]

Servadei, Annette (pno)
Brahms, J.:Pno Music (misc)—Intermezzo Opp. 117/1; Pieces, Op, 118/2, & Op. 119/1; Rhap., Op. 79/2; Waltzes, Op. 39/2 & 15 *(rec Apr.–May 1990)* IMP Classics ▲ PCD 949 [DDD]
Dohnányi, E. von:Pno Music—Vars & Fugue on a Theme by E.G., Op. 4; Passacaglia in e♭, Op. 6; 4 Piano Pieces, Op. 2 Continuum ▲ CON 1064 [DDD]
Mendelssohn, F.:Pno Music (misc)—Andante & Rondo, Op. 14; Kinderstück, Op. 72, No. 2; Scherzo, Op. 16, No. 2; Songs Without Words, Op. 19, No. 1 & Op. 30, No. 2; Duetto, Op. 38, No. 6; Spring Song, Op. 62, No. 6; Prelude, Op. 35, No. 1; Venetian Gondola Song, Op. 19, No. 6 *(rec 4–5/90)* IMP Classics ▲ PCD 949 [DDD]
Schumann, R.:Pno Music (misc)—Arabesque, Op. 18; Vogel als Prophet, Op. 82, No. 7; Aufschwung, Op. 12, No. 2; Fantasie Tanz, Op. 124, No. 5; Romance, Op. 28, No. 2; Intermezzo, Op. 26, No. 4; Thema *(rec 4–5/90)* IMP Classics ▲ PCD 949 [DDD]
Sibelius, J.:Impromptu Pno Continuum ▲ CON 1058
Sibelius, J.:Pno Music—Valse triste; Oeillet, Op. 85/2; March, Op. 5/3; Romance, Op. 24/9; Air de danse, Op. 34/2; Kavaljeren; Valse, Op. 5/1; Mandolinato; Gavotte, Op. 94/6; Romance, Op. 24/2; Valsette, Op. 40/1; Humoresque, Op. 40/3; Berceuse, Op. 40/5; Polonaise, Op. 40/10; Bells, Op. 65; Musical Box, Op. 76/9; Kleiner Walzer, Op. 97/3; Rondoletto, Op. 40; The Oarsman, Op. 103/3; Petite marche, Op. 99/8; Valse lyrique, Op. 96a; Esquisse, Op. 76/1; Danse, Op. 94/1; Étude, Op. 76/2; Nocturne, Op. 24/8; Romance, Op. 101/1; Finlandia, Op. 26/7 Continuum ▲ CON 1072 [DDD]
Sibelius, J.:Pno Music—Son., Op. 12; Kylikki, Op. 41; 3 Sons., Op. 67; Rondinos, Op. 68; 4 Lyric Pieces, Op. 74 Continuum ▲ CON 1060
Sibelius, J.:Pno Music—10 Pieces Opp. 24 & 34 Continuum ▲ CON 1058
Sibelius, J.:Pno Music—Valse triste, Op. 44; Spagnuolo; Till trånaden; Mandolinato; Morceau romantique; Kavaljeren; Pensées lyriques, Op. 40; 6 Finnish Folk Songs; 10 Piano Pieces, Op. 58 Continuum ▲ CON 1059

Serviarian-Kuhn, Dora (pno)
Khachaturian, A.:Con Pno, w. L. Tjeknavorian (cnd), Armenian PO ASV ▲ ASV 964

Sessions, J. (vc)
Kahn, E.I.:Nenia judaeis qui hac aetate perierunt, w. T. Gunther (pno) CRI ▲ CD 563 [DDD]

Šesták, Peter (va)—see also ORCHESTRAS & ENSEMBLES Albrecht String Quartet
Godár, V.:Déploration sur la mort de Witold Lutoslawski, w. Eleonóra Škutová-Slaničková (pno), Peter Biely (vn), Ivana Pristašová (vn), Jozef Lupták (vc) *(rec Residence of Slovak Composers, Apr 1996)* Slovart ▲ SR 0018–2–131 [DDD]
Godár, V.:Ricercar, w. Eleonóra Škutová-Slaničková (pno), Ivana Pristašová (vn), Jozef Lupták (vc) *(rec Residence of Slovak Composers, Apr 1996)* Slovart ▲ SR 0018–2–131 [DDD]

Seth-Smith, Imogen (trb vl/b vl)—see ORCHESTRAS & ENSEMBLES English Fantasy

Seton, Laura (vn)
Bourland, R.:Sax Qnt, w. Al Regni (s sax), Mark Feldman (vn), Lois Martin (va), Beverly Davidson (vc) Open Loop ▲ 034 [DDD]

Setrak, M. (pno)
Bizet, G.:Pno Music—Nocturnes; Variations chromatiques; Caprices; Valses; Sérénade; La Chasse fantastique; Romance sans paroles; Trois Esquisses musicales; Marine; Magasin des familles; Les Chants du Rhin; Quatre Préludes Musique d'abord 2–▲ HMA 1905223/24

Severinsen, Doc (flgl)
Trumpet Spectacular, w. E. Kunzel (cnd), Cincinnati Pops Orch Telarc ▲ CD 80223 [DDD] ■ CS 30223 (D)

Sevirance, Nanci (va)—see ORCHESTRAS & ENSEMBLES Porter String Quartet

Sewell, L. (vc)—see ORCHESTRAS & ENSEMBLES Lark String Quartet

Seyfarth, Walter (cl)—see ORCHESTRAS & ENSEMBLES Berlin Philharmonic Wind Quintet

Seykora, Fred (vc)
Kellaway, R.:Music of, w. Chuck Domanico (electric bass), Roger Kellaway (pno/perc), Emil Richards (mar/perc), Joe Porcaro (perc), Bob Zimmitti (perc)—Thinking of You; Un canto per la pace [A Song for Peace]; Love of my Life; Eleventide; In My Heart; Eve; Windows; Winter [Parts 1–3] *(rec Ocean Way Recording Studio, Los Angeles, CA, May 1–5, 1993)* Angel ▲ CDC 54903 [DDD]
Kellaway, R.:Music of, w. Roger Kellaway (pno/perc), Chuck Domanico (elec b), Emil Richards (mar/perc), Joe Porcaro (perc), Bob Zimmitti (perc)—Thinking of You; Un canto per la pace [A Song for Peace]; Love of my Life; Eleventide; In My Heart; Eve; Windows; Winter [Parts 1–3] *(rec Ocean Way Recording Studio, Los Angeles, CA, May 1–5, 1993)* EMI Classics ▲ CDC 54903 [DDD]
Roccisano, J.:Sonorities, w. V. Morosco (sax), J. Porcaro (perc) Protone ■ CSPR 153

Sfetsas, Christos (vc)
Karaindrou, E.:Film Music—Fairytale; Parade; Return; Song [all from Happy Homecoming, Comrade; w. Vangelis Skouras (Fr hn), Aliki Krithari (hp), Andreas Tsekouras (acc), Eleni Karaindrou (pno), Nelli Semitekolo (pno), Anthis Sokratis (tpt), Lefteris Chalkiadakis (cnd)]; Wandering in Alexandria (2 vers) [both from Wandering; w. Tassos Diakoyiorgis (santouri), Nelli Semitekolo (prepared pno), Anthis Sokratis (tpt), Nikos Guinos (cl), Katerina Ktona (hpd)] ECM ▲ 78118–21429–2 [AAD]
Karaindrou, E.:The Suspended Step of the Stork, w. Vangelis Christopoulos (ob), Ada Rouva (hp), Nikos Spinoulas (hn), Andreas Tsekouras (acc), Dimitris Vraskos (vn), L. Chalkiadakis (cnd), *(orch unknown) (rec Sound, Athens, Apr & Aug 1991)* ECM ▲ 78118–21456–2 [AAD]

Sgrizzi, Luciano (hpd)
Monteverdi, C.:Music of, w. Egidio Roveda (vc), E. Loehrer (cnd), Lugano Chamber Society Orch, Lugano Chamber Society Chorus—Altri Canti di Marte; Le Combat de Tancrede et Clorinde; Lamento Della Ninfa; Perche T'en Fuggi, O Fillide; Hor Ch'el Ciel e la Terra Accord ▲ ACD 220882
Scarlatti, D.:Sons Kbd—24 sels Accord ▲ ACD 220322 [AAD]

Sgrizzi, Luciano (pno)
Schobert, J.:Music of, w. C. Ganchini (vn), V. Méjean (vn), Philipp Bosbach (vc)—Qts. in f, Op. 7/2 & in E♭, Op. 14/1; Sons. in d & A, Op. 14/4 & 5; Trios in D & B♭, Op. 16/1 & 4 Musique d'Abord ▲ HMA 1901294

Shadd, M. (perc)
Foss, L.:Thirteen Ways of Looking at a Blackbird, w. E. LaBruce (mez), C. Meves (fl), A. Brovan (pno) [E] *(rec 1989–90)* Koss Classics ▲ KC 1006 [DDD]

Shaffer, Elaine (fl)
Mozart, W.A.:Con 1 Fl, w. E. Kurtz (cnd), Philharmonia Orch Royal Classics ▲ ROY 6450
Mozart, W.A.:Con Fl Hp, w. Marilyn Costello (hp), Y. Menuhin (cnd), Philharmonia Orch Royal Classics ▲ ROY 6450
Telemann, G.P.:Suite in a Fl, w. Y. Menuhin (cnd), Philharmonia Orch *(rec Abbey Road Studio 1, London, June 1963)* EMI Classics ▲ CDK 65340 [ADD]

Shafran, Daniel (vc)
Davïdov, K.Y.:Con 2 Vc, w. E. Mravinsky (cnd), Leningrad PO *(rec Large Hall, Moscow Conservatory, May 2, 1949)* Russian Compact Disc ▲ RDCD 10914 (m) [AAD]
Dvořák, A.:Con Vc, w. N. Järvi (cnd), Estonian SO *(rec 1978)* Multisonic (Russian Treasure) ▲ 31 0180
Rachmaninoff, S.:Son Vc, w. Yakov Flier (pno) Multisonic ▲ MUL 310354
Schumann, R.:Con Vc, w. K. Kondrashin (cnd), Russian State SO *(rec 1962)* Multisonic ("Russian Treasure" series) ▲ 31 0180

Shaham, Gil (vn)
Barber, S.:Con Vn, w. A. Previn (cnd), London SO Deutsche Grammophon ▲ 439886–2 [DDD]
Beethoven, L. van:Romances Vn, Orpheus CO *(rec Performing Arts Ctr, State Univ of NY, Purchase, NY, Dec 1995)* Deutsche Grammophon ▲ 449923–2 [DDD]
Bruch, M.:Con 1 Vn, w. G. Sinopoli (cnd), Philharmonia Orch Deutsche Grammophon ▲ 427656–2 [DDD]
Dvořák, A.:Romance Vn, Orpheus CO *(rec Performing Arts Ctr, State Univ of NY, Purchase, NY, Dec 1995)* Deutsche Grammophon ▲ 449923–2 [DDD]
Dvořák, A.:Romantic Pieces, Op. 75, w. Orli Shaham (pno) Deutsche Grammophon ▲ 449 820–2
Dvořák, A.:Son Vn, w. Orli Shaham (pno) Deutsche Grammophon ▲ 449 820–2
Dvořák, A.:Sonatina Vn, w. Orli Shaham (pno) Deutsche Grammophon ▲ 449 820–2
Elgar, E.:Salut d'amour, Orpheus CO *(rec Performing Arts Ctr, State Univ of NY, Purchase, NY, Dec 1995)* Deutsche Grammophon ▲ 449923–2 [DDD]
Franck, C.:Son Vn, w. G. Oppitz (pno) Deutsche Grammophon ▲ 429729–2 [DDD]
Korngold, E.W.:Con Vn, w. A. Previn (cnd), London SO Deutsche Grammophon ▲ 439886–2
Kreisler, F.:Vn Pieces, Orpheus CO—Schön Rosmarin; Liebesfreud; Liebesleid [all orchd Clark McAlister] *(rec Performing Arts Ctr, State Univ of NY, Purchase, NY, Dec 1995)* Deutsche Grammophon ▲ 449923–2 [DDD]
Mendelssohn, F.:Con in e Vn & Orch, Op. 64, w. G. Sinopoli (cnd), Philharmonia Orch Deutsche Grammophon ▲ 427656–2
Paganini, N.:Con 1 Vn, w. G. Sinopoli (cnd), New York PO Deutsche Grammophon ▲ 429786–2 [DDD]
Prokofiev, S.:Cons Vn (comp), w. A. Previn (cnd), London SO *(rec Henry Wood Hall, London, June 1995)* Deutsche Grammophon ▲ 447758–2 [DDD]
Prokofiev, S.:Son solo Vn, Op. 115 *(rec Henry Wood Hall, London, June 1995)* Deutsche Grammophon ▲ 447758–2 [DDD]
Ravel, M.:Tzigane, w. G. Oppitz (pno) Deutsche Grammophon ▲ 429729–2 [DDD]
Saint-Saëns, C.:Con 3 Vn, w. G. Sinopoli (cnd), New York PO Deutsche Grammophon ▲ 429786–2 [DDD]
Saint-Saëns, C.:Son 1 Vn, w. G. Oppitz (pno) Deutsche Grammophon ▲ 429729–2 [DDD]
Sarasate, P. de:Spanish Dances, Orpheus CO—Romanza Andaluza, Op. 22/1 [orchd Otto Hohn] *(rec Performing Arts Ctr, State Univ of NY, Purchase, NY, Dec 1995)* Deutsche Grammophon ▲ 449923–2 [DDD]
Sarasate, P. de:Zigeunerweisen, w. L. Foster (cnd), London SO Deutsche Grammophon ▲ 431815–2 [DDD]
Sibelius, J.:Con Vn, w. G. Sinopoli (cnd), Philharmonia Orch Deutsche Grammophon ▲ 437540–2
Tchaikovsky, P.:Con Vn, w. G. Sinopoli (cnd), Philharmonia Orch Deutsche Grammophon ▲ 437540–2
Tchaikovsky, P.:Sérénade mélancolique, Orpheus CO *(rec Performing Arts Ctr, State Univ of NY, Purchase, NY, Dec 1995)* Deutsche Grammophon ▲ 449923–2 [DDD]
Vivaldi, A.:Cons Vn, Op. 8/1–4, "The Four Seasons", Orpheus CO Deutsche Grammophon ▲ 439933–2 ■ 439933–4
Wieniawski, H.:Con 1 Vn, w. L. Foster (cnd), London SO Deutsche Grammophon ▲ 431815–2 [DDD]
Wieniawski, H.:Con 2 Vn, w. L. Foster (cnd), London SO Deutsche Grammophon ▲ 431815–2 [DDD]
Wieniawski, H.:Légende, w. L. Foster (cnd), London SO Deutsche Grammophon ▲ 431815–2 [DDD]

Shaham, Hagai (vn)—see ORCHESTRAS & ENSEMBLES Aviv String Quartet

Shaham, Orli (pno)
Dvořák, A.:Romantic Pieces, Op. 75, w. Gil Shaham (vn) Deutsche Grammophon ▲ 449 820–2
Dvořák, A.:Son Vn, w. Gil Shaham (vn) Deutsche Grammophon ▲ 449 820–2
Dvořák, A.:Sonatina Vn, w. Gil Shaham (vn) Deutsche Grammophon ▲ 449 820–2

Shakhovskaya, Natalia (vc)
Boccherini, L.:Con Vc, G.482, w. L. Markiz (cnd), *(orch unknown) (rec 1973)* Russian Compact Disc ▲ RCD 16203 [ADD]
Schumann, R.:Con Vc, w. L. Markiz (cnd), *(orch unknown) (rec 1976)* Russian Compact Disc ▲ RCD 16203 [ADD]
Shostakovich, D.:Con 1 Vc, w. G. Rozhdestvensky (cnd), Moscow RSO IMP ("BBC Radio Classics" series) ▲ IMP 5691702
Tchaikovsky, P.:Vars on a Rococo Theme, w. K. Kondrashin (cnd), Moscow State SO *(rec 1963)* Russian Compact Disc ▲ RCD 16203 [ADD]

Shakin, Vladimir (pno)
Beethoven, L. van:Con 1 Pno, w. A. Titov (cnd), New Classical Orch Infinity Digital ▲ QK 66723 [DDD]
Beethoven, L. van:Con 4 Pno, w. A. Titov (cnd), New Classical Orch Infinity Digital ▲ QK 66723 [DDD]
Beethoven, L. van:Rondo a capriccio, "Rage Over a Lost Penny", w. Vladimir Shakin (pno) or Valery Vishnevsky (pno) Audiophile Classics ▲ 101.003
Beethoven, L. van:Son 4 Pno *(rec St. Petersburg, 1992)* Audiophile Classics ▲ 101.002 [DDD]
Beethoven, L. van:Son 7 Pno Audiophile Classics ▲ 101.003
Beethoven, L. van:Son 8 Pno, "Pathétique" Audiophile Classics ▲ 101.003
Beethoven, L. van:Son 9 Pno Audiophile Classics ▲ 101.003
Chopin, F.:Pno Music (misc)—Barcarolle in F#, Op. 60; 3 Mazurkas, Op. 63; Polonaise-fant. in A♭, Op. 61; Berceuse in D♭, Op. 57; 3 Mazurkas, Op. 59 Infinity Digital ▲ QK 57257 [DDD]
Schubert, Franz:Impromptus Pno, D.899 Infinity Digital ▲ QK 64386 [DDD]

Shames, Jonathan (pno)
Asia, D.:Qt Pno, w. Bridge Ensemble Koch International Classics ▲ KIC 7313–2 [DDD]
Asia, D.:Son Pno, "Scherzo" Koch International Classics ▲ KIC 7313–2 [DDD]

Shames, Jonathan (pno) (cont.)
Finzi, G.:Interlude Ob & Strs, w. W. Rapier (ob), R. Diaz (va), A. Diaz (vc), T. Dimitriades (str) *(rec live Oct. 1, 1989)* Boston Records ▲ BR 1001
Hindemith, P.:Trauermusik, w. E. Shumsky (va) Ambassador ▲ ARC 1011 [DDD]

Shames, S. L. (pno)
Bloch, E.:Suite hébraïque, w. E. Shumsky (va) Ambassador ▲ ARC 1011 [DDD]
Hindemith, P.:Son Va & Pno, Op. 11/4, w. E. Shumsky (va) Ambassador ▲ ARC 1011 [DDD]
Hindemith, P.:Son Va & Pno, Op. 11/4, w. E. Shumsky (va) Ambassador ▲ ARC 1011 [DDD]

Shameyeva, N. (hp)
Damase, J.–M.:Sonatine Hp, w. Vera Dulova (hp) [arr for 2 harps] *(rec 1975)* Russian Compact Disc ("Talents of Russia" series) ▲ RCD 16204 [AAD]

Shamir, B. (vn)—see ORCHESTRAS & ENSEMBLES Daniel String Quartet

Shamvill, Regina (pno)
Schumann, R.:Con Pno, w. A. Manzano (cnd), Ecuador National SO *(rec live, Sucre National Theater, Quito, Ecuador, May 20, 1994)* Gallo ▲ CD 859 [DDD]

Shank, Bud (fl)
Dring, M.:Pastel Panche, w. Bill Perkins (sax/fl), Ray Brown (bass), Leigh Kaplan (pno), Shelley Manne (perc)Shank Perkins Brown—Teal for Two; Muave Mood; Lime Clash Cambria ▲ CD 1084 [ADD]
Dring, M.:Shades of Dring, w. Bill Perkins (sax/fl), Ray Brown (bass), Leigh Kaplan (pno), Shelley Manne (perc)—In the Pink; Hallelujah Red; Brown and Out; Hello Yellow; Saxy Blue Cambria ▲ CD 1084 [ADD]
Kosins, M.S.:Love Letters:A Dialogue, w. P. Terry (hp), B. Badgley (vc) *(rec 1980)* Centaur ▲ CRC 2105 [ADD]
Kosins, M.S.:Winter Moods *(rec 1980)* Centaur ▲ CRC 2105 [ADD]

Shank, Leslie (vn)
Corelli, A.:Concerti grossi, Op. 6, w. R. Tecco (vn), J. Koestenbaum (vc), C. Hogwood (cnd), St. Paul CO—No. 2 *(rec May 1992)* London ▲ 440376–2
Corelli, A.:Trio Sons, Op. 3, w. R. Tecco (vn), L. James (org) *(rec Jan. 1993)* London ▲ 440376–2
Holst, G.:A Fugal Con, w. J. Bogorad (vn), K. Greenbank (vn), R. Tecco (vn), J. Koestenbaum (vc), C. Hogwood (cnd), St. Paul CO *(rec May 1992)* London ▲ 440376–2
Holst, G.:Savitri, w. R. Tecco (vn), J. Koestenbaum (vc), C. Hogwood (cnd), St. Paul CO *(rec May 1992)* London ▲ 440376–2
Tippett, M.:Fant Concertante on a Theme of Corelli, w. R. Tecco (vn), J. Koestenbaum (vc), C. Hogwood (cnd), St. Paul CO *(rec May 1992)* London ▲ 440376–2

Shank, Nadine (pno)
American-Jewish Art Songs, w. Paulina Stark (sop) Centaur ▲ CRC 2108
Ben-Haim, P.:Songs without Words, w. Lynn Klock (sax) *(rec Eastman Theater, Eastman School of Music)* Open Loop ▲ OL 021
Bozza, E.:Aria Sax, w. Lynn Klock (a sax) *(rec Eastman School of Music, 1993–94)* Open Loop ▲ 033 [DDD]
Classical Play-along, Vol. 5 Open Loop ▲ OL 017
Glazunov, A.:Con Sax, w. Lynn Klock (a sax) [arr sax & pno] *(rec Eastman School of Music, 1993–94)* Open Loop ▲ 033 [DDD]
Hartley, W.S.:Son Br Sax, w. Lynn Klock (br sax) *(rec Eastman Theater, Eastman School of Music)* Open Loop ▲ OL 021
Heiden, B.:Son A Sax, w. Lynn Klock (a sax) *(rec Eastman School of Music, 1993–94)* Open Loop ▲ 033 [DDD]
Ibert, J.:Aria Cl & Pno, w. Lynn Klock (a sax) [arr for sax & pno] *(rec Eastman School of Music, 1993–94)* Open Loop ▲ 033 [DDD]
Ibert, J.:Concertino da camera, w. Lynn Klock (a sax) [arr for sax & pno] *(rec Eastman School of Music, 1993–94)* Open Loop ▲ 033 [DDD]
Rueff, J.:Concertino, w. Lynn Klock (a sax) [arr for sax & pno] *(rec Eastman School of Music, 1993–94)* Open Loop ▲ 033 [DDD]
Tansman, A.:Sonatine Bn, w. Lynn Klock (sax) *(rec Eastman Theater, Eastman School of Music)* Open Loop ▲ OL 021
Telemann, G.P.:Sonate metodiche, w. Lynn Klock (sax)—No. 4 in c *(rec Kilbourne Hall, Aug. 14, 1994)* Open Loop ▲ OL 021
Tomasi, H.:Chant Corse, w. Lynn Klock (sax) *(rec Eastman Theater, Eastman School of Music)* Open Loop ▲ OL 021
Vintage Flora, w. Lynn Klock (sax) Open Loop ▲ OL 007

Shankar, Ravi (sitar)
Shankar, R.:Con Sitar, w. A. Previn (cnd), London SO EMI Classics ("Studio" series) ▲ CDM 69121
Shankar, R.:Morning Love, w. J.–P. Rampal (fl) EMI Classics ("Studio" series) ▲ CDM 69121
Shankar, R.:Music of Angel ▲ CDC 55617

Shanley, G. (fl)
Ginastera, A.:Duo Fl, w. P. Christ (ob) Crystal ▲ CD 321
Hovhaness, A.:Tzaikerk, w. E. Shapiro (vn), J. Peters (bn) Crystal ■ C 800
Still, W.G.:Miniatures, w. P. Christ (ob), S. Davis (pno) Crystal ■ C 321
Still, W.G.:Miniatures, w. P. Christ (ob), S. Davis (pno) Crystal ▲ CD 321

Shannon, Robert (pno)
Copland, A.:Duo Fl, w. Gregory Fulkerson (vn) *(rec RCA Recording Studios, New York City)* New World ▲ 80313–2
Harbison, J.:Son 1 Pno, "Roger Sessions In Memoriam" Bridge ▲ BCD 9036 [DDD]
Ives, C.:Son 2 Pno Bridge ▲ BCD 9036 [DDD]
Ives, C.:Sons Vn, w. G. Fulkerson (vn) Bridge 2–▲ BCD 9024 [DDD]
Machover, T.:Bounce *(rec Oct. 3 & 5, 1993)* Bridge ▲ BCD 9040 [DDD]
Machover, T.:Chansons d'amour *(rec Oct. 3 & 5, 1993)* Bridge ▲ BCD 9040 [DDD]

Shao, Kathy (hpd/org)
Handel, G.F.:Sons Ob, w. Gonzalo X. Ruiz (ob), Michael Eagan (archlt), Shelley Taylor (vc)—in B♭, after HWV 365; in g, HWV 364; in d, HWV 359a; in B♭, HWV 357; in a, after HWV 367b; in F, HWV 363a; in c, HWV 366 Well-Tempered ▲ WTP 5174 [DDD]

Shao, S. (vc)
Van Appledorn, M.J.:Ayre, w. G.J. Schenk (vn), J. Ingolfsson (vn), C.–J. Chang (va), D. Foster (va), M. Ingolfsson (vc) CRS ▲ CD 9257

Shapira, Ittai (vn)
Debussy, C.:Son Vn, w. Michael Abramovich (pno) Meridian ▲ MER 84284 [DDD]
Encore:Pieces for Violin & Piano, w. Jeremy Denk (pno) Meridian ▲ MER 84314 [DDD]
Janácek, L.:Son Vn, w. Michael Abramovich (pno) Meridian ▲ MER 84284 [DDD]
Strauss, R.:Son Vn, w. Michael Abramovich (pno) Meridian ▲ MER 84284 [DDD]

Shapiro, Bernard (ob)
Dresher, P.:Channels Passing, w. P. Taub (fl), C. Sereque (cl), R. Pressley (tpt), S. Dempster (trbn), E.M. Gray (vn), W. Gray (vc) *(rec 1983–84)* New Albion ▲ NA 053

Shapiro, Eudice (vn)
Harrison, L.:Con Vn, w. W. Kraft (cnd), Los Angeles Percussion Ensemble *(rec 1975)* Crystal ▲ CD850
Hovhaness, A.:Tzaikerk, w. G. Shanley (fl), J. Peters (bn) Crystal ■ C 800
Stravinsky, I.:Vn Pno Music, w. R. Berkowitz (pno)—Suite d'apres des themes fragments et morceaux de Pergolesi; Variation d'Apollon; Berceuse & Scherzo from "Firebird"; Chanson Russe from "Mavra"; Ballade from "Fairy's Kiss"; Danse Russe from "Pétrouchka" Crystal ▲ CD302
Toch, E.:Son Vn, w. R. Berkowitz (pno) Crystal ▲ CD302

Shapiro, Lois (pno)
Barber, S.:Son Vc, w. Rhonda Rider (vc) *(rec Campion Center, Weston, MA, Aug 3–4, 1993)* Centaur ▲ CRC 2267 [DDD]
Carter, E.:Son Vc, w. Rhonda Rider (vc) *(rec Campion Center, Weston, MA, Aug 3–4, 1993)* Centaur ▲ CRC 2267 [DDD]
Dohnányi, E. von:Son Vn, w. C. Lieberman (vn) AFKA ▲ SK 503
Kovách, A.:Trio 2, w. C. Lieberman (vn), R. Feldman (vc) AFKA ▲ SK 503
Shifrin, S.:Son Vc, w. Rhonda Rider (vc) *(rec Campion Center, Weston, MA, Aug 3–4, 1993)* Centaur ▲ CRC 2267 [DDD]
Styles, w. Pieter Wispelwey (vc), Paul Komen (pno), Florilegium Channel Classics ▲ CCS 395

Shapiro, M. (vc)
Copland, A.:Duo Fl, w. L. Zucker (fl) Cantilena ▲ 660022 [DDD]
Lebaron, A.:Lamentation/Invocation, w. A. Shearer (sgr), R. Yamins (sgr), N. Kellman (perc), L. Bouchard (tpt), New Music Consort [E] Mode ▲ 30

Shapiro, Madeleine (vc)—see ORCHESTRAS & ENSEMBLES New Music Consort

Shapiro, Marc (pno)
An American Flute Recital, w. Laurel Zucker (fl) Cantilena ▲ 660022 [DDD]
Bloch, E.:Suite modale, w. L. Zucker (fl) Cantilena ▲ 660022 [DDD]
Bloch, E.:Suite modale, w. Laurel Zucker (fl) Cantilena ▲ 66011-2 [DDD]
Kennan, K.W.:Night Soliloquy, w. Laurel Zucker (fl) Cantilena ▲ 660022 [DDD]
Kingman, D.:Scénario musical 2, w. Laurel Zucker (fl) Cantilena ▲ 660022 [DDD]
Kingman, D.:Scénario musical 2, w. Laurel Zucker (fl) Innova ▲ INNOVA 504
Lewis, P.S.:Little Trio, w. J. McKenzie (fl), L. Granger (vc) New Albion ▲ NA 060 [DDD]
Lewis, P.S.:Through the Mountain, w. L. Granger (vc) New Albion ▲ NA 060 [DDD]
Romances for Flute & Piano, w. Laurel Zucker (fl) *(rec Cunningham Chapel, Belmont CA)* Cantilena ▲ C 660062 [DDD]
Wilder, A.:Son 2 Fl, w. L. Zucker (fl) Cantilena ▲ 660022 [DDD]

Shapiro, Sandra (pno)
Schumann, R.:Andante & Vars Hn, w. Thomas Hecht (pno), Gerald Appleman (vc), Alan Stepansky (vc), L. William Kuyper (Fr hn) *(rec Performing Arts Ctr/Purchase College–State Univ of NY Recital Hall, May 8, 1995)* Elysium ▲ GRK 709 [DDD]
Schumann, R.:Fantasiestücke Cl, w. Stanley Drucker (cl) *(rec Performing Arts Ctr/Purchase College–State Univ of NY Recital Hall, May 8, 1995)* Elysium ▲ GRK 709 [DDD]
Schumann, R.:Märchenerzählungen, w. Stanley Drucker (cl), Dorian Rence (va) *(rec Performing Arts Ctr/Purchase College–State Univ of NY Recital Hall, May 8, 1995)* Elysium ▲ GRK 709 [DDD]

Shapiro, Susanne (hpd)
Soler, P.A.:Sons Hpd—M.1; R.1, 6, 8, 13, 18, 21, 31, 45, 100, 103, 106, 113, 118 PROdigital ▲ CTG 1066 [DDD]

Sharon, Boaz (pno)
Koechlin, C.:Chansons pour Gladys, w. C. LeBlanc (sop) Hyperion ▲ CDA 66243 [DDD]
Koechlin, C.:Rondels, w. C. LeBlanc (sop)—Op. 1/2-5 & Op. 8/2,4,5 [F] Hyperion ▲ CDA 66243 [DDD]
Koechlin, C.:Songs, w. C. LeBlanc (sop)—Si tu le veux, Op. 5/5; Aux temps des fées, Op. 7/4; Déclin d'amour, Op. 13/1; La Chanson des Ingénues, Op. 22/1; Le Cortège d'Amphitrite, Op. 31/2; Le repas préparé, Op. 31/5; Amphise et Melitta, Op. 31/6; Améthyste, Op. 35/2; Hymne à Vénus, Op. 68/1 [F] Hyperion ▲ CDA 66243 [DDD]
Milhaud, D.:Pno Music—3 valses [from Madame Bovary]; L'album de Madame Bovary; 4 Sketches (Esquisses); 3 rag-caprices; Satie (ed. Milhaud):5 grimaces; Polka [from 'L'eventail de Jeanne']; Tango des Fratellini Unicorn-Kanchana ▲ DKP CD 9155

Sharon, Rena (pno)
Gounod, C.:Mélodies (6), w. James Sommerville (hn) Marquis Classics ▲ MAR 157 [DDD]
Reinecke, C.:Nocturne Hn, Op. 112, w. James Sommerville (hn) Marquis Classics ▲ MAR 157 [DDD]
Reinecke, C.:Trio Ob, w. James Mason (ob), James Sommerville (hn) Marquis Classics ▲ MAR 157 [DDD]
Schumann, R.:Adagio & Allegro Hn, w. James Sommerville (hn) Marquis Classics ▲ MAR 157 [DDD]
Sibelius, J.:Music for Vn Pno, w. Y. Yaron (vn)—Opp. 78/1-4, 79/6, 81/1-3 & 5 *(rec Feb. 1976 & July 1977)* Finlandia ▲ 4509-95853-2 [AAD]
Silver Sounds for Flute, w. Kathleen Rudolph (fl) Musica Viva ▲ MVCD 1069 [DDD]

Sharp, Elliot (cl)
Sharp, E.:Intifada, w. Soldier String Quartet Tzadik ("Composer" series) ▲ TZA 7016 [DDD]

Sharp, Elliott (gtr)
Sharp, E.:X-topia, w. Soldier String Quartet Tzadik ("Composer" series) ▲ TZA 7016 [DDD]

Sharp, Elliott (pno)
Sharp, E.:Mapping Newport Classics ▲ NPD 85504 [DDD]

Sharp, Elliott (syn)
Sharp, E.:KILIAIVI Newport Classics ▲ NPD 85504

Sharp, John (vc)
Strauss, R.:Don Quixote, w. D. Barenboim (cnd), Chicago SO *(rec in Orchestra Hall, Chicago, 5/28/91)* Erato ▲ 2292-45625-2 [DDD]
Tchaikovsky, P.:Souvenir de Florence, w. R. Solomonow (va), Vermeer String Quartet *(rec May–Oct., 1993)* Cedille ▲ CDR 90000 017 [DDD]

Sharp, P. (hn)—see ORCHESTRAS & ENSEMBLES Berlin German Opera Orch Soloists

Sharpe, Kevin (pno)
White, J.:Music for Vn, w. Janna Lower (vn) Opus One ▲ CD 167 [DDD]

Sharpe, Robert (org)
Christmas from Lichfield, w. [cnd:Andrew Lumsden], Lichfield Cathedral Choir Nimbus ▲ NI 5496

Sharrow, Leonard (bn)
Mozart, W.A.:Con Bn, w. A. Toscanini (cnd), NBC SO RCA Gold Seal ▲ 09026-60286-2 ■ 09026-60286-4

Shaughnessy, R. (cl)
Karg-Elert, S.:Jugend, w. D. Worthen (fl), R. Menual (hn), J. Weber (pno) Leonarda ▲ LE 335 [DDD]

Shavel, Adel (hpd)
Handel, G.F.:Cants, w. M. Zakai (cta), A. Biron (fl)—"Mal palpita il cor" [I] Koch International Classics ▲ KIC 7021-2 [DDD] ■ 3-7021-4 (D)

Shaw, Briony (vn)
Vivaldi, A.:Cons for 2 Vns, w. Iona Brown (vn), Johnathan Rees (vn), Ralph de Souza (vn), I. Brown (cnd), Academy of St. Martin in the Fields—Nos. 3 & 10 *(rec London, Sept 1995)* Hänssler Classic ▲ CD 98.017 [DDD]

Shaw, Clyde (vc)—see also ORCHESTRAS & ENSEMBLES Audubon String Quartet
Dohnányi, E. von:Serenade, w. David Salness (vn), Doris Lederer (va) *(rec LSU Recital Hall, Louisiana State Univ, Baton Rouge, July 23–25, 1995)* Centaur ▲ CRC 2309 [DDD]

Shaw, Julia (hp)
Dances for 2 Harps, w. Nora Bumanis (hp) CBC Records ("Musica Viva" series) ▲ MVCD 1062 [DDD]

Shaw, Katheryn (vn)
Hovhaness, A.:Sextet Rcr, w. J. Tyson (rcr), J. Starkman (vn), J. Cosart (va), A. Robbins (vc), F. Conover Fitch (hpd) Titanic ▲ Ti 169 [DDD]
Something for Recorder & Strings, w. John Tyson (rcr), Frances Conover Fitch (hpd), Jane Starkman (vn), Jann Cosart (va), Alice Robbins (vc), Tom Coleman (db) Titanic ▲ Ti 169 [DDD]

Shaw, R. (hpd)
Blow, J.:No, Lesbia, no, you ask in vain, w. B. Borden (sop) [E] Globe ▲ GLO 5029 [DDD]

Shawn, Allen (pno)
Chambers, W.M.:Ten Grand, w. Ursula Oppens (pno), Walter Hilse (pno), Bennett Lerner (pno), Nurit Tiles (pno), Aleck Karis (pno), Edmund Niemann (pno), Joseph Kubera (pno), Martin Goldray (pno), Elizabeth di Filice (pno), Geisel (cnd) Newport ▲ NPD 85553
Shawn, A.:Eclogue Pnos, w. E. Wright (pno) Opus One ▲ CD 157
Shawn, A.:Trio Cl, w. D. Krakauer (cl), M. Neuman (vc) Opus One ▲ CD 157
Shawn, A.:Winter Sketchbook, w. J. Jenner (vn) Opus One ▲ CD 157

Shchedrin, Rodion (pno)
Shchedrin, R.:Con 1 Pno, w. E. Svetlanov (cnd), USSR SO Russian Disc ▲ RUS 11129 [AAD]
Shchedrin, R.:Con 3 Pno, w. E. Svetlanov (cnd), USSR SO Russian Disc ▲ RUS 11129 [AAD]

Shchmitov, Alexei (pno)
Rubinstein, A.:Son 2 Vc, w. Alla Vasilieva (vc) *(rec State House for Radio Broadcasting, May 1994)* Russian Disc ▲ RD CD 10038 [AAD]

Shea, David (cl)
Kulesha, G.:Political Implications, w. Indiana Trio Crystal ▲ CD 734

Shearing, George (pno)
Get Happy!, w. King's Singers, Neil Swainson (db) EMI Classics ▲ CDC 54190 [DDD] ■ 4DS 54190 (D)

Shebalin, D. (va)—see ORCHESTRAS & ENSEMBLES Borodin String Quartet

Shebanova, Tatyana (pno)
Chopin, F.:Largo *(rec Dec. 3–5, 1990)* Canyon ▲ EC 3638-2 [DDD]
Chopin, F.:Prelude in A♭ *(rec Dec. 3–5, 1990)* Canyon ▲ EC 3638-2 [DDD]
Chopin, F.:Preludes, Op. 28 *(rec Dec. 3–5, 1990)* Canyon ▲ EC 3638-2 [DDD]
Chopin, F.:Prelude, Op. 45 *(rec Dec. 3–5, 1990)* Canyon ▲ EC 3638-2 [DDD]
Chopin, F.:Waltzes *(rec Toyama, Japan, Dec. 4–6, 1990)* Canyon Classics ▲ 3635 [DDD]

Shedrin, S. (ob)—see ORCHESTRAS & ENSEMBLES Collegium dell'Arte

Sheen, Graham (bn)
Vivaldi, A.:Con Ob Bn, w. C. Nicklin (ob), N. Marriner (cnd), Academy of St. Martin in the Fields Philips ▲ 412892-2 [DDD]

Shehan, Steve (perc)
East/West, w. Pinhas, Richard (syns/gtr), Norman Spinrad (voc), Dominique E. (voc), Patrick Gauthier (syn), G. Grunblatt (syn), François Auger (perc), Didier Batard (bass gtr) Cuneiform ▲ Rune 31

Shehori, Mordecai (org)
Mozart, W.A.:Andante Mechanical Org, K.616 Connoisseur Society ▲ CD 4189 [DDD]

Shehori, Mordecai (pno)
Beethoven, L. van:Son 2 Pno Connoisseur Society ▲ CD 4189 [DDD]
Liszt, F.:Rhap espagnole Connoisseur Society ▲ CD 4189 [DDD]
Liszt, F.:Song Transcriptions—Chopin:Six Polish Songs Connoisseur Society ▲ CD 4189 [DDD]
Mozart, W.A.:Adagio Pno, K.540 Connoisseur Society ▲ CD 4189 [DDD]
Mozart, W.A.:Fant Pno, K.397 Connoisseur Society ▲ CD 4189 [DDD]
Mozart, W.A.:Rondo Pno, K.485 Connoisseur Society ▲ CD 4189 [DDD]

Shell, Roger (vc)
Vivaldi, A.:Trio Sons Gtr Vn, w. P. Press (gtr), P. Peabody (vn), E. Brewer (hpd)—(2) in C, RV.82 & in g, RV.85 ESS.A.Y ▲ CD 1004 [DDD] ■ C 1004 (D)
Vivaldi, A.:Trio Sons Vn Lt, w. Paul Peabody (vn), Peter Press (gtr), Edward Brewer (hpd) ESS.A.Y ▲ ESS 1004 [DDD]

Shelley, Howard (pno)
Alwyn, W.:Con 1 Pno, w. R. Hickox (cnd), London SO Chandos ▲ CHAN 9155 [DDD]
Alwyn, W.:Con 2 Pno, w. R. Hickox (cnd), London SO Chandos ▲ CHAN 9196
Chopin, F.:Barcarolle Pno Chandos ▲ CHAN 9175 [DDD]
Chopin, F.:Berceuse Chandos ▲ CHAN 9018 [DDD]
Chopin, F.:Fant Chandos ▲ CHAN 9018 [DDD]
Chopin, F.:Impromptus Chandos ▲ CHAN 9175 [DDD]
Chopin, F.:Preludes, Op. 28 ASV Quicksilva ▲ ASQ 6095 [ADD]
Chopin, F.:Preludes, Op. 28 IMP Classics ▲ PCD 862 [DDD]
Chopin, F.:Scherzos Chandos ▲ CHAN 9018 [DDD]
Chopin, F.:Son Pno, Op. 35 IMP Classics ▲ PCD 862 [DDD]
Chopin, F.:Son Pno, Op. 58 Chandos ▲ CHAN 9175 [DDD]
Dickinson, P.:Con Pno, w. D. Atherton (cnd), BBC SO EMI ▲ CDC7 47584 [DDD]
Gershwin, G.:Con Pno, w. Y. P. Tortelier (cnd), Philharmonia Orch Chandos ▲ CHAN 9092 [DDD]
Gershwin, G.:"I Got Rhythm" Vars, w. Y. P. Tortelier (cnd), BBC PO Chandos ▲ CHAN 9325 [DDD]
Gershwin, G.:Porgy & Bess (suite), "Catfish Row Suite", w. Y. P. Tortelier (cnd), BBC PO Chandos ▲ CHAN 9325 [DDD]
Gershwin, G.:Rhap in Blue, w. Y. P. Tortelier (cnd), Philharmonia Orch Chandos ▲ CHAN 9092 [DDD]
Gershwin, G.:Second Rhap, w. Y. P. Tortelier (cnd), Philharmonia Orch Chandos ▲ CHAN 9092 [DDD]
Hindemith, P.:The Four Temperaments, w. Y. P. Tortelier (cnd), BBC PO Chandos ▲ CHAN 9124 [DDD]
Mendelssohn, F.:Capriccio brillante, London Mozart Players Chandos ▲ CHAN 9215 [DDD]
Mendelssohn, F.:Con 1 Pno, London Mozart Players Chandos ▲ CHAN 9215 [DDD]
Mendelssohn, F.:Con 2 Pno, London Mozart Players Chandos ▲ CHAN 9215 [DDD]
Mozart, W.A.:Con 9 Pno, w. H. Shelley (cnd), London Mozart Players Chandos ▲ CHAN 9068 [DDD]
Mozart, W.A.:Con 12 Pno, w. H. Shelley (cnd), London Mozart Players Chandos ▲ CHAN 9256 [DDD]
Mozart, W.A.:Con 13 Pno, w. H. Shelley (cnd), London Mozart Players Chandos ▲ CHAN 9326 [DDD]
Mozart, W.A.:Con 14 Pno, w. H. Shelley (cnd), London Mozart Players Chandos ▲ CHAN 9137 [DDD]
Mozart, W.A.:Con 17 Pno, w. H. Shelley (cnd), London Mozart Players Chandos ▲ CHAN 9068 [DDD]
Mozart, W.A.:Con 19 Pno, w. H. Shelley (cnd), London Mozart Players Chandos ▲ CHAN 9256 [DDD]
Mozart, W.A.:Con 20 Pno, w. H. Shelley (cnd), London Mozart Players Chandos ▲ CHAN 8992 [DDD]
Mozart, W.A.:Con 21 Pno, w. H. Shelley (cnd), City of London Sinfonia IMP ▲ IMP 2007
Mozart, W.A.:Con 21 Pno, w. H. Shelley (cnd), London Mozart Players Chandos ▲ CHAN 9404 [DDD]
Mozart, W.A.:Con 22 Pno, w. H. Shelley (cnd), London Mozart Players Chandos ▲ CHAN 9404 [DDD]
Mozart, W.A.:Con 23 Pno, w. H. Shelley (cnd), London Mozart Players Chandos ▲ CHAN 8992 [DDD]
Mozart, W.A.:Con 24 Pno, w. H. Shelley (cnd), City of London Sinfonia IMP ▲ IMP 2007
Mozart, W.A.:Con 24 Pno, w. H. Shelley (cnd), London Mozart Players Chandos ▲ CHAN 9326 [DDD]
Mozart, W.A.:Con 27 Pno, w. H. Shelley (cnd), London Mozart Players Chandos ▲ CHAN 9137 [DDD]
Rachmaninoff, S.:Cons Pno (comp), w. B. Thomson (cnd), Scottish National Orch Chandos 2-▲ CHAN 8882/83 [DDD]
Rachmaninoff, S.:Con 1 Pno, w. B. Thomson (cnd), Royal Scottish National Orch Chandos ▲ CHAN 9192 [DDD]
Rachmaninoff, S.:Con 2 Pno, w. B. Thomson (cnd), Royal Scottish National Orch Chandos ▲ CHAN 9193 [DDD]
Rachmaninoff, S.:Con 3 Pno, w. B. Thomson (cnd), Royal Scottish National Orch Chandos ▲ CHAN 9193 [DDD]
Rachmaninoff, S.:Con 4 Pno, w. B. Thomson (cnd), Royal Scottish National Orch Chandos ▲ CHAN 9192 [DDD]
Rachmaninoff, S.:Études-tableaux, Opp. 33 & 39 Hyperion ▲ CDA 66091
Rachmaninoff, S.:Pno Music (comp solo piano) Hyperion 8-▲ CDS 44041/48
Rachmaninoff, S.:Pno Music (misc)—solo piano transcriptions of works by Bach *(Prelude, Gavotte & Gigue)*, Bizet *(Minuet from L'Arlésienne)*, Kreisler *(Liebesleid; Liebesfreud)*, Mussorgsky *(Hopak)*, Rimsky-Korsakov *(Flight of the bumble bee)*, Schubert *(Wohin?)*, et al. Hyperion ▲ CDA 66486
Rachmaninoff, S.:Rhapsody on a Theme of Paganini, w. B. Thomson (cnd), Scottish National Orch Chandos 2-▲ CHAN 8882/83 [DDD]
Rachmaninoff, S.:Rhapsody on a Theme of Paganini, w. B. Thomson (cnd), Royal Scottish National Orch Chandos ▲ CHAN 9192 [DDD]
Rachmaninoff, S.:Son 2 Pno [1913 version] Hyperion ▲ CDA 66198 [DDD]
Rachmaninoff, S.:Songs, w. Sergei Leiferkus (bar)—At the Gates of the Holy Cloister; Nothing Shall I Say to You; Song of the Disenchanted; Do You Remember the Evening?; Were You Hiccoughing, Natasha?; O, No, I Beg You, Do Not Leave!, Op. 4/1; Morning, Op. 4/2; In the Silence of the Secret Night, Op. 4/3; Sing Not, O Lovely One, Op. 4/4; My Child, Your Beauty Is That of a Flower, Op. 8/2; Thoughts, Reflection, Op. 8/3; I Was with Her, Op. 14/4; You Are So Loved By All, Op. 14/6; She Is as Beautiful as Midday, Op. 14/9; Spring Torrents, Op. 14/11; It Is Time, Op. 14/12; Fate, Op. 21/1; By a Fresh Grave, Op. 21/2; Lilacs, Op. 21/5; Before the Icon, Op. 21/10; I Am No Prophet, Op. 21/11; All Was Taken from Me, Op. 26/2; We Shall Rest, Op. 26/3; Christ Is Risen, Op. 26/6; Yesterday We Met, Op. 26/13; All Passes, Op. 26/15; Letter to K.S. Stanislavsky; In the Soul of Each of Us, Op. 34/2; The Raising of Lazarus, Op. 34/6; You Knew Him, Op. 34/9; The Herald, Op. 34/11; From the Gospel of John *(rec St. Michael's Church, Highgate, London, Sept 19–20, 1994 & Jan 30)* Chandos ▲ CHAN 9374 [DDD]

Shelley, Howard (pno) (cont.)

Rachmaninoff, S.:Songs, w. Joan Rodgers (sop), Maria Popescu (mez), Alexandre Naomenko (ten), Sergei Leiferkus (bar)—At the Gates of the Holy Cloister; Nothing Shall I Say to You; Again You Are Bestirred, My Heart; April! A Festive Day in the Spring; Dusk Was Falling; Song of the Disenchanted; The Flower Died; Do You Remember the Evening?; O, No, I Beg You, Do Not Leave, Op. 4/1; Morning, Op. 4/2; In the Silence of the Secret Night, Op. 4/3; Sing not, O Lovely One, Op. 4/4; Oh, My Field, Op. 4/5; It Wasn't Long Ago, My Friend, Op. 4/6; Water Lily, Op. 8/1; My Child, Your Beauty Is That of a Flower, Op. 8/2; Thoughts, Reflection, Op. 8/3; I Fell in Love, to My Sorrow, Op. 8/4; A Dream, Op. 8/5; Prayer, Op. 8/6; I Await You, Op. 14/1; Small Island, Op. 14/2; How Fleeting Is Delight in Love, Op. 14/3; I Was with Her, Op. 14/4; Summer Nights, Op. 8/5; You Are so Loved by All, Op. 14/6; Do Not Believe Me, Friend, Op. 14/7; Oh, Do Not Grieve, Op. 14/8; She Is as Beautiful as Midday, Op. 14/9; In My Soul, Op. 14/10; Spring Torrents, Op. 14/11; It Is Time, Op. 14/12 — Chandos ▲ CHAN 9405

Rachmaninoff, S.:Songs, w. Joan Rodgers (sop), Maria Popescu (mez), Alexandre Naoumenko (ten), Sergei Leiferkus (bass)—Letter to K. S. Stanislawsky; The Muse, Op. 34/1; In the Soul of Each of Us, Op. 34/2; The Storm, Op. 34/3; A Passing Breeze, Op. 34/4; Arion, Op. 35/5; The Raising of Lazarus, Op. 34/6; It Cannot Be, Op. 34/7; Music, Op. 34/8; You Knew Him, Op. 34/9; I Remember This Day, Op. 34/10; The Herald, Op. 34/11; What Happiness, Op. 34/12; Dissonance, Op. 34/13; Vocalise, Op. 34/14; From the Gospel of St. John; At Night in My Garden, Op. 38/1; To Her, Op. 38/2; Daisies, Op. 38/3; The Pied Piper, Op. 38/4; Sleep, Op. 38/5; A-oo, Op. 38/6; A Prayer; All Glory to God — Chandos ▲ CHAN 9477

Rachmaninoff, S.:Songs, Joan Rodgers (sop) *(Lilacs, Op. 21/5; Fragment from a. Musset, Op. 21/6; How Peaceful, Op. 21/7; I Am Not a Prophet, Op. 21/11; How Pained I Am, Op. 21/12; Let Us Leave, My Sweet, Op. 26/5; I Am Again Alone, Op. 26/9; At My Window, Op. 26/10; Night Is Sorrowful, Op. 26/12)*, Maria Popescu (mez) *(Night; On the Death of a Siskin, Op. 21/8; Before the Icon, Op. 21/10; There Are Many Sounds, Op. 26/1; All Was Taken from Me, Op. 26/2; Christ Is Risen, Op. 26/6; To My Children, Op. 26/7; Yesterday We Met, Op. 26/13; The Ring, Op. 26/14)*, Alexandre Naoumenko (ten) *(Twilight, Op. 21/3; They Replied, Op. 21/4; Melody, Op. 1/9; I Beg for Mercy, Op. 26/8; The Fountain, Op. 26/11)*, Sergei Leiferkus (bass) *(Were You Hiccoughing, Natasha; Fate, Op. 21/1; By a Fresh Grave, Op. 21/2; We Shall Rest, Op. 26/3; 2 Farewells, Op. 26/4; All Passes, Op. 26/15)* — Chandos ▲ CHAN 9451

Rachmaninoff, S.:Suite 1 for 2 Pnos, w. H. MacNamara (pno) — Hyperion ▲ CDA 66375 [DDD]
Rachmaninoff, S.:Suite 2 for 2 Pnos, w. H. MacNamara (pno) — Hyperion ▲ CDA 66375 [DDD]
Rachmaninoff, S.:Symphonic Dances, w. H. MacNamara (pno) — Hyperion ▲ CDA 66375 [DDD]
Schubert, Franz:Son Pno, D.784 — Amon Ra ▲ CD-SAR 13 [DDD]
Schubert, Franz:Son Pno, D.894 — Amon Ra ▲ CD-SAR 13 [DDD]
Schumann, R.:Carnaval Pno — Chandos ▲ CHAN 8814 [DDD]
Schumann, R.:Kinderszenen — Chandos ▲ CHAN 8814 [DDD]
Szymanowski, K.:Sym 4, w. V. Sinaisky (cnd), BBC PO — Chandos ▲ CHAN 9478
Tippett, M.:Con Pno, w. R. Hickox (cnd), Bournemouth SO — Chandos ▲ CHAN 9333 [DDD]
Vaughan Williams, R.:Con Pno, w. B. Thomson (cnd), London SO — Chandos ▲ CHAN 8941 [DDD]
Vaughan Williams, R.:Epithalamion, w. S. Roberts (b-bar), D. Willcocks (cnd), London PO, Bach Choir — EMI Classics ▲ CDM 64730

Shelly, Frances (fl)—see ORCHESTRAS & ENSEMBLES Shelly/Egler Duo

Shelter, N. (pno)

Brahms, J.:Songs, w. J. Loibl (bar)—15 songs — FSM ▲ FCD 97201 [DDD]
Schubert, Franz:Songs (misc), w. J. Loibl (bar), E. Werba (pno)—13 Goethe-Lieder — FSM ▲ FCD 97202 [DDD]
Schumann, R.:Songs, w. P. Schreier (ten)—Liederkreis, Op. 39; 2 Gypsy Songs; other songs — Berlin Classics ▲ BER 2111 [ADD]
Schumann, R.:Songs, w. P. Schreier (ten)—Lieder, Opp. 25, 37 & 40; other songs — Berlin Classics ▲ BER 2112 [ADD]
Schumann, R.:Songs, w. P. Schreier (ten)—Dichterliebe; Liederkreis, Op. 24; Lieder nach Heine — Berlin Classics ▲ BER 2110 [ADD]
Schumann, R.:Songs, w. P. Schreier (ten)—Kerner Lieder, Op. 35; 6 Lieder, Op. 90 — Berlin Classics ▲ BER 2113 [ADD]
Wolf, H.:Songs (misc), w. J. Loibl (bar), E. Werba (pno)—10 Goethe-Lieder — FSM ▲ FCD 97202 [DDD]
Wolf, H.:Songs (misc), w. J. Loibl (baritone)—14 Songs — FSM ▲ FCD 97201 [DDD]

Shelton, M. (vn)

Soler, P.A.:Qnt 1 Hpd, w. D. Schrader (hpd), C. Verrette (vn), P. Slowik (va), J. M. Rozendaal (vc) *(rec Oct. & Dec. 1992)* — Cedille ▲ CDR 90000 013 [DDD]
Soler, P.A.:Qnt 2 Hpd, w. D. Schrader (hpd), C. Verrette (vn), P. Slowik (va), J. M. Rozendaal (vc) *(rec Oct. & Dec. 1992)* — Cedille ▲ CDR 90000 013 [DDD]
Soler, P.A.:Qnt 3 Hpd, w. D. Schrader (hpd), C. Verrette (vn), P. Slowik (va), J. M. Rozendaal (vc) *(rec Oct. & Dec. 1992)* — Cedille ▲ CDR 90000 013 [DDD]

Sheludyakov, Anatoli (pno)

Eshpai, A.Y.:Son 1 Vn, w. Levon Ambartsumian (vn) *(rec Large Hall, Moscow Conservatory, July 10 & 12, 1989)* — Russian Compact Disc ▲ RDCD 10001 [DDD]
Khachaturian, K.:Son Vn, w. Levon Ambartsumian (vn) *(rec Large Hall, Moscow Conservatory, July 10 & 12, 1989)* — Russian Compact Disc ▲ RDCD 10001 [DDD]
Prokofiev, S.:Son Vn, Op. 94bis, w. Levon Ambartsumian (vn) *(rec Large Hall, Moscow Conservatory, July 10 & 12, 1989)* — Russian Compact Disc ▲ RDCD 10001 [DDD]
Schnittke, A.:Son 2 Vn, w. Levon Ambartsumian (vn) *(rec Large Hall, Moscow Conservatory, July 10 & 12, 1989)* — Russian Compact Disc ▲ RDCD 10001 [DDD]
Vainberg, M.:Children's Notebooks — Olympia ▲ OLY 581 [DDD]
Vainberg, M.:Trio Pno, w. Irina Tkachenko (vn), Tatiana Zavarskaya (vc) — Olympia ▲ OLY 581 [DDD]

Shemer, David (hpd)

Baroque Favorites, w. B. Kol (rcr), A. Brodo (vc) — PWK Classics ▲ PWK 1138 [DDD]

Shenderovich, Evgeni (pno)

Rachmaninoff, S.:Aleko (sels), w. E. Nesterenko (bass)—1 aria — Russian Disc ▲ RUS 11 372 [DDD]
Rachmaninoff, S.:Songs, w. E. Nesterenko (bass)—5 songs — Russian Disc ▲ RUS 11 372 [DDD]
Sviridov, G.:Songs, w. E. Nesterenko (bass)—Approaching Izhory — Russian Disc ▲ RUS 11 372 [DDD]
Tchaikovsky, P.:Songs, w. E. Nesterenko (bass)—17 songs — Russian Disc ▲ RUS 11 372 [DDD]

Sheng, Charlotte (pno)

Mather, B.:Elegy, w. Robert Cram (fl), David Hutchenreuther (vc), Jonathan Wade (perc) — Centrediscs ▲ CMC 5094 [DDD]

Shepherd, Mark (org)

Magnificat & Nunc Dimittis, Vol. 3, w. [cnd:Andrew Lumsden], Lichfield Cathedral Choir — Priory ▲ PRI 505 [DDD]

Shepherd, Scott (perc)

La Montaine, J.:Lessons of Christmas, w. Polly Jo Baker (sop), David Griffith (ten), Carol Baum (hp), J. Montaine (cnd), Fredonia Singers — Fredonia Discs ▲ FDCD 14

Sheppard, Craig (pno)

Favorite Songs, w. Renato Bruson (bar) *(rec live, Wigmore Hall, London)* — Chandos ("Collect" series) ▲ CHAN 6551 [ADD]
Jolivet, A.:Concertino Tpt, w. W. Marsalis (tpt), E.-P. Salonen (cnd), Philharmonia Orch — CBS ▲ MK 42096 [DDD]
Prokofiev, S.:Mélodies, w. Mayumi Fujikawa (vn) — ASV ▲ ASV 667
Prokofiev, S.:Son Vn, Op. 94bis, w. Mayumi Fujikawa (vn) — ASV ▲ ASV 667
Prokofiev, S.:Son 1 Vn, w. Mayumi Fujikawa (vn) — ASV ▲ ASV 667

Sheppard, Peter (vn)

Cui, C.:Kaleidoscope, w. Aaron Shorr (pno) — Olympia ▲ OLY 456 [DDD]
Cui, C.:Son Vn, w. Aaron Shorr (pno) — Olympia ▲ OLY 456 [DDD]
Hallgrímsson, H.:Offerto — Eye of the Storm ▲ EOS 5004 [DDD]
Haydn, M.:Con Vn & Orch, w. Parnassus Ensemble — Meridian ▲ CDE 84243 [DDD]
Haydn, M.:Con Vn, P.53, w. Parnassus Ensemble — Meridian ▲ CDE 84243 [DDD]
Haydn, M.:Divert Vns, Va & Db, w. Parnassus Ensemble — Meridian ▲ CDE 84243 [DDD]
Telemann, G.P.:Fants Vn — Meridian ▲ MER 84266 [DDD]

Sheppard, Susan (vc)—see also ORCHESTRAS & ENSEMBLES L'École d'Orphée

Telemann, G.P.:Sons Ob, w. Paul Goodwin (ob), John Toll (hpd), Nigel North (thb/archlt) — Harmonia Mundi ▲ HMU 907152
Vivaldi, A.:Sons Ob, w. P. Goodwin (ob), G. Hennessey (ob), J. Holloway (vn), C. Lawson (cl), N. North (archlt/gtr), F. Eustace (bn), J. Toll (hpd/org)—RV.53, 58, 81 & 779 — Harmonia Mundi USA ▲ HMU 907104

Sherba, John (vn)—see also ORCHESTRAS & ENSEMBLES Kronos Quartet

Riley, T.:In C, w. Bruce Ackley, Steve Adams, Don R. Baker, Chris Brown, George Brooks, Steve Coughlin, Blake Derby, Bill Douglass, Mihr'un'Nisa Douglass, Hank Dutt, David Harrington, Don Howe, Joan Jeanrenaud, Alden Jenks, Warner Jepson, Henry Kaiser, Jaron Lanier, Bill Maginnis, George Marsh, Shabda Owens, Jon Raskin, Gyan Riley, Terry Riley, Gino Robair, John Sackett, Ramón Sender, Toyji Tomita, Danny Tunick, William Winant, Evan Ziporyn *(rec Jan. 14, 1990)* — New Albion ▲ NA 071

Sheridan, Mark (vc)—see ORCHESTRAS & ENSEMBLES English Piano Trio

Sherman, Russell (pno)

Beethoven, L. van:Bagatelles (24)—Op. 119 — Pro Arte ▲ CDD 261 [DDD]
Beethoven, L. van:Con 1 Pno, w. V. Neumann (cnd), Czech PO — Pro Arte ▲ CDD 259 [DDD]
Beethoven, L. van:Con 2 Pno, w. V. Neumann (cnd), Czech PO — Pro Arte ▲ CDD 260 [DDD]
Beethoven, L. van:Con 3 Pno, w. V. Neumann (cnd), Czech PO — Pro Arte ▲ CDD 260 [DDD]
Beethoven, L. van:Con 4 Pno, w. V. Neumann (cnd), Czech PO — Pro Arte ▲ CDD 259 [DDD]
Beethoven, L. van:Con 5 Pno, "Emperor", w. V. Neumann (cnd), Czech PO — Pro Arte ▲ CDD 261 [DDD]
Beethoven, L. van:Sons Pno (comp)—Nos. 1, 2, 9, 16, 30 & 32 — GM 2-▲ GM 2050CD
Beethoven, L. van:Sons Pno (comp) — GM Recordings 2-▲ GMR 2050
Beethoven, L. van:Son 1 Pno *(rec 1993-94)* — GM 2-▲ GM 2050 CD [DDD]
Beethoven, L. van:Son 9 Pno *(rec 1993-94)* — GM 2-▲ GM 2050 CD [DDD]
Beethoven, L. van:Son 16 Pno *(rec 1993-94)* — GM 2-▲ GM 2050 CD [DDD]
Beethoven, L. van:Son 21 Pno, "Waldstein" *(rec 1993-94)* — GM 2-▲ GM 2050 CD [DDD]
Beethoven, L. van:Son 30 Pno *(rec 1993-94)* — GM 2-▲ GM 2050 CD [DDD]
Beethoven, L. van:Son 32 Pno *(rec 1993-94)* — GM 2-▲ GM 2050 CD [DDD]
Berg, A.:Chamber Con, w. R. Kollsch (vn), G. Schuller (cnd), New England Conservatory Ensemble — GM ▲ GM 2033 CD
Chopin, F.:Barcarolle Pno — Pro Arte ▲ CDD 311 [DDD]
Chopin, F.:Preludes, Op. 28 — Pro Arte ▲ CDD 311 [DDD]
Gershwin, G.:Music of, w. Kunzel, Schuller (cnd), Rochester Pops Orch, Orch of St. Luke—American in Paris; Con in F; Rhap in Blue; etc. — Pro Arte ▲ CDM 814; ■ PCD 814
Grieg, E.:Music of, w. J. Silverstein (vn), A. Gerhardt (cnd), Utah SO, London Royal Promenade Orch—Peer Gynt Suites 1 & 2; Holberg Suite; Piano Concerto (1st movt.) — Pro Arte ▲ CDM 811; ■ PCD 811
Haydn, J.:Sons Pno—4 Sonatas—in c, H.XVI/20; in b, H.XVI/32; in D, H.XVI/42; in Eb, H.XVI/52 — Albany ▲ TROY 031-2 [DDD]
Liszt, F.:Études d'exécution transcendante, S.139 — Albany ▲ TROY 028-2 [DDD]
Liszt, F.:Pno Music (misc)—Hungarian Melody; Réminiscences de Don Juan; Réminiscences de Lucia di Lammermoor; Soirée de Vienne No. 6 *(rec 6/87)* — Pro Arte ▲ CDD 380 [DDD]
Liszt, F.:Son Pno *(rec 6/87)* — Pro Arte ▲ CDD 380 [DDD]
Schubert, Franz:Son Pno, D.850 — Albany ▲ TROY 084 [DDD]
Schubert, Franz:Son Pno, D.960 — Albany ▲ TROY 084 [DDD]
Wolpe, S.:Form *(rec Rutgers Presbyterian Church, New York City)* — New World ▲ 80308-2

Shermont, Robert (vn)

Albrechtsberger, J.G.:Concertino 5 Instrs, w. Armando Ghitalla (tpt), Jean Cauhape (va), Alfred Zighera (vc), James Weaver (pno) *(rec Dec 1963 & Jan 1964)* — Crystal ▲ CD 760

Sherry, Fred (vc)—see also ORCHESTRAS & ENSEMBLES Chamber Music Northwest members, Bargemusic, Lincoln Center Chamber Music Society members, Tashi

Barker, T.E.:Trikhýalo, w. R. Schulte (vn), M. Amory (va) *(rec Nov. 1992)* — CRI ▲ CD 661 [DDD]
Beethoven, L. van:Folksong Arrs, w. Arturo Delmoni (vn), New York Vocal Arts Ensemble [Beverly Myers (sop), Katherine Benfer (mez), James Archie Worley (ten), John Kramer (bar), Raymond Beegle (pno)]—Highlander's Lament; Chase of the Wolf; The Soldier in a Foreign Land; The Pulse of an Irishman; Lochnagar; O Swiftly Glides the Bonny Boat; O Might I but my Patrick Love; Kak Pashli; Bolero; Ridder Stigs Runekast; When Mortals all to Rest Retire; Faithful Johnie; Charlie is my Darling; Glencoe; Come Fill, Fill, my Good Fellow; Auld Lang Syne *(rec SUNY Purchase Performing Arts Center, Theatre C, Sept 11-13, 1995)* — Arabesque ▲ Z6672 [DDD]
Carter, E.:Son Fl, w. H. Sollberger (fl), C. Kuskin (ob), P. Jacobs (hpd) — Elektra/Nonesuch ▲ 79183-2
Cordero, R.:Qnt Fl, w. John Wion (fl), Arthur Bloom (cl), Kees Kooper (vn), Mary Louise Boehm (pno) — Albany ▲ TROY 153 [DDD]
Crumb, G.:Vox balaenae, w. Z. Mueller (fl), J. Gemmell (pno) — New World ▲ NW 357-2
Davidovsky, M.:Divert Vc, w. G. Rothman (cnd), Riverside SO — New World ▲ NW 383-2 [DDD]
Dembski, S.:Trio, w. R. Schulte (vn), A. Feinberg (pno) — CRI ▲ CD 570 [DDD]
Diamond, D.:Qnt Cl, w. Lawrence Sobol (cl), Linda Moss (va), Louise Schulman (va), Timothy Eddy (vc) *(rec RCA Studio A, New York City)* — New World ▲ 80508-2
Lerdahl, F.:Waltzes, w. R. Schulte (vn), S. Nickrenz (va), D. Palme (db) — CRI ▲ CD 580 [ADD/DDD]
Luening, O.:Trio Fl, Vc & Pno, w. Harvey Sollberger (fl), Charles Wuorinen (pno) — CRI ("American Masters" series) ▲ CD 716 [ADD]
Maggio, R.:Qts for 2 Fls & 2 Vcs, w. Bart Feller (fl), Kathleen Nester (fl), Jonathan Spitz (vc), B. Lubman (cnd) *(rec St. Peter's Church, Chelsea, New York, May 22, 1995)* — CRI ▲ CD 720 [DDD]
Mamlok, U.:Stray Birds, w. P. Bryn-Julson (sop), H. Sollberger (fl) — CRI ■ C 301
Palmer, R.:Qnt Cl, w. A. Bloom (cl), K. Kooper (vn), P. Doktor (va), Mary Louise Boehm (pno) — Albany ▲ TROY 153
Rochberg, G.:Trio Pno, w. Mary Louise Boehm (pno), Kees Kooper (vn) — Albany ▲ TROY 153
Rorem, N.:Bright Music, w. M. Martin (fl), A.-M. Schub (pno), A. Kavafian (vn), I. Kavafian (vn) — New World ▲ 80416-2 [DDD]
Rorem, N.:Winter Pages, w. T. Palmer (cl), F. Morelli (bn), I. Kavafian (vn), C. Wadsworth (pno) — New World ▲ 80416-2 [DDD]
Schubert, Franz:Qt 12 Strs, w. I. Kavafian (vn), A. Kavafian (vn), P. Neubauer (va) — Omega ▲ OCD 1015 [DDD]
Schubert, Franz:Qnt Strs, D.956, w. A. Kavafian (vn), I. Kavafian (vn), P. Neubauer (va), L. Parnas (vc) — Omega ▲ OCD 1015 [DDD]
Wilson, R.:Lord Chesterfield to His Son — Albany ▲ TROY 074 [DDD]
Wilson, R.:Music Vn, w. Y. Matsuda (vn) — CRI ▲ CD 602 [ADD]
Wolpe, S.:Qt Ob, w. S. Taylor (ob), D. Kennedy (perc), A. Karis (pno) *(rec Nov. 9-10, 1991)* — Koch ▲ KIC 7112 [DDD]
Wolpe, S.:Trio in 2 Parts Fl, w. H. Sollberger (fl), C. Wuorinen (pno) *(rec Nov. 9-10, 1991)* — Koch ▲ KIC 7112 [DDD]
Wuorinen, C.:Album Leaf, w. C. Macomber (vn) — Koch International Classics ▲ KIC 7242-2 [DDD]
Wuorinen, C.:Archangel, w. D. Taylor (trbn), B. Hudson (vn), C. Zeavin (vn), L. Schulman (va) *(rec March 31, 1981)* — Koch International Classics ▲ KIC 7110-2 [DDD]
Wuorinen, C.:Chamber Con Vc, w. C. Wuorinen (cnd), Group for Contemporary Music — Music & Arts ▲ CD 801 [ADD]
Wuorinen, C.:Fast Fant Vc, w. C. Wuorinen (pno) — New World ▲ NW 385-2 [DDD]
Wuorinen, C.:Five, w. C. Wuorinen (cnd), Orch of St. Luke *(rec Feb. 9, 1990)* — Koch International Classics ▲ KIC 7110-2 [DDD]
Wuorinen, C.:Fortune, w. A. R. Kay (cl), C. Macomber (vn), J. Winn (pno) — Koch International Classics ▲ KIC 7242-2 [DDD]
Wuorinen, C.:Qt 3 Strs, w. B. Hudson (vn), C. Zeavin (vn), L. Martin (va) — New World ▲ NW 385-2 [DDD]
Wuorinen, C.:Tashi, w. J. Kopperud (cl), C. Macomber (vn), J. Winn (pno) — Koch International Classics ▲ KIC 7242-2 [DDD]
Wuorinen, C.:Trio Vn, w. R. Schulte (vn), J. Winn (pno) *(rec Sept. 11-13, 1991)* — Koch International Classics ▲ KIC 7123-2 [DDD]
Wuorinen, C.:Variations II Vc — Koch International Classics ▲ KIC 7242-2 [DDD]

Sherry, Jonathan (pno)
Talma, L.:The Leaden Echo & the Golden Echo, w. Eleanor Clark (sop), Gregg Smith (cnd), Gregg Smith Singers Vox Box ("The American Composers" series) 3-▲ CDX 3037
Sherwin, Doron David (cnt/perc/sgr)—see ORCHESTRAS & ENSEMBLES La Reverdie
Sherwin, Doron David (cnt)—see ORCHESTRAS & ENSEMBLES Conserto Vago
Shetler, Norman (pno)
Christmas Lieder, w. Peter Schreier (ten) Eurodisc ▲ 69013-2-RG [ADD]
Peter Screier:From Boy Alto of the Dresden Kreuzchor to Lyric Tenor, w. Peter Schreier (alt/ten), Rudolf Mauersberger (pno/cnd), Walter Olbertz (pno), various orchs *(rec ca. 1950)* Berlin Classics 4-▲ BER 9041 [ADD]
Schubert, Franz:Schwanengesang, w. S. Lorenz (bar) [G] Capriccio ▲ 10097 [DDD]
Schumann, R.:Liederkreis, Op. 24, w. J. Loibl (bar) [G] FSM ▲ FCD 97719 [DDD]
Schumann, R.:Spanische Liebeslieder, w. M. Shirai (mez), M. Lipovsek (mez), J. Protschka (ten), M. Hölle (bass), N. Deutsch (pno) [G] Capriccio ▲ CDC 10079
Shevchuk, Konstantin (bn)
Ustvolskaya, G.:Composition 3, w. Natalia Danilina (fl), Maria Osipova (fl), Inna Rodina (fl), Michail Tokarev (fl), Kirill Sokolov (bn), Dmitrii Krasnik (bn), Arsenii Makarov (bn), Galina Sandovskaya (pno), O. Malov (cnd) *(rec St. Petersburg Radio House, Jan. 1994)* Megadisc ▲ 7867
Shewan, Paul (tpt)
Shewan, S.:Magnificat, w. Erin Stedman (sop), Kimberly Higgins (alt), Robert Dingman (ten), Alexander Burgess (bar), Barbara Hull (tpt), Nanita Wilson (hn), Scott Emmons (trbn), Kirk Kettinger (tuba), Ann Musser Honeywell (org) Albany ▲ TROY 149 [DDD]
Shewan, S.:The Voice of the Lord in the Storm, w. Erin Stedman (sop), Kimberly Higgins (alt), Robert Dingman (ten), Alexander Burgess (bar), Barbara Hull (tpt), Nanita Wilson (hn), Scott Emmons (trbn), Kirk Kettinger (tuba), Ann Musser Honeywell (org) Albany ▲ TROY 149 [DDD]
Shewan, Stephen (pno)
Shewan, S.:The Widow's Lament in Springtime, w. Jill Richardson (sop), Amy Anderson (ob), Rebecca Patterson (vc) Albany ▲ TROY 149 [DDD]
Sheynkman, Emanuil (balalaika)
Tubin, E.:Con Balalaika, w. N. Järvi (cnd), Swedish RSO BIS ▲ CD 351 [DDD]
Shibuya, Y. (pno)
Shinohara, M.:Cooperation, w. A. Nishigata (shamisen), K. Mitsuhashi (shakuhachi), M. Akao (fue), S. Yaotani (hichiriki), K. Ishikawa (sho), C. Fukunaga (koto), J. Ueda (biwa), M. Yoshizawa (kokyu), I. Tsuji (oboe), T. Takahashi (cl), G. Kitamura (tpt), A. Murata (trbn), S. Eiso (perc), S. Ueki (vn), S. Katsuta (vc), K. Komatsu (cnd) *(rec live Casals Hall, Tokyo, Mar. 5, 1994)* Camerata ▲ 30CM 375 [DDD]
Shick, Steven (perc)
Delio, T.:Music of, w. John Fonville (fl), Aleck Karis (pno), Jacques Linder (pno), Sandra Sprecher (pno)—anti-paysage for Fl, Perc, Pno & Tape; Of for Tape; Though for solo Pno; so again for Tape; on again for Tape; of again for Tape *(rec Univ of CA, San Diego, Univ of Maryland, Catonsville & Washington D.C.)* Neuma ▲ 45090 [DDD]
Shida, Tomiko (vn)—see ORCHESTRAS & ENSEMBLES Brussels String Quartet
Shields, Roger (pno)
Piano Music in America, 1900–1945 Vox Box 3-▲ CD3X 3027 [ADD]
Shifrin, David (cl)—see also ORCHESTRAS & ENSEMBLES Lincoln Center Chamber Music Society members, Chamber Music Northwest members
Bartók, B.:Contrasts, w. Ik-Hwan Bae (vn), W. Doppmann (pno) Delos ▲ CD 3043 [DDD]
Beethoven, L. van:Qnt Pno, Ob, Cl, Hn & Bn, w. C. Rosenberger (pno), A. Vogel (ob), K. Munday (bn), R. Graham (hn) Delos ▲ DCD 3024 [DDD]
Brahms, J.:Qnt Cl, w. Chamber Music Northwest Delos ▲ DE 3066 [DDD]
Brahms, J.:Sons Cl (comp), w. C. Rosenberger (pno) Delos ▲ DCD 3025 [DDD]
Brahms, J.:Trio Cl, w. C. Carr (vc), D. Golub (pno) Arabesque ▲ Z 6608
Copland, A.:Con Cl, w. G. Schwarz (cnd), New York Chamber SO EMI Classics (American Composer Series) ▲ CDM 64305
Copland, A.:Con Cl, w. G. Schwarz (cnd), New York Chamber SO EMI Classics ▲ CDC 49095 [DDD]
Drattell, D.:Con Cl, "Fire Dances", w. G. Schwarz (cnd), Seattle SO *(rec Seattle Opera House, June 17, 1994)* Delos ▲ DE 3159 [DDD]
Messiaen, O.:Quatuor pour la fin du temps, w. Ik-Hwan Bae (vn), W. Lash (vc), W. Doppmann (pno) Delos ▲ CD 3043 [DDD]
Mozart, W.A.:Con Cl, w. G. Schwarz (cnd), Mostly Mozart Festival Orch Delos ▲ DCD 3020 [DDD]
Mozart, W.A.:Qnt Cl, K.581, w. Chamber Music Northwest Delos ▲ DCD 3020 [DDD]
Mozart, W.A.:Qnt Pno, K.452, w. C. Rosenberger (pno), A. Vogel (ob), K. Munday (bn), R. Graham (hn) Delos ▲ DCD 3024 [DDD]
Nielsen, C.:Qnt Ww, w. R. Wilson (fl), A. Vogel (ob), D. Jolley (hn), J. Feves (bn) *(rec July 1-4, 1992)* Delos ▲ DE 3136 [DDD]
Poulenc, F.:Sxt Pno, w. André Previn (pno), Elizabeth Mann (fl), Steve Taylor (ob), Dennis Godburn (bn), Richard Todd (hn) *(rec Manhattan Center Studios, New York City, Apr. 7-8, 1993)* RCA Red Seal ▲ 09026-68181-2 [DDD]
Prokofiev, S.:Qnt Ob, w. A. Vogel (ob), P. Frank (vn), S. Tenebom (va), E. Meyer (db) *(rec July 1-4, 1992)* Delos ▲ DE 3136 [DDD]
Ravel, M.:Intro & Allegro, w. B. Allen (hp), Wilson (fl), Tokyo String Quartet EMI Classics ▲ CDC 47520
Schumann, R.:Fantasiestücke Cl, w. C. Rosenberger (pno) Delos ▲ DCD 3025 [DDD]
Songs & Arias, w. Bejun Mehta (trb), Carol Rosenberger (pno) Delos ▲ DCD 3019 [DDD]
Shillito, Christina (vc)—see also ORCHESTRAS & ENSEMBLES Pro Arte String Trio
Weber, C.M. von:Trio Fl, w. Clive Conway (fl), Christine Croshaw (pno) Meridian ▲ MER 84260 [DDD]
Shimazu, Norifumi (perc)—see ORCHESTRAS & ENSEMBLES Bugaku Percussion Ensemble
Shimizu, Takashi (vn)
Brahms, J.:Con Vn, w. S. Baudo (cnd), London SO Platz ▲ PLZ 574 [DDD]
Brahms, J.:Tragic Ov, w. S. Baudo (cnd), London SO Platz ▲ PLZ 574 [DDD]
Shimon, I. (va)—see ORCHESTRAS & ENSEMBLES Daniel String Quartet
Shimonoto, Ayumi (shamisen/sgr)
Takahashi, Y.:Music of, w. Vladimir Tonkha (nar), Kazuko Takada (shamisen/sgr), Yumiko Tanaka (b shamisen), Ko Ishikawa (mouth org), Kishiko Suzumi (va), Yuji Takahashi (pno)—Sugagaki Kuzushi; Mimi No Ho; Kagehime No Michiyuki; Yubi-Tomyo [Finger Light] Tzadik ▲ TZA 7010 [DDD]
Shin, Dongsok (positiv org)
Telemann, G.P.:Con Tpt Strs in D, w. Edward Carroll (tpt/pic tpt), Diane Bruce (vn), Elizabeth Field (vn), Annabelle Hoffman (vc), Edward Brewer (hpd/positiv org) *(rec Rye Presbyterian Church)* Helicon Classics ▲ HE 1009
Telemann, G.P.:Musique héroïque, w. Edward Carroll (tpt/pic tpt), Diane Bruce (vn), Elizabeth Field (vn), Annabelle Hoffman (vc), Edward Brewer (hpd/positiv org) *(rec Rye Presbyterian Church)* Helicon Classics ▲ HE 1009
Telemann, G.P.:Sons Tpt, w. Edward Carroll (tpt/pic tpt), Diane Bruce (vn), Elizabeth Field (vn), Annabelle Hoffman (vc), Edward Brewer (hpd/positiv org) *(rec Rye Presbyterian Church)* Helicon Classics ▲ HE 1009
Telemann, G.P.:Trio Sons, w. Edward Carroll (tpt/pic tpt), Diane Bruce (vn), Elizabeth Field (vn), Annabelle Hoffman (vc), Edward Brewer (hpd/positiv org) *(rec Rye Presbyterian Church)* Helicon Classics ▲ HE 1009
Shin'ar, Jonathan (pno)
Chopin, F.:Ballades Pno (comp) IMP ("Classics" series) ▲ IMP 6700992
Chopin, F.:Scherzos—Nos. 1-3 IMP ("Classics" series) ▲ IMP 6700992
Prokofiev, S.:Son 1 Pno IMP Masters ▲ IMPMCD 67 [DDD]
Prokofiev, S.:Son 2 Pno IMP Masters ▲ IMPMCD 67 [DDD]
Prokofiev, S.:Son 3 Pno IMP Masters ▲ IMPMCD 67 [DDD]
Scriabin, A.:Son 1 Pno IMP Masters ▲ IMPMCD 67 [DDD]
Scriabin, A.:Son 5 Pno IMP Masters ▲ IMPMCD 67 [DDD]
Shingles, Stephen (va)
Debussy, C.:Son Fl, w. W. Bennett (fl), S. Kanga (hp) Chandos ▲ CHAN 8621 [DDD]
Shinohara, Beni (vn)—see ORCHESTRAS & ENSEMBLES Porter String Quartet

Shinohe, Seiki (cl)
Beethoven, L. van:Trio 7 Pno, w. J. Adler (pno), D. Schwalke (vc) Classic Studio Berlin ▲ CS 10 308 [DDD]
Brahms, J.:Trio Cl, w. D. Schwalke (vc), J. Adler (pno) Classic Studio Berlin ▲ CS 10 308 [DDD]
Reger, M.:Sons Cl, Op. 49, w. J. Adler (pno)—No. 2 *(rec 1986)* Classic Studio Berlin ▲ CS 10908 [DDD]
Reger, M.:Son Cl, Op. 107, w. J. Adler (pno) *(rec 1986)* Classic Studio Berlin ▲ CS 10908 [DDD]
Shinozaki, Ayako (hp)
Lyrical Melodies of Japan, w. András Adorján ás (fl) Denon ("Repertoire" series) ▲ CO 8114 [DDD]
Silent Night:Beautiful Christmas Melodies, w. Ayako Shinozaki (hp) Sony Classical ▲ SFK 62677 ■ SFT 62677
Shioi, Luli (elec bass/sgr)
Sato, M.:Improvs, w. Michihiro Sato (tsugaru shamisen), Bill Frisell (elec gtr), Fred Frith (elec gtr), Tenko (sgr), Mark Miller (elec bass), Nicolas Collins (elec), Christian Marclay (turntables), Steve Coleman (sax), Tom Cora (vc), Joey Baron (perc), Mark Dresser (elec bass), Gerry Hemingway (perc), Toh Ban Djan [Ikue Mori (perc), Luli Shioi (elec bass/sgr)], Semantics [Elliott Sharp (electric gtr/bass), Samm Bennett (perc), Ned Rothenberg (sax)]—23 improvisations with various accompaniment combinations *(rec Baby Monster Studio, NY, Apr. 11-16, 1988)* Hat Hut ▲ hat ART CD 6015 [ADD]
Shiokawa, Yuuko (vn)
Janácek, L.:Son Vn, w. A. Schiff (pno) *(rec July 21-30, 1992)* London ▲ 440313-2 [DDD]
Mozart, W.A.:Trio Pno, K.502, w. András Schiff (pno), Miklos Perényi (vc) Teldec ▲ TEL 99205 [DDD]
Mozart, W.A.:Trio Pno, K.542, w. András Schiff (pno), Miklos Perényi (vc) Teldec ▲ TEL 99205 [DDD]
Shiran, O. (vn)
Klein, G.:Fant & Fugue, w. M. Kugel (vn), C. Leiman (vn), F. Nemirovsky (vc) *(rec June 21, July 5 & 20, 199)* Koch International Classics ▲ KIC 7230-2 [DDD]
Klein, G.:Trio Vn, w. M. Kugel (va), F. Nemirovsky (vc) *(rec June 21, July 5 & 20, 199)* Koch International Classics ▲ KIC 7230-2 [DDD]
Shirao, T. (va)—see ORCHESTRAS & ENSEMBLES Freiburg Baroque Soloists
Shirato, Fumio (db)—see ORCHESTRAS & ENSEMBLES Orches Trio
Shirato, N. (pno)
Delz, C.:Qt Pno, w. C. Delz (pno), F. Gauwerky (pno), A. Hempel (pno), J. Krist (pno) Grammont ▲ CTSP 18-2 [ADD]
Shirato, Noriko (vn)—see ORCHESTRAS & ENSEMBLES Orches Trio
Shirinsky, Alexander (vn)
Brahms, J.:Sons Vn (comp), w. N. Rozova (pno) Olympia ▲ OLY 285 [DDD]
Fine Night, w. Shirinsky, Alexander (vn), Natalia Rozova (pno) Mezhdunarodnaya Kniga ▲ MK 417030 [DDD]
Medtner, N.:Music for Vn & Pno, w. D. Galynin (pno)—Sonata No. 1 in b, Op. 21; Sonata No. 2 in G, Op. 44; Sonata No. 3 in e, Op. 57; Nocturnes, Op. 16; Canzonas, Op. 43; Danzas, Op. 43 MK 2-▲ MKA 417109 [DDD]
Shirinsky, Sergei (vc)—see also ORCHESTRAS & ENSEMBLES Beethoven String Quartet
Borodin, A.:Trio Pno, w. Emil Gilels (pno), Dmitry Tsyganov (vn) Multisonic ▲ MUL 310266
Shirinsky, Vasily (vn)—see ORCHESTRAS & ENSEMBLES Beethoven String Quartet
Shirotori, Mari (harm)—see ORCHESTRAS & ENSEMBLES Stanislas Ensemble
Shislov, A. (vn)—see ORCHESTRAS & ENSEMBLES Shostakovich String Quartet
Shornsheim, C. (hpd)
Devienne, F.:Sons Ob, Op. 70, w. B. Glaetzner (ob), S. Pank (vc) Berlin Classics ▲ BER 1017 [DDD]
Devienne, F.:Sons Ob, Op. 71, w. B. Glaetzner (ob), S. Pank (vc) Berlin Classics ▲ BER 1017 [DDD]
Shorr, Aaron (pno)
Cui, C.:Kaleidoscope, w. Peter Sheppard (vn) Olympia ▲ OLY 456 [DDD]
Cui, C.:Son Vn, w. Peter Sheppard (vn) Olympia ▲ OLY 456 [DDD]
Shorter, Lloyd (E hn)
Davidson, T.:Blue Dawn (The Promised Fruit), w. Carol Brown (fl), Charles Holdeman (bn), Charles Abramovic (pno) CRI ▲ CD 681 [DDD]
Davidson, T.:Lullaby, w. Marshall Taylor (sax), Carol Brown (fl), Charles Holdeman (bn), Charles Abramovic (pno) CRI ▲ CD 681 [DDD]
Shostac, David (fl)
Silverman, F.-E.:Speaking Alone New World ▲ NW 355-2 [DDD]
Shostakovich, Dmitri (pno)
Shostakovich, D.:Con 1 Pno, w. L. Vaillant (tpt), A. Cluytens (cnd), French National Orch EMI Classics ▲ CDC 54606
Shostakovich, D.:Con 1 Pno, w. A. Gauk (cnd), Moscow PO *(rec 1957)* Russian Disc ▲ RUS 15 005 [AAD]
Shostakovich, D.:Con 1 Pno, w. J. Thompson (tpt), M. Shostakovich (cnd), Montreal Musici Chandos ▲ CHAN 8357 [DDD]
Shostakovich, D.:Con 2 Pno, w. A. Cluytens (cnd), French National Orch EMI Classics ▲ CDC 54606
Shostakovich, D.:Con 2 Pno, w. S. Samosud (cnd), Moscow PO *(rec 1957)* Russian Disc ▲ RUS 15 005 [AAD]
Shostakovich, D.:Con 2 Pno, w. M. Shostakovich (cnd), Montreal Musici Chandos ▲ CHAN 8443 [DDD]
Shostakovich, D.:From Jewish Folk Poetry, w. N. Doralik (sop), Z. Dolukhovna (mez), A. Masennikov (ten) *(rec 1956)* Russian Disc ▲ RUS 15 015 [ADD]
Shostakovich, D.:Pirogov Suite—3 Fantastic Dances EMI Classics ▲ CDC 54606
Shostakovich, D.:Preludes & Fugues Pno, w. A. Cluytens (cnd), French National Orch EMI Classics ▲ CDC 54606
Shostakovich, D.:Preludes Pno, Op. 34, w. L. Kogan (vn) [arr. w. violin]—sels. *(rec 1956)* Multisonic ("Russian Treasures" series) ▲ 31 0179
Shostakovich, D.:Qnt Pno, w. Beethoven String Quartet *(rec 1940)* Multisonic ("Russian Treasures" series) ▲ 31 0179
Shostakovich, D.:Qnt Pno, w. Beethoven String Quartet Vanguard Classics ▲ OVC 8077 [ADD]
Shostakovich, D.:Son Vc, w. M. Rostropovich (vc) *(rec 1959)* Multisonic ("Russian Treasures" series) ▲ 31 0179
Shostakovich, D.:Son Vc, w. M. Rostropovich (vc) *(rec 1958)* Russian Disc ▲ RUS 15 005 [AAD]
Shpiegelman, Ilya (va)
Mozart, W.A.:Serenata Notturna, w. Alexander Mayorov (vn), Irina Belskaya (vn), Sergey Kirichenko (db), A. Rudin (cnd), Musica Viva CO *(rec Moscow Conservatory Great Hall, 1996)* Russian Compact Disc ▲ RCD 30201 [DDD]
Shraybman, Vladimir (pno)
Ravel, M.:Pavane pour une infante défunte Multisonic ▲ MUL 310355
Schumann, R.:Märchenbilder, w. Rudolf Barshay (va) Multisonic ▲ MUL 310355
Shröder, J. (vn)—see ORCHESTRAS & ENSEMBLES Paris Quartet
Shrude, Marlyn (pno)
Albright, W.:Son A Sax, w. J. Sampen (a sax) Capstone ▲ CPS 8603
Babbitt, M.:Images, w. J. Sampen (sax) Neuma ▲ 45080 [DDD]
Shrude, M.:Renewing the Myth, w. J. Sampen (sax) Neuma ▲ 450-80 [DDD]
Subotnick, M.:In 2 Worlds, w. J. Sampen (sax) Neuma ▲ 450-80 [DDD]
Wuorinen, C.:Divert Sax, w. J. Sampen (a sax) Neuma ▲ 450-80 [DDD]
Shrut, Arlene (pno)
Mendelssohn, Fanny:Songs, w. L. Kolb (sop)—6 Lieder, Op. 1; 6 Lieder, Op. 7; 6 Lieder, Op. 9; 5 Lieder, Op. 10; Heimweh; Italien; Nonne; Sehnsucht; Verlust [G] Centaur ▲ CRC 2120 [DDD]
Schubert, Franz:Songs (misc), w. D. Lichti (bar)—Harfenspieler I-III, D.478-480 [G] Dorian ▲ DOR 90131 [DDD]
Schumann, R.:Songs, w. D. Lichti (bar)—Gesange des Harfners (3), Op. 98a, Nos. 4,6 & 8 [G] Dorian ▲ DOR 90131 [DDD]
Wolf, H.:Goethe-Lieder (sels), w. D. Lichti (bar)—Harfenspieler I-III; Cophtisches Lieder I-II; Der Rattenfänger; Prometheus; Anakreons Grab; Königlich Gebet [G] Dorian ▲ DOR 90131 [DDD]
Wolf, H.:Songs (misc), w. D. Lichti (bar)—Drei Gedichte von Michelangelo [G] Dorian ▲ DOR 90131 [DDD]

▲ = CD ♦ = Enhanced CD Δ = MD ■ = Cassette Tape □ = DCC

Shtarkman, Alexander (pno)
Brahms, J.:Ballades, Op. 10 — Russian Disc ▲ RDCD 10061 [DDD]
Liszt, F.:Fant on 2 themes from Mozart's *Le nozze di Figaro* — Russian Disc ▲ RDCD 10061 [DDD]
Liszt, F.:Rhap espagnole — Russian Disc ▲ RDCD 10061 [DDD]

Shuhan, Alex (hn/pno)
Bernstein, L.:Dance Suite Chamber Ensemble, w. Will Rudd (tpt/flgl), Bob Thompson (tpt/flgl), Mark Kellogg (trbn/eup), Charles Villarrubia (tuba), David Gluck (dr/perc) *(rec Cliff Temple Baptist Church, Dallas, TX)* — D'Note Classics ▲ DND 1007 [DDD]
Corea, C.:Children's Songs, w. Will Rudd (tpt/flgl), Bob Thompson (tpt/flgl), Mark Kellogg (trbn/eup), Charles Villarrubia (tuba), David Gluck (dr/perc)—Nos 6 & 11 [arr Gluck/Shuhan] *(rec Cliff Temple Baptist Church, Dallas, TX)* — D'Note Classics ▲ DND 1007 [DDD]
Gershwin, G.:Porgy & Bess (sels), w. Will Rudd (tpt/flgl), Bob Thompson (tpt/flgl), Mark Kellogg (trbn/eup), Charles Villarrubia (tuba), David Gluck (dr/perc)—Summertime [arr Thompson] *(rec Cliff Temple Baptist Church, Dallas, TX)* — D'Note Classics ▲ DND 1007 [DDD]
Gluck, C.W.:Nicole, w. Will Rudd (tpt/flgl), Bob Thompson (tpt/flgl), Mark Kellogg (trbn/eup), Charles Villarrubia (tuba), David Gluck (dr/perc) *(rec Cliff Temple Baptist Church, Dallas, TX)* — D'Note Classics ▲ DND 1007 [DDD]
Khachaturian, A.:Gayane (suites), w. Will Rudd (tpt/flgl), Bob Thompson (tpt/flgl), Mark Kellogg (trbn/eup), Charles Villarrubia (tuba), David Gluck (dr/perc)—Sabre Dance [arr Gluck]; Lullaby; Dance of the Rose Maidens [both arr Villarrubia] *(rec Cliff Temple Baptist Church, Dallas, TX)* — D'Note Classics ▲ DND 1007 [DDD]
McCarthy, D.:American Dance Music, w. Will Rudd (tpt/flgl), Bob Thompson (tpt/flgl), Mark Kellogg (trbn/eup), Charles Villarrubia (tuba), David Gluck (dr/perc) *(rec Cliff Temple Baptist Church, Dallas, TX)* — D'Note Classics ▲ DND 1007 [DDD]
Scheidt, S.:Instr Music, w. Will Rudd (tpt/flgl), Bob Thompson (tpt/flgl), Mark Kellogg (trbn/eup), Charles Villarrubia (tuba), David Gluck (dr/perc)—Centone No. 5 [trans Verne Reynolds] *(rec Cliff Temple Baptist Church, Dallas, TX)* — D'Note Classics ▲ DND 1007 [DDD]

Shukayev, Leonid (vc)—see ORCHESTRAS & ENSEMBLES St. Petersburg String Quartet, St. Petersburg Trio

Shukov, Igor (pno)
Beethoven, L. van:Andante, WoO 57, "Andante favori" *(rec Munich, Mar 8, 1992)* — Live Classics ▲ LCL 551 [DDD]
Prokofiev, S.:Son 2 Pno *(rec Herkulessaal der Residenz, Munich, Mar. 30, 1993)* — Live Classics ▲ LCL 541 [DDD]
Prokofiev, S.:Son 9 Pno *(rec Munich, Mar 18, 1994)* — Live Classics ▲ LCL 551 [DDD]
Schubert, Franz:Impromptus Pno (comp)—Op. 142/3 *(rec Munich, Mar 8, 1992)* — Live Classics ▲ LCL 551 [DDD]
Schubert, Franz:Moments musicaux—No. 3 *(rec Munich, Mar 8, 1992)* — Live Classics ▲ LCL 551 [DDD]
Schubert, Franz:Son Pno, D.784 *(rec Munich, Mar 8, 1992)* — Live Classics ▲ LCL 551 [DDD]
Scriabin, A.:Etudes Pno, Op. 65 *(rec Herkulessaal der Residenz, Munich, Mar. 30, 1993)* — Live Classics ▲ LCL 541 [DDD]
Scriabin, A.:Preludes Pno (misc) *(rec Herkulessaal der Residenz, Munich, Mar. 30, 1993)* — Live Classics ▲ LCL 541 [DDD]
Scriabin, A.:Son 7 Pno *(rec Herkulessaal der Residenz, Munich, Mar. 30, 1993)* — Live Classics ▲ LCL 541 [DDD]
Scriabin, A.:Son 9 Pno *(rec Herkulessaal der Residenz, Munich, Mar. 30, 1993)* — Live Classics ▲ LCL 541 [DDD]
Scriabin, A.:Vers la flamme *(rec Herkulessaal der Residenz, Munich, Mar. 30, 1993)* — Live Classics ▲ LCL 541 [DDD]

Shulman, A. (pno)
Delius, F.:Music of, w. I. Brown (pno)—works for cello & piano—Creole Dance (from *Koanga*); 3 Pieces (from *Hassan*); Romance; Summer Night on the Water *(rec 9/87)* — Continuum ▲ CCD 1025

Shulman, Amy (hp)—see also ORCHESTRAS & ENSEMBLES Kent/Shulman Duo
Matson, S.:i–5, w. P. Kent (vn), M. Newman (vn), R. Tischer (va), E. Duke-Kirkpatrick (vc), B. Morgenthaler (db) *(rec Aug. 29–30, 1992)* — Audioquest ▲ AQCD 1013
Matson, S.:Range, w. Catherine Robbin (mez), Susan Greenberg (fl), Joseph Stone (fl), Glen Garrett (cl), Suren Karapetyan (hn), Peter Kent (vn), Kazi Pitelka (va), Sebastian Toettcher (vc), Don Ferrone (db), Doug Livingston (gtr/mand), John Schneider (gtr), Terry Schoenig (perc), S. Matson (cnd) *(rec Schnee Studio, Universal City, CA, Mar 12, 1995)* — New Albion ▲ NA 091

Shulman, Andrew (vc)—see also ORCHESTRAS & ENSEMBLES Britten String Quartet, Ambache Chamber Ensemble members, Ambache Chamber Ensemble
Delius, F.:Son Vc & Pno, w. I. Brown (pno) *(rec 9/87)* — Continuum ▲ CCD 1025
Dyson, G.:Music of, w. I. Brown (pno)—Prelude, Fantasy & Chaconne; 2 Pieces *(rec 9/87)* — Continuum ▲ CCD 1025
Haydn, J.:Divert Hn, Vn & Vc, H.IV/5, w. Michael Thompson (hn), Christopher Warren-Green (vn) — Nimbus ▲ NI 5010
Vivaldi, A.:Cons Vc, w. C. Warren-Green (cnd), London CO—RV 401 — Virgin Classics ▲ 59600 [DDD]

Shulman, Nora (fl)
Mozart, W.A.:Con Fl Hp, w. J. Loman (hp), M. Bernardi (cnd), CBC Vancouver SO — CBC ("SM 5000" series) ▲ SMCD 5133 [DDD]
Weinzweig, J.:Divert 1 Fl, w. V. Feldbrill (cnd), *(orch unknown)* *(rec live, Walter Hall, Univ. of Toronto, Mar. 11, 1993)* — Centrediscs ▲ CMC 5295 [DDD]

Shulman, Suzanne (fl)
Françaix, J.:Heure du berger Orch, w. James Mason (ob), James Campbell (cl), James Sommerville (hn), James McKay (bn), André Laplante (pno) *(rec Glenn Gould Studio, CBC Toronto, Mar. 26–27, 1994)* — CBC ("Musica Viva" series) ▲ MVV 1089 [DDD]
Glick, S.I.:Suite Hébraïque 5, w. J. Campbell (cl), A. Dawes (vn), D. Domb (vc) — CBC ("Musica Viva" series) ▲ MVCD 1046 [DDD]
Ravel, M.:Intro & Allegro, w. E. Goodman (hp), S. McCartney (cl), Amadeus Ensemble members — CBC ("Musica Viva" series) ▲ MVCD 1054 [DDD]
Wagner, R.:Siegfried Idyll, w. T. Holowach (vn), M. Skazinetsky (vn), L. Toman (va), R. Laurie (vc), C. Elliott (db), T. Maloney (cl), J. Valdepenas (cl), J. Fetherston (cl), S. Mosher (bn), S. Wilson (hn), R. Cohen (hn), J. Cowell (tpt), G. Gould (cnd) *(rec July 27–29 & Sept. 8, 198)* — Sony Classical ▲ SMK 52650 [ADD]

Shuman, Mark (vc)
Handel, G.F.:Sons Ob, w. Malylin Zupniik (ob), Raymond Leppard (hpd)—in a, B♭, e, g & g — ASV ▲ ASV 663 [DDD]
Telemann, G.P.:Sons Ob, w. M. Zupniik (ob), R. Leppard (hpd)—4 Sonatas—Nos. 1 in c, 3 in F & 6 in g; & Sonata in B♭ — ASV ▲ ASV 663 [DDD]

Shumsky, E. (va)
Beale, J.:Ballade, w. E. Shumsky (cnd), Pacific Rim Soloists — Ambassador ▲ ARC 1011 [DDD]
Bloch, E.:Suite hébraïque, w. S. L. Shames (pno) — Ambassador ▲ ARC 1011 [DDD]
Hindemith, P.:Son Va & Pno, Op. 11/4, w. S. L. Shames (pno) or J. Shames (pno) — Ambassador ▲ ARC 1011 [DDD]
Hindemith, P.:Trauermusik, w. J. Shames (pno) — Ambassador ▲ ARC 1011 [DDD]
Kreisler, F.:Praeludium & Allegro, w. *(pno unknown)*, E. Shumsky (cnd), Pacific Rim Soloists — Ambassador ▲ ARC 1011 [DDD]

Shumsky, Oscar (vn)
Bach, J.S.:Arias, w. Lois Marshall (sop), Maureen Forrester (alt), Richard Lewis (ten), Norman Farrow (b-bar), Brian Priestman (cnd), *(chorus unknown)*—Arias Nos. 32, 42, 120a, 132, & 182; Duet from Cant. 205 — Vox Box 2–▲ CDX 5127 [ADD]
Bach, J.S.:Cons Vn (comp), Scottish CO — Nimbus ▲ NI 5325 [DDD]
Bach, J.S.:Con Vn & Ob, w. R. Miller (ob), Scottish CO — Nimbus ▲ NI 5325 [DDD]
Bach, J.S.:Con for 2 Vns, w. J. Tunnell (vn), Scottish CO — Nimbus ▲ NI 5325 [DDD]
Beethoven, L. van:Con Vn, Op. 61, w. A. Davis (cnd), Philharmonia Orch — ASV Quicksilva ▲ QS 6080 [DDD]

Shumsky, Oscar (vn) (cont.)
Beethoven, L. van:Romances Vn, w. A. Davis (cnd), Philharmonia Orch—Op. 50 — ASV Quicksilva ▲ QS 6080 [DDD]
Glazunov, A.:Con Vn, w. N. Järvi (cnd), Scottish National Orch — Chandos ▲ CHAN 8596 [DDD]
Mozart, W.A.:Con 4 Vn, w. Y. P. Tortelier (cnd), Scottish CO — Nimbus ▲ NI 5009
Mozart, W.A.:Con 5 Vn, w. Y. P. Tortelier (cnd), Scottish CO — Nimbus ▲ NI 5009
Ysaÿe, E.:Sons Vn — Nimbus ▲ NI 5039
Ysaÿe, E.:Sons Vn — Nimbus ▲ NI 7715 [DDD]

Shumway, David (vc)
Mahin, B.:Cyclic Maneuvers — Capstone ▲ CPS 8611
Mahin, B.:Cyclic Maneuvers — Capstone ▲ CPS 8061

Shure, Leonard (pno)
Beethoven, L. van:Con 5 Pno, "Emperor", w. L. Fleisher (cnd), New England Conservatory Orch *(rec live, Jordan Hall, Dec 15, 1982)* — Audiofon ▲ CD 72018
Beethoven, L. van:Vars on a waltz by Diabelli, Op. 120 — Audiofon ▲ CD 72001
Schubert, Franz:Son Pno, D.958 — Audiofon ▲ CD 72010
Schubert, Franz:Son Pno, D.960 — Audiofon ▲ CD 72010
Schumann, R.:Fant Pno *(rec live, Jordan Hall, Dec 15, 1982)* — Audiofon ▲ CD 72018

Shure, Paul (vn)—see ORCHESTRAS & ENSEMBLES Los Angeles String Quartet, Hollywood String Quartet

Shustin, Alexander (vn)
Ustvolskaya, G.:Duet Vn, w. Oleg Malov (pno) *(rec St. Petersburg Radio House, Oct. & Nov. 1994)* — Megadisc ▲ 7863
Ustvolskaya, G.:Son Vn, w. Oleg Malov (pno) *(rec St. Petersburg Radio House, Oct. & Nov. 1994)* — Megadisc ▲ 7865
Ustvolskaya, G.:Trio Cl, w. Adil Feodorov (cl), Oleg Malov (pno) *(rec St. Petersburg Radio House, Oct. & Nov. 1994)* — Megadisc ▲ 7865

Shütz, G. (pno)
Raff, J.:Chaconne 2 Pnos, w. T. Hitzlberger (pno) — CPO ▲ CPO 999106 [DDD]
Reinecke, C.:Pno Music, w. T. Hitzlberger (pno)—La belle Griseldis in F, Op. 94; Andante & Variations in E♭, Op. 6; Impromptu in A, Op. 66 — CPO ▲ CPO 999106 [DDD]
Rheinberger, J.:Duo Pnos, w. T. Hitzlberger (pno) — CPO ▲ CPO 999106 [DDD]

Sice, Robert van (mar/perc)
Wood, James:Spirit Festival with Lamentations, w. Percussive Rotterdam — Mode ▲ MOD 51 [DDD]
Wood, James:Spirit Festival with Lamentations, w. Percussive Rotterdam *(rec Steurbaut Sound Recording Centre, Gent, Belgium, June 26, 1993)* — mode ▲ mode 51
Wood, James:Village Burial with Fire Mar, w. Percussive Rotterdam — Mode ▲ MOD 51 [DDD]

Sichermann, Erich (va)
Fauré, G.:Qt 1 Pno, w. J. Eymar (pno), G. Kehr (vn), B. Braunholz (vc) *(rec 1966)* — Vox Box 2–▲ CDX 5073 [ADD]
Fauré, G.:Qt 2 Pno, w. J. Eymar (pno), G. Kehr (vn), B. Braunholz (vc) *(rec 1966)* — Vox Box 2–▲ CDX 5073 [ADD]
Fauré, G.:Qnts Pno & Strs, Opp. 89 & 115, w. J. Eymar (pno), G. Kehr (vn), W. Neuhaus (vn), B. Braunholz (vc) *(rec 1970)* — Vox Box 2–▲ CDX 5073 [ADD]

Sidener, Michele (va)
Summerdays:From the Musical Masterworks Festival at Old Lyme, w. Sheir Greenawald (sop), Beverly Hoch (sop), John Koch (ten), Aloysia Friedman (vn), Norman Krieger (cnd), Norman Krieger (pno) — Well-Tempered Productions ▲ WTP 5173 [DDD]

Siebens, Etienne (db)
Biber, H. von:Harmonia artificiosa-ariosa, w. M. Lindal (vn), B. Sargent (vn), M. van der Velden (viol), M. Spányi (hpd)—Partitas 3 & 5 *(rec Feb. 4–6, 1993)* — BIS ▲ CD 608 [DDD]
Biber, H. von:Mystery (or Rosary) Sons, w. M. Lindal (vn), M. van der Velden (viol), M. Spányi (hpd)—No. 10 *(rec Feb. 4–6, 1993)* — BIS ▲ CD 608 [DDD]
Biber, H. von:Sons Vn & Continuo, w. M. Lindal (vn), L. Swarts (vc), M. Spányi (hpd) *(rec Feb. 4–6, 1993)* — BIS ▲ CD 608 [DDD]
Biber, H. von:Son violino solo representativa, w. M. Lindal (vn), L. Swarts (vc), M. Spányi (hpd) *(rec Feb. 4–6, 1993)* — BIS ▲ CD 608 [DDD]

Sieber, Daniel (tpt)
Daetwyler, J.:Dialogue Tpt, w. H. Gertschen (org) — Gallo ▲ CD 548 [AAD]

Sieber, Wolfgang (org)—see ORCHESTRAS & ENSEMBLES Timporg Trio

Siebert, Ellen (vl)
Out of the Orient Crystall Skyes, w. Nancy Zylstra (sop), Margriet Tindemans (vl), Jillion Stopples Dupree (hpd/org), Michael Sand (baroque vn/vl), Linda Melsted (baroque vn), Olga Hauptmann (baroque va), Russell Paige (vl) — Wildboar ▲ WLBR 8901 [DDD]

Siebert, Judith Kehler (pno)
Nishimura, A.:Heterophony, w. Shirley Sawatzky (pno), B. Tovey (cnd), Winnipeg SO *(rec Winnipeg, Manitoba, Mar. 16 & 18, 1993)* — CBC ("SM 5000" series) ▲ SMCD 5141 [DDD]

Siebert, Renée (fl)
Haydn, J.:Trios Fls & Vc, "London Trios", w. Laurel Zucker (fl), Samuel Magill (vc) *(rec Concordia College)* — Cantilena ▲ 66013-2 [DDD]
Mozart, W.A.:Andante Fl, K.315/285a, w. J. Faerber (cnd), Württemberg CO — Vox Box 3–▲ CD3X 3003 [ADD]
Mozart, W.A.:Cons Fl, w. J. Faerber (cnd), Württemberg CO — Vox Box 3–▲ CD3X 3003 [ADD]
Mozart, W.A.:Con Fl Hp, w. C. Michel (hp), J. Faerber (cnd), Württemberg CO — Vox Box 3–▲ CD3X 3003 [ADD]
Mozart, W.A.:Qts Fl, w. R. Friend (vn), W. Trampler (va), G. Neikrug (vc) — Vox Box 3–▲ CD3X 3003 [ADD]
Mozart, W.A.:Rondo Fl, K.Anh.184, w. J. Faerber (cnd), Württemberg CO — Vox Box 3–▲ CD3X 3003 [ADD]
Mozart, W.A.:Sons Fl Hpd (comp), w. J. Norell (hpd) — Vox Box 3–▲ CD3X 3003 [ADD]
Shatin, J.:Ruah Fl, w. R. Black (cnd), Prism CO — CRI ▲ CD 605 [DDD]

Siebler, Ulrike (fl)
Tailleferre, G.:Forlane, w. A. Gassenhuber (pno) *(rec Dec. 1992)* — Troubadisc ▲ TRO 01406 [DDD]
Tailleferre, G.:Image, w. D. Marshall (cl), H. Stralendorf (cel), A. Gassenhuber (pno), Fanny Mendelssohn String Quartet *(rec Dec. 1992)* — Troubadisc ▲ TRO 01406 [DDD]

Siefert, O. (trbn)—see ORCHESTRAS & ENSEMBLES Datura Trombone Quartet

Siegel, J. (pno)
Gershwin, G.:Con Pno, w. L. Slatkin (cnd), St. Louis SO — Vox Box 2–▲ CDX 5007 [ADD]
Gershwin, G.:"I Got Rhythm" Vars, w. L. Slatkin (cnd), St. Louis SO — Vox Box 2–▲ CDX 5007 [ADD]
Gershwin, G.:Rhap in Blue, w. L. Slatkin (cnd), St. Louis SO — Vox Box 2–▲ CDX 5007 [ADD]
Gershwin, G.:Second Rhap, w. L. Slatkin (cnd), St. Louis SO — Vox Box 2–▲ CDX 5007 [ADD]

Siegel, Richard (hpd)
Telemann, G.P.:Son Bn, w. Maurice Allard (bn) *(rec Lutheran Church of la Villette, Sept 13 & 17, 1983)* — Studio SM ▲ 2527
Telemann, G.P.:Son in a Vc, w. Etienne Peclard (vc) *(rec Lutheran Church of la Villette, Sept 13 & 17, 1983)* — Studio SM ▲ 2527
Telemann, G.P.:Suite Ob, w. Reynald Parrot (ob), Maurice Allard (bn) *(rec Lutheran Church of la Villette, Sept 13 & 17, 1983)* — Studio SM ▲ 2527

Siegele, P. (org)
Mahler, G.:Bach Orchestral Works, w. M.-U. Senn (fl), P. Schwarz (hpd), P. Ruzicka (cnd), Berlin RSO — Koch Schwann ▲ 3-1204-2 [ADD]

Sieger, Joseph (pno)
Favorite Encores, w. Mischa Elman (vn) *(rec 1959 & 1966)* — Vanguard Classics ▲ OVC 8029
Kreisler, F.:Vn Pieces, w. M. Elman (vn)—Caprice viennois; La Gitana; Liebesfreud; Rondino on a Theme of Beethoven; Schön Rosmarin; 4 arrs. of works by Dvořák *(Slavonic Dances 1 & 2; Slavonic Fantasie in b)* & Tartini *(Variations on a Theme of Corelli)*; 7 works in the styles of other composers *(Allegretto in the style of Boccherini; La précieuse...Couperin; Sicilienne & Rigaudon...Francoeur; Malagueña...Granados; Andantino...Martini; Preghiera...Martini; Preludium & Allegro...Pugnani)* *(rec 1960 & 1966)* — Vanguard Classics ▲ OVC 8028

Siegers, Antonia (va)—see ORCHESTRAS & ENSEMBLES Acht Ensemble

INSTRUMENT.

Siegmeister, E. (pno)
Siegmeister, E.:Con Cl, w. J. Brymer (cl), London SO *(rec 1973)* Premier ("Composer" series) ▲ PRCD 1010 [ADD]
Siegmeister, E.:Con Fl, w. P. Lloyd (fl), London SO *(rec 1973)* Premier ("Composer" series) ▲ PRCD 1010 [ADD]
Siewers, Maria Isabel (gtr)
Guastavino, C.:Balicento ASV ▲ ASV 933 [DDD]
Guastavino, C.:Cantilena ASV ▲ ASV 933 [DDD]
Guastavino, C.:Cantos Populares (3), w. Stamic String Quartet members ASV ▲ ASV 933 [DDD]
Guastavino, C.:Jeromita Linares, w. Stamic String Quartet ASV ▲ ASV 933 [DDD]
Guastavino, C.:Sante Fé Antiguo ASV ▲ ASV 933 [DDD]
Sifler, Paul (org)
Sifler, P.:Yuletide Echoes Fredonia Discs ▲ FDCD 14
Siflies, George (cl)
Brahms, J.:Qnt Cl, w. J. Korman (vn), J. Beiler (vn), D. Barnes (va), J. Sant'Ambrogio (vc) *(rec 1975–79)* Vox Box 3–▲ CD3X 3014 [ADD]
Mozart, W.A.:Qnt Cl, K.581, w. J. Korman (vn), J. Lind Jones (vn), J. Korman (va), J. Sant'Ambrogio (vc) *(rec 1975–79)* Vox Box 3–▲ CD3X 3014 [ADD]
Sigl, Peter (vc)
Vivaldi, A.:Con for 2 Vcs, w. M. Peters (vc), M. Haselböck (cnd), Vienna Academy [period instrs] Novalis ▲ 150074 [DDD]
Signorini, Lucia (vc)
Casella, A.:Son 2 Vc Nuova Era ▲ NUO 7191 [DDD]
Cilea, F.:Son Vc, w. F. Nicolosi (pno) Nuova Era ▲ NUO 7191 [DDD]
Hindemith, P.:Kammermusik 3, w. F. Trinca (cnd), Naples Accademic Musicale Solisti Nuova Era ▲ 7075 [DDD]
Hindemith, P.:Son Vc, Op. 25/3 Nuova Era ▲ 7075 [DDD]
Paganini, N.:Qts (15) Vn, w. R. Ricci (vn), A. Vismara (va), S. Cardi (gtr)—No. 7 Bongiovanni ▲ GB 5507 [DDD]
Paganini, N.:Terzetto concertante Va, w. A. Vismara (va), S. Cardi (gtr) Bongiovanni ▲ GB 5507 [DDD]
Paganini, N.:Terzetto Vn, w. R. Ricci (vn), S. Cardi (gtr) Bongiovanni ▲ GB 5507 [DDD]
Reger, M.:Suites Vc Nuova Era ▲ 7016 [DDD]
Respighi, O.:Adagio con variazioni Vc Pno, w. F. Nicolosi (pno) Nuova Era ▲ NUO 7191 [DDD]
Sigurbjörnsson, Thorkell (pno)
Sigurbjörnsson, T.:Intrada, w. Gunnar Egilson (cl), Ingvar Jónasson (va) Music from Iceland ▲ ITM 702 [ADD]
Sigurbjörnsson, T.:Nocturnes, w. Unnur María Ingólfsdóttir (vn) Music from Iceland ▲ ITM 702 [ADD]
Sigurdsson, Elisabeth (pno)
Stolarczyk, W.:Earth Air Fire Water, w. Amalie Malling (pno), John Damgaard (pno), Anne Øland (pno), Teddy Teirup (pno), Friedrich Gürtler (pno), Rosalind Bevan (pno), Poul Rosenbaum (pno), Rodolfo Llambias (pno), Bella Horn-Ribera (pno), Anders Riber (pno), Thomas Tronheim (pno), Elsebeth Broderson (pno), Erik Kaltoft (pno), Jørgen Hald Nielsen (pno), Aino Gilemann (pno), Birgit Kjær (pno), Jørgen Thomsen (pno), Gunhild Donslund (pno), Henrik Bo Hansen (pno), Lone Karlsson (pno), Erik Fessel (pno), Lasse Nilsson (pno), Janos Ferenczi (pno), Erik Bach (pno), Axel Momme (pno), Arne de Cros Dich (pno), Sven Micha Slot (pno), Hanne Bramsen Buhl (pno), Lili Olesen (pno), Susannah Carlsson (pno), Ulla Erml (pno), Vagn Sørensen (pno), Leif Greibe (pno), Bodil Krogh (pno), Kirsten Ottosen (pno), Inger Bergenholz (pno), Karsten Gylendorf (pno), Bjønr Elkjær (pno), Jacob Bjørn Jensen (pno), Jørgen Kaad (pno), Anne Marie Hjelm (pno), Carl Ulrik Munk Andersen (pno), Poul Lumbye (pno), Oluf Hildebrandt Nielsen (pno), Joachim Olsson (pno), Peter Pade Ramsøe Jacobsen (pno), Astrid Pollmann (pno), Jette Borsch (pno), Kirsten Karlshøj (pno), Maria Teresa Assing (pno), Allan Dahl Hansen (pno), Johan Hugossen (pno), Tine Fenger Pederson (pno), Arne Jørgen Fæø (pno), Anja Høgsted (pno), Anne Sophie Parbo (pno), Inga Lindmark (pno), Teresa Drabik Stathakis (pno), Anne Ruth Ferenczi (pno), Irene Hasager (pno), Yuka Ichikawa (pno), Birgitte Baur (pno), Malene Thastum (pno), Jens E. Rasmussen (pno), Birgitte Zielke (pno), Claus Zielke (pno), Stefan Kasch (pno), Bin Qiao (pno), Inger Johanne Teirup (pno), Lindy Rosborg (pno), Liisa Heininen (pno), David Højer (pno), Ellen Refstrup (pno), Thomas K. Søorensen (pno), Erik Kure (pno), Michael Rauff (pno), Jan beck Eriksson (pno), Tanja Zapolski (pno), Vibeke Skagbo (pno), Pål Eide Lindtner (pno), Ha-Young Sul (pno), Benedicte Palko (pno), Inke Kesseler (pno), Anne Marie Meineche (pno), Sverre Larsen (pno), Kasper Peter Bach (pno), Elisabetta Eliseo (pno), Olga Magieres (pno), Carl Erik Kühl (pno), Thorkild Borup Nielsen (pno), Valeria Zanini (pno), Lars Stenhoft (perc), Dennis Boel (perc), Winnie Dahlgren (perc), Susanne Vind (perc), Claus Byrith (elec), Anne Marie Storm (elec), J. Ribera (cnd) *(rec live, Koldinghaus Castle, Denmark, May 2, 1996)* Danica ▲ DCD 1996
Sigurdsson, Thorsteinn Gauti (pno)
Thórarinsson, L.:Styr, w. H. Leifsson (cnd), Iceland SO Music from Iceland ▲ ITM 705
Siirala, Jussi (pno)
Creston, P.:Son Sax, w. Pekka Savijoki (a sax) *(rec Nacka Aula, Nacka, Sweden, May 2, 1980)* BIS ▲ CD 52 [AAD]
Hindemith, P.:Son Alto Hn, w. Pekka Savijoki (a sax) *(rec Nacka, Sweden, May 3, 1980)* BIS ▲ CD 159 [AAD]
Maurice, P.:Tableaux de Provence, w. P. Savijoki (sax) BIS ▲ CD 209 [AAD]
Siki, Béla (pno)
Saint-Saëns, C.:Carnival of the Animals, w. Géza Anda (pno), I. Markevitch (cnd), Philharmonia Orch *(rec Jan 1954)* Testament ▲ SBT 1071
Sikorski, Christian (vn)—see ORCHESTRAS & ENSEMBLES Sikorsi String Quartet
Sikovetsky, Julian (vn)
Sibelius, J.:Con Vn, w. N. Anosov (cnd), Czech PO (original 1903/04 version) Supraphon ▲ SUP 3005
Silberschlag, Jeff (tpt)—see also ORCHESTRAS & ENSEMBLES Maryland Bach Aria Group members
Gould, M.:Cinerama Holiday—Souvenirs of Paris; On the Boulevard [both arr Gould for solo tpt] *(rec Seattle Opera House, June 13, 1994)* Delos ▲ DE 3166 [DDD]
Gould, M.:Festive Music, w. G. Schwarz (cnd), Seattle SO—Interlude *(rec Seattle Opera House, June 13, 1994)* Delos ▲ DE 3166 [DDD]
Silberstein, Myron (pno)
Bloch, E.:In the Night *(rec Music Hall, Tarrytown, NY, Nov 7 & 8, 1994)* Connoisseur Society ▲ CD 4208
Bloch, E.:Son Pno *(rec Music Hall, Tarrytown, NY, Nov 7 & 8, 1994)* Connoisseur Society ▲ CD 4208
Franck, C.:Danse lente *(rec Music Hall, Tarrytown, NY, Nov 7 & 8, 1994)* Connoisseur Society ▲ CD 4208
Franck, C.:Prélude, choral et fugue *(rec Music Hall, Tarrytown, NY, Nov 7 & 8, 1994)* Connoisseur Society ▲ CD 4208
Giannini, V.:Prelude & Fughetta *(rec Music Hall, Tarrytown, NY, Nov 7 & 8, 1994)* Connoisseur Society ▲ CD 4208
Giannini, V.:Vars on Cantus Firmus *(rec Music Hall, Tarrytown, NY, Nov 7 & 8, 1994)* Connoisseur Society ▲ CD 4208
Silbert, G. (pno)
Bach, J.S.:Goldberg Vars Bequest ▲ BCSC 10007 [DDD]
Silfies, George (cl)
Mozart, W.A.:Qnt Pno, K.452, w. W. Klien (pno), P. Bowman (ob), G. Berry (bn), R. Pandolfi (hn) *(rec 1975–79)* Vox Box 3–▲ CD3X 3014 [ADD]
Mozart, W.A.:Trio Cl, K.498, w. T. Dumm (va), P. Paul (pno) *(rec 1975–79)* Vox Box 3–▲ CD3X 3014 [ADD]
Sillito, Kenneth (vn)—see also ORCHESTRAS & ENSEMBLES Academy of St. Martin in the Fields Chamber Ensemble
Bach, J.S.:Con for 2 Vns, w. Hugh Bean (vn), A. Davidson (cnd), England Virtuosi Classics for Pleasure ("Silver Doubles" series) 2–▲ CFP CDCFP 4769 [ADD]
Hommages, w. Margaret Fingerhut (pno), Margaret Cable (mez), William Bennett (fl), Clifford Benson (pno) Chandos ▲ CHAN 8578 [DDD]
Saint-Saëns, C.:Fant Vn, w. S. Kanga (hp) Chandos ▲ CHAN 8621 [DDD]
Sillito, Kenneth (vn) (cont.)
Spohr, L.:Potpourri 2 Chandos ▲ CHAN 9424
Vaughan Williams, R.:Con accademico, w. B. Thomson (cnd), London SO Chandos ▲ CHAN 8633 [DDD]
Vivaldi, A.:Cons for 2 Vns, w. P. Zukerman (vn), P. Zukerman (cnd), English CO—(2) in a, RV.522; in d, RV.565 *(rec 1971)* Sony Classical ("Essential Classics" series) ▲ SBK 48273 [ADD] ■ SBT 48273
Walton, W.:Qt Pno, w. H. Milne (pno), R. Smissen (va), S. Orton (vc) Chandos ▲ CHAN 8999 [DDD]
Walton, W.:Son Vn & Pno, w. H. Milne (pno) Chandos ▲ CHAN 8999 [DDD]
Sillman, J. (org)
Mozart, W.A.:Arias, w. B. Hendricks (sop), N. Marriner (cnd), Academy of St. Martin in the Fields, Academy Chorus EMI Classics ▲ CDC 49283
Siloti, Alexander (pno)
Private Recordings Pearl ▲ PEA 9993 (m) [AAD]
Silva, Miguel da (va)—see also ORCHESTRAS & ENSEMBLES Ysaÿe String Quartet
Britten, H.:Phantasy Qt, w. François Leleux (ob), Guillaume Sutre (vn), Marc Coppey (vc) Harmonia Mundi France ("Les Nouveaux Interprètes" series) ▲ HMN 911556
Music at the Time of Beaumarchais, w. Montserrat Figueras (sop), Lawrence Monteyro (sop), Raphel Oleg (vn), Christophe Coin (vc), Marc Coppey (vc), José Miguel Moreno (gtr), Paul Badura-Skoda (pno), Philippe Cassard (pno), Eric Le Sage (pno), Bob Van Asperen (h Valois ▲ V 4767
Silva, Paul da (pno)
Dvořák, A.:Ballad, w. Kirstin Fife (vn) *(rec Castle Oaks Studio, Calabasas, CA)* Raptoria Caam ▲ RCD 1006
Dvořák, A.:Notturno, w. Kirstin Fife (vn) *(rec Castle Oaks Studio, Calabasas, CA)* Raptoria Caam ▲ RCD 1006
Janácek, L.:Dumka, w. Kirstin Fife (vn) *(rec Castle Oaks Studio, Calabasas, CA)* Raptoria Caam ▲ RCD 1006
Janácek, L.:Romance Vn & Pno, w. Kirstin Fife (vn) *(rec Castle Oaks Studio, Calabasas, CA)* Raptoria Caam ▲ RCD 1006
Janácek, L.:Son Vn, w. Kirstin Fife (vn) *(rec Castle Oaks Studio, Calabasas, CA)* Raptoria Caam ▲ RCD 1006
Smetana, B.:From the Homeland, w. Kirstin Fife (vn) *(rec Castle Oaks Studio, Calabasas, CA)* Raptoria Caam ▲ RCD 1006
Silva, Rohan de (pno)
Bartók, B.:Romanian Folk Dances Pno, w. K. Nikkanen (vn) [arr. for violin & piano Zoltán Szekely] *(rec 9/90)* Collins Classics ▲ 12032 [DDD]
Franck, C.:Son Vn, w. A. A. Meyers (vn) RCA Red Seal ▲ 09026-61283-2
Strauss, R.:Son Vn, w. A. Meyers (vn) RCA Red Seal ▲ 09026-61283-2
Silvanská, Ada (vn)
Jirásek, J.:Katharsis, w. Václav Slivanský (fl), Lubomír Herza (vc), Renata Jelínková (hpd) *(rec St. Virgin Mary Church, Strahov)* Arta ▲ 0054 [DDD]
Silvansky, Sergei (pno)
Bacewicz, G.:Partita Vn, w. Arnold Belnick (vn) *(rec Univ of Southern California, July 1995)* Cambria ▲ CD 1052 [DDD]
Bacewicz, G.:Son 3 Vn & Pno, w. Arnold Belnick (vn) *(rec Univ of Southern California, July 1995)* Cambria ▲ CD 1052 [DDD]
Bacewicz, G.:Son 4 Vn & Pno, w. Arnold Belnick (vn) *(rec Univ of Southern California, July 1995)* Cambria ▲ CD 1052 [DDD]
Bacewicz, G.:Son 5 Vn & Pno, w. Arnold Belnick (vn) *(rec Univ of Southern California, July 1995)* Cambria ▲ CD 1052 [DDD]
Silver, Bonnie (hpd)
Boccherini, L.:Qnts Gtr & Strs, w. N. Kraft (gtr)—in D, G.448 [arr. Kraft & Silver for guitar & harpsichord] Chandos ▲ CHAN 8937 [DDD]
Haydn, J.:Qts Strs, Op. 2, w. Norbert Kraft (gtr) [arr. by the performers for guitar & harpsichord]—Op. 2/2 Chandos ▲ CHAN 8937 [DDD]
Rodrigo, J.:Fant para un gentilhombre, w. N. Kraft (gtr) [arr. by the performers for guitar & harpsichord] Chandos ▲ CHAN 8937 [DDD]
Vivaldi, A.:Con Lt, w. N. Kraft (gtr) [arr. by the performers for guitar & harpsichord] Chandos ▲ CHAN 8937 [DDD]
Silverman, Ethan (bn)—see ORCHESTRAS & ENSEMBLES Speculum Musicae
Silverman, Robert (pno)
Bach, J.S.:Das wohltemperierte Klavier—Book 1:Prelude in e♭; Fugue in d#; Prelude in D♭; Fugue in E♭ *(rec live in Albuquerque, NM)* Stereophile 2–▲ STPH 005–2 [ADD]
Baker, M.C.:Con Pno, w. K. Akiyama (cnd), Vancouver CO—additional piano works by Baker CBC ("SM 5000" series) ▲ SMCD 5107
Beethoven, L. van:Son 30 Pno Marquis ▲ RVCD 1901 [DDD]
Beethoven, L. van:Son 31 Pno Marquis ▲ RVCD 1901 [DDD]
Beethoven, L. van:Son 32 Pno Marquis ▲ RVCD 1901 [DDD]
Brahms, J.:Intermezzos Pno, Op. 117 *(rec Jan. 29 & 30, 1990)* Stereophile ▲ STPH 003–2 [ADD/AAD]
Brahms, J.:Pieces Pno, Op. 118 CBC ("Musica Viva" series) ▲ MVCD 1028
Brahms, J.:Rhaps Pno, Op. 79—No. 1 CBC ("Musica Viva" series) ▲ MVCD 1028
Brahms, J.:Son 3 Pno *(rec Jan. 29 & 30, 1990)* Stereophile ▲ STPH 003–2 [ADD]
Brahms, J.:Vars on a Hungarian Song CBC ("Musica Viva" series) ▲ MVCD 1028
Chopin, F.:Barcarolle Pno *(rec live in Albuquerque, NM, Nov. 6 & 8, 1992 & Nov. 5)* Stereophile 2–▲ STPH 005–2 [ADD]
Chopin, F.:Scherzos—No. 3 in c#, Op. 39 *(rec live, Albuquerque, NM, Nov. 6 & 8, 1992 & Nov. 5)* Stereophile 2–▲ STPH 005–2 [ADD]
Chopin, F.:Waltzes—in c#, Op. 64/2 *(rec live, Albuquerque, NM, Nov. 6 & 8, 1992 & Nov. 5)* Stereophile 2–▲ STPH 005–2 [ADD]
Franck, C.:Miniatures (11) CBC ("Musica Viva" series) ▲ MVCD 1061 [DDD]
Franck, C.:Prélude, aria et final CBC ("Musica Viva" series) ▲ MVCD 1061 [DDD]
Franck, C.:Prélude, choral et fugue CBC ("Musica Viva" series) ▲ MVCD 1061 [DDD]
Franck, C.:Prélude, fugue et var CBC ("Musica Viva" series) ▲ MVCD 1061 [DDD]
Liszt, F.:Pno Music (misc)—Son Pno in b, S.178; La lugubre gondola I & II; Annés de Pèlerinage, First Year:Switzerland:Vallée d'Oberman, Orage; Leibstraum *(rec Albuquerque, NM, Nov 2–5, 1993)* Stereophile ▲ STPH 0082 [DDD]
Schubert, Franz:Moments musicaux *(rec live in Albuquerque, NM, Nov. 6 & 8, 1992 & Nov. 5)* Stereophile 2–▲ STPH 005–2 [ADD]
Schumann, R.:Son Pno, Op. 14 *(rec live in Albuquerque, NM, Nov. 6 & 8, 1992 & Nov. 5)* Stereophile 2–▲ STPH 005–2 [ADD]
Silverman, Tracy (vn)—see ORCHESTRAS & ENSEMBLES Turtle Island String Quartet
Silvers, James (pno)
Lovenstein, J.:Music of, w. Mary Brockenbrough (sop), Laura Sanders (sop), Barton Green (ten), Rockland Osgood (ten), David Murray (bar), Benjamin Sears (bar), Jonathan Lovenstein (pno), Heather O'Donnell (pno), James Silvers (pno), Rocy Reider (fl), Jason Horowitz (vn), Adrianna Hulscher (vn), James Johnston (vn), Mimi Ragson (vn), Peter Landeen (vc), Reinmar Seidler (vc)—Blake Songs; other works Titanic ▲ Ti 221 [DDD]
Silverstein, Joseph (vn)—see also ORCHESTRAS & ENSEMBLES Lincoln Center Chamber Music Society members
Barber, S.:Con Vn, w. C. Ketchum (cnd), Utah SO Pro Arte ▲ CDD 241
Beach, A.M.C.:Music for Vn & Pno, w. V. Eskin (pno)—Oh Mistress Mine, Op. 37/1; Romance, Op. 23; Three Pieces, Op. 40 (La captive; Berceuse; Mazurka); Lento espressivo, Op. 125 Northeastern ▲ NR 9004-CD
Beethoven, L. van:Con Vn, Op. 61, w. J. Silverstein (cnd), Utah SO Pro Arte ▲ CDD 228 [DDD]
Beethoven, L. van:Con Vn, Op. 61, w. J. Silverstein (cnd), Utah SO Pro Arte ▲ CDS 588 [DDD]
Beethoven, L. van:Die Weihe des Hauses (ov), w. J. Silverstein (cnd), Utah SO Pro Arte ▲ CDS 588 [DDD]
Brahms, J.:Con Vn, w. C. Ketchum (cnd), Utah SO Pro Arte ▲ CDS 3431
Brahms, J.:Con Vn, w. J. Silverstein (cnd), Utah SO Pro Arte ▲ CDD 271

▲ = CD ♦ = Enhanced CD ∆ = MD ■ = Cassette Tape □ = DCC

Silverstein, Joseph (vn) (cont.)
Dohnányi, E. von:Serenade, w. P. Neubauer (va), G. Hoffman (vc) *(rec Apr. 14, 1993)* Delos ▲ DE 3151 [DDD]
Dvořák, A.:Con Vn, w. J. Silverstein (cnd), Utah SO Pro Arte ▲ CDD 389
Foote, A.:Pieces Vn & Pno, Op. 9, w. V. Eskin (pno) Northeastern ▲ NR 206–CD
Foote, A.:Trio 2, w. V. Eskin (pno), J. Eskin (vc) Northeastern ▲ NR 206–CD
Grieg, E.:Music of, w. Russell Sherman (pno), A. Gerhardt (cnd), Utah SO, London Royal Promenade Orch—Peer Gynt Suites 1 & 2; Holberg Suite; Piano Concerto (1st movt.) Pro Arte ▲ CDM 811; ▮ PCD 811
Kodály, Z.:Serenade for 2 Vns & Va, w. A. Kavafian (vn), P. Neubauer (va) *(rec Feb. 22, 1993)* Delos ▲ DE 3151 [DDD]
Mendelssohn, F.:Con in e Vn & Orch, Op. 64, w. J. Silverstein (cnd), Utah SO Pro Arte ▲ CDD 187 [DDD]
Mendelssohn, F.:Music of, w. S. Comissiona (cnd), Houston SO, Utah SO—Violin Concerto in e, Op. 64; Midsummer Night's Dream (overture); etc. Pro Arte ▲ CDM 815 ▮ PCD 815
Schumann, C.:Trio Pno, w. C. Carr (vc), V. Jochum (pno) Tudor ▲ TUD 788 [DDD]
Vivaldi, A.:Cons Vn, Op. 8/1–4, "The Four Seasons", w. S. Ozawa (cnd), Boston SO Telarc ▲ CD 80070 [DDD] ▮ CS 30070 (D)

Silverthorne, Paul (va)
Beethoven, L. van:Serenade Strs, Op. 8, w. C. Conway (vn), G. Garcia (vc) [flute, viola, guitar arr.] Meridian ▲ CDE 84199
Brahms, J.:Sons Cl (comp), w. J. Jacobson (pno) Meridian ▲ CDE 84190
Brahms, J.:Songs, Op. 91, w. S. Walker (mez), J. Jacobson (pno) [G] Meridian ▲ CDE 84190
Britten, H.:Elegy Va EMI Classics ("Anglo-American Chamber Music" series) ▲ CDC 55398
Elgar, E.:Qnt Pno Strs, w. Israela Margalit (pno), Alexander Barantschick (vn), Janice Graham (vn), Moray Welsh (vc) EMI Classics ("Anglo-American Chamber Music" series) ▲ CDC 55403
Haydn, J.:Qts Fl, w. Clive Conway (fl), Nona Liddell (vn), Charles Tunnell (vc) Meridian ▲ CDE 84118
Knussen, O.:"...upon one note", w. Michael Collins (cl), Clio Gould (vn), Christopher van Kampen (vc), John Constable (pno) *(rec Henry Wood Hall & All Hollows Gospel Oak, London, Oct & Dec 1995)* Deutsche Grammophon ▲ 449 572–2 [DDD]
Kreutzer, J.:Grand Trio, w. C. Conway (fl), G. Garcia (gtr) Meridian ▲ CDE 84199
Lazarof, H.:Oct Strs, w. Yukiko Kamei (vn), Peter Marsh (vn), Yoko Matsuda (vn), Miwako Watanabe (vn), Milton Thomas (va), Godfried Hoogeveen (vc), David Speltz (vc), H. Lazarof (cnd) Laurel ▲ LR 843 [DDD]
Matthews, C.:Suns Dance, w. Sebastian Bell (pic), Gareth Hulse (ob), Michael Collins (b cl), John Orford (ctbn), Michael Thompson (hn), Nona Liddell (vn), Joan Atherton (vn), Christopher van Kampen (vc), Robin McGee (db) *(rec All Saint's Church, Petersham, Oct 1992)* Deutsche Grammophon ▲ 447067–2 [DDD]
Molino, F.:Trio Fl, Op. 45, w. C. Conway (fl), G. Garcia (gtr) Meridian ▲ CDE 84199
Rózsa, M.:Con Va, w. J. Sedares (cnd), New Zealand SO Koch International Classics ▲ KIC 7304 [DDD]
Schnittke, A.:Trio Strs, w. M. Marinkovic (vn), T. Hugh (vc) ASV ▲ ASV 868 [DDD]
Schubert, Franz:Qt Fl, w. C. Conway (fl), G. Garcia (gtr), C. Tunnell (vc) Meridian ▲ CDE 84118
Walton, W.:Qt Pno, w. *(pianist unknown)*, Janice Graham (vn), Moray Welsh (vc) EMI Classics ("Anglo-American Chamber Music" series) ▲ CDC 55404

Silvmark, Johan (perc)
Larsson, M.:Clockworks, w. Love Derwinger (pno), Rolan Pöntinen (pno), Stockholm Chamber Brass *(rec Studio 2, Swedish Radio, Nov. 13, 1994)* BIS ▲ CD 699 [DDD]
Stravinsky, I.:L'Histoire du soldat (sels), w. Stockholm Chamber Brass—Tango; Waltz; Ragtime [all arr. Joakim Agnas for Brass] *(rec Danderyd Grammar School Gymnasium, June 26–30, 1994)* BIS ▲ CD 699 [DDD]
Stravinsky, I.:Ragtime, w. Stockholm Chamber Brass [arr. Joakim Agnas for Brass Qnt] *(rec Danderyd Grammar School Gymnasium, June 26–30, 1994)* BIS ▲ CD 699 [DDD]

Šimandl, Josef (vc)
Schubert, Franz:Qnt Strs, D.956, w. Josef Suk (vn), Jiří Baxa (vn), Ladislav Černý (va), Saša Večtomov (vc) *(rec live, 1971)* Praga ▲ PR 250055

Simcisko, Viktor (vn)
Purcell, H.:Sons (12) Vns, Z.790–801, w. Elisabeth Selig–Plaskurova (vn), Dusan Dockal (vc), Marica Dobiasova (hpd)—Nos. 1–3 *(rec Bratislava, 1994)* Discover International ▲ DI 920251 [DDD]
Purcell, H.:Sons (10) Vns, Z.802–811, w. Elisabeth Selig–Plaskurova (vn), Dusan Dockal (vc), Marica Dobiasova (hpd)—Nos. 2, 3, 5, 6 & 9 *(rec Bratislava, 1994)* Discover International ▲ DI 920251 [DDD]
Romberg, A.:Qnts Fl, w. V. Brunner (fl), M. Telecky (va), J. Cút (va), J. Alexander (vc) Trevak ▲ TRE 40007 [DDD]
Sperger, J.:Trios, w. M. Jukovic (fl), V. Dufka (ob), M. Telecky (va), J. Alexander (vc), sels. unknown Trevak ▲ TRE 40002 [DDD]
Zimmermann, A.:Cassations, w. V. Brunner (fl), J. Brunner (fl), J. Vondra (hn), P. Sivanic (hn), M. Tedla (vn), M. Telecky (va), J. Alexander (vc)—in G, D & D Trevak ▲ TRE 40008 [DDD]

Simcock, Ian (org)
Duruflé, M.:Mass, "Cum jubilo", w. Aaron Webber (trb), Simon Keenlyside (bar), Natalie Clein (vc), James O'Donnell (cnd), Westminster Cathedral Choir Hyperion ▲ CDA 66757
Duruflé, M.:Motets on Gregorian Chants, Op. 10, w. Aaron Webber (trb), Simon Keenlyside (bar), Natalie Clein (vc), J. O'Donnell (cnd), Westminster Cathedral Choir Hyperion ▲ CDA 66757
Duruflé, M.:Notre Père, w. Aaron Webber (trb), Simon Keenlyside (bar), Natalie Clein (vc), J. O'Donnell (cnd), Westminster Cathedral Choir Hyperion ▲ CDA 66757
Duruflé, M.:Requiem, w. Aaron Webber (trb), Simon Keenlyside (bar), Natalie Clein (vc), J. O'Donnell (cnd), Westminster Cathedral Choir Hyperion ▲ CDA 66757
Masterpieces of Mexican Polyphony, w. [cnd:James O'Donnell], Westminster Cathedral Choir, Andrew Watts (dulcian), Andrew Lawrence–King (hp) Hyperion ▲ CDA 66330 [DDD]
Pott, F.:Passion Sym Priory 2–▲ PRI 390 [DDD]
Poulenc, F.:Choral Music, w. J. O'Donnell (cnd), Westminster Cathedral Choir—Quatre petites prières de St. Francois d'Assise; Quatre motets pour un temps de pénitence; Quatre motets pour le temps de Noël; Salve Regina; Exultate Deo; Litanies à la Vierge Noire Hyperion ▲ CDA 66664
Poulenc, F.:Mass, w. J. O'Donnell (cnd), Westminster Cathedral Choir Hyperion ▲ CDA 66664
Tavener, J.:Lamentation, Last Prayer & Exultation, w. P. Rozario (sop) Collins Classics ▲ COL 1428 [DDD]

Simmonds, P. (hpd)—see ORCHESTRAS & ENSEMBLES Trio Basiliensis

Simmons, Peter (bn)
Talma, L.:Let's Touch the Sky, w. Rebecka Troxler (fl), Gerard Reuter (ob), Gregg Smith (cnd), Gregg Smith Singers Vox Box ("The American Composers" series) 3–▲ CDX 3037

Simmons, Raymond (tpt)
Gershwin, G.:Rhap in Blue, w. B. Griffiths (vn), P. Whittaker (cl), D. James (trbn), A. Litton (pno), H. Fisher (dr), A. Litton (cnd), Royal PO [original big band orchestration] RPO ▲ RPO 5011 [DDD]

Simms, John (pno)
Bartók, B.:Son for 2 Pnos, w. J. Avery (pno), T. L. Davis (perc), S. Schick (perc) Music & Arts ▲ CD 648 [AAD/ADD]

Simões, Nailson (tpt/flgl)—see ORCHESTRAS & ENSEMBLES Brasil Brass Quintet

Simola, Reino (cl)—see ORCHESTRAS & ENSEMBLES Helsinki Wind Quintet

Simon, A. (ob)
Beethoven, L. van:Qnt Ob, 3 Hns & Bn, w. R. Woodhams (hn), G. Stilfies (hn), G. Berry (hn), R. Pandolfi (bn) *(rec 1975–79)* Vox Box 3–▲ CD3X 3014 [ADD]

Simon, Abbey (pno)
Brahms, J.:Vars on a Theme by Paganini Vox Box 3–▲ CD3X 3020 [ADD]
Chasins, A.:Pno Transcriptions—Trans of Gluck's Melodie (Dance of the Blessed Spirits) [from *Orfeo ed Euridice*] *(rec 1980)* Allegretto ▲ ACD 8204
Chopin, F.:Andante Spianato & Grande Polonaise, w. H. Beissel (cnd), Hamburg SO Vox Box 2–▲ CDX 5002 [ADD]
Chopin, F.:Con 1 Pno, w. H. Beissel (cnd), Hamburg SO Vox Box 2–▲ CDX 5002 [ADD]
Chopin, F.:Con 2 Pno, w. H. Beissel (cnd), Hamburg SO Vox Box 2–▲ CDX 5002 [ADD]
Chopin, F.:Études (24) *(rec 1976)* Vox Box 2–▲ CDX 5167

Simon, Abbey (pno) (cont.)
Chopin, F.:Grand Fant on Polish Airs, w. H. Beissel (cnd), Hamburg SO Vox Box 2–▲ CDX 5002 [ADD]
Chopin, F.:Krakowiak, w. H. Beissel (cnd), Hamburg SO Vox Box 2–▲ CDX 5002 [ADD]
Chopin, F.:Nocturnes *(rec Elite Recordings, NYC, 1982)* Vox Box 2–▲ CDX 5146
Chopin, F.:Scherzos—in b♭, Op. 31 Special Music Co. ("Classics of the Heart" series) ▲ SCD 5197
Chopin, F.:Vars on Mozart's *La ci darem la mano*, w. H. Beissel (cnd), Hamburg SO Vox Box 2–▲ CDX 5002 [ADD]
Chopin, F.:Waltzes *(rec 1974)* Vox Box 2–▲ CDX 5167
Godowsky, L.:Transcriptions & Paraphrases—Paraphrase on Johann Strauss' "Die Fledermaus"; Transcription of Albéniz's Triana [from *Iberia*] *(rec 1980)* Allegretto ▲ ACD 8204
Liszt, F.:Transcriptions & Paraphrases—Transcription of Mozart's Don Juan Fantasy *(rec 1980)* Allegretto ▲ ACD 8204
Rachmaninoff, S.:Cons Pno (comp), w. L. Slatkin (cnd), St. Louis SO Vox Box 2–▲ CDX 5008 [ADD]
Rachmaninoff, S.:Pno Transcriptions—Trans of Kreisler:Liebesleid & Liebesfreud; Mendelssohn:Scherzo [from *A Midsummer Night's Dream*]; Mussorgsky:Hopak [from *The Fair at Sorochinsk*]; Rimsky–Korsakov:The Flight of the Bumblebee [from *Tsar Saltan*] *(rec 1980)* Allegretto ▲ ACD 8204
Rachmaninoff, S.:Rhapsody on a Theme of Paganini, w. L. Slatkin (cnd), St. Louis SO Vox Box 2–▲ CDX 5008 [ADD]
Ravel, M.:Con Pno (left hand), w. L. de Froment (cnd), Luxembourg RSO Vox Box 2–▲ CDX 5032 [ADD]
Ravel, M.:Con in G Pno, w. L. de Froment (cnd), Luxembourg RSO Vox Box 2–▲ CDX 5031 [ADD]
Ravel, M.:Pno Music—complete works for solo piano Vox Box 2–▲ CDX 5012 [ADD]
Schumann, R.:Arabeske Pno Dante ▲ PSG 9649
Schumann, R.:Carnaval Pno *(rec Elite Recordings, NYC, 1970)* Allegretto ▲ ACD 8192
Schumann, R.:Fant Pno *(rec Elite Recordings, NYC, 1970)* Allegretto ▲ ACD 8192
Schumann, R.:Kinderszenen Dante ▲ PSG 9649
Schumann, R.:Kreisleriana Dante ▲ PSG 9649
Schumann, R.:Vars on A–B–E–G–G Dante ▲ PSG 9649

Simon, Béla (pno)
Sarasate, P. de:Caprice basque, w. Lajos Csury (vn) Classical Diamonds ▲ 4007 [DDD]
Sarasate, P. de:Carmen Fant, w. Lajos Csury (vn) [arr for vn & pno] Classical Diamonds ▲ 4007 [DDD]
Sarasate, P. de:Spanish Dances, w. Lajos Csury (vn) Classical Diamonds ▲ 4007 [DDD]
Sarasate, P. de:Zigeunerweisen, w. Lajos Csury (vn) Classical Diamonds ▲ 4007 [DDD]

Simon, Jan (pno)
Brahms, J.:Son 2 Pno Supraphon ▲ SUP 111844 [DDD]
Brahms, J.:Waltzes Pno, Op. 39—sels. Supraphon ▲ SUP 111844 [DDD]
Chopin, F.:Mazurkas—Op. 17, Nos. 1–4 Supraphon ▲ 11 1545–2 [DDD]
Chopin, F.:Preludes, Op. 28 Supraphon ▲ 11 1545–2 [DDD]
Chopin, F.:Son Pno, Op. 35 Supraphon ▲ 11 1545–2 [DDD]

Šimon, Jan (trb vl)—see ORCHESTRAS & ENSEMBLES Pro Arte Antiqua Prague

Simon, László (pno)
Clementi, M.:Sons Pno—Son. in F, Op. 36/2; Son. in f♯, Op. 26/2 *(rec Feb. 11, 1979)* BIS ▲ CD 36 [DDD]
Frumerie, G. de:Vars & Fugue Pno, w. S. Westerberg (cnd), Stockholm PO Caprice ▲ CAP 21400 [AAD]
Kodály, Z.:Marosszék Dances *(rec Sept. 19–20, 1981)* BIS ▲ CD 194 [AAD]
Kodály, Z.:Méditation sur un motif de Claude Debussy *(rec Sept. 19–20, 1981)* BIS ▲ CD 194 [AAD]
Kodály, Z.:Pieces (7) Pno *(rec Sept. 19–20, 1981)* BIS ▲ CD 194 [AAD]
Liszt, F.:Années de pèlerinage 1 *(rec Sept. 19–20, 1981)* BIS ▲ CD 194 [AAD]
Liszt, F.:Études d'exécution transcendante, S.139 BIS ▲ CD 369
Liszt, F.:Sonetti del Petrarca Pno *(rec Sept. 19–20, 1981)* BIS ▲ CD 194 [AAD]

Simonacci, Giancarlo (pno)
Dashow, J.:Some Dream Songs, w. J. Logue (sop), M. Buffa (vn)—[E] CRI ▲ CD 578 [DDD]

Simoncini, Alessandro (vn)—see ORCHESTRAS & ENSEMBLES Giovane Quartetto Italiano

Simoncini, Luca (vc)—see ORCHESTRAS & ENSEMBLES Giovane Quartetto Italiano

Simonin, Christine (ondes martinot)
Koechlin, C.:Premier album de Lilian, w. Kathrin Graf (sop), Philippe Racine (fl), Daniel Cholette (pno) Accord ▲ ACD 201232 [DDD]
Koechlin, C.:Second album de Lilian, w. Philippe Racine (fl), Daniel Cholette (pno) Accord ▲ ACD 201232 [DDD]
Koechlin, C.:Vers le soleil for Ondes Martinot Accord ▲ ACD 201232 [DDD]

Simonot, Geneviève (vn)
Chausson, E.:Con Vn, Pno & Str Qt, w. R. Daugareil (vn), R. Pasquier (vn), B. Pasquier (va), R. Pidoux (vc), J.–C. Pennetier (pno) Harmonia Mundi Plus ▲ HMP 3901135

Simonsen, Henrik (db)
Vesth, T.:Music of, w. Jan Sommer (gtr), Nils Sylvest Jeppesen (vc), Per Friman (vn), Gert–Inge Andersson (va), Berit Spaelling (hp), Bent Larsen (fl), Bjorn Nielsen (ob), Svend Rasmussen (cl)—Cuddling Rain; Waltz the Blue Sea; Kaspers Lullaby; Autumn Sunshine; Red Fox Hunting Tea Party; Off White Eternity; Tartan Fl Danica ▲ DCD 8142

Simonsen, K. (b gtr)—see ORCHESTRAS & ENSEMBLES Antifonale Chamber Ensemble

Simpson, D. (vc)—see ORCHESTRAS & ENSEMBLES Aeolian String Quartet

Simpson, David (vc)
Klein, G.:Duo Vn & Vc, w. Serge Garcia (vn) Arion ▲ ARN 68272 [DDD]
Klein, G.:Four Movements, w. Serge Garcia (vn), Sona Khochafian (vn), Françoise Gnéri (va) Arion ▲ ARN 68272 [DDD]
Klein, G.:Movements Str Qt, w. Serge Garcia (vn), Sona Khochafian (vn), Françoise Gnéri (va) Arion ▲ ARN 68272 [DDD]
Scelsi, G.:Duo Vn, w. Carmen Fournier (vn) Accord ▲ ACD 200742 [DDD]

Simpson, Derek (vc)—see also ORCHESTRAS & ENSEMBLES London Chamber Players
Purcell, H.:Chamber Music, w. Alberto Lysy (vn), Robert Masters (vn), Yehudi Menuhin (vn), Cecil Arnowitz (va), Walter Gerhard (va), Ambrose Gauntlett (vl), Roy Jesson (hpd/org)—Trio Sons Nos. 2 in C, 6 in G & 8 in G; Fants Nos. 4 in g, 7 in c, 8 in d & 13 in F, "Upon One Note" EMI Classics ("Baroque" series) ▲ CDK 65734
Purcell, H.:Dido & Aeneas (sels), w. Victoria de los Angeles (sop—Dido), Heather Harper (sop—Belinda), Sibyl Michelow (sop), Elizabeth Robson (sop), Colin Tilney (hpd), J. Barbirolli (cnd), English CO, Ambrosian Singers—Ov.; Shake the Cloud; Ah! Ah! Belinda; When Monarchs Unite; But Ere We This Perform; But Death, Alas! I Cannot Shun...When I am Laid in Earth; With Drooping Wings *(rec Abbey Road Studio 1, London, Aug. 1965)* EMI Classics ▲ CDK 65341 [ADD]
Purcell, H.:Fants, w. Alberto Lysy (vn), Robert Masters (vn), Yehudi Menuhin (vn), Cecil Arnowitz (va), Walter Gerhard (va), Ambrose Gauntlett (vl), Roy Jesson (hpd/org)—Nos. 4 in g, 7 in c, 8 in d, 13 in F EMI Classics ▲ CDK 65734
Purcell, H.:Sons (22) Vns, w. Alberto Lysy (vn), Robert Masters (vn), Yehudi Menuhin (vn), Cecil Aronowitz (va), Walter Gerhard (va), Ambrose Gauntlett (vl), Roy Jesson (hpd/org)—Nos. 2, 6, & 8 EMI Classics ▲ CDK 65734

Simpson, Robert (org)
Music for Horn & Organ, w. Steve Gross (hn) *(rec 1987)* ACA Digital ▮ CM20002–2

Simpson, Rosalind (hp)—see also ORCHESTRAS & ENSEMBLES Peter Garland Ensemble
Garland, P.:Cantares de la Frontera ¿What Next? ▲ WN 0008 [DDD] ▮ F

Sims, Zoot (sax)
Schwartz, C.:Mother! Mother!, w. Clark Terry (tpt), A. Weisberg (cnd), Contemporary Chamber Ensemble Pablo Today ▮ 52312–115

Sinclair, David (db)
Telemann, G.P.:Cons (misc), w. Masahiro Arita (trns fl/pic), Eric Hoeprich (chl), Hans Peter Westermann (ob), Dane Roberts (db), La Stravaganza Cologne—in E for Transverse Flute, Oboe d'amore, Viola d'amore, Strings & Continuo; in e for Transverse Flute, Violin, Strings & Continuo; in D for Transverse Flute, Strings & Continuo; in E♭ for Strings & Continuo; in G for Transverse Flute, Chalumeau, Oboe, 2 Double Basses, Strings & Continuo *(rec Cologne, May 30–June 3, 1994)* Denon ("Aliare" series) ▲ CO 78933 [DDD]

INSTRUMENT.

Sinclair, David (vle)—see ORCHESTRAS & ENSEMBLES Ricercar Consort
Sinclair, Diane Bruce (vn)—see also ORCHESTRAS & ENSEMBLES New York Camerata
Cory, E.:Pas de Quatre, w. Jayn Rosenfeld (fl), Charles Forbes (vc), Meg Bachman Vas (pno), New York Camerata — Soundspells ▲ CD 116 [DDD]
Sindelar, V. (fl)—see ORCHESTRAS & ENSEMBLES Scarborough Chamber Players
Sindelar, V. (fl/pic)—see ORCHESTRAS & ENSEMBLES Scarborough Chamber Players
Singer, Jeanne (pno)
Singer, J.:Songs & Song Cycles, w. A. Miskell (ten), F. Hechtel (sop)—American Indian Song Suite; Arno is Deep; From Petrarch; Hannah; Memoria; Lost Garden; Old Wild Woman; Query to the Creator; Songs from Later Years (song cycle); Wry Rimes (song cycle) [E] — Cambria ▲ CD 1051
Singer, J.:To Stir a Dream:American Poets in Song, w. F. Hechtel (sop), A. Miskell (ten) — Cambria ▲ CMB 1051 [DDD]
Singer, Margaret (pno)
Flury, R.:Con 1 Pno, w. U.J. Flury (cnd), Czech SO *(rec Filmové Studio, Prague, Apr 22–23, 1994)* — Gallo ▲ CD 865 [DDD]
Flury, R.:Con 2 Pno, w. U.J. Flury (cnd), Czech SO *(rec Filmové Studio, Prague, Apr 22–23, 1994)* — Gallo ▲ CD 865 [DDD]
Singleton, Philip (va)
Schoenberg, A.:Pierrot lunaire, w. Leslie Boucher (nar), Julie Stone (fl/pic), Tod Kerstetter (cl/b cl), Andrew Carlson (vn), Juanita Karpf (vc), F. Joseph Lozier (pno) *(rec Roswell United Methodist Church, Roswell, GA, July 20, Aug. 2 & Sept. 1)* — ACA Digital ▲ CM 20027
Zwilich, E.T.:Passages, w. Leslie Boucher (sop), Julie Stone (fl/pic), Tod Kerstetter (cl/b cl), Andrew Carlson (vn), Juanita Karpf (vc), F. Joseph Lozier (pno), Joanna Parks (perc), Shannon O'Kelley (perc) *(rec Roswell United Methodist Church, Roswell, GA, July 20, Aug. 2 & Sept. 1)* — ACA Digital ▲ CM 20027
Sinnhoffer, Ingo (vn)—see ORCHESTRAS & ENSEMBLES Sinnhoffer String Quartet members
Šintál, Michal (ob)
Holst, G.:A Fugal Con, w. J. Harvan (fl), G. Brand (cnd), European Winds — Albany ▲ TROY 120 [DDD]
Respighi, O.:Liriche su parole di poeti armeni, w. Denisa Šlepkovská (mez), Vladimír Havran (fl), Gabriel Koncer (cl), Ivan Viskup (b cl), Ivan Paulicka (bn), Frantisek Kovács (trbn), Katarína Vavreková (hp), M. Adriano (cnd) [arr. for chamber group by Adriano] *(rec Slovak Radio Concert Hall, Bratislava, Jan. 4–9, Feb. 19 & June)* — Marco Polo ▲ 8.223595 [DDD]
Siorenko, V. (vn)
Bach, J.S.:Con for 2 Vns, w. A. Schulrufer (vn), A. Steinlucht (cnd), Mozarteum Orch — Infinity Digital ▲ QK 57217 [DDD]
Sipahi, Omer (vn)
Weber, C.M. von:Qnt Cl, w. L. Fuchs (cl), M. Solms (vn), D. Morice (va), P. Caldwell (vc) — Gallo ▲ CD 570 [DDD]
Sirbu, M. (pno)
Enescu, G.:Son 1 Vn, w. M. Sirbu (vn) — Dynamic ▲ CD 41
Enescu, G.:Son 2 Vn, w. M. Sirbu (vn) — Dynamic ▲ CD 41
Enescu, G.:Son 3 Vn, w. M. Sirbu (vn) — Dynamic ▲ CD 41
Sirbu, Mariana (vn)
Enescu, G.:Son 1 Vn, w. M. Sirbu (pno) — Dynamic ▲ CD 41
Enescu, G.:Son 2 Vn, w. M. Sirbu (pno) — Dynamic ▲ CD 41
Enescu, G.:Son 3 Vn, w. M. Sirbu (pno) — Dynamic ▲ CD 41
Franck, C.:Andantino quietoso, w. M. Sarbu (pno) — Dynamic 2–▲ CD 21/1-2 [DDD]
Franck, C.:Gran Duo, w. M. Sarbu (pno) — Dynamic 2–▲ CD 21/1-2 [DDD]
Franck, C.:Son Vn, w. M. Sarbu (pno) — Dynamic 2–▲ CD 21/1-2 [DDD]
Širc, Jan (vc)—see ORCHESTRAS & ENSEMBLES Czech String Trio
Sirc, Jan (vc)
Mysliveček, J.:Sons en Trio, w. Radomír Sirc (vc), Václav Hoskovec (db), Robert Hugo (hpd) — Studio Matous ▲ MAT 19 [DDD]
Sirc, Radomír (vc)
Mysliveček, J.:Sons en Trio, w. Jan Sirc (vc), Václav Hoskovec (db), Robert Hugo (hpd) — Studio Matous ▲ MAT 19 [DDD]
Sirguey, Gaït (pno)
Gounod, C.:Songs, w. Darynn Zimmer (sop), R. Wilson (cnd), New York Solisti—Les Deux pigeons; Le Soir; Le Temps des roses; L'Absent; Viens! Les Gazons sont verts! *(rec American Academy of Arts & Letters, New York City, Jan 20–22 & May 27–28, 19)* — New Albion ▲ NA 078
Massenet, J.:Songs, w. Darynn Zimmer (sop), R. Wilson (cnd), New York Solisti—Oh! Si les fleurs avaient des yeux; Crépuscule; Souvenez-vous, vierge Marie!; C'est l'amour — New Albion ▲ NA 078
Sirodeau, Christophe (pno)
Segerstam, L.:A"on m...på..m-poème"-now..., w. Pia Segerstam (vc) *(rec Paris, Feb 28, 1996)* — BIS ▲ CD 792 [DDD]
Segerstam, L.:At the Border, w. Pia Segerstam (vc) *(rec Paris, Mar 1, 1996)* — BIS ▲ CD 792 [DDD]
Segerstam, L.:Thoughts 1976 *(rec Paris, Feb 28, 1996)* — BIS ▲ CD 792 [DDD]
Segerstam, L.:Zweixly con ped...adagissimo con nostalgia!, w. Nikolaos Samaltanos (pno) *(rec Paris, Feb 28, 1996)* — BIS ▲ CD 792 [DDD]
Sirokay, Zsuzanna (pno)
Beerhalter, A.:Vars on "Im tiefen Keller sitz' ich hier", w. H. R. Stalder (basset horn) *(rec 1981)* — Jecklin-Disco ▲ JD 560-2 [ADD]
Berr, F.:Fant 17, w. H. R. Stalder (cl) *(rec 1975)* — Jecklin-Disco ▲ JD 578-2 [ADD]
Boieldieu, F.-A.:Sons (9) Pno, w. H. R. Stalder (cl)— Sonata in E♭ [arr for cl & pno] *(rec 1975)* — Jecklin-Disco ▲ JD 578-2 [ADD]
Cavallini, E.:Adagio & Tarantella, w. H.R. Stalder *(rec 1975)* — Jecklin-Disco ▲ JD 578-2 [ADD]
Czerny, C.:Intro, Vars & Finale, w. Peter-Lukas Graf (fl) — Jecklin ▲ JEC 577 [ADD]
Czerny, C.:Rondoletto concertant, w. Peter-Lukas Graf (fl) — Jecklin ▲ JEC 577 [ADD]
Danzi, F.:Son Bas Hn, w. H.R. Stalder (cl) *(rec 1981)* — Jecklin-Disco ▲ JD 560-2 [ADD]
Kuhlau, F.:Intro & Rondo on "Ah! quand il gèle" from *Le Colporteur*, w. Peter-Lukas Graf (fl) *(rec 1982)* — Jecklin ▲ JEC 577 [ADD]
Molique, W.B.:Intro, Andante & Polonaise, w. Peter-Lukas Graf (fl) — Jecklin ▲ JEC 577 [ADD]
Ponchielli, A.:Il Convegno, w. H. R. Stalder (cl) [adapted for 2 clarinets & piano] *(rec 1975)* — Jecklin-Disco ▲ JD 578-2 [ADD]
Ries, F.:Fant on themes from "Mosè in Egitto", w. Peter-Lukas Graf (fl) — Jecklin ▲ JEC 577 [ADD]
Sirucek, Jerry (ob)—see ORCHESTRAS & ENSEMBLES Musica Sonora, Baroque Chamber Players
Siskovic, Crtomir (vn)
Kogoj, M.:Music of, w. Emanuele Arciuli (pno)—Andante in E; Prelude; Portrait; 7 Pieces; Piano [complete collection] — Stradivarius ▲ STV 33342
Sitkovetsky, Dmitri (vn)
Bach, J.S.:Cons Vn (comp), w. Vaclav Hudacek (vn), D. Sitkovetsky (cnd), Prague Virtuosi — Supraphon ▲ SUP 3085
Bach, J.S.:Con Vn & Ob, w. Vaclav Hudacek (vn), D. Sitkovetsky (cnd), Prague Virtuosi — Supraphon ▲ SUP 3085
Bach, J.S.:Con for 2 Vns, w. Vaclav Hudacek (vn), D. Sitkovetsky (cnd), Prague Virtuosi — Supraphon ▲ SUP 3085
Bach, J.S.:Goldberg Vars, w. Caussé (va), Maisky (vc) [string Trio version arr. Dmitri Sitkovetsky] — Orfeo ▲ 138851 ■ 138851
Bach, J.S.:Goldberg Vars, w. D. Sitkovetsky (cnd), New European Strings [arr. Sitkovetsky] — Elektra/Nonesuch ▲ 79341-2 ■ 79341-4
Bach, J.S.:Sons & Partitas Vn, BWV 1001-1006 — Orfeo 2–▲ 130852
Bartók, B.:Con 1 Vn, w. L. Pešek (cnd), Philharmonia Orch — Virgin Classics ▲ CDC 45118
Bartók, B.:Con 2 Vn, w. L. Pešek (cnd), Philharmonia Orch — Virgin Classics ▲ CDC 45118
Beethoven, L. van:Romances Vn, w. N. Marriner (cnd), Academy of St. Martin in the Fields — Virgin Classics ▲ CDC 45001
Beethoven, L. van:Trio 6 Pno, "Archduke", w. G. Oppitz (pno), D. Geringas (vc) — Novalis ▲ 150008 [DDD]
Beethoven, L. van:Trio 9 Pno, "Kakadu", w. G. Oppitz (pno), D. Geringas (vc) — Novalis ▲ 150008 [DDD]

Sitkovetsky, Dmitri (vn) (cont.)
Brahms, J.:Con Vn, w. N. Marriner (cnd), Academy of St. Martin in the Fields *(rec Henry Wood Hall, London, May 4–6, 1995)* — Hänssler Classic ("Academy" series) ▲ CD 98.934 [DDD]
Elgar, E.:Con Vn, w. Y. Menuhin (cnd), Royal PO — Virgin Classics ▲ CDC 45065
Grieg, E.:Sons Vn, Opp. 8, 13 & 45, w. B. Davidovich (pno) — Orfeo ▲ 047831 [DDD]
Kreisler, F.:Transcriptions, w. B. Canino (pno) — Orfeo ▲ 048831 [DDD]
Mendelssohn, F.:Con in e Vn & Orch, Op. 64, w. N. Marriner (cnd), Academy of St. Martin in the Fields *(rec Henry Wood Hall, London, May 4–6, 1995)* — Hänssler Classic ("Academy" series) ▲ CD 98.934 [DDD]
Mozart, W.A.:Cons Vn, w. D. Sitkovetsky (cnd), English CO—Nos. 4–5 — Novalis ▲ 150007 [DDD]
Prokofiev, S.:Mélodies, w. P. Gililov (pno) — Virgin Classics ▲ CDC 59023
Prokofiev, S.:Son solo Vn, Op. 115 — Virgin Classics ▲ CDC 59023
Prokofiev, S.:Son Vn, Op. 94bis, w. P. Gililov (pno) — Virgin Classics ▲ CDC 59023
Prokofiev, S.:Son 1 Vn, w. P. Gililov (pno) — Virgin Classics ▲ CDC 59023
Ravel, M.:Berceuse sur le nom de Gabriel Fauré, w. B. Davidovich (pno) — Orfeo ▲ 108841 [DDD] ■ M 108841A (D)
Ravel, M.:Son Vn Pno, w. B. Davidovich (pno) — Orfeo ▲ 108841 [DDD] ■ M 108841A (D)
Ravel, M.:Sonate posthume, w. B. Davidovich (pno) — Orfeo ▲ 108841 [DDD] ■ M 108841A (D)
Ravel, M.:Tzigane, w. B. Davidovich (pno) [violin-piano version] — Orfeo ▲ 108841 [DDD] ■ M 108841A (D)
Schoenberg, A.:Chamber Sym 1, w. A. Andorjan (fl), E. Brunner (cl), D. Geringas (vc), G. Oppitz (pno) [Webern's 1923 arr. for Flute, Clarinet, Violin, Cello & Piano] — Tudor ▲ 717 [DDD]
Schubert, Franz:Trio 1 Pno, w. G. Oppitz (pno), D. Geringas (vc) — Novalis ▲ 150002
Schubert, Franz:Trio 2 Pno, w. G. Oppitz (pno), D. Geringas (vc) — Novalis ▲ 150003
Shostakovich, D.:Con 1 Vn, w. A. Davis (cnd), BBC SO — Virgin Classics ▲ CDC 59601
Shostakovich, D.:Con 2 Vn, w. A. Davis (cnd), BBC SO — Virgin Classics ▲ CDC 59601
Spohr, L.:Songs Bar, Op. 154, w. D. Fischer-Dieskau (bar), H. Höll (pno) [G] — Orfeo ▲ 103841 [DDD] ■ M 103841A
Sitkovetsky, Julian (vn)
Glazunov, A.:Con Vn, w. K. Kondrashin (cnd), Moscow Youth Orch *(rec 1952)* — Arlecchino ▲ ARL110
Sibelius, J.:Con Vn, w. K. Kondrashin (cnd), Moscow Youth Orch *(rec 1952)* — Arlecchino ▲ ARL110
Sitsky, Larry (pno)
Contemporary Australian Piano Music — Move ▲ MD 3066
Siva, Miguel da (va)
Beethoven, L. van:Qts Pno, WoO 36, w. Philippe Cassard (pno), Raphael Oleg (vn), Marc Copey (vc) — Valois 2–▲ V 4715
Beethoven, L. van:Qt Pno, Op. 16, w. Philippe Cassard (pno), Raphael Oleg (vn), Marc Copey (vc) — Valois 2–▲ V 4715
Sivanič, Peter (hn)
Scarmolin, A.L.:Sym 2, w. Stanislav Bicák (bn), Miroslav Herák (vc), J. E. Suben (cnd), Slovak RSO Bratislava *(rec Bratislava, Jan 23–25, 1995)* — New World ▲ 80502-2
Zimmermann, A.:Cassations, w. V. Brunner (fl), J. Brunner (fl), J. Vondra (hn), V. Simcisko (vn), M. Tedla (vn), M. Telecky (va), J. Alexander (vc)—in G, D & D — Trevak ▲ TRE 40008 [DDD]
Sivelöv, Niklas (pno)
Berwald, F.:Con Pno, w. O. Kamu (cnd), Helsingborg SO *(rec Helsingborg Concert Hall, Helsingborg, Sweden, May 15–21 & May 30 – June)* — Naxos ▲ 8.553052 [DDD]
Sivils, Timothy (perc)
Argento, D.:I Hate & I Love, w. Joe Pereira (perc), Robert Shaw (cnd), Robert Shaw Festival Singers *(rec Church of St. Pierre, Gramat, France, July 26–28, 1994)* — Telarc ▲ CD 80408 [DDD]
Sivonen, Ilkka (pno)—see also ORCHESTRAS & ENSEMBLES Sinfonia Lahti Chamber Ensemble members
Kokkonen, J.:Opus sonorum, w. U. Söderblom (cnd), Lahti SO — BIS ▲ CD 508 [DDD]
Siwy, André (vn)
Martinů, B.:Con 2 for 2 Vns, w. Yaga Siwy (vn), R. Barshaï (cnd), Belgian Radio-TV French SO *(rec 1989)* — Discover International ▲ DI 920161 [DDD]
Prokofiev, S.:Son for 2 Vns, w. Yaga Siwy (vn), R. Barshaï (cnd), Belgian Radio-TV French SO *(rec 1989)* — Discover International ▲ DI 920161 [DDD]
Szymanowski, K.:Con 2 Vn, w. R. Barshaï (cnd), Belgian Radio-TV French SO *(rec 1989)* — Discover International ▲ DI 920161 [DDD]
Siwy, Yaga (vn)
Martinů, B.:Con 2 for 2 Vns, w. André Siwy (vn), R. Barshaï (cnd), Belgian Radio-TV French SO *(rec 1989)* — Discover International ▲ DI 920161 [DDD]
Prokofiev, S.:Son for 2 Vns, w. André Siwy (vn), R. Barshaï (cnd), Belgian Radio-TV French SO *(rec 1989)* — Discover International ▲ DI 920161 [DDD]
Six, Jack (db)—see also ORCHESTRAS & ENSEMBLES Dave Brubeck Quartet
Berlin, I.:Songs, w. Francis Thorne (pno/sgr)—Top Hat, White Tie & Tails; Remember; This Year's Kisses; Isn't This a Lovely Day; Everybody Step; Change Partners; There's No Business Like Show Business; When That Midnight Choo-Choo Leaves for Alabam'; No Strings; Slumming on Park Avenue; Soft Lights & Sweet Music; They Say It's Wonderful; I'll See You in C-U-B-A; Always; How Deep is the Ocean; Society Bear; I'm Putting All My Eggs in One Basket; I Used to Be Color Blind — CRI ▲ CD 557 [ADD]
Sjöberg, Carl (vn)—see ORCHESTRAS & ENSEMBLES Con Sordino Chamber Group
Sjöberg, Pär (ob)
Mats Aberg, w. Mats Aberg (org) *(rec Jan. 28, 1983)* — BIS ▲ CD 229 [DDD]
Sjöblom, Klas (ob)—see ORCHESTRAS & ENSEMBLES Danish Wind Octet, Scandinavian Wind Quintet
Sjöblom, Klas (ob/E hn)
Maegaard, J.:Musica Riservata II, w. Jesper Helmuth Madsen (cl), Jørgen Bove (sax), Peter Andersen (bn) *(rec Copenhagen, 1995–96)* — Marco Polo/Dacapo ▲ 8.224050 [DDD]
Sjögren, B. (baroque va)—see ORCHESTRAS & ENSEMBLES Musica Holmiae
Sjögren, B. (va da bracchio)—see ORCHESTRAS & ENSEMBLES Musica Holmiae
Sjøgren, Kim (vn)
Kuhlau, F.:Qnts Fl, w. Eyvind Rafn (fl), Georg Svendsen Andersen (va), Bjarne Boye Rasmussen (va), Lars Holm Johansen (vc) *(rec Torpen Kapel, Humlebaek, Nordsjaelland, Denmark, Aug 1985)* — Naxos ▲ 8.553303 [DDD]
Mozart, W.A.:Con 3 Vn, w. M. Schønwandt (cnd), Copenhagen Collegium Musicum — BIS ▲ CD 282 [DDD]
Mozart, W.A.:Con 5 Vn, w. M. Schønwandt (cnd), Copenhagen Collegium Musicum — BIS ▲ CD 282 [DDD]
Nielsen, C.:Con Vn, w. M. Schønwandt (cnd), Danish National RSO — Chandos ▲ CHAN 8894 [DDD]
Skaggs, Lawrence (vc)—see ORCHESTRAS & ENSEMBLES McPherson Trio
Skála, Pavel (perc)—see also ORCHESTRAS & ENSEMBLES Prague Percussion Project
Jirásek, J.:Labyrinth, w. Jan Jirásek (voice/syn), Irmela Nolte (fl) *(rec Audiostudio of Czech Radio, Prague)* — Arta ▲ 0054 [DDD]
Skanavi, Vladimir (pno)
A Collection Of 19th Century Songs, w. Natalia Gerasimova (mez) — Art & Electronics ▲ AED 68020 [DDD]
Skarba, H. (trbn)
Bruckner, A.:Motets, w. H. P. Blochwitz (ten), H. Breika (trbn), H. Weimer (trbn), S. Rommelspacher (org), Freiburg Vocal Ensemble—Os justi; Afferentur regi; Christus factus est; Tota pulchra es Maria; Vexilla regis prodeunt; Ecce sacerdos magnus; Pange lingua; Locus iste; Ave Maria; Virga Jesse floruit — Entrée ▲ 0039 [ADD]
Skareng, Per (gtr)
Bach, J.S.:Sons & Partitas Vn, BWV 1001-1006—Son No. 1, BWV 1001 [trans Per Skareng & Gordon Crosskey] — Caprice ▲ CAP 21392 [AAD]
Carlstedt, J.:Swedish Dances (2) — Caprice ▲ CAP 21392 [AAD]
Frumerie, G. de:Vars on a Swedish Folk Tune — Caprice ▲ CAP 21392 [AAD]
Giuliani, M.:Rossiniana—No. 1 — Caprice ▲ CAP 21392 [AAD]
Lauro, A.:Gtr Music—2 waltzes Carora & Angostura; Suite Venezolana — Caprice ▲ CAP 21392 [AAD]
Sagreras, J.S.:El Colibri — Caprice ▲ CAP 21392 [AAD]
Tárrega, F.:Recuerdos de la Alhambra — Caprice ▲ CAP 21392 [AAD]

▲ = CD ♦ = Enhanced CD Δ = MD ■ = Cassette Tape □ = DCC

Skavavi, Katia (vc)
Brahms, J.:Trio Cl, w. Michel Lethiec (cl), Truls Mork (pno) Lyrinx ▲ LYX 123 [DDD]

Skazinetsky, Mark (vn)
Catherine Wilson & Friends:Classical Potpourri, w. Catherine Wilson (pno), Norman Hathaway (va), Jack Mendelsohn (vc), Joel Quarrington (db) Doremi ▲ DHR 71111
Wagner, R.:Siegfried Idyll, w. T. Holowach (vn), L. Toman (va), R. Laurie (vc), C. Elliott (db), S. Shulman (fl), T. Maloney (cl), J. Valdepenas (cl), J. Fetherston (cl), S. Mosher (bn), S. Wilson (hn), R. Cohen (hn), J. Cowell (tpt), G. Gould (cnd) *(rec July 27–29 & Sept. 8, 198)* Sony Classical ▲ SMK 52650 [ADD]

Skeaping, Roderick (vn)
Purcell, H.:Songs, w. A. Deller (ct), W. Kuijken (vl), J. Ryan (vl), W. Christie (hpd), R. Elliott (hpd)—An Evening Hymn; Fairest Isle; From Rosy Bow'rs; I Attempt From Love's Sickness; If Music Be the Food of Love; Not All My Torments; O Lead Me to Some Peaceful Gloom; O Solitude; The Plaint; Retired From My Dear Astrea's Sight; Sweeter Than Roses; Thrice Happy Lovers *(rec April 1979)* Harmonia Mundi ▲ HML 590249

Skelly, Michael (pno)
Richter, M.:Landscapes of the Mind II, w. D. Heifetz (vn) Leonarda ▲ LE 337

Skelton, Logan (pno)
Dankner, S.:Sextet, w. V. Poullette (vn), E. Tanner (vn), M. Gyurik (va), A. Nisbet (vc), R. Kassinger (db) Albany ▲ TROY 067
Dankner, S.:Son Vn, w. Susan Doering (vn) *(rec Loyola Univ.)* Centaur ▲ CRC 2247
Thomson, V.:Synthetic Waltzes, w. K. Lyman (pno) *(rec Oct. 10 & 11, 1992 & Jan.)* Centaur ▲ CRC 2180 [DDD]

Skerjanc, Edvard (vn)
Vivaldi, A.:Con for 2 Vns Vc, R.565, w. E. Turovsky (vn), A. Aubut (vc), Y. Turovsky (cnd), Montreal Musici—RV.542 in F Chandos ▲ CHAN 8651 [DDD]

Skernick, Abraham (va)—see also ORCHESTRAS & ENSEMBLES Musica Sonora
Loeffler, C.M.:Rhaps, w. J. Mack (ob), E. Podis (pno) Crystal ■ C 323
Loeffler, C.M.:Rhaps, w. J. Mack (ob), E. Podis (pno) Crystal ▲ CD323
Mozart, W.A.:Qt Ob, K.370, w. J. Mack (ob), D. Majeske (vn), S. Geber (vc) Crystal ▲ CD323 ■ C 323
Mozart, W.A.:Sinf concertante Vn, K.364, w. R. Druian (vn), G. Szell (cnd), Cleveland Orch *(rec 1963)* CBS ▲ MYK 37810 [AAD] ■ MYT 37810

Skigin, Semion (pno)
Glinka, M.:Songs, w. Sergei Leiferkus (bar)—A Farewell to St. Petersburg; Elegy; The Fire of Longing Burns in My Heart; I Recall a Wonderful Moment; Doubt; Mary; How Sweet It Is to Be with You; Say Not That It Grieves the Heart *(rec All Saints' Church, Petersham, Surrey, England, Apr 26–27, 1995)* Conifer Classics ▲ 75605-51264-2 [DDD]
Mussorgsky, M.:nursery, w. Sergei Leiferkus (bar) Conifer Classics ▲ 75605-51229-2 [DDD]
Mussorgsky, M.:Songs & Dances, w. Sergei Leiferkus (bar) Conifer Classics ▲ 75605-51229-2 [DDD]
Mussorgsky, M.:Songs (misc), w. Sergei Leiferkus (bar)—The Puppet Show; Forgotten; The Seminarist; Savishna; The Billy-Goat; Song of Mephistopheles Conifer Classics ▲ 75605-51229-2 [DDD]
Mussorgsky, M.:Songs (misc), w. Sergei Leiferkus (bar)—Cruel Death [Epitaph]; The Misunderstood One; Misfortune; The Spirit of Heaven; Pride; Is Spinning Man's Work?; Vision; Trouble; On the Dnieper; Yeryomushka's Cradle Song; The Feast; The Classicist; From My Tears *(rec All Saints' Church, Petersham, Surrey, Apr 26–29, 1995)* Conifer Classics ▲ 75605-51248-2 [DDD]
Mussorgsky, M.:Sunless, w. Sergei Leiferkus (bar) *(rec All Saints' Church, Petersham, Surrey, Apr 26–29, 1995)* Conifer Classics ▲ 75605-51248-2 [DDD]
Tchaikovsky, P.:Songs, w. Sergei Leiferkus (bar)—I Bless You, Forests; It Was in the Early Spring; Death; None But the Lonely Heart; Reconciliation; Sleep, Poor Friend; Dusk Fell on the Earth; The Love of a Dead Man; My Genius, My Angel, My Friend; Why?; A Tear Trembles; Frenzied Nights; Not a Word, O My Friend; I Should Like in a Single Word; Do Not Believe It, My Friend; On the Golden Cornfields; No Response, or Ord, or Greeting; Amid the Din of the Ball; Don Juan's Serenade *(rec All Saints' Church, Petersham, Surrey, Sept 4–10, 1995)* Conifer Classics ("The Complete Song Edition" series) ▲ 75605-51266-2 [DDD]
Tchaikovsky, P.:Songs, w. Nina Rautio (sop)—If Only I Had Known; He Loved Me So Much; Do Not Leave Me; The Canary; Zemfira's Song; Gypsy's Song; The Fearful Minute; It Is Both Bitter & Sweet; To Forget So Soon; Was I Not a Little Blade of Grass?; Take My Heart Away; Cradle Song; Tell Me, What in the Shade of the Branches; Evening; The Mild Stars Shone for Us; Wait!; At Bedtime; Does the Day Reign? [R] *(rec All Saint's Church, Petersham, Surrey, Sept 1995 & Jan 1996)* Conifer Classics ▲ 51267 [DDD]

Skinnarmo, Eilev (vn)—see ORCHESTRAS & ENSEMBLES Busoni String Quartet

Skinner, Noel (pno)
Stoll, D.:Son Pnos, w. D. Ward (pno) Meridian ▲ MER 84245 [DDD]

Skjoldan, Erik (pno)
Borup-Jørgensen, A.:Pno Music—Winter Pieces (1959); Raindrop Interludes (1992–94); Summer Intermezzi (1971); Epigrams (1976); Thalattal Thalattal (1987–88) Point ▲ PCD 5117
Borup-Jørgensen, A.:Songs, w. Helene Gjerris (sop)—O Barn; Verirrt; Sehnsucht; Über die Heide; Ende des Herbstes; Schluszstück Point ▲ PCD 5117
Brask, P.:Etudes (11) Pno *(rec May 1984)* Classico ▲ CLASSCD 107
Brask, P.:Son Va, w. G.-I. Andersson (va) *(rec Dec. 1992)* Classico ▲ CLASSCD 107
Brask, P.:Sonatina Pno *(rec Dec. 1992)* Classico ▲ CLASSCD 107
Brask, P.:Suite Pno *(rec Dec. 1992)* Classico ▲ CLASSCD 107

Skocic, Adalbert (vc)—see ORCHESTRAS & ENSEMBLES Vienna Chamber Ensemble members

Skoczen-Staniszewska, M. (hp)
McLeod, J.:Gokstad Ship, w. J. Manning (sop), J. McLeod (cnd), Polish Radio-TV SO Vienna Modern Masters ▲ VMM 3026 [DDD]

Skorodin, Elain (vn)
Women at an Exposition, w. Sunny Joy Langton (sop), Susanne Mentzer (mez), Kimberly Schmidt (pno) *(rec Nov. 1991)* Koch International Classics ▲ KIC 7240 [ADD]

Skott, Morten (gtr)—see also ORCHESTRAS & ENSEMBLES Danish Guitar Duo
The Danish Guitar Duo, w. Soren Bodker Madsen (gtr) Point ▲ PCD 5107
Jolivet, A.:Sérénade for 2 Gtrs, w. Per Dybro Sørensen (gtr) *(rec Fruering Kirke, Denmark)* Paula ▲ PACD 63 [DAD]

Skoumal, Adam (pno)
Dvořák, A.:Songs, w. Milada Cechalová (sop), Stanislav Predota (ten)—Evening Songs, Opp. 3, 9 & 31; Songs, Op. 2; The Orphan, Op. 5; Rosemary; 2 Songs on Folk Poems, Op. posth.; 4 Songs, Op. 6; 3 Modern Greek Poems, Op. 50; 4 Songs, Op. 82 Studio Matous ▲ MAT 24 [DDD]
Janácek, L.:Moravian Folk Poetry, w. Eva Truplová (sop), Stanislav Predota (ten) Studio Matou ▲ MAT 15 [DDD]
Janácek, L.:Vocal Music, w. Eva Struplová (sop), Stanislav Predota (ten), Hanus Barton (pno), L. Cerny (cnd), *(ensemble unknown)*, Milan Uherek (cnd), Severácek Children's Choir—Little Queens; Folk Poetry from Hukvaldy; Folk Nocturnes; Nursery Rhymes Studio Matous ▲ MAT 16 [DDD]
Reicha, A.:Grand quatator concertant, w. Prague Wind Quintet members Studio Matous ▲ MAT 25 [DDD]
Reicha, A.:Son Pno, Op. 43 Studio Matous ▲ MAT 25 [DDD]

Skouras, Vangelis (hn)
Karaindrou, E.:Film Music, w. Jan Garbarek (t sax), Vangelis Christopoulos (ob), Anthis Sokratis (tpt), Nikos Guinos (cl), Tassos Diakoyiorgis (santouri), Petros Protopapas (fl), Andreas Tsekouras (acc), Christos Sfetsas (vc), Eleni Karaindrou (pno/voc), L. Chalkiadakis (cnd), *(ensemble unknown)*—Farewell Theme; Scream; Improv. On Farewell & Waltz Theme; Farewell Theme II [all from The Beekeeper; w. Jan Garbarek (ten sax), Tassos Diakoyiorgis (satouri), Vassilis Dertilis (kbd), Eleni Karaindrou (pno), Lefteris Chalkiadakis (cnd)]; Elegy for Rosa; Rosa's Song (text:Christofis) [both from Rosa; w. Vangelis Skouras (Fr hn), Petros Protopapas (fl), Alekos Christidis (timp), Eleni Karaindrou (voc), Lefteis Chalkiadakis (cnd)]; Fairytale; Parade; Return; Song [all from Happy Homecoming, Comrade; w. Vangelis Skouras (Fr hn), Christos Sfetsas (vc), Aliki Krithari (hp), Andreas Tsekouras (acc), Eleni Karaindrou (pno), Nelli Semitekolo (pno), Anthis Sokratis (tpt), Lefteris Chalkiadakis (cnd)]; Wandering in Alexandria (2 vers) [both from Wandering; w. Tassos Diakoyiorgis (santouri), Nelli Semitekolo (prepared pno), Anthis Sokratis (tpt), Nikos Guinos (cl), Katerina Ktona (hpd), Christos Sfetsas (vc)]; The Journey [from Voyage to Cythera]; Adagio [from Landscape in the Mist] [both w. Vangelis Christopoulos (ob), str orch, Lefteris Chalkiadakis (cnd)] ECM ▲ 78118-21429-2 [AAD]

Skov, Susanne (pno)
Barber, S.:Prayers of Kierkegaard, w. J. Koch (pno), C. Bjørkøe (pno), Safri Duo, La Camerata Danica ▲ DCD 8154

Skovajsa, Jiri (pno)
Novák, V.:Qnt Pno, w. Kubín String Quartet *(rec Ostrava Radio Studio, Czech Republic, June 12 & 13 & Nov. 27, 1)* Centaur ▲ CRC 2191 [DDD]

Skovlund, Verner (va)
Olsen, P.R.:Concertino Cl, w. Jens Schou (cl), Peder Elbaek (vn), Svend Winsløv (vc), Rosalind Bevan (pno) *(rec PAULA's Recording Hall, 1984)* Paula ▲ PACD 36 [AAD]
Olsen, P.R.:Qt 2 Strs, w. Peder Elbaek (vn), Jørgen Larsen (vn), Svend Winsløv (vc) *(rec PAULA's Recording Hall, 1984)* Paula ▲ PACD 36 [AAD]

Skowronski, Vincent P. (vn)
Bach, J.S.:Sons & Partitas Vn, BWV 1001–1006—Partita No. 2 in d Skowronski Classical ▲ S:CR-01 [AAD]
Hindemith, P.:Son Vn, Op. 31/2 Skowronski Classical ▲ S:CR-01 [AAD]
Ysaÿe, E.:Sons Vn, Sons 2 & 5 Skowronski Classical ▲ S:CR-01 [AAD]

Skuce, Peter (hp/org/perc)—see ORCHESTRAS & ENSEMBLES Dufay Collective

Skudlik, Johannes (org)
Orgel & Trompete in Landsberg, w. Klaus-Ulrich Dann (tpt) Ambitus ▲ AMB 97870 [DDD]
Sacred Horn Music, w. Allgäuer Horn Ensemble, U. Köbl (hn), M. Neukirchner (hn), C. Wulkopf (cta) Ars Produktion ▲ FCD 368304

Škutová-Slaničková, Eleonóra (pno)
Godár, V.:Déploration sur la mort de Witold Lutoslawski, w. Peter Biely (vn), Ivana Pristašová (vn), Peter Šesták (va), Jozef Lupták (vc) *(rec Residence of Slovak Composers, Apr 1996)* Slovart ▲ SR 0018-2-131 [DDD]
Godár, V.:Ricercar, w. Ivana Pristašová (vn), Peter Šesták (va), Jozef Lupták (vc) *(rec Residence of Slovak Composers, Apr 1996)* Slovart ▲ SR 0018-2-131 [DDD]
Godár, V.:Talisman, w. Peter Krajniak (vn), Jozef Lupták (vc) *(rec Residence of Slovak Composers, Apr 1996)* Slovart ▲ SR 0018-2-131 [DDD]

Skytt, Rozalina (hp)
Rangström, T.:Vauxhall, w. Bengt Christiansson (fl), Lars Olof Loman (ob), Lars Almgren (cl), Sven Aarflot (bn), Rolf Bengtsson (hn), Rune Bodin (trbn), O. Vänskä (cnd), Stockholm PO *(rec Stockholm Concert Hall, Jan. 16 & 18, 1985)* Caprice ▲ CAP 21195 [DDD]

Slaato, Annette (va)—see ORCHESTRAS & ENSEMBLES Copenhagen Contemporary Players

Slaatto, Helge (vn)
Bentzon, N.V.:Duo Concertante, w. F. Reinecke (db) Ambitus ▲ 97845 [DDD]
Biber, H. von:Son violino solo representativa, w. F. Reinecke (db) Ambitus ▲ 97845 [DDD]
Sanri, E.:Settings of Visual Poems & a Visual Phantasie, w. F. Reinecke (db) Ambitus ▲ 97845 [DDD]
Vogt, H.:Sonatina Vn, w. F. Reinecke (db) Ambitus ▲ 97845 [DDD]
Yun, I.:Together, w. F. Reinecke (db) Ambitus ▲ 97845 [DDD]

Slagter, Jacob (hn)
Brahms, J.:Trio Hn, w. Guarneri Trio Prague members Ottavo ▲ OTT 29134 [DDD]
Mozart, W.A.:Cons Hn, w. J. Kussmaul (cnd), Amsterdam Mozart Players—No. 1 [Allegro]; Nos. 2–4 Canal Grande ▲ CG 9211 [DDD]
Mozart, W.A.:Rondo Hn, K.514 (compl'd Süssmayer), w. J. Kussmaul (cnd), Amsterdam Mozart Players Canal Grande ▲ CG 9211 [DDD]

Slatkin, Felix (vn)—see ORCHESTRAS & ENSEMBLES Hollywood String Quartet, Hollywood String Quartet members

Slatkin, Leonard (pno)
Bernstein, L.:Anniversaries (7) Pno—Nathalie Koussevitzky, No. 5, "In Memoriam" RCA Red Seal ▲ 09026-61581-2

Slatkine, Muriel (pno)
Brahms, J.:Son 2 Vc, w. G. Leclerc (vc) Gallo ▲ CD 509
Schubert, Franz:Son Arpeggione, w. G. Leclerc (vc) Gallo ▲ CD 509

Slaughter, Susan (tpt)
Barber, S.:Capricorn Con, w. Jacob Berg (fl), Peter Bowman (ob), L. Slatkin (cnd), St. Louis SO *(rec Powell Symphony Hall, St. Louis, MO, May 7, 1995)* RCA Red Seal ▲ 09026-68283-2 [DDD]

Slávik, Ján (vc)—see also ORCHESTRAS & ENSEMBLES Moyzes String Quartet
Corelli, A.:Sons 2 Vns, Opp. 1–4 (sels), w. A. Hölbling (vn), Q. Hölbling (vn), D. Ruso (hpd)—Op. 1, No. 6; Op. 2, No. 4; Op. 4, No. 9 *(rec Oct. 21–23, 1990)* Naxos ▲ 8.550619 [DDD]
Geminiani, F.:Sons (12) Vn, Vne & Hpd, w. A. Hölbling (vn), Q. Hölbling (vn), D. Ruso (hpd) *(rec Oct. 21–23, 1990)* Naxos ▲ 8.550619 [DDD]
Porpora, N.A.:Sinf da camera, w. A. Hölbling (vn), Q. Hölbling (vn), D. Ruso (pno)—No. 6 only *(rec Oct. 21–23, 1990)* Naxos ▲ 8.550619 [DDD]
Pugnani, G.:Trio Sons, Op. 1, w. A. Hölbling (vn), Q. Hölbling (vn), D. Ruso (pno)—No. 3 *(rec Oct. 21–23, 1990)* Naxos ▲ 8.550619 [DDD]
Schmidt, F.:Qnt Cl, w. A. Janoska (cl), D. Ruso (pno), F. Török (vn), A. Lakatos (va) Marco Polo ▲ 8.223415
Schmidt, F.:Qnt Cl, w. A. Jánoska (cl), S. Mucha (vn), A. Lakatos (va), D. Ruso (pno) Marco Polo ▲ 8.223414
2 Violins & 1 Guitar II, w. Hölbling, Anna (vn), Quido Hölbling (vn), Jozef Zsapka (gtr) *(rec 1992)* Naxos ▲ 8.550645 [DDD]

Slawinska, B. (vc)
Marcello, B.:Sons Vc, w. Lusia Duron (hpd) Producciones Fonograficas ▲ PFCD 232

Slawson, Brian (mar)
Bach, J.S.:Jesu bleibet meine Freude CBS ▲ MK 39704 ■ MT 39704
Bach, J.S.:Music of CBS ▲ MK 39704
Handel, G.F.:Solomon (arrival of the queen of Sheba) CBS ▲ MK 39704 ■ MT 39704
Pachelbel, J.:Canon CBS ▲ MK 39704 ■ MT 39704
Vivaldi, A.:Music of CBS ▲ MK 39704 ■ MT 39704

Slawson, Brian (perc)
Bach on Wood CBS ▲ MK 39704
Distant Drums CBS ▲ MK 42666 [ADD]

Slenczynska, R. (pno)
Chopin, F.:Ballades Pno (comp) *(rec live, Oct. 18, 1988)* ACA Digital Recording ■ CM20010-10 (CrO2)
Chopin, F.:Études (24)—Op. 10 *(rec live Oct. 18, 1988)* ACA Digital Recording ■ CM20010-10 (CrO2)
Liszt, F.:Études d'exécution transcendante d'après Paganini, S.140—No. 3, "La Campanella" *(rec live Oct. 18, 1988)* ACA Digital Recording ■ CM20010-10 (CrO2)
Poulenc, F.:Pièces Pno—Hymne only *(rec live Oct. 18, 1988)* ACA Digital Recording ■ CM20010-10 (CrO2)
Ravel, M.:Jeux d'eau *(rec live 10/18/88)* ACA Digital Recording ■ CM20010-10 (CrO2)

Slepicka, C. (bn)
Danzi, F.:Sinf concertante, w. K. F. Schmid (cl), J.-P Rouchon (cnd), Maurice Ravel CO
Divertimento ▲ DIV 31008 [DDD]
Hoffmeister, F.A.:Con Cl, Bn & Orch, w. K. F. Schmid (cl), J.-P Rouchon (cnd), Maurice Ravel CO
Divertimento ▲ DIV 31008 [DDD]
Vogel, J.C.:Sinf concertante Cl, w. K. F. Schmid (cl), J.-P. Rouchon (cnd), Maurice Ravel CO
Divertimento ▲ DIV 31008 [DDD]

Slepokourov, Sergei (org)
Sergei Slepokourov Russian Compact Disc ▲ RCD 16222

Slivanská, Ada (vn)—see ORCHESTRAS & ENSEMBLES Quartetto con Flauto

Slivansky, Václav (fl)—see also ORCHESTRAS & ENSEMBLES Quartetto con Flauto
Jirásek, J.:Katharsis, w. Ada Silvanská (vn), Lubomír Herza (vc), Renata Jelínková (hpd) *(rec St. Virgin Mary Church, Strahov)* Arta ▲ 0054 [DDD]

Slochteren, Koen van (ob)
Trumpet & Organ:Oboe & Organ, w. Alan Stringer (tpt), Simon C. Jansen (org) Vivace ▲ 575

Slocum, W. (hn)
Beethoven, L. van:Son Hn, w. R. Fusco (pno) Dana Recording Project ▲ DRP 2
Dukas, P.:Villanelle, w. R. Fusco (pno) Dana Recording Project ▲ DRP 2
Hindemith, P.:Son Hn, w. R. Fusco (pno) Dana Recording Project ▲ DRP 2
Rollin, R.:The Raven & thr First Men, w. J. Turk (tuba), R. Rollin Dana Recording Project ▲ DRP 4

Slokar, Branimir (alt trbn)
Hummel, J.N.:Vars Ob, w. P. Angerer (cnd), Pforzheim CO Claves ■ C 906

Slokar, Branimir (trbn)
Arutiunian, A.:Con Trbn, w. L. Shambadal (cnd), Berlin Sinfonia *(rec Villa Siemens, Berlin, Feb 5–9, 1996)*
Claves ▲ CD 50-9606 [DDD]
Bloch, E.:Sym Trbn, w. L. Shambadal (cnd), Berlin Sinfonia *(rec Villa Siemens, Berlin, Feb 5–9, 1996)*
Claves ▲ CD 50-9606 [DDD]
Daetwyler, J.:Dialogue concertant, w. C. Eisenhoffer (hp) Gallo ▲ CD 578 [DAD]
Daetwyler, J.:Rêverie du Soir, w. C. Eisenhoffer (hp) Gallo ▲ CD 578 [DAD]
David, Ferdinand:Concertino Trbn, w. J.-M. Auberson (cnd), Lausanne CO Claves ▲ CD 8407 [DDD]
Divertimenti for Trombone & Orchestra, w. Southwest German CO [cnd:Paul Angerer]
Claves ▲ CD 906 [ADD]
Grondahl, L.:Con Trbn, w. L. Shambadal (cnd), Berlin Sinfonia *(rec Villa Siemens, Berlin, Feb 5–9, 1996)*
Claves ▲ CD 50-9606 [DDD]
Rota, N.:Con Trbn, w. L. Shambadal (cnd), Berlin Sinfonia *(rec Villa Siemens, Berlin, Feb 5–9, 1996)*
Claves ▲ CD 50-9606 [DDD]
Tomasi, H.:Con Trbn, w. J.-M. Auberson (cnd), Lausanne CO Claves ▲ CD 8407 [DDD]
Wagenseil, G.C.:Con Trbn, w. J.-M. Auberson (cnd), Lausanne CO Claves ▲ CD 8407 [DDD]

Slot, Sven Micha (pno)
Stolarczyk, W.:Earth Air Fire Water, w. Amalie Malling (pno), John Damgaard (pno), Anne Øland (pno), Teddy Teirup (pno), Friedrich Gürtler (pno), Rosalind Bevan (pno), Poul Rosenbaum (pno), Rodolfo Llambias (pno), Bella Horn-Ribera (pno), Anders Riber (pno), Elisabeth Sigurdsson (pno), Thomas Tronheim (pno), Elsebeth Broderson (pno), Erik Kaltoft (pno), Jørgen Hald Nielsen (pno), Aino Gilemann (pno), Birgit Kjær (pno), Jørgen Thomsen (pno), Gunhild Donslund (pno), Henrik Bo Hansen (pno), Lone Karlsson (pno), Erik Fessel (pno), Lasse Nilsson (pno), Janos Ferenczi (pno), Erik Bach (pno), Axel Momme (pno), Arne de Cros Dich (pno), Hanne Bramsen Buhl (pno), Lili Olesen (pno), Susannah Carlsson (pno), Ulla Erml (pno), Vagn Sørensen (pno), Leif Greibe (pno), Bodil Krogh (pno), Kirsten Ottosen (pno), Inger Bergenholz (pno), Karsten Gylendorf (pno), Bjønr Elkjær (pno), Jacob Bjørn Jensen (pno), Jørgen Kaad (pno), Anne Marie Hjelm (pno), Carl Ulrik Munk Andersen (pno), Poul Lumbye (pno), Oluf Hildebrandt Nielsen (pno), Joachim Olsson (pno), Peter Pade Ramsøe Jacobsen (pno), Astrid Pollmann (pno), Jette Borsch (pno), Kirsten Karlshøj (pno), Maria Teresa Assing (pno), Allan Dahl Hansen (pno), Johan Hugossen (pno), Tine Fenger Pederson (pno), Arne Jørgen Fæø (pno), Anja Høgsted (pno), Anne Sophie Parbo (pno), Inga Lindmark (pno), Teresa Drabik Stathakis (pno), Anne Ruth Ferenczi (pno), Irene Hasager (pno), Yuka Ichikawa (pno), Birgitte Baur (pno), Malene Thastum (pno), Jens E. Rasmussen (pno), Birgitte Zielke (pno), Claus Zielke (pno), Stefan Kasch (pno), Bin Qiao (pno), Inger Johanne Teirup (pno), Lindy Rosborg (pno), Liisa Heininen (pno), David Højer (pno), Ellen Refstrup (pno), Thomas K. Søorensen (pno), Erik Kure (pno), Michael Rauff (pno), Jan beck Eriksson (pno), Tanja Zapolski (pno), Vibeke Skagbo (pno), Pål Eide Lindtner (pno), Ha-Young Sul (pno), Benedicte Palko (pno), Inke Kesseler (pno), Anne Marie Meineche (pno), Sverre Larsen (pno), Kasper Peter Bach (pno), Elisabetta Eliseo (pno), Olga Magieres (pno), Carl Erik Kühl (pno), Thorkild Borup Nielsen (pno), Valeria Zanini (pno), Lars Stenhoft (perc), Dennis Boel (perc), Winnie Dahlgren (perc), Susanne Vind (perc), Claus Byrith (elec), Anne Marie Storm (elec), J. Ribera (cnd) *(rec live, Koldinghaus Castle, Denmark, May 2, 1996)* Danica ▲ DCD 1996

Slowick, Kenneth (vc)
Schubert, Franz:Qnt Strs, D.956, w. L. Rautenberg (vn), J. Gatwood (vn), S. Dann (va), A. Bylsma (vc)
Sony Classical ("Vivarte" series) ▲ SK 46669

Slowik, Kenneth (vc)—see also ORCHESTRAS & ENSEMBLES Smithsonian Chamber Players
Beethoven, L. van:Son 1 Vc, w. J. Weaver (pno) Smithsonian Collection ▲ ND 0323
Beethoven, L. van:Son 1 Vc, w. J. Weaver (pno) Smithsonian Collection 6-▲ ND 0320
Beethoven, L. van:Son 2 Vc, w. J. Weaver (pno) Smithsonian Collection 6-▲ ND 0320
Beethoven, L. van:Son 2 Vc, w. J. Weaver (pno) Smithsonian Collection ▲ ND 0323
Boccherini, L.:Fugues, G.73, w. A. Bylsma (vc)—in c, G.2; in B♭, G.8; in F, G.9 *(rec Sept. 6–7, 1992)*
Sony Classical ▲ SK 53362 [DDD]
Boccherini, L.:Sons (34) Vc, w. A. Bylsma (vc), B. Van Asperen (hpd)—in c, G.2; in B♭, G.8; in F, G.9 *(rec Sept. 6–7, 1992)* Sony Classical ▲ SK 53362 [DDD]
Dotzauer, F.:Pieces Vc, Op. 104, w. Anner Bylsma (vc), Steven Doane (vc) *(rec New York City, Jan. 19–22, 1994)* Sony Classical ("Vivarte" series) ▲ SK 64307 [DDD]
Dotzauer, F.:Qnt Strs, w. Vera Beths (vn), Jody Gatwood (vn), Lisa Rautenberg (va), Anner Bylsma (vc) *(rec New York City, Jan. 19–22, 1994)* Sony Classical ("Vivarte" series) ▲ SK 64307 [DDD]
Mozart, W.A.:Qt Fl, K.285, w. Cristopher Krueger (fl), J. Schröder (vn), J. Griffin (va) [period instrs]
Smithsonian Collection 5-▲ ND 031
Mozart, W.A.:Qts Pno, w. J. Weaver (pno), J. Schröder (vn), J. Griffin (va) [period instrs]
Smithsonian Collection 5-▲ ND 031
Mozart, W.A.:Qnt Hn, K.407, w. L. Greer (hn), J. Schröder (vn), J. Griffin (vn), M. Graybeal (va) [period instrs] Smithsonian Collection 5-▲ ND 031
Mozart, W.A.:Qnt Hn, K.407, w. L. Greer (hn), J. Schröder (vn), J. Griffin (vn), M. Graybeal (va) [period instrs] Smithsonian Collection ▲ ND 039

Slowik, Kenneth (vl)—see ORCHESTRAS & ENSEMBLES Smithsonian Chamber Players

Slowik, P. (va)
Soler, P.A.:Qnt 1 Hpd, w. D. Schrader (hpd), C. Verrette (vn), M. Shelton (vn), J. M. Rozendaal (vc) *(rec Oct. & Dec. 1992)* Cedille ▲ CDR 90000 013 [DDD]
Soler, P.A.:Qnt 2 Hpd, w. D. Schrader (hpd), C. Verrette (vn), M. Shelton (vn), J. M. Rozendaal (vc) *(rec Oct. & Dec. 1992)* Cedille ▲ CDR 90000 013 [DDD]
Soler, P.A.:Qnt 3 Hpd, w. D. Schrader (hpd), C. Verrette (vn), M. Shelton (vn), J. M. Rozendaal (vc) *(rec Oct. & Dec. 1992)* Cedille ▲ CDR 90000 013 [DDD]

Small, Elisabeth (vn)
Loewe, C.:Grand Duo, w. Alan Mandel (pno) *(rec Belmont Univ., Studio A, Dec. 15–18, 1994)*
Premier ▲ PRCD 1037 [DDD]
Röntgen, J.:Son Vn, w. Alan Mandel (pno) *(rec Belmont Univ., Studio A, Dec. 15–18, 1994)*
Premier ▲ PRCD 1037 [DDD]

Small, Haskell (pno)
Gershwin, G.:Pno Music—Con. in F; American in Paris; Lullaby; Three Quarter Blues [arrs. H. Small]
Centaur ▲ CRC 2174

Small, Jonathan (ob)
Vaughan Williams, R.:Con Ob, w. V. Handley (cnd), Royal Liverpool PO
Classics for Pleasure ("Eminence" series) ▲ CDEMX 2179 [DDD]

Small, Mark (gtr)
The Water Is Wide, w. Robert Torres (gtr) Channel Classics ▲ CD 3301

Smalley, Roger (pno)
Boyd, A.:Angklung *(rec Studio 620, ABC Perth, Mar 1991)* Tall Poppies ▲ TP 60 [DDD]
Edwards, R.:Kumari *(rec Studio 620 Perth, Mar 1991)* Tall Poppies ▲ TP 51 [DDD]
Edwards, R.:Kumari *(rec Studio 620, ABC Perth, Mar 1991)* Tall Poppies ▲ TP 60 [DDD]
Edwards, R.:Monos II *(rec Studio 620, ABC Perth, Mar 1991)* Tall Poppies ▲ TP 60 [DDD]
Hannan, M.:Resonances I *(rec Studio 620, ABC Perth, Mar 1991)* Tall Poppies ▲ TP 60 [DDD]
Lumsdaine, D.:Ruhe Sanfte, sanfte Ruh' *(rec Studio 200, ABC Sydney, June 1994)*
Tall Poppies ▲ TP 60 [DDD]
Smalley, R.:Con Pno, w. D. Masson (cnd), West Australian SO Vox Australis ▲ VAST 003-2
Smalley, R.:Pieces I–V Pno *(rec Studio 200, ABC Sydney, June 1994)* Tall Poppies ▲ TP 60 [DDD]
Sutherland, M.:Voices I *(rec Studio 620, ABC Perth, Mar 1991)* Tall Poppies ▲ TP 60 [DDD]

Smart, Gary (pno)
Brotons, S.:Son da Con Tpt, w. B. Theurer (tpt) *(rec 5/91)* Capstone ▲ CPS 8612 CD [DDD]
Smart, G.:Music of, w. B. Theurer (tpt), M. Smart (sop), Franciscan Quartet—Trumpeter Swan; Fanfare, Invocation & Alleluia Capstone ▲ CPS 8612 CD [DDD]
Theurer, B.:Music of, w. B. Theurer (tpt), S. Jones (tpt)—Feste; Fant Capstone ▲ CPS 8612 CD [DDD]

Smebye, Einar Henning (pno)
Brahms, J.:Songs, w. Tove Traesdal (mez)—8 songs, Op. 57 Victoria ▲ VCD 19106
Grieg, E.:Sons Vn, Opp. 8, 13 & 45, w. T. Tønnesen (vn) *(rec June 1993)* Victoria ▲ VCD 19070
Grieg, E.:Songs, w. Tove Traesdal (mez)—6 German Songs, Op. 48 Victoria ▲ VCD 19106
Heise, P.:Songs, w. Tove Traesdal (mez)—Gudrun's Grief [Dengang var Gudrn beredt til døoden; Hos sad jarlers aedle hustruer; Da sagde Herborg; Da sagde Gullrönd; Engang Gudrun end ham skuede; Saa var min Sigurd] Victoria ▲ VCD 19106
Ravel, M.:Histoires naturelles, w. Tove Traesdal (mez) Victoria ▲ VCD 19106
Saeverud, H.:Pno Music—5 Capriccios, Op. 1; Easy Pieces, Op. 14; Silju Dance, Op. 17; Easy Pieces, Op. 18 Victoria ▲ VCD 19084
Saeverud, H.:Pno Music—Siljustøl:Suites No. 1, Op. 21, No. 2, Op. 22, No. 3, Op. 24 & No. 4, Op. 25
Victoria ▲ VCD 19085
Saeverud, H.:Pno Music—Peer Gynt (sels.), Op. 28; 6 Sonatinas, Op. 30 Victoria ▲ VCD 19086
Schnittke, A.:Son 2 Vn, w. Lars-Erik ter Jung (vn) Simax ▲ PSC 1115
Szymanowski, K.:Myths, w. Lars-Erik ter Jung (vn) Simax ▲ PSC 1115
20th Century Works for Solo Trumpet or Trumpet & Piano, w. Ole Edvard Antonsen (tpt)
Simax ▲ PSC 1041 [DDD]

Smedvig, Rolf (tpt)—see also ORCHESTRAS & ENSEMBLES Empire Brass Quintet
Bach, J.S.:Brandenburg Con 2, w. J. Ling (cnd), Scottish CO Telarc ▲ CD 80227 [DDD]
Bach, J.S.:Suite 2 Orch, w. J. Ling (cnd), Scottish CO Telarc ▲ CD 80227 [DDD]
Bellini, V.:Con in E♭ Ob, w. J. Ling (cnd), Scottish CO Telarc ▲ CD 80232 [DDD] ■ CS 30232 (D)
Ceremonial Music for Trumpet & Symphonic Organ, w. Michael Murray (org)
Telarc ▲ CD 80341 [DDD]
Haydn, J.:Con Tpt, w. J. Ling (cnd), Scottish CO Telarc ▲ CD 80232 [DDD] ■ CS 30232 (D)
Hummel, J.N.:Con in E♭ Tpt, S.49, w. J. Ling (cnd), Scottish CO
Telarc ▲ CD 80232 [DDD] ■ CS 30232 (D)
Mozart, L.:Con Tpt, w. J. Ling (cnd), Scottish CO Telarc ▲ CD 80227 [DDD]
Tartini, G.:Con Tpt, w. J. Ling (cnd), Scottish CO Telarc ▲ CD 80232 [DDD] ■ CS 30232 (D)
Telemann, G.P.:Con Tpt Strs in D, w. J. Ling (cnd), Scottish CO Telarc ▲ CD 80227 [DDD]
Torelli, G.:Con Tpt, w. J. Ling (cnd), Scottish CO Telarc ▲ CD 80232 [DDD] ■ CS 30232 (D)

Smendzianka, Regina (pno)
Chopin, F.:Berceuse *(rec Warsaw, 1959–60)* Polskie Nagrania 2-▲ PNCD 307 A/B
Chopin, F.:Pno Music (misc)—Berceuse in D♭, Op. 57; Barcarolle in F♯, Op. 60; Tarantella in A♭, Op. 43; Ecossaises (3), Op. 72/3; Marche Funèbre in c, Op. 72/2; Marche Funèbre in c, Op. 72/2; Contredanse in G♭; Cantabile in B♭; Fugue in a; Moderato (Albumblatt) in 2 Bourrées [No. 1 in G, No. 2 in A]; Printemps in g; Galop Marquis in A♭; Fant in f, Op. 49 *(rec Polish Radio, Nov 23–27, 1991)*
Canyon Classics ▲ 141 [DDD]
Chopin, F.:Waltzes *(rec Warsaw, 1959–61)* Polskie Nagrania ▲ PNCD 302
Paderewski, I.J.:Fant polonaise, w. R. Bader (cnd), Cracow PO *(rec 1991)*
Koch Schwann ▲ 3-1145-2 [DDD]

Smeyers, David (b cl)
Blank, A.:Bicinium III, w. B. Zelinsky (cl) *(rec Sept. 24–26, 1990)* Pro Viva ▲ ISPV 164 CD [DDD]

Smeyers, David (cl)
Betz, S.:Sprache ist k-eine Handlung, w. B. Zelinsky (cl) *(rec Sept. 24–26, 1990)*
Pro Viva ▲ ISPV 164 CD [DDD]
Clarinet Counterpoints, w. Beate Zelinsky (cl) CPO ▲ CPO 999116 [DDD]
Glynn, G.:Mannheimer Duos, w. B. Zelinsky (cl) *(rec Sept. 24–26, 1990)*
Pro Viva ▲ ISPV 164 CD [DDD]
Hamary, A.:Graffiti, w. B. Zelinsky, D. Smeyers *(rec Sept. 24–26, 1990)*
Pro Viva ▲ ISPV 164 CD [DDD]
Lachenmann, H.:Allegro sostenuto, w. B. Wambach (pno), M. Bach (vc) CPO ▲ CPO 999102-2 [DDD]
Lachenmann, H.:Dal niente CPO ▲ CPO 999102-2 [DDD]
Stahmer, K.H.:Porcelain Music, w. B. Zelinsky (cl) *(rec Sept. 24–26, 1990)*
Pro Viva ▲ ISPV 164 [DDD]

Smidt, Ulfert (org)
Martin, F.:Passacaglia Org [Wöhl-Orgel der Petrikirche zu Cuxhaven] *(rec Sept 1994–Mar 1995)*
Thorofon ▲ CTH 2261 [DDD]

Smietana, Krzysztof (vn)
Fauré, G.:Berceuse Vn, w. J. Blakely (pno) Meridian ▲ MER 84259 [DDD]
Fauré, G.:Sicilienne, w. J. Blakely (pno) Meridian ▲ MER 84259 [DDD]
Fauré, G.:Son 1 Vn, w. J. Blakely (pno) Meridian ▲ MER 84259 [DDD]
Fauré, G.:Son 2 Vn, w. J. Blakely (pno) Meridian ▲ MER 84259 [DDD]

Smiles, Julian (vc)—see ORCHESTRAS & ENSEMBLES Australia Ensemble

Smiley, Mariko (vn)—see ORCHESTRAS & ENSEMBLES Aurora String Quartet

Smirnoff, Joel (vn)—see also ORCHESTRAS & ENSEMBLES Juilliard String Quartet, Boehm Quintet members
Berger, A.:Duos, w. C. Oldfather (pno), J. Krosnick (vc), G. Kalish (pno), P. Lanini (ob), D. Stewart (cl)—Duo No. 1 for Violin & Piano (1948); Duo for Cello & Piano (1951); Duo for Oboe & Clarinet (1952) New World ▲ NW 360-2 [DDD]
Brody, M.:Voices Vn CRI ▲ CD 594 [DDD]
Gruenberg, L.:Rhap Vn, w. C. Oldfather (pno) GM ▲ GM 2015CD
Gruenberg, L.:White Lilacs, w. C. Oldfather (pno) GM ▲ GM 2015CD
Tower, J.:Platinum Spirals CRI ▲ CD 582 [DDD]

Smirnoff, Joel (vn/va)—see ORCHESTRAS & ENSEMBLES Collage New Music Ensemble

Smirnov, E. (pno)
Bartók, B.:Sons (2) Vn & Pno, w. G. Kremer (vn) Hungaroton ▲ HCD 11655

Smirnov, Evgeni (vn)
Artyomov, V.:Gurian Hymn, w. T. Gridenko (vn), Y. Adjemova (vn), D. Kitayenko (cnd), Moscow PO
Olympia ▲ OLY 515 [DDD]

Smirnov, Yuri (hpd/pno)
Schnittke, A.:Con grosso 1, w. Gidon Kremer (vn), Tatiana Grindenko (vn), H. Schiff (cnd), CO of Europe
Deutsche Grammophon ("Digital Midprice" series) ▲ 445520-2

Smirnova, Eva (pno)
Chopin, F.:Nocturnes—2 Nocturnes, Op. 62 Infinity Digital ▲ QK 57257 [DDD]

Smirnova, Lisa (pno)
Bach, J.S.:Sons Fl, BWV 1030–35, w. Benjamin Schmidt (vn) [arr Robert Schumann for pno]
MD + G ▲ MDG 3330614
Paganini, N.:Caprices Vn, w. Benjamin Schmid (vn) [arr Robert Schumann for vn & pno]
MD + G ▲ MDG 3330674

Smissen, Robert (va)—see also ORCHESTRAS & ENSEMBLES Academy of St. Martin in the Fields Chamber Ensemble, Ambache Chamber Ensemble
Matiegka, W.T.:Grand Trio Vn, Va & Gtr, w. H. Williams (vn), D. Chivers (gtr) Erasmus ▲ WVH 086

Smissen, Robert (va) (cont.)
Matiegka, W.T.:Serenade Fl, Va & Gtr, w. E. Frank (fl), D. Chivers (gtr) Erasmus ▲ WVH 086
Walton, W.:Qt Pno, w. H. Milne (pno), K. Sillito (vn), S. Orton (vc) Chandos ▲ CHAN 8999 [DDD]
Smit, Leo (pno)
Copland, A.:Pno Music—The Cat & The Mouse; 3 Moods; Petite Portrait; Passacaglia; 4 Piano Blues; Sentimental Melody; Piano Vars. Sunday Afternoon Music; The Young Pioneers; Son. for Piano; Midsummer Nocturne; Fant.; Down a Country Lane; In Evening Air; Night Thoughts; 2 Pieces Sony Classical 2-▲ SM2K 66345
Copland, A.:Songs (misc), w. J. DeGaetani (mez)—Zion's Walls; At the River; Simple Gifts; 3 Moods; Night Thoughts; 12 Poems of Emily Dickinson; The Little Horses *(rec 1981)* Bridge ▲ BCD 9046 [ADD]
Smith, (pno)
Mozart, W.A.:Sons Vn Pno (misc), w. J. Heifetz (vn)—K.378 RCA Gold Seal ▲ 7869-2 (m/s) [ADD] ■ 7869-4 (m/s)
Smith, Brooks (pno)
Brahms, J.:Hungarian Dances Pno 4-Hands, w. J. Heifetz (vn)—Nos. 11,17 & 20 [arr. violin & piano] RCA Gold Seal ▲ 7965-2-RG [ADD]
Grieg, E.:Son 2 Vn, w. Jascha Heifetz (vn) *(rec Radio Recorders, Hollywood, Dec 15, 1955)* RCA Gold Seal 2-▲ 09026-61740-2 (m) [ADD]
Griffes, C.T.:Poem Fl, w. G. Woodward (fl) [arr fl & pno] Stereophile ▲ STPH 001-2 [AAD]
Music of France, w. Jascha Heifetz (vn) RCA Gold Seal ▲ 7707-2 RC [ADD]
Prokofiev, S.:Son Fl, w. G. Woodward (fl) Stereophile ▲ STPH 001-2 [AAD]
Reinecke, C.:Son Fl, w. G. Woodward (fl) Stereophile ▲ STPH 001-2 [AAD]
Schumann, R.:Romances Ob, w. G. Woodward (fl) Stereophile ▲ STPH 001-2 [AAD]
Smith, C. (fl)
Ravel, M.:Daphins et Chloé, w. Y. Levi (cnd), Atlanta SO, Atlanta Sym Chorus *(rec May 24-25, 1993)* Telarc ▲ CD 80352 [DDD]
Smith, Chris (gittern/oud)—see ORCHESTRAS & ENSEMBLES Altramar Medieval Music Ensemble
Smith, Chris (lt/gittern)—see ORCHESTRAS & ENSEMBLES Altramar Medieval Music Ensemble
Smith, Cyril (pno)
Arnold, M.:Con for 2 Pnos, w. P. Sellick (pno), M. Arnold (cnd), City of Birmingham SO EMI Classics ▲ CDM 64044-2
Fauré, G.:Dolly, w. P. Sellick (pno) Nimbus ▲ NI 5178 (m) [AAD]
Franck, C.:Prélude, choral et fugue, w. P. Sellick (pno) [piano duet version] Nimbus ▲ NI 5178 (m) [AAD]
Mendelssohn, F.:Allegro brillant, w. P. Sellick (pno) Nimbus ▲ NI 5178 (m) [AAD]
Schubert, Franz:Fant Pno, D.940, w. P. Sellick (pno) Nimbus ▲ NI 5178 (m) [AAD]
Schubert, Franz:Son Pno, D.617, w. P. Sellick (pno) Nimbus ▲ NI 5178 (m) [AAD]
Smith, D. (hn)
Vivaldi, A.:Cons for 2 Hns, w. A. Spanjer (hn), R. Kapp (cnd), Philharmonia Virtuosi—RV.538 ESS.A.Y ▲ CD 1022 [DDD]
Smith, D. (vc)—see ORCHESTRAS & ENSEMBLES Amelite Consortium
Smith, Daniel (bn)
Bach, Joh. Christian:Con Bn, w. P. Ledger (cnd), English CO ASV Quicksilva ▲ ASQ 6177
Bassoon Bon-Bons, w. Royal PO [cnd:Ettore Stratta], English CO [cnd:Philip Ledger], Coull String Quartet, Roger Vignoles (pno) ASV ▲ ASV 2052 [DDD]
Bravo Bassoon, w. Jonathan Still (pno), Caravaggio Ensemble ASV ▲ ASV 2078 [DDD]
Danzi, F.:Qts Bn, Op. 40, w. Coull String Quartet members—No. 3 in B♭ ASV ▲ ASV 613 [DDD]
English Music for Bassoon & Piano, w. Roger Vignoles (pno) ASV ▲ ASV 535
Graupner, C.:Con Bn, w. P. Ledger (cnd), English CO ASV Quicksilva ▲ ASQ 6177
Hargrave, H.:Con 4 Bn, w. P. Ledger (cnd), English CO ASV ▲ ASV 681 [DDD]
Hargrave, H.:Con 4 Bn, w. P. Ledger (cnd), English CO ASV Quicksilva ▲ ASQ 6177
Hertel, J.W.:Con Bn, w. P. Ledger (cnd), English CO ASV Quicksilva ▲ ASQ 6177
Jacob, G.:Suite Bn, w. Coull String Quartet ASV ▲ ASV 613
Reicha, A.:Qnt Bn, w. Coull String Quartet ASV ▲ ASV 613
Vivaldi, A.:Cons Bn, w. P. Ledger (cnd), English CO—Nos. 4, 10, 12, 15, 18, 22, 25, 28 [RV 474, 500, 499, 487, 467, 486, 491, 466] ASV ▲ ASV CD 971
Vivaldi, A.:Cons Bn, w. P. Ledger (cnd), English CO—Concerti RV.469, 470, 474, 476, 487, 494 ASV ▲ ASV 571 [DDD]
Vivaldi, A.:Cons Bn, w. P. Ledger (cnd), English CO—No. 26 in C, R.479 ASV Quicksilva ▲ ASQ 6177
Vivaldi, A.:Cons Bn, w. T. Ninić (cnd), Zagreb Solisti—Concerti RV.471, 475, 490, 492, 495, 496 ASV ▲ ASV 734 [DDD]
Vivaldi, A.:Cons Bn, w. T. Ninić (cnd), Zagreb Solisti—Concerti RV.480, 484, 489, 493, 503, 504 ASV ▲ ASV 751 [DDD]
Vivaldi, A.:Cons Bn, w. P. Ledger (cnd), English CO—Concerti RV.466, 467, 486, 491, 499, 500 ASV ▲ ASV 565 [DDD]
Vivaldi, A.:Cons Bn, w. T. Ninić (cnd), Zagreb Solisti—Concerti RV.473, 478, 483, 485, 497, 498, 502 ASV ▲ ASV 752 [DDD]
Vivaldi, A.:Cons Bn, w. Ravinia Chamber Ensemble—5 selections Crystal ■ C 344
Smith, Dave (pno)
Black Christmas:Spirituals in the African-American Tradition, w. Vanessa Ayers (mez), Thomas Young (ten), Robert Mosley (bar), Ronald Isaac (cnd) ESS.A.Y ▲ ESS 1011 [DDD]
New Music for Multi-Tracked Clarinets, w. Roger Heaton (cl/a cl/b cl/ctb cl), S. Limbrick (perc) Clarinet Classics ▲ CC 0009
Smith, David (vc)
Bach, Joh. Christian:Con Bn, w. P. Ledger (cnd), English CO ASV ▲ ASV 681 [DDD]
Graupner, C.:Con Bn, w. P. Ledger (cnd), English CO ASV ▲ ASV 681 [DDD]
Hertel, J.W.:Con Bn, w. P. Ledger (cnd), English CO ASV ▲ ASV 681 [DDD]
Smith, Dennis (trbn)
All-American Trombone, w. Oakland Univ Wind Sym [cnd:James Dawson] Coronet ▲ COR 400-7 ■ LPC 4007
Pryor, A.:Trbn & Band Music, w. Dawson (cnd), Oakland Univ Wind Sym Coronet ▲ COR 400-7 ■ LPC 4007
Smith, Edward (hpd)—see ORCHESTRAS & ENSEMBLES Clemencic Consort
Smith, Erik (hpd)
Stradella, A.:Vocal Music, w. G. Dagnino (bass), S. Piccollo (sop), M. Mazzara (alt), R. Balconi (ct), E. Velardi (cnd), Alessandro Stradella Consort—Sinfonia in E from the Cantata "Crudo Mar"; Toccata in a for Harpsichord; Exultate in Deo Fideles, Motet for Bass Solo & Violins; Si Apra al Riso Ogni Labbro, Cantata for 3 Voices & Strings [I,L] Bongiovanni ▲ GB 2123 [DDD]
Smith, Fenwick (fl)
Cage, J.:Ryoanji for 4 Soloists, w. Anthony D'Amico (db), Michael Miller (ob), Petur Eiriksson (b trbn), S. Drury (cnd), New England Conservatory Avant-Garde Ensemble *(rec New England Conservatory of Music, Boston, MA, Mar. 4 & 6, 1991)* Mode ▲ MODE 41
Copland, A.:Duo Fl, w. R. Hodgkinson (pno) Northeastern ("Classical Arts" series) ▲ NR 227-CD
Copland, A.:Threnodies I & II, w. S. Chase (vn), K. Murdock (va), R. Thomas (vc) Northeastern ("Classical Arts" series) ▲ NR 227-CD
Copland, A.:Vocalise, w. R. Hodgkinson (pno) Northeastern ("Classical Arts" series) ▲ NR 227-CD
Foote, A.:At Dusk, w. R. Thomas (vc), C. Yeats (harp) Northeastern ("Classical Arts" series) ▲ NR 227-CD
Foote, A.:Nocturne, w. L. Chang (vn), V. Uritzky (vn), K. Murdock (va), B. Coppock (vc) Northeastern ("Classical Arts" series) ▲ NR 227-CD
Foote, A.:Pieces Ob & Pno, Op. 31, w. R. Hodgkinson (pno) Northeastern ("Classical Arts" series) ▲ NR 227-CD
Foote, A.:Sarabande & Rigaudon, w. M. Thompson (va), R. Hodgkinson (pno) Northeastern ("Classical Arts" series) ▲ NR 227-CD
Harbison, J.:Duo Fl & Pno, w. Randall Hodgkinson (pno) *(rec Kresge Auditorium, between 1988 & 1994)* Archetype ▲ 60104 [DDD]
Koechlin, C.:Morceau de lecture, w. M. Amlin (pno) Hyperion ▲ CDA 66414 [DDD]
Koechlin, C.:Pieces Fl & Pno, Op. 149, w. M. Amlin (pno) [F] Hyperion ▲ CDA 66414 [DDD]

Smith, Fenwick (fl) (cont.)
Koechlin, C.:Pieces Fl, Op. 157, w. M. Amlin (pno) Hyperion ▲ CDA 66414 [DDD]
Koechlin, C.:Premier album de Lilian, w. J. West (sop), M. Amlin (pno) [F] Hyperion ▲ CDA 66414 [DDD]
Koechlin, C.:Son Fl & Pno, w. M. Amlin (pno) Hyperion ▲ CDA 66414 [DDD]
Koechlin, C.:Son for 2 Fls, w. L. Buyse (fl) Hyperion ▲ CDA 66414 [DDD]
Schulhoff, E.:Concertino Fl, w. M. Ludwig (va), E. Barker (db)—Andante con moto moderato; Furiant; Andante; Rondino *(rec May 1992)* Northeastern ▲ NR 248-CD
Schulhoff, E.:Son Fl, w. S. Pinkas (pno)—Allegro moderato; Scherzo; Allegro giocoso; Aria; Andante; Rondo-Finale; Allegro molto gajo *(rec June 1992)* Northeastern ▲ NR 248-CD
Seasons Remembered 2, w. Judith Lynn Stillman (pno), Toby Appel (va), John Deak (db), Eliot Porter (db), Diaz Trio [David Kim (vn), Roberto Diaz (va), Andres Diaz (vc)], Lutz Rath (vc), Ruth Waterman (vn) North Star ▲ 9837-40052-2 ■ 9837-40052-4
Thomson, V.:Rapsodico Northeastern ▲ NR 240-CD
Thomson, V.:Serenade, w. S. Leventhal (vn) Northeastern ▲ NR 240-CD
Vivaldi, A.:Con for 2 Fls, w. W. Bennett (fl), N. Marriner (cnd), Academy of St. Martin in the Fields Philips ▲ 412892-2 [DDD]
Warren, E.R.:Singing Earth, w. N. Gibson (sop), E. R. Warren (pno)—The wind sings welcome; Summer stars; Tawny days; Great memories [E] Cambria ▲ CD 1028 [DDD]
Warren, E.R.:Songs Sop, w. N. Gibson (sop), E. R. Warren (pno)—22 songs [E] Cambria ▲ CD 1028 [DDD]
Smith, H. (sax)
Miller, E.J.:Fant-Con in 3 Movts A Sax, w. R. Ponto (cnd), Oberlin Wind Ensemble Opus One ▲ CD 154
Miller, E.J.:Seven Sides of a Crystal, w. R. Ponto (cnd), Oberlin Wind Ensemble Opus One ▲ CD 154
Smith, Hazel (vn)—see ORCHESTRAS & ENSEMBLES australYSIS members
Smith, Henry Charles (trbn)
Hindemith, P.:Son Trbn, w. G. Gould (pno) *(rec 1976)* Sony Classical ("Glenn Gould Edition" series) 2-▲ SM2K 52671 [ADD]
Smith, Hopkinson (lt)
Bach, J.S.:Lt Music Astrée 2-▲ E 7721 [AAD]
Bach, J.S.:Suites Vc, BWV 1007-1012—BWV 1010 & 1012 [arr. Smith for lute] *(rec Oct 1992)* Astrée ▲ E 8744 [DDD]
Gallot, J.:Lt Music—Suite in f#; Suite in a; Pièces in F; Pièces in d; Chaconne in C Astrée ▲ E 8528
Gaultier, D.:La Rhétorique des dieux—Suite No. 1 in D, No. 2 in A & No. 12 in a Astrée ▲ E 7778 [AAD]
Gaultier, E.:Lt Music—3 suites; La cascade Astrée ▲ E 8703 [DDD]
Kapsberger, G.G.:Libro I d'intavolatura di lauto Astrée ▲ E 8553
Mouton, C.:Pieces de luth (sels)—Book 1—9 pieces in a; Book 2—8 pieces in f# & 4 pieces in A Astrée ▲ E 7728 [AAD]
Weiss, S.L.:Lt Music—Sonata in a; Fantasia in C; Sonata in f#; Tombeau sur la mort de M. Comte de Logy Astrée ▲ E 8718 [DDD]
Smith, Hopkinson (lt/thb/gtr)
Baroque Music for Recorder, w. Conrad Steinmann (rcr), Monica Huggett (baroque vn), Jordi Savall (vl), Pere Ros (vl), Claude Flagel (h-g), Johann Sonnleitner (hpd) Claves ▲ CD 508103 [ADD]
Smith, Hopkinson (thb)
Marais, M.:Pièces de viole [Book 3] (sels), w. J. Savall (bass vl), T. Koopman (hpd) Astrée ▲ E 8761
Smith, Hopkinson (vih)
Milán, L. de:Maestro (sels)—sel. of 16 solo instrumental works—fantasias, etc.—for the vihuela da mano Astrée ▲ E 7748 [AAD]
Milán, L. de:Maestro (sels), w. M. Figueras (sop)—sel. of 16 sonetos, villancicos & romances, sung in Castilian, Portuguese & Italian Astrée ▲ E 7777 [AAD]
Mudarra, A.:Libros de musica (sels), w. Montserrat Figueras (sop)—Book 3:Si me llaman a mi; Si viesse e melevasse; La vita fugge; O gelosia d'amanti; Triste estava el rey David; Israel, mira tus montes; Beatus ille; Dulces exuviae; Regia qui mesto Por asperos caminos; Que llanto son aquestos; Claros y frescos rios; Isabel, perdiste la tu faxa; Gentil cavallero; Recuerde el alma dormida Astrée 2-▲ E 8533
Narváez, L. de:Seys libros—21 works (14 fantasias, etc.) Astrée ▲ E 8706 [DDD]
Smith, Hopkinson (vih/gtr)
Mudarra, A.:Libros de musica Astrée ▲ E 8740
Smith, J. (instr)
Debussy, C.:Danses sacrée et profane, w. Y. Kondonassis (hp), F. Cohen (cl), M. Chalifour (vn), W.-F. Gu (va), S. Konopka (va), R. Weiss (vc), T. Sperl (db) *(rec Nov. 23-25, 1992)* Telarc ▲ CD 80361 [DDD]
Smith, Jai (perc)
Hays, S.:Dreaming the World, w. Thomas Bruckner (bar), Sal Basile (voc), Jennifer López (voc), John Schaffer (voc), Sorrel Hays (voc), Joseph Kubera (pno), John Kennedy (perc), Charles Wood (perc), Maya Gunji (perc), Eric Kivnick (perc) New World ▲ 805202 [DDD]
Smith, James (gtr)
An American Collage Vol. II, w. Conctanoo Koono (pno), Ayke Agus (pno), Anita Swearingen (pno), Michael Lang (pno), Diane Lang Bryan (cl), Sherry Kloss (vn), Laila Padorr (fl), Victor Morosco (a sax) Protone ▲ PR 1114 [DDD]
Smith, James Russell (perc)
York, W.:Native Songs, w. N. Armstrong (sop), S. Sylvan (bar), S. Downey (sgr), R. Woodhouse (sgr), P. Friedland (fl), J. Fischer (pno) *(rec May 1987)* New World ▲ 80439-2
Smith, Jane (org)
Maslanka, D.:Mass, w. Lydia Catherine Easley (sop), Charles Roe (bar), G.I. Hanson (cnd), Univ of Arizona Wind Orch, Univ of Arizona Sym Choir, Arizona Chamber Choir, Tuscon Boys' Chorus *(rec St. Thomas the Apostle Church, Tuscon, Arizona, Apr 29-30, 1996)* Albany 2-▲ TROY 221-22 [DDD]
Smith, Joseph (pno)
American Piano, Vol. 4:Rhythmic Moments Premier ▲ PRCD 1028 [DDD]
Arlen, H.:Pno Music—Bonbon; Ode; Rhythmic moments Premier ▲ PRCD 1028 [DDD]
Burleigh, H.T.:Songs, w. Hilda Harris (mez), Philip Creech (ten), Steven Cole (ten), Arthur Woodley (bass)—Now Sleeps the Crimson Petal; Promis' Lan'; Ethiopia Saluting the Colors; Lovely Dark & Lonely One; Love Watches; Almona; O, Night of Dream & Wonder; His Helmet's Blaze; I Hear His Footsteps, Music Sweet; Thou Art Weary; This is Nirvana; Ahmed's Song of Farewell; Through Moanin' Pines; The Frolic; In de Col' Moonlight; A Jubilee; On Bended Knees; A New Hiding-Place; Worth While; The Jungle Flower; Kashmiri Song; Among the Fuchsias; Till I Wake; By an' By; Ev'ry Time I Feel de Spirit; Deep River; Oh, Didn't it Rain; Swing Low, Sweet Chariot; Wade in de Water; Heav'n, Heav'n Premier ▲ PRCD 1041 [DDD]
Foster, S.C.:Pno Music—Old Folks at Home; Santa Anna's retreat; Village bells polka Premier ▲ PRCD 1028 [DDD]
Gershwin, G.:Pno Music—Novelette in fourths; Rubato; Sleepless night Premier ▲ PRCD 1028 [DDD]
Herbert, V.:Pno Music—La coquette Premier ▲ PRCD 1028 [DDD]
Joplin, S.:Pno Music—Bethna Premier ▲ PRCD 1028 [DDD]
Let My Song Fill Your Heart:A Remembrance of the American Concert Song, w. Maryanne Telese (sop), Arthur Woodley (bass), Peter Howard (pno) Premier ▲ PR 1002
Levant, O.:Sonatina Premier ▲ PRCD 1028 [DDD]
Smith, Joshua (fl)
Ravel, M.:Intro & Allegro, w. Y. Kondonassis (hp), F. Cohen (cl), M. Chalifour (vn), W.-F. Gu (va), S. Konopka (va), R. Weiss (vc), T. Sperl (db) *(rec Nov. 23-25, 1992)* Telarc ▲ CD 80361 [DDD]
Ravel, M.:Pavane pour une infante défunte, w. Y. Kondonassis (hp), F. Cohen (cl), M. Chalifour (vn), W.-F. Gu (va), S. Konopka (va), R. Weiss (vc), T. Sperl (db) [arr. by Kondonassis] *(rec Nov. 23-25, 1992)* Telarc ▲ CD 80361 [DDD]
Smith, Kate (vn)
Berg, O.:Odd Trio, w. T. Tureski (mar), W. Beauvais (gtr) Centaur ▲ CRC 2167 [DDD]
Smith, Kenneth (fl)
British Flute Music, Vol. 1:Summer Music, w. Paul Rhodes (pno) ASV ▲ ASV 739 [DDD]

INSTRUMENT.

Smith, Kenneth (fl) (cont.)
British Flute Music, Vol. 2:Folk & Fantasy, w. Paul Rhodes (pno) ASV ▲ ASV 768 [DDD]
British Flute Music, Vol. 3:The Reed of Pan, w. Paul Rhodes (pno) ASV ▲ ASV 862 [DDD]
Golden Flute, w. Paul Rhodes (pno) ASV ▲ ASV CD 2102
Walking in the Air:21 Favorites for Flute, w. Paul Rhodes (pno) ASV ("White Line" series) ▲ ASV 2072
Smith, L. (org)
Avshalomov, J.:Prophecy, w. C. Matheson (ten), J. Dexter (cnd), Mid-America Chorale CRI ▲ CD 667 [ADD]
Smith, L. (vc)—see ORCHESTRAS & ENSEMBLES Huntingdon Trio
Smith, N. (hn)—see ORCHESTRAS & ENSEMBLES Wisconsin Brass Quintet
Smith, Penelope (pno)—see ORCHESTRAS & ENSEMBLES Classic Trio
Smith, Peter (pno)
Drumming, w. Evelyn Glennie (perc) *(rec Whitfield Street Studios, London, Dec 11-15, 1994)* Catalyst ▲ 09026-68195-2 [DDD]
Liszt, F.:Transcriptions & Paraphrases—Soirées Vienne, Valses-Caprices d'aprés Schubert Meridian ▲ MER 84247 [DDD]
Smith, Philip (tpt)
Orchestral Excerpts for Trumpet Summit ▲ DCD 144 [DDD]
Zwilich, E.T.:Con Tpt, w. Z. Mehta (cnd), New York PO Ensemble New World ▲ NW 372-2 [DDD]
Smith, R. (pno)—see ORCHESTRAS & ENSEMBLES Huntingdon Trio
Smith, Rheta (ob)
Zaimont, J.L.:Dance/Inner Dance, w. Kathleen Nester (fl), Theodore Mook (vc) *(rec SUNY Purchase, Theatre C, Jan 8-10 & Feb 20, 1995)* Arabesque ▲ ARA 6667 [DDD]
Smith, Robert Edward (hpd)
Bach, J.S.:Kbd Music (misc)—Chromatic Fant & Fugue, BWV 903; Cappricio upon the Departure of His Beloved Brother; Con Hpd, BWV 972; 6 Preludes for Beginners; Toccata in D, BWV 912 *(rec Hartford, CT, June 8-9, 1992)* Wildboar ▲ WLBR 9501 [DDD]
Bach, J.S.:Kbd Music (misc) Wildboar ▲ WLBR 9502
Smith, Roger (vc)—see ORCHESTRAS & ENSEMBLES Academy of St. Martin in the Fields Chamber Ensemble
Smith, Ronald (pno)
Alkan, C.-V.:Etudes (12) in major keys—No. 5, "Allegro barbaro" *(rec Abbey Road Studios, London, Jan 10-12, 1977)* APR 2-▲ APR 7031 [ADD]
Alkan, C.-V.:Etudes (12) in minor keys *(rec Abbey Road Studios, London, Jan 10-12, 1977)* APR 2-▲ APR 7031 [ADD]
Alkan, C.-V.:Petites fants *(rec Abbey Road Studios, London, Jan 10-12, 1977)* APR 2-▲ APR 7031 [ADD]
Alkan, C.-V.:Preludes Pno, Op. 31—No. 8, "La chanson de la folle au bord du mer" *(rec Abbey Road Studios, London, Jan 10-12, 1977)* APR 2-▲ APR 7031 [ADD]
Balakirev, M.:Son Pno Nimbus ▲ NI 5187 [DDD]
Beethoven, L. van:Son 8 Pno, "Pathétique" Nimbus ▲ NI 5034 [DDD]
Beethoven, L. van:Son 14 Pno, "Moonlight Son" Nimbus ▲ NI 5034 [DDD]
Beethoven, L. van:Son 23 Pno, "Appassionata" Nimbus ▲ NI 5034 [DDD]
Beethoven, L. van:Sym 7 [Liszt's solo piano arr.] Nimbus ▲ NI 5013
Busoni, F.:Chaconne Pno Nimbus ▲ NI 5013
Chopin, F.:Études (24) Nimbus ▲ NI 5223 [DDD]
Mussorgsky, M.:Pictures at an Exhibition Nimbus ▲ NI 5187 [DDD]
Scriabin, A.:Son 9 Pno Nimbus ▲ NI 5187 [DDD]
Smith, S. (vn)—see ORCHESTRAS & ENSEMBLES Audubon String Quartet
Smith, Steve (vn)—see ORCHESTRAS & ENSEMBLES Smith String Quartet
Smith, Tim (b cl)
Hyla, L.:We Speak Etruscan, w. Tim Berne (br sax) *(rec Dec. 18, 1994)* New World ▲ 80491-2
Smith, Trefor (pno)
Kirchner, T.:Adagio quasi Fant Koch Schwann ▲ SCH 313962 [DDD]
Kirchner, T.:Frühlingsrhuss Koch Schwann ▲ SCH 313962 [DDD]
Kirchner, T.:Preludes Pno Koch Schwann ▲ SCH 313962 [DDD]
Smith, Wadada Leo (tpt/flgl/fls/bells)
Smith, W.L.:Music of, w. Robin Lorentz (vn), Erika Duke (vc), Dorothy Stone (fl/pic), Martin Walker (cl), Vicki Ray (pno/cel), Mika Noda (vib/bells/timp), David Philipson (perc/bells)—Another Wave More Waves; Double Thunderbolt; Tao-Njia; and others Tzadik ("Composer" series) ▲ TZA 7017 [DDD]
Smith, Wilhelmina (vc)—see ORCHESTRAS & ENSEMBLES Windham String Quartet
Smith, Wilma (vn)
Tcherepnin, I.:Flores musicales, w. Peggy Pearson (ob), Ivan Tcherepnin (psaltery/org/elecs) *(rec Harvard Univ. Electronic Music Studio, Oct. & Dec. 1981)* CRI ▲ CD 684 [ADD]
Smith Toney, Kelly (vn)
Constantinides, D.:Vocal Music, w. Cynthia Dewey (nar), Angela DeVerger (sop), Evelyn Petros (sop), Susan Faust Straley (sop), Eugenia Epperson (fl), Richard Jernigan (cl), Hye-Yun Chung (hp), Stephen Brown (pno), John Raush (perc), D. Constantinides (cnd), Louisiana State Univ New Music Ensemble—Reflections IV for Sop, Fl, Hp & Pno; Intimations [1 Act Opera]; 4 Songs on Poems by Sappho; Mutability for Sop & Str Qt.; 4 Greek Songs Vestige ▲ 04
Smits, Raphaëlla (gtr)
Bach, J.S.:Sons & Partitas Vn, BWV 1001-1006—BWV 1002, 1004 & 1005 *(rec Vereenigde Doopsgezinde Kerk, Haarlem, The Netherlands, Oct 1993)* Accent ▲ 93100 D [DDD]
Barrios, A.:Gtr Music—Choro de Saudade; Una Limosa par el Amor de Dios (Gran Tremolo); Vals, Op. 8, No. 4 Accent ▲ 8966 [DDD]
Bennett, Richard Rodney:Impromptus (5) Accent ▲ 8966 [DDD]
Burkhart, F.:Passacaglia Gtr Accent ▲ 8966 [DDD]
Copper, L.:Gtr Music—Grande Sérenade, Op. 30; Les Soirées d'Auteuil, Op. 23/7 (from Sept Morseaux Episodiques); Reverie, Op. 53/1 (from Six Pièces Originales) *(rec Dec. 1991)* Accent 2-▲ 9182 [DDD]
Giuliani, M.:Grand Ov Accent ▲ 8863 [DDD]
Giuliani, M.:Gtr Music—La Chasse-Rondeau, Op. 109; Variazioni, Op. 112 Accent ▲ 8863 [DDD]
Lyrical 20th Century Guitar Music Accent ▲ 8966 [DDD]
Martin, F.:Pièces brèves Gtr Accent ▲ 8966 [DDD]
Mertz, K.J.:Gtr Music—La Rimembranza; Le Gondolier, Op. 65/3; Pianto dell'Amante; Souvenir de Choulhoff-Mazurka; Ständchen; Liebesbotschaft; Le Carneval de Venice Accent ▲ 8863 [DDD]
Morel, Jorge:Sonatina Gtr Accent ▲ 8966 [DDD]
Sor, F.:Etudes—Op. 6/11; Op. 35/22; Op. 31/12 *(rec Dec. 1991)* Accent 2-▲ 9182 [DDD]
Sor, F.:Fants Gtr—Op. 59 *(rec Dec. 1991)* Accent 2-▲ 9182 [DDD]
Sor, F.:Vars on a Theme of Mozart—Op. 59 *(rec Dec. 1991)* Accent 2-▲ 9182 [DDD]
Turina, J.:Son Gtr Accent ▲ 8966 [DDD]
Weiss, S.L.:Lt Music—Sarabande in C; Bourrée in a; Tombeau sur la mort de M. Cajetan Baron d'Hartig, arrivée le 25 de mars 1719; Tombeau sur la mort de M. Comte D'Logy, arrivée 1721; Capricio in D *(rec Vereenigde Doopsgezinde Kerk, Haarlem, The Netherlands, Oct. 1993)* Accent ▲ 93100 D [DDD]
Smits, Reitze (bc)—see ORCHESTRAS & ENSEMBLES New Consort
Smola, Oldřich (va)
Domazlicky, F.:Czech Folk Songs, w. Z. Jiroušek (vn), J. Mráček (vn), P. Mišejka (vc), J. Karas (cnd), Disman Radio Children's Ensemble *(rec June 1992)* Channel Classics ▲ CCS 5193 [DDD]
Smuraglia, Maria (gtr)
Merchi, J.B.:Duets Gtrs, w. Carlo Mascilli Migliorini (gtr) Entrée ▲ 0073
Smykal, Jaroslav (pno)
Auric, G.:Imaginées II, w. M. Nyikos (vc) Koch Schwann ▲ CD 310059 [DDD]
Honegger, A.:Son Vc, w. M. Nyikos (vc) Koch Schwann ▲ CD 310 059 [DDD]
Honegger, A.:Sonatina Cl, w. M. Nyikos (vc) Koch Schwann ▲ CD 310 059 [DDD]
Milhaud, D.:Elégie, w. M. Nyikos (vc) Koch Schwann ▲ CD 310 059 [DDD]
Milhaud, D.:Son Vc, w. M. Nyikos (vc) Koch Schwann ▲ CD 310 059 [DDD]
Poulenc, F.:Son Vc, w. M. Nyikos (vc) Koch Schwann ▲ CD 310 059 [DDD]

Smylie, Dennis (b cl)
Martino, D.:Strata CRI ▲ CD 693 [ADD]
Smylie, Dennis (cl)
Martino, D.:Triple Con, w. Anand Devendra (cl), Leslie Thimmig (cl), H. Sollberger (cnd), Group for Contemporary Music *(rec Dec 1978)* Albany ▲ TROY 168 [DDD]
Snedeker, Jeffery (hn)
Bordogni, G.:Allegro vivace, w. Marilyn Willbanks (pno) *(rec Univ of MA, Amherst, July 31-Aug 4, 1995)* Snedeker ▲ 001
Bordogni, G.:Andantino, w. Marilyn Willbanks (pno) *(rec Univ of MA, Amherst, July 31-Aug 4, 1995)* Snedeker ▲ 001
Dauprat, L.-F.:Melodie Hns, w. Richard Seraphinoff (hn), Marilyn Willbanks (pno) *(rec Univ of MA, Amherst, July 31-Aug 4, 1995)* Snedeker ▲ 001
Gallay, J.-F.:Grand Caprice, w. Marilyn Willbanks (pno) *(rec Univ of MA, Amherst, July 31-Aug 4, 1995)* Snedeker ▲ 001
Gallay, J.-F.:Solo 11 Hn, w. Marilyn Willbanks (pno) *(rec Univ of MA, Amherst, July 31-Aug 4, 1995)* Snedeker ▲ 001
Gallay, J.-F.:Vocalises (3), w. Marilyn Willbanks (pno) *(rec Univ of MA, Amherst, July 31-Aug 4, 1995)* Snedeker ▲ 001
Panseron, A.:Andantino Hn, w. Marilyn Willbanks (pno) *(rec Univ of MA, Amherst, July 31-Aug 4, 1995)* Snedeker ▲ 001
Rossini, G.:Prelude, Theme & Vars Hn, w. Marilyn Willbanks (pno) *(rec Univ of MA, Amherst, July 31-Aug 4, 1995)* Snedeker ▲ 001
Saint-Saëns, C.:Romances Hn, w. Marilyn Willbanks (pno)—Op. 36 *(rec Univ of MA, Amherst, July 31-Aug 4, 1995)* Snedeker ▲ 001
Snell, Keith (pno)
Saint-Saëns, C.:Carnival of the Animals, w. A. Nel (pno), R. Stamp (cnd), Academy of London Orch Virgin Classics ▲ 59533 [DDD]
Snider, Leslie (vc)
Fauré, G.:Trio, w. H. Lipsky (vn), M. Koslovsky (pno) Analekta ▲ ATM 29704
Granados, E.:Trio Pno, w. H. Lipsky (vn), M. Koslovsky (pno) Analekta ▲ ATM 29704
Snijders, John (pno)—see also ORCHESTRAS & ENSEMBLES Ives Ensemble members
Cage, J.:Two⁶, w. Josje ter Haar (vn) *(rec Theater Romein, Leeuwarden, the Netherlands, Jan 14-17, 1996)* Hat Art ("Hat NOW." series) 2-▲ 6192 [DDD]
Snítil, Václav (vn)
Milhaud, D.:Son 2 Vn, w. J. Hála (pno) *(rec 1987)* Supraphon ▲ 110103-2 [DDD]
Ravel, M.:Son Vn Pno, w. J. Hála (pno) *(rec 1987)* Supraphon ▲ 110103-2 [DDD]
Roussel, A.:Son 1 Vn, w. Josef Hála (pno) *(rec 1987)* Supraphon ▲ 110103-2 [DDD]
Smetana, B.:From the Homeland, w. Petr Messiereur (vn), Josef Hála (pno) or Jarmila Kozderková (pno) Panton ▲ PAN 811202
Suk, J.:Ballade Vn, w. Petr Messiereur (vn), Josef Hála (pno), Jarmila Kozderková (pno) Panton ▲ PAN 811202
Suk, J.:Fant Vn, w. V. Válek (cnd), Prague SO Panton ▲ PAN 811212
Snitker, Ronald (bn/ctbn)
A Double Reed Consort, w. Wizardsl, Iowa Double Reed Consort [Lissa Stolz (ob), Debra Hawk-Burt (ob/e hn), Ronald Tyree (bn), Trevor Johnson (hpd)] *(rec Clapp Recital Hall, Univ. of Iowa, Iowa City, Jan. 1993 & May 1994)* CRS Master ▲ CRS 9460
Snitkovsky, Semyon (vn)
Glazunov, A.:Con Vn, w. G. Rozhdestvensky (cnd), USSR Large SO Vox Box 2-▲ CDX 5118 [ADD]
Snowden, Jonathan (fl)—see also ORCHESTRAS & ENSEMBLES Michael Thompson Wind Quintet
Bizet, G.:L'Arlésienne (suites), w. J. Delacôte (cnd), Royal PO Tring ▲ TRP 49 [DDD]
Rózsa, M.:Son Fl Silva Classics ▲ SIL 6006 [DDD]
Doyle, P.:Sense & Sensibility, w. Jane Eaglen (sop), Richard Morgan (ob), Robert Hill (cl), Tony Hymas (pno), R. Ziegler (cnd), *(orch unknown)* *(rec Air Studios, Lyndhurst Hall)* Sony Classical ▲ SK 62258 [DDD]
Snyder, Barry (pno)—see also ORCHESTRAS & ENSEMBLES Eastman Trio
Adler, S.:Duo Son, w. Natalya Antonova (pno) Gasparo ▲ GS 298 [DDD/DAD]
Bolcom, W.:Dance Portraits (3) *(rec 1995)* Vox Classics ▲ VOX 7509
Britten, H.:Son Vc, w. Steven Doane (vc) *(rec Eastman Theater, Rochester, NY, Jan 14-15 & Apr 10-11, 19)* Bridge ▲ BCD 9056 [DDD]
Bridge, F.:Mélodie Vn, w. Steven Doane (vc) *(rec Eastman Theater, Rochester, NY, Jan 14-15 & Apr 10-11, 19)* Bridge ▲ BCD 9056 [DDD]
Bridge, F.:Scherzetto Vc, w. Steven Doane (vc) *(rec Eastman Theater, Rochester, NY, Jan 14-15 & Apr 10-11, 19)* Bridge ▲ BCD 9056 [DDD]
Bridge, F.:Son Vc, w. Steven Doane (vc) *(rec Eastman Theater, Rochester, NY, Jan 14-15 & Apr 10-11, 19)* Bridge ▲ BCD 9056 [DDD]
Bridge, F.:Spring Song, w. Steven Doane (vc) *(rec Eastman Theater, Rochester, NY, Jan 14-15 & Apr 10-11, 19)* Bridge ▲ BCD 9056 [DDD]
Clarke, R.:Son Vc, w. Pamela Frame (vc) Koch International Classics ▲ KIC 7281 [DDD]
Copland, A.:Son Vn & Pno, w. Z. Zeitlin (vn) Gasparo ▲ GS 279
Crawford, R.:Son Vn & Pno, w. Catherine Tait (vn) Gasparo ▲ GS 300
Dohnányi, E. von:Rhaps, Op. 11 Pro Arte ▲ CDD 240 ■ PCD 240
Dohnányi, E. von:Ruralia hungarica Pno Pro Arte ▲ CDD 240 ■ PCD 240
Druckman, J.:Duo Vn & Pno, w. Z. Zeitlin (vn) Gasparo ▲ GS 279
Fauré, G.:Music for Vc & Pno, w. S. Doane (vc)—Sérénade, Op. 98; Sicilienne, Op. 78; Élégie, Op. 24; Sonatas, Opp. 109 & 117; Romance, Op. 69; Mourceau de lecture (w. Kurt Fowler, 2nd cello); Papillon, Op. 77; Après un rêve, Op. 7/1 Bridge ▲ BCD 9038 [DDD]
Jaffe, S.:Double Son for 2 Pnos, w. A. Nel (pno) *(rec Nov. 22 & 23, 1991)* Bridge ▲ BCD 9047 [DDD]
Mamlok, U.:Designs, w. Catherine Tait (vn) Gasparo ▲ GS 300
Mamlok, U.:Son Vn, w. Catherine Tait (vn) Gasparo ▲ GS 300
Mozart, W.A.:Con 26 Pno, w. D. Zinman (cnd), Rochester PO *(rec 1978)* Vox Box 3-▲ CDX 3010 [ADD]
Reynolds, V.:Son Vn, w. Z. Zeitlin (vn) Gasparo ▲ GS 279
Talma, L.:Son Vn, w. Catherine Tait (vn) Gasparo ▲ GS 300
Zwilich, E.T.:Son in 3 Movts, w. Catherine Tait (vn) Gasparo ▲ GS 300
Snyder, John (didjeridu/waterphone)
Lockwood, A.:Thousand Year Dreaming, w. Art Baron (conch shell/trbn/didjeridu), Liby Van Cleve (ob/E hn), Jon Gibson (didjeridu), J.D. Parran (cl), Michael Publiese (perc), Scott Robinson (conch shell/perc), Charles Wood (tam-tam, stones), Peter Zummo (trbn/didjeridu) ¿What Next? ▲ WN 0010
Snyder, Patricia (org)
Sowerby, L.:Songs, w. Ronald Stalford (org), Con Vivium—18 Christmas Songs Albany ▲ TROY 187 [DDD]
Soames, Victoria (cl)
Bärmann, H.J.:Air Varié, w. J. Drake (pno) Clarinet Classics ▲ CC 0003
Bärmann, H.J.:Qnt 3 Cl, w. Duke String Quartet Clarinet Classics ▲ CC 0003
The Best of Classical Song, w. Ritchie, Elizabeth (sop), Jennifer Purvis (pno) IMP Classics ▲ PCD 987 [DDD]
Mendelssohn, F.:Concert Pieces, w. R. Heaton (cl), J. Drake (pno)—Nos. 1 & 2 Clarinet Classics ▲ CC 0003
Müller, I.:Qt 2 Cl, w. Mühlfeld Ensemble Clarinet Classics ▲ CC 0006 [ADD]
Paer, F.:Una voce al cor mi parta, w. E. Ritchie (sop), J. Purvis (pno) Clarinet Classics ▲ CC 0006 [ADD]
Les Six Works for Clarinet & Piano, w. Soame, Victoria (cl), Julius Drake (pno) *(rec 1989)* Clarinet Classics ▲ CC 0001 [DDD]
Spohr, L.:Faust (sels), w. E. Ritchie (sop), J. Purvis (pno)—Ich bin allein Clarinet Classics ▲ CC 0006 [ADD]

▲ = CD ♦ = Enhanced CD Δ = MD ■ = Cassette Tape □ = DCC

Soames, Victoria (cl) (cont.)
Spohr, L.:Songs (misc), w. E. Ritchie (sop), J. Purvis (pno)—6 deutsche Lieder, Op. 103 Clarinet Classics ▲ CC 0006 [ADD]
Spohr, L.:Vars in B♭ on a Theme from *Alruna,* w. J. Purvis (pno) Clarinet Classics ▲ CC 0006 [ADD]
Weber, C.M. von:Melody Cl, w. J. Drake (pno) Clarinet Classics ▲ CC 0003
Weber, C.M. von:Qnt Cl, w. Duke String Quartet Clarinet Classics ▲ CC 0003
Weber, C.M. von:Vars on a Theme from *Silvana* Cl, w. J. Drake (pno) Clarinet Classics ▲ CC 0003

Soares, Ferdananda (pno)
Brahms, J.:Hungarian Dances Pno 4-Hands, w. Inger Södergren (pno)—Nos. 1, 2, 5, 17 *(rec 1991)* Approche ▲ CAL 6219 [DDD]
Brahms, J.:Liebeslieder Waltzes Pno 4-Hands, w. Inger Södergren (pno) *(rec 1991)* Approche ▲ CAL 6219 [DDD]
Brahms, J.:Neue Liebeslieder Waltzes, w. Inger Södergren (pno)—Op. 65a *(rec 1991)* Approche ▲ CAL 6219 [DDD]
Brahms, J.:Waltzes Pno, Op. 39, w. Inger Södergren (pno) *(rec 1991)* Approche ▲ CAL 6219 [DDD]

Sobol, Deborah (pno)
Bernstein, L.:Son Cl, w. Larry Combs (cl) *(rec Bennett Hall, Highland Park, IL, Jan. 18, 24 & 25, 1994)* Summit ▲ DCD 172 [DDD]
Brahms, J.:Son 2 Vn, w. L. Combs (cl) [clarinet & piano trans. Kent Kennan] Summit ▲ DCD 125 [DDD]
Copland, A.:Son Vn & Pno, w. Larry Combs (cl) [trans. for clarinet] *(rec Bennett Hall, Highland Park, IL, Jan. 18, 24 & 25, 1994)* Summit ▲ DCD 172 [DDD]
Gershwin, G.:Preludes (3) Pno *(rec Bennett Hall, Highland Park, IL, Jan. 18, 24 & 25, 1994)* Summit ▲ DCD 172 [DDD]
Larry Combs:Clarinet, w. Larry Combs (cl) Summit ▲ DCD 125 [DDD]
Prokofiev, S.:Son Vn, Op. 94bis, w. L. Combs (cl) [clarinet & piano trans. by Kent Kennan] Summit ▲ DCD 125 [DDD]
Scriabin, A.:Preludes Pno (misc), w. L. Combs (cl) [clarinet & piano transcriptions by Willard Elliot]—Op. 11, No. 23; Op. 15, No. 2; Op. 16, Nos. 1–5 Summit ▲ DCD 125 [DDD]
Songs of the Romantic Age, w. Patrice Michaels Bedi (sop) *(rec Chicago, June 20–22 & 27, 1994)* Cedille ▲ CDR 90000 019 [DDD]

Sobol, Lawrence (cl)
Diamond, D.:Qnt Cl, w. Long Island Chamber Ensemble Grenadilla ■ GSC 1007
Diamond, D.:Qnt Cl, w. Linda Moss (va), Louise Schulman (va), Timothy Eddy (vc), Fred Sherry (vc) *(rec RCA Studio A, New York City)* New World ▲ 80508-2
Harris, R.:Con Cl, w. P. Basquin (pno), Long Island Chamber Ensemble Grenadilla ■ GSC 1007
Hovhaness, A.:Firdausi, w. Agostini (hp), Boyar (perc) Grenadilla ■ GSC 1008
Hovhaness, A.:O Lady Moon, w. Barbara Martin (sop), Elizabeth Rodgers (pno) Grenadilla ■ GSC 1073
Hovhaness, A.:Saturn, w. Kate Hurney (sop), Martin Berkovsky (pno) Crystal ▲ CD 808
Husa, K.:Evocations of Slovakia, w. L. Schulman (va), T. Eddy (vc) Grenadilla ■ GSC 1008
Macdowell, E.:Pieces Cl, w. P. Basquin (pno) Grenadilla ■ GSC 1008

Soddeman, Fritz (org)
The Klais Organ in St. Mary's Cathedral, Hildesheim *(rec Sept. 17–19, 1991)* Calig ▲ CAL 50909 [DDD]

Soderberg, Marta (va)
Veeneman, C.:The Wiry Concord, w. Susan Werner (banjo), Forrest Covington (hammered dlc/cimbalom), Georganne Assat (hp), Donald Martin Jenni (hpd), Mark Johnson (hpd), Barbara Phillips Farley (pno), James Austin (pno), James Knutson (perc), Patrick Doyle (perc), Steven Butters (perc), James Popejoy (perc), M. Geary (cnd) Capstone ▲ SCI 6

Söderblom, Jan (vn)
Gothoni, R.:The Bull & His Herdsman:A Zen Story from Ancient China, w. Soile Isokoski (sop), Jorma Hynninen (bar), Ilari Angervo (va), Jan-Erik Kustafsson (vc), Heini Kärkkäinen (pno), R. Gothoni (cnd) Ondine ▲ ODE 832 [DDD]
Grieg, E.:Sons Vn, Opp. 8, 13 & 45, w. I. Tateno (pno)—Op. 45 *(rec Aug. 27–30, 1991)* Finlandia ▲ 4509-95867-2 [DDD]

Södergren, Inger (pno)
Beethoven, L. van:Son 30 Pno Approche ▲ 6648
Beethoven, L. van:Son 31 Pno Approche ▲ 6648
Beethoven, L. van:Son 32 Pno Approche ▲ 6648
Brahms, J.:Hungarian Dances Pno 4-Hands, w. Fernanda Soares (pno)—Nos. 1, 2, 5, 17 *(rec 1991)* Approche ▲ CAL 6219 [DDD]
Brahms, J.:Liebeslieder Waltzes Pno 4-Hands, w. Fernanda Soares (pno) *(rec 1991)* Approche ▲ CAL 6219 [DDD]
Brahms, J.:Neue Liebeslieder Waltzes, w. Fernanda Soares (pno)—Op. 65a *(rec 1991)* Approche ▲ CAL 6219 [DDD]
Brahms, J.:Waltzes Pno, Op. 39, w. Fernanda Soares (pno) *(rec 1991)* Approche ▲ CAL 6219 [DDD]

Sofronitsky, Vladimir (pno)
Prokofiev, S.:Pieces Pno, Op. 52 *(rec between 1953–55)* Russian Disc ▲ RUS 15001 [DDD]
Prokofiev, S.:Sarcasms *(rec between 1953–55)* Russian Disc ▲ RUS 15001 [DDD]
Prokofiev, S.:Son 7 Pno *(rec between 1953–55)* Russian Disc ▲ RUS 15001 [DDD]
Prokofiev, S.:Tales of an Old Grandmother *(rec between 1953–55)* Russian Disc ▲ RUS 15001 [DDD]
Prokofiev, S.:Visions fugitives—sels *(rec between 1953–55)* Russian Disc ▲ RUS 15001 [DDD]
Rachmaninoff, S.:Études-tableaux, Opp. 33 & 39 Arlecchino ARL
Rachmaninoff, S.:Moments musicaux Arlecchino ARL
Rachmaninoff, S.:Pno Music (misc)—Préludes, Opp. 3/2, 23/4 & 6; Études, Op. 39/4–6 *(rec 1946–1951)* Multisonic ▲ 31 0181
Rachmaninoff, S.:Preludes Pno Arlecchino ARL
Schumann, R.:Carnaval Pno Arlecchino ▲ ARL12
Schumann, R.:Fant Pno Arlecchino ▲ ARL1
Schumann, R.:Impromptus on a Theme by Clara Wieck Pno, Op. 5 Arlecchino ▲ ARL1
Schumann, R.:Kreisleriana Arlecchino ▲ ARL1
Schumann, R.:Papillons Arlecchino ▲ ARL12
Schumann, R.:Son 1 Pno Arlecchino ▲ ARL12
Scriabin, A.:Pno Music (misc)—Preludes, Opp. 11/1, 39/2 & 3, 48/2; Impromptu, Op. 12/2; Etudes, Opp. 8/7, 42/4 & 6 *(rec 1946–1951)* Multisonic ▲ 31 0181
Scriabin, A.:Son 3 Pno *(rec 1946–1951)* Multisonic ▲ 31 0181

Soh, Tomotada (vn)
Bruch, M.:Adagio appassionato, w. H. Griffiths (cnd), Royal PO Gallo ▲ CD 692
Bruch, M.:In memoriam, w. H. Griffiths (cnd), Royal PO Gallo ▲ CD 692
Bruch, M.:Romance Vn, w. H. Griffiths (cnd), Royal PO Gallo ▲ CD 692

Sohm, Richard (perc)
Bartók, B.:Son for 2 Pnos, w. G. Sándor (pno), R. Reinhardt (pno), O. Schad (perc) *(rec 1965)* Vox Box ("Legends" series) 2-▲ CDX2 5506 [ADD]

Soifertis-Lukjanenko, Evgenni (pno)
Prokofiev, S.:Son 6 Pno Partridge ▲ 1127-2 [DDD]
Shostakovich, D.:Preludes Pno, Op. 34 Partridge ▲ 1127-2 [DDD]

Sokal, Harry (s sax)
Rüegg, M.:Music of, w. Lauren Newton (sgr), Wolfgang Puschnig (fl/s sax), Roman Schwaller (t sax), Karl Fian (tpt), Christian Radovan (trbn), Woody Schabata (vib)—Reflections on Aubade; Reflections on Méditation; Reflections on Sévère Réprimande; Reflections on Idylle; Reflections on Gnossiennes Nos. 1 & 2; Satie ist mir im traum 3x nicht erschienen *(rec Vienna, Sept. 20–22, 1983 & Mar.)* Hat Hut ("NOW." series) ▲ hat ART CD 6024 [ADD]

Sokal, Harry (sax)
Satie, E.:Gnossiennes Pno, w. Lauren Newton (sgr)—No. 3 [arr. voice & instruments] *(rec Vienna, Sept. 21, 1983)* Hat Hut ("NOW." series) ▲ hat ART CD 6024 [ADD]

Sokol, Ivan (org)
Saint-Saëns, C.:Sym 3, w. B. Rezucha (cnd), Slovak PO Vivace 3-▲ E 321 [DDD]

Sokol, Mark (vn)—see ORCHESTRAS & ENSEMBLES Concord String Quartet

Sokol, Michael (vn)
Rochberg, G.:Duo Concertante, w. N. Fischer (vc) CRI ■ ACS 6013

Sokolov, Dmitrii (db)
Ustvolskaya, G.:Composition 2, w. Igo Propischin (db), Leonid Kolosov (db), Vitalii Goryachev (db), Vladimir Vulih (db), Vyacheslav Kovalenko (db), Alexei Peresipkin (db), Vladimir Nefedov (db), Valerii Javnertchik (perc), Galina Sandovskaya (pno), O. Malov (cnd) *(rec St. Petersburg Radio House, Jan. 1994)* Megadisc ▲ 7867

Sokolov, Grigory (pno)
Bach, J.S.:The Art of the Fugue Opus 111 2-▲ OPS 52-9116/17
Bach, J.S.:Partitas Hpd, BWV 825–830—BWV 826 Opus 111 2-▲ OPS 52-9116/17
Beethoven, L. van:Vars on a waltz by Diabelli, Op. 120 Opus 111 ▲ OPS 42-9106
Brahms, J.:Ballades, Op. 10 Opus 111 ▲ OPS 30-103
Brahms, J.:Son 3 Pno Opus 111 ▲ OPS 30-103
Chopin, F.:Preludes, Op. 28 Opus 111 ▲ OPS 30-9006
Prokofiev, S.:Son 9 Pno Opus 111 ▲ OPS 40-9104
Rachmaninoff, S.:Preludes Pno, Opp 23 & 32—Op. 23/4 Opus 111 ▲ OPS 40-9104
Scriabin, A.:Son 3 Pno Opus 111 ▲ OPS 40-9104
Scriabin, A.:Son 9 Pno Opus 111 ▲ OPS 40-9104

Sokolov, Ivan (pno)
Ustvolskaya, G.:Preludes Pno *(rec Oct 3–5, 1995)* Triton 2-▲ 17014 [DDD]
Ustvolskaya, G.:Sons Pno *(rec Oct 3–5, 1995)* Triton 2-▲ 17014 [DDD]

Sokolov, Kirill (bn)
Ustvolskaya, G.:Composition 3, w. Natalia Danilina (fl), Maria Osipova (fl), Inna Rodina (fl), Michail Tokarev (fl), Dmitrii Krasnik (bn), Arsenii Makarov (bn), Konstantin Shevchuk (bn), Galina Sandovskaya (pno), O. Malov (cnd) *(rec St. Petersburg Radio House, Jan. 1994)* Megadisc ▲ 7867

Sokolov, Vladimir (cl)
Rubinstein, A.:Qnt Pno, w. A. Nasedkin (pno), V. Zverov (fl), A. Demim (hn), S. Krasavin (bn) Russian Disc ("The A. Rubinstein Edition" series) ▲ RUS 11 061 [ADD]

Sokratis, Anthis (tpt)
Karaindrou, E.:Film Music, w. Jan Garbarek (t sax), Vangelis Christopoulos (ob), Anthis Sokratis (tpt), Nikos Guinos (cl), Tassos Diakoyiorgis (santouri), Vangelis Skouras (hn), Petros Protopapas (fl), Andreas Tsekouras (acc), Christos Sfetsas (vc), Eleni Karaindrou (pno/voc), L. Chalkiadakis (cnd), *(ensemble unknown)*—Farewell Theme; Scream; Improv. On Farewell & Waltz Theme; Farewell Theme II [all from The Beekeeper; w. Jan Garbarek (ten sax), Tassos Diakoyiorgis (satouri), Vassilis Dertilis (kbd), Eleni Karaindrou (pno), Lefteris Chalkiadakis (cnd)]; Elegy for Rosa; Rosa's Song (text:Christofis) [both from Rosa; w. Vangelis Skouras (Fr hn), Petros Protopapas (fl), Alekos Christidis (timp), Eleni Karaindrou (voc), Lefteis Chalkiadakis (cnd)]; Fairytale; Parade; Return; Song [all from Happy Homecoming, Comrade; w. Vangelis Skouras (Fr hn), Christos Sfetsas (vc), Aliki Krithari (hp), Andreas Tsekouras (acc), Eleni Karaindrou (pno), Nelli Semitekolo (pno), Lefteris Chalkiadakis (cnd)]; Wandering in Alexandria (2 vers) [both from Wandering; w. Tassos Diakoyiorgis (santouri), Nelli Semitekolo (prepared pno), Anthis Sokratis (tpt), Nikos Guinos (cl), Katerina Ktona (hpd), Christos Sfetsas (vc)]; The Journey [from Voyage to Cythera]; Adagio [from Landscape in the Mist] [both w. Vangelis Christopoulos (ob), str orch, Lefteris Chalkiadakis (cnd)] ECM ▲ 78118-21429-2 [AAD]

Solberger, Harvey (fl)
Wuorinen, C.:Variations I Fl Music & Arts ▲ CD 800 [ADD]
Wuorinen, C.:Variations II Fl Music & Arts ▲ CD 800 [ADD]

Soldan, Ursula (vn)
Reger, M.:Cantatas, w. V. Schweizer (sop), A. Hellmann (alt), R. Julius Koch (ob), R. Hellmann, B. Banz (va), C. Hellmann (vc), C. Fink (db), H. Bilgram (org), D. Hellmann (cnd), Mainz Bach Choir Entrée ▲ 0049 [ADD]

Soldier, David (vn)—see also ORCHESTRAS & ENSEMBLES Soldier String Quartet
Jenkins, L.:Monkey on the Dragon, w. Leroy Jenkins (vn), Henry Threadgill (fl), Don Byron (cl), Marth Ehrlich (b cl), Janet Frice (bn), Vincent Chancey (hn), Frank Gordon (tpt), Jeff Hoyer (trbn), Jane Henry (vn) Ron Lawrence (va), Mary Wooton (vc), Lindsey Horner (db), Thurman Barker (traps), Myra Melford (pno), T. Léon (cnd) *(rec live, Merkin Concert Hall, New York City, Apr. 9, 1992)* CRI ("eXchange" series) ▲ CD 663 [DDD]

Soler, Àngel (pno)
Casanovas, J.:Joan Miró, w. Anna Ricci (mez) *(rec Albert Moraleda Studio, 1993–95)* Edicions Albert Moraleda 2-▲ 032D [DDD]
Cercós, J.:Songs, w. Anna Ricci (mez)—Sanglot, sanglot, pur sanglot! [from Les Fenêtres] *(rec Albert Moraleda Studio, 1993–95)* Edicions Albert Moraleda 2-▲ 032D [DDD]
Cerdà, A.:Tres letras asturianas, w. Anna Ricci (mez) *(rec Albert Moraleda Studio, 1993–95)* Edicions Albert Moraleda 2-▲ 032D [DDD]
Giró, J.:Chansons françaises (3), w. Anna Ricci (mez)—Sérénade *(rec Albert Moraleda Studio, 1993–95)* Edicions Albert Moraleda 2-▲ 032D [DDD]
Quadreny, J.M.M.:Cançons de bressol, w. Anna Ricci (mez) *(rec Albert Moraleda Studio, 1993–95)* Edicions Albert Moraleda 2-▲ 032D [DDD]

Sollberger, Harvey (fl)
Carter, E.:Son Fl, w. C. Kuskin (ob), F. Sherry (vc), P. Jacobs (hpd) Elektra/Nonesuch ▲ 79183-2
Chou Wen-Chung:Cursive, w. Charles Wuorinen (pno) CRI ▲ CD 691 [ADD]
Luening, O.:Trio Fl, Vc & Pno, w. Fred Sherry (vc), Charles Wuorinen (pno) CRI ("American Masters" series) ▲ CD 716 [ADD]
Mamlok, U.:Stray Birds, w. P. Bryn-Julson (sop), F. Sherry (vc) CRI ■ C 301
Reynolds, R.:Transfigured Wind 4 Neuma ▲ 45074 [ADD/DDD]
Roussakis, N.:Short Pieces Fls, w. Sophie Sollberger (fl) *(rec 1975)* CRI ▲ CD 709 [DDD]
Sollberger, H.:Riding the Wind II, III, IV Neuma ▲ 450-81
Westergaard, P.:Divert on Discobbolos Fragments, w. Charles Wuorinen (pno) CRI ▲ CD 696 [ADD]
Wilson, R.:Music Fl CRI ▲ CD 602 [ADD]
Wolpe, S.:Trio in 2 Parts Fl, w. F. Sherry (vc), C. Wuorinen (pno) *(rec Nov. 9–10, 1991)* Koch ▲ KIC 7112 [DDD]

Sollberger, Sophie (fl)
Roussakis, N.:Short Pieces Fls, w. Harvey Sollberger (fl) *(rec 1975)* CRI ▲ CD 709 [DDD]

Sollenberger, Jay (tpt)—see ORCHESTRAS & ENSEMBLES Missouri Brass Quintet

Söllscher, Göran (gtr)
Rodrigo, J.:Concierto de Aranjuez, Orpheus CO Deutsche Grammophon ▲ 429232-2 [DDD] □ 429232-5
Rodrigo, J.:Fant para un gentilhombre, Orpheus CO Deutsche Grammophon ▲ 429232-2 [DDD] □ 429232-5
Villa-Lobos, H.:Con Gtr, Orpheus CO Deutsche Grammophon ▲ 429232-2 [DDD]

Solms, Marianne (vn)
Weber, C.M. von:Qnt Cl, w. L. Fuchs (cl), O. Sipahi (vn), D. Morice (va), P. Caldwell (vc) Gallo ▲ CD 570 [DDD]

Solodchin, G. (vn)—see ORCHESTRAS & ENSEMBLES Delmé String Quartet

Solokov, Dmitri (pno)
Chopin, F.:Preludes, Op. 28 *(rec Melodija Studio, St. Petersburg, Russia, June 2–4, 1995)* Elysium ▲ GRK 711 [DDD]
Mussorgsky, M.:Pictures *(rec Melodija Studio, St. Petersburg, Russia, June 2–4, 1995)* Elysium ▲ GRK 711 [DDD]

Solomon (pno)
Bach, J.S.:Italian Con APR ▲ APR 7030 [ADD]
Beethoven, L. van:Con 1 Pno, w. H. Menges (cnd), Philharmonia Orch EMI Classics ("The Artist Profile" series) 2-▲ CDZB 67735
Beethoven, L. van:Con 3 Pno, w. A. Boult (cnd), BBC SO *(rec Bedford Grammar School, Aug 8, 9 & 12, 1944)* Dutton Laboratories ▲ DUT 7015 [ADD]
Beethoven, L. van:Con 3 Pno, *(orch unknown)* Memories ("Golden" series) 2-▲ MEM 3005

Solomon (pno) (cont.)
Beethoven, L. van:Con 3 Pno, w. H. Menges (cnd), Philharmonia Orch EMI Classics ("Artist Profile" series) 2-▲ CDZB 67735
Beethoven, L. van:Con 3 Pno, *(cnd & orch unknown)* EMI Classics 2-▲ ZDHB 65503
Beethoven, L. van:Con 4 Pno, *(cnd & orch unknown)* EMI Classics 2-▲ ZDHB 65503
Beethoven, L. van:Con 5 Pno, "Emperor", *(cnd & orch unknown)* EMI Classics 2-▲ ZDHB 65503
Beethoven, L. van:Son 3 Pno APR ▲ APR 7030 [ADD]
Beethoven, L. van:Son 14 Pno, "Moonlight Son" *(rec 1956)* APR 2-▲ APR 7030
Beethoven, L. van:Son 14 Pno, "Moonlight Son" EMI Classics 2-▲ ZDHB 65503
Beethoven, L. van:Son 27 Pno *(rec 1951–56)* EMI Classics ▲ ZDBH 64708
Beethoven, L. van:Son 27 Pno, w. H. Menges (cnd), Philharmonia Orch EMI Classics ("The Artist Profile" series) 2-▲ CDZB 67735
Beethoven, L. van:Sons 28–32 Pno, "The Late Sons" *(rec 1951–56)* EMI Classics ▲ ZDBH 64708
Beethoven, L. van:Trio 6 Pno, "Archduke", w. H. Holst (vn), A. Pini (vc) APR ▲ APR 5503 [ADD]
Beethoven, L. van:Trio 7 Pno, w. Henry Holst (vn), Anthony Pini (vc) *(rec Abbey Road, Studio No. 3)* Dutton Laboratories ▲ DUT 7015 [ADD]
Brahms, J.:Fants Pno, Op. 116, No. 4 in E *(rec 1956)* APR 2-▲ APR 7030
Brahms, J.:Intermezzos Pno, Op. 117—in E♭ *(rec 1956)* APR 2-▲ APR 7030
Brahms, J.:Pieces Pno, Op. 118, No. 6 in e♭ *(rec 1956)* APR 2-▲ APR 7030
Brahms, J.:Rhaps Pno, Op. 79, in b *(rec 1956)* APR 2-▲ APR 7030
Brahms, J.:Son 3 Pno *(rec London, 1952)* Testament ▲ SBT 1084
Brahms, J.:Vars & Fugue on a Theme by Handel—10 Vars. APR ▲ APR 5503 [ADD]
Chopin, F.:Fant *(rec 1956)* APR 2-▲ APR 7030
Chopin, F.:Nocturnes, No. 1 *(rec 1956)* APR 2-▲ APR 7030
Chopin, F.:Pno Music (misc)—Études—in F, Op. 10/8; in A♭ & F, Op. 25/1 & 3; Fantaisie in f, Op. 49; two Polonaises—in A, Op. 40 & in A♭, Op. 53 *(rec 1932 & 1934 for Columbia)* Pearl ▲ PEA 9478 (m) [AAD]
Chopin, F.:Pno Music (misc)—Études in f, f & F, Opp. 10/9, 25/2 & 25/3; Nocturne No. 8 in D♭, Op. 27/2; Berceuse in D♭, Op. 57 APR ▲ APR 5503 [ADD]
Chopin, F.:Scherzos—No. 2 *(rec 1956)* APR 2-▲ APR 7030
Grieg, E.:Con Pno, Op. 16, w. H. Menges (cnd), Philharmonia Orch EMI Classics ("Artist Profile" series) 2-▲ CDZB 67735
Liszt, F.:Album d'un voyageur—Au bord d'une source *(rec London, 1932)* Testament ▲ SBT 1084
Liszt, F.:Études de concert (3) Pno—La leggierezza *(rec London, 1932)* Testament ▲ SBT 1084
Liszt, F.:Hungarian Rhaps—No. 15 *(rec London, 1932)* Testament ▲ SBT 1084
Liszt, F.:Pno Music (misc)—Au bord d'une source; Étude de concert, "La leggierezza"; Hungarian Rhapsody No. 15 *(rec 1930 & 1932 for Columbia)* Pearl ▲ PEA 9478 (m) [AAD]
Schumann, R.:Carnaval Pno *(rec London, 1952)* Testament ▲ SBT 1084
Schumann, R.:Con Pno, w. H. Menges (cnd), Philharmonia Orch EMI Classics ("The Artist Profile" series) 2-▲ CDZB 67735
Tchaikovsky, P.:Con 1 Pno, *(cnd & orch unknown)* Memories 2-▲ MEM CD 3009
Tchaikovsky, P.:Con 1 Pno, w. H. Harty (cnd), Hallé Orch *(rec 1930 for Columbia Records)* Pearl ▲ GEMMCD 9478 (m) [AAD]

Solomon, Ashley (fl/rcr)
Il Flauto Dolce:Italian Music from 3 Centuries, w. Jan Spencer (vc), Terence Charlston (hpd/org) Meridian ▲ MER 84292 [DDD]

Solomon, Nanette (pno)
Character Sketches:Solo Piano Works by 7 American Women Leonarda ▲ LE 334 [DDD]

Solomon, Peter (hpd)
Mieg, P.:Septet, w. Günter Rumpel (fl), Simon Fuchs (ob), Primroz Novsak (vn), Marius Ungareanu (va), Carolyn Hopkins Marti (vc), Ronald Dangel (db) *(rec 1993)* Jecklin ▲ JS 314-2 [DDD]

Solomon, Yonty (pno)
Beethoven, L. van:Son 1 Vc, w. T. Hugh (vc) IMP Masters ▲ IMPMCD 80 [DDD]
Beethoven, L. van:Son 2 Vc, w. T. Hugh (vc) IMP Masters ▲ IMPMCD 80 [DDD]
Beethoven, L. van:Son 3 Vc, w. T. Hugh (vc) IMP Masters ▲ IMPMCD 80 [DDD]
Grieg, E.:Son Vc, w. T. Hugh (vc) IMP Masters ▲ IMPMCD 72 [DDD]
Grieg, E.:Songs, w. T. Hugh (vc)—Jeg elsker dig, Op. 5/3 IMP Masters ▲ IMPMCD 72 [DDD]
Sorabji, K.S.:Le Jardin parfumé Altarus ▲ CD 9037

Solomonow, Rami (va)
Tchaikovsky, P.:Souvenir de Florence, w. J. Sharp (vc), Vermeer String Quartet *(rec May–Oct., 1993)* Cedille ▲ CDR 90000 017 [DDD]

Solothurski, Chaim (va)
Vanhal, J.B.:Divert Strs, w. R. Mehne (vn), G. Dzwiza (db), K. Stoll (db) Signum ▲ X 45-00

Solovyev, Vissarion (va)—see ORCHESTRAS & ENSEMBLES Taneyev String Quartet

Solow, Jeffrey (vc)
Arensky, A.:Trio 1 Pno, w. M. Golabek (pno), A. Cardenes (vn) Delos ▲ DE 3056 [DDD]
Lazarof, H.:Duo Vc & Pno, w. J. Lowenthal (pno) Laurel ▲ LR 845CD [AAD]
Lazarof, H.:Duo Solitaire, w. Yukiko Kamei (vn) Laurel ▲ LR 856 [DDD]
Lazarof, H.:Momenti Laurel ▲ LR 845CD [AAD]
Lazarof, H.:Trio Pno, Vn & Vc, w. J. Lowenthal (pno), Y. Matsudo (vn) Laurel ▲ LR 845CD [AAD]
Levitch, L.:Qt Fl, Va, Vc & Pno, w. Sheridan Stokes (fl), Sven Reher (va), Irma Vallecillo-Gray (pno) Cambria ▲ CD 1059 [ADD]
Levitch, L.:Qnt Fl, w. Sheridan Stokes (fl), Kathleen Lenski (vn), Miwako Watanabe (vn), Paul Polivnick (va) Cambria ▲ CD 1059 [ADD]
Tchaikovsky, P.:Trio Pno, w. M. Golabek (pno), A. Cardenes (vn) Delos ▲ DE 3056 [DDD]

Sølstein, P. (hn)
Rasmussen, S.:Music of, w. W. Gaffron (vn), A. Turner (vc), E. Dalsgarð (fl), A. Klett (cl), J. Andreasen (pno), S.A. Johansen (cnd), *(orch unknown)*—"Warnings I"—The Naked Destruction Tutl ▲ FKT 4

Solti, Georg (pno)
Bartók, B.:Son for 2 Pnos, w. M. Perahia (pno), D. Corkhill (perc), E. Glennie (perc) CBS ▲ MK 42625 [DDD]
Brahms, J.:Vars on a Theme by Haydn, w. M. Perahia (pno)— Op. 56b [2-piano vers.] CBS ▲ MK 42625 [DDD]
Brahms, J.:Vars on a Theme of Robert Schumann, Op. 23, w. A. Schiff (pno) London ▲ 425110-2 [DDD]
Mozart, W.A.:Con 7 Pnos, w. D. Barenboim (pno), A. Schiff (pno), G. Solti (cnd), English CO London ▲ 430232-2 [DDD]
Mozart, W.A.:Con 20 Pno, w. G. Solti (cnd), English CO London ▲ 430232-2 [DDD]
Strauss, R.:Songs, w. K. Te Kanawa (sop)—Malven; Hat gesagt; Muttertandelei; Madrigal; Ständchen; Schlechtes Wetter; Allerseelen; Die Nacht; Cäcilie; All mein Gedanken; Begegnung; Morgen; Zueignung [G] London ▲ 430511-2 [DDD]

Soltz, Gabriela (fl)—see ORCHESTRAS & ENSEMBLES Consort Fontegara

Solum, Geir (hn)
Grieg, E.:Lyric Pieces, w. B. Hoff (bass), B. Fiskum (cnd), Trondheim Soloists—Op. 68/4 & 5 [arr Grieg for orch] Victoria ▲ VCD 19072

Solum, John (alt fl)
Wilson, R.:Persuasions, w. A. Burton (sop), B. Uribe (pno), M. Schachman (ob/E hn), G. Dejean (bn/ctbn) Albany ▲ TROY 074 [DDD]

Solum, John (fl)
Bach, J.S.:Sons Fl, BWV 1030–35, w. I. Kipnis (hpd), B. Bogatin (vc)—BWV 1030-1035 [period instrs] Arabesque ▲ Z 6589
Bach, J.S.:Trio Son Fl, Vn & Hpd, w. J.-M. Schwarz (vn), I. Kipnis (hpd), E. Potash (vc) [period instrs] Arabesque ▲ ARA 6640 [DDD]
Beeson, J.:Fant, Ditty & Fughettas, w. Richard Wyton (fl) *(rec Skinner Recital Hall, Vassar College, Poughkeepsie, NY, Mar 24–26, 1994)* CRI ▲ CD 712 [DDD]
Kupferman, M.:Abstractions *(rec Skinner Recital Hall, Vassar College, Poughkeepsie, NY, Mar 24–26, 1994)* CRI ▲ CD 712 [DDD]
Laderman, E.:Epigrams & Canons, w. Richard Wyton (baroque fl) *(rec Skinner Recital Hall, Vassar College, Poughkeepsie, NY, Mar 24–26, 1994)* CRI ▲ CD 712 [DDD]

Solum, John (fl) (cont.)
Luening, O.:Fantasias Baroque Fl *(rec Skinner Recital Hall, Vassar College, Poughkeepsie, NY, Mar 24–26, 1994)* CRI ▲ CD 712 [DDD]
Nowak, L.:Suite Fl, w. Igor Kipnis (hpd) *(rec Skinner Recital Hall, Vassar College, Poughkeepsie, NY, Mar 24–26, 1994)* CRI ▲ CD 712 [DDD]
Telemann, G.P.:Musique de Table, w. E. Potash (vl), I. Kipnis (hpd) [played on period instrument] Arabesque ▲ ARA 6640 [DDD]
Vivaldi, A.:Cons Fl (misc), w. I. Kipnis (hpd), I. Kipnis (cnd), Connecticut Early Music Festival Ensemble [period instrs]—Concerto in D, RV.428, "Il Gardellino" Chesky ▲ CD 78 [DDD]

Solum, John (trns fl)
Bach, J.S.:Trio Son for 2 Fls, BWV 1039, w. R. Wyton (trns fl), E. Potash (vc), I. Kipnis (hpd) [period instrs] Arabesque ▲ ARA 6640 [DDD]
Handel, G.F.:Trio Sons, w. Judson Griffin (vn), Arthur Fiacco (vc), Igor Kipnis (hpd)—in c, H.386a Epiphany ▲ EP 7
Handel, G.F.:Trio Sons, w. J.-M. Schwarz (vn), E. Potash (vc) [period instrs]—in G, Op. 2/1, HWV 389; in F, Op. 2/4, HWV 386b Arabesque ▲ ARA 6640 [DDD]
The Instrument of Kings:A Program of 18th Century Music for Flute & Keyboard, w. Igor Kipnis (hpd/pno), Arthur Fiacco (vc) *(rec Jan. 17–21, 1994)* Epiphany ▲ EP 2
Telemann, G.P.:Musique de Table, w. A. Fiacco (vc), I. Kipnis (hpd)—solo in b for Fl & Bc Epiphany ▲ EP 7

Soly, Genevieve (hpd)
Bach, J.S.:Cons solo Hpd, BWV 972–987 [the organ at Notre-Dame-de-la-Défense Church, Montreal]—BWV 972 & 974 Analekta Fleur de Lys ▲ FL 2 3001
Bach, J.S.:Sons Fl, BWV 1030–35, w. Jean-Pierre Pinet (fl)—BWV 1030 & 1032 *(rec Oct 1995)* Analekta Fleur de Lys ▲ FL 23061 [DDD]
Bach, J.S.:Sons Vn Hpd, BWV 1014-1019, w. Chantal Rémillard (vn)—BWV 1015 & 1018 *(rec Oct 1995)* Analekta Fleur de Lys ▲ FL 23061 [DDD]

Soly, Genevieve (org)
Bach, J.S.:Cons Org, BWV 592–597 [the organ at Notre-Dame-de-la-Défense Church, Montreal]—BWV 592 & 593 Analekta Fleur de Lys ▲ FL 2 3001
Bach, J.S.:Org Music (misc)—Cons in d, BWV 588; in G, BWV 592; in a, BWV 593; in D, BWV 972; in d, BWV 974 Analekta ▲ ATM 29726
Handel, G.F.:Cons (16) Org, w. Carl Philipp Ensemble Analekta Fleur de Lys ▲ FL 2 3026
Handel, G.F.:Cons (16) Org, w. Carl Philipp Ensemble Analekta Fleur de Lys ▲ FL 2 3029
Vivaldi, A.:Cons Vn Org, w. E. Turovsky (vn), Y. Turovsky (cnd), Montreal Musici—RV.542 in F Chandos ▲ CHAN 8651 [DDD]
Walther, Joh. G.:Org Music—Con del Sig Luigi Manzia; Con del Sigr. Meck in e, LV.133 Analekta ▲ ATM 29726
Walther, Joh. G.:Org Music [organ at Notre-Dame-de-la-Défense Church, Montreal]—Con. del Sig L. Manzia; Con. del Sigr. Meck Analekta Fleur de Lys ▲ FL 2 3005

Sólyom, Janos (pno)
Sibelius, J.:Songs, w. B. Nilsson (sop)—Våren flyktar hastigt, Op. 13/4; Se'n har jag ej fragat mera, Op. 17/1; Illalle, Op. 17/6; Svarta rosor, Op. 36/1; Säf, säf, susa, Op. 36/4; Den första kyssen, Op. 37/1; Var det en dröm?, Op. 37/4; Flickan kom ifran sin älsklings möte, Op. 37/5; På verandan vid havet, Op. 38/2; Im Feld ein Mädchen singt, Op. 50/3 *(rec 1975)* BIS ▲ CD 15 [AAD]
Strauss, R.:Songs, w. B. Nilsson (sop)—Zueignung, Op. 10/1; Allerseelen, Op. 10/8; Ständchen, Op. 17/2; Ruhe, meine Seele, Op. 27/1; Cäcilie, Op. 27/2; Befreit, Op. 39/4; Wiegenlied, Op. 41/1 [G] *(rec 1975)* BIS ▲ CD 15 [AAD]

Somary, Johannes (org)
Handel, G.F.:Ezio, w. Julianne Baird (sop—Fulvia), Jennifer Lane (mez—Onoria), D'Anna Fortunato (cta—Ezio), Raymond Pellerin (alt—Emperor), Frederick Urrey (ten—Massimo), Nathaniel Watson (bar—Varo), R.A. Clark (cnd), Manhattan CO *(rec St. Jean Baptiste Church, New York, Mar. 1994)* Vox Classics 2-▲ VOX 27503 [DDD]

Sombart, Elizabeth (pno)
Desbrière, J.:Pièces Etranges (5), w. P. Gallois (fl) Thésis ▲ THC 82012 [DDD]
Fauré, G.:Fant Fl, w. P. Gallois (fl) Thésis ▲ THC 82012 [DDD]
Fauré, G.:Sicilienne, w. P. Gallois (fl) [flute-piano version] Thésis ▲ THC 82012 [DDD]
Messiaen, O.:La Merle noir, w. P. Gallois (fl) Thésis ▲ THC 82012 [DDD]
Mozart, W.A.:Son 8 Pno Quantum ▲ QM 6908 [DDD]
Mozart, W.A.:Son 11 Pno Quantum ▲ QM 6908 [DDD]
Mozart, W.A.:Vars Pno, K.265 Quantum ▲ QM 6908 [DDD]
Poulenc, F.:Son Fl, w. P. Gallois (fl) Thésis ▲ THC 82012 [DDD]
Roussel, A.:Joueurs de flûte, w. P. Gallois (fl) Thésis ▲ THC 82012 [DDD]

Somenzi, Massimo (pno)
Dvořák, A.:From the Bohemian Forest, w. E. Bellio (pno) *(rec 5/91)* Giulia 2-▲ GS 201004 [DDD]
Dvořák, A.:Legends, Op. 59, w. E. Bellio (pno) *(rec 5/91)* Giulia 2-▲ GS 201004 [DDD]
Dvořák, A.:Slavonic Dances (comp), w. E. Bellio (pno) [piano 4-hands] *(rec 5/91)* Giulia 2-▲ GS 201004 [DDD]

Somer, Hilde (pno)
Ginastera, A.:Con Pno, w. E. Märzendorfer (cnd), Vienna PO Phoenix ▲ PHCD 110 [AAD]
Ginastera, A.:Son 1 Pno Phoenix ▲ PHCD 110 [AAD]
Janácek, L.:Capriccio, w. J. Rudel (cnd), Caramoor Festival Orch Phoenix ▲ PHCD 109 [AAD]
Janácek, L.:Concertino Pno, w. J. Rudel (cnd), Caramoor Festival Orch Phoenix ▲ PHCD 109 [AAD]

Sommati, Pier Domenico (vn)
Paganini, N.:Divertimenti carnevaleschi, w. Stefan Milenkovich (vn), Riccardo Agosti (vc) *(rec Dynamic's, Genova, Feb 22–24, 1995)* Dynamic ▲ CD 105 [DDD]
Paganini, N.:In cuor più non mi sento, w. Stefan Milenkovich (vn), Riccardo Agosti (vc) *(rec Dynamic's, Genova, Feb 22–24, 1995)* Dynamic ▲ CD 105 [DDD]

Sommer, Jan (gtr)—see also ORCHESTRAS & ENSEMBLES Duo Musica, Molino Trio
Molino, F.:Trio Duos, Op. 16, w. B. Larsen (fl) *(rec Feb. 22–23, 1993)* Classico ▲ CLASSCD 106
Molino, F.:Trio Duos, Op. 61, w. B. Larsen (fl) *(rec Feb. 22–23, 1993)* Classico ▲ CLASSCD 106
Molino, F.:Trio Fl, Op. 4/1, w. B. Larsen (fl), L. Grunth (va) *(rec Feb. 22–23, 1993)* Classico ▲ CLASSCD 106
Molino, F.:Trio Fl, Op. 45, w. B. Larsen (fl), L. Grunth (va) *(rec Feb. 22–23, 1993)* Classico ▲ CLASSCD 106
Piazzolla, A.:Histoire du tango, w. B. Larsen (fl) Classico ▲ CLASSCD 101
Vesth, T.:Music of, w. Nils Sylvest Jeppesen (vc), Per Friman (vn), Gert-Inge Andersson (va), Berit Spaelling (hp), Bent Larsen (fl), Bjorn Nielsen (ob), Svend Rasmussen (cl), Henrik Simonsen (db)—Cuddling Rain; Waltz the Blue Sea; Kaspers Lullaby; Autumn Sunshine; Red Fox Hunting Tea Party; Off White Eternity; Tartan Fl Danica ▲ DCD 8142

Sommer, Raphael (vc)—see ORCHESTRAS & ENSEMBLES Solomon Trio

Sommer-Link, F. (vn)
Viotti, G.B.:Con 22 Vn, w. L. Graham (cnd), American Promenade Orch Klavier ▲ KCD 11053 [DDD]

Sommerville, James (hn)
Françaix, J.:Heure du berger Orch, w. Suzanne Shulman (fl), James Mason (ob), James Campbell (cl), James McKay (bn), André Laplante (pno) *(rec Glenn Gould Studio, CBC Toronto, Mar. 26–27, 1994)* CBC ("Musica Viva" series) ▲ MVV 1089 [DDD]
Gounod, C.:Mélodies (6), w. Rena Sharon (pno) Marquis Classics ▲ MAR 157 [DDD]
Nielsen, C.:Serenata in vano, w. James Campbell (cl), James McKay (bn), Tsuyoshi Tsutsumi (vc), Joel Quarrington (db) *(rec Glenn Gould Studio, CBC Toronto, Mar. 26–27, 1994)* CBC ("Musica Viva" series) ▲ MVV 1089 [DDD]
Reinecke, C.:Nocturne Hn, Op. 112, w. Rena Sharon (pno) Marquis Classics ▲ MAR 157 [DDD]
Reinecke, C.:Trio Ob, w. James Mason (ob), Rena Sharon (pno) Marquis Classics ▲ MAR 157 [DDD]
Schumann, R.:Adagio & Allegro Hn, w. Rena Sharon (pno) Marquis Classics ▲ MAR 157 [DDD]
Strauss, R.:Till Eulenspiegels lustige Streiche, w. James Campbell (cl), James McKay (bn), Martin Beaver (vn), Joel Quarrington (db)—[arr. Franz Hasenöhrl as Einmal Anders! (frolic for 5 instruments; 1954)] *(rec Glenn Gould Studio, CBC Toronto, Mar. 26–27, 1994)* CBC ("Musica Viva" series) ▲ MVV 1089 [DDD]

Son, Dang Thai (pno)
Chopin, F.:Andante Spianato & Grande Polonaise, w. Krystian Zimerman (pno) [2 versions] Polskie Nagrania ▲ PNCD 008 [ADD]
Chopin, F.:Barcarolle Pno Analekta ▲ AN 27703
Chopin, F.:Barcarolle Pno LaserLight ▲ 14 224
Chopin, F.:Nocturnes Analekta 2-▲ AN 27701-2
Chopin, F.:Pno Music (misc), w. Martha Argerich (pno), Vladimir Ashkenazy (pno), Stanislav Bunin (pno), Halina Czerny-Stefanska (pno), Jan Ekier (pno), Yuval Fichman (pno), Kemal Gekic (pno), Adam Harasiewicz (pno), Krzysztof Jablonski (pno), Louis Kentner (pno), Jean-Marc Luisada (pno), Garrick Ohlsson (pno), Ivo Pogorelich (pno), Maurizio Pollini (pno)—includes Ballade (Nos. 1 & 2); Barcarolle, Op. 60; Concerto Nos. 1 & 2; Études (Op. 10, Nos. 1, 5, 8, 10 & 12 & Op. 25, No. 10, 18 & 25); Grand valse brillante; Impromptus (Nos. 3 & 4); Mazurkas (Op. 24, Nos. 1-4; Op. 30, Nos. 1-4; Op. 50, No. 32; Op. 59, Nos. 1-3); Nocturnes (Op. 9, No. 3; Op. 37, No. 12; Op. 48, No. 13; Op. 55, No. 16)Polonaise (Op. 40, Nos. 3 & 4; Op. 44, No. 5; Op. 53, No. 6; Op. 61, No. 7); Preludes (Op. 28 Nos. 13-18, 21-24 & Op. 45, No. 25); Scherzos (Nos. 1-3); Sonatas (Nos. 2 & 3); Waltzes (No. 1 & 6) LaserLight 5-▲ 15 961 [ADD/DDD]
Chopin, F.:Preludes, Op. 28 Analekta ▲ AN 27703
Chopin, F.:Prelude, Op. 45 Analekta ▲ AN 27703
Chopin, F.:Waltzes Analekta ▲ AN 27704

Son, Eun Soo (pno)
Rachmaninoff, S.:Con 2 Pno, w. M. Ermler (cnd), Moscow PO Russian Disc ▲ RUS 10011 [DDD]

Soné, Mayako (hpd)
Bach, J.S.:English Suites—BWV 807, 808 & 811 Erato ▲ 2292-45789-2
Scarlatti, D.:Sons Kbd—in C, G, C, G, d, A, A, A, E, A, A, D & G; Fandango in d *(rec Notre Dame du Liban Church, Paris, Feb. 23-25, 1993)* Erato ▲ 4509-94806-2 [DDD]

Song, Ju-Ying (pno)
Bartók, B.:Improvs (8) on Hungarian Peasant Songs, w. J.-Y. Song *(rec New York, June 20 & 21, 1994)* Pro Piano ▲ PPR 224503 [DDD]
Debussy, C.:Etudes *(rec New York, June 20 & 21, 1994)* Pro Piano ▲ PPR 224503 [DDD]
Viñao, E.:Etudes Pno—Nos. 1-3 & 5 [all from Book 1] *(rec Academy of Arts & Letters, New York, Nov 14-15, 1995)* Pro Piano ("Pianist's Perspective Recording" series) ▲ PPR 224511
Viñao, E.:Trio Pno, w. Mark Steinberg (vn), Maria Kitsopoulos (vc) *(rec Academy of Arts & Letters, New York, Nov 14-15, 1995)* Pro Piano ("Pianist's Perspective Recording" series) ▲ PPR 224511

Sonies, Barbara (vn)—see ORCHESTRAS & ENSEMBLES Philadelphia Trio, Penn Contemporary Players

Sonnen, F. (vn)—see ORCHESTRAS & ENSEMBLES La Primavera String Ensemble

Sonnenschmidt, Jürgen (org)
Draeseke, F.:Mysterium:Christus, w. C. Bischoff (sop), A. Vogel (sop), E. Dersen (alt), K. Markus (ten), H.J. Ritzerfeld (ten), P. Langshaw (bar), B. Kämpff (bass), U.-R. Follert (cnd), Breslau State PO, Evangelical Boys' Choir Palatine, Heilbronn Vocal Ensemble, Palatine Kurrende Bayer 5-▲ 100175/79

Sonnetheil, Jürgen (org)
Rheinberger, J.:Sons Org—No. 2, Op. 65 & No. 4, Op. 98 *(rec Peine, May 1995-July 1996)* CPO ▲ 999351-2 [DDD]
Rheinberger, J.:Songs, w. Gotthold Schwarz (bar)—Religious Songs (6), Op. 157; Elegaic Songs (2), Op. 128 *(rec Peine, May 1995-July 1996)* CPO ▲ 999351-2 [DDD]

Sonnleitner, Johann (hpd)
Baroque Music for Recorder, w. Conrad Steinmann (rcr), Monica Huggett (baroque vn), Hopkinson Smith (lt/thb/gtr), Jordi Savall (vl), Pere Ros (vl), Claude Flagel (h-g) Claves ▲ CD 508103 [ADD]
Handel, G.F.:German Arias, H.202-210, w. Elisabeth Speiser (sop), Kathy Gohl (vn), Jap Schröder (vn) [G] *(rec 1984)* Jecklin-Disco ▲ JD 589-2 [ADD]
Roman, J.H.:Sons Fl, w. Jaap Schröder (vn)—No. 12 in D *(rec Studio 2, Radiohuset, Stockholm, May 7 & 8, 1986)* Musica Sveciae ▲ MS 406 [DDD]
Roman, J.H.:Sons Hpd—No. 9 in d *(rec Studio 2, Radiohuset, Stockholm, May 7 & 8, 1986)* Musica Sveciae ▲ MS 406 [DDD]

Sønstevold, Knut (bn)
Crusell, B.H.:Con 2 Cl, w. K.-I. Stevensson (cl), I. Olsen (hn), O. Kamu (cnd), Swedish RSO Musica Sveciae ▲ MSV 527 [DDD]
Crusell, B.H.:Intro, Theme & Vars on a Swedish Air, w. K.-I. Stevensson (cl), I. Olsen (hn), K. Sönstevold (bn), O. Kamu (cnd), Swedish RSO Musica Sveciae ▲ MSV 527 [DDD]
Crusell, B.H.:Sinf concertante, w. K.-I. Stevensson (cl), I. Olsen (hn), K. Sönstevold (bn), O. Kamu (cnd), Swedish RSO Musica Sveciae ▲ MSV 527 [DDD]
Hindemith, P.:Son Bn, w. E. Knardahl (pno) [arr bn & pno] *(rec Nacka, Sweden, April 15, 1978)* BIS ▲ CD 159 [AAD]
Mozart, W.A.:Con Bn, w. S. Comissiona (cnd), Swedish RSO Caprice ▲ CAP 21411 [DDD]
Strauss, R.:Duet-Concertino, w. P. Meyer (cl), E.-P. Salonen (cnd), New Stockholm CO CBS ▲ MK 44702 [DDD]
The Virtuoso Bassoon BIS ▲ CD 122 [AAD]
Zelenka, J.D.:Trio Sons Obs, w. B. Glaetzner (ob), I. Goritzki (ob), A. Beyer (vn), S. Pank (vl), W. H. Bernstein (hpd) Berlin Classics 2-▲ BER 1070 [DDD]
Zelenka, J.D.:Trio Sons Obs, w. Burkhard Glaetzer (ob), Ingo Goritzki (ob), Achim Beyer (vn), Siegfried Pank (va), Walter-Heinz Bernstein (hpd) Berlin Classics 4-▲ BER 1150 [DDD]

Soós, Adrienne (pno)
Debussy, C.:L'Enfant prodigue, w. Ivo Haag (pno)—Symphonie [arr for 2 Pnos] Pan Classics ▲ 510076 [DDD]
Debussy, C.:Épigraphes antiques, w. Ivo Haag (pno) [arr for 2 Pnos] Pan Classics ▲ 510076 [DDD]
Debussy, C.:Petite suite, w. Ivo Haag (pno) [arr for 2 Pnos] Pan Classics ▲ 510076 [DDD]
Debussy, C.:Triomphe de Bacchus, w. Ivo Haag (pno) [arr for 2 Pnos] Pan Classics ▲ 510076 [DDD]
Koechlin, C.:Sonatines françaises, w. Ivo Haag (pno)—No. 1 Pan Classics ▲ 510076 [DDD]
Koechlin, C.:Suite for 2 Pnos, w. Ivo Haag (pno) Pan Classics ▲ 510076 [DDD]

Soper, Lee (tpt)
Baroque Trumpetissimo, w. David Bilger (tpt), Stephen Burns (tpt), Edward Carroll (tpt), Alex Holton (tpt), Raymond Mase (tpt), Timothy Morrison (tpt), Lee Soper (tpt), Atsuko Sato (bn), Ben Harms (timp), Edward Brewer (org/hpd), Philharmonia Virtuosi [cnd:Richard Kapp] ESS.A.Y ▲ ESS 1035 [DDD]

Sopkin, George (vc)—see ORCHESTRAS & ENSEMBLES Fine Arts String Quartet members, Fine Arts String Quartet

Sora, Giovanni (cl)
Mercadante, S.:Sinf concertante 1, w. Luca Truffelli (fl), Roberto Saltini (cl), Andrea Mastini (cnt), C.F. Sedazzari (cnd), Camerata Schubert Bongiovanni ▲ GB 2199 [DDD]
Mercadante, S.:Sinf concertante 3, w. Luca Truffelli (fl), Roberto Saltini (cl), Andrea Mastini (cnt), C.F. Sedazzari (cnd), Camerata Schubert Bongiovanni ▲ GB 2199 [DDD]

Sørensen, Gert (perc)
Nørholm, I.:Chamber Music, w. B. Rørbeck (vn), J. Christiansen (gtr), N. Ullner (vc), P. Salo (pno/hpd), Kuhlau Flute Quartet—Before Silence, Op. 83; Contrast-Continuum, Op. 70; Guitar Sonata No. 2; The Orthodox Dream; So to Say, Op. 74; Turbulens-Laminar, Op. 93; Variants, Op. 19 *(rec 9/90)* Kontrapunkt ▲ 32065 [DDD]

Sørensen, Gert (perc/kbd/cmpt)
Nørgård, P.:Music for Perc, w. Palle Mikkelborg (perc), Per Nørgård (kbd/vocals)—Waves; Isternia; I Ching; Energy Fields Forever; Nemo Dynamo; Bulan; Circus City Marco Polo ("dacapo" series) ▲ 8.224024-25 [DDD]

Sørensen, Gert (vib)
Schnittke, A.:Voices of Nature, w. Stefan Parkman (cnd), Danish National Radio Choir Chandos ▲ CHAN 9480

Sørensen, Hans (hn)
Nielsen, C.:Qnt Ww, w. H.G. Jespersen (fl), S.C. Felumb (ob), A. Oxenvad (cl), K. Larsson (bn) *(rec Jan. 24 & 25, 1936)* Clarinet Classics ▲ CC 0002
Nielsen, C.:Serenata in vano, w. A. Oxenvad (cl), K. Larsson (bn), L. Jensen (vc), L. Hegner (db) *(rec Feb. 2, 1937)* Clarinet Classics ▲ CC 0002

Sørensen, Lars Algot (ob)—see ORCHESTRAS & ENSEMBLES Copenhagen Wind Quintet

Sørensen, Per Dybro (gtr)
Borup-Jörgensen, A.:Music of—Morceaux; Old Chinese Poems [w. Agnete Christiansen (mez)]; Preambula; Songs on Texts by Sarvig [w. Marianne Lund (sop)]; Fr Gitarre; Praeludien; Poésies pour la Dame à la Licorne [w. Karl Petersen (gtr)] *(rec Fruering Kirke, 1993)* Paula ▲ PACD 81 [DAD]
Davies, P.M.:Hill Runes *(rec Fruering Kirke, Denmark)* Paula ▲ PACD 63 [DAD]
Davies, P.M.:Lullaby for Ilian Rainbow *(rec Fruering Kirke, Denmark)* Paula ▲ PACD 63 [DAD]
Davies, P.M.:Son Gtr *(rec Fruering Kirke, Denmark)* Paula ▲ PACD 63 [DAD]
Jolivet, A.:Concert Etudes Gtr *(rec Fruering Kirke, Denmark)* Paula ▲ PACD 63 [DAD]
Jolivet, A.:Sérénade for 2 Gtrs, w. Morten Skott (gtr) *(rec Fruering Kirke, Denmark)* Paula ▲ PACD 63 [DAD]
Jolivet, A.:Tombeau de Robert de Visée *(rec Fruering Kirke, Denmark)* Paula ▲ PACD 63 [DAD]

Sørensen, Vagn (pno)
Stolarczyk, W.:Earth Air Fire Water, w. Amalie Malling (pno), John Damgaard (pno), Anne Øland (pno), Teddy Teirup (pno), Friedrich Gürtler (pno), Rosalind Bevan (pno), Poul Rosenbaum (pno), Rodolfo Llambias (pno), Bella Horn-Ribera (pno), Anders Riber (pno), Elisabeth Sigurdsson (pno), Thomas Tronheim (pno), Elsebeth Broderson (pno), Erik Kaltoft (pno), Jørgen Hald Nielsen (pno), Aino Gilemann (pno), Birgit Kjær (pno), Jørgen Thomsen (pno), Gunhild Donslund (pno), Henrik Bo Hansen (pno), Lone Karlsson (pno), Erik Fessel (pno), Lasse Nilsson (pno), Janos Ferenczi (pno), Erik Bach (pno), Axel Momme (pno), Arne de Cros Dich (pno), Sven Micha Slot (pno), Hanne Bramsen Buhl (pno), Lili Olesen (pno), Susannah Carlsson (pno), Ulla Erml (pno), Leif Greibe (pno), Bodil Krogh (pno), Kirsten Ottosen (pno), Inger Bergenholz (pno), Karsten Gylendorf (pno), Bjørn Elkjær (pno), Jacob Bjørn Jensen (pno), Jørgen Kaad (pno), Anne Marie Hjelm (pno), Carl Ulrik Munk Andersen (pno), Poul Lumbye (pno), Oluf Hildebrandt Nielsen (pno), Joachim Olsson (pno), Peter Pade Ramsøe Jacobsen (pno), Astrid Pollmann (pno), Jette Borsch (pno), Kirsten Karlshøj (pno), Maria Teresa Assing (pno), Allan Dahl Hansen (pno), Johan Hugossen (pno), Tine Fenger Pederson (pno), Arne Jørgen Fæø (pno), Anja Høgsted (pno), Anne Sophie Parbo (pno), Inga Lindmark (pno), Teresa Drabik Stathakis (pno), Anne Ruth Ferenczi (pno), Irene Hasager (pno), Yuka Ichikawa (pno), Birgitte Baur (pno), Malene Thastum (pno), Jens E. Rasmussen (pno), Birgitte Zielke (pno), Claus Zielke (pno), Stefan Kasch (pno), Bin Qiao (pno), Inger Johanne Teirup (pno), Lindy Rosborg (pno), Liisa Heininen (pno), David Højer (pno), Ellen Refstrup (pno), Thomas K. Søorensen (pno), Erik Kure (pno), Michael Rauff (pno), Jan beck Eriksson (pno), Tanja Zapolski (pno), Vibeke Skagbo (pno), Pål Eide Lindtner (pno), Ha-Young Sul (pno), Benedicte Palko (pno), Inke Kesseler (pno), Anne Marie Meineche (pno), Sverre Larsen (pno), Kasper Peter Bach (pno), Elisabetta Eliseo (pno), Olga Magieres (pno), Carl Erik Kühl (pno), Thorkild Borup Nielsen (pno), Valeria Zanini (pno), Lars Stenhoft (perc), Dennis Boel (perc), Winnie Dahlgren (perc), Susanne Vind (perc), Claus Byrith (elec), Anne Marie Storm (elec), J. Ribera (cnd) *(rec live, Koldinghaus Castle, Denmark, May 2, 1996)* Danica ▲ DCD 1996

Soria Jr., Samuel (org)
In Sweet Rejoicing Music for Christmas:Ars Antique Choralis, Vol 3, w. [cnd:Richard Proulx], Cathedral Singers, Mary Hickey (fl), Jeri-Lou Aike (vn), Elizabeth Anderson (vc) *(rec Oct. 17-19 & 24-26, 1993)* GIA ▲ CD 323 ■ CS 323

Soriano, Gonzalo (pno)
Falla, M. de:Noches en los jardines de España, w. R. Frühbeck de Burgos (cnd), New Philharmonia Orch EMI Classics ▲ CDM 64746

Soriano, Joaquin (pno)
Falla, M. de:Con Hpd, w. J. Serebrier (cnd), English CO ASV ▲ ASV 775
Falla, M. de:Noches en los jardines de España, w. J. Serebrier (cnd), English CO ASV ▲ ASV 775
Turina, J.:Rapsodia sinfónica, w. J. Serebrier (cnd), English CO ASV ▲ ASV 775

Sorin, C. (db)
Bolcom, W.:Sons (2) for 2 Pnos, Bass & Perc, w. E. Ax (pno), C. Bolling (pno), C. Cordelette (perc) CBS ▲ MK 45646 [DDD]
Bolling, C.:Suite 2 Fl, w. J.-P. Rampal (fl), C. Bolling (pno), C. Cordelette (perc) CBS ▲ MK 42318 [DDD] ■ FMT 42318 (D)

Sorkin, Leonard (vn)—see ORCHESTRAS & ENSEMBLES Fine Arts String Quartet, Fine Arts String Quartet members

Soroga, Pieralba (pno)
In Recital, w. Nicolai Gedda (ten) Fonè ▲ 85F 02-6 [ADD]

Soroka, Solomia (vn)
Martinů, B.:Qnt Strs, w. Charmian Gadd (vn), Rainer Moog (va), Theodore Kuchar (va), Young-Chang Cho (vc) *(rec Australian Festival of Chamber Music, July 1994)* Naxos ▲ 8.553916 [DDD]

Sortoretti, Christine (hpd)
The Lausanne Vocal Ensemble Euterpe in Concert, w. [cnd:Christophe Gesseney], Euterpe, Yves Rechsteiner (org), C. Delafontaine (pic), Marianne Amrein (fl douce/perc) Gallo ▲ CD 766 [DDD]

Sosa, Raoul (pno)
Lipatti, D.:Sonatine Pno Analekta ▲ CLCD 2016
Moszkowski, M.:Études Analekta ▲ CLCD 2016
Scriabin, A.:Pieces Pno Left-Hand, Op. 9 Analekta ▲ CLCD 2016
Sosa, R.:Son 1 Pno Analekta ▲ CLCD 2016

Sosinska, Marta (pno)
Chopin, F.:Barcarolle Pno *(rec National Philharmonic, Warsaw, 1981)* Polskie Nagrania ▲ PNCD 016
Chopin, F.:Fant *(rec National Philharmonic, Warsaw, 1984)* Polskie Nagrania ▲ PNCD 016
Chopin, F.:Polonaise-fant Polskie Nagrania ▲ PNCD 008 [ADD]
Chopin, F.:Son Pno, Op. 35 *(rec National Philharmonic, Warsaw, 1984)* Polskie Nagrania ▲ PNCD 016
Chopin, F.:Son Pno, Op. 58 *(rec National Philharmonic, Warsaw, 1981)* Polskie Nagrania ▲ PNCD 016

Sotkovetsky, J. (vn)
Glazunov, A.:Con Vn, w. K. Kondrashin (cnd), Moscow Youth Orch *(rec 1952)* Russian Disc ▲ RUS 15 009 [AAD]
Khachaturian, A.:Con Vn, w. Niyazi (cnd), Romanian Radio Orch *(rec 1954)* Russian Disc ▲ RUS 15 009 [AAD]

Soucy, Dominique (fl)
Kraft, L.:Cloud Studies, w. Lisa Maron (pic), Margaret Swinchoski (pic), Tanya Dusevic (fl), Adrienne Flynn (fl), Christina Jennings (fl), Zara Lawler (fl), Joseph Piscitelli (fl), Michelle Ryang (fl), Diane Taublieb (fl), Laurel Ann Maurer (alt fl), Richard Wyton (alt fl), J. Solum (cnd) *(rec Skinner Recital Hall, Vassar College, Poughkeepsie, NY, Mar 24-26, 1994)* CRI ▲ CD 712 [DDD]

Soufflard, Serge (va)
Mozart, W.A.:Sinf concertante Vn, K.364, w. Philip Bride (vn), K. Redel (cnd), French Instrumental Ensemble *(rec Apr. 9 & 10, 1990)* Pierre Verany ▲ PVY 730024 [DDD]

Soule, Richard (fl/pic)—see ORCHESTRAS & ENSEMBLES Sierra Winds

Soustrot, Bernard (tpt)
Gervaise, C.:Danceries, w. François-Henri Houbart (org)—7 sels Forlane ▲ FRL 16732 [DDD]
Handel, G.F.:Cons (16) Org, w. F. Houbart (org)—No. 13 in F [The Cuckoo & the Nightingale] Forlane ▲ FRL 16732 [DDD]
Handel, G.F.:Messiah, w. Patricia Schuman (sop), Lucia Valentini Terrani (alt), Bruce Ford (ten), Gwynne Howell (bass), C. Scimone (cnd), Venice Solisti, John McCarthy (cnd), Ambrosian Singers *(rec S. Francisco Church, Schio, Italy, June 23-30, 1989)* Arts 2-▲ 471052 [DDD]
Haydn, J.:Con Tpt, w. L. Sagrestano (cnd), Prague Musici Accord ▲ ACD 220462 [DDD]
Hummel, J.N.:Con in E♭ Tpt, S.49, w. M. Soustrot (cnd), Loire PO Pierre Verany ▲ PV 788011 [DDD]
Jolivet, A.:Con 2 Tpt, w. M. Soustrot (cnd), Loire PO Pierre Verany ▲ PV 788011 [DDD]
Loeillet, J.-B.:Sons (misc), w. François-Henri Houbart (org)—in d for Tpt & Org Forlane ▲ FRL 16732 [DDD]
Omourtet, J.-J.:Première Suite, w. François-Henri Houbart (org) Forlane ▲ FRL 16732 [DDD]
Telemann, G.P.:Musique héroïque, w. François-Henri Houbart (org) Forlane ▲ FRL 16732 [DDD]
Trumpet & Organ, w. Soustrot, Bernared (tpt), François-Henri Houbart (org) Pierre Verany ("Favourites" series) ▲ 730012 [DDD]
Trumpet & Organ, w. Soustrot, Bernared (tpt), François-Henri Houbart (org) Pierre Verany ▲ 789103 [DDD]

Soustrot, Bernard (tpt) (cont.)
Vivaldi, A.:Con for 2 Tpts, w. Maurice André (tpt), N. Marriner (cnd), Academy of St. Martin in the Fields Classics for Pleasure ("Eminence" series) ▲ CFP 2235
South, Philip (perc)
Bremner, A.:In the Shrubbery, w. Judy Glen (nar), David Miller (pno), Gerard Willems (pno), Roland Peelman (cnd), Song Company *(rec Studio 200, ABC Ultimo Centre, Apr 1993)* Tall Poppies ▲ TP 064 [DDD]
Edwards, R.:Flower Songs, w. David Hewitt (perc), Roland Peelman (cnd), Song Company *(rec Studio 200, ABC Ultimo Centre, Apr 1993)* Tall Poppies ▲ TP 064 [DDD]
Souza, Cristina da (pno)
Clementi, M.:Pno Music (comp), w. Aldo Antognazzi (pno), Christian Badian (pno), Eduardo Cazaban (pno), Dao Di Renzo (pno), Pablo Lavandera (pno), Yi Fang Huang (vn), Silvina Cardenas (fl), Nestor Herzbaum (fl)—Sons (6) for Pno, Op. 2, Nos. 1, 3 & 5 (w. flutes); Duets (3) for Piano 4-Hands, Op. 3, Nos. 2 & 3; Sons (3) for Pno & Vn, Op. 3, No. 4 Aura Classics ▲ AU 32287
Souza, Ralph de (vn)—see also ORCHESTRAS & ENSEMBLES Schubert Ensemble of London
Vivaldi, A.:Cons for 2 Vns, w. Iona Brown (vn), Johnathan Rees (vn), Briony Shaw (vn), I. Brown (cnd), Academy of St. Martin in the Fields—Nos. 3 & 10 *(rec London, Sept 1995)* Hänssler Classic ▲ CD 98.017 [DDD]
Soveral, Madalena (pno)
Denisov, E.:Pieces (3) Pno 4-Hands, w. O. Delangle (pno), J.-L. Haguenauer (pno) *(rec Jan. 1990)* Pierre Verany ▲ PV.790112 [DDD]
Sovijoki, J. (gtr)
Ponce, M.:Thème, varié et finale *(rec Dec. 10-11, 1983)* BIS ▲ CD 255 [AAD]
Soyer, David (vc)—see also ORCHESTRAS & ENSEMBLES Guarneri String Quartet
Boccherini, L.:Qnts Gtr, G.445-453, w. A. Diaz (gtr), A. Schneider (vn), F. Galimir (vn), M. Tree (va)—in C, G.446 *(rec 1965)* Vanguard Classics ▲ OVC 8006 [ADD]
Boccherini, L.:Qnts Strs, w. A. Schneider (vn), F. Galimir (vn), M. Tree (va), L. Harrell (vc)—Op. 13, No. 5 *(rec 1965)* Vanguard Classics ▲ OVC 8006 [ADD]
Dvořák, A.:Qnt Pno, Op. 81, w. P. Serkin (pno), F. Galimir (vn), A. Schneider (vn), M. Tree (va) *(rec 1965)* Vanguard Classics ▲ OVC 8003 [ADD]
Mozart, W.A.:Qts Pno, w. P. Serkin (pno), A. Schneider (vn), M. Tree (va) *(rec 1965)* Vanguard Classics ▲ OVC 8007 [ADD]
Schubert, Franz:Qnt Pno, D.667, w. P. Serkin (pno), A. Schneider (vn), M. Tree (va), J. Levine (db) *(rec 1964)* Vanguard Classics ▲ OVC 8005 [ADD]
Spada, Pietro (pno)
Bartók, B.:Romanian Christmas Carols *(rec Rome, Italy, July 19 & 26, 1986)* Arts ▲ 47284-2 [DDD]
Beethoven, L. van:Con 6 Pno, w. A. Gibson (cnd), Philharmonia Orch ASV ▲ ASV 911 [DDD]
Beethoven, L. van:Fant Pno, Op. 80, "Choral Fant", w. A. Gibson (cnd), Philharmonia Orch ASV ▲ ASV 911 [DDD]
Beethoven, L. van:Rondo Pno, WoO 6, w. A. Gibson (cnd), Philharmonia Orch ASV ▲ ASV 911 [DDD]
Catalani, A.:Pno Music—Impressioni; Scherzo-tarantella; Ricordo di Lugano; Notturno; others ASV ▲ ASV 921 [DDD]
Catalani, A.:Pno Music—Tempo di Valzer; Serenata ASV ▲ ASVCD 956
Clementi, M.:Orchestral Music (comp), w. F. d' Avalos (cnd), Philharmonia Orch—Piano Con.; Minuetto Pastorale; 2 Symphonies, Op. 18 ASV ▲ ASV 802
Clementi, M.:Sons Pno—Op. 1/1-4; Op. 2/2; Son in a♭ *(rec Rome, Italy, Jan 1981 & Mar 1983)* Arts Music ▲ 447223-2 [DDD]
Clementi, M.:Sons Pno—Op. 2/4 & 6 *(rec Rome, Italy, Jan 1981 & Mar 1983)* Arts Music ▲ 447224-2 [DDD]
Clementi, M.:Sons Pno, w. Giorgio Cozzolino (pno)—Op.7/1-3; Op. 8/1-3 *(rec Rome, Italy, 1981-83)* Arts ▲ 447225-2 [DDD]
Clementi, M.:Sons Pno, w. Giorgio Cozzolino (pno)—Op. 9/1-3; Op. 10/1-3; Op. 11/1 *(rec Rome, Italy, 1981-83)* Arts ▲ 447226-2 [DDD]
Clementi, M.:Sons Pno, w. Giorgio Cozzolino (pno)—Op. 12/1-5 *(rec Rome, Italy, 1981-83)* Arts ▲ 47227-2 [DDD]
Clementi, M.:Sons Pno 4-Hands, w. Giorgio Cozzolino (pno)—Op. 1/6 *(rec Rome, Italy, Jan 1981 & Mar 1983)* Arts Music ▲ 447223-2 [DDD]
Clementi, M.:Sons Pno 4-Hands, w. Giorgio Cozzolino (pno)—Op. 3/1-3 & Op. 6/1 *(rec Rome, Italy, Jan 1981 & Mar 1983)* Arts Music ▲ 447224-2 [DDD]
Field, J.:Nocturnes Pno (misc)—Nos 1-15 *(rec Rome, Italy, June 1986)* Arts ▲ 47181-2 [DDD]
Field, J.:Pno Music—The Favorite Hornpipe Danced by Madame De Caro; Go to the Devil & Shake Yourself; The 2 Slaves Dances in Black Beard [all arr as rondos]; Rondo Speed the Plough; Rondos [from Cons 1-4]; Rondos in A & A♭ *(rec Rome, Italy, June 1989 & Apr 1990)* Arts Music ▲ 47179-2 [DDD]
Field, J.:Pno Music (comp)—Nocturnes 16-19; 4 Fants *(rec Rome, Italy, June 1986 & July 1989)* Arts ▲ 47182-2 [DDD]
Field, J.:Pno Music (comp) Arts 6-▲ 47380-2 [DDD]
Field, J.:Pno Music (comp), w. Giorgio Cozzolino (pno)—Waltzer; Polonaise; Marche triomphale; Prelude; Largo; 3 Valses; 2 Quadrilles; Anglaise; 4 Exercises; Poco Adagio (from Con 2 Pno); Andante inédite; Rondeau; Air russe varié; Grande valse en forme de Rondeau; Andante; Danse des ours *(rec Rome, Italy, Apr 1989-Apr 1990)* Arts ▲ 47183-2 [DDD]
Field, J.:Pno Music (comp)—Rondos (from Pno Cons No. 5 & 6); Come Again, Come Again Rondo; Rondoletto; Fal Lal La Vars; Since Them I'm Doomed Vars; Logie of Buchan Vars;Kamarinskaya Vars; Air du Bon Roi Henry IV Vars; Chanson Russe Variée Vars; Within a Mile of Edinboro Town Vars *(rec Rome, Italy, Nov 1989-July 1990)* Arts ▲ 471802 [DDD]
Field, J.:Sons Pno (comp) *(rec Rome, Italy, Mar & Oct 1989)* Arts Music ▲ 47178-2 [DDD]
Liszt, F.:Wiehnachtsbaum *(rec Rome, Italy, July 19 & 26, 1986)* Arts ▲ 47284-2 [DDD]
Martucci, G.:Pno Music, w. Giorgio Cozzolino (pno)—Fant in d, Op. 32; Fant on Un Ballo in Maschera, Op. 8; Theme & Vars in E♭, Op. 58 ASV ▲ ASVCD 956
Paisiello, G.:Cons Hpd, St. Cecilia CO—Nos. 1, 3, 4 & 7 *(rec Roma, Italy, Mar 8-14, 1992)* Arts ▲ 741202 [DDD]
Paisiello, G.:Cons Hpd, St. Cecilia CO—Nos. 2, 5, 6 & 8 *(rec Roma, Italy, Mar 8-14, 1992)* Arts ▲ 471212 [DDD]
Piano Festival *(rec Roma, Italy, Apr 1984)* Arts ▲ 447198-2 [DDD]
Rendano, A.:Allegro ASV ▲ ASVCD 956
Salieri, A.:Cons Pno, w. P. Spada (cnd), Philharmonia Orch ASV ▲ ASV 955
Schumann, R.:Carnaval Pno *(rec Roma, Italy, May 1991)* Arts ▲ 447125-2 [DDD]
Schumann, R.:Kreisleriana *(rec Roma, Italy, May 1991)* Arts ▲ 447125-2 [DDD]
Spaelling, Berit (hp)
Vesth, T.:Music of, w. Jan Sommer (gtr), Nils Sylvest Jeppesen (vc), Per Friman (vn), Gert-Inge Andersson (va), Bent Larsen (fl), Bjorn Nielsen (ob), Svend Rasmussen (cl), Henrik Simonsen (db)—Cuddling Rain; Waltz the Blue Sea; Kaspers Lullaby; Autumn Sunshine; Red Fox Hunting Tea Party; Off White Eternity; Tartan Fl Danica ▲ DCD 8142
Spaendonck, Ronald van (cl)
Hindemith, P.:Die junge Magd, w. Lucienne Van Deyck (mez), Marc Grauwels (fl), Gaggini String Quartet Syrinx ▲ 95101
Hindemith, P.:Kleine Kammermusik, w. Marc Grauwels (fl), Juris van den Hauwe (ob), et al. Syrinx ▲ 95101
Spaeter, Matthias (archlt)—see also ORCHESTRAS & ENSEMBLES Il Divertimento, Concerto Soave, La Fenice Ensemble
Piccinini, A.:Music of, w. Christina Pluhar (thb)—Toccatas II, VI, XI, XIII, XVI & XX; Aria Francese & Corrente; Ricercar Primo; Chiaconne in partite varie; Saravanda alla Francesca; Aria di Feorenze; Toccata a dui Liuti; Aria II; Passacaglia; Baletto in Diverse partite a requisitione dell' illustrissimo conte Alessandro Bentivoglio; Aria di Sarabanda in varie partite; Chiacona Mariona L'Empreinte Digitale ▲ ED 13057
Spaeter, Matthias (thb)
Roman, J.H.:Sacred Music, w. G. Ryhming (sop), K. Ottesen (vc), E. Nordenfelt (hpd/org)—Psalms 4, 5, 81, 103, 124 & 125; Mon coeur tressaille de joie; Oiseaux, animaux sauvages; Mes prères, hâtez-vous; Dieu, Dieu de to Gallo ▲ CD 764 [DDD]

Spalding, Albert (vn)
Albert Spalding Biddulph ▲ LAB 054 [ADD]
Mendelssohn, F.:Con in e Vn & Orch, Op. 64, w. E. Ormandy (cnd), Philadelphia Orch *(rec 12/20/41 for Victor, prev)* Biddulph ▲ LAB 054 [ADD]
Mozart, W.A.:Sinf concertante Vn, K.364, w. W. Primrose (va), F. Stiedry (cnd), New Friends of Music Orch *(rec May 28, 1941)* Pearl ▲ PEA 9045 [AAD]
Spohr, L.:Con 8 Vn, w. E. Ormandy (cnd), Philadelphia Orch *(rec 5/9/38)* Biddulph ▲ LAB 054 [ADD]
Spangenberg, M. (cl)
Strauss, R.:Beauty & the Beast, w. K. Nagel (bn) Amati ▲ 9205
Strauss, R.:Duet-Concertino, w. K. Nagel (bn), Polish Chamber PO Amati ▲ 9205
Spang-Hanssen, Ulrik (org)
Buxtehude, D.:Org Music (comp) *(rec 1990-93)* Classico 6-▲ CD 143/8
Hartmann, J.P.E.:Org Music, w. Aarhus Brass Quintet—Fant in a; Funeral March for Thorvaldsen; Fant in f, Op. 20; Funeral March for Oblenschlaeger; Andante for Brass & Org; Son in g, Op. 58; Good Friday-Easter Morning, Op. 43; Funeral March for N.P. Nielsen; Festive tones [Opening Music for the University's Jubilee in 1879] *(rec Arhus Cathedral, Feb-May 1995)* Classico ▲ 127
Trombone & Organ Music, w. Niels-Ole Bo Johansen (trbn) Classico ▲ 122
Spanhove, Bart (rcr)—see ORCHESTRAS & ENSEMBLES Flanders Recorder Quartet
Spanjer, A. (hn)
Vivaldi, A.:Cons for 2 Hns, w. D. Smith (hn), R. Kapp (cnd), Philharmonia Virtuosi—RV.538 ESS.A.Y ▲ CD 1022 [DDD]
Spano, Robert (pno)
Bresgen, C.:Son Fl, w. J. Bentley (fl) Capstone ▲ CPS 8605
Genzmer, H.:Son Fl, w. J. Bentley (fl) Capstone ▲ CPS 8605
Hindemith, P.:Pieces (8) Fl & Pno, w. J. Bentley (fl) Capstone ▲ CPS 8605
Hindemith, P.:Son Cl, w. J. Bentley (cl) Capstone ▲ CPS 8605
Raphael, G.:Son Fl, w. J. Bentley (fl) Capstone ▲ CPS 8605
Zupko, R.:Fluxus II Capstone ▲ CPS 8603
Spanoghe, Jenny (vn)—see also ORCHESTRAS & ENSEMBLES Gaggini String Quartet
Gistelinck, E.:Music of, w. Daniel Blumenthal (pno)—Music for René for Vn & Pno, Op. 35; Clowns for Pno, Op. 45; 3 Songs for Children for Vn & Pno, Op. 49; Kleine Treurmuziek voor Che for Pno, Op. 22/a; Horizon 250 for Vn & Pno, Op. 46; 5 Preludes for a Little Boy for Pno, Op. 29; Prelude 6 for Pno, Op. 34; Lullaby for Nathaly for Vn & Pno, Op. 31 *(rec BRTN, Studio 4, Brussels)* René Gailly ▲ CD 87113 [DDD]
Legley, V.:Burlesque, w. Daniel Blumenthal (pno) *(rec BRTN, Studio 4, Brussels)* René Gailly ▲ CD 87114 [DDD]
Legley, V.:Drie Meisjes, w. Daniel Blumenthal (pno) *(rec BRTN, Studio 4, Brussels)* René Gailly ▲ CD 87114 [DDD]
Legley, V.:Romance, w. Daniel Blumenthal (pno) *(rec BRTN, Studio 4, Brussels)* René Gailly ▲ CD 87114 [DDD]
Legley, V.:Son Vn *(rec BRTN, Studio 4, Brussels)* René Gailly ▲ CD 87114 [DDD]
Legley, V.:Son Vn & Pno, w. Daniel Blumenthal (pno) *(rec BRTN, Studio 4, Brussels)* René Gailly ▲ CD 87114 [DDD]
Spanoghe, Vivian (vc)
Devreese, G.:Concertino Vc, w. F. Devreese (cnd), Brussels Belgian Radio-TV PO [1992 version] *(rec Brussels, 1993)* Marco Polo ▲ 8.223680 [DDD]
Jongen, J.:Son Vc, w. Andre de Groote (pno) *(rec Brussels Royal Conservatory Concert Hall, Aug 1995)* Talent ▲ DOM 291035 [DDD]
Shostakovich, D.:Con 1 Vc, w. E. Tabakov (cnd), Sofia Soloists CO *(rec 1984)* Talent ▲ DOM 2910 11 [AAD]
Shostakovich, D.:Con 2 Vc, w. E. Tabakov (cnd), Sofia Soloists CO *(rec 1984)* Talent ▲ DOM 2910 11 [AAD]
Tournemire, C.:Poème Vc, w. Andre de Groote (pno) *(rec Brussels Royal Conservatory Concert Hall, Aug 1995)* Talent ▲ DOM 291035 [DDD]
Vierne, L.:Son Vc, w. Andre de Groote (pno) *(rec Brussels Royal Conservatory Concert Hall, Aug 1995)* Talent ▲ DOM 291035 [DDD]
Spányi, Miklós (hpd)
Bach, C.P.E.:Cons Hpd & Strs, w. Concerto Armonico *(rec Angyalföld Reformed Church, Dec 15-17, 1994)* BIS ▲ CD 707 [DDD]
Bach, C.P.E.:Cons Hpd & Strs, w. P. Szüts (cnd), Concerto Armonico Budapest—in g, H.409; in A, H.411; in D, H.421 *(rec Angyalföld Reformed Church, Budapest, Hungary, Oct 29-30, 1995)* BIS ▲ CD 767 [DDD]
Bach, C.P.E.:Cons Hpd & Strs, w. P. Szüts (cnd), Concerto Armonico Budapest—in d, H.427 (W.23); in c, H.441 (W.31); in F, H.443 (W.33) [period instrs] Hungaroton ▲ HCD 31159 [DDD]
Bach, C.P.E.:Kbd Music, w. Concerto Armonico [period instrs]—Cons in G, A & F, H.406, 410 & 415 *(rec Angyalföld Reformed Church, Budapest, Hungary, Nov 17-19, 1994)* BIS ▲ CD 708 [DDD]
Biber, H. von:Harmonia artificiosa-ariosa, w. M. Lindal (vn), B. Sargent (vn), M. van der Velden (viol), E. Siebens (db)—Partitas 3 & 5 *(rec Feb. 4-6, 1993)* BIS ▲ CD 608 [DDD]
Biber, H. von:Mystery (or Rosary) Sons, w. M. Lindal (vn), M. van der Velden (viol), E. Siebens (db)—No. 10 *(rec Feb. 4-6, 1993)* BIS ▲ CD 608 [DDD]
Biber, H. von:Sons Vn & Continuo, w. M. Lindal (vn), L. Swarts (vc), E. Siebens (db) *(rec Feb. 4-6, 1993)* BIS ▲ CD 608 [DDD]
Biber, H. von:Son violino solo representativa, w. M. Lindal (vn), L. Swarts (vc), E. Siebens (db) *(rec Feb. 4-6, 1993)* BIS ▲ CD 608 [DDD]
Spányi, Miklós (org)
Monteverdi, C.:Music of, w. B. Máté (vc), S. Benyus (db), I. Szabó (thb), Monteverdi Chamber Choir—Laudate pueri, Lauda Ierusalem, Nisi Dominus Hungaroton ▲ HCD 31273 [DDD]
Sparf, Nils-Erik (va)
Britten, H.:Lachrymae, w. P. Csaba (cnd), New Stockholm CO [F] BIS ▲ CD 435 [DDD]
Sparf, Nils-Erik (vn)
Aulin, T.:Four Watercolors, w. B. Forsberg (pno) Musica Sveciae ▲ MSV 616 [DDD]
Brahms, J.:Sons Vn (comp), w. E. Westenholz (pno) BIS ▲ CD 212 [AAD]
Chausson, E.:Chanson perpétuelle, w. Anne Sofie von Otter (mez), Ulf Forsberg (vn), Matti Hirvikangas (va), Mats Lindström (vc), Bengt Forsberg (pno) *(rec Stockholm, Nov 1994)* Deutsche Grammophon ▲ 447 752-2 [DDD]
Delage, M.:Poèmes hindous, w. Anne Sofie von Otter (mez), Andreas Alin (fl), Peter Rydström (fl/pic), Ulf Bjurenhed (ob/E hn), Lars Paulsson (cl), Per Billman (cl/b cl), Ulf Forsberg (vn), Matti Hirvikangas (va), Mats Lindström (vc), Lisa Viguier (hp) *(rec Stockholm, Nov 1994)* Deutsche Grammophon ▲ 447 752-2 [DDD]
Fauré, G.:La bonne chanson, w. Anne Sofie von Otter (mez), Ulf Forsberg (vn), Matti Hirvikangas (va), Mats Lindström (vc), Tomas Gertonsson (db), Bengt Forsberg (pno) *(rec Stockhom, Nov 1994)* Deutsche Grammophon ▲ 447 752-2 [DDD]
Kallstenius, E.:Son Vn Musica Sveciae ▲ MSV 616 [DDD]
Mozart, W.A.:Sinf concertante Vn, K.364, w. B. Lysell (vn), J.-O. Wedin (cnd), Stockholm Sinfonietta BIS ▲ CD 205
Nilsson, T.:Music of, w. Ingmari Landin (alt), Lars Sjögren (ten), Lage Wedin (bass), Jerker Halldén (fl), Hans-Ola Ericsson (org), Anders Loguin (perc), Torsten Nilsson (cnd), Gustaf Sjökvist (cnd), Swedish Radio Chorus—Ordinarium Missae; Balthasar/Daniel; Drei Gedichte Phono Suecia ▲ PHN 40 [AAD]
Poulenc, F.:Rapsodie nègre, w. Anne Sofie von Otter (mez), Andreas Alin (fl), Lars Paulsson (cl), Ulf Forsberg (vn), Matti Hirvikangas (va), Mats Lindström (vc), Bengt Forsberg (pno) *(rec Stockhom, Nov 1994)* Deutsche Grammophon ▲ 447 752-2 [DDD]
Ravel, M.:Trois poèmes de Stéphane Mallarmé, w. Anne Sofie von Otter (mez), Peter Rydström (fl/pic), Andreas Alin (fl), Lars Paulsson (cl), Per Billman (cl/b cl), Ulf Forsberg (vn), Matti Hirvikangas (va), Mats Lindström (vc), Bengt Forsberg (pno) *(rec Stockholm, Nov 1994)* Deutsche Grammophon ▲ 447 752-2 [DDD]
Roman, J.H.:Bröllopsmusik, w. C. Högmann (sop), P. Mattei (b-bar), E. Ericson (cnd), Drottningholm Baroque Ensemble *(rec 1992)* Musica Sveciae ▲ MSCD 413 [DDD]
Roman, J.H.:Cons (3) Vn, w. Orpheus Chamber Ensemble BIS ▲ CD 284 [DDD]

▲ = CD ♦ = Enhanced CD Δ = MD ■ = Cassette Tape □ = DCC

Sparf, Nils-Erik (vn) (cont.)
Roman, J.H.:Songs, w. S. Rydén (sop), K. Ottesen (vc), S. Överg (thb/lt/gtr), B. Gäfvert (org/hpd)—Thet är en kostelig ting; 4 Songs from *Vårbetraktelser* [text by Jacob Freese]:Mit hierta rörs af frögd/I foglar, vilde djur/Min andagt/Gud, alla härars Gud; Ihr Augen worzu nutzt ihr mir [w. E. Nordenfelt (harpsichord)]; Sein eigen Hertze fressen [w. Nordenfelt]; Kom tysta enslighet; La Ragion gli affetti ascolta; The Happy Man; For the Few Hours; Herren lofver af Himlen hög [Ps. 148]; 5 Songs by Olof von Dalin:Ata litet, dricka vatten/At ju mungen har idag/Födas, gråta dij och lindas/Är det hela tidsfördrifvet/Den är lycklig född til Verlden; Herre när jag tig hafver; Jag förtröstar på Herran; Gud, jag will sjunga om din makt *(rec May 9–11 & July 10, 1994)* Swedish Society ▲ SCD 1066
Sibelius, J.:Danses champêtres, w. B. Forsberg (pno) *(rec Danderyd Grammar School, Sweden, May 21–23, 1993)* BIS ▲ CD 625 [DDD]
Sibelius, J.:Music for Vn Pno, w. B. Forsberg (pno)—Two Pieces, Op. 2 (original version); Two Pieces, Op. 2 (revised version); Scène d'amour from Scaramouche, Op. 71; Two Pieces (Serious Melodies), Op. 77; Four Pieces, Op. 78; Six Pieces, Op. 79 BIS ▲ CD 525 [DDD]
Sibelius, J.:Novelette, w. B. Forsberg (pno) *(rec Danderyd Grammar School, Sweden, May 21–23, 1993)* BIS ▲ CD 625 [DDD]
Sibelius, J.:Pieces Vn Pno, Op. 81, w. B. Forsberg (pno) *(rec Danderyd Grammar School, Sweden, May 21–23, 1993)* BIS ▲ CD 625 [DDD]
Sibelius, J.:Pieces Vn Pno, Op. 115, w. B. Forsberg (pno) *(rec Danderyd Grammar School, Sweden, May 21–23, 1993)* BIS ▲ CD 625 [DDD]
Sibelius, J.:Pieces Vn Pno, Op. 116, w. B. Forsberg (pno) *(rec Danderyd Grammar School, Sweden, May 21–23, 1993)* BIS ▲ CD 625 [DDD]
Sibelius, J.:Sonatina Vn, w. B. Forsberg (pno) BIS ▲ CD 525 [DDD]
Stenhammar, W.:Son Vn, w. B. Forsberg (pno) Musica Sveciae ▲ MSV 616 [DDD]
Tubin, E.:Son Vn, w. Roland Pöntinen (pno) BIS ▲ CD 269 [AAD]
Vivaldi, A.:Con Lt, w. T. Galli (va), J. Lindberg (cnd), Drottningholm Baroque Ensemble BIS ▲ CD 290 [DDD]
Vivaldi, A.:Cons Vn, Op. 8/1–4, "The Four Seasons", w. Drottningholm Baroque Ensemble BIS ▲ CD 275 [DDD] ▲ MD 275
Vivaldi, A.:Trio Sons Vn Lt, w. J. Lindberg (lt), K. Ottesen (vc), M. Wieslander (hpd) BIS ▲ CD 290 [DDD]
Wirén, D.:Con Vn, w. S. Comissiona (cnd), Stockholm PO Caprice ▲ CAP 21326 [DDD/AAD]

Sparke, Kevin (perc)—see also ORCHESTRAS & ENSEMBLES World Casio Quartet
First, D.:The Good Book's (Accurate) Jail of Escape Dust Coordinates 2, w. Matt Sullivan (ob), Chris Jepperson (cl), Annemarie Wiesner (vn), Gary Trosclair (tpt), Elaine Kaplinsky (kbd syn), Chad Henderson (teahouse gtr/b gtr), David First (e-bow gtr/teahouse gtr/Distortion gtr/kbd syn/programming) *(rec Baby Monster Studios, NYC, May 1992)* O. O. Discs ▲ OO 23 [DDD]

Sparks, Paul (mand)
Vivaldi, A.:Con for 2 Mands, w. N. Woodhouse (mand), L. Friedman (cnd), St. Andrew Camerata Omega ▲ OCD 1012 [DDD]

Sparnaay, Harry (b cl)—see also ORCHESTRAS & ENSEMBLES Het Trio
Bruynèl, T.:Intra Donemus ▲ NEAR 01 [DDD]
Janácek, L.:Youth, w. Fodor Quintet Ottavo ▲ OTT 69031 [DDD]
Musiana 95:Electroacoustic Music from Denmark & Japan, w. Ensemble from the East, Trio Sparnaay/Kooistra/Abe, Hanne Andersen, Sofia Asunción Claro, Mari Kimura (hp/vn), Thomas Sandberg Classico ▲ CLASSCD 139 [DDD]

Sparnaay, Harry (cl)
Ladder of Escape I Attacca ▲ BABEL 8945-1 [DDD]

Spasovski, R. (pno)
Satie, E.:Pno Music (misc)—3 Gnossiennes; Nocturnes; Je te veux; Airs a faire fuir; Les trois valses distinguees du precieux degoute; 3 Gymnopedies; Danses de travers; 3 Sarabandes; Avant-dernieres pensees; Poudre d'or Pro Arte ▲ CDD 3439

Später, M. (lt)
Reicha, A.:Vars & Fant on Mozart's "Se vuol ballare", w. J.-P. Rampal (fl), I. Stern (vn), M. Rostropovich (vc) Sony Classical ▲ SK 44568 [DDD]
Telemann, G.P.:Qt Fl, w. J.-P. Rampal (fl), I. Stern (vn), M. Rostropovich (vc) Sony Classical ▲ SK 44568 [DDD]

Speach, Bernadette (pno)
Speach, B.:a page upon which.. Avant ▲ 02

Speidel, Sontraud (pno)—see also ORCHESTRAS & ENSEMBLES Trenkner-Speidel Piano Duo
Bruckner, A.:Sym 3, "Wagner", w. Evelinde Trenker (pno) [arr. Mahler & Krzyzanowski for Pno Duet] MD + G ▲ MDG 3300591 [DDD]

Speller, Frank (org)
Speller, F.:Choral Music, w. P. Gardner (cnd), Univ of Texas Concert Chorale—Mass of Saint Louis [chorus & organ]; Gloria Patri [chorus & organ]; Hail Mary [Chorus a cappella] Albany ▲ TROY 049-2 [DDD]
Speller, F.:Org Music [Visser-Rowland tracker organ, Univ. of Texas at Austin]—Toccata, "The Majesty of Christ"; Four Chorale Preludes; Prelude & Fugue in A♭, "Ecumenical"; Psalm 19, "The heavens declare the glory of God"; Four Biblical Dances; Te Deum Albany ▲ TROY 049-2 [DDD]

Speltz, David (vc)
Lazarof, H.:Oct Strs, w. Yukiko Kamei (vn), Peter Marsh (vn), Yoko Matsuda (vn), Miwako Watanabe (vn), Paul Silverthorne (va), Milton Thomas (va), Godfried Hoogeveen (vc), H. Lazarof (cnd) Laurel ▲ LR 843 [DDD]

Spencer, Charles (pno)
Brahms, J.:Songs, w. M. Lipovsek (mez), D. Geringas (vc)—Gestillte Sehnsucht; Geistliches Wiegenlied; Wie Melodien zieht es; Immer leiser wird mein Schlummer; Klage; Auf den Kirchhofe; Der Tod, das ist die kühle Nacht; Wir wandelten; Es schauen die Blumen; Von ewiger Liebe; Die Mainacht; Wie bist du, mein Königin; Wenn du nur zuweilen lächelst; Es träumte mir; Unbewegte laue luft; Im Garten am Seegestade; Lerchengesang; Serenade; Abendregen; Dort in den Weiden steht ein Haus; Da unten im Tale; Och Moder, ich well en Ding han *(rec Apr. 29–May 1, 1992)* Sony Classical ▲ SK 52490 [DDD]
Rossini, G.:Arias, w. Cecilia Bartoli (mez)—Beltà crudele *(rec 1990)* London ▲ 448300-2 [DDD]; ■ 448300-4
Rossini, G.:Songs, w. C. Bartoli (mez) [I] London ▲ 430518-2 [DDD]
Schubert, Franz:Songs (misc), w. G. Janowitz (sop)—15 songs—D.296, 297, 457, 491, 504, 514, 543, 547, 672, 833, 861, 866/2, 881, 917, 938 [G] Nuova Era ▲ 6860 [DDD]

Spencer, Jan (vc)
Il Flauto Dolce:Italian Music from 3 Centuries, w. Ashley Solomon (fl/rcr), Terence Charlston (hpd/org) Meridian ▲ MER 84292 [DDD]

Spencer, Patricia (fl)
The Now & Present Flute, w. L. Hall (pno) *(rec SUNY Purchase, June 3–5, 20, 1993)* Neuma ▲ 450-88
Tower, J.:Black Topaz, w. Stephen Gosling (pno), Laura Flax (cl), Chris Gekker (tpt), Mike Powell (trbn), Jonathan Haas (perc), Deborah Moore (perc) *(rec American Academy of Arts & Letters, New York City, Sept. 26–28, 1994)* New World ▲ 80470-2
Tower, J.:Hexachords CRI ▲ CD 582 [DDD]

Spencer, Robert (fl)
Alfred Deller, w. Alfred Deller (ct), Harold Lester (hpd/org), Desmond Dupré (gtr) *(rec between 1965 & 1979)* Memoire Vive ▲ 262004 [ADD]

Spencer, Robert (lt)
Dowland, J.:Dances Lt Musique d'Abord ▲ HMA 1901076
Dowland, J.:Lt Music Harmonia Mundi France 2-▲ HMC 90244, HMC 90245
Dowland, J.:Solo Lute Music Harmonia Mundi ▲ HMT 790245
Dowland, J.:Songs, w. Alfred Deller (ct) Harmonia Mundi ▲ HMT 790245

Spencer, Robert (thb/baroque gtr)
The Early Guitar, w. James Tyler (lt/baroque gtr/mand), Paul Elliott (ten), Monica Huggett (baroque vn), Jane Ryan (b vl/baroque vc) Saga Classics ▲ 3356 [ADD]

Spengler, Félix (pno)
Kawanagh, I.C.:Pno Music—Serenata Cubana; El volorio; No bailes más; Invitación; Improvisada; Tres golpes Piu Mosso ▲ VAPPIU001
Lecuona, E.:Pno Music—La comparsa; Mo hables más; Y la negra bailaba; Ahí viene el chino; Danza negra; En tres pour quatro; La Malagueña Piu Mosso ▲ VAPPIU001
Robredo, M.S.:Pno Music—La Tedezco; El Pañuelo de Pepa; Los ojos de Pepa; Recuerdos tristes; Las quejas; La niña bonita; El Somatén; Pero por qué? Piu Mosso ▲ VAPPIU001

Spengler, Jean de (vc)—see ORCHESTRAS & ENSEMBLES Stanislas Ensemble

Spengler, Michael (vl)—see also ORCHESTRAS & ENSEMBLES Hedos Ensemble
Blavet, M.:Sons Trns Fl, w. Hans-Joachim Fuss (trns fl), Nicolau de Figueiredo (hpd)—Op. 2/2–4 & 6; Sonataterza; Son seconda [both from Op. 3] Pan Classics ▲ CD 510089 [DDD]

Sperer, E. (org)
French Music for Choir & 2 Organs, w. [cnd:Franz Brandl], Munich Madrigal Choir, W. Englhardt (org) FSM ▲ 97735 [DDD]

Spering, Christoph (org)
Rossini, G.:Péchés de vieillesse (sels), w. M. Castets (sop), M. Georg (mez), J.-L. Maurette (ten), M. Brodard (bar), R. Nolte (bass), E. Kalvelage (pno), M. Jorand (perc), Cologne Chorus Musicus—Toast pour le nouvel an, Roméo, La Grande Coquette, Un sou, Chanson de Zora, La Nuit de Noël, Le Dodo des enfants, Le Lazzarone, Adieux à la vie!, Soupirs et sourire, L'Orpheline du Tyrol, Choeur de chasseurs démocrates; *Morceaux réservés*—Ave Maria, Les Amants de Séville, Le Chant des Titans, Chant funèbre [F] *(rec Aug. 1992)* Opus 111 ▲ OPS 30-70 [DDD]

Sperl, Thomas (db)
Debussy, C.:Danses sacrée et profane, w. Y. Kondonassis (hp), F. Cohen (cl), M. Chalifour (vn), W.-F. Gu (va), S. Konopka (va), R. Weiss (vc), J. Smith (instr) *(rec Nov. 23–25, 1992)* Telarc ▲ CD 80361 [DDD]
Ravel, M.:Intro & Allegro, w. Y. Kondonassis (hp), J. Smith (fl), F. Cohen (cl), M. Chalifour (vn), W.-F. Gu (va), S. Konopka (va), R. Weiss (vc) *(rec Nov. 23–25, 1992)* Telarc ▲ CD 80361 [DDD]
Ravel, M.:Pavane pour une infante défunte, w. Y. Kondonassis (hp), J. Smith (fl), F. Cohen (cl), M. Chalifour (vn), W.-F. Gu (va), S. Konopka (va), R. Weiss (vc) [arr. by Kondonassis] *(rec Nov. 23–25, 1992)* Telarc ▲ CD 80361 [DDD]

Speyer, Louis (hn)
Berlioz, H.:La Damnation de Faust, w. Suzanne Danco (sop), David Poleri (ten), Martial Singher (bar), Donald Gramm (bass), McHenry Boatwright (bass), Joseph de Pasquale (va), C. Munch (cnd), Boston SO, Harvard Glee Club, Radcliffe Choral Society *(rec Feb 1954)* RCA Victor Gold Seal 8-▲ 0902-668444-2 [ADD]

Spicer, Kelly (bn)—see ORCHESTRAS & ENSEMBLES Cincinnati Contemporary Music Ensemble

Spiegelberg, Daniel (pno)
Beethoven, L. van:Son 1 Vc, w. D. Markevitch (vc) *(rec 2/91)* Gallo ▲ CD 673 [ADD]
Beethoven, L. van:Son 2 Vc, w. D. Markevitch (vc) Gallo ▲ CD 673 [ADD]
Beethoven, L. van:Son 3 Vc, w. D. Markevitch (vc) *(rec 2/91)* Gallo ▲ CD 672 [ADD]
Beethoven, L. van:Son 5 Vc, w. D. Markevitch (vc) Gallo ▲ CD 673 [ADD]
Beethoven, L. van:Son Hn, w. D. Markevitch (vc) *(rec 2/91)* Gallo ▲ CD 673 [ADD]
Beethoven, L. van:Trio Strs, Op. 3, w. D. Markevitch (vc) *(rec 2/91)* Gallo ▲ CD 672 [ADD]
Martin, F.:Pno Music—Guitare [4 pièces brèves] (1933); Danse grave (1940); Eight Preludes (1947–48); Clair de lune (1952); Etude rythmique (1965); Esquisse (1965); Fantaisie sur des Rythmes Flamenco (1973) Gallo ▲ CD 636 [AAD]

Spiegeleir, Olivier de (pno)
Beethoven, L. van:Allegretto, WoO 56 Pavane ▲ ADW 7230 [DDD]
Beethoven, L. van:Bagatelles (24) Pavane ▲ ADW 7230 [DDD]
Beethoven, L. van:Bagatelle, WoO 59, "Für Elise" Pavane ▲ ADW 7230 [DDD]
Beethoven, L. van:Presto Pavane ▲ ADW 7230 [DDD]
Debussy, C.:Pno Music (misc)—The Little Shepherd; The Snow Is Dancing; Des pas sur la neige; La vent dans la plaine; Brouillards; Bruyères; Clair de lune; Reflets dans l'eau; jardins sous la pluie Pavane ▲ 7332
Liszt, F.:Pno Music (misc)—Eglogue; Au lac de Wallenstadt; Au bord d'une source; Orage; Nuages gris; Feux-follets; Murmures de la forêt; Ronde des lutins Pavane ▲ 7332

Spiegelman, Joel (elec hpd)
Kupferman, M.:Mask of Electra, w. Jan De Gaetani (mez), Ronald Roseman (ob) Soundspells ▲ SP 112 [ADD]

Spiegelman, Joel (hpd)
Bach, J.S.:Goldberg Vars—a free interpretation on the Kurzweil 250 digital synthesizer EastWest Records America ▲ 90927-2 ■ 90927-4

Spierer, Leon (vn)
Holewa, H.:Trio Vn, Va & Vc, w. Ulrich Fritze (va), Jörg Baumann (vc) Phono Suecia ▲ PHN 49 [ADD]
Martinů, B.:Sonatina for 2 Vns, w. Fredell Lack (vn), Timothy Hester (pno) *(rec Dudley Recital Hall, Univ of Houston School of Music, Aug 18–20, 1993)* Centaur ▲ CRC 2276 [DDD]
Rosenberg, H.:Con 2 Vn, w. A. Jansons (cnd), Stockholm PO Caprice ▲ CAP 21367 [DDD]
Söderlundh, L.B.:Con Vn, w. A. Jansons (cnd), Stockholm PO Caprice ▲ CAP 21367 [DDD]

Spieth, Noëlle (hpd)—see also ORCHESTRAS & ENSEMBLES Isabella D'Este
Couperin, L.:Suites Hpd—in F, d, g, a, C, F, d, G & D Adès 2-▲ ADE 202372 [DDD]
Rebel, J.-F.:Sons 2 or 3 Parts, w. Frédéric Martin (vn), Odile Edouard (vn), Christine Plumbeau (vl), Eric Bellocq (thb)—Nos. 1–7 [L'immortelle; L'apollon; Tombeau de monsieur de Lully; La venus; La flore; La pallas; La junon] Adda ▲ ADD 581265 [DDD]

Spikay, Deborah (hp)
Atterberg, K.:Chamber Music, w. E. Pérényi (vn), A. Kiss (vn), I. Prunyi (pno), S. Falvay (pno), G. Kertész (vc)—Son. in b for Violin, Op. 27; Höstballader, Op. 15; Valse monotone in C; Rondeau Rétrospectif, Op. 26; Trio Concertante in g, Op. 57 Marco Polo ▲ 8.223404

Spiller, Anton (vn)—see also ORCHESTRAS & ENSEMBLES Koeckert String Quartet
Villa-Lobos, H.:Trio 1 Vn, w. J. Humeston (vc), M. Duphil (pno) Marco Polo ▲ 8.223182
Villa-Lobos, H.:Trio 3 Vn, w. J. Humeston (vc), M. Duphil (pno) Marco Polo ▲ 8.223182

Spillman, Herndon (org)
Berlinski, H.:The Burning Bush Titanic ▲ Ti 205 [DDD]
Clérambault, L.N.:Premier livre d'orgue contents deux suites—Suite du premier ton; Suite du deuxième ton Titanic ▲ Ti 204 [DDD]
A Diversity of Riches Titanic ▲ Ti 205 [DDD]
Duruflé, M.:Org Music (comp) [the organ of Pithiviers, France]—Scherzo, Op. 2; Prélude, adagio et choral varié sur le "Veni Creator," Op. 4; Suite, Op. 5; Prélude et fugue sur le nom d'Alain, Op. 7; Prelude on the Introit of the Epiphany; Fugue on the Theme of the Carillon of Hours of the Cathedral of Soissons Titanic ▲ Ti 200 [AAD]
Duruflé, M.:Org Music (sels)—Suite, Op. 5 Titanic ▲ Ti 204 [DDD]
Duruflé, M.:Suite Org Titanic ▲ Ti 204 [DDD]
Fax, M.:Pieces (3) Org Titanic ▲ Ti 205 [DDD]
Guthrie, J.M.:Vars on "Herzlich tut mich Verlangen" Titanic ▲ Ti 205 [DDD]
Hampton, C.:Dances (5) Org Titanic ▲ Ti 205 [DDD]
Kerr, T.:Anguished American Easter, 1968 Titanic ▲ Ti 205 [DDD]
Messiaen, O.:L'Ascension Org Titanic ▲ Ti 204 [DDD]
Messiaen, O.:Org Music (sels)—L'Ascension Titanic ▲ Ti 204 [DDD]
Persichetti, V.:Chorale Prelude Org Titanic ▲ Ti 205 [DDD]
300 Years of French Glory Titanic ▲ Ti 168 [DDD]

Spillman, Robert (pno)
Dutilleux, H.:Songs (4), w. Patrick Mason (bar) Bridge ▲ BRI 9058 [DDD]
Fauré, G.:La bonne chanson, w. Patrick Mason (bar) Bridge ▲ BRI 9058 [DDD]
Mozart, W.A.:Songs, w. T. Ringholz (sop)—Abendempfindung; Als Luise die Briefe; An die Bescheidenheit; An die Einsamkeit; An die Freundschaft; An die Hoffnung; Die betrogene Welt; Geheime Liebe; Gesellenreise; Die kleine Spinnerin; Lied der Freiheit; Das Lied der Trennung; Das Traumbild; Das Veilchen; Die Verschweigung; Der Zauberer; Die Zufriedenheit [G] *(rec Sept. 1986)* Arabesque ▲ Z 6576 [DDD]
Poulenc, F.:La Fraîcheur et le feu, w. Patrick Mason (bar) Bridge ▲ BRI 9058 [DDD]

INSTRUMENT.

Spillman, Robert (pno) (cont.)
Ravel, M.:Histoires naturelles, w. Patrick Mason (bar) Bridge ▲ BRI 9058 [DDD]
Welcher, D.:Abeja Blanca, w. Jan De Gaetani (mez), Philip West (E hn) Bridge ▲ BCD 9048 [ADD]
Spindler, R. (pno)
Van De Vate, N.:Pieces Pno Vienna Modern Masters ▲ VMM 2003 [DDD]
Van De Vate, N.:Son 1 Pno Vienna Modern Masters ▲ VMM 2003 [DDD]
Spinelli, Alberto (pno)
Mendelssohn, F.:Allegro brillant, w. Giuseppe Modugno (pno) Nuova Era ▲ NUO 7204 [DDD]
Mendelssohn, F.:Duo concertant, w. Giuseppe Modugno (pno) Nuova Era ▲ NUO 7204 [DDD]
Mendelssohn, F.:Fant Pno Duet, w. Giuseppe Modugno (pno) Nuova Era ▲ NUO 7204 [DDD]
Mendelssohn, F.:Vars Pno 4-Hands, w. Giuseppe Modugno (pno) Nuova Era ▲ NUO 7204 [DDD]
Spinks, Charles (org)
Scarlatti, A.:Domine refugium factus, w. Keith Majoram (bass), Marylin Sansom (vc), R. Norrington (cnd), Schütz Choir London *(rec 1973)* London 2-▲ 443868-2 [ADD]
Scarlatti, A.:O magnum mysterium, w. Keith Majoram (bass), Marylin Sansom (vc), Roger Norrington (cnd), Schütz Choir London *(rec 1973)* London 2-▲ 443868-2 [ADD]
Scarlatti, D.:Stabat mater, w. Keith Majoram (bass), Marylin Sansom (vc), R. Norrington (cnd), Schütz Choir London *(rec 1973)* London 2-▲ 443868-2 [ADD]
Spinoulas, Nikos (hn)
Karaindrou, E.:The Suspended Step of the Stork, w. Vangelis Christopoulos (ob), Ada Rouva (hp), Christos Sfetsas (vc), Andreas Tsekouras (acc), Dimitris Vraskos (vn), L. Chalkiadakis (cnd), *(orch unknown) (rec Sound, Athens, Apr & Aug 1991)* ECM ▲ 78118-21456-2 [AAD]
Spiri, Anthony (hpd/pno)
Boccherini, L.:Sons (5) Vc & Db, w. J. Berger (vc), A. Posch (vc), J. Bleicher (org) ebs ▲ ebs 6011 [DDD]
Spiri, Anthony (pno)
Reger, M.:Albumblatt & Tarantella, w. K. Leister (cl) Camerata 2-▲ 25CM-371-2
Reger, M.:Sons Cl, Op. 49, w. K. Leister (cl) Camerata 2-▲ 25CM-371-2
Reger, M.:Son Cl, Op. 107, w. K. Leister (cl) Camerata 2-▲ 25CM-371-2
Spitz, Jonathan (vc)—see also ORCHESTRAS & ENSEMBLES Leonardo Trio
Cohn, J.:Serenade, w. M. Granados (fl), E. Kiesewetter (vn) *(rec Sept. 1992)* XLNT ▲ CD 18007 [DDD]
Maggio, R.:Qts for 2 Fls & 2 Vcs, w. Bart Feller (fl), Kathleen Nester (fl), Fred Sherry (vc), B. Lubman (cnd) *(rec St. Peter's Church, Chelsea, New York, May 22, 1995)* CRI ▲ CD 720 [DDD]
Spitzer, Laura (pno)
Baley, V.:Nocturnal 5 *(rec Madhatter Studios, Los Angeles)* Cambria ▲ CMB 1077 [DDD]
Diamond, D.:Partita Ob, Bn & Pno, w. S. Caplan (ob), K. Wolfe (bn) Cambria ▲ 1091 [DDD]
Schubert, Franz:Duetsche Messe, w. R. Hansmann (sop), M. Lipovšek (mez), J. Reinprecht (ten), F. Wolf (cnd), St. Augustin Orch, St. Augustin Chorus Preiser ▲ 93325
Spitznagel, Astrid (pno)
Encores, w. Ludwig Streicher (db) Orfeo ▲ C 225911 A [DDD]
Spivakov, Vladimir (vn)
Bach, J.S.:Con Fl, Vn & Hpd, w. E. Duran (fl), S. Bezrodny (hpd), V. Spivakov (cnd), Moscow Virtuosi RCA Red Seal ▲ 7991-2-RC [DDD]
Bach, J.S.:Cons Vn (comp), w. Moscow Solisti Virtuosi RCA Red Seal ▲ 09026-61582-2
Bach, J.S.:Con in d Vn, w. Moscow Solisti Virtuosi RCA Red Seal ▲ 09026-61582-2
Bach, J.S.:Con in D Vn, w. Moscow Solisti Virtuosi RCA Red Seal ▲ 09026-61582-2
Bach, J.S.:Con Vn & Ob, w. A. Utkin (ob), V. Spivakov (cnd), Moscow Virtuosi RCA Red Seal ▲ 7991-2-RC [DDD]
Bach, J.S.:Con for 2 Vns, w. A. Futer (vn), V. Spivakov (cnd), Moscow Virtuosi RCA Red Seal ▲ 7991-2-RC [DDD]
Bach, J.S.:Con for 3 Vns, w. A. Futer (vn), B. Garlitsky (vn), V. Spivakov (cnd), Moscow Virtuosi RCA Red Seal ▲ 7991-2-RC [DDD]
Basic 100, Vol. 80, w. Moscow Virtuosi RCA Victor ▲ 09026-68457-2 ■ 09026-68457-4
The Bells of St. Genevieve & Other Baroque Favorites, w. J. Levine (cnd), English CO, James Galway (fl), Pinchas Zukerman (vn), Canadian Brass, et al. RCA Victor ▲ 09026-61002-2 [DDD] ■ 09026-61002-4 (CrO2) □ 09026-61002-5
Brahms, J.:Con Vn, w. Y. Temirkanov (cnd), Royal PO RCA Red Seal ▲ 09026-61696-2
Brahms, J.:Con Vn & Vc, "Double Con", w. A. Kniazev (vc), Y. Temirkanov (cnd), Royal PO RCA Red Seal ▲ 09026-61696-2
Brahms, J.:Scherzo Vn, w. M. Rudy (pno) RCA Red Seal ▲ 09026-61390-2 [DDD]
Brahms, J.:Sons Vn (comp), w. M. Rudy (pno) RCA Red Seal ▲ 09026-61390-2 [DDD]
Hartmann, K.A.:Con funèbre, w. V. Spivakov (cnd), Moscow Virtuosi RCA Red Seal ▲ 60370-2-RC [DDD]
Haydn, J.:Con 1 Vn, w. V. Spivakov (cnd), Moscow Virtuosi RCA Red Seal ▲ 7948-2-RC [DDD] ■ 7948-4-RC (CrO2)
It Ain't Necessarily So & Other Violin Miniatures, w. Sergei Bezrodny (pno) RCA Red Seal ▲ 09026-60861-2
It's Peaceful Here, w. Sergei Bezrodny (pno) RCA Red Seal ▲ 09026-62524-2
Mozart, W.A.:Con 2 Vn, w. V. Spivakov (cnd), Moscow Virtuosi RCA Red Seal ▲ 09026-60152-2 [DDD]
Mozart, W.A.:Con 3 Vn, w. V. Spivakov (cnd), Moscow Virtuosi RCA Red Seal ▲ 09026-60152-2 [DDD]
Mozart, W.A.:Con 5 Vn, Moscow Virtuosi RCA ("Basic 100" series) ▲ 09026-68457-2 ■ 09026-68457-4
Mozart, W.A.:Con 5 Vn, w. V. Spivakov (cnd), Moscow Virtuosi RCA Red Seal ▲ 09026-60152-2 [DDD]
Mozart, W.A.:Concertone Vns, w. B. Garlitski (vn), Moscow Virtuosi RCA Red Seal ▲ 09026-60467-2
Mozart, W.A.:Sinf concertante Vn, K.364, w. S. Mintz (va), Moscow Virtuosi RCA Red Seal ▲ 09026-60467-2
Mozart, W.A.:Sinf concertante Vn, K.364, Moscow Virtuosi RCA ("Basic 100" series) ▲ 09026-68457-2 ■ 09026-68457-4
Penderecki, K.:Capriccio Vn, w. V. Spivakov (cnd), Moscow Virtuosi RCA Red Seal ▲ 60370-2-RC [DDD]
Prokofiev, S.:Con 1 Vn, w. Y. Temirkanov (cnd), Royal PO RCA Red Seal ▲ 09026-60990-2
Schnittke, A.:Con Pno, w. V. Krainev (pno), Moscow Virtuosi RCA Red Seal ▲ 09026-60466-2
Schnittke, A.:Suite in the Old Style, w. E. Kissin (pno) RCA Red Seal ▲ 60370-2-RC [DDD]
Sibelius, J.:Con Vn, w. Y. Temirkanov (cnd), St. Petersburg PO *(rec Coventry, England & St. Petersburg, Russia, Nov 10, 1992 & Jan 17, 19)* RCA Red Seal ▲ 09026-61701-2 [DDD]
Stravinsky, I.:Con Vn, w. V. Spivakov (cnd), Moscow Virtuosi RCA Red Seal ▲ 60370-2-RC [DDD]
Tchaikovsky, P.:Con Vn, w. Y. Temirkanov (cnd), Royal PO RCA Red Seal ▲ 09026-60990-2
Vivaldi, A.:Cons Vn (misc), w. V. Spivakov (cnd), Moscow Virtuosi—(2) in e, RV.278 & in a, RV.357 RCA Red Seal ▲ 60369-2 [DDD] ■ 60369-4 (CrO2)
Vivaldi, A.:Cons Vn, Op. 8/1-4, "The Four Seasons", w. V. Spivakov (cnd), Moscow Virtuosi RCA Red Seal ▲ 60369-2 [DDD] ■ 60369-4 (CrO2)
Vivaldi, A.:Con for 2 Vns Vc, R.565, w. A. Fouter (vn), M. Milman (vc), V. Spivakov (cnd), Moscow Virtuosi RCA Red Seal ▲ 60240-2-RC [DDD]
Spivakovsky, Tossy (vn)
Sibelius, J.:Con Vn, w. T. Hannikainen (cnd), London SO *(rec Walthamstow Assembly Hall, London)* Everest ▲ EVC 9035 [AAD]
Tchaikovsky, P.:Con Vn, w. W. Goehr (cnd), London SO *(rec Walthamstow Assembly Hall, London)* Everest ▲ EVC 9035 [AAD]
Tchaikovsky, P.:Souvenir d'un lieu cher, w. W. Goehr (cnd), London SO—Mélodie [arr vn & orch] *(rec Walthamstow Assembly Hall, London)* Everest ▲ EVC 9035 [AAD]
Spoliansky, Mischa (pno)
Richard Tauber Sings Lieder:12 German Folk Songs, w. Richard Tauber (ten) *(rec 1926)* Pearl ▲ PEA 9370 (m) [AAD]
Schubert, Franz:Winterreise, w. R. Tauber (ten)—12 selections—Nos. 1, 5, 6, 8, 11, 13, 15, 18, 20, 21, 22, 24 [G] *(rec 6/20/27 for Parlophone-Od)* Pearl ▲ PEA 9370 (m) [AAD]

Sponberg, Atle (vn)
Bibalo, A.:Son Vn Norway Music ▲ SOL 10913 [DDD]
Halvorsen, J.:Passacaglia & Sarabande con variazioni, w. Øystein Birkeland (vc) [arr for Vn & Vc] Simax ▲ PSC 1104
Kodály, Z.:Duo Vn & Vc, w. Øystein Birkeland (vc) Simax ▲ PSC 1104
Meyers, R.:Je vous chante Norway Music ▲ SOL 10913 [DDD]
Olsen, S.:Village Songs, w. Baekkelund (cnd), Gjovik Sinfonietta Norway Music ▲ BD 7026
Ravel, M.:Son Vn Vc, w. Øystein Birkeland (vc) Simax ▲ PSC 1104
Spong, Jon (pno)
Griffes, C.T.:Songs, w. Milnes (bar)—An den Wind; Am Kreuzweg wird begraben; Meeres Stille; Auf geheimem Waldespfade; Song of the Dagger New World ▲ NW 273-2 [ADD]
Sporrong, P. (vn)—see ORCHESTRAS & ENSEMBLES Berlin Spectrum Ensemble members
Spotti, Renata (vn)
Schubert, Franz:Son Vn, D.574, w. Massimo Palumbo (pno) Enterprise ("Tiziano" series) ▲ ENT TZ 96009 [DDD]
Schubert, Franz:Sonatinas Vn, w. Massimo Palumbo (pno) Enterprise ("Tiziano" series) ▲ ENT TZ 96009 [DDD]
Spranger, Irene (fl)
Hasse, J.A.:Con Fl, w. A. Manze (cnd), Concerto Copenhagen *(rec Aug. 8-10, 1992)* Chandos ("Chaconne" series) ▲ CHAN 0535 [DDD]
Scheibe, J.A.:Con Fl in D, w. A. Manze (cnd), Concerto Copenhagen *(rec Aug. 8-10, 1992)* Chandos ("Chaconne" series) ▲ CHAN 0535 [DDD]
Sprecher, Sandra (pno)
Delio, T.:Music of, w. John Fonville (fl), Steven Shick (perc), Aleck Karis (pno), Jacques Linder (pno)—anti-paysage for Fl, Perc, Pno & Tape; Of for Tape; Though for solo Pno; so again for Tape; on again for Tape; of again for Tape *(rec Univ of CA, San Diego, Univ of Maryland, Catonsville & Washington D.C.)* Neuma ▲ 45090 [DDD]
Sprenger, H. (va)—see ORCHESTRAS & ENSEMBLES Berlin String Quintet
Spring, Christian (pno)
Berceuses, Lullabies & Wiegenlieder Gallo ▲ CD 564 [DDD]
Fröhlich, F.T.:Choral Music, w. E. Speiser (sop), P. Steiner (ten), J. Krattiger (bass), B. Billeter (pno), Winterthur Vocal Ensemble [G] *(rec 1988)* Jecklin-Disco ▲ JD 627-2 [ADD]
Music of Springtime Gallo ▲ CD 656 [DDD]
Spring, Matthew (lt/h-g/lira da braccio/vi/gittern)—see ORCHESTRAS & ENSEMBLES Sirinu
Spring, Robert (cl)
Dragon's Tongue Summit ▲ DCD 166 [DDD]
Tower, J.:Breakfast Rhythms, w. A. Weisberg (cnd), Ensemble 21 Summit ▲ DCD 124 [DDD]
Tower, J.:Clarinet Con, w. E. Sellheim (pno) Summit ▲ DCD 124 [DDD]
Tower, J.:Fant Cl, w. E. Sellheim (pno) Summit ▲ DCD 124 [DDD]
Tower, J.:Wings Summit ▲ DCD 124 [DDD]
Springfels, Mary (va)
Blow, J.:Songs, w. Christine Brandes (sop), N. McGegan (cnd), Arcadian Academy Harmonia Mundi USA ▲ HMU 907167
Purcell, H.:Music of, w. Christine Brandes (sop), N. McGegan (cnd), Arcadian Academy Harmonia Mundi France ▲ HMU 907167
Rosenmüller, J.:Music of, w. Ellen Hargis (sop), Paul O'Dette (thb), D. Douglass (cnd), King's Noyse—Suite in C [from Studentenmusik]; Jubilent aethera; Son X à 5; Son VII à 4; In te, Domine, speravi; Son XI à 5; Son IV à 3; Ach Herr, strafe mich nicht in deinem Zorn; Son III à 2; Leiber Herre Gott, Wecke uns auf Harmonia Mundi ▲ HMU 907179
Springfels, Mary (vi)
Bach, J.S.:Sons Fl, BWV 1030-35, w. J. See (baroque fl), D. Moroney (hpd)—includes alternate manuscript solo flute version of BWV 1033 Harmonia Mundi USA 2-▲ HMU 907024/25 2-
Bach, J.S.:Sons Vn, w. J. See (baroque fl), D. Moroney (hpd)—BWV 1020 [doubtful; trans. for flute & continuo] Harmonia Mundi USA 2-▲ HMU 907024/25 2-
Dance Songs of Renaissance England, w. Folger Consort, M. Bleeke, T. Chancey, W. Gillespie, M. Springfels, B. Wissick *(rec Jan. 24, 1988)* Folger Consort ▲ BDCD1 9004 [DDD]
Purcell, H.:Pavan 3 for 2 Vns, w. N. McGegan (cnd), Arcadian Academy *(rec Sept 18-21, 1994)* Harmonia Mundi France ▲ HMU 907167
Purcell, H.:Sons for 2 Vns (misc), w. N. McGegan (cnd), Arcadian Academy—in B♭ & in F *(rec Sept 18-21, 1994)* Harmonia Mundi France ▲ HMU 907167
Purcell, H.:Songs, w. D. Minter (ct), P. O'Dette (archlt), M. Meyerson (hpd/org)—Be Welcome Then, Great Sir; Celia Has a Thousand Charmes; Crown the Altar; The Fatal Hour Comes On Apace; From Silent Shades; Hark! How All Things; Hark! the Echoing Air; Here the Dieties Approve; I Attempt From Love's Sickness to Fly; If Musick be the Food of Love; Lord, What is Man; Musick For A While; Not All My Torments; Now That the Sun Hath Veil'd His Light; O Solitude; Sleep, Adam, Sleep; Sweeter Than Roses; Thrice Happy Lovers; 'Tis Nature's Voice [E] Harmonia Mundi USA ▲ HMU 907035
Three Parts upon a Ground, w. John Hollowy (vn), Stanley Ritchie (vn), Andrew Manze (vn), Nigel North (lt), John Toll (hpd/org) Harmonia Mundi USA ▲ HMU 907091
Springuel, C. (va)
Beethoven, L. van:Vars on Grétry's romance "Un fièvre brûlante", WoO 72, w. M. Grauwels (fl), B. Bessler (vn), G. H. (hp), Y. Stormes (gtr) Syrinx ▲ 94101 [DDD]
Spohr, L.:Son 4 Vn, w. M. Grauwels (fl), B. Bessler (vn), G. H. (hp), Y. Stormes (gtr) Syrinx ▲ 94101 [DDD]
Sprúdzs, Uldis (vn)—see ORCHESTRAS & ENSEMBLES Riga String Quartet
Spruijt, Wim (gtr)
Theodorakis, M.:Songs, w. Peter Goedhart (bar)—Ballad of Mauthausen; Songs (4) from "Epitaph"; Romancero Gitano [after Garcia Lorca] [arr Stephen Dodgson for voc & gtr] Erasmus ▲ WVH 167
Spurr, Phyllis (pno)
Brahms, J.:Songs, w. K. Ferrier (cta) [G] Danacord ▲ DACOCD 301 (m)
Srdic, Nikola (cl)—see ORCHESTRAS & ENSEMBLES Tickmayer Formatio
Stabrawa, Daniel (vn)—see ORCHESTRAS & ENSEMBLES Philharmonia String Quartet, Berlin Philharmonia String Quartet
Stacy, Thomas (E hn)
Hampton, C.:Vars on "Amazing Grace", w. H. Huff (org) *(rec Aug. 26, 1993)* Catalyst ▲ 09026-61979-2 ■ 09026-61979-4
Hodkinson, S.:The Edge of the Olde One, w. P. Phillips (cnd), Eastman Musica Nova New World ▲ 80489-2
Hodkinson, S.:The Edge of the Olde One, w. P. Phillips (cnd), Eastman Musica Nova Grenadilla ■ GSC 1054
Persichetti, V.:Con E Hn, w. V. Persichetti (cnd), New York String Orch New World ▲ 80489-2
Rorem, N.:Con E Hn, w. M. Palmer (cnd), Rochester PO *(rec Eastman Theater, Rochester, NY, Oct. 8, 1994)* New World ▲ 80489-2
Skrowaczewski, S.:Con E Hn, w. S. Skrowaczewski (cnd), Minnesota Orch Phoenix ▲ PHCD 120 [AAD]
Stadelmann, Christian (vn)—see ORCHESTRAS & ENSEMBLES Philharmonia String Quartet, Berlin Philharmonia String Quartet
Stadler, Sergei (vn)
Petrov, A.:Con Vn, w. Y. Temirkanov (cnd), Leningrad State Phil Academic SO *(rec Grand Hall of the Leningrad State PO)* Russian Compact Disc ▲ RCD 26601
Schubert, Franz:Intro & Vars Fl on "Tröckne Blumen", w. F. Gottlieb (pno) [violin & piano] Art & Electronics ▲ AED 10478 [DDD]
Schumann, R.:Son 1 Vn, w. F. Gottlieb (pno) Art & Electronics ▲ AED 10478 [DDD]
Strauss, R.:Son Vn, w. F. Gottlieb (pno) Art & Electronics ▲ AED 10478 [DDD]
Stadlmair, Vincent (vc)—see ORCHESTRAS & ENSEMBLES Franz Schubert String Quartet
Stadlmayer, Andreas (vn)
Bach, J.S.:Cons Vn (comp), w. T. Karolski (cnd), Camerata Romana Vivace ▲ E 506
Bach, J.S.:Con for 2 Vns, w. T. Brodzky (vn), T. Karolski (cnd), Camerata Romana Vivace ▲ E 506
Stadtfeld, D. Sanford (rcr)—see ORCHESTRAS & ENSEMBLES The Whole Noyse

▲ = CD ♦ = Enhanced CD Δ = MD ■ = Cassette Tape □ = DCC

Stadtherr, Karel (vn)—see also ORCHESTRAS & ENSEMBLES Vlach String Quartet
Dvořák, A.:Terzetto, w. Jana Vlacková (vn), Petr Verner (va) *(rec Martínek Studio, Prague, 1995)* Naxos ▲ 8.553373 [DDD]

Staege, Roswitha (fl)
Yun, I.:Con Fl, w. H. Zender (cnd), Saarbrück RSO *(rec Saarbrück Radio Studio, May 1985)* Camerata ▲ 30CM 109 [AAD]
Yun, I.:Salomo *(rec Saarbrück Radio Studio, May 1985)* Camerata ▲ 30CM 109 [AAD]

Staerk, Ulrich (pno)
Langgaard, R.:Songs, w. Anne Margrethe Dahl (sop)—5 Lieder [text Rittershaus]; Lieder von Goethe; 5 Lieder [text Eichendorff/Heine]; Marienlied [text Eichendorff]; Waldeslieder [text Redwitz]; Aus alten Märchen [text Heine]; Lyriches Intermezzo von Heinrich Heine; Wer zum ersten Male liebt [text Heine] *(rec Frederiksdal Castle, Lolland, Sept. 4-6, 1994)* Marco Polo ("dacapo" series) ▲ 8.224011 [DDD]

Staff, David (tpt)
Purcell, H.:Son Tpt, w. R. Glenton (cnd), Orch of the Golden Age *(rec Manchester Grammar School, England, May 13 & 14, 1995)* Naxos ▲ 8.553444 [DDD]
Purcell, H.:Te Deum & Jubilate, w. Jeni Bern (sop), Susan Bisatt (sop), William Purefoy (ct), Christopher Robson (ct), Ian Honeyman (ten), Thomas Guthrie (bass), R. Glenton (cnd), Orch of the Golden Age, Golden Age Choir *(rec Manchester Grammar School, England, May 13 & 14, 1995)* Naxos ▲ 8.553444 [DDD]
Torelli, G.:Tpt Music, w. P.-O. Lindeke (tpt), E. Tarr (tpt), G. Cassone (tpt), S. Vartolo (cnd), San Petronio Cappella Musicale Orch—Sinfs., G.1, 2, 8, 10, 11, 26, 29, 30, 31, 33; Sons. G.3–6, 13, 15–25; Con. G.27 Bongiovanni 3–▲ GB 5523/25

Stahl, Eckhard (vc)
Clarke, R.:Son Vc, w. V. Mokrosch (pno) Bayer ▲ BR 100 200CD [DDD]
Firsova, E.:Son Vc, w. V. Mokrosch (pno) Bayer ▲ BR 100 200CD [DDD]
Fromm–Michaels, I.:Suite Vc Bayer ▲ BR 100 200CD [DDD]

Staicu, Paul (hn)
Mozart, W.A.:Cons Hn, w. P. Staicu (cnd), Ciprian Porumbescu Conservatory Camerata CO Electrecord ▲ ELCD 107 [AAD]

Staier, Andreas (hpd)
Bach, C.P.E.:Con Hpd & Strs, H.474, w. T. Hengelbrock (cnd), Freiburg Baroque Orch Deutsche Harmonia Mundi ▲ 77187-2 [DDD]
Bach, J.S.:Chromatic Fant & Fugue Deutsche Harmonia Mundi ▲ 77039–2–RC [ADD]
Bach, J.S.:Chromatic Fant & Fugue *(rec Seewen, Switzerland, Apr. 15–17, 1988)* Deutsche Harmonia Mundi ▲ 05472–77330–2 [DDD]
Bach, J.S.:Fants Hpd—in a, BWV 904 *(rec Seewen, Switzerland, Apr. 15–17, 1988)* Deutsche Harmonia Mundi ▲ 05472–77330–2 [DDD]
Bach, J.S.:Fants Hpd—BWV 904, 906, 917, 919, 921, 922 Deutsche Harmonia Mundi ▲ 77039–2–RC [ADD]
Bach, J.S.:Italian Con *(rec Beethovenhaus, Bonn, Germany, Apr 14–29, 1993)* Deutsche Harmonia Mundi 3–▲ 05472–77306–2 [DDD]
Bach, J.S.:Italian Con *(rec Beethovenhaus, Bonn, Apr. 14–29, 1993)* Deutsche Harmonia Mundi ▲ 05472–77330–2 [DDD]
Bach, J.S.:Partitas Hpd, BWV 825–830 *(rec Beethovenhaus, Bonn, Germany, Apr 14–29, 1993)* Deutsche Harmonia Mundi 3–▲ 05472–77306–2 [DDD]
Bach, J.S.:Partitas Hpd, BWV 825–830—in D, BWV 828 *(rec Beethovenhaus, Bonn, Apr. 14–29, 1993)* Deutsche Harmonia Mundi ▲ 05472–77330–2 [DDD]
Bach, J.S.:Partita Hpd, BWV 831, "Ov nach französischer Art" *(rec Beethovenhaus, Bonn, Germany, Apr 14–29, 1993)* Deutsche Harmonia Mundi 3–▲ 05472–77306–2 [DDD]
Bach, J.S.:Preludes & Fugues Hpd—BWV 894, 901, 902 Deutsche Harmonia Mundi ▲ 77039–2–RC [ADD]
Delight in Disorder, w. Pedro Memelsdorff (rcr) Deutsche Harmonia Mundi ▲ 05472–77318–2 [DDD]
Haydn, J.:Sons Pno—5 Sonatas, H.XVI/48–52 Deutsche Harmonia Mundi ▲ 77160–2–RC [DDD]
Scarlatti, D.:Sons Kbd—K.108, 118, 119, 141, 198, 203, 454, 455, 490–492, 501, 502, 516–519 Deutsche Harmonia Mundi ▲ 05472–77224–2
Scarlatti, D.:Sons Kbd—K.69, 113–116, 208, 209, 215, 216, 246, 247, 394, 395, 414, 415, 426, 427 & 513 Teldec ▲ TEL 12601 [DDD]
Schubert, Franz:Songs (misc), w. Christoph Prégardien (ten)—Am Flusse; Trost in Tränen; 4 Lieder, Op. 3; Sehnsucht; Die Liebe; Lieder, Op. 5; 3 Gesänge des Harfners; 3 Lieder, Op. 19; An die entferne; Versunken; An der Mond; 3 Lieder, Op. 32 [all after Goethe] Deutsche Harmonia Mundi ▲ 05472–77342–2 [DDD]

Staier, Andreas (pno)
Dussek, J.L.:Con Pno Op. 22, Concerto Cologne *(rec German Radio, Cologne, Nov 24–28, 1992)* Capriccio ▲ 10 444 [DDD]
Dussek, J.L.:Con Pno Op. 49, Concerto Cologne *(rec German Radio, Cologne, Nov 24–28, 1992)* Capriccio ▲ 10 444 [DDD]
Dussek, J.L.:Sons Pno—Fant & Fugue, Op. 55; Son, Op. 64 [Le Retour à Paris]; Elégie Harmonique, Op. 61 *(rec Beethovenhaus Bohn, Kammermusiksaal, Sept 14–18, 1994)* Deutsche Harmonia Mundi ▲ 05472–77334–2 [DDD]
Dussek, J.L.:The Sufferings of the Queen of France, w. Jean–Michel Forest (speaker—Marie–Antoinette) *(rec German Radio, Cologne, Nov 24–28, 1992)* Capriccio ▲ 10 444 [DDD]
Mendelssohn, F.:Songs, w. Christopher Prégardien (ten)—6 Songs, including Auf Flügeln des Gesanges Deutsche Harmonia Mundi ▲ 05472–77319–2
Schubert, Franz:Pieces Pno, D.946 Teldec ▲ TEL 11084 [DDD]
Schubert, Franz:Die Schöne Müllerin, w. C. Prégardien (ten) Deutsche Harmonia Mundi ▲ 05472–77273–2
Schubert, Franz:Schwanengesang, w. Christopher Prégardien (ten) Deutsche Harmonia Mundi ▲ 05472–77319–2
Schubert, Franz:Son Pno, D.845 Teldec ▲ TEL 11084 [DDD]
Schubert, Franz:Songs (misc), w. C. Prégardien (ten)—Songs of Schiller poems Deutsche Harmonia Mundi ▲ 05472–77296–2 [DDD]
Schumann, R.:Con Pno, w. P. Herreweghe (cnd), Champs Elysées Theater Orch [J. B. Streicher fortepno, ca. 1850] Harmonia Mundi ▲ HMC 901555
Schumann, R.:Dichterliebe, w. Christopher Prégardien (ten) Deutsche Harmonia Mundi ▲ 05472–77319–2

Stairs, Michael (org)
A Longwood Gardens Christmas:Longwood Gardens Organ, Vol. 3 Direct–to–Tape Recording ▲ DTR 9102CD [DDD] ■ DTR 8705
Longwood Gardens Organ, Vol. 5 Direct–to–Tape Recording ▲ DTR 8605 [DDD]

Stakian, A. A. (vn)
Bach, J.S.:Sons & Partitas Vn, BWV 1001–1006—Partita in d, BWV 1004 Gallo ▲ CD 510 [ADD]
Hindemith, P.:Son Vn, Op. 31/1 Gallo ▲ CD 510 [ADD]
Jolivet, A.:Suite rhapsodique Gallo ▲ CD 510 [ADD]
Martinon, J.:Son 6 Vn Gallo ▲ CD 510 [ADD]

Stalenowski, S. (vn)
Wieniawski, H.:Vn & Pno Music, w. M. Paderewski (pno)—Souvenir de Poznan & Mazurka in a, Op. 3/1 & 2; Polonaise de Concert in D, Op. 4; Souvenir de Moscou, Op. 6; Romance sans parole et Rondo élégant, Op. 9; La Champêtre & Chanson polonaise, Op. 12/1 & 2; Scherzo tarantelle in g, Op. 16; Légende, Op. 17; Obertas & La ménétrier, Op. 19/1 & 2; Polonaise brillante in A, Op. 21 Pavane ▲ ADW 7213 [DDD]

Stalder, Hans–Rudolf (bas hn)
Beerhalter, A.:Vars on "Im tiefen Keller sitz' ich hier", w. Z. Sirokay (pno) *(rec 1981)* Jecklin–Disco ▲ JD 560–2 [ADD]
Mozart, W.A.:Adagio Bas Hns, K.410/440d, w. E. Schmid (bas hn), P. Meyer (bn) *(rec 1978)* Jecklin–Disco ▲ JD 549–2 [ADD]
Mozart, W.A.:Adagio Cls, K.411, w. K. Leister (cl), P. Geisler (cl), H. Hofer (bas hn), E. Schmid (bas hn) *(rec 1978)* Jecklin–Disco ▲ JD 549–2 [ADD]

Stalder, Hans–Rudolf (bas hn) (cont.)
Mozart, W.A.:Adagio E Hn, w. K. Leister (cl), H. Hofer (bas hn), E. Schmid (bas hn) [arr. Raymond Meylan for clarinet & basset horn] *(rec 1978)* Jecklin–Disco ▲ JD 549–2 [ADD]

Stalder, Hans–Rudolf (chl)
The Viola d'Amore:In Numerous Voices, w. Dorothea Jappe (va d'amore), Konrad Hünteler (trns fl), Herbert Hoever (vn), Michael Jappe (vl/vc), Rolf Junghanns (hpd/pno) Adagio ▲ ADG 91016

Stalder, Hans–Rudolf (cl)
Berr, F.:Fant 17, w. Z. Sirokay (pno) *(rec 1975)* Jecklin–Disco ▲ JD 578–2 [ADD]
Boieldieu, F.–A.:Sons (9) Pno, w. Z. Sirokay (pno)— Sonata in E♭ [arr for cl & pno] *(rec 1975)* Jecklin–Disco ▲ JD 578–2 [ADD]
Crusell, B.H.:Duos (3) for 2 Cls, w. H. Hofer (cl)—No. 2 *(rec 1975)* Jecklin–Disco ▲ JD 578–2 [ADD]
Danzi, F.:Son Bas Hn, w. Z. Sirokay (pno) *(rec 1981)* Jecklin–Disco ▲ JD 560–2 [ADD]
Kreutzer, C.:Das Mühlrad, w. E. Speiser (sop), R. Junghanns (kbd) [period instrs] *(rec 1984)* Jecklin–Disco ▲ JD 587–2 [ADD]
Kreutzer, C.:Trio for 2 Cls & Va, w. E. Schmid (cl), D. Jappe (va) [period instrs] *(rec 1984)* Jecklin–Disco ▲ JD 587–2 [ADD]
Kreutzer, C.:Trio Pno, Cl & Bn, w. R. Junghanns (kbd), W. Stiftner (bn) [period instrs] *(rec 1984)* Jecklin–Disco ▲ JD 587–2 [ADD]
Krommer, F.:Sinf Concertante, w. P.–L. Graf (fl), T. Wicky (vn), Capriccio Ensemble Tudor ▲ 757 [DDD]
Lehmann, H.U.:Tractus, w. U. Burkhard (fl), P. Fuchs (ob) *(rec Jan. 13, 1978)* Grammont ▲ CTS P 4–2
Mendelssohn, F.:Concert Pieces, w. H. Leuthold (bas hn), J. von Vintschger (pno) *(rec 1981)* Jecklin–Disco ▲ JD 560–2 [ADD]
Mozart, W.A.:Diverts Bas Hns, K.Anh.229, w. H. Hofer (cl), H. Leuthold (bas hn) [arr. for 3 basset horns]—No. 1 *(rec 1978)* Jecklin–Disco ▲ JD 549–2 [ADD]
Mozart, W.A.:Notturnos Sops, w. E. Speiser (sop), V. Gohl (cta), K. Widmer (bass), R. Kubli (bas hn), H. Leuthold (bas hn) [l] *(rec 1968)* Jecklin–Disco ▲ JD 549–2 [ADD]
Mozart, W.A.:Più non si trovano, w. E. Speiser (sop), V. Gohl (cta), K. Widmer (bass), R. Kubli (bas hn), H. Leuthold (bas hn) [l] *(rec 1968)* Jecklin–Disco ▲ JD 549–2 [ADD]
Ponchielli, A.:Il Convegno, w. Z. Sirokay (pno) [adapted for 2 clarinets & piano] *(rec 1975)* Jecklin–Disco ▲ JD 578–2 [ADD]
Ravel, M.:Intro & Allegro, w. Ursula Holliger (hp), Perter–Lukas Graf (fl), Zurich CO Claves ▲ CD 50280 [ADD]
Reinecke, C.:Intro & Allegro appassionato, w. J. von Vintschger (pno) *(rec 1987)* Jecklin–Disco ▲ JD 602–2 [ADD]
Reinecke, C.:Son Fl, w. J. von Vintschger (pno) *(rec 1987)* Jecklin–Disco ▲ JD 602–2 [ADD]
Reinecke, C.:Trio Pno, Op. 274, w. J. Hefti (hn), J. von Vintschger (pno) *(rec 1987)* Jecklin–Disco ▲ JD 602–2 [ADD]
Rossini, G.:Fant Cl, w. J. von Vintschger (pno) *(rec 1975)* Jecklin–Disco ▲ JD 578–2 [ADD]
Schnyder von Wartensee, X.:Con for 2 Cls, w. T. Friedli (cl), Capriccio Ensemble Tudor ▲ 757 [DDD]
Spohr, L.:Fant & Vars on a Theme of Danzi, w. Zurich Chamber Players *(rec 1972, 1975 & 1982)* Jecklin–Disco ▲ JD 536–2 [ADD]
Spohr, L.:Vars in B♭ on a Theme from *Alruna*, w. J. von Vintschger (pno) *(rec 1972, 1975 & 1982)* Jecklin–Disco ▲ JD 536–2 [ADD]
Weber, C.M. von:Grand duo concertant Cl, w. J. von Vintschger (pno) *(rec 1972, 1975 & 1982)* Jecklin–Disco ▲ JD 536–2 [ADD]
Weber, C.M. von:Intro, Theme & Vars Cl, w. Zurich Chamber Players *(rec 1972, 1975 & 1982)* Jecklin–Disco ▲ JD 536–2 [ADD]
Weber, C.M. von:Vars on a Theme from *Silvana* Cl, w. J. von Vintschger (pno) *(rec 1972, 1975 & 1982)* Jecklin–Disco ▲ JD 536–2 [ADD]

Stalder, Hans–Rudolf (hp)
Backofen, J.G.:Concertante Hp, w. U. Holliger (bas hn), A. Schmid (vc) *(rec 1981)* Jecklin–Disco ▲ JD 560–2 [ADD]

Staley, Jim (trbn)—see ORCHESTRAS & ENSEMBLES Tone Road Ramblers

Stalford, Ronald (org)
Sowerby, L.:Songs, w. Patricia Snyder (org), Con Vivium—18 Christmas Songs Albany ▲ TROY 187 [DDD]

Stallman, Robert (fl)
The American Flute, w. David Buechner (pno) ASV ▲ ASV 869 [DDD]
Blavet, M.:Sons Trns Fl, w. Edwin Swanborn (hpd), Karl Bennion (vc)—Op. 2/2, 4 & 6; Op. 3/2, 4 & 6 VAI Audio ▲ VAIA 1101
Dodgson, S.:Con Fl, w. R. Zollman (cnd), Northern Sinfonia of England *(rec St Nicholas Hospital, Newcastle–upon–Tyne, Oct 23–24, 1992)* Biddulph ▲ LAW 013 [DDD]
Handel, G.F.:Sons Fl, w. Karl Bennion (vc), Edwin Swanborn (hpd), Op. 1, Nos. 1, 2, 4, 5, 7, 9 & 11 VAI Audio ▲ VAIA 1091
Incantations:20th Century Works for Solo Flute *(rec Church of the Good Shepherd, New York City, May 24–27, 1994)* Vai Audio ▲ VAIA 1112 [DDD]
Kraft, L.:O Primavera, w. R. Roseman (ob), E. Gilmore (cl) *(rec 1989–1990)* Centaur ▲ CRC 2079 [ADD]
Leclair, J.–M.:Sons Vn (Books 1–4), w. E. Swanborn (hpd), K. Bennon (vc)—Opp. 2/1, 3 & 11; 9/2 & 7 *(rec Mar. 21–24, 1993)* VAI Audio ▲ VAIA 1068 [DDD]
McKinley, W.T.:Con Fl, w. R. Black (cnd), Prism Orch Owl ▲ OWL 34 [DDD]
Vivaldi, A.:Cons Fl, Op. 10, w. J. Lubbock (cnd), St. John's Smith Square Orch ASV ▲ ASV 733 [DDD]

Stamm, Peter (pno)
Eisler, H.:Songs, w. Wolfgang Holzmair (bar)—sels from Eisler's Hollywood Songbook Koch Schwann ▲ SCH CD 313222
Reger, M.:Songs, w. Iris Vermillion (mez)—Es schläft ein stiller Garten, Op. 98/4; Winterahnung, Op. 4/3; Im April, Op. 4/4; Ein Paar, Op. 55/9; Nelken, Op.15/3; Hat gesagt–Bleibt's nicht dabei, Op.75/12; Die blunten Kühe, Op. 70/4; Schlummerlied; Flötenspierlerin, Op. 88/3; Totensprache, Op. 62/12; Leise, leise weht irh Lüfte, Op. 97/2; Der bescheidene Schäfer, Op. 97/4; Mittag, Op. 76/35; Vor der Liebe, Op. 76/32; Waldeinsamkeit, Op. 76/3; Der verliebte Jäger, Op. 76/13; Traum durch dir Dämmerung, Op. 35/3; Aeolscharfe, Op. 75/11; Ein Drängen, Op. 97/3; Einsamkeit, Op. 75/18; An die Hoffnung, Op. 124 *(rec Jan & Nov 1995)* CPO ▲ 999317–2 [DDD]

Stamper, Richard (vn)
Arensky, A.:Trio 1 Pno, w. V. Ashkenazy (pno), C. Jackson (vc) *(rec Nov 1990)* Naxos ▲ 8.550467 [DDD]
Tchaikovsky, P.:Trio Pno, w. V. Ashkenazy (pno), C. Jackson (vc) *(rec Nov. 1990)* Naxos ▲ 8.550467 [DDD]

Stan, Mircea (trbn)
Braxton, A.:Composition 144, w. Anthony Braxton (fl/s sax/a sax), Seppo Baron Paakkunainen (fl/t sax/br sax), Pentti Lahti (fl/s sax/a sax), Pepa Päivinen (fl/t sax/sop sax/b cl), Mikko–Ville Luolajan–Mikkola (vn), Teppo Hauta–aho (db/vc), Jukka Wasama (dr) *(rec Järvenpää House, Järvenpää, Finland, Nov 7, 1988)* Leo ▲ LR 233
Braxton, A.:Composition 145, w. Anthony Braxton (fl/s sax/a sax), Seppo Baron Paakkunainen (fl/t sax/br sax), Pentti Lahti (fl/s sax/a sax), Pepa Päivinen (fl/t sax/sop sax/b cl), Mikko–Ville Luolajan–Mikkola (vn), Teppo Hauta–aho (db/vc), Jukka Wasama (dr) *(rec Järvenpää House, Järvenpää, Finland, Nov 7, 1988)* Leo ▲ LR 233

Stancul, Jasminka (pno)
Beethoven, L. van:Con 1 Pno, w. A. Rahbari (cnd), Slovak Radio New PO Discover International ▲ DICD 920104 [DDD]
Beethoven, L. van:Con 2 Pno, w. A. Rahbari (cnd), Slovak Radio New PO Discover International ▲ DICD 920104 [DDD]
Beethoven, L. van:Con 3 Pno, w. A. Rahbari (cnd), Slovak Radio New PO Discover International ▲ DICD 920121 [DDD]
Beethoven, L. van:Con 4 Pno, w. A. Rahbari (cnd), Slovak Radio New PO Discover International ▲ DICD 920121 [DDD]
Beethoven, L. van:Con 5 Pno, "Emperor", w. A. Rahbari (cnd), BRTN PO Brussels Discover International ▲ DICD 920160 [DDD]
Beethoven, L. van:Son 32 Pno Discover International ▲ DICD 920160 [DDD]

INSTRUMENT.

Stancul, Jasminka (pno) (cont.)
Schubert, Franz:Trio Pno, D.28, w. Werner Hink (vn), Fritz Dolezal (vc) *(rec Apr & June 1995)* Camerata ▲ 30 CM 342 [DDD]
Schubert, Franz:Trio 1 Pno, w. Werner Hink (vn), Fritz Dolezal (vc) *(rec Apr & June 1995)* Camerata ▲ 30 CM 342 [DDD]
Stanczyk, Anna Maria (pno)
24 Classic Hits Polskie Nagrania Edition ▲ ECD 060 [DDD]
Standaart, Peter (fl)
Wyner, Y.:Memorial Music, w. Susan Davenny Wyner (sop), Mary Posses (fl), Jonathan Drexler (fl) *(rec Dwight Chapel, Yale University, 1975)* CRI ("American Masters" series) ▲ CD 701 [ADD]
Standage, Silas (org)
Stairway to Heaven, w. [cnd:Richard Marlow], Trinity College Choir Cambridge, Richard Pearce (org), Philip Rushforth (org) *(rec Trinity College Chapel, Cambridge)* Conifer Classics ▲ 75605-51521-2 [DDD]
Standage, Simon (va)
Telemann, G.P.:Con Va, w. S. Standage (cnd), Collegium Musicum 90 *(rec Goldsmiths' College, Apr 24-26, 1995)* Chandos ("Chaconne" series) ▲ CHAN 0593
Standage, Simon (vn)—see also ORCHESTRAS & ENSEMBLES Salomon String Quartet
Bach, J.S.:Con Fl, Vn & Hpd, w. L. Beznosiuk (fl), T. Pinnock (hpd), T. Pinnock (cnd), English Concert Archiv ▲ 413731-2 [DDD]
Bach, J.S.:Cons Vn (comp), w. S. Standage (cnd), Collegium Musicum 90 Chandos ("Chaconne" series) ▲ CHAN 0594
Bach, J.S.:Con Vn & Ob, w. D. Reichenberg (ob), T. Pinnock (cnd), English Concert Archiv ▲ 413731-2 [DDD]
Bach, J.S.:Con for 2 Vns, w. Micaela Comberti (vn), S. Standage (cnd), Collegium Musicum 90 Chandos ("Chaconne" series) ▲ CHAN 0594
Bach, J.S.:Con for 3 Vns, w. Micaela Comberti (vn), Miles Golding (vn), S. Standage (cnd), Collegium Musicum 90 Chandos ("Chaconne" series) ▲ CHAN 0594
Guillemain, L.-G.:Son Vn, w. L. U. Mortensen (hpd) Chandos ("Chaconne" series) ▲ CHAN 0531 [DDD]
Haydn, J.:Con 1 Vn, w. T. Pinnock (cnd), English CO Archiv ▲ 427316-2 [DDD]
Haydn, J.:Con 3 Vn, w. T. Pinnock (cnd), English Concert Archiv ▲ 427316-2 [DDD]
Haydn, J.:Con 4 Vn, w. T. Pinnock (cnd), English Concert Archiv ▲ 427316-2 [DDD]
Leclair, J.-M.:Cons Vn, Op. 7, w. S. Standage (cnd), Collegium Musicum 90—No. 1 Chandos ("Early Music" series) ▲ CHAN 0589 [DDD]
Leclair, J.-M.:Cons Vn, Op. 7, w. S. Standage (cnd), Collegium Musicum 90—Nos. 2 in D & 5 in a Chandos ("Chaconne" series) ▲ CHAN 0551 [DDD]
Leclair, J.-M.:Cons Vn, Op. 10, w. S. Standage (cnd), Collegium Musicum 90—Nos. 1 in B♭ & 5 in e Chandos ("Chaconne" series) ▲ CHAN 0551 [DDD]
Leclair, J.-M.:Cons Vn, Op. 10, w. S. Standage (cnd), Collegium Musicum 90—Nos. 3, 4 & 6 Chandos ("Early Music" series) ▲ CHAN 0589 [DDD]
Leclair, J.-M.:Sons Vn (Books 1-4), w. L. U. Mortensen (hpd)—Sonata in a, Op. 5/7; Sonata in A, Op. 9/4 Chandos ("Chaconne" series) ▲ CHAN 0531 [DDD]
Marcello, A.:Cons Vn, w. S. Standage (cnd), Collegium Musicum 90 Chandos ("Chaconne" series) ▲ CHAN 0563 [DDD]
Marcello, A.:Con Vn, w. S. Standage (cnd), Collegium Musicum 90 Chandos ("Chaconne" series) ▲ CHAN 0563 [DDD]
Mondonville, J.-J.C. de:Son Hpd, Op. 3/5, w. L. U. Mortensen (hpd) Chandos ("Chaconne" series) ▲ CHAN 0531 [DDD]
Mozart, W.A.:Adagio Vn, K.261, w. C. Hogwood (cnd), Academy of Ancient Music L'Oiseau-Lyre 2-▲ 433045-2 [DDD]
Mozart, W.A.:Cons Vn, w. C. Hogwood (cnd), Academy of Ancient Music—Nos. 1-5 L'Oiseau-Lyre 2-▲ 433045-2 [DDD]
Mozart, W.A.:Rondo Vn, K.373, w. C. Hogwood (cnd), Academy of Ancient Music L'Oiseau-Lyre 2-▲ 433045-2 [DDD]
Mysliveček, J.:Trio Fl, w. Andreas Kröper (fl), Thomas Fritzsch (vc) *(rec Evangelic Church, Korunní, Prague, Jan 1994)* Arta ▲ LC 4789 [DDD]
Pichl, V.:Divert Fl, w. Andreas Kröper (fl), Thomas Fritzsch (vc) *(rec Evangelic Church, Korunní, Prague, Jan 1994)* Arta ▲ LC 4789 [DDD]
Reicha, A.:Grand Trio Fl, w. Andreas Kröper (fl), Thomas Fritzsch (vc) *(rec Evangelic Church, Korunní, Prague, Jan 1994)* Arta ▲ LC 4789 [DDD]
Telemann, G.P.:Con Fl Vn in e, w. R. Brown (fl), S. Standage (cnd), Collegium Musicum 90 Chandos ("Chaconne" series) ▲ CHAN 0519 [DDD]
Telemann, G.P.:Cons for 2 Fls, w. R. Brown (fl), S. Peasgood (fl), J. Coe (vc), S. Standage (cnd), Collegium Musicum 90—(1) in D Chandos ("Chaconne" series) ▲ CHAN 0512 [DDD]
Telemann, G.P.:Cons in a & E Vn, w. S. Standage (cnd), Collegium Musicum 90 Chandos ("Chaconne" series) ▲ CHAN 0519 [DDD]
Telemann, G.P.:Cons in f# & G Vn, w. S. Standage (cnd), Collegium Musicum 90 Chandos ("Chaconne" series) ▲ CHAN 0512 [DDD]
Telemann, G.P.:Con in G for 2 Vns, w. M. Comberti (vn), S. Standage (cnd), Collegium Musicum 90 Chandos ("Chaconne" series) ▲ CHAN 0512 [DDD]
Telemann, G.P.:Duos, Collegium Musicum 90—Canonic Duos Chandos ("Chaconne" series) ▲ CHAN 0549 [DDD]
Vivaldi, A.:Cons Ob, w. D. Reichenberg (ob), T. Pinnock (cnd), English CO—R.548 Archiv ▲ 415674-2 [DDD]
Vivaldi, A.:Con Ob Vns, w. A. Robson (ob), M. Comberti (vn), S. Standage (cnd), Collegium Musicum 90 Chandos ("Chaconne" series) ▲ CHAN 0528 [DDD]
Vivaldi, A.:Cons Vn (misc), w. S. Standage (cnd), Collegium Musicum 90 *(rec April 1992)* Chandos ("Chaconne" series) ▲ CHAN 0530 [DDD]
Vivaldi, A.:Cons Vn, Op. 3/1-12, "L'estro armonico", w. T. Pinnock (cnd), English CO Archiv 2-▲ 423094-2 [DDD]
Vivaldi, A.:Cons Vn, Op. 4, "La stravaganza", w. T. Pinnock (cnd), English CO Archiv 2-▲ 429753-2 [DDD]
Vivaldi, A.:Cons Vn, Op. 8/1-4, "The Four Seasons", w. T. Pinnock (cnd), English CO Archiv ▲ 400045-2 [DDD]
Vivaldi, A.:Cons Vn, Op. 8/1-4, "The Four Seasons", w. T. Pinnock (cnd), English CO CRD ▲ 3325
Vivaldi, A.:Cons for 2 Vns, w. E. Wilcock (vn), T. Pinnock (cnd), English CO—R.516 Archiv ▲ 415674-2 [DDD]
Stanese, Liviu (va)—see ORCHESTRAS & ENSEMBLES Enesco String Quartet
Stang, Alexander (vn)
Mozart, W.A.:Con 3 Vn, w. L. Korkhin (cnd), Orch del'Arte Infinity Digital ▲ 64331 [DDD]
Ustvolskaya, G.:Octet Obs, w. Nicolay Neretin (ob), Piotr Tosenko (ob), Olga Ribaltchenko (vn), Valentin Lukin (vn), Nikolay Tkachenko (vn), Valerii Znamenskii (timp), Oleg Malov (pno), O. Malov (cnd) *(rec St. Petersburg Radio House, Oct. & Nov. 1994)* Megadisc ▲ 7865
Vivaldi, A.:Cons Ob Vn, w. C. Oshinakaev (ob), L. Korkhin (cnd), Renaissance CO—in B♭, RV.548 Infinity Digital ▲ QK 57244 [DDD]
Vivaldi, A.:Cons Vn (misc), w. L. Korkhin (cnd), Renaissance CO Infinity Digital ▲ QK 57217 [DDD]
Stangaard, Frode (pno)
Nielsen, T.:Paessagi, w. Erik Kaltoft (pno) Point ▲ PCD 5089
Stangler, Ferdinand (va)
Schmidt, F.:Qnt Cl, w. A. Prinz (cl), J. Demus (pno), A. Kamper (vn), W. Resel (vc) *(rec 1965)* Preiser ▲ 93383 [ADD]
Schmidt, F.:Qnt Pno, w. J. Demus (pno), A. Kamper (vn), W. Hink (vn), W. Resel (vc) *(rec 1965)* Preiser ▲ 93383 [ADD]
Stanic, Jelka (vn)
Vivaldi, A.:Cons Vn (misc), w. A. Janigro (cnd), Zagreb Solisti—RV.179 in C *(rec 1964)* Vanguard Classics ("The Bach Guild" series) ▲ OVC 2006 [ADD]
Stanick, Gerald (va)—see ORCHESTRAS & ENSEMBLES Fine Arts String Quartet
Stanick, Toni (vn)
Armanini, M.:Con Vn, w. J. Zoltek (cnd), Bohuslav Martinů PO Chroma ▲ CHR CD 10001 [DDD]

Stanis, Sharon (vn)—see ORCHESTRAS & ENSEMBLES Lafayette String Quartet
Stansell, John (org)
Mendelssohn & Co Classic Masters ▲ CMCD 1035
Stantchev, Ognian (va)
Mozart, W.A.:Adagio & Rondo Glass Armonica, w. A. Atanasov (org), L. Oshavkova (fl), C. T. Kasmetski (ob), N. Bespalov (vc) Divertimento ▲ DIV 31020 [DDD]
Stanzeleit, Susanne (vn)
Bantock, G.:Son 3 Vn, w. Gusztáv Fenyő (pno) *(rec St. Michael's Church, Highgate, London)* United ▲ CAL 88031 [DDD]
Dunhill, T.:Son Vn, w. Gusztáv Fenyő (pno) *(rec St. Michael's Church, Highgate, London)* United ▲ CAL 88031 [DDD]
Dvořák, A.:Ballad, w. Julian Jacobson (pno) Meridian ▲ MER 84274 [DDD]
Dvořák, A.:Mazurek, w. Julian Jacobson (pno) Meridian ▲ MER 84274 [DDD]
Dvořák, A.:Notturno, w. Julian Jacobson (pno) Meridian ▲ MER 84274 [DDD]
Dvořák, A.:Romance Vn, w. Julian Jacobson (pno) Meridian ▲ MER 84274 [DDD]
Dvořák, A.:Romantic Pieces, Op. 75, w. Julian Jacobson (pno) Meridian ▲ MER 84281 [DDD]
Dvořák, A.:Rondo, w. Julian Jacobson (pno) Meridian ▲ MER 84281 [DDD]
Dvořák, A.:Slavonic Dances (sels), w. Julian Jacobson (pno) Meridian ▲ MER 84281 [DDD]
Dvořák, A.:Son Vn, w. Julian Jacobson (pno) Meridian ▲ MER 84274 [DDD]
Dvořák, A.:Sonatina Vn, w. Julian Jacobson (pno) Meridian ▲ MER 84281 [DDD]
Dvořák, A.:Zigeunermelodien, Op. 55, w. Julian Jacobson (pno)—No. 4 [Songs My Mother Taught Me] Meridian ▲ MER 84281 [DDD]
Stanford, C.V.:Son 1 Vn, w. Gusztáv Fenyő (pno) *(rec St. Michael's Church, Highgate, London)* United ▲ CAL 88031 [DDD]
Staples, Sheryl (vn)
Romances et Méditations, w. Kurt Leuders (org), John Novacek (pno) Arkay ▲ ARK 6097
Rorem, N.:The Santa Fe Songs, w. Kurt Ollman (bar), Heiichiro Ohyama (va), Peter Rejto (vc), Lydia Artymiw (pno) *(rec live, Tucson Chamber Music Festival, Mar 12, 1995)* Arizona Friends of Chamber Music ▲ 1995 [DDD]
Starck, Claude (vc)
Chopin, F.:Son Vc, w. R. Requejo (pno) Claves ▲ CD 703
Saint-Saëns, C.:Con 1 Vc, w. P.-L. Graf (cnd), English CO *(rec EMI Studio London, 1975)* Claves ▲ CD 50501 [ADD]
Stamitz, C.:Con 1 Vc, w. P. Angerer (cnd), Southwest German CO Pforzheim *(rec Pforzheim, 1981)* Claves ("Favor Collection" series) ▲ CLF 8105 [ADD]
Stamitz, C.:Con 2 Vc, w. P. Angerer (cnd), Southwest German CO Pforzheim *(rec Pforzheim, 1981)* Claves ("Favor Collection" series) ▲ CLF 8105 [ADD]
Stamitz, C.:Con 3 Vc, w. P. Angerer (cnd), Southwest German CO Pforzheim *(rec Pforzheim, 1981)* Claves ("Favor Collection" series) ▲ CLF 8105 [ADD]
Vivaldi, A.:Sons Vc, w. I. Ahlgrimm (hpd), M. Frey (vc)—Op. 14/1-5; Son in a, RV.44; Sons in B♭, E♭ & g Tudor 2-▲ 709 [ADD]
Starin, Stefani (alt fl)
Pugliese, J.:Freeze, w. Dean Drummond (zmz), Dominic Donato (zmz), James Pugliese (Yamaha DX711) *(rec New York City, May 29, 1992)* Mode ▲ MODE 33
Starin, Stefani (fl)
Jenkins, L.:Dream of Dreams of Home, w. T. Buckner (bar), L. Jenkins (va) Lovely Music ▲ LCD 3022 [DDD]
Starin, Stefani (fl/khaen)
Lockwood, A.:The Angel of Repose, w. T. Buckner (bar) Lovely Music ▲ LCD 3022 [DDD]
Starker, János (vc)
Bach, C.P.E.:Con Vc, H.439, w. Santa Fe Festival Orch Delos ▲ DE 3197 [DDD]
Bach, J.S.:Sons Vl, BWV 1027-1029, w. G. Sébok (hpd)—BWV 1027 & 1028 Mercury Living Presence 2-▲ 432756-2 [ADD]
Bach, J.S.:Suites Vc, BWV 1007-1012 Mercury Living Presence 2-▲ 432756-2 [ADD]
Baker, D.:Singers of Songs/Weavers of Dreams, w. George Gaber (perc) *(rec Indiana Univ Opera House, Bloomington, 1980)* Laurel ▲ LR 817
Baker, D.:Son Vc, w. Alain Planès (pno) *(rec Indiana Univ Opera House, Bloomington, 1980)* Laurel ▲ LR 817
Bartók, B.:Con Va, w. L. Slatkin (cnd), St. Louis SO RCA Red Seal ▲ 60717-2-RC [DDD] ■ 60717-4-RC (CrO2)
Bartók, B.:Rhap 1 Vc, w. Gyorgy Sebok (pno) Mercury Living Presence ▲ 434358-2
Beethoven, L. van:Con Vn, Vc & Pno, "Triple Con", w. H. Szeryng (pno), L. Grychtolowna (pno), H. Dressel (cnd), Folkwang CO Philips ("Duo" series) 2-▲ 442580-2
Boccherini, L.:Con Vc, G.480, w. Santa Fe Festival Orch Delos ▲ DE 3197 [DDD]
Bottermund, H.:Vars (many) [his own arr. of selected vars.] Delos ▲ DCD 1015
Brahms, J.:Con Vn & Vc, "Double Con", w. E. Verhey (vn), A. Joó (cnd), Amsterdam PO Erasmus ▲ WVH 034 [DDD]
Brahms, J.:Con Vn & Vc, "Double Con", w. Henryk Szeryng (vn), B. Haitink (cnd), Royal Concertgebouw Orch Philips ("Solo" series) ▲ 446194-2
Brahms, J.:Son 1 Vc, w. R. Buchbinder (pno) RCA Red Seal ▲ 09026-61562-2
Brahms, J.:Son 1 Vc, w. Gyorgy Sebok (pno) Mercury Living Presence ▲ 434377-2
Brahms, J.:Son 2 Vc, w. Gyorgy Sebok (pno) Mercury Living Presence ▲ 434377-2
Brahms, J.:Son in D Vc, w. S. Neriki (pno) RCA Red Seal ▲ 09026-60598-2 [DDD]
Brahms, J.:Trio 1 Pno, w. J. Katchen (pno), J. Suk (vn) London ▲ 421152-2 [ADD]
Brahms, J.:Trio 2 Pno, w. J. Katchen (pno), J. Suk (vn) London ▲ 421152-2 [ADD]
Bruch, M.:Kol Nidrei, w. A. Dorati (cnd), London SO Mercury Living Presence ▲ 432001-2 [ADD]
Chopin, F.:Intro & Polonaise, "Polonaise brilliante", w. Gyorgy Sebok (pno) Mercury Living Presence ▲ 434358-2
Chopin, F.:Son Vc, w. Gyorgy Sebok (pno) Mercury Living Presence ▲ 434358-2
Couperin, F.:Pièces en Concert, w. Santa Fe Festival Orch [trans. Paul Bazelaire] Delos ▲ DE 3197 [DDD]
Debussy, C.:Son Vc, w. Gyorgy Sebok (pno) Mercury Living Presence ▲ 434358-2
Diamond, D.:Kaddish, w. G. Schwarz (cnd), Seattle SO Delos ▲ DE 3103 [DDD]
Dohnányi, E. von:Konzertstück, w. G. Schwarz (cnd), Seattle SO Delos ▲ DE 3095 [DDD]
Dvořák, A.:Con Vc, w. A. Dorati (cnd), London SO Mercury Living Presence ▲ 432001-2 [ADD]
Dvořák, A.:Con Vc, w. L. Slatkin (cnd), St. Louis SO RCA Red Seal ▲ 60717-2-RC [DDD] ■ 60717-4-RC (CrO2)
Haydn, J.:Con 1 Vc, w. G. Schwarz (cnd), Scottish CO Delos ▲ DCD 3062
Haydn, J.:Con 2 Vc, w. G. Schwarz (cnd), Scottish CO Delos ▲ DE 3063 [DDD]
Hindemith, P.:Con Vc, w. D. R. Davies (cnd), Bamberg SO *(rec Sinfonie an der Regnitz, Bamberg, July 19-21, 1994)* RCA Red Seal ▲ 09026-68027-2 [DDD]
Janos Starker Plays, w. Gyorgy Sebok (pno) *(rec Apr. 16 & 17, 1963 - June)* Mercury Living Presence ▲ 434344-2
Janson, J.-B.-A.:Cons Vc, w. Santa Fe Festival Orch—Concerto in D Delos ▲ DE 3197 [DDD]
Kodály, Z.:Duo Vn & Vc, w. J. Gingold (vn) Delos ▲ DCD 1015
Kodály, Z.:Son Vc, Op. 8 Delos ▲ DCD 1015
Lalo, E.:Con Vc, w. S. Skrowaczewski (cnd), London SO Mercury Living Presence ▲ 432010-2 [ADD]
Martinů, B.:Sons Vc, w. R. Firkusny (pno) RCA Red Seal ▲ 09026-61220-2
Martinů, B.:Vars on a Theme by Rossini, w. Gyorgy Sebok (pno) Mercury Living Presence ▲ 434358-2
Mendelssohn, F.:Son 2 Vc, w. Gyorgy Sebok (pno) Mercury Living Presence ▲ 434377-2
Mendelssohn, F.:Vars concertantes, w. Gyorgy Sebok (pno) Mercury Living Presence ▲ 434358-2
Mennin, P.:Con Vc, w. J. Mester (cnd), Louisville Orch *(rec 1969)* Albany ("First Edition Encores" series) ▲ TROY 044-2 [AAD]
Popper, D.:Vc & Pno Music, w. S. Neriki (pno)—Papillon; Gnomentanz; Wiegenlied; Elfentanz; Spinning Song; Tarantelle; & 14 others Delos ▲ DCD 3065 [DDD]
Rachmaninoff, S.:Son Vc, w. S. Neriki (pno) RCA Red Seal ▲ 09026-60598-2 [DDD]
Saint-Saëns, C.:Con 1 Vc, w. A. Dorati (cnd), London SO Mercury Living Presence ▲ 432010-2 [ADD]

▲ = CD ♦ = Enhanced CD Δ = MD ■ = Cassette Tape □ = DCC

Starker, János (vc) (cont.)

Schumann, R.:Adagio & Allegro Hn, w. R. Buchbinder (pno)—No. 1 in e RCA Red Seal ▲ 09026-61562-2

Schumann, R.:Con Vc, w. D. R. Davies (cnd), Bamberg SO *(rec Sinfonie an der Regnitz, Bamberg, July 19–21, 1994)* RCA Red Seal ▲ 09026-68027-2 [DDD]

Schumann, R.:Con Vc, w. S. Skrowaczewski (cnd), London SO Mercury Living Presence ▲ 432010-2 [ADD]

Schumann, R.:Fantasiestücke Cl, w. S. Neriki (pno) [cello-piano trans.] RCA Red Seal ▲ 09026-60598-2 [DDD]

Starer, R.:Con Vc, w. L. Botstein (cnd), Boston Pro Arte CO *(rec Feb. 17, 1991)* CRI ▲ CD 618 [DDD]

Starker Encore Album Denon ▲ CO 8117 [DDD]

Strauss, R.:Don Quixote, w. L. Slatkin (cnd), Bavarian RSO RCA Red Seal ▲ 09026-60561-2 [DDD]

Villa-Lobos, H.:Fant Vc, w. E. de Carvalho (cnd), Paraiba SO Delos ▲ DE 1017 [DDD]

Virtuoso Music for Cello, w. Starker, Janos (vc) Denon ▲ CO 8118 [DDD]

Vivaldi, A.:Con for 2 Vcs, w. Parisot (vc), E. de Carvalho (cnd), Paraiba SO—Finale Delos ▲ DE 1018 [DDD]

Vivaldi, A.:Cons Vn (misc), w. Santa Fe Festival Orch—in D, RV.230 [trans. for vc] Delos ▲ DE 3197 [DDD]

Weiner, L.:Hungarian Wedding Dance, w. Gyorgy Sebok (pno) Mercury Living Presence ▲ 434358-2

Starkman, Jane (vn)

Hovhaness, A.:Sextet Rcr, w. J. Tyson (rcr), K. Shaw (vn), J. Cosart (va), A. Robbins (vc), F. Conover Fitch (hpd) Titanic ▲ Ti 169 [DDD]

Something for Recorder & Strings, w. John Tyson (rcr), Frances Conover Fitch (hpd), Katheryn Shaw (vn), Jann Cosart (va), Alice Robbins (vc), Tom Coleman (db) Titanic ▲ Ti 169 [DDD]

Starkman, Naum (pno)

Beethoven, L. van:Con 5 Pno, "Emperor", w. M. Gorenstein (cnd), Russian SO *(rec Moscow Conservatory Great Hall, May & June, 1995)* PopeMusic ▲ PM 10042 [DDD]

Beethoven, L. van:Son 14 Pno, "Moonlight Son" *(rec Moscow Conservatory Great Hall, May & June, 1995)* PopeMusic ▲ PM 10042 [DDD]

Starks, T. (syn)

Copland, A.:Appalachian Spring Pro Arte ▲ CDS 3436 [DDD]

Copland, A.:Fanfare for the Common Man Pro Arte ▲ CDS 3436 [DDD]

Copland, A.:Midday Thoughts Pro Arte ▲ CDS 3436 [DDD]

Copland, A.:Our Town Pno Pro Arte ▲ CDS 3436 [DDD]

Copland, A.:Proclamation Pro Arte ▲ CDS 3436 [DDD]

Copland, A.:The Tender Land (suite) Pro Arte ▲ CDS 3436 [DDD]

Starobin, David (gtr)—see also ORCHESTRAS & ENSEMBLES Boehm Quintet members, Contemporary Chamber Ensemble

Copper, L.:Gtr Music—Caprice sur l'air espagnol, Op. 13; La romanesca *(rec Nov. 1992)* GHA ▲ GHA 126.022

Crumb, G.:Quest, w. Speculum Musicae Bridge ▲ 9069

Giuliani, M.:Grand Ov Bridge ▲ BCD 9029 [DDD]

Giuliani, M.:Gtr Music—Grand Overture, Op. 61; Six Variations on an Original Theme, Op. 20; Variations on Cavatina "De calma oh ciel," Op. 101; 2 Preludes, Op. 83. Nos. 5 & 6; 8 sels. from Opp. 14 (Six Rondeaux progressives), 46 (Choix de mes Fleurs chéries) & 51 (Leçons progressives) [19th Cent gtr] Bridge ▲ BCD 9029 [DDD]

Giuliani, M.:Vars on an Original Theme Bridge ▲ BCD 9029 [DDD]

Giuliani, M.:Variazioni sulla Cavatina favorita, "De calma oh ciel" Bridge ▲ BCD 9029 [DDD]

Jemnitz, S.:Trio Gtr, Vn & Va, w. B. Hudson (vn), K. Kashkashian (va) Bridge ▲ BCD 9004 ■ BC5-7004

Kolb, B.:Looking for Claudio CRI ▲ CD 576 [ADD]

Kurtág, G.:The Little Predicament, w. S. Palma (pic), S. Taylor (trbn) Bridge ▲ BCD 9004 ■ BC5-7004

Machover, T.:Bug-Mudra, w. O. Fader (elec gtr), D. Kennedy (perc), T. Machover (elec) *(rec live, Tokyo)* Bridge ▲ BCD 9022 [DDD]

New Music with Guitar Bridge ▲ BRI 9009 [AAD]

New Music with Guitar, Vol. 4 Bridge ▲ BRI 9022 [DDD]

Regondi, G.:Etudes Bridge ▲ BCD 9039 [DDD]

Regondi, G.:Gtr Music—Introduction et Caprice; Rêvier *(rec Feb. & May, 1994)* Bridge ▲ BCD 9055 [DDD]

Regondi, G.:Intro et caprice *(rec Nov. 1992)* GHA ▲ GHA 126.022

Regondi, G.:Les Oiseaux, w. D. Rogers (conc) Bridge ▲ BCD 9039 [DDD]

Roxbury, R.:Songs of Walt Whitman, w. P. Mason (bar), S. Palma (fl) [E] Bridge ▲ BCD 9022 [DDD]

Ruders, P.:Etude & Ricercare *(rec MasterSound Astoria, June 1995)* Bridge ▲ BCD 9057 [DDD]

Ruders, P.:Psalmodies, w. D. Palma (cnd), Speculum Musicae Bridge ▲ BCD 9037 [DDD]

Saxton, R.:Night Dance Bridge ▲ BCD 9022 [DDD]

Searle, H.:2 Practical Cats, w. P. Mason (bar), S. Palma (fl), T. Eddy (vc) [E] Bridge ▲ BCD 9022 [DDD]

A Song from the East:Russian & Hungarian Music with Guitar Bridge ▲ BRI 9004 ■ BC5-7004

Sor, F.:Gtr Music—Menuet, Op. 11/12; Etude, Op. 6/9; Septième fantaisie et variations brillantes, Op. 30; Larghetto, Op. 35/3; Andantino, Op. 31/13; Souvenirs d'une soirée à Berlin, Op. 56 *(rec Nov. 1992)* GHA ▲ GHA 126.022

Sor, F.:Souvenir de Russie, w. O. Fader (gtr) Bridge ▲ BCD 9004 ■ BC5-7004

Starobin, M.:Chase Bridge ▲ BCD 9022 [DDD]

Sugár, R.:Hungarian Children's Songs Bridge ▲ BCD 9004 ■ BC5-7004

Ung, C.:Tall Wind, w. Joan Heller (sop), Keith Underwood (fl), Robert Atherholt (ob), Chris Finckel (vc), A. Weisberg (cnd) *(rec Vanguard Recording Studio, New York, 1982)* CRI ▲ CRI 710 [DDD/ADD]

Starobin, David (mand)

Rorem, N.:Hearing, w. R. Rees (sop), K. Wheeler (mez), M. Galloway (ten), R. Hilley (bar), R. Wagner (cl), J. Hamlin (tpt), D. Davidson (vn), K. Askew (va), J. Babich (db), P. Suits (pno), D. Druckman (perc), G. Smith (cnd) Premier ▲ PRCD 1035 [ADD]

Starodumov, Evgeni (gtr)

Khandoshkin, I.:Son 1 Vn Russian Compact Disc ▲ RCD 15008 [AAD]

Vyssolsky, M.T.:Vars on Russian folk song "The Spinner" Russian Compact Disc ▲ RCD 15008 [AAD]

Starreveld, Harrie (fl)—see also ORCHESTRAS & ENSEMBLES Het Trio

Bland, W.:Qt Fl, Cl, Vn & Pno, w. C. Neidich (cl), C. Macomber (vn), R. Eckhardt (pno) Bridge ▲ BCD 9013 [DDD]

Bland, W.:Warm Country Night, w. R. Eckhardt (pno) Bridge ▲ BCD 9013 [DDD]

Bruynèl, T.:Le jardin, w. Karin van der Poel (voc), Annelie de Man (hpd) Donemus ▲ NEAR 01 [DDD]

Kolb, B.:Extremes, w. T. Kooistra (vc) New World ▲ 80422-2 [DDD]

Yun, I.:Qt Fls, w. R. de Reede (fl), T. Roorda (fl), M. Takahashi (fl) Attacca ▲ BABEL 9056-3 [DDD]

Starreveld, Harrie (fl/pic)

Harvey, J.:Nataraja, w. René Eckhardt (pno) Bridge ▲ BCD 9031 [DDD]

Statkiewicz, Edward (vn)

Bacewicz, G.:Son 4 Vn & Pno, w. A. Utrecht (pno) Olympia ▲ OLY 392 [ADD]

Bergsma, W.:Con Vn, w. Z. Szostak (cnd), Polish Radio-TV SO *(rec 1969)* Vox Box ("The American Composers" series) 2-▲ CDX 5158

Statom, Brendan (db)

Gilles Apap & the Transylvanian Mountain Boys, w. Gilles Apap (vn), Jean-Marc Apap (va), Chris Judge (gtr) Sony Classical ▲ SK 62374

Stattleman, David (perc)—see ORCHESTRAS & ENSEMBLES Altramar Medieval Music Ensemble

Stauch, Markus (db)

Jochen Kowalski:Aria from Berlin's Operatic History, w. Jochen Kowalski (ct), C. Schornsheim (hpd), R. Alpermann (hpd), H. Friedrich (vc), Berlin CO [cnd:M. Pommer] Berlin Classics ▲ BER 1050 [DDD]

Staudigl, Freddy (tpt/pic)—see ORCHESTRAS & ENSEMBLES Brassissimo Vienna

Stav, A. (cl)—see ORCHESTRAS & ENSEMBLES Oslo Wind Ensemble

Stavicek, Jiri (bn)

Burkhard, W.:Serenade Fl, Op. 77, w. S. Gärtner (fl), W. Meienberg (cl), M. Gugel (hn), M. Paccagnella (hp), H. Schneeberger (vn), C. Schiller (va), B. Wyganth (db) *(rec between 1985 & 1989)* Jecklin-Disco ▲ JD 647-2 [ADD]

Stavrache, C. (hp)

Vivaldi, A.:Cons Diverse Instrs, w. G. Vicari (mand), C. de Filippis (mand), J. Wummer (fl), R. Morris (fl), W. Vacchiano (tpt), N. Prager (tpt), E. Brenner (b ob), A. Wurtzler (hp), J. Gorigliano (vn), L. Varga (vc), L. Bernstein (cnd), New York PO—in C, RV.558 *(rec Dec. 15, 1958)* Sony Classical ("Leonard Bernstein:The Royal Edition" series) ▲ SMK 47642 [ADD]

Steblov, Alexei (vc)—see ORCHESTRAS & ENSEMBLES Talan String Quartet

Stec, Gregorz (ob)

Arnaud, L.:Well Tempered Oboist, w. M. Mitsumoto (cnd), Cracow RSO *(rec Krakow, Poland, Sept. 20–22, 1993)* Cambria ▲ CMB 1074 [DDD]

Steck, William (vn)

Adler, S.:Close Encounters, w. Y. Caruthers (vc) Gasparo ▲ GS 297

Adler, S.:Double Portrait, w. C. Lewis (pno) Gasparo ▲ GS 297

Adler, S.:Etudes Vn, "Meadowmountetudes" Gasparo ▲ GS 297

Adler, S.:Little Suite, w. C. Lewis (pno) Gasparo ▲ GS 297

Adler, S.:Music of, w. G. Peachey (pno), C. Lewis (pno), Y. Caruthers (vc)—Sons. 2–4; Etudes (4), "Meadowmountetudes"; Double Portrait; Little Suite; Close Encounters Gasparo ▲ GS 297 [DDD/ADD]

Adler, S.:Sons Vn, w. G. Peachey (pno)—Son. No. 2; Sons. Nos. 3 & 4 [w. C. Lewis] Gasparo ▲ GS 297

Adler, S.:Trio 1 Pno, w. Cary Lewis (pno), Dorothy Lewis (vc) Gasparo ▲ GS 298 [DDD/DAD]

Weber, C.M. von:Sons Vn, w. Lambert Orkis (pno) *(rec Glendale Baptist Church, Nashville, TN)* Gasparo ▲ GAS 263 [DDD]

Weber, C.M. von:Vars on a Norwegian Air Vn, w. Lambert Orkis (pno) *(rec Glendale Baptist Church, Nashville, TN)* Gasparo ▲ GAS 263 [DDD]

Steele-Perkins, Crispian (nat tpt)

The Art of James Bowman, w. James Bowman (ct), Downshire Players of London, King's Consort, Music's Re-creation Meridian ▲ MER 84332

Steele-Perkins, Crispian (tpt)

American Music Sampler, w. Jill Gomez (sop), Helen McQueen (E hn), Wayne Marshall (pno), City of London Sinfonia [cnd:R. Hickox] Virgin Classics 2-▲ CDC 59089

Copland, A.:Quiet City, w. H. McQueen (E hn), R. Hickox (cnd), City of London Sinfonia Virgin Classics ▲ 59520 [DDD]

The King's Trumpeter:Music for Trumpet & Organ from King's College Cambridge, w. Stephen Cleobury (org) Priory ▲ PRCD 189 [DDD]

Music for Trumpet and Orchestra, w. Tafelmusik [cnd:J. Lanon] *(rec Mar. 30–Apr. 1, 1993)* Sony Classical ("Vivarte" series) ▲ SK 53365 [DDD]

Scarlatti, A.:Cants, w. Deborah York (sop), James Bowman (ct), R. King (cnd), King's Consort—3 cants Hyperion ▲ CDA 66875

Six Trumpet Concertos, w. English CO [cnd:Anthony Halstead] IMP Classics ("Masters" series) ▲ PCD 821 [DDD]

Trumpet Voluntary, w. Stephen Burns (tpt), Gerald Gifford (org) ASV ("Quicksilva" series) ▲ ASV 6081 [ADD/DDD]

Vivaldi, A.:Cons Diverse Instrs, w. Joanna Graham (bn), Ruth McDowall (cl), David Rix (ct), Deborah Davis (fl), Duke Dobing (fl), Tim Caister (hn), Stephen Stirling (hn), Christopher Hooker (ob), Helen McQueen (ob), Michael Meekes (tpt), Nicholas Kraemer (hpd), N. Kraemer (cnd), London Sinfonietta—Cons. in F, RV.539; in C, RV.533; in D, RV.122; in C, RV.537; in C, RV.560; in F, RV.538; in G, RV.545 *(rec All Saints Church, East Finchley, Oct. 1994 & Jan. 1995)* Naxos ("Vivaldi Collection" series) ▲ 8.553204 [DDD]

Vivaldi, A.:Con for 2 Tpts, w. M. Meeks (tpt), N. Ward (vn), A. Watkinson (vn), A. Watkinson (cnd), City of London Sinfonia Virgin Classics ▲ CDZ 59651

Steenhoven, Karel van (rcr)—see ORCHESTRAS & ENSEMBLES Amsterdam Loeki Stardust Quartet

Steen-Nøkleberg, Einar (pno)

Beethoven, L. van:Sons Vc (comp), w. R. Metzmacher (vc) Brioso 2-▲ BR 100

Beethoven, L. van:Vars on "Ein Mädchen oder Weibchen" from Mozart's *Die Zauberflöte*, w. R. Metzmacher (vc)—No. 3 Brioso 2-▲ BR 100

Beethoven, L. van:Vars on "See, the Conquering Hero Comes" from Handel's *Judas Maccabaeus*, w. R. Metzmacher (vc)—No. 1 Brioso 2-▲ BR 100

Beethoven, L. van:Vars on "Bei Männern" from Mozart's *Die Zauberflöte*, w. R. Metzmacher (vc)—No. 2 Brioso 2-▲ BR 100

Borgstrom, H.:Hamlet, w. K. Andersen (cnd), Bergen PO NKF ▲ NKFCD 50026 [DDD]

Brahms, J.:Sons Vc (comp), w. R. Metzmacher (vc) Brioso ▲ BR 101

Brahms, J.:Songs, w. S. Carlsen (b-bar) Victoria ▲ VCD 19073

Grieg, E.:Peer Gynt, w. Stefan Schioll (cnd), Norwegian State Institute of Music Chamber Choir *(rec Lindeman Hall, Norwegian State Academy of Music, Oslo, Feb 12–14, 1994)* Naxos ▲ 8.553398 [DDD]

Grieg, E.:Pno Music (comp)—4 Album Leaves, Op. 28; Poetic Tone-pictures, Op. 3; Iceland [from Melodies of Norway, EG 108]; Pictures from Everyday-life [Humoresques, Op. 19]; Prayer [from Sigurd Jorsalfar, Op. 56/1]; Ballade, Op. 24 *(rec Lindeman Hall, Norwegian State Academy of Music, Oslo, Aug 6–9, 1993)* Naxos ▲ 8.550883 [DDD]

Grieg, E.:Pno Music (comp)—From Holberg's Time [from Suite in the Olden Style, Op. 40]; I Went to Bed So Late [from Melodies of Norway, EG 108]; 6 Norwegian Mountain Melodies, EG 108A; Morning Mood [from Peer Gynt Suite No. 1]; Slåtter, Op. 72 *(rec Lindeman Hall, Norwegian State Academy of Music, Oslo, Aug 10–12, 1993)* Naxos ▲ 8.550884 [DDD]

Grieg, E.:Pno Music (comp)—Agitato; Albumblade; The Entry of the Boyars [from Johan Halvorsen]; Norwegian Dances, Op. 35; Dance of the Mountain King's Daughter [from Peer Gynt]; Sigurd Jorsalfar [3 transcriptions for pno]; Waltz Caprices *(rec Lindeman Hall, Norwegian State Academy of Music, Oslo, Feb 12–14, 1994)* Naxos ▲ 8.553398 [DDD]

Grieg, E.:Pno Music (comp)—Piano Pieces, EG 105; Elegiac Melodies, Op. 34 [trans]; Norwegian Melodies Nos. 6 & 22; Melodies, Op. 53; Transcriptions of Songs, Op. 41; Nordic Melodies, Op. 63; Piano Pieces, EG 110–12 *(rec Lindeman Hall, Norwegian State Academy of Music, Oslo, Mar 7–9, 1994)* Naxos ▲ 8.553399 [DDD]

Grieg, E.:Pno Music (comp)—Canon à 4 voci, EG 179; At the Halfdan Kjerulf Statue, EG 167; Larvikspolka, EG 101; Norweigan Melodies Nos. 87 & 146; Transcriptions of Songs, Op. 52; 23 Small Pieces, EG 104; Con in b [frag] *(rec Lindeman Hall, Norwegian State Academy of Music, Oslo, Apr 12–14, 1994)* Naxos ▲ 8.553400 [DDD]

Grieg, E.:Pno Music (comp)—Improvisations on 2 Norwegian Folk-Songs; Ballad to St Olaf [from Melodies of Norway, EG 108]; 25 Norwegian Folk-Songs & Dances; The 1st Meeting, Op. 52/2; 19 Norwegian Folk-Songs *(rec Lindeman Hall, Norwegian State Academy of Music, Oslo, Aug 3–5, 1993)* Naxos ▲ 8.550882 [DDD]

Grieg, E.:Pno Music (comp)—Son in e, Op. 7; Funeral March in memory of Rikard Nordraak, EG 107; 4 Pno Pieces, Op. 1; The Sirens' Enticement [from Melodies of Norway, EG 108]; Stimmungen [Moods], Op. 73; I Love You, Op. 41/3; Humoresques, Op. 6 *(rec Lindeman Hall, Norwegian State Academy of Music, Oslo, July 31–Aug 2, 1993)* Naxos ▲ 8.550881 [DDD]

Grieg, E.:Son Pno *(rec Lindeman Hall, Norwegian State Academy of Music, Oslo, Apr 12–14, 1994)* Naxos ▲ 8.553400 [DDD]

Mahler, G.:Des Knaben Wunderhorn, w. Anne Gjevang (alt)—Um schlimme Kinder artig zu machen; Ablösung im Sommer; Zu Strassburg auf der Schanz'; Starke Einbildungskraft; Scheiden und Meiden; Verlorne Müh'; Irdische Leben; Rheinlegendchen; Lob des hohen Verstands *(rec Jar Church, Sept 1995)* Victoria ▲ VCD 19069

Mussorgsky, M.:Songs (misc), w. S. Carlsen (b-bar) Victoria ▲ VCD 19073

Pfitzner, H.:Songs, w. Anne Gjevang (alt)—Hast du von den Fischerkinden das alte Märchen vernommen?; Velassene Mägdlein; Denk es, o Seele; Ist der Himmel im Lenz so blau? *(rec Jar Church, Sept 1995)* Victoria ▲ VCD 19069

Schubert, Franz:Songs (misc), w. S. Carlsen (b-bar) Victoria ▲ VCD 19073

Schumann, R.:Songs, w. S. Carlsen (bs-bar) Victoria ▲ VCD 19073

Werfel, A.M.:Songs, w. Anne Gjevang (alt)—Stille Stadt; In meines Vaters Garten; Laue Sommernacht; Bei dir ist es Traut; Ich wandle unter Baumen *(rec Jar Curch, Sept 1995)* Victoria ▲ VCD 19069

Steen–Nøkleberg, Einar (pno) (cont.)
Zemlinsky, A. von:Songs, w. Anne Gjevang (alt)—3 Schwestern; Mädchen mit den verbundenen Augen; Lied der Jungfrau; Als ihr Geliebter schied; Und kehrt er einst Heim; Sie kam zum Schloss gegangen *(rec Jar Curch, Sept 1995)* Victoria ▲ VCD 19069

Steer, Michael (db)
Still, W.G.:Folk Suites, w. A. Still (fl), S. De Witt Smith (pno), New Zealand String Quartet—No. 1 Koch International Classics ▲ KIC 7192 [DDD]
Still, W.G.:Instrumental Music, w. A. Still (fl), S. De Witt Smith (pno), New Zealand String Quartet—Quit Dat Fool'nish; Summerland Koch International Classics ▲ KIC 7192 [DDD]
Still, W.G.:Music of, w. S. DeWitt Smith (pno), A. Still (fl), New Zealand String Quartet—Summerland; Quit dat Fool'nish; Pastorela; Folk Suite 1; Suite for Violin & Piano [Movts. I & II]; Prelude for Flute, String Qnt. & Piano *(rec May 1993)* Koch International Classics ▲ KIC 7192 [DDD]
Still, W.G.:Pastorela, w. S. De Witt Smith (pno) Koch International Classics ▲ KIC 7192 [DDD]
Still, W.G.:Preludes Fl, w. A. Still (fl), S. De Witt Smith (pno), New Zealand String Quartet Koch International Classics ▲ KIC 7192 [DDD]
Still, W.G.:Suite Vn, w. S. De Witt Smith (pno), New Zealand String Quartet Koch International Classics ▲ KIC 7192 [DDD]

Stefanato, Angelo (vn)
Vivaldi, A.:Cons for 4 Vns, w. Luigi Ferro (vn), Franco Gulli (vn), Edmondo Malanotte (vn), R. Fasano (cnd), Rome Virtuosi—in b, Op. 3/10 *(rec Opéra de Rome, July & August, 1959)* EMI Classics ▲ CDK 65338 [ADD]

Stefano, Dario de (vc)—see ORCHESTRAS & ENSEMBLES Paganini String Quartet

Stefanski, Andrzej (pno)
Szymanowski, K.:Masques *(rec Warsaw, 1968)* Polskie Nagrania ▲ PLN 066 [ADD]
Szymanowski, K.:Son 2 Pno *(rec Warsaw, 1968)* Polskie Nagrania ▲ PLN 066 [ADD]

Stefanski, Ludwik (pno)
Chopin, F.:Polonaises, w. Halina Czerny–Stefanska (pno)—Youthful Polonaises [in g, B, A, g#, B♭ & G♭]; Polonaises, Op. 71 [in d, B♭ & f] *(rec Warsaw, 1960)* Polskie Nagrania ▲ PNCD 306 A
Chopin, F.:Rondos Pno & 4–Hands, w. Halina Czerny–Stefanska (pno) *(rec Warsaw, 1960)* Polskie Nagrania ▲ PNCD 310

Stefek, Miroslav (hn)
Mozart, W.A.:Con Hn, K.447, w. K. Ančerl (cnd), Czech PO *(rec 1952–1966)* Supraphon ▲ CD 111935 [AAD]
Mozart, W.A.:Sinf concertante Ob, K.Anh.9, w. Frantisek Hanták (ob), Milos Kopecky (cl), Karel Vacek (bn), *(orch unknown)* Supraphon ▲ SUP 3053

Stegall, G. (pno)
Jongen, J.:Pno Music—Deux Pièces [Clair de lune; Soleil à midi], Op. 33; Sarabande triste, Op. 58; Seven selections from Treize (13) Préludes, Op. 69 [Angoisse; Giovinezza; Papillons noirs; Nostalgique; Appassionata; Pour danser; Air du fêtes]; Suite en forme de sonate, Op. 60 Klavier ▲ KCD 11032 [DDD]

Stegenga, Herre–Jan (vc)
Berens, H.:Trio Strs, w. J.–J. Kantarow (vn), V. Mendelssohn (va) Erasmus ▲ WVH 017 [DDD]
Brahms, J.:Qnt Cl, w. W. Boeykens (cl), J.–J. Kantarow (vn), A. Czifra (vn), V. Mendelssohn (va) Erasmus ▲ WVH 017 [DDD]
Roussel, A.:Chamber Music, w. Paul Verhey (fl/pic), Frank van den Brink (cl), Hans Roerade (ob), Jos de Lange (bn), Jet Röling (pno), Schoenberg String Quartet—Trio for Fl, Va & Vc, Op. 40; Qt for Strs, Op. 45; Andante & Scherzo for Fl & Pno, Op. 51; Pipe for Pic & Pno; Trio for Strs, Op. 58; Music from Elpenor for Fl & Str Qt, Op. 59; Andante from an unfinished Ww Trio for Ob, Cl & Bn Olympia ▲ OLY 460 [DDD]

Stehli–Altwegg, G. (cembalo)
Haller, H.:Inventions (6), w. W. Zumsteg (fl) Grammont ▲ CTSP 10–2 [ADD]

Steigerwalt, Gary (pno)
Muller & Steigerwalt, w. Dana Muller (pno) *(rec Aug.–Sept. 1991)* Centaur ▲ CRC 2127 [DDD]
Piston, W.:Concertino Pno, w. R. Capp (cnd), New York Philharmonia Virtuosi *(rec 1976)* Vox Box ("The American Composers" series) 2–▲ CDX 5158
Schubert, Franz:Pieces Pno, D.946 Centaur ▲ CRC 2199
Schubert, Franz:Son Pno, D.850 Centaur ▲ CRC 2199

Stein, Alexandre (vc)
Boccherini, L.:Son 7 Vc & Hp, w. Françoise Stein (hp) *(rec Neumünster Church, Zurich, Switzerland, May 12–14, 1982)* Doron ▲ DRC 3025 [ADD]
Duport, J.–L.:Nocturne concertant 3, w. Françoise Stein (hp) *(rec Neumünster Church, Zurich, Switzerland, May 12–14, 1982)* Doron ▲ DRC 3025 [ADD]
Spohr, L.:Son 5 Vn, w. Françoise Stein (hp) *(rec Neumünster Church, Zurich, Switzerland, May 12–14, 1982)* Doron ▲ DRC 3025 [ADD]

Stein, Cléna (db)
Boismortier, J.B. de:Sons, Op. 26, w. Kim Walker (bn), Darryl Nixon (hpd)—Sonata No. 4 Gallo ▲ CD 367 [ADD]
Boismortier, J.B. de:Sons, Op. 50, w. Kim Walker (bn), Darryl Nixon (hpd)—Sonata Nos. 1,2,4 & 5 Gallo ▲ CD 367 [ADD]

Stein, Edmund (vn)—see ORCHESTRAS & ENSEMBLES Thouvenel String Quartet

Stein, Françoise (hp)
Boccherini, L.:Son 7 Vc & Hp, w. Alexandre Stein (vc) *(rec Neumünster Church, Zurich, Switzerland, May 12–14, 1982)* Doron ▲ DRC 3025 [ADD]
Duport, J.–L.:Nocturne concertant 3, w. Alexandre Stein (vc) *(rec Neumünster Church, Zurich, Switzerland, May 12–14, 1982)* Doron ▲ DRC 3025 [ADD]
Spohr, L.:Son 5 Vn, w. Alexandre Stein (vc) *(rec Neumünster Church, Zurich, Switzerland, May 12–14, 1982)* Doron ▲ DRC 3025 [ADD]

Stein, Joan (pno)
Rosner, A.:Son 1 Vc, w. Maxine Neuman (vc) *(rec SUNY, Stony Brook)* Albany ▲ TROY 163 [DDD]

Stein, Leonard (pno)
Cage, J.:Music for..., w. Joan La Barbara (sop), William Winant (perc) *(rec Central Park Summerstage, New York City, July 23, 1992)* Music & Arts ▲ CD 875 [DDD]
Cage, J.:Songs, w. J. La Barbara (sop), W. Winant (perc)—A Flower (1950); Mirakus (1984); Eight Whiskus (1984); The Wonderful Widow of Eighteen Springs (1942); Nowth upon Nacht (1984); Sonnekus (1985); Forever and Sunsmell (1942); Solos for Voice [from Songbooks] Nos. 49, 52 & 67 (1970); Music for Two (by One) (1984) New Albion ▲ NA 035 [DDD]

Stein, Leonard (pno/perc)
Cage, J.:Four [6], w. Joan La Barbara (sop/perc), John Cage (voice/perc), William Winant (perc) *(rec Central Park Summerstage, New York City, July 23, 1992)* Music & Arts ▲ CD 875 [DDD]

Stein, Richard (pno)
Scarlatti, D.:Sons Kbd—14 selections Erasmus ▲ WVH 148

Steinbach, Falko (pno)
Bartók, B.:Son Pno *(rec 1990)* Ambitus ▲ 97862 [DDD]
Brahms, J.:Fants Pno, Op. 116 Ambitus ▲ 97862 [DDD]
Brahms, J.:Vars on a Theme of Robert Schumann, Op. 9 Ambitus ▲ 97882 [DDD]
Eisler, H.:Son 3 Pno *(rec 1990)* Ambitus ▲ 97862 [DDD]
Schumann, R.:Romances Pno Ambitus ▲ 97882 [DDD]
Schumann, R.:Son 2 Pno Ambitus ▲ 97882 [DDD]

Steinberg, Julie (pno)
Cage, J.:Nocturne, w. D. Abel (vn) New Albion ▲ NA 036 [DDD]
Cage, J.:Pno Music Music & Arts ▲ MUA CD 937
Dresher, P.:Double Ikat, w. D. Abel (vn), W. Winant (perc) *(rec 1992)* New Albion ▲ NA 053
Harrison, L.:May Rain, w. John Duykers (ten), William Winant (perc) New Albion ▲ NA 055
Hovhaness, A.:Invocations to Vahakn, w. W. Winant (perc) New Albion ▲ NA 036 [DDD]

Steinberg, Julie (pno/prepared pno/hmc/bass dr/vn/dog whistle)
Curran, A.:Schtyx, w. D. Abel (vn/hi–hat/dog whistle), W. Winant (perc/vn/dog whistle) CRI ▲ CD 668 [DDD]

Steinberg, Mark (vn)—see also ORCHESTRAS & ENSEMBLES Continuum Chamber Ensemble
Moss, L.:Songs of the Earth, w. Nan Hughes (mez), David Krakauer (cl), Joel Sachs (pno), Cheryl Seltzer (pno) Capstone ▲ CPS 8619
Viñao, E.:Trio Pno, w. Ju–Ying Song (pno), Maria Kitsopoulos (vc) *(rec Academy of Arts & Letters, New York, Nov 14–15, 1995)* Pro Piano ("Pianist's Perspective Recording" series) ▲ PPR 224511

Steinbrecher, J. (bn)
Lachner, F.P.:Octet, w. S. Meyer (cl), N. Frisch (hn), Chalumeau Quintet Ambitus ▲ 97825 [DDD]

Steinbrecher, Karl (bn)
Lutoslawski, W.:Die Strohkette, w. Barbara Miller (sop), Oksana Sowiak (mez), Robert Dohn (fl), Willy Schnell (ob), Martin Klose (cl), Hartmut Stute (cl), A. Grüber (cnd) Vox Box 2–▲ CDX 5133

Steiner, Karl (pno)
Music of the 2nd Generation of the 2nd Viennese School Centaur 2–▲ CRC 2241/42 [ADD]

Steinerová, Bozena (pno)
Tchaikovsky, P.:Con 1 Pno, w. O. Trhlík (cnd), Prague RSO Panton ▲ PAN 811208

Steinfatt, Rudiger (pno)
Henselt, A. von:Pno Music—Ballad in B♭, Op. 31; Introduction & Variations on a Theme by Donizetti, Op. 1; Grande Valse, "L'aurore boréale," Op. 30; Rondo serioso; Valse mélancolique, Op. 36; Scherzo in b, Op. 9; Toccatina in c, Op. 25; Pensée fugitive, Op. 5; Four Impromptus (in c, Op. 7; in f, Op. 17; in b♭, Op. 34; in b, Op. 37) Koch Schwann ▲ CD 310 023 [ADD]

Steinhardt, Arnold (vn)—see also ORCHESTRAS & ENSEMBLES Guarneri String Quartet
Bauer, M.:Son Va, w. V. Eskin Northeastern ■ NR 222–C
Beach, A.M.C.:Compositions, w. Lincoln Mayorga (pno) Sheffield Lab ▲ SLS 10063
Boulanger, L.:Cortège, w. V. Eskin (pno) Northeastern ■ NR 222–C
Boulanger, L.:Nocturne, w. V. Eskin (pno) Northeastern ■ NR 222–C
Chaminade, C.:Romanza appassionata, w. V. Eskin (pno) Northeastern (Classical Arts) ■ NR 222–C
Chaminade, C.:Sérénade espagnole, w. V. Eskin (pno) Northeastern (Classical Arts) ■ NR 222–C
Dvořák, A.:Romantic Pieces, Op. 75, w. L. Mayorga (pno) Sheffield Lab ("Audiophile Reference" series) ▲ 10039–2
Dvořák, A.:Romantic Pieces, Op. 75, w. Lincoln Mayorga (pno) Sheffield Lab ▲ SLS 10039
Dvořák, A.:Sonatina Vn, w. L. Mayorga (pno) Sheffield Lab ("Audiophile Reference" series) ▲ 10039–2
Dvořák, A.:Sonatina Vn, w. L. Mayorga (pno) *(rec Culver City, CA, Nov 30– Dec 1, 1985)* Sheffield Lab ("Salon" series) ▲ SLS 501
Dvořák, A.:Sonatina Vn, w. Lincoln Mayorga (pno) Sheffield Lab ▲ SLS 10039
Grieg, E.:Son 3 Vn, w. Lincoln Mayorga (pno) Sheffield Lab ▲ SLS 10063
Grieg, E.:Son 3 Vn, w. L. Mayorga (pno) *(rec Culver City, CA, Nov 30– Dec 1, 1985)* Sheffield Lab ("Salon" series) ▲ SLS 501
Herbert, V.:A la Valse, w. Lincoln Mayorga (pno) Sheffield Lab ▲ SLS 10063
Herbert, V.:A la Valse, w. L. Mayorga (pno) *(rec Culver City, CA, Nov 30– Dec 1, 1985)* Sheffield Lab ("Salon" series) ▲ SLS 501
Kreisler, F.:Apple Blossoms (sels), w. Lincoln Mayorga (pno)—Who Can Tell?; Miniature Viennese March; Syncopation; Cavatina; Hungarian Dance Sheffield Lab ▲ SLS 10063
Kreisler, F.:Vn Pieces, w. L. Mayorga (pno)—Miniature Viennese March; Syncopation; Who can tell? [all from the operetta Apple Blossoms]; Cavatina; Hungarian Dance in f *(rec Culver City, CA, Nov 30– Dec 1, 1985)* Sheffield Lab ("Salon" series) ▲ SLS 501
Strauss, R.:Son Vn, w. L. Mayorga (pno) Sheffield Lab ("Audiophile Reference" series) ▲ 10039–2
Strauss, R.:Son Vn, w. Lincoln Mayorga (pno) Sheffield Lab ▲ SLS 10039
Tailleferre, G.:Son 1 Vn, w. V. Eskin (pno) Northeastern ■ NR 222–C

Steinhauser, Severin (cym)
Hauser, F.:Die Welle, w. Martin André Grütter (cym/tamtam), Roli Fischer (cym), Barbara Frey (cym), Cyril Lützelschwab (cym), Lukas Rohner (cym), Hans Ulrich (cym), Ruud Wiener (cym), Michael Erni (timp), Fran Lorkovic (timp), F. Hauser (cnd) *(rec Studio DRS, Basel, Switzerland, Nov. 6, 1988)* Hat Hut ▲ hat ART CD 6017 [ADD]

Steinkraus, Helmut (fl)
Bach, J.S.:Cant 204, w. Elisabeth Speiser (sop), Willi Schnell (ob), Dietmar Keller (ob), Susanne Lautenbacher (vn), R. Ewerhart (cnd), Württemberg CO *(rec 1966)* Vox Box 3–▲ CD3X 3039
Bach, J.S.:Cant 209, w. Elisabeth Speiser (sop), Martin Galling (hpd), R. Ewerhart (cnd), Württemberg CO *(rec 1966)* Vox Box 3–▲ CD3X 3039

Steinmann, Conrad (rcr)
Baroque Music for Recorder, w. Monica Huggett (baroque vn), Hopkinson Smith (lt/thb/gtr), Jordi Savall (vl), Pere Ros (vl), Claude Flagel (h–g), Johann Sonnleitner (hpd) Claves ▲ CD 508103 [ADD]
Sammartini, G.:Cons Rcr, w. C. Banchini (cnd), Ensemble 415—in F Musique d'Abord ▲ HMA 1901245 [DDD]
Vivaldi, A.:Cons Flautino, w. H. Müller–Brühl (cnd), Capella Clementina [period instrs]—RV.444 & 445 *(rec Schloss Hohenems, Austria)* Claves ("Favor Collection" series) ▲ CLF 0804–9 [ADD]
Vivaldi, A.:Cons Fl, Op. 10, w. H. Müller–Brühl (cnd), Capella Clementina [period instrs]—No. 2 in g [La notte] *(rec Schloss Hohenems, Austria)* Claves ("Favor Collection" series) ▲ CLF 0804–9 [ADD]
Vivaldi, A.:Cons Rcr, w. H. Müller–Brühl (cnd), Capella Clementina [period instrs]—in c, RV.441 *(rec Schloss Hohenems, Austria)* Claves ("Favor Collection" series) ▲ CLF 0804–9 [ADD]

Steisner, Martin (perc)—see ORCHESTRAS & ENSEMBLES Kroumata Percussion Ensemble

Steljes, Cynthia (ob/E hn)—see ORCHESTRAS & ENSEMBLES Gelato Quartet

Stelzner, Rainer (pno)
Brahms, J.:Liebeslieder Waltzes SATB, w. M. Creed (pno), U. Gronostay (cnd), Berlin RIAS Chamber Choir [G] *(rec March 1984)* Koch Treasure ▲ 31616–2 [ADD]

Stenberg, Kathryn (vn)—see ORCHESTRAS & ENSEMBLES Stratos

Stengaard, Frode (org)
Nielsen, C.:Preludes Org, Op. 51—Nos. 11, 13, 14, 18, 21 & 27 Rondo Grammofon ▲ RCD 8335
Nielsen, C.:Songs, w. Lars Thodberg Bertelsen (bar)—I Drive Forth Through Joyful Radiance; O For a Thousand Voices; The Great White Flock We See; This Is the Day Which the Lord Has Made; I Will Love You, Who Are My Strength; Draw Me Towards You, Jesus; Deeply the Year Draws to a Close; Peace Be with You, One & All!; Be of Good Cheer! Once Again; Peace & Happiness; The Peace of God is More than Guardian Angels; If You Have Put Your Hand to the Plough of the Lord; The Lord Says Are You Weary; I Know a Little Heaven; When I Consider the Time & Hour; Christians, Open Your Eyes!; O Christianity!; Whichever Way You Go; Let the Heavens Resound; Undaunted, However My Fortune; Jesus, Let My Heart Receive; Our Lord is a Mighty King; Are You Down–Hearted, Dear Friend; Like Dew on Mown Fields; Strange to Say Rondo Grammofon ▲ RCD 8335
Nielsen, C.:Songs, w. Eva Hess Thaysen (sop), Mette Ejsing (alt), John Laursen (ten), Lars Thodberg Bertelsen (bar), Tove Lønskov (pno)—Little Helle; Sir Oluf's Song; Dance–Song; Dawn [all from the play Sir Oluf He Rides]; The Storm Wages over the Dark Waters; My Girl Is as Fair as Amber; The Day the Eagle was Ready to Fly; A Mother was Told at the Feast; The Thistle Crop Looks Promising; Once When Death was Awaited; So Bitter was My Heart; Like a Venturous Fleet at Anchor [all from the play The Mother]; The Sign & the Word of the Cross; Of All the Flowers that Grow on Earth; As the Golden Sun Breaks Through; There is a Path; It Is No Great Struggle; Daffodil, Why Are You Here? [all from Hymns & Sacred Songs]; The Sun Springs Out Like a Rose [from the play Cosmus]; The Great Master Comes; See My Fragile Web; Our Eyes May Rejoice; When Summer's Song is Sung; Earth in Whose Embrace [all from 20 Popular Melodies]; Of What are You Singing? [The Lark]; Teach Me, O Stars of Night [both from 4 Popular Melodies]; Italian Shepherd's Song; We Love You, Our Lofty North!; Vocalise; The Power that Gave Me My Little Song [all from Amor & the Poet]; May Song [Merrily, with Joyful Song!] Rondo Grammofon ▲ RCD 8329

Stengenga, Herre–Jan (vc)
Roussel, A.:Chamber Music, w. Paul Verhey (fl), Hans Roerade (ob), Herman Jeurissen (hn), Jean–Jacques Kantorow (vn), Jet Röling (pno) Olympia ▲ OLY 458 [DDD]

Stensgaard, Kai (mar)
Marimba Classic Danacord ▲ DACOCD 304 [ADD]
Tchaikovsky, P.:Album pour enfants [trans. for solo marimba]—Sweet dreams; Mazurka; The doll's burial; Waltz Danacord ▲ DACOCD 304 [DDD]

Stenske, David (vn)

Jacob, G.:Qnt Cl, w. Daniel Geeting (cl), Melissa Phelps-Beckstead (vn), Richard Rintoul (va), Joyce Geeting (vc) *(rec Memorial Chapel, Univ. of Redlands, Redlands, CA, Mar. 5, Apr. 30 & June 30)* PROdigital ▲ PRO 9226 [DDD]

Stenzl, Hans-Peter (pno)—see ORCHESTRAS & ENSEMBLES Stenzl Piano Duo

Stenzl, Volker (pno)—see also ORCHESTRAS & ENSEMBLES Stenzl Piano Duo

Brahms, J.:Hungarian Dances Pno 4-Hands, w. Hans Peter (pno)—Nos. 1-6 *(rec live)* Ars Musici ▲ AM 1130 [DDD]

Brahms, J.:Serenade 1 Orch, w. Hans Peter (pno) [arr J. Brahms for pno 4-hands] *(rec live)* Ars Musici ▲ AM 1130 [DDD]

Brahms, J.:Vars on a Theme of Robert Schumann, Op. 23, w. Hans Peter (pno) *(rec live)* Ars Musici ▲ AM 1130 [DDD]

Brahms, J.:Waltzes Pno, Op. 39, w. Hans Peter (pno)—No. 15 *(rec live)* Ars Musici ▲ AM 1130 [DDD]

Britten, H.:Introduction & Rondo alla burlesca & Mazurka elegiaca, w. Hans Peter (pno)—No. 1 *(rec Düsseldorf, Jan. 29 & Feb. 1, 1990)* Ars Musici ▲ AM 1088-2 [DDD]

Lutoslawski, W.:Vars on a Theme of Paganini for 2 Pnos, w. Hans Peter (pno) *(rec Düsseldorf, Jan. 29 & Feb. 1, 1990)* Ars Musici ▲ AM 1088-2 [DDD]

Ravel, M.:La Valse, w. Hans Peter (pno) *(rec Düsseldorf, Jan. 29 & Feb. 1, 1990)* Ars Musici ▲ AM 1088-2 [DDD]

Schubert, Franz:Fant Pno, D.940, w. H. Peter (pno) Ars Musici ▲ AM 1087-2

Schubert, Franz:Son Pno 4-Hands, D.812, w. H. Peter (pno) Ars Musici ▲ AM 1087-2

Stravinsky, I.:Con Pnos, w. Hans Peter (pno) *(rec Düsseldorf, Jan. 29 & Feb. 1, 1990)* Ars Musici ▲ AM 1088-2 [DDD]

Štepán, Pavel (pno)

Dvořák, A.:Qnt Pno, Op. 81, w. Smetana String Quartet *(rec 1966)* Testament ▲ SBT 1074

Kabalevsky, D.:Con 3 Pno, w. A. Klima (cnd), Prague RSO Sound ▲ 3437 [AAD]

Prokofiev, S.:Con 3 Pno, w. A. Klima (cnd), Prague SO Sound ▲ CD 3437

Saint-Saëns, C.:Carnival of the Animals, w. I. Hurnik (pno), M. Turnovsky (cnd), Prague SO Supraphon Collection ▲ 11 0646-2 [ADD]

Suk, J.:Episodes Supraphon ▲ SUP 0031 [ADD]

Suk, J.:Lullabies Supraphon ▲ SUP 0031 [ADD]

Suk, J.:Pno Music Supraphon ▲ SUP 0032

Suk, J.:Pno Music—Suite, Op. 21; Spring, Op. 22a; Summer Moods, Op. 22b; About Mother, Op. 28 Supraphon ▲ SUP 112233 [DDD]

Suk, J.:Qnt Pno, w. Suk String Quartet Supraphon (pn▲ SUP 111532 [DDD]

Suk, J.:Things Lived & Dreamt Supraphon ▲ SUP 0031 [ADD]

Stepansky, Alan (vc)

Barber, S.:Son Vc, w. Israela Margalit (pno) EMI Classics ("Anglo-American Chamber Music" series) ▲ CDC 55400

Copland, A.:Qt Pno, w. Israela Margalit (pno), Glenn Dicterow (vn), Rebecca Young (va) EMI Classics ("Anglo-American Chamber Music" series) ▲ CDC 55405

Korngold, E.W.:Trio Pno, w. Israela Margalit (pno), Glenn Dicterow (vn) EMI Classics ("Anglo-American Chamber Music" series) ▲ CDC 55401

Schumann, R.:Andante & Vars Hn, w. Thomas Hecht (pno), Sandra Shapiro (pno), Gerald Appleman (vc), L. William Kuyper (Fr hn) *(rec Performing Arts Ctr/Purchase College-State Univ of NY Recital Hall, May 8, 1995)* Elysium ▲ GRK 709 [DDD]

Stephens, Alison (mand)

Music for Mandolin, w. Sue Mossop (mand), Poppy Holden (sop), Richard Burnett (pno) Amon Ra ▲ CDSAR 53 [DDD]

Stephens, Patrick (pno)

Bizet, G.:Songs, w. V. Cole (ten)—J'aime l'amour!; Chanson d'avril; Absence; La chanson du fou [F] *(rec Apr. 8-10, 1993)* Delos ▲ DE 3131 [DDD]

Hahn, R.:Songs, w. V. Cole (ten)—Le rossignol des lilas; A Chloris; Si mes vers avaient des ailes; L'Heure exquise; Cantique; D'Une prison; Infidelité; Paysage; Le souvenir d'avoir chanté [F] *(rec Apr. 8-10, 1993)* Delos ▲ DE 3131 [DDD]

Massenet, J.:Songs, w. V. Cole (ten)—Ouvre tes yeux bleus; Elégie; Berceuse; Sonnet; Nuit d'espagne; Stances; Vous aimerez demain *(rec Apr. 8-10, 1993)* Delos ▲ DE 3131 [DDD]

Mysteries Beyond:Songs & Chants in Praise of Mary, w. [cnd:Dennis Keene], Voices of Ascension, V. Cole (ten), Kathleen Bride (hp), M. Kruczek (org) *(rec Apr. 17, 28-30, 1993)* Delos ▲ DE 3138 [DDD]

Vinson Cole, w. Vinson Cole (ten) Connoisseur Society ▲ CD 4184 [DDD]

Stephens, Suzanne (cl)

Stockhausen, K.:Tierkreis Cl, w. K. Pasveer (fl), M. Stockhausen (tpt/pno) Acanta ▲ CD 43201 [DDD]

Stephenson, Blake (cl)—see ORCHESTRAS & ENSEMBLES Essex Winds Woodwind Quintet

Stephenson, Michael (s sax)—see ORCHESTRAS & ENSEMBLES New Century Saxophone Quartet

Stephenson, William (pno)

Busoni, F.:Pno Music—Suite Campestre; 2 transcriptions of Chorale Preludes by Bach; Klavierstück, Op. 33Gb/4, Fant. in modo antico; Nach der Wendung, "Elegy No. 1"; Macchiote Modiovali; Sonatinas 4 & 6; Berceuse, "Elegy No. 7" Olympia ▲ OLY 461 [DDD]

Liszt, F.:Années de pèlerinage 1 Olympia ▲ OCD 265 [DDD]

Liszt, F.:Années de pèlerinage 2 Olympia ▲ OLY 277 [DDD]

Liszt, F.:Études d'exécution transcendante, S.139 Olympia ▲ OLY 277 [DDD]

Liszt, F.:Harmonies poétiques et religieuses—Funérailles Olympia ▲ OCD 265 [DDD]

Stepina, Agne (vc)—see ORCHESTRAS & ENSEMBLES Riga String Quartet

Stepner, Daniel (vn)—see ORCHESTRAS & ENSEMBLES Lydian String Quartet, Boston Museum Trio members, Boston Museum Trio

Sterczynski, Jerzy (pno)

Chopin, F.:Con 2 Pno, w. A. Natanek (cnd), New Polish PO *(rec Warsaw, 1994)* Selene ▲ CD 9405.21 [DDD]

Chopin, F.:Mazurkas, w. Aga Winska (sop)—Op. 6/1 & 4, Op. 7/1 & 3, Op. 24/1 & 2, Op. 33/2 & 3, Op. 50/1 & 2, Op. 67/1 & Op. 68/2 [all arr Viardot]; Op. 17/1 & 4 [arr Bordese] *(rec Rzeszow, June 28-30, 1995)* Selene ▲ CD 9504.27 [DDD]

Chopin, F.:Nocturnes—Op. 9/1 *(rec Rzeszow, June 28-30, 1995)* Selene ▲ CD 9504.27 [DDD]

Chopin, F.:Pno Music (misc)—Son, Op. 35; Var in E [Hexameron]; Vars in E; Vars brillantes, Op. 12; Allegretto; Galop Marquis; Bourrées in G & A; Cantabile; Contredanse; Fugue; Wiosna [Spring]; Largo; Moderato; Marche funèbre; Écossaises Nos. 1-3 *(rec Rzeszow & Warsaw, 1993 & 1989)* Selene ▲ CD 9401.17 [DDD]

Chopin, F.:Polonaises—Op. 26/1 & 2; Op. 40/1 & 2; Op. 44; Op. 53; Op. 61 *(rec Rzeszow, 1992)* Selene ▲ CD 9309.16 [DDD]

Chopin, F.:Polonaises *(rec Rzeszow, 1992)* Selene 2-▲ CD 9202.4-5 [DDD]

Chopin, F.:Preludes, Op. 28—Nos. 7 & 20 [2 versions] *(rec Rzeszow, June 28-30, 1995)* Selene ▲ CD 9504.27 [DDD]

Chopin, F.:Waltzes *(rec Rzeszow)* Selene ▲ CD 9305.12 [DDD]

Dobrzynski, I.F.:Con Pno, w. A. Natanek (cnd), New Polish PO *(rec Warsaw, 1994)* Selene ▲ CD 9405.21 [DDD]

Liszt, F.:Transcriptions & Paraphrases—Tchaikovsky:Polonaise [from Eugene Onegin] *(rec Rzeszow, Mar 7-8, 1993)* Selene ▲ CD 9308.15 [DDD]

Tchaikovsky, P.:Nutcracker Suite *(rec Rzeszow, Mar 7-8, 1993)* Selene ▲ CD 9308.15 [DDD]

Tchaikovsky, P.:Les Saisons *(rec Rzeszow, Mar 7-8, 1993)* Selene ▲ CD 9308.15 [DDD]

Sterling, Gene (perc)—see ORCHESTRAS & ENSEMBLES Just Strings Ensemble

Sterling, Victor (perc)—see ORCHESTRAS & ENSEMBLES New Generation

Sterman, A. (fl/sop sax)—see ORCHESTRAS & ENSEMBLES Philip Glass Ensemble

Sterman, Andrew (fl/pic/s sax/b cl)—see ORCHESTRAS & ENSEMBLES Philip Glass Ensemble

Stern, Isaac (vn)

Bach, C.P.E.:Trio Son Fl, H.586, w. J.-P. Rampal (fl), J. Ritter (hpd) CBS ▲ MK 37813 [DDD]

Bach, Joh. Christian:Trio Fl, Vn & Vc, w. J.-P. Rampal (fl), M. Rostropovich (vc) Sony Classical ▲ SK 44568 [DDD]

Stern, Isaac (vn) (cont.)

Bach, J.C.F:Son Fl, HW.VIII/1-2, w. J.-P. Rampal (fl), J. Ritter (hpd)—in C CBS ▲ MK 37813 [DDD]

Bach, J.S.:Con 1 Vn, London SO CBS ▲ MK 42258

Bach, J.S.:Con 1 Vn, w. I. Stern (cnd), London SO CBS ▲ MYK 38487 [ADD] ■ MYT 38487

Bach, J.S.:Con 1 Vn, *(orch unknown)* Sony Classical ▲ SMK 66471

Bach, J.S.:Con 1 Vn, w. P. Casals (cnd), Prades Festival Orch *(rec June 16, 1950)* Sony Classical ("The Casals Edition" series) ▲ SMK 58982 [ADD]

Bach, J.S.:Con 2 Vn, w. A. Schneider (cnd), English CO CBS ▲ MYK 38487 [ADD] ■ MYT 38487

Bach, J.S.:Con 2 Vn, w. A. Schneider (cnd), English CO CBS ▲ MK 42258

Bach, J.S.:Con 2 Vn, *(orch unknown)* Sony Classical ▲ SMK 66471

Bach, J.S.:Con Vn & Ob, w. H. Gomberg (ob), L. Bernstein (cnd), New York PO CBS ▲ MK 42258

Bach, J.S.:Con Vn & Ob, w. H. Gomberg (ob), L. Bernstein (cnd), New York PO CBS ■ MGT 39798

Bach, J.S.:Con Vn & Ob, w. Harold Gomberg (ob), *(orch unknown)* Sony Classical ▲ SMK 66471

Bach, J.S.:Con Vn & Ob, w. M. Tabuteau (ob), P. Casals (cnd), Prades Festival Orch *(rec June 5, 1950)* Sony Classical ("The Casals Edition" series) ▲ SMK 58982

Bach, J.S.:Con for 2 Vns, w. I. Perlman (vn), Z. Mehta (cnd), New York PO CBS ▲ MK 36692 [DDD]

Bach, J.S.:Con for 2 Vns, w. I. Perlman (vn), Z. Mehta (cnd), New York PO CBS ▲ MYK 38487 ■ MYT 38487

Bach, J.S.:Con for 2 Vns, w. Itzhak Perlman (vn), Z. Mehta (cnd), New York PO Sony Classical ▲ SMK 66471

Bach, J.S.:Con for 2 Vns, w. P. Zukerman (vn), St. Paul CO CBS ▲ MK 37278 [DDD]

Bach, J.S.:Con for 2 Vns, w. P. Zukerman (vn), P. Zukerman (cnd), St. Paul CO CBS ▲ MK 42258

Bach, J.S.:Con for 2 Vns, w. I. Perlman (vn), Z. Mehta (cnd), New York PO CBS ■ MGT 39798

Bach, J.S.:A Musical Offering, w. J.-P. Rampal (fl), J. Ritter (hpd), L. Parnas (vc)—trio, section 8] CBS ▲ MK 37813 [DDD]

Bach, J.S.:Sons Vn, BWV 1023, w. Alexander Zakin (pno) Sony Classical ▲ SMK 68361 [ADD]

Bach, J.S.:Sons Vn Hpd, BWV 1014-1019, w. Alexander Zakin (pno)—in E, BWV 1016 Sony Classical ▲ SMK 68361 [ADD]

Bach, J.S.:Sons Vn, BWV 1020, w. Alexander Zakin (pno) Sony Classical ▲ SMK 68361 [ADD]

Bach, J.S.:Trio Son Fl, Vn & Hpd, w. J.-P. Rampal (fl), J. Ritter (hpd) CBS ▲ MK 37813 [DDD]

Bartók, B.:Con 2 Vn, w. L. Bernstein (cnd), New York PO Sony Classical ▲ SMK 47511 [ADD]

Bartók, B.:Rhaps (2) Vn & Orch, w. L. Bernstein (cnd), New York PO Sony Classical ▲ SMK 47511 [ADD]

Bartók, B.:Sons (2) Vn & Pno, w. Alexander Zakin (pno) Sony Classical ▲ SMK 64535 [ADD]

Beethoven, L. van:Con Vn, Op. 61, w. D. Barenboim (cnd), New York PO CBS ▲ MK 42256 [ADD]

Beethoven, L. van:Con Vn, Op. 61, w. D. Barenboim (cnd), New York PO Odyssey ▲ MBK 42613 [ADD]

Beethoven, L. van:Con Vn, Op. 61, w. L. Bernstein (cnd), New York PO CBS 2-■ MGT 31418

Beethoven, L. van:Con Vn, Op. 61, w. L. Bernstein (cnd), New York PO Sony Classical ▲ SMK 47521 [ADD]

Beethoven, L. van:Con Vn, Op. 61, w. Ormandy (cnd), *(orch unknown)* Sony Classical 2-▲ SM2K 66941

Beethoven, L. van:Con Vn, Vc & Pno, "Triple Con", w. Leonard Rose (vc), Eugene Istomin (pno), Ormandy (cnd), *(orch unknown)* Sony Classical 2-▲ SM2K 66941

Beethoven, L. van:Con Vn, Vc & Pno, "Triple Con", w. L. Rose (vc), E. Istomin (pno), E. Ormandy (cnd), Philadelphia Orch Sony Classical ("Essential Classics" series) ▲ SBK 46549 [ADD] ■ SBT 46549

Beethoven, L. van:Con Vn, Vc & Pno, "Triple Con", w. L. Rose (vc), E. Istomin (pno), E. Ormandy (cnd), Philadelphia Orch Sony Classical ("Essential Classics" series) 3-▲ SB3K 48397

Beethoven, L. van:Qt Pno, Op. 16, w. E. Ax (pno), J. Laredo (va), Y. Ma (vc) *(rec Mar. 9-12, 1992)* Sony Classical ▲ SK 53339 [DDD]

Beethoven, L. van:Romances Vn, w. S. Ozawa (cnd), Boston SO CBS ▲ MK 37204 [DDD]

Beethoven, L. van:Sons Vn (comp), w. Eugene Istomin (pno) Sony Classical 3-▲ SM3K 64524 [ADD/DDD]

Beethoven, L. van:Sons Vn (comp), w. E. Istomin (pno)—Nos. 1-4 & 9 CBS 2-▲ M2K 39680 [DDD]

Beethoven, L. van:Sons Vn (comp), w. E. Istomin (pno)—Nos. 5-8 & 10 CBS 2-▲ M2K 39681 [DDD]

Beethoven, L. van:Son 10 Vn, w. M. Hess (pno) *(rec 14th Edinburgh Festival, Aug. 28, 1960)* Music & Arts 3-▲ CD 779 [AAD]

Beethoven, L. van:Trio 1 Pno, w. Eugene Istomin (pno), Leonard Rose (vc) Sony Classical ("Isaac Stern:A Life in Music" series) 2-▲ SM2K 64510

Beethoven, L. van:Trio 2 Pno, w. Eugene Istomin (pno), Leonard Rose (vc) Sony Classical ("Isaac Stern:A Life in Music" series) 2-▲ SM2K 64510

Beethoven, L. van:Trio 3 Pno, w. Eugene Istomin (pno), Leonard Rose (vc) Sony Classical ("Isaac Stern:A Life in Music" series) 2-▲ SM2K 64510

Beethoven, L. van:Trio 4 Pno, "Ghost", w. Eugene Istomin (pno), Leonard Rose (vc) Sony Classical ("Isaac Stern:A Life in Music" series) 2-▲ SM2K 64513

Beethoven, L. van:Trio 4 Pno, "Ghost", w. E. Istomin (pno), L. Rose (vc) Sony Classical ("Essential Classics" series) ▲ SBK 53514 ■ SBT 53514

Beethoven, L. van:Trio 6 Pno, "Archduke", w. Eugene Istomin (pno), Leonard Rose (vc) Sony Classical ("Isaac Stern:A Life in Music" series) 2-▲ SM2K 64513

Beethoven, L. van:Trio 6 Pno, "Archduke", w. E. Istomin (pno), L. Rose (vc) Sony Classical ("Essential Classics" series) ▲ SBK 53514 ■ SBT 53514

Beethoven, L. van:Trio 8 Pno, w. Eugene Istomin (pno), Leonard Rose (vc) Sony Classical ("Isaac Stern:A Life in Music" series) 2-▲ SM2K 64510

Beethoven, L. van:Trio 9 Pno, "Kakadu", w. Eugene Istomin (pno), Leonard Rose (vc) Sony Classical ("Isaac Stern:A Life in Music" series) 2-▲ SM2K 64513

Beethoven, L. van:Trio Pno, Op. 44, w. Eugene Istomin (pno), Leonard Rose (vc) Sony Classical ("Isaac Stern:A Life in Music" series) 2-▲ SM2K 64510

Bloch, E.:Baal Shem, "3 Pictures of Chassidic Life", w. Alexander Zakin (pno) Sony Classical ▲ SMK 64533 [ADD]

Bloch, E.:Nigun, w. Alexander Zakin (pno) *(rec 1948)* CBS 4-▲ M4K 42003 (m/s) [ADD]

Bloch, E.:Son 1 Vn, w. Alexander Zakin (pno) Sony Classical ▲ SMK 64533 [ADD]

Boccherini, L.:Qnts Strs, w. Cho-Liang Lin (vn), Jaime Laredo (va), Yo-Yo Ma (vc), Sharon Robinson (vc)—Qnt in E for Strs, Op. 13/5 Sony Classical ▲ SK 53983

Boccherini, L.:Qnt Strs, G.275, w. Cho-Liang Lin (vn), Jaime Laredo (va), Yo-Yo Ma (vc), Sharon Robinson (vc) Sony Classical ▲ SK 53983

Brahms, J.:Con Vn, w. Mehta, Barenboim (cnd), New York PO Sony Classical 2-▲ SM2K 66941

Brahms, J.:Con Vn, w. Z. Mehta (cnd), New York PO Odyssey 3-▲ MB3K 45828

Brahms, J.:Con Vn, w. E. Ormandy (cnd), Philadelphia Orch CBS 2-■ MGT 31418

Brahms, J.:Con Vn, w. E. Ormandy (cnd), Philadelphia Orch *(rec 1959)* CBS ▲ MK 42257 [AAD]

Brahms, J.:Con Vn, w. E. Ormandy (cnd), Philadelphia Orch Sony Classical ("Essential Classics" series) ▲ SBK 46335 [ADD] ■ SBT 46335

Brahms, J.:Con Vn & Vc, "Double Con", w. Leonard Rose (vc), Mehta, Barenboim (cnd), New York PO Sony Classical 2-▲ SM2K 66941

Brahms, J.:Con Vn & Vc, "Double Con", w. L. Rose (vc), E. Ormandy (cnd), Philadelphia Orch Sony Classical ("Essential Classics" series) ▲ SBK 46335 [ADD] ■ SBT 46335

Brahms, J.:Con Vn & Vc, "Double Con", w. Yo-Yo Ma (vc), C. Abbado (cnd), Chicago SO CBS ▲ MK 42387 [DDD]

Brahms, J.:Qts Pno (comp), w. E. Ax (pno), J. Laredo (va), Yo-Yo Ma (vc) Sony Classical 2-▲ S2K 45846 [DDD] 2-■ S2T 45846 (D)

Brahms, J.:Qts Pno (comp), w. Emanuel Ax (pno), Jaime Laredo (va), Yo-Yo Ma (vc) Sony Classical ("Isaac Stern:A Life in Music" series) 3-▲ SM3K 64520

Brahms, J.:Qt 3 Pno, w. E. Ax (pno), J. Laredo (va), Yo-Yo Ma (vc) CBS ▲ MK 42387 [DDD]

Brahms, J.:Sextet Strs, Op. 18, w. C.-L. Lin (vn), J. Laredo (va), M. Tree (va), Yo-Yo Ma (vc), S. Robinson (vc) Sony Classical 2-▲ S2K 45820

Brahms, J.:Sextet Strs, Op. 18, w. A. Schneider (vn), M. Katims (va), M. Thomas (va), P. Casals (vc), M. Foley (vc) *(rec Prades, France, June 23-July 3, 1952)* Sony Classical ("The Casals Edition" series) ▲ SMK 58994 [ADD]

Brahms, J.:Sextet Strs, Op. 18, w. A. Schneider (vn), M. Katims (va), M. Thomas (va), P. Casals (vc), M. Foley (vc) *(rec 1952)* Sony Masterworks ("Portrait" series) ▲ MPK 44851 [ADD]

Stern, Isaac (vn) (cont.)
Brahms, J.:Sextet Strs, Op. 36, w. Cho-Liang Lin (vn), J. Laredo (va), M. Tree (va), Yo-Yo Ma (vc), S. Robinson (vc) Sony Classical 2-▲ S2K 45820
Brahms, J.:Sons Vn (comp), w. Y. Bronfman (pno) *(rec Dec. 18-19, 1991)* Sony Classical ▲ SK 53107 [DDD]
Brahms, J.:Sons Vn (comp), w. Alexander Zakin (pno) Sony Classical ▲ SMK 64531 [ADD]
Brahms, J.:Son 2 Vn, w. M. Hess (pno) *(rec 14th Edinburgh Festival, Aug. 28, 1960)* Music & Arts 3-▲ CD 779 [AAD]
Brahms, J.:Trios (3) Pno, w. Eugene Istomin (pno), Leonard Rose (vc) Sony Classical ("Isaac Stern:A Life in Music" series) 3-▲ SM3K 64520
Brahms, J.:Trio 1 Pno, w. M. Hess (pno), P. Casals (vc) *(rec Prades, France, June 23-July 3, 1952)* Sony Classical ("The Casals Edition" series) ▲ SMK 58994 [ADD]
Bruch, M.:Con 1 Vn, w. E. Ormandy (cnd), Philadelphia Orch CBS ▲ MYK 37811 [ADD] ■ MYT 37811
Bruch, M.:Con 1 Vn, w. Ormandy, Rostropovich (cnd), Philadelphia Orch, National SO Washington D.C. Sony Classical ▲ SMK 66830
Bruch, M.:Con 1 Vn, w. E. Ormandy (cnd), Philadelphia Orch CBS ▲ MK 42256 [ADD]
Celebration:Life With Music CBS 4-▲ M4K 42003 (m/s) [ADD]
Copland, A.:Son Vn & Pno, w. Alexander Zakin (pno) Sony Classical ▲ SMK 64533 [ADD]
Davies, P.M.:Con Vn, w. A. Previn (cnd), Royal PO CBS ▲ MK 42449 [DDD]
Debussy, C.:Son Vn, w. Alexander Zakin (pno) Sony Classical ▲ SMK 64532 [ADD]
Dutilleux, H.:L'Arbre de songes, w. L. Maazel (cnd), French National Orch CBS ▲ MK 42449 [DDD]
Dvořák, A.:Con Vn, w. E. Ormandy (cnd), Philadelphia Orch CBS ▲ MK 42257 [AAD]
Dvořák, A.:Con Vn, w. E. Ormandy (cnd), Philadelphia Orch Sony Classical (Essential Classics) ▲ SBK 46337 [ADD] ■ SBT 46337
Early Recordings *(rec 1945-46)* Pearl ▲ PEA CD 9248
Enescu, G.:Son 3 Vn, w. Alexander Zakin (pno) Sony Classical ▲ SMK 64532 [ADD]
Fauré, G.:Qt 1 Pno, w. E. Ax (pno), J. Laredo (vn), Y.-Y. Ma (vc) Sony Classical ▲ SK 48066 [DDD]
Fauré, G.:Qt 2 Pno, w. E. Ax (pno), J. Laredo (vn), Y.-Y. Ma (vc) Sony Classical ▲ SK 48066 [DDD]
Franck, C.:Son Vn, w. Alexander Zakin (pno) Sony Classical ▲ SMK 64532 [ADD]
Handel, G.F.:Sons Vn & Kbd, w. Alexander Zakin (pno)—No. 3 Sony Classical ▲ SMK 68361 [ADD]
Haydn, J.:Con 1 Vn, w. Alexander Zakin (hpd), I. Stern (cnd), Columbia CO Sony Classical 2-▲ SM2K 64528 [ADD/DDD]
Haydn, J.:Con 1 Vn, w. I. Stern (cnd), Columbia String Orch *(rec 11/12/47; mono)* CBS 4-▲ M4K 42003 (m/s) [ADD]
Haydn, J.:Diverts Vn, Va & Vc, H.IV/6-11, w. Jean-Pierre Rampal (fl), Msitslav Rostropovich (vc)—Nos. 2 & 6 CBS ▲ MK 37786 [DDD]
Haydn, J.:Trios Fls & Vc, "London Trios", w. Jean-Pierre Rampal (fl), Mstislav Rostropovich (vc) CBS 4-▲ M4K 42003 (m/s) [ADD]
Haydn, J.:Trios Fls & Vc, "London Trios", w. Jean-Pierre Rampal (fl), Mstislav Rostropovich (vc) CBS ▲ MK 37786 [DDD]
Haydn, J.:Trios Pno, Vn & Vc, w. Eugene Istomin (pno), Leonard Rose (vc)—H.XV/10 CBS 4-▲ M4K 42003 (m/s) [ADD]
Haydn, J.:Trios Pno, Vn & Vc, w. Eugene Istomin (pno), Leonard Rose (vc)—No. 20 Sony Classical ("Isaac Stern:A Life in Music" series) 2-▲ SM2K 64516
Hindemith, P.:Son in C Vn & Pno, w. Alexander Zakin (pno) Sony Classical ▲ SMK 64533 [ADD]
Humoresque:20 Favorite Violin Encores CBS ▲ MDK 45816
Isaac Stern:A Life in Music Sony Classical 12-▲ SM12K 67195
Isaac Stern Presents Encores with Orchestra Sony Classical ("Isaac Stern:A Life in Music" series) ▲ SMK 64537
60th Anniversary Celebration CBS ▲ MK 36692
Lalo, E.:Sym espagnole, w. E. Ormandy (cnd), Philadelphia Orch CBS ▲ MYK 37811 [ADD] ■ MYT-37811
Mendelssohn, F.:Con in e Vn & Orch, Op. 64, w. E. Ormandy (cnd), Philadelphia Orch CBS ▲ MYK 36724 ■ MYT 36724
Mendelssohn, F.:Con in e Vn & Orch, Op. 64, w. S. Ozawa (cnd), Boston SO CBS ▲ MK 37204 [DDD]
Mendelssohn, F.:Con in e Vn & Orch, Op. 64, w. K. Ancerl (cnd), Prague SO Multisonic ("Prague Spring Collection" series) ▲ 31 0104 [ADD]
Mendelssohn, F.:Con in e Vn & Orch, Op. 64, w. E. Ormandy (cnd), Philadelphia Orch Sony Classical ("Essential Classics" series) ▲ SBK 46542 [ADD] ■ SBT 46542
Mendelssohn, F.:Con in e Vn & Orch, Op. 64, w. E. Ormandy (cnd), Philadelphia Orch CBS ▲ MLK 39452 ■ MT 39452
Mendelssohn, F.:Trio 1 Pno, w. Eugene Istomin (pno), Leonard Rose (vc) Sony Classical ("Isaac Stern:A Life in Music" series) ▲ SMK 64519
Mendelssohn, F.:Trio 2 Pno, w. Eugene Istomin (pno), Leonard Rose (vc) Sony Classical ("Isaac Stern:A Life in Music" series) ▲ SMK 64519
Mozart, W.A.:Adagio Vn, K.261, w. G. Szell (cnd), Cleveland Orch Sony Classical 3-▲ SM3K 66475
Mozart, W.A.:Adagio Vn, K.261, w. A. Schneider (cnd), English CO CBS 2-▲ M2K 42494 [ADD]
Mozart, W.A.:Cons Vn—Nos 1 & 5 [w. G. Szell (cnd), Columbia SO]; No. 3 [w. G. Szell (cnd), Cleveland Orch]; Nos 2 & 4 [w. A. Schneider (cnd), English CO] Odyssey 2-▲ MB2K 45614
Mozart, W.A.:Cons Vn—Nos 1 & 5 [w. G. Szell (cnd), Columbia SO]; No. 3 [w. G. Szell (cnd), Cleveland Orch]; Nos 2 & 4 [w. A. Schneider (cnd), English CO] CBS 2-▲ M2K 42494 [ADD]
Mozart, W.A.:Cons Vn, w. G. Szell (cnd), Cleveland Orch—Nos. 1-5 Sony Classical 3-▲ SM3K 66475
Mozart, W.A.:Con 4 Vn, w. A. Schneider (cnd), English CO CBS ▲ MYK 37808 [ADD] ■ MYT 37808
Mozart, W.A.:Con 5 Vn, w. G. Szell (cnd), Columbia SO CBS ▲ MYK 37808 [ADD] ■ MYT 37808
Mozart, W.A.:Concertone Vns, w. Pinchas Zukerman (vn), G. Szell (cnd), English CO Sony Classical 3-▲ SM3K 66475
Mozart, W.A.:Music of, w. Ferruccio Furlanetto (bass), N. Marriner (cnd), Academy of St. Martin in the Fields, Canadian Brass—Eine kleine Nachtmusik; Syms 38 & 41; sels from Die Zauberflöte; plus others Sony Classical ("Greatest Hits" series) ▲ MLK 62682 ■ MLT 62682
Mozart, W.A.:Qts Fl, w. J-P. Rampal (fl), S. Accardo (vn), M. Rostropovich (vc) CBS ▲ MK 42320 [DDD]
Mozart, W.A.:Qts Fl, w. J.-P. Rampal (fl), A. Schneider (vn), L. Rose (vc) Odyssey ▲ MBK 42601
Mozart, W.A.:Qts Pno, w. Eugene Istomin (pno), Milton Katims (va), Leonard Rose (vc)—No. 2 Sony Classical ("Isaac Stern:A Life in Music" series) 2-▲ SM2K 64516
Mozart, W.A.:Rondo Vn, K.373, w. U. Schneider (cnd), English CO CBS 2-▲ M2K 42494 [ADD]
Mozart, W.A.:Rondo Vn, K.373, w. G. Szell (cnd), Cleveland Orch Sony Classical 3-▲ SM3K 66475
Mozart, W.A.:Serenade Vn, K.250, w. J.-P. Rampal (cnd), Franz Liszt CO *(rec Italian Institute, Budapest, Apr. 13-15, 1994)* Sony Classical ▲ SK 66270 [DDD]
Mozart, W.A.:Serenade Vn, K.250, w. A. Schneider (cnd), English CO—Rondeau CBS 2-▲ M2K 42494 [ADD]
Mozart, W.A.:Sinf concertante Vn, K.364, w. W. Primrose (va), P. Casals (cnd), Perpignan Festival Orch *(rec Perpignan, France, July 5-8, 1951)* Sony Classical ("The Casals Edition" series) ▲ SMK 58983 [ADD]
Mozart, W.A.:Sinf concertante Vn, K.364, w. P. Zukerman (va), Z. Mehta (cnd), New York PO CBS ▲ MK 36692 [DDD]
Mozart, W.A.:Sinf concertante Vn, K.364, w. P. Zukerman (va), D. Barenboim (cnd), English CO *(rec 1971)* CBS 4-▲ M4K 42003 (m/s) [ADD]
Mozart, W.A.:Sinf concertante Vn, K.364, w. G. Szell (cnd), Cleveland Orch Sony Classical 3-▲ SM3K 66475
Mozart, W.A.:Sons Vn Pno (comp), w. Yefim Bronfman (pno)—K.304, 377, 481 & 547 Sony Classical ▲ SK 61962
Mozart, W.A.:Sons Vn Pno (comp), w. Y. Bronfman (pno)—in C, K.296; in B♭, K.454; in A, K.526 *(rec Mar. 13-16, 1993)* Sony Classical ▲ SK 53972 [DDD]
Mozart, W.A.:Sons Vn Pno (misc), w. Yefim Bronfman (pno)—K. 302, 303, 305, 376, 380 Sony Classical ▲ SK 64309
Mozart, W.A.:Trios Fl, w. J.-P. Rampal (fl), M. Rostropovich (vc) Sony Classical ▲ SK 44568 [DDD]
Prokofiev, S.:Cons Vn (comp), w. Z. Mehta (cnd), New York PO CBS ▲ MK 42439 [DDD]

Stern, Isaac (vn) (cont.)
Prokofiev, S.:Cons Vn (comp), w. E. Ormandy (cnd), Philadelphia Orch CBS ▲ MYK 38525 [ADD] ■ MYT 38525
Prokofiev, S.:Con 2 Vn, w. L. Bernstein (cnd), New York PO *(rec 1957; mono)* CBS 4-▲ M4K 42003 (m/s) [ADD]
Prokofiev, S.:Son Vn, Op. 94bis, w. Alexander Zakin (pno) Sony Classical ▲ SMK 64534 [ADD]
Prokofiev, S.:Son 1 Vn, w. Alexander Zakin (pno) Sony Classical ▲ SMK 64534 [ADD]
Rameau, J.P.:Pièces de clavecin en concert, w. J. S. Ritter (hpd), J.-P. Rampal (fl) Sony Classical ▲ SK 45868 [DDD]
Ravel, M.:Tzigane, w. E. Ormandy (cnd), Philadelphia Orch *(rec 1957)* CBS 4-▲ M4K 42003 (m/s) [ADD]
Reicha, A.:Vars & Fant on Mozart's "Se vuol ballare", w. J.-P. Rampal (fl), M. Rostropovich (vc), M. Später (lt) Sony Classical ▲ SK 44568 [DDD]
Saint-Saëns, C.:Introduction & Rondo capriccioso, w. E. Ormandy (cnd), Philadelphia Orch *(rec 1957)* CBS 4-▲ M4K 42003 (m/s) [ADD]
Sarasate, P. de:Zigeunerweisen, w. *(other artist unknown)* *(rec Hollywood, for the soundtrack of the 1947 Warner Bros. film "Humoresque," 8/14/46)* CBS 4-▲ M4K 42003 (m/s) [ADD]
Schubert, Franz:Fant Vn, D.934, w. Daniel Barenboim (pno) Sony Classical 2-▲ SM2K 64528 [ADD/DDD]
Schubert, Franz:Qnt Strs, D.956, w. A. Schneider (vn), M. Katims (va), P. Casals (vc), P. Tortelier (vc) *(rec Prades, France, July 1-2, 1952)* Sony Classical ("The Casals Edition" series) ▲ SMK 58992 [ADD]
Schubert, Franz:Qnt Strs, D.956, w. A. Schneider (vn), M. Katims (va), P. Casals (vc), P. Tortelier (vc) *(rec 1952)* CBS 4-▲ M4K 42003 (m/s) [ADD]
Schubert, Franz:Qnt Strs, D.956, w. Cho-Liang Lin (vn), Jaime Laredo (va), Yo-Yo Ma (vc), Sharon Robinson (vc) Sony Classical ▲ SK 53983
Schubert, Franz:Qnt Strs, D.956, w. Cho-Liang Lin (vn), Jaime Laredo (va), Yo-Yo Ma (vc), Sharon Robinson (vc) Sony Classical ▲ SK 53983
Schubert, Franz:Rondo Vn, D.895, w. Daniel Barenboim (pno) Sony Classical 2-▲ SM2K 64528 [ADD/DDD]
Schubert, Franz:Son Vn, D.574, w. Daniel Barenboim (pno) Sony Classical 2-▲ SM2K 64528 [ADD/DDD]
Schubert, Franz:Sonatinas Vn, w. M. Hess (pno) *(rec 14th Edinburgh Festival, Aug. 28, 1960)* Music & Arts 3-▲ CD 779 [AAD]
Schubert, Franz:Sonatinas Vn, w. Daniel Barenboim (pno) Sony Classical 2-▲ SM2K 64528 [ADD/DDD]
Schubert, Franz:Trio 1 Pno, w. Eugene Istomin (pno), Leonard Rose (vc) Sony Classical ("Isaac Stern:A Life in Music" series) 2-▲ SM2K 64516
Schubert, Franz:Trio 2 Pno, w. Eugene Istomin (pno), Leonard Rose (vc) Sony Classical ("Isaac Stern:A Life in Music" series) 2-▲ SM2K 64516
Schumann, R.:Qt Pno, Op. 47, w. E. Ax (pno), J. Laredo (va), Y. Ma (vc) *(rec Mar. 9-12, 1992)* Sony Classical ▲ SK 53339 [DDD]
Shostakovich, D.:Trio 2 Pno, w. Yo Yo Ma (vc), E. Ax (pno) CBS ▲ MK 44664 [DDD]
Sibelius, J.:Con Vn, w. E. Ormandy (cnd), Philadelphia Orch Sony Classical ▲ SMK 66829
Tartini, G.:Sons Vn & Continuo, w. Alexander Zakin (pno)— in g, Op. 1/10, "Didone abbandonata" Sony Classical ▲ SMK 68361 [ADD]
Tchaikovsky, P.:Con Vn, w. L. Bernstein (cnd), New York PO *(rec Mar. 3, 1975)* Sony Classical ▲ SMK 47637 [ADD]
Tchaikovsky, P.:Con Vn, w. E. Ormandy (cnd), Philadelphia Orch CBS ▲ MYK 36724 ■ MYT 36724
Tchaikovsky, P.:Con Vn, w. E. Ormandy (cnd), Philadelphia Orch Sony Classical ▲ SMK 66829
Tchaikovsky, P.:Serenade Strs, w. L. Bernstein (cnd), New York PO *(rec Oct. 22, 1970)* Sony Classical ▲ SMK 47637 [ADD]
Tchaikovsky, P.:Sérénade mélancolique, w. E. Ormandy (cnd), Philadelphia Orch Sony Classical ▲ SMK 66830
Tchaikovsky, P.:Souvenir d'un lieu cher, w. E. Ormandy (cnd), Philadelphia Orch—Méditation [arr Glazunov] Sony Classical ▲ SMK 66830
Telemann, G.P.:Qt Fl, w. J.-P. Rampal (fl), M. Rostropovich (vc), M. Später (lt) Sony Classical ▲ SK 44568 [DDD]
Vivaldi, A.:Cons Fl Vn, w. J.-P. Rampal (fl), J. Rolla (cnd), Franz Liszt CO Sony Classical ▲ SK 45867 [DDD] ■ ST 45867 (D)
Vivaldi, A.:Cons Vn, Op. 8/1-4, "The Four Seasons", w. I. Stern (cnd), Jerusalem Music Center CO Odyssey ▲ MBK 42526
Vivaldi, A.:Cons for 2 Vns, w. D. Oistrakh (vn), E. Ormandy (cnd), Philadelphia Orch *(rec 1955-6)* CBS 4-▲ M4K 42003 (m/s) [ADD]
Vivaldi, A.:Cons for 2 Vns, w. J.-P. Rampal (fl), J.-P. Rampal (cnd), Jerusalem Music Center CO—RV.514 CBS ▲ MK 38982
Vivaldi, A.:Cons for 2 Vns, w. P. Zukerman (vn), P. Zukerman (cnd), St. Paul CO—1—in A CBS ▲ MK 37278 [DDD]
Vivaldi, A.:Con for 3 Vns, w. P. Zukerman (vn), I. Perlman (vn), Z. Mehta (cnd), New York PO CBS ▲ MK 36692 [DDD]
Waxman, F.:Carmen Fant, w. F. Waxman (cnd), *(orch unknown)* *(rec Hollywood for the soundtrack of the 1947 Warner Bros. film Humoresque, 8/14/46)* CBS 4-▲ M4K 42003 (m/s) [ADD]
Webern, A.:Pieces Vn, w. Charles Rosen (pno) Sony Classical ▲ SMK 64535 [ADD]
Wieniawski, H.:Con 2 Vn, w. E. Ormandy (cnd), Philadelphia Orch Sony Classical ▲ SMK 66830
Wieniawski, H.:Con 2 Vn, w. E. Kurtz (cnd), New York PO *(rec Carnegie Hall, 3/27/46)* CBS 4-▲ M4K 42003 (m/s) [ADD]

Stern, Kay (vn)—see also ORCHESTRAS & ENSEMBLES Lark String Quartet, Phoenix Trio
Cowell, H.:Set of 5, w. Josephine Gandolfi (pno), Rick Kvistad (perc) Koch International Classics ▲ KIC 7205 [DDD]
Miller, E.J.:Beyond the Wheel, w. E. London (cnd), Cleveland Chamber SO GM ▲ GM 2045

Stern, Wendy (fl)—see ORCHESTRAS & ENSEMBLES Flute Force

Sternat, Mathilde (vc)
Boccherini, L.:Qnts Fl, G.437-442, w. Jean-Pierre Rampal (fl), Bruno Pasquier (vn), Régis Pasquier (vn), Roland Pidoux (vc concertante)—1-3, 5 & 6 Sony Classical ▲ SK 62679

Sternberg, Will (gtr/tapes)
Exquisite Corpses from P.S. 122, w. Watson, David (shears/stick vn/gtr/tpt), Judy Dunaway (gtr/balloons), Anthony Coleman (sampler), Raissa St. Pierre (drums), Guy Yarden (vn/pno), Leslie Ross (bn), Linda Austin (gtr), Bruce Kaplan (gtr), Doug Henderson (peckhorn/bass/toy pno), Sue Ann Harkey (gtr), Cinnie Cole (sampler), et al. ¿What Next? ▲ WN 0002 [ADD]

Sternfield, Allan (pno)
Klein, G.:Son Pno *(rec June 21, July 5 & 20, 199)* Koch International Classics ▲ KIC 7230-2 [DDD]

Sterrett, T. O. (pno)
Aldridge, R.:Prisoner, w. Albert Regni (s sax) Open Loop ▲ 034 [DDD]
Aldridge, R.:Qt for an Outdoor Festival, w. Al Regni (s sax), Mark Feldman (vn), Beverly Lauridsen (vc) Open Loop ▲ 034 [DDD]
Bourland, R.:Stone Qt, w. Al Regni (sax), Lois Martin (va), Beverly Lauridsen (vc) Open Loop ▲ 034 [DDD]

Steuart, Richard (tpt)
Biber, H. von:Son Tpt, 2 Vns, Vc, w. Oldrich Vlcek (vn), Sylvie Hessova (vn), Ivo Anyz (va), Vaclav Jirovec (vc) *(rec Prague, Nov. 1994)* Discover International ▲ DI 920244 [DDD]
Finger, G.:Son Tpt & Vn, w. Prague Virtuosi *(rec Prague, Nov. 1994)* Discover International ▲ DI 920244 [DDD]
Finger, G.:Son Tpt, Vn & Ob, w. Sylvie Hessova (vn), Oldrich Vlcek (vn), Milan Hruby (ob) *(rec Prague, Nov. 1994)* Discover International ▲ DI 920244 [DDD]
Neruda, J.B.G.:Con Tpt, w. Prague Virtuosi *(rec Prague, Nov. 1994)* Discover International ▲ DI 920244 [DDD]
Vejvanovsky, P.J.:Son à 4, w. Prague Virtuosi *(rec Prague, Nov. 1994)* Discover International ▲ DI 920244 [DDD]

Steuber, Lillian (pno)
Ferguson, H.:Son 1 Vn, w. J. Heifetz (vn) RCA Gold Seal ▲ 7872-2-RG (m/s) [ADD]

864

▲ = CD ♦ = Enhanced CD Δ = MD ■ = Cassette Tape □ = DCC

Steuber, Lillian (pno) (cont.)
Khachaturian, K.:Son Vn, w. J. Heifetz (vn) RCA Gold Seal ▲ 7872-2-RG (m/s) [ADD]
Rachmaninoff, S.:Rhapsody on a Theme of Paganini, w. Jack Richard Crossan (pno) [two-piano arr.] Janus ■ JAN 1107-1 (CrO2)

Steuermann, Eduard (pno)
Schoenberg, A.:Con Pno, w. H. Scherchen (cnd), Hessian RSO *(rec 1954)* Arkadia ▲ 768 [ADD]

Stevens, Andy (cl)
Encore, w. [cnd:Duain Wolfe], Colorado Children's Chorale, Rick Chinski (gtr), Robert Davine (acc), Laurie Kahler (pno), Samuel Lancaster (pno), Barry Oliver (pno), Marylin Preston (fl), Karen Yonovitz (fl), Peter Cooper (ob), Lionel Young (vn), Basil Vendreys (va), Wayne Templeman (vc), Charle *(rec Denver Center Media)* Colorado Children's Chorale ▲ 001

Stevens, Bruce (org)
Bruce Stevens Raven ▲ OAR 280 [DDD]
Historic Organs of New Orleans, w. George Bozeman (org), James S. Darling (org), Jesse E. Eschbach (org), Gerald D. Frank (org), John Gearhart (org), James Hammann (org), Frederick Hohman (org), Lenora McCroskey (org), Mary Gifford Matthys (org), Lorenz Maycher (org), Donald Messer (org) *(rec June 1989)* Organ Historical Society 2-▲ OHS 89
Rheinberger, J.:Miscellaneen—No. 6 Raven ▲ OAR 140 CD [DDD]
Rheinberger, J.:Sons Org—No. 3 in G, Op. 88, "Pastoral"; No. 11 in d, Op. 148; No. 12 in D♭, Op. 154 Raven ▲ OAR 140 CD [DDD]
Rheinberger, J.:Sons Org—No. 2 in A♭, Op. 65, "Fantaisie-Sonata"; No. 6 in e♭, Op. 119; No. 8 in e, Op. 132 Raven ▲ OAR 180 CD [DDD]
Rheinberger, J.:Sons Org—No. 16 in g#, Op. 175; No. 17 in B, Op. 181, "Fantaisie-Sonata"; No. 20 in F, Op. 196, "Zur Friedensfeier" Raven ▲ OAR 220 [DDD]

Stevens, Cyrus (vn)
Imbrie, A.W.:To a Traveler, w. Alan R. Kay (cl), Edmund Niemann (pno) *(rec Sept. 24, 1993)* New World ▲ 80441-2

Stevens, Delores (pno)
Brahms, J.:Son in D Vc, w. P. Hatch (vc) PROdigital ▲ VM 5308 [DDD]
Enescu, G.:Concertpiece Va, w. P. Hatch (va) PROdigital ▲ VM 5308 [DDD]
Joachim, J.:Hebrew Melodies, w. P. Hatch (va) PROdigital ▲ VM 5308 [DDD]
19th Century Viola Music, w. Peter Hatch (va) PROdigital ▲ PROVM 5308 [DDD]
Sitt, H.:Album Leaves Va, w. P. Hatch (va) PROdigital ▲ VM 5308 [DDD]

Stevens, Denis (baroque va)—see ORCHESTRAS & ENSEMBLES In Nomine Players

Stevens, J. (tuba)—see also ORCHESTRAS & ENSEMBLES Wisconsin Brass Quintet
Penn, W.:Essays Tuba, w. Louwenaar (hpd) CRI ■ C 367

Stevens, Leigh Howard (mar)
Debussy, C.:Children's Corner Delos ▲ DE 3142 [DDD]
Khachaturian, A.:Album of Children's Pieces—The Adventures of Ivan Delos ▲ DE 3142 [DDD]
Schumann, R.:Album für die Jugend—Humming Song, Soldier's March; The Wild Rider; Knecht Ruprecht; May, Sweet May, Roundelay; No. 26; Remembrance; No. 30 Delos ▲ DE 3142 [DDD]
Tchaikovsky, P.:Album pour enfants—Song of the Lark; Morning Prayer; The Hobby Horse; Italian Song; German Song; Waltz; Neapolitan Dance-Song; Mazurka; The Doll's Burial; The New Doll; Nursery Tale; Sweet Dreams Delos ▲ DE 3142 [DDD]

Stevens, Thomas (tpt)
Bozza, E.:Badinage, w. Z. Carno (pno) Crystal ■ C 367
Bozza, E.:Caprice, w. Z. Carno (pno) Crystal ■ C 367
Bozza, E.:Lied Tpt & Pno, w. Z. Carno (pno) Crystal ■ C 367
Campo, F.:Times Crystal ▲ CD 667
Chou Wen-Chung:Soliloquy of a Bhiksuni, w. M. Peters (perc), Los Angeles Brass Society Crystal ▲ CD 667
Hovhaness, A.:Avak, the Healer, w. Marni Nixon (sop), E. Gold (cnd), Crystal CO Crystal ■ C 800
Hovhaness, A.:Avak, the Healer, w. Marni Nixon (sop), E. Gold (cnd), Crystal CO Crystal ▲ CD 806
Hovhaness, A.:Prayer of St. Gregory, w. E. Gold (cnd), Crystal CO Crystal ■ C 800
Ibert, J.:Impromptu Tpt & Pno, w. Z. Carno (pno) Crystal ■ C 367
Kupferman, M.:The Fires of Prometheus Crystal ▲ CD 667
Lazarof, H.:Spectrum, w. H. Lazarof (cnd), Utah SO CRI ▲ CD 588 [ADD]
Poulenc, F.:Son Tpt, w. J. Cerminaro (hn), R. Sauer (trbn) Crystal ■ C 367
Revueltas, S.:Little Serious Pieces, w. Westwood Wind Quintet members Crystal ▲ CD 667
Reynolds, V.:Signals, w. R. Bobo (tuba), Los Angeles Brass Society Crystal ▲ CD 667
Ropartz, G.:Andante & Allegro, w. Z. Carno (pno) Crystal ■ C 367
Saint-Saëns, C.:Spt Tpt, w. André Previn (pno), Julie Rosenfeld (vn), Ani Kavafian (vn), Toby Hoffman (va), Carter Brey (vc), Jack Kulowitsch (db) *(rec Manhattan Center Studios, New York City, May 25-26, 1993)* RCA Red Seal ▲ 09026-68181-2 [DDD]
Thomas Stevens, w. Zito Carno (pno) Crystal ▲ CD 665
Thomas Stevens, Trumpet Crystal ▲ CD 761
Tomasi, H.:Triptyque, w. Z. Carno (pno) Crystal ■ C 367

Stevenson, Doris (pno)
Brahms, J.:Sons Vc (comp), w. N. Rosen (vc) John Marks ▲ JMR 5 [DDD]
Mendelssohn, F.:Lied ohne Worte Vc, w. N. Rosen (vc) John Marks ▲ JMR 5 [DDD]
Orientale:Romantic Music for Cello, w. Nathaniel Rosen (vc), Arturo Delmoni (vn) North Star ▲ NS 0027
Reverie:Romantic Music for Quiet Times, w. Nathaniel Rosen (vc), Kaaren Erickson (sop), Arturo Delmoni (vn) John Marks Records ▲ JMR 10
Schumann, R.:Fantasiestücke Cl, w. N. Rosen (vc) John Marks ▲ JMR 5 [DDD]
Shostakovich, D.:Son Vc, w. C. Prieto (vc) IMP Classics ▲ IMPPCD 1084 [DDD]

Stevenson, Robert W. (b cl)
Symonds, N.:Persuasion, w. Joseph Macerollo (acc) *(rec Glenn Gould Studio, CBC Toronto, Mar 17, 1994 & Mar 13 & 2)* CBC ▲ MVCD 1096 [DDD]

Stevenson, Ronald (pno)
Bottesini, G.:Fants & Vars, w. Joseph Banowetz (pno) *(rec Genoa, May 2-5, 1994)* Dynamic ▲ CDS 122 [DDD]
Busoni, F.:Fant contrappuntistica Pno 4-Hands, w. Joseph Banowetz (pno) Altarus ▲ CD 9044
Busoni, F.:Finnländische Volksweisen, w. Joseph Banowetz (pno) Altarus ▲ CD 9044
Busoni, F.:Fugue on the folksong *O du lieber Augustin*, w. Joseph Banowetz (pno) Altarus ▲ CD 9044
Busoni, F.:Pno Music—Toccata; Var on a Chopin Prelude; Prelude & Etude in Arpeggios; Tanzwaltzer [tran von Zadora]; Epilogue from "An die Jugend" Altarus ▲ AIR CD 9041
Cathedrals in Sound, w. Stevenson, Ronald (pno) Altarus ▲ CD 9043
Grainger, P.:Pno Music (misc)—Hill-Song No. 1 [arr. Stevenson]; Songs (14) of the North; 3 Scotch Folksongs [arr. Stevenson]; Scotch Strathspey & Reel Altarus ▲ CD 9040
Grainger, P.:Rosenkavalier-Ramble—tran & fant on Strauss' Rosenkavalier Altarus ▲ AIRCD 9042
Mozart, W.A.:Fant Mechanical Org, w. Joseph Banowetz (pno) [arr Busoni for pno 4-hands] Altarus ▲ CD 9044
Stevenson, R.:Passacaglia on DSCH Altarus ▲ CD 9091
Stevenson, R.:Prelude, Fugue & Fant Altarus ▲ CD 9091
Stevenson, R.:Prelude, Fugue & Fantasy on Themes from Busoni's *Doktor Faust* Altarus ▲ AIR CD 9041
Stevenson, R.:Recitative & Air Pno Altarus ▲ CD 9091
Stevenson, R.:Transcriptions Pno—transcriptions and fantasias from:Busoni:Doktor Faust; Berg:Wiegenlied aus Wozzeck; Bush:Minstrel's Lay; Britten:Peter Grimes Altarus ▲ AIRCD 9042

Stevensson, Kjell-Inge (cl)
Crusell, B.H.:Con 2 Cl, w. I. Olsen (hn), K. Sönstevold (bn), O. Kamu (cnd), Swedish RSO Musica Sveciae ▲ MSV 527 [DDD]
Crusell, B.H.:Intro, Theme & Vars on a Swedish Air, w. I. Olsen (hn), K. Sönstevold (bn), O. Kamu (cnd), Swedish RSO Musica Sveciae ▲ MSV 527 [DDD]
Crusell, B.H.:Sinf concertante, w. I. Olsen (hn), K. Sönstevold (bn), O. Kamu (cnd), Swedish RSO Musica Sveciae ▲ MSV 527 [DDD]
Rautavaara, E.:Sonetto Cl, w. E. Knardahl (pno) *(rec June 10, 1976)* BIS ▲ CD 66 [AAD]

Stevensson, Kjell-Inge (cl) (cont.)
The Virtuoso Clarinet, w. Kjell Fagéus (cl), Eva Knardahl (pno), Mats Persson (pno) *(rec Nacka Aula, Nacka, Sweden, June 10-12, 1976 & Sept.)* BIS ▲ CD 62 [AAD]

Števove, Miloš (hn)
Mozart, W.A.:Cons Hn, w. J. Kopelman (cnd), Capella Istropolitana *(rec Nov. 1988)* Naxos ▲ 8.550148 [DDD]

Stewart, Charles (vn)—see ORCHESTRAS & ENSEMBLES Chilingirian String Quartet

Stewart, David (trbn)
Gough, O.:Currulao, w. Beverly Davison (vn), Roger Heaton (cl), Bruce Nockles (tpt), John Pigneguy (hn), Tracey Goldsmith (acc), Orlando Gough (kbd), Paul Clarvis (perc) *(rec London, 1995)* Catalyst ▲ 0902-668332-2 [DDD]

Stewart, David (vn)
Macdonald, A.:Con Vn, w. S. Streatfeild (cnd), Manitoba CO *(rec St. Matthews Anglican Church, Winnipeg, Manitoba, Sept. 4-9, 1994)* BIS ▲ CD 698 [DDD]

Stewart, Don (cl)
Berger, A.:Duos, w. J. Smirnoff (vn), C. Oldfather (pno), J. Krosnick (vc), G. Kalish (pno), P. Lanini (ob)—Duo No. 1 for Violin & Piano (1948); Duo for Cello & Piano (1951); Duo for Oboe & Clarinet (1952) New World ▲ NW 360-2 [DDD]

Stewart, G. (gtr)—see ORCHESTRAS & ENSEMBLES San Francisco Guitar Quartet

Stewart, Jan (vn)
Starer, R.:Elegy for a Woman Who Died Too Young, w. Steven Honigberg (vc) Albany ▲ TROY 157 [DDD]

Stewart, Laurent (hpd)
Frescobaldi, G.:Hpd Music—Toccatas; Partitas; Canzonas; Balletos Pierre Verany ▲ 794032 [DDD]

Stewart, Laurent (org)
Palestrina, G.:Sacred Music, w. Catherine Greuillet (sop), Thierry Gregoire (alt), Pierre Sciema (alt), Bruno Boterf (ten), Joel Suhubiette (ten), Jean-Luc Baudoin (ten), Jean-Claude Sarragosse (bass), Françoise Lasserre (cnd), Champagne-Ardenne Akademia Regional Vocal Ensemble—Ave maria; Salve regina; Vergine bella; Vergine saggia; Virgine pura; Virgine santa; Vergine sola; Vergine chiara; Vergine, quante lagrime; Vergine, tale è terra; Ave mundi spes; Ave regina coelorum; Alma redemptoris mater; Regina coleli laetare; Salve regina; Magnificat; others *(rec Convent of the Annunciation Dominican Church, Paris, Jan., 1994)* Pierre Verany ▲ PVY 794041 [DDD]

Stewart, Mark (bass gtr)
Andriessen, L.:Hoketus, w. Katherine Pendry (panpipes), James Poke (panpipes), Evan Ziporyn (a sax), Richard Craig (a sax), Steven Schick (congas), Amy Knoles (congas), Lisa Moore (Fender Rhodes), Damian LeGassick (Fender Rhodes), Cees van Zeeland (pno), Gerard Bouwhuis (pno), Robert Black (bass gtr), *(rec Air Recording Studios, Lyndhurst Hall, Hampstead, London, June 29-July 3, 1994)* Sony Classical ▲ SK 66483 [DDD]

Stewart, Mark (elec gtr)
Andriessen, L.:Hout, w. Evan Ziporyn (t sax), Steven Schick (perc), Lisa Moore (pno) *(rec Air Recording Studios, Lyndhurst Hall, Hampstead, London, June 29-July 3, 1994)* Sony Classical ▲ SK 66483 [DDD]
Wolfe, J.:Lick, w. Evan Ziporyn (s sax), Steven Schick (perc), Lisa Moore (pno), Maya Beiser (vc), Robert Black (db) *(rec Air Recording Studios, Lyndhurst Hall, Hampstead, London, June 29-July 3, 1994)* Sony Classical ▲ SK 66483 [DDD]

Stewart, Mark (gtr)—see ORCHESTRAS & ENSEMBLES Bang on a Can, Bang on a Can members

Stewart, Murray (org)
Franck, C.:Org Music (comp) [organ at Haderslev Cathedral, Denmark] [Disc One]—Grande pièce symphonique; Pastorale; Trois Chorales; [Disc Two]—Prélude, Fugue & Variation; Fantaisie in A; Cantabile; Pièce héroïque; Fantaisie in C; Prière; Final *(rec 1980)* Kontrapunkt 2-▲ 32053/54 [ADD]
Vierne, L.:Pièces en style libre—2 pieces Kontrapunkt ▲ 32067 [ADD]
Vierne, L.:Sym 1 Org—2 pieces Kontrapunkt ▲ 32067 [ADD]

Stewart, Murray (vn)
Howells, H.:Orchestral Music, w. K. Stott (pno), V. Handley (cnd), Royal Liverpool PO—Concerto for String Orchestra (1938); Concerto No. 2 in c for Piano & Orchestra (1925); Three Dances for Violin & Orchestra (1915) *(rec Feb. 1991 & Mar. 1992)* Hyperion ▲ CDA 66610 [DDD]
Jaubert, M.:Film Music, w. M. Plasson (cnd), Toulouse Capitole Orch—Le quai des brumes; Le jour se lève *(rec July 2-5, 1992)* EMI Classics ▲ CDC 54764-2 [DDD]
Kosma, J.:Film Music, w. M. Plasson (cnd), Toulouse Capitole Orch—Les portes de la nuit; Les enfants du paradis:Baptiste *(rec July 2-5, 1992)* EMI Classics ▲ CDC 54764-2 [DDD]

Stewart, Raymond (tuba)—see ORCHESTRAS & ENSEMBLES Meridian Arts Ensemble

Stewart, Victoria (vn)—see ORCHESTRAS & ENSEMBLES Bronx Arts Ensemble

Stidfole, Arthur (bn)
Behrman, D.:On the Other Ocean, w. David Behrman (elec), Maggi Payne (fl), Kim-1 (computer) *(rec Mills College, Oakland, CA, Sep 18, 1977)* Lovely Music ▲ LCD 1041 [ADD]

Stiehler, Helmar (vc)—see ORCHESTRAS & ENSEMBLES Koeckert String Quartet, Stuttgart Piano Trio

Stier, Charles (cl)
Brahms, J.:Sons Cl (comp), w. William Bloomquist (pno) Halcyon 2-▲ HP 30101 [DDD]
Brahms, J.:Son 1 Cl, w. W. Bloomquist (pno) Élan ▲ CD 2224 [DDD]
Brahms, J.:Son 2 Cl, w. W. Bloomquist (pno) Élan ▲ CD 2238 [DDD]
Cameos, w. Stier, Charles (cl), Molly Newton (pno) Élan ▲ CD 2246 [DDD]
Gade, N.W.:Fantasistykker, w. William Bloomquist (pno) Halcyon 2-▲ HP 30101 [DDD]
Gade, N.W.:Fantasistykker, w. W. Bloomquist (pno) Élan ▲ CD 2238 [DDD]
One Halcyon ▲ HP 30104 [DDD]
Reger, M.:Albumblatt & Romanze, w. W. Bloomquist (pno)—Romanze Élan ▲ CD 2238
Reger, M.:Albumblatt & Tarantella, w. William Bloomquist (pno) Halcyon 2-▲ HP 30101 [DDD]
Reger, M.:Albumblatt & Tarantella, w. W. Bloomquist (pno) Élan ▲ CD 2238 [DDD]
Reger, M.:Son Cl, Op. 107, w. W. Bloomquist (pno) Élan ▲ CD 2224 [DDD]
Schumann, R.:Fantasiestücke Cl, w. William Bloomquist (pno) Halcyon 2-▲ HP 30101 [DDD]
Schumann, R.:Fantasiestücke Cl, w. W. Bloomquist (pno) Élan ▲ CD 2238 [DDD]
Weber, C.M. von:Grand duo concertant Cl, w. William Bloomquist (pno) Halcyon 2-▲ HP 30101 [DDD]
Weber, C.M. von:Grand duo concertant Cl, w. W. Bloomquist (pno) Élan ▲ CD 2238 [DDD]

Stifelman, Leslie (pno)
Bowles, P.:Con for 2 Pnos, w. Alan Feinberg (pno), J. Sheffer (cnd), Eos Ensemble *(rec Manhattan Center Studios, New York, Sept 22 & 23, 1995)* Catalyst ▲ 09026-68409-2 [DDD]
Gershwin, G.:Con Pno, w. M. Alsop (cnd), Concordia Orch EMI Classics ▲ CDC 54851
Kernis, A.J.:America(n) (Day) Dreams, w. Kim Barber (mez), Mary Rowell (vn), Leslie Tomkins (va), Tonya Tomkins (vc), Robert Black (db), Kathleen Nester (fl), Larry Guy (cl/b cl), John Dent (tpt), Anthony Cecere (hn), Susan Jolles (hp), Jeffrey Milarsky (perc), M. Barrett (cnd)—A Navajo Blanket; Wednesday at the Waldorf; The Pregnant Dream; The Blue Bottle; "So Long" to the Moon from the Men of Apollo; Epilogue:The Pure Suit of Happiness *(rec Manhattan Center Studios, New York, May 31-June 3, 1995)* New Albion ♦ NA 083CD
Kernis, A.J.:Nocturne, w. Nancy Allen Lundy (sop), John Dent (tpt), Jeff Milarsky (glock), Benjamin Herman (glock), Lisa Moore (pno), M. Barrett (cnd) *(rec Manhattan Center Studios, New York, May 31-June 3, 1995)* New Albion ♦ NA 083CD

Stiftner, W. (bn)
Kreutzer, C.:Trio Pno, Cl & Bn, w. R. Junghanns (kbd), H.-R. Stalder (cl) [period instrs] *(rec 1984)* Jecklin-Disco ▲ JD 587-2 [ADD]

Stiglich, Irina (org)
Musica Sacra, w. Lyubomir Pipkov Sofia Chamber Choir Jade ▲ JAD C095

Stiglich, Irina (pno/org)
Schumann, R.:Choral Music, w. T. Pavlovich (cnd), Vassil Arnaudov Sofia Chamber Choir—Tamburinschlägerin; Waldmädchen; Klosterfräulein; Soldatenbraut; Meerfey; Die Capelle; Rosmarien; Des Knaben Wunderhorn:Jäger Wolgemuth; Das verlassene Mägdlein; Der Bleicherin Nachtlied; In Meeres Mitten ist ein offener Laden; Mailied; Frühlingslied; An die Nachtigall; An den Abendstern; Nänie; Triolett; Spruch; Sommerruh; Chor der Houris aus das Paradies und die Peri; Ländliches Lied; Lied Gega ▲ GD 144 [DDD]

INSTRUMENT.

Stigmer, Jan (vn)
Larsson, L.-E.:Concertinos, w. Per-Ola Lindberg (va), Bjøorg Vaernes (vc), Ingalill Hillerud (db), Joakim Kallhed (pno), Camerata Romana—Nos. 8-12 Intim Musik ▲ INT 31
Roman, J.H.:Cons (4) Vn, w. T. Svedlund (cnd), Camerata Romana—in d & f Intim Musik ▲ INT 32

Stilfies, G. (hn)
Beethoven, L. van:Qnt Ob, 3 Hns & Bn, w. A. Simon (ob), R. Woodhams (hn), G. Berry (hn), R. Pandolfi (bn) *(rec 1975-79)* Vox Box 3-▲ CD3X 3014 [ADD]

Still, Alexa (fl)
Alexa Still, w. New Zealand CO [cnd:Nocholas Braithwaite] Koch International Classics ▲ KIC 7063 [DDD]
Alexa Still "Flute" w. Susan DeWitt Smith (pno) Koch International Classics ▲ KIC 7144 [DDD]
Arnold, M.:Con 1 Fl, w. N. Braithwaite (cnd), New Zealand CO Koch International Classics ▲ KIC 7607
Arnold, M.:Con 2 Fl, w. N. Braithwaite (cnd), New Zealand CO Koch International Classics ▲ KIC 7140 [DDD]
Arnold, M.:Con 2 Fl, w. N. Braithwaite (cnd), New Zealand CO Koch International Classics ▲ KIC 7607
Barber, S.:Canzone Fl & Pno, w. S. DeWitt Smith (pno) Koch International Classics ▲ KIC 7144 [DDD]
Barber, S.:Music of, w. Chicago SO, San Diego CO, Atlantic Sinfonietta, New Zealand SO, Arioso Wind Quintet, Capricorn, Repertory Singers—Capricorn Con; Canzone; Fadograph of a Yestern Scene; Cave of the Heart; Adagio for Strs; Souvenirs; Hermit Songs; To Be Sung on Water; The Lovers; Summer Music Koch International Classics ▲ KIC 7361
Bloch, E.:Two Last Poems...Maybe, w. J. Sedares (cnd), New Zealand SO *(rec Oct. 1993)* Koch International Classics ▲ KIC 7232 [DDD]
Burton, E.:Sonatina Fl, w. S. D. Smith (pno) Koch International Classics ▲ KIC 7144 [DDD]
Copland, A.:Duo Fl, w. S. de Witt Smith (pno) Koch International Classics ▲ KIC 7144 [DDD]
Copland, A.:Vocalise, w. S. DeWitt Smith (pno) Koch International Classics ▲ KIC 7144 [DDD]
Flute Salad, w. Gilbert, Laura (fl), Doriot Dwyer (fl), Bradley Garner (fl), New Zealand CO, London SO Koch Schwann ▲ KIC CD 7602
Hovhaness, A.:Music of, w. Marvin Rosen (pno), Jordania (cnd), Manhattan CO, New Zealand CO, KBS SO—The Prayer of St. Gregory; Elibris; Mystic Flute; Aria, Hymn & Fugue; Mountain Idylls; Gtr Sym; Adagio; Son; Fred the Cat; Aria [from Harotiun] Koch International Classics ▲ KIC 7311 [DDD]
Jacob, G.:Con Fl, w. N. Braithwaite (cnd), New Zealand CO Koch International Classics ▲ KIC 7140 [DDD]
Moross, J.:Con Fl, w. D. Armstrong (cnd), New Zealand CO Koch Schwann ▲ KIC CD 7367
Musgrave, T.:Orfeo II, w. N. Braithwaite (cnd), New Zealand CO Koch International Classics ▲ KIC 7140
Still, W.G.:Folk Suites, w. M. Steer (db), S. De Witt Smith (pno), New Zealand String Quartet—No. 1 Koch International Classics ▲ KIC 7192 [DDD]
Still, W.G.:Instrumental Music, w. S. De Witt Smith (pno)—Quit Dat Fool'nish; Summerland Koch International Classics ▲ KIC 7154
Still, W.G.:Instrumental Music, w. S. De Witt Smith (pno), M. Steer (db), New Zealand String Quartet—Quit Dat Fool'nish; Summerland Koch International Classics ▲ KIC 7192 [DDD]
Still, W.G.:Music of, w. S. DeWitt Smith (pno), M. Steer (db), New Zealand String Quartet—Summerland; Quit dat Fool'nish; Pastorela; Folk Suite 1; Suite for Violin & Piano [Movts. I & II]; Prelude for Flute, String Qnt. & Piano *(rec May 1993)* Koch International Classics ▲ KIC 7192 [DDD]
Still, W.G.:Preludes Fl, w. S. De Witt Smith (pno), M. Steer (db), New Zealand String Quartet Koch International Classics ▲ KIC 7192 [DDD]

Still, Jonathan (pno)
Bravo Bassoon, w. Daniel Smith (bn), Caravaggio Ensemble ASV ▲ ASV 2078 [DDD]

Still, Ray (ob d'amore)
Bach, J.S.:Con Ob d'amore, w. R. Stamp (cnd), Academy of London Orch Virgin Classics ▲ CDZ 59686-2

Still, Ray (ob)
Bach, J.S.:Con Vn & Ob, w. I. Perlman (vn), Israel PO EMI Classics ▲ CDC 47073-2 [DDD]
Marcello, A.:Con Ob & Strs, w. R. Stamp (cnd), Academy of London Orch Virgin Classics ▲ CDZ 59686
Strauss, R.:Con Ob, w. R. Stamp (cnd), Academy of London Orch Virgin Classics ▲ CDZ 59686

Stillman, Judith Lynn (pno)
On the 20th Century, w. Wynton Marsalis (tpt) *(rec Jan. 20-24, 1992)* Sony Classical ▲ SK 47193 [DDD] Δ SM 47193-2 [DDD]; ■ ST 47193-4
Seasons Remembered 2, w. Toby Appel (va), John Deak (db), Eliot Porter (db), Diaz Trio [David Kim (vn), Roberto Diaz (va), Andres Diaz (vc)], Lutz Rath (vc), Fenwick Smith (fl), Ruth Waterman (vn) North Star ▲ 9837-40052-2 ■ 9837-40052-4

Stilz, Manfred (vc)—see ORCHESTRAS & ENSEMBLES Ravel Trio
Legrand, H.:Andante, w. E. Berchot (pno) Arcobaleno ▲ SBCD 7300

Stinders, Herman (hpd)
17th & 18th Century Chamber Music, w. Pieter-Jan Belder (rcr), René Schiffer (baroque vc) *(rec Nov. 1991)* Erasmus ▲ WVH 058 [DDD]

Stinders, Herman (org)
Esteves, J.R.:Missa a oito voces, w. Erik van Nevel (cnd), Currende Vocal Ensemble [L] Accent ▲ 9069 [DDD]
Scarlatti, D.:Stabat mater, w. Erik van Nevel (cnd), Currende Vocal Ensemble [L] Accent ▲ 9069 [DDD]
Wert, G. de:Sacred Music, w. E. Van Nevel (cnd), Concerto Palatino Choir, Currende Vocal Ensemble—Missa Dominicalis; sels. from *Motectorum quinque vocum, liber primus, Il secondo libro de motetti a cinque voci & Modulationem cum sex vocibus, liber primus* Accent ▲ 9291 [DDD]

Stingl, Anton (lt)
Music for Lute, Guitar & Mandolin, w. Konrad Ragossnig (gtr), Michael Schäffer (lt), Karl Scheit (gtr), Leo Witoszinskyj (gtr), William Matthews (gtr), Paul Grund (mand), Artur Rumetsch (mand), Edith Bauer-Slais (mand), Elfriede Kunschak (mand) Vox Box 3-▲ CD3X 3022
Vivaldi, A.:Cons Diverse Instrs, w. J. Faerber (cnd), Württemberg CO—in D for Lt & Strs Special Music Co. ("Classics of the Heart" series) ▲ SCD 5198

Stinton, Jennifer (fl)
An American Recital, w. Malcolm Martineau (pno) Collins Classics ▲ COL 1385 [DDD]
Bach, C.P.E.:Cons Fl, w. J. Lubbock (cnd), St. John's Smith Square Orch—in d, A & G Collins Classics ▲ COL 1373 [DDD]
Beethoven, L. van:Son 5 Vn, "Spring", w. M. Martineau (pno) Collins Classics ▲ COL 1347
The Concerto Collection, w. English CO [cnd:Steuart Bedford], Philharmonia Orch [cnd:Tamás Vásáry] Collins Classics 2-▲ COL 7005 [DDD]
Honegger, A.:Con da camera, w. G. Browne (E hn), S. Bedford (cnd), Scottish CO Collins Classics ▲ 12102 [DDD]
Honegger, A.:Con da camera, w. G. Browne (E hn), S. Bedford (cnd), Scottish CO Collins Classics 2-▲ 70052 [DDD]
Ibert, J.:Con Fl, w. S. Bedford (cnd), Scottish CO Collins Classics ▲ 12102 [DDD]
Ibert, J.:Con Fl, w. G. Browne (E hn), S. Bedford (cnd), Scottish CO Collins Classics 2-▲ 70052 [DDD]
Mozart, W.A.:Con Fl, K.314, w. T. Vásáry (cnd), Philharmonia Orch Collins Classics 2-▲ 70052 [DDD]
Mozart, W.A.:Con Fl Hp, w. A. Brewer (hp), T. Vásáry (cnd), Philharmonia Orch Collins Classics 2-▲ 70052 [DDD]
Nielsen, C.:Con Fl, w. S. Bedford (cnd), Scottish CO Collins Classics ▲ 12102 [DDD]
Nielsen, C.:Con Fl, w. S. Bedford (cnd), Scottish CO Collins Classics 2-▲ 70052 [DDD]
Poulenc, F.:Son Fl, w. S. Bedford (cnd), Scottish CO [orchd. by Lennox Berkeley] Collins Classics ▲ 12102 [DDD]
Poulenc, F.:Son Fl, w. S. Bedford (cnd), Scottish CO [orchd. by Lennox Berkeley] Collins Classics 2-▲ 70052 [DDD]
Rodrigo, J.:Concierto pastorale, w. T. Vásáry (cnd), Philharmonia Orch Collins Classics 2-▲ 70052 [DDD]
Romantic Works for Flute & Harp, w. Aline Brewer (hp) Collins Classics ▲ COL 1008 [DDD]
Schubert, Franz:Intro & Vars Fl on "Tröckne Blumen", w. M. Martineau (pno) Collins Classics ▲ COL 1347
Schubert, Franz:Son Arpeggione, w. M. Martineau (pno) Collins Classics ▲ COL 1347

Stinton, Jennifer (fl) (cont.)
Vivaldi, A.:Cons Fl (misc), w. H. Christophers (cnd), Royal Concertgebouw CO—RV.440 Collins Classics ▲ COL 1324 [DDD]
Vivaldi, A.:Cons Fl, Op. 10, w. H. Christophers (cnd), Royal Concertgebouw CO Collins Classics ▲ COL 1324 [DDD]

Stirling, Michael (vc)
Zimmermann, B.A.:Présence, w. Hermann Kretzschmar (pno), Peter Rundel (vn) *(rec Frankfurt, May 1-4 & Oct 24-25, 1992)* RCA Red Seal ▲ 09026-61181-2 [DDD]

Stirling, Stephen (hn)
Vivaldi, A.:Cons Diverse Instrs, w. Joanna Graham (bn), Ruth McDowall (cl), David Rix (ct), Deborah Davis (fl), Duke Dobing (fl), Tim Caister (hn), Christopher Hooker (ob), Helen McQueen (ob), Michael Meekes (tpt), Crispian Steele-Perkins (tpt), Nicholas Kraemer (hpd), N. Kraemer (cnd), London Sinfonietta—Cons. in F, RV.539; in C, RV.533; in D, RV.122; in C, RV.537; in C, RV.560; in F, RV.538; in G, RV.545 *(rec All Saints Church, East Finchley, Oct. 1994 & Jan. 1995)* Naxos ("Vivaldi Collection" series) ▲ 8.553204 [DDD]

Stivín, Jiří (flautino)
Vivaldi, A.:Cons Fl (misc), w. J. Válek (fl), J. Novotny (fl), *(orch unknown)*—Flute Concerti, RV.108, 533, & in F; Flautino Concerti, RV.443, 444 & 445 Naxos ▲ 8.550385 [DDD]

Stivín, Jiří (rcr)
Telemann, G.P.:Con Rcr, Fl, w. Jiří Válek (fl), M. Munclinger (cnd), Prague CO Supraphon ▲ SUP 3039
Telemann, G.P.:Cons Rcr, w. Pro Arte Antiqua Prague—in C Arta ▲ ARTA 0058 [DDD]
Telemann, G.P.:Cons Rcr, Vl, w. Petr Hejny (va), Pro Arte Antiqua Prague—in a Arta ▲ ARTA 0058 [DDD]
Telemann, G.P.:Con in a for 2 Rcrs, w. Miloslav Klement (rcr), M. Munclinger (cnd), Prague CO Supraphon ▲ SUP 3039
Telemann, G.P.:Fantasias Rcr—Nos. 1, 3, 8 & 10 Supraphon ▲ SUP 3039
Telemann, G.P.:Suite Rcr, w. R. Edlinger (cnd), Capella Istropolitana Naxos ▲ 8.550156 [DDD] Δ 7.550156 [DDD]
Telemann, G.P.:Suite Rcr, w. M. Munclinger (cnd), Prague CO Supraphon ▲ SUP 3039
Telemann, G.P.:Trio Sons, w. Petr Hejny (va), Pro Arte Antiqua Prague—in g & F for Rcr, Vl & Bc Arta ▲ ARTA 0058 [DDD]
Vivaldi, A.:Cons Diverse Instrs, w. Václav Hudeček (cl), Ludomír Brabec (pno), G. Delogu (cnd), Janáček CO, Prague CO—in C for 2 Rcrs, 2 Bns, 2 Vns, 2 Gtrs, Vc, Strings & Cont, RV.558; in d for Vn, Gtr, Strs & Cont, RV.540; in F for Vn, Gtr, Strs & Cont, RV.542; in a for Rcr, Strs & Cont, RV.108; in C for 2 Vns, 2 Gtrs, 2 Fls, 2 Rcrs, 2 Strs & 2 Conts, RV.565 Supraphon ▲ SUP 3023

St. John, Lara (vn)
Bach, J.S.:Sons & Partitas Vn, BWV 1001-1006—Partita No. 2 in d, BWV 1004; Son No. 3 in C, BWV 1005 Well-Tempered Productions ▲ WTP 5180

Stobart, Henry (rcr/bgp/vl/shawm/pipe/tabor)—see ORCHESTRAS & ENSEMBLES Sirinu

Stobart, James (hn)
Böck, A.:Pieces (4), w. G. Langenstein (hn), G. Dzwiza (db), K. Stoll (db) Signum ▲ X 45-00 [DDD]

Stochl, Frédéric (db)
Rebotier, J.:La musique adoucit les sons Adès ▲ ADE 204472 [DDD/AAD]

Stockhausen, Markus (tpt)
Kagel, M.:Nah und Fern, w. Andreas Adam (tpt), Marco Blaauw (tpt), Achim Gorsch (tpt), Arie Abbenes (car), M. Kagel (cnd) Montaigne ▲ MO 782062
Stockhausen, K.:Oberlippentanz Acanta ▲ CD 43201 [DDD]

Stockhausen, Markus (tpt/flgl)
Stockhausen, M.:Music of, w. Simon Stockhausen (syn/sax), Jo Thönes (dr/perc)—Bells; Kitchen; Passacaglia; The Heaven Open; Thunderstorm; Gamelan; Outer Space; Ping Pong; Sound Duo; Fireworks; Yeah!; 2 Brothers; Grand Finale; Daydream; Miles Mute?; Desert Wind; Spirit; Boomerang Largo ▲ CD 5133 [DDD]

Stockhausen, Markus (tpt/pno)
Stockhausen, K.:Tierkreis Cl, w. S. Stephens (cl), K. Pasveer (fl) Acanta ▲ CD 43201 [DDD]

Stockhausen, Simon (syn/sax)
Stockhausen, M.:Music of, w. Markus Stockhausen (tpt/flgl), Jo Thönes (dr/perc)—Bells; Kitchen; Passacaglia; The Heaven Open; Thunderstorm; Gamelan; Outer Space; Ping Pong; Sound Duo; Fireworks; Yeah!; 2 Brothers; Grand Finale; Daydream; Miles Mute?; Desert Wind; Spirit; Boomerang Largo ▲ CD 5133 [DDD]

Stöckigt, Siegfried (pno)
Albert, E. d':Con 2 Pno, w. G. Herbig (cnd), Berlin SO Berlin Classics ▲ BER 9179
Dessau, P.:Guernica Berlin Classics ▲ BER 9181
Dessau, P.:Son Pno Berlin Classics ▲ BER 9181
Dessau, P.:Sonatine Pno, w. H. Kegel (cnd), Dresden PO Berlin Classics ▲ BER 9181
Dessau, P.:Studien (12) Pno—9 Studien Berlin Classics ▲ BER 9181
Gershwin, G.:Con Pno, w. K. Masur (cnd), Dresden PO Berlin Classics ("Masur Edition" series) ▲ BER 9158
Gershwin, G.:Rhap in Blue, w. Kurt Hiltawsky (cl), K. Masur (cnd), Dresden PO Berlin Classics ("Masur Edition" series) ▲ BER 9158
Gershwin, G.:Rhap in Blue, w. K. Masur (cnd), Leipzig Gewandhaus Orch Deutsche Grammophon ("Resonance" series) ▲ 427203-2 [ADD] ■ 427203-4

Stockmeier, Wolfgang (org)
David, J.N.:Org Music—Fantasia super "L'homme armé"; Fantasy & Fugue in C; Fantasy & Fugue in e; Introduction & Passacaglia on "Wach auf, wach auf, du deutsches Land"; Partita on "Da Jesus am Kreuze stand" CPO ▲ CPO 999042-2 [DDD]
Karg-Elert, S.:Org Music—Sinfonische Kanzone, Op. 85/1; Sinfonischer Choral, "Jesu meine Freude," Op. 87/2; Sinfonie, Op. 143 CPO ▲ CPO 999033-2 [DDD]
Karg-Elert, S.:Org Music—Chorale Improvisations, Op. 65/25, 44, 54, 56, 58, 59 & 63; Fantasia & Fugue, Op. 39b; Improvisation, Op. 34b; Kaleidoscope, Op. 11; Sequenz I, W.8 CPO ▲ CPO 999034-2 [DDD]
Karg-Elert, S.:Org Music CPO ▲ CPO 999035-2 [DDD]
Karg-Elert, S.:Org Music—Chorale Improvisations, Op. 65/1, 5, 16, 20, 21, 40 & 49; Homage to Handel; Sequenz II, W.12; Triptych, Op. 141 CPO ▲ CPO 999036-2 [DDD]
Karg-Elert, S.:Org Music CPO ▲ CPO 999119 [DDD]
Pepping, E.:Org Music—Partita on the chorale "Wie schön leuchtet der Morgenstern" (1933); Concerto II (1941); Four Fugues (1942); Partita, "Ach wie flüchtig, ach wie nichtig" (1953) CPO ▲ CPO 999039-2 [DDD]
Rheinberger, J.:Characteristic Pieces CPO ▲ CPO 999040-2 [DDD]
Rheinberger, J.:Fughettas (book 1) CPO ▲ CPO 999040-2 [DDD]
Rheinberger, J.:Fughettas (book 2) CPO ▲ CPO 999041-2 [DDD]
Rheinberger, J.:Meditations CPO ▲ CPO 999041-2 [DDD]
Rheinberger, J.:Miscellaneen CPO ▲ CPO 999089-2 [DDD]
Scheidt, S.:Org Music—Organ Works from Tabulatura Nova (1624); Credo in unum deum; Passamezzo in a; Cantica Sacra; Fuga in G; Psalmus sub Communione CPO ▲ CPO 999105 [DDD]
Walther, Joh. G.:Org Music—Walther's complete "free" organ music, numbering 22 compositions: 14 Concerto Arrangements for solo organ of works by other composers [Albinoni, Torelli, Telemann, et al.], in 3-5 movements each; 4 Preludes & Fugues; Fugue in F; Toccata & Fugue in C; Concerto in C; Alcuni Variationi (after Corelli) CPO 3-▲ CPO 999131-2 [DDD]

Stockton, Ann Mason (hp)
Debussy, C.:Danses sacrée et profane, w. F. Slatkin (cnd), Concert Arts Strings Testament ▲ TESSBT 1053 (m) [ADD]
Nostalgique, w. Felix Slatkin (cnd) Crystal ▲ CD 171
Ravel, M.:Intro & Allegro, w. Arthur Gleghorn (fl), Mitchell Lurie (cl), Hollywood String Quartet Testament ▲ TESSBT 1053 (m) [ADD]

Stokes, Christopher (org)
Vivaldi, A.:Beatus vir, R.597, w. Carys-Anne Lane (sop), Jayne Whitaker (sop), Christine Swain (ob), Robert Glenton (vc), N. Ward (cnd), Northern CO, Oxford Schola Cantorum *(rec St. Peter's Church, Hale, Cheshire, Mar. 14, 1994)* Naxos ▲ 8.550767 [DDD]

Stokes, Christopher (org) (cont.)
Vivaldi, A.:Gloria, RV.589, w. Anna Crookes (sop), Jayne Whitaker (sop), Caroline Trevor (alt), Christine Swain (ob), Robert Glenton (vc), N. Ward (cnd), Northern CO, Oxford Schola Cantorum *(rec St. Peter's Church, Hale, Cheshire, Dec. 3, 1993)* Naxos ▲ 8.550767 [DDD]
Stokes, Sheridan (fl)
Boccherini, L.:Sons Pno, Op. 5, w. Bess Karp (hpd) [arr for Fl & Hpd] *(rec Brentwood, CA, 1973)* Orion ▲ 7821-2 [AAD]
Lazarof, H.:Trio Wind Instruments, w. J. Winter (ob), G. Gray (cl) Laurel ▲ LR 845CD [AAD]
Levitch, L.:Qt Fl, Va, Vc & Pno, w. Sven Reher (va), Jeffrey Solow (vc), Irma Vallecillo-Gray (pno) Cambria ▲ CD 1059 [ADD]
Levitch, L.:Qnt Fl, w. Kathleen Lenski (vn), Miwako Watanabe (vn), Jeffrey Solow (vc), Paul Polivnick (va) Cambria ▲ CD 1059 [ADD]
Stokman, Abraham (pno)
Ran, S.:Hyperbolae *(rec 1979-91)* CRI ▲ CD 609 [ADD/DDD]
Stoll, Klaus (db)
Barrière, F.:Son Vc & Db, w. Joerg Baumann (vc) Camerata ▲ 32CM 5
Böck, A.:Pieces (4), w. G. Langenstein (hn), J. Stobart (hn), G. Dzwiza (db) Signum ▲ X 45-00 [DDD]
Boismortier, J.B. de:Sons, Op. 40, w. J. Baumann (vc)—No. 2 Koch Schwann ▲ SCH 313382 [ADD/DDD]
Bottesini, G.:Grande con for 2 Dbs, w. W. Güttler (db), M. Bamert (cnd), Berlin RSO Koch Schwann ▲ CD 311042 [DDD]
Bottesini, G.:Grandi Duetti for 2 Db, w. G. Dzwiza (db)—Nos. 1 & 2 Signum ▲ X 45-00 [DDD]
Couperin, F.:Con Vc, w. Joerg Baumann (vc) Camerata ▲ 32CM 5
Mozart, W.A.:Duo Bn Vc, w. Joerg Baumann (vc) Camerata ▲ 32CM 5
Mozart, W.A.:Son Bn Vc, w. J. Baumann (vc) Camerata ▲ 25CM 373
Rossini, G.:Duet Vc, w. Joerg Baumann (vc) Camerata ▲ 32CM 5
Vanhal, J.B.:Divert Strs, w. R. Mehne (vn), C. Solothurski (va), G. Dzwiza (db) Signum ▲ X 45-00
Stoll, V. (trbn)—see ORCHESTRAS & ENSEMBLES Datura Trombone Quartet
Stolper, M. (fl)
Nielsen, C.:Con Fl, w. D. Kober (cnd), Chicago CO Centaur ▲ CRC 2024 [DDD]
Stoltzman, Lucy Chapman (vn)
Bartók, B.:Contrasts, w. R. Stoltzman (cl), R. Goode (pno) RCA Red Seal ▲ 60170-2-RC [DDD]
Harrison, L.:Suite Vn, Pno & Small Orch, w. Keith Jarrett (pno), R. Hughes (cnd), Ensemble New World ▲ NW 366-2 [DDD]; ■ NW 366-4 (D)
Ives, C.:Largo, w. R. Stoltzman (cl), R. Goode (pno) RCA Red Seal ▲ 60170-2-RC [DDD]
Stravinsky, I.:L'Histoire du soldat Suite Vn, w. R. Stoltzman (cl), R. Goode (pno) RCA Red Seal ▲ 60170-2-RC [DDD]
Stoltzman, Richard (cl)
Bartók, B.:Contrasts, w. L. C. Stoltzman (vn), R. Goode (pno) RCA Red Seal ▲ 60170-2-RC [DDD]
Basic 100, Vol. 55, w. James Galway (fl), Marisa Robles (hp) RCA Victor ▲ 09026-68024-2 ■ 09026-68024-4
Beethoven, L. van:Trio 7 Pno, w. R. Serkin (pno), A. Meunier (vc) Sony Classical ▲ SMK 47296 [ADD]
Begin Sweet World RCA Victor ▲ RCD1-7124 ■ AMK1-7124
Bernstein, L.:Prelude, Fugue & Riffs Cl, w. L. Leighton Smith (cnd), London SO RCA Red Seal ▲ 09026-61360-2 [DDD]
Bernstein, L.:Son Cl, w. Irma Vallecillo (pno) *(rec Mechanics Hall, Worcester, MA, Jan 6-8, 1994)* RCA Red Seal ▲ 09026-62685-2 [DDD]
Brahms, J.:Qnt Cl, w. Tokyo String Quartet RCA Red Seal ▲ 09026-68049-2
Brahms, J.:Sons Cl (comp), w. R. Goode (pno) RCA Gold Seal ▲ 60036-2-RG [DDD]
Brasil, w. Stoltzman, Richard (cl), Gary Burton (vib), Eddie Gomez (db), Danny Gottlieb (perc) RCA Victor ▲ 60708-2-RC [DDD] ■ 60708-4-RC (CrO2)
Carol of the Drum, w. Chieftains, Emily Mitchell (hp), Michala Petri (rcr), James Galway (fl), Hampton String Quartet, Royal PO, Boys' Choir of Harlem RCA Victor ▲ 09026-61839-2 ■ 09026-61839-4
Copland, A.:Con Cl, w. L. Leighton Smith (cnd), London SO RCA Red Seal ▲ 09026-61360-2 [DDD]
Corigliano, J.:Con Cl, w. L. Leighton Smith (cnd), London SO RCA Red Seal ▲ 09026-61360-2 [DDD]
Ebony, w. Woody Herman's Thundering Herd RCA Red Seal ▲ 6486-2-RC [DDD]
English Music for Clarinet & String Orchestra, w. Guildhall String Ensemble [cnd:Robert Salter] RCA Red Seal ▲ 60437-2-RC [DDD] ■ 60437-4-RC
Englund, S.E.:Con Cl, w. L. Foss (cnd), Berlin SO *(rec Jesus-Christus-Kirche, Berlin, May 10-14, 1993)* RCA Red Seal ▲ 09026-61902-2 [DDD]
Erb, D.:Con Cl, w. C. Comet (cnd), Grand Rapids SO *(rec DeVos Hall, Grand Rapids, MI, May 22, 1994)* Koss Classics ▲ KC 3002 [DDD]
Finzi, G.:Con Cl, w. R. Salter (cnd), Guildhall String Ensemble RCA Red Seal ▲ 60437-2-RC [DDD]; ■ 60437-4-RC (CrO2)
Fisher, C.:Sonatine Cl, w. Irma Vallecillo (pno) *(rec Mechanics Hall, Worcester, MA, Jan 6-8, 1994)* RCA Red Seal ▲ 09026-62685-2 [DDD]
Foss, L.:Con Cl, w. L. Foss (cnd), Berlin SO *(rec Jesus-Christus-Kirche, Berlin, May 10-14, 1993)* RCA Red Seal ▲ 09026-61902-2 [DDD]
Gershwin, G.:Preludes (3) Pno, w. Irma Vallecillo (pno) *(rec Mechanics Hall, Worcester, MA, Jan 6-8, 1994)* RCA Red Seal ▲ 09026-62685-2 [DDD]
Harkl, w. Stoltzman, Richard (cl), Eddie Gomez (perc), Jeremy Wall (kbd), Dave Samuels (vib), Bill Douglas (bn), Harlem Boys Choir RCA Victor ▲ 09026-61272-2 [DDD] ■ 09026-61272-4 (CrO2)
Hyman, R.:Clarinata, w. Irma Vallecillo (pno) *(rec Mechanics Hall, Worcester, MA, Jan 6-8, 1994)* RCA Red Seal ▲ 09026-62685-2 [DDD]
Innervoices, w. Judy Collins (sgr) RCA Victor ▲ 7888-2-RC [DDD]
Ives, C.:Largo, w. L. Chapman Stoltzman (vn), R. Goode (pno) RCA Red Seal ▲ 60170-2-RC [DDD]
Ives, C.:Songs, w. R. Goode (pno) [arr. for clarinet & piano]—The things our fathers loved; Walking; Like a sick eagle; Ann Street - Broadway; The cage; The see'r; The Housatonic at Stockbridge; In the mornin'; Serenity RCA Red Seal ▲ 60170-2-RC [DDD]
McKinley, W.T.:Con 2 Cl, w. L. Foss (cnd), Berlin SO *(rec Jesus-Christus-Kirche, Berlin, May 10-14, 1993)* RCA Red Seal ▲ 09026-61902-2 [DDD]
McKinley, W.T.:Son Cl, w. Irma Vallecillo (pno) *(rec Mechanics Hall, Worcester, MA, Jan 6-8, 1994)* RCA Red Seal ▲ 09026-62685-2 [DDD]
Mozart, W.A.:Andante Fl, K.315/285a, w. A. Schneider (cnd), Mostly Mozart Festival Orch RCA Gold Seal ▲ 60035-2-RG [DDD]
Mozart, W.A.:Con Bn, w. A. Schneider (cnd), English CO [trans. Stoltzman] RCA Gold Seal ▲ 60379-2-RG [ADD] ■ 60379-4-RG
Mozart, W.A.:Con Cl, English CO RCA Red Seal ▲ 60723-2 [DDD] ■ 60723-4 (CrO2)
Mozart, W.A.:Con Cl, w. A. Schneider (cnd), English CO RCA Gold Seal ▲ 60379-2-RG [ADD] ■ 60379-4-RG
Mozart, W.A.:Con Cl, English CO RCA Victor ▲ 09026-68024-2; ■ 09026-68024-2
Mozart, W.A.:Qnt Cl, K.581, w. Tokyo String Quintet RCA Red Seal ▲ 60723-2 [DDD] ■ 60723-4 (CrO2)
New York Counterpoint RCA Victor ▲ 5944-2-RC [DDD]
Noël, w. Canadian Brass, Canadian Brass Jazz All-Stars, Angel Romero (gtr), *(children's choir unknown)*, Harolyn Blackwell (sop), Jerry Hadley (ten), King's Singers, James Galway (fl) *(rec Apr. 17-20, 1994)* RCA Victor ▲ 09026-62683-2 ■ 09026-62683-4
O Holy Night:Christmas Favorites, w. James Galway (fl), Michala Petri (rcr), Emily Mitchell (hp), Canadian Brass, Boston Pops Orch [cnd:Arthur Fiedler] RCA Victor ▲ 09026-61836-2 ■ 09026-61836-4
Out Classics, w. Ofra Harnoy (vc), Peter Serkin (pno), Leonard Slatkin (cnd), London PO, et al. RCA Red Seal ▲ 09026-68261-2 ■ 09026-68261-4
Poulenc, F.:Son Cl Pno, w. I. Vallecillo (pno) RCA Red Seal ▲ 60198-2-RC [DDD] ■ 60198-4-RC (CrO2)
Ravel, M.:Intro & Allegro, w. Hedi Lehwalder (hp), James Galway (fl), Tokyo String Quartet RCA Red Seal ▲ 09026-62552-2
Romance, w. Nancy Allen (hp), Irma Vallecillo (pno) RCA Red Seal ▲ 60198-2-RC [DDD]

Stoltzman, Richard (cl) (cont.)
Rossini, G.:Theme & Vars Cl, w. A. Schneider (cnd), Mostly Mozart Festival Orch RCA Gold Seal ▲ 60035-2-RG [DDD]
Rowles, J.:The Peacocks, w. Irma Vallecillo (pno) *(rec Mechanics Hall, Worcester, MA, Jan 6-8, 1994)* RCA Red Seal ▲ 09026-62685-2 [DDD]
Saint-Saëns, C.:Son Cl, w. I. Vallecillo (pno) RCA Red Seal ▲ 60198-2-RC [DDD] ■ 60198-4-RC (CrO2)
Schubert, Franz:Sonatinas Vn, w. R. Goode (pno)—D.384 & D.385 RCA Red Seal ▲ 6772-2-RC [DDD]
Schumann, R.:Fantasiestücke Cl, w. R. Goode (pno) RCA Red Seal ▲ 6772-2-RC [DDD]
Schumann, R.:Romances Ob, w. R. Goode (pno) RCA Red Seal ▲ 6772-2-RC [DDD]
Spirits, w. Stoltzman, Richard (cl), Eddie Gomez (db), David Torn (gtr), Dave Samuels (vib), Bill Douglas (bn), King's Singers RCA Victor ▲ 09026-68416-2 ■ 09026-68416-4
Stock, D.:Yerusha, w. D. Stock (cnd), Pittsburgh New Music Ensemble *(rec Levy Hall, Rodef Shalom Temple, Pittsburgh, Feb. 11, 1990)* Northeastern ("Contemporary" series) ▲ NR 255 [DDD]
Stravinsky, I.:Ebony Con, Woody Herman's Thundering Herd RCA Red Seal ▲ 09026-61360-2 [DDD]
Stravinsky, I.:L'Histoire du soldat Suite Vn, w. L. Chapman Stoltzman (vn), R. Goode (pno) RCA Red Seal ▲ 60170-2-RC [DDD]
Takemitsu, T.:Fantasma Cantos, w. T. Otaka (cnd), BBC Welsh National SO RCA Red Seal ▲ 09026-62537-2
Takemitsu, T.:Music of, w. Tashi, Y. Nagano (mez), H. Ibe (gtr), M. Nagasako (hp), K. Abe (vib), Y. Takahashi (pno), R. Noguchi (fl), M. Hamada (lt), T. Koizumi (picc), S. Ueki (vn), Y. Hattori (vc), P. Serkin (pno), Ozawa, Wakasugi (cnd), Boston SO—Quatrain; Stanza I; Sacrifice; Ring; Valeria; A Flock Descends into the Pentagonal Garden Deutsche Grammophon ("20th Century Classics" series) ▲ 423253-2 [ADD]
Takemitsu, T.:Quatrain II, w. T. Otaka (cnd), BBC Welsh National SO RCA Red Seal ▲ 09026-62537-2
Takemitsu, T.:Waterways, w. T. Otaka (cnd), BBC Welsh National SO RCA Red Seal ▲ 09026-62537-2
Takemitsu, T.:Waves, w. T. Otaka (cnd), BBC Welsh National SO RCA Red Seal ▲ 09026-62537-2
Weber, C.M. von:Con 1 Cl, w. A. Schneider (cnd), Mostly Mozart Festival Orch RCA Gold Seal ▲ 60035-2-RG [DDD]
Weber, C.M. von:Qnt Cl, w. Tokyo String Quartet RCA Red Seal ▲ 09026-68049-2
Stolz, Lissa (ob)
A Double Reed Consort, w. Wizards!, Iowa Double Reed Consort [Lissa Stolz (ob), Debra Hawk-Burt (ob/e hn), Ronald Tyree (bn), Ronald Snitker (bn/ctbn), Trevor Johnson (hpd)] *(rec Clapp Recital Hall, Univ. of Iowa, Iowa City, Jan. 1993 & May 1994)* CRS Master ▲ CRS 9460
Stolze, Kurt-Heinz (hpd)
Bach, J.S.:Con for 4 Hpds, w. M. Galling (hpd), H. Bilgram (hpd), F. Lehrndorfer (hpd), G. Kehr (cnd), Mainz CO Vox Box 2-▲ CDX 5040
Rinaldo di Capua:La Zingara, w. Annalisa Monkewitz (sop—Nisa), Rodolfo Malacarne (ten—Tagliaborse), Laerte Malaguti (bass—Calcante), Josef Ulsamer (vl), G. Kehr (cnd), Mainz CO Dynamic ▲ CD 141 [ADD]
Stolzman, R. (cl)—see ORCHESTRAS & ENSEMBLES Tashi
Stone, Colin (pno)
Prokofiev, S.:Pno Music (misc)—Romeo & Juliet, Op. 75 [10 pieces]; Contredance, Op. 96/2; Mephisto Waltz, Op. 96/3; Intermezzo, Op. 52/1; Rondo, Op. 52/2; Etude, Op. 52/3; Hamlet; The Love for 3 Oranges; CinDerella [10 pieces] *(rec All Saints, Petersham, Jan 17-19, 1994)* United ▲ CAL 88028 [DDD]
Stone, Diana (müttertrompette)
Schulhoff, E.:Son erotica Supraphon ▲ SUP 112170 [DDD]
Stone, Dorothy (fl)—see also ORCHESTRAS & ENSEMBLES California EAR Unit
Alexander, K.:And the Whole Air Is Tremulous New World ▲ 80456-2
Babbitt, M.:None but the Lonely Fl New World ▲ 80456-2
Cage, J.:Ryoanji Fl, w. Arthur Jarvinen (perc) New World ▲ 80456-2
Feldman, Morton:Why Patterns, w. G. Mowrey (pno), A. Jarvinen (perc) *(rec 10/90)* New Albion ▲ NA 039 [DDD]
Mosko, S.L.:for Morton Feldman, w. Erika Duke-Kirkpatrick (vc), Gaylord Mowrey (pno) New World ▲ 80456-2
Mosko, S.L.:Indigenous Music 2, *(cnd & orch unknown)* [for solo flute] New World ▲ 80456-2
Stone, Dorothy (fl/pic)
Smith, W.L.:Music of, w. Robin Lorentz (vn), Erika Duke (vc), Martin Walker (cl), Wadada Leo Smith (tpt/flgl/fls/bells), Vicki Ray (pno/cel), Mika Noda (vib/bells/timp), David Philipson (perc/bells)—Another Wave More Waves; Double Thunderbolt; Tao-Njia; and others Tzadik ("Composer" series) ▲ TZA 7017 [DDD]
Stone, Dorothy (fls)
Feldman, Morton:Trio Fls New World ▲ 80456-2
Stone, Joseph (fl)
Carter, E.:Syringa, w. P. Suits (pno) CRI ▲ CD 648 [ADD]
Matson, S.:Range, w. Catherine Robbin (mez), Susan Greenberg (fl), Glen Garrett (cl), Suren Karapetyan (hn), Peter Kent (vn), Kazi Pitelka (va), Sebastian Toettcher (vc), Don Ferrone (db), Doug Livingston (gtr/mand), John Schneider (gtr), Amy Shulman (hp), Terry Schoenig (perc), S. Matson (cnd) *(rec Schnee Studio, Universal City, CA, Mar 12, 1995)* New Albion ▲ NA 091
Stone, Julie (fl)
Nielson, L.:Black Magic, w. Martha Thomas (pno) *(rec Atlanta, GA, July 5, 1993)* ACA Digital Recording ▲ CM 20027
Stone, Julie (fl/pic)
Schoenberg, A.:Pierrot lunaire, w. Leslie Boucher (nar), Tod Kerstetter (cl/b cl), Andrew Carlson (vn), Philip Singleton (va), Juanita Karpf (vc), F. Joseph Lozier (pno) *(rec Roswell United Methodist Church, Roswell, GA, July 20, Aug. 2 & Sept. 1)* ACA Digital ▲ CM 20027
Zwilich, E.T.:Passages, w. Leslie Boucher (sop), Tod Kerstetter (cl/b cl), Andrew Carlson (vn), Philip Singleton (va), Juanita Karpf (vc), F. Joseph Lozier (pno), Joanna Parks (perc), Shannon O'Kelley (perc) *(rec Roswell United Methodist Church, Roswell, GA, July 20, Aug. 2 & Sept. 1)* ACA Digital ▲ CM 20027
Stone, Richard (lt)
Weiss, S.L.:Lt Music—Sonatas for Lute in A, c, B♭ Titanic ▲ TI 213 [DDD]
Stone, Richard (thb/lt)—see ORCHESTRAS & ENSEMBLES Tempesta di Mare
Stone, Terrell (gallichone)
Brescianello, G.A.:Sons (18) Gallichone—Sons 1-9 *(rec Padua, Italy, Aug 30-31 & Sept 1-2, 199)* Dynamic ▲ CD 151 [DDD]
Stone, Terrell (thb)—see ORCHESTRAS & ENSEMBLES Il Ruggiero, Ensemble Barocco Padua Sans Souci
Stonefelt, Kay (perc)
Cox, C.A.:Studies of Light & Dark (4), w. Cindy Annice Cox (pno) Capstone ▲ SCI 6
Stoop, Ernestine (hp)
Andriessen, H.:Music of, w. Roberta Alexander (sop), Paul Verhey (fl), D. Porcelijn (cnd), Netherlands Radio CO—Miroir de Peine; Magna res est amor; Fiat Domine; Vars & Fugue on a Theme by Kuhnau; Vars on a Theme by Couperin; Chromatic Vars NM Classics ▲ NM 92023
Debussy, C.:Arabesques (2) [trans. for solo harp by F. Cambreling] *(rec Amsterdam & Utrecht, Sept & Nov 1993 & Oct 199)* Globe ▲ GLO 5144 [DDD]
Debussy, C.:Children's Corner, w. Masumi Nagasawa (hp) [trans. for 2 hps by Shigeaki Saegusa] *(rec Amsterdam & Utrecht, Sept & Nov 1993 & Oct 199)* Globe ▲ GLO 5144 [DDD]
Debussy, C.:Clair de lune [trans. for solo hp by V. Coeur] *(rec Amsterdam & Utrecht, Sept & Nov 1993 & Oct 199)* Globe ▲ GLO 5144 [DDD]
Debussy, C.:Danses sacrée et profane, w. E. Spanjaard (cnd), Amsterdam New Sinfonietta *(rec Amsterdam & Utrecht, Sept & Nov 1993 & Oct 199)* Globe ▲ GLO 5144 [DDD]
Debussy, C.:Rêverie [trans. for solo hp by F. Cambreling] *(rec Amsterdam & Utrecht, Sept & Nov 1993 & Oct 199)* Globe ▲ GLO 5144 [DDD]
Debussy, C.:Son Fl, w. Eleonore Pameijer (fl), Prunella Pacey (va) *(rec Amsterdam & Utrecht, Sept & Nov 1993 & Oct 199)* Globe ▲ GLO 5144 [DDD]

INSTRUMENT.

Stoppel, Klaus (vc)
Beethoven, L. van:Duet, WoO 32, "Mit 2 obligaten Augengläsern", w. H. Fukai (va) Signum ▲ X 46-00 [ADD]
Haydn, M.:Divert Va, Vc & Db, w. Hirofumi Fukai (va), G. Dzwiza (db) Signum ▲ X 46-00 [ADD]
Romberg, B.:Trios Va, w. H. Fukai (va), G. Dzwiza (db)—1 trio Signum ▲ X 46-00 [ADD]
Rossini, G.:Duet Vc, w. G. Dzwiza (db) Signum ▲ X 46-00 [ADD]
Storck, Helga (hp)
Spohr, L.:Son 1 Vn, w. K. Guntner (vn) Calig ▲ CAL 50887 [DDD]
Spohr, L.:Son 3 Vn, w. K. Storck (vc) [arr. cello & harp] Calig ▲ CAL 50887 [DDD]
Spohr, L.:Trio Hp, w. K. Guntner (vn), K. Storck (vc) Calig ▲ CAL 50887 [DDD]
Storck, Klaus (vc)
Spohr, L.:Son 3 Vn, w. H. Storck (hp) [arr. cello & harp] Calig ▲ CAL 50887 [DDD]
Spohr, L.:Trio Hp, w. H. Storck (hp), K. Guntner (vn) Calig ▲ CAL 50887 [DDD]
Vivaldi, A.:Cons Vc, w. W. Hofmann (cnd), Seiler CO—RV.401 Deutsche Grammophon ("Musikfest" series) ■ 413682-4
Storgårds, John (vn)
Nordgren, P.H.:Con 4 Vn, w. J. Storgårds (cnd), Wegelius CO Ondine ▲ ODE CD 873
Schumann, R.:Con Vc, w. L. Segerstam (cnd), Tampere PO [arr composer for vn & orch] Ondine ▲ ODE CD 879
Schumann, R.:Con Vn, w. L. Segerstam (cnd), Tampere PO Ondine ▲ ODE CD 879
Storhaug, Teri Fay (hn)
Ost, M.:The Ride Home, w. Julie Schwartz (pno) Meyer ▲ MC 0108
Storhaug, Teri Fay (rcr)
Hoffman, D.:Fant on *Black is the Color of My True Love's Hair*, w. Britt Swenson (vn), Steve Hillesland (vc), Annette Wellin (pno) Meyer ▲ MC 0108
Storms, Yves (gtr)
Barrios, A.:Gtr Music—Prelude; Una limosna por el amor de Diós Syrinx ▲ 94106 [DDD]
Beethoven, L. van:Vars on Grétry's romance "Un fièvre brûlante", WoO 72, w. M. Grauwels (fl), B. Bessler (vn), C. Springuel (va), G. H. (hp) Syrinx ▲ 94101 [DDD]
Brouwer, L.:Gtr Music—Canción de Cuna; Ojos Brujos; Estudios sencillos I-X Syrinx ▲ 94106 [DDD]
Cardoso, J.:Gtr Music—Prelude; Tema Negro; Milonga; Vals Peruano Syrinx ▲ 94106 [DDD]
Guimarães, J.:Sons de Carrilhões Syrinx ▲ 94106 [DDD]
Lauro, A.:Gtr Music—Vals; El Marabino; Vals Criollo; Aire de Joropo Syrinx ▲ 94106 [DDD]
Marc Grauwels & Friends, w. Marc Grauwels (fl), Marie-Noelle de Callataÿ (sop), Hiroko Masaki (sop), Dennis James (glass hmc), Ingrid Procureur (hp), Yvietta Matison (va), Mark Drobinsky (vc), Alain De Rijckere (bn), Daniel Blumenthal (pno), Frank Michiels (perc), Belgian RSO, W Syrinx 2-▲ 96101 [DDD]
Piazzolla...Shanker, w. Marc Grauwels (fl) Syrinx ▲ CSR 91103 [DDD]
Schubert, Franz:Qt Fl, w. M. Grauwels (fl), Y. Matison (va), M. Drobinsky (vc) Syrinx ▲ 93105 [DDD]
Sojo, V.E.:Pieces from Venezuela Syrinx ▲ 94106 [DDD]
Sor, F.:Vars on a Theme of Mozart Syrinx ▲ 94101 [DDD]
Spohr, L.:Son 4 Vn, w. M. Grauwels (fl), B. Bessler (vn), C. Springuel (va), G. H. (hp) Syrinx ▲ 94101 [DDD]
Traeg, A.:Son Fl, w. M. Grauwels (fl) Syrinx ▲ 94101 [DDD]
Villa-Lobos, H.:Chôro 1 Syrinx ▲ 94106 [DDD]
Villa-Lobos, H.:Gtr Music—Etudes 1, 8 & 11; Preludes 1, 3 & 5; Valsa-chôro *(rec 1991)* Pavane ▲ ADW 7256 [DDD]
Villa-Lobos, H.:Songs, w. A. de Brégan (sop)—Canção do Poeta; Duas Paisagens; Canção de Cristal Xangô; Samba Clássico; Jardim Fanado; Vôo; Dinga-Donga; Canção do Carreiro; Bachianas Brasileiras No. 5; Canide Ioune [Port] Pavane ▲ ADW 7256 [DDD]
Stotijn, Haakon (ob)—see ORCHESTRAS & ENSEMBLES Alma Musica Ensemble
Stott, Kathryn (pno)
Chabrier, E.:Pno Music (misc), w. Elizabeth Burley (pno)—10 Pièces pittoresques; Impromptu; 5 morceaux pour pno; 3 valses romantiques Unicorn-Kanchana ▲ DKP CD 9158
Chopin, F.:Pno Music (misc) *(rec Snape Maltings, Aldeburgh, Suffolk, Dec 20, 1988 & Jan 18, 19)* Conifer Classics 2-▲ 75605-51753-2 [DDD]
Debussy, C.:Images (6) Pno—Set 1 *(rec Faculty of Music Concert Hall, Cambridge, Jan 8-9, 1987)* Conifer Classics 2-▲ 75605-51755-2 [DDD]
Debussy, C.:Pno Music (misc)—Arabesques, Ballade slave, Isle joyeuse, Plus que lente, Rêverie *(rec Faculty of Music Concert Hall, Cambridge, Jan 8-9, 1987)* Conifer Classics 2-▲ 75605-51755-2 [DDD]
Debussy, C.:Suite bergamasque *(rec Faculty of Music Concert Hall, Cambridge, Jan 8-9, 1987)* Conifer Classics 2-▲ 75605-51755-2 [DDD]
Fauré, G.:Ballade Pno, w. Y. P. Tortelier (cnd), BBC PO Chandos ▲ CHAN 9416 [DDD]
Fauré, G.:Pno Music—Barcarolles Nos. 2-7, 11 & 12; Impromptus Nos. 1-3 & 6; Mazurka in B♭; Nocturnes Nos. 1, 4, & 8-11; 3 Romances sans paroles; Valse-caprice No. 4 Conifer Classics 2-▲ 75605-51751-2 [DDD]
Howells, H.:Orchestral Music, w. M. Stewart (vn), V. Handley (cnd), Royal Liverpool PO—Concerto for String Orchestra (1938); Concerto No. 2 in c for Piano & Orchestra (1925); Three Dances for Violin & Orchestra (1915) *(rec Feb. 1991 & Mar. 1992)* Hyperion ▲ CDA 66610 [DDD]
Liszt, F.:Liebesträume *(rec Haberdashers' Aske's School, Elstree, Apr 1989 & Feb 1990)* Conifer Classics 2-▲ 75605-51753-2 [DDD]
Liszt, F.:Sonetti del Petrarca Pno *(rec Haberdashers' Aske's School, Elstree, Apr 1989 & Feb 1990)* Conifer Classics 2-▲ 75605-51753-2 [DDD]
Lloyd, G.:Con 3 Pno, w. G. Lloyd (cnd), BBC PO Albany ▲ TROY 019-2 [DDD] ■ TROY 019-4 (D)
Lloyd, G.:Con 4 Pno, w. G. Lloyd (cnd), London SO *(rec 1984)* Albany ▲ AR 004-2 [DDD] ■ AR 004-4 (D)
Lloyd, G.:The Lily-Leaf & the Grasshopper *(rec 1984)* Albany ▲ AR 004-2 [DDD] ■ AR 004-4 (D)
Lloyd, G.:The Transformation of That Naked Ape Albany ▲ AR 004-2 [DDD] ■ AR 004-4 (D)
Nyman, M.:Con Pno, w. M. Nyman (cnd), Royal Liverpool Orch Argo ▲ 443382-2 [DDD]
Ravel, M.:Gaspard de la nuit *(rec St. George's Church, Brandon Hill, Bristol, July 30-31, 1990)* Conifer Classics 2-▲ 75605-51755-2 [DDD]
Ravel, M.:Jeux d'eau *(rec St. George's Church, Brandon Hill, Bristol, July 30-31, 1990)* Conifer Classics 2-▲ 75605-51755-2 [DDD]
Ravel, M.:Pavane pour une infante défunte *(rec St. George's Church, Brandon Hill, Bristol, July 30-31, 1990)* Conifer Classics 2-▲ 75605-51755-2 [DDD]
Ravel, M.:Sonatine Pno *(rec St. George's Church, Brandon Hill, Bristol, July 30-31, 1990)* Conifer Classics 2-▲ 75605-51755-2 [DDD]
Ravel, M.:Le Tombeau de Couperin *(rec St. George's Church, Brandon Hill, Bristol, July 30-31, 1990)* Conifer Classics 2-▲ 75605-51755-2 [DDD]
Shostakovich, D.:Qnt Pno, w. London Musici String Quartet Conifer Classics ▲ 75605-51194-2
Ustvolskaya, G.:Composition 3, London Musici Conifer Classics ▲ 75605-51194-2
Ustvolskaya, G.:Octet Obs, London Musici Conifer Classics ▲ 75605-51194-2
Stouffer, Bradley (perc)—see ORCHESTRAS & ENSEMBLES Eastman Percussion Ensemble members
Stoune, M. (fl)
Glazer, S.:Con Fl, w. J. Sudduth (cnd), Texas Tech Univ Symphonic Band Opus One ▲ 147
Stout, Gordon (mar)
Adler, S.:Dialogs (9) Eup, w. B. Bowman (eup) Crystal ■ C393
Brian Bowman, w. Brian Bowman (eup), Marjorie Lee (pno) Crystal ■ C393
Kupferman, M.:Sound Phantoms 7, w. S. Mauk (sax) Soundspells ▲ SP 103
Reynolds, R.:Autumn Island Neuma ▲ 450-72 [DDD]
Stout, Gordon (perc)—see ORCHESTRAS & ENSEMBLES Eastman Percussion Ensemble members
Stout, R. (vn)—see ORCHESTRAS & ENSEMBLES Apple Hill Chamber Players
Stoytcheva, Anna (pno)
Bond, V.:Batucada Gega ▲ GD 197 [DDD]
Bond, V.:Other Selves, w. Georgy Valtchev (vn), Christo Tanev (vc) Gega ▲ GD 197 [DDD]
Bond, V.:Rage Gega ▲ GD 197 [DDD]
Bond, V.:Son Vc, w. Christo Tanev (vc) Gega ▲ GD 197 [DDD]

Strabbioli, Edoardo Maria (pno)
Ysaÿe, E.:Poème élégiaque Vn & Pno, w. Frank Peter Zimmermann (vn) EMI Classics ▲ CDC 55255
Ysaÿe, E.:Rêve d'enfant, w. Frank Peter Zimmermann (vn) EMI Classics ▲ CDC 55255
Stradner, Christoph (vc)
Goldmark, K.:Son Vc, w. Charles Owen (pno)—Andante *(rec Chapel of Palais Liechtenstein, Vienna, July 1995)* Dorian ▲ DOR 80145 [DDD]
Strauss, R.:Son Vc, w. Charles Owen (pno) *(rec Chapel of Palais Liechtenstein, Vienna, July 1995)* Dorian ▲ DOR 80145 [DDD]
Suk, J.:Ballade & Serenade, w. Charles Owen (pno) *(rec Chapel of Palais Liechtenstein, Vienna, July 1995)* Dorian ▲ DOR 80145 [DDD]
Webern, A.:Little Pieces Vc, w. Charles Owen (pno) *(rec Chapel of Palais Liechtenstein, Vienna, July 1995)* Dorian ▲ DOR 80145 [DDD]
Webern, A.:Pieces Vc, w. Charles Owen (pno) *(rec Chapel of Palais Liechtenstein, Vienna, July 1995)* Dorian ▲ DOR 80145 [DDD]
Webern, A.:Son Vc, w. Charles Owen (pno) *(rec Chapel of Palais Liechtenstein, Vienna, July 1995)* Dorian ▲ DOR 80145 [DDD]
Strahl, Tomasz (vc)
Bruzdowicz, J.:Trio dei Due Mondi, w. Robert Szreder (vn), Boguslaw Jan Strobel (pno) Pavane ▲ ADW 7335 [DDD]
Chopin, F.:Grand Duo, w. Edward Wolanin (pno) *(rec Warsaw Philharmony Hall, May 29, 1994)* Canyon Classics ▲ 238
Chopin, F.:Intro & Polonaise, "Polonaise brilliante", w. Edward Wolanin (pno) *(rec Warsaw Philharmony Hall, May 29, 1994)* Canyon Classics ▲ 238
Chopin, F.:Son Vc, w. Edward Wolanin (pno) *(rec Warsaw Philharmony Hall, May 15, 1994)* Canyon Classics ▲ 238
Stralendorf, H. (cel)
Tailleferre, G.:Image, w. U. Siebler (fl), D. Marshall (cl), A. Gassenhuber (pno), Fanny Mendelssohn String Quartet *(rec Dec. 1992)* Troubadisc ▲ TRO 01406 [DDD]
Strange, David (vc)
Haydn, J.:Die Schöpfung, w. Helena Döse (sop—Eva), Lucia Popp (sop—Gabriel), Werner Hollweg (ten—Uriel), Benjamin Luxon (bar—Adam), Kurt Moll (bass—Raphael), Jack McCormack (db), Antál Dorati (hpd), A. Dorati (cnd), Royal PO, Brighton Festival Chorus *(rec Kingsway Hall, London, Dec 1976)* London 2-▲ 443027-2 [ADD]
Strasser, Tamas (va)
Carreño, T.:Qt Strs, w. J. Roche (vn), R. Zelnick (vn), C. Heller (vc) Vox Box 2-▲ CDX 5029 [ADD]
Ullmann, V.:Dialogues III, w. Y.N. Kim (vn) Innova ▲ MN 108
Ultan, L.:Dialogues III, w. Y.N. Kim (vn) Innova ▲ MN 108
Straszynski, Andrzey (vn)
Saint-Saëns, C.:Con 3 Vn, w. V. Brodsky (cnd), Polish National RSO Katowice *(rec Katowice, Poland, Aug 4-8, 1988)* Arts ▲ 4471402 [DDD]
Saint-Saëns, C.:Havanaise Vn, w. V. Brodsky (cnd), Polish National RSO Katowice *(rec Katowice, Poland, Aug 4-8, 1988)* Arts ▲ 4471402 [DDD]
Saint-Saëns, C.:Introduction & Rondo capriccioso, w. V. Brodsky (cnd), Polish National RSO Katowice *(rec Katowice, Poland, Aug 4-8, 1988)* Arts ▲ 4471402 [DDD]
Stratman, M. (pno)
Belden, G.:Gilgamesh, w. S. D. Belden (cta), T. Heavner (perc) [E] Capstone ▲ CPS 8613
Stratta, Ettore (pno)
Gershwin, G.:Rhap in Blue, w. E. Stratta (cnd), Festival Orch Kem-Disc ▲ 1008 [DDD]
Straub, Bernhard (bn)—see ORCHESTRAS & ENSEMBLES Avalon Wind Quintet
Strauch, Pierre (vc)
Lachenmann, H.:Allegro sostenuto, w. Pierre-Laurent Aimard (pno), Alain Damiens (cl) Accord ▲ ACD 202082 [DDD]
Lachenmann, H.:Pression Accord ▲ ACD 202082 [DDD]
Straumer, R. (vn)
Mauersberger, R.:Qt Strs, w. A. Priebst (vc) *(rec June 1991)* Thorofon ▲ CTH 2112 [DDD]
Mauersberger, R.:Trio Pno, w. W. Apel (pno), A. Priebst (vc) *(rec June 1991)* Thorofon ▲ CTH 2112 [DDD]
Štraus, Ivan (vn)—see also ORCHESTRAS & ENSEMBLES Suk String Quartet
Korte, O.:Philosophical Dialogues, w. Walter Delahunt (pno) *(rec Martinů Hall of Liechtenstein Palace in Prague, Mar 11 & 12, 1995)* Panton ▲ 811398-2 [DDD]
Strauss, Michael (va)
Finko, D.:Con Va, w. J. Freeman (cnd), Orch 2001 *(rec Lang Concert Hall, Swarthmore College)* CRI ▲ CD 723 [DDD]
Musgrave, T.:Orfeo III, w. Pamela Guidetti (fl), Mei Chen Liao Cope (vn), Igor Szwec (vn), Lori Barnett (vc), Miles B. Davis (db), J. Freeman (cnd) *(rec Lang Concert Hall, Swarthmore College)* CRI ▲ CD 723 [DDD]
Strauss, Richard (pno)
Strauss, R.:Songs, w. R. Hutt (ten)—Breit über mein Haupt, Op. 19/2; Morgen, Op. 27/4 [G] *(rec 1921)* Pearl 2-▲ GEMMCDS 9365 (m) [AAD]
Strauss, R.:Songs, w. H. Konetzni (sop—4 solo songs), A. Dermota (ten—6 solo songs), A. Poell (bar—6 solo songs)—Opp. 21/2, 21/3, 69/5, 88/2 *(Konetzni)*; Opp. 15/5, Op. 17/1, 21/1, 32/2, 37/1, 49/2 *(Dermota)*; Opp. 19/1, 21/4, 27/1, 27/3, 36/1, 48/5 *(Poell)* [G] *(rec 1943)* Preiser ▲ 93261 (m) [AAD]
Strauss, R.:Songs, w. M. Reining (sop—6 solo songs), L. Piltti (sop—7 solo songs), A. Dermota (ten—8 solo songs)—Opp. 10/1, 27/2, 29/1, 37/3, 41/1, 48/1 *(Reining)*; Opp. 15/5, 17/2, 21/1, 29/2, 48/2, 48/3, 49/1 *(Piltti)*; Opp. 10/1, 10/3, 17/1, 19/2, 21/2, 27/3, 32/1, 37/2 *(Dermota)* [G] *(rec Vienna, Apr. 1942)* Preiser ▲ 93262 (m) [AAD]
Strauss, Thomas (org)
Barockmusik für Posaunen und Gesang, w. Datura Trombone Quartet, A. Scharinger (db), C. Weigel (baroque vc), J. Gagelmann (perc), R. Haeger (perc) Ars Musici ▲ AM 1094 [DDD]
Stravinsky, Igor (pno)
Stravinsky, I.:Capriccio, w. E. Ansermet (cnd), Walther Straram Orch EMI Classics 2-▲ ZDCB 54607
Stravinsky, I.:Chants du rossignol et Marche, w. S. Dushkin (vn) EMI Classics 2-▲ ZDCB 54607
Stravinsky, I.:Duo Concertant, w. Samuel Dushkin (vn) Memories ▲ MEM 3004
Stravinsky, I.:Pétrouchka (russian dance), w. S. Dushkin (vn) [arr Samuel Dushkin for Violin & Piano] EMI Classics 2-▲ ZDCB 54607
Stravinsky, I.:Pno-Rag-Music EMI Classics 2-▲ ZDCB 54607
Stravinsky, I.:Pno-Rag-Music, w. I. Stravinsky (cnd), New York Philharmonic SO IMP (Golden Legacy) ▲ IMPGLRS 107 [ADD]
Stravinsky, I.:Serenade Pno EMI Classics 2-▲ ZDCB 54607
Stravinsky, I.:Suite italienne Vc, w. S. Dushkin (vn) EMI Classics 2-▲ ZDCB 54607
Stravinsky, I.:Vn Pno Music, w. Samuel Dushkin (vn)—Berceuse de l'oiseau de feu; Scherzo de l'oiseau de feu; Dance Russe; Serenata at Scherzino de la Suite Italienne; Air du Rossignol; Marche Chinoise du Rossignol Memories ▲ MEM 3004
Stravinsky, Marius (va)
Gubaidulina, S.:Meditation on a Bach Chorale, w. Elisabeth Chojnacka (hpd), Hanna Weinmeister (vn), Elvira Bekova (vn), Alfia Bekova (vc), Alois Posch (db) *(rec Lockenhaus Festival, Austria, 1995)* BIS ▲ CD 810 [DDD]
Stravinsky, Soulima (pno)
Chabrier, E.:Pièces pittoresques—Sous Bois; Mauresque; Scherzo. Valse *(rec Univ of Illinois, Champagne-Urbana, 1960's)* Centaur ▲ CRC 2226 [ADD]
Debussy, C.:Etudes *(rec Univ of Illinois, Champagne-Urbana, 1960's)* Centaur ▲ CRC 2226 [ADD]
Ravel, M.:Sonatine *(rec Univ of Illinois, Champagne-Urbana, 1960's)* Sterling ▲ CRC 2226 [ADD]
Strawson, G. (pno)—see ORCHESTRAS & ENSEMBLES Piano Circus
Street, Alfred Erick (gtr)
Villa-Lobos, H.:Chôro 1 Arion ▲ ARN 68029 [DDD]
Villa-Lobos, H.:Etudes Gtr—Nos. 4,7,8 & 11 Arion ▲ ARN 68029 [DDD]
Villa-Lobos, H.:Gavotta-Chôro Arion ▲ ARN 68029 [DDD]

▲ = CD ♦ = Enhanced CD Δ = MD ■ = Cassette Tape □ = DCC

Street, Alfred Erick (gtr) (cont.)
Villa-Lobos, H.:Preludes Gtr — Arion ▲ ARN 68029 [DDD]
Strehle, Wilfred (va)
Brahms, J.:Son 1 Cl, w. Karina Wisniewska (pno) — Nimbus ▲ NI 5473 [DDD]
Dvořák, A.:Sonatina Vn, w. Karina Wisniewska (pno) [arr for viola Lipka & Hallman] — Nimbus ▲ NI 5473 [DDD]
Hindemith, P.:Duet Va & Vc, w. Wolfgang Boettcher (vc) — Nimbus ▲ NI 5473 [DDD]
Hindemith, P.:Son Va & Pno, Op. 11/4, w. Karina Wisniewska (pno) — Nimbus ▲ NI 5473 [DDD]
Hindemith, P.:Trauermusik, w. Karina Wisniewska (pno) [arr for viola & piano] — Nimbus ▲ NI 5473 [DDD]
Strehle, Wilfried (va)—see ORCHESTRAS & ENSEMBLES Brandis String Quartet
Streicher, Dieter (vn)
Brahms, J.:Trio Hn, w. Sebastian Weigle (hn), Claudius Tanski (pno) — MD + G ▲ MDG 3010595 [DDD]
Streicher, Ludwig (db)
Encores, w. Astrid Spitznagel (pno) — Orfeo ▲ C 225911 A [DDD]
Streicher, W.-D. (vn)—see ORCHESTRAS & ENSEMBLES Parnassus Trio
Streit, D. (cnt)
Ducommun, S.:Petit Concert, w. P. Lehmann (tpt), J. Henry (trbn) — Gallo ▲ CD 654 [DDD]
Strieby, Lawrence (hn)
Hindemith, P.:Son Alto Hn, w. T. Lichtman (pno) — Summit 2-▲ DCD 115 [DDD] 2-■ DCD 115
Hindemith, P.:Son for 4 Hns, w. T. Bacon (hn), A. D. Krehbiel (hn), G. Williams (hn) — Summit 2-▲ DCD 115 [DDD] 2-■ DCD 115
Strieder, Willie (tpt)
Van Appledorn, M.J.:Incantations, w. J. Garret (pno) — Opus One ▲ CD 162
Van Appledorn, M.J.:Rhap, w. Gail Barber (hp) *(rec Texas Tech Univ., Hemmle Recital Hall, Lubbock Texas, Feb. 16, 1994)* — Opus One ▲ CD 169
Strijkers, Piet (b vi/perc)—see ORCHESTRAS & ENSEMBLES Romanesque
Strijkers, Piet (vl)—see ORCHESTRAS & ENSEMBLES Paul Rans Ensemble, Ricercar Consort
Stringer, Alan (tpt)
Haydn, J.:Con Tpt, w. N. Marriner (cnd), Academy of St. Martin in the Fields — London ("Serenata" series) ▲ 430633-2 [ADD]
Trumpet & Organ:Oboe & Organ, w. Simon C. Jansen (org), Koen van Slochteren (ob) — Vivace ▲ 575
Strizich, Robert (gtr)
Harrison, L.:Canticle 3, w. L. Miller (ocarina), William Winant, et al. (perc), D.R. Davies (cnd) — MusicMasters ▲ 7051-2-C [DDD]
Strobel, Boguslaw Jan (pno)
Antheil, G.:Son 1 Vn, w. Robert Szreder (vn) — Pavane ▲ ADW 7335 [DDD]
Antheil, G.:Son 2 Vn, w. Robert Szreder (vn) — Pavane ▲ ADW 7335 [DDD]
Bruzdowicz, J.:Son Vn Pno, "Spring in America", w. Robert Szreder (vn) — Pavane ▲ ADW 7335 [DDD]
Bruzdowicz, J.:Trio dei Due Mondi, w. Robert Szreder (vn), Tomasz Strahl (vc) — Pavane ▲ ADW 7335 [DDD]
Lutoslawski, W.:Partita Vn & Pno, w. R. Szreder (vn) — Pavane ▲ ADW 7283 [DDD]
Paderewski, I.J.:Son Vn, w. R. Szreder (vn) — Pavane ▲ ADW 7283 [DDD]
Szymanowski, K.:Son Vn, w. R. Szreder (vn) — Pavane ▲ ADW 7283 [DDD]
Strong, David (pno)
Hindemith, P.:Son Pno 4-Hands, w. Bernard Roberts (pno) *(rec Nimbus Foundation Concert Hall, May 17-19)* — Nimbus 2-▲ NI 5459/60 [DDD]
Hindemith, P.:Son for 2 Pnos, w. Bernard Roberts (pno) *(rec Nimbus Foundation Concert Hall, May 17-19)* — Nimbus 2-▲ NI 5459/60 [DDD]
Štros, Jan (vc)—see ORCHESTRAS & ENSEMBLES Suk String Quartet
Strosser, Emmanuel (pno)
Brahms, J.:Son for 2 Pnos, w. Claire Desert (pno) — FNAC Music ▲ 592351
Brahms, J.:Vars on a Theme of Robert Schumann, Op. 23, w. Claire Desert (pno) — FNAC Music ▲ 592351
Chausson, E.:Duos, "La nuit" & "Le réveil", w. D. Collot (sop), B. Vinson (mez), J. Bouillat (ten), G. Wieclaw (bass), C. Desert (pno), J. Sourisse (cnd), Jean Sourisse Ensemble, Audite Nova Vocal Ensemble — FNAC Music ▲ 592224 [DDD]
Debussy, C.:Songs, w. D. Collot (sop), B. Vinson (mez), J. Bouillat (ten), G. Wieclaw (bass), C. Desert (pno), J. Sourisse (cnd), Jean Sourisse Ensemble, Audite Nova Vocal Ensemble—3 chansons de Chateau D'Orleans — FNAC Music ▲ 592224 [DDD]
Fauré, G.:Madrigal, w. D. Collot (sop), B. Vinson (mez), J. Bouillat (ten), G. Wieclaw (bass), C. Desert (pno) — FNAC Music ▲ 592224 [DDD]
Fauré, G.:Pavane Orch, w. D. Collot (sop), B. Vinson (mez), J. Bouillat (ten), G. Wieclaw (bass), C. Desert (pno), J. Sourisse (cnd), Jean Sourisse Ensemble, Audite Nova Vocal Ensemble — FNAC Music ▲ 592224 [DDD]
Fauré, G.:Songs, w. D. Collot (sop), B. Vinson (mez), J. Bouillat (ten), G. Wieclaw (bass), C. Desert (pno), J. Sourisse (cnd), Jean Sourisse Ensemble, Audite Nova Vocal Ensemble—Le Ruisseau, Op. 22; Puisqu'ici bas, Op. 10/1, Les Djinns, Op. 12 — FNAC Music ▲ 592224 [DDD]
Poulenc, F.:Son Ob, w. François Leleux (ob) — Harmonia Mundi France ("Les Nouveaux Interprètes" series) ▲ HMN 911556
Poulenc, F.:Trio Ob, w. François Leleux (ob), Jean-François Duquesnoy (bn) — Harmonia Mundi France ("Les Nouveaux Interprètes" series) ▲ HMN 911556
Ravel, M.:Songs, w. D. Collot (sop), B. Vinson (mez), J. Bouillat (ten), G. Wieclaw (bass), C. Desert (pno), J. Sourisse (cnd), Jean Sourisse Ensemble, Audite Nova Vocal Ensemble—3 a capella songs — FNAC Music ▲ 592224 [DDD]
Saint-Saëns, C.:Choral Music, w. D. Collot (sop), B. Vinson (mez), J. Bouillat (ten), G. Wieclaw (bass), C. Desert (pno), J. Sourisse (cnd), Jean Sourisse Ensemble, Vocal Audite Nova Ensemble—Calme des nuits, Op. 68/1; Les fleurs et les arbres, Op. 68/2; Salterelle, Op. 74 — FNAC Music ▲ 592224 [DDD]
Strub, Max (vn)
Pfitzner, H.:Duo Vn, w. L. Hoelscher (vc), H. Pfitzner (cnd), Berlin State Opera Orch — Preiser ▲ 90029 (m) [AAD]
Stuart, Mark (vc/gtr/ mand)—see ORCHESTRAS & ENSEMBLES Gangster Band
Stuart, Thaddeus James (org)
Bruckner, A.:Choral Music, w. R. Shewan (cnd), Roberts Wesleyan College Brass Ensemble, Roberts Wesleyan College Chorale—Ave Maria I [w. E. Stedman (sop), J. Richardson (mez)]; Ave Maria II; Aequale; Afferentur regi; Aequale II; Germanenzug [w. J. Richardson (ten), B. Clicker (ten)]; Inveni David; Tröstern Musik; Tota pulchra es Maria [w. C. Jones (ten)]; Or justi meditabitur; Ave Maria III [w. A. Mosher (bar)]; Christus factus est pro nobis; Ecce sacerdos magnus; Ave Regina coelorum; Virga Jesse floruit; Vexilla regis prodeunt; Das deutsche Lied *(rec Apr. 19-21, 1991)* — Albany ▲ TROY 063 [DDD]
Stubbings, Paul (org)
Paul Stubbings Plays the Organ of St. Martin in the Fields — Arkay ▲ ARK 6154
Stubbs, Stephen (baroque lt)
Kellner, J.C.:Lt Works—Fantasias in C, in A, in D, in d, in F, in A; Aria; Campanella; Courante; Sarabande; Gigue; Gavotte; Rondeau; Gigue; Pastorel; Passepied; Chaconne — CPO ▲ CPO 999097 [DDD]
Stubbs, Stephen (chit/vih)
Virtuoso Solo Music for Cornetto, w. Bruce Dickey (cornetto), Erin Headley (vl), Andrew Lawrence-King (double hp/Renaissance hp) — Accent ▲ 9173 [DDD]
Stubbs, Stephen (lt)—see also ORCHESTRAS & ENSEMBLES Tragicomedia
Airs & Dances of Shakespeare's Time, w. C. Mendoze (cnd), Musica Antiqua Ensemble, John Elwes (ten) — Pierre Verany ▲ 787092 [DDD]
Bach, J.S.:Anna Magdalena Bach Notebook, w. Tragicomedia — Teldec ("Das alte Werke" series) ▲ 91183
Hamburg Baroque (Songs), w. Tuula Nienstedt (mez), Andrew Lawrence-King (baroque hp) *(rec 1989)* — Ambitus ▲ AMB 97837
Moulinié, E.:Airs Lt, w. Suzie Le Blanc (sop)—Book 1 *(rec Quebec, July 1995)* — CBC ▲ 1095 [DDD]
Stubbs, Stephen (lt/voc)
Proensa, w. Paul Hillier (bass), Andrew Lawrence-King (hp/voc), Erin Headley (vielle) — ECM New Series ▲ 78118-21368-2 [DDD]
Stucka, Gary (vc)
Elgar, E.:Romance Bn, w. Bruce Grainger (bn), Gail Niwa (pno) *(rec DePaul Univ. Concert Hall, Chicago, Sept 1992)* — Centaur ▲ CRC 2244 [DDD]
Haydn, M.:Divert Vn, Vc & Db, w. David Taylor (vn), Jerry Fuller (db) *(rec WTMT Studio 1, Jan 24, 1993)* — Musical Arts Society ▲ MAS 41595 [DDD]
Mozart, W.A.:Duo Bn Vc, w. Bruce Grainger (bn) *(rec DePaul Univ. Concert Hall, Chicago, Sept 1992)* — Centaur ▲ CRC 2244 [DDD]
Romberg, B.:Trios Va, w. Li-Kuo Chang (va), Jerry Fuller (db)—No. 1 in e *(rec WTMT Studio 1, Jan 24, 1993)* — Musical Arts Society ▲ MAS 41595 [DDD]
Stucki, Madeleine (pno)
Chaminade, C.:Pno Music (misc)—Etude mélodique, Op. 118; Danse créole, Op. 94; Lolita; Automne; Poème Provençal, Op. 127; 6 Romances sans paroles, Op. 76; Pêcheurs de nuit; Autrefois; Arabesque; Callirhoë *(rec Swiss Radio DRS Studio, Bern, June 21-22, 1994)* — Relief ▲ CR 931039 [DDD]
Stucky, Rodney (gtr)
Handel, D.:A Recitative Gtr — Vienna Modern Masters ▲ VMM 2019 [DDD]
Studer, Michael (pno)
Liszt, F.:Songs, w. G. Westphal (sgr)—Lenore; Der blinde Sänger; Der traurige Mönch; Des toten Dichters Liebe [G] *(rec 1982)* — Jecklin-Disco ▲ JD 570-2 [ADD]
Nietzsche, F.:Pno Music, w. G. Westphal (nar)—Das zerbrochene Ringlein [G] *(rec 1982)* — Jecklin-Disco ▲ JD 570-2 [ADD]
Strauss, R.:Songs, w. G. Westphal (voc)—Das Schloss am Meere [G] *(rec 1982)* — Jecklin-Disco ▲ JD 570-2 [ADD]
Studky, Rodney (gtr)
Handel, D.:Barge Music, w. Bradley Garner (a fl), Jon Pascolini (db), Russell Burge (perc), Allen Otte (perc) — Vienna Modern Masters ▲ VMM 2019 [DDD]
Studt, Richard (vn)
Bach, J.S.:Con 2 for 3 Hpds, w. Carmel Kaine (vn), Ronald Thomas (vn), Christopher Hogwood (bc), Nicholas Kraemer (bc), N. Marriner (cnd), Academy of St. Martin in the Fields [trans for 3 vn] *(rec St. John's, Smith Square, London, Aug 1974 & Feb 1975)* — Boston Skyline ▲ BSD 127 [ADD]
Stuermer, Daryl (gtr)
Vivaldi, A.:Cons Vn, Op. 8/1-4, "The Four Seasons", w. Jerome Franke (vn), Karine Garibova (vn), Pasquale Laurino (vn), Olga Miliaeva (va), Roza Borisova (vc), Mika Hennessy (db), Melanie Panush (ham dlc), Stanislav Venglevski (bayan), Mike Kashou (arabic tabla), Ed Paloucek (celtic fid), Gary Bottoni (highland pipe), Dubuffet String Quartet *(rec July-Sept 1995)* — EarthBeat! ▲ 35270-2 [DDD]
Stuhr-Rommereim, John (hpd)—see ORCHESTRAS & ENSEMBLES Musica Humana
Stuhr-Rommereim, Rebecca (baroque fl)—see ORCHESTRAS & ENSEMBLES Musica Humana
Stultz, Richard (pno)
Angels Are Everywhere!, w. [cnd:Marie Stultz], Treble Chorus of New England, Tanya Kodinsk (pno/org) — AFKA ▲ SK 539
Stumacher, E. (pno)—see ORCHESTRAS & ENSEMBLES Apple Hill Chamber Players
Stumpf, T. (pno)
Cogan, R.:Polyutterances, w. J. Heller (sop) — Neuma ▲ 450-89
Fussell, C.C.:Songs, w. J. Heller (sop)—Goethe Lieder — Neuma ▲ 450-89
Stumpf, T.:Lear's Daughters, w. J. Heller (sop) — Neuma ▲ 450-89
Sturrock, Kathron (pno)
Bliss, A.:Interludes (2) Pno — Chandos ▲ CHAN 8770 [DDD]
Bliss, A.:Masks — Chandos ▲ CHAN 8770 [DDD]
Bliss, A.:Son Va, w. E. Vardi (va) — Chandos ▲ CHAN 8770 [DDD]
Bliss, A.:Toccata — Chandos ▲ CHAN 8770 [DDD]
Bliss, A.:Triptych — Chandos ▲ CHAN 8770 [DDD]
Brahms, J.:Sons Vn (comp), w. N. Wakabayashi (vn) — IMP Classics ▲ IMPPCD 1050 [DDD]
Jolivet, A.:Fantaise-Caprice, w. Anna Noakes (fl) — ASV ("French Chamber Music" series) ▲ ASV 948
Jolivet, A.:Son Fl, w. Anna Noakes (fl) — ASV ("French Chamber Music" series) ▲ ASV 948
Stute, Hartmut (cl)
Lutoslawski, W.:Die Strohkette, w. Barbara Miller (sop), Oksana Sowiak (mez), Robert Dohn (fl), Willy Schnell (ob), Martin Klose (cl), Karl Steinbrecher (bn), A. Grüber (cnd) — Vox Box 2-▲ CDX 5133
Stutz, Elissa (pno)
Baley, V.:Nocturnal 6 *(rec Univ. of Nevada, Las Vegas)* — Cambria ▲ CMB 1077 [DDD]
Stutz, Reiner (gtr)
Reiner Stutz — FSM ("Fono" series) ▲ 97723
Stuurop, Alda (vn)
Bach, C.P.E.:Trio Son Fl, H.367, w. Wilbert Hazelzet (fl), Richte van der Meer (vc), Jacques Ogg (hpd) *(rec Utrecht, Sept 1993)* — Globe ▲ GLO 5110 [DDD]
Bach, C.P.E.:Trio Son Fl, H.371, w. Wilbert Hazelzet (fl), Richte van der Meer (vc), Jacques Ogg (hpd) *(rec Utrecht, Sept 1993)* — Globe ▲ GLO 5110 [DDD]
Bach, C.P.E.:Trio Son Fl, H.570, w. Wilbert Hazelzet (fl), Richte van der Meer (vc), Jacques Ogg (hpd) *(rec Utrecht, Sept 1993)* — Globe ▲ GLO 5110 [DDD]
Bach, C.P.E.:Trio Son Fl, H.574, w. Wilbert Hazelzet (fl), Richte van der Meer (vc), Jacques Ogg (hpd) *(rec Utrecht, Sept 1993)* — Globe ▲ GLO 5110 [DDD]
Bach, C.P.E.:Trio Son for 2 Fls, H.580, w. Kate Clarke (fl), Wilbert Hazelzet (fl), Richte van der Meer (vc), Jacques Ogg (hpd) *(rec Utrecht, Sept 1993)* — Globe ▲ GLO 5110 [DDD]
Sublet, P. (pno)—see ORCHESTRAS & ENSEMBLES Meister Consort
Sublet, Pierre (cel)
Dünki, J.-J.:Tétraptéron O-IV, w. P. Clemann (pno), J.-J. Dünki (clvd), S. Reymond (hpd) *(rec Sept. 18, 1992)* — Jecklin ▲ JS 289-2 [ADD]
Suchanov, Vadim (pno)
Brahms, J.:Son for 2 Pnos, w. Valery Afanassiev (pno) *(rec Musica-Théâtre, La Chaux-de-Fonds, Oct. 31-Nov. 2, 1994)* — Denon ▲ DEN 78976 [DDD]
Brahms, J.:Souvenir de la Russie, w. Valery Afanassiev (pno) *(rec Musica-Théâtre, La Chaux-de-Fonds, Oct. 31-Nov. 2, 1994)* — Denon ▲ DEN 78976 [DDD]
Suderburg, Robert (pno)
Suderburg, R.:Chamber Music VII, w. Charles Schlueter (tpt) *(rec Symphony Hall, Boston, MA, Sept. 1994)* — Vox Classics ▲ VOX 7513 [DDD]
Suderburg, R.:Chamber Music VIII, w. Charles Schlueter (tpt) *(rec Symphony Hall, Boston, MA, Sept. 1994)* — Vox Classics ▲ VOX 7513 [DDD]
Suderburg, R.:Night Set, w. S. Dempster (trbn) — Delfon ▲ DRS 2127 [DDD]
Suesse, Dana (pno)
Suesse, D.:Music of, w. Cy Coleman (pno)—Coctail Suite; Jazz Concerto in D for Combo & Orch (arr for 2 pnos); plus others *(rec 1940-56)* — Pearl ▲ PEA 9202 [ADD]
Suesse, D.:Music of, w. Cy Coleman (pno), Robert Barlow (hp), F. Fennell (cnd), American SO, All City Concert Choir—Con Romantico for Pno & Orch; A Little Light Music; Young Man with Harp for Hp & Orch; The Blues [from Con in 3 Rhythms]; Coronach for Hp & Orch; Jazz Con for Combo & Orch; The Night Is Young & You're So Beautiful for Orch & Chorus *(rec Carnegie Hall, Dec 1974)* — Premier ▲ PRCD 1055
Suftin, Isha (acc)
O'Rourke, J.:Terminal Pharmacy, w. Tony Burr (cl), Jeff Cortazzo (b trbn), John McEntire (dr), Rob Prosser (acc), Mike Dockter (vc), Hattie Franck (vc), Robert Keck (vc), Mary LaBreque (vc), Dan Loch (vc), Stan Saderk (vc), Lisa Hemmer (fl), Sue Oberg (fl), Wendi Lev (fl), Jim Vanden (fl), Jim O'Rourke (gtr), Steve Braack (elec) — Tzadik ▲ TZA 7011 [DDD]
Sugahara, Atsushi (mar)
Ichiyanagi, T.:Portrait of Forest *(rec Chichibu Myuzu Park Ongaku-do, Oct 5-6, 1995)* — Camerata ▲ 30CM 414 [DDD]
Sugahara, Atsushi (perc)
Fukushi, N.:Anima of a Tree *(rec Chichibu Myuzu Park Ongaku-do, Oct 5-6, 1995)* — Camerata ▲ 30CM 414 [DDD]

INSTRUMENT.

Sugahara, Atsushi (perc) (cont.)
Ikebe, S.-I.:Monovalence IV *(rec Chichibu Myuzu Park Ongaku-do, Oct 5-6, 1995)* Camerata ▲ 30CM 414 [DDD]
Ishii, M.:Thirteen Drums *(rec Chichibu Myuzu Park Ongaku-do, Oct 5-6, 1995)* Camerata ▲ 30CM 414 [DDD]
Kitazume, M.:Shadows III-A *(rec Chichibu Myuzu Park Ongaku-do, Oct 5-6, 1995)* Camerata ▲ 30CM 414 [DDD]
Takahashi, Y.:The Wolf *(rec Chichibu Myuzu Park Ongaku-do, Oct 5-6, 1995)* Camerata ▲ 30CM 414 [DDD]

Sugahara, Atsushi (timp)
Ichiyanagi, T.:Rhythm Gradation *(rec Chichibu Myuzu Park Ongaku-do, Oct 5-6, 1995)* Camerata ▲ 30CM 414 [DDD]

Sugitani, Shoko (pno)
Schumann, C.:Con Pno, w. G. Oskamp (cnd), Berlin SO Verdi Classics ▲ AU 32 107
Schumann, R.:Con Pno, w. G. Oskamp (cnd), Berlin SO Verdi Classics ▲ AU 32 107

Suite, Bill (E hn)
Scelsi, G.:Anahit, w. Paul Zukofsky (vn), Julie Bogorad (fl), Peggy Russell (fl), Courtney Westcott (fl), Lawrence McDonald (cl), Joan Waryha (cl), Jean Hansen (b cl), Nita VanPelt (sax), Bob Zobal (tpt), John Carter (trbn), Martin Lydecker (trbn), Stan Cortman (hn), Robert Ward (hn), William Curry (va), Jody Rowitsch (va), Irene Wade (va), Anne Fagerburg (vc), John Gockel (vc), Sue Manz (bass), Steven Stearman (bass) *(rec Oberlin Conservatory of Music, Oct 8, 1973)* CP² ▲ CP2 108 [AAD]

Suits, Paul (pno)
Carter, E.:Syringa, w. J. Stone (fl) CRI ▲ CD 648 [ADD]
Rorem, N.:Hearing, w. R. Rees (sop), K. Wheeler (mez), M. Galloway (ten), R. Hilley (bar), R. Wagner (cl), J. Hamlin (tpt), D. Starobin (mand), D. Davidson (vn), K. Askew (va), J. Babich (db), D. Druckman (perc), G. Smith (cnd) Premier ▲ PRCD 1035 [ADD]

Suk, Josef (va)
Berlioz, H.:Harold in Italy, w. D. Fischer-Dieskau (cnd), Czech PO *(rec 1976)* Supraphon ▲ 11 0708-2 [ADD]
Bruch, M.:Trios Cl, Va & Pno, Op. 83, w. Ludmila Peterková (cl), Josef Hála (pno) Supraphon ▲ SUP 3014
Dvořák, A.:Qnt Strs, Op. 97, w. Smetana String Quartet Supraphon ▲ SUP 111469 [DDD]
Dvořák, A.:Sextet, w. J. Schuchro (vc), Smetana String Quartet Supraphon ▲ SUP 111469 [DDD]
Martinů, B.:Rhap-Con Va, w. V. Neumann (cnd), Czech PO Supraphon ▲ SUP 111969 [AAD]
Mozart, W.A.:Trio Cl, K.498, w. Ludmila Peterková (cl), Josef Hála (pno) Supraphon ▲ SUP 3014

Suk, Josef (vn)—see also ORCHESTRAS & ENSEMBLES Suk Trio
Bach, J.S.:Brandenburg Cons, w. J. Suk (cnd), Suk CO *(rec 1989)* Vanguard Classics 2-▲ OVC 7002/03 [DDD]
Bach, J.S.:Cons Vn (comp), w. V. Smetáček (cnd), Prague SO *(rec 1966)* Supraphon Collection ▲ 11 0642-2 [ADD]
Bach, J.S.:Con Vn & Ob, w. J. Adamus (ob), J. Vlach (cnd), Suk CO Supraphon ▲ 10 4127 [DDD]
Bach, J.S.:Con Vn & Ob, w. J. Adamus (ob), J. Vlach (cnd), Suk CO *(rec 1985)* Supraphon Collection ▲ 11 0642-2 [ADD]
Bach, J.S.:Con for 2 Vns, w. M. Kosina (vn), J. Vlach (cnd), Suk CO *(rec 1982)* Supraphon ▲ 110281-2 [AAD]
Bach, J.S.:Con for 2 Vns, w. L. Jásek (vn), V. Smetáček (cnd), Prague SO *(rec 1965)* Supraphon Collection ▲ 11 0642-2 [ADD]
Bartók, B.:Con 1 Vn, w. L. Pešek (cnd), Czech PO *(rec live, Czech Radio broadcasts, 1985)* Praga ▲ PR 250099
Bartók, B.:Con 1 Vn, w. J. Ferencsik (cnd), Czech PO *(rec live, Prague, 2/23/79)* Supraphon ▲ 11 0706-2 [ADD]
Bartók, B.:Duos (44), w. A. Gertler (vn) Sound ▲ CD 3444
Beethoven, L. van:Con Vn, Op. 61, w. M. Sargent (cnd), BBC SO IMP ("BBC Radio Classics" series) ▲ IMP 5691612
Beethoven, L. van:Con Vn, Op. 61, w. A. Boult (cnd), New Philharmonia Orch EMI Classics ▲ CDE 67765
Beethoven, L. van:Romances Vn, w. N. Marriner (cnd), Academy of St. Martin in the Fields EMI Classics ▲ CDE 67765
Beethoven, L. van:Romances Vn, w. N. Marriner (cnd), Academy of St. Martin in the Fields Klavier ▲ KCD 11035 [DDD]
Benda, G.A.:Sons for 2 Vns, w. Shizuka Ishikawa (vn), Jitka Vlasankova (vc), Josef Hala (hpd) Lotos ▲ CD 0027 [DDD]
Berg, A.:Con Vn, w. V. Neumann (cnd), Czech PO *(rec 1980)* Supraphon ▲ 11 0706-2 [ADD]
Berlioz, H.:Rêverie et caprice, w. V. Smetáček (cnd), Prague SO *(rec 1977)* Supraphon ▲ 11 0708-2 [ADD]
Berlioz, H.:Rêverie et caprice, w. V. Smetáček (cnd), Prague SO Supraphon Collection ▲ 11 0639-2 [ADD]
Brahms, J.:Trio Hn, w. P. Damm (hn), W. Genuit (pno) Acanta ▲ CD 43270 [DDD]
Brahms, J.:Trio 1 Pno, w. J. Katchen (pno), J. Starker (vc) London ▲ 421152-2 [ADD]
Brahms, J.:Trio 2 Pno, w. J. Katchen (pno), J. Starker (vc) London ▲ 421152-2 [ADD]
Bruch, M.:Con 1 Vn, w. K. Ančerl (cnd), Czech PO Supraphon Collection ▲ 11 0639-2 [ADD]
Dvořák, A.:Ballad, w. Josef Hála (pno) Supraphon ▲ SUP 111466
Dvořák, A.:Con Vn, w. K. Ančerl (cnd), Czech PO Supraphon Collection ▲ 11 0601-2 [ADD]
Dvořák, A.:Con Vn, w. K. Ančerl (cnd), Czech PO Vivace 3-▲ E 325 [ADD/DDD]
Dvořák, A.:Con Vn, w. K. Ančerl (cnd), Czech PO *(rec live, July 30, 1963)* Orfeo d'or ("Festspiel Dokumente" series) ▲ 395951
Dvořák, A.:Con Vn, w. K. Ančerl (cnd), Czech PO Supraphon ("Czech Philharmonic Series") ▲ SUP 111928 [ADD]
Dvořák, A.:Con Vn, w. M. Sargent (cnd), BBC SO IMP ("BBC Radio Classics" series) ▲ IMP 5691612
Dvořák, A.:Notturno, w. Josef Hála (pno) [arr vn & pno] Supraphon ▲ SUP 111466
Dvořák, A.:Qts Pno Strs, Opp. 23 & 87, w. J. Hála (pno), J. Kodousek (va), J. Chuchro (vc)—Op. 23 & Op. 87 Supraphon ▲ 11 1464-2 [DDD]
Dvořák, A.:Romance Vn, w. K. Ančerl (cnd), Czech PO Vivace 3-▲ E 325 [ADD/DDD]
Dvořák, A.:Romance Vn, w. K. Ančerl (cnd), Czech PO Supraphon ("Czech Philharmonic Series") ▲ SUP 111928 [ADD]
Dvořák, A.:Romantic Pieces, Op. 75, w. Josef Hála (pno) Supraphon ▲ SUP 111466
Dvořák, A.:Son Vn, w. Josef Hála (pno) Supraphon ▲ SUP 111466
Dvořák, A.:Sonatina Vn, w. Josef Hála (pno) Supraphon ▲ SUP 111466
Dvořák, A.:Sonatina Vn, w. Jan Panenka (pno) Supraphon ▲ SUP 110270 [AAD]
Fauré, G.:Son 2 Vn, w. Josef Hala (pno) *(rec Domovina Studio, Prague, Sept. 23-24, 1994)* Discover International ▲ DI 920306 [DDD]
Franck, C.:Son Vn, w. Josef Hala (pno) *(rec Domovina Studio, Prague, Sept. 23-24, 1994)* Discover International ▲ DI 920306 [DDD]
Janácek, L.:Con Vn, w. V. Neumann (cnd), Czech PO Supraphon ▲ SUP 111965 [DDD]
Janácek, L.:Son Vn, w. Jan Panenka (pno) Supraphon ▲ SUP 110270 [AAD]
Jewels of Baroque Music, w. Aleš Bárta (org) Lotos ▲ LT 0009 [DDD]
Josef Suk Plays Famous Violin Encores, w. Josef Hala (pno) Supraphon ▲ SUP 111311 [DDD]
Kodály, Z.:Adagio Vn, w. Pierre Fournier (vc), André Navarra (vc), Tatjana Sadovskaja (pno) Praga ▲ PR 250065
Kodály, Z.:Duo Vn & Vc, w. Pierre Fournier (vc), André Navarra (vc) Praga ▲ PR 250065
Locatelli, P.:Sons Vn, Op. 8, w. Shizuka Ishikawa (vn), Jitka Vlasankova (vc), Josef Hala (hpd)—Trio Son Lotos ▲ CD 0027 [DDD]
Lovely Time, w. Josef Hála (pno) Lotos ▲ CD 0026 [DDD]
Lovely Time 1, w. Suk CO Lotos ▲ LT 0002 [DDD]
Lovely Time 2, w. Suk CO Lotos ▲ LT 0004 [DDD]
Martinů, B.:Con 1 Vn, w. V. Neumann (cnd), Czech PO Supraphon ▲ SUP 111969 [AAD]
Martinů, B.:Con 2 Vn, w. V. Neumann (cnd), Czech PO Supraphon ▲ 11 0702-2 [ADD]
Martinů, B.:Con 2 Vn, w. V. Neumann (cnd), Czech PO Supraphon ▲ SUP 111969 [AAD]
Martinů, B.:Madrigal Stanzas, w. J. Hála (pno) Supraphon ▲ 11 0099-2 [DDD]

Suk, Josef (vn) (cont.)
Martinů, B.:Son 2 Vn, w. J. Hála (pno) Supraphon ▲ 11 0099-2 [DDD]
Martinů, B.:Son 3 Vn, w. J. Hála (pno) Supraphon ▲ 11 0099-2 [DDD]
Mendelssohn, F.:Con in e Vn & Orch, Op. 64, w. K. Ančerl (cnd), Czech PO Supraphon Collection ▲ 11 0639-2 [ADD]
Mozart, W.A.:Adagio Vn, w. T. Hanuš (cnd), Prague Chamber PO Lotos ▲ CD 0031 [DDD]
Mozart, W.A.:Adagio Vn, K.261, w. L. Hlaváček (cnd), Prague CO Eurodisc 3-▲ 69255-2-RG [ADD]
Mozart, W.A.:Adagio Vn, K.261, w. N. Marriner (cnd), Academy of St. Martin in the Fields Klavier ▲ KCD 11035 [DDD]
Mozart, W.A.:Arias, w. Helen Donath (sop), Dieter Klöcker (cl), Karl-Otto Hartmann (bn), K. Donath (cnd), Suk CO—Cor Sincerum; Jesus Amor Meus; Mens Sancta Deo [2 versions]; Jesu Dulcis Memoria; Salve Regina; Domine Deus Salutis Meae; Plasmator Deus; Die Hoffnung dient zum Stabe *(rec Cultural House, Prague, June 3-10, 1987)* Panton ▲ PAN 810860
Mozart, W.A.:Cons Vn, w. L. Hlaváček (cnd), Prague CO Eurodisc 3-▲ 69255-2-RG [ADD]
Mozart, W.A.:Con 2 Vn, w. J. Suk (cnd), Suk CO Vanguard Classics ▲ OVC 7001 [DDD]
Mozart, W.A.:Con 3 Vn, w. J. Suk (cnd), Suk CO Vanguard Classics ▲ OVC 7001 [DDD]
Mozart, W.A.:Rondo Vn, K.269, w. L. Hlaváček (cnd), Prague CO Eurodisc 3-▲ 69255-2 [ADD]
Mozart, W.A.:Rondo Vn, K.373, w. N. Marriner (cnd), Academy of St. Martin in the Fields Klavier ▲ KCD 11035 [DDD]
Mozart, W.A.:Rondo Vn, K.373, w. L. Hlaváček (cnd), Prague CO Eurodisc 3-▲ 69255-2 [ADD]
Mozart, W.A.:Sinf concertante Vn, K.364, w. T. Kakuska (va), J. Suk (cnd), Suk CO *(rec 1989)* Vanguard Classics ▲ OVC 7001 [DDD]
Music From the Heart of Europe, w. Lubomir Brabec (gtr), Rudolf Firkušny (pno), Vaclav Neumann (cnd), Jiří Belohlávek (cnd), Panocha Quartet, Czech PO, Prague CO, Prague Musica Antiqua, et al. Supraphon ▲ SUP 0063 [DDD]
Ravel, M.:Sonate posthume, w. Josef Hála (pno) *(rec Domovina Studio, Prague, Sept. 23-24, 1994)* Discover International ▲ DI 920306 [DDD]
Rudolph [Archduke Of Austria]:Vars Vn, w. S. Kagan (pno) Koch International Classics ▲ KIC 7082-2 [DDD]
Schubert, Franz:Qnt Strs, D.956, w. Jiří Baxa (vn), Ladislav Černy (va), Saša Večtomov (vc), Josef Simandl (vc) *(rec live, 1971)* Praga ▲ PR 250055
Schubert, Franz:Rondo Vn, D.438, w. N. Marriner (cnd), Academy of St. Martin in the Fields Klavier ▲ KCD 11035 [DDD]
Smetana, B.:From the Homeland, w. Jan Panenka (pno) Supraphon ▲ SUP 110270 [AAD]
Suk, J.:Fant Vn, w. K. Ančerl (cnd), Czech PO *(rec 1965)* Supraphon Collection ▲ 11 0601-2 [ADD]
Suk, J.:Fant Vn, w. K. Ančerl (cnd), Czech PO Supraphon ("Czech Philharmonic Series") ▲ SUP 111928 [ADD]
Suk, J.:Pieces Vn Pno, w. Jan Panenka (pno) Supraphon ▲ SUP 110270 [AAD]
Suk, J.:Qt Pno, w. J. Panenka (pno), J. Talich (va), M. Fukačová (vc) Supraphon ▲ SUP 111532 [DDD]
Tartini, G.:Trio Sons, w. Shizuka Ishikawa (vn), Jitka Vlasankova (vc), Josef Hala (hpd)—Op. 3/2; Op. 8/1 & 3; Son in D Lotos ▲ CD 0027 [DDD]
Vivaldi, A.:Cons Ob Vn, w. J. Adamus (ob), J. Vlach (cnd), Suk CO—R.576 Supraphon ▲ 10 4127 [DDD]
Vivaldi, A.:Cons Vn (misc), w. J. Vlach (cnd), Suk CO—R.230 Supraphon ▲ 10 4127 [DDD]
Vivaldi, A.:Cons Vn, Op. 3/1-12, "L'estro armonico", w. J. Vlach (cnd), Suk CO—No. 9 in D *(rec June 16-19, 1985)* Supraphon ("Collection" series) ▲ 11 0685-2 [ADD]
Vivaldi, A.:Cons Vn, Op. 8/1-4, "The Four Seasons", w. L. Haváček (cnd), Prague CO Supraphon ▲ 110281-2 [AAD]
Vivaldi, A.:Cons Vn, Op. 8/1-4, "The Four Seasons", w. L. Haváček (cnd), Prague CO *(rec Apr 13-16, 1975)* Supraphon ("Collection" series) ▲ 110685-2 [ADD]
Vivaldi, A.:Cons for 2 Vns, w. O. Vlček (vn), Prague Virtuosi—RV.509 in c, RV.514 in d, RV.522 in a, RV.523 in a, RV.524 in B♭ Supraphon ▲ 11 1271-2 [DDD]
Vivaldi, A.:Cons for 2 Vns, w. O. Vlček (vn), Prague Virtuosi—RV. 505, RV. 515, RV. 519, RV. 530 Supraphon ▲ SUP 11 1819 [DDD]
Zelenka, J.D.:Con à 8, w. Jana Brozková (ob), Ludmila Vybíralová (vn), Ivo Laniar (vc), Jaroslav Kubita (bn), F. Vajnar (cnd), Suk CO *(rec Studio Martínek, Prague, May 15-17 & Nov. 8-13, 19)* Panton 2-▲ PAN 811235 [DDD]

Suk, Josef (vn/va)
Martinů, B.:Con 1 Vn, w. V. Neumann (cnd), Czech PO Supraphon ▲ 11 0702-2 [ADD]
Mozart, W.A.:Sinf concertante Vn, K.364, w. V. Neumann (cnd), Czech PO Panton ▲ PAN 811206
Rudolph [Archduke Of Austria]:Son Vn, w. S. Kagan Koch International Classics ▲ KIC 7082-2 [DDD]

Sukarlan, Amanda (pno)
Loevendie, T.:Strides Vienna Modern Masters ("Distinguished Performers III" series) ▲ VMM 2016 [DDD]
Loevendie, T.:Toccata Vienna Modern Masters ("Distinguished Performers III" series) ▲ VMM 2016 [DDD]
Loevendie, T.:Walk Vienna Modern Masters ("Distinguished Performers III" series) ▲ VMM 2016 [DDD]

Sukova, Eva (pno)
Classical Piano Favorites Lydian ▲ LYD 18023 [DDD]

Sulem, Jean (va)—see ORCHESTRAS & ENSEMBLES Rosamunde String Quartet

Sulem-Bialobroda, Agnès (vn)—see ORCHESTRAS & ENSEMBLES Rosamunde String Quartet

Sulich, Stephen (pno)
Delius, F.:Songs, w. R. Golden (sop)—18 songs, composed 1888-1895 [E,F,G]—The bird's story; Twilight fancies; Young Venevil; Three Songs by Percy Shelley (1891); Four Poems of Paul Verlaine (1895); The homeward way; Cradle song; Hidden love; Dreamy nights; Nachtigall; Am schönsten Sonnerabend war's; Sehnsucht; Beim Sonnenuntergang Koch International Classics ▲ KIC 7043-2 [DDD]

Sulli, G. del (fl)—see ORCHESTRAS & ENSEMBLES Seicentonovecento Ensemble

Sullivan, Matthew (ob)—see also ORCHESTRAS & ENSEMBLES Musicians' Accord, Quintet of the Americas
First, D.:The Good Book's (Accurate) Jail of Escape Dust Coordinates 2, w. Chris Jepperson (cl), Annemarie Wiesner (vn), Gary Trosclair (tpt), Elaine Kaplinsky (kbd syn), Chad Henderson (teahouse gtr/b gtr), Kevin Sparke (perc), David First (e-bow gtr/teahouse gtr/Distortion gtr/kbd syn/programming) *(rec Baby Monster Studios, NYC, May 1992)* O. O. Discs ▲ OO 23 [DDD]

Sullivan, Matthew (ob/E Hn/Yamaha WX-7 wind controller)—see ORCHESTRAS & ENSEMBLES First Avenue

Sullivan, Taimur (sax)
Melby, J.:Alto Rhap, w. Debra Richtmeyer (sax), Paul Martin Zonn (cl), Wilma Zonn (ob) Zuma ▲ ZMA 105
Melby, J.:Con Cl & Tape, w. Paul Martin Zonn (cl), Debra Richtmeyer (sax), Wilma Zonn (ob) Zuma ▲ ZMA 105
Zonn, P.M.:Cloning of Wilma Zonn Ww, w. Paul Martin Zonn (cl), Wilma Zonn (ob), Debra Richtmeyer (sax) Zuma ▲ ZMA 105
Zonn, P.M.:Nimbus III Ww, w. Paul Martin Zonn (cl), Wilma Zonn (ob), Debra Richtmeyer (sax) Zuma ▲ ZMA 105
Zonn, P.M.:Shadow of the Condor Ww, w. Paul Martin Zonn (cl), Wilma Zonn (ob), Debra Richtmeyer (sax) Zuma ▲ ZMA 105

Sultan, Grete (pno)
Bach, J.S.:Goldberg Vars *(rec Finch Junior College, NY, 1959)* Concord Concerto 2-▲ CCD 42030 [ADD]
Cage, J.:Etudes Australes (comp) *(rec New York City, Aug. 1978 & Nov.-Dec. 198)* Wergo 3-▲ WER 6152-2 [AAD]
Cage, J.:Music of Changes—Book 1 *(rec Syracuse Univ, Syracuse, NY, 1974)* Concord Concerto 2-▲ CCD 42030 [ADD]
Cage, J.:The Perilous Night *(rec Town Hall, New York City, 1969)* Concord Concerto 2-▲ CCD 42030 [ADD]
Debussy, C.:Etudes—Nos. 7-11 *(rec New York City, 1967)* Concord Concerto 2-▲ CCD 42030 [ADD]

▲ = CD ♦ = Enhanced CD Δ = MD ■ = Cassette Tape □ = DCC

Sultan, Grete (pno) (cont.)
Schoenberg, A.:Pieces Pno, Op. 23 *(rec Brooklyn College, Brooklyn, NY, 1990)* Concord Concerto 2-▲ CCD 42030 [ADD]
Schoenberg, A.:Piece Pno, Op. 33a *(rec Philips Collection, Washington, D.C., 1971)* Concord Concerto 2-▲ CCD 42030 [ADD]

Sultanov, Alexei (pno)
Chopin, F.:Andante Spianato & Grande Polonaise Teldec ▲ 2292-46463-2 ZK
Chopin, F.:Ballades Pno (comp)—Op. 52 Teldec ▲ 2292-46463-2 ZK
Chopin, F.:Polonaises—Polonaise héroïque, Op. 53 Teldec ▲ 2292-46463-2 ZK
Chopin, F.:Scherzos Teldec ▲ 2292-46463-2 ZK
Rachmaninoff, S.:Con 2 Pno, w. M. Shostakovich (cnd), London SO Teldec (Digital Experience) ▲ 9031-77601-2 AW [DDD] ■ 9031-77601-4
Sensual Classics II, w. C. Katsaris (pno), Brodsky Quartet, London SO [cnd:M. Shostakovich], New York PO [cnd:Z. Mehta], BBC SO [cnd:A. Davis], Leipzig Gewandhaus Orch [cnd:K. Masur], 12 Cellos of the Berlin PO [cnd:A. Jordan, E. Inbal], et al. Teldec ▲ 92014-2 ■ 92014-4
Tchaikovsky, P.:Con 1 Pno, w. M. Shostakovich (cnd), London SO Teldec ("Digital Experience" series) ▲ 9031-77601-2 AW [DDD]

Sultanov, N. (pno)
Doppler, A.F.:Fant pastorale hongroise, w. S. Kutluer (fl) Gallo ▲ CD 810 [DDD]
Genin, Pierre A.:The Carnival in Venice, w. S. Kutluer (fl) Gallo ▲ CD 810 [DDD]
Melikov, A.:Fants of Komde, w. S. Kutluer (fl) Gallo ▲ CD 810 [DDD]
Morlacchi, F.:Pastore Svizzero, w. S. Kutluer (fl) Gallo ▲ CD 810 [DDD]
Poulenc, F.:Son Fl, w. S. Kutluer (fl) Gallo ▲ CD 810 [DDD]

Sulzen, Donald (pno)
Brahms, J.:Ballads & Romances, Op. 75, w. Julie Kaufmann (sop), Marilyn Schmeige (mez)—2 sels Orfeo ▲ 369961 [DDD]
Brahms, J.:Duets, Op. 20, w. Julie Kaufmann (sop), Marilyn Schmeige (mez) Orfeo ▲ 369961 [DDD]
Brahms, J.:Duets, Op. 61, w. Julie Kaufmann (sop), Marilyn Schmeige (mez) Orfeo ▲ 369961 [DDD]
Brahms, J.:Duets, Op. 66, w. Julie Kaufmann (sop), Marilyn Schmeige (mez) Orfeo ▲ 369961 [DDD]
Brahms, J.:Romances & Songs, Op. 84, w. Julie Kaufmann (sop), Marilyn Schmeige (mez)—3 sels Orfeo ▲ 369961 [DDD]
Brahms, J.:Songs, w. Julie Kaufmann (sop), Marilyn Schmeige (mez) Orfeo ▲ 369961 [DDD]
Fauré, G.:La Chanson d'Eve, w. Marilyn Schmiege (mez) Orfeo ▲ 347941 [DDD]
Fauré, G.:Le Jardin clos, w. Marilyn Schmiege (mez) Orfeo ▲ 347941 [DDD]
Fauré, G.:Mélodies 'de Venise', Op. 58, w. Marilyn Schmiege (mez) Orfeo ▲ 347941 [DDD]
My Heritage, w. Jo Ann Pickens (sop) Koch Schwann ▲ SCH 314472 [DDD]

Sumi, Seiko (pno)
Fontyn, J.:Zephyr, w. M. Tanaka (bn) Thorofon ▲ CTH 2099 [DDD]
Hindemith, P.:Son Bn, w. M. Tanaka (bn) Thorofon ▲ CTH 2099 [DDD]
The Magic Bassoon, w. Tanaka, Masahito (bn) Thorofon ▲ CTH 2099 [DDD]
Saint-Saëns, C.:Son Bn, w. M. Tanaka (bn) Thorofon ▲ CTH 2099 [DDD]
Weber, C.M. von:Andante & Rondo ungarese Bn, w. M. Tanaka (bn) Thorofon ▲ CTH 2099 [DDD]

Summer, Mark (vc)—see ORCHESTRAS & ENSEMBLES Turtle Island String Quartet

Summerly, Jeremy (org)
Weelkes, T.:Anthems, w. Gary Cooper (org), Oxford Camerata—Hosanna to the son of David; Give ear, O Lord; All people clap your hands; What joy so true; O Lord, grant the king a long life; Lord, to thee I make my mooan; All laud and praise; Lachrimae Pavan (Morley); A remembrance of my friend Thomas Morley; Passymeasures Pavan (Morley); Gloria in excelsis Deo; When David hear; Give the king thy judgements; O Lord, arise; O how amiable are thy dwellings; Most mighty and all-knowing Lord; Alleluia, I heard a voice *(rec Chapel of Hertford College, Oxford, Jan 3-4, 1995)* Naxos ▲ 8.553209 [DDD]

Sun, Christina (erhu)
Gisberg:Music of, w. Christine Bard (perc), Jeff O'Malley (nar), Jacqueline Leclair (ob), Quentin Chiappetta (sampler/pno/cpsr), Reuben Radding (bass instrument), Gisburg (voice/fl/cpsr)—Opening; No Stranger Not At All; Imaginary Movielandscape 1; Portrait; "Jowohl"; Mein Herz hat nicht vergessen [tango]; Ritual; Dying Takes Its Time; Fruits; Mic' N Drums Tzadik ("The Composers" series) ▲ TZA 7007 [DDD]

Sun, Elisabeth (pno)
Debussy, C.:Chansons de Bilitis, w. S. Nigoghossian (mez) [F] Quantum ▲ QM 6912 [DDD]
Debussy, C.:Epigraphes antiques, w. M. J. Truys (pno) Quantum ▲ QM 6912 [DDD]

Sun, Elisabeth (cel)
Debussy, C.:Chansons de Bilitis (recitation), w. A. Lochner (nar), A. Adorjan (fl), M. Larrieu (fl), S. Mildonian (hp), Y. Nagae (hp) [F] Quantum ▲ QM 6912 [DDD]

Sund, Hakan (pno)
Orhängen, w. Elisabeth Söderström (sop), Clas Pehrsson (rec) *(rec June 15-18, 1981)* BIS ▲ CD 187 [AAD]

Sundberg, B. (hn)—see ORCHESTRAS & ENSEMBLES Musica Holmiae

Sundholm, Stewart (hn)
Polosi, L.:Triptych, w. Roxanne Joyner (tpt), Michael Plant (trbn) Opus One ▲ CD 160

Sundling, Wille (vn)—see ORCHESTRAS & ENSEMBLES Crafoord String Quartet

Sung, Hugh (pno)
Aaron Rosand:Romances for Violin & Piano, w. Aaron Rosand (vn) Vox ("Classics" series) ▲ VOX 7505 [DDD]
Brahms, J.:Hungarian Dances Pno 4-Hands, w. A. Rosand (vn) [Joseph Joachim's 1871 & 1880 arr.] Biddulph ▲ LAW 003 [DDD]
Brahms, J.:Sons Vn (comp), w. Aaron Rosand (vn) *(rec Philadelphia, Jan 1992)* Vox Classics ▲ VOX 7535 [DDD]
Handel, G.F.:Sons Vn & Kbd, w. Aaron Rosand (vn)—includes Andante from Flute Sonata in B minor (Op. 1 No. 9) *(rec Jan. 9 & 10, 1992)* Biddulph ▲ LAW 004 [DDD]
Joachim, J.:Romance Vn, w. A. Rosand (vn) Biddulph ▲ LAW 003 [DDD]
Maggio, R.:Barcarole, w. Scott St. John (vn), John Koen (vc), Don Liuzzi (perc), J. Higdon (cnd) *(rec Settlement Music School, Germantown, PA, June 17, 1995)* CRI ▲ CD 720 [DDD]

Sung, Hyun-Jung (vc)
Boccherini, L.:Fugues, G.73, w. J. Berger (vc), M. Galling (pno) ebs ▲ EBS 6032 [DDD]
Boccherini, L.:Sons (34) Vc, w. J. Berger (vc), M. Galling (pno)—G.6, 565, 571 & 572 ebs ▲ EBS 6032 [DDD]

Sung, Li Chin (gtr/syn/perc/voc)
Sung, L.C.:Music of, w. Ah Chuen (voc)—Grandfather 1; Garden; Point of Death; Dream On; Give Up; Known; Treasure; Speed Game; Buddha; Mad Birds; East. West; Silence; Suffocation; Shame; Wake up & Death; Jump; Grandfather 3; Run; Ear Games; Grandfather 4; Yin 1; Grandfather 2; Muzzy; and others *(rec 1992-95)* Tzadik ("Composer" series) ▲ TZA 7014 [DDD]

Supové, Kathleen (pno)
Childs, M.E.:Kilter, w. Anthony de Mare (pno) XI Compact Discs ▲ XI 114
Epstein, M.:Waterbowls *(rec Nov. 14-17, 1992)* CRI ("Emergency Music" series) ▲ CD 653 [DDD]
Foss, L.:Solo Pno *(rec Nov. 14-17, 1992)* CRI ▲ CD 653 [DDD]
Lang, D.:While Nailing at Random *(rec Nov. 14-17, 1992)* CRI ("Emergency Music" series) ▲ CD 653 [DDD]
Macbride, D.:Chartres CRI ▲ CD 640 [DDD]
Rzewski, F.:North American Ballads *(rec Nov. 14-17, 1992)* CRI ("Emergency Music" series) ▲ CD 653 [DDD]
Scelsi, G.:Incantations Pno Neuma ▲ 450-72 [DDD]
Woolf, R.:Dancétudes *(rec Nov. 14-17, 1992)* CRI ("Emergency Music" series) ▲ CD 653 [DDD]
York, W.:Reminiscence 2, w. J. D. Fredericks (fl), I. Greitzer (cl) *(rec May 1987)* New World ▲ 80439-2

Surmélian, Hasmig (pno)
Hovhaness, A.:Music of, w. Annie Jodry (vn), J.-J. Werner (cnd), Léon Barzin Orch—Lousadzak [Coming of Light] for Pno & Str Orch; Saris for Vn & Pno; Oror for Vn & Pno; Shatakh for Vn & Pno; Shatakh II; Khirgiz Suite for Vn & Pno; A Khirgiz Tala; Khirgiz III; Con No. 2 for Vn & Str Orch *(rec Paris, May 1995)* Media 7 ▲ MA 951001 [DDD]

Sushanskaya, Rimma (vn)
Dvořák, A.:Romance Vn, w. W. Boughton (cnd), English String Orch IMP ("Concert Classics" series) ▲ IMP PCD 1103
Prokofiev, S.:Son Vn, Op. 94bis, w. R. Vignoles (pno) IMP Masters ▲ IMP MCD 58 [DDD]
Shostakovich, D.:Son Vn, w. R. Vignoles (pno) IMP Masters ▲ IMP MCD 58 [DDD]

Suske, Karl (va)
Kaminski, H.:Qnt Strs, w. New Leipzig String Quartet *(rec Radio DRS 2 Studio, Zurich, Jan.-Mar. 1994)* Christophorus ▲ CHR 77148 [DDD]

Suske, Karl (vn)
Bach, J.S.:Sons & Partitas Vn, BWV 1001-1006 *(rec 1983-88)* Berlin Classics 2-▲ BER CD 9275
Beethoven, L. van:Con. Vn, WoO 5, w. H. Bongartz (cnd), Leipzig Gewandhaus Orch Berlin Classics ▲ BER 2078 [DDD]
Beethoven, L. van:Romances Vn, w. H. Bongartz (cnd), Leipzig Gewandhaus Orch—in G Berlin Classics ▲ BER 2078 [DDD]
Reger, M.:Con in Olden Style, w. Heinz Schunk (vn), O. Suitner (cnd), Berlin Staatskapelle Berlin Classics ▲ BER 9123
Vivaldi, A.:Sons Ob, w. B. Glaetzner (ob), I. Goritzki (ob), A. Bayer (vn), T. Reinhardt (bn), S. Pank (vl), C. Schornsheim (org/hpd)—RV.28, 34, 53, 81 & 779 Capriccio ▲ CD 10143 [DDD] ■ CAS 27153 (CrO2)

Suslin, Alexander (perc)—see ORCHESTRAS & ENSEMBLES Astraea

Suslin, Vikot (perc)—see ORCHESTRAS & ENSEMBLES Astraea

Sussman, D. (vc)
Bach, J.S.:Sons Fl, BWV 1030-35, w. P. Fried (fl), M. Kroll (hpd) Golden Tone ▲ GTCD 001 ■ GTC 001

Sussman, David (gtr)
Flute Flavors, w. Paul Fried (fl), Christopher O'Riley (pno), Ronald Feldman (vc) Golden Tone ▲ GTCD 002

Sussman, Michael (cl)
Macchia, S.:Chamber Con 3, w. J. Tanner (fl/alt fl), F. Cohen (ob/E hn), D. Fedora (bn), L. Klock (hn), V. Kadlubkiewicz (vn), J. Messina (db), P. Tanner (perc) *(rec July 1992)* Gasparo ▲ GS 226 [DDD]
Spratlan, L.:Night Music, w. V. Kadlubkiewicz (vn), J. Kelley (perc) *(rec July 1992)* Gasparo ▲ GS 226 [DDD]

Süssmut, Gernot (vn)—see ORCHESTRAS & ENSEMBLES Petersen String Quartet

Süssmuth, Gernot (vn)
Schulhoff, E.:Duo Vn, w. Hans-Jakob Eschenburg (vc) *(rec Berlin, June 6-8 & Nov 7-8, 1994)* Capriccio ▲ 10 539 [DDD]

Sutherland, Donald (org)
Liszt, F.:Ave Maria von Arcadelt, w. P. Gustaf Mitchell (trbn) [at St. Patrick's Church Org, Washington, DC] Gothic ▲ G 49080 [DDD]
Liszt, F.:Evocation à la Chapelle Sixtine, w. P. Gustaf Mitchell (trbn) [at St. Patrick's Church Org, Washington, DC] Gothic ▲ G 49080 [DDD]
Liszt, F.:Fant & Fugue on "Ad nos, ad salutarem undam" Org, w. P. Gustaf Mitchell (trbn) [at St. Patrick's Church Org, Washington, DC] Gothic ▲ G 49080 [DDD]
Liszt, F.:Org Music—Vars on "Weinen, Klagen, Sorgen, Zagen"; Ave Maria von Arcadelt; Evocation à la Chapelle Sixtine; Cujus animam [w. P. Gustaf Mitchell (trbn)]; Fant & Fugue on the chorale "Ad nos, ad sulutarem undam"[Lively-Fulcher org] *(rec St. Patrick's Church, Washington, D.C.)* Gothic ▲ G 49080 [DDD]
Liszt, F.:Transcriptions & Paraphrases, w. P. Gustaf Mitchell (trbn)—Cujus animam [from Stabat mater; at St. Patrick's Church Org, Washington, DC] Gothic ▲ G 49080 [DDD]
Liszt, F.:Vars on "Weinen, Klagen, Sorgen, Zagen", S.179, w. P. Gustaf Mitchell (trbn) [at St. Patrick's Church Org, Washington, DC] Gothic ▲ G 49080 [DDD]

Sutherland, Donald (pno)
Starer, R.:Anna Margarita's Will, w. P. Bryn-Johnson (sop), K. Kraber (fl), S. Kates (vc), P. Ingraham (hn) *(rec 1980)* CRI ▲ CD 612 [ADD]

Sutherland, Pete (fid)
Man with the Wooden Flute, w. Chris Norman (fl), Robin Bullock (gtr/cittern/fid), Ann Marie Morgan (vl) Dorian ▲ DOR 90166 [DDD]

Sutherland, Robin (hpd)
Handel, G.F.:Sons Fl, w. Laurel Zucker (fl)—(7) in e, g, a, G, C, b & F, Op. 1/1b, 2, 4, 5, 7, 9 & 11 Cantilena ▲ 66005-2 [DDD]

Sutherland, Robin (pno)
Bach, J.S.:Goldberg Vars d'Note 2-▲ DND 1013
Bach, J.S.:Goldberg Vars d'Note 2-▲ DND 1013 [ADD]
Chaminade, C.:Concertino Fl, w. Laurel Zucker (fl) Cantilena ▲ 66011-2 [DDD]
Chaminade, C.:Concertino Fl, w. Laurel Zucker (fl) Cantilena ▲ C 660012 [DDD]
Handel, G.F.:Sons Fl, w. Laurel Zucker (fl)—Op. 1/2, 4, 5, 7, 9, 11 & 16; Op. 7/7 *(rec Cunningham Chapel, Belmont, CA)* Cantilena ▲ C 660052 [DDD]
Laurel Zucker:Virtuoso Flutist, w. Laurel Zucker (fl) Cantilena ▲ 660012 [DDD]
Lewis, P.S.:Delicate Sky, w. Nadya Tichman (vn), Jack Van Geem (perc) *(rec St. Stephen's Church, Belvedere, CA, Oct 1994 & June 1995)* New Albion ▲ NA 079
Lewis, P.S.:Sun Music *(rec St. Stephen's Church, Belvedere, CA, Oct 1994 & June 1995)* New Albion ▲ NA 079
Poulenc, F.:Son Fl, w. Laurel Zucker (fl) Cantilena ▲ C 660012 [DDD]
Prokofiev, S.:Son Fl, w. L. Zucker (fl) Cantilena ▲ 660012 [DDD]
Prokofiev, S.:Son Fl, w. Laurel Zucker (fl) Cantilena ▲ C 660012 [DDD]
Schumann, R.:Adagio & Allegro Hn, w. F. Cooley (tuba) [trans. for tuba] Summit ▲ DCD 156 [DDD]
Schumann, R.:Fantasiestücke Cl, w. F. Cooley (tuba) [trans. for tuba] Summit ▲ DCD 156 [DDD]
Schumann, R.:Märchenbilder, w. F. Cooley (tuba) [trans. for tuba] Summit ▲ DCD 156 [DDD]
Schumann, R.:Romances Ob, w. F. Cooley (tuba) [trans. for tuba] Summit ▲ DCD 156 [DDD]
Trombonology, w. Lawrence, Mark (trbn) *(rec Little Bridges Hall, Claremont College, Pomona, CA)* d'Note Classics ▲ DND 1012 [DDD]

Sutherland, Shelagh (kbd)
Fitkin, G.:Frame, w. G. Fitkin (kbd), Smith String Quartet Argo ▲ 433690-2 [DDD]
Fitkin, G.:Huah, w. G. Fitkin (kbd), Smith String Quartet Argo ▲ 433690-2 [DDD]
Fitkin, G.:Slow, w. G. Fitkin (kbd), Smith String Quartet Argo ▲ 433690-2 [DDD]

Sutre, Guillaume (vn)
Britten, H.:Phantasy Qt, w. François Leleux (ob), Miguel Da Silva (va), Marc Coppey (vc) Harmonia Mundi France ("Les Nouveaux Interprètes" series) ▲ HMN 911556

Sutte, Jack (tpt)
Rorem, N.:Studies for 11, w. E. Ostling (fl), K. Lord (ob), G. Raden (cl), S. Copes (vn), C.-J. Chang (va), J. Lastrapes (vc), K. Englichova (hp), R. Uchida (pno), A. LaFargue (perc), R. Laveille (perc), R. Milanov (cnd) New World ▲ 80445-2

Sutter, Christian (db)
Kancheli, G.:Exil, w. Catrin Demenga (sop), Maacha Deubner (sop), Natalia Pschenitschnikova (a fl/b fl), Ruth Killius (va), Rebecca Firth (vc) *(rec Propstei St. Gerold, Basel, May 1994)* ECM New Series ▲ 78118-21535-2 [DDD]

Suwanai, Akiko (vn)
Tchaikovsky, P.:Con Vn, w. D. Kitayenko (cnd), Moscow PO Teldec ▲ 2292-46010-2 [DDD]

Suys, Filip (vn)
Crumb, G.:Black Angels (Images I), w. Marleen Ydiers (vn), Annemarie Vercauteren (va), Arne Deforce (vc), Johan Vandermaelen (elec) *(rec Steurbaut Sound Recording Ctr)* René Gailly ▲ CD87 118 [DDD]
Mozetich, M.:Qt Strs, w. Marleen Ydiers (vn), Annemarie Vercauteren (va), Arne Deforce (vc) *(rec Steurbaut Sound Recording Ctr)* René Gailly ▲ CD87 118 [DDD]

Suzuki, Haruo (perc)—see ORCHESTRAS & ENSEMBLES Bugaku Percussion Ensemble

Suzuki, Hidemi (vc)
Bach, J.S.:Cant 49, w. N. Argenta (sop), K. Mertens (bass), M. Ponseele (ob), S. Kuijken (vn), P. Hantaï (org), La Petite Bande Accent ▲ ACC 9395 D [DDD]

INSTRUMENT.

Suzuki, Hidemi (vc) (cont.)
Bach, J.S.:Cant 58, w. N. Argenta (sop), K. Mertens (bass), M. Ponseele (ob), S. Kuijken (vn), P. Hantaï (org), La Petite Bande — Accent ▲ ACC 9395 D [DDD]
Bach, J.S.:Cant 82, w. N. Argenta (sop), K. Mertens (bass), M. Ponseele (ob), S. Kuijken (vn), P. Hantaï (org), La Petite Bande — Accent ▲ ACC 9395 D [DDD]
Boccherini, L.:Sons (34) Vc, w. R. Zipperling (vc), G. Penson (hpd)—Son. duets in B♭, G.8, in E♭, G.10, in A, G.13, in C G.17 & in B♭, G.565 — Ricercar ▲ RIC 122107
Defense de la Basse Viole contre les Enterprises du Violon et les Pretentions du Violoncelle [Defense of the Bass Viol against the Enterprise of the Violin & the Pretension of the Cello], w. Philippe Pierlot (b vl), François Fernandez (vn), Ricercar Consort — Ricercar ▲ RIC 93005
Handel, G.F.:Sons Vn, w. Ryo Terakado (baroque vn), Kaori Uemura (vl), Christophe Rousset (hpd)—in d, HWV 359a; in A, HWV 361; in G, HWV 364a; in D, HWV 371; Violin movt in a, HWV 408; Violin movt (Allegro) in c, HWV 412 — Denon/PCM Digital ▲ DEN 75858 [DDD]
Leclair, J.–M.:Sons Vn (Books 1–4), w. R. Terakado (baroque vn), K. Uemura (va da gamba), C. Rousset (hpd)—"Troisieme livre" (Book 3), Op. 5 *(rec Feb. 26–Mar. 9, 1993)* — Denon/PCM Digital ▲ DEN 75720 [DDD]

Suzuki, Ichiro (gtr)
Britten, H.:Nocturnal Gtr *(rec House St. Gregorius, Oct 14 & 15, 1980)* — Camerata ▲ 25CM 413 [AAD]
Carulli, F.:Fantasy on Themes from Bellini's *Il pirata*, w. B. Fromanger (fl) — Forlane ▲ FOR 16635 [AAD]
Castelnuovo-Tedesco, M.:Con 1 Gtr, w. H. Yazaki (cnd), Gunma SO *(rec Shibukawa Shimin–kaikan, May 2, 1980)* — Camerata ▲ 25CM 413 [AAD]
Diabelli, A.:Pieces (3) Fl & Gtr, w. B. Fromanger (fl) — Forlane ▲ FOR 16635 [DDD]
Giuliani, M.:Grand Son Fl, w. B. Fromanger (fl) — Forlane ▲ FOR 16635 [DDD]
Hayashi, H.:Hamon *(rec Iruma Shimin–kaikan, May 1, 1977)* — Camerata ▲ 25CM 413 [AAD]
Moreno Torroba, F.:Pièces caractéristiques *(rec Iruma Shimin–kaikan, May 1, 1977)* — Camerata ▲ 25CM 413 [AAD]
Paganini, N.:Sons Fl, w. B. Fromanger (fl)—Centone di Sonate (Sonate 1), Op. 64; Sonata No. 4 in A — Forlane ▲ FOR 16635 [DDD]
Sor, F.:Vars on a Theme of Mozart *(rec House St. Gregorius, Oct 14–15, 1980)* — Camerata ▲ 25CM 413 [AAD]
Tambourin, w. Larrieu, Maxence (fl) *(rec Imaichi Public Hall, Nakamichi Research Center, Kodaira city & House St. Gregorius, Higashi–Kurume city)* — Camerata ▲ 32CM 148

Suzuki, Shinichi (vn)
Franck, C.:Son Vn, w. Manfred Gurlitt (pno) *(rec ca 1928)* — Symposium ▲ 1156

Suzumi, Kishiko (va)
Takahashi, Y.:Music of, w. Vladimir Tonkha (nar), Kazuko Takada (shamisen/sgr), Yumiko Tanaka (b shamisen), Ko Ishikawa (mouth org), Ayumi Shimonoto (shamisen/sgr), Yuji Takahashi (pno)—Sugagaki Kuzushi; Mimi No Ho; Kagehime No Michiyuki; Yubi–Tomyo [Finger Light] — Tzadik ▲ TZA 7010 [DDD]

Suzumi, Kishiko (vn)
Ichiyanagi, T.:Scenes II, w. K. Kimura (pno) — Camerata ▲ 32CM 52
Nørholm, I.:Con Vn, w. T. Vetö (cnd), Aalborg SO — Kontrapunkt ▲ 32099 [DDD]

Svanberg, K. (pno)
Grieg, E.:Norwegian Folk Songs, Op. 66 — Swedish Society ▲ SCD 1048
Nielsen, C.:Pieces Pno, Op. 3 — Swedish Society ▲ SCD 1048
Sibelius, J.:Pieces Pno, Op. 75 — Swedish Society ▲ SCD 1048
Stenhammar, W.:Son Pno — Swedish Society ▲ SCD 1048

Svard, Lois (pno)
Ashley, R.:Van Cao's Meditation — Lovely Music ▲ LCD 3051 [DDD]
Duckworth, W.E.:Imaginary Dances — Lovely Music ▲ LCD 3051 [DDD]
Tyranny, G.:Nocturne with & without Memory — Lovely Music ▲ LCD 3051 [DDD]

Svejkovsky, Josef (tpt)
Trumpet & Organ, w. Karel Hron (org) — Multisonic ▲ MUL 310192 [DDD]

Svendsen, Asger (bn)—see also ORCHESTRAS & ENSEMBLES Collegium Musicum Soloists
Roussel, A.:Chamber Music, w. Majken Bjerno (sop), Toke Lund Christiansen (fl), Bjørn Carl Nielsen (ob), Niels Thomsen (cl), Per Jacobsen (hn), Ketil Christensen (tpt), Anne Søe Hansen (vn), Zwi Carmelli (va), Piotr Zelazny (va), Niels Ullner (vc), Michael Dabelsteen (db), Tine Rehling (hp), Morten Mogensen (pno), Per Salo (pno), Per Jensen (perc)—Divertissement, Op. 6; Trio, Op. 40; Joueurs de Flute, Op. 27; Serenade, Op. 30; Le marchand de sable qui passe, Op. 13; Andante et scherzo, Op. 13; 2 poèmes de ronsard, Op. 26; Aria; Elpenor, Op. 59; Pipe — Kontrapunkt 2–▲ KPT 32218 [DDD]

Svendsen, Troels (vn)
Biber, H. von:Mystery (or Rosary) Sons, w. Wim ten Have (vn), Karen Englund (hpd)—No. 4 *(rec Strandmarks Church, Copenhagen, Denmark, Sept 1994)* — Rondo Gramophon ▲ RCD 8343 [DDD]
Biber, H. von:Son à 3 for 2 Vns, B Trbn, w. Wim ten Have (vn), Mogens Andresen (b trbn), Karen Englund (hpd) *(rec Strandmarks Church, Copenhagen, Denmark, Sept 1994)* — Rondo Gramophon ▲ RCD 8343 [DDD]
Purcell, H.:Pavans, Z.748–751, w. Wim ten Have (vn), Karen Englund (hpd)—in B♭, Z.750 *(rec Strandmarks Church, Copenhagen, Denmark, Sept 1994)* — Rondo Gramophon ▲ RCD 8343 [DDD]
Schmelzer, J.H.:Polish Bagpipes, w. Wim ten Have (vn), Karen Englund (hpd) *(rec Strandmarks Church, Copenhagen, Denmark, Sept 1994)* — Rondo Gramophon ▲ RCD 8343 [DDD]
Telemann, G.P.:Fants Vn—No. 12 in a *(rec Strandmarks Church, Copenhagen, Denmark, Sept 1994)* — Rondo Gramophon ▲ RCD 8343 [DDD]
Telemann, G.P.:Son Polonese, w. Wim ten Have (va), Karen Englund (hpd) *(rec Strandmarks Church, Copenhagen, Denmark, Sept 1994)* — Rondo Gramophon ▲ RCD 8343 [DDD]

Svensson, Kerstin (vn)
Söderlundh, L.B.:Allegro Concertante, w. Jeffrey Lee (vn), T. Svedlund (cnd), Örebro CO — Intim Musik ▲ INT 36

Svetlanov, Evgeni (pno)
Medtner, N.:Nocturnes Vn, w. A. Labko (vn)—No. 3 in c — Russian Disc ▲ RUS 11017 [DDD]
Medtner, N.:Qnt Pno, w. Borodin String Quartet — Russian Disc ▲ RUS 11019 [DDD]
Medtner, N.:Son 1 Vn, w. A. Labko (vn) — Russian Disc ▲ RUS 11017 [DDD]
Medtner, N.:Son 2 Vn, w. A. Labko (vn) — Russian Disc ▲ RUS 11019 [DDD]
Medtner, N.:Son 3 Vn, w. A. Labko (vn) — Russian Disc ▲ RUS 11017 [DDD]
Rachmaninoff, S.:Trio élégiaque 2, w. Leonid Kogan (vn), Fedor Luzanov (vc) — Russian Disc ▲ RUS 10046 [AAD]
Svetlanov, E.:Con Pno, w. M. Shostakovich (cnd), USSR Radio–TV Large SO — Russian Disc ▲ RUS 11 043 [ADD]

Svetlanova, Nina (pno)
Ippolitov–Ivanov, M.:Poems of Tagore, w. Z. Dolukhanova (mez) *(rec 1952–66)* — Russian Disc ▲ RUS 15 015 [ADD]
Kabalevsky, D.:Joyful Songs, w. Z. Dolukhanova (mez) *(rec 1952–66)* — Russian Disc ▲ RUS 15 015 [ADD]
Shchedrin, R.:Solfeggi, w. Z. Dolukhanova (sop) *(rec 1971)* — Russian Disc ▲ RUS 11 030 [AAD]

Švihliková, V. (hpd)
Benda, F.:Son Fl & Hpd, w. J.–P. Rampal (fl) *(rec 1955)* — Supraphon ▲ 111308–2 [AAD]

Svitzer, Henrik (fl)
Hoffmeister, F.A.:Trios for 2 Fls & Vc, w. Bent Larsen (fl), Niels Ullner (vc) — Classico ▲ CLASSCD 119
Maegaard, J.:Canon, w. Toke Lund Christiansen (fl), Ulla Miilmann Jørgensen (fl) *(rec Copenhagen, 1995–96)* — Marco Polo/Dacapo ▲ 8.224050 [DDD]

Svoboda, František (bn)
Mozart, W.A.:Qnt Pno, K.452, w. P. Serkin (pno), A. Genovese (ob), H. Wright (cl), R. Sebring (hn) *(rec Aug. 1992)* — Boston Records ▲ BR 1004

Svyatkin, Alexander (pno)
Rachmaninoff, S.:Con 2 Pno, w. A. Anichanov (cnd), St. Petersburg State SO — Audiophile Classics ▲ 101.037
Tchaikovsky, P.:Con 1 Pno, w. A. Anichanov (cnd), St. Petersburg State SO *(rec St. Petersburg, 1992 & 1993)* — Audiophile Classics ▲ 101.024 [DDD]

Svyatkin, Alexander (pno) (cont.)
Tchaikovsky, P.:Con 2 Pno, w. A. Anichanov (cnd), St. Petersburg State SO *(rec St. Petersburg, 1992 & 1993)* — Audiophile Classics ▲ 101.024 [DDD]

Swain, Christine (ob)
Vivaldi, A.:Beatus vir, R.597, w. Carys–Anne Lane (sop), Jayne Whitaker (sop), Robert Glenton (vc), Christopher Stokes (org), N. Ward (cnd), Northern CO, Oxford Schola Cantorum *(rec St. Peter's Church, Hale, Cheshire, Mar. 14, 1994)* — Naxos ▲ 8.550767 [DDD]
Vivaldi, A.:Gloria, RV.589, w. Anna Crookes (sop), Jayne Whitaker (sop), Caroline Trevor (alt), Robert Glenton (vc), Christopher Stokes (org), N. Ward (cnd), Northern CO, Oxford Schola Cantorum *(rec St. Peter's Church, Hale, Cheshire, Dec. 3, 1993)* — Naxos ▲ 8.550767 [DDD]

Swainson, Neil (db)
Get Happy!, w. King's Singers, George Shearing (pno) — EMI Classics ▲ CDC 54190 [DDD] ■ 4DS 54190 (D)

Swallow, J. (trbn)
Berio, L.:Sequenza V — GM ▲ 2009CD
Hoddinott, A.:Ritornelli, w. A. Weisberg (cnd), Ensemble — GM ▲ 2009CD
Milhaud, D.:Concertino d'hiver, w. G. Schuller (cnd), *(orch unknown)* — GM ▲ 2009CD
Schuller, G.:Eine kleine Posaunenmusik, w. G. Schuller (pno), *(ensemble unknown)* — GM ▲ 2009CD
Stravinsky, I.:L'Histoire du soldat Suite Vn, w. G. Tarack (vn), C. Russo (cl), T. Weis (tpt), J. Levine (db), Loren Glickman (bn), R. Desroches (perc), L. Stokowski (cnd) — Vanguard Classics ▲ SVC 1 [AAD]

Swallow, Keith (pno)
Bax, A.:Son Cl & Pno, w. J. Hilton (cl) — Chandos ▲ CHAN 8683 [DDD]
Debussy, C.:Première rapsodie, w. J. Hilton (cl), clarinet & piano — Chandos ("Collect" series) ▲ CHAN 6589 [DDD]
Milhaud, D.:Duo concertante Cl & Pno, w. J. Hilton (cl) — Chandos ("Collect" series) ▲ CHAN 6589 [DDD]
Poulenc, F.:Son Cl Pno, w. J. Hilton (cl) — Chandos ("Collect" series) ▲ CHAN 6589 [DDD]
Ravel, M.:Pièce en forme de Habanera, w. J. Hilton (cl) — Chandos ("Collect" series) ▲ CHAN 6589 [DDD]
Roussel, A.:Aria Cl, w. J. Hilton (cl) — Chandos ("Collect" series) ▲ CHAN 6589 [DDD]
Saint–Saëns, C.:Son Cl, w. J. Hilton (cl) — Chandos ("Collect" series) ▲ CHAN 6589 [DDD]
Vaughan Williams, R.:Studies in English Folk–Song, w. J. Hilton (cl) — Chandos ▲ CHAN 8683 [DDD]
Weber, C.M. von:Grand duo concertant Cl, w. J. Hilton (cl) — Chandos ▲ CHAN 8366 [DDD]
Weber, C.M. von:Vars on a Theme from *Silvana* Cl, w. J. Hilton (cl) — Chandos ▲ CHAN 8366 [DDD]

Swanborn, Edwin (hpd)
Blavet, M.:Sons Trns Fl, w. Robert Stallman (fl), Karl Bennion (vc)—Op. 2/2, 4 & 6; Op. 3/2, 4 & 6 — VAI Audio ▲ VAIA 1101
Handel, G.F.:Sons Fl, w. Robert Stallman (fl), Karl Bennion (vc), Op. 1, Nos. 1, 2, 4, 5, 7, 9 & 11 — VAI Audio ▲ VAIA 1091
Leclair, J.–M.:Sons Vn (Books 1–4), w. R. Stallman (fl), K. Bennon (vc)—Opp. 2/1, 3 & 11; 9/2 & 7 *(rec Mar. 21–24, 1993)* — VAI Audio ▲ VAIA 1068 [DDD]

Swann, Frederic (org)
Bach, J.S.:Passacaglia & Fugue Org — Gothic ▲ G 49049 [DDD]
Farnam, L.:Toccata on "O Filii et Filiae" *(rec Riverside Church, New York)* — Gothic ▲ G 49082
Franck, C.:Chorals Org, M.38–40 *(rec Riverside Church, New York)* — Gothic ▲ G 49082
Franck, C.:Chorals Org, M.38–40—No. 1 — Gothic ▲ G 49049 [DDD]
Franck, C.:Pièce héroïque *(rec Riverside Church, New York)* — Gothic ▲ G 49082
Gigout, E.:Grand–Choeur Dialogue *(rec Riverside Church, New York)* — Gothic ▲ G 49082
Karg–Elert, S.:Symphonic Chorale 1 *(rec Riverside Church, New York)* — Gothic ▲ G 49082
Langlais, J.:Hymne d'Actions de grâces "Te Deum" *(rec Riverside Church, New York)* — Gothic ▲ G 49082
Mendelssohn, F.:Sons Org—No. 1 — Gothic ▲ G 49049 [DDD]
Wright, M.S.:Intro, Passacaglia & Fugue — Gothic ▲ G 49049 [DDD]

Swann, Jeffrey (pno)
Beethoven, L. van:Son 27 Pno *(rec Dec. 10–14, 1993)* — Arkadia–Akademia ▲ 140 [DDD]
Beethoven, L. van:Son 28 Pno *(rec Dec. 10–14, 1993)* — Arkadia–Akademia ▲ 140 [DDD]
Beethoven, L. van:Son 29 Pno, "Hammerklavier" *(rec Dec. 10–14, 1993)* — Arkadia–Akademia ▲ 140 [DDD]
Boulez, P.:Son 3 Pno—performs 2 versions — Music & Arts ▲ CD 763 [DDD]
Bruckner, A.:Son 2 Vn, w. R. Cani (vn) *(rec Milan, Dec. 16–18, 1993)* — Arkadia–Akademia ▲ 143 [DDD]
Busoni, F.:Indianische Fant Pno, w. G.–F. Masini (cnd), Montpellier PO — Arkadia–Akademia ▲ 126 [DDD]
Busoni, F.:Konzertstück Pno, w. G.–F. Masini (cnd), Montpellier PO — Arkadia–Akademia ▲ 126 [DDD]
Chopin, F.:Nocturnes—2 nocturnes; sels unknown *(rec Jungle Studios, Milan, July 14–16, 1995)* — Agora Musica ▲ 024 [DDD]
Chopin, F.:Waltzes *(rec Jungle Studios, Milan, July 14–16, 1995)* — Agora Musica ▲ 024 [DDD]
Debussy, C.:Etudes — Music & Arts ▲ CD 608 [DDD]
Fauré, G.:Préludes, Op. 103 — Music & Arts ▲ CD 608 [DDD]
Liszt, F.:Années de pèlerinage (comp) — Arkadia–Akademia 2–▲ 108 [DDD]
Liszt, F.:Apparitions d'après Lamartine—Nos. 1 & 2 — Arkadia–Akademia ▲ 113 [DDD]
Liszt, F.:Consolations — Arkadia–Akademia ▲ 113 [DDD]
Liszt, F.:Csárdás Pno — Arkadia–Akademia ▲ 113 [DDD]
Liszt, F.:Csárdás macabre — Arkadia–Akademia ▲ 113 [DDD]
Liszt, F.:Historical Hungarian Portraits — Arkadia–Akademia ▲ 113 [DDD]
Liszt, F.:Hungarian Rhaps—Nos. 5 & 12 — Arkadia–Akademia ▲ 113 [DDD]
Liszt, F.:Hungarian Rhaps—Nos. 18 & 19 — Music & Arts ▲ CD 245 [DDD]
Liszt, F.:Mephisto Waltz 3 Pno — Music & Arts ▲ CD 245 [DDD]
Liszt, F.:Pno Music (misc)—late piano pieces — Music & Arts ▲ CD 245 [DDD]
Liszt, F.:Venezia e Napoli — Arkadia–Akademia 2–▲ 108 [DDD]
Martucci, G.:Con 1 Pno, w. M. de Bernart (cnd), Montpellier PO — Arkadia–Akademia ▲ 111 [DDD]
Martucci, G.:Con 2 Pno, w. M. de Bernart (cnd), Montpellier PO — Arkadia–Akademia ▲ 111 [DDD]
Moszkowski, M.:Operatic Paraphrase on Venusberg — Arkadia–Akademia ▲ 112 [DDD]
Moszkowski, M.:Per Aspera — Arkadia–Akademia ▲ 112 [DDD]
Piano Works — Arkadia–Akademia ▲ 112 [DDD]
Respighi, O.:Son Vn, w. R. Cani (vn) *(rec Milan, Dec. 16–18, 1993)* — Arkadia–Akademia ▲ 143 [DDD]
Rossini, G.:Péchés de vieillesse (sels)—15 selections — Arkadia–Akademia ▲ 103 [DDD]
Wuorinen, C.:Son 2 Pno—performs 2 versions — Music & Arts ▲ CD 763 [DDD]

Swanton, Philip (org)
Festal Music for 3 Organs & for Organ 4–Hands, w. Annerös Hulliger (org), A. Marcon (org) — Koch Schwann ▲ SCH 310472 [DDD]
Festliche Musik für zwei Orgeln, w. Annerös Hulliger (org) — Koch Schwann ▲ SCH 312842 [DDD]

Swarthout, Elizabeth (pno)—see ORCHESTRAS & ENSEMBLES Elson–Swarthout Duo

Swarts, Lucia (vc)
Biber, H. von:Sons Vn & Continuo, w. M. Lindal (vn), E. Siebens (db), M. Spányi (hpd) *(rec Feb. 4–6, 1993)* — BIS ▲ CD 608 [DDD]
Biber, H. von:Son violino solo representativa, w. M. Lindal (vn), E. Siebens (db), M. Spányi (hpd) *(rec Feb. 4–6, 1993)* — BIS ▲ CD 608 [DDD]
Corelli, A.:Sons Vn, Op. 5, w. Ryo Terakado (baroque vn), Siebe Henstra (hpd/org)—Nos. 7–12 *(rec Oud–Katholieke Kerk, The Hague, Netherlands, Aug 8–10, 1994)* — Denon ▲ CO 78820 [DDD]
Mozart, W.A.:Church Sons, w. Yasuko Uyama–Bouvard (org), Manfred Kramer (vn), Maria Lindal (vn), Richard Myron (db)—K.67, 144, 145, 241, 244, 245, 274, 328 & 336 — Adda ▲ ADD 581274 [DDD]

Swartz, (sax)
Duckworth, W.E.:Thirty–One Days — Lovely Music ▲ LCD 2032 [ADD]

Swartz, Jennifer (hp)
Somers, H.:Suite Hp, w. V. Feldbrill (cnd), National Arts Center Canada Orch *(rec St. Joseph's Church, Ottawa, July 6–7, 1995)* — CBC ▲ 5162 [DDD]

▲ = CD ♦ = Enhanced CD Δ = MD ■ = Cassette Tape □ = DCC

Swearingen, Anita (pno)
An American Collage Vol. II, w. Constance Keene (pno), Ayke Agus (pno), Michael Lang (pno), Diane Lang Bryan (cl), James Smith (gtr), Sherry Kloss (vn), Laila Padorr (fl), Victor Morosco (a sax) — Protone ▲ PRCD 1114 [DDD]
Copland, A.:Duo Fl, w. Padorr (fl) — Protone ■ CSPR 114
Copland, A.:Vocalise, w. Padorr (fl) — Protone ■ CSPR 114
Dello Joio, N.:The Developing Flutist, w. Padorr (fl) — Protone ■ CSPR 114
Piston, W.:Son Fl, w. Padorr (fl) — Protone ■ CSPR 114

Swedrup, Patrick (vn)—see also ORCHESTRAS & ENSEMBLES Tale String Quartet
Jolivet, A.:Fl Music (comp), w. Manuela Wiesler (fl), Erica Goodman (hp), Håkan Olsson (va), Helena Nilsson (vc), Christian Davidsson (bn), Roland Pöntinen (pno), P. Järvi (cnd), Tapiola Sinfonietta, Kroumata Percussion Ensemble—Alla rustica for Fl & Hp; Chant de Linos for Fl, Hp & Str Trio; Pastorales de Noël for Fl, Bn & Hp; Con for Fl & Strs; Suite en concert for Fl & 4 Perc Players; Fant-Caprice for Fl & Pno; Cabrioles for Fl & Pno *(rec Danderyd Grammar School, Sweden, Tapiola Hall, Tapiola, Finland, Gothenburg Concert Hall, Sweden & Studio 2, Radiohuset, Stockholm, Sweden)* — BIS ▲ CD 739 [DDD]
Lindblad, A.F.:Qnt Strs, w. Peter Olofsson (vn), Tony Bauer (va), Jonal Lindgård (va), Lars Frykholm (vc) — Musica Sveciae ▲ MSV 522 [DDD]
Penderecki, K.:Qt Cl, w. M. Fröst (cl), I. Kierkegaard (va), H. Nilsson (vc) *(rec Feb. 18-20, 1994)* — BIS ▲ CD 652 [DDD]
Randel, A.:Qt Strs, w. Peter Olofsson (vn), Tony Bauer (va), Jonal Lindgård (va), Lars Frykholm (vc) — Musica Sveciae ▲ MSV 522 [DDD]
Schnittke, A.:Con grosso 3, w. T. Olsson (vn), L. Markiz (cnd), Stockholm CO — BIS ▲ CD 537 [DDD]

Swensen, Joseph (vn)
Bach, J.S.:Sons Vn, w. J. Gibbons (hpd)—not advised of selections — RCA Red Seal ▲ 09026-60563-2
Beethoven, L. van:Serenade Fl, Op. 25, w. J. Galway (fl), P. Neubauer (va) — RCA Red Seal ▲ 7756-2-RC [DDD] ■ 7756-4-RC
Giuliani, M.:Serenade Vn, w. E. Anderson (vc), K. Yamashita (gtr) — RCA Red Seal ▲ 09026-60237-2
Sibelius, J.:Con Vn, w. J.-P. Saraste (cnd), Finnish RSO — RCA Red Seal ▲ 09026-60444-2
Sibelius, J.:Humoresques, w. J.-P. Saraste (cnd), Finnish RSO — RCA Red Seal ▲ 09026-60444-2
Sibelius, J.:Serenades Vn, w. J.-P. Saraste (cnd), Finnish RSO — RCA Red Seal ▲ 09026-60444-2

Swenson, Britt (vn)
Hoffman, D.:Fant on *Black is the Color of My True Love's Hair*, w. Teri Fay Storhaug (rcr), Steve Hillesland (vc), Annette Wellin (pno) — Meyer ▲ MC 0108

Swenson, I. (vn)
Hanson, H.:Con da Camera, w. B. Preston (vn), C. Wiersma (vn), M. Lambros (va), Elizabeth Anderson (vc) — Albany ▲ TROY 129 [DDD]

Swierstra, Stass (va)
Schubert, Franz:Qt Fl, w. M. Root (fl), F. Jacobs (gtr), V. De Hoog (vc) — Globe ▲ GLO 5040 [DDD]

Swift, (cl)
Dreyfus, G.:Trio Fl, w. Ridell (fl), G. Dreyfus (bn) — Move ▲ MD 3071
Sutherland, M.:Little Suite, w. Dodd (fl), G. Dreyfus (bn) — Move ▲ MD 3071
Weiss, A.:Petite suite Fl, w. Ridell (fl), G. Dreyfus (bn) — Move ▲ MD 3071

Swimberghe, Hedwig (cl)—see ORCHESTRAS & ENSEMBLES Belgian Wind Quintet

Swinchoski, Margaret (pic)
Kraft, L.:Cloud Studies, w. Lisa Maron (pic), Tanya Dusevic (fl), Adrienne Flynn (fl), Christina Jennings (fl), Zara Lawler (fl), Joseph Piscitelli (fl), Michelle Ryang (fl), Dominique Soucy (fl), Diane Taublieb (fl), Laurel Ann Maurer (alt fl), Richard Wyton (alt fl), J. Solum (cnd) *(rec Skinner Recital Hall, Vassar College, Poughkeepsie, NY, Mar 24-26, 1994)* — CRI ▲ CD 712 [DDD]

Swist, Christopher (perc)
Cage, J.:But What About The Noise...?, w. Craig Bitterman, Eberhard Blum, Patti Cudd, Thomas Furminger, Erik Oña *(rec Slee Concert Hall, Univ. at Buffalo, NY, May 28 - June 1, 1995)* — Hat Art ("Hat Now" series) ▲ 6179 [DDD]

Świtała, Wojciech (pno)
Chopin, F.:Andante Spianato & Grande Polonaise — Polish Radio Katowice ("Stale Xport" series) ▲ PRK 007
Chopin, F.:Andante Spianato & Grande Polonaise *(rec Nov. 27, 1992)* — REM ▲ REM 311187 [DDD]
Chopin, F.:Ballades Pno (comp)—Op. 47 — Polish Radio Katowice ("Stale Xport" series) ▲ PRK 007
Chopin, F.:Scherzos—Opp. 20 & 31 — Polish Radio Katowice ("Stale Xport" series) ▲ PRK 007
Chopin, F.:Son Pno, Op. 35 — Polish Radio Katowice ("Stale Xport" series) ▲ PRK 007

Swope, Mary Alice (vc)
Rutter, J.:Requiem, w. Karyn List (sop), Kathy Farmer (fl), Barbara Cook (ob), Julie Albertson (hp), Tom Alderman (org), Jennifer Mautz (timp), Mike Del Campo (perc), Michael O'Neal (cnd), Michael O'Neal Singers *(rec Roswell United Methodist Church, Atlanta, GA, Mar 27, 1995)* — ACA Digital Recording ▲ CM 20048 [DDD]

Syer, J. (pno)—see ORCHESTRAS & ENSEMBLES New Works Calgary Ensemble

Sykes, Belinda (voc/shawms/bagpipe)—see ORCHESTRAS & ENSEMBLES Ensemble Saraband

Sykes, Debra (cym)
Dempster, S.:Music of, w. Stuart Dempster (trbn/didjeridu/conch), Jay Bulen (trbn), Jeff Domoto (trbn), Moe Escobedo (trbn/didjeridu/conch), Scott Higbee (trbn), Gretchen Hopper (trbn), Nathaniel Irby-Oxford (trbn), Chad Kirby (trbn/conch), Dave Marriott (trbn), Greg Powers (trbn)—Conch Calling; Morning Light; Didjerilayover; Secret Currents; Melodic Communion; Shell Shock; Cloud Landings *(rec Fort Worden, Port Townsend, WA, June 18, 1994)* — New Albion ▲ NA 076

Sykes, Peter (hpd)
Couperin, F.:L'Art de toucher le clavecin—Septieme Prelude *(rec Music Room, Cambridge, Sept. 13-14, 1993)* — Titanic ▲ TI 229
Couperin, F.:Hpd Music—Septieme Prelude [from L'art de toucher le clavecin]; Les moissoneurs; Les langueurs tendres; Le gazoüillement; La bersan; Les baricades misterieuses; Les bergeries; La commère; Le moucheron [all from Sixieme Ordre]; La muse naissante; L'enfantine; L'adolescente; Les délices [all from Les petits ages] — Titanic ▲ TIC 229
Couperin, F.:Pièces de clavecin (sels)—Sixieme Ordre; Les Petits Ages *(rec Music Room, Cambridge, Sept. 13-14, 1993)* — Titanic ▲ TI 229
Rameau, J.P.:Hpd Music (misc)—Allemande; Courante; Sarabande; Les trois mains; Fanfarinette; La triomphante; Gavotte; Doubles 1-6 [all from Pièces de clavecin]; Les cyclopes — Titanic ▲ TIC 229
Rameau, J.P.:Pièces de clavecin avec une méthode sur la mécanique des doigts—Les Cyclopes; Pièces de Clavecin *(rec Music Room, Cambridge, Sept. 13-14, 1993)* — Titanic ▲ TI 229

Sykes, Peter (org)
From the Heartland — Titanic ▲ Ti 181 [DDD]
Holst, G.:The Planets [Great Skinner Org, Girard College, Philadelphia] [trans Sykes] — Raven ▲ OAR 380 [DDD]
A Nantucket Organ Tour *(rec Sept 18-20, 1994)* — Raven ▲ OAR 320 [DDD]

Sykora, Adolf (vn)—see ORCHESTRAS & ENSEMBLES Janáček String Quartet

Sykora, Vaclav Jan (hpd)
The Harpsichord in Czech Music of the 18th Century, w. Josef Hála (hpd) — Panton ▲ PAN 811038

Sylvest, Nils (vc)
Rachmaninoff, S.:Son Vc, w. T. Lonskov (pno) — Canzone ▲ KPTCAN 33009 [DDD]
Strauss, R.:Ariadne auf Naxos, w. T. Lonskov (pno) [arr. for cello] — Canzone ▲ KPTCAN 33009 [DDD]
Strauss, R.:Son Vc, w. T. Lonskov (pno) — Canzone ▲ KPTCAN 33009 [DDD]

Sylvester, Robert (vc)—see ORCHESTRAS & ENSEMBLES Eastman Trio, Kohon String Quartet

Sylvestre, Brigitte (hp)
Boucourechliev, A.:Les Archipels, w. Elisabeth Chojnacka (hpd), Françoise Rieunier (org), Roland Auzet, Jean-Pierre Drouet (perc), Hakon Austbö (pno), Françoise-Frédéric Guy (pno), Claude Helffer (pno), Georges Pludermacher (pno), Ysaÿe String Quartet, Les Pléiades Ensemble — Musique Francaise d'Aujourd'hui ("Collection MFA-Radio France" series) ▲ MFA 216001
Kagel, M.:Zwei Akte:Grand Duo, w. M. Riessler (sax) — Montaigne ▲ MO 782003 [DDD]

Sylvestre, Gaston (perc)—see ORCHESTRAS & ENSEMBLES Le Cercle Trio

Syme, David (pno)
Gershwin, G.:Con Pno, w. H. de la Fuente (cnd), Mineria SO — JB Records ▲ 1006-2 ■ 1006-4

Syme, David (pno) (cont.)
Gershwin, G.:"I Got Rhythm" Vars, w. H. de la Fuente (cnd), Mineria SO — JB Records ▲ 1006-2 ■ 1006-4
Gershwin, G.:Rhap in Blue, w. H. de la Fuente (cnd), Mineria SO — IMP Classics ▲ IMPPCD 1057 [DDD]
Gershwin, G.:Rhap in Blue, w. H. de la Fuente (cnd), Mineria SO — JB Records ▲ 1006-2 ■ 1006-4

Synkova, Milada (hpd)
Mozart, W.A.:Così fan tutte (sels), w. Joanna Borowska (sop—Fiordiligi), Priti Coles (sop—Despina), Rohangiz Yachmi (mez—Dorabella), John Dickie (ten—Ferrando), Andrea Martin (bar—Guglielmo), Peter Mikulaš (bass—Don Alfonso), J. Wildner (cnd), Capella Istropolitana, Slovak Phil Chorus—Ov.; [Act I] La mia Dorabella capace non è; È la fede della femmine; Una bella serenata; Ah guarda, sorella; Vorrei dir, e cor non ho; Sento, o Dio; Bella vita militar!; Soave sia il vento; Smanie implacabili; In uomini, in soldati; Alla bella Despinetta; Come Scoglio; Non siate ritrosi; Un'aura amorosa; [Act II] Una donna a quindici anni; Prenderò quel brunettino; La mano a me date; Ei parte...senti...ah no!; Donne mie la fate a tanti a tanti; Fra gle amplessi; Fortunato l'uom che prende *(rec Slovak Philharmonic Moyzes Hall, Bratislava, Feb.-Apr. 1990)* — Naxos ▲ 8.553172 [DDD]

Syré, W. (org)
Tunder, F.:Org Music [complete surviving works]—nine Chorale-Fantasies, -Motets & -Preludes; five Preludes; Canzona in g — Motette 2-▲ DCD 11081 [DDD]

Syrier, Remy (org)
de Grigny, N.:Org Music [Severin Organ at Maastricht]—Veni Creator en taille à 5; Fugue à 5; Duo; Récit de Cromorne; Dialogue fur les Grands Jeux; A solis ortus cardine; Fugue à 5; Trio; Point d'Orgue sur les Grands Jeux — René Gailly ▲ CD 87071 [DDD]
Marchand, L.:Pieces Org [Severin Organ at Maastricht]—[Book 1] Plein Jeu; Fugue; Trio; Basse de Trompette; Quatuor; Tierce en taille; Duo; Récit; Tierce en taille; Basse de Trompette ou de Cromorne; Fond d'Orgue; Dialogue; [Book 3] Dialogue — René Gailly ▲ CD 87071 [DDD]

Syrinx, (fl)
Bach, J.S.:Suite 2 Orch, w. E. de Stoutz (cnd), Zurich CO *(rec 1986)* — Analekta ▲ AN2-8501 [DDD] ■ AN4-8501
Boccherini, L.:Con in D Fl, w. E. de Stoutz (cnd), Zurich CO *(rec 1986)* — Analekta ▲ AN2-8501 [DDD] ■ AN4-8501

Syrus, David (hpd)
Rossini, G.:Tancredi, w. Veronica Cangemi (sop—Roggiero), Eva Mei (sop—Amenaide), Vasselina Kasarova (mez—Tancredi), Melinda Paulsen (cta—Isaura), Ramón Vargas (ten—Argirio), Harry Peeters (bass—Orbazzano), Janos Maté (vn), Gottfried Greiner (vc), Ingo Nawra (db), R. Abbado (cnd), Munich RSO, Bavarian Radio Chorus *(rec Studio 1, Munich, July 17-30, 1995)* — RCA Red Seal 3-▲ 09026-68349-2 [DDD]

Szabadi, Vilmos (vn)
Bartók, B.:Con 1 Vn, w. A. Ligeti (cnd), Hungarian State Orch *(rec Budapest, Dec. 17-21, 1992 & Jan. 2)* — Hungaroton ("Classic" series) ▲ HCD 31543 [DDD]
Bartók, B.:Con 2 Vn, w. A. Ligeti (cnd), Hungarian State Orch *(rec Budapest, Dec. 17-21, 1992 & Jan. 2)* — Hungaroton ("Classic" series) ▲ HCD 31543 [DDD]
Bartók, B.:Son Vn *(rec 1993)* — Hungaroton ▲ HCD 31558 [DDD]
Bartók, B.:Son in e Vn & Pno, w. Márta Gulyás (pno) *(rec 1993)* — Hungaroton ▲ HCD 31558 [DDD]
The Virtuoso Violin, w. Márta Gulyás (pno) — White Label ▲ HRC 180 [ADD]

Szabó, Csilla (pno)
Brahms, J.:Qt 1 Pno, w. P. Kolmós (vn), G. Németh (va), K. Botvay (vc) *(rec 1972-74)* — Hungaroton 2-▲ HCD 11597/98 [ADD]

Szabó, Géza (vc)
Constantinescu, P.:Byzantine Vars, w. E. Acél (cnd), Oradea PO *(rec 1983)* — Olympia ▲ OCD 415 [AAD]

Szabó, István (lt/thb/gtr/man/koboz/saz baglama/sgr)—see ORCHESTRAS & ENSEMBLES Vagantes

Szabó, István (thb)
Monteverdi, C.:Music of, w. M. Spányi (org), B. Máté (vc), S. Benyus (db), Monteverdi Chamber Choir—Laudate pueri, Lauda Ierusalem, Nisi Dominus — Hungaroton ▲ HCD 31273 [DDD]

Szabó, M. (vn)—see ORCHESTRAS & ENSEMBLES Danubius Quartet

Szabó, Paul (vc)
Beethoven, L. van:Septet Strs, w. Ildikó Hegyi (vn), Győző Máthé (va), István Tóth (db), Jozsef Balogh (cl), Jenő Keveházi (hn), József Vajda (bn) *(rec Scottish Church, Budapest, Apr. 21-23 & May 29-31, 1)* — Naxos ▲ 8.553090 [DDD]
Beethoven, L. van:Sxt Hns, Op. 81b, w. Jenő Keveházi (hn), János Keveházi (hn), Ildikó Hegyi (vn), Péter Popa (vn), Győző Máthé (va) *(rec Scottish Church, Budapest, Apr. 21-23 & May 29-31, 1)* — Naxos ▲ 8.553090 [DDD]

Szabo, Tamás (vn)—see ORCHESTRAS & ENSEMBLES Kodály String Quartet

Szász, T. (pno)
Beethoven, L. van:Son 21 Pno, "Waldstein" — Bainbridge ▲ BCD 6275 [DDD]
Beethoven, L. van:Son 32 Pno — Bainbridge ▲ BCD 6275 [DDD]

Szathmary, Zsigmond (org)
Bach, J.S.:Org Music (misc)—Schübler Chorales, BWV 645-650; Fantasia & Fugue in g, BWV 542; Fugue in g, BWV 578; Passacaglia & Fugue in c, BWV 582; Prelude & Fugue in E♭, BWV 552; Toccata & Fugue in d, BWV 565 — RCA Silver Seal ▲ 60785-2-RV [ADD] ■ 60785-4-RV

Szczepaniak-Lamy, Joanna (pno)
Haydn, J.:Sons Pno—in D & e — Pierre Verany ▲ PVY 795102

Szczepanska, Ewa (va)
Penderecki, K.:Sinfonietta, w. R. Kabara (vn), D. Imietowski (vc), Cracow Chamber Players — Vienna Modern Masters ▲ VMM 3023 [DDD]

Szebenyi, Janós (fl)
Devienne, F.:Con Fl, w. J. Sándor (cnd), Budapest PO — Vivace ▲ E 562 [ADD]
Haydn, M.:Con Fl, P.54, w. J. Sándor (cnd), Budapest PO — Vivace ▲ E 562 [ADD]
Mozart, W.A.:Qts Fl, w. A. Kiss (vn), L. Bársony (va), K. Botvay (vc) — White Label ▲ HRC 128 [ADD]
Rosetti, F.A.:Con Fl, w. J. Sándor (cnd), Budapest PO — Vivace ▲ E 562 [ADD]

Szecsődi, Ferenc (vn)
Erkel, F.:Duo brillant en forme de fantaisie sur des airs hongrois concertant, w. I. Kassai (pno) — Marco Polo ▲ 8.223317

Szegedi, Erno (pno)
Dohnányi, E. von:Qnt 2 Pno, w. Tátrai String Quartet — Hungaroton ▲ HCD 11624 [ADD]
Dohnányi, E. von:Sextet, w. B. Kovács (cl), F. Tarjáni (hn), Tátrai String Quartet members — Hungaroton ▲ HCD 11624 [ADD]

Szehng, H. (vn)
Bartók, B.:Con 1 Vn, w. Davis, Haitink (cnd), Royal Concertgebouw Orch, London SO, BBC SO — Philips 2-▲ 438812-2

Szekeley, E. (vn)
Willey, J.:Some Connections, w. D. Schene (pno) — CRI ▲ CD 562 [DDD]

Székely, István (pno)
Beethoven, L. van:Son 8 Pno, "Pathétique" — LaserLight ▲ 15 628 [DDD]
Chopin, F.:Con 1 Pno, w. G. Németh (cnd), Budapest SO — Naxos ▲ 8.550123 [DDD] △ 7.550123 [DDD]
Chopin, F.:Con 1 Pno, w. G. Németh (cnd), Budapest SO *(rec Italian Institute, Budapest, Mar 29-Apr 1, 1988)* — Naxos 4-▲ 8.504011 [DDD]
Chopin, F.:Con 2 Pno, w. G. Németh (cnd), Budapest SO — Naxos ▲ 8.550123 [DDD] △ 7.550123 [DDD]
Chopin, F.:Con 2 Pno, w. G. Németh (cnd), Budapest SO *(rec Italian Institute, Budapest, Mar 29-Apr 1, 1988)* — Naxos 4-▲ 8.504011 [DDD]
Chopin, F.:Études (24) — Lydian ▲ LYD 18064 [DDD]
Chopin, F.:Pno Music (misc), w. T. Irinsky (pno), B. Szokolay (pno), I. Zaritzkaya (pno)—includes Ballade No. 3; Barcarolle, Op. 60; Berceuse, Op. 57; Piano Con. 2 (larghetto); Etude, Op. 10/3; Fantaisie-Impromptu, Op. 66; Mazurka, Op. 33/2; Nocturne, Op. 9/2; Polonaise-Fantaisie, Op. 61; Prelude, Op. 28/15; Scherzo, Op. 31; Piano Son. 2 (finale); Waltz, Op. 64/1 — Naxos ▲ 8.551104 [DDD]
Chopin, F.:Son Pno, Op. 35 — Lydian ▲ LYD 18062

INSTRUMENT.

Székely, István (pno) (cont.)
Chopin, F.:Son Pno, Op. 58 — Lydian ▲ LYD 18062
Chopin, F.:Waltzes — Lydian ▲ LYD 18063

Szelecsenyi, Norbert (pno)
Pierné, G.:Son Vn, w. I. Matuz (fl) — Marco Polo ▲ 8.223189
Pierné, G.:Trio Pno, w. B. Bánfalvi (vn), K. Vass (vc) — Marco Polo ▲ 8.223189

Szeles, P. (vc)
Terényi, E.:Baroque Rhap, w. G. Dudea (cnd), Tîrgu Mures Philharmonic CO — Electrecord ▲ ELCD 124 [AAD]
Terényi, E.:Vivaldiana, w. G. Costea, E. Botár, C. Mandeal, Cluj–Napoca CO *(Vivaldiana)*, Costea, et al. *(Gallant Dances)*, P. Szeles, G. Dudea, Tîrgu Mures Phil. CO *(Baroque Rhap.)*, "G. Dima" Conservatory Percussion Ensemble of Cluj–Napoca *(Swing Suite)* — Electrecord ▲ ELCD 124 [AAD]

Szell, George (pno)
Brahms, J.:Qnt Pno, w. Budapest String Quartet *(rec Coolidge Auditorium, Library of Congress, Oct 11, 1945)* — Bridge ▲ BCD 9062
Mozart, W.A.:Qts Pno, w. Budapest String Quartet members *(rec 1946)* — Sony Masterworks ("Portrait" series) ▲ MPK 47685 [ADD]
Mozart, W.A.:Sons Vn Pno (misc), w. R. Druian (vn)—K.296 & 301 *(rec 1967)* — Sony Masterworks ("Portrait" series) ▲ MPK 47685 [ADD]
Schubert, Franz:Qnt Pno, D.667, w. Georges Moleux (db), Budapest String Quartet members *(rec Coolidge Auditorium, Library of Congress, May 16, 1946)* — Bridge ▲ BCD 9062

Szendrey–Karper, Lázló (gtr)
Guitar Recital — White Label ▲ HRC 146 [ADD]
Schubert, Franz:Qt Fl, w. Z. Jeney (fl), P. Lukács (va), Banda (vc) — White Label ▲ HRC 146 [ADD]

Szenthelyi, Judit (pno)
Dohnányi, E. von:Ruralia hungarica Vn, w. Miklós Szenthelyi (vn) *(rec Nov 27–28, 1995)* — Hungaroton ▲ HCD 31639 [DDD]
Dohnányi, E. von:Son Vn, w. Miklós Szenthelyi (vn) *(rec Nov 27–28, 1995)* — Hungaroton ▲ HCD 31639 [DDD]
Kodály, Z.:Adagio, w. Miklós Szenthelyi (vn) *(rec Nov 27–28, 1995)* — Hungaroton ▲ HCD 31639 [DDD]
Kodály, Z.:Epigrams, w. Miklós Szenthelyi (vn) *(rec Nov 27–28, 1995)* — Hungaroton ▲ HCD 31639 [DDD]
Kodály, Z.:Háry János (sels), w. Miklós Szenthelyi (vn)—Intermezzo [arr J. Szigeti] *(rec Nov 27–28, 1995)* — Hungaroton ▲ HCD 31639 [DDD]
Liszt, F.:Grand duo concertant on Lafont's *Le Marin*, w. Miklós Szenthelyi (vn) *(rec Nov 27–28, 1995)* — Hungaroton ▲ HCD 31639 [DDD]

Szenthelyi, Miklos (vn)
Beethoven, L. van:Con 6 Pno, w. G. Györványi–Ráth (cnd), Hungarian State Orch — Capriccio ▲ 10 912 [DDD]
Beethoven, L. van:Con 6 Pno, w. G. Györványi–Ráth (cnd), Hungarian State Orch — Laserlight ▲ 15 515
Beethoven, L. van:Con Vn, Op. 61, w. G. Györványi–Ráth (cnd), Hungarian State Orch — LaserLight ▲ 15 515 [DDD]
Beethoven, L. van:Romances Vn, w. G. Györványi–Ráth (cnd), Hungarian State Orch — Capriccio ▲ 10 912 [DDD]
Beethoven, L. van:Romances Vn, w. G. Györványi–Ráth (cnd), Hungarian State Orch — Laserlight ▲ 15 515
Bruch, M.:Con 1 Vn, w. J. Sándor (cnd), Budapest PO — Laserlight ▲ 15 615
Dohnányi, E. von:Ruralia hungarica Vn, w. Judit Szenthelyi (pno) *(rec Nov 27–28, 1995)* — Hungaroton ▲ HCD 31639 [DDD]
Dohnányi, E. von:Son Vn, w. Judit Szenthelyi (pno) *(rec Nov 27–28, 1995)* — Hungaroton ▲ HCD 31639 [DDD]
Dvořák, A.:Romance Vn, w. T. Pál (cnd), Hungarian State Orch — LaserLight ▲ 15 517 [DDD]
Dvořák, A.:Romance Vn, w. T. Pál (cnd), Hungarian State Orch — LaserLight ▲ 15 824 [DDD]
Khachaturian, A.:Spartacus (sels), w. L. Kovács (cnd), Miskolc SO — Classical Diamonds ▲ 4008 [ADD]
Kodály, Z.:Adagio, w. Judit Szenthelyi (pno) *(rec Nov 27–28, 1995)* — Hungaroton ▲ HCD 31639 [DDD]
Kodály, Z.:Epigrams, w. Judit Szenthelyi (pno) *(rec Nov 27–28, 1995)* — Hungaroton ▲ HCD 31639 [DDD]
Kodály, Z.:Háry János (sels), w. Judit Szenthelyi (pno)—Intermezzo [arr J. Szigeti] *(rec Nov 27–28, 1995)* — Hungaroton ▲ HCD 31639 [DDD]
Liszt, F.:Grand duo concertant on Lafont's *Le Marin*, w. Judit Szenthelyi (pno) *(rec Nov 27–28, 1995)* — Hungaroton ▲ HCD 31639 [DDD]
Paganini, N.:Centone di sonate, w. D. Benkö (gtr)—Nos. 1–4 — Hungaroton ▲ HCD 31478 [DDD]
Paganini, N.:Duetto amoroso Vn, w. D. Benkö (gtr) — Hungaroton ▲ HCD 31478 [DDD]
Paganini, N.:Sons Vn & Gtr, w. D. Benkö (gtr)—Son. concertata in A, Son. per novene (No. 2) in E & Son. in A, Op. 3/1 — Hungaroton ▲ HCD 31478 [DDD]
Tchaikovsky, P.:Valse–Scherzo Vn, Hungarian SO — Capriccio ▲ 10 924 [DDD]

Szeryng, Henryk (vn)
Bach, J.S.:Cons Vn (comp), w. N. Marriner (cnd), Academy of St. Martin in the Fields — Philips ▲ 422250–2 [ADD]
Bach, J.S.:Con for 2 Vns, w. J.–L. Garcia (vn), H. Szeryng (cnd), English CO *(rec live, Queen Elizabeth Hall, London Feb 26, 1972)* — Intaglio ▲ INCD 7201 [ADD]
Bach, J.S.:Con for 2 Vns, w. M. Hasson (vn), N. Marriner (cnd), Academy of St. Martin in the Fields—Air & Suite No. 3, BWV 1068 — Philips ▲ 422250–2 [ADD]
Bach, J.S.:Con for 2 Vns, w. M. Hasson (vn), N. Marriner (cnd), Academy of St. Martin in the Fields — Philips 2–▲ 426462–2 [ADD]
Beethoven, L. van:Con Vn, Op. 61, w. B. Haitink (cnd), Royal Concertgebouw Orch — Philips ("Solo" series) ▲ 442398–2
Beethoven, L. van:Romances Vn, w. B. Haitink (cnd), Royal Concertgebouw Orch — Philips ▲ 446521–2
Beethoven, L. van:Romances Vn, w. B. Haitink (cnd), Royal Concertgebouw Orch — Philips ("Solo" series) ▲ 442398–2
Beethoven, L. van:Sons Vn (comp), w. Ingrid Haebler (pno)—Nos. 1–5 — Philips ▲ 446521–2
Beethoven, L. van:Sons Vn (comp), w. Ingrid Haebler (pno)—Nos. 6–10 — Philips ▲ 446524–2
Beethoven, L. van:Son 5 Vn, "Spring", w. A. Rubinstein (pno) — RCA Gold Seal ▲ 09026–61861–2
Beethoven, L. van:Son 8 Vn, w. A. Rubinstein (pno) — RCA Gold Seal ▲ 09026–61861–2
Beethoven, L. van:Son 8 Vn, w. A. Rubinstein (pno) — RCA Gold Seal ▲ 6264–2–RG [ADD]
Beethoven, L. van:Son 9 Vn, "Kreutzer", w. A. Rubinstein (pno) — RCA Gold Seal ▲ 09026–61861–2
Beethoven, L. van:Trios Pno (comp), w. W. Kempff (pno), P. Fournier (vc)—Opp. 1,70 & 97 — Deutsche Grammophon 3–▲ 415879–2 [ADD]
Beethoven, L. van:Trio 4 Pno, "Ghost", w. W. Kempff (pno), P. Fournier (vc) — Deutsche Grammophon ("Galleria" series) ▲ 429712–2 [ADD]
Beethoven, L. van:Trio 6 Pno, "Archduke", w. W. Kempff (pno), P. Fournier (vc) — Deutsche Grammophon ("Galleria" series) ▲ 429712–2 [ADD]
Berg, A.:Con Vn, w. J. Krenz (cnd), Polish National SO *(rec Warsaw, 1958)* — Prelude ▲ PRE 2148 [ADD]
Berg, A.:Con Vn, w. R. Kubelik (cnd), Bavarian RSO *(rec live 1975)* — Artists ▲ FED 59 [ADD]
Berg, A.:Con Vn, w. R. Kubelik (cnd), Bavarian RSO — Deutsche Grammophon ("20th Century Classics" series) ▲ 431740–2 [ADD]
Brahms, J.:Con Vn, w. B. Haitink (cnd), Royal Concertgebouw Orch — Philips ("Solo" series) ▲ 446194–2
Brahms, J.:Con Vn, w. A. Dorati (cnd), London SO — Mercury Living Presence ▲ 434318–2 [ADD]
Brahms, J.:Con Vn, w. B. Haitink (cnd), Royal Concertgebouw Orch — Philips ▲ 416438–2 [ADD]
Brahms, J.:Con Vn & Vc, "Double Con", w. Janos Starker (vc), B. Haitink (cnd), Royal Concertgebouw Orch — Philips ("Solo" series) ▲ 446194–2
Brahms, J.:Son 1 Vn, w. A. Rubinstein (pno) — RCA Gold Seal ▲ 6264–2–RG [ADD]
Brahms, J.:Son 3 Vn, w. A. Rubinstein (pno) — RCA Gold Seal ▲ 6264–2–RG [ADD]
Brahms, J.:Trio 1 Pno, w. A. Rubinstein (pno), P. Fournier (vc) *(rec 1972)* — RCA Red Seal ▲ 6260–2–RC [ADD]

Szeryng, Henryk (vn) (cont.)
Brahms, J.:Trio 2 Pno, w. A. Rubinstein (pno), P. Fournier (vc) *(rec 1972)* — RCA Red Seal ▲ 6260–2–RC [ADD]
Gluck, C.W.:Melodie, w. Charles Reiner (pno) *(rec Feb. 13–14, 1963)* — Mercury Living Presence ▲ 434351–2
Halffter, C.:Con Vn, w. E. Bátiz (cnd), Mexico City PO — ASV ▲ ASV 871 [DDD]
Henryk Szeryng, w. London SO [cnd:A. Dorati] — Mercury Living Presence ▲ 434339–2
Khachaturian, A.:Con Vn, *(orch unknown)* *(rec 1958–63)* — Arlecchino ▲ ARL117
Khachaturian, A.:Con Vn, w. A. Dorati (cnd), London SO — Mercury Living Presence ▲ 434318–2 [ADD]
Kreisler, F.:Vn Pieces, w. Charles Reiner (pno)—Caprice Viennois; Schön Rosmarin; Liebesleid; Liebesfreud; Recitativo & Scherzo; Tempo di Minuetto; Praeludium & Allegro; Chanson Louis XIII & Pavane; Tambourin Chinois; Menuet; The Old Refrain; Rondino [on a theme by Beethoven]; Allegretto [in the style of Boccherini] *(rec Jan. 22–23, 1963)* — Mercury Living Presence ▲ 434351–2
Leclair, J.–M.:Sons Vn (Books 1–4), w. Charles Reiner (pno)—No. 3 in D *(rec Feb. 13–14, 1963)* — Mercury Living Presence ▲ 434351–2
Locatelli, P.:The Labyrinth, w. Charles Reiner (pno) *(rec Feb. 13–14, 1963)* — Mercury Living Presence ▲ 434351–2
Mozart, W.A.:Con 3 Vn, w. H. Szeryng (cnd), English CO *(rec live, Queen Elizabeth Hall, London, Feb. 26, 1972)* — Intaglio ▲ INCD 7201 [ADD]
Mozart, W.A.:Con 5 Vn, w. R. Kubelik (cnd), Bavarian RSO *(rec live 1975)* — Artists ▲ FED 59 [ADD]
Ponce, M.:Con Vn, w. J. Krenz (cnd), Polish National SO *(rec Warsaw, 1958)* — Prelude ▲ PRE 2148 [ADD]
Ponce, M.:Con Vn, w. E. Batiz (cnd), *(orch unknown)* — ASV ▲ ASV 866 [DDD]
Ponce, M.:Con Vn, w. E. Bátiz (cnd), Royal PO — ASV ▲ ASV 952
Prokofiev, S.:Con 2 Vn, w. J. Krenz (cnd), Polish National SO *(rec Warsaw, 1958)* — Prelude ▲ PRE 2148 [ADD]
Prokofiev, S.:Con 2 Vn, *(orch unknown)* *(rec 1958–63)* — Arlecchino ▲ ARL117
Schubert, Franz:Trio 1 Pno, w. A. Rubinstein (pno), E. Fournier (vc) — RCA Gold Seal ▲ 6262–2–RG [ADD]
Schumann, R.:Trio 1 Pno, w. A. Rubinstein (pno), P. Fournier (vc) — RCA Gold Seal ▲ 6262–2–RG [ADD] ■ 6262–4–RG (CrO2)
Sibelius, J.:Con Vn, w. J. Barbirolli (cnd), Helsinki CO *(rec live Royal Festival Hall, London)* — Intaglio ▲ INCD 7201 [ADD]
Szymanowski, K.:Con 2 Vn, *(orch unknown)* *(rec 1958–63)* — Arlecchino ▲ ARL117
Szymanowski, K.:Con 2 Vn, w. A. Rodzinski (cnd), Rome RAI SO *(rec 1958)* — Stradivarius 2–▲ DAT 12306 [ADD]
Tchaikovsky, P.:Con Vn, w. C. Munch (cnd), Boston SO — RCA ■ ALK1–4493
Vivaldi, A.:Music of, w. Salvatore Accardo (vn), Frederico Agostini (vn), Heinz Holliger (ob), Ida Levin (vn), Aurele Nicolet (fl), Massimo Paris (va d'amore), Angel Romero (gtr), Celedonio Romero (gtr), Celine Romero (gtr), Pinchas Zukerman (vn), Academy of St. Martin in the Fields, English CO, I Musici, Naples Weekly International Soloists, St. Paul CO, Dresden Staatskapelle—The Four Seasons [Winter]; Con in D for Gtr [Largo]; Con in D for Fl, "Il gardellino" [Cantabile]; Con in C for Diverse Insts [Andante molto]; Con in g for Strs [Andante molto]; Con in D for 2 Vns & 2 Vcs [Largo]; Con in g for Ob, Vn, Ww & Strs [Larghetto]; Con in a for Gtr, "L'estro armonico" [Largo]; Con in F for 3 Vns [Andante]; Con in F for Fl [Largo]; Con in d for Va D'Amore [Largo]; Con in E for Vn & Strs, "Il riposo" [Allegro]; Con in G for Ob, Bn & Strs [Largo]; Con in B♭ for Vn & Strs [Largo]; Con in A for Gtr & Strs [Larghetto]; Con in E for Vn & Strs, "L'amoroso" [Allegro]; Con in G for Fl [Largo]; Con in A for Vn [Larghetto]; Con in c for Vn & Strs, "Il sospetto" [Andante]; Con in a for 2 Obs & Strs [Largo]; Con in g for Orch [Largo non molto]; Con in a for Vn [Largo]; Con in C for Ob [Adagio]; Con in g for Fl, "La notte" [Largo] — Philips ▲ 454051–2 ■ 454 051–4

Szeverényi, Ilona (hpd)
Bach, C.P.E.:Fants Kbd— in E♭, H.339 *(rec 1994)* — Hungaroton ▲ HCD 4004 [DDD]
Bach, J.S.:Chromatic Fant & Fugue *(rec 1994)* — Hungaroton ▲ HCD 4004 [DDD]
Bach, J.S.:Sons & Partitas Vn, BWV 1001–1006—BWV 1004 *(rec 1994)* — Hungaroton ▲ HCD 4004 [DDD]
Bach, J.S.:Suites Vc, BWV 1007–1012—in d, BWV 1008 *(rec 1994)* — Hungaroton ▲ HCD 4004 [DDD]

Szidon, Roberto (pno)
Gershwin, G.:Con Pno, w. E. Downes (cnd), London PO — Deutsche Grammophon ("Resonance" series) ▲ 427203–2 [ADD] ■ 427203–4
Liszt, F.:Hungarian Rhaps — Deutsche Grammophon ("Galleria" series) 2–▲ 423925–2 [ADD]
Schumann, R.:Adagio & Allegro Hn, w. Jenny Abel (vn) — Ars Musici 2–▲ 1038
Schumann, R.:Dichterliebe, w. T. Quasthoff (bass) [G] — RCA Red Seal ▲ 09026–61225–2
Schumann, R.:Fant Pno — Ars Musici 2–▲ 1038
Schumann, R.:Fantasiestücke Cl, w. Jenny Abel (vn) — Ars Musici 2–▲ 1038
Schumann, R.:Liederkreis, Op. 39, w. T. Quasthoff (bass) [G] — RCA Red Seal ▲ 09026–61225–2
Schumann, R.:Märchenbilder, w. Jenny Abel (vn) — Ars Musici 2–▲ 1038
Schumann, R.:Romances Ob, w. Jenny Abel (vn) — Ars Musici 2–▲ 1038
Schumann, R.:Son 1 Vn, w. Jenny Abel (vn) — Ars Musici 2–▲ 1038
Schumann, R.:Son 2 Vn, w. Jenny Abel (vn) — Ars Musici 2–▲ 1038
Schumann, R.:Son 3 Vn, w. Jenny Abel (vn) — Ars Musici 2–▲ 1038
Schumann, R.:Songs, w. T. Quasthoff (bass)—Die Fünf Lieder, Op. 53; Belsazar, Op. 57 [G] — RCA Red Seal ▲ 09026–61225–2
Schumann, R.:Stücke im Volkston, w. Jenny Abel (vn) — Ars Musici 2–▲ 1038
Villa–Lobos, H.:Son 1 Vn, w. Jenny Abel (vn) — Bayer ▲ BR 100119 [DDD]
Villa–Lobos, H.:Son 2 Vn, w. Jenny Abel (vn) — Bayer ▲ BR 100119 [DDD]
Villa–Lobos, H.:Son 3 Vn, w. Jenny Abel (vn) — Bayer ▲ BR 100119 [DDD]

Szigeti, Florin (vn)—see ORCHESTRAS & ENSEMBLES Enesco String Quartet

Szigeti, Joseph (vn)
The Art of Joseph Szigeti, Vol. 1, w. Kurt Ruhrseitz (pno) — Biddulph 2–▲ LAB 005–6 (m) [AAD]
The Art of Joseph Szigeti, Vol. 2 — Biddulph 2–▲ LAB 007–8 (m) [AAD]
Bach, J.S.:Arioso Ob, w. W. Goehr (cnd), *(orch unknown)* [arr. for violin & orch.] *(rec 1937)* — Biddulph ▲ LAB 064 [AAD]
Bach, J.S.:Brandenburg Con 5, w. E. Istomin (pno), J. Wummer (cl), P. Casals (cnd), Prades Festival Orch *(rec June 10–12, 1950)* — Sony Classical ("The Casals Edition" series) ▲ SMK 58982 [ADD]
Bach, J.S.:Con Vn, BWV 1052, w. F. Stiedry (cnd), New Friends of Music Orch *(rec 1940)* — Biddulph ▲ LAB 064 [AAD]
Bach, J.S.:Con for 2 Vns, w. C. Flesch (vn), W. Goehr (cnd), *(orch unknown)* *(rec 1937)* — Pearl ▲ PEA 9938 (m) [AAD]
Bach, J.S.:Sons & Partitas Vn, BWV 1001–1006—Son No. 1 in g, BWV 1001 — Iron Needle ▲ 1321 [ADD]
Bach, J.S.:Sons & Partitas Vn, BWV 1001–1006—BWV 1001, 1003 & 1006 — Music & Arts ▲ CD 774 [AAD]
Bach, J.S.:Sons & Partitas Vn, BWV 1001–1006—Son No. 1 in g, BWV 1001 — Grammofono 2000 ▲ GRM 78630
Bach, J.S.:Sons & Partitas Vn, BWV 1001–1006—Sons. Nos. 1 & 2 *(rec 1928–1937)* — Music & Arts 2–▲ CD 813 [AAD]
Bach, J.S.:Sons & Partitas Vn, BWV 1001–1006 *(rec July & Oct 1955)* — Vanguard Classics 2–▲ OVC 8021/22 [ADD]
Bartók, B.:Contrasts, w. B. Goodman (cl), Bartók (pno) *(rec 1940)* — Hungaroton 6–▲ HCD 12326/31 (m) [ADD]
Bartók, B.:Contrasts, w. B. Goodman (cl), Bartók (pno) *(rec 1940)* — Sony Masterworks ("Portrait" series) ▲ MPK 47676 [ADD]
Bartók, B.:Contrasts, w. B. Goodman (cl), Bartók (pno) — CBS ▲ MK 42227 ■ MYT 42227

▲ = CD ♦ = Enhanced CD Δ = MD ■ = Cassette Tape □ = DCC

Szigeti, Joseph (vn) (cont.)
Bartók, B.:Pno Music, w. B. Bartók (pno), V. Medgyaszay (sop), M. Basilides (cta), F. Székelyhidy (ten), B. Goodman (cl), D. Bartók Pásztory (pno), H. J. Baker, E. J. Rubsam (perc)—studio, broadcast & piano roll recordings of music by Bartók, Kodály, Beethoven, Debussy, Liszt & Scarlatti, chronologically arranged from ca. 1920 through 1945—Sonatina; 6 Romanian Folk Dances; Evening in Transylvania; 8 sels. from 15 Hungarian Peasant Songs; Suite, Op. 14 (both the issued & test recordings); Allegro barbaro; 5 sels. from 2 Romanian Dances, 3 Burlesques, 10 Easy Pieces & 14 Bagatelles; & 4 Sons. by D. Scarlatti (test recordings); 8 sels. from 15 Hungarian Peasant Songs; 4 sels. from 9 Little Piano Pieces, Petite Suite & 3 Rondos on Folk Melodies; & "Sursum corda" from Liszt's Années de pèlerinage; 20 Hungarian Folk Songs; 5 Hungarian Folk Tunes; 8 Hungarian Folksongs; Hungarian Folk Tunes; 6 Romanian Folk Dances; Rhap. 1 Violin & Piano; Contrasts for Clarinet, Violin & Piano; 2 sels. from Mikrokosmos; 32 sels. from Mikrokosmos; Rhap. 1; Son. No. 2; Beethoven's "Kreutzer" Son.; Debussy's Son. 3; Son. 2 Pianos & Percussion; Petite Suite; 3 Hungarian Folk Tunes; 11 sels. from Improvs. on Hungarian Peasant Songs; Mikrokosmos; 3 Rondos on Folk Melodies; 9 Little Piano Pieces; 14 Bagatelles; 15 sels. from For Children & 2 sels. from 10 Easy Pieces — Hungaroton 6–▲ HCD 12326/31 (m) [ADD]
Bartók, B.:Rhaps Vn & Pno, Sz.86 & 89, w. B. Bartók (pno) [two performances of No. 1] *(rec 1940)* — Hungaroton 6–▲ HCD 12326/31 (m) [ADD]
Bartók, B.:Rhaps Vn & Pno, Sz.86 & 89, w. B. Bartók (pno) *(rec 1940)* — Vanguard Classics ▲ OVC 8008 [AAD]
Bartók, B.:Son 2 Vn & Pno, w. B. Bartók (pno) *(rec 1940)* — Hungaroton 6–▲ HCD 12326/31 (m) [ADD]
Bartók, B.:Son 2 Vn & Pno, w. B. Bartók (pno) *(rec 1940)* — Vanguard Classics ▲ OVC 8008 [AAD]
Bartók, B.:Songs, w. *(vocalists unknown)*, B. Bartók (pno) — EMI Classics ▲ CDC 55031
Beethoven, L. van:Con Vn, Op. 61, w. B. Walter (cnd), New York PO *(rec 1947)* — Sony Masterworks ("Portrait" series) ▲ MPK 52536 (m) [AAD]
Beethoven, L. van:Con Vn, Op. 61, w. B. Walter (cnd), British SO *(rec 1932)* — Iron Needle ▲ 1302 (m) [ADD]
Beethoven, L. van:Con Vn, Op. 61, w. B. Walter (cnd), *(orch unknown)* *(rec 1928–1937)* — Music & Arts 2–▲ CD 813 [AAD]
Beethoven, L. van:Con Vn, Op. 61, w. B. Walter (cnd), British SO *(rec 1932)* — Pearl ▲ PEA 9345 (m) [AAD]
Beethoven, L. van:Sons Vn (comp), w. C. Arrau (pno) — Vanguard Classics 4–▲ OVC 8060/63 (m) [ADD]
Beethoven, L. van:Son 5 Vn, "Spring", w. M. Horszowski (pno) *(rec 1953)* — Sony Masterworks ("Portrait" series) ▲ MPK 52536 (m) [AAD]
Beethoven, L. van:Son 5 Vn, "Spring", w. A. Schnabel (pno) *(rec live Apr. 1948)* — Pearl ▲ PEA 9026 [AAD]
Beethoven, L. van:Son 5 Vn, "Spring", w. Claudio Arrau (pno) — Enterprise ("Sirio" series) ▲ ENT SO 530012
Beethoven, L. van:Son 6 Vn, w. M. Horszowski (pno) *(rec 1953)* — Sony Masterworks ("Portrait" series) ▲ MPK 52569 (m) [ADD]
Beethoven, L. van:Son 9 Vn, "Kreutzer", w. B. Bartók (pno) *(rec live, Library of Congress, Washington D.C. 4/13/40)* — Hungaroton 6–▲ HCD 12326/31 (m) [ADD]
Beethoven, L. van:Son 9 Vn, "Kreutzer", w. B. Bartók (pno) *(rec 1940)* — Vanguard Classics ▲ OVC 8008 [AAD]
Beethoven, L. van:Son 9 Vn, "Kreutzer", w. Claudio Arrau (pno) — Enterprise ("Sirio" series) ▲ ENT SO 530012
Beethoven, L. van:Son 10 Vn, w. A. Schnabel (pno) *(rec live Apr. 1948)* — Pearl ▲ PEA 9026 [AAD]
Berg, A.:Con Vn, w. D. Mitropoulos (cnd), NBC SO *(rec live 12/30/45)* — Intaglio ▲ IND 706–1 [ADD]
Bloch, E.:Con Vn, w. C. Munch (cnd), Paris Conservatory Societé des Concerts Orch *(rec 1939 for Columbia Records)* — Pearl ▲ PEA 9938 (m) [AAD]
Bloch, E.:Nigun, w. M. Abravanel (cnd), Los Angeles PO [violin & orchestra version] — Music & Arts 4–▲ CD 720–4 [AAD]
Bloch, E.:Nigun, w. K. Ruhrseitz (pno) *(rec 1928 for Columbia Records)* — Pearl ▲ PEA 9938 (m) [AAD]
Bloch, E.:Son 1 Vn, w. C. Bussotti (pno) — Music & Arts 4–▲ CD 720–4 [AAD]
Brahms, J.:Con Vn, w. D. Mitropoulos (cnd), New York PO *(rec 1948)* — Legend ▲ LGD 135 [ADD]
Brahms, J.:Con Vn, w. H. Harty (cnd), Hallé Orch *(rec 1928 for Columbia)* — Pearl ▲ PEA 9345 (m) [AAD]
Brahms, J.:Con Vn, w. E. Ormandy (cnd), Philadelphia Orch *(rec 1945; from Columbia LP ML)* — Sony Masterworks ("Portrait" series) ▲ MPK 52535 (m) [ADD]
Brahms, J.:Con Vn, w. H. Harty (cnd), Hallé Orch *(rec 1928–1937)* — Music & Arts 2–▲ CD 813 [AAD]
Brahms, J.:Son 3 Vn, w. Egon Petri (pno) — Iron Needle ▲ 1321 [ADD]
Brahms, J.:Son 3 Vn, w. E. Petri (pno) *(rec 1928–1937)* — Music & Arts 2–▲ CD 813 [AAD]
Brahms, J.:Son 3 Vn, w. Egon Petri (pno) — Grammofono 2000 ▲ GRM 78630
Brahms, J.:Trio 2 Pno, w. M. Hess (pno), P. Casals (vc) *(rec 1952)* — Sony Masterworks ("Portrait" series) ▲ MPK 52535 (m) [ADD]
Brahms, J.:Trio 2 Pno, w. Myra Hess (pno), Pablo Casals (vc) *(rec Prades, June 16, 1952)* — Sony Classical ▲ SMK 66571 [ADD]
Busoni, F.:Divert Fl, w. T. Scherman (cnd), Little Orch Society *(rec 1954)* — Sony Masterworks ("Portrait" series) ▲ MPK 52537 (m) [ADD]
Busoni, F.:Son 2 Vn, w. Clara Haskil (pno) — Music & Arts 4–▲ CD 720–4 [AAD]
Busoni, F.:Son 2 Vn, w. M. Horszowski (pno) *(rec 1956)* — Sony Masterworks ("Portrait" series) ▲ MPK 52537 (m) [ADD]
The Complete HMV Recordings — Biddulph ▲ LAB 043 [ADD]
Corelli, A.:La Follia, w. O. Klemperer (cnd), Los Angeles PO — Grammofono 2000 ▲ GRM 78643
Corelli, A.:Son Vn, Op. 5/12, "La Follia", w. A. Farkas (pno) *(rec 1940)* — Sony Masterworks (Portrait) ▲ MPK 52569 (m) [ADD]
Debussy, C.:Clair de lune, w. A. Földes (pno) *(rec 1942)* — Sony Masterworks (Portrait) ▲ MPK 52569 (m) [ADD]
Debussy, C.:Son Vn, w. B. Bartók (pno) *(rec live, Library of Congress, Washington D.C. 4/13/40)* — Hungaroton 6–▲ HCD 12326/31 (m) [ADD]
Debussy, C.:Son Vn, w. B. Bartók (pno) *(rec 1940)* — Vanguard Classics ▲ OVC 8008 [AAD]
Handel, G.F.:Sons Vn, w. Nikita Magaloff (pno)—No. 4 in d, HWV 364 — Grammofono 2000 ▲ GRM 78630
Handel, G.F.:Sons Vn, w. Nikita Magaloff (pno)—in d — Iron Needle ▲ 1321 [ADD]
Hindemith, P.:Son in E Vn & Pno, w. C. Bussotti (pno) — Sony Masterworks ("Portrait" series) ▲ MPK 52569 (m) [ADD]
Ives, C.:Sons Vn, w. A. Foldes (pno), No. 4 *(rec 1942)* — CRI ■ ACS 6014
Lalo, E.:Aubade, w. A. Farkas (pno) *(rec 1941)* — Sony Masterworks ("Portrait" series) ▲ MPK 52569 (m) [ADD]
Mendelssohn, F.:Con in e Vn & Orch, Op. 64, w. T. Beecham (cnd), London PO — EMI Classics ▲ CDH 64562
Mendelssohn, F.:Con in e Vn & Orch, Op. 64, w. T. Beecham (cnd), London PO *(rec 1933 for Columbia)* — Pearl ▲ PEA 9377 (m) [AAD]
Mozart, W.A.:Con 3 Vn, w. D. Mitropoulos (cnd), New York PO *(rec 1949)* — Legend ▲ LGD 135 [ADD]
Mozart, W.A.:Con 3 Vn, w. B. Walter (cnd), NBC SO *(rec live 1951)* — Music & Arts 4–▲ CD 720–4 [AAD]
Mozart, W.A.:Con 4 Vn, w. T. Beecham (cnd), London PO *(rec Oct. 8, 1934 for Columbia)* — Pearl ▲ PEA 9377 (m) [AAD]
Mozart, W.A.:Divert Hns Strs, K.287, w. M. Goberman (cnd), *(orch unknown)* *(rec 1938; orig. issued as Col)* — Biddulph ▲ LAB 064 [ADD]
Mozart, W.A.:Sons Vn Pno (misc), w. A. Schnabel (pno)—K.481 *(rec live Apr. 1948)* — Pearl ▲ PEA 9026 [AAD]
Mozart, W.A.:Sons Vn Pno (misc), w. N. Magaloff (pno)—Son. No. 21 *(rec 1928–1937)* — Music & Arts 2–▲ CD 813 [AAD]
Mozart, W.A.:Sons Vn Pno (misc), w. Nikita Magaloff (pno)—No. 21 in e, K.304 — Grammofono 2000 ▲ GRM 78630
Mozart, W.A.:Sons Vn Pno (misc)—K.296, 301–306, 376–380 & 526 [w. Horszowski]; 454, 481 [w. George Szell] *(rec 1955)* — Vanguard Classics 4–▲ OVC 8036/39 (m/s) [ADD]

Szigeti, Joseph (vn) (cont.)
Mozart, W.A.:Sons Vn Pno (misc), w. Nikita Magaloff (pno)—in e, K.304 — Iron Needle ▲ 1321 [ADD]
Prokofiev, S.:Con 1 Vn, w. T. Beecham (cnd), London PO — EMI Classics ▲ CDH 64562
Prokofiev, S.:Con 1 Vn, w. T. Beecham (cnd), London PO *(rec 8/25/35 for Columbia)* — Pearl ▲ PEA 9377 (m) [AAD]
Ravel, M.:Son Vn Pno, w. C. Bussotti (pno) *(rec 1953)* — Sony Masterworks ("Portrait" series) ▲ MPK 52569 (m) [ADD]
The Recordings with Béla Bartók & Andor Foldes, w. Béla Bartók (pno), Benny Goodman (cl) *(rec 1940–41)* — Biddulph ▲ BID LAB 070 [ADD]
Schubert, Franz:Fant Vn, D.934, w. J. Levine (pno) *(rec 1949)* — Sony Masterworks ("Portrait" series) ▲ MPK 52538 (m) [ADD]
Schubert, Franz:Rondo Vn, D.895, w. C. Bussotti (pno) *(rec 1952; from Columbia LP ML)* — Sony Masterworks ("Portrait" series) ▲ MPK 52538 (m) [ADD]
Schubert, Franz:Rondo Vn, D.895, w. N. Magaloff (pno) *(rec 1928–1937)* — Music & Arts 2–▲ CD 813 [AAD]
Schubert, Franz:Sonatina Vn, D.384, w. A. Földes (pno) *(rec 1942; from Columbia LP ML)* — Sony Masterworks ("Portrait" series) ▲ MPK 52538 (m) [ADD]
Schumann, R.:Trio 1 Pno, w. M. Horszowski (pno), R. von Tobel (vc) *(rec live 1956)* — Music & Arts 4–▲ CD 689 (m) [AAD]
A Szigeti Recital — Sony Masterworks ("Portrait" series) ▲ MPK 52569 (m) [ADD]
Tartini, G.:Con Vn, D.45, w. W. Goehr (cnd), New Friends of Music Orch—in d, D.45 *(rec 1937)* — Biddulph ▲ LAB 064 [ADD]
Tartini, G.:Sons Vn & Continuo, w. Kurt Ruhrseitz (pno)—No. 12 in G, Op. 2 — Grammofono 2000 ▲ GRM 78630
Tartini, G.:Sons Vn & Continuo, w. Kurt Ruhrseitz (pno)—in G — Iron Needle ▲ 1321 [ADD]
Tchaikovsky, P.:Valse sentimentale, w. H. Kaufman (pno) *(rec 1944)* — Sony Masterworks (Portrait) ▲ MPK 52569 (m) [ADD]

Szilvasy, Láezió (vc)
Schubert, Franz:Qnt Strs, D.956, w. Tátrai String Quartet — White Label ▲ HRC 056

Szokolay, Balázs (pno)
Bartók, B.:Mikrokosmos—23 selections *(rec May 30–June 4, 1989)* — Naxos ▲ 8.550451 [DDD]
Bartók, B.:Pno Music—Allegro barbaro:3 Hungarian Folksongs from the Csik District; 15 Hungarian Peasant Songs; Sonatina; 3 Rondos on Slovak Folktunes; 6 Dances in Bulgarian Rhythm *(rec May 30–June 4, 1989)* — Naxos ▲ 8.550451 [DDD]
Chopin, F.:Pno Music (misc), w. T. Irinsky (pno), I. Szekely (pno), I. Zaritzkaya (pno)—includes Ballade No. 3; Barcarolle, Op. 60; Berceuse, Op. 57; Piano Con. 2 (larghetto); Etude, Op. 10/3; Fantaisie-Impromptu, Op. 66; Mazurka, Op. 33/2; Nocturne, Op. 9/2; Polonaise-Fantaisie, Op. 61; Prelude, Op. 28/15; Scherzo, Op. 31; Piano Son. 2 (finale); Waltz, Op. 64/1 — Naxos ▲ 8.551104 [DDD]
Clementi, M.:Sons Pno—in G, Op. 25/2; in f#, Op. 25/5; in D, Op. 37/2; in B♭, Op. 24/2; 6 Progressive Sonatinas, Op. 36/1–6 *(rec Italian Cultural Institute, Budapest, June 28–July 4, 1990)* — Naxos ▲ 8.550452 [DDD]
Grieg, E.:Lyric Pieces *(rec Dec. 13, 16–19, 1991)* — Naxos ▲ 8.550577 [DDD]
Grieg, E.:Lyric Pieces—Opp. 12/1 & 6; 38/5; 54/1, 4 & 5; 57/4 & 6; 62/3, 4 & 6; 65/1, 2, 3 & 4; 68/2, 4 & 5; 71/1 *(rec Feb. 13 & 16–19, 1990)* — Naxos ▲ 8.550650 [DDD]
Grieg, E.:Lyric Pieces—Opp. 12/1, 2, 5 & 7; 38/2, 3, 4, 5, 6, 7 & 8; 43/2; 47/1, 2, 3 & 4; 54/2; 57/5; 65/1; 68/1, 3 & 6; 71/1, 2, 3, 4, 5, 6 & 7 — Naxos ▲ 8.550450 [DDD]
The Romance Collection *(rec Italian Institute, Sept 9–11, 1987)* — Naxos 4–▲ 8.504005 [DDD]
Romantic Piano Favorites, Vol. 1 — Naxos ▲ 8.550052 [DDD]
Romantic Piano Favorites, Vol. 5 *(rec. Jan. 20–28, 1988)* — Naxos ▲ 8.550168 [DDD]
Romantic Piano Favorites, Vol. 6 *(rec. Apr. 25–June 30, 1988)* — Naxos ▲ 8.550215 [DDD]

Szor, Terry (tpt)—see ORCHESTRAS & ENSEMBLES Musicians' Accord

Szpilman, Wladyslaw (pno)
Chopin, F.:Intro & Polonaise, "Polonaise brilliante", w. Tadeusz Wronski (vn) *(rec Warsaw, 1961)* — Polskie Nagrania ▲ PNCD 309
Chopin, F.:Trio Pno, w. Tadeusz Wronski (vn), Aleksander Ciechanski (vc) *(rec Warsaw, 1961)* — Polskie Nagrania ▲ PNCD 309

Szreder, Robert (vn)
Antheil, G.:Son 1 Vn, w. Boguslaw Jan Strobel (pno) — Pavane ▲ ADW 7335 [DDD]
Antheil, G.:Son 2 Vn, w. Boguslaw Jan Strobel (pno) — Pavane ▲ ADW 7335 [DDD]
Bacewicz, G.:Son 2 Vn *(rec 1991)* — Pavane ▲ ADW 7266 [DDD]
Bruzdowicz, J.:Epigrams (5) Vn *(rec 1991)* — Pavane ▲ ADW 7266 [DDD]
Bruzdowicz, J.:Son Vn, "Il Ritorno" *(rec 1991)* — Pavane ▲ ADW 7266 [DDD]
Bruzdowicz, J.:Son Vn Pno, "Spring in America", w. Boguslaw Jan Strobel (pno) — Pavane ▲ ADW 7335 [DDD]
Bruzdowicz, J.:Trio dei Due Mondi, w. Tomasz Strahl (vc), Boguslaw Jan Strobel (pno) — Pavane ▲ ADW 7335 [DDD]
Lutoslawski, W.:Partita Vn & Pno, w. B. J. Strobel (pno) — Pavane ▲ ADW 7283 [DDD]
Paderewski, I.J.:Son Vn, w. B. J. Strobel (pno) — Pavane ▲ ADW 7283 [DDD]
Prokofiev, S.:Son solo Vn, Op. 115 — Pavane ▲ ADW 7266 [DDD]
Szymanowski, K.:Son Vn, w. B. Jan Strobel (pno) — Pavane ▲ ADW 7283 [DDD]

Szreter, Karol (pno)
Tartini, G.:Son Vn "Devil's Trill", w. M. Rostal (vn) — Symposium ▲ 1079

Sztankovits, Béla (gtr)
Rossini, G.:Il barbiere di Siviglia, w. I. Kertesi (sop—Berta), S. Ganassi (mez—Rosina), R. Vargas (ten—Almaviva), A. Romero (bar—Dr. Bartolo), R. Servile (bar—Figaro), F. de Grandis (bass—Basilio), K. Sárkány (bass—Fiorello), A. Déri (pno), W. Humburg (cnd), Failoni CO, Hungarian Radio Chorus *(rec Nov. 16–28, 1992)* — Naxos 3–▲ 8.660027/29 [DDD]
Vivaldi, A.:Cons for 2 Gtrs, w. Zoltán Tokos (gtr), Budapest Strings *(rec Unitarian Church, Budapest, Nov. 1991)* — Naxos ▲ 8.553028 [DDD]
Vivaldi, A.:Con for 2 Mands, w. Zoltán Tokos (gtr), Budapest Strings *(rec Unitarian Church, Budapest, Nov 1991)* — Naxos ▲ 8.553028 [DDD]
Vivaldi, A.:Con for 2 Vns, RV.523, w. Zoltán Tokos (gtr), Budapest Strings [arr 2 gtrs] *(rec Unitarian Church, Budapest, Nov. 1991)* — Naxos ▲ 8.553028 [DDD]

Sztompka, Henryk (pno)
Chopin, F.:Mazurkas—Opp. 6, 7, 17, 24, 30, 33 & 41 *(rec Warsaw, 1959–60)* — Polskie Nagrania ▲ PNCD 313 A
Chopin, F.:Mazurkas—Opp. 50, 56, 59, 63, 67, 68 & posth. *(rec Warsaw, 1959)* — Polskie Nagrania ▲ PNCD 313 B

Szucs, Ferenc (vc)
Damase, J.-M.:Qnt Fl, Hp & Strs, w. Anna Noakes (fl), Gillian Tingay (hp), Richard Friedman (vn), Jane Atkins (vl) — ASV ▲ ASV 898 [DDD]
Damase, J.-M.:Trio Fl, w. Anna Noakes (fl), Gillian Tingay (hp) — ASV ▲ ASV 898 [DDD]

Szücs, Loránt (pno)
Bartók, B.:Mikrokosmos, w. K. Zempléni (pno) — Hungaroton 3–▲ HCD 31154/56 [ADD]

Szücs, Mihály (vn)
Bartók, B.:Contrasts, w. B. Kovács (cl), E. Tusa (pno) *(rec 1965)* — Hungaroton ▲ HCD 31554 [ADD]
Bartók, B.:Duos (44), w. W. Wilkomirska (vn) — Hungaroton 3–▲ HCD 31154/56 [ADD]

Szüts, Péter (vn)—see ORCHESTRAS & ENSEMBLES Trio Cristofori, Eder String Quartet

Szwec, Igor (vn)
Musgrave, T.:Orfeo III, w. Pamela Guidetti (fl), Mei Chen Liao Cope (vn), Michael Strauss (va), Lori Barnett (vc), Miles B. Davis (db), J. Freeman (cnd) *(rec Lang Concert Hall, Swarthmore College)* — CRI ▲ CD 723 [DDD]

Tabacco, Giorgio (hpd)
The Piemontese School of the 18th Century, w. Enrico Gatti (vn), Antonio Mosca (vc) — Symphonia ▲ SYM 92S13 [DDD]
Pugnani, G.:Ovs, w. L'Astrée Ensemble—No. 1 in D; No. 3 in B — Symphonia ▲ SY 93S21

Tabe, Kyoko (pno)
Encore *(rec Swiss Radio DRS, Studio Zurich, May 9–12, 1994)* — Denon ▲ CO 78928 [DDD]

Tabe, Kyoko (pno) (cont.)
Liszt, F.:Paraphrase on Verdi's Quartet *(rec Iwai Civic Concert Hall, Apr. 5-7, 1995)* Denon ▲ DEN 78960 [DDD]
Liszt, F.:Son Pno *(rec Iwai Civic Concert Hall, Apr. 5-7, 1995)* Denon ▲ DEN 78960 [DDD]
Liszt, F.:Sonetti del Petrarca Pno *(rec Iwai Civic Concert Hall, Apr. 5-7, 1995)* Denon ▲ DEN 78960 [DDD]
Mendelssohn, F.:Lieder ohne Worte Pno—Op.19/1-6; Op. 30/1, 2 & 6; Op. 38/2 & 5; Op. 53/1-5; Op. 62/1, 3, 5 & 6; Op. 67/2, 4 & 5; Op. 85/2; Op. 102/3 *(rec Apr. 13-15, 1993)* Denon/PCM Digital ▲ CO 75657 [DDD]
Mozart, W.A.:Con 9 Pno, w. J. López-Cobos (cnd), Lausanne CO *(rec Musica Théatre, La Chaux-de-Fonds, June 10-11, 1995)* Denon ▲ CO-78833 [DDD]
Mozart, W.A.:Con 24 Pno, w. J. López-Cobos (cnd), Lausanne CO *(rec Musica Théatre, La Chaux-de-Fonds, June 10-11, 1995)* Denon ▲ CO-78833 [DDD]
Yoshimatsu, T.:Pleiades Dances Denon ▲ DEN 18002

Taboloff, Gregory (pno)
Rare Russian Masterpieces Better Music ▲ BMC 2001 [DDD]

Tabuteau, Marcel (ob)
Bach, J.S.:Con Vn & Ob, w. I. Stern (vn), P. Casals (cnd), Prades Festival Orch *(rec June 5, 1950)* Sony Classical ("The Casals Edition" series) ▲ SMK 58982
Mozart, W.A.:Qt Ob, K.370, w. A. Pernel (vn), K. Tuttle (va), P. Tortelier (vc) *(rec live June 1953)* Music & Arts 4-▲ CD 689 (m) [AAD]

Tacchi, N. (bn)—see ORCHESTRAS & ENSEMBLES Stanislas Ensemble

Tacchino, Gabriel (pno)
Chopin, F.:Ballades Pno (comp)—in g, Op. 23 Pierre Verany ▲ PVY 730017 [DDD]
Chopin, F.:Fant Pierre Verany ▲ PVY 730017 [DDD]
Chopin, F.:Preludes, Op. 28 Pierre Verany ▲ PVY 730017 [DDD]
Chopin, F.:Scherzos—in b, Op. 20 Pierre Verany ▲ PVY 730017 [DDD]
Favorite Piano, w. Daniel Adni (pno), A. Brownridge (pno), J. Février (pno), M. Lympany (pno), J. Ogdon (pno) Classics for Pleasure ▲ CDCFP 4622 [ADD/DDD]
Franck, C.:Qnt Pno, w. Athenaeum Enesco String Quartet Pierre Verany ▲ PV.792032 [DDD]
Gershwin, G.:Con Pno, w. L. Foster (cnd), Monte Carlo PO Erato ("Bonsai" series) ▲ 2292-45929-2 ▮ 2292-45929-4
Gershwin, G.:Rhap in Blue, w. L. Foster (cnd), Monte Carlo PO Erato ("Bonsai" series) ▲ 2292-45929-2 ▮ 2292-45929-4
Poulenc, F.:Aubade Pno, w. G. Prêtre (cnd), Monte Carlo PO EMI Classics ▲ CDM 64714
Poulenc, F.:Con Pno, w. G. Prêtre (cnd), Monte Carlo PO EMI Classics ▲ CDM 64714
Poulenc, F.:Con for 2 Pnos, w. B. Ringeissen (pno), G. Prêtre (cnd), Monte Carlo PO EMI Classics ▲ CDM 64714
Prokofiev, S.:Cons Pno (comp), w. L. de Froment (cnd), Luxembourg RSO *(rec 1972-77)* Vox Box 3-▲ CD3X 3000 [ADD]
Prokofiev, S.:Con 1 Pno, w. L. de Froment (cnd), Luxembourg RSO *(rec 1972)* Allegretto ▲ ACD 8168 [ADD] ▮ ACS 8168
Prokofiev, S.:Con 2 Pno, w. L. de Froment (cnd), Luxembourg RSO *(rec 1977)* Allegretto ▲ ACD 8168 [ADD] ▮ ACS 8168
Prokofiev, S.:Con 3 Pno, w. L. de Froment (cnd), Luxembourg RSO *(rec 1977)* Allegretto ▲ ACD 8168 [ADD] ▮ ACS 8168
Prokofiev, S.:March & Scherzo Pno—March *(rec 10/90)* Pierre Verany ▲ PV.791022 [DDD]
Prokofiev, S.:Prelude Pno *(rec 10/90)* Pierre Verany ▲ PV.791022 [DDD]
Prokofiev, S.:Romeo & Juliet Pno *(rec 10/90)* Pierre Verany ▲ PV.791022 [DDD]
Prokofiev, S.:Son 2 Pno *(rec 10/90)* Pierre Verany ▲ PV.791022 [DDD]
Prokofiev, S.:Son 3 Pno *(rec 10/90)* Pierre Verany ▲ PV.791022 [DDD]
Satie, E.:Pno Music (misc)—Croquis et Agaceries d'un Gros Bonhomme en Bois; Piccadilly; Rag-Time Parade; Six Gnossiennes; Sonatine Bureaucratique; Trois Gymnopédies; Les Trois Valses Distinguées du Precieux Degouté; Valse "Je te veux"; Veritables Preludes Flasques Pierre Verany ▲ PV.789105 [DDD]

Tachezi, Herbert (hpd/org)
Boyce, W.:Syms, Op. 2, w. A. Janigro (cnd), Zagreb Solisti *(rec Grossesaal, Musikverein, Vienna, 1965)* Vanguard Classics ▲ SVC 46 [ADD]

Tachezi, Herbert (org)
Bach, J.S.:Passacaglia & Fugue Org Teldec ("Digital Experience" series) ▲ 9031-74780-2 [DDD] ▮ 9031-74780-4
Bach, J.S.:Preludes & Fugues, BWV 531-552—BWV 542 & 552 Teldec ("Digital Experience" series) ▲ 9031-74780-2 [DDD] ▮ 9031-74780-4
Bach, J.S.:Toccata, Adagio & Fugue Org, BWV 564 Teldec ("Digital Experience" series) ▲ 9031-74780-2 [DDD] ▮ 9031-74780-4
Bach, J.S.:Toccata & Fugue Org, BWV 565 Teldec ("Digital Experience" series) ▲ 9031-74780-2 [DDD] ▮ 9031-74780-4
Handel, G.F.:Cons (16) Org, w. N. Harnoncourt (cnd), Vienna Concentus Musicus Teldec ▲ 4509-91188-2

Tachezi, Herbert (pno)
Gabrieli, G.:Music of, w. R. Clemenic (rcr), A. Heiller (hpd), E. Appia (cnd), Gabrieli Festival Orch, Gabrieli Festival Chorus—Processional & Ceremonial Music from Sacrae Symphoniae [1597, 1615] & Concerti [1587]; originally released as Bach Guild BGS 5004)—Sancta et immaculata virginitas; O magnum mysterium; Nunc dimittis; Angelus ad pastores; O Jesu mi dulcissime; Exaudi Deus; Hodie completi sunt; O Domine Jesu Christe; Canzona Quarti Toni a 15 (ricercar); Inclina Domine *(rec Vienna, Feb. 1958)* Vanguard Classics ("The Bach Guild" series) ▲ OVC 2007 [ADD]
Haydn, J.:Con Org & Strs, H.XVIII/2, w. N. Harnoncourt (cnd), Vienna Concentus Musicus Teldec ▲ 2292-44196-2
Haydn, J.:Il Mondo della Luna (ov), w. N. Harnoncourt (cnd), Vienna Concentus Musicus Teldec ▲ 2292-44196-2

Tachibana, Chiharu (fl)
Sauguet, H.:Sonatine Fl, w. Shizuyo Takeda (pno) Sonpact ▲ SPT 96017 [DDD]

Tacke, Mathias (vn)—see also ORCHESTRAS & ENSEMBLES Vermeer String Quartet
Kurtág, G.:Scenes from a Novel, w. C. Whittlesey (sop), T. Fichter (db), M. Fábián (cimbalom) *(rec Jan. 7-9, 1992)* Sony Classical ▲ SK 53290 [DDD]

Taddei, G. (db)—see ORCHESTRAS & ENSEMBLES Seicentonovecento Ensemble

Taddei, Jacques (org)
Landowski, M.:Adagio Cantabile, w. Steliana Calos (sop), Pompei Harasteanu (bass), Dominique de Williencourt (vc), R. Georgescu (cnd), Timisoara PO, Timisoara Chorus *(rec Mar. 16-18, 1993)* Chamade ▲ 5611 [DDD]
Landowski, M.:Leçons de Ténèbres, w. Steliana Calos (sop), Pompei Harasteanu (bass), Dominique de Williencourt (vc), R. Georgescu (cnd), Timisoara PO, Timisoara Chorus *(rec Mar. 16-18, 1993)* Chamade ▲ 5611 [DDD]

Tadenuma, Akemi (pno)
Noda, T.:In the Garden, w. Sonoko Numata (vn) *(rec Saitama Geijyutsu Gekijo Music Hall, Apr 26, 1995)* Camerata ▲ 30CM 409 [DDD]
Noda, T.:In the Garden, w. Sonoko Numata (vn) Camerata ▲ 30CM 344
Takemitsu, T.:Hika, w. Sonoko Numata (vn) *(rec Saitama Geijyutsu Gekijo Music Hall, Apr 26, 1995)* Camerata ▲ 30CM 409 [DDD]
Yamada, K.:Music of, w. Sonoko Numata (vn)—Lullaby [from the Chugoku Area]; Red Dragonfly *(rec Saitama Geijyutsu Gekijo Music Hall, Apr 26, 1995)* Camerata ▲ 30CM 409 [DDD]

Taga, Kumie (vn)—see ORCHESTRAS & ENSEMBLES Akiko Tatsumi String Quartet

Tagliavini, Luigi (org)
Gherardeschi, G.:Messa Org Fonè ▲ FON 93F 22 [DDD]

Tahmizian, Emma (pno)
Prokofiev, S.:Mélodies, w. L. Gilbert (fl) [arr. Gilbert] *(rec Jan. 1991)* Koch International Classics ▲ KIC 7105 [DDD]
Prokofiev, S.:Son Fl, w. L. Gilbert (fl) *(rec Jan. 1991)* Koch International Classics ▲ KIC 7105 [DDD]

Tahmizian, Emma (pno) (cont.)
Prokofiev, S.:Visions fugitives, w. L. Gilbert (fl) [arr. Howard Harrison for Flute & Piano] *(rec Jan. 1991)* Koch International Classics ▲ KIC 7105 [DDD]

Tahmizian, S. (pno)
American Flute, Vol. 1, w. Zizi Mueller (fl), Yuval Waldman (vn), Jesse Levine (va) Premier ▲ PRCD 1029 [DDD]

Taillard, Pierre-André (b cl)
Mozart, W.A.:Con Cl, Concerto Cologne Capriccio Δ 70375

Tainton, Carol (hpd)
Reichardt, J.F.:Con Vn Hpd, w. *(violinist unknown)* Koch Schwann ▲ SCH 313422 [ADD]

Tainton, Carol (pno)
Ruzicka, P.:Chamber Music, w. Matthias Lorenz (vc), Hamburg String Quartet MD + G ▲ MDG 6250549
Stephan, R.:Music for 7 Stringed Instrs, w. B. Hartog (vn), I. Schliephake (vn), S. Passaggio (va), G. Donderer (vc), A. Akahoshi (db), M. Schmidt (hp) *(rec 1983)* Koch Schwann ▲ CD 311 122 [ADD]

Tait, Catherine (vn)
Crawford, R.:Son Vn & Pno, w. Barry Snyder (pno) Gasparo ▲ GS 300
Mamlok, U.:Designs, w. Barry Snyder (pno) Gasparo ▲ GS 300
Mamlok, U.:From My Garden Gasparo ▲ GS 300
Mamlok, U.:Son Vn, w. Barry Snyder (pno) Gasparo ▲ GS 300
Milhaud, D.:Suite Vn, w. King (cl), I. Hobson (pno) Arabesque ▲ Z 6569 [DDD]
Talma, L.:Son Vn, w. Barry Snyder (pno) Gasparo ▲ GS 300
Zwilich, E.T.:Son in 3 Movts, w. Barry Snyder (pno) Gasparo ▲ GS 300

Tait, Mararet (vc)—see ORCHESTRAS & ENSEMBLES Aurora String Quartet

Tait, Margaret (vc)—see ORCHESTRAS & ENSEMBLES Aurora String Quartet

Takacs, P. (pno)
Miller, E.J.:Going Home, w. L. McDonald (cl) Opus One ▲ 138
Miller, E.J.:Seven Sides of a Crystal, w. L. McDonald (cl) Opus One ▲ 138

Takada, Kazuko (hikomono)
Fujieda, M.:Music of, w. Mamoru Fujueda (cmpt), Makiko Sakurai (shomyo/Buddhist chant), Mineko Grimmer (audible sculptures), Kodo Uesugi (fukimono), Toshiyuki Matsukura (uchimono), Satoshi Sakai (uchimono), Koshin Ebihara (jumon)—The Night Chant III; Wind Chant; Cocoon Chant; Duct Chant; Falling Chant; The Night Chant I Tzadik ("The Composers" series) ▲ TZA 7003 [DDD]

Takada, Kazuko (shamisen/sgr)
Takahashi, Y.:Music of, w. Vladimir Tonkha (nar), Yumiko Tanaka (b shamisen), Ko Ishikawa (mouth org), Kishiko Suzumi (va), Ayumi Shimonoto (shamisen/sgr), Yuji Takahashi (pno)—Sugagaki Kuzushi; Mimi No Ho; Kagehime No Michiyuki; Yubi-Tomyo [Finger Light] Tzadik ▲ TZA 7010 [DDD]

Takagi, Yukiko (pno)
McPhee, C.:Balinese Ceremonial Music, w. Stephen Drury (pno), D. R. Davies (cnd), Brooklyn PO MusicMasters ("Classics" series) ▲ 01612-67159-2

Takahashi, Aki (pno)
Feldman, Morton:For John Cage, w. Y. Toyoshima (vn) O.O. Imports 2-▲ ALCD 41
Feldman, Morton:Pno Music—Pno Piece 1955; Two Intermissions; Illusions; Extensions 3; Pno Piece to Phillip Guston; Palais de Mari Mode ▲ MODE 54
Feldman, Morton:Triadic Memories O.O. Imports ▲ ALCD 33

Takahashi, Machiko (fl)
Yun, I.:Qt Fls, w. R. de Reede (fl), T. Roorda (fl), H. Starreveld (fl) Attacca ▲ BABEL 9056-3 [DDD]

Takahashi, Machiko (fl/pic)
Schoenberg, A.:The Cabaret Songs, w. Yumi Nara (sop), Izumi Okubo (vn/va), Vincent Jacquemin (cl/b cl), François Deppe (vc), Brigitte Foccroulle (pno), J.-P. Peuvion (cnd), Liège New Music Ensemble [arr Patrick Davin for Salon Orch] Adda ▲ ADD 581273 [DDD]
Schoenberg, A.:Pierrot lunaire, w. Yumi Nara (sop), Izumi Okubo (vn/va), Vincent Jacquemin (cl/b cl), François Deppe (vc), Brigitte Foccroulle (pno), J.-P. Peuvion (cnd), Liège New Music Ensemble Adda ▲ ADD 581273 [DDD]

Takahashi, T. (cl)
Shinohara, M.:Cooperation, w. A. Nishigata (shamisen), K. Mitsuhashi (shakuhachi), M. Akao (fue), S. Yaotani (hichiriki), K. Ishikawa (sho), C. Fukunaga (koto), J. Ueda (biwa), M. Yoshizawa (kokyu), I. Tsuji (ob), G. Kitamura (tpt), A. Murata (trbn), S. Eiso (perc), S. Ueki (vn), S. Katsuta (vc), Y. Shibuya (pno), K. Komatsu (cnd) *(rec live Casals Hall, Tokyo, Mar. 5, 1994)* Camerata ▲ 30CM 375 [DDD]
Shinohara, M.:Tabiyuki, w. A. Ogawa (mez), M. Kakagawa (fl), I. Tsuji (ob), K. Okazaki (fagotto), G. Kitamura (tpt), A. Murata (trbn), S. Eiso (perc), S. Ueki (vn), A. Nakakoji (va), S. Katsuta (vc), M. Komuro (contrabass), K. Komatsu (cnd) *(rec live Casals Hall, Tokyo, Mar. 5, 1994)* Camerata ▲ 30CM 375 [DDD]

Takahashi, Yuji (pno)
Feldman, Morton:False Relationships & the Extended Ending, w. M. Raimondi (vn), S. Barab (vc), P. Jacobs (pno), M. Feldman (cnd) *(rec 6/8/70)* CRI ▲ CD 620 [ADD]
Hayashi, H.:The Second Sym, "Canciones", w. T. Otaka (cnd), Tokyo PO Camerata ▲ 32CM 297
Messiaen, O.:Etudes (4) de Rhythme Denon ▲ CO 1052 [DDD]
Rzewski, F.:The People United Will Never Be Defeated O.O. Imports ▲ ALCD 19
Satie, E.:Pno Music (comp)—3 Gnossiennes; 5 Nocturnes; 3 Gymnopédies; Prélude de la porte héroïque du ciel; Je te veux; 3 pièces froides (Air à faire fuir); 3 pièces froides (danses de travers; Rag-time parade Denon ▲ 7485 [DDD]
Tada, E.:Sym 2 Pno (The Min-On Contemporary Music Festival '85"), w. T. Otaka (cnd), Tokyo PO Camerata ▲ 32CM 297
Takahashi, Y.:Music of, w. Vladimir Tonkha (nar), Kazuko Takada (shamisen/sgr), Yumiko Tanaka (b shamisen), Ko Ishikawa (mouth org), Kishiko Suzumi (va), Ayumi Shimonoto (shamisen/sgr)—Sugagaki Kuzushi; Mimi No Ho; Kagehime No Michiyuki; Yubi-Tomyo [Finger Light] Tzadik ▲ TZA 7010 [DDD]
Takemitsu, T.:Music of, w. Tashi, Y. Nagano (mez), H. Ibe (gtr), M. Nagasako (hp), K. Abe (vib), Y. Takahashi (pno), R. Noguchi (fl), M. Hamada (lt), T. Koizumi (picc), S. Ueki (vn), Y. Hattori (vc), R. Stoltzman (cl), P. Serkin (pno), Ozawa, Wakasugi (cnd), Boston SO—Quatrain; Stanza I; Sacrifice; Ring; Valeria; A Flock Descends into the Pentagonal Garden Deutsche Grammophon ("20th Century Classics" series) ▲ 423253-2 [ADD]
Xenakis, I.:Herma Denon ▲ CO 1052 [DDD]
Yun, I.:Gasa, w. Akiko Tatsumi (vn) *(rec Shibukawa City Auditorium, May 26, 1988)* Camerata ▲ 30CM 70 [AAD]

Takao, Naoko (pno)
Gibson, R.:Haiku (4), w. Sally Gibson Dorer (vc) Capstone ▲ CPS 8621

Takase, Yoshiko (pno)
Togawa, Y.:Kaze No Ha Vienna Modern Masters ("Distinguished Performers III" series) ▲ VMM 2016 [DDD]

Takeda, Shizuyo (pno)
Sauguet, H.:Sonatine Fl, w. Chiharu Tachibana (fl) Sonpact ▲ SPT 96017 [DDD]

Takezawa, Kyoko (vn)
Barber, S.:Con Vn, w. L. Slatkin (cnd), St. Louis SO *(rec Powell Symphony Hall, St. Louis, MO, Apr 24, 1994)* RCA Red Seal ▲ 09026-68283-2 [DDD]
Bartók, B.:Con 2 Vn, w. M. Tilson Thomas (cnd), London SO RCA Red Seal ▲ 09026-61675-2
Elgar, E.:Con Vn, w. C. Davis (cnd), Bavarian RSO RCA Red Seal ▲ 09026-61612-2
Elgar, E.:Intro & Allegro, w. C. Davis (cnd), Bavarian RSO RCA Red Seal ▲ 09026-61612-2
Mendelssohn, F.:Con in d Vn & Strs, w. C. P. Flor (cnd), Bamberg SO RCA Red Seal ▲ 09026-62512-2
Mendelssohn, F.:Con in e Vn & Orch, Op. 64, w. C. P. Flor (cnd), Bamberg SO RCA Red Seal ▲ 09026-62512-2
Recital, w. Phillip Moll (pno) RCA Red Seal ▲ 09026-60704-2

Takita, Michiko (koto)
Nakagawa, I.:Lied, w. Masami Nakagawa (fl) *(rec Iruma City Auditorium, Sept. 9, 1987)* Camerata ▲ 32CM 118 [DDD]

▲ = CD ♦ = Enhanced CD Δ = MD ▮ = Cassette Tape ◻ = DCC

Takova-Baynova, Anna (vn)
Minkus, L.:Ballets, w. Valentina Raicheva (hp), B. Spassov (cnd), Sofia National Opera Orch—La bayadère (sels.) (1877); Paquita (complete) (1846) *(rec Studio I, Bulgarian National Radio, Sofia, Feb 1994)* Capriccio ▲ 10 544 [DDD]

Tal, Yaara (pno)—see also ORCHESTRAS & ENSEMBLES Tal & Groethuysen Duo
Czerny, C.:Pno Music (4–Hands), w. A. Groethuysen (pno)—Grand Sonate brillante, Op. 10; Ouverture caracteristique et brillante, Op. 54; Grand Sonate, Op. 178; Fantaisie, Op. 226 Sony Classical ▲ SK 45936 [DDD]
Gouvy, T.:Aubade, w. A. Groethuysen (pno) Sony Classical ▲ SK 53110
Gouvy, T.:Ghiribizzi, w. A. Groethuysen (pno) Sony Classical ▲ SK 53110
Gouvy, T.:Morceaux, Op. 59, w. A. Groethuysen (pno)—Nos. 1 & 2 Sony Classical ▲ SK 53110
Gouvy, T.:Scherzo, Op. 77/1, w. A. Groethuysen (pno) Sony Classical ▲ SK 53110
Gouvy, T.:Son Pno 4–Hands, Op. 36, w. A. Groethuysen (pno) Sony Classical ▲ SK 53110
Gouvy, T.:Son Pno 4–Hands, Op. 49, w. A. Groethuysen (pno) Sony Classical ▲ SK 53110
Gouvy, T.:Son Pno 4–Hands, Op. 51, w. A. Groethuysen (pno) Sony Classical ▲ SK 53110
Hummel, J.N.:Nocturne, w. A. Groethuysen (pno) Koch Schwann ▲ CD 310017 [DDD]
Hummel, J.N.:Sons Pno 4–Hands, w. A. Groethuysen (pno) Koch Schwann ▲ CD 310017 [DDD]

Talanov, Alexander (vn)—see ORCHESTRAS & ENSEMBLES Talan String Quartet

Talanov, Vladimir (vn)—see ORCHESTRAS & ENSEMBLES Talan String Quartet

Talbot, John (pno)
Moeran, E.J.:Son Vn, w. Donald Scotts (vn) Chandos ▲ CHAN 8465 [ADD]

Talich Jr., Jan (va)—see also ORCHESTRAS & ENSEMBLES Talich String Quartet
Dvořák, A.:Qnt Strs, Op. 97, w. Stamitz String Quartet Bayer ▲ 100184 [DDD]
Mozart, W.A.:Duos Vn, w. Jan Talich Sr. (vn) Calliope ▲ CAL 9230
Mozart, W.A.:Sinf concertante Vn, K.364, w. Jan Talich Sr. (vn), K. Redel (cnd), Talich CO Calliope ▲ CAL 9230
Suk, J.:Qt Pno, w. J. Panenka (pno), J. Suk (vn), M. Fukačová (vc) Supraphon ▲ SUP 111532 [DDD]

Talich Sr, Jan (vn)
Mozart, W.A.:Duos Vn, w. Jan Talich Jr. (va) Calliope ▲ CAL 9230
Mozart, W.A.:Sinf concertante Vn, K.364, w. Jan Talich Jr. (va), K. Redel (cnd), Talich CO Calliope ▲ CAL 9230

Talipin, Oleg (bn)
Vivaldi, A.:Cons Bn, w. L. Korkhin (cnd), Renaissance CO—in a, RV.497 Infinity Digital ▲ QK 57244 [DDD]

Talisman, Evgeni (org)
And Life of the Future Century, w. Lina Mkrtchyan (cta), Leningrad Chamber Choir Multisonic ("Russian Stars on Classics" series) ▲ MUL 310053 [DDD]

Talitman, Rachel (hp)
Spohr, L.:Son 3 Vn, w. Sergiu Schwartz (vn) Arcobaleno ▲ AAOC 93642
Spohr, L.:Son 4 Vn, w. Sergiu Schwartz (vn) Arcobaleno ▲ AAOC 93642
Spohr, L.:Son 5 Vn, w. Sergiu Schwartz (vn) Arcobaleno ▲ AAOC 93642

Tallini, Arturo (gtr)—see ORCHESTRAS & ENSEMBLES Trio Chitarristico

Talmi, Er'ella (fl)
Avni, T.:Collage, w. Y. Amihai (sgr), Milo [Leon Malloy] (perc) Symposium ▲ 1110
Debussy, C.:Son Fl, w. G. Levertov (vn), A. Giles (hp) PWK Classics ▲ PWK 1141 [DDD]
Donizetti, G.:Son Fl & Pno, w. M. Frager (pno) Stradivari Classics ▲ SCD 6042 [DDD]
Moscheles, I.:Son Fl, w. M. Frager (pno) Stradivari Classics ▲ SCD 6042 [DDD]
Ravel, M.:Intro & Allegro, w. A. Giles (hp), A. Arnheim (cl), R. Kaminkovsky (vn), R. Mozes (vn), Y. Kaminkovsky (va), Y. Alperin (vc) PWK Classics ▲ PWK 1141 [DDD]
Schubert, Franz:Intro & Vars Fl on "Tröckne Blumen", w. M. Frager (pno) Stradivari Classics ▲ SCD 6042 [DDD]
Virtuoso Flute, w. Yoav Tamil (pno) PWK Classics ▲ PWK 1133 [DDD]

Talò, Elena (vn)—see ORCHESTRAS & ENSEMBLES I Filarmonici

Talvi, Ilkka (vn)
Albert, S.:In Concordiam, w. G. Schwarz (cnd), Seattle SO Delos ▲ DE 3059 [DDD]
Creston, P.:Partita Fl, w. S. Goff (fl), G. Schwarz (cnd), Seattle SO *(rec 3/1/91)* Delos ▲ DE 3114 [DDD]
Diamond, D.:Con 2 Vn, w. G. Schwarz (cnd), Seattle SO *(rec Sept. 11, 1991)* Delos ▲ DE 3119 [DDD]

Tamagawa, Kiyochi (cel)
Debussy, C.:Chansons de Bilitis (recitation), w. L. Jeffrey (fl), M. Meisenbach (fl), W. Dudley (hp), M. Golden (hp)—no speaker *(rec 6 & 8/91)* Centaur ▲ CRC 2114 [DDD]

Tamayo, Lidia (hp)
Schifrin, L.:Tangos, w. Marisa Canales (fl) Urtext ▲ URT 1 [DDD]

Tamil, Yoav (pno)
Virtuoso Flute, w. Er'ella Talmi (fl) PWK Classics ▲ PWK 1133 [DDD]

Tamir, Alexander (pno)
Brahms, J.:Neue Liebeslieder Waltzes, w. B. Eden (pno)—65a CRD ▲ 3413 [ADD]
Brahms, J.:Sym 3, w. B. Eden (pno) [2–piano version] CRD ▲ 3414
Brahms, J.:Vars on a Theme by Haydn, w. B. Eden (pno)—Op. 56b CRD ▲ 3413 [ADD]
Brahms, J.:Vars on a Theme of Robert Schumann, Op. 23, w. B. Eden (pno) CRD ▲ 3414
Brahms, J.:Waltzes Pno, Op. 39, w. B. Eden (pno) [piano duet versions] CRD ▲ 3413 [ADD]
Dances around the World, w. Eden, Bracha (pno) PWK Classics ▲ PWK 1134 [DDD]

Tamminga, Liuwe (org)
Golin, G.:Ricercare—No. XVII *(rec Italy)* Tactus ▲ TC 540001 [DDD]
Palestrina, G.:De Beata Marie, w. Sergio Vartolo (cnd), San Petronio Capella Musicale Soloists *(rec Verona Cathedral, Jan 1995)* Bongiovanni 2–▲ GB 5556/57–2 [DDD]
Palestrina, G.:Masses, w. Sergio Vartolo (cnd), San Petronio Cappella Musicale Soloists—Missas in Duplicibus Minoribus I & II *(rec 1995)* Bongiovanni ▲ GB 5558 [DDD]
Parabosco, G.:Ricercares—Nos. XVIII, XXI *(rec Italy)* Tactus ▲ TC 540001 [DDD]
Perti, G.A.:Liturgy for Good Friday, w. Patrizia Vaccari (sop), Maura Pederzoli (sop), Cristina Calzolari (sop), Alida Oliva (sop), Claudia Bugli (sop), Lucia Bagnoli (alt), Cinzia Meneghel (alt), Renzo Bez (alt), Alessandro Carmignani (alt), Michel van Goethem (alt), Mauro Collina (ten), Vincenzo Di Donato (ten), Paolo Fanciullacci (ten), Giovanni Caccamo (ten), Paolo Da Col (ten), Sergio Foresti (bass), Marco Scavazza (bass), Luca Ferracin (bass), Paride Montanari (bass), Sergio Vartolo (org), S. Vartolo (cnd), Bologna San Petronio Capella Musicale Orch—Omnes amici mei; De lamentatione Jeremiae Prophetae:Heth. Cogitavit; Velum templi; Vinea mea; De lamentatione Jeremiae Prophetae:Lamed. Matribus suis; Tamquam ad latronem; Tenebrae factae sunt; Animam meam; Tradiderunt me; Jesum tradidit; De lamentatione Jeremiae Prophetae:Aleph. Ego vir; Caligaverunt *(rec St. Petronio Basilica, Bologna, Mar 28–31, 1995)* Naxos ▲ 8.553321 [DDD]
Segni, J.:Ricercares—Nos. III, IV, VI, VIII, IX, XI, XII, XIII, XV, XVI *(rec Italy)* Tactus ▲ TC 540001 [DDD]
Willaert, A.:Ricercares—Nos. I, X, XIV [from Musica Nova (1540)] *(rec Italy)* Tactus ▲ TC 540001 [DDD]

Tan, Melvyn (hpd)
Oboe Collection, w. Robin Canter (ob), Anthony Pleeth (vc), Richard Burnett (pnos), James Wood (perc) Amon Ra ▲ CDSAR 22 [DDD]

Tan, Melvyn (pno)
Beethoven, L. van:Allegretto, WoO 53 [period instrument] Virgin Classics ("Veritas Edition" series) ▲ CDM 61161
Beethoven, L. van:Andante, WoO 57, "Andante favori" [period instrument] Virgin Classics ("Veritas Edition" series) ▲ CDM 61161
Beethoven, L. van:Bagatelle, WoO 59, "Für Elise" [period instrument] Virgin Classics ("Veritas Edition" series) ▲ CDM 61161
Beethoven, L. van:Music of, w. Anthony Pleeth (vc) Hyperion 2–▲ CDD 22004
Beethoven, L. van:Son 21 Pno, "Waldstein" [period instrument] Virgin Classics ("Veritas Edition" series) ▲ CDM 61160

Tan, Melvyn (pno) (cont.)
Beethoven, L. van:Son 23 Pno, "Appassionata" [period instrument] Virgin Classics ("Veritas Edition" series) ▲ CDM 61160
Beethoven, L. van:Son 26 Pno, "Les Adieux" [period instrument] Virgin Classics ("Veritas Edition" series) ▲ CDM 61160
Beethoven, L. van:Vars on an Original Theme, Op. 34 [period instrument] Virgin Classics ("Veritas Edition" series) ▲ CDM 61161
Beethoven, L. van:Vars on "God Save the King", WoO 78 EMI Classics ▲ CDC 54526
Davis, C.:Pride & Prejudice, w. C. Davis (cnd), *(orch unknown)* Angel ▲ CDQ 36090
Donizetti, G.:Songs, w. I. Caddy (bass–bar), A. Halstead (hn), S. Comberti (vc)—Canto d'Ugolino; L'amor funesto; Trovatore in caricatura; Spirito di Dio; Viva il matrimonio; Le renégat; Noé—scène du Déluge; Le départ pour la chasse; On coeur pour abri; La hart [I, F] *(rec 8/84 & 12/85)* Meridian ▲ CDE 84183
Mendelssohn, F.:Assai tranquillo, w. Steven Isserlis (vc) RCA Red Seal ▲ 09026–62553–2
Mendelssohn, F.:Son 1 Vc, w. Steven Isserlis (vc) RCA Red Seal ▲ 09026–62553–2
Mendelssohn, F.:Son 2 Vc, w. Steven Isserlis (vc) RCA Red Seal ▲ 09026–62553–2
Mendelssohn, F.:Vars concertantes, w. Steven Isserlis (vc) RCA Red Seal ▲ 09026–62553–2
Mozart, W.A.:Con 9 Pno, w. New Mozart Ensemble Virgin Classics ▲ CDC 45012
Mozart, W.A.:Con 18 Pno, w. N. McGegan (cnd), Philharmonia Baroque Orch *(rec Walnut Creek Regional Center for the Arts, Feb 27–28 & Mar 2, 1995)* Harmonia Mundi France ▲ HMU 907138
Mozart, W.A.:Con 19 Pno, w. N. McGegan (cnd), Philharmonia Baroque Orch *(rec Walnut Creek Regional Center for the Arts, Feb 27–28 & Mar 2, 1995)* Harmonia Mundi France ▲ HMU 907138
Mozart, W.A.:Con 27 Pno, w. New Mozart Ensemble Virgin Classics ▲ CDC 45012
Schubert, Franz:Moments musicaux [period instrument] Virgin Classics ("Veritas Edition" series) ▲ CDM 61161
Schubert, Franz:Pieces Pno, D.946 [period instrument] Virgin Classics ("Veritas Edition" series) ▲ CDM 61161
Weber, C.M. von:Konzertstück Pno, w. R. Norrington (cnd), London Classical Players EMI Classics ▲ CDC 55348
Weber, C.M. von:Sym 2, w. R. Norrington (cnd), London Classical Players EMI Classics ▲ CDC 55348

Tanaka, C. (vn)
Yashiro, A.:Qt Strs, w. S. Muto (vn), T. Uzuka (va), K. Yasuda (vc) Camerata ▲ 30CM 51
Yashiro, A.:Trio Pno, w. H. Puig–Robert (pno), K. Yasuda (vc) Camerata ▲ 30CM 51

Tanaka, Masahito (bn)
Bassoon Fantasia Pavane ▲ ADW 7252 [DDD]
Fontyn, J.:Zephyr, w. S. Sumi (pno) Thorofon ▲ CTH 2099 [DDD]
Hindemith, P.:Son Bn, w. S. Sumi (pno) Thorofon ▲ CTH 2099 [DDD]
Kaneta, C.:Ambivalence IV Thorofon ▲ CTH 2099 [DDD]
The Magic Bassoon, w. Seiko Sumi (pno) Thorofon ▲ CTH 2099 [DDD]
Saint–Saëns, C.:Son Bn, w. Seiko Sumi (pno) Thorofon ▲ CTH 2099 [DDD]
Weber, C.M. von:Andante & Rondo ungarese Bn, w. S. Sumi (pno) Thorofon ▲ CTH 2099 [DDD]
Yun, I.:Monolog Thorofon ▲ CTH 2099 [DDD]

Tanaka, Naoko (vn)
Baksa, R.:Qnt Ob & Strs, w. B. Lucarelli (ob), M. Yanagita (vn), S. Winterbottom (va), T. Hoyle (vc) Capstone ▲ CPS 8610
Weill, K.:Con Vn, w. J. Rudel (cnd), Orch of St. Luke MusicMasters ▲ 7007–2–C [DDD]

Tanaka, Yoko (pno)
Miyoshi, A.:Collection of Songs, w. M. Asai (pno), F. Kuyiyama (cnd), Chorale OMP Camerata ▲ 32CM–28
Miyoshi, A.:Poems of Animals, w. A. Miyoshi (nar), F. Kuyiyama (cnd), Chorale OMP Camerata ▲ 32CM–28
Miyoshi, A.:Symphonic Choral Poem, w. A. Miyoshi (nar), M. Asai (pno), F. Kuyiyama (cnd), Chorale OMP Camerata ▲ 32CM–28

Tanaka, Yumiko (shamisen)
Miki, M.:Music of, w. K. Mitsuhashi (shakuhachi), N. Yoshimura (koto), Masur (cnd), Tokyo Metropolitan SO, Tokyo PO, Leipzig Gewandhaus Orch—Jo No Kyoju; Prelude for Shakuhachi, Koto & Strings; Ha No Kyoku; Con. for Koto & Orch.; Kyu no Kyoku; Sym. for Two Worlds Camerata 2–▲ 30CM 223/24
Takahashi, Y.:Music of, w. Vladimir Tonkha (nar), Kazuko Takada (shamisen/sgr), Ko Ishikawa (mouth org), Kishiko Suzumi (va), Ayumi Shimonoto (shamisen/sgr), Yuji Takahashi (pno)—Sugagaki Kuzushi; Mimi No Ho; Kagehime No Michiyuki; Yubi–Tomyo [Finger Light] Tzadik ▲ TZA 7010 [DDD]

Tanamura, Mazumi (va)
Brahms, J.:Sons Cl (comp), w. Takashi Hironaka (pno) Camerata ▲ 30CM 377
Dietrich, A.:Allegro, w. Takashi Hironaka (pno) [trans Tanamura for Va & Pno] Camerata ▲ 30CM 377

Tanenbaum, David (gtr)
Bolcom, W.:Seasons Neuma ▲ 45084
Brouwer, L.:Estudios Sencillos GSP Recordings 2–▲ GSP 1000CD [ADD] 2–■ GSP 1000C
Carcassi, M.:Etudes Gtr, Op. 60 GSP Recordings 2–▲ GSP 1000CD [ADD] 2–■ GSP 1000C
Currier, M.:Son Gtr Neuma ▲ 45084
Curtis–Smith, C.:Great Am Gtr Solo, "GAGS!" Neuma ▲ 45084
Davies, P.M.:Son Gtr New Albion ▲ NA 032 [ADD]
Harrison, L.:Music for Hp—Serenade for Frank Wigglesworth; Avalokiteshvara; Music for Bill & Me; Jahla; Sonata in Ishartum; Beverly's Troubador Piece; A Waltz for Evelyn Hinrichsen New Albion ▲ NA 055
Harrison, L.:Serenade Gtr, w. William Winant (perc) New Albion ▲ NA 055
Henze, H.–W.:An eine Äolsharfe, w. H. W. Henze (cnd), Ensemble Modern Ars Musici ▲ 0859
Henze, H.–W.:Royal Winter Music *(rec 1/4–5/85)* Audiofon ▲ CD 72029
Johanson, B.:Morta dulce Cano Neuma ▲ 45084
Kernis, A.J.:100 Greatest Dance Hits, w. Chester String Quartet *(rec Manhattan Center Studios, New York, May 31–June 3, 1995)* New Albion ♦ NA 083CD
Korde, S.:Time Grids Neuma ▲ 45084
Lewis, P.S.:Beaming Contrasts, w. Alexander String Quartet New Albion ▲ NA 060 [DDD]
Manuel Barrueco Plays Lennon & McCartney, w. Manuel Barrueco (gtr), London SO [cnd:Jeremy Lubbock] Angel ▲ CDC 55228
Piazzolla, A.:Las cuatro estaciones porteñas New Albion ▲ NA 065
Piazzolla, A.:Milonga del angel New Albion ▲ NA 065
Piazzolla, A.:La muerte del angel New Albion ▲ NA 065
Piazzolla, A.:Pieces Gtr New Albion ▲ NA 065
Pure Barrueco, w. Manuel Barrueco (gtr), London SO [cnd:Jeremy Lubbock] EMI Classics ▲ CDC 55315
Reich, S.:Electric Counterpoint New Albion ▲ NA 032 [ADD]
Sierra, R.:Triptico, w. Shanghai String Quartet New Albion ▲ NA 032 [ADD]
Sor, F.:Etudes—Op. 6, Nos. 1,2,3,6,8,9,11; Op. 29, Nos. 13,17,22,23; Op. 31, Nos. 16,19,20,21; Op. 35, Nos. 13,16,17,22 GSP Recordings 2–▲ GSP 1000CD [ADD] 2–■ GSP 1000C
Takemitsu, T.:All in Twilight New Albion ▲ NA 032 [ADD]
Tippett, M.:The Blue Gtr New Albion ▲ NA 032 [ADD]

Tanenbaum, J. (perc)—see ORCHESTRAS & ENSEMBLES Relâche Ensemble

Tanev, Christo (vc)
Bond, V.:Dreams of Flying, w. Georgy Valtchev (vn), Nikolai Gagov (vn), Valentin Gerov (va) Gega ▲ GD 197 [DDD]
Bond, V.:Other Selves, w. Georgy Valtchev (vn), Anna Stoytcheva (pno) Gega ▲ GD 197 [DDD]
Bond, V.:Son Vc, w. Anna Stoytcheva (pno) Gega ▲ GD 197 [DDD]

Tanfield, Peter (vn)—see ORCHESTRAS & ENSEMBLES Dussek Piano Trio

Tang, Achim (db)—see ORCHESTRAS & ENSEMBLES Bantam Orch

Tanguy, Jean Michel (fl)—see ORCHESTRAS & ENSEMBLES Belgian Wind Quintet

Tanner, Eric (vn)
Dankner, S.:Sextet, w. L. Skelton (pno), V. Poullette (vn), M. Gyurik (va), A. Nisbet (vc), R. Kassinger (db) Albany ▲ TROY 067

Tanner, Joanne (fl/alt fl)
Macchia, S.:Chamber Con 3, w. M. Sussman (cl), F. Cohen (ob/E hn), D. Fedora (bn), L. Klock (hn), V. Kadlubkiewicz (vn), J. Messina (db), P. Tanner (perc) *(rec July 1992)* Gasparo ▲ GS 226 [DDD]
Tanner, Paul (perc)—see ORCHESTRAS & ENSEMBLES Nova Ensemble
Tanner, Peter (perc)
Macchia, S.:Chamber Con 3, w. J. Tanner (fl/alt fl), M. Sussman (cl), F. Cohen (ob/E hn), D. Fedora (bn), L. Klock (hn), V. Kadlubkiewicz (vn), J. Messina (db) *(rec July 1992)* Gasparo ▲ GS 226 [DDD]
Tan-Nicholson, Pamela (pno)
Brahms, J.:Scherzo Vn, w. Vasko Vassilev (vn) Harmonia Mundi France ("Les Nouveaux Interprètes" series) ▲ HMN 911576
Brahms, J.:Sons Vn (comp), w. Vasko Vassilev (vn) Harmonia Mundi France ("Les Nouveaux Interprètes" series) ▲ HMN 911576
Tanosaki, Kazuko (pno)
Matsuo, M.:Hirai V, w. E. Michael Richards (cl), M. Matsuo (cnd), Hamilton College Orch Opus One ▲ CD 156
Tanski, Claudius (pno)
Brahms, J.:Trio Cl, w. Dieter Klöcker (cl), Christoph Henkel (vc) MD + G ▲ MDG 3010595 [DDD]
Brahms, J.:Trio Hn, w. Sebastian Weigle (hn), Dieter Streicher (vn) MD + G ▲ MDG 3010595 [DDD]
Busoni, F.:Bach Transcriptions—Wachet auf, ruft uns die Stimme; Ich ruf zu Dir, Herr [Andante]; Toccata & Fugue in d, BWV 565 MD + G ▲ L 3436 [DDD]
Busoni, F.:Elegies (7) Pno—Nos. 3–6 MD + G ▲ L 3436 [DDD]
Busoni, F.:Sonatina 2 Pno, w. C. Tanski MD + G ▲ L 3436 [DDD]
Busoni, F.:Toccata Pno MD + G ▲ L 3436 [DDD]
Czerny, C.:Grande Sérénade Concertante, w. Consortium Classicum MD + G ("Gold" series) ▲ MDG 3010518 [DDD]
Czerny, C.:Nonet, w. Consortium Classicum MD + G ("Gold" series) ▲ MDG 3010518 [DDD]
Draeseke, F.:Son Pno Altarus ▲ CD 9030
Draeseke, F.:Son Pno MD + G ▲ L 3514 [DDD]
Liszt, F.:Mosonyis Grabgeleit MD + G ▲ L 3514 [DDD]
Liszt, F.:Son Pno MD + G ▲ L 3514 [DDD]
Liszt, F.:Son Pno Altarus ▲ CD 9030
Reger, M.:Qt Pno, w. Mannheim String Quartet MD + G ▲ MDG CD 3360715
Reubke, J.:Son Pno MD + G ▲ MDG 3120344 [DDD]
Smetana, B.:Pno Music (complete)—Scherzo-Polka, Op. 5/1; Polkas (3), Op. 7; am Meeresufer, Op. 17; Bömische Tänze; Rêves; Andante in E♭ MD + G ▲ MGD CD 3120483
Tantzov, Oleg (cl)
Hindemith, P.:Qt Cl, Vn, Vc & Pno, w. Mikhail Tzinman (vn), Natalya Savinova (vc), Victor Yampolsky (pno) *(rec Mosfilm Studio, Dec 1994)* Triton ▲ 17005 [DDD]
Hindemith, P.:Qnt Cl, w. Moscow Contemporary Music Ensemble *(rec Mosfilm Studio, Dec 1994)* Triton ▲ 17005 [DDD]
Hindemith, P.:Son Cl, w. Victor Yampolsky (pno) *(rec Mosfilm Studio, Dec 1994)* Triton ▲ 17005 [DDD]
Tanyel, Seta (pno)
Arutiunian, A.:Armenian Rhap, w. J. Brown (pno) Chandos ▲ CHAN 8466 [DDD]
Bax, A.:Pno Music for 2 Pnos, w. J. Brown (pno)—Moy Mell (1917); Hardanger (1927); The Poisoned Fountain (1928); The Devil that Tempted St. Anthony (1929); Red Autumn (1931) Chandos ▲ CHAN 8603 [DDD]
Bax, A.:Son for 2 Pnos, w. J. Brown (pno) Chandos ▲ CHAN 8603 [DDD]
Chopin, F.:Mazurkas—Opp. 17/4, 24/2 & 33/4 Collins Classics ▲ COL 1330 [DDD]
Chopin, F.:Polonaises—Op. 44 Collins Classics ▲ COL 1330 [DDD]
Chopin, F.:Preludes, Op. 28 Collins Classics ▲ COL 1330 [DDD]
Chopin, F.:Scherzos—Op. 31 Collins Classics ▲ COL 1330 [DDD]
Franck, C.:Symphonic Vars, w. J. Kaspszyk (cnd), Philharmonia Orch *(rec 9/90)* Collins Classics ▲ 11582 [DDD]
Khachaturian, A.:Suite 2 Pnos, w. Jeremy Brown (pno) Chandos ▲ CHAN 8466 [DDD]
Moszkowski, M.:Pno Music—Fant-impromptu, Op. 6; 3 Etudes de concert, Op. 24; Isoldes Tod 3 mouvment; 3 Morceaux, Op. 73; Grande valse de concert, Op. 88 Collins Classics ▲ COL 1473
Moszkowski, M.:Pno Music—Chanson Bohème de L'Opera Carmen de Georges Bizet; Baracrolle aus Hoffmann Erzählungen; Reverie, Expansion, En Automne, Air de Ballet from Op. 36; Serenata, Op. 15/1; Tarentella, Op. 27/2; Albumblatt, Op. 2; Poeme de Mai, Op. 67; Nocturne, Minuetto, Au Crepuscule, Danse Russe, Op. 68; La jongleuse, Op. 52/4 Collins Classics ▲ COL 1412 [DDD]
Poulenc, F.:Capriccio Pnos, w. Brown (pno) Chandos ▲ CHAN 8519 [DDD]
Poulenc, F.:Elégie Pnos, w. Brown (pno) Chandos ▲ CHAN 8519 [DDD]
Poulenc, F.:L'Embarquement pour Cythère, w. Brown (pno) Chandos ▲ CHAN 8519 [DDD]
Poulenc, F.:Son Pno 4-Hands, w. Brown (pno) Chandos ▲ CHAN 8519 [DDD]
Poulenc, F.:Son for 2 Pnos, w. Brown (pno) Chandos ▲ CHAN 8519 [DDD]
Scharwenka, X.:Pno Music (comp)—4 Polish Dances, Op. 58; Scherzo in G, Op. 40; Barcarolle in e, Op. 14; 2 Pieces, Op. 22; Theme & Variations, Op. 48 Collins Classics ▲ COL 1365 [DDD]
Scharwenka, X.:Qt Pno, w. Levon Chilingirian (vn), Ivo-Jan Van Der Werff (va), Garbis Atmacayan (vc) Collins Classics ▲ COL 1419 [DDD]
Scharwenka, X.:Serenade Vn, w. Lydia Mordkovitch (vn) Collins Classics ▲ COL 1448 [DDD]
Scharwenka, X.:Son Vc, w. Colin Carr (vc) Collins Classics ▲ COL 1448 [DDD]
Scharwenka, X.:Son Vn, w. Lydia Mordkovitch (vn) Collins Classics ▲ COL 1448 [DDD]
Scharwenka, X.:Trio 1 Pno, w. Lydia Mordkovitch (vn), Colin Carr (vc) Collins Classics ▲ COL 1448 [DDD]
Scharwenka, X.:Trio 2 Pno, w. Levon Chilingirian (vn), Garbis Atmacayan (vc) Collins Classics ▲ COL 1419 [DDD]
Shostakovich, D.:Concertino for 2 Pnos, w. Jeremy Brown (pno) Chandos ▲ CHAN 8466 [DDD]
Shostakovich, D.:Suite for 2 Pnos, w. Jeremy Brown (pno) Chandos ▲ CHAN 8466 [DDD]
Tanzini, (pno)
Casella, A.:Scarlattiana, w. G. Albrecht (cnd), Berlin RSO Koch Schwann ▲ CD 311054 [DDD]
Tao, Patricia (pno)—see ORCHESTRAS & ENSEMBLES Guild Piano Trio
Tapaninen, Juhani (bn)—see ORCHESTRAS & ENSEMBLES Helsinki Wind Quintet
Tappert, Johannes (gtr)
French Sonatas of the 18th Century, w. Birgit Schmieder (ob) MD + G ▲ MDG 6170631
Tapping, Roger (va)—see also ORCHESTRAS & ENSEMBLES Takács String Quartet, Allegri String Quartet
Debussy, C.:Chamber Music, w. William Bennett (fl), David Campbell (cl), James Campbell (cl), Nicholas Daniel (ob), Robert Makell (hn), Richard Watkins (hn), Robin Kennard (bn), Rachel Gough (bn), Simon Haram (sax), Ieuan Jones (hp), Clifford Benson (pno), Julius Drake (pno), John York (pno)—Rapsodie for Eng hn; Syrinx; Première rapsodie; Son for Fl, Va & Hp; Le petit nègre; Petite pièce; Rapsodie for Sax *(rec All Saints' Church, East Finchley, London, Jan 12–20, 1994)* Cala 2-▲ CACD 1017 [DDD]
Saint-Saëns, C.:Chamber Music, w. W. Bennett (fl), D. Campbell (cl), J. Campbell (cl), N. Daniel (ob), R. Makell (hn), R. Watkins (hn), R. Kennard (bn), R. Gough (bn), S. Haram (sax), I. Jones (hp), C. Benson (pno), J. Drake (pno), J. York (pno)—Odelette, Op. 162; Son for Cl, Op. 167; Feuillet d'album, Op. 81; Son for Bn, Op. 168; Caprice on Danish & Russian Airs, Op. 79; Son for Ob, Op. 166; Romance in D♭, Op. 37; Tarantelle, Op. 6 *(rec All Saints' Church, East Finchley, London, Jan 12–20, 1994)* Cala 2-▲ CACD 1017 [DDD]
Tarack, Gerald (vn)—see also ORCHESTRAS & ENSEMBLES Bronx Arts Ensemble
Grieg, E.:Sons Vn, Opp. 8, 13 & 45, w. D. Hancock (pno) Bridge ▲ BCD 9026 [ADD]
Stravinsky, I.:L'Histoire du soldat Suite Vn, w. C. Russo (cl), T. Weis (tpt), J. Levine (db), Loren Glickman (bn), J. Swallow (trbn), R. Desroches (perc), L. Stokowski (cnd) Vanguard Classics ▲ SVC 1 [AAD]
Tarantiles, A. (hp)
Wallach, J.:Mourning Madrigals, w. K. Birnbaum (sop), F. Urrey (ten), C. Abraham (fl) [E] Capstone ▲ CPS 8613

Tarasov, A. (gtr)
Babadjanyan, A.:Music of, w. A. Arutiunyan (pno), Arno Babadjanyan (pno), B. Chekmenyov (gtr), A. Nikolayev (perc), Silantiev, Mavisakhalyan (cnd), All-Union Radio-TV Sym Variety Orch, Armenian Radio-TV Orch—Nocturne; Prelude & Vagarshapat Dance; Capriccio; Polyphonic Son; Exprompt; Armenian Rhap; Elegy in Commemoration of A. Khachaturyan; 6 Pictures; Melody & Humoresque; Fant on Give Me My Music Back; Fant on Dum spiro spero; Fant on Winer Love; Fant on Call Me; Piece for the Pno & Orch [Dreams] *(rec 1953–83)* Russian Compact Disc ("Talents of Russia" series) ▲ RCD 16251 [ADD]
Tarasov, Sergei (pno)
Schubert, Franz:Son Pno, D.664 Art & Electronics ▲ AED 68018 [DDD]
The Young Tarasov Art & Electronics ▲ AED 68018 [DDD]
Tarasova, Marina (vc)
Davïdov, K.Y.:Con 1 Vc, w. K. Krimets (cnd), Davydov SO Olympia ▲ OLY 571 [DDD]
Davïdov, K.Y.:Con 2 Vc, w. K. Krimets (cnd), Davydov SO Olympia ▲ OLY 571 [DDD]
Davïdov, K.Y.:Pieces Vc & Pno, Op. 17, w. Alexander Polezhaev (pno) Olympia ▲ OLY 571 [DDD]
Davïdov, K.Y.:Salonstücke, Op. 30, w. Alexander Polezhaev (pno) Olympia ▲ OLY 571 [DDD]
Kabalevsky, D.:Con 1 Vc, w. V. Dudarova (cnd), Russian SO Olympia ▲ OLY 292 [DDD]
Kabalevsky, D.:Con 2 Vc, w. V. Dudarova (cnd), Russian SO Olympia ▲ OLY 292 [DDD]
Kabalevsky, D.:Improvisation Vn, w. V. Dudarova (cnd), Russian SO Olympia ▲ OLY 292 [DDD]
Kabalevsky, D.:In Memory of Sergei Prokofiev, w. Alexander Polezhaev (pno) *(rec Moscow, 1993)* Olympia ▲ OCD 294 [DDD]
Kabalevsky, D.:Major-Minor Studies *(rec Moscow, 1993)* Olympia ▲ OCD 294 [DDD]
Kabalevsky, D.:Rondo Vn, w. V. Dudarova (cnd), Russian SO Olympia ▲ OLY 292 [DDD]
Kabalevsky, D.:Son Vc, w. Alexander Polezhaev (pno) *(rec Moscow, 1993)* Olympia ▲ OCD 294 [DDD]
Khachaturian, A.:Con Vc, w. V. Dudarova (cnd), Russian SO Olympia ▲ OLY 539 [DDD]
Khachaturian, A.:Con-Rhap Vc, w. V. Dudarova (cnd), Russian SO Olympia ▲ OLY 539 [DDD]
Miaskovsky, N.:Con Vc, w. Y. Samoilov (cnd), Moscow New Opera Orch Olympia ▲ OLY 530 [DDD]
Miaskovsky, N.:Son 1 Vc, w. Alexander Polezhaev (pno) Olympia ▲ OLY 530 [DDD]
Miaskovsky, N.:Son 2 Vc, w. Alexander Polezhaev (pno) Olympia ▲ OLY 530 [DDD]
Tarcha, Carlos (perc)—see ORCHESTRAS & ENSEMBLES Duo Dialogos
Tardiff, Paul (pno)
Copland, A.:Duo Vn, w. Fritz Gearhart (vn) Koch International Classics ▲ KIC 7268
Cowell, H.:Suite Vn, w. Fritz Gearhart (vn) Koch International Classics ▲ KIC 7268
Dello Joio, N.:Vars & Capriccio, w. Fritz Gearhart (vn) Koch International Classics ▲ KIC 7268
Still, W.G.:Suite Vn, w. Fritz Gearhart (vn) Koch International Classics ▲ KIC 7268
Tarjáni, Ferenc (hn)
Dohnányi, E. von:Sextet, w. E. Szegedi (pno), B. Kovács (cl), Tátrai String Quartet members Hungaroton ▲ HCD 11624 [ADD]
Durkó, Z.:Iconography 2, w. A. Mihály (cnd), Budapest Chamber Ensemble *(rec 1972)* Hungaroton ▲ HCD 31654 [AAD]
Kocsár, M.:Con—in memoriam ZH, w. M. Kocsár (cnd), Franz Liszt CO Hungaroton ▲ HCD 31188 [DDD]
Tarling, Judith (va)—see ORCHESTRAS & ENSEMBLES Revolutionary Drawing Room String Quartet
Tarlton, Philip (bn)
Danzi, F.:Sextet Ob, w. Richard Berry (hn), Michael Thompson (hn), John Bradburg (cl), Robert Hill (cl), John Price (bn)—version for Harmonie ensemble *(rec St. Paul's Church, Rusthall, Kent, England, June 1994)* Naxos ▲ 8.553076 [DDD]
Tarpley, Joel (hn)
Cohn, J.:Music of, w. M. Piccinini (fl), M. Dine (ob), J. Manasse (cl), M. Finn (bn), N. Akamatsu (db), S. Alderking (pno)—Wind Quintet, Op. 36b (1981); Goldfinch Variations for Wind Trio, Op. 61 (1984); Little Overture for Wind Quartet, Op. 59 (1982); Suite Champêtre for Wind Quintet (after Rameau), Op. 47 (1968) XLNT ■ C 2
Cohn, J.:Music of, w. M. Piccinini (fl), M. Dine (ob), J. Manasse (cl), M. Finn (bn), N. Akamatsu (db), S. Alderking (pno)—Wind Quintet, Op. 36b (1981); Little Overture for Wind Quintet, Op. 59 (1982); Sonatina for Clarinet & Piano, Op. 56 (1981); Sonata Romantica for Double Bass & Piano, Op. 18 (1952); Sonata Robusta for Bassoon & Piano, Op. 55 (1980); Sonata for Flute & Piano, Op. 52 (1974); Goldfinch Variations for Three Treble Instruments, Op. 61 (1984) *(rec 1985)* XLNT ▲ CD 18006 [ADD]
Tarr, Edward (tpt)
Alexius, C.:Sonatina Tpt, w. E. Westenholz (pno) BIS ▲ CD 152 [AAD]
Baroque Masterpieces for Trumpet & Organ, Vol. 1, w. M. Ullrich Kent (tpt), et al. Elektra/Nonesuch ■ 71279-4
Cellier, A.:Thème et variations sur le Psaume 149 du Psautier de la Réforme, "Chantez à Dieu chanson nouvelle", w. E. Westenholz (pno) BIS ▲ CD 152 [AAD]
Fux, J.J.:Plaudite, sonat tuba, w. M. Klietmann (ten), P. Németh (cnd), Capella Savaria [period instrs] [L] Hungaroton ▲ HCD 31134 [DDD]
Gershwin, G.:Rhap in Blue, w. E. Westenholz (pno) [trumpet-piano trans. by T. Dokshitser] BIS ▲ CD 152 [AAD]
Guyonnet, J.:La Cantate interrompue, w. F. Rochaix (nar), S. Stenhammar (sop), S. Seban (pno), G. Calame (pno), E. Séjourne (perc), P. Geiss (tpt), B. Nilsson (tpt), H. Ries (trbn), H. Rückert (trbn), J.-M. Collet, J. Guyonnet (cnd), Geneva Collegium Academicum [F] *(rec Nov. 15, 1986)* Grammont ▲ CTSP 30-2
Haydn, J.:Con Tpt, w. J. Rolla (cnd), Franz Liszt CO Christophorus ▲ CD 74557 [DDD]
Hindemith, P.:Son Tpt, w. E. Westenholz (pno) *(rec Holte, Denmark, Sept. 20, 1979)* BIS ▲ CD 159 [AAD]
Holmboe, V.:Triade, w. E. Westenholz (org) BIS ▲ CD 78 [AAD/DDD]
Hummel, J.N.:Con in E Tpt, w. J. Rolla (cnd), Franz Liszt CO Christophorus ▲ CD 74557 [DDD]
Italian Masterworks for Organ & Trumpet, w. Irmtraud Krüger (org), N. Eklund (tpt), C. Frigerio (vc) Christophorus ▲ CHR 77145 [DDD]
Kreutzer, C.:Vars for Chromatic Tpt, w. J. Rolla (cnd), Franz Liszt CO Christophorus ▲ CD 74557 [DDD]
Martinů, B.:Sonatina Tpt, w. E. Westenholz (pno) BIS ▲ CD 152 [AAD]
Millares, A.:Fant for A♭ Tpt, w. J. Rolla (cnd), Franz Liszt CO Christophorus ▲ CD 74557 [DDD]
Neruda, J.B.G.:Con Tpt, w. J. Rolla (cnd), Franz Liszt CO Christophorus ▲ CD 74557 [DDD]
The Princely Trumpet, w. Franz Liszt CO Christophorus ▲ CD 74559 [DDD]
The Silver Trumpets of Lisbon & Lusitanian Organ Music, w. Edward Tarr Trumpet Ensemble, Irmtraud Krüger (org) MD + G ▲ L 3348 [DDD]
Torelli, G.:Tpt Music, w. P.-O. Lindeke (tpt), D. Staff (tpt), G. Cassone (tpt), S. Vartolo (cnd), San Petronio Cappella Musicale Orch—Sinfs., G.1, 2, 8, 10, 11, 26, 29, 30, 31, 33; Sons. G.3–6, 13, 15–25; Con. G.27 Bongiovanni 3-▲ GB 5523/25
Weiner, S.:Phantasy 1 Tpt, w. E. Westenholz (org) BIS ▲ CD 152 [AAD]
Werner, F.:Duo Tpt, w. E. Westenholz (pno) BIS ▲ CD 152 [AAD]
Tartak, Marvin (cel)—see ORCHESTRAS & ENSEMBLES San Francisco Contemporary Music Players
Tartak, Marvin (pno)—see ORCHESTRAS & ENSEMBLES San Francisco Contemporary Music Players
Tasa, David (tpt)
Eben, Petr:Vitraux, w. G. Augst (org) Gallo ▲ CD 604 [AAD]
Taskov, Krassimir (pno)
Bruch, M.:Fant for 2 Pnos, w. V. Georgieva (pno) Gega ▲ GD 139 [DDD]
Busoni, F.:Fant contrappuntistica Pno, w. V. Georgieva (pno) Gega ▲ GD 139 [DDD]
Martinů, B.:Fant for 2 Pnos, w. V. Georgieva (pno) Gega ▲ GD 139 [DDD]
Mozart, W.A.:Fant Pno, K.396, w. V. Georgieva (pno) Gega ▲ GD 139 [DDD]
Taskov, K.:Fant for 2 Pnos, w. V. Georgieva (pno) Gega ▲ GD 139 [DDD]
Tast, William (fl)
Mozart, W.A.:Andante Fl, K.315/285a, w. H. Haenchen (cnd), C.P.E. Bach CO LaserLight ▲ 15 875 [DDD]
Mozart, W.A.:Cons Fl, w. H. Haenchen (cnd), C.P.E. Bach CO LaserLight ▲ 15 873 [DDD]
Mozart, W.A.:Cons Fl, w. H. Haenchen (cnd), C.P.E. Bach CO LaserLight ▲ 14 037 [DDD]

878 ▲ = CD ♦ = Enhanced CD Δ = MD ■ = Cassette Tape □ = DCC

Tast, William (fl) (cont.)
Mozart, W.A.:Concertone Vns, w. Katharina Hanstedt (hp), H. Haenchen (cnd), C.P.E. Bach CO
Berlin Classics ▲ BER 2004
Tatanusitch, Vladimir (hn)—see ORCHESTRAS & ENSEMBLES Collegium dell'Arte
Tate, Grady (dr)
Clair de Lune & Sister Moon, w. Thomas Young (ten), Jay Leonhart (bass), Mike Renzi (pno) *(rec Nola Recording Studio, NYC, Oct 21 & 23, 1996)* Ocean ▲ OR 104
Jazz Meets the Symphony:Works of Lalo Schifrin, w. London PO, Ray Brown (db)
Atlantic ▲ 82506-2 P ■ 82506-4 P
Previn, A.:Honey & Rue, w. Kathleen Battle (sop), Chris Gekker (tpt), James Pugh (trbn), Rufus Reid (bass), A. Previn (cnd), Orch of St. Luke's Deutsche Grammophon ▲ 437787-2 ■ 437 787-4
Tateno, Izumi (pno)
Finnish Miniatures for Cello, w. Erkki Rautio (vc) *(rec Jan. 3 & 7, 1991)*
Finlandia ▲ 4509-95871-2 [DDD]
Finnish Piano Miniatures *(rec Sep. 18, & Dec. 30, 1991)* Finlandia 2-▲ 4509-95870-2 [DDD]
Grieg, E.:Son Vc, w. E. Rautio (vc) *(rec Aug. 27-30, 1991)* Finlandia ▲ 4509-95867-2 [DDD]
Grieg, E.:Son Pno *(rec Aug. 27-30, 1991)* Finlandia ▲ 4509-95867-2 [DDD]
Grieg, E.:Sons Vn, Opp. 8, 13 & 45, w. J. Söderblom (vn)—Op. 45 *(rec Aug. 27-30, 1991)*
Finlandia ▲ 4509-95867-2 [DDD]
Mamiya, M.:Con III Pno, w. K. Akiyama (cnd), Tokyo SO *(rec live Tokyo Metropolitan Theater, Large Hall, June 23, 1993)* Camerata ▲ 32CM 319 [DDD]
Merikanto, O.:Music of, w. Eeva-Jiisa Saarinen (mez), Jorma Hynninen (bar), Sauli Tiilikainen (bar), Kaija Saaikettu (vn), Erkki Rautio (vc), Pertti Eerola (pno), Ralf Gothoni (pno), Raija Kerppo (pno), Tauno Satomaa (cnd), Candomino Choir—Summer Evening (waltz); Valse lente; Romance; On the Highest Tree-Top; Annina; Bye, Bye Lullabye; The Weeping Flute; At Sea; Hey My Heart; Where Rustling Birches Bend; Play Softly, the Tune of Mourning; Fairy Tale by the Fireside; Idyll; Scherzo, Op. 6/4; O Dost Thou Remember That Hymn; Lade Ladoga; Why Do I Sing; The Thunderbird; The Happy Ones; Summer Evening's Idyll Finlandia ▲ FIN 500432 [AAD/DDD]
Palmgren, S.:Pno Music—Illusion, Op. 1/2; Intermezzo, Op. 3/4; Sonette, Op. 4/3; Barcarole, Op. 14; Spring, Op. 27; Youth, Op. 28; Finnish Rhythms, Op. 31; 2 Pieces from Spring, Op. 47; 3 Pno Pieces, Op. 54; Snowflakes, Op. 57/2 Finlandia ▲ FIN 98991 [DDD]
Palmgren, S.:Preludes (24) Pno *(rec Sept. 7, 1992)* Finlandia ▲ 4509-95868-2 [DDD]
Palmgren, S.:Son Pno *(rec Sept. 7, 1992)* Finlandia ▲ 4509-95868-2 [DDD]
Sibelius, J.:Sonatina Vn, w. Y. Arai (vn) *(rec Apr. 1980)* Finlandia ▲ 4509-95853-2 [AAD]
Tátrai, (vn)
Kodály, Z.:Serenade for 2 Vns & Va, w. Várkonyi (vn), G. Konrád (va) Hungaroton ▲ HCD 31046
Tatsumi, Akiko (vn)—see also ORCHESTRAS & ENSEMBLES Akiko Tatsumi String Quartet
Yun, I.:Contrasts Vn *(rec Shibukawa City Auditorium, May 26, 1988)* Camerata ▲ 30CM 70 [AAD]
Yun, I.:Gasa, w. Yuji Takahashi (pno) *(rec Shibukawa City Auditorium, May 26, 1988)*
Camerata ▲ 30CM 70 [AAD]
Yun, I.:Königliches Thema *(rec Shibukawa City Auditorium, May 26, 1988)*
Camerata ▲ 30CM 70 [AAD]
Tattaglia, John (va)
Reger, M.:Serenade, Op. 141a, w. R. Willoughby (fl), M. McDonald (vn)
Gasparo Gallante ▲ GG 1003 [AAD]
Taub, Paul (fl)—see also ORCHESTRAS & ENSEMBLES New Performance Group of the Cornish Institute
Dresher, P.:Channels Passing, w. B. Shapiro (ob), C. Sereque (cl), R. Pressley (tpt), S. Dempster (trbn), E.M. Gray (vn), W. Gray (vc) *(rec 1983–84)* New Albion ▲ NA 053
Giteck, J.:Lenningrad Spring, w. *(other artists unknown)* New Albion ▲ NA 054
Lam, B.-C.:Another Spring, w. Walter Gray (vc), Bun-Ching Lam (pno) CRI ▲ CD 726 [DDD]
Taub, Paul (pic)
Lam, B.-C.:Bittersweet Music I CRI ▲ CD 726 [DDD]
Taub, Robert (pno)
Babbitt, M.:Pno Music (comp)—3 Compositions (1947–48); Duet (1956); Semi-simple Vars (1956); Partitions (1957); Post-partitions (1966); Tableaux (1973); Reflections for Piano & Synthesized Tape (1974); Canonical Form (1983); Lagniappe (1985) Harmonia Mundi France ▲ HMC 905160
Beethoven, L. van:Sons Pno (comp)—Nos. 1, 2, 9, 10, 13, 14, 21 & 24; Son quasi una fant *(rec Institute for Advanced Study, Princeton, NJ, Nov. 1994 & Jan. 1995)*
Vox Classics 2-▲ VOX 27514 [DDD]
Beethoven, L. van:Sons Pno (comp)—Nos. 4, 18, 19, 20, 22, 23 & 27 *(rec Nov 1995–Jan 1996)*
Vox Classics 2-▲ VOX2 7532 [DDD]
Beethoven, L. van:Son 5 Pno *(rec Wolfensohn Hall, Institute for Advanced Study, Princeton, NJ, Mar & Nov 1995)* Vox Classics 2-▲ VOX2 7529
Beethoven, L. van:Son 6 Pno *(rec Wolfensohn Hall, Institute for Advanced Study, Princeton, NJ, Mar & Nov 1995)* Vox Classics 2-▲ VOX2 7529
Beethoven, L. van:Son 7 Pno *(rec Wolfensohn Hall, Institute for Advanced Study, Princeton, NJ, Mar & Nov 1995)* Vox Classics 2-▲ VOX2 7529
Beethoven, L. van:Son 8 Pno, "Pathétique" *(rec Wolfensohn Hall, Institute for Advanced Study, Princeton, NJ, Mar & Nov 1995)* Vox Classics 2-▲ VOX2 7529
Beethoven, L. van:Son 16 Pno *(rec Wolfensohn Hall, Institute for Advanced Study, Princeton, NJ, Mar & Nov 1995)* Vox Classics 2-▲ VOX2 7529
Beethoven, L. van:Son 28 Pno *(rec Wolfensohn Hall, Institute for Advanced Study, Princeton, NJ, Mar & Nov 1995)* Vox Classics 2-▲ VOX2 7529
Persichetti, V.:Con Pno, w. C. Dutoit (cnd), Philadelphia Orch New World ▲ NW 370-2 [DDD]
Powell, Mel:Duplicates, w. A. Feinberg (pno), D.A. Miller (cnd), Los Angeles PO
Harmonia Mundi USA ▲ HMU 907096
Sessions, R.:Con Pno, w. P.L. Dunkel (cnd), Westchester PO *(rec Jan. 17, 1994)*
New World ▲ 80443-2
Taube, G. (vn)
Taube, E.:Där blaser, w. S. Forssén (pno), Gothenburg Chamber Choir Prophone ▲ PCD 003
Taube, Michael (pno)
The Columbia Recordings, Vol. 2, w. Jacqueline Du Pré (vc), Theo van der Pas (pno), Gerald Moore (pno), Wolfgang Rebner (pno) *(rec 1930–1939)* Pearl ▲ PEA 9443 (m) [AAD]
Tauber, Charles (pno)
Sarasate, P. de:Vn & Pno Music, w. Charles Castleman (vn), Barbara Lister-Sink (pno)—Faust Fant.; Carmen; Zigeunerweisen; Les Adieux; Zapateado; Malaguena; Romance; others
Music & Arts ▲ CD 855 [DDD]
Taubl, Norbert (cl)—see ORCHESTRAS & ENSEMBLES Vienna Chamber Ensemble members
Taublieb, Diane (fl)
Kraft, L.:Cloud Studies, w. Lisa Maron (pic), Margaret Swinchoski (pic), Tanya Dusevic (fl), Adrienne Flynn (fl), Christina Jennings (fl), Zara Lawler (fl), Joseph Piscitelli (fl), Michelle Ryang (fl), Dominique Soucy (fl), Laurel Ann Maurer (alt fl), Richard Wyton (alt fl), J. Solum (cnd) *(rec Skinner Recital Hall, Vassar College, Poughkeepsie, NY, Mar 24-26, 1994)* CRI ▲ CD 712 [DDD]
Taubman, Leo (pno)
The Voices of Living Stereo, Vol. 2, w. Eileen Farrell (sop), Birgit Nilsson (sop), Roberta Peters (sop), Leontyne Price (sop), Galina Vishnevskaya (sop), Rosalind Elias (mez), Shirley Verrett (mez), Marian Anderson (cta), Maureen Forrester (cta), Sergio Franchi (ten), Mario Lanza (ten), Richard Lewis (ten), Jan Pee, Alexander Dedyukhin (pno), Franz Rupp (pno), George Trovillo (pno), Charles Wadsworth (pno), Boston Pops Orch [cnd:Arthur Fiedler], Boston SO [cnd:Charles Munch], Chicago SO [cnd:Fritz Reiner], RCA Victor Orch, RCA Victor Chorus [cnd:Wa *(rec Boston & Chicago & New York & Rome, 1957-1964)* RCA Living Stereo ▲ 09026-68167-2 [ADD]
Taussig, E. (pno)
Schubert, Franz:Qnt Pno, D.667, w. R. Ricci (vn), M. Virizly (vc), E. Klemmstein (va), G. Karr (db)
One-Eleven ▲ URS 92010
Tavares, Gustavo (vc)
Graziani, C.:Sons Vc, Op. 3, w. Antonio Meneses (vc), Rosana Lanzelotte (hpd)
Sanctus 2-▲ 002/003 [DDD]
Tavener, John (pno)
Tavener, J.:Melina, w. P. Rozario (sop) Collins Classics ▲ COL 1428 [DDD]
Tavener, John (pno) (cont.)
Tavener, J.:Mini Song Cycle, w. P. Rozario (sop) Collins Classics ▲ COL 1428 [DDD]
Tavernier, Michel (bn)
Klein, G.:Divert Ob, w. Jean-Pierre Arnaud (ob), Jean-Marc Liet (ob), Rémi Lerner (cl), Christian Rocca (cl), Amaury Wallez (bn), Éric Karcher (hn), Philippe Queyraud (hn) Arion ▲ ARN 68272 [DDD]
Tawaststjerna, Erik T. (pno)
Sibelius, J.:Pno Music—3 Lyric Pieces, Op. 41; 6 Impromptus, Op. 5; Sonata in F, Op. 12; 6 Finnish Folksongs (1903) BIS ▲ CD 153
Sibelius, J.:Pno Music—10 Pieces, Op. 24; 10 Pieces, Op. 34 BIS ▲ CD 169
Sibelius, J.:Pno Music—10 Pieces, Op. 58; Pensées lyriques, Op. 40 BIS ▲ CD 195
Sibelius, J.:Pno Music—3 Sonatinas, Op. 67; 2 Rondinos, Op. 68; 4 Lyric Pieces, Op. 74; 13 Pieces, Op. 76 BIS ▲ CD 196
Sibelius, J.:Pno Music—5 Pieces, Op. 75; 5 Pieces, Op. 85; 6 Pieces, Op. 94; 6 Bagatelles, Op. 97
BIS ▲ CD 230
Sibelius, J.:Pno Music—8 Pieces, Op. 99; 5 Romantic Pieces, Op. 101; 5 Pieces, Op. 103; 5 Esquisses, Op. 114; Morceau romantique (1925); Kavaljaren (1900) BIS ▲ CD 278
Sibelius, J.:Pno Transcriptions (comp) BIS ▲ CD 367
Sibelius, J.:Pno Transcriptions (comp) BIS ▲ CD 366
Sibelius, J.:Qnt Pno, w. Sibelius Academy String Quartet *(rec Jan. 1985)*
Finlandia ▲ 4509-95858-2 [DDD]
Taweel, Neville (vn)
Stravinsky, I.:Pastorale, w. Derek Wickens (ob), Leonard Brain (E hn), Thomas Kelly (cl), John Price (bn), L. Stokowski (cnd), Royal PO *(rec Kingsway Hall, London, England, June 16–17, 1969)*
London ("Phase 4 Stereo" series) ▲ 443898-2 [ADD]
Taylor, David (lt)—see also ORCHESTRAS & ENSEMBLES Echos Muse
Dowland, J.:Lt Music—Lachrimae; Tarleton's Riserrectione *(rec 1/91)* Arabesque ▲ Z 6622 [DDD]
Taylor, Andrew Kohji (pno)
Bach, J.S.:Con 1 for 2 Hpds, w. Alfred Genovese (ob), P. van Haeren (cnd), New England CO [orig Bach version for Ob & Vn] *(rec Campion Center, Weston, MA, Feb 1993)* Boston Records ▲ BR 1007
Mozart, W.A.:Con 3 Vn, w. P. van Haeren (cnd), New England CO *(rec Campion Center, Weston, MA, Feb 1993)* Boston Records ▲ BR 1007
Taylor, Bobby (ob)—see ORCHESTRAS & ENSEMBLES Blair Woodwind Quintet
Taylor, David (b trbn)
Dlugoszewski, L.:Duende Quidditas, w. Lucia Dlugoszewski (pno) *(rec live, Solomon R. Guggenheim Museum, Oct 23, 1983)* New World ▲ 80494-2
Ewazen, E.:Dagon II *(rec Chelsea Sound Studios, NYC, Jan 22, 1981)* New World ▲ 80494-2
Franzetti, C.:Concertino Bass Trbn, w. Lois Colin (hp), Carlos Franzetti (pno), C. Franzetti (cnd), Modus Chamber Ensemble *(rec Hip Pocket Studios, New York)* Premier ▲ PRCD 1044 [DDD]
Liebman, D.:Remembrance, w. Bill Blount (cl), Stephen Taylor (ob), Alan Cox (fl), Dennis Godburn (bn)
New World ▲ 80494-2
Rzewski, F.:Moonrise with Memories, w. David Carp (kazoo), Bill Blount (cl), Allan Dean (tpt), Louise Schulman (vn), Robert Wolinsky (gtr), Bill Moersch (mar/dlc) *(rec RCA Studios, NYC, June 4, 1981)*
New World ▲ 80494-2
Taylor, David (trbn)
Lieberson, P.:King Gesar, w. Yo-Yo Ma (vc), Emanuel Ax (pno), Peter Serkin (pno), Omar Ebrahim (nar), Andras Adorjan (fl), Deborah Marshall (cl), William Purvis (hn), Stefan Huge (perc)
Sony Classical ▲ SK 57971
Stravinsky, I.:Octet, w. M. Parloff (fl), D. Schiffrin (cl), F. Morelli (bn), S. Heinneman (bn), R. Mase (tpt), C. Gekker (tpt), R. Borror (trbn), G. Schuller (cnd) *(rec Sep. 1991)* GM ▲ GM 2030
Wigglesworth, F.:Psalm 148, w. Kathy Fink (fl), Elizabeth Brown (fl), Jeanne Wilson (fl), Kevin James (trbn), D. Schuler (cnd), Church of St. Luke in the Fields Choir CRI ▲ C 733 [DDD]
Wuorinen, C.:Archaeopteryx, w. C. Wuorinen (cnd), St. Luke's Chamber Ensemble *(rec June 14–17, 1991)* Koch International Classics ▲ KIC 7110-2 [DDD]
Wuorinen, C.:Archangel, w. B. Hudson (vn), C. Zeavin (vn), L. Schulman (va), F. Sherry (vc) *(rec March 31, 1981)* Koch International Classics ▲ KIC 7110-2 [DDD]
Wuorinen, C.:Trio Bass Trbn, w. D. Braynard (tuba), D. Palma (db) *(rec Sept. 11–13, 1991)*
Koch International Classics ▲ KIC 7123-2 [DDD]
Taylor, David (vn)
Haydn, M.:Divert Vn, Vc & Db, w. Gary Stucka (vc), Jerry Fuller (db) *(rec WTMT Studio 1, Jan 24, 1993)*
Musical Arts Society ▲ MAS 41595 [DDD]
Vanhal, J.B.:Divert Strs, w. Li-Kuo Chang (va), Jerry Fuller (db) *(rec WTMT Studio 1, Jan 24, 1993)*
Musical Arts Society ▲ MAS 41595 [DDD]
Taylor, J. (bn)—see ORCHESTRAS & ENSEMBLES American Brass Quintet
Taylor, John (org)
Carr, I.:Music of, w. I. Carr (tpt/flgl)—12 works inspired by Shakespeare *(rec May 30–31, 1992)*
Celestial Harmonies ▲ 13064-2
Taylor, Joseph Paul (elec/syn)
Sharp, E.:20 Below, w. Anthony Coleman (toy pno/org), Wayne Horvitz (syn), Zeena Parkins (org/syn), Gwen Toth (reed org), David Weinstein (org/syn) Newport Classics ▲ NPD 85504
Taylor, Marshall (sax)—see also ORCHESTRAS & ENSEMBLES Relâche Ensemble
Davidson, T.:Lullaby, w. Carol Brown (fl), Lloyd Shorter (E hn), Charles Holdeman (bn), Charles Abramovic (pno) CRI ▲ CD 681 [DDD]
Davidson, T.:Transparent Victims CRI ▲ CD 681 [DDD]
Taylor, Martin (gtr)
Just One of Those Things, w. Stéphane Grappelli (vn) EMI Classics ▲ CDM 69172
Taylor, Paul Arden (E hn)
Copland, A.:Quiet City, w. John Wallace (tpt), W. Boughton (cnd), English SO
Nimbus ▲ NI 5246 [DDD]
Copland, A.:Quiet City, w. John Wallace (tpt), W. Boughton (cnd), English SO
Nimbus ▲ NI 4002 [ADD/DDD]
Taylor, Shelley (vc)—see also ORCHESTRAS & ENSEMBLES Zephyrus, Zephyrus members
Handel, G.F.:Sons Ob, w. Gonzalo X. Ruiz (ob), Michael Eagan (archlt), Kathy Shao (hpd/org)—in Bb, after HWV 365; in g, HWV 364; in d, HWV 359a; in Bb, HWV 357; in a, after HWV 367b; in F, HWV 363a; in c, HWV 366 Well-Tempered ▲ WTP 5174 [DDD]
Taylor, Shirien (vn)
Haydn, J.:Diverts Fl, Vn & Vc, w. Laurel Zucker (fl), Samuel Magill (vc)—in D, H.IV/6; in G, H.IV/7; H.IV/8 *(rec Concordia College)* Cantilena ▲ 66013-2 [DDD]
Mozart, W.A.:Qts Fl, w. Laurel Zucker (fl), Mary Hammann (va), Sam Magill (vc)—K.285, 285b & 298 *(rec Academy of Arts & Letters, New York City, June 11, 1994)* Cantilena ▲ C 660072 [DDD]
Taylor, Stephen (ob)
Bach, J.S.:Con Vn & Ob, w. P. Peabody (vn), R. Kapp (cnd), Philharmonia Virtuosi
ESS.A.Y ▲ CD 1002 [DDD] ■ C 1002 (D)
Liebman, D.:Remembrance, w. David Taylor (b trbn), Bill Blount (cl), Alan Cox (fl), Dennis Godburn (bn)
New World ▲ 80494-2
Poulenc, F.:Sxt Pno, w. André Previn (pno), Elizabeth Mann (fl), David Shifrin (cl), Dennis Godburn (bn), Richard Todd (hn) *(rec Manhattan Center Studios, New York City, Apr. 7–8, 1993)*
RCA Red Seal ▲ 09026-68181-2 [DDD]
Wolpe, S.:Qt Ob, w. F. Sherry (vc), D. Kennedy (perc), A. Karis (pno) *(rec Nov. 9–10, 1991)*
Koch ▲ KIC 7112 [DDD]
Taylor, Stewart (trbn)
Kurtág, G.:The Little Predicament, w. S. Palma (pic), D. Starobin (gtr)
Bridge ▲ BCD 9004 ■ BC5-7004
Martin, F.:Ballade Trbn (or T Sax), w. B. Berman (pno) Gallo ▲ CD 633 [DDD]
Taylor, V. (pno)—see ORCHESTRAS & ENSEMBLES Videmus members
Taylor, Virginia (fl)
Taylor & Kain, w. Timothy Kain (gtr) Tall Poppies ▲ TP 3 [DDD]
Taylor, William (hp)—see ORCHESTRAS & ENSEMBLES Rowallan Consort
Tchaikovsky, Boris (pno)
Tchaikovsky, B.:Son Vc, w. A. Vasilieva (vc) Russian Disc ▲ RUS 11 026 [ADD]

INSTRUMENT.

Tchakerian, Sonick (vn)—see ORCHESTRAS & ENSEMBLES Trio Italiano
Tchaplygina, Alla (vc)—see ORCHESTRAS & ENSEMBLES Moscow Ancient Music Ensemble members
Tchavdarov, Zahari (va)
Bashmakov, L.:Con da camera, w. Gunilla von Bahr (pic/fl), Paavo Pohjola (vn), Mona Nordin (vn), Elemér Lavotha (vc) *(rec Grünewald Hall, Stockholm, Sweden, May 11, 1974)* BIS ▲ CD 11 [AAD]
Hindemith, P.:Son Va & Pno, Op. 25/4 *(rec Feb. 14, 1977)* BIS ▲ CD 81 [AAD]
Pergament, M.:Pezzo, w. G. von Bahr (fls), P. Pohjola (vn), Z. Zirchev (vn), U. Vrethammar (vc) *(rec Jan. 25, 1973)* BIS ▲ CD 37 [AAD]
Reger, M.:Suites Va—Suite No. 1 in g *(rec Feb. 14, 1977)* BIS ▲ CD 81 [AAD]
Shostakovich, D.:Son Va, w. A. Zaharieva (pno) *(rec Jan. 15, 1977)* BIS ▲ CD 81 [AAD]
Tchekina, Tatiana (pno)
Schnittke, A.:Trio Pno, w. Oleh Krysa (vn), Torleif Thedéen (vc) *(rec Malmö Concert Hall, Sweden, May 12–14, 1994)* BIS ▲ CD 697 [DDD]
Schulhoff, E.:Son 1 Vn, w. Oleh Krysa (vn) *(rec Danderyd Grammar School, Sweden, Dec 10–11, 1994)* BIS ▲ CD 679 [DDD]
Tchicai, John (t sax/sgr/perc)
Blak, K.:Con Grotto, w. Lennart Kullgren (gtr/fl/sgr/perc), Anders Hagberg (fl/perc/sgr), Kristian Blak (pno/perc/sgr), Anders Jormin (bass instr/perc/sgr), Karin Korpelainen (perc/sgr), Sharon Weiss (perc/kaval) *(rec Lidargjógv, Sandoy, Aug. 1984)* Tutl ▲ HJF 33
Tchinakajev, Chanjafi (ob)
Bach, J.S.:Con Vn & Ob, w. Mikhail Gantvarg (vn), M. Gantvarg (cnd), St. Petersburg Soloists Audiophile Classics ▲ 101.021
Tchutchov, Victor (pno)
Mozart, W.A.:Qnt Pno, K.452, w. L. Oshavkova (fl), C. T. Kasmetski (ob), P. Radev (cl), S. Kunchev (hn) Divertimento ▲ DIV 31020 [DDD]
Teachey, Philip (ob)
Mozart, W.A.:Qnt Pno, K.452, w. Landon Bilyeu (pno), Charles West (cl), Bruce Hammel (bn), Alan Paterson (hn) Klavier ▲ KCD 11072 [DDD]
Teal, Christian (vn)—see ORCHESTRAS & ENSEMBLES Blair String Quartet
Tebbet, Roger (org)
Alain, J.:Vars sur un thème de Jannequin Amphion ▲ PHI 139 [DDD]
Dubois, T.:Toccata Org Amphion ▲ PHI 139 [DDD]
Dupré, M.:Vars sur un vieux Noël Amphion ▲ PHI 139 [DDD]
Franck, C.:Chorals Org, M.38–40—No. 1 in E Amphion ▲ PHI 139 [DDD]
Widor, C.M.:Sym 5 Org Amphion ▲ PHI 139 [DDD]
TeBrake, N. (vn)
Bach, J.S.:Cons Vn (comp), w. J. Schröder (vn), S. Ritchie, R. Brown, J. Griffin, M. Lutszke, M. Willems, A. Fuller *(rec June 6–8, 1986)* Reference ▲ RR 23 CD [DDD]
Vivaldi, A.:Cons for 2 Vns, w. J. Schröder (vn), S. Ritchie (vn), R. Brown (vn), J. Griffin (va), M. Lutszke (vc), M. Willems (db), A. Fuller (hpd) *(rec June 6–8, 1986)* Reference ▲ RR 23 CD [DDD]
Tecco, Romuald (vn)
Copland, A.:Qt Pno, w. D.R. Davies (pno), K. Harrison (va), L. Duckles (vc) MusicMasters ▲ 7026-2-C [DDD]
Copland, A.:Son Vn & Pno, w. D.R. Davies (pno) MusicMasters ▲ 7026-2-C [DDD]
Copland, A.:Vitebsk:Study on a Jewish Theme, w. L. Duckles (vc), D.R. Davies (pno) MusicMasters ▲ 7026-2-C [DDD]
Corelli, A.:Concerti grossi, Op. 6, w. L. Shank (vn), J. Koestenbaum (vc), C. Hogwood (cnd), St. Paul CO—No. 2 *(rec May 1992)* London ▲ 440376-2
Corelli, A.:Trio Sons, Op. 3, w. L. Shank (vn), L. James (org) *(rec Jan. 1993)* London ▲ 440376-2
Harrison, L.:Grand Duo, w. Dennis Russell Davies (pno) *(rec. Cabrillo Music Festival, Santa Cruz, CA, 1988)* MusicMasters ▲ 7073-2-C [DDD]
Holst, G.:A Fugal Con, w. J. Bogorad (vn), K. Greenbank (vn), L. Shank (vn), J. Koestenbaum (vc), C. Hogwood (cnd), St. Paul CO *(rec May 1992)* London ▲ 440376-2
Holst, G.:Savitri, w. L. Shank (vn), J. Koestenbaum (vc), C. Hogwood (cnd), St. Paul CO *(rec May 1992)* London ▲ 440376-2
Tippett, M.:Fant Concertante on a Theme of Corelli, w. L. Shank (vn), J. Koestenbaum (vc), C. Hogwood (cnd), St. Paul CO *(rec May 1992)* London ▲ 440376-2
Tedesco, Edmondo (cl)
Petrassi, G.:Grand septuor Cl, w. A. Molino (cnd), Compania Stradivarius ▲ STR 33347
Tedla, M. (vn)
Zimmermann, A.:Cassations, w. V. Brunner (fl), J. Brunner (fl), J. Vondra (hn), P. Sivanic (hn), V. Simcisko (vn), M. Telecky (va), J. Alexander (vc)—in G, D & D Trevak ▲ TRE 40008 [DDD]
Tees, Stephen (va)—see also ORCHESTRAS & ENSEMBLES Academy of St. Martin in the Fields Chamber Ensemble
Alwyn, W.:Pastoral Fant, w. R. Hickox (cnd), City of London Sinfonia Chandos ▲ CHAN 9065 [DDD]
Tavener, J.:To a Child Dancing in the Wind, w. P. Rozario (sop), K. Lukas (fl), H. Tunstall (hp) Collins Classics ▲ COL 1428 [DDD]
Teglbjærg, Christen Stubbe (pno)
Schierbeck, P.:Songs, w. Henriette Bonde-Hansen (sop)—I Danmark; Alverden går omkring; Sommerklange og Vintertoner; Fjerne Melodier; Fem Sange; Nakjælen *(rec Copenhagen, June 1995)* Marco Polo/Dacapo ▲ 8.224017 [DDD]
Teherani, Kevan (perc)
Strauss (I), Joh.:Radetzky March, w. Ralf Kircher (perc), Rudolf Schmidinger (perc), Brassissimo Vienna *(rec Pfarrkirche Staatz, Nov 29–Dec 2, 1993)* Brassissimo ▲ BVR 2328517 [DDD]
Strauss (II), Joh.:Music of, w. Ralf Kircher (perc), Rudolf Schmidinger (perc), Brassissimo Vienna—Maskenball-Quadrille; Unter Donner und Blitz; Etwas Kleines; Kaiserwalzer; Annenpolka; Waldmeister-Ov; Leichtes Blut; Auf der Jagd; Pizzikato-Polka [composed w. Josef Strauss]; Elyen a Magyar; Perpetuum Mobile; Fledermaus-Ov *(rec Pfarrkirche Staatz, Nov 29–Dec 2, 1993)* Brassissimo ▲ BVR 2328517 [DDD]
Strauss, Josef:Music of, w. Ralf Kircher (perc), Rudolf Schmidinger (perc), Brassissimo Vienna—Ohne Sorgen; Moulinet-Polka; Pizzikato-Polka [composed w. Johann Strauss II]; Feuerfest *(rec Pfarrkirche Staatz, Nov 29–Dec 2, 1993)* Brassissimo ▲ BVR 2328517 [DDD]
Teikari, Jouko (ob)—see ORCHESTRAS & ENSEMBLES Helsinki Wind Quintet
Teirup, Teddy (pno)
Stolarczyk, W.:Earth Air Fire Water, w. Amalie Malling (pno), John Damgaard (pno), Anne Øland (pno), Friedrich Gürtler (pno), Rosalind Bevan (pno), Poul Rosenbaum (pno), Rodolfo Llambias (pno), Bella Horn-Ribera (pno), Anders Riber (pno), Elisabeth Sigurdsson (pno), Thomas Tronheim (pno), Elsebeth Broderson (pno), Erik Kaltoft (pno), Jørgen Hald Nielsen (pno), Aino Gilemann (pno), Birgit Kjær (pno), Jørgen Thomsen (pno), Gunhild Donslund (pno), Henrik Bo Hansen (pno), Lone Karlsson (pno), Erik Fessel (pno), Lasse Nilsson (pno), Janos Ferenczi (pno), Erik Bach (pno), Axel Momme (pno), Arne de Cros Dich (pno), Sven Micha Slot (pno), Hanne Bramsen Buhl (pno), Lili Olesen (pno), Susannah Carlsson (pno), Ulla Erml (pno), Vagn Sørensen (pno), Leif Greibe (pno), Bodil Krogh (pno), Kirsten Ottosen (pno), Inger Bergenholz (pno), Karsten Gylendorf (pno), Bjørn Elkjær (pno), Jacob Bjørn Jensen (pno), Jørgen Kaad (pno), Anne Marie Hjelm (pno), Carl Ulrik Munk Andersen (pno), Poul Lumbye (pno), Oluf Hildebrandt Nielsen (pno), Joachim Olsson (pno), Peter Pade Ramsøe Jacobsen (pno), Astrid Pollmann (pno), Jette Borsch (pno), Kirsten Karlshøj (pno), Maria Teresa Assing (pno), Allan Dahl Hansen (pno), Johan Hugossen (pno), Tine Fenger Pederson (pno), Arne Jørgen Fæø (pno), Anja Høgsted (pno), Anne Sophie Parbo (pno), Inga Lindmark (pno), Teresa Drabik Stathakis (pno), Anne Ruth Ferenczi (pno), Irene Hasager (pno), Yuka Ichikawa (pno), Birgitte Baur (pno), Malene Thastum (pno), Jens E. Rasmussen (pno), Birgitte Zielke (pno), Claus Zielke (pno), Stefan Kasch (pno), Bin Qiao (pno), Inger Johanne Teirup (pno), Lindy Rosborg (pno), Liisa Heininen (pno), David Højer (pno), Ellen Refstrup (pno), Thomas K. Søorensen (pno), Erik Kure (pno), Michael Rauff (pno), Jan beck Eriksson (pno), Tanja Zapolski (pno), Vibeke Skagbo (pno), Pål Eide Lindtner (pno), Ha-Young Sul (pno), Benedicte Palko (pno), Inke Kesseler (pno), Anne Marie Meineche (pno), Sverre Larsen (pno), Kasper Peter Bach (pno), Elisabetta Eliseo (pno), Olga Magieres (pno), Carl Erik Kühl (pno), Thorkild Borup Nielsen (pno), Valeria Zanini (pno), Lars Stenhoft (perc), Dennis Boel (perc), Winnie Dahlgren (perc), Susanne Vind (perc), Claus Byrith (elec), Anne Marie Storm (elec), J. Ribera (cnd) *(rec live, Koldinghaus Castle, Denmark, May 2, 1996)* Danica ▲ DCD 1996
Telecky, Milan (va)
Romberg, A.:Qnts Fl, w. V. Brunner (fl), V. Simcisko (vn), J. Cút (va), J. Alexander (vc) Trevak ▲ TRE 40007 [DDD]
Sperger, J.:Trios, w. M. Jukovic (fl), V. Dufka (ob), V. Simcisko (vn), J. Alexander (vc), sels. unknown Trevak ▲ TRE 40002 [DDD]
Zimmermann, A.:Cassations, w. V. Brunner (fl), J. Brunner (fl), J. Vondra (hn), P. Sivanic (hn), V. Simcisko (vn), M. Tedla (vn), J. Alexander (vc)—in G, D & D Trevak ▲ TRE 40008 [DDD]
Tellefsen, Arve (vn)
Debussy, C.:Son Vn, w. Hans Pålsson (pno) *(rec Nacka Aula, Nacka, Sweden, Apr. 28, 1975)* BIS ▲ CD 28 [AAD]
Elling, C.:Con Vn, w. M. Jansons (cnd), Oslo PO NKF ▲ NKFCD 50021
Fauré, G.:Trio, w. F. Helmerson (vc), H. Pålsson (pno) *(rec Apr. 26–27, 1975)* BIS ▲ CD 35 [AAD]
Franck, C.:Son Vn, w. H. Pålsson (pno) *(rec Oct. 24, 1975)* BIS ▲ CD 35 [AAD]
Nielsen, C.:Con Vn, w. Y. Menuhin (cnd), Royal PO Virgin Classics ("Ultraviolet" series) ▲ CUV 61136
Prokofiev, S.:Son Vc, w. F. Helmerson (vc), H. Pålsson (pno) *(rec June 13, 1975)* BIS ▲ CD 35 [AAD]
Shostakovich, D.:Trio 2 Pno, w. H. Palsson (pno), F. Helmerson (vc) BIS ▲ CD 26 [AAD]
Stenhammar, W.:Sentimental Romances, w. S. Westerberg (cnd), Swedish RSO Caprice ▲ CAP 21358
Valen, F.:Con Vn, w. C. Eggen (cnd), Norwegian Broadcasting Orch Simax ▲ PSC 3116
Tellini, D. (vn)
Milesi, P.:Modi 1, w. D. Cassamagnaghi (fl), F. Pomarico (ob), A. Bianchi (cl), L. Dosso (bn), G. Govi (vn), M. Ravasio (va), S. Righini (vc), P. Rizzi (db), C. Vignani (hpd), J. Scully (perc), P. Milesi (cnd) Cuneiform ▲ RUNE 63
Telmányi, Emil (vn)
Brahms, J.:Hungarian Dances Pno 4-Hands, w. G. Vásárhelyi (pno)—No. 1 in g [arr. for violin & piano] *(rec Berlin April 1939)* Danacord ▲ DACOCD 343 (m) [AAD]
Brahms, J.:Scherzo Vn, w. G. Vásárhelyi (pno) *(rec April 1939, Berlin)* Danacord ▲ DACOCD 343 (m) [AAD]
Brahms, J.:Son 1 Vn, w. G. Vásárhelyi (pno) *(rec Berlin, April 1939)* Danacord ▲ DACOCD 343 (m) [AAD]
Brahms, J.:Son 2 Vn, w. G. Vásárhelyi (pno) *(rec Berlin, April 1939)* Danacord ▲ DACOCD 343 (m) [AAD]
Telrup, Teddy (pno)
Lauridsen, L.:From My Dreamworld Rondo Grammofon ▲ RCD 8316
Lauridsen, L.:From My Walking Tours Rondo Grammofon ▲ RCD 8316
Lauridsen, L.:Trio Vn, Va & Pno, w. Niels Øllegaard (vn), Henrik Krarup (va) Rondo Grammofon ▲ RCD 8316
Temianka, Henri (vn)
Arensky, A.:Trio 1 Pno, w. E. Joyce (pno), A. Sala (vc) *(rec 1938)* Biddulph 2-▲ LAB 059/60 [ADD]
Indy, V. d':Son Vn, w. Albert Dominguez (pno) *(rec Loas Angeles, CA, 1973)* Orion ▲ 7820-2 [AAD]
Lalo, E.:Son Vn *(rec Los Angeles, CA, 1973)* Orion ▲ 7820-2 [AAD]
The Parlophone Recordings *(rec 1935–39)* Biddulph 2-▲ LAB 059/60 [ADD]
Schubert, Franz:Rondo Vn, D.438, Temianka CO *(rec 1937)* Biddulph 2-▲ LAB 059/60 [ADD]
Sibelius, J.:Humoresques, w. H. Temianka (cnd), Temianka CO—Op. 89/4 *(rec 1937)* Biddulph 2-▲ LAB 059/60 [ADD]
Tempel, Thomas (E hn)
Copland, A.:Quiet City, w. G. Bordner (tpt), H. Wolff (cnd), St. Paul CO Teldec ▲ 2292-46314-2 [DDD]
Templeman, Wayne (vc)
Encore, w. Colorado Children's Chorale, Duain Wolfe (cnd), Rick Chinski (gtr), Robert Davine (acc), Laurie Kahler (pno), Samuel Lancaster (pno), Barry Oliver (pno), Marylin Preston (fl), Karen Yonovitz (fl), Peter Cooper (ob), Andy Stevens (cl), Lionel Young (vn), Basil Vendreys (va), Wayne Templeman (vc), Charle *(rec Denver Center Media)* Colorado Children's Chorale ▲ 001
Tenenbaum, Alexandr (vn)—see ORCHESTRAS & ENSEMBLES Philharmonia Virtuosi
Tenenbaum, Mela (vn)—see also ORCHESTRAS & ENSEMBLES Philharmonia Virtuosi
Locatelli, P.:L'arte del violino, w. R. Kapp (cnd), Kiev Pro Musica, Philharmonia Virtuosi—Nos. 1–6 *(rec Kiev, Ukraine, Oct. 1994–95)* ESS.A.Y ▲ CD 1043/44 [DDD]
Tea Time:A Collection of Favorites for Violin & Piano, w. Anton Nel (pno) *(rec Purchase College, Recital Hall, Sept 1994)* ESS.A.Y. ▲ 1042 [DDD]
Vivaldi, A.:Cons Vn (misc), w. R. Kapp (cnd), Philharmonia Virtuosi—Cons for Vn & 2 Orchs *(rec Recital Hall, Purchase College, Purchase, NY, Oct. 22 & 23, 1995)* ESS.A.Y ▲ CD 1046 [DDD]
Tenenbom, Steven (va)
Prokofiev, S.:Qnt Ob, w. A. Vogel (ob), D. Shifrin (cl), P. Frank (vn), E. Meyer (db) *(rec July 1–4, 1992)* Delos ▲ DE 3136 [DDD]
Schubert, Franz:Qnt Strs, D.956, w. P. Frank (vn), F. Galimir (vn), P. Wiley (vc), J. Lichten (vc) Sony Classical ▲ SMK 45901 [ADD/DDD] ▮ SMT 45901
Vivaldi, A.:Cons Va d'amore, w. R. Kapp (cnd), Philharmonia Virtuosi—RV.394 ESS.A.Y ▲ CD 1022 [DDD]
Tenisch, Markus (org)
Holliger, H.:Alb-Chehr, w. Oswald Brumann (bass), Sabine Gertschen (dlc), Edmund Volken (dlc), Elmar Schmid (cl), Klaus Schmid (cl), Marcel Volken (Swiss org), Paul Locher (vn), Franziskus Abgottspon (nar) ECM New Series ▲ 78118-21540-2 [DDD]
Tennant, Scott (gtr)—see also ORCHESTRAS & ENSEMBLES Los Angeles Guitar Quartet
Guitar Recital GHA ▲ 126.011
Moreno Torroba, F.:Suite castellana GHA ▲ 126.034
Rodrigo, J.:Gtr Music—Por los Campos de España; Pajaros de Primavera; Tiento Antiguo; Piezas Pequeñas (3); Invocation et Danse GHA ▲ 126.026
Teodorescu, Mihai (fl)
Enescu, G.:Dectet Ww, w. N. Alexandru (fl), C. Silvestri (cnd) Electrecord ▲ ELCD 122 [AAD]
Enescu, G.:Oct Strs, w. N. Alexandru (fl), C. Silvestri (cnd) Electrecord ▲ ELCD 122 [AAD]
Teplyakov, Ilya (vn)—see ORCHESTRAS & ENSEMBLES St. Petersburg String Quartet
Tepponen, Sakari (vn)
Sibelius, J.:Swanwhite (incidental), w. Pauli Pietiläinen (org), O. Vänskä (cnd), Lahti SO *(rec Church of the Cross, Lahti, Finland, Jan 8–12, 1996)* BIS ▲ CD 815 [DDD]
Terakado, Ryo (va)
Bach, W.F.:Duets (3) Vas, w. Francois Fernandez (va) *(rec 1992)* Ricercar 2-▲ 089125/26
Mozart, W.A.:Qnt Strs, K.515, w. Kuijken String Quartet Denon ▲ DEN 78850 [DDD]
Mozart, W.A.:Qnt Strs, K.516, w. Kuijken String Quartet Denon ▲ DEN 78850 [DDD]
Terakado, Ryo (vn)—see also ORCHESTRAS & ENSEMBLES Ricercar Consort
Biber, H. von:Mystery (or Rosary) Sons, w. Siebe Henstra (hpd/org), Kaori Uemura (viol)—Passacaglia; Son. 6 *(rec Oud-Katholieke Kerk, The Hague, Netherlands, Aug. 11–12, 15–17, 1994)* Denon ▲ CO 78946 [DDD]
Biber, H. von:Sons Vn & Continuo, w. Siebe Henstra (hpd/org), Kaori Uemura (viol)—V in e [from 8 vn sons.]; VI in c; VIII in a *(rec Oud-Katholieke Kerk, the Hague, Netherlands, Aug. 11–12, 15–17, 1994)* Denon ▲ CO 78946 [DDD]
Biber, H. von:Son violino solo representativa, w. Siebe Henstra (hpd/org), Kaori Uemura (viol) *(rec Oud-Katholieke Kerk, the Hague, Netherlands, Aug. 11–12, 15–17, 1994)* Denon ▲ CO 78946 [DDD]
Clérambault, L.N.:Cants, w. Noémi Rime (sop), Jean-Paul Fouchécourt (ten), Nicolas Riveng (bass), Hiro Kurosaki (vn), Marc Hantaï (fl), Eric Bellocq (thb), Elisabeth Matiffa (b vl), Bruno Croscet (basse de vn), W. Christie (cnd), Les Arts Florissants—Pyrame et Tisbé, La Muse de l'opéra ou les Caractères Lyriques, La Mort d'Hercule, Orphée Musique d'Abord ▲ HMA 1901329
Corelli, A.:Sons Vn, Op. 5, w. Siebe Henstra (hpd/org), Lucia Swarts (baroque vc)—Nos. 7–12 *(rec Oud-Katholieke Kerk, The Hague, Netherlands, Aug 8–10, 1994)* Denon ▲ CO 78820 [DDD]
Handel, G.F.:Sons Vn, w. H. Suzuki (baroque vc), Kaori Uemura (vl), Christophe Rousset (hpd)—in d, HWV 359a; in A, HWV 361; in G, HWV 364a; in D, HWV 371; Violin movt in a, HWV 408; Violin movt (Allegro) in c, HWV 412 Denon/PCM Digital ▲ DEN 75858 [DDD]

▲ = CD ♦ = Enhanced CD Δ = MD ▮ = Cassette Tape □ = DCC

Terakado, Ryo (vn) (cont.)
Leclair, J.-M.:Sons Vn (Books 1–4), w. K. Uemura (va da gamba), H. Suzuki (vc), C. Rousset (hpd)—"Troisieme livre" (Book 3), Op. 5 *(rec Feb. 26–Mar. 9, 1993)* Denon/PCM Digital ▲ DEN 75720 [DDD]
Rameau, J.P.:Pièces de clavecin en concert, w. Christophe Rousset (hpd), Kaori Uemura (vl) Harmonia Mundi ▲ HMX 2901418
Telemann, G.P.:Qts, Book 4, w. Masahiro Arita (trns fl), Kaori Uemura (vl), Cristophe Rousset (hpd) Denon ▲ DEN 78844 [DDD]
Tercieux, Thomas (vn)—see ORCHESTRAS & ENSEMBLES Rosamunde String Quartet
Terekiev, Victoria (pno)
Donizetti, G.:Larghetto, Theme & Vars, w. M. Belli (vn) Nuova Era 2-▲ 7100/01 [DDD]
Malipiero, G.F.:Pno Music—Preludi autunnali; Maschere che passano; Barlumi; Poemetti lunari Nuova Era ▲ NUO 7150 [DDD]
Rossini, G.:Prelude, Theme & Vars Hn, w. S. Baroncini (hn) Nuova Era 2-▲ 7100/01 [DDD]
Terjung, Uta (vn)—see ORCHESTRAS & ENSEMBLES Sikorsi String Quartet
Terranova, C. (kbd)
Blanchard, P.:Music of, w. P. Blanchard (vn), V. Pagliarin (vn), C. Mouton (bass), L. Robin (dr), M. Garay (perc)—Isidora; Koid'9; Perdoname; Folklores; Train de sables; Lithops; Marguesas Keys; Bodas de sangue *(rec Nov. 1992)* OMD ▲ CD 1538 [DDD]
Terroni, Raphael (pno)
Coates, E.:Songs, w. B. Rayner (bar)—I Heard You Singing; Bird Songs of Eventide; Homeward to You; and Today Ours ASV ("White Line" series) ▲ ASV 2081
Terry, Clark (tpt)
Schwartz, C.:Mother! Mother!, w. Zoot Sims (sax), A. Weisberg (cnd), Contemporary Chamber Ensemble Pablo Today ■ 52312-115
Terry, Patricia (hp)
Kosins, M.S.:Love Letters:A Dialogue, w. B. Shank (fl), B. Badgley (vc) *(rec 1980)* Centaur ▲ CRC 2105 [ADD]
Tertis, Lionel (va)
Bach, J.S.:Chaconne *(rec 1925)* Pearl ▲ PEA 9918 (m) [AAD]
Bax, A.:Son Va & Pno, w. A. Bax (pno) *(rec 1929)* Pearl ▲ PEA 9918 (m) [AAD]
Brahms, J.:Son 2 Cl, w. H. Cohen (pno) *(rec 1933)* Pearl ▲ PEA 9918 (m) [AAD]
Delius, F.:Son 2 Vn & Pno, w. G. Reeves (pno) *(rec 1929)* Pearl ▲ PEA 9918 (m) [AAD]
Halvorsen, J.:Passacaglia & Sarabande con variazioni, w. A. Sammons (vn) *(rec 5/27/29 for Columbia Reco)* Biddulph ▲ LAB 023 [ADD]
Mendelssohn, F.:Trio 2 Pno, w. W. Murdoch (pno), A. Sammons (vn) [violin-viola-piano arr.] *(rec 12/9/25 for Columbia Reco)* Biddulph ▲ LAB 023 [ADD]
Mozart, W.A.:Sinf concertante Vn, K.364, w. A. Sammons (vn), H. Harty (cnd), London PO *(rec Apr. 30, 1933 for Columbi)* Biddulph ▲ LAB 023 [ADD]
Terwilliger, E. (hn)
Strauss, R.:Con 1 Hn, w. E. Terwilliger (cnd), Polish Chamber PO Amati ▲ 9205
Terwilliger, William (vn)
Starer, R.:Duo Vn, w. Andrew Cooperstock (pno) Albany ▲ TROY 152 [DDD]
Tesař, Zdenek (cl)
Beethoven, L van:Sxt Winds, Op. 71, w. V. Kyzivát (cl), Z. Tylšar (hn), B. Tylšar (hn), F. Herman (bn), V. Horák (bn) Supraphon ▲ 11 1445-2 [DDD]
Tessmann, Volker (bn)—see ORCHESTRAS & ENSEMBLES Acht Ensemble
Tétard, Albert (vc)
Boulez, P.:Messagesquisse, w. et al. Erato ▲ 2292-45493-2 [DDD]
Tetard, Albert (vc)
Messiaen, O.:Quatuor pour la fin du temps, w. C. Desurmont (cl), L. Yordanoff (vn), D. Barenboim (pno) Deutsche Grammophon ("20th Century Classics" series) ▲ 423247-2 [ADD]
Teti, Carol (org)
Historic Organs of New Orleans, w. George Bozeman (org), James S. Darling (org), Jesse E. Eschbach (org), Gerald D. Frank (org), John Gearhart (org), James Hammann (org), Frederick Hohman (org), Lenora McCroskey (org), Mary Gifford Matthys (org), Lorenz Maycher (org), Donald Messer (org) *(rec June 1989)* Organ Historical Society 2-▲ OHS 89
Tetley-Kardos, Richard (pno)
Glazunov, A.:Son 1 Pno Audiofon ▲ CD 72052
Reger, M.:Improvs Audiofon ▲ CD 72052
Reger, M.:Intermezzi Audiofon ▲ CD 72052
Strauss, R.:Serenade Ww [arr pno] Audiofon ▲ CD 72052
Tetzlaff, Christian (vn)
Bartók, B.:Con 2 Vn, w. M. Gielen (cnd), London PO Virgin Classics ▲ CDC 59062
Bartók, B.:Son Vn Virgin Classics ▲ CDC 59062
Dvořák, A.:Con Vn, w. L. Pešek (cnd), Czech PO Virgin Classics ▲ CDC 45022
Haydn, J.:Con 1 Vn, w. H. Schiff (cnd), Northern Sinfonia of England Virgin Classics ▲ CDC 59065
Haydn, J.:Con 3 Vn, w. H. Schiff (cnd), Northern Sinfonia of England Virgin Classics ▲ CDC 59065
Haydn, J.:Con 4 Vn, w. H. Schiff (cnd), Northern Sinfonia of England Virgin Classics ▲ CDC 59065
Janáček, L.:Con Vn, w. L. Pešek (cnd), Philharmonia Orch Virgin Classics ▲ 59076 [DDD]
Lalo, E.:Sym espagnole, w. L. Pešek (cnd), Czech PO Virgin Classics ▲ CDC 45022
Mozart, W.A.:Rondo Vn, K.373, w. H. Schiff (cnd), Northern Sinfonia of England Virgin Classics ▲ CDC 59065
Weill, K.:Con Vn, w. C. Tetzlaff (cnd), German Chamber PO Winds Virgin Classics ▲ CDC 45056
Tetzlaff, Tanja (vc)
Gabrielli, D.:Ricercares Vc—Nos. 1, 2, & 5–7 *(rec Vienna, Apr 16, 1994)* Camerata ▲ 30CM 365 [DDD]
Haydn, J.:Con 1 Vc, w. B. Perrenoud (cnd), Vienna CO *(rec Vienna, Feb 4–7, 1994)* Camerata ▲ 30CM 365 [DDD]
Haydn, J.:Con 2 Vc, w. B. Perrenoud (cnd), Vienna CO *(rec Vienna, Feb 4–7, 1994)* Camerata ▲ 30CM 365 [DDD]
Teufel, Edgar (pno)
Duparc, H.:Songs, w. C. Dagois (cta)—La vie antérieure; Le manoir de Rosemonde; Extase; Au pays où se fait la guerre; Soupir; Lamento; Phidylé Bayer ▲ 100170
Fauré, G.:Songs, w. C. Dagois (cta)—Fleur jetée; Le secret; Clair de lune; Au bord de l'eau; Automne; Mandoline; Après un rêve; Prison Bayer ▲ 100170
Teuffel, Gunter (va)
Hindemith, P.:Die Serenaden, w. Ruth Ziesak (sop), Lajos Lencses (ob), Ansgar Schneider (vc) CPO ▲ CPO 999332
Hindemith, P.:Trio Pno, w. Shoshana Rudiakov (pno), Lajos Lencses (heckelphone) CPO ▲ CPO 999332
Teutsch, Götz (vc)
Tal, J.:Else-Hommage, w. C. Gayer (sop), J. Bliese (nar), H. Ganz (va), N. Hauptmann (hn), K. Helwig (pno), J. Tal (cnd) Academy ▲ ACA 8506 [ADD]
Teutsch, R. (hn)
Telemann, G.P.:Con for 3 Horns, w. I. James (hn), T. Abramovici (hn), V. Czarnecki (cnd), Southwest German CO Pforzheim ebs ▲ ebs 6092 [DDD]
Telemann, G.P.:Suite for 4 Hns, w. I. James (hn), T. Abramovici (hn), A. Lewis (hn), V. Czarnecki (cnd), Southwest German CO Pforzheim ebs ▲ ebs 6092 [DDD]
Tezlaff, A. (fl)—see also ORCHESTRAS & ENSEMBLES Albert Schweitzer Wind Quintet
Yun, I.:Sori *(rec Dec. 1991)* CPO ▲ CPO 999184 [DDD]
Thal, Herbert (tpt)
Vivaldi, A.:Con Vn Obs, RV.563, w. H. Zickler (tpt), G. Kehr (cnd), Mainz CO Allegretto ▲ ACD 8098 [ADD] ■ ACS 8098
Thalben-Ball, George (pno/org)
Master Ernest Lough, w. Lough, Master Ernest (trb), London Temple Church Choir Pearl ▲ PEA 9211 (m) [AAD]

Thalheim, Armin (clvd)
Bach, C.P.E.:Sons Hpd—6 sons from Essay on the True Art of Playing Keyboard Instruments Berlin Classics ▲ BER 9198
Thalheim, Armin (hpd)
Bach, C.P.E.:Sons Fl, w. Haupt (fl), Pank (vl)—in e, H.551 (W.124); in G, H.554 (W.127); in a, H.555 (W.128); in D, H.556 (W.129); in G, H.564 (W.133); in G, H.548 (W.134) Capriccio ▲ 10101
Bach, J.S.:Aria variata alla maniera italiana Capriccio ▲ CDC 10034 [DDD]
Bach, J.S.:Capriccio Departure Capriccio ▲ CDC 10034 [DDD]
Bach, J.S.:Toccatas Hpd, BWV 910–16—BWV 915, 916 Capriccio ▲ CDC 10034 [DDD]
Thalmann, K. (db)
Lauber, J.:Con Db, w. O. Henzold (cnd), AML Lucerne SO Gallo ▲ CD 838
Tharichen, Werner (timp)
Virtuoso Kettledrum Concertos, w. Berlin RSO [cnd:Urus Lajovic] Koch Schwann ▲ SCH 311052
Thatcher, Helen (vc)—see ORCHESTRAS & ENSEMBLES Sorrel String Quartet
Thedéen, Torleif (vc)—see also ORCHESTRAS & ENSEMBLES Stockholm Arts Trio
Bloch, E.:Schelomo, w. L. Markiz (cnd), Malmö SO *(rec Aug. 23, 1990)* BIS ▲ CD 576 [DDD]
Britten, H.:Suites Vc (comp) BIS ▲ CD 446 [DDD]
Elgar, E.:Con Vc, w. L. Markiz (cnd), Malmö SO BIS ▲ CD 486 [DDD]
Gubaidulina, S.:Rejoice, w. O. Krysa (vn) BIS ▲ CD 566 [DDD]
Kokkonen, J.:Con Vc, w. O. Vänskä (cnd), Lahti SO BIS ▲ CD 468 [DDD]
Prokofiev, S.:Son Vc, w. R. Pöntinen (pno) BIS ▲ CD 386 [DDD]
Rachmaninoff, S.:Son Vc, w. R. Pöntinen (pno) BIS ▲ CD 386 [DDD]
Russian Cello Music, w. Thedeen, Torleif (vc), Roland Pontinen (pno) BIS ▲ CD 336
Sallinen, A.:The Nocturnal Dances of Don Juanquixote, w. O. Vänskä (cnd), Tapiola Sinfonietta BIS ▲ CD 560 [DDD]
Schnittke, A.:Con 1 Vc, w. L. Segerstam (cnd), Danish National RSO BIS ("BIS Twins" series) 2-▲ CD 437/507
Schnittke, A.:Con 1 Vc, w. L. Segerstam (cnd), Danish National RSO BIS ▲ CD 507 [DDD]
Schnittke, A.:Con 2 Vc, w. L. Markiz (cnd), Malmö SO BIS ▲ CD 567 [DDD]
Schnittke, A.:Con grosso 2, w. O. Krysa (vn), L. Markiz (cnd), Malmö SO BIS ▲ CD 567 [DDD]
Schnittke, A.:Hymns Vc, w. Entcho Rdoukanov (db), Christian Davidsson (bn), Ingegerd Fredlund (hp), M. Kamata (hpd), Anders Holdar (tubular bells/timp), Anders Loguin (tubular bells) BIS ("BIS Twins" series) 2-▲ CD 437/507
Schnittke, A.:Hymns Vc, w. E. Radoukanov (db), C. Davidsson (bn), I. Fredlund (hp), M. Kamata (hpd), A. Holdar (tubular bells / timp), A. Loguin (tubular bells) BIS ▲ CD 507 [DDD]
Schnittke, A.:Klingende Buchstaben BIS ("BIS Twins" series) 2-▲ CD 437/507
Schnittke, A.:Klingende Buchstaben BIS ▲ CD 507 [DDD]
Schnittke, A.:Stille Musik Vn, w. Oleh Krysa (vn) *(rec Danderyd Grammar School, Sweden, Sept. 19, 1992)* BIS ▲ CD 697 [DDD]
Schnittke, A.:Trio Pno, w. Tatiana Tchekina (pno), Oleh Krysa (vn) *(rec Malmö Concert Hall, Sweden, May 12–14, 1994)* BIS ▲ CD 697 [DDD]
Schulhoff, E.:Duo, w. Oleh Krysa (vn) *(rec Malmö Concert Hall, Sweden, May 12, 1994)* BIS ▲ CD 679 [DDD]
Schulhoff, E.:Son Vc, w. Stefan Bojsten (pno) *(rec Danderyd Grammar School, Sweden, May 11, 1996)* BIS ▲ CD 679 [DDD]
Schumann, R.:Con Vc, w. L. Markiz (cnd), Malmö SO BIS ▲ CD 486 [DDD]
Shostakovich, D.:Con 1 Vc, w. J. DePreist (cnd), Malmö SO *(rec June 15–16, 1993)* BIS ▲ CD 626 [DDD]
Shostakovich, D.:Con 2 Vc, w. J. DePreist (cnd), Malmö SO *(rec Oct. 8–9, 1992)* BIS ▲ CD 626 [DDD]
Theis, Günter (ob/ob d'amore)—see ORCHESTRAS & ENSEMBLES Freiburg Baroque Soloists
Thelander, Kristin Pederson (hn)
Beethoven, L. van:Son Hn, w. C. lei Post (pno) *(rec Sept. 28–30, 1991)* Crystal ▲ CD 677
Dauprat, L.-F.:Son Hn & Pno, w. C. lei Post (pno) *(rec Sept. 28–30, 1991)* Crystal ▲ CD 677
From a Woman's Perspective:Art Songs by Women Composers, w. K. Eberle (mez), R. Guy (pno) Vienna Modern Masters ▲ VMM 2005 [DDD]
Krufft, N. von:Son in E Hn & Pno, w. C. lei Post (pno) *(rec Sept. 28–30, 1991)* Crystal ▲ CD 677
Kuhlau, F.:Andante & Polacca, w. C. lei Post (pno) *(rec Sept. 28–30, 1991)* Crystal ▲ CD 677
Oestreich, C.:Andante Hn, w. C. Post (pno) *(rec Sept. 28–30, 1991)* Crystal ▲ CD 677
Thelen, Ursula (fl)—see ORCHESTRAS & ENSEMBLES Cologne Flautando
Then-Bergh, I. (vn)—see also ORCHESTRAS & ENSEMBLES Munich Piano Trio
Schubert, Franz:Trio 1 Pno, w. M. Schäfer (pno), C. Hellmann (vc) *(rec Studio 3 des BR, Mar. 28–31, 1994)* Calig ▲ CAL 50931 [DDD]
Schubert, Franz:Trio 2 Pno, w. M. Schäfer (pno), C. Hellmann (vc) *(rec Studio 3 des BR, Mar. 28–31, 1994)* Calig ▲ CAL 50931 [DDD]
Theodore, David (ob)
Holst, G.:Choral Music, w. R. Truman (vc), S. Williams (hp), Holst Singers—The Princess; Light Leaves Whisper; Ave Maria; Jesu, Thou the Virgin-born; A Welcome Song; In Youth is Pleasure; Two Eastern Pictures; Bring us in Good Ale; Lully My Liking; Of One That Is So Fair and Bright; Diverus and Lazarus; Terly Terlow; This Have I Done for My True Love; Six Choral Folksongs; Twelve Welsh Folksongs; O Spiritual Pilgrim Hyperion ▲ CDA 66705 [DDD]
Mozart, W.A.:Con Ob, K.314, w. R. Hickox (cnd), City of London Sinfonia Chandos ▲ CHAN 9051 [DDD]
Salieri, A.:Con Fl, w. S. Milan (fl), R. Hickox (cnd), City of London Sinfonia Chandos ▲ CHAN 9051 [DDD]
Vaughan Williams, R.:Con Ob, w. B. Thomson (cnd), London SO Chandos ▲ CHAN 8594 [DDD]
Theofanidis, Chris (pno)
Thofanidis, C.:Suite Fl, w. Karen Bennett (fl) Albany ▲ TROY 158 [DDD]
Theurer, Britton (tpt)
Brotons, S.:Son da Con Tpt, w. G. Smart (pno) *(rec 5/91)* Capstone ▲ CPS 8612 CD [DDD]
Eakin, C.:Capriccio Tpt, "Here, There & Everywhere" *(rec 5/91)* Capstone ▲ CPS 8612 CD [DDD]
Schwartz, E.:Sinf Juxta, w. E. Schwartz (pno), S. Jones (tpt), S. Barnhart (perc) Capstone ▲ CPS 8612 CD [DDD]
Smart, G.:Music of, w. M. Smart (sop), G. Smart (pno), Franciscan Quartet—Trumpeter Swan; Fanfare, Invocation & Alleluia Capstone ▲ CPS 8612 CD [DDD]
Theurer, B.:Music of, w. S. Jones (tpt), G. Smart (pno)—Feste; Fant Capstone ▲ CPS 8612 CD [DDD]
Thevet, Lucien (hn)
Poulenc, F.:Elégie Hn, w. Francis Poulenc (pno) Adès ▲ ADE 202522 [AAD]
Thiago de Mello, Guadencio (perc)
Love Songs & Lullabies, w. Sharon Isbin (gtr), Benita Valente (sop), Thomas Allen (bar), Julia Bogorad (fl) Virgin Classics ▲ 59226
Thibaud, Jacques (vn)
Bach, J.S.:Brandenburg Con 5, w. A. Cortot (pno), A. Cortot (cnd), Paris Ecole Normale CO *(rec 1930)* Music Memoria ▲ 30321
Bach, J.S.:Brandenburg Con 5, w. A. Cortot (pno), R. Cortet (fl), Paris Conservatory Societé des Concerts Orch *(rec May 16, 1932)* Biddulph ▲ LAB 028 [ADD]
Bach, J.S.:Con 2 Vn, w. T. Ortmans (cnd), studio orch *(rec 1924)* Biddulph ▲ LAB 024 [ADD]
Beethoven, L. van:Son 9 Vn, "Kreutzer", w. A. Cortot (pno) *(rec 5/27–28/29)* Biddulph ▲ LAB 028 [ADD]
Beethoven, L. van:Son 9 Vn, "Kreutzer", w. A. Cortot (pno) *(rec May 1929)* EMI Classics 3-▲ 64057 (m) [ADD]
Beethoven, L. van:Trio 7 Pno, w. A. Cortot (pno), P. Casals (vc) *(rec Nov.–Dec. 1928)* EMI Classics 3-▲ 64057-2 (m) [ADD]
Beethoven, L. van:Trio 9 Pno, "Kakadu", w. A. Cortot (pno), P. Casals (vc) *(rec July 6, 1926)* EMI Classics 3-▲ 64057 (m) [ADD]
Brahms, J.:Con Vn & Vc, "Double Con", w. P. Casals (vc), A. Cortot (cnd), Barcelona Pau Casals Orch *(rec between May 11–12, 1929)* Koch Historic 2-▲ 7705-2 [ADD]

INSTRUMENT.

Thibaud, Jacques (vn) (cont.)

Brahms, J.:Con Vn & Vc, "Double Con", w. P. Casals (vc), A. Cortot (cnd), Barcelona Pau Casals Orch — Pearl 4–▲ PEAS 9935 (m) [AAD]
Brahms, J.:Con Vn & Vc, "Double Con", w. P. Casals (vc), A. Cortot (cnd), Barcelona Pau Casals Orch *(rec 1929 for HMV)* — Pearl ▲ PEA 9363 (m) [AAD]
Brahms, J.:Con Vn & Vc, "Double Con", w. Pablo Casals (vc), A. Cortot (cnd), Barcelona Pau Casals Orch — Dutton Laboratories ▲ DUT 5006 [ADD]
Brahms, J.:Con Vn & Vc, "Double Con", w. P. Casals (vc), A. Cortot (cnd), Barcelona Pau Casals Orch *(rec May 1929)* — EMI Classics 3–▲ 64057-2 (m) [ADD]
The 1922–23 HMV & 1924 Victor Recordings, w. Thibaud, Jacques (vn), Harold Craxton (pno), Alfred Cortot (pno), Jesús-Maria Sanromá (pno) — Biddulph ▲ LAB 014 [ADD]
The 1924–27 HMV Recordings, w. Thibaud, Jacques (vn) — Biddulph ▲ LAB 024 [ADD]
Chausson, E.:Con Vn, Pno & Str Qt, w. A. Cortot (pno), *(string quartet unknown) (rec 1931)* — Biddulph ▲ LAB 029 [ADD]
Chausson, E.:Con Vn, Pno & Str Qt, w. Alfred Cortot (pno), *(ensemble unknown)* — Memories ▲ MEM CD 4605
The Complete Solo Recordings, w. Swiss Romande Orch [cnd:J. Levine] *(rec 1929–36)* — APR 2–▲ APR 7028 [ADD]
Debussy, C.:Music of, w. A. Cortot (pno)—Minstrels — EMI Classics ▲ CDH 63032
Debussy, C.:Son Vn, w. A. Cortot (pno) *(rec 1929 for HMV)* — Music Memoria ▲ 30321
Debussy, C.:Son Vn, w. A. Cortot (pno) *(rec 1929 for HMV)* — Pearl ▲ PEA 9348 (m) [AAD]
Debussy, C.:Son Vn, w. A. Cortot (pno) — EMI Classics ▲ CDH 63032
Debussy, C.:Son Vn, w. A. Cortot (pno) *(rec 1929 for HMV)* — Biddulph ▲ LHW 006 [ADD]
Fauré, G.:Berceuse Vn, w. A. Cortot (pno) *(rec 1931, from HMV DB1653)* — Biddulph ▲ LAB 029 [ADD]
Fauré, G.:Berceuse Vn, w. A. Cortot (pno) — EMI Classics ▲ CDH 63032
Fauré, G.:Berceuse Vn, w. Alfred Cortot (pno) — Memories ▲ MEM CD 4605
Fauré, G.:Qt 2 Pno, w. Marguerite Long (pno), Maurice Vieux (va), Pierre Fournier (vc) *(rec June 10, 1940)* — Iron Needle 2–▲ IN 1342/43 (m) [ADD]
Fauré, G.:Qt 2 Pno, w. Marguerite Long (pno), Maurice Vieux (va), Pierre Fournier (vc) *(rec June 10, 1940)* — Enterprise ("Strings" series) ▲ ENT QT 99302
Fauré, G.:Son 1 Vn, w. A. Cortot (pno) — EMI Classics ▲ CDH 63032
Fauré, G.:Son 1 Vn, w. Alfred Cortot (pno) *(rec ca 1928)* — Symposium ▲ 1156
Franck, C.:Son Vn, w. Alfred Cortot (pno) — Biddulph ▲ LHW 027
Franck, C.:Son Vn, w. A. Cortot (pno) — EMI Classics ▲ CDH 63032
Grand Seigneur du Violon Français *(rec 1929–34)* — Music Memoria ▲ 30321
Haydn, J.:Trios Pno, Vn & Vc, w. Alfred Cortot (pno), Pablo Casals (vc)—No. 25 only *(rec 6/20/27)* — Biddulph ▲ LAB 028 [ADD]
Mendelssohn, F.:Trio 1 Pno, w. Alfred Cortot (pno), Pablo Casals (vc) *(rec June 1927)* — Iron Needle 2–▲ IN 1342/43 (m) [ADD]
Mendelssohn, F.:Trio 1 Pno, w. A. Cortot (pno), P. Casals (vc) *(rec 1927 for HMV)* — Biddulph ▲ LHW 002 [ADD]
Mendelssohn, F.:Trio 1 Pno, w. A. Cortot (pno), P. Casals (vc) *(rec June 1927)* — EMI Classics 3–▲ 64057-2 (m) [ADD]
Mozart, W.A.:Con 23 Pno, w. P. Gaubert (cnd), Paris SO — Biddulph ▲ LAB 114
Mozart, W.A.:Con 5 Vn, w. C. Munch (cnd), Paris Conservatory Societé des Concerts Orch — Biddulph ▲ LAB 114
Mozart, W.A.:Con 6 Vn, w. M. Sargent (cnd), *(orch unknown) (rec 1926 HMV recording)* — Biddulph ▲ LAB 016 [ADD]
Mozart, W.A.:Sons Vn Pno (misc), w. Marguérite Long (pno) — Biddulph ▲ LAB 114
Schubert, Franz:Trio 1 Pno, w. Alfred Cortot (pno), Pablo Casals (vc) — Memories ▲ MEM CD 4605
Schubert, Franz:Trio 1 Pno, w. A. Cortot (pno), P. Casals (vc) *(rec 1926)* — EMI Classics 3–▲ 64057-2 (m) [ADD]
Schumann, R.:Trio 1 Pno, w. A. Cortot (pno), P. Casals (vc) *(rec 1928 for HMV)* — Biddulph ▲ LHW 004 [ADD]
Schumann, R.:Trio 1 Pno, w. A. Cortot (pno), P. Casals (vc) *(rec 1928 for HMV)* — EMI Classics 3–▲ 64057-2 (m) [ADD]

Thibaud, Pierre (tpt)

Albrechtsberger, J.G.:Concertino Tpt, w. K. Toyoda (cnd), Gunma SO *(rec Tone–Numata Public Hall, Japan, Sept 8–9, 1981)* — Camerata ▲ 32CM 168 [DDD]
Haydn, J.:Con Tpt, w. K. Toyoda (cnd), Gunma SO *(rec Tone–Numata Public Hall, Japan, Sept 8–9, 1981)* — Camerata ▲ 32CM 168 [DDD]
Jolivet, A.:Concertino Tpt, w. Henriette Puig-Roget (pno), K. Toyoda (cnd), Gunma SO *(rec Tone–Numata Public Hall, Japan, Sept 8–9, 1981)* — Camerata ▲ 32CM 168 [DDD]

Thibaudet, Jean-Yves (ondes Martenot)

Messiaen, O.:Turangalîla-sym, w. T. Harada (pno), R. Chailly (cnd), Royal Concertgebouw Orch *(rec March 1992)* — London ▲ 436626-2 [DDD]

Thibaudet, Jean-Yves (pno)

Brahms, J.:Vars on a Theme by Paganini—Book I; Book II *(rec Henry Wood Hall, London, England, Jul 1994)* — London ▲ 444338-2 [DDD]
Chausson, E.:Con Vn, Pno & Str Qt, w. J. Bell (vn), Takács String Quartet — London ▲ 425860-2 [DDD]
Debussy, C.:Arabesques (2) — London 2–▲ 452022-2
Debussy, C.:Estampes — London 2–▲ 452022-2
Debussy, C.:L'Isle joyeuse — London 2–▲ 452022-2
Debussy, C.:Pour le piano — London 2–▲ 452022-2
Debussy, C.:Preludes Pno — London 2–▲ 452022-2
Debussy, C.:Son Vn, w. J. Bell (vn) — London ▲ 421817-2 [DDD]
Fauré, G.:Son 1 Vn, w. J. Bell (vn) — London ▲ 421817-2 [DDD]
Franck, C.:Son Vn, w. J. Bell (vn) — London ▲ 421817-2 [DDD]
Grieg, E.:Intermezzo, w. T. Mørk (vc) — Virgin Classics ▲ CDC 45034
Grieg, E.:Son Vc, w. T. Mørk (vc) — Virgin Classics ▲ CDC 45034
Liszt, F.:Cons Pno, w. C. Dutoit (cnd), Montreal SO — London ▲ 433075-2 [DDD] □ 433075-5
Liszt, F.:Fant on Hungarian Folk Tunes, w. C. Dutoit (cnd), Montreal SO — London ▲ 433075-2 [DDD]
Liszt, F.:Totentanz, w. C. Dutoit (cnd), Montreal SO — London ▲ 433075-2 [DDD]
Liszt, F.:Transcriptions & Paraphrases—Verdi's Rigoletto:Paraphrase de concert; Donizetti's Lucia et Parisina:Valse de concert on 2 motifs; Gounod's Faust:Valse de l'opera; Tchaikovsky's Eugene Onegin:Polonaise; Wagner's Der fliegende Holländer:Spinning Chorus; Tannhäuser:O du mein holder Abenstern; Lohengrin:Lohengrin's Admonition; Tristan und Isolde:Isoldes Liebestod; Mozart's Le nozze di Figaro:Fant. on 2 motifs [expanded Busoni] *(rec May 18–20, 1992)* — London ▲ 436736-2 [DDD]
Miaskovsky, N.:Con Vc, w. Truls Mørk (vc) [arr vc & pno] — Virgin Classics ▲ CDC 45119
Rachmaninoff, S.:Con 1 Pno, w. V. Ashkenazy (cnd), Cleveland Orch *(rec Severance Hall, Cleveland, Ohio, Apr 25, 1994)* — London ▲ 448219-2
Rachmaninoff, S.:Con 2 Pno, w. V. Ashkenazy (cnd), Cleveland Orch — London ▲ 440653-2 [DDD]
Rachmaninoff, S.:Con 2 Pno, w. V. Ashkenazy (cnd), Cleveland Orch *(rec Severance Hall, Cleveland, Ohio, Apr 25, 1994)* — London ▲ 448219-2
Rachmaninoff, S.:Con 3 Pno, w. V. Ashkenazy (cnd), Cleveland Orch *(rec Severance Hall, Cleveland, Ohio, Apr 25, 1994)* — London ▲ 448219-2 [DDD]
Rachmaninoff, S.:Pieces Vc, w. Truls Mørk (vc) — Virgin Classics ▲ CDC 45119
Rachmaninoff, S.:Rhapsody on a Theme of Paganini, w. V. Ashkenazy (cnd), Cleveland Orch — London ▲ 440653-2 [DDD]
Rachmaninoff, S.:Son Vc, w. Truls Mørk (vc) — Virgin Classics ▲ CDC 45119
Rachmaninoff, S.:Vocalise, w. Truls Mørk (vc) [arr vc & pno] — Virgin Classics ▲ CDC 45119
Ravel, M.:Gaspard de la nuit — London ▲ 448618-2
Ravel, M.:Jeux d'eau — London ▲ 448618-2
Ravel, M.:Menuet sur le nom d'Haydn — London ▲ 448618-2
Ravel, M.:Miroirs — London ▲ 448618-2
Ravel, M.:Pavane pour une infante défunte — London ▲ 448618-2
Ravel, M.:Pno Music — London 2–▲ 433515-2 [DDD]

Thibaudet, Jean-Yves (pno) (cont.)

Ravel, M.:Prélude Pno — London ▲ 448618-2
Schubert, Franz:Impromptus Pno (comp)—2 sels — London ▲ 455 011-2 ■ 455 011-4
Schumann, R.:Arabeske Pno *(rec Henry Wood Hall, London, England, Jul 1994)* — London ▲ 444338-2 [DDD]
Schumann, R.:Sym Etudes [1852 version revised in 1861 to include Etudes II & IX from 1837 version]—also Symphonic Etudes, Appendix [first published 1873] *(rec Henry Wood Hall, London, England, Jul 1994)* — London ▲ 444338-2 [DDD]
Sibelius, J.:Malinconia, w. T. O. Mørk (vc) — Virgin Classics ▲ CDC 45034
Sibelius, J.:Pieces Vn, w. T. Mørk (vc) — Virgin Classics ▲ CDC 45034
Wolf, H.:Mörike-Lieder (sels), w. B. Fassbaender (mez)—Zum neuen Jahr; Gebet; Fubreise; Auf einer wanderung;Peregrina 1 & 2; Lebe wohl; Verborgenheit; Auf ein altes Bild; Schlafendes Jesuskind; An den Schlaf; Das verlassene Mägdlein; In der Frühe; Gesang Weylas; Im Frühling; Denk es, o Seele!; Dr Gärtner; Begegnung; Nimmersatte Liebe; Der Knabe und das Immlein; Bei einer Trauung; Storchenbotschaft; SelbstgestUandnis; Jägerlied; Der Feulerreiter — London ▲ 440208-2 [DDD]

Thielemans, Toots (hmc)

Red Square Blue Russian Composers, w. Hersch, Fred (pno), James Newton (fl), Phil Woods (a sax), Erik Friedlander (vc), Steve La Spina (bass), Jeff Hirshfield (drums) — Angel ▲ CDC 54743

Thielmann, Christel (vl)

Baroque Sonatas & Canzonas for Recorder, Harpsichord & Gamba, w. Peter Hannan (rcr), Colin Tilney (hpd) — CBC Records ("SM 5000" series) ▲ SMCD 5049 [DDD]
Baroque Sonatas & Canzonas for Recorder, Harpsichord & Viol, w. Peter Hannan (rcr), Colin Tilney (hpd) — CBC Records ("SM 5000" series) ▲ SMCD 5049 [DDD]

Thienes, Ernst (pno)—see ORCHESTRAS & ENSEMBLES Innsbruck Salon Quintet

Thiergärtner, Jürgen (baroque gtr)—see ORCHESTRAS & ENSEMBLES Gervasio Duo

Thiers, Marleen (va)—see ORCHESTRAS & ENSEMBLES Kuijken String Quartet

Thimmig, L. (winds)—see ORCHESTRAS & ENSEMBLES Mother Mallard

Thimmig, Leslie (cl)

Martino, D.:Triple Con, w. Anand Devendra (cl), Dennis Smylie (cl), H. Sollberger (cnd), Group for Contemporary Music *(rec Dec 1978)* — Albany ▲ TROY 168 [DDD]

Thiollier, François-Joël (pno)

Busoni, F.:Con Pno, Op. 39, w. M. Schønwandt (cnd), Nice PO — Kontrapunkt ▲ 32057 [DDD]
Falla, M. de:Noches en los jardines de España, w. A. Wit (cnd), Polish National RSO Katowice *(rec Polish Radio Concert Hall, Katowice, Nov. 29–Dec. 2, 1993)* — Naxos ▲ 8.550753 [DDD]
Famous Piano Music *(rec Temple Saint Marcel, Paris, Nov 28–Dec 1, 1994)* — Naxos 4–▲ 8.504010 [DDD]
Fauré, G.:Ballade Pno, w. A. de Almeida (cnd), Irish National SO *(rec May 10–11, 1993)* — Naxos ▲ 8.550754 [DDD]
Franck, C.:Symphonic Vars, w. A. de Almeida (cnd), Irish National SO *(rec May 10–11, 1993)* — Naxos ▲ 8.550754 [DDD]
Gershwin, G.:An American in Paris [solo piano arr.] — Thésis ▲ THC 82001
Gershwin, G.:The George Gershwin Songbook — Thésis ▲ THC 82001
Gershwin, G.:Pno Music—Impromptu in two keys; Rialto Ripples — Thésis ▲ THC 82001
Gershwin, G.:Preludes (3) Pno — Thésis ▲ THC 82001
Gershwin, G.:Rhap in Blue [arr. for solo piano] — Thésis ▲ THC 82001
Indy, V. d':Sym on a French Mountain Air, w. A. de Almeida (cnd), Irish National SO *(rec May 10–11, 1993)* — Naxos ▲ 8.550754 [DDD]
Onslow, G.:Sons Vc, w. Pierre Franck (va) — Pierre Verany ▲ PVY 796032 [DDD]
Rachmaninoff, S.:Pno Music (comp solo piano)—Prelude, Op. 3, No. 2; Preludes (23), Op. 23 & Op. 32; Sonatas No. 1 in d, Op. 28 & No. 2 in b♭ *(original 1913 version)*, Op. 36 — Thésis 2–▲ THC 82004
Rachmaninoff, S.:Pno Music (comp solo piano)—Études-Tableaux, Op. 33 & Op. 39; Trois Nocturnes (1887–88); ten miscellaneous pieces (Polka; Prelude; Fragments; Morceaux de fantaisie; Canon; Prelude in G; Oriental; Lilacs; Daisies; Lento); nine transcriptions (Le vol; Berceuse; Gopak; Wohin; Liebesfreud; Prelude; Liebesleid; Menuet; Scherzo) — Thésis 2–▲ THC 82005
Rachmaninoff, S.:Pno Music (comp solo piano)—Moments Musicaux, Op. 16; Variations on a Theme by...Chopin, Op. 22 & Corelli, Op. 42; Four Pieces (ca. 1888); Morceaux de fantaisie, Op. 3; Morceaux de salon, Op. 10 — Thésis 2–▲ THC 82006
Ravel, M.:Con Pno (left hand), w. A. Wit (cnd), Polish National RSO Katowice *(rec Concert Hall of the Polish Radio in Katowice, Nov. 29–Dec. 2, 1993)* — Naxos ▲ 8.550753 [DDD]
Ravel, M.:Con in G Pno, w. A. Wit (cnd), Polish National RSO Katowice *(rec Polish Radio Concert Hall, Katowice, Nov. 29–Dec. 2, 1993)* — Naxos ▲ 8.550753 [DDD]
Ravel, M.:Pno Music—La parade; Pavane pour une infante défunte; Sérénade grotesque; A la manière de Chabrier; A la manière de Borodine; Menuet antique; Jeux d'eau; Menuet sur le nom de Haydn; Prélude; Sonatine; Miroirs *(rec Studio Ned Music, Boulogne, France, Nov. 18–19, 1993)* — Naxos ▲ 8.550683 [DDD]
Ravel, M.:Pno Music—Valses nobles et sentimentales; Gaspard de la nuit; Le tombeau de Couperin; La Valse *(rec Studio Ned Music, Boulogne, France, Jan. 1994)* — Naxos ▲ 8.553008 [DDD]

Thiry, Louis (org)

Messiaen, O.:Org Music (comp) — Calliope 3–▲ CAL 9926/28

Thomas, Andrew (hpd)

Schubel, M.:Christmas Treat, w. David Moore (vc) — Opus One ▲ CD 151

Thomas, Dwight (org)

Berlin, I.:Music of—Alexander's Ragtime Band; Let's Face the Music; This Is the Army; Change Partners; Always; Heat Wave; Annie Get Your Gun; Puttin' on the Ritz; With You; Me; Top Hat Medely; Slumming on Park Avenue; Russian Lullaby; Give Me Your Tired/God Bless America [w. Betty White (cnd), Indianapolis Sym Choir] — Newport Classics ▲ NCD 60078

Thomas, Geoffrey (hpd)

Vivaldi, A.:Cons Ob, w. S. Schilli (ob), D. Jonas (ob), G. Kósa (hpd), J. Kis Domonkos (vc), Nagy, Morandi (cnd), Failoni CO—RV 450, 452, 453, 454, 534, 535 & 536 *(rec Dec. 1992)* — Naxos ▲ 8.550859 [DDD]

Thomas, Ireen (vih)

The Art of Spanish Variations, w. Toyohiko Satoh (lt/vih) — Channel Classics ▲ CCS 3091 [DDD]

Thomas, Jacquelin (vc)—see ORCHESTRAS & ENSEMBLES Brodsky String Quartet

Thomas, James (org)

Berkeley, L.:Chichester Service, w. Alan Thurlow (cnd), Chichester Cathedral Choir — Priory ▲ PRI 570 [DDD]
Berkeley, L.:The Lord Is My Shepherd, w. Alan Thurlow (cnd), Chichester Cathedral Choir — Priory ▲ PRI 570 [DDD]
Burgon, G.:Songs of the Creation, w. Alan Thurlow (cnd), Chichester Cathedral Choir — Priory ▲ PRI 570 [DDD]
Harvey, J.:God Is Our Refuge, w. Alan Thurlow (cnd), Chichester Cathedral Choir — Priory ▲ PRI 570 [DDD]
Howells, H.:Chichester Service, w. Alan Thurlow (cnd), Chichester Cathedral Choir — Priory ▲ PRI 570 [DDD]
Lloyd, R.:Chichester Mass, w. Alan Thurlow (cnd), Chichester Cathedral Choir — Priory ▲ PRI 570 [DDD]
Walker, R.:Here, O My Lord, I See Thee Face to Face, w. Alan Thurlow (cnd), Chichester Cathedral Choir — Priory ▲ PRI 570 [DDD]

Thomas, Jeffrey (hpd)

Bach, J.S.:Con for 4 Hpds, w. John Butt (hpd), Phebe Craig (hpd), Johathan Dimmock (hpd), J. Thomas (cnd), American Bach Soloists — Koch International Classics ▲ KIC 7237 [DDD]

Thomas, John Charles (tube tpt/ram's horn)

Mostel, R.:Swiftly, w. Dan Erkkila (shakuhachi/ram's horn/Tibetan thighbone trumpets), Geoffrey Gordon (perc), Tibetan Singing Bowl Ensemble *(rec live, WNYC Studios, Sept 18, 1987)* — Digital Fossils ▲ 10009-2 [DDD]

Thomas, Ladd (org)

Britten, H.:War Requiem, w. *(vocalists unknown)*, W. Hall (cnd), Vienna Festival SO, William Hall Chorale — Klavier ■ KC 544

Thomas, Ladd (org) (cont.)
Britten, H.:War Requiem, w. Jeanine Altmeyer (sop), Douglas Lawrence (ten), Michael Sells (bar), W. Hall (cnd), William Hall Orch, William Hall Chorale, Columbus Boys' Choir
Klavier ▲ KCD 11017 [ADD]
Thomas, Linda Lee (pno)
The Expressive Oboe, w. Roger Cole (ob) Musica Viva ▲ MVCD 1070 [DDD]
Thomas, Martha (pno)
Nielson, L.:Black Magic, w. Julie Stone (fl) *(rec Atlanta, GA, July 5, 1993)*
ACA Digital Recording ▲ CM 20027
Thomas, Michael (hn)
Haydn, J.:Con 1 Hn, w. C. Warren-Green (cnd), London CO
Virgin Classics ("Ultraviolet" series) ▲ CUV 61235
Thomas, Michael (vn)—see ORCHESTRAS & ENSEMBLES Brodsky String Quartet
Thomas, Milton (va)
Bernstein, L.:Music of, w. J. Norman (sop), K. Te Kanawa (sop), J. Anderson (sop), F. von Stade (mez), C. Ludwig (mez), T. Troyanos (mez), J. Carreras (ten), D. Garrison (ten), J. Hadley (ten), T. Hampson (bar), T. Daly (sgr), G. Kremer (vn), M. Rostropovich (vc), L. Bernstein (cnd), *(orch unknown)*—various popular works Deutsche Grammophon ▲ 439251-2 ■ 439251-4
Brahms, J.:Sextet Strs, Op. 18, w. I. Stern (vn), A. Schneider (vn), M. Katims (va), P. Casals (vc), M. Foley (vc) *(rec 1952)* Sony Masterworks ("Portrait" series) ▲ MPK 44851 [ADD]
Brahms, J.:Sextet Strs, Op. 18, w. I. Stern (vn), A. Schneider (vn), M. Katims (va), P. Casals (vc), M. Foley (vc) *(rec Prades, France, June 23–July 3, 1952)*
Sony Classical ("The Casals Edition" series) ▲ SMK 58994 [ADD]
Lazarof, H.:Cadence II *(rec 1970)* CRI ▲ CD 631
Lazarof, H.:Continuum, w. S. Plummer (vn), L. Lesser (vc) *(rec 1970)* CRI ▲ CD 631
Lazarof, H.:Oct Strs, w. Yukiko Kamei (vn), Peter Marsh (vn), Yoko Matsuda (vn), Miwako Watanabe (vn), Paul Silverthorne (va), Godfried Hoogeveen (vc), David Speltz (vc), H. Lazarof (cnd)
Laurel ▲ LR 843 [DDD]
Lazarof, H.:Volo, w. H. Lazarof (cnd), *(ensemble unknown)* *(rec 1st Methodist Church, Los Angeles, CA)*
Laurel ▲ LR 844 [DDD]
Mozart, W.A.:Qts Pno, w. W. Kapell (pno), A. Grumiaux (vn), P. Tortelier (vc)—K.493 *(rec live June 1, 1953)* Music & Arts 4-▲ CD 689 (m) [AAD]
Spohr, L.:Double Qt 1, w. J. Heifetz (vn), I. Baker (vn), P. Amoyal (vn), P. Rosenthal (vn), A. Harshman (va), G. Piatigorsky (vc), L. Lesser (vc) RCA Gold Seal ▲ 7870-2-RG (m/s) [ADD]
Thomas, Patricia (pno)—see also ORCHESTRAS & ENSEMBLES Zemlinsky Trio
Maggini, E.:Canto XVII, w. Werner Zumsteg (fl) *(rec RTSI, Rete 2, Dec 1993)*
Jecklin ▲ JS 311-2 [DDD]
Thomas, Ronald (vc)
Copland, A.:Threnodies I & II, w. F. Smith (fl), S. Chase (vn), K. Murdock (va)
Northeastern ("Classical Arts" series) ▲ NR 227-CD
Foote, A.:At Dusk, w. F. Smith (fl), C. Yeats (harp) Northeastern ("Classical Arts" series) ▲ NR 227-CD
Schoenberg, A.:Verklärte Nacht, w. S. Chase (vn), L. Chang (vn), M. Thompson (va), S. Ansel (va), M. Djokic (vc) *(rec Methuen, MA, Dec. 1990)* Northeastern ▲ NOR 249 [DDD]
Shostakovich, D.:Son Vc, w. M. Lee (pno) *(rec Weston, MA, Jan. 1993)*
Northeastern ▲ NOR 245 [DDD]
Shostakovich, D.:Trio 2 Pno, w. R. Hodgkinson (pno), S. Chase (vn) *(rec Methuen, MA, Jan. 1990)*
Northeastern ▲ NOR 245 [DDD]
Tchaikovsky, P.:Souvenir de Florence, w. A. Delmoni (vn), L. Chang (vn), M. Thompson (va), S. Ansel (va), M. Reynolds (vc) *(rec Weston, MA, Jan. 1993)* Northeastern ▲ NOR 249 [DDD]
Thomas, Ronald (vn)
Bach, J.S.:Con 2 for 3 Hpds, w. Carmel Kaine (vn), Richard Studt (vn), Christopher Hogwood (bc), Nicholas Kraemer (bc), N. Marriner (cnd), Academy of St. Martin in the Fields [trans for 3 vn] *(rec St. John's, Smith Square, London, Aug 1974 & Feb 1975)* Boston Skyline ▲ BSD 127 [ADD]
Vivaldi, A.:Cons Vn, Op. 8/1-12, "Il cimento dell'armonia e dell'inventione", w. R. Thomas (cnd), Bournemouth Sinfonietta—Nos. 7-12 Chandos ("Collect" series) ▲ CHAN 6578 [ADD]
Vivaldi, A.:Cons Vn, Op. 8/1-4, "The Four Seasons", w. Bournemouth Sinfonietta
Chandos ("Collect" series) ▲ CHAN 6510 [ADD]
Thomas, Stephan (org)
Derungs, G.A.:Con da chiesa, w. Karl Raas (org), Peter Schneider (vib), Adrian Schilling (timp), M. Schwarz (cnd), St. Gallen Collegium Musicum Musiques Suisses ▲ 6125 [DDD]
Thomas, Susan (fl)
Vienna Nocturne:The Mair-Davis Duo & Friends Play Waltzes & Sonatas of the Golden Age, w. Mair-Davis Duo, Theodore Arm (vn), Mary Lou Rylands (vc) North Star ▲ NS0034 [DDD]
Vienna Nocturne:The Mair-Davis Duo & Friends Play Waltzes & Sonatas of the Golden Age, w. Mair-Davis Duo, Theodore Arm (vn), Mary Lou Rylands (vc) North Star ▲ NS0034 [DDD]
Thomas, Werner (vc)
Fauré, G.:Son 1 Vc, w. C. Piazzini (pno) Calig ▲ CAL 50881 [DDD]
Grotchaninoff, A.:Vc & Pno Music, w. C. Piazzini (pno)—Fantasia; Nocturne, Op. 86; Sonata in E, Op. 113 Calig ▲ CAL 50881 [DDD]
Gretchaninoff, A.:Suite Vc, w. A. Symeonides (cnd), Bamberg SO Koch Schwann ▲ 311008 [DDD]
Khachaturian, A.:Con Vc, w. A. Symeonides (cnd), Bamberg SO Koch Schwann ▲ 311008 [DDD]
Rachmaninoff, S.:Son Vc, w. C. Piazzini (pno) *(rec Dec. 21-22, 1987)* Calig ▲ CAL 50871 [DDD]
Rubinstein, A.:Cons Vc, w. Y. Ahronovitch (cnd), Bamberg SO
Koch Schwann ▲ CD 311 103 [DDD] ■ MC 211 103 (D)
Saint-Saëns, C.:Chant saphique, w. C. Piazzini (pno) *(rec Dec. 22-23, 1986)*
Calig ▲ CAL 50862 [DDD]
Saint-Saëns, C.:Son 1 Vc, w. C. Piazzini (pno) *(rec Dec. 22-23, 1986)* Calig ▲ CAL 50862 [DDD]
Saint-Saëns, C.:Son 2 Vc, w. C. Piazzini (pno) *(rec Dec. 22-23, 1986)* Calig ▲ CAL 50862 [DDD]
Strauss, R.:Son Vc, w. C. Piazzini (pno) *(rec Dec. 21-22, 1987)* Calig ▲ CAL 50871 [DDD]
Thomas-Mifune, Werner (vc)
Brahms, J.:Son 2 Vc, w. Carmen Piazzini (pno) Koch Schwann ▲ SCH 318232
Brahms, J.:Son in D Vc, w. Carmen Piazzini (pno) Koch Schwann ▲ SCH 318232
Dvořák, A.:Con Vc, w. R. Krečmer (cnd), Bamberg SO Koch Schwann ▲ SCH 311462 [DDD]
Dvořák, A.:Con Vc & Pno, w. R. Krečmer (cnd), Bamberg SO Koch Schwann ▲ SCH 311462 [DDD]
Ghedini, G.F.:Con for 2 Vcs, w. A. Meneses (vc), G. Schmöhe (cnd), Bamberg SO *(rec 1/90)*
Koch Schwann ▲ 311106 H1 [DDD]
Harmonies Du Soir:Virtuoso Romantic Cello Music, w. Munich CO [cnd:Hans Stadlmair]
Orfeo ▲ C 131851-A [DDD]
Magic Cello Calig ▲ CAL 50967 [ADD]
Reger, M.:Suites Vc *(rec Dec. 9-11, 1992)* Calig ▲ CAL 50921 [DDD]
Romberg, B.:Con Vcs, w. A. Meneses (vc), G. Schmöhe (cnd), Bamberg SO
Koch Schwann ▲ 311106 H1 [DDD]
Schubert, Franz:Son Arpeggione, w. Carmen Piazzini (pno) Calig ▲ CAL 50949 [DDD]
Schumann, R.:Adagio & Allegro Hn, w. Carmen Piazzini (pno) Calig ▲ CAL 50949 [DDD]
Schumann, R.:Fantasiestücke Cl, w. Carmen Piazzini (pno) Calig ▲ CAL 50949 [DDD]
Schumann, R.:Romances Ob, w. Carmen Piazzini (pno) Calig ▲ CAL 50949 [DDD]
Taneyev, S.:Canzona Cl, w. M. Tang (cnd), Bavarian RSO Koch Schwann ▲ 3-1135-2 [DDD]
Taneyev, S.:Suite de Concert, w. M. Tang (cnd), Bavarian RSO [arr vc & orch]
Koch Schwann ▲ 3-1135-2 [DDD]
Thomasz, Stefan (db)
Dittersdorf, K.D. von:Con Db, w. N. Boboc (cnd), Arad PO Olympia (Explorer) ▲ OCD 405 [AAD]
5 Centuries of German Music in Transylvania, w. H. Andreescu (cnd), Bucharest Virtuosi, Georgeta Stoleriu (sop), Adrian Petrescu (ob), René Cristian Popescu (vn), Gabriel Bala (va), Nicolae Licaret (hpd)
Electrecord ▲ ELC EDC 168 [DDD]
Thompson, Bob (tpt/flgl)
Bernstein, L.:Dance Suite Chamber Ensemble, w. Will Rudd (tpt/flgl), Alex Shuhan (hn/pno), Mark Kellogg (trbn/eup), Charles Villarrubia (tuba), David Gluck (dr/perc) *(rec Cliff Temple Baptist Church, Dallas, TX)* D'Note Classics ▲ DND 1007 [DDD]
Thompson, Bob (tpt/flgl) (cont.)
Corea, C.:Children's Songs, w. Will Rudd (tpt/flgl), Alex Shuhan (hn/pno), Mark Kellogg (trbn/eup), Charles Villarrubia (tuba), David Gluck (dr/perc)—Nos 6 & 11 [arr Gluck/Shuhan] *(rec Cliff Temple Baptist Church, Dallas, TX)* D'Note Classics ▲ DND 1007 [DDD]
Gershwin, G.:Porgy & Bess (sels), w. Will Rudd (tpt/flgl), Alex Shuhan (hn/pno), Mark Kellogg (trbn/eup), Charles Villarrubia (tuba), David Gluck (dr/perc)—Summertime [arr Thompson] *(rec Cliff Temple Baptist Church, Dallas, TX)* D'Note Classics ▲ DND 1007 [DDD]
Gluck, C.W.:Nicole, w. Will Rudd (tpt/flgl), Alex Shuhan (hn/pno), Mark Kellogg (trbn/eup), Charles Villarrubia (tuba), David Gluck (dr/perc) *(rec Cliff Temple Baptist Church, Dallas, TX)*
D'Note Classics ▲ DND 1007 [DDD]
Khachaturian, A.:Gayane (suites), w. Will Rudd (tpt/flgl), Alex Shuhan (hn/pno), Mark Kellogg (trbn/eup), Charles Villarrubia (tuba), David Gluck (dr/perc)—Sabre Dance [arr Gluck]; Lullaby; Dance of the Rose Maidens [both arr Villarrubia] *(rec Cliff Temple Baptist Church, Dallas, TX)*
D'Note Classics ▲ DND 1007 [DDD]
McCarthy, D.:American Dance Music, w. Will Rudd (tpt/flgl), Alex Shuhan (hn/pno), Mark Kellogg (trbn/eup), Charles Villarrubia (tuba), David Gluck (dr/perc) *(rec Cliff Temple Baptist Church, Dallas, TX)*
D'Note Classics ▲ DND 1007 [DDD]
Scheidt, S.:Instr Music, w. Will Rudd (tpt/flgl), Alex Shuhan (hn/pno), Mark Kellogg (trbn/eup), Charles Villarrubia (tuba), David Gluck (dr/perc)—Centone No. 5 [trans Verne Reynolds] *(rec Cliff Temple Baptist Church, Dallas, TX)* D'Note Classics ▲ DND 1007 [DDD]
Thompson, Carol (hp)
The Enchanted Isles:Harp Music of Ireland, Scotland, England & Wales Dorian ▲ DOR 90120 [DDD]
The Peacock's Feather:A Celtic Quest *(rec Troy Savings Bank Music Hall, Troy, NY, Feb 1996)*
Dorian ▲ DOR 90240 [DDD]
Thompson, Chester (dr)
Duke, G.:Muir Woods Suite, w. George Duke (pno), Stanley Clarke (bass), Paulinho Dacosta (perc), E. Stratta (cnd), Lille National Orch *(rec live, Montreaux Music Festival, Montreaux, Switzerland, July 12, 1993)* Warner Bros ▲ 9 46132-2 [DDD]
Thompson, Claude (org)
Fauré, G.:Cantique de Jean Racine, w. *(orch unknown)*, Claude Thompson (cnd), Petits Chanteurs de Trois-Rivières [F] REM ▲ 311148 XCD [DDD]
Fauré, G.:Messe basse, w. *(orch unknown)*, Claude Thompson (cnd), Petits Chanteurs de Trois-Rivières [L]
REM ▲ 311148 XCD [DDD]
Fauré, G.:Motets, w. *(orch unknown)*, Claude Thompson (cnd), Petits Chanteurs de Trois-Rivières—Ave Maria; Ave Maria, Op. 67, No. 2; Ave Maria, Op. 93; Ave verum; Ecce fidelis servus; Maria Mater gratiae; O Salutaris; Salve Regina; Sancta Mater; Tantum ergo; Tantum ergo, Op. 55; Tantum ergo, Op. 65, No. 2; Tu es Petrus [L] REM ▲ 311148 XCD [DDD]
Thompson, Don (tin whistle/ob)
Partch, H.:Yankee Doodle Fant, w. Lola Harding (sop), Hilmar Luckhardt (tin whistle), Lee Hoiby (flex-a-tones), Harry Partch (chromelodeon) *(rec 1945)* Innova 4-▲ 401
Thompson, J. (elec bass)
Lebaron, A.:Dish, w. D. Ohrenstein (sop), M. Rowell (vn), P. Bush (pno/syn), J. Cirker (dr), B. Ruyle (perc) *(rec Feb. & Apr. 1993)* CRI ("Emergency Music" series) ▲ CD 654 [DDD]
Thompson, James (tpt)
Forsyth, M.:Con Tpt, w. R. Armenian (cnd), Kitchener-Waterloo SO *(rec May 23, 1991 & June 1, 19)*
CBC ("SM 5000" series) ▲ SMCD 5130 [DDD]
Shostakovich, D.:Con 1 Pno, w. D. Shostakovich Jr (pno), M. Shostakovich (cnd), Montreal Musici
Chandos ▲ CHAN 8357 [DDD]
Vivaldi, A.:Con for 2 Tpts, w. R. Early (tpt), Y. Turovsky (cnd), Montreal Musici
Chandos ▲ CHAN 8651 [DDD]
Thompson, L. R. (b cl)
Folio, C.:Developing Hues, w. C. Folio (fl) Capstone ▲ CPS 8615
Thompson, Marcus (va)
Bartók, B.:Con Va, w. P. Freeman (cnd), Slovenian RSO Centaur ▲ CRC 2150
Bloch, E.:Suite Va & Pno, w. P. Freeman (cnd), Slovenian RSO Centaur ▲ CRC 2150
Dohnányi, E. von:Qnt 2 Pno, w. A. Wolf (pno), R. Lefkowitz (vn), C. Lieberman (vn), D. Finch (vc)
AFKA ▲ SK 503
Foote, A.:Sarabande & Rigaudon, w. F. Smith (fl), R. Hodgkinson (pno)
Northeastern ("Classical Arts" series) ▲ NR 227-CD
Schoenberg, A.:Verklärte Nacht, w. S. Chase (vn), L. Chang (vn), S. Ansel (va), R. Thomas (vc), M. Djokic (vc) *(rec Methuen, MA, Dec. 1990)* Northeastern ▲ NOR 249 [DDD]
Taneyev, S.:Qnt Pno Strs, w. J. Lowenthal (pno), P. Rosenthal (vn), Y. Kamei (vn), S. Kates (vc)
Arabesque ▲ Z 6539 [DDD]
Tchaikovsky, P.:Souvenir de Florence, w. A. Delmoni (vn), L. Chang (vn), S. Ansel (va), R. Thomas (vc), M. Reynolds (vc) *(rec Weston, MA, Jan. 1993)* Northeastern ▲ NOR 249 [DDD]
Thompson, Michael (hn)—see also ORCHESTRAS & ENSEMBLES Michael Thompson Wind Quintet
Brahms, J.:Trio Hn, w. R. Dubinsky (vn), L. Edlina (pno) Chandos ▲ CHAN 8606 [DDD]
Britten, H.:Canticles I-V, w. M. Chance (ct), A. Rolfe-Johnson (ten), A. Opie (bar), R. Vignoles (pno), S. Williams (hp) Hyperion ▲ CDA 66498
Britten, H.:Serenade, Op. 31, w. A. Rolfe-Johnson (ten), B. Thomson (cnd), Scottish National Orch [E]
Chandos ▲ CHAN 8657 [DDD]
Danzi, F.:Sextet Ob, w. Richard Berry (hn), John Bradbury (cl), Robert Hill (cl), John Price (bn), Philip Tarlton (bn)—version for Harmonie ensemble *(rec St. Paul's Church, Rusthall, Kent, England, June 1994)* Naxos ▲ 8.553076 [DDD]
Gough, O.:Saeta, w. Pepe de la Matrona (voc), Bruce Nockles (tpt), John Pigneguy (hn), David Purser (trbn), Orlando Gough (kbd) *(rec London, 1995)* Catalyst ▲ 0902-668332-2 [DDD]
Haydn, J.:Cons Hn, w. C. Warren-Green (cnd), Philharmonia Orch Nimbus ▲ NI 5010
Haydn, J.:Con for 2 Hns, w. Richard Watkins (hn), C. Warren-Green (cnd), Philharmonia Orch
Nimbus ▲ NI 5018
Haydn, J.:Divert Hn, Vn & Vc, H.IV/5, w. Christopher Warren-Green (vn), Andrew Shulman (vc)
Nimbus ▲ NI 5010
Mason, B.:Double Con, w. D. Purser (trbn), D. Mason (cnd), London Sinfonietta
Bridge ▲ BCD 9045 [DDD]
Matthews, C.:Suns Dance, w. Sebastian Bell (pic), Gareth Hulse (ob), Michael Collins (b cl), John Orford (ctbn), Michael Thompson (hn), Nona Liddell (vn), Joan Atherton (vn), Paul Silverthorne (va), Christopher van Kampen (vc), Robin McGee (db) *(rec All Saint's Church, Petersham, Oct 1992)*
Deutsche Grammophon ▲ 447067-2 [DDD]
Mozart, L.:Con Hn, w. C. Warren-Green (cnd), Philharmonia Orch Nimbus ▲ NI 5018
Rosetti, F.A.:Cons Hn, w. C. Warren-Green (cnd), Philharmonia Orch—Con. in d Nimbus ▲ NI 5018
Vivaldi, A.:Cons for 2 Hns, w. R. Watkins (hn), C. Warren-Green (cnd), Philharmonia Orch—RV.539
Nimbus ▲ NI 5018
Thompson, Nicholas (tpt)
Telemann, G.P.:Cons Tpts, w. Mark Bennett (tpt), Michael Harrison (tpt), Paul Goodwin (ob), Lorraine Wood (ob), T. Pinnock (cnd), English Concert—in D *(rec Henry Wood Hall, London, Mar 1993)*
Archiv Produktion ▲ 439893-2 [DDD]
Thompson, R. (org)
Campbell, A.:Arabesques Innova ▲ MN 108
Thompson, Robert (bn)
Andriessen, J.:Concertino Bn, w. G. Simon (cnd), English CO Wind Ensemble
Chandos ▲ CHAN 9278 [DDD]
Downey, J.:The Edge of Space, w. G. Simon (cnd), London SO Chandos ▲ CHAN 9278 [DDD]
Jacob, G.:Con Bn, w. G. Simon (cnd), English CO Chandos ▲ CHAN 9278 [DDD]
Thompson, Susan (pno)
Foss, L.:Fant Rondo
Vienna Modern Masters ("Distinguished Performers III" series) ▲ VMM 2016 [DDD]
Thomsen, Joakim Dam (ob)—see ORCHESTRAS & ENSEMBLES Boreas Wind Quintet

INSTRUMENT.

Thomsen, Jørgen (pno)
Stolarczyk, W.:Earth Air Fire Water, w. Amalie Malling (pno), John Damgaard (pno), Anne Øland (pno), Teddy Teirup (pno), Friedrich Gürtler (pno), Rosalind Bevan (pno), Poul Rosenbaum (pno), Rodolfo Llambias (pno), Bella Horn-Ribera (pno), Anders Riber (pno), Elisabeth Sigurdsson (pno), Thomas Tronheim (pno), Elsebeth Broderson (pno), Erik Kaltoft (pno), Jørgen Hald Nielsen (pno), Aino Gilemann (pno), Birgit Kjær (pno), Gunhild Donslund (pno), Henrik Bo Hansen (pno), Lone Karlsson (pno), Erik Fessel (pno), Lasse Nilsson (pno), Janos Ferenczi (pno), Erik Bach (pno), Axel Momme (pno), Arne de Cros Dich (pno), Sven Micha Slot (pno), Hanne Bramsen Buhl (pno), Lili Olesen (pno), Susannah Carlsson (pno), Ulla Erml (pno), Vagn Sørensen (pno), Leif Greibe (pno), Bodil Krogh (pno), Kirsten Ottosen (pno), Inger Bergenholz (pno), Karsten Gylendorf (pno), Bjønr Elkjær (pno), Jacob Bjørn Jensen (pno), Jørgen Kaad (pno), Anne Marie Hjelm (pno), Carl Ulrik Munk Andersen (pno), Poul Lumbye (pno), Oluf Hildebrandt Nielsen (pno), Joachim Olsson (pno), Peter Pade Ramsøe Jacobsen (pno), Astrid Pollmann (pno), Jette Borsch (pno), Kirsten Karlshøj (pno), Maria Teresa Assing (pno), Allan Dahl Hansen (pno), Johan Hugossen (pno), Tine Fenger Pederson (pno), Arne Jørgen Fæø (pno), Anja Høgsted (pno), Anne Sophie Parbo (pno), Inga Lindmark (pno), Teresa Drabik Stathakis (pno), Anne Ruth Ferenczi (pno), Irene Hasager (pno), Yuka Ichikawa (pno), Birgitte Baur (pno), Malene Thastum (pno), Jens E. Rasmussen (pno), Birgitte Zielke (pno), Claus Zielke (pno), Stefan Kasch (pno), Bin Qiao (pno), Inger Johanne Teirup (pno), Lindy Rosborg (pno), Liisa Heininen (pno), David Højer (pno), Ellen Refstrup (pno), Thomas K. Søorensen (pno), Erik Kure (pno), Michael Rauff (pno), Jan beck Eriksson (pno), Tanja Zapolski (pno), Vibeke Skagbo (pno), Pål Eide Lindtner (pno), Ha-Young Sul (pno), Benedicte Palko (pno), Inke Kesseler (pno), Anne Marie Meineche (pno), Sverre Larsen (pno), Kasper Peter Bach (pno), Elisabetta Eliseo (pno), Olga Magieres (pno), Carl Erik Kühl (pno), Thorkild Borup Nielsen (pno), Valeria Zanini (pno), Lars Stenhoft (perc), Dennis Boel (perc), Winnie Dahlgren (perc), Susanne Vind (perc), Claus Byrith (elec), Anne Marie Storm (elec), J. Ribera (cnd) *(rec live, Koldinghaus Castle, Denmark, May 2, 1996)* Danica ▲ DCD 1996

Thomsen, Niels (cl)—see also ORCHESTRAS & ENSEMBLES Collegium Musicum Soloists
Brahms, J.:Sons Cl (comp), w. E. Westenholz (pno) Kontrapunkt ▲ 32078 [DDD]
Gade, N.W.:Fantasistykker, w. E. Westenholz (pno) Kontrapunkt ▲ 32078 [DDD]
Holmboe, V.:Chamber Con 3, w. H. Koivula (cnd), Danish Radio Concert Orch *(rec Danish Radio Studio 2, June & Sept 1996)* Marco Polo/Dacapo ▲ 8.224038 [DDD]
Nielsen, C.:Con Cl, w. M. Schønwandt (cnd), Danish National RSO Chandos ▲ CHAN 8894 [DDD]
Nielsen, C.:Qnt Ww, w. James Galway (fl), Björn Carl Nielsen (ob), Jens Tofte-Hansen (bn), Björn Fosdal (hn) *(rec Vangede Church, Copenhagen, Mar 16, 1985)* RCA Red Seal ▲ 07863-56359-2 [ADD]
Roussel, A.:Chamber Music, w. Majken Bjerno (sop), Toke Lund Christiansen (fl), Bjørn Carl Nielsen (ob), Per Jacobsen (hn), Asger Svendsen (bn), Ketil Christensen (tpt), Anne Søe Hansen (vn), Zwi Carmelli (va), Piotr Zelazny (va), Niels Ullner (vc), Michael Dabelsteen (db), Tine Rehling (hp), Morten Mogensen (pno), Per Salo (pno), Per Jensen (perc)—Divertissement, Op. 6; Trio, Op. 40; Joueurs de Flute, Op. 27; Serenade, Op. 30; Le marchand de sable qui passe, Op. 13; Andante et scherzo, Op. 13; 2 poèmes de ronsard, Op. 26; Aria; Elpenor, Op. 59; Pipe Kontrapunkt 2-▲ KPT 32218 [DDD]

Thomson, George (va)—see ORCHESTRAS & ENSEMBLES Earplay members

Thomson, P. (pno)
Liszt, F.:De Profundis, w. K. Stratton (cnd), Hungarian State Orch [Michael Maxwell version] Hungaroton ▲ HCD 31525 [DDD]
Liszt, F.:Fant on Themes from Beethoven's *Ruins of Athens*, w. K. Stratton (cnd), Hungarian State Orch Hungaroton ▲ HCD 31525 [DDD]
Liszt, F.:Wandererfantasie, w. K. Stratton (cnd), Hungarian State Orch Hungaroton ▲ HCD 31525 [DDD]

Thon, Thomas (org)
Eben, Petr:Job Supraphon ▲ SUP 0181

Thönes, Jo (dr/perc)
Stockhausen, M.:Music of, w. Markus Stockhausen (tpt/flgl), Simon Stockhausen (syn/sax)—Bells; Kitchen; Passacaglia; The Heaven Open; Thunderstorm; Gamelan; Outer Space; Ping Pong; Sound Duo; Fireworks; Yeah!; 2 Brothers; Grand Finale; Daydream; Miles Mute?; Desert Wind; Spirit; Boomerang Largo ▲ CD 5133 [DDD]

Thorby, Pamela (rcr)—see ORCHESTRAS & ENSEMBLES Palladian Ensemble

Thoreson, D. (pno)
Messiaen, O.:La Merle noir, w. C. Hall (fl) ACA Digital Recording ▲ CM 20024
Messiaen, O.:Poèmes pour Mi, w. T. Hopkin (sop) ACA Digital Recording ▲ CM 20024

Thornblade, Rebecca (vc)—see ORCHESTRAS & ENSEMBLES Meaux String Quartet

Thornburg, Scott (tpt)—see ORCHESTRAS & ENSEMBLES New York Trumpet Ensemble

Thornburgh, Elaine (hpd)
Byrd, W.:Kbd Music—My Lady Nevell's Ground; O Mistress mine; John come kiss me now; Passamezzo Pavan & Galliard; The Carman's Whistle; Walsingham; Hugh Aston's Ground; Fortune; Sellinger's Round Koch International Classics ▲ KIC 7057-2 [DDD]
Scarlatti, D.:Sons Kbd—K.52, 211, 212, 248, 249, 261-264, 318, 319, 347, 348, 416, 417 & 490-492 Koch International Classics ▲ KIC 7014-2 [DDD] ■ 3-7014-4 (D)

Thorndycraft, Rosemary (ten vl/b vl)—see ORCHESTRAS & ENSEMBLES English Fantasy

Thorndycroft, Rosemary (b vl/h-g)
Old English Nursery Rhymes, w. Vivien Ellis (sop), Tim Laycock (sgr), Broadside Band [Jeremy Barlow (rcrs/perc), Sharon Lindo (vns/rcr), George Weigand (lt/mandore/cittern/gtr), Ben Sansom (vn), Marilyn Sansom (vc)] *(rec Valley Recordings, Littleton-on-Severn, Feb 1996)* Saydisc ▲ CDSDL 419

Thorne, Francis (pno)
Thorne, F.:Rhapsodic Vars 1, w. W. Strickland (cnd), Polish National RSO Katowice CRI ▲ CD 586 [ADD]

Thorne, Francis (pno/sgr)
Berlin, I.:Songs, w. Jack Six (db)—Top Hat, White Tie & Tails; Remember; This Year's Kisses; Isn't This a Lovely Day; Everybody Step; Change Partners; There's No Business Like Show Business; When That Midnight Choo-Choo Leaves for Alabam'; No Strings; Slumming on Park Avenue; Soft Lights & Sweet Music; They Say It's Wonderful; I'll See You in C-U-B-A; Always; How Deep is the Ocean; Society Bear; I'm Putting All My Eggs in One Basket; I Used to Be Color Blind CRI ▲ CD 557 [ADD]

Thorp, William (vn)—see ORCHESTRAS & ENSEMBLES Extempore String Ensemble

Thorson, Ingryd (pno)
Dvořák, A.:Pno Music, w. J. Thurber (pno)
Poulenc, F.:Con for 2 Pnos, w. J. Thurber (pno), F. Rasmussen (cnd), Aarhus SO Olympia ▲ OLY 364 [DDD]

Thorspecken, Cornelia (fl)
A Distant Mirror, w. C. Hacke (pno) Bayer ▲ 100246 [DDD]

Threadgill, Henry (fl)
Jenkins, L.:Monkey on the Dragon, w. Leroy Jenkins (vn), Henry Threadgill (fl), Don Byron (cl), Marth Ehrlich (b cl), Janet Frice (bn), Vincent Chancey (hn), Frank Gordon (tpt), Jeff Hoyer (trbn), David Soldier (vn), Jane Henry (vn) Ron Lawrence (va), Mary Wooton (vc), Lindsey Horner (db), Thurman Barker (traps), Myra Melford (pno), T. Léon (cnd) *(rec live, Merkin Concert Hall, New York City, Apr. 9, 1992)* CRI ("eXchange" series) ▲ CD 663 [DDD]
Jenkins, L.:Panorama 1, w. Leroy Jenkins (vn), Don Byron (cl), marty Ehrlich (b cl), Vincent Chancey (hn) *(rec live, Merkin Concert Hall, New York City, Apr. 9, 1992)* CRI ("eXchange" series) ▲ CD 663 [DDD]

Thunemann, Klaus (bn)—see also ORCHESTRAS & ENSEMBLES Musiktage Mondsee Ensemble
Albinoni, T.:Sinf (6) e con (6) à 5, Op. 2, w. H. Holliger (ob), I Musici—Nos. 5 & 6 Philips ▲ 432115-2 [DDD]
Beethoven, L. van:Qnt Pno, Ob, Cl, Hn & Bn, w. A. Brendel (pno), H. Holliger (ob), E. Brunner (cl), H. Baumann (hn) Philips ▲ 420182-2 [DDD]
Danzi, F.:Concertino Cl, w. E. Brunner (cl), H. Stadlmair (cnd), Munich CO Tudor ▲ 718 [DDD]
Hummel, J.N.:Con Bn, w. N. Marriner (cnd), Academy of St. Martin in the Fields Philips ▲ 432081-2 [DDD]
Mozart, W.A.:Con Bn, w. N. Marriner (cnd), Academy of St. Martin in the Fields Philips ▲ 422390-2 [DDD]
Mozart, W.A.:Con Bn, w. E. de Stoutz (cnd), Zurich CO *(rec Kirche Altstetten/ZH, June 1982)* Claves ▲ CD 508205 [DDD]

Thunemann, Klaus (bn) (cont.)
Mozart, W.A.:Duo Bn Vc, w. S. Orton (vc) Philips ▲ 422390-2 [DDD]
Mozart, W.A.:Qnt Pno, K.452, w. A. Brendel (pno), H. Holliger (ob), E. Brunner (cl), H. Baumann (hn) Philips ▲ 420182-2 [DDD]
Poulenc, F.:Trio Ob, w. I. Goritzki (ob), R. Requejo (pno) Claves ▲ CD 9020 [DDD]
Saint-Saëns, C.:Son Bn, w. R. Requejo (pno) Claves ▲ CD 9020 [DDD]
Stamitz, C.:Con Cl Bn, w. E. Brunner (cl), H. Stadlmair (cnd), Munich CO Tudor ▲ 718 [DDD]
Strauss, R.:Duet-Concertino, w. T. Friedli (cl), M. Aeschbacher (cnd), Lausanne CO Claves ▲ CD 9010 [DDD]
Telemann, G.P.:Con in F Rcr Bn, w. M. Petri (rcr), I. Brown (cnd), Academy of St. Martin in the Fields Philips ▲ 410041-2 [DDD]
Vivaldi, A.:Cons Bn, I Musici—RV.471 in C; RV.481 in d; RV.493 in G; RV.496 in g; RV.500 in a; RV.504 in B♭, "La Notte" Philips ▲ 432124-2 [DDD]
Vivaldi, A.:Cons Bn, I Musici—RV.473, 483, 485, 492, 497, 503 Philips ▲ 416355-2 [DDD]
Weber, C.M. von:Andante & Rondo ungarese Bn, w. N. Marriner (cnd), Academy of St. Martin in the Fields Philips ▲ 432081-2 [DDD]
Weber, C.M. von:Con Bn, w. N. Marriner (cnd), Academy of St. Martin in the Fields Philips ▲ 432081-2 [DDD]

Thurber, Julian (pno)
Dvořák, A.:Pno Music, w. I. Thorson (pno)
Poulenc, F.:Con for 2 Pnos, w. I. Thorson (pno), F. Rasmussen (cnd), Aarhus SO Olympia ▲ OLY 364 [DDD]

Thuri, Frantisek Xaver (hpd)
Stamitz, J.W.A.:Cons Org, w. Alena Veselá (org), V. Válek (cnd), Dvořák CO Supraphon ("Mannheim" series) ▲ SUP CD 3094
Zelenka, J.D.:Trio Sons Obs, w. Jana Brozková (ob), Vojtech Jouza (ob), Jan Jouza (vn), Jaroslav Kubita (bn), Václav Hoskovec (db)—Nos. 1-3 Studio Matous ▲ MAT 8 [DDD]
Zelenka, J.D.:Trio Sons Obs, w. Jana Brozková (ob), Vojtech Jouza (ob), Jaroslav Kubita (bn), Václav Hoskovec (db)—Nos. 4-6, ZWV 181 Studio Matous ▲ MAT 9 [DDD]

Thurzo, Alexandru Iosif (va)
Haydn, M.:Con Org, w. Ectarina Botár (hpd), E. Acél (cnd), Oradea PO Olympia ("Explorer" series) ▲ OCD 406 [AAD]

Thwaites, Penelope (pno)
Grainger, P.:Songs, w. Stephen Varcoe (bar)—The Lost Lady Found; Creeping Jane; Bold William Taylor; 6 Dukes Went a-Fishin'; The British Waterside; The Pretty Maid Milking Her Cow; Hard Hearted Barb'ra; Willow, Willow; Shallow Brown; Bonnie George Campbell; Drowned; Leezie Lindsay; Willie's Gone to Melville Castle; Lukannon; Northern Ballad; Ride with an Idle Whip; The Men of the Sea; Merciful Town; Soldier, Soldier; Sailor's Chanty; The Secret of the Sea Chandos ("The Grainger Edition" series) ▲ CHAN 9503

Thyresson, M. (org)
Pergament, M.:Kol Nidre, w. L. Rosenblüth (bar), E. Ericson (cnd), Stockholm Royal Conservatory Chamber Choir BIS ▲ CD 1 [AAD]
Rosenblüth, L.:Jewish Liturgical Music, w. L. Rosenblüth (cant), G. von Bahr (fl), A. Vitolius (org), E. Ericson (cnd), Stockholm Royal Conservatory Chamber Choir—Psalms 93 & 155, plus 5 settings for High Holidays, Rosh Hashanah, Sabbath & Yom Kippur BIS ▲ CD 1 [AAD]

Tichener, Meg (va)
Curran, A.:VSTG, w. D. Abel (vn), S. Wood (vn), D. Weinschelbaum (vc) CRI ▲ CD 668 [DDD]

Tichman, Nadya (vn)
Lewis, P.S.:Delicate Sky, w. Jack Van Geem (perc), Robin Sutherland (pno) *(rec St. Stephen's Church, Belvedere, CA, Oct 1994 & June 1995)* New Albion ▲ NA 079

Tichman, Nina (pno)
Bartók, B.:Sons (2) Vn & Pno, w. Ida Bieler (vn) MD + G ("Ensemble Villa Musica" series) ▲ MDG 3040666
Copland, A.:Blues *(rec Apr. 8-10 & May 4-5, 1992)* Wergo ▲ WER 6211-2 [DDD]
Copland, A.:Pno Music—3 Moods; Petit Portrait; Midsummer Nocturne; The Cat and the Mouse *(rec Apr. 8-10 & May 4-5, 1992)* Wergo ▲ WER 6211-2 [DDD]
Copland, A.:Pno Music—Passacaglia; Fant. Wergo ▲ WER 6212-2
Copland, A.:Son Pno *(rec Apr. 8-10 & May 4-5, 1992)* Wergo ▲ WER 6211-2 [DDD]
Copland, A.:Vars Pno *(rec Apr. 8-10 & May 4-5, 1992)* Wergo ▲ WER 6211-2 [DDD]

Tickmayer, Steven Kovaks (pno/harm/perc)—see ORCHESTRAS & ENSEMBLES Tickmayer Formatio

Tidwell, Burton (org)
With Pipes & Voices, w. Beverly Hoch (sop), Zion Evangelical Church Choir Wooster OH Arkay ▲ ARK 6150 [DDD]

Tidyman, David (hpd)
La Sensible:Harpsichord Music from the 16th-20th Century *(rec Apr. 1994)* Taskin Digital ▲ TC 22852-01 [DDD]

Tiefenbach, Peter (org/pno)
Opening Day, w. Wendy Humphreys (sop), Stuart Laughton (tpt), Wendy Humphreys (Celtic hp), William O'Meara (org) Doremi ▲ 9301 [DDD]

Tiensuu, Jukka (hpd)
Bashmakov, L.:Inventions (4), w. Matti Rantanen (acc) Finlandia ▲ FIN 54404 [DDD]
Tiensuu, J.:Arsenic & Old Lace, w. Arditti String Quartet Montaigne ▲ MO 782033

Tietov, (hp)
Debussy, C.:Danses sacrée et profane, w. L. Slatkin (cnd), St. Louis SO Telarc ▲ CD 80071 [DDD]

Tikker, T. (org)
Tournemire, C.:Fresques syms sacrées Arkay ▲ AR 6118 [DDD]
Tournemire, C.:Symphonie Sacrée Arkay ▲ AR 6118 [DDD]
Tournemire, C.:Symphonie-Choral Arkay ▲ AR 6118 [DDD]

Tilbury, John (pno)
Berg, A.:Early Songs, w. Roswitha Trexler (sop) Berlin Classics ▲ BER 9049 [DDD]

Tiles, Nurit (pno)
Chambers, W.M.:Ten Grand, w. Ursula Oppens (pno), Walter Hilse (pno), Bennett Lerner (pno), Aleck Karis (pno), Edmund Niemann (pno), Joseph Kubera (pno), Martin Goldray (pno), Allen Shawn (pno), Elizabeth di Filice (pno), Geisel (cnd) Newport ▲ NPD 85553
Dresher, P.:This Same Temple, w. Edward Neimann (pno) Lovely Music ▲ LCD 2011 [DDD]

Tillard, Francoise (pno)
Mahler, G.:Songs, w. Hanna Schaer (mez)—Erinnurung; Frühlingsmorgen; Ablösung im sommer; Nicht wiedersehen; Ich ging mit lust; Hans und Grete; Starke einbildungskraft; Zu straburg auf der schanz'; Ausl Ausl; Scheiden und meiden; Das irdische Leben; Wer hat dies Liedlein erdacht?; Des Antonius von padua fischpredigt Adda ▲ ADD 581208
Mendelssohn, Fanny:Trio Pno, w. E. Popa (vn), R. Maillard (vc) *(rec June 16-19, 1992)* Opus 111 ▲ OPS 30-71
Werfel, A.M.:Songs, w. Hanna Schaer (mez)—Die stille Stadt; In meins Vaters Garten; Laue Sommernacht; Bei dir ist es traut; Ich wandle unter Blumen Adda ▲ ADD 581208

Tilles, Nurit (pno)—see also ORCHESTRAS & ENSEMBLES Double Edge
Lang, D.:Music of, w. J. Rozen (elec tuba), D. Lang (nar), E. Niemann (pno), R. Schulte (vn), U. Oppens (pno), L. Vaillancourt (cnd), Le Nouvel Ensemble Moderne—Are You Experienced?; Orpheus Over & Under; Spud; Illumination Rounds CRI ▲ CD 625 [DDD]

Tillmanns, Hans Helmut (org)
Bach, J.S.:Toccata & Fugue Org, BWV 565 Koch Schwann ▲ 315003 [DDD]
Bruhns, N.:Preludes & Fugues (4) Org—in G Koch Schwann ▲ 315003 [DDD]
Buxtehude, D.:Org Music (misc)—Nun komm, der heiden Heiland; Gelobet seist du, Jesu Christ; Lobt Gott, ihr Christen allzugleich; Puer natus in Bethlehem; Ciacona in c; Ciacona in e; Prelude & Fugue in e; Toccata in d [at the Buxtehude Org, Torrlösa, Sweden] Koch Schwann ▲ 315003 [DDD]

Tilly, Rolf (tpt)
Britten, H.:Fanfare for St. Edmundsbury, w. B. Nilsson (tpt), J. Hjelm (tpt) BIS ▲ CD 31 [AAD]

Tilney, Colin (hpd)
Bach, J.S.:Cons for 3 Hpds (comp), w. C. Rousset (hpd), D. Moroney (hpd), C. Hogwood (cnd), Academy of Ancient Music L'Oiseau-Lyre ▲ 433053-2 [DDD]

▲ = CD ♦ = Enhanced CD Δ = MD ■ = Cassette Tape □ = DCC

Tilney, Colin (hpd) (cont.)
- Bach, J.S.:Con for 4 Hpds, w. C. Rousset (hpd), D. Moroney (hpd), C. Hogwood (hpd), C. Hogwood (cnd), Academy of Ancient Music — L'Oiseau-Lyre ▲ 433053-2 [DDD]
- Bach, J.S.:English Suites — Music & Arts 2-▲ CD 777 [DDD]
- Bach, J.S.:Toccatas Hpd, BWV 910-16 — Dorian ▲ DOR 90115 [DDD]
- Baroque Sonatas & Canzonas for Recorder, Harpsichord & Gamba, w. Peter Hannan (rcr), Christel Thielmann (va da gamba) — CBC Records ("SM 5000" series) ▲ SMCD 5049 [DDD]
- Baroque Sonatas & Canzonas for Recorder, Harpsichord & Viol, w. Peter Hannan (rcr), Christel Thielmann (vl) — CBC Records ("SM 5000" series) ▲ SMCD 5049 [DDD]
- Elizabethan Songs & Dances, w. Tilney, Colin (hpd) — CBC Records ("Musica Viva" series) ▲ MVCD 1021 [DDD]
- Fanfarinette:Music for the French Harpsichord — Musica Viva ▲ MVCD 1034 [DDD]
- Frescobaldi, G.:Hpd Music [early 18th-century Italian brass-strung hpd]—Toccata Prima (from Toccatas:Book 2, 1627); Capriccio sopra in Bassa Fiamenga (from Capricci Fatti sopra Diversi Soggetti:Book 1, 1624); Gagliarde 1-5 (1627); Capriccio di Durezze (1624); Partite sopra l'aria della Romanesca (from Toccate e Partite d'Intavolutura di Cimbalo:Book 1, 1616/1637); Canzona Quarta (1627); Ancidetemi pur d'Archadelt passaggiato (1627); Correnti 1-4 (1616); Partite sopra Ciaccona (1627); Corrente & Ciaccona (1637); Partite sopra Passacagli (1627); Cento Partite sopra Passacagli (1637); Toccata Nona (1616) — Dorian ▲ DOR 90124 [DDD]
- Go from My Window *(rec Nov. 1993)* — Dorian ▲ DOR 90195 [DDD]
- Hannan, Peter:Generic Music, w. Peter Hannan (rcr) — CBC ("Musica Viva" series) ▲ MVCD 1055 [DDD]
- Musica Dolce, w. Julianne Baird (sop) — Dorian ▲ DOR 90123 [DDD]
- Purcell, H.:Dido & Aeneas (sels), w. Victoria de los Angeles (sop—Dido), Heather Harper (sop—Belinda), Sibyl Michelow (sop), Elizabeth Robson (sop), Derek Simpson (vc), J. Barbirolli (cnd), English CO, Ambrosian Singers—Ov.; Shake the Cloud; Ah! Ah! Belinda; When Monarchs Unite; But Ere We This Perform; But Death, Alas! I Cannot Shun...When I am Laid in Earth; With Drooping Wings *(rec Abbey Road Studio 1, London, Aug. 1965)* — EMI Classics ▲ CDK 65341 [ADD]
- Scarlatti, D.:Sons Kbd—16 Sonatas — Music & Arts ▲ CD 907 [DDD]
- Scarlatti, D.:Sons Kbd—K.2, 9, 12, 18, 21, 30, 84, 86, 87, 159, 175, 277, 278, 302, 314, 315, 334, 337, 418 — Dorian ▲ DOR 90103 [DDD]
- Songs of Love & War:Italian Dramatic Songs of the 17th & 18th Centuries, w. Julianne Baird (sop), Myron Lutzke (vc) — Dorian ▲ DOR 90104 [DDD]
- Vivaldi, A.:Sons Vc, w. O. Harnoy (vc)—RV.40, 41, 43, 45, 46, 47 — RCA Red Seal ▲ 09026-60430-2 ■ 09026-60430-4

Tilney, Colin (pno)
- Mozart, W.A.:Pno Music (misc)—12 Variations in B♭, K.500 & minuet in D, K.355; Das Lied der Trennung, K.519; Die Zufriedenheit, K.473; Abendempfindung an Laura, K.523; Das Veilchen, K.476; Das Traumbild, K.530; Die Vershweigung, K.518; Der Frühling, K.597; Die kleine Spinnerin, K.531 — Dorian ▲ DOR 90173 [DDD]
- Mozart, W.A.:Songs, w. J. Baird (sop)—Als Luise die Briefe, K.520; An Chloe, K.524; Lied zur Gesellenreise, K.468; Oiseaux, si tous les ans, K.307; Dans un bois solitaire, K.308; Ridente la calma, K.152; Sei du mein Trost, K.391; Ich würd' auf meinem Pfad, K.390; Der Zauberer, K.472; Die Alte, K.517 — Dorian ▲ DOR 90173 [DDD]

Tilson Thomas, Michael (pno)
- Gershwin, G.:Music of — CBS ▲ MK 39699 [DDD]
- Gershwin, G.:Preludes (3) Pno — CBS ▲ MK 39699 [DDD]
- Gershwin, G.:Preludes (3) Pno — CBS ▲ MK 42516 [ADD/DDD] ■ FMT 42516
- Gershwin, G.:Rhap in Blue, w. M. Tilson Thomas (cnd), Los Angeles PO — CBS ▲ MK 39699 [DDD]
- Gershwin, G.:Second Rhap, w. M. Tilson Thomas (cnd), Los Angeles PO — CBS ▲ MK 39699 [DDD]

Timm, Jürnjacob (vc)
- Albert, E. d':Con Vc, w. C.P. Flor (cnd), Berlin SO — Berlin Classics ▲ BER 9179
- Beethoven, L. van:Con Vn, Vc & Pno, "Triple Con", w. C. Funke (vn), Rösel (pno), H. Kegel (cnd), Dresden PO — Capriccio ▲ 10150 [DDD]
- Schumann, R.:Con Vc, w. K. Masur (cnd), Leipzig Gewandhaus Orch — Berlin Classics ▲ BER CD 9151
- Tchaikovsky, P.:Vars on a Rococo Theme, w. K. Masur (cnd), Leipzig Gewandhaus Orch — Berlin Classics ▲ BER CD 9151

Timmons, J. (pno)
- Bergsma, W.:Pno Music—Tangents; 3 Fants.; Piano Vars. — Laurel ▲ LR 852 [AAD]

Timofeyeva, Lyubov (pno)
- Tchaikovsky, P.:Trio Pno, w. M. Fedotov (vn), K. Rodin (vc) — MK ▲ 417001 [DDD]

Tinarelli, Marco (db)
- Haydn, J.:Lo Speziale, w. Gil Manuel Beltran (ten—Sempronio), Daniela Broganelli (sgr—Volpino), Cinzia Forte (sgr—Grilletta), Paolo Pellegrini (sgr—Mengone), Maurizio Gambini (vc), Gabriele Catalucci (hpd), F. Maestri (cnd), In Canto CO *(rec 1993)* — Bongiovanni 2-▲ GB 2171/72 [DDD]
- Sarro, D.N.:Son Fl, w. U. Giani (fl), E. Rohrmann (vc), G. Catalucci (hpd) *(rec Dec. 8, 1992)* — Bongiovanni ▲ GB 2147 [DDD]

Tindall, Blair (ob)
- Franzetti, C.:Con Ob, w. Allison Brewster Franzetti (pno), C. Franzetti (cnd), Modus Chamber Ensemble *(rec Hip Pocket Studios, New York)* — Promior ▲ PRCD 1044 [DDD]

Tindemans, Margriet (fid)—see ORCHESTRAS & ENSEMBLES Kuijken Consort

Tindemans, Margriet (rcr/vn/vl)—see ORCHESTRAS & ENSEMBLES Echos Muse

Tindemans, Margriet (vl)
- Hildegard Of Bingen:Ordo virtutum, w. B. Thornton (cnd), Sequentia — Editio Classica 2-▲ 77051-2-RG [DDD] 2-■ 77051-4-RG (CrO2)
- Jacquet De La Guerre, E.:Sons Vn, w. Ingrid Matthews (vn), Byron Schenkman (hpd) — Wildboar ▲ WLBR 9601 [DDD]
- Jacquet De La Guerre, E.:Suites Hpd, w. Ingrid Matthews (vn), Byron Schenkman (hpd)—Prélude in a; Toccata; Chaconne "L"Inconstante" — Wildboar ▲ WLBR 9601 [DDD]
- Out of the Orient Crystall Skyes, w. Nancy Zylstra (sop), Jillion Stopples Dupree (hpd/org), Michael Sand (baroque vn/vl), Linda Melsted (baroque vn), Olga Hauptmann (baroque va), Ellen Siebert (vl), Russell Paige (vl) — Wildboar ▲ WLBR 8901 [DDD]
- Volans, K.:White Man Sleeps Hpds, w. Robert Hill (hpd), Kevin Volans (hpd), Robyn Schulkowsky (perc) *(rec West German Radio, Cologne & Watershed Recording Studio, London, Apr 20, 1984 & July 27, 1)* — United ▲ CAL 88034 [ADD]

Ting, Liuh-Wen (va)—see ORCHESTRAS & ENSEMBLES Continuum Chamber Ensemble

Tingay, Gillian (hp)
- Damase, J.-M.:Qnt Fl, Hp & Strs, w. Anna Noakes (fl), Richard Friedman (vn), Jane Atkins (vl), Ferenc Szucs (vc) — ASV ▲ ASV 898 [DDD]
- Damase, J.-M.:Son Fl & Hp, w. Anna Noakes (fl) — ASV ▲ ASV 898 [DDD]
- Damase, J.-M.:Trio Fl, w. Anna Noakes (fl), Ferenc Szucs (vc) — ASV ▲ ASV 898 [DDD]
- Damase, J.-M.:Vars on *Early Morning*, w. Anna Noakes (fl) — ASV ▲ ASV 898 [DDD]
- Fantaisie for Flute & Harp, w. Anna Noakes (fl) — ASV ▲ ASV 2101
- Jolivet, A.:Alla rustica, w. Anna Noakes (fl) — ASV ("French Chamber Music" series) ▲ ASV 948
- Jolivet, A.:Petite suite, w. Anna Noakes (fl), Jonathan Barritt (va) — ASV ("French Chamber Music" series) ▲ ASV 948

Tinnefeld, Hans-Joachim (b gtr)
- Weill, K.:Songs, w. Sara Musinowski (sgr), Stefan Weinzierl (pno)—September Song; Listen to My Song; Mon Ami, My Friend; It Never Was You; One Life to Live; My Ship; I'm a Stranger Here Myself; Foolish Heart; Speak Low; Sing Me Not a Ballad; Lonely House; Trouble Man; Stay Well; Lost in the Stars — Signum ▲ SIG X85-00 [DDD]

Tinney, Hugh (pno)
- Fleischmann, A.:Qnt Pno, w. Vanbrugh String Quartet *(rec St. Georges, Bristol, Ireland, May 17-19, 1995)* — Marco Polo ("Irish Composer" series) ▲ 8.223888 [DDD]
- Liszt, F.:Harmonies poétiques et religieuses — Meridian ▲ MER 84240 [DDD]
- Mendelssohn, F.:Cons 2 Pnos, w. Benjamin Frith (pno), P. Ó. Duinn (cnd), RTE Sinfonietta *(rec Dublin, Oct 1995)* — Naxos ▲ 8.553416 [DDD]

Tinturin, Noëlle Compinsky (pno)—see ORCHESTRAS & ENSEMBLES Tinturin Duo

Tinturin, Peter (gtr)—see ORCHESTRAS & ENSEMBLES Tinturin Duo

Tipo, Maria (pno)
- Bach, J.S.:Goldberg Vars — EMI Classics ▲ CDC 47546
- Bach, J.S.:Partitas Hpd, BWV 825-830—Nos. 1, 2 & 4 — EMI Classics ▲ CDC 54463
- Bach, J.S.:Partitas Hpd, BWV 825-830—Nos. 3, 5 & 6 — EMI Classics ▲ CDC 54464
- Chopin, F.:Nocturnes — EMI Classics ▲ ZDCB 55073
- Clementi, M.:Sons Pno—Op. 8/1, 13/6, 25/5 & 40/3 — EMI Classics ▲ CDC 54766
- Mozart, W.A.:Con 21 Pno, w. J. Perlea (cnd), Vienna SO — Vox Box ("Legends" series) 2-▲ CDX2 5515 [ADD]
- Mozart, W.A.:Con 23 Pno, w. A. Jordan (cnd), Paris Orchestral Ensemble — EMI Classics ▲ CDC 54234
- Mozart, W.A.:Con 25 Pno, w. J. Perlea (cnd), Vienna SO — Vox Box ("Legends" series) 2-▲ CDX2 5515 [ADD]
- Mozart, W.A.:Con 27 Pno, w. A. Jordan (cnd), Paris Orchestral Ensemble — EMI Classics ▲ CDC 54234
- Scarlatti, D.:Sons Kbd — Vox Box ("Legends" series) 2-▲ CDX2 5515 [ADD]

Tirimo, Martin (pno)
- Chopin, F.:Con 1 Pno, w. F. Glushchenko (cnd), Philharmonia Orch — Conifer Classics ▲ 75605-51247-2 [DDD]
- Chopin, F.:Con 2 Pno, w. F. Glushchenko (cnd), Philharmonia Orch — Conifer Classics ▲ 75605-51247-2 [DDD]
- Debussy, C.:Estampes — IMP ("Classics" series) ▲ IMP 6700182
- Debussy, C.:Etudes — IMP ("Classics" series) ▲ IMP 6700182
- Debussy, C.:L'Isle joyeuse — IMP ("Classics" series) ▲ IMP 6700182
- Debussy, C.:Preludes Pno (sels)—24 sels — IMP ("Classics" series) ▲ IMP 6700792
- Rachmaninoff, S.:Études-tableaux, Opp. 33 & 39, w. Y. Levi (cnd), Philharmonia Orch — Classics for Pleasure ▲ CDCFP 9017 [DDD]
- Rachmaninoff, S.:Rhapsody on a Theme of Paganini, w. Y. Levi (cnd), Philharmonia Orch — Classics for Pleasure ▲ CDCFP 9017 [DDD]
- Tippett, M.:Con Pno, w. M. Tippett (cnd), BBC PO — Nimbus ▲ NI 5301 [DDD]

Tirincanti, Gaspare (cl)
- Brahms, J.:Sons Cl (comp), w. Maurizio Deoriti (pno) — Stradivarius ▲ STV SIP 27 [DDD]
- Brahms, J.:Trio Cl, w. Marco Boni (vc), Maurizio Deoriti (pno) — Stradivarius ▲ STV SIP 27 [DDD]

Tirino, Thomas (pno)
- Lecuona, E.:Pno Music—Andalucia [Suite Española]; Ante El Escorial; Zambra Gitana; Aragonesa; Granada; Zambra; San Francisco El Grande; Aragón [Vals España]; Preludio en la Noche; La Habanera; Mazurka en Glissando; Canto del Guajiro; 3 Miniatures; Canto Siboney; Noche Azul *(rec Patrych Sound Studios, New York City, 1994-95)* — BIS ▲ CD 754 [DDD]
- Lecuona, E.:Pno Music—Rapsodia Argentina for Pno & Orch [arr Bartos/Tirino; w Michael Bartos (cnd), Polish National RSO]; Diary of a Child; Adiós a las Trincheras; Cuba & America; Black Cat; Cuba at Arms; El Somrero de Yarey:Suite; Quasi Bolero (song trans); Dame de tus Rosas (song trans); Waltzes:Crisantemo, Vals del Sena, Locura, Barba-Azul, Vals de los Mares, Ojos Triunfadores, Bésame, Soñaba Contigo, Voilà — BIS ▲ CD 774 [DDD]
- Lecuona, E.:Pno Music—Danzas Afro-Cubanas; Danzas Cubanas Típicas; Échate pa'allá María!; Valses Fantásticos; Vals del Nilo; Gardenia; Porcelana China; Polka de los Enanos; Noches de Estrellas; Yo te Quiero Siempre — BIS ▲ CD 794 [DDD]
- Lecuona, E.:Rapsodia Cubana, w. M. Bartos (cnd), Polish National RSO Katowice — BIS ▲ CD 794 [DDD]
- Lecuona, E.:Rapsodia negra, w. M. Bartos (cnd), Polish National RSO Katowice *(rec Centre of Culture, Katowice, Poland, Feb 27, 1993)* — BIS ▲ CD 754 [DDD]
- Macdowell, E.:Con 1 Pno, w. V. Kazandjiev (cnd), Bulgarian RSO — Centaur ▲ CRC 2149 [DDD]
- Macdowell, E.:Con 2 Pno, w. V. Kazandjiev (cnd), Bulgarian RSO — Centaur ▲ CRC 2149 [DDD]

Tironi, Paloma (hp)
- Respighi, O.:Gli uccelli, w. Stefano Mancini (fl), Alberto Cesaraccio (ob), Antonio Puglia (cl), Stefano Melis (cel), R. Tigani (cnd), Sassari SO *(rec Rome, Oct 11-14, 1994)* — Bongiovanni ▲ GB 2166 [DDD]

Tischer, R. (va)
- Matson, S.:i-5, w. A. Shulmann (hp), P. Kent (vn), M. Newman (vn), E. Duke-Kirkpatrick (vc), B. Morgenthaler (db) *(rec Aug. 29-30, 1992)* — Audioquest ▲ AQCD 1013
- Matson, S.:Steel Chords, w. D. Livingston (gtr), P. Kent (vn), M. Newman (vn), J. Derouin (vn), C. Moussas (vn), E. Duke-Kirkpatrick (vc), B. Morgenthaler (db), S. Matson (cnd) *(rec Aug. 29-30, 1992)* — Audioquest ▲ AQCD 1013

Tisdel, Scott (vc)
- Sierra, R.:Fantasías, w. William Helmers (cl), Stefanie Jacob (pno) — CRI ▲ CD 724 [DDD]
- Sierra, R.:Piezas Características, w. William Helmers (b cl), Catherine Schubilske (vn), Dennis Najoom (tpt), Stefanie Jacob (pno), Thomas Wetzel (perc), N. Gittleman (cnd) — CRI ▲ CD 724 [DDD]

Titov, Alexander (pno)
- Gounod, C.:Ave Maria, w. V. Stenkina (alt) — Infinity Digital ▲ QK 57254 [DDD]
- Gounod, C.:Ave Maria, w. Valeria Stenkina (alt) — Infinity Digital ▲ QK 69255 [DDD]
- Schubert, Franz:Ave Maria! Jungfrau mild!, w. V. Stenkina (alt) — Infinity Digital ▲ QK 57254 [DDD]
- Schubert, Franz:Ave Maria! Jungfrau mild!, w. Valeria Stenkina (alt) — Infinity Digital ▲ QK 69255 [DDD]

Titterington, David (org)
- Eben, Petr:Job, w. H. Lee (nar) [E] — Multisonic ▲ 31 0095-2 [DDD]

Titze, Karl Maria (vn)
- Pfitzner, H.:Qnt Pno, w. W. Kamper (pno), A. Kamper (vn), E. Weis (va), F. Kvarda (vc) — Preiser ▲ 93111 (m) [AAD]

Tkachenko, Irina (vn)
- Vainberg, M.:Trio Pno, w. Anatoli Sheludyakov (pno), Tatiana Zavarskaya (vc) — Olympia ▲ OLY 581 [DDD]

Tkachenko, Nikolay (vn)
- Ustvolskaya, G.:Octet Obs, w. Nicolay Neretin (ob), Piotr Tosenko (ob), Alexander Stang (vn), Olga Ribaltchenko (vn), Valentin Lukin (vn), Valerii Znamenskii (timp), Oleg Malov (pno), O. Malov (cnd) *(rec St. Petersburg Radio House, Oct. & Nov. 1994)* — Megadisc ▲ 7865

Tkanov, Y. (va)
- Ravel, M.:Pavane pour une infante défunte, w. Vera Dulova (hp) [arr. V. Borisovsky] *(rec 1992)* — Russian Compact Disc ("Talents of Russia" series) ▲ RCD 16206 [AAD]

Tlatlik, Zygmunt (bn)
- Scarmolin, A.L.:Sym 3, w. J. E. Suben (cnd), Polish National RSO Katowice *(rec Katowice, Poland, Sept 25, 1993)* — New World ▲ 80502-2

Tluck, B. (vc)—see ORCHESTRAS & ENSEMBLES Orfeo Trio

Tluck, Eugen (va)
- Suder, J.:Qt Pno, w. Orfeo Trio — Calig ▲ CAL 50880 [DDD]

Tobel, R. von (vc)
- Schumann, R.:Trio 1 Pno, w. M. Horszowski (pno), J. Szigeti (vn) *(rec live 1956)* — Music & Arts 4-▲ CD 689 (m) [AAD]

Tobias, Alex (perc)
- Shea, D.:Hsi-Yu Chi, w. Sim Cain (perc), Hideki Kato (bass instrument), Wu Man (pipa), Zeena Parkins (hp/pno/acc), Jim Pugliese (perc), Mark Ribot (gtr/banjo), David Shea (sampler/pno/turntables), Alex Tobias (celtic dr/misc.), Rebecca Wilson (screaming), John Zorn (a sax) — Tzadik ("The Composers" series) ▲ TZA 7005 [DDD]

Toccafondi, Anna (pno)
- Castelnuovo-Tedesco, M.:Songs, w. Leonardo de Lisi (ten)—Coplas, Op. 7/1; Chansons Grises; "1830", Op. 36; Poems de la Pléïade, Op. 79; Shakespeare Songs Op. 24/1; Poesia Svedese, Op. 189; Sera, Op. 23; Sonetto di Dante, Op. 101; Sonetti del Petrarca, Op. 74; L'infinito, Op. 22; Piccino Picciò, Op. 26 — Vocalia ▲ VOC 001 [DDD]

Tocco, James (pno)
- Copland, A.:Blues — Pro Arte ▲ CDD-183
- Copland, A.:Danzón Cubano, w. H. Foss (pno) — Pro Arte ▲ CDD-183
- Copland, A.:Pno Music—3 Episodes from "Our Town"; 4 Episodes from "Rodeo"; 4 Piano Blues — Pro Arte ▲ CDD-183
- Copland, A.:Vars Pno — Pro Arte ▲ CDD-183
- Corigliano, J.:Con Pno, w. L. Leighton Smith (cnd), Louisville Orch — Louisville ▲ LCD 008 [ADD]

Tocco, James (pno) (cont.)
Griffes, C.T.:De profundis — Gasparo ▲ GS 233
Griffes, C.T.:Fant Pieces, Op. 6 — Gasparo 4–▲ GS 1007
Griffes, C.T.:Fant Pieces, Op. 6 — Gasparo ▲ GS 232
Griffes, C.T.:Legend Pno — Gasparo 4–▲ GS 1007
Griffes, C.T.:Legend Pno — Gasparo ▲ GS 234
Griffes, C.T.:Pno Music—Roman Sketches, Op. 7; Preludes (1919); De Profundis; Son Pno; 3 Tone-Pictures, Op. 5 — Gasparo 4–▲ GS 1007
Griffes, C.T.:The Pleasure Dome of Kubla Khan — Gasparo ▲ GS 234
Griffes, C.T.:The Pleasure Dome of Kubla Khan — Gasparo 4–▲ GS 1007
Griffes, C.T.:Preludes (3) Pno — Gasparo ▲ GS 231
Griffes, C.T.:Rhap Pno — Gasparo ▲ GS 232
Griffes, C.T.:Rhap Pno — Gasparo 4–▲ GS 1007
Griffes, C.T.:Roman Sketches, Op. 7 — Gasparo ▲ GS 231
Griffes, C.T.:Son Pno — Gasparo ▲ GS 233
Griffes, C.T.:Tone-Pictures, Op. 5 — Gasparo ▲ GS 234
Macdowell, E.:Sea Pieces — Gasparo ▲ GS 234
Macdowell, E.:Sons Pno (comp) — Gasparo 4–▲ GS 1007
Macdowell, E.:Son 2 Pno — Gasparo ▲ GS 233
Macdowell, E.:Son 3 Pno — Gasparo ▲ GS 232
Macdowell, E.:Son 4 Pno — Gasparo ▲ GS 231
Orrego-Salas, J.:Mobili, w. Kim Kashkashian (va) *(rec Musical Arts Ctr, Bloomington, IN, Apr 3, 1987)* — Indiana Univ School of Music ▲ IUSM 02
Rachmaninoff, S.:Suite 2 for 2 Pnos, w. Ruth Laredo (pno) *(rec St. Hugo of the Hills Catholic Church, Bloomfield Hills, MI)* — Gasparo ▲ GAS 313
Schulhoff, E.:Jazz Etudes Pno *(rec Lockenhaus Festival, 1986)* — ECM New Series 2–▲ 78118-21347-2 [DDD]
Stravinsky, I.:Con Pno Ww, w. H.R. Reynolds (cnd), Detroit Chamber Winds — Koch International Classics ▲ KIC 7211
Stravinsky, I.:Pno-Rag-Music, w. H.R. Reynolds (cnd), Detroit Chamber Winds — Koch International Classics ▲ KIC 7211
Stravinsky, I.:Le Sacre du printemps Pno, w. Ruth Laredo (pno) *(rec St. Hugo of the Hills Catholic Church, Bloomfield Hills, MI)* — Gasparo ▲ GAS 313

Toda, Yayoi (vn)
Keuris, T.:Con 2 Vn, w. D. Porcelijn (cnd), Netherlands Radio CO — Emergo ▲ EC 3940 [DDD]

Todd, J. (vc)—see ORCHESTRAS & ENSEMBLES Coull String Quartet

Todd, Richard (hn)
Poulenc, F.:Sxt Pno, w. André Previn (pno), Elizabeth Mann (fl), Steve Taylor (ob), David Shifrin (cl), Dennis Godburn (bn) *(rec Manhattan Center Studios, New York City, Apr. 7–8, 1993)* — RCA Red Seal ▲ 09026-68181-2 [DDD]
Schuller, G.:Con 1 Hn, w. G. Schuller (cnd), Saarbrück RSO — GM ▲ GM 2044

Toet, Charles (sackbut)
Cavalli, P.F.:Vespero della beata Vergine Maria, w. Barbara Borden (sop), Emily van Evera (sop), Markus Brutscher (ten), Mark Padmore (ten), Rodrigo del Pozo (ten), Gerd Türk (ten), Harry van der Kamp (bass), Peter Zimpel (sgr), Bruce Dickey (sackbut), Concerto Palatino, Schola Cantorum Basiliensis — Harmonia Mundi France ("Documenta" series) 2–▲ HMC 905219/20

Toettcher, Sebastian (vc)—see also ORCHESTRAS & ENSEMBLES Viklarbo Chamber Ensemble
Matson, S.:Range, w. Catherine Robbin (mez), Susan Greenberg (fl), Joseph Stone (fl), Glen Garrett (cl), Suren Karapetyan (hn), Peter Kent (vn), Kazi Pitelka (va), Don Ferrone (db), Doug Livingston (gtr/mand), John Schneider (gtr), Amy Shulman (hp), Terry Schoenig (perc), S. Matson (cnd) *(rec Schnee Studio, Universal City, CA, Mar 12, 1995)* — New Albion ▲ NA 091

Tofani, C. (vn)—see ORCHESTRAS & ENSEMBLES Seicentonovecento Ensemble

Tofte-Hansen, Jens (bn)
Nielsen, C.:Qnt Ww, w. James Galway (fl), Bjõrn Carl Nielsen (ob), Niels Thomsen (cl), Bjõrn Fosdal (hn) *(rec Vangede Church, Copenhagen, Mar 16, 1985)* — RCA Red Seal ▲ 07863-56359-2 [ADD]

Tog, Henning (bn)—see ORCHESTRAS & ENSEMBLES Berlin Philharmonic Wind Ensemble

Togni, Camillo (pno)
Togni, C.:La Guirlande du blois, w. Dorothy Dorow (sop) — Stradivarius ▲ STV DTM 90002 [ADD]
Togni, C.:Son Fl, w. Severino Gazzelloni (fl) — Stradivarius ▲ STV DTM 90002 [ADD]

Tognon, Paolo (baroque bn)—see ORCHESTRAS & ENSEMBLES Ensemble Barocco Padua Sans Souci, Consorto Vago

Tokarev, Michail (fl)
Ustvolskaya, G.:Composition 3, w. Natalia Danilina (fl), Maria Osipova (fl), Inna Rodina (fl), Kirill Sokolov (bn), Dmitrii Krasnik (bn), Arsenii Makarov (bn), Konstantin Shevchuk (bn), Galina Sandovskaya (pno), O. Malov (cnd) *(rec St. Petersburg Radio House, Jan. 1994)* — Megadisc ▲ 7867

Tokarev, Michail (pic)
Ustvolskaya, G.:Composition 1, w. Alexei Arbuszov (tuba), Oleg Malov (pno) *(rec St. Petersburg Radio House, Jan. 1994)* — Megadisc ▲ 7867

Toker, Gustavo (band)
Piazzolla, A.:Music of, w. Juan Pablo Dobal (pno), Aurelia Saxophone Quartet—Escualo; Adio Nonino; Caliente; Astor que Estas en Los Cielos; Contrabajeando; Cuatro Estaciones Porteñas; Vayamos al Diablo; Four, for Tango; Milonga del Angel; Contrabajissimo; Michelangelo 70; Fuga y Misterio; Variaciones de la Fuga *(rec live, De Rode Hoed, Amsterdam, June 26, 1994)* — Etcetera ▲ KTC 1186

Tokos, Monika (gtr)
Concierto de Aranjuez, w. Jürgen Rost (gtr), Budapest Strings [cnd:Bela Banfalvi] — LaserLight ▲ 15602 [DDD]

Tokos, Zoltán (gtr)
Boccherini, L.:Qnts Gtr & Strs, w. Danubius Quartet—Qnts., G.451 & 453; Qnt. G.275 [w. György Éder (cello)] *(rec August 1992)* — Naxos ▲ 8.550731 [DDD]
Boccherini, L.:Qnts Gtr & Strs, w. Danubius Quartet—in D, G.448, G.449 & in G, G.450 *(rec Aug. 1–4, 1991)* — Naxos ▲ 8.550552 [DDD]
Rodrigo, J.:Concierto de Aranjuez, w. B. Bánfalvi (cnd), Budapest Strings — Laserlight ▲ 15 602 [DDD]
Vivaldi, A.:Cons for 2 Gtrs, w. Béla Sztankovits (gtr), Budapest Strings *(rec Unitarian Church, Budapest, Nov. 1991)* — Naxos ▲ 8.553028 [DDD]
Vivaldi, A.:Con for 2 Mands, w. Béla Sztankovits (gtr), Budapest Strings *(rec Unitarian Church, Budapest, Nov 1991)* — Naxos ▲ 8.553028 [DDD]
Vivaldi, A.:Con for 2 Vns, RV.523, w. Béla Sztankovits (gtr), Budapest Strings [arr 2 gtrs] *(rec Unitarian Church, Budapest, Nov. 1991)* — Naxos ▲ 8.553028 [DDD]

Tol, Hans (rcr)—see ORCHESTRAS & ENSEMBLES La Fontegara Amsterdam, La Dada

Toll, John (hpd)—see also ORCHESTRAS & ENSEMBLES Musica Secreta
Stanley, J.:Cons Org, Op. 10, w. London Baroque—Concerto No. 4 in c — Amon Ra ▲ CD-SAR 14 [DDD]
Telemann, G.P.:Sons Ob, w. Paul Goodwin (ob), Susan Sheppard (vc), Nigel North (thb/archlt) — Harmonia Mundi ▲ HMU 907152
Vivaldi, A.:Cons Diverse Instrs, w. M. Verbruggen (rcr), P. Goodwin (ob), J. Holloway (vn), D. Godburn (bn), S. Comberti (vc)—7 Concerti—in D, RV.84; in a, RV.86; in D, RV.94; in D, "Las Pastorella," RV.95; in F, RV.99; in g, RV.103; in g, RV.105 — Harmonia Mundi USA ▲ HMU 907046

Toll, John (hpd/org)—see also ORCHESTRAS & ENSEMBLES Romanesca
Three Parts upon a Ground, w. John Hollowy (vn), Stanley Ritchie (vn), Andrew Manze (vn), Mary Springfels (vl), Nigel North (lt) — Harmonia Mundi USA ▲ HMU 907091
Vivaldi, A.:Son Fl Ob, RV.59, w. C. Lawson (chl) [arr rcr & va bastarda] — Harmonia Mundi USA ▲ HMU 907104
Vivaldi, A.:Sons Ob, w. P. Goodwin (ob), G. Hennessey (ob), J. Holloway (vn), C. Lawson (cl), N. North (archlt/gtr), S. Sheppard (vc), F. Eustace (bn)—RV.53, 58, 81 & 779 — Harmonia Mundi USA ▲ HMU 907104

Tollefson, Arthur (pno)
Still, W.G.:Folk Suites, w. Leonard Garrison (fl), Robert Umiker (cl), Samuel Magill (vc) — Cambria ▲ CD 1060 [ADD]

Tollefson, Arthur (pno) (cont.)
Still, W.G.:Romance Sax, w. Robert Umiker (a sax) — Cambria ▲ CD 1060 [ADD]

Tolley, R. (tpt)
Van Appledorn, M.J.:Cornucopia — CRS ▲ CD 9153

Tolpygo, Mikhail (va)
Martinů, B.:Rhap-Con Va, w. E. Chivzhel (cnd), State SO *(rec 1990)* — Consonance ▲ 81-0003 [DDD]

Toman, Larry (va)
Wagner, R.:Siegfried Idyll, w. T. Holowach (vn), M. Skazinetsky (vn), L. Toman (va), R. Laurie (vc), C. Elliott (db), S. Shulman (fl), T. Maloney (cl), J. Valdepenas (cl), J. Fetherston (cl), S. Mosher (bn), S. Wilson (hn), R. Cohen (hn), J. Cowell (tpt), G. Gould (cnd) *(rec July 27–29 & Sept. 8, 198)* — Sony Classical ▲ SMK 52650 [ADD]

Tomas, Markus (pno)
Zaidel-Rudolph, J.:Virtuoso I — Claremont ▲ GSE 1532

Tomás, Pilar (hpd)
Anglebert, J.-H. d':Kbd Music—Suite No. 3 in d *(rec Madrid, Oct 4–9, 1990)* — RNE/Spanish National Radio ▲ M3/08 [DDD]
Clérambault, L.N.:Suite Hpd *(rec Madrid, Oct 4–9, 1990)* — RNE/Spanish National Radio ▲ M3/08 [DDD]
Couperin, F.:Pièces de clavecin (sels)—Ordre XXVI *(rec Madrid, Oct 4–9, 1990)* — RNE/Spanish National Radio ▲ M3/08 [DDD]

Tomasek, J. (vn)
Shostakovich, D.:Con 2 Vn, w. C. Mackerras (cnd), Prague RSO — Praga ▲ PR 250052

Tomasi, W. (b fl)—see ORCHESTRAS & ENSEMBLES Vienna Flautists

Tomaszewski, Tomasz (vn)—see also ORCHESTRAS & ENSEMBLES Berlin German Opera Orch Soloists
Martinů, B.:La Revue de Cuisine (sels), w. G. Lösch (vc), R. Schönemann (cl), V. Knappe (bn), A. Lange (tpt), S. Schubert-Weber (pno)—Suite for Violin, Cello, Clarinet, Bassoon, Trumpet & Piano — FSM-Adagio ▲ FCD 97 219

Tomšič, Dubravka (pno)
Bach, J.S.:Italian Con — PMG ("Vienna Master" series) ▲ CD 160202 [DDD]
Bach, J.S.:Partitas Hpd, BWV 825–830—BWV 825 — PMG ("Vienna Master" series) ▲ CD 160202 [DDD]
Bach, J.S.:Toccatas Hpd, BWV 910–16—BWV 912 — PMG ("Vienna Master" series) ▲ CD 160202 [DDD]
Beethoven, L. van:Con 1 Pno, w. A. Nanut (cnd), Ljubljana RSO — PMG ("Vienna Master" series) ▲ CD 160220 [DDD]
Beethoven, L. van:Con 1 Pno, w. A. Nanut (cnd), Philharmonia Slavonica — Vivace 3–▲ E 323 [DDD]
Beethoven, L. van:Con 3 Pno, w. A. Nanut (cnd), Philharmonia Slavonica — Vivace 3–▲ E 323 [DDD]
Beethoven, L. van:Con 3 Pno, w. A. Nanut (cnd), Ljubljana RSO — PMG ("Vienna Master" series) ▲ CD 160221 [DDD]
Beethoven, L. van:Con 5 Pno, "Emperor", w. A. Nanut (cnd), Ljubljana SO — Allegretto ▲ ACD 8193
Beethoven, L. van:Son 8 Pno, "Pathétique" — Vivace 3–▲ E 330 [ADD/DDD]
Beethoven, L. van:Son 8 Pno, "Pathétique" — PMG ("Vienna Master" series) ▲ CD 160203 [DDD]
Beethoven, L. van:Son 14 Pno, "Moonlight Son" — Vivace 3–▲ E 330 [ADD/DDD]
Beethoven, L. van:Son 14 Pno, "Moonlight Son" — PMG ("Vienna Master" series) ▲ CD 160203 [DDD]
Beethoven, L. van:Son 21 Pno, "Waldstein" — PMG ("Vienna Master" series) ▲ CD 160203 [DDD]
Beethoven, L. van:Son 21 Pno, "Waldstein" — Vivace 3–▲ E 330 [ADD/DDD]
Beethoven, L. van:Son 23 Pno, "Appassionata" — Koch International Classics ▲ KIC 7066-2 [DDD]
Beethoven, L. van:Son 26 Pno, "Les Adieux" — Koch International Classics ▲ KIC 7066-2 [DDD]
Beethoven, L. van:Son 31 Pno — Koch International Classics ▲ KIC 7066-2 [DDD]
Brahms, J.:Con 1 Pno, Ljubljana RSO — Critics Choice 2–▲ CCD 944 [DDD]
Brahms, J.:Con 2 Pno, Ljubljana RSO — Critics Choice 2–▲ CCD 944 [DDD]
Chopin, F.:Con 1 Pno, w. M. Munih (cnd), Ljubljana SO — Allegretto ▲ ACD 8198
Chopin, F.:Fant — PMG (Vienna Master) ▲ CD 160206 [DDD]
Chopin, F.:Impromptus — PMG (Vienna Master) ▲ CD 160206 [DDD]
Chopin, F.:Nocturnes—Op. 27, Nos. 1 & 2; Op. 37, Nos. 1 & 2 — PMG (Vienna Master) ▲ CD 160206 [DDD]
Favorite Encores — Stradivari Classics ▲ SCD 6065 [DDD] ■ SMC 6065 (D)
Grieg, E.:Con Pno, Op. 16, w. A. Lizzio (cnd), Philharmonia Slavonica — Vivace 2–▲ G 117/118 [DDD]
Grieg, E.:Con Pno, Op. 16, w. A. Lizzio (cnd), Philharmonia Slavonica — Vivace 3–▲ E 322 [DDD]
The Mozart Collection, w. Joze Banic (bn), Pietro Cavaliere (cl), Ruda Kosi (hp), Joze Falout (hn), Ljubljana SO [cnd:Anton Nanut, Marko Munih, Alexander Pitamic, Mihail Glinka] — Stradivari Classics ("Treasury of Great Classics" series) 5–▲ S5D 61000 [DDD] 5–■ S5C 61000 (D)
Mozart, W.A.:Con 26 Pno, w. A. Nanut (cnd), Ljubljana SO — Allegretto ▲ ACD 8198
Mozart, W.A.:Sons Pno—No. 4 in E♭, K.282 & No. 14 in c, K.457 — Koch International Classics ▲ KIC 7040-2 [DDD]
Rachmaninoff, S.:Rhapsody on a Theme of Paganini, w. A. Nanut (cnd), Ljubljana SO — Vox Box 3–▲ CD3X 3020 [ADD]
Scarlatti, D.:Sons Kbd—L.103, 104, 118, 210, 349, 352, 366, 383, 387, 391, 396, 413, 487 — PMG ("Vienna Master" series) ▲ CD 160106 [DDD]
Schumann, R.:Con Pno, w. A. Lizzio (cnd), Philharmonia Slavonica — Vivace 3–▲ E 322 [DDD]

Tomes, Susan (pno)—see also ORCHESTRAS & ENSEMBLES Florestan Trio
Brahms, J.:Sons Vn (comp), w. K. Osostowicz (vn) — Hyperion ▲ CDA 66465
Fauré, G.:Son 1 Vn, w. K. Osostowicz (vn) — Hyperion ▲ CDA 66277
Fauré, G.:Son 2 Vn, w. K. Osostowicz (vn) — Hyperion ▲ CDA 66277
Martinů, B.:Sonatina for 2 Vns, w. K. Osostowicz (vn), E. Kovacic (vn) — Hyperion ▲ CDA 66473 [DDD]
Milhaud, D.:Son for 2 Vns, w. K. Osostowicz (vn), E. Kovacic (vn) — Hyperion ▲ CDA 66473 [DDD]
Saint-Saëns, C.:Carnival of the Animals, w. I. Brown (pno), Nash Ensemble — Virgin Classics ▲ 59514 [DDD]
Weir, J.:Chamber Music, w. William Howard (pno), Petra Casen (hpd), Domus Chamber Ensemble, Schubert Ensemble—Distance & Enchantment; The Bagpiper's Trio; I Broke Off a Golden Branch; El Rey de Francia; The Art of Touching the Keyboard; The King of France; Ardnamurchan Point — Collins Classics ▲ COL 1453

Tomfohrde, Ruth (pno)
Carter, E.:Elegy Va, w. L. Wheeler (va) — Albany ▲ TROY 141 [DDD]
Heiden, B.:Son Va, w. Lawrence Wheeler (va) — Albany ▲ TROY 141 [DDD]
Martinů, B.:Son 3 Vc, w. A. Elliott (vc) — Koch International Classics ▲ KIC 7064-2 [DDD]

Tomiinari, Yuichi (hn)—see ORCHESTRAS & ENSEMBLES Orphée Piano & Wind Quintet

Tomioka, Kazuo (s sax/a sax)
Ikebe, S.-I.:Energeia, w. Shin-ichi Iwamoto (t sax), H. Iwaki (cnd), New Japan PO — Camerata ▲ 30CM 351 [DDD]

Tomita, Isao (synths)
Wild Classics:A Celebration of Animals & Nature, w. James Galway (fl), Ofra Harnoy (vc), Martin Hoherman (vc), Emily Mitchell (hp), Michael Dussek (pno), Samuel Lipman (pno), Leo Litwin (pno), Gerhard Oppitz (pno), Isao Tomita (synths), Boston Pops Orch [cnd:Arthur Fiedler], Chicago SO [cnd:Fritz Reiner] — RCA Red Seal ▲ 09026-68483-2 ■ 09026-68483-4

Tomita, Toyoji (trbn)
Brown, C.:Lava, w. William Winant (perc), Tom Dill (tpt), Peter Wahrhaftig (tuba), Chris Brown (elecs)—Crack; Eruption; Fountain; River; Crest; Pahoehoe — Tzadik ("The Composers" series) ▲ TZA 7002 [DDD]
Riley, T.:In C, w. Bruce Ackley, Steve Adams, Don R. Baker, Chris Brown, George Brooks, Steve Coughlin, Blake Derby, Bill Douglass, Mihr'un'Nisa Douglass, Hank Dutt, David Harrington, Don Howe, Joan Jeanrenaud, Alden Jenks, Warner Jepson, Henry Kaiser, Jaron Lanier, Bill Maginnis, George Marsh, Shabda Owens, Jon Raskin, Gyan Riley, Terry Riley, Gino Robair, John Sackett, Ramón Sender, John Sherba, Danny Tunick, William Winant, Evan Ziporyn *(rec Jan. 14, 1990)* — New Albion ▲ NA 071

Tomkins, Leslie (va)
Kernis, A.J.:America(n) (Day) Dreams, w. Kim Barber (mez), Mary Rowell (vn), Tonya Tomkins (vc), Robert Black (db), Kathleen Nester (fl), Larry Guy (cl/b cl), John Dent (tpt), Anthony Cecere (hn), Leslie Stifelman (pno), Susan Jolles (hp), Jeffrey Milarsky (perc), M. Barrett (cnd)—A Navajo Blanket; Wednesday at the Waldorf; The Pregnant Dream; The Blue Bottle; "So Long" to the Moon from the Men of Apollo; Epilogue:The Pure Suit of Happiness *(rec Manhattan Center Studios, New York, May 31–June 3, 1995)* New Albion ♦ NA 083CD

Tomkins, Tonya (vc)
Beethoven, L. van:Trio Pno, Op.38, w. S. Hoogland (pno), E. Hoeprich (cl) Koch International Classics ▲ KIC 7015–2 [DDD] ■ 3–7015–4 (D)
Glinka, M.:Trio pathétique, w. E. Hoeprich (cl), S. Hoogland (fortepno) Koch International Classics ▲ KIC 7015–2 [DDD] ■ 3–7015–4 (D)
Kernis, A.J.:America(n) (Day) Dreams, w. Kim Barber (mez), Mary Rowell (vn), Leslie Tomkins (va), Robert Black (db), Kathleen Nester (fl), Larry Guy (cl/b cl), John Dent (tpt), Anthony Cecere (hn), Leslie Stifelman (pno), Susan Jolles (hp), Jeffrey Milarsky (perc), M. Barrett (cnd)—A Navajo Blanket; Wednesday at the Waldorf; The Pregnant Dream; The Blue Bottle; "So Long" to the Moon from the Men of Apollo; Epilogue:The Pure Suit of Happiness *(rec Manhattan Center Studios, New York, May 31–June 3, 1995)* New Albion ♦ NA 083CD

Tomlinson, Charles (db)—see ORCHESTRAS & ENSEMBLES Musicians' Accord

Tommasini, Anthony (pno)
Thomson, V.:Portraits, w. S. Leventhal (vn), J. Miller (vc), F.T. Cohen (ob), R. Haroutunian (bn)—Selected Portraits (13) for Pno (1935–42); Five Ladies for Vn & Pno (1930; 1940; 1983); A Portrait of 2, for Ob, Bn & Pno (1984); 3 Portraits for Pno (1940; arr Samuel Dushkin in 1947 for Vn & Pno); Etude for Vc & Pno:A Portrait of Frederic James (1966); Lili Hastings for Vc & Pno (1983) Northeastern ▲ NR 240–CD
Thomson, V.:Son Vn, w. S. Leventhal (vn) Northeastern ▲ NR 240–CD

Tomter, Lars Anders (va)
Brahms, J.:Sons Cl (comp), w. L. O. Andsnes (pno) Broadway Angel ▲ CDC 59154
Schumann, R.:Märchenbilder, w. L. O. Andsnes (pno) Broadway Angel ▲ CDC 59154
Walton, W.:Con Va, w. P. Daniel (cnd), English Northern Philharmonia *(rec Leeds Town Hall, Apr 5 & 6, 1995)* Naxos ▲ 8.553402 [DDD]

Toney, Kelly Smith (vn)—see ORCHESTRAS & ENSEMBLES Louisiana State Univ New Music Ensemble

Tonkha, Vladimir (vc)
Gubaidulina, S.:Silenzio, w. Friedrich Lips (bayan), Gidon Kremer (vn) *(rec Lockenhaus Festival, Austria, 1995)* BIS ▲ CD 810 [DDD]

Tønnesen, Terje (vn)
Grieg, E.:Sons Vn, Opp. 8, 13 & 45, w. E. H. Smebye (pno) *(rec June 1993)* Victoria ▲ VCD 19070

Tooten, Luc (vc)—see ORCHESTRAS & ENSEMBLES Arriaga String Quartet

Toperczer, Peter (pno)
Rossini, G.:Petite messe solennelle, w. Livia Aghova (sop), Marta Benackova (mez), Gil Manuel Beltran (ten), Peter Mikulas (bass), Raphaele Cortesi (pno), Josef Ksica (harm), Romano Gandolfi (cnd), Prague Chamber Choir *(rec Domovina Studios, Prague, Sept. 10–12, 1994)* Discover International 2–▲ DI 920324–5 [DDD]
Saint-Saëns, C.:Carnival of the Animals, w. M. Lapsansky (pno), O. Lenárd (cnd), Czech-Slovak RSO Bratislava Naxos ▲ 8.550499 [DDD]
Tchaikovsky, P.:Con 1 Pno, w. J. Belohlávek (cnd), Prague SO *(rec live, Smetana Hall, Municipal House, Prague, Mar 15, 1978)* Panton ("60 Years of the Prague SO" series) ▲ PAN 811374 [ADD]

Topolski, Zlatko (vn)
Hummel, J.N.:Son Vn & Pno, Op. 5/1, w. Hans Kann (pno) *(rec 1973)* Tuxedo ▲ TUXCD 1026

Torán, Silvia (pno)
Chopin, F.:Pno Music (misc)—Ballades Nos. 1 & 4; Mazurkas Nos. 22–25; Nocturnes Nos. 7 & 8; Polonaise No. 7 ASV Quicksilva ▲ ASQ 6142 [DDD]
Chopin, F.:Son Pno, Op. 58 ASV Quicksilva ▲ ASQ 6142 [DDD]

Torchinsky, Abe (tuba)
Hindemith, P.:Son Bass Tuba, w. Glenn Gould (pno) *(rec 1975)* Sony Classical ("Glenn Gould Edition" series) 2–▲ SM2K 52671 [ADD]

Torciani, Luca (vn)—see ORCHESTRAS & ENSEMBLES Flautarte Quartet

Tordesillas, José (pno)
Arie Antiche, w. Alfredo Kraus (ten) Nimbus ▲ NI 5102 [DDD]

Torelli, Francesca (lt/thb/sop)
Melli, D.M.:Music of—Rapii bacio gradito; Amarilli crudele; Languisco e moro; Tu fuggi o vita; O Rosetta; O Filli; Dolcissimo sostegno; Tu pasci Armilla; Pazzerella voi sete; Se di farmi morire; Presso un fiume tranquillo; Giovinetta vezzosetta; Viver io fortunato; Ho visto al pianto mio; I bei legami *(rec Chiesa di Rossena Reggio Emilia, Italy, Aug 1995)* Tactus ▲ TC 600002 [DDD]
Melli, P.P.:Music of—Capriccio il gran Matias; Correntes [La Glisente; L'Alfonsina; La Strasinata; La Inamorata]; Volta [La Furiosa]; Volta sopra una battaglia; Capriccios [Il Favorito; Il Ciarlino; Il gran Monarca]; Gagliarda [La Savia] *(rec Chiesa di Rossena Reggio Emilia, Italy, Aug 1995)* Tactus ▲ TC 600002 [DDD]

Torén, Torvald (org)
Dupré, M.:Evocation Proprius ▲ PRCD 9003
Dupré, M.:Preludes & Fugues, Op. 36 Proprius ▲ PRCD 9003
Dupré, M.:Sym-Passion, "The World Awaiting the Saviour" Proprius ▲ PRCD 9003
Duruflé, M.:Org Music (comp)—Scherzo, Op. 2; Suite, Op. 5; Prélude et fugue sur le nom d'Alain, Op. 7 Proprius ▲ PRCD 9059

Torgé, Christer (trbn)
Nilsson, T.:Concertino Trbn, w. Hans Fagius (org) *(rec Österåker Church, Åkersberga, Sweden, Apr 25–26, 1979)* BIS ▲ CD 138 [AAD]

Torger, Arne (pno)
Bäck, S.-E.:Expansive Preludes Caprice ▲ CAP 21490

Torgersen, Torleif (pno)
Thoresen, L.:Pno Music—4 Inventions in Memoriam Fartein Valen; Arise!; Sun Glitter; Stages of the Inner Dialogue Simax ▲ PSC 1105 [DDD]
Valen, F.:Gavotte & Musette Simax ▲ PSC 1105 [DDD]
Valen, F.:Intermezzo Simax ▲ PSC 1105 [DDD]
Valen, F.:Pieces Pno Simax ▲ PSC 1105 [DDD]
Valen, F.:Vars Pno Simax ▲ PSC 1105 [DDD]

Torke, Michael (pno)
Torke, M.:Music of, w. D. Miller (cnd), London Sinfonietta—The Yellow Pages (1985); Adjustable Wrench; Rust; Slate; Vanada Argo ▲ 430209–2 [DDD]

Torn, David (gtr)
Spirits, w. Stoltzman, Richard (cl), Eddie Gomez (db), Dave Samuels (vib), Bill Douglas (bn), King's Singers RCA Victor ▲ 09026–68416–2 ■ 09026–68416–4

Törnqvist, Lillian (hp)—see ORCHESTRAS & ENSEMBLES Trio Rococo

Török, František (vn)—see ORCHESTRAS & ENSEMBLES Moyzes String Quartet
Schmidt, F.:Qnt Cl, w. A. Janoska (cl), D. Ruso (pno), A. Lakatos (va), J. Slávik (vc) Marco Polo ▲ 8.223415

Torre, Rey de la (gtr)
Spanish Music Elektra/Nonesuch ■ 71233–4

Torres, Robert (gtr)
The Water Is Wide, w. Mark Small (gtr) Channel Classics ▲ CD 3301

Tortelier, Maud (vc)
Vivaldi, A.:Con for 2 Vcs, w. P. Tortelier (vc), P. Ledger (cnd), London Mozart Players *(rec 11/79)* EMI ("Studio" series) ▲ CDM 769835–2 [ADD]
Vivaldi, A.:Con Vn Vcs, w. J. F. Manzone (vn), P. Tortelier (vc), P. Ledger (cnd), London Mozart Players *(rec 11/79)* EMI ("Studio" series) ▲ CDM 769835–2 [ADD]

Tortelier, Paul (vc)
Couperin, L.:Pièces en concert, w. Y. P. Tortelier (cnd), Scottish CO [arr. by Paul Bazelaire from various short Couperin works] *(rec 6/76)* EMI (Studio) ▲ CDM 763118–2 [ADD]

Tortelier, Paul (vc) (cont.)
Dvořák, A.:Rondo, w. C. Groves (cnd), Royal PO MCA Classics ▲ MCAD 6295 [DDD] ■ MCAC 6295 (D)
Dvořák, A.:Rondo, w. C. Groves (cnd), Royal PO *(rec 1989)* RPO ▲ RPO 7005 [DDD]
Dvořák, A.:Rondo, w. C. Groves (cnd), Royal PO IMP ("Masters" series) ▲ IMP 6600112 [DDD]
Elgar, E.:Con Vc, w. C. Groves (cnd), Royal PO IMP ("Masters" series) ▲ IMP 6600112 [DDD]
Elgar, E.:Con Vc, w. C. Groves (cnd), Royal PO *(rec 1989)* RPO ▲ RPO 7005 [DDD]
Elgar, E.:Con Vc, w. C. Groves (cnd), Royal PO MCA Classics ▲ MCAD 6295 [DDD] ■ MCAC 6295 (D)
Elgar, E.:Con Vc, w. M. Sargent (cnd), BBC SO Testament ▲ TES SBT 2025 [ADD]
Hindemith, P.:Con Vc, w. K. Ančerl (cnd), Czech PO Supraphon ▲ SUP 111955 [AAD]
Mozart, W.A.:Qt Ob, K.370, w. M. Tabuteau (ob), A. Pernel (vn), K. Tuttle (va) *(rec live June 1953)* Music & Arts 4–▲ CD 689 (m) [AAD]
Mozart, W.A.:Qts Pno, w. W. Kapell (pno), A. Grumiaux (vn), M. Thomas (va)—K.493 *(rec live June 1, 1953)* Music & Arts 4–▲ CD 689 (m) [AAD]
Schubert, Franz:Qnt Strs, D.956, w. I. Stern (vn), A. Schneider (vn), M. Katims (va), P. Casals (vc) *(rec 1952)* CBS 4–▲ M4K 42003 (m/s) [ADD]
Schubert, Franz:Qnt Strs, D.956, w. I. Stern (vn), A. Schneider (vn), M. Katims (va), P. Casals (vc) *(rec Prades, France, July 1–2, 1952)* Sony Classical ("The Casals Edition" series) ▲ SMK 58992 [ADD]
Schumann, R.:Con Vc, w. H. Abendroth (cnd), Leipzig RSO Berlin Classics ("Dokumente" series) ▲ BER 2052 [ADD]
Tchaikovsky, P.:Vars on a Rococo Theme, w. C. Groves (cnd), Royal PO IMP ("Masters" series) ▲ IMP 6600112 [DDD]
Tchaikovsky, P.:Vars on a Rococo Theme, w. C. Groves (cnd), Royal PO MCA Classics ▲ MCAD 6295 [DDD] ■ MCAC 6295 (D)
Tchaikovsky, P.:Vars on a Rococo Theme, w. C. Groves (cnd), Royal PO *(rec 1989)* RPO ▲ RPO 7005 [DDD]
Vivaldi, A.:Cons Vc, w. P. Ledger (cnd), London Mozart Players—RV.400, 401, 424 *(rec 11/79)* EMI ("Studio" series) ▲ CDM 769835–2 [ADD]
Vivaldi, A.:Con for 2 Vcs, w. M. Tortelier (vc), P. Ledger (cnd), London Mozart Players *(rec 11/79)* EMI ("Studio" series) ▲ CDM 769835–2 [ADD]
Vivaldi, A.:Con Vn Vcs, w. J. F. Manzone (vn), M. Tortelier (vc), P. Ledger (cnd), London Mozart Players *(rec 11/79)* EMI ("Studio" series) ▲ CDM 769835–2 [ADD]
Walton, W.:Con Vc, w. A. Boult (cnd), London PO *(rec live, Royal Festival Hall, London 1967)* Intaglio ▲ INCD 7281 [ADD]

Tortelier, Yan Pascal (vn)
Chausson, E.:Poème Vn, w. Y.P. Tortelier (cnd), Ulster Orch Chandos ▲ CHAN 8952 [DDD]
Ravel, M.:Tzigane, w. Y.P. Tortelier (cnd), Ulster Orch Chandos ▲ CHAN 8972 [DDD]
Satie, E.:Choses vues à droite et à gauche, w. A. Ciccolini (pno) Virgin Classics 2–▲ CDZB 62877
Violin Favourites Chandos ▲ CHAN 6608 [DDD]

Tortolano, William (vn)
Biber, H. von:Mystery (or Rosary) Sons, w. Charles Krigbaum (org) GIA 2–▲ GIA 286

Toschmakow, Juri (vn)
Lalo, E.:Romance-sérénade, w. N. Athinäos (cnd), Frankfurt State Orch Signum ▲ X66–00 [DDD]

Tosenko, Peter (ob)
Ustvolskaya, G.:Octet Obs, w. Nicolay Neretin (ob), Alexander Stang (vn), Olga Ribaltchenko (vn), Valentin Lukin (vn), Nikolay Tkachenko (vn), Valerii Znamenskii (timp), Oleg Malov (pno), O. Malov (cnd) *(rec St. Petersburg Radio House, Oct. & Nov. 1994)* Megadisc ▲ 7865
Vivaldi, A.:Cons for 2 Obs, w. C. Oshinakaev (ob), L. Korkhin (cnd), Renaissance CO—in a, RV.536 Infinity Digital ▲ QK 57244 [DDD]

Tosheva, Angela (pno)
Arnaoudov, G.:Incarnation dans la Lumière *(rec Salle Bulgaria, Sofia, Bulgaria, Jan 1995)* Concord Concerto ▲ CCD 42032 [DDD]
Arnaoudov, G.:"Un pan de ciel au milieu du silence..." *(rec Salle Bulgaria, Sofia, Bulgaria, Jan 1995)* Concord Concerto ▲ CCD 42032 [DDD]
Arnaoudov, G.:Partita I *(rec Salle Bulgaria, Sofia, Bulgaria, Jan 1995)* Concord Concerto ▲ CCD 42032 [DDD]
Arnaoudov, G.:Svarog Ritual *(rec Salle Bulgaria, Sofia, Bulgaria, Jan 1995)* Concord Concerto ▲ CCD 42032 [DDD]

Tosi, Monica (va)
Dragonetti, D.:Qnt Strs, w. Ubaldo Fioravanti (db), Piero Toso (vn), Giancarlo di Vacri (va), Mario Finotti (vc) *(rec Sala San Bovo, Padova, Italy, Jan 17–19, 1995)* Dynamic ▲ CD 133 [DDD]

Toso, P. (vc)
Boulez, P.:Messagesquisse, w. B. Licther (vc), A. Loudos (vc), B. Feigenwinter (vc), M. Keller (vc), F. Schiltknecht (vc), J. Wyttenbach (cnd) *(rec Switzerland, June 1993)* ECM New Series 2–▲ 78118–21520–2 [DDD]

Toso, Piero (vn)
Dragonetti, D.:Qnt Strs, w. Ubaldo Fioravanti (db), Giancarlo di Vacri (va), Monica Tosi (va), Mario Finotti (vc) *(rec Sala San Bovo, Padova, Italy, Jan 17–19, 1995)* Dynamic ▲ CD 133 [DDD]
Vivaldi, A.:Cons Vn (misc), w. J.-C. Malgoire (cnd), Venice Solisti—(2) RV.179 & RV.212a Sony Classical ("Essential Classics" series) ▲ SBK 47662 ■ SBT 47662
Vivaldi, A.:Cons Vn, Op. 8/1–12, "Il cimento dell'armonia e dell'inventione", w. C. Scimone (cnd), Venice Solisti—Nos. 1-6 & 8 Erato ("Bonsai" series) ▲ 2292–45945–2 ■ 2292–45945–4

Totenberg, Roman (vn)
Bartók, B.:Rhaps (2) Vn & Orch, w. V. Golschmann (cnd), Vienna State Opera Orch—No. 1 *(rec 1961)* Vanguard Classics ▲ OVC 4046 [ADD]
Bloch, E.:Con Vn, w. V. Golschmann (cnd), Vienna State Opera Orch *(rec 1961)* Vanguard Classics ▲ OVC 4046 [ADD]
Brahms, J.:Con Vn, w. A. Wit (cnd), Polish National RSO Katowice Titanic ▲ Ti 163 [DDD]
Lipinski, K.J.:Con 2 Vn, w. A. Wit (cnd), Polish National RSO Katowice Titanic ▲ Ti 163 [DDD]

Toth, Andro (vc)—see also ORCHESTRAS & ENSEMBLES Oberlin Trio
White, J.:Introit, Illusions, Ritual & Dance, w. M. Rosen (cnd), Oberlin Percussion Group Opus One ▲ CD 167 [DDD]

Tóth, Erika (vn)—see ORCHESTRAS & ENSEMBLES Éder String Quartet

Toth, Gwen (reed org)
Sharp, E.:20 Below, w. Anthony Coleman (toy pno/org), Wayne Horvitz (syn), Zeena Parkins (org/syn), Joseph Paul Taylor (elec/syn), David Weinstein (org/syn) Newport Classics ▲ NPD 85504

Tóth, István (db)
Beethoven, L. van:Septet Strs, w. Ildikó Hegyi (vn), Győző Máthé (va), Péter Szabó (vc), Jozsef Balogh (cl), Jenő Keveházi (hn), József Vajda (bn) *(rec Scottish Church, Budapest, Apr. 21–23 & May 29–31, 1)* Naxos ▲ 8.553090 [DDD]
Schubert, Franz:Adagio & Rondo concertante Vn, w. J. Jandó (pno), Kodály String Quartet *(rec Dec. 2–4, 1991)* Naxos ▲ 8.550658 [DDD]
Schubert, Franz:Qnt Pno, D.667, w. J. Jandó (pno), Kodály String Quartet *(rec Dec. 2–4, 1991)* Naxos ▲ 8.550658 [DDD]

Tóth, István (rcr/fl/gemshn/sgr)—see ORCHESTRAS & ENSEMBLES Vagantes

Toth, Jon (vn)
Brahms, J.:Sextet Strs, Op. 36, w. P. Carmirelli (vn), P. Naegele (va), C. Levine (va), F. Arico (vc), D. Reichenberger (vc) Sony Classical ▲ SMK 46249 [ADD] ■ SMT 46249

Toth, June de (pno)
Bartók, B.:Allegro barbaro Eroica ▲ JDT 30000
Bartók, B.:Burleskes, Op. 8c Eroica ▲ JDT 3002 [DDD]
Bartók, B.:Dirges Eroica ▲ JDT 30000
Bartók, B.:For Children—42 Hungarian Folk Songs Eroica ▲ JDT 3002 [DDD]
Bartók, B.:Hungarian Peasant Songs Eroica ▲ JDT 30000
Bartók, B.:Sketches (7) Eroica ▲ JDT 30000
Bartók, B.:Son Pno Eroica ▲ JDT 30000
Bartók, B.:Suite Pno Eroica ▲ JDT 3002 [DDD]

Tóth, Zoltán (va)—see also ORCHESTRAS & ENSEMBLES Éder String Quartet, Ravel String Quartet
Liszt, F.:Music of, w. A. Kiss (n), E. Banda (vc), M. Perényi (vc), H. Lubik (hp), I. Lantos (pno/org), S. Margittay (harm)—Angelus; La lugubre gondola; Epithalam; Am Grabe Richard Wagners; Romance oubliée; Elégies 1 & 2; Offertorium; Benedictus Hungaroton ▲ HCD 11798 [DDD]
Totsiou, Anni (pno)
Rachmaninoff, S.:Suite 1 for 2 Pnos, w. Lola Totsiou (pno) Orata ▲ ORA ML 183 [ADD]
Scriabin, A.:Fant 2 Pnos, w. Lola Totsiou (pno) Orata ▲ ORA ML 183 [ADD]
Shostakovich, D.:Suite for 2 Pnos, w. Lola Totsiou (pno) Orata ▲ ORA ML 183 [ADD]
Totsiou, Lola (pno)
Rachmaninoff, S.:Suite 1 for 2 Pnos, w. Anni Totsiou (pno) Orata ▲ ORA ML 183 [ADD]
Scriabin, A.:Fant 2 Pnos, w. Anni Totsiou (pno) Orata ▲ ORA ML 183 [ADD]
Shostakovich, D.:Suite for 2 Pnos, w. Anni Totsiou (pno) Orata ▲ ORA ML 183 [ADD]
Touboul, C. (pno)—see ORCHESTRAS & ENSEMBLES Ophir Trio
Toulson, Smith (cl)—see also ORCHESTRAS & ENSEMBLES Pennsylvania Wind Quintet
Swack, I.:Profiles, w. J. Zagst (vn), L. Feldman (vc) Opus One ▲ 149
Tournon, Sylvie (fl)—see ORCHESTRAS & ENSEMBLES Stanislas Ensemble
Tournus, M. (vc)—see ORCHESTRAS & ENSEMBLES French String Trio
Touvron, Guy (cnt)
Arban, J.-B.:Cavatina & Vars, w. Nelly Cottin (pno) *(rec Feb 1996)* Ligia Digital ▲ 0105040 [DDD]
Arban, J.-B.:Fants Verdi, w. Nelly Cottin (pno)—Fant No. 1 on Il Trovatore; Fant brillante on Don Carlos; Fant brillante on I vespri siciliani; Fant on La forza del destino; Fant on Rigoletto; Fant on La traviata *(rec Feb 1996)* Ligia Digital ▲ 0105040 [DDD]
Touvron, Guy (tpt)
Albinoni, T.:Cons à 5 Obs, Op. 9, w. Maurice André (tpt), J. Faerber (cnd), Württemberg CO—No. 9 in C [played on tpts] *(rec Eglise Evangélique, Heilbronn, May 1979)* EMI Classics ▲ CDK 65337 [ADD]
Basic 100, Vol. 39, w. Al Hirt (tpt) RCA Victor ▲ 09026-61857-2 ■ 09026-61857-4
Carnival in Venice, w. Venice Soloists [cnd:Claudio Scimone] RCA Red Seal ▲ 09026-61815-2
Constant, M.:Alleluias, w. E. Krapp (org) RCA Red Seal ▲ 09026-61186-2
Dialogue, w. Olivier Vernet (org) *(rec Sept. 1992)* Ligia Digital ▲ LIDI 0105002-92 [DDD]
Eben, Petr:Windows, w. E. Krapp (org) RCA Red Seal ▲ 09026-61186-2
Fantasia for Trumpet & Organ, w. Luigi Celeghin (org) *(rec Church of Sts Felice & Fortunato di Noale, Venice, Oct 29 & 30, 1995)* Bongiovanni ▲ GB 5589 [DDD]
Genzmer, H.:Son Tpt, w. E. Krapp (org) RCA Red Seal ▲ 09026-61186-2
Haydn, J.:Con Tpt, Prague CO RCA Red Seal ▲ 09026-60858-2
Haydn, M.:Con in C Tpt, Prague CO RCA Red Seal ▲ 09026-60858-2
Hummel, J.N.:Con in E♭ Tpt, S.49, Prague CO RCA Red Seal ▲ 09026-60858-2
Hummel, J.N.:Con in E♭ Tpt, S.49, Prague CO RCA Victor ▲ 09026-61857-2; ■ 09026-61857-4
Jolivet, A.:Arioso barocco, w. E. Krapp (org) RCA Red Seal ▲ 09026-61186-2
Langlais, J.:Chorales Tpt & Org, w. E. Krapp (org)—Nos. 1, 2, 4 & 7 only RCA Red Seal ▲ 09026-61186-2
Molter, J.M.:Cons Tpt, w. G. Messler (tpt), J. Faerber (cnd), Württemberg CO RCA Red Seal ▲ 09026-61200-2
Molter, J.M.:Con 2 Tpt, w. J. Faerber (cnd), Württemberg CO RCA Victor ▲ 09026-61857-2; ■ 09026-61857-4
Molter, J.M.:Con 3 Tpt, w. J. Faerber (cnd), Württemberg CO RCA Victor ▲ 09026-61857-2; ■ 09026-61857-4
Neruda, J.B.G.:Con Tpt, Prague CO RCA Red Seal ▲ 09026-60858-2
Touyère, Raymond (hpd)
Couperin, F.:Pièces de clavecin (sels)—6e ordre; 11e ordre; 12e ordre Gallo ▲ CD 854 [ADD]
Purcell, H.:Suites Hpd *(rec Collège St-Louis à Genève, May-June 1972)* Gallo ▲ CD 852 [ADD]
Touyère, Raymond (pno)
Récital de Musique Française, w. Touyère, Raymond (pno) *(rec Eglise St-Paul à Genève, Mar 1974)* Gallo ▲ CD853 [ADD]
Touzet, Lucette (pno)
Couperin, G.-F.:Music of, w. Pascale Bonnier (pno), Blandine Virard (pno)—Vars on Ah! Ça Ira Adda ▲ ADD 581114
Jadin, L.E.:Sons Pno 4-Hands, Op. 2, w. Pascale Bonnier (pno), Blandine Virard (pno)—No. 1 Adda ▲ ADD 581114
Méhul, E.-N.:Sons Hpd, Op. 1, w. Pascale Bonnier (pno), Blandine Virard (pno)—No. 3 Adda ▲ ADD 581114
Rigel, H.-J.:Kbd Music, w. Pascale Bonnier (pno), Blandine Virard (pno)—Son No. 3, Op. 3 Adda ▲ ADD 581114
Tapray, J.F.:Sons Hpd, Op. 24, w. Pascale Bonnier (pno), Blandine Virard (pno)—No. 3 Adda ▲ ADD 581114
Tower, Joan (pno)
Tower, J.:Très lent, w. André Emelianoff (vc) *(rec American Academy of Arts & Letters, New York City, Sept. 26-28, 1994)* New World ▲ 80470-2
Townhill, Dennis (org)
Leighton, K.:Org Music *(rec St. Mary's Cathedral, Edinburgh)* Priory 3-▲ PRI 326 [DDD]
Townsend, Dave (E conc)
Portrait of a Concertina, w. Nick Hooper (gtr) Saydisc ■ SDLC 351 (D)
Toyama, Keiko (pno)
Beethoven, L. van:Son 7 Vn, w. Werner Hink (vn) *(rec Japan, Oct 6, 1994)* Camerata ▲ 30 CM 416 [DDD]
Beethoven, L. van:Son 10 Vn, w. Werner Hink (vn) *(rec Japan, Oct 6, 1994)* Camerata ▲ 30 CM 416 [DDD]
Chopin, F.:Intro & Polonaise, "Polonaise brilliante", w. Maurice Gendron (vc) *(rec Iruma-shi Shimin Kaikan, June 1981)* Camerata ▲ 25CM 366
Chopin, F.:Son Vc, w. Maurice Gendron (vc) *(rec Iruma-shi Shimin Kaikan, June 1981)* Camerata ▲ 25CM 366
Lalo, E.:Son Vc, w. Maurice Gendron (vc) *(rec Honjo Bunka-kaikan, Sept 1985)* Camerata ▲ 25CM 366
Mozart, W.A.:Qnt Pno, K.452, w. Günther Passin (ob), Yuji Murai (cl), Gottfried Langenstein (hn), Koji Okazaki (bn) *(rec Shibukawa Shimin Kaikan, Sept 1, 1981)* Camerata ▲ 32CM 180 [DDD]
Mozart, W.A.:Trio Cl, K.498, w. Peter Schmidl (cl), Klaus Peisteiner (va) *(rec Tsukuba Nova Hall, Oct 12, 1990)* Camerata ▲ 32CM 180 [DDD]
Schubert, Franz:Sonatinas Vn, w. Werner Hink (vn) *(rec Higashimatsuyama City Hall, Saitama, Japan & Baumgartner Studio, Vienna)* Camerata ▲ 32CM 42
Toyoda, Koji (vn)
Ysaÿe, E.:Son Vns, w. Gerard Jarry (vn) Koch Schwann ▲ SCH 317212 [DDD]
Toyoshima, Yasushi (vn)
Feldman, Morton:For John Cage, w. A. Takahashi (pno) O.O. Imports 2-▲ ALCD 41
Tozer, Geoffrey (pno)
Bach, J.S.:Clavierbüchlein for Anna Magdalena Bach (sels)—Polonaises in F & G; Musette in D; March in E♭; Bist du bei mir (aria); Gib dich zufrieden und sei stille (chorale) *(rec Sydney, Australia, Feb 1988)* Tall Poppies ▲ TP 001 [DDD]
Bartók, B.:For Children—sels.:Play; Children's dance; #12; Old Hungarian tune; Soldier's song; #19; #21; #25; Drunkard's song; Jeering song *(rec Sydney, Australia, Feb 1988)* Tall Poppies ▲ TP 001 [DDD]
Bartók, B.:Little Pieces—Minuetto *(rec Sydney, Australia, Feb 1988)* Tall Poppies ▲ TP 001 [DDD]
Bartók, B.:Mikrokosmos—Vol. V:Merry Andrew, No. 139; Peasant dance, No. 128 *(rec Sydney, Australia, Feb 1988)* Tall Poppies ▲ TP 001 [DDD]
Busoni, F.:Bach Transcriptions—Prelude & Fugue in D, BWV 532 Chandos ▲ CHAN 9394
Busoni, F.:Fant nach J. S. Bach Pno Chandos ▲ CHAN 9394
Busoni, F.:Indianisches Tagebuch 1 Chandos ▲ CHAN 9394

Tozer, Geoffrey (pno) (cont.)
Busoni, F.:Pno Music—Sonatina super Carmen; Exeunt omnes [from Stücke]; All'Italia; Berceuse [both from Elegien]; Turandots Frauengemach; Gigue, Bolero & Vars [from An die Jügend] Chandos ▲ CHAN 9394
Busoni, F.:Sonatina 2 Pno Chandos ▲ CHAN 9394
Busoni, F.:Toccata Pno Chandos ▲ CHAN 9394
Korngold, E.W.:Son 1 Pno Chandos ▲ CHAN 9389 [DDD]
Korngold, E.W.:Son 2 Pno Chandos ▲ CHAN 9389 [DDD]
Korngold, E.W.:Son 3 Pno Chandos ▲ CHAN 9389 [DDD]
Liszt, F.:Cons Pno, w. N. Järvi (cnd), Swiss Romande Orch Chandos ▲ CHAN 9360 [DDD]
Liszt, F.:Symphonic Poems, w. N. Järvi (cnd), Swiss Romande Orch—Nos. 3 & 6 Chandos ▲ CHAN 9360 [DDD]
Liszt, F.:Transcriptions & Paraphrases—Alyabiev:The Nightingale; Bellini:Réminiscences de Norma; Chopin:Chants polonais (6) for Pno; Liszt:Loreley; Rossini:Cujus animam [from Air du stabat mater]; Schumann:Widmung; Frühlingsnacht; Spohr:Die Rose; Verdi:Concert Paraphrase [from Rigoletto]; Wagner:Spinning Chorus [from The Flying Dutchman] Chandos ▲ CHAN 9471
Medtner, N.:Con 1 Pno, w. N. Järvi (cnd), London PO Chandos 2-▲ CHAN 9040 [DDD]
Medtner, N.:Con 2 Pno, w. N. Järvi (cnd), London PO Chandos 2-▲ CHAN 9040 [DDD]
Medtner, N.:Con 3 Pno, w. N. Järvi (cnd), London PO Chandos 2-▲ CHAN 9040 [DDD]
Medtner, N.:Pno Music (comp)—Sonata in g, Op. 22; Sonata reminiscenza in a, Op. 38/1; Dancing Fairy Tale, Op. 48/1; Fairy Tale (1915); Fairy Tale in f, Op. 26/3; Fairy Tale in g#, Op. 31/3; Fairy Tale in e, Op. 34/2; Fairy Tale in d, Op. 51/1; Funeral March, Op. 31/2; The Organ Grinder, Op. 54/3; Russian Fairy Tale, Op. 42/1 Chandos ▲ CHAN 9050 [DDD]
Medtner, N.:Pno Music (misc)—Sonata Triad, Op. 11; Forgotten Melodies, Op. 38/2-7; Fairy Tales, Op. 51/2-6 Chandos ▲ CHAN 9153 [DDD]
Medtner, N.:Son 1 Vn, w. L. Mordkovitch (vn) Chandos ▲ CHAN 9293 [DDD]
Medtner, N.:Son 2 Vn, w. L. Mordkovitch (vn) Chandos ▲ CHAN 9293 [DDD]
Medtner, N.:Son-Ballade Chandos 2-▲ CHAN 9040 [DDD]
Mozart, W.A.:Pno Music (misc)—Minuets:K.1, K.2, K.4, K.61; Allegro, K.3; Pno piece, K.33B *(rec Sydney, Australia, Feb 1988)* Tall Poppies ▲ TP 001 [DDD]
Prokofiev, S.:Music for Children—Morning; Promenade; Tarantella; Regrets; March; Grasshoppers; Playing tag *(rec Sydney, Australia, Feb 1988)* Tall Poppies ▲ TP 001 [DDD]
Rawsthorne, A.:Con 1 Pno, w. M. Bamert (cnd), London PO Chandos ▲ CHAN 9125 [DDD]
Rawsthorne, A.:Con 2 Pno, w. M. Bamert (cnd), London PO Chandos ▲ CHAN 9125 [DDD]
Rawsthorne, A.:Con Pnos, w. T.-A. Cislowski (pno), M. Bamert (cnd), London PO Chandos ▲ CHAN 9125 [DDD]
Respighi, O.:Con in modo misolidio, w. E. Downes (cnd), BBC PO *(rec Jan. 7 & 8, 1994)* Chandos ▲ CHAN 9285 [DDD]
Respighi, O.:Con Pno, w. E. Downes (cnd), BBC PO *(rec Jan. 7 & 8, 1994)* Chandos ▲ CHAN 9285 [DDD]
Respighi, O.:Toccata Pno, w. E. Downes (cnd), BBC PO Chandos ▲ CHAN 9311 [DDD]
Rimsky-Korsakov, N.:Con Pno, w. D. Kitayenko (cnd), Bergen PO Chandos ▲ CHAN 9229 [DDD]
Rimsky-Korsakov, N.:Russian Easter Festival, w. D. Kitayenko (cnd), Bergen PO Chandos ▲ CHAN 9229 [DDD]
Rimsky-Korsakov, N.:Sadko Orch, Op. 5, w. D. Kitayenko (cnd), Bergen PO Chandos ▲ CHAN 9229 [DDD]
Rimsky-Korsakov, N.:Sym 3, w. D. Kitayenko (cnd), Bergen PO Chandos ▲ CHAN 9229 [DDD]
Schubert, Franz:Scherzo Pno, D.593/1 *(rec Sydney, Australia, Feb 1988)* Tall Poppies ▲ TP 001 [DDD]
Schumann, R.:Album für die Jugend (sels)—A little piece; The poor orphan; A hunter's song; A wild horseman; Little folk song; The merry peasant; A spring song; The little morning wanderer; #22; Italian sailor's song; Wintertime; Sheherazade *(rec Sydney, Australia, Feb 1988)* Tall Poppies ▲ TP 001 [DDD]
Stravinsky, I.:Capriccio, w. N. Järvi (cnd), Swiss Romande Orch Chandos ▲ CHAN 9238 [DDD]
Tchaikovsky, P.:Album pour enfants—The song of the peasant; The organ grinder; German song *(rec Sydney, Australia, Feb 1988)* Tall Poppies ▲ TP 001 [DDD]
Tchaikovsky, P.:Con 3 Pno, w. N. Järvi (cnd), London PO *(rec June 7 & 8, 1991)* Chandos ▲ CHAN 9130 [DDD]
Tchaikovsky, P.:Sym 7, w. N. Järvi (cnd), London PO *(rec June 7 & 8, 1991)* Chandos ▲ CHAN 9130 [DDD]
Tracey, Bradford (hpd)
Fux, J.J.:Partitas Kbd—in g FSM-Adagio ▲ FCD 91 626
Kerll, J.C.:Kbd Music—Toccata III FSM-Adagio ▲ FCD 91 626
Purcell, H.:Suites Hpd Adagio ▲ ADG 91627
Wagenseil, G.C.:Diverts Kbd—in F FSM-Adagio ▲ FCD 91 626
Tracey, Bradford (org)
Kerll, J.C.:Org Music—Toccata I in d; Canzona I in d; Ciacona in C FSM-Adagio ▲ FCD 91 626
Pachelbel, J.:Org Music—Ciacona in C FSM-Adagio ▲ FCD 91 626
Tracey, Bradford (pno)
Beethoven, L. van:Songs, w. James Griffett (ten), Franzjosef Maier (vn), Rudolf Mandalka (vc)—To the Aeolian Harp; Sally in Our Alley; The Soldier; Sympathy; The Farewell Song; Come, Darby Dear, Easy; The Shepherd's Song; The British Light Dragoons Ars Musici ▲ 1142 [ADD]
Haydn, J.:Canzonettas, w. James Griffett (ten)—Nos. 25-36 Teldec ▲ TEL SEL 97503 [ADD]
Haydn, J.:Songs, w. James Griffett (ten), Franzjosef Maier (vn), Rudolf Mandalka (vc)—Will Ye Got to Flanders; The Glancing of Her Apron; Jockie & Sandy; O Can Ye Sew Cushions; Margret's Ghost; Up in the Morning Early; Barbara Allen; Green Grow the Rashes; Lizae Baillie; Blue Bonnets Ars Musici ▲ 1142 [ADD]
Tracey, Bradford (pno/hpd)
Haydn, J.:Pno Music—Andante con variazioni, H.XVII/6; Divertimento Nos. 6 & 12; Sonatas 28 & 50 Adagio ▲ ADG 91635 [ADD]
Tracey, Bradford (vir)
Farnaby, G.:Kbd Music Adagio ▲ ADG 91614
Tracey, Ian (org)
Guilmant, A.:Sym 1, w. Y. P. Tortelier (cnd), BBC PO Chandos ▲ CHAN 9271 [DDD]
Liverpool Encores Mirabilis ▲ MRCD901 [DDD]
Poulenc, F.:Con Org, w. Y.P. Tortelier (cnd), BBC PO Chandos ▲ CHAN 9271 [DDD]
Widor, C.M.:Sym 5 Org Chandos ▲ CHAN 9271 [DDD]
Tradatti, Ana Maria (pno)
Zyman, S.:Son Fl, w. Marisa Canales (fl) Urtext ▲ URT 1 [DDD]
Traficante, Valerie (pno)
Fauré, G.:Ballade Pno, w. J. Serebrier (cnd), Royal PO IMP ("Classics" series) ▲ IMP 6700782
Indy, V. d':Sym on a French Mountain Air, w. J. Serebrier (cnd), Royal PO IMP ("Classics" series) ▲ IMP 6700782
Saint-Saëns, C.:Con 2 Pno, w. J. Serebrier (cnd), Royal PO IMP ("Classics" series) ▲ IMP 6700782
Traikova, Maya (pno)
Prokofiev, S.:Romeo & Juliet Pno Arcobaleno ▲ AAOC 9396
Prokofiev, S.:Son 2 Pno Arcobaleno ▲ AAOC 9396
Prokofiev, S.:Son 3 Pno Arcobaleno ▲ AAOC 9396
Tramier, Brigitte (hpd)
Baroque Music for Lute, Guitar & Harpsichord, w. Jean Michel Robert (lt/gtr) Koch Schwann ▲ SCH 315442 [DDD]
Trampler, Walter (va)
Bainbridge, S.:Con Va, w. M. Tilson Thomas (cnd), London Sinfonietta Continuum ▲ CCD 1020
Brahms, J.:Qts Pno (comp), w. Beaux Arts Trio Philips ▲ 454017-2
Brahms, J.:Qnt 1 Strs, w. Juilliard String Quartet Sony Classical ▲ SK 68476
Brahms, J.:Qnt 2 Strs, w. Chamber Music Northwest Delos ▲ DE 3066 [DDD]
Brahms, J.:Qnt 2 Strs, w. Juilliard String Quartet Sony Classical ▲ SK 68476
Diamond, D.:Qnt Cl, w. D. Schifrin (cl), P. Neubauer (va), H. Cheifetz (vc), W. Lash (vc) *(rec 6 & 7/90)* Delos ▲ 3088 [DDD]

Trampler, Walter (va) (cont.)
Herrmann, B.:Souvenirs de Voyage, w. D. Schifrin (cl), P. Frank (vn), T. Arm (vn), W. Lash (vc) *(rec 6 & 7/90)* Delos ▲ 3088 [DDD]
Imbrie, A.W.:Serenade Fl, w. L. DiTullio (fl), L. Brandwynne (pno) *(rec Aug. 17, 1971; originally)* CRI ▲ CD 632 [ADD]
Mozart, W.A.:Qts Fl, w. R. Siebert (fl), R. Friend (vn), G. Neikrug (vc) Vox Box 3-▲ CD3X 3003 [ADD]
Mozart, W.A.:Qnts Strs, w. Budapest String Quartet Sony Classical 3-▲ SM3K 46527
Schoenberg, A.:Verklärte Nacht, w. Yo Yo Ma (vc), Juilliard String Quartet [arr. for string sextet] Sony Classical ▲ SK 47690 [DDD]
Wernick, R.:Con Va, "Do Not Go Gentle...", w. L. Botstein (cnd), Boston Pro Arte CO *(rec Oct. 7, 1989)* CRI ▲ CD 618 [DDD]
Wilson, R.:Son Va, w. B. Uribe (pno) Albany ▲ TROY 074 [DDD]

Trávniček, Jiri (vn)—see ORCHESTRAS & ENSEMBLES Janáček String Quartet

Trede-Boettcher, Ursula (hpd)
Austin, E.:Lighthouse 1 Capstone ▲ CPS 8625
Austin, E.:Music of, w. Jeananne Albee (pno), Jerome Reed (pno), Mary Lou Rylands (vc), Markus Lücke (cl), Sibylle Dotzauer (pno), Constitution Brass, Gerald Kegelmann (cnd), Heidelberg State Music School Chamber Choir—To Begin for Brass Qnt; Klavier Double for Pno & Tape; Circling for Vc & Pno; Lighthouse I for solo Hpd; Gathering Threads for solo Cl; Zodiac Suite for Pno; An Die Nachgeborenen [To Those Born Later] Capstone ▲ CPS 8625

Trede-Boettcher, Ursula (pno)
Alotin, Y.:Sonatina Vn, w. Marianne Boettcher (vn) Bayer ▲ 100169 [DDD]
Beau, L.A. le:Son Vn, w. Marianne Boettcher (vn) Bayer ▲ 100169 [DDD]
Bloch, A.:Suplicazioni Vc, w. Wolfgang Boettcher (vc) Pro Viva ▲ ISPV 172
Boulanger, L.:D'un matin de printemps Fl & Pno, w. Marianne Boettcher (vn) Bayer ▲ 100169 [DDD]
Danzi, M.:Son 1 Vn, w. Marianne Boettcher (vn) Bayer ▲ 100169 [DDD]
Dinescu, V.:Echos I Bayer ▲ 100169 [DDD]
Mendelssohn, Fanny:Adagio, w. Marianne Boettcher (vn) Bayer ▲ 100169 [DDD]

Tredici, David del (pno)
del Tredici, D.:Fant Pieces *(rec 1987)* CRI ▲ CD 649 [DDD]
del Tredici, D.:Scherzo, w. Robert Helps (pno) CRI ("American Masters" series) ▲ CD 689 [DDD]
Helps, R.:Etudes CRI ("American Masters" series) ▲ CD 717 [ADD]
Josten, W.:Con sacro I-II, w. L. Stokowski (cnd), American SO CRI ▲ CD 597 [ADD]

Tree, M. (vn)
Brahms, J.:Trio Hn, w. M. Bloom (hn), R. Serkin (pno) Sony Classical ▲ SMK 46249 [ADD] ■ SMT 46249

Tree, Michael (va)—see also ORCHESTRAS & ENSEMBLES Guarneri String Quartet
Boccherini, L.:Qnts Gtr, G.445–453, w. A. Diaz (gtr), A. Schneider (vn), F. Galimir (vn), D. Soyer (vc)—in C, G.448 *(rec 1965)* Vanguard Classics ▲ OVC 8006 [ADD]
Boccherini, L.:Qnts Strs, w. A. Schneider (vn), F. Galimir (vn), D. Soyer (vc), L. Harrell (vc)—Op. 13, No. 5 *(rec 1965)* Vanguard Classics ▲ OVC 8006 [ADD]
Brahms, J.:Sextet Strs, Op. 18, w. I. Stern (vn), C.-L. Lin (vn), J. Laredo (va), Yo-Yo Ma (vc), S. Robinson (vc) Sony Classical 2-▲ S2K 45820
Brahms, J.:Sextet Strs, Op. 36, w. I. Stern (vn), Cho-Liang Lin (vn), J. Laredo (va), Yo-Yo Ma (vc), S. Robinson (vc) Sony Classical 2-▲ S2K 45820
Dvořák, A.:Qnt Pno, Op. 81, w. P. Serkin (pno), F. Galimir (vn), A. Schneider (vn), D. Soyer (vc) *(rec 1965)* Vanguard Classics ▲ OVC 8003 [ADD]
Mozart, W.A.:Qts Pno, w. P. Serkin (pno), A. Schneider (vn), D. Soyer (vc) *(rec 1965)* Vanguard Classics ▲ OVC 8007 [ADD]
Schubert, Franz:Qnt Pno, D.667, w. P. Serkin (pno), A. Schneider (vn), D. Soyer (vc), J. Levine (db) *(rec 1964)* Vanguard Classics ▲ OVC 8005 [ADD]

Trefny, Marcus (vc)—see ORCHESTRAS & ENSEMBLES Vienna Piano Trio

Treger, Alexander (vn)
Levitch, L.:Fant Ob, w. Greg Donovetsky (ob), Kenneth Burward-Hoy (va), Janice Foy (vc) Cambria ▲ CD 1059 [ADD]

Trenkner, Evelinde (pno)—see also ORCHESTRAS & ENSEMBLES Trenkner-Speidel Piano Duo
Bruckner, A.:Sym 3, "Wagner", w. Sontraud Speidel (pno) [arr. Mahler & Krzyzanowski for Pno Duet] MD + G ▲ MDG 3300591 [DDD]
Mahler, G.:Sym 6, w. S. Zenker (pno) [trans. for piano 4-Hands in 1906 by Alexander von Zemlinsky] *(rec 4/91)* MD + G ▲ L 3400 [DDD]
Mahler, G.:Sym 7, w. S. Zenker (pno) [arr. for piano duo by Alfredo Casella] MD + G ▲ L 3445 [DDD]

Trentin, Franco (gtr)
Bach, J.S.:Lt Music—Prelude, BWV 999; Fugue, BWV 1000 Gallo ▲ CD 820 [DDD]
Bolling, C.:Con Gtr, w. Ivo Antognini (pno), Rino Rossi (db), Matteo Mazza (dr) Gallo ▲ CD 820 [DDD]
Cimarosa, D.:Sons (50) Kbd—C.30, 35, 39 & 56 [all arr Trentin for gtr] Gallo ▲ CD 820 [DDD]
Trentin, F.:Gtr Music—Pequeño Paquito; Notturno; Introduzione e Tango su temi di Gade/Matos Rodriguez; Serenata nello stille spagnolo; Lullaby for Amel Gallo ▲ CD 820 [DDD]

Trentin, O. (bn)—see ORCHESTRAS & ENSEMBLES Venice New Quintet

Trepel, Shirley (vc)—see ORCHESTRAS & ENSEMBLES Shepherd String Quartet

Trepte, Paul (org)
The Psalms of David, Vol. 8:Praise the Lord O My Soul, w. Ely Cathedral Choir, Paul Trepte (cnd), David Price (org) Priory ▲ PRI 460 [DDD]
Stanford, C.V.:Church Music, w. Donald Hunt (cnd), Worcester Cathedral Choir—Magnificat & Nunc dimittis in A, Op. 12; Motets, Op. 38, Nos. 1–3 & Op. 135, Nos. 1 & 3; Motet, "O living will"; Anthems, Op. 123 & Op. 145; Anthem, "The Lord is my shepherd" [E,L] Hyperion ▲ CDA 66030 [DDD]

Tretick, Stephanie (vn)—see ORCHESTRAS & ENSEMBLES II Quattro

Trevisani, Raffaele (fl)
Dvořák, A.:Sonatina Vn, w. Paola Girardi (pno) Stradivarius ▲ STV 33321 [DDD]
Franck, C.:Son Vn, w. P. Girardi (pno) Stradivarius ▲ STR 33321
Franck, C.:Son Vn, w. Paola Girardi (pno) Stradivarius ▲ STV 33321 [DDD]
Prokofiev, S.:Son Fl, w. Paola Girardi (pno) Stradivarius ▲ STV 33321 [DDD]

Triebskorn, Walter (cl)
Busoni, F.:Concertino Cl, w. C.A. Bunte (cnd), Berlin SO Vox Box 2-▲ CDX 5133

Trige, A. (bn)—see ORCHESTRAS & ENSEMBLES Danish Wind Octet

Trigg, William (perc)—see ORCHESTRAS & ENSEMBLES New Music Consort, Musicians' Accord members
Cage, J.:Music for 4 for Perc, w. K. Grossman (perc), C. Nappi (perc), M. Pugliese (perc) *(rec in concert at Merkin Concert Hall, New York City, 4/4/89)* Mode ▲ 25
Kassel, R.:Res Facta, w. S. Berkowitz (cl) Mode ▲ 23
Lebaron, A.:Con for Active Frogs, w. G. Cartwright (voc), D. Shea (voc), J. Staley (voc), A. LeBaron (cnd), New Music Consort [E] Mode ▲ 30
Lebaron, A.:Rite of the Black Sun, w. F. Cassara (zmz), P. Guerguerian (perc), M. Pugliese (perc), C. Heldrich (cnd), New Music Consort Mode ▲ 30

Trimborn, Roswitha (cem)—see ORCHESTRAS & ENSEMBLES Capella Clementina

Trimborn, Roswitha (hpd)
Mozart, W.A.:Con Pno, K.107, *(orch unknown)* Koch Schwann ▲ SCH 313422 [ADD]

Trinicanti, Gaspare (cl)
Brahms, J.:Sons Cl (comp), w. M. Deoriti (pno) *(rec June 1993)* Sipario Dischi ▲ CS 27 C
Brahms, J.:Trio Cl, w. M. Boni (vc), M. Deoriti (pno) *(rec June 1993)* Sipario Dischi ▲ CS 27 C

Triplett, Robert (org)
Dupré, M.:Pieces Org, Op. 18 Centaur ▲ CRC 2030 [DDD]
Dupré, M.:Sym-Passion, "The World Awaiting the Saviour" Centaur ▲ CRC 2030 [DDD]
Martin, F.:Passacaglia Org Centaur ▲ CRC 2030 [DDD]
Roger-Ducasse, J.:Pastoral Org Centaur ▲ CRC 2030 [DDD]

Tristano, Luciano (fl)
Petrassi, G.:Ala, w. Mario Ancillotti (fl), Leonardo Bartelloni (pno) Koch Schwann ▲ SCH 315242
Petrassi, G.:Dialogo angelico, w. Mario Ancillotti (fl) Koch Schwann ▲ SCH 315242

Tritle, Kent (org)
Boëllmann, L.:Suite gothique [1993 N.P. Mander Org, Church of St. Ignatius Loyola, New York City]—Toccata *(rec July 26–28, 1994)* Epiphany ▲ EP 4 [DDD]
Brahms, J.:Chorale Preludes, Op. 122 [1993 N.P. Mander Org, Church of St. Ignatius Loyola, New York City]—Op. 122/2, 3, 5 & 8 *(rec July 26–28, 1994)* Epiphany ▲ EP 4 [DDD]
Bruckner, A.:Prelude & Fugue Org [1993 N.P. Mander Org, Church of St. Ignatius Loyola, New York City] *(rec July 26–28, 1994)* Epiphany ▲ EP 4 [DDD]
Franck, C.:Cantabile Epiphany ▲ EP 7
Franck, C.:Cantabile [1993 N.P. Mander Org, Church of St. Ignatius Loyola, New York City] *(rec July 26–28, 1994)* Epiphany ▲ EP 4 [DDD]
Franck, C.:Pièce héroïque [1993 N.P. Mander Org, Church of St. Ignatius Loyola, New York City] *(rec July 26–28, 1994)* Epiphany ▲ EP 4 [DDD]
Liszt, F.:Prelude & Fugue on the name B-A-C-H [1993 N.P. Mander Org, Church of St. Ignatius Loyola, New York City] *(rec July 26–28, 1994)* Epiphany ▲ EP 4 [DDD]
Mendelssohn, F.:Sons Org [1993 N.P. Mander Org, Church of St. Ignatius Loyola, New York City]—No. 3 *(rec July 26–28, 1994)* Epiphany ▲ EP 4 [DDD]
St. Ignatius Loyola, w. Tritle, Kent (org) Gothic ▲ GOT 49068 [DDD]
Widor, C.M.:Sym 6 Org [Mander tracker organ, Church of St. Ignatius Loyola New York City]—2nd movt. Epiphany ▲ EP 4
Widor, C.M.:Sym 9 Org [Mander tracker organ, Church of St. Ignatius Loyola New York City]—Andante Sostenuto Epiphany ▲ EP 4

Tritt, William (pno)
Champagne, C.:Danse villageoise, w. P. Oundjian (pno) CBC ("Musica Viva" series) ▲ MVCD 1060 [DDD]
Debussy, C.:Son Vn, w. P. Oundjian (vn) CBC ("Musica Viva" series) ▲ MVCD 1060 [DDD]
Dela, M.:Sonatine, w. P. Oundjian (vn) CBC ("Musica Viva" series) ▲ MVCD 1060 [DDD]
Gershwin, G.:Con Pno, w. E. Kunzel (cnd), Cincinnati Pops Orch Telarc ▲ CD 80166 [DDD] ■ CS 30166 (D)
Gershwin, G.:"I Got Rhythm" Vars, w. E. Kunzel (cnd), Cincinnati Pops Orch Telarc ▲ CD 80166 [DDD] ■ CS 30166 (D)
Gershwin, G.:Rhap in Blue, w. B. Brott (cnd), Hamilton PO CBC ("SM 5000" series) ▲ SMCD 5111 [DDD]
Gershwin, G.:Rhap in Blue, w. E. Kunzel (cnd), Cincinnati Jazz Orch [original jazz band orchestration of 1924, including 48 bars, mostly solo piano, cut prior to the premiere] Telarc ▲ CD 80166 [DDD] ■ CS 30166 (D)
Gershwin, G.:Rialto Ripples Rag, w. E. Kunzel (cnd), Cincinnati Pops Orch Telarc ▲ CD 80166 [DDD] ■ CS 30166 (D)
Gershwin, G.:Second Rhap, w. B. Brott (cnd), Hamilton PO CBC ("SM 5000" series) ▲ SMCD 5111 [DDD]
Gottschalk, L.M.:Grande Tarantelle, w. E. Kunzel (cnd), Cincinnati Pops Orch Telarc ▲ CD 80112 [DDD]
Gould, M.:Interplay Pno, w. E. Kunzel (cnd), Cincinnati Pops Orch Telarc ▲ CD 80112 [DDD]
Messiaen, O.:Thème et vars, w. P. Oundjian (vn) CBC ("Musica Viva" series) ▲ MVCD 1060 [DDD]
Miniatures, w. Hammer, Moshe (vn), Tsuyoshi Tsutsumi (vc) CBC Records ("Musica Viva" series) ▲ MVCD 1043 [DDD]
Movie Love Themes, w. E. Kunzel (cnd), Cincinnati Pops Orch Telarc ▲ CD 80243 [DDD] ■ CS 30243 (D)
Ravel, M.:Son Vn Pno, w. P. Oundjian (vn) CBC ("Musica Viva" series) ▲ MVCD 1060 [DDD]

Trog, Henning (bn)—see ORCHESTRAS & ENSEMBLES Berlin Philharmonic Wind Quintet

Troi, Irène (vn)—see ORCHESTRAS & ENSEMBLES Limoges Baroque Ensemble Soloists

Trompler, Christian (va)
Mozart, W.A.:Sinf concertante Vn, K.364, w. Thorsten Rosenbusch (vn), H. Haenchen (cnd), C.P.E. Bach CO Berlin Classics ▲ BER 2003 [DDD]

Trondhjem, Thomas (pno)
Kuhlau, F.:Son Pno, Op. 34 Rondo Grammofon ▲ RCD 8341
Kuhlau, F.:Sons Pno, Op. 46 Rondo Grammofon ▲ RCD 8341
Kuhlau, F.:Vars on a Danish Air, Op. 14 Rondo Grammofon ▲ RCD 8341
Kuhlau, F.:Vars on the Norwegian Air "God dag, Rasmus Hansen", Op. 15 Rondo Grammofon ▲ RCD 8341
Kuhlau, F.:Vars on a Danish Song, Op. 22 Rondo Grammofon ▲ RCD 8341

Tröndle, H. (pno)—see ORCHESTRAS & ENSEMBLES Orfeo Trio

Tronheim, Thomas (pno)
Stolarczyk, W.:Earth Air Fire Water, w. Amalie Malling (pno), John Damgaard (pno), Anne Øland (pno), Teddy Teirup (pno), Friedrich Gürtler (pno), Rosalind Bevan (pno), Poul Rosenbaum (pno), Rodolfo Llambias (pno), Bella Horn-Ribera (pno), Anders Riber (pno), Elisabeth Sigurdsson (pno), Elsebeth Broderson (pno), Erik Kaltoft (pno), Jørgen Hald Nielsen (pno), Aino Gilemann (pno), Birgit Kjær (pno), Jørgen Thomsen (pno), Gunhild Donslund (pno), Henrik Bo Hansen (pno), Lone Karlsson (pno), Erik Fessel (pno), Lasse Nilsson (pno), Janos Foronczi (pno), Erik Bach (pno), Axel Momme (pno), Arne de Croo Dich (pno), Sven Micha Slot (pno), Hanne Bramsen Buhl (pno), Lili Olesen (pno), Susannah Carlsson (pno), Ulla Erml (pno), Vagn Sørensen (pno), Leif Greibe (pno), Bodil Krogh (pno), Kirsten Ottosen (pno), Inger Bergenholz (pno), Karsten Gylendorf (pno), Bjørn Elkjær (pno), Jacob Bjørn Jensen (pno), Jørgen Kaad (pno), Anne Marie Hjelm (pno), Carl Ulrik Munk Andersen (pno), Poul Lumbye (pno), Oluf Hildebrandt Nielsen (pno), Joachim Olsson (pno), Peter Pade Ramsøe Jacobsen (pno), Astrid Pollmann (pno), Jette Borsch (pno), Kirsten Karlshøj (pno), Maria Teresa Assing (pno), Allan Dahl Hansen (pno), Johan Hugossen (pno), Tine Fenger Pederson (pno), Arne Jørgen Fæø (pno), Anja Høgsted (pno), Anne Sophie Parbo (pno), Inga Lindmark (pno), Teresa Drabik Stathakis (pno), Anne Ruth Ferenczi (pno), Irene Hasager (pno), Yuka Ichikawa (pno), Birgitte Baur (pno), Malene Thastum (pno), Jens E. Rasmussen (pno), Birgitte Zielke (pno), Claus Zielke (pno), Stefan Kasch (pno), Bin Qiao (pno), Inger Johanne Teirup (pno), Lindy Rosborg (pno), Liisa Heininen (pno), David Højer (pno), Ellen Refstrup (pno), Thomas K. Søorensen (pno), Erik Kure (pno), Michael Rauff (pno), Jan beck Eriksson (pno), Tanja Zapolski (pno), Vibeke Skagbo (pno), Pål Eide Lindtner (pno), Ha-Young Sul (pno), Benedicte Palko (pno), Inke Kesseler (pno), Anne Marie Meineche (pno), Sverre Larsen (pno), Kasper Peter Bach (pno), Elisabetta Eliseo (pno), Olga Magieres (pno), Carl Erik Kühl (pno), Thorkild Borup Nielsen (pno), Valeria Zanini (pno), Lars Stenhoft (perc), Dennis Boel (perc), Winnie Dahlgren (perc), Susanne Vind (perc), Claus Byrith (elec), Anne Marie Storm (elec), J. Ribera (cnd) *(rec live, Koldinghaus Castle, Denmark, May 2, 1996)* Danica ▲ DCD 1996

Troperczer, P. (pno)
Tchaikovsky, P.:Con 1 Pno, w. B. Rezucha (cnd), Slovak PO Stradivari Classics ▲ SCD 6017 [DDD] ■ SMC 6017 (D)

Tropp, Vladimir (pno)
Medtner, N.:Second Improvisation Denon ▲ CO 78772
Rachmaninoff, S.:Morceaux de fant Denon ▲ DEN 18003
Schumann, C.:Variations on a Theme by Robert Schumann Denon ▲ DEN 78775 [DDD]
Schumann, R.:Carnaval Pno Denon ▲ DEN 78775 [DDD]
Schumann, R.:Humoreske Pno Denon ▲ DEN 78775 [DDD]
Scriabin, A.:Preludes Pno, Op. 11 Denon ▲ DEN 78772
Tchaikovsky, P.:Les Saisons Denon ▲ DEN 18003

Trosclair, Gary (tpt)
First, D.:The Good Book's (Accurate) Jail of Escape Dust Coordinates 2, w. Matt Sullivan (ob), Chris Jepperson (cl), Annemarie Wiesner (vn), Elaine Kaplinsky (kbd syn), Chad Henderson (teahouse gtr/b gtr), Kevin Sparks (perc), David First (e-bow gtr/teahouse gtr/Distortion gtr/kbd syn/programming) *(rec Baby Monster Studios, NYC, May 1992)* O. O. Discs ▲ OO 23 [DDD]

Tröster, Michael (gtr)—see also ORCHESTRAS & ENSEMBLES Capriccioso Duo
Castelnuovo-Tedesco, M.:Sérénade, w. D. Hopf (gtr), J. Przybylski (cnd), Warsaw SO *(rec Aug. 1992)* Thorofon ▲ CTH 2171 [DDD]
Moreno Torroba, F.:Concierto de Castilla, w. J. Przybylski (cnd), Warschauer SO *(rec Aug. 1992)* Thorofon ▲ CTH 2171 [DDD]

INSTRUMENT.

Tröster, Michael (gtr) (cont.)
Rodrigo, J.:Concierto de Aranjuez, w. J. Przybylski (cnd), Warschauer SO *(rec Aug. 1992)* Thorofon ▲ CTH 2171 [DDD]

Troster, Michael (gtr)
Villa-Lobos, H.:Chôro 1 Thorofon ▲ CTH 2052 [DDD]
Villa-Lobos, H.:Etudes Gtr Thorofon ▲ CTH 2052 [DDD]
Villa-Lobos, H.:Preludes Gtr Thorofon ▲ CTH 2052 [DDD]
Villa-Lobos, H.:Suite populaire brésilienne Thorofon ▲ CTH 2052 [DDD]

Tröster-Weyhofen, Gertrud (mand)
Baumann, H.:Con Capriccioso, w. G. Vogt (cnd), Bavarian State Youth Plucked Instrument Orch Thorofon ▲ CTH 2146 [DDD]
Behrend, S.:Serenade Mand, w. G. Vogt (cnd), Bavarian State Youth Plucked Instrument Orch Thorofon ▲ CTH 2146 [DDD]
Mandolin Concerti, w. Bavarian State Youth Plucked Instrument Orch [cnd:Gerhard Vogt] Thorofon ▲ CTH 2146 [DDD]
Starck, A.:Con Mand, w. G. Vogt (cnd), Bavarian State Youth Plucked Instrument Orch Thorofon ▲ CTH 2146 [DDD]
Tober-Vogt, E.:Carnival of Venice, w. G. Vogt (cnd), Bavarian State Youth Plucked Instrument Orch Thorofon ▲ CTH 2146 [DDD]
Vivaldi, A.:Con Mand, RV.425, w. G. Vogt (cnd), Bavarian State Youth Plucked Instrument Orch Thorofon ▲ CTH 2146 [DDD]

Trotter, Linda (vn)
Banfield, W.:Cone Tone, w. Velda Kelly (vn), Charlotte Givens (va), Tim Holley (vc) Innova ▲ 510 [DDD]

Trotter, Thomas (org)
Choral Evensong for Ascension Day, w. King's College Choir Cambridge, Philip Ledger (cnd) EMI Classics ▲ CDM 65102
A Festival of Lessons & Carols from King's, w. King's College Choir Cambridge EMI Classics ("Studio" series) ▲ CDM 63180 [ADD] ■ EG 63180
The Grand Organ of Birmingham Town Hall Hyperion ▲ CDA 66216 [DDD]
Janáček, L.:Slavonic Mass, w. N. Troitskaya (sop), E. Randova (cta), K. Kaludov (ten), S. Leiferkas (bass), C. Dutoit (cnd), Montreal SO, Montreal Sym Chorus London ▲ 436211-2
Music for Holy Week, w. King's College Choir Cambridge, Philip Ledger (cnd) EMI Classics ▲ CDM 65103

Trovillo, George (pno)
Opera Arias & Songs, w. Eileen Farrell (sop), Philharmonia Orch [cnd:Thomas Schippers] Testament ▲ SBT 1073
The Voices of Living Stereo, Vol. 2, w. Eileen Farrell (sop), Birgit Nilsson (sop), Roberta Peters (sop), Leontyne Price (sop), Galina Vishnevskaya (sop), Rosalind Elias (mez), Shirley Verrett (mez), Marian Anderson (cta), Maureen Forrester (cta), Sergio Franchi (ten), Mario Lanza (ten), Richard Lewis (ten), Jan Pee, Alexander Dedyukhin (pno), Franz Rupp (pno), Leo Taubman (pno), Charles Wadsworth (pno), Boston Pops Orch [cnd:Arthur Fiedler], Boston SO [cnd:Charles Munch], Chicago SO [cnd:Fritz Reiner], RCA Victor Orch, RCA Victor Chorus [cnd:Wa *(rec Boston & Chicago & New York & Rome, 1957-1964)* RCA Living Stereo ▲ 09026-68167-2 [ADD]

Troxler, Rebecca (fl)
Johnson, H.:Serenade Fl, w. M. Votta (cl) Albany ▲ TROY 061 [DDD]
Johnson, H.:Trio Fl, Ob & Pno, w. M. W. McCracken (ob), E. A. Holding (pno) Albany ▲ TROY 061 [DDD]
Talma, L.:Let's Touch the Sky, w. Gerard Reuter (ob), Peter Simmons (bn), Gregg Smith (cnd), Gregg Smith Singers Vox Box ("The American Composers" series) 3-▲ CDX 3037

Trüb, Isabelle (pno)
Hindemith, P.:A Frog He Went a-Courting, w. Niall Brown (vc) *(rec Théâtre de Poche, Vevey Mar 11-12, 1995)* Doron ▲ DRC 3024 [DDD]
Hindemith, P.:Kleine Son Vc, w. Niall Brown (vc) *(rec Théâtre de Poche, Vevey Mar 11-12, 1995)* Doron ▲ DRC 3024 [DDD]
Hindemith, P.:Leichte Stücke, w. Niall Brown (vc) *(rec Théâtre de Poche, Vevey Mar 11-12, 1995)* Doron ▲ DRC 3024 [DDD]
Hindemith, P.:Pieces (3) Vc & Pno, w. Niall Brown (vc) *(rec Théâtre de Poche, Vevey Mar 11-12, 1995)* Doron ▲ DRC 3024 [DDD]

Trubashnik, Senia (ob)
Glick, S.I.:Son Ob, w. V. Tyron (pno) CBC ("Musica Viva" series) ▲ MVCD 1046 [DDD]
Vivaldi, A.:Cons Ob, w. K. Redel (cnd), Luxembourg RSO, 1 concerto—in d Forlane ▲ FOR 16548 [AAD]
Vivaldi, A.:Cons Ob, w. K. Redel (cnd), Luxembourg Radio-TV SO—in d Forlane ▲ FRL 16644 [AAD]

Trudel, Alain (trbn)
Alain Trudel, w. Guy Few (pno) Analekta ▲ CLCD 2015

Truffelli, Luca (fl)
Mercadante, S.:Fant concertante on Themes from Orazi e Curiazi, w. Gian-Luca Petrucci (fl d'amore), C.F. Sedazzari (cnd), Camerata Schubert Bongiovanni ▲ GB 2199 [DDD]
Mercadante, S.:Sinf concertante 1, w. Roberto Saltini (cl), Giovanni Sora (cl), Andrea Mastini (cnt), C.F. Sedazzari (cnd), Camerata Schubert Bongiovanni ▲ GB 2199 [DDD]
Mercadante, S.:Sinf concertante 2, w. Roberto Saltini (cl), Andrea Mastini (cnt), C.F. Sedazzari (cnd), Camerata Schubert Bongiovanni ▲ GB 2199 [DDD]
Mercadante, S.:Sinf concertante 3, w. Roberto Saltini (cl), Giovanni Sora (cl), Andrea Mastini (cnt), C.F. Sedazzari (cnd), Camerata Schubert Bongiovanni ▲ GB 2199 [DDD]

Trull, Natalia (pno)
Rachmaninoff, S.:Con 3 Pno, w. A. Anichanov (cnd), St. Petersburg State SO Audiophile Classics ▲ 101.038

Truman, Robert (vc)
Holst, G.:Choral Music, w. D. Theodore (ob), S. Williams (hp), Holst Singers—The Princess; Light Leaves Whisper; Ave Maria; Jesu, Thou the Virgin-born; A Welcome Song; In Youth is Pleasure; Two Eastern Pictures; Bring us in Good Ale; Lully My Liking; Of One That Is So Fair and Bright; Diverus and Lazurus; Terly Terlow; This Have I Done for My True Love; Six Choral Folksongs; Twelve Welsh Folksongs; O Spiritual Pilgrim Hyperion ▲ CDA 66705 [DDD]

Trusler, J. (vn)—see ORCHESTRAS & ENSEMBLES Delmé String Quartet

Truys, Marie-Josèphe (pno)—see also ORCHESTRAS & ENSEMBLES Cecilia Piano Quartet
Debussy, C.:Epigraphes antiques, w. E. Sun (pno) Quantum ▲ QM 6912 [DDD]

Tryon, Valerie (pno)—see also ORCHESTRAS & ENSEMBLES Rembrandt Trio
The Cantorial Voice of the Cello, w. Coenraad Bloemendal (vc), Andrés Díaz (vc), Andrew Mark (vc) *(rec Troy Savings Bank Music Hall, Troy, NY, May 1994)* Dorian ▲ DOR 90208 [DDD]
Chopin, F.:Ballades Pno (comp) *(rec Humbercrest United Church, Toronto)* CBC ("Musica Viva" series) ▲ MVCD 1092 [DDD]
Chopin, F.:Scherzos *(rec Humbercrest United Church, Toronto)* CBC ("Musica Viva" series) ▲ MVCD 1092 [DDD]
Dances & Romances for Violin, w. Moshe Hammer (vn), William Beauvais (gtr) Musica Viva ▲ MVCD 1071 [DDD]
Debussy, C.:Songs, w. Claudette Leblanc (sop)—Nuits d'toiles; Beau soir; Musique; Mandoline; Ariettes oubliées; Deux romances; Fêtes galantes Nos. 1 & 2; Proses lyriques; Noël des enfants qui n'ont plus de maisons Unicorn-Kanchana ▲ DKP 9133 [DDD]
The Joy of Piano *(rec. Jan. 27-29, 1992)* Musica Viva ▲ MVV 1065 [DDD]

Trythall, Richard (pno)
Ives, C.:Son 2 Pno, w. Lauren Weiss (fl) *(rec Villa Aurelia, American Academy, Rome, Dec 1992 & Sept 1995)* Centaur ▲ 2285 [DDD]
Ives, C.:Studies Pno—No. 2 "Varied Air & Variations"; No. 9, "The Anti-Abolitionist Riots"; No. 21, "Some South-Paw Pitching" *(rec Villa Aurelia, American Academy, Rome, Dec 1992 & Sept 1995)* Centaur ▲ 2285 [DDD]
Ives, C.:Three-Page Son *(rec Villa Aurelia, American Academy, Rome, Dec 1992 & Sept 1995)* Centaur ▲ 2285 [DDD]

Trythall, Richard (pno) (cont.)
Trythall, R.:Pno Music—Arabesque 2; Fantasy; Insieme; Solo Aspen ▲ APN 30301-CD ■ APN 30301-C

Tsachor, Uriel (pno)
Barber, S.:Son Vc, w. Emanuel Gruber (vc) Arcobaleno ▲ AAOC 9326
Britten, H.:Son Vc, w. Emanuel Gruber (vc) Arcobaleno ▲ AAOC 9326
Reger, M.:Son Vn Pno, Op. 139, w. A. Hardy (vn) Olympia ▲ OLY 357 [DDD]
Romantic Piano Pearls Divox ▲ CDX 25207 [DDD]
Schnittke, A.:Son Vc, w. Emanuel Gruber (vc) Arcobaleno ▲ AAOC 9326
Schumann, R.:Bunte Blätter Arcobaleno ▲ SBCD 8900 [DDD]
Schumann, R.:Humoreske Pno Arcobaleno ▲ SBCD 8900 [DDD]
Strauss, R.:Son Vn, w. A. Hardy (vn) Olympia ▲ OLY 357 [DDD]

Tschopp, Sybille (vn)
Eine klingende Musikgeschichte des Kantons Luzern [A Resonant Music History of Lucerne Canton], w. R. Baumgartner (cnd), Lucerne Festival Strings, Karin Krauer (va) Gallo ▲ CD 727 [ADD]

Tsekouras, Andreas (acc)
Karaindrou, E.:Film Music, w. Jan Garbarek (t sax), Vangelis Christopoulos (ob), Anthis Sokratis (tpt), Nikos Guinos (cl), Tassos Diakoyiorgis (santouri), Vangelis Skouras (hn), Petros Protopapas (fl), Christos Sfetsas (vc), Eleni Karaindrou (pno/voc), L. Chalkiadakis (cnd), *(ensemble unknown)*—Farewell Theme; Scream; Improv. On Farewell & Waltz Theme; Farewell Theme II [all from The Beekeeper; w. Jan Garbarek (ten sax), Tassos Diakoyiorgis (satouri), Vassilis Dertilis (kbd), Eleni Karaindrou (pno), Lefteris Chalkiadakis (cnd)]; Elegy for Rosa; Rosa's Song (text:Christofis) [both from Rosa; w. Vangelis Skouras (Fr hn), Petros Protopapas (fl), Alekos Christidis (timp), Eleni Karaindrou (voc), Lefteis Chalkiadakis (cnd)]; Fairytale; Parade; Return; Song [all from Happy Homecoming, Comrade; w. Vangelis Skouras (Fr hn), Christos Sfetsas (vc), Aliki Krithari (hp), Andreas Tsekouras (acc), Eleni Karaindrou (pno), Nelli Semitekolo (pno), Anthis Sokratis (tpt), Lefteris Chalkiadakis (cnd)]; Wandering in Alexandria (2 vers) [both from Wandering; w. Tassos Diakoyiorgis (santouri), Nelli Semitekolo (prepared pno), Anthis Sokratis (tpt), Nikos Guinos (cl), Katerina Ktona (hpd), Christos Sfetsas (vc)]; The Journey [from Voyage to Cythera]; Adagio [from Landscape in the Mist] [both w. Vangelis Christopoulos (ob), str orch, Lefteris Chalkiadakis (cnd)] ECM ▲ 78118-21429-2 [AAD]
Karaindrou, E.:The Suspended Step of the Stork, w. Vangelis Christopoulos (ob), Ada Rouva (hp), Christos Sfetsas (vc), Nikos Spinoulas (hn), Dimitris Vraskos (vn), L. Chalkiadakis (cnd), *(orch unknown) (rec Sound, Athens, Apr & Aug 1991)* ECM ▲ 78118-21456-2 [AAD]

Tsessos, M. (gtr)
Castelnuovo-Tedesco, M.:Con 1 Gtr, w. V. Altschuler (cnd), St. Petersburg Philharmony CO Infinity Digital ▲ QK 64335 [DDD]
Villa-Lobos, H.:Con Gtr, w. V. Altschuler (cnd), St. Petersburg Philharmony CO Infinity Digital ▲ QK 64335 [DDD]
Vivaldi, A.:Cons Gtr, w. V. Altschuler (cnd), St. Petersburg Philharmony CO Infinity Digital ▲ QK 64335 [DDD]

Tsiganov, Dmitri (vn)—see ORCHESTRAS & ENSEMBLES Beethoven String Quartet

Tsinman, Mikhail (vn)
Medtner, N.:Son 1 Vn, w. Victor Yampolsky (pno) *(rec Mosfilm Studio, Jan & Feb 1996)* Triton ▲ 17009 [DDD]
Medtner, N.:Son 2 Vn, w. Victor Yampolsky (pno) *(rec Mosfilm Studio, Jan & Feb 1996)* Triton ▲ 17009 [DDD]

Ts'ong, Fou (pno)
Chopin, F.:Barcarolle Pno Sony Classical ("Essential Classics" series) ▲ SBK 53515 ■ SBT 53515
Chopin, F.:Berceuse Sony Classical ("Essential Classics" series) ▲ SBK 53515 ■ SBT 53515
Chopin, F.:Con 1 Pno, w. M. Tang (cnd), Sinfonia Varsovia Collins Quest ▲ COL 3015 [DDD]
Chopin, F.:Con 2 Pno, w. M. Tang (cnd), Sinfonia Varsovia Collins Quest ▲ COL 3015 [DDD]
Chopin, F.:Fant Sony Classical ("Essential Classics" series) ▲ SBK 53515 ■ SBT 53515
Chopin, F.:Mazurkas—2 Mazurkas (1826); Opp. post. 67/1-4 & 68/1-3; Opp. 6, 7, 17, 24, 30, 33, 41, 50, 56, 59, 63 Sony Classical ▲ SB2K 53246 [DDD]
Chopin, F.:Nocturnes Sony Classical ▲ SB2K 53249 [ADD]
Chopin, F.:Polonaise-fant Sony Classical ("Essential Classics" series) ▲ SBK 53515 ■ SBT 53515
Mozart, W.A.:Con 7 Pnos, w. V. Ashkenazy (pno), D. Barenboim (pno), Philharmonia Orch London 2-▲ 421577-2 [ADD]
Mozart, W.A.:Con 9 Pno, w. F. Ts'ong (cnd), Polish CO IMP Masters ▲ IMPMCD 84 [DDD]
Mozart, W.A.:Con 12 Pno, w. F. Ts'ong (cnd), Polish CO IMP Masters ▲ IMPMCD 84 [DDD]
Mozart, W.A.:Con 18 Pno, w. J. Maksymiuk (cnd), Polish CO Vivace ▲ E 572 [ADD]
Mozart, W.A.:Con 21 Pno, w. F. Ts'ong (cnd), Sinfonia Varsovia IMP Masters ▲ IMPMCD 74 [DDD]
Mozart, W.A.:Con 22 Pno, w. F. Ts'ong (cnd), Sinfonia Varsovia IMP Masters ▲ IMPMCD 79 [DDD]
Mozart, W.A.:Con 24 Pno, w. F. Ts'ong (cnd), Sinfonia Varsovia IMP Masters ▲ IMPMCD 79 [DDD]
Mozart, W.A.:Con 25 Pno, w. J. Maksymiuk (cnd), Polish CO Vivace ▲ E 572 [ADD]
Mozart, W.A.:Con 27 Pno, w. F. Ts'ong (cnd), Sinfonia Varsovia IMP Masters ▲ IMPMCD 74 [DDD]

Tsubota, Mitsuru (vn)—see ORCHESTRAS & ENSEMBLES St. Luke's Chamber Ensemble

Tsuji, I. (ob)
Shinohara, M.:Cooperation, w. A. Nishigata (shamisen), K. Mitsuhashi (shakuhachi), M. Akao (fue), S. Yaotani (hichiriki), K. Ishikawa (sho), C. Fukunaga (koto), J. Ueda (biwa), M. Yoshizawa (kokyu), T. Takahashi (cl), G. Kitamura (tpt), A. Murata (trbn), S. Eiso (perc), S. Ueki (vn), S. Katsuta (vc), Y. Shibuya (pno), K. Komatsu (cnd) *(rec live Casals Hall, Tokyo, Mar. 5, 1994)* Camerata ▲ 30CM 375 [DDD]
Shinohara, M.:Tabiyuki, w. A. Ogawa (mez), M. Kakagawa (fl), T. Takahashi (cl), K. Okazaki (fagotto), G. Kitamura (tpt), A. Murata (trbn), S. Eiso (perc), S. Ueki (vn), A. Nakakoji (va), S. Katsuta (vc), M. Komuro (contrabass), K. Komatsu (cnd) *(rec live Casals Hall, Tokyo, Mar. 5, 1994)* Camerata ▲ 30CM 375 [DDD]

Tsuji, Y. (perc/shak/sgr)—see ORCHESTRAS & ENSEMBLES Far East Side Band

Tsuruta, Kinshi (biwa)
Takemitsu, T.:Music of, w. K. Yokoyama (shakuhachi), Y. Horigome (cnd), Tokyo Metropolitan SO—Far Calls, Coming, Far! (1980); Requiem for Strings (1957); Nov. Steps (1967); Visions (1989) Denon/PCM Digital ▲ DEN 79441 [DDD]

Tsutsumi, Tsuyoshi (vc)
Martinů, B.:La Revue de Cuisine, w. James Campbell (cl), James McKay (bn), Guy Few (tpt), Moshe Hammer (vn), André Laplante (pno) *(rec Glenn Gould Studio, CBC Toronto, Mar. 26-27, 1994)* CBC ("Musica Viva" series) ▲ MVV 1089 [DDD]
Miniatures, w. Moshe Hammer (vn), William Tritt (pno) CBC Records ("Musica Viva" series) ▲ MVCD 1043 [DDD]
Nielsen, C.:Serenata in vano, w. James Campbell (cl), James McKay (bn), James Sommerville (hn), Joel Quarrington (db) *(rec Glenn Gould Studio, CBC Toronto, Mar. 26-27, 1994)* CBC ("Musica Viva" series) ▲ MVV 1089 [DDD]

Tsutusmi, Tsuyoshi (vc)
Beethoven, L. van:Sons Vc (comp), w. R. Turini (pno) *(rec May 28-31, 1980)* Sony Classical 2-▲ SB2K 53240 [ADD]
Beethoven, L. van:Vars on "Ein Mädchen oder Weibchen" from Mozart's *Die Zauberflöte*, w. R. Turini (pno) *(rec May 28-31, 1980)* Sony Classical 2-▲ SB2K 53240 [ADD]
Beethoven, L. van:Vars on "Bei Männern" from Mozart's *Die Zauberflöte*, w. R. Turini (pno) *(rec May 28-31, 1980)* Sony Classical 2-▲ SB2K 53240 [ADD]

Tsyganov, Dmitry (vn)
Borodin, A.:Trio Pno, w. Emil Gilels (pno), Sergey Shirinsky (vc) Multisonic ▲ MUL 310266

Tubery, Jean (cnt/muet/rcr)—see ORCHESTRAS & ENSEMBLES La Fenice Ensemble

Tubery, Jean (hn)
Cavalli, P.F.:Vespero della beata Vergine Maria, w. F. Lasserre (cnd), La Fenice Ensemble, Akademia Pierre Verany 2-▲ PVY 796042 [DDD]

Tuckwell, Barry (hn)
Banks, D.:Trio Hn, w. B. Langbein (vn), M. Jones (pno) *(rec 4/87)* Tudor ▲ 771 [DDD]
Barry Tuckwell, w. Academy of St. Martin in the Fields [cnd:Neville Marriner], English CO EMI Classics ("Doublefforte" series) 2-▲ CDFB 69395
Brahms, J.:Trio Hn, w. B. Langbein (vn), M. Jones (pno) *(rec 4/87)* Tudor ▲ 771 [DDD]
Brahms, J.:Trio Hn, w. I. Perlman (vn), V. Ashkenazy (pno) London ▲ 414128-2 [ADD]

▲ = CD ♦ = Enhanced CD Δ = MD ■ = Cassette Tape □ = DCC

Tuckwell, Barry (hn) (cont.)
Britten, H.:Serenade, Op. 31, w. P. Pears (ten), B. Britten (cnd), London SO [E] London ▲ 417153-2 [ADD]
Haydn, J.:Cons Hn, w. N. Marriner (cnd), Academy of St. Martin in the Fields London ("Serenata" series) ▲ 430633-2
Herzogenberg, H. von:Trio Pno, Ob & Hn, w. Ingo Goritzki (ob), Ricardo Requejo (pno) Claves ▲ CD 803
Holloway, R.:Con Hn, w. M. Bamert (cnd), Scottish CO Collins Classics ▲ COL 1439 [DDD]
Knussen, O.:Con Hn, w. O. Knussen (cnd), London Sinfonietta *(rec Henry Wood Hall & All Hollows Gospel Oak, London, Oct & Dec 1995)* Deutsche Grammophon ▲ 449 572-2 [DDD]
Koechlin, C.:Morceau de lecture, w. Daniel Blumenthal (pno) [arr hn & pno] ASV ▲ ASVCD 716
Koechlin, C.:Petites Pièces, w. B. Langbein (vn), M. Jones (pno) *(rec 4/87)* Tudor ▲ 771 [DDD]
Koechlin, C.:Pieces Hn & Pno, w. Daniel Blumenthal (pno) ASV ▲ ASVCD 716
Koechlin, C.:Son Hn, w. Daniel Blumenthal (pno) ASV ▲ ASVCD 716
Mozart, W.A.:Con "0" Hn, w. B. Tuckwell (cnd), Philharmonia Orch *(rec July 1990)* Collins Classics ▲ 11532 [DDD]
Mozart, W.A.:Cons Hn, w. N. Marriner (cnd), Academy of St. Martin in the Fields EMI Classics ▲ CDM 69569
Mozart, W.A.:Cons Hn, w. B. Tuckwell (cnd), English CO London ▲ 410284-2 [DDD]
Mozart, W.A.:Cons Hn, w. B. Tuckwell (cnd), Philharmonia Orch *(rec July 1990)* Collins Classics ▲ 11532 [DDD]
Mozart, W.A.:Con Movt Hn, K.494a, w. B. Tuckwell (cnd), Philharmonia Orch *(rec July 1990)* Collins Classics ▲ 11532 [DDD]
Mozart, W.A.:Rondo Hn, K.371, w. N. Marriner (cnd), Academy of St. Martin in the Fields EMI Classics ▲ CDM 69569
Reinecke, C.:Trio Ob, w. I. Goritzki (ob), R. Requejo (pno) Claves ▲ CD 803
Romantic Trios, w. Joan Sutherland (sop), Richard Bonynge (cnd) London ▲ 421552-2 LH [ADD]
Strauss, R.:Das Alphorn, w. M. McLaughlin (sop), V. Ashkenazy (pno) London ▲ 430370-2 [DDD]
Strauss, R.:Andante Hn, w. V. Ashkenazy (pno) London ▲ 430370-2 [DDD]
Strauss, R.:Con 1 Hn, w. V. Ashkenazy (cnd), Royal PO London ▲ 430370-2 [DDD]
Strauss, R.:Con 2 Hn, w. V. Ashkenazy (cnd), Royal PO London ▲ 430370-2 [DDD]
Strauss, R.:Intro, Theme & Vars, w. V. Ashkenazy (pno) London ▲ 430370-2 [DDD]

Tuckwell, Barry (nat hn)
Koechlin, C.:Sonneries for 2, 3 or 4 Hunting Hns ASV ▲ ASVCD 716

Tudón, Raúl (perc)—see ORCHESTRAS & ENSEMBLES Tambuco Camerata

Tudor, David (pno)
Cage, J.:Pno Music—Music for Pno, No. 52-56 *(rec Nov 25, 1956)* Hat Hut ("Now" series) ▲ CD 6181 [ADD]
Cardew, C.:Son 3 Pno *(rec Sept 20, 1958)* Hat Hut ("Now" series) ▲ CD 6181 [ADD]
Evangelisti, F.:Proiezioni sonore *(rec Sept 14, 1958)* Hat Hut ("Now" series) ▲ CD 6181 [ADD]
Nilsson, B.:Quantitäten *(rec Sept 14, 1958)* Hat Hut ("Now" series) ▲ CD 6181 [ADD]
Pousseur, H.:Impromptu et Vars II *(rec Sept 14, 1958)* Hat Hut ("Now" series) ▲ CD 6181 [ADD]
Wolff, C.:Duo for Pianists I, w. John Cage (pno)—2 versions *(rec Oct 1, 1960)* Hat Hut ("Now" series) ▲ CD 6181 [ADD]
Wolff, C.:For Pno *(rec Sept 14, 1958)* Hat Hut ("Now" series) ▲ CD 6181 [ADD]
Wolpe, S.:Passacaglia *(rec Esoteric Studios, NY, 1954)* Hat Hut ▲ CD 6182 [AAD]
Wolpe, S.:Son Vn, w. Frances Magnes (vn) *(rec Esoteric Studios, NY, 1954)* Hat Hut ▲ CD 6182 [AAD]

Tukiainen, Seppo (vn)—see ORCHESTRAS & ENSEMBLES Sibelius Academy String Quartet

Tuláček, Tomáš (vn)
Tučapský, A.:The 7 Sorrows, w. Nigel Perrin (cnd), Bath Camerata *(rec St. George's Brandon Hill, Bristol, Jan 28, 1996)* SOMM ▲ SOMMCD 205 [DDD]

Tulbure, Traian (hn)
Schumann, R.:Konzertstück Hns, w. V. Oprea (hn), D. Lung (hn), A. Marc (hn), C. Mandeal (cnd), Cluj-Napoca PO Electrecord ▲ ELCD 107 [AAD]

Tullio, Louise di (fl)
Bedings, H.:Ballade Fl & Hp, w. S. McDonald (hp) Klavier ▲ KCD 11019 [ADD]
Dring, M.:Dances Fl & Pno, w. Leigh Kaplan (pno)—WIB Waltz; Sarabande; Tango Cambria ▲ CD 1084 [ADD]
Lauber, J.:Medieval Dances, w. S. McDonald (hp) Klavier ▲ KCD 11019 [ADD]
Masters of Flute & Harp, w. Susann McDonald (hp) Klavier ▲ KCD 11019 [ADD]
Masters of Flute & Harp, Vol. 1, w. Susann McDonald (hp) Klavier ■ KC 556
Masters of Flute & Harp, Vol. 2, w. Susann McDonald (hp) Klavier ■ KC 560
Persichetti, V.:Serenade 10 Fl, w. S. McDonald (hp) Klavier ▲ KCD 11019 [ADD]
Sonatas for Flute & Harp, w. Susann McDonald (hp) Klavier ▲ KCD 11015 [ADD]

Tullio, V. di (pno)
Casals, P.:Song of the Birds, w. L. A. Greco (vc) Orion ▲ CDA 8901 [AAD] ■ OC 8802
Riddle, N.:Son Vc, w. L. A. Greco (vc) Orion ▲ CDA 8901 [AAD] ■ OC 8802

Tůma, Jaroslav (hpd)
Jirásek, J.:Zoe *(rec Studio 1, Czech Radio, Pizen)* Arta ▲ 0054 [DDD]

Tůma, Jaroslav (org)
Bach, J.S.:Org Mass Supraphon ▲ SUP 3176
Biber, H. von:Mystery (or Rosary) Sons, w. Gabriela Demeterová (vn) Supraphon ▲ SUP CD 3155
Carolling, w. Benačková, Gabriela (sop), Lubomír Vraspír (ten), Bambini di Praga [cnd:Jaroslav Krček], Prague Brass Quintet Supraphon ▲ SUP 111417 [DDD]
Handel, G.F.:Cons (16) Org, w. O. Vlček (cnd), Prague Virtuosi—Nos 1-12 Supraphon 3-▲ SUP 11 1494 [DDD]
Historic Organs of Bohemia, Vol. 2 Supraphon ▲ SUP 3175
Muffat, G.:Apparatus Panton ▲ PAN 811016

Tumeo, Claudio (tt)—see ORCHESTRAS & ENSEMBLES Collegium Pro Musica

Tunick, Danny
Riley, T.:In C, w. Bruce Ackley, Steve Adams, Don R. Baker, Chris Brown, George Brooks, Steve Coughlin, Blake Derby, Bill Douglass, Mihr'un'Nisa Douglass, Hank Dutt, David Harrington, Don Howe, Joan Jeanrenaud, Alden Jenks, Warner Jepson, Henry Kaiser, Jaron Lanier, Bill Maginnis, George Marsh, Shabda Owens, Jon Raskin, Gyan Riley, Terry Riley, Gino Robair, John Sackett, Ramón Sender, John Sherba, Toyji Tomita, Danny Tunick, William Winant, Evan Ziporyn *(rec Jan. 14, 1990)* New Albion ▲ NA 071

Tunis, A. (pno)
Debussy, C.:Son Vn, w. A. Dubeau (vn) *(rec 1988)* Analekta Fleur de Lys ▲ FL 2 3021 [DDD] ■ AN4-8702
Fauré, G.:Son 1 Vn, w. Angèle Dubeau (vn) Analekta ▲ AN 28701
Fauré, G.:Son 1 Vn, w. A. Dubeau (vn) *(rec 1988)* Analekta Fleur de Lys ▲ FL 2 3021 [DDD] ■ AN4-8702
Leclair, J.-M.:Sons Vn (Books 1-4), w. Angèle Dubeau (vn)—Op. 9/3 Analekta ▲ AN 28701
Leclair, J.-M.:Sons Vn (Books 1-4), w. A. Dubeau (vn) [arr for vn & pno]— Op. 9/3 *(rec 1988)* Analekta Fleur de Lys ▲ FL 2 3021 [DDD] ■ AN4-8702
Rachmaninoff, S.:Son Vc, w. Desmond Hoebig (vc) CBC ▲ MVCD 1093 [DDD]
Rachmaninoff, S.:Vocalise, w. Desmond Hoebig (vc) [trans Leonard Rose for vc & pno] CBC ▲ MVCD 1093 [DDD]
Shostakovich, D.:Son Vc, w. Desmond Hoebig (vc) CBC ▲ MVCD 1093 [DDD]

Tunnell, Charles (vc)
Haydn, J.:Qts Fl, w. Clive Conway (fl), Nona Liddell (vn), Paul Silverthorne (va) Meridian ▲ CDE 84118
Hummel, J.N.:Adagio, Vars & Rondo on "Schöne Minka", w. C. Croshaw (pno), C. Conway (fl) Meridian ▲ MER 84217
Hummel, J.N.:Son Vc, w. C. Croshaw (pno) Meridian ▲ MER 84217
Schubert, Franz:Qt Fl, w. C. Conway (fl), P. Silverthorne (va), G. Garcia (gtr) Meridian ▲ CDE 84118

Tunnell, John (vn)
Bach, J.S.:Con for 2 Vns, w. Jaime Laredo (vn), J. Laredo (cnd), Scottish CO IMP ("Classics" series) ▲ IMP 6700402

Tunnell, John (vn) (cont.)
Bach, J.S.:Con for 2 Vns, w. O. Shumsky (vn), Scottish CO Nimbus ▲ NI 5325 [DDD]

Tunnicliffe, Richard (vc)—see also ORCHESTRAS & ENSEMBLES Locatelli Trio
Rossini, G.:Sons Str Qt, w. E. Wallfisch (vn), M. Marcus (vn), C.-C. Nwanoku (db) Hyperion ▲ CDA 66595

Tunstall, Helen (hp)
Britten, H.:Gloriana (choral dances), w. I. Partridge (ten), H. Christophers (cnd), The Sixteen *(rec 1 & 4/91)* Collins Classics ▲ 12862 [DDD]
Spratling, H.:Choral Music, w. Tracey Chadwell (sop), Susan Bullock (sop), Jeffery Dyball (hp), John Hatton (org), J. Rennert (cnd), Parnassus String Ensemble, Spratling Choir—Mass of the Holy Spirit; O Salutaris Hostia; Tantum Ergo; Sinf Str Orch; Son Hp; O Magnum Mysterium; In Paradisum *(rec St. Mary Magdelene, Paddington, May 15-17, 1988)* SOMM ▲ SOMMCD 206 [ADD]
Tavener, J.:To a Child Dancing in the Wind, w. P. Rozario (sop), K. Lukas (fl), S. Tees (va) Collins Classics ▲ COL 1428 [DDD]

Turban, Ingolf (vn)
Bruch, M.:Con 2 Vn, w. L. Shambadal (cnd), Bamberg SO *(rec Mar. 1992)* Claves ▲ CD 9318 [DDD]
Busoni, F.:Con Vn, w. L. Shambadal (cnd), Bamberg SO *(rec Mar. 1992)* Claves ▲ CD 9318 [DDD]
Grieg, E.:Sons Vn, Opp. 8, 13 & 45, w. Jean-Jacques Dunki (pno) Claves ▲ 50-8808
Hartmann, K.A.:Son 1 Vn Claves ▲ CD 9518 [DDD]
Hartmann, K.A.:Son 2 Vn Claves ▲ CD 9518 [DDD]
Hartmann, K.A.:Suite 1 Vn Claves ▲ CD 9518 [DDD]
Hartmann, K.A.:Suite 2 Vn Claves ▲ CD 9518 [DDD]
Paganini, N.:Caprices Vn, w. Giovanni Bria (pno) [arr. R. Schumann for violin & piano] Claves ▲ CD 9416 [DDD]
Respighi, O.:Con all'antica, w. M. Viotti (cnd), English CO Claves ▲ CD 9017 [DDD]
Respighi, O.:Pastorale Vn, w. M. Viotti (cnd), English CO Claves ▲ CD 9017 [DDD]
Strauss, R.:Con Vn, w. L. Shambadal (cnd), Bamberg SO *(rec Mar. 1992)* Claves ▲ CD 9318 [DDD]
Tartini, G.:Sons Vn & Continuo, w. Y. Savary (vc), U. Deutschler (hpd)—Sonata in A, "Pastorale" (B A16); Sonata in C (B C11); Sonata in E (B E6); Sonata in g, "Devil's Trill" (B G5); Sonata in g, "Didone abbandonata" (B G10) Claves ▲ CD 9110 [DDD]

Tureck, Rosalyn (pno)
Bach, J.S.:Adagio Clvd VAI Audio ▲ VAIA 1041
Bach, J.S.:Adagio Clvd *(rec Great Hall of the Philharmonic, July 5, 1995)* VAI Audio ▲ VAIA 1131 [DDD]
Bach, J.S.:Aria variata alla maniera italiana VAI Audio ▲ VAIA 1041
Bach, J.S.:Aria variata alla maniera italiana *(rec Great Hall of the Philharmonic, July 5, 1995)* VAI Audio ▲ VAIA 1131 [DDD]
Bach, J.S.:Capriccio Departure VAI Audio ▲ VAIA 1041
Bach, J.S.:Capriccio Departure *(rec Great Hall of the Philharmonic, July 5, 1995)* VAI Audio ▲ VAIA 1131 [DDD]
Bach, J.S.:Chromatic Fant & Fugue VAI Audio 2-▲ VAIA 1024-2 [DDD]
Bach, J.S.:Chromatic Fant & Fugue VAI Audio ▲ VAIA 1041
Bach, J.S.:Chromatic Fant & Fugue *(rec Great Hall of the Philharmonic, July 5, 1995)* VAI Audio ▲ VAIA 1131 [DDD]
Bach, J.S.:Clavierbüchlein for Anna Magdalena Bach (sels)—Musette in D (S. Anh. 126) only *(rec Great Hall of the Philharmonic, July 5, 1995)* VAI Audio ▲ VAIA 1131 [DDD]
Bach, J.S.:English Suites—BWV 808 *(rec live, Town Hall, New York, 1948)* VAI Audio ▲ VAIA 1085
Bach, J.S.:English Suites—BWV 808 VAI Audio ▲ VAIA 1051 [ADD]
Bach, J.S.:Fants Hpd VAI Audio ▲ VAIA 1041
Bach, J.S.:Goldberg Vars VAI Audio ▲ VAIA 1029 [AAD]
Bach, J.S.:Italian Con VAI Audio ▲ VAIA 1086 F
Bach, J.S.:Italian Con VAI Audio ▲ VAIA 1051 [ADD]
Bach, J.S.:Music of—Prelude & Fugue, BWV 866; Gigue [from Partita, BWV 825]; Vars 28 & 29; Musette in D; Gigue [from English Suite No. 3] ; Allegro [from Son in d, BWV 964] VAI Audio ▲ VAIA 1086
Bach, J.S.:Partitas Hpd, BWV 825-830—BWV 825, 826, 830 VAI Audio ▲ VAIA 1040
Bach, J.S.:Partitas Hpd, BWV 825-830 VAI Audio ▲ VAIA 1086 F
Bach, J.S.:Partitas Hpd, BWV 825-830—No. 2 in c only *(rec Great Hall of the Philharmonic, July 5, 1995)* VAI Audio ▲ VAIA 1131 [DDD]
Bach, J.S.:Preludes Hpd, BWV 933-38, "Little Preludes" *(rec live, Town Hall, New York, 1948)* VAI Audio ▲ VAIA 1085
Bach, J.S.:Sons (5) Kbd—in d, BWV 964 VAI Audio ▲ VAIA 1051 [ADD]
Bach, J.S.:Sons (5) Kbd—BWV 964 *(rec live, Town Hall, New York, 1948)* VAI Audio ▲ VAIA 1085 F
Bach, J.S.:Toccatas Hpd, BWV 910-16—BWV 12 VAI Audio ▲ VAIA 1041
Bach, J.S.:Das wohltemperierte Klavier—Prelude & Fugues in C, c, C#, G [BWV 846, 847, 872, 884] VAI Audio ▲ VAIA 1051 [ADD]
Bach, J.S.:Das wohltemperierte Klavier—Prelude & Fugues, BWV 855, 880, 849 *(rec live, Town Hall, New York, 1948)* VAI Audio ▲ VAIA 1085
Bach, J.S.:Das wohltemperierte Klavier—Prelude & Fugue in B♭, BWV 866 VAI Audio ▲ VAIA 1041
Bach, J.S.:Das wohltemperierte Klavier—Prelude in e♭ only *(rec Great Hall of the Philharmonic, July 5, 1995)* VAI Audio ▲ VAIA 1131 [DDD]
Brahms, J.:Vars & Fugue on a Theme by Handel VAI Audio 2-▲ VAIA 1024-2 [DDD]
Busoni, F.:Chaconne Pno VAI Audio 2-▲ VAIA 1024-2 [DDD]
Dallapiccola, L.:Studi (2) Vn, w. Ruggiero Ricci (vn) *(rec NY, May 2, 1952)* VAI Audio ▲ VAIA 1124 [ADD]
Diamond, D.:Son 1 Pno *(rec NY, Dec 8, 1948)* VAI Audio ▲ VAIA 1124 [ADD]
Liszt, F.:Grandes études de Paganini, S.141—Nos. 1, 2 & 6 VAI Audio ▲ VAIA 1086
Live at the Teatro Colón *(rec live, Aug. 14, 1992)* VAI Audio 2-▲ VAIA 1024-2 [DDD]
Mendelssohn, F.:A Midsummer Night's Dream (sels) [arr. Hutcheson for pno] VAI Audio ▲ VAIA 1086
Schubert, Franz:Moments musicaux VAI Audio 2-▲ VAIA 1024-2 [DDD]
Schubert, Franz:Moments musicaux—No. 2 VAI Audio ▲ VAIA 1086
Schuman, W.:Con Pno, w. D. Saidenberg (cnd), Saidenberg Little Sym *(rec NY, Jan 13, 1943)* VAI Audio ▲ VAIA 1124 [ADD]

Tureski, Trevor (perc)
Berg, O.:Odd Trio, w. K. Smith (vn), W. Beauvais (gtr) Centaur ▲ CRC 2167 [DDD]
Berg, O.:Peter Quince at the Clavier, w. J. Relyea (bass), L. Freedman (E♭ & B♭ cl), J. Hess (pno) Centaur ▲ CRC 2167 [DDD]

Turetschek, Gerhard (ob)
Mozart, W.A.:Con Ob, K.314, w. K. Böhm (cnd), Vienna PO Deutsche Grammophon ▲ 429816-2 [ADD] ■ 429816-4

Turetzky, Bertram (db)
Erickson, R.:Ricercar à 3 *(rec 1987-91)* CRI ▲ CD 616 [DDD]
Reynolds, R.:Whispers out of Time, w. J. Négyesy (vn), Liu (va), P. Farrell (vc), H. Sollberger (cnd), San Diego SO Ensemble New World ▲ NW 80401-2 [DDD]
Smith, S.S.:Notebook, w. J. Fonville (fl), E. Harkins (tpt), P. Hoffmann (pno) O.O. Discs ▲ OO 11 [DDD]

Turini, Ronald (pno)
Beethoven, L. van:Sons Vc (comp), w. T. Tsutsumi (vc) *(rec May 28-31, 1980)* Sony Classical 2-▲ SB2K 53240 [ADD]
Beethoven, L. van:Vars on "Ein Mädchen oder Weibchen" from Mozart's *Die Zauberflöte*, w. T. Tsutsumi (vc) *(rec May 28-31, 1980)* Sony Classical 2-▲ SB2K 53240 [ADD]
Beethoven, L. van:Vars on "Bei Männern" from Mozart's *Die Zauberflöte*, w. T. Tsutsumi (vc) *(rec May 28-31, 1980)* Sony Classical 2-▲ SB2K 53240 [ADD]

Turk, J. (tuba)
Amato, B.:Two Together, w. D. Orhenstein (sop) Dana Recording Project ▲ DRP 4
Largent, E.:Shorts, w. E. Largent (pno) Dana Recording Project ▲ DRP 4
Penn, W.:Essays Tuba Dana Recording Project ▲ DRP 4
Rollin, R.:The Raven & thr First Men, w. W. Slocum (hn), R. Rollin Dana Recording Project ▲ DRP 4
Smith, Glenn:Forowen, w. L. Turk (pic) Dana Recording Project ▲ DRP 4

INSTRUMENT.

Turk, L. (pic)
Smith, Glenn:Forowen, w. J. Turk (tuba) Dana Recording Project ▲ DRP 4

Turkovič, Milan (bn)—see also ORCHESTRAS & ENSEMBLES Lincoln Center Chamber Music Society members
Beethoven, L. van:Duos, WoO 27, w. Karl Leister (cl)—in B♭ *(rec Studio Baumgarten, Vienna, June 30–July 1, 1994)* Camerata ▲ 30CM 370 [DDD]
Brahms, J.:Son Bn, w. Karl Engel (pno) Camerata ▲ 32CM 66
Elgar, E.:Romance Bn, w. Ferenc Bognar (pno) *(rec Studio Baumgarten, Vienna, June 30–July 1, 1994)* Camerata ▲ 30CM 370 [DDD]
Françaix, J.:Divert Bn, w. M. Sieghart (cnd), Stuttgart CO Orfeo ▲ 223911 [DDD]
Gershwin, G.:Porgy & Bess (sels), w. M. Sieghart (cnd), Stuttgart CO [suite arr. for bassoon & orchestra] Orfeo ▲ 223911 [DDD]
Glinka, M.:Trio pathétique, w. Karl Leister (cl), Ferenc Bognar (pno) *(rec Studio Baumgarten, Vienna, June 30–July 1, 1994)* Camerata ▲ 30CM 370 [DDD]
Haydn, M.:Concertino Bn & Orch, w. M. Sieghart (cnd), Stuttgart CO Orfeo ▲ 223911 [DDD]
Hindemith, P.:Kleine Kammermusik, w. Wolfgang Schulz (fl), Hansjörg Schellenberger (ob), Karl Leister (cl), Günter Högner (hn) Sony Classical ▲ SK 64400
Hindemith, P.:Son Bn, w. Ferenc Bognár (pno) Sony Classical ▲ SK 64400
Ibert, J.:Carignane, w. Karl Engel (pno) Camerata ▲ 32CM 66
Mendelssohn, F.:Concert Pieces, w. Karl Leister (cl)—No. 2 *(rec Studio Baumgarten, Vienna, June 30–July 1, 1994)* Camerata ▲ 30CM 370 [DDD]
Mozart, W.A.:Con Bn, w. M. Sieghart (cnd), Stuttgart CO Orfeo ▲ 223911 [DDD]
Poulenc, F.:Son Cl Bn, w. Karl Leister (cl) Camerata ▲ 30CM 370
Saint-Saëns, C.:Son Bn, w. Karl Engel (pno) Camerata ▲ 32CM 66
Schumann, R.:Romances Ob, w. Karl Engel (pno) Camerata ▲ 32CM 66
Strauss, R.:Duet-Concertino, w. E. Brunner (cl), M. Graf (hp), L. Zagrosek (cnd), Bamberg SO Koch Schwann ▲ CD 311065 [DDD]
Villa-Lobos, H.:Ciranda das sete notas, w. M. Sieghart (cnd), Stuttgart CO Orfeo ▲ 223911 [DDD]
Vivaldi, A.:Cons Bn, w. Italian Solisti—RV.478 in C; RV.480 in c; RV.484 in e; RV.501 in B♭, "La Notte" Denon ▲ CO 77528 [DDD]

Turley, Barry (org)
Barry Turley, Organist Gothic ▲ GOT 49040 [DDD]
Franck, C.:Chorals Org, M.38–40 [Angerstein & Associates Org, Phillips Memorial Baptist Church, Cranston, RI] AFKA ▲ SK 511
Franck, C.:Chorals Org, M.38–40 [Angerstein & Associates Organ, Phillips Memorial Baptist Church, Cranston, RI] Afka ▲ SK 511
Vierne, L.:Sym 2 Org [Angerstein & Associates Organ, Phillips Memorial Baptist Church, Cranston, RI] AFKA ▲ SK 511
Vierne, L.:Sym 2 Org [Angerstein & Associates Org, Phillips Memorial Baptist Church, Cranston, RI] AFKA ▲ SK 511

Turnagoel, Ihsan (gtr)
Gragnani, F.:Qt for 2 Gtrs, w. S. Prunnbauer (gtr), D. Klöcker (cl), H. Ganz (va) *(rec Sept. 1984)* Koch Treasure ▲ 31612-2 [ADD]

Turnbell, Elizabeth (va)—see ORCHESTRAS & ENSEMBLES Pro Arte String Trio

Turner, A. (vc)
Rasmussen, S.:Music of, w. W. Gaffron (vn), E. Dalsgarð (fl), A. Klett (cl), P. Sólstein (hn), J. Andreasen (pno), S.Á. Johansen (cnd), *(orch unknown)*—"Warnings I"—The Naked Destruction Tutl ▲ FKT 4

Turner, Kerry (hn)—see ORCHESTRAS & ENSEMBLES American Horn Quartet

Turner, M. (vc/voc)
Song, J.:Improvs, w. J. Song (Kayagum & voc [right channel]), M. Turner (vc & voc [left channel])—Reclusive Prayer; Love & Fear; Dancing Dead; Colours; Harbor My Distant Whisper; Genealogy; Frontier Guard; Precious Few; Han River Elegy; Squirm und Drag; Stories O.O. Discs ▲ OO 10 [DDD]

Turnnard, V. (pno)
Vaughan Williams, R.:Songs, w. J. Shirley-Quirk (bar)—Linden Lea Saga Classics ▲ 3353 [ADD]

Turnovsky, S. (bn)
Mozart, W.A.:Con Bn, w. J. Wildner (cnd), Vienna Mozart Academy Naxos ▲ 8.550345 [DDD]

Turnquist, Melody (org)
Albright, W.:Jericho, w. K. Benjamin (tpt) Gothic ▲ G 49067 [DDD]
Eben, Petr:Windows, w. K. Benjamin (tpt) Gothic ▲ G 49067 [DDD]
Hamelin, P.:Sonata ben melodico, w. K. Benjamin (tpt) Gothic ▲ G 49067 [DDD]
Nelhybel, V.:Metamorphosis, w. K. Benjamin (tpt) Gothic ▲ G 49067 [DDD]
Starer, R.:Preludes Tpt, w. K. Benjamin (tpt) Gothic ▲ G 49067 [DDD]

Turovsky, Eleanora (vn)
Bach, Joh. Christian:Sinf concertante, T.284/4, w. Y. Turovsky (vc), Y. Turovsky (cnd), Montreal Musici Chandos ▲ CHAN 8470 [DDD]
Glière, R.:Pieces Vn, Op. 39, w. Y. Turovsky (vc) Chandos ▲ CHAN 8652 [DDD]
Honegger, A.:Sonatina Vns & Vc, w. Yuli Turovsky (vc) Chandos ▲ CHAN 8358 [DDD]
Kodály, Z.:Duo Vn & Vc, w. Y. Turovsky (vc) Chandos ▲ CHAN 8427 [DDD]
Martinů, B.:Duo Vn & Vc, w. Y. Turovsky (vc) Chandos ▲ CHAN 8358 [DDD]
Miaskovsky, N.:Son 2 Vc, w. L. Edlina (pno) Chandos ▲ CHAN 8523 [DDD]
Prokofiev, S.:Ov on Hebrew Themes, w. R. Golani (va), J. Campbell (cl), Borodin Trio [orig. chamber version] Chandos ▲ CHAN 8924 [DDD]
Prokofiev, S.:Son for 2 Vns, w. Y. Turovsky (vc) [violin & cello arr. by David Oistrakh] Chandos ▲ CHAN 8652 [DDD]
Ravel, M.:Son Vn Vc, w. Y. Turovsky (vc) Chandos ▲ CHAN 8358 [DDD]
Rivier, J.:Sonatine, w. Y. Turovsky (vc) Chandos ▲ CHAN 8358 [DDD]
Shostakovich, D.:Preludes Pno, Op. 34, w. P. Pettinger (pno) [arr. for violin & piano]— 19 preludes, omitting Nos. 4,7,9,14 & 23 Chandos ▲ CHAN 8555 [DDD]
Stravinsky, I.:Suite italienne Vc, w. Y. Turovsky (vc) [vn & vc arr. Katherine Rife] Chandos ▲ CHAN 8652 [DDD]
Tcherepnin, A.:Duo, w. Y. Turovsky (vc) Chandos ▲ CHAN 8652 [DDD]
Vivaldi, A.:Cons Ob Vn, w. T. Baskin (ob), Y. Turovsky (cnd), Montreal Musici—RV.548 Chandos ▲ CHAN 8651 [DDD]
Vivaldi, A.:Cons Vn Org, w. G. Soly (org), Y. Turovsky (cnd), Montreal Musici—RV.542 in F Chandos ▲ CHAN 8651 [DDD]
Vivaldi, A.:Con for 2 Vns Vc, R.565, w. E. Skerjanc (vn), A. Aubut (vc), Y. Turovsky (cnd), Montreal Musici—RV.542 in F Chandos ▲ CHAN 8651 [DDD]

Turovsky, Yuli (vc)—see also ORCHESTRAS & ENSEMBLES Borodin Trio
Arensky, A.:Trio 1 Pno, w. Edlina (pno), Dubinsky (vn) Chandos ▲ CHAN 8477 [DDD]
Bach, Joh. Christian:Con Vc, w. Y. Turovsky (cnd), Montreal Musici Chandos ▲ CHAN 8470 [DDD]
Bach, Joh. Christian:Sinf concertante, T.284/4, w. E. Turovsky (vn), Y. Turovsky (cnd), Montreal Musici Chandos ▲ CHAN 8470 [DDD]
Bach, J.S.:Suites Vc, BWV 1007–1012 *(rec Aug 1991)* Chandos 2–▲ CHAN 9034/35 [DDD]
Beethoven, L. van:Trio 7 Pno, w. L. Edlina (pno), J. Campbell (cl) Chandos ▲ CHAN 8655 [DDD]
Bloch, E.:From Jewish Life, w. Y. Turovsky (cnd), Montreal Musici—Prayer [trans. A. Antonini]; Suppliation & Jewish Song [trans. P. Purich for cello & orch.] Chandos ▲ CHAN 8800 [DDD]
Bloch, E.:Méditation hébraïque, w. Y. Turovsky (cnd), Montreal Musici [vc & orch. trans. Peter Purich] Chandos ▲ CHAN 8800 [DDD]
Bloch, E.:Nigun, w. Y. Turovsky (cnd), Montreal Musici [vc & orch. trans. Peter Purich] Chandos ▲ CHAN 8800 [DDD]
Boccherini, L.:Adagio & Allegro, Montreal Musici Chandos ▲ CHAN 8768 [DDD]
Boccherini, L.:Con Vc, G.482, w. Y. Turovsky (cnd), Montreal Musici Chandos ▲ CHAN 8470 [DDD]
Boccherini, L.:Con in D Vc, w. Y. Turovsky (cnd), Montreal Musici Chandos ▲ CHAN 8408 [DDD]
Brahms, J.:Trio Cl, w. J. Campbell (cl), L. Edlina (pno) Chandos ▲ CHAN 8606 [DDD]
Cassadó, G.:Con Vc, Montreal Musici Chandos ▲ CHAN 8768 [DDD]
Debussy, C.:Son Vc, w. L. Edlina (pno) Chandos ▲ CHAN 8458
Glazunov, A.:Chant du ménéstrel, w. P. Pettinger (pno) Chandos ▲ CHAN 8555 [DDD]

Turovsky, Yuli (vc) (cont.)
Glazunov, A.:Elégie Vc, w. P. Pettinger (pno) Chandos ▲ CHAN 8555 [DDD]
Glazunov, A.:Serenade espagnole, w. P. Pettinger (pno) Chandos ▲ CHAN 8555 [DDD]
Glière, R.:Pieces Vn, Op. 39, w. E. Turovsky (vn) Chandos ▲ CHAN 8652 [DDD]
Glinka, M.:Trio pathétique, w. R. Dubinsky (vn), L. Edlina (pno) Chandos ▲ CHAN 8477 [DDD]
Haydn, J.:Divert Vc & Str Orch, Montreal Musici Chandos ▲ CHAN 8768 [DDD]
Honegger, A.:Sonatina Vns & Vc, w. Elanora Turovsky (vn) Chandos ▲ CHAN 8358 [DDD]
Kodály, Z.:Duo Vn & Vc, w. E. Turovsky (vn) Chandos ▲ CHAN 8427 [DDD]
Kodály, Z.:Son Vc, Op. 8 Chandos ▲ CHAN 8427 [DDD]
Martinů, B.:Duo Vn & Vc, w. E. Turovsky (vn) Chandos ▲ CHAN 8358 [DDD]
Mozart, W.A.:Con Vc, Montreal Musici Chandos ▲ CHAN 8768 [DDD]
Prévost, A.:Improvisation II Vc Analekta ▲ UMM 103
Prévost, A.:Son 1 Vc, w. J. Vaillancourt (pno) Analekta ▲ UMM 103
Prévost, A.:Son 2 Vc, w. J. Vaillancourt (pno) Analekta ▲ UMM 103
Prokofiev, S.:Chout (suite), w. P. Pettinger (pno) [cello & piano arr.] Chandos ▲ CHAN 8555 [DDD]
Prokofiev, S.:Music of, w. P. Pettinger (pno)—Adagio from *Cinderella*; Dance from *Romeo & Juliet*; Waltz from *(Tale of the Stone Flower* Chandos ▲ CHAN 8555 [DDD]
Prokofiev, S.:Son Vc, w. L. Edlina (pno) Chandos ▲ CHAN 8340 [DDD]
Prokofiev, S.:Son for 2 Vns, w. E. Turovsky (vn) [violin & cello arr. by David Oistrakh] Chandos ▲ CHAN 8652 [DDD]
Rachmaninoff, S.:Son Vc, w. L. Edlina (pno) Chandos ▲ CHAN 8523 [DDD]
Ravel, M.:Son Vn Vc, w. E. Turovsky (vn) Chandos ▲ CHAN 8358 [DDD]
Rivier, J.:Sonatine, w. E. Turovsky (vn) Chandos ▲ CHAN 8358 [DDD]
Shostakovich, D.:Son Vc, w. L. Edlina (pno) Chandos ▲ CHAN 8340 [DDD]
Stravinsky, I.:Suite italienne Vc, w. E. Turovsky (vn) [vn & vc arr. Katherine Rife] Chandos ▲ CHAN 8652 [DDD]
Tartini, G.:Con in D Vc, Montreal Musici Chandos ▲ CHAN 8768 [DDD]
Tcherepnin, A.:Duo, w. E. Turovsky (vn) Chandos ▲ CHAN 8652 [DDD]
Vivaldi, A.:Cons Vc, w. Y. Turovsky (cnd), Montreal Musici—RV.413, 424 Chandos ▲ CHAN 8408 [DDD]
Vivaldi, A.:Con for 2 Vcs, w. A. Aubut (vc), Y. Turovsky (cnd), Montreal Musici Chandos ▲ CHAN 8408 [DDD]

Turrini, Liliana Medici (org)
Italian Organ Music *(rec 1992)* Bongiovanni ▲ GB 5034-2 [DDD]

Turriziani, Angelo (org)
L'Organo Veneziano Pierre Verany ▲ 785095 [DDD]
Zipoli, D.:Son d'intavolatura Org L'Empreinte Digitale ▲ ED 13001

Tusa, Antonio (vc)
Brahms, J.:Qnt Pno, w. Clara Haskil (pno), Peter Rybar (vn), Clemens Dahinden (vn), Heinz Wigand (va) Doron 2–▲ DRC 4007/8 [ADD]
Brahms, J.:Sextet Strs, Op. 36, w. Peter Rybar (vn), Clemens Dahinden (vn), Heinz Wigand (va), Oskar Kromer (va), Carl-Heinz Jucker (vc) Doron 2–▲ DRC 4007/8 [ADD]

Tusa, Eszsébet (pno)
Bartók, B.:Contrasts, w. B. Kovács (cl), M. Szücs (vn) *(rec 1965)* Hungaroton ▲ HCD 31554 [ADD]
Bartók, B.:Little Pieces *(rec 1967)* Hungaroton ▲ HCD 31554 [ADD]
Bartók, B.:Out of Doors *(rec 1967)* Hungaroton ▲ HCD 31554 [ADD]
Bartók, B.:Out of Doors Hungaroton ▲ HCD 31051
Bartók, B.:Son Pno *(rec 1968)* Hungaroton ▲ HCD 31554 [ADD]
Bartók, B.:Son Pno Hungaroton ▲ HCD 31051
Bartók, B.:Suite Pno *(rec 1966)* Hungaroton ▲ HCD 31554 [ADD]

Tuttle, Karen (va)
Mozart, W.A.:Qt Ob, K.370, w. M. Tabuteau (ob), A. Pernel (vn), P. Tortelier (vc) *(rec live June 1953)* Music & Arts 4–▲ CD 689 (m) [AAD]

Tuuk, Jonathan (org)
Works for Cathedral Spaces, w. Grand Rapids Chamber Choir [cnd:Larry G. Biser] Pro Organo ▲ POCD 7015

Tverskaya, Olga (pno)
Brahms, J.:Son 1 Vc, w. Peter Bruns (vc) Opus 111 ▲ OPS 30-144
Brahms, J.:Son 2 Vc, w. Peter Bruns (vc) Opus 111 ▲ OPS 30-144
Haydn, J.:Songs, w. Mhairi Lawson (sop), Oleg Kogan (vc), Rachel Podger (vn) Opus 111 ▲ OPS 30-121
Schubert, Franz:Moments musicaux Opus 111 ▲ OPS 30-139
Schubert, Franz:Son Pno, D.959 Opus 111 ▲ OPS 30-139
Schubert, Franz:Son Vn, D.574, w. Fabio Biondi (vn) Opus 111 ▲ OPS 30-126
Schubert, Franz:Sonatinas Vn, w. Fabio Biondi (vn) Opus 111 ▲ OPS 30-126

Tvrdík, Ivan (vc)
Respighi, O.:Toccata Pno, w. Konstantin Scherbakov (pno), H. Griffiths (cnd), Slovak RSO Bratislava *(rec Concert Hall of the Slovak Radio, Bratislava, Sept. 19–22, 1994)* Naxos ▲ 8.553207 [DDD]

Tvrzský, Jaroslav (org)
Dvořák, A.:Ave maris stella, w. Eva Randová (mez) *(rec Dvořák Hall of Rudolfinum Prague, Sept. 4–6, 1989)* Panton ▲ PAN 811241 [DDD]
Dvořák, A.:Hymnus ad laudes in festo Sanctae Trinitatis, w. Eva Randová (mez) *(rec Dvořák Hall of Rudolfinum Prague, Sept. 4–6, 1989)* Panton ▲ PAN 811241 [DDD]

Tyler, Guy (db)
Gisberg:Music of, w. Gisburg (sgr/fl), Jeff O'Malley (nar), Midori Seiler (vn), Ron Lawrence (va), Anthony Coleman (pno), Christine Bard (perc)—Low-End; Since You Have Left; The Woman Is Perfected; Sharks; Night & Wind; Saturnspacemonsters Walking on a Sandy Surface; Old Moon in Winter; Never Saw the Stars So Bright; Habe Die Liebe Verschlafen; W.A.L.S.H. Tzadik ▲ TZA CD 7019 [DDD]

Tyler, James (lt/baroque gtr/mand)
The Early Guitar, w. Paul Elliott (ten), Monica Huggett (baroque vn), Jane Ryan (b vl/baroque vc), Robert Spencer (thb/baroque gtr) Saga Classics ▲ 3356 [ADD]
Music for Merchants & Monarchs Saga Classics ▲ 3365 [ADD]
Music of the Renaissance Virtuosi, w. Nigel North (lt/ thb/cittern), Douglas Wootton (lt/bandora), Jane Ryan (b vl) Saga Classics ▲ 3350 [ADD]
Music of the Renaissance Virtuosi Elektra/Nonesuch ■ N5-71389

Tyler, James (mand)
Vivaldi, A.:Con for 2 Mands, w. R. Jeffrey (mand), T. Pinnock (cnd), English CO Archiv ▲ 415674-2 [DDD]
Vivaldi, A.:Con for 2 Mands, w. Wootton (mand), N. Marriner (cnd), Academy of St. Martin in the Fields Philips ▲ 412892-2 [DDD]

Tylšar, Bedřich (hn)
Barsanti, F.:Con grosso, w. Z. Tylšar (hn), L. Pešek (cnd), Dvořák CO Supraphon ▲ 103907-2 [DDD]
Beethoven, L. van:Qnt Ob, 3 Hns & Bn, w. J. Mihule (ob), Z. Tylšar (hn), R. Beránek (hn), F. Herman (bn) Supraphon ▲ 11 1445-2 [DDD]
Beethoven, L. van:Sxt Hns, Op. 81b, w. Z. Tylšar (hn), L. Pešek (cnd), Dvořák CO Supraphon ▲ 103907-2 [DDD]
Beethoven, L. van:Sxt Winds, Op. 71, w. V. Kyzivát (cl), Z. Tesař (cl), Z. Tylšar (hn), F. Herman (bn), V. Horák (bn) Supraphon ▲ 11 1445-2 [DDD]
Fiala, J.:Con for 2 Hns, w. Z. Tylšar (hn), F. Vajnar (cnd), Capella Istropolitana Naxos ▲ 8.550459 [DDD]
Handel, G.F.:Con for 2 Vns & 2 Hns, w. P. Mareš (vn), J. Opsitos (vn), Z. Tylšar (F hn), L. Pešek (cnd), Dvořák CO Supraphon ▲ 103907-2 [DDD]
Mozart, W.A.:Divert Hns Strs, K.247, w. Z. Tylšar (hn), Stamic String Quartet Supraphon ▲ 111523-2 [DDD]
Mozart, W.A.:Divert Hns Strs, K.287, w. Z. Tylšar (hn), Stamic String Quartet Supraphon ▲ 111524-2 [DDD]
Mozart, W.A.:Divert Hns Strs, K.334, w. Z. Tylšar (hn), Stamic String Quartet Supraphon ▲ 11 1525-2 [DDD]

Tylšar, Bedřich (hn) (cont.)
Mozart, W.A.:Musikalischer Spass, w. Z. Tylšar (hn), L. Pešek (cnd), Dvořák CO Supraphon ▲ 103907-2 [DDD]
Pokorny, F.X.:Con Hns, w. Z. Tylšar (hn), F. Vajnar (cnd), Capella Istropolitana Naxos ▲ 8.550459 [DDD]
Reicha, A.:Trios Hns, Op. 93, w. Z. Tylšar (hn), F. Herman (bn) [arr Fr hns & bn] Supraphon ▲ 11 1445-2 [DDD]
Reicha, A.:Trios Hns, Op. 82, w. Z. Tylšar (hn), Z. Divoký (hn) Supraphon ▲ 11 1446-2 [DDD]
Rosetti, F.A.:Con for 2 Hns, w. Z. Tylšar (hn), F. Vajnar (cnd), Capella Istropolitana—Concerti in A♭ & E♭ Naxos ▲ 8.550459 [DDD]
Telemann, G.P.:Cons (misc), w. L. Kyselak (va), Z. Tylšar (hn), A. Hoelbling (vn) O. Hoelbling (vn), A. Jablokov (vn), R. Edlinger (cnd), Capella Istropolitana—Viola Con. in G; Concerto in F for 3 Violins; Concerto for 2 Horns Naxos ▲ 8.550156 [DDD] ∆ 7.550156 [DDD]

Tylšar, Zdenek (hn)
Barsanti, F.:Con grosso, w. B. Tylšar (hn), L. Pešek (cnd), Dvořák CO Supraphon ▲ 103907-2 [DDD]
Beethoven, L. van:Qnt Ob, 3 Hns & Bn, w. J. Mihule (ob), B. Tylšar (hn), R. Beránek (hn), F. Herman (bn) Supraphon ▲ 11 1445-2 [DDD]
Beethoven, L. van:Sxt Hns, Op. 81b, w. B. Tylšar (hn), L. Pešek (cnd), Dvořák CO Supraphon ▲ 103907-2 [DDD]
Beethoven, L. van:Sxt Winds, Op. 71, w. V. Kyzivát (cl), Z. Tesař (cl), B. Tylšar (hn), F. Herman (bn), V. Horák (bn) Supraphon ▲ 11 1445-2 [DDD]
Fiala, J.:Con for 2 Hns, w. B. Tylšar (hn), F. Vajnar (cnd), Capella Istropolitana Naxos ▲ 8.550459 [DDD]
Handel, G.F.:Con for 2 Vns & 2 Hns, w. P. Mareš (vn), J. Opsitos (vn), B. Tylšar (F hn), L. Pešek (cnd), Dvořák CO Supraphon ▲ 103907-2 [DDD]
Mahler, G.:Sym 5, w. Miroslav Kejmar (tpt), V. Neumann (cnd), Czech PO *(rec House of Artists, Prague, Mar 1993)* Canyon Classics ▲ 3616
Mozart, W.A.:Cons Hn, w. O. Vlček (cnd), Prague CO *(rec live Sept. 1982)* Supraphon ▲ 103619-2 [DDD]
Mozart, W.A.:Divert Hns Strs, K.247, w. B. Tylšar (hn), Stamic String Quartet Supraphon ▲ 111523-2 [DDD]
Mozart, W.A.:Divert Hns Strs, K.287, w. B. Tylšar (hn), Stamic String Quartet Supraphon ▲ 111524-2 [DDD]
Mozart, W.A.:Divert Hns Strs, K.334, w. B. Tylšar (hn), Stamic String Quartet Supraphon ▲ 11 1525-2 [DDD]
Mozart, W.A.:Musikalischer Spass, w. B. Tylšar (hn), L. Pešek (cnd), Dvořák CO Supraphon ▲ 103907-2 [DDD]
Pokorny, F.X.:Con Hns, w. B. Tylšar (hn), F. Vajnar (cnd), Capella Istropolitana Naxos ▲ 8.550459 [DDD]
Reicha, A.:Trios Hns, Op. 93, w. B. Tylšar (hn), F. Herman (bn) [arr Fr hns & bn] Supraphon ▲ 11 1445-2 [DDD]
Reicha, A.:Trios Hns, Op. 82, w. B. Tylšar (hn), Z. Divoký (hn) Supraphon ▲ 11 1446-2 [DDD]
Rosetti, F.A.:Con for 2 Hns, w. B. Tylšar (hn), F. Vajnar (cnd), Capella Istropolitana—Concerti in A♭ & E♭ Naxos ▲ 8.550459 [DDD]
Stamitz, C.:Con Hn in E♭, w. F. Vajnar (cnd), Prague CO Supraphon ▲ 11 1424-2 [DDD]
Telemann, G.P.:Cons (misc), w. L. Kyselak (va), B. Tylšar (hn), A. Hoelbling (vn) O. Hoelbling (vn), A. Jablokov (vn), R. Edlinger (cnd), Capella Istropolitana—Viola Con. in G; Concerto in F for 3 Violins; Concerto for 2 Horns Naxos ▲ 8.550156 [DDD] ∆ 7.550156 [DDD]

Tynkkynen, Marjut (acc)
Suilamo, H.:BIAS, w. Lea Pekkala (vc) Finlandia ▲ FIN 12179 [DDD]

Tyranny, "Blue" Gene (clavinet)
Ashley, R.:Yellow Man with Heart with Wings, w. R. Ashley (English voc/all instrs except clavinet), G. Grenier (Spanish voc) Lovely Music ▲ LCD 1003 [ADD]

Tyranny, "Blue" Gene (kbd)
Tyranny, G.:Free Delivery—The Intermediary with a Rendition of Stardust (1983); Sunrise or Sunset in Texas (1983); The Country Boy Country Dog Intro (1984); The Intermediary Following Traces of the Song (1988); Five Takes on the Nocturne With and Without Memory (1989) Lovely Music ▲ LCD 1064 [ADD]

Tyranny, "Blue" Gene (pno/polymoog/other instrs)
Ashley, R.:Private Parts (The Record), w. Robert Ashley (voc) Lovely Music ▲ LCD 1001 [ADD]

Tyree, Ronald (bn)
A Double Reed Consort, w. Wizards!, Iowa Double Reed Consort *(rec Clapp Recital Hall, Univ. of Iowa, Iowa City, Jan. 1993 & May 1994)* CRS Master ▲ CRS 9460

Tyron, V. (pno)
Addinsell, R.:Warsaw Con, w. B. Brott (cnd), Toronto Festival Pops Orch Pro Arte ▲ CDD 422 [DDD]
Glick, S.I.:Son Ob, w. S. Trubashnik (ob) CBC ("Musica Viva" series) ▲ MVCD 1046 [DDD]
Glick, S.I.:Suite Hébraïque 1, w. J. Campbell (cl) CBC ("Musica Viva" series) ▲ MVCD 1046 [DDD]
Hooray for Hollywood, w. B. Brott (cnd), Toronto Festival Pops Orch Pro Arte ▲ CDD 422 [DDD]

Tyson, John (rcr)
Boismortier, J.B. de:Con Rec & Strs, w. *(ensemble unknown)* Titanic ▲ Ti 169 [DDD]
Cooke, A.:Con Rcr Titanic ▲ Ti 169 [DDD]
Hovhaness, A.:Sextet Rcr, w. J. Starkman (vn), K. Shaw (vn), J. Cosart (va), A. Robbins (vc), F. Conover Fitch (hpd) Titanic ▲ Ti 169 [DDD]
Lovenstein, J.:Fant Rcr, w. *(ensemble unknown)* Titanic ▲ Ti 169 [DDD]
Something for Recorder & Strings, w. Frances Conover Fitch (hpd), Jane Starkman (vn), Katheryn Shaw (vn), Jann Cosart (va), Alice Robbins (vc), Tom Coleman (db) Titanic ▲ Ti 169 [DDD]
Vivaldi, A.:Cons Rcr, *(orch unknown)*—Concerto in c Titanic ▲ Ti 169 [DDD]

Tyson, John (rcr/pipe/tabor)—see ORCHESTRAS & ENSEMBLES Renaissonics

Tzinman, Mikhail (vn)
Hindemith, P.:Qt Cl, Vn, Vc & Pno, w. Oleg Tantzov (cl), Natalya Savinova (vc), Victor Yampolsky (pno) *(rec Mosfilm Studio, Dec 1994)* Triton ▲ 17005 [DDD]

Ubukata, Bruce (pno)
Brahms, J.:Liebeslieder Waltzes SATB, w. Kathleen Brett (sop), Catherine Robbin (mez), Benjamin Butterfield (ten), Russell Braun (bar), Stephen Ralls (pno) *(rec Glenn Gould Studio, CBC Toronto, Dec. 7-9, 1993)* CBC ("Musica Viva" series) ▲ MVCD 1077 [DDD]
Greer, J.:All Around the Circle, w. Kathleen Brett (sop), Catherine Robbin (mez), Benjamin Butterfield (ten), Russell Braun (bar), Stephen Ralls (pno) CBC ▲ MVV 1077 [DDD]
Greer, J.:All Around the Circle, w. Kathleen Brett (sop), Catherine Robbin (mez), Benjamin Butterfield (ten), Russell Braun (bar), Stephen Ralls (pno) *(rec Glenn Gould Studio, CBC Toronto, Dec. 7-9, 1993)* CBC ("Musica Viva" series) ▲ MVCD 1077 [DDD]
Schumann, R.:Spanische Liebeslieder, w. Kathleen Brett (sop), Catherine Robbin (mez), Benjamin Butterfield (ten), Russell Braun (bar), Stephen Ralls (pno) CBC ("Musica Viva" series) ▲ MVCD 1077 [DDD]
Somers, H.:Songs from the Newfoundland Outports, w. Elmer Iseler (cnd), Elmer Iseler Singers *(rec Flora McRae Eaton Memorial Auditorium & St. Anne's Anglican Church, Toronto)* Centrediscs ▲ CMC 5495 [DDD]

Uchida, Mitsuko (pno)
Beethoven, L. van:Con 3 Pno, w. K. Sanderling (cnd), Royal Concertgebouw Orch Philips ▲ 446082-2
Beethoven, L. van:Con 4 Pno, w. K. Sanderling (cnd), Royal Concertgebouw Orch [live recording] Philips ▲ 446082-2
Chopin, F.:Son Pno, Op. 35 Philips ▲ 420949-2 [DDD]
Chopin, F.:Son Pno, Op. 58 Philips ▲ 420949-2 [DDD]
Debussy, C.:Etudes Philips ▲ 422412-2 [DDD] ▫ 422412-5
Mozart, W.A.:Adagio Pno, K.540 Philips ▲ 412616-2 [DDD]
Mozart, W.A.:Allegro & Andante & Rondo Philips ▲ 412122-2 [DDD]
Mozart, W.A.:Complete Mozart Edition, w. Ingrid Haebler (pno), Ton Koopman (hpd) Philips 5-▲ 422518-2 [ADD]
Mozart, W.A.:Complete Mozart Edition Philips 5-▲ 422517-2 [ADD]
Mozart, W.A.:Cons Pno, w. J. Tate (cnd), English CO Philips 9-▲ 438207-2

Uchida, Mitsuko (pno) (cont.)
Mozart, W.A.:Con 5 Pno, w. J. Tate (cnd), English CO Philips ▲ 432082-2 [DDD]
Mozart, W.A.:Con 6 Pno, w. J. Tate (cnd), English CO Philips ▲ 432082-2 [DDD]
Mozart, W.A.:Con 8 Pno, w. J. Tate (cnd), English CO Philips ▲ 432086-2 [DDD]
Mozart, W.A.:Con 9 Pno, w. J. Tate (cnd), English CO Philips ▲ 432086-2 [DDD]
Mozart, W.A.:Con 11 Pno, w. J. Tate (cnd), English CO Philips ("Digital Classics" series) ▲ 422458-2 [DDD]
Mozart, W.A.:Con 12 Pno, w. J. Tate (cnd), English CO Philips ("Digital Classics" series) ▲ 422458-2 [DDD]
Mozart, W.A.:Con 13 Pno, w. J. Tate (cnd), English CO Philips ▲ 422359-2 [DDD]
Mozart, W.A.:Con 14 Pno, w. J. Tate (cnd), English CO Philips ▲ 422359-2 [DDD]
Mozart, W.A.:Con 15 Pno, w. J. Tate (cnd), English CO Philips ▲ 426305-2 [DDD]
Mozart, W.A.:Con 16 Pno, w. J. Tate (cnd), English CO Philips ▲ 426305-2 [DDD]
Mozart, W.A.:Con 17 Pno, w. J. Tate (cnd), English CO Philips ▲ 422592-2 [DDD]
Mozart, W.A.:Con 18 Pno, w. J. Tate (cnd), English CO Philips ▲ 422348-2 [DDD]
Mozart, W.A.:Con 19 Pno, w. J. Tate (cnd), English CO Philips ▲ 422348-2 [DDD]
Mozart, W.A.:Con 20 Pno, w. J. Tate (cnd), English CO Philips ▲ 416381-2 [DDD] ▫ 416381-5
Mozart, W.A.:Con 20 Pno, w. J. Tate (cnd), English CO Philips ("Insignia" series) ▲ 434164-2 [DDD]
Mozart, W.A.:Con 21 Pno, w. J. Tate (cnd), English CO Philips ▲ 416381-2 [DDD] ▫ 416381-5
Mozart, W.A.:Con 22 Pno, w. J. Tate (cnd), English CO Philips ▲ 420187-2 [DDD]
Mozart, W.A.:Con 23 Pno, w. J. Tate (cnd), English CO Philips ▲ 420187-2 [DDD]
Mozart, W.A.:Con 23 Pno, w. J. Tate (cnd), English CO Philips ("Insignia" series) ▲ 434164-2 [DDD]
Mozart, W.A.:Con 24 Pno, w. J. Tate (cnd), English CO Philips ▲ 422331-2 [DDD]
Mozart, W.A.:Con 25 Pno, w. J. Tate (cnd), English CO Philips ▲ 422331-2 [DDD]
Mozart, W.A.:Con 26 Pno, w. J. Tate (cnd), English CO Philips ("Digital Classics" series) ▲ 420951-2 [DDD]
Mozart, W.A.:Con 27 Pno, w. J. Tate (cnd), English CO Philips ("Digital Classics" series) ▲ 420951-2 [DDD]
Mozart, W.A.:Fant Pno, K.397 Philips ▲ 412123-2 [DDD]
Mozart, W.A.:Fant Pno, K.475 Philips ▲ 412617-2 [DDD]
Mozart, W.A.:Gigue Pno, K.574 Philips ▲ 412616-2 [DDD]
Mozart, W.A.:Pno Music (misc)—Fant. in c, K.475; Sons. K.457, 533/494, 545, 576; Rondo K.411, Fant., K.397; 10 Vars. K.455; Adagio K.540 Philips 2-▲ 432989-2 [DDD]
Mozart, W.A.:Qnt Pno, K.452, w. J. Tate (cnd), English CO Wind Ensemble Philips ▲ 422592-2 [DDD]
Mozart, W.A.:Rondo Pno, K.485 Philips ▲ 420185-2 [DDD]
Mozart, W.A.:Rondo Pno, K.511 Philips ▲ 412122-2 [DDD]
Mozart, W.A.:Rondo Pno Orch, K.382, w. J. Tate (cnd), English CO Philips ▲ 432082-2 [DDD]
Mozart, W.A.:Son 1 Pno Philips ▲ 412617-2 [DDD]
Mozart, W.A.:Son 2 Pno Philips ("Digital Classics" series) ▲ 420186-2 [DDD]
Mozart, W.A.:Son 3 Pno Philips ("Digital Classics" series) ▲ 420186-2 [DDD]
Mozart, W.A.:Son 4 Pno Philips ("Digital Classics" series) ▲ 420186-2 [DDD]
Mozart, W.A.:Son 5 Pno Philips ("Digital Classics" series) ▲ 420186-2 [DDD]
Mozart, W.A.:Son 6 Pno Philips ▲ 420185-2 [DDD]
Mozart, W.A.:Son 7 Pno Philips ▲ 412741-2 [DDD]
Mozart, W.A.:Son 8 Pno Philips ▲ 412741-2 [DDD]
Mozart, W.A.:Son 9 Pno Philips ▲ 412741-2 [DDD]
Mozart, W.A.:Son 10 Pno Philips ▲ 412616-2 [DDD]
Mozart, W.A.:Son 11 Pno Philips ▲ 412123-2 [DDD]
Mozart, W.A.:Son 12 Pno Philips ▲ 412123-2 [DDD]
Mozart, W.A.:Son 13 Pno Philips ▲ 412616-2 [DDD]
Mozart, W.A.:Son 14 Pno Philips ▲ 412617-2 [DDD]
Mozart, W.A.:Son 15 Pno Philips ▲ 412122-2 [DDD]
Mozart, W.A.:Son 16 Pno Philips ▲ 420185-2 [DDD]
Mozart, W.A.:Son 17 Pno Philips ▲ 412617-2 [DDD]
Schumann, R.:Carnaval Pno Philips ▲ 442777-2
Schumann, R.:Kreisleriana Philips ▲ 442777-2

Uchida, Reiko (pno)
Rorem, N.:Studies for 11, w. E. Ostling (fl), K. Lord (ob), G. Raden (cl), J. Sutte (tpt), S. Copes (vn), C.-J. Chang (va), J. Lastrapes (vc), K. Englichova (hp), A. LaFargue (perc), R. Laveille (perc), R. Milanov (cnd) New World ▲ 80445-2

Udagawa, Hideko (vn)
Brahms, J.:Con Vn, w. C. Mackerras (cnd), London SO Chandos ▲ CHAN 8974 [DDD]
Bruch, M.:Con 1 Vn, w. C. Mackerras (cnd), London SO Chandos ▲ CHAN 8974 [DDD]
Chausson, E.:Poème Vn, w. K. Klein (cnd), London PO IMP ("Classics" series) ▲ IMP 6700312
Glazunov, A.:Con Vn, w. K. Klein (cnd), London PO IMP ("Classics" series) ▲ IMP 6700312
The Heart of the Violin Concerto, w. Ernst Kovacic (vn), Jaime Laredo (vn), Anne Akiko Meyers (vn), Elmar Oliveira (vn) Pickwick ("The Orchid" series) ▲ PICORCD 11013
Saint-Saëns, C.:Etudes Pno, Op. 52, w. K. Klein (cnd), London PO—Caprice en forme de valse [trans Ysaye] IMP ("Classics" series) ▲ IMP 6700312
Sarasate, P. de:Spanish Dances, w. K. Klein (cnd), London PO—Romanze andaluza, Op. 22/1 IMP ("Classics" series) ▲ IMP 6700312
Tchaikovsky, P.:Souvenir d'un lieu cher, w. K. Klein (cnd), London PO IMP ("Classics" series) ▲ IMP 6700312

Udow, Michael (perc)
Cahn, W.:...Won't You Join the Dance, w. James VanDenmark (db) Nexus ▲ 10339 [DDD]

Ueda, J. (biwa)
Shinohara, M.:Cooperation, w. A. Nishigata (shamisen), K. Mitsuhashi (shakuhachi), M. Akao (fue), S. Yaotani (hichiriki), K. Ishikawa (sho), C. Fukunaga (koto), M. Yoshizawa (kokyu), I. Tsuji (oboe), T. Takahashi (cl), G. Kitamura (tpt), A. Murata (trbn), S. Eiso (perc), S. Ueki (vn), S. Katsuta (vc), Y. Shibuya (pno), K. Komatsu (cnd) *(rec live Casals Hall, Tokyo, Mar. 5, 1994)* Camerata ▲ 30CM 375 [DDD]

Ueda, J. (satsuma-biwa/voc)
Offermans, W.:How to Survive in Paradise II, w. W. Offermans (fl/b fl) Gallo ▲ CD 732 [DDD]
Offermans, W.:Voice & Noise, w. W. Offermans (fl/b fl) Gallo ▲ CD 732 [DDD]

Ueki, Saburo (vn)
Shinohara, M.:Cooperation, w. A. Nishigata (shamisen), K. Mitsuhashi (shakuhachi), M. Akao (fue), S. Yaotani (hichiriki), K. Ishikawa (sho), C. Fukunaga (koto), J. Ueda (biwa), M. Yoshizawa (kokyu), I. Tsuji (oboe), T. Takahashi (cl), G. Kitamura (tpt), A. Murata (trbn), S. Eiso (perc), S. Katsuta (vc), Y. Shibuya (pno), K. Komatsu (cnd) *(rec live Casals Hall, Tokyo, Mar. 5, 1994)* Camerata ▲ 30CM 375 [DDD]
Shinohara, M.:Tabiyuki, w. A. Ogawa (mez), M. Kakagawa (fl), I. Tsuji (ob), T. Takahashi (cl), K. Okazaki (fagotto), G. Kitamura (tpt), A. Murata (trbn), S. Eiso (perc), A. Nakakoji (va), S. Katsuta (vc), M. Komuro (contrabass), K. Komatsu (cnd) *(rec live Casals Hall, Tokyo, Mar. 5, 1994)* Camerata ▲ 30CM 375 [DDD]
Takemitsu, T.:Music of, w. Tashi, Y. Nagano (mez), H. Ibe (gtr), M. Nagasako (hp), K. Abe (vib), Y. Takahashi (pno), R. Noguchi (fl), M. Hamada (lt), T. Koizumi (picc), Y. Hattori (vc), R. Stoltzman (cl), P. Serkin (pno), Ozawa, Wakasugi (cnd), Boston SO—Quatrain; Stanza I; Sacrifice; Ring; Valeria; A Flock Descends into the Pentagonal Garden Deutsche Grammophon ("20th Century Classics" series) ▲ 423253-2 [ADD]

Uemura, Kaori (vl)—see also ORCHESTRAS & ENSEMBLES Orlando Gibbons Viol Ensemble, Ricercar Consort
Biber, H. von:Mystery (or Rosary) Sons, w. Ryo Terakado (baroque vn), Siebe Henstra (hpd/org)—Passacaglia; Son. 6 *(rec Oud-Katholieke Kerk, The Hague, Netherlands, Aug. 11-12, 15-17, 1994)* Denon ▲ CO 78946 [DDD]
Biber, H. von:Sons Vn & Continuo, w. Ryo Terakado (vn), Siebe Henstra (hpd/org)—V in e [from 8 vn sons.]; VI in c; VIII in a *(rec Oud-Katholieke Kerk, the Hague, Netherlands, Aug. 11-12, 15-17, 1994)* Denon ▲ CO 78946 [DDD]
Biber, H. von:Son violino solo representativa, w. Ryo Terakado (baroque vn), Siebe Henstra (hpd/org) *(rec Oud-Katholieke Kerk, the Hague, Netherlands, Aug. 11-12, 15-17, 1994)* Denon ▲ CO 78946 [DDD]

Uemura, Kaori (vl) (cont.)
Handel, G.F.:Sons Vn, w. Ryo Terakado (baroque vn), H. Suzuki (baroque vc), Christophe Rousset (hpd)—in d, HWV 359a; in A, HWV 361; in G, HWV 364a; in D, HWV 371; Violin movt in a, HWV 408; Violin movt (Allegro) in c, HWV 412 Denon/PCM Digital ▲ DEN 75858 [DDD]
Leclair, J.-M.:Sons Vn (Books 1–4), w. R. Terakado (baroque vn), H. Suzuki (vc), C. Rousset (hpd)—"Troisieme livre" (Book 3), Op. 5 *(rec Feb. 26–Mar. 9, 1993)* Denon/PCM Digital ▲ DEN 75720 [DDD]
Marais, M.:Pièces de viole [Book 5], w. W. Kuijken (vl), R. Kohnen (hpd)—Suite in g; Chaconne in G; Dialogue; Le Jeu du Volant; Le Tableau de l'Operation de la Taille; Suite in a; La Poitevine Accent ▲ 78744 [DDD]
Rameau, J.P.:Pièces de clavecin en concert, w. Christophe Rousset (hpd), Ryo Terakado (vn) Harmonia Mundi ▲ HMX 2901418
Telemann, G.P.:Qts, Book 4, w. Masahiro Arita (trns fl), Ryo Terakado (baroque vn), Cristophe Rousset (hpd) Denon ▲ DEN 78844 [DDD]

Uesugi, Kodo (fukimono)
Fujieda, M.:Music of, w. Mamoru Fujueda (cmpt), Makiko Sakurai (shomyo/Buddhist chant), Mineko Grimmer (audible sculptures), Kazuko Takada (hikimono), Toshiyuki Matsukura (uchimono), Satoshi Sakai (uchimono), Koshin Ebihara (jumon)—The Night Chant III; Wind Chant; Cocoon Chant; Duct Chant; Falling Chant; The Night Chant I Tzadik ("The Composers" series) ▲ TZA 7003 [DDD]

Ughi, Uto (vn)
Bach, J.S.:Sons & Partitas Vn, BWV 1001–1006 RCA Red Seal 2-▲ 09026-60971-2
Basic 100, Vol. 76, w. Santa Cecilia CO [cnd:Leonard Friedman] RCA Victor ▲ 09026-68453-2 ■ 09026-68453-4
Beethoven, L. van:Con Vn, Op. 61, w. W. Sawallisch (cnd), London SO RCA Gold Seal ("Papillon Collection" series) ▲ 6536-2-RG [ADD/DDD]
Brahms, J.:Con Vn, w. W. Sawallisch (cnd), Philharmonia Orch RCA Silver Seal ▲ 60479-2-RV [DDD] ■ 60479-4-RV (CrO2)
Bruch, M.:Con 1 Vn, w. W. Sawallisch (cnd), Philharmonia Orch RCA Silver Seal ▲ 60479-2-RV [DDD] ■ 60479-4-RV (CrO2)
Dvořák, A.:Con Vn, w. L. Slatkin (cnd), Philharmonia Orch RCA Red Seal ▲ 60431-2-RC [DDD]
Dvořák, A.:Romance Vn, w. L. Slatkin (cnd), Philharmonia Orch RCA Red Seal ▲ 60431-2-RC [DDD]
Dvořák, A.:Romantic Pieces, Op. 75 [not clear from release copy if this is performed with piano or orchestra] RCA Red Seal ▲ 60431-2-RC [DDD]
Mendelssohn, F.:Con in e Vn & Orch, Op. 64, w. G. Prêtre (cnd), London SO RCA gold Seal ("Papillon Collection" series) ▲ 6536-2-RG [ADD/DDD]
Paganini, N.:Con 1 Vn, w. L. Friedman (cnd), St. Cecilia CO RCA ("Basic 100" series) ▲ 09026-68453-2 ■ 09026-68453-4
Paganini, N.:Con 2 Vn, w. L. Friedman (cnd), St. Cecilia CO RCA ("Basic 100" series) ▲ 09026-68453-2 ■ 09026-68453-4
Paganini, N.:Con 2 Vn, w. U. Ughi (cnd), St. Cecilia CO RCA Red Seal ▲ 7844-2 RC [DDD]
Paganini, N.:Con 4 Vn, w. U. Ughi (cnd), St. Cecilia CO RCA Red Seal ▲ 7844-2 RC [DDD]

Ugorski, Anatol (pno)
Mussorgsky, M.:Pictures at an Exhibition Deutsche Grammophon ▲ 435616-2 [DDD]
Stravinsky, I.:Scenes Pno Deutsche Grammophon ▲ 435616-2 [DDD]

Uhl, Oswald (vc)
Strauss, R.:Don Quixote, w. R. Strauss (cnd), Bavarian State Orch *(rec 1940–41)* Preiser 2-▲ PRE 90205 [ADD]

Uittenbosch, Anneke (hpd)
Bach, J.S.:Cons for 3 Hpds (comp), w. G. Leonhardt (hpd), A. Curtis (hpd), G. Leonhardt (cnd), Leonhardt Consort Teldec 3-▲ 2292-42726-2 [ADD]
Bach, J.S.:Con for 4 Hpds, w. E. Müller (hpd), G. Leonhardt (hpd), J. van Wering (hpd), G. Leonhardt (cnd), Leonhardt Consort Teldec 3-▲ 2292-42726-2 [ADD]

Uittenbosch, Anneke (hpd/org)
Sweelinck, J.P.:Kbd Music—More palatino; Ick voer al over Rhijn; Fant Chromatica in d; Est-ce Mars; Onder een linde groen; Toccata in a; Poolse Dans; Malle Sijmen; Pavana Lachrimae; Pavana hispanica; Toccata in a; Echo Fant; Mein junges Leben hat ein End *(rec Amsterdam & Oegstgeest, Oct 1989)* Globe ▲ GLO 6035 [DDD]

Uitti, Frances-Marie (vc)
Cage, J.:A Dip in the Lake Etcetera ▲ KTC 2016
Cage, J.:Etudes Boreales Etcetera 2-▲ KTC 2016
Cage, J.:Lecture on Nothing Etcetera ▲ KTC 2016
Cage, J.:Solo Vc Etcetera ▲ KTC 2016
Cage, J.:26' 1.1499" Etcetera ▲ KTC 2016
Cage, J.:Vars I–IV—I, II & III Etcetera ▲ KTC 2016
Scelsi, G.:Music of, w. Joëlle Léandre (sgr/db), Nicolas Isherwood (bass), Giancarlo Schiaffini (trbn/tuba), Karin Schmeer (hp), Robyn Schulkowsky (tamtam)—Maknongan for Low-Registered Instrument (1976) [3 versions:bass, double bass, tuba]; Tre pezzi for Trombone (1956); Wo Ma for Bass (1960); C'est bien la nuit for Double Bass (1972); Le réveil profond for Double Bass (1977); Et Maintenant, c'est a vous a jouer for Cello & Double Bass (1974); Okanagon for Harp, Double Bass & Tamtam (1968); Mantram for Double Bass (1987) *(rec Sendesaal, Hessen Radio, Frankfurt, Feb. 8–9, May 18–21 & Aug)* Hat Hut ("NOW." series) ▲ hat ART CD 6124 [DDD]
Stiebler, E.:Sequenz II *(rec Sender Freies Berlin, Feb 11, 1994)* Hat Hut ("Now" series) ▲ CD 6169 [DDD]
Stiebler, E.:Trio '89, w. Marianne Schroeder (pno), Robyn Schulkowsky (perc) *(rec Sender Freies Berlin, Feb 13, 1994)* Hat Hut ("Now" series) ▲ CD 6169 [DDD]

Ulanowsky, Paul (pno)
Bach, J.S.:Songs, w. L. Lehmann (sop)—Bist du bei mir Claremont ▲ GSE78 50 57
Brahms, J.:Songs, w. L. Lehmann (sop)—Wie bist du, meine Königin; Wir wandelten; An die Nachtigall; Erlaube mir, fein's Mädchen; Da unten im Tale; Feinsliebchen, du sollst mir nicht barfuss geh'n; Die Mainacht; Sonntag; Oliebliche Wangen; Auf dem Kirchhofe Claremont ▲ GSE78 50 57
The Complete 1941 Radio Recital Cycle, w. Lotte Lehmann (sop) *(rec Nov. & Dec. 1941)* Eklipse 2-▲ EKR 18
Kreisler, F.:Vn Pieces, w. L. Kaufman (vn)—trans. of works by Rimsky-Korsakov *(Hymn to the Sun)*, Tchaikovsky *(Andante cantabile)*, Trad. *(Londonderry Air)* Cambria ▲ CD 1063 [ADD]
The New York Farewell Recital (1951), w. Lotte Lehmann (sop) *(rec 1951)* VAI Audio ▲ VAIA 1038
Schubert, Franz:Songs (misc), w. L. Lehmann (sop)—Der Erlkönig Claremont ▲ GSE78 50 57
Schumann, R.:Songs, w. L. Lehmann (sop)—Der Nussbaum; Aufträge; Du bist wie eine Blume; Widmung Claremont ▲ GSE78 50 57
Songs & Waltzes from Vienna, w. Lotte Lehmann (sop) *(rec 1941)* Sony Masterworks (Portrait) ▲ MPK 47682 [ADD]
Strauss, R.:Songs, w. L. Lehmann (sop)—Ständchen; Morgen; Allerseelen; Zueignung Claremont ▲ GSE78 50 57
Wolf, H.:Songs (misc), w. L. Lehmann (sop)—Frühling übers Jahr; In der Frühe; Auf ein altes bild; Heimweh; Auch kleine Dinge; Peregrina I Claremont ▲ GSE78 50 57

Ulbrich, Rudolf (vn)
Eisler, H.:Chamber Music, w. Joachim Zindler (va), Clemens Diller (vc) Berlin Classics ▲ BER CD 9231

Ullén, Fredrik (pno)
Ligeti, G.:Kbd Music—Bagatelles (3) for David Tudor; Chromatische Phantasie; Duo Capricci; Études, Books I & II; Invention *(rec Swedish Broadcasting Co. Studio 2, Stockholm, Sweden, Mar 1–2, 1995)* BIS ▲ CD 783 [DDD]

Ullery, Charles (bn)
Daugherty, M.:Bounce I, w. K. Wolfe (bn) Opus One ▲ 138
Russell, A.:Suite Concertante, w. Floyd Cooley (tuba), Janet Ketchum (fl), James Kanter (cl), Earle Dumler (ob), Arthur David Krehbiel (hn) Crystal ▲ CD 120

Ullmann, Elisabeth (org)
Mozart, W.A.:Church Sons, w. P. Angerer (cnd), Concilium Musicum MD + G ▲ L 3298 [DDD]
Muffat, G.:Apparatus MD + G ("Gold" series) 2-▲ MDG 3200529 [DDD]
Orgellandschaft Wien MD + G ▲ O 3343 [DDD]

Ullner, Niels (vc)—see also ORCHESTRAS & ENSEMBLES Copenhagen Contemporary Players
Hoffmeister, F.A.:Trios for 2 Fls & Vc, w. Bent Larsen (fl), Henrik Svitzer (fl) Classico ▲ CLASSCD 119
Nørholm, I.:Chamber Music, w. T. L. Christiansen (fl), B. Rørbech (vn), M. Vitek (vn), H. Olsen (va), I. Olsen (gtr), A. Øland (pno)—Essai Prismatique; Medusa's Shadow; Mosaic; Prelude to My Wintermorning; Sonata Quasi Variazioni *(rec 2/89)* Kontrapunkt ▲ 32019 [DDD]
Nørholm, I.:Chamber Music, w. B. Rørbeck (vn), J. Christiansen (gtr), P. Salo (pno/hpd), G. Sørensen (perc), Kuhlau Flute Quartet—Before Silence, Op. 83; Contrast-Continuum, Op. 70; Guitar Sonata No. 2; The Orthodox Dream; So to Say, Op. 74; Turbulens-Laminar, Op. 93; Variants, Op. 19 *(rec 9/90)* Kontrapunkt ▲ 32065 [DDD]
Nystroem, G.:Sinf concertante, w. P. Järvi (cnd), Malmö SO *(rec Malmö Concert Hall, Sweden, Aug. 16–18, 1994)* BIS ▲ CD 682 [DDD]
Roussel, A.:Chamber Music, w. Majken Bjerno (sop), Toke Lund Christiansen (fl), Bjørn Carl Nielsen (ob), Niels Thomsen (cl), Per Jacobsen (hn), Asger Svendsen (bn), Ketil Christensen (tpt), Anne Søe Hansen (vn), Zwi Carmelli (va), Piotr Zelazny (va), Michael Dabelsteen (db), Tine Rehling (hp), Morten Mogensen (pno), Per Salo (pno), Per Jensen (perc)—Divertissement, Op. 6; Trio, Op. 40; Joueurs de Flute, Op. 27; Serenade, Op. 30; Le marchand de sable qui passe, Op. 13; Andante et scherzo, Op. 13; 2 poèmes de ronsard, Op. 26; Aria; Elpenor, Op. 59; Pipe Kontrapunkt 2-▲ KPT 32218 [DDD]
Schubert, Franz:Qt Fl, w. T. L. Christiansen (fl), H. Olsen (va), I. Olsen (gtr) Kontrapunkt ▲ 32024 [DDD]

Ullrich, Dietmar (hn)—see ORCHESTRAS & ENSEMBLES Sabine Meyer Wind Ensemble

Ullrich, M. (tpt)
Baroque Masterpieces for Trumpet & Organ, Vol. 1, w. E. Tarr (tpt), Kent, et al. Elektra/Nonesuch ■ 71279-4

Ulmer, (pno)
Debussy, C.:Preludes Pno Protone 2-■ CSPR 151/52

Ulrich, Hans (cym)
Hauser, F.:Die Welle, w. Martin André Grütter (cym/tamtam), Roli Fischer (cym), Barbara Frey (cym), Cyril Lützelschwab (cym), Lukas Rohner (cym), Severin Steinhauser (cym), Hans Ulrich (cym), Ruud Wiener (cym), Michael Erni (timp), Fran Lorkovic (timp), F. Hauser (cnd) *(rec Studio DRS, Basel, Switzerland, Nov. 6, 1988)* Hat Hut ▲ hat ART CD 6017 [ADD]

Ulrich, K. H. (fl)
Mozart, W.A.:Adagio & Rondo Glass Armonica, w. B. Hoffmann (glass armonica), H. Hucke (ob), E. Nippes (va), H. Plumacher (vc) Allegretto ▲ ACD 8174 [ADD] ■ ACS 8174
Naumann, J.G.:Qt Glass Hmc, w. B. Hoffmann (glass hmc), E. Nippes (va), H. Plumacher (vc) Allegretto ▲ ACD 8174 [ADD] ■ ACS 8174

Ulrich, Rudolf (baroque tpt)
Bach Trumpet Gala, Vol. 1, w. Peter Epp (baroque tpt), Arnold Mehl (baroque tpt), Munich Bach Trumpet Ensemble, Franz Lehrndorfer (org) Ars Musici ▲ 0869

Ulsamer, Josef (vl)
Rinaldo di Capua:La Zingara, w. Annalisa Monkewitz (sop—Nisa), Rodolfo Malacarne (ten—Tagliaborse), Laerte Malaguti (bass—Calcante), Kurt-Heinz Stolze (hpd), G. Kehr (cnd), Mainz CO Dynamic ▲ CD 141 [ADD]

Ulydert, Marja (cl)—see ORCHESTRAS & ENSEMBLES Ives Ensemble members

Umble, James (a sax)
Brown, N.K.:Déjeuner sur l'herbe, w. D. Orhenstein (sop), K. Thomas Umble (fl), R. Fusco (pno) Dana Recording Project ▲ DRP 5 [DDD]
Chambers, E.:Rothko-Tobey Continuum Cambria ▲ CD 1088
Eychenne, M.:Cantilène et Danse, w. Cleveland Duo Dana Recording Project ▲ DRP 5 [DDD]
Turok, P.:Improvisations Vn, w. S. Warner (vn), R. Fusco (pno) Dana Recording Project ▲ DRP 5 [DDD]

Umble, K. Thomas (fl)
Brown, N.K.:Déjeuner sur l'herbe, w. D. Orhenstein (sop), J. Umble (a sax), R. Fusco (pno) Dana Recording Project ▲ DRP 5 [DDD]

Umemura, Yuko (pno)
Ifukube, A.:Lullabies (3) Among the Native Tribes on the Island of Sakhalin, w. Kyoko Hirata (sop) Camerata ▲ 32CM 290
Ifukube, A.:Son Vn, w. Takeshi Kobyayashi (vn) Camerata ▲ 32CM 290

Umiker, Robert (a sax)
Still, W.G.:Romance Sax, w. Arthur Tollefson (pno) Cambria ▲ CD 1060 [ADD]

Umiker, Robert (cl)
Still, W.G.:Folk Suites, w. Leonard Garrison (fl), Samuel Magill (vc), Arthur Tollefson (pno) Cambria ▲ CD 1060 [ADD]

Underhill, Nicholas (pno)
Viens, M.:York, Maine *(rec Manhattan School of Music)* MMC ▲ MMC 2019 [DDD]

Underwood, Dale (sax)—see also ORCHESTRAS & ENSEMBLES East Coast Saxophone Quartet
Classic Pastiche Open Loop ▲ OL 009
Soliloquy, w. Texas Tech Univ Wind Ensemble [cnd:James Sudduth] Open Loop ▲ OL 013
Van Appledorn, M.J.:Liquid Gold, w. R. Chiles (pno) Opus One ▲ 147

Underwood, J. (va)—see ORCHESTRAS & ENSEMBLES Delmé String Quartet

Underwood, Keith (fl)
Biscardi, C.:Tenzone, w. Robert Dick (fl), Robert Weirich (pno) *(rec Sprague Hall, Yale Univ., New Haven, CT, 1978)* CRI ▲ CD 686 [ADD]
Ung, C.:Tall Wind, w. Joan Heller (sop), Robert Atherholt (ob), David Starobin (gtr), Chris Finckel (vc), A. Weisberg (cnd) *(rec Vanguard Recording Studio, New York, 1982)* CRI ▲ CRI 710 [DDD/ADD]

Underwood, Keith (fl/rec)—see ORCHESTRAS & ENSEMBLES Jazzantiqua

Ung, Susan Lee Pounders (va)
Ung, C.:Khse Buon Va *(rec Kerr Center, Tempe, AZ, Jan 29, 1991)* CRI ▲ CRI 710 [DDD/ADD]

Ungar, Jay (vn)
Gohl, M.:The West, w. Nana Vasconcelos (sgr), Seamus Eagan (sgr), Molly Mason (gtr), *(other artists unknown)*, M. Gohl (cnd), Black Elk Voices Sony Classical ▲ SK 62727 ■ ST 62727

Ungár, Tamás (pno)
Conyngham, B.:Southern Cross, w. Robert Davidovici (vn), G. Simon (cnd), London SO *(rec St Jude-on-the-Hill, Hampstead Garden Suburb, London, Apr 2–4, 1990)* Cala ▲ CACD 1008 [DDD]
Mussorgsky, M.:Pictures at an Exhibition, w. G. Simon (cnd), Philharmonia Orch [arr Lawrence Leonard, 1977] *(rec All Hallows Church, Gospel Oak, London, Feb 21–24 & Apr 8–10, 199)* Cala ▲ CACD 1012 [DDD]

Ungár, Tamás (pno/syn)
Conyngham, B.:Monuments, w. G. Simon (cnd), London SO *(rec St Jude-on-the-Hill, Hampstead Garden Suburb, London, Apr 2–4, 1990)* Cala ▲ CACD 1008 [DDD]

Ungareanu, Marius (va)
Mieg, P.:Septet, w. Peter Solomon (hpd), Günter Rumpel (fl), Simon Fuchs (ob), Primroz Novsak (vn), Carolyn Hopkins Marti (vc), Ronald Dangel (db) *(rec 1993)* Jecklin ▲ JS 314-2 [DDD]

Unger, Johannes (org)
Mauersberger, R.:Geh aus, mein Herz, und suche Freude, w. Sabine Dicke (sop), Dorothea Schmidt (sop), Friederike Urban (sop), Annette Bassenge (alt), Christiane Fischer (alt), Sabine Hering (alt), Wolfgang Unger (dir), Thüringian Academic Sing Circle Thorofon ▲ CTH 2245 [DDD]

Ungereanu, Mihal (pno)
Gerber, R.:Con for 2 Pnos, w. S. Petrescu (pno), M. Cichirdan (cnd), Craiova PO Gallo ▲ CD 580 [AAD]

Ungerer, G. (pno)
Kirchner, T.:Pno Music—Preludes (18), Op. 9 (16 selections); Songs Without Words, Op. 13/1–7 *(rec 1987)* Jecklin-Disco ▲ JD 618-2 [DDD]

Uninsky, Alexandre (pno)
Chopin, F.:Berceuse Philips ("Duo" series) 2-▲ 442574-2
Chopin, F.:Impromptus Philips ("Duo" series) 2-▲ 442574-2
Chopin, F.:Mazurkas—57 mazurkas Philips ("Duo" series) 2-▲ 442574-2

Unwin, Nicholas (pno)
Tippett, M.:Son 1 Pno Chandos ▲ CHAN 9468
Tippett, M.:Son 2 Pno Chandos ▲ CHAN 9468
Tippett, M.:Son 3 Pno Chandos ▲ CHAN 9468

▲ = CD ♦ = Enhanced CD Δ = MD ■ = Cassette Tape ◻ = DCC

Uosek, Jiri (vc)—see ORCHESTRAS & ENSEMBLES Prague Chamber Ensemble
Urbain, Luc (fl)
Boismortier, J.B. de:Suites Fl, Op. 35—Nos. 3, 5, 6 *(rec 1993)* Approche ▲ CAL 6865 [ADD/DDD]
Mozart, W.A.:Qts Fl, w. French CO Soloists Approche ▲ 6625
Urban, Martin (tuba)—see ORCHESTRAS & ENSEMBLES Brassissimo Vienna
Urban, Ulrich (pno)
Reger, M.:Aus meinem Tagebuch—Vol. 1 Koch Schwann ▲ SCH 310332 [DDD]
Schulhoff, E.:Little Round Dances Koch Schwann ▲ SCH 311862 [DDD]
Schulhoff, E.:Son 3 Pno Koch Schwann ▲ SCH 311862 [DDD]
Schulhoff, E.:Variations on an Original Dorian Theme & Fugato Koch Schwann ▲ SCH 311862 [DDD]
Urban-Stivers, Carol (pno)—see ORCHESTRAS & ENSEMBLES Sierra Winds
Uremura, K. (vl)
Couperin, F.:Nouveaux Concerts, "Les Goûts-réunis", w. W. Kuijken (vl), R. Kohnen (hpd)—Nos. 12 & 13 *(rec June 1992)* Accent ▲ 9288 D [DDD]
Couperin, F.:Pièces de violes avec la bass chifrée, w. W. Kuijken (vl), R. Kohnen (hpd) *(rec June 1992)* Accent ▲ 9288 D [DDD]
Uriarte, Begoña (pno)—see also ORCHESTRAS & ENSEMBLES Uriarte-Mrongovius Duo
Ogermann, C.:Music for 2 Pnofortes, w. K.-H. Mrongovius (pno) Mobile Fidelity ▲ MFCD 786 [DDD]
Schubert, Franz:Allegro Moderato & Andante Pno 4-Hands, w. Karl-Hermann Mrongovius (pno) Calig ▲ CAL 50950 [DDD]
Schubert, Franz:Andantino Varie, w. Karl-Hermann Mrongovius (pno) Calig ▲ CAL 50950 [DDD]
Schubert, Franz:Fant Pno, D.940, w. Karl-Hermann Mrongovius (pno) Calig ▲ CAL 50950 [DDD]
Schubert, Franz:Ländler Pno, D.814, w. Karl-Hermann Mrongovius (pno) Calig ▲ CAL 50950 [DDD]
Schubert, Franz:Marches militaires, D.733, w. Karl-Hermann Mrongovius (pno) Calig ▲ CAL 50950 [DDD]
Schubert, Franz:Vars on an Original Theme Pno 4-Hands, w. Karl-Hermann Mrongovius (pno) Calig ▲ CAL 50950 [DDD]
Uriash, Igor (pno)
Beethoven, L. van:Son 1 Pno *(rec St. Petersburg, 1992)* Audiophile Classics ▲ 101.001 [DDD]
Beethoven, L. van:Son 2 Pno *(rec St. Petersburg, 1992)* Audiophile Classics ▲ 101.001 [DDD]
Uribe, B. (pno)
Wilson, R.:Con Pno, w. L. Botstein (cnd), Boston Pro Arte CO *(rec Feb. 16, 1992)* CRI ▲ CD 618 [DDD]
Wilson, R.:Eclogue CRI ▲ CD 602 [ADD]
Wilson, R.:Fixations Albany ▲ TROY 074 [DDD]
Wilson, R.:Persuasions, w. A. Burton (sop), J. Solum (alt fl), M. Schachman (ob/E hn), G. Dejean (bn/ctbn) Albany ▲ TROY 074 [DDD]
Wilson, R.:Son Va, w. W. Trampler (va) Albany ▲ TROY 074 [DDD]
Uriol, Jose Luis Gonzalez (org)
Bruna, P.:Org Music MP Classics 3-▲ 11019/21
Uritzky, Viacheslav (vn)
Foote, A.:Nocturne, w. F. Smith (fl), L. Chang (vn), K. Murdock (va), B. Coppock (vc) Northeastern ("Classical Arts" series) ▲ NR 227-CD
Ursuleasa, Mihaela (pno)
Beethoven, L. van:Con 5 Pno, "Emperor", w. J. López-Cobos (cnd), Lausanne CO *(rec Théatre de Vevey, Sept 1995)* Claves ▲ CD 9520 [DDD]
Mozart, W.A.:Con 9 Pno, w. J. López-Cobos (cnd), Lausanne CO *(rec Théatre de Vevey, Sept 1995)* Claves ▲ CD 9520 [DDD]
Uryash, Igor (pno)
Grieg, E.:Con Pno, Op. 16, w. A. Titov (cnd), New Philharmonia Orch Infinity Digital ▲ QK 57227 [DDD]
Schumann, R.:Con Pno, w. A. Titov (cnd), New Philharmony Orch Infinity Digital ▲ QK 57227 [DDD]
Uryvayev, Sergei (pno)—see also ORCHESTRAS & ENSEMBLES St. Petersburg Trio
Beethoven, L. van:Con 3 Pno, w. A. Titov (cnd), St. Petersburg Classical Music Studio Orch Infinity Digital ▲ QK 57222 [DDD]
Beethoven, L. van:Son 3 Pno *(rec St. Petersburg, 1992)* Audiophile Classics ▲ 101.001 [DDD]
Mozart, W.A.:Con 19 Pno, w. A. Titov (cnd), St. Petersburg Classical Music Studio Orch Infinity Digital ▲ QK 64333 [DDD]
Mozart, W.A.:Con 20 Pno, w. A. Titov (cnd), St. Petersburg New PO Infinity Digital ▲ QK 57232 [DDD]
Mozart, W.A.:Con 21 Pno, w. A. Titov (cnd), St. Petersburg New PO Infinity Digital ▲ QK 57232 [DDD]
Utagawa, A. (fl)—see ORCHESTRAS & ENSEMBLES Les Joueurs de Flute
Utesch, Peter (bn)—see ORCHESTRAS & ENSEMBLES Sebon Quartet
Utkin, Alexei (ob)
Bach, J.S.:Con Vn & Ob, w. V. Spivakov (vn), V. Spivakov (cnd), Moscow Virtuosi RCA Red Seal ▲ 7991-2-RC [DDD]
Vivaldi, A.:Cons for 2 Obs, w. M. Evstigneev (ob), V. Spivakov (cnd), Moscow Virtuosi—RV.535 RCA Red Seal ▲ 60240-2-RC [DDD]
Utrecht, Aleksandra (pno)
Bacewicz, G.:Son 4 Vn & Pno, w. E. Statkiewicz (vn) Olympia ▲ OLY 392 [ADD]
Uyama-Bouvard, Yasuko (org)
Gabrieli, G.:Sacrae symphoniae, w. Toulouse Saqueboutiers, A Sei Voci Adda ▲ ADD 242292
Mozart, W.A.:Adagio & Allegro Adda ▲ ADD 581274 [DDD]
Mozart, W.A.:Andante Mech Org Adda ▲ ADD 581274 [DDD]
Mozart, W.A.:Church Sons, w. Manfred Kramer (vn), Maria Lindal (vn), Lucia Swarts (vc), Richard Myron (db)—K.67, 144, 145, 241, 244, 245, 274, 328 & 336 Adda ▲ ADD 581274 [DDD]
Mozart, W.A.:Fant Mechanical Org Adda ▲ ADD 581274 [DDD]
Uyldert, Marja (cl)—see ORCHESTRAS & ENSEMBLES Ives Ensemble members
Uzuka, Toshiyuki (va)
Yashiro, A.:Qt Strs, w. C. Tanaka (vn), S. Muto (vn), K. Yasuda (vc) Camerata ▲ 30CM 51
Vacas, Conchi (fl)
Debussy, C.:Son Fl, w. Alison Montoya (va), Zoraida Avila (hp) *(rec Madrid, Oct 1-3 1990)* RNE/Spanish National Radio ▲ M3/06 [DDD]
Falla, M. de:Psyché, w. Elena Montaña (sop), Zoraida Avila (hp), Wen-Yu Ku (vn), Alison Montoya (va), Gloria Cuerda (vc) *(rec Madrid, Oct 1-3 1990)* RNE/Spanish National Radio ▲ M3/06 [DDD]
Ginastera, A.:Cantos del Tucumán, w. Elena Montaña (sop), Wen-Yu Ku (vn), Zoraida Avila (hp), Conchi Sangregorio (perc) *(rec Madrid, Oct 1-3 1990)* RNE/Spanish National Radio ▲ M3/06 [DDD]
Guibert, A.:The Bath Tub, w. Elena Montaña (sop), Wen-Yu Ku (vn), Alison Montoya (va), Gloria Cuerda (vc), Zoraida Avila (hp) *(rec Madrid, Oct 1-3 1990)* RNE/Spanish National Radio ▲ M3/06 [DDD]
Roussel, A.:Sérénade, w. Wen-Yu Ku (vn), Alison Montoya (va), Gloria Cuerda (vc), Zoraida Avila (hp) *(rec Madrid, Oct 1-3 1990)* RNE/Spanish National Radio ▲ M3/06 [DDD]
Vacchiano, William (tpt)
Scriabin, A.:Sym 4, w. D. Mitropoulos (cnd), New York PO *(rec 1953)* Theorema ▲ TH 121132
Shostakovich, D.:Con 1 Pno, w. A. Previn (pno), L. Bernstein (cnd), New York PO *(rec Apr. 8, 1962)* Sony Classical ▲ SMK 47618 [ADD]
Vivaldi, A.:Cons Diverse Instrs, w. G. Vicari (mand), C. de Filippis (mand), J. Wummer (fl), R. Morris (fl), N. Prager (tpt), E. Brenner (b ob), C. Stavrache (hp), A. Wurtzler (hp), J. Gorigliano (vn), L. Varga (vc), L. Bernstein (cnd), New York PO—in C, RV.558 *(rec Dec. 15, 1958)* Sony Classical ("Leonard Bernstein:The Royal Edition" series) ▲ SMK 47642 [ADD]
Vacek, Karel (bn)
Mozart, W.A.:Sinf concertante Ob, K.Anh.9, w. Frantisek Hanták (ob), Milos Kopecky (cl), Miroslav Stefek (hn), *(orch unknown)* Supraphon ▲ SUP 3053
Váchalová, Barbora (hp)—see also ORCHESTRAS & ENSEMBLES Prague Chamber Ensemble
Matejů, Z.:Stele of Forbiddance, w. Kamil Dolezal (cl) Panton ▲ PAN 811397
Matejů, Z.:Stele of Forbiddance, w. Kamil Dolezal (cl) *(rec Martínek Studio, Prague, Jan 13, 16, 17, 24 & Feb)* Panton ▲ 811397-2 [DDD]
Vachon, Mario (pno)—see ORCHESTRAS & ENSEMBLES Duo Campion-Vachon
Vachulka, Ladislav (org)
Reicha, A.:Te Deum, w. Marta Boháčová (sop), Oldřich Lindauer (ten), Karel Průša (bass), V. Smetáček (cnd), Prague SO, Kühn Chorus *(rec Cathedral of the Ascension of the Virgin, Karlov, Prague, 1970)* Panton ▲ PAN 800242 [AAD]
Vacri, Giancarlo di (va)
Dragonetti, D.:Qt 4 Strs, w. Stefano Furini (vn), Pietro Juvarra (vn), Teodora Campagnaro (vc) *(rec Sala San Bovo, Padova, Italy, Jan 17-19, 1995)* Dynamic ▲ CD 133 [DDD]
Dragonetti, D.:Qnt Strs, w. Ubaldo Fioravanti (db), Piero Toso (vn), Monica Tosi (va), Mario Finotti (vc) *(rec Sala San Bovo, Padova, Italy, Jan 17-19, 1995)* Dynamic ▲ CD 133 [DDD]
Vad, Knud (org)
Bach, J.S.:Org Music (misc), w. J. E. Hansen (org), H. Otto (org), H. Rilling (org)—Toccata & Fugue in d, BWV 565; Fugue in g, BWV 578; Passacaglia & Fugue in c, BWV 582; Fantasia & Fugue in g, BWV 542; Chorales, BWV 147, 583, 608, 622, 645 Denon ▲ CO 8009 [DDD]
Vadrot, Didier (sax)
Sauguet, H.:Sonatine bucolique, w. Catherine Garnier (pno) Sonpact ▲ SPT 96017 [DDD]
Vaernes, Berit (vn)—see ORCHESTRAS & ENSEMBLES Vertavo String Quartet
Vaernes, Bjørg (vc)—see also ORCHESTRAS & ENSEMBLES Vertavo String Quartet
Larsson, L.-E.:Concertinos, w. Jan Stigmer (vn), Per-Ola Lindberg (va), Ingalill Hillerud (db), Joakim Kallhed (pno), Camerata Romana—Nos. 8-12 Intim Musik ▲ INT 31
Vagnini, S. (org/hpd//t fl)—see ORCHESTRAS & ENSEMBLES Il Cortegiano
Vahle, Petra (va)
Denisov, E.:Con for 2 Vas, w. N. Imai (va), A. de Man (hpd), L. Markiz (cnd), Amsterdam New Sinfonietta *(rec 6/91)* BIS ▲ CD 518 [DDD]
Tubin, E.:Va & Pno Music, w. V. Rumessen (pno)—Sonata for Alto Saxophone & Piano [version for viola & piano] (1951); Sonata for Viola & Piano (1965) BIS 2-▲ CD 541/42 [DDD]
Vaidman, Vera (vn)
Dvořák, A.:Sonatina Vn, w. E. Krasovsky (pno) PWK Classics ▲ PWK 1137 [DDD]
Romantic Strings, w. Vaidman, Vera (vn), Emanuel Krasovsky (pno) PWK Classics ▲ PWK 1137 [DDD]
Schubert, Franz:Sonatina Vn, D.385, w. E. Krasovsky (pno) PWK Classics ▲ PWK 1137 [DDD]
Vaillancourt, J.-E. (pno)
McPhee, C.:Balinese Ceremonial Music, w. L. Vaillancourt (pno) Ummus ▲ UMM 104
Vaillancourt, Joan (pno)
Prévost, A.:Improvisation Pno Analekta ▲ UMM 103
Prévost, A.:Improvisation Voc, w. *(soloist unknown)* Analekta ▲ UMM 103
Prévost, A.:Son 1 Vc, w. Y. Turovsky (vc) Analekta ▲ UMM 103
Prévost, A.:Son 2 Vc, w. Y. Turovsky (vc) Analekta ▲ UMM 103
Vaillancourt, Lorraine (pno)
McPhee, C.:Balinese Ceremonial Music, w. J.-E. Vaillancourt (ano) Ummus ▲ UMM 104
Vaillant, Ludovic (tpt)
Shostakovich, D.:Con 1 Pno, w. D. Shostakovich (pno), A. Cluytens (cnd), French National Orch EMI Classics ▲ CDC 54606
Vainberg, M. (pno)
Vainberg, M.:Sons Vc, w. A. Vasilieva (vc) Russian Disc ▲ RUS 11 026 [ADD]
Väinmaa, Lauri (pno)
Sisask, U.:Starry Sky Cycle Finlandia ▲ 4509-95880-2 [DDD]
Vajda, József (bn)
Beethoven, L. van:Qnt Ob, 3 Hns & Bn, w. Ottó Rácz (ob), Jenő Keveházi (hn), János Keveházi (hn), Sándor Berki (hn) Naxos ▲ 8.553090 [DDD]
Beethoven, L. van:Qnt Pno, Ob, Cl, Hn & Bn, w. J. Jandó (pno), J. Kiss (ob), B. Kovács (cl), J. Keveházi (hn) *(rec Dec. 1-4, 1990)* Naxos ▲ 8.550511 [DDD]
Beethoven, L. van:Septet Strs, w. Ildikó Hegyi (vn), Győző Máthé (va), Péter Szabó (vc), István Tóth (db), Jozsef Balogh (cl), Jenő Keveházi (hn) *(rec Scottish Church, Budapest, Apr. 21-23 & May 29-31, 1)* Naxos ▲ 8.553090 [DDD]
Kocsár, M.:Elegia, w. M. Kocsár (cnd), Franz Liszt CO Hungaroton ▲ HCD 31188 [DDD]
Mozart, W.A.:Qnt Hn, K.407, w. J. Jandó (pno), J. Kiss (ob), B. Kovács (cl), J. Keveházi (hn) *(rec Dec. 1-4, 1990)* Naxos ▲ 8.550511 [DDD]
Telemann, G.P.:Con in F Rcr Bn, w. L. Czidra (rcr), J. Rolla (cnd), Franz Liszt CO White Label ▲ HRC 042
Vajo, Marek (tpt)
Purcell, H.:Son Tpt, w. Jaroslav Halíř (tpt), Radek Nemec (tpt), Jan Vobořil (hn), Jiří Nauš (trbn), Lubomír Maryška (tuba), Pavel Černy (org), Oldřich Šatava (timp) [trans. F. Antonín Vaigl] *(rec Mirror Chapel of the Prague Klementinum, Mar 26, 1995)* Panton ▲ 811368-2 [DDD]
Vakarelis, Janis (pno)
Gershwin, G.:Con Pno, w. H. Lewis (cnd), Royal PO RPO ▲ RPO 5012 [DDD]
Liszt, F.:Con 2 Pno, w. W. Rowicki (cnd), Royal PO RPO Records Impact ▲ 5001 [DDD]
Prokofiev, S.:Con 3 Pno, w. W. Rowicki (cnd), Royal PO RPO Records Impact ▲ 5001 [DDD]
Valach, Jan (org)
Franck, C.:Sym in d [performer's trans. for solo organ] Koch Schwann ▲ CD 311098 [DDD]
Valanctus, Rimantas (lure)
Habbestad, K.:The Articles of Norwegian Christian Law, w. Ståle Bjørnhaug (nar), Adomas Kontautas (lure), Zigmas Kazlauskas (lure), Marius Balcytis (lure) Norway Music ▲ 2912
Valdepeñas, Joaquin (cl)—see also ORCHESTRAS & ENSEMBLES Amici Quartet
Bernstein, L.:Son Cl, w. P. Parr (pno) CBC ("Musica Viva" series) ▲ MVCD 1016 [DDD]
Debussy, C.:Petite pièce, w. P. Parr (pno) CBC ("Musica Viva" series) ▲ MVCD 1016 [DDD]
Lutoslawski, W.:Dance Preludes Cl, Hp, Pno, Perc & Strs, w. P. Parr (pno) CBC ("Musica Viva" series) ▲ MVCD 1016 [DDD]
Morawetz, O.:Son Cl, w. P. Parr (pno) CBC ("Musica Viva" series) ▲ MVCD 1016 [DDD]
Morawetz, O.:Weaver, w. M. DuBois (ten), P. Parr (pno) Centrediscs ▲ CDCCD 3589 [DDD]
Mozart, W.A.:Con Cl, w. J.-L. Garcia (cnd), English CO Summit ▲ DCD 131 [DDD]
Penderecki, K.:Miniatures Cl, w. P. Parr (pno) CBC ("Musica Viva" series) ▲ MVCD 1016 [DDD]
Schubert, Franz:Der Hirt auf dem Felsen, w. E. Wiens (sop), R. Jansen (pno) CBC ("Musica Viva" series) ▲ MVCD 1053 [DDD]
Thrower, J.:Improv on a Blue Theme, w. M. Bernardi (cnd), CBC Vancouver SO CBC ("SM 5000" series) ▲ SMCD 5094 [DDD]
Wagner, R.:Siegfried Idyll, w. T. Holowach (vn), M. Skazinetsky (vn), L. Toman (va), R. Laurie (vc), C. Elliott (db), S. Shulman (fl), T. Maloney (cl), J. Valdepenas (cl), J. Fetherston (cl), S. Mosher (bn), S. Wilson (hn), R. Cohen (hn), J. Cowell (tpt), G. Gould (cnd) *(rec July 27-29 & Sept. 8, 198)* Sony Classical ▲ SMK 52650 [ADD]
Weber, C.M. von:Grand duo concertant Cl, w. P. Parr (pno) CBC ("Musica Viva" series) ▲ MVCD 1016 [DDD]
Valdés, Pedro (perc)—see ORCHESTRAS & ENSEMBLES New Generation
Válek, Jirí (fl)
Bach, J.S.:Suite 2 Orch, w. J. Suk (cnd), Suk CO Vanguard Classics 2-▲ OVC 7002/03 [DDD]
Hindemith, P.:Son Fl, w. Josef Hála (pno) Supraphon ▲ SUP 0096 [DDD]
Martinů, B.:Son Fl & Pno, w. Josef Hála (pno) Supraphon ▲ SUP 0096 [DDD]
Mozart, W.A.:Andante Fl, w. V. Válek (cnd), Czech Phil CO *(rec House of Artists, Prague, Feb 1-3, 1996)* Canyon Classics 2-▲ 336
Mozart, W.A.:Cons Fl, w. V. Válek (cnd), Czech Phil CO *(rec House of Artists, Prague, Feb 1-3, 1996)* Canyon Classics 2-▲ 336
Mozart, W.A.:Con Fl, K.313, w. V. Neumann (cnd), Czech PO Supraphon Collection ▲ 11 0636-2 [ADD]
Mozart, W.A.:Con Fl Hp, w. H. Müllerová (hp), R. Edlinger (cnd), Capella Istropolitana *(rec 1988)* Naxos ▲ 8.550159 [DDD]
Mozart, W.A.:Con Fl Hp, w. Hana Müllerová-Jouzová (hp), V. Válek (cnd), Czech Phil CO *(rec House of Artists, Prague, Feb 1-3, 1996)* Canyon Classics 2-▲ 336
Poulenc, F.:Son Fl, w. Josef Hála (pno) Supraphon ▲ SUP 0096 [DDD]
Prokofiev, S.:Son Fl, w. Josef Hála (pno) Supraphon ▲ SUP 0096 [DDD]
Reicha, A.:Qts Fl, w. Jan Buble (vn), Jan Marek (va), Ladislav Pospfsil (vc) Panton ▲ PAN 811003

INSTRUMENT.

Válek, Jirí (fl) (cont.)
Richter, F.X.:Cons Fl, w. V. Válek (cnd), Dvořák CO—in E & D Supraphon ▲ SUP 111872 [DDD]
Stamitz, A.:Con Fls, w. R. Pivoda (fl), F. Vajnar (cnd), Prague CO Supraphon ▲ 11 1424-2 [DDD]
Stamitz, C.:Cons Fl, w. V. Válek (cnd), Dvořák CO—In D & G Supraphon ▲ SUP 111872 [DDD]
Telemann, G.P.:Con Rcr, Fl, w. Jiří Stivín (rcr), M. Munclinger (cnd), Prague CO Supraphon ▲ SUP 3039
Vivaldi, A.:Cons Fl (misc), w. J. Novotny (fl), J. Stivín (flautino), *(orch unknown)*—Flute Concerti, RV.108, 533, & in F; Flautino Concerti, RV.443, 444 & 445 Naxos ▲ 8.550385 [DDD]

Válek, Martin (vn)—see ORCHESTRAS & ENSEMBLES Apollo String Quartet

Valenca, Rosihna de (gtr)
Chevalier, C.:Music of, w. Teca Calazans (sgr), Ze-Luis (sgr), Regina Machado (sgr), Nigel Scragg (fl/a sax), Jean-Yves Candela (pno), Wilson das Neves (perc), Regina Machado (perc), Silvano Michelino (perc)—Comme d'habitude; Couleur café; Une histoire d'amour; Les feuilles mortes; Les moulins de mon coeur; Syracuse; Je t'aimerai; Ces petits rien; La valse des lilas; L'absent; Que reste-il de nos amours; Un homme et une femme *(rec Studio Bastille)* Iris ▲ 010 [DDD]

Valent, Miloš (vn)
Benda, G.A.:Scherzi Notturni, w. Peter Zajíček (vn), Musica Aeterna Bratislava *(rec Moyzes Hall of the Slovak Philharmonic, Apr & June 1995)* Slovart ▲ SR 0013-2-131 [DDD]
Bodino, S.:Sons, w. Peter Zajíček (vn), Peter Király (vc), Pascal Dubreuil (hpd), Musica Aeterna—Sons 1-6 *(rec Castle of Tonky, Slovakia, Apr 1994)* Slovart ▲ SR 0008-2-131 [DDD]

Valenti, Fernando (hpd)
Bach, J.S.:Brandenburg Con 5, w. Anshel Brusilow (vn), William Kincaid (fl), L. Stokowski (cnd), Philadelphia Orch *(rec Feb 25, 1960)* Sony Classical ("Masterworks Heritage" series) 2-▲ MH2K 62345 [ADD]

Valentine, Colette (pno)
Ewazen, E.:"...to cast a shadow again", w. William Sharp (bar), Chris Gekker (tpt) *(rec Recital Hall, SUNY Purchase, 1993)* Well-Tempered Productions ▲ WTP 5172 [DDD]
Let Us Break Bread together, w. Jones, Harold (fl) Leonarda ▲ LE 333 [DDD]

Valentini, Giovanni (pno)
Donizetti, G.:Music for Pno 4-Hands, w. L. Bavaj (pno)—La solita suonata; Una delle più matte; Sons. in D, C, G & A; Polacca in G Bongiovanni ▲ GB 5515 [DDD]

Valentini, Romano (pno)
Berio, L.:Pezzi (2) Vn, w. C. Chiarappa (vn) Denon/PCM Digital ▲ CO 75448

Valetti, Pablo (vn)
Deutsche Barocklieder, w. Andreas Scholl (ct), Alix Verzier (vc), Markus Markl (hpd), Karl Ernst Schroder (lt), Friederike Heumann (va), Juan Manuel Quintana (va), Stephanie Pfister (vn) Harmonia Mundi France ▲ HMC 901505

Valetti, Pablo (vn)—see ORCHESTRAS & ENSEMBLES Rare Fruits Council

Valle, F. della (vn)
Campana, J.L.:Je est un autre..., w. J. Geoffroy (perc) Skarbo ▲ SKR3923 [DDD]
Malec, I.:Attacca, w. J. Geoffroy (perc) Skarbo ▲ SKR3923 [DDD]
Tanguy, E.:Towards, w. J. Geoffroy (perc) Skarbo ▲ SKR3923 [DDD]
Tosi, D.:Phonic Design, w. J. Geoffroy (perc) Skarbo ▲ SKR3923 [DDD]

Vallecillo-Gray, Irma (pno)
Bernstein, L.:Son Cl, w. Richard Stoltzman (cl) *(rec Mechanics Hall, Worcester, MA, Jan 6-8, 1994)* RCA Red Seal ▲ 09026-62685-2 [DDD]
Fisher, C.:Sonatine Cl, w. Richard Stoltzman (cl) *(rec Mechanics Hall, Worcester, MA, Jan 6-8, 1994)* RCA Red Seal ▲ 09026-62685-2 [DDD]
Gershwin, G.:Preludes (3) Pno, w. Richard Stoltzman (cl) *(rec Mechanics Hall, Worcester, MA, Jan 6-8, 1994)* RCA Red Seal ▲ 09026-62685-2 [DDD]
Hyman, R.:Clarinata, w. Richard Stoltzman (cl) *(rec Mechanics Hall, Worcester, MA, Jan 6-8, 1994)* RCA Red Seal ▲ 09026-62685-2 [DDD]
Ives, C.:Largo, w. E. Sato (vn), D. Schifrin (cl) *(rec 6 & 7/90)* Delos ▲ 3088 [DDD]
Levitch, L.:Qt Fl, Va, Vc & Pno, w. Sheridan Stokes (fl), Sven Reher (va), Jeffrey Solow (vc) Cambria ▲ CD 1059 [ADD]
Loeffler, C.M.:Rhaps, w. A. Vogel (ob), P. Neubauer (va) *(rec July 1-4, 1992)* Delos ▲ DE 3136 [DDD]
McKinley, W.T.:Son Cl, w. Richard Stoltzman (cl) *(rec Mechanics Hall, Worcester, MA, Jan 6-8, 1994)* RCA Red Seal ▲ 09026-62685-2 [DDD]
Paul Sperry Sings American Cycles & Sets, w. Paul Sperry (ten) Albany ▲ TROY 058 [DDD]
Paul Sperry Sings an American Sampler:From Billings to Bolcom, w. Paul Sperry (ten) Albany ▲ TROY 081 [DDD]
Paul Sperry Sings Romantic American Songs, w. Paul Sperry (ten) Albany ▲ TROY 043-2 [ADD]
Paulus, S.:Artsongs, w. P. Sperry (ten) [E] Albany ▲ TROY 036-2 [DDD]
Poulenc, F.:Son Cl Pno, w. R. Stoltzman (cl) RCA Red Seal ▲ 60198-2-RC [DDD] ■ 60198-4-RC (CrO2)
Romance, w. Richard Stoltzman (cl), Nancy Allen (hp) RCA Red Seal ▲ 60198-2-RC [DDD]
Rowles, J.:The Peacocks, w. Richard Stoltzman (cl) *(rec Mechanics Hall, Worcester, MA, Jan 6-8, 1994)* RCA Red Seal ▲ 09026-62685-2 [DDD]
Saint-Saëns, C.:Son Cl, w. R. Stoltzman (cl) RCA Red Seal ▲ 60198-2-RC [DDD] ■ 60198-4-RC (CrO2)
Songs of an Innocent Age, w. Paul Sperry (ten) Albany ▲ TROY 034-2 [ADD]

Valli, Mauro (vc)
Dussek, J.L.:Trio Son Pno, Op. 65, w. Paolo Bidoli (pno), Francesca Pagnini (fl) Enterprise ("Tiziano" series) ▲ ENT TZ 96002 [DDD]
Kalkbrenner, F.:Son Fl, w. Francesca Pagnini (fl), Paolo Bidoli (pno) Enterprise ("Tiziano" series) ▲ ENT TZ 96002 [DDD]
Kreutzer, C.:Son Fl, Vc & Pno, w. Francesca Pagnini (fl), Paolo Bidoli (pno) Enterprise ("Tiziano" series) ▲ ENT TZ 96002 [DDD]

Vallon, M. (bn)—see ORCHESTRAS & ENSEMBLES Biedermeier Quintet members, Biedermeier Quintet

Valmond, (vn)
Valmond, J.:Con Vn, L'Estro Armonico Gallo ▲ CD 493

Valo, Jari (vn)
Eliasson, A.:Con Vn, Ostrobothnian CO Caprice ▲ CAP 21422

Valsta, Tapani (pno)
Kokkonen, J.:Qnt Pno, w. Sibelius Academy String Quartet BIS ▲ CD 458 [DDD]

Valsta, Tapani (pno/org)
Masterpieces for Cello, w. Noras, Arto (vc) Finlandia ▲ 4509-95883-2 [AAD]

Valtchev, Georgy (vn)
Bond, V.:Dreams of Flying, w. Nikolai Gagov (vn), Valentin Gerov (va), Christo Tanev (vc) Gega ▲ GD 197 [DDD]
Bond, V.:Other Selves, w. Christo Tanev (vc), Anna Stoytcheva (pno) Gega ▲ GD 197 [DDD]
Bond, V.:Weddings & Bar Mitzvahs Gega ▲ GD 197 [DDD]

Van, (gtr)
Argento, D.:Letters from Composers, w. V. Sutton (ten) [E] CRI ■ C 291

Van Cleve, Libby (elec ob)
Vees, J.:Tattooed Barbie, w. Jack Vees (elec gtr/drm machine) CRI ("Emergency Music" series) ▲ CD 730 [DDD]

Van Cleve, Libby (ob)
Hatzis, C.:Byzantium, w. Exultate Chamber Singers *(rec 1993)* Centrediscs ▲ CMCCD 4693 [DDD]

Van Cleve, Libby (ob/E hn)
Lockwood, A.:Thousand Year Dreaming, w. Art Baron (conch shell/trbn/didjerido), Liby Van Cleve (ob/E hn), Jon Gibson (didjeridu), J.D. Parran (cl), Michael Publiese (perc), Scott Robinson (conch shell/perc), John Snyder (didjeridu/waterphone), Charles Wood (tam-tam, stones), Peter Zummo (trbn/didjeridu) ¿What Next? ▲ WN 0010

Van Appledorn, Mary Jeanne (syn)
Van Appledorn, M.J.:Freedom of Youth, w. Lori Berg (nar) Capstone ▲ CPS 8618

Vanasco, Francesca (vc)
Wheeler, T.:The Dancing Bird, w. V. Rice (elec bass), T. Wheeler (perc) Albany ▲ TROY 114

Van Asperen, Bob (hpd)
Bach, C.P.E.:Sons Fl, w. B. Kuijken (fl)—in E♭, H.545; in G, H.509; in C, H.515; in B♭, H.578; in D, H.505; in g, H.542.5; in B♭, H.543; in C, H.504; in G, H.508; in E, H.506 *(rec Feb 24-Mar 12, 1993)* Sony Classical 2-▲ S2K 53964 [DDD]
Bach, J.S.:The Art of the Fugue, w. G. Leonhardt (hpd) Editio Classica 2-▲ 77013-2-RG [ADD]
Boccherini, L.:Sons (34) Vc, w. A. Bylsma (vc), K. Slowik (vc)—in c, G.2; in B♭, G.8; in F, G.9 *(rec Sept. 6-7, 1992)* Sony Classical ▲ SK 53362 [DDD]
Handel, G.F.:Chaconne Hpd Sony Classical ("Vivarte" series) ▲ SK 68260
Handel, G.F.:Suites Hpd—Passacaille; Suites 1, 2, 5 & 8 Sony Classical ("Vivarte" series) ▲ SK 68260
The Harpsichord in the Netherlands:1580-1712 Sony Classical ("Vivarte" series) ▲ SK 46349
Music at the Time of Beaumarchais, w. Montserrat Figueras (sop), Lawrence Monteyro (sop), Raphel Oleg (vn), Miguel da Silva (va), Christophe Coin (vc), Marc Coppey (vc), José Miguel Moreno (gtr), Paul Badura-Skoda (pno), Philippe Cassard (pno), Eric Le Sage (pno) Valois ▲ V 4767
Soler, P.A.:Hpd Music (comp) Astrée 12-▲ E 8780
Telemann, G.P.:Der Getreue Music-Meister (sels), w. W. Van Hauwe (rcr), W. Möller (vc)—Sonata in f for recorder & continuo Globe ▲ GLO 5016 [ADD]
Telemann, G.P.:Kleine Kammermusik, w. W. Van Hauwe (rcr)—Partita No. 4 in g Globe ▲ GLO 5016 [ADD]
Telemann, G.P.:Sonate metodiche, w. W. Van Hauwe (fl), W. Möller (vc)—Son No. 10 in B♭ for voice flute & continuo Globe ▲ GLO 5016 [ADD]

Van Asperen, Bob (org)
Bach, J.C.F.:Son Vc, w. A. Bylsma (vc pic) Sony Classical ("Vivarte" series) ▲ SK 45945
Bach, J.S.:Sons Vl, BWV 1027-1029, w. A. Bylsma (vc pic) Sony Classical ("Vivarte" series) ▲ SK 45945
Frescobaldi, G.:Music Vc, w. A. Bylsma (vc), L. Schifes—Canzone VIII, XV, XVI; Ricercari I-VII; Canon Deutsche Harmonia Mundi ▲ 7978-2-RC [DDD]
Haydn, J.:Ave regina, w. Marie-Claude Vallin (sop), B. Weil (cnd), L'Archibudelli, Tölz Boys' Choir *(rec Bad Tolz, Germany, Jan. 2-4, 1993)* Sony Classical ("Vivarte" series) ▲ SK 53368 [DDD]
Haydn, J.:Lauda Sion, w. Ab Koster (nat hn), Knut Hasselmann (nat hn), B. Weil (cnd), L'Archibudelli, Tölz Boys' Choir *(rec Bad Tolz, Germany, Jan. 2-4, 1993)* Sony Classical ("Vivarte" series) ▲ SK 53368 [DDD]
Haydn, J.:Libera me, Domine, w. B. Weil (cnd), L'Archibudelli, Tölz Boys' Choir *(rec Bad Tolz, Germany, Jan. 2-4, 1993)* Sony Classical ("Vivarte" series) ▲ SK 53368 [DDD]
Haydn, J.:Mass 4, Missa 'Sunt bona mixta malis', w. Anner Bylsma (vc), Anthony Woodrow (db), B. Weil (cnd), Tölz Boys' Choir *(rec Bad Tolz, Germany, June 6, 1992)* Sony Classical ("Vivarte" series) ▲ SK 53368 [DDD]
Haydn, J.:Non nobis, Domine, w. Anner Bylsma (vc), Anthony Woodrow (db), B. Weil (cnd), Tölz Boys' Choir *(rec Bad Tolz, Germany, June 4, 1992)* Sony Classical ("Vivarte" series) ▲ SK 53368 [DDD]
Jacchini, G.M.:Sons Vc, w. A. Bylsma (vc), L. Schifes (continuo instr)—Op. 1/7 & 8; Op. 3/9 & 10 Deutsche Harmonia Mundi ▲ 7978-2-RC [DDD]

Van Asperen, Bob (org/hpd/cnd)
Chamber Music for Trumpet & Winds, w. Wolfgang Basch (tpt) Deutsche Harmonia Mundi ▲ 7976-2-RC [DDD]

Vance, Scott (b cl)
Krumm, P.:Con B Cl, w. B. Childs (cnd), Univ of Redlands Chamber Ensemble Opus One ▲ CD 170 [DDD]

Van Demark, James (db)
Cahn, W.:...Won't You Join the Dance, w. Michael Udow (perc) Nexus ▲ 10339 [DDD]
Schubert, Franz:Qnt Pno, D.667, w. J. O'Conor (pno), Cleveland String Quartet members Telarc ▲ CD 80225 [DDD]

Vanden, Jim (fl)
O'Rourke, J.:Terminal Pharmacy, w. Tony Burr (cl), Jeff Cortazzo (b trbn), John McEntire (dr), Rob Prosser (acc), Isha Suftin (acc), Mike Dockter (vc), Hattie Franck (vc), Robert Keck (vc), Mary LaBreque (vc), Dan Loch (vc), Stan Saderk (vc), Lisa Hemmer (fl), Sue Oberg (fl), Wendi Lev (fl), Jim O'Rourke (gtr), Steve Braack (elec) Tzadik ▲ TZA 7011 [DDD]

Vanden Eynden, Jean-Claude (pno)
Brahms, J.:Liebeslieder Waltzes SATB, w. Greta De Reyghere (sop), Lucienne Van Deyck (mez), Guy De Mey (ten), Huub Claessens (bass), Luc Devos (pno) *(rec Consevatoire Royal, Liège, 1994)* Ricercar ▲ 153138
Brahms, J.:Neue Liebeslieder Waltzes, w. Greta De Reyghere (sop), Lucienne Van Deyck (mez), Guy De Mey (ten), Huub Claessens (bass), Luc Devos (pno) *(rec Consevatoire Royal, Liège, 1994)* Ricercar ▲ 153138
Brahms, J.:Waltzes Pno, Op. 39, w. Luc Devos (pno) *(rec Consevatoire Royal, Liège, 1994)* Ricercar ▲ 153138
de Greef, A.:Con 1 Pno, w. P. Bartholomée (cnd), Liège PO EMI Classics ▲ CDM 65075
Franck, C.:Grand Con 2 Pno, w. E. Doneux (cnd), Belgian RSO Koch Schwann ▲ CD 311111 [DDD] ■ MC 211111 (D)
Franck, C.:Vars brillantes sur la ronde favorite de Gustave III, w. E. Doneux (cnd), Belgian RSO Koch Schwann ▲ CD 311111 [DDD] ■ MC 211111 (D)
Lekeu, G.:Son Vn, w. P. Hirshhorn (vn) Ricercar ▲ RIS 104091 [DDD]
Vieuxtemps, H.:Duo concertant on themes from Weber's Oberon, w. Thérèse-Maria Gilissen (va) [arr va & pno] *(rec Studio 2 Flagey RTBF, Brussels, June 1985)* Pavane ▲ ADW 7340 [DDD]
Vieuxtemps, H.:Elégie, w. Thérèse-Maria Gilissen (va) *(rec Studio 2 Flagey RTBF, Brussels, June 1985)* Pavane ▲ ADW 7340 [DDD]

Van der Pas, Theo (pno)
Beethoven, L. van:Vars on "Bei Männern" from Mozart's *Die Zauberflöte*, w. E. Feuermann (vc) *(rec 1937)* Pearl ▲ PEA 9442 (m) [AAD]
Beethoven, L. van:Vars on "Bei Männern" from Mozart's *Die Zauberflöte*, w. E. Feuermann (vc) *(rec 7/11/34)* EMI Classics ▲ CDH 64250-2 (m) [ADD]
Brahms, J.:Son 1 Vc, w. E. Feuermann (vc) *(rec 1934)* Biddulph ▲ LAB 011 [ADD]
Brahms, J.:Son 1 Vc, w. E. Feuermann (vc) *(rec 1934)* Pearl ▲ PEA 9443 (m) [AAD]
The Columbia Recordings, Vol. 1, w. Emanuel Feuermann (vc), Malcolm Sargent (cnd), *(orch unknown) (rec 1934-1937)* Pearl ▲ PEA 9442 (m) [AAD]
The Columbia Recordings, Vol. 2, w. Jacqueline Du Pré (vc), Michael Taube (pno), Gerald Moore (pno), Wolfgang Rebner (pno) *(rec 1930-1939)* Pearl ▲ PEA 9443 (m) [AAD]

Vanderwerf, Paul (vn)—see ORCHESTRAS & ENSEMBLES Ad Hoc String Quartet

Vandeville, Jacques (E hn)
Koechlin, C.:Suite E Hn Arion ▲ ARN 68286 [DDD]
Koechlin, C.:Symphonic Pieces, w. Jean-Michel Louchart (pno)—Au loin [arr for E hn & Pno] Arion ▲ ARN 68286 [DDD]

Vandeville, Jacques (ob d'amore)
Koechlin, C.:Le Repos de Tityre Arion ▲ ARN 68286 [DDD]

Vandeville, Jacques (ob)
Jolivet, A.:Rhapsodie à 7, w. J.-L. Petit (cnd), Avray CO, Millière String Trio REM ▲ REM 311196 [DDD]
Jolivet, A.:Suite liturgique, w. S. Davené (sop) , *(not advised of cellist or harpist)* REM ▲ REM 311196 [DDD]
Koechlin, C.:Son Ob, w. Jean-Michel Louchart (pno) Arion ▲ ARN 68286 [DDD]

Vandeville, Jacques (ob/ob d'amore/E hn)
Koechlin, C.:Pieces Ob & Pno, w. Jean-Michel Louchart (pno) Arion ▲ ARN 68286 [DDD]

Vandewalle, Daan (pno)
Ives, C.:Son 2 Pno, w. Paul Klinck (vn), Bert Jacobs (fl) *(rec Steurbaut Sound Recording Centre)* René Gailly ▲ CD 87078 [DDD]
Ives, C.:Studies Pno—Nos. 9 & 21-23 *(rec Steurbaut Sound Recording Centre)* René Gailly ▲ CD 87078 [DDD]

Van Dewater, P. (vn)
Polishook, M.:The Tribute, w. M. Gibson (vn), M. Ewing (va), D. Assael (vc) Vienna Modern Masters ▲ VMM 2008 [DDD]

896 ▲ = CD ♦ = Enhanced CD Δ = MD ■ = Cassette Tape □ = DCC

Van Doeselaar, Leo (org)
Flute & Organ, w. Eleonore Pameijer (fl) Vivace ▲ E 539 [ADD]
Hindemith, P.:Kammermusik (comp), w. R. Brautigam (pno), L. Harrell (vc), K. Kulka (vn), K. Kashkashian (va), N. Blume (va d'amore), R. Chailly (cnd), Royal Concertgebouw Orch—No. 1 for Small Orchestra, Op. 24/1 (1922); No. 2 (Piano Concerto) for Piano & 12 Instruments, Op. 36/1 (1924); No. 3 (Cello Concerto), foe Cello & 10 Instruments, Op. 36/2 (1925); No. 4 (Violin Concerto) for Violin & Large Orchestra, Op. 36/3 (1925); No. 5 (Viola Concerto) for Viola & Large Chamber Orchestra, Op. 36/4 (1927); No. 6 (Viola d'amore Concerto) for Viola d'amore & Chamber Orchestra, Op. 46/1 (1927); No. 7 (Organ Concerto) for Organ & chamber Orchestra, Op. 46/2 (1927) London 2-▲ 433816-2 [DDD]
Liszt, F.:Fant & Fugue on "Ad nos, ad salutarem undam" Org Channel Classics ▲ CG 9429
Liszt, F.:Prelude & Fugue on the name B-A-C-H Channel Classics ▲ CG 9429
Mendelssohn, F.:Ave Maria, w. H. Lamy (ten), P. Herreweghe (cnd), Ghent Collegium Vocale Harmonia Mundi France ▲ HMC 901272 [DDD]
Noordt, A. van:Tabulature Book NM Classics ▲ NM 92024

Van Doeselaar, Leo (pno)
Liszt, F.:Am Grabe Richard Wagners Channel Classics ▲ CG 9429
Schubert, Franz:Fant Pno, D.940, w. W. Jordans (pno) Globe ▲ GLO 5049 [DDD]
Schubert, Franz:Intro & Vars Fl on "Tröckne Blumen", w. M. Root (fl) Globe ▲ GLO 5040 [DDD]
Schubert, Franz:Marches caractéristiques, w. W. Jordans (pno)—No. 1 Globe ▲ GLO 5049 [DDD]
Schubert, Franz:Rondo Pno, D.951, w. W. Jordans (pno) Globe ▲ GLO 5049 [DDD]
Schubert, Franz:Vars on an Original Theme Pno 4-Hands, w. W. Jordans (pno) Globe ▲ GLO 5049 [DDD]
Verhulst, J.:Songs, w. Annegeer Stumphius (sop), Nico Van der Meel (ten)—25 sels NM Classics ▲ NM 92029

Vandré, Philipp (prepared pno)
Cage, J.:Sons & Interludes [on a Steinway "O"-type piano] *(rec Frankfurt, Dec 17-18, 1994)* Mode ▲ mode 50 [DDD]

Vanek, Lumír (bn)—see ORCHESTRAS & ENSEMBLES Prague Wind Quintet

Vanek, Lumír (bn)
Martinů, B.:Madrigals Ob, w. Jurij Likin (ob), Vlastimil Mareš (cl) *(rec Studio Martínek, Prague, Mar 3, 1995)* Panton ("Protokol XX" series) ▲ 811348-2 [DDD]
Martinů, B.:Les Rondes, w. Jurij Likin (ob), Vlastimil Mareš (cl), Vladislav Kozderka (tpt), Jana Herojnová (vn), Pavel Kutman (vn), Ivan Klánsky (pno) *(rec Studio Martínek, Prague, Mar 3, 1995)* Panton ("Protokol XX" series) ▲ 811348-2 [DDD]
Martinů, B.:Sxt Fl, Ob, Cl, 2 Bns & Pno, w. Jan Riedlbauch (fl), Jurij Likin (ob), Vlastimil Mareš (cl), Svatopluk Čech (bn), Ivan Klánsky (pno) *(rec Studio Martínek, Prague, Mar 3, 1995)* Panton ("Protokol XX" series) ▲ 811348-2 [DDD]

Vanessa-Mae, (vn)
Bach, J.S.:Sons & Partitas Vn, BWV 1001-1006—Partita No. 3 in E Angel ▲ CDC 55395 ■ 4DS 55395
Beethoven, L. van:Romances Vn, w. V. Fedotov (cnd), London SO—in F, Op. 50 Angel ▲ CDC 55395 ■ 4DS 55395
Brahms, J.:Scherzo Vn Angel ▲ CDC 55395 ■ 4DS 55395
Bruch, M.:Scottish Fant Vn, w. V. Fedotov (cnd), London SO [arr Vanessa-Mae] Angel ▲ CDC 55395 ■ 4DS 55395

Vangi, M. (fl)
Martini, G.B.:Music for Fls, w. M. Mercelli (fl), N. Guidetti (fl), G. Perrucci (fl)—(2 works for 2 Flutes) Sonata in C; Sonata in D; (3 works for 2 Flutes & Continuo) Allegro in C; Allegro & Rondo in C; Pastorale in C Bongiovanni ▲ GB 5517 [DDD]

Van Hessel, Richard (fl/rcr/gittern)—see ORCHESTRAS & ENSEMBLES The Whole Noyse

Vanhove, Frank (fl)
Maes, J.:Arabesque & Scherzo, w. G. Oskamp (cnd), Royal Flanders PO *(rec Elisabeth Hall, Antwerp, July 1994)* Marco Polo ("Anthology of Flemish Music" series) ▲ 8.223741 [DDD]

Van Oosten, Ben (org)
Vierne, L.:Syms Org (comp)—Nos. 4-6 MD + G 2-▲ L 3213/14 [DDD]
Vierne, L.:Syms Org (comp)—Nos. 1-3 MD + G 2-▲ L 3211/12 [DDD]
Widor, C.M.:Syms Org, Op. 13—Op. 13/1 & 2 MD + G ▲ L 3401 [DDD]
Widor, C.M.:Sym 3 Org MD + G ▲ L 3402 [DDD]
Widor, C.M.:Sym 4 Org MD + G ▲ L 3402 [DDD]
Widor, C.M.:Sym 5 Org [Cavaillé-Coll Org, St. Ouen, Rouen] MD + G ▲ MDG 3160403 [DDD]
Widor, C.M.:Sym 6 Org [Cavaillé-Coll Org, St. Ouen, Rouen] MD + G ▲ MDG 3160403 [DDD]
Widor, C.M.:Sym 7 Org MD + G ▲ L 3404 [DDD]
Widor, C.M.:Sym 8 Org [Cavaille-Coll org] *(rec St. Ouen, Rouen, France)* MD + G ▲ MDG 3160405
Widor, C.M.:Sym 9 Org MD + G ▲ L 3404 [DDD]

Vanoosthuyse, Eddy (cl)
Mozart, W.A.:Qnt Cl, K.581, w. Vilnius String Quartet *(rec Vilnius Recording Studio, Vilnuis, Lithuania, Mar 1995)* Infinity Digital ▲ QK 69270 [DDD]
Weber, C.M. von:Qnt Cl, w. Vilnius String Quartet *(rec Vilnius Recording Studio, Vilnuis, Lithuania, Mar 1995)* Infinity Digital ▲ QK 69270 [DDD]

Van Paassen, Marius (pno)
The Animal in 20th Century Piano Music Attacca ▲ BABEL 8950-3 [DDD]
Rubinstein, A.:Prelude Pno Attacca ▲ CD 8741
Rubinstein, A.:Son 4 Pno Attacca ▲ CD 8741
Rubinstein, A.:Vars on "Yankee Doodle" Attacca ▲ CD 8741

VanPelt, Nita (sax)
Scelsi, G.:Anahit, w. Paul Zukofsky (vn), Julie Bogorad (fl), Peggy Russell (fl), Courtney Westcott (fl), Lawrence McDonald (cl), Joan Waryha (cl), Jean Hansen (b cl), Bill Suite (E hn), Bob Zobal (tpt), John Carter (trbn), Martin Lydecker (trbn), Stan Cortman (hn), Robert Ward (hn), William Curry (va), Jody Rowitsch (va), Irene Wade (va), Anne Fagerburg (vc), John Gockel (vc), Sue Manz (bass), Steven Stearman (bass) *(rec Oberlin Conservatory of Music, Oct 8, 1973)* CP² ▲ CP2 108 [AAD]

Vapi, Emilio (fl)
Gragnani, F.:Gtr Music, w. Marco Riboni (gtr), Leopoldo Saracino (gtr), Andrea Pecola (vn), Anna Maria Giaquinta (cl), Andrea Bellato (vc)—Qt in A for Vn, Cl & 2 Gtrs, Op. 8; Duet No. 1 in A for Vn & Gtr; Trio in D for Fl, Vn & Gtr, Op. 13; Duet No. 2 in A for Vn & Gtr; Sxt in A for Fl, Cl, Vn, 2 Gtrs & Vc, Op. 9 Stradivarius ▲ STV 33385 [DDD]

Vardeli, Konstantin (vn)—see ORCHESTRAS & ENSEMBLES Georgian State String Quartet

Vardi, Arie (pno)
Children's Corner PWK Classics ▲ PWK 1132 [DDD]
Mozart, W.A.:Con 6 Pno, w. A. Vardi (cnd), Israel CO PWK Classics ▲ PWK 1144 [AAD]
Mozart, W.A.:Con 21 Pno, w. A. Vardi (cnd), Israel CO PWK Classics ▲ PWK 1144 [AAD]

Vardi, Emmanuel (va)
Bliss, A.:Son Va, w. K. Sturrock (pno) Chandos ▲ CHAN 8770 [DDD]
Brahms, J.:Sons Cl (comp), w. C. Carey (pno) Finnadar ■ 90519-4

Varga, István (cl)
Truscott, H.:Son 1 Cl, w. Melinda Lugossy (pno) *(rec Alpha-Line Studio, Festetich Castle, Budapest, 1994)* Marco Polo ▲ 8.223727 [DDD]

Varga, Jason (perc)
Snyder, R.:Enneagram Studies, w. Eric Ginsberg (cl), Stephen Krahn (pno), Chris Casart (perc), Rick Schaefer (perc), Kelly Scheef (perc), Scott Zimmerman (perc) Coronet ▲ COR 400-9

Varga, Laszlo (vc)—see also ORCHESTRAS & ENSEMBLES Borodin Trio
Haydn, J.:Life & Music of, w. A. Dorati (cnd), Bamberg SO—narration with selected excerpts from Syms. Nos. 11, 45, 82, 94, 96, 100, 101 & 104; Con. for Harpsichord; Mass No. 2, "Great Organ Mass"; Son. No. 48; Con. No. 1 for Violin; Qt. No. 76/3; Baryton Divert. 107; Musical Clock; Con. for Trumpet; Philemon and Baucis; Con. No. 2 for Horns; Mass in D♭; The Creation; Austrian National Anthem; plus the complete Con. No. 2 in D for Cello & Orch., H.VIIb/2 (Op.101) Vox Music Masters ("Music Masters" series) ▲ MMD 8508 [ADD] ■ MMC 8508
Kupferman, M.:Aristo Vars, w. K. Rosenak (pno) Soundspells ▲ CD 105

Varga, Laszlo (vc) (cont.)
Kupferman, M.:Blue Son, w. K. Rosenak (pno) Soundspells ▲ CD 105
Kupferman, M.:Con Vc, Tape & Orch, w. S. Landau (cnd), Music for Westchester SO *(rec 1975)* Vox Box ("The American Composers" series) 2-▲ CDX 5158
Kupferman, M.:Dark Orpheus, w. W. Anderson (gtr) Soundspells ▲ CD 105
Kupferman, M.:Night Voices, w. K. Rosenak (pno), W. Anderson (gtr) Soundspells ▲ CD 105
Prokofiev, S.:Sym-Con Vc, w. L. de Froment (cnd), Luxembourg RSO Vox Box 3-▲ CD3X 3000 [ADD]
Saint-Saëns, C.:Allegro appassionato, w. L. de Froment (cnd), Luxembourg RSO Vox Box 2-▲ CDX 5084 [ADD]
Saint-Saëns, C.:Con 1 Vc, w. L. de Froment (cnd), Luxembourg RSO Vox Box 2-▲ CDX 5084 [ADD]
Saint-Saëns, C.:Con 2 Vc, w. S. Landau (cnd), Westphalia SO Vox Box 2-▲ CDX 5084 [ADD]
Schumann, R.:Andante & Vars Hn, w. P. Frankl (pno), A. Schiff (pno), O. Hegedüs (vc), A. Halstead (hn) Vox Box 3-▲ CD3X 3001 [ADD]
Schumann, R.:Con Vc, w. S. Landau (cnd), Westphalia SO Vox Box 2-▲ CDX 5027 [ADD]
Tchaikovsky, P.:Vars on a Rococo Theme, w. S. Köhler (cnd), Stuttgart PO Vox Box 3-▲ CD3X 3026 [ADD]
Vivaldi, A.:Cons Diverse Instrs, w. G. Vicari (mand), C. de Filippis (mand), J. Wummer (fl), R. Morris (fl), W. Vacchiano (tpt), N. Prager (tpt), E. Brenner (b ob), C. Stavrache (hp), A. Wurtzler (hp), J. Gorigliano (vn), L. Varga (vc), L. Bernstein (cnd), New York PO—in C, RV.558 *(rec Dec. 15, 1958)* Sony Classical ("Leonard Bernstein:The Royal Edition" series) ▲ SMK 47642 [ADD]

Varga, Zoltán (timp/perc)
Cornologia, w. Budapest Festival Horn Quartet, Dimitris Politis (gtr), Ferenc Gayer (db/bass gtr), János Weszely (dr), Sándor Balogh (pno) *(rec Hungaroton Classic Studio, Feb 15-16, 1996)* Hungaroton ▲ HCD 31652 [ADD/DDD]

Vargera, Josefina (vn)—see ORCHESTRAS & ENSEMBLES Delius String Quartet

Varhule, Joseph (mazda mar)
Partch, H.:Bless This Home, w. Harry Partch (voc/adapted va), Vincenzo Prockelo (ob), Danlee Mitchell (kithara/harmonic canon), J. Garvey (cnd) *(rec Univ of Illinois, 1961)* Innova 4-▲ 401

Várjon, Dénes (pno)
Beethoven, L. van:Son 12 Pno, "Funeral March" Capriccio ▲ CD 10714 [DDD]
Beethoven, L. van:Son 21 Pno, "Waldstein" Capriccio ▲ CD 10714 [DDD]
Beethoven, L. van:Son 24 Pno Capriccio ▲ CD 10714 [DDD]
Beethoven, L. van:Son 26 Pno, "Les Adieux" Capriccio ▲ CD 10714 [DDD]
Brahms, J.:Pieces Pno, Op. 118—No. 5 in F, "Romance" LaserLight ▲ 14 224
Chopin, F.:Nocturnes—in D♭, Op. 27/2 LaserLight ▲ 14 224
Liszt, F.:Via Crucis, w. I. Prunyi (pno), J. Dobra (cnd), Tomkins Vocal Ensemble [L] *(rec 2/91)* Hungaroton ▲ HCD 31424 [DDD]
Mozart, W.A.:Con 7 Pnos, w. J. Jandó (pno), M. Antal (pno), Concentus Hungaricus [arr. Mozart for 2 pianos & orch.] *(rec Jan. 7-10, 1991)* Naxos ▲ 8.550210 [DDD]
Mozart, W.A.:Con 10 Pnos, w. J. Jandó (pno), M. Antal (cnd), Concentus Hungaricus *(rec Jan. 7-10, 1991)* Naxos ▲ 8.550210 [DDD]
Schumann, R.:Albumblätter *(rec Phoenix Studio, Budapest, Jan. 17-20, 1994)* Naxos ▲ 8.550849 [DDD]
Schumann, R.:Bunte Blätter *(rec Mar. 1992)* Naxos ▲ 8.550680 [DDD]
Schumann, R.:Fant Pno *(rec Mar. 1992)* Naxos ▲ 8.550680 [DDD]
Schumann, R.:Impromptus on a Theme by Clara Wieck Pno, Op. 5 *(rec Phoenix Studio, Budapest, Jan. 17-20, 1994)* Naxos ▲ 8.550849 [DDD]
Schumann, R.:Intermezzos *(rec Phoenix Studio, Budapest, Jan. 17-20, 1994)* Naxos ▲ 8.550849 [DDD]
Schumann, R.:Romances Pno *(rec Phoenix Studio, Budapest, Jan. 17-20, 1994)* Naxos ▲ 8.550849 [DDD]

Várkonyi, (vn)
Kodály, Z.:Serenade for 2 Vns & Va, w. Tátrai (vn), G. Konrád (va) Hungaroton ▲ HCD 31046

Varsano, Daniel (pno)
Satie, E.:Pno Music (misc), w. D. Varsano (pno) P. Entremont (pno) Sony Classical ("Essential Classics" series) ▲ SBK 48283 [ADD] ■ SBT 48283

Varshavsky, Mark (vc)
A Century of Italian Music from Scarlatti to Paganini, w. Christine Lacoste (vc) Ducale ▲ DUC 19 [DDD]

Varsi, Dinorah (pno)
Brahms, J.:Pno Music (misc), w. Stephen Bishop Kovacevich (pno), Adam Harasiewicz (pno)—Opp. 79, 116, 117, 118 & 119; Vars. on themes by Handel, Op. 24 & Paganini, Op. 35 Philips ("Duo" series) 2-▲ 442589-2
Schumann, R.:Son 2 Pno Philips ("Solo" series) ▲ 442653-2

Vartolo, Sergio (hpd)
Frescobaldi, G.:Capricci Kbd Tactus 2-▲ TC 580691
Frescobaldi, G.:Fiori musicali [1657 Fedrigotti organ at St. Francesca Romana in Ferrara]—the 3 organ masses; some sels. preceded by versions sung by chorus Tactus 2-▲ TC 580690
Luzzaschi, L.:Madrigali, w. H. Alfonso (sop), C. Miatello (sop), M. Pennichi (sop) Musique d'Abord ▲ HMA 1001136

Vartolo, Sergio (hpd/org)
Frescobaldi, G.:Toccate e partite d'intavolatura—Book 2 Tactus 3-▲ TC 580681 [DDD]

Vartolo, Sergio (org)
Cavazzoni, G.:Org Music [from Libro Secondo]—3 Organ Masses (Missa Apostolorum; Missa de Beata Vergine; Missa Dominicalis) Tactus 2-▲ TC 510390
Perti, G.A.:Liturgy for Good Friday, w. Patrizia Vaccari (sop), Maura Pederzoli (sop), Cristina Calzolari (sop), Alida Oliva (sop), Claudia Bugli (sop), Lucia Bagnoli (alt), Cinzia Meneghel (alt), Renzo Bez (alt), Alessandro Carmignani (alt), Michel van Goethem (alt), Mauro Collina (ten), Vincenzo Di Donato (ten), Paolo Fanciullacci (ten), Giovanni Caccamo (ten), Paolo Da Col (ten), Sergio Foresti (bass), Marco Scavazza (bass), Luca Ferracin (bass), Paride Montanari (bass), Liuwe Tamminga (org), S. Vartolo (cnd), Bologna San Petronio Capella Musicale Orch—Omnes amici mei; De lamentatione Jeremiae Prophetae:Heth. Cogitavit; Velum templi; Vinea mea; De lamentatione Jeremiae Prophetae:Lamed. Matribus suis; Tamquam ad latronem; Tenebrae factae sunt; Animam meam; Tradiderunt me; Jesum tradidit; De lamentatione Jeremiae Prophetae:Aleph. Ego vir; Caligaverunt *(rec St. Petronio Basilica, Bologna, Mar 28-31, 1995)* Naxos ▲ 8.553321 [DDD]
Preludes a la fugue K617 ▲ 7039
Zipoli, D.:Son d'intavolatura Org Tactus ▲ TC 682602

Varty, Alex (gtr)
Oswald, J.:Parade, w. John Oswald (kbd/a sax/elec), Paul Plimley (kbd), Cora Risdall (baby) ReR ▲ CMCD [DDD]

Vas, Meg Bachman (pno)—see ORCHESTRAS & ENSEMBLES New York Camerata

Vásárhelyi, Georg (pno)
Brahms, J.:Hungarian Dances Pno 4-Hands, w. E. Telmányi (vn)—No. 1 in g [arr. for violin & piano] *(rec Berlin April 1939)* Danacord ▲ DACOCD 343 (m) [AAD]
Brahms, J.:Scherzo Vn, w. E. Telmányi (vn) *(rec April 1939, Berlin)* Danacord ▲ DACOCD 343 (m) [AAD]
Brahms, J.:Son 1 Vn, w. E. Telmányi (vn) *(rec Berlin, April 1939)* Danacord ▲ DACOCD 343 (m) [AAD]
Brahms, J.:Son 2 Vn, w. E. Telmányi (vn) *(rec Berlin, April 1939)* Danacord ▲ DACOCD 343 (m) [AAD]

Vásáry, Tamás (pno)
Chopin, F.:Con 1 Pno, w. J. Semkow (cnd), Berlin PO Deutsche Grammophon ("Resonance" series) ▲ 429515-2 [ADD]
Chopin, F.:Con 1 Pno, w. T. Vásáry (cnd), Northern Sinfonia of England ASV ("Quicksilva" series) ▲ ASQ 6141 [DDD]
Chopin, F.:Con 2 Pno, w. T. Vásáry (cnd), Northern Sinfonia of England ASV ("Quicksilva" series) ▲ ASQ 6141 [DDD]
Chopin, F.:Con 2 Pno, w. J. Kulka (cnd), Berlin PO Deutsche Grammophon ("Resonance" series) ▲ 429515-2 [ADD]

Vásáry, Tamás (pno) (cont.)
Chopin, F.:Con 2 Pno, w. T. Vásáry (cnd), Northern Sinfonia of England
ASV Quicksilva ▲ QS 6003 [ADD]
Chopin, F.:Nocturnes—15 nocturnes
Deutsche Grammophon ("Resonance" series) ▲ 429154-2 [ADD] ■ 429154-4
Debussy, C.:L'Isle joyeuse Deutsche Grammophon ("Resonance" series) ▲ 429517-2 [ADD]
Debussy, C.:Masques Deutsche Grammophon ("Resonance" series) ▲ 429517-2
Debussy, C.:La Plus que lente Deutsche Grammophon ("Resonance" series) ▲ 429517-2 [ADD]
Debussy, C.:Suite bergamasque Deutsche Grammophon ("Resonance" series) ▲ 429517-2 [ADD]
Honegger, A.:Concertino Pno & Orch, w. T. Vásáry (cnd), Bournemouth Sinfonietta
Chandos ▲ CHAN 8993 [DDD]
Mozart, W.A.:Con 26 Pno, w. T. Vásáry (cnd), Berlin PO Deutsche Grammophon ▲ 429810-2 [ADD]
Mozart, W.A.:Fant Mechanical Org, w. P. Frankl (pno) [arr. for piano duet] ASV ▲ ASV 799 [DDD]
Mozart, W.A.:Fugue Pno, K.401, w. P. Frankl (pno) [duet version] ASV ▲ ASV 799 [DDD]
Mozart, W.A.:Pno Music 4-Hands, w. P. Frankl (pno)—Sons., K.357, 358 & 521; & 2 shorter works
ASV ▲ ASV 792
Mozart, W.A.:Son Pno 4-Hands, K.19d, w. P. Frankl (pno) ASV ▲ ASV 799 [DDD]
Mozart, W.A.:Son Pno 4-Hands, K.381, w. P. Frankl (pno) ASV ▲ ASV 799 [DDD]
Mozart, W.A.:Son Pno 4-Hands, K.497, w. P. Frankl (pno) ASV ▲ ASV 799 [DDD]
Rachmaninoff, S.:Con 1 Pno, w. Y. Ahronovitch (cnd), London SO
Deutsche Grammophon ■ 415922-2
Rachmaninoff, S.:Con 2 Pno, w. Y. Ahronovitch (cnd), London SO
Deutsche Grammophon ■ 415922-4
Schumann, R.:Con Pno, w. T. Vásáry (cnd), Northern Sinfonia of England
ASV Quicksilva ▲ QS 6003 [ADD]

Vasilaki, Y. (va)—see ORCHESTRAS & ENSEMBLES Florida String Quartet

Vasiliev, Victor (hpd)—see ORCHESTRAS & ENSEMBLES Baroque Chamber Ensemble

Vasilieva, Alla (vc)
Rubinstein, A.:Son 1 Vc, w. Mikhail Muntyan (pno) *(rec State House for Radio Broadcasting, May 1994)*
Russian Disc ▲ RD CD 10038 [AAD]
Rubinstein, A.:Son 2 Vc, w. Alexei Shchmitov (pno) *(rec State House for Radio Broadcasting, May 1994)*
Russian Disc ▲ RD CD 10038 [AAD]
Tchaikovsky, B.:Son Vc, w. B. Tchaikovsky (pno) Russian Disc ▲ RUS 11 026 [ADD]
Vainberg, M.:Sons Vc, w. M. Vainberg (pno) Russian Disc ▲ RUS 11 026 [ADD]

Vasilykov, Vadim (bells)
Schnittke, A.:Suite in the Old Style, w. Igor Boguslavsky (va), Alla Litvinenko (hpd), Viktor Grishin (vib), Viktor Gabinsky (mar) [arr. unknown] *(rec 1989)* Consonance ▲ 81-0009 [DDD]

Vasquez, Joen (vn)—see also ORCHESTRAS & ENSEMBLES Il Quattro
Kauffman, I.:D.S. al Fine, w. Brian Reagin (vn), Irvin Kauffman (gtr) Alanna ▲ ALA 5552

Vass, Katalin (vc)
Pierné, G.:Trio Pno, w. N. Szelecsenyi (pno), B. Bánfalvi (vn) Marco Polo ▲ 8.223189

Vassallo, Eduardo (vc)—see ORCHESTRAS & ENSEMBLES Tango 7

Vassilakis, Dimitri (pno)
Aubain, J.:Son Tpt, w. P. Vigneron (pno) *(rec Nov 1991)* Quantum ▲ QM 6921 [DDD]
Enescu, G.:Légende, w. P. Vigneron (tpt) *(rec Nov. 1991)* Quantum ▲ QM 6921 [DDD]
Hubeau, J.:Son for Chromatic Tpt, w. P. Vigneron (tpt) *(rec Nov. 1991)* Quantum ▲ QM 6921 [DDD]
Lantier, P.:Son Tpt, w. P. Vigneron (tpt) *(rec Nov. 1991)* Quantum ▲ QM 6921 [DDD]
Schmitt, F.:Suite Tpt, w. P. Vigneron (tpt) *(rec Nov. 1991)* Quantum ▲ QM 6921 [DDD]

Vassilev, Vasko (vn)
Brahms, J.:Scherzo Vn, w. Pamela Tan-Nicholson (pno)
Harmonia Mundi France ("Les Nouveaux Interprètes" series) ▲ HMN 911576
Brahms, J.:Sons Vn (comp), w. Pamela Tan-Nicholson (pno)
Harmonia Mundi France ("Les Nouveaux Interprètes" series) ▲ HMN 911576

Vassiliades, Christopher (pno)
Kupferman, M.:The Canticles of Ulysses—Maestoso - allegro Molto; Lento; Lento Espressivo ed Agitato; Allegretto con molto appassionato; Finale:Tempestuoso Soundspells ▲ CD 115 [DDD]
Kupferman, M.:Cirrus Soundspells ▲ CD 115 [DDD]
Kupferman, M.:Distances Soundspells ▲ CD 115 [DDD]
Kupferman, M.:Imprints—Doloroso; Rubato Soundspells ▲ CD 115 [DDD]
Kupferman, M.:Infinities Fant Soundspells ▲ CD 115 [DDD]
Kupferman, M.:Partita Soundspells ▲ CD 115 [DDD]
Kupferman, M.:Pno Music—2 Imprints; Infinities Fant; Partita; Tiananmen Suite; Cirrus; Distances; Pico [...among the smallest particles]; The Canticles of Ulysses Soundspells ▲ CD 115 [DDD]
Kupferman, M.:Pico (...among the smallest particles) Soundspells ▲ CD 115 [DDD]
Kupferman, M.:Tiananmen Suite—Slow and Austere; Real Fast; Broadly; Lyrically; Agitated - Big!
Soundspells ▲ CD 115 [DDD]

Vassiliev, Alexei (vc)
Ustvolskaya, G.:Grand Duet Vc, w. Oleg Malov (pno) *(rec St. Petersburg Radio House, Oct. & Nov. 1994)*
Megadisc ▲ 7863

Vassiliev, Vasko (vn)
Delibes, L.:Coppélia (sels), w. A. Kolodenko (va), K. Nagano (cnd), Lyon Opera Orch
Erato 2-▲ 91730-2

Vaucher, J.-F. (org)
Dupré, M.:Esquisses, Op. 41 [at the organ of Saint-François, Lausanne] Gallo ▲ CD 743 [AAD]
Dupré, M.:Evocation [at the organ of Saint-François, Lausanne] Gallo ▲ CD 743 [AAD]
Dupré, M.:Lamento [at the organ of Saint-François, Lausanne] Gallo ▲ CD 743 [AAD]
Dupré, M.:Les vêpres de la Vierge [at the organ of Saint-François, Lausanne] Gallo ▲ CD 743 [AAD]
Duruflé, M.:Suite Org [at the organ of Saint-François, Lausanne] Gallo ▲ CD 743 [AAD]
Reger, M.:Chorale Fants, Op. 52 [organ of Saint-François, Lausanne]—No. 2, "Wachet auf, ruft uns die Stimme" Gallo ▲ CD 743 [AAD]

Vaucher-Clerc, Germaine (hpd)
Martin, F.:Petite sym concertante, w. E. Hunziker (hp), D. Rosslaud (pno), F. Martin (cnd), Swiss-Italian Orch *(rec Sept. 3, 1970)* Jecklin-Disco ▲ JD 645-2 [ADD]

Vaughan, Denis (hpd)—see ORCHESTRAS & ENSEMBLES London Chamber Players

Vaughn, B. K. (pno)
Harrison, C.:Songs from a Child's Garden, w. B. Ford (sop) [E] CRS ▲ 9255

Vavreková, Katarina (hp)
Respighi, O.:Liriche su parole di poeti armeni, w. Denisa Šlepkovská (mez), Vladimír Havran (fl), Michal Sintál (ob), Gabriel Koncer (cl), Ivan Viskup (b cl), Ivan Paulicka (bn), Frantisek Kovács (trbn), M. Adriano (cnd) [arr. for chamber group by Adriano] *(rec Slovak Radio Concert Hall, Bratislava, Jan. 4-9, Feb. 19 & June)* Marco Polo ▲ 8.223595 [DDD]

Vázonyi, Balint (pno)
Liszt, F.:Hungarian Rhaps—Nos. 2, 3, 5, 6, 11, 13, 15, 17
Allegretto ▲ ACD 8029 [ADD] ■ ACS 8029
13 Piano Reveries, w. Vazsonyi, Balint (pno) Allegretto ▲ ACD 8038 [ADD] ■ ACS 8038

Veazey, Charles (ob)
Tull, F.:Concertino Ob, w. E. Corporon (cnd), North Texas College of Music Chamber Players *(rec Univ. of North Texas Concert Hall, May 8-10, 1995)* Klavier ▲ KCD 11071 [DDD]

Vecchi, Guido (vc)
Jacobi, F.:Psalms, w. W. Strickland (cnd), Oslo PO CRI ("American Masters" series) ▲ CD 703 [ADD]

Vecchioni, Luigi (vn)—see ORCHESTRAS & ENSEMBLES Manfred String Quartet

Vecsey, Franz von (vn)
Beethoven, L. van:Son 3 Vn, w. G. Agosti (pno) *(rec early 1930s)* Pearl ▲ PEA 9498 (m) [AAD]
The Electric Recordings, w. Vecsey, Franz von (vn) Pearl ▲ PEA 9498 (m) [AAD]

Večtomov, Saša (vc)
Schubert, Franz:Qnt Strs, D.956, w. Josef Suk (vn), Jirí Baxa (vn), Ladislav Černý (va), Josef Šimandl (vc) *(rec live, 1971)* Praga ▲ PR 250055

Vedernikova, Olga (vn)
Tchaikovsky, P.:Ballet Music, w. Alexander Dardyikin (vc), Anna Verkholanzeva (hp), A. Vedernikov (cnd), Russian Philharmonia—ballet suites from Swan Lake; Sleeping Beauty; Nutcracker *(rec Moscow Conservatory Large Hall, Feb 1996)* Arts ▲ 47372-2 [DDD]

Veena, Mukha (syn)
Celli, J.:Improvisations, w. J. Celli (reeds, E hn [without reeds], Mukha Veena, Yamaha WX-7 midi breath controller with TX-802), J. H. Kim (komungo, changgo & electric komungo)—Types of Asia for Changgo & English Horn (without reeds); Dasreng for solo Komungo; Mukhan
O.O. Discs ▲ OO 2 [DDD]

Vees, Jack (elec bass/elec)
Vees, J.:SPNFL CRI ("Emergency Music" series) ▲ CD 730 [DDD]
Vees, J.:Surf Music Again CRI ("Emergency Music" series) ▲ CD 730 [DDD]

Vees, Jack (elec gtr/dr machine)
Vees, J.:Tattooed Barbie, w. Libby Van Cleve (elec ob)
CRI ("Emergency Music" series) ▲ CD 730 [DDD]

Vees, Jack (pno/elec)
Vees, J.:Pno Trio CRI ("Emergency Music" series) ▲ CD 730 [DDD]

Vega, Ana (pno)
Cruz, Z. de la:Pulsares RNE/Spanish National Radio ▲ M3/12 [ADD]

Vega, Jorge de la (fl)
Franzetti, C.:Suite Fl, w. Carlos Franzetti (pno), C. Franzetti (cnd), Modus Chamber Ensemble *(rec Hip Pocket Studios, New York)* Premier ▲ PRCD 1044 [DDD]

Veggetti, Stefano (vc)—see also ORCHESTRAS & ENSEMBLES L'Astrée Ensemble
Lanzetti, S.:Sons Vc, w. C. Ronco (vc), D. Petech (hpd), J. Held (bc)—Nos. 5-9, 11 & 12 *(rec 5/91)*
Nuova Era ("Ancient Music" series) ▲ 7048 [DDD]

Végh, Sándor (vn)
Beethoven, L. van:Trio 6 Pno, "Archduke", w. Mieczyslaw Horzowsky (pno), Pablo Casals (vc) *(rec 1956)*
Historical Performers ▲ HPS 31
Reger, M.:Serenades Fl Vn Va, w. Peter-Lukas Graf (fl), Rainer Moog (va) *(rec Kirche Reutigen, Dec 1980)* Claves ▲ CD 508104 [ADD]
Schumann, R.:Trio 3 Pno, w. P. Casals (vc), R. Serkin (pno) *(rec live July 11, 1956)*
Music & Arts 4-▲ CD 688 (m) [AAD]

Vehanen, Kosti (pno)
Sibelius, J.:Songs, w. M. Anderson (cta)—Come away, death; Säv, säv susa, Op. 36/4; Flickan kom ifran sin, Op. 37/5; Aus banger Brust, Op. 50/4; Langsamt som Kvällasskyn, Op. 61/1 [E,G,Sw] *(rec 1936-37)* Pearl ▲ PEA 9405 (m) [AAD]

Veihelmann, Helmut (vc)
Stamitz, C.:Qts Cl, w. E. Brunner (cl), G. Schneider (vn), A. Baader (va)
Koch Schwann ▲ CD 310003 [DDD]

Veil, Bernhard (cl)—see ORCHESTRAS & ENSEMBLES Chalumeau Trio

Veilhan, Jean-Claude (cl)
Molter, J.M.:Cons Cl, w. P. Couvert (cnd), St. Cecilia Academy Orch Rome
Pierre Verany ▲ PV 792011 [DDD]
Vivaldi, A.:Cons Diverse Instrs, w. P. Couvert (cnd), St. Cecilia Academy Orch Rome—in C, R.555; in C, R.556; in C, R.558; in C, R.560; in g, R.577; in B♭, R. 579; in C, R. 599 *(rec Paris, Jan 1996)*
K617 ▲ 7062 [DDD]

Veilhan, Jean-Claude (cl/bas hn)—see ORCHESTRAS & ENSEMBLES Trio di Bassetto

Veillon, M. (hn)
Balissat, J.:Vars (7), w. P. Genet, F. Gottraux (vn), N. Pache (va), M. Jaermann (vc), R. Birnstigl (db), F. Rapin (cl), F. Schmocker (bn), J. Balissat (cnd) Grammont ▲ CTSP 17-2 [ADD]

Veillon, Michel (db)
Gounod, C.:Requiem, w. C. Fleischmann (hp), F. Margot (org), A. Charlet (cnd), Romande Chamber Choir *(rec 1992 & 1993)* Claves ▲ CD 9326 [DDD]

Veis, Daniel (vc)—see also ORCHESTRAS & ENSEMBLES Antonín Dvořák Trio
Dvořák, A.:Con Vc, w. L. Pešek (cnd), Prague RSO Panton ▲ PAN 811211
Hanuš, J.:Son-Rhap, w. Helena Veisová (pno) Panton ▲ PAN 811014
Kabeláč, M.:Son Vc, w. Helena Veisová (pno) Panton ▲ PAN 811014

Veisová, Helena (pno)
Hanuš, J.:Son-Rhap, w. Daniel Veis (vc) Panton ▲ PAN 811014
Kabeláč, M.:Son Vc, w. Daniel Veis (vc) Panton ▲ PAN 811014

Veit, Ingo (vih/lt/gtr)—see ORCHESTRAS & ENSEMBLES Duo Maréll

Veits, Melitta (org)
Haydn, J.:Mass 14, "Harmoniemesse", w. Barbara Martig-Tüller (sop), Ria Bollen (alt), Adalbert Kraus (ten), Kurt Widmer (bass), D. Hellmann (cnd), Southwest German RSO Baden-Baden
Calig ▲ CAL 50490

Velden, Mieneke van der (vl)—see also ORCHESTRAS & ENSEMBLES Royal Consort
Biber, H. von:Harmonia artificiosa-ariosa, w. M. Lindal (vn), B. Sargent (vn), E. Siebens (db), M. Spányi (hpd)—Partitas 3 & 5 *(rec Feb. 4-6, 1993)* BIS ▲ CD 608 [DDD]
Biber, H. von:Mystery (or Rosary) Sons, w. M. Lindal (vn), E. Siebens (db), M. Spányi (hpd)—No. 10 *(rec Feb. 4-6, 1993)* BIS ▲ CD 608 [DDD]

Veleminský, Marek (gtr)—see ORCHESTRAS & ENSEMBLES Prague Guitar Quartet

Velez, Glen (perc)
Dalglish, M.:Hymnody of Earth, w. M. Dalglish (hammer dulcimer/voc), J. Litton (cnd), American Boychoir MusicMasters ▲ 7058-2 [DDD] ■ 01612-67058-4 (D)
Istanpitta II, w. F. Renz (cnd), New York Early Music Ensemble
Lyrichord ("Early Music" series) ▲ LEMS 8022

Veltman, N. (vc)
Linde, B.:Sinf, Op. 23, w. J. Hirokami (cnd), Norrköping SO *(rec Mar. 26, 1993)*
BIS ▲ CD 621 [DDD]

Vena, Claudio (va/acc)—see ORCHESTRAS & ENSEMBLES Gelato Quartet

Venanzi, Henri (pno)
Art Song Heritage of the Americas, w. Kennedy, Frederick (ten) CRS Master ▲ CRS 9662
Spirituals, w. Arroyo, Martina (sop) Centaur ▲ CRC 2060 [DDD]

Vendreys, Basil (va)
Encore, w. [cnd:Duain Wolfe], Colorado Children's Chorale, Rick Chinski (gtr), Robert Davine (acc), Laurie Kahler (pno), Samuel Lancaster (pno), Barry Oliver (pno), Marylin Preston (fl), Karen Yonovitz (fl), Peter Cooper (ob), Andy Stevens (cl), Lionel Young (vn), Basil Vendreys (va), Wayne Templeman (vc), Charle *(rec Denver Center Media)* Colorado Children's Chorale ▲ 001

Vendryes, Basil (va)—see ORCHESTRAS & ENSEMBLES Aurora String Quartet

Vengerov, Maxim (vn)
Bach, J.S.:Chaconne Canyon Classics ▲ 3655
Beethoven, L. van:Son 7 Vn, w. I. Vinogradova (pno) Canyon Classics ▲ 3655
Beethoven, L. van:Son 9 Vn, "Kreutzer", w. A. Markovich (pno) Teldec ▲ 9031-74001-2 ZK
Brahms, J.:Son 2 Vn, w. A. Markovich (pno) Teldec ▲ 9031-74001-2 ZK
Bruch, M.:Con 1 Vn, w. K. Masur (cnd), Leipzig Gewandhaus Orch Teldec ▲ 90875-2
Maxim Vengerov, w. Vengerov, Maxim (vn), Irina Vinogradova (pno) *(rec 1989)*
Biddulph ▲ LAW 001 [DDD]
Mendelssohn, F.:Con in e Vn & Orch, Op. 64, w. K. Masur (cnd), Leipzig Gewandhaus Orch
Teldec ▲ 90875-2
Paganini, N.:Con 1 Vn, w. Z. Mehta (cnd), Israel PO Teldec ▲ 9031-73266-2 ZK
Prokofiev, S.:Con 1 Vn, w. M. Rostropovich (cnd), London SO *(rec London, May 1994)*
Teldec ▲ 92256-2 [DDD]
Saint-Saëns, C.:Havanaise Vn, w. Z. Mehta (cnd), Israel PO Teldec ▲ 9031-73266-2 ZK
Saint-Saëns, C.:Introduction & Rondo capriccioso, w. Z. Mehta (cnd), Israel PO
Teldec ▲ 9031-73266-2 ZK
Schubert, Franz:Fant Vn, D.934, w. I. Vinogradova (pno) Canyon Classics ▲ 3655
Schubert, Franz:Fant Vn, D.934, w. I. Vinogradova (pno) Biddulph ▲ LAW 001 [DDD]

898 ▲ = CD ♦ = Enhanced CD Δ = MD ■ = Cassette Tape □ = DCC

Vengerov, Maxim (vn) (cont.)
Shostakovich, D.:Con 1 Vn, w. M. Rostropovich (cnd), London SO *(rec London, May 1994)* Teldec ▲ 92256-2 [DDD]
Virtuoso Vengerov, w. Vengerov, Maxim (vn) Teldec ▲ 77351-2
Waxman, F.:Carmen Fant, w. I. Vinogradova (pno) Biddulph ▲ LAW 001 [DDD]
Waxman, F.:Carmen Fant, w. I. Vinogradova (pno) Canyon Classics ▲ 3655
Waxman, F.:Carmen Fant, w. Z. Mehta (cnd), Israel PO Teldec ▲ 9031-73266-2 ZK
Venglevski, Stanislav (bayan)
Vivaldi, A.:Cons Vn, Op. 8/1-4, "The Four Seasons", w. Jerome Franke (vn), Karine Garibova (vn), Pasquale Laurino (vn), Olga Miliaeva (va), Roza Borisova (vc), Mika Hennessy (db), Melanie Panush (ham dlc), Stanislav Venglevski (bayan), Mike Kashou (arabic tabla), Daryl Stuermer (gtr), Ed Paloucek (celtic fid), Gary Bottoni (highland pipe), Dubuffet String Quartet *(rec July-Sept 1995)* EarthBeat! ▲ 35270-2 [DDD]
Venzago, Mario (pno)
Janácek, L.:The Diary of One Who Disappeared, w. Clara Wirz (alt), Peter Keller (ten), Mario Venzago (cnd), Lucerne Singers Accord ▲ ACD 220312 [DDD]
Schumann, R.:Andante & Vars Hn, w. Robert Majek (pno), Käthi Gohl (vc), Rama Jucker (vc), Francesco Raselli (hn) Accord ▲ ACD 201572 [AAD]
Schumann, R.:Stücke im Volkston, w. Rama Jucker (vc) Accord ▲ ACD 201572 [AAD]
Verbit, Marthanne (pno)
Antheil, G.:Airplane Son Albany ▲ TROY 146 [DDD]
Antheil, G.:La femme 100 têtes—sels Albany ▲ TROY 146 [DDD]
Antheil, G.:Pno Music—Little Shimmy; Tango from the opera "Transatlantic"; Son.; Valentine Waltzes Albany ▲ TROY 146 [DDD]
Antheil, G.:Son 4 Pno Albany ▲ TROY 146 [DDD]
Antheil, G.:Son Sauvage Albany ▲ TROY 146 [DDD]
Antheil, G.:Pno Music—Airplane Son.; Son. Sauvage; La Femme 100 Têtes after Max Ernst; Little Shimmy; Tango from the opera "Transatlantic"; Son.; Valentine Waltzes Albany ▲ TROY 146 [DDD]
Ornstein, L.:Arabesques Pno Albany ▲ TROY 070 [ADD]
Ornstein, L.:4th Son Pno Albany ▲ TROY 070 [ADD]
Scott, C.:Pno Music—Sonata No.1, Op. 66 (1909); Danse Negre (1908); Lotusland (1905) Albany ▲ TROY 070
Valentines, w. Verbit, Marthanne (pno) Albany ▲ TROY 071 [ADD]
Verbruggen, Marion (rcr)
Bach, J.S.:Sons Fl, BWV 1030-35, w. M. Meyerson (hpd)—BWV 1031 [trans. Verbruggen] Harmonia Mundi USA ▲ HMU 907119
Bach, J.S.:Suites Vc, BWV 1007-1012—Nos. 1-3 *(rec Oct 1991)* Harmonia Mundi USA ▲ HMU 907071
Bach, J.S.:Trio Sons Org, BWV 525-530, w. M. Meyerson (hpd)—BWV 525, 527, 529 & 530 [trans. Verbruggen] Harmonia Mundi USA ▲ HMU 907119
Baroque Chamber Music with Recorder, w. Verbruggen, Marion (rcr), Arion Ensemble Titanic ▲ Ti 177 [DDD]
Eyck, J. van:Der fluyten lust-hof Harmonia Mundi ▲ HMU 907170
The Golden Dream:17th Century Music from the Low Countries, w. M. Springfels (cnd), Newberry Consort, Paul Odette (lt) *(rec Troy Savings Bank Music Hall, Nov 1-3. 1993)* Harmonia Mundi France ▲ HMU 907123
Telemann, G.P.:Con in F Rcr, B Vl, w. S. Cunningham (vl), M. Huggett (cnd), Orch of the Age of Enlightenment *(rec Nov. 2-4, 1992)* Harmonia Mundi USA ▲ HMU 907093
Telemann, G.P.:Con in a for Rcr, Vl, w. S. Cunningham (vl), M. Huggett (cnd), Orch of the Age of Enlightenment *(rec Nov. 2-4, 1992)* Harmonia Mundi USA ▲ HMU 907093
Telemann, G.P.:Suite Rcr, w. M. Huggett (cnd), Orch of the Age of Enlightenment *(rec Nov. 2-4, 1992)* Harmonia Mundi USA ▲ HMU 907093
Vivaldi, A.:Cons Diverse Instrs, w. P. Goodwin (ob), J. Holloway (vn), D. Godburn (bn), J. Toll (hpd), S. Comberti (vc)—7 Concerti—in D, RV.84; in a, RV.86; in D, RV.94; in D, "Las Pastorella," RV.95; in F, RV.99; in g, RV.103; in g, RV.105 Harmonia Mundi USA ▲ HMU 907046
Vivaldi, A.:Con Fl Bn, w. D. Godburn (bn), N. McGegan (cnd), Philharmonia Baroque Orch Harmonia Mundi USA ▲ HMU 907040
Vivaldi, A.:Cons Rcr, w. N. McGegan (cnd), Philharmonia Baroque Orch—(6) in C, RV.443 & in C, RV.444 (sopranino recorder); in F, RV.433, "La Tempesta di Mare"; in F, RV.434; in G, RV.435; in c, RV.441 (alto recorder) Harmonia Mundi USA ▲ HMU 907040
Vivaldi, A.:Cons Vn, Op. 8/1-4, "The Four Seasons", w. Flanders Recorder Quartet [arr for rcrs] Harmonia Mundi France ▲ HMU 907153
Verbruggen, Marion (rcr/fl)
Handel, G.F.:Sons Rcr, w. Ton Koopman (hpd/chest org), Jaap ter Linden (vc)—No. 1 in B♭; No. 2 in g, Op. 1/2; No. 4 in a, Op. 1/4; No. 7 in C, Op. 1/7; No. 9 in d, Op. 1/9; No. 11 in F, Op. 1/11 *(rec Waalse Kerk, Amsterdam, Apr 27-29, 1994)* Harmonia Mundi France ▲ HMU 907151
Vercauteren, Annemarie (va)
Crumb, G.:Black Angels (Images I), w. Filip Suys (vn), Marleen Ydiers (vn), Arne Deforce (vc), Johan Vandermaelen (elec) *(rec Steurbaut Sound Recording Ctr)* René Gailly ▲ CD87 118 [DDD]
Mozetich, M.:Qt Strs, w. Filip Suys (vn), Marleen Ydiers (vn), Arne Deforce (vc) *(rec Steurbaut Sound Recording Ctr)* René Gailly ▲ CD87 118 [DDD]
Vercruysse, R. (instr)—see ORCHESTRAS & ENSEMBLES Quintessens
Verdehr, Walter (vn)—see ORCHESTRAS & ENSEMBLES Verdehr Trio
Verdery, Benjamin (gtr)
Bach, J.S.:Sons & Partitas Vn, BWV 1001-1006—Son No. 2 in a, BWV 1003 [arr Verdery for gtr] Doremi ▲ DHR 2
Bach, J.S.:Suites Vc, BWV 1007-1012—No. 6 in D [arr Verdery for gtr] Doremi ▲ DHR 2
Verdin, Joris (harm)
Franck, C.:Harm Music (misc), w. J. van Immerseel (pno)—12 pieces for solo harmonium, 1 for solo piano, 2 for harmonium & piano *(rec 2/90)* Ricercar ▲ RIC 75057 [DDD]
Lefébure-Wély, L.J.A.:Suites Harmonicorde *(rec Chapelle de Monty-Charneux, May 1995)* Ricercar ▲ RIC 163147
Verdin, Joris (org)
Franck, C.:Org Music (misc)—Pièces in E♭, D♭ & A; Andantino in A♭; Offertoires in f, g, f# & E♭; Préludes pour l'Ave maris stella; Offertoire pour la messe de minuit; Élévation in A; Pastorale in E, Op. 19 Arion ▲ ARN 68276 [DDD]
Verebes, Robert (va)
Bach, J.S.:Chromatic Fant & Fugue [trans Z. Kodaly for va] *(rec Bourcheville, Quebec)* SNE ▲ 564
Bach, J.S.:Sons Vl, BWV 1027-1029, w. Mireille Lagacé (hpd) *(rec Bourcheville, Quebec)* SNE ▲ 564
Barnes, M.:Ballade SNE ▲ 562
Bloch, E.:Meditation & Processional, w. Suzanne Blondin (pno) SNE ▲ 612
Bloch, E.:Suite hébraïque, w. Suzanne Blondin (pno) SNE ▲ 612
Bruch, M.:Romanze Va, w. Suzanne Blondin (pno) SNE ▲ 612
Coulthard, J.:Son Rhap, w. Dale Bartlett (pno) *(rec Boucherville, Quebec)* SNE ▲ 550
Dittersdorf, K.D. von:Son Va, w. Mireille Lagacé (pno) *(rec Montreal)* SNE ▲ 569
Enescu, G.:Concertpiece Va, w. Suzanne Blondin (pno) SNE ▲ 612
Hindemith, P.:Son Va, Op 11/5 SNE 2-▲ 546/7
Hindemith, P.:Son Va, Op. 25/1 SNE ▲ 562
Hindemith, P.:Son Va, Op. 25/1 SNE 2-▲ 546/7
Hindemith, P.:Son in C Va & Pno, w. Dale Bartlett (pno) SNE 2-▲ 546/7
Hindemith, P.:Son Va & Pno, Op. 11/4, w. Dale Bartlett (pno) SNE 2-▲ 546/7
Hindemith, P.:Son Va & Pno, Op. 25/4, w. Dale Bartlett (pno) SNE 2-▲ 546/7
Hummel, J.N.:Son Va, w. Mireille Lagacé (pno) *(rec Montreal)* SNE ▲ 569
Kodály, Z.:Adagio, w. Suzanne Blondin (pno) SNE ▲ 612
Martinů, B.:Son 1 Va, w. Dale Bartlett (pno) *(rec Boucherville, Quebec)* SNE ▲ 550
Mendelssohn, F.:Son Va, w. Dale Bartlett (pno) *(rec Boucherville, Quebec)* SNE ▲ 550
Penderecki, K.:Cadenza SNE ▲ 562
Reger, M.:Suites Va—No. 1 SNE ▲ 562
Schubert, Franz:Son Arpeggione, w. Suzanne Blondin (pno) *(rec Montreal)* SNE ▲ 580

Verebes, Robert (va) (cont.)
Schumann, R.:Märchenbilder, w. Suzanne Blondin (pno) *(rec Montreal)* SNE ▲ 580
Stamitz, C.:Son Va, w. Mireille Lagacé (pno) *(rec Montreal)* SNE ▲ 569
Stravinsky, I.:Elégie SNE ▲ 562
Vanhal, J.B.:Son Va, w. Mireille Lagacé (pno) *(rec Montreal)* SNE ▲ 569
Vaughan Williams, R.:Romance Va, w. Suzanne Blondin (pno) SNE ▲ 612
Vieuxtemps, H.:Capriccio SNE ▲ 562
Vieuxtemps, H.:Elégie, w. Suzanne Blondin (pno) SNE ▲ 612
Vieuxtemps, H.:Son Va, w. Suzanne Blondin (pno) *(rec Montreal)* SNE ▲ 580
Wieniawski, H.:Rêverie, w. Suzanne Blondin (pno) SNE ▲ 612
Vered, Ilana (pno)
Largo I, w. Vladimir Ashkenazy (pno), Alfred Brendel (pno), Alicia de Larrocha (pno), Julius Katchen (pno), András Schiff (pno), et al. Celestial Harmonies ▲ 35509-2 2-■ 35509-4
Largo II, w. Vladimir Ashkenazy (pno), Alfred Brendel (pno), Alicia de Larrocha (pno), Julius Katchen (pno), András Schiff (pno), et al. Celestial Harmonies ▲ 19504-2 ■ 19504-4
Penderecki, K.:Miniatures Vn Pno, w. Gabriel Banat (vn) *(rec Feb 1972)* Vox Box 2-▲ CDX 5142
25 Virtuoso Etudes, w. Vered, Ilana (pno) *(rec Music Hall, Tarrytown, NY, Feb. 1992)* Connoisseur Society ▲ CD 4197
Veress, Claudio (va)
Mozart, W.A.:Trio Cl, K.498, w. A. Morf (cl), I. von Alpenheim (pno) BIS 2-▲ CD 513/14 [DDD]
Schubert, Franz:Adagio & Rondo concertante Vn, w. Arion Trio BIS 4-▲ CD 521/24 [DDD]
Schubert, Franz:Chamber Music Pno, w. A. Cincera (db), Arion Trio BIS 4-▲ CD 521/24 [DDD]
Schubert, Franz:Qnt Pno, D.667, w. A. Cincera (db), Arion Trio BIS 4-▲ CD 521/24 [DDD]
Vergnory-Mion, Claire (cl)
Juon, P.:Chamber Music, w. Jean-François Benatar (va), Pierre Lenert (va), Philippe Nadal (vc), Hélène Calef (pno)—Trio Miniatures for Cl, Vc & Pno; Son in D for Va & Pno, Op. 15; Divert for Cl & 2 Vas, Op. 34; Trio for Cl, Vc & Pno, Op. 17 REM ▲ REM 311267 [DDD]
Verhagen, P. (pno)—see ORCHESTRAS & ENSEMBLES Kegelstaat Trio Amsterdam
Verheul, Koos (fl)
Verhey, T.:Con Fl, w. L. Vis (cnd), Residentie Orch The Hague Olympia ▲ OCD 503 [AAD]
Verhey, Emma (vn)
Beethoven, L. van:Con Vn, Op. 61, w. H. Vonk (cnd), Uttrecht SO Vivace 3-▲ E 324 [ADD/DDD]
Beethoven, L. van:Romances Vn, w. H. Vonk (cnd), Royal PO Vivace 3-▲ E 324 [ADD/DDD]
Bartók, B.:Son 2 Vn & Pno, w. Y. Egorov (pno) *(rec May 25, 1981)* Erasmus ▲ WVH 023 [ADD]
Brahms, J.:Con Vn & Vc, "Double Con", w. J. Starker (vc), A. Joó (cnd), Amsterdam PO Erasmus ▲ WVH 034 [DDD]
Brahms, J.:Son 3 Vn, w. Y. Egorov (pno) *(rec May 25, 1981)* Erasmus ▲ WVH 023 [ADD]
Diepenbrock, A.:Hymne Vn, w. H. Vonk (cnd), Residentie Orch The Hague Chandos ▲ CHAN 8821 [DDD]
Mendelssohn, F.:Con in e Vn & Orch, Op. 64, w. A. Joó (cnd), Budapest SO Sound 2-▲ E 220 [DDD]
Mendelssohn, F.:Con in e Vn & Orch, Op. 64, w. A. Joó (cnd), Budapest SO—Das Konzert, Vol. 1 Vivace 2-▲ G 107/108 [DDD/ADD]
Mendelssohn, F.:Con in e Vn & Orch, Op. 64, w. A. Joó (cnd), Budapest SO Vivace ▲ E 555 [DDD]
Mendelssohn, F.:Con in e Vn & Orch, Op. 64, w. A. Joó (cnd), Budapest SO Vivace 3-▲ E 324 [ADD/DDD]
Mendelssohn, F.:Con in e Vn & Orch, Op. 64, w. A. Joó (cnd), Budapest SO Laserlight ▲ 15 615 [DDD]
Schoeck, O.:Concerto quasi una fantasia, w. *(orch unknown)* Musiques Suisses ▲ 6117
Schubert, Franz:Qnt Pno, D.667, w. D. Dechene (pno), F. Erblich (va), J. DeCroos (vc), P. Jansen (db) Vivace ▲ E 561 [DDD]
Schubert, Franz:Qnt Pno, D.667, w. D. Dechene (pno), F. Erblich (va), J. DeCroos (vc), P. Jansen (db) Laserlight ▲ 15 522 [DDD]
Schubert, Franz:Rondo Vn, D.438, w. Colorado String Quartet Laserlight ▲ 15 522 [DDD]
Schubert, Franz:Rondo Vn, D.438, w. Colorado String Quartet Vivace ▲ E 561 [DDD]
Schubert, Franz:Son Vn, D.574, w. Y. Egorov (pno) *(rec May 25, 1981)* Erasmus ▲ WVH 023 [ADD]
Tchaikovsky, P.:Con Vn, w. A. Joó (cnd), Budapest SO Sound 2-▲ E 220 [DDD]
Tchaikovsky, P.:Con Vn, w. A. Joó (cnd), Budapest SO Vivace 3-▲ E 324 [ADD/DDD]
Tchaikovsky, P.:Con Vn, w. A. Joó (cnd), Budapest SO Vivace ▲ E 555 [DDD]
Tchaikovsky, P.:Con Vn, w. A. Joó (cnd), Budapest SO Laserlight ▲ 15 516
Tchaikovsky, P.:Con Vn, w. A. Joó (cnd), Budapest SO—Das Konzert, Vol. 2 Vivace 2-▲ G 117/118 [DDD]
Tchaikovsky, P.:Con Vn, w. A. Joó (cnd), Budapest SO Capriccio ▲ 10 921 [DDD]
Verhey, Paul (fl)
Andriessen, H.:Music of, w. Roberta Alexander (sop), Ernestine Stoop (hp), D. Porcelijn (cnd), Netherlands Radio CO—Miroir de Peine; Magna res est amor; Fiat Domine; Vars & Fugue on a Theme by Kuhnau; Vars on a Theme by Couperin; Chromatic Vars NM Classics ▲ NM 92023
Roussel, A.:Chamber Music, w. Hans Roerade (ob), Herman Jeurissen (hn), Jean-Jacques Kantorow (vn), Herre-Jan Stengenga (vc), Jet Röling (pno) Olympia ▲ OLY 458 [DDD]
Verhey, Paul (fl/pic)
Roussel, A.:Chamber Music, w. Frank van den Brink (cl), Hans Roerade (ob), Joe de Lange (bn), Herre-Jan Stegenga (vc), Jet Röling (pno), Schoenberg String Quartet—Trio for Fl, Va & Vc, Op. 40; Qt for Strs, Op. 45; Andante & Scherzo for Fl & Pno, Op. 51; Pipe for Pic & Pno; Trio for Strs, Op. 58; Music from Elpenor for Fl & Str Qt, Op. 59; Andante from an unfinished Ww Trio for Ob, Cl & Bn Olympia ▲ OLY 460 [DDD]
Verheye, Jan (db)
Berkeley, M.:For the Savage Messiah, w. Kristof van Gryspeere (pno), Dirk Lievens (vn), Kaat De Cock (va), Stefaan Craeynest (vc) *(rec Steurbaut Sound Recording Ctr)* René Gailly ▲ CD87 118 [DDD]
de Veritch, (va)
Thompson, R.:Suite Ob, w. P. Christ (ob), Atkins (cl) Crystal ▲ CD 321
Thompson, R.:Suite Ob, w. P. Christ (ob), Atkins (cl) Crystal ■ C 321
Verkholanzeva, Anna (hp)
Tchaikovsky, P.:Ballet Music, w. Olga Vedernikova (vn), Alexander Dardyikin (vc), A. Vedernikov (cnd), Russian Philharmonia—ballet suites from Swan Lake; Sleeping Beauty; Nutcracker *(rec Moscow Conservatory Large Hall, Feb 1996)* Arts ▲ 47372-2 [DDD]
Verkoeyen, Jos (vn)—see ORCHESTRAS & ENSEMBLES Gaudeamus String Quartet
Verlet, Blandine (hpd)
Bach, J.S.:Chromatic Fant & Fugue Astrée ▲ E 8565
Bach, J.S.:Fants Hpd—in a, BWV 922 Astrée ▲ E 8565
Bach, J.S.:Fant & Fugue Hpd, BWV 904 Astrée ▲ E 8565
Bach, J.S.:Goldberg Vars Astrée ▲ E 8745
Bach, J.S.:Preludes & Fugues Hpd—in a, BWV 894 Astrée ▲ E 8565
Bach, J.S.:Toccatas Hpd, BWV 910-16—in f BWV 914; in d BWV 913 Astrée ▲ E 8565
Bach, J.S.:Das wohltemperierte Klavier—Book 2 Astrée 2-▲ E 8539
Couperin, L.:Hpd Music Astrée 5-▲ E 8506
Raick, D.:Suites Hpd Koch Schwann ▲ SCH 315602 [DDD]
Verlet, Blandine (pno)
Mozart, W.A.:Sons Vn Pno (misc), w. G. Poulet (vn)—first 16 sons. Philips 2-▲ 438803-2
Vermeulen, Jan (pno)
Mozart, W.A.:Music of, w. Philip Defrancq (ten), Reginaldo Pinheiro (ten), Jan Van Der Crabben (bar), Guy Penson (org), P. Peire (cnd), Collegium Instrumentale Brugense, Capella Brugensis—Zerfliesset heut', geliebte Brüder [song]; Dir Seele des Weltalls [cant]; O heiliges Band der Freundschaft [song]; Die ihr einem Neuen Grade [Maurer-Geselienlied]; Die Maurerfreude [cant]; Maurerische Trauermusik; Die ihr der unermesslichen Weltalls Schöpfer ehrt [Kleine deutsche Kantate]; Laut verkünde unsre Freude [Eine kleine Freimaurerkantate]; Lasst uns mit geschlugnen Händen [hymn]; Ihr unsre neuen Leiter [song] *(rec Studio Steurbaut, Gent, Dec 1992)* René Gailly ▲ 92013 [DDD]
Verna, Markus (perc)—see ORCHESTRAS & ENSEMBLES Percussion Art Quartet
Vernède, Arielle (pno)
Holt, S. ten:Canto ostinato, w. Gerard Bouwhuis (pno), Gene Carl (pno), C. van Zeeland (pno) *(rec live, Jan 10, 1988)* Donemus 3-▲ CV 2/3/4

INSTRUMENT.

Verner, Pavel (ob)
Telemann, G.P.:Cons Ob Orch, w. J. Vlach (cnd), Suk CO—6 Concerti—in c, c, D, d, e & f *(rec 1987)* Supraphon ▲ 11 0122-2 [DDD]
Verner, Pavel (vc)—see ORCHESTRAS & ENSEMBLES Apollo String Quartet
Verner, Petr (va)—see also ORCHESTRAS & ENSEMBLES New Vlach String Quartet, Vlach String Quartet
Dvořák, A.:Terzetto, w. Jana Vlacková (vn), Karel Stadtherr (vn) *(rec Martínek Studio, Prague, 1995)* Naxos ▲ 8.553373 [DDD]
Vernet, Olivier (org)
Bach, J.S.:Org Music (comp)—Preludes & Fugues, BWV 531-533, 535, 549-551 & 566; Preludes, BWV 568 & 569; Chorals, BWV 696/704, 715, 718, 721, 722, 724-726, 728, 729, 732, 735, 737, 738, 741, 1095, 1104, 1107 & 1117; Partitas, BWV 766 & 767; Fant, BWV 570; Fugues, BWV 575, 577 & 578; Fant con Imitazione, BWV 563; Toccata & Fugue, BWV 565; Passacaglia, BWV 582 Ligia Digital 3-▲ CD 0104037/39
Balbastre, C.-B.:Marche des marseillais et l'air Ça ira [Jean-André Silbermann Org, St. Maurice de Soultz Church] *(rec Mar 24-26, 1995)* Ligia Digital ▲ 0104031 [DDD]
Benaut:Mass Org [Jean-André Silbermann Org, St. Maurice de Soultz Church] *(rec Mar 24-26, 1995)* Ligia Digital ▲ 0104031 [DDD]
Buxtehude, D.:Org Music (comp) Ligia Digital 5-▲ 0104025
Buxtehude, D.:Org Music (comp)—Praeludium in g, BuxWV 149; Mit Fried und Freud ich fahr dahin, BuxWV 76; In dulci Jubilo, BuxWV197; Der Tag, der ist so freudenreich, BuxWV 182; Praeludium en d, BuxWV 140; Gelobet siest du, Jesu Christ, BuxWV 188; Praeludium in C, BuxWV 137; Nun komm, der Heiden Heiland, BuxWV 211; Lobt Gott, ihr Christen allzugleich, BuxWV 202; Ciaconna en mi mineur, BuxWV 160; Wie schön leuchtet der Morgenstern, BuxWV 160; Praeludium in A, BuxWV 188; Puer natus in Bethlehem, BuxWV 189; Toccata in d, BuxWV 155 *(rec Apr. 1993)* Ligia Digital ▲ 0104007 [DDD]
Calviere, A.:Pièce unique [Jean-André Silbermann Org, St. Maurice de Soultz Church] *(rec Mar 24-26, 1995)* Ligia Digital ▲ 0104031 [DDD]
Corrette, M.:Org Music [Jean-André Silbermann Org, St. Maurice de Soultz Church]—Pièces de mon Livre de Clavecin qui se peuvent toucher sur l'Orgue *(rec Mar 24-26, 1995)* Ligia Digital ▲ 0104031 [DDD]
Couperin, F.:Messe propre pour les couvents de religieux et religieuses, w. Josep Cabre (cnd), La Fidelissima Schola Gregorienne *(rec Mar 21-24, 1996)* Ligia Digital ▲ 0104041 [DDD]
Dialogue, w. Guy Touvron (tpt) *(rec Sept. 1992)* Ligia Digital ▲ LIDI 0105002-92 [DDD]
Guilain, J.-A.:Pièces d'orgue pour le Magnificat [Jean-André Silbermann Org, St. Maurice de Soultz Church]—Suite du 2nd ton *(rec Mar 24-26, 1995)* Ligia Digital ▲ 0104031 [DDD]
Mendelssohn, F.:Sons Org *(rec Oct. 1992)* Ligia Digital ▲ 0104004 [DDD]
Piroye, C.:Org Music [Jean-André Silbermann Org, St. Maurice de Soultz Church]—La Béatitude *(rec Mar 24-26, 1995)* Ligia Digital ▲ 0104031 [DDD]
Verney, Helen (vc)
Dussek, J.L.:Hp Music, w. Danielle Perrett (hp), James Ellis (vn), Warwick Cole (pno), Gillian Jones (hand-hn)—A Favorite Duet for Hp & Pno, Op. 11; Son in E♭ for Hp, Op. 34/1; Favorite Son for Hp, Vn & Vc, Op. 37; Son in B♭ for Hp, Op. 34/2; Duo for Hp, Pno & Hand-Horn, Op. 38 Meridian ▲ MER 84244 [DDD]
Verney, Laurent (va)
L'Alto Romantique [The Romantic Viola], w. Claire Marie LeGuay (pno) Pierre Verany ▲ 793121 [DDD]
Brahms, J.:Son 1 Cl, w. Nicholas Angelich (pno) Harmonia Mundi France ("Les Nouveaux Interprètes" series) ▲ HMN 911565
Brahms, J.:Son 2 Cl, w. Nicholas Angelich (pno) Harmonia Mundi France ("Les Nouveaux Interprètes" series) ▲ HMN 911565
Viola Nouveau Centrediscs ▲ CMCCD 0883
Verney, Mary (pno)
Beethoven, L. van:Con 1 Pno, w. Hanover Band Nimbus ▲ Ni 5003
Beethoven, L. van:Con 3 Pno, w. Hanover Band [period instrs] Nimbus ▲ NI 5031 [DDD]
Vernizzi, Rino (bn)—see also ORCHESTRAS & ENSEMBLES Rossini Wind Quartet, Italiano Octet
Villa-Lobos, H.:Bachiana brasileira 6, w. Andrea Griminelli (fl) *(rec Chiesa della Misericordia, Torino, Italy, Feb 1987)* Arts Music ▲ 447200-2 [DDD]
Villa-Lobos, H.:Duo Ob, w. Pietro Borgonovo (ob) *(rec Chiesa della Misericordia, Torino, Italy, Feb 1987)* Arts Music ▲ 447200-2 [DDD]
Villa-Lobos, H.:Qt Fl, w. Andrea Griminelli (fl), Pietro Borgonovo (ob), Michele Carulli (cl) *(rec Chiesa della Misericordia, Torino, Italy, Feb 1987)* Arts Music ▲ 447200-2 [DDD]
Villa-Lobos, H.:Qnten forme de chôros, w. Andrea Griminelli (fl), Pietro Borgonovo (ob), Michele Carulli (cl), Francesco Pomarico (E hn) *(rec Chiesa della Misericordia, Torino, Italy, Feb 1987)* Arts Music ▲ 447200-2 [DDD]
Villa-Lobos, H.:Trio Ob, w. Pietro Borgonovo (ob), Michele Carulli (cl) *(rec Chiesa della Misericordia, Torino, Italy, Feb 1987)* Arts Music ▲ 447200-2 [DDD]
Vernon, R. (va)—see ORCHESTRAS & ENSEMBLES Cleveland Orch String Quartet
Verrette, C. (vn)
Soler, P.A.:Qnt 1 Hpd, w. D. Schrader (hpd), M. Shelton (vn), P. Slowik (va), J. M. Rozendaal (vc) *(rec Oct. & Dec. 1992)* Cedille ▲ CDR 90000 013 [DDD]
Soler, P.A.:Qnt 2 Hpd, w. D. Schrader (hpd), M. Shelton (vn), P. Slowik (va), J. M. Rozendaal (vc) *(rec Oct. & Dec. 1992)* Cedille ▲ CDR 90000 013 [DDD]
Soler, P.A.:Qnt 3 Hpd, w. D. Schrader (hpd), M. Shelton (vn), P. Slowik (va), J. M. Rozendaal (vc) *(rec Oct. & Dec. 1992)* Cedille ▲ CDR 90000 013 [DDD]
Verry, François (pno)
Boieldieu, F.-A.:Sons Pno, Op. 4 *(rec Dec 1989)* Media 7 ▲ 2024 [DDD]
Boieldieu, F.-A.:Sons Pno, Op. 4 Adda ▲ ADD 590012 [DDD]
Boieldieu, F.-A.:Son Pno, Op. 6 Adda ▲ ADD 590012 [DDD]
Boieldieu, F.-A.:Son Pno, Op. 6 *(rec Dec 1989)* Media 7 ▲ 2024 [DDD]
Versteegh, Bob (pno)
Contemporary Music for Saxophone, w. Edward-Kelly, J. (sax) Col legno ▲ AU31805
Elias, B.:Pythikos Nomos, w. John-Edward Kelly (sax) Col Legno ▲ AU 31817
Eliasson, A.:Poem, w. John-Edward Kelly (sax) Col Legno ▲ AU 31817
John-Edward Kelly, w. Kelly, John-Edward (sax) Col Legno ▲ AU 31805
Kox, H.:Through a Glass, Darkly, w. John-Edward Kelly (sax) Col Legno ▲ AU 31817
Reiner, K.:Dve Skladby, w. John-Edward Kelly (sax) Col Legno ▲ AU 31817
Verstraelen, Godelieve (pno)
Brod, H.:Nocturne Ob, w. Jan De Maeyer (ob) Arcobaleno ▲ AAOC 9328
Dallier, H.:Fant Caprice, w. Jan De Maeyer (ob) Arcobaleno ▲ AAOC 9328
Demersseman, J.A.:Fant Suisse, w. Jan De Maeyer (ob) Arcobaleno ▲ AAOC 9328
Godard, B.:Scènes écossaise, w. Jan De Maeyer (ob) Arcobaleno ▲ AAOC 9328
Lalliet, T.:Carnival de Venise, w. Jan De Maeyer (ob) Arcobaleno ▲ AAOC 9328
Saint-Saëns, C.:Son Ob, w. J. De Maeyer (ob) Arcobaleno ▲ AAOC 9328
Verzari, Sandro (tpt)
Aldrovandini, G.:Sinf Tpt, w. F. Colusso (cnd), Seicentonovecento Ensemble Bongiovanni ▲ GB 10010 [DDD]
Gabrielli, D.:Con Tpt, w. F. Colusso (cnd), Seicentonovecento Ensemble Bongiovanni ▲ GB 10010 [DDD]
Gabrielli, D.:Sons Tpt, w. F. Colusso (cnd), Seicentonovecento Ensemble—Sons 4, 5, 7 & 8 Tpt Bongiovanni ▲ GB 10010 [DDD]
Torelli, G.:Tpt Music, w. F. Colusso (cnd), Seicentonovecento Ensemble—Concerto; Sinfonia G.2-4 & 8; Sonata G.1 & 5-7 *(rec 9/90)* Bongiovanni ▲ GB 10008 [DDD]
Verzier, Alix (vc)
Deutsche Barocklieder, w. Scholl, Andreas (ct), Markus Markl (hpd), Karl Ernst Schroder (lt), Friederike Heumann (va), Juan Manuel Quintana (va), Stephanie Pfister (vn), Pablo Valetti (vn) Harmonia Mundi France ▲ HMC 901505
Verzoni, Marcello (pno)
Brazillian Piano Music Koch Schwann ▲ SCH 311822 [DDD]
Verzoni, Marcello (pno) (cont.)
Guarnieri, C.M.:Ponteios—6 sels.—Nos. 24,42,44,45,49 & 50 Koch Schwann ▲ CD 310019 [DDD] ■ MC 210019 (D)
Nazareth, E.:Pno Music—Escorregando; Duvidoso; Garoto; Faceira; Apanhel-te cavaquinho; Remando; Bambino; Favorito Koch Schwann ▲ CD 310019 [DDD] ■ MC 210019 (D)
Villa-Lobos, H.:Cirandas Pno—Nos. 13 & 15 Koch Schwann ▲ CD 310019 [DDD] ■ MC 210019 (D)
Vescovo, Pierre del (hn)
Dauprat, L.-F.:Son Hn & Hp, w. Lily Laskine (hp)—Andante Erato ▲ 94801-2
Dukas, P.:Villanelle, w. Jean Hubeau (pno) Erato ▲ 94801-2
Mozart, W.A.:Con Hn, K.495, w. J.-F. Paillard (cnd), Jean-François Paillard CO—Romanza; Rondo Erato ▲ 94801-2
Veselá, Alena (org)
Brixi, F.X.:Cons Org (comp), w. F. Jílek (cnd), Bohuslav Martinů CO—Concerto in G Supraphon Collection ▲ 11 0633-2 [ADD]
Linek, J.:Con Org, w. F. Jílek (cnd), Bohuslav Martinů CO *(rec 1972)* Supraphon Collection ▲ 11 0633-2 [ADD]
Stamitz, J.W.A.:Cons Org, w. V. Válek (cnd), Dvořák CO *(rec 1982)* Supraphon Collection ▲ 11 0633-2 [ADD]
Stamitz, J.W.A.:Cons Org, w. Frantisek Xaver Thuri (hpd), V. Válek (cnd), Dvořák CO Supraphon ("Mannheim" series) ▲ SUP CD 3094
Vesmas, Tamas (pno)
Bartók, B.:Dances (6) Pno Manu ▲ MAN 1443
Bartók, B.:Suite Pno Manu ▲ MAN 1443
Enescu, G.:Son Pno, Op. 24/3 Manu ▲ MAN 1443
Janácek, L.:Son October 1, 1905 Pno Manu ▲ MAN 1443
Prokofiev, S.:Ballade Vc, w. Alexander Ivashkin (vc) *(rec School of Music, Auckland Univ & St. Barnabas Church, Christchurch)* Manu ▲ 1517
Prokofiev, S.:Cinderella (sels), w. Alexander Ivashkin (vc)—Adagio for vc & pno *(rec School of Music, Auckland Univ & St. Barnabas Church, Christchurch)* Manu ▲ 1517
Prokofiev, S.:Son Vc, w. Alexander Ivashkin (vc) *(rec School of Music, Auckland Univ & St. Barnabas Church, Christchurch)* Manu ▲ 1517
Schnittke, A.:Aphorisms Pno *(rec School of Music, Auckland Univ)* Manu ▲ MANU 1480
Schnittke, A.:Son Vc, w. Alexander Ivashkin (vc) Manu ▲ MAN 1480
Schnittke, A.:Son Vc, w. A. Ivashkin (vc) *(rec School of Music, Auckland Univ)* Manu ▲ MANU 1480
Schubert, Franz:Allegretto Pno, D.915 Manu ▲ MAN 1449
Schubert, Franz:Pieces Pno, D.946 Manu ▲ MAN 1449
Schumann, R.:Kinderszenen Manu ▲ MAN 1449
Vester, Frans (fl)
Telemann, G.P.:Con Rcr, Fl, w. F. Brüggen (rcr), A. Rieu (cnd), Amsterdam CO Teldec ▲ 77620-2 [ADD]
Vesterdahl, Anders (acc)
Werner, S.E.:Tango Studies, w. Majken Bell (acc), Heidi Hansen (acc), Carsten Holbek (acc), Hans Jorgen Holbek (acc), Lelo Nika (acc), Morten Rossen (acc) *(rec Danish Accordian Academy, Oct. 1994)* Marco Polo ("dacapo" series) ▲ 8.224006 [DDD]
Vesterman, Helena (pno)
Kessler, M.:Con Pno, w. R. Black (cnd), Slovak RSO Bratislava *(rec Slovak Radio & Television Studios)* MMC ▲ MMC 2009 [DDD]
Vestre, Björne (ob)
Boccherini, L.:Syms, w. S. Prunnbauer (gtr), Jürgen Hollerbuhl (ob), Jörn Maatz (ob), H. Maile (vn), H. Ganz (vn), R. Forest (vc), J. Stárek (cnd), Berlin RIAS Sinfonietta—in C, G.495 (Op. 21/3) *(rec Dec. 1979)* Koch Treasure ▲ 31612-2 [ADD]
Vetter, Joachim (org)
The Large Organ at the St.-Marien-Kirche in Rostock *(rec Nov. 22-24, 1991)* Motette ▲ MOT 11651 [DDD]
Veyron-Lacroix, Robert (hpd)
Bartók, B.:Hungarian Peasant Songs, w. J.-P. Rampal [arr. Arma for flute & keyboard] Odyssey ■ YT 33905
Beethoven, L. van:National Airs with Vars, Op. 107, w. J.-P. Rampal (fl) [pno-fl ver.] Vox Box 2-▲ CDX 5000 [ADD]
Handel, G.F.:Sons Fl, w. Jean-Pierre Rampal (fl)—Op. 1 Odyssey ■ YT 32371
Les introuvables de Dietrich Fischer-Dieskau, w. Dietrich Fischer-Dieskau (bar), Kark Engel (pno), Hertha Klust (pno), Gerald Moore (pno), Aribert Reimann (pno) EMI Classics 6-▲ CDZF 68509
Mozart, W.A.:Sons Fl Hpd (comp), w. J.-P. Rampal (fl) Odyssey ■ YT 32970
20th Century Flute Masterpieces, w. Jean-Pierre Rampal (fl), Lamoureux Orch [cnd:Jean Martinon] Erato 2-▲ 45839-2 [ADD]
Veyron-Lacroix, Robert (pno)
Beethoven, L. van:Serenade Fl, Op. 41, w. J.-P. Rampal (fl) Vox Box 2-▲ CDX 5000 [ADD]
Beethoven, L. van:Son Fl, w. J.-P. Rampal (fl) Vox Box 2-▲ CDX 5000 [ADD]
Beethoven, L. van:Trio Fl, WoO 37, w. J.-P. Rampal (fl), P. Hongne (bn) Vox Box 2-▲ CDX 5000 [ADD]
Poulenc, F.:Son Fl, w. J.-P. Rampal (fl) Odyssey ■ YT 33905
Prokofiev, S.:Son Fl, w. J.-P. Rampal (fl) Odyssey ■ YT 33905
Viard, Maurice (sax)
Debussy, C.:Rapsodie, w. P. Coppola (cnd), London SO Pearl ▲ PEA 9348 (m) [AAD]
Viardo, Vladimir (pno)
Franck, C.:Chorals Org, M.38-40—Nos. 2 & 3 [trans Viardo for Pno] *(rec Academy of Arts & Letters, New York, Nov 12-13, 1995)* Pro Piano ▲ PPR 224509
Franck, C.:Prélude, fugue et var [trans Viardo for Pno] *(rec Academy of Arts & Letters, New York, Nov 12-13, 1995)* Pro Piano ▲ PPR 224509
Liszt, F.:Transcriptions & Paraphrases—Bach:Prelude & Fugue in a, BWV 543 *(rec Academy of Arts & Letters, New York, Nov 12-13, 1995)* Pro Piano ▲ PPR 224509
Medtner, N.:Forgotten Melodies 1, Sonata reminiscenza Elektra/Nonesuch ▲ 79283-2 ■ 79283-4
Medtner, N.:Forgotten Melodies 2—Canzona matinata; Son tragica Elektra/Nonesuch ▲ 79283-2 ■ 79283-4
Medtner, N.:Son Pno, Op. 30 Elektra/Nonesuch ▲ 79283-2 ■ 79283-4
Penderecki, K.:Son Vn, w. Grigori Zhislin (vn) *(rec National Philharmonic Hall, Warsaw, Poland, Nov. 23, 1993)* Sony Classical ▲ SK 66284 [DDD]
Rachmaninoff, S.:Con 2 Pno, w. E. Mata (cnd), Dallas SO Pro Arte ▲ CDD 442
Rachmaninoff, S.:Variations on a Theme by Corelli Elektra/Nonesuch ▲ 79283-2 ■ 79283-4
Shostakovich, D.:Preludes Pno, Op. 34 Elektra/Nonesuch ▲ 79234-2-ZK ■ 79234-4-AW
Shostakovich, D.:Son 2 Pno Elektra/Nonesuch ▲ 79234-2-ZK ■ 79234-4-AW
Vicari, G. (mand)
Vivaldi, A.:Cons Diverse Instrs, w. G. Vicari (mand), C. de Filippis (mand), J. Wummer (fl), R. Morris (fl), W. Vacchiano (tpt), N. Prager (tpt), E. Brenner (b ob), C. Stavrache (hp), A. Wurtzler (hp), J. Gorigliano (vn), L. Varga (vc), L. Bernstein (cnd), New York PO—in C, RV.558 *(rec Dec. 15, 1958)* Sony Classical ("Leonard Bernstein:The Royal Edition" series) ▲ SMK 47642 [ADD]
Vidal, Dominique (cl)
Mozart, W.A.:Qts Cl, w. Millière String Trio Quantum ▲ QM 6905 [DDD] ■ QM 1999 (D)
Vidal, Lluís (hpd)
Falla, M. de:Con Hpd, w. J. Pons (cnd), Barcelona Teatro Lliure CO Harmonia Mundi France ▲ HMC 901432
Vidal, Lluís (pno)
Soler, J.:Chamber Con Pno, w. J. Pons (cnd), Barcelona Teatro Lliure CO Harmonia Mundi France ▲ HMC 905231
Soler, J.:Mahler Lieder, w. Virgínia Parramon (sop), J. Pons (cnd), Barcelona Teatro Lliure CO Harmonia Mundi France ▲ HMC 905231
Vidal, Salvador (cl)
Llanas, A.:Con Cl, w. J.L. Temes (cnd), London PO Discobi ▲ DIS 2008

Viding, Mads (db)
Clausen, T.:Songs (3), w. Thomas Clausen (pno), Jesper Grove Jørgensen (cnd), Lille MUKO Point ▲ PCD 5125

Vidovic, Victor (gtr)
Giuliani, M.:Grand Ov *(rec 3/90)* REM ▲ 311118 XCD [DDD]
Moreno Torroba, F.:Suite castellana *(rec 3/90)* REM ▲ 311118 XCD [DDD]
Ponce, M.:Thème, varié et finale REM ▲ 311118 XCD [DDD]
Scarlatti, D.:Sons Kbd—K.23 & 483 *(rec 3/90)* REM ▲ 311118 XCD [DDD]
Sor, F.:Vars on a Theme of Mozart *(rec 3/90)* REM ▲ 311118 XCD [DDD]

Vieira, Walmir (tuba)—see ORCHESTRAS & ENSEMBLES Brasil Brass Quintet

Viens, Michael C. (pno)
Viens, M.:Color Scope, w. Bruce Fithian (ten) MMC ▲ MMC 2040 [DDD]
Viens, M.:Star Blaze, w. Bruce Fithian (ten) MMC ▲ MMC 2040 [DDD]
Viens, M.:Sundown Voyager, w. Bruce Fithian (ten) MMC ▲ MMC 2040 [DDD]
Viens, M.:Voices in the Still, w. Isabelle Ganz (mez) MMC ▲ MMC 2040 [DDD]

Vierne, Louis (org)
Vierne, L.:Pièces de fant—2 improvisations Andantino EMI Classics ▲ CDC 55037

Viersen, Quirine (vc)
Kox, H.:Con Vc, w. E. Spanjaard (cnd), Netherlands Radio CO NM Classics ▲ NM 92040

Vieux, Maurice (va)
Fauré, G.:Qt 2 Pno, w. Marguerite Long (pno), Jacques Thibaud (vn), Pierre Fournier (vc) *(rec June 10, 1940)* Enterprise ("Strings" series) ▲ ENT QT 99302
Fauré, G.:Qt 2 Pno, w. Marguerite Long (pno), Jacques Thibaud (vn), Pierre Fournier (vc) *(rec June 10, 1940)* Iron Needle 2-▲ IN 1342/43 (m) [ADD]

Vieuxtemps, (pno)
Stravinsky, I.:Les Noces, w. M. Quercia (sop), S. Cooper (mez), P. Capelle (ten), P. Marinov (bass), R. Conil (pno), Arzoumanian (pno), Raynaut (pno), R. Hayrabedian (cnd), Strasbourg Percussion Ensemble, Contemporary Choir Pierre Verany ▲ PV 787032 [DDD]

Vigay, Denis (vc)
Music for Trumpet & Organ, w. Ashton, Graham (tpt), Leslie Pearson (org), John Orford (bn), Gordon Hunt (ob) IMP Classics ▲ PCD 986 [DDD]
Trumpet & Organ:Sonatas & Suites, w. Ashton, Graham (tpt), Leslie Pearson (org), Gordon Hunt (ob), John Orford (bn) IMP ("Classics" series) ▲ IMP 6700922

Vigeland, Nils (pno)
Cage, J.:Winter Music, w. Mats Persson (pno), Steffen Schleiermacher (pno), Kristine Scholz (pno), Eberhard Blum (pic/fl/alt fl)—for 4 pianos; for 4 pianos with flute parts from Atlas Eclipticalis *(rec Sender Freies Berlin & Hessen Radio, Frankfurt, Feb. 10–11, 1992 & June 6)* Hat Hut ("NOW." series) ▲ hat ART CD 6141 [DDD]

Vigeland, Nils (pno/cel)
Feldman, Morton:For Christian Wolff, w. Eberhard Blum (fl) *(rec Sender Freies Berlin, June 16 & 17, 1992)* Hat Hut ("NOW." series) 3-▲ hat ART CD 3-61201/02 [DDD]
Feldman, Morton:For Philip Guston, w. Eberhard Blum (fl/alt fl), Jan Williams (chimes/glock/mar/vib) *(rec Buffalo, NY, Aug. 19–21, 1991)* Hat Hut ("NOW." series) 4-▲ hat ART CD 4-61041/44 [DDD]

Vigh, Andrea (hp)
Romantische Harfe [Romantic Harp] Capriccio ▲ 10474 [DDD]

Vignani, C. (hpd)
Milesi, P.:Modi 1, w. D. Cassamagnaghi (fl), F. Pomarico (ob), A. Bianchi (cl), L. Dosso (bn), G. Govi (vn), D. Tellini (vn), M. Ravasio (va), S. Righini (vc), P. Rizzi (db), C. Vignani (hpd), J. Scully (perc), P. Milesi (cnd) Cuneiform ▲ RUNE 63

Vigne, Aquiles Delle (pno)
Liszt, F.:Son Pno *(rec EMS Studios, Brussels, Sept. 1993)* Discover International ▲ DI 920316 [DDD]
Schumann, R.:Fant Pno *(rec EMS Studios, Brussels, Sept. 1993)* Discover International ▲ DI 920316 [DDD]

Vigneron, Pascal (tpt)
Ancelin, P.:Chant de déploration, w. V. Warnier (org) Quantum ▲ QM 6952
Aubain, J.:Son Tpt, w. D. Vassilakis (pno) *(rec Nov 1991)* Quantum ▲ QM 6921 [DDD]
Chailly, J.:Jeu de quartes, w. V. Warnier (org) Quantum ▲ QM 6952
Delerue, G.:Récit et choral, w. V. Warnier (org) Quantum ▲ QM 6952
Enescu, G.:Légende, w. D. Vassilakis (pno) *(rec Nov. 1991)* Quantum ▲ QM 6921 [DDD]
Hubeau, J.:Son for Chromatic Tpt, w. D. Vassilakis (pno) *(rec Nov. 1991)* Quantum ▲ QM 6921 [DDD]
Jansen, P.:Processionnal en sept tableux, w. V. Warnier (org) Quantum ▲ QM 6952
Jolivet, A.:Arioso barocco, w. V. Warnier (org) Quantum ▲ QM 6952
Landowski, M.:Cahier pour quatre jours, w. V. Warnier (org) Quantum ▲ QM 6952
Lantier, P.:Son Tpt, w. D. Vassilakis (pno) *(rec Nov. 1991)* Quantum ▲ QM 6921 [DDD]
Rivier, J.:Aria Tpt, w. V. Warnier (org) Quantum ▲ QM 6952
Schmitt, F.:Suite Tpt, w. D. Vassilakis (pno) *(rec Nov. 1991)* Quantum ▲ QM 6921 [DDD]

Vignoles, Roger (pno)
Au Jardin des Aveux, w. Langridge, Philip (ten), Ann Murray (mez) Virgin Classics ▲ CDC 59019
Barber, S.:Son Vc, w. R. Kirshbaum (vc) Virgin Classics ▲ 59565 [DDD]
Barber, S.:Songs, w. Thomas Allen (bar)—3 Songs [The Daisies; With Rue My Heart Is Laden; Bessie Bobtail], Op. 2; 3 Songs [Rain Has Fallen; Sleep Now; I Hear an Army], Op. 10; Sure on This Shining Night; Nocturne [both from 4 Songs, Op. 13]; Solitary Hotel [from Despite & Still, Op. 41]; 3 Songs [Now I Have Fed & Eaten up the Rose; A Green Lowland of Pianos; O Boundless, Boundless Evening], Op. 45 Virgin Classics ▲ CDC 45033
Bassoon Bon-Bons, w. Smith, Daniel (bn), Royal PO [cnd:Ettore Stratta], English CO [cnd:Philip Ledger], Coull String Quartet ASV ▲ ASV 2052 [DDD]
Beethoven, L. van:Notturno, w. N. Imai (va) Chandos ▲ CHAN 8664 [DDD]
Brahms, J.:Sons Cl (comp), w. N. Imai (va) Chandos ▲ CHAN 8550 [DDD]
Brahms, J.:Sons Vn (comp), w. G. Pauk (vn) *(rec 7/90)* Ottavo ▲ OTR C79030 [DDD]
Brahms, J.:Songs, w. Sarah Walker (mez)—Gypsy Songs, Op. 103; 6 Mädchenlieder; 2 Gesänge Meridian ▲ MER 84232 [DDD]
Britten, H.:Canticles I–V, w. M. Chance (ct), A. Rolfe-Johnson (ten), A. Opie (bar), S. Williams (hp), M. Thompson (hn) Hyperion ▲ CDA 66498
Britten, H.:Purcell Realizations, w. M. Chance (ct), A. Rolfe-Johnson (ten), A. Opie (bar)—3 Realizations (An evening hymn; Let the dreadful engines; In the black dismal dungeon of despair) Hyperion ▲ CDA 66498
Bruch, M.:Trios Cl, Va & Pno, Op. 83, w. J. Hilton (cl), N. Imai (va) Chandos ▲ CHAN 8776 [DDD]
Butterworth, G.:Songs (6) from *A Shropshire Lad*, w. G. Trew (bar) [E] *(rec 8/79)* Meridian ▲ CDE84185
Cabaret Songs, w. Walker, Sarah (mez) *(rec live 1982 & 1988)* Meridian ▲ 84167
Debussy, C.:Chansons de Bilitis, w. Sarah Walker (mez) Unicorn–Kanchana ▲ UKCD 2078
Debussy, C.:Chansons de France (3), w. Sarah Walker (mez) Unicorn–Kanchana ▲ UKCD 2078
Debussy, C.:Fêtes galantes 2, w. Sarah Walker (mez) Unicorn–Kanchana ▲ UKCD 2078
Dvořák, A.:Zigeunermelodien, Op. 55, w. Sarah Walker (mez) Meridian ▲ MER 84232 [DDD]
Enescu, G.:Chansons (7) de Clément Marot, w. Sarah Walker (mez) Unicorn–Kanchana ▲ UKCD 2078
English Music for Bassoon & Piano, w. Smith, Daniel (bn) ASV ▲ ASV 535
Franck, C.:Son Vn, w. N. Imai (va) [trans. for viola & piano] Chandos ▲ CHAN 8873 [DDD]
Grieg, E.:Son Vc, w. Robert Cohen (vc) CRD ▲ 3391 [ADD]
Gurney, I.:The Western Playland, w. G. Trew (bar), Coull String Quartet [E] Meridian ▲ CDE84185
Kiri in Recital, w. Te Kanawa, Kiri (sop) London ▲ 425820-2 LH [DDD]
Mozart, W.A.:Trio Cl, K.498, w. J. Hilton (cl), N. Imai (va) Chandos ▲ CHAN 8776 [DDD]
Peel, G.:In Summertime on Bredon, w. G. Trew (bar) [E]—When the Lad for Longing Sighs; Reveille; In Summertime on Bredon *(rec 8/79)* Meridian ▲ CDE84185
Prokofiev, S.:Son Vn, Op. 94bis, w. R. Sushanskaya (vn) IMP Masters ▲ IMP MCD 58 [DDD]
Prokofiev, S.:Songs, w. C. Farley (sop)—Five Poems, Op. 23; Five Melodies, Op. 35; Three Children's Songs, Op. 68; Two Russian Songs, Op. 104 [R] ASV ▲ ASV 669 [DDD]
Prokofiev, S.:The Ugly Duckling, w. C. Farley (sop) [R] ASV ▲ ASV 669 [DDD]

Vignoles, Roger (pno) (cont.)
Roussel, A.:Light, w. Sarah Walker (mez) Unicorn–Kanchana ▲ UKCD 2078
Roussel, A.:Mélodies, w. Sarah Walker (mez) Unicorn–Kanchana ▲ UKCD 2078
Roussel, A.:Poèmes chinois, w. Sarah Walker (mez) Unicorn–Kanchana ▲ UKCD 2078
Schubert, Franz:Son Arpeggione, w. N. Imai (vla) Chandos ▲ CHAN 8664 [DDD]
Schubert, Franz:Winterreise, w. T. Allen (bar) Virgin Classics ▲ CDC 59036
Schumann, R.:Frauenliebe und –leben, w. J. van Nes (mez) Ottavo ▲ PLY 89241 [DDD]
Schumann, R.:Märchenbilder, w. N. Imai (va) Chandos ▲ CHAN 8550 [DDD]
Schumann, R.:Märchenerzählungen, w. J. Hilton (cl), N. Imai (va) Chandos ▲ CHAN 8776 [DDD]
The Sea, w. Allen, Thomas (sgr), Sarah Walker (mez) Hyperion ▲ CDA 66165
Shostakovich, D.:Son Vn, w. R. Sushanskaya (vn) IMP Masters ▲ IMP MCD 58 [DDD]
Somervell, A.:The Shropshire Lad, w. G. Trew (bar) [E] *(rec 8/79)* Meridian ▲ CDE84185
Song Recital, w. Masterson, Valerie (sop), Richard Adeney (hp) Pearl ▲ PEA 9590 [DDD]
Tosti, P.F.:Songs, w. D. O'Neill (ten)—15 songs Meridian ▲ CDE 84128
Vieuxtemps, H.:Va Pno Music, w. N. Imai (va)—(complete) Capriccio in c, Op. posth.; Elégie, Op. 30; Sonata in B♭, Op. 36 Chandos ▲ CHAN 8873 [DDD]
Warlock, P.:Songs, w. John Mark Ainsley (ten)—The Wind from the West; To the Memory of a Great Singer; Take, O Take Those Lips away; As Ever I Saw; The Bayley Berith the Bell away; There Is a Lady Sweet & Kind; Lullaby; Sweet Content; Late Summer; The Singer; Rest, Sweet Nymphs; Sleep; A Sad Song; In an Arbour Green; Autumn Twilight; I Held Love's Head; Thou Gav'st Me Leave to Kiss; Yarmouth Fair; Pretty Ring Time; A Prayer to St. Anthony; The Sick Heart; Robin Good-Fellow; Jillian of Berry; Fair & True; Ha'nacker Mill; My Own Country; The First Mercy; The Lover's Maze; Cradle Song; Sing No More Ladies; Passing by; The Contended Lover; The Fox Hyperion ▲ CDA 66736
Weill, K.:Songs, w. C. Farley (sop)—(songs from 1914–1950) including Reiterlied; Speak low; Is it him or is it me; The saga of Jenny; That's him; One life to live; Foolish heart; Matrosen–Tango; Alabama Song; Havanna–Lied; Das schöne Kind; Polly's Lied (Hübsch als es währte); Denn wie man sich bettet, so liegt man; etc. ASV ▲ ASV 790
Wolf, H.:Mörike–Lieder (sels), w. J. van Nes (mez) Ottavo ▲ PLY 89241 [DDD]

Viguier, Lisa (hp)
Delage, M.:Poèmes hindous, w. Anne Sofie von Otter (mez), Andreas Alin (fl), Peter Rydström (fl/pic), Ulf Bjurenhed (ob/E hn), Lars Paulsson (cl), Per Billman (cl/b cl), Nils-Erik Sparf (vn), Ulf Forsberg (vn), Matti Hirvikangas (va), Mats Lindström (vc) *(rec Stockholm, Nov 1994)* Deutsche Grammophon ▲ 447 752-2 [DDD]

Viitasalo, Marita (pno)
Brahms, J.:Sons Cl (comp), w. A.–M. Korsimaa (cl) *(rec Apr. 1993)* Finlandia ▲ 4509-95878-2 [DDD]
Debussy, C.:Preludes Pno—Book 1 Ondine ▲ ODE 723-2 [DDD]
Schubert, Franz:Der Hirt auf dem Felsen, w. S. Isokoski (sop), A.–M. Korsimaa (cl) *(rec Jan. 1993)* Finlandia ▲ 4509-95878-2 [DDD]
Schubert, Franz:Songs (misc), w. S. Isokoski (sop)—Sei mir gegrüsst, Op. 20/1; Nacht und Träume, Op. 43/2; Im Frühling; Gretchen am Spinnrade, Op. 2; Ganymed, Op.19/3; Du bist die Ruh, Op. 59/3; Die junge Nonne, Op. 43/1; Ave Maria, Op. 52/6; Lied der Mignon I, II & III, Op. 62/1–3; Mignons Gegang; Der Hirt auf dem Felsen, Op. 129 [w. A.–M. Korsimaa (clarinet)] *(rec Jan. 18–20, 1993)* Finlandia ▲ 4509-95877-2 [DDD]

Vila, Gerardo (pno/fl)—see ORCHESTRAS & ENSEMBLES Tango 7

Villarrubia, Charles (tuba)
Bernstein, L.:Dance Suite Chamber Ensemble, w. Will Rudd (tpt/flgl), Bob Thompson (tpt/flgl), Alex Shuhan (hn/pno), Mark Kellogg (trbn/eup), David Gluck (dr/perc) *(rec Cliff Temple Baptist Church, Dallas, TX)* D'Note Classics ▲ DND 1007 [DDD]
Corea, C.:Children's Songs, w. Will Rudd (tpt/flgl), Bob Thompson (tpt/flgl), Alex Shuhan (hn/pno), Mark Kellogg (trbn/eup), David Gluck (dr/perc)—Nos 6 & 11 [arr Gluck/Shuhan] *(rec Cliff Temple Baptist Church, Dallas, TX)* D'Note Classics ▲ DND 1007 [DDD]
Gershwin, G.:Porgy & Bess (sels), w. Will Rudd (tpt/flgl), Bob Thompson (tpt/flgl), Alex Shuhan (hn/pno), Mark Kellogg (trbn/eup), David Gluck (dr/perc)—Summertime [arr Thompson] *(rec Cliff Temple Baptist Church, Dallas, TX)* D'Note Classics ▲ DND 1007 [DDD]
Gluck, C.W.:Nicole, w. Will Rudd (tpt/flgl), Bob Thompson (tpt/flgl), Alex Shuhan (hn/pno), Mark Kellogg (trbn/eup), David Gluck (dr/perc) *(rec Cliff Temple Baptist Church, Dallas, TX)* D'Note Classics ▲ DND 1007 [DDD]
Khachaturian, A.:Gayane (suites), w. Will Rudd (tpt/flgl), Bob Thompson (tpt/flgl), Alex Shuhan (hn/pno), Mark Kellogg (trbn/eup), David Gluck (dr/perc)—Sabre Dance [arr Gluck]; Lullaby; Dance of the Rose Maidens [both arr Villarrubia] *(rec Cliff Temple Baptist Church, Dallas, TX)* D'Note Classics ▲ DND 1007 [DDD]
McCarthy, D.:American Dance Music, w. Will Rudd (tpt/flgl), Bob Thompson (tpt/flgl), Alex Shuhan (hn/pno), Mark Kellogg (trbn/eup), David Gluck (dr/perc) *(rec Cliff Temple Baptist Church, Dallas, TX)* D'Note Classics ▲ DND 1007 [DDD]
Scheidt, S.:Instr Music, w. Will Rudd (tpt/flgl), Bob Thompson (tpt/flgl), Alex Shuhan (hn/pno), Mark Kellogg (trbn/eup), David Gluck (dr/perc)—Centone No. 5 [trans Verne Reynolds] *(rec Cliff Temple Baptist Church, Dallas, TX)* D'Note Classics ▲ DND 1007 [DDD]

Villars, Anne-Claude (vn)—see ORCHESTRAS & ENSEMBLES Elyséen String Quartet

Villevielle, Claude (ob)
Garnier, F.–J.:Con Ob, Talich CO Koch Schwann ▲ SCH 314752 [DDD]
Garnier, F.–J.:Sym Concertante 1, w. J. Kolar (ob), Talich CO Koch Schwann ▲ SCH 314752 [DDD]
Garnier, F.–J.:Sym Concertante 2, Talich CO Koch Schwann ▲ SCH 314752 [DDD]
Kreutzer, R.:Con Ob, Talich CO Koch Schwann ▲ SCH 314752 [DDD]
Poulenc, F.:Son Ob, w. Kun Woo Paik (pno) Accord ▲ ACD 205192 [DDD]

Vincent-Vizzutti, Laura (pno)
Tyzik, J.:Elegy, w. Allen Vizzutti (tpt), J. Tyzik (cnd), *(orch unknown)* *(rec Hochstein School of Music, Rochester, New York, July 27–29, 1995)* Summit ▲ 188 [DDD]
Tyzik, J.:Son Tpt, w. Allen Vizzutti (tpt) *(rec Hochstein School of Music, Rochester, New York, July 27–29, 1995)* Summit ▲ 188 [DDD]
Vizzutti, A.:Andante & Capriccio, w. Allen Vizzutti (tpt), J. Tyzik (cnd), *(orch unknown)* *(rec Hochstein School of Music, Rochester, New York, July 27–29, 1995)* Summit ▲ 188 [DDD]
Vizzutti, A.:The Carnival of Venus, w. Allen Vizzutti (tpt) *(rec Hochstein School of Music, Rochester, New York, July 27–29, 1995)* Summit ▲ 188 [DDD]
Vizzutti, A.:Son 1 Tpt, w. Allen Vizzutti (tpt) *(rec Hochstein School of Music, Rochester, New York, July 27–29, 1995)* Summit ▲ 188 [DDD]
Vizzutti, A.:Son 2 Tpt, w. Allen Vizzutti (tpt) *(rec Hochstein School of Music, Rochester, New York, July 27–29, 1995)* Summit ▲ 188 [DDD]

Vincenz, M. (pno)
Wolf-Ferrari, E.:Sons Vn, w. C. Rossi (vn), M. Vincenz (pno)i—No. 1 in g, Op. 1 (1895); No. 2 in a, Op. 10 (1901); No. 3 in E, Op. 27 (1943) Dynamic ▲ CDS 68 [DDD]

Vincenzi, Marco (pno)
Busoni, F.:Son in C Vn, w. C. Rossi (vn) Dynamic ▲ CD 87 [DDD]
Busoni, F.:Son 1 Vn, w. C. Rossi (vn) Dynamic ▲ CD 87 [DDD]
Busoni, F.:Son 2 Vn, w. C. Rossi (vn) Dynamic ▲ CD 87 [DDD]
Vieuxtemps, H.:Vn & Pno Music (sels), w. Ruggiero Ricci (vn)—Fant appassionata; Ballade et Polonaise; Chant d'amour; Désespoir; Souvenir; Rondino; Tarantella; Rêverie; Romance; Hommage à Paganini; Innocence; Yankee Doodle *(rec Dynamic's, Genoa, Italy, May 3–5, 1995)* Dynamic ▲ CDS 112 [DDD]

Vincenzi, Marco (positive org)—see ORCHESTRAS & ENSEMBLES Basso Generale

Vinci, Jan (fl)
Blanchard, P.:Music of, w. J. Brown (gtr), A. Alton (pno)—Lament; Frolic Albany ▲ TROY 086 [DDD]
Fine, V.:Canzones y Dances, w. J. Brown (gtr), A. Alton (pno) Albany ▲ TROY 086
Holland, A.:Poems Without Words, w. J. Brown (gtr), A. Alton (pno) Albany ▲ TROY 086
York, A.:Transilience, w. J. Brown (gtr), A. Alton (pno) Albany ▲ TROY 086

Vinci, Mark (fl)
Brubeck, C.:Songs, w. Frederica von Stade (sop), Jenny Elkus (sgr), Bill Crofut (sgr/banjo), Chris Brubeck (sgr/trbn/pno/db), Frank Brown (cl), Edward Arron (vc), Dan Brubeck (dr/perc)—The Distance between Us; La Paloma azul; Strange Meadowlark; Across Your Dreams; Summer Song; Polly; Blue Rondo–A Tribute to Dave; Autumn in Our Town; Thinking of You Thinking of Me; It's a Raggy Waltz; Heart of Winter; In the Grace of Your Room; Lonely on Both Ends of the Road *(rec Sandisfield, MA; Fantasy Studios, Berkeley, CA)* Telarc ▲ CD 80467 [DDD]
Vinci, Michele (perc)
Petrassi, G.:Serenata Fls, w. M. Berni (fl), A. Vismara (va), F. Fraioli (db), V. de Vita (pno) Bongiovanni ▲ GB 5534 [DDD]
Vind, Niels (tpt)—see ORCHESTRAS & ENSEMBLES Royal Danish Brass
Vindenes, Njal (gtr)
Am, M.:Like a Leaf on the River Victoria ▲ VCD 19063
Asheim, N.H.:Varp Victoria ▲ VCD 19063
Berio, L.:Sequenza XI Victoria ▲ VCD 19063
Britten, H.:Nocturnal Gtr Victoria ▲ VCD 19063
Ginastera, A.:Son Gtr Victoria ▲ VCD 19063
Vineburg, Charlotte (pno)
Hazzan Rishon, Legendary Cantorial Recitativi, Opuses 1 & 2, w. Montefiore, David (cant), V. Zeltser (vn), A. Bacelar (vc), G. Lochner (vc), C. Morrison (va) Behar/Berg 2–▲ 001494
Vines, M. (pno)
Baksa, R.:Earth Elegy, w. R. Lee (tpt) *(rec Brooklyn College, Apr. 1993 & May 1994)* Capstone ▲ CPS 8620 [DDD]
Baksa, R.:Son Tpt, w. R. Lee (tpt) *(rec Brooklyn College, Apr. 1993 & May 1994)* Capstone ▲ CPS 8620 [DDD]
Viñes, Ricardo (pno)
Ricardo Viñes & Francis Planté, w. Francis Planté (pno) *(rec between 1928 & 1936)* Pearl ▲ PEA 9857 [ADD]
Vinogradova, Irina (pno)
Beethoven, L. van:Son 7 Vn, w. M. Vengerov (vn) Canyon Classics ▲ 3655
Maxim Vengerov, w. Maxim Vengerov (vn) *(rec 1989)* Biddulph ▲ LAW 001 [DDD]
Prokofiev, S.:Mélodies, w. Z. Bron (vn) Giulia ▲ GS 201017 [DDD]
Schubert, Franz:Fant Vn, D.934, w. M. Vengerov (vn) Biddulph ▲ LAW 001 [DDD]
Schubert, Franz:Fant Vn, D.934, w. M. Vengerov (vn) Canyon Classics ▲ 3655
Tchaikovsky, P.:Sérénade mélancolique, w. Z. Bron (vn) Giulia ▲ GS 201017 [DDD]
Waxman, F.:Carmen Fant, w. M. Vengerov (vn) Biddulph ▲ LAW 001 [DDD]
Waxman, F.:Carmen Fant, w. M. Vengerov (vn) Canyon Classics ▲ 3655
Vintschger, Isabel von (pno)
Busoni, F.:Pno Music for 2 Pnos, w. J. von Vintschger (pno)—4 pieces *(rec 1982)* Jecklin–Disco ▲ JD 579–2 [ADD]
Mozart, W.A.:Pno Music 4–Hands, w. J. von Vintschger (pno)—Andante & Vars., K. 501; Sons., K.358, 381, 497, 521 *(rec 1969)* Jecklin ▲ J 4405 [ADD]
Reger, M.:Intro, Passacaglia & Fugue Pnos, w. J. von Vintschger (pno) *(rec 1985)* Jecklin–Disco ▲ JD 609–2
Reger, M.:Vars & Fugue on a Theme of Beethoven, w. J. von Vintschger (pno) *(rec 1985)* Jecklin–Disco ▲ JD 609–2
Reger, M.:Vars & Fugue on a Theme by Mozart, w. J. von Vintschger (pno) *(rec 1985)* Jecklin–Disco ▲ JD 609–2
Vintschger, Jürg von (pno)
Busoni, F.:Pno Music for 2 Pnos, w. I. von Vintschger (pno)—4 pieces *(rec 1982)* Jecklin–Disco ▲ JD 579–2 [ADD]
Mendelssohn, F.:Concert Pieces, w. H.R. Stalder (cl), H. Leuthold (bas hn) *(rec 1981)* Jecklin–Disco ▲ JD 560–2 [ADD]
Mozart, W.A.:Pno Music 4–Hands, w. I. von Vintschger (pno)—Andante & Vars., K. 501; Sons., K.358, 381, 497, 521 *(rec 1969)* Jecklin ▲ J 4405 [ADD]
Reger, M.:Intro, Passacaglia & Fugue Pnos, w. I. von Vintschger (pno) *(rec 1985)* Jecklin–Disco ▲ JD 609–2
Reger, M.:Vars & Fugue on a Theme of Beethoven, w. I. von Vintschger (pno) *(rec 1985)* Jecklin–Disco ▲ JD 609–2
Reger, M.:Vars & Fugue on a Theme by Mozart, w. I. von Vintschger (pno) *(rec 1985)* Jecklin–Disco ▲ JD 609–2
Reinecke, C.:Intro & Allegro appassionato, w. H. R. Stalder (cl) *(rec 1987)* Jecklin–Disco ▲ JD 602–2 [ADD]
Reinecke, C.:Son Fl, w. H. R. Stalder (cl) *(rec 1987)* Jecklin–Disco ▲ JD 602–2 [ADD]
Reinecke, C.:Trio Pno, Op. 274, w. H.R. Stalder (cl), J. Hefti (hn) *(rec 1987)* Jecklin–Disco ▲ JD 602–2 [ADD]
Rossini, G.:Fant Cl, w. H.–R. Stalder (cl) *(rec 1975)* Jecklin–Disco ▲ JD 578–2 [ADD]
Spohr, L.:Vars in B♭ on a Theme from *Alruna*, w. H. R. Stalder (cl) *(rec 1972, 1975 & 1982)* Jecklin–Disco ▲ JD 536–2 [ADD]
Weber, C.M. von:Grand duo concertant Cl, w. H. R. Stalder (cl) *(rec 1972, 1975 & 1982)* Jecklin–Disco ▲ JD 536–2 [ADD]
Weber, C.M. von:Vars on a Theme from *Silvana* Cl, w. H. R. Stalder (cl) *(rec 1972, 1975 & 1982)* Jecklin–Disco ▲ JD 536–2 [ADD]
Vio, Andrea (vn)—see ORCHESTRAS & ENSEMBLES Venice String Quartet
Violette, Andrew (pno)
Schubel, M.:Pno Music—B–natural; Miraplex; Everybody's Favourite Rag Opus One ▲ CD 151
Virard, Blandine (pno)
Couperin, G.–F.:Music of, w. Pascale Bonnier (pno), Lucette Touzet (pno)—Vars on Ah! Ça Ira Adda ▲ ADD 581114
Jadin, L.E.:Sons Pno 4–Hands, Op. 2, w. Pascale Bonnier (pno), Lucette Touzet (pno)—No. 1 Adda ▲ ADD 581114
Méhul, E.–N.:Sons Hpd, Op. 1, w. Pascale Bonnier (pno), Lucette Touzet (pno)—No. 3 Adda ▲ ADD 581114
Rigel, H.–J.:Kbd Music, w. Pascale Bonnier (pno), Lucette Touzet (pno)—Son No. 3, Op. 3 Adda ▲ ADD 581114
Tapray, J.F.:Sons Hpd, Op. 24, w. Pascale Bonnier (pno), Lucette Touzet (pno)—No. 3 Adda ▲ ADD 581114
Virizly, M. (vc)
Schubert, Franz:Qnt Pno, D.667, w. E. Taussig (pno), R. Ricci (vn), E. Klemmstein (va), G. Karr (db) One–Eleven ▲ URS 92010
Virzaladze, Elizo (pno)
Brahms, J.:Qnt Pno, w. Borodin String Quartet Teldec ▲ 97461–2
Vischer, Antoniette (hpd)
Ligeti, G.:Continuum Wergo ▲ WER 60045–50
Viscuglia, Felix (cl/a sax)—see ORCHESTRAS & ENSEMBLES Sierra Winds
Vísek, Tomás (pno)
Saudek, V.:Con Pno, w. F. Babicky (cnd), Brno State PO Panton ▲ PAN 811012
Visek, Tomas (pno)
Schulhoff, E.:Pno Music—5 Pittoresken; Partita für Klavier; Jazz Etudes (5); Hot Music; Zehn synkopierte Etüden; Suite dansante en jazz pour piano Supraphon ▲ SUP 11 1870 [DDD]
Schulhoff, E.:Symphonia germanica Supraphon ▲ SUP 112170 [DDD]
Vísek, Tomás (pno)
Simon, L.:Con Pno, w. F. Babicky (cnd), Brno State PO Panton ▲ PAN 811012
Vishnevsky, Valery (pno)
Beethoven, L. van:Rondo a capriccio, "Rage Over a Lost Penny" Audiophile Classics ▲ 101.003
Beethoven, L. van:Son 7 Pno Audiophile Classics ▲ 101.003
Beethoven, L. van:Son 8 Pno, "Pathétique" Audiophile Classics ▲ 101.003
Beethoven, L. van:Son 9 Pno Audiophile Classics ▲ 101.003
Vishnevsky, Valery (pno) (cont.)
Beethoven, L. van:Son 10 Pno Audiophile Classics ▲ 101.004
Beethoven, L. van:Son 11 Pno Audiophile Classics ▲ 101.004
Beethoven, L. van:Son 12 Pno, "Funeral March" Audiophile Classics ▲ 101.004
Tchaikovsky, P.:Morceaux, Op. 9 Audiophile Classics ▲ 101.013
Tchaikovsky, P.:Morceaux, Op. 10 Audiophile Classics ▲ 101.013
Tchaikovsky, P.:Morceaux, Op. 19 Audiophile Classics ▲ 101.013
Tchaikovsky, P.:Souvenir de Hapsal—No. 3 [Chant sans paroles] Audiophile Classics ▲ 101.013
Viskup, Ivan (b cl)
Respighi, O.:Liriche su parole di poeti armeni, w. Denisa Šlepkovská (mez), Vladimír Havran (fl), Michal Sintál (ob), Gabriel Koncer (cl), Ivan Paulicka (bn), Frantisek Kovács (trbn), Katarína Vavreková (hp), M. Adriano (cnd) [arr. for chamber group by Adriano] *(rec Slovak Radio Concert Hall, Bratislava, Jan. 4–9, Feb. 19 & June)* Marco Polo ▲ 8.223595 [DDD]
Vismara, Augusto (va)
Arrigo, G.:Serenata per Andromeda, w. C. Scarponi (pno), V. de Vita (cl), K. Martin (cnd), Musica d'Oggi Bongiovanni ▲ GB 5511 [DDD]
Ghedini, G.F.:Concert Music, w. K. Martin (cnd), Musica d'Oggi Bongiovanni ▲ GB 5511 [DDD]
Paganini, N.:Qts (15) Vn, w. R. Ricci (vn), L. Signorini (vc), S. Cardi (gtr)—No. 7 Bongiovanni ▲ GB 5507 [DDD]
Paganini, N.:Terzetto concertante Va, w. L. Signorini (vc), S. Cardi (gtr) Bongiovanni ▲ GB 5507 [DDD]
Petrassi, G.:Duetto Vn Va, w. A. Salvatore (vn) Bongiovanni ▲ GB 5534 [DDD]
Petrassi, G.:Serenata Fls, w. M. Berni (fl), F. Fraioli (db), V. de Vita (pno), M. Vinci (perc) Bongiovanni ▲ GB 5534 [DDD]
Visser, Wanda (vn)—see ORCHESTRAS & ENSEMBLES Camerata Trajectina
Vita, V. de (cl)
Arrigo, G.:Serenata per Andromeda, w. C. Scarponi (pno), A. Vismara (va), K. Martin (cnd), Musica d'Oggi Bongiovanni ▲ GB 5511 [DDD]
Vita, V. de (pno)
Petrassi, G.:Invenzioni Pnos [solo piano version] Bongiovanni ▲ GB 5534 [DDD]
Petrassi, G.:Serenata Fls, w. M. Berni (fl), A. Vismara (va), F. Fraioli (db), M. Vinci (perc) Bongiovanni ▲ GB 5534 [DDD]
Vitali, Marco (vc)—see ORCHESTRAS & ENSEMBLES Conserto Vago
Vitasalo, Marita (pno)
Sibelius, J.:Pno Music—2 Impromptus, Op. 5; 6 Pieces, Op. 24; 5 Pieces, Op. 34; Pensés lyriques, Op. 40; 5 Pieces, Op. 75; 4 Pieces, Op. 76; 5 Pieces, Op. 85; 3 Bagatelles, Op. 97 *(rec June 29–July 3, 1992)* Finlandia ▲ 4509–95874–2 [DDD]
Vítek, M. (vn)—see ORCHESTRAS & ENSEMBLES Pro Arte Piano Trio
Vitek, Milan (vn)
Nørholm, I.:Chamber Music, w. T. L. Christiansen (fl), B. Rørbech (vn), H. Olsen (va), I. Olsen (gtr), N. Ullner (vc), A. Øland (pno)—Essai Prismatique; Medusa's Shadow; Mosaic; Prelude to My Wintermorning; Sonata Quasi Variazioni *(rec 2/89)* Kontrapunkt ▲ 32019 [DDD]
Vítek, Pavel (va)—see ORCHESTRAS & ENSEMBLES Kubín String Quartet
Vito, Gioconda de (vn)
Brahms, J.:Con Vn, w. P. Van Kempen (cnd), German Opera Orch *(rec live, Berlin, 1941)* Arkadia ▲ 623 [ADD]
Brahms, J.:Con Vn, w. W. Furtwängler (cnd), Berlin PO Music & Arts 4–▲ CD 804 [ADD]
Brahms, J.:Con Vn, w. P. Van Kempen (cnd), Berlin State Orch A Classical Record ▲ ACR38–2
Dvořák, A.:Con Vn, w. P. Van Kempen (cnd), Berlin State Orch A Classical Record ▲ ACR38–2
Vitolius, Andris (org)
Ephros, G.:The Priestly Benediction, w. L. Rosenblüth (cantor) BIS ▲ CD 1 [AAD]
Rosenblüth, L.:Jewish Liturgical Music, w. L. Rosenblüth (cant), G. von Bahr (fl), M. Thyresson (org), E. Ericson (cnd), Stockholm Royal Conservatory Chamber Choir—Psalms 93 & 155, plus 5 settings for High Holidays, Rosh Hashanah, Sabbath & Yom Kippur BIS ▲ CD 1 [AAD]
Vivian, Alan (cl)—see ORCHESTRAS & ENSEMBLES Australia Ensemble
Vizzutti, Allen (tpt)
Tyzik, J.:Blue Rondo, w. J. Tyzik (cnd), *(orch unknown)* *(rec Hochstein School of Music, Rochester, New York, July 27–29, 1995)* Summit ▲ 188 [DDD]
Tyzik, J.:Elegy, w. Laura Vincent–Vizzutti (pno), J. Tyzik (cnd), *(orch unknown)* *(rec Hochstein School of Music, Rochester, New York, July 27–29, 1995)* Summit ▲ 188 [DDD]
Tyzik, J.:Son Tpt, w. Laura Vincent–Vizzutti (pno) *(rec Hochstein School of Music, Rochester, New York, July 27–29, 1995)* Summit ▲ 188 [DDD]
Vizzutti, A.:Andante & Capriccio, w. Laura Vincent–Vizzutti (pno), J. Tyzik (cnd), *(orch unknown)* *(rec Hochstein School of Music, Rochester, New York, July 27–29, 1995)* Summit ▲ 188 [DDD]
Vizzutti, A.:The Carnival of Venus, w. Laura Vincent–Vizzutti (pno) *(rec Hochstein School of Music, Rochester, New York, July 27–29, 1995)* Summit ▲ 188 [DDD]
Vizzutti, A.:Son 1 Tpt, w. Laura Vincent–Vizzutti (pno) *(rec Hochstein School of Music, Rochester, New York, July 27–29, 1995)* Summit ▲ 188 [DDD]
Vizzutti, A.:Son 2 Tpt, w. Laura Vincent–Vizzutti (pno) *(rec Hochstein School of Music, Rochester, New York, July 27–29, 1995)* Summit ▲ 188 [DDD]
Vlachová, Jana (vn)—see also ORCHESTRAS & ENSEMBLES New Vlach String Quartet, Vlach String Quartet
Dvořák, A.:Terzetto, w. Karel Stadtherr (vn), Petr Verner (va) *(rec Martínek Studio, Prague, 1995)* Naxos ▲ 8.553373 [DDD]
Vladar, Stefan (pno)
Beethoven, L. van:Con 1 Pno, w. B. Wordsworth (cnd), Capella Istropolitana *(rec 10/88)* Naxos ▲ 8.550190 [DDD]
Beethoven, L. van:Con 2 Pno, w. B. Wordsworth (cnd), Capella Istropolitana *(rec Slovak Philharmonic Concert Hall, Bratislava, Mar 1988)* Naxos 4–▲ 8.504011 [DDD]
Beethoven, L. van:Con 2 Pno, w. B. Wordsworth (cnd), Capella Istropolitana Naxos ▲ 8.550121 [DDD]
Beethoven, L. van:Con 3 Pno, w. B. Wordsworth (cnd), Capella Istropolitana Naxos ▲ 8.550122 [DDD]
Beethoven, L. van:Con 4 Pno, w. B. Wordsworth (cnd), Capella Istropolitana Naxos ▲ 8.550122 [DDD]
Beethoven, L. van:Con 4 Pno, w. B. Wordsworth (cnd), Capella Istropolitana *(rec Concert Hall, Bratislava, Mar 1988)* Naxos ▲ 8.553266 [DDD]
Beethoven, L. van:Con 5 Pno, "Emperor", w. B. Wordsworth (cnd), Capella Istropolitana *(rec Concert Hall, Bratislava, Mar 1988)* Naxos ▲ 8.553266 [DDD]
Beethoven, L. van:Con 5 Pno, "Emperor", w. B. Wordsworth (cnd), Capella Istropolitana *(rec Slovak Philharmonic Concert Hall, Bratislava, Mar 1988)* Naxos 4–▲ 8.504011 [DDD]
Beethoven, L. van:Con 5 Pno, "Emperor", w. B. Wordsworth (cnd), Capella Istropolitana Naxos ▲ 8.550121 [DDD]
Beethoven, L. van:Rondo Pno, WoO 6 *(rec 10/88)* Naxos ▲ 8.550190 [DDD]
Beethoven, L. van:Son 14 Pno, "Moonlight Son" *(rec Feb 28, 1989)* Camerata ▲ 32CM 104
Brahms, J.:Qnt Pno, w. Artis String Quartet *(rec May 11–13, 1993)* Sony Classical ▲ SK 58954 [DDD]
Chopin, F.:Son Pno, Op. 58 *(rec Feb 28, 1989)* Camerata ▲ 32CM 104
Liszt, F.:Consolations—No. 3 in D♭ *(rec Feb 28, 1989)* Camerata ▲ 32CM 104
Opera Fantasies, w. P.–A. Bidaud (cnd), Mélodia Brass Ensemble Sony Classical ▲ SK 52564
Schmidek, K.:Clock Pieces *(rec Feb 28, 1989)* Camerata ▲ 32CM 104
Schubert, Franz:Fant Pno, D.760, "Wandererfantasie" *(rec Feb 28, 1989)* Camerata ▲ 32CM 104
Schumann, R.:Albumblätter Naxos ▲ 8.550144 [DDD]
Schumann, R.:Arabeske Pno Naxos ▲ 8.550144 [DDD]
Schumann, R.:Qnt Pno, w. Artis String Quartet *(rec May 11–13, 1993)* Sony Classical ▲ SK 58954 [DDD]
Schumann, R.:Sym Etudes Naxos ▲ 8.550144 [DDD]
Vlaeva, Nadejda (pno)
Christoff, D.:Rain Hoods...After the Storm *(rec Salle Bulgaria, Sofia, Bulgaria, June 1995)* Concord Concerto ▲ CCD 42038 [DDD]
Christoff, D.:Son 6 Pno *(rec Salle Bulgaria, Sofia, Bulgaria, June 1995)* Concord Concerto ▲ CCD 42038 [DDD]

▲ = CD ♦ = Enhanced CD Δ = MD ■ = Cassette Tape □ = DCC

Vlaeva, Nadejda (pno) (cont.)
Christoff, D.:Son 7 Pno *(rec Salle Bulgaria, Sofia, Bulgaria, June 1995)* Concord Concerto ▲ CCD 42038 [DDD]
Christoff, D.:Son 8 Pno *(rec Salle Bulgaria, Sofia, Bulgaria, June 1995)* Concord Concerto ▲ CCD 42038 [DDD]
Christoff, D.:Toccata for All Soul's Day *(rec Salle Bulgaria, Sofia, Bulgaria, June 1995)* Concord Concerto ▲ CCD 42038 [DDD]

Vlasák, Frantisek (tpt)
Vivaldi, A.:Cons for 2 Obs, w. J. Kolár (ob), R. Hrabě (ob), J. Hasenöhrl (tpt), O. Vlček (cnd), Prague Virtuosi—Con. in C, RV.559 *(rec 1991)* Emergo ▲ EC 3981 [DDD]
Vivaldi, A.:Con for 2 Tpts, w. J. Hasenöhrl (tpt), O. Vlček (cnd), Prague Virtuosi *(rec 1991)* Emergo ▲ EC 3981 [DDD]

Vlašánková, Jitka (vc)
Benda, G.A.:Sons for 2 Vns, w. Shizuka Ishikawa (vn), Josef Suk (vn), Josef Hala (hpd) Lotos ▲ CD 0027 [DDD]
Locatelli, P.:Sons Vn, Op. 8, w. Shizuka Ishikawa (vn), Josef Suk (vn), Josef Hala (hpd)—Trio Son Lotos ▲ CD 0027 [DDD]
Martinů, B.:Qt Cl, Hn, Vc & Side Drum, w. Vlastimil Mareš (cl), Vladimíra Klánská (hn), Petr Holub (side dr) *(rec Studio Martinek, Prague, Mar 3, 1995)* Panton ("Protokol XX" series) ▲ 811348-2 [DDD]
Tartini, G.:Trio Sons, w. Shizuka Ishikawa (vn), Josef Suk (vn), Josef Hala (hpd)—Op. 3/2; Op. 8/1 & 3; Son in D Lotos ▲ CD 0027 [DDD]

Vlatkovic, Radovan (hn)—see also ORCHESTRAS & ENSEMBLES Musiktage Mondsee Ensemble
Mozart, W.A.:Cons Hn, w. J. Tate (cnd), English CO EMI Classics ▲ CDM 64851
Mozart, W.A.:Music of, w. Alban Berg Quartet, F. P. Zimmermann (vn), A. Dumay (vn), A. S. Mutter (vn), S. Meyer (cl), C. Zacharias (pno), *(sels unknown)* EMI Classics ▲ CDC 54165
Mozart, W.A.:Rondo Hn, K.371, w. J. Tate (cnd), English CO EMI Classics ▲ CDM 64851
Strauss, R.:Con 1 Hn, w. J. Tate (cnd), English CO EMI Classics ▲ CDM 64851

Vlček, Oldřich (vn)
Biber, H. von:Son Tpt, 2 Vns, Vc, w. Richard Steuart (tpt), Sylvie Hessova (vn), Ivo Anyz (va), Vaclav Jirovec (vc) *(rec Prague, Nov. 1994)* Discover International ▲ DI 920244 [DDD]
Finger, G.:Son Tpt, Vn & Ob, w. Richard Steuart (tpt), Sylvie Hessova (vn), Milan Hruby (ob) *(rec Prague, Nov. 1994)* Discover International ▲ DI 920244 [DDD]
Vejvanovsky, P.J.:Harmonia romana, w. Prague Virtuosi *(rec Prague, Nov. 1994)* Discover International ▲ DI 920244 [DDD]
Vejvanovsky, P.J.:Sons & Serenades, w. Vaclav Jirovec (vc), Jan Hasenöhrl (tpt), Jiri Pribyl (trbn), Frantisek Xaver (hpd), Milan Hruby (brass), O. Vlček (cnd), Prague Virtuosi—Intrada; Harmonia romana; Serenada; Offertur ad duos chorus; Son à 4 be mollis; Son paschalis; Son tribus quadrantibus; Son campanarum; Serenada *(rec Lobochovice castle, July 26–28, 1992)* Discover International ▲ DI 920243 [DDD]
Vivaldi, A.:Cons for 2 Vns, w. J. Suk (vn), Prague Virtuosi—RV.509 in c, RV.514 in d, RV.522 in a, RV.523 in a, RV.524 in B♭ Supraphon ▲ 11 1271-2 [DDD]
Vivaldi, A.:Cons for 2 Vns, w. J. Suk (vn), Prague Virtuosi—RV. 505, RV. 515, RV. 519, RV. 530 Supraphon ▲ SUP 11 1819 [DDD]

Vliet, Herman van (org)
Recital Festivo ▲ FECD 104 [DDD]

Vliet, Lien van der (org)
Brons, C.:Litany Org Donemus ▲ CV 16
de Leeuw, T.:Sweelinck-variaties Donemus ▲ CV 16
Raxach, E.:The Looking Glass Donemus ▲ CV 16
Ruiter, W. de:Parten Donemus ▲ CV 16
Schat, P.:Passacaglia & Fugue Donemus ▲ CV 16
Welmer, J.:Sequens Donemus ▲ CV 16

Vlyi, Csilla (vc)—see ORCHESTRAS & ENSEMBLES Affetti Musicali

Vobořil, Jan (hn)
Purcell, H.:Son Tpt, w. Jaroslav Halíř (tpt), Marek Vajo (tpt), Radek Nemec (tpt), Jiří Nauš (trbn), Lubomír Maryška (tuba), Pavel Černy (org), Oldřich Šatava (timp) [trans. F. Antonín Vaigl] *(rec Mirror Chapel of the Prague Klementinum, Mar 26, 1995)* Panton ▲ 811368-2 [DDD]

Vodenicharov, Boyen (pno)
Gershwin, G.:Con Pno, w. J. Alfidi (cnd), Philharmonia Bulgarica Vivace ▲ E 548 [ADD]
Gershwin, G.:Rhap in Blue, w. J. Alfidi (cnd), Philharmonia Bulgarica Vivace ▲ E 548 [ADD]

Vogel, Allan (ob)
Beethoven, L. van:Qnt Pno, Ob, Cl, Hn & Bn, w. C. Rosenberger (pno), D. Shifrin (cl), K. Munday (bn), R. Graham (hn) Delos ▲ DCD 3024 [DDD]
Loeffler, C.M.:Rhaps, w. P. Neubauer (va), I. Vallecillo (pno) *(rec July 1–4, 1992)* Delos ▲ DE 3136 [DDD]
Mozart, W.A.:Don Giovanni (sels), w. Paul Fried (fl)—sels [arr. for fl & ob] *(rec Shadow Mountain Studios, Jan.–Feb. 1995)* Golden Tone ▲ GTCD 004
Mozart, W.A.:Entführung (sels), w. Paul Fried (fl)—How anxious Serail; With tenderness Serail; What Rapture Serail [arr. for fl & ob] *(rec Shadow Mountain Studios, Jan.–Feb. 1995)* Golden Tone ▲ GTCD 004
Mozart, W.A.:Nozze di Figaro (sels), w. Paul Fried (fl)—Tell me fair ladies; Say goodbye; How delightful; Non so piu [arr. for fl & ob] *(rec Shadow Mountain Studios, Jan.–Feb. 1995)* Golden Tone ▲ GTCD 004
Mozart, W.A.:Qnt Pno, K.452, w. C. Rosenberger (pno), D. Shifrin (cl), K. Munday (bn), R. Graham (hn) Delos ▲ DCD 3024 [DDD]
Mozart, W.A.:Zauberflöte (sels), w. Paul Fried (fl)—Vogelfänger; Loveliness beyond; All the world; Till love; How Strong; Du feines; In diesen...; Kindly Voice; Act 1 Finale; Bewahret euch; I'll have revenge [all arr. for Fl & Ob] *(rec Shadow Mountain Studios, Jan.–Feb. 1995)* Golden Tone ▲ GTCD 004
Nielsen, C.:Qnt Ww, w. R. Wilson (fl), D. Shifrin (cl), D. Jolley (hn), J. Feves (bn) *(rec July 1–4, 1992)* Delos ▲ DE 3136 [DDD]
Prokofiev, S.:Qnt Ob, w. D. Shifrin (cl), P. Frank (vn), S. Tenebom (va), E. Meyer (db) *(rec July 1–4, 1992)* Delos ▲ DE 3136 [DDD]

Vogel, Edith (pno)
Beethoven, L. van:Fant Pno, Op. 80, "Choral Fant", w. J. Pritchard (cnd), BBC SO, BBC Sym Chorus, BBC Singers IMP ("BBC Radio Classics" series) ▲ IMP 9132

Vogel, Harald (org)
Bach, J.S.:Canonic Vars on "Von Himmel hoch..." Capriccio ▲ CDC 10040 [DDD]
Bach, J.S.:Org Music (misc)—7 Chorale Preludes; Pastorale, BWV 590; Prelude & Fugue in g, BWV 535; Toccata, Adagio & Fugue in C, BWV 564; Fantasia in G, BWV 572; Fantasia in c Deutsche Harmonia Mundi ▲ 05472-77202-2
Bach, J.S.:Trio Sons Org, BWV 525–530—BWV 529–530 Capriccio ▲ CDC 10040 [DDD]
Bach, J.S.:Trio Sons Org, BWV 525–530—BWV 525–528 Capriccio ▲ CDC 10037 [DDD]
Bach, J.S.:Trio Son Org, BWV 584—BWV 529–530 Capriccio ▲ CDC 10040 [DDD]
Buxtehude, D.:Org Music (comp) [period organs]—Canzona in g, BuxWV 173; Canzonetta in C, BuxWV 167; Chorale Preludes (BuxWV 189, 192, 197, 206, 209, 220, 221, 223); Praeludiums (BuxWV 141, 146, 149); Magnificat primi toni, BuxWV 203; Toccata in d, BuxWV 155 MD + G ▲ L 3424 [DDD]
Buxtehude, D.:Org Music (comp)—includes Durch Adams Fall ist ganz verderbt; Wir danken dir, Herr Jesu Christ; Praeludium in C; Praeludium in g; Fuga in C; Canzona in d MD + G ▲ L 3425 [DDD]
Buxtehude, D.:Org Music (comp)—Canzonetta in G, BuxWV.171; Chaconnes in c, BuxWV.159 & in e, BWV.160; Chorale Preludes, BuxWV.76, 186, 193, 194, 198, 202; Fugue in C, BuxWV.174; Magnificat IX toni, BuxWV.205; Preludes in F, BuxWV.144 & 145; Toccata in F, BuxWV.156 MD + G ▲ L 3270 [DDD]
Buxtehude, D.:Org Music (comp)—includes Magnificat I; Komm heiliger Geist; Praeludium in e; Aria "La Capricciosa"; Auf meinen lieben Gott MD + G ▲ L 3426 [DDD]
Buxtehude, D.:Org Music (comp)—includes Preludium in g; Canzona in C; Ich ruf zu dir; Herr Jesu Christ; Praeludium in a; Nun freut euch, lieben Christen g'mein; Gott der Vater wohn uns bei MD + G ▲ L 3427 [DDD]
Buxtehude, D.:Org Music (comp) MD + G ▲ L 3269 [DDD]

Vogel, Harald (org) (cont.)
Buxtehude, D.:Org Music (comp) [period organs] MD + G ▲ L 3268 [DDD]

Vogelsänger, J. (hpd/org)—see ORCHESTRAS & ENSEMBLES Arcangelo Corelli Trio

Vogler, Jan (vc)
Beethoven, L. van:Sons Vc (comp), w. Bruno Canino (pno)—Nos. 4 & 5, Op. 102 Berlin Classics ▲ BER 1100 [DDD]
Beethoven, L. van:Son 1 Vc, w. Bruno Canino (pno) Berlin Classics ▲ BER 1122
Beethoven, L. van:Son 2 Vc, w. Bruno Canino (pno) Berlin Classics ▲ BER 1122
Beethoven, L. van:Son 3 Vc, w. Bruno Canino (pno) Berlin Classics ▲ BER 1167
Beethoven, L. van:Vars on "Ein Mädchen oder Weibchen" from Mozart's *Die Zauberflöte*, w. Bruno Canino (pno) Berlin Classics ▲ BER 1167
Beethoven, L. van:Vars on "See, the Conquering Hero Comes" from Handel's *Judas Maccabaeus*, w. Bruno Canino (pno) Berlin Classics ▲ BER 1167
Beethoven, L. van:Vars on "Bei Männern" from Mozart's *Die Zauberflöte*, w. Bruno Canino (pno) Berlin Classics ▲ BER 1167
Brahms, J.:Son 2 Vc, w. Bruno Canino (pno) Berlin Classics ▲ BER 1029 [DDD]
Debussy, C.:Son Vc, w. Bruno Canino (pno) Berlin Classics ▲ BER 1029 [DDD]
Rachmaninoff, S.:Vocalise, w. Bruno Canino (pno) Berlin Classics ▲ BER 1029 [DDD]
Schnittke, A.:Son Vc, w. Bruno Canino (pno) Berlin Classics ▲ BER 1029 [DDD]
Schumann, R.:Adagio & Allegro Hn, w. Bruno Canino (pno) Berlin Classics ▲ BER 1122
Schumann, R.:Fantasiestücke Cl, w. Bruno Canino (pno) Berlin Classics ▲ BER 1167
Schumann, R.:Stücke im Volkston, w. Bruno Canino (pno) Berlin Classics ▲ BER 1100 [DDD]

Vogler, Rim (vn)
Schoenberg, A.:Ode to Napoleon, w. Roland Hermann (nar), Frank Reinecke (vn), Stefan Fehlandt (va), Michael Sanderling (vc), Frank-Immo Zichner (pno) *(rec Siemensvilla, Berlin-Lankwitz, Aug. 1994)* EDA ▲ EDA 008-2 [DDD]

Vogt, Bruce (pno)
Brahms, J.:Son 1 Vn, w. L. Pollet (fl) [trans Paul Klengel in D for vc & pno; adapted for fl] Titanic ▲ TI 216
Coulthard, J.:Fanfare Son, w. Louis Ranger (tpt) *(rec Univ of Victoria, May 1994)* Crystal ▲ CD 669
Debussy, C.:Epigraphes antiques, w. L. Pollet (fl) [trans Anthony Summers; adapted] Titanic ▲ TI 216
Handel, G.F.:Sons Vn & Kbd, Op. 1, w. L. Pollet (fl)—in g Titanic ▲ TI 216
Kupferman, M.:Infinities, w. Louis Ranger (tpt)—No. 22 (1967) *(rec Univ of Victoria, May 1994)* Crystal ▲ CD 669
Mozart, W.A.:Sons Vn Pno (misc), w. L. Pollet (fl)—in F, K.376 Titanic ▲ TI 216
Peeters, F.:Son Tpt, w. Louis Ranger (tpt) *(rec Univ of Victoria, May 1994)* Crystal ▲ CD 669
Portriat of the Viola Musica Viva ▲ MVCD 1072 [DDD]

Vogt, Lars (pno)
Grieg, E.:Con Pno, Op. 16, w. S. Rattle (cnd), City of Birmingham SO EMI Classics ▲ CDC 54746
Schumann, R.:Con Pno, w. S. Rattle (cnd), City of Birmingham SO EMI Classics ▲ CDC 54746

Vogt, Michael (tuba)
Glandien, L.:Es Lebe ReR ▲ CMCD [DDD]
Tuba Intim ReR ▲ Tuba 1

Voisin, Roger (tpt)
The Extraordinary Roger Voisin:The Baroque Trumpet MCA Classics 2-▲ MCAD2-9807

Volans, Kevin (hpd)
Volans, K.:Mbira, w. Deborah James (hpd), Robyn Schulkowsky (perc) *(rec West German Radio, Cologne, Apr 20, 1984)* United ▲ CAL 88034 [ADD]
Volans, K.:White Man Sleeps Hpds, w. Robert Hill (hpd), Margriet Tindemans (vl), Robyn Schulkowsky (perc) *(rec West German Radio, Cologne & Watershed Recording Studio, London, Apr 20, 1984 & July 27, 1)* United ▲ CAL 88034 [ADD]

Volken, Edmund (dlc)
Holliger, H.:Alb-Chehr, w. Oswald Brumann (bass), Sabine Gertschen (dlc), Elmar Schmid (cl), Klaus Schmid (cl), Markus Tenisch (Swiss org), Marcel Volken (Swiss org), Paul Locher (vn), Franziskus Abgottspon (nar) ECM New Series ▲ 78118-21540-2 [DDD]

Volken, Marcel (org)
Holliger, H.:Alb-Chehr, w. Oswald Brumann (bass), Sabine Gertschen (dlc), Edmund Volken (dlc), Elmar Schmid (cl), Klaus Schmid (cl), Markus Tenisch (Swiss org), Paul Locher (vn), Franziskus Abgottspon (nar) ECM New Series ▲ 78118-21540-2 [DDD]

Volkman, Dean (perc)
Encore, w. Colorado Children's Chorale,Duain Wolfe (cnd), Rick Chinski (gtr), Robert Davine (acc), Laurie Kahler (pno), Samuel Lancaster (pno), Barry Oliver (pno), Marylin Preston (fl), Karen Yonovitz (fl), Peter Cooper (ob), Andy Stevens (cl), Lionel Young (vn), Basil Vendreys (va), Wayne Templeman (vc), Charle *(rec Denver Center Media)* Colorado Children's Chorale ▲ 001

Volkonsky, André (pno)
Bach, J.S.:Das wohltemperierte Klavier—Book II Lyrinx ▲ LYX 48 [ADD]

Volkov, Alexander (pno)
Brahms, J.:Trio Cl, w. E. Eban (cl), Marcel Bergman (vc) Meridian ▲ CDE 84122

Volkov, Oleg (pno)
All Russian, w. Volkov, Oleg (pno) Brioso ▲ BR 105
Beethoven, L. van:Trio 7 Pno, w. E. Eban (cl), Marcel Bergman (vc) Meridian ▲ CDE 84122
Beethoven, L. van:Vars on a Russian Dance from P. Wranitzky's ballet "Das Waldmachen", WoO 71 Art & Electronics ▲ AED 10319 [DDD]
Haydn, J.:Sons Pno—No. 38 Art & Electronics ▲ AED 10319 [DDD]
Live from Moscow *(rec live, Tchaikovsky Concert Hall, Moscow, May 22, 1994)* Brioso ▲ BR 106
Rachmaninoff, S.:Preludes Pno, Opp 23 & 32—Op. 23, Nos. 1, 2, 5 & 6 Art & Electronics ▲ AED 10319 [DDD]
Rachmaninoff, S.:Son 2 Pno Art & Electronics ▲ AED 10319 [DDD]
Schnittke, A.:Con Pno, w. V. Sinaisky (cnd), Moscow PO Brioso ▲ BR 109
Shostakovich, D.:Con 1 Pno, w. V. Sinaisky (cnd), Moscow PO Brioso ▲ BR 109

Vollenweider, Andreas (kbd)
Pavarotti & Friends 2, w. Luciano Pavarotti (ten), Nancy Gustafson (sop), Bryan Adams (sgr), Michael Kamen (cnd), Leone Mageira (cnd), Bologna Community Theater Orch London ▲ 444460-2 ■ 444460-4

Vollenweider, Hans (org)
Bach, J.S.:Org Music (misc)—Vars canoniques, BWV 769; Chorals de Leipzig, BWV 651–668 Accord 2-▲ ACD 149514

Vollenwyder, Erich (org)
Maggini, E.:Org Music—Via crucis; Ultima verba Christi; Patmos *(rec 1984)* Jecklin ▲ JS 287-2 [DDD]

Volpov, Alexander (vc)—see ORCHESTRAS & ENSEMBLES Classic Trio

Vonderthann, Andreas (perc)—see ORCHESTRAS & ENSEMBLES Karl Peinkofer Percussion Ensemble

Vondra, J. (hn)
Zimmermann, A.:Cassations, w. V. Brunner (fl), J. Brunner (fl), P. Sivanic (hn), V. Simcisko (vn), M. Tedla (vn), M. Telecky (va), J. Alexander (vc)—in G, D & D Trevak ▲ TRE 40008 [DDD]

Vorholz, Dieter (vn)
Bach, J.S.:Con for 2 Vns, w. S. Lautenbacher (vn), G. Kehr (cnd), Mainz CO Allegretto ▲ ACD 8057 [ADD] ■ ACS 8057
Bach, J.S.:Con for 2 Vns, w. S. Lautenbacher (vn), G. Kehr (cnd), Mainz CO *(rec 1958)* Vox Box 3-▲ CD3X 3008 [ADD]
Bach, J.S.:Life & Music of, w. S. Lautenbacher (vn), G. Kehr (cnd), Mainz CO—narration with selected excerpts from Brandenburg Cons. Nos. 2, 3, 4 & 5, BWV 1047–50; Cants. Nos. 57 & 211; Chorale Prelude, BWV 645; Con. No. 2 for Violin, BWV 1042; Inventions, BWV 785; Italian Con., BWV 971; Toccata & Fugue, BWV 565; Mass in b, BWV 232; Wohltemperierte Klavier [Bk. 1], BWV 846; St. Matthew Passion, BWV 244; St. John Passion, BWV 245; Con. for 2 Violins, BWV 1043; Passacaglia & Fugue, BWV 582; Magnificat, BWV 243; plus complete versions of Con. for 2 Violins, BWV 1043 & Con. for Violin, BWV 1042 Vox Music Masters ("Music Masters" series) ▲ MMD 8500 [ADD] ■ MMC 8500

INSTRUMENT.

Vos, W. (xyl)
Saint-Saëns, C.:Carnival of the Animals, w. D. Wayenberg (vn), H. Oudenaarden (vn), J. Hagen (fl), H. de Fraaf (cl), H. Krul (db), M. Dekkers (acc), Daniel String Quartet *(rec Rotterdam, May 28, 1985)* Erasmus ▲ WHV 001 [DDD]
Vosgerchian, L. (pno)
Schubert, Franz:Son Pno, D.960 Titanic ▲ Ti 210 [DDD]
Schumann, R.:Kreisleriana Titanic ▲ Ti 210 [DDD]
Voss, Angela (trb vl/ten vl)—see ORCHESTRAS & ENSEMBLES English Fantasy
Voss, Hermann (va)—see ORCHESTRAS & ENSEMBLES Melos String Quartet
Vostrelov, Yuri (bayan)
Yuri Vostrelov:Russian Performing School *(rec 1975–88)* Russian Compact Disc ▲ RCD 16201
Votapek, Ralph (pno)
Corigliano, J.:Son Vn & Pno, w. John Corigliano, Sr. (vn) *(rec Steinway Hall, NYC, Mar 1, 1966)* CRI ▲ CD 659 [ADD]
Poulenc, F.:Aubade Pno, w. S. Richman (cnd), Harmonie Ensemble/New York Music & Arts ▲ CD 649 [DDD]
Votava, Jan (trbn)
Bruckner, A.:Mass 3, w. Dagmar Masková (sgr), Vladimír Nacházel (sgr), Jiří Novotný (sgr), Jiří Seiler (sgr), Jiří Uherek (sgr), Eva Zbytovská (sgr), Josef Kšica (org), Josef Pancík (cnd), Prague Chamber Choir Orfeo ▲ 327 951 [DDD]
Bruckner, A.:Motets, w. Dagmar Masková (sgr), Vladimír Nacházel (sgr), Jiří Novotný (sgr), Jiří Seiler (sgr), Jiří Uherek (sgr), Eva Zbytovská (sgr), Josef Kšica (org), Josef Pancík (cnd), Prague Chamber Choir—Locus iste; Afferentur regi; Ave Maria (2); Pange lingua; Pange lingua (phrygisch); Tantum ergo (2); Libera me; Os iusti; Virga jesse; Vexilla regis; Christus factus est; Tota pulchra es Maria; Ecce sacerdos magnus Orfeo ▲ 327 951 [DDD]
Vote, Jeanne Fryberger (hpd)—see ORCHESTRAS & ENSEMBLES Maryland Bach Aria Group members
Votta, Michael (cl)
Johnson, H.:Serenade Fl, w. R. Troxler (fl) Albany ▲ TROY 061 [DDD]
Vraskos, Dimitris (vn)
Karaindrou, E.:The Suspended Step of the Stork, w. Vangelis Christopoulos (ob), Ada Rouva (hp), Christos Sfetsas (vc), Nikos Spinoulas (hn), Andreas Tsekouras (acc), L. Chalkiadakis (cnd), *(orch unknown) (rec Sound, Athens, Apr & Aug 1991)* ECM ▲ 78118-21456-2 [AAD]
Vrethammar, Ulla (vc)
Pergament, M.:Pezzo, w. G. von Bahr (fls), P. Pohjola (vn), Z. Zirchev (vn), Z. Tchavdarov (va) *(rec Jan. 25, 1973)* BIS ▲ CD 37 [AAD]
Vries, Han de (ob)
Albinoni, T.:Cons Obs, w. Alma Music Amsterdam EMI Classics ▲ CDC 54664
Andriessen, L.:Anachrony 2, w. H. Williams (cnd), Netherlands Ballet Orch *(rec Amsterdam Music Theater, Oct 3–6, 1994)* Donemus ▲ CV 54 [DDD]
Ravel, M.:Pièce en forme de Habanera, w. G. Simon (cnd), Philharmonia Orch [orchd. by Arthur Hoérée] *(rec St. Jude-on-the-Hill, Hampstead, London, Feb 8–12, 1991)* Cala ▲ CACD 1005 [DDD]
Schat, P.:Thema, w. P. Schat (cnd), Netherlands Wind Ensemble Donemus ▲ CV 19
Telemann, G.P.:Cons Ob Orch, Alma Music Amsterdam EMI Classics ▲ CDC 54664
Vrsajkov, Milan (vc)—see ORCHESTRAS & ENSEMBLES Tickmayer Formatio
Vuataz, R. (pno)
Bach, J.S.:Trio Sons Org, BWV 525–530, w. R. Cotutiù (fl) [trans Cotutiù & Vataz for fl & pno] Gallo ▲ CD 611 [ADD]
Vulih, Vladimir (db)
Ustvolskaya, G.:Composition 2, w. Igo Propischin (db), Leonid Kolosov (db), Vitalii Goryachev (db), Vladimir Vulih (db), Vyacheslav Kovalenko (db), Alexei Peresipkin (db), Dmitrii Sokolov (db), Vladimir Nefedov (db), Valerii Javnertchik (perc), Galina Sandovskaya (pno), O. Malov (cnd) *(rec St. Petersburg Radio House, Jan. 1994)* Megadisc ▲ 7867
Vulp, Urmas (vn)—see ORCHESTRAS & ENSEMBLES Tallinn String Quartet
Vybíralová, Ludmila (vn)
Zelenka, J.D.:Con à 8, w. Jana Brozková (ob), Josef Suk (vn), Ivo Laniar (vc), Jaroslav Kubita (bn), F. Vajnar (cnd), Suk CO *(rec Studio Martinek, Prague, May 15–17 & Nov. 8–13, 19)* Panton 2–▲ PAN 811235 [DDD]
Vyzrálek, Josef (vn)—see ORCHESTRAS & ENSEMBLES Bohuslav Martinů Philharmonic String Quartet
Waal, Rian de (pno)
Godowsky, L.:Pno Music—Passacaglia [44 Variations, Cadenza & Fugue on the opening of Schubert's "Unfinished" Symphony] (1927); 3 Schubert Song Transcriptions:Das Wandern, Gute Nacht & Ungeduld (from Twelve Schubert Songs, 1926); Ballet Music from Rosamunde & Moment Musical No. 3 in f [Schubert] (1922); Kunstlerleben (from Symphonic Metamorphosis on Themes by Johann Strauss, 1905); Invitation to the Dance [Weber] (a contrapuntal arr., ca. 1905); Alt-Wien (1919) Hyperion ▲ CDA 66496 [DDD]
Wachenfeld, Kristin (hpd)
Bach, J.S.:Das wohltemperierte Klavier—Book 1 *(rec Oct 1990)* Ambitus 2–▲ 383847 [DDD]
Wachowski, Gerd (org)
Festive Organ Music MD + G ▲ CD 3128
Pachelbel, J.:Org Music MD + G ▲ MDG CD 6060273
Wachsenegger, Jörg (cl)—see ORCHESTRAS & ENSEMBLES Vienna Lanner Ensemble
Wächter, Edmund (fl)
Bach, J.S.:Trio Son for 2 Fls, BWV 1039, w. Elisabeth Weinzierl (fl), Eva Schieferstein (hpd) Entrée ▲ 0081 [DDD]
Buffardin, P.G.:Trio Son Fl, w. Elisabeth Weinzierl (fl), Eva Schieferstein (hpd) [arr for 2 flutes & bc] Entrée ▲ 0081 [DDD]
Hasse, J.A.:Trio Sons Fls, Op. 3, w. Elisabeth Weinzierl (fl), Ulrich Fuchs (vc)—Trio Son No. 6 in D Entrée ▲ 0081 [DDD]
Haydn, J.:Trios Fls & Vc, "London Trios", w. Elizabeth Weinzier (fl), Ulrich Fuchs (vc) Christophorus ▲ CHR 77146 [DDD]
Hoffmeister, F.A.:Trios for 2 Fls & Vc, w. E. Weinzierl (fl), U. Fuchs (vc) Christophorus ▲ CHR 77146 [DDD]
Quantz, J.J.:Trio Son Fls, w. Elisabeth Weinzierl (fl), Ulrich Fuchs (vc) Entrée ▲ 0081 [DDD]
Vivaldi, A.:Trio Son Fls, w. Elisabeth Weinzierl (fl), Ulrich Fuchs (vc) Entrée ▲ 0081 [DDD]
Wächter, Peter (vn)—see also ORCHESTRAS & ENSEMBLES Vienna String Quintet, Vienna Phil Trio
Schmidt, F.:Qnt Cl, w. E. Ottensamer (cl), R. Keuschnig (pno), J. Hell (vn), P. Pecha (va), R. Wallfisch (vc) *(rec Jan. 7, 1991)* Orfeo ▲ 287921 [DDD]
Schmidt, F.:Qnt Pno, w. R. Keuschnig (pno), J. Hell (vn), P. Pecha (va), G. Iberer (vc) *(rec Jan. 7, 1991)* Orfeo ▲ 287921 [DDD]
Wächter, Waltraut (vn)
Weill, K.:Con Vn, w. M. Pommer (cnd), Leipzig RSO Ondine ▲ ODE 771-2 [DDD]
Wade, Irene (va)
Scelsi, G.:Anahit, w. Paul Zukofsky (vn), Julie Bogorad (fl), Peggy Russell (fl), Courtney Westcott (fl), Lawrence McDonald (cl), Joan Waryha (cl), Jean Hansen (b cl), Bill Suite (e hn), Nita VanPelt (sax), Bob Zobal (tpt), John Carter (trbn), Martin Lydecker (trbn), Stan Cortman (hn), Robert Ward (hn), William Curry (va), Jody Rowitsch (va), Anne Fagerburg (vc), John Gockel (vc), Sue Manz (bass), Steven Stearman (bass) *(rec Oberlin Conservatory of Music, Oct 8, 1973)* CP² ▲ CP2 108 [AAD]
Wade, Jonathan (perc)
Mather, B.:Elegy, w. Robert Cram (fl), David Hutchenreuther (vc), Charlotte Sheng (pno) Centrediscs ▲ CMC 5094 [DDD]
Wade, Patsy (pno)
Barber, S.:Songs, w. S. Mabry (mez)—O Boundless, Boundless; A Green Lowland; Now Have I Fed [E] Owl ▲ OWL 35 [DAD]
Goosen, F.:At Casterbridge Fair, w. S. Mabry (mez)—three songs:After the Club-Dance; The Inquiry; A Wife Waits Owl ▲ OWL 35 [DAD]
Goosen, F.:Garland, w. S. Mabry (mez) Owl ▲ OWL 35 [DAD]

Wadsworth, Charles (pno)
Rorem, N.:Winter Pages, w. T. Palmer (cl), F. Morelli (bn), I. Kavafian (vn), F. Sherry (vc) New World ▲ 80416-2 [DDD]
The Voices of Living Stereo, Vol. 2, w. Eileen Farrell (sop), Birgit Nilsson (sop), Roberta Peters (sop), Leontyne Price (sop), Galina Vishnevskaya (sop), Rosalind Elias (mez), Shirley Verrett (mez), Marian Anderson (cta), Maureen Forrester (cta), Sergio Franchi (ten), Mario Lanza (ten), Richard Lewis (ten), Jan Pee, Alexander Dedyukhin (pno), Franz Rupp (pno), Leo Taubman (pno), George Trovillo (pno), Boston Pops Orch [cnd:Arthur Fiedler], Boston SO [cnd:Charles Munch], Chicago SO [cnd:Fritz Reiner], RCA Victor Orch, RCA Victor Chorus [cnd:Wa *(rec Boston & Chicago & New York & Rome, 1957–1964)* RCA Living Stereo ▲ 09026-68167-2 [ADD]
Wagemans, Michel (pno)
Brahms, J.:Sons Cl (comp), w. Peter Hatch (va) *(rec Elder Forest Studios, Elder Forest, CA)* PROdigital ▲ PRO 6215 [DDD]
Granados, E.:Son Vn, w. J. Palomares (vn) PROdigital ▲ PRO 1229 [DDD]
Grieg, E.:Sons Vn, Opp. 8, 13 & 45, w. Joaquín Palomares (vn) *(rec Elder Forest Studios, Elder Forest, CA)* PROdigital ▲ PRO 1314 [DDD]
Mompou, F.:Impresiones intimas PROdigital ▲ PRO 5162 [DDD]
Mompou, F.:Paisajes PROdigital ▲ PRO 5162 [DDD]
Mompou, F.:Variaciones sobre un tema PROdigital ▲ PRO 5162 [DDD]
Turina, J.:El poema de una sanluqueña, w. J. Palomares (vn) PROdigital ▲ PRO 1229 [DDD]
Turina, J.:Son 1 Vn, w. J. Palomares (vn) PROdigital ▲ PRO 1229 [DDD]
Turina, J.:Son 2 Vn, w. J. Palomares (vn) PROdigital ▲ PRO 1229 [DDD]
Wager, Mattias (org)
Duruflé, M.:Mass, "Cum jubilo", w. P. Mattei (bar), St. Jacobs Chamber Choir *(rec Nov. 9–12, 1992)* BIS ▲ CD 602 [DDD]
Duruflé, M.:Requiem, w. P. Hofman (ten), P. Mattei (bar), E. Lavotha (vc), St. Jacobs Chamber Choir *(rec Nov. 9–12, 1992)* BIS ▲ CD 602 [DDD]
Wagner, A. (pno)
Mendelssohn, F.:Songs, w. W. Holzmair (bar)—21 songs (from Opp. 9, 19a, 34, 47, 57, 71, 86 & 99) [G] *(rec 1985)* Preiser ▲ 93368 [ADD]
Wagner, Bob (bn)
Zaimont, J.L.:Sky Curtains, w. Kathleen Nester (fl), Daniel Gilbert (cl), Lois Martin (va), Christopher Finkel (vc) *(rec SUNY Purchase, Theatre C, Jan 8–10 & Feb 20, 1995)* Arabesque ▲ ARA 6667 [DDD]
Wagner, J. (vn)
Berlioz, H.:Rêverie et caprice, w. M. Schønwandt (cnd), Berlin SO, Ernst Senff Chorus, Berlin Radio Choir Kontrapunkt 2–▲ KPT 32143 [DDD]
Wagner, Mattias (org)
Bach, J.S.:Cons Org, BWV 592–597—BWV 596 Opus 3 ▲ 19506 [AAD]
Wagner, R. (cl)
Rorem, N.:Hearing, w. R. Rees (sop), K. Wheeler (mez), M. Galloway (ten), R. Hilley (bar), J. Hamlin (tpt), D. Starobin (mand), D. Davidson (vn), K. Askew (va), J. Babich (db), P. Suits (pno), D. Druckman (perc), G. Smith (cnd) Premier ▲ PRCD 1035 [ADD]
Wagner, Robert (bn)—see also ORCHESTRAS & ENSEMBLES Boehme Quintet
Wilson, R.:Con Bn, w. L. Botstein (cnd), Boston Pro Arte CO CRI ▲ CD 575 [DDD]
Wahlberg, Ingrid (pno)
Genishta, J.:Nocturnes (3) Vc, w. A. Ivashkin (vc)—1 Nocturne Manu ▲ MAN 1426 [DDD]
Glazunov, A.:Elégie Vc, w. A. Ivashkin (vc) Manu ▲ MAN 1426 [DDD]
Glazunov, A.:Serenade espagnole, w. A. Ivashkin (vc) [trans vc & pno] Manu ▲ MAN 1426 [DDD]
Mosolov, A.:Legenda, w. A. Ivashkin (vc) Manu ▲ MAN 1426 [DDD]
Rimsky-Korsakov, N.:Serenade Vc, w. A. Ivashkin (vc) Manu ▲ MAN 1426 [DDD]
Roslavets, N.:Dance of the White Girls, w. A. Ivashkin (vc) Manu ▲ MAN 1426 [DDD]
Russian Elegy, w. Ivashkin, Alexander (vc) Manu ▲ MAN 1426 [DDD]
Shostakovich, D.:Moderato Vc, w. A. Ivashkin (vc) Manu ▲ MAN 1426 [DDD]
Wahlberg, Paul (fl)—see ORCHESTRAS & ENSEMBLES Musica Domestica
Wahlin, Mikael (org)
Dupré, M.:Préludes & Fugues, Op. 7 Caprice ▲ CAP 21404 [DDD]
Fleury, A.:Prelude, Andante & Toccata Caprice ▲ CAP 21404 [DDD]
Jongen, J.:Little Prelude Caprice ▲ CAP 21404 [DDD]
Jongen, J.:Toccata Org Caprice ▲ CAP 21404 [DDD]
Krenek, E.:Sons Pno—Op. 92/1 Caprice ▲ CAP 21404 [DDD]
Reger, M.:Intro & Passacaglia Caprice ▲ CAP 21404 [DDD]
Reger, M.:Pieces Org, Op. 69—No. 4 [Moment Musical] Caprice ▲ CAP 21404 [DDD]
Wahrhaftig, Peter (tuba)—see also ORCHESTRAS & ENSEMBLES San Francisco Contemporary Music Players
Brown, C.:Lava, w. William Winant (perc), Toyoji Tomita (trbn), Tom Dill (tpt), Chris Brown (elecs)—Crack; Eruption; Fountain; River; Crest; Pahoehoe Tzadik ("The Composers" series) ▲ TZA 7002 [DDD]
Curran, A.:Why Is This Night Different Than All Other Nights?, w. Roy Malan (vn), Donald Haas (acc), Alvin Curran (pno), William Winant (perc) Tzadik ("The Composers" series) ▲ TZA 7001 [DDD]
Waiman, Mikhail (vn)
Tchaikovsky, P.:Con Vn, w. G. Rozhdestvensky (cnd), Leningrad PO IMP ("BBC Radio Classics" series) ▲ IMP 9134
Wait, Mark (pno)
Stravinsky, I.:Capriccio, w. R. Craft (cnd), Orch of St. Luke MusicMasters ▲ 01612-67158-2
Waites, Althea (pno)
Bland, E.:Sketches Set 7 *(rec July 25 & Aug. 6, 1990)* Cambria ▲ 1097 [DDD]
Bonds, M.:Troubled Water *(rec July 25 & Aug. 6, 1990)* Cambria ▲ 1097 [DDD]
Price, F.B.:Cotton Dance Cambria ▲ 1097 [DDD]
Price, F.B.:Dances in the Canebrakes *(rec July 25, 1990; Aug. 6, 19)* Cambria ▲ 1097 [DDD]
Price, F.B.:The Old Boatman Cambria ▲ 1097 [DDD]
Price, F.B.:Son Pno Cambria ▲ 1097 [DDD]
Still, W.G.:3 Visions Cambria ▲ CD 1097 [DDD]
Waitzman, Daniel (fl)—see ORCHESTRAS & ENSEMBLES Bell'Arte Trio
Wajt, Mark (pno)
Stravinsky, I.:L'Histoire du soldat, w. Catherine Ciesinski (mez), Jon Humphries (ten), David Evitts (bar), R. Craft (cnd), Orch of St. Luke, Gregg Smith Singers MusicMasters ▲ 01612-67152-2
Wakabayashi, Nobu (vn)
Brahms, J.:Sons Vn (comp), w. K. Sturrock (pno) IMP Classics ▲ IMPPCD 1050 [DDD]
Wakamatsu, Natsumi (vn)
Rameau, J.P.:Pièces de clavecin en concert, w. C. Arita (hpd), W. Kuijken (vl), M. Arita (trns fl/pic) Denon ▲ CO 79045 [DDD]
Vivaldi, A.:Con Fl Ob, RV.107, w. M. Arita (fl), M. Homma (ob), K. Dosaka (bn), Bach-Mozart Ensemble Tokyo *(rec June 22–26, 1992)* Denon ▲ CO 75198 [DDD]
Wakefield, David (hn)—see also ORCHESTRAS & ENSEMBLES American Brass Quintet
Balada, L.:Son Winds, w. J. Aley (tpt), R. Borror (tenor trbn), R. Biddlecome (bass trbn), American Brass Quintet New World ▲ 80442-2
Wakefield, Thomas (pno)
Beethoven, L. van:Con 3 Pno [trans. for solo piano Wakefield] Symposium ▲ 1062
Liszt, F.:Pno Music (misc)—March héroique dans le genre hongroise; Grand galop chromatique; Hexameron Vars on the March from Bellini's "I Puritani" [comp with Thalberg, Pixis, Herz, Czerny & Chopin] Symposium ▲ SYM 1091
Liszt, F.:Transcriptions & Paraphrases—Rossini:William Tell Ov; Schubert:Serenade; Ave Maria; Donizetti:Lucia di Lammermoor [w. Penny Losemore (pno)]; Bellini:Reminiscences de Norma Symposium ▲ SYM 1091

▲ = CD ♦ = Enhanced CD Δ = MD ■ = Cassette Tape □ = DCC

Walace, Brett (vc)
A Colorado Kind of Christmas, w. Colorado Children's Chorale,Duain Wolfe (cnd), Mike Fitzmaurice (db), Rod Garnet (fl), William Hill (perc), Deborah Schmit-Lobis (pno), Mary Louise Burke (pno), Laurie Kahler (pno), Helen Hope (hp) *(rec Denver Center Media)* Colorado Children's Chorale ▲ XMAS
Walasek, Wojciech (vc)—see ORCHESTRAS & ENSEMBLES Wilanów String Quartet
Walcha, Helmut (org)
Organ Works Archiv ("Galleria" series) ▲ 431551-2 AGA
Wald, Herbert (pno)
Beethoven, L. van:Son 17 Pno, "Tempest" Stradivari Classics ▲ SCD 6006 [DDD] ■ SMC 6006 (D)
Beethoven, L. van:Son 23 Pno, "Appassionata" Stradivari Classics ▲ SCD 6006 [DDD] ■ SMC 6006 (D)
Waldeland, H. (pno)
Grieg, E.:Ballade Pno Swedish Society ▲ SCD 1030
Grieg, E.:Lyric Pieces Swedish Society ▲ SCD 1030
Stenhammar, W.:Late Summer Nights Swedish Society ▲ SCD 1032
Waldeland, Hege (vc)—see also ORCHESTRAS & ENSEMBLES Trio Con Brio
Jersild, J.:Fant e canto affetuoso, w. Lena Bust Nielsen (fl), Jesper Helmuth Madsen (cl), Sonja Gislinge (hp) Paula ▲ PACD 75 [DAD]
Walden, Stanley (cl)—see ORCHESTRAS & ENSEMBLES New York Woodwind Soloists
Walden, Timothy (vc)
Tippett, M.:Con Orch, w. R. Hickox (cnd), Bournemouth SO Chandos ▲ CHAN 9384 [DDD]
Waldman, Yuval (vn)
American Flute, Vol. 1, w. Zizi Mueller (fl), Jesse Levine (va), S. Tahmizián (pno) Premier ▲ PRCD 1029 [DDD]
Bach, J.S.:Cant 20, w. José Cueto (vn), Jennifer Rende (va), Gail Kruvand (db), Maryland Bach Aria Group members—Wacht auf Crystal ▲ CD 705 [DDD]
Bach, J.S.:Cant 82, w. José Cueto (vn), Jennifer Rende (va), Gail Kruvand (db), Maryland Bach Aria Group members *(rec St. Peter's Church, Hale, Cheshire, Mar 14, 1994)* Naxos ▲ 8.550763 [DDD]
Bach, J.S.:Cant 110, w. José Cueto (vn), Jennifer Rende (va), Gail Kruvand (db), Maryland Bach Aria Group members—Wachtet auf Crystal ▲ CD 705 [DDD]
Bach, J.S.:Con Vn & Ob, w. V. Brewer (ob), J. Somary (cnd), Amor Artis Orch Omega ▲ OCD 1013 [DDD]
Newman, Anthony:Chamber Music, w. M. Mills (pno), P.J. Bacchus (fl), D. Wan, Flute Force, Laurentian String Quartet—Qnt for Piano & Strings, "Easter"; Qt for 4 Flutes; Introduction & Toccata for Flute & Piano; Vars & Toccata for Violin Newport Classic ▲ NCD 60032 [DDD]
Stradella, A.:Sinf alla Serenata, w. José Cueto (vn), Jennifer Rende (va), Gail Kruvand (db), Maryland Bach Aria Group members Crystal ▲ CD 705 [DDD]
Torelli, G.:Son Tpt, G.1, w. José Cueto (vn), Jennifer Rende (va), Gail Kruvand (db), Maryland Bach Aria Group members Crystal ▲ CD 705 [DDD]
Vivaldi, A.:Cons Bn, w. José Cueto (vn), Jennifer Rende (va), Gail Kruvand (db), Maryland Bach Aria Group members—in B♭, RV.501, "La notte" Crystal ▲ CD 705 [DDD]
Vivaldi, A.:Cons Vn, Op. 8/1-4, "The Four Seasons", w. J. Somary (cnd), Amor Artis Orch Omega ▲ OCD 1013 [DDD]
Waldner, T. (dr)
Pfiffner, E.:Cambiamenti concertanti, w. D. Doherty (ob), Basel Serenata *(rec March 1992)* Pro Viva ▲ ISPV 170 [DDD]
Waldner, Thomas (perc)—see ORCHESTRAS & ENSEMBLES Basel Perc Trio
Walevska, Christine (vc)
Dvořák, A.:Con Vc, w. A. Gibson (cnd), London PO IMP Collectors Series ▲ IMPX 9035
Haydn, J.:Con 1 Vc, w. E. de Waart (cnd), English CO Philips 2-▲ 438797-2
Haydn, J.:Con 2 Vc, w. E. de Waart (cnd), English CO Philips 2-▲ 438797-2
Tchaikovsky, P.:Vars on a Rococo Theme, w. A. Gibson (cnd), London PO IMP Collectors Series ▲ IMPX 9035
Walker, Frances (pno)
Coleridge-Taylor, S.:Negro Melodies—At the Dawn of Day; The Stones Are Very Hard; Take Nabandji; They Will Not Lend Me a Child; Song of Conquest; Warrior's Song; Oloba; The Bamboula; The Angels Changed My Name; Deep River; Didn't My Lord Deliver Daniel?; Don't Be Weary, Traveller; Going Up; I'm Troubled inMind; I Was Down A-Yonder; Let Us Cheer the Weary Traveller; Many Thousand Gone; My Lord Delivered Daniel; Oh, He Raise a Poor Lazarus; Pilgrim's Song; Run, Mary, Run; Sometimes I Feel Like a Motherless Child; Steal Away; Wade in the Water *(rec St. Albans, NY, Apr 2 & 3, 1978)* Orion ▲ 7806-2 [AAD]
Walker, George (pno)
Beethoven, L. van:Son 26 Pno, "Les Adieux" *(rec Montclair, NJ, May 1994)* Albany ▲ TROY 117 [DDD]
Brahms, J.:Waltzes Pno, Op. 39—No. 15 *(rec Montclair, NJ, May 1994)* Albany ▲ TROY 117 [DDD]
Chopin, F.:Barcarolle Pno *(rec Montclair, NJ, May 1994)* Albany ▲ TROY 117 [DDD]
Chopin, F.:Mazurkas—No. 2 in f *(rec Montclair, NJ, May 1994)* Albany ▲ TROY 117 [DDD]
Scarlatti, D.:Sons Kbd in E, L.23; in A, L.23; in B♭, L.39, in d, L.300; in E, L.430; in G, L.490; *(rec Montclair, NJ, May 1994)* Albany ▲ TROY 117 [DDD]
Schubert, Franz:Moments musicaux—No. 3 in f *(rec Montclair, NJ, May 1994)* Albany ▲ TROY 117 [DDD]
Walker, G.:Son Vc, w. Italo Babini (vc) Albany ▲ TROY 154 [DDD]
Walker, G.:Son 1 Pno *(rec Montclair, NJ, May 1994)* Albany ▲ TROY 117 [DDD]
Walker, G.:Son 2 Pno Albany ▲ TROY 154 [DDD]
Walker, G.:Son 1 Vn, w. Gregory Walker (vn) Albany ▲ TROY 154 [DDD]
Walker, Gregory (vn)
Kaleidoscope:Music by African-American Women, w. Helen Walker-Hill (pno) *(rec Marshall Auditorium, Haveford College, PN, Dec 1993 & Mar 1994)* Leonarda ▲ LE 339 [DDD]
Walker, G.:Son 1 Vn, w. George Walker (pno) Albany ▲ TROY 154 [DDD]
Walker, Jane (fl)
Paccione, P.:...Like Spring, w. Dyann Scheele (fl) Capstone ▲ SCI 6
Walker, John (org)
At the Riverside Church, New York City Gothic ▲ GOT 18517
Dupré, M.:Sym-Passion, "The World Awaiting the Saviour" Gothic ▲ G 18517
John Walker & the Riverside Organ Pro Organo ▲ POCD 7016
To Behold the Fair Beauty, w. Shadyside Presbyterian Church Chancel Choir Pro Organo ▲ POCD 7043 [DDD]
Walker, Kim (bn)
Boismortier, J.B. de:Sons, Op. 26, w. Darryl Nixon (hpd), Cléna Stein (db)—Sonata No. 4 Gallo ▲ CD 367 [ADD]
Boismortier, J.B. de:Sons, Op. 50, w. Darryl Nixon (hpd), Cléna Stein (db)—Sonata Nos. 1,2,4 & 5 Gallo ▲ CD 367 [ADD]
Devienne, F.:Qts Bn, Op. 73, w. Alexander String Quartet members Gallo ▲ CD 472 [DDD]
Gerber, R.:Con Bn, w. M. Cichirdan (cnd), Craiova PO Gallo ▲ CD 620 [AAD]
Hummel, J.N.:Con Bn, w. J. Glover (cnd), London Mozart Players Gallo ▲ CD 499 [DDD]
Mozart, W.A.:Con Bn, w. J. Glover (cnd), London Mozart Players Gallo ▲ CD 499 [DDD]
Strauss, R.:Duet-Concertino, w. D. Ashkenazy (cl), V. Ashkenazy (cnd), Berlin RSO London ▲ 436415-2 [DDD]
Wolf-Ferrari, E.:Suite-concertino Bn, w. J. Glover (cnd), London Mozart Players Gallo ▲ CD 499 [DDD]
Walker, Martin (cl)—see also ORCHESTRAS & ENSEMBLES Viklarbo Chamber Ensemble
Cox, R.:Music of, w. Amelite Consortium—When April May *(rec April & May 1992)* Raptoria Caam ▲ RCD 1001
Fink, M.J.:Music of, w. Amelite Consortium—Thread of Summer *(rec April & May 1992)* Raptoria Caam ▲ RCD 1001
Fox, J.:Music of, w. Amelite Consortium—Between the Wheels *(rec April & May 1992)* Raptoria Caam ▲ RCD 1001
Newman, M.:Colores de Mexico *(rec Mad Hatter Studios)* Raptoria Caam ▲ RCD 1007

Walker, Martin (cl) (cont.)
Newman, M.:Music of, w. Amelite Consortium—Ornitholites *(rec April & May 1992)* Raptoria Caam ▲ RCD 1001
Smith, W.L.:Music of, w. Robin Lorentz (vn), Erika Duke (vc), Dorothy Stone (fl/pic), Wadada Leo Smith (tpt/flgl/fls/bells), Vicki Ray (pno/cel), Mika Noda (vib/bells/timp), David Philipson (perc/bells)—Another Wave More Waves; Double Thunderbolt; Tao-Njia; and others Tzadik ("Composer" series) ▲ TZA 7017 [DDD]
Walker, M.:Music of, w. Amelite Consortium—Interlude I & II *(rec April & May 1992)* Raptoria Caam ▲ RCD 1001
Walker, Nina (pno)
Argentinian Songs, w. Raúl Giménez (ten) Nimbus ▲ NI 5107 [DDD]
Balakirev, M.:Pno Music—Reminiscences of Glinka's *A Life for the Tsar*, Mazurkas 6 & 7; Nocturne 2; Polka in f♯; Scherzo 2; Spanish Melody; The Spinner; Tarantella; Waltzes 2 & 4; Valse mélancholique; Valse de concert ASV ▲ ASV 940
Brahms, J.:Ernste Gesänge, w. S. Gehrman (bass) [G] Nimbus ▲ NI 5024 [AAD]
Brahms, J.:Songs, w. S. Gehrman (bass) [G] Nimbus ▲ NI 5024 [AAD]
Mussorgsky, M.:Songs & Dances, w. S. Gehrman (bass) Nimbus ▲ NI 1414 [ADD]
Rossini, G.:Les Soirées musicales, w. J. Anderson (sop), K. Bouleyn (sop), R. Giménez (ten), A. Corbelli (bar) [I] Nimbus ▲ NI 5132 [DDD]
Schubert, Franz:Pno Music (4-hands), w. Adrian Farmer (pno)—Marches militaire in D, G & B♭, D.733; Polonaises (6) for Pno 4-Hands, D.824; Variations on a theme in B♭, D.968 Nimbus ▲ NI-5485 [DDD]
Schubert, Franz:Polonaises Pno, D.599, w. Adrian Farmer (pno) *(rec Concert Hall of the Nimbus Foundation, Dec. 14-16, 1994)* Nimbus ▲ NI 5443 [DDD]
Schubert, Franz:Rondo Pno, D.608, w. Adrian Farmer (pno) *(rec Concert Hall of the Nimbus Foundation, Dec. 14-16, 1994)* Nimbus ▲ NI 5443 [DDD]
Schubert, Franz:Die Schöne Müllerin, w. S. Gehrman (bass) [E] Nimbus ▲ NI 5023 [AAD]
Schubert, Franz:Die Schöne Müllerin, w. S. Gehrman (bass) [G] Nimbus ▲ NI 5253 [ADD]
Schubert, Franz:Schwanengesang, w. S. Gehrman (bass) [G] Nimbus ▲ NI 5022
Schubert, Franz:Son Pno, D.617, w. Adrian Farmer (pno) *(rec Concert Hall of the Nimbus Foundation, Dec. 14-16, 1994)* Nimbus ▲ NI 5443 [DDD]
Schubert, Franz:Songs (misc), w. S. Gehrman (bass)—7 songs [G] Nimbus ▲ NI 5022
Schubert, Franz:Songs (misc), w. S. Gehrman (bass)—5 songs [G] Nimbus ▲ NI 5024 [AAD]
Schubert, Franz:Vars on a French Song Pno 4-Hands, D.624, w. Adrian Farmer (pno) *(rec Concert Hall of the Nimbus Foundation, Dec. 14-16, 1994)* Nimbus ▲ NI 5443 [DDD]
Schubert, Franz:Winterreise, w. S. Gehrman (bass) [E] Nimbus ▲ NI 5282 [ADD]
Schumann, R.:Dichterliebe, w. S. Gehrman (bass) [G] Nimbus ▲ NI 5024 [AAD]
Walker, Timothy (gtr)
Britten, H.:Canticles I-V, w. P. Esswood (ct), J. Griffett (ten), J. Ridgway (pno)—Canticle II IMP Masters ▲ IMPMCD 57 [DDD]
Britten, H.:Folksong Arrs, w. P. Esswood (ct), J. Griffett (ten), J. Ridgway (pno) IMP Masters ▲ IMPMCD 57 [DDD]
Britten, H.:Songs from the Chinese, w. P. Esswood (ct), J. Griffet (ten) IMP Masters ▲ IMPMCD 57 [DDD]
Day's End:The Soft Sound of Spanish Guitar, w. Eduardo Fernández (gtr), William Gómez (gtr), Nicola Hall (gtr), John Williams (gtr) London ▲ 448 560-2
Henze, H.-W.:Chamber Music, w. N. Jenkins (ten), B. Jones (cnd), Scharoun Ensemble Koch Schwann ▲ CD 310004 [DDD]
Walker, Urs (vn)
Keller, A.:Der enthüllte Stern, w. D. Fueter (sop), K. Graf (sop), A. K. Graf (fl), L. Pellerin (ob), E. Schmid (cl), C. Schiller (va), P. Demenga (vc), P. Hug-Rutti (hp), F. Eberle (dr) [G] Grammont ▲ CTSP 19-2 [ADD]
Keller, A.:Ewiger Augenblick, w. D. Fueter (sop), K. Graf (sop), A. K. Graf (fl), E. Schmid (cl), D. Isler (cel), P. Hug-Rutti (hp), P. Demenga (vc) [G] Grammont ▲ CTSP 19-2 [ADD]
Koechlin, C.:Paysages et marines, w. Kiyoshi Kasai (fl), Elmar Schmid (cl), Alexandru Gavrilovici (vn), Christoph Schiller (va), Patrick Demenga (vc) Accord ▲ ACD 201092 [DDD]
Ringger, R.U.:Memories 2, w. L. Akerlund (sop), M. Ziegler (fl), P. Zaugg (hp), D. Pezzoti (vc), F. Mohr, R.U. Ringger [G] Grammont ▲ CTSP 29-2 [ADD]
Ringger, R.U.:Memories of Tomorrow, w. L. Akerlund (sop), M. Ziegler (fl), P. Zaugg (hp), D. Pezzoti (vc), F. Mohr, R.U. Ringger [G] Grammont ▲ CTSP 29-2 [ADD]
Walker-Hill, Helen (pno)
Kaleidoscope:Music by African-American Women, w. Gregory Walker (vn) *(rec Marshall Auditorium, Haveford College, PN, Dec 1993 & Mar 1994)* Leonarda ▲ LE 339 [DDD]
Wall, Jeremy (kbd)
Harkl, w. Richard Stoltzman (cl), Eddie Gomez (perc), Dave Samuels (vib), Bill Douglas (bn), Harlem Boys Choir RCA Victor ▲ 09026-61272-2 [DDD] ■ 09026-61272-4 (CrO2)
Wallace, Frank (vih/bar)
Ay e Mil Centaur ▲ CRC 2112
Wallace, Frank (vih/bar/fl)
The Art of Flemish Song in the Courts of Europe, w. Live Oak, Nancy Knowles (sop) Centaur ▲ CRC 2109
Wallace, John (tpt)
Arias for Soprano & Trumpet, w. Helen Field (sop), Philharmonia Orch [cnd:Simon Wright] Nimbus ▲ NI 5123 [DDD]
Classical Trumpet Concertos, w. Philharmonia Orch [cnd:Simon Wright] Nimbus ▲ NI 5121 [DDD]
Copland, A.:Quiet City, w. Paul Arden Taylor (E hn), W. Boughton (cnd), English SO Nimbus ▲ NI 4002 [ADD/DDD]
Copland, A.:Quiet City, w. Paul Arden Taylor (E hn), W. Boughton (cnd), English SO Nimbus ▲ NI 5246 [DDD]
Davies, P.M.:Con Tpt, w. P. M. Davies (cnd), Scottish National Orch Collins Classics ▲ 11812 [DDD]
Fasch, J.F.:Con Tpt & Ob d'amore, w. C. Warren-Green (cnd), Philharmonia Orch *(rec July 13-15, 1988)* Nimbus ▲ NI 7016 [DDD]
Gabrieli & His Contemporaries, w. Wallace Collection [cnd:John Wallace] Nimbus ▲ NI 5236-2 [DDD]
Haydn, J.:Con Tpt, w. C. Warren-Green (cnd), Philharmonia Orch *(rec Dec. 19-20, 1983)* Nimbus ▲ NI 7016 [DDD]
Haydn, J.:Con Tpt, w. C. Warren-Green (cnd), Philharmonia Orch Nimbus ▲ NI 5010
Haydn's Trumpet Concerto & Other Classical Concerti, w. Philharmonia Orch Nimbus ▲ NI 7016 [DDD]
Hindemith, P.:Concert Music Pno, Brass & Hps, w. R. Kapil (pno), S. Wright (cnd), Philharmonia Orch, Wallace Collection Nimbus ▲ NI 5103 [DDD]
Hummel, J.N.:Con in E♭ Tpt, S.49, w. C. Warren-Green (cnd), Philharmonia Orch Nimbus ▲ NI 5065 [DDD]
Hummel, J.N.:Con in E Tpt, w. C. Warren-Green (cnd), Philharmonia Orch *(rec June 23-25, 1986)* Nimbus ▲ NI 7016 [DDD]
Italian Trumpet Spectacular Nimbus ▲ NI 1405 [DDD]
John Wallace Directing the Wallace Collection & Leeds Festival Chorus Nimbus ▲ NI 5175 [DDD]
Man:The Measure of All Things—Italian Baroque Trumpet Music, w. Philharmonia Orch [cnd:C. Warren-Green] Nimbus ▲ NI 5017 [DDD]
Neruda, J.B.G.:Con Tpt, w. C. Warren-Green (cnd), Philharmonia Orch Nimbus ▲ NI 5065 [DDD]
Neruda, J.B.G.:Con Tpt, w. C. Warren-Green (cnd), Philharmonia Orch *(rec July 13-15, 1988)* Nimbus ▲ NI 7016 [DDD]
Rule Britannia, w. Edmund Barha (ten), Wallace Collection, Leeds Festival Chorus, English String Orch [cnd:William Boughton] Nimbus ▲ NI 5155 [DDD]
T for Trumpeter:Trumpet Concertos & Fanfares, w. Wallace Collection, Philharmonia Orch [cnd:Christopher Warren-Green] Nimbus ▲ NI 5065 [DDD]
Telemann, G.P.:Cons Tpt, w. W. Boughton (cnd), English String Orch—Concerto in D for Trumpet & Strings; 2 Concerti in D for Trumpet & Orchestra; Concerti in E♭ for 2 Trumpets & Strings & in D for 3 Trumpets & Orchestra; Suite in D for Trumpet & Strings; Overture in D for 2 Trumpets & Orchestra; Sinfonia in F for Trumpet, Recorder, 3 Trombones & Orchestra Nimbus ▲ NI 5189 [DDD]

INSTRUMENT.

Wallace, John (tpt) (cont.)
Trumpet Music from the Italian Baroque, w. Wallace Collection, Philharmonia Orch [cnd:Simon Wright] Nimbus ▲ NI 5079 [DDD]
Vačkář, D.C.:Jazz Con, w. Radoslav Kapil (pno), S. Wright (cnd), Wallace Collection, Philharmonia Orch members Nimbus ▲ NI 5103 [DDD]
Vivaldi Concerti & Baroque Trumpet Music, w. Philharmonia Orch Nimbus ▲ NI 7012 [DDD]
Weber, F.D.:Vars Tpt, w. C. Warren-Green (cnd), Philharmonia Orch *(rec June 23-25, 1986)* Nimbus ▲ NI 7016 [DDD]
Weber, F.D.:Vars Tpt, w. C. Warren-Green (cnd), Philharmonia Orch Nimbus ▲ NI 5065 [DDD]

Wallace, S. M. (org)
Scott, K.L.:The Wind of Heaven, w. H. Rubin (vn), K. Lee Scott (cnd), Lee Scott Singers VQR Digital ▲ QR 2051 [DDD]

Wallendorf, Klaus (hn)—see also ORCHESTRAS & ENSEMBLES Consortium Classicum, Berlin PO Horns
Lieder der Romantik, w. Dietrich Fischer-Dieskau (bar), Dieter Klöcker (cl), Hartmut Höll (pno) Orfeo ▲ 153861

Wallenstein, Alfred (vc)
Strauss, R.:Don Quixote, w. T. Beecham (cnd), New York PO *(rec 4/7/32)* Pearl 3-▲ PEA 9922 (m) [AAD]

Waller, Anne (gtr)
Songs, Dances & Fantasy, w. Jerry Fuller (db), Frederick Ockwell (pno), Kenneth Dorsch (hpd), William Ferris (pno), Steve Hartman (hp), Thomas Potter (bar), John Vorrasi (ten) Musical Arts Society ▲ CD 41589 [AAD] ■ CS 41589

Waller, Susan (fl)
Bowles, P.:Son Fl, w. Irene Herrmann (pno) Koch International Classics ▲ KIC 7343 [DDD]

Wallez, Amaury (bn)
Françaix, J.:Divert Bn, w. Carl Stamitz Ensemble Pierre Verany ▲ PVY 792102 [DDD]
Françaix, J.:Octet, w. J.-L. Sajot (cl), Carl Stamitz Ensemble Pierre Verany ▲ PVY 792102 [DDD]
Klein, G.:Divert Ob, w. Jean-Pierre Arnaud (ob), Jean-Marc Liet (ob), Rémi Lerner (cl), Christian Rocca (cl), Michel Tavernier (bn), Éric Karcher (hn), Philippe Queyraud (hn) Arion ▲ ARN 68272 [DDD]
Poulenc, F.:Sxt Pno, w. P. Rogé (pno), P. Gallois (fl), M. Bourgue (ob), M. Portal (cl), A. Cazalet (hn) London ▲ 421581-2 [DDD]
Poulenc, F.:Trio Ob, w. M. Bourgue (ob), P. Rogé (pno) London ▲ 421581-2 [DDD]

Wallez, Florian (va)—see ORCHESTRAS & ENSEMBLES Denis Clavier String Quartet

Wallez, Jean-Pierre (vn)
Beethoven, L. van:Con Vn, Op. 61, w. J.-C. Casadesus (cnd), Lille National Orch Forlane ▲ FRL 54 [DDD]
Beethoven, L. van:Romances Vn, w. J.-C. Casadesus (cnd), Lille National Orch Forlane ▲ FRL 54 [DDD]
Stravinsky, I.:L'Histoire du soldat, w. Georges Descrieres (nar), D. Debart (cnd), Basse Normandie Instrumental Ensemble Forlane ▲ FRL 16580 [DDD]
Vivaldi, A.:Cons Vn, Op. 8/1-4, "The Four Seasons", w. J.-P. Wallez (cnd), Paris Orchestral Ensemble Forlane ▲ FRL 16644 [AAD]

Wallfisch, Elizabeth (vn)—see also ORCHESTRAS & ENSEMBLES Purcell Quartet, Locatelli Trio
Albinoni, T.:Sonate da chiesa, Op. 4, w. Locatelli Trio Hyperion 2-▲ CDA 66831/32
Albinoni, T.:Trattenimenti armonici per camera, w. Locatelli Trio Hyperion 2-▲ CDA 66831/32
Bach, J.S.:Con Fl, Vn & Hpd, w. Lisa Beznosiuk (fl), Paul Nicholson (hpd), E. Wallfisch (cnd), Orch of the Age of Enlightenment Virgin Classics ▲ CD 45190
Bach, J.S.:Con 2 for 3 Hpds, Orch of the Age of Enlightenment [trans. for violin & strings] Virgin Classics ▲ CDC 59319
Bach, J.S.:Cons Vn (comp), Orch of the Age of Enlightenment Virgin Classics ▲ CDC 59319
Bach, J.S.:Con Vn, BWV 1052, w. E. Wallfisch (cnd), Orch of the Age of Enlightenment Virgin Classics ▲ CDC 45095
Bach, J.S.:Con Vn, BWV 1058, w. E. Wallfisch (cnd), Orch of the Age of Enlightenment Virgin Classics ▲ CDC 45095
Bach, J.S.:Con Vn & Ob, w. A. Robson (ob), E. Wallfisch (cnd), Orch of the Age of Enlightenment Virgin Classics ▲ CDC 45095
Bach, J.S.:Con for 2 Vns, w. *(2nd vn unknown)*, Orch of the Age of Enlightenment Virgin Classics ▲ CDC 59319
Biber, H. von:Harmonia artificiosa-ariosa, w. Purcell Quartet Chandos ("Chaconne" series) 2-▲ CHAN 0575/76 [DDD]
Bloch, E.:Suite hébraïque, w. L. Wallfisch (pno) ebs ▲ EBS 6044 [ADD]
Brooks, J.:Con 1 Vn, w. P. Holman (cnd), Parley of Instruments Hyperion ▲ CDA 66865
Haydn, J.:Con 1 Vn, w. Orch of the Age of Enlightenment Virgin Classics ▲ CDC 59266
Haydn, J.:Con 4 Vn, w. Orch of the Age of Enlightenment Virgin Classics ▲ CDC 59266
Leclair, J.-M.:Cons Vn, Op. 7, w. N. Kraemer (cnd), Raglan Baroque Players—No. 2 in D United ▲ CAL 88009 [DDD]
Linley, T.:Con Vn, w. P. Holman (cnd), Parley of Instruments Hyperion ▲ CDA 66865
Locatelli, P.:L'arte del violino, w. N. Kraemer (cnd), Raglan Baroque Players Hyperion 3-▲ CDA 66721/23
Locatelli, P.:Concerti grossi, w. Nicholas Kraemer (hpd), Raglan Baroque Players Hyperion 2-▲ CDA 66981/2
Mysliveček, J.:Cons Vn, w. R. Goodman (cnd), Brandenburg Orch—in B♭ Hyperion ▲ CDA 66840
Rossini, G.:Sons Str Qt, w. M. Marcus (vn), R. Tunnicliffe (vc), C.-C. Nwanoku (db) Hyperion ▲ CDA 66595
Schubert, Franz:Rondo Vn, D.438, w. R. Goodman (cnd), Brandenburg Orch Hyperion ▲ CDA 66840
Shaw, T.:Con Vn, w. P. Holman (cnd), Parley of Instruments Hyperion ▲ CDA 66865
Spohr, L.:Con 8 Vn, w. R. Goodman (cnd), Brandenburg Orch Hyperion ▲ CDA 66840
Viotti, G.B.:Con 22 Vn, w. R. Goodman (cnd), Brandenburg Orch Hyperion ▲ CDA 66840
Vivaldi, A.:Cons Vn, Op. 8/1-4, "The Four Seasons", w. P. Rapson (hpd), P. Rapson (cnd), Fiori Musicali Meridian ▲ CDE 84195
Vivaldi, A.:Cons for 2 Vns, w. M. Huggett (vn), N. Kraemer (cnd), Raglan Baroque Players—Concerto in G, RV.516 Veritas 2-▲ VCD 7 90803-2 [DDD] 2-■ VCD 7 90803-4 (D)
Wesley, S.:Con 2 Vn, w. P. Holman (cnd), Parley of Instruments Hyperion ▲ CDA 66865

Wallfisch, Ernst (va)—see also ORCHESTRAS & ENSEMBLES Wallfisch Duo
Bloch, E.:Pieces (2) Va, w. L. Wallfisch (pno) ebs ▲ EBS 6044 [ADD]
Bloch, E.:Suite Va ebs ▲ EBS 6044 [ADD]
Bloch, E.:Suite Va & Pno, w. L. Wallfisch (pno) ebs ▲ EBS 6044 [ADD]
Malipiero, G.F.:Dialogo 5, w. S. Comissiona (cnd), Jerusalem SO Bayer ▲ BR 200028 [ADD]
Paganini, N.:Son large Va, w. F. Allers (cnd), Northwest German PO Bayer ▲ BR 200028 [ADD]
Vanhal, J.B.:Con Va, w. J. Faerber (cnd), Württemberg CO Bayer ▲ BR 200028 [ADD]
Weber, C.M. von:Andante & Rondo ungarese Va, w. W. Brückner-Rüggeberg (cnd), North German RSO Bayer ▲ BR 200028 [ADD]
Weber, C.M. von:Vars on *A Schüsserl und a Reind'rl* Va, w. W. Brückner-Rüggeberg (cnd), North German RSO Bayer ▲ BR 200028 [ADD]

Wallfisch, Lory (pno)—see also ORCHESTRAS & ENSEMBLES Wallfisch Duo
Bloch, E.:Pieces (2) Va, w. E. Wallfisch (va) ebs ▲ EBS 6044 [ADD]
Bloch, E.:Suite hébraïque, w. E. Wallfisch (vn) ebs ▲ EBS 6044 [ADD]
Bloch, E.:Suite Va & Pno, w. E. Wallfisch (va) ebs ▲ EBS 6044 [ADD]
Enescu, G.:Son Vc, w. Julius Berger (vc) Ebs ▲ 6043 [DDD]
Enescu, G.:Son Pno, Op. 24/1 Ebs ▲ 6043 [DDD]

Wallfisch, Peter (pno)
Brahms, J.:Sons Vc (comp), w. R. Wallfisch (vc) Chandos ▲ CHAN 8615 [DDD]
Bridge, F.:Son Vc, w. R. Wallfisch (vc) Chandos ▲ CHAN 8499 [DDD]
Delius, F.:Son Vc & Pno, w. R. Wallfisch (vc) Chandos ▲ CHAN 8499 [DDD]
Leighton, K.:Alleluia pascha nostrum, w. R. Wallfisch (vc) *(rec May 14 & 15, 1992)* Chandos ▲ CHAN 9132 [DDD]
Leighton, K.:Fant on an American Hymn-tune, w. J. Hilton (cl), R. Wallfisch (vc) *(rec May 14 & 15, 1992)* Chandos ▲ CHAN 9132 [DDD]
Leighton, K.:Son Pno *(rec May 14 & 15, 1992)* Chandos ▲ CHAN 9132 [DDD]

Wallfisch, Peter (pno) (cont.)
Leighton, K.:Vars Pno *(rec May 14 & 15, 92)* Chandos ▲ CHAN 9132 [DDD]
Schumann, R.:Adagio & Allegro Hn, w. R. Wallfisch (vc) Chandos ▲ CHAN 8528 [DDD]
Schumann, R.:Albumblätter Chandos ▲ CHAN 8528 [DDD]

Wallfisch, Raphael (vc)
Barber, S.:Con Vc, w. G. Simon (cnd), English CO Chandos ▲ CHAN 8322 [DDD]
Bax, A.:Con Vc (1932), w. B. Thomson (cnd), London PO Chandos ▲ CHAN 8494 [DDD]
Bax, A.:Rhapsodic Ballad Chandos ▲ CHAN 8499 [DDD]
Bliss, A.:Con Vc, w. V. Handley (cnd), Ulster Orch Chandos ▲ CHAN 8818 [DDD]
Bloch, E.:From Jewish Life, w. L. Hendry (pno) Chandos ("Collect" series) ▲ CHAN 6552 [DDD]
Brahms, J.:Con Vn & Vc, "Double Con", w. L. Mordkovitch (vn), N. Järvi (cnd), London SO Chandos ▲ CHAN 8667 [DDD]
Brahms, J.:Sons Vc (comp), w. P. Wallfisch (pno) Chandos ▲ CHAN 8615 [DDD]
Britten, H.:Sym Vc, w. S. Bedford (cnd), English CO Chandos ▲ CHAN 8363 [DDD]
Bridge, F.:Son Vc, w. P. Wallfisch (pno) Chandos ▲ CHAN 8499 [DDD]
Delius, F.:Con Vc, w. C. Mackerras (cnd), Royal Liverpool PO Classics for Pleasure ("Eminence" series) ▲ CDEMX 2185 [DDD]
Delius, F.:Double Con, w. Tasmin Little (vn), C. Mackerras (cnd), Royal Liverpool PO Classics for Pleasure ("Eminence" series) ▲ CDEMX 2185 [DDD]
Delius, F.:Son Vc & Pno, w. P. Wallfisch (pno) Chandos ▲ CHAN 8499 [DDD]
Dohnányi, E. von:Konzertstück, w. C. Mackerras (cnd), London SO Chandos ▲ CHAN 8662 [DDD]
Dvořák, A.:Con Vc, w. C. Mackerras (cnd), London SO Chandos ▲ CHAN 8662 [DDD]
Dvořák, A.:Pieces (5) Vc, w. L. Hendry (pno)—Polonaise in A; Rondo in g; Silent Woods; Slavonic Dances, Op. 46/3 & 8 Chandos ("Collect" series) ▲ CHAN 6552 [DDD]
Finzi, G.:Con Vc, w. V. Handley (cnd), Royal Liverpool PO Chandos ▲ CHAN 8471 [DDD]
Glazunov, A.:Chant du ménéstrel, w. B. Thomson (cnd), London PO Chandos ▲ CHAN 8579 [DDD]
Glazunov, A.:Chant du ménéstrel, w. B. Thomson (cnd), London PO Chandos ("Collect" series) ▲ CHAN 6552 [DDD]
Hindemith, P.:Con Vc, w. Y. P. Tortelier (cnd), BBC PO Chandos ▲ CHAN 9124 [DDD]
Honegger, A.:Chamber Music (comp), w. D.-S. Kang (vn), J.-P. Audoli (vn), P.-H. Xuereb (va), J. Rossi (db), P. Devoyon (pno)—Sonatine for 2 Violins (1920); Sonatine for Violin & Cello (1932); Sonata for Cello & Piano (1920); Sonata for Viola & Piano (1920); Trio in f for Violin, Cello & Piano (1914); Paduana for Solo Cello (1945); Prelude for Double Bass & Piano (1932) Timpani ▲ IC1009 [DDD]
Honegger, A.:Chamber Music (comp), w. D.-S. Kang (vn), P.-H. Xuereb (va), M. Arrignon (cl), A. Marion (fl), A. Haraldsdottir (fl), C. Moreaux (ob), T. Caens (tpt), M. Becquet (trbn), P. Zanlonghi (hp), P. Devoyon (pno), F. Kondo (mez), Ludwig String Quartet—Sonatine for Clarinet & Piano (1921-22); Rapsodie for 2 Flutes, Clarinet & Piano (1917); Danse de la Chèvre for Solo Flute (1921); Romance for Flute & Piano (1953); Petite Suite for 2 Flutes & Piano (1934); Trois Contrepoints for Piccolo, Oboe, Violin & Cello (1922); Intrada for Trumpet & Piano (1947); Hommage du trombone exprimant la tristesse de l'auteur absent for Trombone & Piano (1925); J'avais un fidèle amant for String Quartet (1929); Chanson de Ronsard & 3 Chansons de la petite Sirène for Mezzo, Flute & String Quartet (1924); Introduction et Danse for Flute, Harp & String Trio [undated]; Colloque for Flute, Celesta, Violin & Viola [undated] Timpani ▲ IC1010 [DDD]
Ireland, J.:Son Vc, w. John York (pno) *(rec St. Martin's Church, East Woodhay, Berkshire, Mar. 16 & 17, 1994)* Marco Polo ▲ 8.223718 [DDD]
Kabalevsky, D.:Con 2 Vc, w. B. Thomson (cnd), London PO Chandos ▲ CHAN 8579 [DDD]
Khachaturian, A.:Con Vc, w. B. Thomson (cnd), London PO Chandos ▲ CHAN 8579 [DDD]
Leighton, K.:Alleluia pascha nostrum, w. P. Wallfisch (pno) *(rec May 14 & 15, 1992)* Chandos ▲ CHAN 9132 [DDD]
Leighton, K.:Con Vc, w. B. Thomson (cnd), Scottish National Orch Chandos ▲ CHAN 8741 [DDD]
Leighton, K.:Fant on an American Hymn-tune, w. J. Hilton (cl), P. Wallfisch (pno) *(rec May 14 & 15, 1992)* Chandos ▲ CHAN 9132 [DDD]
Leighton, K.:Veris gratia, w. George Caird (ob), V. Handley (cnd), Royal Liverpool PO Chandos ▲ CHAN 8471 [DDD]
Martinů, B.:Concertino Vc, Ww, Pno & Perc, w. J. Belohlávek (cnd), Czech PO Chandos ▲ CHAN 9015 [DDD]
Martinů, B.:Con 1 Vc, w. J. Belohlávek (cnd), Czech PO [1955 version] Chandos ▲ CHAN 9015 [DDD]
Martinů, B.:Con 2 Vc, w. J. Belohlávek (cnd), Czech PO Chandos ▲ CHAN 9015 [DDD]
Maw, N.:Son Notturna, w. W. Boughton (cnd), English String Orch *(rec Concert Hall of the Nimbus Foundation, Wyastone Leys, Monmouth, Nov 7-8, 1995)* Nimbus ▲ NI 5471 [DDD]
Moeran, E.J.:Con Vc, w. N. del Mar (cnd), Bournemouth Sinfonietta Chandos ▲ CHAN 8456 [DDD]
Moeran, E.J.:Son Vc *(rec St. Martin's Church, East Woodhay, Berkshire, Mar. 16 & 17, 1994)* Marco Polo ▲ 8.223718 [DDD]
Prokofiev, S.:Sym-Con Vc, w. N. Järvi (cnd), Scottish National Orch Chandos ▲ CHAN 8508 [DDD]
Respighi, O.:Adagio con variazioni Vc Orch, w. T. Vásáry (cnd), Bournemouth Sinfonietta Chandos ▲ CHAN 8913 [DDD]
Rubbra, E.:Son Vc *(rec St. Martin's Church, East Woodhay, Berkshire, Mar. 16 & 17, 1994)* Marco Polo ▲ 8.223718 [DDD]
Schmidt, F.:Qnt Cl, w. E. Ottensamer (cl), R. Keuschnig (pno), J. Hell (vn), P. Wächter (vn), P. Pecha (va) *(rec Jan. 7, 1991)* Orfeo ▲ 287921 [DDD]
Schumann, R.:Adagio & Allegro Hn, w. P. Wallfisch (pno) Chandos ▲ CHAN 8528 [DDD]
Shostakovich, D.:Con 1 Vc, w. G. Simon (cnd), English CO Chandos ▲ CHAN 8322 [DDD]
Stanford, C.V.:Irish Rhaps, w. L. Mordkovitch (vn), V. Handley (cnd), Ulster Orch Chandos 2-▲ CHAN 7002/03 [DDD]
Stanford, C.V.:Irish Rhap 3, w. V. Handley (cnd), Ulster Orch Chandos ▲ CHAN 8861 [DDD]
Strauss, R.:Don Quixote, w. N. Järvi (cnd), Scottish National Orch Chandos ▲ CHAN 8631 [DDD]
Strauss, R.:Romanze Vc, w. N. Järvi (cnd), Scottish National Orch Chandos ▲ CHAN 8631 [DDD]
Tavener, J.:Eternal Memory, w. J. Brown (cnd), Royal PO Royal Philharmonic Collection ▲ TRP 48 [DDD]
Tavener, J.:The Protecting Veil, w. J. Brown (cnd), Royal PO Royal Philharmonic Collection ▲ TRP 48 [DDD]
Tavener, J.:Thrinos Royal Philharmonic Collection ▲ TRP 48 [DDD]
Tchaikovsky, P.:Pezzo capriccioso, w. G. Simon (cnd), English CO Chandos ("Collect" series) ▲ CHAN 6552 [DDD]
Tchaikovsky, P.:Songs, w. G. Simon (cnd), English CO—Was I not a blade of grass?, Op. 47/7; Christ had a garden, Op. 54/5 [orchd. Tchaikovsky] Chandos ("Collect" series) ▲ CHAN 6552 [DDD]
Vivaldi, A.:Cons Vc, w. N. Kraemer (cnd), London Sinfonietta—in F, RV.412; in a, RV.419; in D, RV.404; in C, RV.399; in d, RV.406; in C, RV.398; in F, RV.410 *(rec Conway Hall, London, Apr. 1994)* Naxos ("Vivaldi Collection" series) ▲ 8.550907 [DDD]
Vivaldi, A.:Cons Vc, w. N. Kraemer (cnd), London Sinfonietta—in E♭, RV.408; in g, RV.531; in G, RV.413; in c, RV.401; in a, RV.422; in C, RV.400 *(rec All Saints Church, East Finchley & Conway Hall, London, Apr., May & Sept. 1994)* Naxos ("Vivaldi Collection" series) ▲ 8.550908 [DDD]
Vivaldi, A.:Cons Vc, w. N. Kraemer (cnd), London Sinfonietta—in B♭, RV.423; in c, RV.402; in a, RV.418; in D, RV.403; in b, RV.424; in d, RV.407; in e, RV.409 *(rec All Saints Church, East Finchley & Conway Hall, London, Apr., May & Sept. 1994)* Naxos ("Vivaldi Collection" series) ▲ 8.550909 [DDD]
Vivaldi, A.:Cons Vc, w. N. Kraemer (cnd), London Sinfonietta—in g, RV.416; in F, RV.411; in d, RV.405; in a, RV.420; in G, RV.414; in g, RV.417; in a, RV.421 *(rec All Saints Church, East Finchley & Conway Hall, London, Apr., May & Sept. 1994)* Naxos ("Vivaldi Collection" series) ▲ 8.550910 [DDD]
Walton, W.:Con Vc, w. B. Thomson (cnd), London PO Chandos ▲ CHAN 8959 [DDD]
Walton, W.:Passacaglia Vc *(rec 1986)* Chandos ▲ CHAN 8959 [DDD]
Walton, W.:Passacaglia Vc Chandos ▲ CHAN 8499 [DDD]

Wallfisch, W. (va)
Mozart, W.A.:Qt Pno, K.493, w. M. Horszowski (pno), Y. Menuhin (vn), P. Casals (vc) *(rec live, Prades Festival, July 7, 1956)* Music & Arts 4-▲ CD 688 (m) [AAD]

Wallin, Annika (bn)
Vanhal, J.B.:Con Bns, w. Arne Nilsson (bn), J.-P. Saraste (cnd), Umeå Sinfonietta BIS ▲ CD 288 [DDD]

906

▲ = CD ♦ = Enhanced CD ∆ = MD ■ = Cassette Tape ◻ = DCC

Wallin, Lennart (pno)
Burkhard, W.:Son Vn, w. Martin Gelland (vn) *(rec Tonhallen, Sundsvall/Sweden & Holmsund Church, Aug 24–27 & Sept 8, 1995)* Vienna Modern Masters ▲ VMM 2017 [DDD]
Jelinek, H.:Zahme Xenien, w. Martin Gelland (vn) *(rec Tonhallen, Sundsvall/Sweden & Holmsund Church, Aug 24–27 & Sept 8, 1995)* Vienna Modern Masters ▲ VMM 2017 [DDD]
Sapp, A.D.:And the Bombers Went Home, w. Martin Gelland (vn) *(rec Tonhallen, Sundsvall/Sweden & Holmsund Church, Aug 24–27 & Sept 8, 1995)* Vienna Modern Masters ▲ VMM 2017 [DDD]
Schoeck, O.:Son Vn, Op. 22, w. Martin Gelland (vn) *(rec Tonhallen, Sundsvall/Sweden & Holmsund Church, Aug 24–27 & Sept 8, 1995)* Vienna Modern Masters ▲ VMM 2017 [DDD]
Strauss, R.:Allegretto Vn, w. Martin Gelland (vn) *(rec Tonhallen, Sundsvall/Sweden & Holmsund Church, Aug 24–27 & Sept 8, 1995)* Vienna Modern Masters ▲ VMM 2017 [DDD]
Wyshnegradsky, I.:Chant douloureux et étude, w. Martin Gelland (vn) *(rec Tonhallen, Sundsvall/Sweden & Holmsund Church, Aug 24–27 & Sept 8, 1995)* Vienna Modern Masters ▲ VMM 2017 [DDD]

Wallin, Ulf (vn)
Dohnányi, E. von:Con 1 Vn, w. A. Francis (cnd), Frankfurt RSO *(rec HR Studio 1, Nov 28–Dec 2, 1995)* CPO ▲ CPO 999308-2 [DDD]
Hindemith, P.:Son in C Vn & Pno, w. Roland Pöntinen (pno) *(rec Musikaliska Akademien, Stockholm, Sweden, Aug 22–25, 1995)* BIS ▲ CD 761 [DDD]
Hindemith, P.:Son in E Vn & Pno, w. Roland Pöntinen (pno) *(rec Musikaliska Akademien, Stockholm, Sweden, Aug 22–25, 1995)* BIS ▲ CD 761 [DDD]
Hindemith, P.:Son Vn & Pno, Op. 11/1, w. Roland Pöntinen (pno)—complete son & fragment of a finale *(rec Musikaliska Akademien, Stockholm, Sweden, Aug 22–25, 1995)* BIS ▲ CD 761 [DDD]
Hindemith, P.:Son Vn & Pno, Op. 11/2, w. Roland Pöntinen (pno) *(rec Musikaliska Akademien, Stockholm, Sweden, Aug 22–25, 1995)* BIS ▲ CD 761 [DDD]
Linde, B.:Con Vn, w. J. Hirokami (cnd), Norrköping SO *(rec Jan. 22 & 23, 1993)* BIS ▲ CD 621 [DDD]
Linde, B.:Music of, w. Love Derwinger (pno)—DansFantasi for Vn & Pno, Op. 7; Danse for Vn & Xyl [w. Johan Silvmark (xyl)]; Son for Vn & Pno, Op. 15/2; 2 Duets for 2 Vns [w. Ulf Johansson (vn)]; Son for Vn & Pno, Op. 10; Romantic Melody for Vn & Pno *(rec Musikaliska Akademien, Stockholm, Sweden, Apr 1994)* BIS ▲ CD 631 [DDD]
Schnittke, A.:Gratulationsrondo, w. R. Pöntinen (pno) BIS ▲ CD 527 [DDD]
Schnittke, A.:Son 1 Vn, w. R. Pöntinen (pno) BIS ▲ CD 527 [DDD]
Schnittke, A.:Son 2 Vn, w. R. Pöntinen (pno) BIS ▲ CD 527 [DDD]
Schnittke, A.:Stille Nacht Vn, w. R. Pöntinen (pno) BIS ▲ CD 527 [DDD]
Schnittke, A.:Suite in the Old Style, w. R. Pöntinen (pno) BIS ▲ CD 527 [DDD]
Schumann, R.:Fantasiestücke Cl, w. A. Kuyumjian (pno) [violin & piano arr.] *(rec 1990)* Koch Schwann ▲ SCH 311852 [DDD]
Schumann, R.:Märchenbilder, w. A. Kuyumjian (pno) [violin & piano version] *(rec 1990)* Koch Schwann ▲ SCH 311852 [DDD]
Stenhammar, W.:Sentimental Romances, w. P. Järvi (cnd), Malmö SO BIS ▲ CD 550 [DDD]

Waln, Ronald (fl)—see ORCHESTRAS & ENSEMBLES Georgia Woodwind Quintet

Walser, Herbert (nat tpt)
Weichlein, R.:Encaenia musices, w. Gunar Letzbor (vn), Daniel Sepec (vn), Herbert Lindsberger (va), Christoph Bitzinger (va), Michael Oman (vl), Gaetano Nasillo (vc), Roberto Sensi (vn), Andreas Lackner (nat tpt), Norbert Kirchner (hpd/org), G. Letzbor (cnd), Ars Antiqua Austria—Sons. Nos. I in C, II in g, III in a, IV in E, V in C & VI in F Symphonia ▲ SY 93S23

Walser, U. (tpt)
Handel, G.F.:Messiah, w. Ruth Holton (sop), Vanessa Williamson (mez), James Griffett (ten), Lawrence Albert (bass), M. Brown (cnd), Gioia della Musica, Bmensky Akademicky Sbor Allegro 2–▲ ALGDPCD 1068 [DDD]

Walsh, Colin (org)
Great European Organs, Vol. 15, w. Stephen Cleobury (org) Priory ▲ PRCD 281 [DDD]
Vierne, L.:Sym 2 Org [Lincoln Cathedral Organ] Priory ▲ PRI 446 [DDD]
Vierne, L.:Sym 3 Org [Lincoln Cathedral Organ] Priory ▲ PRI 446 [DDD]

Walsh, Diane (pno)
Aitken, H.:Rosa de Fuego CRI ▲ CD 595 [DDD]
Beach, A.M.C.:Invocation, w. Curtis Macomber (vn) Koch International Classics ▲ KIC 7223 [DDD]
Beach, A.M.C.:Romance, w. Curtis Macomber (vn) Koch International Classics ▲ KIC 7223 [DDD]
Beach, A.M.C.:Son Vn, w. Curtis Macomber (vn) Koch International Classics ▲ KIC 7223 [DDD]
Corigliano, J.:Son Vn & Pno, w. Curtis Macomber (vn) Koch International Classics ▲ KIC 7223 [DDD]

Walsh, Michele (vn)
Schultz, Andrew:Mephisto, w. Sonia Croucher (fl), Karen Schaupp (gtr), Belinda Kendall-Smith (bass), G. Roberts (cnd), Perihelion Ensemble members *(rec Nickson Room, Music Dept, Univ of Queensland, Australia, Dec 1994)* Tall Poppies ▲ TP 065 [DDD]

Walstad, Sidsel (hp)
Haug, H.:Dialogue, w. Willy Postma (hp) Victoria ▲ VCD 19049 [DDD]

Walta, Jaring (vn)
Van Baaren, K.:Septet Vn, w. J. de Wit (fl), F. Minderaa (ob), et al. Olympia ▲ OCD 505 [AAD]

Walter, Alfred (pno)
Furtwängler, W.:Songs, w. Guido Pikal (ten), A. Walter (cnd), Frankfurt on the Oder PO, Frankfurt on the Oder Phil Chorus—Der traurige Jäger; Der Schatzgräber; Geduld; Auf dem See; Du sendest, Freund, mir Lieder; Erinnerung; Das Vaterland; Möwenflug; Lied; Erinnerung; Der Soldat *(rec Maison de la Radio Bruxelles, Oct. 7–8, 1993)* Marco Polo ▲ 8.223546 [DDD]

Walter, Bruno (pno)
Kathleen Ferrier Edition, Vol. 9, w. Kathleen Ferrier (cta) London ▲ 433476-2 LM [ADD]
Mozart, W.A.:Con 20 Pno, w. B. Walter (cnd), NBC SO *(rec live, New York, Mar 11, 1939)* Grammofono 2000 ▲ GRM 78622
Mozart, W.A.:Con 20 Pno, w. B. Walter (cnd), Vienna PO EMI Classics ("Great Recordings of the Century" series) 3–▲ CDHC 63912
Mozart, W.A.:Con 20 Pno, w. B. Walter (cnd), Vienna PO *(rec 1937, from Victor M 420)* Pearl ▲ PEA 9940 (m) [AAD]
Mozart, W.A.:Con 20 Pno, w. B. Walter (cnd), Vienna PO *(rec May 7, 1937; from HMV DB)* Preiser ▲ 90141 (m) [AAD]
Wagner, R.:Wesendonck Songs, w. Kirsten Flagstad (sop) *(rec live, 1952)* Historical Performers ▲ HPS 27
Wagner, R.:Wesendonck Songs, w. Kirsten Flagstad (sop) *(rec live, 1952)* Legend ▲ LGD 119
Wagner, R.:Wesendonck Songs, w. Kirsten Flagstad (sop) *(rec 1944–52)* Music & Arts ▲ CD 838 [AAD]

Walter, Johannes (fl)
Virtuoso Flute Music Berlin Classics ▲ BER 9161

Walter, Mary (hp)
Hindemith, P.:Concert Music Pno, Brass & Hps, w. T. Lichtmann (pno), P.L. Jenks (hp), Summit Brass Summit 2–▲ DCD 115 [DDD] 2–■ DCD 115

Walter, Naum (pno)
Falla, M. de:Canciones populares españolas (7), w. Marina Yashvili (vn)—El paño moruno; Nana; Canción; Polo; Asturiana; Jota [all arr P. Kokhansky for vn & pno] *(rec 1975)* Russian Compact Disc ("Talents of Russia" series) ▲ RCD 16252 [ADD]
Paganini, N.:Cantibile in D, w. Marina Yashvili (vn) [arr for vn & pno] *(rec 1975)* Russian Compact Disc ("Talents of Russia" series) ▲ RCD 16252 [ADD]
Paganini, N.:Moto perpeuto in C, w. Marina Yashvili (vn) [arr for vn & pno] *(rec 1975)* Russian Compact Disc ("Talents of Russia" series) ▲ RCD 16252 [ADD]

Walters, Edward (cl)
Moss, L.:Miracles, w. James McDonald (ten), Ruth Ann McDonald (pno) *(rec Peabody Conservatory of Music, Baltimore, MD)* Capstone ▲ CPS 8619

Walters, J. (Italianate triple hp)—see ORCHESTRAS & ENSEMBLES Kithara

Walters, Mark (figl)
Wilby, P.:Flight, w. G. Cutt (cnd), Grimethorpe Colliery Band *(rec Dec 1993)* Doyen ▲ CD 029 [DDD]

Walterskirchen, Gerhard (org)
Haydn, M.:Requiem in c, w. Siglinde Damisch (sop), Gabriele Schreckenbach (mez), Chris Merritt (ten), Hans Udo Müller (pno), E. Hinreiner (cnd), Salzburg RSO, Mozart Choir *(rec June 1981)* Koch Treasure ▲ 31608-2 [ADD]

Walther, Geraldine (va)
Hindemith, P.:Der Schwanendreher, w. H. Blomstedt (cnd), San Francisco SO London ▲ 433809-2 [DDD]

Walton, Chris (pno)
Donizetti, G.:Arias, w. Otto Linsi (ten)—Eterno amore e fè; Me voglio fa' na casa; Il barcaiolo Gallo ▲ CD 886 [ADD]
Puccini, G.:Arias, w. Otto Linsi (ten)—Terra e mare; Storiella d'amore; Avanti Urania!; Sole e amore Gallo ▲ CD 886 [ADD]
Rotoli, A.:Songs, w. Otto Linsi (ten)—La gondola nera; Ho sognato; Il tuo pensiero Gallo ▲ CD 886 [ADD]
Tosti, P.F.:Songs, w. Otto Linsi (ten)—Io voglio amarti; L'ultima canzone; La serenata; Marechiare; Ideale; Non t'amo più; Rosa; April Serenata popolare Gallo ▲ CD 886 [ADD]
Verdi, G.:Arias, w. Otto Linsi (ten)—Stornello; Non t'accostare all'urna; Brindisi Gallo ▲ CD 886 [ADD]

Walzel, M. (hn)
Van Appledorn, M.J.:Patterns, w. A. Brittin (hn), J. Whitaker (hn), L. Dawson (hn), H. Landers (hn) Opus One ▲ CD 162

Wambach, Bernhard (pno)
Lachenmann, H.:Allegro sostenuto, w. D. Smeyers (cl), M. Bach (vc) CPO ▲ CPO 999102-2 [DDD]
Lachenmann, H.:Ein Kinderspiel CPO ▲ CPO 999102-2 [DDD]
Rihm, W.:Lieder, w. R. Salter (bar), F. Lang (drum), M. Rosenthal (drum)—Vier Gedichte aus Atemwende [text by Paul Celan] for Voice & Piano (1973); Hölderlin-Fragmente for Voice & Piano (1976–7); Neue Alexanderlieder [5 poems by Ernst Herbeck] for Baritone & Piano 1979); Wölfli-Liederbuch for Baritone, Piano & 2 Drums (1980–81) [G] CPO ▲ CPO 999049-2 [ADD]
Stockhausen, K.:Klavierstücke I–VIII Koch Schwann ▲ CD 310016 [DDD]
Stockhausen, K.:Klavierstück IX Koch Schwann ▲ CD 310009 [DDD]
Stockhausen, K.:Klavierstück X Koch Schwann ▲ CD 310009 [DDD]
Stockhausen, K.:Klavierstück XI [first & second versions] Koch Schwann ▲ CD 310009 [DDD]
Stockhausen, K.:Klavierstück XII Koch Schwann ▲ CD 310015 [DDD]
Stockhausen, K.:Klavierstück XIII Koch Schwann ▲ CD 310015 [DDD]
Stockhausen, K.:Klavierstück XIV Koch Schwann ▲ CD 310015 [DDD]

Wan, D.
Newman, Anthony:Chamber Music, w. M. Mills (pno), P.J. Bacchus (fl), Y. Waldman (vn), D. Wan, Flute Force, Laurentian String Quartet—Qnt for Piano & Strings, "Easter"; Qt for 4 Flutes; Introduction & Toccata for Flute & Piano; Vars & Toccata for Violin Newport Classic ▲ NCD 60032 [DDD]

Wanami, Takayoshi (vn)
Brahms, J.:Con Vn, w. A. Leaper (cnd), London PO IMP Classics ▲ IMP PCD 1062 [DDD]
Bruch, M.:Con 1 Vn, w. A. Fistoulari (cnd), New Philharmonia Orch *(rec ca. 1977)* Chandos ("Collect" series) ▲ CHAN 6558 [ADD]
Schumann, R.:Con Vn, w. A. Leaper (cnd), London PO IMP Classics ▲ IMP PCD 1062 [DDD]
Tchaikovsky, P.:Con Vn, w. A. Fistoulari (cnd), New Philharmonia Orch *(rec ca. 1977)* Chandos ("Collect" series) ▲ CHAN 6558 [ADD]

Wandel, S. (cl)
Schacht, T. von:Cons Cl, w. D. Kloecker (cl), O. Link (cl), H. Stadlmair (cnd), Bamberg SO—in D & B for 1 Clarinet; in B for 2 Clarinets; in B for 3 Clarinets *(rec May 11–15, 1992)* Orfeo ▲ 290931 [DDD]

Wandel, Waldemar (cl)
Mozart, W.A.:Don Giovanni, w. Gernot Schmalfub (ob), Christian Hartmann (ob), Dieter Klöcker (cl), Sara Willis (hn), Christian Auer (hn), Karl-Otto Hartmann (bn), Eberhard Buschmann (bn), Jürgen Normann (db), Consortium Classicum Bayer ▲ BR 100 135 [DDD]

Wang, Jian (vc)
Barber, S.:Son Vc, w. C. Rosenberger (pno) Delos ▲ DE 3097 [DDD]
Chopin, F.:Intro & Polonaise, "Polonaise brilliante", w. C. Rosenberger (pno) Delos ▲ DE 3097 [DDD]
Chopin, F.:Son Vc, w. C. Rosenberger (pno) Delos ▲ DE 3097 [DDD]
Presenting Jian Wang, w. Carol Rosenberger (pno) Delos ▲ DE 3097 [DDD]
Schumann, R.:Adagio & Allegro Hn, w. C. Rosenberger (pno) Delos ▲ DE 3097 [DDD]

Wang, S. (pno)
Ince, K.:Cross Scintillations, w. C.-L. Lin (vn) *(rec Milwaukee, Sept. 1992 & Oct. 1993)* Northeastern ("Contemporary" series) ▲ NR 254

Wanger, Fredrik (pno)
All American Trombone, w. Barron, Ronald (trbn), Harvard Univ Wind Ensemble, Atlantic Brass Quintet *(rec Sanders Theater, Harvard Univ; Symphony Hall, Boston; Morse Auditorium, Boston Univ, Nov 7, Dec 8–9, 1995; Jan)* Boston Brass ▲ BB 1003
Hindemith, P.:Leichte Stücke, w. R. Barron (trbn) [tran for trbn & pno] Boston Brass ▲ BB 1002CD ■ BB 1002CT
Hindemith, P.:Son Alto Hn, w. R. Barron (trbn) Boston Brass ▲ BB 1002CD ■ BB 1002CT
Hindemith, P.:Son Trbn, w. R. Barron (trbn) Boston Brass ▲ BB 1002CD ■ BB 1002CT

Warburton, Thomas (pno)
Albright, W.:Chromatic Dances *(rec UNC, Chapel Hill, June 1980)* CRI ▲ CRI 674 [ADD]
Albright, W.:Grand Son in Rag *(rec Duke Univ, Durham, NC, May 1992)* CRI ▲ CRI 674 [DDD]
Albright, W.:Pianoàgogo *(rec UNC, Chapel Hill, June 1980)* CRI ▲ CRI 674 [ADD]
Albright, W.:Sphaera *(rec Duke Univ, Durham, NC, May 1992)* CRI ▲ CRI 674 [DDD]
Hoiby, L.:Bermudas, w. Terry Rhodes (sop), Ellen Williams (mez), Hsiao-mei Ku (vn), Jonathan Bagg (va), Fred Raimi (vc) Albany ▲ TROY 172 [DDD]

Ward, Cecily (vn)—see ORCHESTRAS & ENSEMBLES Stratos

Ward, David (pno)
Mozart, W.A.:Allegro & Andante Meridian ▲ CDE 84197
Mozart, W.A.:Allegro in Son form Meridian ▲ CDE 84197
Mozart, W.A.:Fant Pno, K.475 Meridian ▲ CDE 84197
Mozart, W.A.:Minuet Pno, K.355 Meridian ▲ CDE 84197
Mozart, W.A.:Son 14 Pno Meridian ▲ CDE 84197
Mozart, W.A.:Vars Pno, K.500 Meridian ▲ CDE 84197
Stoll, D.:Qt Pno, w. Pro Arte String Trio Meridian ▲ MER 84245 [DDD]
Stoll, D.:Son Pno Meridian ▲ MER 84245 [DDD]
Stoll, D.:Son Pnos, w. N. Skinner (pno) Meridian ▲ MER 84245 [DDD]

Ward, Jeremy (bn)
Bach, Joh. Christian:Con Bn, w. A. Halstead (cnd), Hanover Band *(rec Rosslyn Hill Chapel, London, Mar–Apr 1995)* CPO ▲ CPO 999347-2 [DDD]

Ward, Laura (pno)
Bach, J.S.:Sons Fl, BWV 1030–35, w. H. Sargous (ob)—BWV 1030 [in g for oboe] Crystal ▲ CD 327 [DDD]
Pasculli, A.:Grand Con Ob, w. H. Sargous (ob) Crystal ▲ CD 327 [DDD]
Wolpe, S.:Son Ob, w. H. Sargous (ob) Crystal ▲ CD 327 [DDD]

Ward, Mark (vc)
Ward, R.:Arioso & Tarantelle, w. Margo Garrett (pno) Albany ▲ TROY 204 [DDD]

Ward, Maxwell (baroque va)—see ORCHESTRAS & ENSEMBLES In Nomine Players

Ward, Nicholas (vn)
Vivaldi, A.:Con for 2 Tpts, w. C. Steele-Perkins (tpt), M. Meeks (tpt), A. Watkinson (vn), A. Watkinson (cnd), City of London Sinfonia Virgin Classics ▲ CDZ 59651

Ward, Robert (hn)
Scelsi, G.:Anahit, w. Paul Zukofsky (vn), Julie Bogorad (fl), Peggy Russell (fl), Courtney Westcott (fl), Lawrence McDonald (cl), Joan Waryha (cl), Jean Hansen (b cl), Bill Suite (e hn), Nita VanPelt (sax), Bob Zobal (tpt), John Carter (trbn), Martin Lydecker (trbn), Stan Cortman (hn), William Curry (va), Jody Rowitsch (va), Irene Wade (va), Anne Fagerburg (vc), John Gockel (vc), Sue Manz (bass), Steven Stearman (bass) *(rec Oberlin Conservatory of Music, Oct 8, 1973)* CP² ▲ CP2 108 [AAD]

INSTRUMENT.

Wardman, Vicci (va)—see ORCHESTRAS & ENSEMBLES Sorrel String Quartet
Ward-Steinman, David (pno)
Ward-Steinman, D.:Fragments from Sappho, w. P. Curtin (sop), D. Baron (fl), D. Glazer (cl) [E] CRI ■ C 238
Warnecke, Mary (pno)
Chopin, F.:Études (24)—Op. 25/1, 2, 7 & 12 *(rec Studio 200, ABC Ultimo Centre, Sydney, May 1994)* Tall Poppies ▲ TP 62 [DDD]
Chopin, F.:Nocturnes—Op. 72/1 *(rec Studio 200, ABC Ultimo Centre, Sydney, May 1994)* Tall Poppies ▲ TP 62 [DDD]
Liszt, F.:Consolations—No. 3 *(rec Studio 200, ABC Ultimo Centre, Sydney, May 1994)* Tall Poppies ▲ TP 62 [DDD]
Liszt, F.:Études de concert (2) Pno—No. 2 *(rec Studio 200, ABC Ultimo Centre, Sydney, May 1994)* Tall Poppies ▲ TP 62 [DDD]
Liszt, F.:Études de concert (3) Pno—No. 3 *(rec Studio 200, ABC Ultimo Centre, Sydney, May 1994)* Tall Poppies ▲ TP 62 [DDD]
Liszt, F.:Liebesträume—No. 3 *(rec Studio 200, ABC Ultimo Centre, Sydney, May 1994)* Tall Poppies ▲ TP 62 [DDD]
Schubert, Franz:Impromptus Pno, D.899 *(rec Studio 200, ABC Ultimo Centre, Sydney, May 1994)* Tall Poppies ▲ TP 62 [DDD]
Warner, C. G. (pno)—see ORCHESTRAS & ENSEMBLES Cleveland Duo
Warner, S. (vn)—see also ORCHESTRAS & ENSEMBLES Cleveland Duo
Turok, P.:Improvisations Vn, w. J. Umble (sax), R. Fusco (pno) Dana Recording Project ▲ DRP 5 [DDD]
Warnier, V. (org)
Ancelin, P.:Chant de déploration, w. P. Vigneron (tpt) Quantum ▲ QM 6952
Chailly, J.:Jeu de quartes, w. P. Vigneron (tpt) Quantum ▲ QM 6952
Delerue, G.:Récit et choral, w. P. Vigneron (tpt) Quantum ▲ QM 6952
Jansen, P.:Processionnal en sept tableux, w. P. Vigneron (tpt) Quantum ▲ QM 6952
Jolivet, A.:Arioso barocco, w. P. Vigneron (tpt) Quantum ▲ QM 6952
Landowski, M.:Cahier pour quatre jours, w. P. Vigneron (tpt) Quantum ▲ QM 6952
Rivier, J.:Aria Tpt, w. P. Vigneron (tpt) Quantum ▲ QM 6952
Warren, Dan (tpt)
Nimmons, P.:Con Tpt, w. R. Armenian (cnd), Kitchener-Waterloo SO *(rec May 23, 1991 & June 1, 19)* CBC ("SM 5000" series) ▲ SMCD 5130 [DDD]
Warren, E. R. (pno)
Warren, E.R.:Singing Earth, w. N. Gibson (sop), F. Smith (fl)—The wind sings welcome; Summer stars; Tawny days; Great memories [E] Cambria ▲ CD 1028 [DDD]
Warren, E.R.:Songs Sop, w. N. Gibson (sop), F. Smith (fl)—22 songs [E] Cambria ▲ CD 1028 [DDD]
Warren, Geoff (fl)—see ORCHESTRAS & ENSEMBLES australYSIS members
Warren-Green, Christopher (vn)
Haydn, J.:Divert Hn, Vn & Vc, H.IV/5, w. Michael Thompson (hn), Andrew Shulman (vc) Nimbus ▲ NI 5010
Mozart, W.A.:Con 5 Vn, w. C. Warren-Green (cnd), London CO Virgin Classics ("Ultraviolet" series) ▲ CUV 61132
Strauss, R.:Ein Heldenleben, w. A. Joó (cnd), Philharmonia Orch *(rec London, June 1984)* Arts ▲ 47240-2 [DDD]
Strauss, R.:Der Rosenkavalier (suite), w. A. Joó (cnd), Philharmonia Orch *(rec London, June 1984)* Arts ▲ 47240-2 [DDD]
Tchaikovsky, P.:Swan Lake, w. J. Lanchbery (cnd), Philharmonia Orch Classics for Pleasure 2-▲ CDCFP 4727 [DDD]
Vaughan Williams, R.:The Lark Ascending, w. C. Warren-Green (cnd), London CO Virgin Classics ▲ 59546 [DDD]
Vivaldi, A.:Cons for 2 Vns, w. R. Furniss (vn), C. Warren-Green (cnd), London CO—RV.522 in a Virgin Classics ▲ 59609 [DDD]
Vivaldi, A.:Con for 3 Vns, w. A. Balanescu (vn), E. Layton (vn), C. Warren-Green (cnd), London CO—RV.551 in F Virgin Classics ▲ 59609 [DDD]
Vivaldi, A.:Cons for 4 Vns, w. R. Furniss (vn), T. Bowes (vn), B. Davison (vn), C. Warren-Green (cnd), London CO—RV.580 in b Virgin Classics ▲ 59609 [DDD]
Warshaw, A. (vn)—see ORCHESTRAS & ENSEMBLES Seicentonovecento Ensemble
Waryha, Joan (cl)
Scelsi, G.:Anahit, w. Paul Zukofsky (vn), Julie Bogorad (fl), Peggy Russell (fl), Courtney Westcott (fl), Lawrence McDonald (cl), Jean Hansen (b cl), Bill Suite (e hn), Nita VanPelt (sax), Bob Zobal (tpt), John Carter (trbn), Martin Lydecker (trbn), Stan Cortman (hn), Robert Ward (hn), William Curry (va), Jody Rowitsch (va), Irene Wade (va), Anne Fagerburg (vc), John Gockel (vc), Sue Manz (bass), Steven Stearman (bass) *(rec Oberlin Conservatory of Music, Oct 8, 1973)* CP² ▲ CP2 108 [AAD]
Wasama, Jukka (dr)
Braxton, A.:Composition 144, w. Anthony Braxton (fl/s sax/a sax), Seppo Baron Paakkunainen (fl/t sax/br sax), Pentti Lahti (fl/s sax/a sax), Pepa Päivinen (fl/t sax/sop sax/b cl), Mircea Stan (trbn), Mikko-Ville Luolajan-Mikkola (vn), Teppo Hauta-aho (db/vc) *(rec Järvenpää House, Järvenpää, Finland, Nov 7, 1988)* Leo ▲ LR 233
Braxton, A.:Composition 145, w. Anthony Braxton (fl/s sax/a sax), Seppo Baron Paakkunainen (fl/t sax/br sax), Pentti Lahti (fl/s sax/a sax), Pepa Päivinen (fl/t sax/sop sax/b cl), Mircea Stan (trbn), Mikko-Ville Luolajan-Mikkola (vn), Teppo Hauta-aho (db/vc) *(rec Järvenpää House, Järvenpää, Finland, Nov 7, 1988)* Leo ▲ LR 233
Washington Jr., Grover (sax)
So Many Stars, w. Kathleen Battle (sop), Antonio Hart (sax), Tom Harrell (flgl), James Carter (b cl), Cyrus Chestnut (pno), Jon Herrington (gtr), Romero Lubambo (gtr), Ira Coleman (elec bass), Christian McBride (elec bass), Cyro Baptista (perc), Steven Berrios (perc) *(rec Hit Factory, Clinton Recording Studios, R.P.M. Sound Studios, Unique Recording Studios, Power Station)* Sony Classical ▲ SK 68473 [DDD]
Wasiółka, Marian (vc)—see also ORCHESTRAS & ENSEMBLES Wilanów String Quartet
Lutoslawski, W.:Grave, w. Maciej Paderewski (pno) Accord ▲ ACD 201142 [DDD]
Wasmuth, Robert (pno)
Boeck, A. de:Cantilena, w. Edmond Baeyens (vc) *(rec Belgian Radio-TV Concerthall, Feb 8, 1982)* Phaedra ▲ 492 002 [ADD]
Wasowski, Andrzej (pno)
Chopin, F.:Mazurkas—Opp. 6, 7, 17, 24, 30, 33, 41, 50, 56, 59, 63, 67, 68 & 2 Mazurkas in a, Op. posth. *(rec Henry Wood Hall, London, Aug 2, 6 & 7, 1980)* Concord Concerto 2-▲ CCD 42036 [ADD]
Chopin, F.:Nocturnes *(rec Henry Wood Hall, London, Sept 30–Oct 1, 1989)* Concord Concerto 2-▲ 42044-2 [DDD]
Wassenius, Magnus (va)—see ORCHESTRAS & ENSEMBLES Ferro String Quartet
Wasserman, Ellen (pno)
Rokeach, M.:Son Vn, w. N. Rubin (vn) Capstone ▲ CPS 8615
Wassmer, Claude (bn)—see also ORCHESTRAS & ENSEMBLES Ricercar Consort
Vivaldi, A.:Cons Bn, St. Cecilia Academy Orch Rome [period instrs] Pierre Verany ▲ PVY 793042 [DDD]
Vivaldi, A.:Sons Fl, w. Jean-Christophe Frisch (trns fl), Christine Plubeau (vl), Pascale Boquet (archlt), Alessandro de Marchi (hpd)—in F, d, e, g, c, D & g Adda ▲ ADD 241882
Watanabe, Miwako (vn)—see also ORCHESTRAS & ENSEMBLES Sequoia String Quartet, Francesco Trio
Lazarof, H.:Oct Strs, w. Yukiko Kamei (vn), Peter Marsh (vn), Yoko Matsuda (vn), Paul Silverthorne (va), Milton Thomas (va), Godfried Hoogeveen (vc), David Speltz (vc), H. Lazarof (cnd) Laurel ▲ LR 843 [DDD]
Levitch, L.:Qnt Fl, w. Sheridan Stokes (fl), Kathleen Lenski (vn), Jeffrey Solow (vc), Paul Polivnick (va) Cambria ▲ CD 1059 [ADD]
Watanabe, Yasuo (pno)
Hachimura, Y.:The Logic of Distraction, w. T. Otaka (cnd), Tokyo Metropolitan SO *(rec live, Tokyo Bunka-Kaikan, Large Hall, May 24, 1980)* Camerata ▲ 32CM-292 [AAD]
Waterbury, Susan (vn)
Erb, D.:Qt 2 Strs, w. A. Fullard (vn), E. Eckert (va), M. Peckham (vc) Albany ▲ TROY 092 [DDD]
Waterman, E. (fl)—see ORCHESTRAS & ENSEMBLES SONOR Ensemble of Univ of California San Diego members
Waterman, Robert (vn)
Granados, E.:Romanza, w. D. Riva (pno) Centaur ▲ CRC 2043 [DDD]
Granados, E.:Serenade for 2 Vns, w. J. Pitchon (vn), D. Riva (pno) Centaur ▲ CRC 2043 [DDD]
Seasons Remembered 2, w. Judith Lynn Stillman (pno), Toby Appel (va), John Deak (db), Eliot Porter (db), Diaz Trio [David Kim (vn), Roberto Diaz (va), Andres Diaz (vc)], Lutz Rath (vc), Fenwick Smith (fl) North Star ▲ 9837-40052-2 ■ 9837-40052-4
Watillon, Sophie (vl)—see also ORCHESTRAS & ENSEMBLES Ricercar Consort, Romanesque
de Machy, S.:Suite in d, w. P. Pierlot (vl), R. Lislevand (thb) Ricercar ▲ RIC 118100 [DDD]
de Machy, S.:Suite in G, w. P. Pierlot (vl), R. Lislevand (thb) Ricercar ▲ RIC 118100 [DDD]
du Buisson:Suite Vls, w. P. Pierlot (vl), R. Lislevand (thb) Ricercar ▲ RIC 118100 [DDD]
Marais, M.:Tombeau pour Monsieur de Ste Colombe, w. P. Pierlot (vl), R. Lislevand (thb) Ricercar ▲ RIC 118100 [DDD]
Watkin, David (vc)
Beethoven, L. van:Son 2 Vc, w. Howard Moody (pno) Chandos ("Chaconne" series) ▲ CHAN 0561
Beethoven, L. van:Son 3 Vc, w. Howard Moody (pno) Chandos ("Chaconne" series) ▲ CHAN 0561
Beethoven, L. van:Son 5 Vc, w. Howard Moody (pno) Chandos ("Chaconne" series) ▲ CHAN 0561
Boccherini, L.:Sons (5) Vc & Db, w. Richard Lester (vc), Chi-Chi Nwanoku (db)—Sons. in c, A, E♭, C, & B♭ Hyperion ▲ CDA 66719
The English Nightingale, w. Piers Adams (rcrs), Howard Beach (hpd/pno) Albany ▲ TROY 088-2 [DDD]
Vivaldi, A.:Con for 2 Vcs, w. J. Coe (vc), S. Standage (cnd), Collegium Musicum 90 Chandos ("Chaconne" series) ▲ CHAN 0528 [DDD]
Vivaldi, A.:Sons Vc, w. Helen Ghough (vc), David Miller (archlt/gtr/thb), Robert King (hpd/org)—Sonatas in E♭, RV.39; e, RV.40; F, RV.41; g, RV.42; a, RV.43; a, RV.44; B♭, RV.45; B♭, RV.46; B♭, RV.47 Hyperion 2-▲ CDA 66881/82
Watkins, Ármin (pno)
Bartók, B.:Romanian Folk Dances Pno, w. Antony Cooke (vc)—Joc Cu Bâtă; Brâul; Pe Loc; Buciumeana; Poarcă Românească; Măruntel [all arr Luigi Silva for Vc & Pno] *(rec Capitol Records, Hollywood, CA)* PROdigital ▲ PRO 7192 [DDD]
Dohnányi, E. von:Son Vc, w. Antony Cooke (vc) *(rec Capitol Records, Hollywood, CA)* PROdigital ▲ PRO 7192 [DDD]
Hubay, J.:Hullámzó Balaton, w. Antony Cooke (vc) [arr Antony Cooke & Armin Watkins for Vc & Pno] *(rec Capitol Records, Hollywood, CA)* PROdigital ▲ PRO 7192 [DDD]
Kodály, Z.:Chorale Preludes, w. Antony Cooke (vc) *(rec Capitol Records, Hollywood, CA)* PROdigital ▲ PRO 7192 [DDD]
Watkins, David (pno)
Berg, A.:Son Pno ACA Digital Recording ■ CM20008-8 (CrO2)
Helps, R.:Portrait ACA Digital Recording ■ CM20008-8 (CrO2)
Martin, F.:Preludes ACA Digital Recording ■ CM20008-8 (CrO2)
Stravinsky, I.:Pno Music—Four Études, Op. 7 ACA Digital Recording ■ CM20008-8 (CrO2)
Watkins, David (vc)—see ORCHESTRAS & ENSEMBLES Veracini Trio
Watkins, Howard (pno)
Banfield, W.:Prophetess II, w. Louise Toppin (sgr) Innova ▲ 510 [DDD]
Watkins, Paul (vc)
Takemitsu, T.:Orion & Pleiades, w. T. Otaka (cnd), BBC Welsh National SO *(rec Brangwyn Hall, Swansea, Wales, Nov 7–8, 1995)* BIS ▲ CD 760 [DDD]
Watkins, Richard (hn)
Arnold, M.:Con Hn, w. M. Stephenson (cnd), London Musici Conifer Classics ▲ 75605-51228-2
Debussy, C.:Chamber Music, w. William Bennett (fl), David Campbell (cl), James Campbell (cl), Nicholas Daniel (ob), Robert Makell (hn), Robin Kennard (bn), Rachel Gough (bn), Simon Haram (sax), Ieuan Jones (hp), Clifford Benson (pno), Julius Drake (pno), John York (pno), Roger Tapping (va)—Rapsodie for Eng hn; Syrinx; Première rapsodie; Son for Fl, Va & Hp; Le petit nègre; Petite pièce; Rapsodie for Sax *(rec All Saints' Church, East Finchley, London, Jan 12–20, 1994)* Cala 2-▲ CACD 1017 [DDD]
Glière, R.:Con Hn, w. E. Downes (cnd), BBC PO Chandos ▲ CHAN 9379 [DDD]
Haydn, J.:Con for 2 Hns, w. Michael Thompson (hn), C. Warren-Green (cnd), Philharmonia Orch Nimbus ▲ NI 5018
Mozart, W.A.:Cons Hn, w. R. Hickox (cnd), City of London Sinfonia IMP Classics ▲ PCD 865 [DDD]
Mozart, W.A.:Con Hn, K.412, w. R. Hickox (cnd), City of London Sinfonia IMP ▲ PCD 2013
Mozart, W.A.:Con Hn, K.417, w. R. Hickox (cnd), City of London Sinfonia IMP ▲ PCD 2013
Mozart, W.A.:Con Hn, K.447, w. R. Hickox (cnd), City of London Sinfonia IMP ▲ PCD 2013
Mozart, W.A.:Con Hn, K.495, w. R. Hickox (cnd), City of London Sinfonia IMP ▲ PCD 2013
Mozart, W.A.:Rondo Hn, K.371, w. R. Hickox (cnd), City of London Sinfonia IMP ▲ PCD 2013
Mozart, W.A.:Rondo Hn, K.371, w. R. Hickox (cnd), City of London Sinfonia IMP Classics ▲ PCD 865 [DDD]
Poulenc, F.:Chamber Music, w. Peter Sidhom (bar), William Bennett (fl), David Campbell (cl), James Campbell (cl), Nicholas Daniel (ob), Rachel Gough (bn), Peter Carter (vn), Chris West (db), Ieuan Jones (hp), Clifford Benson (pno), Julius Drake (pno), John York (pno)—Son for Ob; L'invitation au château; Villanelle; Son 2 Cls; Trio; Sxt; Son for Cl & Bn; Rapsodie nègre; Son for Cl; Mouvements perpétuels; Son for Fl *(rec All Saints' Church, East Finchley, London, Jan 12–20, 1994)* Cala ▲ CACD 1018 [DDD]
Saint-Saëns, C.:Chamber Music, w. W. Bennett (fl), D. Campbell (cl), J. Campbell (cl), N. Daniel (ob), R. Makell (hn), R. Kennard (bn), R. Gough (bn), S. Haram (sax), I. Jones (hp), C. Benson (pno), J. Drake (pno), J. York (pno), R. Tapping (va)—Odelette, Op. 162; Son for Cl, Op. 167; Feuillet d'album, Op. 81; Son for Bn, Op. 168; Caprice on Danish & Russian Airs, Op. 79; Son for Ob, Op. 166; Romance in D♭, Op. 37; Tarantelle, Op. 6 *(rec All Saints' Church, East Finchley, London, Jan 12–20, 1994)* Cala 2-▲ CACD 1017 [DDD]
Simpson, R.:Qt Hn, w. P. Lowbury (vn), C. Dearnley (vc), C. Green Armytage (pno) Hyperion ▲ CDA 66695
Simpson, R.:Trio Hn, w. P. Lowbury (vn), C. Green Armytage (pno) Hyperion ▲ CDA 66695
Smyth, E.:Con Vn Hn, w. Sophie Langdon (vn), O. de la Martinez (cnd), BBC PO Chandos ▲ CHAN 9449
Tomlinson, E.:Rhapsody & Rondo, w. E. Tomlinson (cnd), Slovak RSO Bratislava *(rec 1992)* Marco Polo ("British Light Music" series) ▲ 8.223513 [DDD]
Vivaldi, A.:Cons for 2 Hns, w. M. Thompson (hn), C. Warren-Green (cnd), Philharmonia Orch—RV.539 Nimbus ▲ NI 5018
Watkins, Sara (ob)
Britten, H.:Insect Pieces (2), w. P. Ledger (pno) Meridian ▲ 84119
Britten, H.:Metamorphoses Ob Meridian ▲ 84119
Watkinson, Andrew (vn)
Vivaldi, A.:Con for 2 Tpts, w. C. Steele-Perkins (tpt), M. Meeks (tpt), N. Ward (vn), A. Watkinson (cnd), City of London Sinfonia Virgin Classics ▲ CDZ 59651
Vivaldi, A.:Cons Vn, Op. 8/1–4, "The Four Seasons", w. A. Watkinson (cnd), City of London Sinfonia Virgin Classics ▲ CDZ 59651
Watne, Åshild (lyre)
Habbestad, K.:Song-Dance, w. Odd Lund (goat's hn), T. Mikkelsen (cnd), Scapoli, Oslo Phil Women's Chamber Choir Norway Music ▲ 2912
Watson, David (shears/stick vn/gtr/tpt)
Exquisite Corpses from P.S. 122, w. Judy Dunaway (gtr/balloons), Anthony Coleman (sampler), Raissa St. Pierre (drums), Guy Yarden (vn/pno), Leslie Ross (bn), Linda Austin (gtr), Bruce Kaplan (gtr), Doug Henderson (peckhorn/bass/toy pno), Sue Ann Harkey (gtr), Cinnie Cole (sampler), et al. ¿What Next? ▲ WN 0002 [ADD]
Watson, Eric (pno)
Ives, C.:Son 1 Pno Accord ▲ ACD 201862 [DDD]

▲ = CD ♦ = Enhanced CD ∆ = MD ■ = Cassette Tape □ = DCC

Watson, Eric (pno) (cont.)
Ives, C.:Songs, w. Nicholas Isherwood (bass), Marie-Noëlle André-Combes (pno)—Tom Sails Away; Ann Street; Thoreau; Maple Leaves; The Cage; 1, 2, 3; Evening; Serenity; A Unison Chant; The New River; The White Gulls; Slugging a Vampire; West London [A Sonnet]; From the Incantation; Charlie Rutlage; Slow March; The Indians; Walt Whitman [from 20th Stanza]; Afterglow; His Exaltation; At the River; In the Mornin'; The Camp Meeting; The Circus Band; From Paracelsus; Premonitions; On the Counter; A Sea Dirge; Like a Sick Eagle; Soliloquy [or A Study in 7th & Other Things]; Memories; The One Way; Remembrance; A Farewell to Land Accord ▲ ACD 201812 [DDD]
Ives, C.:Studies Pno—No. 9, "The Anti-Abolitionist Riots"; No. 20 Accord ▲ ACD 201862 [DDD]
Ives, C.:Three-Page Son Accord ▲ ACD 201862 [DDD]
Watson, Ian (hpd)
Vivaldi, A.:Cons Vn, Op. 3/1-12, "L'estro armonico", w. J.L. Garcia (vn), M. Eade (vn), I. Watson (cnd), English CO Virgin Classics ▲ CDZ 59656
Watson, Ian (hpd/org)
Corelli, A.:Concerti grossi, Op. 6, w. M. Eade (vn), J.L. Garcia (vn), W. Bennett (fl), N. Black (ob), English CO—No. 2 in F Virgin Classics ▲ CDZ 59656
Watson, Ian (org)
Albinoni, T.:Adagio Org, w. J.L. Garcia (vn), M. Eade (vn), English CO Virgin Classics ▲ CDZ 59656
Lloyd Webber, W.S.:Mass Org & Choir, w. R. Hickox (cnd), Richard Hickox Singers [L] ASV ▲ ASV 584 [DDD]
Mozart, W.A.:Church Sons, w. R. King (cnd), King's Consort Hyperion ▲ CDA 66377 [DDD]
Watson, Ian (pno)
Contemporary Trumpet Music, w. Graham Ashton (tpt/flgl), T. Fry (perc) Virgin Classics ▲ CDC 45003
Watson, James (tpt)
Trumpet & Soprano in Duet, w. J. Partridge (sop) ASV ▲ ASV 2088 [DDD]
Watson, K. (perc)
Shifrin, L.:Journeys Label "X" ▲ LXCD 11 [AAD]
Watson, Pamela (fl)
Handel, D.:The Poems of Our Climate, w. Sheryl Woods (sop), Brian Delay (gtr), Val Griffen (vc), Anton Nel (pno), Jack Brennan (perc), James Culley (perc), Allen Otte (perc), G. Samuel (cnd) Vienna Modern Masters ▲ VMM 2019 [DDD]
Watters, Clarence (org)
Dupré, M.:Org Music—Vêpres du Commun—Ave Maris Stella; Cortège et Litanie, Op. 19; Le chemin de la croix, Op. 29—2 sels. AFKA ▲ SK 508 [ADD]
Dupré, M.:Préludes & Fugues, Op. 7—Prelude & Fugue No. 2; Fugue from No. 3 AFKA ▲ SK 508 [ADD]
Dupré, M.:Vars sur un vieux Noël AFKA ▲ SK 508 [ADD]
Widor, C.M.:Sym 9 Org AFKA ▲ SK 508 [ADD]
Watts, André (pno)
Beethoven, L van:Son 13 Pno EMI Classics ▲ CDM 64600
Beethoven, L van:Son 14 Pno, "Moonlight Son" EMI Classics ▲ CDM 64600
Beethoven, L van:Son 23 Pno, "Appassionata" EMI Classics ▲ CDM 64600
Brahms, J.:Con 2 Pno, w. L. Bernstein (cnd), New York PO Sony Classical ▲ SMK 47539 [ADD]
Chopin, F.:Con 2 Pno, w. T. Schippers (cnd), New York PO Sony Classical (Essential Classics) ▲ SBK 46336 [ADD] ■ SBT 46336
Chopin, F.:Pno Music (misc)—Ballade No. 1; Études in C# & A♭; Nocturnes in C# & c EMI Classics ▲ CDC 54151
Chopin, F.:Son Pno, Op. 35 EMI Classics ▲ CDC 54151
Haydn, J.:Sons Pno—H.XVI/48 *(rec live, 4/6/88)* EMI Classics ▲ CDM 64598
Liszt, F.:Con 1 Pno, w. L. Bernstein (cnd), New York PO *(rec 1964)* Sony Classical ("Bernstein:The Royal Edition" series) ▲ SMK 47571 [ADD]
Liszt, F.:Con 1 Pno, w. A. Litton (cnd), Dallas SO *(rec Meyerson Symphony Center, Dallas, Texas, July 9–10, 1995)* Telarc ▲ CD 80429 [DDD]
Liszt, F.:Con 2 Pno, w. A. Litton (cnd), Dallas SO *(rec Meyerson Symphony Center, Dallas, Texas, July 9–10, 1995)* Telarc ▲ CD 80429 [DDD]
Liszt, F.:Études d'exécution transcendante d'après Paganini, S.140 Sony Classical ("Essential Classics" series) ▲ SBK 62664 ■ SBT 62664
Liszt, F.:Études d'exécution transcendante d'après Paganini, S.140 CBS ▲ MLK 39450 ■ MT 39450
Liszt, F.:Pno Music (misc)—Au Lac De Wallenstadt; Hungarian Rhapsody No. 13; Les Jeux d'eau à la Villa D'Este; Il Penseroso; Six Grand Etudes After Paganini EMI Classics ▲ CDM 64599
Liszt, F.:Pno Music (misc)—Bagatelle ohne Tonart; Nuages Gris; En Rêve; Schlaflos, Frage und Antwort; Un Sospiro; Transcendental Etude No. 10; Valse Oublié No. 1 EMI Classics ▲ CDM 64601
Liszt, F.:Son Pno EMI Classics ▲ CDM 64601
Macdowell, E.:Con 2 Pno, w. A. Litton (cnd), Dallas SO *(rec Meyerson Symphony Center, Dallas, Texas, July 9–10, 1995)* Telarc ▲ CD 80429 [DDD]
Mozart, W.A.:Son 12 Pno *(rec live Apr. 6, 1988)* EMI Classics ▲ CDM 64598
Rachmaninoff, S.:Con 3 Pno, w. S. Ozawa (cnd), New York PO *(rec Oct. 1, 1969)* Sony Classical ("Essential Classics" series) ▲ SBK 53512 [ADD] ■ SBT 53512
Saint-Saëns, C.:Con 2 Pno, w. Y. Levi (cnd), Atlanta SO *(rec Symphony Hall, Woodruff Arts Center, Atlanta, GA, Nov. 21, 1994)* Telarc ▲ CD 80386 [DDD]
Schubert, Franz:Fant Pno, D.760, "Wandererfantasie" EMI Classics ▲ CDC 54153
Schubert, Franz:Son Pno, D.664 EMI Classics ▲ CDC 54153
Schubert, Franz:Son Pno, D.784 *(rec live 4/6/88)* EMI Classics ▲ CDM 64598
Tchaikovsky, P.:Con 1 Pno, w. L. Bernstein (cnd), New York PO *(rec Mar. 12, 1973)* Sony Classical ▲ SMK 47630 [ADD]
Tchaikovsky, P.:Con 1 Pno, w. Y. Levi (cnd), Atlanta SO *(rec Symphony Hall, Woodruff Arts Center, Atlanta, GA, Aug. 1, 1994)* Telarc ▲ CD 80386 [DDD]
Watts, Andrew (bn)
Bassoon Collection, w. Frances Eustace (bn), Paul Nicholson (kbds), Jennifer Ward Clarke (vc) Amon Ra ▲ CDSAR 35 [DDD]
Vivaldi, A.:Cons Diverse Instrs, w. Le Nouveau Quartet—6 concerti for various combinations of flute, violin, bassoon, cello & continuo (R.83 in c; R.84 in D; R.91 in D; R.96 in d; R.100 in F; R.106 in g) Amon Ra ▲ CD-SAR 47 [DDD]
Watts, Andrew (dulcian)
Masterpieces of Mexican Polyphony, w. Westminster Cathedral Choir, James O'Donnell (cnd), Andrew Lawrence-King (hp), Iain Simcock (org) Hyperion ▲ CDA 66330 [DDD]
Watts, Ernie (sax)
Symphonic Boleros, w. V. Lewis (cnd), Royal PO, Ettore Stratta (cnd), Sal Marquez (tpt), Clare Fischer (pno), Jorge Callandrelli (pno), Brian Monroney (gtr) Teldec ▲ 91180-2 ■ 91180-4
Watts, Eugene (trbn)—see ORCHESTRAS & ENSEMBLES Canadian Brass
Watts, Jane (org)
Great European Organs, Vol. 7 Priory ▲ PRCD 237 [DDD]
Great European Organs, Vol. 18 Priory ▲ PRCD 286 [DDD]
Great European Organs, Vol. 19 Priory ▲ PRCD 294 [DDD]
Jones, D.:A Refusal to Mourn [Klais Org, St. John's Smith Square, London] Priory ▲ PRI 491 [DDD]
Langlais, J.:Paraphrases grégoriennes [Klais Org, St. John's Smith Square, London] Priory ▲ PRI 491 [DDD]
Langlais, J.:Sym 1 [Klais Org, St. John's Smith Square, London] Priory ▲ PRI 491 [DDD]
Preston, S.:Alleluyas [Klais Org, St. John's Smith Square, London] Priory ▲ PRI 491 [DDD]
Preston, S.:Fant Org [Klais Org, St. John's Smith Square, London] Priory ▲ PRI 491 [DDD]
Waumbach, B. (pno)
Zimmermann, B.A.:Enchiridion CPO ▲ CPO 999198 [DDD]
Zimmermann, B.A.:Intercommunicazione, w. M. Bach (vc) CPO ▲ CPO 999198 [DDD]
Wayenberg, Daniel (pno)
Chopin, F.:Pno Music (misc)—Nocturne in F#, Op. 15/1; Waltz in E♭, Op. 18 [Grande valse brillante]; Ballade No. 3 in A♭, Op. 47; Etude in c, Op. 10/12; Fant-Impromptu in c#, Op. 66; Waltz in D♭, Op. 64/1 [Minute Waltz]; Mazurka in a, Op. 17/4; Scherzo No. 2 in b♭, Op. 31; Prelude in D♭, Op. 28/15 [Raindrop Prelude]; Ballade No. 1 in g, Op. 23; Mazurka in D, Op. 33/2; Polonaise in A♭, Op. 53 IMP ("Classics" series) ▲ IMP 6700142

Wayenberg, Daniel (pno) (cont.)
Franck, C.:Qnt Pno, w. Daniel String Quartet *(rec Rotterdam, May 28, 1985)* Erasmus ▲ WHV 001 [DDD]
Poulenc, F.:Con for 2 Pnos, w. H. Oudenaarden (pno), G. Oskamp (cnd), Limburg SO *(rec Nov. 1992 & May 1993)* Erasmus ▲ WVH 099 [DDD]
Saint-Saëns, C.:Carnival of the Animals, w. H. Oudenaarden (pno), J. Hagen (fl), H. de Fraaf (cl), H. Krul (db), W. Vos (xyl), M. Dekkers (acc), Daniel String Quartet *(rec Rotterdam, May 28, 1985)* Erasmus ▲ WHV 001 [DDD]
Saint-Saëns, C.:Carnival of the Animals, w. H. Oudenaarden (pno), G. Oskamp (cnd), Limburg SO *(rec Nov. 1992 & May 1993)* Erasmus ▲ WVH 099 [DDD]
Weait, Christopher (bn)
Telemann, G.P.:Canonic Son 2 Bn, w. Margaret Barstow (vc) D'Note Classics ▲ DND 1008 [DDD]
Telemann, G.P.:Fants Bn—Nos. 1 in C; 3 in d; 8 in g [w. Margaret Barstow (vc)]; 10 in a D'Note Classics ▲ DND 1008 [DDD]
Telemann, G.P.:Qt Bn Fls, w. Katherine Borst (fl), Craig J. Kirchhoff (fl), Nelson Harper (hpd) D'Note Classics ▲ DND 1008 [DDD]
Telemann, G.P.:Son Bn, w. Nelson Harper (hpd) D'Note Classics ▲ DND 1008 [DDD]
Telemann, G.P.:Trio Sons, w. *(artist unknown)* Christopher Weait (bn), Nelson Harper (hpd)—in F for Fl, Bn & Bc D'Note Classics ▲ DND 1008 [DDD]
Weaver, James (hpd)—see also ORCHESTRAS & ENSEMBLES Oberlin Baroque Ensemble
Bach, J.S.:Cons solo Hpd, BWV 972-987 Smithsonian Collection 5-▲ ND 0380 [DDD]
Bach, J.S.:Cons solo Hpd, BWV 972-987—BWV 974 Smithsonian Collection ▲ ND 0383 [DDD]
Bach, J.S.:Italian Con Smithsonian Collection 5-▲ ND 0380 [DDD]
Bach, J.S.:Italian Con Smithsonian Collection ▲ ND 0383 [DDD]
Bach, J.S.:Partitas Hpd, BWV 825-830 [1745 Dulcken harpsichord] Smithsonian Collection 6-■ NC 007
Bach, J.S.:Partita Hpd, BWV 831, "Ov nach französischer Art" Smithsonian Collection 5-▲ ND 0380 [DDD]
Bach, J.S.:Partita Hpd, BWV 831, "Ov nach französischer Art" Smithsonian Collection ▲ ND 0383 [DDD]
Weaver, James (org)—see also ORCHESTRAS & ENSEMBLES Smithsonian Chamber Players
Leighton, K.:Prelude, Scherzo & Passacaglia Gothic ▲ G 49060 [DDD]
Weaver, James (pno)
Albrechtsberger, J.G.:Concertino 5 Instrs, w. Armando Ghitalla (tpt), Robert Shermont (vn), Jean Cauhape (va), Alfred Zighera (vc) *(rec Dec 1963 & Jan 1964)* Crystal ▲ CD 760
Beethoven, L van:Son 1 Vc, w. K. Slowik (vc) Smithsonian Collection 6-▲ ND 0320
Beethoven, L van:Son 1 Vc, w. K. Slowik (vc) Smithsonian Collection ▲ ND 0323
Beethoven, L van:Son 2 Vc, w. K. Slowik (vc) Smithsonian Collection 6-▲ ND 0320
Beethoven, L van:Son 2 Vc, w. K. Slowik (vc) Smithsonian Collection ▲ ND 0323
Mozart, W.A.:Qts Pno, w. J. Schröder (vn), J. Griffin (va), K. Slowik (vc0 [period instrs] Smithsonian Collection 5-▲ ND 031
Mozart, W.A.:Trio Cl, K.498, w. L. McDonald (cl), J. Griffin (va) [period instrs] Smithsonian Collection 5-▲ ND 031
Weaver, John (org)
John Weaver Performs... Gothic ▲ GOT 49060 [DDD]
Webb, Charles H. (pno)
Kreisler, F.:Vn Pieces, w. J. Gingold (vn) *(rec 1976)* Music & Arts ▲ CD 286 [AAD]
Webb, Hugh (hp)
Child of Light, w. , Elysian Singers London, Matthew Greenall (cnd), Matthew Morley (org) Continuum ▲ CON 1043 [DDD]
Music for Christmas, w. Elysian Singers London, Matthew Greenall (cnd), Matthew Morley (org) Continuum ▲ CCD 1043
Weber, Barton (pno)
Boehm, T.:Compositions Fl, w. A. Adorján (fl), W. Bennett (fl), U. Burkhard (fl), M. Debost (fl), I. Grafenauer (fl), A. Nicolet (fl)—works for Flute & Piano *(Andante pastorale, from Souvenir des Alpes; Elegie in A♭, Op. 47; Fantaisie sur un air allemand, Op. 22; Fantaisie in A♭ on a Theme by Schubert; Grande Polonaise in D, Op. 16; Variations on Nel cor più non mi sento)*; works for Flute Ensemble *(Duettino in D, Pièce facile in C & Romanza in F [Nos. 66–68]; plus a six-flute ensemble performance of the 2nd movt. from Boismortier's Flute Concerto No. 1 in G)* *(rec live, Cuvilliés Theater, Munich 11/27/81)* Orfeo ▲ 018821 [DDD]
Strauss, R.:Con 2 Hn, w. Johannes Ritzkowsky (hn), Wolfgang Sawallisch (pno) *(rec Kleine Konzertsall, Gasteig, Germany, Mar 22–23, 1988)* Arts ▲ 47261-2 [DDD]
Weber, Ekkehard (vl)—see ORCHESTRAS & ENSEMBLES Trio Basiliensis
Weber, Janice (pno)
Karg-Elert, S.:Impressions exotiques, w. D. Worthen (fl) Leonarda ▲ LE 335 [DDD]
Karg-Elert, S.:Jugend, w. D. Worthen (fl), R. Shaughnessy (cl), R. Menual (hn) Leonarda ▲ LE 335 [DDD]
Karg-Elert, S.:Son Fl, Op. 121, w. D. Worthen (fl) Leonarda ▲ LE 335 [DDD]
Karg-Elert, S.:Suite pointillistique, w. D. Worthen (fl) Leonarda ▲ LE 335 [DDD]
Rachmaninoff, S.:Pno Transcriptions—Siloti:Prelude in g#; Bach:Partita Prelude in E for Violin; Liszt:Hungarian Rhapsody, No. 2 (w. Rachmaninoff's own cadenza); Rachmaninoff:Polka de W.R.; Dance of the Gypsy Men (from his student opera Aleko); Italian Polka (w. Bradel Michel [trumpet]); Lilacs; Kreisler:Liebeslied; Liebesfreund; Rimsky-Korsakov:Bumble Bee IMP Classics ▲ IMPPCD 1051 [DDD]
Weber, Jürgen (va)—see ORCHESTRAS & ENSEMBLES German String Trio
Weber, Katharina (pno)
Eisler, H.:Pno Music (misc), w. Christoph Keller (pno)—5 frühe Klavierstücke; 2 kleine Klavierstücke; Andante; Kleine Musik zum abreagieren sentimentaler Stimmungen; Klavierstücke für Kinder, Op. 31; Sieben Klavierstücke, Op. 32; Sonatine [Gradus ad Parnassum], Op. 44; 3 Fugen; Improvisation für Ernst Bloch; Rachmaninoff Parodie; Die Mutter Ov [2 Pnos]; Ov 1940 [2 Pnos] Accord ▲ ACD 201612 [DDD]
Weber, Kurt (cl)
Schubert, Franz:Der Hirt auf dem Felsen, w. E. Mathis (sop), K. Engel (pno) [G] Novalis ▲ 150026 [DDD]
Vogel, W.:Sonances, w. H. Peter-Indermühle (fl), H. Elhorst (ob), I. Backer (bn), K. Hanke (hn), U. Lehmann (vn), L. Dober (vn), H. Forster (va), M. Liechti (vc), R. Tschupp (cnd) Grammont ▲ CTSP 14-2 [ADD]
Weber, M. (cl)
Wyttenbach, J.:Lamentoroso, w. L. Akerlund (sop), H. Bissegger (cl), N. Calame (cl), M. Maurer (cl), E. Molinari (cl), H. Zwahlen (cl) *(rec May 19–20, 1990)* Grammont ▲ CTSP 37-2 [ADD]
Weber, Rudolf (va)
Holzbauer, I.:Nocturni Fl, w. R. Frei (db), Winterthur Baroque Quintet *(rec 1969)* Jecklin-Disco ▲ JD 4406-2 [ADD]
Holzbauer, I.:Qnt Fl, w. Winterthur Baroque Quintet *(rec 1969)* Jecklin-Disco ▲ JD 4406-2 [ADD]
Weber, Stephen (pno)
Weber, S.:Etudes Pno *(rec Texas Tech Univ., Hemmle Recital Hall, Lubbock, TX, Feb. 1994)* Opus One ▲ CD 169
Weber, Tamas (vc)
Gerber, R.:Sarabande, w. Dagmar Clottu (pno) Gallo ▲ CD 861 [ADD]
Webersinke, Amadeus (pno)
Beethoven, L van:Con 6 Pno, w. K. Masur (cnd), Leipzig Gewandhaus Orch Berlin Classics ▲ BER 2077 [ADD]
Reger, M.:Con Pno, w. G. Herbig (cnd), Dresden PO Berlin Classics ▲ BER 9104 [ADD]
Webster, C. (pno)
Words of Love, w. Laplante, Bruno (bar), F. Duval (sop) Analekta ▲ AN29401 [DDD] ■ AN4-9401
Webster, Martin (hn)
Joan Lippincott & Philadelphia Brass, w. Joan Lippincott (org), Philadelphia Brass Gothic ▲ GOT 49072 [DDD]

INSTRUMENT.

Webster, Michael (cl)
Martino, D.:A Set CRI ▲ CD 693 [ADD]
Weckler, Ellen (pno)
Banfield, W.:4 Persons, w. Fred Ormand (cl), Harry Sargous (ob), Lynette Diers Cohen (bn) Innova ▲ 510 [DDD]
Wedd, Patrick (hpd)
Geminiani, F.:The Enchanted Forest, w. Elizabeth Wilcock (vn), Stanley Ritchie (vn), Susie Napper (vc), Janet See (fl), Barbara Kallaur (fl), J.E. Gardiner (cnd), CBC Vancouver SO CBC ▲ 5163 [DDD]
Wedd, Patrick (org)
Coulthard, J.:Music to St. Cecilia, w. M. Bernardi (cnd), Calgary PO CBC ("SM 5000" series) ▲ SMCD 5113 [DDD]
Jongen, J.:Symphonie Concertante, w. M. Bernardi (cnd), Calgary PO CBC ("SM 5000" series) ▲ SMCD 5113 [DDD]
Poulenc, F.:Con Org, w. M. Bernardi (cnd), Calgary PO CBC ("SM 5000" series) ▲ SMCD 5113 [DDD]
Wedemeier, Ulrich (lt/gtr)
Heudelinne, L.:Suites de pièces, w. Simone Eckert (treble vl), Karl-Ernst Went (hpd), Hermann Hickethler (vl) Christophorus ▲ 77181 [DDD]
Weems, Nancy (pno)
Rosner, A.:Of Numbers & of Bells, w. Timothy Hester (pno) *(rec Dudley Recital Hall, Univ. of Houston)* Albany ▲ TROY 163 [DDD]
Wegner, Ellen (hp)
Boccherini, L.:Son Fl & Hp, w. Hans-Jörg Wegner (fl) *(rec June 1994)* Thorofon ▲ CTH 2243 [DDD]
Ciardi, C.:Il Pifferaro, w. Hans-Jörg Wegner (fl) *(rec June 1994)* Thorofon ▲ CTH 2243 [DDD]
Donizetti, G.:Son Fl & Hp, w. Hans-Jörg Wegner (fl) *(rec June 1994)* Thorofon ▲ CTH 2243 [DDD]
Rossini, G.:Allegretto Hp *(rec June 1994)* Thorofon ▲ CTH 2243 [DDD]
Rossini, G.:Andante con variazioni Fl, w. Hans-Jörg Wegner (fl) *(rec June 1994)* Thorofon ▲ CTH 2243 [DDD]
Rossini, G.:Son Hp *(rec June 1994)* Thorofon ▲ CTH 2243 [DDD]
Rota, N.:Sarabande & Toccata *(rec June 1994)* Thorofon ▲ CTH 2243 [DDD]
Rota, N.:Son Fl, w. Hans-Jörg Wegner (fl) *(rec June 1994)* Thorofon ▲ CTH 2243 [DDD]
Wegner, Hans-Jörg (fl)—see also ORCHESTRAS & ENSEMBLES Trio Cantabile
Boccherini, L.:Son Fl & Hp, w. Ellen Wegner (hp) *(rec June 1994)* Thorofon ▲ CTH 2243 [DDD]
Ciardi, C.:Il Pifferaro, w. Ellen Wegner (hp) *(rec June 1994)* Thorofon ▲ CTH 2243 [DDD]
Donizetti, G.:Son Fl & Hp, w. Ellen Wegner (hp) *(rec June 1994)* Thorofon ▲ CTH 2243 [DDD]
Flöten Fantasien [Flute Fantasies], w. Christiane Kroeker (pno) *(rec Aug. 1992)* Thorofon ▲ CTH 2187 [DDD]
Mercadante, S.:Vars Fl—9 sels *(rec June 1994)* Thorofon ▲ CTH 2243 [DDD]
Rossini, G.:Andante con variazioni Fl, w. Ellen Wegner (hp) *(rec June 1994)* Thorofon ▲ CTH 2243 [DDD]
Rota, N.:Son Fl, w. Ellen Wegner (hp) *(rec June 1994)* Thorofon ▲ CTH 2243 [DDD]
Wegner, Uwe (pno)
Grondahl, A.:Songs, w. Tuula Nienstedt (alt)—Madonnas Svaner; Valborgsnat paa Havet; Der skreg en Fugi; Middelhavsnat; Storm *(rec Friedrich-Ebert Halle, Hamburg, Sept. 20-26, 1982)* Entrée ▲ 0068 [ADD]
Kinkel, J.:Songs, w. Tuula Nienstedt (alt)—An den Mond, Op. 7/5; Die Zigeuner, Op. 7/6; Die Lorelei, Op. 7/4; Die Geister haben's vernommen, Op. 6/3 *(rec Friedrich-Ebert Halle, Hamburg, Sept. 20-26, 1982)* Entrée ▲ 0068 [ADD]
Mendelssohn, Fanny:Songs, w. Tuula Nienstedt (alt)—Die frühen Gräber, Op. 9/4; Die Mainacht, Op. 9/6; Das Heimweh; Italien; Sehnsucht *(rec Friedrich-Ebert Halle, Hamburg, Sept. 20-26, 1982)* Entrée ▲ 0068 [ADD]
Schumann, C.:Songs, w. Tuula Nienstedt (alt)—Was weinst du, Blümlein, Op. 23/1; Liebst du um Schönheit, Op. 12; Sie liebten sich beide, Op. 13/2; Er ist gekommen in Sturm und Regen, Op. 12; Das ist ein Tag, der klingen mag, Op. 23/5 *(rec Friedrich-Ebert Halle, Hamburg, Sept. 20-26, 1982)* Entrée ▲ 0068 [ADD]
Wegren, T. J. (pno)
Wegren, T.J.:Vignettes Innova ▲ MN 107
Wehle, Reiner (bas hn)—see ORCHESTRAS & ENSEMBLES Sabine Meyer Wind Ensemble
Wehle, Reiner (cl)—see ORCHESTRAS & ENSEMBLES Kontraste Ensemble, Trio di Clarone
Mozart, W.A.:Qnt Cl, K.581, w. Mannheim String Quartet Novalis ▲ 150006 [DDD]
Wehr, David Allen (pno)
American 20th Century Piano Music Chandos ▲ CHAN 8751 [DDD]
Chopin, F.:Nocturnes *(rec Music Hall, Tarrytown, NY, Aug 25-27, 1995)* Connoisseur Society 2-▲ CD 4211 [DDD]
Griffes, C.T.:Fant Pieces, Op. 6 *(rec Music Hall, Tarrytown, NY, Nov 21-2, 1994)* Connoisseur Society ▲ CD 4205
Griffes, C.T.:Roman Sketches, Op. 7 *(rec Music Hall, Tarrytown, NY, Nov 21-2, 1994)* Connoisseur Society ▲ CD 4205
Griffes, C.T.:Son Pno *(rec Music Hall, Tarrytown, NY, Nov 21-2, 1994)* Connoisseur Society ▲ CD 4205
Liszt, F.:Transcriptions & Paraphrases—Transcriptions of Wagner:Valhalla [from Das Rheingold]; Senta's Ballad [from Der fliegende Holländer]; Am stillen Herd [from Die Meistersinger von Nürnberg]; Solemn March to the Holy Grail [from Parsifal]; Fant. on Themes from Rienzi; Elsa's Dream [from Lohengrin]; Evening Star; Entry of the Guest [both from Tannhäuser] *(rec Tarrytown Music Hall, Aug. 1993)* Connoisseur Society ▲ CD 4199
Wei, Yang (pipa)
Gu, G.:Vars Pipa *(rec Shanghai, Jan 1994)* Marco Polo ("Chinese Composers" series) ▲ 8.223951 [DDD]
Weichert, Caroline (pno)
Shostakovich, D.:Preludes & Fugues Pno Accord 2-▲ ACD 202032 [DDD]
Weichert, Gregor (pno)
Beethoven, L. van:National Airs with Vars, Op. 107 Accord ▲ ACD 200092 [DDD]
Liszt, F.:Pno Music (misc)—Chaconne et sarabande d'almira, S.181; Polonaise d'eugène onegin, S.429; Vars sur "Weinen, Klagen, Sorgen", S.180; Réminiscences de "La Juive", S.409; Epithalame, S.526; In Festo Transfigurationis, S.188; Mazurka, S.384 Accord ▲ ACD 220332
Schubert, Franz:Sons Pno (comp)—in c, D.958; in C, D.279; in c#, D.655; in A♭, D.557 Accord ▲ ACD 220622 [DDD]
Schubert, Franz:Sons Pno (comp)—in E, D.459; in A, D.959 Accord ▲ ACD 220592 [DDD]
Schubert, Franz:Sons Pno (comp)—D.157, 279, 459, 557, 575, 664, 784, 958, 959 & 960 Accord 4-▲ ACD 200872 [DDD]
Schubert, Franz:Sons Pno (comp)—in a, D.537; in e, D.566; in E♭, D.568; in f#, D.571/570; in C, D.613; in f, D.625; in C, D.840; in a, D.845; in D, D.850; in G, D.894 Accord 4-▲ ACD 200862 [DDD]
Schubert, Franz:Son Pno, D.157 Accord ▲ ACD 149155 [DDD]
Schubert, Franz:Son Pno, D.537 Accord ▲ ACD 220542 [DDD]
Schubert, Franz:Son Pno 4-Hands, D.812, w. Annie Gicquel (pno) Accord ▲ ACD 200212 [AAD]
Schubert, Franz:Son Pno, D.575 Accord ▲ ACD 149155 [DDD]
Schubert, Franz:Son Pno, D.613 Accord ▲ ACD 220542 [DDD]
Schubert, Franz:Son Pno, D.625 Accord ▲ ACD 221032
Schubert, Franz:Son Pno, D.784 Accord ▲ ACD 149155 [DDD]
Schubert, Franz:Son Pno, D.840 Accord ▲ ACD 221022
Schubert, Franz:Son Pno, D.845 Accord ▲ ACD 220542 [DDD]
Schubert, Franz:Son Pno, D.850 Accord ▲ ACD 221022
Schubert, Franz:Son Pno, D.894 Accord ▲ ACD 221032
Schubert, Franz:Vars on an Original Theme Pno 4-Hands, w. Annie Gicquel (pno) Accord ▲ ACD 200212 [AAD]
Ullmann, V.:Sons Pno CPO ▲ CPO 999087-2 [DDD]
Wölfl, J.:Sons Pno—in F; in c; in E Accord ▲ ACD 201202 [DDD]
Weichsel, Y. (rcr)—see ORCHESTRAS & ENSEMBLES Il Parnaso Musicale

Weidmann, Markus (bn)
Blacher, B.:Songs, w. Katharina Richter (sop), Cornelia Wosnitza (sop), Markus Köhler (bar), Horst Göbel (pno), Chatschatur Kanajan (vn), Piotr Prysiasnik (vn), Fred Günther (va), Ithay Khen (vc), Christian Peters (sax)—3 Chansons; Ungereimtes; 4 Lieder; Nebel; 13 Ways of Looking at a Blackbird; 5 Sinnsprüche Omars des Zeltmachers; 3 Psalmen; Aprèslude; Francesca da Rimini; Jazz-Koloraturen Signum ▲ SIG X73-00 [DDD]
Weidner-Zajac, Elzbeta (pno)
Lutoslawski, W.:Bucolics *(rec Sept. 1993)* Dorian Discovery ▲ DIS 80121 [DDD]
Szymanowski, K.:Masques *(rec Sept. 1993)* Dorian Discovery ▲ DIS 80121 [DDD]
Szymanowski, K.:Mazurkas—Nos. 1-4 *(rec Sept. 1993)* Dorian Discovery ▲ DIS 80121 [DDD]
Szymanowski, K.:Preludes Pno, Op. 1—Nos. 1, 2 & 5 *(rec Sept. 1993)* Dorian Discovery ▲ DIS 80121 [DDD]
Zarebski, J.:Grand polonaise *(rec Sept. 1993)* Dorian Discovery ▲ DIS 80121 [DDD]
Zarebski, J.:Pno Music—Lullaby, Op. 22; Tarantelle, Op. 25 *(rec Sept. 1993)* Dorian Discovery ▲ DIS 80121 [DDD]
Weigand, George (lt/mandore/cittern/gtr)—see also ORCHESTRAS & ENSEMBLES Extempore String Ensemble
Old English Nursery Rhymes, w. Vivien Ellis (sop), Tim Laycock (sgr), Broadside Band *(rec Valley Recordings, Littleton-on-Severn, Feb 1996)* Saydisc ▲ CDSDL 419
Weigel, Achim (vl)
Boismortier, J.B. de:Suites Fl, Op. 35, w. B. Böhm (trns fl/rcr), J. Hübscher (lt/baroque gtr) CPO ▲ CPO 999048-2 [DDD]
Mahin, B.:Of Mice & Men Capstone ▲ CPS 8061
Weigel, Clemens (vc)
Barockmusik für Posaunen und Gesang, w. Datura Trombone Quartet, A. Scharinger (db), T. Strauss (org), J. Gagelmann (perc), R. Haeger (perc) Ars Musici ▲ AM 1094 [DDD]
Weigel, Michael (bn)
Milhaud, D.:Cataloque de fleurs, w. Ulrike Sonntag (sop), Irmela Nolte (fl), Deborah Marshall (cl), Renate Eggebrecht (vn), Stefan Berg (va), Friedemann Kupsa (vc), Arpat György (db) *(rec Ludwigsburg, Germany, Jan. 1995)* Troubadisc ▲ TROCD 01410 [DDD]
Milhaud, D.:Machines agricoles, w. Ulrike Sonntag (sop), Irmela Nolte (fl), Deborah Marshall (cl), Renate Eggebrecht (vn), Stefan Berg (va), Friedemann Kupsa (vc), Arpat György (db) *(rec Ludwigsburg, Germany, Jan. 1995)* Troubadisc ▲ TROCD 01410 [DDD]
Weigel, Wolfgang (gtr)
Dinescu, V.:Figuren II, w. Reinbert Evers (gtr)—2 versions *(rec SDR Studio Villa Berg, Apr 1992)* Pro Viva ▲ ISPV 165 [DDD]
Jung, H.:Topografien, w. Reinbert Evers (gtr) *(rec SDR Studio Villa Berg, Apr 1992)* Pro Viva ▲ ISPV 165 [DDD]
Kučera, V.:Festivals of the Imagination, w. Reinbert Evers (gtr) *(rec SDR Studio Villa Berg, Apr 1992)* Pro Viva ▲ ISPV 165 [DDD]
Like Fire Burning:Contemporary Music for 2 Guitars, w. Evers, Reinbert (gtr) *(rec Apr. 1992)* DA Music U.S.A. ▲ ISPV 165 CD [DDD]
Nickerson, J.:Like Fire Burning, w. Reinbert Evers (gtr) *(rec SDR Studio Villa Berg, Apr 1992)* Pro Viva ▲ ISPV 165 [DDD]
Stahmer, K.H.:Notturni lugubri e capricciosi, w. Reinbert Evers (gtr) *(rec SDR Studio Villa Berg, Apr 1992)* Pro Viva ▲ ISPV 165 [DDD]
Weiger, Mark (ob/ob d'amore)—see ORCHESTRAS & ENSEMBLES Wizards!
Weigl, Wolfgang (gtr)
Castelnuovo-Tedesco, M.:Con 1 Gtr, w. P. Schmelzer (cnd), Prague Virtuosi Koch Schwann ▲ SCH 310392 [DDD]
New Spanish Guitar Music Koch Schwann ▲ SCH 310150 [DDD]
Ponce, M.:Concierto del sur, w. P. Schmelzer (cnd), Prague Virtuosi Koch Schwann ▲ SCH 310392 [DDD]
Villa-Lobos, H.:Con Gtr, w. P. Schmelzer (cnd), Prague Virtuosi Koch Schwann ▲ SCH 310392 [DDD]
Weigle, Friedemann (va)—see ORCHESTRAS & ENSEMBLES Petersen String Quartet
Weigle, Sebastian (hn)
Brahms, J.:Trio Hn, w. Dieter Streicher (vn), Claudius Tanski (pno) MD + G ▲ MDG 3010595 [DDD]
Mozart, W.A.:Con Hn, K.412, w. J.-P. Weigle (cnd), Dresden PO LaserLight ▲ 15 874
Mozart, W.A.:Cons Hn, w. J.-P. Weigle (cnd), Dresden PO—No. 1 [Rondo]; Nos. 2-4 LaserLight ▲ 15 874
Mozart, W.A.:Con Movt Hn, K.370b, w. J.-P. Weigle (cnd), Dresden PO LaserLight ▲ 15 874
Mozart, W.A.:Con Movt Hn, K.494a, w. J.-P. Weigle (cnd), Dresden PO LaserLight ▲ 15 874
Mozart, W.A.:Rondo Hn, K.371, w. J.-P. Weigle (cnd), Dresden PO LaserLight ▲ 15 874
Mozart, W.A.:Sinf concertante Ob, K.Anh.9, w. Andreas Lorenz (ob), Eckart Konigstedt (bn), Klaus Kirbach (hpd), H. Haenchen (cnd), C.P.E. Bach CO Berlin Classics ▲ BER 2004
Weijenberg, J. van (vn)
Beethoven, L. van:Son 2 Vn, w. N. Murai (pno) *(rec Jan. 1989)* Eufoda ▲ 1130 [DDD]
Beethoven, L. van:Son 5 Vn, "Spring", w. N. Murai (pno) *(rec Jan. 1989)* Eufoda ▲ 1130 [DDD]
Beethoven, L. van:Son 10 Vn, w. N. Murai (pno) Eufoda ▲ 1130 [DDD]
Brahms, J.:Sons Vn (comp), w. N. Murai (pno) Eufoda ▲ 1156 [DDD]
Mozart, W.A.:Sons Vn Pno (misc), w. N. Murai (pno)—in G, K.301; in e, K.304; in G, K.379; in B, K.454 Eufoda ▲ EUF 1182 [DDD]
Weil, Terence (vc)
Falla, M. de:Con Hpd, w. R. Puyana (hpd), D. Sandeman (fl), N. Black (ob), T. King (cl), R. Cohen (vn), C. Mackerras (cnd) *(rec 1969)* Philips ("Spanish" series) ▲ 432829-2 [ADD]
Weiler, Ella Lou (va)
The Maestros Tea Party:Mr. Einstein Visits the Queen, w. Mary Jane Rupert (pno), Diana Salomon (vn), Patricia Wenzel (vn), Fern Meyers (vc), Gerhard Finkenbeiner (glass armonica), Vera Meyer (glass armonica) *(rec Euphoria Sound Studio, Revere, MA)* Cultured Kids ▲ unknown ■ 120012FM-4
Weilerstein, Donald (vn)—see also ORCHESTRAS & ENSEMBLES Weilerstein Duo
Bloch, E.:Suite 1 Vn Arabesque ▲ Z 6605
Bloch, E.:Suite 2 Vn Arabesque ▲ Z 6606
Weilerstein, Vivian Hornik (pno)—see ORCHESTRAS & ENSEMBLES Weilerstein Duo
Weimer, H. (trbn)
Bruckner, A.:Motets, w. H. P. Blochwitz (ten), H. Skarba (trbn), H. Breika (trbn), S. Rommelspacher (org), Freiburg Vocal Ensemble—Os justi; Afferentur regi; Christus factus est; Tota pulchra es Maria; Vexilla regis prodeunt; Ecce sacerdos magnus; Pange lingua; Locus iste; Ave Maria; Virga Jesse floruit Entrée ▲ 0039 [ADD]
Weinberger, Bruce (sax)—see ORCHESTRAS & ENSEMBLES Rascher Saxophone Quartet
Weiner, Lazar (pno)
The Yiddish Art Song, w. Leon Lishner (bass) *(rec mid-1970s)* Omega Classics ▲ OCD 3010 [ADD]
Weiner, Stanley (va)
Weiner, S.:Con Va, w. J. Stulen (cnd), Hilversum NOS Radio Orch *(rec 1987)* Koch Schwann ▲ SCH 313372 [ADD/DDD]
Weiner, Susan (ob)
Albinoni, T.:Con in C Tpt, w. Gerard Schwarz (tpt), Ronald Roseman (ob), Virginia Brewer (ob), Ronald MacCourt (bn), William Scribner (bn), Edward Brewer (hpd) Vox Box 2-▲ CDX 5124 [ADD]
Hertel, J.W.:Con à cinque, w. Gerard Schwarz (tpt), Ronald Roseman (ob), Virginia Brewer (ob), Ronald MacCourt (bn), William Scribner (bn), Edward Brewer (hpd) Vox Box 2-▲ CDX 5124 [ADD]
Purcell, H.:Come Ye Sons of Art, w. Laura Goetz (ob), Davis Brooks (vn), Lisa Brooks (vn), Jann Cosart (va), Mary Burke (vl), Vance Reese (db), Thomas Gerber (hpd), Henry H. Leck (cnd), Indianapolis Children's Choir [arr. Maurice Blower] *(rec The Lodge, May & June 1995)* VAI Audio ▲ VAIA 1130 [DDD]
Purcell, H.:Fly, Bold Rebellion (sels), w. Laura Goetz (ob), Davis Brooks (vn), Lisa Brooks (vn), Jann Cosart (va), Mary Burke (vl), Vance Reese (db), Thomas Gerber (hpd), Henry H. Leck (cnd), Indianapolis Children's Choir—Be Welcome Then, Great Sir [arr. Steven Rickards] *(rec The Lodge, May & June 1995)* VAI Audio ▲ VAIA 1130 [DDD]

Weiner, Susan (ob) (cont.)
Purcell, H.:King Arthur (sels), w. Laura Goetz (ob), Davis Brooks (vn), Lisa Brooks (vn), Jann Cosart (va), Mary Burke (vl), Vance Reese (db), Thomas Gerber (hpd), Henry H. Leck (cnd), Indianapolis Children's Choir—Fairest Isle [arr. Steven Rickards] *(rec The Lodge, May & June 1995)* VAI Audio ▲ VAIA 1130 [DDD]
Telemann, G.P.:Cons Tpt, w. Gerard Schwarz (tpt), Ronald Roseman (ob), Virginia Brewer (ob), Ronald MacCourt (bn), William Scribner (bn), Edward Brewer (hpd) Vox Box 2–▲ CDX 5124 [ADD]

Weinland, Jay
Brooke, N.:Obomobile, w. Brandon Adrien, Jennifer Baker, Karen Birch, Daniel Cate, Judy Christy, Richard Cochran, Jessica Cooper, Leslie Dominguez, Erin Hannigan, Dorothy Knight, Jason Lichtenwalter, Jay Moore, Hwa-Ling Russell, Toyin Spellman, Sarah Weiner Opus One ▲ CD 160

Weinmeister, Gabriele (vn)
Killmayer, W.:Qt Strs, w. C. Altenburger (vn), B. Westphal (va), J. Berger (vc) CPO ▲ CPO 999020-2 [DDD]
Killmayer, W.:Trio for 2 Vns & Vc, w. C. Altenburger (vn), J. Berger (vc) CPO ▲ CPO 999020-2 [DDD]

Weinmeister, Hanna (vn)
Gubaidulina, S.:Meditation on a Bach Chorale, w. Elisabeth Chojnacka (hpd), Elvira Bekova (vn), Marius Stravinsky (va), Alfia Bekova (vc), Alois Posch (db) *(rec Lockenhaus Festival, Austria, 1995)* BIS ▲ CD 810 [DDD]
Suslin, V.:Capriccio über die Abreise, w. Gidon Kremer (vn) *(rec Lockenhaus Festival, Austria, 1995)* BIS ▲ CD 810 [DDD]

Weinschelbaum, Dina (vc)
Curran, A.:VSTG, w. D. Abel (vn), S. Wood (vn), M. Tichener (va) CRI ▲ CD 668 [DDD]

Weinstein, David (org/syn)
Sharp, E.:20 Below, w. Anthony Coleman (toy pno/org), Wayne Horvitz (syn), Zeena Parkins (org/syn), Joseph Paul Taylor (elec/syn), Gwen Toth (reed org) Newport Classics ▲ NPD 85504

Weinstock, Frank (pno)
Handel, D.:Fl City, w. Bradley Garner (fl) Vienna Modern Masters ▲ VMM 2019 [DDD]
Handel, D.:Trio Ob, w. Sara Lambert Bloom (ob), Benjamin Jew (E hn) Vienna Modern Masters ▲ VMM 2019 [DDD]
Kramer, J.D.:Atlanta Licks, w. L. Raley, P. Rehfeldt, H. Farberman (cnd), London PO, Atlanta Chamber Players Leonarda ▲ LE 332
Kramer, J.D.:Music for Pno 3, w. L. Raley, P. Rehfeldt, H. Farberman (cnd), London PO, Atlanta Chamber Players Leonarda ▲ LE 332
Kramer, J.D.:Music for Pno 5, w. L. Raley, P. Rehfeldt, H. Farberman (cnd), London PO, Atlanta Chamber Players Leonarda ▲ LE 332
Kramer, J.D.:Musica Pro Musica, w. L. Raley, P. Rehfeldt, H. Farberman (cnd), London PO, Atlanta Chamber Players Leonarda ▲ LE 332
Kramer, J.D.:Renascence, w. L. Raley, P. Rehfeldt, H. Farberman (cnd), London PO, Atlanta Chamber Players Leonarda ▲ LE 332

Weintraub, Barbara (pno)
Farrenc, J.-L.:Trio Vn, w. K. Hoover (fl), C. Brey (vc) Leonarda ■ LE 304
Ulehla, L.:Elegy, w. K. Hoover (fl), C. Brey (vc) Leonarda ■ LE 304

Weinzier, Elizabeth (fl)
Haydn, J.:Trios Fls & Vc, "London Trios", w. Edmund Wächter (fl), Ulrich Fuchs (vc) Christophorus ▲ CHR 77146 [DDD]

Weinzierl, Elizabeth (fl)
Bach, J.S.:Trio Son for 2 Fls, BWV 1039, w. Edmund Wächter (fl), Eva Schieferstein (hpd) Entrée ▲ 0081 [DDD]
Buffardin, P.G.:Trio Son Fl, w. Edmund Wächter (fl), Eva Schieferstein (hpd) [arr for 2 flutes & bc] Entrée ▲ 0081 [DDD]
Hasse, J.A.:Trio Sons Fls, Op. 3, w. Edmund Wächter (fl), Ulrich Fuchs (vc)—Trio Son No. 6 in D Entrée ▲ 0081 [DDD]
Hoffmeister, F.A.:Trios for 2 Fls & Vc, w. E. Wächter (fl), U. Fuchs (vc) Christophorus ▲ CHR 77146 [DDD]
Lotti, A.:Trio Son Fl, w. Ulrich Fuchs (vc), Eva Schieferstein (hpd) Entrée ▲ 0081 [DDD]
Quantz, J.J.:Trio Son Fls, w. Edmund Wächter (fl), Ulrich Fuchs (vc) Entrée ▲ 0081 [DDD]
Vivaldi, A.:Trio Son Fls, w. Edmund Wächter (fl), Ulrich Fuchs (vc) Entrée ▲ 0081 [DDD]

Weinzierl, Stefan (pno)
Weill, K.:Songs, w. Sara Musinowski (sgr), Hans-Joachim Tinnefeld (b gtr)—September Song; Listen to My Song; Mon Ami, My Friend; It Never Was You; One Life to Live; My Ship; I'm a Stranger Here Myself; Foolish Heart; Speak Low; Sing Me Not a Ballad; Lonely House; Trouble Man; Stay Well; Lost in the Stars Signum ▲ SIG X85-00 [DDD]

Weir, Gillian (org)
Messiaen, O.:Org Music (comp) Collins Classics 7–▲ COL 7031 [DDD]
Saint-Saëns, C.:Sym 3, w. Y.P. Tortelier (cnd), Ulster Orch Chandos ▲ CHAN 8822 [DDD]
Scherzo Koss Classics ▲ KC 1013 [DDD]
Stanford, C.V.:Concert Piece Org, w. V. Handley (cnd), Ulster Orch Chandos ▲ CHAN 8861 [DDD]

Weirich, Robert (pno)
Beach, A.M.C.:Pieces Vn, Op. 40, w. Pamela Frame (vc) Koch International Classics ▲ KIC 7281 [DDD]
Beach, A.M.C.:Son Vn, w. Pamela Frame (vc) [arr. Frame] Koch International Classics ▲ KIC 7281 [DDD]
Biscardi, C.:Mestiere *(rec Pick-Staiger Concert Hall, Northwestern Univ., Evanston, IL, Aug. 1981)* CRI ▲ CD 686 [ADD]
Biscardi, C.:Tenzone, w. Robert Dick (fl), Keith Underwood (fl) *(rec Sprague Hall, Yale Univ., New Haven, CT, 1978)* CRI ▲ CD 686 [ADD]

Weis, Erich (va)
Pfitzner, H.:Qnt Pno, w. W. Kamper (pno), A. Kamper (vn), K. M. Titze (vn), F. Kvarda (vc) Preiser ▲ 93111 (m) [AAD]
Pfitzner, H.:Sxt Cl, w. L. Wlach (cl), A. Kamper (vn), F. Kvarda (vc), J. Hermann (db), W. Kamper (pno) Preiser ▲ 93111 (m) [AAD]

Weis, T. (tpt)
Stravinsky, I.:L'Histoire du soldat Suite Vn, w. G. Tarack (vn), C. Russo (cl), J. Levine (db), Loren Glickman (bn), J. Swallow (trbn), R. Desroches (perc), L. Stokowski (cnd) Vanguard Classics ▲ SVC 1 [AAD]

Weisberg, Arthur (bn)—see also ORCHESTRAS & ENSEMBLES New York Woodwind Quintet, New York Woodwind Quintet members
Telemann, G.P.:Qt Bn, w. S. Baron (fl), R. Roseman (ob), E. Brewer (hpd)—in d Elektra/Nonesuch ■ 71352-4

Weise, Manfred (cl)
Strauss, R.:Duet-Concertino, w. W. Liebscher (bn), R. Kempe (cnd), Dresden Staatskapelle EMI Classics 3–▲ CDZC 64342

Weiser, Dan (pno)—see ORCHESTRAS & ENSEMBLES Upper Valley Duo

Weisflog, Thomas (org)
Sowerby, L.:Forsaken of Man, w. Alicia Clark (sop), Judith Compton (alt), Thomas Potter (bass), Paul Grizzell (bass), Matthew Greenberg (bass), Bruce Hall (sgr), John Vorassi (sgr), William Ferris (cnd), William Ferris Chorale *(rec St. Thomas the Apostle Church, Chicago, June 1990)* New World ▲ 803942 [AAD]

Wei-shan, Liu (guzheng)
Chen, Y.:Music of, w. Zhao Yang-qin (yangqin), Chen Jie-bing (erhu), Min Xiao-fen (pipa), J. Falletta (cnd), Women's PO, Chanticleer—Duo Ye No. 2; Sym 2; Ge Xu; Chinese Myths Cant; Pan Gu Creates Heaven & Earth; Nu Wa Creates Human Beings; Weaving Maid & Cowherd; Song of Weaving Maid & Cowherd *(rec Skywalker Sound, San Rafael, CA, June 1996)* New Albion ▲ NA 090

Weisman, Vladimir (vn)—see ORCHESTRAS & ENSEMBLES Claremont String Quartet

Weismeyer, Roger (ob)
Bowles, P.:Scènes d'Anabase, w. Brian Staufenbiel (ten), Irene Herrmann (pno) Koch International Classics ▲ KIC 7343 [DDD]
Bowles, P.:Son Ob & Cl, w. Mark Brandenburg (cl) Koch International Classics ▲ KIC 7343 [DDD]

Weiss, Alan (pno)
Alkan, C.-V.:Pno Music—Grande Sonate; Les Festin D'Esope; Miniatures Fidelio ▲ FID 8839 [DDD]
Mozart, W.A.:Con 10 Pnos, w. R. Firkušný (pno), D. Zinman (cnd), Rochester PO *(rec 1978)* Vox Box 3–▲ CD3X 3010 [ADD]
Mozart, W.A.:Pno Music 4-Hands, w. R. Firkusny (pno)—Andante & Vars., K.501; Fugue, K.426; Sons., K.19d, 357, 358, 381, 448, 497, 521 *(rec 1978–79)* Vox Box 3–▲ CD3X 3010 [ADD]

Weiss, Catherine (vn)—see ORCHESTRAS & ENSEMBLES Purcell Quartet

Weiss, Jeanne (pno)—see also ORCHESTRAS & ENSEMBLES Weiss Duo
Haydn, J.:Con Org, Vn & Strs, H.XVIII/6, w. Sidney Weiss (vn), S. Weiss (cnd), Crystal CO Crystal ▲ CD 511 ■ C 511
Mendelssohn, F.:Con in d Vn, Pno & Strs, w. S. Weiss (vn), S. Weiss (cnd), Crystal CO Crystal ▲ CD 511 ■ C 511

Weiss, Kenneth (hpd)
Bach, J.S.:Goldberg Vars L'Empreinte Digitale ▲ ED 13065
Mondonville, J.-J.C. de:Pièces de clavecin, Op. 3, w. Walter Reiter (vn) Meridian ▲ MER 84302 [DDD]
Mondonville, J.-J.C. de:Pièces de clavecin, Op. 5, w. Linda Perillo (sop), Walter Reiter (vn) Meridian ▲ MER 84302 [DDD]

Weiss, Lauren (fl)
Ives, C.:Son 2 Pno, w. Richard Trythall (pno) *(rec Villa Aurelia, American Academy, Rome, Dec 1992 & Sept 1995)* Centaur ▲ 2285 [DDD]
Lifchitz, M.:Canto de paz, w. L. Vardaman (sop), G. Kitzis (vn), N. Ives (vc), M. Lifchitz (pno) Opus One ▲ 149
Lifchitz, M.:Yellow Ribbons, w. M. Lifchitz (pno), M. Lifchitz (cnd), North/South Consonance Ensemble—Nos. 1 (1981) & 21 (1984) Opus One ▲ 149

Weiss, Liselotte (pno)
Liselotte Weiss *(rec Apr. 30–May 1, 1975)* BIS ▲ CD 23 [AAD]

Weiss, M. (sax)
Moser, R.:Wal, w. I. Roth (sax), B. Beaufreton (sax), J.-G. Koerper (sax), P. Egholm (sax), M. Venzago (cnd), Basel SO Grammont ▲ CTSP 12-2 [ADD]

Weiss, Richard (vc)
Debussy, C.:Danses sacrée et profane, w. Y. Kondonassis (hp), F. Cohen (cl), M. Chalifour (vn), W.-F. Gu (va), S. Konopka (va), T. Sperl (db), J. Smith (instr) *(rec Nov. 23–25, 1992)* Telarc ▲ CD 80361 [DDD]
Ravel, M.:Intro & Allegro, w. Y. Kondonassis (hp), J. Smith (fl), F. Cohen (cl), M. Chalifour (vn), W.-F. Gu (va), S. Konopka (va), T. Sperl (db) *(rec Nov. 23–25, 1992)* Telarc ▲ CD 80361 [DDD]
Ravel, M.:Pavane pour une infante défunte, w. Y. Kondonassis (hp), J. Smith (fl), F. Cohen (cl), M. Chalifour (vn), W.-F. Gu (va), S. Konopka (va), T. Sperl (db) [arr. by Kondonassis] *(rec Nov. 23–25, 1992)* Telarc ▲ CD 80361 [DDD]

Weiss, Sharon (perc/kaval)
Blak, K.:Con Grotto, w. John Tchicai (t sax/sgr/perc), Lennart Kullgren (gtr/fl/sgr/perc), Anders Hagberg (fl/perc/sgr), Kristian Blak (pno/perc/sgr), Anders Jormin (bass instr/perc/sgr), Karin Korpelainen (perc/sgr) *(rec Lídargjógv, Sandoy, Aug. 1984)* Tutl ▲ HJF 33

Weiss, Sidney (vn)—see also ORCHESTRAS & ENSEMBLES Weiss Duo
Haydn, J.:Con Org, Vn & Strs, H.XVIII/6, w. Jeanne Weiss (pno), S. Weiss (cnd), Crystal CO Crystal ▲ CD 511 ■ C 511
Mendelssohn, F.:Con in d Vn, Pno & Strs, w. J. Weiss (pno), S. Weiss (cnd), Crystal CO Crystal ▲ CD 511 ■ C 511

Weiss, Ursula (vn)
Buxtehude, D.:Sons Vn, Vl & Continuo, w. John Holloway (vn), Jaap ter Linden (vl), Mogens Rasmussen (vl), Lars Ulrik Mortensen (hpd/org)—BuxWV 266, 267, 269 & 271–273 *(rec Radio House, Studio 2, Sept 25–28, 1994)* Marco Polo ("dacapo" series) ▲ 8.224005 [DDD]

Weissenberg, Alexis (pno)
Bartók, B.:Con 2 Pno, w. E. Ormandy (cnd), Philadelphia Orch RCA Gold Seal ▲ 09026-61396-2
Brahms, J.:Con 2 Pno, w. P. Maag (cnd), Turin RAI SO Diamante ▲ ARCD 2030 [ADD]
Chopin, F.:Con 2 Pno, w. A. Orizio (cnd), Gaspparo da Salò Orch *(rec live 6/67)* Fonè ▲ 91F05 [ADD]
Chopin, F.:Grand Fant on Polish Airs, w. A. Orizio (cnd), Gasparo da Salò Orch *(rec live 6/67)* Fonè ▲ 91F05 [ADD]
Chopin, F.:Krakowiak, w. A. Orizio (cnd), Gasparo da Salò Orch *(rec live 6/67)* Fonè ▲ 91F05 [ADD]
Chopin, F.:Vars on Mozart's *La ci darem la mano*, w. A. Orizio (cnd), Gasparo da Salò Orch *(rec live 6/67)* Fonè ▲ 91F05 [ADD]
Debussy, C.:Children's Corner Deutsche Grammophon ("Digital Midprice" series) ▲ 445547-2
Debussy, C.:Estampes Deutsche Grammophon ("Digital Midprice" series) ▲ 445547-2
Debussy, C.:La Fille aux cheveaux de lin Pno Deutsche Grammophon ("Digital Midprice" series) ▲ 445547-2
Debussy, C.:L'Isle joyeuse Deutsche Grammophon ("Digital Midprice" series) ▲ 445547-2
Debussy, C.:Music of, w. Leonard Pennario (pno)— also Munch, Boston SO; Reiner, Chicago SO; Morton Gould & His Orch. RCA ■ ALK1-4981
Debussy, C.:La Plus que lente Deutsche Grammophon ("Digital Midprice" series) ▲ 445547-2
Debussy, C.:Suite bergamasque Deutsche Grammophon ("Digital Midprice" series) ▲ 445547-2
Debussy, C.:Suite bergamasque RCA Silver Seal ▲ 09026-60909-2 ■ 09026-60909-4
Franck, C.:Symphonic Vars, w. H. von Karajan (cnd), Berlin PO EMI Classics ▲ CDM 64747
Rachmaninoff, S.:Con 3 Pno, w. G. Prêtre (cnd), Chicago SO RCA Gold Seal ▲ 09026-61396-2
Rachmaninoff, S.:Music of, w. Anna Moffo (sop), Alexander Brailowsky (pno), Leonard Pennario (pno), (cnd) (cnd), *(orch unknown)* RCA ■ 5697-4-RV
Rachmaninoff, S.:Prelude Pno, Op. 3/2 RCA Red Seal ▲ 60568-2-RC [ADD] ■ 60568-4-RC (CrO2)
Rachmaninoff, S.:Preludes Pno, Opp 23 & 32 RCA Red Seal ▲ 60568-2-RC [ADD] ■ 60568-4-RC (CrO2)
Rachmaninoff, S.:Son 1 Pno Deutsche Grammophon ▲ 427499-2 [DDD]
Rachmaninoff, S.:Son 2 Pno Deutsche Grammophon ▲ 427499-2 [DDD]

Weissenborn, Günther (pno)
Mozart, W.A.:Songs, w. Erika Köth (sop) *(rec 1966)* Berlin Classics ▲ BER 9125
Schubert, Franz:Winterreise, w. P. Anders (ten) [G] Acanta ▲ CD 43806 [DDD]

Weitz, Guy (org)
Bach, J.S.:Preludes & Fugues, BWV 531–552—in E♭, BWV 552 Amphion ▲ PHI 132 [ADD]
Franck, C.:Chorals Org, M.38–40—Nos. 1 in E & 3 in a Amphion ▲ PHI 132 [ADD]
Franck, C.:Final Amphion ▲ PHI 132 [ADD]
Liszt, F.:Prelude & Fugue B-A-C-H Amphion ▲ PHI 132 [ADD]
Vierne, L.:Sym 1 Org—Finale Amphion ▲ PHI 132 [ADD]
Weitz, G.:Sym 1—sel from 1st movt. Amphion ▲ PHI 132 [ADD]
Widor, C.M.:Sym 4 Org—Andante cantabile Amphion ▲ PHI 132 [ADD]

Wekre, Frøydis Ree (hn)
Berge, S.:Hornlokk Crystal ▲ CD 678
Clearfield, A.:Songs of the Wolf, w. Andrea Clearfield (pno) Crystal ▲ CD 678
Friedman, S.:Topanga Vars Crystal ▲ CD 678
Frøydis Ree Wekre, Horn, w. Zita Carno (pno), Sequoia String Quartet *(rec 1980 & 1983)* Crystal ▲ CD 377
Madsen, T.:Dream Crystal ▲ CD 678
Madsen, T.:Son Hn, w. Jens Harald Bratlie (pno) Crystal ▲ CD 678
Plagge, W.:Son 3 Hn, w. Wolfgang Plagge (pno) Crystal ▲ CD 678

Welbourne, Todd (pno)
Koykkar, J.:Impulse Northeastern ▲ NR 246-CD

Weldy, Fred (pno)
American Song Recital, w. Lauren Wagner (sop) Channel Classics ▲ CCS 5293 [DDD]

INSTRUMENT.

Welin, Karl-Erik (org)
Nilsson, T.:Out of Earthly Night, w. Gudrun Bruna (sop), Marianne Mellnäs (sop), Kaysa Hälldin (alt), Lars Sjögren (ten), Göran Swartz (bass), Sture Hedin (sgr), Ola Kyhlberg (sgr), Lars Ljungman (sgr), Nils Philipson (sgr), Ulrik Quale (sgr), Nils Spangenberg (sgr), Britta Therén (sgr), Torsten Nilsson (cnd), Oscar's Motet Choir *(rec Oscar's Church, Stockholm, Sweden, Apr 26–27, 1978)* BIS ▲ CD 138 [AAD]
Wellejus, Henning (pno)
Sings Danish Romances, w. Annie Birgit Garde (sop) Danacord ▲ DACOCD 348 [DDD]
Weller, John (vn)
Lam, B.-C.:Last Spring, w. Bun-Ching Lam (pno), Ella Marie Gray (vn), Melissa Hamilton (va), Walter Gray (vc) CRI ▲ CD 726 [DDD]
Wellin, Annette (pno)
Hoffman, D.:Fant on *Black is the Color of My True Love's Hair*, w. Teri Fay Storhaug (rcr), Britt Swenson (vn), Steve Hillesland (vc) Meyer ▲ MC 0108
Wellington, Chris (va)
Bononcini, A.:Stabat Mater, w. Felicity Palmer (sop), Paul Esswood (ct), Philip Langridge (ten), Christopher Keyte (bass), John Scott (org), John Willison (vn), Don McVeigh (va), G. Guest (cnd), Philomusica Antiqua of London, St. John's College Choir Cambridge *(rec 1977)* London 2-▲ 443868-2 [ADD]
Caldara, A.:Crucifixus, w. Felicity Palmer (sop), Paul Esswood (ct), Philip Langridge (ten), Christopher Keyte (bass), John Scott (org), John Willison (vn), Don McVeigh (va), G. Guest (cnd), Philomusica Antiqua of London, St. John's College Choir Cambridge *(rec 1977)* London 2-▲ 443868-2 [ADD]
Lotti, A.:Crucifixus, w. Felicity Palmer (sop), Paul Esswood (ct), Philip Langridge (ten), Christopher Keyte (bass), John Scott (org), John Willison (vn), Don McVeigh (va), G. Guest (cnd), Philomusica Antiqua of London, St. John's College Choir Cambridge *(rec 1977)* London 2-▲ 443868-2 [ADD]
Wells, Alexander (pno)
Britten, H.:Choral Music, w. Skaila Kanga (hp), R. Corp (cnd), New London Children's Choir—Friday Afternoons, Op. 7; Sweet was the Song; King Herod & the Cock; The Oxen; Fancie; The Birds; 3 Two-part Songs; A Walden Trio [Christmas Song of the Women]; A Ceremony of Carols *(rec All Hallows, Gospel Oak, London, Sept. 17–18, 1994)* Naxos ▲ 8.553183 [DDD]
Wells, David (vc)
Kupferman, M.:Con Vc & Jazz Band, w. D. Mattran (cnd), Hartt Jazz Ensemble Soundspells ▲ SP 111 [ADD]
Richter, M.:Qhanri, w. M. Richter (pno) Leonarda ▲ LE 337
Ziffrin, M.:Sono Vc, w. J. Wells (pno) Opus One ▲ 146
Wells, John (pno)
Ziffrin, M.:Sono Vc, w. D. Wells (vc) Opus One ▲ 146
Welsh, Moray (vc)
Bach, J.S.:Son Fl, BWV 1079, w. J. Galway (fl), K.-W. Chung (vn), P. Moll (hpd) RCA Gold Seal ("Papillon Collection" series) ▲ 6517-2-RG [ADD] ■ 6517-4-RG
Bach, J.S.:Trio Son for 2 Fls, BWV 1039, w. J. Galway (fl), K.-W. Chung (vn), P. Moll (hpd) RCA Gold Seal ("Papillon Collection" series) ▲ 6517-2-RG [ADD] ■ 6517-4-RG
Britten, H.:Son Vc, w. John Lenehan (pno) EMI Classics ("Anglo-American Chamber Music" series) ▲ CDC 55398
Delius, F.:Son Vc & Pno, w. Israela Margalit (pno) EMI Classics ("Anglo-American Chamber Music" series) ▲ CDC 55399
Elgar, E.:Qnt Pno Strs, w. Israela Margalit (pno), Alexander Barantschick (vn), Janice Graham (vn), Paul Silverthorne (va) EMI Classics ("Anglo-American Chamber Music" series) ▲ CDC 55403
Grainger, P.:Folk Song Settings, w. Philip Martin (pno), K. Montgomery (cnd), Bournemouth Sinfonietta—Blithe bells; Country gardens; Green bushes; Handel in the Strand; Mock morris; Molly on the shore; My Robin is to the greenwood gone; Shepherd's hey; Spoon River; Walking tune; Youthful rapture; Youthful Suite *(rec ca. 1979)* Chandos ("Collect" series) ▲ CHAN 6542 [ADD]
Howells, H.:Fant Vc & Orch, w. R. Hickox (cnd), London SO Chandos ▲ CHAN 9410 [DDD]
Howells, H.:Threnody, w. R. Hickox (cnd), London SO Chandos ▲ CHAN 9410 [DDD]
McEwen, J.:Hills o' Heather, w. A. Mitchell (cnd), London PO Chandos ▲ CHAN 9345 [DDD]
Walton, W.:Qt Pno, w. *(pianist unknown)*, Janice Graham (vn), Paul Silverthorne (va) EMI Classics ("Anglo-American Chamber Music" series) ▲ CDC 55404
Welsh, Stephen (sax)
Colgrass, M.:Urban Requiem, w. David Fernandez (sax), Tom McCormick (sax), George Weremchuk (sax), G. Green (cnd), Univ of Miami Wind Ensemble *(rec Miami Beach, Feb 1996)* Albany ▲ TROY 212 [DDD]
Welte, M. (org)
M. Welte & Söhne Pneumatic Orchestrions Organ Historical Society ▲ DC 100 [DDD]
Weman, Lena (fl)
Bach, C.P.E.:Sons Fl, w. Hans-Ola Ericsson (org/hpd)—H.504–9; H.515; H.542–3; H.545; H.574; H.578 *(rec Masonic Hall, Uppsala, Sweden & Entrance Hall, Uppsala Cathedral, Sweden; Feb 20–25, 1995)* BIS 2-▲ CD 755/756 [DDD]
Wendland, Peter (vl)
Krieger, J.P.:Trio Sons, w. Mihoko Kimura (vn), Michael Freimuth (thb), Siebe Henstra (hpd/org)—Nos. 1–6 Prezioso ▲ 840.402
Marais, M.:Pièces en trio, w. Ursula Schmidt-Laukamp (rcr), Harald Hoeren (hpd)—No. 3 in D Ars Produktion ▲ ARS 368337
Wenger, Beat (fl)
Klatzow, P.:Chamber Con, w. Jimmy Reinders (cl), Robert Grishkoff (hn), Uliano Marchio (gtr), Lamar Crowson (pno), Barry Jordan (elec org), Peter Hamblin (perc), P. Klatzow (cnd) Claremont ▲ GSE 1524
Wennberg, G. (hn)—see ORCHESTRAS & ENSEMBLES Musica Holmiae
Went, Karl-Ernst (hpd)
Heudelinne, L.:Suites de pièces, w. Simone Eckert (treble vl), Ulrich Wedemeier (lt/Baroque gtr), Hermann Hickethier (vl) Christophorus ▲ 77181 [DDD]
Wentz, Jed (fl)
Bach, J.S.:Sons Fl, BWV 1030–35, w. C. Wuyts (hpd) Fidelio ▲ FID 9210 [DDD]
Wenzel, Patricia (vn)
The Maestros Tea Party:Mr. Einstein Visits the Queen, w. Mary Jane Rupert (pno), Diana Salomon (vn), Ella Lou Weiler (va), Fern Meyers (vc), Gerhard Finkenbeiner (glass armonica), Vera Meyer (glass armonica) *(rec Euphoria Sound Studio, Revere, MA)* Cultured Kids ▲ unknown ■ 120012FM-4
Wenzinger, August (vl)—see ORCHESTRAS & ENSEMBLES Oberlin Baroque Ensemble, August Wenzinger Ensemble
Werba, Erik (pno)
Beethoven, L. van:An die ferne Geliebte, w. Peter Schreier (ten) *(rec Aug 12, 1979)* Orfeo d'or ("Festspiel Dokumente" series) ▲ 399951
Brahms, J.:Songs, w. E. Gruberova (sop)—Opp. 70/1, 85/6, 95/1, 106/2 Orfeo ▲ 066831 [DDD]
Brahms, J.:Songs, w. Irmgard Seefried (sop)—Feinsliebchen; In stiller Nacht; Die Trauernde; Da unten im Tale *(rec Aug 18, 1960)* Orfeo d'or ("Festspiel Dokumente" series) ▲ 398951 (m)
Busoni, F.:Songs, w. Elio Battaglia (bar)—2 Songs [text Byron], Op. 15; Old German Song, Op. 18/1; 2 Songs, Op. 31; 2 Songs, Op. 24; Ave Maria, Op. 1; 5 Songs [text Goethe] Fonit Cetra ("Italia" series) ▲ FCT CDC 84
Dvořák, A.:Songs, w. E. Gruberova (sop)—Liebeslieder, Op. 83 Orfeo ▲ 066831 [DDD]
Dvořák, A.:Zigeunermelodien, Op. 55, w. Peter Schreier (ten) *(rec Aug 12, 1979)* Orfeo d'or ("Festspiel Dokumente" series) ▲ 399951
Mahler, G.:Songs from Rückert, w. M. Lipovšek (mez)—omitting "Blicke mir nicht" [G] Orfeo ▲ 176891 [DDD]
Nicolai Gedda in Recital, w. Nicolai Gedda (ten), *(rec. live at the Salzburg Festival, Aug. 1961)* EMI Classics ▲ CDM 65352
Schreker, F.:Songs, w. M. Lipovšek (mez)—(5) Ich frag' nach dir; Dies aber kann mein Sehnen; Die Dunkelheit sinkt schwer; Sie sind so schön; Einst gibt ein Tag [G] Orfeo ▲ 176891 [DDD]
Schubert, Franz:Die Schöne Müllerin, w. E. Haefliger (ten) *(rec 1967)* Sony Classical ("Essential Classics" series) ▲ SBK 48287 [AAD] ■ SBT 48287

Werba, Erik (pno) (cont.)
Schubert, Franz:Songs (misc), w. J. Loibl (bar), N. Shelter (pno)—13 Goethe-Lieder FSM ▲ FCD 97202 [DDD]
Schubert, Franz:Songs (misc), w. Irmgard Seefried (sop)—Ganymed; Der König von Thule; Gretchen am Spinnrad; Gretchens Bitte; Szene aus Faust; Schäfers Klagelied; Wanderers Nachtlied; Liebhaber in allen Gestalten; Im Frühling; Fischerweise; Widerschein; Der Wanderer an den Mond; Der Tod und das Mädchen; Der Jüngling und der Tod; Das Lied im Grünen; Seligkeit Adès ▲ ADE 203102 [AAD]
Schumann, R.:Frauenliebe und -leben, w. Irmgard Seefried (sop) *(rec Aug 18, 1960)* Orfeo d'or ("Festspiel Dokumente" series) ▲ 398951 (m)
Schumann, R.:Liederkreis, Op. 39, w. Irmgard Seefried (sop)—In der Fremde; Waldesgespräch; Die Stille; Zwielicht; Frühlingsnacht *(rec Aug 18, 1960)* Orfeo d'or ("Festspiel Dokumente" series) ▲ 398951 (m)
Schumann, R.:Myrthen, w. Irmgard Seefried (sop)—Widmung; Die Lotosblume; Lied der Suleika; Der Nussbaum *(rec Aug 18, 1960)* Orfeo d'or ("Festspiel Dokumente" series) ▲ 398951 (m)
Schumann, R.:Songs, w. Irmgard Seefried (sop)—Lieder nach Gedichten der Königin Maria Stuart, Op. 135; Dein Angesicht aus, Op. 127; Meine Rose, Op. 90; Aufträge, Op. 77; Stille Tränen, Op. 35 *(rec Aug 18, 1960)* Orfeo d'or ("Festspiel Dokumente" series) ▲ 398951 (m)
Strauss, R.:Songs, w. M. Lipovšek (mez)—Op. 10, Nos. 1,3 & 4; Op. 27, Nos. 1 & 4 [G] Orfeo ▲ 176891 [DDD]
Strauss, R.:Songs, w. Evelyn Lear (sop)—Ständchen, Op. 17; Morgen, Op. 27; Mein Herz ist stumm, Op. 19; Leises Lied, Op. 39; Allerseelen, Op. 10; Schlechtes Wetter, Op. 69; Ich wollt ein Sträusslein binden, Op. 68; An die Nacht, Op. 68; Säusle, liebe Myrte!, Op. 68; Wie erkenn' ich mein Treulieb, Op. 67; Guten Morgen, Op. 67; Sie trugen ihn, Op. 67; Wiegenlied, Op. 41; Ruhe, meine Seele, Op. 27, Befreit, Op. 39; Leise Lieder, Op. 41a; In der Campagna, Op. 41; Du meines Herzens Krönelein, Op. 21; Blindenklage, Op. 56; Die Georgine, Op. 10; Gefunden, Op. 56; Die Nacht; Op. 10; Schlagende Herzen, Op. 29; Wie sollten wir geheim sie halten, Op. 19; Meinem Kinde, Op. 37; Zueignung, Op. 10 *(rec Salzburg & Vienna, 1964–65)* VAI Audio ▲ VAIA 1080
Strauss, R.:Songs, w. Peter Schreier (ten)—Die Georgine; Die Zeitlose; Ach weh, mir unglückhaftem Mann; Traum durch die Dämmerung; Du meines Herzens Krönelein; Wie sollten wir geheimsam sie halten; Ruhe meine Seele; All' meine Gedanken; Nachtgang; Freundliche Vision; Heimliche Aufforderung; Morgen; Die Nacht; Ständchen *(rec Aug 12, 1979)* Orfeo d'or ("Festspiel Dokumente" series) ▲ 399951
Strauss, R.:Songs, w. E. Gruberova (sop)—10 songs—Opp. 22/1–4; 48/1–2; 68/1,2 & 5; 69/5 Orfeo ▲ 066831 [DDD]
Wolf, H.:Songs (misc), w. M. Lipovšek (mez)—4 Mignon-Lieder [G] Orfeo ▲ 176891 [DDD]
Wolf, H.:Songs (misc), w. J. Loibl (bar), N. Shelter (pno)—10 Goethe-Lieder FSM ▲ FCD 97202 [DDD]
Werba, Michael (bn)—see ORCHESTRAS & ENSEMBLES Vienna Chamber Ensemble members
Werchowska, Marie-Claude (pno)
Balakirev, M.:Scherzo 2 *(rec Auditorium du C.N.R. de Douai, Mar 1–3, 1995)* Ligia Digital ▲ 0103028 [DDD]
Borodin, A.:Petite Suite *(rec Auditorium du C.N.R. de Douai, Mar 1–3, 1995)* Ligia Digital ▲ 0103028 [DDD]
Borodin, A.:Scherzo Pno *(rec Auditorium du C.N.R. de Douai, Mar 1–3, 1995)* Ligia Digital ▲ 0103028 [DDD]
Cui, C.:Berceuse *(rec Auditorium du C.N.R. de Douai, Mar 1–3, 1995)* Ligia Digital ▲ 0103028 [DDD]
Mussorgsky, M.:Pno Music—Scherzo in c#; Niania et moi; Première punition; Impromtu passionné; Plaisanterie enfantine; La couturière; Une larme; Gopak *(rec Auditorium du C.N.R. de Douai, Mar 1–3, 1995)* Ligia Digital ▲ 0103028 [DDD]
Rimsky-Korsakov, N.:Pieces Pno, Op. 11 *(rec Auditorium du C.N.R. de Douai, Mar 1–3, 1995)* Ligia Digital ▲ 0103028 [DDD]
Werder, Manfred (pno)
Tenney, J.:Bridge, w. Erika Radermacher (pno) Hat Hut ("Now" series) ▲ ART CD 6193 [DDD]
Weremchuk, George (sax)
Colgrass, M.:Urban Requiem, w. David Fernandez (sax), Tom McCormick (sax), Stephen Welsh (sax), G. Green (cnd), Univ of Miami Wind Ensemble *(rec Miami Beach, Feb 1996)* Albany ▲ TROY 212 [DDD]
Werff, Ivo-Jan van der (va)—see also ORCHESTRAS & ENSEMBLES Medici String Quartet
Scharwenka, X.:Qt Pno, w. Seta Tanyel (pno), Levon Chilingirian (vn), Garbis Atmacayan (vc) Collins Classics ▲ COL 1419 [DDD]
Wering, J. van (hpd)
Bach, J.S.:Con for 4 Hpds, w. E. Müller (hpd), G. Leonhardt (hpd), A. Uittenbosch (hpd), G. Leonhardt (cnd), Leonhardt Consort Teldec 3-▲ 2292-42726-2 [ADD]
Werke, Frøydis Ree (hn)—see also ORCHESTRAS & ENSEMBLES Prunes
Madsen, T.:Con Hn, w. O.K. Ruud (cnd), Trondheim SO Simax ▲ PSC 1100
Nystedt, K.:Con Hn, w. O.K. Ruud (cnd), Trondheim SO Simax ▲ PSC 1100
Plagge, W.:Con Hn, w. O.K. Ruud (cnd), Trondheim SO Simax ▲ PSC 1100
Werner, Joseph (pno)
Cahn, W.:In Ancient Temple Gardens, w. Bob Becker (xyl/perc) Nexus ▲ 10339 [DDD]
Werner, Lasse (pno)
Segerstam, L.:Rituals in La, w. Leif Segerstam (pno) *(rec Swedish Broadcasting Co. Studio 4, Stockholm, Sweden, Oct 15, 1974)* BIS ▲ CD 20 [AAD]
Werner, Max (vc)—see ORCHESTRAS & ENSEMBLES Gaudeamus String Quartet
Werner, Susan (banjo)
Veeneman, C.:The Wiry Concord, w. Susan Werner (banjo), Forrest Covington (hammered dlc/cimbalom), Georganne Assat (hp), Donald Martin Jenni (hpd), Mark Johnson (hpd), Barbara Phillips Farley (pno), James Austin (pno), Marta Soderberg (va), James Knutson (perc), Patrick Doyle (perc), Steven Butters (perc), James Popejoy (perc), M. Geary (cnd) Capstone ▲ SCI 6
Werthen, Rudolf (vc)
Boccherini, L.:Qnts Strs, I Fiamminghi CO—in C, G.324 (Op. 30/6) Koch Schwann ▲ CD 311184 [ADD/DDD]
Wesenigk, Fritz (tpt)
Honegger, A.:Sym 2, w. H. von Karajan (cnd), Berlin PO *(rec French Church, St. Moritz, Aug 1969)* Deutsche Grammophon ("The Originals" series) ▲ 447435-2 [ADD]
Wesner-Hoehn, Beverly (hp)
Britten, H.:A Ceremony of Carols, w. Henry H. Leck (cnd), Indianapolis Children's Choir *(rec The Lodge, May & June 1995)* VAI Audio ▲ VAIA 1130 [DDD]
Eaton, J.:Ars Poetica, w. Nelda Nelson (sop), Carole Morgan (fl), Daniel Rothmuller (vc), C. Colnot (cnd) *(rec Dec 18, 1986)* Indiana Univ School of Music ▲ 0-253-31842-4
Wesotowska, Anna (pno)
Chopin, F.:Intro, Theme & Vars, w. Krystyna Makowska (pno)—Vars *(rec Warsaw, 1987)* Selene ▲ CD 9404.20 [DDD]
Chopin, F.:Rondo for 2 Pnos, w. Krystyna Makowska (pno) *(rec Warsaw, 1987)* Selene ▲ CD 9404.20 [DDD]
Moniuszko, S.:Pno Music—Concert Polonaise in A; Wedding Mazurka; Polonaise in D; Waltz; Spinner; Contredanses Nos. 1–6; Tramp's Song; Montain Dances [from Halka] [all for Pno Duet; w. Krystyna Makowska (pno)]; The Chimes Aria [from Haunted Manor]; Autumn Song; The Wild-Party Waltz; Waltzes in e♭ & A♭; Bagatelle in g; Song Without Words; Mazurka [Farewell to Vilnius]; Farewell *(rec Warsaw, 1987)* Selene ▲ CD 9404.20 [DDD]
West, (ob)
Gideon, M.:Questions on Nature, w. J. DeGaetani (mez), S. Lipman (pno), Jekofsky (perc) CRI ■ C 343
West, Charles (cl)
Alwyn, W.:Son Cl, w. Susan Grace (pno) *(rec Concert Hall, Virginia Commonwealth University, Richmond, VA)* Klavier ▲ KCD 11073 [DDD]
Bartók, B.:Contrasts, w. Laura Roelofs (vn), Landon Bilyeu (pno) Klavier ▲ KCD 11072 [DDD]
Delmas, M.:Fant italienne, w. Susan Grace (pno) *(rec Concert Hall, Virginia Commonwealth Univ, Richmond, VA)* Klavier ▲ KCD 11073 [DDD]
Faith, R.:Sea Pieces (2), w. Susan Grace (pno) *(rec Concert Hall, Virginia Commonwealth Univ, Richmond, VA)* Klavier ▲ KCD 11073 [DDD]

West, Charles (cl) (cont.)
Genzmer, H.:Sonatine Cl & Pno, w. Susan Grace (pno) *(rec Concert Hall, Virginia Commonwealth Univ, Richmond, VA)* Klavier ▲ KCD 11073 [DDD]
Glinka, M.:Trio pathétique, w. Bruce Hammel (bn), Landon Bilyeu (pno) Klavier ▲ KCD 11072 [DDD]
Lutoslawski, W.:Dance Preludes Cl & Pno, w. Susan Grace (pno) *(rec Concert Hall, Virginia Commonwealth Univ, Richmond, VA)* Klavier ▲ KCD 11073 [DDD]
Mozart, W.A.:Qnt Pno, K.452, w. Landon Bilyeu (pno), Philip Teachey (ob), Bruce Hammel (bn), Alan Paterson (hn) Klavier ▲ KCD 11072 [DDD]
Muczynski, R.:Time Pieces, w. Susan Grace (pno) *(rec Concert Hall, Virginia Commonwealth Univ, Richmond, VA)* Klavier ▲ KCD 11073 [DDD]

West, Chris (db)
Poulenc, F.:Chamber Music, w. Peter Sidhom (bar), William Bennett (fl), David Campbell (cl), James Campbell (cl), Nicholas Daniel (ob), Richard Watkins (hn), Rachel Gough (bn), Peter Carter (vn), Ieuan Jones (hp), Clifford Benson (pno), Julius Drake (pno), John York (pno)—Son for Ob; L'invitation au château; Villanelle; Son 2 Cls; Trio; Sxt; Son for Cl & Bn; Rapsodie nègre; Son for Cl; Mouvements perpétuels; Son for Fl *(rec All Saints' Church, East Finchley, London, Jan 12–20, 1994)* Cala ▲ CACD 1018 [DDD]

West, Philip (E hn)
Welcher, D.:Abeja Blanca, w. Jan De Gaetani (mez), Robert Spillman (pno) Bridge ▲ BCD 9048 [ADD]

Westcott, Courtney (fl)—see also ORCHESTRAS & ENSEMBLES Zephyrus members, Zephyrus
Scelsi, G.:Anahit, w. Paul Zukofsky (vn), Julie Bogorad (fl), Peggy Russell (fl), Lawrence McDonald (cl), Joan Waryha (cl), Jean Hansen (b cl), Bill Suite (e hn), Nita VanPelt (sax), Bob Zobal (tpt), John Carter (trbn), Martin Lydecker (trbn), Stan Cortman (hn), Robert Ward (hn), William Curry (va), Jody Rowitsch (va), Irene Wade (va), Anne Fagerburg (vc), John Gockel (vc), Sue Manz (bass), Steven Stearman (bass) *(rec Oberlin Conservatory of Music, Oct 8, 1973)* CP² ▲ CP2 108 [AAD]

Westenholz, Elisabeth (org)
Holmboe, V.:Triade, w. E. H. Tarr (tpt) BIS ▲ CD 78 [AAD/DDD]
Nielsen, C.:Commotio BIS ▲ CD 131 [AAD]
Nielsen, C.:Preludes Org, Op. 51 BIS ▲ CD 131 [AAD]
Nielsen, C.:Preludes (2) BIS ▲ CD 131 [AAD]
Weiner, S.:Phantasy 1 Tpt, w. E. Tarr (tpt) BIS ▲ CD 152 [AAD]

Westenholz, Elisabeth (pno)—see also ORCHESTRAS & ENSEMBLES Pro Arte Piano Trio
Alexius, C.:Sonatina Tpt, w. E. Tarr (tpt) BIS ▲ CD 152 [AAD]
Beethoven, L. van:Con 1 Pno, w. M. Schønwandt (cnd), Copenhagen Collegium Musicum BIS ▲ CD 429 [DDD]
Beethoven, L. van:Con 2 Pno, w. M. Schønwandt (cnd), Copenhagen Collegium Musicum BIS ▲ CD 349
Beethoven, L. van:Con 3 Pno, w. M. Schønwandt (cnd), Copenhagen Collegium Musicum BIS ▲ CD 429 [DDD]
Beethoven, L. van:Con 4 Pno, w. M. Schønwandt (cnd), Copenhagen Collegium Musicum BIS ▲ CD 349
Beethoven, L. van:Vars on an Original Theme, Op. 34 Kontrapunkt ▲ KPT 32145 [DDD]
Beethoven, L. van:Vars & Fugue Pno, Op. 35, "Eroica"—15 variations Kontrapunkt ▲ KPT 32145 [DDD]
Beethoven, L. van:Vars on an Original Theme, Op. 76 Kontrapunkt ▲ KPT 32118 [DDD]
Beethoven, L. van:Vars on a waltz by Diabelli, Op. 120 Kontrapunkt ▲ KPT 32118 [DDD]
Beethoven, L. van:Vars Pno, WoO 80 Kontrapunkt ▲ KPT 32145 [DDD]
Böhm, T.:Grande polonaise, w. Robert Aitken (fl) BIS ▲ CD 166
Brahms, J.:Sons Vc (comp), w. C. Henkel (vc) BIS ▲ CD 192
Brahms, J.:Son 1 Vc, w. K. B. Dinitzen (vc) Kontrapunkt ▲ KPT 32172 [DDD]
Brahms, J.:Sons Cl (comp), w. N. Thomsen (cl) Kontrapunkt ▲ 32078 [DDD]
Brahms, J.:Sons Vn (comp), w. N. E. Sparf (vn) BIS ▲ CD 212 [AAD]
Cellier, A.:Thème et variations sur le Psaume 149 du Psautier de la Réforme, "Chantez à Dieu chanson nouvelle", w. E. Tarr (tpt) BIS ▲ CD 152 [AAD]
Doppler, A.F.:Fant pastorale hongroise, w. Robert Aitken (fl), Per Oien (fl), Geir Henning Braaten (pno) BIS ▲ CD 166
Fauré, G.:Music for Vc & Pno, w. Kim Bak Dinitzen (vc)—Son No. 1, Op. 109; Elégie, Op. 24; Son No. 2, Op. 117; Après un rêve, Op. 7; Sicilienne, Op. 78; Papillon, Op. 77; Sérénade, Op. 98; Romance, Op. 69; Berceuse, Op. 16 Kontrapunkt ▲ KPT 32220 [DDD]
Gade, N.W.:Fantasistykker, w. N. Thomsen (cl) Kontrapunkt ▲ 32078 [DDD]
Gade, N.W.:Frühlings Fant, w. Anne Margrethe Dahl (sop), Kirsten Dolberg (cta), Gert Hennig-Jensen (ten), Sten Byriel (bass), M. Schønwandt (cnd), Tivoli SO *(rec Tivoli Concert Hall, Apr 29–30, May 4, 1996)* Marco Polo/Dacapo ▲ 8.224051 [DDD]
Gade, N.W.:Music of, w. S. Elbæk (vn)—Volkstanze, Op. 62; Elegie, Op. 19/1; Scherzo, 19/1; Canzonette, Op. 19/3; Abenddämmerung, Op. 34/4; Allegro Vivace in A; Fantasiestücke, Op. 43; Capriccio in a Kontrapunkt ▲ 32164 [DDD]
Gershwin, G.:Rhap in Blue, w. E. Tarr (tpt) [trumpet-piano trans. by T. Dokshitser] BIS ▲ CD 152 [AAD]
Haydn, J.:Qts Strs, Op. 77, "Lobkowitz Qts", w. Toke Lund Christiansen (fl) [arr. for flute & piano]—No. 1 Kontrapunkt ▲ 32071 [DDD]
Haydn, J.:Trios Pno, Fl & Vc, w. Toke Lund Christiansen (fl), Anne Lund Christiansen (vc) Kontrapunkt ▲ 32071 [DDD]
Hindemith, P.:Son Tpt, w. E.H. Tarr (tpt) *(rec Holte, Denmark, Sept. 20, 1979)* BIS ▲ CD 159 [AAD]
Kuhlau, F.:Grand Trio, w. T. L. Christiansen (fl), A. L. Christiansen (vc) [arr fl, vc & pno] Kontrapunkt ▲ 32064 [DDD]
Kuhlau, F.:Sons Fl (comp), w. T. Lund Christiansen (fl)—Sonatas Op. 64, Op. 69, Op. 71, Op. 83/1–3, Op. 85, Op. 110/1–3 Kontrapunkt 3–▲ 32114/16 [DDD]
Martinů, B.:Sonatina Tpt, w. E. Tarr (tpt) BIS ▲ CD 152 [AAD]
Martinů, B.:Trio Fl, w. T.L. Christiansen (fl), A. L. Christiansen (vc) Kontrapunkt ▲ 32064 [DDD]
Mozart, W.A.:Con 20 Pno, w. M. Schønwandt (cnd), Copenhagen Collegium Musicum BIS ▲ CD 283 [DDD]
Mozart, W.A.:Con 23 Pno, w. M. Schønwandt (cnd), Copenhagen Collegium Musicum BIS ▲ CD 283 [DDD]
Nielsen, C.:Pno Music—Five Piano Pieces, Op. 3; Symphonic Suite, Op. 8; Humoresque-Bagatelles, Op. 11; Festive Prelude (1899); Chaconne, Op. 32; Theme & Variations, Op. 40; Suite, "The Luciferian," Op. 45; Piano Music for Great & Small, Op. 53, Vols. 1 & 2; Three Piano Pieces, Op. 59; Piano Piece in C (1931); Dream of "Silent Night" (1905) *(rec 1980)* BIS 2–▲ CD 167/68 [AAD]
Prokofiev, S.:Mélodies, w. N. Madojan (vn) Kontrapunkt ▲ KPT 32185 [DDD]
Prokofiev, S.:Son Vn, Op. 94bis, w. N. Madojan (vn) Kontrapunkt ▲ KPT 32185 [DDD]
Prokofiev, S.:Son 1 Vn, w. N. Madojan (vn) Kontrapunkt ▲ KPT 32185 [DDD]
Schubert, Franz:Son Arpeggione, w. T. L. Christiansen (fl) [flute-piano version] Kontrapunkt ▲ 32024 [DDD]
Schumann, R.:Adagio & Allegro Hn, w. K. Bak Dinitzen (vc) Kontrapunkt ▲ KPT 32172 [DDD]
Strauss, R.:Son Vc, w. K. Bak Dinitzen (vc) Kontrapunkt ▲ KPT 32172 [DDD]
Taffanel, P.:Fant on Freischütz, w. Robert Aitken (fl), or Per Oien (fl), Geir Henning Braaten (pno) BIS ▲ CD 166
Werner, F.:Duo Tpt, w. E. Tarr (tpt) BIS ▲ CD 152 [AAD]

Westenholz, Peter (pno)
Brahms, J.:Songs, w. Hanne Stavad (cta), Morten Zeuthen (vc)—Von ewiger Liebe, Op. 43/1; Die Mainacht, Op. 43/2 Danica ▲ DCD 8143
Brahms, J.:Songs, Op. 91, w. Hanne Stavad (cta), Morten Zeuthen (vc) Danica ▲ DCD 8143
Heise, P.:Songs, w. Hanne Stavad (cta), Morten Zeuthen (vc)—Gudrans Sorg [song cycle] Danica ▲ DCD 8143
Lutoslawski, W.:Songs, w. Hanne Stavad (cta), Morten Zeuthen (vc)—5 Songs after poems by Illakowicz Danica ▲ DCD 8143
Nielsen, C.:Songs, w. Hanne Stavad (cta), Morten Zeuthen (vc)—Det bodes der for Af Op. 6; I Seraillets Have Af Op. 4; Har Dagen sauket al sin sorg Af Op. 4 Danica ▲ DCD 8143
Nørgård, P.:Short Songs, w. Hanne Stavad (cta), Morten Zeuthen (vc) Danica ▲ DCD 8143

Westenholz, Peter (pno) (cont.)
Schubert, Franz:Songs (misc), w. Hanne Stavad (cta), Morten Zeuthen (vc)—Der Tod und das Mädchen, D.531; Ganymed, D.544; Lachen und Weinen, D.777; Seligkeit, D.433; Wanderes nachlied II, D.768 Danica ▲ DCD 8143

Westerheide, Reinhold (gtr)
A Lady Shaves Her Legs, w. A. De Man (hpd) Erasmus ▲ WVH 072 [DDD]

Westerhof, Erik (gtr)—see ORCHESTRAS & ENSEMBLES Groningen Guitar Duo

Westermann, Hans Peter (ob)
Bach, C.P.E.:Con Ob, H.468, w. T. Hengelbrock (cnd), Freiburg Baroque Orch Deutsche Harmonia Mundi ▲ 77187-2 [DDD]
Telemann, G.P.:Cons (misc), w. Masahiro Arita (trns fl/pic), Eric Hoeprich (chl), Dane Roberts (db), David Sinclair (db), La Stravaganza Cologne—in E for Transverse Flute, Oboe d'amore, Viola d'amore, Strings & Continuo; in e for Transverse Flute, Violin, Strings & Continuo; in D for Transverse Flute, Strings & Continuo; in E♭ for Strings & Continuo; in G for Transverse Flute, Chalumeau, Oboe, 2 Double Basses, Strings & Continuo *(rec Cologne, May 30–June 3, 1994)* Denon ("Aliare" series) ▲ CO 78933 [DDD]

Westin, Lori (hn)
Orchestral Excerpts for Horn, w. Arthur David Krehbiel (hn) *(rec Aug. & Sept. 1992)* Summit ▲ DCD 141 [DDD]

Westlake, Nigel (cl)
Edwards, R.:The Tower of Remoteness, w. David Bollard (pno) *(rec Sir John Clancy Auditorium, Univ of NSW, July 1990)* Tall Poppies ▲ TP 51 [DDD]
Schubert, Franz:Der Hirt auf dem Felsen, w. J. Bates (sop), D. Bollard (pno), Australia Ensemble [G] *(rec July 1991)* Tall Poppies ▲ TP 011 [DDD]
Songs of Sea & Sky, w. David Bollard (pno) Tall Poppies ▲ TP 4 [DDD]

Westphal, Barbara (va)
Brahms, J.:Scherzo Vn, w. U. Oppens (pno) [trans Westphal for va & pno] Bridge ▲ BCD 9021 [DDD]
Brahms, J.:Sons Cl (comp), w. U. Oppens (pno) Bridge ▲ BCD 9021 [DDD]
Killmayer, W.:Qt Pno, w. S. Mauser (pno), C. Altenburger (vn), J. Berger (vc) CPO ▲ CPO 999020-2 [DDD]
Killmayer, W.:Qt Strs, w. C. Altenburger (vn), G. Weinmeister (vn), J. Berger (vc) CPO ▲ CPO 999020-2 [DDD]

Westphal, Vérène (vc)
Denisov, E.:Son A Sax & Vc, w. Claude Delangle (a sax) *(rec Paris, July 1995)* BIS ▲ CD 765 [DDD]
Karasikov, V.:Casus in terminus, w. Claude Delangle (a sax), Odile Delangle (pno) *(rec Paris, July 1995)* BIS ▲ CD 765 [DDD]
Vustin, A.:Musique pour l'ange, w. Claude Delangle (t sax), Jean Geoffroy (vib) *(rec Paris, July 1995)* BIS ▲ CD 765 [DDD]

Weszely, János (dr)
Cornologia, w. Budapest Festival Horn Quartet, Zoltán Varga (timp/perc), Dimitris Politis (gtr), Ferenc Gayer (db/bass gtr), Sándor Balogh (pno) *(rec Hungaroton Classic Studio, Feb 15–16, 1996)* Hungaroton ▲ HCD 31652 [ADD/DDD]

Wetter-Smith, Brooks de (fl)
Foss, L.:Pieces (3) Fl & Pno, w. Stephan Seebass (pno) Crystal ▲ CD 318
Gaubert, P.:Son 1 Fl, w. Stephan Seebass (pno) Crystal ▲ CD 318
Pierné, G.:Son Vn, w. Stephan Seebass (pno) Crystal ▲ CD 318
Reynolds, V.:Son Fl, w. Stephan Seebass (pno) Crystal ▲ CD 318

Wetzel, Thomas (perc)
Sierra, R.:Piezas Características, w. William Helmers (b cl), Catherine Schubilske (vn), Scott Tisdel (vc), Dennis Najoom (tpt), Stefanie Jacob (pno), N. Gittleman (cnd) CRI ▲ CD 724 [DDD]

Wey-Ervin, Peggy (E hn)
Gerber, R.:Con E Hn, w. T. Loosli (cnd), Bern Sinfonietta Gallo ▲ CD 862 [ADD]

Weyhofen, Gertrud (mand)—see ORCHESTRAS & ENSEMBLES Capriccioso Duo

Wharton, Geoffry (vn)
Kagel, M.:Blue's Blue:A Musico-Ethnological Reconstruction, w. M. Kagel (voice/glass tpt), M. Riessler (cl/sax), T. Ross (gtr) Montaigne ▲ MO 782003 [DDD]
Kagel, M.:Rrrrrrr... Cl, Vn & Pno, w. M. Riessler (cl), K. Becker (pno) Montaigne ▲ MO 782003 [DDD]

Wheater, Tim (fl)
The Dreamer:Romances for Alto Flute, Vol. 2, w. M. Hoppe (pno) Bainbridge ▲ BBR 6300 ■ BBR 6300

Wheatly, Michael (vn)—see ORCHESTRAS & ENSEMBLES Cincinnati Contemporary Music Ensemble

Wheeler, Lawrence (va)
Carter, E.:Elegy Va, w. R. Tomfohrde (pno) Albany ▲ TROY 141 [DDD]
Creston, P.:Suite Va, w. R. Tomfohrde (vc) Albany ▲ TROY 141 [DDD]
Heiden, B.:Son Va, w. Ruth Tomfohrde (pno) Albany ▲ TROY 141 [DDD]
Rochberg, G.:Son Va, w. L. Wheeler, R. Tomfohrde Albany ▲ TROY 141 [DDD]

Wheeler, Thad (perc)
Silver, S.:Dance Converging, w. Lois Martin (va), William Purvis (hn), Lisa Moore (pno) *(rec Recital Hall, Music Division, SUNY, Purchase, New York, Apr 12, 1995)* CRI ▲ CD 708 [DDD]
Wheeler, T.:The Dancing Bird, w. F. Vanasco (vc), V. Rice (elec bass) Albany ▲ TROY 114

Wheldon, Roy (vl)—see also ORCHESTRAS & ENSEMBLES American Baroque
Abel, C.F.:Pieces (27) Vl—Adagio; Allegro moderato New Albion ▲ NA 059
Wheldon, R.:Music for Vl—Fanfare; Galax; Prelude & Divisions on She's So Heavy; Twin Rows New Albion ▲ NA 059
Wheldon, R.:Qt after Abel [2nd movt. by F.C. Abel] New Albion ▲ NA 059

Whistler, Simon (va)—see also ORCHESTRAS & ENSEMBLES Hausmusik
Mozart, W.A.:Qnts Strs, w. Salomon String Quartet Hyperion 2–▲ CDD 22005

Whitaker, J. (hn)
Van Appledorn, M.J.:Patterns, w. A. Brittin (hn), M. Walzel (hn), L. Dawson (hn), H. Landers (hn) Opus One ▲ CD 162

Whitcombe, Michael (sax)—see also ORCHESTRAS & ENSEMBLES Prism Saxophone Quartet
Ibert, J.:Concertino da camera, w. D. Barra (cnd), San Diego CO Koch International Classics ▲ KIC 7094-2 [DDD]

White, Harry (sax)—see ORCHESTRAS & ENSEMBLES Rascher Saxophone Quartet

White, J. (pno)—see also ORCHESTRAS & ENSEMBLES Gavin Bryars Ensemble
Erb, D.:Son Hpd, w. Koch String Quartet CRI ▲ CD 593 [ADD/DDD]

White, Robert (bgp)
The Spirits of England & France, Vol. 2, w. Emma Kirkby (sop), Pavlo Beznosiuk (fid), Nick Bicat (perc), Gothic Voices [cnd:Christopher Page] Hyperion ▲ CDA 66773

White, Tim (perc)—see ORCHESTRAS & ENSEMBLES Nova Ensemble

Whitehead, William (org)
Magnificat & Nunc Dimittis, Vol. 6, w. Rochester Cathedral Choir, Roger Sayer (cnd) Priory ▲ PRI 529 [DDD]
Sowerby, L.:Org Music [Great Organ of Washington Cathedral]—Carrillon, A Wedding Processional Resmiranda ▲ Resmiranda 8004
Sowerby, L.:Sym Org [Great Organ of Washington Cathedral] Resmiranda ▲ Resmiranda 8004

Whitehouse, Brooks (vc)—see ORCHESTRAS & ENSEMBLES Guild Piano Trio

Whitelaw, John (hpd)
Byrd, W.:Kbd Music—Bells; Ut, Re, Mi, Fa, Sol, La; Jhon Come Kisse Me Now; A Medley; Praeludium to Ye Fancie Fantasia; My Ladye Nevells Grownde; Munsers Almaine; Horne Pipe; 3rd Pavian, Galliarde to the Same; 10th Pavian, Galliarde to the Same; Passings Mesures Pavian, Galliarde to the Same *(rec Ghent, Belgium)* Talent ▲ DOM 291022 [ADD/DDD]

Whiteley, John Scott (org)
European Organ Tour, w. Graham Barber (org), Marc Rochester (org), Kimberly Marshall (org) *(rec 1983–88)* Priory ▲ PRCD 903
Guillou, J.:Toccata Org [Org of York Minster] Priory ▲ PRI 487
Jongen, J.:Org Music Priory ▲ PRI 324 [DDD]
Jongen, J.:Org Music Priory ▲ PRI 382 [DDD]
Malengreau, P.:Symphonie de la Passion [Org of York Minster] Priory ▲ PRI 487

Whiteley, John Scott (org) (cont.)
Peeters, F.:Org Music [Org of York Minster]—Suite [4 pieces] Priory ▲ PRI 487
Pierné, G.:Pastorale Org [Org of York Minster] Priory ▲ PRI 487
Widor, C.M.:Org Music [Org of York Minster]—Scherzo in E [La chasse] Priory ▲ PRI 487

Whiting, Nicholas (vn)
Haydn, J.:Sym 96, "Miracle", w. Hugh Bean (vn), John Anderson (ob), L. Slatkin (cnd), Philharmonia Orch *(rec Abbey Road Studio No. 1, London, Aug 1993)* RCA Red Seal ▲ 09026-68424-2 [DDD]

Whitney, Gloria (pno)—see ORCHESTRAS & ENSEMBLES Eaken Piano Trio

Whitney, John (pno)—see ORCHESTRAS & ENSEMBLES John Whitney Trio

Whittaker, P. (cl)
Gershwin, G.:Rhap in Blue, w. B. Griffiths (vn), R. Simmons (tpt), D. James (trbn), A. Litton (pno), H. Fisher (dr), A. Litton (cnd), Royal PO [original big band orchestration] RPO ▲ RPO 5011 [DDD]

Wiame, Benny (tpt)
Hovhaness, A.:Prayer of St. Gregory, w. R. Werthen (cnd), I Fiamminghi CO *(rec Basilica of Bonne Espérance, Vellereille-les-Brayeux, Belgium, Aug. 18–20, 1994)* Telarc ▲ CD 80392 [DDD]

Wick, Tilmann (vc)
Carter, E.:Son Vc, w. H. Rhee (pno) MD + G ▲ L 3397 [DDD]
Miaskovsky, N.:Son 2 Vc, w. H. Rhee (pno) MD + G ▲ L 3397 [DDD]
Poulenc, F.:Son Vc, w. H. Rhee (pno) MD + G ▲ L 3397 [DDD]

Wicke, B. (org)—see also ORCHESTRAS & ENSEMBLES Bonn Telemann Ensemble
Rinck, J.C.H.:Con Org *(rec 1992)* FSM ▲ FCD 97759 [DDD]
Rosier, N.-C.:Son Vn, w. N. Scheer (vn), T. Habel-Thormé (rcr) *(rec 1992)* FSM ▲ FCD 97759 [DDD]
Telemann, G.P.:Son Bn, w. M. Séché (bn) *(rec 1992)* FSM ▲ FCD 97759 [DDD]

Wickens, Derek (ob)—see also ORCHESTRAS & ENSEMBLES Michael Thompson Wind Quintet
Bach, Joh. Christian:Sinf concertante Fl, w. J. Galway (fl), W. Armon (vn), N. Jones (vc), L. Jones (cnd), London Little Orch Elektra/Nonesuch ■ 71165-4
Handel, G.F.:Royal Fireworks Music, w. Alan Civil (hn), John Wilbraham (tpt), Harold Lester (hpd), J. Somary (cnd), English CO *(rec Conway Hall, London, 1973)* Vanguard Classics ▲ SVC 47 [AAD]
Handel, G.F.:Water Music (comp), w. Alan Civil (hn), John Wilbraham (tpt), Harold Lester (hpd), J. Somary (cnd), English CO *(rec Conway Hall, London, 1973)* Vanguard Classics ▲ SVC 47 [AAD]
Stravinsky, I.:Pastorale, w. Neville Taweel (vn), Leonard Brain (E hn), Thomas Kelly (cl), John Price (bn), L. Stokowski (cnd), Royal PO *(rec Kingsway Hall, London, England, June 16–17, 1969)* London ("Phase 4 Stereo" series) ▲ 443898-2 [ADD]

Wicks, Camilla (vn)
Beethoven, L. van:Con Vn, Op. 61, w. B. Walter (cnd), New York PO *(rec 1950)* Legend ▲ LGD 114 [ADD]

Wicks, D. (va)
Lentz, G.:Caeli enarrant...IV, w. Georges Lentz (vn), J. Booth (vn), P. Morrison (vc) Tall Poppies ▲ TP 35

Wicky, Anton (alphn)
Music for Alphorn, Organ & Cello, w. H. Keller (org), Alfred Richter (vc) Koch Schwann ▲ SCH 310812 [DDD]

Wicky, T. (vn)
Krommer, F.:Sinf Concertante, w. P.-L. Graf (fl), H. R. Stalder (cl), Capriccio Ensemble Tudor ▲ 757 [DDD]

Widihofer, Johann (hn)
Brahms, J.:Choral Music, w. A. Korondi (sop), G. Mossyrsch (hp), J. Keiding (hn), E. Ortner (cnd), Arnold Schoenberg Choir—Lieder und Romanzen, Op. 93a; 3 Gesänge, Op. 42; 7 Lieder, Op. 62; 5 Gesänge, Op. 104; 4 Gesänge, Op. 17 Teldec ▲ 4509-92058-2 [DDD]

Widlund, Mats (pno)
Peterson-Berger, W.:Pno Music—Gratulation; Flöjtspel pa Peneios; I skymningen; Intag i Sommarhagen; Langt bort i skogarna; Nachspiel; Serenad; Under asparna; Villa d'Este *(rec 1989)* Musica Sveciae ▲ MSCD 613 [AAD]
Sjögren, E.:Pno Music—I skogen; Morgonvandring; Novellettes Nos. 1–3; Pa sjön Musica Sveciae ▲ MSCD 613 [AAD]
Söderlundh, L.B.:Suite from Havãng, w. T. Svedlund (cnd), Örebro CO Intim Musik ▲ INT 36
Stenhammar, W.:Pno Music (misc)—Andante quasi adagio ur Sonat g; Fantasies, Nos. 1–3; Intermezzo *(rec 1989)* Musica Sveciae ▲ MSCD 613 [AAD]
Wirén, D.:Con Pno, w. P. Sakari (cnd), Swedish CO Caprice ▲ CAP 21513

Widmann, Carolin (vn)
Orff, C.:Schulwerk (complete), w. Godela Orff (nar), Sonja Korkeala (vn), Markus Zahnhausen (rcr), Karl Peinkofer (perc), Andreas Schumacher (perc), Wilfried Hiller (perc/mar), Martin Ruhland (mar), Munich Hochschule Madrigal Choir—Wessobrun Prayer for a capella Choir; 2 Pieces for a capella Choir; 8 Pieces for 2 Vns; Mater et filia for women's a capella Choir; Devotional Yodel for male a capella Choir; 5 Pieces for Sop, Rcr & Perc; Death for Nar., Wood Bells, Bass Xyl & Tam-Tam; Omnia tempus habent for mixed Choir, Timp & Little Dr; Rubato, molto allegro, rubato; Abenlied for Nar, Bass Metallophon, Bass Xyl, Large Dr & Wine Glass; 5 Pieces for Fl & Perc; Devotional Yodel for male Choir [version 2]; 7 Pieces for 2 Xyl *(rec Munich, 1994–95)* Celestial Harmonies ▲ 13105-2
Orff, C.:Schulwerk (complete), w. Godela Orff (nar), Marina Koppelstetter (mez), Sabina Lehmann (vc), Markus Zahnhausen (rcr), Karl Peinkofer Percussion Ensemble—4 Pieces for Xylophone; 5 Little Canons; 4 Dance Pieces; Songs & Instrumental Pieces; 3 Pieces for Fl & Perc; Songs & Dances; 2 Time Change Dances for Vn & Vc; 7 Folk Dances; Music for the Night *(rec Munich, 1994–95)* Celestial Harmonies ▲ 13104-2

Widner, Marc (pno)
McPhee, C.:Kambing Slem, w. R. Aitken (fl) CBC ("Musica Viva" series) ▲ MVCD 1057 [DDD]
McPhee, C.:Lagoe Sesoeloelingan Ardja, w. R. Aitken (fl) CBC ("Musica Viva" series) ▲ MVCD 1057 [DDD]

Widor, Charles-Marie (org)
Widor, C.M.:Sym 5 Org—5th movement, Toccata EMI Classics ▲ CDC 55037
Widor, C.M.:Sym 9 Org EMI Classics ▲ CDC 55037

Wieder-Atherton, Sonia (vc)
Ibert, J.:Con Vc, w. B. Desgraupes (cnd), Erwartung Ensemble Adda ▲ ADD 581263 [DDD]
Kodály, Z.:Duo Vn & Vc, w. Raphael Oleg (vn) Valois ▲ V 4716
Martinů, B.:Duet Vn & Vc, w. Raphael Oleg (vn) Valois ▲ V 4716
Martinů, B.:Duo Vn & Vc, w. Raphael Oleg (vn) Valois ▲ V 4716

Wiegand, A. (fl)—see ORCHESTRAS & ENSEMBLES Debussy Trio

Wiel, Mark van de (b cl)
Birtwistle, H.:Linoi 1, w. Alison Rhind (pno) Olympia ▲ OLY 484 [DDD]
Mozart, W.A.:Con Cl, w. J. Clayton (cnd), Chetham's CO Olympia ▲ OLY 484 [DDD]
Sssmayr, F.X.:Con Movt Bas Cl, w. J. Clayton (cnd), Chetham's CO Olympia ▲ OLY 484 [DDD]
Woolrich, J.:Si va Facendo Notte, w. J. Clayton (cnd), Chetham's CO Olympia ▲ OLY 484 [DDD]

Wiencek, Daniel (pno)—see ORCHESTRAS & ENSEMBLES Bowed Piano Ensemble

Wiener, Jean (pno)
Satie, E.:Pno Music (comp), w. Jean-Joël Barbier (pno)—Prélude de la porte heroïque du ciel; Poudre d'or; Aperçus désagréables [quatre mains]; En habit de cheval [quatre mains]; Heures séculaires et instanées; Cinq nocturnes; Premier menuet; Fête donnée par les chevaliers normands en l'honneur d'une jeune demoiselle; Passacaille; Songe creux; Prélude en tapisserie; Nouvelles pièces froides; Deux rêveries nocturnes; Préludes falsques [Pour un chien] Accord ▲ ACD 200902 [AAD]

Wiener, Ruud (cym)
Hauser, F.:Die Welle, w. Martin André Grütter (cym/tamtam), Roli Fischer (cym), Barbara Frey (cym), Cyril Lützelschwab (cym), Lukas Rohner (cym), Severin Steinhauser (cym), Hans Ulrich (cym), Michael Erni (timp), Fran Lorkovic (timp), F. Hauser (cnd) *(rec Studio DRS, Basel, Switzerland, Nov. 6, 1988)* Hat Hut ▲ hat ART CD 6017 [ADD]

Wieringa, K. (pno)
Feldman, Morton:Untitled Composition, w. R. Berman (vc) *(rec 1990)* Attacca ▲ Babel 9160-3 [DDD]

Wiersma, Calvin (vn)
Hanson, H.:Con da Camera, w. B. Preston (vn), I. Swenson (vn), M. Lambros (va), Elizabeth Anderson (vc) Albany ▲ TROY 129 [DDD]

Wiesel, Arnan (pno)
Ichiyanagi, T.:Flowers Blooming in Summer, w. Alice Giles (hp) Koch Schwann ▲ SCH 317652
Koch, J.:Toccata Hp & Pno, w. Alice Giles (hp) Koch Schwann ▲ SCH 317652
Mogot, G.:Prélude, w. Alice Giles (hp) Koch Schwann ▲ SCH 317652
Salzedo, C.:Son Hp, w. Alice Giles (hp) Koch Schwann ▲ SCH 317652
Turina, J.:Theme & Vars, Op. 100, w. Alice Giles (hp) Koch Schwann ▲ SCH 317652
Zagwijn, H.:Van de Jaargetijden, w. Alice Giles (hp) Koch Schwann ▲ SCH 317652

Wieslander, Maria (hpd)
Vivaldi, A.:Trio Sons Vn Lt, w. N.-E. Sparf (vn), J. Lindberg (lt), K. Ottesen (vc) BIS ▲ CD 290 [DDD]

Wieslander, Maria (org)
Carissimi, G.:Ferma lascia ch'io parli, w. Lena Nordin (sop), Sven Åberg (chit), Chrichan Larsson (vc), Nanette Nowels-Stenholm (pno), M. Guidarini (cnd), *(orch unknown)* Swedish Society ▲ SCD 1076
Donizetti, G.:Maria Stuarda (sels), w. Lena Nordin (sop), Carina Morling (mez), Ingus Petterssons (ten), Anders Bergström (bar), Tord Wallström (bar), Sven Åberg (chit), Chrichan Larsson (vc), Nanette Nowels-Stenholm (pno), M. Guidarini (cnd), *(orch unknown)* Swedish Society ▲ SCD 1076

Wiesler, Manuela (fl)
Amirov, F.:Pieces (6) Fl, w. R. Pöntinen (pno) BIS ▲ CD 419 [DDD]
Bäck, S.-E.:Son Fl Caprice ▲ CAP 21490
Chaminade, C.:Concertino Fl, w. P. Auguin (cnd), Helsingborg SO *(rec 6/91)* BIS ▲ CD 529 [DDD]
Debussy, C.:Syrinx BIS ▲ CD 459 [DDD]
Denisov, E.:Pieces (4) Fl, w. R. Pöntinen (pno) BIS ▲ CD 419 [DDD]
Denisov, E.:Son Fl, w. R. Pöntinen (pno) BIS ▲ CD 419 [DDD]
Françaix, J.:Con Fl, w. P. Auguin (cnd), Helsingborg SO *(rec 6/91)* BIS ▲ CD 529 [DDD]
Françaix, J.:Suite Fl BIS ▲ CD 459 [DDD]
Harrison, L.:Con 1 Fl, w. Kroumata Percussion Ensemble BIS ▲ CD 272 [DDD]
Hvoslef, K.:Sextet Fl & Perc, w. Kroumata Percussion Ensemble *(rec 3/19/89)* BIS ▲ CD 512 [DDD]
Ibert, J.:Con Fl, w. P. Auguin (cnd), Helsingborg SO *(rec 6/91)* BIS ▲ CD 529 [DDD]
Jolivet, A.:Ascèses *(rec June 18, 1992)* BIS ▲ CD 549 [DDD]
Jolivet, A.:Chant de Linos, w. R. Pöntinen (pno) *(rec Mar. 1992)* BIS ▲ CD 549 [DDD]
Jolivet, A.:Con Fl, w. P. Järvi (cnd), Tapiola Sinfonietta *(rec June 4 & 9, 1993)* BIS ▲ CD 630 [DDD]
Jolivet, A.:Fl Music (comp), w. Erica Goodman (hp), Patrik Swedrup (vn), Håkan Olsson (va), Helena Nilsson (vc), Christian Davidsson (bn), Roland Pöntinen (pno), P. Järvi (cnd), Tapiola Sinfonietta, Kroumata Percussion Ensemble—Alla rustica for Fl & Hp; Chant de Linos for Fl, Hp & Str Trio; Pastorales de Noël for Fl, Bn & Hp; Con for Fl & Strs; Suite en concert for Fl & 4 Perc Players; Fant-Caprice for Fl & Pno; Cabrioles for Fl & Pno *(rec Danderyd Grammar School, Sweden, Tapiola Hall, Tapiola, Finland, Gothenburg Concert Hall, Sweden & Studio 2, Radiohuset, Stockholm, Sweden)* BIS ▲ CD 739 [DDD]
Jolivet, A.:Incantations (5) Fl *(rec June 18, 1992)* BIS ▲ CD 549 [DDD]
Jolivet, A.:Incantation Fl *(rec June 18, 1992)* BIS ▲ CD 549 [DDD]
Jolivet, A.:Son Fl, w. R. Pöntinen (pno) *(rec Mar. 1992)* BIS ▲ CD 549 [DDD]
Jolivet, A.:Suite en concert, w. Kroumata Percussion Ensemble BIS ▲ CD 272 [DDD]
Manuela Plays French Solo Flute Music BIS ▲ CD 459 [DDD]
Marais, M.:Vars on *Folies d'Espagne* BIS ▲ CD 459 [DDD]
Martin, F.:Ballade Fl, w. Julius Jacobson (pno) *(rec Malmö Concert Hall, Sweden, Apr 1990)* BIS ▲ CD 71 [DDD]
Mouquet, J.:Flûte, w. P. Auguin (cnd), Helsingborg SO *(rec 6/91)* BIS ▲ CD 529 [DDD]
Prokofiev, S.:Son Fl, w. R. Pöntinen (pno) BIS ▲ CD 419 [DDD]
The Russian Flute BIS ▲ CD 419 [DDD]
Sandström, S.-D.:Free Music, w. Kroumata Percussion Ensemble BIS ▲ CD 512 [DDD]
Sigurbjörnsson, T.:Calaïs *(rec Denmark, Aug 1 & 4, 1995)* BIS ▲ CD 709 [DDD]
Sigurbjörnsson, T.:Calaïs Music from Iceland ▲ ITM 702 [ADD]
Sigurbjörnsson, T.:Columbine, w. T. Vetö (cnd), South Jutland SO *(rec Denmark, Aug 1 & 4, 1995)* BIS ▲ CD 709 [DDD]
Sigurbjörnsson, T.:Eurydice, w. T. Vetö (cnd), South Jutland SO *(rec Denmark, Aug 1 & 4, 1995)* BIS ▲ CD 709 [DDD]
Sigurbjörnsson, T.:Liongate, w. T. Vetö (cnd), South Jutland SO *(rec Denmark, Aug 1 & 4, 1995)* BIS ▲ CD 709 [DDD]
Taktakishvili, O.:Son Fl, w. R. Pöntinen (pno) BIS ▲ CD 419 [DDD]
To Manuela BIS ▲ CD 456 [DDD]
Tomasi, H.:Sonatine Fl BIS ▲ CD 459 [DDD]

Wiesmeyer, Roger (ob)
Mozart, W.A.:Adagio Rondo, w. Carol Adee (fl), Noriko Kishi (vc), Kurt Rohde (va), J. Meredith (cnd), Sonos Handbell Ensemble Well-Tempered Productions ▲ WTP 5182 [DDD]

Wiesner, Annemarie (vn)
First, D.:The Good Book's (Accurate) Jail of Escape Dust Coordinates 2, w. Matt Sullivan (ob), Chris Jepperson (cl), Gary Trosclair (tpt), Elaine Kaplinsky (kbd syn), Chad Henderson (teahouse gtr/b gtr), Kevin Sparke (perc), David First (e-bow gtr/teahouse gtr/Distortion gtr/kbd syn/programming) *(rec Baby Monster Studios, NYC, May 1992)* O. O. Discs ▲ OO 23 [DDD]

Wiesner, Daniel (pno)
Enescu, G.:Légende, w. Jaroslav Halíř (tpt) *(rec Martínek Studio, Prague, Jan 23 & 26, 1995)* Panton ▲ 811368-2 [DDD]
Françaix, J.:Sonatine Tpt & Pno, w. Jaroslav Halíř (tpt) *(rec Martínek Studio, Prague, Jan 23 & 26, 1995)* Panton ▲ 811368-2 [DDD]
Janácek, L.:Capriccio, w. Jan Riedlbauch (fl/pic), Vladislav Kozderka (tpt), Jan Fišer (tpt), Václav Ferebauer (trbn), Jan Hynčica (trbn), Antonín Keller (trbn), Jiří Novotny (ten tuba), L. Svárovský (cnd) *(rec Martinek Studio in Prague, Jan 9, Feb 27, Mar 20, 19)* Panton ▲ 811393-2 [DDD]
Janácek, L.:Son October 1, 1905 Pno *(rec Martinek Studio in Prague, Jan 9, Feb 27, Mar 20, 19)* Panton ▲ 811393-2 [DDD]
Smetana, B.:Czech Dances Studio Matou ▲ MAT 14 [DDD]
Smetana, B.:The Moldau, w. Petr Jirikovsk (pno) [arr for Pno 4-Hands] Studio Matou ▲ MAT 14 [DDD]

Wiesner, Dietrich (fl)
Kagel, M.:Pan, w. Arditti String Quartet *(rec 7/89)* Montaigne ▲ MO 789004 [DDD]

Wiest, W. (trbn)—see ORCHESTRAS & ENSEMBLES Berlin German Opera Orch Soloists

Wigand, Heinz (va)
Brahms, J.:Qnt Pno, w. Clara Haskil (pno), Peter Rybar (vn), Clemens Dahinden (vn), Antonio Tusa (vc) Doron 2-▲ DRC 4007/8 [ADD]
Brahms, J.:Sextet Strs, Op. 36, w. Peter Rybar (vn), Clemens Dahinden (vn), Oskar Kromer (va), Carl-Heinz Jucker (vc), Antonio Tusa (vc) Doron 2-▲ DRC 4007/8 [ADD]

Wiget, Ueli (pno)
Henze, H.-W.:Requiem, w. H. Hardenberger (tpt), I. Metzmacher (cnd), Ensemble Modern *(rec Sept. 11, 1993)* Sony Classical ▲ SK 58972 [DDD]
Ligeti, G.:Con Pno, w. P. Eötvös (cnd), Ensemble Modern *(rec Aug. 4–5, 1990)* Sony Classical ▲ SK 58945 [DDD]

Wiggins, Web (hpd/org)—see ORCHESTRAS & ENSEMBLES Tempesta di Mare

Wilk, Jonas (tpt)—see ORCHESTRAS & ENSEMBLES Royal Danish Brass

Wijnkoop, Alexander van (vn)—see also ORCHESTRAS & ENSEMBLES Bern String Quartet
Rameau, J.P.:Music of, w. Kathrin Graf (sop), Peter-Lukas Graf (fl), Michio Kobayashi (hpd/pno)—Rossignols amoureux *(rec Protestant Chuch Seon, 1976)* Claves ("Favor Collection" series) ▲ CD 604 [ADD]

Wiklander, Kurt (org)
Wiklander, K.:Music of, w. Mats Rondin (vc), Eyvind Sand Kjeldsen (vn)—Toccata on the Easter Introitus for Org; 2 Chorales from Dalecarlia for Org; Fant. for Vc & Org; 4 Miniatures for Org; Meditation in Folk Style on B-A-C-H for Vn & Org; 3 Organ Chorales on Sacred Folk-Tunes in the Swedish Chorale; Fant. for Org on O Christ Who Art Light & Day; Scherzo Ostinato; Meditation for Org BIS ▲ CD 659

Wikomirska, Wanda (vn)
Szymanowski, K.:Con 1 Vn, w. W. Rowicki (cnd), Warsaw PO Polskie Nagrania ▲ PLN 64 [ADD]
Szymanowski, K.:Con 2 Vn, w. W. Rowicki (cnd), Warsaw PO Polskie Nagrania ▲ PLN 64 [ADD]
Szymanowski, K.:Roxana's Song, w. Tadeusz Chmielewski (pno) Polskie Nagrania ▲ PLN 64 [ADD]

▲ = CD ♦ = Enhanced CD Δ = MD ■ = Cassette Tape □ = DCC

Wikomirska, Wanda (vn) (cont.)
Szymanowski, K.:Son Vn, w. Tadeusz Chmielewski (pno) Polskie Nagrania ▲ PLN 64 [ADD]

Wikström, Inger (pno)
Mozart, W.A.:Adagio Pno, K.540 Proprius ▲ PRCD 9054
Mozart, W.A.:Trio Pno, K.502, w. B. Lysell (vc), O. Karlsson (vc) Proprius ▲ PRCD 9054
Mozart, W.A.:Trio Pno, K.542, w. B. Lysell (vn), O. Karlsson (vc) Proprius ▲ PRCD 9054
Shostakovich, D.:Concertino for 2 Pnos, w. I. Wikström, *(pno unknown)* Swedish Society ▲ SCD 1031
Shostakovich, D.:Fantastic Dances Swedish Society ▲ SCD 1031
Shostakovich, D.:From the Bedbug Swedish Society ▲ SCD 1031
Shostakovich, D.:Preludes Pno, Op. 34 Swedish Society ▲ SCD 1031
Shostakovich, D.:Son 2 Pno Swedish Society ▲ SCD 1031

Wilbraham, John (tpt)
Handel, G.F.:Royal Fireworks Music, w. Derek Wickens (ob), Alan Civil (hn), Harold Lester (hpd), J. Somary (cnd), English CO *(rec Conway Hall, London, 1973)* Vanguard Classics ▲ SVC 47 [AAD]
Handel, G.F.:Water Music (comp), w. Derek Wickens (ob), Alan Civil (hn), Harold Lester (hpd), J. Somary (cnd), English CO *(rec Conway Hall, London, 1973)* Vanguard Classics ▲ SVC 47 [AAD]
Hovhaness, A.:Prayer of St. Gregory, w. A. Hovhaness (cnd), Polyphonia Orch Crystal ▲ CD 807
Hovhaness, A.:Sym 24, w. Martyn Hill (ten), Sax (vn), A. Hovhaness (cnd), National PO London, John Alldis Choir [E] *(rec 1974)* Crystal ▲ CD 803 [ADD]
Purcell, H.:Son Tpt, w. R. Leppard (cnd), English CO CBS ▲ MDK 44644 [DDD] ■ MDT 44644 (D)

Wilcock, Elizabeth (vn)
Geminiani, F.:The Enchanted Forest, w. Stanley Ritchie (vn), Susie Napper (vc), Janet See (fl), Barbara Kallaur (fl), Patrick Wedd (hpd), J.E. Gardiner (cnd), CBC Vancouver SO CBC ▲ 5163 [DDD]
Vivaldi, A.:Cons for 2 Vns, w. S. Standage (vn), T. Pinnock (cnd), English CO—R.516 Archiv ▲ 415674-2 [DDD]

Wild, Bettina (fl)
Schulhoff, E.:Double Con Fl, w. Aleksandar Madzar (pno), A. Delfs (cnd), German CO *(rec Freie Waldorfschule, Bremen, Oct 1994)* London ▲ 444819-2 [DDD]

Wild, Earl (org)
Bach, J.S.:Fant & Fugue Org, BWV 542, w. *(rec Jan 1985)* Onyx ▲ 104 [DDD]

Wild, Earl (pno)
The Art of the Transciption—Live from Carnegie Hall Audiofon 2-▲ CD72008-2
Balakirev, M.:Fant on themes from Glinka's *A Life for the Czar (rec Webster Hall, New York City, June 9, 1969)* Elan ▲ CD 2266 [ADD]
Basic 100, Vol. 30, w. Arthur Fiedler (cnd), Boston Pops Orch RCA Victor ▲ 09026-61727-2 ■ 09026-61727-4
Beethoven, L. van:Son 11 Pno Dell'Arte ▲ CD DBS 7004
Beethoven, L. van:Son 18 Pno Dell'Arte ▲ CD DBS 7004
Beethoven, L. van:Sym 1 *(rec Jan. 1985)* Onyx ▲ 104 [DDD]
Brahms, J.:Ballades, Op. 10 Vanguard Classics ▲ OVC 4034 [ADD]
Brahms, J.:Vars on a Theme by Paganini Vanguard Classics ▲ OVC 4034 [ADD]
Chopin, F.:Ballades Pno (comp) Chesky ▲ CD44 [DDD]
Chopin, F.:Con 1 Pno, w. M. Sargent (cnd), Royal PO *(rec October 9 & 10, 1965)* Chesky ▲ CD93 [ADD]
Chopin, F.:Études (24) Chesky ▲ CD77 [DDD]
Chopin, F.:Nouvelles études Chesky ▲ CD77 [DDD]
Chopin, F.:Scherzos Chesky ▲ CD44 [DDD]
Collins, E.J.:Pno Music—All God's Chillun' Got Wings; Cowboy's Breakdown; Didn't My Lord Deliver Daniel?; Gospel Train; Lil' David Play On Yo' Harp; Passacaglia; Tango; Valse Eccentrique; Valse Heroique; Valse Limpide; Valse Pensive; Valse Romantique; Variations On an Irish Tune *(rec Nov. 1988)* CRI ▲ CD 644 [DDD]
Copland, A.:Con Pno, w. A. Copland (cnd), Symphony of the Air Vanguard Classics ▲ OVC 4029 [ADD]
Copland, A.:Con Pno, w. A. Copland (cnd), Symphony of the Air *(rec 1961)* Vanguard Classics ▲ SVC 3 [AAD]
Dohnányi, E. von:Capriccio Chesky ▲ CD 13
Dohnányi, E. von:Vars on a Nursery Song, w. C. von Dohnányi (cnd), New Philharmonia Orch Chesky ▲ CD 13
Fauré, G.:Ballade Pno, w. C. Gerhardt (cnd), London National PO *(rec March 28, 1967)* Chesky ▲ CD93 [ADD]
Franck, C.:Symphonic Vars, w. M. Freccia (cnd), RCA Victor SO *(rec 1968)* Chesky ▲ CD 87 [ADD]
Gershwin, G.:An American in Paris, w. Benny Goodman (cl), A. Toscanini (cnd), NBC SO Enterprise ("The Radio Years" series) ▲ ENT RY 60
Gershwin, G.:Con Pno, w. A. Fiedler (cnd), Boston Pops Orch RCA Gold Seal ▲ 6519-2-RG [ADD] ■ 6519-4-RG (CrO2)
Gershwin, G.:Con Pno, w. A. Fiedler (cnd), Boston Pops Orch RCA Victor ▲ 09026-61727-2; ■ 09026-61727-4 (CrO2)
Gershwin, G.:Con Pno, w. J. Giunta (cnd), Des Moines SO Chesky ▲ CD 98 [DDD]
Gershwin, G.:"I Got Rhythm" Vars, w. A. Fiedler (cnd), Boston Pops Orch RCA Gold Seal ▲ 6519-2-RG [ADD] ■ 6519-4-RG (CrO2)
Gershwin, G.:Pno Music [performers trans. of works by Gershwin]—Fantasy on Porgy and Bess; Improvisation in the form of a Theme & Three Variations on "Someone To Watch Over Me"; Seven Virtuoso Etudes (I got rhythm; Oh, lady, be good!; Liza; Embraceable you; Somebody loves me; Fascinatin' rhythm; The man I love) Chesky ▲ CD 32 [DDD]
Gershwin, G.:Rhap in Blue, w. A. Fiedler (cnd), Boston Pops Orch RCA Victor ▲ 09026-61727-2; ■ 09026-61727-4 (CrO2)
Gershwin, G.:Rhap in Blue, w. A. Fiedler (cnd), Boston Pops Orch RCA Gold Seal ▲ 6519-2-RG [ADD] ■ 6519-4-RG (CrO2)
Gershwin, G.:Rhap in Blue, w. Benny Goodman (cl), A. Toscanini (cnd), NBC SO Iron Needle ▲ 1306
Gershwin, G.:Rhap in Blue, w. Benny Goodman (cl), A. Toscanini (cnd), NBC SO *(rec Nov. 1, 1942)* Vintage Jazz Classics ▲ VJC 1034
Gershwin, G.:Rhap in Blue, w. Benny Goodman (cl), A. Toscanini (cnd), NBC SO Enterprise ("The Radio Years" series) ▲ ENT RY 60
Grieg, E.:Con Pno, Op. 16, w. R. Leibowitz (cnd), Royal PO *(rec 1962)* Chesky ▲ CD50 [ADD]
Liszt, F.:Con 1 Pno, w. M. Sargent (cnd), Royal PO *(rec October 9 & 10, 1962)* Chesky ▲ CD93 [ADD]
Liszt, F.:Études d'exécution transcendante d'après Paganini, S.140—No. 2 in E♭ Vanguard Classics ▲ OVC 4034 [ADD]
Liszt, F.:Fant on Hungarian Folk Tunes, w. R. Stanger (cnd), Royal PO *(rec 1963)* Chesky ▲ CD50 [ADD]
Liszt, F.:Pno Music (misc)—Gnomenreigen; Mephisto Polka; Mephisto Waltz; Reminiscences de Robert le Diable (Valse infernale); Reminiscences de Don Juan (after Mozart); Waltzes from Gounod's Faust Vanguard Classics ▲ OVC 4035 [ADD]
Liszt, F.:Transcriptions & Paraphrases—Chopin:Meine Freuden; Liszt—Die Loreley; Schumann—Frühlingsnacht; Widmung; Wagner—Spinning Chorus Onyx ▲ 104 [DDD]
Macdowell, E.:Con 2 Pno, w. M. Freccia (cnd), RCA Victor SO *(rec 1967)* Chesky ▲ CD 76 [ADD]
Medtner, N.:Pno Music (misc)—Second Improvisation (Theme & 16 Variations on "The Mermaid's Song"), Op. 47 (1926); Sonate-Idylle, Op. 56 (1937); Vergessene Weisen (Forgotten Melodies), Op. 39 (1819-20) Chesky ▲ AD 1 [DDD]
Menotti, G.C.:Con Pno, w. J. Mester (cnd), Symphony of the Air *(rec 1961)* Vanguard Classics ▲ SVC 3 [AAD]
Menotti, G.C.:Con Pno, w. J. Mester (cnd), Symphony of the Air Vanguard Classics ▲ OVC 4029 [ADD]
Paderewski, I.J.:Con Pno, w. A. Fiedler (cnd), London SO *(rec Barking Town Hall, London, England, Sept 6, 1970)* Elan ▲ CD 2266 [ADD]
Rachmaninoff, S.:Cons Pno (comp), w. J. Horenstein (cnd), Royal PO Chandos 2-▲ CHAN 8521/22 [ADD]
Rachmaninoff, S.:Con 1 Pno, w. J. Horenstein (cnd), Royal PO Chandos ("Collect" series) ▲ CHAN 6605 [ADD]
Rachmaninoff, S.:Con 1 Pno, w. J. Horenstein (cnd), Royal PO *(rec 1965)* Chesky ▲ CD 41 [ADD]

Wild, Earl (pno) (cont.)
Rachmaninoff, S.:Con 2 Pno, w. J. Horenstein (cnd), Royal PO Chandos ("Collect" series) ▲ CHAN 6507 [ADD]
Rachmaninoff, S.:Con 2 Pno, w. J. Horenstein (cnd), Royal PO *(rec 1966)* Chesky ▲ CD 2 ■ CC 2
Rachmaninoff, S.:Con 3 Pno, w. J. Horenstein (cnd), Royal PO Chandos ("Collect" series) ▲ CHAN 6507 [ADD]
Rachmaninoff, S.:Con 3 Pno, w. J. Horenstein (cnd), Royal PO *(rec 1965)* Chesky ▲ CD 76 [ADD]
Rachmaninoff, S.:Con 4 Pno, w. J. Horenstein (cnd), Royal PO Chandos ("Collect" series) ▲ CHAN 6605 [ADD]
Rachmaninoff, S.:Con 4 Pno, w. J. Horenstein (cnd), Royal PO *(rec 1965)* Chesky ▲ CD 41 [ADD]
Rachmaninoff, S.:Rhapsody on a Theme of Paganini, w. J. Horenstein (cnd), Royal PO Chandos 2-▲ CHAN 8521/22 [ADD]
Rachmaninoff, S.:Rhapsody on a Theme of Paganini, w. J. Horenstein (cnd), Royal PO Chandos ("Collect" series) ▲ CHAN 6605 [ADD]
Rachmaninoff, S.:Rhapsody on a Theme of Paganini, w. J. Horenstein (cnd), Royal PO *(rec 1965)* Chesky ▲ CD 41 [ADD]
Rachmaninoff, S.:Songs [solo piano trans by Earl Wild]—Floods of Spring; Midsummer Eve; Little Island; Where Beauty Dwells; In the Silent Night; Vocalise; On the Death of a Linnet; The Muse; O, Cease Thy Singing; To the Children; Dreams; Sorrow in Springtime *(rec 7/82)* Dell'Arte ▲ CDDBS 7001
Rachmaninoff, S.:Songs [3 solo piano trans by Earl Wild]—Oh, do not grieve; Floods of spring; In the silent night Chesky ▲ CD58 [DDD]
Rachmaninoff, S.:Variations on a Theme by Chopin Chesky ▲ CD58 [DDD]
Rachmaninoff, S.:Variations on a Theme by Corelli Chesky ▲ CD58 [DDD]
Rachmaninoff, S.:Vocalise [solo piano trans. by Earl Wild] Chesky ▲ CD58 [DDD]
The Romantic Master:13 Transcriptions for Solo Piano Sony Classical ▲ SK 62036
Saint-Saëns, C.:Con 2 Pno, w. M. Freccia (cnd), RCA Victor SO *(rec 1967)* Chesky ▲ CD50 [ADD]
Scharwenka, X.:Con 1 Pno, w. E. Leinsdorf (cnd), Boston SO *(rec Symphony Hall, Boston, MA, Jan 20, 1969)* Elan ▲ CD 2266 [ADD]
Schumann, R.:Papillons *(rec 1/84)* Dell'Arte ▲ CDDBS 7005
Schumann, R.:Pno Music (misc)—Fantasiestücke, Op. 12, No. 2 (Aufschwung); Romance, Op. 28, No. 2; Waldscenen (Vogel als Prophet) *(rec 1/84)* Dell'Arte ▲ CDDBS 7005
Tausig, C.:Trans & Arr—Invitation to the Dance [Weber]; Marche Militaire [Schubert] Chesky ▲ CD 2
Tchaikovsky, P.:Con 1 Pno, w. A. Fistoulari (cnd), Royal PO Chesky ▲ CD 13
Transcriptions Onyx 2-▲ 104 [DDD]
The Virtuoso Piano Vanguard Classics ▲ OVC 4033 [ADD]
Wild, E.:Variations on an American Theme, w. J. Giunta (cnd), Des Moines SO Chesky ▲ CD 98 [DDD]

Wild, Ulrike (hpd/org)—see ORCHESTRAS & ENSEMBLES Scaramouche

de Wilde, (cl)
Mozart, W.A.:Con Cl, w. E. van Beinum (cnd), Royal Concertgebouw Orch Philips ■ 411174-4

Wilde, Barry (vn)
Reger, M.:Serenades Fl, Opp. 77a & 141a, w. A. Noakes (fl), G. Robertson (va) ASV ▲ ASV 875 [DDD]

Wilde, David (pno)
Reizenstein, F.:Son Vn, w. E. Gruenberg (vn) Continuum ▲ CCD 1024
Wilson, T.:Con Pno, w. B. Thomson (cnd), Scottish National Orch Chandos ▲ CHAN 8626 [DDD]

Wiley, Peter (vc)—see also ORCHESTRAS & ENSEMBLES Beaux Arts Trio
Beethoven, L. van:Trio 9 Pno, "Kakadu", w. R. Serkin (pno), Y. Horigome (vn) Sony Classical ▲ SMK 47296 [ADD]
Schubert, Franz:Qnt Strs, D.956, w. P. Frank (vn), F. Galimir (vn), S. Tenenbom (va), J. Lichten (vc) Sony Classical ▲ SMK 45901 [ADD/DDD] ■ SMT 45901

Wiley, W. (perc)
Van De Vate, N.:Music for Va, w. M.-K. Johnson (va), E. Zuckerman (pno) Vienna Modern Masters ▲ VMM CD 2001 [ADD]

Wilhelm, David (pno)—see ORCHESTRAS & ENSEMBLES Bowed Piano Ensemble

Wilhelm, Karl (org)
In Quires & Places Where They Sing, w. Te Deum Singers, [cnd:R. Birney-Smith] Te Deum ▲ TDR-CD004

Wilkie, Matthew (bn)—see ORCHESTRAS & ENSEMBLES CO of Europe Soloists

Wilkinson, Bernhardur (fl)—see ORCHESTRAS & ENSEMBLES Reykjavik Wind Quintet

Wilkinson, H. (org)
Banks, H.C.:Beyond the Aurora Por Organo ▲ POCD 7044 [DDD]
Karg-Elert, S.:Org Music—Choral Improvisation on "In Dulci Jubilo," Op. 75/2; Ave Maria, from Cathedral Windows, Op. 106/2; Fugue, Canzona & Epilogue from 3 Symphonic Canzonas, Op. 85/3 Pro Organo ▲ POCD 7044 [DDD]
Vierne, L.:Sym 2 Org—Scherzo movt. Pro Organo ▲ POCD 7044 [DDD]
Willan, H.:Intro, Passacaglia & Fugue Pro Organo ▲ POCD 7044 [DDD]

Wilkinson, R. (vielle/rcr)
Codax, M.:Cantigas d'amigo (7), w. H. Newnham (ct/perc), R. Bandt (rcr/fl/psalter/perc), J. Griffiths (lt/gtr morisca) Vox Australis ▲ VAST 005-2
Codax, M.:Music of, w. H. Newnham (ct/perc), R. Bandt (rcr/fl/psalter/perc), J. Griffiths (lt/gtr morisca)—L'Autrier Jost' una Sebissa; Istanpitta Gaetta; Bel m'es Quant Son Li Fruit Madur; Slatarello Vox Australis ▲ VAST 005-2

Wilkomirska, Maria (pno)
Chopin, F.:Son Vc, w. Kazimierz Wilkomirski (vc) *(rec Warsaw, 1959-60)* Polskie Nagrania 2-▲ PNCD 301 A/B
Chopin, F.:Sons Pno (comp) *(rec Warsaw, 1959-60)* Polskie Nagrania 2-▲ PNCD 301 A/B

Wilkomirska, Wanda (vn)
Bacewicz, G.:Son 4 Vn & Pno, w. P. Dan (pno) *(rec 1988)* Ambitus ▲ 97830 [DDD]
Bargielski, Z.:Neo-Sonatina, w. P. Dan (pno) *(rec 1988)* Ambitus ▲ 97830 [DDD]
Bartók, B.:Duos (44), w. M. Szücs (vn) Hungaroton 3-▲ HCD 31154/56 [ADD]
Karlowicz, M.:Con Vn, w. W. Rowicki (cnd), Warsaw Philharmonic SO *(rec National Philharmonic Concert Hall, Warsaw, 1963)* Polskie Nagrania ▲ PNCD 142 [DDD]
Paderewski, I.J.:Son Vn, w. P. Dan (pno) *(rec 1988)* Ambitus ▲ 97830 [DDD]
Szymanowski, K.:Con 1 Vn, w. W. Rowicki (cnd), Warsaw Philharmonic SO *(rec National Philharmonic Concert Hall, Warsaw, 1961)* Polskie Nagrania ▲ PNCD 142 [DDD]
Zarycki, A.:Mazurka Vn, w. P. Dan (pno) *(rec 1988)* Ambitus ▲ 97830 [DDD]

Wilkomirski, Kazimierz (vc)
Chopin, F.:Son Vc, w. Maria Wilkomirska (pno) *(rec Warsaw, 1959-60)* Polskie Nagrania 2-▲ PNCD 301 A/B

Willbanks, Marilyn (pno)
Bordogni, G.:Allegro vivace, w. Jeffery Snedeker (hn) *(rec Univ of MA, Amherst, July 31-Aug 4, 1995)* Snedeker ▲ 001
Bordogni, G.:Andantino, w. Jeffery Snedeker (hn) *(rec Univ of MA, Amherst, July 31-Aug 4, 1995)* Snedeker ▲ 001
Dauprat, L.-F.:Melodie Hns, w. Jeffery Snedeker (hn), Richard Seraphinoff (hn) *(rec Univ of MA, Amherst, July 31-Aug 4, 1995)* Snedeker ▲ 001
Gallay, J.-F.:Grand Caprice, w. Jeffery Snedeker (hn) *(rec Univ of MA, Amherst, July 31-Aug 4, 1995)* Snedeker ▲ 001
Gallay, J.-F.:Solo 11 Hn, w. Jeffery Snedeker (hn) *(rec Univ of MA, Amherst, July 31-Aug 4, 1995)* Snedeker ▲ 001
Gallay, J.-F.:Vocalises (3), w. Jeffery Snedeker (hn) *(rec Univ of MA, Amherst, July 31-Aug 4, 1995)* Snedeker ▲ 001
Panseron, A.:Andantino Hn, w. Jeffery Snedeker (hn) *(rec Univ of MA, Amherst, July 31-Aug 4, 1995)* Snedeker ▲ 001
Rossini, G.:Prelude, Theme & Vars Hn, w. Jeffery Snedeker (hn) *(rec Univ of MA, Amherst, July 31-Aug 4, 1995)* Snedeker ▲ 001
Saint-Saëns, C.:Romances Hn, w. Jeffery Snedeker (hn)—Op. 36 *(rec Univ of MA, Amherst, July 31-Aug 4, 1995)* Snedeker ▲ 001

Willems, Gerard (pno)—see also ORCHESTRAS & ENSEMBLES Mozartrois
Bremner, A.:In the Shrubbery, w. Judy Glen (nar), David Miller (pno), Philip South (perc), Roland Peelman (cnd), Song Company *(rec Studio 200, ABC Ultimo Centre, Apr 1993)* Tall Poppies ▲ TP 064 [DDD]

Willens, Michael (db)—see also ORCHESTRAS & ENSEMBLES Jazzantiqua, Old Fairfield Academy Orch members
Vivaldi, A.:Cons for 2 Vns, w. J. Schröder (vn), S. Ritchie (vn), N. TeBrake (vn), R. Brown (vn), J. Griffin (va), M. Lutszke (vc), A. Fuller (hpd) *(rec June 6-8, 1986)* Reference ▲ RR 23 CD [DDD]
Vivaldi, A.:Sinf, RV.116, w. J. Schröder (vn), S. Ritchie (vn), J. Griffin (va), M. Lutszke (vc), A. Fuller (hpd) *(rec June 6-8, 1986)* Reference ▲ RR 23 CD [DDD]

Willett, Dan (ob)—see ORCHESTRAS & ENSEMBLES Missouri Quintet

Williams, B. (va)
Bax, A.:Elegiac Trio, w. M. Meisenbach (fl), M. Golden (hp) *(rec 6 & 8/91)* Centaur ▲ CRC 2114 [DDD]

Williams, Davey (gtr)
Lebaron, A.:The E. & O. Line (sels), w. Louise Cloutier (mez—Eurydice/Vendors), Hugh Panero (ten—Hermes), Lawrence Hamilton (bar—Orpheus/Men), Frank London (tpt), Marcus Rojas (tuba), Myra Melford (pno/kbd), Fred Hopkins (elec bass), Thurman Barker (dr), A. LeBaron (cnd)—Juke Joint Jam Session; Eurydice Meets Hermes; Eurydice's Death [Funeral Band]; Eurydice's River Journey; Orpheus Laments [Looked Away] *(rec Coolidge Auditorium, Library of Congress, 1987)* Mode ▲ Mode 42

Williams, G. (vc)
Mageau, M.J.:Triple Con, w. A. Lorenz (vn), W. Lorenz (pno), Petronsky (cnd), Slovak RSO Bratislava Vienna Modern Masters ▲ VMM 3001 [DDD]

Williams, Gail (hn)
Hindemith, P.:Son Hn, w. T. Lichtman (pno) Summit 2–▲ DCD 115 [DDD] 2–■ DCD 115
Hindemith, P.:Son for 4 Hns, w. T. Bacon (hn), A. D. Krehbiel (hn), L. Strieby (hn) Summit 2–▲ DCD 115 [DDD] 2–■ DCD 115
Mozart, W.A.:Cons Hn, w. A. Schneider (cnd), CO of Europe ASV ("CO of Europe" series") ▲ CDCOE 805 [DDD]
Rochberg, G.:Trio Cl, w. L. Combs (cl), M. A. Covert (pno) Crystal ■ C 731
Schuller, G.:Romantic Son Cl, w. L. Combs (cl), M. A. Covert (pno) Crystal ■ C 731
20th Century Settings for Horn Summit ▲ DCD 139 [DDD]

Williams, Hildburg (vn)
Matiegka, W.T.:Grand Trio Vn, Va & Gtr, w. R. Smissen (va), D. Chivers (gtr) Erasmus ▲ WVH 086

Williams, Huw Tregelles (org)
Celebration:Christmas Fanfares & Carols, w. BBC Welsh Chorus, [cnd:John Hugh Thomas], Welsh Guards Fanfare Trumpeters, Aled Jones (nar) Nimbus ▲ NI 5310 [DDD]
Magnificat & Nunc Dimittis, Vol. 7, w. Hereford Cathedral Choir, Roy Massey (cnd) Priory ▲ PRI 535 [DDD]
The Spirit of Christmas Present, w. Kansas City Chorale [cnd:Charles Bruffy], BBC Welsh Chorus [cnd:John Hugh Thomas], Welsh Guards Fanfare Trumpeters, Christ Church Cathedral Choir [cnd:Stephen Darlington], Gulbenkian Orch [cnd:Michel Swierczewski], English St Nimbus ▲ NI 7034 [DDD]

Williams, Jan (perc)
Brown, E.:Music of, w. Eberhard Blum (fl)—1991 [versions 1 & 2]; For Ann [versions 1 & 2]; 1980 [versions 1 & 2] [all from Folio II] *(rec Slee Concert Hall, Buffalo, New York, June 1-2, 1995)* Hat Hut ("Now" series) ▲ CD 6176 [DDD]
Brown, E.:Music of, w. Eberhard Blum (fl/sound objects), Steffen Schleiermacher (pno/cel)—4 Systems; Hodograph 1, Versions 1 & 2; Octet 1 *(rec Hessen Radio, Frankfurt, Dec. 16-17, 1993)* Hat Hut ("NOW." series) ▲ hat ART CD 6146 [DDD]
Cage, J.:composed Improvisation *(rec Hessen Radio, Frankfurt, Dec. 16-17, 1993)* Hat Hut ("NOW." series) ▲ hat ART CD 6146 [DDD]
Cage, J.:Ryoanji, w. John Patrick Thomas (voc), Gudrun Reschke (ob), Eberhard Blum (fl), Iven Hausmann (trbn), Robert Black (db) *(rec Akademie der Künste, Berlin, June 22, 1995)* Hat Hut ("Now" series) ▲ hat ART CD 6183 [DDD]
Cage, J.:Vars I-IV, w. Eberhard Blum (fl)—Vars III [version 1 for perc; version 2 for fl & sound objects] *(rec Slee Concert Hall, Buffalo, New York, June 1-2, 1995)* Hat Hut ("Now" series) ▲ CD 6176 [DDD]
Cage, J.:Vars I-IV, w. Eberhard Blum (fl/sound objects)—Var II *(rec Hessen Radio, Frankfurt, Dec. 16-17, 1993)* Hat Hut ("NOW." series) ▲ hat ART CD 6146 [DDD]
Feldman, Morton:For Philip Guston, w. Eberhard Blum (fl/alt fl), Nils Vigeland (pno/cel) *(rec Buffalo, NY, Aug. 19-21, 1991)* Hat Hut ("NOW." series) 4–▲ hat ART CD 4-61041/44 [DDD]
Feldman, Morton:The King of Denmark *(rec Hessen Radio, Frankfurt, Dec. 16-17, 1993)* Hat Hut ("NOW." series) ▲ hat ART CD 6146 [DDD]
Feldman, Morton:Why Patterns, w. E. Blum (fl), M. Feldman (vn) *(rec 12/17/78)* CRI ▲ CD 620 [ADD]
Foss, L.:Curriculum Vitae with Time Bomb, w. B. Schimmel (acc) *(rec 1989-90)* Koss Classics ▲ KC 1006 [DDD]
Foss, L.:Paradigm, w. J. Grassel (electric gtr), S. Basson (bn), R. Dagon (cl), L. Anderson (vn) *(rec 1989-90)* Koss Classics ▲ KC 1006 [DDD]
Garcia, O.J.:Metallic Images O.O. Discs ▲ OO 6 [DDD]
Vigeland, N.:Progress, w. M. Pugliese (perc) *(rec in concert at Merkin Concert Hall, New York City, 4/4/89)* Mode ▲ 25
Wolff, C.:Edges, w. Eberhard Blum (fl)—Realization for Fl & Perc [Versions 1 & 2] *(rec Slee Concert Hall, Buffalo, New York, June 1-2, 1995)* Hat Hut ("Now" series) ▲ CD 6176 [DDD]
Wolff, C.:Exercises, w. Eberhard Blum (fl), Roland Dahinden (trbn), Steffen Schleiermacher (pno) *(rec Hessischer Radio, Frankfurt, Aug 6-7, 1994)* Hat Hut ("Now" series) ▲ CD 6167 [DDD]

Williams, John (gtr)
Albéniz, I.:Gtr Music—Asturias; Cordoba; Granada; Majorca CBS ▲ MDK 45648 [DDD] ■ MDT 45648 (D)
Albéniz, I.:Gtr Music—includes Asturias; Cadiz; Cordoba; Granada; Seville; Tango CBS ▲ MK 36679 [DDD]
Albéniz, I.:Iberia Suite, w. P. Daniel (cnd), London SO [3 sections arr. Steve Gray for solo gtr & orch] Sony Classical ▲ SK 48480 [DDD]
Bach, J.S.:Con 2 Vn, w. K. Sillito (cnd), Academy of St. Martin in the Fields—& Andante from Sonata BWV 1003 [arr. Williams] CBS ▲ MK 39560 [DDD]
Bach, J.S.:Lt Music—BWV 995, 996, 997 & 1006a CBS ▲ MK 42204
Bach, J.S.:Suite Lt, BWV 995—BWV 995 & 997 London ("Weekend Classics" series) ▲ 433022-2 [AAD]
The Baroque Album CBS ▲ MK 44518 [ADD] ■ MT 44518
Carulli, F.:Serenade for 2 Gtrs, w. J. Bream (gtr) RCA ■ ARK1-0456
Castelnuovo-Tedesco, M.:Con 1 Gtr, w. C. Groves (cnd), English CO CBS 2–▲ M2K 44791 [ADD/DDD]
Day's End:The Soft Sound of Spanish Guitar, w. Eduardo Fernández (gtr), William Gómez (gtr), Nicola Hall (gtr), Timothy Walker (gtr) London ▲ 448 560-2
Echoes of London CBS ▲ MK 42119 [DDD]
Fragments of a Dream, w. Inti-Illimani (flamenco gtr), Paco Peña (flamenco gtr) CBS ▲ MK 44574 [ADD] ■ FMT 44574
Giuliani, M.:Con 1 Gtr, English CO CBS 2–▲ M2K 44791 [ADD/DDD]
Giuliani, M.:Con 1 Gtr, English CO Sony Classical ("Essential Classics" series) ▲ SBK 48168; ■ SBT 48168
Giuliani, M.:Son Vn, w. I. Perlman (vn) CBS ▲ MK 34508 [AAD] ■ MT 34508
Giuliani, M.:Vars on a Theme by Handel *(rec New York City, Nov 17, 1965)* Sony Classical ("Essential Classics" series) ▲ SBK 62425 [ADD] ■ SBT 62425
Giuliani, M.:Variazioni Concertanti, w. J. Bream (gtr) RCA ■ ARK1-0456
Granados, E.:Valses poeticos (7) [trans. for solo guitar] Sony Classical ▲ SK 48480 [DDD]
The Great Guitar Concertos CBS 2–▲ M2K 44791 [ADD/DDD]
Greatest Hits CBS ■ MT 31407

Williams, John (gtr) (cont.)
Guitar Concertos, w. English CO [cnd:Daniel Barenboim] Odyssey 2–▲ MB2K 45610
The Guitar Is the Song CBS ▲ MK 37825 [AAD]
Guitar Recital London ("Two-Fers" series) 2–▲ 452173-2 (m)
Handel, G.F.:Cons (16) Org—Op. 4, No. 5 [arr. Williams] CBS ▲ MK 39560 [DDD]
Iberia Sony Classical ▲ SK 48480 [DDD]
John Williams & Friends, w. Carlos Bonell (gtr), Brian Gascoigne (mar/vib), Morris Pert (mar/vib), Keith Marjoram (db) CBS ▲ MK 35108 [AAD]
John Williams in Seville, w. Williams, John (gtr) *(rec Nov. 10-18, 1992)* Sony Classical ▲ SK 53359 [DDD] ■ ST 53359
Julian & John together, w. Julian Bream (gtr) RCA Gold Seal ▲ 09026-61450-2 ■ 09026-61450-4
Julian & John together Again, w. Julian Bream (gtr) RCA Gold Seal ▲ 09026-61452-2 ■ 09026-61452-4
Latin American Guitar Music Sony Classical ("Essential Classics" series) ▲ SBK 47669 ■ SBT 47669
Llobet, M.:Gtr Music—Canciones populares Catalanas (1899-1918) Sony Classical ▲ SK 48480 [DDD]
Lucky to Be Me, w. Jessye Norman (sop) Philips ▲ 422401-2 PH ■ 422401-4 PH
The Mantis & the Moon:Guitar Duets from around the World, w. Timothy Kain (gtr) Sony Classical ▲ SK 62007
Marcello, A.:Con Ob & Strs [arr. Williams] CBS ▲ MK 39560 [DDD]
Music of Takemitsu Sony Classical ▲ SK 46720
Pachelbel, w. Jean-Pierre Rampal (fl), Igor Kipnis (hpd), Raymond Leppard (cnd), Canadian Brass, E. Power Biggs (org), et al. Sony Classical ("Greatest Hits" series) ▲ MLK 62680 ■ MLT 62680
Paganini, N.:Cantabile, w. I. Perlman (vn) CBS ▲ MK 34508 [AAD] ■ MT 34508
Paganini, N.:Caprices Vn—No. 24 in A *(rec New York City, May 21-22, 1964)* Sony Classical ("Essential Classics" series) ▲ SBK 62425 [ADD] ■ SBT 62425
Paganini, N.:Son concertata, w. I. Perlman (vn) CBS ▲ MK 34508 [AAD] ■ MT 34508
Paganini, N.:Sons Vn & Gtr, w. I. Perlman (vn)—Op. 64/1 CBS ▲ MK 34508 [AAD] ■ MT 34508
Paganini, N.:Sons Vn & Gtr, Op. 3, w. I. Perlman (vn)—No. 6 CBS ▲ MK 34508 [AAD] ■ MT 34508
Ponce, M.:Concierto del sur, w. A. Previn (cnd), London SO CBS 2–▲ M2K 44791 [ADD/DDD]
A Portrait of John Williams, w. Leslie Pearson (hpd/org continuo) CBS ▲ MK 37791
Rodrigo, J.:Concierto de Aranjuez, w. L. Frémaux (cnd), Philharmonia Orch CBS 2–▲ M2K 44791 [ADD/DDD]
Rodrigo, J.:Concierto de Aranjuez, w. L. Frémaux (cnd), Philharmonia Orch CBS ▲ MDK 45648 [DDD] ■ MDT 45648 (D)
Rodrigo, J.:Concierto de Aranjuez, w. D. Barenboim (cnd), English CO CBS ▲ MK 33208
Rodrigo, J.:Concierto de Aranjuez, w. E. Ormandy (cnd), Philadelphia Orch Sony Classical ("Essential Classics" series) ▲ SBK 48168 ■ SBT 48168
Rodrigo, J.:Concierto de Aranjuez, w. C. Groves (cnd), English CO CBS ▲ MYK 36717
Rodrigo, J.:Fant para un gentilhombre, w. C. Groves (cnd), English CO Sony Classical ("Essential Classics" series) ▲ SBK 48168 ■ SBT 48168
Rodrigo, J.:Fant para un gentilhombre, w. L. Frémaux (cnd), Philharmonia Orch CBS ▲ MDK 45648 [DDD] ■ MDT 45648 (D)
Rodrigo, J.:Fant para un gentilhombre, w. L. Frémaux (cnd), Philharmonia Orch CBS 2–▲ M2K 44791 [ADD/DDD]
Rodrigo, J.:Invocación y danza Sony Classical ▲ SK 48480 [DDD]
Scarlatti, D.:Sons Kbd—in E, K.380; in A, K.208; in a, K.175, in A, K.322; in d, K.213; in D, K.159 *(rec London, 1971)* Sony Classical ("Essential Classics" series) ▲ SBK 62425 [ADD] ■ SBT 62425
Spanish Guitar Favorites CBS ▲ MK 44794 [ADD] ■ MT 44794
Spanish Guitar Favourites London ("Weekend Classics" series) ▲ 421165-2 ■ 421165-4
Spanish Guitar Music Sony Classical ("Essential Classics" series) ▲ SBK 46347 [ADD] ■ SBT 46347
Speach, B.:Music of, w. J. Schanzer, L. Krech (trbn), A. de Mare (pno), Michael Pugliese (perc), T. Davis (speaker), et al., B. Speach (cnd), Bowery Ensemble—Moto for Trombone, Percussion & Piano (1982); Pensées for Guitar (1983); Trajet for Trombone & Percussion (1983); Sonata for Piano (1986); Shattered Glass for Percussion (1987); Telepathy (Poetry/Music Suite) for Speaker, Contrabas Mode ▲ 16
Spirit of the Guitar:Music of the Americas CBS ▲ MK 44898 [ADD]
Strictly Virtuosity, w. Andrés Segovia (gtr) Takoma ▲ CDP 72899
Takemitsu, T.:Music of, w. E.-P. Salonen (cnd), London Sinfonietta—Vers, l'arc-en-ceil, Palma for Guitar, Oboe & Orch.; To the Edge of Dream for Guitar & Orch. Sony Classical ▲ SMK 53473
Takemitsu, T.:Music of, w. S. Bell (fl), G. Hulse (ob), E.-P. Salonen (cnd), London Sinfonietta—To the Edge of Dream (for Guitar & Orchestra); Vers, L'arc-en-ciel, Palma (for Guitar & Oboe); Toward the Sea (for Alto Flute & Guitar); Folios (for solo Guitar); 12 Songs for Guitar (selections) Sony Classical ▲ SK 46720
Villa-Lobos, H.:Con Gtr, w. D. Barenboim (cnd), English CO CBS ▲ MK 33208
Villa-Lobos, H.:Con Gtr, w. D. Barenboim (cnd), English CO CBS 2–▲ M2K 44791 [ADD/DDD]
Villa-Lobos, H.:Preludes Gtr *(rec London, 1974)* Sony Classical ("Essential Classics" series) ▲ SBK 62425 [ADD] ■ SBT 62425
Vivaldi, A.:Cons Gtr, w. J. Rolla (cnd), Franz Liszt CO [solo parts trans. for guitar]—Violin Concerti, RV.230, R.345 & R.356; Concerto for 2 Mandolins (w. Ben Verdery, 2nd guitar); Concerto for Lute & 2 Violins, RV.93; Concerto for Viola d'amore & Lute, RV.540 (w. N. Blum, viola d'amore); Trio for Violin & Lute, RV.82 (w. J. Rolla, violin) Sony Classical ▲ SK 46556 [DDD]
Vivaldi, A.:Con Lt, w. English CO Sony Classical ("Essential Classics" series) ▲ SBK 48168 ■ SBT 48168
Vivaldi, A.:Con Lt, w. English CO CBS 2–▲ M2K 44791 [ADD/DDD]
Vivaldi, A.:Con in A Mand, w. English CO CBS 2–▲ M2K 44791 [ADD/DDD]

Williams, L. (va)
Beethoven, L. van:Serenade Fl, Op. 25, w. S. Milan (fl), L. Chilingirian (vn) Chandos ▲ CHAN 9108 [DDD]

Williams, R. (vn)—see ORCHESTRAS & ENSEMBLES Valcour String Quartet

Williams, Robert (bn)
Kosins, M.S.:Songs of the Seeker, w. J. Carradine (nar), A. Kavafian (vn), T. D. Barna (pno) *(rec 1980)* Centaur ▲ CRC 2105 [ADD]

Williams, Roger Bevan (org)
Arne, T.:Favourite Cons (6), w. A. Shepherd (cnd), Cantilena Chandos 2–▲ CHAN 8604/05 [DDD]

Williams, Sioned (hp)
Britten, H.:Canticles I-V, w. M. Chance (ct), A. Rolfe-Johnson (ten), A. Opie (bar), R. Vignoles (pno), M. Thompson (hn) Hyperion ▲ CDA 66498
Holst, G.:Choral Music, w. D. Theodore (ob), R. Truman (vc), Holst Singers—The Princess; Light Leaves Whisper; Ave Maria; Jesu, Thou the Virgin-born; A Welcome Song; In Youth is Pleasure; Two Eastern Pictures; Bring us in Good Ale; Lully My Liking; Of One That Is So Fair and Bright; Diverus and Lazurus; Terly Terlow; This Have I Done for My True Love; Six Choral Folksongs; Twelve Welsh Folksongs; O Spiritual Pilgrim Hyperion ▲ CDA 66705 [DDD]
Nielsen, C.:Fog is Lifting, w. James Galway (fl) *(rec Wilshire United Church, Hollywood, CA, Dec 2, 1986)* RCA Red Seal ▲ 07863-56359-2 [ADD]

Willencourt, Dominique de (vc)
Debussy, C.:Son Vc, w. Anne Queffélec (pno) Forlane ▲ FRL 16585 [DDD]
Fauré, G.:Elégie, w. Anne Queffélec (pno) Forlane ▲ FRL 16585 [DDD]
Fauré, G.:Papillon, w. Anne Queffélec (pno) Forlane ▲ FRL 16585 [DDD]
Fauré, G.:Romance Vc, w. Anne Queffélec (pno) Forlane ▲ FRL 16585 [DDD]
Fauré, G.:Sérénade, w. Anne Queffélec (pno) Forlane ▲ FRL 16585 [DDD]
Fauré, G.:Sicilienne, w. Anne Queffélec (pno) Forlane ▲ FRL 16585 [DDD]
Franck, C.:Son Vn, w. Anne Queffélec (pno) [arr for Vc & Pno] Forlane ▲ FRL 16585 [DDD]
Haydn, J.:Trios Pno, Fl & Vc, w. R. Mamou (pno), Shigenori Kudo (fl) Pavane ▲ ADW 7202 [DDD]
Landowski, M.:Adagio Cantabile, w. Steliana Calos (sop), Pompei Harasteanu (bass), Jacques Taddei (org), R. Georgescu (cnd), Timisoara PO, Timisoara Chorus *(rec Mar. 16-18, 1993)* Chamade ▲ 5611 [DDD]

Williencourt, Dominique de (vc) (cont.)
Landowski, M.:Leçons de Ténèbres, w. Steliana Calos (sop), Pompei Harasteanu (bass), Jacques Taddei (org), R. Georgescu (cnd), Timisoara PO, Timisoara Chorus *(rec Mar. 16–18, 1993)* Chamade ▲ 5611 [DDD]

Willis, Andrew (pno)
Ibert, J.:Chamber Music, w. Sue Ann Kahn (fl), Eleanor Lawrence (fl), Peggy Schecter (fl), Rie Schmidt (fl), David Krakauer (cl), Lauren Goldstein (bn), Curtis Macomber (vn), Susan Jolles (hp), Frederic Hand (gtr)—2 Mouvements; Aria; Histoires; Pastoral; Aria; Entr'acte Albany ▲ TROY 145 [DDD]
Ibert, J.:Jeux, w. Sue Ann Kahn (fl) Albany ▲ TROY 145 [DDD]
Kraft, L.:Fant 2 Fl & Pno, w. S. A. Kahn (fl) Capstone ▲ CPS 8609 CD
Luening, O.:Third Short Son Fl, w. Sue Ann Kahn (fl) CRI ■ C 531
Luening, O.:Third Short Son Fl, w. Sue Ann Kahn (fl) CRI ("American Masters" series) ▲ CD 716 [ADD]
Rochberg, G.:Between 2 Worlds, w. S. A. Kahn (fl) CRI ■ C 531
Schickele, P.:Spring Serenade, w. S. A. Kahn (fl) CRI ■ C 531

Willis, Arthur (pno)
Ibert, J.:Music of, w. C. Schadeberg (sop), Sue Ann Kahn (fl), E. Lawrence (fl), P. Schechter (fl), R. Schmidt (fl), David Krakauer (cl), L. Goldstein (bn), Curtis Macomber (vn), Susan Jolles (hp), Frederick Hand (gtr)—Entr'acte; Jeux; Sonatine; 2 Movements; 2 Interludes; Aria; Pièce for solo Fl; Histoires; 2 Stèles orientées; Pastoral; Aria; Entr'acte Albany ▲ TROY 145

Willis, Sara (hn)
Mozart, W.A.:Don Giovanni, w. Gernot Schmalfub (ob), Christian Hartmann (ob), Dieter Klöcker (cl), Waldemar Wandel (cl), Christian Auer (hn), Karl-Otto Hartmann (bn), Eberhard Buschmann (bn), Jürgen Normann (db), Consortium Classicum Bayer ▲ BR 100 135 [DDD]

Willison, David (pno)
Alwyn, W.:Rhap Pno, w. Quartet of London members Chandos ▲ CHAN 8440 [DDD]
Beautiful Dreamer (& other Parlour Favorites), w. Benjamin Luxon (bar), Delmé String Quartet, et al. Omega Classics ▲ OCD 3005 [DDD]
Butterworth, G.:Bredon Hill & Other Songs, w. B. Luxon (bar) [E] Chandos ▲ CHAN 8831 [DDD]
Butterworth, G.:Songs (6) from *A Shropshire Lad*, w. A. R. Johnson (ten) IMP Classics ▲ IMPPCD 1065 [DDD]
Butterworth, G.:Songs (6) from *A Shropshire Lad*, w. B. Luxon (bar) [E] Chandos ▲ CHAN 8831 [DDD]
Gurney, I.:Songs, w. B. Luxon (bar)—20 songs:Carol of the Skiddaw Yowes; The apple orchard; The fields are full; The twa corbies; Severn Meadows; Desire in spring; Ha'nacker Mill; Down by the Salley Gardens; The scribe; Hawk & Buckle; On the Downs; The fiddler of Dooney; In Flanders; The folly of being comforted; I praise the tender flower; Black Stichel; An epitaph; By a bierside; Cranham Woods; Sleep [E] Chandos ▲ CHAN 8831 [DDD]
I Love My Love:A Collection of British Folk Songs, w. Benjamin Luxon (bar) Chandos ▲ CHAN 8946 [DDD]
Ireland, J.:Songs, w. A. R. Johnson (ten)—The Land of Lost Content & others IMP Classics ▲ IMPPCD 1065 [DDD]
Quilter, R.:Songs, w. B. Luxon (bar)—five song groups:Three Shakespeare Songs, Op. 6; To Julia, Op. 8; Seven Elizabethan Lyrics, Op. 12; Four Songs, Op. 14; Three Songs of William Blake, Op. 20; *eight individual songs*—Love's philosophy, Op. 3/1; Now sleeps the crimson petal, Op. 3/2; At close of day; Go, lovely rose, Op. 24/3; Arab love song, Op. 25/4; Music, when soft voices die, Op. 25/5; In the bud of the morninG o, Op. 25/6; I arise from dreams of thee, Op. 29 [E] Chandos ▲ CHAN 8782 [DDD]
Schubert, Franz:Die Schöne Müllerin, w. B. Luxon (bar) [G] Chandos ▲ CHAN 8725 [DDD]
Schubert, Franz:Schwanengesang, w. B. Luxon (bar) [G] Chandos ▲ CHAN 8721 [DDD]
A Ticket To Heaven (& other Parlour Favorites), w. Benjamin Luxon (bar), Delmé String Quartet, et al. Omega Classics ▲ OCD 3006 [DDD]
Vaughan Williams, R.:The House of Life, w. B. Luxon (bar) [E] Chandos ▲ CHAN 8475 [DDD]
Vaughan Williams, R.:In the Spring, w. Luxon, Willison [E] Chandos ▲ CHAN 8475 [DDD]
Vaughan Williams, R.:Linden Lea, w. B. Luxon (bar) [E] Chandos ▲ CHAN 8475 [DDD]
Vaughan Williams, R.:Poems by Fredegond Shove, w. B. Luxon (bar) [E] Chandos ▲ CHAN 8475 [DDD]
Vaughan Williams, R.:Songs of Travel, w. A. R. Johnson (ten) IMP Classics ▲ IMPPCD 1065 [DDD]
Vaughan Williams, R.:Songs of Travel, w. B. Luxon (bar) [E] Chandos ▲ CHAN 8475 [DDD]
Vaughan Williams, R.:Tired, w. B. Luxon (bar) [E] Chandos ▲ CHAN 8475 [DDD]
Warlock, P.:Songs Bar, w. B. Luxon (bar)—32 songs [E] Chandos ▲ CHAN 8643 [DDD]

Willison, John (vn)
Bononcini, A.:Stabat Mater, w. Felicity Palmer (sop), Paul Esswood (ct), Philip Langridge (ten), Christopher Keyte (bass), John Scott (org), Chris Wellington (va), Don McVeigh (va), G. Guest (cnd), Philomusica Antiqua of London, St. John's College Choir Cambridge *(rec 1977)* London 2–▲ 443868–2 [ADD]
Caldara, A.:Crucifixus, w. Felicity Palmer (sop), Paul Esswood (ct), Philip Langridge (ten), Christopher Keyte (bass), John Scott (org), Chris Wellington (va), Don McVeigh (va), G. Guest (cnd), Philomusica Antiqua of London, St. John's College Choir Cambridge *(rec 1977)* London 2–▲ 443868–2 [ADD]
Lotti, A.:Crucifixus, w. Felicity Palmer (sop), Paul Esswood (ct), Philip Langridge (ten), Christopher Keyte (bass), John Scott (org), Chris Wellington (va), Don McVeigh (va), G. Guest (cnd), Philomusica Antiqua of London, St. John's College Choir Cambridge *(rec 1977)* London 2–▲ 443868–2 [ADD]

Willner, Sarah (va samples)
Dresher, P.:Water Dreams, w. Paul Dresher (elec) Lovely Music ▲ LCD 2011 [ADD]

Willoughby, Robert (fl)
Pierné, G.:Canzonetta Fl, w. W. Price (vc) Gasparo Gallante ▲ GG 1003 [AAD]
Pierné, G.:Son da camera Fl, w. Catherina Meints (vl), W. Price (pno) Gasparo Gallante ▲ GG 1003 [AAD]
Reger, M.:Serenade, Op. 141a, w. M. McDonald (vn), J. Tattaglia (va) Gasparo Gallante ▲ GG 1003 [AAD]
Reger, M.:Suite Vn Pno, w. W. Price (pno) [arr. unknown] Gasparo Gallante ▲ GG 1003 [AAD]
Roussel, A.:Trio Fl, w. K. Plummer (va), C. Meints (vc) Gasparo Gallante ▲ GG 1003 [AAD]

Wills, Arthur (org)
Albinoni, T.:Adagio Org [Org of Ely Cathedral] [arr. Giazotto] Meridian ▲ MER 84305
Blow, J.:Org Music [Org of Ely Cathedral]—Voluntaries in A & G Meridian ▲ MER 84305
Lemmens, N.J.:Org Music [Org of Ely Cathedral]—The Storm [Grand Fant in e] Meridian ▲ MER 84305
Purcell, H.:Voluntaries Org [Org of Ely Cathedral]—Z.720 Meridian ▲ MER 84305
Wagner, R.:Die Walküre (ride of the valkyries) [Org of Ely Cathedral] [arr for Org] Meridian ▲ MER 84305
Widor, C.M.:Marche pontificale [Org of Ely Cathedral] Meridian ▲ MER 84305
Wills, A.:Variations on Amazing Grace [Org of Ely Cathedral] Meridian ▲ MER 84305

Wills, Simon (trbn)
Bruckner, A.:motets, w. Richard Cheetham (trbn), Adrian Lane (trbn), Steven Saunders (trbn), Matthew Morley (org), Robert James (cnd), James St. Bride's Church Choir—Os justi; Locus iste; Libera me [in f, 1854]; Ave maria; Ecce sacerdos; Vexilla regis; Salvum fac populum tuum [1884]; Afferentur regi; Pange lingua; Tota pulchra es [Daniel Norman (tenor)]; Virga Jesse; Inveni David; Iam lucis orto sidere [Hymnus, 1868]; Tantum ergo [in D, 1988]; Christus factus est *(rec St. Bride's Church, Fleet Street, London, Jan. 27–29, 1994)* Naxos ▲ 8.550956 [DDD]

Willson, M. (shiva)
Shields, A.:Apocalypse, w. A. Shields (voc/kbd/syn—The Woman, the Seaweed & Chorus), J. Matus (elec gtr) CRI ▲ CD 647 [DDD]

Wilson, (fl)
Ravel, M.:Intro & Allegro, w. B. Allen (hp), D. Shifrin (cl), Tokyo String Quartet EMI Classics ▲ CDC 47520

Wilson, A. (cl)
McLeod, J.:The Dramatic Landscape, w. C. Rundell (cnd), Royal Northern College of Music Wind Orch Vienna Modern Masters ▲ VMM 3026 [DDD]

Wilson, Anna (fl)
Ward, R.:Serenade for Mallarmé, w. Jonathan Bagg (va), Fred Raimi (vc), Jane Hawkins (pno) Albany ▲ TROY 204 [DDD]

Wilson, C. (lt/Renaissance gtr/baroque gtr)—see ORCHESTRAS & ENSEMBLES Kithara

Wilson, Catherine (pno)—see also ORCHESTRAS & ENSEMBLES Catherine Wilson Trio
Catherine Wilson & Friends:Classical Potpourri, Mark Skazinetsky (vn), Norman Hathaway (va), Jack Mendelsohn (vc), Joel Quarrington (db) Doremi ▲ DHR 71111
Duets:Ofra Harnoy & Friends, w. Ofra Harnoy (vc), Michael Dussek (pno), Orford String Quartet, Maureen Forrester (cta), Andrew Davis (pno), Jeanne Baxtresser (fl), Paul Brodie (sax), Shauna Rolston (vc), Armin Strings, Canadian Piano Trio, Adele Armin (vn) Mastersound ▲ MST 30 [DDD]
Salut d'Amour, w. Ofra Harnoy (vc), Helena Bowkun (pno), Michael Dussek (pno) RCA Red Seal ▲ 60697–2–RC [AAD/DDD]

Wilson, Christopher (lt)
Byrd, W.:Songs, w. Michael Chance (ct), Fretwork—If women could be fair; Lullaby, my sweet little baby; Ah silly soul; Ye sacred muses Virgin Classics ▲ 59586 [DDD]
Crema, G.M. da:Lt Music—Ricercar tredecimo; Ricercar duodecimo; Saltarello ditto Bel flor; Saltarello ditto El Giorgio; Saltarello ditto El Maton; Con lacrime e sospiri; Lasciar il velo; Ricercar sexto; Ricercar quinto; De vous servir; Ricercar decimoquarto; O felici occhi miei; Pass'e mezo ala bolognesa; Saltarello ala bolognesa; Ricercar decimoquinto *(rec Sommerset, England, Feb 1994)* Naxos ("Early Music" series) ▲ 8.550778 [DDD]
Dall'Aquila, M.:Lt Music—Ricercars Nos. 15, 16, 18, 19, 22, 24, 28, 33, 70 & 101; La traditora; Priambolo No. 71; Amy souffrez; Ricercar/Fants Nos. 7, 26 & 29; La cara cosa *(rec Sommerset, England, Feb 1994)* Naxos ("Early Music" series) ▲ 8.550778 [DDD]
Dowland, J.:The First Booke of Songs or Ayres, w. Paul Agnew (ten)—Awake sweet love thou art returnd; Goe crystall teares; If my complaints could passions move; Come again:sweet love doth now invite; Can she excuse my wrongs with vertues cloak?; Deare, if you change, ile never chuse again; All ye whom love or fortune hath betraid; Sleep wayward thoughts Metronome ▲ MET CD 1010 [DDD]
Dowland, J.:The First Booke of Songs or Ayres, w. R. Müller (ten) ASV ("Gaudeamus" series) ▲ CDGAU 135 [DDD]
Dowland, J.:Lachrimae, or Seaven Teares, w. Fretwork EMI Classics ▲ CDC 45005
Dowland, J.:The Second Booke of Songs or Ayres, w. Paul Agnew (ten)—Flow my teares fall from your springs; If fluds of teares could cleanse my follies past; Fine knacks for Ladies, cheape, choise, brave and new; I saw my Lady weepe; Tymes eldest sonne, old age the heire of ease; Then sit thee downe, & say thy Nunc demittis; When others sings Venite exultemus; Come ye heavie states of night; Shall I sue, shall I seeke for grace; Sorrow sorrow stay, lend true repentant teares Metronome ▲ MET CD 1010 [DDD]
Dowland, J.:Songs, w. Michael Chance (ct), Fretwork—Goe nightly cares, the enemy to rest; Lasso vita mia, mi fu morire Virgin Classics ▲ 59586 [DDD]
Music for Viols, w. Fretwork, P. Nicholson (kbd), M. Chance (alt) Virgin Classics ▲ CDZ 59691
Rosa Elizabeth Lute Music Virgin Classics ▲ CDC 59034
Vihuela Music of the Spanish Renaissance Virgin Classics ▲ CDC 59596

Wilson, Christopher (vih)
Milán, L. de:Maestro—Fants 3, 5, 7, 10, 18, 21, 26, 35; Pavana 5; Tiento 1 *(rec St. Andrew's Church, Toddington, Gloucestershire, Aug 7–9, 1995)* Naxos ▲ 8.553523 [DDD]
Narváez, L. de:Seis Libros—Fant del quinto tono; Fant del tercer tono; Fant del segundo tono; Cum sancto spiritu; Ya se asienta el Ramiro; Paseavase el rey Moro; Fant del primer tono; O gloriosa domina; Conde Claros *(rec St. Andrew's Church, Toddington, Gloucestershire, Aug 7–9, 1995)* Naxos ▲ 8.553523 [DDD]

Wilson, Christopher (vihs/lts/gtrs)
From a Spanish Palace Songbook:Music from the Time of Columbus, w. Philpot, Margaret (alt), Shirley Rumsey (vihs/lts/gtrs) Hyperion ▲ CDA 66454 [DDD]

Wilson, Glen (hpd)
Bach, J.S.:Partita Fl, BWV 1013, w. W. van Hauwe (rcr), W. Möller (vc), T. Satoh (lt)—in c *(rec 1988)* Channel Classics ▲ CCS 4492 [DDD]
Escher, R.:Chamber Music, w. Jacques Zoon (fl), Herman De Boer (cl), Bart Schneemann (ob), Zoltan Benyacs (va), Dmitri Ferschtman (vc)—includes Le Tombeau de Ravel; Trio for Strings; Trio for Cl, Va & Pno NM Classics ▲ NM 92026
Haydn, J.:Arianna a Naxos, w. Carolyn Watkinson (cta) [I] *(rec 6/90)* Virgin Classics ▲ 59033 [DDD]
Haydn, J.:Canzonettas, w. Carolyn Watkinson (cta)—Nos. 25, 27–32, 36, 41, 42 [E] *(rec June 1990)* Virgin Classics ▲ 59033 [DDD]
Platti, G.B.:Sons Fl, w. B. Böhm (trns fl), R. Zipperling (vc) CPO ▲ CPO 999021–2 [DDD]
Scarlatti, D.:Sons Kbd—14 sonatas Teldec ▲ 46419–2
Telemann, G.P.:Rcr Music (misc), w. W. van Hauwe (ob), W. Möller (vc), T. Satoh (lt)—Fantasies Nos. 1 & 8; Partita No. 5 in e; Son. d; Son. D; Trio Son. in B♭ *(rec 1988)* Channel Classics ▲ CCS 4492 [DDD]

Wilson, J. (hn)
Gottschalk, A.:Section for 4 Hns, w. T. Bacon (hn), N. Goodearl (hn), J. Graber (hn), R. Brown (timp) Summit ▲ DCD 135 [DDD]

Wilson, J. Eric (sop sax)—see ORCHESTRAS & ENSEMBLES Resounding Winds Saxophone Quartet

Wilson, James (vc)—see ORCHESTRAS & ENSEMBLES Shanghai String Quartet

Wilson, Jeanne (fl)
Wigglesworth, F.:Psalm 148, w. Kathy Fink (fl), Elizabeth Brown (fl), Kevin James (trbn), David Taylor (trbn), D. Schuler (cnd), Church of St. Luke in the Fields Choir CRI ▲ C 733 [DDD]

Wilson, K.-L. (pic)
Dun, T.:In Distance, w. G. Benet (pno), T. Dun (dr) *(rec June 4, 1992)* CRI ▲ CD 655 [DDD]

Wilson, Mescal (pno)
Szymanowski, K.:Sym 4, w. D. Burkh (cnd), Janáček PO Centaur ▲ CRC 2153

Wilson, Nancy (vn)
Jane's Hand:The Jane Austen Songbooks, w. Julianne Baird (sop), Elizabeth Henreckson-Farnum (sop), Lorie Gratis (mez), Daniel Pincus (ten), Philip Anderson (ten), Martil Dillon (ten), Peter Segal (bar gtr), Mary Jane Newman (pno/hpd), Anthony Newman (pno) Vox Classics ▲ VOX 7537 [DDD]

Wilson, Nanita (hn)
Shewan, S.:Magnificat, w. Erin Stedman (sop), Kimberly Higgins (alt), Robert Dingman (ten), Alexander Burgess (bar), Paul Shewan (tpt), Barbara Hull (tpt), Scott Emmons (trbn), Kirk Kettinger (tuba), Ann Musser Honeywell (org) Albany ▲ TROY 149 [DDD]
Shewan, S.:The Voice of the Lord in the Storm, w. Erin Stedman (sop), Kimberly Higgins (alt), Robert Dingman (ten), Alexander Burgess (bar), Paul Shewan (tpt), Barbara Hull (tpt), Scott Emmons (trbn), Kirk Kettinger (tuba), Ann Musser Honeywell (org) Albany ▲ TROY 149 [DDD]

Wilson, Ransom (fl)—see also ORCHESTRAS & ENSEMBLES Lincoln Center Chamber Music Society members
Corigliano, J.:Irish Folk Songs (3), w. R. White (ten) RCA Gold Seal ▲ 60395–2–RG [ADD]
Devienne, F.:Sinf concertante for 2 Fls, w. J.-P. Rampal (fl), C. Scimone (cnd), Venice Solisti *(rec 1976)* Erato ▲ 2292–45836–2 [ADD]
Flutes, w. Robison, Paula (fl), Carol Wincenc (fl) New World ▲ 80403–2 [DDD]
Nielsen, C.:Qnt Ww, w. A. Vogel (ob), D. Shifrin (cl), D. Jolley (hn), J. Feves (bn) *(rec July 1–4, 1992)* Delos ▲ DE 3136 [DDD]
Schwantner, J.:Black Anemones, w. B. Zeger (pno) New World ▲ 80403–2 [DDD]
Schwantner, J.:A Play of Shadows, w. A. Neale (cnd), New York CO Solisti New World ▲ 80403–2 [DDD]
Viotti, G.B.:Sym Concertante Fls, w. J.-P. Rampal (fl), C. Scimone (cnd), Venice Solisti *(rec 1976)* Erato ▲ 45836–2 [ADD]

Wilson, S. (vc)—see ORCHESTRAS & ENSEMBLES Alexander String Quartet

Wilson, Scott (hn)
Wagner, R.:Siegfried Idyll, w. T. Holowach (vn), M. Skazinetsky (vn), L. Toman (va), R. Laurie (vc), C. Elliott (db), S. Shulman (fl), T. Maloney (cl), J. Valdepenas (cl), J. Fetherston (cl), S. Mosher (bn), R. Cohen (hn), J. Cowell (tpt), G. Gould (cnd) *(rec July 27–29 & Sept. 8, 198)* Sony Classical ▲ SMK 52650 [ADD]

Wilson, Todd (org)
Bach, Joh. Christian:Sons & Duets Kbd 4-Hands, w. David Higgs (org)—No. 6 [National City Christian Church organs, Washington D.C.] *(rec Jan 11–13, 1995)* Delos ▲ DE 3175 [DDD]
Bonnet, J.:Vars de Concert Delos ▲ DE 3123 [DDD]

Wilson, Todd (org) (cont.)
Dello Joio, N.:Antiphonal Fant on a Theme of Vincenzo Albrici, w. T. Russell (cnd), Naples PO D'Note Classics ▲ DND 1002
Demessieux, J.:Chorale Preludes (12) on Gregorian Themes—3 selections—Adeste fideles; Attende Domine; Rorarte coeli Delos ▲ DE 3123 [DDD]
Dupré, M.:Org Music—Cortège et Litanie, Op. 19/2 Delos ▲ DE 3123 [DDD]
Duruflé, M.:Org Music (comp) [Schudi organ, St. Thomas Aquinas, Dallas, Texas]—Scherzo, Op. 2; Prélude, adagio et choral varié sur le "Veni Creator," Op. 4; Suite, Op. 5; Prélude et fugue sur le nom d'Alain, Op. 7; Prelude on the Introit of the Epiphany; Fugue on the Theme of the Carillon of Hours of the Cathedral of Soissons Delos ▲ DCD 3047
Hampton, C.:Alexander Vars, w. David Higgs (org) [National City Christian Church Orgs, Washington D.C.] *(rec Jan 11–13, 1995)* Delos ▲ DE 3175 [DDD]
In a Quiet Cathedral *(rec Mar. 29–31, 1993)* Delos 2-▲ DE 3145 [DDD]
Ives, C.:Vars on *America* D'Note Classics ▲ DND 1002
Jongen, J.:Son heroïca Delos ▲ DE 3123 [DDD]
Langlais, J.:Thème & Vars Delos ▲ DE 3123 [DDD]
Mozart, W.A.:Adagio & Allegro Mechanical Org, w. David Higgs (org) [National City Christian Church Orgs, Washington D.C.] *(rec Jan 11–13, 1995)* Delos ▲ DE 3175 [DDD]
Mozart, W.A.:Adagio & Fugue Strs, w. David Higgs (org)—Adagio [trans David Fuller for 2 orgs; National City Christian Church organs, Washington D.C.] *(rec Jan 11–13, 1995)* Delos ▲ DE 3175 [DDD]
Plays Virtuoso French Organ Music Delos ▲ DE 3123 [DDD]
Saint-Saëns, C.:Danse macabre, w. David Higgs (org) [trans C. Dikinson & C. Mathewson Lockwood for 2 orgs; National City Christian Church organs, Washington D.C.] *(rec Jan 11–13, 1995)* Delos ▲ DE 3175 [DDD]
Wagner, R.:Die Walküre (ride of the valkyries), w. David Higgs (org) [trans C. Dikinson & C. Mathewson Lockwood for 2 orgs; National City Christian Church organs, Washington D.C.] *(rec Jan 11–13, 1995)* Delos ▲ DE 3175 [DDD]
Widor, C.M.:Sym 10 Org Delos ▲ DE 3123 [DDD]

Wiltschinsky, Peter (gtr)—see ORCHESTRAS & ENSEMBLES Hill/Wiltschinsky Guitar Duo

Wiman, Federico (pno)
Clementi, M.:Pno Music (comp), w. Aldo Antognazzi (pno), Christian Badian (pno), Jose Maria Brusco (pno), Daniela Lanzillo (pno), J. Rotter (cnd), Württemberg PO—Con in C for Pno; Sons (6) for Pno, Op. 1, Nos. 1–3; "Son inedita" in A♭ Aura Classics ▲ AU 32070

Wimmer, Thomas (va da gamba)
Vivaldi, A.:Sons Vn, w. Marco Ambrosini (va d'amore), Riccardo Delfino (va da rota)—RV.23, 53 & 58 Preiser ▲ PRE 90276
Vivaldi, A.:Sons for 2 Vns, Op. 1, w. Marco Ambrosini (va d'amore), Riccardo Delfino (va da rota)—No. 12 [La Follia] Preiser ▲ PRE 90276

Wimunc-Pearson, B. (pno)
Gubaidulina, S.:Sounds of the Forest, w. T. Lane (fl) Zuma Records ▲ ZMA 104
Ives, C.:Son 3 Vn, w. T. Lane (fl) [trans. Lane] Zuma Records ▲ ZMA 104
Nielsen, C.:Children Are Playing, w. T. Lane (fl) Zuma Records ▲ ZMA 104
Nielsen, C.:Fog Is Lifting, w. T. Lane (fl) Zuma Records ▲ ZMA 104

Winant, William (perc)—see also ORCHESTRAS & ENSEMBLES San Francisco Contemporary Music Players
Braxton, A.:Composition 107 (sels), w. A. Braxton (saxes), D. Rosenboom (pno) Centaur ▲ CRC 2110 [DDD]
Brown, C.:Lava, w. Toyoji Tomita (trbn), Tom Dill (tpt), Peter Wahrhaftig (tuba), Chris Brown (elecs)—Crack; Eruption; Fountain; River; Crest; Pahoehoe Tzadik ("The Composers" series) ▲ TZA 7002 [DDD]
Cage, J.:Four [6], w. Joan La Barbara (sop/perc), John Cage (voice/perc), Leonard Stein (pno/perc) *(rec Central Park Summerstage, New York City, July 23, 1992)* Music & Arts ▲ CD 875 [DDD]
Cage, J.:Music for..., w. Joan La Barbara (sop), Leonard Stein (pno) *(rec Central Park Summerstage, New York City, July 23, 1992)* Music & Arts ▲ CD 875 [DDD]
Cage, J.:Songs, w. J. La Barbara (sop), L. Stein (pno)—A Flower (1950); Mirakus (1984); Eight Whiskus (1984); The Wonderful Widow of Eighteen Springs (1942); Nowth upon Nacht (1984); Sonnekus (1985); Forever and Sunsmell (1942); Solos for Voice [from Songbooks] Nos. 49, 52 & 67 (1970); Music for Two (by One) (1984) New Albion ▲ NA 035 [DDD]
Curran, A.:Schtyx, w. D. Abel (vn/hi-hat/dog whistle), J. Steinberg (pno/prepared pno/hmc/bass dr/vn/dog whistle) CRI ▲ CD 668 [DDD]
Curran, A.:Why Is This Night Different Than All Other Nights?, w. Roy Malan (vn), Donald Haas (acc), Peter Wahrhaftig (tuba), Alvin Curran (pno) Tzadik ("The Composers" series) ▲ TZA 7001 [DDD]
Dresher, P.:Double Ikat, w. D. Abel (vn), J. Steinberg (pno) *(rec 1992)* New Albion ▲ NA 053
Feldman, Morton:Rothko Chapel, w. D. Dietrich (sop), D. Abel (vn), K. Rosenak (pno), Philip Brett (cnd), Univ of California at Berkeley Chamber Chorus *(rec 10/90)* New Albion ▲ NA 039 [DDD]
Harrison, L.:Ariadne, w. L. Miller (ocarina) MusicMasters ▲ 7051-2-C [DDD]
Harrison, L.:Canticle 3, w. L. Miller (ocarina), R. Strizich (gtr), D.R. Davies (cnd) MusicMasters ▲ 7051-2-C [DDD]
Harrison, L.:Fugue Perc, w. Dan Kennedy (perc), D. Rosenthal (perc), T. Manley (perc) New Albion ▲ NA 055
Harrison, L.:May Rain, w. John Duykers (ten), Julie Steinberg (pno) New Albion ▲ NA 055
Harrison, L.:Serenade Gtr, w. David Tanenbaum (gtr) New Albion ▲ NA 055
Harrison, L.:Song of Quetzalcoatl, w. Dan Kennedy (perc), D. Rosenthal (perc), T. Manley (perc) New Albion ▲ NA 055
Hovhaness, A.:Invocations to Vahakn, w. J. Steinberg (pno) New Albion ▲ NA 036 [DDD]
Lewis, P.S.:Journey to Still Water Pond, w. Alexander String Quartet New Albion ▲ NA 060 [DDD]
Riley, T.:In C, w. Bruce Ackley, Steve Adams, Don R. Baker, Chris Brown, George Brooks, Steve Coughlin, Blake Derby, Bill Douglass, Mihr'un'Nisa Douglass, Hank Dutt, David Harrington, Don Howe, Joan Jeanrenaud, Alden Jenks, Warner Jepson, Henry Kaiser, Jaron Lanier, Bill Maginnis, George Marsh, Shabda Owens, Jon Raskin, Gyan Riley, Terry Riley, Gino Robair, John Sackett, Ramón Sender, John Sherba, Toyji Tomita, Danny Tunick, Evan Ziporyn *(rec Jan. 14, 1990)* New Albion ▲ NA 071
Rosenboom, D.:A Precipice in Time, w. D. Rosenboom (elec), A. Braxton (sax), et al. Centaur ▲ CRC 2110 [DDD]
Zorn, J.:Elegy, w. Mike Patton (sgr), Barbara Chaffe (fl), David Abel (vn), Scummy (gtr), David Shea (turntables), David Slusser (sound effects) Tzadik ▲ TZA 7302 [ADD]
Zorn, J.:Kristallnacht, w. David Krakauer (cl/b cl), Frank London (tpt), Mark Feldman (vn), Marc Ribot (gtr), Mark Dresser (electric bass), Anthony Coleman (kbd) Tzadik ▲ TZA 7301 [ADD]

Wincenc, Carol (fl)
Bach, J.S.:Suite 1 Orch, w. H. Rilling (cnd), Oregon Bach Festival CO Hänssler Classic ▲ HAN 98984 [DDD]
Flute Music of Barber, Copland, Cowell, Del Tredici, Foss, Griffes Elektra/Nonesuch ▲ 79114-2
Flutes, w. Paula Robison (fl), Ransom Wilson (fl) New World ▲ 80403-2 [DDD]
Foss, L.:Renaissance Con, w. L. Foss (cnd), Brooklyn PO New World ▲ NW 375-2 [DDD]
Mozart, W.A.:Qts Fl, w. Emerson String Quartet members Deutsche Grammophon ▲ 431770-2 [DDD]
Mozart, W.A.:Rondo Fl Str Trio, w. Emerson String Quartet members Deutsche Grammophon ▲ 431770-2 [DDD]
Ravel, M.:Intro & Allegro, w. V. McKeand (hp), D. Campbell (cl), Allegri String Quartet Virgin Classics ▲ CDZ 59695
Ravel, M.:Le Tombeau de Couperin, w. V. McKeand (hp), D. Campbell (cl), Allegri String Quartet Virgin Classics ▲ CDZ 59695
Rochberg, G.:Slow Fires of Autumn, w. Allen (hp) CRI ■ ACS 6013
Schoenfield, P.:Achat Sha'alti, w. P. Schoenfield (pno) New World ▲ 80403-2 [DDD]
Schoenfield, P.:Klezmer Rondos, w. D. Webster (bar), A. Neale (cnd), New York CO Solisti New World ▲ 80403-2 [DDD]
Schoenfield, P.:Ufaratsta, w. P. Schoenfield (pno) New World ▲ 80403-2 [DDD]
Tower, J.:Snow Dreams, w. Sharon Isbin (gtr) *(rec American Academy of Arts & Letters, New York City, Sept. 26–28, 1994)* New World ▲ 80470-2

Wingreen, Harriet (pno)
Crawford, R.:Songs (5), w. L. Field (sop) [E] *(rec 1987)* Cambria ▲ CD 1037 [DDD]
Flowering of Vocal Music in America, 1767–1823, w. Susan Belling (sop), Cynthia Clarey (sop), Barbara Wallace (sop), Debra Vanderlinde (sop), D'Anna Fortunato (mez), Evelyn Petros (mez), Charles Bressler (ten), Richard Anderson (bar), James Tyeska (bar), Joseph McKee (bass), Cynthia Otis (hp), Leonard Rav New World ▲ 80467-2
Gideon, M.:Morning Songs (4) of Childhood on Hebrew Texts, w. L. Field (sop) [He] *(rec 1987)* Cambria ▲ CD 1037 [DDD]
In Recital, Vol. 2, w. Julius Baker (fl) *(rec live 1983)* VAI Audio ▲ VAIA 1033
Price, F.B.:Songs, w. L. Field (sop)—Travel's End; To My Little Son; Night; To the Dark Virgin [E] *(rec 1987)* Cambria ▲ CD 1037 [DDD]
Riegger, W.:Con Pno, w. New Art Wind Quintet CRI ▲ CD 572 [ADD]
Rogers, P.:Sonja, w. L. Field (sop)—5 songs [E] *(rec 1987)* Cambria ▲ CD 1037 [DDD]
Van De Vate, N.:Songs for the 4 Parts of the Night, w. L. Field (sop) [E] *(rec 1987)* Cambria ▲ CD 1037 [DDD]

Winhardt, Peter (pno)
Brahms, J.:Songs, w. Eckart Runge (vc)—Liebestreu [arr E. Runge for cello & piano] *(rec July 10–11 & Nov 14–15)* Ars Musici ▲ AMP 5061-2 [DDD]
Debussy, C.:Son Vc, w. Eckart Runge (vc) *(rec July 10–11 & Nov 14–15)* Ars Musici ▲ AMP 5061-2 [DDD]
Fauré, G.:Papillon, w. Eckart Runge (vc) *(rec July 10–11 & Nov 14–15)* Ars Musici ▲ AMP 5061-2 [DDD]
Messiaen, O.:Quatour, w. Eckart Runge (vc) [5th movt, "The Glorification of Jesus' Eternity"] *(rec July 10–11 & Nov 14–15)* Ars Musici ▲ AMP 5061-2 [DDD]
Schumann, R.:Fantasiestücke Cl, w. Eckart Runge (vc) *(rec July 10–11 & Nov 14–15)* Ars Musici ▲ AMP 5061-2 [DDD]
Strauss, R.:Son Vc, w. Eckart Runge (vc) *(rec July 10–11 & Nov 14–15)* Ars Musici ▲ AMP 5061-2 [DDD]

Winiarczyk, S. (ob)
Caprioli, A.:Serenata per Francesca, w. V. Fuchsberger (sgr), G. Schneider (vn), A. Aigmüller (dr), R. Crow (instr), R. Huber (instr), K. Ager (cnd), Austrian Ensemble for New Music *(rec 1987)* Pro Viva ▲ ISPV 148 CD [ADD]
Mozart, W.A.:Cassation, K.63, w. G. Hölscher (ob), R. Schnepps (hn), H. Nerat (hn), Salzburg CO *(rec March 28–30, 1992)* Naxos ▲ 8.550609 [DDD]
Mozart, W.A.:Cassation, K.99/63a, w. G. Hölscher (ob), R. Schnepps (hn), H. Nerat (hn), Salzburg CO *(rec March 28–30, 1992)* Naxos ▲ 8.550609 [DDD]
Mozart, W.A.:Cassation, K.100/62a, w. G. Hölscher (ob), R. Schnepps (hn), H. Nerat (hn), Salzburg CO *(rec March 28–30, 1992)* Naxos ▲ 8.550609 [DDD]

Winiger, Daniel (org)
Ave Maria, w. Zurich Boys' Choir, [cnd:Alphons von Aarburg], Daniel Perret (trb), Frieder Lang (ten), Alain Clément (bass), Praxedis Rütti (hp), Andrej Lütschg (vn) Tudor ▲ TUD 7029 [DDD]

Winkler, Michael-Christfried (org)
Das Orgelwerk Berlin Classics ▲ BER 1044 [DDD]
Saint-Saëns, C.:Oratorio de Noël, w. Ute Selbig (sop), Elisabeth Wilke (mez), Annette Markert (cta), Armin Ude (ten), Egbert Junghans (bar), Jutta Zoff (hp), M. Flämig (cnd), Dresden PO, Dresden Kreuz Choir *(rec Dresden, Mar & Apr 1987)* Capriccio ▲ 10216 [DDD]

Winn, James (pno)—see also ORCHESTRAS & ENSEMBLES New York New Music Ensemble members
Black, R.:Foramen habet! Bridge ▲ BCD 9061 [DDD]
A Jenny Lind Recital, w. Elizabeth Parcells (sop) Northeastern ("Classical Arts" series) ▲ NOR 237 ■ NR 237-C
Wuorinen, C.:Double Solo, w. W. Purvis (hn), B. Hudson (vn) *(rec Oct. 17, 1991)* Koch International Classics ▲ KIC 7123-2 [DDD]
Wuorinen, C.:Fortune, w. A. R. Kay (cl), C. Macomber (vn), F. Sherry (vc) Koch International Classics ▲ KIC 7242-2 [DDD]
Wuorinen, C.:Tashi, w. J. Kopperud (cl), C. Macomber (vn), F. Sherry (vc) Koch International Classics ▲ KIC 7242-2 [DDD]
Wuorinen, C.:Trio Hn Continued, w. W. Purvis (hn), B. Hudson (vn) *(rec Sept. 11–13, 1991)* Koch International Classics ▲ KIC 7123-2 [DDD]
Wuorinen, C.:Trio Vn, w. R. Schulte (vn), F. Sherry (vc) *(rec Sept. 11–13, 1991)* Koch International Classics ▲ KIC 7123-2 [DDD]

Winne, Jan de (fl)
Haydn, J.:Trios Pno, Fl & Vc, w. Guy Penson (hpd), Roel Dieltiens (vc) Eufoda ▲ EUF 1185 [DDD]

Winograd, Peter (vn)—see ORCHESTRAS & ENSEMBLES American String Quartet

Winokur, Ken (perc)
Field, K.:Music of, w. Ken Field (sax/perc/syn/fl), Karen Aqua (perc), Mike Rivard (elec bass), John Fleagle (voice), Karen Gruber (perc)—A Space in a Place; Om on the Range; Takuskanskan; 5 Saxophones in Search of Meaning; Sanity; Perpetual Motion; Thoughts Unspoken; Berrendo; Sympathetic Magic; The Missing Soul; When I Fall in Love *(rec The Henge, Roswell, NM, Wellspring Sound, Concord, MA, The Chicken Loft, Cambridge, MA & The Basement, Cambridge, MA, 1988–1995)* O.O. Discs ▲ OO 25

Winschermann, Helmut (ob)
Bach, J.S.:Con Ob, BWV 1053, w. H. Winschermann (cnd), German Bach Soloists *(rec Münster zu Heilsbronn, 1965)* Musicaphon ▲ 51351 [AAD]
Bach, J.S.:Con Vn & Ob, w. Georg Friedrich Hendel (vn), H. Winschermann (cnd), German Bach Soloists Musicaphon ▲ 51357 [AAD]
Mozart, W.A.:Complete Mozart Edition, w. Daniel Chorzempa (org), German Bach Soloists Philips 2-▲ 422521-2 [ADD]
Telemann, G.P.:Kleine Kammermusik, w. Hans-Martin Linde (fl), Ferdinand Conrad (rcr), Susanne Lautenbacher (vn), Johannes Koch (vl), Hugo Ruf (hpd) *(rec Südwest-Tonstudio H. Jansen, Stuttgart, Jan. 1966)* Musicaphon ▲ 51539 [ADD]

Winsløv, Svend (vc)—see also ORCHESTRAS & ENSEMBLES Danish Trio
Bentzon, N.V.:Qt Cl, w. John Kruse (cl), Bjarbe Hansen (vn), Rastko Roknic (va) *(rec Det Fynske Musikkonservatorium, 1993)* Paula ▲ PACD 78 [DAD]
Olsen, P.R.:Concertino Cl, w. Jens Schou (cl), Peder Elbaek (vn), Verner Skovlund (va), Rosalind Bevan (pno) *(rec PAULA's Recording Hall, 1984)* Paula ▲ PACD 36 [AAD]
Olsen, P.R.:Qt 2 Strs, w. Peder Elbaek (vn), Jørgen Larsen (vn), Verner Skovlund (va) *(rec PAULA's Recording Hall, 1984)* Paula ▲ PACD 36 [AAD]
Olsen, P.R.:Trio II Pno, w. Peder Elbaek (vn), Rosalind Bevan (pno) *(rec PAULA's Recording Hall, 1984)* Paula ▲ PACD 36 [AAD]

Winstin, Robert Ian (pno)
Piano Art *(rec Aug. 18–21 1993)* E.R.M. ▲ ERM 6661 [DDD]
Winstin Sampler:A Fabulous Collection from 3 Albums E.R.M. ▲ CCC 111 [ADD]
Winstin, R.I.:Con 1 Pno, w. Virtual Orch E.R.M. ▲ CCC 6660 [DDD]
Winstin, R.I.:Episodes, w. A. L. Glise (gtr) E.R.M. ▲ CCC 6659 [DDD]
Winstin, R.I.:Music of, w. Virtual Orch—In Memoria:J.S. Bach; Nursery Rhymes E.R.M. ▲ CCC 6660 [DDD]
Winstin, R.I.:Pno Music—Three Pieces for Piano; Piano Attacks E.R.M. ▲ CCC 6659 [DDD]
Winstin, R.I.:Sym 4, w. Virtual Orch E.R.M. ▲ CCC 6660 [DDD]

Winter, (org)
Bach, J.S.:Toccata & Fugue Org, BWV 538, "Dorian" PMG ("Vienna Master" series) ▲ CD 160117 [DDD]

Winter, Geoffrey (hn)—see ORCHESTRAS & ENSEMBLES American Horn Quartet

Winter, Helmut (org)
Bach, J.S.:Fant Org, BWV 572 PMG ("Vienna Master" series) ▲ CD 160117 [DDD]

Winter, John (ob)
Lazarof, H.:Trio Wind Instruments, w. S. Stokes (fl), G. Gray (cl) Laurel ▲ LR 845CD [AAD]

▲ = CD ♦ = Enhanced CD △ = MD ■ = Cassette Tape □ = DCC

Winter, O. (org)
Bach, J.S.:Chorale Preludes Org—BWV 653, 659, 664 PMG ("Vienna Master" series) ▲ CD 160117 [DDD]
Bach, J.S.:Preludes & Fugues, BWV 531–552—BWV 547 PMG ("Vienna Master" series) ▲ CD 160117 [DDD]
Bach, J.S.:Trio Sons Org, BWV 525–530—BWV 528 PMG ("Vienna Master" series) ▲ CD 160117 [DDD]

Winter, Otto (ob)
Baur, J.:Con romano, w. H.–M. Schneidt (cnd), Bamberg SO Thorofon ▲ CTH 2270

Winterbottom, S. (va)
Baksa, R.:Qnt Ob & Strs, w. B. Lucarelli (ob), N. Tanaka (vn), M. Yanagita (vn), T. Hoyle (vc) Capstone ▲ CPS 8610

Winter-Jones, Kristin (fl)
Gibson, R.:Calling Capstone ▲ CPS 8621

Winther, Elena (pno)
Milhaud, D.:Le Bal martiniquais, w. V. Pleshakov (pno) Sonpact ▲ SPT 92004 [DDD]
Milhaud, D.:Concertino d'automne, w. V. Pleshakov (pno), A. de Almeida (cnd), Ensemble Sonpact ▲ SPT 92004 [DDD]
Milhaud, D.:Fant pastorale, w. V. Pleshakov (pno) [two-piano arr.] Sonpact ▲ SPT 92004 [DDD]
Milhaud, D.:Scaramouche for 2 Pnos, w. V. Pleshakov (pno) Sonpact ▲ SPT 92004 [DDD]
Milhaud, D.:Les Songes, Op. 237, w. V. Pleshakov (pno) Sonpact ▲ SPT 92004 [DDD]
Milhaud, D.:Suite for 2 Pnos, w. V. Pleshakov (pno), A. de Almeida (cnd), Ensemble Sonpact ▲ SPT 92004 [DDD]

Winunguj, George (didjeridu)
Dreyfus, G.:Sextet, w. Adelaide Wind Quintet Southern Cross ▲ SCCD 1024 [AAD]

Wion, John (fl)
Cordero, R.:Qnt Fl, w. Arthur Bloom (cl), Kees Kooper (vn), Fred Sherry (vc), Mary Louise Boehm (pno) Albany ▲ TROY 153 [DDD]

Wirssaladze, Elisso (pno)
Beethoven, L. van:Son 3 Vc, w. Natalia Gutman (vc) *(rec Schliersee, July 9, 1992)* Live Classics ▲ LCL 622 [DDD]
Beethoven, L. van:Trio 7 Pno, w. Eduard Brunner (cl), Natalia Gutman (vc) *(rec Wildbad Kreuth, July 3, 1992)* Live Classics ▲ LCL 622 [DDD]
Brahms, J.:Pieces Pno, Op. 119 *(rec Liederhalle Stuttgart, Apr. 15, 1991)* Live Classics ▲ LCL 321 [DDD]
Brahms, J.:Son 1 Vc, w. Natalia Gutman (vc) *(rec Kreuth Musikfest, July 9/16, 1992)* Live Classics ▲ 621
Brahms, J.:Son 1 Pno *(rec Wigmore Hall, London, Oct. 16, 1993)* Live Classics 2–▲ 341/2
Chopin, F.:Waltzes *(rec Liederhalle Stuttgart, Apr. 15, 1991)* Live Classics ▲ LCL 321 [DDD]
Grieg, E.:Son Vc, w. Natalia Gutman (vc) *(rec Kreuth Musikfest, July 9/16, 1992)* Live Classics ▲ 621
Liszt, F.:Études de concert (3) Pno *(rec Wigmore Hall, London, Oct. 16, 1993)* Live Classics 2–▲ 341/2
Liszt, F.:Mephisto Waltz 1 Orch *(rec Wigmore Hall, London, Oct. 16, 1993)* Live Classics 2–▲ 341/2
Liszt, F.:Transcriptions & Paraphrases—Der Erlkönig [Schubert] *(rec Wigmore Hall, London, Oct. 16, 1993)* Live Classics 2–▲ 341/2
Liszt, F.:Transcriptions & Paraphrases—Schumann:Widmung *(rec June 11, 1994)* Live Classics ▲ LCL 352 [DDD]
Mozart, W.A.:Fant Pno, K.475 *(rec Munich, Jan 15, 1995)* Live Classics ▲ LCL 351 [DDD]
Mozart, W.A.:Romance *(rec Liederhalle Stuttgart, Apr. 15, 1991)* Live Classics ▲ LCL 321 [DDD]
Mozart, W.A.:Son 14 Pno *(rec Munich, Jan 15, 1995)* Live Classics ▲ LCL 351 [DDD]
Mozart, W.A.:Vars Pno, K.264 *(rec Munich, Jan 15, 1995)* Live Classics ▲ LCL 351 [DDD]
Prokofiev, S.:Sarcasms *(rec Liederhalle Stuttgart, Apr. 15, 1991)* Live Classics ▲ LCL 321 [DDD]
Prokofiev, S.:Son 8 Pno *(rec Munich, Jan 15, 1995)* Live Classics ▲ LCL 351 [DDD]
Prokofiev, S.:Toccata Pno *(rec Liederhalle Stuttgart, Apr. 15, 1991)* Live Classics ▲ LCL 321 [DDD]
Schubert, Franz:Moments musicaux—No. 2 *(rec Wigmore Hall, London, Oct. 16, 1993)* Live Classics 2–▲ 341/2
Schubert, Franz:Son Pno, D.850 *(rec Wigmore Hall, London, Oct. 16, 1993)* Live Classics 2–▲ 341/2
Schumann, R.:Arabeske Pno *(rec Mar 4, 1995)* Live Classics ▲ LCL 352 [DDD]
Schumann, R.:Fant Pno *(rec June 11, 1994)* Live Classics ▲ LCL 352 [DDD]
Schumann, R.:Son 1 Pno *(rec June 11, 1994)* Live Classics ▲ LCL 352 [DDD]
Schumann, R.:Waldscenen—Der Vogel als Prophet [The Bird as Prophet] *(rec Liederhalle Stuttgart, Apr. 15, 1991)* Live Classics ▲ LCL 321 [DDD]

Wirtz, Tiny (pno)
Reicha, A.:Fugues CPO 2–▲ CPO 999065–2 [DDD]
Zimmermann, B.A.:Capriccio Pno Koch Schwann ▲ SCH 314462 [DDD]
Zimmermann, B.A.:Enchiridion Koch Schwann ▲ SCH 314462 [DDD]
Zimmermann, B.A.:Extemporale Koch Schwann ▲ SCH 314462 [DDD]
Zimmermann, B.A.:Konfigurationen Koch Schwann ▲ SCH 314462 [DDD]
Zimmermann, B.A.:Unpublished Pieces Koch Schwann ▲ SCH 314462 [DDD]

Wiseman, Sarah (vc)—see ORCHESTRAS & ENSEMBLES Illinois Performers' Workshop Ensemble

Wishart, Stevie (vn/elecs/h-g/sgr)—see ORCHESTRAS & ENSEMBLES Machine for Making Sense

Wisniewska, Karina (pno)
Brahms, J.:Son 1 Cl, w. Wilfried Strehle (va) Nimbus ▲ NI 5473 [DDD]
Dvořák, A.:Sonatina Vn, w. Wilfried Strehle (va) [arr for viola Lipka & Hallman] Nimbus ▲ NI 5473 [DDD]
Hindemith, P.:Son Va & Pno, Op. 11/4, w. Wilfried Strehle (va) Nimbus ▲ NI 5473 [DDD]
Hindemith, P.:Trauermusik, w. Wilfried Strehle (va) [arr for viola & piano] Nimbus ▲ NI 5473 [DDD]

Wispelwey, Pieter (vc)
Bach, J.S.:Suites Vc, BWV 1007–1012 Channel Classics 2–▲ CCS 1090 [DDD]
Brahms, J.:Sons Vc (comp), w. P. Komen (pno) *(rec Sept. 1992)* Channel Classics ▲ CCS 5493 [DDD]
Crumb, G.:Son Vc Globe ▲ GLO 5089 [DDD]
Escher, R.:Son Vc Globe ▲ GLO 5089 [DDD]
Kodály, Z.:Son Vc, Op. 8 Globe ▲ GLO 5089 [DDD]
Reger, M.:Caprice & Kleine Romanze, w. Paolo Giacometti (pno) Channel Classics ▲ CCS 9596
Reger, M.:Suites Vc Channel Classics ▲ CCS 9596
Reger, M.:Suite Vn Pno, w. Paolo Giacometti (pno)—3rd movt. Channel Classics ▲ CCS 9596
Reger, M.:Wiegenlied, Capriccio & Burla, w. Paolo Giacometti (pno)—Wiegenlied Channel Classics ▲ CCS 9596
Schubert, Franz:Son Arpeggione, w. Paolo Giacometti (pno) Channel Classics ▲ CCS 9696
Schubert, Franz:Sonatinas Vn, w. Paolo Giacometti (pno) [trans P. Wispelwey for vc & pno] Channel Classics ▲ CCS 9696
Smit, L.:Concertino Vc, w. E. Spanjaard (cnd), Netherlands Radio CO NM Classics ▲ NM 92040
Styles, w. Paul Komen (pno), Lois Shapiro (pno), Florilegium Channel Classics ▲ CCS 395

Wissick, Brent (vl)
Dance Songs of Renaissance England, w. Folger Consort, M. Bleeke, T. Chancey, W. Gillespie, M. Springfels *(rec Jan. 24, 1988)* Folger Consort ▲ BDCD1 9004 [DDD]

Wissick, Brent (vl/baroque vc)
Purcell, H.:Songs, w. S. Sanford (sop), R. Erickson (hpd/org)—Tis Nature's Voice; Strike the Viol; Ye Gentle Spirits; Round O'; From Rosy Bowers; Hornpipe; Let Us Dance; Hard, the Echoing Air; Ah, How Sweet It Is Albany ▲ TROY 127

Wisskirchen, Paul (org)
Eben, Petr:Con 2 Org, "Symphonia gregoriana", w. V. Hempfling (cnd), Halle Handel Festival Orch Motette ▲ CD 40151 [DDD]
Peeters, F.:Con Org Orch, w. Cologne Youth Orch Motette ▲ MOT CD 40161 [DDD]

Wit, Jolle de (fl)
Van Baaren, K.:Septet Vn, w. J. Walta (vn), F. Minderaa (ob), et al. Olympia ▲ OCD 505 [AAD]

Witoszinskyj, Leo (gtr)
Music for Lute, Guitar & Mandolin, w. Ragossnig, Konrad (gtr), Anton Stingl (lt), Michael Schäffer (lt), Karl Scheit (gtr), William Matthews (gtr), Paul Grund (mand), Artur Rumetsch (mand), Edith Bauer-Slais (mand), Elfriede Kunschak (mand) Vox Box 3–▲ CD3X 3022

Witsenburg, Edward (hp)
Riotte, J.P.:Notturno, w. E. Sebestyen (vn) Koch Schwann ▲ SCH 313392 [ADD/DDD]

Witten, David (pno)
Ponce, M.:Pno Music—Prelude & Fugue on a theme of Handel; Full Moon; 4 Mexican Dances; Intermezzo; Intro, Prelude & Fugue on a theme of J.S. Bach; In Spite of Everything [Dance for the Left Hand Alone]; Scherzino Mexicano; Prelude & Fugue for the Left Hand Alone; 2 Concert Etudes; Notturno; Mexican Ballade *(rec Paine Hall, Harvard Univ, Cambridge, MA, Jan 1994 & Jan 1995)* Marco Polo ("Latin-American Classics" series) ▲ 8.223609 [DDD]

Wittenberg, Jan (vn)—see ORCHESTRAS & ENSEMBLES Gaudeamus String Quartet

Wittgenstein, Paul (pno)
Ravel, M.:Con Pno (left hand), *(cnd & orch unknown)* Memories 2–▲ MEM CD 3009

Witthoeft, Cornelius (pno)
Scheidel-Austin, E.:Sonnets from the Portuguese, w. Melinda Liebermann (sop) Capstone ▲ CPS 8618

Wittig, William (fl)
Songs of the Nightingale, w. Emerson, Karen Smith (sop), Martin Katz (pno) *(rec Sweeney Concert Hall, Sage Hall, Smith College, Northampton, MA, Jan 3–5, 1994)* Centaur ▲ 2232 [DDD]

Wittmann, Andreas (ob)—see ORCHESTRAS & ENSEMBLES Berlin Philharmonic Wind Ensemble, Berlin Philharmonic Wind Quintet

Witt Smith, Susan de (pno)
Alexa Still "Flute", w. Alexa Still (fl) Koch International Classics ▲ KIC 7144 [DDD]
Barber, S.:Canzone Fl & Pno, w. A. Still (fl) Koch International Classics ▲ KIC 7144 [DDD]
Bloch, E.:Con grosso 1, w. D. Barra (cnd), San Diego CO Koch International Classics ▲ KIC 7196 [DDD]
Burton, E.:Sonatina Fl, w. A. Still (fl) Koch International Classics ▲ KIC 7144 [DDD]
Copland, A.:Duo Fl, w. A. Still (fl) Koch International Classics ▲ KIC 7144 [DDD]
Copland, A.:Vocalise, w. A. Still (fl) Koch International Classics ▲ KIC 7144 [DDD]
Songs of War & Peace, w. Leoni Men's Chorus,Diane Loomer (cnd), Christopher Gaze (nar), Philip Crewe (perc), Salvador Ferreras (perc) Skylark ▲ 9501 [DDD]
Still, W.G.:Folk Suites, w. A. Still (fl), M. Steer (db), New Zealand String Quartet—No. 1 Koch International Classics ▲ KIC 7192 [DDD]
Still, W.G.:Instrumental Music, w. A. Still (fl)—Quit Dat Fool'nish; Summerland Koch International Classics ▲ KIC 7154
Still, W.G.:Instrumental Music, w. A. Still (fl), M. Steer (db), New Zealand String Quartet—Quit Dat Fool'nish; Summerland Koch International Classics ▲ KIC 7192 [DDD]
Still, W.G.:Music of, w. A. Still (fl), M. Steer (db), New Zealand String Quartet—Summerland; Quit dat Fool'nish; Pastorela; Folk Suite 1; Suite for Violin & Piano [Movts. I & II]; Prelude for Flute, String Qnt. & Piano *(rec May 1993)* Koch International Classics ▲ KIC 7192 [DDD]
Still, W.G.:Pastorela, w. M. Steer (db) Koch International Classics ▲ KIC 7192 [DDD]
Still, W.G.:Preludes Fl, w. A. Still (fl), M. Steer (db), New Zealand String Quartet Koch International Classics ▲ KIC 7192 [DDD]
Still, W.G.:Suite Vn, w. M. Steer (db), New Zealand String Quartet Koch International Classics ▲ KIC 7192 [DDD]

Wizansky, J. (pno)
Lees, B.:Son 1 Vn, w. E. Orner (vn) Albany ▲ TROY 138 [DDD]
Lees, B.:Son 2 Vn, w. E. Orner (vn) Albany ▲ TROY 138 [DDD]
Lees, B.:Son 3 Vn, w. E. Orner (vn) Albany ▲ TROY 138 [DDD]

Wjuniski, Ilton (hpd)
Bach, C.P.E.:Sons Fl, w. M. Faust (fl)—in D, H.505 (W.83) *(rec May 1991)* GM ▲ GM 2037
Bach, J.C.F:Son Fl, HW.VIII/1–2, w. M. Faust (fl)—in d *(rec May 1991)* GM ▲ GM 2037
Bach, J.S.:Sons Fl, BWV 1030–35, w. M. Faust (fl)—BWV 1030–1032 *(rec May 1991)* GM ▲ GM2036
Bach, J.S.:Sons Vn, w. M. Faust (vn)—BWV 1020 [doubtful; trans. for flute & continuo] *(rec May 1991)* GM ▲ GM 2037
Bach, J.S.:Trio Son Fl, BWV 529, w. M. Faust (fl) *(rec May 1991)* GM ▲ GM2036
Mozart, W.A.:Sons Fl Hpd (misc), w. M. Faust (fl)—K.14, 57, 304 & 379 *(rec Oct. 6, 1991)* GM ▲ GM2038
Mozart, W.A.:Sons Fl Hpd (misc), w. M. Faust (fl)—in F, K.13 *(rec May 1991)* GM ▲ GM2037

Wlach, Leopold (cl)
Pfitzner, H.:Sxt Cl, w. A. Kamper (vn), E. Weis (va), F. Kvarda (vc), J. Hermann (db), W. Kamper (pno) Preiser ▲ 93111 (m) [AAD]

Wlosok, Pavel (pno)
Whitacre, E.:Ghost Train Triptych, w. James Riggs (sax), E. Corporon (cnd), North Texas College of Music Wind Sym Klavier ▲ KCD 11077 [DDD]

Wobisch, Helmut (tpt)
The Virtuoso Trumpet, w. Zagreb Soloists [cnd:Antonio Janigro] *(rec 1961)* Vanguard Classics ("The Bach Guild" series) ▲ OVC 2008 [ADD]

Wodnicki, Adam (pno)
Austin, L.:Sinf Concertante:A Mozartean Episode, w. T. Clark (cnd), *(orch unknown)* Centaur ▲ CRC 2029 [DDD]
Austin, L.:Son Concertante, w. T. Clark (cnd), *(orch unknown)* Centaur ▲ CRC 2029 [DDD]
Clark, T.:Peninsula Centaur ▲ CRC 2029 [DDD]
Schwantner, J.:And the Mountians Rising Nowhere, w. E. Corporon (cnd), North Texas College of Music Wind Sym Klavier ▲ KCD 11079 [DDD]
Subotnick, M.:Trembling, w. R. Davidovici (vn), J. La Barbara (recorded voc), L. Austin ("Ghost" elec) *(rec Dec. 1992)* Centaur ▲ CRC 2170 [DDD]
Winsor, P.:Dulcimer Dream, w. A. Wodnicki (pno) Centaur ▲ CRC 2029 [DDD]

Wohlfahrt, Sebastian (va)—see ORCHESTRAS & ENSEMBLES Sikorsi String Quartet

Wohlmacher, J. (vc)
Volkmann, R.:Con Vc, w. W. A. Albert (cnd), Northwest German PO CPO 2–▲ CPO 999151 [DDD]

Wohlmacher, William (cl)
Barati, G.:Trio Cl, w. Stacy Phelps-Wetzel (vn), Lawrence Granger (vc) *(rec Emeryville Recording Company, Emeryville, CA, 1994)* Centaur ▲ CRC 2286 [DDD]

Woitach, Richard (pno)
Dvořák, A.:Zigeunermelodien, Op. 55, w. Jon Vickers (ten)—My Song Resounds, My Song of Love; Yon Lies the Moon, So Far, So Still; Dark in Flowing Linen; Soaring Ever Upward *(rec live, New York, Apr. 30, 1967)* VAI Audio ▲ VAIA 1032 [ADD]
Handel, G.F.:Messiah (sels), w. Jon Vickers (ten)—Behold & See If There Be; But Thou Didst Not Leave His Soul in Hell *(rec live, New York, Apr. 30, 1967)* VAI Audio ▲ VAIA 1032 [ADD]
Purcell, H.:Songs, w. Jon Vickers (ten)—Sweeter than Roses; There's Not a Swain of the Plain; Not All of My Torments; Man Is for the Woman Made *(rec live, New York, Apr. 30, 1967)* VAI Audio ▲ VAIA 1032 [ADD]
Scarlatti, A.:Cants, w. Jon Vickers (ten) Richard Woitach (pno)—Cara e dolce; Difesa non ha; O dolcissima speranza; La speranza; Toglietemi la vita ancor *(rec live, New York, Apr. 30, 1967)* VAI Audio ▲ VAIA 1032 [ADD]
Schumann, R.:Dichterliebe, w. Jon Vickers (ten) *(rec live, New York, Apr. 30, 1967)* VAI Audio ▲ VAIA 1032 [ADD]

Wojtera, A. (perc)
Mahin, B.:Of Mice & Men Capstone ▲ CPS 8611
Mahin, B.:Shadows, w. Elizabeth Curtis (sop), Caryl Conger (pno) Capstone ▲ CPS 8611
Mahin, B.:Shadows, w. E. Curtis (sop), C. Conger (pno) Capstone ▲ CPS 8061

Wojtowicz, Christian (vc)
Kay, D.:Tasmania Sym, w. R. Mills (cnd), Tasmanian SO Vox Australis ▲ VAST 013

Wolanin, Edward (pno)
Chopin, F.:Grand Duo, w. Tomasz Strahl (vc) *(rec Warsaw Philharmony Hall, May 29, 1994)* Canyon Classics ▲ 238
Chopin, F.:Intro & Polonaise, "Polonaise brilliante", w. Tomasz Strahl (vc) *(rec Warsaw Philharmony Hall, May 29, 1994)* Canyon Classics ▲ 238
Chopin, F.:Son Vc, w. Tomasz Strahl (vc) *(rec Warsaw Philharmony Hall, May 15, 1994)* Canyon Classics ▲ 238
Chopin, F.:Vars on a Theme from *La Cenerentola*, w. Grzegorz Olkiewicz (fl) *(rec Warsaw Philharmony Hall, May 15, 1994)* Canyon Classics ▲ 238

Wolf, Andrew (pno)
Dohnányi, E. von:Qnt 2 Pno, w. R. Lefkowitz (vn), C. Lieberman (vn), M. Thompson (va), D. Finch (vc) AFKA ▲ SK 503

Wolf, Gerhard (perc)
Helmschrott, R.:Cross & Freedom, w. Helmut Schatz, Nancy Gibson (sop), Frieder Aurich (ten), Matthias Weichert (bass), Manfred Ball (nar), Anett Baumann (vn), Frank Philliptsch, Linda Robbins, Martin Homann (perc), Robert M. Helmschrott (org), H.-C. Rademann (cnd), Munich Trombone Quartet, Dresden Chamber Choir Vienna Modern Masters ▲ VMM 3027 [DDD]

Wolf, Jan (gtr)
20th Century Works for Solo Guitar, w. Wolf, Jan (gtr) Partridge ▲ 1115-2 [ADD]

Wolf, M. (va)
Mozart, W.A.:Qnt Strs, K.515, w. Alban Berg String Quartet EMI Classics ▲ CDC 49085 [DDD]

Wolf, Marie (ob/rcr)
Vivaldi, A.:Cons Ob, w. P. Németh (cnd), Capella Savaria—RV.450, 454, 457, 442, 535, 545 & 557 *(rec 1991)* Musique d'Abord ▲ HMA 1903018

Wolfe, Kristin (bn)
Daugherty, M.:Bounce I, w. C. Ullery (bn) Opus One ▲ 138
Diamond, D.:Partita Ob, Bn & Pno, w. S. Caplan (ob), L. Spitzer (pno) Cambria ▲ 1091 [DDD]

Wolfe, P. (org)
Music of the Middle Ages, Vol. 7, w. French Ars Antiqua, Russell Oberlin (ct), Charles Bressler (ten), R. Price (ten), G. Meyers (bar), M. Blackman (vl) Lyrichord ▲ LYR 8007 [ADD]

Wolff, Christian (synclavier)
Wolff, C.:Mayday Materials Centaur ▲ CRC 2052 [DDD]

Wolff, Christian (vc)—see ORCHESTRAS & ENSEMBLES Manfred String Quartet

Wolff, Ernst Victor (pno)
Wolf, H.:Songs (misc), w. A. Kipnis, (bass), Coenraad V. Bos (pno), Gerald Moore (pno)—Grenzen der Menschheit; Um Mitternacht; Sterb' ich, so hüllt in Blumen meine Glieder; Michelangelo-Lieder I-III *[w. Bos, rec. 1933-4]*; Cophtisches Lied I; Der Musikant; Der Soldat I; Der Schreckenberger *[w. Moore, rec. 1935]*; Wie glänzt der helle Mond; Nun lasst uns Frieden schliessen; Wir haben beide lange Zeit geschwiegen; Geselle, woll'n wir uns in Kutten hüllen; Heb' auf dein blondes Haupt; Wie viele Zeit verlor ich; Was für ein Lied soll dir gesungen werden *[w. Wolff, rec. 1934]* *[rec "Hugo Wolf Society," 1933-35]* Music & Arts 2-▲ CD 661 (m) [AAD]
Wolf, H.:Songs (misc), w. A. Kipnis, (bass), Coenraad V. Bos (pno), Gerald Moore (pno)—Grenzen der Menschheit; Um Mitternacht; Sterb' ich, so hüllt in Blumen meine Glieder; Michelangelo-Lieder I-III *[w. Bos, rec. 1933-4]*; Cophtisches Lied I; Der Musikant; Der Soldat I; Der Schreckenberger *[w. Moore, rec. 1935]*; Wie glänzt der helle Mond; Nun lasst uns Frieden schliessen; Wir haben beide lange Zeit geschwiegen; Geselle, woll'n wir uns in Kutten hüllen; Heb' auf dein blondes Haupt; Wie viele Zeit verlor ich; Was für ein Lied soll dir gesungen werden *[w. Wolff, rec. 1934]* *(rec 1933-35)* Preiser 2-▲ 89204 (m) [AAD]

Wolfgang, Randall (ob)
Mozart, W.A.:Con Ob, K.314, w. Orpheus CO Deutsche Grammophon 3-▲ 431665-2 [DDD]
Mozart, W.A.:Con Ob, K.314, w. Orpheus CO Deutsche Grammophon ▲ 423623-2 [DDD]

Wolford, Dale (sax)
More Than Sax:Baroque, Blues & Beyond, w. Stephanie Friedman (mez), Ivan Rosenblum (pno) *(rec Belmont, CA & Richmond, CA, Aug. 17-20, 1993 & Jan. 2)* Gliddon ▲ GP 001 [DDD]

Wolford, Dale (sax/syn)
Weill, K.:Songs, w. Pamela Alexander (sop), Ivan Rosenblum (kbd)—Complainte de la Seine; Le Roi d'Aquitaine; Youkali; Je ne t'aime pas; Le train du Ciel; Scène au Dancing; Es regnet; Der Abschiedsbrief; Pirate Jenny; Barbara Song; Die Muschel von Margate; Nanna's Lied; What Did She Get, That Soldier's Wife?; Surabaya Johnny *(rec Bay View Studios, Richmond, CA)* Laurel ▲ LR 855

Wolfsthal, Josef (vn)
Beethoven, L. van:Con Vn, Op. 61, w. M. Gurlitt (cnd), Berlin PO [includes cadenzas by Joachim] Symposium ▲ SYM 1141
Beethoven, L. van:Con Vn, Op. 61, w. M. Gurlitt (cnd), Berlin PO *(rec 1928 for Polydor)* Pearl ▲ PEA 9387 (m) [AAD]
Beethoven, L. van:Romances Vn, Berlin State Opera Orch—Op. 50 *(rec ca. 1925 for Polydor)* Pearl ▲ PEA 9387 (m) [AAD]
Mozart, W.A.:Con 5 Vn, w. F. Weissmann (cnd), Berlin State Opera Orch *(rec 1928 for Parlophone)* Pearl ▲ PEA 9387 (m) [AAD]

Wolinsky, Robert (gtr)
Rzewski, F.:Moonrise with Memories, w. David Taylor (b trbn), David Carp (kazoo), Bill Blount (cl), Allan Dean (tpt), Louise Schulman (vn), Bill Moersch (mar/dlc) *(rec RCA Studios, NYC, June 4, 1981)* New World ▲ 80494-2

Wolk, B. (vn)
Bach, J.S.:Sons & Partitas Vn, BWV 1001-1006 [trans. violin-guitar of BWV 1002 & 1004] FSM-Fono ▲ 97712 [DDD]

Wolk, Burkhard (gtr)—see ORCHESTRAS & ENSEMBLES Albéniz Guitar Duo

Wollenweber, D. (ob)
Lachner, F.P.:Nonet, w. A. Duisberg (fl), P. Prieditis (cl), P. Douglas (hn), M. Postinghel (bn), I. Grünkorn (vn), M. Gieler (va), T. Ruge (vc), F. Heidenreich (db) *(rec June 10, 1991)* Thorofon ▲ CTH 2132 [DDD]

Wollesen, Kenny (perc)
Waits, T.:The Black Rider:The Casting of Magic Bullets, w. Angelika Thomas (sgr—Anne), Annette Paulmann (sgr—Kätchen), Sona Cervena (sgr—Bird/Messenger/Spoonwoman), Monika Tahal (sgr—Witness/Bird/Shrink/Wilhelm's Double/Skeleton), Susi Eisenkolb (sgr—Bridesmaid/Pegleg's Double), Heinz Vossbrink (sgr—Kuno), Dominique Horwitz (sgr—Pegleg), Gerd Kunath (sgr—Bertram), Stefan Kurt (sgr—Wilhelm), Klaus Schreiber (sgr—Robert/Man on Stag/Georg Schmid), Jörg Holm (Old Uncle/Duke), Jan Moritz Steffen (sgr—Young Kuno/Bird/Shrink/Skeleton), Tom Waits (voc/caliope/org/chamberlain/mar/emax/gtr/train whistle), Ralph Carney (sax/b cl/bar hn), Bill Douglas (bass gtr) Island ▲ 314518559-2

Wollny, Klaus (gtr)
Music for 2 Guitars, w. Bernard Hebb (gtr) Entrée ▲ 0054 [ADD]

Wolosoff, Bruce (pno)
Busoni, F.:Elegies (7) Pno Music & Arts ▲ CD 293 [DDD]
Busoni, F.:Son Pno, Op. 20a Music & Arts ▲ CD 293 [DDD]

Wolpe, Katharina (pno)
Hamilton, I.:Le Jardin de Monet Symposium ▲ 1121
Hamilton, I.:Palinodes Symposium ▲ 1121
Schoenberg, A.:Pno Music—Three Pieces, Op. 11; Six Pieces, Op. 19; Five Pieces, Op. 23; Suite, Op. 25; Piano Piece, Opp. 33a & 33b Symposium ▲ 1107
Wolpe, S.:Passacaglia *(rec Sept. 30, Oct. 1 & Dec. 1)* Largo ▲ 5120 [DDD]
Wolpe, S.:Pno Music (misc)—Early Piece; Studies, Part 1; 2 Studies, Part 2; Form for Piano; Farm IV *(rec Sept. 30, Oct. 1 & Dec. 1)* Largo ▲ 5120 [DDD]
Wolpe, S.:Zemach Suite *(rec Sept. 30, Oct. 1 & Dec. 1)* Largo ▲ 5120 [DDD]

Wolters, Rainer (vn)
Bach, J.S.:Con Fl, Vn & Hpd, w. J. Galway (fl), U. Deutschler (hpd), J. Faerber (cnd), Württemberg CO RCA Red Seal ▲ 09026-60900-2 ■ 09026-60900-4 □ 09026-60900-5

Woo, Betty (pno)
Kingman, D.:Dances & Ghost Dances, w. Justin Blasdale (pno) Innova ▲ INNOVA 504

Wood, Barbara (bn)—see ORCHESTRAS & ENSEMBLES Missouri Quintet

Wood, Charles (perc)
Hays, S.:Dreaming the World, w. Thomas Bruckner (bar), Sal Basile (voc), Jennifer López (voc), John Schaffer (voc), Sorrel Hays (voc), Joseph Kubera (pno), John Kennedy (perc), Maya Gunji (perc), Eric Kivnick (perc), Jai Smith (perc) New World ▲ 805202 [DDD]
Lockwood, A.:Thousand Year Dreaming, w. Art Baron (conch shell/trbn/didjeridu), Liby Van Cleve (ob/E hn), Jon Gibson (didjeridu), J.D. Parran (cl), Michael Publiese (perc), Scott Robinson (conch shell/perc), John Snyder (didjeridu/waterphone), Peter Zummo (trbn/didjeridu) ¿What Next? ▲ WN 0010

Wood, Graham (vn)
Souvenir, w. David Bollard (pno) *(rec Sir John Clancy Auditorium, Univ of NSW, Sydney, June 1993)* Tall Poppies ▲ TP 56 [DDD]

Wood, Gregory (vc)
Ashford, R.:Because, w. Mayumi Plumohira (vn), Catherine Bush (vn), Bruce Plumohira (va) Nigel Classics ▲ NC 10101
Ashford, R.:Rise & Fall & Peaceful Rest, w. Mary Boyd (pno), Mayumi Plumohira (vn) Nigel Classics ▲ NC 10101
Ashford, R.:Short & Suite, w. Mayumi Plumohira (vn) Nigel Classics ▲ NC 10101
Ashford, R.:Summer's End, w. Mayumi Plumohira (vn), Catherine Bush (vn), Bruce Plumohira (va) Nigel Classics ▲ NC 10101
Ashford, R.:Vn & Vc Music, w. Mayumi Plumohira (vn)—Young & Old Together; Far & Near Love Song; Young & Old Together Nigel Classics ▲ NC 10101

Wood, James (perc)
Oboe Collection, w. Canter, Robin (ob), Anthony Pleeth (vc), Melvyn Tan (hpd), Richard Burnett (pnos) Amon Ra ▲ CDSAR 22 [DDD]

Wood, Lorraine (ob)
Telemann, G.P.:Cons Tpts, w. Mark Bennett (tpt), Michael Harrison (tpt), Nicholas Thompson (tpt), Paul Goodwin (ob), T. Pinnock (cnd), English Concert—in D *(rec Henry Wood Hall, London, Mar 1993)* Archiv Produktion ▲ 439893-2 [DDD]

Wood, Ross (org)
The Sounds of Trinity:2 Organs with Brass & Timpani, w. Brian Jones (org), *(other musicians unknown)* Arkay ■ 4116
With Heart & Voice, w. Trinity Choir, Brian Jones (cnd) *(rec Trinity Church, Boston, June 6, 7 & 9, 1994)* Gothic ▲ GOT 49071 [DDD]

Wood, Sharon (vn)
Curran, A.:VSTG, w. D. Abel (vn), M. Tichener (va), D. Weinschelbaum (vc) CRI ▲ CD 668 [DDD]

Woodcock, David (pno)
24 Aspects of an Amorous Nature, w. Peter Jeffes (ten) Symposium ▲ SYM 1183

Woodhams, Richard (ob)
Beethoven, L. van:Qnt Ob, 3 Hns & Bn, w. A. Simon (ob), G. Stilfies (hn), G. Berry (hn), R. Pandolfi (bn) *(rec 1975-79)* Vox Box 3-▲ CD3X 3014 [ADD]
Herschel, W.:Music of, w. D. Jerome (cnd), Mozart Festival Orch—Cons in C & E♭ for Ob; Chamber Sym Newport Classic ▲ NPD 85612 [DDD]
Strauss, R.:Con Ob, w. W. Sawallisch (cnd), Philadelphia Orch EMI Classics ▲ CDC 56149
Strauss, R.:Ein Heldenleben, w. W. Sawallisch (cnd), Philadelphia Orch EMI Classics ▲ CDC 56149

Woodhouse, Nigel (mand)
Vivaldi, A.:Con for 2 Mands, w. P. Sparks (mand), L. Friedman (cnd), St. Andrew Camerata Omega ▲ OCD 1012 [DDD]

Woodhouse, Violet Gordon (hpd)
Great Virtuosi of the Harpsichord, Vol. III, w. Violet Gordon Woodhouse (hpd) Pearl ▲ PEA CD 9242

Woodrow, Anthony (db)
Haydn, J.:Mass 4, Missa 'Sunt bona mixta malis', w. Anner Bylsma (vc), Bob Van Asperen (org), B. Weil (cnd), Tölz Boys' Choir *(rec Bad Tolz, Germany, June 6, 1992)* Sony Classical ("Vivarte" series) ▲ SK 53368 [DDD]
Haydn, J.:Non nobis, Domine, w. Anner Bylsma (vc), Bob Van Asperen (org), B. Weil (cnd), Tölz Boys' Choir *(rec Bad Tolz, Germany, June 4, 1992)* Sony Classical ("Vivarte" series) ▲ SK 53368 [DDD]
Vivaldi, A.:Sons Vc, w. R. Dieltiens (vc), R. Kohnen (hpd)—(3) in b♭ & g (from Op. 14); in e Accent ▲ 9181 [DDD]

Woods, P. (cl)
Bliss, A.:Qnt Cl, w. Audubon String Quartet Telarc ▲ CD 80205 [DDD]

Woods, Pamela (ob)
Bax, A.:Qnt Ob, w. Audubon String Quartet Telarc ▲ CD 80205 [DDD]
Britten, H.:Phantasy Qt, w. Audubon String Quartet members Telarc ▲ CD 80205 [DDD]

Woods, Phil (a sax)
Red Square Blue Russian Composers, w. Hersch, Fred (pno), James Newton (fl), Toots Thielemans (hmc), Erik Friedlander (vc), Steve La Spina (bass), Jeff Hirshfield (drums) Angel ▲ CDC 54743

Woods, Rex (pno)
Donald Knaub, w. Donald Knaub (b trbn) Crystal ■ C680
Hidas, F.:Rhap B Trbn & Pno, w. D. Knaub (b trbn) Crystal ■ C680
Jacob, G.:Cameos, w. D. Knaub (bass trbn) [bass trombone & piano arr.] Crystal ■ C680

Woodside, Mary (vn)
Derungs, M.:Music of, w. M. Stern (cnd), Zurich Tonhalle Orch—Con for Vn; Giarsun; Con for Rcr, Db, Hpd & Strs; Scene teatrali for Ww Oct Grammont ▲ CTSP 51-2

Woodward, G. (fl)
Griffes, C.T.:Poem Fl, w. B. Smith (pno) [arr fl & pno] Stereophile ▲ STPH 001-2 [AAD]
Prokofiev, S.:Son Fl, w. B. Smith (pno) Stereophile ▲ STPH 001-2 [AAD]
Reinecke, C.:Son Fl, w. B. Smith (pno) Stereophile ▲ STPH 001-2 [AAD]
Schumann, R.:Romances Ob, w. B. Smith (pno) Stereophile ▲ STPH 001-2 [AAD]

Wooley, Robert (hpd)
Böhm, G.:Hpd Music—Capriccio in D; Prelude, Fugue & Postlude in g; Suites in c, f, E♭, & F Meridian ▲ CDE 84087
Seixas, C. de:Sons Kbd—No. 7 from 25 Sonatas; & Nos. 12, 14, 24, 27, 32, 34, 47, 50, 57 & 78 from 80 Sonatas Amon Ra ▲ CD-SAR 43 [DDD]

Wooley, Robert (org)
Gibbons, O.:Org Music (comp), w. R. Wooley (cnd), St. John's College Choir Cambridge [Dallam Organ, Ploujean]—Fant. No. 3 in d for Double Organ; Fant. No. 1 in d; Prelude No. 1 in a; Fant. No. 5 in g; Prelude No. 3 in d; Fant. No. 6 in a; Fant. No. 9 in C; Prelude No. 2 in C; Fant. No. 7 in a; Fant. No. 4 in d; Fant. No. 2 in d; Prelude No. 4 in a; Fant. No. 10 in C; Fant. No. 8 in a; If ye be risen again with Christ; Oh Lord, in thy wrath rebuke me not; Almighty God, who by thy son; O clap your hands; We praise thee, Oh Father; So God loved the world; O God the King of Glory Chandos ("Chaconne" series) ▲ CHAN 0559 [DDD]
Organ Music Chandos ▲ CHAN 0553 [DDD]
Purcell, H.:Org Music—Voluntaries in d, Z.718 & in G, Z.720 Chandos ▲ CHAN 8763 [DDD]

Wooley, Robert (pno)
Bach, Joh. Christian:Sons Kbd, Op. 17 Chandos ("Chaconne" series) ▲ CHAN 0543 [DDD]

Woolley, Robert (hpd)—see ORCHESTRAS & ENSEMBLES Purcell Quartet

Woolley, Scot (pno)
Korngold, E.W.:Der Ring des Polykrates (incidental music)—Potpourri Koch International Classics ▲ KIC 7277 [DDD]
Korngold, E.W.:Der Schneemann [arr pno] Koch International Classics ▲ KIC 7277 [DDD]

Woolweaver, Scott (va)—see also ORCHESTRAS & ENSEMBLES Griffin Music Ensemble
Kirchner, L.:Qt 1 Strs, w. M. Beaulieu (vn), C. Hoener (vn), A. Mark (vc) Albany ▲ TROY 137 [DDD]
Kirchner, L.:Qt 2 Strs, w. M. Beaulieu (vn), C. Hoener (vn), A. Mark (vc) Albany ▲ TROY 137 [DDD]
Kirchner, L.:Qt 3 Strs, w. M. Beaulieu (vn), C. Hoener (vn), A. Mark (vc) Albany ▲ TROY 137 [DDD]

Wooten, Mary (vc)—see ORCHESTRAS & ENSEMBLES Sirius String Quartet

▲ = CD ♦ = Enhanced CD Δ = MD ■ = Cassette Tape □ = DCC

Wooton, Mary (vc)—see also ORCHESTRAS & ENSEMBLES Soldier String Quartet
Jenkins, L.:Monkey on the Dragon, w. Leroy Jenkins (vn), Henry Threadgill (fl), Don Byron (cl), Marth Ehrlich (b cl), Janet Frice (bn), Vincent Chancey (hn), Frank Gordon (tpt), Jeff Hoyer (trbn), David Soldier (vn), Jane Henry (vn) Ron Lawrence (va), Lindsey Horner (db), Thurman Barker (traps), Myra Melford (pno), T. Léon (cnd) *(rec live, Merkin Concert Hall, New York City, Apr. 9, 1992)* CRI ("eXchange" series) ▲ CD 663 [DDD]

Wootton, Douglas (lt/bandora)
Music of the Renaissance Virtuosi, w. James Tyler (lt/baroque gtr/mand), Nigel North (lt/ thb/cittern), Jane Ryan (b vl) Saga Classics ▲ 3350 [ADD]

Wootton, Douglas (mand)
Vivaldi, A.:Con for 2 Mands, w. J. Tyler (mand), N. Marriner (cnd), Academy of St. Martin in the Fields Philips ▲ 412892-2 [DDD]

Wöpke, Peter (vc)—see ORCHESTRAS & ENSEMBLES Sinnhoffer String Quartet members

Work, George (vc)—see also ORCHESTRAS & ENSEMBLES Ames Piano Quartet
Strauss, R.:Qt Pno, w. W. David (pno), M. Darlington (vn), L. Burkhalter (va) *(rec Oct. 1991)* Dorian ▲ DOR 90167 [DDD]
Widor, C.M.:Qt Pno, w. W. David (pno), M. Darlington (vn), L. Burkhalter (va) *(rec Oct. 1991)* Dorian ▲ DOR 90167 [DDD]

Worth, T. A. (org)
Delius, F.:Hassan—Serenade[arr. E. Fenby]; Fennimore & Gerda [arr. R. Hebble] Direct-to-Tape Recording ▲ DTR 9301CD
Delius, F.:Songs [arr. R. Hebble]—Sleigh Ride Direct-to-Tape Recording ▲ DTR 9301CD
Franck, C.:Grande pièce symphonique Direct-to-Tape Recording ▲ DTR 9301CD
Mozart, W.A.:Fant Mechanical Org Direct-to-Tape Recording ▲ DTR 9301CD

Worthen, D. (fl)
Karg-Elert, S.:Impressions exotiques, w. J. Weber (pno) Leonarda ▲ LE 335 [DDD]
Karg-Elert, S.:Jugend, w. R. Shaughnessy (cl), R. Menual (hn), J. Weber (pno) Leonarda ▲ LE 335 [DDD]
Karg-Elert, S.:Son Fl, Op. 121, w. J. Weber (pno) Leonarda ▲ LE 335 [DDD]
Karg-Elert, S.:Suite pointillistique, w. J. Weber (pno) Leonarda ▲ LE 335 [DDD]

Wortman, Kurt (perc)
An Empire Brass Christmas, w. Empire Brass Quintet, Laurie Monohan (sgr), Brian Jones (perc) Telarc ▲ CD 80416 [DDD]
Passage, 138 B.C.-A.D. 1611, w. Empire Brass Quintet, Laurie Monahan (sgr), M. Collver (sgr), Pete Maunu (acoustic/elec/12string gtr), Doug Lunn (fretless bass), D. Goldblatt (syn) *(rec Lenox, MA & Los Angeles, CA May 27-29 & June 28-July)* Telarc ▲ CD 80355 [DDD]

Woshakiwsky, G. (va)—see ORCHESTRAS & ENSEMBLES New World String Quartet

Woudenberg, Pierre (cl)
Brahms, J.:Qnt Cl, w. Schoenberg String Quartet Koch Schwann ▲ SCH 311502
Reger, M.:Qnt Cl, w. Schoenberg String Quartet Koch Schwann ▲ SCH 311502

Woytowicz, Boleslaw (pno)
Chopin, F.:Études (24) *(rec Warsaw, 1959)* Polskie Nagrania ▲ PNCD 304
Chopin, F.:Nouvelles études *(rec Warsaw, 1959)* Polskie Nagrania ▲ PNCD 304
Chopin, F.:Prelude, Op. 45 *(rec Warsaw, 1959)* Polskie Nagrania ▲ PNCD 303

Wright, Brian (lt)
Shakespearian Songbook, w. James Griffett (ten) Carlton ("Musick's Monument" series) ▲ MSK 6500022

Wright, David (cl)
Mason, D.G.:Son Cl (or Vn), w. G. Davis (pno) Centaur ▲ CRC 2067 [DDD]
Reger, M.:Sons Cl, Op. 49, w. G. Davis (pno)—No. 1 Centaur ▲ CRC 2067 [DDD]
Saint-Saëns, C.:Son Cl, w. G. Davis (pno) Centaur ▲ CRC 2067 [DDD]
Weber, C.M. von:Grand duo concertant Cl, w. G. Davis (pno) Centaur ▲ CRC 2067 [DDD]

Wright, Elisabeth (hpd)
Bach, J.S.:Sons Fl, BWV 1030-35, w. Kim Pineda (trns fl), Elisabeth Reed (vc)—Nos. 1 in b, 3 in A, 5 in e & 6 in E Focus ▲ FOCUS 944 [DDD]

Wright, Elisabeth (pno)
Adler, S.:Trio 2 Pno, w. Veronica Kadlubkiewicz (vn), Roy Christensen (vc) Gasparo ▲ GS 298 [DDD/DAD]
Shawn, A.:Eclogue Pnos, w. A. Shawn (pno) Opus One ▲ CD 157

Wright, Gavin (vn)
Battiato, F.:L'Ombra della Luce, w. Franco Battiato (voc), Antonio Ballista (pno), Roger Chase (va), Filippo Destrieri (kbd/computer), Anthony Pleeth (vc), G. Pio (cnd), London Astarte Orch Hemisphere ▲ 837234-2
Battiato, F.:Povera Patria, w. Franco Battiato (voc), Antonio Ballista (pno), Roger Chase (va), Filippo Destrieri (kbd/computer), Anthony Pleeth (vc), G. Pio (cnd), London Astarte Orch Hemisphere ▲ 837234-2
Battiato, F.:Le Sacre Sinfonie del Tiempo, w. Franco Battiato (voc), Antonio Ballista (pno), Roger Chase (va), Filippo Destrieri (kbd/computer), Anthony Pleeth (vc), G. Pio (cnd), London Astarte Orch Hemisphere ▲ 837234-2

Wright, Harold (cl)
Brahms, J.:Qnt Cl, w. Boston Sym Chamber Players Philips ▲ 442149-2
Brahms, J.:Sons Cl (comp), w. P. Serkin (pno) *(rec Aug. 1992)* Boston Records ▲ BR 1005
Coleridge-Taylor, S.:Qnt Cl & Strs, w. Hawthorne String Quartet *(rec 9/90)* Koch International Classics ▲ KIC 7056-2 [DDD]
Mozart, W.A.:Qnt Cl, K.581, w. Marlboro Festival Ensemble Odyssey 3-▲ MB3K 45827
Mozart, W.A.:Qnt Cl, K.581, w. Marlboro Festival Ensemble *(rec 1968)* Sony Classical ▲ SMK 46252 [ADD]
Mozart, W.A.:Qnt Cl, K.581, w. Boston Sym Chamber Players Philips ▲ 442149-2
Mozart, W.A.:Qnt Pno, K.452, w. P. Serkin (pno), A. Genovese (ob), R. Sebring (hn), F. Svoboda (bn) *(rec Aug. 1992)* Boston Records ▲ BR 1004
Schubert, Franz:Der Hirt auf dem Felsen, w. B. Valente (sop), R. Serkin (pno) [G] Sony Classical ("Essential Classics" series) ▲ SBK 48176 ■ SBT 48176
Schubert, Franz:Der Hirt auf dem Felsen, w. B. Valente (sop), R. Serkin (pno) [G] *(rec 1960)* Sony Classical ▲ SMK 45901 [ADD/DDD] ■ SMT 45901
Schumann, R.:Fantasiestücke Cl, w. H. Goldsmith (pno) Music & Arts ▲ CD 690-1 [AAD]
Schumann, R.:Fantasiestücke Cl, w. P. Serkin (pno) *(rec Aug. 1992)* Boston Records ▲ BR 1005
Schumann, R.:Märchenerzählungen, w. N. Imai (va), H. Goldsmith (pno) Music & Arts ▲ CD 690-1 [AAD]

Wright, Keith (org)
Heaven & Earth Are Full of Thy Glory, w. [cnd:Jonathan Bielby], Wakefield Cathedral Choir Priory ▲ PRCD 341 [DDD]
Stanford, C.V.:Church Music, w. J. Lancelot (cnd), Durham Cathedral Choir—complete morning and evening canticles for holy communion Priory ▲ PRI 437 [DDD]

Wright, Lawrence (tpt)
Joan Lippincott & Philadelphia Brass, w. Joan Lippincott,(org), Philadelphia Brass Gothic ▲ GOT 49072 [DDD]

Wright, Michael (db)
Schnittke, A.:Sym 7, w. Nigel Seaman (tuba), David Buckland (ctbn), T. Otaka (cnd), BBC Welsh National SO *(rec Brangwyn Hall, Swansea, Wales, July 26-27, 1995)* BIS ▲ CD 747 [DDD]

Wright, Peter (org)
Bairstow, E.C.:Choral Music, w. Philip Moore (cnd), Guildford Cathedral Choir—Blessed City, Heavenly Salem Priory ▲ PRI 6 [DDD]
Barié, A.:Pièces (3) Org [Lewis Organ, Southwark Cathedral] Priory ▲ PRI 406 [DDD]
Barié, A.:Sym Org [Lewis Organ, Southwark Cathedral] Priory ▲ PRI 406 [DDD]
Blitheman, J.:In pace, w. Philip Moore (cnd), Guildford Cathedral Choir Priory ▲ PRI 6 [DDD]
Byrd, W.:Church Music, w. Philip Moore (cnd), Guildford Cathedral Choir—Christe Qui Lux Es et Dies Priory ▲ PRI 6 [DDD]

Wright, Peter (org) (cont.)
Dupré, M.:Le tombeau de Titelouze [at the Lewis Organ, Southwark Cathedral] Priory ▲ PRI 406 [DDD]
Duruflé, M.:Motets on Gregorian Chants, Op. 10, w. Philip Moore (cnd), Guildford Cathedral Choir Priory ▲ PRI 6 [DDD]
Moore, P.:All Wisdom, w. Philip Moore (cnd), Guildford Cathedral Choir Priory ▲ PRI 6 [DDD]
Tallis, T.:Church Music, w. Philip Moore (cnd), Guildford Cathedral Choir—Te Lucis Ante Terminum Priory ▲ PRI 6 [DDD]
Victoria, T.L. de:Sacred Choral Music, w. Philip Moore (cnd), Guildford Cathedral Choir—Magnificat, VII Tone Priory ▲ PRI 6 [DDD]

Wright, R. Douglas (trbn)—see ORCHESTRAS & ENSEMBLES Empire Brass Quintet

Wrigley, Yolande (pno)
Bax, A.:Folk Tale, w. B. Gregor-Smith (vc) ASV ▲ ASV 896 [DDD]
Bax, A.:Legend-Son, w. B. Gregor-Smith (vc) ASV ▲ ASV 896 [DDD]
Bax, A.:Son Vc & Pno, w. B. Gregor-Smith (vc) ASV ▲ ASV 896 [DDD]
Bax, A.:Sonatina Vc & Pno, w. B. Gregor-Smith (vc) ASV ▲ ASV 896 [DDD]
Bridge, F.:Son Vc, w. B. Gregor-Smith (vc) ASV ▲ ASV 796
Chopin, F.:Son Vc, w. Bernard Gregor-Smith (vc) ASV Quicksilva ▲ ASQ 6178
Debussy, C.:Son Vc, w. B. Gregor-Smith (vc) ASV ▲ ASV 796
Dohnányi, E. von:Son Vc, w. B. Gregor-Smith (vc) ASV ▲ ASV 796
Rachmaninoff, S.:Son Vc, w. Bernard Gregor-Smith (vc) ASV Quicksilva ▲ ASQ 6178

Write, Desmond (pno)
Ireland, J.:Pno Music—April; The Darkened Valley; London Pieces [Chelsea Reach; Ragamuffin; Soho Forenoons]; 3 Pastels [A Grecian Lad; The Bad Bishop; Puck's Birthday]; In Those Days [Daydream; Meridian; A Sea Idyll]; Preludes [The Undertone-Obsession; The Holy Boy; Fire of Spring; The Towing Path; Summer Evening]; Green Ways [The Cherry Tree; Cypress; The Palm & May] Classics for Pleasure ▲ CFP 4674

Wronski, Tadeusz (vn)
Chopin, F.:Intro & Polonaise, "Polonaise brilliante", w. Wladyslaw Szpilman (pno) *(rec Warsaw, 1961)* Polskie Nagrania ▲ PNCD 309
Chopin, F.:Trio Pno, w. Wladyslaw Szpilman (pno), Aleksander Ciechanski (vc) *(rec Warsaw, 1961)* Polskie Nagrania ▲ PNCD 309
Turski, Z.:Con 1 Vn, w. S. Wislocki (cnd), Warsaw Philharmonic SO *(rec 1962)* Olympia ▲ OCD 327 [AAD]

Wu, Mia (vn)
Dashow, J.:Trio 4/3, w. Lutz Rath (vc), Sylvia Kahan (pno) *(rec Studio Wonderland, Rome, June 1993)* Pro Viva ▲ ISPV 177 CD [DDD]
Lennon, J.A.:Ballade Belliss', w. C. Seltzer (pno) CRI ▲ CD 599 [ADD/DDD]
Lennon, J.A.:Translations, w. R. Rosales (sop), D. Krakauer (cl), J. Sachs (pno) CRI ▲ CD 599 [ADD/DDD]

Wu, S.-C. (pno)
Müller-Zurich, P.:Cons Va Pno, w. C. Schiller (va) Grammont ▲ CTSP 20-2

Wührer, Friedrich (pno)
Schumann, R.:Con Pno, w. H. Abendroth (cnd), Berlin Radio Orch Berlin Classics ("Dokumente" series) ▲ BER 2052 [ADD]

Wullschleger, B. (lt)—see ORCHESTRAS & ENSEMBLES Lautentrio Ricardo Correa

Wulp, G. van der (bn)
Vivaldi, A.:Con Ob Bn, w. P. Frankenberg (ob), M. Haselböck (cnd), Vienna Academy [period instrs] Novalis ▲ 150074 [DDD]

Wummer, John (fl)
Babbitt, M.:Composition for 4 Instrs, w. Drucker (cl), March (vn), McCall (vc) CRI ■ C 138
Bach, J.S.:Brandenburg Con 5, w. E. Istomin (pno), J. Szigeti (vn), P. Casals (cnd), Prades Festival Orch *(rec June 10-12, 1950)* Sony Classical ("The Casals Edition" series) ▲ SMK 58982 [ADD]
Debussy, C.:Son Fl, w. Milton Katims (va), Laura Newell (hp) Ambassador ▲ ARC 1013
Vivaldi, A.:Cons Diverse Instrs, w. G. Vicari (mand), C. de Filippis (mand), R. Morris (fl), W. Vacchiano (tpt), N. Prager (tpt), E. Brenner (b ob), C. Stavrache (hp), A. Wurtzler (hp), J. Gorigliano (vn), L. Varga (vc), L. Bernstein (cnd), New York PO—in C, RV.558 *(rec Dec. 15, 1958)* Sony Classical ("Leonard Bernstein:The Royal Edition" series) ▲ SMK 47642 [ADD]
Vivaldi, A.:Cons Fl (misc), w. L. Bernstein (cnd), New York PO—in c, RV.441 *(rec Dec. 15, 1958)* Sony Classical ("Leonard Bernstein:The Royal Edition" series) ▲ SMK 47642 [ADD]

Wunderlich, Heinz (org)
Bach, J.S.:Passacaglia & Fugue Org Elektra/Nonesuch ■ 71252-4
Bach, J.S.:Preludes & Fugues, BWV 531-552—BWV 548 Elektra/Nonesuch ■ 71252-4
Bach, J.S.:Toccata & Fugue Org, BWV 540 Elektra/Nonesuch ■ 71252-4
Bach, J.S.:Toccata & Fugue Org, BWV 565 Elektra/Nonesuch ■ 71252-4

Wunrow, Theresa Elder (hp)
Piston, W.:Capriccio Hp, w. G. Schwarz (cnd), Seattle SO Delos ▲ DE 3106 [DDD]
Piston, W.:Fant E Hn, w. G. Danielson (E hn), G. Schwarz (cnd), Seattle SO *(rec Jan. 27-28, 1992)* Delos ▲ DE 3126 [DDD]

Wuorinen, Charles (pno)
Chou Wen-Chung:Cursive, w. Harvey Sollberger (fl) CRI ▲ CD 691 [ADD]
Luening, O.:Trio Fl, Vc & Pno, w. Harvey Sollberger (fl), Fred Sherry (vc) CRI ("American Masters" series) ▲ CD 716 [ADD]
Rochberg, G.:La Bocca della verità, w. J. Ostryniec (ob) CRI ■ ACS 6013
Westergaard, P.:Divert on Discobbolos Fragments, w. Harvey Sollberger (fl) CRI ▲ CD 696 [ADD]
Wolpe, S.:Trio in 2 Parts Fl, w. H. Sollberger (fl), F. Sherry (vc) *(rec Nov. 9-10, 1991)* Koch ▲ KIC 7112 [DDD]
Wuorinen, C.:Duo Vn, w. Paul Zukofsky (vn) New World ▲ 80517-2
Wuorinen, C.:Fast Fant Vc, w. F. Sherry (vc) New World ▲ NW 385-2 [DDD]

Wurlitzer, Ulrich (cl)—see also ORCHESTRAS & ENSEMBLES Bonaventura Ensemble
Bernstein, L.:Son Cl, w. New Munich Piano Trio Orfeo ▲ 326931 [DDD]

Würtz, Klára (pno)
Bartók, B.:Pno Music—13 sels. from 15 Hungarian Peasant Songs, Sz.71; Suite, Op. 14; Burleske, Op. 8; Romanian Folkdances, Sz.56; 6 sels. from Mikrokosmos; Son., Sz.80; 3 Hungarian Folksongs from the Cxik District, Sz.35a *(rec Oct. 1993)* Globe ▲ GLO 5111 [DDD]

Würtzler, Astrid von (hp)
Coolidge, P.S.:Rhap Hp, w. S. Landau (cnd), Westphalian SO Recklinghausen *(rec 1975)* Vox Box ("The American Composers" series) 2-▲ CDX 5157
Vivaldi, A.:Cons Diverse Instrs, w. G. Vicari (mand), C. de Filippis (mand), J. Wummer (fl), R. Morris (fl), W. Vacchiano (tpt), N. Prager (tpt), E. Brenner (b ob), C. Stavrache (hp), A. Wurtzler (hp), J. Gorigliano (vn), L. Varga (vc), L. Bernstein (cnd), New York PO—in C, RV.558 *(rec Dec. 15, 1958)* Sony Classical ("Leonard Bernstein:The Royal Edition" series) ▲ SMK 47642 [ADD]

Wustman, John (pno)
Berg, A.:Songs, Op. 2, w. B. Fassbaender (mez) [G] Acanta ▲ 43579
Brahms, J.:Liebeslieder Waltzes SATB, w. N. Mackenzie (pno), Robert Shaw Festival Singers [G] *(rec Aug. 6-7, 1992)* Telarc ▲ CD 80326 [DDD]
Brahms, J.:Neue Liebeslieder Waltzes, w. N. Mackenzie (pno), Robert Shaw Festival Singers [G] *(rec Aug. 6-7, 1992)* Telarc ▲ CD 80326 [DDD]
Brahms, J.:Songs, w. N. Mackenzie (pno), Robert Shaw Festival Singers—7 Abendlieder [G] *(rec Aug. 6-7, 1992)* Telarc ▲ CD 80326 [DDD]
French & Italian Art Songs, w. Carol Loverde (sop) Centaur ▲ CRC 2151
In Recital at Philharmonic Hall, w. Birgit Nilsson (sop) *(rec Lincoln Center, New York, 1967)* Melodram ▲ CDM 18027 (m) [AAD]
Mahler, G.:Des Knaben Wunderhorn, w. B. Fassbaender (mez)—6 sels. [G] Acanta ▲ 43579
Ogermann, C.:Tagore-Lieder, w. B. Fassbaender (mez)—set of 7 songs [G] Acanta ▲ 43579
Pavarotti at Carnegie Hall, w. Luciano Pavarotti (ten) London ▲ 421526-2 [DDD] ■ 421526-4 (D)

Wuyts, Christiane (hpd)
Bach, J.S.:Sons Fl, BWV 1030-35, w. J. Wentz (fl) Fidelio ▲ FID 9210 [DDD]
The Boutmy Dynasty Arcobaleno ▲ SBCD 5800

Wyatt, S. A. (syn/elec)
Wyatt, S.A.:Still Hidden Laughs — Centaur ▲ CRC 2045 [DDD]

Wyganth, Béatrice (db)
Burkhard, W.:Serenade Fl, Op. 77, w. S. Gärtner (fl), W. Meienberg (cl), J. Stavicek (bn), M. Gugel (hn), M. Paccagnella (hp), H. Schneeberger (vn), C. Schiller (va) *(rec between 1985 & 1989)* — Jecklin-Disco ▲ JD 647-2 [ADD]

Wynberg, Simon (gtr)
Ferrer, J.:Gtr Music—Belle (Andante & Gavotte); La danse de Naïades; L'Etudiant de Salamanque; Vals — Chandos ▲ CHAN 8512 [DDD]
Fossa, F. de:Trios, Op. 18, w. M. Beaver (vn), B. Epperson (vc) *(rec St. John's Church, Elora, Ontario, Mar. 23-25, 1993)* — Naxos ▲ 8.550760 [DDD]
Paganini, N.:Cantabile, w. S. St. John (vn) *(rec Mar. 1993)* — Naxos ▲ 8.550690 [DDD]
Paganini, N.:Cantabile & Waltz, w. S. St. John (vn) *(rec Mar. 1993)* — Naxos ▲ 8.550759 [DDD]
Paganini, N.:Duetto amoroso Vn, w. S. St. John (vn) *(rec Mar. 1993)* — Naxos ▲ 8.550759 [DDD]
Paganini, N.:Son concertata, w. S. St. John (vn) *(rec Mar. 1993)* — Naxos ▲ 8.550690 [DDD]
Paganini, N.:Son large Va, w. S. St. John (vn) [arr. for viola & guitar] *(rec Mar. 1993)* — Naxos ▲ 8.550759 [DDD]
Paganini, N.:Sons Vn & Gtr, Op. 2, w. S. St. John (vn) *(rec Mar. 1993)* — Naxos ▲ 8.550759 [DDD]
Paganini, N.:Sons Vn & Gtr, Op. 3, w. S. St. John (vn) *(rec Mar. 1993)* — Naxos ▲ 8.550690 [DDD]
Paganini, N.:Vars on "Baracaba", w. S. St. John (vn) *(rec Mar. 1993)* — Naxos ▲ 8.550690 [DDD]
Paganini, N.:Vars di bravura, w. S. St. John (vn) *(rec Mar. 1993)* — Naxos ▲ 8.550759 [DDD]
Summertime:Music for Oboe & Guitar, w. John Anderson (ob) — Chandos ("Collect" series) ▲ CHAN 6581 [DDD]
Zani Deferranti, M.A.:Gtr Music—Fantaisie variée sur la Romance d'Otello "Assisaà piè," Op. 7; Six Mélodies Nocturnes Originales, Op. 41a (Nos. 1-4 only); Ronde des fées, Op. 2; Exercice, Op. 50, No. 14; Nocturne sur la dernière pensée de Weber, Op. 40 — Chandos ▲ CHAN 8512 [DDD]

Wyner, Yehudi (pno)
Fine, I.:Childhood Fables for Grownups, w. S. Davenny Wyner (sop) [E] — CRI ▲ CD 574 [ADD]
Wyner, Y.:Concert Duo Vn, w. Matthew Raimondi (vn) — CRI ("American Masters" series) ▲ CD 701 [ADD]

Wyre, J. (perc)—see ORCHESTRAS & ENSEMBLES Nexus

Wyrick, Eric (vn)
Handel, G.F.:Trio Sons, w. S. Machamer (vib), Gerald Ranck (hpd/pno) [performer trans. for vibraphone, violin & piano]—Op. 2, No. 3 for 2 Violins & Keyboard — Ashlar ▲ 1009
Kraft, L.:Inventions & Airs, w. E. Gilmore (cl), A. Karis (pno) *(rec 1989-1990)* — Centaur ▲ CRC 2079 [ADD]
Leclair, J.-M.:Son 3 for 2 Vns, w. S. Machamer (vn) [performer trans. for vibraphone & violin] — Ashlar ▲ 1009
Vibrant Baroque, w. Steven Machamer (vib), Gerald Ranck (pno) — Ashlar Records ▲ 1009

Wyss, Gérard (pno)
Bach, J.S.:Sons Vl, BWV 1027-1029, w. E. Nyffenegger (vc) — Divox ▲ CDX 25206 [ADD]
Brahms, J.:Romanzen aus Tieck's *Magelone*, w. W. Holzmair (bar), W. Quadflieg (spkr) [G] — Tudor 2-▲ 761 [DDD]
Brahms, J.:Sons Vc (comp), w. E. Nyffenegger (vc) — Divox ▲ CDX 25202 [ADD]
Brahms, J.:Songs, w. Edith Mathis (sop)—Von ewiger Liebe, Op. 43; Dein blaues Auge, Op. 59; Meine Liebe ist grün, Op. 63/5; Anklänge, Op.7/3; Volkslied, Op. 7/4; Die Trauernde, Op. 7/5; Klage, Op. 69/1; Das Mädchen, Op. 95/1; Spanisches Lied, Op. 6/1; Nachtwandler, Op. 86/3; Therese, Op. 86/1; Bei dir sind meine Gedanken, Op. 95/2; Sehnsucht, Op. 14/8; Gold überwiegt die Liebe, Op. 48/4; Schön war, das ich dir weihte, Op. 95/7; Klage, Op. 105/3; Regenlied; Mädchenlied, Op. 107/5; An die Nachtigall, Op. 46/4; Wie Melodien zieht es mir, Op. 105/1; Wiegenlied, Op. 49/4 *(rec Swiss Radio DRS, Studio Bern, May 20-22, 1994)* — Denon ▲ CO 78947 [DDD]
Chopin, F.:Son Vc, w. E. Nyffenegger (vc) — Divox ▲ CDX 25204 [ADD]
Duparc, H.:Chanson triste, w. Wolfgang Holzmair (bar) — Philips ▲ 446 686-2
Duparc, H.:Extase, w. Wolfgang Holzmair (bar) — Philips ▲ 446 686-2
Duparc, H.:L'Invitation au voyage, w. Wolfgang Holzmair (bar) — Philips ▲ 446 686-2
Duparc, H.:Le Manoir de Rosemonde, w. Wolfgang Holzmair (bar) — Philips ▲ 446 686-2
Duparc, H.:Sérénade, w. Wolfgang Holzmair (bar) — Philips ▲ 446 686-2
Duparc, H.:Soupir, w. Wolfgang Holzmair (bar) — Philips ▲ 446 686-2
Fauré, G.:La bonne chanson, w. Wolfgang Holzmair (bar) — Philips ▲ 446 686-2
Fauré, G.:Mélodies 'de Venise', Op. 58, w. Wolfgang Holzmair (bar)—4 sels — Philips ▲ 446 686-2
Fauré, G.:Mirages, w. Wolfgang Holzmair (bar) — Philips ▲ 446 686-2
Fauré, G.:Poèmes d'un jour, w. Wolfgang Holzmair (bar) — Philips ▲ 446 686-2
Flury, U.J.:Suite nostalgique, w. U. J. Flury (vn) *(rec Radio Studio, Bern, Apr. 29, 1977)* — Gallo ▲ CD 802 [ADD]
Franck, C.:Son Vn, w. E. Nyffenegger (vc) [trans. for cello & piano] — Divox ▲ CDX 25204 [ADD]
Francoeur, F.:Sons (22) Vn & Continuo, w. E. Nyffenegger (vc)—in E — Divox ▲ CDX 25206 [ADD]
Grieg, E.:Son Vc, w. E. Nyffenegger (vc) — Divox ▲ CDX 25204 [ADD]
Janácek, L.:Fairy Tale, w. E. Nyffenegger (vc) — Divox ▲ CDX 25205 [ADD]
Kosma, J.:Le Ménagerie de Tristan, w. Ursula Wick (mez) — Gallo ▲ CD 831
Locatelli, P.:Son Vc, w. E. Nyffenegger (vc) — Divox ▲ CDX 25206 [ADD]
Lully, J.-B.:Passacaglia Vc & Pno, w. E. Nyffenegger (vc) — Divox ▲ CDX 25206 [ADD]
Mendelssohn, F.:Son 1 Vc, w. E. Nyffenegger (vc) — Divox ▲ CDX 25203 [ADD]
Mendelssohn, F.:Son 2 Vc, w. E. Nyffenegger (vc) — Divox ▲ CDX 25203 [ADD]
Mussorgsky, M.:Songs & Dances, w. Anton Diakov (bass) — Accord 2-▲ ACD 202152 [DDD]
Pfitzner, H.:Son Vc, w. E. Nyffenegger (vc) — Divox ▲ CDX 25205 [ADD]
Ponchielli, A.:Capriccio Ob, w. Omar Zoboli (ob) — Accord ▲ ACD 220682 [AAD]
Ponchielli, A.:Paolo et Virginia, w. Antony Morf (cl), Thomas Füri (vn) — Accord ▲ ACD 220682 [AAD]
Ponchielli, A.:Qt Fl, w. Heinrich Keller (fl), Omar Zoboli (ob), Bruno Furlanetto (E♭ cl), Antony Morf (cl) — Accord ▲ ACD 220682 [AAD]
Ponchielli, A.:Romances (misc), w. Eva Csapó (sop)—Un Sogno; Dimenticar Ben Mio; L'Orfana; La Povera — Accord ▲ ACD 220682 [AAD]
Poulenc, F.:Songs, w. Ursula Wick (mez)—Les chemins de l'amour; Le bestaire — Gallo ▲ CD 831
Ravel, M.:Mélodies populaires grecques, w. Wolfgang Holzmair (bar) — Philips ▲ 446 686-2
Satie, E.:Songs, w. Ursula Wick (mez)—Air du rat; Spleen; La grenouille américane; Air du poète; Chanson du chat; La diva de l'empire; Je te veux; Allons-y chochotte — Gallo ▲ CD 831
Schubert, Franz:Fant Vn, D.934, w. R. Oleg (vn) — Denon/PCM Digital ▲ DEN 75636 [DDD]
Schubert, Franz:Rondo Vn, D.895, w. R. Oleg (vn) — Denon/PCM Digital ▲ DEN 75636 [DDD]
Schubert, Franz:Son Arpeggione, w. E. Nyffenegger (vc) — Divox ▲ CDX 25202 [ADD]
Schubert, Franz:Son Arpeggione, w. R. Oleg (va) — Denon/PCM Digital ▲ DEN 75636 [DDD]
Schubert, Franz:Songs (misc), w. W. Holzmair (bar)—21 songs [G] — Tudor ▲ 762 [DDD]
Schumann, R.:Liederkreis, Op. 39, w. Edith Mathis (sop) *(rec Swiss Radio DRS, Studio Bern, May 20-22, 1994)* — Denon ▲ CO 78947 [DDD]
Schumann, R.:Stücke im Volkston, w. E. Nyffenegger (vc) — Divox ▲ CDX 25203 [ADD]
Strauss, R.:Son Vc, w. E. Nyffenegger (vc) — Divox ▲ CDX 25205 [ADD]
Wiener, J.:Songs, w. Ursula Wick (mez)—Septpetites histoires; Polka; 29-40 chantefleurs — Gallo ▲ CD 831

Wytko, Joseph (sax)
Creston, P.:Son Sax, w. W. Cosand (pno) — ACA Digital Recording ▲ CM 20012
Demars, J.:Seventh Healing Song of John Joseph (Blue) — ACA Digital Recording ▲ CM 20012-2
Maurice, P.:Tableaux de Provence, w. W. Cosand (pno) — ACA Digital Recording ▲ CM 20012

Wyton, Richard (a fl)
Kraft, L.:Cloud Studies, w. Lisa Maron (pic), Margaret Swinchoski (pic), Tanya Dusevic (fl), Adrienne Flynn (fl), Christina Jennings (fl), Zara Lawler (fl), Joseph Piscitelli (fl), Michelle Ryang (fl), Dominique Soucy (fl), Diane Taublieb (fl), Laurel Ann Maurer (a fl), J. Solum (cnd) *(rec Skinner Recital Hall, Vassar College, Poughkeepsie, NY, Mar 24-26, 1994)* — CRI ▲ CD 712 [DDD]

Wyton, Richard (fl)
Beeson, J.:Fant, Ditty & Fughettas, w. John Solum (fl) *(rec Skinner Recital Hall, Vassar College, Poughkeepsie, NY, Mar 24-26, 1994)* — CRI ▲ CD 712 [DDD]

Wyton, Richard (fl) (cont.)
Laderman, E.:Epigrams & Canons, w. John Solum (baroque fl) *(rec Skinner Recital Hall, Vassar College, Poughkeepsie, NY, Mar 24-26, 1994)* — CRI ▲ CD 712 [DDD]

Wyton, Richard (trns fl)
Bach, J.S.:Trio Son for 2 Fls, BWV 1039, w. J. Solum (trns fl), E. Potash (vc), I. Kipnis (hpd) [period instrs] — Arabesque ▲ ARA 6640 [DDD]

Wyttenbach, Janka (pno)
Keller, A.:Songs Bar & Pno, w. K. Widmer (bass) [G] — Grammont ▲ CTSP 19-2 [ADD]
Schmid, E.:Gesänge der Zeit, w. K. Widmer (bass) [G] *(rec. Oct. 31, 1975)* — Grammont ▲ CTSP 33-2 [ADD]
Schmid, E.:Rhap Cl, w. R. Gmür (cl) *(rec Dec. 16, 1986)* — Grammont ▲ CTSP 33-2 [ADD]
Schmid, E.:Songs from Sonnets by Michelangelo-Rilke, w. K. Widmer (bass) [G] *(rec. Oct. 31, 1975)* — Grammont ▲ CTSP 33-2 [ADD]

Xaver, Frantisek (hpd)
Vejvanovsky, P.J.:Sons & Serenades, w. Vaclav Jirovec (vc), Jan Hasenöhrl (tpt), Jiri Pribyl (trbn), Milan Hruby (brass), Oldrich Vlcek (vn), O. Vlček (cnd), Prague Virtuosi—Intrada; Harmonia romana; Serenada; Offertur ad duos chorus; Son à 4 de mollis; Son paschalis; Son tribus quadrantibus; Son campanarum; Serenada *(rec Lobochovice castle, July 26-28, 1992)* — Discover International ▲ DI 920243 [DDD]

Xiao-fen, Min (pipa)
Chen, Y.:Music of, w. Liu Wei-shan (guzheng), Zhao Yang-qin (yangqin), Chen Jie-bing (erhu), J. Falletta (cnd), Women's PO, Chanticleer—Duo Ye No. 2; Sym 2; Ge Xu; Chinese Myths Cant; Pan Gu Creates Heaven & Earth; Nu Wa Creates Human Beings; Weaving Maid & Cowherd; Song of Weaving Maid & Cowherd *(rec Skywalker Sound, San Rafael, CA, June 1996)* — New Albion ▲ NA 090

Xiaohui, Ma (erhu)
Gu, G.:Con Erhu, "Gazing at the Moon", w. G. Guanren (cnd), Shanghai Chinese Folk Orch *(rec Shanghai, Jan 1994)* — Marco Polo ("Chinese Composers" series) ▲ 8.223951 [DDD]

Xiao-Mei, Zhu (pno)
Scarlatti, D.:Sons Kbd—K.531, 98, 124, 125, 87, 27, 533, 32, 141, 142, 25, 69, 481, 386, 128, 39, 113 *(rec Prague Academy of Music, Nov 15, 1995)* — Memoire Vive ▲ 262022 [ADD]
Schubert, Franz:Allegretto Pno, D.915 *(rec Prague Academy of Music, Jan 14, 1994)* — Memoire Vive ▲ 262022 [ADD]

Xuereb, Pierre-Henri (va)
Honegger, A.:Chamber Music (comp), w. D.-S. Kang (vn), J.-P. Audoli (vn), R. Wallfisch (vc), J. Rossi (db), P. Devoyon (pno)—Sonatine for 2 Violins (1920); Sonatine for Violin & Cello (1932); Sonata for Cello & Piano (1920); Sonata for Viola & Piano (1920); Trio in f for Violin, Cello & Piano (1914); Paduana for Solo Cello (1945); Prelude for Double Bass & Piano (1932) — Timpani ▲ IC1009 [DDD]
Honegger, A.:Chamber Music (comp), w. D.-S. Kang (vn), R. Wallfisch (vc), M. Arrignon (cl), A. Marion (fl), A. Haraldsdottir (fl), C. Moreaux (ob), T. Caens (tpt), M. Becquet (trbn), P. Zanlonghi (hp), P. Devoyon (pno), F. Kondo (mez), Ludwig String Quartet—Sonatine for Clarinet & Piano (1921-22); Rapsodie for 2 Flutes, Clarinet & Piano (1917); Danse de la Chèvre for Solo Flute (1921); Romance for Flute & Piano (1953); Petite Suite for 2 Flutes & Piano (1934); Trois Contrepoints for Piccolo, Oboe, Violin & Cello (1922); Intrada for Trumpet & Piano (1947); Hommage du trombone exprimant la tristesse de l'auteur absent for Trombone & Piano (1925); J'avais un fidèle amant for String Quartet (1929); Chanson de Ronsard & 3 Chansons de la petite Sirène for Mezzo, Flute & String Quartet (1924); Introduction et Danse for Flute, Harp & String Trio [undated]; Colloque for Flute, Celesta, Violin & Viola [undated] — Timpani ▲ IC1010 [DDD]

Xue-Wei, (vn)
Brahms, J.:Con Vn, w. I. Bolton (cnd), London PO — ASV ▲ ASV 748
Bruch, M.:Con 1 Vn, w. K. Bakels (cnd), Philharmonia Orch — ASV ▲ ASV 680 [DDD]
Headington, C.:Con Vn, w. J. Glover (cnd), London PO — ASV ▲ ASV 780 [DDD]
Mendelssohn, F.:Con in e Vn & Orch, Op. 64, w. I. Bolton (cnd), London PO — ASV ▲ ASV 748
Saint-Saëns, C.:Con 3 Vn, w. K. Bakels (cnd), Philharmonia Orch — ASV ▲ ASV 680 [DDD]
Saint-Saëns, C.:Introduction & Rondo capriccioso, w. J. Lenehan (pno) [arr. violin & piano] — ASV ▲ ASV 892 [DDD]
Saint-Saëns, C.:Son 1 Vn, w. J. Lenehan (pno) — ASV ▲ ASV 892 [DDD]
Saint-Saëns, C.:Son 2 Vn, w. J. Lenehan (pno) — ASV ▲ ASV 892 [DDD]
Strauss, R.:Con Vn, w. J. Glover (cnd), London PO — ASV ▲ ASV 780 [DDD]
Tchaikovsky, P.:Con Vn, w. S. Accardo (cnd), Philharmonia Orch — ASV ▲ ASV 713 [DDD]
Tchaikovsky, P.:Sérénade mélancolique, w. S. Accardo (cnd), Philharmonia Orch — ASV ▲ ASV 713 [DDD]
Tchaikovsky, P.:Souvenir d'un lieu cher, w. S. Accardo (cnd), Philharmonia Orch—Mélodie [arr vn & orch] — ASV ▲ ASV 713 [DDD]
Tchaikovsky, P.:Valse-Scherzo Vn, w. S. Accardo (cnd), Philharmonia Orch — ASV ▲ ASV 713 [DDD]

Xunfa, Yu (bamboo fl)
Zhu, J.:Sym 4, w. C. Peng (cnd), Shanghai PO *(rec Shanghai, China, Jan 1994)* — Marco Polo ("Chinese Composers" series) ▲ 8.223941 [DDD]

Yablonskaya, Oxana (pno)
Beethoven, L. van:Son 7 Pno — In Sync ▮ C 4127
Beethoven, L. van:Son 8 Pno, "Pathétique" — In Sync ▮ C 4127
Brahms, J.:Sons Vc (comp), w. D. Yablonski (vc) — Arcobaleno ▲ SBCD 9400 [DDD]
Rachmaninoff, S.:Pno Music (misc)—Daisies, Op. 38/3; Études-tableaux, Op. 33/6 & 8; Lilacs, Op. 21/5; Moments musicaux, Op. 16/4 & 5; Morceaux de fantaisie, Op. 3/1; Morceaux de salon, Op. 10/2 & 3; Preludes for Pno, Op. 32/6, 8, 10, 12 — Connoisseur Society ▲ CD 4194
Rachmaninoff, S.:Pno Transcriptions—Mendelssohn:Scherzo from "A Midsummer Night's Dream" — Connoisseur Society ▲ CD 4194
Rachmaninoff, S.:Variations on a Theme by Corelli — Connoisseur Society ▲ CD 4194
Tchaikovsky, P.:Morceaux, Op. 51 *(rec Fisher Hall, Santa Rosa, CA, May 12 & 13, 1994)* — Naxos ▲ 8.553063 [DDD]
Tchaikovsky, P.:Son Pno, Op. 37 *(rec Fisher Hall, Santa Rosa, CA, May 12 & 13, 1994)* — Naxos ▲ 8.553063 [DDD]

Yablonski, Dimitri (vc)
Brahms, J.:Sons Vc (comp), w. O. Yablonskaya (pno) — Arcobaleno ▲ SBCD 9400 [DDD]

Yamahata, Renie (hp)
Debussy, C.:Danses sacrée et profane, w. T. Briccetti (cnd), Prague Virtuosi *(rec Korunni Studios, Prague, Oct. 31-Nov. 3, 1994)* — Discover International ▲ DI 920281 [DDD]
Fauré, G.:Fant Fl, w. Angela Jones (fl) *(rec Korunni Studios, Prague, Oct. 31-Nov. 3, 1994)* — Discover International ▲ DI 920281 [DDD]
Fauré, G.:Impromptu Hp *(rec Korunni Studios, Prague, Oct. 31-Nov. 3, 1994)* — Discover International ▲ DI 920281 [DDD]
Ravel, M.:Intro & Allegro, w. Angela Jones (fl), T. Briccetti (cnd), Prague Virtuosi *(rec Korunni Studios, Prague, Oct. 31-Nov. 3, 1994)* — Discover International ▲ DI 920281 [DDD]
Saint-Saëns, C.:Fant Vn, w. A. Jones (fl) *(rec Korunni Studios, Prague, Oct. 31-Nov. 3, 1994)* — Discover International ▲ DI 920281 [DDD]

Yamamoto, Yasuhiro (ob)—see ORCHESTRAS & ENSEMBLES Orphée Piano & Wind Quintet

Yamamura, Yasuo (perc)—see ORCHESTRAS & ENSEMBLES Bugaku Percussion Ensemble

Yamashita, Kazuhito (gtr)
Bach, J.S.:Sons & Partitas Vn, BWV 1001-1006 [arr. Yamashita for guitar] — Crown Classics ▲ CRC 8001 [DDD]
Boccherini, L.:Qnts Gtr & Strs, w. Tokyo String Quartet—in D, G.448 & in G, G.450 — RCA Red Seal ▲ 60421-2-RC [DDD]
Carulli, F.:Con Gtr, Janáček CO — RCA Red Seal ▲ 5914-2-RC [DDD]
Castelnuovo-Tedesco, M.:Con 1 Gtr, w. L. Slatkin (cnd), London PO — RCA Red Seal ▲ 60355-2-RC [DDD]
Castelnuovo-Tedesco, M.:Con 2 Gtr, w. L. Slatkin (cnd), London PO — RCA Red Seal ▲ 60355-2-RC [DDD]
Castelnuovo-Tedesco, M.:Con for 2 Gtrs, w. N. Yamashita (gtr), L. Slatkin (cnd), London PO — RCA Red Seal ▲ 60355-2-RC [DDD]
Castelnuovo-Tedesco, M.:Qnt Gtr & Str, w. Tokyo String Quartet — RCA Red Seal ▲ 60421-2-RC [DDD]

▲ = CD ♦ = Enhanced CD Δ = MD ▮ = Cassette Tape ◻ = DCC

Yamashita, Kazuhito (gtr) (cont.)
Cimarosa, D.:Serenade Fl & Gtr, w. J. Galway (fl) *(rec CBS Studios, London, June 23-25, 1986)* RCA Gold Seal ▲ 61448-2
Debussy, C.:Passepied, w. N. Yamashita (gtr) RCA Red Seal ▲ 6777-2-RC [DDD]
Debussy, C.:Petite suite, w. N. Yamashita (gtr) RCA Red Seal ▲ 6777-2-RC [DDD]
Dvořák, A.:Sym 9, "From the New World" [solo guitar trans.] RCA Red Seal ▲ 7929-2-RC [DDD]
Françaix, J.:Divert 2 Gtr, w. N. Yamashita (gtr) RCA Red Seal ▲ 6777-2-RC [DDD]
Giuliani, M.:Grand Duo Concertant, Op. 52, w. J. Galway (fl) RCA Red Seal ▲ 09026-60237-2
Giuliani, M.:Grand Duo Concertant Fl, w. J. Galway (fl) *(rec CBS Studios, London, June 23-25, 1986)* RCA Gold Seal ▲ 61448-2
Giuliani, M.:Grand Son Fl, w. J. Galway (fl) RCA Red Seal ▲ 09026-60237-2
Giuliani, M.:Serenade Vn, w. J. Swensen (vn), E. Anderson (vc) RCA Red Seal ▲ 09026-60237-2
Kazuhito Yamashita Plays His Favorites *(rec June 4-5, 1991)* Crown Classics ▲ CRC 8007 [DDD]
Mozart, W.A.:Don Giovanni (sels), w. N. Yamashita (gtr)—Nella bionda egli ha l'usanza; Giovinette, che fate all'amore; La ci darem la mano; Dalla sua pace; Deh! vieni alla finestra, o mio tesoro Crown Classics ▲ CRCC 8008 [DDD]
Mozart, W.A.:Nozze di Figaro (sels), w. N. Yamashita (gtr)—Voi che sapete; Non più andrai; L'ho perduta, me meschina! *(rec Aug. 22-23, 1991)* Crown Classics ▲ CRCC 8008 [DDD]
Mozart, W.A.:Zauberflöte (sels), w. N. Yamashita (gtr)—Der Vogelfänger bin ich ja; Dies Bildnis ist bezauberend schön; Bei Männern, welche Liebe fühlen; Zum Ziele führt dich diese Bahn; Das klingt so herrlich; O Isis und Osiris Crown Classics ▲ CRCC 8008 [DDD]
Music of Spain RCA Red Seal ▲ 5913-2-RC [DDD]
Paganini, N.:Son concertata, w. J. Galway (fl) *(rec CBS Studios, London, June 23-25, 1986)* RCA Gold Seal ▲ 61448-2
Rimsky-Korsakov, N.:Scheherazade, w. N. Yamashita (gtr) RCA Red Seal ▲ 6777-2-RC [DDD]
Rodrigo, J.:Concierto de Aranjuez, w. James Galway (fl), J.-F. Paillard (cnd), Jean-François Paillard CO RCA Gold Seal ▲ 09026-68428-2 ■ 09026-68428-4
Rossini, G.:Andante con variazioni Va, w. J. Galway (fl) *(rec CBS Studios, London, June 23-25, 1986)* RCA Gold Seal ▲ 61448-2
Stravinsky, I.:The Firebird Suite [solo gtr trans.] RCA Red Seal ▲ 7929-2-RC [DDD]
Vivaldi, A.:Con Lt, Janáček CO RCA Red Seal ▲ 5914-2-RC [DDD]

Yamashita, Naoko (gtr)
Castelnuovo-Tedesco, M.:Con for 2 Gtrs, w. K. Yamashita (gtr), L. Slatkin (cnd), London PO RCA Red Seal ▲ 60355-2-RC [DDD]
Debussy, C.:Passepied, w. K. Yamashita (gtr) RCA Red Seal ▲ 6777-2-RC [DDD]
Debussy, C.:Petite suite, w. K. Yamashita (gtr) RCA Red Seal ▲ 6777-2-RC [DDD]
Françaix, J.:Divert 2 Gtr, w. K. Yamashita (gtr) RCA Red Seal ▲ 6777-2-RC [DDD]
Giuliani, M.:Con 1 Gtr, Janáček CO RCA Red Seal ▲ 5914-2-RC [DDD]
Mozart, W.A.:Don Giovanni (sels), w. K. Yamashita (gtr)—Nella bionda egli ha l'usanza; Giovinette, che fate all'amore; La ci darem la mano; Dalla sua pace; Deh! vieni alla finestra, o mio tesoro Crown Classics ▲ CRCC 8008 [DDD]
Mozart, W.A.:Nozze di Figaro (sels), w. K. Yamashita (gtr)—Voi che sapete; Non più andrai; L'ho perduta, me meschina! *(rec Aug. 22-23, 1991)* Crown Classics ▲ CRCC 8008 [DDD]
Mozart, W.A.:Zauberflöte (sels), w. K. Yamashita (gtr)—Der Vogelfänger bin ich ja; Dies Bildnis ist bezauberend schön; Bei Männern, welche Liebe fühlen; Zum Ziele führt dich diese Bahn; Das klingt so herrlich; O Isis und Osiris Crown Classics ▲ CRCC 8008 [DDD]
Rimsky-Korsakov, N.:Scheherazade, w. K. Yamashita (gtr) RCA Red Seal ▲ 6777-2-RC [DDD]

Yamashita, Stomu (syn/perc)
Yamash'Ta, S.:Sea & Sky, w. Sen Izumi (syn), Takashi Kokobu (syn), Muse Orch Kuckuck ▲ CD 072 ■ MC 072

Yamazaki, H. (perc)
Fukushi, N.:Chromosphere, w. J. Arase (perc), M. Okada (perc), S. Sato (perc), S. Yoshihara (perc), T. Otaka (cnd), Tokyo PO *(rec live Tokyo Bunka-Kaikan, Large Hall, May 30, 1981)* Camerata ▲ 32CM 293 [AAD]

Yampolsky, Viktor (pno)—see also ORCHESTRAS & ENSEMBLES Moscow Contemporary Music Ensemble
Bach, J.S.:Sons Vn, w. Leonid Kogan (vn)—in b, BWV 1014 Multisonic ▲ MUL 310354
David Oistrakh, w. David Oistrakh (vn), Lev Oborin (pno) Vanguard Classics 3-▲ OVC 4080/02 [ADD]
Hindemith, P.:Kammermusic 2, w. A. Vinogradov (cnd), Moscow Contemporary Music Ensemble Triton ▲ 17010 [DDD]
Hindemith, P.:Qt Cl, Vn, Vc & Pno, w. Oleg Tantzov (cl), Mikhail Tzinman (vn), Natalya Savinova (vc) *(rec Mosfilm Studio, Dec 1994)* Triton ▲ 17005 [DDD]
Hindemith, P.:Son Cl, w. Oleg Tantzov (cl) *(rec Mosfilm Studio, Dec 1994)* Triton ▲ 17005 [DDD]
Medtner, N.:Nocturnes *(rec Mosfilm Studio, Jan & Feb 1996)* Triton ▲ 17009 [DDD]
Medtner, N.:Son 1 Vn, w. Mikhail Tsinman (vn) *(rec Mosfilm Studio, Jan & Feb 1996)* Triton ▲ 17009 [DDD]
Medtner, N.:Son 2 Vn, w. Mikhail Tsinman (vn) *(rec Mosfilm Studio, Jan & Feb 1996)* Triton ▲ 17009 [DDD]
Mosolov, A.:Pieces Bn, w. Alexander Popov (bn) *(rec Mosfilm Studio, Jan 1995)* Triton ▲ 17004 [DDD]
Mosolov, A.:Pieces Ob, w. Petr Fedkov (ob) *(rec Mosfilm Studio, Jan 1995)* Triton ▲ 17004 [DDD]

Yanagita, Masako (vn)—see also ORCHESTRAS & ENSEMBLES Jennings String Quartet
Baksa, R.:Qnt Ob & Strs, w. B. Lucarelli (ob), N. Tanaka (vn), S. Winterbottom (va), T. Hoyle (vc) Capstone ▲ CPS 8610
Colgrass, M.:Concert Masters, w. Ronald Oakland (vn), Robert Rudie (vn), K. Akiyama (cnd), American SO *(rec 1977)* Vox Box ("The American Composers" series) 2-▲ CDX 5158

Yanchenko, Oleg (org)
Artyomov, V.:Lamentations, w. D. Kitayenko (cnd), Moscow PO Olympia ▲ OLY 515 [DDD]

Yang, Wen-Sinn (vc)
Janácek, L.:Pno Music, w. Gilead Mishory (pno), András Adorján (pic), Saschko Gawriloff (vn)—Son. for Vn & Pno; Allegro for Vn & Pno; Romance for Vn & Pno; Dumka for Vn & Pno; Tema Con Vars. for Pno; Fairy Tale for Vc & Pno; Presto for Vc & Pno; March of the Bluebreasts for Pic & Pno; Music for Excercises w. Clubs for Pno; In Memoriam for Pno; Reminiscence for Pno Tudor ▲ TUD 7003 [DDD]

Yang-qin, Zhao (yangqin)
Chen, Y.:Music of, w. Liu Wei-shan (guzheng), Chen Jie-bing (erhu), Min Xiao-fen (pipa), J. Falletta (cnd), Women's PO, Chanticleer—Duo Ye No. 2; Sym 2; Ge Xu; Chinese Myths Cant; Pan Gu Creates Heaven & Earth; Nu Wa Creates Human Beings; Weaving Maid & Cowherd; Song of Weaving Maid & Cowherd *(rec Skywalker Sound, San Rafael, CA, June 1996)* New Albion ▲ NA 090

Yankelev, J. (vn)—see ORCHESTRAS & ENSEMBLES New World String Quartet

Yanuchevskaia, Macha (vc)
Scarlatti, A.:Cants & Duets, w. Véronique Dietschy (sop), Alain Zaepffel (ct), Marianne Muller (vl), Aline Zylberajch (hpd/org), Yasurnori Imamura (thb)—Il Sonno; Clori e Mirtillo; Marcantonio e Cleopatra; Doralbo e Niso Adès ▲ ADE 202172 [DDD]

Yaotani, S. (hichiriki)
Shinohara, M.:Cooperation, w. A. Nishigata (shamisen), K. Mitsuhashi (shakuhachi), M. Akao (fue), S. Yaotani (hichiriki), K. Ishikawa (sho), C. Fukunaga (koto), J. Ueda (biwa), M. Yoshizawa (kokyu), I. Tsuji (oboe), T. Takahashi (cl), G. Kitamura (tpt), A. Murata (trbn), S. Eiso (perc), S. Ueki (vn), S. Katsuta (vc), Y. Shibuya (pno), K. Komatsu (cnd) *(rec live Casals Hall, Tokyo, Mar. 5, 1994)* Camerata ▲ 30CM 375 [DDD]

Yarbrough, Joan (pno)
Britten, H.:Introduction & Rondo alla burlesca & Mazurka elegiaca, w. R. Cowan (pno)—No. 1 Centaur ▲ CRC 2095 [DDD]
Britten, H.:Scottish Ballad, w. R. Cowan (pno), P. Freeman (cnd), Berlin RSO Centaur ▲ CRC 2095 [DDD]
Bruch, M.:Con for 2 Pnos, w. Robert Cowan (pno), P. Freeman (cnd), Moscow PO *(rec Moscow Radio Union, Feb 28, 1994)* Centaur ▲ CRC 2227 [DDD]
Milhaud, D.:Con for 2 Pnos, w. Robert Cowan (pno), P. Freeman (cnd), Royal PO *(rec Henry Wood Hall, London, Sept 26, 1977)* Centaur ▲ CRC 2227 [DDD]

Yarbrough, Joan (pno) (cont.)
Milhaud, D.:Scaramouche for 2 Pnos, w. Robert Cowan (pno) *(rec Moscow Radio Union, Mar 2, 1994)* Centaur ▲ CRC 2227 [DDD]
Vaughan Williams, R.:Con Pno, w. R. Cowan (pno), P. Freeman (cnd), Berlin RSO Centaur ▲ CRC 2095 [DDD]

Yarbrough, P. (va)—see ORCHESTRAS & ENSEMBLES Alexander String Quartet

Yarden, Guy (vn/pno)
Exquisite Corpses from P.S. 122, w. Watson, David (shears/stick vn/gtr/tpt), Judy Dunaway (gtr/balloons), Anthony Coleman (sampler), Raissa St. Pierre (drums), Guy Yarden (vn/pno), Leslie Ross (bn), Linda Austin (gtr), Bruce Kaplan (gtr), Doug Henderson (peckhorn/bass/toy pno), Sue Ann Harkey (gtr), Cinnie Cole (sampler), et al. ¿What Next? ▲ WN 0002 [ADD]

Yardley, D. (pno)
Rahbee, D.G.:Novellette *(rec The Music Room)* Seda ▲ 333 [DDD]

Yaron, Yuval (vn)
Achron, J.:Vn & Pno Music, w. Hélène Jeanney (pno)—Hebrew Melody, Op. 33; Hebrew Lullaby Accord ▲ ACD 205462 [DDD]
Bach, J.S.:Sons & Partitas Vn, BWV 1001-1006 Accord 2-▲ ACD 200562 [DDD]
Bistritzky, Z.:Fantastic Dream, w. Hélène Jeanney (pno) Accord ▲ ACD 205462 [DDD]
Bloch, E.:Abodah, "God's Worship", w. Hélène Jeanney (pno) Accord ▲ ACD 205462 [DDD]
Bloch, E.:Baal Shem, "3 Pictures of Chassidic Life", w. Hélène Jeanney (pno) Accord ▲ ACD 205462 [DDD]
Bruch, M.:Kol Nidrei, w. Hélène Jeanney (pno) Accord ▲ ACD 205462 [DDD]
Elman, M.:Vn Arrs, w. Hélène Jeanney (pno)—Eili Eili [Yiddish Melody] Accord ▲ ACD 205462 [DDD]
Ravel, M.:Kaddisch, w. Hélène Jeanney (pno) Accord ▲ ACD 205462 [DDD]
Sibelius, J.:Music for Vn Pno, w. R. Sharon (pno)—Opp. 78/1-4, 79/6, 81/1-3 & 5 *(rec Feb. 1976 & July 1977)* Finlandia ▲ 4509-95853-2 [AAD]
Ysaÿe, E.:Sons Vn Accord ▲ ACD 200922 [DDD]

Yashvili, Marina (vn)
Brahms, J.:Hungarian Dances Pno 4-Hands, w. Taisiya Schpiller (pno)—Nos. 1, 7, 16 & 17 [arr J. Joachim for vn & pno] *(rec 1975)* Russian Compact Disc ("Talents of Russia" series) ▲ RCD 16252 [ADD]
Brahms, J.:Son 2 Vn, w. Igor Chernyshov (pno) *(rec 1991)* Russian Compact Disc ("Talents of Russia" series) ▲ RCD 16252 [ADD]
Brahms, J.:Songs, w. Taisiya Schpiller (pno)—Contemplation in D♭ [arr J. Heifitz for vn & pno] *(rec 1991)* Russian Compact Disc ("Talents of Russia" series) ▲ RCD 16252 [ADD]
Falla, M. de:Canciones populares españolas (7), w. Naum Walter (pno)—El paño moruno; Nana; Canción; Polo; Asturiana; Jota [all arr P. Kokhansky for vn & pno] *(rec 1975)* Russian Compact Disc ("Talents of Russia" series) ▲ RCD 16252 [ADD]
Paganini, N.:Cantibile in D, w. Naum Walter (pno) [arr for vn & pno] *(rec 1975)* Russian Compact Disc ("Talents of Russia" series) ▲ RCD 16252 [ADD]
Paganini, N.:Moto perpeuto in C, w. Naum Walter (pno) [arr for vn & pno] *(rec 1975)* Russian Compact Disc ("Talents of Russia" series) ▲ RCD 16252 [ADD]

Yasinitsky, Ann Marie (fl)
Jolivet, A.:Chant de Linos, w. Gerald Berthiaume (pno) Vienna Modern Masters ▲ VMM 2013 [DDD]

Yasuda, K. (vc)
Yashiro, A.:Qt Strs, w. C. Tanaka (vn), S. Muto (vn), T. Uzuka (va) Camerata ▲ 30CM 51
Yashiro, A.:Trio Pno, w. H. Puig-Robert (pno), C. Tanaka (vn) Camerata ▲ 30CM 51

Yasukawa, Kazuko (pno)
Yashiro, A.:Suite Classique, w. K. Kanazawa (pno) Camerata ▲ 30CM 50

Yates, Catherine (vn)—see ORCHESTRAS & ENSEMBLES Sorrel String Quartet

Yates, Sophie (hpd)
Bach, J.S.:Italian Con Chandos ("Chaconne" series) ▲ CHAN 0598
Couperin, F.:Pièces de clavecin (sels)—4th order [from Book 1]; 6th order [from Book 2]; 26th order [from Book 4] Chandos ("Chaconne" series) ▲ CHAN 0598
Daquin, L.-C.:Pièces de clavecin (sels)—3rd suite [from Book 1] Chandos ("Chaconne" series) ▲ CHAN 0598
Duphly, J.:Pièces de clavecin (4 books)—La Pothoüin (rondeau) [from Book 4] Chandos ("Chaconne" series) ▲ CHAN 0598
Handel, G.F.:The Harmonious Blacksmith Chandos ("Chaconne" series) ▲ CHAN 0598
Purcell, H.:Music of—Suites No. 1, Z.660; No. 2, Z.661; No. 3, Z.662; No. 4, Z.663; No. 5, Z.666; No. 6, Z.667; No. 7, Z.668; No. 8, Z.669; Ground in Gamut, Z.645; Prelude; Suite of Lessons, Z.665; A New Ground, Z.T682; Saraband w. Division, Z.654; Grounds, Z.D221 & Z.D222; Round O, Z.T684 Chandos ("Early Music" series) ▲ CHAN 0587 [DDD]
Rameau, J.P.:Nouvelles suites—La Poule; Gavotte & Vars Chandos ("Chaconne" series) ▲ CHAN 0598
Rameau, J.P.:Pièces de clavecin avec une méthode sur la mécanique des doigts—Les Cyclopes (rondeau) Chandos ("Chaconne" series) ▲ CHAN 0598
Scarlatti, D.:Sons Kbd—K.24 & K.513 Chandos ("Chaconne" series) ▲ CHAN 0598
Spanish & Portuguese Harpsichord Chandos ▲ CHAN 0560 [DDD]

Yates, Sophie (vir)
Byrd, W.:Songs, w. Fretwork, Robert Hollingworth (cnd), I Fagiolini—Attollite port; Triumph with pleasant melody; O Lord, how vain; All in a Garden Green; Domine secundum actum meum; Truth at the first; Who likes to love; Wolsey's Wilde; Da mihi auxilium; Farewell, false love; O Mistrys Myne; Miserere mihi, Domine; My mind to me a kingdom is; La volta; Ad Dominum cum tribularer Chandos ("Chaconne" series) ▲ CHAN 0578 [DDD]
English Virginals Music Chandos ▲ CHAN 0574 [DDD]

Ydiers, Marleen (vn)
Crumb, G.:Black Angels (Images I), w. Filip Suys (vn), Annemarie Vercauteren (va), Arne Deforce (vc), Johan Vandermaelen (elec) *(rec Steurbaut Sound Recording Ctr)* René Gailly ▲ CD87 118 [DDD]
Mozetich, M.:Qt Strs, w. Filip Suys (vn), Annemarie Vercauteren (va), Arne Deforce (vc) *(rec Steurbaut Sound Recording Ctr)* René Gailly ▲ CD87 118 [DDD]

Yeager, Paul (vn)
Samuel, G.:Transformations, w. K. Sassmannshaus (cnd), Starling CO *(rec Corbett Auditorium, College-Conservatory of Music, Univ. of Cincinnati, OH, Sept 25, 1994)* Centaur ▲ CRC 2238 [DDD]

Yeats, Caitriona (hp)
Foote, A.:At Dusk, w. F. Smith (fl), R. Thomas (vc) Northeastern ("Classical Arts" series) ▲ NR 227-CD

Yegorov, Pavel (pno)
Schumann, R.:Carnaval Pno Infinity Digital ▲ QK 57264 [DDD]
Schumann, R.:Kinderszenen Infinity Digital ▲ QK 57264 [DDD]

Yeh, John Bruce (cl)
Bernstein, L.:Prelude, Fugue & Riffs Cl, w. DePaul Univ Jazz Ensemble *(rec May 1-3, 1993)* Reference ▲ RR 55 CD [DDD]
Blackwood, E.:Son Cl *(rec WFMT Chicago, Feb. 19-21, 1995)* Cedille ▲ CDR 90000 022 [DDD]
Blackwood, E.:Sonatina Pic Cl *(rec WFMT Chicago, Feb. 19-21, 1995)* Cedille ▲ CDR 90000 022 [DDD]
Gould, M.:Derivations, w. DePaul Univ Jazz Ensemble *(rec May 1-3, 1993)* Reference ▲ RR 55 CD [DDD]
Nielsen, C.:Con Cl, w. D. Kober (cnd), Chicago CO Centaur ▲ CRC 2024 [DDD]
Prokofiev, S.:Son Fl, w. D. Kober (cnd), Chicago CO [arr. Kennan as Con. for Clarinet & Orch.] Centaur ▲ CRC 2154
Reger, M.:Son Cl, Op. 107, w. Easley Blackwood (pno) *(rec WFMT Chicago, Feb. 19-21, 1995)* Cedille ▲ CDR 90000 022 [DDD]
Shaw, A.:Con Cl, w. J.B. Yeh, DePaul Univ Jazz Ensemble *(rec May 1-3, 1993)* Reference ▲ RR 55 CD [DDD]
Stravinsky, I.:Ebony Con, w. DePaul Univ Wind Ensemble *(rec May 1-3, 1993)* Reference ▲ RR 55 CD [DDD]

Yenney, H. (vn)—see ORCHESTRAS & ENSEMBLES Griffin Music Ensemble

Yeo, Douglas (trbn)
Hindemith, P.:Stücke (4) Bn & Vc, w. R. Barron (trbn) [arr. for tenor & bass trombones] Boston Brass ▲ BB 1002CD ■ BB 1002CT
In The Family, w. Ronald Barron (trbn), Marianne Gedigian (fl), Ann Hobson Pilot (hp), Edwin Barker (bass), Thomas Gauger (perc) *(rec Morse Auditorium, Boston Univ, Dec 1995)* Boston Brass ▲ BB 1004
Yeo, Richard (vc)—see ORCHESTRAS & ENSEMBLES Ad Hoc String Quartet
Yepes, Narciso (gtr)
Bacarisse, S.:Concertino Gtr, w. R. Frühbeck de Burgos (cnd), London SO Deutsche Grammophon ▲ 435845-2
Boccherini, L.:Qnts Gtr & Strs, w. Melos String Quartet—Op. 50/4, 7 & 9 Deutsche Grammophon ("Resonance" series) ▲ 429512-2 [ADD]
Fantasy, Deutsche Grammophon ("Musikfest" series) ■ 415439-4
Guitar Duos, w. Godelieve Monden (gtr) RCA Red Seal ▲ 09026-60764-2
Guitarra Española:Albéniz + Deutsche Grammophon ▲ 435843-2
Guitarra Española:Rodrigo, Aranjuez,w. Spanish NationalRadio-TV SO [cnd:O. Alonso], London SO [cnd:R. Frühbeck de Burgos] Deutsche Grammophon ▲ 435845-2
Guitarra Española:Tárrega + Deutsche Grammophon ▲ 435844-2
Rodrigo, J.:Concierto de Aranjuez, w. L.A. Garcia-Navarro (cnd), Philharmonia Orch Deutsche Grammophon ▲ 415349-2 [ADD]
Rodrigo, J.:Concierto de Aranjuez, w. O. Alonso (cnd), Spanish National Radio-TV SO Deutsche Grammophon ▲ 435845-2 [ADD]
Rodrigo, J.:Fant para un gentilhombre, w. L.A. Garcia-Navarro (cnd), English CO Deutsche Grammophon ▲ 415349-2 [ADD]
Vivaldi, A.:Con Lt, w. P. Kuentz (cnd), Kuentz CO Deutsche Grammophon ("Resonance" series) ▲ 429528-2 [ADD] ■ 429528-4
Vivaldi, A.:Con Va d'amore Lt, w. M. Frasca-Colombier (vn), P. Kuentz (cnd), Kuentz CO Deutsche Grammophon ("Resonance" series) ▲ 429528-2 [ADD] ■ 429528-4
World of the Spanish Guitar, Vol. 1 London ■ 417043-4
World of the Spanish Guitar, Vol. 2 London ■ 417046-4
Yepes, N.:Gtr Music—Jeux interdits; Danse espagnole, No. 10; Rondo; Son; Recuerdos de la alhambra; Alborada [Petite boîte]; Leyenda; Danse espagnole, No. 4; Gavotte; Homenaje a Debussy [Hommage pour le tombeau de Claude Debussy]; Farruca; Rumores de la caleta; En los trigales; 2 menuets Accord ▲ ACD 222032 [AAD]
Yesilcay, Mehmet Cemal (lt/perc)—see ORCHESTRAS & ENSEMBLES Ensemble Saraband
Yin, Cheng-Zong (pno)
Yellow River Con, w. A. Leaper (cnd), Bratislava RSO Marco Polo ▲ 8.223412 [DDD]
Ying, Tian (pno)
Chopin, F.:Fant *(rec Mar 19–20, 1996)* Arizona Friends of Chamber Music ▲ YING [ADD]
Mozart, W.A.:Rondo Pno K.511 *(rec Mar 19–20, 1996)* Arizona Friends of Chamber Music ▲ YING [ADD]
Rachmaninoff, S.:Variations on a Theme by Corelli *(rec Mar 19–20, 1996)* Arizona Friends of Chamber Music ▲ YING [ADD]
Ravel, M.:Gaspard de la nuit *(rec Mar 19–20, 1996)* Arizona Friends of Chamber Music ▲ YING [ADD]
Schumann, R.:Toccata Pno *(rec Mar 19–20, 1996)* Arizona Friends of Chamber Music ▲ YING [ADD]
Ylönen, Marko (vc)
Nordgren, P.H.:Hate-Love, w. J. Kangas (cnd), Ostrobothnian CO Ondine ▲ ODE 737-2 [DDD]
Rautavaara, E.:Con Vc, w. M. Pommer (cnd), Helsinki PO Ondine ▲ ODE 819 [DDD]
Yoken, David (pno)
Smith, S.S.:Here & There, w. J. Fonville (fl), D. Savage (bn) O.O. Discs ▲ OO 11 [DDD]
Yokoyama, Katsuya (shak)
Noda, T.:Mutation, w. Toshi Fujita (koto), Mikiko Haga (koto), Chieko Mori (koto), T. Otaka (cnd), Tokyo Metropolitan SO *(rec live, Tokyo Bunka-Kaikan, Large Hall, May 24, 1980)* Camerata ▲ 32CM-292 [AAD]
Takemitsu, T.:Music of, w. K. Tsuruta (biwa), Y. Horigome (cnd), Tokyo Metropolitan SO—Far Calls, Coming, Far! (1980); Requiem for Strings (1957); Nov. Steps (1967); Visions (1989) Denon/PCM Digital ▲ DEN 79441 [DDD]
Yokoyama, Yukio (pno)
Chopin, F.:Études (24) *(rec Japan)* Sony Classical ▲ SK 62605
Yonovitz, Karen (fl)
Encore, w. [cnd:Duain Wolfe], Colorado Children's Chorale, Rick Chinski (gtr), Robert Davine (acc), Laurie Kahler (pno), Samuel Lancaster (pno), Barry Oliver (pno), Marylin Preston (fl), Karen Yonovitz (fl), Peter Cooper (ob), Andy Stevens (cl), Lionel Young (vn), Basil Vendreys (va), Wayne Templeman (vc), Charle *(rec Denver Center Media)* Colorado Children's Chorale ▲ 001
Yoo, Scott (vn)
Prokofiev, S.:Con 2 Vn, w. E. de Carvalho (cnd), Paraiba SO Delos ▲ DE 1018 [DDD]
Yordanoff, Luben (vn)
Messiaen, O.:Quatuor pour la fin du temps, w. C. Desurmont (cl), A. Tetard (vc), D. Barenboim (pno) Deutsche Grammophon ("20th Century Classics" series) ▲ 423247-2 [ADD]
York, Andrew (gtr)—see also ORCHESTRAS & ENSEMBLES Los Angeles Guitar Quartet
Greif, M.:Clear Day, w. Matthew Greif (gtr) *(rec Mission San Luis Rey)* Metro ▲ MCD 59601
York, A.:Gtr Music—3 Dances; 8 Dreamscapes; 3 Dilineations; 8 Discernments; 3 Diagrams *(rec Nov. 1993)* GSP Recordings ▲ GSP 1007
York, Donald (syn)
Hand, F.:Music of, w. Nancy Donaruma (vc), Jazzantiqua—Cantigas de Santa Maria; Rose Liz; Bachiaras; Tourdion; Lady Carey's Fant; Chaconne; Toby & Lynn MusicMasters ▲ 01612-65150-2
York, John (pno)
Berg, A.:Pieces (4) Cl, w. J. Campbell (cl) Crystal ■ C331
Debussy, C.:Chamber Music, w. William Bennett (fl), David Campbell (cl), James Campbell (cl), Nicholas Daniel (ob), Robert Makell (hn), Richard Watkins (hn), Robin Kennard (bn), Rachel Gough (bn), Simon Haram (sax), Ieuan Jones (hp), Clifford Benson (pno), Julius Drake (pno), Roger Tapping (va)—Rapsodie for Eng hn; Syrinx; Première rapsodie; Son for Fl, Va & Hp; Le petit nègre; Petite pièce; Rapsodie for Sax *(rec All Saints' Church, East Finchley, London, Jan 12–20, 1994)* Cala 2-▲ CACD 1017 [DDD]
Ireland, J.:Son Vc, w. Raphael Wallfisch (vc) *(rec St. Martin's Church, East Woodhay, Berkshire, Mar. 16 & 17, 1994)* Marco Polo ▲ 8.223718 [DDD]
James Campbell, w. James Campbell (cl) Crystal ■ C331
Lekeu, G.:Son Vn, w. Detlef Hahn (vn) ASV ("Quicksilva" series) ▲ ASQ 6158 [DDD]
Poulenc, F.:Chamber Music, w. Peter Sidhom (bar), William Bennett (fl), David Campbell (cl), James Campbell (cl), Nicholas Daniel (ob), Richard Watkins (hn), Rachel Gough (bn), Peter Carter (vn), Chris West (db), Ieuan Jones (hp), Clifford Benson (pno), Julius Drake (pno)—Son for Ob; L'invitation au château; Villanelle; Son 2 Cls; Trio; Sxt; Son for Cl & Bn; Rapsodie nègre; Son for Cl; Mouvements perpétuels; Son for Fl *(rec All Saints' Church, East Finchley, London, Jan 12–20, 1994)* Cala ▲ CACD 1018 [DDD]
Poulenc, F.:Son Cl Pno, w. J. Campbell (cl) Crystal ■ C331
Ravel, M.:Son Vn Pno, w. Detlef Hahn (vn) ASV ("Quicksilva" series) ▲ ASQ 6158 [DDD]
Saint-Saëns, C.:Chamber Music, w. W. Bennett (fl), D. Campbell (cl), J. Campbell (cl), N. Daniel (ob), R. Makell (hn), R. Watkins (hn), R. Kennard (bn), R. Gough (bn), S. Haram (sax), I. Jones (hp), C. Benson (pno), J. Drake (pno), R. Tapping (va)—Odelette, Op. 162; Son for Cl, Op. 167; Feuillet d'album, Op. 81; Son for Bn, Op. 168; Caprice on Danish & Russian Airs, Op. 79; Son for Ob, Op. 166; Romance in D♭, Op. 37; Tarantelle, Op. 6 *(rec All Saints' Church, East Finchley, London, Jan 12–20, 1994)* Cala 2-▲ CACD 1017 [DDD]
Saint-Saëns, C.:Son 1 Vn, w. D. Hahn (vn) ASV ("Quicksilva" series) ▲ ASQ 6158 [DDD]
Schumann, R.:Fantasiestücke Cl, w. J. Campbell (cl) Crystal ■ C331
Yoshida, Hiromi (shô)
Peebles, S.:Tomoé, w. Ikuo Kakehashi (perc/kbd), Sarah Peebles (kbd/elec/perc/shô) *(rec live, Shukôji Temple, Kawasaki, Sept 25, 1993)* Innova ▲ 506
Yoshihara, Sumire (perc)
Fukushi, N.:Chromosphere, w. J. Arase (perc), M. Okada (perc), S. Sato (perc), H. Yamazaki (perc), T. Otaka (cnd), Tokyo PO *(rec live Tokyo Bunka-Kaikan, Large Hall, May 30, 1981)* Camerata ▲ 32CM 293 [AAD]
Ishii, M.:Search in Grey *(rec Iruma Shimin Kaikan, Japan, Feb. 1979)* Camerata ▲ 32CM 313 [AAD]
Noda, T.:Ecologue, w. M. Nakagawa (fl) Camerata ▲ 32CM 58
Nørgård, P.:Waves *(rec Iruma Shimin Kaikan, Japan, Feb. 1979)* Camerata ▲ 32CM 313 [AAD]
Stockhausen, K.:Zyklus *(rec Iruma Shimin Kaikan, Japan, Feb. 1979)* Camerata ▲ 32CM 313 [AAD]
Yoshimura, Nanae (koto)
Miki, M.:Music of, w. K. Mitsuhashi (shakuhachi), Y. Tanaka (shamisen), Masur (cnd), Tokyo Metropolitan SO, Tokyo PO, Leipzig Gewandhaus Orch—Jo No Kyoju; Prelude for Shakuhachi, Koto & Strings; Ha No Kyoku; Con. for Koto & Orch.; Kyu no Kyoku; Sym. for Two Worlds Camerata 2-▲ 30CM 223/24
Minami, S.:Coloration-Project III, w. K. Mitsuhashi (shak) *(rec Iruma City Auditorium, Dec. 14, 1990)* Camerata ▲ 32CM 189 [DDD]
Nishimura, A.:Nanae, w. K. Mitsuhashi (shak) *(rec Iruma City Auditorium, Dec. 14, 1990)* Camerata ▲ 32CM 189 [DDD]
Satoh, S.:Kamu-Ogi-Guoto, w. K. Mitsuhashi (shakuhachi fl) *(rec Iruma City Auditorium, Dec. 14, 1990)* Camerata ▲ 32CM 189 [DDD]
Yoshimatsu, T.:Moyura, w. K. Mitsuhashi (shak) *(rec Iruma City Auditorium, Dec. 14, 1990)* Camerata ▲ 32CM 189 [DDD]
Yuasa, J.:Cosmos Haptic 3, w. K. Mitsuhashi (shak) *(rec Iruma City Auditorium, Dec. 14, 1990)* Camerata ▲ 32CM 189 [DDD]
Yoshino, Naoko (hp)
Duos for Flute & Harp, w. Shigenori Kudo (fl) Sony Classical ▲ SK 48033
Handel, G.F.:Con Hp, w. Berlin PO Virtuosi—Allegro moderato Sony Classical ▲ MLK 62369 [ADD/DDD]
Mozart, W.A.:Con Fl Hp, w. S. Coles (fl), Y. Menuhin (cnd), English CO Virgin Classics ▲ 59075 [DDD]
Mozart, W.A.:Con Fl Hp, w. S. Coles (fl), Y. Menuhin (cnd), English CO Virgo ▲ CDZ 61108 [DDD]
Yoshizawa, M. (kokyu)
Shinohara, M.:Cooperation, w. A. Nishigata (shamisen), K. Mitsuhashi (shakuhachi), M. Akao (fue), S. Yaotani (hichiriki), K. Ishikawa (sho), C. Fukunaga (koto), J. Ueda (biwa), M. Yoshizawa (kokyu), I. Tsuji (oboe), T. Takahashi (cl), G. Kitamura (tpt), A. Murata (trbn), S. Eiso (perc), S. Ueki (vn), S. Katsuta (vc), Y. Shibuya (pno), K. Komatsu (cnd) *(rec live Casals Hall, Tokyo, Mar. 5, 1994)* Camerata ▲ 30CM 375 [DDD]
Yossifov, Dragomir (pno)
Nikolov, L.:Son 2 Pno 4-Hands, w. Tsvetana Ivanova (pno) Gega ▲ GD 149 [DDD]
Yost, Kelly (pno)
Piano Reflections:A Gentle Selection of Reflective Light Classics Channel Productions ▲ CD 1684
Quiet Colors:Gentle Light Piano Classics Channel Productions ▲ CD 1691 ■ CS 1691
Roses & Solitude Channel Productions ▲ CD 1696
Young, Charles Rochester (ten sax)—see ORCHESTRAS & ENSEMBLES Resounding Winds Saxophone Quartet
Young, Charlie (a sax)—see ORCHESTRAS & ENSEMBLES East Coast Saxophone Quartet
Young, Crawford (lt)—see also ORCHESTRAS & ENSEMBLES Project Ars Nova Ensemble
Musica Humana, w. Françoise Atlan (mez), John Fleagle (ten/hp), Anonymous 4, Ensemble Discantus, Ensemble Gilles Binchois, Ensemble Organum, Gothic Voices, Greece Byzantine Choir, Hilliard Ensemble, Musica Nova, et al. L'Empreinte Digitale ▲ ED 13047
Young, Emma (vn)
Prokofiev, S.:Son for 2 Vns, w. L. Mordkovitch (vn) Chandos ▲ CHAN 8988 [DDD]
Schnittke, A.:Praeludium in memoriam Dmitri Shostakovich, w. L. Mordkovitch (vn) Chandos ▲ CHAN 8988 [DDD]
Young, La Monte (pno)
Young, L.:The Well-Tuned Pno *(rec 1981)* Gramavision 5-▲ R255-79452 ■ R45H 79452
Young, Landon (perc)—see ORCHESTRAS & ENSEMBLES Peter Garland Ensemble
Young, Lionel (vn)
Encore, w. [cnd:Duain Wolfe], Colorado Children's Chorale, Rick Chinski (gtr), Robert Davine (acc), Laurie Kahler (pno), Samuel Lancaster (pno), Barry Oliver (pno), Marylin Preston (fl), Karen Yonovitz (fl), Peter Cooper (ob), Andy Stevens (cl), Basil Vendreys (va), Wayne Templeman (vc), Charle *(rec Denver Center Media)* Colorado Children's Chorale ▲ 001
Young, Richard (va)—see also ORCHESTRAS & ENSEMBLES Vermeer String Quartet
Copland, A.:Qt Pno, w. Israela Margalit (pno), Glenn Dicterow (vn), Alan Stepansky (vc) EMI Classics ("Anglo-American Chamber Music" series) ▲ CDC 55405
Corigliano, J.:Soliloquy, w. Stanley Drucker (cl), Kerry McDermott (vn), Lisa Kim (vn), Gerald Appleman (vc) Cala Records ("New York Legends" series) ▲ CAL CACD 509 [DDD]
Youngstrom, Kenton (gtr)—see ORCHESTRAS & ENSEMBLES Falla Trio
Ysaÿe, Eugène (vn)
The Complete Violin Recordings *(rec Columbia Studios, 1912–19)* Sony Classical ("Masterworks Heritage" series) ▲ MHK 62337 [ADD]
Eugène Ysaÿe, w. Camille Decreus (pno) Symposium ▲ SYM 1045
Eugène Ysaÿe:The Complete Recordings *(rec 1912)* Opal ▲ CD 9851 (m) [AAD]
The Great Violinists Series One-Eleven ▲ URS 50100 [ADD]
Yudina, Maria (pno)
Bartók, B.:Mikrokosmos Melodiya ("Russian Piano School" series) ▲ 74321-25176-2
Beethoven, L. van:Vars & Fugue Pno, Op. 35, "Eroica" *(rec 1961)* Russian Disc ▲ RUS 15010 [AAD]
Beethoven, L. van:Vars on a waltz by Diabelli, Op. 120 *(rec 1961)* Russian Disc ▲ RUS 15010 [AAD]
Berg, A.:Son Pno Melodiya ("Russian Piano School" series) ▲ 74321-25176-2
Brahms, J.:Intermezzos Pno, Op. 117 Arlecchino ARL
Brahms, J.:Rhaps Pno, Op. 79—No. 2 Arlecchino ARL
Brahms, J.:Vars & Fugue on a Theme by Handel Arlecchino ARL
Haydn, J.:Sons Pno—in E♭, H.XIV/52 *(rec 1948)* Arlecchino ▲ ARL120
Hindemith, P.:Sons Pno—No. 3 Melodiya ("Russian Piano School" series) ▲ 74321-25176-2
Krenek, E.:Son 2 Pno Melodiya ("Russian Piano School" series) ▲ 74321-25176-2
Mozart, W.A.:Adagio Pno, K.540 *(rec 1948)* Arlecchino ▲ ARL120
Mozart, W.A.:Con 20 Pno, USSR RSO *(rec 1948)* Arlecchino ▲ ARL120
Mozart, W.A.:Rondo Pno, K.511 *(rec 1948)* Arlecchino ▲ ARL120
Mussorgsky, M.:Pictures Arlecchino ARL
Prokofiev, S.:Les Choses en soi Arlecchino ARL
Shostakovich, D.:Son 2 Pno Arlecchino ARL
Stravinsky, I.:Serenade Pno Melodiya ("Russian Piano School" series) ▲ 74321-25176-2
Szymanowski, K.:Preludes Pno, Op. 1 *(rec 1956–57)* Arlecchino ▲ ARLA 59
Taneyev, S.:Qnt Pno Strs, w. Beethoven String Quartet *(rec 1956–57)* Arlecchino ▲ ARLA 59
Yuen, Wong On (erhu)
Chen, P.:Pieces (5) Erhu, w. Y.W. Sie (cnd), Hong Kong PO—Colourful Clouds Chasing the Moon; Scenes from Tibet; Morning-Star Lily in Flower; Song of Tong Mountain; Song of the Horse-head Fiddle *(rec Tsuen Wan Town Hall, May 25–28, 1987)* Marco Polo ("Chinese Composers" series) ▲ 8.223927 [DDD]
Yuen, Wong On (gaohu)
Chen, P.:Fant on Cantonese Themes, w. Y.W. Sie (cnd), Hong Kong PO *(rec Tsuen Wan Town Hall, May 25–28, 1987)* Marco Polo ("Chinese Composers" series) ▲ 8.223927 [DDD]
Yuguchi, Miwa (pno)
Ichiyanagi, T.:Cloud Atlas—Nos I–III *(rec Jan 8–9, 1996)* Thorofon ▲ CTH 2324 [DDD]

▲ = CD ♦ = Enhanced CD Δ = MD ■ = Cassette Tape □ = DCC

Yuguchi, Miwa (pno) (cont.)
Otaka, H.:Sonatine Pno *(rec Jan 8–9, 1996)* Thorofon ▲ CTH 2324 [DDD]
Takemitsu, T.:Litany *(rec Jan 8–9, 1996)* Thorofon ▲ CTH 2324 [DDD]
Takemitsu, T.:Uninterrupted Rests *(rec Jan 8–9, 1996)* Thorofon ▲ CTH 2324 [DDD]
Terauchi, S.:The Phoenix Hall and Eight Putto-Figures Worshipping the Sacrifice Ceremony in the Clouds *(rec Jan 8–9, 1996)* Thorofon ▲ CTH 2324 [DDD]
Yashiro, A.:Son Pno *(rec Jan 8–9, 1996)* Thorofon ▲ CTH 2324 [DDD]

Yui, Micah (pno)
Bloch, E.:Con symphonique, w. D. Amos (cnd), London SO Laurel ▲ LR 851CD [ADD]
Bloch, E.:Scherzo fantasque, w. D. Amos (cnd), London SO Laurel ▲ LR 851CD [ADD]

Yun, Qu (zheng)
High Mountain & Flowing Water Yellow River ▲ 82002 [DDD]

Yurigin-Klevke, Vladimir (pno)
Cui, C.:Romances (16), w. V. Sharonova (sop) Russian Disc ▲ RUS 11 021 [DDD]
Dargomyzhsky, A.:Romances (11), w. V. Sharonova (sop) Russian Disc ▲ RUS 11021 [DDD]

Zabaleta, Nicanor (hp)
Handel, G.F.:Con Hp, w. P. Kuentz (cnd), Kuentz CO Deutsche Grammophon ▲ 427206–2 [AAD]
La harpe du siècle:Hommage a Nicanor Zabaleta w. Berlin PO [cnd:Ernst Märzendorfer], Berlin RSO, Paul Kuentz CO [cnd:Paul Kuentz] Deutsche Grammophon ("Double" series) 2–▲ 439693–2
Mozart, W.A.:Con Fl Hp, w. W. Schulz (fl), K. Böhm (cnd), Vienna PO Deutsche Grammophon ▲ 413552–2 [ADD]
Mozart, W.A.:Con Fl Hp, w. W. Schulz (fl), K. Böhm (cnd), Vienna PO Deutsche Grammophon ▲ 429815–2 [ADD]
Mozart, W.A.:Con Fl Hp, w. Karlheinz Zoeller (fl), E. Märzendorfer (cnd), Berlin PO Deutsche Grammophon ▲ 427206–2 [AAD]
Nicanor Zabaleta Ermitage ▲ ERM 134 [ADD]
Rodrigo, J.:Concert-Serenade, w. E. Märzendorfer (cnd), Berlin RSO Deutsche Grammophon ("Resonance" series) ▲ 427214–2 [ADD]

Zabatnikov, Nikolai (vn)—see also ORCHESTRAS & ENSEMBLES Beethoven String Quartet
Schnittke, A.:Qt 2 Strs, w. A. Krysa (vn), F. Dnizhinin (va), Y. Altman (vc) Vox Box 2–▲ CDX 5121 [ADD]

Zabka, Lidia (hn)
Rodrigo, J.:Concierto de Aranjuez, w. David Russell (gtr), W. Michniewski (cnd), Sinfonia Varsovia Polskie Nagrania ▲ PNCD 103 [DDD]

Zaccaria, Zeno (hpd)—see ORCHESTRAS & ENSEMBLES Il Ruggiero

Zaćek, Jan (gtr)
Debussy, C.:Children's Corner, w. R. Jackman (gtr)—[trans. for guitar] Supraphon ▲ SUP 111845 [DDD]
Mussorgsky, M.:Pictures at an Exhibition, w. R. Jackman (gtr) [trans. for guitar] Supraphon ▲ SUP 111845 [DDD]

Zacharias, Christian (pno)
Beethoven, L. van:Cons Pno (comp), w. H. Vonk (cnd), Dresden Staatskapelle EMI Classics ▲ ZDMC 63937
Beethoven, L. van:Con Vn, Vc & Pno, "Triple Con", w. U. Hoelscher (vn), H. Schiff (vc), K. Masur (cnd), Leipzig Gewandhaus Orch EMI Classics ▲ ZDMC 63937
Beethoven, L. van:Qnt Pno, Ob, Cl, Hn & Bn, w. Sabine Meyer Wind Ensemble EMI Classics ▲ CDC 55013
Mozart, W.A.:Con 20 Pno, w. D. Zinman (cnd), Bavarian RSO EMI Classics ▲ CDC 49899
Mozart, W.A.:Con 21 Pno, w. D. Zinman (cnd), Bavarian RSO EMI Classics ▲ CDC 49899
Mozart, W.A.:Music of, w. Alban Berg Quartet, F. P. Zimmermann (vn), A. Dumay (vn), A. S. Mutter (vn), S. Meyer (cl), R. Vlatkovi (hn), *(sels unknown)* EMI Classics ▲ CDC 54165
Mozart, W.A.:Qnt Pno, K.452, w. Sabine Meyer Wind Ensemble EMI Classics ▲ CDC 55013

Zacher, Gerd (org)
Kagel, M.:Marches to Miss the Victory Koch Schwann ▲ SCH 313922 [ADD]
Kagel, M.:"Rrrrrrr......" Org Koch Schwann ▲ SCH 313922 [ADD]
Kagel, M.:Sankt-Bach-Passion, w. Anne Sofie von Otter (mez), Hans Peter Blochowitz (ten), Roland Hermann (bar), Peter Roggisch (nar), M. Kagel (cnd), South German RSO, Limburg Cathedral Boys' Chorus, Hamburg North German Choir Montaigne ▲ MO 782044
Ligeti, G.:Etude 1 Org *(rec mid-1968)* Vox Box 2–▲ CDX 5142
Ligeti, G.:Volumina Org *(rec mid-1968)* Vox Box 2–▲ CDX 5142

Zadra, Riccardo (pno)
Bizet, G.:Pno Music—Vars chromatiques; Casilda; Premier nocturne; Danse bohémienne; Extase; Grande valse de concert; Danse d'almées; Chants du rhin; Chanson provençale; Carnaval Gallo ▲ CD 821

Zaffaroni, D. (bn)
Savinio, A.:Album 1914, w. L. Castellani (sop), A. Jona (sgr), B. Canino (pno/cel) Stradivarius ▲ STR 33309 [DDD]

Zagorovskaya, Tatiana (pno)
Beethoven, L. van:Son 5 Pno *(rec St. Petersburg, 1992)* Audiophile Classics ▲ 101.002 [DDD]
Beethoven, L. van:Son 6 Pno *(rec St. Petersburg, 1992)* Audiophile Classics ▲ 101.002 [DDD]
Grieg, E.:Con Pno, Op. 16, w. A. Kantorov (cnd), St. Petersburg State SO Audiophile Classics ▲ 101.020 [DDD]

Zagst, J. (vn)
Swack, I.:Profiles, w. S. Toulson (cl), L. Feldman (vc) Opus One ▲ 149

Zahab, Roger (vn)
Cage, J.:Harmonies Vn & Kbd, w. Eric Moe (pno/hpd/org)—also includes condensed version Koch International Classics ▲ KIC 7130 [DDD]
Zahab, R.:Verging Lightfall, w. Eric Moe (pno/hpd/org) Koch International Classics ▲ KIC 7130 [DDD]

Zahardnik, Bohuslav (cl)
Mozart, W.A.:Qnt Cl, K.581, w. Karel Rehak (va), Talich String Quartet Calliope 3–▲ CAL 9231.3 [DDD]

Zaharieva, Albena (pno)
Shostakovich, D.:Son Va, w. Z. Tchavdarov (va) *(rec Jan. 15, 1977)* BIS ▲ CD 81 [AAD]

Zähl, Jovita (pno)
Brown, E.:Corroboree, w. Duo Degenhardt-Kent Mode ▲ 19

Zahnhausen, Markus (rcr)
Orff, C.:Schulwerk (complete), w. Godela Orff (nar), Marina Koppelstetter (mez), Carolin Widmann (vn), Sabina Lehrmann (vc), Karl Peinkofer Percussion Ensemble—4 Pieces for Xylophone; 5 Little Canons; 4 Dance Pieces; Songs & Instrumental Pieces; 3 Pieces for Fl & Perc; Songs & Dances; 2 Time Change Dances for Vn & Vc; 7 Folk Dances; Music for the Night *(rec Munich, 1994–95)* Celestial Harmonies ▲ 13104–2
Orff, C.:Schulwerk (complete), w. Godela Orff (nar), Carolin Widmann (vn), Sonja Korkeala (vn), Karl Peinkofer (perc), Andreas Schumacher (perc), Wilfried Hiller (perc/mar), Martin Ruhland (mar), Munich Hochschule Madrigal Choir—Wessobrun Prayer for a capella Choir; 2 Pieces for a capella Choir; 8 Pieces for 2 Vns; Mater et filia for women's a capella Choir; Devotional Yodel for male a capella Choir; 5 Pieces for Sop, Rcr & Perc; Death for Nar., Wood Bells, Bass Xyl & Tam-Tam; Omnia tempus habent for mixed Choir, Timp & Little Dr; Rubato, molto allegro, rubato; Abenlied for Nar, Bass Metallophon, Bass Xyl, Large Dr & Wine Glass; 5 Pieces for Fl & Perc; Devotional Yodel for male Choir [version 2]; 7 Pieces for 2 Xyl *(rec Munich, 1994–95)* Celestial Harmonies ▲ 13105–2

Zahradnik, Bohuslav (cl)
Mozart, W.A.:Qnt Cl, K.581, w. Talich String Quartet Calliope ▲ CAL 9628
Mozart, W.A.:Qnt Cl, K.581, w. Talich String Quartet Calliope ▲ CAL 9232 [DDD]
Mozart, W.A.:Qnt Cl, K.581, w. Talich String Quartet *(rec 1980–85)* Calliope ▲ CAL 6628 [ADD]
Stamitz, C.:Con 11 Cl, w. F. Vajnar (cnd), Prague CO Supraphon ▲ 11 1424–2 [DDD]

Zaidenshnir, I. (vn)—see ORCHESTRAS & ENSEMBLES Northern Crown Soloists Ensemble

Zaimont, Judith L. (pno)
Zaimont, J.L.:Pno Music—Suite Impressions (3); Evening; June; July; August; September [all from Calendar Collections]; Piano Rags (2); Snazzy Son [w. Doris Lang Kosloff (pno)]; Nocturne "La Fin de siècle" 4-Tay ▲ 4001 [DDD]

Zaiser, Uwe (tpt)
Arnold, M.:Qnt Brass, w. Peter Leiner (tpt), Sjön Scott (hn), Jochen Scheerer (posaune), Ralf Rudolph (tuba) Bayer ▲ BR 100251 [DDD]
Crespo, E.:Suite Americana 1, w. Peter Leiner (tpt), Sjön Scott (hn), Jochen Scheerer (posaune), Ralf Rudolph (tuba) Bayer ▲ BR 100251 [DDD]
Ewald, V.:Qnt 1 Brass, w. Peter Leiner (tpt), Sjön Scott (hn), Jochen Scheerer (trbn), Ralf Rudolph (tuba) Bayer ▲ BR 100251 [DDD]
Horovitz, J.:Music Hall Suite, w. Peter Leiner (tpt), Sjön Scott (hn), Jochen Scheerer (posaune), Ralf Rudolph (tuba) Bayer ▲ BR 100251 [DDD]
Koetsier, J.:Qnt Brass, w. Peter Leiner (tpt), Sjön Scott (hn), Jochen Scheerer (posaune), Ralf Rudolph (tuba) Bayer ▲ BR 100251 [DDD]

Zajíček, Peter (vn)
Benda, G.A.:Scherzi Notturni, w. Miloš Valent (vn), Musica Aeterna Bratislava *(rec Moyzes Hall of the Slovak Philharmonic, Apr & June 1995)* Slovart ▲ SR 0013–2–131 [DDD]
Bodino, S.:Sons, w. Miloš Valent (vn), Peter Királ (vc), Pascal Dubreuil (hpd), Musica Aeterna—Sons 1–6 *(rec Castle of Tonky, Slovakia, Apr 1994)* Slovart ▲ SR 0008–2–131 [DDD]

Zak, Jakov (pno)
Bazelaire, P.:Suite française, w. S. Heled (vc) InSync ■ C 4154
Berg, A.:Songs, Op. 2, w. M. Zakai (cta) [G] Koch International Classics ▲ KIC 7021–2 [DDD] ■ 3–7021–4 (D)
Boëllmann, L.:Son Vc, w. S. Heled (vc) InSync ■ C 4153
Castelnuovo-Tedesco, M.:Notturno sull'acqua & Scherzino, w. S. Heled (vc) InSync ■ C 4153
Castelnuovo-Tedesco, M.:Toccata, w. S. Heled (vc) InSync ■ C 4153
Cilea, F.:Son Vc, w. S. Heled (vc) InSync ■ C 4154
Mahler, G.:Songs, w. M. Zakai (cta)—6 early songs:Ablösung im Sommer; Erinnerung; Frühlingsmorgen; Phantasie; Schneiden und Meiden; Serenade [G] Koch International Classics ▲ KIC 7021–2 [DDD] ■ 3–7021–4 (D)
Milhaud, D.:Elégie, w. S. Heled (vc) InSync ■ C 4154
Rare Cello Music, w. Heled, Simca (vc), Daniel Edni (pno), Jonathan Feldman (pno), Michael Levin (pno), Alexander Peskanov (pno) *(rec 1976, 1982, 1983, 1985, 1)* Classico ▲ CLASSCD 153
Ravel, M.:Chansons madécasses, w. M. Zakai (cta), A. Biron (fl), M. Haran (vc) [F] Koch International Classics ▲ KIC 7021–2 [DDD] ■ 3–7021–4 (D)
Rossini, G.:Fant Cl, w. G. Dembinsky (cl) PWK Classics ▲ PWK 1142 [DDD]
Schumann, R.:Fantasiestücke Cl, w. G. Dembinsky (cl) PWK Classics ▲ PWK 1142 [DDD]
Tcherepnin, A.:Son Vc, w. S. Heled (vc) InSync ■ C 4154
Weber, C.M. von:Grand duo concertant Cl, w. G. Dembinsky (cl) PWK Classics ▲ PWK 1142 [DDD]
Weber, C.M. von:Vars on a Theme from *Silvana* Cl, w. G. Dembinsky (cl) PWK Classics ▲ PWK 1142 [DDD]
Webern, A.:Songs from *Der siebente Ring*, Op. 3, w. M. Zakai (cta) [G] Koch International Classics ▲ KIC 7021–2 [DDD] ■ 3–7021–4 (D)

Zakin, Alexander (hpd)
Haydn, J.:Con 1 Vn, w. Isaac Stern (vn), I. Stern (cnd), Columbia CO Sony Classical 2–▲ SM2K 64528 [ADD/DDD]

Zakin, Alexander (pno)
Bach, J.S.:Sons Vn, BWV 1023, w. Isaac Stern (vn) Sony Classical ▲ SMK 68361 [ADD]
Bach, J.S.:Sons Vn Hpd, BWV 1014–1019, w. Isaac Stern (vn)—in E, BWV 1016 Sony Classical ▲ SMK 68361 [ADD]
Bach, J.S.:Sons Vn, BWV 1020, w. Isaac Stern (vn) Sony Classical ▲ SMK 68361 [ADD]
Bartók, B.:Sons (2) Vn & Pno, w. Isaac Stern (vn) Sony Classical ▲ SMK 64535 [ADD]
Bloch, E.:Baal Shem, "3 Pictures of Chassidic Life", w. Isaac Stern (vn) Sony Classical ▲ SMK 64533 [ADD]
Bloch, E.:Nigun, w. Issac Stern (vn) *(rec 1948)* CBS 4–▲ M4K 42003 (m/s) [ADD]
Bloch, E.:Son 1 Vn, w. Isaac Stern (vn) Sony Classical ▲ SMK 64533 [ADD]
Brahms, J.:Sons Vn (comp), w. Isaac Stern (vn) Sony Classical ▲ SMK 64531 [ADD]
Copland, A.:Son Vn & Pno, w. Isaac Stern (vn) Sony Classical ▲ SMK 64533 [ADD]
Debussy, C.:Son Vn, w. Isaac Stern (vn) Sony Classical ▲ SMK 64532 [ADD]
Enescu, G.:Son 3 Vn, w. Isaac Stern (vn) Sony Classical ▲ SMK 64532 [ADD]
Franck, C.:Son Vn, w. Isaac Stern (vn) Sony Classical ▲ SMK 64532 [ADD]
Handel, G.F.:Sons Vn & Kbd, w. Isaac Stern (vn)—No. 3 Sony Classical ▲ SMK 68361 [ADD]
Hindemith, P.:Son in C Vn & Pno, w. Isaac Stern (vn) Sony Classical ▲ SMK 64533 [ADD]
Prokofiev, S.:Son Vn, Op. 94bis, w. Isaac Stern (vn) Sony Classical ▲ SMK 64534 [ADD]
Prokofiev, S.:Son 1 Vn, w. Isaac Stern (vn) Sony Classical ▲ SMK 64534 [ADD]
Tartini, G.:Sons Vn & Continuo, w. Isaac Stern (vn)— in g, Op. 1/10, "Didone abbandonata" Sony Classical ▲ SMK 68361 [ADD]

Zaliyailo, Zinon (vc)
Vivaldi, A.:Con for 2 Vcs, w. S. Raldugin (vc), L. Korkhin (cnd), Renaissance CO Infinity Digital ▲ QK 57244 [DDD]

Zaltsman, E. (vn)
Avni, T.:Love under a Different Sun, w. E. Berendsen (sgr), M. Meltzer (fl), S. Magen (vc) Symposium ▲ 1110

Zaluski, Iwo (pno)
Oginski, M.K.:Polonaises Pno—18 sels Olympia ▲ OLY 345 [DDD]
Zaluski, K.B.:Pno Music—2 Nocturnes; Funeral March; 3 Mazurkas Olympia ▲ OLY 345 [DDD]

Zamborsky, Stanislav (pno)
Grieg, E.:Con Pno, Op. 16, w. R. Stankovsky (cnd), Philharmonia Cassovia *(rec House of Arts, Kosice, Nov. 13–14, 1990)* Lydian ▲ 18106 [DDD]

Zamfir, Gheorghe (pan fl)
Classics by Candlelight Philips ▲ 826806–2
Colors Philips ▲ 846028–2 PM [AAD/DDD] ■ 846028–4 PM
Dances Of Romance Philips ▲ 432988–2 PH [DDD]
Fantasy Philips ("Mercury" series) ▲ 824898–2
Glorious Pipes Philips □ 426057–5
Greatest Hits LaserLight ▲ 15117
Harmony Philips ▲ 830627–2 PH [DDD] ■ 830627–4 PH (D)
The Lonely Shepherd Philips ("Mercury" series) ▲ 822787–2 ■ 822787–4
Master of the Panflute:Greatest Hits Delta ▲ 11016
Music by Candlelight Philips ▲ 810010–2
Opéra:Favorite Melodies from Opera Philips ▲ 518424–2
A Return to Romance Philips ▲ 836056–2 EH [AAD] ■ 836056–4 EH
Romance of the Pan Flute Philips ▲ 810966–2 PH ■ 832150–4 EH
Zamfir Christmas at Notre Dame Basilica Philips ▲ 314510309–2 PH [DDD]
Zamfir Himself Philips ▲ 412221–2
Zamfir, Vol. 1 LaserLight ▲ 15227
Zamfir, Vol. 2 LaserLight ▲ 15232
Zamfir, G.:Black Waltz, w. L. Foster (cnd), Monte Carlo PO Philips ▲ 412221–2 [DDD]
Zamfir, G.:Con 1 Panpipes, w. L. Foster (cnd), Monte Carlo PO Philips ▲ 412221–2 [DDD]
Zamfir, G.:Couleurs d'automne, w. L. Foster (cnd), Monte Carlo PO Philips ▲ 412221–2 [DDD]
Zamfir, G.:Music of, w. M. Cellier (org)—34 (sels.) Analekta 3–▲ AN 28401–3 [AAD]
Zamfir, G.:Rhap du printemps, w. L. Foster (cnd), Monte Carlo PO Philips ▲ 412221–2 [DDD]

Zamkochian, Berj (org)
Bach, J.S.:Preludes & Fugues, BWV 531–552 *(rec Methuen Memorial Music Hall, Methuen, MA)* ZC Music ▲ 111594 ■ 111594T
Brody, J.:Intro, Passacaglia & Double Fugue *(rec Methuen Memorial Music Hall, Methuen, MA)* ZC Music ▲ 111594 ■ 111594T
Brody, J.:Metamorphosis Org *(rec Methuen Memorial Music Hall, Methuen, MA)* ZC Music ▲ 111594 ■ 111594T
Mendelssohn, F.:Sons Org—No. 1 in f *(rec Austin Organ, St. Joseph's Cathedral, Hartford, CT)* ZC Music ▲ 040795 [ADD]

Zamkochian, Berj (org) (cont.)
Mozart, W.A.:Andante Mechanical Org, K.616 *(rec Methuen Memorial Music Hall, Methuen, MA)* ZC Music ▲ 111594 ▮ 111594T
Poulenc, F.:Con Org, w. C. Munch (cnd), Boston SO RCA Gold Seal ▲ 60817-2-RG [ADD] ▮ 60817-4-RG (CrO2)
Reger, M.:Pieces Org, Op. 145—No. 3 [Weihnachten] *(rec Austin Organ, St. Joseph's Cathedral, Hartford, CT)* ZC Music ▲ 040795 [ADD]
Reubke, J.:Son Org *(rec Klais Organ, Ruhr, St. Mariä Geburt Mülheim, Germany)* ZC Music ▲ 040795 [ADD]
Saint-Saëns, C.:Sym 3, w. C. Munch (cnd), Boston SO RCA Gold Seal ▲ 60817-2-RG [ADD] ▮ 60817-4-RG (CrO2)
Saint-Saëns, C.:Sym 3, w. C. Munch (cnd), Boston SO *(rec 1956 & 1959)* RCA Living Stereo ▲ 09026-61500-2
Vartabet, G.:Org Music—Hymn of Vesting [2 settings]; Who is Like Unto the Lord Our God?; Holy, Holy, Holy; Christ in Our Midst; Lord Have Mercy; Prayer for the Catholicos; At This Time... *(rec Methuen Memorial Music Hall, Methuen, MA, Nov. 16, 1994)* ZC Music ▲ 111694 [DDD] ▮ 111694T
Yegmalian, M.:Org Music—The Lord's Prayer; Holy, Holy, Holy; Amen, Holy Father; Christ is Sacrificed *(rec Methuen Memorial Music Hall, Methuen, MA, Nov. 16, 1994)* ZC Music ▲ 111694 [DDD] ▮ 111694T

Zanardi, Carlo (baroque vc)—see ORCHESTRAS & ENSEMBLES Ensemble Barocco Padua Sans Souci
Zanardi, Carlo (vc)—see ORCHESTRAS & ENSEMBLES Ensemble Barocco Padua Sans Souci
Zander, Ingo (vc)—see ORCHESTRAS & ENSEMBLES Acht Ensemble

Zander, P. (hpd)
Japanese Melodies, w. Yo-Yo Ma(vc), M. Mamiya, Pro Musica Nipponia CBS ▲ MK 39703 ▮ FMT 39703

Zander, P. (pno)
Paganini, N.:Intro & Vars on "Dal tuo stellato soglio", w. Yo-Yo Ma (vc) [arr. Silva] CBS ▲ MK 37280 [DDD]

Zandmane, Inara (pno)
Vasks, P.:Landscapes of a Burnt-Out Earth *(rec Riga Recording Studio, Latvia, Dec 1995)* Conifer Classics ▲ 51272 [DDD]

Zanelli, R. (hp)
Mozart, W.A.:Con Fl Hp, w. P. Janovsky (fl), A. Lizzio (cnd), Mozart Festival Orch Vivace 3-▲ E 315 [DDD]

Zanin, Angelo (vc)—see ORCHESTRAS & ENSEMBLES Venice String Quartet

Zanini, Valeria (pno)
Pade, S.:Con Pno, w. P. Erös (cnd), Aalborg SO Point ▲ PCD 5083 [ADD]

Zank, Gerhard (vc)—see also ORCHESTRAS & ENSEMBLES New Munich Piano Trio, Munich Piano Trio, Bonaventura Ensemble
Arensky, A.:Trio 1 Pno, w. H. Lechler (pno), A. Lazar (vn) *(rec Mar 23-26, 1992)* Calig ▲ CAL 50913 [DDD]
Arensky, A.:Trio 2 Pno, w. H. Lechler (pno), A. Lazar (vn) *(rec Mar 23-26, 1992)* Calig ▲ CAL 50913 [DDD]

Zanlonghi, Gilbert (vc)—see also ORCHESTRAS & ENSEMBLES Monnaie Piano Trio
Lekeu, G.:Qt Pno, Vn, Va & Vc, w. D. Blumenthal (pno), T. Adamopoulos (vn), C. Desjardins (va) Koch Schwann ▲ CD 310185 [DDD]
Lekeu, G.:Son Vc, w. D. Blumenthal (pno) Koch Schwann ▲ CD 310185 [DDD]

Zanlonghi, Pascale (hp)
Honegger, A.:Chamber Music (comp), w. D.-S. Kang (vn), P.-H. Xuereb (va), R. Wallfisch (vc), M. Arrignon (cl), A. Marion (fl), A. Haraldsdottir (fl), C. Moreaux (ob), T. Caens (tpt), M. Becquet (trbn), P. Devoyon (pno), F. Kondo (mez), Ludwig String Quartet—Sonatine for Clarinet & Piano (1921-22); Rapsodie for 2 Flutes, Clarinet & Piano (1917); Danse de la Chèvre for Solo Flute (1921); Romance for Flute & Piano (1953); Petite Suite for 2 Flutes & Piano (1934); Trois Contrepoints for Piccolo, Oboe, Violin & Cello (1922); Intrada for Trumpet & Piano (1947); Hommage du trombone exprimant la tristesse de l'auteur absent for Trombone & Piano (1925); J'avais un fidèle amant for String Quartet (1929); Chanson de Ronsard & 3 Chansons de la petite Sirène for Mezzo, Flute & String Quartet (1924); Introduction et Danse for Flute, Harp & String Trio [undated]; Colloque for Flute, Celesta, Violin & Viola [undated] Timpani ▲ IC1010 [DDD]

Zanon, Ricardo (pno)
Clementi, M.:Pno Music (comp), w. Federico Aldao (pno), Aldo Antognazzi (pno), Ana Chavez (pno), Lorena Di Florio (pno), Marcela Paludi (pno)—Sons (6) for Pno, Op. 1, Nos. 4-6; Sons (6) for Pno, Op. 2, Nos. 2, 4 & 6 Aura Classics ▲ AU 32072

Zanten, Nanette van (fid/hp cithara)—see ORCHESTRAS & ENSEMBLES Wayal Duo

Zapf, Gerd (tpt)
Trumpet & Organ, w. Roland Muhr (org) *(rec Oct. 14-15 & 21-22, 1983)* Calig ▲ CAL 50832 [DDD]

Zaratzian, H. (va)
Rieti, V.:Partita Hpd, w. S. Marlowe (hpd), S. Baron (fl), R. Roseman (ob), C. Libove (vn), A. Ajemian (vn), C. McCraken (vc) CRI ▲ CD 601 [ADD]

Zaritskaya, Irina (pno)
Chopin, F.:Pno Music (misc), w. T. Irinsky (pno), I. Szekely (pno), B. Szokolay (pno)—includes Ballade No. 3; Barcarolle, Op. 60; Berceuse, Op. 57; Piano Con. 2 (larghetto); Etude, Op. 10/3; Fantaisie-Impromptu, Op. 66; Mazurka, Op. 33/2; Nocturne, Op. 9/2; Polonaise-Fantaisie, Op. 61; Prelude, Op. 28/15; Scherzo, Op. 31; Piano Son. 2 (finale); Waltz, Op. 64/1 Naxos ▲ 8.551104 [DDD]
Kabalevsky, D.:Preludes Pno, Op. 38—Nos. 1, 2, 6, 8, 20 & 24 Entrée ▲ 0061
Kabalevsky, D.:Son 3 Pno Entrée ▲ 0061
Scriabin, A.:Poèmes Pno, Op. 32 Entrée ▲ 0061
Scriabin, A.:Preludes Pno, Op. 16 Entrée ▲ 0061
Scriabin, A.:Son 2 Pno Entrée ▲ 0061

Zaslav, Bernard (va)—see also ORCHESTRAS & ENSEMBLES Kohon String Quartet, Zaslav Duo
Downey, J.:A Dolphin, w. D. Nelson (ten), Bourachoff (fl), B. Burda (perc), J. Downey (pno) Gasparo ▲ GS 276 ▮ GS 276C

Zaslav, Naomi (pno)—see ORCHESTRAS & ENSEMBLES Zaslav Duo

Zaugg, Priska (hp)
Ringger, R.U.:Memories 2, w. L. Akerlund (sop), M. Ziegler (fl), U. Walker (vn), D. Pezzoti (vc), F. Mohr, R.U. Ringger [G] Grammont ▲ CTSP 29-2 [ADD]
Ringger, R.U.:Memories of Tomorrow, w. L. Akerlund (sop), M. Ziegler (fl), U. Walker (vn), D. Pezzoti (vc), F. Mohr, R.U. Ringger [G] Grammont ▲ CTSP 29-2 [ADD]

Zavarskaya, Tatiana (vc)
Vainberg, M.:Trio Pno, w. Anatoli Sheludyakov (pno), Irina Tkachenko (vn) Olympia ▲ OLY 581 [DDD]

Zavelberg, Irmgard (vn)—see ORCHESTRAS & ENSEMBLES Rubin String Quartet
Zavelberg, Ulrike (vc)—see ORCHESTRAS & ENSEMBLES Rubin String Quartet
Zavelberg, Ulrike (vn)—see ORCHESTRAS & ENSEMBLES Meininger Trio

Zawinul, Joe (kbd)
Zawinul, J.:Stories of the Danube, w. Bruhan Ocal (voc/perc), Walter Grassman (dr), C. Richter (cnd), Brno State PO Philips ▲ 454143-2

Zayas, Juana (pno)
Chopin, F.:Etudes (24) Music & Arts ▲ CD 891 [DDD]

Zazofsky, Peter (vn)—see also ORCHESTRAS & ENSEMBLES Muir String Quartet
Van Rossum, F.:Con 1 Vn, w. P. Bartholomée (cnd), Liège PO *(rec Feb. 9-12, 1993)* Chamade ▲ 5615 [DDD]
Van Rossum, F.:Con 2 Vn, w. P. Bartholomée (cnd), Liège PO *(rec Feb. 9-12, 1993)* Chamade ▲ 5615 [DDD]

Zbinden, J.-F. (pno)
Zbinden, J.-F.:Con da camera Pno, w. V. Desarzens (cnd), Lausanne CO Grammont ▲ CTSP 3-2 [ADD]
Zbinden, J.-F.:Jazz Sonatine Grammont ▲ CTSP 3-2 [ADD]

Zeavin, Carol (vn)—see also ORCHESTRAS & ENSEMBLES Group for Contemporary Music String Quartet
Wuorinen, C.:Archangel, w. D. Taylor (trbn), B. Hudson (vn), L. Schulman (va), F. Sherry (vc) *(rec March 31, 1981)* Koch International Classics ▲ KIC 7110-2 [DDD]
Wuorinen, C.:Qt 3 Strs, w. B. Hudson (vn), L. Martin (va), F. Sherry (vc) New World ▲ NW 385-2 [DDD]

Zecchi, Carlo (pno)
Michelangeli:The First Recordings/Zecchi:Great Recordings *(rec 1935-38)* Pearl 2-▲ PEA 9086 [ADD]

Zechlin, Dieter (pno)
Brahms, J.:Liebeslieder Waltzes SATB, w. Barbara Hoene (sop), Gisela Pohl (alt), Armin Ude (ten), Siegfried Lorenz (bar), Klaus Bässler (pno), W.-D. Hauschild (cnd), Berlin RSO Berlin Classics ▲ BER 9269
Brahms, J.:Neue Liebeslieder Waltzes, w. Barbara Hoene (sop), Gisela Pohl (alt), Armin Ude (ten), Siegfried Lorenz (bar), Klaus Bässler (pno), W.-D. Hauschild (cnd), Berlin RSO Berlin Classics ▲ BER 9269

Zedníček, Jiří (vc)—see ORCHESTRAS & ENSEMBLES Kubín String Quartet

Zeeland, Cees van (pno)
Andriessen, L.:Hoketus, w. Katherine Pendry (panpipes), James Poke (panpipes), Evan Ziporyn (a sax), Richard Craig (a sax), Steven Schick (congas), Amy Knoles (congas), Lisa Moore (Fender Rhodes), Damian LeGassick (Fender Rhodes), Gerard Bouwhuis (pno), Robert Black (bass gtr), Mark Stewart (bass gtr) *(rec Air Recording Studios, Lyndhurst Hall, Hampstead, London, June 29-July 3, 1994)* Sony Classical ▲ SK 66483 [DDD]
Andriessen, L.:De Staat, w. G. Bouwhuis (pno) Attacca ▲ BABEL 8949-2 [DDD]
Holt, S. ten:Canto ostinato, w. Gerard Bouwhuis (pno), Gene Carl (pno), A. Vernède (pno) *(rec live, Jan 10, 1988)* Donemus 3-▲ CV 2/3/4
Ives, C.:Three Quarter-Tone Pieces, w. G. Bouwhuis (pno) *(rec Jan. 1992)* Channel Classics ▲ CCS 4592 [DDD]
Martland, S.:Drill, w. Gerard Bouwhuis (pno) *(rec Maltings, Snape, Suffolk, Mar 26, 1989)* Catalyst ▲ 09026-68397-2 [DDD]
Messiaen, O.:Visions de l'Amen, w. G. Bouwhuis (pno) *(rec Jan. 1992)* Channel Classics ▲ CCS 4592 [DDD]
Stravinsky, I.:Agon, w. G. Bouwhuis (pno) [Stravinsky's 2-piano arr.] Attacca ▲ BABEL 8949-2 [DDD]
Wagenaar, D.:Music of, w. Gerard Bouwhuis (pno), Netherlands Wind Ensemble, The Hague Percussion Group—La Volta; Stadium; Solenne; Liederen; Metrum Donemus ▲ CV 29
Zeeland, C. van:Initials, w. G. Bouwhuis (pno) *(rec Jan. 1992)* Channel Classics ▲ CCS 4592 [DDD]

Zeeland, Cees van (prepared pno)
Cage, J.:Dances (3) for 2 Prepared Pnos, w. G. Bouwhuis (prepared pno) Attacca ▲ BABEL 8949-2 [DDD]

Zeeuw, Chantal de (org)
Beauverlet-Charpentier, J.-M.:Org Music Pierre Verany 2-▲ PV.785032/33 [DDD]
Benaut:Mass Org Pierre Verany 2-▲ PV.785032/33 [DDD]
Couperin, G.-F.:Org Music Pierre Verany 2-▲ PV.785032/33 [DDD]
Liszt, F.:Fant & Fugue on "Ad nos, ad salutarem undam" Org Pierre Verany ▲ PV.783041 [ADD]
Liszt, F.:Prelude & Fugue B-A-C-H Pierre Verany ▲ PV.783041 [ADD]
A Triumphal Display of French Organ Music from the Revolution to the Empire Pierre Verany 2-▲ 785032/33 [DDD]

Zeeuw, Chantal de (pno)
Liszt, F.:Vars on "Weinen, Klagen, Sorgen, Zagen", S.179 Pierre Verany ▲ PV.783041 [ADD]

Zeger, Brian (pno)
McKinley, W.T.:Qt 1 Pno, w. Broyhill Chamber Ensemble *(rec Appalachian State Univ, July 1995)* MMC ▲ MMC 2041 [DDD]
Schwantner, J.:Black Anemones, w. R. Wilson (fl) New World ▲ 80403-2 [DDD]

Zehetmair, Thomas (vn)
Bach, J.S.:Cons Vn (comp), w. Amsterdam Bach Soloists Berlin Classics ▲ BER 1114 [DDD]
Bach, J.S.:Con Vn, BWV 1052, w. Amsterdam Bach Soloists Berlin Classics ▲ BER 1114 [DDD]
Bach, J.S.:Con Vn, BWV 1058, w. Amsterdam Bach Soloists Berlin Classics ▲ BER 1114 [DDD]
Bach, J.S.:Sons & Partitas Vn, BWV 1001-1006 Teldec 2-▲ 9031-76138-2
Bartók, B.:Con 1 Vn, w. I. Fischer (cnd), Budapest Festival Orch Berlin Classics ▲ BER 1134 [DDD]
Bartók, B.:Con 2 Vn, w. I. Fischer (cnd), Budapest Festival Orch Berlin Classics ▲ BER 1134 [DDD]
Beethoven, L. van:Romances Vn, w. T. Zehetmair (cnd), Philharmonia Orch Teldec ("M Line" series) ▲ 97448-2
Berg, A.:Chamber Con, w. O. Maisenberg (pno), H. Holliger (cnd), CO of Europe Teldec ▲ 2292-46019-2 [DDD]
Berg, A.:Con Vn, w. H. Holliger (cnd), Philharmonia Orch Teldec ("M Line" series) ▲ 97449-2
Hartmann, K.A.:Con funèbre, w. H. Holliger (cnd), Philharmonia Orch Teldec ("M Line" series) ▲ 97449-2
Janácek, L.:Con Vn, w. H. Holliger (cnd), Philharmonia Orch Teldec ▲ 2292-46449-2 ZK
Janácek, L.:Con Vn, w. H. Holliger (cnd), Philharmonia Orch Teldec ("M Line" series) ▲ 97449-2
Mozart, W.A.:Adagio Vn, K.261, w. T. Zehetmair (cnd), Philharmonia Orch Teldec ("M Line" series) ▲ 97448-2
Mozart, W.A.:Con 1 Vn, w. T. Zehetmair (cnd), Philharmonia Orch Teldec ▲ 2292-46341-2
Mozart, W.A.:Con 2 Vn, w. T. Zehetmair (cnd), Philharmonia Orch Teldec ▲ 2292-46340-2 [DDD]
Mozart, W.A.:Con 3 Vn, w. T. Zehetmair (cnd), Philharmonia Orch Teldec ▲ 2292-46340-2 [DDD]
Mozart, W.A.:Con 4 Vn, w. T. Zehetmair (cnd), Philharmonia Orch Teldec ▲ 2292-46341-2
Mozart, W.A.:Con 5 Vn, w. T. Zehetmair (cnd), Philharmonia Orch Teldec ▲ 2292-46340-2 [DDD]
Mozart, W.A.:Con 7 Vn, w. T. Zehetmair (cnd), Philharmonia Orch Teldec ▲ 2292-46341-2
Mozart, W.A.:Qt Pno, K.478, w. Alfred Brendel (pno), Tabea Zimmermann (va), Richard Duven (vc), Peter Riegelbauer (db) Philips ▲ 446001-2
Mozart, W.A.:Rondo Vn, K.269, w. T. Zehetmair (cnd), Philharmonia Orch Teldec ("M Line" series) ▲ 97448-2
Mozart, W.A.:Rondo Vn, K.373, w. T. Zehetmair (cnd), Philharmonia Orch Teldec ("M Line" series) ▲ 97448-2
Paganini, N.:Caprices Vn Teldec ▲ 76259-2
Schubert, Franz:Qnt Pno, D.667, w. Alfred Brendel (pno), Tabea Zimmermann (va), Richard Duven (vc), Peter Riegelbauer (db) Philips ▲ 446001-2
Shostakovich, D.:Qt 13 Strs, w. G. Kremer (vn), N. Imai (va), B. Pergamentschikow (vc) *(rec Lockenhaus Festival, 1985)* ECM New Series 2-▲ 78118-21347-2 [DDD]
Szymanowski, K.:Caprices, w. Silke Avehaus (pno) EMI Classics ▲ CDC 55607
Szymanowski, K.:Con 1 Vn, w. S. Rattle (cnd), City of Birmingham SO EMI Classics ▲ CDC 55607
Szymanowski, K.:Con 2 Vn, w. S. Rattle (cnd), City of Birmingham SO EMI Classics ▲ CDC 55607
Szymanowski, K.:Romance, w. Silke Avehaus (pno) EMI Classics ▲ CDC 55607
Zimmermann, B.A.:Son Vn *(rec Feb & July 1995)* ECM New Series ▲ ECM 1571 [DDD]

Zehnder, Jean-Claude (org)
Bach, J.S.:Org Music (misc)—2 Choralbearbeitungen über Allein Gott in der Höh sei Ehr, BWV 711 & 717; Prelude & Fugue, BWV 531 *(rec Pere Casulleras, CH-Waldenburg 1992)* Jecklin ▲ JS 309-2 [DDD]
Erbach, C.:Kbd Music—Ricercar tertii toni *(rec Pere Casulleras, CH-Waldenburg 1992)* Jecklin ▲ JS 309-2 [DDD]
Pachelbel, J.:Org Music—Nun lob mein Seel den Herren [Choralvorspiel]; Choralsatz; Fuga super Dies sind die heilgen zehn Gebot; Choralsatz von M. Praetorius *(rec Pere Casulleras, CH-Waldenburg 1992)* Jecklin ▲ JS 309-2 [DDD]

Zeibig, W. (db)
Ludwig Güttler:Trompete, Corno da Caccia, Posthorn, w. Güttler, Ludwig (tpt), Virtuosi Saxoniae, F. Kircheis (hpd), J. Bischof (vc) *(rec 1988-92)* Berlin Classics ▲ BER 1053 [DDD]

Zeijl, Jaap (va)
Berg, A.:Adagio, w. Hans-Udo Heinzmann (fl), Malte Lammers (ob), Walter Hermann (cl), Heinrich Horlein (vn), Seven Forsberg (vc), Willi Beyer (db), Jurgen Lamke (pno), Werner Hagen (pno), Volker Kneip (perc) [arr chamber ensemble] Koch Schwann ▲ SCH CD 311912

▲ = CD ♦ = Enhanced CD Δ = MD ▮ = Cassette Tape □ = DCC

Zeijl, Jaap (va) (cont.)
Busoni, F.:Berceuse élégiaque, w. Hans-Udo Heinzmann (fl), Malte Lammers (ob), Walter Hermann (cl), Heinrich Horlein (vn), Seven Forsberg (vc), Willi Beyer (db), Jurgen Lamke (pno), Werner Hagen (pno), Volker Kneip (perc) [arr Stein for chamber ensemble] Koch Schwann ▲ SCH CD 311912
Debussy, C.:Prélude à l'après-midi d'un faune, w. Hans-Udo Heinzmann (fl), Malte Lammers (ob), Walter Hermann (cl), Heinrich Horlein (vn), Seven Forsberg (vc), Willi Beyer (db), Jurgen Lamke (pno), Werner Hagen (pno), Volker Kneip (perc) [arr Sachs for chamber ensemble] Koch Schwann ▲ SCH CD 311912
Schoenberg, A.:Chamber Sym 1, w. Hans-Udo Heinzmann (fl), Malte Lammers (ob), Walter Hermann (cl), Heinrich Horlein (vn), Seven Forsberg (vc), Willi Beyer (db), Jurgen Lamke (pno), Werner Hagen (pno), Volker Kneip (perc) [arr Webern for chamber ensemble] Koch Schwann ▲ SCH CD 311912

Zeitlin, Zvi (vn)—see also ORCHESTRAS & ENSEMBLES Eastman Trio
Adler, S.:Canto III Gasparo ▲ GS 279
Copland, A.:Son Vn & Pno, w. B. Snyder (pno) Gasparo ▲ GS 279
Druckman, J.:Duo Vn & Pno, w. B. Snyder (pno) Gasparo ▲ GS 279
Foss, L.:Early Song, w. L. Foss (pno) Gasparo ▲ GS 279
Reynolds, V.:Son Vn, w. B. Snyder (pno) Gasparo ▲ GS 279
Schoenberg, A.:Con Vn, w. R. Kubelik (cnd), Bavarian RSO Deutsche Grammophon ("20th Century Classics" series) ▲ 431740-2 [DDD]

Zejfart, Pavel (vn)—see also ORCHESTRAS & ENSEMBLES Panocha String Quartet, Musiktage Mondsee Ensemble
Dvořák, A.:Qnt Strs, Op. 77, w. J. Panocha (vn), M. Sehnoutka (va), J. Kulhan (vc), P. Nejtek (db) Supraphon ▲ SUP 11 1461 [DDD]

Zelazny, Piotr (va)
Roussel, A.:Chamber Music, w. Majken Bjerno (sop), Toke Lund Christiansen (fl), Bjørn Carl Nielsen (ob), Niels Thomsen (cl), Per Jacobsen (hn), Asger Svendsen (bn), Ketil Christensen (tpt), Anne Søe Hansen (vn), Zwi Carmelli (va), Niels Ullner (vc), Michael Dabelsteen (db), Tine Rehling (hp), Morten Mogensen (pno), Per Salo (pno), Per Jensen (perc)—Divertissement, Op. 6; Trio, Op. 40; Joueurs de Flute, Op. 27; Serenade, Op. 30; Le marchand de sable qui passe, Op. 13; Andante et scherzo, Op. 13; 2 poèmes de ronsard, Op. 26; Aria; Elpenor, Op. 59; Pipe Kontrapunkt 2-▲ KPT 32218 [DDD]

Zelenka, Milan (gtr)
Castelnuovo-Tedesco, M.:Con 1 Gtr, Prague CO Supraphon ▲ SUP 0038
Castelnuovo-Tedesco, M.:Con 2 Gtr, Prague CO Supraphon ▲ SUP 0038
Homenaje a Andrés Segovia [Hommage to Segovia] Supraphon ▲ SUP 111855 [DDD]
Paganini, N.:Grand Son Vn, w. P. Messiereur (vn) *(rec 1983)* Supraphon ▲ 10 3647-2 [AAD]
Paganini, N.:Son concertata, w. P. Messiereur (vn) *(rec 1983)* Supraphon ▲ 10 3647-2 [AAD]
Paganini, N.:Terzetto Vn, w. P. Messiereur (vn), E. Rattay (vc) *(rec 1983)* Supraphon ▲ 10 3647-2 [AAD]

Zelenka, Rudolf (pno)
Kozeluch, L.:Original Scottish Airs, w. J. Griffett (ten), J. Krejci (vn), P. Hejny (vc) [arr. J. Griffett; lyrics by Robert Burns]—Nae gentle dames; Here's a health to ane I lo'e dear; Ye banks and braes of bonie Doon; Blythe, blythe and merry was she; Lord Gregory; My Nannie's awa'; And ye shall walk in silk attire; Turn again, thou fair Eliza; Contented wi' little; The day returns; On a bank of flowers; Adieu ye streams; All Water; My love she's but a lassie yet; True hearted was he, the sad swain o' the Yarrow; She's fair and fause; O this is no my aine lassie; The Tears of Scotland Campion ▲ 1322 [DDD]

Zelickman, R. (cl)—see ORCHESTRAS & ENSEMBLES SONOR Ensemble of Univ of California San Diego members

Zelinsky, Beate (cl)
Betz, S.:Sprache ist k-eine Handlung, w. D. Smeyers (cl) *(rec Sept. 24-26, 1990)* Pro Viva ▲ ISPV 164 CD [DDD]
Blank, A.:Bicinium III, w. D. Smeyers (b cl) *(rec Sept. 24-26, 1990)* Pro Viva ▲ ISPV 164 CD [DDD]
Clarinet Counterpoints, w. David Smeyers (cl) CPO ▲ CPO 999116 [DDD]
Glynn, G.:Mannheimer Duos, w. D. Smeyers (cl) *(rec Sept. 24-26, 1990)* Pro Viva ▲ ISPV 164 CD [DDD]
Hamary, A.:Graffiti, w. D. Smeyers *(rec Sept. 24-26, 1990)* Pro Viva ▲ ISPV 164 CD [DDD]
Stahmer, K.H.:Porcelain Music, w. D. Smeyers (cl) *(rec Sept. 24-26, 1990)* Pro Viva ▲ ISPV 164 [DDD]

Zelles, Allison (hp)—see ORCHESTRAS & ENSEMBLES Altramar Medieval Music Ensemble

Zelnick, Robert (vn)
Carreño, T.:Qt Strs, w. J. Roche (vn), T. Strasser (va), C. Heller (vc) Vox Box 2-▲ CDX 5029 [ADD]

Zeltser, Mark (pno)
Beethoven, L. van:Con Vn, Vc & Pno, "Triple Con", w. A. S. Mutter (vn), Yo-Yo Ma (vc), H. von Karajan (cnd), Berlin PO Deutsche Grammophon ▲ 415276-2 [ADD]

Zeltser, Villi (vn)
Hazzan Rishon, Legendary Cantorial Recitativi, Opuses 1 & 2, w. David Montefiore (cant), C. Vineburg (pno), A. Bacelar (vc), G. Lochner (vc), C. Morrison (va) Behar/Berg 2-▲ 001494

Zeltsman, Nancy (mar)—see also ORCHESTRAS & ENSEMBLES Marimolin
Aldridge, R.:Combo Platter, w. Albert Regni (s sax), Sharon Leventhal (vn) Open Loop ▲ 034 [DDD]
Woodcuts GM Recordings ▲ GM 2043 CD

Zeman, Dietmar (bn)
Mozart, W.A.:Con Bn, w. K. Böhm (cnd), Vienna PO Deutsche Grammophon ▲ 429816-2 [ADD] ■ 429816-4

Zemlin, L. (gtr)—see ORCHESTRAS & ENSEMBLES San Francisco Guitar Quartet

Zempléni, Kornél (pno)
Bartók, B.:Mikrokosmos, w. L. Szücs (pno)—Szücs (Vols. 1-4); Zempléni (Vols. 5 & 6) Hungaroton 3-▲ HCD 31154/56 [ADD]

Zenatý, Ivan (vn)
Albinoni, T.:Cons à 5 Obs, Op. 9, w. Z. Dejmek (cnd), Janáček CO—No. 10 in F *(rec Aug 19-21, 1992)* Supraphon ▲ SUP 111568 [DDD]
Dvořák, A.:Ballad, w. A. Kubalek (pno) Dorian ▲ DOR 90171 [DDD]
Dvořák, A.:Con Vn, w. B. Kulinsky (cnd), Prague PO Multisonic ▲ 31 0156 [DDD]
Dvořák, A.:Mazurek, w. A. Kubalek (pno) Dorian ▲ DOR 90171 [DDD]
Dvořák, A.:Mazurek, w. O. Vlček (cnd), Prague Virtuosi *(rec Domovina Studio, Prague, Aug. 23-25, 1994)* Discover International ▲ DI 920265 [DDD]
Dvořák, A.:Romance Vn, w. O. Vlček (cnd), Prague Virtuosi *(rec Domovina Studio, Prague, Aug. 23-25, 1994)* Discover International ▲ DI 920265 [DDD]
Dvořák, A.:Romantic Pieces, Op. 75, w. A. Kubalek (pno) Dorian ▲ DOR 90171 [DDD]
Dvořák, A.:Son Vn, w. A. Kubalek (pno) Dorian ▲ DOR 90171 [DDD]
Dvořák, A.:Sonatina Vn, w. A. Kubalek (pno) Dorian ▲ DOR 90171 [DDD]
Grieg, E.:Son 1 Vn, w. Antonin Kubalek (pno) *(rec Troy Savings Bank Music Hall, Troy, New York, Oct 1995)* Dorian ▲ DOR 90234 [DDD]
Grieg, E.:Son 2 Vn, w. Antonin Kubalek (pno) *(rec Troy Savings Bank Music Hall, Troy, New York, Oct 1995)* Dorian ▲ DOR 90234 [DDD]
Grieg, E.:Son 3 Vn, w. Antonin Kubalek (pno) *(rec Troy Savings Bank Music Hall, Troy, New York, Oct 1995)* Dorian ▲ DOR 90234 [DDD]
Ivan Zenatý:Violin Multisonic ▲ MUL 310194 [DDD]
Janácek, L.:Con Vn, w. F. Jílek (cnd), Brno State PO *(rec Jan. 22-25, 1992)* Supraphon ▲ 111522-2 [DDD]
Kalabis, V.:Son Vn, w. Milan Langer (pno) *(rec Martínek Studio in Prague, Jan 23 & 26 & Feb 13 & 14)* Panton ▲ 811398-2 [DDD]
Martinů, B.:Son in C Vn, w. Milan Langer (pno) Panton ▲ PAN 810965
Martinů, B.:Son in d Vn, w. Milan Langer (pno) Panton ▲ PAN 810965
Martinů, B.:Sonatina Vn, w. Milan Langer (pno) Panton ▲ PAN 810965
Mendelssohn, F.:Con in d Vn & Strs, w. P. Altrichter (cnd), Prague SO Supraphon ▲ SUP 111808 [DDD]
Mendelssohn, F.:Con in e Vn & Orch, Op. 64, w. P. Altrichter (cnd), Prague SO Supraphon ▲ SUP 111808 [DDD]
Mysliveček, J.:Con in C Vn, w. O. Vlček (cnd), Prague Virtuosi *(rec Domovina Studio, Prague, Aug. 23-25, 1994)* Discover International ▲ DI 920265 [DDD]

Zenatý, Ivan (vn) (cont.)
Pergolesi, G.B.:Con Vn, w. Z. Dejmek (cnd), Janáček CO *(rec Aug. 19-21, 1992)* Supraphon ▲ SUP 111568 [DDD]
Schulhoff, E.:Melody Vn, w. Josef Hála (pno) Supraphon ▲ SUP 112168 [DDD]
Schulhoff, E.:Son 1 Vn, w. Josef Hála (pno) Supraphon ▲ SUP 112168 [DDD]
Schulhoff, E.:Son 2 Vn, w. Josef Hála (pno) Supraphon ▲ SUP 112168 [DDD]
Schulhoff, E.:Suite Vn, w. Josef Hála (pno) Supraphon ▲ SUP 112168 [DDD]
Suk, J.:Fairy Tale, w. B. Kulínský (cnd), Prague PO *(rec Sept. 1990)* Multisonic ▲ 31 0045-2 [DDD]
Suk, J.:Fant Vn, w. B. Kalinsky (cnd), Prague SO Multisonic ▲ 31 0156 [DDD]
Torelli, G.:Con grossi, w. Z. Dejmek (cnd), Janáček CO—No. 7 in d for Violin & Orch. *(rec Aug. 19-21, 1992)* Supraphon ▲ SUP 111568 [DDD]
Vanhal, J.B.:Con Vn, w. O. Vlček (cnd), Prague Virtuosi *(rec Domovina Studio, Prague, Aug. 23-25, 1994)* Discover International ▲ DI 920265 [DDD]
Vivaldi, A.:Cons Vn, Op. 4, "La stravaganza", w. Z. Dejmek (cnd), Janáček CO—Nos. 2 & 3 *(rec Aug. 19-21, 1992)* Supraphon ▲ SUP 111568 [DDD]

Zenker, Silvia (pno)
Mahler, G.:Sym 6, w. E. Trenkner (pno) [trans. for piano 4-Hands in 1906 by Alexander von Zemlinsky] *(rec 4/91)* MD + G ▲ L 3400 [DDD]
Mahler, G.:Sym 7, w. E. Trenkner (pno) [arr. for piano duo by Alfredo Casella] MD + G ▲ L 3445 [DDD]

Zentgraf, Hans (vc)
Reger, M.:Suites Vc *(rec Sept 1993)* MD + G ▲ MDG 6120558

Zenziper, Arkadi (pno)
Mozart, W.A.:Sons Pno Vn Vc, w. E. Haupt (fl), F. Dittmann (vc)—K.15 LaserLight ▲ 15 878 [DDD]

Zeppezauer, Erik (db)
Bibalo, A.:Invenzione Evolutiva Norway Music ▲ SOL 10913 [DDD]
Meyers, R.:Elegiac Memories, w. A. Brunsvik (pno) Norway Music ▲ SOL 10913 [DDD]

Zerer, Wolfgang (hpd)
Barsanti, F.:Sons Rcr, Op. 1, w. Hans Maria Kneihs (rcr) *(rec Studio Baumgarten, Vienna, Jan 7-9, 1986)* Camerata ▲ 32CM 131 [DDD]
Loeillet, J.-B.:Sons Various Instruments, Op. 2, w. Hans Maria Kneihs (rcr)—No. 5 in c *(rec Studio Baumgarten, Vienna, Jan 7-9, 1986)* Camerata ▲ 32CM 131 [DDD]
Philidor, P.:Suite Rcr, Op. 1/5, w. Hans Maria Kneihs (rcr) *(rec Studio Baumgarten, Vienna, Jan 7-9, 1986)* Camerata ▲ 32CM 131 [DDD]

Zertsalova, Natalia (pno)—see also ORCHESTRAS & ENSEMBLES Igor Oistrakh Trio
Mozart, W.A.:Sons Vn Pno (misc), w. I. Oistrakh (vn)—in C, K.296; in G, K.301; in D♭, K.302; in C, K.303; in e, K.304; in A, K.305; in D, K.306; in F, K.376; in F, K.377 Vox Box 2-▲ CDX 5128 [DDD]
Prokofiev, S.:Mélodies, w. I. Oistrakh (vn) Allegretto ▲ ACD 8188 [DDD] ■ ACS 8188
Ravel, M.:Son Vn Pno, w. I. Oistrakh (vn) Allegretto ▲ ACD 8188 [DDD] ■ ACS 8188
Schubert, Franz:Fant Vn, D.934, w. I. Oistrakh (vn) Allegretto ▲ ACD 8188 [DDD] ■ ACS 8188

Zes, A. (ob)—see ORCHESTRAS & ENSEMBLES Collegium dell'Arte

Zetterqvist, Mats (vn)
Peterson-Berger, W.:Romance Vn, w. S. Köhler (cnd), Swedish RSO Musica Sveciae ▲ MSCD 630 [DDD]

Zeuthen, Morten (vc)—see also ORCHESTRAS & ENSEMBLES Kontra String Quartet
Bach, J.S.:Suites Vc, BWV 1007-1012 Classico ▲ CLASSCD 104/5
Brahms, J.:Songs, w. Hanne Stavad (cta), Peter Westenholz (pno)—Von ewiger Liebe, Op. 43/1; Die Mainacht, Op. 43/2 Danica ▲ DCD 8143
Brahms, J.:Songs, Op. 91, w. Hanne Stavad (cta), Peter Westenholz (pno) Danica ▲ DCD 8143
Glass, L.:Romance Vc, w. Amalie Malling (pno) *(rec Copenhagen, Mar & June 1996)* Marco Polo/Dacapo ▲ 8.224052 [DDD]
Glass, L.:Son Vc, w. Amalie Malling (pno) *(rec Copenhagen, Mar & June 1996)* Marco Polo/Dacapo ▲ 8.224052 [DDD]
Grainger, P.:La Scandinavie, w. Amalie Malling (pno) *(rec Copenhagen, Mar & June 1996)* Marco Polo/Dacapo ▲ 8.224052 [DDD]
Hamerik, A.:Concert-Romanze, w. Amalie Malling (pno) [arr for vc & pno] *(rec Copenhagen, Mar & June 1996)* Marco Polo/Dacapo ▲ 8.224052 [DDD]
Heise, P.:Chamber Music, w. A. Malling (pno), Kontra String Quartet—Quintet in F for Piano & Strings (1869); Cello Sonata in a (1867); 2 Fantasy Pieces for Cello & Piano Marco Polo/Dacapo ▲ DCCD 9113 [DDD]
Heise, P.:Songs, w. Hanne Stavad (cta), Peter Westenholz (pno)—Gudrans Sorg [song cycle] Danica ▲ DCD 8143
Lutoslawski, W.:Songs, w. Hanne Stavad (cta), Peter Westenholz (pno)—5 Songs after poems by Illakowicz Danica ▲ DCD 8143
Nielsen, C.:Songs, w. Hanne Stavad (cta), Peter Westenholz (pno)—Det bodes der for Af Op. 6; I Seraillets Have Af Op. 4; Har Dagen sauket al sin sorg Af Op. 4 Danica ▲ DCD 8143
Nørgård, P.:Short Songs, w. Hanne Stavad (cta), Peter Westenholz (pno) Danica ▲ DCD 8143
Schubert, Franz:Songs (misc), w. Hanne Stavad (cta), Peter Westenholz (pno)—Der Tod und das Mädchen, D.531; Ganymed, D.544; Lachen und Weinen, D.777; Seligkeit, D.433; Wanderers nachlied II, D.768 Danica ▲ DCD 8143
Sehested, H.:Fant Pieces, w. Amalie Malling (pno) *(rec Copenhagen, Mar & June 1996)* Marco Polo/Dacapo ▲ 8.224052 [DDD]

Zeyen, M. M. (pno)
Bach, J.S.:Music of, w. L. A. Greco (vc)—arr. by Silto/Casals for cello & piano:Jesu, meine Freude; Andante from Son. Violin in A, BWV 1003; Adagio from Organ Toccata in C; Air from Orchestral Suite in D Orion ▲ CDA 8901 [AAD] ■ OC 8802
Barber, S.:Son Vc, w. L. A. Greco (vc) Orion ▲ CDA 8901 [AAD] ■ OC 8802

Zheng, H. (vc)
Tchaikovsky, P.:Vars on a Rococo Theme, w. P. Olefsky (cnd), English CO Amatius Classics ▲ ACCD 1002 [DDD]
Tcherepnin, A.:Mystère, w. P. Olefsky (cnd), Amatius Orch of New York Amatius Classics ▲ ACCD 1002 [DDD]
Vivaldi, A.:Con for 2 Vcs, w. P. Olefsky (vc), P. Olefsky (cnd), English CO Amatius Classics ▲ ACCD 1001 [DDD]

Zhislin, Grigori (va)
Van De Vate, N.:Con Va, w. J. M. Florencio (cnd), Polish Radio-TV SO Vienna Modern Masters ▲ VMM 3023 [DDD]

Zhislin, Grigori (vn)
Penderecki, K.:Son Vn, w. Vladimir Viardo (pno) *(rec National Philharmonic Hall, Warsaw, Poland, Nov. 23, 1993)* Sony Classical ▲ SK 66284 [DDD]

Zhuk, Valentin (vn)
Ryabov, V.:Con da passacaglia, w. V. Igolinsky (vn), S. Kravchenko (vn), T. Sergeyeva (kbd) MCA Classics/Melodiya ▲ MLD 32131 [AAD] ■ MLC 32131
Strauss, R.:Con Vn, w. A. Lazarev (cnd), USSR Radio-TV Large SO Audiophile Classics ▲ APL 101519

Zhvania, Nodar (va)—see ORCHESTRAS & ENSEMBLES Georgian State String Quartet

Zichner, Frank-Immo (pno)
Schoenberg, A.:Ode to Napoleon, w. Roland Hermann (nar), Rim Vogler (vn), Frank Reinecke (vn), Stefan Fehlandt (va), Michael Sanderling (vc) *(rec Siemensvilla, Berlin-Lankwitz, Aug. 1994)* EDA ▲ EDA 008-2 [DDD]

Zickler, Heinz (tpt)
Vivaldi, A.:Con Vn Obs, RV.563, w. H. Thal (tpt), G. Kehr (cnd), Mainz CO Allegretto ▲ ACD 8098 [ADD] ■ ACS 8098

Ziegler, Fiona (vn)
Broadstock, B.:Eheu Fugaces, w. Marilyn Richardson (sop), Christine Draeger (fl), Roslyn Dunlop (cl), Susan Blake (vc), David Miller (pno), Daryl Pratt (perc) Vox Australis ▲ VAST018-2 [DDD]

Ziegler, Matthias (fl)
Ringger, R.U.:Long, long ago Grammont ▲ CTSP 29-2 [ADD]

INSTRUMENT.

Ziegler, Matthias (fl) (cont.)
Ringger, R.U.:Memories 2, w. L. Akerlund (sop), P. Zaugg (hp), U. Walker (vn), D. Pezzoti (vc), F. Mohr, R.U. Ringger [G] Grammont ▲ CTSP 29-2 [ADD]
Ringger, R.U.:Memories of Tomorrow, w. L. Akerlund (sop), P. Zaugg (hp), U. Walker (vn), D. Pezzoti (vc), F. Mohr, R.U. Ringger [G] Grammont ▲ CTSP 29-2 [ADD]
Ziegler, Pablo (pno)
Piazzolla, A.:Music of, w. F.S. Paz (vn), Horacio Malivicino (elec gtr), Hector Console (db), A. Piazolla (band)—Verando porteño; Lunfardo; Milonga del angel; Muerte del angel; Astor's Speech; La camorra; Mumuki; Adios Nonino; Contra bajissmo; Michelangelo; Concierto para quinteto *(rec Sept. 6, 1987)* Chesky ▲ JD 107 [DDD]
Piazzolla, A.:Music of, w. Emanuel Ax (pno)—Revirado; Fuga y misterio; Milonga del ángel; Decarissimo; Soledad; La muerte del ángel; Adiós Nonino; Libertango; Verano porteño; Michelangelo; Buenos Aires hora cero; Tangata [arr 2 pnos Pablo Ziegler] *(rec Am Acad of Arts & Letters, NY, June 19–20, 1996)* Sony Classical ▲ SK 62728 [DDD]
Zienkowski, Edward (vn)
Karlowicz, M.:Con Vn, w. T. Ukigaya (cnd), Pomorska PO *(rec 1988–89)* Thorofon ▲ CTH 2046 [DDD]
Zigante, Frédéric (gtr)
Giuliani, M.:Gtr Music—Vars Gtr, Opp. 87, 101, 102, 146 *(rec Ivrea, Italy, July 1992)* Arts ▲ 47147-2 [DDD]
Giuliani, M.:Rossiniana—Nos. 1–4 *(rec Ivrea, Italy, July 1992)* Arts ▲ 47146-2 [DDD]
Giuliani, M.:Rossiniana—Nos. 5 & 6 *(rec Ivrea, Italy, July 1992)* Arts ▲ 47147-2 [DDD]
Paganini, N.:Gtr Music—Sons 1-16 *(rec Torino, Italy, 1988–89)* Arts ▲ 47192-2 [DDD]
Paganini, N.:Gtr Music—Sons 17-37 *(rec Torino, Italy, 1988–89)* Arts ▲ 47193-2 [DDD]
Paganini, N.:Gtr Music—Grande Son, M.S.3; Son, M.S. 87; Son, M.S. 104; Sonatine, M.S. 85; Andantino, M.S. 99; Rondoncino, M.S.94; Andanatino, M.S.102; Marcia, M.S.96; Valtz, M.S.96; Valtz, M.S.92; Allegretto, M.S.90; Allgretto, M.S.86; Andantino, M.S.88; Valtz M.S.100 & Trio, M.S.101; Andantino, M.S.97; Marziale, M.S.105; Allegretto, M.S.91; Andantino, M.S.89; Sinf della Lodovisia, M.S.98 *(rec Torino, Italy, 1988–89)* Arts ▲ 47194-2 [DDD]
Paganini, N.:Gtr Music—Ghiribizzi, M.S.43, Nos. 1–43 *(rec Turin, Italy, 1988–89)* Arts ▲ 47195-2 [DDD]
Villa-Lobos, H.:Gtr Music—Chôro No. 1; 12 Études; Simples; 5 Préludes; Suite Populaire Brésilienne; Etude No. 10 [1928 version] Stradivarius ▲ STV 33378 [DDD]
Zighera, Alfred (vc)
Albrechtsberger, J.G.:Concertino 5 Instrs, w. Armando Ghitalla (tpt), Robert Shermont (vn), Jean Cauhape (va), James Weaver (pno) *(rec Dec 1963 & Jan 1964)* Crystal ▲ CD 760
Zigmund, Jiri (va)—see ORCHESTRAS & ENSEMBLES Wilhan String Quartet
Zilberstein, Lilya (pno)
Brahms, J.:Intermezzos Pno, Op. 117 Deutsche Grammophon ▲ 431123-2 [DDD]
Brahms, J.:Pieces Pno, Op. 118 Deutsche Grammophon ▲ 431123-2 [DDD]
Brahms, J.:Vars on a Theme by Paganini Deutsche Grammophon ▲ 431123-2 [DDD]
Grieg, E.:Con Pno, Op. 16, w. N. Järvi (cnd), Gothenburg SO Archiv ▲ 437549-2
Liszt, F.:Années de pèlerinage 2—No. 7, "Dante Sonata" Deutsche Grammophon ▲ 435385-2 [DDD]
Schubert, Franz:Son Pno, D.850 Deutsche Grammophon ▲ 435385-2 [DDD]
Zill, H.-M. (fl)
Karg-Elert, S.:Fl & Pno Music, w. H.-D. Meyer-Moortgat (pno)—Sinfonische Kanzone, Op. 114; Sonata in B, Op. 121; Impression exotiques, Op. 134; Suite pointillistique, Op. 135; Sonata appassionata, Op. 140 Ambitus ▲ 97833 [DDD]
Zimansky, Robert (vn)
Bloch, E.:Baal Shem, "3 Pictures of Chassidic Life", w. Christoph Keller (pno) Accord ▲ ACD 220342 [AAD]
Reger, M.:Son Vn Pno, Op. 72, w. Christoph Keller (pno) Accord ▲ ACD 200002 [DDD]
Reger, M.:Son Vn Pno, Op. 84, w. Christoph Keller (pno) Accord ▲ ACD 200002 [DDD]
Scelsi, G.:L'Âme Ailée Accord ▲ ACD 200622 [DDD]
Scelsi, G.:L'Âme Ouverte Accord ▲ ACD 200622 [DDD]
Scelsi, G.:Divertimenti—No. 3 Accord ▲ ACD 200622 [DDD]
Scelsi, G.:Trio Strs, w. Christoph Schiller (va), Patrick Demenga (vc) Accord ▲ ACD 200622 [DDD]
Schmid, E.:Sonatine II, w. C. Keller (pno) *(rec Nov. 29, 1987)* Grammont ▲ CTSP 33-2 [ADD]
Schumann, R.:Son 1 Vn, w. Christoph Keller (pno) Accord ▲ ACD 220532 [DDD]
Schumann, R.:Son 2 Vn, w. Christoph Keller (pno) Accord ▲ ACD 220532 [DDD]
Schumann, R.:Son 3 Vn, w. Christoph Keller (pno) Accord ▲ ACD 220532 [DDD]
Szymanowski, K.:Con 1 Vn, w. D. Burkh (cnd), Janáček PO Centaur ▲ CRC 2153
Zimbalist, Efrem (vn)
Bach, J.S.:Con for 2 Vns, w. F. Kreisler (vn), *(orch unknown) (rec 1915)* Pearl 2-▲ PEA 9996 [AAD]
Warren, E.R.:Good Morning, America!, w. E. Zimbalist, Jr. (nar), S. Kawalla (cnd), Cracow Polish Radio-TV SO, Cracow Polish Radio-TV Chorus [E] Cambria ▲ CD 1042 [DDD]
Zimdars, Richard (pno)
Anderson, Tommy Joe:Son 3 Sax, w. K. Fischer (sax) *(rec 1988)* ACA Digital Recording ▲ CM 20003
Baker, C.:Omaggi e Fant Tuba, w. D. Randolph (tuba) ACA Digital Recording ▲ CM 20018
Bassett, L.:Duo Concertante, w. K. Fischer (a sax) *(rec 1988)* ACA Digital Recording ▲ CM 20003
Contrasts in Contemporary Music, w. David Randolph (tuba), P. Randolph (pno) *(rec July–Aug. 1991)* ACA Digital ▲ CM 20018
Harris, R.:American Ballads (6)—Nos. 1 & 2 Albany ▲ TROY 105 [DDD]
Harris, R.:Pno Music—Suite; True Love Don't Weep; Toccata; Little Suite Albany ▲ TROY 105 [DDD]
Harris, R.:Son Pno Albany ▲ TROY 105 [DDD]
Heiden, B.:Diversion, w. Kenneth Fischer (sax) *(rec 1988)* ACA Digital Recording ▲ CM 20003
Zimerman, Krystian (pno)
Bacewicz, G.:Son 2 Pno Olympia ▲ OLY 392 [ADD]
Beethoven, L. van:Cons Pno (comp), w. Zimerman, Bernstein (cnd), Vienna PO *(rec 1989)* Deutsche Grammophon 3-▲ 435467-2 [DDD]
Brahms, J.:Con 1 Pno, w. L. Bernstein (cnd), Vienna PO Deutsche Grammophon ▲ 413472-2 [DDD]
Brahms, J.:Con 2 Pno, w. L. Bernstein (cnd), Vienna PO Deutsche Grammophon ▲ 415359-2 [DDD]
Chopin, F.:Andante Spianato & Grande Polonaise, w. Dang Thai Son (pno) [2 versions] Polskie Nagrania ▲ PNCD 008 [ADD]
Chopin, F.:Ballades Pno (comp) Deutsche Grammophon ▲ 423090-2 [DDD]
Chopin, F.:Barcarolle Pno Deutsche Grammophon ▲ 423090-2 [DDD]
Chopin, F.:Con 1 Pno, w. C.M. Giulini (cnd), Los Angeles PO Deutsche Grammophon ▲ 415970-2 [ADD]
Chopin, F.:Con 2 Pno, w. C.M. Giulini (cnd), Los Angeles PO Deutsche Grammophon ▲ 415970-2 [ADD]
Chopin, F.:Con 2 Pno, w. H. von Karajan (cnd), Berlin PO *(rec Sept. 1, 1980)* Exclusive ▲ EXL 41 [AAD]
Chopin, F.:Fant Deutsche Grammophon ▲ 423090-2 [DDD]
Debussy, C.:Preludes Pno Deutsche Grammophon ▲ 435773-2
Grieg, E.:Con Pno, Op. 16, w. H. von Karajan (cnd), Berlin SO *(rec Sept. 1981)* Deutsche Grammophon ▲ 439015-2 [DDD]
Liszt, F.:Cons Pno, w. S. Ozawa (cnd), Boston SO Deutsche Grammophon ▲ 423571-2 [DDD]
Liszt, F.:Harmonies poétiques et religieuses—Funérailles Deutsche Grammophon ▲ 431780-2 [DDD]
Liszt, F.:Pno Music (misc)—Nuage gris; La lugubre gondola No. 2 Deutsche Grammophon ▲ 431780-2 [DDD]
Liszt, F.:Son Pno Deutsche Grammophon ▲ 431780-2 [DDD]
Liszt, F.:Totentanz, w. S. Ozawa (cnd), Boston SO Deutsche Grammophon ▲ 423571-2 [DDD]
Lutoslawski, W.:Con Pno, w. W. Lutoslawski (cnd), BBC SO Deutsche Grammophon ▲ 431664-2 [DDD]
Respighi, O.:Son Vn, w. K. W. Chung (vn) Deutsche Grammophon ▲ 427617-2 [DDD]
Schumann, R.:Con Pno, w. H. von Karajan (cnd), Berlin SO *(rec Sept. 1981)* Deutsche Grammophon ▲ 439015-2 [DDD]
Strauss, R.:Son Vn, w. K.-W. Chung (vn) Deutsche Grammophon ▲ 427617-2 [DDD]

Zimerman, Krystian (pno) (cont.)
Stravinsky, I.:Les Noces, w. A. Mory (sop), P. Parker (mez), J. Mitchinson (ten), P. Hudson (bass), M. Argerich (pno), H. Francesch (pno), C. Katsaris (pno), L. Bernstein (cnd), English Bach Festival Orch, English Bach Festival Chorus [R] Deutsche Grammophon ("20th Century Classics" series) ▲ 423251-2 [ADD]
Zimmer, Stefan (cl)—see ORCHESTRAS & ENSEMBLES Avalon Wind Quintet
Zimmerman, Gabriele (fl)
Bach, J.S.:Cant 212, "Peasant Cant", w. Ursula Buckel (sop), Claus Ocker (bass), Peter Buck (vc), Martin Galling (hpd), R. Ewerhart (cnd), Württemberg CO *(rec 1965)* Vox Box 3-▲ CD3X 3039
Zimmerman, Knut (vn)
Christmas Concertos, w. M. Erxleben (cnd), New Berlin SO, Michael Erxlaben (vn), Hans-Peter Kirchberg (org) Capriccio ▲ 10442 [DDD]
Zimmerman, Scott (perc)
Snyder, R.:Enneagram Studies, w. Eric Ginsberg (cl), Stephen Krahn (pno), Chris Casart (perc), Rick Schaefer (perc), Kelly Scheef (perc), Jason Varga (perc) Coronet ▲ COR 400-9
Zimmerman, Ulrich (cl)
Brahms, J.:Qnt Cl, w. Enesco String Quartet Intaglio ▲ ING 763 [ADD]
Mozart, W.A.:Qnt Cl, K.581, w. Enesco String Quartet Intaglio ▲ ING 763 [ADD]
Zimmermann, Frank Peter (vn)
Beethoven, L. van:Con Vn, Vc & Pno, "Triple Con", w. Robert Cohen (vc), Wolfgang Manz (pno), J.-P. Saraste (cnd), English CO Classics for Pleasure ("Silver Doubles" series) 2-▲ CFP CDCFP 4775 [ADD/DDD]
Mozart, W.A.:Adagio Vn, w. J. Faerber (cnd), Württemberg CO EMI Classics 2-▲ CDFB 69355
Mozart, W.A.:Cons Vn, w. J. Faerber (cnd), Württemberg CO—Nos. 1-5 EMI Classics 2-▲ CDFB 69355
Mozart, W.A.:Music of, w. Alban Berg Quartet, A. Dumay (vn), A. S. Mutter (vn), S. Meyer (cl), R. Vlatkovi (hn), C. Zacharias (pno), *(sels unknown)* EMI Classics ▲ CDC 54165
Mozart, W.A.:Rondo in B♭ Vn, w. J. Faerber (cnd), Württemberg CO EMI Classics 2-▲ CDFB 69355
Mozart, W.A.:Rondo Vn, K.373, w. J. Faerber (cnd), Württemberg CO EMI Classics 2-▲ CDFB 69355
Prokofiev, S.:Con 2 Vn, w. M. Jansons (cnd), Philharmonia Orch EMI Classics ▲ CDC 54454
Saint-Saëns, C.:Con 3 Vn, w. M. Jansons (cnd), Oslo PO EMI Classics ▲ CDC 55184
Sibelius, J.:Con Vn, w. M. Jansons (cnd), Philharmonia Orch EMI Classics ▲ CDC 54454
Ysaÿe, E.:Poème élégiaque Vn & Pno, w. Edoardo Maria Strabbioli (pno) EMI Classics ▲ CDC 55255
Ysaÿe, E.:Rêve d'enfant, w. Edoardo Maria Strabbioli (pno) EMI Classics ▲ CDC 55255
Ysaÿe, E.:Sons Vn EMI Classics ▲ CDC 55255
Zimmermann, Tabea (va)
Franck, C.:Qnt Pno, w. A Rabinovitch (pno), K. Bennion (vn), L. Hagen (vn), C. Hagen (vc) *(rec Lockenhaus Fest, 1984)* ▲
Mozart, W.A.:Qt Pno, K.478, w. Alfred Brendel (pno), Thomas Zehetmair (vn), Richard Duven (vc), Peter Riegelbauer (db) Philips ▲ 446001-2
Saint-Saëns, C.:Carnival of the Animals, w. M. Argerich (pno), N. Freire (pno), G. Kremer (vn), I. van Keulen (vn), M. Maisky (vc), et al. Philips ("Digital Classics" series) ▲ 416841-2 [DDD]
Schubert, Franz:Qnt Pno, D.667, w. Alfred Brendel (pno), Thomas Zehetmair (vn), Richard Duven (vc), Peter Riegelbauer (db) Philips ▲ 446001-2
Veress, S.:Trio, w. H. Schneeberger (vn), T. Demenga (vc) ECM New Series ▲ 78118-21477-2 [DDD]
Zimmermann, B.A.:Antiphonen, w. H. Zender (cnd), Ensemble Modern *(rec Frankfurt, May 1–4 & Oct 24–25, 1992)* RCA Red Seal ▲ 09026-61181-2 [DDD]
Zimmermann, Willi (vn)—see ORCHESTRAS & ENSEMBLES Winterthur String Quartet
Zimmitti, Bob (perc)
Kellaway, R.:Music of, w. Fred Seykora (vc), Chuck Domanico (electric bass), Roger Kellaway (pno/perc), Emil Richards (mar/perc), Joe Porcaro (perc)—Thinking of You; Un canto per la pace [A Song for Peace]; Love of my Life; Eleventide; In My Heart; Eve; Windows; Winter [Parts 1–3] *(rec Ocean Way Recording Studio, Los Angeles, CA, May 1–5, 1993)* EMI Classics ▲ CDC 54903 [DDD]
Zindler, Joachim (va)
Eisler, H.:Chamber Music, w. Rudolf Ulbrich (vn), Clemens Diller (vc) Berlin Classics ▲ BER CD 9231
Zinger, Pablo (pno)
Guastavino, C.:Songs, w. U. Espaillat (ten)—Desde que te conocí; Viniendo de Chilecito; En los surcos del amor; Mi garganta; Cuando acaba de llover; Préstame tu pañuelito; Ya me voy a retirar; Las puertas de la mañana; Piececitos; Cita; Se equivocó la paloma; Jardín de amores; A volar!; Nana del niño malo; La novia; Geografía Física; Alpuente de la golodrinal; Elegía; La rosa y el sauce; Pueblito, mi pueblo *(rec May 1992)* New Albion ▲ NA 058
Surinach, C.:Doppio Concertino, w. P. Zinger (cnd), Bronx Arts Ensemble *(rec 1992)* New World ▲ 80428-2
Surinach, C.:Flamenco cyclothymia, w. I. Chorberg (vn) *(rec 1992)* New World ▲ 80428-2
Surinach, C.:Qt Pno, w. I. Chorberg (vn), Bronx Arts Ensemble *(rec 1992)* New World ▲ 80428-2
Ziółko, Leszek (vc)—see ORCHESTRAS & ENSEMBLES Tutti e solo
Ziporyn, Evan (b cl)
Wigglesworth, F.:Summer Music CRI ▲ C 733 [DDD]
Ziporyn, E.:Tsmindao Ghmerto *(rec The Hit Factory, New York, Oct 4–8, 1995)* Sony Classical ▲ SK 62254 [DDD]
Ziporyn, Evan (cl)—see ORCHESTRAS & ENSEMBLES Bang on a Can
Ziporyn, Evan (s sax)
Wolfe, J.:Lick, w. Mark Stewart (elec gtr), Steven Schick (perc), Lisa Moore (pno), Maya Beiser (vc), Robert Black (db) *(rec Air Recording Studios, Lyndhurst Hall, Hampstead, London, June 29–July 3, 1994)* Sony Classical ▲ SK 66483 [DDD]
Ziporyn, Evan (sax)
Andriessen, L.:Hoketus, w. Katherine Pendry (panpipes), James Poke (panpipes), Richard Craig (a sax), Steven Schick (congas), Amy Knoles (congas), Lisa Moore (Fender Rhodes), Damian LeGassick (Fender Rhodes), Cees van Zeeland (pno), Gerard Bouwhuis (pno), Robert Black (bass gtr), Mark Stewart (bass gtr) *(rec Air Recording Studios, Lyndhurst Hall, Hampstead, London, June 29–July 3, 1994)* Sony Classical ▲ SK 66483 [DDD]
Riley, T.:In C, w. Bruce Ackley, Steve Adams, Don R. Baker, Chris Brown, George Brooks, Steve Coughlin, Blake Derby, Bill Douglass, Mihr'un'Nisa Douglass, Hank Dutt, David Harrington, Don Howe, Joan Jeanrenaud, Alden Jenks, Warner Jepson, Henry Kaiser, Jaron Lanier, Bill Maginnis, George Marsh, Shabda Owens, Jon Raskin, Gyan Riley, Terry Riley, Gino Robair, John Sackett, Ramón Sender, John Sherba, Toyji Tomita, Danny Turick, William Winant *(rec Jan. 14, 1990)* New Albion ▲ NA 071
Ziporyn, E.:Kekembangan, w. Chris Jonas (sax), Randy McKean (sax), Dan Plonsey (sax), Sekar Jaya Gamelan Orch New World ▲ 804302
Ziporyn, Evan (t sax)
Andriessen, L.:Hout, w. Mark Stewart (elec gtr), Steven Schick (perc), Lisa Moore (pno) *(rec Air Recording Studios, Lyndhurst Hall, Hampstead, London, June 29–July 3, 1994)* Sony Classical ▲ SK 66483 [DDD]
Zipperling, Rainer (vc)
Boccherini, L.:Sons (34) Vc, w. H. Suzuki (vc), G. Penson (hpd)—Son. duets in B♭, G.8, in E♭, G.10, in A, G.13, in C G.17 & in B♭, G.565 Ricercar ▲ RIC 122107
Platti, G.B.:Sons Fl, w. B. Böhm (trns fl), G. Wilson (hpd) CPO ▲ CPO 999021-2 [DDD]
Sainte-Colombe, M. de:Concerts for 2 B Vls, w. P. Pierlot (vl)—No. 44, "Tombeau Les Regrets" Ricercar ▲ RIC 118100 [DDD]
Sainte-Colombe, M. de:Fant en rondeau, w. P. Pierlot (vl) Ricercar ▲ RIC 118100 [DDD]
Sainte-Colombe, M. de:Tombeau, w. P. Pierlot (vl) Ricercar ▲ RIC 118100 [DDD]
Zirchev, Z. (vn)
Pergament, M.:Pezzo, w. G. von Bahr (fls), P. Pohjola (vn), Z. Tchavdarov (va), U. Vrethammar (vc) *(rec Jan. 25, 1973)* BIS ▲ CD 37 [AAD]
Zisman, Daniel (vn)—see ORCHESTRAS & ENSEMBLES Tango 7
Zito, Ronnie (dr)—see ORCHESTRAS & ENSEMBLES John Whitney Trio
Zitterbart, Ralph (pno)
Galbraith, N.:Con 1 Pno, w. K. Lockhart (cnd), Cincinnati CO *(rec Emory Theater, Cincinnati, OH, Jan 24, 1994)* Ocean ▲ OR 101 [DDD]

▲ = CD ♦ = Enhanced CD Δ = MD ■ = Cassette Tape □ = DCC

Zitterbart, Ralph (pno) (cont.)
Galbraith, N.:Con 1 Pno, w. K. Lockhart (cnd), Cincinnati CO — Ocean ▲ ORC 101

Zivkovic, Nebojša Jovan (mar/vib)
Milhaud, D.:Con Mar, w. E. Theis (cnd), Austrian Chamber Sym *(rec Casino Zögernitz, Vienna, June 6–19, 1995)* — Musicaphon ▲ M 56809 [DDD]

Zivoni, Yossi (vc)
Mendelssohn, F.:Son in F Vc, w. A. Goldstone (pno) — Meridian ▲ MER 84229 [DDD]

Zivoni, Yossi (vn)
Bach, J.S.:Sons & Partitas Vn, BWV 1001–1006—Sons Nos. 1 in g & 3 in C; Partita No. 1 in b — Meridian ▲ MER 84283 [DDD]
Mendelssohn, F.:Son Vn (1820), w. A. Goldstone (pno) — Meridian ▲ MER 84229 [DDD]
Mendelssohn, F.:Son Vn, Op. 4, w. A. Goldstone (pno) — Meridian ▲ MER 84229 [DDD]

Zizzo, Alicia (pno)
Gershwin, G.:Con Pno, w. M. Charry (cnd), George Gershwin Festival Orch *(rec 6/90)* — Pro Arte/Fanfare ▲ CDD 514 [DDD]
Gershwin, G.:Lullaby *(rec 6/90)* — Pro Arte/Fanfare ▲ CDD 514 [DDD]
Gershwin, G.:Pno Music—Pno Preludes; Pno Suite [from Blue Monday Blues]; 7 Miniatures in Gershwin's Hand; Rhap in Blue — IMP ("Masters" series) ▲ IMP 6600052
Gershwin, G.:Rhap in Blue, w. M. Charry (cnd), George Gershwin Festival Orch *(rec 6/90)* — Pro Arte/Fanfare ▲ CDD 514 [DDD]

Zlatníková, Kateřina (cimbalom)
Stravinsky, I.:L'Histoire du soldat Suite Ensemble, w. J. Novotný (fl), K. Krautgartner (cl), L. Pešek (cnd), Prague Chamber Harmony *(rec May 18–22, 1964)* — Supraphon ("Collection" series) ▲ 11 0672–2 [ADD]

Zmudzinski, Tadeusz (pno)
Szymanowski, K.:Sym 4, w. K. Stryja (cnd), Polish State PO — Marco Polo ▲ 8.223290 [DDD]
Szymanowski, K.:Sym 4, w. W. Rowicki (cnd), Warsaw PO — Polskie Nagrania ▲ PLN 62 [ADD]

Znamenskii, Valerii (timp)
Ustvolskaya, G.:Octet Obs, w. Nicolay Neretin (ob), Piotr Tosenko (ob), Alexander Stang (vn), Olga Ribaltchenko (vn), Valentin Lukin (vn), Nikolay Tkachenko (vn), Oleg Malov (pno), O. Malov (cnd) *(rec St. Petersburg Radio House, Oct. & Nov. 1994)* — Megadisc ▲ 7865

Zobel, Bob (tpt)
Scelsi, G.:Anahit, w. Paul Zukofsky (vn), Julie Bogorad (fl), Peggy Russell (fl), Courtney Westcott (fl), Lawrence McDonald (cl), Joan Waryha (cl), Jean Hansen (b cl), Bill Suite (e hn), Nita VanPelt (sax), John Carter (trbn), Martin Lydecker (trbn), Stan Cortman (hn), Robert Ward (hn), William Curry (va), Jody Rowitsch (va), Irene Wade (va), Anne Fagerburg (vc), John Gockel (vc), Sue Manz (bass), Steven Stearman (bass) *(rec Oberlin Conservatory of Music, Oct 8, 1973)* — CP² ▲ CP2 108 [AAD]

Zoboli, Omar (ob)
Fröhlich, F.T.:Divert Ob, w. *(pno unknown)* — Musiques Suisses ▲ 6116
Ponchielli, A.:Capriccio Ob, w. Gérard Wyss (pno) — Accord ▲ ACD 220682 [AAD]
Ponchielli, A.:Qt Fl, w. Heinrich Keller (fl), Bruno Furlanetto (E♭ cl), Antony Morf (cl), Gérard Wyss (pno) — Accord ▲ ACD 220682 [AAD]
Wolf–Ferrari, E.:Concertino E hn, w. R. Maxym (cnd), Folkwang CO — Koch Schwann ▲ CD 310113 [DDD]
Wolf–Ferrari, E.:Idillio–Concertino, w. R. Maxym (cnd), Folkwang CO — Koch Schwann ▲ CD 310113 [DDD]

Zoernig, L. (vc)
Crumb, G.:Vox balaenae, w. J. Schlefer (fl), S. Moltisanti (pno) — Zuma Records ▲ ZMA 102

Zoff, Jutta (hp)
Saint–Saëns, C.:Oratorio de Noël, w. Ute Selbig (sop), Elisabeth Wilke (mez), Annette Markert (cta), Armin Ude (ten), Egbert Junghans (bar), Michael–Christfield Winkler (org), M. Flämig (cnd), Dresden PO, Dresden Kreuz Choir *(rec Dresden, Mar & Apr 1987)* — Capriccio ▲ 10216 [DDD]
Virtuoso Harp Music, w. Zoff, Jutta (hp) — Berlin Classics ▲ BER 2018 [ADD]

Zöller, Karlheinz (fl)
Bach, C.P.E.:Son Fl, H.562 — EMI Classics ("Baroque" series) ▲ CDK 65733
Mozart, W.A.:Cons Fl, w. B. Klee (cnd), English CO — Deutsche Grammophon ▲ 429815–2 [ADD]
Mozart, W.A.:Con Fl Hp, w. Nicanor Zabaleta (hp), E. Märzendorfer (cnd), Berlin PO — Deutsche Grammophon ▲ 427206–2 [AAD]

Zon, A. van (tpt)
Vivaldi, A.:Con for 2 Tpts, w. E. Carroll (tpt), H. Friesen (cnd), Concerto Rotterdam *(rec Apr. 26–27, 1988)* — Erasmus ▲ WVH 005 [DDD]

Zonn, Paul Martin (cl)
Melby, J.:Alto Rhap, w. Debra Richtmeyer (sax), Taimur Sullivan (sax), Wilma Zonn (ob) — Zuma ▲ ZMA 105
Melby, J.:Con Cl & Tape, w. Debra Richtmeyer (sax), Taimur Sullivan (sax), Wilma Zonn (ob) — Zuma ▲ ZMA 105
Zonn, P.M.:Cloning of Wilma Zonn Ww, w. Wilma Zonn (ob), Debra Richtmeyer (sax), Taimur Sullivan (sax) — Zuma ▲ ZMA 105
Zonn, P.M.:Nimbus III Ww, w. Wilma Zonn (ob), Debra Richtmeyer (sax), Taimur Sullivan (sax) — Zuma ▲ ZMA 105
Zonn, P.M.:Shadow of the Condor Cl — Zuma Records ▲ ZMA 105 [DDD]
Zonn, P.M.:Shadow of the Condor Ww, w. Wilma Zonn (ob), Debra Richtmeyer (sax), Taimur Sullivan (sax) — Zuma ▲ ZMA 105

Zonn, Wilma (ob)
Melby, J.:Alto Rhap, w. Debra Richtmeyer (sax), Taimur Sullivan (sax), Paul Martin Zonn (cl) — Zuma ▲ ZMA 105
Melby, J.:Con Cl & Tape, w. Paul Martin Zonn (cl), Debra Richtmeyer (sax), Taimur Sullivan (sax) — Zuma ▲ ZMA 105
Zonn, P.M.:Cloning of Wilma Zonn Ob — Zuma Records ▲ ZMA 105 [DDD]
Zonn, P.M.:Cloning of Wilma Zonn Ww, w. Paul Martin Zonn (cl), Debra Richtmeyer (sax), Taimur Sullivan (sax) — Zuma ▲ ZMA 105
Zonn, P.M.:Nimbus III Ww, w. Paul Martin Zonn (cl), Debra Richtmeyer (sax), Taimur Sullivan (sax) — Zuma ▲ ZMA 105
Zonn, P.M.:Shadow of the Condor Ww, w. Paul Martin Zonn (cl), Debra Richtmeyer (sax), Taimur Sullivan (sax) — Zuma ▲ ZMA 105

Zoon, Jacques (fl)
Escher, R.:Air pour charmer un lézard *(rec Singelkerk, Amsterdam, Aug 14–15, 1995)* — NM Classics ▲ 92059 [DDD]
Escher, R.:Chamber Music, w. Herman De Boer (cl), Bart Schneemann (ob), Zoltan Benyacs (va), Dmitri Ferschtman (vc), Glen Wilson (hpd)—includes Le Tombeau de Ravel; Trio for Strings; Trio for Cl, Va & Pno — NM Classics ▲ NM 92026
Escher, R.:Son Fl, w. Bernd Brackman (pno) *(rec Singelkerk, Amsterdam, Aug 14–15, 1995)* — NM Classics ▲ 92059 [DDD]
Geraedts, J.:Sonatine Fl, w. Bernd Brackman (pno) *(rec Singelkerk, Amsterdam, Aug 14–15, 1995)* — NM Classics ▲ 92059 [DDD]
Keuris, T.:Aria Fl & Pno, w. Bernd Brackman (pno) *(rec Singelkerk, Amsterdam, Aug 14–15, 1995)* — NM Classics ▲ 92059 [DDD]
Loevendie, T.:Music Fl & Pno, w. Bernd Brackman (pno) *(rec Singelkerk, Amsterdam, Aug 14–15, 1995)* — NM Classics ▲ 92059 [DDD]
Maderna, B.:Hyperion, w. P Walmsley–Clark (sop), B. Ganz (nar), P. Eötvös (cnd), Asko Ensemble, Les Jeunes Solistes Vocal Ensemble — Montaigne 2–▲ MO 782014 [DDD]
Pijper, W.:Son Fl, w. Bernd Brackman (pno) *(rec Singelkerk, Amsterdam, Aug 14–15, 1995)* — NM Classics ▲ 92059 [DDD]
Ravel, M.:Daphnis et Chloé, w. R. Chailly (cnd), Royal Concertgebouw Orch, Martin Wright (cnd), Netherlands Radio Chorus *(rec Grotezaal, Concertgebouw, Amsterdam, Feb 17 & 18, 1994)* — London ▲ 443934–2 [DDD]
Schulhoff, E.:Double Con Fl, w. Monica Gutman (pno), I. Yinon (cnd), Bavarian Chamber PO — Koch Schwann ▲ SCH 313712 [DDD]

Zorn, Günter (ob)—see ORCHESTRAS & ENSEMBLES Sebon Quartet

Zorn, John (a sax)
Shea, D.:Hsi–Yu Chi, w. Sim Cain (perc), Hideki Kato (bass instrument), Wu Man (pipa), Zeena Parkins (hp/pno/acc), Jim Pugliese (perc), Mark Ribot (gtr/banjo), David Shea (sampler/pno/turntables), Alex Tobias (celtic dr/misc.), Rebecca Wilson (screaming) — Tzadik ("The Composers" series) ▲ TZA 7005 [DDD]

Zsapka, Jozef (gtr)
2 Violins & 1 Guitar II, w. Hölbling, Anna (vn), Quido Hölbling (vn), Ján Slávik (vc) *(rec 1992)* — Naxos ▲ 8.550645 [DDD]

Zsigmondy, Denes (vn)
Bartók, B.:Son Vn — Klavier ▲ KCD 11056 [ADD]
Bartók, B.:Son 1 Vn & Pno, w. Anneliese Nisse (pno) — Klavier ▲ KCD 11056 [ADD]
Bartók, B.:Son 2 Vn & Pno, w. Anneliese Nisse (pno) — Klavier ▲ KCD 11056 [ADD]
The Romantic Violin, w. Anneliese Nissen (pno), Vienna Kohonaden Orch [cnd:Hans Hagen] — Klavier ▲ KCD 11037 [ADD]

Zubicky, Gregor (ob)
Bozza, E.:Fant pastoral, w. M. Hirvonen (pno) — Simax ▲ PSC 1057 [DDD]
Deslandres, A.E.M.:Intro et Polonaise, w. M. Hirvonen (pno) — Simax ▲ PSC 1057 [DDD]
Dutilleux, H.:Son Ob, w. M. Hirvonen (pno) — Simax ▲ PSC 1057 [DDD]
The French Oboe — Simax ▲ PSC 1057 [DDD]
Grovlez, G.:Sarabande et Allegro, w. M. Hirvonen (pno) — Simax ▲ PSC 1057 [DDD]
Poulenc, F.:Trio Ob, w. P. Hannisdal (bn), M. Hirvonen (pno) — Simax ▲ PSC 1057 [DDD]
Saint–Saëns, C.:Son Ob, w. M. Hirvonen (pno) — Simax ▲ PSC 1057 [DDD]

Zucker, Laurel (fl)
An American Flute Recital, w. M. Shapiro (pno) — Cantilena ▲ 660022 [DDD]
Bach, J.S.:Ov Fl, BWV 1067, Erkel CO *(rec Hungaroton Classic Studio)* — Cantilena ▲ C 660092 [DDD]
Bach, J.S.:Son in a Fl *(rec Hungaroton Classic Studio)* — Cantilena ▲ C 660092 [DDD]
Bloch, E.:Suite modale, w. M. Shapiro (pno) — Cantilena ▲ 660022 [DDD]
Bloch, E.:Suite modale, w. Marc Shapiro (pno) — Cantilena ▲ 66011–2 [DDD]
Chaminade, C.:Concertino Fl, w. Robin Sutherland (pno) — Cantilena ▲ 66011–2 [DDD]
Chaminade, C.:Concertino Fl, w. Robin Sutherland (pno) — Cantilena ▲ C 660012 [DDD]
Copland, A.:Duo Fl, w. M. Shapiro (vc) — Cantilena ▲ 660022 [DDD]
Debussy, C.:Syrinx — Cantilena ▲ C 660012 [DDD]
Fauré, G.:Fant Fl, w. Richard Cionco (pno) *(rec California State Univ Recital Hall, Sacramento)* — Cantilena ▲ 66011–2 [DDD]
Giuliani, M.:Duettino, w. Richard Savino (gtr) — Cantilena ▲ 66012–2 [DDD]
Giuliani, M.:Grand Son Fl, w. Richard Savino (gtr) — Cantilena ▲ 66012–2 [DDD]
Giuliani, M.:Qual Mesto Gemito, w. Richard Savino (gtr) — Cantilena ▲ 66012–2 [DDD]
Giuliani, M.:Serenade Fl, w. Richard Savino (gtr) — Cantilena ▲ 66012–2 [DDD]
Handel, G.F.:Sons Fl, w. Robin Sutherland (hpd)—(7) in e, g, a, G, C, b & F, Op. 1/1b, 2, 4, 5, 7, 9 & 11 — Cantilena ▲ 66005–2 [DDD]
Handel, G.F.:Sons Fl, w. Robin Sutherland (pno)—Op. 1/2, 4, 5, 7, 9, 11 & 16; Op. 7/7 *(rec Cunningham Chapel, Belmont, CA)* — Cantilena ▲ C 660052 [DDD]
Haydn, J.:Diverts Fl, Vn & Vc, w. Shirien Taylor (vn), Samuel Magill (vc)—in D, H.IV/6; in G, H.IV/7; H.IV/8 *(rec Concordia College)* — Cantilena ▲ 66013–2 [DDD]
Haydn, J.:Trios Fls & Vc, "London Trios", w. Renée Siebert (fl), Samuel Magill (vc) *(rec Concordia College)* — Cantilena ▲ 66013–2 [DDD]
Kennan, K.W.:Night Soliloquy, w. Marc Shapiro (pno) — Cantilena ▲ 660022 [DDD]
Kingman, D.:Scénario musical 2, w. Marc Shapiro (pno) — Cantilena ▲ 660022 [DDD]
Kingman, D.:Scénario musical 2, w. Marc Shapiro (pno) — Innova ▲ INNOVA 504
Laurel Zucker:Virtuoso Flutist, w. R. Sutherland (pno) — Cantilena ▲ 660012 [DDD]
Mozart, W.A.:Cons Fl, w. Z. Dorman (cnd), Israel PO members *(rec Israel Conservatory, Tel–Aviv)* — Cantilena ▲ 66011–2 [DDD]
Mozart, W.A.:Cons Fl, w. Z. Dorman (cnd), Israel PO members *(rec Israel Conservatory of Music, Tel–Aviv)* — Cantilena ▲ C 660102 [DDD]
Mozart, W.A.:Qts Fl, w. Shirien Taylor (vn), Mary Hammann (va), Sam Magill (vc)—K.285, 285b & 298 *(rec Academy of Arts & Letters, New York City, June 11, 1994)* — Cantilena ▲ C 660072 [DDD]
Mozart, W.A.:Qt Fl, K.Anh.171, w. Z. Dorman (cnd), Israel PO members—in C, K.285b *(rec Israel Conservatory of Music, Tel–Aviv)* — Cantilena ▲ C 660102 [DDD]
Poulenc, F.:Son Fl, w. Robin Sutherland (pno) — Cantilena ▲ C 660012 [DDD]
Prokofiev, S.:Son Fl, w. R. Sutherland (pno) — Cantilena ▲ 660012 [DDD]
Prokofiev, S.:Son Fl, w. Robin Sutherland (pno) — Cantilena ▲ C 660012 [DDD]
Romances for Flute & Piano, w. Zucker, Laurel (fl), Marc Shapiro (pno) *(rec Cunningham Chapel, Belmont CA)* — Cantilena ▲ C 660062 [DDD]
Serenades for Flute & Harp, w. Sara Cutler (hp) — Cantilena ▲ C 660082
Song of the Wild — Cantilena ▲ 66004–2 [DDD]
Telemann, G.P.:Suite in a Fl, Erkel CO *(rec Hungaroton Classic Studio, Budapest)* — Cantilena ▲ 66011–2 [DDD]
Telemann, G.P.:Suite in a Fl, Erkel CO *(rec Hungaroton Classic Studio)* — Cantilena ▲ C 660092 [DDD]
Wilder, A.:Son 2 Fl, w. M. Shapiro (pno) — Cantilena ▲ 660022 [DDD]
Zucker, L.:Aviary — Cantilena ▲ 660022 [DDD]
Zucker, L.:Effect Out — Cantilena ▲ 660022 [DDD]
Zucker, L.:Shining — Cantilena ▲ 660022 [DDD]

Zuckerman, E. (pno)
Van De Vate, N.:Music for Va, w. M.–K. Johnson (va), W. Wiley (perc) — Vienna Modern Masters ▲ VMM CD 2001 [ADD]

Zukerman, Eugenia (fl)
Bach, C.P.E.:Qts (3) Fl, w. P. Zukerman (va), A. Newman (hpd)—H.538 [fl, vi & fortepno version] — BOMR 2–▲ 617505 [DDD] 2–■ 517504 (D)
Bach, J.C.F.:Son Fl, HW.VIII/1–2, w. A. Newman (pno)—in D — BOMR 3–▲ 617505 [DDD] 2–■ 517504 (D)
Bach, J.S.:Brandenburg Con 5, w. P. Zukerman (vn), A. Newman (hpd), Howard (vc) — BOMR 3–▲ 617505 [DDD] 2–■ 517504 (D)
Bach, J.S.:Con Fl, Vn & Hpd, w. P. Zukerman (vn), A. Newman (hpd), Howard (vc) — BOMR 3–▲ 617505 [DDD] 2–■ 517504 (D)
Bach, J.S.:A Musical Offering, w. P. Zukerman (vn), A. Newman (pno), Howard (vc) — BOMR 3–▲ 617505 [DDD] 2–■ 517504 (D)
Beach, A.M.C.:Theme & Vars, w. Shanghai String Quartet *(rec Church of the Ascension, New York, Oct 19–22, 1994)* — Delos ▲ DE 3173 [DDD]
Foote, A.:Scherzo, w. Shanghai String Quartet *(rec Church of the Ascension, New York, Oct 19–22, 1994)* — Delos ▲ DE 3173 [DDD]
Ginastera, A.:Impresiones de la Puna, w. Shanghai String Quartet *(rec Church of the Ascension, New York, Oct 19–22, 1994)* — Delos ▲ DE 3173 [DDD]
Incantation *(rec 1st Congregational Church, LA, June 9–12, 1996)* — Delos ▲ DE 3184 [DDD]
Mozart, W.A.:Cons Fl, w. P. Zukerman (cnd), English CO *(rec London, June 22–24, 1977)* — Sony Classical ("Essential Classics" series) ▲ SBK 62424 [ADD] ■ SBT 62424

Zukerman, George (bn)
Weber, C.M. von:Con Bn, w. J. Faerber (cnd), Württemberg CO *(rec 1965)* — Allegretto ▲ ACD 8189

Zukerman, Pinchas (va)
Bach, C.P.E.:Qts (3) Fl, w. E. Zukerman (fl), A. Newman (hpd)—H.538 [fl, vi & fortepno version] — BOMR 2–▲ 617505 [DDD] 2–■ 517504 (D)
Bartók, B.:Con Va, w. L. Slatkin (cnd), St. Louis SO — RCA Red Seal ▲ 60749–2–RC [DDD] ■ 60749–4–RC
Beethoven, L. van:Qnt Strs, Op. 29, w. Tokyo String Quartet — RCA Red Seal 3–▲ 09026–61284–2
Beethoven, L. van:Serenade Strs, Op. 8, w. I. Perlman (vn), L. Harrell (vc) — EMI Classics 2–▲ ZDCB 54198
Beethoven, L. van:Trio Strs, Op. 3, w. I. Perlman (vn), L. Harrell (vc) — EMI Classics 2–▲ ZDCB 54198
Beethoven, L. van:Trios Strs, Op. 9, w. I. Perlman (vn), L. Harrell (vc) — EMI Classics 2–▲ ZDCB 54198
Berlioz, H.:Harold in Italy, w. C. Dutoit (cnd), Montreal SO — London ▲ 421193–2 [DDD]

INSTRUMENT.

Zukerman, Pinchas (va) (cont.)
Brahms, J.:Sons Cl (comp), w. D. Barenboim (pno) Deutsche Grammophon ▲ 437248-2 [ADD]
Brahms, J.:Sons Cl (comp), w. M. Neikrug (pno) RCA Red Seal ▲ 09026-61276-2
Brahms, J.:Songs, Op. 91, w. M. Horne (mez), M. Neikrug (pno) [G] RCA Red Seal ▲ 09026-61276-2
Mozart, W.A.:Duos Vn, w. I. Perlman (vn) RCA Red Seal ▲ 60735-2 [DDD] ■ 60735-4 (CrO2)
Mozart, W.A.:Sinf concertante Vn, K.364, w. I. Perlman (vn), Z. Mehta (cnd), Israel PO Deutsche Grammophon ▲ 415486-2 [DDD]
Mozart, W.A.:Sinf concertante Vn, K.364, w. I. Stern (vn), D. Barenboim (cnd), English CO *(rec 1971)* CBS 4-▲ M4K 42003 (m/s) [ADD]
Mozart, W.A.:Sinf concertante Vn, K.364, w. I. Stern (vn), Z. Mehta (cnd), New York PO CBS ▲ MK 36692 [DDD]
Schumann, R.:Märchenbilder, w. Marc Neikrug (pno) RCA Red Seal 2-▲ 09026-68052-2
Telemann, G.P.:Con in a for Rcr, Vl, w. M. Petri (rcr), P. Zukerman (cnd), St. Paul CO Philips ("Digital Classics" series) ▲ 420243-2 [DDD]

Zukerman, Pinchas (vn)
Bach, Joh. Christian:Sinf concertante, T.284/4, w. Yo-Yo Ma (vc), P. Zukerman (cnd), St. Paul CO CBS ▲ MK 39964
Bach, J.S.:Brandenburg Con 5, w. E. Zukerman (fl), A. Newman (hpd), Howard (vc) BOMR 3-▲ 617505 [DDD] 2-■ 517504 (D)
Bach, J.S.:Con Fl, Vn & Hpd, w. E. Zukerman (fl), A. Newman (hpd), Howard (vc) BOMR 3-▲ 617505 [DDD] 2-■ 517504 (D)
Bach, J.S.:Cons Vn (comp), w. P. Zukerman (cnd), English CO CBS ■ MGT 39798
Bach, J.S.:Cons Vn (comp), w. P. Zukerman (cnd), English CO RCA Red Seal ▲ 60718-2-RC [DDD] ■ 60718-4-RC (CrO2) □ 09026-60718-5
Bach, J.S.:Cons Vn (comp), w. P. Zukerman (cnd), English CO *(rec 1971)* Sony Classical ("Essential Classics" series) ▲ SBK 48273 [ADD] ■ SBT 48273
Bach, J.S.:Con 2 Vn, w. P. Zukerman (cnd), St. Paul CO Philips ▲ 416389-2 [DDD]
Bach, J.S.:Con Vn, BWV 1058, w. P. Zukerman (cnd), English CO RCA Red Seal ▲ 60718-2-RC [DDD] ■ 60718-4-RC (CrO2) □ 09026-60718-5
Bach, J.S.:Con Vn, BWV 1058, w. D. Barenboim (cnd), English CO EMI Classics ▲ CDC 47856-2
Bach, J.S.:Con Vn & Ob, w. R. Killmer (ob), St. Paul CO CBS ▲ MK 37278 [DDD]
Bach, J.S.:Con for 2 Vns, w. Midori (vn), P. Zukerman (cnd), St. Paul CO Philips ▲ 416389-2 [DDD]
Bach, J.S.:Con for 2 Vns, w. I. Perlman (vn), D. Barenboim (cnd), English CO EMI Classics ▲ CDC 47856-2
Bach, J.S.:Con for 2 Vns, w. I. Stern (vn), St. Paul CO CBS ▲ MK 37278 [DDD]
Bach, J.S.:Con for 2 Vns, w. I. Stern (vn), P. Zukerman (cnd), St. Paul CO CBS ▲ MK 42258
Bach, J.S.:Con for 2 Vns, w. J.-L. Garcia (vn), P. Zukerman (cnd), English CO RCA Red Seal ▲ 60718-2-RC [DDD] ■ 60718-4-RC (CrO2) □ 09026-60718-5
Bach, J.S.:A Musical Offering, w. E. Zukerman (fl), A. Newman (pno), Howard (vc) BOMR 3-▲ 617505 [DDD] 2-■ 517504 (D)
Bach, J.S.:Sons Vn, w. A. Newman (hpd)—BWV 1023 BOMR 2-▲ 617505 [DDD] 2-■ 517504 (D)
Bartók, B.:Con 2 Vn, w. L. Slatkin (cnd), St. Louis SO RCA Red Seal ▲ 60749-2-RC [DDD] ■ 60749-4-RC
Beethoven, L. van:Con Vn, Op. 61, w. D. Barenboim (cnd), Chicago SO Deutsche Grammophon ▲ 435099-2 [ADD]
Beethoven, L. van:Con Vn, Op. 61, w. Z. Mehta (cnd), Los Angeles PO RCA Red Seal ▲ 09026-61219-2 ■ 09026-61219-4 □ 09026-61219-5
Beethoven, L. van:Romances Vn, w. P. Zukerman (cnd), St. Paul CO Philips ▲ 420168-2 [DDD]
Beethoven, L. van:Sons Vn (comp), w. M. Neikrug (pno) RCA Red Seal 4-▲ 09026-60991-2
Beethoven, L. van:Son 2 Vn, w. D. Barenboim (pno) *(rec Sept. 9, 1971)* Ermitage ▲ ERM 125 [ADD]
Beethoven, L. van:Son 3 Vn, w. D. Barenboim (pno) *(rec Sept. 9, 1971)* Ermitage ▲ ERM 125 [ADD]
Beethoven, L. van:Son 5 Vn, "Spring", w. D. Barenboim (pno) EMI Classics ▲ CDM 64631
Beethoven, L. van:Son 5 Vn, "Spring", w. M. Neikrug (pno) RCA Red Seal ▲ 09026-61561-2
Beethoven, L. van:Son 8 Vn, w. D. Barenboim (pno) *(rec Sept. 9, 1971)* Ermitage ▲ ERM 125 [ADD]
Beethoven, L. van:Son 8 Vn, w. D. Barenboim (pno) EMI Classics ▲ CDM 64631
Beethoven, L. van:Son 9 Vn, "Kreutzer", w. D. Barenboim (pno) EMI Classics ▲ CDM 64631
Beethoven, L. van:Son 9 Vn, "Kreutzer", w. M. Neikrug (pno) RCA Red Seal ▲ 09026-61561-2
Beethoven, L. van:Son 10 Vn, w. M. Neikrug (pno) RCA Red Seal ▲ 09026-61219-2 ■ 09026-61219-4 □ 09026-61219-5
Beethoven, L. van:Trios Pno (comp), w. D. Barenboim (pno), J. Du Pré (vc) EMI Classics ("Studio" series) 3-▲ ZDMC 63124 [ADD]
Beethoven, L. van:Trio 3 Pno, w. D. Barenboim (pno), J. Du Pré (vc) *(rec live, Brighton Festival 1970)* Arkadia 2-▲ 589 [ADD]
Beethoven, L. van:Trio 5 Pno, w. D. Barenboim (pno), J. Du Pré (vc) *(rec live, Brighton Festival 1970)* Arkadia 2-▲ 589 [ADD]
Beethoven, L. van:Trio 5 Pno, w. D. Barenboim (pno), J. Du Pré (vc) EMI Classics 2-▲ ZDMB 69707
Beethoven, L. van:Trio 6 Pno, "Archduke", w. D. Barenboim (pno), J. Du Pré (vc) *(rec live, Brighton Festival 1970)* Arkadia 2-▲ 589 [ADD]
The Bells of St. Genevieve & Other Baroque Favorites, w. J. Levine (cnd), English CO, James Galway (fl), Vladimir Spivakov (vn), Canadian Brass, et al. RCA Victor ▲ 09026-61002-2 [DDD] ■ 09026-61002-4 (CrO2) □ 09026-61002-5
Berg, A.:Chamber Con, w. Daniel Barenboim (pno), P. Boulez (cnd), Ensemble InterContemporain Deutsche Grammophon ("The Originals" series) ▲ 447405-2
Berg, A.:Con Vn, w. P. Boulez (cnd), London SO Sony Classical ("Pierre Boulez Edition" series) ▲ SMK 68331
Bolling, C.:Suite Vn, w. Claude Bolling Trio Milan ▲ 73138-35647-2 ■ 73138-35467-2
Brahms, J.:Con Vn, w. Z. Mehta (cnd), Los Angeles PO *(rec Dorothy Chandler Pavilion, Los Angeles, Apr 1-2, 1994)* RCA Red Seal ▲ 09026-68046-2 [DDD]
Brahms, J.:Con Vn & Vc, "Double Con", w. L. Harrell (vc), Z. Mehta (cnd), New York PO Odyssey 3-▲ MB3K 45828
Brahms, J.:Scherzo Vn, w. D. Barenboim (pno) Deutsche Grammophon ▲ 437248-2 [ADD]
Brahms, J.:Scherzo Vn, w. Marc Neikrug (pno) *(rec Manhattan Center Studios, New York, Mar 8, 1993)* RCA Red Seal ▲ 09026-61697-2 [DDD]
Brahms, J.:Sons Vn (comp), w. Marc Neikrug (pno) *(rec Manhattan Center Studios, New York, Apr 30 & Aug 14-15, 1992)* RCA Red Seal ▲ 09026-61697-2 [DDD]
Bruch, M.:Con 1 Vn, w. Z. Mehta (cnd), Los Angeles PO Odyssey ▲ MBK 44717 ■ YT 44717
Bruch, M.:Con 1 Vn, w. Z. Mehta (cnd), Los Angeles PO *(rec 1977)* Sony Classical ("Essential Classics" series) ▲ SBK 48274 [ADD] ■ SBT 48274
Bruch, M.:Con 1 Vn, w. Z. Mehta (cnd), London PO *(rec Henry Wood Hall, London, Sept 24-25, 1992)* RCA Red Seal ▲ 09026-68046-2 [DDD]
Debussy, C.:Son Vn, w. Marc Neikrug (pno) RCA Red Seal ▲ 09026-62697-2
Elgar, E.:Con Vn, w. L. Slatkin (cnd), St. Louis SO RCA Red Seal ▲ 09026-61672-2 ■ 09026-61672-4
Fauré, G.:Son 1 Vn, w. Marc Neikrug (pno) RCA Red Seal ▲ 09026-62697-2
Franck, C.:Son Vn, w. Marc Neikrug (pno) RCA Red Seal ▲ 09026-62697-2
Haydn, J.:Con 1 Vn, w. P. Zukerman (cnd), National Arts Center Canada Orch RCA Red Seal ▲ 09026-60797-2
Haydn, J.:Con 4 Vn, w. P. Zukerman (cnd), National Arts Center Canada Orch RCA Red Seal ▲ 09026-60797-2
Haydn, J.:Sinf concertante, w. Ralph Kirshbaum (vc), P. Zukerman (cnd), English SO RCA Red Seal ▲ 09026-62696-2
Lalo, E.:Sym espagnole, w. Z. Mehta (cnd), Los Angeles PO Odyssey ▲ MBK 44717 ■ YT 44717
Lalo, E.:Sym espagnole, w. Z. Mehta (cnd), Los Angeles PO *(rec 1977)* Sony Classical ("Essential Classics" series) ▲ SBK 48274 [ADD] ■ SBT 48274
Leclair, J.-M.:Sons for 2 Vns, Op. 3, w. I. Perlman (vn)—No. 4 in F RCA Red Seal ▲ 60735-2-RC [DDD] ■ 60735-4-RC (CrO2)
Mendelssohn, F.:Athalie (sels), w. L. Bernstein (cnd), New York PO—War March of the Priests *(rec Oct. 26, 1967)* Sony Classical ▲ SMK 47592 [ADD]

Zukerman, Pinchas (vn) (cont.)
Mendelssohn, F.:Con in e Vn & Orch, Op. 64, w. L. Bernstein (cnd), New York PO *(rec Feb. 6, 1969)* Sony Classical ▲ SMK 47592 [ADD]
Mendelssohn, F.:Con in e Vn & Orch, Op. 64, w. P. Zukerman (cnd), St. Paul CO Philips ▲ 412212-2 [DDD]
Mozart, W.A.:Adagio Vn, K.261, w. P. Zukerman (cnd), St. Paul CO CBS ▲ MDK 44654 [DDD] ■ MDT 44654 (D)
Mozart, W.A.:Cons Vn, w. P. Zukerman (cnd), St. Paul CO—Nos. 1-3 CBS ▲ MDK 44653 [DDD] ■ MDT 44653 (D)
Mozart, W.A.:Cons Vn, w. P. Zukerman (cnd), St. Paul CO—Nos. 4 & 5 CBS ▲ MDK 44654 [DDD] ■ MDT 44654 (D)
Mozart, W.A.:Cons Vn, w. P. Zukerman (cnd), St. Paul CO—Nos. 1-3 Sony Classical ("Essential Classics" series) ▲ SBK 46539 [ADD] ■ SBT 46539
Mozart, W.A.:Cons Vn, w. P. Zukerman (cnd), St. Paul CO—Nos. 4 & 5 Sony Classical ("Essential Classics" series) ▲ SBK 46540 [ADD] ■ SBT 46540
Mozart, W.A.:Concertone Vns, w. I. Perlman (vn), Z. Mehta (cnd), Israel PO Deutsche Grammophon ▲ 415486-2 [DDD]
Mozart, W.A.:Concertone Vns, w. Isaac Stern (vn), G. Szell (cnd), English CO Sony Classical 3-▲ SM3K 66475
Mozart, W.A.:Qnt Strs, K.515, w. Tokyo String Quartet RCA Red Seal ▲ 09026-60940-2
Mozart, W.A.:Rondo Vn, K.269, w. P. Zukerman (cnd), St. Paul CO CBS ▲ MDK 44647 [DDD]
Mozart, W.A.:Rondo Vn, K.373, w. P. Zukerman (cnd), St. Paul CO CBS ▲ MDK 44654 [DDD] ■ MDT 44654 (D)
Mozart, W.A.:Sons Vn Pno (comp), w. M. Neikrug (pno)—K.9, 26, 31, 196 & 547 RCA Red Seal ▲ 09026-60744-2
Mozart, W.A.:Sons Vn Pno (misc), w. M. Neikrug (pno)—K.28, 30, 304 & 526 RCA Red Seal ▲ 09026-60742-2
Mozart, W.A.:Sons Vn Pno (misc), w. M. Neikrug (pno)—K.301, 306 & 378 RCA Red Seal ▲ 09026-60743-2 [DDD]
Mozart, W.A.:Sons Vn Pno (misc), w. M. Neikrug (pno)—K.8, 377, 379 RCA Red Seal ▲ 60447-2 [DDD] ■ 60447-4 (CrO2)
Mozart, W.A.:Sons Vn Pno (misc), w. M. Neikrug (pno)—K.27, 303 & 454 RCA Red Seal ▲ 60740-2 [DDD]
Mozart, W.A.:Vars Vn Pno, K.359, w. M. Neikrug (pno) RCA Red Seal ▲ 60740-2 [DDD]
Mozart, W.A.:Vars Vn Pno, K.360, w. M. Neikrug (pno) RCA Red Seal ▲ 60447-2 [DDD] ■ 60447-4 (CrO2)
Schubert, Franz:Sonatinas Vn, w. D. Barenboim (pno)—Nos. 2 & 3 *(rec Sept. 9, 1971)* Ermitage ▲ ERM 125 [ADD]
Schumann, R.:Fantasiestücke Cl, w. Marc Neikrug (pno) RCA Red Seal 2-▲ 09026-68052-2
Schumann, R.:Romances Ob, w. Marc Neikrug (pno) RCA Red Seal 2-▲ 09026-68052-2
Schumann, R.:Son 1 Vn, w. Marc Neikrug (pno) RCA Red Seal 2-▲ 09026-68052-2
Schumann, R.:Son 2 Vn, w. Marc Neikrug (pno) RCA Red Seal 2-▲ 09026-68052-2
Tchaikovsky, P.:Con Vn, w. A. Dorati (cnd), London SO *(rec 1968)* Odyssey ▲ MBK 46268 [ADD] ■ YT 46268
Tchaikovsky, P.:Con Vn, w. Z. Mehta (cnd), Israel PO CBS ▲ MDK 44643 [DDD] ■ MDT 44643 (D)
Tchaikovsky, P.:Con Vn, w. Z. Mehta (cnd), Israel PO CBS ▲ MK 39563 [DDD]
Telemann, G.P.:Duet Rcr & Vn, w. M. Petri (rcr), P. Zukerman (cnd), St. Paul CO Philips ("Digital Classics" series) ▲ 420243-2 [DDD]
Vieuxtemps, H.:Con 5 Vn, w. C. Mackerras (cnd), London SO *(rec 1969)* Sony Classical ("Essential Classics" series) ▲ SBK 48274 [ADD] ■ SBT 48274
Vivaldi, A.:Cons Vn (misc), w. P. Zukerman (cnd), Los Angeles PO—Concerto in a, RV.356 *(rec 1976)* Sony Classical ("Essential Classics" series) ▲ SBK 48273 [ADD] ■ SBT 48273
Vivaldi, A.:Cons Vn (misc), w. P. Zukerman (cnd), St. Paul CO—RV.199 Philips ▲ 416389-2 [DDD]
Vivaldi, A.:Cons Vn (misc), w. P. Zukerman (cnd), English CO RCA Red Seal ▲ 09026-68433-2
Vivaldi, A.:Cons Vn, Op. 8/1-12, "Il cimento dell'armonia e dell'inventione", w. P. Zukerman (cnd), English CO—Nos. 5-12 Sony Classical ("Essential Classics" series) ▲ SBK 53513 ■ SBT 53513
Vivaldi, A.:Cons Vn, Op. 8/1-4, "The Four Seasons", w. P. Zukerman (cnd), St. Paul CO CBS ▲ MDK 44644 [DDD] ■ MDT 44644 (D)
Vivaldi, A.:Cons Vn, Op. 8/1-4, "The Four Seasons", w. P. Zukerman (cnd), St. Paul CO CBS ▲ MK 36710 [DDD] ■ IMT 36710 (D)
Vivaldi, A.:Cons Vn, Op. 8/1-4, "The Four Seasons", w. P. Zukerman (cnd), English CO CBS ▲ MYK 38478 [ADD] ■ MYT 38478
Vivaldi, A.:Cons for 2 Vns, w. I. Stern (vn), P. Zukerman (cnd), St. Paul CO—1—in A CBS ▲ MK 37278 [DDD]
Vivaldi, A.:Cons for 2 Vns, w. K. Sillito (vn), P. Zukerman (cnd), English CO—(2) in a, RV.522; in d, RV.565 *(rec 1971)* Sony Classical ("Essential Classics" series) ▲ SBK 48273 [ADD] ■ SBT 48273
Vivaldi, A.:Con for 3 Vns, w. I. Perlman (vn), I. Stern (vn), Z. Mehta (cnd), New York PO CBS ▲ MK 36692 [DDD]
Vivaldi, A.:Music of, w. Salvatore Accardo (vn), Frederico Agostini (vn), Heinz Holliger (ob), Ida Levin (vn), Aurele Nicolet (fl), Massimo Paris (va d'amore), Angel Romero (gtr), Celedonio Romero (gtr), Celine Romero (gtr), Henryk Szeryng (vn), Academy of St. Martin in the Fields, English CO, I Musici, Naples Weekly International Soloists, St. Paul CO, Dresden Staatskapelle—The Four Seasons [Winter]; Con in D for Gtr [Largo]; Con in D for Fl, "Il gardellino" [Cantabile]; Con in C for Diverse Insts [Andante molto]; Con in g for Strs [Andante molto]; Con in D for 2 Vns & 2 Vcs [Largo]; Con in g for Ob, Vn, Ww & Strs [Larghetto]; Con in a for Gtr, "L'estro armonico" [Largo]; Con in F for 3 Vns [Andante]; Con in F for Fl [Largo]; Con in d for Va D'Amore [Largo]; Con in E for Vn & Strs, "Il riposo" [Allegro]; Con in G for Ob, Bn & Strs [Largo]; Con in B♭ for Vn & Strs [Largo]; Con in A for Gtr & Strs [Larghetto]; Con in E for Vn & Strs, "L'amoroso" [Allegro]; Con in G for Fl [Largo]; Con in A for Vn [Larghetto]; Con in c for Vn & Strs, "Il sospetto" [Andante]; Con in a for 2 Obs & Strs [Largo]; Con in g for Orch [Largo non molto]; Con in a for Vn [Largo]; Con in C for Ob [Adagio]; Con in g for Fl, "La notte" [Largo] Philips ▲ 454051-2 ■ 454 051-4

Zukerman, Pinchas (vn/va)
Schoenberg, A.:Pierrot lunaire, w. Y. Minton (speaker), L. Harrell (vc), D. Barenboim (pno), M. Debost (fl/pic), A. Pay (cl/b cl), P. Boulez (cnd) *(rec June 20-21, 1977)* Sony Classical ▲ SMK 48466 [ADD]

Zukofsky, Paul (vn)
Brandt, H.:Quombex *(rec Paul Hall, Julliard School of Music, June 3, 1972)* CP² ▲ CP2 108 [AAD]
Cage, J.:Cheap Imitation CP2 Recordings ▲ CP2 103
Cage, J.:Chorals Vn CP2 Recordings ▲ CP2 103
Cage, J.:Freeman Etudes Vn CP2 Recordings ▲ CP2 102
Cage, J.:Nocturne, w. Gilbert Kalish (pno) *(rec Paul Hall, Julliard School of Music, May 21, 1972)* CP² ▲ CP2 108 [AAD]
Feldman, Morton:For John Cage, w. M. Schroeder (pno) CP2 Recordings ▲ 101 [DDD]
Feldman, Morton:Spring of Chosroes, w. U. Oppens (pno) CP2 Recordings ▲ CP2 102 [ADD]
Feldman, Morton:Vertical Thoughts II, w. Gilbert Kalish (pno) *(rec Paul Hall, Julliard School of Music, May 21, 1972)* CP² ▲ CP2 108 [AAD]
Glass, Philip:The Photographer, w. Philip Glass Ensemble CBS ▲ MK 37849 ■ PMT 37849
Glass, Philip:Strung Out *(rec Big Apple Recording Studio, New York City, June 29, 1976)* CP² ▲ CP2 108 [AAD]
Ichiyanagi, T.:Con Vn, w. T. Otaka (cnd), Tokyo PO Camerata ▲ 32CM 295
Martino, D.:Fant-Vars Pno CRI ▲ CD 693 [ADD]
Martino, D.:Trio Cl, w. Arthur Bloom (cl), Gilbert Kalish (pno) CRI ▲ CD 693 [ADD]
Scelsi, G.:Anahit, w. Julie Bogorad (fl), Peggy Russell (fl), Courtney Westcott (fl), Lawrence McDonald (cl), Joan Waryha (cl), Jean Hansen (b cl), Bill Suite (e hn), Nita VanPelt (sax), Bob Zobal (tpt), John Carter (trbn), Martin Lydecker (trbn), Stan Cortman (hn), Robert Ward (hn), William Curry (va), Jody Rowitsch (va), Irene Wade (va), Anne Fagerburg (vc), John Gockel (vc), Sue Manz (bass), Steven Stearman (bass) *(rec Oberlin Conservatory of Music, Oct 8, 1973)* CP² ▲ CP2 108 [AAD]
Schnabel, A.:Son solo Vn *(rec Rutgers Church, New York City, June 13 & 21, 1983)* CP² ▲ CP² 110 [DDD]

930

▲ = CD ♦ = Enhanced CD △ = MD ■ = Cassette Tape □ = DCC

Zukofsky, Paul (vn) (cont.)
  Schnabel, A.:Son Vn Pno, w. Ursula Oppens (pno)   CP2 Recordings ▲ CP2 102
  Schuman, W.:Con Vn, w. M. Tilson Thomas (cnd), Boston SO
                       Deutsche Grammophon ("20th Century Classics" series) ▲ 429860-2 [ADD]
  Sessions, R.:Con Vn, w. G. Schuller (cnd), French Radio-TV PO   CRI ▲ CD 676 [ADD]
  Wolpe, S.:Second Piece Vn *(rec Paul Hall, Julliard School of Music, May 21, 1972)*
                       CP² ▲ CP2 108 [AAD]
  Wuorinen, C.:Con Amplified Vn, w. J. Dixon (cnd), Univ of Iowa SO   Music & Arts ▲ CD 801 [ADD]
  Wuorinen, C.:Duo Vn, w. Charles Wuorinen (pno)   New World ▲ 80517-2
  Xenakis, I.:Mikka *(rec Big Apple Recording Studio, New York City, June 29, 1976)*
                       CP² ▲ CP2 108 [AAD]
  Xenakis, I.:Mikka S *(rec Big Apple Recording Studio, New York City, June 29, 1976)*
                       CP² ▲ CP2 108 [AAD]

Zummo, Peter (trbn)
  Hamilton, T.:Off-Hour Wait State, w. Thomas Buckner (voc), Roscoe Mitchell (a sax), Ralph Samuelson (shak), Tom Hamilton (syn/elec), Jonathan Haas (perc)   O.O. Discs ▲ OO 26 [DDD]

Zummo, Peter (trbn/didjeridu)
  Lockwood, A.:Thousand Year Dreaming, w. Art Baron (conch shell/trbn/didjeridu), Liby Van Cleve (ob/E hn), Jon Gibson (didjeridu), J.D. Parran (cl), Michael Pubilese (perc), Scott Robinson (conch shell/perc), John Snyder (didjeridu/waterphone), Charles Wood (tam-tam, stones)
                       ¿What Next? ▲ WN 0010

Zumsteg, Julie (vc)
  Bloch, E.:From Jewish Life, w. D. Schrader (pno)—Prayer *(rec June 2 & 3, 1992)*
                       Centaur ▲ CRC 2140 [DDD]

Zumsteg, Werner (fl)
  Haller, H.:Inventions (6), w. G. Stehli-Altwegg (cembalo)   Grammont ▲ CTSP 10-2 [ADD]
  Honegger, A.:Danse de la chèvre   Nimbus ▲ NI 5327 [ADD]
  Maggini, E.:Canto V *(rec RTSI, Rete 2, Dec 1993)*   Jecklin ▲ JS 311-2 [DDD]
  Maggini, E.:Canto XVII, w. Patricia Thomas (pno) *(rec RTSI, Rete 2, Dec 1993)*
                       Jecklin ▲ JS 311-2 [DDD]
  Maggini, E.:Disegni, w. Walther Giger (gtr) *(rec RTSI, Rete 2, Dec 1993)*   Jecklin ▲ JS 311-2 [DDD]
  Maggini, E.:Ikaros *(rec RTSI, Rete 2, Dec 1993)*   Jecklin ▲ JS 311-2 [DDD]
  Maggini, E.:Der Schwarze Vogel *(rec RTSI, Rete 2, Dec 1993)*   Jecklin ▲ JS 311-2 [DDD]
  Maggini, E.:Trilogie der bemalte Vogel *(rec RTSI, Rete 2, Dec 1993)*   Jecklin ▲ JS 311-2 [DDD]
  Maggini, E.:Zwischen Himmel und Erde, w. Jeannette Fischer (sop)—Als ob die Nacht; Im Wärmezirkel; Komm ich weiss; Greift ein Engel; So wie du daliegst; Er sagte; Als ob ein Jubel; Wenn die Tische; Gib mir die Hand *(rec RTSI, Rete 2, Dec 1993)*   Jecklin ▲ JS 311-2 [DDD]

Zupnik, Marilyn (ob)
  Handel, G.F.:Sons Ob, w. Mark Shuman (vc), Raymond Leppard (hpd)—in a, B♭, e, g & g
                       ASV ▲ ASV 663 [DDD]
  Telemann, G.P.:Sons Ob, w. M. Shuman (vc), R. Leppard (hpd)—4 Sonatas—Nos. 1 in c, 3 in F & 6 in g; & Sonata in B♭   ASV ▲ ASV 663 [DDD]

Zurawlew, Jerzy (pno)
  Chopin, F.:Fant *(rec Warsaw, 1959-60)*   Polskie Nagrania ▲ PNCD 314

Zürcher, Martin (rcr)
  Telemann, G.P.:Der Getreue Music-Meister (sels), w. H. Barbé (hpd)—2 Sonatas *(rec 1970)*
                       Jecklin-Disco ▲ JEC CD 4403 [ADD]
  Telemann, G.P.:Kleine Kammermusik, w. H. Barbé (hpd) *(rec 1970)*
                       Jecklin-Disco ▲ JEC CD 4403 [ADD]

Zusman, Natalia (pno)
  Bach, J.S.:Con 1 for 2 Hpds, w. I. Heifetz (pno), E. Blank (cnd), Russian CO
                       Sonora ▲ SO 22564CD [DDD]
  Borodin, A.:Tarantella, w. Inna Heifetz (pno) *(rec Tsai Performance Center, Boston)*
                       Sonora ▲ SO 22566 [DDD]
  Glière, R.:Pieces for 2 Pnos, Op. 41, w. Inna Heifetz (pno) *(rec Tsai Performance Center, Boston)*
                       Sonora ▲ SO 22566 [DDD]
  Schnittke, A.:The Revisionist's Tale, w. Inna Heifetz (pno) *(rec Tsai Performance Center, Boston)*
                       Sonora ▲ SO 22566 [DDD]
  Shostakovich, D.:Concertino for 2 Pnos, w. Inna Heifetz (pno) *(rec Tsai Performance Center, Boston)*
                       Sonora ▲ SO 22566 [DDD]

Zuyeva, Elizaveta (ob)
  Aschaffenburg, W.:Con Ob, w. E. London (cnd), Russian State SO   New World ▲ 805112 [DDD]

Zverov, Valentin (fl)
  Rubinstein, A.:Qnt Pno, w. A. Nasedkin (pno), V. Sokolov (cl), A. Demim (hn), S. Krasavin (bn)
                       Russian Disc ("The A. Rubinstein Edition" series) ▲ RUS 11 061 [ADD]

Zwahlen, H. (cl)
  Wyttenbach, J.:Lamentoroso, w. L. Akerlund (sop), H. Bissegger (cl), N. Calame (cl), M. Maurer (cl), E. Molinari (cl), M. Weber (cl) *(rec May 19-20, 1990)*   Grammont ▲ CTSP 37-2 [ADD]

Zwart, Titia (vl)
  Philidor, P.:Music of, w. W. Hazelet (trns fl), K. Clark (trns fl), M. Fentross (lt/thb), J. Ogg (hpd)—Trios 1 & 2 in G & e for 2 Flutes & Continuo; Suite No. 3 in D for 2 Flutes; Suites Nos. 5, 6 & 12 in e, b & D for Flute & Continuo *(rec June 1993)*   Globe ▲ GLO 5107 [DDD]

Zweden, J. van (vn)
  Vivaldi, A.:Cons Vn, Op. 8/1-4, "The Four Seasons", w. J. W. de Vriend (cnd), Combattimento Consort Amsterdam   Fidelio ▲ FID 8841 [DDD]

Zweig, Mimi (vn)
  Shostakovich, D.:Qnt Pno, w. J. Horner (va), Borodin Trio   Chandos ▲ CHAN 8342 [DDD]

Zweistra, Ageet (vc)
  Vivaldi, A.:Sons Vc, w. E. Ferre (baroque gtr)—(3) in E♭, RV.39; in g, RV.42; in a, RV.44
                       L'Oiseau-Lyre ▲ 433052-2 [DDD]

Zwiauer, Florian (vn)—see ORCHESTRAS & ENSEMBLES Franz Schubert String Quartet
Zwicker, J. (baroque vc)—see ORCHESTRAS & ENSEMBLES Il Parnaso Musicale
Zwicky, Conrad (org)
  Mozart, W.A.:Sons Fl Hpd (comp), w. Regula Schwarzenbach (fl) [arr for fl & org] *(rec Jan-Mar 1996)*
                       Jecklin ▲ JD 7082 [DDD]

Zwilich, J. (vn)
  Zwilich, E.T.:Son in 3 Movts, w. J. Gemmell (pno)   CRI ▲ CD 621 [ADD]

Zylberajch, Aline (hpd)—see also ORCHESTRAS & ENSEMBLES Les Nièces de Rameau
  Bach, C.P.E.:Sons Hpd, H.24-29, "Prussian" *(rec Dec 1992)*   Ligia Digital ▲ 0101005 [DDD]

Zylberajch, Aline (hpd/org)
  Scarlatti, A.:Cants & Duets, w. Véronique Dietschy (sop), Alain Zaepffel (ct), Marianne Muller (vl), Macha Yanuchevskaia (vc), Yasurnori Imamura (thb)—Il Sonno; Clori e Mirtillo; Marcantonio e Cleopatra; Doralbo e Niso   Adès ▲ ADE 202172 [DDD]

CHORAL GROUPS

A Capella Portugesa
O. Rees (cnd)
Holy Week at the Chapel of the Dukes of Braganza — Hyperion ▲ CDA 66867
Masters of the Royal Chapel, Lisbon, w. Stephen Farr (org) — Hyperion ▲ CDA 66725
Music from Renaissance Coimbra — Hyperion ▲ CDA 66735
A Sei Voci
Gabrieli, G.:Sacrae symphoniae, w. Yasuko Uyama–Bouvard (org), Toulouse Saquebouties — Adda ▲ ADD 242292
Helfer, C. d':Missa pro defunctis, w. B. Fabre–Garrus (cnd), Toulouse Saquebouties, Psallette de Lorraine — Astrée ▲ E 8521
Josquin Desprez:Sacred Music—Missa de beata virgine; Memor esto verbi tui; Christum ducem; Deploration sur la mort d'Ockeghem; Planxit autem David — Forlane ▲ FRL 16552 [DDD]
Salve Regina:Musiques festives mariales du grégorien au 17ème siècle, w. Jean Boyer (org) — Accord ▲ ACD 205072 [DDD]
B. Fabre–Garrus (cnd)
Allegri, G.:Motets — Astrée ▲ E 8524
Allegri, G.:Motets—De ore prudentis; Repleti sunt omnes — Astrée ▲ E 8552 [DDD]
Allegri, G.:Il Salmo Miserere mei Deus — Astrée ▲ E 8524
Allegri, G.:Vidi tubam magnam — Astrée ▲ E 8524
Bencini, P.P.:Vesperae Beatae Virginis in Sancto Petro Romae — Astrée ▲ E 8540
Escaich, T.:Ad Ultimas Laudes — Chamade ▲ CHCD 5638 [DDD]
Janequin, C.:Chansons—Il estoit une fillette; Ung gay bergier; Plus ne suys; Le chant des oyseaux; Pavane et gaillard; Ce tendron si doulce; Martin menoit son pourceau; Suyvez tousjours l'amoureuse entreprise; Puisque mon coeur; Ung jour que madame; Toutes les nuictz; Fy, fy, mettez les hors; Tétin refaict plus blanc; Si ung petet de vostre bien; L'amour, la mort, la vie; Une nonnain for belle; J'ai double deuil' Tourdion "C'est grand plaisir"; La guerre — Astrée ("Auvidis" series) ▲ E 8571
Jommelli, N.:Sacred Music—Miserere; Vesperae in Sancto Petro Romae — Astrée 2–▲ E 8590
Josquin Desprez:Missa de Beata Virgine — Astrée ▲ E 8560
Josquin Desprez:Motets—O Virgo Prudentissima; Stabat mater Dolorosa; Ave Maria; Inviolata, Integra est Casta es Maria; Tu solis — Astrée ▲ E 8560
Aachen Boys' Choir
Mendelssohn, F.:Die Hochzeit des Camacho, w. R. Hofman (sop—Quiteria), A. Ulbrich (mez—Lucinda), S. Weir (ten—Basilio), H. Rhys–Evans (ten—Vivaldo), N. van der Meel (ten—Camacho), W. Wild (bar—Carrasco), U. Malmberg (bass—Sancho Panza), U. Cold (bass—Don Quixote), J. van Immerseel (cnd), Anima Eterna Orch, Chor Modus Novus [G] *(rec Sept. 19–22, 1992)* — Channel Classics 2–▲ CCS 5593 [DDD]
F. ter Wey (cnd)
Hindemith, P.:Madrigals *(rec Aachen, Nov 27, 1993)* — CPO ▲ CPO 999345–2 [DDD]
Hindemith, P.:Mass *(rec Aachen, Nov 27, 1993)* — CPO ▲ CPO 999345–2 [DDD]
Aachen Carmina Mundi
H. Nickoll (cnd)
Distler, H.:Mörike–Chorliederbuch — ebs ▲ ebs 6077 [DDD]
Distler, H.:Mörike–Chorliederbuch—Vol. 1, nearly complete; 19 secular songs for mixed chorus [G] — ebs ▲ ebs 6074 [DDD]
Aarau New Canton School Choir
Bertoni, F.:Orfeo ed Euridice, w. Jeannette Fischer (sop—Euridice), Julia Juon (mez—Orfeo), Steve Davislim (ten—Imeneo), R. Tschupp (cnd), Aargauer SO *(rec Zurich Radio Studio, Oct 30–Nov 1, 1994)* — Jecklin ▲ JEC 700
Aargauer Chamber Choir
Wehrli, W.:Ein weltliches Requiem, w. R. Amsler (sop), D. Labusch (cta), B. Hunziker (ten), R. Strebel (bass), K. Girod (cnd), Aargauer CO *(rec live Jan. 12, 1992)* — Jecklin ▲ JS 276–2 [DDD]
Aarhus Music Students Chamber Choir
Mathiassen:Choral Music—4 Sange; 2 Sange; Lille Almanak; I Danmarks Forundringsskød — Point ▲ PCD 5112
Aarhus Sym Chorus
Gade, N.W.:Korsfarerne, w. Rorholm (mez), Westi (ten), Cold (bass), F. Rasmussen (cnd), Aarhus SO [Da] — BIS ▲ CD 465 [DDD]
Aarhus Univ Chamber Choir
Monteverdi, C.:Madrigals—[from Book 5] Ecco Silvio; Ma se con la pietá; Dorinda, ah diró; Ecco piegando; Ferir quel petto, Silvio; [from Book 6] Incenente spoglie; Ditelo, o fiumi; Dara la notte; Ma te racoglie, o Ninfa; O chiome d'or; Dunque, amte reliquie — Point ▲ PCD 5112
Abbé Damien Poisblaud Choir
Gregorian Chant, w. Thoronet Abbey Choir — Pavane ▲ ADW 7239 [DDD]
Abendmusik Chorus
Parker, H.:Hora novissima, w. A. Soranno (sop), J. Simson (mez), K. Hall (b–bar), D. Andersen (b–bar), J. Levick (cnd), Nebraska CO, Nebraska Wesleyan Univ Choir — Albany 2–▲ TROY 124/25
Academic Choral Society
Kokkonen, J.:Erekhtheion, w. S. Vihavainen (sop), W. Grönroos (bar), O. Vänskä (cnd), Lahti SO [Fin] — BIS ▲ CD 498 [DDD]
Kokkonen, J.:Requiem (in memoriam Maija Kokkonen), w. Satu Vihavainen (sop), Jorma Hynninen (bar), U. Söderblom (cnd), Helsinki PO — Finlandia ▲ FIN 53353 [DDD]
Academy Chorus
Handel, G.F.:Coronation Anthems (4) for George II, w. N. Marriner (cnd), Academy of St. Martin in the Fields [E] — Philips ▲ 412733–2 [DDD]
Mozart, W.A.:Arias, w. B. Hendricks (sop), J. Sillman (org)., N. Marriner (cnd), Academy of St. Martin in the Fields — EMI Classics ▲ CDC 49283
Mozart, W.A.:Ave verum corpus, w. K. Te Kanawa (sop), A. Sofie von Otter (mez), A. R. Johnson (ten), R. Lloyd (bass)., N. Marriner (cnd), Academy of St. Martin in the Fields *(rec London, Mar. 10–12, 1993)* — Philips ▲ 438999–2
Mozart, W.A.:Missa, K.427, w. L. Marshall (sop), F. Palmer (sop), A. Rolfe Johnson (ten), G. Howell (bass), N. Marriner (cnd), Academy of St. Martin in the Fields [L] — Philips ▲ 420891–2 [ADD]
Mozart, W.A.:Requiem, w. S. McNair (sop), C. Watkinson (cta), F. Araiza (ten), R. Lloyd (b–bar), N. Marriner (cnd), Academy of St. Martin in the Fields [L] — Philips ▲ 432087–2 [DDD]
Vivaldi, A.:Gloria, RV.589, w. B. Hendricks (sop), A. Murray (mez), J. Rigby (mez), U. Heilmann (ten), J. Hynninen (bar), N. Marriner (cnd), Academy of St. Martin in the Fields — EMI Classics ▲ CDC 54283
Walton, W.:Henry V (shakespeare senario), w. Christopher Plummer (nar), N. Marriner (cnd), Academy of St. Martin in the Fields [E] — Chandos ▲ CHAN 8892 [DDD]
Academy of Ancient Music Chorus
Haydn, J.:L'Anima del filosofo, or Orfeo ed Euridice, w. Cecilia Bartoli (mez), Uwe Heilmann (ten), Ildebrando d'Arcangelo (bass), C. Hogwood (cnd), Academy of Ancient Music — L'oiseau Lyre ▲ 452 668–2
Mozart, W.A.:Clemenza, w. Barbara Bonney (sop—Servilia), Cecilia Bartoli (mez—Sesto), Della Jones (mez—Vitellia), Diana Montague (mez—Annio), Uwe Heilman (ten—Tito), Giles Cachemaille (bar—Publio), C. Hogwood (cnd), Academy of Ancient Music — London ("Editions de l'oiseau–lyre" series) 2–▲ 444131–2 [DDD]
Academy of Ancient Music Vocal Ensemble
Telemann, G.P.:Don Quichotte der Löwenritter, w. M. Schneider (cnd), Bremen La Stagione — CPO ▲ CPO 999210
Academy of Catholic Theology Choir
Górecki, H.–M.:Euntes ibant et flebant — Polskie Nagrania Edition ▲ ECD 036
Górecki, H.–M.:Pryzbadz Duchu Swiety — Polskie Nagrania Edition ▲ ECD 036
Górecki, H.–M.:Swiety, Swiety, Swiety — Polskie Nagrania Edition ▲ ECD 036
Górecki, H.–M.:Zdrowas badz Mayja — Polskie Nagrania Edition ▲ ECD 036
Luciuk, J.:O, ziemio polska — Polskie Nagrania Edition ▲ ECD 036
Academy of Catholic Theology Choir (cont.)
Luciuk, J.:Oremus — Polskie Nagrania Edition ▲ ECD 036
Lukaszewski, P.:Angelus Domini — Polskie Nagrania Edition ▲ ECD 036
Lukaszewski, P.:Ave Maria — Polskie Nagrania Edition ▲ ECD 036
Paciorkiewicz, T.:Ave Regina caelorum — Polskie Nagrania Edition ▲ ECD 036
Paciorkiewicz, T.:Ziemia trudnej jednosci — Polskie Nagrania Edition ▲ ECD 036
Sawa, M.:Gloria Tibi Trinitas — Polskie Nagrania Edition ▲ ECD 036
Twardowski, R.:Hosanna — Polskie Nagrania Edition ▲ ECD 036
Academy of Music Chorus
Giordano, U.:Andrea Chénier, w. Montserrat Caballé (sop), Franco Corelli (ten), R. de Carlo (sgr), D. Dondi (sgr), G. Ellsworth (sgr), J. Fair (sgr), R. Falk (sgr), S. Felter (sgr), E. Green (sgr), H. Hicks (sgr), H. Krauss (sgr), L. Miller (sgr), N. Riggins (sgr), H. Salerno (sgr), A. Guadagno (cnd), Academy of Music Orch — Great Opera Performances 2–▲ GOP 766
Academy of St. Martin in the Fields Chorus
Charpentier, M.–A.:Magnificat, w. D. Upshaw (sop), A. Murray (mez), E. Robinson (mez), J. Aler (ten), K. Moll (bass), N. Marriner (cnd), Academy of St. Martin in the Fields — EMI Classics ▲ CDC 54284
Charpentier, M.–A.:Te Deum in C, w. D. Upshaw (sop), A. Murray (mez), E. Robinson (mez), J. Aler (ten), K. Moll (bass), N. Marriner (cnd), Academy of St. Martin in the Fields — EMI Classics ▲ CDC 54284
Handel, G.F.:Messiah, w. Elly Ameling (sop), Anna Reynolds (alt), Philip Langridge (ten), Gwynne Howell (bass), N. Marriner (cnd), Academy of St. Martin in the Fields *(rec St John's, Smith Square, London, Jan & July 1976)* — London ("Double Decker" series) 2–▲ 444824–2 [ADD]
Handel, G.F.:Messiah, w. Elly Ameling (sop), Anna Reynolds (mez), Philip Langridge (ten), Gwynne Howell (bass), N. Marriner (cnd), Academy of St. Martin in the Fields [E] — Argo ■ 421234–4
Mozart, W.A.:Missa, K.427, w. K. Te Kanawa (sop), A. Sofie von Otter (mez), A. R. Johnson (ten), R. Lloyd (bass), N. Marriner (cnd), Academy of St. Martin in the Fields *(rec London, Mar. 10–12, 1993)* — Philips ▲ 438999–2
Mozart, W.A.:Requiem, w. I. Cotrubas (sop), H. Watts (cta), R. Tear (ten), J. Shirley–Quirk (bar), N. Marriner (cnd), Academy of St. Martin in the Fields [L] — London ▲ 417746–2 [ADD]
Accademia di Santa Cecilia Chorus—see St. Cecilia Academy Chorus Rome
Accademia Monteverdiana Chorus
Gay, J.:The Beggar's Opera (sels), w. P. Clark (sop), A. Jenkins (sop), M. Cable (mez), E. Lane (mez), S. Minty (mez), E. Fleet (sgr), P. Hall (ten), V. Midgley (ten), N. Rogers (ten), J. Noble (bar), D. Stevens (cnd), Accademia Monteverdiana Orch—59 songs *(rec Aug. 1978)* — Koch Treasure ▲ 31621–2 [ADD]
L'Accent Grave Vocal Ensemble
Lefébure–Wély, L.J.A.:Music of, w. Sylvie de May (sop), Catherine Ravenne (alt), Xavier Bisaro (org), Vincent Genvrin (org), La Lyre Seraphique—Adoremus et procidamus; Marche en mib majeur; Adoro te [alterné]; Tantum ergo; Sacris solemnis; Elévation en la mineur; Marche en ut majeur; Noël varié, offertoire pour le jour de Noël; Sanctus; O Salutaris; Pastorale en sol majeur; Agnus Dei; Communion en fa majeur; Domine salvum; Missum redemptorem; Sortie en sib majeur et Cloches — Media 7 ▲ 005 [DDD]
Accentus Chamber Choir
Bach, J.S.:Cant 6, w. Barbara Schlick (sop), Andreas Scholl (ct), Christoph Prégardien (ten), Gotthold Schwarz (bass), C. Coin (cnd), Limoges Baroque Ensemble — Astrée ▲ E 8555
Bach, J.S.:Cant 41, w. Barbara Schlick (sop), Andreas Scholl (ct), Christoph Prégardien (ten), Gotthold Schwarz (bass), C. Coin (cnd), Limoges Baroque Ensemble — Astrée ▲ E 8555
Bach, J.S.:Cant 68, w. Barbara Schlick (sop), Andreas Scholl (ct), Christoph Prégardien (ten), Gotthold Schwarz (bass), C. Coin (cnd), Limoges Baroque Ensemble — Astrée ▲ E 8555
L. Equilbey (cnd)
Poulenc, F.:Choral Music—7 Chansons; Un soir de neige; Les petites voix; Chansons Françaises *(rec Dec. 3 & 5, 1993)* — Pierre Verany ▲ PVY 794042 [DDD]
Ravel, M.:Chansons *(rec Dec. 3 & 5, 1993)* — Pierre Verany ▲ PVY 794042 [DDD]
Ad Libitum Vocal Quartet
Haydn, J.:Vocal Trios & Qts, w. Christine Gerbaud (mez), Denis Dumas (ten), Alain Golven (bar)—Everything in Its Time; Eloquence; The Old Man; Harmony in Marriage; Against Arrogance; The Instant; From the Song of Thanksgiving to God; The Warning; Evening Hymn to God *(rec July 1995)* — Pierre Verany ▲ PVY 795102
Adirondack Children's Choir
Smith, Gregg:Prayer for Peace, w. G. Smith (cnd), Adirondack CO, Gregg Smith Singers, Adirondack Festival Chorus — Premier ("Composer" series) ▲ PRCD 1020 [ADD/DDD]
Adirondack Festival Chorus
Smith, Gregg:Magnificat, w. R. Rees (sop), G. Smith (cnd), Adirondack CO, Gregg Smith Singers — Premier ("Composer" series) ▲ PRCD 1020 [ADD/DDD]
Smith, Gregg:Prayer for Peace, w. G. Smith (cnd), Adirondack CO, Gregg Smith Singers, Adirondack Children's Choir — Premier ("Composer" series) ▲ PRCD 1020 [ADD/DDD]
Smith, Gregg:Vars on a Bach Chorale, w. G. Smith (cnd), Adirondack CO, Gregg Smith Singers — Premier ("Composer" series) ▲ PRCD 1020 [ADD/DDD]
Aeolian Singers
Herrmann, B.:Moby Dick, w. John Amis (ten), Robert Bowman (ten), David Kelly (bass), Michael Rippon (bass), London PO [E] — Unicorn–Kanchana ▲ UKCD 2061
Aix–en–Provence Festival Chorus
Gilles, J.:Mess des morts, w. A. Azema (sop), J. Nirouët (alt), W. Hite (ten), P. Mason (bar), J. Cohen (cnd), Boston Camerata, Ensemble de Tambours Provençaux — Erato ▲ 2292–45989–2
Mozart, W.A.:Così fan tutte, w. M. Adani (sop), T. Stich–Randall (mez), T. Berganza (mez), L. Alva (ten), A. Cortis (ten), R. Panerai (bar), H. Rosbaud (cnd), Paris Conservatory Societé des Concerts Orch [I] *(rec live, Aix–en–Provence, July 26, 1957)* — Melodram 3–▲ MEL 37084 [AAD]
Akademia
Cavalli, P.F.:Antiphons to the Blessed Virgin — Pierre Verany ▲ PVY 793052 [DDD]
Cavalli, P.F.:Missa pro defunctis — Pierre Verany ▲ PVY 793052 [DDD]
Cavalli, P.F.:Vespero della beata Vergine Maria, w. Jean Tubery (hn), F. Lasserre (cnd), La Fenice Ensemble — Pierre Verany 2–▲ PVY 796042 [DDD]
Akademie Chamber Choir
Bach, J.S.:Christmas Oratorio, w. E. Roon (sop), D.H. Braun (mez), E. Majkut (ten), W. Berry (bass), L. Dutoit (echo), B. Seidlhofer (hpd), J. Nebois (org), F. Grossmann (cnd), Vienna SO — Vox Box 2–▲ CDX 5096 [ADD]
Beethoven, L. van:Missa Solemnis, w. Ilona Steingruber (sop), Else Schuerhoff (alt), Ernst Majkut (ten), Otto Wiener (bass), O. Klemperer (cnd), Vienna SO *(rec Vienna, 1950)* — Vox Legends 2–▲ CDX2 5527
F. Grossmann (cnd)
Akademie Chamber Choir & Vienna SO, w. Vienna SO, Elisabeth Roon (sop), Laurence Dutoit (sop), Daagmar Herrmann–Braun (cta), Erich Majkut (ten), W. Berry (bass) — Vox 90s ■ V9–9903
Aks Dorian Chorale
Talma, L.:La Corona [E] — CRI ■ C 187
Albemarle Consort of Voices
Handel, G.F.:Dixit Dominus, w. *(soloists unknown)*, J. Litton (cnd), Eighteenth Century Ensemble, American Boychoir — MusicMasters ▲ 01612–67084–2 [DDD]
Hymn, w. American Boychoir, St. Luke's Chamber Ensemble — Angel ▲ CDC 55064; ■ 4DS 55064
Vivaldi, A.:Dixit Dominus, w. J. Litton (cnd), Eighteenth Century Ensemble, American Boychoir — MusicMasters ▲ 01612–67084–2 [DDD]

▲ = CD ♦ = Enhanced CD Δ = MD ■ = Cassette Tape □ = DCC

Jeff Alexander Choir
Three Tenors of the Golden Age, w.Jussi Björling (ten), Mario Lanza (ten), Jan Peerce (ten), John Corigliano (vn), Constantine Callinicos (pno), Frederick Schauwecker (pno), RCA Victor Orch [cnd:Renato Cellini, Constantine Callinicos, Erich Leinsdorf, Sylvan Levin, Maximilian Pilzer, Frieder Weissmann], Rome Opera Orch, Rome Opera Chorus
RCA Gold Seal ▲ 09026-68531-2 [ADD] ■ 09026-68531-4

Alexandrov Red Army Choir
The Sacred War:The Alexandrov Red Army Choir Today, Vol. 2
Mezhdunarodnaya Kniga ▲ MKA 437121 [DDD]

I. Agafonnikov (cnd)
Victory Day:The Alexandrov Red Army Choir Today, Vol. 3 *(rec 1992)*
Mezhdunarodnaya Kniga ▲ MK 437122 [DDD]

Alfelder Vocal Ensemble
Handel, G.F.:Te Deum, "Caroline", w. Mieke van der Sluis (sop), Graham Pushee (alt), Harry Van Berne (ten), Harry van der Kamp (bass), W. Helbich (cnd), Bremen Baroque Orch
CPO ▲ CPO 999244 [DDD]
Handel, G.F.:The Ways of Zion Do Mourn, w. Mieke van der Sluis (sop), Graham Pushee (alt), Harry van Berne (ten), Harry van der Kamp (bass), W. Helbich (cnd), Bremen Baroque Orch
CPO ▲ CPO 999244 [DDD]

Alfonso X El Sabio Group
L.L. Virumbrales (cnd)
Cabezón, A. de:Vocal Music, w. Felipe Lopez (org)—Libro de Canto Nuevo
RNE/Spanish National Radio ▲ AME 004
Martin Y Coll, A.:Vocal Music, w. Felipe Lopez (org)—Flores de Musica
RNE/Spanish National Radio ▲ AME 004

All City Concert Choir
Suesse, D.:Music of, w. Cy Coleman (pno), Dana Suesse (pno), Robert Barlow (hp), F. Fennell (cnd), American SO—Con Romantico for Pno & Orch; A Little Light Music; Young Man with Harp for Hp & Orch; The Blues [from Con in 3 Rhythms]; Coronach for Hp & Orch; Jazz Con for Combo & Orch; The Night Is Young & You're So Beautiful for Orch & Chorus *(rec Carnegie Hall, Dec 1974)*
Premier ▲ PRCD 1055

All Saints Boys' Choir
Harrison, Dobson, Smithers (cnd)
Now Make We Merthe, w. Purcell Consort of Voices, London Brass Ensemble *(rec May 1965, Dec. 21-22, 196)*
Boston Skyline ▲ BSD 121 [ADD]

Alla Francesca
Ciconia, J.:Vocal & Instrumental Consort Music, w. Alta—Mercé o morte; Una panthera; Gli alti col dançor; O Padua, sidus preclarum; Ben che da vui; Sus une fontayne; Caçando un giorno; Quod jactatur; Poy che morir; Venecle, mundi splendor; O rosa bella; Chi, vole amar; O felix temptum jubila; Chi nel servir antico; Deduto sey; Aler m'en veus; O virum omaimoda; Gloria; Regina gloriosa
Opus 111 ▲ OPS 30-101 [DDD]
Llibre Vermell de Montserrat
Opus 111 ▲ OPS 30-131
G. Lesne (cnd)
Coincy, G. de:Les Miracles de Nostre-Dame
Opus 111 ▲ OPS 30-146

John Alldis Choir
Beethoven, L. van:Fant Pno, Op. 80, "Choral Fant", w. D. Barenboim (pno), O. Klemperer (cnd), New Philharmonia Orch [G]
EMI Classics ("Studio" series) 3-▲ CDMC 63360 [ADD]
Beethoven, L. van:Fant Pno, Op. 80, "Choral Fant", w. D. Barenboim (pno), O. Klemperer (cnd), New Philharmonia Orch [G]
EMI Classics ("Studio" series) 2-▲ CDMB 69538 [ADD]
Berlioz, H.:Tristia, w. C. Davis (cnd), London SO [F]
Philips ▲ 416431-2 [ADD]
Holst, G.:A Choral Fant, w. J. Coster (mez), A. Boult (cnd), London PO *(rec Aug. 30, 1967)*
Intaglio ▲ ING 740 [ADD]
Hovhaness, A.:Sym 24, w. Martyn Hill (ten), John Wilbraham (tpt), Sax (vn), A. Hovhaness (cnd), National PO London [E] *(rec 1974)*
Crystal ▲ CD 803 [ADD]
Leoncavallo, R.:Pagliacci, w. M. Caballé (sop), P. Domingo (ten), S. Milnes (bar), N. Santi (cnd), London SO
RCA Gold Seal 2-▲ 09026-60865-2 [ADD]
Massenet, J.:Thaïs, w. Beverly Sills (sop—Thaïs), Nicolai Gedda (ten—Nicias), Sherrill Milnes (bar—Athanaël), L. Maazel (cnd), New Philharmonia Orch
EMI Classics 2-▲ CDMB 65479
Mozart, W.A.:Complete Mozart Edition, w. C. Eda-Pierre (sop), N. Burrowes (sop), R. Tear (ten), S. Burrows (ten), C. Davis (cnd), Academy of St. Martin in the Fields
Philips 2-▲ 422538-2 [ADD]
Mozart, W.A.:Così fan tutte, w. M. Price (sop), L. Popp (sop), Y. Minton (mez), L. Alva (ten), G. Evans (bar), H. Sotin (bass), O. Klemperer (cnd), New Philharmonia Orch
EMI Classics 3-▲ CDMC 63845
Mozart, W.A.:Missa, K.427, w. I. Cotrubas (sop), K. Te Kanawa (sop), W. Krenn (ten), H. Sotin (bass), R. Leppard (cnd), New Philharmonia Orch [L]
EMI Classics ▲ CDC 47385
Mozart, W.A.:Nozze di Figaro, w. H. Harper (sop), J. Blegen (sop), T. Berganza (mez), D. Fischer-Dieskau (bar), G. Evans (bar), D. Barenboim (cnd), English CO [I]
EMI Classics ("Studio" series) 3-▲ CDMC 63646 [ADD]
Mozart, W.A.:Nozze di Figaro, w. E. Söderström (sop), R. Grist (sop), T. Berganza (mez), G. Evans (bar), O. Klemperer (cnd), New Philharmonia Orch
EMI Classics 3-▲ CDMC 63849
Mozart, W.A.:Requiem, w. H. Donath (sop), Y. Minton (mez), A. Davies (ten), G Nienstedt (bass), C. Davis (cnd), BBC SO [L]
Philips ▲ 420353-2 [ADD]
Puccini, G.:La Bohème, w. M. Caballé (sop), J. Blegen (sop), P. Domingo (ten), S. Milnes (bar), R. Raimondi (bass), G. Solti (cnd), London PO [I]
RCA Red Seal 2-▲ RCD2-0371 2-■ ARK2-0371
Puccini, G.:Il tabarro, w. L. Price (sop), P. Domingo (ten), S. Milnes (bar), E. Leinsdorf (cnd), New Philharmonia Orch
RCA Gold Seal 2-▲ 09026-60865-2 [ADD]
Puccini, G.:Tosca, w. L. Price (sop), P. Domingo (ten), S. Milnes (bar), Z. Mehta (cnd), New Philharmonia Orch [I]
RCA Victrola 2-▲ RCD2-0105
Puccini, G.:Turandot, w. J. Sutherland (sop), M. Caballé (sop), L. Pavarotti (ten), N. Ghiaurov (bass), Z. Mehta (cnd), London PO [I]
London 2-▲ 414274-2 [ADD]
Rossini, G.:Il barbiere di Siviglia, w. Beverly Sills (sop), Fedora Barbieri (mez), Nicolai Gedda (ten), Renato Capecchi (bar), Sherill Milnes (bar), Ruggero Raimondi (bass), J. Levine (cnd), London SO
EMI Classics 2-▲ CDMB 66040
Vivaldi, A.:Gloria, RV.589, w. V. Negri (cnd), English CO
Philips ▲ 420648-2 [ADD]
Vivaldi, A.:Lauda Jerusalem, w. V. Negri (cnd), English CO
Philips ▲ 420648-2 [ADD]
Vivaldi, A.:Sacred Choral Music, w. V. Negri (cnd), English CO—Lauda Jerusalem, RV.609; Introduzione al Gloria, RV.642; Gloria, RV.589; Laudate pueri, RV.602; Laudate Dominum, RV.606 [L]
Philips ▲ 420648-2 [ADD]
J. Alldis (cnd)
Stravinsky, I.:Choral Music, w. O.G. Blarr (cnd), Ensemble 1971—eleven various a cappella & vocal-instrumental works, sung in English, Latin & Russian:Introitus T.S. Eliot in memoriam (1965); Pater noster (1926); Ave Maria (1934); Credo (1932); Elegy for J.F.K. (1964); In memoriam Dylan Thomas (1954); Tres sacrae cantiones di Gesualdo (1960); Anthem (1962); Pastorale
Koch Schwann ▲ CD 313 050 [ADD]

John Alldis Choir Male Voices
Brahms, J.:Alto Rhap, w. Janet Baker (mez), A. Boult (cnd), London PO
EMI Classics ("Doublefforte" series) 2-▲ CDFB 68655

Allegri Singers
L. Halsey (cnd)
Warlock, P.:Choral Music
Continuum ▲ CON 1053 [DDD]

Allmänna Sången
C.R. Alin (cnd)
Orff, C.:Carmina burana, w. Lena Nordin (sop), Hans Dornbusch (ten), Peter Mattei (bar), Love Derwinger (pno), Roland Pöntinen (pno), Kroumata Percussion Ensemble, Uppsala Choir School Children's Chorus [chamber version] *(rec Uppsala Univ Hall, Uppsala, Sweden, June 9-11, 1995)*
BIS ▲ CD 734 [DDD]

Alpe Adria Chorus
Rousseau, J.-J.:Le Devin du village, w. Kirchner (sgr), Choy (sgr), Müller de Vries (sgr), R. Clemencic (cnd), Alpe Adria Ensemble [F]
Nuova Era 2-▲ 7106/07 [DDD]

Alsfeld Vocal Ensemble
Eybler, J.L.E. von:Requiem mit Libera, w. B. Schlick (sop), H. van der Kamp (bass), W. Helbich (cnd), Steintor Barock Bremen
CPO ▲ CPO 999234 [DDD]
Telemann, G.P.:Hamburger Admiralitätsmusik, w. Mieke van der Sluis (sop—Hammonia), Graham Pushee (ten—Themis), Rufus Müller (ten—Mercurius), Klaus Mertens (bass—Neptunius), David Thomas (bass—Mars), Michael Schopper (bass—Albis), W. Helbich (cnd), Bremen Baroque Orch *(rec Nov 9, 1995)*
CPO 2-▲ CPO 999373-2 [DDD]
W. Helbich (cnd)
Bach, J.S.:Motets (misc)—BWVAnh.159-65
CPO ▲ CPO 999235 [DDD]
Festive Motets from the 16th Century
Koch Schwann ▲ SCH 313012 [DDD]
Lassus, O. de:Madrigals
Teldec ("Das alte Werke" series) ▲ 93685
Lassus, O. de:Motets
Teldec ("Das alte Werke" series) ▲ 93685
Nucius, J.:Missa super
MD + G ▲ MDG 3340454

Alta
Ciconia, J.:Vocal & Instrumental Consort Music, w. Alla Francesca—Mercé o morte; Una panthera; Gli alti col dançor; O Padua, sidus preclarum; Ben che da vui; Sus une fontayne; Caçando un giorno; Quod jactatur; Poy che morir; Venecle, mundi splendor; O rosa bella; Chi, vole amar; O felix temptum jubila; Chi nel servir antico; Deduto sey; Aler m'en veus; O virum omaimoda; Gloria; Regina gloriosa
Opus 111 ▲ OPS 30-101 [DDD]

Altra Voce
Ryelandt, J.:Agnus Dei, w. Ingrid Kapelle (sop), Lucienne van Deyck (mez), Joseph Cornwell (ten), Huub Claessens (bass), Stephan Macleod (bass), G. Llewellyn (cnd), Royal Flanders PO, Audite Nova *(rec live, Elisabeth Hall, Antwerp, Holland, Dec 9, 1994)*
Marco Polo 2-▲ 8.223785/86 [DDD]

Ama Deus Ensemble Chorus
Handel, G.F.:Messiah, w. Julianne Baird (sop), Jennifer Lane (mez), David Price (ten), Kevin Deas (b-bar), V. Radu (cnd), Ama Deus Ensemble [period instruments; 1749 Covent Garden version]
Vox Classics 2-▲ VOX2 7502 [DDD]

Amarillis Vocal Ensemble
Marx, K.:When Jesus Left His Mother, w. F. Staehelin (sgr), W. Pailer (bass), C. Näf (cnd), Amarillis Instrumental Ensemble, Feld Evangelistic Kantorei [G] *(rec 6/89)*
FSM ▲ FCD 97737 [DDD]

Ambrosian Chorus
Cherubini, L.:Requiem Mass in c, w. R. Muti (cnd), Philharmonia Orch
EMI Classics 2-▲ CDFB 68613
Debussy, C.:Nocturnes, w. P. Thomas (cnd), Philharmonia Orch
CBS ▲ MDK 44645 [DDD] ■ MDT 44645 (D)
Giordano, U.:Andrea Chénier, w. A. Gulin (sop—Maddalena), C. Bergonzi (ten—Andrea Chenier), S. Milnes (bar—Gérard), A. Guadagno (cnd), New Philharmonia Orch *(rec live, London, 2/8/70)*
Myto 2-▲ 2 MCD 91750 [ADD]
Hovhaness, A.:Lady of Light, w. Patricia Clark (sop), Leslie Fyson (bar), A. Hovhaness (cnd), Royal PO
Crystal ▲ CD 806
Kern, J.:Show Boat, w. F. von Stade (mez), T. Stratas (sop), J. Hadley (ten), B. Hubbard (bar), P. O'Hara (sgr), K. Burns (mez), N. Kulp (sgr), J. McGlinn (cnd), London Sinfonietta [original orchd Robert Russell Bennett]—also includes 45 minutes of music intended for the original performance but never included, plus music from revivals and films [1988 studio cast]
Angel 3-▲ A23 49108 [DDD]
Lerner, A.J.:Brigadoon, w. J. McGlinn (sgr), London Sinfonietta [1992 studio cast]
Broadway Angel ▲ CDQ 54481 ■ 4DQ 54481
Mahler, G.:Sym 3, w. H. Watts (cta), G. Solti (cnd), London SO, Wandsworth School Boys' Choir [G]
London 2-▲ 414254-2 [ADD]
Night & Day, w. Hampson, Thomas (bar), John McGlinn (cnd), London SO
EMI Classics ▲ CDC 54203 [DDD] ■ 4DS 54203 (D)
Porter, C.:Anything Goes, w. F. von Stade (mez), J. McGlinn (sgr), K. Criswell (sop), C. Groenendaal (sgr), J. Gilford (sgr), London SO [original 1934 Broadway version w. original orchestration by Robert Russell Bennett & Hans Spialek]
Angel ▲ CDC 49848-2 [DDD]
Puccini, G.:Le Villi, w. R. Scotto (sop), P. Domingo (ten), T. Gobbi (bar), L. Nucci (bar), L. Maazel (cnd), London National PO [I]
CBS ▲ MK 36669 [ADD]
Purcell, H.:Dido & Aeneas, w. Helen Donath (sop—Belinda), Shirley Verrett (sop—Dido), Oralia Dominguez (mez—Sorceress), Carmen Lavani (alt—A Spirit), Margaret Lensky (cta—2nd Witch), Carlo Gaifa (ten—A Sailor), Dan Jordacescu (bar—Aeneas), Rosina Cavicchioli (sgr—A Woman), Lilia Teresita Reyes (sgr—1st Witch), R. Leppard (cnd), Turin RAI SO *(rec Torino, May 20, 1971)*
Arkadia ▲ 619 [ADD]
Rossini, G.:La Cenerentola, w. C. Malone (sop), F. Palmer (sop), A. Baltsa (mez), F. Araiza (ten), S. Alaimo (bar), J. del Carlo (bass), R. Raimondi (bass), N. Marriner (cnd), Academy of St. Martin in the Fields
Philips ("Digital Classics" series) 3-▲ 420468-2 [DDD]
Verdi, G.:Requiem Mass, w. Renata Scotto (sop), Agnes Baltsa (mez), Veriano Luchetti (ten), Evgeny Nesterenko (bass), R. Muti (cnd), Philharmonia Orch
EMI Classics 2-▲ CDFB 68613

Ambrosian Light Opera Chorus
Home Sweet Home, w. Sutherland, Joan (sop), Richard Bonynge (cnd), New Philharmonia Orch
London ▲ 425048-2 LC [ADD]
Operetta Gala, w. Sutherland, Joan (sop), Richard Bonynge (cnd), New Philharmonia Orch, Swiss Romande Orch
London ("Opera Gala" series) ▲ 421880-2 LA [ADD]

Ambrosian Male Voice Chorus
Bruckner, A.:Helgoland, w. W. Morris (cnd), Symphonica of London
IMP Classics ▲ IMP 1042 [DDD]
Wagner, R.:Das Liebesmahl der Apostel, w. W. Morris (cnd), Symphonica of London [G]
IMP Classics ▲ IMP 1042 [DDD]

Ambrosian Opera Chorus
Bel Canto, w. Battle, Kathleen (sop), Benno Campanella (cnd), London PO
Deutsche Grammophon ▲ 435866-2 ■ 435866-4
Bellini, V.:Beatrice di Tenda, w. J. Sutherland (sop), L. Pavarotti (ten), R. Bonynge (cnd), London SO
London ("Grand Opera" series) 3-▲ 433706-2 [ADD]
Bellini, V.:Norma, w. M. Caballé (sop), F. Cossotto (mez), P. Domingo (ten), R. Raimondi (bass), C.F. Cillario (cnd), London PO [I]
RCA Gold Seal 3-▲ 6502-2-RG [ADD]
Bizet, G.:Carmen, w. I. Cotrubas (sop), T. Berganza (mez), P. Domingo (ten), S. Milnes (bar), C. Abbado (cnd), London SO [F]
Deutsche Grammophon 3-▲ 419636-2 [ADD]
Bizet, G.:Carmen (sels), w. I. Cotrubas (sop), T. Berganza (mez), P. Domingo (ten), S. Milnes (bar), C. Abbado (cnd), London SO [F]
Deutsche Grammophon ▲ 435401-2 [ADD]
Boito, A.:Mefistofele, w. M. Caballé (sop), P. Domingo (ten), N. Treigle (bass), J. Rudel (cnd), London SO [I]
EMI Classics 2-▲ CDCB 49522 [ADD]
Charpentier, G.:Louise, w. I. Cotrubas (sop), J. Berbié (mez), P. Domingo (ten), M. Sénéchal (ten), G. Bacqier (bar), G. Prêtre (cnd), New Philharmonia Orch [F]
Sony Classical 3-▲ S3K 46429 [ADD]
Donizetti, G.:Don Pasquale, w. M. Freni (sop), G. Winbergh (ten), S. Bruscantini (bar), L. Nucci (bar), R. Muti (cnd), Philharmonia Orch
EMI Classics 2-▲ CDCB 47068
Donizetti, G.:Don Pasquale, w. Beverly Sills (sop), Alfredo Kraus (ten), Alan Titus (bar), Donald Gramm (b-bar), S. Caldwell (cnd), London SO
EMI Classics 2-▲ CDMB 66030
Donizetti, G.:Don Pasquale (sels), w. M. Freni (sop), G. Winbergh (ten), S. Bruscantini (bar), L. Nucci (bar), R. Muti (cnd), Philharmonia Orch
EMI Classics ▲ CDC 54490
Donizetti, G.:Lucia di Lammermoor, w. M. Caballé (sop), A. Murray (mez), C. H. Ahnsjö (ten), V. Bello (ten), J. Carreras (ten), V. Sardinero (bar), S. Ramey (bass), J. López-Cobos (cnd), New Philharmonia Orch
Philips 2-▲ 426563-2
Donizetti, G.:Lucia di Lammermoor, w. E. Gruberová (sop), A. Kraus (ten), D. Lloyd (ten), R. Bruson (bar), Royal PO *(rec 1983)*
EMI Classics ▲ CDMB 64622
Gershwin, G.:Ovs, w. J. McGlinn (cnd), New Princess Theater Orch, London Sinfonietta National PO—A Damsel in Distress; Girl Crazy; Of Thee I Sing; Tip-Toes; Primrose; Stiff Upper Lip; Oh, Kay!
EMI Classics ("Doublefforte" series) 2-▲ CDFB 68589
Gluck, C.W.:Orfeo ed Euridice, w. E. Gruberova (sop), Marshall (sop), A. Baltsa (mez), R. Muti (cnd), Philharmonia Orch
Angel ("Studio" series) 2-▲ CDMB 63637 [DDD]
Gounod, C.:Faust, w. J. Sutherland (sop), F. Corelli (ten), N. Ghiaurov (bass), R. Bonynge (cnd), London SO [F]
London ("Grand Opera" series) 3-▲ 421240-2 [AAD]
Great Operatic Duets, w. Caballé, Montserrat (sop), Shirley Verrett (mez), Anton Guadagno (cnd), New Philharmonia Orch
RCA Gold Seal ▲ 60818-2-RG [ADD]

Ambrosian Opera Chorus (cont.)

Handel, G.F.:Semele, w. Kathleen Battle (sop), Sylvia McNair (sop), Marylin Horne (mez), Michael Chance (ct), John Aler (ten), Samuel Ramey (bass), J. Nelson (cnd), English CO Deutsche Grammophon 3-▲ 435782-2 –

Kern, J.:Show Boat, w. P. O'Hara (sop), T. Stratas (sop), K. Burns (mez), F. von Stade (mez), D. Garrison (ten), J. Hadley (ten), B. Hubbard (bar), J. McGlinn (cnd), London Sinfonietta, Ambrosian Singers EMI Classics 3-▲ A23 49108

Kern, J.:Show Boat, w. P. O'Hara (sop), T. Stratas (sop), K. Burns (mez), F. von Stade (mez), D. Garrison (ten), J. Hadley (ten), B. Hubbard (bar), J. McGlinn (cnd), London Sinfonietta EMI Classics ▲ ZDC 49847

Leoncavallo, R.:Pagliacci, w. M. Caballé (sop), R. Scotto (sop), A. Varnay (mez), J. Hamari (mez), J. Carreras (ten), M. Manuguerra (bar), T. Allen (bar), K. Nurmela (bar), U. Benelli (bar), R. Muti (cnd), Philharmonia Orch EMI Classics 2-▲ CDMB 63650

Leoncavallo, R.:Pagliacci (sels), w. R. Scotto (sop), J. Carreras (ten), K. Nurmela (bar), R. Muti (cnd), Philharmonia Orch EMI Classics ("Studio" series) ▲ CDM 63933 ■ EG 63933

Mascagni, P.:Cavalleria rusticana (sels), w. M. Caballé (sop), J. Carreras (ten), R. Muti (cnd), Philharmonia Orch EMI Classics ("Studio" series) ▲ CDM 63933 ■ EG 63933

Massenet, J.:Cendrillon, w. R. Welting (sop), F. von Stade (mez), N. Gedda (ten), J. Bastin (bass), J. Rudel (cnd), Philharmonia Orch [F] CBS 2-▲ M2K 35194 [ADD]

Massenet, J.:Manon, w. B. Sills (sop), N. Gedda (ten), G. Souzay (bar), G. Bacquier (bar), J. Rudel (cnd), New Philharmonia Orch [F] EMI Classics ("Studio" series) 3-▲ CDMC 69831 [ADD]

Meyerbeer, G.:Les Huguenots, w. J. Sutherland (sop), M. Arroyo (sop), H. Tourangeau (mez), A. Vrenios (ten), D. Cossa (bar), G. Bacquier (bar), N. Ghiuselev (bass), R. Bonynge (cnd), New Philharmonia Orch London ("Grand Opera" series) 4-▲ 430549-2 [AAD]

Meyerbeer, G.:Le Prophète, w. Renata Scotto (sop), Marilyn Horne (mez), James McCracken (ten), Jerome Hines (bass), H. Lewis (cnd), Royal PO [F] CBS 3-▲ M3K 34340 [ADD]

Mozart, W.A.:Così fan tutte, w. K. Mattila (sop), E. Szmytka (sop), A. S. von Otter (mez), F. Araiza (ten), T. Allen (bar), J. van Dam (b-bar), N. Marriner (cnd), Academy of St. Martin in the Fields [I] Philips 3-▲ 422381-2 [DDD]

Mozart, W.A.:Don Giovanni, w. S. Sweet (sop), K. Mattila (sop), M. McLaughlin (sop), F. Araiza (ten), T. Allen (bar), S. Alaimo (b-bar), R. Lloyd (bass), N. Marriner (cnd), Academy of St. Martin in the Fields Philips 3-▲ 432129-2 [DDD]

Mozart, W.A.:Nozze di Figaro, w. L. Popp (sop), B. Hendricks (sop), A. Baltsa (mez), G. Raimondi (ten), J. Van Dam (bar), N. Marriner (cnd), Academy of St. Martin in the Fields [I] Philips 3-▲ 416370-2 [DDD]

Mozart, W.A.:Nozze di Figaro (sels), w. L. Popp (sop), B. Hendricks (sop), A. Baltsa (mez), G. Raimondi (ten), J. van Dam (b-bar), N. Marriner (cnd), Academy of St. Martin in the Fields [I] Philips ▲ 416870-2 [DDD]

Mozart, W.A.:Zauberflöte, w. K. Te Kanawa (sop), C. Studer (sop), E. Lind (sop), F. Araiza (ten), O. Bär (bar), S. Ramey (bass), N. Marriner (cnd), Academy of St. Martin in the Fields [G] Philips 2-▲ 426276-2 [DDD]

Opera Arias, w. Ramey, Samuel (bass), D. Renzetti (cnd), Philharmonia Orch Philips ▲ 420184-2 PH [DDD] ■ 420184-4

Puccini, G.:Madama Butterfly, w. M. Freni (sop), T. Berganza (mez), J. Carreras (ten), J. Pons (bar), G. Sinopoli (cnd), Philharmonia Orch [I] Deutsche Grammophon 3-▲ 423567-2 [DDD]

Puccini, G.:Manon Lescaut, w. M. Caballé (sop—Manon Lescaut), P. Domingo (ten—Des Grieux), R. Tear (ten—Edmondo), V. Sardinero (bar—Lescaut), N. Mangin (bass—Geronte), B. Bartoletti (cnd), New Philharmonia Orch EMI Classics ▲ CDMB 64852

Puccini, G.:La Rondine, w. M. Nicolesco (sop), K. Te Kanawa (sop), P. Domingo (ten), D. Rendall (ten), L. Nucci (bar), L. Maazel (cnd), London SO [I] CBS 2-▲ M2K 37852 [DDD]

Puccini, G.:Tosca, w. R. Scotto (sop), P. Domingo (ten), R. Bruson (bar), J. Levine (cnd), Philharmonia Orch [I] EMI Classics 2-▲ CDCB 49364 [DDD]

Puccini, G.:Tosca (sels), w. R. Scotto (sop), P. Domingo (ten), R. Bruson (bar), J. Levine (cnd), Philharmonia Orch EMI Classics ▲ CDC 54324

Ravel, M.:L'Enfant et les sortilèges, w. Arleen Augér (sop), Marilyn Richardson (sop), Jane Berbié (mez), Linda Finnie (mez), Jocelyne Taillon (mez), Davenny Wyner (mez), Philip Langridge (ten), Philippe Huttenlocher (bar), Jules Bastin (bass), A. Previn (cnd), London SO Classics for Pleasure ("Eminence" series) ▲ CFP 2241

Rossini, G.:Arias, w. M. Horne (mez), H. Lewis (cnd), Royal PO, Swiss Romande Orch [I] London ▲ 421306-2 [ADD]

Rossini, G.:Guillaume Tell, w. M. Caballé (sop), M. Mesplé (sop), C. Burles (ten), N. Gedda (ten), G. Bacquier (bar), G. Howell (bass), L. Gardelli (cnd), Royal PO EMI Classics 4-▲ CDMD 69951

Rossini, G.:Mosè in Egitto, w. J. Anderson (sop), S. Nimsgern (b-bar), R. Raimondi (bass), C. Scimone (cnd), Philharmonia Orch [I] Philips 2-▲ 420109-2 [ADD]

Rossini, G.:Otello, w. F. von Stade (mez), J. Carreras (ten), S. Fisichella (ten), S. Ramey (bass), J. López-Cobos (cnd), Philharmonia Orch [I] Philips 2-▲ 432456-2 [ADD]

Rossini, G.:Semiramide, w. C. Studer (sop), J. Larmore (mez), F. Lopardo (ten), S. Ramey (bass), I. Marin (cnd), London SO Deutsche Grammophon ▲ 437797-2

Rossini, G.:Semiramide, w. J. Sutherland (sop), M. Horne (mez), Myers (sgr), Grant (sgr), R. Bonynge (cnd), New Philharmonia Orch [I] *(rec live at the Theatre Royal, Drury Lane, 2/9/69)* Arkadia 2-▲ 579 (m) [ADD]

Rossini, G.:The Siege of Corinth, w. B. Sills (sop), S. Verrett (mez), J. Diaz (bass), T. Schippers (cnd), London SO [I] *(rec London, 1974)* EMI Classics 3-▲ CDMC 64335

Rossini, G.:Il turco in Italia, w. M. Caballé (sop), E. Dara (bar), L. Nucci (bar), S. Ramey (bass), R. Chailly (cnd), National PO London [I] CBS 2-▲ M2K 37859 [DDD]

Shostakovich, D.:Lady Macbeth of Mtsensk, w. G. Vishnevskaya (sop), B. Finnilä (mez), N. Gedda (ten), A. Haugland (bass), M. Rostropovich (cnd), London PO [R], EMI Classics 2-▲ CDCB 49955 [ADD]

Verdi, G.:Otello, w. G. Jones (sop—Desdemona), A. di Stasio (mez—Emilia), J. McCracken (ten—Otello), P. de Palma (ten—Cassio), D. Fischer-Dieskau (bar—Iago), J. Barbirolli (cnd), New Philharmonia Orch EMI Classics ▲ CDMB 65296

Verdi, G.:Rigoletto, w. Beverly Sills (sop), Sherill Milnes (bar), Alfredo Kraus (bar), Samuel Ramy (bass), J. Rudel (cnd), Philharmonia Orch EMI Classics 2-▲ CDMB 724356603721

J. McCarthy (cnd)

Bertoni, F.:Orfeo ed Euridice, w. Cecilia Gasdia (sop—Euridice), Delores Ziegler (mez—Orfeo), Bruce Ford (ten—Imeneo), C. Scimone (cnd), Venice Solisti *(rec Vicenza, Italy, Aug 3-7, 1990)* Arts Music ▲ 47118-2 [DDD]

Ambrosian Singers

Amazing Grace, w. Norman, Jessye (sop), Dalton Baldwin (pno), Geoffrey Parsons (pno), Christopher Bowers-Broadbent (org), Alexander Gibson (cnd), Willis Patterson (cnd), Royal PO Philips ▲ 432546-2 PH [DDD] ■ 432546-4 PH

Bach, J.S.:St. Matthew Passion, w. E. Ameling (sop), B. Finnilä (cta), E. Haefliger (ten), S. McCoy (ten), B. Luxon (bar), B. McDaniel (bar), J. Somary (cnd), English CO *(rec 1977)* Vanguard Classics 3-▲ OVC 4060/62 [ADD]

Bach, J.S.:St. Matthew Passion (sels), w. E. Ameling (sop), B. Finnilä (cta), E. Haefliger (ten), S. McCoy (ten), B. Luxon (bar), B. McDaniel (bar), J. Somary (cnd), English CO Vanguard Classics ▲ OVC 4063 [ADD]

Beethoven, L. van:Choral Music, w. M. Tilson Thomas (cnd), London SO—Elegiac Song, Op. 118; Opferlied, Op. 121b; Bundeslied, Op. 122 CBS ▲ MK 33509 [ADD]

Beethoven, L. van:König Stephen (incidental music), w. M. Tilson Thomas (cnd), London SO CBS ▲ MK 33509 [ADD]

Beethoven, L. van:Meeresstille und glückliche Fahrt, w. M. Tilson Thomas (cnd), London SO CBS ▲ MK 33509 [ADD]

Beethoven, L. van:Sym 9, "Choral Sym", w. Gillian Webster (sop), Catherine Wyn-Rogers (cta), Martyn Hill (ten), Robert Hayward (bar), R. Leppard (cnd), Royal PO Tring ("Royal Philharmonic Collection" series) ▲ TRP 51 [DDD]

Berlioz, H.:La Damnation de Faust, w. J. Veasey (mez), N. Gedda (ten), G. Bastin (bar), C. Davis (cnd), London SO, London Sym Chorus [F] Philips 2-▲ 416395-2 [ADD]

Bliss, A.:The Olympians, w. R. Woodland (sop), S. Minty (mez), T. Hemsley (bar), R. Herincx (bass), B. Fairfax (cnd), Polyphonia Orch *(rec 1972)* Intaglio 2-▲ ING 755 [ADD]

Ambrosian Singers (cont.)

Bliss, A.:The world is charged with the grandeur of God, w. A. Bliss (cnd), London SO Wind & Brass Ensemble Lyrita ▲ SRCD 225 [ADD]

Brahms, J.:Ein Deutsches Requiem, w. M. Price (sop), S. Ramey (bar), A. Previn (cnd), Royal PO [G] Teldec ("Digital Experience" series) ▲ 9031-75862-2 AW [DDD] ■ 9031-75862-4

Brahms, J.:Schicksalslied, w. W. Sawallisch (cnd), London PO EMI Classics ▲ CDC 54359

Britten, B.:Billy Budd, w. P. Pears (ten), P. Glossop (bar), J. Shirley-Quirk (bar), B. Luxon (bar), M. Langdon (bass), O. Brannigan (bass), B. Britten (cnd), London SO [E] London 3-▲ 417428-2 [ADD]

Cherubini, L.:Requiem Mass in c, w. R. Muti (cnd), New Philharmonia Orch EMI Classics ▲ CDC 49678

Christmas Album, w. Schwarzkopf, Elisabeth (sop), Charles Mackerras, Philharmonia Orch *(rec 1957)* EMI Classics ("Studio" series) ▲ CDM 63574 [ADD]

Delius, F.:An Arabesk, w. Thomas Allen (bar), Royal PO Unicorn-Kanchana ▲ UK 2076

Delius, F.:Music of, w. Robert Tear (ten), J. Barbirolli (cnd), Hallé Orch, London SO—Brigg Fair; In a Summer Garden; On Hearing the First Cuckoo in Spring; Summer Night on the River; A Song before Sunrise; Intermezzo & Serenade [from Hassan]; La Calinda; Late Swallows; Intermezzo [from Fennimore & Gerda]; The Walk to Paradise Garden; Prelude [from Irmelin]; A Song of Summer; Appalachia; rehearsal of Appalachia EMI Classics ▲ ZDMB 65119

Delius, F.:Songs of Farewell, Royal PO Unicorn-Kanchana ▲ UK 2076

Donizetti, G.:Lucia di Lammermoor (sels), w. E. Gruberova (sop), A. Agache (ten), A. Miles (bass), R. Bonynge (cnd), London SO—Oh giusto cielo...Il dolce suono; Ohimè! sorge il tremendo fantasma; S'avanza Enrico; Spargi d'amore pianto Teldec ▲ 4509-93691-2 [DDD]

Duruflé, M.:Requiem, w. B. Bonney (soprano), J. Larmore (mezzo-soprano), T. Hampson (bass-baritone), Ambrosian Singers, M. Legrand (cnd), Philharmonia Orch, Teldec ▲ 90879-2

Fauré, G.:Requiem, w. B. Bonney (sop), J. Larmore (mez), T. Hampson (bass-bar), M. Legrand (cnd), Philharmonia Orch Teldec ▲ 90879-2

Grieg, E.:Peer Gynt, w. L. Popp (sop), N. Marriner (cnd), Academy of St. Martin in the Fields EMI Classics ▲ CDC 47003 [DDD]

Handel, G.F.:Coronation Anthems (4) for George II, w. Y. Menuhin (cnd), Menuhin Festival Orch *(rec St. Augustine's Church, Maida Vale, London, Oct. 1969)* EMI Classics ▲ CDK 65336 [ADD]

Handel, G.F.:Messiah, w. Elisabeth Harwood (sop), Janet Baker (mez), Paul Esswood (ct), Robert Tear (ten), Raimund Herincx (bass), C. Mackerras (cnd), English CO [E] Angel ("Studio" series) ▲ CDM 69040

Handel, G.F.:Messiah, w. Joan Sutherland (sop), Huguette Tourangeau (mez), Werner Krenn (ten), Tom Krause (bar), R. Bonynge (cnd), English CO [E] London ("Serenata" series) 2-▲ 433740-2 [ADD]

Handel, G.F.:Messiah, w. Elisabeth Harwood (sop), Janet Baker (mez), Paul Esswood (ct), Robert Tear (ten), Raimund Herincx (bass), C. Mackerras (cnd), English CO [E] Angel ("Studio" series) 2-▲ CDMB 62748 [ADD]

Handel, G.F.:Solomon (sels), w. Y. Menuhin (cnd), Menuhin Festival Orch—From the Censer Curling Rise [chorus] *(rec St. Augustine's Church, Maida Vale, London, Oct. 1969)* EMI Classics ▲ CDK 65336 [ADD]

Holst, G.:The Planets, w. S. Rattle (cnd), Philharmonia Orch Classics for Pleasure ("Eminence" series) ▲ CDEMX 9513 [DDD]

Kern, J.:Show Boat, w. P. O'Hara (sop), T. Stratas (sop), K. Burns (mez), F. von Stade (mez), D. Garrison (ten), J. Hadley (ten), B. Hubbard (bar), J. McGlinn (cnd), London Sinfonietta, Ambrosian Opera Chorus EMI Classics 3-▲ A23 49108

Ketèlbey, A.W.:Music of, w. J. Temperley (mez), V. Mdegley (ten), L. Pearson (pno), J. Lanchbery (cnd), Philharmonia Orch—In a Persian Market; In a Monastery Garden; Chal Romano; In the Mystic Land of Egypt; The Clock and the Dresden Figures; Bells across the Meadows; In a Chinese Temple; In the Moonlight; Sanctuary of the Heart Classics for Pleasure ▲ CDCFP 4637 [ADD]

Lehár, F.:Die lustige Witwe (sels), w. J. Sutherland (sop), R. Resnik (mez), W. Krenn (ten), R. Bonynge (cnd), National PO London—overture & highlights from Acts 1 & 2 London ("Opera Gala" series) ▲ 421884-2 [ADD]

Mahler, G.:Das Klagende Lied, w. T. Zylis-Gara (sop), A. Reynolds (mez), A. Kaposy (ten), W. Morris (cnd), New Philharmonia Orch [G] *(rec 1967)* Nimbus ▲ NI 5085 [AAD]

Mahler, G.:Das Klagende Lied, w. T. Zylis-Gara (sop), A. Reynolds (mez), A. Kaposy (ten), W. Morris (cnd), New Philharmonia Orch IMP Classics ▲ IMPCD 1053 [DDD]

Mahler, G.:Sym 3, w. N. Procter (cta), J. Horenstein (cnd), London SO, Wandsworth School Boys' Choir [G] Unicorn-Kanchana ("Souvenir" series) 2-▲ UKCD 2006/07 [ADD]

Mahler, G.:Sym 8, w. W. Morris (cnd), Symphonica of London, New Philharmonia Chorus IMP Classics 2-▲ IMP DPCD 1019 [DDD]

Mendelssohn, F.:A Midsummer Night's Dream (comp), w. A. Augér (sop), A. Murray (mez), N. Marriner (cnd), Philharmonia Orch [E] Philips ▲ 411106-2 [DDD]

Newman, Alfred:Film Music, w. C. Gerhardt (cnd), National PO London, Grenadier Guards Band RCA ▲ 0184-2-RG [ADD] ■ 0184-4-RG

Original Scores from the MGM Classics, w. E. Bernstein (cnd), Royal PO Chandos ("7000" series) ▲ CHAN 7053

Puccini, G.:Madama Butterfly, w. R. Scotto (sop), P. Domingo (ten), I. Wixell (bar), L. Maazel (cnd), Philharmonia Orch [I] CBS 2-▲ M2K 35181 [AAD]

Puccini, G.:Mass, w. J. Carreras (ten), H. Prey (bar), C. Scimone (cnd), *(orch unknown)* Erato ▲ 96367-2

Purcell, H.:Dido & Aeneas, w. J. Norman (sop), M. McLaughlin (sop), T. Allen (bar), R. Leppard (cnd), English CO [E] Philips ▲ 416299-2 [DDD]

Purcell, H.:Dido & Aeneas, w. Victoria de los Angeles (sop—Dido), Heather Harper (sop—Belinda), Patricia Johnson (mez—Sorceress), Peter Glossup (bar—Aeneas), J. Barbirolli (cnd), English CO EMI Classics 2-▲ ZDM 65664

Purcell, H.:Dido & Aeneas (sels), w. Victoria de los Angeles (sop—Dido), Heather Harper (sop—Belinda), Sibyl Michelow (sop), Elizabeth Robson (sop), Derek Simpson (vc), Colin Tilney (hpd), J. Barbirolli (cnd), English CO—Ov.; Shake the Cloud; Ah! Ah! Belinda; When Monarchs Unite; But Ere We This Perform; But Death, Alas! I Cannot Shun...When I am Laid in Earth; With Drooping Wings *(rec Abbey Road Studio 1, London, Aug. 1965)* EMI Classics ▲ CDK 65341 [ADD]

Purcell, H.:Hail. Bright Cecilia, w. April Cantelo (sop), Alfred Deller (alt), Wilfred Brown (ten), Maurice Bevan (bar), M. Tippett (cnd), Kalmar CO Vanguard Classics ▲ OVC 8020 [ADD]

Rameau, J.P.:Les Fêtes d'Hébé, w. Ursula Connors (sop), R. Leppard (cnd), English CO EMI Classics ("Baroque" series) ▲ CDK 65732

Rodgers, R.:Carousel, w. B. Cook (sop), S. Ramey (bass), S. Brightman (sop), M. Forrester (cta), et al., P. Geminiani (cnd), Royal PO [1987 studio cast] MCA Classics ▲ MCAD 6209 [DDD] ■ MCAC 6209

Rossini, G.:Arias, w. R. Blake (ten), M. Valdes (cnd), London SO—8 arias from Armida, Ermione, Gazza ladra, Otello, Ricciardo e Zoraide, Semiramide, Zelmira [I] Arabesque ▲ Z 6612

Rossini, G.:Arias, w. R. Blake (ten), J. McCarthy (cnd), London SO [I] Arabesque ▲ Z 6582

Rossini, G.:Semiramide, w. J. Sutherland (sop), M. Horne (mez), J. Serge (ten), J. Rouleau (bass), S. Malas (bass), R. Bonynge (cnd), London SO [I] *(rec 1966)* London 3-▲ 425481-2 [ADD]

Rózsa, M.:Film Music, w. C. Gerhardt (cnd), National PO London RCA ("Classic Film Scores" series) ▲ 0911-2 RG ■ 0911-4 RG

Songs of Praise, w. I. Marin (cnd), London SO Deutsche Grammophon ▲ 435387-2 GH [DDD]

Steiner, M.:Film Music, w. C. Gerhardt (cnd), National PO RCA ▲ 0136-2-RG [ADD] ■ 0136-4-RG

Thomas, A.:Hamlet, w. J. Anderson (sop—Ophelie), D. Graves (mez—Gertrude), G. Kunde (ten—Laerte), T. Hampson (bar—Hamlet), S. Ramey (bass—Claudius), A. de Almeida (cnd), London PO EMI Classics 3-▲ CDCC 54820

Treasures of Operetta II, w. Hill Smith, Marilyn (sop), Peter Morrison (bar), Chandos Concert Orch [cnd:Stuart Barry] Chandos ▲ CHAN 8561 [DDD]

Verdi, G.:Attila, w. C. Deutekom (sop), G. Raimondi (ten), C. Bergonzi (ten), S. Milnes (bar), L. Gardelli (cnd), Royal PO Philips 2-▲ 426115-2

Verdi, G.:Il corsaro, w. M. Caballé (sop), J. Norman (sop), J. Carreras (ten), L. Gardelli (cnd), New Philharmonia Orch [I] Philips 2-▲ 426118-2 [ADD]

Verdi, G.:Un giorno di regno, w. J. Norman (sop), F. Cossotto (mez), J. Carreras (ten), I. Wixell (bar), V. Sardinero (bar), W. Ganzarolli (bar), P. Elvin (bass), A. Cassinelli (bass), L. Gardelli (cnd), Royal PO Philips 2-▲ 422429-2 [ADD]

▲ = CD ♦ = Enhanced CD Δ = MD ■ = Cassette Tape □ = DCC

Ambrosian Singers (cont.)
Verdi, G.:I lombardi alla prima crociata, w. C. Deutekom (sop), D. Malvisi (sop), M. Aparici (sop), P. Domingo (ten), G. Raimondi (ten), M. Lo Monaco (ten), M. Dean (b-bar), C. Grant (bass), L. Gardelli (cnd), Royal PO Philips 2-▲ 422420-2 [ADD]
Verdi, G.:La traviata, w. E. Gruberova (sop), N. Shicoff (ten), G. Zancanaro (bar), C. Rizzi (cnd), London SO Teldec 2-▲ 9031-76348-2 PL
Vienna, City of My Dreams, w. Domingo, Plácido (ten), English CO [cnd:J. Rudel] EMI Classics ▲ CDC 47398
Wagner, R.:Tannhäuser (sels), w. K. Te Kanawa (sop), W. Meier (mez), R. Kollo (ten), H. Hagegard (bar), M. Janowski (cnd), Philharmonia Orch Teldec ▲ 46336-2 ■ 46336-4
Wagner, R.:Tannhäuser (sels), w. K. Te Kanawa (sop), R. Kollo (ten), Håkan Hagegård (bar), W. Meier (mez), M. Holle (bass), M. Janowski (cnd), Philharmonia Orch; music from film soundtrack for Meeting Venus Teldec ▲ 2292 46336-2 [DDD] ■ 2292 46336-4 □ 2292 46336-5

C. McCarthy (cnd)
Bizet, G.:Carmen (sels), w. Teresa Berganza (mez—Carmen), Plácido Domingo (ten—Don José), C. Abbado (cnd), London SO, George Watson's College Boys' Chorus—C'est toi? C'est moi Deutsche Grammophon ▲ 447270-2 [ADD] ■ 447 270-4

J. McCarthy (cnd)
Handel, G.F.:Messiah, w. Patricia Schuman (sop), Lucia Valentini Terrani (alt), Bruce Ford (ten), Gwynne Howell (bass), Bernard Soustrot (tpt), C. Scimone (cnd), Venice Solisti *(rec S. Francisco Church, Schio, Italy, June 23-30, 1989)* Arts 2-▲ 471052 [DDD]
Handel, G.F.:Messiah, w. Patricia Schuman (sop), Lucia Valentini Terrani (alt), Bruce Ford (ten), Gwynne Howell (bass), C. Scimone (cnd), Venice Solisti *(rec Schio, Italy, June 23-30, 1989)* Arts 2-▲ 47105-2 [DDD]

Amburgo Radio Chorus
Schoenberg, A.:Moses und Aaron (sels), w. H. Rosbaud (cnd), Amburgo RSO—Danza del Vitello d'Oro Stradivarius ▲ STV 10022 [ADD]

American Boychoir
Bernstein, L.:Chichester Psalms, w. J. Litton (cnd), American SO [He] MusicMasters ▲ 7049-2-C
Davidson, C.:I Never Saw Another Butterfly, w. J. Litton (cnd), American SO—[E] MusicMasters ▲ 7049-2-C
Handel, G.F.:Dixit Dominus, w. *(soloists unknown)*, J. Litton (cnd), Eighteenth Century Ensemble, Albemarle Consort of Voices MusicMasters ▲ 01612-67084-2 [DDD]
Hymn, w. Albemarle Consort of Voices, St. Luke's Chamber Ensemble Angel ▲ CDC 55064; ■ 4DS 55064
In the Spirit:Sacred Music for Christmas, w. Norman, Jessye (sop), St. Luke's Orch [cnd:David Robertson], Riverside Church Choir, St. Barnabas Adult Choir, St. Thomas Men & Boys Choir Philips ▲ 454640-2 ■ 454640-4
A Joyous Christmas:Trumpets Sound, Voices Ring, w. Atlantic Brass Quintet MusicMasters ▲ 01612-67076-2 [DDD]
Mahler, G.:Sym 3, w. Jessye Norman (sop), S. Ozawa (cnd), Boston SO, Tanglewood Festival Chorus Philips ▲ 434909-2
Vivaldi, A.:Dixit Dominus, w. J. Litton (cnd), Eighteenth Century Ensemble, Albemarle Consort of Voices MusicMasters ▲ 01612-67084-2 [DDD]

J. Litton (cnd)
Dalglish, M.:Hymnody of Earth, w. M. Dalglish (hammer dulcimer/voc), G. Velez (perc) MusicMasters ▲ 7058-2 [DDD] ■ 01612-67058-4 (D)

American Concert Choir
Bach, J.S.:Cant 198, w. Marnie Nixon (sop), Elaine Bonazzi (mez), Nico Castel (ten), Peter Binder (bar), R. Craft (cnd), Columbia SO Sony Classical ("Essential Classics" series) 2-▲ SB2K 62656
Bloch, E.:America, w. L. Stokowski (cnd), Symphony of the Air *(rec 4/60)* Vanguard Classics ▲ OVC 8014 [ADD]

American Festival Chorus
Harris, R.:Sym 4, "Folksong Sym", w. V. Golschmann (cnd), American Festival Orch *(rec 1960; originally released)* Vanguard Classics ▲ OVC 4076 [ADD]

American Opera Society Chorus
Bellini, V.:I Capuleti e i Montecchi, w. L. Hurley (sop), G. Simionato (mez), R. Cassily (ten), E. Flagello (bass), A. Gamson (cnd), American Opera Society Orch [I] *(rec live, New York 10/14/58)* Melodram ("Connaisseur" series) 2-▲ CDM 27509 [ADD]
Bellini, V.:Il pirata, w. M. Callas (sop), P. M. Ferraro (ten), C. Ego (bar), N. Rescigno (cnd), American Opera Society Orch [I] *(rec live, New York 1/27/59)* Melodram 2-▲ MEL 26013
Bellini, V.:Il pirata, w. M. Callas (sop—Imogene), P. M. Ferraro (ten—Gualterio), Constantine Ego (bar—Ernesto), N. Rescigno (cnd), American Opera Society Orch *(rec 1959)* EMI Classics ▲ CDMB 64938
Bellini, V.:La straniera, w. M. Caballé (sop), B. M. Casoni (cta), A. Zambon (ten), A. Guadagno (cnd), American Opera Society Orch *(rec 1969)* Melodram 2-▲ MLO 270111 [ADD]
Berlioz, H.:Les Troyens, w. R. Resnik (mez—Dido), E. Steber (sop—Cassandra), R. Cassily (ten—Aeneas), R. Lawrence (cnd), American Opera Society Orch *(rec live, Carnegie Hall, 12/29/59 & 1/12/60)* VAI Audio 3-▲ VAIA 1006-3 [ADD]
Catalani, A.:La Wally, w. R. Tebaldi (sop), C. Bergonzi (ten), P. Glossop (bar), F. Corena (bass), F. Cleva (cnd), American Opera Society Orch *(rec Mar. 13, 1968)* Intaglio 2-▲ ING 764 [ADD]

American Repertory Singers
L. Nestor (cnd)
Ferko, F.:The Hildegard Motets—O Verbum Patris; O splendidissima gemma; Hodie aperuit; O factura Dei; O ignus Spiritus Paracliti; Laus Trinitati; O vos angeli; O speculum columbe; Nunc gaudeant *(rec St. Patrick's Church, Washington, DC, Apr 25 & 26, 1995)* ARSIS ▲ CD 102 [DDD]
Ferko, F.:Marian Motets (6)—Motet for the Immaculate Conception of the Blessed Virgin Mary; Motet for the Nativity of the Mother of God; Motet for the Annunciation; Motet for Mary, Mother of God; Motet for the Falling Asleep of the Mother of God; O frondens virga *(rec St. Patrick's Church, Washington, DC, Apr 25 & 26, 1995)* ARSIS ▲ CD 102 [DDD]
Thompson, R.:Choral Music—The Peaceable Kingdom; Bitter-Sweet; The Best of Rooms; Alleluia; Odes of Horace; The Last Invocation *(rec St. Patrick's Church in the City, Washington, DC)* ARSIS ▲ CD 103 [DDD]

American Voices
Oliveros, P.:In Memoriam Mr. Whitney, w. P. Oliveros (voc/acc) *(rec Connecticut, Mar. 10, 1991)* Mode ▲ MODE 40

American Youth Chorus
Kodály, Z.:Te Deum, w. L. Stokowski (cnd), American Youth SO *(rec 1968)* Music & Arts ▲ CD 771 [AAD]

Ametsa D'Irun Choir
Schubert, Franz:Mass 5, w. S. Chilcott (sop), R. Cyrille (alt), Vonk (ten), G. Schwarz (bass), R. Delcroix (cnd), Basque Bayonne-Côte Orch [L] Forlane ▲ FOR 16649 [DDD]

Amor Artis Chorale
Handel, G.F.:Acis & Galatea, w. J. Baird (sop), L. Hirst (mez), S. Oosting (ten), J. Ostendorf (b-bar), J. Somary (cnd), Amor Artis Orch [E] Newport Classic 2-▲ NC 60045 [DDD]
Handel, G.F.:Judas Maccabaeus, w. Heather Harper (sop), Helen Watts (cta), Alexander Young (ten), John Shirley-Quirk (bass), J. Somary (cnd), English CO [E] *(rec 1979)* Vanguard Classics 2-▲ OVC 4071/72 [ADD]
Handel, G.F.:Judas Maccabaeus (sels), w. Heather Harper (sop), Helen Watts (cta), Alexander Young (ten), John Shirley-Quirk (bar), J. Somary (cnd), English CO Vanguard Classics ▲ OVC 4073 [ADD]
Handel, G.F.:Messiah, w. Margaret Price (sop), Yvonne Minton (mez), Alexander Young (ten), Justino Diaz (bass), J. Somary (cnd), English CO [E] *(rec 1970)* Vanguard Classics ▲ OVC 4020 [ADD]
Handel, G.F.:Messiah, w. Margaret Price (sop), Yvonne Minton (mez), Alexander Young (ten), Justino Diaz (bass), J. Somary (cnd), English CO [E] *(rec 1970)* Vanguard Classics 2-▲ OVC 4018/19 [ADD]
Handel, G.F.:Theodora, w. H. Harper (sop), M. Lehane (mez), M. Forrester (cta), A. Young (ten), J. Lawrenson (bar), J. Somary (cnd), English CO [E] *(rec 1968)* Vanguard Classics 2-▲ OVC 4074/5 [ADD]

Amor Artis Chorale (cont.)
Mozart, W.A.:Requiem, w. Lorna Haywood (sop), D'Anna Fortunado (mez), Partick Romero (ten), John Cheek (bass), J. Sommary (cnd), Amor Artis Orch [period instrs] *(rec St. Jean Baptiste Church, New York City, Mar 1996)* Vox Classics ▲ VOX 7534 [DDD]
Saint-Saëns, C.:Requiem, w. Hewes (sgr), Weld (sgr), MacMaster (sgr), Watson (sgr), J. Somary (cnd), Amor Artis Orch *(rec live)* Premier ▲ PRCD 1025 [DDD]

Ampleforth Abbey Monks' Choir
Vision of Peace:The Way of the Monk *(rec Ampleforth Abbey, Apr 25-28, 1994 & Apr 5-7)* Omega ▲ OCD 1017 [DDD]

Amsterdam Baroque Choir
Biber, H. von:Requiem à 15, w. E. Bongers (sop), A. Grimm (sop), K. Wessel (alt), P. de Groot (alt), M. Reyans (ten), S. Davies (ten), R. Steur (bass), K.-J. de Koning (bass), T. Koopman (cnd), Amsterdam Baroque Orch Erato ▲ 91725
Biber, H. von:Vesperae longiores ac breviores una cum litaniis Laurentanis, w. E. Bongers (sop), A. Grimm (sop), K. Wessel (alt), P. de Groot (alt), M. Reyans (ten), S. Davies (ten), R. Steur (bass), K.-J. de Koning (bass), T. Koopman (cnd), Amsterdam Baroque Orch Erato ▲ 91725
Purcell, H.:The Fairy Queen, w. C. Bott (sop), J. Thomas (ten), M. Schopper (bass), T. Koopman (cnd), Amsterdam Baroque Orch Erato 2-▲ 98507-2

Amsterdam Phil Chorus
Beethoven, L. van:Fant Pno, Op. 80, "Choral Fant", w. Lili Kraus (pno), G. Rivoli (cnd), Amsterdam PO FNAC Music ("Via Classics" series) ▲ 642316

Amsterdam Schola Cantorum
The Ecclesiastical Year in Gregorian Chant Sony Classical ("Essential Classics" series) ▲ SBK 47670 ■ SBT 47670

Amsterdam Toonkunst Choir
Verdi, G.:Requiem Mass, w. I. Auez (sop), L. Fischer (cta), L. van Tulder (ten), H. Schey (bar), C. Schuricht (cnd), Royal Concertgebouw Orch *(rec live, Amsterdam, Nov. 2, 1939)* Archipon 2-▲ ARC 3.2/3 (m) [ADD]

Ancient Consort Singers
J. Alexander (cnd)
Spanish Renaissance Music from the Old & New World, w. Ancient Instrumental Ensemble [cnd:Ron Purcell] *(rec 1980)* Entrée ▲ 0007-2 [ADD]

Angel Vocal Ensemble
Guardian Angel:Songs & Prayers PHD ▲ PHD 570014

Angelicum de Puebla
B.J. Echenique (cnd)
Padilla, J.G. de:Maitines de Natividad, w. Schola Cantorum Urtext ▲ URT 2004 [DDD]

Anonymous 4 [Ruth Cunningham, Marsha Genensky, Susan Hellauer, Johanna Rose]
An English Ladymass:Medieval Chant & Polyphony Harmonia Mundi ▲ HMU 907080 ■ HMU 407080
The Lily & the Lamb:Chant & Polyphony from Medieval England Harmonia Mundi France ▲ HMU 907125 ■ HMU 407125
Love's Illusion:Courtly Love Songs of Medieval France from the Montpellier Codex Harmonia Mundi USA ▲ HMU 907109 ■ HMU 407109
Musica Humana, w. Françoise Atlan (mez), John Fleagle (ten/hp), Crawford Young (lt), Ensemble Discantus, Ensemble Gilles Binchois, Ensemble Organum, Gothic Voices, Greece Byzantine Choir, Hilliard Ensemble, Musica Nova, et al. L'Empreinte Digitale ▲ ED 13047
On Yoolis Night:Medieval Carols & Motets *(rec Nov. 23-25, 1992)* Harmonia Mundi USA ▲ HMU 907099 ■ HMU 407099
A Star in the East:Medieval Hungarian Christmas Music Harmonia Mundi ▲ HMU 907139 ■ HMU 407139

M. Wright (cnd)
Einhorn, R.:Voices of Light, w. Susan Narucki (sop), Corrie Pronk (alt), Frank Hameleers (ten), Henk van Heijnsbergen (b-bar), Ronald Hoogeveen (vn), Harm Bakker (vl), Michael Feves (vl), Naomi Hirschfeld (vl), S. Mercurio (cnd), Netherlands Radio PO, Netherlands Radio Chorus *(rec Music Center of the Netherlands Radio & TV, Aug 23-25, 1995)* Sony Classical ▲ SK 62006 [DDD]

Gus Anton Concert Choir
Schubert, Franz:Choral Part-Songs [w. vocal soloists, hn qt, pno] Koch Schwann ▲ CD 314022 & 314023 [ADD]

Ardwyn Singers
Mahler, G.:Sym 2, w. Benita Valente (sop), Maureen Forrester (cta), G. Kaplan (cnd), London SO, BBC Welsh Chorus, Cardiff Polyphonic Choir, Dyfed Choir Conifer Classics 2-▲ 75605-51277-2 [DDD]

Arena di Verona Chorus
Donizetti, G.:Requiem Mass, w. L. Pavarotti (ten), M. Cortez (ten), R. Bruson (bar), P. Washington (bass), G. Fackler (cnd), Arena di Verona Orch London ("Ovation" series) ▲ 425043-2 [ADD]
Verdi, G.:Don Carlos, w. M. Caballé (sop), F. Cossotto (mez), P. Domingo (ten), P. Cappuccilli (bar), G. Petkov (bar), E. Inbal (cnd), Arena di Verona Orch [I] *(rec live 7/2/69)* Melodram 3-▲ MEL 37057 (m) [AAD]
Verdi, G.:Ernani, w. I. Ligabue (sop), F. Corelli (ten), P. Cappuccilli (bar), R. Raimondi (bass), O. de Fabritiis (cnd), Arena di Verona Orch *(rec live, Verona 7/15/72)* Golden Age of Opera 2-▲ GAO 131/32 [ADD]
Verdi, G.:Nabucco, w. Monica Pick-Hieronimi (sop), Anna Schiatti (sop), Mina Blum (sop), Angelo Casertano (ten), Gilberto Maffezzoni (ten), Paolo Gavanelli (bass), Paata Burchuladze (bass), Franco Federici (bass), A. Guadagno (cnd), Arena di Verona Orch *(rec Berlin, Spring 1996)* Koch Schwann 2-▲ SCH CD 364272

Guido d'Arezzo Chorus
Salieri, A.:Axur, Re d'Ormus, w. A. Martin (bar), E. Mei (sop), C. Rayam (ten), E. Nova (bass), A. Vespasiani (mez), M. Valenti (sop), R. Clemencic (cnd), Guido d'Arezzo Orch [I] *(rec live 1989)* Nuova Era 3-▲ 6852/54 [DDD]

Argenteul Vittoria Choir
P. Piquemal, Marco (cnd)
Fauré, G.:Messe basse, w. B. Thomas (cnd), Bernard Thomas CO, Michel Piquemal Vocal Ensemble, Petits Chanteurs de Paris Forlane ▲ FRL 16536 [DDD]
Fauré, G.:Requiem, w. B. Thomas (cnd), Bernard Thomas CO, Michel Piquemal Vocal Ensemble, Petits Chanteurs de Paris Forlane ▲ FRL 16536 [DDD]

Arizona Chamber Choir
Maslanka, D.:Mass, w. Lydia Catherine Easley (sop), Charles Roe (bar), Jane Smith (org), G.I. Hanson (cnd), Univ of Arizona Wind Orch, Univ of Arizona Sym Choir, Tuscon Boys' Chorus *(rec St. Thomas the Apostle Church, Tuscon, Arizona, Apr 29-30, 1996)* Albany 2-▲ TROY 221-22 [DDD]

Arizona State Univ Choirs
J. DeMars (cnd)
Demars, J.:An American Requiem, w. Joni Killian (sop), Linda Childs (mez), George Killian (ten), Robert La France (b-bar) *(rec Phoenix Symphony Hall, Jan 17, 1994)* Renaissance ▲ 94001 [DDD]

Armed Forces Radio Chorus
Verdi, G.:Rigoletto (sels), w. Zinka Milanov (sop), A. Toscanini (cnd), NBC SO—V'ho ingannato *(rec 1938-1944)* Minerva ▲ MN A15 [ADD]

M. Constant (cnd)
Ohana, M.:Signes *(rec 1968)* Erato ("Musifrance" series) ▲ 2292-45503-2 [ADD/DDD]

Armée Française Choir
In Honor of the 50th Anniversary of the End of the War, w. Republican Guard Orch of Harmony Socadisc ▲ 895766

Armenian Choir Sofia
B. Papazian (cnd)
Armenian Liturgical Chants Jade ▲ JAD C 056

Armenian Church School Girls' Choir Old Jerusalem
Fleischer, T.:In the Mountains of Armenia, w. V. Lepejian (nar), C. Maovsessian (cl) Opus One ▲ Cd 158 [DDD]

Ronald Arnatt Chorale
Holst, G.:The Planets, w. W. Susskind (cnd), St. Louis SO, Missouri Singers Vox Box 2-▲ CDX 5105 [ADD]

CHORAL GROUPS

Vassil Arnaudov Sofia Chamber Choir
T. Pavlovich (cnd)
Schumann, R.:Choral Music, w. I.Stiglich (pno/org)—Tamburnischlägerin; Waldmädchen; Klosterfräulein; Soldatenbraut; Meerfey; Die Capelle; Rosmarien; Des Knaben Wunderhorn:Jäger Wolgemuth; Das verlassene Mägdlein; Der Bleicherin Nachtlied; In Meeres Mitten ist ein offener Landen; Mailied; Frühlingslied; An die Nachtigall; An den Abendstern; Nänie; Triolett; Spruch; Sommerruh; Chor der Houris aus das Paradies und die Peri; Ländliches Lied; Lied Gega ▲ GD 144 [DDD]
I. Stiglich (cnd)
Nightingales, w. T. Pavlovitch (pno/org) Gega ▲ GD 195
Gunther Arndt Chorus
Lehár, F.:Paganini (sels), w. Melitta Muszely (sop), Rudolf Schock (ten), Siegfried Borries (vn), W. Schmidt-Boelcke (cnd), FFB Orch Emperor Operetta ▲ KO 86343
Lehár, F.:Schön ist die Welt (sels), w. Renate Holm (sop), Rudolf Schock (ten), F. Fox (cnd), FFB Orch Emperor Operetta ▲ KO 86344

Ars Laeta Vocal Group
Martin, F.:Requiem, w. E. Speiser (sop), R. Bollen (cta), E. Tappy (ten), P. Lagger (bass), A. Luy (org), F. Martin (cnd), Swiss-Italian Orch, Union Chorale, Choir of Our Lady of Lausanne *(rec live, May 4, 1973)* Jecklin-Disco ▲ JD 631-2 [ADD]
Ars Pulcherrima Artium Chorus
Grétry, A.-E.-M.:Denys le tyran, w. S. Donzelli (sgr), R. Franceschetto (sgr), C. Di Segni (ten), B. De Simone (bar), F. Vizioli (cnd), Italian International Orch [F] *(rec live, Fermo, Palazzo Sassatelli, 1989)* Memories ▲ DR 3106 [DDD]
Arte Antica
M. Jaenike (cnd)
Pergolesi, G.B.:Vocal Music, w. A. Miskell (ten)—Laudate Pueri; Messa Solenne; Salve Regina for High Voice; Salve Regina for 2 High Voices & Orchestra; Ten Part Mass in G (sels.) Cambria ▲ 1039 [ADD]
Les Arts Florissants Chorus
Lully, J.-B.:Atys, w. Agnès Mellon (sop), Guillemette Laurens (mez), Guy de Mey (ten), Jean-François Gardeil (bar), W. Christie (cnd), Les Arts Florissants [F] Harmonia Mundi France 3-▲ HMC 901257/59 [DDD];
Rameau, J.P.:Nélée et Myrthis, w. A. Mellon (sop—Myrthis), D. Michel-Dansac (sop—Maid), C. Pelon (sop—Maid), F. Semellaz (sop—Corinne), J. Corréas (bass—Nélée), W. Christie (cnd), Les Arts Florissants [F] *(rec 5/91)* Harmonia Mundi France ▲ HMC 901381
Rameau, J.P.:Pygmalion, w. A. Mellon (sop—Céphise), D. Michel-Dansac (sop—La Statue), S. Piau (sop—L'Amour), H. Crook (ten—Pygmalion), W. Christie (cnd), Les Arts Florissants [F] *(rec 5/91)* Harmonia Mundi France ▲ HMC 901381
Asko Choir
Boogman, W.:La Disciplina Dei sentimenti, w. Charlotte Riedijk (nar), Jan Panis (sound projection), Hans Tutschku (sound projection), M. Foster (cnd), Asko Ensemble *(rec Muziekcentrum Vredenburg Utrecht, Netherlands, Dec 17, 1993)* Donemus ▲ CV 57 [DDD]
Athens Sym Chorus
Glanville-Hicks, P.:Nausicaa, w. Teresa Stratas (sop—Nausicaa), Sophia Steffan (cta—Queen Arete), Michalis Heliotis (ten—Antinous/Priest), George Moutsios (ten—Eurymachus), Edward Ruhl (ten—Phemius), George Tsantikos (ten—Clytoneus), Vassilis Koundouris (bar—Messenger), John Modenos (bar—Aethon), Spiro Malas (bass—King Alcinous), C. Surinach (cnd), Athens SO *(rec Athens Festival, 1961)* CRI ▲ CD 695 [ADD]
Glanville-Hicks, P.:Nausicaa (sels), w. Teresa Stratas (sop), Spiro Malas (bass), Michalis Helii (sgr), Michalis Heliots (sgr), George Moutsio (sgr), Edward Ruhl (sgr), Sophia Steffan (sop), George Tsantikos (sgr), C. Surinach (cnd), Athens SO CRI ▲ CD 695 [ADD]
Atherstone Choral Society
Showtime, w. Royal Engineers Orch Bandleader ▲ BND 5084 [DDD]
Athestis Chorus
F.M. Bressan (cnd)
Battiato, F.:Messa Arcaica, w. Akemi Sakamoto (mez), Franco Battiato (voc), Filippo Destrieri (kbd/cmpt), Carlo Guaitoli (pno), Angelo Privitera (kbd/cmpt), A. Ballista (cnd), Italian Virtuosi Hemisphere ▲ 837234-2
Beethoven, L. van:Sym 9, "Choral Sym", w. P. Maag (cnd), Padua & Venice CO *(rec Basilica di S. Antonio, Padova, Italy, Dec 20, 1994)* Arts Music ▲ 47248-2 [DDD]
Atlanta Chamber Chorus
Bach, J.S.:Magnificat, BWV 243, w. P. Jensen (sop), D. Upshaw (sop), M. Simpson (mez), D. Gordon (ten), W. Stone (bar), R. Shaw (cnd), Atlanta SO Telarc ▲ CD 80194 [DDD]
Bach, J.S.:Mass in b, BWV 232, w. S. McNair (sop), G. Simpson (mez), D. Ziegler (mez), J. Aler (ten), W. Stone (bar), T. Paul (bass), R. Shaw (cnd), Atlanta SO [L] Telarc 2-▲ CD 80233 [DDD]
Haydn, J.:Die Schöpfung, w. Dawn Upshaw (sop), Jon Humphrey (ten), John Cheek (bass), R. Shaw (cnd), Atlanta SO [E] Telarc 2-▲ CD 80298 [DDD]
Vivaldi, A.:Gloria, RV.589, w. D. Upshaw (sop), P. Jensen (sop), M. Simpson (mez), D. Gordon (ten), W. Stone (bar), R. Shaw (cnd), Atlanta SO Telarc ▲ CD 80194 [DDD]
Atlanta Choral Guild
The Joy of Christmas, w. Newman, Anthony (org), Chestnut Brass Company [cnd:William Noll], Choral Guild of Atlanta Brass & Percussion, Benjamin Harms (timp), Walter Huff (org) Sony Classical ▲ SFK 62698 ■ SFT 62698
Atlanta Sym Chorus
Beethoven, L. van:Elegischer Gesang, "Sanft wie du lebtest", w. R. Shaw (cnd), Atlanta SO [chorus & string orch. performance] Telarc ▲ CD 80248 [DDD]
Beethoven, L. van:Mass, Op. 86, w. H. Schellenberg (mez), M. Simpson (mez), J. Humphrey (ten), M. Myers (ten), R. Shaw (cnd), Atlanta SO [L] Telarc ▲ CD 80248 [DDD]
Beethoven, L. van:Meeresstille und glückliche Fahrt, w. R. Shaw (cnd), Atlanta SO [G] Telarc ▲ CD 80248 [DDD]
Beethoven, L. van:Missa Solemnis, w. S. McNair (sop), Janice Taylor (mez), J. Aler (ten), T. Krause (bar), R. Shaw (cnd), Atlanta SO [L] Telarc 2-▲ CD 80150 [DDD]
Beethoven, L. van:Sym 9, "Choral Sym", w. B. Valente (sop), F. Kopleff (cta), J. Hadley (ten), J. Cheek (bass), R. Shaw (cnd), Atlanta SO Pro Arte ▲ CDD 245 [DDD]
Berlioz, H.:Requiem, "Grande Messe des Morts", w. J. Aler (ten), R. Shaw (cnd), Atlanta SO [L] Telarc 2-▲ CD 80109-2 [DDD]
Bernstein, L.:Chichester Psalms, w. R. Shaw (cnd), Atlanta SO [He] Telarc ▲ CD 80181 [DDD]
Bernstein, L.:Missa brevis, w. D. L. Ragin (ct), R. Shaw (cnd), Atlanta SO [L] Telarc ▲ CD 80181 [DDD]
Boito, A.:Mefistofele (sels), w. Cheek (sgr), R. Shaw (cnd), Atlanta SO—Prologue [I] Telarc 2-▲ CD 80109-2 [DDD]
Borodin, A.:Prince Igor (Polovtsian dances), w. R. Shaw (cnd), Atlanta SO [R] Telarc ▲ CD 80039 [DDD]
Brahms, J.:Alto Rhap, w. M. Horne (mez), R. Shaw (cnd), Atlanta SO [G] Telarc ▲ CD 80176 [DDD]
Brahms, J.:Ein Deutsches Requiem, w. A. Augér (sop), R. Stilwell (bar), R. Shaw (cnd), Atlanta SO [G] Telarc 2-▲ CD 80092 [DDD]
Brahms, J.:Gesang der Parzen, w. R. Shaw (cnd), Atlanta SO [G] Telarc ▲ CD 80176 [DDD]
Brahms, J.:Nänie, w. R. Shaw (cnd), Atlanta SO [G] Telarc ▲ CD 80176 [DDD]
Brahms, J.:Schicksalslied, w. R. Shaw (cnd), Atlanta SO [G] Telarc ▲ CD 80176 [DDD]
Britten, B.:War Requiem, w. L. Haywood (sop), A. Rolfe-Johnson (ten), B. Luxon (bar), R. Shaw (cnd), Atlanta SO [L] Telarc 2-▲ CD 80157 [DDD]
Choral Masterpieces, w. R. Shaw (cnd), Atlanta SO Telarc ▲ CD 80119 [DDD]
Christmas Favorites with Robert Shaw, w. R. Shaw (cnd), Atlanta SO Vox 90s ■ V9-9901
Christmas with Robert Shaw, w. R. Shaw (cnd), Atlanta SO Allegretto ▲ ACD 8409 [ADD]
Duruflé, M.:Requiem, w. Blegen, Morris, Shaw, Atlanta SO [L] Telarc ▲ CD 80135 [DDD]
Dvořák, A.:Te Deum, w. R. Shaw (cnd), Atlanta SO [L] Telarc ▲ CD 80287 [DDD]
Fauré, G.:Requiem, w. J. Blegen (sop), J. Morris (bass), R. Shaw (cnd), Atlanta SO [L] Telarc ▲ CD 80135 [DDD]
Glass, Philip:Itaipu, w. R. Shaw (cnd), Atlanta SO Sony Classical ▲ SK 46352 [DDD]

Atlanta Sym Chorus (cont.)
Grand & Glorious:Great Operatic Choruses, w. R. Shaw (cnd), Atlanta SO, A. Howard (asst choral cnd) Telarc ▲ CD 80333 [DDD]
Handel, G.F.:Messiah, w. Kaaren Erickson (sop), Sylvia McNair (sop), Alfreda Hodgson (cta), Jon Humphrey (ten), Richard Stilwell (bar), R. Shaw (cnd), Atlanta SO [E] Telarc ▲ CD 80103 [DDD]; ■ CS 30103 (D)
Handel, G.F.:Messiah, w. Kaaren Erickson (sop), Sylvia McNair (sop), Alfreda Hodgson (cta), Jon Humphrey (ten), Richard Stilwell (bar), R. Shaw (cnd), Atlanta SO [E] Telarc 2-▲ CD 80093-2 [DDD]
Hindemith, P.:When Lilacs Last In The Dooryard Bloom'd, w. Jan DeGaetani (mez), William Stone (bar), R. Shaw (cnd), Atlanta SO [E] Telarc ▲ CD 80132 [DDD]
Janácek, L.:Slavonic Mass, w. C. Brewer (sop), M. Simpson (mez), K. Dent (ten), R. Roloff (bass), R. Shaw (cnd), Atlanta SO [Sla] Telarc ▲ CD 80287 [DDD]
Mahler, G.:Sym 8, w. R. Shaw (cnd), Atlanta SO [G] Telarc ▲ CD 80267 [DDD]
The Many Moods of Christmas, w. R. Shaw (cnd), Atlanta SO Telarc ▲ CD 80087 [DDD] ■ CS 30087 (D)
Mendelssohn, F.:Elijah, w. Barbara Bonney (sop), Henriette Schellenberg (sop), Florence Quivar (mez), Marietta Simpson (mez), Reid Bartelme (trb), Jerry Hadley (ten), Richard Clement (ten), Thomas Hampson (bar), Thomas Paul (bar), R. Shaw (cnd), Atlanta SO [E] *(rec Symphony Hall, Woodruff Arts Center, Atlanta, GA, Nov. 5-7, 1994)* Telarc 2-▲ CD 80389 [DDD]
Mozart, W.A.:Missa, K.427, w. Edith Wiens (sop), Delores Ziegler (mez), John Aler (ten), William Stone (bar), R. Shaw (cnd), Atlanta SO [L] Telarc 2-▲ CD 80150 [DDD]
Mozart, W.A.:Requiem, w. A. Augér (sop), D. Ziegler (mez), J. Hadley (ten), T. Krause (bar), R. Shaw (cnd), Atlanta SO [L] Telarc ▲ CD 80128 [DDD]
Orff, C.:Carmina burana, w. J. Blegen (sop), W. Brown (ten), H. Hagegård (bar), R. Shaw (cnd), Atlanta SO [G, L] Telarc ▲ CD 80056 [DDD]
Poulenc, F.:Stabat mater, w. C. Goerke (sop), R. Shaw (cnd), Atlanta SO *(rec Atlanta, Nov. 7-8, 1993)* Telarc ▲ CD 80362 [DDD]
Rachmaninoff, S.:The Bells, w. R. Shaw (cnd), Atlanta SO *(rec Atlanta, Nov 4-5, 1995)* Telarc ▲ CD 80365 [DDD]
Ravel, M.:Daphins et Chloé, w. C. Smith (fl), Y. Levi (cnd), Atlanta SO *(rec May 24-25, 1993)* Telarc ▲ CD 80352 [DDD]
Ravel, M.:Pavane pour une infante défunte, w. Y. Levi (cnd), Atlanta SO *(rec May 24-25, 1993)* Telarc ▲ CD 80352 [DDD]
Schubert, Franz:Mass 2, w. D. Upshaw (sop), D. Gordon (ten), W. Stone (bass), R. Shaw (cnd), Atlanta SO [L] Telarc ▲ CD 80212 [DDD]
Schubert, Franz:Mass 6, w. B. Valente (sop), M. Simpson (mez), J. Humphrey (ten), G. Siebert (ten), M. Myers (ten), R. Shaw (cnd), Atlanta SO [L] Telarc ▲ CD 80212 [DDD]
Stravinsky, I.:Sym of Psalms, w. R. Shaw (cnd), Atlanta SO [L] Telarc ▲ CD 80254 [DDD]
Szymanowski, K.:Stabat Mater, w. C. Goerke (sop), M. Simpson (mez), V. Ledbetter (bar), R. Shaw (cnd), Atlanta SO *(rec Atlanta, Nov. 7-8, 1993)* Telarc ▲ CD 80362 [DDD]
Verdi, G.:Choruses, w. R. Shaw (cnd), Atlanta SO—from Aida, Don Carlos, Macbeth, Nabucco, Otello [I] Telarc 2-▲ CD 80152 [DDD] 2-■ CS 30152 (D)
Verdi, G.:Requiem Mass, w. V. Dunn (sop), D. Curry (cta), J. Hadley (ten), P. Plishka (bass), R. Shaw (cnd), Atlanta SO [L] Telarc 2-▲ CD 80152 [DDD] 2-■ CS 30152 (D)
Verdi, G.:Te Deum, w. R. Shaw (cnd), Atlanta SO [G] Telarc 2-▲ CD 80092 [DDD]
Verdi, G.:Te Deum, w. R. Shaw (cnd), Atlanta SO [L] Telarc 2-▲ CD 80109-2 [DDD]
Walton, W.:Belshazzar's Feast, w. W. Stone (bar), R. Shaw (cnd), Atlanta SO [E] Telarc ▲ CD 80181 [DDD]

Audite Nova
Chausson, E.:Duos, "La nuit" & "Le réveil", w. D. Collot (sop), B. Vinson (mez), J. Bouillat (ten), G. Wieclaw (bass), E. Strosser (pno), C. Desert (pno), J. Sourisse (cnd), Jean Sourisse Ensemble FNAC Music ▲ 592224 [DDD]
Debussy, C.:Songs, w. D. Collot (sop), B. Vinson (mez), J. Bouillat (ten), G. Wieclaw (bass), C. Desert (pno), E. Strosser (pno), J. Sourisse (cnd), Jean Sourisse Ensemble—3 chansons de Chateau D'Orleans FNAC Music ▲ 592224 [DDD]
Fauré, G.:Pavane Orch, w. D. Collot (sop), B. Vinson (mez), J. Bouillat (ten), G. Wieclaw (bass), C. Desert (pno), E. Strosser (pno), J. Sourisse (cnd), Jean Sourisse Ensemble FNAC Music ▲ 592224 [DDD]
Fauré, G.:Songs, w. D. Collot (sop), B. Vinson (mez), J. Bouillat (ten), G. Wieclaw (bass), C. Desert (pno), E. Strosser (pno), J. Sourisse (cnd), Jean Sourisse Ensemble—Le Ruisseau, Op. 22; Puisqu'ici bas, Op. 10/1, Les Djinns, Op. 12 FNAC Music ▲ 592224 [DDD]
Ravel, M.:Songs, w. D. Collot (sop), B. Vinson (mez), J. Bouillat (ten), G. Wieclaw (bass), E. Strosser (pno), C. Desert (pno), J. Sourisse (cnd), Jean Sourisse Ensemble—3 a capella songs FNAC Music ▲ 592224 [DDD]
Ryelandt, J.:Agnus Dei, w. Ingrid Kapelle (sop), Lucienne van Deyck (mez), Joseph Cornwell (ten), Huub Claessens (bass), Stephan Macleod (bass), G. Llewellyn (cnd), Royal Flanders PO, Altra Voce *(rec live, Elisabeth Hall, Antwerp, Holland, Dec 9, 1994)* Marco Polo 2-▲ 8.223785/86 [DDD]
Augsburg Cathedral Boys' Choir
Diabelli, A.:Pastoralmesse, w. R. Kammler (cnd), Munich Residenz CO Ars Musici ▲ AM 0967 [ADD]
Kempter, K.:Pastoralmesse, w. R. Kammler (cnd), Munich Residenz CO Ars Musici ▲ AM 0967 [ADD]
Mozart, W.A.:Missae Breves, w. R. Kammler (cnd), Collegium Aureum—in G, K.49; in d, K.65; in F, K.192; in D, K.194; in C, K.220; in Bb, K.275; in C, K.258; in C, K.259 [L] Deutsche Harmonia Mundi 2-▲ 77090-2-RC [DDD]
Schubert, Franz:Deutsche Messe, w. Alexander Seitz (trb), Robert Wörle (ten), Ulrich Streckmann (bass), R. Kammler (cnd), Munich Residenz CO Calig ▲ CAL 50952 [DDD]
Schubert, Franz:Mass 2, w. Alexander Seitz (trb), Robert Wörle (ten), Ulrich Streckmann (bass), R. Kammler (cnd), Munich Residenz CO Calig ▲ CAL 50952 [DDD]
R. Kammler (cnd)
Lassus, O. de:Motets—Gustate et videt; Exultate justi in Domino; Ave verum; Alma redemptoris mater; Laetentur coeli—Tunc exaltabunt; Tui sunt coeli; Confitebor tibi Domine; Vexilla regis; Surrexit pastor bonus Ars Musici ▲ 1084 [DDD]
Lassus, O. de:Vinum bonum Ars Musici ▲ 1084 [DDD]
Austrian Radio Chorus
Alcalay, L.:Una strofa di Dante, w. B. Maderna (cnd), Austrian RSO Vienna Modern Masters ▲ VMM 3020 [AAD]
Bellini, V.:Beatrice di Tenda, w. E. Gruberová (sop—Beatrice), V. Kasarova (mez—Agnese), D. Bernardini (ten—Orombello), B. Robinšak (ten—Anichino), I. Morosov (ten—Filippo Maria Visconti), D. Sumegi (bass—Rizzardo), P. Steinberg (cnd), Austrian RSO [I] *(rec live, Vienna Concert House 1/30 & 2/1/92)* Nightingale Classics 2-▲ NC 070560-2 [DDD]
Cornelius, P.:Der Barbier von Bagdad, w. S. Jurinac (sop), H. Rössl-Majdan (mez), E. Majkut (ten), R. Schock (ten), A. Poell (bass-bar), G. Frick (bass), H. Hollreiser (cnd), Austrian RSO [G] *(rec live Vienna, 1952)* Verona 2-▲ 27050/51 (m) [AA
Cornelius, P.:Der Barbier von Bagdad, w. S. Jurinac (sop), H. Rössl-Majdan (mez), E. Majkut (ten), R. Schock (ten), A. Poell (bass-bar), G. Frick (bass), H. Hollreiser (cnd), Austrian RSO *(rec live Vienna 1952)* Melodram 2-▲ MEL 27050 (m) [AAD]
Einem, G. von:Dantons Tod, w. K. Laki (sop), I. Mayr (mez), H. Hiestermann (ten), W. Hollweg (ten), T. Adam (bass-bar), K. Rydl (bass), L. Zagrosek (cnd), Austrian RSO [G] *(rec live, Salzburg, 8/13/83)* Orfeo 2-▲ 102842 [ADD]
Gluck, C.W.:Paride ed Elena, w. I. Cotrubas (sop), S. Greenberg (sop), Fontana (sgr), F. Bonisolli (ten), L. Zagrosek (cnd), Austrian RSO [I] *(rec 1983)* Orfeo 2-▲ 118842 [DDD]
Handel, G.F.:Acis & Galatea [arr Mozart], w. E. Mathis (sop), R. Gambill (ten), A R. Johnson (ten), R. Lloyd (b-bar), P. Schreier (cnd), Austrian RSO [E] Orfeo 2-▲ 133852 [DDD]
Kaufmann, D.:Heiligenlegende, w. H. M. Kneihs (speaker), G. König (rcr), E. Ortner (cnd), Austrian RSO Vienna Modern Masters ▲ VMM 3020 [AAD]
Meyerbeer, G.:Les Huguenots, w. Jeanette Scovotti (sop—Urbain), Rita Shane (sop—Marguerite de Valois), Enriqueta Tarrès (sop—Valentine), Nicolai Gedda (ten—Raoul de Nangis), Justino Diaz (bass—Marcel), Dimiter Petkov (bass—Le Comte de Saint-Bris), E. Märzendorfer (cnd), Austrian RSO *(rec Vienna, Feb 17, 1971)* Myto 2-▲ MCD 961141
Operetta Recital, w. Weikl, Bernd (bar), Austrian Radio Orch, Austrian Radio Chorus [cnd:Kurt Eichorn] Orfeo ▲ 077831

 ▲ = CD ♦ = Enhanced CD Δ = MD ■ = Cassette Tape ☐ = DCC

Austrian Radio Chorus (cont.)
Verdi, G.:I due Foscari, w. K. Ricciarelli (sop), E. Connell (sop), J. Carreras (ten), V. Bello (ten), M. Antoniak (ten), P. Cappuccilli (bar), S. Ramey (bass), F. Handlos (bass), L. Gardelli (cnd), Austrian RSO Philips 2-▲ 422426-2 [ADD]
Wagner, R.:Das Liebesverbot, w. H. Zadek (cta), L. Sorell (mez), A. Dermota (ten), K. Equiluz (ten), L. Welter (bar), Imdahl (sgr), R. Heger (cnd), Austrian RSO *(rec live, Vienna, 1962)* Melodram 2-▲ MEL 27052 [AAD]

Avignon Vocal Ensemble
Barbieri, L.:Surgite pastores, w. S. Vartolo (cnd), St. Petronio Cappella Musicale, St. Petronio Voci Bianche Chorus, Tölz Boys' Choir *(rec Oct. 3–5, 1991)* Tactus ▲ TC 551801
Campra, A.:Tancrède, w. C. Dussaut (sop—Herminie), A. Arapian (ten—Argant), J. Bona (bar—Tancrède), C. Zaffini (cnd), Provence Instrumental Ensemble—highlights *(rec 1986)* Pierre Verany ▲ PV.786111 [ADD]
Franceschini, P.:Sacred Music, w. S. Vartolo (cnd), San Petronio Cappella Musicale—Dixit Dominus a 8 for Trumpet & Violin; Laudate a Pueri a 6 for Trumpet & Violins *(rec Oct. 3–5, 1991)* Tactus ▲ TC 650001
Perti, G.A.:Messa e salmi concertati, w. S. Vartolo (cnd), San Petronio Cappella Musicale Orch, San Petronio Voci Bianche Chorus, Tölz Boys' Choir *(rec Oct. 3–5, 1991)* Tactus ▲ TC 551801
Rota, A.:Missarum liber primus, w. S. Vartolo (cnd), San Petronio Cappella Musicale Orch, San Petroni Voci Bianche Chorus, Tölz Boys' Choir *(rec Oct. 3–5, 1991)* Tactus ▲ TC 551801
Trombetti, A.:Il primo libro de motetti accomodati per cantare e far concerti, w. S. Vartolo (cnd), St. Petronio Cappella Musicale, St. Petronio Voci Bianche Chorus, Tölz Boys' Choir *(rec Oct. 3–5, 1991)* Tactus ▲ TC 551801

Ay-Kherel Ensemble
Janssen, G.:Noach, w. Claron McFadden (sop—Noach's Wife), Lieuwe Visser (bass—Noach), Huib Rooymans (nar), L. Vis (cnd), New Artis Orch, Mondriaan Quartet *(rec Amsterdam, June 20–21, 1994)* Donemus 2-▲ CV 42/43

Azuoliukas Choir
V. Miskinis (cnd)
Duruflé, M.:Mass, "Cum jubilo" Jade ▲ 28667-2
Poulenc, F.:Laudes de Saint Antoine de Padoue Jade ▲ 28667-2
Poulenc, F.:Quatre petites prières de Saint François d'Assise Jade ▲ 28667-2

Azusa Pacific Univ Choir
Amen:A Gospel Celebration, w. Central State Univ Chorus, Cincinnati Pops Chorale, Jennifer Holliday (sgr), Maureen McGovern (sgr), Lou Rawls (sgr), Cincinnati Pops Orch [cnd:Erich Kunzel] *(rec Feb. 28–Mar. 1, 1993)* Telarc ▲ CD 80315 [DDD] ■ CD 80315

Bach Choir
Bach, J.S.:St. Matthew Passion, w. F. Lott (sop), A. Hodgson (cta), R. Tear (ten), J. Shirley-Quirk (bar), S. Roberts (bar), D. Willcocks (cnd), Thames CO [E] ASV Quicksilva 3-▲ ASQ 324 [ADD]
Bennett, Richard Rodney:Spells, w. J. Manning (sop), D. Willcocks (cnd), Philharmonia Orch [E] Continuum ▲ CCD 1030
Vaughan Williams, R.:Epithalamion, w. S. Roberts (b-bar), H. Shelley (pno), D. Willcocks (cnd), London PO EMI Classics ▲ CDM 64730
Vaughan Williams, R.:Riders to the Sea, w. M. Davies (cnd), London PO EMI Classics ▲ CDM 64730
Walton, W.:Belshazzar's Feast, w. G. Howell (bass), D. Willcocks (cnd), Philharmonia Orch [E] Chandos ▲ CHAN 8760 [DDD]
Walton, W.:Coronation Te Deum, w. J. Scott (org), D. Willcocks (cnd), Philharmonia Orch [L] Chandos ▲ CHAN 8760 [DDD]
Walton, W.:Gloria, w. A. Gunson (cta), N. Mackie (ten), S. Roberts (bar), D. Willcocks (cnd), Philharmonia Orch [L] Chandos ▲ CHAN 8760 [DDD]
Walton, W.:In Honour of the City of London, w. D. Willcocks (cnd), Philharmonia Orch [E] Chandos ▲ CHAN 8998 [DDD]

D. Willcocks (cnd)
Family Carols, w. Fanfare Trumpeters of the Royal Military School of Music, Graham Ashton Brass Ensemble, John Scott (org) Chandos ▲ CHAN 8973 [DDD]
Gabrieli, G.:Choral Music, w. Wilbraham Brass Soloists, King's College Choir Cambridge EMI Classics ("Doublefforte" series) 2-▲ CDFB 68631
Scheidt, S.:Choral Music, w. Wilbraham Brass Soloists, King's College Choir Cambridge EMI Classics ("Doublefforte" series) 2-▲ CDFB 68631
Schütz, H.:Choral Music, w. Wilbraham Brass Soloists, King's College Choir Cambridge EMI Classics ("Doublefforte" series) 2-▲ CDFB 68631
Walton, W.:Choral Music—Where does the uttered music go? (1946); Antiphon (1977); Jubilate Deo (1972) Chandos ▲ CHAN 8998 [DDD]
Walton, W.:Christmas Carol Settings—Mae we joy now in this feast (1931); What cheer? (1961); All this time (1970); King Herod and the Cock (1978) Chandos ▲ CHAN 8998 [DDD]

Bach Collegium Chorus
Bach, J.S.:Cant 6 Hänssler Classic 4-▲ HAN 98837 [AAD]
Bach, J.S.:Cant 31 Hänssler Classic 4-▲ HAN 98837 [AAD]
Bach, J.S.:Cant 34 Hänssler Classic 4-▲ HAN 98837 [AAD]
Bach, J.S.:Cant 42 Hänssler Classic 4-▲ HAN 98837 [AAD]
Bach, J.S.:Cant 43 Hänssler Classic 4-▲ HAN 98837 [AAD]
Bach, J.S.:Cant 108 Hänssler Classic 4-▲ HAN 98837 [AAD]
Bach, J.S.:Cant 128 Hänssler Classic 4-▲ HAN 98837 [AAD]
Bach, J.S.:Cant 172 Hänssler Classic 4-▲ HAN 98837 [AAD]
Bach, J.S.:Cant 175 Hänssler Classic 4-▲ HAN 98837 [AAD]
Bach, J.S.:Cant 182 Hänssler Classic 4-▲ HAN 98837 [AAD]
Bach, J.S.:Cant 184 Hänssler Classic 4-▲ HAN 98837 [AAD]
Bach, J.S.:Easter Oratorio Hänssler Classic 4-▲ HAN 98837 [AAD]
Cherubini, L.:Requiem Mass 2, w. H. Rilling (cnd), Stuttgart Gächinger Kantorei Hänssler Classic 2-▲ HAN 98981 [DDD]
Haydn, J.:Mass 10, "Kriegsmesse", "Paukenmesse", w. Gächinger Kantorei Hänssler Classic 2-▲ HAN 98981 [DDD]

Bach Guild Chorus
Bach, J.S.:Cant 78, w. T. Stich-Randall (sop), D. Hermann (sop), A. Dermota (ten), H. Braun (bar), F. Prohaska (cnd), Bach Guild Orch [G] *(rec May 1954)* Vanguard Classics ("The Bach Guild" series) ▲ OVC 2009 [ADD]
Bach, J.S.:Cant 106, "Actus tragicus", w. T. Stich-Randall (sop), D. Hermann (sop), A. Dermota (ten), H. Braun (bar), F. Prohaska (cnd), Bach Guild Orch [G] *(rec May 1954)* Vanguard Classics ("The Bach Guild" series) ▲ OVC 2009 [ADD]

Back Bay Chorale
Kyr, R.:Unseen Rain, w. B. Taylor (cnd), Project Ars Nova Ensemble *(rec 1st & 2nd Church, Boston, MA, Feb. 1993)* New Albion ▲ NA 075
Paine, J.K.:St. Peter, w. J. Ommerlé (sop), A. Fortunato (mez), P. Kelly (ten), D. Evitts (bar), G. Schuller (cnd), Boston Pro Arte CO [E] *(rec live in concert at Sanders Theater, Cambridge, Mass., 5/21/89)* GM 2-▲ 2027CD 2

Baltimore Sym Chorus
Berlioz, H.:Hymne des Marseillais, w. S. McNair (sop), R. Leech (ten), D. Zinman (cnd), Baltimore SO Telarc ▲ CD 80164 [DDD]
Ives, C.:Holidays, w. D. Zinman (cnd), Baltimore SO *(rec Joseph Meyerhoff Symphony Hall, Baltimore, MD, Sept 1994)* Argo ▲ 444860-2 [DDD]

Bamberg Oratorio Chorus
Hoffmann, E.T.A.:Aurora, w. Thomas Rieger (trb), Maltraud Meier (mez), Siegfried Schulze (bass), Koch (sgr), Ohlmann (sgr), H. Dechant (cnd), Bamberg Youth Orch Bayer 3-▲ 100276-78

Bamberg RIAS Chorus
Smetana, B.:The Bartered Bride, w. P. Lorengar (sop), F. Wunderlich (ten), G. Frick (bass), R. Kempe (cnd), Bamberg SO [G] *(rec ca. 1963)* EMI Classics ("Studio" series) 2-▲ CDMB 64002

Bamberg Sym Chorus
Bruckner, A.:Missa solemnis, w. C. Oelze (sop), C. Schubert (alt), J. Dümüller (ten), R. Hagen (bass), K. A. Rickenbacher (cnd), Bamberg SO Virgin Classics ▲ CDC 59060

Bamberg Sym Chorus (cont.)
Bruckner, A.:Psalm 112, w. C. Oelze (sop), C. Schubert (alt), J. Dümüller (ten), R. Hagen (bass), K. A. Rickenbacher (cnd), Bamberg SO Virgin Classics ▲ CDC 59060
Bruckner, A.:Psalm 114, w. C. Oelze (sop), C. Schubert (alt), J. Dümüller (ten), R. Hagen (bass), K. A. Richenbacher (cnd), Bamberg SO Virgin Classics ▲ CDC 59060
Bruckner, A.:Psalm 150, w. C. Oelze (sop), C. Schubert (alt), J. Dümüller (ten), R. Hagen (bass), K. A. Rickenbacher (cnd), Bamberg SO Virgin Classics ▲ CDC 59060
Donizetti, G.:Requiem Mass, w. C. Studer (sop), H. Müller-Molinari (mez), A. Baldin (ten), J. P. Bogart (bass), J.-H. Rootering (bass), M. A. G. Martinez (cnd), Bamberg SO [L] Orfeo ▲ 172881 [DDD]
Mozart, W.A.:Entführung, w. S. Greenberg (sop), J. Thames (sop), J. Van Der Schaaf (ten), W. Gahmlich (ten), K. Rydl (bass), M. Viotti (cnd), Frankfurt RSO LaserLight ▲ 14117 [DDD]
Mozart, W.A.:Entführung, w. S. Greenburg (sop), J. Thames (sop), J. van der Schaaf (ten), W. Gahmlich (ten), K. Rydl (bass), Trissenaar (sgr), M. Viotti (cnd), Frankfurt RSO Capriccio 2-▲ 10 403/04
Reger, M.:Psalm 100, w. H. Stein (cnd), Bamberg SO Koch Schwann ▲ SCH 312092 [DDD]
Reger, M.:Die Weihe der Nacht, w. H. Stein (cnd), Bamberg SO Koch Schwann ▲ SCH 312092 [DDD]

Bambini di Praga
Carolling, w. Beňačková, Gabriela (sop), Lubomír Vraspír (ten), Bambini di Praga [cnd:Jaroslav Krček], Tuma (org), Prague Brass Quintet Supraphon ▲ SUP 111417 [DDD]
Orff, C.:Carmina burana, w. Zdena Kloubová (sop), Vladimir Dolezal (ten), Ivan Kusnjer (bar), G. Delogu (cnd), Prague SO, Kühn Choir *(rec live, Prague, Dec 12, 1995)* Supraphon ▲ SUP 3160
Suk, J.:Songs, Op. 15, w. B. di Praga, L. Čermáková (pno), J. Saroun (pno), B. Kulínský (cnd)—Žal; Tuzba; Společný hrob; Pastýři na jaro; Diviná voda; Vily; Pastýř a pastyřka; Zpominky; Choutka po vdaní; Kéž byVedeli [Cz] Multisonic ▲ 31 0111-2 [DDD]

B. Kulínský (cnd)
Ave Maria:Famous Sacred Choral Works, w. Prague SO Youth Chorus Multisonic ▲ MUL 310163 [DDD]
Dvořák, A.:Moravian Duets, Opp. 20, 32 & 38, w. L. Čermáková (pno) Multisonic ▲ 31 0111-2 [DDD]

Bancroft's School Chorus
Humperdinck, E.:Hänsel und Gretel, w. E. Schwarzkopf (sop), E. Grümmer (sop), A. Felbermayer (sop), M. von Ilosvay (mez), E. Schürhoff (mez), J. Metternich (bar), H. von Karajan (cnd), Philharmonia Orch, Loughton High School Chorus [G] *(rec 1953)* EMI Classics ("Studio" series) 2-▲ CDMB 69293 (m) [ADD]

Barcelona Children's Choir
Albéniz, I.:Pepita Jiménez (suite), w. Susan Chilcott (sop), Francesc Garrigosa (ten), Barcelona Children's Choir, J. Pons (cnd), Barcelona's Free Theater CO Harmonia Mundi France ▲ HMC 901537

Barcelona Gran Teatro de Liceo Chorus
Bellini, V.:Norma, w. Caballé (soprano—Norma), F. Cossotto (mez), B. Prevedi (ten), J. Carreras (ten), I. Vinco (bass), C. F. Cillario (cnd), Barcelona Teatro Liceo Orch [I] *(rec live, Barcelona 1/11/70)* Melodram 2-▲ CDM 27089 [ADD]
Bizet, G.:Les Pêcheurs de perles, w. A. Maliponte (sop—Leila), A. Kraus (ten—Nadir), S. Bruscantini (bar—Zurga), C. F. Cillario (cnd), Barcelona Teatro Liceo Orch Bongiovanni 2-▲ GB 516/17 [ADD]
Massenet, J.:Hérodiade, w. M. Caballé (sop—Salomé), D. Vejzovic (mez—Hérodiade), J. Carreras (ten—Jean), J. Pons (bar—Hérode), E. Serra (bar—Vitellius), V. Esteve (bar—High Priest), R. Kennedy (bass—Phanuel), J. Delacôte (cnd), Barcelona Teatro Liceo Orch *(rec Jan. 6, 1984)* Legato Classics 2-▲ LCD 182 [ADD]
Meyerbeer, G.:L'Africiane, w. Montserrat Caballe (sop—Selika), Christine Weidinger (sop—Inez), Miriam Ucelay (mez—Anna), Placido Domingo (ten—Vasco de Gama), Guillermo Sarabia (bar—Nelusko), Juan Thomas (b-bar—High Priest of Brahma), Dimiter Petkov (bass—Don Pedro), Juan Pons (bass—Don Diego), Eduardo Soto (bass—Grand Inquisitor), A. de Almeida (cnd), Barcelona Teatro Liceo Orch *(rec Barcelona, Nov 27, 1977)* Legato Classics 2-▲ LCD 208-2 [ADD]
Rimsky-Korsakov, N.:The Legend of the Invisible City of Kitzeh (sels), w. A. Coates (cnd), Barcelona Teatro Liceo Orch—Village Wedding Procession [Act 2]; The Battle of Kerzhenets [Act 3] *(rec Liceo Theater, Barcelona, 1928)* Claremont ▲ GSE 785061
Verdi, G.:La forza del destino (sels), w. Raina Kabalvanska (sop), Carlo Bergonzi (ten), I. Savini (cnd), Barcelona Teatro Liceo Orch *(rec live, Nov 13, 1972)* Arkadia ▲ 499

Bari Teatro Petruzzelli Chorus
Bellini, V.:I Puritani, w. K. Ricciarelli (sop), E. Jankovic (mez), C. Merritt (ten), C. Gaifa (ten), A. Riva (bass), R. Scandiuzzi (bass), G. Ferro (cnd), Sicilian SO *(rec Apr. 10, 1986)* Cetra Classic ▲ CDC 20 [ADD]
Bellini, V.:I Puritani, w. Katia Ricciarelli (sop), Eleonora Jankovic (mez), Juan Luque Carmona (ten), Carlo Gaifa (ten), Chris Merritt (ten), Roberto Scandiuzzi (bass), G. Ferro (cnd), Sicilian SO Fonit Cetra ("Digital Operas" series) 3-▲ FCT CDC 20

Baroque Choir
Odes on the Death of Henry Purcell, w. Holman, Goodman (cnd), Parley of Instruments, Baroque Orch, R. Holton (sop), R. Covey-Crump (ten), C. Daniels (ten), S. Birchall (bass) Hyperion ▲ CDA 66578 [DDD]

Baroque Choral Guild
Bach, J.S.:Cant 56, w. W. Parker (bass), N. McGegan (cnd), Arcadian Academy [G] Harmonia Mundi USA ("Nightingale" series) ▲ HMN 907601
Bach, J.S.:Cant 82, w. W. Parker (bar), N. McGegan (cnd), Arcadian Academy [G] Harmonia Mundi USA ("Nightingale" series) ▲ HMN 907601

Baroque Music Chorus
Telemann, G.P.:Der Tag des Gerichts, w. Patrice Michaels Bell (sop), Sandra Walker (mez), Karen Brunssen (mez), Bruce Fowler (ten), Kurt R. Hansen (ten), William Stone (bar), Douglas Anderson (bar), T. Wikman (cnd), Music of the Baroque Orch *(rec live, St. Paul's United Church of Christ, Feb 23, 1992)* Music of the Baroque 2-▲ MB 107

Bartók Chorus
Górecki, H.-M.:Beatus Vir, w. Tamás Altorjay (bar), T. Pál (cnd), Fricsay SO Stradivarius ▲ STV 33324 [DDD]
Górecki, H.-M.:Beatus Vir, w. T. Altorjay (bar), T. Pál (cnd), Fricsay SO Stradivarius ▲ STR 33324 [DDD]
Górecki, H.-M.:Sym 2, "Copernican Sym", w. E. Soós (sop), T. Altorjay (bar), T. Pál (cnd), Fricsay SO Stradivarius ▲ STR 33324 [DDD]

Basel Boys' Choir
Schütz, H.:Danket dem Herren, denn er ist freundlich, w. H.-M. Linde (cnd), Basel Schola Cantorum Instrumental Ensemble, Chiaroscuro Ensemble EMI Classics ("Baroque" series) ▲ CDK 65736

Basel Madrigalists
Gesellige Zeit:German Lieder, Madrigals & Instrumental Music of the 16th & 17th Centuries, w. Basel Ensemble Galliarda [cnd:Fritz Näf] Musicaphon ▲ 506803

F. Näf (cnd)
Brahms, J.:Motets Op. 74—Op. 74/1 (1877) Musiques Suisses ▲ 6124 [DDD]
Burkhard, W.:Sacred Music, w. Paolo Vignoli (ten)—Die Sintflut; Christi Leidensverkundigung; Das Ezzolied Ars Musici ▲ 1146
Eisler, H.:Gegen den Krieg Musiques Suisses ▲ 6124 [DDD]
Gesellige Zeit:German Songs, Madrigals & Instrumental Music from the 16th & 17th Centuries, w. Basel Ensemble Galliarda *(rec Reformed Church, CH-Arlesheim, Feb. 13–15, 1987)* Musicaphon ▲ 56803
Josquin Desprez:Missa, "Da Pacem" Musiques Suisses ▲ 6124 [DDD]
Resinarius, B.:Verleih uns Frieden genädiglich Musiques Suisses ▲ 6124 [DDD]
Schütz, H.:Verleih uns Frieden genädiglich Musiques Suisses ▲ 6124 [DDD]

Bastille Opera Chorus
Berlioz, H.:Béatrice et Bénédict (sels), w. Kathleen Battle (sop), M.-W. Chung (cnd), Bastille Opera Orch—Je vais le voir *(rec Salle Gounod, Bastille Opera, Paris, Nov 1993 & June 1994)* Deutsche Grammophon ▲ 447114-2 [DDD]
Saint-Saëns, C.:Samson et Dalila, w. W. Meier (mez), P. Domingo (ten), S. Ramey (bass), A. Fondary (bar), M.-W. Chung (cnd), Bastille Opera Orch EMI Classics 2-▲ CDCB 54470
Shostakovich, D.:Lady Macbeth of Mtsensk, w. M. Ewing (sop), E. Zaremba (mez), P. Langridge (ten), H. Zednik (ten), A. Haugland (bass), A. Kotcherga (bass), K. Moll (bass), S. Larin (bass), M.-W. Chung (cnd), Bastille Opera Orch Deutsche Grammophon 2-▲ 437511-2

CHORAL GROUPS

Bath Camerata
N. Perrin (cnd)
Tučapský, A.:Lauds *(rec St. George's Brandon Hill, Bristol, Jan 28, 1996)*
SOMM ▲ SOMMCD 205 [DDD]
Tučapský, A.:Lenten Motets *(rec St. George's Brandon Hill, Bristol, Jan 28, 1996)*
SOMM ▲ SOMMCD 205 [DDD]
Tučapský, A.:The Sacrifice, w. Stephen Foulkes (bar), Colin Hunt (org) *(rec Wells Cathedral, Jan 27, 1996)* SOMM ▲ SOMMCD 205 [DDD]
Tučapský, A.:The 7 Sorrows, w. Tomáš Tuláček (vn) *(rec St. George's Brandon Hill, Bristol, Jan 28, 1996)* SOMM ▲ SOMMCD 205 [DDD]

Bath Festival Chorus
Mahler, G.:Das Klagende Lied, w. J. Rodgers (sop), L. Finnie (cta), H. P. Blochwitz (ten), R. Hickox (cnd), Bournemouth SO, Waynflete Singers Chandos ▲ CHAN 9247 [DDD]

Bavarian Chorus
Handel, G.F.:Judas Maccabaeus, w. Agnes Giebel (sop), Julianna Falk (cta), Fritz Wunderlich (ten), L. Welter (bar), Pöld (sgr), R. Kubelik (cnd), Bavarian RSO [G] *(rec live 10/25/63)*
Melodram 2-▲ MEL 28026 [AAD]
Nicolai, O.:Lustigen Weiber, w. Erika Köth (sop), Hertha Töpper (mez), Maria Rogner (sgr), Hans Günter Nöcker (b-bar), Kim Borg (bass), Naan Pödl (sgr), F. Rieger (cnd), Bavarian RSO *(rec 1960's)*
Pantheon 2-▲ PHE 6660 (m)

Bavarian Radio Boys' Chorus
Bach, J.S.:Christmas Oratorio, w. E. Ameling (sop), B. Fassbaender (mez), H. Laubenthal (ten), H. Prey (bar), E. Jochum (cnd), Tölz SO—highlights Philips ("Silver Line" series) ▲ 422252-2 [ADD]

Bavarian Radio Chorus
Bach, J.S.:Mass in b, BWV 232, w. E. Jochum (cnd), Bavarian RSO—Kyrie eleison *(rec Herkulessaal, Munich, Mar. & Apr. 1980)* EMI Classics ▲ CDK 65334 [ADD]
Bach, J.S.:Mass in b, BWV 232, w. L. Marshall (sop), H. Töpper (mez), P. Pears (ten), K. Borg (bass), E. Jochum (cnd), Bavarian RSO Philips 2-▲ 438739-2
Bach, J.S.:Mass in b, BWV 232, w. Helen Donath (sop), Brigitte Fassbaender (cta), Claes H. Ahnsjö (ten), Roland Hermann (bar), Robert Holl (bass), E. Jochum (cnd), Bavarian RSO
EMI Classics ("Doublefforte" series) 2-▲ CDFB 68640
Beethoven, L. van:Fidelio, w. Elizabeth Norberg-Schulz (sop—Marzelline), Deborah Voigt (sop—Lenore), Ben Heppner (ten—Florestan), Michael Schade (ten—Jaquino), Günter von Kannaten (b-bar—Don Pizarro), Matthias Hölle (bass—Rocco), Thomas Quasthoff (bass—Don Fernando), C. Davis (cnd), Bavarian RSO, Bavarian State Opera Men's Chorus *(rec Herkulessaal der Residenz, Munich, May 15-25, 1995)* RCA Victor 2-▲ 09026-68344-2 [DDD]
Beethoven, L. van:Missa Solemnis, w. L. Orgonasova (sop), J. Rappé (ten), J.-H. Rootering (bass), C. Davis (cnd), Bavarian RSO RCA Red Seal 2-▲ 09026-60967-2
Beethoven, L. van:Sym 9, "Choral Sym", w. L. Bernstein (cnd), Bavarian RSO members, Dresden State Orch members, Kirov Theatre Orch members, London SO members, New York PO members, Orch de Paris members, Berlin Radio Chorus, Dresden Philharmonie Children's Chorus [G] *(rec live, Schauspielhaus, East Berlin, 12/25/89)* Deutsche Grammophon ▲ 429861-2 [DDD] ■ 429861-4
Bellini, V.:I Capuleti e i Montecchi (sels), w. Vesselina Kasarova (mez), F. Haider (cnd), Munich RSO—Se Romeo t'uccise un figlio RCA Red Seal ▲ 0902-668522-2 [DDD]
Bellini, V.:I Puritani, w. Edita Gruberova (sop), Katia Lytting (mez), Justin Lavender (ten), Carlo Tuand (ten), Ettore Kim (bar), Francesco Ellero d'Artegna (bass), Dankwart Siegele (bass), F. Luisi (cnd), Munich RSO Nightingale Classics 3-▲ NIG 70562
Berlioz, H.:Roméo et Juliette, w. Olga Borodina (mez), Thomas Moser (ten), Alastair Miles (bass), C. Davis (cnd), Vienna PO Philips ▲ 442134-2
Bialas, G.:Aus der Matratzengruft, w. H.-M. Schneidt (cnd), Bavarian RSO
CPO 2-▲ CPO 999204 [DDD]
Brahms, J.:Alto Rhap, w. N. Stutzmann (mez), C. Davis (cnd), Bavarian RSO
RCA Red Seal ▲ 09026-61201-2
Brahms, J.:Alto Rhap, w. A. Hodgson (cta), B. Haitink (cnd), Bavarian RSO [G] Orfeo ▲ 025821 [DDD]
Brahms, J.:Begräbnisgesang, w. B. Haitink (cnd), Bavarian RSO [G] Orfeo ▲ 025821 [DDD]
Brahms, J.:Ein Deutsches Requiem, w. M. Price (sop), T. Allen (bar), W. Sawallisch (cnd), Bavarian RSO [G] Orfeo ▲ 039101
Brahms, J.:Ein Deutsches Requiem, w. A. M. Blasi (sop), B. Terfel (b-bar), E. Schloter (org), C. Davis (cnd), Bavarian RSO [G] RCA Red Seal ▲ 09026-60868-2
Brahms, J.:Gesang der Parzen, w. B. Haitink (cnd), Bavarian RSO [G] Orfeo ▲ 025821 [DDD]
Brahms, J.:Gesang der Parzen, w. C. Davis (cnd), Bavarian RSO RCA Red Seal ▲ 09026-61201-2
Brahms, J.:Marienlieder, w. C. Davis (cnd), Bavarian RSO RCA Red Seal ▲ 09026-61201-2
Brahms, J.:Nänie, w. B. Haitink (cnd), Bavarian RSO [G] Orfeo ▲ 025821 [DDD]
Brahms, J.:Nänie, w. C. Davis (cnd), Bavarian RSO RCA Red Seal ▲ 09026-61201-2
Brahms, J.:Schicksalslied, w. C. Davis (cnd), Bavarian RSO RCA Red Seal ▲ 09026-61201-2
Bruckner, A.:Mass 1, w. E. Mathis (sop), M. Schiml (mez), W. Ochman (ten), K. Ridderbusch (bass), E. Jochum (cnd), Bavarian RSO Deutsche Grammophon ("The Originals" series) 2-▲ 447409-2
Bruckner, A.:Mass 1, w. E. Mathis (sop), M. Schiml (sop), W. Ochman (ten), K. Ridderbusch (bass), E. Jochum (cnd), Bavarian RSO [L] Deutsche Grammophon 4-▲ 423127-2 [ADD]
Bruckner, A.:Mass 2, w. E. Jochum (cnd), Bavarian RSO [L]
Deutsche Grammophon 4-▲ 423127-2 [ADD]
Bruckner, A.:Mass 2, w. E. Jochum (cnd), Bavarian RSO
Deutsche Grammophon ("The Originals" series) 2-▲ 447409-2
Bruckner, A.:Mass 3, w. K. Mattila (sop), M. Lipovšek (mez), T. Moser (ten), K. Moll (bass), C. Davis (cnd), Bavarian RSO [L] Philips ▲ 422358-2 [DDD]
Bruckner, A.:Mass 3, w. M. Stader (sop), C. Hellmann (mez), E. Haefliger (ten), K. Borg (bass), E. Jochum (cnd), Bavarian RSO Deutsche Grammophon ("The Originals" series) 2-▲ 447409-2
Bruckner, A.:Mass 3, w. M. Stader (sop), A. Hellmann (alt), E. Haefliger (ten), K. Borg (bass), E. Jochum (cnd), Bavarian RSO [L] Deutsche Grammophon 4-▲ 423127-2 [ADD]
Busoni, F.:Doktor Faust, w. H. Hillebrecht (sop), W. Cochran (ten), D. Fischer-Dieskau (bar), K. C. Kohn (bass), F. Leitner (cnd), Bavarian RSO [G]
Deutsche Grammophon ("20th Century Classics" series) 3-▲ 427413-2 [ADD]
Catalani, A.:La Wally, w. E. Marton (sop), F. Araiza (ten), A. Titus (bar), F. Ellero d'Artegna (bass), P. Steinberg (cnd), Munich RSO [I] Eurodisc 2-▲ 69073-2-RC [DDD] ■ 69073-4-RC (CrO2)
Donizetti, G.:Anna Bolena (sels), w. Carol Vaness (sop), Melinda Paulsen (cta), Dennis O'Neill (ten), Anton Rosner (ten), Ambrogio Riva (bass), R. Abbado (cnd), Munich RSO—Final Scene & Aria [from Act II] *(rec Studio 1, Bavaria, Apr 13-17, 1993)* RCA Red Seal ▲ 09026-61828-2 [DDD]
Donizetti, G.:Arias, w. Vesselina Kasarova (mez), F. Haider (cnd), Munich RSO—Sposa a Percy...per questa fiamma indomita [from Anna Bolena]; Fia dunque vero...O mio Fernando [from La Favorita]
RCA Red Seal ▲ 0902-668522-2 [DDD]
Donizetti, G.:Don Pasquale, w. E. Mei (sop), T. Allen (bar), R. Abbado (cnd), Munich RSO
RCA Red Seal 2-▲ 09026-61924-2
Donizetti, G.:La fille du régiment, w. Edita Gruberová (sop), Rosa Laghezza (mez), Deon van der Walt (sgr), Philippe Fourcade (bass), François Castel (sgr), M. Panni (cnd), Munich RSO
Nightingale Classics 2-▲ NIG 70566
Dostal, N.:Clivia (sels), w. Sari Barabas (sop), Heinz Hoppe (ten), W. Schubert (cnd), Graunke SO
Emperor Operetta ▲ KO 86352
Egk, W.:Peer Gynt, w. J. Perry (sop), N. Sharp (sop), C. Wulkopf (mez), H. Hopf (ten), R. Hermann (bar), H. Wallberg (cnd), Munich RSO [G] Orfeo 2-▲ 005822 [DDD]
Gluck, C.W.:Alceste, w. J. Norman (sop), N. Gedda (ten), B. Weikl (bar), T. Krause (bar), S. Nimsgern (b-bar), S. Baudo (cnd), Bavarian RSO [French version] Orfeo 3-▲ 027823 [DDD]
Gluck, C.W.:Alceste (sels), w. J. Norman (sop), N. Gedda (ten), B. Weikl (bar), T. Krause (bar), S. Nimsgern (b-bar), S. Baudo (cnd), Bavarian RSO Orfeo ▲ 027901 [DDD]
Gluck, C.W.:Iphigénie en Tauride, w. S. Jurinac (sop), F. Wunderlich (ten), H. Prey (bar), K. Engen (bass), R. Kubelik (cnd), Bavarian RSO [1781 J.B. von Alxinger-Gluck German-language version] *(rec live, Munich 1965)* Myto 2-▲ 2 MCD 91544 [ADD]
Gluck, C.W.:Iphigénie en Tauride, w. P. Lorengar (sop), F. Bonisolli (ten), D. Fischer-Dieskau (bar), W. Grönroos (bar), L. Gardelli (cnd), Bavarian RSO [F] Orfeo 2-▲ 052832 [DDD]

Bavarian Radio Chorus (cont.)
Gluck, C.W.:Orfeo ed Euridice (sels), w. Vesselina Kasarova (mez), F. Haider (cnd), Munich RSO—Che farò senza Euridice! RCA Red Seal ▲ 0902-668522-2 [DDD]
Gounod, C.:Faust, w. K. Te Kanawa (sop), F. Araiza (ten), E. Nesterenko (bass), C. Davis (cnd), Bavarian RSO [F] Philips 3-▲ 420164-2 [DDD]
Handel, G.F.:Giulio Cesare in Egitto, w. Lucia Popp (sop), Christa Ludwig (mez), Fritz Wunderlich (ten), Walter Berry (bass), F. Leitner (cnd), Munich PO Melodram 3-▲ MEL 37059 [AAD]
Handel, G.F.:Giulio Cesare in Egitto, w. Lucia Popp (sop), Christa Ludwig (mez), Fritz Wunderlich (ten), Walter Berry (bass), F. Leitner (cnd), Munich PO [G] *(rec live, Munich 7/1-5/65)*
Verona 3-▲ 27035/37 [AAD]
Handel, G.F.:Rinaldo (sels), w. Vesselina Kasarova (mez), F. Haider (cnd), Munich RSO—Or la tromba in suon festante RCA Red Seal ▲ 0902-668522-2 [DDD]
Handel, G.F.:Serse, w. Ingeborg Hallstein (sop), Fritz Wunderlich (ten), et al., R. Kubelik (cnd), Bavarian RSO [G] *(rec 10/22-28/62)* Verona 3-▲ 27032/34 (m) [AAD]
Haydn, J.:Mass 3, "Cäcilienmesse", w. Lucia Popp (sop), Doris Soffel (mez), Rudolf Laubenthal (ten), Kurt Moll (bass), R. Kubelik (cnd), Bavarian RSO [L] Orfeo 2-▲ 032822 [DDD]
Haydn, J.:Mass 3, "Cäcilienmesse", w. Maria Stader (sop), Marga Höffgen (cta), Richard Holm (ten), Josef Greindl (bass), E. Jochum (cnd), Bavarian RSO Deutsche Grammophon 2-▲ 437383-2 [ADD]
Haydn, J.:Mass 10, "Kriegsmesse", "Paukenmesse", w. Judith Blegen (sop), Brigitte Fassbaender (mez), Claes Hakan Ahnsjö (ten), Hans Sotin (bass), L. Bernstein (cnd), Bavarian RSO [L]
Philips ▲ 412734-2 [DDD]
Haydn, J.:Die Schöpfung, w. Margaret Marshall (sop), Lucia Popp (sop), Vinson Cole (ten), Bernd Weikl (bar), Gwynne Howell (bass), R. Kubelik (cnd), Bavarian RSO
Orfeo 2-▲ 150852 [DDD] 2-■ 150852 (D)
Hindemith, P.:Mathis der Maler, w. Urszula Koszut (sop), Trudeliese Schmidt (mez), Rose Wagemann (mez), William Cochran (ten), Donald Grobe (ten), James King (ten), Manfred Schmidt (ten), Dietrich Fischer-Dieskau (bar), Gerd Feldhoff (bass), Alexander Malta (bass), Peter Meven (bass), Karl Kreile (sgr), R. Kubelik (cnd), Bavarian RSO EMI Classics 2-▲ CDCC 55237
Kelterborn, R.:Songs for 4 Winds & Chorus, w. T. Jones (trbn), M. Hoffmann (wind instr), W. Mittelbach (wind instr), G. Pettinger (wind instr), G. Kember (cnd) *(rec May 13, 1983)*
Grammont ▲ CTSP 35-2 [ADD]
Killmayer, W.:Yolimba, w. M. Venuti (sop—Yolimba), A. Titus (bar—Möhringer), P. Schneider (cnd), Munich RSO [G] Orfeo ▲ 257921 [DDD]
Korngold, E.W.:Violanta, w. E. Martón (sop), S. Jerusalem (ten), W. Berry (bass), M. Janowski (cnd), Munich RSO [G] CBS ▲ MK 35909 [ADD]
Kubelík, R.:Inventions & Interludes, w. R. Kubelík (cnd), Bavarian RSO *(rec Prague, 1993)*
Panton ▲ PAN 811225
Lehár, F.:Friederike (sels), w. Helen Donath (sop), Gabriele Fuchs (sop), Adolf Dallapozza (ten), H. Wallberg (cnd), Munich RSO Emperor Operetta ▲ KO 86344
Lehár, F.:Das Land des Lächelns (sels), w. Renate Holm (sop), Anneliese Rothenberger (sop), Nicolai Gedda (ten), W. Mattes (cnd), Graunke SO Emperor Operetta ▲ KO 86341
Lehár, F.:Die lustige Witwe (sels), w. Erika Koth (sop), Anneliese Rothenberger (sop), Nicolai Gedda (ten), Robert Ilosfalvy (ten), W. Mattes (cnd), Graunke SO Emperor Operetta ▲ KO 86343
Leoncavallo, R.:La Bohème, w. Lucia Popp (sop), Alexandrina Milcheva (mez), Franco Bonisolli (ten), Bernd Weikl (bar), H. Wallberg (cnd), Munich RSO [I] Orfeo 2-▲ 023822 [DDD]
Lincke, P.:Frau Luna (sels), w. Ingeborg Hallstein (sop), Renata Tebaldi (sop), Willi Brokmeier (ten), W. Schmidt-Boelcke (cnd), Bavarian RSO [G] Acanta ▲ CD 42484 [DDD]
Lortzing, A.:Zar und Zimmermann (sels), w. Lucia Popp (sop), Adalbert Kraus (ten), Hermann Prey (bar), Fritz Krenn (bass), Karl Ridderbusch (bass), H. Wallberg (cnd), Bavarian RSO [G]
Acanta 2-▲ CD 42424 [DDD]
Mad Scenes, w. Gruberova, Edita (sop), Munich RSO [cnd:Fabio Luisi]
Nightingale Classics ▲ NIG CD 110560
Mahler, G.:Syms, w. R. Kubelik (cnd), Bavarian RSO Deutsche Grammophon 10-▲ 429042-2 [ADD]
Marschner, H.A.:Der Vampyr, w. Arleen Augér (sop), Donald Grobe (ten), Roland Hermann (bar), Nikolas Hillebrand (bass), F. Rieger (cnd), Bavarian RSO *(rec live, Munich, 1974)*
Enterprise ("Documents" series) 2-▲ ENT 1009
Mascagni, P.:Iris, w. I. Tokody (sop), P. Domingo (ten), J. Pons (bar), G. Patanè (cnd), Munich RSO
CBS 2-▲ M2K 45526
Mendelssohn, F.:A Midsummer Night's Dream (comp), w. Edith Mathis (sop), Brigitte Fassbaender (mez), O. Klemperer (cnd), Bavarian RSO *(rec live, May 23, 1969)* Originals ▲ ORI SH 917
Mozart, W.A.:Arias, w. Vesselina Kasarova (mez), F. Haider (cnd), Munich RSO—Voi che sapete che cosa è amor [from Le nozze di Figaro]; Batti, batti, o bel Masetto [from Don Giovanni]
RCA Red Seal ▲ 0902-668522-2 [DDD]
Mozart, W.A.:Ave verum corpus, w. L. Bernstein (cnd), Bavarian RSO *(rec live April 1990)*
Deutsche Grammophon ▲ 431791-2 [DDD] □ 431791-5
Mozart, W.A.:Don Giovanni, w. J. Varady (sop), A. Augér (sop), E. Mathis (sop), T. Moser (ten), A. Titus (bar), R. Panerai (bar), R. Scholze (bass), J.-H. Rootering (bass), R. Kubelik (cnd), Bavarian RSO [I]
Eurodisc 3-▲ 7798-2 [DDD]
Mozart, W.A.:Exsultate, w. A. Augér (sop), L. Bernstein (cnd), Bavarian RSO *(rec live April 1990)*
Deutsche Grammophon ▲ 431791-2 [DDD] □ 431791-5
Mozart, W.A.:Missa, K.427, w. Arleen Augér (sop), Heather Harper (sop), Horst Lubenthal (ten), Ulrik Cold (bass), S. Celibidache (cnd), Stuttgart RSO, Southwest German Radio Chorus *(rec live, 1980's)*
Topazio ▲ TOP 26045
Mozart, W.A.:Missa, K.427, w. A. Augér (sop), F. von Stade (mez), F. Lopardo (ten), C. Hauptmann (bass), L. Bernstein (cnd), Bavarian RSO *(rec live April 1990)*
Deutsche Grammophon ▲ 431791-2 [DDD] □ 431791-5
Mozart, W.A.:Requiem, w. A. M. Blasi (sop), M. Lipovšek (mez), U. Heilmann (ten), J.-H. Rootering (bass), C. Davis (cnd), Bavarian RSO [L]
RCA Red Seal ▲ 09026-60599-2 [DDD] ■ 09026-60599-4 (CrO2) □ 09026-60599-5
Mozart, W.A.:Requiem, w. M. McLaughlin (sop), M. Ewing (sop), J. Hadley (ten), C. Hauptmann (bass), L. Bernstein (cnd), Bavarian RSO [L] Deutsche Grammophon ▲ 427353-2 [DDD]
Mozart, W.A.:Zauberflöte, w. L. Popp (sop), E. Gruberova (sop), S. Jerusalem (ten), W. Brendel (bar), R. Bracht (bass), B. Haitink (cnd), Bavarian RSO [G] EMI Classics 3-▲ CDCC 47951 [DDD]
Mozart, W.A.:Zauberflöte (sels), w. L. Popp (sop), E. Gruberova (sop), S. Jerusalem (ten), W. Brendel (bar), R. Bracht (bass), B. Haitink (cnd), Bavarian RSO [G] EMI Classics ▲ CDC 47008 [DDD]
Mussorgsky, M.:Boris Godunov, w. Martha Mödl (sop—Marina Mniszek), Lotte Schädle (sop—Xenia), Dorothea Siebert (mez—Fyodor), Hertha Töpper (mez—Xenia's wet-nurs), Karl Hermann Bennert (Boyer Khrushchyov), Lorenz Fehenberger (ten—Prince Shuysky), Hans Hopf (ten—Grigory), Karl Ostertag (ten—Missail), Hans Hotter (b-bar—Boris Godunov), Hermann Uhde (bar—Andrey Shchelkalov), Kurt Böhme (bass—Varlaam), Kim Borg (bass—Pimen), Kieth Engen (bass—Lewicki), Adolf Keil (bass—Nikitich), Benno Kusche (bar—Rangoni), Heinz Maria Linz (bass—Czernikowski), E. Jochum (cnd), Bavarian RSO *(rec Munich, May 1957)* Myto 3-▲ MCD 953131
Orff, C.:Der Mond—Ein kleines Welttheater, w. Karl Erb (nar), Paul Kuen (ten—Lad 3), Josef Knapp (bar—Lad 2), Benno Kusche (bar—Lad 1), Georg Hann (bass—St. Peter), Georg Wieter (bass—Lad 4), Rudolf Wünzer (bass—The Farmer), Karl Hanft (sgr—Innkeeper), Willy Rösner (sgr—The Major), R. Alberth (cnd), Bavarian RSO *(rec Studio 1, Bavarian Radio, Jan. 19-20, 1950)*
Calig ▲ CAL 50948 (m) [ADD]
Puccini, G.:Turandot (sels), w. Ben Heppner (ten), R. Abbado (cnd), Munich RSO—Nessun dorma *(rec Residenz Herkulesaal, Munich, Sept. 27-Oct. 3, 1993 & J)*
RCA Red Seal ▲ 09026-62504-2 [DDD]
Rossini, G.:Arias, w. Vesselina Kasarova (mez), F. Haider (cnd), Munich RSO—Nacqui all'affanno e al pianto [from La cenerentola]; Una voce poco fa [from Il barbiere di Siviglia]; Amici in ogni evento...Pensa alla patria [from L'Italiana in Algeri] RCA Red Seal ▲ 0902-668522-2 [DDD]
Rossini, G.:Tancredi, w. Veronica Cangemi (sop—Roggiero), Eva Mei (sop—Amenaide), Vasselina Kasarova (mez—Tancredi), Melinda Paulsen (cta—Isaura), Ramón Vargas (ten—Argirio), Harry Peeters (bass—Orbazzano), Janos Maté (vn), Gottfried Greiner (vc), Ingo Nawra (db), David Syrus (hpd), R. Abbado (cnd), Munich RSO *(rec Studio 1, Munich, July 17-30, 1995)*
RCA Red Seal 3-▲ 09026-68349-2 [DDD]

938 ▲ = CD ♦ = Enhanced CD Δ = MD ■ = Cassette Tape □ = DCC

Bavarian Radio Chorus (cont.)

Saint-Saëns, C.:Samson et Dalila, w. J. Carreras (ten), A. Baltsa (mez), Summers (bar), Estes (bass), Burchuladze (bass), C. Davis (cnd), Bavarian RSO Philips 2-▲ 426243-2 [DDD]

Schubert, Franz:Mass 4, w. H. Donath (sop), B. Fassbaender (mez), F. Araiza (ten), D. Fischer-Dieskau (bar), W. Sawallisch (cnd), Bavarian RSO [L] EMI Classics ("Studio" series) ▲ CDM 69222

Schubert, Franz:Mass 5, w. L. Popp (sop), B. Fassbaender (mez), A. Dallapozza (ten), D. Fischer-Dieskau (bar), W. Sawallisch (cnd), Bavarian RSO [L] EMI Classics ("Studio" series) ▲ CDM 69222

Schubert, Franz:Mass 6, w. C.M. Giulini (cnd), Bavarian RSO *(rec live, Munich)* Sony Classical ▲ SK 69290

Schubert, Franz:Mass 6, w. H. Donath (sop), B. Fassbaender (mez), F. Araiza (ten), D. Fischer-Dieskau (bar), W. Sawallisch (cnd), Bavarian RSO [L] EMI Classics ("Studio" series) ▲ CDM 69223

Schubert, Franz:Offertorium, D.963, w. P. Schreier (ten), W. Sawallisch (cnd), Bavarian RSO [L] EMI Classics ("Studio" series) ▲ CDM 69223

Schubert, Franz:Tantum ergo, D.962, w. L. Popp (sop), B. Fassbaender (mez), A. Dallapozza (ten), D. Fischer-Dieskau (bar), W. Sawallisch (cnd), Bavarian RSO [L] EMI Classics ("Studio" series) ▲ CDM 69223

Smetana, B.:The Bartered Bride, w. Dorothea Siebert (sop), Dagmar Hermann (mez), Maria von Ilosvay (mez), Hans Braun (bar), Kurt Böhme (bass), J. Keilberth (cnd), Bavarian RSO *(rec 1958)* Pantheon 2-▲ PHE 6652 (m)

Smetana, B.:Dalibor, w. Sándor Kónya (ten), Franz Crass (bass), Gerd Nienstedt (bass), R. Kubelik (cnd), Bavarian RSO *(rec live, Munich, 1969)* Serenissima 2-▲ SER 360169

Smetana, B.:Dalibor (sels), w. F. Weathers (sop), S. Konya (ten), G. Nienstedt (bass), R. Kubelik (cnd), Bavarian RSO—nine solo, duet & trio arias featuring tenor Sandor Konya as Dalibor, from Acts 1-3 *(rec live, Munich, 1968)* Myto 2-▲ 2 MCD 92465 [ADD]

Strauss (II), Joh.:Die Fledermaus, w. L. Popp (sop), E. Lind (sop), A. Baltsa (mez), P. Domingo (ten), W. Brendel (bar), K. Rydl (bass), P. Domingo (cnd), Munich RSO [G] EMI Classics 2-▲ CDCB 47480

Strauss, R.:Elektra, w. C. Studer (sop), E. Marton (sop), M. Lipovsek (mez), H. Winkler (ten), B. Weikl (bar), W. Sawallisch (cnd), Bavarian RSO EMI Classics 2-▲ CDCB 54067

Strauss, R.:Feuersnot, w. J. Varady (sop), B. Weikl (bar), H. Berger-Tuna (bass), H. Fricke (cnd), Munich RSO [G] Acanta 2-▲ 43530-1-2 [DDD]

Strauss, R.:Die Frau ohne Schatten, w. C. Studer (sop), U. Vinzing (sop), H. Schwarz (mez), R. Kollo (ten), A. Muff (bass), Schmidt (sgr), W. Sawallisch (cnd), Bavarian RSO [G] EMI Classics ▲ CDC 54494 [DDD]

Strauss, R.:Die Frau ohne Schatten, w. C. Studer (sop), U. Vinzing (sop), H. Schwarz (mez), R. Kollo (ten), A. Muff (bass), Schmidt (sgr), W. Sawallisch (cnd), Bavarian RSO [uncut version] [G] EMI Classics 3-▲ CDCC 49074 [DDD]

Stravinsky, I.:Oedipus Rex, w. J. Norman (sop), T. Moser (ten), S. Nimsgern (b-bar), R. Bracht (bass), C. Davis (cnd), Bavarian RSO [L] Orfeo ▲ 071831 [DDD] ■ 071831 (D)

Suder, J.:Leider machen Leute, w. P. Coburn (sop), K. König (ten), M. Morgan (bar), W. Probst (bar), U. Mund (cnd), Bamberg SO [G] Orfeo 2-▲ 124862 [DDD]

Verdi, G.:Alzira, w. M. Cotrubas (sop), F. Araiza (ten), R. Bruson (bar), L. Gardelli (cnd), Munich RSO [I] Orfeo 2-▲ 057832 [DDD]

Verdi, G.:Falstaff, w. S. Sweet (sop), M. Horne (mez), F. Lopardo (ten), R. Panerai (bar), A. Titus (bar), C. Davis (cnd), Bavarian RSO RCA Red Seal 2-▲ 09026-60705-2 [DDD]

Verdi, G.:Macbeth (sels), w. Carol Vaness (sop), Marisca Mulder (sop), Ambrogio Riva (bass), R. Abbado (cnd), Munich RSO—Grand Sleepwalking Scene [from Act IV] *(rec Studio 1, Bavaria, Apr 13-17, 1993)* RCA Red Seal ▲ 09026-61828-2 [DDD]

Verdi, G.:Otello (sels), w. Carol Vaness (sop), Melinda Paulsen (cta), R. Abbado (cnd), Munich RSO—Canzone del salice; Ave Maria [both from Act IV] *(rec Studio 1, Bavaria, Apr 13-17, 1993)* RCA Red Seal ▲ 09026-61828-2 [DDD]

Verdi, G.:Requiem Mass, w. C. Vaness (sop), F. Quivar (mez), D. O'Neill (ten), C. Colombara (bass), C. Davis (cnd), Bavarian RSO RCA Red Seal 2-▲ 09026-60902-2

Verdi, G.:La traviata (sels), w. Carol Vaness (sop), Dennis O'Neill (ten), R. Abbado (cnd), Munich RSO—Final Scene & Aria [from Act I] *(rec Studio 1, Bavaria, Apr 13-17, 1993)* RCA Red Seal ▲ 09026-61828-2 [DDD]

Verdi, G.:Il trovatore (sels), w. Carol Vaness (sop), Dennis O'Neill (ten), Anton Rosner (ten), R. Abbado (cnd), Munich RSO—Scene, Aria & Miserere [from Act IV] *(rec Studio 1, Munich, Apr 13-17, 1993)* RCA Red Seal ▲ 09026-61828-2 [DDD]

Wagner, R.:Die Feen, w. L. E. Gray (sop), K. Lövaas (sop), K. Láki (sop), Anderson (sop), R. Alexander (sop), R. Hermann (bar), K. Moll (bass), W. Sawallisch (cnd), Bavarian RSO [G] *(rec live, Munich Opera Fest. 1983)* Orfeo 3-▲ 062833 [DDD]

Wagner, R.:Lohengrin, w. Sharon Sweet (sop—Elsa), Eva Marton (sop—Ortrud), Ben Heppner (ten—Lohengrin), Anton Rosner (ten—Nobleman), Heinrich Weber (ten—Nobleman), Jan-Hendrik Rootering (bar—Heinrich der Vögler), Sergei Leiferkus (bar—Friedrich von Telramund), Bryn Terfel (b-bar—King's Herald), Barbara Fleckenstein (sgr—Page), Atsuko Suzuki (sgr—Page), Gisela Ulmann (sgr—Page), Marion Rambausek (sgr—Page), Dankwart Siegele (sgr—Nobleman), Jürgen Weiss (sgr—Nobleman), C. Davis (cnd), Bavarian SO, Bavarian State Opera Chorus *(rec Residenz Herkulesaal, Munich, May 14-28, 1994)* RCA Red Seal 3-▲ 09026-62646-2 [DDD]

Wagner, R.:Die Meistersinger von Nürnberg, w. G. Janowitz (sop), B. Fassbaender (mez), S. Kónya (ten), G. Unger (ten), T. Stewart (bar), F. Crass (bass), T. Hemsley (bass), R. Kubelik (cnd), Bavarian RSO [G] *(rec live, Munich, Oct. 1967)* Myto 4-▲ 4 MCD 92569 [ADD]

Wagner, R.:Die Meistersinger von Nürnberg, w. Gundula Janowitz (sop), Brigitte Fassbaender (mez), Sándor Kónya (ten), Gerhard Unger (ten), Thomas Helmsey (bar), Thomas Stewart (bar), Franz Crass (bass), R. Kubelik (cnd), Bavarian RSO *(rec 1967)* Calig 4-▲ 5097174 [ADD]

Wagner, R.:Tristan und Isolde (sels), w. H. Behrens (sop), Y. Minton (mez), P. Hofmann (ten), B. Weikl (bass), L. Bernstein (cnd), Bavarian RSO Philips ▲ 438501-2

Weber, C.M. von:Der Freischütz, w. Irmgard Seefried (sop), Rita Streich (sop), Richard Holm (ten), Eberhard Wächter (bar), Kurt Böhme (b-bar), E. Jochum (cnd), Bavarian RSO Deutsche Grammophon 2-▲ 439717-2 [ADD]

Weinberger, J.:Schwanda der Dudelsackpfeifer, w. L. Popp (sop), G. Killebrew (mez), S. Jerusalem (ten), H. Prey (bar), S. Nimsgern (bass), H. Wallberg (cnd), Munich RSO [F] CBS 3-▲ M3K 36926 [ADD]

M. Gläser (cnd)

Humperdinck, E.:Königskinder, w. Dagmar Schellenberger (sop—Goose girl), Marilyn Schmiege (cta—Witch), Thomas Moser (ten—King's Son), Heinrich Weber (ten—Broommaker), Dietrich Henschel (bar—Fiddler), Andreas Kohn (bass—Woodcutter), F. Luisi (cnd), Munich RSO *(rec live, Munich Herkulessaal, Mar 22-24, 1996)* Calig 3-CAL 5096870 [DDD]

Wagner, R.:Lohengrin (sels), w. Eva Marton (sop—Ortrud), Sharon Sweet (sop—Elsa von Brabant), Barbara Fleckenstein (sgr—Page), Marion Rambausek (sgr—Page), Atsuko Suzuki (sgr—Page), Gisela Ulmann (sgr—Page), Ben Heppner (ten—Lohengrin), Anton Rosner (ten—Nobleman), Heinrich Weber (ten—Nobleman), Sergei Leiferkus (bar—Friedrich von Telramund), Bryn Terfel (b-bar—King's Herald), Jan-Hendrik Rootering (bass—Henry the Fowler), Dankwart Siegele (sgr—Nobleman), Jürgen Weiss (sgr—Nobleman), C. Davis (cnd), Bavarian RSO, Bavarian State Opera Chorus—Seht! Seht! [from Act 1, Scene 2]; Nun sei bedankt, mein lieber Schwan!; Wenn ich im Kampfe für dich siege; Welch holde Wunder muss ich sehen?; Nun höret mich und achtet wohl; Durch Gottes Sieg ist jetzt dein Leben mein [all from Act 1, Scene 3]; Treulich geführt ziehet dahin [from Act 3, Scene 1]; Wie hehr erkenn' ich unsrer Liebe Wesen!; Höchstes Vertrau'n hast du mir schon zu danken; Weh' nun ist all' unser Glück dahin! [all from Act 3, Scene 2]; In fernem Land, unnahbar euren Schritten [from Act 3, Scene 3] *(rec Munich, Mar 14-28, 1994)* RCA Red Seal ▲ 09026-68239-2 [DDD]

E. Jochum (cnd)

Bruckner, A.:Motets, w. R. Holm (ten)—Locus iste; Ave Maria; Virga Jesse; Os justi; Pange lingua; Christus factus est pro nobis; Vexilla regis; Afferentur regi; Tota pulchra es Maria (w. Holm); Ecce sacerdos [L] Deutsche Grammophon 4-▲ 423127-2 [ADD]

H. Mende (cnd)

Kelemen, M.:Passionato, w. Karl-Bernhard Sebon (fl) *(rec Munich, Germany, May 18, 1979)* BIS ▲ CD 742 [AAD]

Bavarian State Chorus

Strauss, R.:Der Rosenkavalier, w. Claire Watson (sop—Feldmarschallin), Lucia Popp (sop—Sophie), Annelie Waas (sop—Marianne), Brigitte Fassbaender (mez—Octavian), Margaretthe Bence (ct—Annina), David Thaw (ten—Valzacchi), Karl Ridderbusch (bass—Baron Ochs), Benno Kusche (bass—Herr von Faninal), Albrecht Peter (bass—Police Inspector), C. Kleiber (cnd), Bavarian State Orch *(rec live, Münchner Festspiele, July 20, 1974)* Arkadia 3-▲ 486 [ADD]

Wagner, R.:Arias & Scenes, w. Julia Varady (sop), Peter Seiffert (ten), D. Fischer-Dieskau (cnd), Bavarian State Orch—Lohengrin:Ov; 'Wedding March & Chorus'; Tannhäuser:'Dich, teure Halle'; Ov Act 2; 'Gepriesen sei die Stunde'; Walküre:'Ein Schwert verhiess mir der Vater' EMI Classics ▲ CDC 56138

Wagner, R.:Das Liebesverbot, w. Pamela Coburn (sop—Mariana), Friedrich Lenz (ten—Antonio), Hermann Prey (bar—Friedrich), Keith Engen (bass—Angelo), Raimund Grumbach (bass—Danieli/Wirt), Wolfgang Fassler (sgr—Luzio), Sabine Haas (sgr—Isabella/Claudios Schwester), Alfred Kuhn (sgr—Brighella/Chef der Sbirren), Hermann Sapell (sgr—Pontio Pilato), Robert Schunk (sgr—Claudio), Marianne Seibel (sgr—Dorella), W. Sawallisch (cnd), Bavarian State Orch *(rec July 9, 1983)* Orfeo d'or 3-▲ 345953

Bavarian State Opera Chorus

Beethoven, L. van:Fidelio, w. S. Jurinac (sop), M. Stader (sop), H. Peerce (ten), H. Knappertsbusch (cnd), Bavarian State Opera Orch [G] *(rec ca. 1961)* MCA Classics 2-▲ MCAD2-9809 [AAD]

Janácek, L.:Jenůfa, w. H. Hillebrecht (sop), A. Varnay (sop), W. Cochran (ten), Cox (sgr), R. Kubelik (cnd), Bavarian State Opera Orch [G] *(rec live in Munich, Mar. 17, 1970)* Myto 2-▲ 2 MCD 90422 [ADD]

Massenet, J.:Chérubin, w. D. Upshaw (sop), F. von Stade (mez), M. Anderson (cta), S. Ramey (bass), P. Steinberg (cnd), Munich RSO RCA Red Seal 2-▲ 09026-60593-2 [DDD]

Orff, C.:Antigonae, w. Christel Goltz (sop), Paul Kuen (ten), Karl Ostertag (ten), Benno Kusche (bar), Hermann Uhde (bar), N. Barth (bar), G. Solti (cnd), Bavarian State Opera Orch *(rec Prinzregententheater, Jan. 12, 1951)* Orfeo d'or 2-▲ 407952

Puccini, G.:La Bohème, w. Trude Eipperle (sop), Hildegarde Ranczak (sop), Alfons Fügel (ten), Carl Kronenberg (bar), Georg Hann (bass), Georg Wieter (bass), Emil Graf (sgr), Otto Hillerbrandt (sgr), Karl Schmidt (sgr), C. Krauss (cnd), Bavarian State Opera Orch *(rec 1940)* Preiser 2-▲ PRE 90275

Strauss, R.:Die ägyptische Helena, w. Annelies Kupper (sop—Aithra), Leonie Rysanek (sop—Helena), Ira Malaniuk (cta—Omniscient Seashell), Bernd Aldenhoff (ten—Menelas), Richard Holm (ten—Da-ud), Hermann Uhde (bar—Altair), J. Keilberth (cnd), Bavarian State Opera Orch *(rec Munich Opera Festival, Prince Regent Theater, Aug 10, 1956)* Orfeo d'or 2-▲ 424962

Strauss, R.:Die ägyptische Helena, w. L. Rysanek (sop), A. Kupper (sop), B. Aldenhoff (ten), H. Uhde (bar), J. Keilberth (cnd), Bavarian State Opera Orch [G] *(rec live, Munich, 8/27/56)* Melodram 2-▲ MEL 27066 (m) [AAD]

Strauss, R.:Feuersnot, w. Maud Cunitz (sop—Diemut), Antonia Fahberg (sop—Elsbeth), Irmgard Barth (mez—Wigelis), Liselotte Nölser (sgr—Margret), Karl Ostertag (ten—Schweiker), Marcel Cordes (bar—Kunrad), Kieth Engen (bass—Kofel), Karl Hoppe (bass—Hämerlein), Max Proebstl (bass—Ortolf), Georg Wieter (bass—Jörg), R. Kempe (cnd), Bavarian State Opera Orch *(rec Munich Opera Festival, Prince Regent Theater, Aug 14, 1958)* Orfeo d'or 2-▲ 423962

Strauss, R.:Der Rosenkavalier, w. Erika Köth (sop—Sophie), Annelie Waas (sop—Marianne), Claire Watson (sop—Marschallin), Hertha Töpper (mez—Octavian), Brigitte Fassbaender (cta—Annina), Gerhard Stolze (ten—Valzacchi), Fritz Wunderlich (ten—Singer), Otto Wiener (bar—Faninal), Kurt Böhme (bass—Baron), J. Keilberth (cnd), Bavarian State Opera Orch *(rec Munich Opera Festival, National Theater, May 21, 1965)* Orfeo d'or 3-▲ 425963

Strauss, R.:Der Rosenkavalier, w. Adele Kern (sop), Viorica Ursuleac (sop), Georgine von Milinkovic (mez), Georg Hann (bass), Ludwig Weber (bass), C. Krauss (cnd), Bavarian State Opera Orch *(rec Munich, June 1942)* Preiser 3-▲ PRE 90218

Verdi, G.:La traviata (sels), w. T. Stratas (sop), F. Wunderlich (ten), H. Prey (bar), G. Patanè (cnd), Bavarian State Opera Orch—substantial selections from Acts 1-3 *(rec live, Munich, 3/28/65)* Myto 2-▲ 2 MCD 91648 [ADD]

Wagner, R.:Der fliegende Holländer, w. Viorica Ursuleac (sop), Luise Willer (mez), Karl Ostertag (ten), Hans Hotter (b-bar), Georg Hann (bass), C. Krauss (cnd), Bavarian State Opera Orch *(rec Mar 13-16, 1944)* Preiser 2-▲ PRE 90250 [ADD]

Wagner, R.:Götterdämmerung, w. Birgit Nilsson (sop—Brünnhilde), Leonie Rysanek (sop—Gutrune), Gerda Sommerschuh (sop—Woglinde), Elisabeth Lindermeier (sop—Wellgunde), Ruth Michaelis (sop—Flohilde), Marianne Schech (sop—Dritte Norne), Ira Malaniuk (mez—Waltraute), Irmgarth Barth (mez—Erste Norne), Hertha Töpper (mez—Zweite Norne), Bernd Aldenhoff (ten—Siegfried), Hermann Uhde (bar—Gunther), Gottlob Frick (bass—Hagen), H. Knappertsbusch (cnd), Bavarian State Opera Orch *(rec live, Prinzregententheater, Sept. 1, 1955)* Orfeo 4-▲ 356944 (m)

Wagner, R.:Götterdämmerung (sels), w. A. Varnay (sop), E. Grümmer (sop), B. Aldenhoff (ten), H. Uhde (bar), G. Frick (bass), J. Greindl (bass), H. Knappertsbusch (cnd), Bavarian State Opera Orch, Bayreuth Festival Orch, Bayreuth Festival Chorus [G] *(rec live 1955 & 1957)* Melodram 4-▲ MEL 46106 (m) [AAD]

Wagner, R.:Lohengrin, w. Sharon Sweet (sop—Elsa), Eva Marton (sop—Ortrud), Ben Heppner (ten—Lohengrin), Anton Rosner (ten—Nobleman), Heinrich Weber (ten—Nobleman), Jan-Hendrik Rootering (bar—Heinrich der Vögler), Sergei Leiferkus (bar—Friedrich von Telramund), Bryn Terfel (b-bar—King's Herald), Barbara Fleckenstein (sgr—Page), Atsuko Suzuki (sgr—Page), Gisela Ulmann (sgr—Page), Marion Rambausek (sgr—Page), Dankwart Siegele (sgr—Nobleman), Jürgen Weiss (sgr—Nobleman), C. Davis (cnd), Bavarian SO, Bavarian Radio Chorus *(rec Residenz Herkulesaal, Munich, May 14-28, 1994)* RCA Red Seal 3-▲ 09026-62646-2 [DDD]

Wagner, R.:Die Meistersinger von Nürnberg, w. C. Studer (sop—Eva), B. Heppner (ten—Walther von Stolzing), B. Weikl (bar—Hans Sachs), S. Lorenz (b-bar—Sixtus Beckmesser), K. Moll (bass—Veit Pogner), W. Sawallisch (cnd), Bavarian State Opera Orch EMI Classics ▲ CDCD 55142

Wagner, R.:Rienzi, der Letzte der Tribunen, w. Cheryl Studer (sop—Irene), René Kollo (ten—Rienzi), Friedrich Lenz (ten—Gesandte), Norbert Orth (ten—Baroncelli), Bodo Brinkmann (bar—Paolo Orsini), Keith Engen (bass—Cecco del Vecchio), Raimund Grumbach (bass—Gesandte), Jan-Hendrik Rootering (bass—Steffano Colonna), Carmen Anhorn (sgr—Ein Friedensbote), Karl Helm (sgr—Kardinal Orvieto), John Janssen (sgr—Adriano), Alfred Kuhn (sgr—Gesandte), Hans Wilbrink (sgr—Gesandte), W. Sawallisch (cnd), Bavarian State Opera Orch *(rec live, July 6, 1983)* Orfeo d'or 3-▲ 346953

Wagner, R.:Tannhäuser, w. Nadine Secunde (sop), Waltraude Meier (mez), Rene Kollo (ten), Bernd Weikl (bar), Z. Mehta (cnd), Bavarian State Opera Orch *(rec live, Munich, 1994)* Serenissima 3-▲ SER 360166

Wagner, R.:Tannhäuser (sels), w. Sylvia Sass (sop), Reiner Goldberg (ten), Hermann Prey (bar), Bavarian State Opera Orch—Ov; Venusberg Bacchanal; Dich, teure halle, grüß' ich wieder; Freudig begrüßen wir die edle Halle; Intro; die Pilger sind's - Beglückt darf nun dich, o Heimat, ich schauen; plus others Laserlight ▲ 14211 [DDD]

Wagner, R.:Tristan und Isolde, w. Helena Braun (sop—Isolde), Margarete Klose (mez—Brangäne), Günther Treptow (ten—Tristan), Paul Kuen (ten—Ein Hirte), Albrecht Peter (bar—Melot), Fritz Richard Bender (bar—Ein Steuermann), Ferdinand Frantz (b-bar—König Marke), Paul Schöffler (b-bar—Kurwenal), H. Knappertsbusch (cnd), Bavarian State Opera Orch *(rec live, Prinzregententheater, July 23, 1950)* Orfeo 3-▲ 355

M. Gläser, U. Mehrpohl (cnd)

Wagner, R.:Lohengrin (sels), w. Eva Marton (sop—Ortrud), Sharon Sweet (sop—Elsa von Brabant), Barbara Fleckenstein (sgr—Page), Marion Rambausek (sgr—Page), Atsuko Suzuki (sgr—Page), Gisela Ulmann (sgr—Page), Ben Heppner (ten—Lohengrin), Anton Rosner (ten—Nobleman), Heinrich Weber (ten—Nobleman), Sergei Leiferkus (bar—Friedrich von Telramund), Bryn Terfel (b-bar—King's Herald), Jan-Hendrik Rootering (bass—Henry the Fowler), Dankwart Siegele (sgr—Nobleman), Jürgen Weiss (sgr—Nobleman), C. Davis (cnd), Bavarian RSO, Bavarian Radio Chorus—Seht! Seht! [from Act 1, Scene 2]; Nun sei bedankt, mein lieber Schwan!; Wenn ich im Kampfe für dich siege; Welch holde Wunder muss ich sehen?; Nun höret mich und achtet wohl; Durch Gottes Sieg ist jetzt dein Leben mein [all from Act 1, Scene 3]; Treulich geführt ziehet dahin [from Act 3, Scene 1]; Wie hehr erkenn' ich unsrer Liebe Wesen!; Höchstes Vertrau'n hast du mir schon zu danken; Weh' nun ist all' unser Glück dahin! [all from Act 3, Scene 2]; In fernem Land, unnahbar euren Schritten [from Act 3, Scene 3] *(rec Munich, Mar 14-28, 1994)* RCA Red Seal ▲ 09026-68239-2 [DDD]

Bavarian State Opera Men's Chorus
Beethoven, L. van:Fidelio, w. Elizabeth Norberg-Schulz (sop—Marzelline), Deborah Voigt (sop—Lenore), Ben Heppner (ten—Florestan), Michael Schade (ten—Jaquino), Günter von Kannaten (b-bar—Don Pizarro), Matthias Hölle (bass—Rocco), Thomas Quasthoff (bass—Don Fernando), C. Davis (cnd), Bavarian RSO, Bavarian Radio Chorus *(rec Herkulessaal der Residenz, Munich, May 15-25, 1995)* RCA Victor 2-▲ 09026-68344-2 [DDD]
Beethoven, L. van:Fidelio (sels), w. L. Rysanek (sop), I. Seefried (sop), E. Haefliger (ten), F. Lenz (ten), D. Fischer-Dieskau (bar), K. Engen (bass), G. Frick (bass), F. Fricsay (cnd), Bavarian State Orch—Overture, various arias & scenes, finale [G], IMP Collectors Series ▲ IMPX 9021 [AAD]

Bayreuth Chorus
Fun at the Festspielhaus, w. A. Kulling (cnd), Festspiel Orch members Campion ▲ RRCD 1328 [ADD]

Bayreuth Festival Chorus
Beethoven, L. van:Syms (comp), w. E. Schwarzkopf (sop), E. Höngen (mez), H. Hopf (ten), O. Edelmann (bass), W. Furtwängler (cnd), Vienna PO, Bayreuth Festival Orch *(rec 1948-54)* EMI Classics 5-▲ CDHE 63606
Beethoven, L. van:Sym 9, "Choral Sym", w. K. Böhm (cnd), Bayreuth Festival Orch Melodram ▲ CDM 18005
Beethoven, L. van:Sym 9, "Choral Sym", w. W. Furtwängler (cnd), Bayreuth Festival Orch EMI Classics ▲ CDH 69801
Wagner, R.:Choruses, w. E. Schärtel (mez), J. Greindl (bass), W. Pitz (cnd), Bayreuth Festival Orch—choruses from Lohengrin, Götterdämmerung, Parsifal, Fliegende Holländer, Tannhäuser, Meistersinger Deutsche Grammophon ("Resonance" series) ▲ 429169-2 [ADD]
Wagner, R.:Der fliegende Holländer, w. A. Varnay (sop), J. Traxel (ten), G. London (bar), A. van Mill (bass), J. Keilberth (cnd), Bayreuth Festival Orch [G] *(rec live, Bayreuth, 7/25/56)* Myto 2-▲ 2 MCD 93175
Wagner, R.:Der fliegende Holländer, w. L. Rysanek (sop), G. London (bar), J. Greindl (bass), W. Sawallisch (cnd), Bayreuth Festival Orch [G] *(rec live, Bayreuth 1959)* Melodram 2-▲ MEL 26101
Wagner, R.:Der fliegende Holländer, w. A. Varnay (sop), W. Windgassen (ten), H. Uhde (bar), L. Weber (bass), H. Knappertsbusch (cnd), Bayreuth Festival Orch [G] *(rec live)* Arkadia 2-▲ 421 [ADD]
Wagner, R.:Der fliegende Holländer, w. L. Balsev (sop), R. Schunk (ten), S. Estes (bass), M. Salminen (bass), W. Nelsson (cnd), Bayreuth Festival Orch Philips 2-▲ 434599-2 [DDD]
Wagner, R.:Der fliegende Holländer, w. Maria Müller (sop), Joel Berglund (ten), Franz Völker (ten), Ludwig Hoffmann (bass), R. Kraus (cnd), Bayreuth Festival Orch *(rec live, Bayreuth, July 18, 1942)* Preiser 2-▲ PRE 90232 [ADD]
Wagner, R.:Götterdämmerung, w. G. Jones (sop), H. Jung (mez), F. Mazura (bar), H. Becht (bar), P. Boulez (cnd), Bayreuth Festival Orch [G] Philips 4-▲ 434424-2 [DDD]
Wagner, R.:Götterdämmerung, w. M. Fuchs (sop), H. Scheppan (sop), S. Svanholm (ten), R. Burg (bar), F. Dalberg (bass), K. Elmendorff (cnd), Bayreuth Festival Orch *(rec July 21, 1942)* Preiser 4-▲ PRE 90164 [AAD]
Wagner, R.:Götterdämmerung (sels), w. A. Varnay (sop), E. Grümmer (sop), B. Aldenhoff (ten), H. Uhde (bar), G. Frick (bass), J. Greindl (bass), H. Knappertsbusch (cnd), Bavarian State Opera Orch, Bayreuth Festival Orch, Bavarian State Opera Chorus [G] *(rec live 1955 & 1957)* Melodram 4-▲ MEL 46106 (m) [AAD]
Wagner, R.:Lohengrin, w. E. Connell (sop), N. Armstrong (sop), P. Hofmann (ten), L. Roar (bass), B. Weikl (bass), S. Vogel (bass), W. Nelsson (cnd), Bayreuth Festival Orch CBS 3-▲ M3K 38594
Wagner, R.:Lohengrin, w. C. Studer (sop), P. Frey (ten), M. Schenk (bass), P. Schneider (cnd), Bayreuth Festival Orch, Philips 32-▲ 434420-2 [ADD/DDD]
Wagner, R.:Lohengrin, w. C. Studer (sop), P. Frey (ten), M. Schenk (bass), P. Schneider (cnd), Bayreuth Festival Orch [G] Philips 4-▲ 434602-2 [DDD]
Wagner, R.:Lohengrin, w. B. Nilsson (sop), A. Varnay (sop), W. Windgassen (ten), H. Uhde (bar), E. Jochum (cnd), Bayreuth Festival Orch *(rec live, Bayreuth 1954)* Melodram 3-▲ MEL 36104
Wagner, R.:Lohengrin, w. L. Rysanek (sop), A. Varnay (sop), S. Kónya (ten), E. Blanc (bar), A. Cluytens (cnd), Bayreuth Festival Orch [G] *(rec live, 7/23/58)* Myto 3-▲ MCD 89002 (m) [ADD]
Wagner, R.:Lohengrin, w. E. Steber (sop), A. Varnay (sop), W. Windgassen (ten), H. Uhde (bar), J. Greindl (bass), J. Keilberth (cnd), Bayreuth Festival Orch *(rec live, Bayreuth Festival, 1953)* Teldec ("Historic" series) 4-▲ 93674
Wagner, R.:Lohengrin (sels), w. Maria Müller (sop), Margarete Klose (mez), Franz Völker (ten), Joseph von Manowarda (bass), W. Furtwängler (cnd), Bayreuth Festival Orch—Prelude to Act III; Operatic sels. *(rec 1931)* Grammofono 2000 ▲ GRM 78515 [ADD]
Wagner, R.:Lohengrin (sels), w. C. Studer (sop), G. Schnaut (sop), P. Frey (ten), M. Schenk (bass), P. Schneider (cnd), Bayreuth Festival Orch Philips ▲ 438500-2
Wagner, R.:Die Meistersinger von Nürnberg, w. E. Grümmer (sop), W. Windgassen (ten), T. Adam (b-bar), J. Greindl (bass), H. Knappertsbusch (cnd), Bayreuth Festival Orch [G] *(rec live, Bayreuth, 1960)* Melodram 4-▲ MEL 46103
Wagner, R.:Die Meistersinger von Nürnberg, w. E. Schwarzkopf (sop), I. Malaniuk (cta), H. Hopf (ten), G. Unger (ten), E. Kunz (bar), O. Edelmann (b-bar), F. Dalberg (bass), H. von Karajan (cnd), Bayreuth Festival Orch [G] *(rec 1951)* EMI Classics ("Great Recordings of the Century" series) 4-▲ CDHD 63500 (m) [ADD]
Wagner, R.:Die Meistersinger von Nürnberg, w. Hannelore Bode (sop), Jean Cox (ten), Klaus Hirte (bar), Karl Ridderbusch (bass), Hans Sotin (bass), S. Varviso (cnd), Bayreuth Festival Orch [1974] [G] Philips 4-▲ 434611-2 [ADD]
Wagner, R.:Die Meistersinger von Nürnberg, w. Hannelore Bode (sop), Jean Cox (ten), Klaus Hirte (bar), Karl Ridderbusch (bass), Hans Sotin (bass), S. Varviso (cnd), Bayreuth Festival Orch [1974] Philips 32-▲ 434420-2 [ADD/DDD]
Wagner, R.:Die Meistersinger von Nürnberg, w. H. Scheppan (sop), L. Suthaus (ten), E. Kunz (bar), P. Schöffler (b-bar), H. Abendroth (cnd), Bayreuth Festival Orch *(rec 1943)* Preiser ▲ PRE 90174 [AAD]
Wagner, R.:Die Meistersinger von Nürnberg, w. L. Della Casa (sop), I. Malaniuk (cta), H. Hopf (ten), O. Edelmann (b-bar), K. Böhme (bass), H. Knappertsbusch (cnd), Bayreuth Festival Orch [G] *(rec live, 1952)* Arkadia 4-▲ 440 (m) [ADD]
Wagner, R.:Die Meistersinger von Nürnberg, w. Maria Müller (sop), Max Lorenz (ten), Jaro Prohaska (bar), Josef Greindl (bass), Bayreuth Festival Orch *(rec live, July-Aug 1943)* Grammofono 2000 4-▲ GRM 78602
Wagner, R.:Die Meistersinger von Nürnberg, w. E. Schwarzkopf (sop), E. Kunz (ten), O. Edelmann (b-bar), H. von Karajan (cnd), Bayreuth Festival Orch *(rec 1951)* Arkadia 4-▲ 224
Wagner, R.:Die Meistersinger von Nürnberg (sels), w. W. Windgassen (ten), H. Hotter (b-bar), A. Cluytens (cnd), Bayreuth Festival Orch—Monologue & Duet from Act 3 [G] *(rec live, 1957)* Arkadia 4-▲ 440 (m) [AAD]
Wagner, R.:Parsifal, w. W. Meier (mez), P. Hofmann (ten), F. Mazura (bar), S. Estes (bass), H. Sotin (bass), M. Salminen (bass), J. Levine (cnd), Bayreuth Festival Orch [1985] [G] Philips 4-▲ 434616-2 [DDD]
Wagner, R.:Parsifal, w. I. Dalis (mez), J. Thomas (ten), G. London (bar), H. Hotter (b-bar), G. Neidlinger (b-bar), H. Knappertsbusch (cnd), Bayreuth Festival Orch [1962] [G] Philips 4-▲ 416390-2 [ADD]
Wagner, R.:Parsifal, w. G. Jones (sop), J. King (ten), T. Stewart (bar), D. McIntyre (b-bar), K. Ridderbusch (bass), F. Crass (bass), P. Boulez (cnd), Bayreuth Festival Orch [G] *(rec 1970)* Deutsche Grammophon 3-▲ 435718-2 [ADD]
Wagner, R.:Parsifal (sels), w. Fritz Wolff (ten), Alexander Kipnis (bass), Muck, Wagner (cnd), Bayreuth Festival Orch [1927]—Transformation Scene, Grail Scene, Flower Maidens Scene, Prelude to Act 3, Good Friday Music InSync ■ C 4137 (m)
Wagner, R.:Parsifal (sels), w. K. Muck (cnd), Bayreuth Festival Orch—Festival of 1927, Act 1 & "Flower Maidens" scene from Act 2); Pistor, Brongeest, Hofmann, Berlin State Opera Orch. & Cho. (Act 3—1928) Opal ▲ CDS 9843 (m) [ADD]
Wagner, R.:Das Rheingold, w. H. Schwarz (mez), H. Zednik (ten), H. Becht (bar), D. McIntyre (b-bar), P. Boulez (cnd), Bayreuth Festival Orch [G] Philips 2-▲ 434421-2 [DDD]
Wagner, R.:Das Rheingold, w. E. Grümmer (sop), R. Gorr (mez), A. Andersson (ten), S. Konya (ten), T. Adam (b-bar), H. Hotter (b-bar), J. Greindl (bass), H. Knappertsbusch (cnd), Bayreuth Festival Orch [G] *(rec live 1958)* Arkadia 2-▲ 441 [AAD]

Bayreuth Festival Chorus (cont.)
Wagner, R.:Das Rheingold, w. L. Finnie (mez—Fricka), G. Clark (ten—Loge), J. Tomlinson (bar—Wotan), B. Brinkmann (bar—Donner), D. Barenboim (cnd), Bayreuth Festival Orch [G] Teldec 2-▲ 4509-91185-2
Wagner, R.:Das Rheingold, w. P. Brivkalne (sop), I. Malaniuk (cta), R. Siewert (cta), Fritz (sgr), Pflanzl (ten), S. Björling (bar), W. Faulhaber (bass), L. Weber (bass), F. Dalberg (bass), H. von Karajan (cnd), Bayreuth Festival Orch [G] *(rec live 8/1/51)* Melodram 2-▲ MEL 26107 (m) [AAD]
Wagner, R.:Das Rheingold, w. E. Schwarzkopf (sop), I. Malaniuk (cta), W. Windgassen (ten), S. Björling (bar), Pflanzl (sgr), H. von Karajan (cnd), Bayreuth Festival Orch [G] *(rec live, 1951)* Arkadia 2-▲ 216 (m) [ADD]
Wagner, R.:Der Ring des Nibelungen, w. Gré Brouwenstein (sop—Freia/Sieglinde), Ilse Hollweg (sop—Waldvogel), Gerda Lammers (sop—Ortlinde), Paula Lenchner (sop—Wellgunde/Gerhilde), Hilde Scheppan (sop—Helmwige), Astrid Varnay (sop—Brünnilde/3rd Norn), Lore Wissmann (sop—Woglinde), Maria von Ilosvay (mez—Flosshilde/Schwertleite/2nd Norn), Louise Charlotte Kamps (mez—Siegrune), Jean Madeira (mez—Erda/Rossweisse/1st Norn), Georgine von Milinkovic (mez—Fricka/Grimgerde), Elisabeth Schärtel (mez—Waltraute), Paul Kuën (ten—Mime), Ludwig Suthaus (ten—Loge), Josef Traxel (ten—Froh), Wolfgang Windgassen (ten—Siegmund/Siegfried), Alfons Herwig (bar—Donner), Hermann Uhde (bar—Gunther), Hans Hotter (b-bar—Wotan), Gustav Neidlinger (b-bar—Alberich), Josef Griendl (bass—Fasolt/Hunding/Hagen), Arnold van Mill (bass—Fafner), H. Knappertsbusch (cnd), Bayreuth Festival Orch *(rec live, Bayreuth, Aug 13-17, 1956)* Golden Melodram 14-▲ GM 1.001 [ADD]
Wagner, R.:Der Ring des Nibelungen, w. G. Jones (sop), H. Schwarz (mez), T. Altmeyer (ten), L. Hofmann (bass), D. McIntyre (b-bar), P. Boulez (cnd), Bayreuth Festival Orch Philips 32-▲ 434420-2 [ADD/DDD]
Wagner, R.:Der Ring des Nibelungen, w. B. Nilsson (sop), L. Rysanek (sop), K. Dvoraková (sop), M. Mödl (sop), A. Burmeister (mez), V. Soukupova (mez), E. Wohlfahrt (ten), W. Windgassen (ten), T. Stewart (bar), T. Adam (b-bar), G. Neidlinger (b-bar), K. Böhme (bass), G. Nienstedt (bass), K. Böhm (cnd), Bayreuth Festival Orch [G] *(rec live, 1966-67)* Philips 14-▲ 420325-2 [ADD]
Wagner, R.:Siegfried, w. A. Varnay (sop), R. Siewert (cta), B. Aldenhoff (ten), P. Kuen (ten), S. Björling (bar), H. Pflanzl (bass), F. Dalberg (bass), H. von Karajan (cnd), Bayreuth Festival Orch [G] *(rec live 1951)* Melodram 4-▲ MEL 46106 (m) [AAD]
Wagner, R.:Siegfried, w. G. Jones (sop), H. Zednik (ten), H. Becht (bar), D. McIntyre (b-bar), P. Boulez (cnd), Bayreuth Festival Orch [G] Philips 3-▲ 434423-2 [DDD]
Wagner, R.:Siegfried, w. B. Nilsson (sop), W. Windgassen (ten), E. Wohlfahrt (ten), T. Adam (b-bar), G. Neidlinger (b-bar), K. Böhm (cnd), Bayreuth Festival Orch [G] Philips 4-▲ 412483-2 [ADD]
Wagner, R.:Siegfried, w. A. Varnay (sop), W. Windgassen (ten), A. Andersson (ten), G. Stoltze (ten), H. Hotter (b-bar), J. Greindl (bass), H. Knappertsbusch (cnd), Bayreuth Festival Orch [G] *(rec live 1958)* Arkadia 4-▲ 443 [AAD]
Wagner, R.:Siegfried (sels), w. A. Varnay (sop), B. Aldenhoff (ten), H. Knappertsbusch (cnd), Bayreuth Festival Orch—Act 3 Scene 3 [G] *(rec live 1957)* Arkadia 4-▲ 443 [AAD]
Wagner, R.:Tannhäuser, w. G. Brouwenstijn (sop), R. Vinay (ten), D. Fischer-Dieskau (bar), J. Greindl (bass), J. Keilberth (cnd), Bayreuth Festival Orch *(rec live, Bayreuth, 1954)* Melodram 3-▲ MEL 36105
Wagner, R.:Tannhäuser, w. V. de Los Angeles (sop), G. Bumbry (mez), W. Windgassen (ten), G. Stolze (ten), D. Fischer-Dieskau (bar), T. Adam (b-bar), J. Greindl (bass), F. Crass (bass), W. Sawallisch (cnd), Bayreuth Festival Orch [G] *(rec 1961)* Myto 3-▲ MCD 93277
Wagner, R.:Tannhäuser, w. A. Silja (sop), G. Bumbry (mez), W. Windgassen (ten), E. Wächter (bar), J. Greindl (bass), W. Sawallisch (cnd), Bayreuth Festival Orch [Dresden version with Paris Venusberg music] [G] Philips 3-▲ 434607-2 [ADD]
Wagner, R.:Tristan und Isolde, w. B. Nilsson (sop), C. Ludwig (mez), W. Windgassen (ten), E. Wächter (bar), M. Talvela (bass), K. Böhm (cnd), Bayreuth Festival Orch [G] Philips 3-▲ 434425-2 [ADD]
Wagner, R.:Tristan und Isolde, w. C. Ligendza (sop—Isolde), Y. Minton (mez—Brangäne), H. Brilioth (ten—Tristan), K. Moll (bass—King Mark), C. Kleiber (cnd), Bayreuth Festival Orch *(rec Bayreuth Festival, 1975)* Exclusive 3-▲ EXL 54 [ADD]
Wagner, R.:Tristan und Isolde, w. M. Mödl (sop), R. Vinay (ten), H. Hotter (b-bar), H. von Karajan (cnd), Bayreuth Festival Orch *(rec 1955)* Arkadia 4-▲ 528 (m) [AAD]
Wagner, R.:Tristan und Isolde, w. B. Nilsson (sop), C. Ludwig (mez), W. Windgassen (ten), E. Wächter (bar), M. Talvela (bass), K. Böhm (cnd), Bayreuth Festival Orch [G] *(rec Bayreuth Festival, 1966)* Deutsche Grammophon 3-▲ 419889-2 [ADD]

BBC Children's Chorus
Vaughan Williams, R.:A Song of Thanksgiving, w. *(nar unknown)*, E. Suddaby (sop), A. Boult (cnd), BBC SO Intaglio ▲ ING 757 [ADD]

BBC Choral Society
Beethoven, L. van:Cant on the Death of the Emperor Joseph II, w. K. Te Kanawa (sop), Y. Newman (mez), D. Barrett (bar), M. Langdon (bass), C. Davis (cnd), BBC SO, BBC Chorus [G] *(rec live Oct. 7, 1970)* Intaglio ▲ INCD 7361 [ADD]
Berkeley, L.:Magnificat, w. A. Boult (cnd), London PO, BBC Chorus *(rec live, Royal Albert Hall, London, 1969)* Intaglio ▲ INCD 7281 [ADD]
Brahms, J.:Gesang der Parzen, w. H. Harper (sop), H. Prey (bar), P. Boulez (cnd), BBC SO *(rec live July 20, 1973)* Memories 2-▲ HR 4493/94 [ADD]
Delius, F.:Appalachia, w. John Noble (bar), C. Groves (cnd), London PO, BBC Chorus, Goldsmith's Choral Union, London Phil Choir IMP ("BBC Radio Classics" series) ▲ IMP 9133
Mahler, G.:Sym 2, w. Rae Woodland (sop), Janet Baker (mez), L. Stokowski (cnd), London SO, BBC Chorus, Goldsmith's Choral Union, Harrow Choral Society *(rec 1963)* Music & Arts ▲ CD 885 [AAD]
Mahler, G.:Sym 2, w. F. Palmer (sop), T. Troyanos (alt), P. Boulez (cnd), BBC SO, London Phil Choir Enterprise 2-▲ LV 915/916
Mozart, W.A.:Requiem, w. Jennifer Smith (sop), Helen Watts (cta), Ian Partridge (ten), Stafford Dean (bass), M. Atzmon (cnd), BBC Welsh National SO IMP ("BBC Radio" series) ▲ IMP 5691452
Vaughan Williams, R.:Sym 1, w. Elaine Blighton (sop), John Cameron (bar), M. Sargent (cnd), BBC SO, BBC Chorus, Christchurch Harmonic Choir New Zealand *(rec 1965)* IMP ("BBC Radio" series) ▲ IMP 5691502

BBC Chorus
Beethoven, L. van:Cant on the Death of the Emperor Joseph II, w. K. Te Kanawa (sop), Y. Newman (mez), D. Barrett (bar), M. Langdon (bass), C. Davis (cnd), BBC SO, BBC Choral Society [G] *(rec live Oct. 7, 1970)* Intaglio ▲ INCD 7361 [ADD]
Berkeley, L.:Magnificat, w. A. Boult (cnd), London PO, BBC Choral Society *(rec live, Royal Albert Hall, London, 1969)* Intaglio ▲ INCD 7281 [ADD]
Delius, F.:Appalachia, w. John Noble (bar), C. Groves (cnd), London PO, BBC Choral Society, Goldsmith's Choral Union, London Phil Choir IMP ("BBC Radio Classics" series) ▲ IMP 9133
Handel, G.F.:Messiah, w. Dora Labbette (sop), Muriel Brunskill (cta), Hubert Eisdell (ten), Harold Williams (bar), T. Beecham (cnd), BBC SO *(rec 1927)* Pearl 2-▲ PEA 9456 [DDD]
Mahler, G.:Sym 2, w. Rae Woodland (sop), Janet Baker (mez), L. Stokowski (cnd), London SO, BBC Choral Society, Goldsmith's Choral Union, Harrow Choral Society *(rec 1963)* Music & Arts ▲ CD 885 [AAD]
Vaughan Williams, R.:Sym 1, w. Elaine Blighton (sop), John Cameron (bar), M. Sargent (cnd), BBC SO, BBC Choral Society, Christchurch Harmonic Choir New Zealand *(rec 1965)* IMP ("BBC Radio" series) ▲ IMP 5691502

BBC Concert Chorus
Verdi, G.:La forza del destino, w. Martina Arroyo (sop—Donna Leonora), Janet Coster (mez—Preziosilla), Kenneth Bowen (ten—Trabuco), Kenneth Collins (ten—Don Alvaro), Peter Glossop (bar—Don Carlo), Roderick Kennedy (bass—Marquis), J. Matheson (cnd), BBC Concert Orch *(rec live, early 1980's)* Exclusive 2-▲ EXL 80 [ADD]
Verdi, G.:I vespri siciliani, w. J. Brumaire (sop), P. Bowden (mez), Bonhomme (sgr), Taylor (sgr), Baran (sgr), M. Rossi (cnd), BBC Concert Orch [original French version] *(rec live, London, 5/10/69)* Arkadia 3-▲ 456 [ADD]

BBC Northern Singers
Liszt, F.:A Faust Sym, w. J. Mitchinson (ten), J. Horenstein (cnd), BBC Northern SO *(rec live)* Intaglio ▲ INCD 7141 [ADD]

BBC Northern Singers (cont.)

Liszt, F.:A Faust Sym, w. J. Mitchinson (ten), J. Horenstein (cnd), BBC Northern SO *(rec live Apr. 1972)* Music & Arts ▲ CD 744 [AAD]

Vaughan Williams, R.:The Pilgrim's Progress, w. Delyth Jones (sop), Elsa Kendal (cta), Charles Groves (ten), Robin Leggate (ten), V. Handley (cnd), BBC Northern SO IMP ("BBC Radio Classics" series) ▲ IMP 5691662

Vaughan Williams, R.:5 Tudor Portraits, w. P. Walker (sop), F. Harrison (alto), A. Boult (cnd), BBC SO Intaglio ▲ ING 757 [ADD]

BBC Singers

Beethoven, L. van:Fant Pno, Op. 80, "Choral Fant", w. Edith Vogel (pno), J. Pritchard (cnd), BBC SO, BBC Sym Chorus IMP ("BBC Radio Classics" series) ▲ IMP 9132

Beethoven, L. van:Missa Solemnis, w. Ileana Cotrubas (sop), Kathleen Kuhlmann (mez), Robert Tear (ten), Gwynne Howell (bass), J. Pritchard (cnd), BBC SO IMP ("BBC Radio Classics" series) ▲ IMP 5691552

Boulez, P.:e.e. cummings ist der Dichter, w. P. Boulez (cnd), Ensemble InterContemporain Erato ▲ 2292-45648-2 [DDD]

Boulez, P.:Le Soleil des eaux, w. P. Bryn-Julson (sop), P. Boulez (cnd), BBC SO [F] Erato ▲ 2292-45494-2 [DDD]

Boulez, P.:Le Visage Nuptial, w. P. Bryn-Julson (sop), E. Laurence (alt), P. Boulez (cnd), BBC SO [F] Erato ▲ 2292-45494-2 [DDD]

Delius, F.:A Song of the High Hills, w. G. Rozhdestvensky (cnd), BBC SO, BBC Sym Chorus IMP ("BBC Radio Classics" series) ▲ IMP 9133

Elgar, E.:The Music Makers, w. Sarah Walker (mez), N. del Mar (cnd), BBC SO, BBC Sym Chorus IMP ("BBC Radio Classics" series) ▲ IMP 5691672

Fauré, G.:Pavane Orch, w. S. Joly (cnd), BBC Concert Orch IMP ("BBC Radio" series) ▲ IMP 5691482

Ives, C.:Choral Music, w. Chrisopher Hughes (org), S. Cleobury (cnd), Duke String Quartet, New London Orch members—Psalms 54, 67, 90 & 135; Easter Carol; Crossing the Bar; The Celestial Country Collins Classics ▲ COL 1479

Last Night of the Proms, w. Bryn Terfel (bar), Evelyn Glennie (mar), Andrew Davis (cnd), BBC SO, BBC Sym Chorus *(rec Royal Albert Hall, Sep. 10, 1994)* Teldec ▲ 97868-2 [DDD]

Mussorgsky, M.:Sorochintsy Fair (sels), w. David Wilson Johnson (bar), G. Rozhdestvensky (cnd), BBC SO, BBC Sym Chorus [E] IMP ("BBC Radio Classics" series) ▲ IMP 9139

Poulenc, F.:Gloria Sop, w. Janice Watson (sop), Y. P. Tortelier (cnd), BBC PO Chandos ▲ CHAN 9341 [DDD]

Poulenc, F.:Stabat mater, w. Janice Watson (sop), Y. P. Tortelier (cnd), BBC PO Chandos ▲ CHAN 9341 [DDD]

Reich, S.:The Desert Music, w. P. Eötvös (cnd), BBC SO IMP ("BBC Radio Classics" series) ▲ IMP 5691692

Scarlatti, D.:Stabat mater, w. J. Kennard (sop), P. Taylor (ten), J. Poole (cnd) *(rec 1976)* Sony Classical ("Essential Classics" series) ▲ SBK 48282 [AAD] ■ SBT 48282

Schoenberg, A.:Die glückliche Hand, w. S. Nimsgern (b-bar), P. Boulez (cnd), BBC SO *(rec Mar. 12, 1981)* Sony Classical ▲ SMK 48464 [ADD]

Schoenberg, A.:Die Jakobsleiter, w. P. Boulez (cnd), BBC SO, Ensemble InterContemporain Sony Classical ▲ SMK 48462 [ADD]

Schoenberg, A.:Moses und Aaron, w. R. Cassilly (ten), G. Reich (nar), P. Boulez (cnd), BBC SO, Ensemble InterContemporain *(rec Nov. 30–Dec. 06, 1974)* Sony Classical 2-▲ SM2K 48456 [ADD]

Szymanowski, K.:Sym 3, w. Philip Langridge (ten), A. Panufnik (cnd), BBC SO, BBC Sym Chorus IMP ("BBC Radio Classics" series) ▲ IMP 9124

Tavener, J.:Akathist of Thanksgiving, w. J. Bowman (ct), T. Wilson (ten), M. Baker (org), M. Neary (cnd), BBC SO, Westminster Abbey Choir *(rec Jan. 21, 1994)* Sony Classical ▲ SK 64446 [DDD]

Vaughan Williams, R.:Sancta civitas, w. Gareth Roberts (ten), Brian Rayner Cook (bar), G. Rozhdestvensky (cnd), BBC SO, BBC Sym Chorus IMP ("BBC Radio Classics" series) ▲ IMP 9125

Webern, A.:music of, w. Christiane Oelze (sop), Gerald Finley (bar), P. Boulez (cnd), Berlin PO—Sym, Op. 21; Cants, Opp. 29 & 31; 3 Songs; Das Augenlicht; Vars, Op. 30; 5 Pieces Deutsche Grammophon ▲ 447 765-2

Wild Classics:A Celebration of Animals & Nature, w. James Galway (fl), Ofra Harnoy (vc), Martin Hoherman (vc), Emily Mitchell (hp), Michael Dussek (pno), Samuel Lipman (pno), Leo Litwin (pno), Gerhard Oppitz (pno), Isao Tomita (synths), Boston Pops Orch [cnd:Arthur Fiedler], Chicago SO [cnd:Fritz Reiner] RCA Red Seal ▲ 09026-68483-2 ■ 09026-68483-4

Cooke, Pritchard (cnd)

Walton, W.:Belshazzar's Feast, w. Stephen Roberts (bar), C. Mackerras (cnd), English CO, BBC Sym Chorus, London Phil Choir IMP ("BBC Radio Classics" series) ▲ IMP 5691612

B. Holten (cnd)

Górecki, H.-M.:Totus tuus *(rec St Paul's Church, Knightsbridge, London, Nov 27, 1993)* United ▲ CAL 88021 [DDD]

Pärt, A.:Magnificat Collins Classics ▲ COL 1472

Pärt, A.:Magnificat-Antiphones Collins Classics ▲ COL 1472

Pärt, A.:Summa Collins Classics ▲ COL 1472

Penderecki, K.:Choral Music—Agnus Dei *(rec St Paul's Church, Knightsbridge, London, Nov 27, 1993)* United ▲ CAL 88021 [DDD]

Szamotul, W.:Polish Psalms & Hymns *(rec St Paul's Church, Knightsbridge, London, Nov 27, 1993)* United ▲ CAL 88021 [DDD]

Szymanowski, K.:Kurpian Songs, w. Helen Miles (sop), Vernon Kirk (ten) *(rec St Paul's Church, Knightsbridge, London, Nov 27, 1993)* United ▲ CAL 88021 [DDD]

Tormis, V.:Choral Music—Curse upon Iron; Karelian Destiny Collins Classics ▲ COL 1472

S. Joly (cnd)

Bantock, G.:Atlanta in Calydon *(rec St. Paul's Church, Knightsbridge, London, Oct 3-4, 1995)* Albany ▲ TROY 180 [DDD]

Bantock, G.:Vanity of Vanities *(rec Oct 6, 1995)* Albany ▲ TROY 180 [DDD]

Davies, P.M.:Choral Music—Westerlings; 1 Star at Last; House of Winter; Sea Runes; Apple Basked [Apple Blossom]; A Hoy Calendar; Shepherds of Hoy; Corpus Christie, with Cat & Mouse; Lullabye for Lucy Collins Classics ▲ COL 1463

Tavener, J.:Choral Music, w. Christopher Bowers-Broadbent (org)—Thunder Entered Her; The Lamb; The Tiger; Hymn to the Mother of God; Hymn for the Dormition of the Mother of God; Responorium in memoriam Annon Lee Silver; Song for Athene; Eonia; God is With Us *(rec live, St Giles, Cripplegate, Jan 22, 1994)* United ▲ CAL 88023 [DDD]

A. Lawrence (cnd)

Grainger, P.:Brigg Fair, w. Gareth Roberts (ten) IMP ("BBC Radio Classics" series) ▲ IMP 9128

J. Poole (cnd)

Duparc, H.:Benedicat vobis Dominus, w. Margaret Phillips (org) IMP ("BBC Radio" series) ▲ IMP 5691482

Martin, F.:Mass, w. Margaret Phillips (org) IMP ("BBC Radio" series) ▲ IMP 5691482

Swayne, G.:Cry NM Classics ▲ NMCD 016

BBC Sym Chorus

Bach, J.S.:Mass in b, BWV 232, w. A. Giebel (sop), J. Baker (mez), N. Gedda (ten), H. Prey (bar), F. Crass (bass), O. Klemperer (cnd), New Philharmonia Orch [L] EMI Classics ("Studio" series) 2-▲ ZDMB 63364-2 [ADD]

Beethoven, L. van:Fant Pno, Op. 80, "Choral Fant", w. Edith Vogel (pno), J. Pritchard (cnd), BBC SO, BBC Singers IMP ("BBC Radio Classics" series) ▲ IMP 9132

Berlioz, H.:Benvenuto Cellini, w. J. Carlyle (sop), J. Veasey (mez), K. Lewis (ten), Kentish, Cameron, Bushby, Garrard, Ward, A. Dorati (cnd), BBC SO [E] *(rec live, Royal Festival Hall, 1964)* Music & Arts 2-▲ CD 618 (m) [AAD]

Borodin, A.:Prince Igor (sels), w. Margaret Field (sop), G. Simon (cnd), Philharmonia Orch Off-stage Brass—Suite [orchd Glazunov & Rimsky-Korsakov] *(rec All Hallows Church, Gospel Oak, London)* Cala ▲ CAL 1011 [DDD]

Boulanger, L.:Choral Music, w. J. Price (sop), N. Boulanger (cnd), BBC SO—Psalm 24 (1916); Pie Jesu (1918) *(rec live Nov. 1968, London)* Intaglio ▲ INCD 703-1 [ADD]

BBC Sym Chorus (cont.)

Boulanger, L.:Du fond de l'abîme, w. B. Greevy (mez), I. Partridge (ten), N. Boulanger (cnd), BBC SO *(rec live, London Nov. 1968)* Intaglio ▲ INCD 703-1 [ADD]

Britten, B.:Spring Sym, w. Eiddwen Harrhy (sop), Linda Finnie (cta), Robert Tear (ten), G. Rozhdestvensky (cnd), BBC SO, London Voices, Southend Boys' Choir IMP ("BBC Radio Classics" series) ▲ IMP 5691752

Debussy, C.:Jeux, w. P. Boulez (cnd), BBC SO, Paris Conservatory Société des Concerts Orch Originals 2-▲ ORISH 855

Delius, F.:Appalachia, w. T. Beecham (cnd), London PO *(rec Jan. 6, 7 & 31, 1938)* Dutton Laboratories ▲ CDLX 7011 [ADD]

Delius, F.:Brigg Fair:An English Rhapsody, w. E. Nørby (bar), T. Beecham (cnd), Royal PO *(rec 1955)* Sony Masterworks (Portrait) ▲ MPK 47680 [ADD]

Delius, F.:Hassan, w. L. Fry (bar), T. Beecham (cnd), Royal PO *(rec 1955-56)* Sony Masterworks (Portrait) ▲ MPK 47680 [ADD]

Delius, F.:A Mass of Life, w. K. Te Kanawa (sop), P. Bowden (mez), R. Dowd (ten), J. Shirley-Quirk (bar), N. del Mar (cnd), BBC SO *(rec live, London 5/3/71)* Intaglio 2-▲ INCD 702-2 [ADD]

Delius, F.:Sea Drift, w. B. Boyce (bar), T. Beecham (cnd), Royal PO *(rec 1954)* Sony Masterworks (Portrait) ▲ MPK 47680 [ADD]

Delius, F.:A Song of the High Hills, w. G. Rozhdestvensky (cnd), BBC SO, BBC Singers IMP ("BBC Radio Classics" series) ▲ IMP 9133

Elgar, E.:The Music Makers, w. J. Rigby (mez), A. Davis (cnd), BBC SO *(rec London, Aug. 1993)* Teldec ▲ 92374-2 [DDD]

Elgar, E.:The Music Makers, w. Sarah Walker (mez), N. del Mar (cnd), BBC SO, BBC Singers IMP ("BBC Radio Classics" series) ▲ IMP 5691672

Fauré, G.:Requiem, w. J. Price (sop), J. Carol Case (bar), N. Boulanger (cnd), BBC SO *(rec live, London Nov. 1968)* Intaglio ▲ INCD 703-1 [ADD]

Gerhard, R.:La Peste, w. Michael Lonsdale (nar), E. Colomer (cnd), Spanish National Youth Orch Auvidis Montaigne ▲ MO 782101

Gounod, C.:Faust, w. M. Licette (sop—Margarita), D. Vane (sop—Siebel), M. Brunskill (cta—Martha), H. Nash (ten—Faust), H. Williams (b-bar—Valentine), R. Easton (bass—Mephistopheles), R. Carr (bass—Wagner), T. Beecham (cnd), BBC SO Dutton Laboratories 2-▲ CDAX 2001 [ADD]

Holst, G.:First Choral Sym, w. H. Harper (sop), M. Sargent (cnd), BBC SO *(rec Jan. 3, 1964)* Intaglio ▲ ING 740 [ADD]

Last Night of the Proms, w. Bryn Terfel (bar), Evelyn Glennie (mar), Andrew Davis (cnd), BBC SO, BBC Singers *(rec Royal Albert Hall, Sep. 10, 1994)* Teldec ▲ 97868-2 [DDD]

Mahler, G.:Das Klagende Lied, w. Teresa Cahill (sop), Janet Baker (mez), Robert Tear (ten), Gwynne Howell (bass), G. Rozhdestvensky (cnd), BBC SO IMP ("BBC Radio" series) ▲ IMP 5691412

Mahler, G.:Sym 2, w. Felicity Palmer (sop/mez), Tatiana Troyanos (mez), P. Boulez (cnd), BBC SO, Paris Conservatory Société des Concerts Orch Originals 2-▲ ORISH 855

Massenet, J.:Sapho, w. Jenny Hill (sop), Laura Sarti (mez), Bernard Dickerson (ten), Alexander Oliver (ten), Neilson Taylor (bar), George Macpherson (bass), Milla Andrew (sgr), B. Keefe (cnd), BBC SO *(rec live, 1973)* Memories 2-▲ MEM 4601 [AAD]

Mozart, W.A.:Complete Mozart Edition, w. J. Norman (sop), M. Freni (sop), Y. Minton (mez), I. Wixell (bar), C. Davis (cnd), BBC SO Philips 3-▲ 422540-2 [ADD]

Mozart, W.A.:Missa, K.317, w. C. Davis (cnd), BBC SO Philips 2-▲ 438800-2

Mozart, W.A.:Missa, K.427, w. C. Davis (cnd), BBC SO Philips 2-▲ 438800-2

Mozart, W.A.:Requiem, w. Elsie Morison (sop), Monica Sinclair (cta), Alexander Young (ten), Marian Nowakowski (bass), T. Beecham (cnd), Royal PO *(rec 1958)* Theorema ▲ TH 121151

Mozart, W.A.:Requiem, w. *(soloists unknown)*, C. Davis (cnd), BBC SO Philips 2-▲ 438800-2

Mussorgsky, M.:Sorochintsy Fair (sels), w. David Wilson Johnson (bar), G. Rozhdestvensky (cnd), BBC SO, BBC Singers [E] IMP ("BBC Radio Classics" series) ▲ IMP 9139

Prokofiev, S.:Poems, w. G. Rozhdestvensky (cnd), BBC SO IMP ("BBC Radio" series) ▲ IMP 5691462

Saxton, R.:I Will Awake the Dawn, w. M. Bamert (cnd), BBC SO Collins Classics ▲ 12832

Schoenberg, A.:A Survivor from Warsaw, w. G. Reich (nar), P. Boulez (cnd), BBC SO *(rec 1976)* Sony Classical 2-▲ S2K 44571 [ADD/DDD]

Schubert, Franz:Fant Vn, D.934, w. J.-L. Poulet (vn), N. Lee (pno) Arion 2-▲ ARN 268006 [AAD]

Szymanowski, K.:Sym 3, w. Philip Langridge (ten), A. Panufnik (cnd), BBC SO, BBC Singers IMP ("BBC Radio Classics" series) ▲ IMP 9124

Testimonies of War:Kriegszeugnisse, 1914-45, w. London PO [cnd:N. Sheriff], Berlin RSO [cnd:B. Goldschmidt], Poznán PO [cnd:A. Borejko] Largo 2-▲ 5130 [DDD]

Tippett, M.:A Child Of Our Time, w. Jill Gomez (sop), Helen Watts (cta), Kenneth Wooliam (ten), John Shirley-Quirk (bar), G. Rozhdestvensky (cnd), BBC SO IMP ("BBC Radio Classics" series) ▲ IMP 9130

Tippett, M.:The Mask of Time, w. F. Robinson (sop), S. Walker (mez), R. Tear (ten), J. Cheek (bass), A. Davis (cnd), BBC SO EMI Classics ▲ ZDMB 64111

Vaughan Williams, R.:Dona nobis pacem, w. R. Flynn (sop), R. Henderson (bar), R. Vaughan Williams (cnd), BBC SO [E,L] *(rec 11/36, broadcast transcri)* Pearl ▲ GEMMCD 9342 (m) [AAD]

Vaughan Williams, R.:Sancta civitas, w. Gareth Roberts (ten), Brian Rayner Cook (bar), G. Rozhdestvensky (cnd), BBC SO, BBC Singers IMP ("BBC Radio Classics" series) ▲ IMP 9125

Wagner, R.:Der fliegende Holländer, w. A. Silja (sop), E. Kozub (ten), T. Adam (b-bar), M. Talvela (bass), O. Klemperer (cnd), New Philharmonia Orch [G] EMI Classics ("Studio" series) 3-▲ CDMC 63344 [ADD]

Wagner, R.:Der fliegende Holländer, w. Anja Silja (sop—Senta), Anneliese Burmeister (mez—Mary), Ernst Kozub (ten—Erik), Gerhard Unger (ten—Steersman), Theo Adam (bass—Dutchman), Martti Talvela (bass—Daland), O. Klemperer (cnd), New Philharmonia Orch EMI Classics 3-▲ CDCC 55179

Cooke, Pritchard (cnd)

Walton, W.:Belshazzar's Feast, w. Stephen Roberts (bar), C. Mackerras (cnd), English CO, BBC Singers, London Phil Choir IMP ("BBC Radio Classics" series) ▲ IMP 5691612

S. Jackson (cnd)

Daniel-Lesur, D.J.Y.:Le cantique des cantiques ASV ▲ ASV 900 [DDD]

Daniel-Lesur, D.J.Y.:In paradisum ASV ▲ ASV 900 [DDD]

Daniel-Lesur, D.J.Y.:Messe du Jubilé ASV ▲ ASV 900 [DDD]

Daniel-Lesur, D.J.Y.:Vie interieure ASV ▲ ASV 900 [DDD]

Rütti, C.:Choral Music—O Magnum Mysterium; Nunc Dumittis; Missa Angelorum; Magnificat; Alpha et Omega ASV ▲ ASV CD 954

BBC Sym Men's Chorus

Stokowski, L.:Transcriptions Orch, w. Ian Boughton (ten), G. Simon (cnd), Philharmonia Orch—Borodin:Requiem *(rec All Hallows Church, Gospel Oak, London)* Cala ▲ CAL 1011 [DDD]

BBC Sym Women's Chorus

Debussy, C.:Ibéria, w. L. Stokowski (cnd), London SO EMI Classics ("Full Dimensional Sound" series) ▲ CDM 65422

Holst, G.:The Planets, w. A. Davis (org), A. David (cnd), BBC SO *(rec London, Dec. 1993)* Teldec ▲ 94541-2 [DDD]

BBC Theater Chorus

Cherubini, L.:Les Deux journées, w. J. Micheau (sop), M. Davies (ten), P. Gianotti (ten), E. Regnier (ten), C. Paul (bar), T. Beecham (cnd), Royal PO *(rec live, London Dec. 19, 1947)* Intaglio 2-▲ INCD 7342 [ADD]

BBC Welsh Choral Society

Mozart, W.A.:Ave verum, w. M. Atzmon (cnd), BBC Welsh National SO IMP ("BBC Radio" series) ▲ IMP 5691452

Mozart, W.A.:Maurerische Trauermusik, w. M. Atzmon (cnd), BBC Welsh National SO IMP ("BBC Radio" series) ▲ IMP 5691452

BBC Welsh National Chorus

Hughes, O.A.:Dewi Saint, w. Yvonne Kenny (sop), Martyn Hill (ten), David Wilson-Johnson (bar), O. A. Hughes (cnd), BBC Welsh National SO [E] Chandos ▲ CHAN 8890 [DDD]

Mahler, G.:Sym 2, w. Benita Valente (sop), Maureen Forrester (cta), G. Kaplan (cnd), London SO, Ardwyn Singers, Cardiff Polyphonic Choir, Dyfed Choir Conifer Classics 2-▲ 75605-51277-2 [DDD]

Rubbra, E.:The Morning Watch, w. R. Hickox (cnd), BBC Welsh National SO Chandos ▲ CHAN 9441

BBC Welsh National Chorus (cont.)
Rubbra, E.:Sym 9, w. Lynne Dawson (sop), Della Jones (alt), Stephen Roberts (bar), R. Hickox (cnd), BBC Welsh National SO — Chandos ▲ CHAN 9441
The Spirit of Christmas Present, w. Kansas City Chorale [cnd:Charles Bruffy], BBC Welsh Chorus [cnd:John Hugh Thomas], Huw Tregelles Williams (org), Welsh Guards Fanfare Trumpeters, Christ Church Cathedral Choir [cnd:Stephen Darlington], Gulbenkian Orch [cnd:Michel Swierczewski], et al. — Nimbus ▲ NI 7034 [DDD]
Tavener, J.:We Shall See Him As He Is, w. P. Rozario (sop), J. M. Ainsley (ten), A. Murgatroyd (ten), R. Hickox (cnd), BBC Welsh National SO [E] — Chandos ▲ CHAN 9128 [DDD]
J.H. Thomas (cnd)
Celebration:Christmas Fanfares & Carols, w. Welsh Guards Fanfare Trumpeters, Huw Tregelles Williams (org), Aled Jones (nar) — Nimbus ▲ NI 5310 [DDD]

Bec-Hellouin Abbey Monks' Choir
Le Temps de Noël, w. En-Calcat Abbey Monks' Choir, Ligugé Abbey Monks' Choir, Timadeuc Abbey Monks' Choir, Les Peres de Chevilly — Studio SM 2-▲ 1219.10
Venite Adoremus, w. Citeaux Abbey Monks' Choir & Séminaristes de la Cathédrale Abbey Monks' Choir Strasbourg — Studio SM ▲ 121698

Beecham Choral Society
Beethoven, L. van:Mass, Op. 86, w. T. Beecham (cnd), Royal PO — EMI Classics ▲ CDM 64385
Beethoven, L. van:Sym 9, "Choral Sym", w. I. Borkh (sop), R. Siewert (cta), R. Lewis (ten), L. Weber (bass), R. Leibowitz (cnd), Royal PO [G] *(rec 6/61)* — Chesky ▲ CD66 [ADD]
Delius, F.:Sea Drift, w. *(soloist unknown)*, T. Beecham (cnd), Royal PO — EMI Classics 2-▲ ZDMB 64386
Mozart, W.A.:Arias, w. I. Hollweg (sop), L. Marshall (sop), L. Simoneau (ten), G. Unger (ten), G. Frick (bass), T. Beecham (cnd), Royal PO — EMI Classics 2-▲ CDHB 63715
Mozart, W.A.:Entführung, w. I. Hollweg (sop), L. Marshall (sop), L. Simoneau (ten), G. Unger (ten), G. Frick (bass), T. Beecham (cnd), Royal PO — EMI Classics 2-▲ CDHB 63715
Ravel, M.:Daphnis et Chloé (suite 1), w. G. Gilbert (fl), G. Prêtre (cnd), Royal PO *(rec Apr. 8 & 9, 1963)* — Chesky ▲ CD 101 [ADD]
Ravel, M.:Daphnis et Chloé (suite 2), w. G. Gilbert (fl), G. Prêtre (cnd), Royal PO *(rec Apr. 8 & 9, 1963)* — Chesky ▲ CD 101 [ADD]
Wagner, R.:Tannhäuser (sels), w. J. Horenstein (cnd), Royal PO—Bacchanale *(rec 1962)* — Chesky ▲ CD 19
T. Beecham (cnd)
Beethoven, L. van:Die Ruinen von Athen (incidental music) — EMI Classics ▲ CDM 64385

Belarus State Capella Chorus Minsk
Benguerel, X.:Libre Vermell, w. Natalia Rudnjewa (mez), L. Kramer (cnd), Belarus Minsk State PO — Koch Schwann 2-▲ SCH 314132

Belcanto Ensemble Frankfurt
Rühm, G.:foetus — Koch Schwann ("Aulos" series) ▲ 314322 [DDD]
Rühm, G.:Schöpfung — Koch Schwann ("Aulos" series) ▲ 314322 [DDD]
Rühm, G.:Sprechquartette — Koch Schwann ("Aulos" series) ▲ 314322 [DDD]
Stahmer, K.H.:Geburtstagskanon für John Cage — Pro Viva ▲ ISPV 167 [DDD]
Stahmer, K.H.:Klanglabyrinthe — Pro Viva ▲ ISPV 167 [DDD]
Stahmer, K.H.:Der Stoff, aus dem die Stille ist — Pro Viva ▲ ISPV 167 [DDD]
D. Spohr (cnd)
Stahmer, K.H.:Hommage à Daidalos, w. Elmar Daucher (steinklänge) *(rec Munich, Oct 1989)* — Pro Viva ▲ ISPV 159 [DDD]
Vetter, M.:Music of, w. Elmar Daucher (steinklänge)—Music aus Stein [improvisation]; Steinklänge *(rec Munich, Oct 1989)* — Pro Viva ▲ ISPV 159 [DDD]

Belfast Cathedral Choir
D. Drinkell (cnd)
Peace I Leave With You:A Sequence of Music for the Holy Eucharist, w. Ian Barber (org) *(rec Belfast Cathedral, Northern Ireland)* — Guild ▲ GMCD 7126 [DDD]

Belfast Philharmonic Society Chorus
Ravel, M.:Daphins et Chloé, w. Y.P. Tortelier (cnd), Ulster Orch, Renaissance Singers — Chandos ▲ CHAN 8893 [DDD]

Belgian Radio-TV Chorus
Lehár, F.:Der Graf von Luxemburg (sels), w. *(soloists unknown)*, A. Sibert (cnd), Belgian Radio-TV Orch — Studio SM ▲ 2222
Lehár, F.:Das Land des Lächeins (sels), w. *(soloists unknown)*, A. Sibert (cnd), Belgian Radio-TV Orch — Studio SM ▲ 2222
Lehár, F.:Die lustige Witwe, w. Teresa Stich-Randall (mez—Missia Palmieri), Monique Stiot (mez—Manon), Germaine Duclos (sgr—Praskovia), Linda Felder (sgr—Olga), Christiane Jacquin (sgr—Nadia), Jeannette Levasseur (sgr—Sylviane), Henri Legay (ten—Camille de Coutançon), Joseph Peyron (ten—Kromsky), Robert Destain (sgr—Baron Popoff), Michel Fauche (sgr—Pristich), Gérard Friedmann (sgr—Lerida), Jacques Gilet (sgr—Bogdanowitch), Jean Guy Henneveux (sgr—Prince Danilo), Serge Klin (sgr—Figg), Jacques Villa (sgr—D'Estillac), A. Sibert (cnd), Belgian Radio-TV Orch *(rec Grand Auditorium, Belgium, Apr 30, 1970)* — Studio SM 2-▲ 2160 [AAD]
Strauss (II), Joh.:Eine Nacht in Venedig (sels), w. *(artists unknown)*, A. Sibert (cnd), Belgian Radio-TV Orch — Studio SM ▲ 2222
Verdi, G.:Aida, w. Jessye Norman (sop), Yannula Pappas (mez), Walter Alberti (bar), Luigi Roni (b-bar), N. Sanzogno (cnd), Belgian Radio-TV Orch *(rec live, Paris, May 4, 1973)* — Agorá ("Phoenix" series) 2-▲ 507

Belgrade National Opera Chorus
Mussorgsky, M.:Boris Godunov, w. Cangalovic (sgr), Djokic (sgr), Milosevic (sgr), Petrovic (sgr), D. Miladinovic (cnd), Belgrade National Opera Orch *(rec live, La Fenice Theater, Venice, Jan. 3, 1967)* — Arkadia 3-▲ 492
Tchaikovsky, P.:Mazeppa, w. Bakocevic (sgr), Cakarevic (sgr), Cangalovic (sgr), N. Mitic (bar), O. Danon (cnd), Belgrade National Opera Orch [R] *(rec live, Berlin, 9/27/69)* — Myto 2-▲ 2 MCD 90527 [ADD]

Belgrade Radio-TV Chorus
V. Ilic (cnd)
Serbian Orthodox Christmas Carols — Jade ▲ JAD C 039
M. Jagust (cnd)
Mokranjac, S.:Liturgy, w. V. Mikic (bass) — Jade ▲ JAD C 021
Mokranjac, S.:Requiem, w. V. Mikic (bass) — Jade ▲ JAD C 021
V. Kranjcevic (cnd)
Mokranjac, S.:Easter Liturgy — Jade ▲ JADC 045

Belloc Abbey Monks' Choir
Jour de Pâques/Jour de Joie, w. J. Colson (cnd), Belloc Abbey Monks' SO — Studio SM ▲ 12 22 03 [ADD]

Belmont Chorale
S.H. Kelly (cnd)
Hairston, J.:Spirituals (20) — Gasparo ▲ GS 269 ■ GS 274C
Jester Hairston:Spirituals — Gasparo ▲ GSCD 269 ■ GS 269C
Pinkham, D.:Choral Music—sels. from Wedding Cantata; Psalm 46; Small Passion; Uncommon Prayers; Festival Jubilate; A Curse, a Lament and a Vision; 13 Motets — Gasparo ▲ GS 288
Ward, R.:Choral Music, w. Linda Ford (org)—In His Last Days; Let Us Heed the Voice Within [both from Images of God]; Earth Shall Be Fair; When Christ Rode Into Jerusalem; Concord Hymn; Sweet Freedom's Song; Ballad of Boston Bay; Epitaphs; Let Music Swell the Breeze — Gasparo ▲ GS 303

Berkeley Chamber Singers
Harrison, L.:Gamelan Music, w. Musicians of the Gamelan Si Betty—Homage to Pacifica; Philemon & Baukis; Cornish Lancaran; Gending Alexander; Bubaran Robert — MusicMasters ▲ 01612-67091-2 [DDD]

Berkshire Boys' Choirs
L. Bernstein (cnd)
Bernstein, L.:Mass, w. Norman Scribner — CBS 2-▲ M2K 44593 [ADD]

Berlin Academy of Arts Chamber Choir
Haydn, J.:Die Schöpfung, w. Edith Mathis (sop), Christoph Prégardien (ten), Harald Stamm (bass), M. Atzmon (cnd), World SO, Pécs Chamber Choir, Shin-Yuh Kai Choir [G] *(rec Basilica San Francesco in Assisi, as part of the IPPNW "Hiroshima Concert 1990")* — BIS 2-▲ CD 493/94 [DDD]

Berlin Ars Nova Ensemble
P. Schwarz (cnd)
Goldschmidt, B.:Belsatzar *(rec June 1990)* — Largo ▲ 5115 [DDD]
Goldschmidt, B.:Letzte Kapitel, w. A. Marks (pno) *(rec June 1990)* — Largo ▲ 5115 [DDD]

Berlin Carl Maria von Weber Men's Choir
Dessau, P.:Haggada, w. Sabine Ritterbusch (sop), Renate Spingler (sop), Yvi Jänicke (alt), Peter Galliard (ten—Rabbi Tarfon/Jude/ten solo), Gabriel Sadé (ten—Pharaoh), Jochen Schmeckenbechier (bar—Rabbi Jehoschua), Bernd Weikl (bar—Moses), Matthias Hölle (bass—Speaker/Rabbi Akiwa), Alfred Muff (bass—Father/Rabbi Eleasar), Johann Tilli (bass—Rabbi Elieser/bass solo), G. Albrecht (cnd), Hamburg State PO, Hamburg Alsterspatzen, North German Radio Chorus [G] *(rec Musikhalle, Hamburg, Sept 4 & 5, 1994)* — Capriccio 2-▲ 10590/91 [DDD]

Berlin Cathedral Boys' Choir
Orff, C.:Carmina burana, w. E. Gruberova (sop), J. Aler (ten), T. Hampson (bar), S. Ozawa (cnd), Berlin PO, Shin-Yuh Kai Chorus [G, L] — Philips ▲ 422363-2 [DDD] ▯ 422363-5

Berlin Cathedral Choir
Mahler, G.:Sym 2, w. G. Bindernagel (sop), E. Leisner (cta), O. Fried (cnd), Berlin State Opera Orch *(rec 1923 for Polydor)* — Pearl 2-▲ PEAS 9929 (m) [AAD]
R. Bader (cnd)
Mozart, W.A.:Schuldigkeit, w. A. Augér (sop), K. Láki (sop), S. Geszty (sop), W. Hollweg (ten), C. H. Ahnsjö (ten) [G] *(rec 1980)* — Koch Schwann 2-▲ CD 313065 [ADD]

Berlin Chamber Chorus
Bach, J.S.:Cant 201, w. Maria Cristina Kiehr (sop), Andreas Scholl (ct), James Taylor (ten), Kurt Azeberger (ten), Roman Trekel (bar), Peter Lika (bass), R. Jacobs (cnd), Berlin Academy for Early Music — Harmonia Mundi France 2-▲ HMC 901544.45
Bach, J.S.:Cant 205, w. Efrat Ben-Nunn (sop), Katharina Kammerloher (alt), Christoph Prégardien (ten), Klaus Häger (bass), R. Jacobs (cnd), Berlin Academy for Early Music — Harmonia Mundi France 2-▲ HMC 901544.45
Bach, J.S.:Cant 213, w. Efrat Ben-Nun (sop), Andreas Scholl (ct), James Taylor (ten), Klaus Häger (bass), R. Jacobs (cnd), Berlin Academy for Early Music — Harmonia Mundi France 2-▲ HMC 901544.45
Mozart, W.A.:Missa brevis, K.258, w. Regina Schudel (sop), Ulla Groenewold (cta), Peter Maus (ten), Berthold Possemeyer (bar), U. Gronostay (cnd), Berlin Radio Sinfonietta [L] — Koch Schwann ▲ CD 313 021 [ADD/DDD]

Berlin Chorus
Straus, O.:Ein Walzertraum (sels), w. Melita Muszely (sop), Lisa Otto (sop), Rudolf Schock (ten), Bruno Fritz (bar), W. Schüchter (cnd), Berlin Orch — Emperor Operetta ▲ KO 86346

Berlin Doctors' Choir
Brahms, J.:Alto Rhap, w. S. Onegin (mez), K. Singer (cnd), Berlin State Opera Orch [G] *(rec 1929 from HMV 78 rpm discs)* — Preiser ("Lebendige Vergangenheit" series) ▲ 89027 (m) [AAD]

Berlin German Opera Chorus
Bellini, V.:Beatrice di Tenda, w. L. Aliberti (sop), C. Capasso (treble), M. Thompson (ten), P. Gavanelli (bass), F. Luisi (cnd), Berlin German Opera Orch — Berlin Classics 2-▲ BER 1042 [DDD]
Bellini, V.:Il pirata, w. Lucia Aliberti (sop), Roberto Frontali (sgr), Stuart Neill (sgr), José Guadalupe Reyes (sgr), M. Viotti (cnd), Berlin German Opera Orch — Berlin Classics 2-▲ BER 1115 [DDD]
Dallapiccola, L.:Ulisse, w. C. Gayer (sop), E. Saedén (bar), V. von Halem (bass), A. Bernard (sgr), L. Maazel (cnd), Berlin German Opera Orch *(rec live, Berlin 9/28/68)* — Stradivarius 2-▲ STR 10063 [ADD]
Flotow, F. von:Martha, w. Erna Berger (sop), Peter Anders (ten), Eugene Fuchs (bar), Josef Greindl (bass), J. Schüler (cnd), Berlin German Opera Orch — Phonographe 2-▲ PHG 5050
Opera Choruses, w. G. Sinopoli (cnd), Berlin German Opera Orch — Deutsche Grammophon [DDD] ▯ 415283-5
Orff, C.:Carmina burana, w. Gundula Janowitz (sop), Gerhard Stolze (ten), Dietrich Fischer-Dieskau (bar), E. Jochum (cnd), Berlin German Opera Orch *(rec Ufa-Studio, Berlin, Oct 1967)* — Deutsche Grammophon ▲ 447437-2 [ADD]
Schumann, R.:Scenes from Goethe's "Faust", w. Lore Hoffman (sop), Walther Ludwig (ten), Karl Schmitt-Walter (bar), H. Schmidt-Isserstedt (cnd), Berlin German Opera Orch — Enterprise ("The Radio Years" series) 2-▲ ENT RY 66
Verdi, G.:La traviata, w. P. Lorengar (sop), S. Malagu (mez), G. Aragall (ten), D. Fischer-Dieskau (bar), L. Maazel (cnd), Berlin German Opera Orch — London ("Double Decker" series) 2-▲ 443000-2
Wagner, R.:Parsifal, w. Gotthelf Pistor (ten), Cornelius Bronsgeest (bar), Ludwig Hofmann (bass), K. Muck (cnd), Berlin German Opera Orch — Preiser ▲ PRE 90270
Wagner, R.:Parsifal (sels), w. E. Larcen (sop), H. Reimar (ten), C. Hartmann (bar), L. Weber (bass), H. Knappertsbusch (cnd), Berlin German Opera Orch—Act 3 *(rec 1943)* — Enterprise ("Document" series) ▲ ENTLV 943 [ADD]
Wagner, R.:Parsifal (sels), w. Carl Hartmann (ten), Hans Reinmar (bar), Ludwig Weber (bass), Elsa Laren (sgr), H. Knappertsbusch (cnd), Berlin German Opera Orch—complete Act 3 *(rec Berlin, March 31, 1942)* — Grammofono 2000 ▲ GRM 78555

Berlin HDK Chamber Choir
Doráti, A.:Jesus oder Barabbas?, w. W. Quadflieg (nar), M. Fischer-Dieskau (cnd), New Berlin CO, Czech PO members [G] *(rec live 1992)* — BIS ▲ CD 578 [DDD]
C. Grube (cnd)
Doráti, A.:Pater Noster *(rec live 1992)* — BIS ▲ CD 578 [DDD]

Berlin Phil Chorus
Mahler, G.:Sym 8, w. Majken Bjerno (sop), Henriette Bonde-Hansen (sop), Inga Nielsen (sop), Kirsten Dolberg (alt), Anne Gjevang (alt), Raimo Sirkiä (ten), Jorma Hynninen (bar), Carsten Stabell (bass), L. Segerstam (cnd), Danish National RSO, Copenhagen Boys' Choir, Danish National Radio Choir — Chandos 2-▲ CHAN 9305/06 [DDD]
Wolf, H.:Christnacht, w. U. Gronostay (cnd), Berlin RSO — Koch Schwann ▲ SCH 313013 [DDD]

Berlin Radio Chamber Choir
Mozart, W.A.:Missa [longa], K.262, w. Regina Schudel (sop), Ulla Groenewold (cta), Peter Maus (ten), Berthold Possemeyer (bar), U. Gronostay (cnd), Berlin Radio Sinfonietta [L] — Koch Schwann ▲ CD 313 021 [ADD/DDD]

Berlin Radio Children's Choir
Schütz, H.:Schwannengesang, w. J. Kowalski (alt), W. Marschall (ten), D. Knothe (cnd), Berlin Soloists, Dreseden Capella Sagittariana — Berlin Classics 2-▲ BER 1071 [DDD]

Berlin Radio Chorus
Bach, C.P.E.:Magnificat, w. V. Hruba-Freiberger (sop), B. Bornemann (alt), P. Schreier (ten), O. Bär (bar), H. Haenchen (cnd), C.P.E. Bach CO — Berlin Classics ▲ BER 1011 [DDD]
Beethoven, L. van:Cant on the Death of the Emperor Joseph II, w. Markus Schäfer (ten), Alan Titus (bar), Bodil Arnesen (sop), K.A. Rickenbacher (cnd), Berlin RSO — Koch Schwann ▲ SCH 314352 [DDD]
Beethoven, L. van:Di Flamme lodert, Op. 121, w. Bodil Arnesen (sop), K.A. Rickenbacher (cnd), Berlin RSO — Koch Schwann ▲ SCH 314852
Beethoven, L. van:Di Flamme lodert, Op. 121b, w. Bodil Arnesen (sop), K.A. Rickenbacher (cnd), Berlin RSO — Koch Schwann ▲ SCH 314852
Beethoven, L. van:In allen guten Stunden, w. Bodil Arnesen (sop), K.A. Rickenbacher (cnd), Berlin RSO — Koch Schwann ▲ SCH 314852
Beethoven, L. van:Leonore Prohaska, w. K.A. Rickenbacher (cnd), Berlin RSO — Koch Schwann ▲ SCH 314852
Beethoven, L. van:Meeresstille und glückliche Fahrt, w. K.A. Rickenbacher (cnd), Berlin RSO — Koch Schwann ▲ SCH 314852
Beethoven, L. van:Missa Solemnis, w. Julia Varady (sop), Iris Vermillion (mez), Vinson Cole (ten), Rene Pape (bass), Kolja Blacher (vn), G. Solti (cnd), Berlin PO — London ▲ 444337-2 [DDD]

▲ = CD ♦ = Enhanced CD Δ = MD ■ = Cassette Tape ▯ = DCC

Berlin Radio Chorus (cont.)

Beethoven, L. van:Music of, w. K.A. Rickenbacher (cnd), Berlin RSO—Wo sich die Pulse jugendlich jagen Koch Schwann ▲ SCH 314852

Beethoven, L. van:Syms (comp), w. H. Kegel (cnd), Dresden PO, Leipzig Radio Chorus Capriccio 7–▲ 10 455

Beethoven, L. van:Sym 9, "Choral Sym", w. L. Bernstein (cnd), Bavarian RSO members, Dresden State Orch members, Kirov Theatre Orch members, London SO members, New York PO members, Orch de Paris members, Bavarian Radio Chorus, Dresden Philharmonie Children's Chorus [G] *(rec live, Schauspielhaus, East Berlin, 12/25/89)* Deutsche Grammophon ▲ 429861–2 [DDD] ■ 429861–4

Beethoven, L. van:Die Weihe des Hauses (incidental music), w. Sylvia McNari (sop), Byrn Terfel (bar), Bruno Ganz (narr), C. Abbado (cnd), Berlin PO *(rec Great Hall, Philharmonie, Berlin)* Deutsche Grammophon ▲ 447748–2 [DDD]

Berlioz, H.:Lélio, "Le retourà la vie", w. M. Rabsilber (ten), B. Grabowski (bar), H.–P. Minetti (nar), R. Reuter (cnd), Berlin Comic Opera Orch [F; narration G] Berlin Classics ▲ BER 2149 [DDD]

Berlioz, H.:Rêverie et caprice, w. J. Wagner (vn), M. Schønwandt (cnd), Berlin SO, Ernst Senff Chorus Kontrapunkt 2–▲ KPT 32143 [DDD]

Brahms, J.:Gesang der Parzen, w. C. Abbado (cnd), Berlin PO Deutsche Grammophon ▲ 431790–2 [DDD] □ 431790–5

Brahms, J.:Nänie, w. C. Abbado (cnd), Berlin PO Deutsche Grammophon ▲ 435349–2 [DDD]

Braunfels, W.:Die Vögel, w. Helen Kwon (sop—Nightingale), Wolfgang Holzmair (bar—Hoopoe), Matthias Gorne (b-bar—Prometheus), Michael Krause (sgr—Loyal Friend), Endrik Wottrich (sgr—Good Hope), L. Zagrosek (cnd), Berlin German SO London ("Entartete Musik" series) ▲ 448 679–2

Bruch, M.:Die Flucht der heiligen Familie, w. U. Gronostay (cnd), Berlin RSO [G] Koch Schwann ▲ CD 313013 [DDD]

Bruch, M.:Gruss an die heilige Nacht, w. G. Schreckenbach (mez), U. Gronostay (cnd), Berlin RSO [G] Koch Schwann ▲ CD 313013 [DDD]

Cherubini, L.:Requiem Mass in c, w. C.P. Flor (cnd), Berlin SO RCA Red Seal ▲ 60059–2–RC [DDD]

Cornelius, P.:Der Cid, w. Gertrud Ottenthal (sop), Ronnie Johansen (sgr), Robert Schunk (ten), Albert Dohmen (bar), Michael Schopper (bass), Endrik Wottrich (sgr), G. Kuhn (cnd), Berlin RSO Koch Schwann 2–▲ SCH 315222

Dvořák, A.:Requiem Mass, w. Elisabeth Rose (sop), Gertraud Prenzlow (cta), Peter Schreier (ten), Theo Adam (bass), K. Ančerl (cnd), Berlin RSO Forlane 2–▲ FRL 16636 [AAD]

Gershwin, G.:Porgy & Bess (sels), w. R. Alexander (sop), S. Estes (bass), L. Slatkin (cnd), Berlin RSO [E] Philips ▲ 412720–2 [DDD]

Goldschmidt, B.:Der gewaltige Hahnrei, w. R. Alexander (sop), M. Posselt (sop), H. Lawrence (sop), R. Wörle (ten), M. Kraus (ten), M. Petzold (ten), C. Otelli (bar), L. Zagrosek (cnd), German SO London ▲ 440850–2 [DDD]

Goldschmidt, B.:Mediterranean Songs, w. R. Alexander (sop), M. Posselt (sop), H. Lawrence (sop), R. Wörle (ten), M. Kraus (ten), M. Petzold (ten), C. Otelli (bar), L. Zagrosek (cnd), German SO London ▲ 440850–2 [DDD]

Gounod, C.:Faust, w. H. Singstreu (sop—Margarete), H. Rosvaenge (ten—Faust), M. Bohnen (bass—Mephistopheles), H. Steiner (cnd), Berlin RSO *(rec 1938)* Myto 2–▲ MCD 94196

Handel, G.F.:L'Allegro, Il Penseroso ed il Moderato, w. V. Hruba–Freiberger (sop), D. Schellenberger–Ernst (sop), J. Kowalski (alt), F.Kapellmann (bass), Rabsilber (sgr), R. Reuter (cnd), Berlin Comic Opera Orch Berlin Classics 2–▲ BER 1147 [DDD]

Handel, G.F.:Judas Maccabaeus, w. Gundula Janowitz (sop), Hertha Töpper (alt), Peter Schreier (ten), Ernest Haefliger (ten), Theo Adam (bass), Siegfried Vogel (bass), H. Koch (cnd), Berlin RSO Berlin Classics 2–▲ BER 9112

Haydn, J.:Die Schöpfung, w. Regina Werner (sop), Peter Schreier (ten), Theo Adam (bass), H. Koch (cnd), Berlin RSO Berlin Classics 2–▲ BER CD 9115

Hindemith, P.:Das Unaufhörliche, w. Ulrike Sonntag (sop), Robert Wörle (ten), Siegfried Lorenz (bar), Artur Korn (bass), L. Zagrosek (cnd), Berlin RSO Wergo 2–▲ WER 66032

Liszt, F.:A Faust Sym, w. J. Zhang (ten), E. Inbal (cnd), Berlin RSO Denon ▲ CO 75634 [DDD]

Mahler, G.:Sym 8, w. Sylvia McNair (sop), Andrea Rost (sop), Cheryl Studer (sop), Anne Sofie von Otter (mez), Rosemarie Lang (cta), Peter Seiffert (ten), Bryn Terfel (bar), Jan–Hendrik Rootering (bass), C. Abbado (cnd), Berlin PO, Prague Phil Chorus, Tölz Boys' Choir Deutsche Grammophon ("4D Audio" series) 2–▲ 445843–2

Mendelssohn, F.:Die Hochzeit des Camacho, w. R. Schudel (sop—Quiteria), C. Swanson (sop—Lucinda), C. Bieber (ten—Basilio), W. Mok (ten—Vivaldo), V. Horn (ten—Camacho), R. Lukas (bar—Carrasco), J. Becker (bass—Sancho Panza), W. Murray (bass—Don Quixote), B. Klee (cnd), Berlin RSO [G] Koch Schwann 2–▲ 314042 [DDD]

Mozart, W.A.:Entführung, w. S. Barabas (sop), R. Streich (sop), A. Dermota (ten), H. Krebs (ten), J. Greindl (bass), F. Fricsay (cnd), Berlin RSO [G] *(rec Jesus–Christuskirche, Berlin–Dahlem, Dec. 19–21, 1949)* Myto 2–▲ 2 MCD 92361 [ADD]

Mozart, W.A.:Missa, K.427, w. A. Augér (sop), B. Bonney (sop), H.–P. Blochwitz (ten), Robert Holl (bass), C. Abbado (cnd), Berlin PO [L] Sony Classical ▲ SK 46671 [DDD]

Mussorgsky, M.:Boris Godunov, w. V. Valente (sop—Xenia), E. Gorochovskaya (mez—Nurse), L. Nichiteanu (mez—Fyodor), E. Zarmeba (mez—Hostess), M. Lipovšek (cta—Marina), P. Langridge (ten—Prince Shuisky), H. Wildhaber (ten—Misail), A. Fedin (ten—Simpleton), S. Leiferkus (bar—Rangoni), A. Kotcherga (bass—B. Godounov), A. Shagidullin (bass—Shchelkalov), S. Ramey (bass—Pimen), S. Larin (bass—Girgory), G. Nikolsky (bass—Varlaam), C. Abbado (cnd), Berlin PO, Tölz Boys' Choir, Slovak Phil Chorus *(rec Nov. 7–30, 1993)* Sony Classical 3–▲ S3K 58977 [DDD]

Nono, L.:Canto sospeso, w. B. Bonney (sop), S. Otto (alt), M. Torzewski (ten), S. Lothar (nar), B. Ganz (nar) *(rec Dec. 9–11, 1992)* Sony Classical ▲ SK 53360 [DDD]

Orff, C.:Carmina burana, w. *(soloists unknown)*, H. Kegel (cnd), Leipzig RSO, Dresden Children's Choir, Leipzig Radio Chorus Berlin Classics 2–▲ BER 2047 [ADD]

Orff, C.:Catulli Carmina, w. *(soloists unknown)*, H. Kegel (cnd), Leipzig RSO, Dresden Children's Choir, Leipzig Radio Chorus Berlin Classics 2–▲ BER 2047 [ADD]

Orff, C.:Trionfo di Afrodite, w. *(soloists unknown)*, H. Kegel (cnd), Leipzig RSO, Dresden Children's Choir, Leipzig Radio Chorus Berlin Classics 2–▲ BER 2047 [ADD]

Pfitzner, H.:Der blumen Rache, w. Yvi Jänicke (cta), Yvonne Wiedstruck (sgr), Yaron Windmüller (voc), R. Reuter (cnd), Berlin RSO CPO ▲ CPO 999158 [DDD]

Pfitzner, H.:Das dunkle Reich, w. Yvi Jänicke (cta), Yvonne Wiedstruck (voc), Yaron Windmüller (voc), R. Reuter (cnd), Berlin RSO CPO ▲ CPO 999158 [DDD]

Pfitzner, H.:Fons salutifer, w. Yvi Jänicke (cta), Yvonne Wiedstruck (voc), Yaron Windmüller (voc), R. Reuter (cnd), Berlin RSO CPO ▲ CPO 999158 [DDD]

Ravel, M.:Daphins et Chloé, w. M. Schønwandt (cnd), Berlin SO Kontrapunkt ▲ KPT 32152 [DDD]

Righini, V.:Te Deum, w. G. Resick (sop), M. Schiml (sop), R. Wohlers (ten), V. von Halem (bass), G. Albrecht (cnd), Berlin RSO [L] Koch Schwann ▲ CD 313052 [ADD]

Rossini, G.:La Cenerentola, w. B. Casoni (mez), U. Benelli (ten), S. Bruscantini (bar), A. Mariotti (bass), P. Bellugi (cnd), Berlin RSO [I] Acanta 2–▲ CD 43271 [DDD]

Schubert, Franz:Alfonso und Estrella, w. E. Mathis (sop), M. Falewicz (sop), P. Schreier (ten), H. Prey (bar), D. Fischer–Dieskau (bar), T. Adam (b-bar), O. Suitner (cnd), Berlin Staatskapelle Berlin Classics 3–▲ BER 2156 [ADD]

Schubert, Franz:Sacred Music, w. M. Hajossyova (sop), P. Schreier (ten), D. Knothe (cnd), Berlin RSO—Offertorium, D.963; Offertorium, D.223; Tantum ergo, D.962; Psalm 23, D.706; An die Sonne, D.439; Offertorium, D.136; Salve Regina, D.106; Salve Regina, D.386; Psalm 92, D.953; Chor der Engel, D.440 [G,L] Capriccio ▲ 10096 [DDD]

Schubert, Franz:Stabat mater, w. G. Zeumer (sop), D. Ellenbeck (ten), E. G. Schramm (bass), R. Bader (cnd), Berlin RSO Koch Schwann ▲ CD 313 055 [ADD]

Schumann, R.:Genoveva, w. E. Moser (sop), P. Schreier (ten), D. Fischer–Dieskau (bar), S. Lorenz (b-bar), K. Masur (cnd), Leipzig Gewandhaus Orch Berlin Classics ("Eterna" series) 2–▲ BER 2056 [ADD]

Shostakovich, D.:Alone, w. Swetlana Katchur (sop), Wladimir Kazatchouk (ten), M. Jurowski (cnd), Berlin RSO *(rec Jesus Christ Church, Berlin–Dahlem, Sept 19–22, 1995)* Capriccio ▲ 10562 [DDD]

Spohr, L.:Mass in C, w. *(artists unknown)* CPO ▲ CPO 999149 [DDD]

Spohr, L.:Psalms, w. *(artists unknown)* CPO ▲ CPO 999149 [DDD]

Berlin Radio Chorus (cont.)

Spontini, G.:Olympia, w. J. Varady (sop), S. Toczyska (mez), F. Tagliavini (ten), D. Fischer–Dieskau (bar), G. Fortune (bass), J. Becker (bass), G. Albrecht (cnd), Berlin RSO [Paris version] Orfeo 2–▲ 137862 [DDD]

Strauss (II), Joh.:Die Fledermaus, w. R. Streich (sop), A. Schlemm (mez), P. Anders (ten), H. Krebs (ten), F. Fricsay (cnd), Berlin RSO [G] *(rec live, Berlin, 11/8/49)* Melodram 2–▲ MEL 29001 (m) [AAD]

Theodorakis, M.:Sym 3, w. Els Bolkestein (sop), H. Rögner (cnd), Berlin Comic Opera Orch Berlin Classics 2–▲ BER 1128 [ADD]

Verdi, G.:Falstaff, w. E. Norberg–Schulz (sop—Nannetta), L. Serra (sop—Alice), S. Graham (mez—Meg Page), M. Lipovsek (cta—Miss Quickly), K. Begley (ten—Dr. Caius), P. Conti (ten—Ford), M. Luperi (ten—Pistol), J. Van Dam (b-bar—Falstaff), P. LeFebvre (bass—Bardolph), G. Solti (cnd), Berlin PO London ▲ 440650–2 [DDD]

Wagner, R.:Die Meistersinger von Nürnberg (sels), w. K. Wessel (alt), E. Kunz (bar), G. Hann (bass), A. Rother (cnd), Berlin RSO—Act 2 Preiser ▲ PRE 90168 [AAD]

Weber, C.M. von:Abu Hassan, w. E. Schwarzkopf (sop), E. Witte (ten), M. Bohnen (bass), L. Ludwig (cnd), Berlin RSO [G] *(rec Germany 1941)* Forlane ▲ FOR 16572 (m) [AAD]

Weber, C.M. von:Abu Hassan, w. Elisabeth Schwarzkopf (sop), Erich Witte (ten), Michael Bohnen (bass), L. Ludwig (cnd), Berlin RSO Grammofono 2000 ▲ GRM 78650

Weber, C.M. von:Der Freischütz, w. R. Ziesack (sop), S. Sweet (sop), A. Schmidt (bar), M. Hölle (bass), M. Janowski (cnd), German SO RCA Red Seal 2–▲ 09026–62538–2

Wolf, H.:Christnacht, w. S. Inou–Heller (sop), M.–L. Wilke (mez), K. Thiem (bar), U. Gronostay (cnd), Berlin RSO [G] Koch Schwann ▲ CD 313013 [DDD]

R. Gritton (cnd)

Schoenberg, A.:Die Jakobsleiter, w. Barbara Kilduff (sop—Seele 1), Jadwiga Rappé (cta—Sterbende), Wilfried Gahmlich (ten—Aufrührerischer), Cornelius Hauptmann (ten—Gabriel), Keith Lewis (ten—Berfener), Kurt Azesberger (bar—Mönch), Barbara Fuchs (sgr—Seele 2), Matteo de Monti (sgr—Ringender), Bjorn Waag (sgr—Auserwählter), E. Inbal (cnd), Frankfurt RSO *(rec Alte Oper, Frankfurt, Sept 6–9, 1994)* Denon ▲ CO 78977 [DDD]

D. Knothe (cnd)

Reger, M.:Geistliche Gesänge, Op. 110 Berlin Classics ("Eterna" series) ▲ BER 2017 [ADD]

Reger, M.:Geistliche Gesänge, Op. 138—Nos. 1–4 Berlin Classics ("Eterna" series) ▲ BER 2017 [ADD]

Berlin Radio Women's Chorus

Liszt, F.:Dante Sym, w. D. Barenboim (cnd), Berlin PO Teldec ▲ 77340

Berlin RIAS Chamber Choir

Busoni, F.:Turandot, w. C. Lindsley (sop), J. Protschka (ten), R. Wörle (ten), R. Pape (bass), G. Albrecht (cnd), Berlin RSO Capriccio ▲ 60039 [DDD]

Handel, G.F.:Choruses, w. M. Creed (cnd), RIAS Sinfonietta—choruses from Messiah, Israel in Egypt, Jephtha, Samson Capriccio ▲ 10245 [DDD]

Haydn, J.:Mass 10, "Kriegsmesse", "Paukenmesse", w. Sylvia McNair (sop), Delores Ziegler (mez), Hans–Peter Blochwitz (ten), Andreas Schmidt (bar), J. Levine (cnd), Berlin SO Deutsche Grammophon ▲ 435853–2

Meyerbeer, G.:Gli amori di Teolinda, w. Julia Varady (sop), J. Fadle (cl), G. Albrecht (cnd), Berlin RSO [I] Orfeo ▲ 054831 [DDD]

Mozart, W.A.:Ave verum corpus, w. M. Creed (cnd), Berlin RSO [L] Capriccio ▲ 10169 [DDD]

Mozart, W.A.:Così fan tutte (sels), w. L. Cuberli (sop), J. Rodgers (sop), C. Bartoli (mez), J. Tomlinson (bass), D. Barenboim (cnd), Berlin PO Erato ▲ 94821

Mozart, W.A.:Don Giovanni (sels), w. L. Cuberli (sop), J. Rodgers (sop), J. Tomlinson (bass), F. Furlanetto (bass), D. Barenboim (cnd), Berlin PO Erato ▲ 94823

Mozart, W.A.:Litaniae Lauretanae, K.195, w. Maria Stader (sop), G. König (cnd), Berlin RIAS SO Deutsche Grammophon 2–▲ 437383–2

Mozart, W.A.:Missa, K.317, w. S. McNair (sop), D. Ziegler (mez), H.P. Blochwitz (ten), A. Schmidt (bar), J. Levine (cnd), Berlin SO Deutsche Grammophon ▲ 435853–2

Mozart, W.A.:Missa, K.427, w. Maria Stader (sop), G. König (cnd), Berlin RIAS SO Deutsche Grammophon 2–▲ 437383–2

Mozart, W.A.:Missa solemnis, K.139, w. M. Lindsay (sop), G. Schreckenbach (mez), W. Hollweg (ten), W. Grönroos (bar), M. Creed (cnd), Berlin RSO [L] LaserLight ▲ 15 883 [DDD]

Mozart, W.A.:Missa solemnis, K.139, w. M. Lindsay (sop), G. Schreckenbach (mez), W. Hollweg (ten), W. Grönroos (bar), M. Creed (cnd), Berlin RSO [L] Capriccio ▲ 10169 [DDD]

Mozart, W.A.:Nozze di Figaro (sels), w. L. Cuberli (sop), J. Rodgers (sop), C. Bartoli (mez), A. Schmidt (bar), D. Barenboim (cnd), Berlin PO Erato ▲ 94822

Mozart, W.A.:Requiem, w. Edith Wiens (sop), Gabriele Schreckenbach (mez), Aldo Baldin (ten), Gerhard Faulstich (bar), U. Gronostay (cnd), Berlin RSO [L] LaserLight ▲ 15 882 [DDD]

Mozart, W.A.:Sacred Music, w. M. Creed (cnd), Berlin RSO—Misericordias Domini, K.222; Inter natos mulierum, K.72; Sancta Maria, mater Dei, K.273; Venite populi, K.260 [L] LaserLight ▲ 15 883 [DDD]

Mozart, W.A.:Sacred Music, w. M. Creed (cnd), Berlin RSO—sels. from Ave verum corpus, K.618; Exsultate, jubilate, K.165; Misericordias Domini, K.222; Missa solemnis, K.139; Requiem; Venite populi, K.260; Vesperae de Domenica, K.321; Vesperae solennes de confessore, K.339 LaserLight ▲ 15 654 [DDD]

Mozart, W.A.:Sacred Music, w. M. Creed (cnd), Berlin RSO—Misericordias Domini, K.222; Inter natos mulierum, K.72; Sancta Maria, mater Dei, K.273; Venite populi, K.260 [L] Capriccio ▲ 10169 [DDD]

Mozart, W.A.:Vesperae de Dominica, w. Maria Stader (sop), G. König (cnd), Berlin RIAS SO Deutsche Grammophon 2–▲ 437383–2

Mozart, W.A.:Vesperae solennes, w. Maria Stader (sop), G. König (cnd), Berlin RIAS SO Deutsche Grammophon 2–▲ 437383–2

Mozart, W.A.:Zauberflöte (sels), w. E. Lear (sop), R. Peters (sop), L. Otto (sop), F. Wunderlich (ten), F. Lenz (ten), D. Fischer–Dieskau (bar), F. Crass (bass), K. Böhm (cnd), Berlin PO—Scenes & Arias Deutsche Grammophon ▲ 429825–2 [ADD] ■ 429825–4

Schubert, Franz:Fierrabras, w. H. Plümacher (cta), F. Wunderlich (ten), R. Wolansky (bar), O. von Rohr (bass), H. Müller–Kray (cnd), Bern State Orch, South Swiss Radio Chorus—abridged performance *(rec 1959)* Myto ▲ MCD 89001 [ADD]

Schulhoff, E.:The Flames, w. Jane Eaglen (sop—Donna Anna, Nun, Woman, Marguerite), Carola Höhn (sop—Shadow), Celina Lindsley (sop—Shadow), Regina Schudel (sop—Shadow), Iris Vermillion (mez—La Morte), Christiane Berggold (alt—Shadow), Kaja Borris (alt—Shadow), Elvira Dressen (alt—Shadow), Kurt Westi (ten—Don Juan), Johann–Werner Prein (bass—Commendatore), Gerd Wolf (bass—Harlequin), J. Mauceri (cnd), Berlin German SO *(rec Jesus–Christus Church, Berlin Dahlem, Oct 1993/Apr 1994)* London 2–▲ 444630–2 [DDD]

Schumann, R.:Manfred, w. *(soloists unknown)*, G. Albrecht (cnd), Berlin RSO Koch Schwann ▲ SCH 310892 [DDD]

Shostakovich, D.:The Fall of Berlin (sels), w. M. Jurowski (cnd), Berlin German SO *(rec Church of Jesus Christ, Berlin–Dahlem, Germany, Mar 4–6, 1991)* Capriccio ▲ 10 405 [DDD]

Shostakovich, D.:Maxim Trilogy (sels), w. M. Jurowski (cnd), Berlin German SO—Youth of Maxim, Op. 41 (1934–5); Return of Maxim, Op. 45 (1936–7); Vyborg District, Op. 50 (1938) *(rec Room 1, German Radio Berlin, June 13–4, 1994)* Capriccio ▲ 10 561 [DDD]

Shostakovich, D.:Suite from Golden Mountains, w. M. Jurowski (cnd), Berlin German SO *(rec Room 1, German Radio Berlin, June 13–4, 1994)* Capriccio ▲ 10 561 [DDD]

Shostakovich, D.:Zoya (sels), w. M. Jurowski (cnd), Berlin German SO *(rec Church of Jesus Christ, Berlin–Dahlem, Germany, Mar 4–6, 1991)* Capriccio ▲ 10 405 [DDD]

Verdi, G.:Requiem Mass, w. Maria Stader (sop), Marjana Radev (mez), Helmut Krebs (ten), Kim Borg (bass), F. Fricsay (cnd), Berlin RIAS SO, St. Hedwig Cathedral Choir *(rec Jesus–Christus Church, Berlin, Sept 1953)* Deutsche Grammophon ("The Originals" series) ▲ 447442–2 [ADD]

Wagner, R.:Der fliegende Holländer, w. Annelies Kupper (sop—Senta), Sieglinde Wagner (mez—Mary), Ernst Haefliger (ten—Steersman), Wolfgang Windgassen (ten—Erik), Josef Metternich (ten—Dutchman), Josef Greindl (bass—Daland), F. Fricsay (cnd), Berlin RIAS SO *(rec 1953)* Deutsche Grammophon 2–▲ 439714–2 (m) [ADD]

Weill, K.:The Threepenny Opera, w. U. Lemper (sop), Milva (sgr), S. Tremper (sgr), H. Dernesch (mez), R. Kollo (ten), M. Adorf (sgr), W. Reichmann (sgr), J. Mauceri (cnd), Berlin RIAS Sinfonietta [G] London ▲ 430075–2 [DDD]

Berlin RIAS Chamber Choir (cont.)
M. Creed (cnd)
Brahms, J.:Songs [sels unknown] Harmonia Mundi ▲ HMC 901592
Krenek, E.:Lamentatio Jeremiae Prophatae Harmonia Mundi France ▲ HMC 901551
Poulenc, F.:Mass Harmonia Mundi ▲ HMC 901588
Poulenc, F.:Motets (4) pour le temps de Noël Harmonia Mundi ▲ HMC 901588
Poulenc, F.:Motets (4) pour un temps de pénitence Harmonia Mundi ▲ HMC 901588
U. Gronostay (cnd)
Brahms, J.:Liebeslieder Waltzes SATB, w. M. Creed (pno), R. Stelzner (pno) [G] *(rec March 1984)* Koch Treasure ▲ 31616-2 [ADD]
Brahms, J.:Zigeunerlieder, w. P. Moll (pno) [G] *(rec March 1984)* Koch Treasure ▲ 31616-2 [ADD]
Cornelius, P.:Requiem, "Seele, vergiss sie nicht..." [G] *(rec 1978)* Koch Schwann ▲ 3-1086-2 [ADD]
Reger, M.:Geistliche Gesänge, Op. 110—No. 1, "Mein Odem ist schwach" [G] *(rec 1978)* Koch Schwann ▲ 3-1086-2 [ADD]

Berlin RIAS Men's Chamber Choir
Liszt, F.:Cantico del sol di Dan Francesco d'Assisi, w. Walton Grönroos (bar), G. Albrecht (cnd), Berlin RSO Koch Schwann ▲ CD 311 055

Berlin RIAS Women's Chamber Choir
Zemlinsky, A. von:Der Geburtstag der Infantin, w. B. Haldas (sop), I. Nielsen (sop), K. Riegel (ten), D. Weller (bass), G. Albrecht (cnd), Berlin RSO [G] Koch Schwann ▲ CD 314 013 [DDD]

Berlin School of the Arts Chamber Choir
C. Grube (cnd)
Distler, H.:Mörike-Chorliederbuch *(rec Lindenkirche Wilmersdorf, 1993)* Thorofon ▲ CTH 2231 [DDD]

Berlin Singakademie
Beethoven, L. van:Die Geschöpfe des Prometheus (sels), w. M. Argerich (pno), C. Abbado (cnd), Berlin PO *(rec May 23-25, 1993)* Sony Classical ▲ SK 53978 [DDD]
Liszt, F.:Prometheus, w. M. Argerich (pno), C. Abbado (cnd), Berlin PO *(rec May 23-25, 1993)* Sony Classical ▲ SK 53978 [DDD]
Scriabin, A.:Sym 5, w. M. Argerich (pno), C. Abbado (cnd), Berlin PO *(rec May 23-25, 1993)* Sony Classical ▲ SK 53978 [DDD]

Berlin State Chorus
Dessau, P.:Puntila, w. Annelies Brumeister (mez—Lsins), Erich Witte (ten—Fredrick), Reiner Süss (bar—Johannes Puntila), P. Dessau (cnd), Berlin State Opera Orch *(rec Berlin, May 1988)* Berlin Classics 2-▲ BER 2184 [ADD]
Lortzing, A.:Der Wildschütz, oder Die Stimme der Natur, w. Edith Mathis (sop), Peter Schreier (ten), Gottfried Hornik (bar), Hans Sotin (bass), B. Klee (cnd) *(rec Berlin, 1982)* Berlin Classics 2-▲ BER 1143 [ADD]

Berlin State Opera Chorus
Beethoven, L. van:Sym 9, "Choral Sym", w. A. Marc (sop), I. Vermillion (mez), S. Jerusalem (ten), F. Struckmann (bar), D. Barenboim (cnd), Berlin State Opera Orch Erato ▲ 94353-2
Cherubini, L.:Médée (sels), w. I. Borkh (sop—Medea), L. Suthaus (ten—Giasone), V. Gui (cnd), Berlin State Opera Orch—3 soprano arias & 3 duets *(rec live, Berlin 1958)* Melodram 2-▲ CDM 27087 [ADD]
Dessau, P.:Einstein, w. Peter Schreier (ten), Theo Adam (bass), Reiner Suss (bass), O. Suitner (cnd), Berlin Staatskapelle Berlin Classics 2-▲ BER CD 9109
Lortzing, A.:Der Waffenschmied, w. E. Ebert (sop—Marie), G. Prenzlow (mez—Mariens), H. Neukirch (ten—Georg), G. Leib (bar—Ritter), H. Krämer (bass—Hans), H. Fricke (cnd), Berlin State Opera Orch Berlin Classics ("Eterna" series) ▲ BER 2036-2 [ADD]
Matthus, S.:Mirabeau, w. Carola Höhn (sop—Marie Antoinette), Carola Fischer (cta—Eveline Le Jay), Peter-Jürgend Schmidt (ten—Ludwig XVI), Jürgen Freier (bar—Honoré-Gabriel de Riqueti), Gerd Wolf (bass—Victor Riqueti), H. Fricke (cnd), Berlin State Opera Orch *(rec Berlin, 1989)* Berlin Classics 2-▲ BER 1075 [DDD]
Nicolai, O.:Lustigen Weiber, w. I. Bielke (sop), M. L. Schilp (mez), W. Ludwig (ten), G. Hann (bass), W. Streinz (bass), A. Rother (cnd), Berlin RSO *(rec May 2, 1943)* Preiser 2-▲ PRE 90208 [ADD]
Nicolai, O.:Lustigen Weiber, w. H. Donath (sop), E. Mathis (sop), H. Schwarz (mez), K. Ludwig (ten), K.-E. Mercker (ten), P. Schreier (ten), C. Dormoy (bar), B. Weikl (bar), K. Moll (bass), S. Vogel (bass), B. Klee (cnd), Berlin Staatskapelle *(rec July 3, 1976)* Berlin Classics ("Eterna" series) ▲ BER 2046-2 [ADD]
Nicolai, O.:Lustigen Weiber, w. H. Donath (sop), E. Mathis (sop), H. Schwarz (cta), P. Schreier (ten), K. Moll (bass), B. Klee (cnd), Berlin Staatskapelle Berlin Classics 2-▲ BER 2115 [ADD]
Pfitzner, H.:Palestrina, w. C. Nossek (sop), R. Long (mez), P. Schreier (ten), S. Lorenz (bar), E. Wlaschiha (bass), O. Suitner (cnd), Berlin Staatskapelle Berlin Classics ▲ BER 1001
Verdi, G.:Aida (sels), w. Hilde Scheppan (sop), Margarete Klose (cta), Helge Roswaenge (ten), Hans Hotter (bar), A. Rother (cnd), Berlin Radio Orch [G] *(rec Nov. 21, 1942)* Preiser ▲ PRE 90219 [ADD]
Verdi, G.:Rigoletto, w. E. Berger (sop), R. Jacobs (alt), H. Roswaenge (ten), H. Schlusnus (bass), J. Greindl (bass), R. Heger (cnd), Berlin State Opera Orch [G] *(rec 11/20-22/44)* Preiser 2-▲ 90036 (m) [AAD]
Verdi, G.:La traviata, w. M. Freni (sop), F. Bonisolli (ten), S. Bruscantini (bar), L. Gardelli (cnd), Berlin State Opera Orch [I] Acanta 2-▲ CD 41644 [DDD]
Verdi, G.:Il trovatore, w. R. Kabaivanska (sop), M. Cortez (ten), F. Bonisolli (ten), G. Zancanaro (bar), B. Bartoletti (cnd), Berlin State Opera Orch [I] Acanta 2-▲ CD 43301 [DDD]
Wagner, R.:Die Meistersinger von Nürnberg (sels), w. E. Marherr-Wagner (mez), R. Hutt (ten), K. Jöken (bar), F. Schorr (b-bar), E. List (bass), L. Schützendorf (sgr), L. Blech (cnd), Berlin State Opera Orch—Act 1:Hilf Gott! Will ich denn Schuster sein?; Das schöne Fest, Johannistag; Act 2:Johannistag! Johannistag!; Hab' ich heut' Singstund'?; Jerum! Jerum!; Act 3:Gleich, Meister! Hier!; Grüss' Gott, mein Evchen...Weilten die Stern' im lieblichen Tanz...O Sachs! Mein Freund!; Sankt Krispin, lobet ihn!; Silentium!...Wach' auf!; Verachtet mir die Meister nicht [G] *(rec Staatsoper unter den Linden, 5/22/28)* Pearl ▲ PEA 9340 (m) [AAD]
Wagner, R.:Rienzi, der Letzte der Tribunen (sels), w. Hilde Scheppan (sop), Margarete Klose (cta), Max Lorenz (ten), Jaro Prohaska (bar), A. Rother (cnd), Berlin State Opera Orch *(rec 1941)* Preiser ▲ PRE 90223 [ADD]
Wagner, R.:Tannhäuser, w. E. Grümmer (sop), M. Schech (sop), H. Hopf (ten), F. Wunderlich (ten), D. Fischer-Dieskau (bar), G. Frick (bass), F. Konwitschny (cnd), Berlin State Opera Orch [G] EMI Classics ("Studio" series) 3-▲ CDMC 63214 [ADD]
Wagner, R.:Tristan und Isolde (acts 2 & 3), w. E. Schlüter (sop), M. Klose (cta), L. Suthaus (ten), J. Prohaska (ten), G. Frick (bass), W. Furtwängler (cnd), Berlin State Opera Orch [G] *(rec live, Berlin, 10/3/47)* Arkadia 2-▲ 358 [ADD]

Berlin State Opera Chorus members
Graun, K.H.:Cesare e Cleopatra, w. Janet Williams (sop), Debora Beronesi (sop), Lynne Dawson (sop), Curtis Rayam (ten), R. Jacobs (cnd), Concerto Cologne Serenissima 3-▲ SER 360171 [DDD]

Berlin Vocal Ensemble
B. Stegmann (cnd)
Distler, H.:Mörike-Chorliederbuch, w. Christiane Kreis (sop), Juliane Mechler (alt), Hendrik Ritter (ten) *(rec Herrenberg, Jan 2-4, 1992)* Musicaphon ▲ BM 56820

Bern Bach Choir
T. Loosli (cnd)
Suter, H.:Le Laudi di San Francesco d'Assisi, w. A. Michael (sop), J. Winklet (alt), A. Baldin (ten), J. Will (bass), P. Laubschet (org), Bern SO, Sekundar School Children's Choir Ars Musici ▲ AM 1015-2 [DDD]

Bern Chamber Choir
Galuppi, B.:Magnificat, w. Ana-Maria Miranda (sop), J. E. Dähler (cnd), Southwest German CO Pforzheim *(rec Berner Münster, Dec 1977)* Claves ▲ CD 50801 [ADD]
Vivaldi, A.:Gloria, RV.589, w. Ana-Maria Miranda (sop), Ria Bollen (alt), J. E. Dähler (cnd), Southwest German CO Pforzheim *(rec Berner Münster, Dec 1977)* Claves ▲ CD 50801 [ADD]
Zelenka, J.D.:Requiem in c, w. *(soloists unknown)*, J. E. Dähler (cnd), Bern CO [L] Claves ▲ CD 8501 [DDD]

Bern Gabrieli Chorus
Burkhard, W.:Mass, Op. 85, w. K. Beidler (sop), M. Brodard (bass), H. Gafner (cnd), Bern SO Jecklin ▲ JD 687

Bern Vocal Ensemble
Mozart, W.A.:Missa Solemnis, w. Christa Goetze (sop), Anna Schaffner (alt), Barnhard Gärtner (ten), Rudolf Rosen (bass), Philippe Laubscher (org), F. Pantillon (cnd), Bieler SO, Pro Arte Chorale Gallo ▲ CD 893 [DDD]
Pantillon, F.:Bethlehem, w. Christa Goetze (sop), Rudolf Rosen (nar), Philippe Laubscher (org), F. Pantillon (cnd), Bieler SO, Pro Arte Chorale Gallo ▲ CD 893 [DDD]
F. Pantillon (cnd)
Pantillon, F.:Missa brevis di San Pedro, w. Philippe Laubscher (org) *(rec La Salle Musica de La Chaux-de-Fonds)* Gallo ▲ CD 884 [DDD]
Pantillon, F.:Le Noël des Bergers, w. Christa Gaetze (sop), Philippe Laubscher (org) *(rec La Salle Musica de La Chaux-de-Fonds)* Gallo ▲ CD 884 [DDD]

Bernese Chorus
Keiser, R.:Passions Oratorium, w. J. Bise (sop), M. Conrad (cta), G. Jelden (ten), U. Gilgen (bass), J.E. Dähler (cnd), Bernese Orch [G] *(rec Feb. 1971)* Claves 2-▲ CD 9223/24 [ADD]

Bethlehem Bach Choir
Bach, J.S.:Cant 56, w. D. Lichti (b-bar), G. Funfgeld (cnd), Bach Festival Orch [G] Dorian ▲ DOR 90127 [DDD]
Bach, J.S.:Cant 63, w. S. McNair (sop), J. Taylor (mez), D. Gordon (ten), D. Lichti (b-bar), G. Funfgeld (cnd), Bach Festival Orch—plus Sanctus from Mass in b, BWV 232 [G] Dorian ▲ DOR 90113 [DDD]
Bach, J.S.:Cant 65, w. D. Gordon (ten), D. Lichti (b-bar), G. Funfgeld (cnd), Bach Festival Orch [G] Dorian ▲ DOR 90113 [DDD]
Bach, J.S.:Cant 140, w. H. Schellenberg (sop), D. Gordon (ten), D. Lichti (b-bar), G. Funfgeld (cnd), Bach Festival Orch [G] Dorian ▲ DOR 90127 [DDD]
G. Funfgeld (cnd)
Bach, J.S.:Motets (misc) [G]—Ich lasse dich nicht, du segnest mich denn, BWV Anh.159 [G] Dorian ▲ DOR 90127 [DDD]

Beverly Hills All Saints' Episcopal Church Choir
T. Foster (cnd)
Hymns through the Ages, w. Craig Phillips (org) *(rec All Saints' Church, Beverly Hills, Feb 12, 14, 16 & Mar 2, 1)* Gothic ▲ GOT 49074
Silence & Music, w. C. Phillips (org) *(rec May 30-June 3, 1993)* Gothic ▲ GOT 49064

Bielefeld Opera Chorus
Spohr, L.:Faust, w. C. Taha (sop), M. Vier (b-bar), E. von Jordis (bass), G. Moull (cnd), Bielefeld PO [1852 version] *(rec live, June 1993)* CPO 2-▲ CPO 999247 [DDD]

Bielefeld Phil Chorus
Krenek, E.:Der Sprüng über den Schatten, w. D. Amos (sop), L. Kemeny (sop), S. MacLean (mez), J. Dürmüller (ten), U. Neuweiler (ten), J. Pflieger (bar), T. Brüning (sgr), D. de Villiers (cnd), Bielefeld PO [G] *(rec live, May 1989)* CPO 2-▲ CPO 999082-2 [DDD]

Bilbao Choral Society
J.L. Ocejo (cnd)
Ramirez, A.:Misa Criolla, w. J. Carreras (ten), A. Ramirez (kbd), Laredo Instrumental Ensemble, Laredo Choral Salvé Philips ("Digital Classics" series) ▲ 420955-2 [DDD] □ 420955-5
Ramirez, A.:Navidad en Verano, w. J. Carreras (ten), A. Ramirez (kbd), Laredo Instrumental Ensemble, Laredo Choral Salvé Philips ("Digital Classics" series) ▲ 420955-2 [DDD] □ 420955-5
Ramirez, A.:Navidad nuestra, w. J. Carreras (ten), A. Ramirez (kbd), Laredo Instrumental Ensemble, Laredo Choral Salvé Philips ("Digital Classics" series) ▲ 420955-2 [DDD] □ 420955-5

Binchois Consort [Mark Chambers (sgr), Fergus McLusky (sgr), Edwin Simpson (ten), Matthew Vine (ten), Andrew Carwood (ten), Chris Watson (ten)]
A. Kirkman (cnd)
Dufay, G.:Missa de St. Anthonii de Padua Hyperion ▲ CDA66854

Bismarck Mandan Civic Chorus
Walth, G.:A Musical Feast, w. Julie Schwartz (pno), G. Walth (cnd) Meyer ▲ MC 0108

Black Elk Voices
Gohl, M.:The West, w. Nana Vasconcelos (sgr), Seamus Eagan (sgr), Jay Ungar (vn), Molly Mason (gtr), *(other artists unknown)*, M. Gohl (cnd) Sony Classical ▲ SK 62727 ■ ST 62727

Blackburn Cathedral Choir
D. Cooper (cnd)
Wood, C.:Music of, w. David Goodenough (org)—Magnificat in E♭; O Most Merciful; God Omnipotent Reigneth; I Will Arise; Father All-Holy; Nunc Dimittis in c; Prelude & Fugue in g; Summer Ended; Haec Dies; Tis The Day of Resurrection; An Easter Carol; Prelude on the Hymn Tune St. Mary; Great Lord of Lords; Oculi Omnium; Prelude on the Hymn Tune York; Expectans Expectavi; Magnificat in F [Collegium Regale] Priory ▲ PRI 484 [DDD]

Blagovest Choral Ensemble
The Lord Is My Light:Russian Sacred Music Multisonic ("Russian Stars on Classics" series) ▲ MUL 310051 [DDD]

Nicole Bianchi Vocal Ensemble
Bach, J.C.F:Die Auferweckung Lazarus, w. Véronique Dietschy (sop), Consuelo Caroli (mez), John Elwes (ten), Philippe Cantor (bar), G. Bezzina (cnd), Nice Baroque Ensemble Adda ▲ ADD 581182 [DDD]

Bmensky Akademicky Sbor
Handel, G.F.:Messiah, w. Ruth Holton (sop), Vanessa Williamson (mez), James Griffett (ten), Lawrence Albert (bass), U. Walser (tpt), M. Brown (cnd), Gioia della Musica Allegro 2-▲ ALGDPCD 1068 [DDD]
Handel, G.F.:Messiah (sels), w. Ruth Holton (sop), Vanessa Williamson (mez), James Griffett (ten), L. Albert (bass), M. Brown (cnd), Gioia della Musica Allegro ▲ ALG PCD 1078 [DDD]

Böblingen Bach Choir
Mozart, W.A.:Requiem, w. U. Buckel (sop), M. Bence (cta), H.-U. Mielsch (ten), E. Wollitz (bass), R. Bader (cnd), Stuttgart PO Allegretto ▲ ACD 8060 [ADD] ■ ACS 8060

Bodra-Smyana Children's Choir
Mahler, G.:Sym 3, w. Brigitte Pretschner (alt), E. Tabakov (cnd), Sofia PO, Bulgarian National Chorus *(rec Bulgarian Concert Hall, Sofia, Apr 1990)* Capriccio 15-▲ 49043 [DDD]
Monteverdi, C.:Madrigals, w. Kralev, Kazandjiev (cnd), Madrigal Chamber Ensemble, Sofia CO Soloists—Ogni Amante e Guerrier; Si, Si Ch'io V'Amo; O Come Vaghi; O Viva Fiamma; Io Son Pur Vezzosetta Pastorella; Ardo e Scoprir; Chiomo d'Oro; Baci Soavi e Cari; Bel Pastor [Dialogo di Ninfa e Pastore] Forlane ▲ FRL 16546 [DDD/AAD]
Schütz, H.:Motets (misc), w. Sofia Soloists CO, Madrigal Chamber Ensemble—Herr, Wenn ich Nur Dich Habe; Herr, Nun Lässest du Deiner in Frieden fahren Forlane ▲ FRL 16546 [DDD/AAD]
Schütz, H.:Musicalische Exequien, w. Sofia Soloists CO, Madrigal Chamber Ensemble Forlane ▲ FRL 16546 [DDD/AAD]

Simón Bolívar Orfeón Univ Schola Cantorum
Estévez, A.:Florentino, el que cantó con el diablo, w. I. Alvarez (ten), W. Alvarado (bar), E. Mata (cnd), Simón Bolívar SO [L] *(rec 2 & 6/90)* Dorian Discovery ▲ DIS 80101 [DDD]

Bologna Chorus
Bellini, V.:I Capuleti e i Montecchi, w. M. Rinaldi (sop), G. Aragall (ten), L. Pavarotti (ten), N. Zaccaria (bass), C. Abbado (cnd), Residentie Orch The Hague *(rec live, Amsterdam 6/30/66)* Melodram 2-▲ MEL 27001
Bellini, V.:I Capuleti e i Montecchi, w. M. Rinaldi (sop—Giulietta), G. Aragall (ten—Romeo), L. Pavarotti (ten—Tebaldo), N. Zaccaria (bass—Capellio), C. Abbado (cnd), Residentie Orch The Hague [I] *(rec live, Amsterdam 6/30/66)* Verona 2-▲ 28001/2

Bologna Teatro Comunale Chorus
Donizetti, G.:La favorita, w. F. Cossotto (mez), L. Pavarotti (ten), G. Bacquier (bar), N. Ghiaurov (bass), R. Bonynge (cnd), Bologna Teatro Comunale Orch London 3-▲ 430038-2 [ADD]
Donizetti, G.:La fille du régiment, w. L. Serra (sop), M. Tagliasacchi (sop), W. Matteuzzi (ten), E. Dara (bar), B. Campanella (cnd), Bologna Teatro Comunale Orch [I] *(rec live, 2/16-26/89)* Nuova Era 2-▲ 6791/92 [DDD]

▲ = CD ♦ = Enhanced CD Δ = MD ■ = Cassette Tape □ = DCC

Bologna Teatro Comunale Chorus (cont.)

Donizetti, G.:Maria Stuarda, w. J. Sutherland (sop), H. Tourangeau (mez), L. Pavarotti (ten), R. Soyer (bar), J. Morris (bass), R. Bonynge (cnd), Bologna Teatro Comunale Orch [I] London 2-▲ 425410-2 [ADD]

Donizetti, G.:Pia de' Tolomei, w. B. Rigacci (cnd), Bologna Teatro Comunale Orch Melodram 3-▲ CDM 37017

Rossini, G.:Arias, w. J. Anderson (sop), D. Gatti (cnd), Bologna Teatro Comunale Orch—arias from La Donna Del Lago, Semiramide, Otello, Guillaume Tell, Ermione, Il viaggio a Reims [I] London ▲ 436377-2 [DDD]

Rossini, G.:Armida, w. R. Fleming (sop), C. Bosi (ten), B. Fowler (ten), J. Francis (ten), D. Kaasch (ten), G. Kunde (ten), I. Zennaro (ten), I. D'Arcangelo (bass), S. Zadvorny (bass), D. Gatti (cnd), Bologna Teatro Comunale Orch *(rec Pesaro, Italy, Aug. 6-17, 1993)* Sony Classical 3-▲ S3K 58968 [DDD]

Rossini, G.:Il barbiere di Siviglia, w. C. Bartoli (mez), W. Matteuzzi (ten), L. Nucci (bar), P. Burchuladze (bass), G. Patanè (cnd), Bologna Teatro Comunale Orch [I] London 3-▲ 425520-2 [DDD]

Rossini, G.:Il barbiere di Siviglia (sels), w. C. Bartoli (mez), W. Matteuzzi (ten), L. Nucci (bar), P. Burchuladze (bass), G. Patanè (cnd), Bologna Teatro Comunale Orch London ▲ 440289-2 [DDD]

Rossini, G.:La Cenerentola, w. C. Bartoli (mez—Cenerentola), F. Costa (mez—Clorinda), G. Banditelli (cta—Tisbe), W. Matteuzzi (ten—Don Ramiro), A. Corbelli (bar—Dandini), E. Dara (bar—Don Magnifico), M. Pertusi (bass—Alidoro), R. Chailly (cnd), Bologna Teatro Comunale Orch *(rec June 22-July 2, 1992)* London 2-▲ 436902-2 [DDD]

Rossini, G.:La Cenerentola (sels), w. Cecilia Bartoli (mez), R. Chailly (cnd), Bologna Teatro Comunale Orch—Nacqui all'affanno...Non più mesta *(rec 1992)* London ▲ 448300-2 [DDD]; ■ 448300-4

Verdi, G.:Un ballo in maschera, w. Leyla Gencer (sop), Adriana Lazzarini (mez), Carlo Bergonzi (ten), Mario Zanasi (bar), O. de Fabritiis (cnd), Bologna Teatro Comunale Orch *(rec live, Nov 28, 1961)* Arkadia 2-▲ 622

Verdi, G.:Macbeth, w. Grace Bumbry (mez—Lady Macbeth), Luciano Saldari (ten—Macduff), Paride Venturi (ten—Malcolm), Renato Bruson (bar—Macbeth), Agostino Ferrin (bass—Banquo), A. Gatto (cnd), Bologna Teatro Comunale Orch *(rec Bologna, Mar. 18, 1975)* Golden Age of Opera 2-▲ GAO 185/86 [ADD]

Verdi, G.:Rigoletto (sels), w. J. Anderson (sop), S. Verrett (mez), L. Pavarotti (ten), L. Nucci (bar), N. Ghiaurov (bass), R. Chailly (cnd), Bologna Teatro Comunale Orch London ▲ 436097-2 [DDD]

Bolshoi Theater Children's Choir

Historical Anthology of Russian Religious Chants, w. Drevnerousski Rospev Male Choir, Yourlov Academic Choir, Rybin Male Choir, St. Petersburg Cappella Russian Season ▲ LDC 288071

A. Zaboronok (cnd)

Kastalski, A.:Chants of the Russian Orthodox Church, w. A. Zaboronok (cnd) Collins Classics ▲ COL 1443

Kastalski, A.:Liturgy of St. John Chrysostom Russian Season ("Russian Season" series) ▲ LDC 288013 [DDD]

Kastalski, A.:Liturgy of St. John Chrysostom Collins Classics ▲ COL 1443

Rachmaninoff, S.:Choruses, Op. 15, w. V. Krainev (pno) Russian Season ("Russian Season" series) ▲ LDC 288013 [DDD]

Bolshoi Theater Chorus

Borodin, A.:Prince Igor, w. Elana Obraztsova (mez—Konchakovna), Tatiana Tugarinova (mez—Yaroslavna), Vladimir Atlantov (ten—Vladimir Igoryevich), Artur Eisen (bass—Vladimir Galitsky), Ivan Petrov (bass—Igor Svyatoslavich), Alexander Vedernikov (bass—Konchak), M. Ermler (cnd), Bolshoi Theater Orch *(rec Moscow, 1969)* Melodiya ("The Russian Opera" series) 3-▲ 74321-29346-2 [ADD]

Glinka, M.:Russlan & Ludmilla, w. Nina Fomina (sop—Gorislava), Bela Rudenko (sop—Ludmilla), Tamara Sinyavskaya (mez—Ratmir), Boris Morozov (bass—Farlaf), Evgeny Nesterenko (bass—Russlan), Valeri Yaroslavtsev (bass—Svetozar), Y. Simonov (cnd), Bolshoi Theater Orch *(rec Moscow, 1978-1979)* Melodiya ("The Russian Opera" series) 3-▲ 74321-29348-2 [ADD]

Mussorgsky, M.:Boris Godounov, w. Georgi Nelepp (ten), Maxim Mikhailov (bass), Mark Reizen (bass), *(other soloists unknown)*, N. Golovanov (cnd), Bolshoi Theater Orch *(rec 1948)* Arlecchino 3-▲ ARL121/23

Mussorgsky, M.:Boris Godunov, w. Irina Arkhipova (mez—Marina Mnishek), Evgenya Verbitskaya (mez—Nurse to Xenia), Valentina Klepatskaya (sgr—Fyodor), Tamara Sorokina (sgr—Xenia), Anton Grigoryev (ten—Simpleton), Vladimir Ivanovsky (ten—Grigory, the Pretender), Gyorgy Shulpin (bar—Prince Shuisky), Alexey Geleva (bass—Varlaam), Ivan Petrov (bass—Boris Godounov), Mark Reshetin (bass—Pimen), Alexi Ivanov (sgr—Andrei Shchelkalov), Evgeny Kibkalo (sgr—Rangoni), A. Melik-Pashayev (cnd), Bolshoi Theater Orch *(rec Moscow, 1962)* Melodiya ("The Russian Opera" series) 3-▲ 74321-29349-2 [ADD]

Popular Scenes From Russian Operas, w. A. Tchistiakov (cnd), Bolshoi Theater Orch, *(soloists unknown)* Russian Season ▲ LDC 288022 [DDD]

Prokofiev, S.:War & Peace, w. Galina Vishnevskaya (sop—Natasha Rostovoa), Irina Arkhipova (mez—Hélène Bezukhova), Evgenya Verbitskaya (mez—Marya Akhrosimova), Alexi Maslennikov (ten—Anatole Kuragin), Vladimir Petrov (ten—Pierre Bezukhov), Pavel Lisitsian (bar—Napoleon), Alexi Krivchenya (bass—Field-Marshall Kutuzov), Evgeny Kibkalo (sgr—Prince Andrei Bolkonsky), A. Melik-Pashayev (cnd), Bolshoi Theater Orch *(rec Moscow, 1961)* Melodiya ("The Russian Opera" series) 3-▲ 74321-29350-2 [ADD]

Russian Opera Choruses, w. A. Lazarev (cnd), Bolshoi Theater Orch Erato ▲ 91723-2 [DDD]

Shchedrin, R.:Dead Souls, w. Larisa Avdeyeva (mez—Korobochka), Galina Borisova (mez—Plyushkin), Alexi Maslennikov (ten—Selifan), Vladislav Piavko (ten—Nozdryov), Vitali Vlasov (ten—Manilov), Boris Morozov (bass—Sobakevich), Alexander Voroshilo (sgr—Chichikov), Y. Temirkanov (cnd), Bolshoi Theater Orch, Moscow Chamber Choir *(rec Moscow, 1982)* Melodiya ("The Russian Opera" series) 2-▲ 74321-29347-2 [ADD]

Tchaikovsky, P.:Eugene Onegin, w. G. Vishnevskaya (sop), L. Avdeyeva (mez), S. Lemeshev (ten), Belov (sgr), Petrov (sgr), B. Khaikin (cnd), Bolshoi Theater Orch [R] *(rec ca. early '60s for Melodi)* Legato Classics 2-▲ LCD 163-2 (m) [ADD]

Tchaikovsky, P.:Queen of Spades, w. T. Milachkina (sop), V. Levko (mez), V. Atlantov (ten), M. Ermler (cnd), Bolshoi Theater Orch [R] Philips 3-▲ 420375-2 [ADD]

Tchaikovsky, P.:Queen of Spades, w. Elena Smolenskaya (sop), Evgenya Verbitskaya (mez), Georgi Nelepp (ten), Pavel Lisitsian (bar), A. Melik-Pashayev (cnd), Bolshoi Opera Orch Arlecchino 3- ARL

Boni Pueri Boys' Choir

J. Skopal (cnd)

Jirásek, J.:Kyrie eleison *(rec City Music Hall, Hradec Králové)* Arta ▲ 0054 [DDD]

Jirásek, J.:Missa Propria *(rec Music Hall, Hradec Králové, Czech Republic, 1994)* Catalyst ▲ 09026-68331-2 [DDD/ADD]

Bordeaux Grand Théâtre Municipal Chorus

Ravel, M.:L'Enfant et les sortilèges, w. M. Lagrange (sop), E. Vidal (sop), M. Damonte (mez), M. Mahé (mez), A. Chedel (cta), L. Pezzino (ten), M. Barrard (bar), V. le Texier (b-bar), A. Lombard (cnd), Bordeaux-Aquitaine National Orch [F] Valois ▲ V 4670

Bordeaux Madrigal

Milhaud, D.:Ani maamin, un chant perdu et retrouvé, w. Sharon Cooper (sop—la Voix), Anna Parus (mez), Bernard Freyd (nar—Isaac), Michel Hermon (nar—le Récitant), Michael Lonsdale (nar—Abraham), Jean Négroni (nar—Jacob), P. Méfano (cnd), Ensemble 2E2M Arion ▲ ARN 68275 [DDD]

Boston Baroque Chorus

Handel, G.F.:Messiah, w. Karen Clift (sop), Catherine Robbin (mez), Bruce Fowler (ten), Victor Ledbetter (bar), M. Pearlman (cnd), Boston Baroque Orch [E] Telarc 2-▲ CD 80322 [DDD]

Boston Baroque Chorus (cont.)

Handel, G.F.:Messiah (sels), w. Karen Clift (sop), Catherine Robbin (mez), Bruce Fowler (ten), Victor Ledbetter (bar), M. Pearlman (cnd), Boston Baroque Orch—Sinfonia; Comfort ye, my people; Every valley shall be exalted; And the glory of the Lord; And He shall purify; Behold, a virgin shall conceive; O thou that tellest good tidings to Zion; For unto us a Child is born; Rejoice greatly, O daughter of Zion; His yoke is easy; All we like sheep; Lift up your heads; The Lord gave the word; Their sound is gone out; Why do the nations?; Let us break their bonds asunder; He that dwelleth in heaven; Thou shalt break them; Hallelujah; I know that my Redeemer liveth; Since by man came death; Behold, I tell you a mystery; The trumpet shall sound; Then shall be brought to pass; O death, where is thy sting?; But thanks be to God; Worthy is the Lamb...Amen *(rec May 18-22, 1992)* Telarc ▲ CD 80348 [DDD]

Boston Camerata

An American Christmas Erato ▲ 4509-92874-2

Musique Judéo-Baroque Musique d'Abord ▲ HMA 1901021

Rossi, S.:The Songs of Solomon [He] Musique d'Abord ▲ HMA 1901021 [ADD]

Saladin, L.:Canticum hebraicum [He] Musique d'Abord ▲ HMA 1901021 [ADD]

J. Cohen (cnd)

The American Vocalist:Spirituals & Folk Hymns, 1850-1870 Erato ▲ 2292-45818-2 ■ 2292-45818-4 AW

Gilles, J.:Mess des morts, w. A. Azema (sop), J. Nirouët (alt), W. Hite (ten), P. Mason (bar), Ensemble de Tambours Provençaux, Aix-en-Provence Festival Chorus Erato ▲ 2292-45989-2

Lamentations, w. Schola Cantorum of Boston [cnd:Frederick Jodry] *(rec Campion Center, Boston, Apr. 1994)* Erato ▲ 4509-98480-2 [DDD]

A Medieval Christmas Elektra/Nonesuch ▲ 71315-2 [ADD]

Musique Judeo-Baroque Harmonia Mundi ▲ HMA 190.1021 [ADD]

New Britain:The Roots of American Folksong Erato ▲ 2292-45474-2 ZK [DDD]

Nueva Espña:Close Encounters in the New World (1590-1690), w. Boston Shawn and Sackbut Ensemble, Women's Choir of the Church Les Amis de la Sagesse, Schola Cantorum of Boston Erato ▲ 45977-2

A Renaissance Christmas Elektra/Nonesuch ▲ 79134-2 ■ 79134-4

A Renaissance Christmas Allegretto ▲ ACD 8405 [ADD]

The Sacred Bridge Erato ▲ 2292-45513-2 [DDD]

Sing We Noël:Christmas Music From England & Early America Elektra/Nonesuch ▲ 71354-2

Tristan & Iseult Erato ▲ 2292-45348-2 ZK

Tristan et Iseult:A Medieval Romance in Music & Poetry, w. Azema, Anne (sop), Ellen Hargis (sop), Henri Ledroit (alt), William Hite (ten), Richard Morrison (bass), Andrea von Ramm (sgr) Erato ▲ 98482-2

Boston Cecilia

Pinkham, D.:Advent Cant, w. C. Baum (hp), Ariel Wind Quintet *(rec Dec. 1992)* Koch International Classics ▲ KIC 7180 [DDD]

Pinkham, D.:Christmas Cant, w. J. D. Christie (org), Lenox Brass *(rec Dec. 1992)* Koch International Classics ▲ KIC 7180 [DDD]

Pinkham, D.:Wedding Cant, w. C. Swistro (sop), T. W. Bridge (ten), B. Bruns (pno) *(rec Dec. 1992)* Koch International Classics ▲ KIC 7180 [DDD]

Boston Early Music Festival Chorus

Mozart, W.A.:Laut verkünde unsre Freude, w. W. Hite (ten), W. Bastian (ten), W. Sharp (bar), A. Parrott (cnd), Boston Early Music Festival Orch [G] Denon ▲ CO 77152 [DDD]

Mozart, W.A.:Requiem, w. J. Bryden (sop), M. Westbrook-Geha (mez), W. Hite (ten), S. Richardson (bar), A. Parrott (cnd), Boston Early Music Festival Orch [L] Denon ▲ CO 77152 [DDD]

Boston Gay Men's Chorus

R. Barney (cnd)

Visions:Words for the Future AFKA ▲ SK 426

Boston Sym Chorus

Mendelssohn, F.:A Midsummer Night's Dream (comp), w. E. Leinsdorf (cnd), Boston SO RCA Victrola ▲ 7816-2-RV [ADD] ■ 7816-4-RV

Mendelssohn, F.:A Midsummer Night's Dream (sels), w. E. Leinsdorf (cnd), Boston SO RCA Silver Seal ▲ 09026-60910-2 ■ 09026-60910-4

Boston Univ Women's Chorus

Bartók, B.:Music of, w. J. Baird (sop), Crofut Consort—various works based upon Rumanian, Ruthenian, Bulgarian & Hungarian folksongs, lullabies, & dances Albany ▲ TROY 046 [DDD]

Kodály, Z.:Songs, w. J. Baird (sop), Crofut Consort—Ave Maria; The Gypsy; Evening Song Albany ▲ TROY 046 [DDD]

Botho Lucas Chorus

Fall, L.:Die Dollarprinzessin (sels), w. Sari Barabas (sop), Christine Gorner (sop), Harry Friedauer (ten), Heinz Hoppe (ten), C. Michalski (cnd), Graunke SO Emperor Operetta ▲ KO 86353

Maurice Bourbon Male Chorus Ensemble

C. Ravier (cnd)

Ravier, C.:Liturgie pour un Dieu mort, w. Guillemette Laurens (mez), Gérard Iglesia (gtr), *(ensemble unknown)* Memoire Vive ▲ 262023

Bournemouth Chorus

Delius, F.:Sea Drift, w. B. Terfel (bass-bar), R. Hickox (cnd), Bournemouth SO Chandos ▲ CHAN 9214 [DDD]

Delius, F.:Songs of Farewell, w. B. Terfel (bass-bar), R. Hickox (cnd), Bournemouth SO Chandos ▲ CHAN 9214 [DDD]

Delius, F.:Songs of Sunset, w. S. Burgess (mez), B. Terfel (bass-bar), R. Hickox (cnd), Bournemouth SO Chandos ▲ CHAN 9214 [DDD]

Vaughan Williams, R.:Flos Campi, w. F. Riddle (va), N. del Mar (cnd), Bournemouth Sinfonietta Chandos ("Collect" series) ▲ CHAN 6545 [ADD]

Bournemouth Sym Chorus

Walton, W.:Belshazzar's Feast, w. Bryn Terfel (b-bar), A. Litton (cnd), Bournemouth SO, L'Inviti, Waynflete Singers *(rec Winchester Cathedral, Feb 1995)* London ▲ 448134-2 [DDD]

Brandeis Univ Chamber Chorus

A. Lucier (cnd)

Ashley, R.:She Was a Visitor Lovely Music ▲ LCD 1002 [AAD]

Brasseur Choir

Fauré, G.:Requiem, w. V. de los Angeles (sop), D. Fischer-Dieskau (bar), A. Cluytens (cnd), Paris Conservatory Societé des Concerts Orch [L] EMI Classics ▲ CDC 47836

Elisabeth Brasseur Chorale

Boulanger, L.:Du fond de l'abîme, w. Oralia Dominguez (ct), Raymond Amade (ten), J. J. Grunenwald (org), I. Markevitch (cnd), Lamoureux Orch *(rec Salle Pleyel, Paris)* Everest ▲ EVC 9034 [AAD]

Boulanger, L.:Psalm 24, w. J. J. Grunenwald (org), I. Markevitch (cnd), Lamoureux Orch *(rec Salle Pleyel, Paris)* Everest ▲ EVC 9034 [AAD]

Boulanger, L.:Psalm 129, w. Pierre Mollet (bar), I. Markevitch (cnd), Lamoureux Orch *(rec Salle Pleyel, Paris)* Everest ▲ EVC 9034 [AAD]

Boulanger, L.:Vieille prière bouddhique, w. Michel Sénéchal (ten), I. Markevitch (cnd), Lamoureux Orch *(rec Salle Pleyel, Paris)* Everest ▲ EVC 9034 [AAD]

Honegger, A.:Le Roi David, w. Henri Doublier (nar), Jacqueline Brumaire (sop), Denise Scharley (alt), Jacques Pottier (ten), S. Baudo (cnd), Paris Opera Orch Accord ▲ ACD 200822 [AAD]

Mozart, W.A.:Entführung, w. Teresa Stich-Randall (mez), Nicolai Gedda (ten), Michel Sénéchal (ten), Carmen Prieto (sgr), H. Rosbaud (cnd), Paris Conservatory Societé des Concerts Orch *(rec Aix-en-Provence Festival, France, 1954)* Agorá ("Phoenix" series) 2-▲ 512

Brassus Chorale

A. Charlet (cnd)

Gounod, C.:Mass 2, w. F. Margot (org) *(rec 1992 & 1993)* Claves ▲ CD 9326 [DDD]

Bratislava Chamber Chorus

Delibes, L.:Lakmé, w. A. Ruffini (sop), S. Lazzarini (mez), G. Morino (ten), B. Praticò (bar), C. Piantini (cnd), Italian International Orch [F] Nuova Era 2-▲ 7096/97 [DDD]

Mascagni, P.:Messa di Gloria, w. Carlo Allemano (ten), Domenico Colaianni (bar), M. Letonja (cnd), Italian International Opera Orch Nuova Era ▲ NUO CD 7270

Bratislava Chamber Chorus (cont.)

Mercadante, S.:Caritea, regina di Spagna, w. Nana Gordaze (sgr), Sonia Lee (sgr), Jacek Laszczkowski (sgr), Nicolas Rivenq (bar), Gregory Bonfatti (sgr), Ayhan Ustuk (sgr), G. Carella (cnd), Italian International Opera Orch *(rec Italy, 1995)* Nuova Era 3-▲ NUO 7258

Rossini, G.:Demetrio e Polibio, w. Christine Weidinger (sop—Lisinga), Sara Mingardo (cta—Siveno), Anna Laura Longo (sgr—Olmira), Dalmacio Gonzales (ten—Demetrio/Eumene), Giorgio Surjan (bass—Polibio), Martino Fullone (sgr—Onao), M. Carraro (cnd), Graz SO *(rec live, Martina Franca Opera Festival, Italy, July 27, 1992)* Dynamic 2-▲ CDS 171/1-2 [DDD]

Bratislava Children's Choir

Bizet, G.:Carmen, w. D. Palade (sop), G. Alperyn (mez), G. Lamberti (ten), A. Titus (bar), et al., A. Rahbari (cnd), Czech-Slovak RSO Bratislava, Slovak Phil Chorus [F] Naxos 3-▲ 8.660005/07 [DDD]

Bizet, G.:Carmen (sels), w. D. Palade (sop—Micaëla), A. Liebeck (sop—Frasquita), G. Alperyn (mez—Carmen), D. Schaechter (mez—Mercédès), G. Lamberti (ten—Don José), M. Dvorsky (ten—Remandado), J. Durco (ten—Cancairo), A. Titus (bar—Escamillo), V. Chmelo (bar—Morales), D. Rigosa (bass—Zuniga), A. Rahbari (cnd), Czech-Slovak RSO Bratislava, Slovak Phil Chorus *(rec July 1990)* Naxos ▲ 8.550727 [DDD]

Puccini, G.:La Bohème, w. L. Orgonasova (sop), C. Gonzales (mez), J. Welch (ten), F. Previati (bar), W. Humburg (cnd), *(orch unknown)* [I] Naxos 2-▲ 8.660003/04 [DDD]

Puccini, G.:La Bohème (sels), w. Luba Orgonasova (sop—Mimi), Carmen Gonzales (sop—Musetta), Jonathan Welch (ten—Rudolfo), Fabio Previati (bar—Marcello), Boaz Senator (bar—Schaunard), Ivan Urbas (bass—Colline), Jiri Sulzenko (bass—Alcindoro), W. Humburg (cnd), Czech-Slovak RSO Bratislava, Slovak Phil Chorus *(rec Concert Hall, Czecho-Slovak Radio, Bratislava, Apr. 23–May 4, 1990)* Naxos ▲ 8.553151 [DDD]

Bratislava Chorus

Operatic Arias, w. Hermann Prey (bar), Bratislava Phil [cnd:Kurt Wöss] Capriccio ▲ 10054 [DDD]

Strauss (II), Joh.:Die Fledermaus (sels), w. Ariane Calix (sop—Ida), Gabriele Fontana (sop—Rosalinde), Brigitte Karwautz (sop—Adele), Rohangiz Yachmi-Caucig (cta—Orlofsky), John Dickie (ten—Eisenstein), Josef Hopferwieser (ten—Alfred), Erich Wessner (ten—Dr. Blind), Andrea Martin (bar—Falke), Alfred Werner (bar—Frank), J. Wildner (cnd), Czech-Slovak RSO Bratislava—Ov.; [Act I] Täubchen, das entflattert ist...; Ach, ich darf nicht hin zu dir; Nein, mit solchen Advokaten; Komm mit mir zum Souper; So muss allein ich bleiben; Trinke, Liebchen, trinke schnell; [Act II] Ein Souper heut' uns winkt; Ich lade gern mir Gäste ein; Mein Herr Marquis, ein Mann wie Sie; Dieser Anstand, so manierlich; Klänge der Heimat; Im Feuerstrom der Reben; Marianka komm und tanz me hier; [Act III] Entr'acte; Spiel' ich die Unschuld vom Lande; O Fledermaus, o Fledermaus *(rec Slovak Radio Concert Hall, Bratislava)* Naxos ▲ 8.553171 [DDD]

Strauss (II), Joh.:Orchestral Music, w. J. Wildner (cnd), Slovak RSO Bratislava—Entrance March [from Der Zigeunerbaron]; Romance from Gounod's Faust [arr. Johann Strauss]; Kaiser-Alexander-Huidigungs-Marsch [arr. Kulling]; Ballet Music [from Indigo und die vierzig Räuber; arr. Schönherr]; Jubilee Waltz; Faust-Quadrille [from Gounod's Faust; arr. Kulling]; Kaiser Franz Joseph-Jubiläums-Marsch [unconfirmed]; Farewell to America Waltz; Sounds from Boston [both arr. Cohen]; Ballet Music [from Die Fledermaus]; Processional March [from Eine Nacht in Venedig] *(rec Bratislava Slovak Radio Concert Hall, Feb 1–4, 1994)* Marco Polo ▲ 8.223247 [DDD]

Van Appledorn, M.J.:Rising Night after Night, w. O. Dohnányi (cnd), Slovak RSO Bratislava Vienna Modern Masters ▲ VMM 3004 [DDD]

L. Holásek (cnd)

Handel, G.F.:Messiah (sels), w. J. Krček (cnd), Capella Istropolitana—choruses *(rec 9/89)* Naxos ▲ 8.550317 [DDD]; Δ 7.550317 [DDD]

Bratislava Phil Chorus

Dvořák, A.:The Spectre's Bride, Op. 69, w. Jitka Sobehartova (sop), Jiri Kubik (ten), Jan Markvart (bar), P. Tiboris (cnd), Bohuslav Martinů PO [Cz] *(rec Nov. 26–30, 1993)* Elysium ▲ GRK 700 [DDD]

Breda Sacred Choir

Cantryn, Veldhoven (cnd)

Bach, J.S.:St. Matthew Passion, w. B. Schlick (sop), K. Wessel (alto), G. de Mey (ten), C. Pregardien (ten), P. Kooy (bass), T. Koopman (cnd), Amsterdam Baroque Orch, Netherlands Bach Society Boys' Choir Erato ▲ 2292-45814-2

Bregenz Festival Choir

Strauss (II), Joh.:Eine Nacht in Venedig, w. E. Réthy (sop), M. Schober (sop), R. Boesch (bar), K. Friedrich (ten), A. Jerger (b-bar), K. Preger (ten), A. Paulik (cnd), Vienna SO [G] *(rec 1951)* Koch Schwann ▲ 3-1272-2 [ADD]

Brewer Chorus

Handel, G.F.:Joshua, w. Julianne Baird (sop), D'Anna Fortunato (mez), John Aler (ten), John Ostendorf (b-bar), R. Palmer (cnd), Brewer CO [period instruments] Newport Classic 2-▲ NPD 85515/1-2 [DDD]

Brighton Festival Chorus

Bax, A.:Enchanted Summer, w. A. Williams-King (sop), L. McWhirter (sop), V. Handley (cnd), Royal PO [E] Chandos ▲ CHAN 8625 [DDD]

Bax, A.:Fatherland, w. M. Hill (ten), V. Handley (cnd), Royal PO [E] Chandos ▲ CHAN 8625 [DDD]

Bax, A.:Walsinghame, w. L. McWhirter (sop), M. Hill (ten), V. Handley (cnd), Royal PO [E] Chandos ▲ CHAN 8625 [DDD]

Beethoven, L. van:Sym 9, "Choral Sym", w. Y. Menuhin (cnd), Royal PO [soloists:R. Falcon, K. McKellar-Ferguson, R. Margison] RPO ▲ RPO 7001 [DDD]

Haydn, J.:Die Schöpfung, w. Helena Döse (sop—Eva), Lucia Popp (sop—Gabriel), Werner Hollweg (ten—Uriel), Benjamin Luxon (bar—Adam), Kurt Moll (bass—Raphael), Jack McCormack (db), David Strange (vc), Antál Dorati (hpd), A. Dorati (cnd), Royal PO *(rec Kingsway Hall, London, Dec 1976)* London 2-▲ 443027-2 [ADD]

Leeds Castle Classics, w. Royal PO, Carl Davis (cnd), Royal Artillery Band RPO Records ▲ RPO 7018 [DDD]

Lloyd, G.:A Symphonic Mass, w. G. Lloyd (cnd), Bournemouth SO Albany ▲ TROY 100 [DDD]

Orff, C.:Carmina burana, w. N. Burrowes (sop), L. Devos (ten), J. Shirley-Quirk (bar), A. Dorati (cnd), Royal PO [G,L] London ▲ 417714-2 [ADD]

Orff, C.:Carmina burana, w. Norma Burrowes (sop), Louis Devos (ten), John Shirley-Quirk (bar), A. Dorati (cnd), Royal PO, Southend Boys' Choir *(rec Kingsway Hall, London, Feb 1976)* London ("Phase 4 Stereo" series) ▲ 444105-2 [ADD]

Shostakovich, D.:Song of the Forest, w. M. Kotliarov (ten), N. Storoyev (bass), V. Ashkenazy (cnd), Royal PO, New London Children's Choir London ▲ 436762-2 [DDD]

L. Heltay (cnd)

Kodály, Z.:Missa Brevis London ("Enterprise" series) ▲ 433080-2 [ADD]

Kodály, Z.:Pange lingua London ("Enterprise" series) ▲ 433080-2 [ADD]

Martin, F.:In terra pax, w. Judith Howarth (sop), Della Jones (cta), Martyn Hill (ten), Roderick Williams (bar), Stephen Roberts (bass), M. Bamert (cnd), London PO Chandos ▲ CHAN 9465

I. Kertesz (cnd)

Kodály, Z.:Psalmus hungaricus, w. L. Kozma (ten) London ("Enterprise" series) ▲ 433080-2 [ADD]

Brighton Festival Women's Chorus

Holst, G.:The Planets, w. A. Previn (cnd), Royal PO *(rec 4/14–15/86)* Telarc ▲ CD 80133 [DDD] ■ CS 30133 (D)

Bristol Bach Choir

G. Jenkins (cnd)

Bristol Bach Choir Priory ▲ PRCD 352 [DDD]

Mathias, W.:A Royal Garland [E] Priory ▲ PRCD 352 [DDD]

Welcome Yule Saydisc ▲ CDSDL 375 [DDD]

Bristol Cathedral Choir

M. Archer (cnd)

Brahms, J.:Motets (comp), w. A. Pinel (org)—Op. 30 & Op. 110/2 [G] Meridian ▲ CDE 84188

Bruckner, A.:Motets [L] Meridian ▲ CDE 84188

Dvořák, A.:Mass, w. Coupe (trb), S. Taylor (ct), P. Cave (ten), S. Foulkes (bass), A. Pinel (org) [L] Meridian ▲ CDE 84188

Bristol Cathedral Special Choirs

Elgar, E.:Choral Songs (sels), w. A. Pinel (org)—Ave Verum Corpus; Benedictus in F; Give Unto the Lord, O Ye Mighty; Great is the Lord; Hear Thy Children, Gentle Jesus; Imperial March; Psalm 67; Spirit of the Lord; Te Deum in F [E,L] *(rec 8/88)* Meridian ▲ CDE 84168

Britten Singers

Britten, B.:Cant misericordium, w. J. M. Ainsley (ten), S. Varcoe (bar), R. Hickox (cnd), City of London Sinfonia [L] Chandos ▲ CHAN 8997 [DDD]

Finzi, G.:Requiem da Camera, w. S. Varcoe (bar), R. Hickox (cnd), City of London Sinfonia [E] Chandos ▲ CHAN 8997 [DDD]

Holst, G.:Psalms 86 & 148, w. J. Alley (org), R. Hickox (cnd), City of London Sinfonia [E] Chandos ▲ CHAN 8997 [DDD]

A. Calabrese (cnd)

Britten, B.:Flower Songs ACA Digital Recording ▲ CM 20039

Britten, B.:Rejoice in the Lamb, w. Susan Ashe (sop), Cynthia Calabrese (alt), Victor Floyd (ten), Charles Sprawls (bass) ACA Digital Recording ▲ CM 20039

Britten, B.:Te Deum, w. Elizabeth Arnold (sop) ACA Digital Recording ▲ CM 20039

Hindemith, P.:Chansons ACA Digital Recording ▲ CM 20039

Rorem, N.:Madrigals ACA Digital Recording ▲ CM 20039

R. Hickox (cnd)

Britten, B.:Chorale on an Old French Carol [E] Chandos ▲ CHAN 8997 [DDD]

Britten, B.:Deus in adjutorium meum [L] Chandos ▲ CHAN 8997 [DDD]

Brnensky Academy Choir

Mozart, W.A.:Requiem, w. E. Mirgova (sop), M. Kozená (cta), J. Griffett (ten), J. Klecker (bass), A. Kroper (cnd), Prague Concertino Nutturno Allegro ▲ ALG PCD 1022 [DDD]

Brnensky Academy Chorus Sbor

Brown, Kröper (cnd)

Hallelujah, w. Pro Cantione Antiqua, Prague Gioio della Musica IMP Classics ("Allegro" series) ▲ ALGPCD 1094 [DDD]

Brno Czech Phil Chorus

P. Fiala (cnd)

Dvořák, A.:Stabat Mater, w. Eva Jenisova (sop), Hana Stolfova-Bandova (cta), Vladimir Dolezal (ten), Jiri Sulzenka (bass), L. Svárovsky (cnd), Czech PO Supraphon 2-▲ SUP CD 3093

Janácek, L.:Music of, w. Zuzana Lapciková (sop), Pavla Dittmannová (cta), Petr Julícek (te), L. Svárovsky (cnd), Brno State PO—Rákos Rákoczy (ballet); folk songs, choruses & dances Supraphon ▲ SUP CD 3129

Brno Janáček Opera Chorus

Janácek, L.:The Beginning of a Romance, w. F. Jílek (cnd), Brno Janáček Opera Orch Multisonic ▲ MUL 310245

Janácek, L.:Fate, w. Magdaléna Hajóssyová (sop), Vladimir Krejčík (ten), Vilém Přibyl (ten), F. Jílek (cnd), Brno Janáček Opera Orch Supraphon ▲ SUP 0045 [AAD]

Janácek, L.:Jenůfa, w. G. Beňačková (sop—Jenufa), N. Kniplová (mez—Kostelnička Buryja), V. Krejčík (ten—Steva Buryja), V. Přibyl (ten—Laca Klemen), F. Jílek (cnd), Brno Janáček Opera Orch [Cz] *(rec 1977–8)* Supraphon 2-▲ 10 2751-2 [AAD]

Smetana, B.:The Kiss, w. Eva Deplotová (sop), Libuše Márová (mez), Leo Marian Vodička (ten), F. Vajnar (cnd), Brno Janáček Opera Orch Supraphon 2-▲ SUP 112180 [AAD]

Brno Radio Chorus

Janácek, L.:Šárka, w. A. Nováková (sop), A. Jurecka (ten), J. Válka (ten), K. Kunc (bass), B. Bakala (cnd), Brno RSO *(rec live, 1953)* Multisonic ("Prague Spring Collection" series) ▲ 31 0154 [ADD]

Brooklyn Boys' Choir

Mahler, G.:Syms, w. J. Blegen (sop), B. Hendricks (sop), M. Price (sop), G. Zeumer (sop), H. Wittek (trb), A. Baltsa (mez), C. Ludwig (mez), K. Riegel (ten), H. Prey (bar), A. Schmidt (bar), J. Van Dam (b-bar), L. Bernstein (cnd), New York PO, Royal Concertgebouw Orch, Vienna PO, Westminster Choir, New York Choral Artists, Vienna Boys' Choir, Vienna State Opera Chorus, Vienna Singverein Deutsche Grammophon 13-▲ 435162-2 [DDD]

Mahler, G.:Sym 3, w. C. Ludwig (mez), L. Bernstein (cnd), New York PO, New York Choral Artists [G] Deutsche Grammophon 2-▲ 427328-2 [DDD]

Brooklyn Phil Chorus

Reich, S.:The Desert Music, w. Reich, Tilson Thomas (cnd), Brooklyn PO, Ensemble Elektra/Nonesuch ▲ 79101-2 [DDD] ■ 79101-4 (D)

Nigel Brooks Chorale

Tanner, J.:Boy with Goldfish, w. L. Siu (sgr), M. Elliott (sgr), L. Holdridge (cnd), London SO Albany ▲ TROY 053 [DDD]

Bruges Cantores Oratorio Choir

Beethoven, L. van:Sym 9, "Choral Sym", w. M. Gauci (sop), A. Rahbari (cnd), Brussels Belgian Radio-TV PO Discover International ▲ DICD 920151 [DDD]

Brünn Czech Phil Chorus

Hummel, J.N.:Alma virgo, w. Amanda Halgrimson (sop), Susan McAdoo (mez), Helmut Wildhaber (ten), Petr Mikuláš (bass), Jan Engel (bass), M. Haselböck (cnd), Vienna Academy Koch Schwann ▲ SCH CD 317792

Hummel, J.N.:Mass in E♭, Op. 80, w. Amanda Halgrimson (sop), Susan McAdoo (mez), Helmut Wildhaber (ten), Petr Mikuláš (bass), Jan Engel (bass), M. Haselböck (cnd), Vienna Academy Koch Schwann ▲ SCH CD 317792

Hummel, J.N.:Quod quod in orbe, w. Amanda Halgrimson (sop), Susan McAdoo (mez), Helmut Wildhaber (ten), Petr Mikuláš (bass), Jan Engel (bass), M. Haselböck (cnd), Vienna Academy Koch Schwann ▲ SCH CD 317792

Brussels Belgian Radio-TV Chorus

Messiaen, O.:La Transfiguration de Notre Seigneur Jésus-Christ, w. Ludwig van Gijsegem (ten), Yvonne Loriod (pno), R. de Leeuw (cnd), Hilversum RSO Montaigne 2-▲ MO 782040

Brussels Choral Society

Jongen, J.:Mass, Op. 130, w. J. Hughes (org), T. Cunningham (cnd), Luc Capouillez Brass Ensemble [L] Pavane ▲ ADW 7242 [DDD]

T. Cunningham (cnd)

Van Nuffel, J.:Motets [L] Pavane ▲ ADW 7242 [DDD]

Brussels Polyphonia Choir

Honegger, A.:Sémiramis, w. V. Ivanov (vn), M. Kemmer (sgr), L. Hager (cnd), RTL SO, Namur Belgium French Community Symphonic Choir *(rec Nov. 16–20, 1992)* Timpani ▲ 1C 1016 [DDD]

Tournemire, C.:Sym 6, w. Daniel Galvez-Vallero (ten), P. Bartholomée (cnd), Liège PO Valois ▲ V 4757

Brussels Radio-TV Chorus

Franck, C.:Messe solennelle, w. L. Devos (ten), P. Bartholomée (cnd), Brussels Radio-TV Instrumentalists [L] *(rec 1976)* Koch Schwann ▲ 3-1044-2 [ADD]

Bucharest George Enescu Phil Chorus

Constantinescu, P.:The Nativity, w. E. Petrescu (sop), M. Kessler (mez), V. Teodorian (ten), H. Bömches (bass), M. Basarab (cnd), Bucharest George Enescu PO *(rec 1977)* Olympia ▲ OCD 402 [AAD]

Bucharest Madrigal Choir

M. Constantin (cnd)

Byzantine Orthodox Vespers and Matutin Koch Schwann ▲ SCH 312472 [DDD]

Bucharest Opera & Ballet Theater Chorus

Leoncavallo, R.:Pagliacci, w. Arta Florescu (sop—Nedda), Cornel Stavru (ten—Canio), Valentin Teodorian (ten—Beppe), Nicolae Herlea (bar—Tonio), Ladislau Konya (bar—Silvio), M. Popa (cnd), Bucharest Opera & Ballet Theater Orch *(rec 1966)* Vox Box 2-▲ CDX 5161

Mascagni, P.:Cavalleria rusticana, w. Marina Krilovici (sop—Santuzza), Viorica Cortez (mez—Lola), Milka Nistor (mez—Lucia), Cornel Stavru (ten—Turiddu), David Ohanesian (bar—Alfio), M. Popa (cnd), Bucharest Opera & Ballet Theater Orch *(rec 1966)* Vox Box 2-▲ CDX 5161

Bucknell Rooke Chapel Choir

Duckworth, W.E.:Southern Harmony, w. Gregg Smith Singers Lovely Music ▲ LCD 2033 [ADD]

▲ = CD ♦ = Enhanced CD Δ = MD ■ = Cassette Tape ◻ = DCC

Budapest Academic Choral Society
G. Hollerung (cnd)
Karai, J.:Choral Music—De profundis; Lament for a Flower [w. Flóra Koós (sop)]; A Spring Night; Evening Waterfall; Night; Stabat Mater; Ave Maria II; How It Rains; Ave maris stella; Alleluja [w. Péter Drucker (ten)]; Hodie Christus natus est; Spring Rejoicing [w. József Karai (pno)] *(rec Blessed Eusebius Catholic Church, Budapest)* Hungaroton ▲ HCD 31348 [DDD]
Budapest Children's Choir
Silent Night, w. Imre Kovacs (fl), Hedy Lubik (hp), Ferenc Gergely (org), Frigyes Hidas (org), Gabor Lehotka (org), Hungarian State Orch CO, Csanyi (cnd), Szekeres (cnd), Budapest Madrigal Choir Hungaroton ▲ HCD 16598
Budapest Chorus
Kodály, Z.:Psalmus hungaricus, w. J. Simándy (ten), A. Dorati (cnd), Hungarian State Orch [Hun] Hungaroton ▲ HCD 11392
Kodály, Z.:Psalmus hungaricus, w. József Simándy (ten), A. Dorati (cnd), Hungarian State Orch, Hungarian Radio-TV Children's Chorus Hungaroton ▲ HCD 31503 [ADD]
Schumann, R.:Requiem, Op. 148, w. E. Andor (sop), Barlay (sgr), Korondy (sgr), J. Gregor (bass), M. Forrai (cnd), Hungarian State Orch [L] Hungaroton ▲ HCD 11809
Schumann, R.:Requiem Mignon, w. E. Andor (sop), Barlay (sgr), Korondy (sgr), J. Gregor (bass), M. Forrai (cnd), Hungarian State Orch [L] Hungaroton ▲ HCD 11809
M. Forrai (cnd)
Beethoven, L. van:Syms (comp), w. Éva Andor (sop), Márta Szirmay (cta), György Korondi (ten), Sándor Sólyom-Nagy (bar), J. Ferencsik (cnd), Hungarian State Orch *(rec 1969, 1971, 1974–76)* Classical Diamonds 6-▲ 4013-18 [ADD]
Budapest Lyon Chorus
Massenet, J.:Grisélidis, w. Michèle Command (sop), Brigitte Desnoues (sop), Jean-Luc Viala (ten), Didier Henry (bar), Maurice Sieyes (bar), Christian Treguier (bar), Jean-Philippe Courtis (bass), Claire Larcher (sgr), P. Fournillier (cnd), Franz Liszt SO Koch Schwann 2-▲ SCH 312702 [DDD]
Budapest Madrigal Choir
Caldara, A.:Magnificat, w. M. Szücs (sop), K. Takács (cta), D. Gulyás (ten), T. Bátor (bass), F. Szekeres (cnd), Budapest Strings [L] Hungaroton ▲ HCD 31259 [DDD]
Sammartini, G.B.:Magnificat in B♭, w. Szücs (sop), Takács (alt), Gulyás (ten), Bátor (bass), F. Szekeres (cnd), Budapest Strings [L] Hungaroton ▲ HCD 31259 [DDD]
Silent Night, w. Imre Kovacs (fl), Hedy Lubik (hp), Ferenc Gergely (org), Frigyes Hidas (org), Gabor Lehotka (org), Hungarian State Orch CO, Csanyi (cnd), Szekeres (cnd), Budapest Children's Choir Hungaroton ▲ HCD 16598
Vivaldi, A.:Magnificat, RV.610, w. T. Takács (mez), D. Gulyás (ten), T. Bátor (bass), R. Szücs (bass), F. Szekeres (cnd), Budapest Strings [L] Hungaroton ▲ HCD 31259 [DDD]
Vivaldi, A.:Magnificat, RV.611, w. T. Takács (mez), J. Németh (mez), Bátori (sgr), Kovács (sgr), Szökefalvi-Nagy (sgr), F. Szekeres (cnd), Budapest Strings [L] Hungaroton ▲ HCD 31259 [DDD]
Vivaldi, A.:L'Olimpiade (sels), w. M. Zempléni (sop), T. Takács (mez), Horváth (sgr), Káplán (sgr), L. Miller (bar), I. Gáti (bar), K. Kováts (bass), F. Szekeres (cnd), Hungarian State Orch [I] White Label ▲ HRC 073 [ADD]
G. Czigány (cnd)
Vivaldi, A.:Juditha triumphans devicta Holofernes barbarie, w. Margit László (sop—Abra), Zsuzsa Barlay (cta—Juditha), József Réti (ten—Servo), Zsolt Bende (bar—Holofernes), József Dene (bar—Ozias), F. Szekeres (cnd), Hungarian State Orch, 1968 Classical Diamonds ▲ CLD 4022-23 [ADD]
Budapest National Opera Chorus
Wayditch, G. von:The Caliph's Magician, w. Júlia Pászthi (sop—Eunuch), Sándor Palcso (ten—The Emir), István Rozsos (ten—Nawab), Zsolt Bende (bar—The Magician), Arpád Kishegyi (sgr—Djinn), András Nagy-Soljom (sgr—The Caliph), Csaba Ötvös (sgr—Djinn), Csilla Ötvös (sgr—Odalisk), A. Kórodi (cnd), Budapest National Opera Orch *(rec 1975)* VAI Audio 2-▲ VAIA 1095-2 [ADD]
Budapest Phil Chorus
Beethoven, L. van:Sym 9, "Choral Sym", w. E. Andor (sop), H. Szirmay (cta), G. Korondy (ten), S. Solyom-Nagy (bar), J. Ferencsik (cnd), Hungarian PO Laserlight ▲ 15 905
Budapest Radio Chorus
Wagner, R.:Der fliegende Holländer, w. I. Haubold (sop—Senta), M. Schiml (mez—Nurse), P. Seiffert (ten—Erik), J. Hering (ten—Helsman), A. Muff (bar—The Dutchman), E. Knodt (bass—Sea Capt.), P. Steinberg (cnd), Vienna ORF SO [G] *(rec Sept. 1992)* Naxos 2-▲ 8.660025/26 [DDD]
Budapest Schola Cantorum
Werner, G.J.:Vesperae de Apostolis, w. Ágnes Dobszay (sop), Péter Patay (cta), Tamás Bubnó (ten), Péter Cser (bass), J. Mezei (cnd), Vienna-Szász CO *(rec St. Columba's Presbyterian Church, Budapest, June 12–15, 1995)* Hungaroton ▲ HCD 31646 [DDD]
Werner, G.J.:Vesperae de Confessoris, w. Éva Bodrogi (sop), Regina Fülöp (cta), Kornél Pechan (ten), Péter Cser (bass), János Mezei (org), J. Mezei (cnd), Vienna-Szász CO *(rec St. Columba's Presbyterian Church, Budapest, June 12–15, 1995)* Hungaroton ▲ HCD 31646 [DDD]
Budapest Sym Chorus
Liszt, F.:Dante Sym, w. G. Lehel (cnd), Budapest SO Hungaroton ▲ HCD 11918
Liszt, F.:Missa solemnis, w. V. Kincses (mez), T. Takács (mez), G. Korondy (ten), J. Gregor (bass), A. Ferencsik (cnd), Budapest SO [L] Hungaroton ▲ HCD 11861
Buenos Aires Teatro Colón Chorus
Bellini, V.:Norma, w. J. Sutherland (sop), F. Cossotto (mez), C. Craig (ten), I. Vinco (bass), R. Bonynge (cnd), Buenos Aires Teatro Colón Orch *(rec live 7/2/69)* Ediciones Teatro Colon 3-▲ ETC 101 [AAD]
Donizetti, G.:Lucia di Lammermoor, w. B. Sills (sop), A. Kraus (ten), G. Mastromei (bar), V. de Narke (bass), J.E. Martini (cnd), Buenos Aires Teatro Colón Orch *(rec 1968)* Arkadia 2-▲ 474
Franzetti, C.:Aubade, w. C. Franzetti (cnd), Buenos Aires Orch *(rec Ion Studios, Buenos Aires, Argentina, 1985)* Premier ▲ PRCD 1044 [DDD]
Offenbach, J.:Les Contes d'Hoffmann, w. H. Harper (sop), Bakocevic (sgr), M. Mesplé (sop), S. Kónya (ten), G. Bacquier (bar), P. Maag (cnd), Buenos Aires Teatro Colón Orch [F] *(rec live, Buenos Aires 8/3/70)* Melodram 2-▲ MEL 27090 [ADD]
Rossini, G.:Il barbiere di Siviglia, w. T. Berganza (mez), R. Casellato (ten), S. Bruscantini (bar), G. Tozzi (bass), B. Bartoletti (cnd), Buenos Aires Teatro Colón Orch [I] *(rec 1969)* Golden Age of Opera 2-▲ GAO 149/50
Verdi, G.:Rigoletto, w. Renata Scotto (sop—Gilda), Stella Maris Silva (sop—Giovanna), Martha Carrizo (mez—Page), Carmen de la Mata (mez—Countess Ceprano), Noemi Souza (cta—Maddalena), Horacio Mastrango (ten—Borso), Richard Tucker (ten—Duke of Mantua), Cornell MacNeil (bar—Rigoletto), Riccardo Yost (bar—Marullo), Guerrino Boschetti (bass—Usher), Tulio Gagliardo (bass—Count Ceprano), Victor de Narké (bass—Monterone), William Wilderman (bass—Sparafucile), F. Previtali (cnd), Buenos Aires Teatro Colón Orch *(rec Colon Theater, Buenos Aires, Aug. 22, 1967)* Legato Classics 2-▲ LCD 198-2
Wagner, R.:Der fliegende Holländer, w. M. Lawrence (sop), F. Destal (bar), A. Kipnis (bass), F. Busch (cnd), Buenos Aires Teatro Colón Orch [G] *(rec live broadcast 9/19/36)* Pearl 2-▲ PEAS 9910 (m) [ADD]
Wagner, R.:Tristan und Isolde (sels), w. K. Flagstad (sop), V. Ursuleac (sop), S. Svanholm (ten), H. Hotter (b-bar), E. Kleiber (cnd), Buenos Aires Teatro Colón Orch—highlights from Acts 1–3 [G] *(rec live, 1948)* Melodram 2-▲ MEL 25007 (m) [AAD]
Buffalo Opera Sacra Chorus
Honegger, A.:Christophe Colomb, w. E. Knecht (speaker—Queen Isabella), S. Rawson (speaker—The Magician), N. Garvey (speaker—Christopher Columbus), A. Furnival (speaker—King Ferdinand), D. McCabe (bar), C. Peltz (cnd), Buffalo Opera Sacra Orch [E] *(rec Buffalo, New York, Oct. 30–31, 1992)* Mode ▲ MOD 35 [DDD]
Bulgaria Male Voices
M. Verhoeff (cnd)
Male Voices of Bulgaria Koch Schwann ▲ SCH 314892
Bulgarian A Capella Choir
Rachmaninoff, S.:All-Night Vigil Sound ▲ CD 3448
Bulgarian Mixed Choir
M. Popsavov (cnd)
Orthodox Wedding Ceremony & New Year's Celebrations, w. Kamenov, Hristo (ten), S. Markov (bass) *(rec 1993)* Jade ▲ JAD C 108
Bulgarian National Chorus
Beethoven, L. van:Fidelio (sels), w. Boris Christoff (bass), E. Gracis (cnd), Bulgarian RSO—Aria of Piazarro Forlane ▲ FRL 16651 [AAD]
Gluck, C.W.:Iphigénie en Aulide (sels), w. Boris Christoff (bass), E. Gracis (cnd), Bulgarian RSO—Récitatif & Aria of Agamemnon Forlane ▲ FRL 16651 [AAD]
Gounod, C.:Faust (sels), w. Alexandrina Pendachanska (sop—Margarethe), Giuseppe Sabbatini (ten—Faust), György Melis (bar—Valentin), Nicolai Ghiaurov (bass—Méphistophélès), Nikola Ghiuselev (bass—Méphistophélès), Berlin RSO, Vienna SO, Hungarian State Opera Orch, Bulgarian RSO, Sofia SO, Bulgarian National Chorus Radio Choir—Intro; Vien ou bière; O sainte médaille...Avant de quitter ces lieux; Le veau d'or [all from Act 2]; Quel trouble inconnu me pénètre!...Salut! demeure chaste et pure; Je voudrais bien savoir...Il était un roi de Thule; Un bouquet!...O Dieu! que de bijoux [both from Act 3]; Gloire immortelle de nos aieux; Vous qui faites l'endormie [both from Act 4]; Intermezzo; Walpurgis Night [both from Act 5] Laserlight ▲ 14209 [DDD]
Gretchaninoff, A.:Liturgica Domestica for St. John Chrysostom, w. B. Christoff (bass) Jade ▲ JAD C062
Kalomiris, M.:Sym 1, w. B. Fidetzis (cnd), Sophia PO Orata ▲ ORAML 62
Mahler, G.:Sym 2, w. Tiha Genova (sop), Vessela Zorova (alt), E. Tabakov (cnd), Sofia PO *(rec Bulgarian Concert Hall, Sofia, Jan 1987)* Capriccio 15-▲ 49043 [DDD]
Mahler, G.:Sym 3, w. Brigitte Pretschner (alt), E. Tabakov (cnd), Sofia PO, Bodra Smyana Children's Choir *(rec Bulgarian Concert Hall, Sofia, Apr 1990)* Capriccio 15-▲ 49043 [DDD]
Mahler, G.:Sym 8, w. Lyudmila Hadzhieva (sop), Maria Temeshi (sop), Darina Takova (sop), Tamara Takac (alt), Boryana Tabakova (alt), Janos Bandi (ten), Pal Kovacs (bar), Tamash Syule (bass), E. Tabakov (cnd), Sofia PO, Bulgarian National Radio Chorus, Bulgarian National Radio Children's Choir *(rec National Palace of Culture, Sofia, June 1991)* Capriccio 15-▲ 49043 [DDD]
Mascagni, P.:Cavalleria rusticana (sels), w. G. Robev (cnd), Sofia PO—Easterchorus Forlane ▲ FRL 16668 [ADD]
Monteverdi, C.:Arias & Duets, w. Boris Christoff (bass), E. Gracis (cnd), Bulgarian RSO—Aria of Seneca [from The Coronation of Poppee] Forlane ▲ FRL 16651 [AAD]
Mozart, W.A.:Arias, w. Boris Christoff (bass), E. Gracis (cnd), Bulgarian RSO—Cosi dunque tradisci Forlane ▲ FRL 16651 [AAD]
Petridis, P.:Con grosso Ww, w. B. Fidetzis (cnd), Sophia PO Orata ▲ ORAML 62
Puccini, G.:Tosca (sels), w. G. Robev (cnd), Sofia PO Forlane ▲ FRL 16668 [ADD]
Rameau, J.P.:Dardanus (sels), w. Boris Christoff (bass), E. Gracis (cnd), Bulgarian RSO—Aria of Antenor Forlane ▲ FRL 16651 [AAD]
Rimsky-Korsakov, N.:Snow Maiden, w. Stefka Evstatieva (sop—Kupava), Elena Zemenkova (sop—Snow Maiden), Alexandrina Milcheva (mez—Spring Fairy), Vessela Zorova (mez—wife), Stefka Mineva (alt—Lehl), Avram Andreev (ten—Tsar), Lyubomir Dyakovski (ten—Cottager, Sprite), Lyubomir Videnov (bar—Misgir), Nicola Ghiuselev (bass—King), S. Angelov (cnd), Bulgarian RSO *(rec Sofia, 1985)* Capriccio 3-▲ 10749-51 [DDD]
Tchaikovsky, P.:Eugene Onegin (sels), w. Alexandrina Pendachanska (sop), Nicolai Ghiaurov (bass), Lyubomir Diakovski (sgr), Niko Isakov (sgr), Dresden State Orch—Intro; Peasant's Chorus & Dance; Scene & Aria of Olga; Scene & Quartet; Letter Scene; plus others Laserlight ▲ 14210 [DDD]
Tchaikovsky, P.:Queen of Spades, w. S. Evstatieva (sop), P. Dilova (mez), I. Konsulov (bar), Mazulok (bass), E. Tchakarov (cnd), Sofia Festival Orch [R] Sony Classical 3-▲ S3K 45720
Verdi, G.:Aida (sels), w. G. Robev (cnd), Sofia PO—Triumphal March Forlane ▲ FRL 16668 [ADD]
Verdi, G.:Don Carlos (sels), w. G. Robev (cnd), Sofia PO—Act 3 Finale Forlane ▲ FRL 16668 [ADD]
Verdi, G.:La forza del destino (sels), w. G. Robev (cnd), Sofia PO Forlane ▲ FRL 16668 [ADD]
Verdi, G.:Macbeth (sels), w. Boris Christoff (bass), E. Gracis (cnd), Bulgarian RSO—Recitative & Aria of Banco Forlane ▲ FRL 16651 [AAD]
Verdi, G.:Nabucco (sels), w. G. Robev (cnd), Sofia PO—Chorus of the Hebrew Slaves Forlane ▲ FRL 16668 [ADD]
Verdi, G.:La traviata (sels), w. G. Robev (cnd), Sofia PO—Matadore Chorus; Gypsies Chorus Forlane ▲ FRL 16668 [ADD]
Verdi, G.:Il trovatore (sels), w. G. Robev (cnd), Sofia PO—Bohemian Chorus Forlane ▲ FRL 16668 [ADD]
Wagner, R.:Lohengrin (sels), w. G. Robev (cnd), Sofia PO—Bride-Chorus Forlane ▲ FRL 16668 [ADD]
Wagner, R.:Tannhäuser (sels), w. G. Robev (cnd), Sofia PO—Entrance of the Knights Forlane ▲ FRL 16668 [ADD]
Weber, C.M. von:Der Freischütz (sels), w. G. Robev (cnd), Sofia PO—The Hunters' Chorus Forlane ▲ FRL 16668 [ADD]
M. Popsavov (cnd)
Mystery of the East:Music from Russian Churches & Monasteries, w. Rybin Choir Moscow, Sofia Orthodox Ensemble, Bulgarian National Choir [cnd:Georgi Robev] Capriccio ▲ 10 597 [DDD]
G. Robev (cnd)
Rachmaninoff, S.:All-Night Vigil *(rec Alexander Nevsky Cathedral, Sofia, Russia)* Capriccio ▲ 10 524 [DDD]
Bulgarian National Chorus Radio Choir
Gounod, C.:Faust (sels), w. Alexandrina Pendachanska (sop—Margarethe), Giuseppe Sabbatini (ten—Faust), György Melis (bar—Valentin), Nicolai Ghiaurov (bass—Méphistophélès), Nikola Ghiuselev (bass—Méphistophélès), Berlin RSO, Vienna SO, Hungarian State Opera Orch, Bulgarian RSO, Sofia SO, Bulgarian National Chorus—Intro; Vien ou bière; O sainte médaille...Avant de quitter ces lieux; Le veau d'or [all from Act 2]; Quel trouble inconnu me pénètre!...Salut! demeure chaste et pure; Je voudrais bien savoir...Il était un roi de Thule; Un bouquet!...O Dieu! que de bijoux [both from Act 3]; Gloire immortelle de nos aieux; Vous qui faites l'endormie [both from Act 4]; Intermezzo; Walpurgis Night [both from Act 5] Laserlight ▲ 14209 [DDD]
Bulgarian National Phil Chorus
Nicola Ghiuselev, w. Ghiuselev, Nicola (bass), Sofia SO [cnd:Metodii Matakiev] Gega ▲ GD 200 [DDD]
Pergolesi, G.B.:Stabat mater, w. T. Genova (sop), Bozhkova (sgr), V. Kazandjiev (cnd), Bulgarian PO [L] Vivace 2-▲ 140141 [ADD/DDD]
Bulgarian National Radio Children's Choir
Mahler, G.:Sym 8, w. Lyudmila Hadzhieva (sop), Maria Temeshi (sop), Darina Takova (sop), Tamara Takac (alt), Boryana Tabakova (alt), Janos Bandi (ten), Pal Kovacs (bar), Tamash Syule (bass), E. Tabakov (cnd), Sofia PO, Bulgarian National Chorus, Bulgarian National Radio Chorus *(rec National Palace of Culture, Sofia, June 1991)* Capriccio 15-▲ 49043 [DDD]
Puccini, G.:Tosca, w. Raina Kabaivanska (sop—Floria Tosca), Nazzareno Antinori (ten—Mario Cavaradossi), Roumen Doikov (ten—Spoletta), Enzo Dara (bar—Casare Angelotti/Il sagrestano), Nelson Portella (bar—Il Barone Scarpia), Stoyan Balabanov (bass—Sciarrone/Un carceriere), Borislav Peev (sgr—Un Pastore), G. Bellini (cnd), Sofia PO, Svetoslav Obrenetov Bulgarian National Chorus *(rec Sophia, Bulgaria, Nov 14–27, 1982)* Arts Music ▲ 47158-2 [DDD]
Bulgarian National Radio Chorus
Mahler, G.:Sym 8, w. Lyudmila Hadzhieva (sop), Maria Temeshi (sop), Darina Takova (sop), Tamara Takac (alt), Boryana Tabakova (alt), Janos Bandi (ten), Pal Kovacs (bar), Tamash Syule (bass), E. Tabakov (cnd), Sofia PO, Bulgarian National Chorus, Bulgarian National Radio Children's Choir *(rec National Palace of Culture, Sofia, June 1991)* Capriccio 15-▲ 49043 [DDD]
Recital, w. Christoff, Boris (bass), Ettore Gracis (cnd), Bulgarian RSO Forlane ▲ FOR 16651 [AAD]
Bulgarian Radio Men's Chorus
M. Milkov (cnd)
Slavonic Orthodox Liturgy, Vol. 2, w. Bulgarian Svetoslav Obretenov Choir [cnd:G. Robev] Harmonia Mundi ▲ HMA 190.105 [AAD] ■
Bulgarian Radio-TV Chorus
Orff, C.:Catulli Carmina, w. E. Stoyanova (sop), K. Kaludov (ten), M. Milkov (cnd), Bulgarian Radio-TV SO [L] *(rec live in Sofia, 1988)* Forlane ▲ FOR 16610 [DDD]
M. Milkov (cnd)
Britten, B.:Missa brevis [L] *(rec live in Sofia, 1989)* Forlane ▲ FOR 16610 [DDD]

CHORAL GROUPS

Bulgarian Svetoslav Obretenov Choir
G. Robev (cnd)
Bulgarian Svetoslav Obretenov Choir
Grande Liturgie Orthodoxe Slave — Harmonia Mundi France ▲ HMC 90101
Slavonic Orthodox Liturgy, Vol. 1 — Harmonia Mundi ▲ HMC 90.101 [ADD] ▮
Vol. 2, w. Bulgarian Radio Men's Choir [cnd:M. Milkov] — Harmonia Mundi ▲ HMA 190.105 [AAD] ▮
William Byrd Choir
G. Turner (cnd)
Lôbo, D.:Sacred Music—Requiem, "Missa pro defunctis" (1621); Motet, "Auvidi vocem de caelo" [L] — Hyperion ▲ CDA 66218 [DDD]
Magalhães, F. de:Missa dilectus meus [L] — Hyperion ▲ CDA 66218 [DDD]
Magalhães, F. de:Motet, "Commissa mea pavesco" [L] — Hyperion ▲ CDA 66218 [DDD]
Stéphane Caillet Vocal Ensemble
Messe de Sainte-Cécile, w. Eve Payeur (perc) — ARB ▲ 1417
Calabria Francesca Cilea Chorus
Coccia, C.:Caterina di Guisa, w. C. Apollonio (sop), N. Ciliento (mez), M. Leonardi (ten), S. Antonucci (bar), M. de Bernart (cnd), Italian PO *(rec Oct. 30 & Nov. 3, 1990)* — Bongiovanni 2-▲ GB 2117/18 [DDD]
California Bach Society Chorus
Bach, J.S.:Cant 118, w. E. Flath (org), E. Flath (cnd), California Bach Society CO, Valley Choral Society [G] — Bainbridge ▲ BCD 2502 [DDD]
Kobialka, D.:Antiphony Across..., w. E. Flath (org), E. Flath (cnd), California Bach Society CO, Valley Choral Society — Bainbridge ▲ BCD 2502 [DDD]
California Boys' Choir
Bach, J.S.:The Art of the Fugue (sels), w. L. Foss (cnd), Sheffield Ensemble [arr. William Malloch] — Sheffield Lab ▲ SLS 502
Calw Aurelius Boys' Choir Soloists
Hiller, W.:Schulamit, w. Regina Klepper (sop), Edeltraud Knabel (alt), Michael Schopper (bass), Elisabeth Woska (nar), Waltraut Mastrogiovanni-Kraxner (shofar), H.R. Zöbeley (cnd), Munich Residenz Orch, Munich Percussion Ensemble, Munich Motet Choir — Wergo ▲ WER 6280-2
Cambridge Chorus
S. Cleobury (cnd)
Tallis, T.:Spem in alium — Argo ▲ 425199-2 [DDD]
Cambridge Schola Gregoriana
M. Berry (cnd)
Gregorian Chant:The Ceremony of the Shepherds & Midnight Mass, w. King's College Choir Cambridge *(rec Private Chapel, Arundel Castle, Jan 1995)* — Herald ▲ HAVPCD 180 [DDD]
12th Century Chant, w. Winchester Cathedral Chorus — Herald ▲ HAVPCD 168
Cambridge Singers
Christmas Day in the Morning, w. Stephen Varcoe (bar), City of London Sinfonia [cnd:John Rutter] — Collegium ▲ COLCD 121 ▮ COLCS 121
Poulenc, F.:Gloria Sop, w. D. Deam (sop), J. Rutter (cnd), City of London Sinfonia [L] — Collegium ▲ COLCD 108 [DDD] ▮ COLC 108 (D)
Poulenc, F.:Litanies à la vierge noire, w. J. Rutter (cnd), City of London Sinfonia [L] — Collegium ▲ COLCD 108 [DDD] ▮ COLC 108 (D)
Rutter, J.:Anthems, w. J. Rutter (cnd), City of London Sinfonia—10 anthems [E] — Collegium ▲ COLCD 100 [DDD] ▮ COLC 100 (D)
Rutter, J.:Anthems, w. J. Rutter (cnd), City of London Sinfonia—I Will Lift Up Mine Eyes" [E] — Collegium ▲ COLCD 103 [DDD] ▮ COLC 103 (D)
Rutter, J.:Church Music, w. J. Rutter (cnd), City of London Sinfonia—Te Deum; Be thou my vision; I believe in springtime; Lord, make me an instrument of thy peace; O be joyful in the Lord; All creatures of our God and King; A choral fanfare; As the bridegroom to his chosen; Christ the Lord is risen again; Thy perfect love; The Lord is my light and my salvation; Go forth into the world in peace; Now thank we all our God — Collegium ▲ COLCD 112 [DDD] ▮ COLC 112 (D)
Rutter, J.:Gloria, w. J. Rutter (cnd), Philip Jones Brass Ensemble [L] — Collegium ▲ COLCD 100 [DDD] ▮ COLC 100 (D)
Rutter, J.:Requiem, w. C. Ashton (sop), D. Deam (sop), J. Rutter (cnd), City of London Sinfonia [E,L] — Collegium ▲ COLCD 103 [DDD] ▮ COLC 103 (D)

J. Rutter (cnd)
A Banquet of Voices:Music for Mulitple Choirs, w. H. Gough (baroque vc), W. Hunt (violone), W. Marshall (chamber org) *(rec London, Feb. 1993)* — Collegium ▲ COLCD 123
Brother Sun, Sister Moon — American Gramaphone ▲ AGCD 588 ▮ AGC 588
Christmas Night:Carols of the Nativity, w. City of London Sinfonia — Collegium ▲ COLCD 106 [DDD] ▮ COLC 106 (D)
Faire Is the Heaven:Music of the English Church — Collegium ▲ COLCD 107 [AAD] ▮ COLC 107
Fauré, G.:Cantique de Jean Racine, w. John Scott (org) [F] — Collegium ▲ COLCD 109 [DDD] ▮ COLC 109 (D)
Fauré, G.:Messe basse (in 3 movts), w. D. Deam (sop), J. Scott (org) [L] — Collegium ▲ COLCD 109 [DDD] ▮ COLC 109 (D)
Fauré, G.:Motets—3 motets [L] — Collegium ▲ COLCD 109 [DDD] ▮ COLC 109 (D)
Fauré, G.:Requiem, w. C. Ashton (sop), S. Varcoe (bar), City of London Sinfonia members [1893 ver.] [L] — Collegium ▲ COLCD 109 [DDD] ▮ COLC 109 (D)
Flora Gave Me Fairest Flowers — Collegium ▲ COLCD 105 [DDD] ▮ COLC 105 (D)
Olde English Madrigals & Folk Songs — American Gramaphone ▲ AGCD 500 ▮ AGC 500
Palestrina, G.:The Song of Songs *(rec Nov. 1993)* — Collegium ▲ COLCD 122 [DDD]
Poulenc, F.:Ave verum corpus [L] — Collegium ▲ COLCD 108 [DDD] ▮ COLC 108 (D)
Poulenc, F.:Exultate Deo [L] — Collegium ▲ COLCD 108 [DDD] ▮ COLC 108 (D)
Poulenc, F.:Motets (4) pour le temps de Noël [L] — Collegium ▲ COLCD 108 [DDD] ▮ COLC 108 (D)
Poulenc, F.:Motets (4) pour un temps de pénitence [L] — Collegium ▲ COLCD 108 [DDD] ▮ COLC 108 (D)
Poulenc, F.:Salve regina [L] — Collegium ▲ COLCD 108 [DDD] ▮ COLC 108 (D)
Stillness & Sweet Harmony — Collegium ▲ COL 502
There Is Sweet Music — Collegium ▲ COLCD 104 [DDD] ▮ COLC 104 (D)
Cambridge Taverner Choir
O. Rees (cnd)
What Is Our Life?:Renaissance Laments & Elegies *(rec Charterhouse Chapel, Mar 1995)* — Herald ▲ HAVPCD 187 [DDD]
Cambridge Univ Chamber Choir
T. Brown (cnd)
Barber, S.:Songs—Reincarnations; Under the Willow Tree; The Virgin Martyrs; A Stopwatch and an Ordnance Map; Agnus Dei; Two Choruses from *Antony & Cleopatra*; Twelfth Night; The Monk & His Cat; Sure on this shining night; Heaven-Haven; Let down the bars, O Death; To be Sung on the Water — Gamut Classics ▲ GAM 535 [DDD]
Britten, B.:A.M.D.G. (Ad Majorem Dei Gloriam) — Gamut Classics ▲ GAM 529 [DDD]
Britten, B.:Sacred & Profane — Gamut Classics ▲ GAM 529 [DDD]
Cambridge Univ. Chamber Choir — Gamut Classics ▲ GAM 529 [DDD]
Sacred & Profane — Gamut Classics ▲ IMCD 703 [DDD]
Cambridge Univ Musical Society Chorus
Schütz, H.:Lobet den Herrn in seinem Heiligtum, w. D. Willcocks (cnd), Wilbraham Brass Soloists, King's College Choir Cambridge — EMI Classics ("Baroque" series) ▲ CDK 65736
Cambridge Voices
Rütti, C.:Verena, die Quelle, w. Silja Walter (nar), I. Moore (cnd), Cambridge Instrumental Ensemble — Herald 2-▲ HAVPCD 186 [DDD]

I. Moore (cnd)
Rütti, C.:Choral Music, w. Veronica Henderson (vc)—O magnum mysterium; Lieder; Der Liebe; Fortis ut mors; Osculetur; Que tu es belle, ma bien-aimée; Ich schlief, doch mein Herz; Behold; Thou Hast Ravished My Heart; In meinem Garten; Vater Unser; Gloria (Missa Angelorum) *(rec St. Cyriac's Church, Swaffham Prior, Mar, 1995)* — Herald ▲ HAVPCD 183 [DDD]

Camerata Chamber Choir
P. Enevold (cnd)
Holmboe, V.:Benedic Domino [L] — BIS ▲ CD 78 [ADD/DDD]
Nielsen, C.:Motets [L] — BIS ▲ CD 131 [AAD]
Camerata Nova
Lassus, O. de:Choral Music, w. L. Taglioni (cnd), Camerata Nova Instrumental Ensemble—Villanelle alla Napoletana — Stradivarius ▲ STV 33374
Camerata Silesia Singers Ensemble
Branca, G.:Sym 9, "L'eve future", w. C. von Borries (cnd), Polish National RSO Katowice *(rec Polish National RSO Concert Hall, Katowice, Poland, Oct. 1994)* — Point Music ▲ 446505-2
Camerata Singers
Bartók, B.:Village Scenes, w. P. Boulez (cnd), New York PO, Schola Cantorum — Sony Classical ("Pierre Boulez Edition" series) ▲ SMK 45837
Bernstein, L.:Chichester Psalms, w. L. Bernstein (cnd), New York PO [He] — CBS ▲ MK 44710 [ADD]
Haydn, J.:Die Schöpfung, w. Judith Raskin (sop), Alexander Young (ten), John Reardon (bar), L. Bernstein (cnd), New York PO [G] *(rec 1966)* — Sony Classical ("Bernstein:The Royal Edition" series) 2-▲ SM2K 47560 [ADD]
Mennin, P.:Sym 4, w. A. Kaplan (cnd), Camerata SO — Phoenix ▲ PHCD 107 [AAD]
Rossini, G.:Stabat Mater, w. M. Arroyo (sop), B. Wolff (mez), T. del Bianco (ten), J. Diaz (bass), T. Schippers (cnd), New York PO — Sony Classical ▲ SB2K 53252
Starer, R.:Ariel, Visions of Isaiah, w. R. Peters (sop), J. Patrick (bar), A. Kaplan (cnd), Camerata Singers *(rec 1972)* — CRI ▲ CD 612 [ADD]
Canadian Opera Company Chorus
Rossini, G.:Ermione (sels), w. R. Bradshaw (cnd), Canadian Opera Company Orch—Sinf *(rec George Weston Recital Hall, Ford Centre for the Performing Arts, North York, Ontario, Dec 20-23, 1994)* — CBC ("SM 5000" series) ▲ SM5 5148 [DDD]
Rossini, G.:Giunone, w. Wendy Nielsen (sop—Giunone), R. Bradshaw (cnd), Canadian Opera Company Orch *(rec George Weston Recital Hall, Ford Centre for the Performing Arts, North York, Ontario, Dec 20-23, 1994)* — CBC ("SM 5000" series) ▲ SM5 5148 [DDD]
Rossini, G.:Mosè in Egitto (sels), w. Wendy Nielsen (sop—Elcia), Anita Krause (mez—Amenosi), Richard Margison (ten—Aronne), Gary Relyea (b-bar—Mosè), R. Bradshaw (cnd), Canadian Opera Company Orch—Scena, Coro & Preghiera [Dal tuo stellato soglio] *(rec George Weston Recital Hall, Ford Centre for the Performing Arts, North York, Ontario, Dec 20-23, 1994)* — CBC ("SM 5000" series) ▲ SM5 5148 [DDD]
Verdi, G.:Alzira (sels), w. Stephen McClare (ten—Otumbo), Richard Margison (ten—Zamoro), Gary Relyea (b-bar—Alvaro), R. Bradshaw (cnd), Canadian Opera Company Orch—Il prigioniero [prologue] *(rec George Weston Recital Hall, Ford Centre for the Performing Arts, North York, Ontario, Dec 20-23, 1994)* — CBC ("SM 5000" series) ▲ SM5 5148 [DDD]
Verdi, G.:Ernani (sels), w. Richard Margison (ten—Ernani), Gary Relyea (b-bar—Don Silva), R. Bradshaw (cnd), Canadian Opera Company Orch—Conspiracy [An alliance; Let the Lion of Castile Rise Again] *(rec George Weston Recital Hall, Ford Centre for the Performing Arts, North York, Ontario, Dec 20-23, 1994)* — CBC ("SM 5000" series) ▲ SM5 5148 [DDD]
Verdi, G.:Inno delle nazioni, w. Richard Margison (ten—Bardo), R. Bradshaw (cnd), Canadian Opera Company Orch *(rec George Weston Recital Hall, Ford Centre for the Performing Arts, North York, Ontario, Dec 20-23, 1994)* — CBC ("SM 5000" series) ▲ SM5 5148 [DDD]
Verdi, G.:Macbeth (sels), w. R. Bradshaw (cnd), Canadian Opera Company Orch—Scottish Exiles' Chorus [Patria oppressa!] *(rec George Weston Recital Hall, Ford Centre for the Performing Arts, North York, Ontario, Dec 20-23, 1994)* — CBC ("SM 5000" series) ▲ SM5 5148 [DDD]
Verdi, G.:Nabucco (sels), w. R. Bradshaw (cnd), Canadian Opera Company Orch—Chorus of the Hebrew Slaves [Va, pensiero, sull'ali dorate] *(rec George Weston Recital Hall, Ford Centre for the Performing Arts, North York, Ontario, Dec 20-23, 1994)* — CBC ("SM 5000" series) ▲ SM5 5148 [DDD]
Candomino Choir
T. Satomaa (cnd)
Merikanto, O.:Music of, w. Eeva-Jiisa Saarinen (mez), Jorma Hynninen (bar), Sauli Tiilikainen (bar), Kaija Saaikettu (vn), Erkki Rautio (vc), Pertti Eerola (pno), Ralf Gothoni (pno), Raija Kerppo (pno), Izumi Tateno (pno)—Summer Evening (waltz); Valse lente; Romance; On the Highest Tree-Top; Annina; Bye, Bye Lullabye; The Weeping Flute; At Sea; Hey My Heart; Where Rustling Birches Bend; Play Softly, the Tune of Mourning; Fairy Tale by the Fireside; Idyll; Scherzo, Op. 6/4; O Dost Thou Remember That Hymn; Lade Ladoga; Why Do I Sing; The Thunderbird; The Happy Ones; Summer Evening's Idyll — Finlandia ▲ FIN 500432 [AAD/DDD]
Cannes Regional Chorus
Cornelius, P.:Stabat Mater, w. D. Borst (sop), J. Mayeur (cta), J.-L. Viala (ten), F. Vassar (bass-bar), M. Piquemal (cnd), Cannes-Provençe Alpes-Côte d'Azur Regional Orch — Musique d'Abord ▲ HMA 1905206

M. Piquemal (cnd)
Cornelius, P.:Requiem, "Seele, vergiss sie nicht..." — Musique d'Abord ▲ HMA 1905206
Cantata Singers
D. Hoose (cnd)
Fine, I.:The Hour Glass — Elektra/Nonesuch ▲ 79175-2-ZK
Harbison, J.:The Flight into Egypt, w. Roberta Anderson (sop), Sanford Sylvan (bar), Cantata Ensemble [E] — New World ▲ 80395-2 [DDD]
Cantemus
Rossini, G.:Torvaldo e Dorliska, w. A. Buda (sop), F. Pediconi (sop), M. Ciliento (mez), E. Palacio (ten), S. Antonucci (bar), A. Marani (b-bar), M. de Bernart (cnd), Swiss-Italian Orch, Swiss-Italian Radio-TV Chorus *(rec Jan. 11, 1992)* — Arkadia-Akademia 2-▲ 123 [DDD]
D. Szabó (cnd)
Kodály, Z.:Choral Music—31 Children's, Youth & Female Choruses [Hun,L] — Hungaroton ▲ HCD 31291 [DDD]
Canterbury Cathedral Choir
Tallis, T.:Church Music, w. David Flood (org)—Ave Dei patris filia; Ave rosa sine spinis; Salve intermerata virgo *(rec Canterbury Cathedral nave)* — Metronome ▲ 1014 [DDD]
Tallis, T.:Mass "Salve intemerata", w. David Flood (org) *(rec Canterbury Cathedral nave)* — Metronome ▲ 1014 [DDD]
Canterbury Cathedral Choir Lay Clerks
D. Flood (cnd)
Gregorian Chant for the Feast of St. Thomas Canterbury — Metronome ▲ METCD 1003 [DDD]
Canterbury Choral Society
D. Shrock (cnd)
Angels Singing, Nowells Ringing, w. Top Brass, Troubadour Ringers *(rec Watchorn Hall, 1st Presbyterian Church, Oklahoma City, OK, Sept. 24-25)* — Integra Classic ▲ IMCD 944 [DDD]
Canticum
C. Erkens (cnd)
Frescobaldi, G.:Fiori musicali, w. Lorenzo Ghielmi (org)—Toccata avanti la Messa; Kyrie; Gloria; Canzon dopo la Pistola; Credo IV; Recercar dopo il Credo; Sanctus; Toccata per le Levatione; Agnus Dei; Tocatta avanti il Ricercar; Recercar con obligato di cantare; Ite Missa est; Toccata Sesta; Invitatorium:Deus in auditorium; Canzon detta la Pesenti; Antiphon:Jam heims Psalm 112; Capriccio sopra la Bassa Fiamenga; Responsorium breve:Ave Maria, gratia plena; Hymnus:Ave Maris stella; Antiphon:Ave Maria, gratia plena Magnificat primi toni; Benedicamus Domino; Marianische Antiphon:Ave Regina; Capriccio sopra la Girolmeta, *(Milan, Oct 1994)* — Deutsche Harmonia Mundi ▲ 05472-77345-2 [DDD]
Cantores de Cordoba Boys' Choir
Musique à la Cité des Rois, w. Ensemble Elyma *(rec June 30-July 2, 1993)* — K617 ▲ 7035
Cantores de Cordoba Children's Choir
Les Chemins du Baroque (The Paths of the Baroque), w. G. Garrido (cnd), Elyma Vocal Ensemble, Elyma Instrumental Ensemble, Cordoba Children's Choir Garrado, Compañia Musical de las Americas, Maîtrise National de Versailles, La Grande Ecurie et la Chambre du Roy [cnd:Jean-Claude Malgoire], Compañia Musical de las Americas, La Fenice [cnd:Josep Cabré], Ense — K617 ("First 4 volumes of K617" series) ▲ 7042

Cantores de Cordoba Children's Choir (cont.)
Les Chemins du Baroque [The Paths of the Baroque], Vol. 4:Domenico Zipoli's Vepres de San Ignaci, w. G. Garrido (cnd), Buenos Aires Affetti Ensemble — K617 ▲ 7027 [DDD]

Cantores in Ecclesia

M. Howard (cnd)
Purcell, H.:Songs, w. Jean Nibbs (sop), Geoffrey Mitchell (ct), Peter Hall (ten), David Thomas (bass), Margaret Phillips (org)—Hear My Prayer, O Lord; Song of the 3 Children; Remember Not, Lord, Our Offences; Voluntary for Single Organ; Magnificat & Nunc Dimittis in g; Thy Work is a Lantern; Burial Sentences for Queen Mary [Man That is Born of a Woman; In the Midst of Life We Are in Death; Thou Knowest, Lord, the Secrets of Our Hearts]; O God, Thou Art My God; Magnificat & Nunc Dimittis in Bb; Voluntary on the 100th Psalm Tune; Turn Thou Us, O Good Lord; O Give Thanks Unto the Lord [Psalm 106] — IMP ("BBC Radio Classics" series) ▲ IMP 9126

Cantores Minores Wratislavienses

E. Kajdasz (cnd)
Palestrina, G.:Masses—Papae Marcelli; Tu es Petrus *(rec Polish Radio Studio, Wroclaw, 1974 & 1976)* — Polskie Nagrania ▲ PNCD 086 [ADD]
Palestrina, G.:Motets—Tu es Petrus *(rec Polish Radio Studio, Wroclaw, 1976)* — Polskie Nagrania ▲ PNCD 086 [ADD]

Cantus Choro
Vol. 1:Sing out with Joy *(rec St. Patrick's Cathedral, Melbourne)* — Move ▲ MD 3032 [DDD]
Vol. 2:Hymns for All Seasons, w. Melbourne Brass Ensemble *(rec St. Patrick's Cathedral, Melbourne)* — Move ▲ MD 3062 [DDD]

Cantus Sacred Music Ensemble
Gretchaninoff, A.:Liturgica Domestica for St. John Chrysostom — Olympia ▲ OLY 480 [DDD]

L. Arshavskaya (cnd)
Chesnokov, P.:Choral Music—Requiem No. 2, Op. 39; Selected Orthodox Chants — Olympia ▲ OLY 482
Chesnokov, P.:Liturgy of the Presanctified Gifts — Olympia ▲ OLY 493 [DDD]
Chesnokov, P.:Orthodox Chants—Let All Flesh Be Silent; Thou Bringest Joy; The Wise Thief — Olympia ▲ OLY 493 [DDD]
Gretchaninoff, A.:Liturgica Domestica for St. John Chrysostom — Olympia ▲ OLY 447 [DDD]
Paliashvili, Z.P.:Liturgy of St. John — Olympia ▲ OLY 483 [DDD]
Yaitchkov, D.:Choral Music—God is With Us; Praise the Lord O My Soul; O Joyous Light; The Lord Our God; others — Olympia ▲ OLY 488 [DDD]

Canzone Choir
The Danish Song Treasury, Vol. 3 — Kontrapunkt ▲ 32155 [DDD]
Gade, N.W.:Comala, w. F. Rasmussen (cnd), South Jutland SO — Kontrapunkt ▲ KPT 32180 [DDD]
Gade, N.W.:Elverskud, w. L. Balslev (sop), E. Guillaume (mez), M. Melbye (bar), F. Rasmussen (cnd), Collegium Musicum [Da] — Kontrapunkt ▲ 32070 [DDD]
Gade, N.W.:Kalanus, w. M. Rørholm (mez), N. Gedda (ten), L. Mróz (bar), F. Rasmussen (cnd), Collegium Musicum — Kontrapunkt ▲ 32072 [DDD]

F. Rasmussen (cnd)
Danish Golden Age — Kontrapunkt ▲ 32068 [ADD]
The Danish Romanticism:Works for Mixed Choir A Cappella — Kontrapunkt ▲ 32173 [DDD]
Danish Song Treasury — Kontrapunkt ▲ 32073 [DDD]
The Danish Song Treasury, Vol. 4 — Kontrapunkt ▲ KPT 32230
Schumann, R.:Choral Music—Gesänge, Op. 59; Lieder, Op. 55; Romances & Ballades, Opp. 67, 75, 145 & 146 [G] — Kontrapunkt ▲ 32076 [ADD]

Capella Alamire
Busnois, A.:Motets — Titanic ▲ Ti 202 [DDD]
Gombert, N.:Motets — Titanic ▲ Ti 202 [DDD]

P. Urquhart (cnd)
Josquin Desprez:Missa, "L'ami Baudechon" *(rec St. Mary of the Annunciation, Cambridge, MA, June 15, 1992)* — Dorian Discovery ▲ DIS 80131 [DDD]
Josquin Desprez:Motets—Ave maris stella; Descendi in hortum meum; Ecce tu pulchra es; Inviolata, integra et casta es [L] *(rec 1989-91)* — Titanic ▲ Ti 202 [DDD]
Josquin Desprez:Music of—Magnificat; Sine nomine [Credo] [both rec. Immaculate Conception Church, Portsmouth, NH, Dec. 14, 1993 & June 18, 1994]; De tous biens [Credo; rec. St. Mary of the Annunciation, Cambridge, MA, May 25, 1993] — Dorian Discovery ▲ DIS 80131 [DDD]
Motets, 1450–1550 — Titanic ▲ Ti 202
Ockeghem, J.:Sine nomine *(rec St. Mary of the Annunciation, Cambridge, MA, May 11, 1993)* — Dorian Discovery ▲ DIS 80131 [DDD]

Capella Bydgostiensis Pro Musica Antiqua

Galonski, Kajdasz (cnd)
Gorczycki, G.G.:Sacred Choral Music, w. R. Stacewicz (sop), I. Tkaczyk (alt), A. Pagowska (alt), E. Sasiadek (ten), W. Brychcy (bass), Wroclaw Orch, Madrigalists Choir, Polish Radio Chorus—Completorium; In virtute tua; Iudica me deus; Laetatus sum; Missa paschalis [L] *(rec 1966)* — Olympia ▲ OCD 320 [AAD]

Capella Cantorum
Bach, J.S.:Nun Komm, der Heiden Heiland, BWV 61, w. K. Eichhorn (cnd), La Dolcezza Ensemble *(rec Berlin-Wilmersdorf, Aug 8-10, 1995)* — Capriccio ▲ 10721 [DDD]
Erlebach, P.H.:Lobe, lobe den Herrn, w. K. Eichhorn (cnd), La Dolcezza Ensemble, Berlin Baroque Trumpet Ensemble *(rec Berlin-Wilmersdorf, Aug 8-10, 1995)* — Capriccio ▲ 10721 [DDD]
Johnston, B.:Son for Microtonal Pno, w. Robert Miller (pno) — New World ▲ 80203-2
Krieger, J.P.:Gloria in excelsis deo, w. K. Eichhorn (cnd), La Dolcezza Ensemble, Berlin Baroque Trumpet Ensemble *(rec Berlin-Wilmersdorf, Aug 8-10, 1995)* — Capriccio ▲ 10721 [DDD]
Zachow, F.W.:Danksaget dem Vater, w. K. Eichhorn (cnd), La Dolcezza Ensemble *(rec Berlin-Wilmersdorf, Aug 8-10, 1995)* — Capriccio ▲ 10721 [DDD]
Zachow, F.W.:Preiset mit mir den Herren, w. K. Eichhorn (cnd), La Dolcezza Ensemble *(rec Berlin-Wilmersdorf, Aug 8-10, 1995)* — Capriccio ▲ 10721 [DDD]
Zachow, F.W.:Von Himmel kam der Engel Schar, w. K. Eichhorn (cnd), La Dolcezza Ensemble, Berlin Baroque Trumpet Ensemble *(rec Berlin-Wilmersdorf, Aug 8-10, 1995)* — Capriccio ▲ 10721 [DDD]

Capella Cordina
Dufay, G.:Missa Sancti Jacobi, w. A. Planchart (cnd) *(rec Sprague Hall, Yale Univ., May 11-12, 1974* — Lyrichord 2-▲ LEM 8013
Dufay, G.:Se la face ay pale, w. A. Planchart (cnd) *(rec Sprague Hall, Yale Univ., May 11-12, 1974)* — Lyrichord 2-▲ LEM 8013

A. Planchart (cnd)
Morales, C. de:Missa 'L'homme armé' — Lyrichord ▲ LYR 8009 [ADD]
Morales, C. de:Sacred Music—selected chansons — Lyrichord ▲ LYR 8009 [ADD]

Capella Cracoviensis
Pflüger, H.G.:Memento Mori, w. Siegmund Nimsgern (bar), R. Bader (cnd), *(orch unknown)* — Bayer ▲ 800910

K.A. Rickenbacher (cnd)
Milhaud, D.:L'Abandon d'Ariane — Koch Schwann ▲ 3-1139-2 [DDD]
Milhaud, D.:Le Carnaval de Londres — Koch Schwann ▲ 3-1138-2 [DDD]
Milhaud, D.:Chamber Syms — Koch Schwann ▲ 3-1139-2 [DDD]
Milhaud, D.:La Délivrance de Thésée, w. *(soloists unknown)* [F] — Koch Schwann ▲ 3-1139-2 [DDD]
Milhaud, D.:L'Enlèvement d'Europe [F] — Koch Schwann ▲ 3-1139-2 [DDD]
Milhaud, D.:Rag-Caprices — Koch Schwann ▲ 3-1138-2 [DDD]
Milhaud, D.:Saudades do Brasil [composer's orchestral version] — Koch Schwann ▲ 3-1138-2 [DDD]

Capella Ducale
Gabrieli, G.:Music of, w. David Cordier (alt), Wilfried Jochens (ten), Rufus Müller (ten), Gerd Türk (ten), Harry van der Kamp (bass), R. Wilson (cnd), Musica Fiata—Toccata [arr Wilson]; Buccinate in neomenia tuba à 19; Canzon XVII à 12; Dulcis Jesu patris imago [Son con voce à 20]; Timor et remor à 6; Son con 3 Vns; Son XIX à 15; In ecclesiis à 14; Canzon V à 7; Jubilate Deo à 10; Son XVIII à 14; Cantate Domino à 8; Canzon primi toni à 10; Misericordia tua Domine à 12; Canzon X à 8; Toccata primi toni; Magnificat à 33 [reconstructed by Wilson]; Benedictus es Dominus à 8 *(rec St. Osdag Church, Mandelsloh, Germany, June 11-15, 1994)* — Sony Classical ("Vivarte" series) 2-▲ S2K 66254 [DDD]

Capella Ducale (cont.)
Grandi, A.:Sacred Music, w. David Cordier (alt), Wilfried Jochens (ten), Rufus Müller (ten), Gerd Türk (ten), Harry van der Kamp (bass), R. Wilson (cnd), Musica Fiata—Heu mihi [Dialogo à 4]; O quam tu pulchra es; Cantemus Domino; Salvum me fac, Deus [Basso solo] *(rec St. Osdag Church, Mandelsloh, Germany, June 11-15, 1994)* — Sony Classical ("Vivarte" series) 2-▲ S2K 66254 [DDD]
Monteverdi, C.:Selva morale et spirituale (sels), w. R. Wilson (cnd), Cologne Musica Fiata *(rec Nov. 11-13, 1992)* — Sony Classical ▲ SK 53363 [DDD]
Picchi, G.:Canzoni da sonar, w. R. Wilson (cnd), Cologne Musica Fiata *(rec Nov. 11-13, 1992)* — Sony Classical ▲ SK 53363 [DDD]

Capella Fidicinia
Schein, J.H.:Fontana d'Israel, w. M. Flämig (cnd), Capella Fidicinia, Dresden Kreuz Choir — Berlin Classics ▲ BER 9078 [ADD]

M. Flämig (cnd)
Scheidt, S.:Sacred Music, w. Dresden Kreuz Choir—Concertus Sacri *(rec 1989)* — Berlin Classics ▲ BER 9126 [ADD]

G. Grüss (cnd)
Bach, J.S.:Music of — Capriccio ▲ CDC 10029 [DDD]

Capella Gregoriana
Lost in Meditation:Meditative Gregorian Chants — Laserlight ▲ 14158

Capella Hafniensis

O. Kongsted (cnd)
Kronborg Motets — Kontrapunkt ▲ 32106 [DDD]
Lechner, L.:Choral Music—Dieweil Gott ist mein Zuversicht; Kronborg Motets [spurious]; Nach Gottes Willen heb ich an — Kontrapunkt ▲ 32106 [DDD]

Capella Lipsiensis

D. Knothe (cnd)
Jungfrau, eur wankelmut — Berlin Classics ▲ BER 9172
Schütz, H.:Il primo libro de madrigali — Berlin Classics ▲ BER 2102 [ADD]

Capella Piccola

T. Reuber (cnd)
Baroque Cantatas & Motets on Authentic Instruments — Ars Produktion ▲ FCD 368303
Telemann, G.P.:Cants—Du aber, Daniel, gehe hin [period instruments] — Ars Produktion ▲ FCD 368303

Capella Pratensis
Sicut Lilium inter Spinas:In Annunciatione Beate Marie Virginis — Emergo ▲ 3975

La Capella Reial de Catalunya

J. Savall (cnd)
Bach, J.S.:Brandenburg Cons, w. Concert des Nations — Astrée ▲ E 8737
Bach, J.S.:Suites Orch, BWV 1066-1069 — Astrée 2-▲ E 8727
El Cançoner del Duc de Calàbria — Auvidis ▲ E 8582
El Canto de la Sibila II, w. Montserrat Figueras (sop) — Fontalis ▲ 9900
Cererols, J.:Missa de Batalla [L] — Astrée ▲ E 8704 [DDD]
Cererols, J.:Missa pro defunctis [L] — Astrée ▲ E 8704 [DDD]
Guerrero, F.:Sacred Motets, w. Hespèrion XX [period instruments]—Alma Redemptoris mater; Ave Maria (a 4); Ave Maria (a 8); Ave, virgo sanctissima; Beata Dei genitrix, Maria; Duo Seraphim; Gabriel archangelus; Laudate Dominum de caelis; O Altitudo divitiarum; O Domine Jesu Christe I; O Domine Jesu Christe II; O sacrum convivium; Pater Noster; Regina caeli; Salva Regina; Trahe me post te, Virgo Maria [L] *(rec Dec. 1991-Jan. 1992)* — Astrée ▲ E 8766
Martin Y Soler, V.:Una Cosa rara, w. M. A. Peters (sop), M. Figueras (sop), G. Fabuel (sop), E. Palacio (ten), F. Belaza-Leoz (bar), S. Palatchi (bass), F. Garrigosa (bass), I. Fresán (sgr), Concert des Nations [I] *(rec 1991)* — Astrée 3-▲ E 8760 [DDD]
Monteverdi, C.:Madrigals (book 8)—Altri canti d'amor; Gira il nemico; Ballo:volgeno il ciel—movete al mio bel suon; Sinfonia a cinque; Altri canti di marte e di dua schiera; Lamento della ninfa; Sinfonia a sei; Hor che'l ciel e la terra — Astrée ▲ E 8546
Mozart, W.A.:Requiem, w. M. Figueras (sop), C. Schubert (alt), G. Türk (ten), J. Schreckenberger (bass), Le Concert des Nations — Astrée ▲ E 8759
Music at the Time of Beaumarchais, w. Montserrat Figueras (sop), Lawrence Monteyro (sop), Raphel Oleg (vn), Miguel da Silva (va), Christophe Coin (vc), Marc Coppey (vc), José Miguel Moreno (gtr), Paul Badura-Skoda (pno), Philippe Cassard (pno), Eric Le Sage (pno), Bob Van Asperen (hpd), et al. — Valois ▲ V 4767
Savall, J.:Joan of Arc, w. J. Savall (vl), M. Figueras (sop), Hespèrion XX — Harmonia Mundi ▲ K 1006-2 ■ K 51006-4
Victoria, T.L. de:Sacred Choral Music, w. Hespèrion XX—11 Marian works—Ave Maria (a 4); Gaude, Maria Virgo (a 5), 1572; Trahe me post te (a 6), 1583; Salve, Regina (a 8), 1572; Ave Regina caelorum (a 5), 1572; Sancta Maria, succerre miseris (a 4), 1572; Ne timeas, Maria (a 4), 1572; Senex, Puerum portabat (instrumental a 4), 1572; O magnum mysterium (a 4), 1572; Vidi speciosam sicut columbam (a 6), 1572; Magnificat Primi toni (a 8), 1600) [L] *(rec 1992)* — Astrée ▲ E 8767 [DDD]
Vox Aeterna, w. Le Concert des Nations, Hesperion XX — Fontalis ▲ 9902

La Cappella
Fux, J.J.:Dafne in Lauro, w. L. Akerlund (sop), S. Piccollo (sop), M. van der Sluis (sop), G. Lesne (alt), M. Klietmann (ten), R. Clemencic (cnd), Clemencic Consort [I] — Nuova Era ("Ancient Music" series) 2-▲ 6930/31 [DDD]
Keiser, R.:Croesus, w. P. Grigorova (sop), M. Klietmann (ten), S. Mizugushi (bass), R. Clemencic (cnd), Clemencic Consort [G] — Nuova Era ("Ancient Music" series) 2-▲ 6934/35 [DDD]
Torrejón Y Velasco, T. de:La purpura de la rosa, w. M. van der Sluis (sop), P. Mildenhall (sop), J. Benet (ten), A. Martin (bar), R. Clemencic (cnd), Clemencic Consort [Sp] — Nuova Era ("Ancient Music" series) ▲ 6936 [DDD]
Vivaldi, A.:L'Olimpiade, w. L. Meeuwsen (sop), M. van der Sluis (sop), E. von Magnus (alt), G. Lesne (alt), A. Christofelis (alt), W. Oberholtzer (bar), A. Walker Schultze (bass), R. Clemencic (cnd), Clemencic Consort [I] *(rec live, Paris, 2/8-10/90)* — Nuova Era ("Ancient Music" series) 2-▲ 6932/33 [DDD]

Cappella Breda
Hartmann, K.A.:Con funèbre, w. André Gertler (vn), K. Ančerl (cnd), Czech PO — Supraphon ▲ SUP 111955 [AAD]

D. Manneke (cnd)
Bruckner, A.:Choral Music—Christus factus est; Locus iste; Ave Maria — Erasmus ▲ WVH 054 [DDD]
Pärt, A.:Magnificat-Antiphones — Erasmus ▲ WVH 054 [DDD]
Pärt, A.:Missa sillabica — Erasmus ▲ WVH 054 [DDD]
Rachmaninoff, S.:Sacred Music—Ave Maria — Erasmus ▲ WVH 054 [DDD]
Stravinsky, I.:Choral Music—Ave Maria; Pater Noster; Credo — Erasmus ▲ WVH 054 [DDD]

Cappella Nova
Gaudeamus Early Music Sampler, w. Great Consort, His Majesties Sagbutts & Cornetts, Rasumovsky String Quartet, Trio Sonnerie, Cardinall's Musick, Clerks' Group, Ex Cathedra, Gentlemen of the Chappell, Gonville & Caius College Choir Cambridge, et al. — ASV/Gaudeamus ▲ ASV 1002

A. Tavener (cnd)
Angus, J.:Sacred Music—All My Belief & Confidence; Song of Simon — ASV ("Gaudeamus" series) ▲ ASV 136 [DDD]
Johnson, Robert:Sacred Music—Ave Dei Patris filia; Benedican Domino; Domine in virtute tua; Dum transisset; Gaude Maria Virgo; I Give You a New Commandment; Laudes Deo — ASV/Gaudeamus ▲ ASV 154
Peebles, D.:Sacred Music—Psalms 107 & 124; Si quis diligit — ASV ("Gaudeamus" series) ▲ ASV 136 [DDD]

Cappella Palatina

D.B. Columbro (cnd)
Viadana, L. da:Canzonettas 3 Voices — Stradivarius ▲ STV 33387 [DDD]

Cappella Palestrina

M. Michielsen (cnd)
Palestrina, G.:Missa "Pro defunctis" — Erasmus ▲ WVH 042 [DDD]

CHORAL GROUPS

Cardiff Polyphonic Choir
Mahler, G.:Sym 2, w. Benita Valente (sop), Maureen Forrester (cta), G. Kaplan (cnd), London SO, Ardwyn Singers, BBC Welsh Chorus, Dyfed Choir Conifer Classics 2-▲ 75605-51277-2 [DDD]

Cardinall's Musick
Gaudeamus Early Music Sampler, w. Great Consort, His Majesties Sagbutts & Cornetts, Rasumovsky String Quartet, Trio Sonnerie, Cappella Nova, Clerks' Group, Ex Cathedra, Gentlemen of the Chappell, Gonville & Caius College Choir Cambridge, et al. ASV/Gaudeamus ▲ ASV 1002
Ludford, N.:Sacred Music—Missa Lapidaverunt Stephanum; Ave Maria ancilla trinitatis ASV ("Gaudeamus" series) ▲ ASV 140 [DDD]

A. Carwood (cnd)
Fayrfax, R.:Missa 'O quam glorifica' ASV ("Gaudeamus" series) ▲ ASV 142 [DDD]
Fayrfax, R.:Motets—Ave Dei Patris; Orbis Factor ASV ("Gaudeamus" series) ▲ ASV 142 [DDD]
Fayrfax, R.:Songs—Sumwhat Musyng; That Was My Joy; To Complayn Me, Alas ASV ("Gaudeamus" series) ▲ ASV 142 [DDD]
Ludford, N.:Sacred Music—Missa 'Videte miraculum'; Ave cuius concepcio [L] ASV ("Guadeamus" series) ▲ CD GAU 131
Ludford, N.:Sacred Music—Missa Chirsti Virgo dilectissima; Plainsong propers for the Feast of the Annunciation; Domine Jesu Christe ASV ("Gaudeamus" series) ▲ ASV 133 [DDD]
Ludford, N.:Sacred Music—Missa Videte miraculum; Missa Benedicta et venerabilis; Missa Christi virgo dilectissima; Missa Lapidaverunt Stephanum; Ave cuius conceptio; Magnificat Benedictal Domine Ihesu Christe; Ave Maria ancilla trinitatis ASV 4-▲ ASV 426 [DDD]
Ludford, N.:Sacred Music—Missa Benedicta et venerabilis; Gloria; Credo; Sanctus–Benedictus; Agnus Dei; Magnificat benedicta ASV ("Gaudeamus" series) ▲ GAU 132 [DDD]
Merbecke, J.:Ave Dei patris filia ASV ▲ ASV 148
Merbecke, J.:Domine Jesu Christe ASV ▲ ASV 148
Merbecke, J.:Mass "Per arma justiciae" ASV ▲ ASV 148
Merbecke, J.:A Virgin & Mother ASV ▲ ASV 148
Sheppard, J.:Mass "Be Not Afraide"—with Plainsong Propers for the Feast of St. Stephen interspersed [L,E] Meridian ▲ CDE 84220

Carmelite Priory Choir
Carmelite Priory Choir London ("Serenata" series) ▲ 425729-2 [ADD]
Responsories, Hymns, Antiphons, Gospel Tone London ■ 417102-4 LT

Carmina Chamber Choir

P. Hanke (cnd)
Holmboe, V.:Choral Music—2 Border Ballads, Op. 110 Danica ▲ DCD 8151
Nørgård, P.:Danish Songs Danica ▲ DCD 8151
Nørgård, P.:Wie ein Kind Danica ▲ DCD 8151
Schultz, S.S.:Choral Music—Denmark Revisited; Lovely Fragrant Denmark Danica ▲ DCD 8151

H. Nickoll (cnd)
Haentjes, W.:Easter Motets (3) ebs ▲ 6039 [DDD]
Martin, F.:Mass ebs ▲ 6039 [DDD]
Nickoll, H.:Salve regina ebs ▲ 6039 [DDD]
Pärt, A.:Magnificat ebs ▲ 6039 [DDD]
Thompson, R.:Alleluia ebs ▲ 6039 [DDD]

Carnegie Mellon Concert Choir

R. Page (cnd)
Balada, L.:Escenas borrascosas, w. Kay Shackleton-Williams (sop—Isabel), Nancy Maria Balach (mez—Beatriz), Matthew Walley (ten—Colón), J.P. Izquierdo (cnd), Carnegie Mellon PO, Carnegie Mellon Repertory Chorus *(rec Carnegie Music Hall, Pittsburgh, PA, Apr 7–8, 1994)* New World ▲ 80498-2
Balada, L.:Torquemada New World ▲ 80442-2

Carnegie Mellon Repertory Chorus
Balada, L.:Escenas borrascosas, w. Kay Shackleton-Williams (sop—Isabel), Nancy Maria Balach (mez—Beatriz), Matthew Walley (ten—Colón), J.P. Izquierdo (cnd), Carnegie Mellon PO, Carnegie Mellon Concert Choir *(rec Carnegie Music Hall, Pittsburgh, PA, Apr 7–8, 1994)* New World ▲ 80498-2

Carus Quintet
Silcher, F.:Songs, w. Martin Bochinger (ten), Harald Stark (b–bar), Maximilian Benker (b–bar), Michael Albert (bass)—Sehnsucht; Heimliche Liebe; Das Lied vom Nöcken; Die drei Röslein; Schifferlied, Schottischer Bardenchor; Abschied; Waldlied; Werbung; Das Gedenken; Tanzlied; Stirb Lieb und Freud; Herr Ulrich; Wonne des Liebenden; Abschiedsgruss; Der Wirtin Töchterlein; Flug der Liebe; Gut' Nacht *(rec Sandhausen, May 1996)* Bayer ▲ 100089 [DDD]

Catania Teatro Massimo Bellini Chorus
Bellini, V.:Adelson e Salvini, w. A. Nafé (mez), F. Previati (bar), A. Licata (cnd), Catania Teatro Massimo Bellini Orch Nuova Era 2-▲ NUO 7154 [DDD]
Bellini, V.:Bianca e Fernando, w. Y. O. Shin (sop), G. Kunde (ten), W. Coppola (ten), A. Tomicich (bass), A. Licata (cnd), Catania Teatro Massimo Bellini Orch Nuova Era 2-▲ NUO 7076 [DDD]
Bellini, V.:I Puritani, w. A. Maliponte (sop—Elvira), A. di Stasio (sop—Enrichetta di Francia), A. Kraus (ten—Lord Arturo Talbo), A. Pedroni (ten—Bruno Roberton), P. Cappuccilli (bar—Sir Riccardo Forth), R. Raimondi (bass—Sir Giorgio), G. Gavazzeni (cnd), Catania Teatro Massimo Bellini Orch *(rec Feb. 6, 1972)* Ornamenti 2-▲ FE 107 [ADD]
Bellini, V.:I Puritani (sels), w. G. Tucci (sop), L. Pavarotti (ten), A. Protti (bar), R. Raimondi (bass), A. Quadri (cnd), Catania Teatro Massimo Bellini Orch [l] *(rec live, Catania 3/22/68)* Verona 3-▲ 27029/31
Bellini, V.:I Puritani (sels), w. G. Tucci (sop), L. Pavarotti (ten), A. Protti (bar), R. Raimondi (bass), A. Quadri (cnd), Catania Teatro Massimo Bellini Orch [l] *(rec live, Catania 3/22/68)* Melodram ▲ MEL 15001
Bellini, V.:I Puritani (sels), w. Gabriella Tucci (sop—Elvira), Vittorina Magnaghi (mez—Enrichetta di Francia), Luciano Pavarotti (ten—Lord Arturo Talbo), Aldo Protti (bar—Sir Riccardo Forth), Ruggero Raimondi (bass—Sir Giorgio), A. Quadri (cnd), Vincenzo Bellini Theater Orch Budget ("The Greatest Voice in Opera" series) ▲ SYP 106
Bellini, V.:Zaira, w. K. Ricciarelli (sop), A. Papadjakou (cta), R. Vargas (ten), S. Alaimo (ten), P. Olmi (cnd), Catania Teatro Massimo Bellini Orch [l] *(rec live 1990)* Nuova Era 2-▲ 6982/83 [DDD]
Bellini, V.:Zaira (sels), w. K. Ricciarelli (sop), R. Vargas (ten), P. Olmi (cnd), Catania Teatro Massimo Bellini Orch Nuova Era ▲ NUO 7187 [DDD]
Marinuzzi, G.:Jacquerie, w. Ilaria Galgani (sop), Antonio Salvadori (bar), Miro Solman (sgr), Martine Surais (sgr), A. Licata (cnd), Catania Teatro Massimo Bellini Orch *(rec Catania, 1994)* Nuova Era 2-▲ NUO 7200 [DDD]
Massenet, J.:Thaïs, w. R. Kabaivanska (sop), S. Bruscantini (bar), O. de Fabritiis (cnd), Catania Teatro Massimo Bellini Orch [l] *(rec live, 4/3/69)* Golden Age of Opera 2-▲ GAO 121/122 [ADD]
Paisiello, G.:Nina, o sia La pazza per amore, w. M. Bolgan (sop), F. Pediconi (sop), D. Bernardini (ten), F. Musinu (bass), G. Surian (bass), R. Bonynge (cnd), Catania Teatro Massimo Bellini Orch [l] *(rec live 1989)* Nuova Era 2-▲ 6872/73 [DDD]
Verdi, G.:Ernani, w. Licia Galvano (sop—Giovanna), Leyla Gencer (sop—Elvira), Carlo Bergonzi (ten—Ernani), Nino Valori (ten—Don Riccardo), Piero Cappuccilli (bar—Don Carlo), Alessandro Cassis (bar—Jago), Ruggero Raimondi (bass—Don Ruy Gomez de Silva), G. Gavazzeni (cnd), Catania Teatro Massimo Bellini Orch *(rec live, Catania, Jan 15, 1972)* Arkadia 2-▲ 621 [ADD]

Cathedral Choral Society Chorus
Brubeck, D.:To Hope!:A Celebration, w. Shelley Waite (sop), Mark Bleeke (ten), Kevin Deas (b–bar), R. Gloyd (cnd), Cathedral Choral Society Orch, Dave Brubeck Quartet *(rec Washington National Cathedral, Washington, D.C., June 12, 1995)* Telarc ▲ CD 80430 [DDD]

Cathedral of the Sacred Heart Choir Newark
Love Is Come Again, w. David J. Messineo (org) *(rec 1992)* Pro Organo ▲ POCD 7041 [DDD]

Cathedral of the Transfiguration Priests Choir
Ektenia:St. Petersburg Litany Deutsche Grammophon ("4D Audio" series) ▲ 445653-2

Cathedral Singers

R. Proulx (cnd)
Alleluia, Song of Gladness:Ars Antiqua Choralis, Vol. 2:Choral Masterworks from the 15th–18th Centuries, w. Donald Fellows (org) GIA ▲ GIA 299
In Sweet Rejoicing Music for Christmas:Ars Antique Choralis, Vol 3, w. Mary Hickey (fl), Jeri-Lou Aike (vn), Elizabeth Anderson (vc), Samuel Soria Jr. (org) *(rec Oct. 17–19 & 24–26, 1993)* GIA ▲ CD 323 ■ CS 323
Rejoice in the Lord:Ars Antiqua Choralis, Vol. 1:Choral Masterworks from the 15th–18th Centuries, w. Donald Fellows (org) GIA ▲ GIA 290
Sublime Chant:The Art of Gregorian, Ambrosian & Callican Chant Gia ▲ CD 338
This Is the Day:Ars Antiqua Choralis, Vol. 4 Gia ▲ GIA 334

CCM Chamber Choir
Schubert, Franz:Der Graf von Gleichen, w. Gwendolyn Coleman (sop), Karen Driscoll (sop), Tracy Thomas (sop), Brad Diamond (ten), John M. Koch (bar), G. Samuel (cnd), Cincinnati PO *(rec Corbett Auditorium, Univ of Cincinnati, Mar 12–13, 1994)* Centaur 2-▲ 2281/2282 [DDD]

CCM Chorus
Beethoven, L. van:Sym 9, "Choral Sym", w. G. Samuel (cnd), Cincinnati PO Centaur ▲ CRC 2107

Ceneva Motet Chorus
Martin, F.:Le Mystère de la Nativité, w. Elly Ameling (sop), Aafje Heynis (cta), Hugues Cuénod (ten), Louis Devos (ten), Eric Tappy (ten), Pierre Bollet (bar), Derrik Olsen (bar), Charles Clavensy (b–bar), André Vessières (bass), E. Ansermet (cnd), Swiss Romande Orch, Jeunes de l'Eglise Chorus Cascavelle 2-▲ CVL 2006 [ADD]

Central City Opera Chorus
Moore, D.:Ballad of Baby Doe, w. Jan Grissom (sop—Baby Doe), Dana Kreuger (mez—Augusta), Myrna Paris (cta—Mama), Brian Steele (bar—Horace), Mark Freiman (b–bar—W. J. Bryan), J. Moriarty (cnd), Central City Opera Orch *(rec Central City, CO)* Newport Classic 2-▲ NPD 85593/2 [DDD]

Central State Univ Chorus
Amen:A Gospel Celebration, w. Azusa Pacific Univ Choir, Cincinnati Pops Chorale, Jennifer Holliday (sgr), Maureen McGovern (sgr), Lou Rawls (sgr), Cincinnati Pops Orch [cnd:Erich Kunzel] *(rec Feb. 28–Mar. 1, 1993)* Telarc ▲ CD 80315 [DDD] ■ CD 80315

Cetra Chorus
Puccini, G.:Madama Butterfly, w. C. Petrella (sop—Madama Butterfly), M. Masini (mez—Suzuki), M. C. Foscale (sgr—Kate Pinkerton), F. Tagliavini (ten—Pinkerton), M. Caruso (ten—Goro), G. Taddei (bar—Sharpless), A. Albertini (bar—Yamadori), A. Biancardo (bass—Bonze), A. Questa (cnd), Turin RAI Orch *(rec 1953)* Cetra Classic 2-▲ CDO 10 [AAD]

La Chambre du Roy

J.-C. Malgoire (cnd)
Pergolesi, G.B.:Pro Jesu dum vivo Astrée ▲ E 8556

Champagne-Ardenne Akademia Regional Vocal Ensemble

F. Lasserre (cnd)
Palestrina, G.:Sacred Music, w. Catherine Greuillet (sop), Thierry Gregoire (alt), Pierre Sciema (alt), Bruno Boterf (ten), Joel Suhubiette (ten), Jean-Luc Baudoin (ten), Jean-Claude Sarragosse (bass), Laurent Stewart (org)—Ave maria; Salve regina; Vergine bella; Vergine saggia; Virgine pura; Virgine santa; Vergine sola; Vergine chiara; Vergine, quante lagrime; Vergine, tale è terra; Ave mundi spes; Ave regina coelorum; Alma redemptoris mater; Regina coieli laetare; Salve regina; Magnificat; others *(rec Convent of the Annunciation Dominican Church, Paris, Jan., 1994)* Pierre Verany ▲ PVY 794041 [DDD]
Palestrina, G.:The Song of Songs Pierre Verany ▲ PVY 795092

Chandos Choir
Handel, G.F.:Rodelinda, Regina de' Longobardi, w. Joan Sutherland (sop), Janet Baker (mez), Raimund Herincx (bar), C. Farncombe (cnd), Philomusica Orch *(rec 1959)* Memories 2-▲ MEM 4577 [ADD]

Chandos Singers
Treasures of Operetta III, w. Marilyn Hill Smith (sop), Peter Morrison (bar), Chandos Concert Orch [cnd:Stuart Barry] Chandos ▲ CHAN 8759 [DDD]

Chanticleer
Anniversary Album Chanticleer ▲ CHN 8801 ■ CR 8801-C
Byrd, W.:Ave regina [L] Harmonia Mundi France ▲ HMC 905182
Byrd, W.:Gradualia seu cantionum sacrarum, liber secundus—Masses (2) in 5 Parts "In Paschal time" & "On the Assumption of the B.V.M." [L] Harmonia Mundi France ▲ HMC 905182
Byrd, W.:Regina coeli [L] Harmonia Mundi France ▲ HMC 905182
Byrd, W.:Salve regina [L] Harmonia Mundi France ▲ HMC 905182
Chen, Y.:Music of, w. Liu Wei-shan (guzheng), Zhao Yang-qin (yangqin), Chen Jie-bing (erhu), Min Xiao-fen (pipa), J. Falletta (cnd), Women's PO—Duo Ye No. 2; Sym 2; Ge Xu; Chinese Myths Cant; Pan Gu Creates Heaven & Earth; Nu Wa Creates Human Beings; Weaving Maid & Cowherd; Song of Weaving Maid & Cowherd *(rec Skywalker Sound, San Rafael, CA, June 1996)* New Albion ▲ NA 090
Morales, C. de:Sacred Music—includes Missa Mille regretz; Motets, plus others Chanticleer ▲ CHAN 8809
Mysteria *(rec 1993)* Teldec ▲ 99203-2 ■ 99203-4
On the Air:Live Radio Highlights *(rec live 1987–89)* Chanticleer ▲ CHN 8807 [AAD]
Our Heart's Joy:A Chanticleer Christmas Chanticleer ▲ CHN 8803 [DDD] ■ CR 8803-C (D)
Out of This World *(rec St. Paul, Minnesota, Oct. 1993)* Teldec ▲ 96515-2 [DDD]
Palestrina, G.:Motets—Gaude gloriosa; Gaude, B. *(rec San Rafael, CA, June 1994)* Teldec ▲ 4509-94561-2 [DDD]
Palestrina, G.:The Song of Songs—Trahe me; Nigra sum; sed formosa; Surge, amica mea; Quam pulchra es; Veni, dilecte mi *(rec San Rafael, CA, June 1994)* Teldec ▲ 4509-94561-2 [DDD]
Psallite!:A Renaissance Christmas Chanticleer ▲ CHN 8806 [ADD] ■ CHN 306
Rorem, N.:Pilgrim Strangers Chanticleer ▲ CHAN 8804 [DDD]
With a Poet's Eye:New American Choral Music Chanticleer ▲ CHN 8804 [DDD]

J. Jennings (cnd)
Mexican Baroque, w. Chanticleer Sinfonia Teldec ▲ 96353

Chapelle Royale Choir
Beethoven, L. van:Missa Solemnis, w. Rosa Mannion (sop), Birgit Remmert (alt), James Taylor (ten), Cornelius Hauptmann (bass), P. Herreweghe (cnd), Champs Elysées Theater Orch, Collegium Vocale *(rec Auditorium Stravinski de Montreux, Feb. 20–21, 1995)* Harmonia Mundi France ▲ HMC 901557
Brahms, J.:Ein Deutsches Requiem, w. Christiane Oelze (sop), Gerald Finley (bar), P. Herreweghe (cnd), Champs Elysées Theater Orch, Collegium Vocale Harmonia Mundi ▲ HMC 901608 ■ HMC 401608
du Mont, H.:Motets pour la chapelle du roy, w. P. Herreweghe (cnd), La Chapelle Royale Orch—Memorare, Dialogus de anima, Magnificat, Super Flumina Babylonis [L] *(rec July 1981)* Musique d'Abord ▲ HMA 1901077
Fauré, G.:Messe basse, w. P. Herreweghe (cnd), Musique Oblique Ensemble [L] Harmonia Mundi France ▲ HMC 901292
Fauré, G.:Requiem, w. A. Mellon (sop), P. Kooy (bass), P. Herreweghe (cnd), Musique Oblique Ensemble [1893 version] [L] Harmonia Mundi France ▲ HMC 901292
Lalande, M.-R. de:Dies Irae, w. P. Kwella (sop), L. Perillo (sop), H. Crook (ten), H. Lamy (ten), P. Harvey (bar), P. Herreweghe (cnd), La Chapelle Royale Orch [L] Harmonia Mundi France ▲ HMC 901352
Lalande, M.-R. de:Miserere mei, Deus, w. P. Kwella (sop), L. Perillo (sop), H. Crook (ten), H. Lamy (ten), P. Harvey (bar), P. Herreweghe (cnd), La Chapelle Royale Orch [L] Harmonia Mundi France ▲ HMC 901352
Mendelssohn, F.:St. Paul, w. Melanie Diener (sop), Annette Markert (mez), James Taylor (ten), Matthias Görne (bass), P. Herreweghe (cnd), Champs Elysées Theater Orch, Collegium Vocale *(rec Stravinsky Auditorium, Montreaux)* Harmonia Mundi France 2-▲ HMC 901584.85
Monteverdi, C.:Vespro della Beata Vergine, w. A. Mellon (sop), G. Laurens (mez), H. Crook (ten), D. Thomas (bass), P. Herreweghe (cnd), Toulouse Saqueboutiers, Collegium Vocale [L] Harmonia Mundi France 2-▲ HMC 901247/48 [DDD]

▲ = CD ♦ = Enhanced CD Δ = MD ■ = Cassette Tape □ = DCC

Chapelle Royale Choir (cont.)
Mozart, W.A.:Missa, K.427, w. C. Oelze (sop), J. Larmore (mez), S. Weir (ten), P. Kooy (bass), P. Herreweghe (cnd), Champs Élysées Theater Orch, Collegium Vocale
Harmonia Mundi France ▲ HMC 901393
Mozart, W.A.:Missa, K.427, w. Jennifer Larmore (sop), Christiane Oelze (sop), Scot Weir (ten), Peter Kooy (bass), P. Herreweghe (cnd), Champs Élysées Theater Orch, Collegium Vocale
Harmonia Mundi France ▲ HMX 29001393
Weill, K.:Berlin Requiem, w. A. Laiter (ten), P. Kooy (bass), P. Herreweghe (cnd), Musique Oblique Ensemble [G] *(rec May 1992)* Harmonia Mundi France ▲ HMC 901422
P. Herreweghe (cnd)
Couperin, F.:Music of, w. René Jacobs (alt), Gérard Lesne (alt), Kenneth Gilbert (hpd), Christophe Rousset (hpd), W. Christie (cnd), Les Arts Florissants—Hpd pieces; Tenebeae Lessons [sels]
Harmonia Mundi ("Great Baroque Composers" series) 3-▲ HMX 390870.72
Josquin Desprez:Motets [L] Harmonia Mundi France ▲ HMC 901243
Lully, J.-B.:Music of, w. René Jacobs (alt), Gérard Lesne (alt), Kenneth Gilbert (hpd), Christophe Rousset (hpd), W. Christie (cnd), Les Arts Florissants—Hpd Pieces; 'Atys' excerpts; Dies Israe; Petits Motets
Harmonia Mundi ("Great Baroque Composers" series) 3-▲ HMX 390870.72
Mendelssohn, F.:Motets & Psalms, w. Ghent Collegium Vocale—Op. 23/3; 69/1; 78/1, 3; 79/1-6; Psalm 55 [G] *(rec 5/84)* Musique d'Abord ▲ HMA 1901142
Palestrina, G.:Sacred Music—Missa Assumpta est Maria; 7 Motets [L] *(rec 7/80; no texts)*
Ricercar ▲ RIC 8029
Rameau, J.P.:Music of, w. René Jacobs (alt), Gérard Lesne (alt), Kenneth Gilbert (hpd), Christophe Rousset (hpd), W. Christie (cnd), Les Arts Florissants—Pieces; Les Indes Gallantes (sels)
Harmonia Mundi ("Great Baroque Composers" series) 3-▲ HMX 390870.72
Schütz, H.:Kleine geistliche Konzerte (sels)—O lieber Herre Gott, SWV.287; Ich bin die Auferstehung, SWV.324 [G] Harmonia Mundi France ▲ HMC 901261 [DDD]
Schütz, H.:Motets (misc)—SWV.379, 380, 386, 391 [G]
Harmonia Mundi France ▲ HMC 901261 [DDD]
Schütz, H.:Musicalische Exequien [G] Harmonia Mundi France ▲ HMC 901261 [DDD]
Chapelle Royale Vocal Ensemble
Lassus, O. de:The Lamentations of Jeremiah [L] Harmonia Mundi France ▲ HMC 901299
Monteverdi, C.:Messe da capella [L] Harmonia Mundi France ▲ HMC 901355
Monteverdi, C.:Missa in illo tempore [L] Harmonia Mundi France ▲ HMC 901355
Chevetogne Monks' Choir
The Holy & Great Feast of Easter Christophorus ▲ CHR 77156 [DDD]
Russian Monastic Vespers *(rec Monastère de Chevetogne)* Studio SM ▲ D 2455
P. Baer (cnd)
Chants de la Liturgie Slavonne:Service of the Exaltation of the Holy Cross
Musique d'Abord ▲ HMA 190567
The Divine Liturgy:Byzantine-Slavonic Chants Christophorus ▲ 77153 [ADD]
Dormition of the Mother of God Christophorus ▲ 77151 [ADD]
Exaltation of the Cross Christophorus ▲ 77152 [ADD]
Friday Vespers & Saturday Mattins of Holy Week Christophorus ▲ 77155 [ADD]
Holy & Great Thursday Christophorus ▲ 77154 [ADD]
Russian Monastery Vesper Koch Schwann ▲ SCH 313018
Transfiguration of the Lord Christophorus ▲ 77150 [ADD]
Chicago A Cappella
J. Miller (cnd)
Palestrina, G.:Hymns— A solis ortus cardine; Christe redemptor omnium; Hostis Herodis impie *(rec St. Gile's Episcopal Church, Northbrook, Illinois, Mar 2-3, 1996)* Centaur ▲ CRC 2303 [DDD]
Palestrina, G.:Masses—O magnum mysterium *(rec St. Gile's Episcopal Church, Northbrook, Illinois, Mar 2-3, 1996)* Centaur ▲ CRC 2303 [DDD]
Palestrina, G.:Motets—O magnum mysterium *(rec St. Gile's Episcopal Church, Northbrook, Illinois, Mar 2-3, 1996)* Centaur ▲ CRC 2303 [DDD]
Palestrina, G.:Offertories—Jubilate Deo universa terra *(rec St. Gile's Episcopal Church, Northbrook, Illinois, Mar 2-3, 1996)* Centaur ▲ CRC 2303 [DDD]
Chicago Lyric Opera Chorus
Donizetti, G.:Don Pasquale, w. Ileana Cotrubas (sop), Alfredo Kraus (ten), Wladimiro Ganzarolli (bar), Vincente Sardinero (bar), Sutliff (sgr), B. Bartoletti (cnd), Chicago Lyric Opera Orch *(rec live, Chicago, Nov. 2, 1974)* Arkadia 2-▲ 490
Donizetti, G.:La fille du régiment, w. J. Sutherland (sop), R. Resnik (mez), A. Kraus (ten), S. Maias (bass), R. Bonynge (cnd), Chicago Lyric Opera Orch [F] *(rec Nov. 20, 1973)* Myto 2-▲ MCD 93276
J. Nelson (cnd)
Górecki, H.-M.:Amen, w. Chicago Sym Chorus Elektra/Nonesuch ▲ 79348-2 ■ 79348-4
Górecki, H.-M.:Euntes ibant et flebant, w. Chicago Sym Chorus
Elektra/Nonesuch ▲ 79348-2 ■ 79348-4
Górecki, H.-M.:Miserere, w. Chicago Sym Chorus Elektra/Nonesuch ▲ 79348-2 ■ 79348-4
Chicago Sym Chorus
Bach, J.S.:Mass in b, BWV 232, w. F. Lott (sop), A. S. von Otter (mez), H. P. Blochwitz (ten), W. Shimell (bar), G. Howell (b-bar), G. Solti (cnd), Chicago SO London 2-▲ 430353-2 [DDD]
Bach, J.S.:St. Matthew Passion, w. K. Te Kanawa (sop), A. S. von Otter (mez), H. P. Blochwitz (ten), A. Rolfe Johnson (ten), O. Bär (bar), T. Krause (bass), G. Solti (cnd), Chicago SO, Glen Ellyn Children's Chorus [G] London 3-▲ 421177-2 [DDD]
Bach, J.S.:St. Matthew Passion (sels), w. K. Te Kanawa (sop), A. S. von Otter (mez), H. P. Blochwitz (ten), A. Rolfe Johnson (ten), O. Bär (bar), T. Krause (bass), G. Solti (cnd), Chicago SO, Glen Ellyn Children's Chorus [G] London ▲ 425691-2 [DDD]
Barber, S.:The Lovers, w. D. Duesing (bar), A. Schenck (cnd), Chicago SO [E], 10/91)
Koch International Classics ▲ KIC 7125-2 [DDD]
Barber, S.:Prayers of Kierkegaard, w. S. Reese (sop), A. Schenck (cnd), Chicago SO [E], 10/91)
Koch International Classics ▲ KIC 7125-2 [DDD]
Bartók, B.:Cant Profana, "The Giant Stags", w. J. Aler (ten), J. Tomlinson (bass), P. Boulez (cnd), Chicago SO Deutsche Grammophon ▲ 435863-2 [DDD]
Bartók, B.:The Miraculous Mandarin, w. P. Boulez (cnd), Chicago SO *(rec Orchestra Hall, Chicago, Dec 1994)* Deutsche Grammophon ▲ 447747-2 [DDD]
Bartók, B.:Music for Strs, Perc & Cel, w. P. Boulez (cnd), Chicago SO *(rec Orchestra Hall, Chicago, Dec 1994)* Deutsche Grammophon ▲ 447747-2 [DDD]
Beethoven, L. van:Fidelio, w. H. Behrens (sop), S. Ghazarian (sop), P. Hofmann (ten), T. Adam (b-bar), H. Sotin (bass), G. Solti (cnd), Chicago SO [G] London 2-▲ 410227-2 [DDD]
Beethoven, L. van:Syms (comp), w. G. Solti (cnd), Chicago SO [soloists in No. 9:Jessye Norman, Reinhild Runkel, Robert Schunk, Hans Sotin] [G] London 6-▲ 430400-2 [DDD]
Beethoven, L. van:Sym 9, "Choral Sym", w. G. Solti (cnd), Chicago SO [G]
London ▲ 417800-2 [DDD] ■ 417800-4
Beethoven, L. van:Sym 9, "Choral Sym", w. G. Solti (cnd), Chicago SO [soloists P. Lorengar, Y. Minton, S. Burrows, M. Talvela] London ("Jubilee" series) ▲ 430438-2 [ADD]
Berlioz, H.:La Damnation de Faust, w. F. von Stade (mez), K. Riegel (ten), J. Van Dam (b-bar), G. Solti (cnd), Chicago SO London 2-▲ 414680-2 [DDD]
Bernstein, E.:Da, *(orch unknown)* Varèse Sarabande ▲ VSD 5244 ■ VSC 5244
Brahms, J.:Ein Deutsches Requiem, w. K. Battle (sop), H. Hagegard (bar), J. Levine (cnd), Chicago SO [G] *(rec ca. 1984)* RCA Gold Seal ▲ 09026-61349-2 ■ 09026-61349-4
Brahms, J.:Ein Deutsches Requiem, w. K. Te Kanawa (sop), B. Weikl (bar), G. Solti (cnd), Chicago SO [G] London 2-▲ 414627-2 [ADD]
Debussy, C.:Nocturnes, w. Solti, Chicago SO London ▲ 436468-2 [DDD]
Debussy, C.:Prélude à l'après-midi d'un faune, w. G. Solti (cnd), Chicago SO
London ▲ 436468-2 [DDD]
Handel, G.F.:Messiah, w. Kiri Te Kanawa (sop), Anne Gjevang (mez), Richard Lewis (ten), Gwynne Howell (bass), G. Solti (cnd), Chicago SO [E] London 2-▲ 414396-2 [DDD]
Handel, G.F.:Messiah (sels), w. Kiri Te Kanawa (sop), Anne Gjevang (mez), Richard Lewis (ten), Gwynne Howell (bass), G. Solti (cnd), Chicago SO—arias & choruses
London ▲ 430098-2 [DDD] ■ 430098-4

Chicago Sym Chorus (cont.)
Handel, G.F.:Messiah (sels), w. G. Solti (cnd), Chicago SO—choruses [E]
London ("Jubilee" series) ▲ 430734-2 [DDD]
Haydn, J.:Die Schöpfung, w. Ruth Ziesak (sop—Eve & Gabriel), Herbert Lippert (ten—Uriel), Rene Papé (bass—Raphael), Anton Scharinger (bass—Adam), G. Solti (cnd), Chicago SO
London 2-▲ 443445-2 [DDD]
Haydn, J.:Die Schöpfung, w. Norma Burrowes (sop), Rüdger Wohlers (ten), James Morris (bass), G. Solti (cnd), Chicago SO—sels. London ("Jubilee" series) ▲ 430739-2 [DDD]
Holst, G.:The Planets, w. J. Levine (cnd), Chicago SO
Deutsche Grammophon ▲ 429730-2 [DDD] □ 429730-5
Ives, C.:Holidays, w. M. Tilson Thomas (cnd), Chicago SO CBS ▲ MK 42381 [DDD]
Ives, C.:Sym 4, w. M. Tilson Thomas (cnd), Chicago SO—also including choral performances of five American hymns which are quoted by Ives in his Fourth Symphony
Sony Classical ▲ SK 44939 [DDD]
Liszt, F.:A Faust Sym, w. S. Jerusalem (ten), G. Solti (cnd), Chicago SO [G] London ▲ 417399-2 [DDD]
Mahler, G.:Sym 2, w. C .Neblett (sop), M. Horne (mez), C. Abbado (cnd), Chicago SO [G]
Deutsche Grammophon ("Galleria" series) 2-▲ 427262-2 [ADD]
Mahler, G.:Sym 2, w. I. Buchanan (sop), M. Zakai (cta), G. Solti (cnd), Chicago SO [G]
London 2-▲ 410202-2 [DDD]
Orff, C.:Carmina burana, w. J. Anderson (sop), P. Creech (ten), B. Weikl (bar), J. Levine (cnd), Chicago SO [G,L] Deutsche Grammophon ▲ 415136-2 [DDD] ■ 415136-4
Prokofiev, S.:Alexander Nevsky, w. R. Elias (mez), F. Reiner (cnd), Chicago SO [E]
RCA Gold Seal ▲ 60176-2-RG [ADD] ■ 60176-4-RG (CrO2)
Schoenberg, A.:Moses und Aaron, w. B. Bonney (sop), M. Zakai (cta), P. Langridge (ten), F. Mazura (bar), A. Haugland (bass), G. Solti (cnd), Chicago SO, Glen Ellyn Children's Chorus [G]
London 2-▲ 414264-2 [DDD]
Stravinsky, I.:Oedipus Rex, w. F. Quivar (mez), P. Langridge (ten), D. Kaasch (ten), J. Morris, J.-H. Rootering (bass), J. Bastin (bass), J. Levine (cnd), Chicago SO Deutsche Grammophon ▲ 435872-2
Verdi, G.:Choruses, w. G. Solti (cnd), Chicago SO—from Aida, Ballo in maschera, Macbeth, Nabucco, Otello, Requiem, Trovatore [I] London ▲ 430226-2 [DDD] □ 430226-5
Verdi, G.:Otello, w. K. Te Kanawa (sop), L. Pavarotti (ten), L. Nucci (bar), G. Solti (cnd), Chicago SO [I]
London 2-▲ 433669-2 [DDD]
Verdi, G.:Requiem Mass, w. A. Marc (sop), W. Meier (mez), P. Domingo (ten), F. Furlanetto (bass), D. Barenboim (cnd), Chicago SO Erato 2-▲ 96357-2
Wagner, R.:Der fliegende Holländer, w. Martin (sop), A. Kollo (ten), N. Bailey (bar), M. Talvela (bass), G. Solti (cnd), Chicago SO [G] London 2-▲ 414551-2 [ADD]
J. Nelson (cnd)
Górecki, H.-M.:Amen, w. Chicago Lyric Opera Chorus Elektra/Nonesuch ▲ 79348-2 ■ 79348-4
Górecki, H.-M.:Euntes ibant et flebant, w. Chicago Lyric Opera Chorus
Elektra/Nonesuch ▲ 79348-2 ■ 79348-4
Górecki, H.-M.:Miserere, w. Chicago Lyric Opera Chorus Elektra/Nonesuch ▲ 79348-2 ■ 79348-4
G. Solti (cnd)
Wagner, R.:Choruses, w. Vienna State Opera Chorus London ▲ 421865-2 [ADD/DDD]
Chicago Sym Chorus members
The Chorus, w. Mormon Tabernacle Choir, New York Choral Society, Vocal Majority, Westminster Choir, et al. Sony Classical ("Greatest Hits" series) ▲ MLK 62684 ■ MLT 62684
Chichester Cathedral Choir
A. Thurlow (cnd)
Berkeley, L.:Chichester Service, w. James Thomas (org) Priory ▲ PRI 570 [DDD]
Berkeley, L.:The Lord Is My Shepherd, w. James Thomas (org) Priory ▲ PRI 570 [DDD]
Burgon, G.:Songs of the Creation, w. James Thomas (org) Priory ▲ PRI 570 [DDD]
Harvey, J.:God Is Our Refuge, w. James Thomas (org) Priory ▲ PRI 570 [DDD]
Howells, H.:Chichester Service, w. James Thomas (org) Priory ▲ PRI 570 [DDD]
Lloyd, R.:Chichester Mass, w. James Thomas (org) Priory ▲ PRI 570 [DDD]
Walker, R.:Here, O My Lord, I See Thee Face to Face, w. James Thomas (org) Priory ▲ PRI 570 [DDD]
Choeur Contemporain
Ohana, M.:Cantigas, w. M. Quercia (sop), F. Atlan (mez), R. Conil (pno), R. Hayrabedian (cnd), Strasbourg Percussion Ensemble [Sp] Pierre Verany ▲ PV 787032 [DDD]
Chor Modus Novus
Mendelssohn, F.:Die Hochzeit des Camacho, w. R. Hofman (sop—Quiteria), A. Ulbrich (mez—Lucinda), S. Weir (ten—Basilio), H. Rhys-Evans (ten—Vivaldo), N. van der Meel (ten—Camacho), W. Wild (bar—Carrasco), U. Malmberg (bass—Sancho Panza), U. Cold (bass—Don Quixote), J. van Immerseel (cnd), Anima Eterna Orch, Aachen Boys Choir [G] *(rec Sept. 19-22, 1992)*
Channel Classics 2-▲ CCS 5593 [DDD]
Choral Arts Academy Men & Boys' Choir
V. Popov (cnd)
Dmitriev, G.:Vespers (sels) *(rec Large Hall, Moscow Conservatory, Feb 18, 1992)*
Russian Compact Disc ▲ RD CD 10003 [AAD]
Choral Arts Society
Liszt, F.:A Faust Sym, w. C. Bressler (ten), L. Bernstein (cnd), New York PO *(rec 1960)*
Sony Classical ("Bernstein:The Royal Edition" series) ▲ SMK 47570 [ADD]
Mussorgsky, M.:Boris Godunov, w. G. Vishnevskaya (sop), N. Gedda (ten), G. Raimondi (ten), M. Rostropovich (cnd), National SO Washington D.C., Washington Oratorio Society [R]
Erato 3-▲ 2292-45418-2 ZB [DDD]
R. Russell (cnd)
Locklair, D.:Choral Music—Windswept; For Amber Waves; Tapestries; Brief Mass; Changing Perceptions; Epitaph Gasparo ▲ GS 306
Choral Cross-Ties
B. Browne (cnd)
Lauridsen, M.:Les Chansons des roses—Mid-Winter Songs; Madrigali; Les Chansons des Roses *(rec McCready Hall, Taylor-Meade Center, Pacific University, Forest Grove, Oregon)*
Freshwater Classical ▲ FWCL 1052 [DDD] ■ FWCL 1054
Lauridsen, M.:Madrigali on Italian Renaissance Poems—Mid-Winter Songs; Madrigali; Les Chansons des Roses *(rec McCready Hall, Taylor-Meade Center, Pacific University, Forest Grove, Oregon)*
Freshwater Classical ▲ FWCL 1052 [DDD] ■ FWCL 1054
Lauridsen, M.:Mid-Winter Songs—Mid-Winter Songs; Madrigali; Les Chansons des Roses *(rec McCready Hall, Taylor-Meade Center, Pacific University, Forest Grove, Oregon)*
Freshwater Classical ▲ FWCL 1052 [DDD] ■ FWCL 1054
Chorale Caecilia
Gounod, C.:The Seven Sayings of Our Lord Jesus Christ on the Cross Arion ▲ ARN 68239 [AAD]
F. DuBois (cnd)
Gounod, C.:Messe brève 7 aux chapelles Arion ▲ ARN 68239 [AAD]
Chorale Experimentale
Berio, L.:Laborintus II, w. Sanguineti (nar), C. Legrand (sop), J. Baucomont (sop), C. Meunier (cta), L. Berio (cnd), Musique Vivante Ensemble [E,I] Musique d'Abord ▲ HMA 190764
Chorale Mystique
Chants-Mystiques:Hidden Treasures of a Living Tradition, w. Mizrahi, Alberto (ten), Chorale Mystique [cnd:Matthew Lazar] *(rec Jewish Theological Seminary, New York City, Mar & June 1995)*
Polygram Classics ("Opus Magica" series) ▲ 314 520 340-2 [DDD]
Chorale OMP
F. Kuyiyama (cnd)
Miyoshi, A.:Collection of Songs, w. Y. Tanaka (pno), M. Asai (pno) Camerata ▲ 32CM-28
Miyoshi, A.:Poems of Animals, w. A. Miyoshi (nar), Y. Tanaka (pno) Camerata ▲ 32CM-28
Miyoshi, A.:Symphonic Choral Poem, w. A. Miyoshi (nar), Y. Tanaka (pno), M. Asai (pno)
Camerata ▲ 32CM-28
Chorkreis St. Quirinus Rosenheim [G. Hamberger, L. & I. Hamberger, K. Ginthör, T. Hamberger, H. Huber]
Beautiful Marian Songs *(rec Feb. 1983)* Calig ▲ CAL 50807 [DAD]

Chorus Civitas
Vaughan Williams, R.:Epithalamion, w. Edward Scott Hendricks (bar), R. Taylor (cnd), Chorus Civitas CO *(rec The Stockade, Baton Rouge, Apr 24 & 27, 1995)* Centaur ▲ CRC 2299 [DDD]
Vaughan Williams, R.:An Oxford Elegy, w. Gerard Killebrew (nar), R. Taylor (cnd), Chorus Civitas CO *(rec The Stockade, Baton Rouge, Apr 24 & 27, 1995)* Centaur ▲ CRC 2299 [DDD]
Chorus Soranus
Van De Vate, N.:An American Essay, w. C. Marstrand (sop), L. Hovman (alt), O. Støvring Larsen (ten), S. Kawalla (cnd), Koszalin State PO Vienna Modern Masters ▲ VMM 3025 [DDD]
Van De Vate, N.:The Pond Vienna Modern Masters ▲ VMM 3025 [DDD]
Chorus Viennensis
Bach, J.S.:Cant 17, w. P. Esswood (ct), K. Equiluz (ten), M. van Egmond (b-bar), N. Harnoncourt (cnd), Vienna Concentus Musicus [G] Teldec 2-▲ 2292-42501-2 [AAD]
Bach, J.S.:Cant 18, w. P. Esswood (ct), K. Equiluz (ten), M. van Egmond (b-bar), N. Harnoncourt (cnd), Vienna Concentus Musicus [G] Teldec 2-▲ 2292-42501-2 [AAD]
Bach, J.S.:Cant 19, w. P. Esswood (ct), K. Equiluz (ten), M. van Egmond (b-bar), N. Harnoncourt (cnd), Vienna Concentus Musicus [G] Teldec 2-▲ 2292-42501-2 [AAD]
Bach, J.S.:Cant 20, w. P. Esswood (ct), K. Equiluz (ten), M. van Egmond (b-bar), N. Harnoncourt (cnd), Vienna Concentus Musicus [G] Teldec 2-▲ 2292-42501-2 [AAD]
Bach, J.S.:Cant 21, w. P. Esswood (ct), K. Equiluz (ten), W. Wyatt (bass), N. Harnoncourt (cnd), Vienna Concentus Musicus, Vienna Boys' Choir [G] Teldec 2-▲ 2292-42502-2 [AAD]
Bach, J.S.:Cant 24, w. P. Esswood (ct), K. Equiluz (ten), M. van Egmond (b-bar), N. Harnoncourt (cnd), Vienna Concentus Musicus [G] Teldec 2-▲ 2292-42503-2 [AAD]
Bach, J.S.:Cant 25, w. K. Equiluz (ten), M. van Egmond (b-bar), N. Harnoncourt (cnd), Vienna Concentus Musicus [G] Teldec 2-▲ 2292-42503-2 [AAD]
Bach, J.S.:Cant 26, w. P. Esswood (ct), K. Equiluz (ten), S. Nimsgern (b-bar), N. Harnoncourt (cnd), Vienna Concentus Musicus [G] Teldec 2-▲ 2292-42503-2 [AAD]
Bach, J.S.:Cant 27, w. P. Esswood (ct), K. Equiluz (ten), S. Nimsgern (b-bar), N. Harnoncourt (cnd), Vienna Concentus Musicus [G] Teldec 2-▲ 2292-42503-2 [AAD]
Bach, J.S.:Cant 28, w. P. Esswood (ct), K. Equiluz (ten), S. Nimsgern (b-bar), N. Harnoncourt (cnd), Vienna Concentus Musicus [G] Teldec 2-▲ 2292-42504-2 [AAD]
Bach, J.S.:Cant 29, w. P. Esswood (ct), K. Equiluz (ten), M. van Egmond (b-bar), N. Harnoncourt (cnd), Vienna Concentus Musicus [G] Teldec 2-▲ 2292-42504-2 [AAD]
Bach, J.S.:Cant 30, w. P. Esswood (ct), K. Equiluz (ten), M. van Egmond (b-bar), N. Harnoncourt (cnd), Vienna Concentus Musicus [G] Teldec 2-▲ 2292-42504-2 [AAD]
Bach, J.S.:Cant 31, w. K. Equiluz (ten), S. Nimsgern (b-bar), N. Harnoncourt (cnd), Vienna Concentus Musicus [G] Teldec 2-▲ 2292-42505-2 [AAD]
Bach, J.S.:Cant 35, w. P. Esswood (ct), N. Harnoncourt (cnd), Vienna Concentus Musicus [G] Teldec 2-▲ 2292-42506-2 [AAD]
Bach, J.S.:Cant 36, w. P. Esswood (ct), K. Equiluz (ten), R. van der Meer (bass), N. Harnoncourt (cnd), Vienna Concentus Musicus Teldec 2-▲ 2292-42506-2 [AAD]
Bach, J.S.:Cant 37, w. P. Esswood (ct), K. Equiluz (ten), R. van der Meer (bass), N. Harnoncourt (cnd), Vienna Concentus Musicus [G] Teldec 2-▲ 2292-42506-2 [AAD]
Bach, J.S.:Cant 38, w. P. Esswood (ct), K. Equiluz (ten), R. van der Meer (bass), N. Harnoncourt (cnd), Vienna Concentus Musicus [G] Teldec 2-▲ 2292-42506-2 [AAD]
Bach, J.S.:Cant 47, w. R. van der Meer (bass), N. Harnoncourt (cnd), Vienna Concentus Musicus, Vienna Boys' Choir [G] Teldec 2-▲ 2292-42560-2 [AAD]
Bach, J.S.:Cant 49, w. R. van der Meer (bass), N. Harnoncourt (cnd), Vienna Concentus Musicus, Vienna Boys' Choir [G] Teldec 2-▲ 2292-42560-2 [AAD]
Bach, J.S.:Cant 50, w. N. Harnoncourt (cnd), Vienna Concentus Musicus, Vienna Boys' Choir [G] Teldec 2-▲ 2292-42560-2 [AAD]
Beethoven, L. van:Sym 9, "Choral Sym", w. E. Inbal (cnd), Vienna SO, Vienna Singakademie [G] *(rec live, Konzerthaus, 12/30/89 & 1/1/90)* Denon ▲ CO 76646 [DDD]
Mozart, W.A.:Masonic Music, w. C. Prégardien (ten), H. Wildhaber (ten), G. Hornik (bass), P. Schneyder (bass), M. Haselböck (cnd), Vienna Academy—Masonic Cants., K.429, 471, 619, 623 & Songs, K.148, 468, 483, 484 [G] Novalis ▲ 150081 [DDD]
Schubert, Franz:Mass 1, w. B. Weil (cnd), Orch of the Age of Enlightenment, Vienna Boys' Choir Sony Classical ▲ SK 68247
Schubert, Franz:Mass 2, w. B. Weil (cnd), Orch of the Age of Enlightenment, Vienna Boys' Choir Sony Classical ▲ SK 68247
Schubert, Franz:Mass 3, w. Alexander Nader (sop), Thomas Puchegger (sop), Belá Fischer (alt), Georg Leskovich (alt), Jörg Hering (ten), Harry Van der Kamp (bass), Arno Hartmann (org), B. Weil (cnd), Orch of the Age of Enlightenment, Vienna Boys' Choir Sony Classical ("Vivarte" series) ▲ SK 68248
Schubert, Franz:Mass 4, w. Alexander Nader (sop), Thomas Puchegger (sop), Belá Fischer (alt), Georg Leskovich (alt), Jörg Hering (ten), Harry Van der Kamp (bass), Arno Hartmann (org), B. Weil (cnd), Orch of the Age of Enlightenment, Vienna Boys' Choir Sony Classical ("Vivarte" series) ▲ SK 68248
Shostakovich, D.:Sym 5, w. E. Inbal (cnd), Vienna SO *(rec Nov. 26-29, 1990)* Denon/PCM Digital ▲ DEN 75719 [DDD]
Shostakovich, D.:Sym 13, w. R. Holl (bass), E. Inbal (cnd), Vienna SO *(rec May 13-17, 1993)* Denon/PCM Digital ▲ CO 75887 [DDD]
H. Gillesberger (cnd)
Bruckner, A.:Motets, w. Vienna Boys' Choir—Locus iste; Jesse floruit; Os iusti; Christus factus est; Ave Maria Acanta ▲ CD 41232 [DDD]
Gallus, J.:Missa ad imitationem Pater noster, w. Vienna Boys' Choir [L] Acanta ▲ 41303
Gallus, J.:Motets, w. Vienna Boys' Choir—Puer concinite; Repleti sunt [L] Acanta ▲ 41303
Christ Church Boys' Chorus
Britten, B.:War Requiem, w. E. Söderström (sop), R. Tear (ten), T. Allen (bar), S. Rattle (cnd), City of Birmingham SO, City of Birmingham Sym Chorus [E,L] EMI Classics 2-▲ CDC 47033
Christ Church Cathedral Choir Oxford
Bach, J.S.:Magnificat, BWV 243, w. E. Kirkby (sop), J. Nelson (sop), C. Watkinson (cta), P. Elliott (ten), D. Thomas (bass), S. Preston (cnd), Academy of Ancient Music [E♭ version; L] L'Oiseau-Lyre ▲ 414678-2 [ADD]
Britten, B.:A Ceremony of Carols ASV Quicksilva ▲ ASQ 6030 [DDD]
Handel, G.F.:Israel in Egypt, w. Elizabeth Gale (sop), Lillian Watson (sop), James Bowman (alt), Ian Partridge (ten), Tom McDonnell (bass), Alan Watt (bass), S. Preston (cnd), English CO *(rec Chapel of Merton College, Oxford, 1975)* London 2-▲ 443470-2 [ADD]
Handel, G.F.:Israel in Egypt, w. Elizabeth Gale (sop), James Bowman (alt), Ian Partridge (ten), Tom McDonnell (bar), Alan Watt (bass), Watson (sgr), S. Preston (cnd), English CO London ("Jubilee" series) 2-▲ 421602-2 [ADD]
The Spirit of Christmas Present, w. Kansas City Chorale [cnd:Charles Bruffy], BBC Welsh Chorus [cnd:John Hugh Thomas], Huw Tregelles Williams (org), Welsh Guards Fanfare Trumpeters, Christ Church Cathedral Choir [cnd:Stephen Darlington], Gulbenkian Orch [cnd:Michel Swierczewski], et al. Nimbus ▲ NI 7034 [DDD]
Turina, J.:Navidad, w. J. de Udaeta (cnd), Granada City Orch *(rec Centro Cultural Manuel de Falla, Granada, Jan. 28-31, 1993 & Jan. 1)* Claves ▲ CD 9310 [DDD]
Vaughan Williams, R.:Flos Campi, w. R. Best (va), S. Darlington (cnd), English String Orch Nimbus ▲ NI 5166 [DDD]
Vaughan Williams, R.:O Clap Your Hands, w. S. Darlington (cnd), English String Orch Nimbus ▲ NI 5166 [DDD]
Vaughan Williams, R.:The Old 100th Psalm Tune, w. S. Darlington (cnd), English String Orch Nimbus ▲ NI 5166 [DDD]
Vaughan Williams, R.:An Oxford Elegy, w. Jack May (nar), S. Darlington (cnd), English String Orch Nimbus ▲ NI 5166 [DDD]
Vaughan Williams, R.:Te Deum, w. S. Darlington (cnd), English String Orch Nimbus ▲ NI 5166 [DDD]
Vivaldi, A.:Gloria, RV.589, w. P. Kwella (sop), E. Priday (sop), C. Wyn-Rogers (alt), A. Carwood (ten), S. Darlington (cnd), Hanover Band Nimbus ▲ NI 5278 [DDD]
Vivaldi, A.:Gloria, RV.589, w. J. Nelson (sop), E. Kirkby (sop), C. Watkinson (cta), P. Elliott (ten), D. Thomas (bass), S. Preston (cnd), Academy of Ancient Music [L] L'Oiseau-Lyre ▲ 414678-2 [ADD]

Christ Church Cathedral Choir Oxford (cont.)
Vivaldi, A.:Gloria (& Intro), RV.588, w. P. Kwella (sop), E. Priday (sop), C. Wyn-Rogers (alt), A. Carwood (ten), S. Darlington (cnd), Hanover Band Nimbus ▲ NI 5278 [DDD]
Walton, W.:Choral Music—Drop Drop Slow Tears, a Litany; Missa Brevis (Coventry); Chicester Service *(rec July 13-14, 1992)* Nimbus ▲ NI 5346 [DDD]
S. Darlington (cnd)
Blow, J.:Anthems, w. Stephen Farr (org)—The Lord Even the Most Mighty; O Lord, Thou Hast Searched Me *(rec Dorchester Abbey, Oxon, Mar 13-14, 1995)* Nimbus ▲ NI 5454 [DDD]
Byrd, W.:Gradualia seu cantionum sacrarum, liber secundus—Feast of All Saints in 5 Parts [L] Nimbus ▲ NI 5237-2 [DDD]
Byrd, W.:Mass in 3 Parts—performed with the Propers for the Nativity [L] Nimbus ▲ NI 5302 [DDD]
Byrd, W.:Mass in 4 Parts—performed with the Propers for the Feast of Corpus Christi [L] Nimbus ▲ NI 5287 [DDD]
Byrd, W.:Motets—three motets—Laudate Dominum; Laudate pueri; Laudibus in sanctis [L] Nimbus ▲ NI 5237-2 [DDD]
Holst, G.:Choral Music—Antiphon; Bring us in good ale; The Evening watch; In the bleak mid-winter; Lullay, my liking; Masters in this hall; Nunc dimittis; Personent hodie; This have I done for my true love; Wassail song Nimbus ▲ NI 5098 [DDD]
Humfrey, P.:Anthems, w. Stephen Farr (org)—Hear, O Heav'ns *(rec Dorchester Abbey, Oxon, Mar 13-14, 1995)* Nimbus ▲ NI 5454 [DDD]
Lassus, O. de:Choral Music—Missa Qual donna; Missa Octavi toni; Exaltabo te Domine (motet); Tristis est anima mea (motet); De profundis clamavi [L] Nimbus ▲ NI 5150 [DDD]
Locke, M.:Anthems, Motets & Ceremonial Music, w. Stephen Farr (org)—How Doth the City (anthem) *(rec Dorchester Abbey, Oxon, Mar 13-14, 1995)* Nimbus ▲ NI 5454 [DDD]
Martin, F.:Mass Nimbus ▲ NI 5197 [DDD]
Mathias, W.:Church & Choral Music—Royal Wedding Anthem (1981); Missa Aedis Christi (1984); I will celebrate; etc. Nimbus ▲ NI 5243-2 [DDD]
Oxford Church Anthems, w. Farr (org) *(rec Christ Church Cathedral, Oxford, May 23-24, 1994)* Nimbus ▲ NI 5440 [DDD]
Palestrina, G.:Sacred Music—Missa O Sacrum Convivium; O Sacrum Convivium; Coenantibus illis; Magnificat; O Sacrum Convivium *(rec May 10-11, 1993)* Nimbus ▲ NI 5394
Palestrina, G.:Sacred Music—Mass for Pentecost; 5 Motets [L] Nimbus ▲ NI 5100 [DDD]
Poulenc, F.:Mass Nimbus ▲ NI 5197 [DDD]
Purcell, H.:Anthems, w. Stephen Farr (org)—I Will Love Thee; O Lord our Governor; Blessed is He Whose Righteousness; Who Hath Believed; Out of the Deep; Hear Me O Lord *(rec Dorchester Abbey, Oxon, Mar 13-14, 1995)* Nimbus ▲ NI 5454 [DDD]
Tippett, M.:A Child Of Our Time—5 Negro Spirituals *(rec Dorchester Abbey, Oxon, May 14-15, 1990)* Nimbus ▲ NI 7026 [DDD]
Tippett, M.:Choral Music, w. M. Jones (pno)—Bonny at Morn (Northumbrian Folksong for Unison Voices & 3 Recorders); Dance, Clarion Air (Madrigal for 5 Voices); Music (Unison Song for Voices & Piano); Plebs Angelica (Motet for Double Choir); The Weeping Babe (Motet for Soprano & Mixed Choir); Five Nwgro Spirituals (from A Child of Our Time) Nimbus ▲ NI 5266 [DDD]
Tippett, M.:Crown of the Year, w. Medici String Quartet [E] Nimbus ▲ NI 5266 [DDD]
Vaughan Williams, R.:Mass in g [L] Nimbus ▲ NI 5083 [DDD]
Vaughan Williams, R.:Sacred Songs—Valiant for truth; The blessed son of God; No sad thought; Lord, thou has been our refuge; O taste and see [E] Nimbus ▲ NI 5083 [DDD]
Victoria Masses *(rec Dorchester Abbey, Oxford, July 12-13, 1993)* Nimbus ▲ NI 5434 [DDD]
Walton, W.:Choral Music—All this time; Jubilate deo; King Herod and the cock; Make we joy now in this fest; What cheer? Nimbus ▲ NI 5098 [DDD]
Weelkes, T.:Ninth Service & Motets Nimbus ▲ NI 5125 [DDD]
F. Grier (cnd)
Britten, B.:A Ceremony of Carols ASV Quicksilva ▲ QS 6030 [DDD]
Britten, B.:Hymn to St. Cecilia ASV Quicksilva ▲ QS 6030 [DDD]
Britten, B.:Hymn to St. Peter ASV Quicksilva ▲ QS 6030 [DDD]
Britten, B.:A Hymn to the Virgin ASV Quicksilva ▲ QS 6030 [DDD]
Britten, B.:Te Deum ASV Quicksilva ▲ QS 6030 [DDD]
Carols from Christ Church, w. Harry Bicket (org), Frances Kelley (hp) ASV ▲ ASV CD 2097
O for the Wings of a Dove ASV ("Quicksilva" series) ▲ ASV 6019 [ADD]
Scarlatti, D.:Stabat mater [L] Hyperion ▲ CDA 66182 [DDD]
Christ Church Cathedral Men & Boys' Choir Oxford
Fauré, G.:Requiem, w. W. Reguson-Wagstaffe (trb), S. Irwin (bass-bar), F. Burgomeister (cnd), Indianapolis Festival Orch Gothic ▲ G 49062 [DDD]
Howells, H.:Requiem, w. J. Barton (trb), P. Flight (ct), D. Honoré (ten), T. Woody (bar), F. Burgomeister (cnd), Indianapolis Festival Orch Gothic ▲ G 49062 [DDD]
Christchurch Harmonic Choir New Zealand
Vaughan Williams, R.:Sym 1, w. Elaine Blighton (sop), John Cameron (bar), M. Sargent (cnd), BBC SO, BBC Chorus, BBC Choral Society *(rec 1965)* IMP ("BBC Radio" series) ▲ IMP 5691502
Church Les Amis de la Sagesse Women's Choir
Nueva Espña:Close Encounters in the New World (1590-1690), w. J. Cohen (cnd), Boston Camerata, Boston Shawn and Sackbut Ensemble, Schola Cantorum of Boston Erato ▲ 45977-2
Church of St. Luke in the Fields Choir
Wigglesworth, F.:Psalm 148, w. Kathy Fink (fl), Elizabeth Brown (fl), Jeanne Wilson (fl), Kevin James (trbn), David Taylor (trbn), D. Schuler (cnd) CRI ▲ C 733 [DDD]
D. Schuler (cnd)
Wigglesworth, F.:A Short Mass CRI ▲ C 733 [DDD]
Church of the Advent Choir Boston
E. Ho (cnd)
Duo Seraphim:Angel Songs for Christmas AFKA ▲ SK 516
Church of the Resurrection Choir Moscow
Russian Choirs Sing for the Children of Chernobyl, w. Moscow Patriarchate Children's Choir, Korez Convent Choir, Pyuchtize Convent Choir, Zagorsk Monks' Choir, Moscow Religious Academy Choir, Moscow Religious Academy Choir, Dormition of the Virgin Church Choir Koch Schwann ▲ SCH 313322 [ADD/DDD]
Cincinnati Pops Chorale
Amen:A Gospel Celebration, w. Azusa Pacific Univ Choir, Central State Univ Chorus, Jennifer Holliday (sgr), Maureen McGovern (sgr), Lou Rawls (sgr), Cincinnati Pops Orch [cnd:Erich Kunzel] *(rec Feb. 28-Mar. 1, 1993)* Telarc ▲ CD 80315 [DDD] ■ CD 80315
Cincinnati Summer Opera Association Chorus
Bizet, G.:Carmen, w. Cooper (sgr), Dunn (sgr), P. Domingo (ten), F. Guarrera (bar), A. Guadagno (cnd), Cincinnati Summer Opera Association Orch [F] *(rec live 7/19/68)* Melodram 2-▲ MEL 27034 (m) [AAD]
Citeaux Abbey Monks' Choir
Salve Regina, w. Timadeuc Abbey Monks' Choir, Sept-fons Abbey Monks' Choir Studio SM ▲ 12 16 34
Citeaux Abbey Monks' Choir & Séminaristes de la Cathédrale Abbey Monks' Choir Strasbourg
Venite Adoremus, w. Bec-Hellouin Abbey Monks' Choir Studio SM ▲ 121698
City of Birmingham Sym Chorus
Bartók, B.:The Miraculous Mandarin, w. S. Rattle (cnd), City of Birmingham SO EMI Classics ▲ CDC 55094
Beethoven, L. van:Syms (comp), w. W. Weller (cnd), City of Birmingham SO Chandos 5-▲ CHAN 7042
Berlioz, H.:Music of, w. L. Frémaux (cnd), City of Birmingham SO—Ovt., Le carnaval romain, Op. 9; Funeral March for Hamlet, Op. 18/3; Hungarian March; Dance of Sylphs; Minuet of the Will-o'-wisps; Ovt., Benvenuto Cellini, Op. 23; The Trojans (selections) Klavier ■ KC 553
Britten, B.:Ballad of Heroes, w. R. Tear (ten), S. Rattle (cnd), City of Birmingham SO [E] *(rec 7/90)* EMI Classics 2-▲ CDCB 54270 [DDD]
Britten, B.:The Building of the House, w. S. Rattle (cnd), City of Birmingham SO [E] *(rec 7/90)* EMI Classics 2-▲ CDCB 54270 [DDD]
Britten, B.:Canadian Carnival, w. S. Rattle (cnd), City of Birmingham SO *(rec 4/82)* EMI Classics 2-▲ CDCB 54270 [DDD]

▲ = CD ♦ = Enhanced CD Δ = MD ■ = Cassette Tape □ = DCC

City of Birmingham Sym Chorus (cont.)
Britten, B.:Praise We Great Men, w. A. Hargan (sop), M. King (alt), R. Tear (ten), W. White (bass), S. Rattle (cnd), City of Birmingham SO [E] *(rec July, 1990)* EMI Classics 2-▲ ZDCB 54270 [DDD]
Britten, B.:War Requiem, w. E. Söderström (sop), R. Tear (ten), T. Allen (bar), S. Rattle (cnd), City of Birmingham SO, Christ Church Boys' Chorus [E,L] EMI Classics 2-▲ CDC 47033
Haydn, J.:Die Schöpfung, w. Arleen Augér (sop), Philip Langridge (ten), David Thomas (bass), S. Rattle (cnd), City of Birmingham SO [E] EMI Classics 2-▲ CDCB 54159 [DDD]
Janácek, L.:Sinfonietta, w. S. Rattle (cnd), City of Birmingham SO EMI ▲ CDC 47504
Janácek, L.:Slavonic Mass, w. F. Palmer (sop), A. Gunson (mez), M. King (mez), J. Mitchinson (ten), J. Parker-Smith (org), S. Rattle (cnd), City of Birmingham SO EMI ▲ CDC 47504
Mahler, G.:Das Klagende Lied, w. H. Döse (sop), A. Hodgson (cta), R. Tear (ten), S. Rae, S. Rattle (cnd), City of Birmingham SO EMI ▲ CDC 47089
Mahler, G.:Sym 2, w. A. Augér (mez), J. Baker (mez), S. Rattle (cnd), City of Birmingham SO [G] EMI Classics 2-▲ CDCB 47962 [DDD]
Nielsen, C.:Pan & Syrinx, w. S. Rattle (cnd), Philharmonia Orch EMI Classics ▲ CDM 64737
Nielsen, C.:Sym 4, w. S. Rattle (cnd), Philharmonia Orch EMI Classics ▲ CDM 64737
Shostakovich, D.:Sym 13, w. N. Storojev (bass), O. Kamu (cnd), City of Birmingham SO [R] Chandos ▲ CHAN 8540 [DDD]
Sibelius, J.:Sym 5, w. S. Rattle (cnd), Philharmonia Orch EMI Classics ▲ CDM 64737
Szymanowski, K.:Litany to the Virgin Mary, w. E. Szmytka (sop), F. Quivar (cta), J. Garrison (ten), J. Connell (bass), S. Rattle (cnd), City of Birmingham SO EMI Classics ▲ CDC 55121
Szymanowski, K.:Stabat Mater, w. E. Szmytka (sop), F. Quivar (mez), J. Connell (bass), S. Rattle (cnd), City of Birmingham SO EMI Classics ▲ CDC 55121
Szymanowski, K.:Sym 3, w. J. Garrison (ten), S. Rattle (cnd), City of Birmingham SO EMI Classics ▲ CDC 55121
Vaughan Williams, R.:Fant on a Theme by Thomas Tallis, w. N. del Mar (cnd), City of Birmingham SO Klavier ▲ KCD 11034 [DDD]
Vaughan Williams, R.:Norfolk Rhap 1, w. N. del Mar (cnd), City of Birmingham SO Klavier ▲ KCD 11034 [DDD]
Vaughan Williams, R.:Toward the Unknown, w. N. del Mar (cnd), City of Birmingham SO Klavier ▲ KCD 11034 [DDD]
Vaughan Williams, R.:Variants of "Dives & Lazarus", w. N. del Mar (cnd), City of Birmingham SO Klavier ▲ KCD 11034 [DDD]
Walton, W.:Coronation Te Deum, w. L. Frémaux (cnd), City of Birmingham SO EMI Classics ▲ CDM 64201

S. Halsey (cnd)
Delius, F.:Songs—Midsummer Song; On Craig Ddu; 2 Unaccompanied Partsongs; The Splendour Falls; 3 Early Partsongs *(rec St. Paul's Church, Birmingham, June 19-21, 1987)* Conifer Classics 2-▲ 75605-51752-2 [DDD]
Elgar, E.:From the Bavarian Highlands *(rec Birmingham Town Hall, July 19-20, 1986)* Conifer Classics 2-▲ 75605-51752-2 [DDD]
Grainger, P.:Songs—Brigg Fair; Morning Song in the Jungle; Danny Deever; The Peora Hunt; Skye Boat Song; Shallow Brown; Irish Tune from County Derry; Australian Up-Country Song; 6 Dukes Went a' Fishin'; There was a Pig; The Lost Lady Found *(rec St. Paul's Church, Birmingham, June 19-21, 1987)* Conifer Classics 2-▲ 75605-51752-2 [DDD]
Holst, G.:Dirge & Hymeneal *(rec Birmingham Town Hall, July 19-20, 1986)* Conifer Classics 2-▲ 75605-51752-2 [DDD]
Holst, G.:Motets *(rec Birmingham Town Hall, July 19-20, 1986)* Conifer Classics 2-▲ 75605-51752-2 [DDD]
Holst, G.:Partsongs (5), Op. 12 *(rec Birmingham Town Hall, July 19-20, 1986)* Conifer Classics 2-▲ 75605-51752-2 [DDD]

City of London School for Boys Chorus
Britten, B.:Psalm 150, w. R. Hickox (cnd), City of London School for Girls Orch, City of London School for Girls Chorus [E] Chandos ▲ CHAN 8855 [DDD]
Britten, B.:Welcome Ode, w. R. Hickox (cnd), City of London School for Girls Orch, City of London School for Girls Chorus [E] Chandos ▲ CHAN 8855 [DDD]

City of London School for Girls Chorus
Britten, B.:Psalm 150, w. R. Hickox (cnd), City of London School for Girls Orch, City of London School for Boys Chorus [E] Chandos ▲ CHAN 8855 [DDD]
Britten, B.:Welcome Ode, w. R. Hickox (cnd), City of London School for Girls Orch, City of London School for Boys Chorus [E] Chandos ▲ CHAN 8855 [DDD]

Clare College Chapel Choir Cambridge
Carols from Clare College Cambridge, w. J. Rutter (cnd), Clare College Orch EMI Classics ▲ CDM 69950

T. Brown (cnd)
Ave verum:Favorite Parish Anthems Guild ▲ 7109
Compline with Anthems & Motets Gamut Classics ▲ GAM 531 [DDD]
French Choral Music Meridian ▲ 84153
From Tallis to Byrd Gamut Classics ▲ IMCD 701 [DDD]
Parish Anthems Gamut Classics ▲ GAMD 505
Tudor Anthems:From the Oxford Book of Tudor Anthems Gamut Classics ▲ GAM 540 [DDD]

Clare College Choir Cambridge
Purcell, H.:Dido & Aeneas, w. L. Hunt (sop), L. Saffer (sop), D. Deam (sop), C. Brandes (sop), R. Rainero (sop), E. Rabiner (mez), P. Elliot (ten), M. Dean (bar), N. McGegan (cnd), Philharmonia Baroque Orch Harmonia Mundi USA ▲ HMU 907110

T. Brown (cnd)
Berkeley, L.:Choral Music—A Festival Anthem, Op. 21/2; Judica me, Op. 96/1; The Lord is My Shepard, Op. 91/1; Magnificat & Nunc Dimittis, Op. 99; Mass for 5 Voices, Op. 64; Missa Brevis, Op. 57; Salve Regina, Op. 48/1; Thou Hast Made Me, Op. 55/1; Three Latin Motets, Op. 83/1 [L,E] Meridian ▲ MER 84216
Byrd, W.:Anthems—O lux beata; Miserere; O Lord, Give Ear *(rec St. George's Church, Chesterton, June 26-27, 1991)* Guild ▲ 7108 [DDD]
Byrd, W.:Church Music—O lux beata; Miserere mei; O Lord Give Ear Guild ▲ 7108
Josquin Desprez:Church Music—Nunc dimittis Guild ▲ 7108
Josquin Desprez:Motets—Nunc dimittis *(rec St. George's Church, Chesterton, June 26-27, 1991)* Guild ▲ 7108 [DDD]
Sheppard, J.:Church Music—In pace; Salvator mundi; In manus tuas; Libera nos Guild ▲ 7108
Sheppard, J.:Sacred Choral Music—In pace; Salvator mundi; in manus tuas; Libera nos *(rec St. George's Church, Chesterton, June 26-27, 1991)* Guild ▲ 7108 [DDD]
Tallis, T.:Church Music—Te lucis; In manus tuas *(rec St. George's Church, Chesterton, June 26-27, 1991)* Guild ▲ 7108 [DDD]
White, R.:Church Music—Christe qui lux; The Lord Bless Us Guild ▲ 7108
White, R.:Sacred Music—Christe qui lux; The Lord bless us *(rec St. George's Church, Chesterton, June 26-27, 1991)* Guild ▲ 7108 [DDD]

Clarion Concerts Chorus
Cherubini, L.:Mass in d, w. Patricia Wells (sop), Maureen Forrester (cta), George Shirley (ten), Justino Diaz (bass), N. Jenkins (cnd), Clarion Concerts Orch *(rec Vanguard's 23rd Street Recording Studio)* Vanguard Classics ▲ SVC-44 [AAD]
Rossini, G.:La pietra del paragone, w. A. Elgar (sop), B. Wolff (mez), E. Bonazzi (mez), J. Carreras (ten), J. Reardon (bar), R. Murcell (bar), A. Foldi (b-bar), J. Diaz (bass), N. Jenkins (cnd), Clarion Concerts Orch [I] *(rec. ca. 1972)* Vanguard Classics 3-▲ OVC 8043/45 [ADD]

Clarion Music Society Chorus
Dittersdorf, K.D. von:Arcifanfano, King of Fools, or It's Always Too Late to Learn, w. P. Brooks (sop), A. Russell (sop), E. Steber (sop), J. McCollum (ten), J. Sopher (ten), H. Rehfuss (bar), D. Smith (bar), N. Jenkins (cnd), Clarion Music Society Orch [E] *(rec live, New York 1965)* VAI Audio 2-▲ VAIA 1010-2 (m) [ADD]

Clerkes of Oxenford
Sheppard, J.:Missa "Cantate" [L] Calliope ▲ CAL 9621
Sheppard, J.:Motets—Spiritus Sanctus [L] Calliope ▲ CAL 9621

Clerkes of Oxenford (cont.)

D. Wulstan (cnd)
Gibbons, O.:Hymns (13) Calliope ▲ CAL 9611
Gibbons, O.:Responsories (7) Calliope ▲ CAL 9611
The Play of Daniel Calliope ▲ CAL 9848 [ADD]
Sheppard, J.:Sacred Choral Music—Gaude, gaude, gaude Maria; Laudem dicite Deo; In pace; In manus tuas (first setting); Verbum caro Classics for Pleasure ▲ CDCFP 4638 [ADD]
Tallis, T.:Church Music, Messe, "Puer natus est"; Motet, "Suscipe quaeso Domine"; Motet, "Salvator mundi" [L] Calliope ▲ CAL 9623 [ADD]
Tallis, T.:Church Music—O nata lux de lumine; Ecce tempus idoneum; Loquebantur variis linguis; Gaude gloriosa, Classics for Pleasure ▲ CDCFP 4638 [ADD]
Tallis, T.:Messe "Puer natus est" *(rec 1977)* Approche ▲ CAL 6623 [ADD]
Tallis, T.:Motet "Salvator" *(rec 1977)* Approche ▲ CAL 6623 [ADD]
Tallis, T.:Motet "Suscipe quaeso Domine" *(rec 1977)* Approche ▲ CAL 6623 [ADD]
Tallis, T.:Spem in alium [L] Elektra/Nonesuch ■ N5-71378
Tallis, T.:Spem in alium Classics for Pleasure ▲ CDCFP 4638 [ADD]
White, R.:Lamentations of Jeremiah [L] Calliope ▲ CAL 9848 [ADD]
White, R.:Motets [L]—Regina coeli; Portio mea Domine; Domine quis habitavit; Christe qui lux es Calliope ▲ CAL 9623 [ADD]
White, R.:Motets *(rec 1977)* Approche ▲ CAL 6623 [ADD]

Clerks' Group

E. Wickham (cnd)
Barbireau, J.:Osculetur me ASV ("Gaudeamus" series) ▲ ASV CD 153
Binchois, G. de B.D.:De plus en plus se renouvelle ASV ("Gaudeamus" series) ▲ ASV CD 153
Busnois, A.:Music of—Gaude Coelestis Domina; In Hydraulis ASV ▲ ASV 143 [DDD]
Gaudeamus Early Music Sampler, w. Great Consort, His Majesties Sagbutts & Cornetts, Rasumovsky String Quartet, Trio Sonnerie, Cappella Nova, Cardinall's Musick, Ex Cathedra, Gentlemen of the Chappell, Gonville & Caius College Choir Cambridge, et al. ASV/Gaudeamus ▲ ASV 1002
Josquin Desprez:Motets—Illibata Dei Virgo Nutrix ASV ▲ ASV 143 [DDD]
Obrecht, J.:Sacred Music—Humilium Decus ASV ▲ ASV 143 [DDD]
Ockeghem, J.:Gaude Maria ASV ("Gaudeamus" series) ▲ ASV CD 153
Ockeghem, J.:Missa "De plus en plus" ASV ("Gaudeamus" series) ▲ ASV CD 153
Ockeghem, J.:Missa prolationum ASV ▲ ASV 143 [DDD]
Pipelare, M.:Salve Regina ASV ("Gaudeamus" series) ▲ ASV CD 153
Pullois, J.:Flos de spina ASV ▲ ASV 143 [DDD]

Cleveland Orch Chorus
Beethoven, L. van:Sym 9, "Choral Sym", w. C. von Dohnányi (cnd), Cleveland Orch [G] Telarc ▲ CD 80120 [DDD] ■ CS 30120 (D)
Busoni, F.:Con Pno, Op. 39, w. G. Ohlsson (pno), Cleveland Chorus, C. von Dohnányi (cnd), Cleveland Orch [G] Telarc ▲ CD 80207 [DDD]
Mendelssohn, F.:Die erste Walpurgisnacht, w. C. von Dohnányi (cnd), Cleveland Orch [G] Telarc ▲ CD 80184 [DDD]
Orff, C.:Carmina burana, w. J. Blegen (sop), K. Riegel (ten), P. Binder (bar), M. Tilson Thomas (cnd), Cleveland Orch [G, L] CBS ▲ MK 33172 [ADD]

Cluj-Napoca Phil Chorus
Enescu, G.:Sym 3, w. I. Baciu (cnd), Cluj-Napoca PO Marco Polo ▲ 8.223143
Puccini, G.:Madama Butterfly, w. Eugenia Moldoveanu (sop—Madama Butterfly), Mihaela Agachi (mez—Suzuki), Corina Circa (mez—Kate Pinkerton), Emil Gherman (ten—B.F. Pinkerton), Stefan Popescu (ten—Goro), Ioan Soanea (bar—The Bonze/Yakuside), Eduard Tumageanian (bar—Sharpless), Alexandru Kopeczi (bass—Prince Yamadori), Mircea Moisa (bass—Commissioner), P. Popescu (cnd), Satu Mare PO *(rec 1979)* Vox Box 2-▲ CDX 5155

Coeli et Terra Vocal Ensemble
Monteverdi, C.:Missa in illo tempore, w. M. Bourbon (cnd), Paris Métamorphoses Ensemble Arion ▲ ARN 68292 [DDD]
Ockeghem, J.:Missa, "L'homme armé" [L] Arion ▲ ARN 68149 [DDD]

M. Bourbon (cnd)
Scarlatti, D.:Missa quatour vocum Arion ▲ ARN 68292 [DDD]

Collegiate Chorale
Foster, S.C.:Old Folks at Home, w. Arthur Woodley (b-bar), S. Richman (cnd), Harmonie Ensemble/New York [arr Dvořák 1894] Music & Arts ▲ MUA CD 926
Strauss, R.:Friedenstag, w. A. Marc (sop), R. Roloff (bass), R. Bass (cnd), Collegiate Orch [G] *(rec in concert at Carnegie Hall, 11/19/89)* Koch International Classics ▲ KIC 7111-2 [DDD]

Collegium Musicum Judaicum Amsterdam

C. Storosum (cnd)
Music of the Bible *(rec 1981)* Entrée ▲ 0029-2 [ADD]

Collegium Vocale
Bach, J.S.:Cant 106, "Actus tragicus", w. M. Klein (trb), R. Harten (alt), M. van Altena (ten), M. van Egmond (b-bar), Leonhardt Consort, Hanover Boys' Chorus [G] Teldec ▲ 2292-42602-2
Bach, J.S.:Cant 107, w. M. Klein (trb), K. Equiluz (ten), M. van Egmond (b-bar), Leonhardt Consort [G] Teldec 2-▲ 2292-42603-2
Bach, J.S.:Cant 113, w. S. Hennig (trb), D. Bratschke (trb), R. Jacobs (ct), K. Equiluz (ten), M. van Egmond (b-bar), Leonhardt Consort, Hanover Boys' Chorus [G] Teldec 2-▲ 2292-42606-2
Bach, J.S.:Cant 114, w. S. Hennig (trb), R. Jacobs (ct), K. Equiluz (ten), M. van Egmond (b-bar), Leonhardt Consort, Hanover Boys' Chorus [G] Teldec 2-▲ 2292-42606-2
Bach, J.S.:Cant 187, w. M. Emmermann (trb), P. Esswood (ct), M. van Egmond (b-bar), G. Leonhardt (cnd), Leonhardt Consort, Hanover Men & Boys' Chorus [G] Teldec 2-▲ 2292-44179-2 [DDD]
Bach, J.S.:Music of, w. R. Jacobs (ct), G. Murray (org), La Chapelle Royale Orch, Ensemble 415—selections from Cantatas 35, 78 & 82, St. John Passion, St. Matthew Passion, & the Well-tempered Clavier; Chorale Prelude, BWV 622; Flute Sonata, BWV 1034; Toccata & Fugue in d *(rec 1969-88)* Harmonia Mundi Plus ▲ HMP 390801
Gluck, C.W.:Orfeo ed Euridice, w. M. Falewicz (sop), M. Kweksilber (sop), R. Jacobs (alt), S. Kuijken (cnd), La Petite Bande Accent 2-▲ 48223/24 [DDD]
Purcell, H.:Music for the Funeral of Queen Mary Harmonia Mundi France ▲ HMC 901462
Purcell, H.:Te Deum & Jubilate Harmonia Mundi France ▲ HMC 901462

P. Herreweghe (cnd)
Bach, C.P.E.:Auferstehung und Himmelfahrt Jesu, w. H. Martinpelto (sop), C. Prégardien (ten), P. Harvey (bass), Orch of the Age of Enlightenment Virgin Classics ▲ CDC 59069
Bach, J.S.:Cant 43, w. B. Schlick (sop), C. Patriasz (cta), C. Prégardien (ten), P. Kooy (bass) Harmonia Mundi France ▲ HMC 901479
Bach, J.S.:Cant 44, w. B. Schlick (sop), C. Patriasz (cta), C. Prégardien (ten), P. Kooy (bass) Harmonia Mundi France ▲ HMC 901479
Bach, J.S.:Cant 57, w. Vasiljka Jezovšek (sop), Sarah Connolly (cta), Mark Padmore (ten), Peter Kooy (bass) Harmonia Mundi ▲ HMC 901594
Bach, J.S.:Cant 66, w. Barbara Schlick (sop), Kai Wessel (alt), James Taylor (ten), Peter Kooy (bass) Harmonia Mundi France ▲ HMC 901513
Bach, J.S.:Cant 73, w. B. Schlick (sop), H. Crook (ten), P. Kooy (bass), Collegium Vocale Orch Virgin Classics ▲ CDC 59237-2
Bach, J.S.:Cant 80, w. Barbara Schlick (sop), Agnès Mellon (sop), Gérard Lesne (ct), Howard Crook (ten), Peter Kooy (bass), La Chapelle Royale Orch Harmonia Mundi France ▲ HMC 6901326
Bach, J.S.:Cant 105, w. B. Schlick (sop), G. Lesne (mez), H. Crook (ten), P. Kooy (bass), Collegium Vocale Orch Virgin Classics ▲ CDC 59237-2
Bach, J.S.:Cant 110, w. Vasiljka Jezovšek (sop), Sarah Connolly (cta), Mark Padmore (ten), Peter Kooy (bass) Harmonia Mundi ▲ HMC 901594
Bach, J.S.:Cant 122, w. Vasiljka Jezovšek (sop), Sarah Connolly (cta), Mark Padmore (ten), Peter Kooy (bass) Harmonia Mundi ▲ HMC 901594
Bach, J.S.:Cant 131, w. B. Schlick (sop), G. Lesne (mez), H. Crook (ten), P. Kooy (bass), Collegium Vocale Orch Virgin Classics ▲ CDC 59237-2
Bach, J.S.:Easter Oratorio, w. Barbara Schlick (sop), Kai Wessel (alt), James Taylor (ten), Peter Kooy (bass) Harmonia Mundi France ▲ HMC 901513

Collegium Vocale (cont.)
P. Herreweghe (cnd) (cont.)
Bach, J.S.:Magnificat, BWV 243, w. A. Mellon (sop), B. Schlick (sop), G. Lesne (ct), H. Crook (ten), P. Kooy (bass), La Chapelle Royale Orch [L] Harmonia Mundi France ▲ HMC 901326
Bach, J.S.:Mass in b, BWV 232, w. B. Schlick (sop), C. Patriasz (cta), C. Brett (ct), H. Crook (ten), P. Kooy (bass), Collegium Vocale Orch [L] Virgin Classics ("Veritas" series) 2-▲ CDCB 59517-2 [DDD]
Beethoven, L. van:Missa Solemnis, w. Rosa Mannion (sop), Birgit Remmert (alt), James Taylor (ten), Cornelius Hauptmann (bass), Champs Élysées Theater Orch, Chapelle Royale Choir *(rec Auditorium Stravinski de Montreux, Feb. 20-21, 1995)* Harmonia Mundi France ▲ HMC 901557
Brahms, J.:Ein Deutsches Requiem, w. Christiane Oelze (sop), Gerald Finley (bar), Champs Élysées Theater Orch, Chapelle Royale Choir Harmonia Mundi ▲ HMC 901608 ■ HMC 401608
Lully, J.-B.:Armide, w. V. Gens (sop), N. Rime (sop), G. Laurens (mez), H. Crook (ten), G. Ragon (ten), La Chapelle Royale Orch [F] Harmonia Mundi France 2-▲ HMC 901456/57
Mendelssohn, F.:Elijah, w. Champs Élysées Theater Orch, La Chapelle Royale Orch Harmonia Mundi France 2-▲ HMC 901463/64
Mendelssohn, F.:St. Paul, w. Melanie Diener (sop), Annette Markert (mez), James Taylor (ten), Matthias Görne (bass), Champs Élysées Theater Orch, Chapelle Royale Choir *(rec Stravinsky Auditorium, Montreaux)* Harmonia Mundi France 2-▲ HMC 901584.85
Monteverdi, C.:Vespro della Beata Vergine, w. A. Mellon (sop), G. Laurens (mez), H. Crook (ten), D. Thomas (bass), Toulouse Saqueboutiers, Chapelle Royale Choir [L] Harmonia Mundi France 2-▲ HMC 901247/48 [DDD]
Mozart, W.A.:Missa, K.427, w. Jennifer Larmore (sop), Christiane Oelze (sop), Scot Weir (ten), Peter Kooy (bass), Champs Élysées Theater Orch, Chapelle Royale Choir Harmonia Mundi France ▲ HMX 29001393
Mozart, W.A.:Missa, K.427, w. C. Oelze (sop), J. Larmore (mez), S. Weir (ten), P. Kooy (bass), Champs Élysées Theater Orch, Chapelle Royale Choir Harmonia Mundi France ▲ HMC 901393
Renaissance, w. Hesperion XX [cnd:J. Savall], French Polyphonic Ensemble [cnd:C. Ravier] Astrée 3-▲ 8608
Schütz, H.:Geistliche Chor-musik—Herr, auf dich traue ich; O lieber Herre Gott; Schaffe in mir, Gott, eine reines Herz; Die mit Tränen säen; Der Herr schauet von Himmel; Wann unsre Augen schlafen ein; Eile, mich, Gott, zu erretten; So fahr ich hin zu Jesu Christ; Die Himmel erzählen die Ehre Gottes; Unser Wandel ist im Himmel; Ich bin eine rufende Stimme; O süsser, O freundlicher; Herzlich lieb hab ich dich, o Herr; Ich liege und schlafe; Selig sind die Toten; Das ist je gewisslich wahr Harmonia Mundi France ▲ HMC 901534

Collegium Vocale Cologne
Fromme (cnd)
Madrigals Odyssey 2-▲ MB2K 45622

Collegium Vocale Nova Ars Cantandi
Acciai, Cristante (cnd)
Viadana, L. da:Responsoria ad lamentationes, w. Schola Gregoriana Stradivarius 2-▲ STV 33444 [DDD]

Cologne Chamber Choir
Brahms, J.:Kyrie, w. Peter Neumann (org) MD + G ▲ MDG 3320598 [DDD]
Brahms, J.:Missa Canonica, w. Peter Neumann (org) MD + G ▲ MDG 3320598 [DDD]
Durante, F.:Lamentationes Jeremiae Prophetae, w. Mechthild Bach (sop), Monika Frimmer (sop), Margarete Joswig (sgr), P. Neumann (cnd), Collegium Cartusianum CPO ▲ CPO 999325
Klebe, G.:Music of, w. Christian Köhn (pno), Silke-Thora Matthies (pno), J. Jacobs (acc)—Warum hat die sonne einen Aschenrand; Der Schrei; Glockentürme Academy ▲ ACA 8509
Monteverdi, C.:Madrigals, w. P. Neumann (cnd), Cologne Instrumental Ensemble—8 selections from Books 2,5,6 & 8 [I] MD + G ▲ L 3081 [DDD]
Mozart, W.A.:Missa, K.427, w. Monika Frimmer (sop), Barbara Schlick (sop), Christoph Prégardien (ten), Klaus Mertens (bass), P. Neumann (cnd), Collegium Cartusianum Virgin Classics ▲ CDM 61167
Schumann, R.:Mass, w. Peter Neumann (org) MD + G ▲ MDG 3320598 [DDD]
P. Neumann (cnd)
Monteverdi, C.:Madrigals MD + G ▲ MDG 3320081
L. Rovatkay (cnd)
Caldara, A.:Music of—Laetatus Sum (Psalm 121); Salve Regina (Antiphon) *(rec May 23-26, 1987)* Calig ▲ CAL 50875 [DDD]
Durante, F.:Nisi Dominus *(rec May 23-26, 1987)* Calig ▲ CAL 50875 [DDD]
Porpora, N.A.:Psalm 109 *(rec May 23-26, 1987)* Calig ▲ CAL 50875 [DDD]

Cologne Chorus Musicus
Bach, J.S.:St. Matthew Passion, w. C. Spering (cnd), Das Neue Orch [arr. by Mendelssohn] Opus 111 ▲ OPS 30-74
Cherubini, L.:Requiem Mass in c, w. C. Spering (cnd), New Orch Opus 111 ▲ OPS 30-116
Handel, G.F.:Acis & Galatea, w. C. Spering (cnd), Das Neue Orch Opus 111 ▲ OPS 30-74
Handel, G.F.:Acis & Galatea [arr Mozart], w. C. Spering (cnd), Das Neue Orch Opus 111 2-▲ OPS 45-9109/10
Handel, G.F.:Ode for St. Cecilia's Day [arr Mozart], w. C. Spering (cnd), Das Neue Orch [arr. Mozart] [E] Opus 111 ▲ OPS 30-74
Handel, G.F.:Ode for St. Cecilia's Day [arr Mozart], w. C. Spering (cnd), Das Neue Orch Opus 111 2-▲ OPS 45-9109/10
Le Sueur, J.-F.:Oratorios for the Coronation of Napoléon & C. X., w. C. Spering (cnd), Das Neue Orch Opus 111 ▲ OPS 30-74
Le Sueur, J.-F.:Oratorios for the Coronations of the Sovereign Princes of Christendom, w. C. Spering (cnd), Das Neue Orch *(rec Oct. 1992)* Opus 111 ▲ OPS 3089 [DDD]
Mendelssohn, F.:Sym 2, w. S. Isokoski (sop), M. Bach (sop), F. Lang (ten), C. Spering (cnd), Das Neue Orch [period instruments] Opus 111 ▲ OPS 30-98
Romberg, A.:Der Lied von der Glocke, w. B. Schlick (sop), F. Lang (ten), P. Lika (bass), C. Spering (cnd), Das Neue Orch *(rec May 24-27, 1992)* Opus 111 ▲ OPS 30-67 [DDD]
Romberg, A.:Der Lied von der Glocke, w. C. Spering (cnd), Das Neue Orch [G] Opus 111 ▲ OPS 30-74
Rossini, G.:Péchés de vieillesse (sels), w. M. Castets (sop), M. Georg (mez), J.-L. Maurette (ten), M. Brodard (bar), R. Nolte (bass), E. Kalvelage (pno), C. Spering (org), M. Jorand (perc)—Toast pour le nouvel an, Roméo, La Grande Coquette, Un sou, Chanson de Zora, La Nuit de Noël, Le Dodo des enfants, Le Lazzarone, Adieux à la viel, Soupirs et sourire, L'Orpheline du Tyrol, Choeur de chasseurs démocrates; *Morceaux réservés*—Ave Maria, Les Amants de Séville, Le Chant des Titans, Chant funèbre [F] *(rec Aug. 1992)* Opus 111 ▲ OPS 30-70 [DDD]
Rossini, G.:Péchés de vieillesse, w. C. Spering (cnd), Das Neue Orch—Album Français [F] Opus 111 ▲ OPS 30-74
Schubert, Franz:Die Verschworenen, w. *(soloists unkown)*, C. Spering (cnd), Das Neue Orch Opus 111 ▲ OPS 30-167

Cologne Concerto
Trumpet Concerti of the Italian Baroque, w. Friedemann Immer (baroque tpt), Graham Nicholson (baroque tpt), Werner Ehrhard (vn) MD + G ▲ L 3271 [DDD]

Cologne Gürzenich Chorus
Haydn, J.:Die Schöpfung, w. Jeannette van Dijck (sop), Peter Schreier (ten), Theo Adam (bass), Hans Plumacher (vc), Heinz Detering (db), Fritz Lehan (hpd), G. Wand (cnd), Cologne Gürzenich Orch Accord 2-▲ ACD 200422 [AAD]

Cologne Opera Chorus
Weber, C.M. von:Oberon, w. D. Voigt (sop), D. Ziegler (mez), G. Lakes (ten), B. Heppner (ten), J. Conlon (cnd), Cologne PO EMI Classics 2-▲ CDCB 54739

Cologne Radio Chorus
Berlioz, H.:L'Enfance du Christ, w. M. Zimmermann (mez), J. Aler (ten), E. Wilm Schulte (bass), S. Dean (bass), P. Kang (bass), E. Inbal (cnd), Frankfurt RSO [F] Denon 2-▲ CO 76863/4 [DDD]
Cornelius, P.:Stabat Mater, w. B. Scherler (mez), M. Schmidt (ten), S. Nimsgern (bass-bar), R. Didusch (sgr), H. Schernus (cnd), Cologne RSO [L] *(rec 1978)* Koch Schwann ▲ 3-1086-2 [ADD]
Gluck, C.W.:Orfeo ed Euridice, w. Ruth-Margret Pütz (sop), Elisabeth Söderström (sop), Dietrich Fischer-Dieskau (bar), F. Leitner (cnd), Cappella Coloniensis *(rec live, Cologne, Nov. 8, 1964)* Orfeo d'or 2-▲ 391952

Cologne Radio Chorus (cont.)
Handel, G.F.:Alcina, w. J. Sutherland (sop), N. Procter (cta), N. Monti (ten), F. Wunderlich (ten), T. Hemsley (bar), F. Leitner (cnd), Cappella Coloniensis Melodram 3-▲ CDM 37002
Handel, G.F.:Alcina, w. J. Sutherland (sop), N. Proctor (cta), van Dick (sgr), F. Leitner (cnd), Cappella Coloniensis [I] *(rec live, 1959)* Verona 3-▲ 27011/13 (m) [AAD]
Jessel, L.:Schwarzwaldmädel (sels), w. E. Lind (sop), F. Fehringer (ten), B. Kusche (bar), Hofmann (sgr), Schörg (sgr), Schubart (sgr), Marszalek (cnd), Cologne RSO [G] Acanta ▲ CD 42552 [DDD]
Kálmán, I.:Die Csárdásfürstin (sels), w. E. Köth (sop), F. Fehringer (ten), B. Kusche (bar), Heusser (sgr), Hofmann (sgr), Marszalek (cnd), Cologne Radio Orch [G] Acanta ▲ CD 42435 [DDD]
Kálmán, I.:Gräfin Mariza, w. A. Görner (sop), F. Wunderlich (ten), B. Kusche (bar), Hartung (sgr), Hofmann (sgr), Marszalek (cnd), Cologne Radio Orch [G] Acanta ▲ CD 42479 [DDD]
Kreutzer, C.:Das Nachtläger in Granada, w. R. Klepper (sop), M. Pabst (ten), H. Prey (bar), H. Froschauer (cnd), Cologne RSO Capriccio ▲ 60029 [DDD]
Künneke, E.:The Alluring Flame, w. Birgit Fandrey (sgr—Dolores), Christianne Hossfeld (sgr—Lisbeth), Maria Mallé (sgr), Jürgen Sacher (ten—Master), Ralf Lukas (bar—Hoffman), Gerd Grochowski (sgr—1st Neighbor), Gerhard Peters (sgr—Friedrich), Zoran Todorovic (sgr—Jacinto), Theodor Weimer (sgr—2nd Neighbor), P. Falk (cnd), Cologne RSO *(rec Cologne, Nov 7-26, 1994)* Capriccio ▲ 10753 [DDD]
Künneke, E.:Die grosse Sünderin (sels), w. M. Cunitz (sop), R. Schock (ten), Bajew (sgr), Gehly (sgr), Rau (sgr), Schröder (sgr), Weigelt (sgr), Marszalek (cnd), Cologne RSO [G] Acanta ▲ CD 42483 [DDD]
Künneke, E.:Der Vetter aus Dingsda (sels), w. G. Van Jüten (sop), Kollo (ten), B. Kusche (bar), Wolff (sgr), Breck (sgr), Geese, Künneke (cnd), Cologne RSO [G] Acanta ▲ CD 43460 [DDD]
Lehár, F.:Paganini (sels), w. A. Schlemm (mez), Lisolette Losch (sop), P. Anders (ten), Gehly (sgr), Hofmann (sgr), Schneider (sgr), Marszalek (cnd), Cologne RSO [G] Acanta ▲ CD 43810 [DDD]
Mozart, W.A.:Don Giovanni, w. S. Ghazarian (sop), G. Ottenthal (sop), P. Pace (sop), G. Sabbatini (ten), R. Bruson (bar), A. Rinaldi-Miliani (bar), F. De Grandis (bass), N. Ghiuselev (bass), N. Järvi (cnd), Cologne RSO [I] Chandos 3-▲ CHAN 8920/22 [DDD]
Mozart, W.A.:Thamos, w. T. Stich-Randall (mez), A. Deloire (mez), J. Traxel (ten), T. Adam (b-bar), M. Rossi (cnd), Cologne RSO [G] *(rec live, Cologne May 20, 1956)* Melodram 3-▲ CDM 37084 [AAD]
Orff, C.:De temporum fine comoedia, w. C. Ludwig (mez), P. Schreier (ten), J. Greindl (bass), H. von Karajan (cnd), Cologne RSO [L] Deutsche Grammophon ("20th Century Classics" series) ▲ 429859-2 [ADD]
Rossini, G.:La Cenerentola, w. E. Ravaglia (sop), L. V. Terrani (mez), F. Araiza (ten), E. Dara (bar), G. Ferro (cnd), Cappella Coloniensis [I] Sony Classical 2-▲ S2K 46433 [ADD]
Rossini, G.:L'italiana in Algeri, w. L. V. Terrani (mez), L. Rizzi (cta), W. Ganzarolli (bar), E. Dara (bar), G. Ferro (cnd), Capella Coloniensis [period instruments] [I] CBS 2-▲ M2K 39048 [ADD]
Rossini, G.:Stabat Mater, w. E. Grümmer (sop), M. von Ilosvay (mez), C. Ludwig (mez), H. Fehn (bass), F. Fricsay (cnd), Cologne RSO [L] *(rec 1953)* Melodram ▲ CDM 16523 [AAD]
Schoeck, O.:Massimilla Doni, w. E. Mathis (sop), A. Küttenbaum (mez), H. Winkler (ten), H. Stamm (bass), G. Albrecht (cnd), Cologne RSO [G] Koch Schwann 2-▲ CD 314025 [DDD]
Schoenberg, A.:Friede auf Erden *(rec June 26, 1958)* Arkadia ▲ 769 [ADD]
Straus, O.:The Merry Nibelungs, w. Lisa Griffith (sop—Kriemhild), Gudrun Volkert (sop—Brunhilde), Daphne Evangelatos (cta—Ute), Gabriele Henkel (sgr—Giselher), Christine Mann (sgr—Vogel), Hein Heidbüchel (ten—Volker), Martin Gantner (sgr—Gunther), Gerd Grochowski (sgr—Dankwart), Michael Nowak (sgr—Siegfried), Josef Otten (sgr—Hagen), S. Köhler (cnd), Cologne RSO *(rec Cologne, Jan 31-Feb 17, 1995)* Capriccio ▲ 10752 [DDD]
Strauss (II), Joh.:Der Zigeunerbaron (sels), w. S. Jurinac (sop), W. Hollweg (ten), P. Anders (ten), K. Schmitt-Walter (bar), Schneider (sgr), G. Hann (bass), Marszalek (cnd), Cologne RSO [G] Acanta ▲ CD 43807 [DDD]
Verdi, G.:Requiem Mass, w. Gré Brouwenstijn (sop), Oralia Dominguez (mez), Giuseppe Zampieri (ten), Nicola Zaccaria (bass), G. Solti (cnd), Cologne RSO *(rec Nov 17, 1958)* Bella Voce 2-▲ 107.201 [AAD]
Wagner, R.:Lohengrin, w. H. Braun (sop—Ortrud), T. Epperle (sop—Elsa von Brabant), P. Anders (ten—Lohengrin), C. Kronenberg (bar—Frederich von Telramund), J. Greindl (bass—Heinrich der Vogler), R. Kraus (cnd), Cologne RSO *(rec Nov. 1951)* Myto 3-▲ MCD 93485
Weill, K.:Aufstieg und Fall der Stadt Mahagonny, w. A. Silja (sop), A. Schlemm (mez), W. Neumann (ten), T. Lehrberger (ten), K. Hirte (bar), J. Latham-König (cnd), Cologne RSO [G] Capriccio 2-▲ CD 10160/1 [DDD]
B.A. Zimmermann (cnd)
Verdi, G.:Un ballo in maschera, w. Martha Mödl (sop—Ulrica), Walburga Wegner (sop—Amelia), Anny Schlemm (mez—Oscar), Lorenz Fehenberger (ten—Ricardo), Dietrich Fischer-Dieskau (bar—Renato), Wilhelm Schirp (bass—Samuel), Willy Schoneweib (bass—Tom), Gunther Wilhelms (bass—Silvan), Fritz Augustin (sgr—Ein Richter), Friedrich Himmelmann (sgr—Ein Diener Amelia), F. Busch (cnd), Cologne RSO Calig 2-▲ 50946/47 (m) [ADD]

Cologne Vocal Consort
Sonatas & Motets of the Italian Baroque, w. Musica Antiqua Cologne Koch Schwann ▲ SCH 310602 [ADD]

Cologne Youth Chorus
Mendelssohn, Fanny:Oratorio, w. I. Lippitz (sop), Annemarie Fischer-Kunz (cta), H. Hatano (ten), T. Thomaschke (bass), E.M. Blankenburg (cnd), Cologne Youth Orch CPO ▲ CPO 999009-2 [DDD]

Colorado Children's Chorale
Mahler, G.:Sym 8, w. Oksana Krovytska (sop—Magna Peccatrix), Sheila Smith (sop—Una poenitentium), Shauna Southwick (sop—Mater gloriosa), Kristine Jepson (mez—Maria Aegyptiaca), Julie Simson (mez—Mulier Samaritana), Kurt Hansen (ten—Doctor Marianus), Brian Steele (bar—Pater ecstaticus), Eugene Green (b-bar—Pater profundus), R. Olson (cnd), Colorado MahlerFest Orch, Colorado MahlerFest Chorale, Colorado Mormon Chorale *(rec MahlerFest VIII, Boulder, CO, Jan 14-15, 1995)* MahlerFest 2-▲ MF8-1
D. Wolfe (cnd)
A Colorado Kind of Christmas, w. Mike Fitzmaurice (db), Rod Garnet (fl), William Hill (perc), Deborah Schmit-Lobis (pno), Brett Walace (vc), Mary Louise Burke (pno), Laurie Kahler (pno), Helen Hope (hp) *(rec Denver Center Media)* Colorado Children's Chorale ▲ XMAS
Encore, w. Rick Chinski (gtr), Robert Davine (acc), Laurie Kahler (pno), Samuel Lancaster (pno), Barry Oliver (pno), Marylin Preston (fl), Karen Yonovitz (fl), Peter Cooper (ob), Andy Stevens (cl), Lionel Young (vn), Basil Vendreys (va), Wayne Templeman (vc), et al. *(rec Denver Center Media)* Colorado Children's Chorale ▲ 001

Colorado MahlerFest Chorale
Mahler, G.:Sym 8, w. Oksana Krovytska (sop—Magna Peccatrix), Sheila Smith (sop—Una poenitentium), Shauna Southwick (sop—Mater gloriosa), Kristine Jepson (mez—Maria Aegyptiaca), Julie Simson (mez—Mulier Samaritana), Kurt Hansen (ten—Doctor Marianus), Brian Steele (bar—Pater ecstaticus), Eugene Green (b-bar—Pater profundus), R. Olson (cnd), Colorado MahlerFest Orch, Colorado Mormon Chorale, Colorado Children's Chorale *(rec MahlerFest VIII, Boulder, CO, Jan 14-15, 1995)* MahlerFest 2-▲ MF8-1

Colorado Mormon Chorale
Mahler, G.:Sym 8, w. Oksana Krovytska (sop—Magna Peccatrix), Sheila Smith (sop—Una poenitentium), Shauna Southwick (sop—Mater gloriosa), Kristine Jepson (mez—Maria Aegyptiaca), Julie Simson (mez—Mulier Samaritana), Kurt Hansen (ten—Doctor Marianus), Brian Steele (bar—Pater ecstaticus), Eugene Green (b-bar—Pater profundus), R. Olson (cnd), Colorado MahlerFest Orch, Colorado MahlerFest Chorale, Colorado Children's Chorale *(rec MahlerFest VIII, Boulder, CO, Jan 14-15, 1995)* MahlerFest 2-▲ MF8-1

Columbia Pro Cantare Women's Ensemble
Janácek, L.:The Diary of One Who Disappeared, w. S. Love (mez), G. Hirst (ten), Kubalek (pno) [Cz] Arabesque ▲ Z 6513 [DDD]

La Columbina
Encina, J. del:Vocal Music, w. Claudio Cavina (alt), Josep Benet (ten), Josep Cabré (baryton)—Triste España sin ventura; Antonilla es desposada; Tan buen ganadico; Mi libertad en sossiego; Pues que tú, Reina del cielo; Cucú, cucú, cucucú *(rec Vereenigde Doopsgezinde Kerk, Haarlem, The Netherlands, Apr 1995)* Accent ▲ ACC 95111 [DDD]

La Columbina (cont.)
Guerrero, F.:Vocal Music, w. Claudio Cavina (alt), Josep Benet (ten), Josep Cabré (bar)—Niño Dios, d'amour herido; Prado verde y florido; Huyd, huyd; Si tus penas no pruevo; Todo quanto pudo dar *(rec Vereenigde Doopsgezinde Kerk, Haarlem, The Netherlands, Apr 1995)* Accent ▲ ACC 95111 [DDD]
Jeudi Saint dans les Espagnes, w. Maria Cristina Kiehr (sop), Claudio Cavina (ct), Josep Benet (ten), Josep Cabré (bar) Accent ▲ 9394 [DDD]
Romero, M.:Vocal Music, w. Claudio Cavina (alt), Josep Benet (ten), Josep Cabré (bar)—¿A quién contaré mis quejas?; En Belén están mis amores; Como suele el blanco zisne; Soberana María; Las voces del fuego *(rec Vereenigde Doopsgezinde Kerk, Haarlem, The Netherlands, Apr 1995)* Accent ▲ ACC 95111 [DDD]
Vásquez, J.:Vocal Music, w. Claudio Cavina (alt), Josep Benet (ten), Josep Cabré (bar)—A, hermosa, abrime cara de rosa; ¿Con qué la lavaré?; Torna, Mingo, a namorarte; Si no os uviera mirado; En la fuente del rosel; Soledad tengo de tí; Buscad buen amor; O dulce contemplación; De los álamos vengo, madre *(rec Vereenigde Doopsgezinde Kerk, Haarlem, The Netherlands, Apr 1995)* Accent ▲ ACC 95111 [DDD]

Columbus Boychoir
Boito, A.:Mefistofele (sels), w. N. Moscona (bass), A. Toscanini (cnd), NBC SO, Robert Shaw Chorale—Prologue RCA Gold Seal ▲ 60276-2-RG [ADD] ■ 60276-4-RG
Britten, B.:War Requiem, w. Jeanine Altmeyer (sop), Douglas Lawrence (ten), Michael Sells (bar), Ladd Thomas (org), W. Hall (cnd), William Hall Orch, William Hall Chorale Klavier ▲ KCD 11017 [ADD]

Columbus Consort
Christmas in Early America:18th Century Carols & Anthems *(rec June 1993)* Channel Classics ▲ CCS 5693 [DDD]

Con Vivium
Sowerby, L.:Songs, w. Patricia Snyder (org), Ronald Stalford (org)—18 Christmas Songs Albany ▲ TROY 187 [DDD]

Concentus Musicae Antiquae Vocal Group
Astorga, E. d':E pur Cesare ha vinto, w. Elisabetta Battaglia (sop) Nuova Era ("Ancient Music" series) ▲ NUO 7198 [DDD]
Astorga, E. d':Stabat Mater, w. Elisabetta Battaglia (sop), Mapelli (sgr), Narita (sgr), Zaramella (sgr) Nuova Era ("Ancient Music" series) ▲ NUO 7198 [DDD]
Haydn, J.:Stabat Mater, w. R. Lampo (sop), S. Zaramella (alt), V. Martino (ten), P. Turner (bass), D. Ferrari (cnd), Milan Sinfonietta Nuova Era ▲ NUO 7170 [DDD]
Ricci, F.P.:Dies irae, w. D. Ferrari (cnd), Capriccio Italiano Ensemble Nuova Era ▲ NUO 7244
Ricci, F.P.:Miserere, w. D. Ferrari (cnd), Capriccio Italiano Ensemble Nuova Era ▲ NUO 7243
Ricci, F.P.:Stabat Mater, w. D. Ferrari (cnd), Capriccio Italiano Ensemble Nuova Era ▲ NUO 7243

Concentus Vocalis Vienna
H. Böck (cnd)
Bruckner, A.:Motets—Ave Maria; Christus factus est; Os Justi; Tota pulchra; Virga Jesse [L] Koch Schwann ▲ 317008 [ADD]
Distler, H.:Totentanz [G] Koch Schwann ▲ 317008 [ADD]

Concert de Les Arts
V. Alonso (cnd)
Morales, C. de:Sacred Music—Lamentabatur Jacob [motet]; Mille Regretz [chanson & mass] Accord ▲ ACD 204662 [DDD]

Le Concert des Nations
J. Savall (cnd)
Mozart, W.A.:Requiem, w. M. Figueras (sop), C. Schubert (alt), G. Türk (ten), J. Schreckenberger (bass), La Capella Reial de Catalunya Astrée ▲ E 8759
Music at the Time of Beaumarchais, w. Montserrat Figueras (sop), Lawrence Monteyro (sop), Raphel Oleg (vn), Miguel da Silva (va), Christophe Coin (vc), Marc Coppey (vc), José Miguel Moreno (gtr), Paul Badura-Skoda (pno), Philippe Cassard (pno), Eric Le Sage (pno), Bob Van Asperen (hpd), et al. Valois ▲ V 4767
Vox Aeterna, w. La Capella Reial de Catalunya, Hesperion XX Fontalis ▲ 9902

Concert Spirituel Vocal Ensemble
Boismortier, J.B. de:Motets, w. H. Niquet (cnd), Concert Spirituel Orch—Motet à grand choeur; Motet à voix seule mêlés de symphonies Adda ▲ ADD 581255 [DDD]
Campra, A.:Messe de Requiem, w. Véronique Gens (sop), Anne Gotkovski (sop), Jean-Paul Fouchécourt (alt), Joseph Cornwell (ten), Peter Harvey (bar), H. Niquet (cnd), Concert Spirituel Orch Adda ▲ ADD 241952 [DDD]
Campra, A.:Motets, w. Véronique Gens (sop), Anne Gotkovski (sop), Jean-Paul Fouchécourt (alt), Douglas Nasrawi (ten), Peter Harvey (bar), Marcos Loureiro de Sá (bar), Kevin Mallon (vn), H. Niquet (cnd), Concert Spirituel Orch—Te Deum; Notus in Judea Deus; Deus in Nomine Tuo Adda ▲ ADD 241942 [DDD]
Campra, A.:Motets, w. Véronique Gens (sop), Anne Gotkovski (sop), Jean-Paul Fouchécourt (alt), Joseph Cornwell (ten), Peter Harvey (bar), H. Niquet (cnd), Concert Spirituel Orch—Benedictus Dominus Adda ▲ ADD 241952 [DDD]
Campra, A.:Motets, w. Véronique Gens (sop), Anne Gotkovsky (sop), Jean-Paul Fauchecourt (ct), Hervé Lamy (ten), Peter Harvey (bass), H. Niquet (cnd), Concert Spirituel Orch—2 Noster Refugium; Cantato Domino; De Profundis Adda ▲ ADD 243912
Gilles, J.:Sacred Music, w. H. Niquet (cnd), Concert Spirituel Orch—Motet a St. Jean Baptiste; Lamentation du mercredi soir; Lamentation du jeudi soir; Lamentation du vendredi soir Adda ▲ ADD 242322

H. Niquet (cnd)
Campra, A.:Missa, "Cui titulus Ad majorem Dei gloriam" Adda ▲ ADD 243912
Charpentier, M.-A.:A la vierge *(rec Notre-Dame du Liban, Paris, Mar 27-31, 1995)* Naxos ▲ 8.553174 [DDD]
Lully, J.-B.:Motets, w. I. Desrochers (sop), D. Favat (sop), R. Duguay (ct), H. Lamy (ten), P. Harvey (bass)—Te Deum; Miserere; Plaude laetare Gallia *(rec Nov. 22-25, 1993)* FNAC Music ▲ 592308 [DDD]

Concerto Palatino Choir
Biber, H. von:Missa alleluja, w. K. Junghänel (cnd), Gradus ad Parnassum, Vienna Hofburgkapelle Choir Deutsche Harmonia Mundi ▲ 05472-77326-2 [DDD]
Schmelzer, J.H.:Vesperae solennes, w. K. Junghänel (cnd), Vienna Hofburgkapelle Choir, Gradus ad Parnassum Deutsche Harmonia Mundi ▲ 05472-77326-2 [DDD]
Schütz, H.:Symphoniae sacrae 1, w. Barbara Borden (sop), Nele Gramss (sop), Rogers Covey-Crump (ten), John Potter (ten), Douglas Nasrawi (ten), Harry van der Kamp (bass) Accent 2-▲ 9178/79 [DDD]

E. van Nevel (cnd)
Wert, G. de:Sacred Music, w. H. Stinders (org), Currende Vocal Ensemble—Missa Dominicalis; sels. from *Motectorum quinque vocum, liber primus, Il secondo libro de motetti a cinque voci & Modulationem cum sex vocibus, liber primus* Accent ▲ 9291 [DDD]

Concerto Polacco
M. Toporowski (cnd)
Förster, K.:Music of—Sonata *(rec St. Peter & Paul Church, Wroctaw, Poland, Apr 11-18, 1994)* Musicon ▲ MCD 015 [DDD]
Luparini, G.B.:Music of—In martirio crudele *(rec St. Peter & Paul Church, Wroctaw, Poland, Apr 11-18, 1994)* Musicon ▲ MCD 015 [DDD]
Szarzynski, S.S.:Choral Music—Ad hymnos ad cantus; Litania cursoria *(rec St. Peter & Paul Church, Wroctaw, Poland, Apr 11-18, 1994)* Musicon ▲ MCD 015 [DDD]
Wronowicz, M.:Music of—Lauda Sion; In dulci iubilo; De Profundis; Laudate Dominum *(rec St. Peter & Paul Church, Wroctaw, Poland, Apr 11-18, 1994)* Musicon ▲ MCD 015 [DDD]

Concerto Vocale
Bach, J.S.:Music of, w. R. Jacobs (cnd), Ensemble 415—Excerpts from Cants & Passions; Toccata & Fugue in d; excerpts from Well-Tempered Clavier Harmonia Mundi ("Great Baroque Composers" series) 3-▲ HMX 390873.75
Charpentier, M.-A.:Leçons de ténèbres, H. 96-110—3 du jeudi [L] Harmonia Mundi France ▲ HMC 901006

Concerto Vocale (cont.)
Charpentier, M.-A.:Leçons de ténèbres, H. 96-110—1ère leçon du mercredi ('Incipit lamentatio Jeremiae'), 2de leçon du mercredi ('VAU. Et egressus est'), 3ème leçon du mercredi ('JOD. Manum suam') Harmonia Mundi France ▲ HMC 901005 [ADD]
Charpentier, M.-A.:Motets Musique d'Abord ▲ HMA 1901149
Charpentier, M.-A.:Rèpons de chaque jour—In monte Oliveti, Tristis est anima mea, Amicus meus Harmonia Mundi France ▲ HMC 901005 [ADD]
Ferrari, B.:Cants—Queste pugenti spine; Pur ti miro, pur ti godo [I] Harmonia Mundi France ▲ HMC 901129
Handel, G.F.:Cants—Nos. 47, "Parti l'idolo mio," & 56, "Sento là che ristretto" [I] Musique d'Abord ▲ HMA 1901004 [DDD];
Handel, G.F.:Italian Duets (22)—Nos. 12, 13, 18 [I] Musique d'Abord ▲ HMA 1901004 [DDD];
Handel, G.F.:Music of, w. Lorraine Hunt (sop), Kenneth Gilbert (hpd), et al., D. Mintner (cnd), Philharmonia Baroque Orch, Ensemble 415—sels. from Duetto "Tanti strali"; Flavio; Giulio Cesare; Harpsichord Suite No. 5; Nisi Dominus; Susanna; Water Music *(rec 1976-79)* Harmonia Mundi Plus ▲ HMP 390804
Marenzio, L.:Madrigals [I] Musique d'Abord ▲ HMA 1901065
Monteverdi, C.:Lamento d'Arianna [I] Harmonia Mundi France ▲ HMC 901129
Monteverdi, C.:Madrigals [I] Harmonia Mundi France ▲ HMC 901129
Pergolesi, G.B.:Stabat mater, w. S. Henning (trb), R. Jacobs (alt) Harmonia Mundi ("Luxury Edition" series) ▲ HMX 2901119
Schütz, H.:Kleine geistliche Konzerte (sels), w. R. Jacobs (cnd)—4 selections from Op. 9 (1639)—Hodie Christus natus est, SWV 315; Rorate coeli desuper, SWV 322; Joseph, du Sohn David, SWV 323; Sei gegrüsset, Maria, SWV 333 [G,L] Harmonia Mundi France ▲ HMC 901310
Schütz, H.:Kleine geistliche Konzerte (sels) [G,L] Harmonia Mundi France ▲ HMC 901097
Schütz, H.:Symphoniae sacrae 1—sels. [G] Harmonia Mundi France ▲ HMC 901097

R. Jacobs (cnd)
Cavalli, P.F.:Calisto, w. Maria Bayo (sop), Graham Pushee (ct), Simon Keenlyside (bar), Marcello Lippi (bar) Harmonia Mundi France 3-▲ HMC 901515/17
Charpentier, M.-A.:Leçons de ténèbres, H. 96-110, w. J. Nelson (mez), Verkinderen (sgr)—H.105, 106, 110 [L] Harmonia Mundi France ▲ HMC 901007
Handel, G.F.:Music of, Ensemble 415—Suite Hpd in E; Water Music (sels); Opera arias & excerpts Harmonia Mundi ("Great Baroque Composers" series) 3-▲ HMX 390873.75
Monteverdi, C.:Incoronazione, w. D. Borst (sop), Lootens (sop), G. Laurens (mez), J. Larmore (mez), A. Köhler (alt), M. Schopper (bass) [direction & new musical realization by René Jacobs] [I] Harmonia Mundi France 3-▲ HMC 901330/32
Monteverdi, C.:Madrigals—A Dio, Florida bella, from Book 6 [I] Musique d'Abord ▲ HMA 1901084
Monteverdi, C.:Orfeo, w. Efrat Ben Nun (sop—Euridice), Laurence Dale (ten—Orfeo) Harmonia Mundi France ▲ HMC 901553.54
Monteverdi, C.:Ritorno d'Ulisse, w. L. Hunt (sop), C. Högman (sop), B. Fink (cta), D. Vissé (ct), C. Prégardien (ten), G. Tucker (ten), D. Thomas (bass) [I] Harmonia Mundi France 3-▲ HMC 901427/29
Monteverdi, C.:Sacred Vocal Music [L] Musique d'Abord ▲ HMA 1901032
Monteverdi, C.:Vespro della Beata Vergine, w. Barbara Borden (sop), Maria Cristina Kiehr (sop), Andreas Scholl (alt), John Bowen (ten), Andrew Murgatroyd (ten), Victor Torres (bar), Antonio Abete (bass), Jelle Draijer (bass), Netherlands Chamber Choir Harmonia Mundi 2-▲ 901566.67
Schütz, H.:Die Geburt unsers Herren Jesu Christi [G] Harmonia Mundi France ▲ HMC 901310
Schütz, H.:Heute ist Christus [G] Harmonia Mundi France ▲ HMC 901310
Schütz, H.:Historia Harmonia Mundi France ▲ HMC 901311
Schütz, H.:Kleine geistliche Konzerte (sels)—4 selections from Op. 9 (1639)—Hodie Christus natus est, SWV 315; Rorate coeli desuper, SWV 322; Joseph, du Sohn David, SWV 323; Sei gegrüsset, Maria, SWV 333 [G,L] Harmonia Mundi France ▲ HMC 901310
Schütz, H.:Music of, Ensemble 415—Italian Madrigals; 'Nativity' excerpts; Sacred Concerts Harmonia Mundi ("Great Baroque Composers" series) 3-▲ HMX 390873.75
Schütz, H.:Il primo libro de madrigali—Op. 1, Nos. 1-18 Musique d'Abord ▲ HMA 1901162

Concierto Montilla Chorus
Carrion, M.R.:La Tempestad, w. L. Huarte (sop), D. Perez (sop), A. Kraus (ten), F. Kraus (bar), R. Alonso (bass), S. Ramalle (bass), E. Estella (cnd), Concierto Montilla Orch Montilla ▲ MON 3011 [ADD]

Concinite de Louvain Choir
K. Aerts (cnd)
Palestrina, G.:Sacred Music—Impropères du vendredi saint; Ave Regina caelorum; Adoramus te Christe; Pueri Habraeorum; Jesu Res admirabilis; In adventu; Dominus dixit; Alleluia, Dominus dixit; Puer natus est nobis; Allelui, Dies sancti Arion ▲ ARN 68274 [AAD]

Conservatorium Choir
Gounod, C.:Messe solennelle 3 de Pâques, w. D.R. Davies (cnd), Jubilee Orch, St. Mary's Cathedral Choir Walsingham Classics ▲ WAL 8011 [DDD]

Consort of Voices
Bizet, G.:L'Arlésienne, w. R. Haydon Clark (cnd), Consort of London Collins Classics ▲ 11412 [DDD]

Consortium Musicum Chorus
Dvořák, A.:Stabat Mater, w. A. Pusar-Jerik (sop), E. N. Houska (mez), J. Reja (ten), F. Petrusanec (bass), M. Munih (cnd), Consortium Musicum Orch [L] Vivace 2-▲ 140141 [ADD/DDD]

Consortium Vocale
H.M. Borchgrevink (cnd)
Laudes Victoria ▲ VCD 19097

Contemporary Choir
Ohana, M.:Avoaha, w. R. Hayrabedian (cnd), Musicatreize Opus 111 ▲ OPS 30-109
Ohana, M.:Lys de Madrigaux, w. R. Hayrabedian (cnd), Musicatreize Opus 111 ▲ OPS 30-109
Stravinsky, I.:Les Noces, w. M. Quercia (sop), S. Cooper (mez), P. Capelle (ten), P. Marinov (bass), Vieuxtemps (pno), R. Conil (pno), Arzoumanian (pno), Raynaut (pno), R. Hayrabedian (cnd), Strasbourg Percussion Ensemble Pierre Verany ▲ PV 787032 [DDD]

Contorum Choir
Taylor, B.J.:Wuthering Heights, w. Dave Willets (sgr), L. Garrett (sop), C. Carter (sgr), J. Sladdon (sgr), S. Campbell (sgr), Philharmonia Orch Silva America ▲ SSD 1008 ■ SSC 1008

Convent Avenue Concert Choir
Spirituals, w. Conrad, Barbara (mez), Gregory Hopkins (cnd), New England Symphonic Ensemble *(rec Convent Avenue Baptist Church, Harlem, NY & Fisher Hall, Santa Rosa, CA, Mar. 27, 1994 & May 23, 1)* Naxos ▲ 8.553036 [DDD]

Copenhagen Boys' Choir
Janácek, L.:Slavonic Mass, w. T. Kiberg (sop), R. Stene (cta), P. Svensson (ten), U. Cold (bass), C. Mackerras (cnd), Danish National RSO, Danish National Radio Choir Chandos ▲ CHAN 9310 [DDD]
Kodály, Z.:Psalmus hungaricus, w. P. Svensson (ten), C. Mackerras (cnd), Danish National RSO, Danish National Radio Choir Chandos ▲ CHAN 9310 [DDD]
Mahler, G.:Sym 8, w. Majken Bjerno (sop), Henriette Bonde-Hansen (sop), Inga Nielsen (sop), Kirsten Dolberg (alt), Anne Gjevang (alt), Raimo Sirkiä (ten), Jorma Hynninen (bar), Carsten Stabell (bass), L. Segerstam (cnd), Danish National RSO, Berlin Phil Choir, Danish National Radio Choir Chandos 2-▲ CHAN 9305/06 [DDD]
Nielsen, C.:Hymnus Amoris, w. I. Nielsen (sop), A. Elkrog (ten), P. Elming (ten), P. Høyer (bar), J. Ditlevsen (bass), L. Segerstam (cnd), Danish National RSO, Danish National Radio Choir [L] Chandos ▲ CHAN 8853 [DDD]

E. Munk (cnd)
Palestrina, G.:Sacred Music—Missa Papae Marcelli; Motets for the Major Festivals of the Church Year Danica ▲ DCD 8163

Copenhagen Schola Cantorum
Josquin Desprez:Motets—Tu solus; Christe, Fili Dei; Mente tota; Tu pauperum refugium; O Domine Jesu Christe; Qui jacuisti mortuus *(rec 1984 & 1987)* Danacord ▲ DACOCD 390
Victoria, T.L. de:Motets—Eram quasi agnus; Tamquam ad latronem; Cagliaverunt oculi mei; Astiterunt reges terrae; Sepulto Domino; Vere languores; O vos Omnes; Sancta Maria; Senex puerum portabat; Domine, nom sum dignus *(rec 1984; 1987)* Danacord ▲ DACOCD 390

Copenhagen Univ Choir

J.G. Jørgensen (cnd)

Brahms, J.:Motets (misc)—Warum ist da Licht gegeben, Op. 74/1 Point ▲ PCD 5110
Bruckner, A.:Locus iste Point ▲ PCD 5110
Cour, N. la:Missa Brevis Point ▲ PCD 5115
Cour, N. la:Motetti Latini (3) Point ▲ PCD 5115
Dvořák, A.:Mass Point ▲ PCD 5110
Holmboe, V.:Benedic Domino Point ▲ PCD 5115
Holmboe, V.:Laudate Dominum Point ▲ PCD 5115
Holmboe, V.:Speravi in Domino Point ▲ PCD 5115
Reger, M.:Geistliche Gesänge, Op. 110—No. 3 [O Tod, wie bitter bist du] Point ▲ PCD 5110
Rossini, G.:O salutaris hostia Point ▲ PCD 5110

N. Muus (cnd)

Heise, P.:Songs—Drikkevise, No. 80/6; Afsked med Vinteren, No. 80/4; Den vilde Rosenbusk, No. 80/5; De smukke, No. 81/3; I Skoven, No. 81/2; Zigøjnernes Sang ved deres Dronnings Grav, No. 82/5; Maanen smiler, No. 85; Tre Katte, No. 87/4; Jylland, No. 78; Til Bacchus, No. 77 Danica ▲ DCD 8141
Kuhlau, F.:Songs—Rejsesang, Op. 67/2; Aarle Morgen, Op. 82/8; Aftenen, Op. 82/3; Amor, Op. 89/5; Skyen, Op. 82/9; Elskovsguden, Op. 67/4; Ihr Vögel zwitschert, No. 183/1; Anticherubinismus, No. 183/10; Majsang, Op. 67/1 Danica ▲ DCD 8141

T. Vetö (cnd)

Liszt, F.:Missa choralis, w. Irene Graaner (sop), Else Paaske (alt), Kai Hansen (ten), Michael Hansen (bar), Hans Christian Andersen (bass), Niels Henrik Nielsen (org) Point ▲ PCD 5075 [ADD]
Liszt, F.:Salve regina Point ▲ PCD 5075 [ADD]

Coral Ridge Chorus

Bish, D.:A Sym of Hymns, w. Sung Sook Lee (sop), D. Bish (org), D. James Kennedy (nar), R. McMurrin (cnd), Coral Ridge Orch [E] VQR Digital ▲ QR 2041 [DDD]

Cordoba Children's Choir

Les Chemins du Baroque (The Paths of the Baroque), w. G. Garrido (cnd), Elyma Vocal Ensemble, Elyma Instrumental Ensemble, Compañia Musical de las Americas, Maîtrise National de Versailles, La Grande Ecurie et la Chambre du Roy [cnd:Jean-Claude Malgoire], Compañia Musical de las Americas, La Fenice [cnd:Josep Cabré], Ense K617 ("First 4 volumes of K617" series) ▲ 7042
Les Chemins du Baroque (The Paths of the Baroque), Vol. 1:Lima-Plata Jesuit Missions, w. G. Garrido (cnd), Elyma Vocal Ensemble, Elyma Instrumental Ensemble K617 ▲ 7025 [DDD]

E. Sanchez (cnd)

Baroque Music at the Royal Audience of Charcas, w. G. Garrido (cnd), Capella Cisplatina, Elyma Ensemble, Luis Berger Ensemble *(rec Apr 19–24, 1996)* K617 ▲ 7064 [DDD]

Cori Spezzati Vocal Ensemble

O. Opdebeeck (cnd)

Palestrina, G.:Officium tenebrarum, w. Harvé Lamy (ten) Jade 2-▲ JADC 114

Cork Children's Choir

Green, P.:Mass of St. Francis of Assisi, "Let Me Bring Love", w. Bernadette Greevy (mez), Sydney MacEwan (bar), David Budway (pno) Alanna ▲ ALA 5553

Coronation Choir

Vaughan Williams, R.:Festival Te Deum, w. E. Bullock (cnd), Coronation Orch *(rec Westminster Abbey, at the Coronation of King George VI & Queen Elizabeth, 5/12/37)* Pearl ▲ GEMMCD 9342 (m) [AAD]

Corydon Singers

M. Best (cnd)

Barber, S.:Agnus Dei [L] Hyperion ▲ CDA 66219 [DDD]
Beethoven, L. van:Mass, Op. 86, w. Janice Watson (sop), Jean Rigby (mez), John Mark Ainsley (ten), Gwynne Howell (bass), Corydon Orch Hyperion ▲ CDA 66830
Berlioz, H.:L'Enfance du Christ, w. Jean Rigby (mez), John Aler (ten), Gerald Finley (ten), Alastair Miles (bar), Gwynne Howell (bass), Cordon Orch, St. Paul's Cathedral Choir Hyperion 2-▲ CDA 66991/2
Bernstein, L.:Chichester Psalms[He] Hyperion ▲ CDA 66219 [DDD]
Britten, B.:A Boy Was Born, w. Westminster Cathedral Choristers [E] Hyperion ▲ CDA 66126
Britten, B.:Festival Te Deum [E] Hyperion ▲ CDA 66126
Britten, B.:Rejoice in the Lamb [E] Hyperion ▲ CDA 66126
Britten, B.:St. Nicolas, w. Anthony A. Rolfe-Johnson (ten), English CO Hyperion ▲ CDA 66333
Britten, B.:A Wedding Anthem, "Amo ergo sum" [E] Hyperion ▲ CDA 66126
Bruckner, A.:Choral Music, w. Corydon Orch—Aequalis 1 & 2; Libera me; Masses 1–3; Psalm 150; Te Deum Hyperion 3-▲ 44071/3
Bruckner, A.:Mass 1, w. Corydon Orch Hyperion ▲ CDA 66650
Bruckner, A.:Motets—11 [L] Hyperion ▲ CDA 66062
Bruckner, A.:Psalm 112, w. English CO Hyperion ▲ CDA 66245 [DDD]
Bruckner, A.:Psalm 114, w. English CO Hyperion ▲ CDA 66245 [DDD]
Bruckner, A.:Requiem, w. J. Rodgers (sop), C. Denley (mez), M. Davies (ten), M. George (bass), Corydon Singers, English CO Hyperion ▲ CDA 66245 [DDD]
Bruckner, A.:Te Deum, w. *(soloist unknown)*, Corydon Orch Hyperion ▲ CDA 66650
Cherubini, L.:Funeral March, w. Corydon Orch Hyperion ▲ CDA 66805
Cherubini, L.:Requiem Mass in c, w. Corydon Orch Hyperion ▲ CDA 66805
Copland, A.:In the Beginning, w. C. Denley (mez) [E] Hyperion ▲ CDA 66219 [DDD]
Copland, A.:Motets (4)—Help us, O Lord; Have mercy on us; Sing ye praises [E] Hyperion ▲ CDA 66219 [DDD]
Duruflé, M.:Requiem, w. Murray, Allen, English CO [L] Hyperion ▲ CDA 66191 [DDD]
Fauré, G.:Ave Verum, w. J. Scott (org) Hyperion ▲ CDA 66292
Fauré, G.:Cantique de Jean Racine, w. J. Scott (org) Hyperion ▲ CDA 66292
Fauré, G.:Messe basse (in 3 movts), w. M. Seers (sop), J. Scott (org) Hyperion ▲ CDA 66292
Fauré, G.:Requiem, w. I. Poulenard (sop), M. George (bass), English CO [1893 version] Hyperion ▲ CDA 66292
Fauré, G.:Tantum ergo, w. J. Scott (org) Hyperion ▲ CDA 66292
Finzi, G.:Intimations of Immortality, w. John Mark Ainsley (ten), Corydon Orch Hyperion ▲ CDA 66876
Howells, H.:Requiem, w. *(soloists & orch unknown)* [L,E] Hyperion ▲ CDA 66076 [AAD]
Howells, H.:Take Him, Earth for Cherishing [L,E] Hyperion ▲ CDA 66076 [AAD]
Rachmaninoff, S.:Liturgy of St John Chrysostom Hyperion ▲ CDA 66703
Vaughan Williams, R.:Choral Hymns, w. J. Bowen (ten), City of London Sinfonia [E] Hyperion ▲ CDA 66569 [DDD]
Vaughan Williams, R.:Fant on Christmas Carols, w. T. Allen (bar), English CO [E] Hyperion ▲ CDA 66420 [DDD]
Vaughan Williams, R.:Flos Campi, w. N. Imai (va), English CO Hyperion ▲ CDA 66420 [DDD]
Vaughan Williams, R.:Hugh the Dover, w. R. Evans (sop), S. Walker (mez), B. Bottone (ter), N. Jenkins (ten), A. Opie (bar), R. Van Allan (bass), Corydon Orch, New London Children's Choir Hyperion 2-▲ CDA 66901/02
Vaughan Williams, R.:Magnificat, w. C. Wyn-Rogers (alt), City of London Sinfonia [E] Hyperion ▲ CDA 66569 [DDD]
Vaughan Williams, R.:Mass in g [L] Hyperion ▲ CDA 66076 [AAD]
Vaughan Williams, R.:Mystical Songs, w. T. Allen (bar), English CO [E] Hyperion ▲ CDA 66420 [DDD]
Vaughan Williams, R.:The Old 100th Psalm Tune, w. City of London Sinfonia [E] Hyperion ▲ CDA 66569 [DDD]
Vaughan Williams, R.:Sacred Songs, w. J. Howarth (sop), J.M. Ainsley (ten), T. Allen (bar), Corydon Orch—Towards the Unknown Region; Dona nobis pacem; O Clap your hands; Lord, Thou hast been our refuge; 4 Hymns Hyperion ▲ CDA 66655 [DDD]
Vaughan Williams, R.:Serenade to Music, w. English CO [E] Hyperion ▲ CDA 66420 [DDD]
Vaughan Williams, R.:Te Deum [L] Hyperion ▲ CDA 66076 [AAD]
Villa-Lobos, H.:Choral Music, w. Corydon Orch—Missa Sao Sebastiao; Magnificat Alleluia; Bendita Sabedoria; Ave Maria; Pater noster; Cor dulce, cor amabile; Panis angelicus; Praesepe; Sub tuum Hyperion ▲ CDA 66638

Cossack Ensemble

V. Ciolkovitch (cnd)

Russian Songs & Liturgical Choruses Forlane ▲ FRL 19124 [DDD]

Cracow Boys' Choir

Penderecki, K.:St. Luke Passion, w. S. van Osten (sop), S. Roberts (bar), K. Rydl (bass), E. Lubaszenko (narr), K. Penderecki (cnd), Polish National RSO Katowice, Warsaw National Phil Chorus Argo ▲ 430328-2 [DDD]

J. Mentel (cnd)

Mahler, G.:Sym 3, w. Ewa Podles (cta), A. Wit (cnd), Polish National RSO Katowice, Cracow Phil Choir *(rec Concert Hall of the Polish National Radio, Katowice, Nov 12–16, 1994)* Naxos 2-▲ 8.550525-6 [DDD]

Cracow Phil Boys' Choir

Penderecki, K.:The Passion & Death of Our Lord Jesus Christ According to St. Luke, w. Leszek Herdegen (nar), Stefania Woytowicz (sop), Andrzej Hiolski (bar), Bernard Ladysz (bass), H. Czyz (cnd), Cracow PO, Cracow Phil Mixed Choir Polskie Nagrania 2-▲ PNCD 017 A/B
Szymanowski, K.:King Roger, w. B. Zagòrzanka (sop), A. Malewicz-Madey (cta), H. Grychnik (ten), W. Ochman (ten), A. Hiolski (bar), L. A. Mròz (bass), K. Stryja (cnd), Polish State PO Katowice, Polish State Phil Chorus *(rec Apr. 7–9, 1990)* Marco Polo ("Opera Classics" series) 2-▲ 8.223339/40 [DDD]

Cracow Phil Chorus

Nicolai, O.:Te Deum, w. Bozena Betley (sop), Zofie Kilanowicz (sop), Katarztna Suska (cta), Henryk Grychnik (ten), Czeslaw Galka (bar), Jerzy Gruszczynski (bass), R. Bader (cnd), Cracow PO Koch Schwann ▲ SCH CD 310872
Penderecki, K.:The Passion & Death of Our Lord Jesus Christ According to St. Luke, w. Leszek Herdegen (nar), Stefania Woytowicz (sop), Andrzej Hiolski (bar), Bernard Ladysz (bass), H. Czyz (cnd), Cracow PO, Cracow Phil Boys' Chorus Polskie Nagrania 2-▲ PNCD 017 A/B
Suppé, F. von:Requiem, w. Aleksandra Baranska (sop), Katarzyna Suska (cta), Jerzy Knetig (ten), Andrjez Hiolski (bass), R. Bader (cnd), Cracow PO Koch Schwann ▲ SCH CD 312482

J. Mentel (cnd)

Mahler, G.:Sym 3, w. Ewa Podles (cta), A. Wit (cnd), Polish National RSO Katowice, Cracow Boys' Choir *(rec Concert Hall of the Polish National Radio, Katowice, Nov 12–16, 1994)* Naxos 2-▲ 8.550525-6 [DDD]

Cracow Polish Radio-TV Chorus

Mahler, G.:Sym 2, w. H. Lisowska (sop), J. Rappé (ten), A. Wit (cnd), Polish National RSO Katowice *(rec Jan. 9–17, 1993)* Naxos 2-▲ 8.550523/24 [DDD]
Moniuszko, S.:Haunted Manor, w. Bozena Betley-Siradzka (sop—Hanna), Anna Witkowska (sop—Marta/Stara Niewiasta), Wiera Baniewicz (mez—Jadwiga), Aleksandra Imalska (mez—Czesnikowa), Kazimierz Dluha (Grzes), Zdzislaw Nikodem (ten—Damazy), Wieslaw Ochman (ten—Stefan), Andrzej Hiolski (bar—Miecznik), Florian Skulski (bar—Maciej), Leonard Mróz (bass—Zbigniew), Andrzej Saciuk (bass—Skoluba), J. Krenz (cnd), Cracow Polish Radio-TV Orch *(rec Cracovia, 1978)* Agorá Music ("Phoenix" series) 3-▲ 509 [ADD]
Petitgirard, L.:Le Légendaire, w. A. Dumay (vn), L. Petitgirard (cnd), Classic Polonaise PO Orchestre Symphonique France ▲ OSF 49013 [DDD]
Vaughan Williams, R.:Flos Campi, w. J. Kosmala (va), S. Kawalla (cnd), Polish National RSO Cracow Centaur ▲ CRC 2094 [ADD]
Warren, E.R.:Good Morning, America!, w. E. Zimbalist, Jr. (nar), S. Kawalla (cnd), Cracow Polish Radio-TV SO [E] Cambria ▲ CD 1042 [DDD]

Cracow Radio Chorus

Mussorgsky, M.:Boris Godunov, w. N. Gedda (ten—Dmitri), M. Talvela (bass—Boris), J. Semkow (cnd), Cracow RSO EMI Classics ▲ CDCC 54377
Warren, E.R.:Abram in Egypt, w. Thomas Hampson (bar), B. Ferden (cnd), Cracow RSO *(rec Church of the Bernardines, Cracow, Poland, June 21–24, 1993)* Cambria ▲ CD 1095 [DDD]
Warren, E.R.:The Harp Weaver, w. Thomas Hampson (bar), B. Ferden (cnd), Cracow RSO *(rec Church of the Bernardines, Cracow, Poland, June 21–24, 1993)* Cambria ▲ CD 1095 [DDD]
Warren, E.R.:The Sleeping Beauty, w. Maria Venuti (mez—Princess), Thomas Hampson (bar—Prince), Gerd Nienstedt (b-bar—King), David Lutz (pno), B. Ferden (cnd), Cracow RSO *(rec Church of the Bernardines, Cracow, Poland, June 21–24, 1993)* Cambria ▲ CD 1095 [DDD]

Crème de la Crème

Crème de la Crème Sampler Disc Sheffield Lab ▲ CD CRM

Croatian Radio-TV Choir

Monteverdi, C.:Vespro della Beata Vergine, w. L. von Matačić (cnd), Zagreb PO *(rec live, 1974)* Memories 2-▲ MEM 4598

Crystal Cathedral Choir

Swann, F.:Anthems Gothic ▲ G 49048

F. Swann (cnd)

O Magnify the Lord Gothic ▲ GOT 49048

Cuba Coro Exaudi

M.F. Pérez (cnd)

Salas y Castro, E.:Villancicos—Un musiquito nuevo; Pues logra ya; Una nave mercantil; Cándido corderito; Si al ver en el Oriente; Qué niño tan bello; Los bronces se enternezcan; Toquen presto a fuego *(rec Dominican Convent Church of Sant Juan de Letrán, Havana, Cuba, July 17–23, 1995)* Milan ▲ 73138 35746-2 [DDD]

Currende Vocal Ensemble

Carissimi, G.:Oratorios, w. E. van Nevel (cnd), Currende Instrumental Ensemble—Ezechia, Jephte & Vanitas Vanitatum [L] Accent ▲ 9059 [DDD]
Early Music of the Netherlands, 1600–1700, w. Ensemble dell'Anima Eterna, Jos van Immerseel (kbd) Emergo ▲ 3986
Lassus, O. de:Patrocinium musicus cantionum, w. *(soloists unknown)*, E. van Nevel (cnd), Concerto Palatino Accent ▲ 8855
Renaissance:polyfonie uit de Nederlanden *(rec Mar. 13–16, 1986)* Eufoda ▲ EUF 1104

E. van Nevel (cnd)

Esteves, J.R.:Missa a oito voces, w. H. Stinders (org) [L] Accent ▲ 9069 [DDD]
Scarlatti, D.:Stabat mater, w. H. Stinders (org) [L] Accent ▲ 9069 [DDD]
Schütz, H.:Cantiones sacrae—SWV.56–66, 69, 71–75, 78–82 [L] *(rec 2/91)* Accent ▲ 9174
Wert, G. de:Sacred Music, w. H. Stinders (org), Concerto Palatino Choir—Missa Dominicalis; sels. from *Motectorum quinque vocum, liber primus, Il secondo libro de motetti a cinque voci & Modulationem cum sex vocibus, liber primus* Accent ▲ 9291 [DDD]

Czech Chamber Choir

Zelenka, J.D.:Miserere, ZWV 57, w. R. Válek (cnd), Baroque 1994 Ensemble Supraphon ▲ SUP 0052 [DDD]
Zelenka, J.D.:Requiem, ZWV 48, w. R. Válek (cnd), Baroque 1994 Ensemble Supraphon ▲ SUP 0052 [DDD]

Czech Chamber Singers Female Chorus

Janácek, L.:The Diary of One Who Disappeared, w. Véra Soukupová (mez), Stepanka Stepanova (mez), Beno Blachut (ten), Nicolai Gedda (ten), Josef Palenícek (pno), Prague Radio Women's Chorus—contains 2 complete performances *(rec 1984 & 1956)* Supraphon ▲ SUP 0022 [DDD/ADD]

Czech Chorus

Dvořák, A.:Arias & Scenes, w. Miroslav Kopp (ten), Z. Košler (cnd), Czech PO—from The King of Charcoal Burner, The Stubborn L Panton ▲ PAN 811189
Dvořák, A.:Requiem Mass, w. G. Benačková (sop), B. Fassbaender (mez), T. Moser (ten), J.-H. Rootering (bass), W. Sawallisch (cnd), Czech PO [L] Supraphon 2-▲ 10 4241 [DDD]
Dvořák, A.:Requiem Mass, w. Maria Stader (sop), Sieglinde Wagner (cta), Ernst Haefliger (ten), Kim Borg (b-bar), K. Ančerl (cnd), Czech PO Deutsche Grammophon ("Double" series) 2-▲ 437377-2
Dvořák, A.:Rusalka (sels), w. Gabriela Benačková (sop), Vera Soukupová (mez), Richard Novák (bass), V. Neumann (cnd), Czech PO Supraphon ▲ SUP 112252 [DDD]
Honegger, A.:Jeanne d'Arc au bûcher, w. C. Château (sop), A.M. Rodde (sop), H. Brachet (mez), P. Proenza (ten), Z. Jankovsky (ten), F. Loup (bass), S. Baudo (cnd), Czech PO *(rec 1974)* Supraphon 2-▲ 11 0557-2 [AAD]

▲ = CD ♦ = Enhanced CD Δ = MD ∎ = Cassette Tape ◻ = DCC

Czech Chorus (cont.)

Honegger, A.:Le Roi David, w. Christiane Eda–Pierre (sop), Martha Senn (mez), Tibere Raffalli (ten), D. Mesguich (nar), A. Gaillard (nar), S. Baudo (cnd), Czech PO [F] Supraphon 2–▲ 11 0132 [DDD]

Czech Phil Children's Choir

Mahler, G.:Sym 3, w. Marta Benačková (alt), V. Neumann (cnd), Czech PO, Prague Chamber Choir *(rec House of Artists, Prague, Aug–Sept 1994)* Canyon Classics 2–▲ CD 256

Czech Phil Chorus

Beethoven, L. van:Sym 9, "Choral Sym", w. V. Neumann (cnd), Czech PO Supraphon 3–▲ SUP 0546 [AAD]

Borodin, A.:Prince Igor (Polovtsian dances), w. V. Smetáček (cnd), Czech PO Supraphon Collection ▲ 11 0622–2 [ADD]

Chabrier, E.:Gwendoline, w. Adriana Kohútková (sop—Gwendoline), Gérard Garino (ten—Armel), Didier Henry (bar—Harald), J.–P. Pepin (cnd), Slovak PO, Slovak Phil Chorus L'Empreinte Digitale 2–▲ ED 13059

Dvořák, A.:Dmitrij, w. *(soloists unknown)*, G. Albrecht (cnd), Czech PO [Cz] *(rec 1989)* Supraphon 3–▲ 11 1259–2 [DDD]

Dvořák, A.:Music of, w. Frederica von Stade (mez), Itzhak Perlman (vn), Yo–Yo Ma (vc), Rudolf Firkusny (pno), S. Ozawa (cnd), Boston SO—Carnival Ov., Op. 92; Romance in f for Vn & Orch, Op. 11; Klid [Silent Woods] for Vc & Orch, Op. 68/5; Humoresque in G♭, Op. 101/1 & 7; Mesíčku na nebi hlubokém [from Rusalka, Op. 114]; Psalm 149 for Chorus & Orch, Op. 79; Gypsy Songs for Voice & Piano, Op. 55/4 & 5; Allegro [from Trio for Vn, Vc & Pno, Op. 90]; Slavonic Dances, Op. 72/2 & 7 *(rec Smetana Hall, Prague, Dec. 16, 1993)* Sony Classical ("Front Line" series) ▲ SK 46687 [DDD]; ■ ST 46687

Dvořák, A.:St Ludmilla, w. Vera Soukupová (mez), Eva Zikmundová (mez), Beno Blachut (ten), Richard Novák (bass), V. Smetáček (cnd), Prague SO *(rec 1963)* Supraphon 2–▲ SUP 112141 [AAD]

Dvořák, A.:The Spectre's Bride, Op. 110, w. J. Krombholc (cnd), Czech PO *(rec 1961)* Supraphon 2–▲ SUP 111982 [DDD]

Dvořák, A.:Stabat Mater, w. Drahomira Tikalova (sop), Marta Krasova (cta), Beno Blachut (ten), Karel Kalas (bass), V. Talich (cnd), Czech PO *(rec 1952)* Supraphon 2–▲ SUP 111902 [ADD]

Dvořák, A.:Stabat Mater, w. G. Benačková (sop), O. Wenkel (cta), P. Dvorsky (ten), J.–H. Rootering (bass), W. Sawallisch (cnd), Czech PO [L] Supraphon 2–▲ 10 3561–2 [DDD]

Eben, Petr:Con 2 Org, "Symphonia gregoriana", w. K. Klugarova (org), L. Pešek (cnd), Czech PO [Cz] Panton ▲ 81 1141–2911

Eben, Petr:Missa cum populo, w. J. Ksica (org), L. Mátl (cnd), chamber ensemble [Cz] Panton ▲ 81 1141–2911

Fibich, Z.:The Romance of Spring, w. K. Šejna (cnd), Czech PO Supraphon ("Czech Philharmonic" series) ▲ SUP 111920 [AAD]

Hovhaness, A.:Tzaikerk, w. Paul Edmund–Davies (fl), Arnold Kobyliansky (vn), Randy Max (timp), R. Werthen (cnd), I Fiamminghi CO *(rec Basilica of Bonne Espérance, Vellereille–les–Brayeux, Belgium, Aug. 18–20, 1994)* Telarc ▲ CD 80392 [DDD]

Janáček, L.:The Cunning Little Vixen, w. G. Benačková (sop—Goldskin), M. Hajóssyová (sop—Cunning Little Vixen), R. Novák (bass—Forester), V. Neumann (cnd), Czech PO, Kühn Children's Chorus [Cz] *(rec 1979–80)* Supraphon 2–▲ 10 3471–2 [AAD]

Janácek, L.:The Excursions of Mr. Brouček, w. Janá Jonaová (sop), Libuše Márová (mez), Vilém Přibyl (ten), Richard Novák (bass), Czech PO Supraphon 2–▲ SUP 112153 [AAD]

Janácek, L.:Slavonic Mass, w. Gabriela Benacková (sop), Vera Soukupová (cta), Frantisek Livora (ten), Karel Pruss (bass), V. Neumann (cnd), Czech PO Panton ▲ PAN 811217

Janácek, L.:Slavonic Mass, w. *(soloists unknown)*, K. Ančerl (cnd), Czech PO [Cz] *(rec 1960–66)* Supraphon ▲ SUP 11 1930 [AAD]

Janácek, L.:Slavonic Mass, w. *(sloists unknown)*, K. Ančerl (cnd), Czech PO Supraphon Collection ▲ 110609

Janácek, L.:Slavonic Mass, w. Elisabeth Söderström (sop), Drahomira Drobkova (cta), František Livora (ten), Richard Novák (bass), C. Mackerras (cnd), Czech PO Supraphon ▲ SUP 103575 [DDD]

Mahler, G.:Sym 2, w. G. Benačková (sop), E. Randova (mez), V. Neumann (cnd), Czech PO *(rec June 11–16, 1980)* Supraphon ▲ 11 1971–2 [AAD]

Mahler, G.:Sym 3, w. C. Ludwig (mez), V. Neumann (cnd), Czech PO *(rec Dec. 16–19, 1981)* Supraphon 3–▲ 11 1972–2 [DDD]

Mahler, G.:Sym 8, w. V. Neumann (cnd), Czech PO *(rec Feb. 10–14, 1982)* Supraphon 3–▲ 11 1972–2 [DDD]

Martinů, B.:Ariadne, w. C. Lindsley (sop), V. Dolezal (ten), R. Novák (ten), N. Phillips (bar), V. Neumann (cnd), Czech PO [Cz] Supraphon ▲ 10 4395–2 [DDD]

Martinů, B.:Bouquet, w. Libuše Domanínská (sop), Soňa Červená (alt), Lubomír Havlák (ten), Ladislav Mráz (bass), K. Ančerl (cnd), Czech PO *(rec 1967)* Praga ("Karel Ančerl Edition" series) ▲ PR 254061

Martinů, B.:Bouquet, w. K. Ančerl (cnd), Czech PO, Kühn Children's Chorus *(rec 1955–56)* Supraphon ▲ SUP 11 1932 [ADD]

Martinů, B.:The Epic of Gilgamesh, w. M. Machotková (sop), J. Zaradníček (ten), V. Zítek (bar), K. Průša (bass), J. Belohlávek (cnd), Prague SO Supraphon ▲ SUP 11 1824 [ADD]

Martinů, B.:Field Mass, w. Václav Zítek (bar), V. Neumann (cnd), Czech PO Panton ▲ PAN 811217

Martinů, B.:Field Mass, w. I. Kusnjer (bar), M. Kejmar (tpt), B. Kotmel (cnd), Czech PO [Cz] Chandos ▲ CHAN 9138 [DDD]

Martinů, B.:The Greek Passion, w. Helen Field (sop), John Mitchinson (ten), Phillip Joll (b–bar), John Tomlinson (bass), C. Mackerras (cnd), Brno State PO [E] *(rec 1981)* Supraphon 2–▲ 10 3611–2 [DDD]

Mysliveček, J.:Belerofonte, w. C. Lindsleyová (sop), G. Mayová (sop), K. Lakiová (sop), D. Ahlstedt (ten), R. Gimenéz (ten), S. Margita (ten), Z. Peskó (cnd), Prague CO [I] *(rec 1987)* Supraphon 3–▲ 11 0006–2 [DDD]

Novák, V.:Storm, w. Maria Tauberová (sop), Drahomíra Tikalová (sop), Beno Blachut (ten), Ladislav Mráz (bar), J. Krombholc (cnd), Czech PO *(rec 1956)* Supraphon 2–▲ SUP 111982 (m) [DDD]

Novák, V.:Storm, w. Jarmila Zilková (sop), Jarmila Smycková (sop), Frantisek Livora (ten), Z. Košler (cnd), Czech PO Supraphon ▲ SUP CD 3088

Pergolesi, G.B.:Stabat mater, w. Tynes (sop), Turner–Butler (alt), M. Bruni (cnd), Prague CO [L] *(rec 1968)* Supraphon Collection ▲ 11 0620–2 [ADD]

Prokofiev, S.:They Are 7, w. J. Kachel (ten), K. Ančerl (cnd), Czech PO Praga ▲ PR 254004

Ravel, M.:Daphnis et Chloé (suite 2), w. S. Baudo (cnd), Czech PO Sound ▲ CD 3441

Reicha, A.:Der neue Psalm, w. Magdaléna Hajóssyová (sop), Anna Barová (mez), Andreas Schmidt (bar), Karel Průša (bass), L. Mátl (cnd), Dvořák CO Panton ▲ PAN 810758 [DDD]

Reicha, A.:Requiem, w. V. Hrubá–Freiberger (sop), A. Barová (mez), V. Dolezal (ten), L. Vele (bass), L. Mátl (cnd), Dvořák CO [L] Supraphon ▲ 11 0332–2 [DDD]

Roussel, A.:Evocations, w. Marie Mrázová (cta), Zdenek Svehla (ten), Jindřich Jindrák (bar), Z. Košler (cnd), Czech PO Supraphon ▲ SUP 111823 [AAD]

Schoenberg, A.:A Survivor from Warsaw, w. V. Neumann (cnd), Czech PO Supraphon ▲ SUP 0177 [AAD]

Smetana, B.:The Bartered Bride, w. G. Benačková (sop), P. Dvorsky (ten), R. Novak (bass), Z. Košler (cnd), Czech PO [Cz] Supraphon 3–▲ 10 3511–2 [DDD]

Smetana, B.:The Bartered Bride (orch sels), w. Gabriela Benačková (sop), Peter Dvorsky (ten), Miroslav Kopp (ten), Z. Košler (cnd), Czech PO Supraphon ▲ SUP 112251 [DDD]

Smetana, B.:Choral Music, w. Miroslav Švejda (ten), Vratislav Jahna (bar), Jaroslav Horáček (bass), Z. Košler (cnd), Prague SO, Prague Radio Chorus Supraphon ▲ SUP CD 3040

Suk, J.:Epilogue, w. Z. Jehličková (sop), I. Kusnjer (bar), J. Galla (bass), V. Neumann (cnd), Czech PO [Cz] Supraphon ▲ 11 0116–2 [DDD]

Zelenka, J.D.:Missa Gratias agimus tibi, w. J. Jonášová (sop), M. Mrázová (cta), V. Dolezal (ten), P. Mikuláš (bass), J. Belohlávek (cnd), Czech PO [L] Supraphon ▲ 11 0816–2 [DDD]

M. Bruni (cnd)

Palestrina, G.:Stabat mater [L] *(rec 1975)* Supraphon Collection ▲ 11 0620–2 [ADD]

L. Mátl (cnd)

Dvořák, A.:Choral Music, w. J. Kšica (org)—Ave Maria; Ave maris stella; Hymns ad laudes; O sanctissima Supraphon ▲ SUP 11 1430 [DDD]

Dvořák, A.:Mass, w. J. Kasica (org) Supraphon ▲ SUP 11 1430 [DDD]

Czech Phil Chorus (cont.)

L. Mátl (cnd) (cont.)

Janácek, L.:Amarus, w. Kvetoslava Nemeckova (sop), Leo Marian Vodicka (ten), Vaclav Zitek (bar), Jan Hora (org), C. Mackerras (cnd), Czech PO *(rec 1984)* Supraphon ▲ SUP CD 3045

Zelenka, J.D.:Responsoria pro Hebdomada Sancta [L] Supraphon ▲ 11 0816–2 [DDD]

Zelenka, J.D.:Sub tuum praesidium 3 [L] Supraphon ▲ 11 0816–2 [DDD]

J. Veselka (cnd)

Janácek, L.:Slavonic Mass, w. Gabriela Benackova (sop), Eva Randova (cta), Vilem Pribyl (ten), Sergej Kopack (bass), F. Jílek (cnd), Brno State PO *(rec 1979)* Supraphon ▲ SUP CD 3045

Lassus, O. de:Psalmi Davidis poenitentiales Supraphon ▲ SUP 112159 [AAD]

Palestrina, G.:Missa "Hodi Christus" Supraphon ▲ SUP 11 2137 [AAD]

Palestrina, G.:Missa "Papae marcelli" Supraphon ▲ SUP 11 2137 [AAD]

Palestrina, G.:Stabat mater Supraphon ▲ SUP 11 2137 [AAD]

Czech Phil Women's Chorus

Kabeláč, M.:Sym 5, w. L. Domanínská (sop), K. Ančerl (cnd), Czech PO *(rec live)* Panton ▲ 81 1102

Czech Radio–TV Chorus

Bellini, V.:Mass in a, w. Leila Bersiani (sop), Valentina di Cola (sop), Stella Salvati (cta), José Antonio Campo (ten), Carlo Lepore (bass), E. Brizio (cnd), Prague SO *(rec Prague, June 1994)* Studio SM ▲ D 2444

Bellini, V.:Salve Regina in a, w. E. Brizio (cnd), Prague SO *(rec Prague, June 1994)* Studio SM ▲ D 2444

Generali, P.:Sacred Music, w. Leila Bersiani (sop), Valentina di Cola (sop), Emanuela Deffai (mez), Sella Salvati (cta), Paolo Macedonio (ten), Roberto Bencivenga (ten), Carlo Lepore (bass), E. Brizio (cnd), Czech Radio–TV Orch—Magnificat; Domine ad Adjuvandum; Virgam Virtutis; Ecce Virgo; Ave Maria Messe Pastorale; Te Deum *(rec FHS Studios, Prague, 1995)* Studio SM ▲ 2517 [DDD]

Da Camera Choir

E. Kuliberg (cnd)

Nielsen, T.:Black Madrigals Point ▲ PCD 5089

J. Meier (cnd)

Allegri, G.:Miserere [L] Arion ▲ ARN 68003

Byrd, W.:Mass in 4 Parts [L] Arion ▲ ARN 68003

Lassus, O. de:Adoramus te Christe [L] Arion ▲ ARN 68003

Lotti, A.:Miserere [L] Arion ▲ ARN 68003

Victoria, T.L. de:Vere languores nostros [L] Arion ▲ ARN 68003

Dale Warland Singers

Barnett, C.:The Last Invocation Innova ▲ MN 110

Barnett, S.:Songs from Hebrew Poetry Innova ▲ MN 110

Childs, M.E.:Bright Faces Innova ▲ MN 110

Franklin, C.J.:With a Poet's Eye Innova ▲ MN 110

Hodkinson, S.:Expiration Innova ▲ MN 110

Larsen, L.:The Settling Years Innova ▲ MN 110

Paulus, S.:Preludes (4) on Playthings of the Wind Innova ▲ MN 110

D. Warland (cnd)

Allegri, G.:Miserere *(rec St. Paul, MN, Aug 1994)* American Choral Catalog ▲ ACC 120 [DDD]

Barber, S.:Agnus Dei [without accompaniment] *(rec St. Paul, MN, Aug. 1994)* American Choral Catalog ▲ ACC 120 [DDD]

Blue Wheat *(rec Chapel of St. Thomas Aquinas, St. Paul, Aug & Nov 1995)* American Choral Catalog ▲ ACC 122 [DDD]

Carols for Christmas Ten Thousand Lakes ▲ SC 100 [ADD]

December Stillness *(rec Church of the Nativity of Our Lord, St. Paul, MN, Jan. 1995)* American Choral Catalog ▲ ACC 121 [DDD]

Howells, H.:Requiem *(rec St. Paul, MN, Aug. 1994)* American Choral Catalog ▲ ACC 120 [DDD]

Martin, F.:Mass *(rec St. Paul, MN, Aug. 1994)* American Choral Catalog ▲ ACC 120 [DDD]

Dallas Civic Opera Chorus

Donizetti, G.:Lucrezia Borgia, w. L. Gencer (sop), T. Troyanos (mez), J. Carrerras (ten), N. Rescigno (cnd), Dallas Civic Opera Orch *(rec 1973)* Melodram 2–▲ MLO 270109 [ADD]

Dallas Sym Chorus

Gershwin, G.:Porgy & Bess (sels), w. Cynthia Clarey (sop—Serena), Cynthia Haymon (sop—Bess), Damon Evans (ten—Sportin' Life), Gordon Hawkins (bar—Porgy), Andrew Litton (pno), A. Litton (cnd), Dallas SO—Intro/Jasbo Brown; Summertime; A Woman Is a Sometime Thing; Gone, Gone, Gone; My Man's Gone Now; Leavin' for the Promise' Lan'; Oh I Got Plenty O' Nuttin'; Bess, You Is My Woman Now; Oh, I Can't Sit Down; I Ain't Got No Shame; It Ain't Necessarily So; Shame on All You Sinners; I Loves You, Porgy; Hurricane; There's a Boat Dat's Leavin' Soon for New York; Act 3, Scene 3 Orchestral Intro; Good Mornin', Sistuh; Oh Lawd, I'm on My Way! [concert suite arr A. Litton] *(rec Eugene McDermott Hall, Dallas, May 1995)* Dorian ▲ DOR 90223 [DDD]

Mahler, G.:Sym 2, w. S. McNair (sop), J. van Nes (cta), E. Mata (cnd), Dallas SO [G] *(rec 9/89)* Pro Arte 2–▲ CDD 479 [DDD]

Prokofiev, S.:Alexander Nevsky, w. M. Paunova (cta), E. Mata (cnd), Dallas SO *(rec 1992)* Dorian ▲ DOR 90169 [DDD]

Tchaikovsky, P.:Moscow, w. Svetlana Furdui (mez), Vassily Gerello (bar), A. Litton (cnd), Dallas SO *(rec McDermott Hall, Meyerson Center, Dallas, TX, Nov 16–18, 1995)* Delos ("Virtual Reality Recording" series) ▲ DE 3196 [DDD]

Dallas Women's Chorus

T. Seelig (cnd)

Rutter, J.:Church Music, w. J. Martinson (org), Turtle Creek Chorale—Praise Ye the Lord; The Lord Is My Light & My Salvation; All Things Bright & Beautiful; Lord, Make Me an Instrument of Thy Peace *(rec July 28–29, 1993)* Reference ▲ RR 57 CD [DDD]

Rutter, J.:Requiem, w. N. Keith (sop), J. Martinson (org), Turtle Creek Chorale *(rec July 28–29, 1993)* Reference ▲ RR 57 CD [DDD]

Damascenus Choir

Chants of the Eastern Church *(rec 1970)* Entrée ▲ 0005–2 [ADD]

Praise of the Mother of God:Eastern Orthodox Church Music Christophorus ▲ CD 74505

Dana Chorale

G. Smith (cnd)

American Choral Music Dana Recording Project ▲ DRP 1 [DDD]

Danish National Choir

Heise, P.:King & Marshall, w. P. Elming (ten), A. Haugland (bass), C. Christiansen (bass), M. Schønwandt (cnd), Danish National RSO Chandos 3–▲ CHAN 9143 [DDD]

Horneman, C.F.E.:Music of, w. Guido Paevatalu (bar), M. Schønwandt (cnd), Danish National RSO—Gurre; Helteliv; Alladin Ov. Chandos ▲ CHAN 9373 [DDD]

Danish National Radio Chamber Choir

Gade, N.W.:Elverskud, w. E. Johansson (sop), A. Gjevang (cta), P. Elming (ten), D. Kitayenko (cnd), Danish National RSO [Da] Chandos ▲ CHAN 9075 [DDD]

Nielsen, C.:Aladdin, w. M. Ejsing (cta), G. Paevatalu (bar), G. Rozhdestvensky (cnd), Danish National RSO Chandos ▲ CHAN 9135 [DDD]

Nielsen, C.:Motets [L] Chandos ▲ CHAN 8853 [DDD]

Strauss, R.:Choral Music—Der Abend; Hymne; Deutsche Motet; Die Göttin im Puttzimmer; An den Baum Daphne Chandos ▲ CHAN 9223 [DDD]

S. Parkman (cnd)

Gade, N.W.:Songs, Op. 13 [G] Chandos ▲ CHAN 9075 [DDD]

Henze, H.–W.:Orpheus Behind the Wire [E] Chandos ▲ CHAN 8963 [DDD]

Lidholm, I.:...a riveder le stelle [I] Chandos ▲ CHAN 8963 [DDD]

Masters of 20th Century A Cappella Chandos ▲ CHAN 8963 [DDD]

Nørgård, P.:Wie ein Kind, w. *(soloists unknown)* [G] Chandos ▲ CHAN 8963 [DDD]

Pizzetti, I.:Composizioni corali (2) [L] Chandos ▲ CHAN 8964 [DDD]

Pizzetti, I.:Composizioni corali (3) [L] Chandos ▲ CHAN 8964 [DDD]

Pizzetti, I.:Messa di Requiem [L] Chandos ▲ CHAN 8964 [DDD]

Poulenc, F.:Figure humaine [F] Chandos ▲ CHAN 8963 [DDD]

Schoenberg, A.:Friede auf Erden [G] Chandos ▲ CHAN 8963 [DDD]

Danish National Radio Children's Choir
Nielsen, C.:Springtime, w. I. Nielsen (sop), P. Gronlund (ten), S. Byriel (b–bar), L. Segerstam (cnd), Danish National RSO, Danish National Radio Choir [Da] Chandos ▲ CHAN 8853 [DDD]

Danish National Radio Choir
Beethoven, L. van:Sym 9, "Choral Sym", w. Kerstin Lindberg-Torlind (sop), Else Jena (mez), Erik Sjöberg (ten), Holger Byrding (bass), F. Busch (cnd), Danish National RSO Arlecchino ARL
Brahms, J.:Alto Rhap, w. K. Ferrier (cta), F. Busch (cnd), Danish National RSO [G] *(rec 10/6/49)* Danacord ▲ DACOCD 301 (m)
Gluck, C.W.:Alceste (sels), w. K. Flagstad (sop), J. Hye-Knudsen (cnd), Danish Radio Concert Orch—five arias & scenes *(rec live 4/14/57)* Melodram 2-▲ MEL 26514 (m) [AAD]
Janácek, L.:Slavonic Mass, w. T. Kiberg (sop), R. Stene (cta), P. Svensson (ten), U. Cold (bass), C. Mackerras (cnd), Danish National RSO, Copenhagen Boys' Choir Chandos ▲ CHAN 9310 [DDD]
Kodály, Z.:Psalmus hungaricus, w. P. Svensson (ten), C. Mackerras (cnd), Danish National RSO, Copenhagen Boys' Choir Chandos ▲ CHAN 9310 [DDD]
Kuhlau, F.:Elverhøj, w. Bodil Gøbel (sop), Gurli Plesner (cta), Mogens Schmidt Johansen (bar), J. Frandsen (cnd), Danish National RSO *(rec Danish Radio Concert Hall, Aug 1974)* Marco Polo/Dacapo ▲ 8.224053 [AAD]
Kuhlau, F.:Lulu, w. T. Kiberg (sop), A. Frellesvig (sgr), K. von Binzer (ten), R. Saarman (ten), U. Cold (bass), E. Harbo (sgr), M. Schønwandt (cnd), Danish National RSO [Da] Kontrapunkt 3-▲ 32009/11 [DDD]
Langgaard, R.:Sym 14, w. M. Schønwandt (cnd), Danish National RSO *(rec 1979)* Danacord ▲ DACOCD 302
Mahler, G.:Sym 2, w. Tina Kiberg (sop), Kirsten Dolberg (alt), L. Segerstam (cnd), Danish National RSO Chandos 2-▲ CHAN 9266/67 [DDD]
Mahler, G.:Sym 3, w. A. Gjevang (mez), L. Segerstam (cnd), Danish National RSO [G] Chandos 2-▲ CHAN 8970/71 [DDD]
Mahler, G.:Sym 8, w. Majken Bjerno (sop), Henriette Bonde-Hansen (sop), Inga Nielsen (sop), Kirsten Dolberg (alt), Anne Gjevang (alt), Raimo Sirkiä (ten), Jorma Hynninen (bar), Carsten Stabell (bass), L. Segerstam (cnd), Danish National RSO, Copenhagen Boys' Choir, Berlin Phil Choir Chandos 2-▲ CHAN 9305/06 [DDD]
Mussorgsky, M.:Boris Godunov, w. A. Haugland (bass—Boris, Pimen & Varlaam), D. Kitayenko (cnd), Danish Radio Concert Orch [concert version based on Mussorgsky's original 1868–69 version] [R] *(rec live 2/27/86)* Kontrapunkt 2-▲ 32036/37 [DDD]
Nielsen, C.:Choral Music, w. L. Segerstam (cnd), Danish National RSO Chandos ▲ CHAN 8853 [DDD]
Nielsen, C.:Hymnus Amoris, w. I. Nielsen (sop), A. Elkrog (ten), P. Elming (ten), P. Høyer (bar), J. Ditlevsen (bass), L. Segerstam (cnd), Danish National RSO, Copenhagen Boys' Choir [L] Chandos ▲ CHAN 8853 [DDD]
Nielsen, C.:Saul & David, w. T. Kiberg (sop), A. Gjevang (mez), P. Lindroos (ten), K. Westi (ten), C. Christiansen (bass), A. Haugland (bass), J. Klint (bass), N. Järvi (cnd), Danish National RSO [Da] Chandos 2-▲ CHAN 8911/12 [DDD]
Nielsen, C.:Sleep, w. L. Segerstam (cnd), Danish National RSO [Da] Chandos ▲ CHAN 8853 [DDD]
Nielsen, C.:Springtime, w. I. Nielsen (sop), P. Gronlund (ten), S. Byriel (b–bar), L. Segerstam (cnd), Danish National RSO, Danish National Radio Children's Choir [Da] Chandos ▲ CHAN 8853 [DDD]
Nørgård, P.:Sym 3, w. Hedwig Rummel (alt), T. Vetö (cnd), Danish National RSO *(rec live, Danish Radio Concert Hall, 1982)* Marco Polo/Dacapo ▲ 8.224041 [AAD]
Nørgård, P.:Sym 3, w. T. Vetö (cnd), Danish National RSO *(rec live 10/14/82)* Marco Polo/Dacapo ▲ DCCD 8901 [ADD]
Nørholm, I.:Sym 4, w. E. Serov (cnd), Odense SO Kontrapunkt ▲ KPT 32212
Prokofiev, S.:Alexander Nevsky, w. L. Schemtchuk (mez), D. Kitayenko (cnd), Danish National RSO [R] Chandos ▲ CHAN 9001 [DDD]
Rachmaninoff, S.:The Bells, w. E. Ustinova (sop), K. Westi (ten), J. Hynninen (bar), D. Kitayenko (cnd), Danish National RSO Chandos ▲ CHAN 8966 [DDD]
Rachmaninoff, S.:Spring, w. J. Hynninen (bar), D. Kitayenko (cnd), Danish National RSO Chandos ▲ CHAN 8966 [DDD]
Schumann, R.:Der Rose Pilgerfahrt, w. G. Kuhn (cnd), Danish National RSO Chandos ▲ CHAN 9350 [DDD]
Sibelius, J.:Kullervo, w. Siole Isokoski (sop), Raimo Laukka (bar), L. Segerstam (cnd), Danish National RSO Chandos ▲ CHAN 9393 [DDD]
Sørensen, B.:The Echoing Garden, w. Åsa Bäverstam (sop), Martyn Hill (ten), L. Segerstam (cnd), Danish National RSO *(rec live, Danish Radio Concert Hall, 1992 & 1994)* Marco Polo/Dacapo ▲ 8.224039 [DDD]
Tarp, S.E.:Te Deum, w. J. Nelson (cnd), Danish National RSO *(rec Sept. 14, 1988)* Marco Polo ▲ DCCD 9005 [DDD]

P. Enevold (cnd)
Denmark Revisited [Gensyn med Danmark] Danacord ▲ DACOCD 308 [DDD]
Langgaard, R.:The Rose Garden Songs [Da] Danacord ▲ DACOCD 308 [DDD]
Lewkovitch, B.:Danish Madrigals [Da] Danacord ▲ DACOCD 308 [DDD]
Schultz, S.S.:Gensyn med Danmark [Da] Danacord ▲ DACOCD 308 [DDD]

U. Gronostay (cnd)
Bruckner, A.:Choral Music—Afferentur; Ave Maria; Christus factus est; Ecce sacerdos; Locus iste; Os justi; Pange lingua; Tota pulchra es Maria; Vexilla regis; Virga Jesse *(rec 9/85)* Kontrapunkt ▲ 32022 [ADD]
Hindemith, P.:Lieder nach alten Texten Chandos ▲ CHAN 9413 [DDD]
Hindemith, P.:Madrigals—Nos. 2, 5, 7 & 9–11 Chandos ▲ CHAN 9413 [DDD] [DDD]
Hindemith, P.:Mass Chandos ▲ CHAN 9413 [DDD]
Hindemith, P.:Songs on Old Texts Chandos ▲ CHAN 9413 [DDD]
Werner, S.E.:Hommage à Bruckner *(rec 9/85)* Kontrapunkt ▲ 32022 [ADD]

J.G. Jørgensen (cnd)
Koppel, H.D.:Moses, w. Elisabeth Meyer-Topsøe (sop), Kirsten Dolberg (mez), Kurt Westi (ten), Michael Kristensen (ten), Per Høyer (bar), Christian Christiansen (bass), O.A. Hughes (cnd), Danish National RSO *(rec Danish Radio Concert Hall, Mar 1996)* Marco Polo/Dacapo ▲ 8.224046 [DDD]

S. Parkman (cnd)
Jersild, J.:Romantiske korsange Chandos ▲ CHAN 9264 [DDD]
Nordic Light Chandos ▲ CHAN 9464
Nørgård, P.:And Time Chandos ▲ CHAN 9264 [DDD]
Pepping, E.:St. Matthew Passion [G] Chandos ▲ CHAN 8854 [DDD]
Rautavaara, E.:Suite de Lorca Chandos ▲ CHAN 9264 [DDD]
Reger, M.:Geistliche Gesänge, Op. 110 Chandos ▲ CHAN 9298 [DDD]
Sandström, S.-D.:A Cradle Song/The Tyger Chandos ▲ CHAN 9264 [DDD]
Schnittke, A.:Con Chorus Chandos ▲ CHAN 9126 [DDD]
Schnittke, A.:Minnesang Chandos ▲ CHAN 9126 [DDD]
Schnittke, A.:Penitential Psalms, w. Eva Bruun Hansen (sop), Elisabeth Rehling (sop), Annette Simonsen (alt), Maria Streijffert (alt), Karl-Gustav Andersson (ten), Poul Vejbo (ten) Chandos ▲ CHAN 9480
Schnittke, A.:Voices of Nature, w. Gert Sørensen (vib) Chandos ▲ CHAN 9480
Tormis, V.:Invocation of Iron Chandos ▲ CHAN 9264 [DDD]

Danish National Radio Choir Soloists
Reger, M.:Choruses Chandos ▲ CHAN 9298 [DDD]

Dantchenko Moscow Stanislavsky Music Theater Chorus
Kabalevsky, D.:Colas Breugnon (ov), w. N. Isakova (sop), V. Kayevchenko (sop), L. Boldin (bar), N. Gutorovich (bar), G. Dudarev (bass), E. Maksimenko (sgr), G. Zhemchuzhin (cnd), Dantchenko Moscow Stanislavsky Music Theater Orch Olympia 2-▲ OLY 291 [ADD]

Darmstadt Concert Choir
Mangold, C.A.:Abraham, w. Monika Frimmer (sop), Georg Mechthild (mez), B Gärtner (ten), Gerd Türk (ten), Giles Cachemaille (bar), Philadelphia Orch Christophorus 2-▲ 77172
Telemann, G.P.:St. Matthew Passion, w. M. Zedelius (sop), A. Browner (alt), H.P. Blochwitz (ten), W. Schmidt (bar), A. Scharinger (bass), W. Seeliger (cnd), Darmstadt CO Christophorus ▲ 77149 [DDD]

Darmstadt Concert Choir (cont.)

W. Seeliger (cnd)
Brahms, J.:Ots SATB, Op. 64, w. Carmen Piazzini (pno) Entrée ▲ 0080 [ADD]
Mangold, C.A.:Songs—Song in 4 Parts, Op. 22 Entrée ▲ 0080 [ADD]
Mendelssohn, F.:Choruses Entrée ▲ 0080 [ADD]
Schumann, R.:Romanzen und Balladen Entrée ▲ 0080 [ADD]
Wolf, H.:Fröhliche Fahrt Entrée ▲ 0080 [ADD]
Wolf, H.:Grablied Entrée ▲ 0080 [ADD]
Wolf, H.:Im stillen Friedhof, w. Carmen Piazzini (pno) Entrée ▲ 0080 [ADD]

Daughters of St. Paul
A Little Love St. Paul Books & Media ▲ 4472-X ■ 4473-1

Debrecen Kodaly Choir

S. Kamp (cnd)
Franck, C.:Choral Music, w. Mariann Bódi (sop), Attila Wendler (ten), Istvan Rácz (bass)—Quae est ista; Dextera Domini Hungaroton ▲ HCD 31579 [DDD]
Franck, C.:Messe solennelle, w. Attila Wendler (ten), Dezsö Karasszon (org), Andrea Kocsis (hp), Zsolt Molnár (vc), Ferenc Nagy (db) Hungaroton ▲ HCD 31579 [DDD]

Robert DeCormier Chorale
Barber, S.:A Stopwatch & an Ordnance Map, w. V. Golschmann (cnd), Symphony of the Air [E] *(rec ca. 1960)* Vanguard Classics ▲ OVC 4016 [ADD]

Robert DeCormier Singers
Christmas Eve, w. Robert DeCormier Ensemble Arabesque ▲ Z 6527
The First Nowell, w. Robert DeCormier Ensemble Arabesque ▲ Z 6526
A Victorian Christmas, w. Robert DeCormier Ensemble Arabesque ▲ Z 6525

R. DeCormier (cnd)
The Man on the Flying Trapeze:A Celebration of an Era, w. Robert DeCormier Ensemble Arabesque ▲ Z 6588
Oh! You Beautiful Doll, w. Robert DeCormier Ensemble *(rec SUNY/Purchase Performing Arts Center, Feb 5–7, 1996)* Arabesque ▲ Z6675 [DDD]

Delitiae Musicae Vocal Ensemble
Verdelot, P.:Missa Philomena, w. M. Longhini (cnd), Delitiae Musicae Instrumental Ensemble Stradivarius ▲ STV 33405 [DDD]

Deller Consort
Byrd, W.:Mass in 3 Parts, w. A. Deller (ct), N. Jenkins (ten), M. Bevan (bar) [L] Musique d'Abord ▲ HMA 190211
Byrd, W.:Mass in 4 Parts, w. H. Sheppard (sop), A. Deller (ct), N. Jenkins (ten), M. Bevan (bar) [L] Musique d'Abord ▲ HMA 190211
Byrd, W.:Mass in 5 Parts, w. H. Sheppard (sop), A. Deller (ct), J. Buttrey (ten), N. Jenkins (ten), M. Bevan (bar) [L] Musique d'Abord ▲ HMA 190211
A Celebration of Christmas:Carols through the Ages, w. Musica Antiqua of Vienna [cnd:René Clemencic] Vanguard Classics 4-▲ OVC 8050/53 [ADD]
Chant Gregorien Musique d'Abord 3-▲ HMA 190235/37
Dowland, J.:Ayres—sels. Musique d'Abord ▲ HMA 1901076
Elizabethan & Jacobean Music - Airs & Instrumental Music of England, w. N. Harnoncourt (cnd), Consort of Viols [Desmond Dupré (lt), Gustav Leonhardt (hpd), Alfred Deller (ct)] Vanguard Classics ▲ OVC 8102 [ADD]
Gregorian Chant Harmonia Mundi ▲ HMC 90234
Handel, G.F.:Psalms—No. 112, "Laudate pueri," & No. 127, "Nisi Dominus" [L] Musique d'Abord ▲ HMA 1901054
Machaut, G. de:Messe de Nostre Dame Editio Classica ▲ 77064-2-RG [ADD]
Purcell, H.:Love's Goddess Sure Was Blind, w. Stour Music Festival CO [E] Musique d'Abord ▲ HMA 190222
Purcell, H.:Songs [E] Harmonia Mundi France ▲ HMC 90242
Purcell, H.:Welcome to All the Pleasures, w. Stour Music Festival CO [E] Musique d'Abord ▲ HMA 190222

A. Deller (cnd)
Blow, J.:Bring, Shephers, Bring the Kids, w. *(soloists unknown)* [E] Musique d'Abord ▲ HMA 190201
Blow, J.:Chloe Found Amintas [E] Musique d'Abord ▲ HMA 190201
Blow, J.:Ode on the Death of Mr. Henry Purcell [E] Musique d'Abord ▲ HMA 190201
Byrd, W.:Songs—Though Amaryllis Dance; This Sweet & Merry Month *(rec London)* Vanguard Classics ("Alfred Deller Edition" series) ▲ OVC 8103 [ADD]
Buxtehude, D.:Cants—In dulci jubilo; Jubilate Domino [L] Musique d'Abord ▲ HMA 190700 [ADD]
Deller Consort *(rec Reims Cathedral and in Notre Dame, Paris)* Editio Classica ▲ 77064-2-RG [ADD]
The English Madrigal School *(rec Walthamstow Hall, London, July 1955 & July 1958)* Vanguard Classics ("The Bach Guild" series) 2-▲ OVC 2533/34 [ADD]
Gibbons, O.:Instrumental & Vocal Music—Ah, dear heart; Behold thou hast made my days; Great King of Gods; In nomine a 5; Pavan Deleroye; Secret Sins; What is our life [E] *(rec 1970–72)* Musique d'Abord ▲ HMA 190219
Gibbons, O.:Instrumental & Vocal Music—The Silver Swan; What is Our Life?; Ah! Dear Heart; Dainty Fine Bird *(rec London)* Vanguard Classics ("Alfred Deller Edition" series) ▲ OVC 8103 [ADD]
The Holly & the Ivy:Christmas Carols of Old England Vanguard Classics ▲ OVC 8023 (m) [ADD]
Madrigal Masterpieces *(rec 1959)* Vanguard Classics ("The Bach Guild" series) ▲ OVC 2000 [ADD]
Madrigals & Chansons of England, Italy & France Bayer ▲ 100028 [DDD]
Monteverdi, C.:Lamento d'Arianna *(rec Walthamstow Hall, London)* Vanguard Classics ▲ OVC 8100 [ADD]
Monteverdi, C.:Madrigals (book 8), w. Baroque String Ensemble Vanguard Classics ("The Bach Guild" series) ▲ OVC 2519 [ADD]
Pilkington, F.:Vocal Music—Rest, Sweet Nymphs; Diaphenia Like the Daffdowndilly; Have I Found Her; O Softly Singing Lute; Amyntas with His Phyllis Fair *(rec London)* Vanguard Classics ("Alfred Deller Edition" series) ▲ OVC 8103 [ADD]
Purcell, H.:Anthems—Come Ye Sons of Art; Rejoice in the Lamb Always; My Beloved Spake; Welcome to All the Pleasures Vanguard Classics ▲ OVC 8027 [ADD]
Purcell, H.:Catches & Songs [E] Harmonia Mundi France ▲ HMC 90242
Purcell, H.:The Indian Queen, w. King's Musick Harmonia Mundi ("Suite" series) ▲ HMT 790243
Purcell, H.:King Arthur, w. R. Hardy (sop), H. Sheppard (sop), J. Knibbs (cta), A. Deller (ct), M. Deller (alt), P. Elliott (ten), L. Nixon (ten), M. Bevan (bar), N. Beavan (bass), King's Musick [E] Harmonia Mundi France 2-▲ HMC 90252/53
Purcell, H.:My Beloved Spake [E] *(rec 1962)* Vanguard Classics ▲ OVC 8027 [ADD]
Purcell, H.:The Prophetess (sels), w. Vienna Concentus Musicus—instrumental music Vanguard Classics ("The Bach Guild" series) ▲ OVC 2517 [ADD]
Purcell, H.:Rejoice in the Lord Alway [E] *(rec 1962)* Vanguard Classics ▲ OVC 8027 [ADD]
Purcell, H.:Sacred Choral & Vocal Music—In guilty night; Man that is born of a woman Musique d'Abord ▲ HMA 190207 [ADD]
Purcell, H.:Come Ye Sons of Art [E] *(rec 1962)* Vanguard Classics ▲ OVC 8027 [ADD]
Purcell, H.:Te Deum & Jubilate [L] Musique d'Abord ▲ HMA 190207 [ADD]
Purcell, H.:Welcome to All the Pleasures [E] *(rec 1959)* Vanguard Classics ▲ OVC 8027 [ADD]
Shakespeare Songs & Consort Music Harmonia Mundi ▲ HMA 190.202
Tallis, T.:Church Music—Jam lucis orto sidere; Salvator mundi Domine; Deus tuorum militum; Iste confessor; Sermone blando angelus; Jam Christus astra ascenderat; Ex more docti mistico; Te lucis ante terminum [L] Musique d'Abord ▲ HMA 190208 [ADD]
Tallis, T.:The Lamentations of Jeremiah [L] Musique d'Abord ▲ HMA 190208 [ADD]
Tomkins, T.:Instr & Voc Music—Fantasias Nos. 9 & 10; Oyez! Has any found a lad?; I Heard a Voice from Heaven; Pavan; To the shady woods [E] *(rec 1970–72)* Musique d'Abord ▲ HMA 190219
Ward, J.:Madrigals—Retire, My Troubled Soul; Upon a Bank with Roses; Out from the Vale *(rec London)* Vanguard Classics ("Alfred Deller Edition" series) ▲ OVC 8103 [ADD]
Weelkes, T.:Instrumental & Vocal Music—All Laud & Praise; The Cries of London; Fantasy; Lachrimae; O care, thou wilt despatch me; Thule, the period of cosmography; To shorten winter's sadness [E] *(rec 1970–72)* Musique d'Abord ▲ HMA 190219

Les Demoiselles de Saint-Cyr
du Mont, H.:Messes (5) en plain-chant—Messe royale Koch Schwann ▲ SCH 310202 [DDD]
du Mont, H.:Motets—Motets a la vierge Koch Schwann ▲ SCH 310202 [DDD]
E. Mandrin (cnd)
Charpentier, M.-A.:Music of, w. Emmanuel Mandrin (org)—Ave Regina cælorum; Sicut spina rosam; Gaude felix Anna; Magnificat; Quam pulchra es; Omni die dic Mariæ; Alma redemptoris mater; In nativitate; Regina cæli; Alma Dei creatoris; Ego mater agnitionis; Salve Regina; Sub tuum; Litanies de la Vierge; Inviolata integra *(rec Paris, Feb 1995)* FNAC Music ▲ 592036 [DDD]
Clérambault, L.N.:Chants et motets à l'usage de St. Louis à St. Cyr *(rec June 20-24, 1993)* FNAC Music 2-▲ 592316 [DDD]

Detroit Sym Chorus
Debussy, C.:Nocturnes, w. P. Paray (cnd), Detroit SO Mercury Living Presence ▲ 434306-2 [ADD]
Paray, P.:Mass for the 500th Anniversary of the Death of Joan of Arc, w. *(soloists unknown)*, P. Paray (cnd), Detroit SO Mercury Living Presence ▲ 432719-2 [ADD]
Deutsche Opera Chorus
Bach, J.S.:St. Matthew Passion, w. G. Janowitz (sop), C. Ludwig (mez), H. Laubenthal (ten), P. Schreier (ten), W. Berry (bar), D. Fischer-Dieskau (bar), H. von Karajan (cnd), Berlin PO, Vienna Singverein [G] Deutsche Grammophon 3-▲ 419789-2 [ADD]
Berg, A.:Lulu, w. E. Lear (sop—Lulu), P. Johnson (mez—Countess Geschwitz), D. Grobe (ten—Alwa), Fischer-Dieskau (bar—Dr. Schön), K. Böhm (cnd), German Opera Orch [G] *(rec 1968)* Deutsche Grammophon 3-▲ 435705-2 [ADD]
Berg, A.:Wozzeck, w. E. Lear (sop—Marie), F. Wunderlich (ten—Andres), G. Stoltze (ten—The Captain), D. Fischer-Dieskau (bar—Wozzeck), K. Böhm (cnd), German Opera Orch [G] *(rec 1965)* Deutsche Grammophon 3-▲ 435705-2 [ADD]
Bruckner, A.:Psalm 150, w. M. Stader (sop), E. Jochum (cnd), Berlin PO [L] Deutsche Grammophon 4-▲ 423127-2 [ADD]
Bruckner, A.:Te Deum, w. M. Stader (sop), S. Wagner (mez), E. Haefliger (ten), P. Lagger (bass), E. Jochum (cnd), Berlin PO [L] Deutsche Grammophon 4-▲ 423127-2 [ADD]
Debussy, C.:Pelléas et Mélisande, w. N. Denize (mez), F. von Stade (mez), G. Raimondi (ten), R. Stilwell (bar), J. Van Dam (bass-bar), H. von Karajan (cnd), Berlin PO [F] EMI Classics 3-▲ CDCC 49350 [ADD]
Lehár, F.:Die lustige Witwe, w. E. Harwood (sop), T. Stratas (sop), W. Hollweg (ten), R. Kollo (ten), Z. Kelemen (bar), H. von Karajan (cnd), Berlin PO [G] *(rec 1972)* Deutsche Grammophon 2-▲ 435712-2 [ADD]
Mozart, W.A.:Don Giovanni, w. A. Tomowa-Sintow (sop), K. Battle (sop), A. Baltsa (mez), G. Winbergh (ten), S. Ramey (bass), F. Furlanetto (bass), P. Burchuladze (bass), H. von Karajan (cnd), Berlin PO [I] Deutsche Grammophon 3-▲ 419179-2 [DDD]
Mozart, W.A.:Don Giovanni (sels), w. A. Tomowa-Sintow (sop), K. Battle (sop), A. Baltsa (mez), G. Winbergh (ten), S. Ramey (bass), F. Furlanetto (bass), P. Burchuladze (bass), H. von Karajan (cnd), Berlin PO [I] Deutsche Grammophon ▲ 419635-2 [DDD]
Mozart, W.A.:Zauberflöte, w. Edith Mathis (sop), Karin Ott (sop), Janet Perry (sop), Anna Tomowa-Sintow (sop), Agnes Baltsa (mez), Hannah Schwarz (mez), Francisco Araiza (ten), Gottfried Hornik (bar), José Van Dam (b-bar), H. von Karajan (cnd), Berlin PO [G] Deutsche Grammophon 3-▲ 410967-2 [DDD]
Mozart, W.A.:Zauberflöte (sels), w. Edith Mathis (sop), Karin Ott (sop), Janet Perry (sop), Anna Tomowa-Sintow (sop), Agnes Baltsa (mez), Hannah Schwarz (mez), Francisco Araiza (ten), Gottfried Hornik (bar), José Van Dam (b-bar), H. von Karajan (cnd), Berlin PO [G] Deutsche Grammophon ▲ 415287-2 [DDD]
Orff, C.:Carmina burana, w. G. Janowitz (sop), G. Stolze (ten), D. Fischer-Dieskau (bar), G.L. Jochum (cnd), German Opera Orch [G, L] Deutsche Grammophon ("Galleria" series) ▲ 423886-2 [ADD]
Puccini, G.:La Bohème, w. M. Freni (sop), E. Harwood (sop), L. Pavarotti (ten), R. Panerai (bar), H. von Karajan (cnd), Berlin PO [I] London 2-▲ 421049-2 [ADD] 2-■ 421049-4
Puccini, G.:La Bohème (sels), w. M. Freni (sop), E. Harwood (sop), L. Pavarotti (ten), R. Panerai (bar), H. von Karajan (cnd), Berlin PO London ▲ 421245-2 [DDD] ■ 421245-4
Puccini, G.:Tosca, w. K. Ricciarelli (sop), J. Carreras (ten), R. Raimondi (bass), H. von Karajan (cnd), Berlin PO [I] Deutsche Grammophon 2-▲ 413815-2 [ADD]
Strauss, R.:Arias, w. C. Ludwig (mez), W. Berry (b-bar), H. Hollreiser (cnd), German Opera Orch—two of Ariadne's solo arias from Ariadne auf Naxos, duets from Elektra, Frau ohne Schatten, Rosenkavalier [G] *(rec Berlin, 1963-64)* Tessitura ▲ 0049-2 [ADD]
Verdi, G.:Nabucco, w. G. Dimitrova (sop), L. V. Terrani (mez), P. Domingo (ten), P. Cappuccilli (bar), E. Nesterenko (bass), G. Sinopoli (cnd), German Opera Orch [I] Deutsche Grammophon 2-▲ 410512-2 [DDD]
Wagner, R.:Lohengrin, w. A. Tomowa-Sintow (sop), D. Vejzovic (sop), A. Kollo (ten), S. Nimsgern (b-bar), K. Ridderbusch (bass), H. von Karajan (cnd), Berlin PO [G] EMI Classics ("Studio" series) 4-▲ CDMD 69314 [ADD]
Wagner, R.:Die Meistersinger von Nürnberg, w. C. Ligendza (sop), C. Ludwig (mez), P. Domingo (ten), R. Laubenthal (ten), D. Fischer-Dieskau (bar), R. Hermann (bar), P. Lagger (bass), E. Jochum (cnd), German Opera Orch Deutsche Grammophon ("Domingo Edition" series) ▲ 435406-2
Wagner, R.:Die Meistersinger von Nürnberg, w. C. Ligendza (sop), C. Ludwig (mez), P. Domingo (ten), R. Laubenthal (ten), D. Fischer-Dieskau (bar), R. Hermann (bar), P. Lagger (bass), E. Jochum (cnd), German Opera Orch [G] Deutsche Grammophon 4-▲ 415278-2 [ADD]
Wagner, R.:Parsifal, w. D. Vejzovic (sop), P. Hofmann (ten), J. Van Dam (b-bar), S. Nimsgern (b-bar), K. Moll (bass), H. von Karajan (cnd), Berlin PO [G] Deutsche Grammophon 4-▲ 413347-2 [DDD]
Wagner, R.:Tristan und Isolde, w. H. Dernesch (sop), C. Ludwig (mez), J. Vickers (ten), P. Schreier (ten), B. Weikl (bar), W. Berry (bass), K. Ridderbusch (bass), H. von Karajan (cnd), Berlin PO [G] EMI Classics ("Studio" series) 4-▲ CDMD 69319 [ADD]
Dijon Chante Cathedral Children's Choir
Noël Studio SM ("Viva Voce" series) ▲ 1223.67 [DDD]
Disman Radio Children's Choir
J. Karas (cnd)
Domazlicky, F.:Czech Folk Songs, w. Z. Jiroušek (vn), J. Mráček (vn), O. Smola (va), P. Mišejka (vc) *(rec June 1992)* Channel Classics ▲ CCS 5193 [DDD]
Krása, H.:Brunidbár *(rec June 1992)* Channel Classics ▲ CCS 5193 [DDD]
Hugo Distler Chorus
Mozart:Missa Solemnis & Salieri:Te Deum (The Coronation Mass for Leopold II in Prague, September 1791), w. Vienna Academy, Ruth Ziesak (sop), E. von Magnus (mez), H. Wildahaber (ten), G. Hornik (bass), Vienna Hofburg Chapel Choir Novalis ▲ 150087 [DDD]
Dominante Chamber Choir
Bergman, E.:The Singing Tree, w. K. Hannula (sop), C. Hellekant (cta), P. Lindroos (ten), P. Salomaa (bass), S. Tiilikainen (bar), M. Wallén (bass), U. Söderblom (cnd), Finnish National Opera Orch, Tapiola Chamber Choir Ondine 2-▲ ODE 794-2D [DDD]
Dominican Friars of France
A. Gouzes (cnd)
Dominican Liturgy Jade ▲ JAD C 107
Domspatzen Boys' Choir
In Dulci Jubilo, w. James Galway (fl), John Georgiadis (cnd), Munich Radio Orch RCA Red Seal ▲ 60736-2-RC [DDD] ■ 60736-4-RC
Don Cossack Choir
Jaroff (cnd)
Evening Bells Deutsche Grammophon ■ 413257-4 GMF
Dorian Choir
Vaughan Williams, R.:Mystical Songs [E] Manu ▲ 1299
K. Grylls (cnd)
Brahms, J.:Motets (misc)—Opp. 30, 74/1 [G] *(rec 10/91)* Manu ▲ 1299
Howells, H.:Requiem [E] *(rec 10/91)* Manu ▲ 1299
Rautavaara, E.:Suite de Lorca [E] Manu ▲ 1299

Dormagen Boys' Choir
Hasse, J.A.:Miserere in c Orch, w. H. Max (cnd), Das Kleine Konzert, Rhineland Kantorei Capriccio ▲ 10 557 [DDD]
Heinichen, J.D.:Sacred Music, w. H. Max (cnd), Das Kleine Konzert, Rhineland Kantorei—Magnificat in A Capriccio ▲ 10 557 [DDD]
Homilius, G.A.:Vocal Music, w. H. Max (cnd), Das Kleine Konzert, Rhineland Kantorei—Verwundrung, Mitleid, Furcht und Schrecken Capriccio ▲ 10 557 [DDD]
Zelenka, J.D.:Miserere in c, w. H. Max (cnd), Das Kleine Konzert, Rhineland Kantorei Capriccio ▲ 10 557 [DDD]
Dormition of the BVM Church Choir at Monastery of the Virgin
Marienhymnen aus Russland, w. H. Pjotr (cnd), A. Matvey (cnd), Moscow Religious Academy & Seminary, Monastery of the Holy Trinity & St. Sergius Combined Choirs Koch Schwann ▲ SHC 313047 [ADD]
Dormition of the Virgin Church Choir
Russian Choirs Sing for the Children of Chernobyl, w. Moscow Patriarchate Children's Choir, Church of the Resurrection Choir Moscow, Korez Convent Choir, Pyuchtize Convent Choir, Zagorsk Monks' Choir, Moscow Religious Academy Choir, Moscow Religious Academy Choir Koch Schwann ▲ SCH 313322 [ADD/DDD]
Dortmund Univ Chamber Choir
W. Gundlach (cnd)
Distler, H.:Choral-Passion, w. W. Jochens (ten—Evangelist), P. Kooy (bass—Jesus), G. Miehlke (bass—Pilatus) *(rec Mar. 1993)* Thorofon ▲ CTH 2185 [DDD]
Mendelssohn, Fanny:Songs, w. Michaela Krämer (sop), Gerhild Romberger (alt), Alastair Thompson (ten), Gerrit Miehlke (bass), Richard Braun (pno)—Morgendämmerung; Im Herbste; Unter des Laubdachs Hut; Ich stand gelehnet an den Mast; Mitternacht; Abschied; Lockung; Abend; Aus meinen Tränen; Wenn ich in deine Augen seh'; Im wunderschönen Monat Mai; Schöne Fremde; Schweigend sinkt die Nacht hernieder; Nacht liegt auf den fremden Wegen; Hochzeitsbitter; Wandl' ich in dem Wald; Frühzeitiger Frühling; Blumengruss; O Herbst; Schilflied; Feldlied; März; Lichter Mai; Waldruhe; Nachtreigen *(rec Musikhochschule Detmold, Dortmund, Oct 1995)* Thorofon ▲ CTH 2299 [DDD]
Downe House School Choir
Elgar, E.:The Apostles, w. S. Armstrong (sop), H. Watts (cta), R. Tear (ten), J. C. Case (bar), B. Luxon (bar), C. Grant (bass), A. Boult (cnd), London PO, London Phil Chorus [E] EMI Classics ▲ CDMB 64206
Dresden Chamber Choir
Helmschrott, R.:Cross & Freedom, w. Helmut Schatz, Nancy Gibson (sop), Frieder Aurich (ten), Matthias Weichert (bass), Manfred Ball (nar), Anett Baumann (vn), Frank Phillipstch, Linda Robbins, Gerhard Wolf, Martin Homann (perc), Robert M. Helmschrott (org), H.-C. Rademann (cnd), Munich Trombone Quartet Vienna Modern Masters ▲ VMM 3027 [DDD]
H.-C. Rademann (cnd)
Berlinski, H.:Das Gebet Bonhoeffers Vienna Modern Masters ▲ TROCD 01409
Berlinski, H.:Das Gebet Bonhoeffers, w. Nancy Gibson (sop), Matthias Weichert (bass), Olaf Georgi (fl), Bernhard Hentrich (vc), Herman Berlinski (org), Holger Miersch (cel), Martin Homann (perc) Vienna Modern Masters ▲ VMM 3027 [DDD]
Zimmermann, H.W.:Neujahrslied Db, w. Matthias Bohrig (db), Robert M. Helmschrott (org) Vienna Modern Masters ▲ VMM 3027 [DDD]
Zimmermann, U.:Neujahrslied Chorus Vienna Modern Masters ▲ VMM 3027
Dresden Children's Choir
Orff, C.:Carmina burana, w. *(soloists unknown)*, H. Kegel (cnd), Leipzig RSO, Berlin Radio Chorus, Leipzig Radio Chorus Berlin Classics 2-▲ BER 2047 [ADD]
Orff, C.:Catulli Carmina, w. *(soloists unknown)*, H. Kegel (cnd), Leipzig RSO, Berlin Radio Chorus, Leipzig Radio Chorus Berlin Classics 2-▲ BER 2047 [ADD]
Orff, C.:Trionfo di Afrodite, w. *(soloists unknown)*, H. Kegel (cnd), Leipzig RSO, Berlin Radio Chorus, Leipzig Radio Chorus Berlin Classics 2-▲ BER 2047 [ADD]
Dresden Church Choir
Schütz, H.:Die Auferstehung unsres Herren Jesu Christi, w. Peter Schreier (ten), H. Grüss (cnd), Capella Fidicinia Dresden Berlin Classics ▲ BER 9205
Schütz, H.:Choral Music, w. R. Mauersberger (cnd), Capella Fidicinia Dresden *(rec 1970)* Berlin Classics ▲ BER 9187
Schütz, H.:Music of, w. R. Mauersberger (cnd), Dresden PO Instrumental Group Berlin Classics 2-▲ BER 2109 [ADD]
Schütz, H.:Musicalische Exequien, w. R. Mauersberger (cnd), Dresden Instrumental Ensemble Berlin Classics ("Eterna" series) ▲ BER 2037 [ADD]
Schütz, H.:Psalmen Davids, w. H. Otto (org), E.-L. Hammer (vl), W. Jaroslawski (vl), R. Mauersberger (cnd)—Singet dem Herrn ein neues Lied, denn er tut Wunder, Psalm 98; Wohl dem, der nicht wandelt im Rat der Gottlosen, Psalm 1; Warum toben die Heiden, Psalm 2; Jauchzet dem Herrn, alle Welt, dienet dem Herren mit Freuden, Psalm 100; Der Herr ist mein Hirt, mir wird nichts mangeln, Psalm 23; Wie lieblich sind deine Wohnungen, Herr Zebaoth, Psalm 84; Aus der Tiefe ruf' ich, Herr, zu dir, Psalm 130; Ach Herr, Straf mich nicht in deinem Zorn, Psalm 6; Ich hebe meine Augen auf zu den Bergen, Psalm 121; Nun lob, mein Seel, den Herren, SWV 41; Ich danke dem Herrn von ganzem Herzen, Psalm 111 [w. Dresden State Orch. members] *(rec Oct. 1965)* Berlin Classics ▲ BER 2070-2 [ADD]
Schütz, H.:The 7 Words of Jesus Christ on the Cross, w. R. Mauersberger (cnd), *(ensemble unknown)* Berlin Classics ("Eterna" series) ▲ BER 2037 [ADD]

Dresden Church Choirs members
G. Schwarze (cnd)
Hell brennt ein Licht [Bright Burns a Light], w. Carl Maria von Weber School for Music Soloists, Prohlis Church Choir Dresden, Dresden Wind Collegium members Christophorus ▲ 77165 [DDD]
Dresden Kreuz Choir
Bach, J.S.:Mass in b, BWV 232, w. Maria Stader (sop), Sieglinde Wagner (mez), Ernst Haefliger (ten), Theo Adam (b-bar), R. Mauersberger (cnd), Dresden State Orch *(rec 1958)* Berlin Classics ▲ BER 9171
Bach, J.S.:St. Matthew Passion, w. A. Burmeister (mez), P. Schreier (ten), T. Adam (bass), R. & E. Mauersberger (cnd), Leipzig Gewandhaus Orch, St. Thomas Chorus *(rec 1970)* Berlin Classics 3-▲ BER 2144 [ADD]
Humperdinck, E.:Hänsel und Gretel, w. G. Schöter (sop), I. Springer (mez), P. Schrier (ten), T. Adam (bar), O. Suitner (cnd), Dresden Staatskapelle Berlin Classics ("Eterna" series) 2-▲ BER 2007 [ADD]
Mendelssohn, F.:Vom Himmel hoch, w. Ute Selbig (sop), Egbert Junghanns (bar), M. Flämig (cnd), Dresden PO *(rec Dresden, Mar & Apr 1987)* Capriccio ▲ 10216 [DDD]
Monteverdi, C.:Vespro, w. M. Flämig (cnd), Capella Fidicinia Leipzig Berlin Classics 2-▲ BER 9204
Saint-Saëns, C.:Oratorio de Noël, w. Ute Selbig (sop), Elisabeth Wilke (mez), Annette Markert (cta), Armin Ude (ten), Egbert Junghans (bar), Jutta Zoff (hp), Michael-Christfield Winkler (org), M. Flämig (cnd), Dresden PO *(rec Dresden, Mar & Apr 1987)* Capriccio ▲ 10216 [DDD]
Schein, J.H.:Fontana d'Israel, w. M. Flämig (cnd), Capella Fidicinia Berlin Classics ▲ BER 9078 [ADD]
M. Flämig (cnd)
Scheidt, S.:Sacred Music, w. Capella Fidicinia—Concertus Sacri *(rec 1989)* Berlin Classics ▲ BER 9126 [ADD]
Theodorakis, M.:Liturgy 2 for the Young Killed in Wars Berlin Classics 2-▲ BER 1128 [ADD]
R. Mauersberger (cnd)
Rudolf Mauersberger & the Dresden Kreuzchor ebs 2-▲ 6073
Dresden Philharmonie Children's Chorus
Beethoven, L. van:Sym 9, "Choral Sym", w. L. Bernstein (cnd), Bavarian RSO members, Dresden State Orch members, Kirov Theatre Orch members, London SO members, New York PO members, Orch de Paris members, Bavarian Radio Chorus, Berlin Radio Chorus [G] *(rec live, Schauspielhaus, East Berlin, 12/25/89)* Deutsche Grammophon ▲ 429861-2 [DDD] ■ 429861-4
Dresden State Chorus
Beethoven, L. van:Fidelio, w. J. Norman (sop), P. Coburn (sop), R. Goldberg (ten), H.-P. Blochwitz (ten), K. Möll (bass), B. Haitink (cnd), Dresden Staatskapelle Philips ▲ 438496-2

Dresden State Chorus (cont.)
Beethoven, L. van:Fidelio, w. J. Norman (sop), P. Coburn (sop), R. Goldberg (ten), H.–P. Blochwitz (ten), A. Schmidt (bar), E. Wlaschiha (bass), K. Moll (bass), B. Haitink (cnd), Dresden Staatskapelle [G] Philips 2-▲ 426308-2 [DDD]
Beethoven, L. van:Sym 9, "Choral Sym", w. H. Blomstedt (cnd), Dresden Staatskapelle [soloists Edith Wiens, Ute Walther, Reiner Goldberg, Karl–Heinz Stryczek] Capriccio ▲ CDC 10060 [DDD]
Beethoven, L. van:Sym 9, "Choral Sym", w. H. Blomstedt (cnd), Dresden Staatskapelle [soloists Edith Wiens, Ute Walther, Reiner Goldberg, Karl–Heinz Stryczek] LaserLight ▲ 15 826 [DDD]
Mozart, W.A.:Complete Mozart Edition, w. M. Price (sop), L. Serra (sop), R. Tear (ten), P. Schreier (ten), T. Adam (b–bar), K. Moll (bass), C. Davis (cnd), Dresden Staatskapelle Philips 3-▲ 422543-2 [ADD]
Strauss, R.:Ariadne auf Naxos, w. G. Janowitz (sop), R. Kempe (cnd) EMI Classics 2-▲ CDMB 64159
Strauss, R.:Der Rosenkavalier (sels), w. A. Pusar–Jeric (sop), M. Stejskal (sop), A. Jahns (mez), U. Walther (cta), R. Haunstein (bar), T. Adam (b–bar), H. Vonk (cnd), Dresden Staatskapelle [G] *(rec live 2/85)* Denon ▲ CO 8010 [DDD]
Verdi, G.:Rigoletto, w. M. Rinaldi (sop), V. Cortez (mez), F. Bonisolli (ten), R. Panerai (bar), B. Rundgren (b–bar), F. Molinari–Pradelli (cnd), Dresden State Orch [I] Acanta 2-▲ CD 41474 [DDD]
Wagner, R.:Die Meistersinger von Nürnberg, w. H. Donath (sop), R. Hesse (mez), A. Kollo (ten), P. Schreier (ten), T. Adam (b–bar), R. Evans (bass), K. Ridderbusch (bass), H. von Karajan (cnd), Dresden Staatskapelle, Leipzig Radio Chorus [G] EMI Classics 4-▲ CDCD 49683 [ADD]

Dresden State Opera Chorus
Beethoven, L. van:Syms (comp), w. Marga Schiml (sop), Peter Schreier (ten), Theo Adam (b–bar), Helena Doese (sgr), H. Blomstedt (cnd), Dresden Staatskapelle *(rec late 1970's–early 1980's)* Berlin Classics 5-▲ BER 2194 [DDD]
Beethoven, L. van:Syms (comp), w. Helena Doese (sop), Marga Schiml (alt), Peter Schreier (ten), Theo Adam (bass), H. Blomstedt (cnd), Dresden Staatskapelle, Leipzig Radio Choir *(rec Lukaskirche, Dresden, 1975–80)* Berlin Classics 5-▲ 0021942BC [ADD]
Beethoven, L. van:Sym 9, "Choral Sym", w. E. Wiens (sop), U. Walther (cta), R. Goldberg (ten), K.–H. Stryczek (bass), H. Blomstedt (cnd), Dresden Staatskapelle, Dresden Sym Chorus—final chorus Capriccio ▲ 10 914 [DDD]
Bizet, G.:Carmen, w. E. Weidlich (sop), E. Höngen (cta), T. Ralf (ten), J. Herrmann (bar), K. Böhme (bass), K. Böhm (cnd), Dresden State Opera Orch *(rec Dec. 4 & 5, 1942)* Preiser 2-▲ 90152 (m)
Mozart, W.A.:Don Giovanni, w. M. Schech (sop), M. Teschemacher (sop), H. Hopf (ten), M. Ahlersmeyer (bar), K. Böhme (bass), G. Frick (bass), K. Elmendorff (cnd), Saxon State Orch [G] *(rec 1943)* Berlin Classics ("Dokumente" series) 3-▲ BER 2048 [ADD]
Mozart, W.A.:Entführung, w. Rosemarie Ronisch (sop), Jutta Vulpius (sop), Rolf Apreck (ten), Jurgen Forster (ten), Arnold van Mill (bass), O. Suitner (cnd), Dresden State Opera Orch Berlin Classics 2-▲ BER 9116
Strauss, R.:Der Rosenkavalier (sels), w. B. Hendricks (sop), K. Te Kanawa (sop), A. S. von Otter (mez), R. Leech (ten), K. Rydl (bass), B. Haitink (cnd), Dresden Staatskapelle EMI Classics ▲ ZDC 54493
Verdi, G.:La forza del destino, w. G. Bumbry (sop—Leonora), H. Dernesch (sop—Preziosilla), N. Gedda (ten—Alvaro), H. Prey (bar—Don Carlos), G. Frick (bass—Pater Guardian), S. Vogel (bass—Marchese), G. Patanè (cnd), Dresden State Orch *(rec Aug. 1965)* Berlin Classics ("Eterna" series) ▲ BER 2025-2 [ADD]
Wagner, R.:Rienzi, der Letzte der Tribunen, w. S. Wennberg (sop), Martin (sop), A. Kollo (ten), P. Schreier (ten), T. Adam (b–bar), H. Hollreiser (cnd), Dresden State Opera Orch [G] EMI Classics ("Studio" series) 3-▲ CDMB 63980

Dresden Sym Chorus
Beethoven, L. van:Sym 9, "Choral Sym", w. E. Wiens (sop), U. Walther (cta), R. Goldberg (ten), K.–H. Stryczek (bass), H. Blomstedt (cnd), Dresden Staatskapelle, Dresden State Opera Chorus—final chorus Capriccio ▲ 10 914 [DDD]

Drevnerousski Rospev Male Choir
Historical Anthology of Russian Religious Chants, w. Yourlov Academic Choir, Bolshoi Theater Children's Choir, Rybin Male Choir, St. Petersburg Cappella Russian Season ▲ LDC 288071

Drottingholm Court Theater Chorus
Mozart, W.A.:Nozze di Figaro, w. A. Augér (sop), B. Bonney (sop), A. Nafé (mez), H. Hagegard (bar), P. Salomaa (bass), A. Östman (cnd), Drottningholm Court Theater Orch [I] L'Oiseau–Lyre 3-▲ 421333-2 [DDD]
Mozart, W.A.:Zauberflöte, w. B. Bonney (sop—Pamina), S. Jo (sop—Queen of the Night), K. Streit (ten—Tamino), G. Cachemaille (b–bar—Papageno), K. Sigmundsson (bass—Sarastro), A. Östman (cnd), Drottningholm Court Theater Orch L'Oiseau–Lyre 2-▲ 440085-2 [DDD]

René DuClos Chorus
Berlioz, H.:L'Enfance du Christ, w. Victoria de los Angeles (sop), Nicolai Gedda (ten), Roger Soyer (bar), Ernest Blanc (bar), A. Cluytens (cnd), Paris Conservatory Societé des Concerts Orch EMI Classics ("Doublefforte" series) 2-▲ CDFB 68586
Offenbach, J.:Les Contes d'Hoffmann, w. E. Schwarzkopf (sop), G. d'Angelo (sop), V. de los Angeles (sop), N. Gedda (ten), G. London (bar), E. Blanc (bar), A. Cluytens (cnd), Paris Conservatory Societé des Concerts Orch [F] EMI Classics ("Studio" series) 2-▲ CDMB 63222 [ADD]
Saint–Saëns, C.:Samson et Dalila, w. R. Gorr (mez), J. Vickers (ten), E. Blanc (bar), G. Prêtre (cnd), Paris Opera Orch [F] EMI Classics 2-▲ CDCB 47895
Satie, E.:Messe des pauvres, w. G. Litaize (org) Virgin Classics 2-▲ CDZB 62877

G. Prêtre (cnd)
Poulenc, F.:Motets (4) pour un temps de pénitence [L] EMI Classics ▲ CDC 47723 [ADD]

Duisburg State Concert Chorus
Romberg, A.:Der Lied von der Glocke, w. M. Friesenhausen (sop), R. Naber (alt), H. Hopfner (ten), K. Ridderbusch (bass), G. Knüsel (cnd), Essen CO Calig ▲ CAL 50942

Henri Duparc Chorus
Franck, C.:Messe solennelle, w. *(soloists unknown)*, J.–P. Salanne (cnd), Domaine Musical Orch—Domine non secundum Cypres ▲ 2610
Franck, C.:Les Sept paroles du Christ sur la croix, w. *(soloists unknown)*, J.–P. Salanne (cnd), Domaine Musical Orch Cypres ▲ 2610

Durham Cathedral Choir
The Psalms of David, Vol. 3 Priory ▲ PRCD 343 [DDD]

J. Lancelot (cnd)
Stanford, C.V.:Church Music, w. K. Wright (org)—complete morning and evening canticles for holy communion Priory ▲ PRI 437 [DDD]

Düsseldorf Choir

M.–A. Schlingensiepen (cnd)
Weill, K.:Kiddush, w. J. Wagner (ten) Koch Schwann ▲ CD 314 050 [DDD]

H. Schmidt (cnd)
Weill, K.:Choral Music—Legende vom toten Sldaten (1929); Zu Potsdam unter dem Eichen (1928) Koch Schwann ▲ CD 314 050 [DDD]
Weill, K.:Recordare Koch Schwann ▲ CD 314 050 [DDD]

Düsseldorf Municipal Choral Society
Beethoven, L. van:Sym 9, "Choral Sym", w. M. Price (sop), M. Lipovsk (alt), P. Seifert (ten), J.–H. Rootering (bass), W. Sawallisch (cnd), Royal Concertgebouw Orch EMI Classics ▲ CDC 54505
Berlioz, H.:La Damnation de Faust, w. J. Larmor (mez—Marguerite), K. Olsen (ten—Faust), D. Wilson–Johnson (bar—Méphistophélès), H. Claessens (bar—Brander), G. Neuhold (cnd), Flanders Royal PO Bayer 2-▲ 500017/18 [DDD]
Schoenberg, A.:Gurrelieder, w. S. Dunn (sop), B. Fassbaender (mez), S. Jerusalem (ten), P. Haage (ten), H. Becht (bass), H. Hotter (nar), R. Chailly (cnd), Berlin RSO, St. Hedwig's Cathedral Choir [G] London 2-▲ 430321-2 [DDD]

Düsseldorf Sym Chorus
Weill, K.:Berlin Requiem, w. J. Wagner (ten), W. Holzmair (bar), H. Schmidt (cnd), Düsseldorf SO [G] Koch Schwann ▲ CD 314 050 [DDD]

Dutch Radio Chorus
Berlioz, H.:Choral Music, w. G. Garino (tenor), R. van der Meer (bass), L. Visser (bass), J. Fournet (cnd), Dutch RSO—Le cinq mai, Op. 6; L'impériale, Op. 26; La mort d'Orphée; La révolution grecque, scène héroïque Denon ▲ CO 72886 [DDD]

Dutch Radio Phil Chorus
Schreker, F.:Die Gezeichneten, w. M. Schmiege (mez), W. Cochran (ten), S. Cowan (bar), W. Oosterkamp (bass), E. de Waart (cnd), Dutch Radio PO Marco Polo 3-▲ 8.223328/30

Dyfed Choir
Mahler, G.:Sym 2, w. Benita Valente (sop), Maureen Forrester (cta), G. Kaplan (cnd), London SO, Ardwyn Singers, BBC Welsh Chorus, Cardiff Polyphonic Choir Conifer Classics 2-▲ 75605-51277-2 [DDD]

East London Chorus
Bliss, A.:Morning Heroes, w. B. Blessed (nar), M. Kibblewhite (cnd), London PO, Harlow Chorus, Hertfordshire Chorus *(rec All Hallows Church, London, Nov. 16–17, 1991 & Jan 26)* Cala ▲ CACD 1010 [DDD]
Bliss, A.:Prayer for St. Francis of Assisi, w. M. Kibblewhite (cnd), London PO, Harlow Chorus, Hertfordshire Chorus *(rec All Hallows Church, London, Nov. 16–17, 1991 & Jan 26)* Cala ▲ CACD 1010 [DDD]
Essentially Christmas, w. A. Doyle (sop), S. Liley (ten), J. Lister (hp), P. Ayres (org), M. Kibbelwhite (cnd), Locke Brass Consort Koch International Classics ▲ KIC 7202 [DDD]
Rutter, J.:Gloria, Locke Brass Consort Koch Schwann ▲ 3-1266-2 [DDD]

M. Kibblewhite (cnd)
Essentially English, w. Roger Sayer (org) Koch Schwann ▲ SCH 312662 [DDD]

Eastman Chorale
Homespun America, w. DeCormier, Hunsberger (cnd), Eastman Wind Ensemble Vox Box 2-▲ CDX 5088 [ADD]

Eastman Chorale members
Sullivan, A.:HMS Pinafore, w. D. Hays (sop), M. Rawlins (sgr), C. Freeman (ten), E. Schilling (sgr), E. Johnson (cta), M. Elder (cnd), Rochester PO—highlights *(rec 11/89)* Pro Arte ▲ CDd 480 [DDD]
Sullivan, A.:The Mikado, w. D. Hays (sop), M. Rawlins (sgr), C. Freeman (ten), E. Schilling (sgr), E. Johnson (cta), M. Elder (cnd), Rochester PO—highlights *(rec 11/89)* Pro Arte ▲ CDd 480 [DDD]
Sullivan, A.:The Pirates of Penzance, w. D. Hays (sgr), M. Rawlins (sgr), C. Freeman (ten), E. Schilling (sgr), E. Johnson (cta), M. Elder (cnd), Rochester PO—highlights *(rec 11/89)* Pro Arte ▲ CDd 480 [DDD]

Eastman–Rochester Chorus
Hanson, H.:Lament for Beowulf, w. H. Hanson (cnd), Eastman–Rochester Orch Mercury Living Presence ▲ 434302-2 [ADD]

Eastman School of Music Chorus
Hanson, H.:Song of Democracy, w. H. Hanson (cnd), Eastman–Rochester Orch Mercury Living Presence ▲ 432008-2 [ADD]

ECOV Ensemble Members
Tchaikovsky, P.:Iolanta, w. Michaela Gurevich (sop—Iolanta), Jaqueline Miura (sop—Brigitta), Tatjana Tabachuk (mez—Martha), Annette Kuhn (mez—Laura), Ian Denolfo (ten—Godefroy), Keith Alexander Bolves (ten—Alméric), Alexander Ben (bar—Robert), Georg Lehner (bar—Ibn–Hakia), Arutiun Kotchinian (bass—René), Kurt Geysen (bass—Bertrand), H. Rotman (cnd), Warsaw PO *(rec Vooruit Center of the Arts, Ghent, Belgium, Aug 28–29, 1993)* CPO 2-▲ CPO 999456-2 [DDD]

Edinburgh Festival Chorus
Fauré, G.:Pavane Orch, w. S. Armstrong (sop), D. Fischer–Dieskau (bar), Orch de Paris EMI Classics ▲ CDM 64634
Fauré, G.:Requiem, w. S. Armstrong (sop), D. Fischer–Dieskau (bar), Orch de Paris EMI Classics ▲ CDM 64634
Mahler, G.:Sym 2, w. S. Armstrong (sop), J. Baker (mez), L. Bernstein (cnd), London SO *(rec 1974)* Sony Classical ("Bernstein:The Royal Edition" series) 2-▲ SM2K 47573 [ADD]

EIAR Chorus
Bellini, V.:Norma, w. G. Cigna (sop), E. Stignani (mez), G. Breviario (ten), V. Gui (cnd), EIAR Orch [I] *(rec 1936 for Cetra)* Pearl 2-▲ PEAS 9422 (m) [AAD]
Donizetti, G.:Lucia di Lammermoor, w. Lina Pagliughi (sop—Lucia), Maria Vinciguerra (mez—Alisa), Armando Giannotti (ten—Normanno), Muzio Giovannoli (ten—Lord Arturo), Giovanni Malipiero (ten—Edgardo), Giuseppe Manacchini (bar—Lord Enrico), Luciano Neroni (bass—Raimondo), U. Tansini (cnd), EIAR Orch *(rec Turin, 1942)* Melodram 2-▲ IMC 202004 [ADD]
Donizetti, G.:Lucia di Lammermoor, w. Lina Pagliughi (sop—Lucia), Maria Vinciguerra (mez—Alisa), Armando Giannotti (ten—Normanno), Muzio Giovagnoli (ten—Arturo), Giovanni Malipiero (ten—Edgardo), Giuseppe Manacchini (bar—Enrico), Luciano Neroni (bass—Raimondo), U. Tansini (cnd), EIAR Orch *(rec 1938)* Bongiovanni ("Il mito dell'opera" series) 2-▲ GB 1122-2 [ADD]
Verdi, G.:La forza del destino, w. Maria Caniglia (sop), Ebe Stignani (mez), Galliano Masini (ten), Carlo Tagliabue (bar), Tancredi Pasero (bass), G. Marinuzzi (cnd), EIAR Orch *(rec 1941)* Grammofono 2000 ▲ GRM 78567 (m)

A. Consoli (cnd)
Bellini, V.:Norma, w. Gina Cigna (sop—Norma), Ebe Stignani (sop—Adalgisa), Adriana Perris (mez—Clotilde), Giovanni Breviario (ten—Pollione), Emilio Renzi (ten—Flavio), Tancredi Pasero (bass—Oroveso), V. Gui (cnd), EIAR Orch *(rec Aug/Sept 1937)* Arkadia ("The 78's" series) 2-▲ 78010 [ADD]

Eindhovens Chamber Choir
Honegger, A.:Le Roi David, w. Bernard Kruysen (bar), Hanke De Hoogh (nar), Sasja Hunnego (nar), A. Clement (cnd), Eindhovens Instrumental Ensemble [orig version] Emergo ▲ 3974

Einsiedein & Lucerne Choralschola

R. Bannwart (cnd)
Missa in festo Pentecostes, w. K. Graf, E. Schmid, C. Schiller, T. Käser *(rec 1987)* Jecklin ▲ JEC 617-2 [ADD]

Elektra Women's Choir

Edmundson, Loomer (cnd)
Classic Elektra, w. Eric Hominich (pno), Evelyn Creaser–Rumley (vn), Nancy DiNovo (vn), Brenda Fedoruk (fl) Skylark ▲ 9402 [DDD]

Elizabethan Singers

L. Halsey (cnd)
Sir Cristemas, w. Simon Preston (kbd/cnd), Ian Partridge (ten), Susan Longfield (sop), Christopher Keyte (bass) Boston Skyline ▲ BSD 124 [ADD]

Glen Ellyn Children's Chorus
Bach, J.S.:St. Matthew Passion, w. K. Te Kanawa (sop), A. S. von Otter (mez), H. P. Blochwitz (ten), A. Rolfe Johnson (ten), O. Bär (bar), T. Krause (bass), G. Solti (cnd), Chicago SO, Chicago Sym Chorus [G] London 3-▲ 421177-2 [DDD]
Bach, J.S.:St. Matthew Passion (sels), w. K. Te Kanawa (sop), A. S. von Otter (mez), H. P. Blochwitz (ten), A. Rolfe Johnson (ten), O. Bär (bar), T. Krause (bass), G. Solti (cnd), Chicago SO, Chicago Sym Chorus [G] London ▲ 425691-2 [DDD]
Christmas with, w. Chicago Chamber Brass Crystal ▲ CD 430
Schoenberg, A.:Moses und Aaron, w. B. Bonney (sop), M. Zakai (cta), P. Langridge (ten), F. Mazura (bar), A. Haugland (bass), G. Solti (cnd), Chicago SO, Chicago Sym Chorus [G] London 2-▲ 414264-2 [DDD]

Elora Festival Singers

N. Edison (cnd)
Hui, M.:San Rocco, w. Lawrence Cherney (ob), Russell Hartenberger (perc) *(rec St Martin–in–the–Fields Church, Toronto, July 1995)* Centrediscs ▲ CMC 5395 [DDD]

Ely Cathedral Choir
Amner, J.:Sacred Music, w. David Price (org), P. Trepte (cnd), Parley of Instruments—Te Deaum; I Will Sing unto the Lord As Long As I Live; Blessed Be the Lord God; O Ye Little Flock; Magnigicat; Nunc dimitis; Sing, O Heav'ns; Vars. on "O Lord in Thee"; Consider, All Ye Passers by; Hear, O Lord; O Sing unto the Lord Hyperion ▲ CDA 66768
Jackson, F.:Benedictine [L] Gamut Classics ▲ GAM 527 [DDD]
O for the Wings of a Dove, w. Westminster Abbey Choir, Worcester Cathedral Choir Chandos ("Collect" series) ▲ CHAN 6519 [ADD]
Stanford Canticles from Ely Gamut Classics ▲ GAM 527 [DDD]

Ely Cathedral Choir (cont.)

P. Trepte (cnd)

Bairstow, E.C.:Choral Music, w. P. Trepte (cnd) [L]—Lamentation — Gamut Classics ▲ GAM 527 [DDD]

Bairstow, E.C.:Choral Music—Lamentation — Guild ▲ 7116 [DDD]

Carols from Many Lands, w. David Price (org) *(rec Ely Cathedral, Apr 1995)* — Herald ▲ HAVPCD 178 [DDD]

Evensong for St. Etheldreda, w. David Price (org) *(rec Ely Cathedral, Jan 1996)* — Herald ▲ HAPVCD 193 [DDD]

Jackson, F.:Benedictine — Guild ▲ 7116 [DDD]

Noble, T.:Choral Music—Magnificat in A; Nunc Dimittis in A — Guild ▲ 7116 [DDD]

The Psalms of David, Vol. 8:Praise the Lord O My Soul, w. Paul Trepte (org), David Price (org) — Priory ▲ PRI 460 [DDD]

Stanford, C.V.:Church Music—Jubilate in A; Jubilate in C; Magnificat in B♭; Nunc Dimittis in B♭; Te Deum in A; Te Deum in C [L] — Gamut Classics ▲ GAM 527 [DDD]

Stanford, C.V.:Church Music—Jubilate in A; Jubilate in C; Magnificat in B♭; Nunc Dimittis in B♭; Te Deum in A; Te Deum in C — Guild ▲ 7116 [DDD]

A. Wills (cnd)

A Choral Festival, w. G. Gifford (org) — Chandos ("Collect" series) ▲ CHAN 6603 [ADD]

Elyma Vocal Ensemble

Les Chemins du Baroque (The Paths of the Baroque), w. G. Garrido (cnd), Elyma Instrumental Ensemble, Cordoba Children's Choir Garrado, Compañia Musical de las Americas, Maîtrise National de Versailles, La Grande Ecurie et la Chambre du Roy [cnd:Jean–Claude Malgoire], Compañia Musical de las Americas, La Fenice [cnd:Josep Cabré], Ense — K617 ("First 4 volumes of K617" series) ▲ 7042

Les Chemins du Baroque (The Paths of the Baroque), Vol. 1:Lima–Plata Jesuit Missions, w. G. Garrido (cnd), Elyma Instrumental Ensemble, Cordoba Children's Choir — K617 ▲ 7025 [DDD]

Elysian Singers London

Delius, F.:Songs, w. S. Douse (ten), A. Ball (pno) — Continuum ▲ CON 1054

M. Greenall (cnd)

Britten, B.:A Ceremony of Carols — Continuum ▲ CCD 1043

Burgon, G.:But Have Been Found Again — Silva Classics ▲ SIL 6002 [DDD]

Burgon, G.:The Fall of Lucifer, w. J. Bowman (ct), R. Covey–Crump (ten), D. Thomas (bass), G. Burgon (cnd), Endymion Ensemble — Silva Classics ▲ SIL 6002 [DDD]

Burgon, G.:The Fire of Heaven — Silva Classics ▲ SIL 6002 [DDD]

Child of Light, w. Hugh Webb (hp), Matthew Morley (org) — Continuum ▲ CON 1043 [DDD]

Music for Christmas, w. Hugh Webb (hp), Matthew Morley (org) — Continuum ▲ CCD 1043

Poulenc, F.:Motets (4) pour le temps de Noël — Continuum ▲ CCD 1043

Emmanuel College Chapel Choir Cambridge

T. Prosser (cnd)

Veni, Veni, Emmanuel, w. Jonathan Mills (org) — ASV ▲ ASV CD 2104

Emmanuel Music Chorus

Schütz, H.:Motets (misc)—O lieber Herre Gott, SWV 381; Tröstet, tröstet mein Volk SVW 382; Ich bin eine rufende Stimme, SWV 383; Ein Kind ist uns geboren, SWV 384; Das Wort ward Fleisch und wohnet unter uns, SWV 385; Die Himmel erzählen die Ehre Gottes, SWV 386; Herzlich lieb hab' ich dich, O Herr, SWV 387; Das ist je gewisslich wahr und ein treuer wertes Wort, SWV 388; Ich bin ein rechter Weinstock, SWV 389; Unser Wandel ist im Himmel, SWV 390; Selig sind die Toten, SWV 391; Ich weiss, dass mein Erlöser lebt, SWV 393; Ich weiss, dass mein Erlöser lebt, SVW 494 *(rec June 1992)* — Koch International Classics ▲ KIC 7174 [DDD]

C. Smith (cnd)

Schütz, H.:Motets (misc)—Psalm 116, SWV 51; Five Passion Motets, SWV 56–60; Heu, mini Domine, SWV 65; Sicut Moses serpentum in deserto exaltavit, SWV 68; Aspice, Pater, SWV 73–75; Supereminet ominem scientiam, SWV 76–77; So fahr ich hin zu Jesu Christ, SWV 379; Das ist je gewisslich wahr, SWV 388; Unser Wandel ist im Himmel, SWV 390 [G,L] — Koch International Classics ▲ KIC 70852 [DDD]

Emory Univ Concert Choir

A. Calabrese (cnd)

Tomorrow Shall Be My Dancing Day:Christmas at Emory University, w. Timothy Albrecht (org), Jane Flynn (org), Nella Rigell (hp) *(rec Cathedral of St. Philip, Atlanta, GA, Apr. 30 & May 1, 1994)* — ACA Digital ▲ CM 20035

En–Calcat Abbey Monks' Choir

Jounée Monastique — Studio SM ▲ 12 16 38

Requiem:Part 1, w. children's choir — GIA ■ CS 181

Requiem:Part 2, w. children's choir — GIA ■ CS 182

Le Temps de Noël, w. Ligugé Abbey Monks' Choir, Timadeuc Abbey Monks' Choir, Bec–Hellouin Abbey Monks' Choir, Les Peres de Chevilly — Studio SM 2–▲ 1219.10

A Year of Liturgy — Studio SM ▲ 12 19.26

Enchanted Carols

Christmas Music — Saydisc ▲ CDSDL 327 ■ CSAR 327

Englebrekt Church Motet Choir

Lindberg, O.:Choral Pieces *(rec Nov. 2, 1980)* — Sterling ▲ CDS 1013

Englebrekt Church Oratory Choir

Lindberg, O.:Requiem, w. I. Sörenson (sop), E. Thallang (alt), C. Solén (ten), E. Saedén (bass), O. Johansson (org), H. Kyhle (cnd), Stockholm Univ College of Music Orch *(rec Nov. 2, 1980)* — Sterling ▲ CDS 1013

English Bach Festival Chorus

Cavalli, P.F.:Ercole armante, w. Felicity Palmer (sop—Jole), Yvonne Minton (mez—Giunone), Patricia Miller (sgr—Dejanira), Ulrik Cold (bass), M. Corboz (cnd), English Bach Baroque Orch — Erato 3–▲ ERA SEL 12980 [ADD]

Stravinsky, I.:Mass, w. L. Bernstein (cnd), English Bach Festival Orch, Trinity Boys' Choir [L] — Deutsche Grammophon ("20th Century Classics" series) ▲ 423251–2 [ADD]

Stravinsky, I.:Les Noces, w. A. Mory (sop), P. Parker (mez), J. Mitchinson (ten), P. Hudson (bass), M. Argerich (pno), H. Francesch (pno), K. Zimerman (pno), C. Katsaris (pno), L. Bernstein (cnd), English Bach Festival Orch [R] — Deutsche Grammophon ("20th Century Classics" series) ▲ 423251–2 [ADD]

Stravinsky, I.:Sym of Psalms, w. L. Bernstein (cnd), London SO *(rec Apr. 8, 1972)* — Sony Classical ▲ SMK 47628 [ADD]

Stravinsky, I.:Sym of Psalms, w. L. Bernstein (cnd), London SO — CBS ▲ MK 44710 [ADD]

English Bach Festival Singers

Rameau, J.P.:Castor et Pollux, w. P. Jeffes (ten), P. Huttenlocher (bar), C. Farncombe (cnd), English Bach Festival Baroque Orch — Erato 2–▲ 95311–2

Rameau, J.P.:La Princesse de navarre, w. N. McGegan (cnd), English Bach Baroque Orch — Erato ▲ ERA SEL 12986 [ADD]

English Chorale

Scarlatti, A.:Dixit Dominus, w. N. Argenta (sop), I. Attrot (sop), C. Denley (mez), T. Pinnock (cnd), English Concert — Archiv ▲ 423386–2 [DDD]

Sullivan, A.:Music of, w. M. Studholme (sop), J. Allister (cta), E. Bohan (ten), I. Wallace (bar), M. Dods (cnd), London Concert Orch—sels. from Gondoliers; H.M.S. Pinafore; Mikado; Pirates of Penzance — PWK Classics ▲ PWK 1157 [AAD]

English Concert Choir

Handel, G.F.:Acis & Galatea [arr Mozart], w. B. Bonney (sop), J. MacDougall (ten), M. Schäfer (ten), J. Tomlinson (bass), T. Pinnock (cnd), English Concert — London 2–▲ 425792–2

Handel, G.F.:Messiah, w. Arleen Augér (sop), Anne Sofie von Otter (mez), Michael Chance (ct), Howard Crook (ten), John Tomlinson (bass), T. Pinnock (cnd), English CO [E] — Archiv 2–▲ 423630–2 [DDD]

Handel, G.F.:Messiah (sels), w. Arleen Augér (sop), Anne Sofia von Otter (mez), Michael Chance (ct), Paul Crook (ten), John Tomlinson (bass), T. Pinnock (cnd), English CO [E] — Archiv ▲ 427664–2 [DDD] ■ 427664–4

Handel, G.F.:Ode for St. Cecilia's Day, w. Felicity Lott (sop), Anthony Rolfe Johnson (ten), T. Pinnock (cnd), English CO [E] — Archiv ▲ 419220–2 [DDD]

Haydn, J.:Stabat Mater, w. T. Pinnock (cnd), English CO [L] — Archiv ▲ 429733–2 [DDD]

Mozart, W.A.:Exsultate, w. Barbara Bonney (sop), T. Pinnock (cnd), English CO — Archive ▲ 445353–2

English Concert Choir (cont.)

Mozart, W.A.:Missa, K.317, w. Barbara Bonney (sop), Catherine Wyn–Rogers (cta), Jamie MacDougall (ten), Stephen Gadd (bass), T. Pinnock (cnd), English CO — Archive ▲ 445353–2

Mozart, W.A.:Vesperae solennes, w. Barbara Bonney (sop), Catherine Wyn–Rogers (cta), Jamie MacDougall (ten), Stephen Gadd (bass), T. Pinnock (cnd), English CO — Archive ▲ 445353–2

Vivaldi, A.:Gloria, RV.589, w. N. Argenta (sop), I. Attrot (sop), C. Denley (mez), T. Pinnock (cnd), English CO — Archiv ▲ 423386–2 [DDD]

T. Pinnock (cnd)

Gloria — Archiv ▲ 437834–2

English Opera Group Chorus

Adams, J.:The Death of Klinghoffer, w. S. Friedman (mez), S. Sylvan (bar), J. Maddalena (bar), T. Hammons (bar), K. Nagano (cnd), Lyon Opera Orch — Elektra/Nonesuch 2–▲ 79281–2 2–■ 79281–4

Britten, B.:Death in Venice, w. J. Bowman (ct), P. Pears (ten), J. Shirley–Quirk (bar), S. Bedford (cnd), English CO [E] — London 2–▲ 425669–2 [ADD]

Sullivan, A.:The Mikado, w. L. Garrett (sop), J. Rigby (mez), S. Bullock (sop), F. Palmer (sop/mez), B. Bottone (ten), R. Angas (bass), E. Idle (bar), R. Van Allan (bass), M. Richardson (bar), P. Robinson (cnd), English National Opera Orch—sels [E] — MCA Classics ▲ MCAD 6215 [DDD]; ■ MCAC 6215 (D)

Epworth Choir

Wesley, C.:Hymns, w. Methodist Central Hall Choir—20 hymns [E] — Abbey ▲ CDMVP 828 [DDD]

Eric Ericson Chamber Choir

Beethoven, L. van:Missa Solemnis, w. C. Studer (sop), J. Norman (sop), P. Domingo (ten), K. Moll (bass), J. Levine (cnd), Vienna PO, Leipzig Radio Chorus — Deutsche Grammophon 2–▲ 435770–2 [DDD]

Beethoven, L. van:Sym 9, "Choral Sym", w. Jane Eaglen (sop), Waltraud Meier (cta), Ben Heppner (ten), Bryn Terfel (bar), C. Abbado (cnd), Berlin PO, Swedish Radio Chorus *(rec Salzburg Easter Festival, 1996)* — Sony Classical ▲ SK 62634 △ SM 62634

Dallapiccola, L.:Canti di prigionia, w. E.–P. Salonen (cnd), Swedish RSO members, Swedish Radio Choir — Sony Classical ▲ SK 68323

Dallapiccola, L.:Il Prigioniero, w. Phyllis Bryn–Julson (sop), Sven–Erik Alexandersson (ten), Howard Haskin (ten), Jorma Hynninen (bar), Lage Wedin (bar), E.–P. Salonen (cnd), Swedish RSO — Sony Classical ▲ SK 68323

Eliasson, A.:Canto del Vagabondo, w. H. Blomstedt (cnd), Swedish RSO, Swedish Radio Chorus — Caprice ▲ CAP 21402 [AAD]

Eric Ericson Chamber Choir — Caprice ▲ CAP 21461

Roman, J.H.:Funeral Music for Frederik I, w. C. Högmann (sop), E. Ericson (cnd), Drottningholm Baroque Ensemble *(rec 1992)* — Musica Sveciae ▲ MSCD 413 [DDD]

Roman, J.H.:Jubilate, w. C. Högmann (sop), P. Mattei (b–bar), E. Ericson (cnd), Drottningholm Baroque Ensemble *(rec 1992)* — Musica Sveciae ▲ MSCD 413 [DDD]

Roman, J.H.:Te Deum, w. S. Rydén (sop), P.–E. Lindskog (ten), E. Ericson (cnd), Drottningholm Baroque Ensemble *(rec 1992)* — Musica Sveciae ▲ MSCD 413 [DDD]

Sacred Songs, w. Hendricks, Barbara (sop), Eric Ericson (cnd), Stockholm CO — EMI Classics ▲ CDC 54098 [DDD]

Sandström, S.–D.:The High Mass, w. Lena Hoel (sop), Sara Olsson (sop), Siri Torjesen (sop), Marianne Eklöf (mez), Annika Skoglund (mez), Peter Bengtson (org), L. Segerstam (cnd), Swedish RSO *(rec live, Berwald Hall, Stockholm, Nov. 25 & 26, 1994)* — Caprice 2–▲ CAP 22036

Söderman, A.:Poems & Songs, w. P.–M. Nilsson (sop), A. Kilström (pno), A. Lundmark (bar)—13 songs for soprano/piano, choir, or baritone/piano [Sw] — Musica Sveciae ▲ MSCD 525 [DDD]

T. Kaljuste (cnd)

Górecki, H.–M.:Miserere, w. Swedish Radio Choir — Caprice ▲ CAP 21515 [DDD]

Escuola Nacional de Música Chorus

Morales, M.:Ildegonda, w. Violeta Dávalos (sgr—Ildegonda), Grace Echauri (sgr—Idelbene), Raúl Hernàndez (sgr—Rizzardo), Ricardo Santin (sgr—Rolando), F. Lozano (cnd), Carlos Chávez SO — Forlane 2–▲ FRL 16739 [DDD]

Essen Studio Choir

K. Haenisch (cnd)

Nicolai, O.:Psalms—Psalms 31 & 97 — Koch Schwann ▲ SCH CD 310872

Essex Children's Choir

C. Price (cnd)

Krása, H.:Brundibár, w. R. Decormier (cnd), Vermont SO members, Vermont Sym Chorus members *(rec Ira Allen Chapel, Univ of Vermont, Burlington, VT, Jan 28, 1996)* — Arabesque ▲ ARA 6680 [DDD]

Estonia Opera Company Chorus

Tubin, E.:The Parson of Reigi, w. M. Eensalu (sop), Kempe (ten), Maiste (bar), P. Mägi (cnd), Estonia Opera Co Orch — Ondine 2–▲ ODE 783–2D [DDD]

Estonian National Male Choir

E. Klas (cnd)

Tubin, E.:Requiem for Fallen Soldiers, w. Tauts (mez) — Ondine 2–▲ ODE 783–2D [DDD]

Estonian Phil Chamber Choir

Pärt, A.:Berliner Messe, w. T. Kaljuste (cnd), Tallinn CO — ECM New Series ▲ 78118–20003–2

Pärt, A.:Litany, w. David James (ct), Rogers Covey–Crump (ten), John Potter (ten), Gordon Jones (bass), T. Kaljuste (cnd), Tallinn CO *(rec Niguliste Church, Tallinn, Sept 1995)* — ECM New Series ▲ 78118–21592–2 [DDD] ■ 78118–21592–4

Pärt, A.:Magnificat–Antiphones — ECM New Series ▲ 78118–20003–2

Pärt, A.:Silouans Song, w. T. Kaljuste (cnd), Tallinn CO — ECM New Series ▲ 78118–20003–2

Pärt, A.:Te Deum, w. T. Kaljuste (cnd), Tallinn CO — ECM New Series ▲ 78118–20003–2

Tobias, R.:Des Jonah Sendung, w. Pille Lill (sop), Urve Tauts (mez), Peter Svensson (ten), Raimo Laukka (bar), Mati Palm (bass), Ines Maidre (org), N. Järvi (cnd), Estonian State SO, Oratorio Choir, Tallinn Boys' Choir *(rec Estonia Concert Hall, Tallinn, Estonia, June 23–29, 1995)* — BIS 2–▲ CD 731/732 [DDD]

Tüür, E.–S.:Music of, w. T. Kaljuste (cnd), Tallinn CO—Architectonics VI; Passion; Illusion; Chrystallisatio; Requiem — ECM New Series ▲ 78118–21590–2

Tüür, E.–S.:Requiem in memoriam Peeter Lilje, w. Kaia Urb (sop), Tiit Kogermann (ten), T. Kaljuste (cnd), Tallinn CO *(rec Estonia Concert Hall, Tallinn, 1994–95)* — ECM ("ECM New" series) ▲ ECM 1590 [DDD]

T. Kaljuste (cnd)

Tormis, V.:Song Cycles — ECM New Series ▲ 78118–21459–2

European Chamber Chorus

Verdi, G.:Il trovatore, w. S. Bisatt (sop), G. Quinn (bar), D. Hinnells (cnd), European Chamber Opera Orch — ASV 2–▲ ASV 225 [DDD]

Européen Vocal Ensemble

P. Herreweghe (cnd)

Gesualdo, D.C.:Responsoria et alia ad Officium Hebdomadae Sanctae spectantia — Harmonia Mundi ▲ HMT 7901320

Lassus, O. de:Lagrime di San Pietro — Harmonia Mundi France ▲ HMC 901483

Schein, J.H.:Fontana d'Israel — Harmonia Mundi ▲ HMC 901574

Evangelical Boys' Choir Palatine

Draeseke, F.:Mysterium:Christus, w. C. Bischoff (sop), A. Vogel (sop), E. Dersen (alt), K. Markus (ten), H.J. Ritzerfeld (ten), P. Langshaw (bar), B. Kämpff (bass), J. Sonnenschmidt (org), U.–R. Follert (cnd), Breslau State PO, Heilbronn Vocal Ensemble, Palatine Kurrende — Bayer 5–▲ 100175/79

Evangelische Singgemeinde Choirs

K. Knall (cnd)

Kraft, Walter:Christus, w. Anna Senn–Dähler (sop), Barbara Künzler (sop), Barbara Sutter (sop), Christine Guy (alt), Heidi Uhlmann (alt), Daniel Zellweger (alt), Matthias Senn (ten), Mikoto Usami (ten), Wolfgang Pailer (bass), Heinz Suter (bass) *(rec Ostdorf bei Balingen, Oct. 8–11, 1986)* — Cantate 2–▲ 58004 [DDD]

Evoe Choir

Poulenc, F.:Gloria Sop, w. Brigette Fournier (sop), P. Crispini (cnd), European Concerts Orch — Doron ▲ DRC 3022 [DDD]

Poulenc, F.:Litanies à la vierge noire, w. P. Crispini (cnd), European Concerts Orch — Doron ▲ DRC 3022 [DDD]

Ex Cathedra Chamber Choir
Sanctus:Baroque Music for the Nativity, w. J. Skidmore (cnd), Ex Cathedra Baroque Orch ASV/Gaudeamus ▲ ASV CD 166
Ex Cathedra Choir
Lalande, M.-R. de:Cantate Domino...quia mirabilia, Ex Cathedra Baroque Orch ASV ("Gaudeamus" series) ▲ ASV 141 [DDD]
Lalande, M.-R. de:De profundis Orch & Chorus, Ex Cathedra Baroque Orch ASV ("Gaudeamus" series) ▲ ASV 141 [DDD]
Lalande, M.-R. de:Regina coeli, Ex Cathedra Baroque Orch ASV ("Gaudeamus" series) ▲ ASV 141 [DDD]
Lassus, O. de:Sacred Music, w. J. Skidmore (cnd), His Majesties Sagbutts & Cornetts—Sgimus tibi a3; Ave verum corpus a6; Bicinia 3, 9 & 14; Bone Jesu a8; Christus resurgens a5; Justorum animae a5; Laudent Deum a4; Musica De donum a6; Quam pulchra es a6; Salve regina a6; Tristis est anima mea a5; Tui Sunt coeli a8; Vide homo a7; Vinum bonum a8 ASV ("Guadeamus" series) ▲ ASV 150
Sir Christemas ASV ▲ ASV 912 [DDD]
Vivaldi, A.:Sacred Choral Music, w. J. Skidmore (cnd), Baroque Orch—Versicle & Response, RV.593; Beatus Vir, RV.597; Hymn [from *Stabat Mater, RV 621*]; Canticle [from *Magnificat, RV.610*] ASV ("Gaudeamus" series) ▲ ASV 137 [DDD]
Ex Tempore Vocal Ensemble
Telemann, G.P.:Cants, w. Greetje Anthoni (sop), Yves Saelens (ten), Stefan Geyer (bar), F. Heyerick (cnd), Le Mercure Galant Baroque Orch—Der Tod Jesu *(rec Studio Steurbaut, Gent, June 1995)* René Gailly ▲ 92025 [DDD]
Exultate Chamber Singers
Hatzis, C.:Byzantium, w. Libby Van Cleve (ob) *(rec 1993)* Centrediscs ▲ CMCCD 4693 [DDD]
Hatzis, C.:Crucifix, w. Chari Polatos (sgr) *(rec 1993)* Centrediscs ▲ CMCCD 4693 [DDD]
J. Tuttle (cnd)
A Choral Flourish *(rec St. Thomas' Anglican Church, Toronto)* Novadisc ▲ ND 0191
Make We Joy!:Music for Christmas, w. Ian Sadler (org), Great Lakes Brass *(rec St. Thomas' Church, Toronto)* Exultate Chamber Singers ▲ ECS 02
Fabio de Bologne Polyphonic Chorus
B. Manduchi (cnd)
Liszt, F.:Via Crucis, w. Elisa Savani Zamballi (sop), Simone Alberghini (bar), Allesandra Mazzanti (org) [orig version] Studio SM 2-▲ 2515 [DDD]
Gerald Fagan Singers
Handel, G.F.:Messiah, w. Leslie Fagan (sop), Janis Taylor (mez), Mark Dubois (ten), Gary Relyea (b-bar), G. Fagan (cnd), Concert Players Orch, London Fanshawe Symphonic Chorus Doremi 2-▲ 9306 [DDD]
I Fagiolini
All the King's Men, w. Concordia Metronome ▲ MET CD 1012 [DDD]
Insalata, w. E. Kenny (theorbo), D. Burchell (hpd/org), Riona D.(baroque vn), T. Cronin (baroque vn), D. Clasen (bar) Metronome ▲ METCD 1004
R. Hollingworth (cnd)
Byrd, W.:Songs, w. Sophie Yates (virs), Fretwork—Attollite port; Triumph with pleasant melody; O Lord, how vain; All in a Garden Green; Domine secundum actum meum; Truth at the first; Who likes to love; Wolsey's Wilde; Da mihi auxilium; Farewell, false love; O Mistrys Myne; Miserere mihi, Domine; My mind to me a kingdom is; La volta; Ad Dominum cum tribularer Chandos ("Chaconne" series) ▲ CHAN 0578 [DDD]
Farnborough Abbey Choir
A. Noble (cnd)
Duruflé, M.:Sacred Choral Music, w. Nigel Hutchinson (org)—Offertory [Veritas mea]; Communion [Beatus servus] *(rec St. Michael's Abbey, Farnborough, May 1994)* Herald ▲ HAVPCD 179 [DDD]
Langlais, J.:Sacred Choral Music, w. Nigel Hutchinson (org)—Kyrie [Missa in simplicitate]; Gloria [Missa in simplicitate]; Gradual [Iustus ut palma]; Alleluia [Beatus vir]; Sequence [Laetabunda]; Gospel [plainsong]; Credo [Plainsong III]; Offertory [Veritas mea]; Sanctus [Missa in simplicitate]; Benedictus [Missa in simplicitate]; Pater Noster [Plainsong]; Agnus Dei [Missa in simplicitate] *(rec St. Michael's Abbey, Farnborough, May 1994)* Herald ▲ HAVPCD 179 [DDD]
Fathers of Saint-Esprit Chevilly
L. Deiss (cnd)
Ave Maria Studio SM ▲ 12 21.63
Gabriel Fauré Choir
T. Farré-Fizio (cnd)
Tomasi, H.:Songs—12 Chants de L'ile de Corse, 12 Noëls de Nicolas Saboly, Messe de la Nativité [suite de noëls provençaux] Sonpact ▲ SPT 93009 [DDD]
Favre Chorus
Mozart, W.A.:Zauberflöte, w. T. Lemnitz (sop), E. Berger (sop), I. Beilke (sop), H. Roswaenge (ten), H. Tessmer (ten), G. Hüsch (bar), W. Strienz (bass), T. Beecham (cnd), Berlin PO [without dialog; G] *(rec 1937-38 for HMV)* EMI Classics ("Great Recordings of the Century" series) 2-▲ CDHB 61034 (m) [ADD]
Mozart, W.A.:Zauberflöte, w. T. Lemnitz (sop), E. Berger (sop), I. Beilke (sop), H. Roswaenge (ten), H. Tessmer (ten), G. Hüsch (bar), W. Strienz (bass), T. Beecham (cnd), Berlin PO [without dialog; G] *(rec 1937-38 for HMV)* Pearl 2-▲ PEAS 9371 (m) [AAD]
Mozart, W.A.:Zauberflöte, w. T. Lemnitz (sop), E. Berger (sop), I. Beilke (sop), H. Roswaenge (ten), H. Tessmer (ten), G. Hüsch (bar), W. Strienz (bass), T. Beecham (cnd), Berlin PO [without dialog; G] *(rec 1937-38 for HMV)* Melodram 2-▲ MEL 27056 (m) [AAD]
Feld Evangelistic Kantorei
Marx, K.:When Jesus Left His Mother, w. F. Staehelin (sgr), W. Pailer (bass), C. Näf (cnd), Amarillis Instrumental Ensemble, Amarillis Vocal Ensemble [G] *(rec 6/89)* FSM ▲ FCD 97737 [DDD]
La Fenice
Angels, w. Concerto Soave, Ensemble Convivencia, Ensemble Lucidarum, Ensemble Venance Fortunat, Iberian Lyric Ensemble L'Empreinte Digitale ▲ ED 13050
Les Chemins du Baroque (The Paths of the Baroque), w. G. Garrido (cnd), Elyma Vocal Ensemble, Elyma Instrumental Ensemble, Cordoba Children's Choir Garrado, Compañia Musical de las Americas, Maîtrise National de Versailles, La Grande Ecurie et la Chambre du Roy [cnd:Jean-Claude Malgoire], Compañia Musical de las Americas, [cnd:Josep Cabré], et al. K617 ("First 4 volumes of K617" series) ▲ 7042
Les Chemins du Baroque [The Paths of the Baroque], Vol. 3:Mexico:Messe de l'Assomption de la Vierge, w. J. Cabré (cnd), Compañia Musical de las Americas K617 ▲ 7024 [DDD]
Guide des Instruments de la Renaissance, w. Ricercar Consort, Le Tourdion Ricercar 3-▲ 95001
Venetian Dialogues Ricercar ▲ 157142
William Ferris Chorale
W. Ferris (cnd)
Corigliano, J.:Richard Wilbur Settings (2)—L'Invitation au Voyage [Baudelaire; trans Wilbur]; A Black November Turkey [Wilbur] *(rec Chicago, Feb 19, 1988)* CRI ▲ CD 659 [DDD]
Sowerby, L.:Forsaken of Man, w. Alicia Clark (sop), Judith Compton (alt), Thomas Potter (bass), Paul Grizzell (bass), Matthew Greenberg (bass), Bruce Hall (sgr), John Vorassi (sgr), Thomas Weisflog (org) *(rec St. Thomas the Apostle Church, Chicago, June 1990)* New World ▲ 803942 [AAD]
Festival of English Church Music Massed Choir
Live at the Crystal Palace, w. National Brass Band Festival Massed Bands, Handel Festival Choir, Handel Festival Orch, National Union of School Orch, Salvation Army Congress Massed Bands, Non-Conformist Union Festival Choir Beulah ▲ 1 PD 1
La Fidelissima Schola Gregorienne
J. Cabre (cnd)
Couperin, F.:Messe propre pour les couvents de religieux et religieuses, w. Olivier Vernet (org) *(rec Mar 21-24, 1996)* Ligia Digital ▲ 0104041 [DDD]
Finlandia Male Chorus
1939 Finlandia ▲ FACD 588062 (m) [ADD]

Finnish Chamber Chorus
Kortekangas, O.:Grand Hotel, w. E.-L. Saarinen (mez), S. Tiilikainen (bar), K. Laurikainen (speaker), Pohjola, Söderström (cnd), Avantil CO, Tapiola Chorus [Fin] Ondine ▲ ODE 749-2 [ADD]
Finnish National Opera Chorus
Sallinen, A.:Kullervo, w. G. Saarinen (pno), J. Silvasti (ten), J. Hynninen (bar), M. Salminen (bass), U. Söderblom (cnd), Finnish National Opera Orch [Fin] Ondine 3-▲ ODE 780-3T [DDD]
Sibelius, J.:Choral Music, w. E. Klas (cnd), Finnish National Opera Orch—Impromptu for female choir & orchestra, Op. 19 (1902; rev. 1910); Snöfrid for mixed choir & orchestra, Op. 29 (1900); Laulu Lemminkäiselle [Song to Lemminkainen] for male choir & orchestra, Op. 31/1 (1896); Oma maa [Homeland] for mixed choir & orchestra, Op. 92 (1918); Maan virsi [Song to the Earth], cantata for mixed choir & orchestra, Op. 95 (1920); Väinön virsi [Väinö's Song], cantata for mixed choir & orchestra, Op. 110 (1926) [Fin] Ondine ▲ ODE 754-2 [DDD]
Sibelius, J.:Finlandia, w. E. Klas (cnd), Finnish National Opera Orch [composer's version from the 1930s for orchestra with male voice choir; text by V.A. Koskenniemi] [Fin] Ondine ▲ ODE 754-2 [DDD]
Finnish Opera Festival Chorus
Sibelius, J.:The Tempest, w. R. Viljakainen (sop), M. Groop (mez), J. Silvasti (ten), J. Hynninen (bar), S. Tiilikainen (bar), J.-P. Saraste (cnd), Finnish RSO Ondine ▲ ODE 813 [DDD]
Finnish Radio Chamber Choir
E.-O. Söderström (cnd)
Rautavaara, E.:Choral Music, w. *(soloists unknown)*—Sprechchor of Ludus verbalis; Lorca Suite; Nirvana Dharma; plus others Ondine ▲ ODE 851
Finzi Singers
Bax, A.:Choral Music—This Worldes Joie; Mater or filium; Five Greek Folk Songs; I Sing of a Maiden that Is Makeless *(rec Dec. 4-5, 1991)* Chandos ▲ CHAN 9139 [DDD]
Bliss, A.:Choral Music, w. A. Lumsden (org), P. Spicer (cnd), Finzi Wind Ensemble—Shield of Faith for Chorus & Organ (1975); The world is charged with the grandeur of God for Chorus, Winds & Brass (1969); [a cappella works]—Birthday Song for a Royal Child (1959); River Music (1967); Mar Portugues (1973) [E] Chandos ▲ CHAN 8980 [DDD]
Howells, H.:Choral Music—2 Madrigals; Long, Long Ago; The Summer Is Coming; Take Him, Earth for Cherishing *(rec Dec 4-5, 1991)* Chandos ▲ CHAN 9139 [DDD]
Moeran, E.J.:Songs—Songs of Springtime; Phyllida and Corydon Chandos ▲ CHAN 9182 [DDD]
Vaughan Williams, R.:A Vision of Aeroplanes Chandos ▲ CHAN 9019 [DDD]
Walton, W.:Choral Music, w. A. Lumsden (org)—Coronation Te Deum; Set Me as a Seal upon Thy Heart; Jubilate Deo; 4 Christmas Carols; The Twelve; Magnificat and Nunc Dimittis; A Litany; Missa Brevis; Cantico del Sole; Where Does the Uttered Music Go; Antiphon Chandos ▲ CHAN 9222 [DDD]
Walton, W.:Music of, w. Hickox, Thomson (cnd), London PO, Academy of St. Martin in the Fields Chandos 23-▲ CHAN 9426 [DDD]
P. Spicer (cnd)
Elgar, E.:Choral Songs (sels)—3 Part-songs, Op. 18; 5 Part-songs, Op. 45; 4 Part-songs, Op. 53; 2 Part-songs, Op. 71; Death on the Hills, Op. 72; 2 Part-songs, Op. 73; How Calmly the Evening; Weary Wind of the West; Evening Scene; The Prince of Sleep; Go Song of Mine, Op. 57 Chandos ▲ CHAN 9269 [DDD]
Finzi, G.:Choral Music, w. H. Bickett (org)—works for mixed chorus, a cappella & with organ, composed 1926-1954)—Three Short Elegies, Op. 5; Seven Partsongs, Op. 17; Lo, the full, final sacrifice, Op. 26; My lovely one, God is gone up & Welcome sweet & sacred feast (Op. 27, Nos. 1-3); Thou didst delight my eyes, Op. 32; All this night, Op. 33; Let us now praise famous men, Op. 35; Magnificat, Op. 36; White-flowering days, Op. 37 [E] Chandos ▲ CHAN 8936 [DDD]
Holst, G.:Choral Music—Ave Maria, Op. 9b; The Evening-Watch; This Have I Done for My True Love, Op. 34/1; Nunc dimittis; Sing Me the Men, Op. 43/2; O Lady, Leave That Silken Thread; Soft & Gently; The Autumn Is Old; Winter & the Birds Chandos ▲ CHAN 9425
Howells, H.:Choral Music, w. Andrew Lumsden (org)—Te Deum; Thee Will I Love; Haec dies; Blessed Are the Dead; Behold O God Our Defender; Inheritance; Here Is the Little Door; A Spotless Rose; Sing Lullaby; Even Such Is Time; God Is Gone Up; The Scribe Chandos ▲ CHAN 9458
Howells, H.:Choral Music, w. H. Bicket (org)—A Sequence for St. Michael (1961); House of the Mind (motet—1949) [E] Chandos ▲ CHAN 9019 [DDD]
Howells, H.:Choral Music—O salutaris Hostia; Salve Regina; Sweetest of sweets; Come, mysoul; Antiphon; Nunc dimittis; Regina caeli [all composed ca. 1913-19] Chandos ▲ CHAN 9021 [DDD]
Howells, H.:Mass in the Dorian Mode [L] Chandos ▲ CHAN 9021 [DDD]
Howells, H.:Requiem, w. H. Bicket (org) Chandos ▲ CHAN 9019 [DDD]
Stevens, B.:Mass [L] Chandos ▲ CHAN 9021 [DDD]
Tippett, M.:A Child Of Our Time—5 Sprirtuals Chandos ▲ CHAN 9265 [DDD]
Tippett, M.:Choral Music—Dance, Clarion Air; Plebs Angelica; Maginficat & Nunc dimittis [w. Andrew Lumsden (organ)]; The Windhover; The Weeping Babe; The Source; Lullaby for 6 Solo Voices Chandos ▲ CHAN 9265 [DDD]
Tippett, M.:Songs from the British Isles Chandos ▲ CHAN 9265 [DDD]
Vaughan Williams, R.:Choral Music—The Dark eyed Sailor; The Springtime of the Year; Just as the Tide Was Flowing; The Lover's Ghost; Wassail Song; Valiant-for-Truth; O vos omnes; O Taste & See; The Souls of the Righteous; The Turtle Dove Chandos ▲ CHAN 9425
Vaughan Williams, R.:Choral Music, w. H. Bicket (org)—A Vision of Aeroplanes (1955); Lord, Thou hast been our Refuge (motet); Prayer to the Father of Heaven (motet) Chandos ▲ CHAN 9019 [DDD]
Vaughan Williams, R.:Shakespeare Songs Chandos ▲ CHAN 9425
Flanders Opera Choir
Haydn, J.:Die Jahreszeiten, w. Krisztina Láki (sop), Helmut Wildhaber, Peter Lika (bass), S. Kuijken (cnd), La Petite Bande Virgin Classics 2-▲ ZDCB 59268
Florence Maggio Musicale Chorus
Bellini, V.:Norma, w. Jane Eaglen (sop—Norma), Eva Mei (sop—Adalgisa), Vincenzo La Scola (ten—Pollione), Dmitri Kavrakos (bass—Oroveso), R. Muti (cnd), Florence Maggio Musicale Orch *(rec live, Alighieri Theater, Florence, July 1994)* EMI Classics 2-▲ CDCC 55471
Bellini, V.:Il pirata, w. M. Caballé (sop), F. Labò (ten), P. Cappuccilli (bar), F. Capuana (cnd), Florence Maggio Musicale Orch [I] *(rec live, Florence 1967)* Memories 2-▲ HR 4186/87 [ADD]
Bellini, V.:Il pirata, w. M. Caballé (sop), F. Labò (ten), P. Cappuccilli (bar), F. Capuana (cnd), Florence Maggio Musicale Orch [I] *(rec live, Florence 1967)* Melodram 2-▲ MEL 27015
Boito, A.:Mefistofele, w. Daniela Dessi (sop), Alberto Cupido (ten), Samuel Ramey (bass), B. Bartoletti (cnd), Florence Maggio Musicale Orch *(rec live, 1989)* Serenissima 2-▲ SER 360114
Cherubini, L.:Médée, w. M. Callas (sop), F. Barbieri (mez), M. Petri (bar), V. Gui (cnd), Florence Maggio Musicale Orch [I] *(rec 1953)* Arkadia 2-▲ 516 (m) [AAD]
Donizetti, G.:Don Pasquale, w. R. Scotto (sop), L. Alva (ten), W. Alberti (bar), F. Corena (bass), B. Rigacci (cnd), Florence Maggio Musicale Orch [I] *(rec live, Florence 3/1/67)* Claque 2-▲ CLQ 2011 (m)
Donizetti, G.:L'elisir d'amore, w. R. Scotto (sop), C. Bergonzi (ten), P. Cava (ten), G. Taddei (bar), G. Gavazzeni (cnd), Florence Maggio Musicale Orch *(rec live 1967)* Memories 2-▲ HR 4129/30 (s)
Donizetti, G.:Maria Stuarda, w. L. Gencer (sop), S. Verrett (mez), F. Tagliavini (ten), F. Molinari-Pradelli (cnd), Florence Maggio Musicale Orch *(rec 1967)* Memories 2-▲ MEM 4504 [AAD]
Donizetti, G.:Maria Stuarda (sels), w. L. Gencer (sop), S. Verrett (mez), F. Tagliavini (ten), F. Molinari-Pradelli (cnd), Florence Maggio Musicale Orch, 11 arias from Acts 2 & 3 [I] *(rec 5/2/67)* Myto 2-▲ 2 MCD 91137 [ADD]
Leoncavallo, R.:Pagliacci, w. Mietta Sighele (sop), Richard Tucker (ten), Kari Murmela (bar), Walter Alberti (bar), R. Muti (cnd), Florence Maggio Musicale Orch *(rec Florence, 1971)* Memories ▲ MEM 4576 [ADD]
Mascagni, P.:Cavalleria rusticana, w. R. Tebaldi (sop), J. Bjoerling (ten), A. Erede (cnd), Florence Maggio Musicale Orch *(rec Sept. 1957)* London ("Historic" series) ▲ 425985-2 [ADD]
Meyerbeer, G.:Roberto il Diavolo, w. R. Scotto (sop), G. Merighi (sgr), B. Christoff (bass), N. Sanzogno (cnd), Florence Maggio Musicale Orch [I] *(rec live 4/7/68)* Melodram 3-▲ MEL 37024
Meyerbeer, G.:Roberto il Diavolo, w. R. Scotto (sop), G. Merighi (sgr), B. Christoff (bass), N. Sanzogno (cnd), Florence Maggio Musicale Orch [I] *(rec live, 4/7/68)* Arkadia 3-▲ 549 (m) [ADD]

▲ = CD ♦ = Enhanced CD Δ = MD ■ = Cassette Tape □ = DCC

Florence Maggio Musicale Chorus (cont.)

Mozart, W.A.:Nozze di Figaro, w. L. Cherici (sop), K. Mattila (sop), M. McLaughlin (sop), M. Bacelli (mez), N. Curiel (mez), U. Benelli (ten), L. Gallo (bar), A. Nosotti (bass), M. Pertusi (bass), G. Tadeo (bass), Z. Mehta (cnd), Florence Maggio Musicale Orch — Sony Classical ▲ SK 53286

Opera Choruses, w. M. Arena (cnd), Florence Maggio Musicale Orch — Acanta ▲ CD 43540

Puccini, G.:Il trittico, w. M. Freni (sop), E. Souljois (sop), G. Giacomini (ten), R. Alagna (ten), J. Pons (bar), L. Nucci (bar), B. Bartoletti (cnd), Florence Maggio Musicale Orch — London 3-▲ 436261-2 [DDD]

Rossini, G.:La Cenerentola, w. Teresa Berganza (mez), Luigi Alva (ten), Renato Capecchi (bar), Paolo Montarsolo (bass), C. Abbado (cnd), Florence Maggio Musicale Orch *(rec Florence, May 1971)* — Memories 2-▲ MEM 4283 [ADD]

Spontini, G.:Agnes von Hohensaufen, w. L. Udovick (sop), D. Dow (sop), F. Corelli (ten), A. Colzani (bar), G. Guelfi (bar), V. Gui (cnd), Florence Maggio Musicale Orch [I] *(rec live 5/9/54)* — Melodram 2-▲ MEL 27055 (m) [AAD]

Spontini, G.:La vestale, w. R. Scotto (sop), O. Dominguez (mez), F. Tagliavini (ten), M. Picchi (ten), V. Gui (cnd), Florence Maggio Musicale Orch [I] *(rec live 5/5/70)* — Melodram ("Connaisseur" series) 2-▲ CDM 27512 [ADD]

Tchaikovsky, P.:Mazeppa, w. M. Olivero (sop), M. Radev (mez), D. Poleri (ten), E. Bastianini (bar), B. Christoff (bass), J. Perlea (cnd), Florence Maggio Musicale Orch [I] *(rec live 6/6/54)* — Melodram 2-▲ MEL 27070 (m) [AAD]

Verdi, G.:Aroldo, w. A. Stella (sop), G. Penno (ten), A. Protti (bar), F. Novelli (bar), T. Serafin (cnd), Florence Maggio Musicale Orch [I] *(rec live 6/3/53)* — Melodram 2-▲ MEL 27014 (m) [AAD]

Verdi, G.:Don Carlos, w. Anita Cerquetti (sop), Cesare Siepi (b-bar), Ettore Bastianini (bar), Gianni Barbieri (bass), A. Votto (cnd), Florence Maggio Musicale Orch — Melodram 3-▲ CDM 370104

Verdi, G.:Don Carlos, w. A. Cerquetti (sop), F. Barbieri (mez), A. LoForese (ten), E. Bastianini (bar), C. Siepi (b-bar), G. Neri (bass), A. Votto (cnd), Florence Maggio Musicale Orch *(rec July 16, 1956)* — Melodram 3-▲ MLO 670104 [ADD]

Verdi, G.:Ernani (sels), w. Mario del Monaco (ten), D. Mitropoulos (cnd), Florence Maggio Musicale Orch—Merc, diletti amici..Come rugiada al cespite; Dell'esilio nel dolore...O tu che l'alma adora *(rec Firenze, June 14, 1957)* — Melodram ▲ CDI 104006 [ADD]

Verdi, G.:La forza del destino (sels), w. Mario del Monaco (ten), D. Mitropoulos (cnd), Florence Maggio Musicale Orch—La vita è inferno all'infelice; O tu che in seno agli angeli *(rec Firenze, June 14, 1953)* — Melodram ▲ CDI 104006 [ADD]

Verdi, G.:La traviata, w. K. Te Kanawa (sop), A. Kraus (ten), D. Hvorostovsky (bar), Z. Mehta (cnd), Florence Maggio Musicale Orch [I] — Philips 2-▲ 438238-2

Verdi, G.:La traviata, w. J. Sutherland (sop), C. Bergonzi (ten), R. Merrill (bar), J. Pritchard (cnd), Florence Maggio Musicale Orch [I] — London 2-▲ 411877-2 [ADD]

Verdi, G.:La traviata (sels), w. R. Tebaldi (sop), N. Filacuridi (ten), U. Savarese (bar), T. Serafin (cnd), Florence Maggio Musicale Orch *(rec live, Florence 1956)* — Melodram ▲ MEL 15006

Verdi, G.:Il trovatore, w. Antonella Banaudi (sop—Leonora), Barbara Frittoli (sop—Ines), Shirley Verrett (mez—Azucena), Enrico Facini (ten—Un messo), Piero de Palma (ten—Ruiz), Luciano Pavarotti (ten—Marico), Leo Nucci (bar—Il Conte di Luna), Roberto Scaltriti (bar—Un vecchio zingaro), Francesco Ellero d'Artegna (bass—Ferrando), Z. Mehta (cnd), Florence Maggio Musicale Orch *(rec Maggio Musicale Fiorentino Community Theater, June 18–July 2, 1990)* — London 2-▲ 430694-2

Verdi, G.:Il trovatore, w. M. Caballé (sop), G. Tucker (ten), M. Zanasi (bar), T. Schippers (cnd), Florence Maggio Musicale Orch [I] *(rec live 1968)* — Melodram 2-▲ MEL 27035

Verdi, G.:Il trovatore, w. M. Caballé (sop), G. Tucker (ten), M. Zanasi (bar), T. Schippers (cnd), Florence Maggio Musicale Orch *(rec 1968)* — Memories ▲ MEM 4521 [ADD]

Verdi, G.:I vespri siciliani, w. Maria Callas (sop), Boris Christoff (bass), Giorgio Kokolios (sgr), E. Kleiber (cnd), Florence Maggio Musicale Orch *(rec live, Florence, May 26, 1951)* — Enterprise ("Documents" series) 3-▲ ENT LV 996

Florence Teatro Comunale Chorus

Bellini, V.:Norma, w. Margherita Rinaldi (sop—Adalgisa), Renata Scotto (sop—Norma), Giuseppina Arista (mez—Clotilde), Ermanno Mauro (ten—Pollione), Gianfranco Turati (ten—Flavio), Agostino Ferrin (bass—Oroveso), R. Muti (cnd), Florence Teatro Comunale Orch *(rec Florence, Dec 19, 1978)* — Legato Classics 2-▲ LCD 203-2

Bellini, V.:Il pirata, w. Montserrat Caballé (sop—Imogene), Flora Raffanelli (sop—Adele), Flaviano Labò (ten—Gualtiero), Giuseppe Baratti (ten—Itulbo), Piero Cappuccilli (bar—Ernesto), E. Ghiglia (cnd), Florence Teatro Comunale Orch *(rec live, Florence, 1967)* — Melodram 2-▲ IMC 205002 [ADD]

Donizetti, G.:L'elisir d'amore, w. Renata Scotto (sop), Carlo Bergonzi (ten), Giuseppe Taddei (bar), Carlo Cava (bass), G. Gavazzeni (cnd), Florence Teatro Comunale Orch *(rec June 1967)* — Pantheon 2-▲ PHE 6612 (m)

Leoncavallo, R.:Pagliacci, w. M. Sighele (sop), R. Tucker (ten), E. Lorenzi (ten), K. Nurmela (bar), R. Muti (cnd), Florence Teatro Comunale Orch *(rec live, Florence, 1971)* — Foyer ▲ FOY 2050 [AAD]

Rossini, G.:Armida, w. L. Albanese (sop), M. Callas (sop), M. Filippeschi (ten), G. Raimondi (ten), T. Serafin (cnd), Florence Teatro Comunale Orch [I] *(rec live, Florence, 4/26/52)* — Melodram 2-▲ MEL 26024

Rossini, G.:L'italiana in Algeri, w. T. Berganza (sop), L. Zannini (mez), U. Benelli (ten), E. Dara (bar), A. Romero (bar), P. Montarsolo (bass), C. Abbado (cnd), Florence Teatro Comunale Orch *(rec 1973)* — Great Opera Performances ▲ GOP 740

Verdi, G.:Attila, w. M. Roberti (sop—Odabella), G. Limarilli (tenor—Foresto), G. Guelfi (baritone—Ezio), B. Christoff (bass—Attila), B. Bartoletti (cnd), Florence Teatro Comunale Orch *(rec Jan. 12, 1962)* — Myto 2-▲ MCD 93589 [DDD]

Verdi, G.:Un ballo in maschera, w. C. Deutekom (sop), G. Tucker (ten), R. Bruson (bar), R. Muti (cnd), Florence Teatro Comunale Orch *(rec live, Florence 1972)* — Foyer 2-▲ FOY 2047 [AAD]

Verdi, G.:Un ballo in maschera, w. A. Cerquetti (sop), E. Stignani (mez), G. Poggi (ten), E. Bastianini (bar), E. Tieri (cnd), Florence Teatro Comunale Orch [I] *(rec live 1/6/57)* — Standing Room Only 2-▲ SRO 804-2 (m) [ADD]

Verdi, G.:Il trovatore, w. Fiorenza Cossotto (mez), Carlos Cossutta (ten), Agistino Ferrin (bass), R. Muti (cnd), Florence Teatro Comunale Orch *(rec live, 1978)* — Serenissima 2-▲ SER 306101 [ADD]

Verdi, G.:I vespri siciliani, w. M. Callas (sop), Kokolios-Bardi (sgr), E. Mascherini (bar), E. Kleiber (cnd), Florence Teatro Comunale Orch [I] *(rec live 5/26/51)* — Melodram 3-▲ MEL 36020 (m)

Verdi, G.:I vespri siciliani, w. Maria Callas (sop—Duchess), Giorgio Kokolios Bardi (ten—Arrigo), Gino Sarri (ten—Danieli), Enzo Mascherini (bar—Guido di Monforte), Boris Christoff (bass—Giovanni da Procida), Mario Forsini (bass—Count Vaudemont), Bruneo Carmassi (bass—Bethune), E. Kleiber (cnd), Florence Teatro Comunale Orch *(rec live, Florence, 1951)* — Melodram 3-▲ IMC 303016 [ADD]

Florilegium Chamber Choir

J. Rice (cnd)

Musgrave, T.:Madrigals [E, L] — Leonarda ▲ LE 328 [DDD]

Musgrave, T.:Rorate Coeli [E,L] — Leonarda ▲ LE 328 [DDD]

Zaimont, J.L.:Parable [He,E] — Leonarda ▲ LE 328 [DDD]

Zaimont, J.L.:Serenade:To Music [He,E] — Leonarda ▲ LE 328 [DDD]

Fontenay Abbey Monks' Choir

Le Chant de Fontenay, w. I. Reznikoff (sgr) — Studio SM ▲ 12 16 40

Fortnightly Club

Schoenberg, A.:Gurrelieder, w. R. Bampton (sop), P. Althouse (ten), L. Stokowski (cnd), Philadelphia Orch, Princeton Glee Club, Mendelssohn Club Philadelphia *(rec live Apr. 9, 1932)* — Pearl 2-▲ PEA 9066 [AAD]

Fortuna

P. Petersen (cnd)

O Magnum Mysterium:Christmas Motets from Renaissance Europe — Titanic ▲ Ti 211 [DDD]

Frankfurt Children's Choir

Honegger, A.:Jeanne d'Arc au bûcher, w. *soloists unknown*, S. Heinrich (cnd), Polish National RSO Cracow, Hersfelder Festival Choir — Koch Schwann ▲ SCH 312922 [DDD]

Orff, C.:Carmina burana, w. Lisa Griffith (sop), Ulrich Ress (ten), Thomas Mohr (bar), M. Tang (cnd), Royal Flemish PO, Frankfurt Figuralchor, Frankfurt Choral Society, Goethe Academy Children's Choir *(rec Oct. 1993)* — Wergo ▲ WER 6602-2 [DDD]

Frankfurt Choir

Bach, J.S.:Cant 91, w. H. Donath (sop), H. Watts (cta), A. Kraus (ten), W. Schöne (bass), H. Rilling (cnd), Stuttgart Bach Collegium, Württemberg CO, Gächinger Kantorei [G] *(rec Feb 1972)* — Hänssler Classic ▲ 98.822 [AAD]

A. Ickstadt (cnd)

Brahms, J.:Choral Music, w. R. Havenith (pno), Hesse Radio Chorus—4 Quartets for SATB Choir & Piano, Op. 92 [G] — Koch Treasure ▲ 31616-2 [ADD]

Frankfurt Choral Society

Orff, C.:Carmina burana, w. Lisa Griffith (sop), Ulrich Ress (ten), Thomas Mohr (bar), M. Tang (cnd), Royal Flemish PO, Frankfurt Figuralchor, Frankfurt Children's Choir, Goethe Academy Children's Choir *(rec Oct. 1993)* — Wergo ▲ WER 6602-2 [DDD]

Frankfurt Figuralchor

Orff, C.:Carmina burana, w. Lisa Griffith (sop), Ulrich Ress (ten), Thomas Mohr (bar), M. Tang (cnd), Royal Flemish PO, Frankfurt Children's Choir, Frankfurt Choral Society, Goethe Academy Children's Choir *(rec Oct. 1993)* — Wergo ▲ WER 6602-2 [DDD]

Frankfurt Kantorei

Bach, J.S.:Cants (misc), w. H. Rilling (cnd), Stuttgart Bach Collegium, Württemberg CO, Gächinger Kantorei—Cantata Nos. 1, 36, 61, 63, 65, 91, 110, 121, 122, 132, 133, 153, 190 — Hänssler Classic 4-▲ 98.836 [ADD]

Bach, J.S.:Cant 20, w. V. Gohl (mez), M. Kessler (mez), T. Altmeyer (ten), A. Kraus (ten), W. Schöne (bass), H. Rilling (cnd), Stuttgart Bach Collegium — Hänssler Classic ▲ 98.801 [AAD]

Bach, J.S.:Cant 75, w. I. Reichelt, V. Gohl (mez), J. Hamari (cta), A. Baldin (ten), A. Kraus (ten), H.-F. Kunz (bass), H. Rilling (cnd), Stuttgart Bach Collegium [G] *(rec 1970)* — Hänssler Classic ▲ 98.891 [AAD]

Bach, J.S.:Cant 102, w. J.E. Martini (cnd), Frankfurt Baroque Orch — EDA ▲ EDA 002-2 [DDD]

Bach, J.S.:Cant 114, w. G. Schnaut (mez), J. Hamari (cta), K. Equiluz (ten), W. Schöne (bass), H. Rilling (cnd), Stuttgart Bach Collegium, Gächinger Kantorei [G] *(rec 1974)* — Hänssler Classic ▲ 98.814 [AAD]

Bach, J.S.:Cant 122, w. A. Augér (sop), G. Schreckenbach (cta), A. Kraus (ten), N. Tüller (bass), H. Rilling (cnd), Stuttgart Bach Collegium [G] *(rec Feb 1972)* — Hänssler Classic ▲ 98.826 [AAD]

Bach, J.S.:Cant 151, w. N. Gamo-Yamamoto (sop), H. Laurich (cta), A. Kraus (ten), H.-F. Kunz (bass), H. Rilling (cnd), Stuttgart Bach Collegium [G] *(rec Feb 1971)* — Hänssler Classic ▲ 98.825 [AAD]

Bach, J.S.:Cant 162, w. A. Augér (sop), A. Rogers (mez), K. Equiluz (ten), W. Schöne (bass), H. Rilling (cnd), Stuttgart Bach Collegium [G] *(rec Dec 1975 & Mar 1976)* — Hänssler Classic ▲ 98.816 [AAD]

Bach, J.S.:Cant 185, w. A. Augér (sop), H. Laurich (mez), A. Baldin (ten), P. Huttenlocher (bar), H. Rilling (cnd), Stuttgart Bach Collegium — Hänssler Classic ▲ 98.804 [AAD]

Bach, J.S.:Christmas Oratorio, w. J.E. Martini (cnd), Frankfurt Baroque Orch — EDA ▲ EDA 002-2 [DDD]

Bach, J.S.:St. John Passion, w. J.E. Martini (cnd), Frankfurt Baroque Orch — EDA ▲ EDA 002-2 [DDD]

Berlioz, H.:Requiem, "Grande Messe des Morts", w. K. Lewis (ten), E. Inbal (cnd), Frankfurt RSO — Denon 2-▲ CO 73205/06 [DDD]

Handel, G.F.:Solomon, w. J.E. Martini (cnd), Frankfurt Baroque Orch — EDA ▲ EDA 002-2 [DDD]

Monteverdi, C.:Vespro della Beata Vergine, w. J.E. Martini (cnd), Frankfurt Baroque Orch — EDA ▲ EDA 002-2 [DDD]

Mozart, W.A.:Missa, K.427, w. J.E. Martini (cnd), Frankfurt Baroque Orch — EDA ▲ EDA 002-2 [DDD]

Orff, C.:Carmina burana ["Trionfi (trittico teatrale)"], w. Lisa Griffith (sop), Susan Roberts (sop), Frankfurt Singakademie — Wergo 2-▲ WER 6275-2

Orff, C.:Catulli Carmina ["Trionfi (trittico teatrale)"], w. Lisa Griffith (sop), Susan Roberts (sop), Frankfurt Singakademie — Wergo ▲ WER 6275-2

Orff, C.:Catulli Carmina, w. R. Ziesack (sop), M. Schäfer (ten), *(other artists unknown)*, W. Schäfer (cnd) [L] — Koch Schwann ▲ 314 021 [DDD]

Orff, C.:Trionfo di Afrodite ["Trionfi (trittico teatrale)"], w. Lisa Griffith (sop), Susan Roberts (sop), Frankfurt Singakademie — Wergo ▲ WER 6275-2

Zemlinsky, A. von:Der Geburtstag der Infantin, w. Soile Isokoski (sop), Iride Martinez (sgr), Andrew Collis (sgr), David Kuebler (ten), Juanita Lascarro (sgr), Machiko Obata (sgr), Anne Schwanewilms (sgr), Natalie Karl (sgr), Martina Rüping (sgr), J. Conlon (cnd), Gürzenich Orch, Cologne PO *(rec Cologne, Feb 1996)* — EMI Classics 2-▲ CDCB 56208

W. Schäfer (cnd)

Dvořák, A.:Mass, w. D. Röschmann (sop), I. Danz (alt), C. Elsner (ten), J. Mannov (bass), E. Krapp (org) — Ars Musici ▲ AM 1083-2 [DDD]

Stravinsky, I.:Les Noces, w. U. Sonntag (sop), C. Kallisch (cta), M. Schäfer (ten), P. Lika (bass), C. Rausch (bass), et al. [G] — Koch Schwann ▲ 314 021 [DDD]

Frankfurt Music School Chorus

Suter, R.:Die Ballade von des Cortez Leuten, w. P. Schweiger (spkr), R. Tschupp (cnd), Frankfurt RSO — Jecklin ▲ JD 690

Frankfurt on the Oder Phil Chorus

Furtwängler, W.:Geisterchor, w. A. Walter (cnd), Frankfurt on the Oder PO *(rec Konzerthalle C.P.E. Bach, Frankfurt on the Oder, June 22–25 1993)* — Marco Polo ▲ 8.223546 [DDD]

Furtwängler, W.:Religiöser Hymnus, w. *(sop unknown)*, Guido Pikal (ten), A. Walter (cnd), Frankfurt on the Oder PO *(rec Konzerthalle C.P.E. Bach, Frankfurt on the Oder, June 22–25 1993)* — Marco Polo ▲ 8.223546 [DDD]

Furtwängler, W.:Songs, w. Guido Pikal (ten), Alfred Walter (pno), A. Walter (cnd), Frankfurt on the Oder PO—Der traurige Jäger; Der Schatzgräber; Geduld; Auf dem See; Du sendest, Freund, mir Lieder; Erinnerung; Das Vaterland; Möwenflug; Lied; Erinnerung; Der Soldat *(rec Maison de la Radio Bruxelles, Oct. 7–8, 1993)* — Marco Polo ▲ 8.223546 [DDD]

Furtwängler, W.:Te Deum, w. A. Walter (cnd), Frankfurt on the Oder PO *(rec Konzerthalle C.P.E. Bach, Frankfurt on the Oder, June 22–25 1993)* — Marco Polo ▲ 8.223546 [DDD]

Frankfurt Opera House & Museum Choruses

Mahler, G.:Sym 8, w. M. Gielen (cnd), Frankfurt Opera House & Museum Orch *(rec 1981)* — Sony Classical ("Essential Classics" series) ▲ SBK 48281 [ADD] ■ SBT 48281

Frankfurt Radio Chorus

Berlioz, H.:Roméo et Juliette, w. N. Denize (mez), V. Cole (ten), R. Lloyd (bass), E. Inbal (cnd), Frankfurt RSO — Denon 2-▲ CO 73210/11 [DDD]

Brahms, J.:Ein Deutsches Requiem, w. M. Stader (sop), H. Prey (bar), C. Schuricht (cnd), Stuttgart RSO, Stuttgart Radio Chorus *(rec Nov. 7, 1959)* — Archipon ▲ ARCH 2.2CD (m) [ADD]

Franchetti, A.:Cristoforo Colombo, w. R. Ragatzu (sop—Isabella), G. Pasino (mez—Annacoana), M. Berti (ten—Ferdinand), R. Bruson (bar—Cristoforo Colombo), R. Scandiuzzi (bass—Don Roldano Ximenes), M. Viotti (cnd), Frankfurt RSO [I] *(rec live, Alte Oper Frankfurt, 8/30 & 9/2 1991)* — Koch Schwann 3-▲ CD 3-1030-2 [DDD]

Mahler, G.:Sym 3, w. D. Soffel (mez), E. Inbal (cnd), Frankfurt RSO [G] — Denon 2-▲ 7828/29 [DDD]

Frankfurt Singakademie

Mahler, G.:Sym 2, w. M. Puetz (sop), M. Höffgen (cta), C. Schuricht (cnd), Hessian RSO, Hesse Radio Chorus *(rec 1960)* — Originals 2-▲ ORISH 819 [ADD]

Orff, C.:Carmina burana ["Trionfi (trittico teatrale)"], w. Lisa Griffith (sop), Susan Roberts (sop), Frankfurt Kantorei — Wergo 2-▲ WER 6275-2

Orff, C.:Catulli Carmina ["Trionfi (trittico teatrale)"], w. Lisa Griffith (sop), Susan Roberts (sop), Frankfurt Kantorei — Wergo ▲ WER 6275-2

Orff, C.:Trionfo di Afrodite ["Trionfi (trittico teatrale)"], w. Lisa Griffith (sop), Susan Roberts (sop), Frankfurt Kantorei — Wergo ▲ WER 6275-2

Frankfurt Vocal Ensemble

Bach, J.S.:Christmas Oratorio, w. Ruth Ziesak (sop), Monica Groop (alt), Christoph Pregardien (ten), Klaus Mertens (bass), R. Otto (cnd), Concerto Cologne *(rec Festeburgkirche Frankfurt, Jan 9–16, 1991 & May 12–1)* — Capriccio 2-▲ 60025-2 [DDD]

Scarlatti, A.:Passion Oratorio, w. M. Bach (sop), P. Geitner (sop), K. Wessel (alt), M. Schneider (cnd), La Stagione — Capriccio 2-▲ CD 10 411/12

Stradella, A.:The Crucifixion & Death of our Lord Jesus Christ, w. M. Schneider (cnd), La Stagione — Capriccio 2-▲ CD 10 411/12

Stradella, A.:Lamentation for Wednesday the Holy Week, w. M. Schneider, La Stagione — Capriccio 2-▲ CD 10 411/12

Fredonia Singers
J. Montaine (cnd)
La Montaine, J.:Lessons of Christmas, w. Polly Jo Baker (sop), David Griffith (ten), Carol Baum (hp), Scott Shepherd (perc) Fredonia Discs ▲ FDCD 14
Adolf Fredriks Bach Choir
Roman, J.H.:The Sweedish Mass, w. H. Martinpelto (sop), A.-S. von Otter (sop), M. Samuelsson (bar), Drottningholm Baroque Ensemble Proprius ▲ PRCD 9920
Adolf Fredriks Girls' Choir
B. Johansson (cnd)
Cantemus 2:An International Choral Collection, w. Ágnes Gaál (pno) Caprice ▲ CAP 21498
Adolf Fredriks Music School Children's Choir
Stenhammar, W.:Sången, w. Iwa Sörenson (sop), Anne Sofie von Otter (mez), Stefan Dahlberg (ten), Per-Arne Wahlgren (bar), H. Blomstedt (cnd), Swedish RSO, Swedish Radio Chorus, Stockholm State Academy of Music Chamber Choir Caprice ▲ CAP 21358
Freiburg Bach Choir
Brahms, J.:Ein Deutsches Requiem, w. Christiane Oelze (sop), Kevin McMillan (bar), H.M. Beuerle (cnd), Freiburg Bach Orch Ars Musici ▲ 1057 [DDD]
Freiburg Choeur des XVI
Schubertiade:Rétrospective, w. Sine Nomine String Quartet, Lausanne Trio, C. Homberger (ten), S. Kanoff (pno), C. Favre (pno), et al. Gallo ▲ CD 631 [AAD]
Freiburg Soloists Choir
Nono, L.:Prometeo, w. I. Ade-Jesemann (sop), M. Bair-Ivenz (sop), S. Otto (alt), P. Hall (ten), U. Krumbiegel (nar), M. Schadock (nar), C. Abbado (cnd), Berlin PO *(rec May 23-25, 1993)* Sony Classical ▲ SK 53978 [DDD]
Freiburg Vocal Ensemble
Bruckner, A.:Motets, w. H. P. Blochwitz (ten), H. Skarba (trbn), H. Breika (trbn), H. Weimer (trbn), S. Rommelspacher (org)—Os justi; Afferentur regi; Christus factus est; Tota pulchra es Maria; Vexilla regis prodeunt; Ecce sacerdos magnus; Pange lingua; Locus iste; Ave Maria; Virga Jesse floruit Entrée ▲ 0039 [ADD]
Busoni, F.:Con Pno, Op. 39, w. D. Lively (pno), Freiburg Vocal Ensemble, M. Gielen (cnd), Southwest German RSO Baden-Baden Koch Schwann ▲ CD 311 160 [DDD]
W. Schäfer (cnd)
Brahms, J.:Deutsche Volkslieder Amati ▲ AMI 9010 [DDD]
French Army Chorus
Liszt, F.:Requiem, w. Jacques Maresch (ten), Daniel Galvez-Vallejo (ten), Lionel Peintre (bar), Bertrand Bontoux (bass), Francois-Henri Houbart (org), Y. Parmentier (cnd), Republican Guard Brass & Percussion Adès ▲ ADE 203032
Schmitt, F.:Salammbô, w. J. Mercier (cnd), French Isles National Orch Adès ▲ ADE 203592 [DDD]
Y. Parmentier (cnd)
Liszt, F.:Psalm 129, w. Lionel Peintre (bar), Francois-Henri Houbart (org) Adès ▲ ADE 203032
French Jeunesses Musicales Chorale
Charpentier, M.-A.:Magnificat, w. Martha Angelici (sop), Jocelyn Chamonin (sop), André Mallabrera (ct), Rémy Corazza (ten), Georges Abdoun (bar), Jacques Mars (bass), Maurice André (tpt), Marie-Claire Alain (org), L. Martini (cnd), Jean-François Paillard CO *(rec Paris, Mar 15, 1963)* Vanguard Classics ▲ OVC 8075 [ADD]
Charpentier, M.-A.:Te Deum, H. 146, w. Martha Angelici (sop), Jocelyn Chamonin (sop), André Mallabrera (ct), Rémy Corazza (ten), Georges Abdoun (bar), Jacques Mars (bass), Maurice André (tpt), Marie-Claire Alain (org), L. Martini (cnd), Jean-François Paillard CO *(rec Paris, Mar 15, 1963)* Vanguard Classics ▲ OVC 8075 [ADD]
French Musical Society Vocal Group
Verdi, G.:Requiem Mass, w. Leontyne Price (sop), Rosalind Elias (mez), Jussi Björling (ten), Giorgio Tozzi (bass), F. Reiner (cnd), Vienna PO *(rec 1959)* London ("Double Decker" series) 2-▲ 444833-2 [ADD]
French National Chorus
Ravel, M.:Daphins et Chloé, w. E. Inbal (cnd), French National Orch Denon ▲ CO 1796 [DDD]
Ravel, M.:Orchestral Music, w. E. Inbal (cnd), French National Orch Denon/PCM Digital 4-▲ DEN 75001 [DDD]
French National Radio Chorus
Debussy, C.:Nocturnes, w. C. Munch (cnd), French National RSO—Nuages & Fêtes *(rec 1968)* FNAC Music (Via Classique) ▲ 642303
Poulenc, F.:Gloria Sop, w. R. Carteri (sop), G. Prêtre (cnd), French National RSO [L] EMI Classics ▲ CDC 47723 [ADD]
Ravel, M.:L'Enfant et les sortilèges, w. E. Bour (cnd), French National RSO Testament ▲ TESSBT 1044 [ADD]
French Oratorio Choir
Berlioz, H.:Requiem, "Grande Messe des Morts", w. J.-P. Lore (cnd), French Oratorio Orch, Guy Touvron Brass Ensemble *(rec Dec. 7-13, 1987)* Esoldun 2-▲ MOS 1001 [DDD]
Berlioz, H.:Resurrexit, w. J.-P. Lore (cnd), French Oratorio Orch, Guy Touvron Brass Ensemble *(rec June 10, 1987)* Esoldun 2-▲ MOS 1001 [DDD]
Massenet, J.:Eve, w. Michèle Command (sop), Carolyn Sebron (mez), Hervé Lamy (ten), Jean-Philippe Courtis (bass), J.-P. Lore (cnd), French Oratorio Orch Erol 3-▲ 94002-04
Massenet, J.:Marie-Magdeleine, w. Michèle Command (sop), Carolyn Sebron (mez), Hervé Lamy (ten), Jean-Philippe Courtis (bass), J.-P. Lore (cnd), French Oratorio Orch Erol 3-▲ 94002-04
Massenet, J.:Méditation from *Thaïs*, w. J.-P. Lore (cnd), French Oratorio Orch Erol 3-▲ 94002-04
French Radio Chorus
Bizet, G.:Carmen, w. J. Norman (sop), M. Freni (sop), N. Shicoff (ten), S. Estes (bass), S. Ozawa (cnd), French National Orch [F] Philips ▲ 426040-2 [DDD] ■ 426040-4 □ 426040-5
Bizet, G.:Carmen, w. J. Norman (sop), M. Freni (sop), N. Shicoff (ten), S. Estes (bass), S. Ozawa (cnd), French National Orch [F] Philips 3-▲ 422366-2 [DDD]
Bizet, G.:Carmen, w. F. Esham (sop), J. Migenes-Johnson (sop), P. Domingo (ten), R. Raimondi (bass), L. Maazel (cnd), French National Orch [F] Erato 3-▲ 2292-45207-2 ZB [DDD]
Bizet, G.:Ivan IV (sels), w. J. Micheau (sop), H. Legay (ten), M. Sénéchal (ten), M. Roux (bar), G. Tzipine (cnd), French National RSO [F] EMI Classics ("Studio" series) 2-▲ CDMB 69704 [ADD]
Gounod, C.:Messe solennelle de St. Cécile, w. B. Hendricks (sop), L. Dale (ten), J.-P. Lafont (bass), G. Prêtre (cnd), Radio France PO [L] EMI Classics ▲ CDC 47094
Massenet, J.:Hérodiade, w. Nadine Denize (mez), Ernst Blanc (bar), D. Lloyd-Jones (cnd), French Radio Lyric Orch *(rec Paris, Dec 5, 1974)* Agorá ("Phoenix" series) 2-▲ 514
Offenbach, J.:Les Contes d'Hoffmann, w. E. Gruberova (sop), C. Eder (mez), P. Domingo (ten), M. Sénéchal (ten), Schmidt (sgr), G. Bacquier (bar), J. Morris (bass), J. Diaz (bass), S. Ozawa (cnd), French National Orch [F] Deutsche Grammophon 2-▲ 427682-2 [DDD]
J.-P. Kreder (cnd)
Donizetti, G.:Gemma di Vergy, w. Montserrat Caballe (sop—Gemma), Anna Ringart (mez—Ida), Luis Lima (ten—Tamas), Vicente Sardinero (bar—Il Conte), Juan Pons (bar—Guido), Francois Loup (b—Rolando), A. Gatto (cnd), Nouvel PO *(rec live, Salle Pleyet, Paris, Apr 20, 1976)* Agorá Music ("Phoenix" series) 2-▲ 501 [ADD]
French Radio Chorus Soloists
Ropartz, G.:Choral Music, w. Christian Papis (nar), Didier Henry (bar), Vincent Le Texier (b-bar), Christine Lajarrige (pno), Irène Brissot (hp), Eric Lebrun (org), M. Piquemal (cnd), Nancy SO, Vittoria Regional French Choir—Psaume 136; Dimanche; Nocturne; Les Vêpres sonnent; Le Miracle de Saint Nicolas *(rec Salle Poirel, Nancy, Apr. 22-24, 1994)* Marco Polo ▲ 8.223774 [DDD]
French Radio Lyric Chorus
Auber, D.-F.:Le Domino noir, w. J. Micheau (sop), J. Peyron (ten), G. Rey (bar), J. Gressier (cnd), French National RSO Melodram 2-▲ MLO 270110 [ADD]
Audran, E.:La Poupée, w. M. Cariven (cnd), French Radio Lyric Orch Musidisc 2-▲ MUS 202402 [AAD]
Messager, A.:Les Dragons de l'impératrice (sels), w. R. Ellis (cnd), French Radio Lyric Orch Musidisc 2-▲ MUS 202092 [AAD]
French Radio Lyric Chorus (cont.)
Messager, A.:Monsieur Beaucaire, w. J. Gressier (cnd), French Radio Lyric Orch Musidisc 2-▲ MUS 202412 [AAD]
French Radio-TV Chorus
Debussy, C.:Invocation, w. M. Rosenthal (cnd), Paris Opera Orch Adès ▲ ADE 203852 AAD
Debussy, C.:Nocturnes, w. M. Rosenthal (cnd), Paris Opera Orch Adès ▲ ADE 203852 AAD
Debussy, C.:Le Printemps, w. M. Rosenthal (cnd), Paris Opera Orch—Salut printemps version Adès ▲ ADE 203852 AAD
Milhaud, D.:Service sacré, w. Heinz Rehfuss (bar), D. Milhaud (cnd), Paris Opera Orch Accord ▲ ACD 201892 [AAD]
Ravel, M.:Daphins et Chloé, w. M. Rosenthal (cnd), Paris Opera Orch Adès ▲ ADE 140742 [DDD]
French Vittoria Regional Choir
Ropartz, G.:Psalm 129, w. Vincent Le Texier (bar), M. Piquemal (cnd), Jean-Walter Audoli Instrumental Ensemble Accord ▲ ACD 205132 [DDD]
Ropartz, G.:Requiem, w. Catherine Dubosc (sop), Jacqueline Mayeur (mez), Vincent Le Texier (bar), M. Piquemal (cnd), Jean-Walter Audoli Instrumental Ensemble Accord ▲ ACD 205132 [DDD]
M. Piquemal (cnd)
Ropartz, G.:Messe in the Honor of St. Anne, w. François-Henri Houbart (org) Accord ▲ ACD 205132 [DDD]
French Vocal Group
M. Tranchant (cnd)
Marcland, P.:Music of, w. Mercier (cnd), Nouvel PO, Debussy Trio, Ensemble InterContemporain—Versets; Paroles; Failles; Mètres; Variants *(rec 1978-84)* Chamade ▲ CHCD 5636 [DDD]
Messiaen, O.:O sacrum convivium! Arion ▲ ARN 68084
Messiaen, O.:Rechants Arion ▲ ARN 68084
Xenakis, I.:Nuits Arion ▲ ARN 68084
Frideswide Consort
Fayrfax, R.:Maria plena virtute ASV ▲ ASV 145 [DDD]
Fayrfax, R.:Missa 'Tecum principium' ASV ▲ ASV 145 [DDD]
Friends
The Music of Francis Johnson & his Contemporaries:Early 19th-Century Black Composers, w. Chestnut Brass Company MusicMasters ▲ 7029-2-C [DDD]
The Sensual Sound of the Soulful Oboe, w. Lucarelli, Bert (ob) Special Music ▲ SCD 4527 [DDD]
Fynske Chamber Choir
A. Joensen (cnd)
Bach, J.S.:Das Orgelbüchlein, w. Kevin Bowyer (org) [at the Marcussen Org] *(rec St. Hans Church, Odense, Denmark, May 14-17, 1995)* Nimbus 2-▲ NI 5457/58 [DDD]
Gabrieli Festival Chorus
Gabrieli, G.:Music of, w. R. Clemenic (rcr), A. Heiller (hpd), H. Tachezi (pno), E. Appia (cnd), Gabrieli Festival Orch—Processional & Ceremonial Music from Sacrae Symphoniae [1597, 1615] & Concerti [1587]; originally released as Bach Guild BGS 5004)—Sancta et immaculata virginitas; O magnum mysterium; Nunc dimittis; Angelus ad pastores; O Jesu mi dulcissime; Exaudi Deus; Hodie completi sunt; O Domine Jesu Christe; Canzona Quarti Toni a 15 (ricercar); Inclina Domine *(rec Vienna, Feb. 1958)* Vanguard Classics ("The Bach Guild" series) ▲ OVC 2007 [ADD]
Gächinger Kantorei
Bach, Joh. Christian:Amadis des Gaules, w. Sonntag, Hobarth, Verebies, Wagner, Schöne, H. Rilling (cnd), Bach Collegium [G] Hänssler Classic 2-▲ 98.963 [DDD]
Bach, J.S.:Cants (misc), w. H. Rilling (cnd), Stuttgart Bach Collegium, Württemberg CO, Frankfurt Kantorei—Cantata Nos. 1, 36, 61, 63, 65, 91, 110, 121, 122, 132, 133, 153, 190 Hänssler Classic 4-▲ 98.836 [ADD]
Bach, J.S.:Cant 1, w. H. Rilling (cnd), Stuttgart Bach Collegium [G] Hänssler Classic ▲ 98.867 [AAD]
Bach, J.S.:Cant 2, w. H. Watts (cta), A. Baldin (ten), W. Heldwein (bass), H. Rilling (cnd), Stuttgart Bach Collegium Hänssler Classic ▲ 98.801 [AAD]
Bach, J.S.:Cant 3, w. H. Rilling (cnd), Stuttgart Bach Collegium [G] Hänssler Classic ▲ 98.873 [AAD]
Bach, J.S.:Cant 4, w. H. Rilling (cnd), Stuttgart Bach Collegium [G] Hänssler Classic ▲ 98.864 [AAD]
Bach, J.S.:Cant 5, w. A. Augér (sop), C. Watkinson (alt), A. Baldin (ten), W. Schöne (bass), H. Rilling (cnd), Stuttgart Bach Collegium [G] *(rec Feb & Oct 1979)* Hänssler Classic ▲ 98.816 [AAD]
Bach, J.S.:Cant 6, w. H. Rilling (cnd), Stuttgart Bach Collegium [G] Hänssler Classic ▲ 98.862 [AAD]
Bach, J.S.:Cant 7, w. H. Watts (cta), A. Kraus (ten), W. Schöne (bass), H. Rilling (cnd), Stuttgart Bach Collegium Hänssler Classic ▲ 98.802 [AAD]
Bach, J.S.:Cant 8, w. A. Augér (sop), H. Watts (cta), A. Kraus (ten), P. Huttenlocher (bar), H. Rilling (cnd), Stuttgart Bach Collegium [G] *(rec 1979)* Hänssler Classic ▲ 98.813 [AAD]
Bach, J.S.:Cant 9, w. H. Rilling (cnd), Stuttgart Bach Collegium [G] Hänssler Classic ▲ 98.859 [AAD]
Bach, J.S.:Cant 10, w. H. Rilling (cnd), Stuttgart Bach Collegium [G] Hänssler Classic ▲ 98.868 [AAD]
Bach, J.S.:Cant 11, "Ascension Oratorio", w. H. Rilling (cnd), Stuttgart Bach Collegium [G] Hänssler Classic ▲ 98.858 [AAD]
Bach, J.S.:Cant 11, "Ascension Oratorio", w. C. Cuccaro (sop), M. Georg (alt), A. Kraus (ten), A. Schmidt (bass), H. Rilling (cnd), Württemberg CO [G] *(rec 1984)* Hänssler Classic 5-▲ 98.976
Bach, J.S.:Cant 11, "Ascension Oratorio", w. C. Cuccaro (sop), M. Georg (alt), A. Kraus (ten), A. Schmidt (bass), H. Rilling (cnd), Württemberg CO [G] Novalis ▲ 150028 [DDD]
Bach, J.S.:Cant 13, w. H. Rilling (cnd), Stuttgart Bach Collegium [G] Hänssler Classic ▲ 98.874 [AAD]
Bach, J.S.:Cant 14, w. H. Rilling (cnd), Stuttgart Bach Collegium [G] Hänssler Classic ▲ 98.859 [AAD]
Bach, J.S.:Cant 16, w. G. Schreckenbach (cta), P. Schreier (ten), P. Huttenlocher (bar), H. Rilling (cnd), Stuttgart Bach Collegium [G] Hänssler Classic ▲ 98.871 [AAD]
Bach, J.S.:Cant 17, w. H. Rilling (cnd), Stuttgart Bach Collegium [G] Hänssler Classic ▲ 98.868 [AAD]
Bach, J.S.:Cant 19, w. H. Rilling (cnd), Vienna Concentus Musicus [G] Hänssler Classic ▲ 98.869 [AAD]
Bach, J.S.:Cant 21, w. H. Rilling (cnd), Stuttgart Bach Collegium [G] Hänssler Classic ▲ 98.865 [AAD]
Bach, J.S.:Cant 23, w. A. Augér (sop), H. Watts (cta), A. Baldin (ten), N. Tüller (bass), H. Rilling (cnd), Stuttgart Bach Collegium [G] *(rec 1977)* Hänssler Classic ▲ 98.879 [AAD]
Bach, J.S.:Cant 24, w. A. Augér (sop), H. Watts (cta), K. Pugh (cta), A. Kraus (ten), W. Heldwein (bass), W. Schöne (bass), H. Rilling (cnd), Stuttgart Bach Collegium Hänssler Classic ▲ 98.803 [AAD]
Bach, J.S.:Cant 25, w. A. Augér (sop), A. Kraus (ten), P. Huttenlocher (bar), H. Rilling (cnd), Stuttgart Bach Collegium Hänssler Classic ▲ 98.810 [ADD]
Bach, J.S.:Cant 26, w. A. Augér (sop), D. Soffel (sop), A. Kraus (ten), P. Huttenlocher (bar), H. Rilling (cnd), Stuttgart Bach Collegium [G] *(rec 1979 & 1980)* Hänssler Classic ▲ 98.821 [AAD]
Bach, J.S.:Cant 28, w. A. Augér (sop), G. Schreckenbach (cta), A. Kraus (ten), W. Heldwein (bass), H. Rilling (cnd), Stuttgart Bach Collegium [G] *(rec Nov 1981 & Feb 1982)* Hänssler Classic ▲ 98.827 [AAD]
Bach, J.S.:Cant 30, w. H. Rilling (cnd), Stuttgart Bach Collegium [G] Hänssler Classic ▲ 98.860 [AAD]
Bach, J.S.:Cant 32, w. H. Rilling (cnd), Stuttgart Bach Collegium [G] Hänssler Classic ▲ 98.873 [AAD]
Bach, J.S.:Cant 33, w. H. Watts (cta), F. Lang (ten), P. Huttenlocher (bar), H. Rilling (cnd), Stuttgart Bach Collegium Hänssler Classic ▲ 98.811 [AAD]
Bach, J.S.:Cant 34, w. H. Watts (cta), A. Kraus (ten), W. Schöne (bass), Stuttgart Bach Collegium Hänssler Classic ▲ 98.887 [AAD]
Bach, J.S.:Cant 36, w. A. Augér (sop), G. Schreckenbach (cta), P. Schreier (ten), W. Heldwein (bass), H. Rilling (cnd), Stuttgart Bach Collegium [G] *(rec Oct 1980, Feb 1981 & Mar)* Hänssler Classic ▲ 98.823 [AAD]
Bach, J.S.:Cant 37, w. A. Augér (sop), C. Watkinson (mez), A. Kraus (ten), P. Huttenlocher (bar), H. Rilling (cnd), Stuttgart Bach Collegium [G] *(rec 1979)* Hänssler Classic ▲ 98.886 [AAD]
Bach, J.S.:Cant 38, w. A. Augér (sop), H. Watts (cta), L.-M. Harder (ten), P. Huttenlocher (bar), H. Rilling (cnd), Stuttgart Bach Collegium [G] *(rec Feb & Apr 1980)* Hänssler Classic ▲ 98.818 [AAD]
Bach, J.S.:Cant 39, w. A. Augér (sop), G. Schreckenbach (cta), F. Gerishen (bar), H. Rilling (cnd), Stuttgart Bach Collegium Hänssler Classic ▲ 98.802 [AAD]
Bach, J.S.:Cant 41, w. H. Donath (sop), M. Höffgen (mez), A. Kraus (ten), S. Nimsgern (b-bar), H. Rilling (cnd), Stuttgart Bach Collegium [G] Hänssler Classic ▲ 98.870 [AAD]
Bach, J.S.:Cant 43, w. A. Augér (sop), J. Hamari (cta), L.-M. Harder (ten), P. Huttenlocher (bar), H. Rilling (cnd), Stuttgart Bach Collegium [G] *(rec 1981-82)* Hänssler Classic ▲ 98.885 [AAD]

964 ▲ = CD ♦ = Enhanced CD ∆ = MD ■ = Cassette Tape □ = DCC

Gächinger Kantorei (cont.)

Bach, J.S.:Cant 44, w. A. Augér (sop), H. Watts (cta), A. Baldin (ten), W. Schöne (bass), H. Rilling (cnd), Stuttgart Bach Collegium [G] *(rec 1979)* Hänssler Classic ▲ 98.886 [AAD]

Bach, J.S.:Cant 46, w. H. Watts (cta), A. Kraus (ten), W. Schöne (bass), H. Rilling (cnd), Stuttgart Bach Collegium Hänssler Classic ▲ 98.808 [AAD]

Bach, J.S.:Cant 47, w. A. Augér (sop), P. Huttenlocher (bar), H. Rilling (cnd), Stuttgart Bach Collegium [G] *(rec 1982)* Hänssler Classic ▲ 98.815 [AAD]

Bach, J.S.:Cant 48, w. M. Hoffgen (mez), A. Baldin (ten), H. Rilling (cnd), Stuttgart Bach Collegium [G] *(rec 1973)* Hänssler Classic ▲ 98.813 [AAD]

Bach, J.S.:Cant 50, w. H. Rilling (cnd), Stuttgart Bach Collegium [G] Hänssler Classic ▲ 98.857 [AAD]

Bach, J.S.:Cant 51, w. A. Augér (sop), H. Rilling (cnd), Stuttgart Bach Collegium [G] Novalis ▲ 150029 [DDD]

Bach, J.S.:Cant 51, w. H. Rilling (cnd), Stuttgart Bach Collegium [G] Hänssler Classic ▲ 98.855 [AAD]

Bach, J.S.:Cant 52, w. A. Augér (sop), H. Rilling (cnd), Stuttgart Bach Collegium [G] *(rec 1982 & 1983)* Hänssler Classic ▲ 98.821 [AAD]

Bach, J.S.:Cant 55, w. A. Kraus (ten), H. Rilling (cnd), Stuttgart Bach Collegium [G] *(rec 1982)* Hänssler Classic ▲ 98.819 [AAD]

Bach, J.S.:Cant 56, w. D. Fischer-Dieskau (bar), H. Rilling (cnd), Stuttgart Bach Collegium [G] Novalis ▲ 150029 [DDD]

Bach, J.S.:Cant 56, w. D. Fischer-Dieskau (bar), H. Rilling (cnd), Stuttgart Bach Collegium [G] *(rec ca 1986)* Hänssler Classic ▲ 98.903 [AAD]

Bach, J.S.:Cant 56, w. H. Rilling (cnd), Stuttgart Bach Collegium [G] Hänssler Classic ▲ 98.855 [AAD]

Bach, J.S.:Cant 57, w. A. Augér (sop), W. Heldwein (bass), H. Rilling (cnd), Stuttgart Bach Collegium [G] *(rec Nov 1981 & Feb 1982)* Hänssler Classic ▲ 98.825 [AAD]

Bach, J.S.:Cant 58, w. I. Reichelt (sop), W. Schöne (bass), H. Rilling (cnd), Stuttgart Bach Collegium [G] Hänssler Classic ▲ 98.871 [AAD]

Bach, J.S.:Cant 59, w. A. Augér (sop), N. Tüller (bass), H. Rilling (cnd), Stuttgart Bach Collegium [G] *(rec 1976–77)* Hänssler Classic ▲ 98.886 [AAD]

Bach, J.S.:Cant 60, w. H. Watts (cta), A. Kraus (ten), P. Huttenlocher (bar), H. Rilling (cnd), Stuttgart Bach Collegium [G] *(rec 1977 & 1978)* Hänssler Classic ▲ 98.821 [AAD]

Bach, J.S.:Cant 61, w. H. Rilling (cnd), Stuttgart Bach Collegium [G] Hänssler Classic ▲ 98.867 [AAD]

Bach, J.S.:Cant 62, w. I. Nielsen (sop), H. Watts (cta), A. Baldin (ten), P. Huttenlocher (bar), H. Rilling (cnd), Stuttgart Bach Collegium [G] *(rec Feb & Apr 1980)* Hänssler Classic ▲ 98.822 [AAD]

Bach, J.S.:Cant 63, w. A. Augér (sop), J. Hamarī (mez), H. Laurich (cta), A. Kraus (ten), W. Heldwein (bass), W. Schöne (bass), H. Rilling (cnd), Stuttgart Bach Collegium [G] *(rec Feb 1971 & Feb 1981)* Hänssler Classic ▲ 98.823 [AAD]

Bach, J.S.:Cant 64, w. A. Augér (sop), A. Murray (mez), P. Huttenlocher (bar), H. Rilling (cnd), Stuttgart Bach Collegium [G] *(rec Jan 1978 & Mar 1981)* Hänssler Classic ▲ 98.825 [AAD]

Bach, J.S.:Cant 65, w. H. Rilling (cnd), Stuttgart Bach Collegium [G] Hänssler Classic ▲ 98.872 [AAD]

Bach, J.S.:Cant 66, w. G. Schreckenbach (cta), A. Kraus (ten), P. Huttenlocher (bar), W. Schöne (bass), H. Rilling (cnd), Stuttgart Bach Collegium [G] *(rec 1981)* Hänssler Classic ▲ 98.880 [AAD]

Bach, J.S.:Cant 68, w. A. Augèr (sop), P. Huttenlocher (bass), H. Rilling (cnd), Stuttgart Bach Collegium [G] *(rec 1980–81)* Hänssler Classic ▲ 98.890 [AAD]

Bach, J.S.:Cant 70, w. H. Rilling (cnd), Stuttgart Bach Collegium [G] Hänssler Classic ▲ 98.866 [AAD]

Bach, J.S.:Cant 71, w. H. Rilling (cnd), Stuttgart Bach Collegium [G] Hänssler Classic ▲ 98.863 [AAD]

Bach, J.S.:Cant 73, w. H. Rilling (cnd), Stuttgart Bach Collegium [G] Hänssler Classic ▲ 98.874 [AAD]

Bach, J.S.:Cant 74, w. H. Donath (sop), H. Laurich (cta), A. Kraus (ten), P. Huttenlocher (bar), H. Rilling (cnd), Stuttgart Bach Collegium Hänssler Classic ▲ 98.887 [AAD]

Bach, J.S.:Cant 76, w. H. Rilling (cnd), Stuttgart Bach Collegium [G] Hänssler Classic ▲ 98.869 [AAD]

Bach, J.S.:Cant 77, w. H. Donath (sop), J. Hamari (mez), A. Kraus (ten), W. Schöne (bar), H. Rilling (cnd), Stuttgart Bach Collegium Hänssler Classic ▲ 98.809 [AAD]

Bach, J.S.:Cant 78, w. H. Rilling (cnd), Stuttgart Bach Collegium [G] Hänssler Classic ▲ 98.861 [AAD]

Bach, J.S.:Cant 79, w. H. Rilling (cnd), Stuttgart Bach Collegium [G] Hänssler Classic ▲ 98.866 [AAD]

Bach, J.S.:Cant 80, w. A. Augér (sop), G. Schreckenbach (cta), L.–M. Harder (ten), P. Huttenlocher (bar), H. Rilling (cnd), Württemberg CO [G] *(rec 1976 & 1983)* Hänssler Classic ▲ 98.819 [AAD]

Bach, J.S.:Cant 82, w. D. Fischer-Dieskau (bar), H. Rilling (cnd), Stuttgart Bach Collegium [G] *(rec ca 1986)* Hänssler Classic ▲ 98.903 [AAD]

Bach, J.S.:Cant 82, w. D. Fischer-Dieskau (bar), H. Rilling (cnd), Stuttgart Bach Collegium [G] Novalis ▲ 150028 [DDD]

Bach, J.S.:Cant 82, w. H. Rilling (cnd), Stuttgart Bach Collegium [G] Hänssler Classic ▲ 98.855 [AAD]

Bach, J.S.:Cant 85, w. H. Rilling (cnd), Stuttgart Bach Collegium [G] Hänssler Classic ▲ 98.864 [AAD]

Bach, J.S.:Cant 86, w. A. Augér (mez), H. Watts (cta), A. Kraus (ten), W. Heldwein (bass), H. Rilling (cnd), Stuttgart Bach Collegium [G] *(rec 1979)* Hänssler Classic ▲ 98.885 [AAD]

Bach, J.S.:Cant 87, w. J. Hamari (cta), A. Baldin (ten), W. Heldwein (bass), H. Rilling (cnd), Stuttgart Bach Collegium [G] *(rec 1980–81)* Hänssler Classic ▲ 98.885 [AAD]

Bach, J.S.:Cant 89, w. A. Augér (sop), H. Watts (cta), P. Huttenlocher (bar), H. Rilling (cnd), Stuttgart Bach Collegium [G] *(rec Sept & Dec 1977)* Hänssler Classic ▲ 98.818 [AAD]

Bach, J.S.:Cant 90, w. H. Watts (cta), A. Kraus (ten), H. Rilling (cnd), Stuttgart Bach Collegium [G] *(rec 1977 & 1978)* Hänssler Classic ▲ 98.821 [AAD]

Bach, J.S.:Cant 91, w. H. Donath (sop), H. Watts (cta), A. Kraus (ten), W. Schöne (bass), H. Rilling (cnd), Stuttgart Bach Collegium, Württemberg CO, Frankfurt Choir [G] *(rec Feb 1972)* Hänssler Classic ▲ 98.822 [AAD]

Bach, J.S.:Cant 93, w. H. Rilling (cnd), Stuttgart Bach Collegium, Württemberg CO [G] Hänssler Classic ▲ 98.865 [AAD]

Bach, J.S.:Cant 94, w. H. Donath (sop), E. Paaske (cta), A. Baldin (ten), H.–F. Kunz (bass), W. Schöne (bass), H. Rilling (cnd), Stuttgart Bach Collegium, Württemberg CO Hänssler Classic ▲ 98.808 [AAD]

Bach, J.S.:Cant 95, w. A. Augér (sop), A. Kraus (ten), W. Heldwein (bass), H. Rilling (cnd), Stuttgart Bach Collegium, Württemberg CO Hänssler Classic ▲ 98.812 [AAD]

Bach, J.S.:Cant 96, w. H. Donath (sop), M. Höffgen (mez), A. Kraus (ten), S. Nimsgern (b–bar), H. Rilling (cnd), Stuttgart Bach Collegium, Württemberg CO [G] *(rec 1973)* Hänssler Classic ▲ 98.814 [AAD]

Bach, J.S.:Cant 98, w. A. Augér (sop), J. Hamari (cta), L.–M. Harder (ten), W. Heldwein (bass), H. Rilling (cnd), Stuttgart Bach Collegium [G] *(rec Oct 1982 & July 1983)* Hänssler Classic ▲ 98.817 [AAD]

Bach, J.S.:Cant 99, w. A. Augér (sop), H. Watts (cta), L.–M. Harder (ten), J. Bröcheler (bar), H. Rilling (cnd), Stuttgart Bach Collegium [G] *(rec 1979)* Hänssler Classic ▲ 98.813 [AAD]

Bach, J.S.:Cant 100, w. H. Rilling (cnd), Stuttgart Bach Collegium [G] Hänssler Classic ▲ 98.858 [AAD]

Bach, J.S.:Cant 100, w. A. Augér (sop), J. Hamari (cta), A. Kraus (ten), P. Huttenlocher (bar), H. Rilling (cnd), Württemberg CO [G] *(rec 1983–84)* Hänssler Classic 5–▲ 98.976

Bach, J.S.:Cant 101, w. A. Augér (sop), H. Watts (cta), A. Baldin (ten), J. Bröcheler (bar), H. Rilling (cnd), Stuttgart Bach Collegium Hänssler Classic ▲ 98.809 [AAD]

Bach, J.S.:Cant 102, w. E. Randová (mez), K. Equiluz (ten), W. Schöne (bass), H. Rilling (cnd), Stuttgart Bach Collegium Hänssler Classic ▲ 98.809 [AAD]

Bach, J.S.:Cant 104, w. H. Rilling (cnd), Stuttgart Bach Collegium [G] Hänssler Classic ▲ 98.869 [AAD]

Bach, J.S.:Cant 107, w. A. Augér (sop), A. Baldin (ten), J. Bröcheler (bar), H. Rilling (cnd), Stuttgart Bach Collegium Hänssler Classic ▲ 98.805 [AAD]

Bach, J.S.:Cant 108, w. H. Donath (sop), M. Höffgen (mez), K. Equiluz (ten), H.–F. Kunz (bass), H. Rilling (cnd), Stuttgart Bach Collegium [G] *(rec 1980–81)* Hänssler Classic ▲ 98.884 [AAD]

Bach, J.S.:Cant 109, w. G. Schreckenbach (cta), K. Equiluz (ten), H. Rilling (cnd), Stuttgart Bach Collegium [G] *(rec Feb 1981)* Hänssler Classic ▲ 98.818 [AAD]

Bach, J.S.:Cant 110, w. K. Graf (sop), H. Gardow (sop), A. Baldin (ten), W. Schöne (bass), H. Rilling (cnd), Stuttgart Bach Collegium [G] *(rec Jan–Feb 1974)* Hänssler Classic ▲ 98.824 [AAD]

Bach, J.S.:Cant 111, w. H. Rilling (cnd), Stuttgart Bach Collegium [G] Hänssler Classic ▲ 98.874 [AAD]

Bach, J.S.:Cant 112, w. H. Rilling (cnd), Stuttgart Bach Collegium [G] Hänssler Classic ▲ 98.860 [AAD]

Bach, J.S.:Cant 113, w. A. Augér (sop), G. Schreckenbach (cta), A. Kraus (ten), N. Tüller (bass), H. Rilling (cnd), Stuttgart Bach Collegium Hänssler Classic ▲ 98.810 [ADD]

Bach, J.S.:Cant 114, w. G. Schnaut (mez), J. Hamari (cta), K. Equiluz (ten), W. Schöne (bass), H. Rilling (cnd), Stuttgart Bach Collegium, Frankfurt Kantorei [G] *(rec 1974)* Hänssler Classic ▲ 98.814 [AAD]

Bach, J.S.:Cant 115, w. A. Augér (sop), H. Watts (cta), L.–M. Harder (ten), W. Schöne (bass), H. Rilling (cnd), Stuttgart Bach Collegium [G] *(rec 1980)* Hänssler Classic ▲ 98.819 [AAD]

Gächinger Kantorei (cont.)

Bach, J.S.:Cant 116, w. A. Augér (sop), H. Watts (cta), L.–M. Harder (ten), P. Huttenlocher (bar), H. Rilling (cnd), Stuttgart Bach Collegium [G] *(rec 1980)* Hänssler Classic ▲ 98.820 [AAD]

Bach, J.S.:Cant 117, w. M. Georg (mez), A. Kraus (ten), A. Schmidt (bar), H. Rilling (cnd), Stuttgart Bach Collegium [G] Novalis ▲ 150028 [DDD]

Bach, J.S.:Cant 117, w. H. Rilling (cnd), Stuttgart Bach Collegium [G] Hänssler Classic ▲ 98.856 [AAD]

Bach, J.S.:Cant 121, w. A. Augér (sop), D. Soffel (cta), A. Kraus (ten), W. Schöne (bass), H. Rilling (cnd), Stuttgart Bach Collegium [G] *(rec Feb & Apr 1980)* Hänssler Classic ▲ 98.824 [AAD]

Bach, J.S.:Cant 123, w. H. Rilling (cnd), Stuttgart Bach Collegium [G] Hänssler Classic ▲ 98.872 [AAD]

Bach, J.S.:Cant 124, w. H. Rilling (cnd), Stuttgart Bach Collegium [G] Hänssler Classic ▲ 98.872 [AAD]

Bach, J.S.:Cant 126, w. H. Watts (cta), A. Kraus (ten), W. Schöne (bass), H. Rilling (cnd), Stuttgart Bach Collegium [G] *(rec 1980)* Hänssler Classic ▲ 98.878 [AAD]

Bach, J.S.:Cant 127, w. A. Augér (sop), L.–M. Harder (ten), W. Schöne (bass), H. Rilling (cnd), Stuttgart Bach Collegium [G] *(rec 1980)* Hänssler Classic ▲ 98.878 [AAD]

Bach, J.S.:Cant 128, w. G. Schreckenbach (cta), A. Baldin (ten), W. Schöne (bass), H. Rilling (cnd), Stuttgart Bach Collegium [G] *(rec 1980–81)* Hänssler Classic ▲ 98.886 [AAD]

Bach, J.S.:Cant 130, w. N. Harnoncourt (cnd), Vienna Concentus Musicus Teldec 2–▲ 2292–42617–2

Bach, J.S.:Cant 131, w. H. Rilling (cnd), Stuttgart Bach Collegium [G] Hänssler Classic ▲ 98.866 [AAD]

Bach, J.S.:Cant 132, w. A. Augér (sop), H. Watts (cta), K. Equiluz (ten), W. Schöne (bass), H. Rilling (cnd), Stuttgart Bach Collegium [G] *(rec Sept 1976 & Jan & Apr 197)* Hänssler Classic ▲ 98.822 [AAD]

Bach, J.S.:Cant 133, w. A. Augér (sop), D. Soffel (cta), A. Baldin (ten), P. Huttenlocher (bar), H. Rilling (cnd), Stuttgart Bach Collegium [G] *(rec Feb–Mar 1980)* Hänssler Classic ▲ 98.826 [AAD]

Bach, J.S.:Cant 135, w. H. Watts (cta), A. Kraus (ten), P. Huttenlocher (bar), Stuttgart Bach Collegium Hänssler Classic ▲ 98.802 [AAD]

Bach, J.S.:Cant 136, w. H. Watts (cta), K. Equiluz (ten), N. Tüller (bass), H. Rilling (cnd), Stuttgart Bach Collegium Hänssler Classic ▲ 98.806 [AAD]

Bach, J.S.:Cant 137, w. H. Rilling (cnd), Stuttgart Bach Collegium [G] Hänssler Classic ▲ 98.861 [AAD]

Bach, J.S.:Cant 138, w. A. Augér (sop), R. Bollen (cta), A. Baldin (ten), P. Huttenlocher (bar), H. Rilling (cnd), Stuttgart Bach Collegium Hänssler Classic ▲ 98.812 [AAD]

Bach, J.S.:Cant 139, w. I. Nelson (sop), H. Watts (cta), A. Kraus (ten), P. Huttenlocher (bar), H. Rilling (cnd), Stuttgart Bach Collegium [G] *(rec 1979 & 1980)* Hänssler Classic ▲ 98.820 [AAD]

Bach, J.S.:Cant 140, w. A. Augér (sop), A. Baldin (ten), P. Huttenlocher (bar), H. Rilling (cnd), Stuttgart Bach Collegium [G] Novalis ▲ 150029 [DDD]

Bach, J.S.:Cant 140, w. H. Rilling (cnd), Stuttgart Bach Collegium [G] Hänssler Classic ▲ 98.857 [AAD]

Bach, J.S.:Cant 145, w. C. Cuccaro (sop), A. Kraus (ten), A. Schmidt (bass), H. Rilling (cnd), Stuttgart Bach Collegium [G] Novalis ▲ 150029 [DDD]

Bach, J.S.:Cant 145, w. H. Rilling (cnd), Stuttgart Bach Collegium [G] Hänssler Classic ▲ 98.856 [AAD]

Bach, J.S.:Cant 146, w. C. Watkinson (cta), P. Schreier (ten), P. Huttenlocher (bass), H. Rilling (cnd), Stuttgart Bach Collegium [G] *(rec 1973)* Hänssler Classic ▲ 98.884 [AAD]

Bach, J.S.:Cant 147, w. H. Rilling (cnd), Stuttgart Bach Collegium [G] Hänssler Classic ▲ 98.863 [AAD]

Bach, J.S.:Cant 148, w. H. Watts (cta), K. Equiluz (ten), H. Rilling (cnd), Stuttgart Bach Collegium [G] *(rec 1977)* Hänssler Classic ▲ 98.814 [AAD]

Bach, J.S.:Cant 149, w. A. Augér (sop), M. Georg (mez), A. Baldin (ten), P. Huttenlocher (bar), H. Rilling (cnd), Stuttgart Bach Collegium [G] *(rec 1984)* Hänssler Classic ▲ 98.815 [AAD]

Bach, J.S.:Cant 153, w. A. Murray (mez), A. Kraus (ten), W. Heldwein (bass), H. Rilling (cnd), Stuttgart Bach Collegium [G] Hänssler Classic ▲ 98.871 [AAD]

Bach, J.S.:Cant 154, w. H. Rilling (cnd), Stuttgart Bach Collegium [G] Hänssler Classic ▲ 98.872 [AAD]

Bach, J.S.:Cant 155, w. H. Rilling (cnd), Stuttgart Bach Collegium [G] Hänssler Classic ▲ 98.873 [AAD]

Bach, J.S.:Cant 159, w. J. Hamari (cta), A. Baldin (ten), P. Huttenlocher (bar), H. Rilling (cnd), Stuttgart Bach Collegium [G] *(rec 1983)* Hänssler Classic ▲ 98.879 [AAD]

Bach, J.S.:Cant 161, w. H. Laurich (cta), A. Kraus (ten), H. Rilling (cnd), Stuttgart Bach Collegium Hänssler Classic ▲ 98.812 [AAD]

Bach, J.S.:Cant 163, w. A. Augér (sop), H. Watts (cta), A. Kraus (ten), N. Tüller (bass), H. Rilling (cnd), Stuttgart Bach Collegium [G] *(rec 1976 & 1977)* Hänssler Classic ▲ 98.820 [AAD]

Bach, J.S.:Cant 164, w. E. Wiens (sop), J. Hamari (cta), L.–M. Harder (ten), W. Heldwein (bass), H. Rilling (cnd), Stuttgart Bach Collegium Hänssler Classic ▲ 98.811 [AAD]

Bach, J.S.:Cant 169, w. C. Watkinson (cta), H. Rilling (cnd), Württemberg CO [G] *(rec 1983)* Hänssler Classic ▲ 98.815 [AAD]

Bach, J.S.:Cant 170, w. H. Rilling (cnd), Stuttgart Bach Collegium Hänssler Classic ▲ 98.804 [AAD]

Bach, J.S.:Cant 171, w. A. Augér (sop), J. Hamari (cta), A. Badin (ten), W. Heldwein (bass), H. Rilling (cnd), Württemberg CO [G] Hänssler Classic ▲ 98.871 [AAD]

Bach, J.S.:Cant 172, w. H. Rilling (cnd), Stuttgart Bach Collegium [G] Hänssler Classic ▲ 98.864 [AAD]

Bach, J.S.:Cant 174, w. H. Rilling (cnd), Stuttgart Bach Collegium [G] Hänssler Classic ▲ 98.856 [AAD]

Bach, J.S.:Cant 176, w. I. Nielsen (sop), C. Watkinson (cta), W. Hedwein (bass), H. Rilling (cnd), Stuttgart Bach Collegium Hänssler Classic ▲ 98.801 [AAD]

Bach, J.S.:Cant 177, w. A. Augér (sop), J. Hamari (cta), P. Schreier (ten), H. Rilling (cnd), Stuttgart Bach Collegium Hänssler Classic ▲ 98.803 [AAD]

Bach, J.S.:Cant 178, w. G. Schreckenbach (cta), A. Baldin (ten), K. Equiluz (ten), W. Schöne (bass), H. Rilling (cnd), Stuttgart Bach Collegium Hänssler Classic ▲ 98.806 [AAD]

Bach, J.S.:Cant 179, w. A. Augér (sop), K. Equiluz (ten), W. Schöne (bass), H. Rilling (cnd), Stuttgart Bach Collegium Hänssler Classic ▲ 98.808 [AAD]

Bach, J.S.:Cant 180, w. A. Augér (sop), C. Watkinson (cta), A. Kraus (ten), W. Heldwein (sop), H. Rilling (cnd), Stuttgart Bach Collegium [G] *(rec Feb & Oct 1979)* Hänssler Classic ▲ 98.816 [AAD]

Bach, J.S.:Cant 181, w. A. Augér (sop), G. Schnaut (mez), G. Schreckenbach (cta), K. Equiluz (ten), N. Tütler (bass), H. Rilling (cnd), Stuttgart Bach Collegium [G] *(rec 1981)* Hänssler Classic ▲ 98.878 [AAD]

Bach, J.S.:Cant 182, w. D. Soffel (cta), A. Baldin (ten), P. Huttenlocher (bar), H. Rilling (cnd), Stuttgart Bach Collegium [G] *(rec 1975)* Hänssler Classic ▲ 98.880 [AAD]

Bach, J.S.:Cant 183, w. A. Augér (sop), J. Hamari (cta), P. Schreier (ten), W. Heldwein (bass), H. Rilling (cnd), Stuttgart Bach Collegium Hänssler Classic ▲ 98.801 [AAD]

Bach, J.S.:Cant 186, w. A. Augér (sop), H. Watts (cta), K. Equiluz (ten), H. Rilling (cnd), Stuttgart Bach Collegium Hänssler Classic ▲ 98.805 [AAD]

Bach, J.S.:Cant 187, w. M. Friesenhausen (sop), H. Laurich (mez), W. Schöne (bass), H. Rilling (cnd), Stuttgart Bach Collegium Hänssler Classic ▲ 98.806 [AAD]

Bach, J.S.:Cant 188, w. A. Augér (sop), J. Hamari (cta), A. Baldin (ten), W. Heldwein (bass), H. Rilling (cnd), Württemberg CO [G] *(rec June & Sept 1983)* Hänssler Classic ▲ 98.817 [AAD]

Bach, J.S.:Cant 190, w. H. Watts (cta), K. Equiluz (ten), N. Tüller (b–bar), H. Rilling (cnd), Stuttgart Bach Collegium [G] Hänssler Classic ▲ 98.870 [AAD]

Bach, J.S.:Cant 191, w. H. Rilling (cnd), Stuttgart Bach Collegium [G] Hänssler Classic ▲ 98.867 [AAD]

Bach, J.S.:Cant 192, w. H. Rilling (cnd), Stuttgart Bach Collegium [G] Hänssler Classic ▲ 98.863 [AAD]

Bach, J.S.:Cant 195, w. H. Rilling (cnd), Stuttgart Bach Collegium [G] Hänssler Classic ▲ 98.859 [AAD]

Bach, J.S.:Cant 198, w. J. Beckmann (sop), A. Kraus (ten), W. Heldwein (bass), H. Rilling (cnd), Stuttgart Bach Collegium [G] *(rec Sept 1976 & Jan 1977)* Hänssler Classic ▲ 98.827 [AAD]

Bach, J.S.:Cant 200, w. H. Rilling (cnd), Stuttgart Bach Collegium [G] Hänssler Classic ▲ 98.858 [AAD]

Bach, J.S.:Christmas Oratorio, w. A. Augér (sop), J. Hamari (cta), P. Schreier (ten), W. Schöne (bass), H. Rilling (cnd), Stuttgart Bach Collegium [G] *(rec 1984)* Hänssler Classic 5–▲ 98.976

Bach, J.S.:Easter Oratorio, w. A. Augér (sop), J. Hamari (cta), A. Kraus (ten), P. Huttenlocher (bar), H. Rilling (cnd), Stuttgart Bach Collegium [G] *(rec 1980–81)* Hänssler Classic 5–▲ 98.976

Bach, J.S.:Easter Oratorio, w. H. Rilling (cnd), Stuttgart Bach Collegium [G] Hänssler Classic ▲ 98.862 [AAD]

Bach, J.S.:Magnificat, BWV 243, w. A. Augér (sop), A. Murray (mez), H. Watts (cta), A. Kraus (ten), P. Huttenlocher (bar), W. Schöne (bass), H. Rilling (cnd), Stuttgart Bach Collegium *(rec 1979)* Sony Classical ("Essential Classics" series) ▲ SBK 48280 [ADD] ■ SBT 48280

Bach, J.S.:Mass in b, BWV 232, w. *(soloists unknown)*, H. Rilling (cnd), Stuttgart Bach Collegium Odyssey 2–▲ MB2K 45615

Bach, J.S.:Motets (misc), w. H. Rilling (cnd), Stuttgart Bach Collegium [G]—O Jesu Christ, mein's Lebens Licht, BWV 118; Ich lasse dich nicht, du segnest mich denn, BWV Anh.159; Jauchzet dem Herrn, alle Welt, BWV Anh.160; Der Gerechte kommt um, BWV deest Hänssler Classic 2–▲ HR 98.965 [DDD]

Gächinger Kantorei (cont.)
Bach, J.S.:Motets, BWV 225-30, w. H. Rilling (cnd), Stuttgart Bach Collegium [G]
Hänssler Classic 2-▲ HR 98.965 [DDD]
Beethoven, L. van:Missa Solemnis, w. P. Coburn (sop), F. Quivar (cta), A. Baldin (ten), A. Schmidt (bar), H. Rilling (cnd), Stuttgart Bach Collegium [L]
Hänssler Classic 2-▲ CD 98.956 [DDD] 2-■ MC 98.956 (D)
Brahms, J.:Ein Deutsches Requiem, w. D. Brown (sop), G. Cachemaille (bar), H. Rilling (cnd), Stuttgart Bach Collegium [G] Hänssler Classic ▲ 98.966 [DDD]
Bruckner, A.:Mass 3, w. *(soloists unknown)*, H. Rilling (cnd), Stuttgart RSO
Hänssler Classic ▲ HAN 98983 [DDD]
Franck, C.:Les Béatitudes, w. D. Montague (mez), K. Lewis (ten), G. Cachemaille (bar), J. Cheek (bass), H. Rilling (cnd), Stuttgart RSO [F] Hänssler Classic 2-▲ 98.964 [DDD]
Handel, G.F.:Messiah (reorchd Mozart), w. Donna Brown (sop), Cornelia Kallisch (cta), R. Saccà (ten), Alastair Miles (bass), H. Rilling (cnd), Stuttgart Bach Collegium [G]
Hänssler Classic 2-▲ 98.975 [DDD]
Haydn, J.:Die Jahreszeiten, w. *(soloists unknown)*, H. Rilling (cnd), Bach Collegium
Hänssler Classic 2-▲ HAN 98982 [DDD]
Haydn, J.:Mass 10, "Kriegsmesse", "Paukenmesse", w. Bach Collegium Chorus
Hänssler Classic 2-▲ HAN 98981 [DDD]
Haydn, J.:The Seven Last Words of Christ on the Cross, w. Pamela Coburn (sop), Ingeborg Danz (mez), Uwe Heilmann (ten), Andreas Schmidt (bar), H. Rilling (cnd), Stuttgart Bach Collegium [oratorio version] [G] Hänssler Classic ▲ 98.977 [DDD]
Haydn, M.:Requiem in B♭, w. Pamela Coburn (sop), Ingeborg Danz (mez), Andreas Schmidt (bar), H. Rilling (cnd), Stuttgart Bach Collegium [L] Hänssler Classic ▲ 98.977 [DDD]
Mozart, W.A.:Kyrie, K.341, w. H. Rilling (cnd), Stuttgart Bach Collegium [L]
Hänssler Classic 2-▲ 98.979 [DDD]
Mozart, W.A.:Missa, K.427, w. C. Oelze (sop), I. Verebics (sop), S. Weir (ten), O. Widmer (bass), H. Rilling (cnd), Stuttgart Bach Collegium [L] Hänssler Classic 2-▲ 98.979 [DDD]
Mozart, W.A.:Requiem, w. A. Augér (sop), C. Watkinson (cta), S. Jerusalem (ten), S. Nimsgern (b-bar), H. Rilling (cnd), Stuttgart Bach Ensemble [L] Odyssey ▲ MBK 42614 ■ YT 42614
Mozart, W.A.:Requiem, w. C. Oelze (sop), I. Danz (mez), S. Weir (ten), A. Schmidt (bar), H. Rilling (cnd), Stuttgart Bach Collegium [L] Hänssler Classic 2-▲ 98.979 [DDD]
Verdi, G.:Messa per Rossini, w. G. Benačková-Cápova (sop), F. Quivar (mez), J. Wagner (ten), A. Agache (bar), A. Haugland (bass), H. Rilling (cnd), Stuttgart RSO, Prague Phil Chorus [L]
Hänssler Classic 2-▲ CD 98.949 [DDD] 2-■ MC 96.949 (D)

H. Rilling (cnd)
Brahms, J.:Liebeslieder Waltzes SATB [G] Acanta ▲ 43805
Brahms, J.:Neue Liebeslieder Waltzes [G] Acanta ▲ 43805

Ganagobie Abbey Monks' Choir
Couperin, F.:Messe propre pour les couvents de religieux et religieuses, w. L. Jouvet (org)
Jade ▲ JAD C096
Monks of the Abbey at Ganagobie Milan ▲ 73138-35653-2 ■ 73138-35653-4

L. Jouvet (cnd)
du Mont, H.:Messes (5) en plain-chant—Royal Mass Jade ▲ JAD C096

Garda Siochana Choir
P. Green (cnd)
Green, P.:The Man from Galilee, w. F. Patterson (ten) Alanna ▲ ALA 5554 [DDD]

Gavrieli Consort
Palestrina, G.:Missa "Hodi Christus", w. *(soloists unknown)*, P. McCreesh (cnd), Gavrieli Players—Missa, "Hodid Christus natus est" Archiv ▲ 437833-2

Gavril Musicescu Chorus
Enescu, G.:Sym 3, w. A. Lascae (cnd), Moldavian PO Ottavo ▲ OTT 59344 [DDD]

General Motors Sym Chorus
Joseph Schmidt, w. Joseph Schmidt (ten), Berlin RSO [cnd:Rudolf Hindemith, Bruno Seidler-Winkler, Hermann Scherchen, Fritz Stiedry, Max von Schillings], unknown orchestra [cnd:Idris Lewis], General Motors SO, General Motors Sym Chorus [cnd:Erno Rapee, José Iturbi, Oscar Straus], et al.
Koch Schwann ▲ SCH 312572 [ADD]

Geneva Elans Vocal Ensemble
Rossini, G.:Stabat Mater, w. O. Liani (sop), J. Jaques (mez), M. Zamfir (ten), T. Krause (bar), P. Crispini (cnd), Geneva Elans Orch Ensemble [L] Gallo ▲ CD 487

Geneva Grand Théâtre Chorus
Romantic French Arias, w. Joan Sutherland (sop), Richard Bonynge (cnd), Swiss Romande Orch
London ("Opera Gala" series) ▲ 421879-2 LA [ADD]
Rossini, G.:Il barbiere di Siviglia, w. J. Larmore (cta), A. Corbelli (bar), R. Gimeniz (bar), H. Hagegard (bar), S. Ramey (bass), J. López-Cobos (cnd), Lausanne CO [I] Teldec 2-▲ 9031-74885-2
Rossini, G.:Il barbiere di Siviglia (sels), w. B. Frittoli (sop), J. Larmore (mez), R. Giménez (ten), Håkan Hagegård (bar), A. Corbelli (bar), S. Ramey (bass), J. López-Cobos (cnd), Lausanne CO
Teldec ▲ 93693-2

Geneva Univ Chorus
Mendelssohn, F.:Psalm 42, w. Y. Perrin (sop), M. Schwartz (mez), O. Dufour (ten), C. Traube (ten), P. Huttenlocher (bar), C. Ossola (bass), M. Hutin (bass), C. Liang-Sheng (cnd), Geneva SO
Gallo ▲ CD 635 [AAD]
Mendelssohn, F.:Psalm 95, w. Y. Perrin (sop), M. Schwartz (mez), O. Dufour (ten), C. Traube (ten), P. Huttenlocher (bar), C. Ossola (bass), M. Hutin (bass), C. Liang-Sheng (cnd), Geneva SO
Gallo ▲ CD 635 [AAD]
Mendelssohn, F.:Psalm 115, w. Y. Perrin (sop), M. Schwartz (mez), O. Dufour (ten), C. Traube (ten), P. Huttenlocher (bar), C. Ossola (bass), M. Hutin (bass), C. Liang-Sheng (cnd), Geneva SO
Gallo ▲ CD 635 [AAD]

Genoa Teatro Carlo Felice Chorus
Rossini, G.:The Siege of Corinth, w. L. Serra (sop), M. Comencini (ten), D. Raffanti (ten), A. Caforio (bass), M. Lippi (bass), P. Olmi (cnd), Genoa Teatro Carlo Felice Orch, Prague Phil Choir *(rec June 2 & 14, 1992)* Nuova Era 3-▲ 7140/42 [DDD]

Genoa Teatro Comunale Chorus
Donizetti, G.:Torquato Tasso, w. A. D'Auria (sop), L. Serra (sop), N. Ciliento (mez), E. Palacio (ten), R. Coviello (bar), S. Alaimo (bass-bar), A. Riva (bass), M.. Bernart (cnd), Genoa Teatro Comunale Orch [I] *(rec live 10/16/85)* Bongiovanni 3-▲ GB 2028/30 [DDD]
Puccini, G.:La Bohème, w. M. Freni (sop), M. Adani (sop), L. Pavarotti (ten), L. Saccomani (bar), M. Wolf-Ferrari (cnd), Genoa Teatro Comunale Orch *(rec live, Apr 12, 1969)*
Melodram 2-▲ MEL 27031 [AAD]
Puccini, G.:La Bohème, w. M. Freni (sop), M. Adani (sop), L. Pavarotti (ten), L. Saccomani (bar), M. Wolf-Ferrari (cnd), Genoa Teatro Comunale Orch [I] *(rec live 4/12/69)* Verona 2-▲ 27079/80
Puccini, G.:Turandot, w. G. Dimitrova (sop), C. Gasdia (sop), N. Martinucci (ten), R. Scandiuzzi (bass), D. Oren (cnd), Genoa Teatro Comunale Orch [I] *(rec live, 1/20-27/89)*
Nuova Era 2-▲ 6786/87 [DDD]
Puccini, G.:Turandot (sels), w. G. Dimitrova (sop), C. Gasdia (sop), N. Martinucci (ten), R. Scandiuzzi (bass), D. Oren (cnd), Genoa Teatro Comunale Orch [I] Nuova Era ▲ 6871 [DDD]

Gentlemen of the Chappell
Gaudeamus Early Music Sampler, w. Great Consort, His Majesties Sagbutts & Cornetts, Rasumovsky String Quartet, Trio Sonnerie, Cappella Nova, Cardinall's Musick, Clerks' Group, Ex Cathedra, Gonville & Caius College Choir Cambridge, et al. ASV/Gaudeamus ▲ ASV 1002

German Opera Chorus—see Deutsche Opera Chorus

Gesamtleitung
W. Ehmann (cnd)
Schütz, H.:Kleine geistliche Konzerte (sels)—Concertos 8-23 of the 2nd part *(rec Petrikirche, Herford, Feb 1965 & Mar 1966)* Cantate ▲ C 57605 [ADD]

Ghent Collegium Vocale
Bach, J.S.:Cant 66, w. G. Leonhardt (cnd), Leonhardt Consort, Hanover Boys' Chorus [G]
Teldec 2-▲ 2292-42571-2 [AAD]

Ghent Collegium Vocale (cont.)
Bach, J.S.:Cant 67, w. G. Leonhardt (cnd), Leonhardt Consort, Hanover Boys' Chorus [G]
Teldec 2-▲ 2292-42571-2 [AAD]
Bach, J.S.:Cant 73, w. G. Leonhardt (cnd), Leonhardt Consort, Hanover Boys' Chorus [G]
Teldec 2-▲ 2292-42573-2 [ADD]
Bach, J.S.:Cant 74, w. G. Leonhardt (cnd), Leonhardt Consort, Hanover Boys' Chorus [G]
Teldec 2-▲ 2292-42573-2 [ADD]
Bach, J.S.:Cant 75, w. G. Leonhardt (cnd), Leonhardt Consort, Hanover Boys' Chorus [G]
Teldec 2-▲ 2292-42573-2 [ADD]
Bach, J.S.:Cant 90, w. P. Esswood (ct), K. Equiluz (ten), M. van Egmond (b-bar), Leonhardt Consort [G]
Teldec 2-▲ 2292-42578-2 [ADD]
Bach, J.S.:Christmas Oratorio, w. B. Schlick (sop), M. Chance (ct), H. Crook (ten), P. Kooy (bass), P. Herreweghe (cnd), Ghent Collegium Vocale Orch [G]
Virgin Classics (Veritas) 2-▲ ZDCB 59530-2 [DDD]
Bach, J.S.:Masses, BWV 233-36, "Lutheran Masses", w. A. Mellon (sop), G. Lesne (alto), C. Prégardien (ten), P. Kooy (bass), P. Herreweghe (cnd), Ghent Collegium Vocale Orch—BWV 233 & 236
Virgin Classics ▲ CDC 59634
Bach, J.S.:Masses, BWV 233-36, "Lutheran Masses", w. A. Mellon (sop), G. Lesne (alto), C. Prégardien (ten), P. Kooy (bass), P. Herreweghe (cnd), Ghent Collegium Vocale Orch—BWV 234 & 235
Virgin Classics ▲ CDC 59587
Bach, J.S.:Motets, BWV 225-30, w. P. Herreweghe (cnd), La Chapelle Royale Orch
Harmonia Mundi France ▲ HMC 901231
Bach, J.S.:St. John Passion, w. B. Schlick (sop), C. Patriasz (cta), H. Crook (ten), W. Kendall (ten), P. Kooy (bass), P. Lika (bass), P. Herreweghe (cnd), La Chapelle Royale Orch [G]
Harmonia Mundi France 2-▲ HMC 901264/65 [DDD]
Bach, J.S.:St. Matthew Passion, w. B. Schlick (sop), R. Jacobs (ct), H. P. Blochwitz (ten), H. Crook (ten), U. Cold (bass), P. Kooy (bass), P. Herreweghe (cnd), La Chapelle Royale Orch [G]
Harmonia Mundi France 3-▲ HMC 901155/57
Bach, J.S.:St. Matthew Passion (sels), w. A. Mellon (sop), G. Lesne (alto), C. Prégardien (ten), P. Kooy (bass), P. Herreweghe (cnd), Ghent Collegium Vocale Orch Virgin Classics ▲ CDC 59587
Brahms, J.:Motets (misc), w. P. Herreweghe (cnd), La Chapelle Royale Orch—Opp. 29, 74 & 110 [G]
Harmonia Mundi France ▲ HMC 901122
Haydn, J.:Die Schöpfung, w. Krisztina Láki (sop), Neil Mackie (ten), Philippe Huttenlocher (bar), S. Kuijken (cnd), La Petite Bande Accent 2-▲ ACC 58228/29
Mendelssohn, F.:Psalm 42, w. E. Harrhy (sop), H. Lamy (ten), P. Kooy (bass), P. Herreweghe (cnd), La Chapelle Royale Orch [G] Harmonia Mundi France ▲ HMC 901272 [DDD]
Mendelssohn, F.:Psalm 115, w. E. Harrhy (sop), P. Herreweghe (cnd), La Chapelle Royale Orch [G]
Harmonia Mundi France ▲ HMC 901272 [DDD]
Mendelssohn, F.:Verleih uns Frieden, w. P. Herreweghe (cnd), La Chapelle Royale Orch [G]
Harmonia Mundi France ▲ HMC 901272 [DDD]

P. Herreweghe (cnd)
Mendelssohn, F.:Ave Maria, w. H. Lamy (ten), L. van Doeselaar (org)
Harmonia Mundi France ▲ HMC 901272 [DDD]
Mendelssohn, F.:Motets & Psalms, w. Chapelle Royale Choir—Op. 23/3; 69/1; 78/1, 3; 79/1-6; Psalm 55 [G] *(rec 5/84)* Musique d'Abord ▲ HMA 1901142

Jean-Paul Gipon Vocal Ensemble
Lassus, O. de:Officium tenebrarum Jade 2-▲ JADC 102

Glinka Boys' Choir
Petrov, A.:The Creation of the World, w. Y. Temirkanov (cnd), Leningrad State Phil Academic SO *(rec Grand Hall of the Leningrad State PO)* Russian Compact Disc ▲ RCD 26601

Gloriae Dei Cantores
Palestrina, G.:Missa de Beata Marie II Paraclete ▲ GDCD 013 [DDD]
Palestrina, G.:Missa "Descendit angelus" Paraclete ▲ GDCD 013 [DDD]

E.C. Patterson (cnd)
Ascension Day Evensong Paraclete ▲ GDCD 003 ■ GDC 003
Be Glad Then America Paraclete ▲ GDCD 008 ■ GDC 008
Be Glad, Then America, w. James E. Jordan Jr. (org) Paraclete ▲ PCL 8 [DDD] 2-■ PCL 8
Brahms, J.:Motets (misc), w. James E. Jordan Jr. (org)—Es ist das Heil uns kommen her; O Heiland reiss die Himmel auf; Ach, arme Welt, du trügest mich Paraclete ▲ GDCD 023 [DDD]
The Chants of Christmas Paraclete ▲ GDCD 005 [DDD] ■ GDC 005 (D)
The Chants of Easter Paraclete ▲ GDCD 015 [DDD]
Easter Day Mass Paraclete ▲ GDCD 002 ■ GDC 002
Holy Radiant Light:The Sacred Song of Russia, w. Andre Papkov (bass)
Paraclete ▲ PCL 7 [DDD] ■ PCL 7
Mendelssohn, F.:Choral Music, w. James E. Jordan Jr. (org)—Heilig; Zwei Geistliche Choere; Mitten wir in Leben sind; Aus tiefer Noth schrei'ich zu dir; Drei Motteten; Sechs Sprüche
Paraclete ▲ GDCD 023 [DDD]
Music of the Americas, 1492-1992, w. David Chalmers (org), James E. Jordan Jr. (org)
Paraclete 2-▲ PCL 10 [DDD] 2-■ PCL 10
Palestrina, G.:Missa de Beata Marie II Paraclete ■ GDC 013
Palestrina, G.:Missa "Descendit angelus" Paraclete ■ GDC 013
Palestrina, G.:Sacred Music—Super flumina Babylonis; Ad Te levavi oculos meos; Miserere nostri, Domine; Sicut cervus; Sitivit anima mea; Jubilate Deo Paraclete ■ GDC 013
Resurrexi Paraclete ▲ GDCD 006 ■ GDC 006
Rheinberger, J.:Hymns—Tribulationes, Op. 140 Paraclete ▲ GDCD 018 [DDD]
Rheinberger, J.:Mass, Op. 109 Paraclete ▲ GDCD 018 [DDD]
Rheinberger, J.:Mass, Op. 187, w. David Chalmers (org) Paraclete ▲ GDCD 018 [DDD]
Rheinberger, J.:Mass, Op. 190, w. David Chalmers (org) Paraclete ▲ GDCD 018 [DDD]
Rheinberger, J.:Motets—Laudate Dominum; Meditabor; Anima nostra Paraclete ▲ GDCD 018 [DDD]
San Marco 1527-1740, w. David Chalmers (org), James E. Jordan Jr. (org)
Paraclete 2-▲ GDCD 014 [DDD] 2-■ GDC 014 I & II
Sowerby, L.:Choral Music, w. D. Chalmers (org), J. E. Jordan Jr. (org)—Great Is the Lord; Hear My Cry, O God; The Lord Is My Shepherd; How Long Wilt Thou Forget Me; Turn Thou to Thy God; Whoso Dwelleth; An Angel Stood by the Alter Of Paraclete 2-▲ GCCD 016
Sowerby, L.:Great Is the Lord Paraclete 2-▲ PCL 16 [DDD] 2-■ PCL 16
This Worldes Joie, w. James E. Jordan Jr. (org), David Chalmers (pno) *(rec Mechanics Hall, Worcester, MA)* Paraclete ▲ GDCD 020
What Cheer! Paraclete ▲ PCL 9503 [DDD] ■ PCL 9503

Gloucester Cathedral Choir
J. Sanders (cnd)
The Psalms of David, Vol. 5:Praise the Lord ye Servants Priory ▲ PRCD 387 [DDD]

Glyndebourne Festival Chorus
Gershwin, G.:Porgy & Bess, w. C. Haymon (sop—Bess), C. Clarey (sop—Serena), M. Simpson (sop—Maria), D. Evans (ten—Sporting Life), G. Baker (bar—Crown), W. White (bar—Porgy), S. Rattle (cnd), London PO EMI Classics 3-▲ CDCC 49568
Gluck, C.W.:Orfeo ed Euridice (sels), w. A. Ayars (sop), Z. Vlachopoulos (sop), K. Ferrier (cta), F. Stiedry (cnd), Southern PO *(rec 1947)* Enterprise ("Palladio" series) ▲ ENTPD 4171 [ADD]
Lehár, F.:Die lustige Witwe, w. F. Lott (sop), E. Szmytka (sop), J. Aler (ten), T. Hampson (b-bar), D. Bogarde (nar), F. Welser-Möst (cnd), London PO EMI Classics ▲ CDCB 55152
Mozart, W.A.:Così fan tutte, w. I. Souez (sop), L. Helletsgrüber (sop), I. Eisinger (sop), H. Nash (ten), W. Domgraf-Fassbäender (bar), J. Brownlee (bar), F. Busch (cnd), Glyndebourne Festival Orch [I] *(rec 1935)* Pearl 3-▲ PEAS 9406 (m) [AAD]
Mozart, W.A.:Così fan tutte, w. Carol Vaness (sop), Delores Ziegler (mez), C. Watson (cta), J. Aler (ten), D. Duesing (bar), C. Desderi (bar), B. Haitink (cnd), London PO EMI Classics 3-▲ CDCC 47727
Mozart, W.A.:Così fan tutte, w. Irene Eisinger (sop—Despina), Luise Helletsgruber (sop—Dorabella), Ina Souez (sop—Fiordiligi), Heddle Nash (ten—Ferrando), John Brownlee (bass—Don Alfonso), Willi Domgraf-Fassbaender (bass—Guglielmo), F. Busch (cnd), Glyndebourne Festival Orch *(rec June 25-28, 1935)* Arkadia ("The 78's" series) 2-▲ 78011 [ADD]

Glyndebourne Festival Chorus (cont.)
Mozart, W.A.:Don Giovanni, w. C. Vaness (sop), M. Ewing (sop), E. Gale (sop), K. Lewis (ten), T. Allen (bar), R. Van Allan (bass), B. Haitink (cnd), London PO [I] EMI Classics 3–▲ CDCC 47036 [DDD]
Mozart, W.A.:Don Giovanni, w. I. Souez (sop), L. Helletsgrüber (sop), A. Mildmay (sop), K. von Pataky (ten), J. Brownlee (bar), R. Henderson (bar), T. Franklin (bar), S. Baccaloni (bass), F. Busch (cnd), Glyndebourne Festival Orch [I] *(rec 1936, orig. issued by HMV)* Pearl 3–▲ PEAS 9369 (m) [AAD]
Mozart, W.A.:Idomeneo, w. Gundula Janowitz (sop), Enriqueta Tarres (sop), Richard Lewis (ten), Luciano Pavarotti (ten), J. Pritchard (cnd), London PO [I] *(rec live, Royal Albert Hall, London Aug. 17, 1964)* Melodram 2–▲ MEL 27003 (m)
Mozart, W.A.:Idomeneo, w. Gundula Janowitz (sop), Enriqueta Tarres (sop), Richard Lewis (ten), Luciano Pavarotti (ten), J. Pritchard (cnd), London PO [I] *(rec live at Royal Albert Hall, Aug. 17, 1964)* Verona 2–▲ 27038/39 (m) [AAD]
Mozart, W.A.:Idomeneo (sels), w. Gundula Janowitz (sop), Enriqueta Tarres (sop), David Hughes (ten), Richard Lewis (ten), Luciano Pavarotti (ten), Neilson Taylor (bar), Dennis Wicks (bass), J. Pritchard (cnd), London PO Budget ("The Greatest Voice in Opera" series) ▲ SYP 107
Mozart, W.A.:Nozze di Figaro, w. Aulikki Rautawaara (sop), Audrey Mildmay (sop), Constance Willis (mez), John Heddle Nash (ten), Roy Henderson (bar), Willi Domgraf–Fassbaender (bar), F. Busch (cnd), Glyndebourne Festival Orch [I] *(rec 1934–35)* Pearl 2–▲ PEAS 9375 (m) [AAD]
Mozart, W.A.:Nozze di Figaro, w. Luise Helletsgrüber (sop), Audrey Mildmay (sop), Aulikki Rautawaara (sop), Willi Domgraf–Fassbaender (bar), Roy Henderson (bar), F. Busch (cnd), Glyndebourne Festival Orch *(rec 1934)* Grammofono 2000 2–▲ GRM 78624
Mozart, W.A.:Nozze di Figaro, w. S. Jurinac (sop), G. Sciutti (sop), R. Stevens (mez), M. Sinclair (cta), D. McCoshan (ten), H. Cuenod (ten), G. Griffith (bar), S. Bruscantini (b–bar), F. Calabrese (bass), V. Gui (cnd), Glyndebourne Festival Orch Classics for Pleasure ▲ CDCFP 4724 [ADD]
Rossini, G.:Il barbiere di Siviglia, w. V. de los Angeles (sop), L. Alva (ten), C. Cava (bass), I. Wallace (bass), V. Gui (cnd), Royal PO *(rec 1962)* EMI Classics 2–▲ CDMB 64162
Rossini, G.:La Cenerentola, w. A. Noni (sop), F. Cadoni (mez), M. de Gabarain (mez), H. Alan (bass), V. Gui (cnd), Glyndebourne Festival Orch *(rec 1955)* EMI Classics 2–▲ CDMB 64183
Rossini, G.:Le Comte Ory, w. J. Sinclair (sop), M. Sinclair (cta), J. Oncina (ten), M. Roux (bar), V. Gui (cnd), Glyndebourne Festival Orch *(rec 1956)* EMI Classics 2–▲ CDMB 64180
Sullivan, A.:The Gondoliers, w. G. Evans (bar), A. Young (ten), O. Brannigan (bass), R. Lewis (ten), M. Sargent (cnd), Pro Arte Orch EMI Classics 2–▲ CDMB 64394
Sullivan, A.:HMS Pinafore, w. G. Baker (bar), J. Cameron (bar), R. Lewis (ten), M. Sargent (cnd), Pro Arte Orch EMI Classics 2–▲ CDMB 64397
Sullivan, A.:The Mikado, w. O. Brannigan (bass), R. Lewis (ten), G. Evans (bar), I. Wallace (bass), M. Sargent (cnd), Pro Arte Orch EMI Classics 2–▲ CDMB 64403
Sullivan, A.:Music of, w. M. Sargent (cnd), Pro Arte Orch—sels. from The Mikado; The Yoemen of the Guard; Iolanthe; The Gondoliers; The Pirates of Penzance; H.M.S. Pinafore Classics for Pleasure ▲ CDCFP 4238 [ADD]
Sullivan, A.:Patience, w. J. Shaw (bar), T. Anthony (bass), A. Young (ten), G. Baker (bar), M. Sargent (cnd), Pro Arte Orch EMI Classics 2–▲ CDMB 64406
Sullivan, A.:The Pirates of Penzance, w. G. Baker (bar), J. Milligan (b–bar), J. Cameron (bar), R. Lewis (ten), M. Sargent (cnd), Pro Arte Orch EMI Classics 2–▲ CDMB 64409
Sullivan, A.:The Sorcerer (sels), w. G. Baker (bar), E. Morison (sop), J. Cameron (bar), R. Lewis (ten), M. Sargent (cnd), Pro Arte Orch EMI Classics 2–▲ CDMB 64397
Sullivan, A.:The Yeomen of the Guard, w. R. Lewis (ten), A. Young (ten), J. Cameron (bar), M. Sargent (cnd), Pro Arte Orch EMI Classics 2–▲ CDMB 64415

Goethe Academy Children's Choir
Orff, C.:Carmina burana, w. Lisa Griffith (sop), Ulrich Ress (ten), Thomas Mohr (bar), M. Tang (cnd), Royal Flemish PO, Frankfurt Figuralchor, Frankfurt Children's Choir, Frankfurt Choral Society *(rec Oct. 1993)* Wergo ▲ WER 6602–2 [DDD]

Golden Age Choir
Purcell, H.:Odes & Welcome Songs (misc), w. Jeni Bern (sop), Susan Bisatt (sop), William Purefoy (ct), Christopher Robson (ct), Ian Honeyman (ten), Thomas Guthrie (bass), R. Glenton (cnd), Orch of the Golden Age—The noise of foreign wars (fragment) [ed. by Bruce Wood] *(rec Manchester Grammar School, England, May 13 & 14, 1995)* Naxos ▲ 8.553444 [DDD]
Purcell, H.:Raise, Raise the Voice, w. Jeni Bern (sop), Susan Bisatt (sop), William Purefoy (ct), Christopher Robson (ct), Ian Honeyman (ten), Thomas Guthrie (bass), R. Glenton (cnd), Orch of the Golden Age *(rec Manchester Grammar School, England, May 13 & 14, 1995)* Naxos ▲ 8.553444 [DDD]
Purcell, H.:Te Deum & Jubilate, w. Jeni Bern (sop), Susan Bisatt (sop), William Purefoy (ct), Christopher Robson (ct), Ian Honeyman (ten), Thomas Guthrie (bass), David Staff (tpt), R. Glenton (cnd), Orch of the Golden Age *(rec Manchester Grammar School, England, May 13 & 14, 1995)* Naxos ▲ 8.553444 [DDD]
Purcell, H.:Welcome to All the Pleasures, w. Jeni Bern (sop), Susan Bisatt (sop), William Purefoy (ct), Christopher Robson (ct), Ian Honeyman (ten), Thomas Guthrie (bass), R. Glenton (cnd), Orch of the Golden Age *(rec Manchester Grammar School, England, May 13 & 14, 1995)* Naxos ▲ 8.553444 [DDD]

Goldsmith's Choral Union
Delius, F.:Appalachia, w. John Noble (bar), C. Groves (cnd), London PO, BBC Chorus, BBC Choral Society, London Phil Choir IMP ("BBC Radio Classics" series) ▲ IMP 9133
Mahler, G.:Sym 2, w. Rae Woodland (sop), Janet Baker (mez), L. Stokowski (cnd), London SO, BBC Chorus, BBC Choral Society, Harrow Choral Society *(rec 1963)* Music & Arts ▲ CD 885 [AAD]

Gonville & Caius College Choir Cambridge
Gaudeamus Early Music Sampler, w. Great Consort, His Majesties Sagbutts & Cornetts, Rasumovsky String Quartet, Trio Sonnerie, Cappella Nova, Cardinall's Musick, Clerks' Group, Ex Cathedra, Gentlemen of the Chappell, et al. ASV/Gaudeamus ▲ ASV 1002
Hadley, P.:A Cant for Lent ASV ▲ ASV 881 [DDD]
Hadley, P.:Songs—I Sing of a Maiden; A Song for Easter; The Cup of Blessing; My Beloved Spake ASV ▲ ASV 881 [DDD]
Rubbra, E.:Choral Music—3 Motets; 3 Hymn Tunes; Magnificat & Nunc Dimittis ASV ▲ ASV 881 [DDD]
Rubbra, E.:Missa in honorem Sancti Dominici ASV ▲ ASV 881 [DDD]
Wood, C.:St. Mark Passion ASV ▲ ASV 854

G. Webber (cnd)
Janácek, L.:Sacred Music—Mass in E♭; Exaudi Deus; In nomine Jesu; Otce nás [The Lord's Prayer]; Regnum mundi; Suscepimus Deus; Zdrávas Maria ASV ▲ ASV 914 [DDD]
Puccini, G.:Sacred Music—Requiem; Salve Regina; Vexilla Regis ASV ▲ ASV 914 [DDD]
Wesley, S.:Sacred Choral Music ASV/Gaudeamus ▲ ASV 157

Goodman Chamber Choir
Luening, O.:No Jerusalem But This, w. K. Sullivan (sop), Jacqueline Pierce (sop), Paul Sperry (ten), M. Moliterno (bar), P. Wilder (sgr), S. Rosser (sgr), A. Goodman (cnd), Music Project CO [E] *(rec 6/6/90)* CRI ▲ CD 600 [DDD]

Gospel Singers
Soldier, D.:War Prayer, w. Dionne Freeney (alt), Jason White (ten), Wilbur Pauley (bass), R.A. Clark (cnd), Manhattan CO Newport Classic ▲ NPD 85589 [DDD]

Gösta Ohlins Vocal Ensemble
Vind, Vind Lyckliga Vind' Intim Musik ▲ INT 11 [DDD]

Gostelradio Armenia Chamber Choir
T. Ekekian (cnd)
Armenian Choral Music Art & Electronics ▲ AED 10483 [DDD]

Gostelradio Choir
Boiko, R.:Festival Procession, w. E. Svetlanov (cnd), Russian State SO Russian Disc ▲ RUS 11020 [AAD]

Gothenburg Chamber Choir
Taube, E.:Där blaser, w. S. Forssén (pno), G. Taube (vn) Prophone ▲ PCD 003

Gothenburg Chorus
Sibelius, J.:The Maiden in the Tower, w. M. A. Häggander (sop), E. Hagegard (ten), J. Hynninen (bar), T. Kruse (cta), N. Järvi (cnd), Gothenburg SO [Fin] BIS ▲ CD 250 [DDD]

Gothenburg Male Choir
Sibelius, J.:Choral Music, w. N. Järvi (cnd), Gothenburg SO—Sandels, Op. 28; Have you courage?, Op. 31/2; War Song of Tyrtaeus, Op. 31/3; The Origin of Fire, Op. 32; March of the Finnish Cavalry, Op. 91/1; Academic March BIS ▲ CD 314

Gothenburg Sym Chorus
Grieg, E.:Peer Gynt, w. B. Bonney (sop), M. Eklöf (mez), K. M. Sandve (ten), U. Malmberg (bar), N. Järvi (cnd), Gothenburg SO [N] Deutsche Grammophon 2–▲ 423079–2 [DDD]
Grieg, E.:Sigurd Jorsalfar, w. B. Bonney (sop), M. Eklöf (mez), K. M. Sandve (ten), U. Malmberg (bar), N. Järvi (cnd), Gothenburg SO [N] Deutsche Grammophon 2–▲ 423079–2 [DDD]
Prokofiev, S.:The Fiery Angel, w. N. Secunde (sop), R. Engert–Ely (mez), H. Zednik (ten), S. Lorenz (bar), K. Moll (bass), N. Järvi (cnd), Gothenburg SO [R] Deutsche Grammophon 2–▲ 431669–2 [DDD]
Stenhammar, W.:Mid–Winter, w. N. Järvi (cnd), Gothenburg SO [Sw] BIS ▲ CD 438 [DDD]

Gothic Voices
Musica Humana, w. Françoise Atlan (mez), John Fleagle (ten/hp), Crawford Young (lt), Anonymous 4, Ensemble Discantus, Ensemble Gilles Binchois, Ensemble Organum, Greece Byzantine Choir, Hilliard Ensemble, Musica Nova, et al. L'Empreinte Digitale ▲ ED 13047
The Spirits of England & France, Vol. 2, w. Emma Kirkby (sop), Robert White (bgp), Pavlo Beznosiuk (fid), Nick Bicat (perc), Christopher Page (cnd) Hyperion ▲ CDA 66773

C. Page (cnd)
The Castle of Fair Welcome Hyperion ▲ CDA 66194 [DDD]
The Garden of Zephirus Hyperion ▲ CDA 66144 ■
Hildegard Of Bingen:Hymns & Sequences [L] Hyperion ▲ CDA 66039 [DDD] ■ KA 66039 (D)
Machaut, G. de:Ballades, rondeaux, virelais, motets & lais [F,L] Hyperion ▲ CDA 66087 [DDD]
The Missa Caput & the Story of the Salve Regina Hyperion ▲ 66857
The Spirits of England & France, Vol. 1, w. Pavlo Beznosiuk (medieval fid) Hyperion ▲ CDA 66739
The Study of Love:French Songs & Motets of the 14th Century *(rec April & May 1992)* Hyperion ▲ CDA 66619 [DDD]
The Voice in the Garden Hyperion ▲ CDA 66653

Grace Lutheran Church Choir River Forest IL
R. Batastini (cnd)
Taize:Wait for the Lord, w. St. Barbara Roman Catholic Church Choir Brookfield IL GIA ▲ GIA 173

Graduate Chamber Singers
Rouse, C.:Madrigals, w. D. Neuen (cnd), Eastman Musica Nova Ensemble *(rec Eastman Theater, Feb 22, 1984)* Albany ▲ TROY 192 [ADD]

Gradus ad Parnassum
Biber, H. von:Missa alleluja, w. K. Junghänel (cnd), Concerto Palatino Choir, Vienna Hofburgkapelle Choir Deutsche Harmonia Mundi ▲ 05472–77326–2 [DDD]
Schmelzer, J.H.:Vesperae solennes, w. K. Junghänel (cnd), Concerto Palatino Choir, Vienna Hofburgkapelle Choir Deutsche Harmonia Mundi ▲ 05472–77326–2 [DDD]

Graezer Concert Choir
Schmidt, F.:Das Buch mit sieben Siegeln, w. Hertha Töpper (mez), Anton Dermota (ten), Thomas Moser (ten), Robert Holl (bass), A.J. Hochstrasser (cnd), Lower Austria Tonkünst Orch *(rec 1975)* Preiser 2–▲ PRE 93263 [ADD]

Grail Singers
A Women's Celebration of Chant & Harmony *(rec Loveland, OH, Aug. 1–6, 1994)* SKR Classical ▲ SKR 1801

Grajna Choir Minsk
N. Kashuro (cnd)
Arkhangelsky, A.:Choral Music—Pomichlaiu dien strachny Gallo ▲ CD 878 [DAD]
Berezovsky, M.:Cast Me Not Away in the Time of Age Gallo ▲ CD 878 [DAD]
Bortnyansky, D.:Sacred Choral Music—Te Deum Gallo ▲ CD 878 [DAD]
Diletski, N.:Music of—Voskrecenski canon Gallo ▲ CD 878 [DAD]
Dmitriev, A.:Svetlana Gallo ▲ CD 878 [DAD]

Grand Rapids Chamber Choir
Larry G. Biser (cnd)
Works for Cathedral Spaces, w. Jonathan Tuuk (org) Pro Organo ▲ POCD 7015

Grande Ecurie
Jean–Claude Malgoire (cnd)
Great Baroque Favorites, w. R. Leppard (cnd), English CO, Philharmonia Virtuosi [cnd:Richard Kapp], et al. CBS ▲ MYK 38482 ■ MYT 38482

Graunke Chorus
Strauss (II), Joh.:Eine Nacht in Venedig (sels), w. Christine Gorner (sop), Rita Streich (sop), Cesare Curzi (ten), Nicolai Gedda (ten), Christian Oppleberg (bar), F. Allers (cnd), Graunke SO Emperor Operetta ▲ KO 86345

Greek Byzantine Choir
Musica Humana, w. Françoise Atlan (mez), John Fleagle (ten/hp), Crawford Young (lt), Anonymous 4, Ensemble Discantus, Ensemble Gilles Binchois, Ensemble Organum, Gothic Voices, Greece Byzantine Choir, Hilliard Ensemble, Musica Nova, et al. L'Empreinte Digitale ▲ ED 13047

L. Angelopoulos (cnd)
Byzantine Mass & Akathistos Hymn Playasound ▲ PLS 65118 [DDD]
Christmas Hymns Jade ▲ JAD C 097
The Divine Liturgy of St. John Chrysostom Opus 111 ▲ OPS 30–78

Greifswald Cathedral Choir
Buxtehude, D.:Cants, w. H. Flugbeil (cnd), Berlin Bach Orch—Wachet auf, ruft uns die Stimme, BuxWV 101; Jesu, meine Freude, BuxWV 60; Cantate Domino, BuxWV 12; Lauda Sion salvatorem, BuxWV68; Mit Fried und Freud ich fahr dahin, BuxWV 76; Befiehl dem Engel, dass er komm, BuxWV 10 *(rec Berlin, Wuppertal–Barmen, Herford, Apr. 1959, Jan. 1960 & Ju)* Cantate ▲ 57601

Grenoble Vocal Ensemble
Messiaen, O.:Petites liturgies (3) de la Présence Divine, w. S. Cardon (cnd), Grenoble Instrumental Ensemble Forlane 2–▲ FOR 16504/05 [AAD/DDD]

Grimbergen Gregoriaans Abbey Monks' Choir
Gregorian High Days Eufoda ▲ EUF 1179
Hemelvaart en Pinkelsteren Eufoda ▲ EUF 1125 [DDD]
Passie en Pasen Eufoda ▲ EUF 1124 [DDD]
Verrijzenis:Gezangen uit de requiemliturgie Eufoda ▲ EUF 1181 [DDD]

G. van Boesschoten (cnd)
Advent en Kerst Eufoda ▲ EUF 1119 [DDD]

Groot Chorus
Bizet, G.:Les Pêcheurs de perles (sels), w. Erna Spoorenberg (sop), Alain Vanzo (ten), J. Fournet (cnd), Groot Radio PO *(rec Amsterdam, 1963)* Bella Voce 2–▲ 107.208
Gounod, C.:Roméo et Juliette, w. Erna Spoorenberg (sop), Alain Vanzo (ten), J. Fournet (cnd), Groot Radio PO *(rec Amsterdam, Jan 1966)* Bella Voce 2–▲ 107.208

Groot Omroep Choir
Beethoven, L. van:Christus am Ölberg, w. Erna Spoorenberg (sop—Seraph), Fritz Wünderlich (ten—Jesus), Hermann Schey (bass—Petrus), H. Spruit (cnd), Netherlands Radio PO *(rec Mar 8, 1957)* Bella Voce ▲ 7003 [AAD]
Puccini, G.:Manon Lescaut, w. Magda Olivero (sop—Manon), Tine Appelman (mez—Singer), Umberto Borso (ten—Chevalier), Mario Carlin (ten—Edmondo/Dancing Master/Lamplighter), Ferdinando Lidonni (bar—Lescaut), Giovanni Foiani (bass—Geronte/Sergeant/Captain), Joop Ruivenkamp (bass—Innkeeper), F. Vernizzi (cnd), Groot Omroep Orch *(rec Amsterdam, Oct 31, 1964)* Bella Voce 2–▲ BLV 107.221 [AAD]

Grosvenor High School Choir
Debussy, C.:Nocturnes, w. Y.P. Tortelier (cnd), Ulster Orch, Renaissance Singers Chandos ▲ CHAN 8914 [DDD]

Grudgionz Festival Chorus
Puccini, G.:Turnadot (sels), w. Luciano Pavarotti (ten), G.–F. Masini (cnd), Grudgionz Festival Orch—Nessun dorma *(rec live, Apr. 23, 1964)* RCA Gold Seal ▲ 09026–68014–2 [ADD]

CHORAL GROUPS

Grudgionz Opera Theater Chorus
Puccini, G.:Turandot (sels), w. Luciano Pavarotti (ten), G.-F. Masini (cnd), Grudgionz Opera Theater Orch—Nessun dorma *(rec Grudgionz, Apr 23, 1964)* Goldies ▲ GLD 63202 [ADD]

Gruppo di Voci
Carissimi, G.:Motets, w. F. Colusso (cnd), Strumenti Antichi, Sulmona Phil Chorus—Vanitas Vanitatum I & II; Sponsa Canticorum; Tolle Sponsa [L] Bongiovanni ▲ GB 10003 [DDD]

Guildford Cathedral Choir
Maunder, J.H.:From Olivet to Calvary, w. J. Mitchinson (ten), F. Harvey (bar), P. Moorse (org) [E] Classics for Pleasure ▲ CDCFP 4619 [ADD]
Vaughan Williams, R.:Fant on Christmas Carols, w. J. Barrow (bar), B. Rose (cnd), Guildford String Orch [2 Christmas Carol choral arr. Vaughan Williams]—And all in the morning & Wassail Song EMI Classics (Studio) ▲ CDM 64131 2 [ADD]

A. Millington (cnd)
Crucifixus, w. G. Morgan (org) *(rec Guilford Cathedral, July 1993)* Herald ▲ HAVPCD 166 [DDD]

P. Moore (cnd)
Bairstow, E.C.:Choral Music, w. Peter Wright (org)—Blessed City, Heavenly Salem Priory ▲ PRI 6 [DDD]
Blitheman, J.:In pace, w. Peter Wright (org) Priory ▲ PRI 6 [DDD]
Byrd, W.:Church Music, w. Peter Wright (org)—Christe Qui Lux Es et Dies Priory ▲ PRI 6 [DDD]
Duruflé, M.:Motets on Gregorian Chants, Op. 10, w. Peter Wright (org) Priory ▲ PRI 6 [DDD]
Moore, P.:All Wisdom, w. Peter Wright (org) Priory ▲ PRI 6 [DDD]
Tallis, T.:Church Music, w. Peter Wright (org)—Te Lucis Ante Terminum Priory ▲ PRI 6 [DDD]
Victoria, T.L. de:Sacred Choral Music, w. Peter Wright (org)—Magnificat, VII Tone Priory ▲ PRI 6 [DDD]

B. Rose (cnd)
Warlock, P.:Choral Music—Adam lay y-bounden; Bethlehem Down EMI Classics ("Studio" series) ▲ CDM 64131 2 [ADD]

Guildford Choral Society
Holst, G.:A Choral Fant, w. L. Dawson (sop), H. D. Wetton (cnd), Royal PO Hyperion ▲ CDA 66660
Holst, G.:First Choral Sym, w. L. Dawson (sop), H. D. Wetton (cnd), Royal PO Hyperion ▲ CDA 66660
Holst, G.:The Golden Goose, w. H. D. Wetton (cnd), Philharmonia Orch Hyperion ▲ CDA 66784
Holst, G.:King Estmere, w. H. D. Wetton (cnd), Philharmonia Orch Hyperion ▲ CDA 66784
Holst, G.:The Morning of the Year, w. H. D. Wetton (cnd), Philharmonia Orch Hyperion ▲ CDA 66784
Lloyd, G.:A Litany, w. Janice Watson (sop), Jeremy White (bar), G. Lloyd (cnd), Philharmonia Orch *(rec Watford Town Hall, Mar 24-25, 1996)* Albany ▲ TROY 200 [DDD]

Györ Girls' Choir
Bartók, B.:Village Scenes, w. Faragó (sop), Adám (sop), A. Dorati (cnd), Budapest Chamber Ensemble [Slovak] Hungaroton ▲ HCD 31047 [ADD]
Lajtha, L.:Hymns for the Holy Virgin, w. M. Szabó (cnd), Tátrai String Quartet, Liszt Academy of Music Chamber Choir [L,F] Hungaroton ▲ HCD 31453 [ADD]
Lajtha, L.:Madrigals, w. M. Szabó (cnd), Tátrai String Quartet, Liszt Academy of Music Chamber Choir [L,F] Hungaroton ▲ HCD 31453 [ADD]
Lajtha, L.:Magnificat, w. M. Szabó (cnd), Tátrai String Quartet, Liszt Academy of Music Chamber Choir [L,F] Hungaroton ▲ HCD 31453 [ADD]

Hagen Phil Chorus
Schreker, F.:Der ferne Klang, w. E. Grigorescu (sop), T. Harper (ten), M. Halász (cnd), Hagen PO [G] Marco Polo 2-▲ 8.223270/271 [DDD]

Hägersten Motet Choir
Bruckner, A.:Ave Maria, *(accompanist unknown)* Caprice ▲ CAP 21420 [DDD]
Bruckner, A.:Locus iste Caprice ▲ CAP 21420 [DDD]
Bruckner, A.:Mass 2 Caprice ▲ CAP 21420 [DDD]
Frumerie, G. de:Singoalla, w. Y. Ahronovitch (cnd), Stockholm PO Caprice 2-▲ CAP 22023 [DDD]
Poulenc, F.:Motets (4) pour le temps de Noël Caprice ▲ CAP 21420 [DDD]
Poulenc, F.:Un Soir de neige Caprice ▲ CAP 21420 [DDD]

Halifax Choral Society

J. Pryce-Jones (cnd)
The Best of Brass & Voices, w. Britannia Building Society Band [cnd:John Pryce-Jones] *(rec BBC Studio 7, 1995)* Doyen ▲ CD 041 [DDD]

William Hall Chorale
Brahms, J.:Choral Music—Heralds of Love; The Way of Love; Questions; Vars. on the Dance; The Cloistered Nun; Flirtation [G] Klavier ■ KC 559
Britten, B.:War Requiem, w. Jeanine Altmeyer (sop), Douglas Lawrence (ten), Michael Sells (bar), Ladd Thomas (org), W. Hall (cnd), William Hall Orch, Columbus Boys' Choir Klavier ▲ KCD 11017 [ADD]
Britten, B.:War Requiem, w. *(vocalists unknown)*, Ladd Thomas (org), W. Hall (cnd), Vienna Festival SO Klavier ■ KC 544
Schumann, R.:Choral Music—Autumn Song; Were I a Little Bird; To the Nightingale; Dark Twilight; Lovely Blossoms; Love's Grief [G] Klavier ■ KC 559

Peter Hall Company
Mendelssohn, F.:A Midsummer Night's Dream (comp), w. L. Dawson (sop), S. Mentzer (mez), J. Tate (cnd), Rotterdam PO, Toonkunst Chorus EMI Classics 2-▲ CDCB 54348

Hallé State Chorus
Handel, G.F.:Brockes-Passion, w. K. Farkas (sop), M. Zádori (sop), D. Minter (alt), J. Bándi (ten), M. Klietmann (ten), G. de Mey (ten), I. Gáti (bar), N. McGegan (cnd), Capella Savaria [period instruments] [G] Hungaroton 3-▲ HCD 12734/36 [DDD]
Orff, C.:Carmina burana, w. S. Armstrong (sop), P. Hall (ten), B. Rayner Cook (bar), M. Handford (cnd), Hallé Orch Classics for Pleasure ▲ CDCFP 9005 [ADD]
Roylance, D.:Battle of the Atlantic Suite, w. L. Garret (sop), B. Connor (cnd), Hallé Orch Conifer Classics ▲ 74321-15008-2
Telemann, G.P.:Brockes Passion, w. M. Zádori (sop), A. Markert (cta), M. Klietmann (ten), G. De Mey (ten), I. Gáti (bar), N. McGegan (cnd), Capella Savaria [period instruments] Hungaroton 3-▲ HCD 31130/32 [DDD]

Hallenser Madrigal Singers
Vivaldi, A.:Gloria, RV.589, w. L. Güttler (cnd), Virtuosi Saxoniae Berlin Classics ▲ BER 1003 [DDD]
Vivaldi, A.:Magnificat, RV.611, w. L. Güttler (cnd), Virtuosi Saxoniae Berlin Classics ▲ BER 1003 [DDD]
Vivaldi, A.:Motets, w. L. Güttler (cnd), Virtuosi Saxoniae—in D, RV.642, "Ostro picta" Berlin Classics ▲ BER 1003 [DDD]

Hamburg Alsterspatzen
Dessau, P.:Haggada, w. Sabine Ritterbusch (sop), Renate Spingler (sop), Yvi Jänicke (alt), Peter Galliard (ten—Rabbi Tarfon/Jude/ten solo), Gabriel Sadé (ten—Pharaoh), Jochen Schmeckenbecher (bar—Rabbi Jehoschua), Bernd Weikl (bar—Moses), Matthias Hölle (bass—Speaker/Rabbi Akiwa), Alfred Muff (bass—Father/Rabbi Eleasar), Johann Tilli (bass—Rabbi Elieser/bass solo), G. Albrecht (cnd), Hamburg State PO, Berlin Carl Maria Von Weber Men's Choir, North German Radio Chorus [G] *(rec Musikhalle, Hamburg, Sept 4 & 5, 1994)* Capriccio 2-▲ 10590/91 [DDD]

Hamburg Cappella Vocale

M. Behrmann (cnd)
Dramatic Gospel Motets, w. Spandau Kantorei Berlin Hänssler Classic ▲ CD 98.948 [DDD]

Hamburg Chorus
Haydn, J.:Die Jahreszeiten, w. Teresa Stich-Randall (mez), Helmut Kretschmar (ten), Erik Wenk (bass), W. Goehr (cnd), North German RSO *(rec 1966)* FNAC Music 2-▲ 642325

Hamburg Monteverdi Chorus
Monteverdi, C.:Vespro della Beata Vergine, w. L. Marshall (sop), F. Palmer (sop), P. Langridge (ten), K. Equiluz (ten), T. Hampson (bar), A. Korn (bass), N. Harnoncourt (cnd), Vienna Concentus Musicus, Vienna Boys' Chorus [L] Teldec 2-▲ 2292-42671-2
Monteverdi, C.:Vespro della Beata Vergine, w. M. Marshall (sop), F. Palmer (sop), P. Langridge (ten), K. Equiluz (ten), T. Hampson (bar), A. Korn (bass), N. Harnoncourt (cnd), Vienna Concentus Musicus, Vienna Boys' Chorus Teldec 2-▲ 92629-2

Hamburg North German Choir
Kagel, M.:Sankt-Bach-Passion, w. Anne Sofie von Otter (mez), Hans Peter Blochowitz (ten), Roland Hermann (bar), Peter Roggisch (narr), Gerd Zacher (org), M. Kagel (cnd), South German RSO, Limburg Cathedral Boys' Chorus Montaigne ▲ MO 782044

Hamburg State Opera Chorus
Liebermann, R.:Medea, w. Françoise Pollet (sop—Medea), Yvi Jänicke (cta—Chalkiope), Zdena Furmančoková (sgr—Syrinx), Dagmar Hesse (sgr—Aiglaia), Hanne Krogen (sgr—Kore), Michaela Lucas (sgr—Oinone), Renate Spingler (sgr—Silene), Jochen Kowalski (ct—Kreon), Aage Haugland (bass—Jason), G. Albrecht (cnd), Hamburg State PO *(rec live, Hamburg, Germany, Sept 24, 1995)* Musiques Suisses ▲ 6126 [DDD]
Rihm, W.:Die Eroberung von Mexico, w. R. Behle (sop), R. Salter (bar), I. Metzmacher (cnd), Hamburg State PO [G] *(rec live Feb. 9, 1992)* CPO 2-▲ CPO 999185-2 [DDD]
Romberg, S.:The Student Prince (operetta), w. C. Jeffreys (sop), E. Geisen (ten), D. Honig (b-bar), S. Gyártó (cnd), Hamburg State Opera Orch [G] Bayer ▲ 150004
Schnittke, A.:Historia von D. Johann Fausten, w. Hanna Schwarz (mez—Fair Helen), Arno Raunig (alt—Mephostophiles), Eberhard Büchner (ten—Old Man), Jürgen Freier (bar—Dr. Johann Faustus), Jonathan Barreto-Ramos (sgr—Student), Jürgen Fersch (sgr—Student), Eberhard Lorenz (sgr—Erzähler), Christoph Johannes Wendel (sgr—Student), G. Albrecht (cnd), Hamburg State PO *(rec live, Hamburg, Germany)* RCA Red Seal 2-▲ 09026-68413-2
Schreker, F.:Der Schatzgräber, w. G. Schnaut (sop), J. Protschka (ten), H. Helm (bar), H. Stamm (bass), G. Albrecht (cnd), Hamburg State Opera Orch [G] *(rec live 5/89)* Capriccio 2-▲ 60010-2 [DDD]
Schumann, R.:Genoveva, w. J. Faulkner (sop—Genoveva), R. Behle (sop—Margaretha), K. Lewis (ten—Golo), A. Titus (bar—Siegfried), H. Stamm (bass—Hidulfus, Caspar), J. Tilli (bass—Balthasar), G. Albrecht (cnd), Hamburg State PO [G] *(rec 1992)* Orfeo 2-▲ 289932 [DDD]
Spohr, L.:Jessonda, w. J. Varady (sop), R. Behle (sop), T. Moser (ten), D. Fischer-Dieskau (bar), K. Moll (bass), G. Albrecht (cnd), Hamburg State PO [G] Orfeo 2-▲ 240912 [DDD]

Hamrahlid Choir
Leifs, J.:Music of, w. Sigrídur Ella Magnúsdóttir (mez), Ólafur Vignir Albertsson (pno), Sólveig Anna Jónsdóttir (pno), Hjálmar Ragnarsson (pno), Edda Erlendsdóttir (pno), Marteinn Hunger Fridriksson (org), Hildigunnur Halldórsdóttir (vn), Gréta Gudnadóttir (vn), Gudmundur Kristmundsson (va), Sigurdur Halldórsson (vc), Richard Korn (db), Iceland SO, Icelandic Opera Chorus, Langholts Church Graduale Choir—Icelandic Cant, Op. 13/4; Valse Lento, Op. 2/1; Icelandic Dance, Op. 11/2 [Tempo Giusto]; Requiem; Lullaby [After the Riots]; Fairy-Tale in the Wood [from Baldr, Op. 34]; Funeral March; Separation [from Elegy, Op. 53]; Galdra Loftur Ov, Op. 10; Funeral March, Op. 6; Reverie; Reunion [from Elegy, Op. 53]; Fine I, Op. 55; Andante [The Last Supper]; Preludia Organo, Op. 16/3 [In the Church]; The Tear of Stone [from Elegy, Op. 53] Music From Iceland ▲ ITM 605 [DDD]

Cortes, Stefánsson, Ingólfsdóttir (cnd)
Ragnarsson, H.:Music of, w. S. E. Magnúsdóttir (mez), H. Halldórsdóttir (vn), G. Gudnadóttir (vn), G. Kristmundsson (va), S. Halldórsson (vc), R. Korn (db), Ó. V. Albertsson (pno), S. A. Jónsdóttir (pno), H. Ragnarsson (pno), E. Erlendsdóttir (pno), M. H. Fridriksson (org), Sakari, Wilkinson (cnd), Iceland SO, Icelandic Opera Chorus, Langholts Church Graduale Choir—Meine kleine Freundin [In the Ballroom]; Lovers Duet; After the concert; Meine kleine Freundin [Annie listens to the Radio]; Lif's Theme [On the Beach]; Lif's Theme II [Night Prayer]; Composing Ov [Vars I, II & III] Music From Iceland ▲ ITM 605 [DDD]

T. Ingólfsdóttir (cnd)
Leifs, J.:Requiem Music from Iceland ▲ ITM 601
Nordal, J.:Choral Music—Surroundings; Good Advice; Invocation to the Rock; Fair Little Friends Music from Iceland ▲ ITM 601
Ragnarsson, H.:Choral Music—April Night Song Music from Iceland ▲ ITM 601
Sigurbjörnsson, T.:Choral Music—Dance of the Trolls; Spring Resounds; Hear, Heaven's Maker; Recessional Music from Iceland ▲ ITM 601
Sveinsson, A.H.:Choral Music—Good Advice; Madrigaletto; Autumn Pictures Music from Iceland ▲ ITM 601

Handel & Haydn Society Chorus
Mozart, W.A.:Missa, K.427, w. Nancy Armstrong (sop), Dominique Labelle (sop), Jeffery Thomas (ten), Richard Morrison (bass), A. Parrott (cnd), Boston Early Music Festival Orch [L] Denon ▲ CO 79573 [DDD]

Handel Festival Choir
Live at the Crystal Palace, w. National Brass Band Festival Massed Bands, Festival of English Church Music Massed Choir, Handel Festival Orch, National Union of School Orch, Salvation Army Congress Massed Bands, Non-Conformist Union Festival Choir Beulah ▲ 1 PD 1

Hanover Boys' Choir
Bach, J.S.:Cant 32, w. W. Gampert (trb), M. van Egmond (b-bar), G. Leonhardt (cnd), Leonhardt Consort [G] Teldec 2-▲ 2292-42505-2 [AAD]
Bach, J.S.:Cant 33, w. R. Jacobs (ct), M. van Altena (ten), G. Leonhardt (cnd), Leonhardt Consort [G] Teldec 2-▲ 2292-42505-2 [AAD]
Bach, J.S.:Cant 39, w. R. Jacobs (ct), M. van Egmond (b-bar), G. Leonhardt (cnd), Leonhardt Consort [G] Teldec 2-▲ 2292-42556-2 [AAD]
Bach, J.S.:Cant 40, w. R. Jacobs (ct), M. van Altena (ten), M. van Egmond (b-bar), Leonhardt Consort [G] Teldec 2-▲ 2292-42556-2 [AAD]
Bach, J.S.:Cant 52, w. S. Kronwitter (trb), Leonhardt Consort [G] Teldec 2-▲ 2292-42422-2 [AAD]
Bach, J.S.:Cant 55, w. K. Equiluz (ten), G. Leonhardt (cnd), Leonhardt Consort [G] Teldec 2-▲ 2292-42422-2 [AAD]
Bach, J.S.:Cant 56, w. M. Schopper (bass), G. Leonhardt (cnd), Leonhardt Consort [G] Teldec 2-▲ 2292-42422-2 [AAD]
Bach, J.S.:Cant 66, w. G. Leonhardt (cnd), Leonhardt Consort, Ghent Collegium Vocale [G] Teldec 2-▲ 2292-42571-2 [AAD]
Bach, J.S.:Cant 67, w. G. Leonhardt (cnd), Leonhardt Consort, Ghent Collegium Vocale [G] Teldec 2-▲ 2292-42571-2 [AAD]
Bach, J.S.:Cant 73, w. G. Leonhardt (cnd), Leonhardt Consort, Ghent Collegium Vocale [G] Teldec 2-▲ 2292-42573-2 [ADD]
Bach, J.S.:Cant 74, w. G. Leonhardt (cnd), Leonhardt Consort, Ghent Collegium Vocale [G] Teldec 2-▲ 2292-42573-2 [ADD]
Bach, J.S.:Cant 75, w. G. Leonhardt (cnd), Leonhardt Consort, Ghent Collegium Vocale [G] Teldec 2-▲ 2292-42573-2 [ADD]
Bach, J.S.:Cant 106, "Actus tragicus", w. M. Klein (trb), R. Harten (alt), M. van Altena (ten), M. van Egmond (b-bar), Leonhardt Consort, Collegium Vocale [G] Teldec ▲ 2292-42602-2
Bach, J.S.:Cant 113, w. S. Hennig (trb), D. Bratschke (trb), R. Jacobs (ct), K. Equiluz (ten), M. van Egmond (b-bar), Leonhardt Consort, Collegium Vocale [G] Teldec 2-▲ 2292-42606-2
Bach, J.S.:Cant 114, w. S. Hennig (trb), R. Jacobs (ct), K. Equiluz (ten), M. van Egmond (b-bar), Leonhardt Consort, Collegium Vocale [G] Teldec 2-▲ 2292-42606-2
Monteverdi, C.:Vespro della Beata Vergine, w. H. Hennig (cnd), Pro Cantione Antiqua, Musica Fiata, Collegium Aureum Ars Musici 2-▲ 1000 [AAD]
Schütz, H.:Meine Seele erhebt den Herren, w. H. Hennig (cnd), London Baroque, Hilliard Ensemble EMI Classics ("Baroque" series) ▲ CDK 65736
Stravinsky, I.:Babel, w. H. Hennig (cnd), North German Radio PO, Doppeltes Wind Quintet [E & G; 2 versions] *(rec Jan. 5-6, 1993)* Calig ▲ CAL 50918 [DDD]

H. Hennig (cnd)
Charpentier, M.-A.:Messe des morts [L] Calig ▲ CAL 50874 [ADD]
Charpentier, M.-A.:Messe pour le samedi de pâques, w. Ton Koopman (org) [L] Calig ▲ CAL 50874 [ADD]
Kodály, Z.:Pange lingua, w. Tobias Gotting (org) Ars Musici ▲ 1129 [DDD]
Liszt, F.:Missa choralis, w. Tobias Gotting (org) Ars Musici ▲ 1129 [DDD]
Widor, C.M.:Mass, w. Tobias Gotting (org) Ars Musici ▲ 1129 [DDD]

Hanover Chorus
Mozart, W.A.:Requiem, w. G. Janowitz (sop), J. Bernheimer (mez), M. Hill (ten), D. Thomas (bass), R. Goodman (cnd), Hanover Band [period instruments; H.C. Robbins Landon edition] Nimbus 4-▲ NI 1791 [DDD]

▲ = CD ♦ = Enhanced CD ∆ = MD ■ = Cassette Tape □ = DCC

Hanover Chorus (cont.)
Mozart, W.A.:Requiem, w. G. Janowitz (sop), J. Bernheimer (mez), M. Hill (ten), D. Thomas (bass), R. Goodman (cnd), Hanover Band [period instruments; H.C. Robbins Landon's edition; L] Nimbus ▲ NI 5241-2 [DDD]

Hanover Girls' Choir
Hasse, J.A.:Miserere in c Girls' Choir Ars Musici ▲ 1113
Kaleidoscope, w. Pieweck, Katja (sop), Andrea Schnaus (pno) *(rec 1982 & 1993)* Thorofon ▲ CTH 2174 [ADD/DDD]

Hanover Men & Boys' Chorus
Bach, J.S.:Cant 187, w. M. Emmermann (trb), P. Esswood (ct), M. van Egmond (b-bar), G. Leonhardt (cnd), Leonhardt Consort, Collegium Vocale [G] Teldec 2-▲ 2292-44179-2 [DDD]

Hanover St. Godehard Schola Cantorum
Byzantinische Osterliturgie Christophorus ▲ CHR 77125 [ADD]

Hanover Theater School Chamber Choir
Koerppen, A.:Italian Madrigals, w. G. A. Albrecht (cnd), State SO Ars Musici ▲ 1021

G.A. Albrecht (cnd)
Koerppen, A.:Magic Forest Ars Musici ▲ 1021

Hanover Youth Choir

H. Hennig (cnd)
Duruflé, M.:Requiem, w. C. Guber (mez), P. Sefcik (bar), C. O. Beyer (vc), T. Götting (org), Kammerorchester Ars Musici ▲ AM 1098-2 [DDD]
Vierne, L.:Messe solennelle, w. C. Guber (mez), P. Sefcik (bar), T. Götting (org), Hanover CO Ars Musici ▲ AM 1098-2 [DDD]

Harlem Boys' Choir
Carol of the Drum, w. The Chieftains, Emily Mitchell (hp), Richard Stoltzman (cl), Michala Petri (rcr), James Galway (fl), Hampton String Quartet, Royal PO RCA Victor ▲ 09026-61839-2 ■ 09026-61839-4
A Christmas Celebration, w. Kathleen Battle (sop), Leonard Slatkin (cnd), Orch of St. Luke, New York Choral Artists EMI Classics ▲ CDC 47587
Hark!, w. Richard Stoltzman (cl), Eddie Gomez (perc), Jeremy Wall (kbd), Dave Samuels (vib), Bill Douglas (bn) RCA Victor ▲ 09026-61272-2 [DDD] ■ 09026-61272-4 (CrO2)
Pavarotti in Central Park, w. Luciano Pavarotti (ten), New York PO members, Leone Magiera (cnd) London ▲ 444450-2 ■ 444450-4

Harlow Chorus
Bliss, A.:Morning Heroes, w. B. Blessed (nar), M. Kibblewhite (cnd), London PO, East London Chorus, Hertfordshire Chorus *(rec All Hallows Church, London, Nov. 16–17, 1991 & Jan 26)* Cala ▲ CACD 1010 [DDD]
Bliss, A.:Prayer for St. Francis of Assisi, w. M. Kibblewhite (cnd), London PO, East London Chorus, Hertfordshire Chorus *(rec All Hallows Church, London, Nov. 16–17, 1991 & Jan 26)* Cala ▲ CACD 1010 [DDD]

Harmonic Choir
Earth to the Unknown Power, w. David Hykes (sgr) *(rec live, The Kitchen, New York, Nov 10 & 11, 1995)* Catalyst ▲ 09026-68347-2 [DDD]

Harrow Choral Society
Mahler, G.:Sym 2, w. Rae Woodland (sop), Janet Baker (mez), L. Stokowski (cnd), London SO, BBC Chorus, BBC Choral Society, Goldsmith's Choral Union *(rec 1963)* Music & Arts ▲ CD 885 [AAD]

Harvard Glee Club
Berlioz, H.:La Damnation de Faust, w. Suzanne Danco (sop), David Poleri (ten), Martial Singher (bar), Donald Gramm (bass), McHenry Boatwright (bass), Joseph de Pasquale (va), Louis Speyer (hn), C. Munch (cnd), Boston SO, Radcliffe Choral Society *(rec Feb 1954)* RCA Victor Gold Seal 8-▲ 0902-668444-2 [ADD]
Berlioz, H.:La Damnation de Faust, w. S. Danco (sop), D. Poleri (ten), M. Singher (bar), D. Gramm (bass), C. Munch (cnd), Boston SO [F] RCA Gold Seal 2-▲ 7940-2-RG [ADD]
Berlioz, H.:Roméo et Juliette, w. M. Roggero (mez), L. Chabay (ten), Y. Sze (bass), C. Munch (cnd), Boston SO, Radcliffe Choral Society RCA Gold Seal 2-▲ 09026-60681-2
Berlioz, H.:Roméo et Juliette, w. Margaret Roggero (mez), Leslie Chabay (ten), Yi-Kwei Sze (bass), C. Munch (cnd), Boston SO, Radcliffe Choral Society *(rec Feb 1953)* RCA Victor Gold Seal 8-▲ 0902-668444-2 [ADD]
Golden Days, w. Hadley, Jerry (ten), Tony Randall (sgr), Mario Lanza (ten), American Theater Orch [cnd:Paul Gemignani] RCA Victor ▲ 09026-62681-2 ■ 09026-62681-2

Harvard Univ Choir
O Great Joy! Northeastern ▲ NOR 251 [DDD]

M.F. Somerville (cnd)
Alleluia! Sacred Choral Music in New England, w. Nancy B. Granert (org) Northeastern ("Classical Arts" series) ▲ NOR 247
Carols From the Yard *(rec Memorial Church, Harvard Univ., Dec. 1994–Jan. 1995)* Gothic ▲ GOT 49075 [DDD]

Hassler Consort

F. Raml (cnd)
Praetorius, M.:Choral Music—Wachet Auf, ruft uns die Stimme; Nun komm der Heiden Heiland; Puer Natus; Missa gantz Teudsch; Vom Himmel hoch; In dulci Jubilo; Joseph, lieber Joseph mein; Psallite; Der Morgenstern ist augdegrungen; Wie schön leuchtet der Morgenstern; Omnis mundis jocundetur; Singet und klinget MD + G ▲ MDG CD 6140660

Hautecome Monks' Choir
Notre Dame:The Monks of Hautecombe Praise the Blessed Virgin Jade ▲ JAD C 014
St. Benoit Jade ▲ JAD C 013

Haydn Vocal Ensemble
Haydn, J.:Applausus:Jubilaeum virtutis Palatium, w. Rosemary Musoleno (sop—Temperantia), Kirsten Dolberg (mez—Prudentia), Douglas Johnson (ten—Justitia), Desmond Byrne (bass—Fortitudo), Jean-Philippe Courtis (bass—Theologia), P. Fournillier (cnd), Picardie Orch [L] *(rec 9/91)* Opus 111 2-▲ OPS 61-9207/8 [DDD]

Heidelberg Madrigal Choir

G. Kegelmann (cnd)
Boulanger, L.:Choral Music—Les Sirènes (1911); Renouveau (1911); Hymne au Soleil (1912); Soir sur la plaine (1913) [F] Bayer ▲ 100041 [DDD]
Mendelssohn, Fanny:Gartenlieder (6) [G] Bayer ▲ 100041 [DDD]
Mendelssohn, Fanny:Nachtreigen [G] Bayer ▲ 100041 [DDD]
Schumann, C.:Choral Songs [G] Bayer ▲ 100041 [DDD]

Heidelberg State Music School Chamber Choir
Austin, E.:Music of, w. Jeananne Albee (pno), Jerome Reed (pno), Mary Lou Rylands (vc), Ursula Trede-Boettcher (hpd), Markus Lücke (cl), Sibylle Dotzauer (pno), Constitution Brass—To Begin for Brass Qnt; Klavier Double for Pno & Tape; Circling for Vc & Pno; Lighthouse I for solo Hpd; Gathering Threads for solo Cl; Zodiac Suite for Pno; An Die Nachgeborenen [To Those Born Later] Capstone ▲ CPS 8625

Heidelberg-Mannheim State Univ Chamber Choir
Austin, E.:An Die Nachgeborenen, w. Alex Bassermann (sgr), Kirsten Grünenpült (sgr), Veronika Winter (sgr), Sibylle Dotzauer (pno) Capstone ▲ CPS 8625

Heilbronn Vocal Ensemble
Draeseke, F.:Mysterium:Christus, w. C. Bischoff (sop), A. Vogel (sop), E. Dersen (alt), K. Markus (ten), H.J. Ritzerfeld (ten), P. Langshaw (bar), B. Kämpf (bass), J. Sonnenschmidt (org), U.-R. Follert (cnd), Breslau State PO, Evangelical Boys' Choir Palatine, Palatine Kurrende Bayer 5-▲ 100175/79

HelioTrope
The Romance of the Rose:Feminine Voices from Medieval France Koch International Classics ▲ KIC 7103 [DDD]

Helmuth Stapff Group
Christmas in the Erz Mountains, w. M. Wiemann (cnd), Nuremberg Wind Soloists Entrée ▲ 0066

Helsingborg Sym Chorus
Larsson, L.-E.:God in Disguise, w. B. Nordin (sop), H. Hagegård (bar), Jonsson (nar), S. Frykberg (cnd), Helsingborg SO [Sw] BIS ▲ CD 96 [AAD]

Helsingborgs Concert Choir
Söderman, A.:Marshal Stig's Daughters, w. H.-P. Frank (cnd), Helsingborg SO, Mikaeli Chamber Choir, Medlemmar Concert Choir [Sw] Musica Sveciae ▲ MSCD 513

Helsinki Music Institute Choir
Ravel, M.:Intro & Allegro, w. Ann Mason Stockton (hp), Arthur Gleghorn (fl), Mitchell Lurie (cl), Hollywood String Quartet Testament ▲ TESSBT 1053 (m) [ADD]
Sallinen, A.:Songs of Life & Death, w. Jorma Hynninen (bar), O. Kamu (cnd), Helsinki PO Ondine ▲ ODE 844 [DDD]

Helsinki State Academy Male Choir
Sibelius, J.:Kullervo, w. E.-L. Saarinen (mez), J. Hynninen (bar), P. Berglund (cnd), Helsinki PO, Helsinki Univ Male Choir EMI Classics ▲ CDM 65080

Helsinki Univ Chorus
Sibelius, J.:Kullervo, w. M. Rorholm (mez), J. Hynninen (bar), E.-P. Salonen (cnd), Los Angeles PO [Fin] Sony Classical ▲ SK 52563

M. Hyökki (cnd)
Madetoja, L.:Songs—Evening Mood; Most Beautiful of Lands; Autumn Evening; Melancholy; Play, Gravel, Sing, Sand...; Unetar, the Bringer of Sleep; Viipuri March; My Wife's a Winsome Wee Thing; Tibbie Dunbar; March of the Savo Ploughman; Väinölä's Children; De Profundis; As I Set Off One Summer's Night; Elegy Finlandia ▲ FIN 398 [DDD]
Rautavaara, E.:Runo 42, w. *(soloists unknown)* Ondine ▲ ODE 842 [DDD]
Sibelius, J.:Songs Male Choir (comp)—(25) Finlandia-hymni; Rakastava; Kuutamollla; Veljeni vieraılla mailla; Isänmaalle; Sortunut ääni; Terve kuu; Venematka; Saarella palaa; Metsämiehen laulu; Sydämeni laulu; etc. [Fin] Finlandia ▲ 4509-94849-2 [DDD]

Helsinki Univ Male Choir
Sibelius, J.:Kullervo, w. E.-L. Saarinen (mez), J. Hynninen (bar), P. Berglund (cnd), Helsinki PO, Helsinki State Academy Male Choir EMI Classics ▲ CDM 65080

Henry's Eight
White, R.:Music of—Domine, quis habitabit [1 & 3]; Ad te levavi oculos meos; Deus misereatur nostri; Miserere mei, Deus; Appropinquet deprecatio mea; Exaudiat te Dominus; Libera me, Domine, de mort; Aeterna regina caeli Meridian ▲ MER 84313 [DDD]

Hereford Cathedral Choir
The Psalms of David, Vol. 1 Priory ▲ PRCD 290 [DDD]

R. Massey (cnd)
Magnificat & Nunc Dimittis, Vol. 7, w. Huw Williams (org) Priory ▲ PRI 535 [DDD]

Françoise Herr Vocal Ensemble
Rameau, J.P.:Platée, w. J. Smith (sop), G. Ragon (ten), G. de Mey (ten), M. Minkowski (cnd), Louvre Musicians [F] Erato ("Musifrance" series) 2-▲ 2292-45028-2 [DDD]

Hersfelder Festival Choir
Honegger, A.:Jeanne d'Arc au bûcher, w. *soloists unknown*, S. Heinrich (cnd), Polish National RSO Cracow, Frankfurt Children's Choir Koch Schwann ▲ SCH 312922 [DDD]

Hertfordshire Chorus
Bliss, A.:Morning Heroes, w. B. Blessed (nar), M. Kibblewhite (cnd), London PO, East London Chorus, Harlow Chorus *(rec All Hallows Church, London, Nov. 16–17, 1991 & Jan 26)* Cala ▲ CACD 1010 [DDD]
Bliss, A.:Prayer for St. Francis of Assisi, w. M. Kibblewhite (cnd), London PO, East London Chorus, Harlow Chorus *(rec All Hallows Church, London, Nov. 16–17, 1991 & Jan 26)* Cala ▲ CACD 1010 [DDD]

Hespèrion XX
Alfonso El Sabio:Cantigas de Santa Maria [Port] *(rec Feb 1993)* Astrée ▲ E 8508 [DDD]
Llibre Vermell de Montserrat Virgin Classics ("Veritas Edition" series) ▲ CDM 61174

J. Savall (cnd)
Bach, J.S.:The Art of the Fugue Astrée 2-▲ E 2001
El Cancionero de la Colombino:1451-1506 Astrée ▲ E 8763
El Cancionero de Palacio:1474-1516 Astrée ▲ E 8762
Caurroy, E. du:Fants (23) Instrs Astrée ▲ E 7749
Couperin, F.:Les Nations Astrée 2-▲ E 7700
Dowland, J.:Lachrimae, or Seaven Teares Astrée ▲ E 8701 [DDD]
Flecha, M.:Ensaladas—La justa; El fuego & La bomba Astrée ▲ E 7742 [AAD]
Folias & Canarios Astrée ▲ E 8516 [DDD]
Guerrero, F.:Sacred Motets, w. La Capella Reial de Catalunya [period instruments]—Alma Redemptoris mater; Ave Maria (a 4); Ave Maria (a 8); Ave, virgo sanctissima; Beata Dei genitrix, Maria; Duo Seraphim; Gabriel archangelus; Laudate Dominum de caelis; O Altitudo divitiarum; O Domine Jesu Christe I; O Domine Jesu Christe II; O sacrum convivium; Pater Noster; Regina caeli; Salva Regina; Trahe me post te, Virgo Maria [L] *(rec Dec. 1991–Jan. 1992)* Astrée ▲ E 8766
Jenkins, J.:Consort Music, w. M. Behringer (org)—pavans & fantasies Astrée ▲ E 8724
Locke, M.:Consort of Fower Parts Astrée ▲ E 8519
Lope de Vega:Intermedios del Barroco Hispánico, w. Montserrat Figueras (sop) Astrée ▲ E 8729
The Medinaceli Song Book:Music in the Kingdom of Castille During the Age of Philip II [Sp] Astrée ▲ E 8764 [DDD]
Music of Spain EMI Classics ("Studio" series) 2-▲ ZDMB 63431
Mvsicqve de Joye Astrée ▲ E 7724 [AAD]
Purcell, H.:Fants Vls (comp) Astrée ▲ E 8536
Purcell, H.:In Nomines Astrée ▲ E 8536
Rosenmüller, J.:Son da Camera e Sinf Astrée ▲ E 8709
Savall, J.:Joan of Arc, w. J. Savall (vl), M. Figueras (sop), La Capella Reial de Catalunya Harmonia Mundi ▲ K 1006-2 ■ K 51006-4
20 years of Hespèrion XX Astrée ▲ E 8522
Victoria, T.L. de:Sacred Choral Music, w. La Capella Reial de Catalunya—11 Marian works—Ave Maria (a 4); Gaude, Maria Virgo (a 5), 1572; Trahe me post te (a 6), 1583; Salve, Regina (a 8), 1572; Ave Regina caelorum (a 5), 1572; Sancta Maria, succerre miseris (a 4), 1572; Ne timeas, Maria (a 4), 1572; Senex, Puerum portabat (instrumental a 4), 1572; O magnum mysterium (a 4), 1572; Vidi speciosam sicut columbam (a 6), 1572; Magnificat Primi toni (a 8), 1600) [L] *(rec 1992)* Astrée ▲ E 8767 [DDD]

Hesse Radio Chorus
Haydn, J.:Die Jahreszeiten, w. Agnes Giebel (sop—Hanne), Fritz Wünderlich (ten—Lukas), Kieth Engen (bass—Simon), H. Müller-Kray (cnd), Stuttgart South Radio Orch *(rec Schwetzingen, May 24, 1959)* Bella Voce 2-▲ 7204 [AAD]
Ligeti, G.:Requiem, w. Liliana Poli (sop), Barbro Ericson (mez), M. Gielen (cnd), Hessian RSO [L] Wergo ▲ WER 60045-50 [ADD]
Mahler, G.:Sym 2, w. M. Puetz (sop), M. Höffgen (cta), C. Schuricht (cnd), Hessian RSO, Frankfurt Singakademie Choir *(rec 1960)* Originals 2-▲ ORISH 819 [ADD]
Verdi, G.:I vespri siciliani, w. M. Cunitz (sop), H. Roswaenge (ten), H. Schlusnus (bar), O. von Rohr (bass), K. Schröder (cnd), Hessian RSO *(rec 1951)* Myto 2-▲ MCD 93279

A. Ickstadt (cnd)
Brahms, J.:Choral Music, w. R. Havenith (pno), Frankfurt Choir—4 Quartets for SATB Choir & Piano, Op. 92 [G] Koch Treasure ▲ 31616-2 [ADD]

Richard Hickox Singers
Holst, G.:Savitri, w. F. Palmer (sop), P. Langridge (ten), S. Varcoe (bar), R. Hickox (cnd), City of London Sinfonia Hyperion ▲ CDA 66099 [DDD]
Rossini, G.:Arias, w. D. Jones (mez), R. Hickox (cnd), City of London Sinfonia—nine arias, from Adelaide di Borgogna, Barbiere di Siviglia, Bianca e Falliero, Cenerentola, Donna del Lago, Italiana in Algeri, Otello, Signor Bruschino [I] Chandos ▲ CHAN 8865 [DDD]

R. Hickox (cnd)
Lloyd Webber, W.S.:Mass Org & Choir, w. Ian Watson (org) [L] ASV ▲ ASV 584 [DDD]
Lloyd Webber, W.S.:Mass for St Mary Magdalene ASV ▲ ASV 961

Stephen Hill Singers
Doyle, P.:Henry V, w. P. Doyle (bar), S. Rattle (cnd), City of Birmingham SO Angel ▲ CDC 49919 ■ 4DS 49919

CHORAL GROUPS

Stephen Hill Singers (cont.)
Porter, C.:Nymph Errant, w. K. Ballard (sgr), E. Belcourt (sgr), *(other sgrs unknown)*, D. Pippin (cnd), Stephen Hill Orch Angel ▲ CDC 54079
Hilliard Ensemble
Bryars, G.:Glorious Hill ECM New Series ▲ 78118-21533-2 [DDD]
Frye, W.:Choral Music—Trinitatis dies; Gloria; Salve virgo; Credo; O Florens rosa; Sanctus; Agnus dei; Ave regina; Sospitati dedit; Tout a par moi; So ys emprentid; Myn herits lust; Alas, alas is my chief song [L, F & E] *(rec Jan. 1992)* ECM New Series ("New" series) ▲ 78118-21476-2 [DDD]
Gesualdo, D.C.:Tenebrae factae sunt ECM New Series ("New" series) 2-▲ 78118-21215-2 [DDD] ■ 78118-21215-4
A Hilliard Songbook:New Music for Voices, w. Hilliard Ensemble [David James (ct), Rogers Covey-Crump (ten), John Potter (ten), Gordon Jones (bar)] *(rec 1995-96)* ECM New Series 2-▲ 7811-821614-2 [DDD]
Mozart, W.A.:Ave verum corpus, w. S. Cleobury (cnd), Cambridge Classical Players, King's College Choir [L] EMI Classics ▲ CDC 49672 [DDD]
Mozart, W.A.:Vesperae de Dominica, w. L. Dawson (sop), E. James (mez), R. Covey-Crump (ten), P. Hillier (bass), S. Cleobury (cnd), Cambridge Classical Players, King's College Choir [L] EMI Classics ▲ CDC 49672 [DDD]
Mozart, W.A.:Vesperae solennes, w. L. Dawson (sop), E. James (mez), R. Covey-Crump (ten), P. Hillier (bass), S. Cleobury (cnd), Cambridge Classical Players, King's College Choir [L] EMI Classics ▲ CDC 49672 [DDD]
Musica Humana, w. Françoise Atlan (mez), John Fleagle (ten/hp), Crawford Young (lt), Anonymous 4, Ensemble Discantus, Ensemble Gilles Binchois, Ensemble Organum, Gothic Voices, Greece Byzantine Choir, Musica Nova, et al. L'Empreinte Digitale ▲ ED 13047
Palestrina, G.:The Song of Songs Virgin Classics 2-▲ ZDMB 61168
Pärt, A.:Chamber Music, w. Gidon Kremer (vn), *(other artists unknown)*, Stuttgart Brass Ensemble—(works for brass, voice, strings & organ) Arbos; An den Wassern zu Babel; De Profundis; Es sang für langen Jahren; Summa ECM New Series ▲ 78118-21325-2 [DDD]; ■ 78118-21325-4 (D)
Pärt, A.:Miserere, w. Western Wind ECM New Series ▲ 78118-21430-2 [DDD]; ■ 78118-21430-4
Pärt, A.:Stabat Mater, w. Gidon Kremer (vn), *(other artists unknown)* ECM New Series ▲ 78118-21325-2 [DDD]; ■ 78118-21325-4 (D)
Schütz, H.:Meine Seele erhebt den Herren, w. H. Hennig (cnd), London Baroque, Hanover Boys' Choir EMI Classics ("Baroque" series) ▲ CDK 65736
17th & 18th Century Songs & Catches, w. David James (alt), Paul Elliott (ten), Leigh Nixon (ten), Paul Hillier (bass) Saga Classics ▲ EC 3332 [ADD]
P. Hillier (cnd)
Codex Speciálník, w. D. James (ct), R. Covey-Crump (ten), J. Potter (ten), G. Jones (bar) *(rec Gönningen City Church, Jan. 1993)* ECM New Series ▲ 78118-21504-2 [DDD]
Josquin Desprez:Chansons & Motets EMI Classics ▲ CDC 49209
Josquin Desprez:Motets EMI Classics ▲ CDC 49209
Machaut, G. de:Je ne cesse de prier [F] Hyperion ▲ CDA 66358 [DDD]
Machaut, G. de:Ma fin est mon commencement [F] Hyperion ▲ CDA 66358 [DDD]
Machaut, G. de:Messe de Nostre Dame [L] Hyperion ▲ CDA 66358 [DDD]
Medieval English Music Harmonia Mundi ▲ HMA 190.1106
Officium, w. D. James (ct), R. Covey-Crump (ten), J. Potter (ten), G. Jones (bar), J. Gabarek (sop/ten saxs) *(rec Sept. 1993)* ECM New Series ▲ 78118-21525-2
The Old Hall Manuscript EMI Classics ▲ CDC 54111
Pärt, A.:Passio Domini nostri Jesu Christi secundum Joannem, w. L. Dawson (sop), D. James (alt), R. Covey-Crump (ten), J. Potter (ten), G. Jones (bass), M. George (bass), Western Wind Chamber Chorus [L] ECM New Series ▲ 78118-21370-2 [DDD]; ■ 78118-21370-4 (D)
Pérotin:4 & 3 Voice Organa ECM New Series ▲ 78118-21385-2 [DDD]
The Romantic Englishman Duo Records ▲ DUOCD 89009
The Singing Club Harmonia Mundi ▲ HMA 190.1153 ■
Songs for a Tudor King, w. Judith Nelson (sop), David James (ct), Paul Elliott (ten), Leigh Nixon (ten), P. Hillier (bar) Saga Classics ▲ 3378 [ADD]
Spanish & Mexian Renaissance Vocal Music EMI Classics 2-▲ ZDCB 54341
Sumer Is Icumen in:Medieval English Songs & Church Music Harmonia Mundi ▲ HMC 901154
Tallis, T.:The Lamentations of Jeremiah [L] ECM New Series ▲ 78118-21341-2 [DDD]
Hilliard Ensemble members
Pärt, A.:Sarah Was 90 Years Old, w. P. Favre (dr) ECM New Series ▲ 78118-21430-2 [DDD]; ■ 78118-21430-4
Hilversum Chorus
Beethoven, L. van:Missa Solemnis, w. E. Moser (sop), H. Schwarz (mez), A. Kollo (ten), K. Moll (bass), L. Bernstein (cnd), Royal Concertgebouw Orch [L] Deutsche Grammophon 2-▲ 413780-2 [ADD]
Mascagni, P.:Nerone, w. R. Didonè (sop), D. Di Domenico (ten), S. Cowan (bar), M. Dirks (bar), Harry Peeters (bass), Shapero (sgr), Strow-Piccolo (sgr), Tcholakov (sgr), K. Bakels (cnd), Hilversum RSO [I] Bongiovanni 2-▲ GB 2052/53 [DDD]
Hilversum Radio Chorus
Marez Oyens, T. de:Sinf Testimonial, w. K. Montgomery (cnd), Hilversum RSO Donemus ▲ CV 8702 [AAD]
His Majesties Clerkes
Cornago, J.:Missa 'Ayo visto de la mappa mundi' [L] Harmonia Mundi USA ▲ HMU 907083
In a Cold Winter's Night Centaur ▲ CRC 2048
A. Heider (cnd)
News of Great Joy Centaur ▲ CRC 2168
P. Hillier (cnd)
Billings, W.:Anthems & Fuguing Tunes—O praise the Lord of Heaven Is any afflicted; Emmaus; Africa; Funeral anthem (Samuel the Priest); Shiloh; Jordan; I am the Rose of Sharon; Euroclydon; Hear my pray'r; Rutland; David's lamentation; As the Hart panteth; Creation; Brookfield; Easter anthem (The Lord is ris'n indeed) [E] Harmonia Mundi USA ▲ HMU 907048 ■
Hljómeyki Chorus
H. Ragnarsson (cnd)
Ragnarsson, H.:Choral Music—Old Verse; Mass; Ave Maria; April Night Song Music from Iceland ▲ ITM 801
Holland Bach Choir
Bach, J.S.:St. John Passion, w. B. Schlick (sop), K. Ishii (ten), M. van Egmond (b-bar), C. de Wolff (cnd), Royal Concertgebouw Orch members [G] Sound 3-▲ CD 3488/90
Bach, J.S.:St. John Passion, w. C. de Wolff (cnd), Amsterdam CO—Eingangschor Vivace ▲ G 536
Handel, G.F.:Israel in Egypt, w. C. de Wolff (cnd), Amsterdam CO—choruses Vivace ▲ G 536
Handel, G.F.:Judas Maccabaeus (sels), w. C. de Wolff (cnd), Amsterdam CO—choruses Vivace ▲ G 536
Handel, G.F.:Messiah (sels), w. C. de Wolff (cnd), Amsterdam CO—Choruses Vivace ▲ G 536
Holst Singers
Bliss, A.:Pastoral, w. S. Minty (mez), H.D. Wetton (cnd), Holst Orch [E] Hyperion ▲ CDA 66175
Boughton, R.:Bethlehem, w. A.G. Melville (cnd), City of London Sinfonia, New London Children's Choir [adapted] Hyperion ▲ CDA 66690
Britten, B.:Gloriana (choral dances), w. M. Hill (ten), H.D. Wetton (cnd), Holst Orch [ver. for tenor, harp & chorus] Hyperion ▲ CDA 66175
Holst, G.:Choral Hymns from the Rig-Veda, w. H.D. Wetton (cnd), Holst Orch Hyperion ▲ CDA 66175
Holst, G.:Choral Music, w. D. Theodore (ob), R. Truman (vc), S. Williams (hp)—The Princess; Light Leaves Whisper; Ave Maria; Jesu, Thou the Virgin-born; A Welcome Song; In Youth is Pleasure; Two Eastern Pictures; Bring us in Good Ale; Lully My Liking; Of One That Is So Fair and Bright; Diverus and Lazurus; Terly Terlow; This Have I Done for My True Love; Six Choral Folksongs; Twelve Welsh Folksongs; O Spiritual Pilgrim Hyperion ▲ CDA 66705 [DDD]
S. Layton (cnd)
Britten, B.:A Boy Was Born, w. Susan Gritton (sgr), Catherine Wyn-Rogers (sgr), David Goode (org) Hyperion ▲ CDA 66825
Britten, B.:Choral Music, w. Susan Gritton (sgr), Catherine Wyn-Rogers (sgr), David Goode (org)—Christ's Nativity; A Shepherd's Carol; Jubilate in C Hyperion ▲ CDA 66825

Holst Singers (cont.)
S. Layton (cnd) (cont.)
Britten, B.:A Hymn to the Virgin, w. Susan Gritton (sgr), Catherine Wyn-Rogers (sgr), David Goode (org) Hyperion ▲ CDA 66825
Britten, B.:Te Deum, w. Susan Gritton (sgr), Catherine Wyn-Rogers (sgr), David Goode (org) Hyperion ▲ CDA 66825
Vaughan Williams, R.:Songs, w. Ian Bostridge (ten), Michael George (bass)—Loch Lomand; 3 Shakespeare Songs; Alister McAlpine's Lament; An Acre of Land; The Seeds of Love; Ca' the yowes; 5 English Folksongs; The Winter Is Gone; Mannin Veen; Bushes & Briars; Down among the Dead Men; 3 Elizabethan Songs; Greensleeves; Rest; Heart's Music; Come away, Death; The Turtle Dove Hyperion ▲ CDA 66777
Holy Spirit Fathers of Chevilly Choir
L. Deiss (cnd)
Resurrexit GIA ■ CS 222
Honley Male Voice Choir
A Song of Yorkshire, w. S. Lindley (org), Leeds Parish Church Choir Boys' Voices, Sellers Engineering Band [cnd:P. McCann] Chandos Brass ▲ CHAN 4515 [DDD]
Hortus Musicus [Mikael Bellini (alt), Lennart Löwgran (alt), Carl Unander-Scharin (ten), Lars Arvidson (bass), Sven-Anders Benktsson (bass)]
Piae Contiones:Sword Dance Musica Sveciae ▲ MSV 201 [DDD]
The Royal Court of the Vasa Kings, 1523-1611, w. Bellini, Mikael (ct), Lennart Löwgren (ct), Carl Unander-Scharin (ten), Lars Arvidson (bass), Sven-Anders Benktsson (bass), Sven Åberg (six-course Renaissance lt), Tallinn [cnd:Andres Mustonen] Musica Sveciae ▲ MSV 202 [DDD]
Houston Chorale
Orff, C.:Carmina burana, w. L. Stokowski (cnd), Houston SO *(rec 1955)* EMI Classics ("FDS" series) ▲ CDM 65207
Stravinsky, I.:The Firebird Suite, w. L. Stokowski (cnd), Houston SO EMI Classics (FDS Series) ▲ CDM 65207
Houston Grand Opera Chorus
Joplin, S.:Treemonisha, w. G. Schuller (cnd), Houston Grand Opera Orch *(rec 1975)* Deutsche Grammophon 2-▲ 435709-2 [ADD]
Houston Sym Male Chorus
Brahms, J.:Alto Rhap, w. Dunja Vejzovic (mez), C. Eschenbach (cnd), Houston SO Virgin Classics 2-▲ CUVB 61226
Howard Univ Chorus
Handel, G.F.:Choruses, w. G. Simon (cnd), Handel Festival Orch—choruses from 12 oratorios [E] Arabesque ▲ Z 6538 [DDD]
Huddersfield Choral Society
All of the World's Most Beautiful Melodies!, w. McCann, Phillip (cnt), Gordon Langford (cnd), Roy Newsome (cnd), Peter Parkes (cnd), Black Dyke Mills Band, Sellers Engineering Band, Academy of St. Martin in the Fields Chamber Ensemble, Leeds Parish Church Boys Choir Chandos ("Brass" series) 5-▲ CHN 4536(5)
Brian Kay's Sunday Morning:A Selection of Choral & Orchestral Favourites, w. V. Handley (cnd), BBC PO Chandos ("BBC Philharmonic" series) ▲ CHN 7025
A Chistmas Celebration Chandos ▲ CHN 4530 [DDD]
Christmas Fantasy, w. Black Dyke Mills Band Chandos ▲ CHAN 8679 [AAD]
Elgar, E.:The Dream of Gerontius, w. G. Ripley (cta), H. Nash (ten), D. Noble (bar), N. Walker (bass), M. Sargent (cnd), Liverpool PO Testament ▲ TES SBT 2025 [ADD]
Elgar, E.:The Music Makers, w. M. Thomas (cta), M. Sargent (cnd), Leeds Philharmonic Society, London SO, Royal Choral Society *(rec live, Royal Albert Hall April 29, 1965)* Intaglio ▲ INCD 7351 [ADD]
Handel, G.F.:Messiah, w. Elsie Morison (sop), Marjorie Thomas (cta), Richard Lewis (ten), James Milligan (bass), M. Sargent (cnd), Royal Liverpool PO Classics for Pleasure 2-▲ CDCFP 4718 [ADD]
Handel, G.F.:Messiah (sels), w. Elsie Morison (sop), Marjorie Thomas (cta), Richard Lewis (ten), James Milligan (bass), Eric Chadwick (org), M. Sargent (cnd), Royal Liverpool PO Classics for Pleasure ▲ CDCFP 9007 [ADD]
Handel, G.F.:Messiah (reorchd Mozart), w. Felicity Lott (sop), Felicity Palmer (sop), Phillip Langridge (ten), Robert Lloyd (b-bar), C. Mackerras (cnd), Royal PO [E] ASV ▲ ASV CD 960
Mendelssohn, F.:Elijah, w. Isobel Baillie (sop), Gladys Ripley (cta), James Johnston (ten), Harold Williams (b-bar), M. Sargent (cnd), Liverpool PO Dutton Laboratories 2-▲ DUTT 2004 [ADD]
Smyth, E.:The Wreckers, w. Judith Howarth (sop), Anne-Marie Owens (mez), Annemarie Sand (mez), Justin Lavender (ten), Anthony Roden (ten), Peter Sidhom (bar), David Wilson-Johnson (bar), Brian Bannatyne-Scott (bass), O. de la Martinez (cnd), BBC PO *(rec live, Royal Albert Hall, London, July 31, 1994)* Conifer Classics 2-▲ 75605-51250-2
Huddersfield Choral Society Youth Choir
The World's Most Beautiful Melodies, Vol. 5, w. Phillip McCann (cnt), Sellers Engineering Band, S. Lindley (org) Chandos ▲ CHAN 4532 [DDD]
Hungarian Festival Choir
Bach, J.S.:St. Matthew Passion, w. R. Kiss (sop), I. Verebics (sop), Á. Csenki (mez), J. Németh (mez), P. Cser (ten), J. Mukk (ten), I. Gáti (bar), F. Korpás (bar), P. Köves (bass), G. Oberfrank (cnd), Hungarian State SO, Hungarian Radio Children's Choir [G] *(rec Feb 1993)* Naxos 3-▲ 8.550832/34 [DDD]
Hungarian People's Army Male Chorus
Bartók, B.:From Olden Times Hungaroton ▲ HCD 31047 [ADD]
Bartók, B.:Old Hungarian Folksongs (4) Hungaroton ▲ HCD 31047 [ADD]
Bartók, B.:Székely Songs Hungaroton ▲ HCD 31047 [ADD]
Liszt, F.:An die Künstler, w. A. Molnár (ten), T. Daróczi (ten), J. Molday (bar), L. Domahidy Jr. (bass), I. Zámbó (cnd), Hungarian State Orch [G] Hungaroton ▲ HCD 12748 [DDD]
Liszt, F.:Hungaria 1848, w. M. Temesi (sop), A. Molnár (ten), S. Sólyom-Nagy (bar), I. Zámbó (cnd), Hungarian State Orch—composed as a salute to the Hungarian revolution [G] Hungaroton ▲ HCD 12748 [DDD]
Liszt, F.:Hungarian Royal Hymn, w. I. Zámbó (cnd), Hungarian State Orch, Jeunesses Musicales Women's Chorus [Hun] Hungaroton ▲ HCD 12748 [DDD]
Liszt, F.:Requiem, w. Alfonz Bartha (ten), Sándor Palcsó (ten), Zsolt Bende (bar), Pál Kovács (bar), A. Ferencsik (cnd), Hungarian State Orch [L] Hungaroton ▲ HCD 11267
Liszt, F.:Septam sacramenta, w. T. Takács (mez), J. Bándi (ten), G. Kallay (ten), K. Kaváts (bar), Zsuzsa Elekes (org), I. Zámbó (cnd), Hungarian State Orch, Jeunesses Musicales Women's Chorus [L] Hungaroton ▲ HCD 12748 [DDD]
Strauss, R.:Guntram, w. I. Tokody (sop), R. Goldberg (ten), S. Sólyom-Nágy (bar), I. Gáti (bar), E. Queler (cnd), Hungarian State Orch [G] CBS 2-▲ M2K 39737 [DDD]
Pödör, Sapszon, Nagy (cnd)
Verdi, G.:Arias, w. Sylvia Sass (sop), Giorgio Lamberti (ten), Kolos Kováts (bass), Oberfrank, Gardelli (cnd), Budapest MÁV SO, Hungarian State Opera Orch, Hungarian Radio-TV Chorus, Hungarian State Opera Chorus—Vieni, o Levita!...Tu sul labbro [from Nabucco]; Verginil...Il ciel per ora...Sciagurata! Hai tu creduto; Qui posa il fianco [both from I Lombardi]; Che mai vegg'io...Infelice! E tu credevi...; Vigili pure il ciel...Iddio n'ascolti [both from Ernani]; Mentre gonfiarsi l'anima [from Attila]; Studia il passo...Come dal ciel precipital [from Macbeth]; O patria, o cara patria...O tu, Palermo [from I vespri Siciliani]; A te l'estremo addio... [from Simon Boccanegra]; Ella giammai m'amò [from Don Carlo] Hungaroton ("Great Hungarian Voices" series) ▲ HCD 31650 [ADD/DDD]
Hungarian Radio Children's Chorus
Bach, J.S.:St. Matthew Passion, w. R. Kiss (sop), I. Verebics (sop), Á. Csenki (mez), J. Németh (mez), P. Cser (ten), J. Mukk (ten), I. Gáti (bar), F. Korpás (bar), P. Köves (bass), G. Oberfrank (cnd), Hungarian State SO, Hungarian Festival Choir [G] *(rec Feb 1993)* Naxos 3-▲ 8.550832/34 [DDD]
Hungarian Radio Chorus
Bach, J.S.:Cant 51, w. I. Kertesi (sop), J. Pászthy (sop), J. Nemeth (mez), J. Mukk (ten), I. Gáti (bass), M. Antal (cnd), Failoni CO Naxos ▲ 8.550643 [DDD]
Bach, J.S.:Cant 80, w. I. Kertesi (sop), J. Nemeth (alt), J. Mukk (ten), I. Gáti (bass), M. Antal (cnd), Failoni CO *(rec Jan 1992)* Naxos ▲ 8.550642 [DDD]
Bach, J.S.:Cant 147, w. I. Kertesi (sop), J. Nemeth (alt), J. Mukk (ten), I. Gáti (bass), M. Antal (cnd), Failoni CO *(rec Jan 1992)* Naxos ▲ 8.550642 [DDD]
Bach, J.S.:Cant 208, "Hunting Cant", w. I. Kertesi (sop), J. Pászthy (sop), J. Nemeth (mez), J. Mukk (ten), I. Gáti (bass), M. Antal (cnd), Failoni CO Naxos ▲ 8.550643 [DDD]

970 ▲ = CD ♦ = Enhanced CD Δ = MD ■ = Cassette Tape □ = DCC

Hungarian Radio Chorus (cont.)
Cherubini, L.:Médée, w. M. Kalmar (sop), S. Sass (sop), T. Takacs (mez), V. Luchetti (ten), K. Kovats (bass), L. Gardelli (cnd), Budapest SO [I] Hungaroton 2-▲ HCD 11904/05
Donizetti, G.:Anna Bolena, w. Edita Gruberová (sop), Delores Ziegler (mez), Stefano Palatchi (bass), E. Boncompagni (cnd), Hungarian RSO Nightingale Classics 3-▲ NIG 70565
Kodály, Z.:Missa Brevis, w. J. Ferencsik (cnd), Hungarian RSO [L] Hungaroton ▲ HCD 11397
Liszt, F.:A Faust Sym, w. A. Necolescu (ten), F. d' Avalos (cnd), Hungarian State SO IMP Classics ▲ IMP PCD 1071 [DDD]
Liszt, F.:Hungarian Coronation Mass, w. V. Kincses (sop), T. Tákacs (mez), D. Gulyas (ten), L. Polgar (bass), G. Lehel (cnd), Budapest SO [L] Hungaroton ▲ HCD 12148
Rossini, G.:Il barbiere di Siviglia, w. I. Kertesi (sop—Berta), S. Ganassi (mez—Rosina), R. Vargas (ten—Almaviva), A. Romero (bar—Dr. Bartolo), R. Servile (bar—Figaro), F. de Grandis (bass—Basilio), K. Sárkány (bass—Fiorello), A. Déri (pno), B. Sztankovits (gtr), W. Humburg (cnd), Failoni CO *(rec Nov. 16-28, 1992)* Naxos 3-▲ 8.660027/29 [DDD]

Hungarian Radio-TV Chamber Chorus
Durkó, Z.:Altamira, w. G. Lehel (cnd), Budapest SO *(rec 1972)* Hungaroton ▲ HCD 31654 [AAD]

Hungarian Radio-TV Children's Chorus
Kodály, Z.:Psalmus hungaricus, w. József Simándy (ten), A. Dorati (cnd), Hungarian State Orch, Budapest Chorus Hungaroton ▲ HCD 31503 [ADD]

Hungarian Radio-TV Children's Chorus Girls' Voices
J. Reményi (cnd)
Mozart, W.A.:Alma Dei creatoris, w. Ibolya Verebics (sop), Judit Németh (cta), József Mukk (ten), József Moldvay (bar), Gábor Oláh (bar), István Ella (org), Hungarian Radio-TV Male Chamber Choir *(rec Hungaroton Studio, June 14-16, 1991)* Hungaroton ▲ HCD 4003 [DDD]
Mozart, W.A.:Ave verum corpus, w. Ibolya Verebics (sop), Judit Németh (cta), József Mukk (ten), József Moldvay (bar), Gábor Oláh (bar), István Ella (org), Hungarian Radio-TV Male Chamber Choir *(rec Hungaroton Studio, June 14-16, 1991)* Hungaroton ▲ HCD 4003 [DDD]
Mozart, W.A.:Miserere, w. Ibolya Verebics (sop), Judit Németh (cta), József Mukk (ten), József Moldvay (bass), Gábor Oláh (bar/Gregorian intonations), István Ella (org), Hungarian Radio-TV Male Chamber Choir *(rec Hungaroton Studio, June 14-16, 1991)* Hungaroton ▲ HCD 4003 [DDD]
Mozart, W.A.:Misericordias Domini, w. Ibolya Verebics (sop), Judit Németh (cta), József Mukk (ten), József Moldvay (bass), Gábor Oláh (bar/Gregorian intonations), István Ella (org), Hungarian Radio-TV Male Chamber Choir *(rec Hungaroton Studio, June 14-16, 1991)* Hungaroton ▲ HCD 4003 [DDD]
Mozart, W.A.:Missa brevis, K.65, w. Ibolya Verebics (sop), Judit Németh (cta), József Mukk (ten), József Moldvay (bass), Gábor Oláh (bar/Gregorian intonations), István Ella (org), Hungarian Radio-TV Male Chamber Choir *(rec Hungaroton Studio, June 14-16, 1991)* Hungaroton ▲ HCD 4003 [DDD]
Mozart, W.A.:Missa brevis, K.194, w. Ibolya Verebics (sop), Judit Németh (cta), József Mukk (ten), József Moldvay (b), Gábor Oláh (bar/Gregorian intonations), István Ella (org), Hungarian Radio-TV Male Chamber Choir *(rec Hungaroton Studio, June 14-16, 1991)* Hungaroton ▲ HCD 4003 [DDD]
Mozart, W.A.:Sancta Maria, w. Ibolya Verebics (sop), Judit Németh (cta), József Mukk (ten), József Moldvay (bass), Gábor Oláh (bar/Gregorian intonations), István Ella (org), Hungarian Radio-TV Male Chamber Choir *(rec Hungaroton Studio, June 14-16, 1991)* Hungaroton ▲ HCD 4003 [DDD]

Hungarian Radio-TV Chorus
Bartók, B.:Cant Profana, "The Giant Stags", w. József Réti (ten), József Gregor (bass), A. Dorati (cnd), Budapest SO Hungaroton ▲ HCD 31503 [ADD]
Giordano, U.:Fedora, w. V. Kincses (sop), E. Martón (sop), J. Carreras (ten), J. Gregor (bass), G. Patanè (cnd), Hungarian Radio-TV SO [I] CBS 2-▲ M2K 42181 [DDD]
Haydn, M.:Missa Pro Defuncto Archiepiscopo Sigismundo, w. Ibolya Verebics (sop), Judit Németh (mez), Martin Klietmann (ten), József Moldvay (bass), H. Rilling (cnd), Franz Liszt CO [L] Hungaroton ▲ HCD 31022 [DDD]
Haydn, M.:Missa Sancti Francisci, w. Ibolya Verebics (sop), Judit Németh (mez), Martin Klietmann (ten), József Moldvay (bass), H. Rilling (cnd), Franz Liszt CO [L] Hungaroton ▲ HCD 31022 [DDD]
Kacsóh, P.:János Vitéz, w. Mária Gyurkovics (sop), Anna Zentai (sop—Iluska), Tivadar Bilicsi (sgr), Hilda Gobbi (sgr), Sándor Pethes (sgr—Bartolo), Róbert Ilosfalvy (ten—Kukorica), György Melis (bar—Bagó), György Radnai (bar—Strázsamester), László Domahidy (bass—Csősz), E. Lukács (cnd), Hungarian State Opera Orch *(rec Budapest, 1961)* Classical Diamonds 2-▲ CLD 4011-12 [AAD]
Kálmán, I.:Die Csárdásfürstin (sels), w. Erzsébet (sgr), György (sgr), Hanna (sgr), Róbert (sgr), Tamás (cnd), Hungarian Radio-TV SO Hungaroton ▲ HCD 16780 [AAD]
Lehár, F.:Giuditta (sels), w. Katalin Pitti (sop), Győzó Leblanc (sgr), G. Oberfrank (cnd), Budapest SO [Hun] Hungaroton ▲ HCD 16809 [ADD]
Lehár, F.:Das Land des Lächelns (sels), w. Házy (sop), Magda Kalmár (sop), Szimándy (sgr), Bende (sgr), G. Oberfrank (cnd), Budapest SO [Hun] Hungaroton ▲ HCD 16809 [ADD]
Liszt, F.:Christus, w. Veronika Kincses (sop), Tamara Takács (mez), Robert Nagy (ten), Sándor Sólyom-Nagy (bar), László Polgár (bass), A. Dorati (cnd), Hungarian State Orch [L] Hungaroton 3-▲ HCD 12831/33 [DDD]
Mascagni, P.:Amica, w. Katia Ricciarelli (sop), Monica Minarelli (sgr), Elia Padovan (sgr), Fabio Armiliato (sgr), Walter Donati (sgr), M. Pace (cnd), Hungarian Radio-TV SO *(rec Budapest, Nov 1995)* Kicco Classic 2-▲ KC 00296 [DDD]
Puccini, G.:Tosca (sels), w. E. Marton (sop), B. Heja (trb), J. Carreras (ten), F. Cerdesits (ten), J. Pons (bar), J. Nemeth (bar), J. Gregor (bass), M. Tilson Thomas (cnd), Hungarian State Orch *(rec Budapest, Dec. 14-22, 1988)* Sony Classical ("Opera Highlights" series) ▲ SMK 53500 [DDD]
Respighi, O.:Semirama, w. E. Marton (sop), V. Kincses (sop), L. Bartolini (ten), L Miller (bar), L. Polgaar (bass), T. Clementis (bass), L. Gardelli (cnd), Hungarian State Orch [I] Hungaroton 2-▲ HCD 31197/98
Schubert, Franz:Choruses [G] White Label ▲ HRC 057

P. Erdei (cnd)
Mahler, G.:Das Klagende Lied, w. Katalin Szendrényi (sop), Klára Takács (cta), Dénes Gulyás (ten), A. Ligeti (cnd), Budapest SO Classical Diamonds ▲ CLD 4010 [DDD]

J. Ferencsik (cnd)
Kodály, Z.:Choral Music [Hun] Hungaroton ▲ HCD 12352

Pödör, Sapszon, Nagy (cnd)
Verdi, G.:Arias, w. Sylvia Sass (sop), Giorgio Lamberti (ten), Kolos Kováts (bass), Oberfrank, Gardelli (cnd), Budapest MÁV SO, Hungarian State Opera Orch, Hungarian People's Army Male Chorus, Hungarian State Opera Chorus—Vieni, o Levita!...Tu sul labbro [from Nabucco]; Vergini!...Il ciel per ora...Sciagurata! Hai tu creduto; Qui posa il fianco [both from I Lombardi]; Che mai vegg'io...Infelice! E tu credevi...; Vigili pure il ciel...Iddio n'ascolti [both from Ernani]; Mentre gonfiarsi l'anima [from Attila]; Studia il passo...Come dal ciel precipital [from Macbeth]; O patria, o cara patria...O tu, Palermo [from I vespri Siciliani]; A te l'estremo addio... [from Simon Boccanegra]; Ella giammai m'amò [from Don Carlo] Hungaroton ("Great Hungarian Voices" series) ▲ HCD 31650 [ADD/DDD]

F. Sapszon (cnd)
Durkó, Z.:Burial Prayer, w. Attila Fülöp (ten), Endre Ütő (bass), G. Lehel (cnd), Budapest SO *(rec 1975)* Hungaroton ▲ HCD 31654 [AAD]

Hungarian Radio-TV Male Chamber Chorus
J. Reményi (cnd)
Mozart, W.A.:Alma Dei creatoris, w. Ibolya Verebics (sop), Judit Németh (cta), József Mukk (ten), József Moldvay (bar), Gábor Oláh (bar), István Ella (org), Hungarian Radio-TV Children's Chorus Girls' Voices *(rec Hungaroton Studio, June 14-16, 1991)* Hungaroton ▲ HCD 4003 [DDD]
Mozart, W.A.:Ave verum corpus, w. Ibolya Verebics (sop), Judit Németh (cta), József Mukk (ten), József Moldvay (bar), Gábor Oláh (bar), István Ella (org), Hungarian Radio-TV Children's Chorus Girls' Voices *(rec Hungaroton Studio, June 14-16, 1991)* Hungaroton ▲ HCD 4003 [DDD]
Mozart, W.A.:Miserere, w. Ibolya Verebics (sop), Judit Németh (cta), József Mukk (ten), József Moldvay (bass), Gábor Oláh (bar/Gregorian intonations), István Ella (org), Hungarian Radio-TV Children's Chorus Girls' Voices *(rec Hungaroton Studio, June 14-16, 1991)* Hungaroton ▲ HCD 4003 [DDD]
Mozart, W.A.:Misericordias Domini, w. Ibolya Verebics (sop), Judit Németh (cta), József Mukk (ten), József Moldvay (bass), Gábor Oláh (bar/Gregorian intonations), István Ella (org), Hungarian Radio-TV Children's Chorus Girls' Voices *(rec Hungaroton Studio, June 14-16, 1991)* Hungaroton ▲ HCD 4003 [DDD]

Hungarian Radio-TV Male Chamber Chorus (cont.)
J. Reményi (cnd) (cont.)
Mozart, W.A.:Missa brevis, K.65, w. Ibolya Verebics (sop), Judit Németh (cta), József Mukk (ten), József Moldvay (bass), Gábor Oláh (bar/Gregorian intonations), István Ella (org), Hungarian Radio-TV Children's Chorus Girls' Voices *(rec Hungaroton Studio, June 14-16, 1991)* Hungaroton ▲ HCD 4003 [DDD]
Mozart, W.A.:Missa brevis, K.194, w. Ibolya Verebics (sop), Judit Németh (cta), József Mukk (ten), József Moldvay (b), Gábor Oláh (bar/Gregorian intonations), István Ella (org), Hungarian Radio-TV Children's Chorus Girls' Voices *(rec Hungaroton Studio, June 14-16, 1991)* Hungaroton ▲ HCD 4003 [DDD]
Mozart, W.A.:Sancta Maria, w. Ibolya Verebics (sop), Judit Németh (cta), József Mukk (ten), József Moldvay (bass), Gábor Oláh (bar/Gregorian intonations), István Ella (org), Hungarian Radio-TV Children's Chorus Girls' Voices *(rec Hungaroton Studio, June 14-16, 1991)* Hungaroton ▲ HCD 4003 [DDD]

Hungarian State Chorus
Bartók, B.:Bluebeard's Castle, w. E. Martón (sop), S. Ramey (bass), A. Fischer (cnd), Hungarian State Orch [Hun] CBS ▲ MK 44523 [DDD]
Cilea, F.:L'Arlesiana, w. M. Spacagna (sop), E. Zilio (mez), P. Kelen (ten), B. Póka (bar), T. Clementis (bass), C. Rosekrans (cnd), Hungarian State Orch Quintana 2-▲ QUI 903067/68
Giordano, U.:Andrea Chénier, w. E. Martón (sop), J. Carreras (ten), G. Zancanaro (bar), G. Patanè (cnd), Hungarian State Orch [I] CBS 2-▲ M2K 42369 [DDD]
Puccini, G.:Tosca, w. E. Marton (sop), J. Carreras (ten), J. Pons (bar), M. Tilson Thomas (cnd), Hungarian State Orch Sony Classical 2-▲ S2K 45847
Respighi, O.:Belfagor, w. S. Sass (sop), T. Takács (mez), G. Lamberti (ten), L. Miller (bar), L. Polgár (bass), L. Gardelli (cnd), Hungarian State Orch [I] Hungaroton 2-▲ HCD 12850/51 [DDD]
Respighi, O.:La Fiamma, w. I. Tokody (sop), T. Takács (mez), P. Kelen (ten), S. Sólyom-Nagy (bar), L. Gardelli (cnd), Hungarian State Orch [I] Hungaroton 3-▲ HCD 12591/93 [DDD]
Strauss (II), Joh.:Eine Nacht in Venedig (sels), w. J. Scovotti (sop), E. Schary (mez), E. Steiner (mez), C. Bini (ten), F. Stricker (ten), W. Brendel (bar), E. Märzendorfer (cnd), Hungarian State Orch [G] Acanta ▲ CD 43809 [DDD]

G. Ugrin (cnd)
Liszt, F.:Choral Music, w. András Molnár (ten), L. Révész (org)—Ave Maria I, S.20/1; Domine salvum fac regem, S.23; Te Deum laudamus, S.27; Ave maris stella, S.34/1; Inno a Maria Vergine, S.39; Rosario, S.56; In domum Domini ibimus, S.57; Chor der Engel, S.85 [G,I,L] Hungaroton ▲ HCD 31103 [DDD]

Hungarian State Choruses
Mascagni, P.:Lodoletta, w. M. Spacagna (sop), P. Kelen (ten), B. Szilágyi (bar), M. Kálmándi (bar), L. Polgár (bass), C. Rosekrans (cnd), Hungarian State Orch [I] Hungaroton 2-▲ HCD 31307/08 [DDD]

Hungarian State Folk Ensemble Chorus
Csámpai, I.:In Memory of Bihari, w. L. Berki (cnd), Hungarian State Folk Ensemble Orch *(rec 1969)* Hungaroton ▲ HCD 18008 [AAD]
Csenki, I.:Gypsy Dances of Hungary, w. Márta Szobek (sgr), R. Lantos (cnd), Hungarian State Folk Ensemble Orch *(rec 1969)* Hungaroton ▲ HCD 18008 [AAD]
Gulyás, L.:Bottle Dance, w. L. Berki (cnd), Hungarian State Folk Ensemble Orch *(rec 1969)* Hungaroton ▲ HCD 18008 [AAD]
Gulyás, L.:An Evening in the Spinning Room, w. M. Pászti (cnd), Hungarian State Folk Ensemble Orch *(rec 1969)* Hungaroton ▲ HCD 18008 [AAD]
Gulyás, L.:Music from Szék, w. L. Berki (cnd), Hungarian State Folk Ensemble Orch *(rec 1969)* Hungaroton ▲ HCD 18008 [AAD]
Gulyás, L.:Triple Jumping Dance, w. Erzsébet Varga (sgr), R. Lantos (cnd), Hungarian State Folk Ensemble Orch *(rec 1969)* Hungaroton ▲ HCD 18008 [AAD]
Kodály, Z.:Kálló Double Dance, w. M. Pászti (cnd), Hungarian State Folk Ensemble Orch *(rec 1969)* Hungaroton ▲ HCD 18008 [AAD]
Maros, R.:Wedding at Ecser, w. R. Lantos (cnd), Hungarian State Folk Ensemble Orch *(rec 1969)* Hungaroton ▲ HCD 18008 [AAD]

Hungarian State Opera Chorus
Boito, A.:Mefistofele, w. E. Marton (sop), P. Domingo (ten), S. Ramey (bass), G. Patanè (cnd), Hungarian State SO [I] *(rec Budapest, 1988)* Sony Classical 2-▲ S2K 44983 [DDD]
Erkel, F.:Bánk Bán, w. K. Agay (sop), E. Komlóssy (cta), J. Réti (ten), J. Simándy (ten), S. Sólyom-Nagy (bar), J. Ferencsik (cnd), Budapest PO [Hun] *(rec 1969)* Hungaroton 2-▲ HCD 11376/77 [ADD]
Erkel, F.:Hunyadi László, w. M. Kalmár (sop), S. Sass (sop), D. Gulyás (ten), A. Molnar (ten), I. Gáti (bar), S. Sólyom-Nagy (bar), J. Kovács (cnd), Hungarian State Opera Orch [Hun] Hungaroton 3-▲ HCD 12581/83 [DDD]
Gluck, C.W.:Orfeo ed Euridice, w. V. Kincses (sop), M. Zempleni (sop), J. Hamari (mez), E. Lukács (cnd), Hungarian State Opera Orch LaserLight ▲ 14113 [DDD]
Puccini, G.:Madama Butterfly, w. V. Kincses (sop), T. Tákacs (mez), P. Dvorsky (ten), L. Miller (bar), G. Patanè (cnd), Hungarian State Opera Orch [I] Hungaroton 2-▲ HCD 12256/57
Puccini, G.:Suor angelica, w. I. Tokody (sop), Barlay (sgr), B. Póka (bar), L. Gardelli (cnd), Hungarian State Opera Orch [I] Hungaroton ▲ HCD 12490
Rossini, G.:Arias, w. Ewa Podles (mez), P. G. Morandi (cnd), Hungarian State Opera Orch—Cruda sorte! Amor tiranno!; Amici, in ogni evento m'affido a voi...Pensa all patria [both from L'Italiana in Algeri]; Eccomi alfine in Babilonia...Ah! quel giorno ognor rammento [from Semiramide]; Oh patria...Di tanti palpiti [from Tancredi]; Non temer:d'un basso affto [from Maometto II]; Mura felici...Elena! oh tu, che chiamo! [from La donna del lago]; Una voce poco fa [from Il Barbiere di Siviglia]; Nacqui all'affanno, al pianto [from Cinderella] *(rec Italian Institute, Budapest, May 16-22, 1995)* Naxos ▲ 8.553543 [DDD]
Szokolay, S.:Blood Wedding, w. E. Házy (sop), O. Szőnyi (sop), E. Komlóssy (cta), Faragó (sgr), A. Kórodi (cnd), Hungarian State Opera Orch [Hun] Hungaroton 2-▲ HCD 11262/63 [ADD]

A. Katona (cnd)
Donizetti, G.:L'elisir d'amore, w. Alessandra Ruffini (sop—Adina), Mariangela Spotorno (sop—Gianetta), Vincenzo La Scola (ten—Nemorino), Simone Alaimo (bar—Dulcamara), Roberto Frontali (bar—Belcore), P.G. Morandi (cnd), Hungarian State Opera Orch *(rec Budapest, July 1995)* Naxos 2-▲ 8.60045-6 [DDD]
Puccini, G.:Madama Butterfly, w. Maria Spacagna (sop), Sharon Grahm (mez), Vivica Genaux (mez), Richard di Renzi (ten), Richard Markley (ten), Erich Parce (bar), James Butler (bass), C. Rosenkrans (cnd), Hungarian State Opera Orch—3 versions *(rec Italian Institute, Budapest, Sept 5-21, 1995)* Vox Classics 4-▲ VOX4 7525 [DDD]

Pödör, Sapszon, Nagy (cnd)
Verdi, G.:Arias, w. Sylvia Sass (sop), Giorgio Lamberti (ten), Kolos Kováts (bass), Oberfrank, Gardelli (cnd), Budapest MÁV SO, Hungarian State Opera Orch, Hungarian People's Army Male Chorus, Hungarian Radio-TV Chorus—Vieni, o Levita!...Tu sul labbro [from Nabucco]; Vergini!...Il ciel per ora...Sciagurata! Hai tu creduto; Qui posa il fianco [both from I Lombardi]; Che mai vegg'io...Infelice! E tu credevi...; Vigili pure il ciel...Iddio n'ascolti [both from Ernani]; Mentre gonfiarsi l'anima [from Attila]; Studia il passo...Come dal ciel precipital [from Macbeth]; O patria, o cara patria...O tu, Palermo [from I vespri Siciliani]; A te l'estremo addio... [from Simon Boccanegra]; Ella giammai m'amò [from Don Carlo] Hungaroton ("Great Hungarian Voices" series) ▲ HCD 31650 [ADD/DDD]

Donald Hunt Singers
Elgar, E.:Choral Songs (comp), w. D. Hunt (cnd), Worcester Cathedral Choir [E] Hyperion 2-▲ CDA 66271/72 [DDD]

Hymnia Chamber Choir
Wagner, R.:Songs, w. L. Koppel (sop), B. Asker (bar), J. E. Frederiksen (pno)—Seven Faust-Lieder (1832); Der Tannenbaum; Geburtsangrüss an Cosima; Kraft-lied; Adieux de Marie Stuart; Dors mon enfant; Attente; Mignonne; Tout n'est qu'images fugitives; Les deux grenadiers *(rec 1988)* Classico ▲ CLASSCD 102

Iasi Moldova Phil Chorus
Enescu, G.:Vox maris, w. I. Baciu (cnd), Iasi Moldova PO Marco Polo ▲ 8.223142

Icelandic Opera Chorus
Leifs, J.:Iceland Cant, w. P. Sakari (cnd), Iceland SO Chandos ("New Directions" series) ▲ CHN 9433
Leifs, J.:Iceland Ov, w. P. Sakari (cnd), Iceland SO Chandos ("New Directions" series) ▲ CHN 9433

Icelandic Opera Chorus (cont.)
Leifs, J.:Music of, w. Sigridur Ella Magnúsdóttir (mez), Ólafur Vignir Albertsson (pno), Sólveig Anna Jónsdóttir (pno), Hjálmar Ragnarsson (pno), Edda Erlendsdóttir (pno), Marteinn Hunger Fridriksson (org), Hildigunnur Halldórsdóttir (vn), Gréta Gudnadóttir (vn), Gudmundur Kristmundsson (va), Sigurdur Halldórsson (vc), Richard Korn (db), Iceland SO, Langholts Church Graduale Choir, Hamrahlid Choir—Icelandic Cant, Op. 13/4; Valse Lento, Op. 2/1 [Tempo Giusto]; Requiem; Lullaby [After the Riots]; Fairy-Tale in the Wood [from Baldr, Op. 34]; Funeral March; Separation [from Elegy, Op. 53]; Galdra Loftur Ov, Op. 10; Funeral March, Op. 6; Reverie; Reunion [from Elegy, Op. 53]; Fine I, Op. 55; Andante [The Last Supper]; Preludia Organo, Op. 16/3 [In the Church]; The Tear of Stone [from Elegy, Op. 53] Music From Iceland ▲ ITM 605 [DDD]
Rachmaninoff, S.:Monna Vanna, w. S. McCoy (ten), S. Milnes (bar), I. Buketoff (cnd), Iceland SO Chandos ▲ CHAN 8987 [DDD]

Cortes, Stefánsson, Ingólfsdóttir (cnd)
Ragnarsson, H.:Music of, w. S. E. Magnúsdóttir (mez), H. Halldórsdóttir (vn), G. Gudnadóttir (vn), G. Kristmundsson (va), S. Halldórsson (vc), R. Korn (db), Ó. V. Albertsson (pno), S. A. Jónsdóttir (pno), H. Ragnarsson (pno), E. Erlendsdóttir (pno), M. H. Fridriksson (org), Sakari, Wilkinson (cnd), Iceland SO, Hamrahlíd Choir, Langholts Church Graduale Choir—Meine kleine Freundin [In the Ballroom]; Lovers Duet; After the concert; Meine kleine Freundin [Annie listens to the Radio]; Lif's Theme [On the Beach]; Lif's Theme II [Night Prayer]; Composing Ov [Vars I, II & III] Music From Iceland ▲ ITM 605 [DDD]

Icelandic Sym Chorus
Ives, C.:Holidays, w. W. Strickland (cnd), Iceland SO, Tokyo PO, Finnish RSO, Göteborg SO [E] CRI ■ ACS 6014

Ieper Chamber Choir
Negro Spirituals, w. Jeanette Thompson (sop), David Miller (pno) Pavane ▲ ADW 7267 [DDD]

In Dulci Jubilo
Salve Festa Dies:Gregorian Chant for Seasons of the Year *(rec Sept. 11, 1992)* Naxos ▲ 8.550712 [DDD]

A. Turco (cnd)
Ambrosian Chant:Early Christian Chant of the Ambrosian Rite *(rec Parish Church of Quatrelle, Mantua, Italy, May, 1995)* Naxos ▲ 8.553502 [DDD]

Indianapolis Children's Choir
H.H. Leck (cnd)
Britten, B.:The Birds, w. Robert Houghton (pno) *(rec The Lodge, May & June 1995)* VAI Audio ▲ VAIA 1130 [DDD]
Britten, B.:A Ceremony of Carols, w. Beverly Wesner-Hoehn (hp) *(rec The Lodge, May & June 1995)* VAI Audio ▲ VAIA 1130 [DDD]
Purcell, H.:Come Ye Sons of Art, w. Laura Goetz (ob), Sarah Weiner (ob), Davis Brooks (vn), Lisa Brooks (vn), Jann Cosart (va), Mary Burke (vl), Vance Reese (db), Thomas Gerber (hpd) [arr. Maurice Blower] *(rec The Lodge, May & June 1995)* VAI Audio ▲ VAIA 1130 [DDD]
Purcell, H.:Fly, Bold Rebellion (sels), w. Laura Goetz (ob), Sarah Weiner (ob), Davis Brooks (vn), Lisa Brooks (vn), Jann Cosart (va), Mary Burke (vl), Vance Reese (db), Thomas Gerber (hpd)—Be Welcome Then, Great Sir [arr. Steven Rickards] *(rec The Lodge, May & June 1995)* VAI Audio ▲ VAIA 1130 [DDD]
Purcell, H.:King Arthur (sels), w. Laura Goetz (ob), Sarah Weiner (ob), Davis Brooks (vn), Lisa Brooks (vn), Jann Cosart (va), Mary Burke (vl), Vance Reese (db), Thomas Gerber (hpd)—Fairest Isle [arr. Steven Rickards] *(rec The Lodge, May & June 1995)* VAI Audio ▲ VAIA 1130 [DDD]
Purcell, H.:Now That the Sun Hath Veiled His Light, w. Robert Houghton (pno) [arr. W.G. Whitaker] *(rec The Lodge, May & June 1995)* VAI Audio ▲ VAIA 1130 [DDD]

Indianapolis Symphonic Women's Choir
Vaughan Williams, R.:Sym 7, w. D. Labelle (sop), R. Allam (nar), R. Leppard (cnd), Indianapolis SO Koss Classics ▲ KC 2214 [DDD]

Innsbruck Chorus
Brahms, J.:Alto Rhap, w. Maura Moreira (cta), R. Wagner (cnd), Innsbruck SO *(rec Innsbruck, 1963)* Allegretto ▲ ACD 8190
Schumann, R.:Requiem Mignon, w. Christa Lehnert (sop), Edith Mathis (sop), Maura Moreira (cta), Margarete Witte-Waldbauer (alt), Robert Titze (bass), R. Wagner (cnd), Innsbruck SO *(rec Innsbruck, 1963)* Allegretto ▲ ACD 8190

Insieme Vocale Datrocanto
Lassus, O. de:Sacred Music, w. D. Tabbia (cnd), Ricercar Academy—Missa Super Je Suis Deshéritée; Lectiones Matutinae de Nativitate Christi; Lectiones Sacrae ex Libri Hiob; Stabat Mater Dolorosa Stradivarius ▲ STV 33345 [DDD]

Le Institutioni Harmoniche
M. Longhini (cnd)
Carissimi, G.:Vocal Music (misc)—Sciolto Havean Dall'alte Sponde [cant & mass]; Suscitavit Dominus; Exurge cor Meum; Ardens est Cor Nostrum Stradivarius ▲ STV 33344 [DDD]
Monteverdi, C.:Magnificat Secondo [L] Nuova Era ("Ancient Music" series) ▲ 7118 [DDD]
Monteverdi, C.:Messe da capella [L] Nuova Era ("Ancient Music" series) ▲ 7118 [DDD]

Intercession Cathedral Church Choir
N. Bultsevich (cnd)
Rejoice, O Indestructable Fortress & Stronghold of Orthodoxy *(rec Nativity Convent, Grodno, Byelorussia, 1992)* Russian Compact Disc ▲ RCD 15015 [ADD]

International Children's Choir
Children's Songs of the World, w. Edita Gruberova (sop), Rudolfsheimer Children's Choir Nightingale Classics ▲ NIG CD 70660

L'Inviti
Walton, W.:Belshazzar's Feast, w. Bryn Terfel (b-bar), A. Litton (cnd), Bournemouth SO, Bournemouth Sym Chorus, Waynflete Singers *(rec Winchester Cathedral, Feb 1995)* London ▲ 448134-2 [DDD]

Iowa City Boys' Choir
Gaburo, K.:Antiphony IX, w. J. Dixon (cnd), Univ of Iowa SO, Iowa City Girls' Choir Music & Arts ▲ CD 832 [DDD]

Iowa City Girls' Choir
Gaburo, K.:Antiphony IX, w. J. Dixon (cnd), Univ of Iowa SO, Iowa City Boys' Choir Music & Arts ▲ CD 832 [DDD]

Ireland National Sym Chorus
Balfe, M.W.:The Bohemian Girl, w. N. Thomas (sop), P. Power (ten), J. Summers (bar), R. Bonynge (cnd), Irish National SO Argo 2-▲ 433324-2 [DDD]

Elmer Iseler Singers
Bach, J.S.:Chorales, Mainly Mozart Orch—Jesu, joy of man's desiring; Sheep may safely graze; Praise ye, almighty God; Be glory, praise & honor; To Thee our humble praise we sing; etc. CBC ("SM 5000" series) ▲ SMCD 5042C [DDD]
Coulthard, J.:Quebec May, w. E. Iseler (cnd), CBC Vancouver SO—[E,F] CBC ("SM 5000" series) ▲ SMCD 5115 [DDD]
Glick, S.I.:Sing Unto the Lord a New Song, w. E. Iseler (cnd), CBC Vancouver SO [E,Heb] CBC ("SM 5000" series) ▲ SMCD 5115 [DDD]
Holman, D.:Night Music, w. E. Iseler (cnd), CBC Vancouver SO [E] CBC ("SM 5000" series) ▲ SMCD 5115 [DDD]
Somers, H.:Chansons de la Nouvelle-France, w. E. Iseler (cnd), CBC Vancouver SO [F] CBC ("SM 5000" series) ▲ SMCD 5115 [DDD]
Somers, H.:Kyrie, w. Roxolana Roslak (sop), Susan Cooper (mez), Robert Missen (ten), Nelson Lohnes (bass), Timothy Cadan (bass), E. Iseler (cnd), *(orch unknown)* *(rec Flora McRae Eaton Memorial Auditorium & St. Anne's Anglican Church, Toronto)* Centrediscs ▲ CMC 5495 [DDD]
Somers, H.:Limericks, w. Patricia Kern (mez), E. Iseler (cnd), *(orch unknown)* *(rec Flora McRae Eaton Memorial Auditorium & St. Anne's Anglican Church, Toronto)* Centrediscs ▲ CMC 5495 [DDD]

E. Iseler (cnd)
Gloria:Sacred Choral Works CBC Records ("Musica Viva" series) ▲ MVCD 1058 [DDD]
Palestrina, G.:Sacred Music—Ascendo ad patrem; Missa Ascendo ad Patrem; Quem vidistis, pastores; Surge illuminare Jerusalem; Stabat Mater; Assumpta est Maria; Magnificat Primi Toni CBC ("Musica Viva" series) ▲ MVCD 1067 [DDD]

Elmer Iseler Singers (cont.)
E. Iseler (cnd) (cont.)
Somers, H.:Songs from the Newfoundland Outports, w. Bruce Ubukata (pno) *(rec Flora McRae Eaton Memorial Auditorium & St. Anne's Anglican Church, Toronto)* Centrediscs ▲ CMC 5495 [DDD]
Spirituals Marquis Classics ▲ ERAD 115
Welcome Yule! CBC Records ("SM 5000" series) ▲ SMCD 5055 [DDD]

Israel National Choir
Fleischer, T.:Oratorio 1492-1992, w. S. Sperber (cnd), Haifa SO, Rinat & Israel Mandolin Ensemble Vienna Modern Masters ▲ VMM 3013 [DDD]

Istanbul State Opera Chorus
Sinangil, A.D.:Mevlâna Oratorio (sels), w. Leyla Demiris (sop), Isin Güyer (mez), Mesut Iktu (bar), Mustafa Iktu (bass), Kâmil Sekerkaran (fl), A. D. Sinangil (cnd), Istanbul State Opera Orch—Récitatif I; Choral; Récitatif II; V[e] partie Gallo ▲ CD 836 [ADD]

Italian d'Olanda Opera Chorus
Mascagni, P.:Cavalleria rusticana, w. L. Bruna Rasa (sop), M. Meloni (mez), R. Gallo Toscani (mez), A. Melandri (ten), A. Poli (bar), P. Mascagni (cnd), Holland Italian Opera Orch [I] *(rec live at the Royal Theatre in the Hague, 11/7/38)* Bongiovanni ▲ GB 1050 (m) [AAD]

Italian Lyric Chorus
Giordano, U.:Andrea Chénier, w. Renata Tebaldi (sop—Maddalena), Anna di Stasio (mez—Bersi), Amalia Pini (mez—Madelon/Contessa), Mario Del Monaco (ten—Andrea Chenier), Antonio Pirino (ten—L'Incredibile/Abate), Aldo Protti (bar—Carlo Gerard), Arturo La Porta (bass/bar—Mathieu/Fleville), Silvano Pagliuca (bass/bar—Roucher/Fouquier-Tinville), Giorgio Onesti (bass—Dumas/Schmidt/Major-domo), F. Capuana (cnd), Italian Lyric Orch *(rec Tokyo, Oct 1, 1961)* Legato Classics 2-▲ LCD 214-2 [ADD]

Italian Phil Chorus
Manfroce, N.A.:Ecuba, w. A. C. Antonacci (sop), D. di Domenico (ten), F. Piccoli (ten), G. De Bellida (sgr), M. de Bernart (cnd), Italian PO [I] *(rec live 1990)* Bongiovanni 2-▲ GB 2119/20 [DDD]

Italian Vocal Quintet
Gesualdo, D.C.:Madrigali a cinque voci, Books I- VI (comp), w. C. Foti (mez), E. Mazzoni (cta), G. Sarti (bar), D. Nabokov (bass)] Rivoalto ▲ RIV 89123 [ADD]
Gesualdo, D.C.:Madrigali a cinque voci, Books I- VI (comp), w. C. Foti (mez), E. Mazzoni (cta), G. Sarti (bar), D. Nabokov (bass)] Rivoalto ▲ RIV 89121 [ADD]

Ithaca College Concert Choir
Ives, C.:Songs, w. L. Stokowski (cnd), American SO, Gregg Smith Singers—Election (It Strikes Me That); Lincoln, the Great Commoner; Majority (or The Masses); They are there! (A War Song March) [E] *(rec 1967)* Sony Masterworks ("Portrait" series) ▲ MPK 46726 [ADD]

IUP Chorale
Persichetti, V.:Celebrations, w. J. Stamp (cnd), Keystone Wind Ensemble *(rec Fisher Auditorium & Waller Hall, IUP Campus, May 1994, Jan & Feb 1995)* Citadel ▲ CTD 88111 [DDD]

Jacques Moderne Ensemble
J. Suhubiette (cnd)
Gagliano, M. da:Missae, et sacrarum cantionum Calliope ▲ CAL 9292 [DDD]
Gagliano, M. da:Sacrarum cantionum liber secundus Calliope ▲ CAL 9292 [DDD]
Janequin, C.:Chansons—Jouissance vous donnerai; Je file quand Dieu; C'est a grand tort; Basse Dance St. Roch; Laissons amours; Basses dances; Luscescit jam o soccili; Faute d'argent; Un mari se voulant coucher; S'il est ainsi que cognée; Martin menait son porceau; Mon ami m'avait promis; Celle qui vit son mari; La bataille de Marignan *(rec Dec 1994)* Calliope ▲ CAL 9293 [DDD]
Regnart, F.:Novae cantionaes sacrae—Super flumina Babylonis; Tulerunt Dominum meum; Initium lamentationum Hieremiae; Angelus ad pastores; Timor et tremor; Exultate justi; Salve Regina; Lux de caelo; Cum crucifixissent Jesum; In te Domine speravi; Laudate pueri Dominum *(rec Lys St. George, June 1993)* Calliope ▲ CAL 9291 [DDD]

James St. Bride's Church Choir
R. James (cnd)
Bruckner, A.:motets, w. Richard Cheetham (trbn), Adrian Lane (trbn), Steven Saunders (trbn), Simon Wills (trbn), Matthew Morley (org)—Os justi; Locus iste; Libera me [in f, 1854]; Ave maria; Ecce sacerdos; Vexilla regis; Salvum fac populum tuum [1884]; Afferentur regi; Pange lingua; Tota pulchra es [Daniel Norman (tenor)]; Virga Jesse; Inveni David; Iam lucis orto sidere [Hymnus, 1868]; Tantum ergo [in D, 1988]; Christus factus est *(rec St. Bride's Church, Fleet Street, London, Jan. 27-29, 1994)* Naxos ▲ 8.550956 [DDD]

Janáček Opera Chorus
Mahler, G.:Beethoven's Sym 9, w. Leah Anne Myers (sop), Ilene Sameth (mez), James Clark (ten), Richard Conant (bass), P. Tiboris (cnd), Brno State PO Bridge ▲ BCD 9033 [DDD]

J. Pancik (cnd)
Fibich, Z.:Śárka, w. Eva Deplotová (sop), Eva Randová (mez), Vilém Přibyl (ten), Vaclav Zítek (bar), J. Štych (cnd), Brno State PO *(rec 1978)* Supraphon 2-▲ SUP 0036

Japan Children's Chorus
Ikebe, S.-I.:Fairy Tales Written on the Sky Camerata ▲ 30CM 378
Ikebe, S.-I.:Lullabies (6) Camerata ▲ 30CM 378
Ikebe, S.-I.:Poems Engraved on Clay Tablets Camerata ▲ 30CM 378

Jerusalem Rubin Conservatory of Music & Dance Ankor Choir
D. Ben-Yohanan (cnd)
Ankor *(rec Jerusalem Music Ctr, July 1994)* Thorofon ▲ CTH 2306 [DDD]

Eva Jessye Choir
Gershwin, G.:Porgy & Bess, w. A. Brown (sgr), E. Matthews (sgr), H. Jackson (sgr), Todd Duncan (sgr), H. Dowdy (sgr), A. Long (sgr) [1940-1942 original cast] MCA Classics ("Broadway Gold" series) ▲ MCAD 10520 ■ MCAC 10520

Jeunes de l'Eglise Chorus
Martin, F.:Le Mystère de la Nativité, w. Elly Ameling (sop), Aafje Heynis (cta), Hugues Cuénod (ten), Louis Devos (ten), Eric Tappy (ten), Pierre Bollet (bar), Derrik Olsen (bar), Charles Clavensy (b-bar), André Vessières (bass), E. Ansermet (cnd), Swiss Romande Orch, Ceneva Motet Chorus Cascavelle 2-▲ CVL 2006 [ADD]

Les Jeunes Solistes Vocal Ensemble
Maderna, B.:Hyperion, w. P Walmsley-Clark (sop), B. Ganz (nar), J. Zoon (fl), P. Eötvös (cnd), Asko Ensemble Montaigne 2-▲ MO 782014 [DDD]

Jeunesses Musicales Women's Chorus
Liszt, F.:Hungarian Royal Hymn, w. I. Zámbó (cnd), Hungarian State Orch, Hungarian People's Army Male Chorus [Hun] Hungaroton ▲ HCD 12748 [DDD]
Liszt, F.:Septam sacramenta, w. T. Takács (mez), J. Bándi (ten), G. Kallay (ten), K. Kaváts (bar), Zsuzsa Elekes (org), I. Zámbó (cnd), Hungarian State Orch, Hungarian People's Army Male Chorus [L] Hungaroton ▲ HCD 12748 [DDD]

Jewish Congregation Choir Berlin
Kol Nidre:Sacred Music of the Synagogue, w. Gloria Seipelt (alt), Leo Roth (ten), Rudolf Wiebel (bar), Werner Buschnakowski (org), Harry Foss (org), Leipzig RSO members, Leipzig Synagogue Choir EMI Classics ▲ CDM 65457

Jiyske Choir
M. Dahl (cnd)
Malling, O.:Seven Last Words, w. Helge Gramstrup (org) *(rec St. Markus church, Arhus, Oct 1995)* Marco Polo/Dacapo ▲ 8.224023 [DDD]

Eric Jones Chorale
America Sings, w. E. Jones (cnd), Eric Jones Orch London ("Weekend Classics" series) ▲ 433686-2 LC ■ 433686-4 LC

Geraint Jones Singers
Bach, C.P.E.:Magnificat, w. Jennifer Vyvyan (sop), Helen Watts (cta), Wilfred Brown (ten), Thomas Hemsley (bass), G. Jones (cnd), Geraint Jones Orch EMI Classics ("Baroque" series) ▲ CDK 65737

Joyful Company of Singers
Holst, G.:A Choral Fant, w. R. Hickox (cnd), City of London Sinfonia, London Sym Chorus Chandos ▲ CHAN 9437
Holst, G.:Ode to Death, w. R. Hickox (cnd), City of London Sinfonia, London Sym Chorus Chandos ▲ CHAN 9437

972 ▲ = CD ♦ = Enhanced CD Δ = MD ■ = Cassette Tape ▯ = DCC

Joyful Company of Singers (cont.)
Holst, G.:Partsongs (7), Op. 44, w. R. Hickox (cnd), City of London Sinfonia, London Sym Chorus
Chandos ▲ CHAN 9437
P. Broadbent (cnd)
Barber, S.:Choral Music—Agnus Dei; God's Grandeur; Heaven-Haven; Let down the Bars, o Death; The Monk & His Cat; Reincarnations; Sure on This Shining Night; To Be Sung on the Water; Twelfth Night; The Virgin Martyrs ASV ▲ ASV 939
Schuman, W.:Mail Order Madrigals—4 Madrigals ASV ▲ ASV 939
Schuman, W.:Perceptions ASV ▲ ASV 939
Jubilate Choir
Scriabin, A.:Poèmes Pno, Op. 69, w. M. Rudy (pno) Calliope ▲ CAL 9692 [ADD]
A. Riska (cnd)
Fougstedt, N.-E.:Songs—Björkarnas valv; 3 songs to texts by Nils Ferlin; 6 songs to texts by Arvid Mörne; 2 songs to texts by Karin Mandelstam; 3 songs to texts by Bertel Gripenberg; Hjärtats sommar; Smultronbacken; Sommarvisa; Skyn, blomman och en lärka; 3 songs to texts by Jarl Hemmer; Sanctus; Mot löftets strand; I jorden går dolda ådror; Djäknevisa; 2 trad songs; Följ oss sång; Silmien laulu *(rec Tapiola Concert Hall, Finland, Nov 11–12, 1995)* BIS ▲ CD 721 [DDD]
Juilliard Chorus
Beethoven, L. van:Sym 9, "Choral Sym", w. M. Arroyo (sop), R. Sarfaty (mez), N. di Virgilio (ten), N. Scott (bass), L. Bernstein (cnd), New York PO *(rec New York, May 18, 1964)*
Sony Classical ("Bernstein:The Royal Edition" series) ▲ SM 47513 [ADD]
Beethoven, L. van:Sym 9, "Choral Sym", w. L. Bernstein (cnd), New York PO [soloists M. Arroyo, R. Sarfaty, N. deVirgilio, N. Scott] Sony Classical ▲ SMK 47518 [ADD]
Mercadante, S.:Il giuramento, w. P. Wells (sop), B. Wolff (mez), G. Colmagro (bar), M. Molese (sgr), T. Schippers (cnd), Juilliard Orch [I] *(rec live, Spoleto, 6/29/70)* Memories 2-▲ HR 4174/75 (m)
Mercadante, S.:Il giuramento, w. P. Wells (sop), B. Wolff (mez), G. Colmagro (bar), M. Molese (sgr), T. Schippers (cnd), Juilliard Orch [I] *(rec live, Spoleto, 6/29/70)* Myto 2-▲ 2 MCD 90632 [ADD]
Jutland Opera Choir
Holmboe, V.:Sym 4, w. O. A. Hughes (cnd), Aarhus SO BIS ▲ CD 572 [DDD]
Kalken Gregorian Choir
J. Derde (cnd)
Treasury of Gregorian Chant René Gailly ▲ 87112
Kalrup Girls' Choir
J.O. Mortensen (cnd)
A Journey through Seasons in Song Point ▲ PCD 5113
Kansas City Chorale
C. Bruffy (cnd)
The Spirit of Christmas Present, w. BBC Welsh Chorus [cnd:John Hugh Thomas], Huw Tregelles Williams (org), Welsh Guards Fanfare Trumpeters, Christ Church Cathedral Choir [cnd:Stephen Darlington], Gulbenkian Orch [cnd:Michel Swierczewski], English St Nimbus ▲ NI 7034 [DDD]
Kansas City Lyric Opera Chorus
Moore, D.:Devil & Daniel Webster, w. Joyce Guyer (sop—Mary Stone), Benjamin Bongers (ten—Walter Butler), Michael Philip Davis (ten—Simon Girty), Matthew Foerschler (ten—Miser Stephens), Darren Keith Woods (ten—Mr. Scratch), Michael Lanman (bass—Blackbeard Teach), David Soxman (bass—Clerk), Brian Steele (bass—Daniel Webster), John Stephens (bass—Jabez Stone), Andrew Stuckey (bass—King Philip), Robert Gibby Brand (actor), Cary Miller (actor), R. Patterson (cnd), Kansas City SO *(rec Sept 1995)* Newport Classic ▲ NPD 85585 [DDD]
Kantiléna Children's Chorus
Martinů, B.:Špalíček, w. A. Kratochvilová (sop), M. Kopp (ten), R. Novák (bass), F. Jílek (cnd), Brno State PO [Cz] Supraphon 2-▲ 11 0752-2 [DDD]
Kapel Van de Lage Landen
H. van der Kamp (cnd)
Busnois, A.:Missa "O Crux lignum" *(rec Waalse Kerk, Amsterdam, May & Oct 1993)*
Emergo ▲ EC 3954-2
Busnois, A.:Motets—Magnificat; In hydraulis; Regina coeli; Anthoni usque limina *(rec Waalse Kerk, Amsterdam, May & Oct 1993)* Emergo ▲ EC 3954-2
Peter Kay Children's Chorus
Puccini, G.:Tosca, w. Jane Eaglen (sop—Floria Tosca), Charbel Michael (alt—Shepherd Boy), John Daszak (ten—Spoletta), Dennis O'Neill (ten—Mario Cavaradossi), Christopher Booth-Jones (bar—Sciarrone), Ashley Holland (bar—Jailor), Gregory Yurisich (bar—Baron Scarpia), Peter Rose (bass—Cesare Angelotti), Andrew Shore (bass—Sacristan), D. Parry (cnd), Philharmonia Orch, Geoffrey Mitchell Choir Chandos ("Opera in English" series) 2-▲ CHAN 3000
Kharkov Church of the Three Saints Choir
S. Kurilo (cnd)
Nikolsky, A.:Liturgy Russian Compact Disc ▲ RCD 13003
King Singers
Byrd, W.:Songs RCA Red Seal ▲ 09026-68004-2; ■ 09026-68004-4
Tallis, T.:Songs RCA Red Seal ▲ 09026-68004-2; ■ 09026-68004-4
King's College Choir Cambridge
Advent Choral Service EMI Classics ("Studio" series) ▲ CDM 63181 ■ EG 63181
Allegri, G.:Miserere EMI Classics ▲ CDC 47065-2 [DDD]
Arensky, A.:Trio 1 Pno, Rembrandt Trio Dorian ▲ DOR 90146 [DDD]
Bach, J.S.:Cant 7, w. P. Esswood (ct), K. Equiluz (ten), M. van Egmond (b-bar), Leonhardt Consort [G]
Teldec 2-▲ 2292-42498-2 [AAD]
Bach, J.S.:Cant 8, w. P. Esswood (ct), K. Equiluz (ten), G. Kiefer (bar), M. van Egmond (b-bar), Leonhardt Consort [G] Teldec 2-▲ 2292-42498-2 [AAD]
Bach, J.S.:Cant 9, w. P. Esswood (ct), K. Equiluz (ten), M. van Egmond (b-bar), Leonhardt Consort [G]
Teldec 2-▲ 2292-42499-2 [AAD]
Bach, J.S.:Cant 10, w. P. Esswood (ct), K. Equiluz (ten), M. van Egmond (b-bar), Leonhardt Consort [G]
Teldec 2-▲ 2292-42499-2 [AAD]
Bach, J.S.:Cant 12, w. P. Esswood (ct), K. Equiluz (ten), M. van Egmond (b-bar), Leonhardt Consort [G]
Teldec 2-▲ 2292-42500-2 [AAD]
Bach, J.S.:Cant 13, w. P. Esswood (ct), K. Equiluz (ten), M. van Egmond (b-bar), Leonhardt Consort [G]
Teldec 2-▲ 2292-42500-2 [AAD]
Bach, J.S.:Cant 14, w. M. van Altena (ten), M. van Egmond (b-bar), Leonhardt Consort [G]
Teldec 2-▲ 2292-42500-2 [AAD]
Bach, J.S.:Cant 22, w. P. Esswood (ct), K. Equiluz (ten), M. van Egmond (b-bar), Leonhardt Consort [G]
Teldec 2-▲ 2292-42502-2 [AAD]
Bach, J.S.:Cant 23, w. W. Gampert (trb), P. Esswood (ct), M. van Altena (ten), M. van Egmond (b-bar), Leonhardt Consort [G] Teldec 2-▲ 2292-42502-2 [AAD]
Carols from King's EMI Classics ("Classics for Pleasure" series) ▲ CDB 67356
Carols from King's EMI Classics ("Studio" series) ▲ CDM 63179 [ADD] ■ EG 63179
Choral Evensong Live From King's College Cambridge *(rec live 7/91)*
EMI Classics ▲ CDC 54412-2 [DDD]
Choral Favorites Classics for Pleasure ▲ CDCFP 4632 [ADD]
Christmas Music from King's EMI Classics ("Studio" series) ▲ CDM 64130
Deck the Halls:Music for Christmas EMI Classics ("Studio" series) ▲ CDM 64133
Fauré, G.:Messe basse (in 3 movts), w. Arleen Augér (sop), John Butt (org)
Classics for Pleasure ("Eminence" series) ▲ CDEMX 2166 [DDD]
Fauré, G.:Requiem, w. Arleen Augér (sop), Benjamin Luxon (bar), John Butt (org), English CO
Classics for Pleasure ("Eminence" series) ▲ CDEMX 2166 [DDD]
A Festival of Lessons & Carols from King's, w. Thomas Trotter (org)
EMI Classics ("Studio" series) ▲ CDM 63180 [ADD] ■ EG 63180
Haydn, J.:Mass 11, "Nelsonmesse", "Imperial Mass", "Coronation Mass", w. Elizabeth Vaughan (sop), Janet Baker (mez), N. Marriner (cnd), Academy of St. Martin in the Fields
London ("Jubilee" series) ▲ 421146-2 [ADD]
Holst, G.:The Planets, w. J. Judd (cnd), Royal PO *(rec Dec. 1–2, 1991)* Denon ▲ CO 75076 [DDD]
Kings College Choir Cambridge EMI Classics ▲ CDC 47065 [DDD]
Procession with Carols on Advent Sunday EMI Classics ("Studio" series) ▲ CDM 63181 [ADD]

King's College Choir Cambridge (cont.)
Vivaldi, A.:Gloria, RV.589, w. E. Vaughan (sop), J. Baker (mez), N. Marriner (cnd), Academy of St. Martin in the Fields London ("Jubilee" series) ▲ 421146-2 [ADD]
M. Berry (cnd)
Gregorian Chant:The Ceremony of the Shepherds & Midnight Mass, w. Cambridge Schola Gregoriana *(rec Private Chapel, Arundel Castle, Jan 1995)* Herald ▲ HAVPCD 180 [DDD]
S. Cleobury (cnd)
Bernstein, L.:Chichester Psalms EMI Classics ▲ CDC 54188
Britten, B.:A Ceremony of Carols Argo ▲ 433215-2 [DDD]
Copland, A.:In the Beginning EMI Classics ▲ CDC 54188
English Anthems EMI Classics ▲ CDC 54418
Fauré, G.:Requiem, w. A. Murray (mez), O. Bär (bar) English CO EMI Classics ▲ CDC 49880
Górecki, H.-M.:Amen EMI Classics ▲ CDC 55096
Górecki, H.-M.:Totus tuus EMI Classics ▲ CDC 55096
Handel, G.F.:Messiah, w. Lynne Dawson (sop), Hilary Summers (cta), John Mark Ainsley (ten), Alastair Miles (bass), R. Goodman (cnd), Brandenburg Consort [1752 version] Argo 2-▲ 440672-2 [DDD]
Howells, H.:Collegium regale Argo ▲ 430205-2 [DDD]
Ives, C.:Psalm 90 EMI Classics ▲ CDC 54188
Larsen, L.:How It Thrills Us EMI Classics ▲ CDC 54188
Mozart, W.A.:Ave verum corpus, w. Cambridge Classical Players, Hilliard Ensemble [L]
EMI Classics ▲ CDC 49672 [DDD]
Mozart, W.A.:Missa, K.317, w. L. Marshall (sop), A. Murray (mez), R. Covey-Crump (ten), D. Wilson-Johnson (bar), English CO [L] Argo ▲ 411904-2 [DDD]
Mozart, W.A.:Vesperae de Dominica, w. L. Dawson (sop), E. James (mez), R. Covey-Crump (ten), P. Hillier (bass), Cambridge Classical Players, Hilliard Ensemble [L] EMI Classics ▲ CDC 49672 [DDD]
Mozart, W.A.:Vesperae solennes, w. L. Dawson (sop), E. James (mez), R. Covey-Crump (ten), P. Hillier (bass), Cambridge Classical Players, Hilliard Ensemble [L] EMI Classics ▲ CDC 49672 [DDD]
Pärt, A.:The Beatitudes EMI Classics ▲ CDC 55096
Pärt, A.:Magnificat EMI Classics ▲ CDC 55096
Schuman, W.:Carols of Death EMI Classics ▲ CDC 54188
Tallis, T.:The Lamentations of Jeremiah Argo ▲ 425199-2 [DDD]
Tavener, J.:Funeral Ikos EMI Classics ▲ CDC 55096
Tavener, J.:Magnificat & Nunc dimittis EMI Classics ▲ CDC 55096
Guest, Cleobury (cnd)
Vivaldi, A.:Beatus vir, RV. 597, w. St. John's College Choir Cambridge
London ("Double Decker" series) 2-▲ 443455-2
Vivaldi, A.:Dixit Dominus, w. St. John's College Choir Cambridge
London ("Double Decker" series) 2-▲ 443455-2
Vivaldi, A.:Gloria, RV.589, w. St. John's College Choir Cambridge
London ("Double Decker" series) 2-▲ 443455-2
Vivaldi, A.:Gloria (& Intro), RV.588, w. St. John's College Choir Cambridge
London ("Double Decker" series) 2-▲ 443455-2
Vivaldi, A.:Magnificat, RV.611, w. St. John's College Choir Cambridge
London ("Double Decker" series) 2-▲ 443455-2
P. Ledger (cnd)
Bach, C.P.E.:Magnificat, w. F. Palmer (sop), H. Watts (cta), R. Tear (ten), S. Roberts (b-bar), Academy of St. Martin in the Fields London ("Jubilee" series) ▲ 421148-2 [ADD]
Bach, J.S.:Christmas Oratorio, w. Elly Ameling (sop), Janet Baker (mez), Robert Tear (ten), Dietrich Fischer-Dieskau (bar), Academy of St. Martin in the Fields *(rec 1976)*
EMI Classics ("Doublefforte" series) 2-▲ CDFB 69503
Bach, J.S.:Magnificat, BWV 243, w. F. Palmer (sop), H. Watts (cta), R. Tear (ten), S. Roberts (b-bar), Academy of St. Martin in the Fields London ("Jubilee" series) ▲ 421148-2 [ADD]
Britten, B.:A Ceremony of Carols [L] EMI Classics ▲ CDC 47709 [ADD]
Britten, B.:Hymn to St. Cecilia [L] EMI Classics ▲ CDC 47709 [ADD]
Britten, B.:Jubilate Deo [L] EMI Classics ▲ CDC 47709 [ADD]
Britten, B.:Missa brevis [L] EMI Classics ▲ CDC 47709 [ADD]
Britten, B.:Rejoice in the Lamb [E] EMI Classics ▲ CDC 47709 [ADD]
Britten, B.:Te Deum [L] EMI Classics ▲ CDC 47709 [ADD]
Charpentier, M.-A.:Te Deum in C, w. F. Lott (sop), I. Partridge (ten), S. Roberts (bar), P. Ledger (org), Academy of St. Martin in the Fields EMI Classics ▲ CDM 63135
Choral Evensong for Ascension Day, w. Thomas Trotter (org) EMI Classics ▲ CDM 65102
Handel, G.F.:Ode for St. Cecilia's Day, w. Jill Gomez (sop), Robert Tear (ten), English CO
ASV ▲ ASV CD 512
Handel, G.F.:Ode for St. Cecilia's Day, w. Jill Gomez (sop), Robert Tear (ten), English CO [E]
ASV ▲ ASV 512 [DDD]
Monteverdi, C.:Vespro della Beata Vergine, w. Elly Ameling (sop), Norma Burrowes (sop), Charles Brett (ct), Martyn Hill (ten), Anthony Rolfe-Johnson (ten), Robert Tear (ten), Peter Knapp (bass), John Noble (bass), Francis Grier (org/hpd), James Lancelot (org/hpd), Andrew Leach (org/hpd), London Early Music Consort—Nigra sum [con.]; Laudate pueri [psalm]; Sancta Maria [son. sopra]; Magnificat *(rec Chapel of King's College, Cambridge, July & Aug. 1975)* EMI Classics ▲ CDK 65339 [ADD]
Music for Holy Week, w. Thomas Trotter (org) EMI Classics ▲ CDM 65103
Palestrina, G.:Sacred Music—Missa, "Hodie Christus natus est"; Motets
EMI Classics ("Classics for Pleasure" series) ▲ CDM 64045
D. Trendell (cnd)
Gouzes, A.:The Rangueil Mass GIA ▲ CD 371
Gouzes, A.:A Sunday Vigil GIA ▲ CD 371
D. Willcocks (cnd)
Allegri, G.:Miserere London ("Jubilee" series) ▲ 421147-2 [ADD]
Bach, J.S.:Cant 147, w. Academy of St. Martin in the Fields *(rec King's College Chapel, Cambridge, June, 1970)* EMI Classics ▲ CDK 65334 [ADD]
Charpentier, M.-A.:Messe de minuit pour Noël, w. I. Partridge (ten), English CO
EMI Classics ▲ CDM 63135
Fauré, G.:Pavane Orch, w. R. Chilcott (trb), J.C. Case (bar), New Philharmonia Orch [choral ver.]
EMI ▲ CDM 64715
Fauré, G.:Requiem, w. R. Chilcott (trb), J.C. Case (bar), New Philharmonia Orch
EMI Classics ▲ CDM 64715
Gabrieli, G.:Choral Music, w. Wilbraham Brass Soloists, Bach Choir
EMI Classics ("Doublefforte" series) 2-▲ CDFB 68631
Handel, G.F.:Chandos Anthems (11), w. April Cantelo (sop), Ian Partridge (ten), Andrew Davis (org), Academy of St. Martin in the Fields—No. 10 only *(rec Chapel of King's College, Cambridge, 1967)*
London 2-▲ 443470-2 [ADD]
Handel, G.F.:Dixit Dominus (sels), w. Teresa Zylis-Gara (sop), Janet Baker (mez), Robert Tear (ten)—Dixit Dominus [chorus w. solos]; Gloria [chorus] *(rec King's College Chapel, Cambridge, Aug. 1965)* EMI Classics ▲ CDK 65336 [ADD]
Noël *(rec 1958–64)* London ("Double Decker" series) 2-▲ 444848-2 [ADD]
Palestrina, G.:Stabat mater London ("Jubilee" series) ▲ 421147-2 [ADD]
Pergolesi, G.B.:Magnificat in C, w. Elizabeth Vaughan (sop), Janet Baker (cta), Ian Partridge (ten), Christopher Keyte (bass), Academy of St. Martin in the Fields *(rec 1966)*
London 2-▲ 443868-2 [ADD]
Scheidt, S.:Choral Music, w. Wilbraham Brass Soloists, Bach Choir
EMI Classics ("Doublefforte" series) 2-▲ CDFB 68631
Schütz, H.:Choral Music, w. Wilbraham Brass Soloists, Bach Choir
EMI Classics ("Doublefforte" series) 2-▲ CDFB 68631
Schütz, H.:Lobet den Herrn in seinem Heiligtum, w. Wilbraham Brass Soloists, Cambridge Univ Musical Society Chorus EMI Classics ("Baroque" series) ▲ CDK 65736
King's Consort Choir
R. King (cnd)
Blow, J.:Ah, Heaven! What Is't I Hear?, w. J. Bowman (ct), M. Chance (ct) [E]
Hyperion ▲ CDA 66253 [DDD]

King's Consort Choir (cont.)
R. King (cnd) (cont.)
Blow, J.:Ode on the Death of Mr. Henry Purcell, w. J. Bowman (ct), M. Chance (ct) [E] Hyperion ▲ CDA 66253 [DDD]
Handel, G.F.:Coronation Anthems (4) for George II, w. King's Consort—Zadok the Priest *(rec St Jude-on-the-Hill, London, Dec 20-21, 1968)* United ▲ CAL 88002 [DDD]
Handel, G.F.:Joseph & His Brethren, w. Yvonne Kenney (sop), Catherine Denley (mez), Connor Burrowes (trb), James Bowman (ct), John Mark Ainsley (ten), Michael George (bass), King's Consort, New College Choir Oxford Hyperion 3-▲ CDA 67171/3
Purcell, H.:Anthems & Services, w. Tom Seligman (trb), James Bowman (ct), Ashley Stafford (ct), John Mark Ainsley (ten), Andrew Gant (ten), Michael George (bass), Charles Pott (bass), King's Consort—O Sing unto the Lord; My beloved spake *(rec St Jude-on-the-Hill, London, Dec 20-21, 1968)* United ▲ CAL 88002 [DDD]
Purcell, H.:Anthems & Services, w. King's Consort—I will sing thanks unto the Lord as long as I live, Z.22; Kyrie in B♭; Nicene Creed in B♭; Benedictus in B♭; I will give thanks unto the Lord, Z.23; Out of the deep have I called, Z.45 Hyperion ▲ CDA 66707
Telemann, G.P.:Cants, w. J. Bowman (ct)—Easter cantata, "Weg mit Sodoms gift'gen Früchten" [G] Meridian ▲ CDE 84138
Vivaldi, A.:Laudate pueri Dominum, RV.601, w. L. Dawson (sop) [L] *(rec 4/86)* Meridian ▲ CDE 84129
Vivaldi, A.:Sacred Choral Music, w. Catherine Denley (sop), Deborah York (sop), James Bowman (ct) Hyperion ▲ CDA 66779
Vivaldi, A.:Sacred Choral Music, w. Susan Gritton (sop), Catherine Denley (mez), Lynton Atkinson (trb), David Wilson-Johnson (bar), Lisa Milne (sgr)—Magnificat; Lauda, Jerusalem; Kyrie eleison; Credo in unum Deum; Dixit Dominus Hyperion ▲ CDA 66769

King's Musick
Handel, G.F.:Salve Regina, w. Alfred Deller (ct) [L] Musique d'Abord ▲ HMA 1901054
Purcell, H.:The Indian Queen, w. A. Deller (cnd), Deller Consort Harmonia Mundi ("Suite" series) ▲ HMT 790243
A. Deller (cnd)
Purcell, H.:King Arthur, w. R. Hardy (sop), H. Sheppard (sop), J. Knibbs (cta), A. Deller (ct), M. Deller (alt), P. Elliott (ten), L. Nixon (ten), M. Bevan (bar), N. Beavan (bass), Deller Consort [E] Harmonia Mundi France 2-▲ HMC 90252/53

King's School Chapel Choir
Wild Classics:A Celebration of Animals & Nature, w. James Galway (fl), Ofra Harnoy (vc), Martin Hoherman (vc), Emily Mitchell (hp), Michael Dussek (pno), Samuel Lipman (pno), Leo Litwin (pno), Gerhard Oppitz (pno), Isao Tomita (synths), Boston Pops Orch [cnd:Arthur Fiedler], Chicago SO [cnd:Fritz Reiner] RCA Red Seal ▲ 09026-68483-2 ∎ 09026-68483-4

King's Singers
America, w. English CO [cnd:C. Davis] EMI Classics ▲ CDC 49701
DDD Christmas, w. Kathleen Battle (sop), Florence Quivar (mez), Taverner Consort, Taverner Choir, Taverner Players, New York Choral Artists, Toronto Mendelssohn Choir, Empire Brass Angel ▲ CDM 63666
La Dolce Vita, w. Tragicomedia EMI Classics ▲ CDC 54191
Get Happy!, w. George Shearing (pno), Neil Swainson (db) EMI Classics ▲ CDC 54190 [DDD] ∎ 4DS 54190 (D)
Górecki, H.-M.:Totus tuus *(rec Salisbury Cathedral, England, Feb 21-23, 1995)* RCA Red Seal ▲ 09026-68255-2 [DDD]
Josquin Desprez:Motets—Benedicta es, celorum regina; O virgo virginum; O virgo prudentissima; Pater noster, qui es in celis; Absolve quaesumus Dominum RCA Red Seal ▲ 09026-61814-2; ∎ 09026-61814-2
Josquin Desprez:Secular Songs—Vous l'arez, s'il vous plaist; Vous ne l'arez pas; A la mort/Monstra; Nymphes, nappés; En l'ombre d'un buissonet; Regretz san fin; Allégez moy; Pour souhaitter; Mille regretz; Se congié prensCe povre mendiant/Pauper sum ego; Petite camusette; Nymphes de bois; En [A] l'ombre d'un buissonet au matinet; Baisez moy, ma doulce amye RCA Red Seal ▲ 09026-61814-2; ∎ 09026-61814-2
The King's Singers, w. Gordon Langford Trio Chandos ("Collect" series) ▲ CHAN 6562 [ADD]
The King's Singers Believe in Music EMI Classics ▲ CDC 49117
King's Singers' 20th Anniversary Celebration Sampler EMI Classics ▲ CDM 69375
Ligeti, G.:The Ligeti Edition, w. Phyllis Bryn-Julson (sop), Rosemary Hardy (sop), Christiane Oelze (sop), Rose Taylor (mez), Sibylle Ehlert (sgr), Omar Ebrahim (bar), Pierre-Laurent Aimard (pno), E.-P. Salonen (cnd), Philharmonia Orch—Vocal Works; Madrigals; Mysteries; Adventures; Songs; Nonsense Madrigals Sony Classical ▲ SK 62311
A Little Christmas Music, w. Kiri Te Kanawa (sop), City of London Brass Quintet, City of London Sinfonia [cnd:R. Hickox] EMI Classics ▲ CDC 49909
Madrigal History EMI Classics ▲ CDM 69837
Miller, G.:Music of, w. John Pizzarelli (gtr), K. Lockhart (cnd), Boston Pops Orch—Runnin' Wild; A String of Pearls; Moonlight Serenade; Chattanooga Choo-Choo; The Nearness of You; My Blue Heaven; Song of the Volga Boatmen; Sunrise Serenade; Kalamazoo; Serenade in Blue; The Anvil Chorus; St. Louis Blues March; A Nightingale Sang in Berkeley Square; American Patrol; Little Brown Jug; In the Mood *(rec Symphony Hall, Boston, May 30-June 1, 1996)* RCA Victor ▲ 09026-68598-2 [DDD] ∎ 09026-68598-4
My Spirit Sang All Day EMI Classics ▲ CDC 49765
New Day EMI Classics ▲ CDC 49564
Noël, w. Canadian Brass, Canadian Brass Jazz All-Stars, Angel Romero (gtr), *(children's choir unknown)*, Richard Stoltzman (cl), Harolyn Blackwell (sop), Jerry Hadley (ten), James Galway (fl) *(rec Apr. 17-20, 1994)* RCA Victor ▲ 09026-62683-2 ∎ 09026-62683-4
Poole, G.:Wymondham Chants *(rec Salisbury Cathedral, England, Feb 21-23, 1995)* RCA Red Seal ▲ 09026-68255-2 [DDD]
Spirits, w. Stoltzman, Richard (cl), Eddie Gomez (db), David Torn (gtr), Dave Samuels (vib), Bill Douglas (bn) RCA Victor ▲ 09026-68416-2 ∎ 09026-68416-4
Stravinsky, I.:Blessed Virgin *(rec Salisbury Cathedral, England, Feb 21-23, 1995)* RCA Red Seal ▲ 09026-68255-2 [DDD]
Stravinsky, I.:Our Father *(rec Salisbury Cathedral, England, Feb 21-23, 1995)* RCA Red Seal ▲ 09026-68255-2 [DDD]
Sullivan, A.:Music of—sels. from The Mikado, Pirates of Penzance & HMS Pinafore:A British Tar; The Sun Whose Rays; Take a Pair of Sparkling Eyes; The Ghost's High-Noon; Ah, Leave Me Not; A Wand'ring Minstrel I; The Pirate King; Tit Willow; With Cat-Like Tread; Brightly Dawns Our Wedding Day; A More Humane Mikado; Rising Early in the Morning; Gilbert & Sullivan Medley; Patter Matter; Here's a Howdy Do RCA Victor ▲ 09026-61885-2; ∎ 09026-61885-4
This Is - The King's Singers EMI Classics ▲ CDC 49118
A Tribute to the Comedian Harmonists EMI Classics ▲ CDC 47677
Watching the White Wheat EMI Classics ▲ CDC 47506 [ADD]

King's Singers [David Hurley (ct), Nigel Short (ct), Bob Chilcott (ten), Bruce Russell (bar), Philip Lawson (bar), Stephen Connolly (bass)]
Bennett, Richard Rodney:Sermons & Devotions *(rec Salisbury Cathedral, England, Feb 21-23, 1995)* RCA Red Seal ▲ 09026-68255-2 [DDD]
Tavener, J.:Music of—Funeral Ikos; Lamb *(rec Salisbury Cathedral, England, Feb 21-23, 1995)* RCA Red Seal ▲ 09026-68255-2 [DDD]
Tormis, V.:The Bishop & the Pagan *(rec Salisbury Cathedral, England, Feb 21-23, 1995)* RCA Red Seal ▲ 09026-68255-2 [DDD]

Kirov Opera Chorus
Borodin, A.:Prince Igor, w. V. Gergiev (cnd), Kirov Opera Orch *(rec Mariinsky Theatre, St. Petersburg)* Philips 3-▲ 442537-2
Glinka, M.:Russlan & Ludmilla, w. Galina Gorchakova (sop), Larissa Diadkova (cta), Irinia Bogachova (sgr), Anna Netrebko (sgr), Yuri Masurin (ten), Konstantin Pluzhnikov (ten), Mikhail Kit (bar), Gennady Bezzubenkov (bass), Vladimir Ognovenko (bass), V. Gergiev (cnd), Kirov Opera Orch Philips ▲ 456 248-2
Mussorgsky, M.:Khovanshchina, w. Mark Reizen (bass), *(other soloists unknown)*, B. Khaikin (cnd), Kirov Opera Orch *(rec 1947)* Arlecchino 3-▲ ARL103/05

Kirov Opera Chorus (cont.)
Mussorgsky, M.:Khovanshchina, w. O. Borodina (mez), V. Galusin (ten), B. Minjelkiev (bass), Ohotnikav (sgr), V. Gergiev (cnd), Kirov Opera Orch [R] Philips 3-▲ 432147-2 [DDD]
Prokofiev, S.:War & Peace, w. Y. Prokina (sop), O. Borodina (mez), G. Gregoriam (ten), A. Gergalov (bar), V. Gergiev (cnd), Kirov Orch [R] Philips 3-▲ 434097-2
Rimsky-Korsakov, N.:Sadko, w. V. Gergiev (cnd), Kirov Orch Philips 3-▲ 442138-2
Tchaikovsky, P.:Arias, w. Galina Gorchakova (sop), V. Gergiev (cnd), Kirov Orch—Letter Scene [from Eugene Onegin]; Zachem eti sl'ozy [Pique Dame]; Gde zhe ty, moj zjelannyj? [from Sorceress]; Pachudilis' mne butta galasa [from Oprichnik] Philips ▲ 446405-2
Tchaikovsky, P.:Iolanta, w. Galina Gorchakova (sop), Nikolai Gassiev (ten), Gegam Grigorian (ten), Dmitri Hvorostovsky (bar), Nikolai Putilin (bar), Sergei Alexashkin (bass), Gennady Bezzubenkov (bass), Larissa Diadkova (sgr), Olga Korzhenskaya (sgr), Tatyana Kravtsova (sgr), V. Gergiev (cnd), Kirov Opera Orch *(rec Mariinsky Theatre, St. Petersburg)* Philips 2-▲ 442796-2
Tchaikovsky, P.:Queen of Spades, w. M. Gulegina (sop), O. Borodina (mez), G. Grigorian (ten), V. Gergiev (cnd), Kirov Opera Orch Philips ▲ 438141-2
Verdi, G.:Arias, w. Galina Gorchakova (sop), V. Gergiev (cnd), Kirov Orch—Madre, pietosa Vergine; Pace, pace mio dio [both from La Forze del destino]; Qui Radamès verrà—Oh patria mia [from Aida]; Tacea la notte placida—Di tale amor [from Il Trovatore]; Mia madre aveva; Piangea cantando; Ave Maria (Willow Song) [all from Otello] Philips ▲ 446405-2

Bruno Kittel Choir
Beethoven, L. van:Sym 9, "Choral Sym", w. Erna Berger (sop), Gertrude Pitzinger (cta), Walther Ludwig (ten), Rudolf Watzke (bass), W. Furtwängler (cnd), Berlin PO *(rec Queens Hall, London, May 1, 1937)* Music & Arts ▲ CD 818 [ADD]
Beethoven, L. van:Sym 9, "Choral Sym", w. Tilla Briem (sop), Elisabeth Höngen (cta), Peter Anders (ten), Rudolf Watzke (bass), W. Furtwängler (cnd), Berlin PO *(rec 1942)* Grammofono 2000 ▲ GRM 78581
Beethoven, L. van:Sym 9, "Choral Sym", w. O. Fried (cnd), Berlin State Opera Orch [G] *(rec 1928 for Polydor)* Pearl ▲ PEA 9372 (m) [AAD]
Beethoven, L. van:Sym 9, "Choral Sym", w. Tilla Briem (sop), Elisabeth Höngen (cta), Peter Anders (ten), Rudolf Watzke (bass), W. Furtwängler (cnd), Berlin PO *(rec Mar 22, 1942)* Iron Needle 3-▲ IN 1348/50 [ADD]
Beethoven, L. van:Sym 9, "Choral Sym", w. W. Furtwängler (cnd), Berlin PO [G] *(rec live, Berlin 3/24/42)* Arkadia ▲ 357 (m) [ADD]

Kodály Female Choir
Brahms, J.:Choral Music White Label ▲ HRC 057

Komi Republic Russian Chamber Choir
V. Kontarev (cnd)
Nikolsky, A.:Choral Music—Peaceful Light (from the Vespers); Spring, the King of the World, Op. 25/1; In the Sky the Stars, Op. 25/2; The Last Judgment, Op. 25/1; Heroic Song on Ilya Muromets, Op. 27/2; A Grey Dove Flew, Op. 27/4; May God Bless Us, Op. 28/2; Why Has Winter Come to Us?, Op. 28/3; Snowflakes, Op. 28/4; On the Mountain, Op. 29/1; Duckling of the Meadows, Op. 29/2; The Bells Pealed in Novgorod, Op. 29/3; Pribaoutki, Op. 29/4; The Pine Tree, Op. 39/1; Submarine Plants, Op. 39/2; The Seagull, Op. 39/3; The Wounded Eagle, Op. 39/4; The Ssong about the Merchant Kalashnikov, Op. 44/2; Nunc dimittis (from the Vespers) Russian Season ▲ RUS 288116

Koorproject Amerstterdam
M. Michielsen (cnd)
Andriessen, H.:Missa in festo assumptionis, w. A. de Klerk (org) Erasmus ▲ WVH 076 [DDD]
Andriessen, H.:Omaggio a Marenzio, w. A. de Klerk (org) Erasmus ▲ WVH 076 [DDD]
Andriessen, H.:Sonnet de Pierre de Ronsard, w. A. de Klerk (org) Erasmus ▲ WVH 076 [DDD]
Andriessen, H.:Sponsa Christi, w. A. de Klerk (org) Erasmus ▲ WVH 076 [DDD]

Koorproject Rotterdam
Clemens Non Papa, J.:Sacred Music—Sancta Maria à 5 Erasmus ▲ WVH 013 [DDD]
Marenzio, L.:Sacred Music—Laudate Dominum à 8 Erasmus ▲ WVH 013 [DDD]
Opitiis, B. de:Sacred Music—O magnum mysterium Erasmus ▲ WVH 013 [DDD]
Palestrina, G.:Sacred Music—Stabat Materà 8; Kyrie; Gloria; Credo; Sanctus; Benedictus; Agnus Dei Erasmus ▲ WVH 013 [DDD]
Victoria, T.L. de:Sacred Choral Music—Salve Regina Erasmus ▲ WVH 013 [DDD]

Korets Holy Trinity Stauropegion Convent Nuns-precentors Choir
My Soul Doth Magnify the Lord *(rec Korets Convent)* Russian Compact Disc ▲ RCD 15003 [AAD]

Korez Convent Choir
Russian Choirs Sing for the Children of Chernobyl, w. Moscow Patriarchate Children's Choir, Church of the Resurrection Choir Moscow, Pyuchtize Convent Choir, Zagorsk Monks' Choir, Moscow Religious Academy Choir, Moscow Religious Academy Choir, Dormition of the Virgin Church Choir Koch Schwann ▲ SCH 313322 [ADD/DDD]

Kuanas State Choir Lithuania
Beethoven, L. van:Syms (comp), w. Jean Glennon (sop), Dalia Schaechter (cta), Algridas Janutas (ten), Benno Schollum (bass), Y. Menuhin (cnd), Sinfonia Varsovia IMP ("IMG" series) 5-▲ IMP 6800025

Paul Kuentz Choir
Bach, J.S.:Magnificat, BWV 243, w. Hélène Obadia (sop), Brigitte Vinson (sop), Madeleine Jalabert (alt), Hervé Lamy (ten), Philip Langshaw (bass), P. Kuentz (cnd), Paul Kuentz Orch Pierre Verany ▲ PVY 730048
Bach, J.S.:Mass in b, BWV 232, w. Hélène Obadia (sop), Madeleine Jalbert (alt), Adrian Brand (ten), Paul Gay (bass), Eric Aubier (tpt), P. Kuentz (cnd), Paul Kuentz Orch Pierre Verany ▲ PVY 730060 [DDD]
Bach, J.S.:St. John Passion, w. Barbara Schlick (sop), Ingeborg Most (alt), Edrian Brand (ten), Alexander Stevenson (ten), Philip Langshaw (bass), Peter Lika (bass), P. Kuentz (cnd), Paul Kuentz Orch Pierre Verany 2-▲ PVY 730051 [DDD]
Charpentier, M.-A.:Te Deum in C, w. P. Kuentz (cnd), Paul Kuentz Orch Pierre Verany ▲ PVY 730048
Handel, G.F.:Messiah (sels), w. Barbara Schlick (sop), Jean Nirouet (ct), Alexander Stevenson (ten), Philip Langshaw (bass), P. Kuentz (cnd), Paul Kuentz Orch Pierre Verany ▲ PVY 730045
Mozart, W.A.:Missa, K.317, w. Mechtild Georg (sop), Barbara Schlick (sop), Alexander Stevenson (ten), Philip Langshaw (bass), P. Kuentz (cnd), Paul Kuentz Orch Pierre Verany ▲ PVY 730041
Orff, C.:Carmina burana, w. Elisabeth Vidal (sop), Alexander Stevensen (ten), André Cognet (bass), P. Kuentz (cnd), Paul Kuentz Orch, Mouez Armor Chorale, Lorient Conservatory Chorus, Notre Dame College Chorus Pierre Verany ▲ PVY 730044
Verdi, G.:Requiem Mass, w. Mariana Slavova (sop), Joke Kramer (mez), Alexander Stevenson (ten), Peter Lika (bass), P. Kuentz (cnd), Paul Kuentz Orch Pierre Verany 2-▲ PVY 730054 [DDD]
F. Bardot (cnd)
Mozart, W.A.:Zauberflöte, w. Birgit Been (sop), Nathalie Boissy (sop), Marianne Seibel (sop), Renate Springer (sop), Elizabeth Vidal (sop), Eleanor James (mez), Salvador Guzman (ten), Herbert Hechenberger (ten), Wolfgang Newmann (ten), Klaus Häger (bass), Philip Langshaw (bass), Hans-Georg Moser (bass), P. Kuentz (cnd), Paul Kuentz Orch, Maitrise des Hauts-de-Seine members Pierre Verany 2-▲ PVY 730055 [DDD]

Kühn Chamber Choir
Ryba, J.J.:Czech Christmas Mass, w. Richard Novak (ten), L. Pešek (cnd), Dvořák CO Supraphon ▲ SUP 111007 [AAD]

Kühn Chamber Soloists
de Monte, P.:Cara la vita mia, w. P. Kühn (cnd), Symposium Musicum *(rec Martínek Studio, Prague, Jan 17, 19 & 20, 1995)* Panton ▲ 811401-2
de Monte, P.:Missa de Requiem, w. P. Kühn (cnd), Symposium Musicum *(rec Martínek Studio, Prague, Jan 17, 19 & 20, 1995)* Panton ▲ 811401-2
de Monte, P.:Motets, w. P. Kühn (cnd), Symposium Musicum—Domine Deus salutis meae; Ecce ego mitto vos; Quasi cedrus; Non turbetur cor vestrum; Advenit ignis divinus; Sancte Johannes Baptista *(rec Martínek Studio, Prague, Jan 17, 19 & 20, 1995)* Panton ▲ 811401-2
P. Kühn (cnd)
Messiaen, O.:Rechants Supraphon ▲ 11 0404-2 [DDD]
Rossi, S.:The Songs of Solomon, w. Symposium Musicum *(rec Martínek-Studio, Prague, Mar 24-26 & May 3-5, 1994)* Panton 2-▲ PAN 811271 [DDD]

▲ = CD ♦ = Enhanced CD Δ = MD ∎ = Cassette Tape □ = DCC

Kühn Children's Chorus
Janácek, L.:The Cunning Little Vixen, w. G. Benačková (sop—Goldskin), M. Hajóssyová (sop—Cunning Little Vixen), R. Novák (bass—Forester), V. Neumann (cnd), Czech PO, Czech Phil Chorus [Cz] *(rec 1979–80)* Supraphon 2-▲ 10 3471–2 [AAD]
Martinů, B.:Bouquet, w. K. Ančerl (cnd), Czech PO, Czech Phil Chorus *(rec 1955–56)* Supraphon ▲ SUP 11 1932 [ADD]

Kühn Choir
Brixi, F.X.:Missa Interga, w. I. Verebics (sop), C. Borchers (cta), S. Weir (ten), Genhardt (bass), H. Rilling (cnd), Prague CO Supraphon ▲ 11 0092–2 [DDD]
Dvořák, A.:The Jacobin, w. D. Šounová–Broukov (sop), V. Přibyl (ten), K. Berman (bass), J. Pinkas (cnd), Brno State PO Supraphon 2-▲ SUP 11 2190 [AAD]
Dvořák, A.:Vanda (sels), w. Eva Randová (mez), Z. Košler (cnd), Czech PO—Homena, priests & priestesses of the God of Darkness [Act 3, Scene 3]; Bozena, pagan Grand Priest & the people [Act 4, Scene 1] *(rec Dvořák Hall of Rudolfinum Prague, Sept. 4–6, 1989)* Panton ▲ PAN 811241 [DDD]
Fibich, Z.:The Atonement of Tantalus, w. F. Jílek (cnd), Brno State PO Supraphon 6-▲ SUP CD 3037
Fibich, Z.:The Courtship of Pelops, w. J. Krombholc (cnd), Brno State PO Supraphon 6-▲ SUP CD 3037
Fibich, Z.:Hippodamia's Death, w. F. Jílek (cnd), Brno State PO Supraphon 6-▲ SUP CD 3037
Orff, C.:Carmina burana, w. Zdena Kloubová (sop), Vladimír Dolezal (ten), Ivan Kusnjer (bar), G. Delogu (cnd), Prague SO, Bambini di Praga *(rec live, Prague, Dec 12, 1995)* Supraphon ▲ SUP 3160
Ravel, M.:Daphnis et Chloé (suite 2), w. L. Pešek (cnd), Czech PO Supraphon ▲ 10 3633–2 [DDD]
Reicha, A.:Te Deum, w. Marta Boháčová (sop), Oldřich Lindauer (ten), Karel Průša (bass), Ladislav Vachulka (org), V. Smetáček (cnd), Prague SO *(rec Cathedral of the Ascension of the Virgin, Karlov, Prague, 1970)* Panton ▲ PAN 800242 [AAD]
Schnittke, A.:Requiem, w. Zdena Kloubová (sop), Olga Štepánová (alt), Vladimír Dolezal (ten), J. Belohlávek (cnd), Prague SO *(rec live, Smetana Hall, Municipal House, Prague, Dec 19, 1990)* Panton ("60 Years of the Prague SO" series) ▲ PAN 811374 [ADD]

P. Kühn (cnd)
Dvořák, A.:Moravian Duets, Opp. 20, 32 & 38, w. Stanislav Bogunia (pno) Supraphon ▲ 10 4093–2 [DDD]
Grieg, E.:Psalms, Op. 74, w. *(soloist unknown)* Praga ▲ PR 250 048
Krček, J.:Sym 2, w. Radovan Lukavsky (nar), J. Belohlávek (cnd), Czech PO Supraphon ▲ SUP CD 3195
Martinů, B.:Dandelion Romance, w. M. Čejková (sop) [Cz] Supraphon 2-▲ 11 0752–2 [DDD]
Martinů, B.:Legend of the Smoke from Potato Fires, w. *(soloists unknown)*, chamber ensemble Supraphon ▲ SUP 110767 [DDD]
Martinů, B.:Mikeš of the Mountains, w. chamber ensemble Supraphon ▲ SUP 110767 [DDD]
Martinů, B.:Mount of 3 Lights, w. V. Dolezal (ten), R. Novák (bass), P. Haničinec (nar), J. Hora (org), Prague Radio Men's Chorus [Cz] *(rec 2–3/88)* Supraphon ▲ 11 0751–2 [DDD]
Martinů, B.:The Opening of the Wells, w. chamber ensemble Supraphon ▲ SUP 110767 [DDD]
Martinů, B.:The Prophecy of Isaiah, w. N. Romanová (sop), D. Drobková (alto), R. Novák (bass), V. Kozderka (tpt), J. Peruška (va), I. Kiezlich (timp), S. Bogunia (pno), Prague Radio Men's Chorus [Cz] *(rec 2–3/88)* Supraphon ▲ 11 0751–2 [DDD]
Mysliveček, J.:Isacco figura, w. Ilona Czaková (sgr), Hye Jin Kim (sgr), Tatiana Korovina (sgr), Victoria Luchianez (sgr), Vladimír Dolezal (ten), Ivan Kusnjer (bar), I. Parík (cnd), Prague Sinfonietta Supraphon 2-▲ SUP 3209
Slavický, K.:Psalmi, w. Salome Losová (sop), Dagmar Pecková (cta), Vladimír Dolezal (ten), Ludek Vele (bass), Jan Hora (org), *(rec Dvořák Hall of Rudolfinum, Prague, Mar. 14–16, 1989)* Panton ("Protokol XX" series) ▲ PAN 811142 [DDD]
Tomášek, V.J.K.:Coronation Mass, w. Prague CO Supraphon ▲ SUP 112138 [DDD]
Vranicky, A.:Missa, w. Prague CO Supraphon ▲ SUP 112138 [DDD]

Kühn Women's Chorus
Messiaen, O.:Petites liturgies (3) de la Présence Divine, w. J. Loriod (ondes Martenot), Y. Loriod (pno), B. Kulínsky (cnd), Prague SO *(rec Dec. 5–6, 1987)* Supraphon ▲ 11 0404–2 [DDD]

P. KŪumlŪuhn (cnd)
Martinů, B.:Primrose, w. P. Messiereur (vn), S. Bogunia (pno) Supraphon 2-▲ 11 0752–2 [DDD]

Küsnacht Seminar Chamber Choir
K. Scheuber (cnd)
Widmer, E.:Ceremony after a Fire Raid *(rec Feb. 2, 1990)* Grammont ▲ CTSP 32–2 [ADD]

Jean LaForge Ensemble Choir
Auber, D.–F.:Fra Diavolo, w. M. Mesplé (sop—Zerline), J. Berbié (mez—Lady Pamela), N. Gedda (ten—Fra Diavolo), R. Corazza (ten—Lord Cockburn), T. Dran (ten—Lorenzo), J. Bastin (bass—Matheo), M. Soustrot (cnd), Monte Carlo PO EMI Classics ▲ CDCB 54810

La Laguna Univ Choir
Halffter, E.:Dominus pastor meus, w. Susan Chilcott (sop), Claire Powell (mez), Joan Cabero (ten), José Antonio Carril (bass), V. P. Pérez (cnd), Tenerife SO Discobi ▲ DIS 2009 [DDD]
Halffter, E.:Elegia en memoria de S.A.S. Príncipe Pierre de Polignac, w. V. P. Pérez (cnd), Tenerife SO Discobi ▲ DIS 2009 [DDD]

Lahti Chamber Choir
Sibelius, J.:Everyman, w. Lilli Paasikivi (mez), Petri Lehto (ten), Sauli Tiilikainen (bar), Leena Saarenpää (pno), Pauli Pietiläinen (org), O. Vänskä (cnd), Lahti SO *(rec Church of the Cross, Lahti, Finland, Jan 11–13, 1995)* BIS ▲ CD–735 [DDD]

Lahti Opera Chorus
Sibelius, J.:The Tempest, w. O. Vänskä (cnd), Lahti SO BIS ("BIS Twins" series) 2-▲ CD 500/581

Rudolf Lamy Singers
Fall, L.:Der fidele Bauer (sels), w. Sonja Knittel (sop), Brigette Fassbaender (mez), Heinz Hoppe (ten), Fritz Wunderlich (ten), Benno Kusche (bass), C. Michalski (cnd), Graunke SO Emperor Operetta ▲ KO 86353
Fall, L.:Der liebe Augustin (sels), w. Sari Barabas (sop), Christine Gorner (sop), Heinz Hoppe (ten), Benno Kusche (b–bar), C. Michalski (cnd), Graunke SO Emperor Operetta ▲ KO 86352
Lehár, F.:Zigeunerliebe (sels), w. Sari Barabas (sop), Christine Gorner (sop), Harry Friedauer (ten), Heinz Hoppe (ten), C. Michalski (cnd), Graunke SO Emperor Operetta ▲ KO 86342

Landsberg Vocal Ensemble
K. Zepnik (cnd)
Mahler, G.:Songs—Ich bin der Welt abhanden gekommen Ambitus ▲ 97839 [DDD]
Mendelssohn, F.:Psalms (misc)—Warum toben die Heiden, Op. 78/1; Richte mich, Gott, Op. 78/2; Denn er hat seinen Engeln befohlen; Jauchzet dem Herrn alle Welt, Op. 69/2 Ambitus ▲ 97839 [DDD]
Wolf, H.:Geistliche Lieder Ambitus ▲ 97839 [DDD]

Langholts Church Graduale Choir
Leifs, J.:Music of, w. Sigrídur Ella Magnúsdóttir (mez), Ólafur Vignir Albertsson (pno), Sólveig Anna Jónsdóttir (pno), Hjálmar Ragnarsson (pno), Edda Erlendsdóttir (pno), Marteinn Hunger Fridriksson (org), Hildigunnur Halldórsdóttir (vn), Gréta Gudnadóttir (vn), Gudmundur Kristmundsson (va), Sigurdur Halldórsson (vc), Richard Korn (db), Iceland SO, Icelandic Opera Chorus, Hamrahlid Choir—Icelandic Cant, Op. 13/4; Valse Lento, Op. 2/1; Icelandic Dance, Op. 11/2 [Tempo Giusto]; Requiem; Lullaby [After the Riots]; Fairy–Tale in the Wood [from Baldr, Op. 34]; Funeral March; Separation [from Elegy, Op. 53]; Galdra Loftur Ov, Op. 10; Funeral March, Op. 6; Reverie; Reunion [from Elegy, Op. 53]; Fine I, Op. 55; Andante [The Last Supper]; Preludia Organo, Op. 16/3 [In the Church]; The Tear of Stone [from Elegy, Op. 53] Music From Iceland ▲ ITM 605 [DDD]

Cortes, Stefánsson, Ingólfsdóttir (cnd)
Ragnarsson, H.:Music of, w. S. E. Magnúsdóttir (mez), H. Halldórsdóttir (vn), G. Gudnadóttir (vn), G. Kristmundsson (va), S. Halldórsson (vc), R. Korn (db), Ó. V. Albertsson (pno), S. A. Jónsdóttir (pno), H. Ragnarsson (pno), E. Erlendsdóttir (pno), M. H. Fridriksson (org), Sakari, Wilkinson (cnd), Iceland SO, Hamrahlíd Choir, Icelandic Opera Chorus—Meine kleine Freundin [In the Ballroom]; Lovers Duet; After the concert; Meine kleine Freundin [Annie listens to the Radio]; Lif's Theme [On the Beach]; Lif's Theme II [Night Prayer]; Composing Ov [Vars I, II & III] Music From Iceland ▲ ITM 605 [DDD]

Langholtskirkju Choir
J. Stefánsson (cnd)
An Anthology of Icelandic Choir Music BIS ▲ CD 239 [DDD]

Laredo Choral Salvé
J.L. Ocejo (cnd)
Ramirez, A.:Misa Criolla, w. J. Carreras (ten), A. Ramirez (kbd), Laredo Instrumental Ensemble, Bilbao Choral Society Philips ("Digital Classics" series) ▲ 420955–2 [DDD] □ 420955–5
Ramirez, A.:Navidad en Verano, w. J. Carreras (ten), A. Ramirez (kbd), Laredo Instrumental Ensemble, Bilbao Choral Society Philips ("Digital Classics" series) ▲ 420955–2 [DDD] □ 420955–5
Ramirez, A.:Navidad nuestra, w. J. Carreras (ten), A. Ramirez (kbd), Laredo Instrumental Ensemble, Bilbao Choral Society Philips ("Digital Classics" series) ▲ 420955–2 [DDD] □ 420955–5

Orlando di Lasso Ensemble Hanover
Lassus, O. de:Choral Music—Audio dulcis mea à 4; Ave Maria à 5; Ave Maria, alta stirps à 4; Ave Regina coelorum à 5; Ave verus corpus à 6; Magnificat "Ecco ch'io lasso il core"; Missus est Angelus Gabriel à 3–6; O Maria, clausus hortus à 3; Regina coeli laetare à 5; Salve Regina à 4; Salve Regina à 5; Salve Regina à 6; Salve Regina à 8; Sancta Maria, omnes sancti Dei à 5; Tota pulchra es, amica mea à 4; Veni, dilecte mi à 5 *(rec 6/91)* Thorofon ▲ CTH 2130 [DDD]

Laudis Cantores
M. Scapin (cnd)
Mercadante, S.:Requiem brève Bongiovanni ▲ GB 2188
Mercadante, S.:Le Sette parole Bongiovanni ▲ GB 2188

Laulun Ystävät Male Choir
Sibelius, J.:Kullervo, w. K. Mattila (sop), J. Hynninen (bar), N. Järvi (cnd), Gothenburg SO [Fin] BIS ▲ CD 313
Sibelius, J.:Syms (comp), w. K. Mattila (sop), J. Hynninen (bar), N. Järvi (cnd), Gothenburg SO BIS 4-▲ CD 622/24 [ADD]

Lausanne Conservatory Chorus
Bach, J.S.:Cant 172, w. H. Klopfenstein (cnd), Lausanne Conservatory Orch [G] Gallo ▲ CD 630 [AAD]

Lausanne Ensemble of Female Voices
Granato, D.:Motets, w. Marie–Hélène Dupard (sop), Phillipe Despont (org)—Crux, moments de la Passion (1990); Homo Quidam (1960); Récitatifs pour la fin du jour (1978); Messe brève (1994); Improvisations rolloises (1958); Rosa vernans (1960); Mariale (1955); Ex Libro Job (1984); Solfeggio sopra'l Jubilate (1968); Petit Magnificat (1980) Gallo ▲ CD 895 [DDD]

Lausanne Euterpe Vocal Ensemble
C. Gesseney (cnd)
Janácek, L.:Choral Elegy Gallo ▲ CD 784 [DDD]
Janácek, L.:Choruses—Parting; The Dove Gallo ▲ CD 784 [DDD]
Janácek, L.:Mass in E♭, w. Y. Rechsteiner (org) Gallo ▲ CD 784 [DDD]
Janácek, L.:Our Father, w. M. Dvorsky (ten), G. Landini (pno) Gallo ▲ CD 784 [DDD]
Kodály, Z.:Geneva Psalms—Psalms 33, 50, 114, 121, 124, 126 & 150 Gallo ▲ CD 784 [DDD]
The Lausanne Vocal Ensemble Euterpe in Concert, w. Christine Sortoretti (hpd), Yves Rechsteiner (org), C. Delafontaine (pic), Marianne Amrein (fl douce/perc) Gallo ▲ CD 766 [DDD]

Lausanne Israeli Community Male Chorus
Concert de musique liturgique Juive à la synagogue de Lausanne, w. Alain Blum, Antoine D., André Stora, Gueorgui Popov, Jean Akiba, J. Rubin (ft), Oleg Kogan (hp), Christine Fleischmann (hp) Doron ▲ DRC 3003 [DDD]

Lausanne Pro Arte Choir
Bach, J.S.:Cant 67, w. H. Watts (cta), W. Krenn (ten), T. Krause, E. Ansermet (cnd), Swiss Romande Orch London ("Serenata" series) ▲ 433175–2 [ADD]
Bach, J.S.:Cant 130, w. E. Ameling (sop), H. Watts (cta), W. Krenn (ten), T. Krause (bass), E. Ansermet (cnd), Swiss Romande Orch London ("Serenata" series) ▲ 433175–2 [ADD]
Martin, F.:Pilate, w. Ariette Chedel (cta), Eugenia Zareska (mez), Eric Tappy (ten), Derrik Olsen (bar), Jean–Christoph Benoit (bar), E. Ansermet (cnd), Swiss Romande Orch Cascavelle 2-▲ CVL 2006 [ADD]
Stravinsky, I.:Canticum sacrum, w. Irene Friedli (alt), Frieder Lang (ten), N. Järvi (cnd), Swiss Romande Orch Chandos ▲ CHAN 9408 [DDD]
Stravinsky, I.:Chorale Variations on the German Christmas Carol "Vom Himmel hoch da komm' ich her", w. Irene Friedli (alt), Frieder Lang (ten), N. Järvi (cnd), Swiss Romande Orch Chandos ▲ CHAN 9408 [DDD]
Stravinsky, I.:Requiem Canticles, w. Irène Friedli (alt), Michel Brodard (bass), N. Järvi (cnd), Swiss Romande Orch, Romande Chamber Choir Chandos ▲ CHAN 9408 [DDD]
Stravinsky, I.:Sym of Psalms, w. N. Järvi (cnd), Swiss Romande Orch, Romande Chamber Choir Chandos ▲ CHAN 9239 [DDD]

Lausanne Vocal Ensemble
M. Corboz (cnd)
Bach, J.S.:St. John Passion, w. F. Palmer (sop), B. Finnilä (cta), K. Equiluz (ten), W. Krenn (ten), P. Huttenlocher (bar), R. van der Meer (bass), Lausanne CO Erato 2-▲ 2292–45406–2 FD
Bach, J.S.:St. Matthew Passion, w. M. Marshall (sop), C. Watkinson (cta), K. Equiluz (ten), G. Faulstisch (bar), P. Huttenlocher (bar), R. Johnson (bar), Lausanne CO Erato 3-▲ 2292–45375–2 GX
Fauré, G.:Cantique de Jean Racine, w. M. Dami (sop), P. Harvey (bar), Lausanne Instrumental Ensemble [F] *(rec Feb. 14–16, 1992)* FNAC Music ▲ 592097 [DDD]
Fauré, G.:Messe basse (in 3 movts), w. M. Dami (sop), Lausanne Instrumental Ensemble [L] *(rec Feb. 14–16, 1992)* FNAC Music ▲ 592097 [DDD]
Fauré, G.:Motets, w. M. Dami (sop), P. Harvey (bar), Lausanne Instrumental Ensemble—Maria Mater Gratiae, Op. 47; Ave verum, Op. 65/1; Tantum ergo, Op. 65/2; Tu es Petrus; Tantum ergo [L] *(rec Feb. 14–16, 1992)* FNAC Music ▲ 592097 [DDD]
Fauré, G.:Requiem, w. M. Dami (sop), P. Harvey (bar), Lausanne Instrumental Ensemble [L] *(rec Feb. 14–16, 1992)* FNAC Music ▲ 592097 [DDD]
Handel, G.F.:Messiah (reorchd Mozart), w. Audrey Michael (sop), Jard van Nes (cta), Hans–Peter Blochwitz (tenor), Marcus Fink (bass), Lausanne Instrumental Ensemble [G] Erato 2-▲ 2292–45497–2 [DDD]
Martin, F.:Mass Cascavelle ▲ CVL 1025 [DDD]
Mendelssohn, F.:Choral Music—Denn er hat seinen Engeln; Hör mein Bitten [Hymn]; Lass, o Herr, mich Hilfe finden; Deines Kind's Gebet erhöre; Herr, wir traun auf deine Güte *(rec Lausanne Cathedral, Jan. 29–31, 1994)* FNAC Music ▲ 592298 [DDD]
Mendelssohn, F.:Sacred Pieces, w. H–J. Rickenbacher (ten), J–Ch. Geiser (org) *(rec Lausanne Cathedral, Jan. 29–31, 1994)* FNAC Music ▲ 592298 [DDD]
Monteverdi, C.:Magnificat, w. Lausanne Instrumental Ensemble Erato 2-▲ ERA SEL 12981 [ADD/DDD]
Monteverdi, C.:Mass Erato 2-▲ ERA SEL 12981 [ADD/DDD]
Monteverdi, C.:Messe da capella Cascavelle ▲ CVL 1025 [DDD]
Monteverdi, C.:Vespro, w. Lausanne Instrumental Ensemble Erato 2-▲ ERA SEL 12981 [ADD/DDD]

Lausanne Youth Chorus
Falla, M. de:Atlántida, w. Montserrat Caballé (sop), Heinz Rehfuss (bar), E. Ansermet (cnd), Swiss Romande Orch, Swiss Romande Red Chorus, Villamont College Little Chorus Cascavelle ▲ CVL 2005 [ADD]

Louis Lavigueur Vocal Ensemble
Gratton, H.:Imagerie:Christmas Pastoral, w. M. Keable (actor), S. Léonard (actor), J.–L. Millette (actor), M. Laferrière (sop), C. Rioux (mez), B. Levasseur (bar), N. Richard (b–bar), L. Lavigueur (cnd), Louis Lavigueur Instrumental Ensemble [F] *(rec 5/91)* CBC ("SM 5000" series) ▲ SMCD 5109 [DDD]

Lebanon Univ of the Holy Ghost Musical Institute Chorus
Hage, Rouhana (cnd)
Chants of the Maronitic Liturgy Entrée ▲ 0078 [ADD]

Leeds Festival Chorus
Berlioz, H.:Grande Symphonie funèbre et triomphale, w. J. Wallace (cnd), Wallace Collection Nimbus ▲ NI 5175 [DDD]
Mahler, G.:Sym 8, w. L. Bernstein (cnd), London SO *(rec 1966)* Sony Classical ("Bernstein:The Royal Edition" series) 3-▲ SM3K 47581 [ADD]

CHORAL GROUPS

Leeds Festival Chorus (cont.)
Rule Britannia, w. Wallace, John (tpt), Edmund Barha (ten), Wallace Collection, English String Orch [cnd:William Boughton] Nimbus ▲ NI 5155 [DDD]

Leeds Parish Church Choir Boys' Voices
All of the World's Most Beautiful Melodies!, w. Phillip McCann (cnt), Gordon Langford (cnd), Roy Newsome (cnd), Peter Parkes (cnd), Black Dyke Mills Band, Sellers Engineering Band, Academy of St. Martin in the Fields Chamber Ensemble, Huddersfield Choral Society Chandos ("Brass" series) 5–▲ CHN 4536(5)
A Song of Yorkshire, w. Honley Male Voice Choir, S. Lindley (org), Sellers Engineering Band [cnd:P. McCann] Chandos Brass ▲ CHAN 4515 [DDD]

Leeds Phil Chorus
Mozart, W.A.:Missa, K.317, w. Janet Price (sop), Kevin Smith (ct), Anthony Rolfe-Johnson (ten), Graham Titus (bass), M. Davies (cnd), BBC Northern SO IMP ("BBC Radio Classics" series) ▲ IMP 5691552

Lege Artis Chamber Choir
B. Abalyan (cnd)
Arkhangelsky, A.:Psalm 40 Sony Classical ▲ SK 64586
Gretchaninoff, A.:To the Mother of God Sony Classical ▲ SK 64586
Ippolitov-Ivanov, M.:Liturgy of St John Chrysostom Sony Classical ▲ SMK 64091
Ippolitov-Ivanov, M.:Vespers Sony Classical ▲ SMK 64091
Penderecki, K.:Choral Music—Song of the Cherubim Sony Classical ▲ SK 64586
Rachmaninoff, S.:Liturgy of St John Chrysostom *(rec Melodia-Studio, St. Petersburg, Russia, Oct 1993)* Sony Classical ("St. Petersburg Classics" series) ▲ SMK 64092 [DDD]
Rachmaninoff, S.:O Mother of God *(rec Melodia-Studio, St. Petersburg, Russia, Oct 1993)* Sony Classical ("St. Petersburg Classics" series) ▲ SMK 64092 [DDD]
Russian Liturgical Chants Sony Classical ("St. Petersburg Classics" series) ▲ SK 57661 [DDD]
Smirnov, D.:Liturgy of St John Chrysostom—Prayers Sony Classical ▲ SK 64586
Stravinsky, I.:Choral Music—Ave Maria Sony Classical ▲ SK 64586
Tchesnokov, P.:In Days of Battle Sony Classical ▲ SK 64586

Leigh Morris Chorale
Still, W.G.:Music of, w. William Warfield (nar), Yolanda Williams (sop), Hilda Harris (alt), P. Brunelle (cnd), Plymouth Music Series Orch, Plymouth Music Series Chorus—Wailing Woman; Swanee River; And They Lynched Him on a Tree; Miss Sally's Party Collins Classics ▲ COL 1454

Leipzig Central German Radio Choir
Brahms, J.:Schicksalslied, w. C. Abbado (cnd), Berlin PO *(rec Philharmonie, Berlin, Feb. 26–28, 1993)* Sony Classical ▲ SK 53975 [DDD]

Leipzig Choirs
Bach, J.S.:Music of, w. L. Güttler (tpt), M. Lorenz (ten), A. Reiss (ten), P. Schreier (ten), H.-C. Polster (b-bar), M. Pommer (cnd), Leipzig New Bach Collegium Musicum—arias, choruses & chorales Capriccio ▲ CDC 10039 [DDD]

Leipzig Concerto Vocale
Bach, J.S.:Cant 49, w. Barbara Schlick (sop), Andreas Scholl (alt), Christophe Prégardien (ten), Gotthold Schwarz (bass), C. Coin (cnd), Limoges Baroque Ensemble Astrée ▲ E 8530
Bach, J.S.:Cant 115, w. Barbara Schlick (sop), Andreas Scholl (alt), Christophe Prégardien (ten), Gotthold Schwarz (bass), C. Coin (cnd), Limoges Baroque Ensemble Astrée ▲ E 8530
Bach, J.S.:Cant 180, w. Barbara Schlick (sop), Andreas Scholl (alt), Christophe Prégardien (ten), Gotthold Schwarz (bass), C. Coin (cnd), Limoges Baroque Ensemble Astrée ▲ E 8530

Leipzig Gewandhaus Chorus
Debussy, C.:Nocturnes, w. L. Stokowski (cnd), Leipzig Gewandhaus Orch *(rec June 1, 1959)* Music & Arts 2–▲ MUA 280 [AAD]
Mendelssohn, F.:Sym 2, w. B. Bonney (sop), E. Wiens (sop), P. Schreier (ten), K. Masur (cnd), Leipzig Gewandhaus Orch [G] Teldec ▲ 2292-44178-2 ZK [DDD]
Ravel, M.:Rapsodie espagnole, w. L. Stokowski (cnd), Leipzig Gewandhaus Orch *(rec June 1, 1959)* Music & Arts 2–▲ MUA 280 [AAD]

Leipzig Radio Chorus
Beethoven, L. van:Fant Pno, Op. 80, "Choral Fant", w. P. Rösel (pno), H. Kegel (cnd), Dresden PO [G] Capriccio ▲ 10150 [DDD]
Beethoven, L. van:Fant Pno, Op. 80, "Choral Fant", w. G. Kootz (pno), F. Konwitschny (cnd), Leipzig Gewandhaus Orch Berlin Classics ▲ BER 2077 [ADD]
Beethoven, L. van:Leonore (opera), w. Helen Donath (sop), Edda Moser (sop), Eberhard Büchner (ten), Richard Cassilly (ten), Theo Adam (b-bar), Hermann Christian Polster (bass), Karl Ridderbusch (bass), H. Blomstedt (cnd), Dresden Staatskapelle Berlin Classics ▲ BER 1140
Beethoven, L. van:Missa Solemnis, w. Anna Tomowa-Sintow (sop), Annelies Burmeister (alt), Peter Schreier (ten), Hermann Christian Polster (bass), Gerhard Bosse (vn), Hannes Kastner (org), K. Masur (cnd), Leipzig Gewandhaus Orch Berlin Classics ("Masur Edition" series) ▲ BER 9160
Beethoven, L. van:Missa Solemnis, w. C. Studer (sop), J. Norman (sop), P. Domingo (ten), K. Moll (bass), J. Levine (cnd), Vienna PO, Eric Ericson Chamber Chorus Deutsche Grammophon 2–▲ 435770-2 [DDD]
Beethoven, L. van:Syms (comp), w. Helena Doese (sop), Marga Schiml (alt), Peter Schreier (ten), Theo Adam (bass), H. Blomstedt (cnd), Dresden Staatskapelle, Dresden State Opera Chorus *(rec Lukaskirche, Dresden, 1975–80)* Berlin Classics 5–▲ 0021942BC [ADD]
Beethoven, L. van:Syms (comp), w. H. Kegel (cnd), Dresden PO, Berlin Radio Chorus Capriccio 7–▲ 10 455
Beethoven, L. van:Syms (comp), w. I. Wenglor (sop), U. Zollenkopf (cta), Hans Joachim Rotzsch (ten), T. Adam (bass-bar), F. Konwitschny (cnd), Leipzig Gewandhaus Orch *(rec 1959–1961)* Berlin Classics ("Eterna" series) 6–▲ BER 2005 [ADD]
Beethoven, L. van:Sym 9, "Choral Sym", w. Ingeborg Wenglor (sop), Ursula Zollenkopf (alt), Hans Jochim Rotzsch (ten), Theo Adam (bass), F. Konwitschny (cnd), Leipzig Gewandhaus Orch Polskie Nagrania Edition ▲ ECD 028
Beethoven, L. van:Sym 9, "Choral Sym", w. F. Konwitschny (cnd), Leipzig RSO Forlane 2–▲ FOR 16674 [ADD]
Blacher, B.:A Jewish Chronicle, w. Anna Barová (cta), Vladimir Bauer (sgr), H. Kegel (cnd), Leipzig RSO Berlin Classics ▲ BER 9016 [ADD]
Brahms, J.:Ein Deutsches Requiem, w. M. A. Häggander (sop), M. Lorenz (ten), H. Kegel (cnd), Leipzig RSO [G] Capriccio ▲ 10095 [DDD]
Dessau, P.:Die Verurteilung des Lukullus, w. Annelies Burmeister (mez—Das Fischweib), Helmut Melchert (ten—Lukullus), Hans-Joachim Rotzsch (ten—Der Kirschbaumträger), Peter Schreier (ten—Lukullus' Cook), Boris Carmeli (bass—King), H. Kegel (cnd), Leipzig RSO Berlin Classics 2–▲ BER 1073 [ADD]
Gluck, C.W.:Orfeo ed Euridice, w. Ruth-Margaret Pütz (sop), Anneliese Rothenberger (sop), Grace Bumbry (mez), V. Neumann (cnd), Leipzig Opera Orch *(rec Leipzig, 1967)* Berlin Classics 2–▲ BER 9033 [ADD]
Handel, G.F.:Imeneo, w. Sylvia Geszty (sop), Renate Krahmer (sop), Hans-Joachim Rotzsch (ten), Günther Leib (bass), Siegfried Vogel (bass), H.-T. Margraf (cnd), Halle Handel Festival Orch *(rec 1966)* Berlin Classics ▲ BER 9110
Ives, C.:Central Park in the Dark, w. W.-D. Hauschild (cnd), Leipzig RSO Berlin Classics ▲ BER 9008 [ADD]
Ives, C.:Holidays, w. W.-D. Hauschild (cnd), Leipzig RSO Berlin Classics ▲ BER 9008 [ADD]
Mendelssohn, F.:Elijah, w. E. Ameling (sop), A. Burmeister (mez), P. Schreier (ten), T. Adam (b-bar), W. Sawallisch (cnd), Leipzig Gewandhaus Orch Philips 2–▲ 438368-2
Mendelssohn, F.:Elijah, w. E. Ameling (sop), A. Burmeister (mez), P. Schreier (ten), T. Adam (b-bar), W. Sawallisch (cnd), Leipzig Gewandhaus Orch [G] Philips 2–▲ 420106-2 [AAD]
Mozart, W.A.:Apollo et Hyacinthus, w. V. Hruba-Frieberger (sop), A. Raunig (alt), R. Popken (alt), J. Dickie (ten), M. Pommer (cnd), Leipzig RSO Berlin Classics 2–▲ BER 1010 [DDD]
Mozart, W.A.:Bastien und Bastienne, w. D. Schellenberger (sop), R. Eschrig (ten), R. Pape (bass), M. Pommer (cnd), Leipzig RSO Berlin Classics 2–▲ BER 1010 [DDD]
Mozart, W.A.:Idomeneo, w. A. Rothenberger (sop), E. Moser (sop), N. Gedda (ten), A. Dallapozza (ten), P. Schreier (ten), T. Adam (b-bar), H. Schmidt-Isserstedt (cnd), Dresden Staatskapelle EMI Classics ("Studio" series) 3–▲ CDMC 63990

Leipzig Radio Chorus (cont.)
Mozart, W.A.:Missa, K.317, w. E. Mathis (sop), J. Rappé (ten), H. P. Blochwitz (ten), T. Quasthoff (bar), P. Schreier (cnd), Dresden Staatskapelle Philips ▲ 426275-2
Mozart, W.A.:Zauberflöte, w. M. Price (sop—Pamina), L. Serra (sop—Queen of the Night), M. Venuti (sop—Papagena), M. McLaughlin (sop—1st Lady), A. Murray (mez—2nd Lady), H. Schwarz (cta—3rd Lady), F. Höher (trb—1st Boy), M. Diedrich (trb—2nd Boy), F. Klos (trb—3rd Boy), P. Schreier (ten—Tamino), R. Tear (ten—Monostatos), R. Goldberg (ten—1st Armoured Man), K. Moll (bass—Sarastro), H. Rech (bass—2nd Armoured Man), C. Davis (cnd), Dresden Staatskapelle Philips ("Duo" series) 2–▲ 442568-2
Mussorgsky, M.:Boris Godunov (sels), w. Hanne-Lore Kuhse (sop), Peter Schreier (ten), Martin Ritzmann (ten), Theo Adam (b-bar), H. Kegel (cnd), Dresden State Orch Berlin Classics ▲ BER 2032 [ADD]
Orff, C.:Carmina burana, w. *(soloists unknown)*, H. Kegel (cnd), Leipzig RSO, Berlin Radio Chorus, Dresden Children's Choir Berlin Classics 2–▲ BER 2047 [ADD]
Orff, C.:Catulli Carmina, w. *(soloists unknown)*, H. Kegel (cnd), Leipzig RSO, Berlin Radio Chorus, Dresden Children's Choir Berlin Classics 2–▲ BER 2047 [ADD]
Orff, C.:Die Kluge, w. H. Kegel (cnd), Leipzig RSO Berlin Classics 2–▲ BER 2104-2 [ADD]
Orff, C.:Der Mond—Ein kleines Welttheater, w. H. Kegel (cnd), Leipzig RSO Berlin Classics 2–▲ BER 2104-2 [ADD]
Orff, C.:Trionfo di Afrodite, w. *(soloists unknown)*, H. Kegel (cnd), Leipzig RSO, Berlin Radio Chorus, Dresden Children's Choir Berlin Classics 2–▲ BER 2047 [ADD]
Schoenberg, A.:Moses und Aaron, w. Renate Krahmer (sop), Gisela Pohl (cta), Reiner Goldberg (ten), Werner Haseleu (nar), H. Kegel (cnd), Leipzig RSO Berlin Classics 2–▲ BER 1116 [ADD]
Schubert, Franz:Rosamunde, w. Ileana Cotrubas (sop), W. Boskovsky (cnd), Dresden State Opera Orch Berlin Classics ▲ BER 9004 [ADD]
Schubert, Franz:Rosamunde, w. Ameling (sop), K. Masur (cnd), Leipzig Gewandhaus Orch [G] Philips ▲ 412432-2 [DDD]
Schumann, R.:Choral Music, w. H. Neumann (cnd), Leipzig RSO *(rec 1978)* Berlin Classics ▲ BER 9191
Wagner, R.:Die Meistersinger von Nürnberg, w. H. Donath (sop), R. Hesse (mez), A. Kollo (ten), P. Schreier (ten), T. Adam (b-bar), R. Evans (bass), K. Ridderbusch (bass), H. von Karajan (cnd), Dresden Staatskapelle, Dresden State Chorus [G] EMI Classics 4–▲ CDCD 49683 [ADD]
Weber, C.M. von:Euryanthe, w. Jessye Norman (sop), Rita Hunter (sop), Nicolai Gedda (ten), Tom Krause (bar), M. Janowski (cnd), Dresden Staatskapelle Berlin Classics 3–▲ BER 1108 [ADD]
Weber, C.M. von:Kampf und Sieg, w. L. Schmidt-Glänzel (sop), E. Fleischer (cta), G. Lutze (ten), H. Krämer (bar), H. Kegel (cnd), Leipzig RSO [G] Forlane ▲ FOR 16572 (m) [AAD]
H. Neumann (cnd)
Brahms, J.:Choral Music, w. Gunther Opitz (hn), Waldemar Markus (hn), Margarethe Kluvetasch (hp)—Opp. 17, 42, 62 & 104 Berlin Classics ▲ BER CD 9276
Mendelssohn, F.:Choral Music Berlin Classics ▲ BER 9278

Leipzig Radio Men's Chorus
Liszt, F.:A Faust Sym, w. K. Masur (cnd), Leipzig Gewandhaus Orch *(rec 1977–80)* EMI Classics ("Doubleforte" series) 2–▲ CDFB 68595

Leipzig St. Thomas Church Choir
Bach, J.S.:Cant 4, w. Helga Terner (sop), Ortrun Wenkel (cta), Peter Schreier (ten), Eberhard Büchner (ten), H.-J. Rotzsch (cnd), Leipzig Gewandhaus Orch, Leipzig New Bach Collegium Musicum Berlin Classics ▲ BER 2067 [ADD]
Bach, J.S.:Cant 14, w. M. Frimmer (sop), E. Büchner (ten), A. Scheibner (bar), M. Pommer (cnd), Leipzig New Bach Collegium Musicum [G] Capriccio ▲ CDC 10027
Bach, J.S.:Cant 21, w. Arleen Augér (sop), Ortrun Wenkel (cta), Siegfried Jerusalem (ten), Peter Schreier (ten), Theo Adam (b-bar), H.-J. Rotzsch (cnd), New Bach Collegium Musicum Berlin Classics ▲ BER 2175 [ADD]
Bach, J.S.:Cant 29, w. Regina Werner (sop), Heidi Riess (alt), Hans-Joachim Rotzsch (ten), Hermann Christian Polster (bass), H.-J. Rotzsch (cnd), Leipzig Gewandhaus Orch Berlin Classics ▲ BER CD 9055
Bach, J.S.:Cant 31, w. Helga Terner (sop), Ortrun Wenkel (cta), Peter Schreier (ten), Eberhard Büchner (ten), H.-J. Rotzsch (cnd), Leipzig Gewandhaus Orch, Leipzig New Bach Collegium Musicum Berlin Classics ▲ BER 2067 [ADD]
Bach, J.S.:Cant 50, w. Arleen Auger (sop), Ortrun Wenkel (cta), Peter Schreier (ten), Theo Adam (b-bar), H.-J. Rotzsch (cnd), New Bach Collegium Musicum Berlin Classics ▲ BER 2176 [ADD]
Bach, J.S.:Cant 51, w. M. Frimmer (sop), M. Pommer (cnd), Leipzig New Bach Collegium Musicum [G] Capriccio ▲ CDC 10027 [DDD]
Bach, J.S.:Cant 51, w. *(soloists unknown)*, K. Thomas (cnd), Leipzig Gewandhaus Orch Berlin Classics ▲ BER 9200
Bach, J.S.:Cant 54, w. Marga Hoffgen (sop), Hermann Prey (bass), K. Thomas (cnd), Leipzig Gewandhaus Orch Berlin Classics ▲ BER CD 9202
Bach, J.S.:Cant 56, w. Marga Hoffgen (sop), Hermann Prey (bass), K. Thomas (cnd), Leipzig Gewandhaus Orch Berlin Classics ▲ BER CD 9202
Bach, J.S.:Cant 59, w. *(soloists unknown)*, K. Thomas (cnd), Leipzig Gewandhaus Orch Berlin Classics ▲ BER 9200
Bach, J.S.:Cant 71, w. K. Thomas (cnd), Leipzig Gewandhaus Orch Berlin Classics ▲ BER 9203
Bach, J.S.:Cant 79, w. Arleen Augér (sop), Ortrun Wenkel (cta), Peter Schreier (ten), Theo Adam (b-bar), H.-J. Rotzsch (cnd), New Bach Collegium Musicum Berlin Classics ▲ BER 2176 [ADD]
Bach, J.S.:Cant 80, w. Arleen Augér (sop), Ortrun Wenkel (cta), Peter Schreier (ten), Theo Adam (b-bar), H.-J. Rotzsch (cnd), New Bach Collegium Musicum Berlin Classics ▲ BER 2176 [ADD]
Bach, J.S.:Cant 82, w. Marga Hoffgen (sop), Hermann Prey (bass), K. Thomas (cnd), Leipzig Gewandhaus Orch Berlin Classics ▲ BER CD 9202
Bach, J.S.:Cant 111, w. K. Thomas (cnd), Leipzig Gewandhaus Orch Berlin Classics ▲ BER 9203
Bach, J.S.:Cant 119, w. Regina Werner (sop), Heidi Riess (alt), Hans-Joachim Rotzsch (ten), Hermann Christian Polster (bass), H.-J. Rotzsch (cnd), Leipzig Gewandhaus Orch Berlin Classics ▲ BER CD 9055
Bach, J.S.:Cant 134, w. Helga Terner (sop), Ortrun Wenkel (cta), Peter Schreier (ten), Eberhard Büchner (ten), H.-J. Rotzsch (cnd), Leipzig Gewandhaus Orch, Leipzig New Bach Collegium Musicum Berlin Classics ▲ BER 2067 [ADD]
Bach, J.S.:Cant 137, w. Arleen Augér (sop), Ortrun Wenkel (cta), Peter Schreier (ten), Siegfried Jerusalem (ten), Theo Adam (b-bar), H.-J. Rotzsch (cnd), New Bach Collegium Musicum Berlin Classics ▲ BER 2175 [ADD]
Bach, J.S.:Cant 140, w. K. Thomas (cnd), Leipzig Gewandhaus Orch Berlin Classics ▲ BER 9203
Bach, J.S.:Cant 143, w. M. Frimmer (sop), E. Büchner (ten), A. Scheibner (bar), M. Pommer (cnd), Leipzig New Bach Collegium Musicum [G] Capriccio ▲ CDC 10027 [DDD]
Bach, J.S.:Cant 192, w. Arleen Auger (sop), Ortrun Wenkel (cta), Peter Schreier (ten), Theo Adam (b-bar), H.-J. Rotzsch (cnd), New Bach Collegium Musicum Berlin Classics ▲ BER 2176 [ADD]
Bach, J.S.:Magnificat, BWV 243, w. *(soloists unknown)*, K. Thomas (cnd), Leipzig Gewandhaus Orch Berlin Classics ▲ BER 9200
Bach, J.S.:Motets, BWV 225–30, w. K. Thomas (cnd), Leipzig Opera Orch Berlin Classics ▲ BER 9103 [ADD]
Liszt, F.:Dante Sym, w. K. Masur (cnd), Leipzig Gewandhaus Orch EMI Classics 2–▲ CDFB 68598
H.-J. Rotzsch (cnd)
O Jesulein zart:Christmas & Advent Songs Capriccio ▲ 10542 [DDD]

Leipzig St. Thomas Church Choir members
Telemann, G.P.:Cants, w. Reiner Süss (bass)—Der Schulmeister; Trauer-Musik eines kunsterfahrenen Canarienvogels; Sagt, ihr alleerschonsten Lippen; Die Hoffnung ist mein Leben Berlin Classics ▲ BER 9135 [DDD]

Leipzig Synagogue Choir
Kol Nidre:Sacred Music of the Synagogue, w. Gloria Seipelt (alt), Leo Roth (ten), Rudolf Wiebel (bar), Werner Buschnakowski (org), Harry Foss (org), Leipzig RSO members, Jewish Congregation Choir Berlin EMI Classics ▲ CDM 65457

Leipzig Univ Choir
Bach, J.S.:Cant 55, w. P. Schreier (ten), M. Pommer (cnd), Leipzig New Bach Collegium Musicum [G] Capriccio ▲ 10151 [DDD]

Leipzig Univ Choir (cont.)

Bach, J.S.:Cant 55, w. Venceslava Hruba–Freiberger (sop), Peter Schreier (ten), M. Pommer (cnd), New Bach Collegium Musicum — Berlin Classics ▲ BER 1066 [DDD]

Bach, J.S.:Cant 84, w. Venceslava Hruba–Freiberger (sop), Peter Schreier (ten), M. Pommer (cnd), Leipzig New Bach Collegium Musicum — Berlin Classics ▲ BER 1066 [DDD]

Bach, J.S.:Cant 84, w. V. Hruba–Freiberger (sop), M. Pommer (cnd), Leipzig New Bach Collegium Musicum [G] — Capriccio ▲ 10151 [DDD]

Bach, J.S.:Cant 199, w. V. Hruba–Freiberger (sop), M. Pommer (cnd), Leipzig New Bach Collegium Musicum [G] — Capriccio ▲ 10151 [DDD]

Bach, J.S.:Cant 199, w. Venceslava Hruba–Freiberger (sop), Peter Schreier (ten), M. Pommer (cnd), Leipzig New Bach Collegium Musicum — Berlin Classics ▲ BER 1066 [DDD]

Handel, G.F.:The Choice of Hercules, w. Arleen Augér (sop), Venceslava Hruba–Freiberger (sop), Eberhard Büchner (ten), Zäppffel (sgr), M. Pommer (cnd), Leipzig New Bach Collegium Musicum [E] — Capriccio ▲ CDC 10019 [DDD]

Leipzig Vocal Concerto

Bach, J.S.:Cant 85, w. Barbara Schlick (sop), Andreas Scholl (alt), Christoph Prégardien (ten), Gotthold Schwarz (bass), Christophe Coin (piccolo vc/cnd), Leipzig Vocal Concerto, Limoges Baroque Ensemble — Astrée ▲ E 8544

Bach, J.S.:Cant 175, w. Barbara Schlick (sop), Andreas Scholl (alt), Christoph Prégardien (ten), Gotthold Schwarz (bass), Christophe Coin (piccolo vc/cnd), Leipzig Vocal Concerto, Limoges Baroque Ensemble — Astrée ▲ E 8544

Bach, J.S.:Cant 183, w. Barbara Schlick (sop), Andreas Scholl (alt), Christoph Prégardien (ten), Gotthold Schwarz (bass), Christophe Coin (piccolo vc/cnd), Leipzig Vocal Concerto, Limoges Baroque Ensemble — Astrée ▲ E 8544

Bach, J.S.:Cant 199, w. Barbara Schlick (sop), Andreas Scholl (alt), Christoph Prégardien (ten), Gotthold Schwarz (bass), Christophe Coin (piccolo vc/cnd), Leipzig Vocal Concerto, Limoges Baroque Ensemble — Astrée ▲ E 8544

Leningrad Chamber Choir

And Life of the Future Century, w. Lina Mkrtchyan (cta), Evgeni Talisman (org) — Multisonic ("Russian Stars on Classics" series) ▲ MUL 310053 [DDD]

Leningrad Chorus

Mozart, W.A.:Requiem, w. Jitka Pavlová (sop), Polovecova (mez), Vorapajev (ten), Gennadi Bezzubenkov (bass), M. Glinka (cnd), Ljubljana SO [L] — Stradivari Classics ▲ SCD 6003 [DDD] ■ SMC 6003 (D)

Leningrad Glinka Academic Choir

V. Tchernushenko (cnd)

Tchaikovsky, P.:Liturgy of St. John Chrysostom — Audiophile Classics ("Legacy Collection" series) ▲ 101.510

Tchaikovsky, P.:Vesper Service *(rec 1979)* — Consonance ▲ 815003 [AAD]

Leningrad Phil Choir

Shostakovich, D.:Sym 2, w. I. Blazhkov (cnd), Leningrad PO *(rec Nov. 1, 1965)* — Russian Disc ▲ RUS 11195 [AAD]

Shostakovich, D.:Sym 10, w. Y. Temirkanov (cnd), Leningrad PO *(rec Jan. 26, 1973)* — Russian Disc ▲ RUS 11195 [AAD]

Leningrad Religious Academy Student Choir

Hymns for the Holy Week in the Russian Orthodox Church, w. Moscow Patriarchate Publishing Division Choir, Korez Holy Trinity Nunnery Trio — Koch Schwann ▲ SCH 313073 [ADD]

Leningrad State Academy Boys' Chorus

Petrov, A.:The Creation of the World, w. Y. Temirkanov (cnd), Leningrad PO *(rec 1970)* — RCA Gold Seal ▲ 74321-32044-2 [ADD]

Leonarda Ensemble Cologne

E.M. Blankenburg (cnd)

Mendelssohn, Fanny:Gartenlieder (17) [G] — CPO ▲ CPO 999012-2 [DDD]

Leonhard Lechner Chamber Choir

W. Seebacher (cnd)

Lechner, L.:Sacred & Secular Songs—Deutsche Sprüche von Leben und Tod; Das Hohelied Salomonis; Jubilate Deo, omnis terra; Missa prima; Nun schein, du Glanz der Herrlichkeit — Entrée ▲ 0047 [ADD]

Leoni Men's Chorus

D. Loomer (cnd)

Songs of War & Peace, w. Christopher Gaze (nar), Stephen Smith (pno), Philip Crewe (perc), Salvador Ferreras (perc) — Skylark ▲ 9501 [DDD]

Leverkusen Cappella Vocale

Homilius, G.A.:St. Matthew Passion, w. A. Monoyios (sop), U. Groenwald (cta), G. Türk, C. Prégardien (ten), K. Mertens (b-bar), H.-G. Wimmer (bass), Berlin Academy for Early Music — Berlin Classics 2–▲ BER 1046 [DDD]

Lichfield Cathedral Choir

A. Lumsden (cnd)

Christmas from Lichfield, w. Robert Sharpe (org) — Nimbus ▲ NI 5496

Magnificat & Nunc Dimittis, Vol. 3, w. Mark Shepherd (org) — Priory ▲ PRI 505 [DDD]

J. Rees-Williams (cnd)

The Psalms of David, Vol. 4:In Jewry Is God Known — Priory ▲ PRCD 383 [DDD]

Ligugé Abbey Monks' Choir

Chefs-D'Oeuvre Grégoriens No. 1 — Studio SM ▲ 12 16.68

Christus natus est — Studio SM ▲ 121612

Gregorian Easter — GIA ■ CS 180

Laudate Deum — Studio SM ▲ 12 16.74

Misericordia Domini:Eternel est son Amour — Studio SM ▲ 12 22 39 [DDD]

Popular Gregorian Masses — Studio SM ▲ 12 16.60

Popular Masses — GIA ■ CS 178

Le Temps de Noël, w. En-Calcat Abbey Monks' Choir, Timadeuc Abbey Monks' Choir, Bec-Hellouin Abbey Monks' Choir, Les Peres de Chevilly — Studio SM 2–▲ 1219.10

O. Bossard (cnd)

Alleluia:Benedicite Domino — Studio SM ▲ 12 21.00

Lille MUKO

Nielsen, C.:Springtime, w. Inga Nielsen (sop), Kim von Binzer (ten), Jørgen Klint (bass), T. Vetõ (cnd), Odense SO, St. Klemens School Children's Choir — Unicorn-Kanchana ▲ DKPCD 9054

J.G. Jørgensen (cnd)

Clausen, T.:Songs (3), w. Thomas Clausen (pno), Mads Viding (db) — Point ▲ PCD 5125

Holten, B.:Nordisk Suite — Point ▲ PCD 5125

Langgaard, R.:The Rose Garden Songs — Point ▲ PCD 5125

Maegaard, J.:Södergran Songs — Point ▲ PCD 5125

Nørgård, P.:Evening Country — Point ▲ PCD 5125

Sundstrøm, A.:The Falcon & the Little Birds — Point ▲ PCD 5125

Limburg Cathedral Boys' Chorus

Kagel, M.:Sankt-Bach-Passion, w. Anne Sofie von Otter (mez), Hans Peter Blochowitz (ten), Roland Hermann (bar), Peter Roggisch (narr), Gerd Zacher (org), M. Kagel (cnd), South German RSO, Hamburg North German Choir — Montaigne ▲ MO 782044

Puccini, G.:La Bohème, w. Katia Ricciarelli (sop), Francisco Araiza (ten), Angelo Casertano (ten), Stefano Antonucci (bar), Claudio Giombi (bar), Paata Burchuladze (bass), Alfredo Mariotti (bass), Alberto Noli (bass), Andrea Piccinni (bass), Lauren Broglia (sgr), A. Guadagno (cnd), Arena di Verona Orch — Koch Schwann 2–▲ SCH 315922

Lincoln Cathedral Choir

C. Walsh (cnd)

Matins for Ascension Day, w. Andrew Post (org) — Priory ▲ PRI 478 [DDD]

Lira Chamber Chorus

L. Ding (cnd)

Górecki, H.-M.:Broad Waters — Elektra/Nonesuch ▲ 79348-2 ■ 79348-4

Górecki, H.-M.:My Vistula, Grey Vistula — Elektra/Nonesuch ▲ 79348-2 ■ 79348-4

Lisbon Gulbenkian Foundation Chorus

Beethoven, L. van:Mass, Op. 86, w. A. Michael (sop), L. Bizimeche-Eisinger (mez), M. Schaeffer (ten), M. Brodard (bar), M. Corboz (cnd), Lisbon Gulbenkian Foundation Orch [L] — Erato ▲ 2292-45461-2 ZK [DDD]

Beethoven, L. van:Meeresstille und glückliche Fahrt, w. M. Corboz (cnd), Lisbon Gulbenkian Foundation Orch [G] — Erato ▲ 2292-45461-2 ZK [DDD]

Beethoven, L. van:Syms (comp), w. Lynne Dawson (sop), Jard Van Nes (cta), Anthony Rolfe Johnson (ten), Eike Wilm Schulte (bass), F. Brüggen (cnd), Orch of the 18th Century [on Sym. 9] — Philips 5–▲ 442156-2

Bomtempo, J.D.:Messe de requiem consacrée à...Camões, w. Angela Maria Blasi (sop), Liliana Bizineche-Eisinger (mez), Reinaldo Macias (ten), Michel Brodard (bass), M. Corboz (cnd), Lisbon Gulbenkian Foundation Orch *(rec Gulbenkian Foundation Grand Auditorium, June 14-16, 1994)* — FNAC Music ▲ 592302 [DDD]

Carvalho, J. de S.:Te Deum, w. Brigitte Fournier (sop), Naoko Okada (sop), Elisabeth Graf (cta), John Elwes (ten), Michel Brodard (bar), M. Corboz (cnd), Lisbon Gulbenkian Foundation Orch — Cascavelle ▲ CVL 1016 [DDD]

Haydn, J.:Mass 3, "Cäcilienmesse", w. Brigette Fournier (sop), Bernarda Fink (alt), Charles Daniels (ten), Marcus Fink (bass), M. Corboz (cnd), Lisbon Gulbenkian Foundation Orch *(rec July 1993)* — FNAC Music ▲ 592309 [DDD]

Mendelssohn, F.:Lauda Sion, w. M. Corboz (cnd), Lisbon Gulbenkian Foundation Orch — Erato ▲ 94359-2

Mendelssohn, F.:Psalm 98, w. M. Corboz (cnd), Lisbon Gulbenkian Foundation Orch — Erato ▲ 94359-2

Mendelssohn, F.:Psalm 114, w. M. Corboz (cnd), Lisbon Gulbenkian Foundation Orch — Erato ▲ 94359-2

Mendelssohn, F.:St. Paul, w. R. Yakar (sop), B. Baileys (mez), M. Schäfer (ten), T. Hampson (bar), M. Corboz (cnd), Lisbon Gulbenkian Foundation Orch — Erato 2–▲ 45279-2

Nunes, E.:Machina Mundi, w. F. Bollon (cnd), Lisbon Gulbenkian Foundation CO — Montaigne ▲ MO 782020 [DDD]

Lisbon Teatro São Carlos Chorus

Donizetti, G.:Maria di Rohan (sels), w. R. Scotto (sop), G. Merighi (sgr), O. de Fabritiis (cnd), Lisbon Teatro São Carlos Orch—1 soprano aria, "Cupo fatal mestizia" & 1 duet, "Ecco l'ora" [I] *(rec live, Lisbon 3/20/68)* — Melodram (Connaisseur) 2–▲ CDM 27512 [ADD]

Franz Liszt Academy Chamber Chorus

Bartók, B.:Choruses (7), w. A. Dorati (cnd), Budapest SO — Hungaroton ▲ HCD 31047 [ADD]

Lajtha, L.:Hymns for the Holy Virgin, w. M. Szabó (cnd), Tátrai String Quartet, Györ Girls' Choir [L,F] — Hungaroton ▲ HCD 31453 [ADD]

Lajtha, L.:Madrigals, w. M. Szabó (cnd), Tátrai String Quartet, Györ Girls' Choir [L,F] — Hungaroton ▲ HCD 31453 [ADD]

Lajtha, L.:Magnificat, w. M. Szabó (cnd), Tátrai String Quartet, Györ Girls' Choir [L,F] — Hungaroton ▲ HCD 31453 [ADD]

Liverpool Cathedral Choir

Your Favorite Hymns:A Thousand Voices Sing the Finest Songs of Praise — Virgin Classics ▲ 59031

Liverpool Music Group Singers

Donizetti, G.:Emilia di Liverpool (sels), w. A. Cantelo (sop), J. Sutherland (sop), W. McAlpine (ten), D. Dowling (bar), H. Alan (bass), J. Pritchard (cnd), Royal Liverpool PO—13 arias from Act 1, & 4 from Act 2 [I] *(rec live, Liverpool Sept. 1957)* — Myto ▲ 1 MCD 91545 [ADD]

Liverpool Phil Choir

Rule Brittania, w. C. Groves (cnd), Royal Liverpool PO, A. Collins (cta) — Classics for Pleasure ▲ CDCFP 4567 [ADD]

Livorno Teatro La Gran Guardia Chorus

Puccini, G.:Tosca, w. R. Tebaldi (sop—Tosca), F. Corelli (ten—Cavaradossi), A. Colzani (bar—Scarpia), P. L. Latinucci (b-bar—Sacristan), G. Beloni (bass—Angelotti), M. Parenti (cnd), Livorno Teatro La Gran Guardia Orch *(rec live Sept. 21, 1959)* — Legato Classics 2–▲ LCD 171-2 [ADD]

Ljubljana Apz Tone Tomšič Chorus

Globokar, V.:Hallo, Do You Hear Me?, w. V. Globokar (cnd), Slovenian RSO, Slovenian Radio Jazz Quintet — Harmonia Mundi France ▲ HMC 90933

Ljubljana Radio Chorus

Dvořák, A.:Stabat Mater, w. A. P. Jeric (sop), E. N. Houska (mez), J. Reja (ten), F. Petrusanec (bass), M. Munih (cnd), Ljubljana RSO [L] — PMG (Vienna Master) ▲ CD 160104 [DDD]

London Bach Society Choir

P. Steinitz (cnd)

Schütz, H.:The 7 Words of Jesus Christ on the Cross, w. D. McCulloch (cnd), Collegium Sagittarii — Cantate ▲ 57615 [AAD]

London Baroque Chiaroscuro

C. Medlam (cnd)

Monteverdi, C.:Orfeo, w. P. Kwella (sop), E. Kirkby (sop), J. Smith (sop), N. Rogers (ten), S. Varcoe (bar), D. Thomas (bass), N. Rogers (cnd), London Cornett & Sackbutt Ensemble — EMI Classics ▲ CDMB 64947

London Chamber Choir

Handel, G.F.:Messiah (sels), w. Patrizia Kwella (sop), Catherine Denley (mez), John Mark Ainsley (ten), Bryn Terfel (b-bar), M. Stephenson (cnd), London Musici — Conifer Classics ▲ 74321-15354-2

Haydn, J.:Salve regina, H.XXIIIb/2, w. Arleen Auger (sop), Alfreda Hodgson (cta), Anthony Rolfe Johnson (ten), Gwynne Howell (bass), John Birch (db), L. Heltay (cnd), Argo CO *(rec St. Jude's, London, Feb 1979)* — London 2–▲ 443027-2 [ADD]

London Choral Society

Classical Spectacular, w. Royal PO, Michael Reed (cnd), Scots Guards Band, Welsh Guards Band — RPO Records 2–▲ CDRPD 9001 [DDD]

Classical Spectacular 1, w. Royal PO, Michael Reed (cnd), Scots Guards Band, Welsh Guards Band, Musketeers of the Sealed Knot — RPO Records ▲ RPO 5009 [DDD]

Classical Spectacular 2, w. Royal PO, Michael Reed (cnd), Gunnar Gudbjornsson (ten), J. Howard (bar), Scots Guards Band, Welsh Guards Band — RPO Records ▲ CDRPO 5010 [DDD]

Handel, G.F.:Messiah, w. Oliver Johnston (trb), Rae Woodland (sop), Norma Proctor (cta), Paul Esswood (ct), Stephen Roberts (bar), J. Tobin (cnd), English SO [Handel's original orchestration] [E] *(rec 1976)* — Protone ■ CSPR 166/67

S. Layton (cnd)

Hahn, R.:Songs, w. Felicity Lott (sop), Susan Bickley (mez), Ian Bostridge (ten), Stephen Varcoe (bar), Graham Johnson (pno)—[CD 1] Si mes vers avaient des ailes; Paysage; Rêverie; Offrande; Mai; Infidelité; Seule; Les Cygnes; Nocturne; 3 jours de vendange; D'une prison; Séraphine; L'Heure exquise; Fêtes galantes; 12 Rondels; [CD 2] Quand la nuit n'est pas étoilée; Le Plus beau présent; Sur l'eau; Le Rossignol des lilas; A Chloris; Ma jeunesse; Puisque j'ai mis ma lèvre; Etudes Latines; La Nymphe de la Source; Au Rossignol; Je me souviens; Air de la lettre; C'est très vilain d'être infidèle; C'est sa banlieue; Nous avons fait un beau voyage; La Dernière Valse — Hyperion ("The Hyperion French Song Edition" series) 2–▲ CDA 67141/42

London Fanshawe Symphonic Chorus

Handel, G.F.:Messiah, w. Leslie Fagan (sop), Janis Taylor (mez), Mark Dubois (ten), Gary Relyea (b-bar), G. Fagan (cnd), Concert Players Orch, Gerald Fagan Singers — Doremi 2–▲ 9306 [DDD]

London Festival Chorus

Bock, J.:Fiddler on the Roof, w. Molly Picon (sgr), Robert Merrill (bar), S. Black (cnd), London Festival Orch — London ("Phase 4 Stereo" series) ▲ 448 949-2

London Gabrieli Chorus

A Heralding of Battles & Ceremonies, w. London Gabrieli Brass Ensemble — Elektra/Nonesuch ■ 71414-4

Purcell, H.:Music for the Funeral of Queen Mary, London Gabrieli Brass Ensemble — Elektra/Nonesuch ■ 71414-4

London Handel Chorus

Handel, G.F.:The Triumph of Time & Truth, w. James Goodman (trb), Fisher (sop), Emma Kirkby (sop), Charles Brett (ct), Ian Partridge (ten), Stephen Varcoe (bar), D. Darlow (cnd), London Handel Orch [E] — Hyperion 2–▲ CDA 66071/72

CHORAL GROUPS

London Monteverdi Choir
Monteverdi, C.:Vespro della Beata Vergine, w. A. Monoyios (sop), M. Pennicchi (sop), M. Chance (ct), G. Tucker (ten), N. Robson (ten), S. Naglia (ten), B. Terfel (b-bar), A. Miles (bass), J. E. Gardiner (cnd), English Baroque Soloists, His Majesties Sagbutts & Cornetts Archiv 2-▲ 429565-2 [DDD]
London Opera Chorus
Mozart, W.A.:Don Giovanni, w. L. Price (sop), L. Popp (sop), S. Sass (sop), S. Burrows (ten), G. Bacquier (bar), B. Weikl (bar), A. Sramek (bar), K. Moll (bass), G. Solti (cnd), London PO London ("Grand Opera" series) 3-▲ 425169-2 [ADD]
Verdi, G.:La traviata, w. J. Sutherland (sop), L. Pavarotti (ten), M. Manuguerra (bar), R. Bonynge (cnd), National PO London [I] London ▲ 400057-2 [DDD] ■ 400057-4
Verdi, G.:La traviata, w. J. Sutherland (sop), L. Pavarotti (ten), M. Manuguerra (bar), R. Bonynge (cnd), National PO London [I] London 2-▲ 430491-2 [DDD]
London Oratory Junior Choir
Vaughan Williams, R.:A Song of Thanksgiving, w. John Gielgud (nar), L. Dawson (sop), M. Best (cnd), City of London Sinfonia [E] Hyperion ▲ CDA 66569 [DDD]
London Oriana Choir
In Dulci Jubilo:Music for Advent & Christmas ASV ▲ ASV 2096 [DDD]
London Phil Chamber Choir
D. Temple (cnd)
Elgar, E.:Songs, w. J. Brecknock (ten), V. Morris (pno)—20 songs—O Happy Eyes; Love; To Her Beneath Whose Stedfast Star; Is She Not Passing Fair?; Sheperd's Song; Weary Wind of the West; Evening Scene; Windlass Song; Poet's Life; Song of Autumn; Death on the Hills; Serenade; Credo in e; Was it Some Golden Star?; Speak, Music; Lo! Christ the Lord is Risen; O Mightiest of the Mighty; The River; How Calmly the Evening; Good Morrow [E] Meridian ▲ CDE 84173
London Phil Chorus
Bach, J.S.:Mass in b, BWV 232, w. E. Schumann (sop), M. Balfour (cta), W. Widdop (ten), F. Schorr (bar), A. Coates (cnd), London SO [L] *(rec Kingsway Hall, London Mar-Apr 1929)* Pearl 2-▲ PEAS 9900 (m) [AAD]
Bartók, B.:Dance Suite, w. F. Welser-Möst (cnd), London PO EMI Classics ▲ CDC 54858
Bartók, B.:The Miraculous Mandarin, w. F. Welser-Möst (cnd), London PO EMI Classics ▲ CDC 54858
Beethoven, L. van:Fant Pno, Op. 80, "Choral Fant", w. A. Brendel (pno), B. Haitink (cnd), London PO Philips ("Insignia" series) ▲ 434148-2 [DDD]
Beethoven, L. van:Sym 9, "Choral Sym", w. B. Walter (cnd), London PO [G] *(rec live, Royal Albert Hall, London Nov. 13, 1947)* Music & Arts ▲ CD 733 [AAD]
Delius, F.:Appalachia, w. John Noble (bar), C. Groves (cnd), London PO, BBC Chorus, BBC Choral Society, Goldsmith's Choral Union IMP ("BBC Radio Classics" series) ▲ IMP 9133
de Luca, E.:Conquerors of the Ages, London PO Alshire ▲ ALCD 41
Elgar, E.:The Apostles, w. S. Armstrong (sop), H. Watts (cta), R. Tear (ten), J. C. Case (bar), B. Luxon (bar), C. Grant (bass), A. Boult (cnd), London PO, Downe House School Choir [E] EMI Classics ▲ CDMB 64206
Elgar, E.:The Kingdom, w. A. Boult (cnd), London PO EMI Classics 2-▲ ZDMB 64209
Elgar, E.:The Kingdom, w. Y. Kenny (sop), A. Hodgson (alt), C. Gillert (ten), B. Luxon (bass), L. Slatkin (cnd), London PO RCA Red Seal 2-▲ 07863-57862-2
Elgar, E.:The Music Makers, w. L. Finnie (mez), B. Thomson (cnd), London PO [E] Chandos ▲ CHAN 9022 [DDD]
Elgar, E.:Sea Pictures, w. L. Finnie (mez), B. Thomson (cnd), London PO [E] Chandos ▲ CHAN 9022 [DDD]
Handel, G.F.:Music of, w. Pauline Tinsley (sop), James Bowman (ct), Anthony Rolfe-Johnson (ten), David Wilson-Johnson (ten), Simon Preston (org), R. Leppard (cnd), English CO—Zadok the Priest; Eternal Source of Light Divine; Tamerlano Ov; Dead March [from Saul]; When the Ear Heard Her; She Delivered the Poor That Cried; Their Bodies Are Buried in Peace; Glory Be to the Father; As It Was in the Beginning; Con a Due Cori in B♭; Waft Her Angels to the Skies; Con in g for Org, Op. 7/5; Hallelujah Chorus [from The Messiah] IMP ("BBC Radio Classics" series) ▲ IMP 5691522
Kodály, Z.:Psalmus hungaricus, w. Raymond Nilsson (ten), J. Ferencsik (cnd), London PO Everest ▲ EVC 9008 [AAD]
Kodály, Z.:Vars on a Hungarian Folk Song, w. F. Welser-Möst (cnd), London PO EMI Classics ▲ CDC 54858
Mahler, G.:Sym 2, w. F. Palmer (sop), T. Troyanos (alt), P. Boulez (cnd), BBC SO, BBC Choral Society Enterprise 2-▲ LV 915/916
Mahler, G.:Sym 8, w. K. Tennstedt (cnd), London PO, Tiffin School Boys' Chorus [G,L] EMI Classics 2-▲ CDCB 47625 [DDD]
Mozart, W.A.:Requiem, w. F. Lott (sop), D. Jones (mez), K. Lewis (ten), W. White (bar), F. Welser-Möst (cnd), London PO EMI Classics ▲ CDM 63260
Mozart, W.A.:Requiem, w. Felicity Lott (sop), Cella Jones (mez), Keith Lewis (ten), Willard White (bass), David Bell (org), F. Welser-Möst (cnd), London PO Classics for Pleasure ("Eminence" series) ▲ CDEMX 2150 [DDD]
Orff, C.:Carmina burana, w. S. Jo (sop), J. Kowalski (alt), B. Skovhus (bar), Z. Mehta (cnd), London PO, Southend Boys' Choir Teldec ▲ 74886-2
Orff, C.:Carmina burana, w. B. Hendricks (sop), M. Chance (ct), J. Black (bar), F. Welser-Möst (cnd), London PO, St. Alban's Cathedral Choristers [G, L] EMI Classics ▲ CDC 54054 [DDD]
Parry, H.:Invocation, w. L. Dawson (sop), A. Davies (ten), B. Rayner Cook (bar), M. Bamert (cnd), London PO [E] Chandos ▲ CHAN 9025 [DDD]
Parry, H.:The Lotus Eaters, w. D. Jones (mez), M. Bamert (cnd), London PO [E] Chandos ▲ CHAN 8990 [DDD]
Parry, H.:The Soul's Ransom, w. D. Jones (mez), D. Wilson-Johnson (bar), M. Bamert (cnd), London PO [E] Chandos ▲ CHAN 8990 [DDD]
Pettersson, G.A.:Sym 12, w. C.R. Larsson (cnd), Stockholm PO, Univ of Uppsala Choir Caprice ▲ CAP 21369 [AAD]
Prokofiev, S.:Zdravitsa, w. D. Gleeson (cnd), London PO, Geoffrey Mitchell Choir IMP ("Masters" series) ▲ IMP 6600122
Strauss (II), Joh.:Die Fledermaus (sels), w. Wilma Lipp (sop), Gerda Scheyer (sop), Christa Ludwig (mez), Anton Dermota (ten), Walter Berry (bar), Erich Kunz (bar), Eberhard Wachter (bar), O. Ackermann (cnd), Philharmonia Orch Emperor Operetta ▲ KO 86340
Stravinsky, I.:Oedipus Rex, w. M. Lipovsek (mez), A. Rolfe-Johnson (ten), J. Tomlinson (bass), F. Welser-Möst (cnd), London PO EMI Classics ▲ CDC 54445
Stravinsky, I.:Perséphone, w. A. Fournet (nar), A. Rolfe-Johnson (ten), K. Nagano (cnd), London PO, Tiffin Boys' School Choir [F] Virgin Classics 2-▲ 59077 [DDD]
Tchaikovsky, P.:Ode to Joy, w. D. Gleeson (cnd), London PO, Geoffrey Mitchell Choir IMP ("Masters" series) ▲ IMP 6600122
Vaughan Williams, R.:Dona nobis pacem, w. E. Wiens (sop), B. Rayner Cook (bar), B. Thomson (cnd), London PO [L] Chandos ▲ CHAN 8590 [DDD]
Vaughan Williams, R.:Mystical Songs, w. B. Rayner Cook (bar), B. Thomson (cnd), London PO [L] Chandos ▲ CHAN 8590 [DDD]
Vaughan Williams, R.:The Pilgrim's Progress, w. J. Noble (bar), A. Boult (cnd), London PO [E] EMI Classics ▲ CDMB 64212
Vaughan Williams, R.:Sym 1, w. N. Armstrong (sop), J. C. Case (bar), A. Boult (cnd), London PO EMI Classics ▲ CDM 64016
Verdi, G.:Requiem Mass, w. E. Schwarzkopf (sop), C. Ludwig (mez), N. Gedda (ten), N. Ghiaurov (bass), C. M. Giulini (cnd), Philharmonia Orch [L] EMI Classics 2-▲ CDCB 47257 [ADD]
Verdi, G.:quattro pezzi sacri, w. J. Baker (sop), C. M. Giulini (cnd), Philharmonia Orch [I,L] EMI Classics 2-▲ CDCB 47257 [ADD]
Verdi, G.:La traviata, w. Maria Caniglia (sop—Violetta), Maria Huder (mez—Flora), Gladys Palmer (cta—Annina), Octave Dua (ten—Giuseppe), Beniamino Gigli (ten—Alfredo), Booth Hitchen (ten—D'Obigny), Adelio Zagonara (bar—Gastone), Aristide Baracchi (bar—Douphol), Mario Basiola (bar—Germont), Norman Walker (bass—Dr. Grenville), V. Gui (cnd), London PO *(rec Royal Opera House, Covent Garden, May 22, 1939)* Minerva 2-▲ MN A28/29 (m) [ADD]

London Phil Chorus (cont.)
Verdi, G.:La traviata, w. Maria Caniglia (sop), Beniamino Gigli (ten), Mario Basiola (bar), V. Gui (cnd), London PO *(rec Royal Opera House, Covent Garden, May 22, 1939)* Enterprise ("The Fourties" series) 2-▲ ENT 313
Cooke, Pritchard (cnd)
Walton, W.:Belshazzar's Feast, w. Stephen Roberts (bar), C. Mackerras (cnd), English CO, BBC Singers, BBC Sym Chorus IMP ("BBC Radio Classics" series) ▲ IMP 5691612
London Radio Chorus
Beethoven, L. van:Sym 9, "Choral Sym", w. S. McNair (sop), U. Heilmann (ten), J. Van Nes (bar), B. Weikl (bar), K. Masur (cnd), Leipzig Gewandhaus Orch Philips ▲ 432995-2
London Schubert Chorale
S. Layton (cnd)
Schubert, Franz:Songs (comp), w. P. Rozario (sop), J.M. Ainsley (ten), I. Bostridge (ten), M. George (bass), G. Johnson (pno)—Winterlied; Ossians Lied nach dem Falle Nathos; Das Mädchen von Inistore; Als ich sie erröten; Schwangesang; Totenkranz für ein Kind; Die Fröhlichkeit; Der Zufriedene; Alles um Liebe; Geist der Liebe; Dei erste Liebe; Die Täuschung; Liebesrausch; Huldigung; Heidenröslein; Nachtgesang; Der Morgenstern; Der Knappenlied; Trinklied vor der Schlacht; Schwertlied; Begräbnislied; Grablied; Osterlied; Hoffnung; Punschlied; Klage um Ali Bey; Abendständchen; Tische'rlied; Wiegenlied; Die Macht der Liebe; Trinklied, D.183; Trinklied, D.267 Hyperion ▲ CDJ 33020
Schubert, Franz:Songs (misc), w. Lorna Anderson (sop), Catherine Wyn-Rogers (alt), Jamie McDougall (ten) Simon Keenlyside (bar), Graham Johnson (pno)—Das Leben ist ein Traum; Das Grab; Trinklied; Punschlied; Vaterlandslied; Selma und Selmar; Morgenlied; An die Sonne; Hermann und Thusnelda; Cora und die Sonne; Lorna; Genugsamkeit; Der Abend; Das Mädchen aus dem Fremde; Am Rosa (I); Am Rosa (II); An Sie; Gebet während der Schlacht; Das Abendroth; Die drei Sänger; Die Sterne; Cronnan; Furcht der Geliebten; Die Erscheinung; Stolie; Das Bild; Lob des Tokayers Hyperion ▲ CDJ 33022
G. Johnson (cnd)
Schubert, Franz:Songs (comp), w. John Mark Ainsley (ten), Michael George (bass), Simon Keenlyside (bass), Graham Schäfer (sgr)—settings of Goethe's poetry Hyperion ▲ CDJ 33024♦
S. Layton (cnd)
Schubert, Franz:Songs (comp), w. Christine Schäfer (sop), John Mark Ainsley (ten), Richard Jackson (bar), Graham Johnson (pno)—Der Einsame; Des Sängers Habe; Zwei Szenen aus dem Schauspiel Lacrimas (Lied der Delphine; Lied des Florio); Mondenschien (chorale); Gesänge Aus Wilhwlm Meister (Nur wer die Sehnsucht kennt; Hwiss mich nicht reden; So lasst mich scheinen); Totengräberweise; Das Echo; An Silvia; Horch, horch die Lerch'; Trinklied; Wiegenlied; Widerspruch; Der Wanderer an den Mond; Grab und Mond (chorale); Nachthelle; Abschied von der Erde Hyperion ▲ CDJ 33026
London Select Choir
Delius, F.:Koanga (sels), w. T. Beecham (cnd), London PO—Closing scene *(rec Dec. 11, 1934)* Dutton Laboratories ▲ CDLX 7011 [ADD]
London Sinfonietta Chorus
Birtwistle, H.:Meridan, w. M. King (mez), O. Knussen (cnd), London Sinfonietta NM Classics ▲ NMCD 009 [DDD]
Lewis, R.H.:Kantaten, w. J. Constable (pno), R.H. Lewis (cnd) New World ▲ 80444-2
Stravinsky, I.:Cant Sop, w. Y. Kenny (sop), J. Aler (ten), E.-P. Salonen (cnd), London Sinfonietta Sony Classical ▲ SK 46667
Tippett, M.:King Priam, w. Heather Harper (sop—Hecuba), Linda Hirst (sop—Serving Woman), Felicity Palmer (sop—Andromache), Julian Saipe (sop—Paris), Yvonne Minton (mez—Helen), Ann Murray (mez—Nurse), Kenneth Bowen (ten—Hermes), Peter Hall (ten—Young Guard), Philip Langridge (ten—Paris), Robert Tear (ten—Achilles), Thomas Allen (bar—Hector), Norman Bailey (bar—Priam), Stephen Roberts (bar—Patroclus), David Wilson-Johnson (bar—Old Man), D. Atherton (cnd), London Sinfonietta Chandos ▲ CHAN 9406/7 [DDD]
T. Edwards (cnd)
Britten, B.:A Boy Was Born, w. S. Leonard (sop), N. Tibbels (sop), S. Bickley (mez), P. Hall (ten), G. Jess (bass), St. Paul's Cathedral Choristers Virgin Classics ▲ CDC 59136
Britten, B.:Hymn to St. Cecilia, w. S. Leonard (sop), N. Tibbels (sop), S. Bickley (mez), P. Hall (ten), G. Jess (bass), St. Paul's Cathedral Choir Virgin Classics ▲ CDC 59136
Britten, B.:Sonnets of Michelangelo, w. S. Leonard (sop), N. Tibbels (sop), S. Bickley (mez), P. Hall (ten), G. Jess (bass), Choristers of St. Paul's Cathedral Virgin Classics ▲ CDC 59136
Ligeti, G.:The Ligeti Edition—complete a capella Choral Works Sony Classical ▲ SK 62305
London Sym Chorus
The Age of Bel Canto, w. Joan Sutherland (sop), Marilyn Horne (mez), Richard Conrad (bar), London SO [cnd:Richard Bonynge] London ("The Classic Sound" series) ▲ 448594-2
Beethoven, L. van:Fant Pno, Op. 80, "Choral Fant", w. Julius Katchen (pno), P. Gamba (cnd), London SO *(rec 1965)* London 2-▲ 440839-2 [ADD]
Beethoven, L. van:Mass, Op. 86, w. A. Tomwa-Sintow (sop), P. Payne (mez), R. Tear (ten), R. Lloyd (bass), C. Davis (cnd), London SO [G] Philips 2-▲ 438362-2
Beethoven, L. van:Missa Solemnis, w. A. Tomwa-Sintow (sop), P. Payne (mez), R. Tear (ten), R. Lloyd (bass), C. Davis (cnd), London SO [G] Philips 2-▲ 438362-2
Beethoven, L. van:Syms (comp), w. C. Hogwood (cnd), Academy of Ancient Music—[soloists in No. 9:Arleen Augér, Catherine Robbin, Anthony Rolfe Johnson, Gregory Reinhart] L'Oiseau-Lyre 6-▲ 425696-2 [DDD]
Beethoven, L. van:Sym 9, "Choral Sym", w. W. Morris (cnd), London SO [G] IMP Classics ▲ PCD 923 [DDD]
Beethoven, L. van:Sym 9, "Choral Sym", w. P. Monteux (cnd), London SO—w. rehearsal sels. MCA Classics 2-▲ MCAD2-9806
Beethoven, L. van:Sym 9, "Choral Sym", w. L. Stokowski (cnd), London SO [soloists Harper, Watts, Young, & McIntyre] [G] London ("Weekend Classics" series) ▲ 421636-2 [AAD]
Beethoven, L. van:Sym 9, "Choral Sym", w. Alison Hargen (sop), Della Jones (mez), David Rendall (ten), Gwynne Howell (b-bar), W. Morris (cnd), London SO IMP ("LSO" series) ▲ IMP 6900032
Beethoven, L. van:Sym 9, "Choral Sym", w. K. Te Kanawa (sop), E. Jochum (cnd), London SO EMI Classics ▲ CDM 64633
Beethoven, L. van:Sym 9, "Choral Sym", w. Heather Harper (sop), Helem Watts (cta), Alexander Young (ten), Donald McIntyre (bass), L. Stokowski (cnd), London SO *(rec London, Sept 23, 1967)* Music & Arts ▲ MUA CD 943
Bellini, V.:Norma, w. J. Sutherland (sop), M. Horne (mez), J. Alexander (ten), R. Cross (bass), R. Bonynge (cnd), London SO [I] London 3-▲ 425488-2 [ADD]
Bellini, V.:Norma (sels), w. J. Sutherland (sop), M. Horne (mez), J. Alexander (ten), R. Cross (bass), R. Bonynge (cnd), London SO [I] London ("Opera Gala" series) ▲ 421886-2 [ADD]
Berlioz, H.:La Damnation de Faust, w. J. Veasey (mez), N. Gedda (ten), C. Bastin (bar), C. Davis (cnd), London SO, Ambrosian Singers [F] Philips 2-▲ 416395-2 [ADD]
Berlioz, H.:Requiem, "Grande Messe des Morts", w. R. Dowd (ten), C. Davis (cnd), London SO [L] Philips 2-▲ 416283-2 [ADD]
Berlioz, H.:Roméo et Juliette, w. R. Resnik (mez), A. Turp (ten), J. Ward (bar), P. Monteux (cnd), London SO [F] MCA Classics 2-▲ MCAD2-9805
Berlioz, H.:Te Deum, w. F. Tagliavini (ten), C. Davis (cnd), London SO, Wandsworth School Boys' Chorus [L] Philips ▲ 416660-2 [ADD]
Bernstein, L.:Candide (restored), w. J. Anderson (sop), C. Ludwig (mez), D. Jones (mez), J. Hadley (ten), N. Gedda (ten), A. Green (sgr), K. Ollmann (bar), L. Bernstein (cnd), London SO *(rec 1989)* Deutsche Grammophon ▲ 429734-2 [DDD] ■ 429734-4
Bernstein, L.:Candide (restored), w. J. Anderson (sop), C. Ludwig (mez), D. Jones (mez), J. Hadley (ten), N. Gedda (ten), A. Green (sgr), K. Ollmann (bar), L. Bernstein (cnd), London SO Deutsche Grammophon ■ 437328-4
Bernstein, L.:Chichester Psalms, w. R. Hickox (cnd), Royal PO [He] MCA Classics ▲ MCAD 6199 [DDD]
The Best of Richard Hickox, w. R. Hickox (cnd), London SO, Penelope Walmsley-Clark (sop), John Graham-Hall (ten), D. Maxwell (bar), Southend Boys' Choir, London Voices IMP Classics 3-▲ TCD 1073 [DDD]
Brahms, J.:Alto Rhap, w. J. Baker (mez), R. Hickox (cnd), City of London Sinfonia Virgin Classics ▲ CDC 59589

978 ▲ = CD ♦ = Enhanced CD Δ = MD ■ = Cassette Tape □ = DCC

London Sym Chorus (cont.)

Brahms, J.:Ein Deutsches Requiem, w. F. Lott (sop), D. Wilson-Johnson (bar), R. Hickox (cnd), London SO [G] Chandos ▲ CHAN 8942 [DDD]

Britten, B.:Ballad of Heroes, w. M. Hill (ten), R. Hickox (cnd), London SO [E] Chandos 2-▲ CHAN 8983/84 [DDD]

Britten, B.:A Midsummer Night's Dream, w. E. Harwood (sop), J. Veasey (mez), H. Watts (cta), A. Deller (ct), P. Pears (ten), J. Shirley-Quirk (bar), B. Britten (cnd), London SO [E] London 2-▲ 425663-2 [ADD]

Britten, B.:Peter Grimes, w. R. Hickox (cnd), City of London Sinfonia Chandos 2-▲ CHAN 9447/8

Britten, B.:Spring Sym, w. S. Armstrong (sop), J. Baker (mez), R. Tear (ten), A. Previn (cnd), London SO EMI Classics ▲ CDM 64736

Britten, B.:Spring Sym, w. E. Gale (sop), A. Hodgson (cta), M. Hill (ten), R. Hickox (cnd), London SO, Southend Boys' Choir [E] Chandos ▲ CHAN 8855 [DDD]

Britten, B.:War Requiem, w. H. Harper (sop), P. Langridge (ten), J. Shirley-Quirk (bar), R. Elms (org), R. Hickox (cnd), London SO, St. Paul's Cathedral Choristers [E,L] Chandos 2-▲ CHAN 8983/84 [DDD]

Britten, B.:War Requiem, w. G. Vishnevskaya (sop), P. Pears (ten), D. Fischer-Dieskau (bar), B. Britten (cnd), London SO [E,L] London 2-▲ 414383-2 [ADD]

Elgar, E.:The Apostles, w. A. Hargan (sop), A. Hodgson (cta), D. Rendall (ten), S. Roberts (bar), B. Terfel (bass-bar), R. Lloyd (bass), R. Hickox (cnd), London SO [E] Chandos 2-▲ CHAN 8875/76 [DDD]

Elgar, E.:The Black Knight, w. R. Hickox (cnd), London SO Chandos ▲ CHAN 9436

Elgar, E.:Caractacus, w. J. Howarth (sop), A. Davies (ten), S. Roberts (bar), D. Wilson-Johnson (bar), A.R. Miles (bass), R. Hickox (cnd), London SO [E] *(rec 1992)* Chandos 2-▲ CHAN 9156/57 [DDD]

Elgar, E.:The Dream of Gerontius, w. F. Palmer (sop), A. Davies (ten), G. Howell (bass), R. Hickox (cnd), London SO [E] Chandos 2-▲ CHAN 8641/42 [DDD]

Elgar, E.:The Kingdom, w. M. Marshall (sop), F. Palmer (sop), Davies (ten), D. Wilson-Johnson (bar), R. Hickox (cnd), London SO [E] Chandos 2-▲ CHAN 8788/89 [DDD]

Elgar, E.:The Light of Life, w. J. Howarth (sop), L. Finnie (mez), A. Davies (ten), J. Shirley-Quirk (bar), R. Hickox (cnd), London SO Chandos ▲ CHAN 9208 [DDD]

Fauré, G.:Requiem, w. A. Jones (trb), S. Roberts (bar), R. Hickox (cnd), Royal PO [L] MCA Classics ▲ MCAD 6199 [DDD]

Fauré, G.:Requiem, w. M. McLaughlin (sop), G. Howell (bass-bar), S. Celibidache (cnd), London SO *(rec Apr. 1982)* Exclusive ▲ EXL 52 [ADD]

Ferguson, H.:The Dream of the Rood, w. A. Dawson (sop), R. Hickox (cnd), London SO [E] Chandos ▲ CHAN 9082 [DDD]

Handel, G.F.:Messiah, w. Kenneth McKellar (ten), George Malcolm (hpd), Ralph Downes (org), A. Boult (cnd), London SO—And the glory of the Lord; And He shall purify; For unto us a Child is born; Glory to God in the highest; His yoke is easy; Behold the Lamb of God; Surely He hath borne our griefs; And with His stripes we are healed; All we like sheep have gone astray; All they that see Him...He trusted in God; Lift up your heads; The Lord gave the word; Their sound has gone out; Let us break the bonds asunder; Hallelujah; Since by man came death; Worthy is the Lamb...Amen London ▲ 436569-2

Handel, G.F.:Messiah, w. Heather Harper (sop), Helen Watts (cta), John Wakefield (ten), John Shirley-Quirk (bar), C. Davis (cnd), London SO Philips 2-▲ 438356-2

Handel, G.F.:Messiah (sels), w. Sheila. Armstrong (sop), Norma Proctor (cta), Kenneth Bowen (ten), John Cameron (bar), L. Stokowski (cnd), London SO [E] London ("Weekend Classics" series) ▲ 433874-2 [ADD] ■ 433874-4

Handel, G.F.:Messiah (sels), w. L. Siegel (cnd), London PO—Glory to God; And the Glory Laserlight ▲ 15 502 [ADD]

Handel, G.F.:Messiah (sels), w. Joan Sutherland (sop), Grace Bumbry (mez), Kenneth McKellar (ten), Joseph Ward (bar), A. Boult (cnd), London SO—arias & choruses London ("Weekend Classics" series) ▲ 417879-2 [AAD] ■ 417879-4

Haydn, J.:Mass 12, "Theresienmesse", w. Lucia Popp (sop), Rosalind Elias (mez), Robert Tear (ten), Paul Hudson (bass), L. Bernstein (cnd), London SO [L] Sony Classical 2-▲ SM2K 47522 [ADD]

Holst, G.:A Choral Fant, w. R. Hickox (cnd), City of London Sinfonia, Joyful Company of Singers Chandos ▲ CHAN 9437

Holst, G.:The Cloud Messenger, w. D. Jones (mez), R. Hickox (cnd), London SO [E] Chandos ▲ CHAN 8901 [DDD]

Holst, G.:A Dirge for 2 Veterans, w. R. Hickox (cnd), City of London Sinfonia Chandos ▲ CHAN 9437

Holst, G.:The Hymn of Jesus, w. R. Hickox (cnd), London SO [E] Chandos ▲ CHAN 8901 [DDD]

Holst, G.:Ode to Death, w. R. Hickox (cnd), City of London Sinfonia, Joyful Company of Singers Chandos ▲ CHAN 9437

Holst, G.:Partsongs (7), Op. 44, w. R. Hickox (cnd), City of London Sinfonia, Joyful Company of Singers Chandos ▲ CHAN 9437

Holst, G.:The Planets, w. G. Holst (cnd), London SO *(rec 1926 Columbia electrical)* Koch Legacy ▲ 3-7018-2 H1 (m)

Holst, G.:The Planets, w. G. Simon (cnd), London SO LaserLight ▲ 14010 [DDD]

Holst, G.:The Planets, w. G. Holst (cnd), London SO *(rec 1922-24 for Columbia)* Pearl ▲ PEA 9417 (m) [AAD]

Holst, G.:The Planets, w. R. Hickox (cnd), London SO IMP Classics ▲ PCD 890 [DDD]

Holst, G.:Short Festival Te Deum, w. C. Groves (cnd), London PO EMI Classics ▲ CDC 49784

Howells, H.:Missa sabrinensis, w. Janice Watson (sop), Della Jones (cta), Martyn Hill (ten), Donald Maxwell (bar), G. Rozhdestvensky (cnd), London SO Chandos ▲ CHAN 9348 [DDD]

Howells, H.:Stabat mater, w. Neill Archer (ten), G. Rozhdestvensky (cnd), London SO Chandos ▲ CHAN 9314 [DDD]

Ireland, J.:Greater Love Hath No Man, w. P. Bott (sop), B. Tarfel (bass-bar), R. Hickox (cnd), London SO [E] Chandos ▲ CHAN 8879 [DDD]

Ireland, J.:These Things shall Be, w. B. Terfel (bass-bar), R. Hickox 9cnd), London SO [E] Chandos ▲ CHAN 8879 [DDD]

Ireland, J.:Vexilla Regis, w. P. Bott (sop), T. Shaw (mez), J. Oxley (ten), B. Terfel (bass-bar), R. Hickox (cnd), London SO [L] Chandos ▲ CHAN 8879 [DDD]

Ives, C.:Orchestral Set 2, w. L. Stokowski (cnd), London SO *(rec June 18, 1970)* Intaglio ▲ ING 7421 [ADD]

Janácek, L.:Slavonic Mass, w. G. Benačková (sop), F. Palmer (sop), G. Lakes (ten), A. Kotcherga (bass), M. Tilson Thomas (cnd), London SO Sony Classical ▲ SK 47182

Mahler, G.:Das Klagende Lied, w. E. Lear (sop), E. Söderström (sop), G. Hoffman (mez), S. Burrows (ten), E. Haefliger (ten), G. Nienstedt (bass), P. Boulez (cnd), London SO Sony Classical ("Pierre Boulez Edition" series) ▲ SK 45841

Mahler, G.:Songs from Rückert, w. J. Baker (mez), M. Tilson Thomas (cnd), London SO [G] CBS 2-▲ M2K 44553 [DDD]

Mahler, G.:Sym 2, w. B. Valente (sop), M. Forrester (cta), G. Kaplan (cnd), London SO MCA Classics 2-▲ MCAD 11011 [DDD]; 2-■ MCAC 11011 (D)

Mahler, G.:Sym 2, w. H. Harper (sop), H. Watts (cta), G. Solti (cnd), London SO [G] London 2-▲ 425005-2 [ADD]

Mahler, G.:Sym 3, w. J. Baker (mez), M. Tilson Thomas (cnd), London SO [G] CBS 2-▲ M2K 44553 [DDD]

Mendelssohn, F.:Elijah, w. R. Plowright (sop), L. Finnie (mez), J. Budd (trb), A. Davies (ten), J. White (bass), R. Hickox (cnd), London SO [E] Chandos 2-▲ CHAN 8774/75 [DDD]

Mendelssohn, F.:A Midsummer Night's Dream (comp), w. Janice Watson (sop), Delia Wallis (mez), A. Previn (cnd), London SO [E] EMI Classics ▲ CDC 47163

Mendelssohn, F.:Psalm 42, w. J. Baker (mez), R. Hickox (cnd), City of London Sinfonia Virgin Classics ▲ CDC 59589

Mendelssohn, F.:Songs (4) (1830), w. J. Baker (mez), F. Lloyd (hn), R. Masters (hp), R. Hickox (cnd), City of London Sinfonia Virgin Classics ▲ CDC 59589

Messiaen, O.:L'Ascension Orch, w. L. Stokowski (cnd), London SO *(rec June 18, 1970)* Intaglio ▲ ING 7421 [ADD]

Messiaen, O.:O sacrum conviviuml, w. T. Edwards (cnd), London Sinfonietta Virgin Classics ▲ CDC 59051

Messiaen, O.:Petites liturgies (3) de la Présence Divine, w. T. Edwards (cnd), London Sinfonietta Virgin Classics ▲ CDC 59051

Messiaen, O.:Rechants, w. T. Edwards (cnd), London Sinfonietta Virgin Classics ▲ CDC 59051

London Sym Chorus (cont.)

Mozart, W.A.:Ave verum corpus, w. C. Davis (cnd), London SO Philips ▲ 412873-2 [ADD]

Mozart, W.A.:Kyrie, K.341, w. K. Te Kanawa (sop), E. Bainbridge (mez), A. Davies (ten), G. Howell (bass), C. Davis (cnd), London SO [L] Philips ▲ 412873-2

Mozart, W.A.:Requiem, w. Y. Kenny (sop), A. Hodgson (mez), A. Davies (ten), G. Howell (bass), R. Hickox (cnd), Northern Sinfonia of England Virgin Classics ▲ CDZ 59648

Mozart, W.A.:Vesperae solennes, w. K. Te Kanawa (sop), E. Bainbridge (mez), A. Davies (ten), G. Howell (bass), C. Davis (cnd), London SO [L] Philips ▲ 412873-2 [ADD]

Mussorgsky, M.:Orchestral Music, w. C. Abbado (cnd), London SO—Triumphal March; Scherzo in B♭; Destruction of Sennacherib; Joshua Salammbô—Chorus of Priestesses; Khovanshchina—Prelude & Galitsin's Journey; Oedipus in Athens—Chorus of People in the Temple RCA Gold Seal ▲ 09026-61354-2 ■ 902

Orff, C.:Carmina burana, w. Barbara Hendricks (sop), John Aler (ten), Håakan Hagegård (bar), E. Mata (cnd), London SO RCA Victor ▲ 09026-68085-2; ■ 09026-68085-4

Orff, C.:Carmina burana, w. P. Walmsley-Clark (sop), J. Graham-Hall (ten), D. Maxwell (bar), R. Hickox (cnd), London SO [G, L] IMP Classics ▲ PCD 855

Orff, C.:Carmina burana, w. S. Armstrong (sop), G. English (ten), T. Allen (bar), A. Previn (cnd), London SO, St. Clement Danes Boys' Chorus [G, L] EMI Classics ▲ CDC 47411 ■ 4AM 34770

Parry, H.:Blest Pair of Sirens, w. R. Hickox (cnd), London SO Chandos 2-▲ CHAN 8641/42 [DDD]

Parry, H.:I Was Glad, w. R. Hickox (cnd), London SO Chandos 2-▲ CHAN 8641/42 [DDD]

Prokofiev, S.:Alexander Nevsky, w. Elena Obraztsova (mez), C. Abbado (cnd), London SO Deutsche Grammophon ("The Originals" series) ▲ 447419-2

Prokofiev, S.:Alexander Nevsky, w. Elena Obraztsova (mez), C. Abbado (cnd), London SO [R] Deutsche Grammophon ▲ 419603-2 [DDD]

Prokofiev, S.:Alexander Nevsky, w. Elena Obraztsova (mez), C. Abbado (cnd), London SO [R] Deutsche Grammophon 3-▲ 435151-2

Ravel, M.:Daphins et Chloé, w. A. Previn (cnd), London SO EMI Classics ("Studio DDD" series) ▲ CDD 63887 [DDD]

Rossini, G.:Il barbiere di Siviglia, w. T. Berganza (mez), L. Alva (ten), H. Prey (bar), P. Montarsolo (bass), C. Abbado (cnd), London SO [I] Deutsche Grammophon 2-▲ 415695-2 [ADD]

Rossini, G.:La Cenerentola, w. T. Berganza (mez), L. Alva (ten), R. Capecchi (bar), U. Trama (bass), C. Abbado (cnd), London SO [I] Deutsche Grammophon 2-▲ 423861-2 [ADD]

Rossini, G.:Stabat Mater, w. H. Field (sop), D. Jones (mez), A. Davies (ten), R. Earle (bass), R. Hickox (cnd), City of London Sinfonia [L] Chandos ▲ CHAN 8780 [DDD]

Stravinsky, I.:Sym of Psalms, w. M. Tilson Thomas (cnd), London SO *(rec Sept. 13-14, 1991)* Sony Classical ▲ SK 53275 [DDD]

Tippett, M.:The Ice Break, w. H. Harper (sop), S. Sylvan (bar), D. Wilson-Johnson (bar), D. Atherton (cnd), London Sinfonietta [E] Virgin Classics ▲ 59048 [DDD]

Vaughan Williams, R.:Benedictine, w. H. Harper (sop), D. Willcocks (cnd), London SO EMI Classics ▲ CDM 64722

Vaughan Williams, R.:Dona nobis pacem, w. Y. Kenny (sop), B. Terfel (b-bar), R. Hickox (cnd), London SO, St. Paul's Cathedral Choristers EMI Classics ▲ CDC 54788

Vaughan Williams, R.:Sancta civitas, w. P. Langridge (ten), B. Terfel (b-bar), R. Hickox (cnd), London SO, St. Paul's Cathedral Choirsters EMI Classics ▲ CDC 54788

Vaughan Williams, R.:Sym 1, w. F. Lott (sop), J. Summers (bar), B. Haitink (cnd), London SO [E] EMI Classics ▲ CDC 49911 [DDD]

Vaughan Williams, R.:Sym 1, w. H. Harper (sop), J. Shirley-Quirk (bar), A. Previn (cnd), London SO [E] RCA Gold Seal ▲ 60580-2-RG [ADD] ■ 60580-4-RG (CrO2)

Vaughan Williams, R.:Sym 1, w. Y. Kenny (sop), B. Rayner Cook (bar), B. Thomson (cnd), London SO [E] Chandos ▲ CHAN 8764 [DDD]

Vaughan Williams, R.:Toward the Unknown, w. B. Thomson (cnd), London SO [E] Chandos ▲ CHAN 8796 [DDD]

Verdi, G.:Aida, w. Maria Caniglia (sop—Aida), Ebe Stignani (mez—Amneris), Beniamino Gigli (ten—Radamés), Armando Borgioli (bar—Amonasro), T. Beecham (cnd), London SO *(rec Royal Opera House, Covent Garden, May 24, 1939)* Enterprise ("The Radio Years" series) 2-▲ ENT RY 62

Verdi, G.:Requiem Mass, w. Michèle Crider (sop), Markella Hatziano (mez), Gabriel Sadé (ten), Robert Lloyd (bass), R. Hickox (cnd), London SO Chandos ▲ CHAN 9490

Verdi, G.:Rigoletto, w. J. Sutherland (sop), H. Tourangeau (mez), L. Pavarotti (ten), S. Milnes (bar), M. Talvela (bass), R. Bonynge (cnd), London SO [I] London 2-▲ 414269-2 [ADD]

Verdi, G.:La traviata, w. Maria Caniglia (sop—Violetta), Baniamino Gigli (ten—Alfredo), Mario Basiola (bar—Germont), V. Gui (cnd), London SO Enterprise ("The Radio Years" series) 2-▲ ENT RY 64

Wagner, R.:Die Meistersinger von Nürnberg (sels), w. Heather Harper (sop), Helem Watts (cta), Alexander Young (ten), Donald McIntyre (bass), L. Stokowski (cnd), London SO—Suite:Prelude Act III, Dance of the Apprentices, Entrance of the Mastersingers *(rec London, Sept 23, 1967)* Music & Arts ▲ MUA CD 943

Walton, W.:Belshazzar's Feast, w. J. Shirley-Quirk (bar), A. Previn (cnd), London SO *(rec 1972)* EMI Classics ▲ CDM 64723

Walton, W.:Belshazzar's Feast, w. David Wilson-Johnson (bar), R. Hickox (cnd), London SO Classics for Pleasure ("Eminence" series) ▲ CDEMX 2225 [DDD]

Walton, W.:In Honour of the City of London, w. R. Hickox (cnd), London SO Classics for Pleasure ("Eminence" series) ▲ CDEMX 2225 [DDD]

London Sym Chorus members

Beethoven, L. van:Sym 9, "Choral Sym", w. H. Harper (sop), A. Hodgson (cta), R. Tear (ten), G. Howell (bass), R. Hickox (cnd), Northern Sinfonia of England ASV Quicksilva ▲ ASQ 6069 [DDD]

London Temple Church Choir

Master Ernest Lough, w. Ernest Lough (trb), George Thalben-Ball (pno/org) Pearl ▲ PEA 9211 (m) [AAD]

London Voices

Auber, D.-F.:Le Domino noir, w. Sumi Jo (sop), Doris Lamprecht (sop), Martine Olmeda (sop), Isabelle Vernet (sop), Jocelyne Taillon (mez), Bruce Ford (ten), Patrick Power (ten), Gilles Cachemaille (bar), Jules Bastin (bass), R. Bonynge (cnd), English CO London 2-▲ 440646-2

Auber, D.-F.:Gustave III (ballet), w. R. Bonynge (cnd), English CO London 2-▲ 440646-2

Bartók, B.:The Miraculous Mandarin, w. N. Järvi (cnd), Philharmonia Orch *(rec 10/90)* Chandos ▲ CHAN 9029 [DDD]

Beethoven, L. van:Fidelio (sels), w. Evelyn Herlitzius (sop—Leonore), Ruth Ziesak (sop—Marzelline), Stig Andersen (ten—Florestan), Herbert Lippert (ten—Jaquino), Albert Dohmen (bar—Don Pizarro), Andreas Kohn (bass—Don Fernando), Hans Tschammer (bass—Rocco), G. Solti (cnd), World Orch for Peace—Finale Act II *(rec Victoria Hall, Geneva, July 5, 1995)* London ▲ 448901-2 [DDD]

The Best of Richard Hickox, w. R. Hickox (cnd), London SO, London Sym Chorus, Penelope Walmsley-Clark (sop), John Graham-Hall (ten), D. Maxwell (bar), Southend Boys' Choir IMP Classics 3-▲ TCD 1073 [DDD]

Britten, B.:Spring Sym, w. Eiddwen Harrhy (sop), Linda Finnie (cta), Robert Tear (ten), G. Rozhdestvensky (cnd), BBC SO, BBC Sym Chorus, Southend Boys' Choir IMP ("BBC Radio Classics" series) ▲ IMP 5691752

Christmas with Kiri, w. Kiri Te Kanawa (sop), Carl Davis, Philharmonia Orch London ▲ 414632-2 LH [DDD]

Handel, G.F.:Salve Regina, w. Janet Baker (mez), Helen Watts (cta), Robert Tear (ten), Benjamin Luxon (bar), John Shirley-Quirk (bar), R. Leppard (cnd), English CO Erato 3-▲ 2292-45994-2

Holliger, H.:Scardanelli-Zyklus, w. A. Nicolet (fl), H. Holliger (cnd), Ensemble Modern ECM New Series 2-▲ 78118-21472-2 [DDD]

Lloyd, G.:John Socman (sels), w. J. Watson (sop), D. Montague (mez), T. Booth (ten), D. Wilson-Johnson (bar), M. Rivers (bar), M. George (bass), G. Lloyd (cnd), Philharmonia Orch Albany ▲ TROY 131 [DDD]

Massenet, J.:Le Roi de Lahore, w. J. Sutherland (sop), L. Lima (ten), S. Milnes (bar), N. Ghiaurov (bass), R. Bonynge (cnd), National PO London London ("Grand Opera" series) 2-▲ 433851-2 [DDD]

Mozart, W.A.:Ave verum corpus, w. C. P. Flor (cnd), Philharmonia Orch RCA Red Seal ▲ 09026-60812-2

Mozart, W.A.:Missa, K.317, w. Y. Kenny (sop), K. Kuhlmann (mez), K. Lewis (ten), D. Wilson-Johnson (bar), C. P. Flor (cnd), Philharmonia Orch RCA Red Seal ▲ 09026-60812-2

London Voices (cont.)
Shostakovich, D.:Sym 2, w. M. Rostropovich (cnd), London SO *(rec St. Augustine's Church, London, Feb. 8 & 9, 1993)* Teldec ▲ 4509-90853-2 [DDD]
Shostakovich, D.:Sym 3, w. M. Rostropovich (cnd), London SO *(rec St. Augustine's Church, London, Feb. 8 & 9, 1993)* Teldec ▲ 4509-90853-2 [DDD]
Weill, K.:Songs, w. U. Lemper (sop), J. Mauceri (cnd), Berlin RIAS Sinfonietta—Bilbao Song; Surabaya Johnny; Was die Herren Matrosen sagen; Der Song von Mandelay; Das Lied vom Branntweinandler; Youkali; Les filles de Bordeaux; Le train du Ciel; Le grand Lustucru; Le roi d'Aquitaine; J'attends un navire; Tchaikovsky; One Life to Live; This Is New; A Song of Jenny; My Ship London ▲ 436417-2 [DDD]
Weiner, L.:Hungarian Folkdance Suite, w. N. Järvi (cnd), Philharmonia Orch Chandos ▲ CHAN 9029 [DDD]

T. Edwards (cnd)
Veress, S.:Songs of the Seasons ECM New Series ▲ 78118-21555-2 [DDD]

Long Island Choral Association
Schuman, W.:The Mighty Casey, w. R. Rees (sop), T. Bogdan (ten), R. Muenz (b-bar), W. Schuman (cnd), Adirondack CO, Gregg Smith Singers [E] Premier ▲ PRCD 1009 [ADD]

J.-P. Lore Vocal Ensemble
Schubert, Ferdinand:Requiem, w. D. Degos (trb), K. Markus (ten), R. Soyer (bass), J. Galard (org), J.-P. Lore (cnd), French Oratorio Orch, Petits Chanteurs de Notre Dame de la Joie *(rec Nov. 9-11, 1980 & Jan. 25)* Esoldun ▲ MOS 1003 [ADD]
Schubert, Franz:Requiem, w. D. Degos (trb), K. Markus (ten), R. Soyer (bass), J. Galard (org), J.-P. Lore (cnd), French Oratorio Orch, Petits Chanteurs de Notre Dame de la Joie *(rec Nov. 9-11, 1980 & Jan. 25)* Esoldun ▲ MOS 1003 [ADD]

Lorient Conservatory Chorus
Orff, C.:Carmina burana, w. Elisabeth Vidal (sop), Alexander Stevensen (ten), André Cognet (bass), P. Kuentz (cnd), Paul Kuentz Orch, Paul Kuentz Choir, Mouez Armor Chorale, Notre Dame College Chorus Pierre Verany ▲ PVY 730044

Los Angeles Chamber Singers
P. Rutenberg (cnd)
Barber, S.:Songs—Heaven-Haven, Op. 13/1 [1941]; Let down the Bars, O Death, Op. 8/2 [1942]; Reincarnations, Op. 16 [1942]; 2 Songs, Op. 42 [1969] Klavier ▲ KCD 11052 [DDD]
Macdowell, E.:Northern Songs Klavier ▲ KCD 11052 [DDD]
Mechem, K.:Five Centuries of Spring Klavier ▲ KCD 11052 [DDD]
Rutenberg, P.:Ballad of the Buffalo Skinners, w. John Reyheim (ten), Raymond McLeod (bass) [trad.; ed. & expanded Peter Rutenberg] Klavier ▲ KCD 11052 [DDD]
Shenandoah:An American Chorister, 1890-1990 Klavier ▲ KCD 11052 [DDD]
Stevens, H.:Campion Suite Klavier ▲ KCD 11052 [DDD]

Los Angeles Master Chorale
Rodgers, R.:The King & I, w. J. Andrews (sgr—Anna Leonowens), L. Salonga (sgr—Tuptim), B. Kingsley (sgr—The King), P. Bryson (sgr—Lun Tha), M. Horne (mez—Lady Thiang), M. Liufau (sgr—Prince Chulalongkorn), E. Kingsley (sgr—Louis Leonowens), R. Moore (sgr—Sir Edward Ramsay), M. Sheen (sgr—The Kralahome), J. Mauceri (cnd), Hollywood Bowl Orch *(rec Culver City, CA, Apr 1992)* Philips ▲ 438007-2 [DDD]
Verdi, G.:Pezzi sacri, w. Yvonne Minton (mez), Z. Mehta (cnd), Los Angeles PO *(rec 1970)* London ("Double Decker" series) 2-▲ 444833-2 [ADD]

Los Angeles Master Chorale Women's Voices
Cherkassky, S.:Prélude pathétique, w. Shura Cherkassky (pno) Biddulph ▲ LHW 034
Debussy, C.:La Damoiselle élue, w. D. Upshaw (sop), P. Rasmussen (mez), E.-P. Salonen (cnd), Los Angeles PO *(rec Feb. 22, 1993)* Sony Classical ▲ SK 58952 [DDD]

Los Angeles Vocal Arts Ensemble
Brahms, J.:Liebeslieder Waltzes SATB, w. A. Guzelimian (pno), Herrera (pno) [G] Elektra/Nonesuch ▲ 79008-2 [DDD]
Brahms, J.:Neue Liebeslieder Waltzes, w. A. Guzelimian (pno), Herrera (pno) [G] Elektra/Nonesuch ▲ 79008-2 [DDD]

Loughton High School Chorus
Humperdinck, E.:Hänsel und Gretel, w. E. Schwarzkopf (sop), E. Grümmer (sop), A. Felbermayer (sop), M. von Ilosvay (mez), E. Schürhoff (mez), J. Metternich (bar), H. von Karajan (cnd), Philharmonia Orch, Bancroft's School Chorus [G] *(rec 1953)* EMI Classics ("Studio" series) 2-▲ CDMB 69293 (m) [ADD]

Louisville Univ Chorus
R. Spalding (cnd)
Balada, L.:Maria Sabina, w. Hector Cortés (nar—Executioner), Amèrica Dunham (nar—Maria Sabina), Burwell Hardy (nar—Town Crier), Guillermo Helguera (nar—Constable), J. Mester (cnd), Louisville Orch *(rec Feb 5, 1973)* New World ▲ 80498-2

Louvre Choir
Handel, G.F.:Amadigi di Gaula, w. E. Harrhy (sop—Melissa), J. Smith (sop—Oriana), P. Bertin (mez—Orgando), B. Fink (cta—Dardano), N. Stutzmann (cta—Amadigi), M. Minkowski (cnd), Louvre Musicians [I] Erato 2-▲ 2292-45490-2 [DDD]

Emily Lowe Singers
Choral Tapestries:An Anthology of Contemporary American Choral Music Northeastern ("Classical Arts" series) ▲ NOR 241 ■ NR 241-C

Lucca St. Cecilia Choir
Boccherini, L.:Credo & Dixit Dominus, w. G. Cosmi (cnd), Lucca Teatro Comunale Giglio Orch [L] Bongiovanni ▲ GB 2087 [DDD]
Boccherini, L.:Villacicos al nacimiento (9), w. G. Cosmi (cnd), Lucca Teatro Comunale Giglio Orch [L] Bongiovanni ▲ GB 2087 [DDD]

Lucca Teatro Comunale del Giglio Chorus
Catalani, A.:Dejanice, w. C. Basto (sop), M. L. Garbato (sop), O. Garaventa (ten), R. Massis (bar), C. Zardo (bass), J. Latham-König (cnd), Lucca Teatro Comunale del Giglio Orch [I] *(rec 9/6/85)* Bongiovanni 2-▲ GB 2031/32 [DDD]
Catalani, A.:Edmea, w. M. Sokolinska Noto (sop), M. Frusoni (ten), M. Chingari (bar), P. Lefebvre (bass), A. Nosotti (bass), G. Pasella (bass), G. del Vivo (bass), M. de Bernart (cnd), Lucca Teatro Comunale Giglio Orch [I] *(rec live 9/89)* Bongiovanni 2-▲ GB 2093/94 [DDD]
Catalani, A.:Loreley, w. M. Colalillo (sop), M. L. Garbato (sop), P. Visconti (ten), A. Cassis (bar), N. Annovazzi (cnd), Lucca Teatro Comunale del Giglio Orch *(rec live 9/19/82)* Bongiovanni 2-▲ GB 2015/16 [ADD]

Lucerne Boy's Choir
Christmas with Ramón Vargas, w. Ramón Vargas (ten), Vienna Concilium Musicum [cnd:Paul Angerer] *(rec live, Jesuitenkirche in Lucerne, Dec 21, 1995)* Claves ▲ CD 509612 [DDD]

Lucerne Festival Chorus
Beethoven, L. van:Sym 9, "Choral Sym", w. Elisabeth Schwarzkopf (sop), Elsa Cavelti (mez), Ernst Haefliger (ten), Otto Edelmann (bass), W. Furtwängler (cnd), Philharmonia Orch *(rec Aug 22, 1954)* Music & Arts ▲ CD 790 [ADD]
Fauré, G.:Requiem, w. E. Mathis (sop), K. Widmer (bass), J. Fournet (cnd), Swiss Festival Orch *(rec 1984)* Koch Treasure ▲ 31619-2 [DDD]

Lucerne Singers
M. Venzago (cnd)
Janácek, L.:The Diary of One Who Disappeared, w. Clara Wirz (alt), Peter Keller (ten), Mario Venzago (pno) Accord ▲ ACD 220312 [DDD]

Lugano Chamber Society Chorus
Monteverdi, C.:Madrigals, w. Basia Retchitzka (sop), Eric Tappy (ten), Rodolfo Malacarne (ten), Laerte Malaguti (bar), James Loomis (bass), E. Loehrer (cnd), Lugano Chamber Society Orch—8 Madrigali Guerrieri e Amorosi Accord ▲ ACD 220872
Monteverdi, C.:Music of, w. Egidio Roveda (vc), Luciano Sgrizzi (hpd), E. Loehrer (cnd), Lugano Chamber Society Orch—Altri Canti di Marte; Le Combat de Tancrede et Clorinde; Lamento Della Ninfa; Perche T'en Fuggi, O Fillide; Hor Ch'el Ciel e la Terra Accord ▲ ACD 220882

Lugano Chamber Society Chorus (cont.)
Monteverdi, C.:Sacred Vocal Music, w. E. Loehrer (cnd), Lugano Chamber Society Instrumental Ensemble—Magnificat (for 6 voices); Vespro della Beata Vergine; Planctus Mariae; Selva Morale e Spiritual; Cantate Domino; Parnassus Musicus Ferdinandeus di G.B. Bonometti; Ab Aeterno Ordinata Sum; Selva Morale e Spirituale; O Beatae Viae; Symbolae Diversorum Musicorum di L. Calvo; Gloria; Selva Morale e Spirituale Accord ▲ ACD 202802 [ADD]
Palestrina, G.:Sacred Music, w. Luciana Ticinelli-Fattori (sop), Maria Minetto (mez), Laerte Malaguti (bar), James Loomis (bass), E. Loehrer (cnd), Lugano Chamber Society Instrumental Ensemble—Vexilla Regis Prodeunt; Adoramus Te; Laudario Di Cortona Accord ▲ ACD 201562 [AAD]

E. Loehrer (cnd)
Monteverdi, C.:Con Accord ▲ ACD 220892 [AAD]
Palestrina, G.:Stabat mater Accord ▲ ACD 201562 [AAD]

A. Sacchetti (cnd)
Jommelli, N.:La Passione di Gesù Cristo, w. E. Loehrer (cnd), Lugano Chamber Society Orch Accord 2-▲ ACD 204352 [AAD]

Lugo Teatro Comunale Rossini Chorus
Donizetti, G.:Betly, w. S. Rigacci (sop), M. Comencini (ten), R. Scaltriti (bar), B. Rigacci (cnd), Emilia Romagna Arturo Toscanini SO *(rec live, 6/90)* Bongiovanni 2-▲ GB 2091/92 [DDD]
Donizetti, G.:Le Convenienze Teatrali, w. M.A. Peters (sop), A. Cicogna (mez), S. Tedesco (ten), R. Scaltriti (bar), B. Rigacci (cnd), Emilia Romagna Arturo Toscanini SO [I] *(rec live, 6/90)* Bongiovanni 2-▲ GB 2091/92 [DDD]

Lulea Chamber Choir
E. Isacson (cnd)
Modern Music for Choir BIS ▲ CD 4 [AAD]
Rautavaara, E.:Ludus verbalis *(rec Feb. 22, 1974)* BIS ▲ CD 66 [AAD]

Lund Univ Choir
Lund University Choir Sings in Varen BIS ▲ CD 162 [ADD]
Peterson-Berger, W.:En Fjällfärd BIS ▲ CD 162 [ADD]

Lund Univ Male Voice Choir
F. Bohlin (cnd)
Nordic Romance:Songs for Male-Voice Choir *(rec Apr. 23-25, 1982)* BIS ▲ CD 206 [AAD]

Lund's Student Choral Society
Tubin, E.:Ave Maria, w. JanÅke Larson (org), N. Järvi (cnd) BIS ▲ CD 269 [DDD]
Tubin, E.:The Retreating Soldier's Song, w. Roland Rydell (bar), Janåke Larson (pno), N. Järvi (cnd) BIS ▲ CD 269 [DDD]

N. Järvi (cnd)
Tubin, E.:Ave Maria BIS ▲ CD 297 [DDD]
Tubin, E.:Requiem for Fallen Soldiers BIS ▲ CD 297 [DDD]
Tubin, E.:The Retreating Soldier's Song BIS ▲ CD 297 [DDD]

Luxembourg Monks' Choir
Regina Caeli Philips ("Sequenza" series) ■ 420809-4

Lynceus Concert
Gaburo, K.:Enough!—(not enough)—, w. Steven Schick (perc) Music & Arts ▲ CD 832 [DDD]

Lynn Murray Chorus
Bernstein, L.:On the Town, w. M. Martin (sgr), N. Walker (sgr), B. Comden (sgr), A. Green (sgr), Tutti Camarata Orch, Leonard Joy Orch, Lynn Murray Orch MCA Classics ▲ MCAD 10280 (m) [AAD]

Lyon National Chorus
Beethoven, L. van:Christus am Ölberg, w. M. Pick-Hieronimi (sop), J. Anderson (sop), V. von Halem (bass), S. Baudo (cnd), Lyon National Orch [G] Harmonia Mundi France ▲ HMC 905181
Fauré, G.:Cantique de Jean Racine, w. J.-L. Gil (org), E. Krivine (cnd) Denon ▲ CO 77527 2 [DDD]
Fauré, G.:Requiem, w. G. Le Roi (sop), F. Le Roux (bar), E. Krivine (cnd), Lyon National Orch [L] Denon ▲ CO 77527 [DDD]
Kagel, M.:Music of, w. P. Méfano (cnd), Lyon Orch, Ensemble 2E2M—Vox Humana?; Finale; Fürst Igor, Stravinsky Accord ▲ ACD 201262 [DDD]
Mendelssohn, F.:Athalie, w. Danielle Borst (sop), Brigitte Desnoues (sop), Carolyn Watkinson (cta), Jean-Marc Avocat (sgr), Souad Natech (sgr), B. Tetu (cnd), Lorraine PO Koch Schwann ▲ SCH 314282 [DDD]
Poulenc, F.:Litanies à la vierge noire, w. S. Baudo (cnd), Lyon National Orch— Salve; Stabat [F] Harmonia Mundi France ▲ HMC 905149
Poulenc, F.:Stabat mater, w. M. Lagrange (sop), S. Baudo (cnd), Lyon National Orch [L] Harmonia Mundi France ▲ HMC 905149

S. Baudo (cnd)
Poulenc, F.:Salve regina [L] Harmonia Mundi France ▲ HMC 905149

Lyon Regional Conservatory Women's Voice Choir
R. Clément (cnd)
Messiaen, O.:Petites liturgies (3) de la Présence Divine REM ▲ REM 311204 [DDD]

Lyric Opera Center Chorus
Weisgall, H.:Six Characters in Search of an Author, w. E. Byrne (sop—Stepdaughter), S. Foster (sop—Prompter), E. Furtal (sop—Coloratura), J. King (mez—Mezzo), N. Maultsby (mez—Mother), P. LoVerne (cta—Madame Pace), D. Pritchett (alt—Wardrobe Mistress), B. Fowler (ten—Tenore Boffo), K. Anderson (ten—Director), A. Schroeder (bar—Accompanist), P. Zawisza (bar—Stage Manager), R. Orth (bar—Father), G. Lehman (bar—Son), M. Wadsworth (b-bar—Basso Cantante), L. Schaenen (cnd), Chicago Lyric Opera Orch *(rec Chicago, June 14 & 16, 1990)* New World 2-▲ 80454-2

Lyubomir Pipkov Sofia Chamber Choir
Musica Sacra, w. I. Stiglich (org) Jade ▲ JAD C095

Macalester Concert Choir
D. Warland (cnd)
Roussakis, N.:Night Speech *(rec St. Paul, MN, Nov, 1969)* CRI ▲ CD 709 [DDD]

John McCarthy Singers
Tiomkin, D.:Film Music, w. L. Johnson (cnd), London Studio SO—Duel in the Sun; Giant; High Noon; Night Passage; Red River; Rio Bravo Unicorn ("Souvenir" series) ▲ UKCD 2011 [DDD]

McCullough Chorale
D. McCullogh (cnd)
Hailstork, A.:Choral Music—The Lamb; 7 Songs of the Rubaiyat; A Carol for All Children *(rec live, 1991 & 1994)* Albany ▲ TROY 156 [DDD]
Hailstork, A.:Settings from the Song of Soloman—Arise My Beloved; Set Me As a Seal *(rec live, 1991 & 1994)* Albany ▲ TROY 156 [DDD]
Hailstork, A.:Songs of Life & Love—The Cloths of Heaven; I Will Sing of Life; Nocturne *(rec live, 1991 & 1994)* Albany ▲ TROY 156 [DDD]
Hailstork, A.:Spiritual Songs—O Praise the Lord; My Lord What a Moanin'; Crucifixion *(rec live, 1991 & 1994)* Albany ▲ TROY 156 [DDD]

Madrid Radio-TV Chorus
Puccini, G.:Madama Butterfly, w. Montserrat Caballé (sop—Cio-Cio-San), Carmen Rigai (mez—Suzuki), Bernabé Martí (ten—Pinkerton), Diego Monjo (ten—Goro), Juan Rico (ten—Yamadori), Manuel Ausensi (bar—Sharpless), Jose Lemar (bass—Bonze), Antonio Leval (bass—Imperial Commissioner), Alejandro Chiara (bass—Registrar), G. Rivoli (cnd), Madrid Radio-TV Orch *(rec Madrid, June 12, 1968)* Legato Classics 2-▲ LCD 210-2 [ADD]

Madrigal Chamber Choir
M. Constantin (cnd)
The Passion & Ressurrection of Jesus, w. George Oancea (nar) Electrecord ▲ ELC 136 [DDD]

Madrigal Ensemble
Boieldieu, F.-A.:Jean de Paris, w. J.-P. Kreder (cnd), ORTF Lyric Orch Musidisc ▲ MUS 201782 [AAD]

Madrigalists Choir
Galonski, Kajdasz (cnd)
Gorczycki, G.G.:Sacred Choral Music, w. R. Stacewicz (sop), I. Tkaczyk (alt), A. Pagowska (alt), E. Sasiadek (ten), W. Brychcy (bass), Wroclaw Orch, Capella Bydgostiensis Pro Musica Antiqua, Polish Radio Chorus—Completorium; In virtute tua; Iudica me deus; Laetatus sum; Missa paschalis [L] *(rec 1966)* Olympia ▲ OCD 320 [AAD]

Maggio Musicale Florentino Chorus—see Florence Maggio Musicale Chorus

Magic Circle Opera Ensemble
Grana, E.D.:Stones, Time & Elements:A Humanist Requiem, w. M. Brecker (sax), R.A. Clark (cnd), Manhattan CO — Newport Classic ▲ NPT 85573

Magnificat Choir
Ramsey, R.:Choral Music, w. P. Cave (cnd), Magnificat Players—Almighty & Everlasting God; We Humbly Beseech; Go Perjur'd Man!; When David Heard; Te Deum; Nunc Dimittis; How Are the Mighty Fallen; others — ASV ("Gaudeamus" series) ▲ ASV 138 [DDD]

Mainz Bach Choir
Saint-Saëns, C.:Oratorio de Noël, w. V. Schweizer (sop), E. Wiens (sop), H. Jung (mez), F. Melzer (ten), K. Widmer (bass), D. Hellmann (cnd), Mainz Bach Orch *(rec 1976)* — Calig ▲ CAL 50512 [AAD]

D. Hellmann (cnd)
Reger, M.:Cantatas, w. V. Schweizer (sop), A. Hellmann (alt), R. Julius Koch (ob), R. Hellmann, U. Soldan (vn), B. Banz (va), C. Hellmann (vc), C. Fink (db), H. Bilgram (org) — Entrée ▲ 0049 [ADD]

Mainz Cathedral Choir
Missa Russica, w. Russian Monks Choir, Moscow Cathedral Choir, Moscow Holy Synod Boys' Choir [cnd:Victor Popov] — Koch Schwann ▲ SCH 312122 ■ SCH 212124

Maîtrise de Garçons de Colmar

A. Steyer (cnd)
Alain, J.:Music of, w. R. Garreau de Labarre (org)—12 works for organ &/or choir *(rec May 1990)* — K617 ▲ 7005 [DDD]
Duruflé, M.:Motets on Gregorian Chants, Op. 10 *(rec 5/90)* — K617 ▲ 7005 [DDD]

Maîtrise de la Cathédrale
Puccini, G.:Turandot, w. M. Caballé (sop—Turnadot), M. Freni (sop—Liu), J. Carreras (ten—Calaf), M. Sénéchal (ten—Emperor Altoum), V. Sardinero (bar—Ping), P. Plishka (bass—Timur), A. Lombard (cnd), Strasbourg PO, Rhine Opera Chorus — EMI Classics ▲ CDMB 65293

Maîtrise de la Loire

Litsova, Berthelon (cnd)
Arkadiev, M.:Missa brevis, w. Louis Robilliard (org), Saratov Phil Choir — REM ▲ REM 311275 [DDD]
Bortnyansky, D.:Sacred Choral Music, w. Louis Robilliard (org), Saratov Phil Choir—Cons Nos. 34 & 35 — REM ▲ REM 311275 [DDD]
Duruflé, M.:Motets on Gregorian Chants, Op. 10, w. Louis Robilliard (org), Saratov Phil Choir — REM ▲ REM 311275 [DDD]
Mendelssohn, F.:Motets, Op. 39, w. Louis Robilliard (org), Saratov Phil Choir — REM ▲ REM 311275 [DDD]
Poulenc, F.:Litanies à la vierge noire, w. Louis Robilliard (org), Saratov Phil Choir — REM ▲ REM 311275 [DDD]
Tchesnokov, P.:Liturgie 6, w. Louis Robilliard (org), Saratov Phil Choir — REM ▲ REM 311275 [DDD]

Maîtrise de Paris
Bruneau, A.:Lazare, w. Françoise Pollet (sop), Mary Saint-Palais (sop), Sylvie Sullé (mez), Jean-Luc Viala (ten), Laurent Naouri (b-bar), J. Mercier (cnd), French National Orch, Vittoria French Regional Choir — Adès ▲ ADE 204512
Bruneau, A.:Requiem, w. Françoise Pollet (sop), Mary Saint-Palais (sop), Sylvie Sullé (mez), Jean-Luc Viala (ten), Laurent Naouri (b-bar), J. Mercier (cnd), French National Orch, Vittoria French Regional Choir — Adès ▲ ADE 204512

P. Marco (cnd)
Mozart, W.A.:Ave verum corpus, w. Noemi Rime (sop), Christine Batty (mez), Stuart Patterson (ten), Bernard Deletre (bass), G. Vashegyi (cnd), Budapest Orfeo Orch — Pierre Verany ▲ PVY 730058 [DDD]
Mozart, W.A.:Missa, K.317, w. Noemi Rime (sop), Christine Batty (mez), Stuart Patterson (ten), Bernard Deletre (bass), G. Vashegyi (cnd), Budapest Orfeo Orch — Pierre Verany ▲ PVY 730058 [DDD]
Mozart, W.A.:Vesperae solennes, w. Noemi Rime (sop), Christine Batty (mez), Stuart Patterson (ten), Bernard Deletre (bass), G. Vashegyi (cnd), Budapest Orfeo Orch — Pierre Verany ▲ PVY 730058 [DDD]

Maîtrise des Hauts-de-Seine members

F. Bardot (cnd)
Mozart, W.A.:Zauberflöte, w. Birgit Been (sop), Nathalie Boissy (sop), Marianne Seibel (sop), Renate Springer (sop), Elizabeth Vidal (sop), Eleanor James (mez), Salvador Guzman (ten), Herbert Hechenberger (ten), Wolfgang Newmann (ten), Klaus Häger (bass), Philip Langshaw (bass), Hans-Georg Moser (bass), P. Kuentz (cnd), Paul Kuentz Orch, Paul Kuentz Choirs — Pierre Verany 2-▲ PVY 730055 [DDD]

Maîtrise des Petits Chanteurs
Mozart, W.A.:Requiem, w. J.-P. Sarcos (cnd), Palais Royal Orch — Pavane ▲ 7336

Maîtrise Gabriel Fauré
Caplet, A.:Le miroir de Jésus, w. R. Allouche (mez), P. Bender (cnd), Cannes-Provençe Alpes-Côte d'Azur Regional Orch — Sonpact ▲ SPT 94010 [DDD]

Maîtrise National de Versailles
Les Chemins du Baroque (The Paths of the Baroque), w. G. Garrido (cnd), Elyma Vocal Ensemble, Elyma Instrumental Ensemble, Cordoba Children's Choir Garrado, Compañia Musical de las Americas, La Grande Ecurie et la Chambre du Roy [cnd:Jean-Claude Malgoire], Compañia Musical de las Americas, La Fenice [cnd:Josep Cabré], Ense — K617 ("First 4 volumes of K617" series) ▲ 7042

Malmö Chamber Choir
Berwald, F.:Estrella de Soria (sels), w. L. Nordin (sop), K. Dalayman (sgr), S. Smith (sgr), A. Lorentzson (sgr), C. Sköld (sgr), S. Westerberg (cnd), Helsingborg SO — Musica Sveciae ▲ MSV 523 [DDD]
Peterson-Berger, W.:Album of 8 Songs *(rec Mar. 28–29, 1981)* — BIS ▲ CD 181 [AAD]
Ryelandt, J.:Missa 6 vocibus *(rec Mar. 28–29, 1981)* — BIS ▲ CD 181 [AAD]
Söderman, A.:Spiritual Songs *(rec Mar. 28–29, 1981)* — BIS ▲ CD 181 [AAD]

Malmö Radio Chorus
Hallén, A.:Harald der Wiking (act III, final scene), w. M. Meyerson (sgr—Berta), S. Lindström (sgr—Sigrun), A. Ljungholm (sgr—Harald), S. Sjöstedt (sgr—Sigleif), K. Jacobsson (sgr—Gudmund/Torgrim), S. Rybrant (cnd), Malmö SO [G] *(rec 6/6/74)* — Musica Sveciae ▲ MSCD 621 [AAD]

Malmö Sym Chorus
Schnittke, A.:Faust Cant, w. Mikael Bellini (alt), Inger Blom (cta), Louis Devos (ten), Urik Cold (bass), J. DePreist (cnd), Malmö SO — BIS ("BIS Twins" series) 2-▲ CD 437/507

Manchester Cathedral Boys' Choir
Davies, P.M.:The Turn of the Tide, w. P. M. Davies (cnd), BBC PO, Manchester Cathedral Girl's Choir, Manchester Cathedral Voluntary Boys' Choir, Manchester Grammar School Choir — Collins Classics ▲ 13902 [DDD]
Gregson, E.:Missa Brevis Pacem, w. James Keenan (trb), Henry Herford (bar), E. Gregson (cnd), Royal Northern College of Music Wind Orch — Doyen ▲ CD 043 [DDD]

Manchester Cathedral Girls' Choir
Davies, P.M.:The Turn of the Tide, w. P. M. Davies (cnd), BBC PO, Manchester Cathedral Boys' Choir, Manchester Cathedral Voluntary Boys' Choir, Manchester Grammar School Choir — Collins Classics ▲ 13902 [DDD]

Manchester Cathedral Voluntary Boys' Choir
Davies, P.M.:The Turn of the Tide, w. P. M. Davies (cnd), BBC PO, Manchester Cathedral Girl's Choir, Manchester Cathedral Boys' Choir, Manchester Grammar School Choir — Collins Classics ▲ 13902 [DDD]

Manchester Grammar School Choir
Davies, P.M.:The Turn of the Tide, w. P. M. Davies (cnd), BBC PO, Manchester Cathedral Girl's Choir, Manchester Cathedral Boys' Choir, Manchester Cathedral Voluntary Boys' Choir — Collins Classics ▲ 13902 [DDD]

Manhattan Opera Chorus
Bizet, G.:Carmen, w. A. Maliponte (sop), M. Horne (mez), J. McCracken (bar), T. Krause (bar), L. Bernstein (cnd), Metropolitan Opera Orch [F] *(rec 1973)* — Deutsche Grammophon 3-▲ 427440-2 [ADD]

Manhattan School of Music Opera Chorus
Rorem, N.:Miss Julie, w. Theodora Fried (sgr—Miss Julie), Heather Sarris (sgr—Christine, the cook), Laurelyn Watson (sgr—Young Girl), David Blackburn (sgr—Mr. Niels), Mark Mulligan (sgr—Young Boy), Philip Torre (sgr—John, the valet), Judd Ernster (bass), D. Gilbert (cnd), Manhattan School of Music Opera Orch — Newport Classic 2-▲ NPT 85605 [DDD]

Mannheim Chorus Opera
Rihm, W.:Die Hamletmaschine, w. P. Schneider (cnd), Mannheim National Theater Orch [G] — Wergo 2-▲ WER 6195-2

Mantova Teatro Sociale Chorus
Cherubini, L.:Médée, w. M. Olivero (sop), E. Baggiore (sgr), L. Ganbelli (bass), A. Lo Forese (sgr), N. Rescigno (cnd), Mantova Teatro Sociale Orch [I] *(rec live, Mantova 1/23/71)* — Myto 2-▲ 2 MCD 91136 [ADD]

Marburg Bach Choir
Zelenka, J.D.:Missa votiva, w. C. Hampe (sop), E. Graf (cta), J. Duske (ten), J. Gebhardt (bass), W. Wehnert (cnd), Hesse Bach Collegium [L] — Thorofon ▲ CTH 2172 [DDD]

W. Wehnert (cnd)
Brahms, J.:Choral Music—Die Wollust in den Maien; Mit Lust tät ich ausreiten; Wach auf, meins Herzens Schöne; Da unten im Tale; Heimliche Liebe; Abschiedslied; Lebewohl; Des Abends *(rec Marburg)* — Musicaphon ▲ M 56814 [DDD]
Loewe, C.:Choral Music—Im Frühling *(rec Marburg)* — Musicaphon ▲ M 56814 [DDD]
Mendelssohn, F.:Choral Music—Frühlingslied; Frühzeitiger Frühling; Die Waldvögelein; Im Walde; Morgengebet; Abschied vom Walde; Entflieh mit mir; Es fiel ein Reif in der Frühlingsnacht; Auf ihrem Grab *(rec Marburg)* — Musicaphon ▲ M 56814 [DDD]
Reger, M.:Choral Music—Der Gruss; Ich hab' die Nacht geträumet *(rec Marburg)* — Musicaphon ▲ M 56814 [DDD]
Schumann, R.:Choral Music—Zierlich ist des Vogels Tritt im Schnee *(rec Marburg)* — Musicaphon ▲ M 56814 [DDD]
Silcher, F.:Choral Music—Wenn ich ein Vöglein wär; Wenn alle Brünnlein fliessen; Ich weiss nicht, was soll es bedeuten; Nun leb wohl, du kleine Gasse *(rec Marburg)* — Musicaphon ▲ M 56814 [DDD]
Zelenka, J.D.:Missa sanctissimae trinitatis, w. Monika Frimmer (sop), Elisabeth Graf (cta), Markus Brutscher (ten) — Thorofon ▲ CTH 2265

Marchigiana Phil Chorus
Mozart, W.A.:Così fan tutte, w. A. C. Antonacci (sop—Fiordiligi), M. Bacelli (sop—Dorabella), L. Cherici (sop—Despina), R. Decker (ten—Ferrando), A. Dohmen (bar—Gugliemo), S. Bruscantini (bar—Don Alfonso), G. Kuhn (cnd), Marchigiana PO [I] *(rec live, Teatro Lauro Rossi at the Festival di Macerata, Aug. 3, 1990)* — Orfeo 3-▲ 243913 [DDD]

Patrick Marco Vocal Ensemble
Boieldieu, F.-A.:Le Calife de Bagdad, w. N. Monestier (sop), Ouaki (sgr), S. Elloir (sgr), Plantak (sgr), Fokenoy (sgr), B. Thomas (cnd), Bernard Thomas CO [F] — Thésis ▲ THC 82015 [DDD]
Loussier, J.:Lumières, w. Déborah Rees (sop), James Bowman (ct), André Arpino (perc), J.-P. Wallez (cnd), Harmonia Nova Orch *(rec Studio de Miraval, 1957)* — Media 7 ▲ CD 707 [DDD]

Margherita Theater Chorus
Gounod, C.:Faust, w. Renata Scotto (sop—Margherita), Anna di Stasio (mez—Marta), Flaviano Labò (ten—Faust), Edoardo Gimenez (ten—Siebel), Piero Cappuccilli (bar—Valentino), Bruno Grella (bar—Wagner), Ruggero Raimondi (bass—Mefistofele), M. Gusella (cnd), Margherita Theater Orch *(rec Genova, 1970)* — Golden Age of Opera 2-▲ GAO 170/71 [ADD]

Maria Treu Basilica Chorus
Leopold I:Missa pro defunctis, w. G. Kramer (cnd), Convivium Musicum Vindobonense — Preiser ▲ 90067 [ADD]
Werner, G.J.:Requiem, w. G. Kramer (cnd), Convivium Musicum Vindobonense — Preiser ▲ 90067 [ADD]

Marseille Opera Chorus
Verdi, G.:Simon Boccanegra, w. Alberto Cupido (ten), Ned Barth (bar), José Van Dam (b-bar), Manfred Schenk (bass), Daniela Longhi (sgr), Dino Musio (sgr), M. Veltri (cnd), Marseille Opera Orch — Lyrinx 3-▲ LYX 127 [DDD]

Massenet Festival Choir
Massenet, J.:Esclarmonde, w. Denia Mazzola (sop), José Sempere (ten), Christian Tréguier (bar), Hélène Parraguin (sgr), P. Fournillier (cnd), Franz Liszt SO *(rec live, Massenet Festival, Saint-Etienne)* — Koch Schwann 3-▲ SCH 312692 [DDD]

Master Chorale of Orange County
Prokofiev, S.:Alexander Nevsky, w. C. Cairns (mez), A. Previn (cnd), Los Angeles PO [R] — Telarc ▲ CD 80143 [DDD]

W. Hall (cnd)
Duruflé, M.:Motets on Gregorian Chants, Op. 10—Ubi caritas; Tota pulchra es; Tu es Petrus; Tantum ergo — Summit ▲ DCD 134 [DDD] ■ DCD 134
Duruflé, M.:Requiem — Summit ▲ DCD 134 [DDD] ■ DCD 134
Rachmaninoff, S.:All-Night Vigil, w. Jonathan Mack (ten) *(rec Santa Ana High School Auditorium, Santa Ana, CA)* — Klavier ▲ KCD 11065 [DDD]

Michael May Festival Chorus
Falla, M. de:La vida breve, w. A. Nafé (mez), A. Ordóñoz (ton), J. López-Cobos (cnd), Cincinnati SO [Sp] — Telarc ▲ CD 80317 [DDD]
Rodgers, R.:The Sound of Music, w. E. Farrell (sop), F. von Stade (mez), Håkan Hagegård (ten), B. Daniels (sgr), L. D. von Schlanbusch (sgr), et al., E. Kunzel (cnd), Cincinnati Pops Orch [1987 studio cast] — Telarc ▲ CD 80162 [DDD] ■ CS 30162
Rossini, G.:Stabat Mater, w. Sung-Sook Lee (sop), Florence Quivar (mez), Kenneth Riegel (ten), Paul Plishka (bass), T. Schippers (cnd), Cincinnati SO *(rec 1975)* — Vox Box 2-▲ CDX 5141 [ADD]

Michael May Festival Chorus Women's Voices
Busoni, F.:Turandot (suite), w. M. Gielen (cnd), Cincinnati SO *(rec 1983)* — Vox Box 2-▲ CDX 5137 [DDD]

Mazowsze Song & Dance Company
God Saving Poland *(rec Warsaw Music Acad. Concert Hall; Skalka Paulite Church, Cracow; Dec 1980; Apr 1983; Mar 1)* — Polskie Nagrania Edition ▲ ECD 034

Mediatrix Ensemble

J.B. Göschl (cnd)
Hildegard Of Bingen:Sacred Songs—Ave Maria; O clarissima Mater; O splendissima gemma; Hodie aperuit; Quia ergo femina; Cum processit; Cum erubuerint; O frondens virga; O quam magnum; Ave generosa; O virga ac diadema; O tu suavissima virga *(rec June 1996)* — Calig ▲ CAL 50982 [DDD]

Medlemmar Concert Choir
Söderman, A.:Marshal Stig's Daughters, w. H.-P. Frank (cnd), Helsingborg SO, Mikaeli Chamber Choir, Helsingborgs Concert Choir [Sw] — Musica Sveciae ▲ MSCD 513

Mellstock Choir
Under the Greenwood Tree:The Carols & Dances of [Thomas] Hardy's Wessex, w. Mellstock Band — Saydisc ▲ CDSDL 360 [DDD] ■ SDLC 360 (D)

Melodic Choir
Mendelssohn, F.:Elijah (sels), w. A. Coates (cnd), Cape Town SO—Hear Ye Israel, Be Not Afraid — Claremont ▲ GSE 78 50 54

Memphis Boychoir
Shout the Glad Tidings, w. Memphis Chamber Choir, Diane Meredith Belcher (org) *(rec 1992)* — Pro Organo ▲ POCD 7037 [DDD]
What Sweeter Music:Carols for the Year Round, w. Memphis Chamber Choir, Diane Meredith Belcher (org) *(rec 1991)* — Pro Organo ▲ POCD 7031 [DDD]

Memphis Chamber Choir
Shout the Glad Tidings, w. Memphis Boychoir, Diane Meredith Belcher (org) *(rec 1992)* — Pro Organo ▲ POCD 7037 [DDD]
What Sweeter Music:Carols for the Year Round, w. Memphis Boychoir, Diane Meredith Belcher (org) *(rec 1991)* — Pro Organo ▲ POCD 7031 [DDD]

Mendelssohn Club Chorus Philadelphia
Handel, G.F.:Messiah, w. Kathleen Battle (sop), Florence Quivar (mez), John Aler (ten), Samuel Ramey (bass), A. Davis (cnd), Toronto SO [E] — EMI Classics ▲ CDC 49407 [DDD]; ■ 4DS 49407 (D)

Mendelssohn Club Chorus Philadelphia (cont.)
Handel, G.F.:Messiah, w. Kathleen Battle (sop), Florence Quivar (mez), John Aler (ten), Samuel Ramey (bass), A. Davis (cnd), Toronto SO [E] EMI Classics 2-▲ CDCB 49027 [DDD]; ■ 4D2S 49027 (D)
Mendelssohn, F.:Die erste Walpurgisnacht, w. T. Brooks (cnd), New School of Music Orch [G] Arabesque ▲ Z 6533
Mendelssohn, F.:A Midsummer Night's Dream (comp), w. J. Blegen (sop), F. von Stade (mez), E. Ormandy (cnd) [G] RCA Red Seal ▲ RCD1-2084
Moran, R.:Requiem, Philadelphia Concerto Soloists *(rec Chapel of Girard College, Philadelphia & Henry Wood Hall, London)* Argo ▲ 444540-2 [DDD]
Schoenberg, A.:Gurrelieder, w. R. Bampton (sop), P. Althouse (ten), L. Stokowski (cnd), Philadelphia Orch, Fortnightly Club, Princeton Glee Club *(rec live Apr. 9, 1932)* Pearl 2-▲ PEA 9066 [AAD]
T. Brooks (cnd)
Persichetti, V.:Cant 2 Fl, w. E. A. Schultz (fl), J. E. Barnes (perc) New World ▲ 80316-2
Persichetti, V.:Love New World ▲ 80316-2
Persichetti, V.:Mass New World ▲ 80316-2

The Merry Companions
The Art of the Bawdy Song, w. Baltimore Consort *(rec Oct. 1990)* Dorian ▲ DOR 90155 [DDD]

Methodist Central Hall Choir
Wesley, C.:Hymns, w. Epworth Choir—20 hymns [E] Abbey ▲ CDMVP 828 [DDD]

Methodist Ladies' College Chorale
J. Elton-Brown (cnd)
Dreyfus, G.:Music of, w. A. Rawlins (narr), F. Witt (cnd), Mandolin Orch, Melbourne Bassoon Quartet—Germany Teddy (Symphony for Mandolin Orchestra); Auscapes for Women's Chorus; The Adventures of Sebastian the Fox for Narrator & Bassoon Quartet; Larino, Safe Haven (versions for 2 Oboes & English Horn & for Trumpet & Piano); Tender Mercies for Horn & Piano; There is Something of Don Quixote in All of Us for Solo Guitar Move ▲ MD 3129 [DDD]

Mexican National Opera Chorus
Verdi, G.:Simon Boccanegra (sels), w. Celia Garcia (sop—Maria Boccanegra), Mario Filippeschi (ten—Gabriele Adorno), Ignacio Ruffino (ten—Pietro), Leonard Warren (bar—Simon Boccanegra), Roberto Silva (bass—Jacopo Fiesco), Carlo Morelli (bass—Paolo), R. Cellini (cnd), Mexican National Opera Orch *(rec Palacio de las Bellas Artes, Mexico City, July 4, 1950)* Legato Classics ▲ LCD 185-1 [ADD]

Mexico City Chorus
Beethoven, L. van:Sym 9, "Choral Sym", w. Irma Gonzalez (sop), Oralia Dominguez (cta), Flavio Becerra (ten), Roberto Banuelas (bar), F. Lozano (cnd), Mexico City PO Forlane ▲ FRL 18 [AAD]
Schifrin, L.:Cantos Aztecas, w. P. Domingo (ten), N. Storojev (bass), C. Julian (sop), M. Felix (sgr), L. Schifrin (cnd), Mexican State SO [Sp] *(rec live 10/29/88)* Pro Arte ▲ CDD 494 [DDD]

MGM Studio Chorus
Rózsa, M.:Ben-Hur, w. M. Rózsa (cnd), MGM Studio SO *(rec Culver City, CA & Rome, Italy)* Rhino 2-▲ R2 72197

Michaelstein Chamber Choir
H. Siede (cnd)
Telemann, G.P.:Cants, w. Constanze Backes (sop), Mechthild Georg (mez), Klaus Mertens (bar), Andreas Post (sgr), L. Rémy (cnd), Telemann CO—Christmas cantatas, "Siehe, ich verkündige Euch" (1761) & "Der Herr hat offenbaret" (1762) *(rec Apr 28–May 2, 1996)* CPO ▲ CPO 999419-2 [DDD]
Telemann, G.P.:Hirten an der Krippe zu Bethlehem, w. Constanze Backes (sop), Mechthild Georg (mez), Klaus Mertens (bar), Andreas Post (sgr), L. Rémy (cnd), Telemann CO *(rec Apr 28–May 2, 1996)* CPO ▲ CPO 999419-2 [DDD]

Mid-America Chorale
J. Dexter (cnd)
Avshalomov, J.:Prophecy, w. C. Matheson (ten), L. Smith (org) CRI ▲ CD 667 [ADD]

Midi-Pyrénées Children's Choir
Orff, C.:Carmina burana, w. Natalie Dessay (sop), Gérard Lesne (ct), Thomas Hampson (bar), M. Plasson (cnd), Toulouse Capitole Orch, Orféon Donostiarra *(rec Halle-aux-Grains, Toulouse, Dec. 2, 4 & 6, 1994)* EMI Classics ▲ CDC 55392 [DDD]

Mikaeli Chamber Choir
Bach, J.S.:Mass in b, BWV 232, w. C. Högman (sop), M. Groop (mez), H. Crook (ten), P. Salomaa (bass), Drottningholm Baroque Ensemble Proprius 2-▲ PRCD 9070/71
Donizetti, G.:Linda di Chamounix, w. Edita Gruberová (sop), Monica Groop (mez), Don Bernardini (sgr), Ettore Kim (sgr), F. Haider (cnd), Swedish RSO Nightingale Classics 3-▲ NIG 70561
Lundquist, I.T.:Sym 7, w. Anita Soldh (sop), Olle Persson (bar), S. Ehrling (cnd), Swedish RSO Caprice ▲ CAP 21419 [DDD]
Martin, F.:Mass Proprius ▲ PRCD 9965
Pizzetti, I.:Messa di Requiem Proprius ▲ PRCD 9965
Söderman, A.:Marshal Stig's Daughters, w. H.-P. Frank (cnd), Helsingborg SO, Helsingborgs Concert Choir, Medlemmar Concert Choir [Sw] Musica Sveciae ▲ MSCD 513
A. Eby (cnd)
Schnittke, A.:Sym 2, w. Malena Ernman (alt), Mikael Bellini (ct), Göran Eliasson (ten), Torkel Borelius (bass), L. Segerstam (cnd), Royal Stockholm PO *(rec Stockholm Concert Hall, Sweden, Feb. 24–25, 1994)* BIS ▲ CD 667 [DDD]

Milan Chamber Music Choir
M. Bordignon (cnd)
Battiato, F.:Haiku, w. Franco Battiato (voc), Pouran Ghaffarpour (voc), Antonio Ballista (pno), Marco Boni (vc), Guido Corti (cnt), Filippo Destrieri (kbd/computer), John Giblin (bass), Gavin Harrison (dr/perc), Jakko Jakszyk (gtr), Roberto Mazza (ob), Fabrizio Merlini (va), Angelo Privitera (kbd/computer) Hemisphere ▲ 837234-2
Battiato, F.:Ricerca sul Terzo, w. Franco Battiato (voc), Alessio Alba (tamboura), Antonio Ballista (pno), Marco Boni (vc), Debendra Kanti Chakraborty (tabla), Guido Corti (cnt), Filippo Destrieri (kbd/computer), John Giblin (bass), Buddhadeu Das Gupta (sarod), Gavin Harrison (dr/perc), Jakko Jakszyk (gtr), Roberto Mazza (ob), Fabrizio Merlini (va), Angelo Privitera (kbd/computer) Hemisphere ▲ 837234-2

Milan Collegio Vocale Euterpe
Croce, G.:Triaca Musicale, w. A. E. Negri (cnd), Milan Euterpe Collegio Instrumental Ensemble Stradivarius ▲ STR 33308 [DDD]

Milan Euterpe Collegio Vocal Ensemble
Pellegrini, V.:Canzone, w. A. E. Negri (cnd), Milan Euterpe Collegio Instrumental Ensemble Stradivarius ▲ STR 33308 [DDD]

Milan Italian Radio-TV Chorus
Bellini, V.:I Puritani (sels), w. Maria Callas (sop), A. Simonetto (cnd), Milan Italian Radio-TV Orch—Ah! Vieni al Tempio Fonit Cetra ("Martini & Rossi" series) ▲ FCT CDMR 5007
Meyerbeer, G.:L'Africaine (sels), w. Gianni Raimondi (ten), A. Simonetto (cnd), Milan Italian Radio-TV Orch—O Pardiso Fonit Cetra ("Martini & Rossi" series) ▲ FCT CDMR 5007
Rossini, G.:Semiramide (sels), w. Maria Callas (sop), A. Simonetto (cnd), Milan Italian Radio-TV Orch—Bel Raggio Lusinghiero Fonit Cetra ("Martini & Rossi" series) ▲ FCT CDMR 5007
Spontini, G.:La vestale (sels), w. Maria Callas (sop), A. Simonetto (cnd), Milan Italian Radio-TV Orch—Tu Che Invoco con Orrore Fonit Cetra ("Martini & Rossi" series) ▲ FCT CDMR 5007
Thomas, A.:Hamlet (sels), w. Maria Callas (sop), A. Simonetto (cnd), Milan Italian Radio-TV Orch—Vi Voglio Offrire i Fiori Fonit Cetra ("Martini & Rossi" series) ▲ FCT CDMR 5007
Thomas, A.:Mignon (sels), w. Gianni Raimondi (ten), A. Simonetto (cnd), Milan Italian Radio-TV Orch—Ah! Non Credevi Tu Fonit Cetra ("Martini & Rossi" series) ▲ FCT CDMR 5007
Verdi, G.:Luisa Miller (sels), w. Gianni Raimondi (ten), A. Simonetto (cnd), Milan Italian Radio-TV Orch—Quando le Sere al Placido Fonit Cetra ("Martini & Rossi" series) ▲ FCT CDMR 5007

Milan Polyphonic Choir
Petrassi, G.:Coro di morti, w. Antonia Ballista (pno), Bruno Canino (pno), G. Petrassi (cnd), Milan Angelicum Instrumentalists Stradivarius ▲ STV DTM 90001 [ADD]
G. Bertola (cnd)
Mozart, W.A.:Lucio Silla, w. C.F. Cillario (cnd), Milan Angelicum CO Sarx 2-▲ SRX 2019

Milan RAI Chorus
Bach, J.S.:Magnificat, BWV 243, w. L. Marimpietri (sop), N. Panni (sop), A. Reynolds (mez), P. Munteanu (ten), B. Carmeli (bass), H. Scherchen (cnd), Milan RAI SO [L] *(rec live, Apr 5, 1963)* Memories ▲ HR 4160 (m) [ADD]
Cherubini, L.:Pimmalione, w. Mariella Adani (sop), Ilva Ligabue (sop), Gabriella Carturan (mez), Umberto Borghi (sgr), E. Gerelli (cnd), Milan RAI SO Melodram 2-▲ CDM 29501
Cherubini, L.:Pimmalione, w. M. Adani (sop), I. Ligabue (sop), G. Carturan (mez), U. Borghi (sgr), E. Gerelli (cnd), Milan RAI Orch [I] *(rec live 1955)* Melodram ▲ CDM 19501 [AAD]
Cilea, F.:Adriana Lecouvreur, w. Carla Gavazzi (sop), Miti Truccato Pace (mez), Giacinto Prandelli (ten), Saturno Meletti (bar), A. Simonetto (cnd), Milan RAI Lyric Orch Fonit Cetra ("Classic Collection" series) 2-▲ FCT CDO 20
Cilea, F.:Adriana Lecouvreur (sels), w. Margherita Carosio (sop), Agostino Lazzari (ten), E. Piazza (cnd), Milan RAI SO Fonit Cetra ("Martini & Rossi" series) ▲ FCT CDMR 5010
Cilea, F.:L'Arlesiana (sels), w. Margherita Carosio (sop), Agostino Lazzari (ten), E. Piazza (cnd), Milan RAI SO Fonit Cetra ("Martini & Rossi" series) ▲ FCT CDMR 5010
Cimarosa, D.:Giannina e Bernardone, w. D. De Cecco (sop), S. Jurinac (sop), G. Sciutti (sop), M. Carlin (ten), M. Boriello (bar), S. Bruscantini (bar), C. De Antoni (sgr), N. Sanzogno (cnd), Milan RAI SO [I] *(rec live, Milan July 26, 1953)* Melodram 2-▲ CDM 29505 [ADD]
Cimarosa, D.:Gli Orazii e i Curiazzi, w. G. Simionato (mez), A. Vercelli (mez), G. Del Signore (ten), T. Spataro (ten), C. M. Giulini (cnd), Milan RAI SO [I] *(rec live 4/13/52)* Melodram 2-▲ CDM 29500 [AAD]
Donizetti, G.:Anna Bolena, w. Leyla Gencer (sop), Giulieta Simionato (mez), Aldo Bertocci (ten), Plinio Clabassi (bass), G. Gavazzeni (cnd), Milan RAI SO *(rec July 11, 1958)* Agorá Music ("Phoenix" series) 2-▲ 503
Donizetti, G.:Anna Bolena, w. M. Callas (sop—Anna Bolena), G. Simionato (mez—Giovanna Seymour), N. Rossi-Lemeni (bass—Enrico VIII), G. Gavazzeni (cnd), Milan RAI SO *(rec May 14, 1957)* EMI Classics ▲ CDMB 64941
Donizetti, G.:Anna Bolena, w. L. Gencer (sop), G. Simionato (mez), A. Bertocci (ten), P. Clabassi (bass), G. Gavazzeni (cnd), Milan RAI SO *(rec 1958)* Memories 2-▲ MEM 4517 [AAD]
Donizetti, G.:Don Pasquale (sels), w. Margherita Carosio (sop), Agostino Lazzari (ten), E. Piazza (cnd), Milan RAI SO Fonit Cetra ("Martini & Rossi" series) ▲ FCT CDMR 5010
Donizetti, G.:La favorita, w. Gloria Scalchi (mez), Luca Canonici (ten), René Massis (bar), Giorgio Surjan (bass), D. Renzetti (cnd), Milan RAI SO Fonit Cetra ("Ricordi" series) 3-▲ FCT RFCD 2015
Donizetti, G.:La fille du régiment, w. A. Moffo (sop), J. Gardino (mez), G. Campora (ten), G. Fioravanti (bar), F. Mannino (cnd), Milan RAI Orch *(rec live Dec 2, 1960)* Melodram 2-▲ MEL 27018 [ADD]
Donizetti, G.:La fille du régiment, w. Lina Pagliughi (sop), Rina Corsi (mez), Cesare Valletti (ten), Sesto Bruscantini (bar), Eraldo Coda (bar), M. Rossi (cnd), Milan RAI Lyric Orch *(rec 1950)* Cetra Classic 2-▲ CDON 38 [ADD]
Donizetti, G.:Gianni di Parigi, w. L. Serra (sop), E. Zilio (mez), G. Morino (ten), E. Fissore (bar), A. Romero (bar), S. Manga (sgr), C. F. Cillario (cnd), Milan RAI Orch [I] *(rec live)* Nuova Era 2-▲ 6752/53 [DDD]
Donizetti, G.:Lucia di Lammermoor (sels), w. Margherita Carosio (sop), Agostino Lazzari (ten), E. Piazza (cnd), Milan RAI SO Fonit Cetra ("Martini & Rossi" series) ▲ FCT CDMR 5010
Donizetti, G.:Requiem Mass, w. G. Tucci (sop), A. Lazzarini (mez), G. Sinimberghi (ten), I. Sardi (bass), F. Maero (sgr), F. Molinari-Pradelli (cnd), Milan RAI SO [L] *(rec live, Milan 3/21/61)* Memories ▲ HR 4131 [ADD]
Giordano, U.:Fedora, w. Pia Tassinari (sop), Ferruccio Tagliavini (ten), Meletti (sgr), Micheluzzi (sgr), Mascolo (sgr), Jolanda Torriani (sgr), O.. Fabritiis (cnd), Milan RAI SO *(rec live, July 10, 1954)* Arkadia 2-▲ 493
Giordano, U.:Madame Sans-Gêne, w. Magda László (sop—Caterina), Carlo Tagliabue (bar—Napoleone), Renato Berti (sgr—Despréaux), Irene Callaway (sgr—Toniotta/Carolina), Danilo Cestari (sgr—Neipperg/Vinaigre), Maria Luisa Malacchi (sgr—Giulia/Principessa Elisa), Carlo Perucci (sgr—Fouché), Danilo Vega (sgr—Lefebvre), Enzo Viaro (sgr—De Brigode/Gelsomino), A. Basile (cnd), Milan RAI SO *(rec Milan, Aug 10, 1957)* Bongiovanni 2-▲ GB 1129/30
Giordano, U.:Il re (sels), w. Margherita Carosio (sop), Agostino Lazzari (ten), E. Piazza (cnd), Milan RAI SO Fonit Cetra ("Martini & Rossi" series) ▲ FCT CDMR 5010
Humperdinck, E.:Hänsel und Gretel, w. Sena Jurinac (sop), Elisabeth Schwarzkopf (sop), Rita Streich (sop), Vittoria Palombini (mez), Rolando Panerai (bar), Bruna Ronshini (sgr), H. von Karajan (cnd), Milan Italian Radio-TV Orch Stradivarius 2-▲ STV 12314
Humperdinck, E.:Hänsel und Gretel (sels), w. Sena Jurinac (sop—Hänsel), Elisabeth Schwarzkopf (sop—Gretel), Vittoria Palombini (mez—Witch), Rolando Panerai (sgr—Peter), Bruna Ronchini (sgr—Gertrude), H.. Karajan (cnd), Milan RAI SO—[Act 1] Suse, liebe Suse, was raschelt im Stroh; [Act 2] Ein Männlein steht im Walde ganz still und Stumm; Abends, will ich schlafen gehn; [Act 3] Wo bin ich? Wach' ich?; Und bist du dann drin...schwaps!; Die Englein haben's im Traum gesagt; Schunt, o schunt das Wunder an *(rec Milan, Dec. 25, 1954)* Legato Classics 3-▲ LCD 197-3
Leoncavallo, R.:Pagliacci, w. R. Moberg (sop—Nedda), J. Bjoerling (ten—Canio), E. Sundquist (bar—Tonio), L. Gardelli (cnd), Milan RAI SO [Sw] *(rec live, Stockholm, 12/8/54)* Legato Classics ▲ LCD 155-1 [ADD]
Leoncavallo, R.:Pagliacci, w. M. Micheluzzi (sop), F. Corelli (ten), M. Carlin (ten), T. Gobbi (bar), L. Puglisi (bar), A. Simonetto (cnd), Milan RAI Orch *(rec live 9/26/54 from RAI Milan)* HRE ▲ 1001-1 [ADD]
Maderna, B.:Ages, w. B. Maderna (cnd), Milan RAI SO *(rec live, 11/6/72)* Stradivarius ▲ STR 10061 [ADD]
Maria Callas & Gianni Raimondi, w. Callas, Maria (sop), Gianni Raimondi (ten), Milan RAI SO, Milan RAI Chorus [cnd:A. Simonetto] *(rec Milan, Nov. 19, 1956)* Incontri memorabili ("Martini & Rossi Concert" series) ▲ CDMR 5007 [ADD]
Mascagni, P.:L'amico Fritz, w. R. Carteri (sop—Suzel), R. Corsi (mez—Beppe), C. Valletti (ten—Fritz), C. Tagliabue (bar—David), V. Gui (cnd), Milan RAI SO *(rec live, Apr. 25, 1953)* Bongiovanni 2-▲ GB 1098/99 [ADD]
Mascagni, P.:Nerone (sels), w. Margherita Carosio (sop), Agostino Lazzari (ten), E. Piazza (cnd), Milan RAI SO Fonit Cetra ("Martini & Rossi" series) ▲ FCT CDMR 5010
Massenet, J.:Don Quichotte, w. Teresa Berganza (mez), Pina Malgarini (mez), Tommaso Frascati (ten), Carlo Badioli (bass), Boris Christoff (bass), A. Simonetto (cnd), Milan RAI SO Melodram 2-▲ CDM 27027
Mendelssohn, F.:St. Paul, w. A. Giebel (sop), O. Dominguez (mez), Theo Altmeyer (ten), S. Nimsgern (b-bar), R. A. El Hage (bass), R. Muti (cnd), Milan RAI Orch [G] *(rec live, Milan, 12/15/70)* Memories 2-▲ HR 4267/68 (m) [ADD]
Mercadante, S.:Il giuramento (sels), w. M. Vitale (sop), M. Pirazzini (mez), R. Panerai (bar), A. Berdini (bar), A. Simonetto (cnd), Milan RAI Orch [I]—14 scenes & arias *(rec live, Milan, 4/5/51)* Myto 2-▲ 2 MCD 90632 [ADD]
Meyerbeer, G.:Les Huguenots, w. A. Pastori (sop), A. de Cavalieri (mez), G. Lauri-Volpi (ten), G. Taddei (bar), G. Tozzi (bass), N. Zaccaria (bass), T. Serafin (cnd), Milan RAI SO *(rec 1956)* Memories 3-▲ MEM 4566 [ADD]
Mozart, W.A.:Don Giovanni, w. Leyla Gencer (sop—Donn'Elvra), Teresa Stich-Randall (mez—Donn'Anna), Sesto Bruscantini (bar—Leporello), Mario Petri (bar—Don Giovanni), F. Molinari-Pradelli (cnd), Milan RAI SO Stradivarius 3-▲ STV DTM 12321 [ADD]
Paisiello, G.:Fedra, w. O. Beggiato (sop), R. Mattioli (sop), A. Tuccari (sop), L. Udovick (sop), A. Lazzari (ten), A. Questa (cnd), Milan RAI SO *(rec 1958)* Memories 2-▲ MEM 4502 [AAD]
Pannain, G.:Beatrice Cenci (sels), w. Margherita Carosio (sop), Agostino Lazzari (ten), E. Piazza (cnd), Milan RAI SO Fonit Cetra ("Martini & Rossi" series) ▲ FCT CDMR 5010
Petrassi, G.:Salmo IX, w. G. Petrassi (cnd), Milan Italian Radio-TV Orch Stradivarius ▲ STV DTM 90001 [ADD]
Rossini, G.:Il barbiere di Siviglia, w. R. Broilo (sop—Berta), G. Simionato (mez—Rosina), L. Infantino (ten—Almaviva), G. Taddei (bar—Figaro), C. Badioli (bass—Bartolo), A. Cassinelli (bass—Basilio), F. Previtali (cnd), Milan RAI SO *(rec 1950)* Cetra Classic 2-▲ CDO 6 [AAD]
Rossini, G.:Elisabetta, regina d'Inghilterra (sels), w. M. Vitale (sop), L. Pagliughi (sop), G. Campora (ten), Pinno (sgr), A. Simonetto (cnd), Milan RAI SO—six arias [I] *(rec live, 4/27/53)* Myto 2-▲ 2 MCD 90530 [ADD]

982 ▲ = CD ♦ = Enhanced CD Δ = MD ■ = Cassette Tape □ = DCC

Milan RAI Chorus (cont.)
Rossini, G.:L'italiana in Algeri, w. Teresa Berganza (mez), Alvino Misciano (ten), Sesto Bruscantini (bar), Mario Petri (sgr), N. Sanzogno (cnd), Milan RAI SO *(rec June 28, 1957)* Pantheon 2-▲ PHE 6646 (m)
Simionato & Di Stefano, w. Simionato, Giulietta (mez), Giuseppe Di Stefano (ten), Milan RAI Orch, Milan RAI Chorus [cnd:Nino Sanzogno] *(rec Nov. 26, 1956)* Incontri Memorabili ▲ CDMR 5015
Verdi, G.:Ernani, w. Montserrat Caballè (sop), Bruno Prevedi (ten), Peter Glossop (bar), Boris Christoff (bass), G. Gavazzeni (cnd), Milan RAI SO *(rec Milan, Mar. 25, 1969)* Pantheon 2-▲ PHE 6634 (m)
Verdi, G.:Un giorno di regno, w. Lina Pagliughi (sop), Mario Carlin (ten), Juan Oncina (ten), Sesto Bruscantini (bar), Renato Capecchi (bar), Laura Cozzi (sgr), Cristiano Dalamangas (sgr), A. Simonetto (cnd), Milan RAI Lyric Orch *(rec 1951)* Cetra Classic 2-▲ CDON 37 [ADD]
Verdi, G.:Giovanna d'Arco, w. Renata Tebaldi (sop), Carlo Bergonzi (ten), Rolando Panerai (bar), A. Simonetto (cnd), Milan RAI SO *(rec Milan, May 26, 1951)* Pantheon 2-▲ PHE 6610 (m)
Verdi, G.:Giovanna d'Arco, w. R. Tebaldi (sop), C. Bergonzi (ten), R. Panerai (bar), A. Simonetto (cnd), Milan RAI Orch [I] *(rec live)* Melodram 2-▲ 27021
Verdi, G.:I lombardi alla prima crociata, w. Renata Broilo (sop), Maria Vitale (sop), Miriam Pirazzini (mez), Aldo Bertocci (ten), Mario Frosini (sgr), Mario Petri (bass), Bruno Franchi (sgr), Gustavo Gallo (sgr), Renato Pasquali (sgr), M. Wolf-Ferrari (cnd), Milan RAI Lyric Orch *(rec 1954)* Cetra Classic 2-▲ CDON 41 [ADD]
Verdi, G.:Nabucco (sels), w. Margherita Carosio (sop), Agostino Lazzari (ten), E. Piazza (cnd), Milan RAI SO Fonit Cetra ("Martini & Rossi" series) ▲ FCT CDMR 5010
Verdi, G.:La traviata, w. R. Tebaldi (sop), G. Prandelli (ten), G. Orlandini (bar), C. M. Giulini (cnd), Milan RAI Orch *(rec live 5/28/52)* Standing Room Only 2-▲ SRO 810-2 [ADD]
Verdi, G.:Il trovatore, w. Leyla Gencer (sop—Leonora), Laura Londi (sop—Ines), Fedora Barbieri (mez—Azucena), Mario del Monaco (ten—Manrico), Athos cesarini (ten—Ruiz), Walter Artioli (ten—Messanger) Ettore Bastianini (bar—Count Luna), Plinio Clabassi (bass—Ferrando), Sergio Liliani (bass—Gypsy), F. Previtali (cnd), Milan RAI SO *(rec live, Milan, May 29, 1957)* Arkadia 2-▲ 483 [ADD]
Verdi, G.:Il trovatore (sels), w. Mario del Monaco (ten), F. Previtali (cnd), Milan RAI SO—Ah! si, ben mio; Di quella pira *(rec Milan, Apr. 8, 1957)* Melodram ▲ CDI 104006 [ADD]
Verdi, G.:Il trovatore (sels), w. Leyla Gencer (sop—Leonora), Laura Londi (sop—Ines), Athos Cesarini (ten—Ruiz), Mario del Monaco (ten—Manrico), Ettore Bastianini (bar), F. Previtali (cnd), Milan RAI SO *(rec Milan, May 18, 1957)* Agorá Music ("Phoenix" series) 3-▲ 510 [ADD]
Wagner, R.:Tannhäuser (sels), w. Margherita Carosio (sop), Agostino Lazzari (ten), E. Piazza (cnd), Milan RAI SO Fonit Cetra ("Martini & Rossi" series) ▲ FCT CDMR 5010
Zandonai, R.:I cavalieri di Ekebù, w. Fiorenza Cossotto (sop), Gina Longobardo Fiordaliso (sgr), Lando Bartolini (ten), G. Gavazzeni (cnd), Milan RAI SO Fonit Cetra ("Italia" series) 2-▲ FCT CDC 93

Milan Teatro alla Scala Chorus—see La Scala Chorus

Milwaukee Sym Chorus
Beethoven, L. van:Sym 9, "Choral Sym", w. Z. Macal (cnd), Milwaukee SO [soloists:B. Valente, J. Taylor, J. F. West, P. Plishka] *(rec 7/31/89)* Koss Classics ▲ KC 1003 [DDD]
Berlioz, H.:Lélio, "Le retouré la vie", w. W. Klemperer (nar), G. Siebert (ten), W. Diana (bar), Z. Macal (cnd) Koss Classics 2-▲ KC 1012 [DDD]
Foss, L.:With Music Strong, w. L. Foss (cnd), Milwaukee SO *(rec 4/89)* Koss Classics ▲ KC 1004 [DDD]
Prokofiev, S.:Alexander Nevsky, w. J. Taylor (mez), Z. Macal (cnd), Milwaukee SO *(rec Oct. 29, 1990)* Koss Classics ▲ KC 1016 [DDD]
Prokofiev, S.:Lt Kijé Suite, w. Z. Macal (cnd), Milwaukee SO *(rec Oct. 29, 1990)* Koss Classics ▲ KC 1016 [DDD]
Sierra, R.:Idilio, w. Z. Macal (cnd), Milwaukee SO *(rec Mar. 9, 1992)* Koss Classics ▲ KC 1021 [DDD]

Mineria Sym Choir
Orff, C.:Carmina burana, w. Gabriela Herrera (sop), Frank Kelley (ten), Ben Holt (bar), H. de la Fuente (cnd), Mineria SO IMP ("Classic" series) ▲ IMP 2024

Minetto Chorus
Caldara, A.:Il gioco del quadriglio, w. Maria-Grazia Ferraccini (sop), Basia Retchitzka (sop), Elana Rizzieri (sop), Maria Minetto (cta), E. Loehrer (cnd), Lugano Chamber Society Orch Dynamic ▲ CDL 140

Minnesota Bach Society
Beethoven, L. van:Meeresstille und glückliche Fahrt, w. P. Bryn-Julson (sop), S. Skrowaczewski (cnd), Minnesota Orch Vox Box 2-▲ CDX 5099 [ADD]

Minnesota Chorale
Haydn, J.:Die Jahreszeiten, w. Arleen Auger (sop), John Aler (ten), Håkan Hågegard (bar), J. Revzen (cnd), St. Paul CO [G] Koch International Classics 2-▲ KIC 7065-2 [DDD]
Haydn, J.:Die Schöpfung, w. Lynn Dawson (sop), Neil Rosenshein (ten), John Cheek (bass), J. Revzen (cnd), St. Paul CO Albany 2-▲ AR 005-6-2

Minsk Chamber Choir
Shostakovich, D.:Zoya, w. W. Mnatsakanov (cnd), Byelorussian Radio-TV SO *(rec Byelorussian Radio Committe Studio, Minsk, Feb 1995)* Russian Compact Disc ▲ RDCD 10002 [DDD]

I. Matukhov (cnd)
Shostakovich, D.:Alone, w. W. Mnatsakanov (cnd), Byelorussion Radio-TV SO—sels *(rec Byelorussian Radio Committe Studio, Minsk, Nov 1995)* Russian Disc ▲ RDCD 10007 [DDD]

Missouri Singers
Holst, G.:The Planets, w. W. Susskind (cnd), St. Louis SO, Ronald Arnatt Chorale Vox Box 2-▲ CDX 5105 [ADD]

Geoffrey Mitchell Choir
Boughton, R.:The Immortal Hour, w. A. Dawson (sop), D. Wilson-Johnson (bar), R. Kennedy (bass), A. Melville (cnd), English CO [E] Hyperion 2-▲ CDA 66101/02 [DDD]
Donizetti, G.:L'assedio di Calais, w. E. Harrhy (sop), D. Jones (mez), R. Serbo (ten), J. Treleaven (ten), R. Smythe (bar), D. Parry (cnd), Philharmonia Orch Opera Rara 2-▲ OR 9 [DDD]
Donizetti, G.:Emilia di Liverpool, w. Y. Kenny (sop), A. Mason (sop), B. Mills (sop), C. Merritt (ten), S. Bruscantini (bar), G. Dolton (bar), C. Thornton-Holmes (bar), D. Parry (cnd), Philharmonia Orch—complete opera, without dialogue Opera Rara 3-▲ OR 8
Donizetti, G.:L'Eremitaggio di Liverpool, w. Y. Kenny (sop), A. Mason (sop), B. Mills (sop), C. Merritt (ten), S. Bruscantini (bar), G. Dolton (bar), C. Thornton-Holmes (bar), D. Parry (cnd), Philharmonia Orch—complete opera, without dialogue Opera Rara 3-▲ OR 8
Donizetti, G.:Maria Padilla, w. L. McDonall (sop—Maria Padilla), D. Jones (mez—Ines Padilla), G. Clark (ten—Don Ruiz), C. du Plessis (bar—Don Pedro), A. Francis (cnd), London SO [I] *(rec at Henry Wood Hall, London June 1980)* Opera Rara 3-▲ ORC 6
Donizetti, G.:Ugo, conte di Parigi, w. E. Harrhy (sop), Y. Kenny (sop), J. Price (sop), D. Jones (mez), M. Arthur (ten), C. du Plessis (bar), A. Francis (cnd), New Philharmonia Orch Opera Rara 3-▲ ORC 1
Meyerbeer, G.:Il crociato, w. Linda Kitchen (sop), Y. Kenny (sop), R. Platt (sop), D. Montague (mez), D. Jones (mez), B. Ford (ten), U. Benelli (bar), D. Parry (cnd), Royal PO [I] *(rec CTS Studios, Wembley, London, Dec. 1990-June 1991)* Opera Rara 4-▲ OR 10
Prokofiev, S.:Zdravitsa, w. D. Gleeson (cnd), London PO, London Phil Chorus IMP ("Masters" series) ▲ IMP 6600122
Puccini, G.:Tosca, w. Jane Eaglen (sop—Floria Tosca), Charbel Michael (alt—Shepherd Boy), John Daszak (ten—Spoletta), Dennis O'Neill (ten—Mario Cavaradossi), Christopher Booth-Jones (bar—Sciarrone), Ashley Holland (bar—Jailor), Gregory Yurisich (bar—Baron Scarpia), Peter Rose (bass—Cesare Angelotti), Andrew Shore (bass—Sacristan), D. Parry (cnd), Philharmonia Orch, Peter Kay Children's Chorus Chandos ("Opera in English" series) 2-▲ CHAN 3000
Tchaikovsky, P.:Ode to Joy, w. D. Gleeson (cnd), London PO, London Philharmonic Choir IMP ("Masters" series) ▲ IMP 6600122

E. Mlynarski State School of Music Children's Choir
Wojnarowski, Marchwicka (cnd)
Elsner, J.:Passio Domini Nostri Jesu Christi, w. Bozena Harasimowicz (sop), Krzysztof Szmyt (ten), Czeslaw Galka (bar), Bogdan Sliwa (bar), Piotr Nowacki (bass), K. Kord (cnd), Warsaw PO, Warsaw National Phil Chorus *(rec National Philharmonic, Warsaw, 1990)* Polskie Nagrania ▲ PNCD 078 [DDD]

Modeno Teatro Comunale Chorus
Bellini, V.:I Puritani, w. Mirella Freni (sop—Elvira), Rita Bezzi (mez—Enrichetta), Alfredo Kraus (ten—Arturo Talbot), Augusto Pedroni (ten—Sir Bruno Robertson), Attilio d'Orazi (bar—Sir Riccardo Forth), Raffaele Ariè (bass—Sir Giorgio), Bruno Cioni (bass—Lord Gualtiero Walton), N. Verchi (cnd), Modena Teatro Comunale Orch *(rec Modena Teatro Comunale, Dec. 26, 1962)* Legato Classics 2-▲ LCD 195-2 [ADD]
Rossini, G.:La pietra del paragone, w. M. C. Nocentini (sop), A. Trovarelli (mez), H. M. Molinari (cta), P. Barbacini (ten), V. Di Matteo (bar), R. Scaltriti (bar), A. Svab (bar), P. Rumetz (bass), C. Desderi (cnd), Camerata Musicale Orch [I] *(rec 1992)* Nuova Era 2-▲ 7132/33 [DDD]

Modern Madrigal Quartet
Rorem, N.:From an Unknown Past [E] Phoenix ▲ PHCD 108 [AAD]
Rorem, N.:Madrigals [E] Phoenix ▲ PHCD 108 [AAD]

Monastery of the Holy Trinity & St. Sergius Combined Choirs
Marienhymnen aus Russland, w. A. Matvey (cnd), Moscow Religious Academy & Seminary, Dormition of the BVM Church Choir at Monastery of the Virgin [cnd:H. Pjotr] Koch Schwann ▲ SHC 313047 [ADD]

Monte Carlo Phil Chorus
French Opera Arias for Tenor, w. Rockwell Blake (ten), Monte Carlo PO, Monte Carlo Phil Chorus [cnd:Patrick Fournillier] EMI Classics ▲ CDC 55058

Montepulciano Arts Center Chorus
Mascagni, P.:Sì, w. Vivian (sop), A. Felle (sop), Maria Gentile (sop), M.G. Liguori (sop), Nicoletti (sgr), Comas (sgr), S. Sanna (cnd), Montepulciano Arts Center Orch [I] *(rec live, 7/24/87)* Bongiovanni 2-▲ GB 2050/51 [DDD]

Monteverdi Chamber Choir
Caldara, A.:Stabat Mater, w. I. Verebics (sop), É. Lax (mez), G. Kállay (ten), B. Szilágyi (bar), E. Kollár (cnd), Concerto Armonico Budapest [L] Hungaroton ▲ HCD 31273 [DDD]
Monteverdi, C.:Music of, w. M. Spányi (org), B. Máté (vc), S. Benyus (db), I. Szabó (thb)—Laudate pueri, Lauda Ierusalem, Nisi Dominus Hungaroton ▲ HCD 31273 [DDD]
Scarlatti, D.:Mass in g [L] Hungaroton ▲ HCD 31273 [DDD]

E. Kollár (cnd)
Sulyok, I.:Compositions Hungaroton ▲ HCD 31350 [DDD]
Sulyok, I.:Mountains Hungaroton ▲ HCD 31350 [DDD]

Monteverdi Choir Hamburg
Telemann, G.P.:Der Tag des Gerichts, w. R. Alexander (sop), K. Equiliz (ten), M. Van Egmond (bass), N. Harnoncourt (cnd), Vienna Concentus Musicus Teldec 2-▲ 77621-2

Monteverdi Choir London
Bach, J.S.:Cant 27, w. R. Hansmann (sop), H. Watts (cta), K. Equiluz (ten), M. Van Egmond (b-bar), J. Jürgens (cnd), Concerto Amsterdam Teldec (Das alte Werke) ▲ 93687
Bach, J.S.:Cant 36, w. N. Argenta (sop), R. Lang (mez), A. Rolfe Johnson (ten), O. Bär (bar), J. E. Gardiner (cnd), English Baroque Soloists Archiv ▲ 437327-2
Bach, J.S.:Cant 50, w. J. E. Gardiner (cnd), English Baroque Soloists Erato 2-▲ 2292-45979-2
Bach, J.S.:Cant 61, w. N. Argenta (sop), R. Lang (mez), A. Rolfe Johnson (ten), O. Bär (bar), J. E. Gardiner (cnd), English Baroque Soloists Archiv ▲ 437327-2 [DDD]
Bach, J.S.:Cant 62, w. N. Argenta (sop), R. Lang (mez), A. Rolfe Johnson (ten), O. Bär (bar), J. E. Gardiner (cnd), English Baroque Soloists Archiv ▲ 437327-2 [DDD]
Bach, J.S.:Cant 106, "Actus tragicus", w. N. Argenta (sop), M. Chance (ct), A. Rolfe Johnson (ten), S. Varcoe (b-bar), J. E. Gardiner (cnd), English Baroque Soloists [G] Archiv ▲ 429782-2 [DDD]
Bach, J.S.:Cant 118, w. J. E. Gardiner (cnd), English Baroque Soloists Erato 2-▲ 2292-45979-2
Bach, J.S.:Cant 118, w. J. E. Gardiner (cnd), English Baroque Soloists [G] Archiv ▲ 429782-2 [DDD]
Bach, J.S.:Cant 131, w. W. Kendall (ten), S. Varcoe (b-bar), J. E. Gardiner (cnd), English Baroque Soloists Erato ▲ 2292-45988-2
Bach, J.S.:Cant 140, w. R. Holton (sop), A. Rolfe Johnson (ten), S. Varcoe (b-bar), J. E. Gardiner (cnd), English Baroque Soloists [G] Archiv ▲ 431809-2 [DDD]
Bach, J.S.:Cant 147, w. R. Holton (sop), M. Chance (ct), A. Rolfe Johnson (ten), S. Varcoe (b-bar), J. E. Gardiner (cnd), English Baroque Soloists [G] Archiv ▲ 431809-2 [DDD]
Bach, J.S.:Cant 158, w. R. Hansmann (sop), H. Watts (cta), K. Equiluz (ten), M. Van Egmond (b-bar), J. Jürgens (cnd), Concerto Amsterdam Teldec ("Das alte Werke" series) ▲ 93687
Bach, J.S.:Cant 198, w. N. Argenta (sop), M. Chance (ct), A. Rolfe Johnson (ten), S. Varcoe (b-bar), J. E. Gardiner (cnd), English Baroque Soloists [G] Archiv ▲ 429782-2 [DDD]
Bach, J.S.:Cant 198, w. R. Hansmann (sop), H. Watts (cta), K. Equiluz (ten), M. Van Egmond (b-bar), J. Jürgens (cnd), Concerto Amsterdam Teldec (Das alte Werke) ▲ 93687
Bach, J.S.:Christmas Oratorio, w. N. Argenta (sop), A. S. von Otter (mez), H.-P. Blochwitz (ten), O. Bär (bar), J. E. Gardiner (cnd), English Baroque Soloists [G] Archiv 2-▲ 423232-2 [DDD]
Bach, J.S.:Christmas Oratorio (sels), w. J. E. Gardiner (cnd), English Baroque Soloists—arias & choruses Archiv ("3D Baroque" series) ▲ 431703-2 [DDD]
Bach, J.S.:Christmas Oratorio (sels), w. N. Argenta (sop), A. S. von Otter (mez), H.-P. Blochwitz (ten), O. Bär (bar), J. E. Gardiner (cnd), English Baroque Soloists [G] Archiv ▲ 427653-2 [DDD]
Bach, J.S.:Magnificat, BWV 243, w. E. Kirkby (sop) et al., J. E. Gardiner (cnd), English Baroque Soloists [L] Philips ("Digital Classics" series) ▲ 411458-2 [DDD]
Bach, J.S.:Mass in b, BWV 232, w. J. E. Gardiner (cnd), English Baroque Soloists [L] Archiv 2-▲ 415514-2 [DDD]
Bach, J.S.:Motets, BWV 225-30, w. J. E. Gardiner (cnd), English Baroque Soloists Erato 2-▲ 2292-45979-2
Bach, J.S.:St. John Passion, w. J. E. Gardiner (cnd), English Baroque Soloists [G] Archiv 2-▲ 419324-2 [DDD]
Bach, J.S.:St. John Passion (sels), w. J. E. Gardiner (cnd), English Baroque Soloists—arias & choruses Archiv ("3D Baroque" series) ▲ 431703-2 [DDD]
Bach, J.S.:St. Matthew Passion, w. B. Bonney (sop), A. Monoyios (sop), A. S. von Otter (mez), M. Chance (ct), H. Crook (ten), A. Rolfe Johnson (ten), O. Bär (bar), A. Schmidt (bar), C. Hauptmann (bass), J. E. Gardiner (cnd), English Baroque Soloists [G] Archiv 3-▲ 427648-2 [DDD]
Beethoven, L. van:Ah, perfido!, w. C. Margiono (sop), J. E. Gardiner (cnd), Orch Révolutionnaire et Romantique Archiv ▲ 435391-2 [DDD]
Beethoven, L. van:Fant Pno, Op. 80, "Choral Fant", w. Robert Levin (pno), J. E. Gardiner (cnd), Orch Révolutionnaire et Romantique Archiv ▲ 447771-2
Beethoven, L. van:Mass, Op. 86, w. C. Margiono (sop), C. Robbin (mez), W. Kendall (ten), A. Miles (bass), J. E. Gardiner (cnd), Orch Révolutionnaire et Romantique [period instrs] Archiv ▲ 435391-2 [DDD]
Beethoven, L. van:Meeresstille und glückliche Fahrt, w. J. E. Gardiner (cnd), Orch Révolutionnaire et Romantique [period instrs] Archiv ▲ 435391-2 [DDD]
Beethoven, L. van:Missa Solemnis, w. C. Margiono (sop), C. Robbin (mez), W. Kendall (ten), A. Miles (bass), J. E. Gardiner (cnd), English Baroque Soloists [L] Archiv ▲ 429779-2 [DDD] ☐ 429779-5
Berlioz, H.:L'Enfance du Christ, w. A. S. von Otter (mez), Johnson (sgr), G. Cachemaille (bar), J. Van Dam (b-bar), J. Bastin (bass), J.E. Gardiner (cnd), Lyon Opera Orch [F] Erato 2-▲ 2292-45275-2 [DDD]
Berlioz, H.:Messe solennelle Sop, w. Donna Brown (sop), Jean-Luc Viala (ten), Gilles Cachemaille (bar), J. E. Gardiner (cnd), Orch Révolutionnaire et Romantique Philips ▲ 442137-2 ■ 442137-4 ☐ 442137-5
Berlioz, H.:Tristia, w. J. E. Gardiner (cnd), Orch Révolutionnaire et Romantique Philips ▲ 446676-2
Brahms, J.:Choral Music, w. J.E. Gardiner (cnd)—Gesänge (Opp. 17, 42 & 104); Liebeslieder Waltzes, Op. 52; Quartet, Op. 92 [G] Philips ▲ 432152-2 [DDD]
Brahms, J.:Ein Deutsches Requiem, w. C. Margiono (sop), R. Gilfry (bar), J. E. Gardiner (cnd), Orch Révolutionnaire et Romantique [period instrs] Philips ▲ 432140-2 [DDD] ☐ 432140-5
Britten, B.:War Requiem, w. L. Orgonasova (sop), A. Rolfe-Johnson (ten), B. Skovhus (bar), J. E. Gardiner (cnd), North German RSO, North German Radio Chorus, Tölz Boys' Choir Deutsche Grammophon 2-▲ 437801-2
Campra, A.:Messe de Requiem, w. J. Nelson (mez), C. Harris (trb), J.-C. Orliac (ten), S. Roberts (bar), J. E. Gardiner (cnd), English Baroque Soloists Erato ▲ 2292-45993-2

CHORAL GROUPS

Monteverdi Choir London (cont.)

Carissimi, G.:Oratorios, w. J. E. Gardiner (cnd), His Majesties Sagbutts & Cornetts, English Baroque Soloists members—Jepthe, Jonas & Judicum extremum Erato ▲ 2292-45466-2 ZK [DDD]
Debussy, C.:Chansons (3) de Charles d'Orléans, w. J. E. Gardiner (cnd), Orch Révolutionnaire et Romantique Philips ▲ 438149-2
Fauré, G.:Les Djinns, w. J. E. Gardiner (cnd), Orch Révolutionnaire et Romantique Philips ▲ 438149-2
Fauré, G.:Madrigal, w. J. E. Gardiner (cnd), Orch Révolutionnaire et Romantique Philips ▲ 438149-2
Fauré, G.:Requiem, w. *(soloists unknown)*, J. E. Gardiner (cnd), Orch Révolutionnaire et Romantique Philips ▲ 438149-2
Gluck, C.W.:Orfeo ed Euridice, w. S. McNair (sop), C. Sieden (sop), D.L. Ragin (ct), J. E. Gardiner (cnd), English Baroque Soloists Philips ▲ 434093-2
Handel, G.F.:L'Allegro, Il Penseroso ed il Moderato, w. Michael Ginn (trb), Patrizia Kwella (sop), Marie McLaughlin (sop), J. E. Gardiner (cnd), English Baroque Soloists Erato 2-▲ 2292-45377-2 ZA
Handel, G.F.:Coronation Anthems (4) for George II, w. J. E. Gardiner (cnd), English Baroque Soloists—Zadok the Priest; The King Shall Rejoice Philips ▲ 432110-2
Handel, G.F.:Coronation Anthems (4) for George II, w. J.E. Gardiner (cnd), Monteverdi Orch—Anthem No. 1 Erato ▲ 2292-45136-2 ■ 2292-45136-4
Handel, G.F.:Dixit Dominus, w. *(soloists unknown)*, J.E. Gardiner (cnd), Monteverdi Orch Erato ▲ 2292-45136-2 ■ 2292-45136-4
Handel, G.F.:Israel in Egypt, w. Norma Burrowes (sop), Charles Brett (ct), Paul Elliot (sgr), J.E. Gardiner (cnd), Monteverdi Orch Erato 2-▲ 2292-45399-2 ZA
Handel, G.F.:Israel in Egypt, w. Ruth Holton (sop), Elisabeth Friday (sgr), Michael Chance (alt), Philip Salmon (ten), Paul Tindall (sgr), J. E. Gardiner (cnd), English Baroque Soloists Philips ▲ 432110-2
Handel, G.F.:Laudate pueri Dominum, w. Sylvia McNair (sop), J. E. Gardiner (cnd), English Baroque Soloists [G] Philips ▲ 434920-2
Handel, G.F.:Messiah, w. Saul Quirke (trb), Margaret Marshall (sop), Catherine Robbin (mez), Charles Brett (ct), Anthony Rolfe Johnson (ten), Robert Hale (b-bar), J. E. Gardiner (cnd), English Baroque Soloists [E] Philips ▲ 412267-2 [DDD]
Handel, G.F.:Messiah, w. Saul Quirke (trb), Margaret Marshall (sop), Catherine Robbin (mez), Charles Brett (ct), Anthony Rolfe Johnson (ten), Robert Hale (b-bar), J. E. Gardiner (cnd), English Baroque Soloists [E] Philips 3-▲ 411041-2 [DDD]
Handel, G.F.:Saul, w. D. Brown (sop), L. Dawson (sop), D. L. Ragin (ct), J. M. Ainsley (ten), A. Miles (bar), J. E. Gardiner (cnd), English Baroque Soloists Philips 3-▲ 426265-2 3PH [DDD]
Handel, G.F.:Semele, w. Norma Burrowes (sop), Patrizia Kwella (sop), Elizabeth Priday (sop), Catherine Denley (mez), Della Jones (mez), Timothy Penrose (alt), Anthony Rolfe-Johnson (ct), Maldwyn Davies (ten), Robert Lloyd (b-bar), David Thomas (bass), J. E. Gardiner (cnd), English Baroque Soloists Erato 2-▲ 2292-45982-2
Handel, G.F.:Solomon, w. Nancy Argenta (sop), Barbara Hendricks (sop), Carolyn Watkinson (cta), Anthony Rolfe Johnson (ct), J. E. Gardiner (cnd), English Baroque Soloists [E] Philips 2-▲ 412612-2 [DDD]
Handel, G.F.:The Ways of Zion Do Mourn, w. Norma Burrowes (sop), Charles Brett (ct), Paul Elliot (ten), J.E. Gardiner (cnd), Monteverdi Orch Erato 2-▲ 2292-45399-2 ZA
Haydn, J.:Die Jahreszeiten, w. Barbara Bonney (sop), Anthony Rolfe Johnson (ct), Andreas Schmidt (bar), J. E. Gardiner (cnd), English Baroque Soloists [period instruments] Archiv 2-▲ 431818-2 [DDD]
Haydn, J.:Die Jahreszeiten (sels), w. Barbara Bonney (sop), Anthony Rolfe Johnson (ten), Andreas Schmidt (bar), J. E. Gardiner (cnd), English Baroque Soloists—arias & choruses Archiv ▲ 447282-2
Haydn, J.:Die Schöpfung, w. Donna Brown (sop), Sylvia McNair (sop), Michael Schade (ten), Gerald Finley (bar), Rodney Gilfry (bar), J. E. Gardiner (cnd), English Baroque Soloists Archiv ▲ 449 217-2
Lehár, F.:Die lustige Witwe, w. Cheryl Studer (sop), Barbara Bonney (sop), Boje Skovhus (bar), Bryn Terfel (b-bar), J.E. Gardiner (cnd), Vienna PO Deutsche Grammophon ▲ 439911-2
Monteverdi, C.:Orfeo, w. English Baroque Soloists, J. E. Gardiner (cnd), His Majesties Sagbutts & Cornetts Archiv 2-▲ 419250-2 [DDD]
Monteverdi, C.:Vespro della Beata Vergine, w. J. Jürgens (cnd), Camerata Accademica Hamburg [L] Ambitus 2-▲ 383826-2 [DDD]
Mozart, W.A.:Don Giovanni, w. Charlotte Margiono (sop—Donna Elvira), Luba Orgonasova (sop—Donna Anna), Eirian James (mez—Zerlina), Julian Clarkson (alt—Masetto), Christoph Prégardien (ten—Don Ottavio), Rodney Gilfry (bar—Don Giovanni), Ildebrando d'Arcangelo (bass—Leporello), Andrea Silvestrelli (bass—Il Commendatore), J. E. Gardiner (cnd), English Baroque Soloists Deutsche Grammophon ("4D Audio" series) 3-▲ 445870-2
Mozart, W.A.:Entführung, w. L. Orgonasova (sop), C. Sieden (sop), S. Olsen (ten), Uwe Peper (ten), C. Hauptmann (bass), Hans-Peter Minetti (nar), J. E. Gardiner (cnd), English Baroque Soloists [G] Deutsche Grammophon 2-▲ 435857-2
Mozart, W.A.:Exsultate, w. S. McNair (sop), J. E. Gardiner (cnd), English Baroque Soloists [G] Philips ▲ 434920-2
Mozart, W.A.:Idomeneo, w. Sylvia McNair (sop), Hillevi Martinpelto (sop), Anne Sophie von Otter (mez), Anthony Rolfe Johnson (ten), J. E. Gardiner (cnd), English Baroque Soloists Archiv 3-▲ 431674-2 [DDD]
Mozart, W.A.:Missa, K.427, w. S. McNair (sop), D. Montague (mez), A. Rolfe Johnson (ten), C. Hauptmann (bass), J. E. Gardiner (cnd), English Baroque Soloists [newly revised version, ed. Gardiner] [L] Philips ▲ 420210-2 [DDD]
Mozart, W.A.:Nozze di Figaro, w. A. Hagley (sop), H. Martinpelto (sop), R. Gilfrey (bar), B. Terfel (b-bar), J. E. Gardiner (cnd), English Baroque Soloists [G] Archiv 3-▲ 439871-2 [DDD]
Mozart, W.A.:Requiem, w. Barbara Bonney (sop), Anne Sophie von Otter (mez), Hans-Peter Blochwitz (ten), Willard White (bass), J. E. Gardiner (cnd), English Baroque Soloists [L] Philips ▲ 420197-2 [DDD]
Mozart, W.A.:Thamos, w. A. Miles (bass), J. E. Gardiner (cnd), English Baroque Soloists Archiv ▲ 437556-2 [DDD]
Mozart, W.A.:Zauberflöte, w. Constanze Backes (sop—Papagena), Christiane Oelze (sop—Pamina), Susan Roberts (sop—First Lady), Cyndia Sieden (sop—Queen of the Night), Carola Guber (cta—Second Lady), Maria Jonas (cta—Third Lady), Andreas Dieterich (trb—First Boy), Jan Andreas Mendel (trb—Second Boy), Florian Wöller (trb—Third Boy), Uwe Peper (ten—Monostatos), Nicolas Robertson (ten—First Man in Armor), Michael Schade (ten—Tamino), Gerald Finley (bar—Papageno), Noel Mann (bass—Second Man in Armour), Harry Peeters (bass—Sarastro), Detlef Roth (bass—Speaker/First Priest), Robert Burt (speaker—Third Priest), Robert Johnston (speaker—Second Priest), Wolfgang Knauer (speaker—Fourth Priest), Douglas Welbat (speaker—Second Priest), J. E. Gardiner (cnd), English Baroque Soloists *(rec Forum am Schlosspark, Ludwigsburg, July 1995)* Archiv 2-▲ 449166-2
Purcell, H.:Come Ye Sons of Art, w. J.E. Gardiner (cnd), Monteverdi Orch Erato ("Gardiner Purcell Collection" series) ▲ 96553-2
Purcell, H.:Dido & Aeneas, w. Ruth Holton (sop—Belinda), Elisabeth Priday (sop—2nd Woman), Donna Deam (sop—1st Witch), Shauna Beesley (sop—2nd Witch), Teresa Shaw (mez—Sorceress), Carolyn Watkinson (cta—Dido), Jonathan Peter Kenny (alt—Spirit), Paul Tindall (ten—Sailor), George Mosley (bass—Aeneas), J.E. Gardiner (cnd), English Baroque Soloists *(rec Saint George's, Bristol, UK, July 12–14, 1990)* Philips ▲ 432114-2
Purcell, H.:The Fairy Queen, w. J.E. Gardiner (cnd), English Baroque Soloists [E] Archiv 2-▲ 419221-2 [DDD]
Purcell, H.:Hail, Bright Cecilia, w. J. Smith (sop), B. Gordon (alt), A. Stafford (alt), P. Elliot (ten), S. Varcoe (bar), D. Thomas (bass), J.E. Gardiner (cnd), English Baroque Soloists Erato ("Gardiner Purcell Collection" series) ▲ 96554-2
Purcell, H.:The Indian Queen, w. J.E. Gardiner (cnd), English Baroque Soloists Erato ("Gardiner Purcell Collection" series) ▲ 96551-2
Purcell, H.:King Arthur, w. J. Smith (sop), G. Fisher (sop), E. Priday (sop), G. Ross (sop), A. Stafford (alt), P. Elliott (ten), S. Varcoe (bar), J.E. Gardiner (cnd), English Baroque Soloists Erato 2-▲ 2292-45211-2 ZA
Purcell, H.:King Arthur, w. Gillian Fisher (sop), E. Priday (sop), Gill Ross (sop), J. Smith (sop), A. Stafford (alt), P. Elliot (ten), S. Varcoe (bar), J.E. Gardiner (cnd), English Baroque Soloists Erato ("Gardiner Purcell Collection" series) 2-▲ 96552-2
Purcell, H.:Music for the Funeral of Queen Mary, w. J.E. Gardiner (cnd), Monteverdi Orch Erato ("Gardiner Purcell Collection" series) ▲ 96553-2

Monteverdi Choir London (cont.)

Purcell, H.:The Prophetess, or The History of Dioclesian, w. L. Dawson (sop), Gillian Fisher (sop), R. Covey-Crump (ten), P. Elliot (ten), S. Varcoe (bar), M. George (bass), J.E. Gardiner (cnd), Monteverdi Orch Erato ("Gardiner Purcell Collection" series) 2-▲ 96556-2
Purcell, H.:The Tempest, w. J.E. Gardiner (cnd), Monteverdi Orch Erato ("Gardiner Purcell Collection" series) ▲ 96555-2
Purcell, H.:Timon of Athens, w. L. Dawson (sop), Gillian Fisher (sop), R. Covey-Crump (ten), P. Elliot (ten), S. Varcoe (bar), M. George (bass), J.E. Gardiner (cnd), Monteverdi Orch Erato ("Gardiner Purcell Collection" series) 2-▲ 96556-2
Purcell, H.:Welcome to All the Pleasures, w. Ruth Holton (sop), Nicola Jenkin (sop), Michael Chance (alt), Paul Tindall (ten), George Mosly (bass), J.E. Gardiner (cnd), English Baroque Soloists *(rec Saint George's, Bristol, UK, July 12–14, 1990)* Philips ▲ 432114-2
Rameau, J.P.:La Danse, w. J. Gomez (sop), A.-M. Rodde (sop), J.-C. Orliac (ten), J.E. Gardiner (cnd), Monteverdi Orch Erato ▲ 45985-2
Ravel, M.:Chansons, w. J. E. Gardiner (cnd), Orch Révolutionnaire et Romantique Philips ▲ 438149-2
Reger, M.:Orchestral Songs, w. D. Fischer-Dieskau (bar), G. Albrecht (cnd), Hamburg PO, St. Michael's Choir—Der Einsiedler, Op. 144a; Hymnus der Liebe, Op. 136; Requiem, Op. 144b; An die Hoffnung, Op. 124 [G] Orfeo ▲ 209901 [DDD]
Telemann, G.P.:Ino, w. R. Alexander (sop), K. Equiliz (ten), M. Van Egmond (bar), N. Harnoncourt (cnd), Vienna Concentus Musicus Teldec 2-▲ 9031-77621-2
Verdi, G.:Requiem Mass, w. Donna Brown (sop), Luba Orgonasova (sop), Anne Sofie von Otter (mez), Luca Canonici (ten), Alastair Miles (bass), J. E. Gardiner (cnd), Orch Révolutionnaire et Romantique Philips 2-▲ 442142-2

J.E. Gardiner (cnd)

Bach, J.S.:Komm, Jesu, Komm Philips ▲ 446116-2
Brahms, J.:Liebeslieder Waltzes SATB Philips ▲ 432152-2 [DDD]
Gabrieli, G.:Canticle Jubilate Deo Philips ▲ 446116-2
Gluck, C.W.:Iphigénie en Aulide, w. L. Dawson (sop), A. S. von Otter (mez), J. Aler (ten), J. Van Dam (b-bar), Lyon Opera Orch Erato ("Musifrance" series) 2-▲ 2292-45003-2-ZA [DDD]
Jubilate Deo! Philips ▲ 446116-2
Monteverdi, C.:Hor che'l ciel Philips ▲ 446116-2
Monteverdi, C.:Vespro della Beata Vergine London ("Double Decker" series) 2-▲ 443482-2
Poulenc, F.:Figure humaine Philips ▲ 446116-2
Purcell, H.:Anthems & Services—Hear My Prayer, O Lord; O God, Thou Hast Cast Us Out Philips ▲ 446116-2
Purcell, H.:King Arthur (sels), w. J. Smith (sop), G. Fisher (sop), E. Priday (sop), G. Ross (sop), English Baroque Soloists Erato ▲ 45919-2
Saint-Saëns, C.:Choeurs, Op. 68 Philips ▲ 438149-2
Saint-Saëns, C.:Choeurs, Op. 141 Philips ▲ 438149-2
Schütz, H.:Es gingen zweene Menschen hinauf Cantate ▲ 57615 [AAD]
Schütz, H.:Ich beschwere euch Cantate ▲ 57615 [AAD]
Schütz, H.:Mein Sohn, warum hast du uns das getan Cantate ▲ 57615 [AAD]
Schütz, H.:Motets (misc), w. English Baroque Soloists—Freue dich des Weibes, SWV.453; Ist nicht Ephraim mein teurer Sohn, SWV.40; Saul, Saul, was verfolgst du mich, SWV.415; Auf dem Gebirge, SWV.396 [G] Archiv ▲ 423405-2 [DDD]
Schütz, H.:Motets (misc)—Freu dich des Weibes deiner Jugend Philips ▲ 446116-2
Schütz, H.:Musicalische Exequien, w. English Baroque Soloists [G] Archiv ▲ 423405-2 [DDD]
Schütz, H.:Psalms—Wie Lieblich sind deine Wohnung (84) Philips ▲ 446116-2
Schütz, H.:Weib, was weinest du Cantate ▲ 57615 [AAD]
Tavener, J.:The World is Burning Philips ▲ 446116-2
Verdi, G.:Pezzi sacri Philips 2-▲ 442142-2

Monteverdi Choir London members

Holst, G.:The Planets, w. J. E. Gardiner (cnd), Philharmonia Orch Deutsche Grammophon ▲ 445860-2

Montilla Chorus

D. Montorio (cnd)

Coros de zarzuelas, w. Montilla Orch Montilla ▲ MNT 3028

Montpellier Vocal Ensemble

J. Glouzes (cnd)

Laudario di Cortona Jade ▲ JAD C 092

Montreal Sym Chorus

Berlioz, H.:Les Troyens, w. F. Pollet (sop—Dido), D. Voigt (sop—Cassandre), C. Dubosc (sop—Ascagne), H. Perraguin (cta—Anna), G. Lakes (ten—Aeneas), J.-L. Maurette (ten—Iopas), J. M. Ainsley (ten—Hylas), M. P. (ten—Panthee), G. Cross (ten—Sinon), G. Quilico (bar—Chorebe), J.-P. Courtis (b-bar—Narbal), M. Belleau (bass—Ghost of Hector), R. Schirrer (bass—Priam), C. Dutoit (cnd), Montreal SO London 4-▲ 443693-2 [DDD]
Debussy, C.:Nocturnes, w. C. Dutoit (cnd), Montreal SO London ▲ 425502-2 [DDD]
Debussy, C.:Pelléas et Mélisande, w. C. Alliot-Lugaz (sop), F. Golfier (sop), C. Carlson (mez), D. Henry (ten), G. Cachemaille (bar), P. Thau (bass), C. Dutoit (cnd), Montreal SO [F] London 2-▲ 430502-2 [DDD]
Fauré, G.:Pavane Orch, w. C. Dutoit (cnd), Montreal SO London ▲ 421440-2 [DDD] □ 421440-5
Fauré, G.:Requiem, w. K. Te Kanawa (sop), S. Milnes (bar), C. Dutoit (cnd), Montreal SO [L] London ▲ 421440-2 [DDD] □ 421440-5
Janácek, L.:Sinfonietta, w. C. Dutoit (cnd), Montreal SO London ▲ 436211-2
Janácek, L.:Slavonic Mass, w. N. Troitskaya (sop), E. Randova (cta), K. Kaludov (ten), S. Leiferkas (bass), T. Trotter (org), C. Dutoit (cnd), Montreal SO London ▲ 436211-2
Prokofiev, S.:Alexander Nevsky, w. J. van Nes (cta), C. Dutoit (cnd), Montreal SO London ▲ 430506-2 [DDD]
Ravel, M.:Daphins et Chloé, w. C. Dutoit (cnd), Montreal SO London ▲ 400055-2 [DDD]

Montreal Tudor Vocal Ensemble

P. Wedd (cnd)

Choral Works of Quebec CBC Records ("Musica Viva" series) ▲ MVCD 1039 [DDD] ■ MVC 1039 (D)

Montserrat Abbey Monks' Choir

Pange Lingua Studio SM ▲ 12 19 50 [AAD]

Montserrat Monastic Schola

G. Estrada (cnd)

Gregorian Chant Jade ▲ JAD C 005

Moravian Trombone Choir of Downey

Music for All Seasons:Moravian Trombones, w. Los Angeles Philharmonic Trombone Ensemble Crystal ▲ CD 220

Moravian-Academic Choral Society

Janácek, L.:Amarus, w. *(soloists unknown)*, B. Bakala (cnd), Brno RSO, 1954) Panton ▲ PAN 811242
Janácek, L.:Sinfonietta, w. B. Bakala (cnd), Brno RSO *(rec 1955)* Panton ▲ PAN 811264
Janácek, L.:Taras Bulba, w. B. Bakala (cnd), Brno RSO *(rec 1952)* Panton ▲ PAN 811264

Mormon Tabernacle Choir

An American Tribute, w. US Air Force Band, Singing Sergeants CBS ▲ MK 42133 [DDD] ■ MT 42133 (D)
Anvil Chorus:Favorite Opera Choruses, w. Philadelphia Orch CBS ■ MT 07061
Bach, J.S.:Jesu bleibet meine Freude [E] CBS ■ MT 6058
Bach, J.S.:Sheep May Safely Graze [E] CBS ■ MT 6058
Beloved Choruses CBS ■ MT 06058
Bless This House CBS ■ MT 06835
The Chorus, w. New York Choral Society, Vocal Majority, Westminster Choir, Chicago Sym Chorus members, et al. Sony Classical ("Greatest Hits" series) ▲ MLK 62684 ■ MLT 62684
Climb Every Mountain CBS ■ MT 30647
Copland, A.:Canticle of Freedom, w. M. Tilson Thomas (cnd), Utah SO [E] CBS ▲ MK 42140 [DDD] ■ MT 42140 (D)
Copland, A.:Motets (4) [E] CBS ▲ MK 42140 [DDD] ■ MT 42140 (D)
Copland, A.:Old American Songs, w. M. Tilson Thomas (cnd), Utah SO [E] CBS ▲ MK 42140 [DDD] ■ MT 42140 (D)

984 ▲ = CD ◆ = Enhanced CD Δ = MD ■ = Cassette Tape □ = DCC

Mormon Tabernacle Choir (cont.)
Fantasies for 8 Horns, Bayreuth Festival Horns Acanta ▲ 43800
God Bless America *(rec 1961–1976)* Sony Masterworks ▲ MDK 48295 ■ MGT 48295
God Bless America CBS ■ MT 06721
God Of Our Fathers, w. Philadelphia Brass CBS ■ MT 30054
A Grand Night for Singing, w. Milnes, Sherrill (bar), Columbia SO CBS ■ MT 35170
Great Choruses of Bach & Handel, w. Philadelphia Orch CBS ■ MXT 39102
The Great Thanksgiving:Hymns & Songs of Thanks & Brotherhood, w. Frank Asper (org), Alexander Schreiner (org) *(rec Salt Lake City, Utah)* Sony Classical ▲ SMK 61983 ■ SMT 61983
Greatest Hits:22 Best-Loved Favorites *(rec 1958–1985)* Sony Masterworks ▲ MDK 48294 ■ MGT 48294
Greatest Hits, Vol. II CBS ■ MT 07086
Greatest Hits, Vol. III CBS ■ MT 07399
Hallelujah:Famous Choruses London ▲ 443381–2 [DDD]
Handel, G.F.:Messiah, w. Eileen Farrell (sop), Martha Lipton (cta), T. Cunningham (ten), William Warfield (bar), E. Ormandy (cnd), Philadelphia Orch [E] CBS 2–▲ M2K 00607 ■ M2T 00607
Handel, G.F.:Messiah (sels), w. R. Condie (cnd), Royal PO—choruses [E] CBS ▲ MK 32935
Handel, G.F.:Music of, w. Igor Kipnis (hpd), E. Ormandy (cnd), Philadelphia Orch—The Harmonious Blacksmith; See the conquering hero comes & Hallelujah Amen, from Judas Maccabaeus ("Handel's Greatest Hits") CBS ▲ MLK 39441 ■ MT 39441
Hanson, H.:Song of Democracy, w. H. Hanson (cnd), United States Air Force Band [E] CBS ▲ MK 42133 [DDD]
Jesu, Joy Of Man's Desiring:20 Great Bach & Handel Choruses *(rec 1958–1981)* Sony Masterworks ▲ MDK 48296 ■ MGT 48296
Live in Australia ABC Classics ▲ 836 508–2 [DDD]
The Lord Is My Shepherd CBS ■ MT 06019
The Lord's Prayer CBS ■ MT 06068
Make a Joyful Noise:Beloved Choruses, w. Columbia SO [cnd:Jerold Ottley] *(rec Salt Lake City, Utah, Feb 13–14, 1980 & Feb 27–)* Sony Classical ▲ SMK 061984 [DDD] ■ SMT 061984
A Mighty Fortress CBS ■ MT 06162
More Greatest Hits:18 Best Loved Favorites Sony Classical ▲ SMK 61982 ■ SMT 61982
The Mormon Tabernacle Choir Album, w. Philadelphia Orch [cnd:Eugene Ormandy] CBS 2–■ MGT 31081
Old Beloved Songs CBS ■ MT 07012
Rock Of Ages:30 Favorite Hymns *(rec 1960–1969)* Sony Masterworks ▲ MDK 48293 ■ MGT 48293
Simple Gifts, w. Stade, Frederica von (mez), Utah SO [cnd:Joseph Silverstein], John Longhurst (org) London ▲ 436284–2 LH [DDD]
Songs America Loves Best, Vol. 1:Memories CBS ■ MT 35825
Songs from America's Heartland London ▲ 430834–2 [DDD]
Songs of Inspiration, w. Te Kanawa, Kiri (sop), Julius Rudel, Utah SO London ▲ 425431–2 LH [DDD]
Songs of the Civil War & Stephen Foster Favorites *(rec 1960–68)* Sony Masterworks ▲ MDK 48297 ■ MGT 48297
Stars & Stripes Forever CBS ■ MT 32298
Tchaikovsky, P.:Ov 1812, w. E. Ormandy (cnd), Philadelphia Orch, Brass Band CBS ■ MT 30447
Tchaikovsky, P.:Ov 1812, w. E. Ormandy (cnd), Philadelphia Orch Brass Band Odyssey ▲ MBK 39784
Tchaikovsky, P.:Romeo & Juliet, w. E. Ormandy (cnd), Philadelphia Orch Brass Band Odyssey ▲ MBK 39784
This Is My Country CBS ■ MT 06419
This Is Your Land CBS ■ MT 06747
Voices in Harmony, w. Vocal Majority CBS ▲ MK 42380 [DDD] ■ FMT 42380 (D)
When You Wish upon a Star:A Tribute to Walt Disney CBS ▲ MK 37200 [DDD] ■ FMT 37200 (D)

Mormon Youth Chorus
Hanson, H.:Song of Democracy, w. H. Hanson (cnd), Mormon Youth SO *(rec Howard Hanson Festival, Salt Lake Tabernacle, UT, Mar 11, 1972)* Citadel ▲ CTD 88110 [ADD]

Moscow Academy Choir
V. Popov (cnd)
Tchaikovsky, P.:Liturgy of St. John Chrysostom Russian Season ("Russian Season" series) ▲ RUS 288096

Moscow Bolshoi Theater Chorus—see Bolshoi Theater Chorus

Moscow Boys' Cappella
Mahler, G.:Sym 3, w. Olga Alexandrova (mez), E. Svetlanov (cnd), Russian State SO, Russian Academic Choir *(rec Large Hall of the Conservatory, Moscow, Dec. 1994)* Russian Season 2–▲ RUS 288111/12 [DDD]

Moscow Capella
Glazunov, A.:Tsar Iudeyskiy, w. I. Golovshin (cnd), Moscow SO *(rec Mosfilm Studio, Moscow, May 1995)* Naxos ▲ 8.553575 [DDD]

Moscow Cathedral Choir
Missa Russica, w. Russian Monks Choir, Mainzer Cathedral Choir, Moscow Holy Synod Boys' Choir [cnd:Victor Popov] Koch Schwann ▲ SCH 312122 ■ SCH 212124

Moscow Chamber Choir
Shchedrin, R.:Dead Souls, w. Larisa Avdeyeva (mez—Korobochka), Galina Borisova (mez—Plyushkin), Alexi Maslennikov (ten—Selifan), Vladislav Piavko (ten—Nozdryov), Vitali Vlasov (ten—Manilov), Boris Morozov (bass—Sobakevich), Alexander Voroshilo (sgr—Chichikov), Y. Temirkanov (cnd), Bolshoi Theater Orch, Bolshoi Theater Chorus *(rec Moscow, 1982)* Melodiya ("The Russian Opera" series) 2–▲ 74321–29347–2 [ADD]
V. Minin (cnd)
Rachmaninoff, S.:Liturgy of St John Chrysostom Melodiya ("Russian Choral Music" series) ▲ 74321–25187–2 [DDD]
Sviridov, G.:Choral Music—Pushkin's Garland; Con to the Memory of A.A. Yurlov; 3 Choral Pieces of the Music to Tolstoy's Drama Tsar Fyodor Ioannovich Russian Compact Disc ▲ RCD 13005

Moscow Chamber Choral Theater
B. Pevzner (cnd)
Kanty:Russian Choral Music of the 17th & 18th Centuries Russian Season ▲ LDC 288092

Moscow Choral Academy Choir
Rachmaninoff, S.:Spring, w. N. Surikov (bar), A. Tchistiakov (cnd), Moscow Choral Academy Orch Russian Season ("Russian Season" series) ▲ LDC 288069
Tchaikovsky, P.:Moscow, w. N. Terntieva (mez), N. Surikov (bar), A. Tchistiakov (cnd) Russian Season ▲ LDC 288069
A. Tchistiakov (cnd)
Taneyev, S.:Choral Music, w. N. Terentieva (mez), N. Surikov (bar)—St. John's of Damascus Russian Season ▲ LDC 288069

Moscow Choral Academy Men & Children's Choir
V. Popov (cnd)
300 Years of Russian Religious Chants Russian Season ▲ LDC 288066

Moscow Holy Synod Boys' Choir
Missa Russica, w. Russian Monks Choir, Moscow Cathedral Choir, Mainzer Cathedral Choir, Moscow Holy Synod Boys' Choir [cnd:Victor Popov] Koch Schwann ▲ SCH 312122 ■ SCH 212124

Moscow Liturgic Choir
Kiev Christmas Liturgy Erato ▲ 2292–92874–2

Moscow Male Voice Choir
V. Popov (cnd)
Arkhangelsky, A.:Hymns of the Russian Orthodox Church Koch Schwann ▲ SCH 315562
Bortnyansky, D.:Sacred Choral Music Koch Schwann ▲ SCH 315562
Chesnokov, P.:Sacred Choral Music Koch Schwann ▲ SCH 315562
Kastalsky, A.:Sacred Choral Music Koch Schwann ▲ SCH 315562

Moscow New Choir
E. Rastvorova (cnd)
Shvedov, K.:Liturgy of St. John Chrysostom, w. Vladimir Gubsky (sgr) Olympia ▲ OLY 481 [DDD]

Moscow New Choir (cont.)
E. Rastvorova (cnd) (cont.)
Shvedov, K.:Sacred Music—selected Orthodox Chants Olympia ▲ OLY 481 [DDD]
Sviridov, G.:Choruses Olympia ▲ OLY 541 [DDD]
Sviridov, G.:Night Clouds Olympia ▲ OLY 541 [DDD]
Sviridov, G.:Songs of Troubled Times Olympia ▲ OLY 541 [DDD]

Moscow Patriarchal Choir
Early Russian Plain Chant Opus 111 ▲ OPS 30–79
Russian Chant:A Millenium of Chants & Hymns Koch International Classics ▲ KIC 7299 [DDD]
A. Rybakova (cnd)
Arkhangelsky, A.:All Night Vigil Russian Compact Disc ▲ RCD 15004 [AAD]
Arkhangelsky, A.:Hymns of the Russian Orthodox Church—I Think upon the Fearful Day; I Cried unto the Lord with My Voice; We Have No Other Help; Why Hast Thou Cast Me off; Blessed Is He That Considereth the Poor Russian Compact Disc ▲ RCD 15004 [AAD]
Russian Folk Songs Naxos ▲ 8.550781 [DDD]

Moscow Patriarchate Children's Choir
Russian Choirs Sing for the Children of Chernobyl, w. Church of the Resurrection Choir Moscow, Korez Convent Choir, Pyuchtize Convent Choir, Zagorsk Monks' Choir, Moscow Religious Academy Choir, Moscow Religious Academy Choir, Dormition of the Virgin Church Choir Koch Schwann ▲ SCH 313322 [ADD/DDD]

Moscow Patriarchate Publishing Division Choir
Hymns for the Holy Week in the Russian Orthodox Church, w. Korez Holy Trinity Nunnery Trio, Leningrad Religious Academy Student Choir Koch Schwann ▲ SCH 313073 [ADD]

Moscow Religious Academy Choir
Russian Choirs Sing for the Children of Chernobyl, w. Moscow Patriarchate Children's Choir, Church of the Resurrection Choir Moscow, Korez Convent Choir, Pyuchtize Convent Choir, Zagorsk Monks' Choir, Moscow Religious Academy Choir, Dormition of the Virgin Church Choir Koch Schwann ▲ SCH 313322 [ADD/DDD]

Moscow State Boys' Choir
Shostakovich, D.:Song of the Forest, w. V. Ivanovsky (ten), I. Petrov (bass), A. Yulov (cnd), Moscow PO, Yurlov Russian Choir Russian Disc ▲ RUS 11 048 [AAD]
Shostakovich, D.:The Sun Shines on Our Motherland, w. K. Ivanov (cnd), USSR SO, Yurlov Russian Choir Russian Disc ▲ RUS 11 048 [AAD]

Moscow Tchaikovsky Conservatory Chamber Choir Women's Voices
B. Tevlin (cnd)
Suslin, V.:Choruses on Poems by Daniil Kharms *(rec Lockenhaus Festival, Austria, 1995)* BIS ▲ CD 810 [DDD]

Moscow Theological Academy Choir
A. Matfei (cnd)
Hymns to the Mother of God at the Moleben, w. Trinity–St. Sergius Laura Monks' Choir, Nicolai Ivanov (cant), Nicolai Zabelich (cant) *(rec Cathedral of the Dormition, Trinity–St. Sergiy Lavra, June 1987)* Russian Compact Disc ▲ RCD 15002 [AAD]

Motet & Madrigal Posen Chamber Chorus
Rossini, G.:La gazetta, w. Teresa Verdera (sop), Gianpiero Ruggeri (sgr), Kasimierz Sergiel (sgr), Ezio Maria Tisi (sgr), W. Keitel (cnd), Minsk Orch Deutsche Schallplatten ▲ DS 1053

Mouez Armor Chorale
Orff, C.:Carmina burana, w. Elisabeth Vidal (sop), Alexander Stevensen (ten), André Cognet (bass), P. Kuentz (cnd), Paul Kuentz Orch, Paul Kuentz Choir, Lorient Conservatory Chorus, Notre Dame College Chorus Pierre Verany ▲ PVY 730044

Mount Angel Abbey Choir
Chants for the Season RCA Victor ▲ 09026–68007–2 ■ 09026–68007–4
A. Baumgartner (cnd)
On Angels' Wings *(rec Mount Angel Abbey Church, Saint Benedict, OR, Jan 3–6, 1995)* RCA Red Seal ▲ 09026–68244–2 [DDD]

Mozart Choir
Haydn, M.:Requiem in c, w. Siglinde Damisch (sop), Gabriele Schreckenbach (mez), Chris Merritt (ten), Hans Udo Müller (pno), Gerhard Walterskirchen (org), E. Hinreiner (cnd), Salzburg RSO *(rec June 1981)* Koch Treasure ▲ 31608–2 [ADD]
Mozart, W.A.:Missa, K.66, w. P. Wise (sop), M. Aoyama (cta), P. Baillie (ten), H. Müller (bass), E. Hinreiner (cnd), Salzburg Camerata Academica, Salzburg RSO [L] *(rec May 1974)* Koch Treasure ▲ 316182 [ADD]

Munich Bach Choir
Bach, J.S.:Cants (misc), w. K. Richter (cnd), Munich Bach Orch—Nos. 1, 4, 6, 12, 23, 67, 87, 92, 104, 108, 126, 158 & 182 Archiv ▲ 439374–2 [ADD]
Bach, J.S.:Cant 26, w. E. Mathis (sop), P. Schreier (ten), A. Schmidt (bar), D. Fischer-Dieskau (bar), K. Richter (cnd), Munich Bach Orch Archiv ▲ 427130–2 [ADD]
Bach, J.S.:Cant 67, w. P. Pears (ten), K. Engen (bass), K. Richter (cnd), Munich Bach Orch Teldec ▲ 9031–77614–2
Bach, J.S.:Cant 80, w. E. Mathis (sop), T. Schmidt (mez), P. Schreier (ten), D. Fischer-Dieskau (bar), K. Richter (cnd), Munich Bach Orch Archiv ▲ 427130–2 [ADD]
Bach, J.S.:Cant 108, w. P. Pears (ten), K. Engen (bass), K. Richter (cnd), Munich Bach Orch Teldec ▲ 9031–77614–2
Bach, J.S.:Cant 116, w. E. Mathis (sop), T. Schmidt (mez), P. Schreier (ten), D. Fischer-Dieskau (bar), K. Richter (cnd), Munich Bach Orch Archiv ▲ 427130–2 [ADD]
Bach, J.S.:Cant 127, w. P. Pears (ten), K. Engen (bass), K. Richter (cnd), Munich Bach Orch Teldec ▲ 9031–77614–2
Bach, J.S.:Cant 140, w. E. Mathis (sop), P. Schreier (ten), D. Fischer-Dieskau (bar), K. Richter (cnd), Munich Bach Orch [G] Deutsche Grammophon ("Galleria" series) ▲ 419466–2 [ADD]
Bach, J.S.:Magnificat, BWV 243, w. M. Stader (sop), H. Töpper (cta), E. Haefliger (ten), D. Fischer-Dieskau (bar), K. Richter (cnd), Munich Bach Orch [L] Deutsche Grammophon ("Galleria" series) ▲ 419466–2 [ADD]
Bach, J.S.:Mass in b, BWV 232, w. B. Bonney (sop), C. Wulkopf (mez), P. Schrier (ten), A. Scharinger (bass), S. Celibidache (cnd), Munich PO Exclusive ▲ EXL 33 [ADD]
Bach, J.S.:Mass in b, BWV 232, w. A. Stumphius (sop), C. Kallisch (alto), R. Wörle (ten), A. Schmidt (bass), H.–M. Schneidt (cnd), Munich Bach Orch *(rec Mar 21, 1992)* Calig 2–▲ CAL 5029/30 [ADD]
Bach, J.S.:St. John Passion, w. Evelyn Lear (sop), Hertha Töpper (mez), Ernst Haefliger (ten), Hermann Prey (bar), Kieth Engen (bass), K. Richter (cnd), Munich Bach Orch Deutsche Grammophon ("2CD" series) 2–▲ 453 007–2
Bach, J.S.:St. Matthew Passion, w. I. Seefried (sop), A. Fahberg (sop), H. Töpper (alt), E. Haefliger (ten), D. Fischer-Dieskau (bar), K. Engen (bass), M. Proebstl (bass), K. Richter (cnd), Munich Bach Orch Archiv ▲ 439338–2 [ADD]

Munich Bavarian Radio Chorus
Huber, K.:Soliloquia, w. H. Lukomska (sop), S. Klare (mez), D. Ahlstedt (ten), B. McDaniel (bar), H. G. Ahrens (b–bar), H. Zender (cnd), Munich Bavarian RSO [L] *(rec Dec. 17, 1979)* Grammont ▲ CTSP 24–2 [ADD]
Huber, K.:Soliloquia, Part II:Cuius legibus rotantur poli, w. H. Lukomska (sop), S. Klare (mez), D. Ahlstedt (ten), B. McDaniel (bar), H. G. Ahrens (b–bar), H. Zender (cnd), Munich Bavarian RSO [L] *(rec Dec. 17, 1979)* Grammont ▲ CTSP 24–2 [ADD]

Munich Bavarian State Opera Chorus
Strauss (II), Joh.:Der Zigeunerbaron (sels), w. Rita Streich (sop), Grace Bumbry (mez), Biserka Cvejic (mez), Gisela Litz (alt), Nicolai Gedda (ten), Hermann Prey (bar), Kurt Bohme (bass), F. Allers (cnd), Munich Bavarian State Opera Orch Emperor Operetta ▲ KO 86346

Munich Benedictine Abbey Choral School
Munich Benedictine Abbey Choral School Celestial Harmonies ▲ 13094–2
G. Joppich (cnd)
Munich Benedictine Abbey Choral School Archiv ▲ 427120–2 [ADD]

Munich Capella Antiqua
Dufay, G.:Choruses & Songs, w. G. Ruhland (bass) Elektra/Nonesuch ■ 71171–4
Dufay, G.:Hymns, w. G. Ruhland (bass) Elektra/Nonesuch ■ 71171–4

CHORAL GROUPS

Munich Capella Antiqua (cont.)
Dufay, G.:Sacred & Secular Music, w. G. Ruhland (bass) Elektra/Nonesuch ▮ 71171-4
Gregorian Chants, w. [cnd:Konrad Ruhland] Celestial Harmonies ▲ 13094-2
Gregorian Chants for Easter Harmonia Mundi ▲ HMC 905113
Quietude Teldec ▲ 96036 ▮ 96036
Voices of the Middle Ages *(rec 9-67)* Elektra/Nonesuch ▮ 71171-4
N. Harnoncourt (cnd)
Monteverdi, C.:Orfeo, w. R. Hansmann (sop), C. Berberian (sop), L. Kozma (ten), K. Equiluz (bar), M. Van Egmond (bass), Vienna Concentus Musicus Teldec 2-▲ 42494-2
Munich Concerto Vocale
Brixi, F.X.:Missa di Gloria, w. F. Wagner (sop), R. Schneider-Waterberg (alt), B. Hirtreiter (ten), M. Mantaj (bass), C. Hammer (org), W. Kelber (cnd), Munich Monteverdi Orch *(rec 1993)* Calig ▲ CAL 50927 [ADD]
Munich Group for Early Music
M. Zöbeley (cnd)
Daser, L.:Sacred Music, w. Karl Ernst Schröder (lt)—Et verbum caro factum est; Hodie Deus homo factus *(rec Church in Attel, May 27-31, 1995)* ARS Musici ▲ AM 1175-2 [DDD]
Gerle, H.:Motets—Luatentabulatur über Inviolata Ars Musici ▲ AM 1133-2 [DDD]
Isaac, H.:Sacred Music, w. Karl Ernst Schröder (lt)—Puer natus *(rec Church in Attel, May 27-31, 1995)* ARS Musici ▲ AM 1175-2 [DDD]
Lassus, O. de:Motets, w. Karl Ernst Schröder (lt)—Resonet in laudibus; Jubilemus singuli; Verbum caro factum est *(rec Church in Attel, May 27-31, 1995)* ARS Musici ▲ AM 1175-2 [DDD]
Lassus, O. de:Songs, w. Karl Ernst Schröder (lt)—Der Tag, der ist so frewdenreich; Maria voll Genad *(rec Church in Attel, May 27-31, 1995)* ARS Musici ▲ AM 1175-2 [DDD]
Rore, C. de:Sacred Music, w. Karl Ernst Schröder (lt)—Illuxit nunc sacra dies; Hodie Christus natus est *(rec Church in Attel, May 27-31, 1995)* ARS Musici ▲ AM 1175-2 [DDD]
Senfl, L.:Sacred Music, w. Karl Ernst Schröder (lt)—Verbum caro factum est; Puer natus est nobis *(rec Church in Attel, May 27-31, 1995)* ARS Musici ▲ AM 1175-2 [DDD]
Munich Hochschule Madrigal Choir
Orff, C.:Schulwerk (complete), w. Godela Orff (nar), Carolin Widmann (vn), Sonja Korkeala (vn), Markus Zahnhausen (rcr), Karl Peinkofer (perc), Andreas Schumacher (perc), Wilfried Hiller (perc/mar), Martin Ruhland (mar)—Wessobrun Prayer for a capella Choir; 2 Pieces for a capella Choir; 8 Pieces for 2 Vns; Mater et filia for women's a capella Choir; Devotional Yodel for male a capella Choir; 5 Pieces for Sop, Rcr & Perc; Death for Nar., Wood Bells, Bass Xyl & Tam-Tam; Omnia tempus habent for mixed Choir, Timp & Little Dr; Rubato, molto allegro, rubato; Abenlied for Nar, Bass Metallophon, Bass Xyl, Large Dr & Wine Glass; 5 Pieces for Fl & Perc; Devotional Yodel for male Choir [version 2]; 7 Pieces for 2 Xyl *(rec Munich, 1994-95)* Celestial Harmonies ▲ 13105-2
Munich Madrigal Choir
Dupré, M.:Motets, Op. 9 FSM ▲ FCD 97 735 [DDD]
Satie, E.:Messe des pauvres FSM ▲ FCD 97735 [DDD]
Widor, C.M.:Mass FSM ▲ FCD 97735 [DDD]
F. Brandl (cnd)
French Music for Choir & 2 Organs, w. E. Sperer (org), W. Englhardt (org) FSM ▲ 97735 [DDD]
Munich Motet Choir
Bizet, G.:Te Deum, w. Angela Maria Blasi (sop), Christian Elsner (ten), H.R. Zöbeley (cnd), Munich SO *(rec live, Herkulessaal, Munich, Mar 13 & 17, 1996)* Calig ▲ CAL 50956 [DDD]
Cherubini, L.:Masses, w. Monika Wiebe (sop), Helena Jungwirth (alt), Rodrigo Orrego (ten), Wolf Matthias Friedrich (bass), H.R. Zöbeley (cnd), Munich SO—Missa Solemnis Calig ▲ CAL 50914
Gounod, C.:Messe solennelle de St. Cécile, w. Angela Maria Blasi (sop), Christian Elsner (ten), Dietrich Henschel (bar), H.R. Zöbeley (cnd), Munich SO *(rec live, Herkulessaal, Munich, Mar 13 & 17, 1996)* Calig ▲ CAL 50956 [DDD]
Handel, G.F.:Judas Maccabaeus, w. M. Meier-Schmid (sop), Elisabeth von Magnus (alt), Jörg Dürmüller (ten), Robert Wörle (ten), Franz-Josef Selig (bass), T. Fey (cnd), Schlierbach CO [E] Christophorus 2-▲ 77128 [DDD]
Haydn, M.:Missa in honorem Sanctae Ursulae, w. Mechthild Bach (sop), Gabriele Binder (cta), Karl-Heinz Lampe (ten), Joachim Gebhardt (bass), H.R. Zöbeley (cnd), Munich Residenz Orch Calig ▲ CAL 50901 [DDD]
Hiller, W.:Schulamit, w. Regina Klepper (sop), Edeltraud Knabel (alt), Michael Schopper (bass), Elisabeth Woska (nar), Waltraut Mastrogiovanni-Kraxner (shofar), H.R. Zöbeley (cnd), Munich Residenz Orch, Munich Percussion Ensemble, Calw Aurelius Boys' Choir Soloists Wergo ▲ WER 6280-2
Mozart, W.A.:Ave verum corpus, w. H.R. Zöbeley (cnd), Munich Residenz Orch Calig ▲ CAL 50901 [DDD]
Mozart, W.A.:Missa, K.257, w. H.R. Zöbeley (cnd), Munich Residenz Orch *(rec July 17, 1988 & Nov. 3, 1)* Calig ▲ CAL 50872 [DDD]
Mozart, W.A.:Missa solemnis, K.337, w. H.R. Zöbeley (cnd), Munich Residenz Orch *(rec July 17, 1988 & Nov. 3, 1)* Calig ▲ CAL 50872 [DDD]
Mozart, W.A.:Regina coeli, K.276, w. H.R. Zöbeley (cnd), Munich Residenz Orch *(rec July 17, 1988 & Nov. 3, 1)* Calig ▲ CAL 50872 [DDD]
Mozart, W.A.:Regina coeli, K.276, w. J. Banse (sop), H.R. Zöbeley (cnd), Munich Residenz Orch Calig ▲ CAL 50901 [DDD]
Orff, C.:Carmina burana, w. *(soloists unknown)*, H.R. Zöbeley (cnd), Munich Residenz Orch Calig 2-▲ CAL 50937/38
Orff, C.:Catulli Carmina, w. *(soloists unknown)*, H.R. Zöbeley (cnd), Munich Residenz Orch Calig 2-▲ CAL 50937/38
Orff, C.:Dithyrambe, w. *(soloists unknown)*, H.R. Zöbeley (cnd), Munich Residenz Orch Calig 2-▲ CAL 50937/38
Serenades and Ständchen, w. Munich Wind Ensemble Calig ▲ CAL 50890 [DDD]
...und Friede auf Erden, w. Munich Wind Ensemble Calig ▲ CAL 50522 [DDD]
H.R. Zöbeley (cnd)
Schütz, H.:Motets (misc)—Es erhub sich ein Streit im Himmel Entrée ▲ 0048 [ADD]
Schütz, H.:Symphoniae sacrae 3—Komm, heiliger Geist, Herre Gott, SWV 417; Nun danket alle Gott, SWV 418 Entrée ▲ 0048 [ADD]
Munich National Theater Chorus
Mascagni, P.:Cavalleria rusticana, w. Ruth Falcon (sop—Lola), Leonie Rysanek (sop—Santuzza), Astrid Varnay (sop—Mamma Lucia), Plácido Domingo (ten—Turiddu), Benito di Bella (bar—Alfio), N. Santi (cnd), Munich National Theater Orch *(rec Munich, Dec 25, 1978)* Legato Classics ▲ LCD 202-1
Munich Phil Chorus
Beethoven, L. van:Sym 9, "Choral Sym", w. H. Donath (sop), D. Soffel (mez), S. Jerusalem (ten), P. Lika (bass), S. Celibidache (cnd), Munich PO *(rec Mar. 19, 1989)* Exclusive ▲ EXL 15 [AAD]
Ravel, M.:Daphnis et Chloé (suite 1), w. S. Celibidache (cnd), Munich PO *(rec live, Munich, 1970's)* As Disc ▲ ASD 2501
Ravel, M.:Daphnis et Chloé (suite 2), w. S. Celibidache (cnd), Munich PO *(rec live, Munich, 1970's)* As Disc ▲ ASD 2501
Munich Radio Chorus
Albert, E. d':Tiefland, w. Martón, Kollo, Weikl, Moll, M. Janowski (cnd), Munich RSO—[G] Acanta 2-▲ 43481
Gazzaniga, G.:Don Giovanni, w. P. Coburn (sop), J. Kaufmann (sop), J. Aler (ten), R. Swensen (ten), J.-L. Chaignaud (bar), G. von Kannen (bass), A. Scharinger (bass), S. Soltesz (cnd), Munich RSO [I] Orfeo 2-▲ 214902 [DDD]
Gluck, C.W.:Le Cinesi, w. K. Erickson (sop), M. Schiml (sop), A. Milcheva (mez), Moser (sgr), L. Gardelli (cnd), Munich RSO [I] Orfeo ▲ 178891 [DDD] ▮ MC 178891 (D)
Gounod, C.:Roméo et Juliette, w. Susan Graham (sop—Stephano), Ruth Ann Swenson (sop—Juliette), Sarah Walker (mez—Gertrude), Paul Charles Clarke (ten—Tybalt), Placido Domingo (ten—Roméo), Kurt Ollmann (bar—Mercutio), Alastair Miles (bass—Frère Laurent), David Pittman-Jennings (bass—Le Duc), Alain Vernhes (bass—Capulet), L. Slatkin (cnd), Munich RSO *(rec Studio 1, Bavarian Radio, Munich, Nov 29 - Dec 10, 1995)* RCA Red Seal 2-▲ 09026-68440-2 [DDD]
Orff, C.:Der Bernauerin, w. L. Popp (sop), Ostermayer (sgr), Laubenthal (ten), H. Lippert (ten), K. Eichhorn (cnd), Munich RSO [G] Orfeo 2-▲ 255912 [DDD]

Munich Radio Chorus (cont.)
Puccini, G.:Suor angelica, w. L. Popp (sop), M. Lipovšek (mez), G. Patanè (cnd), Munich RSO Eurodisc ▲ 7806-2-RC [DDD]
Spontini, G.:La vestale, w. R. Plowright (sop), G. Pasino (mez), F. Araiza (ten), P. Lefèbvre (ten), A. Cauli (bar), F. de Grandis (bass), G. Kuhn (cnd), Munich RSO [F] Orfeo 2-▲ 256922 [DDD]
Verdi, G.:Oberto, Conte di San Bonifacio, w. G. Dimitrova (sop), R. Baldani (mez), A. Browner (mez), C. Bergonzi (ten), R. Panerai (bar), L. Gardelli (cnd), Munich RSO [I] Orfeo ▲ 175881 [DDD]
Verdi, G.:Oberto, Conte di San Bonifacio, w. G. Dimitrova (sop), R. Baldani (mez), A. Browner (mez), C. Bergonzi (ten), R. Panerai (bar), L. Gardelli (cnd), Munich RSO [I] Orfeo 2-▲ 105842 [DDD] 3-▮ A 105843 F
Munich Residenz Motet Choir
Schütz, H.:Magnificat anima mea, w. H.R. Zöbeley (cnd), Munich Residenz Orch [L] Orfeo ▲ 002811 [DDD]
Schütz, H.:Weihnachtshistorie, w. H.R. Zöbeley (cnd), Munich Residenz Orch [G] Orfeo ▲ 002811 [DDD]
Munich St. Michael's Choir
Diabelli, A.:Pastoralmesse, w. C. Degler (sop), S. Linden (sop), S. Rauschkolb (cta), D. Clayton (ten), H. Müller (bass), E. Ehret (cnd), Munich St. Michael's Orch [L] Koch Schwann ▲ CD 313015 [ADD]
Weber, C.M. von:Missa sancta 2, w. Maria Taborsky (sop), Gerda Kink (alt), Hermann Pöllmann (ten), Hans Huber (bass), Gisela Schindler (org), E. Ehret (cnd), Munich St. Michael's Orch Studio SM ▲ D 2454 [ADD]
Munich Theater Gartnerplatz Chorus
Lehár, F.:Giuditta (sels), w. Anneliese Rothenberger (sop), Nicolai Gedda (ten), W. Mattes (cnd), Graunke SO Emperor Operetta ▲ KO 86342
Strauss (II), Joh.:Wiener Blut (sels), w. Christine Gorner (sop), Anneliese Rothenberger (sop), Nicolai Gedda (ten), W. Mattes (cnd), Graunke SO Emperor Operetta ▲ KO 86345
Münster Cathedral Choir
Haydn, M.:German Masses, w. R. van Husen (ten), M. Flöth (bass), H.-G. Freimuth (cnd), Münster Wind Ensemble—No. 1 Calig ▲ CAL 50824 [ADD]
Schubert, Franz:Duetsche Messe, w. R. van Husen (ten), M. Flöth (bass), H.-G. Freimuth (cnd), Münster Wind Ensemble Calig ▲ CAL 50824 [ADD]
Münster City Theater Chorus
Corghi, A.:Divara—Wasser und Blut, w. Susanna von der Burg (sop—Divara), Suzanne McLeod (mez—Else Windscherer), Eva Lillian Thingboe (mez—Hille Feiken), Robert Schwarts (ten—Lame Man), Heinz Fitz (spkr—Bernd Knipperdollinck), Hanslutz Hildmann (spkr—Jan Matthys), Michael Holm (spkr—Bernhard Rothmann), Christopher Krieg (spkr—Jan van Leiden), W. Humburg (cnd), Münster SO [G] *(rec Grosses Haus, Münster State Theater, Nov. 27-29, 1993)* Marco Polo 2-▲ 8.223706/07 [DDD]
Münsterschwarzach Abbey Monks' Choir
Gregorian Chants for Lent, Passion & Easter Christophorus ▲ CD 77572 [ADD]
Masses for Christmas Archiv ▲ 410658-2 [ADD]
G. Joppich (cnd)
Gregorian Chants for Advent & Christmas Christophorus ▲ CD 77567
Gregorianischer Choral *(rec Münsterschwarzach Abbey, Jan & June 1981 & Jan 198)* Archiv ▲ 447 294-2 [DDD]
Musashino Chorus
Matsuoka, Tomizawa (cnd)
Mahler, G.:Sym 2, w. Junko Ioka (sop), Setsuko Takemoto (mez), T. Asahina (cnd), Osaka PO *(rec Suntory Hall, Tokyo, July 23, 1995)* Canyon Classics 2-▲ 335
Musica Contexta
S. Ravens (cnd)
Midnight Mass for Queen Mary Tudor Herald ▲ HAVPCD 195 [DDD]
Musica Sacra Chorus
Gordon, R.I.:Water Music Catalyst ▲ 09026-61822-2 ▮ 09026-61822-4
Handel, G.F.:Messiah (sels), w. Judith Blegen (sop), Katherine Ciesinski (mez), John Aler (ten), John Cheek (bass), R. Westenburg (cnd), Musica Sacra RCA Silver Seal ▲ 60481-2-RV [DDD]; ▮ 60481-4-RV (CrO2)
Monk, M.:Return Catalyst ▲ 09026-61822-2 ▮ 09026-61822-4
Sherman, K.D.:Graveside Catalyst ▲ 09026-61822-2 ▮ 09026-61822-4
R. Westenburg (cnd)
Hildegard Of Bingen:Sacred Songs—O quam mirabilis; O ecclesia (w. Judith Malafronte); O clarissima mater (w. Judith Malafronte); O tu illustrata *(rec Church of St. Ignatius Loyola, NYC, Apr 26 & 27 & May 15 & 16)* Catalyst ▲ 09026-68329-2
Monk, M.:Songs—Dawn (w. Katie Geissinger & Alexandra Montano); Quarry Weave 1 (w. Thomas Bogdan, James Fredericks & Neil Farrell); Quarry Lullaby (w. Mark Rehnstrom); Quarry Weave 2; Farmer's Song (w. Katie Geissinger); Astronaut Anthem; Nightfall *(rec Church of St. Ignatius Loyola, NYC, Apr 26 & 27 & May 15 & 16)* Catalyst ▲ 09026-68329-2
Musikfreunde Chorus
Mozart, W.A.:Zauberflöte, w. I. Seefried (sop-Pamina), W. Lipp (sop—Queen of the Night), A. Dermota (ten—Tamino), E. Kunz (bar—Papageno), J. Greindl (bass—Sarastro), H. von Karajan (cnd), Vienna PO [without dialogue; G] *(rec 1950)* EMI Classics ("Studio" series) 2-▲ CDHB 69631 (m)
Namur Belgium French Community Symphonic Choir
Honegger, A.:Sémiramis, w. V. Ivanov (vn), M. Kemmer (sgr), L. Hager (cnd), RTL SO, Brussels Polyphonia Choir *(rec Nov. 16-20, 1992)* Timpani ▲ 1C 1016 [DDD]
Namur Chamber Choir
Lassus, O. de:Aurora lucis rutilat, w. P. Cao (cnd), La Fenice Ensemble, Ricercar Consort *(rec St. Lambert à Mozet, Nov 1994)* Ricercar ▲ 155141
Lassus, O. de:Motets, w. P. Cao (cnd), La Fenice Ensemble, Ricercar Consort—Omnes de saba; Da pacem Domine; Timor et tremor; Tui sunt coeli; Surge propera amica mea; Aurora lucis rutilat *(rec St. Lambert à Mozet, Nov 1994)* Ricercar ▲ 155141
Lassus, O. de:Vinum bonum, w. P. Cao (cnd), La Fenice Ensemble, Ricercar Consort *(rec St. Lambert à Mozet, Nov 1994)* Ricercar ▲ 155141
D. Menier (cnd)
Uy, P.:Choral pour la Paix, w. Dinah Bryant (sop), Zeger Vandersteene (ten), Philippe Huttenlocher (bar), Alain Carré (nar), Dominique Cornil (pno), G. Octors (cnd), Wallonie Royal CO *(rec Aulne, Belgium, 1995)* Cypres ▲ 2611 [DDD]
Nancy Concert Royal
R. Depoutot (cnd)
Bach, J.M.:Vocal Music—Sei Lieber Tag Wilkommen; Das Blut Jesu-Christi; Liebster Jesu; Herr, du läbest mich Erfahren; Fürchtet euch nicht; Ach, wie Sehnlich; Unser leben währet siebenzig Jahr; Nun hab'ich Überwunden; Es ist ein grosser Gewinn; Herr, wenn ich nur dich Habe; Halt was du Hast; Auf labt uns; Ich weiss dass mein erlöser Lebt; Herr, ich warte auf dein Heil; Ach, bleiss bei uns Adda ▲ ADD 581111 [DDD]
du Mont, H.:Choral Music—Christus Natus est Nobis; Domine Salvum Fac Regem; Seigneur, ma puissance supreme; Quand L'esprit accable; Tristitia Vestra; Bernardus Doctor; Cantate Domino; Santa Caecilia; In Lecturo Meo; Credidi Propter; O Panis Angelorum; Laudibus Cives; Panis Angelicus; O Domine Deus; Lausemus Dominum; Domine Salvum Fac Regem; Litanies de la vierge Adda ▲ ADD 581034 [DDD]
Nantes Vocal Ensemble
Charpentier, M.-A.:In honorem Sancti Xaverii canticum, w. E. Baudry (sop), C. Dune (sop), G. Ragon (ten), P. Colléaux (cnd), Stradivaria Ensemble [L] Arion ▲ ARN 68037 [DDD]
Charpentier, M.-A.:In nativitatem Domini canticum, w. J.-L. Bindi (bass), P. Colléaux (cnd), Nantes Instrumental Ensemble [L] Arion ▲ ARN 68015 [AAD]
Charpentier, M.-A.:Judicum Salomonis, w. A. Zaepffel (ct), J. Benet (ten), Elwes (ten), G. Ragon (ten), J. Cabré (bar), G. Reinhart (bar), P. Colléaux (cnd), Stradivaria Ensemble [L] Arion ▲ ARN 68037 [DDD]
Gluck, C.W.:Orfeo ed Euridice (sels), w. Alain Zaepffel (alt), D. Cuiller (cnd), Stradivaria Ensemble—Ballo; Che Puro Ciel Adda ▲ ADD 581050

986 ▲ = CD ♦ = Enhanced CD △ = MD ▮ = Cassette Tape ▯ = DCC

Nantes Vocal Ensemble (cont.)

Hasse, J.A.:Il trionfo di Clelia (sels), w. Alain Zaepffel (alt), D. Cuiller (cnd), Stradivaria Ensemble—Resta Cara Adda ▲ ADD 581050

Traetta, T.:Ifigenia in Tauride (sels), w. Alain Zaepffel (alt), D. Cuiller (cnd), Stradivaria Ensemble—Scène avec Shoeurs Adda ▲ ADD 581050

P. Colleaux (cnd)

Handel, G.F.:Samson (sels), w. Alain Zaepffel (alt), D. Cuiller (cnd), Stradivaria Ensemble—The Body Comes; Return Oh God of Hosts Adda ▲ ADD 581050

Handel, G.F.:Theodora (sels), w. Alain Zaepffel (alt), D. Cuiller (cnd), Stradivaria Ensemble—Sweet Rose & Lily; Unhappy, Happy Crew; Kind Heaven; Go Gen'rous Pious Youth Adda ▲ ADD 581050

Piccinni, N.:Tigrane (sels), w. Alain Zaepffel (alt), D. Cuiller (cnd), Stradivaria Ensemble—Ah Cleopatra Adda ▲ ADD 581050

Naples Alessandro Scarlatti Chorus

Scarlatti, A.:La Griselda, w. M. Freni (sop), L. Alva (ten), V. Luchetti (ten), R. Panerai (bar), S. Bruscantini (bar), N. Sanzogno (cnd), Naples Alessandro Scarlatti RAI Orch [I] *(rec live 10/29/70)* Memories 2-▲ HR 4154/55 (m) [ADD]

Naples RAI Chorus

Piccinni, N.:Didon, w. G. Tucci (sop), O. Mori (bass), M. Petri (bass), M. Rossi (cnd), Naples RAI Orch *(rec live 4/16/70)* Arkadia 2-▲ 596 [ADD]

Naples Teatro San Carlo Chorus

Bizet, G.:Les Pêcheurs de perles, w. M. Pobbe (sop), F. Tagliavini (ten), U. Savarese (bar), C. Cava (bass), O. de Fabritiis (cnd), Naples Teatro San Carlo Orch [I] *(rec live 1/4/59)* Melodram 2-▲ MEL 27069 (m) [AAD]

Cilea, F.:Adriana Lecouvreur, w. Magda Olivero (sop), Giulletta Simionato (mez), Franco Corelli (ten), Ettore Bastianini (bar), M. Rossi (cnd), Naples Teatro San Carlo Orch *(rec Naples, Nov 28, 1959)* Agorá Music ("Phoenix" series) 2-▲ 502

Cilea, F.:Adriana Lecouvreur, w. M. Olivero (sop), G. Simionato (mez), F. Corelli (ten), E. Bastianini (bar), M. Rossi (cnd), Naples Teatro San Carlo Orch [I] *(rec live 11/28/59)* Melodram 2-▲ MEL 27009 (m) [AAD]

Cilea, F.:Adriana Lecouvreur, w. L. Gencer (sop—Adriana), A. Lazzarini (mez—Princess), F. Ricciardi (ten—Abbot), A. Zambon (ten—Maurizio), E. Sordello (bar—Michonnet), A. Zerbini (bass—Prince), O. de Fabritiis (cnd), Naples Teatro San Carlo Orch *(rec Dec. 17, 1966)* Golden Age of Opera 2-▲ GAO 143/44 [ADD]

Cilea, F.:Adriana Lecouvreur (sels), w. Renata Tebaldi (sop—Adriana), Piero de Palma (ten—Abate), Gianni Poggi (ten—Mauriczio), Giuseppe Taddei (bar—Michonnet), Augusto Romani (bass—Prince), G. Santini (cnd), Naples Teatro San Carlo Orch—Del sultano Amurate...Io son l'umile ancella; Giusto Cielo! che feci in tal giorno; Salvatemi! salvatemi!...Scostatevi, profani! *(rec San Carlo Theater, Naples, Dec. 26, 1952)* Legato Classics 2-▲ LCD 193-2 [ADD]

Donizetti, G.:Caterina Cornaro, w. L. Gencer (sop), G. Aragall (ten), R. Bruson (bar), L. Risani (sgr), C.F. Cillario (cnd), Naples Teatro San Carlo Orch *(rec live, 5/28/72)* Myto 2-▲ 2 MCD 92153 [ADD]

Donizetti, G.:Caterina Cornaro, w. L. Gencer (sop), G. Aragall (ten), R. Bruson (bar), C.F. Cillario (cnd), Naples Teatro San Carlo Orch [I] *(rec live, Naples 5/28/72)* Memories 2-▲ HR 4448/49 (m) [ADD]

Donizetti, G.:Don Pasquale, w. G. D'Angelo (sop), A. Kraus (ten), R. Capecchi (bar), F. Corena (bass), U. d'Alessio (sgr), A. Erede (cnd), Naples Teatro San Carlo Orch [I] *(rec live in Edinburgh, 9/7/63)* Verona 2-▲ 27023/24 (m) [AAD]

Donizetti, G.:Don Pasquale, w. Gianna D'Angelo (sop), Alfredo Kraus (ten), Renato Capecchi (bar), Fernando Corena (bass), Ugo D'Alessio (sgr), A. Erede (cnd), Naples Teatro San Carlo Orch Great Opera Performances 2-▲ GOP 763

Donizetti, G.:La favorita, w. S. Zanolli (sop), G. Simionato (mez), G. Raimondi (ten), M. Zanasi (bar), N. Zaccaria (bass), F. Previtali (cnd), Naples Teatro San Carlo Orch [I] *(rec live, Naples 5/12/63)* Golden Age of Opera 2-▲ GAO 105/06 [ADD]

Donizetti, G.:Gemma di Vergy, w. Montserrat Caballé (sop—Gemma di Vergy), Biancamaria Casoni (mez—Ida di Greville), Giorgio Lamberti (ten—Tamas), Renato Bruson (bar—Conte di Vergy), Mario Machì (bass—Rolando), Mario Rinaudo (bass—Guido), A. Gatto (cnd), Naples Teatro San Carlo Orch *(rec Naples, Dec. 12, 1975)* Myto 2-▲ 952124

Donizetti, G.:Linda di Chamounix, w. A. Stella (sop), C. Valletti (ten), R. Capecchi (bar), G. Taddei (bar), T. Serafin (cnd), Naples Teatro San Carlo Orch *(rec 1959)* Andromeda ▲ ANR 2509 [ADD]

Donizetti, G.:Lucia di Lammermoor, w. M. Callas (sop), G. Raimondi (ten), R. Panerai (bar), A. Zerbini (bass), F. Molinari-Pradelli (cnd), Naples Teatro San Carlo Orch [I] *(rec live, 3/22/56)* Myto ▲ 2 MCD 90319 (m) [ADD]

Donizetti, G.:Lucia di Lammermoor (sels), w. Christina Deutekom (sop—Lucia), Luciano Pavarotti (ten—Edgardo), Domenico Trimarchi (bar—Enrico Ashton), Silviano Pagliuca (bass—Raimondo Bidebent), C.M. Guilini (cnd), Naples Teatro San Carlo Orch Budget ("The Greatest Voice in Opera" series) ▲ SYP 103

Donizetti, G.:Maria di Rohan, w. F. Previtali (cnd), Naples Teatro San Carlo Orch Melodram 3-▲ CDM 37017

Giordano, U.:Fedora, w. R. Tebaldi (sop), Mizzetti (sgr), G. di Stefano (ten), M. Sereni (bar), A. Basile (cnd), Naples Teatro San Carlo Orch [I] *(rec live, 1961)* Legato Classics 2-▲ LCD 158-2 (m) [ADD]

Gounod, C.:Faust (sels), w. R. Tebaldi (sop), F. Cadoni (mez), M. Filippeschi (ten), R. Panerai (bar), I. Tajo (bass), F. Patanè (cnd), Naples Teatro San Carlo Orch—Act IV, Scenes 1 & 2 & Act V, Scene 2 *(rec live, 4/26/51)* Standing Room Only 2-▲ SRO 810-2 [ADD]

Leoncavallo, R.:Edipo re, w. L. Infantino (ten), G. Fioravanti (bar), G. Malaspina (bar), R. Parodi (cnd), Naples Teatro San Carlo Orch *(rec live, Naples, 1970)* Italian Opera Rarities ▲ IOR 7723 [ADD]

Massenet, J.:Werther, w. E. Ravaglia (sop), B. Casoni (mez), C. Bergonzi (ten), D. Trimarchi (bar), O. de Fabritiis (cnd), Naples Teatro San Carlo Orch [I] *(rec live, Naples, 2/13/69)* Melodram 2-▲ 27058 [AAD]

Mercadante, S.:Elisa e Claudio, w. Virginia Zeani (sop), Agostino Lazzari (ten), Domenico Trimarchi (bar), Ugo Trama (bass), Fiorini (sgr), U. Rapalo (cnd), Naples Teatro San Carlo Orch *(rec live, Naples, 1/31/71)* Melodram 2-▲ MEL 27099 [ADD]

Mozart, W.A.:Don Giovanni, w. M. Caballé (sop), T. Stich-Randall (mez), E. Wächter (bar), E. Kunz (bar), M. Gielen (cnd), Naples Teatro San Carlo Orch [I] *(rec live, Lisbon, 1960)* Standing Room Only 2-▲ SRO 813-2 [ADD]

Pacini, G.:Saffo, w. L. Gencer (sop), F. Mattiucci (mez), T. del Bianco (ten), L. Quilico (bar), F. Capuana (cnd), Naples Teatro San Carlo Orch [I] *(rec live, 4/7/67)* Arkadia 2-▲ 541 (m) [ADD]

Puccini, G.:Turandot (sels), w. L. Gencer (sop), L. Udovich (sop), F. Corelli (ten), O. de Fabritiis (cnd), Naples Teatro San Carlo Orch—Signore ascolta; Il nome che cercate...tu che di gel sei cinta *(rec Jan. 13, 1962)* Golden Age of Opera 2-▲ GAO 143/44 [ADD]

Rossini, G.:Il barbiere di Siviglia (sels), w. R. Scotto (sop), A. di Stasio (mez), A. Kraus (ten), A. Protti (bar), C. Badioli (bass), E. Campi (bass), V. Bellezza (cnd), Naples Teatro San Carlo Orch *(rec July 26, 1958)* Golden Age of Opera 2-▲ GAO 137/38 [ADD]

Rossini, G.:Il barbiere di Siviglia (sels), w. M. Resemba (sop), N. Sabatano (sop), F. de Lucia (ten), F. Novelli (bar), G. Schottler (bass), A. di Tommaso (bass), S. Valentino (bass), S. Sassano (cnd), Naples Teatro San Carlo Orch [I] *(rec 1918 for Phonotype)* Standing Room Only ▲ SRO 819-1 [ADD]

Rossini, G.:La Cenerentola, w. Teresa Berganza (mez), Nicola Monti (ten), Sesto Bruscantini (bar), Mario Petri (bar), Leonardo Monreale (sgr), M. Rossi (cnd), Naples RAI SO *(rec Oct 8, 1958)* Pantheon 2-▲ PHE 6656 (m)

Verdi, G.:Aida, w. A. Stella (sop), F. Barbieri (mez), F. Corelli (ten), A. Colzani (bar), M. Petri (bar), V. Gui (cnd), Naples Teatro San Carlo Orch [I] *(rec live, Naples 11/2/55)* Golden Age of Opera 2-▲ GAO 116/17 [ADD]

Verdi, G.:Aida (sels), w. O. Rovere (sop), E. Stignani (mez), M. Filippeschi (ten), C. Cava (bass), B. McFerrin (sgr), V. Bellezza (cnd), Naples Teatro San Carlo Orch [I] [highlights] *(rec live, Arena Flegrea, Naples, 7/15/56)* Golden Age of Opera ▲ GAO 130 [ADD]

Verdi, G.:Aida (sels), w. A. Cerquetti (sop), E. Nicolai (mez), G. Penno (ten), G. Guelfi (bar), B. Christoff (bass), G. Santini (cnd), Naples Teatro San Carlo Orch [I] [highlights] *(rec live, Naples, July 24, 1954)* Golden Age of Opera ▲ GAO 134 [ADD]

Verdi, G.:Ernani, w. Margherita Roberti (sop), Anna di Stasio (mez), Athos Cesarini (ten), Mario del Monaco (ten), Ettore Bastianini (bar), Mario Rinaudo (bass), Nicola Rossi-Lemeni (bass), F. Previtali (cnd), Naples Teatro San Carlo Orch Melodram 2-▲ CDM 270100

Naples Teatro San Carlo Chorus (cont.)

Verdi, G.:La forza del destino, w. R. Tebaldi (sop), O. Dominguez (mez), F. Corelli (ten), R. Capecchi (bar), E. Bastianini (bar), B. Christoff (bass), F. Molinari-Pradelli (cnd), Naples Teatro San Carlo Orch *(rec Oct. 1 1958)* Melodram 3-▲ MLO 370102 [AAD]

Verdi, G.:La forza del destino (sels), w. R. Tebaldi (sop), F. Corelli (ten), F. Molinari-Pradelli (cnd), Naples Teatro San Carlo Orch *(rec live Mar. 15, 1958)* Legato Classics 2-▲ LCD 171-2 [ADD]

Verdi, G.:Giovanna d'Arco, w. Renata Tebaldi (sop—Giovanna), Gino Penno (ten—Carlo VII), Luciano Della Pergola (ten—Delil), Ugo Savarese (bar—Giacomo), Iginio Ricco (bass—Talbot), G. Santini (cnd), Naples Teatro San Carlo Orch *(rec San Carlo Theater, Naples, Mar. 15, 1951)* Legato Classics 2-▲ LCD 193-2 [ADD]

Verdi, G.:Nabucco, w. M. Callas (sop), G. Bechi (bar), L. Neroni (bass), V. Gui (cnd), Naples Teatro San Carlo Orch [I] *(rec live 12/20/49)* Melodram 2-▲ MEL 26029 (m) [AAD]

Verdi, G.:Rigoletto, w. Cecilia Nunez Albanese (sop—Gilda), Wilma Borrelli (cta—Maddalena), Jaime Aragall (ten—Duke of Mantua), Renato Bruson (bar—Rigoletto), Loris Gambelli (bass—Sparafucile), G. Campanino (cnd), Naples Teatro San Carlo Orch *(rec San Carlo Theatre, Naples, Feb. 1973)* Golden Age of Opera 2-▲ GAO 177-78 [ADD]

Verdi, G.:Rigoletto (sels), w. A. Pastori (sop), Antonioli (ten), C. Tagliabue (bar), U. Rapalo (cnd), Naples Teatro San Carlo Orch [I] *(rec live, Naples, 1/20/56)* The Golden Age of Opera 2-▲ GAO 115 [ADD]

Verdi, G.:Stiffelio, w. A. Gulin (sop—Lina), M. del Monaco (ten—Stiffelio), A. Marchiandi (ten—Raffaele), G. Fioravanti (bar—Stankar), J. Hecht (bass—Jorg), O. de Fabritiis (cnd), Naples Teatro San Carlo Orch *(rec Dec. 26, 1972)* Standing Room Only 2-▲ SRO 169-2

Verdi, G.:La traviata, w. B. Sills (sop), M. Zotti (sop), G. Borelli (mez), A. Kraus (ten), M. Zanasi (bar), A. Ceccato (cnd), Naples Teatro San Carlo Orch *(rec live 1/17/70)* Melodram 2-▲ MEL 27063 (m) [AAD]

Verdi, G.:La traviata, w. Renata Tebaldi (sop—Violetta), Giacinto Prandelli (ten—Alfredo), Carlo Tagliabue (bar—Germont), T. Serafin (cnd), Naples Teatro San Carlo Orch *(rec Arena Flegrea, Naples, July 3, 1954)* Golden Age of Opera 2-▲ GAO 191/192 [ADD]

Verdi, G.:La traviata, w. V. Zeani (sop), G. Raimondi (ten), U. Savarese (bar), A. Questa (cnd), Naples Teatro San Carlo Orch [I] *(rec live, Naples 8/11/57)* Golden Age of Opera 2-▲ GAO 103/04 [ADD]

Verdi, G.:La traviata (sels), w. Anna de Santis (sop—Annina), Renata Tebaldi (sop—Violetta), Giuseppe Campora (ten—Alfredo), Gerardo Gaudioso (bar—Douphol), Giuseppe Taddei (bar—Germont), Antonio Picillo (bass—Grenvil), G. Santini (cnd), Naples Teatro San Carlo Orch—E strano...Ah, fors'e lui; Folliel...Sempre libera; Pero l'attendo...Amami, Alfredo; Invitato a qui seguirmi; Alfredo, Alfredo, di questo core; Teneste la promessa...Addio del passato; Ma se tornando...Ah! Gran Dio! Morir si giovine; Se una pudica vergine *(rec San Carlo Theater, Naples, Jan. 17, 1952)* Legato Classics 2-▲ LCD 193-2 [ADD]

Verdi, G.:Il trovatore, w. M. Callas (sop), C. Elmo (mez), G. Lauri-Volpi (ten), P. Silveri (bar), T. Serafin (cnd), Naples Teatro San Carlo Orch [I] *(rec live, Naples, 1/27/51)* Melodram 2-▲ MEL 26001 (m) [AAD]

Verdi, G.:Il trovatore, w. Maria Callas (sop), Cloe Elmo (cta), Giacomo Lauri-Volpi (ten), Paolo Siveri (sgr), T. Serafin (cnd), Naples Teatro San Carlo Orch *(rec Theatre of San Carlo, Naples, Jan. 27, 1951)* Pantheon 2-▲ PHE 6636 (m)

Wagner, R.:Lohengrin (sels), w. R. Tebaldi (sop—Elsa), E. Nicolai (mez—Ortrud), G. Penno (ten—Lohengrin), G. Guelfi (bar—Telramund), G. Neri (bass—Heinrich), G. Santini (cnd), Naples Teatro San Carlo Orch—8 soprano duets/trio from Acts 1-3 [I] *(rec live, Naples, 12/26/54)* Standing Room Only ▲ SRO 834-1 [ADD]

Wagner, R.:Tannhäuser, w. L. Rysanek (sop), J. Lustig (sgr), M. Cordes (bar), G. Frick (bass), K. Böhm (cnd), Naples Teatro San Carlo Orch [G] *(rec live, Naples, 3/17/56)* Melodram 3-▲ MEL 37073 (m) [AAD]

Wagner, R.:Tannhäuser (sels), w. R. Tebaldi (sop), H. Beirer (ten), C. Tagliabue (bar), B. Christoff (bass), K. Böhm (cnd), Naples Teatro San Carlo Orch—10 soprano solo, duet & ensemble arias Acts 2 & 3 [I; Hans Beirer (Tannhäuser) sings in German] *(rec live, Naples, 3/12/50)* Standing Room Only ▲ SRO 834-1 [ADD]

National Cathedral Choir

R.W. Dirksen (cnd)

Noël:Traditional Christmas Carols & Masterworks of the 20th Century, w. Douglas Major (org) VQR Digital ▲ VQR 2006 [DDD]

National Cathedral Choral Society

The Joy of Christmas, w. Classical Brass Centaur ▲ CRC 2132

National Gallery Vocal Arts Ensemble

G. Manos (cnd)

Four Centuries of Vocal Music Koch International Classics ▲ KIC 7038 [DDD]

National Music Camp High School Choir

Hanson, H.:Sym 7, "A Sea Sym", w. H. Hanson (cnd), World Youth SO Interlochen *(rec live, Kresge Auditorium, Interlochen, Michigan, Aug 7, 1977)* Citadel ▲ CTD 88116 [ADD]

National Phil London Chorus

Leoncavallo, R.:Pagliacci, w. M. Freni (sop), L. Pavarotti (ten), I. Wixell (bar), G. Patanè (cnd), National PO London [I] London 2-▲ 414590-2 [ADD]

Mascagni, P.:Cavalleria rusticana, w. J. Varady (sop), L. Pavarotti (ten), P. Cappuccilli (bar), G. Gacazzeni (cnd), National PO London [I] London 2-▲ 414590-2 [ADD]

Szabelski, B.:Sym 5, w. A. Markowski (cnd), National PO London Olympia ▲ OCD 300 [AAD]

Verdi, G.:Un ballo in maschera, w. M. Price (sop), K. Battle (sop), C. Ludwig (mez), L. Pavarotti (ten), R. Bruson (bar), G. Solti (cnd), National PO London [I] London 2-▲ 410210-2 [DDD]

Verdi, G.:Un ballo in maschera, w. M. Price (sop), K. Battle (sop), C. Ludwig (mez), L. Pavarotti (ten), R. Bruson (bar), G. Solti (cnd), National PO London [I] London ▲ 425529-2 [DDD]

National Reisopera Choir

A. Wise (cnd)

Donizetti, G.:Linda di Chamounix, w. Mariella Devia (sop—Linda), Sonia Ganassi (mez—Pierotto), Francesca Provvisionato (mez—Maddalena), Luca Canonici (ten—Carlo), Alfonso Antoniozzi (bass—Il Marchese di Boisfleury), Petteri Salomaa (bass—Antonio), Boguslaw Fiksinski (sgr—L'intendente), Donato Di Stefano (sgr—Il Prefetto), G. Bellini (cnd), Eastern Netherlands Orch *(rec Muziekcentrum Enschede, Holland, June 24-July 2, 1992)* Arts Music 3-▲ 47151-2 [DDD]

Verdi, G.:Music of, w. G. Bellini (cnd), Orkest van het Oosten—Sinf [from I Vespri Siciliani]; Vedi! le fosche...Chi del gitano i giorni abbella; Or co' dadi...Squilli, echeggi la tromba guerriera [both from Il Trovatore]; Va pensiero, sull'ali dorate; Sinf [both from Nabucco]; Sinf [from La forza del destino]; O Signore, dal tetto natio [from I Lombardi alla prima crociata]; Patria oppressa [from Macbeth]; Si ridesti il Leon di Castiglia [from Ernani]; Sinf [from Aida] *(rec Enschede, Holland, June 18-21, 1990)* Arts Music ▲ 447107-2 [DDD]

National Shrine of the Immaculate Conception Choir Washington D.C.

L. Nestor (cnd)

A Child Is Born:Christmas at the National Shrine, w. organ VQR Digital ▲ VQR 2021 [DDD]

National Youth Chamber Choir

Twentieth Century English Choral Classics IMP Classics ▲ PCD 1077 [DDD]

National Zarzuela Theater Chorus

Romanzas de Zarzuelas, w. Plácido Domingo (ten), Manuel Moreno-Buendía, Madrid SO EMI Classics ▲ CDC 49148 [DDD] ■ 4DS 49148 (D)

NBC Sym Chorus

Puccini, G.:La Bohème, w. L. Albanese (sop), A. McKnight (sop), J. Peerce (ten), F. Valentino (bar), A. Toscanini (cnd), NBC SO [I] RCA Gold Seal 2-▲ 60288-2-RG [ADD] 2-■ 60288-4-RG (CrO2)

Wagner, R.:Die Walküre (act 1/scene 3), w. Rose Bampton (sop), Set Svanholm (ten), A. Toscanini (cnd), NBC SO [G] *(rec rehearsals & performance, New York, 4/4-6/47)* Myto 2-▲ 2 MCD 90316 (m) [ADD]

Nebraska Wesleyan Univ Choir

Parker, H.:Hora novissima, w. A. Soranno (sop), J. Simson (mez), K. Hall (b-bar), D. Andersen (b-bar), J. Levick (cnd), Nebraska CO, Abendmusik Chorus Albany 2-▲ TROY 124/25

Neideraltaicher Scholaren

K. Ruhland (cnd)

The Quintessence of Chant Sony Classical 2-▲ S2K 62805

Néophyte of Rila Choir
D. Daragyozov (cnd)
Pater Noster Jade ▲ JAD C 071
Netherlands Bach Society Boys' Choir
Cantryn, Veldhoven (cnd)
Bach, J.S.:St. Matthew Passion, w. B. Schlick (sop), K. Wessel (alto), G. de Mey (ten), C. Pregardien (ten), P. Kooy (bass), T. Koopman (cnd), Amsterdam Baroque Orch, Breda Sacred Choir Erato ▲ 2292-45814-2
Netherlands Bach Society Choir
Bach, J.S.:St. John Passion, w. B. Schlick (sop), K. Wessel (alto), G. de Mey (ten), G. Turk (ten), K. Mertens (b-bar), P. Kooy (bass), T. Koopman (cnd), Amsterdam Baroque Orch Erato 2-▲ 94675-2
Biber, H. von:Requiem à 15, w. S. Paiu (sgr), B. Lettinga (alt), H. van der Kamp (bass), G. Leonhardt (cnd), Netherlands Bach Society Baroque Orch Deutsche Harmonia Mundi ▲ 05472-77277-2
Biber, H. von:Requiem à 15, w. Marta Almajano (sop), Mieke van der Sluis (sop), John Elwes (ten), Mark Padmore (ten), Frans Huijts (bar), Harry van der Kamp (bass), G. Leonhardt (cnd), Netherlands Bach Society Baroque Orch *(rec Utrecht, Germany, Oct 22-24, 1994)* Deutsche Harmonia Mundi ▲ 05472-77344-2 [DDD]
Mozart, W.A.:Requiem, w. B. Schlick (sop), C. Watkinson (cta), C. Prégardien (ten), H. van der Kamp (bass), T. Koopman (cnd), Amsterdam Baroque Orch [L] Erato ▲ 2292-45472-2 [DDD] ■ 2292-45472-4
Steffani, A.:Stabat Mater, w. Marta Almajano (sop), Mieke van der Sluis (sop), John Elwes (ten), Mark Padmore (ten), Harry van der Kamp (bass), G. Leonhardt (cnd), Netherlands Bach Society Baroque Orch *(rec Utrecht, Germany, Oct 22-24, 1994)* Deutsche Harmonia Mundi ▲ 05472-77344-2 [DDD]
Valls, F.:Scala Arentina Mass, w. S. Paiu (sop), M. van der Sluis (sop), B. Lettinga (alt), D. Cordier (ct), J. Elwes (ten), H. van der Kamp (bass), G. Leonhardt (cnd), Netherlands Bach Society Baroque Orch Deutsche Harmonia Mundi ▲ 05472-77277-2
Netherlands Chamber Choir
Andriessen, L.:De Tijd, w. R. de Leeuw (cnd), Schoenberg Ensemble, The Hague Percussion Group Elektra/Nonesuch ▲ 79291-2 ■ 79291-4
Bach, J.S.:Cant 21, w. G. de Reyghere (mez), R. Jacobs (alt), C. Prégardien (ten), P. Lika (bass), S. Kuijken (vn), S. Kuijken (cnd), La Petite Bande Virgin Classics ▲ CDC 59528
Bach, J.S.:Cant 21, w. G. de Reyghere (mez), C. Prégardien (ten), P. Lika (bass), S. Kuijken (cnd), La Petite Bande [G] Veritas ▲ VC 7 90779-2 [DDD] ■ VC 7 90779-4 (D)
Bach, J.S.:Magnificat, BWV 243, w. G. de Reyghere (sop), R. Jacobs (alt), C. Prégardien (ten), P. Lika (bass), S. Kuijken (vn), S. Kuijken (cnd), La Petite Bande Virgin Classics ▲ CDC 59528
Bach, J.S.:Magnificat, BWV 243, w. G. de Reyghere (sop), R. Jacobs (alt), C. Prégardien (ten), P. Lika (bass), S. Kuijken (vn), S. Kuijken (cnd), La Petite Bande [L] Veritas ▲ VC 7 90779-2 [DDD] ■ VC 7 90779-4 (D)
Bach, J.S.:Mass in b, BWV 232, w. J. Smith (sop), M. Chance (ct), N. van der Meel (ten), H. van der Kamp (bass), F. Brüggen (cnd), Orch of the 18th Century [L] *(rec live)* Philips ("Digital Classics" series) 2-▲ 426238-2 [DDD]
Bach, J.S.:St. John Passion, w. F. Brüggen (cnd), Orch of the 18th Century Philips ▲ 434905-2
Mozart, W.A.:Nozze di Figaro, w. E. Schwarzkopf (sop), G. Sciurri (sop), G. Taddei (bar), H. Prey (bar), C. M. Giulini (cnd), Residentie Orch The Hague [I] *(rec live, Holland Festival, 1961)* Verona 3-▲ 27092/94
Mozart, W.A.:Requiem, w. *(soloists unknown)*, S. Kuijken (cnd), La Petite Bande Accent ▲ 68645
Sweelinck, J.P.:Psalms of David, w. T. Koopman (cnd), Residentie Orch The Hague—Psalms 130 & 150 [F] Olympia ▲ OCD 500 [AAD]
Verdi, G.:Falstaff, w. M. Freni (sop), I. Ligabue (sop), L. Alva (ten), R. Capecchi (bar), F. Corena (bass), C. M. Giulini (cnd), Royal Concertgebouw Orch [I] *(rec live, The Hague 6/20/63)* Verona 2-▲ 27095/96
Webern, A.:Vocal Chamber Music, w. D. Dorow (sop), R. de Leeuw (cnd), Schoenberg Ensemble—(choral songs) Entflieht auf leichten Kähnen, Op. 2 (1908 & 1914 versions); Two Songs, Op. 19 (1926); (songs for solo voice & instrumental chamber ensemble) Two Songs, Op. 8 (1910); Schmerz, immer blick' nach oben (1913); Three Songs (1913-14); Four Songs, Op. 13 (1914-18); Six Songs, Op. 14 (1917-21); Five Sacred Songs, Op. 15 (1917-22); Five Canons, Op. 16 (1923-24); Three Traditional Rhymes, Op. 17 (1924-25); Three Songs, Op. 18 (1925) [G,L] Koch Schwann ▲ CD 314005 [DDD]
W. Christie (cnd)
Bruynèl, T.:Continuation Donemus ▲ NEAR 01 [DDD]
U. Gronostay (cnd)
Cornelius, P.:Requiem, "Seele, vergiss sie nicht..." Globe ▲ GLO 5105 [DDD]
Diepenbrock, A.:Caelestis urbs Jerusalem NM Classics ▲ NM 92039
Draeseke, F.:Grosse Messe *(rec Amsterdam, Nov 1995)* Globe ▲ GLO 5147 [DDD]
Kodály, Z.:Laudes Organi, w. E. Krapp (org) *(rec October 1993)* Globe ▲ GLO 5115 [DDD]
Kodály, Z.:Missa Brevis, w. E. Krapp (org) *(rec October 1993)* Globe ▲ GLO 5115 [DDD]
Krenek, E.:Lamentatio Jeremiae Prophatae [L] Globe ▲ GLO 5085 [DDD]
Lange, D. de:Requiem NM Classics ▲ NM 92039
Liszt, F.:Choral Music, w. D. Fischer-Dieskau (bar)—Es war einmal ein König; Arbeiter Chor; Sankt Christoph; Qui Mariam absolvisti; Rosario; Die Seligkeiten *(rec 10/89)* Globe ▲ GLO 5070 [DDD]
Mendelssohn, F.:Choral Music—27 Part-Songs for Mixed Chorus—Six Lieder, Op. 41; Six Lieder, Op. 48; Six Lieder, Op. 59; 4 Lieder, Op. 100; plus Nos. 1,2,3,4 & 6 from Six Lieder, Op. 88 [G] Globe ▲ GLO 5075 [DDD]
Rheinberger, J.:Mass, Op. 109 *(rec 10/89)* Globe ▲ GLO 5070 [DDD]
Röntgen, J.:Motets—3 sels NM Classics ▲ NM 92039
Schumann, R.:Gesänge Chorus *(rec Amsterdam, Nov 1995)* Globe ▲ GLO 5147 [DDD]
Wolf, H.:Choral Music—Im stillen Friedhof; Grablied; Die Stimme des Kindes, Op. 10; Gottvertrauen; Geistliche Lieder (6); Im Sommer, Op. 13/1; Geistesgruss, Op. 13/2; Mailied, Op. 13/3; Fröhliche Fahrt, Op. 17/1 Globe ▲ GLO 5105 [DDD]
R. Jacobs (cnd)
Monteverdi, C.:Vespro della Beata Vergine, w. Barbara Borden (sop), Maria Cristina Kiehr (sop), Andreas Scholl (alt), John Bowen (ten), Andrew Murgatroyd (ten), Victor Torres (bar), Antonio Abete (bass), Jelle Draijer (bass), Concerto Vocale Harmonia Mundi 2-▲ 901566.67
Kerstens, Leeuw (cnd)
Boehmer, K.:Canto in Modo Nono NM Classics ▲ NM 82025
de Leeuw, T.:Hymnes (5) NM Classics ▲ NM 82025
Schat, P.:Adem NM Classics ▲ NM 82025
T. Koopman (cnd)
Bach, J.S.:Motets, BWV 225-30 Philips ▲ 434165-2 [DDD]
Netherlands Jeugd Chorus
Olthuis, K.:De Naam van de Maan, w. *(soloists unknown)*, R. Kieft (cnd), Netherlands Jeugd SO Composers' Voice 2-▲ CVCD 11/12 [DDD]
Netherlands Opera Chorus
Gluck, C.W.:Orfeo ed Euridice, w. G. Koeman (sop), D. Duval (sop), K. Ferrier (cta), C. Bruck (cnd), Netherlands Opera Orch *(rec live, 1951)* Verona 2-▲ 27016/17 (m) [AAD]
Mozart, W.A.:Nozze di Figaro, w. C. Margiono (sop), B. Bonney (sop), I. Rey (sop), A. Murray (mez, P.-L. Lang (mez), P. Langridge (ten), C. Späth (ten), T. Hampson (bar), K. Moll (bass), A. Scharinger (bass), K. Langan (bass), N. Harnoncourt (cnd), Royal Concertgebouw Orch *(rec Amsterdam, May 1993)* Teldec 3-▲ 90861-2 [DDD]
Strauss (II), Joh.:Die Fledermaus (sels), w. E. Gruberova (sop), B. Bonney (sop), M. Lipovšek (mez), W. Kmentt (ten), W. Hollweg (ten), J. Protschka (ten), C. Boesch (bar), A. Scharinger (bass), N. Harnoncourt (cnd), Royal Concertgebouw Orch Teldec ▲ 42427-2
Verdi, G.:Un ballo in maschera, w. G. Bouwenstijn (sop), E. Ratti (sop), A. Delori (cta), G. Zampieri (ten), F. Molinari-Pradelli (cnd), Netherlands Opera Orch *(rec live 1958)* Globe 2-▲ GLO 5109

Netherlands Opera Chorus (cont.)
W. Maczewski (cnd)
Schoenberg, A.:Moses und Aaron, w. David Pittman-Jennings (nar), Gabriele Fontana (sop—Young Girl), Yvonne Naef (cta—Sick Woman), John Graham-Hall (ten—Young Man/Naked Youth), Pår Lindskog (ten—Youth), Chris Merritt (ten—Aaron), Siegfried Lorenz (bar—Another Man), Michael Devlin (b-bar—Ephraimite), László Polgár (bass—Priest), P. Boulez (cnd), Royal Concertgebouw Orch, Zaans Youth Choir, Waterland Music School *(rec Concertgebouw, Amsterdam, Oct 1995)* Deutsche Grammophon 2-▲ 449 174-2 [DDD]
Netherlands Radio Chorus
Keulen, G. van:Scena, w. D. Porcelijn (cnd), Netherlands Radio PO Donemus ▲ CV 33
Mascagni, P.:Iris, w. M. Olivero (sop), L. Ottolini (ten), R. Capecchi (bar), P. Clabassi (bass), F. Vernizzi (cnd), Netherlands Radio Orch *(rec live, 1963)* Verona 2-▲ 27014/15 [AAD]
Mascagni, P.:Iris, w. M. Olivero (sop), L. Ottolini (ten), R. Capecchi (bar), P. Clabassi (bass), F. Vernizzi (cnd), Netherlands Radio Orch *(rec Amsterdam, 1963)* Great Opera Performances ▲ GPO 708
Mascagni, P.:Il piccolo Marat, w. S. Neves (sop—Mariella), C. Pfeiler (mez—Principessa di Fleury), D. Galvez-Vallejo (ten—Marat), S. Cowan (bar—Soldier), M. Dirks (bar—Il Ladro), F. Vassar (bass—L'Orco), H. Claessens (bass—Spy), K. Bakels (cnd), Netherlands RSO *(rec Feb. 9, 1992)* Bongiovanni 2-▲ GB 2168/69 [DDD]
M. Wright (cnd)
Einhorn, R.:Voices of Light, w. Susan Narucki (sop), Corrie Pronk (alt), Frank Hameleers (ten), Henk van Heijnsbergen (b-bar), Ronald Hoogeveen (vn), Harm Bakker (vl), Michael Feves (vl), Naomi Hirschfeld (vl), S. Mercurio (cnd), Netherlands Radio PO, Anonymous 4 *(rec Music Center of the Netherlands Radio & TV, Aug 23-25, 1995)* Sony Classical ▲ SK 62006 [DDD]
Ravel, M.:Daphins et Chloé, w. Jacques Zoon (fl), R. Chailly (cnd), Royal Concertgebouw Orch *(rec Grotezaal, Concertgebouw, Amsterdam, Feb 17 & 18, 1994)* London ▲ 443934-2 [DDD]
Netherlands Radio Male Chamber Choir
de Leeuw, T.:Antigone, w. Martine Mahe (mez), R. de Leeuw (cnd), Netherlands Radio CO NM Classics ▲ NM 92036
Netherlands Theater Chorus
Massenet, J.:Thérèse, w. J. Piland (sop), H. Haskin (ten), C. van Tassel (bar), L. Vis (cnd), Netherlands PO [F] Canal Grande ▲ CG 9220 [DDD]
Netherlands Women's Chamber Choir
Debussy, C.:Nocturnes, w. E. Krivine (cnd), Lyon National Orch Denon ▲ DEN 78774 [DDD]
Neuilly St-Croix Youth Chorus
Fauré, G.:Choral Music, w. Hervé Lamy (ten), Jean-François Hatton (org), F. Polgár (cnd), Paris Opera Soloists—Requiem, Op. 48 [1893 Version]; Salve Regina, Op. 67/1; Ave Maria, Op. 67/2; Tantum Ergo, Op. 65/2; Ave Verum, Op. 65/1; Cantique de Jean Racine, Op. 11 Adès ▲ ADE 202982
F. Polgár (cnd)
Saint-Saëns, C.:Choral Music, w. H. Lamy (ten), J.-F. Hatton (org), Paris Opera Orch Soloists—Pie Jesu; Ave Verum Adès ▲ ADE 202982
Neuwieder Chamber Chorus
B. Kämpf (cnd)
Duruflé, M.:Requiem, w. M. Palberg (mez), B. Kämpf (bar) [L] Motette ▲ CD 50241 [DDD]
Neve Shir Choir
Fleischer, T.:The Clock Wants to Sleep Opus One ▲ Cd 158 [DDD]
New Amsterdam Singers
American Journey:Poetry & Song in the 20th Century, w. Elizabeth Rodgers (pno) Albany ▲ TROY 108 [DDD]
New Calliope Singers
P. Schubert (cnd)
Druckman, J.:Madrigals (4) [E] *(rec 1990)* CRI ▲ CD 638 [DDD]
New Cantatas & Madrigals *(rec 1990)* CRI ▲ CRI 638 [DDD]
10th Anniversary Anthology of New Choral Chamber Music Finnadar ■ 90850-4
New College Choir Cambridge
Christmas Carols CRD ▲ CD 3443
New College Choir Oxford
Desmarets, H.:Sacred Music, w. Barbara Schlick (sop), Mieke Van der Sluis (sop), Harry Geraerts (ct), Fiori Musicali—Deux grands motets lorrains; Mystères de notre seigneur Jésus-Christ Erato ▲ ERA SEL 98529 [ADD]
Gibbons, O.:Second Service & Anthems CRD ▲ CD 3451 [DDD]
Handel, G.F.:Deborah, w. S. Gritton (sop), Y. Kenny (sop), C. Denley (mez), J. Bowman (alt), M. George (bass), R. King (cnd), King's Consort Hyperion 2-▲ CDA 66841 [DDD]
Handel, G.F.:Joseph & His Brethren, w. Yvonne Kenney (sop), Catherine Denley (mez), Connor Burrowes (trb), James Bowman (ct), John Mark Ainsley (ten), Michael George (bass), R. King (cnd), King's Consort, King's Consort Choir Hyperion 3-▲ CDA 67171/3
Handel, G.F.:Occasional Oratorio, w. Susan Gritton (sop), Lisa Milne (sop), James Brown (ct), John Mark Ainsley (ten), Michael George (bass), R. King (cnd), King's Consort Hyperion 2-▲ CDA 66961/62
Haydn, J.:Die Schöpfung, w. Emma Kirkby (sop), Anthony Rolfe Johnson (ten), Michael George (bass), C. Hogwood (cnd), Academy of Ancient Music [E] L'Oiseau-Lyre 2-▲ 430397-2 [DDD]
Poulenc, F.:Motets (4) pour le temps de Noël [F] CRD ▲ 3462 [DDD]
Purcell, H.:Anthems, w. J. Bowman (ct), R. Covey-Crump (ten), C. Daniels (ten), M. George (b-bar), King's Consort Hyperion ▲ CDA 66656
Purcell, H.:Anthems & Services, w. J. Bowman (ct), R. Covey-Crump (ten), C. Daniels (ten), S. Varcoe (bar), M. George (bass), R. King (cnd), King's Consort—My heart is inditing; The way of God is an undefiled way; Sing unto God; Behold, I bring you glad tidings; Since God so tender a regard; Early, O Lord, my fainting soul; Sleep, Adam, sleep and take thy rest; Awake, ye dead; The earth trembled; Lord not to us but to thy name; O all ye people, clap your hands Hyperion ▲ CDA 66644
Purcell, H.:Anthems & Services, w. James Bowman (ct), Charles Daniels (ten), Michael George (bass), Robert Evans (bass), R. King (cnd), King's Consort—O sing unto the Lord; O praise God in His holiness; Praise the Lord, O Jerusalem; It is a good thing to give thanks; O give thanks unto the Lord; Let mine eyes run down with tears; My beloved spake Hyperion ▲ CDA 66585
Purcell, H.:Anthems & Services, w. James Bowman (ct), Roger Covey-Crump (ten), Michael George (bass), R. King (cnd), King's Consort—Behold, now praise the Lord; Blessed are they that fear the Lord; I will give thanks unto Thee, O Lord; My song shall be always Hyperion ▲ CDA 66609
Purcell, H.:Music of, w. R. King (cnd), King's Consort—When I Am Laid in Earth [w. G. Fisher (sop)]; Welcome, Welcome Glorious Morn; Oh, Fair Cedaria; Hear My Prayer, O Lord; Let Mine Eyes Run down with Tears; The Sparrow and the Gentle Dove; If Music Be the Food of Love; Rejoice in the Lord Alway; Hosanna to the Highest; Thou Knowest, Lord, the Secrets of Our Hearts; Fairest Isle, All Isles Excelling; Mark, How Readily Each Pliant String; Sound the Trumpet; She Loves and Confesses Too; O How Blest Is the Isle; Now that the Sun Hath Veiled His Light (an evening hymn); Vouchsafe, O Lord, to Keep Us This Day; With Rapture of Delight; Hail Bright C. Hyperion ▲ KING 2
Purcell, H.:Odes & Welcome Songs (comp), w. R. King (cnd), King's Consort [E] Hyperion 8-▲ CDS 44031/38 [DDD]
E. Higginbottom (cnd)
Boyce, W.:Anthems & Voluntaries, w. G. Cooper (org)—By the waters of Babylon; I have surely built thee an house; The Lord is King; O give thanks; O praise the Lord; O where shall wisdom be found?; Turn thee unto me; Voluntaries I, IV & VII; Wherewithal shall a young man [E] *(rec 4/91)* CRD ▲ 3483
Byrd, W.:Cantiones sacrae (1589) [L] CRD ▲ CD 3420 [DDD]
Byrd, W.:Cantiones sacrae (1591) [L] CRD ▲ CD 3439 [DDD]
A Ceremony of Carols *(rec New College Chapel, Oxford, Dec. 18-20, 1991)* CRD ▲ CRD 3490 [DDD]
Duruflé, M.:Requiem, w. [L] CRD ▲ 3466 [DDD]
Fauré, G.:Requiem [L] CRD ▲ 3466 [DDD]
Greene, M.:Anthems—10 anthems:How long wilt thou forget me, O Lord?; The King shall rejoice; Let God arise; Lord let me know mine end; O clap your hands; Thou visitest the earth; Voluntary I [E] *(rec 4/91)* CRD ▲ 3483 [DDD]

New College Choir Oxford (cont.)
E. Higginbottom (cnd) (cont.)
Howells, H.:Choral Music—Behold, O God our defender (1953); Missa Aedis Christi (1958); Three Carol–Anthems [Sing Lullaby; Here is the little door; A spotless rose] (1918–20); Where wast thou? (1948) CRD ▲ 3455 [DDD]
Howells, H.:Choral Music—A Sequence for St. Michael (1961); A Hymn for St. Cecilia (1960); House of the Mind (motet—1949); Magnificat & Nunc Dimittis (1977); O Pray for the Peace of Jersalem (1941); King of Glory (1951) CRD ▲ 3454 [DDD]
Josquin Desprez:Music of—Inviolata; Praeter Rerum Seriem; Salve Regina; Stabat Mater Dolorosa; Veni Sancte Spiritus; Virgo Prudentissima; Virgo Salutiferi [L] Meridian ▲ ECD 84093
Lalande, M.–R. de:Confitebor tibi, Domine, w. G. Fisher (sop), O. Johnston (trb), C. Daniels (ct), A. Smith (ten), S. Varcoe (bass), King's Consort [L] Erato (Musifrance) ▲ 2292–45014–2 [DDD]
Lalande, M.–R. de:De profundis solo Voices, Orch & Chorus, w. G. Fisher (sop), O. Johnston (trb), C. Daniels (ct), A. Smith (ten), S. Varcoe (bass), King's Consort [L] Erato (Musifrance) ▲ 2292–45014–2 [DDD]
Lalande, M.–R. de:Miserere, w. G. Fisher (sop), O. Johnston (trb), C. Daniels (ct), A. Smith (ten), S. Varcoe (bass), King's Consort [L] Erato (Musifrance) ▲ 2292–45014–2 [DDD]
Locke, M.:Anthems, Motets & Ceremonial Music, w. Parley of Instruments—Descende caelo cincta sororibus ("The Oxford Ode"); How doth the city sit solitary; Super flumina Babylonis; O be joyful in the Lord, all ye lands; Audi, Domine, clamantes ad te; Lord let me know mine end; Jesu auctor clementie; Be thou exalted, Lord [E,L] Hyperion ▲ CDA 66373 [DDD]
Motets en espace, w. Gervais (cnd), Versailles National Masters, Gary Cooper (org) K617 ▲ 7010 [DDD]
Mozart, W.A.:Litaniae Lauretanae, K.195, w. Hanover Band *(rec July 1992)* K617 ▲ 7028 [DDD]
Mozart, W.A.:Vesperae de Dominica, w. Hanover Band *(rec July 1992)* K617 ▲ 7028 [DDD]
Purcell, H.:Sacred Choral & Vocal Music, w. R. Muller (ten) [E, L] Meridian ▲ CDE 84112
Tallis, T.:Church Music—Gaude gloriosa; Nunc dimittis (from Magnificat); Motets (from Cantiones Sacrae, 1575) CRD ▲ CD 3429 [DDD]
Tomkins, T.:3rd or Great Service, w. D. Burchell (org) *(rec July 16–18, 1990)* CRD ▲ CRD 3467 [DDD]
Wesley, S.S.:Anthems, w. E. Higginbottom (org)—(6 choral anthems & 3 solo organ selections) Ascribe unto the Lord; Blessed be the God and Father; Choral Song & Fugue; Thou will keep him in perfect peace; Wash me thoroughly from my wickedness; Andante in E minor; Cast me not away; Larghetto; The Wilderness [E] CRD ▲ 3463 [DDD]
Wesley, S.S.:Anthems—Ascribe unto the Lord; Blessed Be the God & Father; Thou Wilt Keep Him in Perfect Peace; Wash Me Thoroughly; Cast Me Not Away; Larghetto; The Wilderness CRD ▲ CRD 3463

D. Lumsden (cnd)
Britten, B.:Choral Music, w. J. Morehen (org)—Te Deum in C; Jubilate Deo in C; Antiphon; Hymn to St. Peter Saga Classics ▲ EC 3385
Purcell, H.:Sacred Choral & Vocal Music, w. J. Morehen (org)—Magnificat and Nunc Dimittis in g; O Lord God of Hosts; Praise the Lord, O Jerusalem Saga Classics ▲ EC 3385

New Company
Prokofiev, S.:Eugene Onegin, w. T. West (nar), K. Fuge (sop), P. im Thurn (bar), J. Walker (bass), E. Downes (cnd), Sinfonia 21 Chandos 2–▲ CHAN 9318/19 [DDD]
Schubert, Franz:Songs (comp), w. M. McLaughlin (sop), T. Hampson (bar), G. Johnson (pno), New Company Singers—soprano/piano songs—D.118, 564, 623, 658, 830, 831, 837, 838, 839, 846, 866/1, 866/3, 923; baritone/piano songs—D.293 & 923; baritone & chorus—Szene aus Faust, D.126 [G] Hyperion ▲ CDJ 33013 [DDD]

New England Conservatory Chorus
Berlioz, H.:L'Enfance du Christ, w. Florence Kopleff (cta), Ceasare Valletti (ten), Gérard Souzay (bar), Lucien Oliver (bar), Giorgio Tozzi (bass), C. Munch (cnd), Boston SO *(rec Dec 1956)* RCA Victor Gold Seal 8–▲ 0902–668444–2 [ADD]
Berlioz, H.:L'Enfance du Christ, w. F. Kopleff (cta), C. Valletti (ten), G. Souzay (bar), G. Tozzi (bass), C. Munch (cnd), Boston SO RCA Gold Seal 2–▲ 09026–61234–2
Berlioz, H.:Requiem, "Grande Messe des Morts", w. Léopold Simoneau (ten), C. Munch (cnd), Boston SO *(rec Apr 1959)* RCA Victor Gold Seal 8–▲ 0902–668444–2 [ADD]
Orff, C.:Carmina burana, w. E. Mandac (sop), S. Kolk (ten), S. Milnes (bar), S. Ozawa (cnd), Boston SO [G, L] RCA Gold Seal ▲ 07863–56533–2 [ADD] ■ 07863–56533–4
Rachmaninoff, S.:Prelude Pno, Op. 3/2, w. A. Weissenberg (pno) RCA Red Seal ▲ 60568–2–RC [ADD] ■ 60568–4–RC (CrO2)
Ravel, M.:Daphins et Chloé, w. C. Munch (cnd), Boston SO *(rec 1955)* RCA Gold Seal ▲ 60469–2–RG [ADD]
Roussel, A.:Bacchus et Ariane (suite 2), w. C. Munch (cnd), Boston SO RCA Gold Seal ▲ 60469–2–RG [ADD]

T. Brooks (cnd)
Cogan, R.:Music of, w. J. Heiss (cnd), New England Conservatory Jazz Big Band—Gulf Coast Bound; Fierce Singleness; Events Dancing Music & Arts ▲ CD 892 [DDD]
Escot, P.:Music of, w. J. Heiss (cnd), New England Conservatory Jazz Big Band—Missa Triste; Mirabilis I; Jubilation Music & Arts ▲ CD 892 [DDD]

New England Merrimack College Treble Chorus
M. Stultz (cnd)
Angels Are Everywhere!, w. Tanya Kodinsky (pno), Richard Stultz (pno/org) Afka ▲ SK 539
Rejoice & Sing AFKA ▲ SK 510

New London Chamber Choir
Boulanger, L.:Choral Music, w. M. Hill (ten), A. Ball (pno), J. Wood (cnd)—Les Sireènes; Soir sur la Plaine; Hymne au Soleil; Pour les funérailles d'un soldat Hyperion ▲ CDA 66726
Stravinsky, I.:Abraham & Isaac, w. O. Knussen (cnd), London Sinfonietta Deutsche Grammophon ▲ 447068–2
Stravinsky, I.:The Flood, w. O. Knussen (cnd), London Sinfonietta Deutsche Grammophon ▲ 447068–2
Stravinsky, I.:Requiem Canticles, w. O. Knussen (cnd), London Sinfonietta Deutsche Grammophon ▲ 447068–2
Tabachnik, M.:Le Pacte des Onzes, w. R. Landry (sop), M. Tabachnik (cnd), Ensemble InterContemporain [F] *(rec March 30, 1987)* Grammont ▲ CTSP 26–2 [ADD]
Wuorinen, C.:A Reliquary for Igor Stravinsky, w. O. Knussen (cnd), London Sinfonietta Deutsche Grammophon ▲ 447068–2

J. Wood (cnd)
Boulanger, L.:Renouveau, w. M. Hill (ten), A. Ball (pno) Hyperion ▲ CDA 66726
The Brightest Heaven of Invention:Flemish Polyphony of the High Renaissance Amon Ra ▲ CDSAR 56 [DDD]
Dallapiccola, L.:choral music, w. Julie Moffat (sop), H. Zender (cnd), Ensemble InterContemporain—Canti di Prigionia; Cinque Frammenti di Saffo; Due Liriche di Anacreonte; Sex Carmina Alcaei; Tempus Destruendi; Tempus Aedificandi; Due Cori di Michelangelo Buonarroti il Giovane Erato ▲ ERA 98509 [DDD]
Josquin Desprez:La Déploration de Johannes Ockeghem [L] Amon Ra ▲ CD-SAR 24 [DDD]
Josquin Desprez:Missa, "Hercules Dux Ferrariae" [L] Amon Ra ▲ CD-SAR 24 [DDD]
La Rue, P. de:Missa pro defunctis [L] Amon Ra ▲ CD-SAR 24 [DDD]
Poulenc, F.:Choral Music—Un soir de neige; Chansons françaises; Sept chansons; Chanson à boire; Petites voix; Figure humaine Hyperion ▲ CDA 66798
Stravinsky, I.:Choral Music, w. New London Chamber Ensemble, Voronezh Chamber Choir—Ave Maria [1934 Slavonic version]; Pater Noster [1926 Slavonic version]; Credo [1964 Slavonic version]; The dove descending breaks the air (1962); Introitus:T.S. Eliot in memoriam (1965) Hyperion ▲ CDA 66410 [DDD]
Stravinsky, I.:Les Noces, w. New London Chamber Ensemble, Voronezh Chamber Choir [R] Hyperion ▲ CDA 66410 [DDD]
Stravinsky, I.:Russian Peasant Songs, w. Voronezh Chamber Choir [performing both the original & revised versions] [R] Hyperion ▲ CDA 66410 [DDD]
Stravinsky, I.:Sacrae cantiones [L] Hyperion ▲ CDA 66410 [DDD]

New London Children's Choir
Boughton, R.:Bethlehem, w. A.G. Melville (cnd), City of London Sinfonia, Holst Singers [adapted] Hyperion ▲ CDA 66690
Britten, B.:Choral Music, w. Alexander Wells (pno), Skaila Kanga (hp), R. Corp (cnd)—Friday Afternoons, Op. 7; Sweet was the Song; King Herod & the Cock; The Oxen; Fancie; The Birds; 3 Two–part Songs; A Walden Trio [Christmas Song of the Women]; A Ceremony of Carols *(rec All Hallows, Gospel Oak, London, Sept. 17–18, 1994)* Naxos ▲ 8.553183 [DDD]
Shostakovich, D.:Song of the Forest, w. M. Kotliarov (ten), N. Storoyev (bass), V. Ashkenazy (cnd), Royal PO, Brighton Festival Chorus London ▲ 436762–2 [DDD]
Vaughan Williams, R.:Hugh the Dover, w. R. Evans (sop), S. Walker (mez), B. Bottone (ter), N. Jenkins (ten), A. Opie (bar), R. Van Allan (bass), M. Best (cnd), Corydon Orch, Corydon Singers Hyperion 2–▲ CDA 66901/02

New Moscow Choir
E. Rastvorova (cnd)
Denisov, E.:Choral Music (misc), w. Moscow Ensemble of Contemporary Music Soloists—Choruses from Medea; Peaceful Light; Legends of the Subterranean Waters Russian Season ▲ RUS 288131

New Opera Theater Chorus
Glinka, M.:Russlan & Ludmilla (sels), w. E. Kolobov (cnd), New Opera Theater Orch—Fant on Russian & Ludmilla Russian Compact Disc ▲ RCD 22001

New Orleans Chamber Choir
Ev'ry Time I Feel the Spirit:Spirituals, w. Ragin, Derek Lee (male alt), Moses Hogan (pno), New World Ensemble, Moses Hogan (cnd) Channel Classics ▲ CCS 2991 [DDD]

New Orleans Opera Chorus
Floyd, C.:Markheim, w. Norman Treigle (bass—Markheim), Audrey Schuh (sgr—Tess), Alan Crofoot (sgr—Josiah Creach), William Diard (sgr—Stranger), K. Andersson (cnd), New Orleans Opera Orch *(rec New Orleans, LA, Mar. 31 & Apr. 2, 1966)* VAI Audio ▲ VAIA 1107
Floyd, C.:Susannah, w. Phyllis Curtin (sop—Susannah Polk), Richard Cassilly (ten—Sam Polk), Norman Treigle (bass—Olin Blitch), Marietta Muhs Cosenza (sgr—Mrs. McLean), Marilyn Davidson (sgr—Mrs. Gleaton), Kay Long (sgr—Mrs. Hayes), Jean Young (sgr—Mrs. Ott), Alton Brim (sgr—Elder Hayes), Thomas Carter (sgr—Elder Gleaton), Jack Davis (sgr—Elder McLean), Keith Kaldenberg (sgr—Little Bat McLean), Burton Parker (sgr—Elder Ott), K. Andersson (cnd), New Orleans Opera Orch *(rec Mar 31, 1962)* VAI Audio 2–▲ VAIA 1115–2 [ADD]
Mascagni, P.:Cavalleria rusticana, w. Zinka Milanov (sop—Santuzza), Jean Craft (mez—Lucia), Marietta Cosenza (mez—Lola), Giuseppe Gismondo (ten—Turiddu), Benjamin Rayson (bar—Alfio), R. Cellini (cnd), New Orleans Opera Orch *(rec live, 1963)* VAI Audio ▲ VAIA 1053
Offenbach, J.:Les Contes d'Hoffmann, w. Beverly Sills (sop—Olympia/Giulietta/Antonia/Stella), Edith Evans (mez—Nicklausse/Mother's Voice), Michael Devlin (ten—Spalanzani), André Turp (ten—Hoffmann), Luigi Vellucci (ten—Andrès/Cochenille/Pitichinaccio/Frantz), Donald Bernard (bar—Luther/Schlemil), Norman Treigle (bass—Lindorf/Coppélius/Dapertutto/Dr. Miracle), John West (bass—Crespel), Alton Brim (sgr—Nathanaël), Rodney Hall (sgr—Hermann), K. Andersson (cnd), New Orleans Opera Orch *(rec Feb 27, 1964)* VAI Audio 2–▲ VAIA 1121–2 [ADD]
Puccini, G.:La Bohème, w. Licia Albanese (sop—Mimì), Audrey Schuh (sop—Musetta), Giuseppe di Stefano (ten—Rodolfo), Arthur Cosenza (bar—Schaunard), Giuseppe Valdengo (bar—Marcello), Norman Treigle (bass—Colline), Warren Gadpaille (bass—Benoît/Alcindoro), Thomas Carter (sgr—Parpignol), Harold Crane (sgr—Custom House Official), Steve Harun (sgr—Sergeant), R. Cellini (cnd), New Orleans Opera Orch *(rec Nov 1959)* VAI Audio 2–▲ VAIA 1119–2 [ADD]
Puccini, G.:Madama Butterfly, w. Dorothy Kirsten (sop—Madama Butterfly), Rosalind Nadell (mez—Suzuki), Eileen Ireland (mez—Kate), Daniele Barioni (ten—Pinkerton), Thomas Carter (ten—Goro), Arthur Cosenza (ten—Yamadori), Richard Torigi (bar—Sharpless), Rodney Hall (bass—The Bronze), Harold Crane (bass—Commissioner), R. Cellini (cnd), New Orleans Opera Orch *(rec live, Mar 1960)* VAI Audio 2–▲ VAIA 1054–2
Puccini, G.:Madama Butterfly, w. V. de los Angeles (sop), R. Nadell (mez), B. Faulkner (sgr), W. Fredericks (sgr), J. Thresh (sgr), D. Bernard (sgr), R. Torigi (sgr), A. Cosenza (bar), W. Herbert (cnd), New Orleans Opera Orch *(rec live March 18, 1954)* Legato Classics 2–▲ LCD 168–2 [ADD]
Saint-Saëns, C.:Samson et Dalila, w. Risë Stevens (mez—Dalila), Ramón Vinay (ten—Samson), Thomas Carter (ten—1st Philistine), Tony Lopez (ten—Philistine Messenger), Joseph Mordino (bar—High Priest), Arthur Cosenza (bass—Abimélech), Joseph Knight (bass—2nd Philistine), Ara Berberian (bass—Old Hebrew), R. Cellini (cnd), New Orleans Opera Orch *(rec live, Apr 2, 1960)* VAI Audio 2–▲ VAIA 1055–2 [ADD]
Verdi, G.:Falstaff, w. Vivian Della Chiesa (sop—Alice), Audrey Schuh (sop—Nannetta), Lizabeth Pritchett (mez—Quickly), Evelyn Sachs (mez—Meg), André Turp (ten—Fenton), Virginio Assandri (ten—Caius), Luigi Vellucci (ten—Bardolfo), Leonard Warren (bar—Falstaff), Richard Torigi (bar—Ford), R. Cellini (cnd), New Orleans Opera Orch *(rec live, May 5, 1956)* VAI Audio 2–▲ VAIA 1056–2
Verdi, G.:Il trovatore, w. M. Caballé (sop), P. Domingo (ten), E. Sordello (bar), K. Andersson (cnd), New Orleans Opera Orch [I] *(rec live 3/14/68)* Melodram 2–▲ MEL 27047 [AAD]

New Philharmonia Chorus
Bach, J.S.:Magnificat, BWV 243, w. Anne Pashley (sop), Lucia Popp (sop), Janet Baker (mez), Robert Tear (ten), Thomas Hemsley (bar), D. Barenboim (cnd), New Philharmonia Orch *(rec All Saints, Tooting, London, May 1960)* EMI Classics ▲ CDK 65334 [ADD]
Bach, J.S.:Magnificat, BWV 243, w. L. Popp (sop), A. Pashley (sop), J. Baker (mez), R. Tear (ten), D. Barenboim (cnd), New Philharmonia Orch EMI Classics ▲ CDM 64634–2
Beethoven, L. van:Missa Solemnis, w. E. Söderström (sop), M. Höffgen (cta), W. Kmentt (ten), M. Talvela (bass), O. Klemperer (cnd), New Philharmonia Orch [L] EMI Classics ("Studio" series) 2–▲ CDMB 69538 [ADD]
Brahms, J.:Ein Deutsches Requiem, w. I. Cotrubas (sop), H. Prey (bar), L. Maazel (cnd), New Philharmonia Orch [G] *(rec 1976)* Sony Classical ▲ SK 45853 [ADD]
Mahler, G.:Sym 8, w. W. Morris (cnd), Symphonica of London, Ambrosian Singers IMP Classics 2–▲ IMP DPCD 1019 [DDD]
Mendelssohn, F.:Elijah, w. Gwyneth Jones (sop), Janet Baker (mez), Simon Woolf (trb), Nicolai Gedda (ten), Dietrich Fischer-Dieskau (bar), R. Frühbeck de Burgos (cnd), New Philharmonia Orch, Wandsworth School Boys' Choir *(rec 1968)* EMI Classics ("Doublefforte" series) 2–▲ CDFB 68601
Mozart, W.A.:Così fan tutte, w. L. Price (sop), J. Raskin (sop), T. Troyanos (mez), G. Shirley (ten), S. Milnes (bar), E. Leinsdorf (cnd), New Philharmonia Orch [I] RCA Gold Seal 3–▲ 6677–2 [ADD]
Mozart, W.A.:Don Giovanni, w. C. Watson (sop), C. Ludwig (mez), N. Gedda (ten), N. Ghiaurov (bass), O. Klemperer (cnd), New Philharmonia Orch EMI Classics 3–▲ CDMC 63841
Mozart, W.A.:Requiem, w. E. Mathis (sop), G. Bumbry (mez), G. Shirley (ten), M. Rintzler (bass), R. Frühbeck de Burgos (cnd), New Philharmonia Orch Classics for Pleasure ▲ CDCFP 4399 [ADD]
Orff, C.:Carmina burana, w. L. Popp (sop), G. Unger (ten), R. Wolansky (bar), J. Noble (bar), R. Frühbeck de Burgos (cnd), New Philharmonia Orch EMI Classics ▲ CDM 64328
Vivaldi, A.:Gloria, RV.589, w. T. Berganza (mez), L. Valentini–Terrani (mez), R. Muti (cnd), New Philharmonia Orch [L] EMI Classics ▲ CDC 47990 [ADD]
Vivaldi, A.:Magnificat, RV.611, w. T. Berganza (mez), L. Valentini–Terrani (mez), R. Muti (cnd), New Philharmonia Orch [L] EMI Classics ▲ CDC 47990 [ADD]

New Sadler's Wells Opera Chorus
Sullivan, A.:HMS Pinafore, w. S. Phipps (cnd), New Sadler's Wells Opera Orch [E] MCA Classics 2–▲ MCAD2–11012
Sullivan, A.:Ruddigore, w. S. Phipps (cnd), New Sadler's Wells Opera Orch—premiere rec'g of the original uncut score [E] MCA Classics 2–▲ MCAD2–11010 [DDD]

New York Baroque
E. Milnes (cnd)
Rossi, S.:The Songs of Solomon—Haleluyah haleli nafshi et Adonai; Yigdal; Kaddish; Barchu; Hashkiveinu; Keter; Haleluyah, ashrei ish yare et Adonai; Elohim Hashiveinu; Mizmor l'David; Mizmor l'Asaf; Haleluyah, ode ladonai; Shir lamma'alot, essa einai; Kaddish; Adon Olam; Lamnatstseach binginot mizmor shir; Mizmor shir l'yom hashshabat; Ein Kehloheinu *(rec St. Peter's Episcopal Church, New York City, Jan 26–30, 1996)* PGM ▲ PGM 108 [DDD]

New York Chamber Chorus
Strauss, R.:Der Bürger als Edelmann (suite), w. G. Schwarz (cnd), New York Chamber SO *(rec 11/88)* Pro Arte ▲ CDD 448 [DDD]

CHORAL GROUPS

New York Choral Artists
Beethoven, L. van:Fant Pno, Op. 80, "Choral Fant", w. E. Ax (pno), Z. Mehta (cnd), New York PO
RCA Silver Seal ▲ 09026-61213-2 ■ 09026-61213-4
Beethoven, L. van:Sym 9, "Choral Sym", w. Z. Mehta (cnd), New York PO [soloists Margaret Price, Marilyn Horne, Jon Vickers, Matti Salminen] [G]
RCA Silver Seal ▲ 60477-2-RV [DDD] ■ 60477-4-RV
A Christmas Celebration, w. Kathleen Battle (sop), Leonard Slatkin (cnd), Orch of St. Luke, Harlem Boys Choir EMI Classics ▲ CDC 47587
DDD Christmas, w. Kathleen Battle (sop), Florence Quivar (mez), Taverner Consort, Taverner Choir, Taverner Players, New York Choral Artists, Toronto Mendelssohn Choir, King's Singers, Empire Brass
Angel ▲ CDM 63666
Gershwin, G.:Let 'Em Eat Cake, w. McGovern, J. Gilford (ten), L. Kert (sgr), M. Thomas (cnd), Orch of St. Luke [E] CBS 2-▲ M2K 42522 [DDD]
Gershwin, G.:Of Thee I Sing, w. McGovern, J. Gilford (ten), L. Kert (sgr), M. Thomas (cnd), Orch of St. Luke [E] CBS 2-▲ M2K 42522 [DDD]
Gershwin, G.:Porgy & Bess (sels), w. R. Alexander (sop), G. Baker (bar), Z. Mehta (cnd), New York PO—Introduction & Summertime; A woman is a sometime thing; Overflow; Since I lose my man; The promise' lan'; I got plenty o' nuttin'; Bess, you is my woman now; O, I can't sit down; It ain't necesssarily so; There's a boat dat's leavin' soon for New York; O, Lawd I'm on my way [E]
Teldec ▲ 2292-46318-2 [DDD]
Holst, G.:The Planets, w. Z. Mehta (cnd), New York PO Teldec ▲ 2292-46316-2 [DDD]
Mahler, G.:Syms, w. J. Blegen (sop), B. Hendricks (sop), M. Price (sop), G. Zeumer (sop), H. Wittek (trb), A. Baltsa (mez), C. Ludwig (mez), K. Riegel (ten), H. Prey (bar), A. Schmidt (bar), J. Van Dam (b-bar), L. Bernstein (cnd), New York PO, Royal Concertgebouw Orch, Vienna PO, Westminster Choir, Brooklyn Boys' Choir, Vienna Boys' Choir, Vienna State Opera Chorus, Vienna Singverein
Deutsche Grammophon 13-▲ 435162-2 [DDD]
Mahler, G.:Sym 3, w. C. Ludwig (mez), L. Bernstein (cnd), New York PO, Brooklyn Boys' Chorus [G]
Deutsche Grammophon 2-▲ 427328-2 [DDD]
Schoenberg, A.:Gurrelieder, w. E. Martón (sop), F. Quivar (mez), G. Lakes (ten), H. Hotter (b-bar), Z. Mehta (cnd), New York PO [G] Sony Classical 2-▲ S2K 48077 [DDD]

New York Choral Artists Men's Voices
Shostakovich, D.:Sym 13, w. Y. Yevtushenko (reciter), S. Leiferkus (bass), K. Masur (cnd), New York PO
Teldec ▲ 90848

New York Choral Society
The Chorus, w. Mormon Tabernacle Choir, Vocal Majority, Westminster Choir, Chicago Sym Chorus members, et al. Sony Classical ("Greatest Hits" series) ▲ MLK 62684 ■ MLT 62684
Thompson, R.:Frostiana Koch International Classics ▲ KIC 7283-2 [DDD]
Thompson, R.:The Testament of Freedom, w. R.A. Clark (cnd), Manhattan CO
Koch International Classics ▲ KIC 7283-2 [DDD]

R. DeCormier (cnd)
Songs of Liberty, w. orch BOMR 2-▲ 61-7634 [DDD]

New York City Chorus
Donizetti, G.:Lucrezia Borgia, w. Montserrat Caballé (sop), Jane Berbié (mez), Alain Vanzo (ten), Kostas Paskalis (bar), Arnold Voketaitis (bass-bar), L. D. Clements (sgr), Adib Fazah (sgr), Mauro Lampi (sgr), Vern Shinall (sgr), Jerold Siena (sgr), William Wiederanders (sgr), J. Perlea (cnd), New York City Opera Orch Great Opera Performances 2-▲ GOP 769

New York City Gay Men's Chorus
Christmas Comes Anew Virgin Classics ▲ CDC 59121

G. Miller (cnd)
Love Lives on Virgin Classics ▲ 59663

New York Concert Chorale
Rossini, G.:Music of, w. M. Fortuna (sop), M. Lerner (sop), D. Voigt (sop), M. Horne (mez), K. Kuhlmann (mez), F. von Stade (mez), R. Blake (ten), C. Estep (ten), C. Merritt (ten), T. Hampson (b-bar), H. Runey (b-bar), J. Opalach (bass), S. Ramey (bass), R. Norrington (cnd), Orch of St. Luke's
EMI Classics ▲ CDC 54643

New York Metropolitan Opera Chorus
Barber, S.:Vanessa, w. E. Steber (sop), G. Resnik (sop), R. Elias (mez), N. Gedda (ten), G. Tozzi (bass), D. Mitropoulos (cnd), Metropolitan Opera Orch [E] RCA Gold Seal ▲ 7899-2-RG [ADD]
Bizet, G.:Carmen (sels), w. Risë Stevens (sop), N. Conner (sop), R. Jobin (ten), R. Weede (bar), G. Sébastian (cnd), Metropolitan Opera Orch [F] Odyssey ■ YT 32102 (m)
Donizetti, G.:L'elisir d'amore, w. K. Battle (sop), D. Upshaw (sop), L. Pavarotti (ten), E. Dara (bar), L. Nucci (bar), J. Levine (cnd), Metropolitan Orch Deutsche Grammophon 2-▲ 429744-2 [DDD]
Legendary Three Tenors, w. Enrico Caruso (ten), Beniamino Gigli (ten), John McCormack (ten), Ruggiero Leoncavallo (pno), Edwin Schneider (pno), Metropolitan Opera Orch [cnd:Giulio Setti], Philharmonia Orch, Philharmonia Chorus [cnd:Stanford Robinson] *(rec 1904-1950)*
RCA Gold Seal ▲ 09026-68534-2 [ADD] ■ 09026-68534-4
Mozart, W.A.:Idomeneo, w. Carol Vaness (sop—Elettra), Cecilia Bartoli (mez—Idamante), Heidi Grant Murphy (mez—Ilia), Plácido Domingo (ten— Idomeneo), Thomas Hampson (bar—Arbace), Bryn Terfel (bass-bar—La Voce), J. Levine (cnd), Metropolitan Opera Orch Deutsche Grammophon ▲ 447737-2
Mussorgsky, M.:Boris Godunov, w. Kerstin Thorborg (mez), René Maison (ten), Alexander Kipnis (bass), G. Szell (cnd), New York Metropolitan Opera Orch *(rec live, Feb 13, 1943)*
The Fourties 2-▲ ENT 1505
Offenbach, J.:Les Contes d'Hoffmann, w. L. Amara (sop), R. Peters (sop), R. Stevens (mez), R. Tucker (ten), M. Singher (bar), P. Monteux (cnd), Metropolitan Opera Orch Stradivarius 2-▲ DAT 12302
Offenbach, J.:Les Contes d'Hoffmann, w. Patrice Munsel (sop), Jarmila Novotná (sop), Raoul Jobin (ten), Ezio Pinza (bass), T. Beecham (cnd), Metropolitan Opera Orch *(rec Feb 26, 1944)*
Enterprise ("The Radio Years") 2-▲ ENT-19 (m)
Ponchielli, A.:La Gioconda, w. E. Panizza (cnd), Metropolitan Opera Orch
Symposium 2-▲ SYM 1176/77
Puccini, G.:La Bohème, w. L. Albanese (sop), L. Hurley (sop), C. Bergonzi (ten), C. Harvuot (bar), M. Sereni (bar), N. Scott (bass), E. Flagello (bass), T. Schippers (cnd), New York Metropolitan Opera Orch *(rec Feb. 15, 1958)* Golden Age of Opera 2-▲ GAO 139/40 [ADD]
Puccini, G.:Manon Lescaut, w. M. Freni (sop—Manon), C. Bartoli (mez—Musici I), L. Pavarotti (ten—Des Grieux), R. Vargas (ten—Edmondo), D. Croft (ten—Lescaut), G. Taddei (bar—Geronte), J. Levine (cnd), Metropolitan Opera Orch [I] *(rec 1992)* London ▲ 440200-2 [DDD]
Puccini, G.:Turandot, w. B. Nilsson (sop—Turnadot), A. Moffo (sop—Liù), F. Corelli (ten—Calaf), C. Anthony (ten—Pong), R. Nagy (ten—Pang), F. Guarrera (bar—Ping), B. Giaiotti (bass—Timur), L. Stokowski (cnd), Metropolitan Opera Orch *(rec Mar. 4, 1961)* Datum 2-▲ DAT 12301 [ADD]
Rossini, G.:Il barbiere di Siviglia, w. R. Peters (sop), C. Valletti (ten), R. Merrill (bar), G. Tozzi (bass), F. Corena (bass), E. Leinsdorf (cnd), Metropolitan Opera Orch [I]
RCA Gold Seal 3-▲ 6505-2-RG [ADD] 2-■ 6505-4-RG (CrO2)
Rossini, G.:Il barbiere di Siviglia, w. Roberta Peters (sop—Rosina), Margaret Roggero (mez—Berta), Cesare Valletti (ten—Count Almaviva), Calvin Marsh (bar—Fiorello/Sergeant), Robert Merrill (bar—Figaro), Fernando Corena (bass—Dr. Bartolo), Carlo Tomanelli (bass—Ambrogio), Giorgio Tozzi (bass—Don Basilio), E. Leinsdorf (cnd), Metropolitan Opera Orch *(rec Manhattan Center, New York, Sept 1-11, 1958)* RCA Living Stereo 3-▲ 09026-68552-2 [ADD]
Rossini, G.:Il barbiere di Siviglia (sels), w. R. Peters (sop), C. Valletti (ten), R. Merrill (bar), G. Tozzi (bass), F. Corena (bass), E. Leinsdorf (cnd), Metropolitan Opera Orch
RCA Gold Seal ▲ 60188-2-RG [ADD] ■ 60188-4-RG (CrO2)
Verdi, G.:Aida, w. Gina Cigna (sop), Bruna Castagna (mez), Giovanni Martinelli (ten), Ezio Pinza (bass), E. Panizza (cnd), New York Metropolitan Opera Orch *(rec live, Feb 6, 1937)*
The Fourties 2-▲ ENT 1501
Verdi, G.:Aida, w. A. Millo (sop), D. Zajick (mez), P. Domingo (ten), J. Morris (bass), S. Ramey (bass), J. Levine (cnd), Metropolitan Opera Orch [I]
Sony Classical 3-▲ S3K 45973 [DDD] 3-■ S3T 45973 (D)
Verdi, G.:Aida (sels), w. A. Millo (sop), D. Zajick (mez), P. Domingo (ten), J. Morris (bar), S. Ramey (bass), T. Cook (bass), J. Levine (cnd), Metropolitan Opera Orch *(rec New York, May 18-26, 1990)*
Sony Classical ("Opera Highlights" series) ▲ SMK 53506 [DDD]

New York Metropolitan Opera Chorus (cont.)
Verdi, G.:Don Carlos (sels), w. J. Bunnell (sop), A. Millo (sop), D. Zajick (mez), M. Sylvester (ten), V. Chernov (bar), F. Furlanetto (bass), P. Plishka (bass), J. Levine (cnd), Metropolitan Opera Orch *(rec New York, Apr. 20–May 14, 1992)* Sony Classical ("Opera Highlights" series) ▲ SMK 53507 [DDD]
Verdi, G.:Luisa Miller, w. A. Millo (sop), F. Quivar (mez), P. Domingo (ten), V. Chernov (bar), J. Levine (cnd), Metropolitan Opera Orch Sony Classical 2-▲ S2K 48073
Verdi, G.:Luisa Miller (sels), w. A. Millo (sop), W. White (mez), F. Quivar (cta), P. Domingo (ten), V. Chernov (bar), J.-H. Rootering (bass), P. Plishka (bass), J. Levine (cnd), Metropolitan Opera Orch *(rec New York, May 2-18, 1991)* Sony Classical ("Opera Highlights" series) ▲ SMK 53508 [DDD]
Verdi, G.:Macbeth, w. L. Rysanek (sop), C. Bergonzi (ten), L. Warren (bar), J. Hines (bass), E. Leinsdorf (cnd), Metropolitan Opera Orch [I] RCA Gold Seal 2-▲ 4516-2-RG [ADD]
Verdi, G.:Otello (sels), w. H. Jepson (sop), G. Martinelli (ten), N. Massue (ten), L. Tibbett (bar), W. Pelletier (cnd), Metropolitan Opera Orch—eleven arias & scenes *(rec 1939)*
Pearl ▲ GEMMCD 9914 (m) [AAD]
Verdi, G.:Il trovatore, w. A. Millo (sop), D. Zajick (mez), S. Kelly (cta), P. Domingo (ten), T. Willson (ten), A. Laciura (ten), J. Morris (bass), G. Bater (bass), J. Levine (cnd), Metropolitan Opera Orch *(rec June 18, 1991)* Sony Classical 2-▲ S2K 48070 [DDD]
Wagner, R.:Götterdämmerung, w. H. Behrens (sop), C. Studer (sop), H. Schwarz (mez), R. Goldberg (ten), B. Weikl (bar), E. Wlaschiha (bar), M. Salminen (bass), J. Levine (cnd), Metropolitan Opera Orch
Deutsche Grammophon 4-▲ 429385-2 [DDD]
Wagner, R.:Lohengrin, w. H. Traubel (sop—Elsa), A. Varnay (sop—Ortrud), L. Melchior (ten—Lohengrin), F. Guerrera (bar—Herald), H. Janssen (bar—Telramund), D. Ernster (bass—King Heinrich), F. Stiedry (cnd), Metropolitan Opera Orch *(rec live Jan. 6, 1950)* Danacord 3-▲ DACOCD 322/24 [AAD]
Wagner, R.:Parsifal, w. J. Norman (sop), P. Domingo (ten), E. Wlaschiha (bar), K. Moll (bass), J. Morris (bass), J.-H. Rootering (bass), J. Levine (cnd), Metropolitan Opera Orch
Deutsche Grammophon 4-▲ 437501-2
Wagner, R.:Siegfried, w. H. Behrens (sop), B. Svenden (sop), R. Goldberg (ten), J. Morris (bass), J. Levine (cnd), Metropolitan Opera Orch [G] Deutsche Grammophon 4-▲ 429407-2 [DDD]

R. Hughes (cnd)
Mozart, W.A.:Idomeneo, w. Heidi Grant-Murphy (sop—Ilia), Carol Vaness (sop—Elettra), Cecilia Bartoli (mez—Idamante), Plácido Domingo (ten—Idomeneo), Frank Lopardo (ten—High Priest), Thomas Hampson (bar—Arbace), Bryn Terfel (b-bar—The Voice), J. Levine (cnd), Metropolitan Opera Orch *(rec Manhattan Center Studios, New York, Mar & Apr 1994)*
Deutsche Grammophon 3-▲ 447 737-2 [DDD]

New York Motet Choir
Gottlieb, J.:Sacred Music, w. M. Stone (sop), H. Reps (mez), D. Lefkowitz (ten), H. Stahl (ten), R. Abelson (bar), R. Botton (bar), P. Newman (reader), S. Sturk (cnd), Metropolitan Brass Ensemble
Premier ("Composer" series) ▲ PRCD 1018 [DDD]

New York Opera Chorus
Bernstein, L.:Candide, w. E. Mills (sop), D. Eisler (ten), Lankston (sgr), J. Mauceri (cnd), New York City Opera Orch [E] *(rec 1985)* New World 2-▲ NW 340/41-2 2-■ NW 340/41-4
Donizetti, G.:Parisina, w. Montserrat Caballé (sop), Jérôme Pruett (ten), Louis Quilico (bar), James Morris (bass), E. Queler (cnd), New York City Opera Orch *(rec live, New York 1974)*
Standing Room Only 2-▲ SRO 836-2 [ADD]
Donizetti, G.:Parisina, w. Montserrat Caballé (sop), Jérôme Pruett (ten), Louis Quilico (bar), James Morris (bass), E. Queler (cnd), New York City Opera Orch Pantheon 2-▲ PHE 6638
Donizetti, G.:Roberto Devereux, w. B. Sills (sop), S. Marsee (mez), P. Domingo (ten), L. Quilico (bar), J. Rudel (cnd), New York City Opera Orch *(rec 1970)* Melodram ▲ MLO 270107 [ADD]
Handel, G.F.:Giulio Cesare in Egitto, w. Beverly Sills (sop), Maureen Forrester (cta), Fritz Wolff (ten), Spiro Malas (bass), Norman Treigle (bass), J. Redel (cnd), New York City Opera Orch
RCA Gold Seal 2-▲ 6182-2-RG [ADD]
Massenet, J.:Manon, w. Beverly Sills (sop—Manon), Plácido Domingo (ten—Des Grieux), Nico Castel (ten—Guillot), Richard Fredricks (bar—Lescaut), Robert Hale (bar—De Brétigny), Malcom Smith (bass—Count de Grieux), J. Rudel (cnd), New York City Opera Orch *(rec live, New York, 1969)*
Melodram 2-▲ IMC 205008 [ADD]
Massenet, J.:Manon, w. B. Sills (sop), P. Domingo (ten), R. Fredricks (bar), J. Rudel (cnd), New York City Opera Orch *(rec live, 1969)* Melodram 2-▲ MEL 27054
Puccini, G.:Il tabarro, w. J. Crader (sop), P. Domingo (ten), C. Ludgin (bar), J. Rudel (cnd), New York City Opera Orch *(rec live 1968; stereo)* Melodram ▲ 17048
Verdi, G.:Rigoletto (sels), w. José Carreras (ten), J. Rudel (cnd), New York City Opera Orch—Questa o quella; Ella mi fu rapital...Parmi veder le lagrime; La donna è mobile *(rec New York, Apr 26, 1973)*
Goldies ▲ GLD 63203 [ADD]
Ward, R.:The Crucible, w. P. Brooks (sop), F. Bible (mez), C. Ludgin (bar), E. Buckley (cnd), New York City Opera Orch [E] Albany 2-▲ TROY 025/26-2 [ADD]

New York Oratorio Society
Handel, G.F.:Messiah (reorchd Mozart), w. Andrew Murphy (b-bar), M. Altman (sgr), J. Davidson (sgr), Peter Elvin (sgr), P. Price (sgr), L. Woodside (cnd), Sinfonia Rubinstein [Sinfonia Rubinstein is made up from musicians from the Lodz Philharmonic Orchestra and the Lodz Opera of Poland] [E]
Koch Schwann 2-▲ SC 100308 [DDD]
Verdi, G.:Aroldo, w. M. Caballé (sop), G. Cecchele (ten), J. Pons (bar), E. Queler (cnd), New York Opera Orch, Westchester Choral Society [I] *(rec live, Carnegie Hall 4/8/79)* CBS 2-▲ M2K 35906 [ADD]

New York Phil Chorus
Bach, J.S.:St. Matthew Passion, w. Nadine Conner (sop), Jean Watson (cta), William Hain (ten), Mack Harrell (bar), Herbert Janssen (bar), Lorenzo Alvary (bass), B. Walter (cnd), New York PO—Part I
Minerva ▲ 20
Beethoven, L. van:Fant Pno, Op. 80, "Choral Fant", w. R. Serkin (pno), L. Bernstein (cnd), New York PO
Odyssey ■ YT 42485
Mahler, G.:Sym 3, w. *(soloist unknown)*, D. Mitropoulos (cnd), New York PO
Enterprise ("Documents" series) 2-▲ ENT LV 1000
Mahler, G.:Sym 3, w. M. Lipton (cta), L. Bernstein (cnd), New York PO *(rec 1961)*
Sony Classical ("Bernstein:The Royal Edition" series) 2-▲ SM2K 47576 [ADD]

New York Russian Chamber Chorus

N. Kachanov (cnd)
Yukechev, Y.:Sacred Choral Music, w. Mary Ellen Callahan (sop)—My Heart Is Ready; O, Beauty; Chant; By Candlelight Helicon Classics ▲ HE 1005

New York Schola Cantorum
Ives, C.:Sym 4, w. L. Stokowski (cnd), American SO *(rec 1965)*
Sony Masterworks ("Portrait" series) ▲ MPK 46726 [ADD]
Milhaud, D.:Choëphores, w. Vera Zorina (nar), Virginia Babikian (sop), Irene Jordan (sop), McHenry Boatwright (bar), L. Bernstein (cnd), New York PO
Sony Classical ("Masterworks Heritage" series) ▲ MHK 62352
Puccini, G.:Edgar, w. R. Scotto (sop), G. Killebrew (mez), C. Bergonzi (ten), V. Sardinero (bar), E. Queler (cnd), New York City Opera Orch *(rec in concert at Carnegie Hall, 4/13/77)* CBS 2-▲ M2K 34584

New York Virtuosi Chamber Chorus
Vaughan Williams, R.:Serenade to Music, w. K. Klein (cnd), New York Virtuosi Chamber SO
Allegretto ▲ ACD 8203

New York Virtuoso Singers
Schuman, W.:Carols of Death CRI ▲ CD 615 [DDD]

H. Rosenbaum (cnd)
Dallapiccola, L.:Prima serie dei cori di Michelangelo Buonarroti il giovane CRI ▲ CD 615 [DDD]
Henze, H.-W.:Orpheus Behind the Wire, CRI ▲ CD 615 [DDD]
Perle, G.:Sonnets to Orpheus CRI ▲ CD 615 [DDD]
To Orpheus CRI ▲ CRI 615 [DDD]

990 ▲ = CD ♦ = Enhanced CD Δ = MD ■ = Cassette Tape □ = DCC

New York Vocal Arts Ensemble
Beethoven, L. van:Folksong Arrs, w. Arturo Delmoni (vn), Fred Sherry (vc), Katherine Benfer (mez), James Archie Worley (ten), John Kramer (bar), Raymond Beegle (pno))—Highlander's Lament; Chase of the Wolf; The Soldier in a Foreign Land; The Pulse of an Irishman; Lochnagar; O Swiftly Glides the Bonny Boat; O Might I but my Patrick Love; Kak Pashli; Bolero; Ridder Stigs Runekast; When Mortals all to Rest Retire; Faithful Johnie; Charlie is my Darling; Glencoe; Come Fill, Fill, my Good Fellow; Auld Lang Syne *(rec SUNY Purchase Performing Arts Center, Theatre C, Sept 11–13, 1995)* Arabesque ▲ Z6672 [DDD]
The Great Sentimental Age, w. Gregg Smith Singers Vox Box 2-▲ CDX 5016 [ADD]
Haydn, J.:Vocal Trios & Qts—9 trios & quartets [G] Arabesque ▲ Z 6556
Listen to the Mockingbird Arabesque ▲ Z 6555 [DDD]
Mozart, W.A.:Notturnos Sops [G] Arabesque ▲ Z 6556
Mozart, W.A.:Più non si trovano [G] Arabesque ▲ Z 6556
R. Beegle (cnd)
Strauss (II), Joh.:Waltzes [composer's arrs. for vocal quartet with piano]—Rosen aus dem Süden; G'schichten aus dem Wiener Wald; Wiener Blut; Wein, Weib und Gesang; An der schönen, blauen Donau; Kaiser-Walzer Arabesque ▲ Z 6586
New Zealand Youth Choir
Rózsa, M.:El Cid, w. Tamra Saylor Fine (org), J. Sedares (cnd), New Zealand SO *(rec Symphony House, Wellington, New Zealand, May 1995)* Koch International Classics ▲ KIC 7340 [DDD] ■ KIC 7340
Newark Boys' Chorus
Stravinsky, I.:Perséphone, w. I. Jacob (nar), J. Aler (ten), R. Craft (cnd), Orch of St. Luke, Gregg Smith Singers MusicMasters ▲ 01612–67103–2
Nice Opera Chorus
Debussy, C.:Pelléas et Mélisande, w. E. Manchet (sop—Mélisande), M. Walker (bar—Pelléas), J. Carewe (cnd), Nice PO—no texts [F] *(rec 6/88)* Pierre Verany 2-▲ PV.788093/4 [DDD]
Nice Russian Vocal Quartet
Chants du Grand Carême et de la Semaine Sainte Studio SM ▲ 12 22 83 [DDD]
Hymnesà la Vierge:Orthodox Liturgical Chants Studio SM ▲ 12 22 27 [AAD]
Sacred Chant of the Russian Orthodox Church Studio SM ▲ 12 17.22
Nidarso Cathedral Choir
Jensen, L.I.:The Return, w. A. Bolstad (sop), R. Sterne (alt), H. Bjørkey (ten), I. Gilhuus (ten), P. Vollestad (bar), C. Stabell (bass), O.K. Ruud (cnd), Trondheim SO, Trondheim Sym Chorus Simax 2-▲ PSC 3109
Niederaltaich Benedictine Chorus
Liturgy of the Presanctified Gifts in German, w. Archimandrit Irenäus Tozzke (cnd), Schola Cantorum St. Godehard Hanover Christophorus ▲ 77175
Niederaltaich Scholars
K. Ruhland (cnd)
Ave Maris Stella:Life of the Virgin Mary in Plainsong Sony Classical ("Vivarte" series) ▲ SK 45861
A Christmas Legend *(rec Bavaria, Germany, June 2–4, 1994)* Sony Classical ("Vivarte" series) ▲ SK 66242 [DDD]
Medieval Christmas Music, w. Capella Antiqua Sony Classical ("Vivarte" series) ▲ SK 45946
Motets of the 17th Century, w. K. Ruhland (cnd) *(rec Apr. 13–15, 1992)* Sony Classical ▲ SK 53117 [DDD]
Psalmi et Cantica, 1400–1600 *(rec July 2–4, 1993)* Sony Classical ("Vivarte" series) ▲ SK 53977 [DDD]
Nikikai Chorus
Verdi, G.:Simon Boccanegra, w. M. Nicolesco (sop), G. Sabbatini (ten), R. Bruson (bar), S. Rinaldi-Miliani (bar), R. Scandiuzzi (bass), N. de Angelis (bass), R. Paternostro (cnd), Tokyo SO *(rec live 2/90)* Capriccio 2-▲ 60018–2 [DDD]
Nine Songs Chorus
Dun, T.:Nine Songs, w. T. Dun (cnd), Nine Songs Ensemble [Chinese] CRI ▲ CD 603 [DDD]
Non-Conformist Union Festival Choir
Live at the Crystal Palace, w. National Brass Band Festival Massed Bands, Festival of English Church Music Massed Choir, Handel Festival Choir, Handel Festival Orch, National Union of School Orch, Salvation Army Congress Massed Bands Beulah ▲ 1 PD 1
Noordlimburgs Men's Chorus
Mystery Circles, w. Collegium Instrumentale Brugense Eufoda ▲ EUF 1144 [DDD]
Norbertijnerabdij Averbode
Gregoriaanse Vespers Eufoda ▲ EUF 1135 [DDD]
Nord-Pas-de-Calais Choir
Mozart, W.A.:Requiem, w. Colette Alliot-Lugaz (sop), Dominique Vissé (ct), Martyn Hill (ten), G. Reinhart (bar), J. Malgoire (cnd), La Grande Ecurie et la Chambre du Roy [L] CBS ▲ MDK 44904 [DDD]
North German Figural Choir
Debussy, C.:Chansons (3) de Charles d'Orléans *(rec St. Oldag Church, Mandelsloh, Jan. 1994)* Thorofon ▲ CTH 2217 [DDD]
Poulenc, F.:Songs—Sept chansons; Un soir de neige; Chansons Françaises *(rec St. Oldag Church, Mandelsloh, Jan. 1994)* Thorofon ▲ CTH 2217 [DDD]
Ravel, M.:Chansons *(rec St. Oldag Church, Mandelsloh, Jan. 1994)* Thorofon ▲ CTH 2217 [DDD]
J. Straube (cnd)
Martin, F.:Gesänge des Ariel *(rec St. Osdag, Mandelsloh, Sept 1994–Mar 1995)* Thorofon ▲ CTH 2261 [DDD]
Martin, F.:Mass *(rec St. Osdag, Mandelsloh, Sept 1994–Mar 1995)* Thorofon ▲ CTH 2261 [DDD]
North German Radio Chorus
Bloch, A.:For the Light Is Come, w. M. Schweigmann (nar), P. Schwarz (org), North German RSO Pro Viva ▲ ISPV 169
Britten, B.:War Requiem, w. L. Orgonasova (sop), A. Rolfe-Johnson (ten), B. Skovhus (bar), J. E. Gardiner (cnd), North German RSO, Monteverdi Choir London, Tölz Boys' Choir Deutsche Grammophon 2-▲ 437801–2
Dessau, P.:Haggada, w. Sabine Ritterbusch (sop), Renate Spingler (sop), Yvi Jänicke (alt), Peter Galliard (ten—Rabbi Tarfon/Jude/ten solo), Gabriel Sadé (ten—Pharaoh), Jochen Schmeckenbechier (bar—Rabbi Jehoschua), Bernd Weikl (bar—Moses), Matthias Hölle (bass—Speaker/Rabbi Akiwa), Alfred Muff (bass—Father/Rabbi Eleasar), Johann Tilli (bass—Rabbi Elieser/bass solo), G. Albrecht (cnd), Hamburg State PO, Berlin Carl Maria Von Weber Men's Choir, Hamburg Alsterspatzen [G] *(rec Musikhalle, Hamburg, Sept 4 & 5, 1994)* Capriccio 2-▲ 10590/91 [DDD]
Nono, L.:Epitaffio 3, w. B. Maderna (cnd), North German RSO *(rec live, Hamburg 2/16/53)* Arkadia ▲ 027 [ADD]
Penderecki, K.:Polish Requiem, w. I. Haubold (sop), G. Winogrodska (mez), Z. Terzakis (ten), Smith (sgr), K. Penderecki (cnd), North German RSO [L] *(rec live, Lucerne, 1989)* Deutsche Grammophon 2-▲ 429720–2 [DDD]
Rossini, G.:Stabat Mater, w. Daniela Dessi (sop), Lucia Mazzaria (sop), Gloria Scalchi (mez), Pietro Ballo (ten), Chris Merritt (ten), Anatoli Kotscherga (bass), Roberto Scandiuzzi (bass), G. Gelmetti (cnd), Stuttgart RSO, Southwest German Radio Chorus Serenissima 2-▲ SER 360155 [DDD]
Stravinsky, I.:Chorale Variations on the German Christmas Carol "Vom Himmel hoch da komm' ich her", w. I. Stravinsky (cnd), North German RSO *(rec live, Venice 9/23/58)* Arkadia 2-▲ 766 [ADD]
Stravinsky, I.:Oedipus Rex, w. *(artists unknown)*, I. Stravinsky (cnd), North German RSO *(rec live, Venice, 9/19/58)* Arkadia 2-▲ 766 [ADD]
Stravinsky, I.:Threni, w. I. Stravinsky (cnd), North German RSO [soloists U. Zollenkopf, J. Deroubaix, H. Luenod *[sic]*, R. Robinson, R. Oliver, C. Scharbach] *(rec live, Venice 9/23/58)* Arkadia 2-▲ 766 [ADD]
Verdi, G.:Requiem Mass, w. Lucia Mazzaria (sop), Daniela Dessi (sop), Gloria Scalchi (mez), Pietro Ballo (ten), Chris Merritt (ten), Anatoli Kotscherga (bass), Roberto Scandiuzzi (bass), G. Gelmetti (cnd), Stuttgart RSO, Southwest German Radio Chorus Serenissima 2-▲ SER 360155 [DDD]

North German Radio Chorus (cont.)
Wagner, R.:Lohengrin, w. Maud Cunitz (sop—Elsa), Margarete Klose (mez—Ortrud), Rudolf Schock (ten—Lohengrin), Josef Metternich (bar—Friedrich von Telramund), Gottlob Frick (bass—King Henry), W. Schüchter (cnd), North German RSO, West German Radio Men's Chorus *(rec 1953)* EMI Classics 2-▲ CDHC 65517
Weill, K.:Aufstieg und Fall der Stadt Mahagonny, w. Lotte Lenya (sop), W. Brückner-Rüggeberg (cnd), North German RSO [G] *(rec 1956)* CBS 2-▲ M2K 37874 (m) [ADD]
R. Gritton (cnd)
Bruckner, A.:Motets, w. Datura Trombone Quartet—Ecce Sacerdos Magnus Ars Musici ▲ AM 1154 [DDD]
Candotto, S.:Missa brevis, w. Datura Trombone Quartet Ars Musici ▲ AM 1154 [DDD]
Krol, B.:Von Werden und Vergehen, w. Datura Trombone Quartet Ars Musici ▲ AM 1154 [DDD]
Purcell, H.:Music for the Funeral of Queen Mary, w. Datura Trombone Quartet Ars Musici ▲ AM 1154 [DDD]
Stravinsky, I.:In memoriam Dylan Thomas, w. Robert Chafin (ten), Datura Trombone Quartet Ars Musici ▲ AM 1154 [DDD]
Northern Light Choir
Danova, R.:The Phantom of the Opera on Ice, w. Susannah Glanville (sop), Kathy Dooley (sop), Johnny Logan (ten), Stephen Lee Garden (ten), Mungo Jerry (bar), Nigel Paul (bar), P. Whitfield (cnd), Northern Light SO, Russian Stars on Ice Chorus Plaza ▲ PZA 008
Northern Sinfonia of England Chorus
Bliss, A.:Pastoral, w. D. Jones (mez), R. Hickox (cnd), Northern Sinfonia of England [E] Chandos ▲ CHAN 8886 [DDD]
Northwest Boychoir
Diamond, D.:This Sacred Ground, w. Erich Parce (bar), G. Schwarz (cnd), Seattle SO, Seattle Chorale, Seattle Girls' Choir *(rec Feb. 13, 1994)* Delos ▲ DE 3141 [DDD]
Northwest German Phil Choir
Rossini, G.:Petite messe solennelle, w. G. de la Cruz (sop), M. L. Gilles (cta), H. D. Saretzki (ten), H. G. Grimm (bass), W. A. Albert (cnd), Northwest German PO [orchestral version] [L] *(rec ca. 1970)* Koch Schwann ▲ 3-1345-2 [ADD]
Northwestern Univ Concert Choir
R. Harris (cnd)
Pinkham, D.:Christmas Cant Northwestern Univ School of Music ▲
Norwegian National Opera Chorus
Braein, E.F.:Anne Pedersdotter, w. K. Ekeberg (sop—Anne Pedersdotter), V. Hanssen (mez—Merete Beyer), R. Eriksen (alt—Herlofs-Marte), I. M. Brekke (alt—Bente), K. M. Sandve (ten—Martin Beyer), C. Ehrstedt (ten—Master Olaus), A. Helleland (ten—David), T. Gilje (ten—Jørund), S. A. Thorsen (bar—Master Johannes), S. Carlsen (bass—Absalon Pedersøn Beyer), T. Stensvold (bass—Master Laurentius), G. Oskarsson (bass—Jens Schelderup), P. Andersson (cnd), Norwegian National Opera Orch Simax 2-▲ PSC 3121
Norwegian State Institute of Music Chamber Choir
S. Schioll (cnd)
Grieg, E.:Peer Gynt, w. Einar Steen-Nokleberg (pno) *(rec Lindeman Hall, Norwegian State Academy of Music, Oslo, Feb 12–14, 1994)* Naxos ▲ 8.553398 [DDD]
NOS Radio Chorus
Henkemans, H.:Tre aspetti d'amore, w. B. Haitink (cnd), Royal Concertgebouw Orch Donemus ▲ CV 14
Notre Dame College Chorus
Orff, C.:Carmina burana, w. Elisabeth Vidal (sop), Alexander Stevensen (ten), André Cognet (bass), P. Kuentz (cnd), Paul Kuentz Orch, Paul Kuentz Choir, Mouez Armor Chorale, Lorient Conservatory Chorus Pierre Verany ▲ PVY 730044
Notre-Dame d'Argentan Abbey Monks' Choir
J. Gajard (cnd)
Les Mystères du Rosaire *(rec June 1968)* Jade ▲ 74321-29490-2 [ADD]
Notre-Dame d'Argentan Abbey Nuns' Choir
The Mysteries of the Rosary Jade ▲ 74321 29490-2
Notre-Dame de Fidélité Jouques Abbey Monks' Choir
Gregorian Chants Stradivarius ▲ STV 33302 [DDD]
Nova Schola Gregoriana
Dominica Resurrectionis Arion ▲ ARN 68094
In Passione et Morte Domini *(rec Apr. 1993)* Naxos ▲ 8.550952 [DDD]
A. Turco (cnd)
Adorate Deum *(rec Aug. 3, 1992)* Naxos ▲ 8.550711 [DDD]
Cavazzoni, G.:Choral Music [from Libro Secondo]—Magnificat Quarti Toni; Magnificat Sesti Toni; 8 Hymns (Veni creator spiritus; Exultet coelum laudibus; Pange lingua gloriosi; Iste confessor; Iesu nostra redemptio; Iesu corona virginum; Deus tuorum militum; Hostis herodes impie) Tactus 2-▲ TC 510390
Novopassky Monastery Choir
Russian Requiem *(rec live, 1992)* Koch Schwann ▲ SCH 312172 [DDD]
Oakham School Chapel Choir
D. Woodcock (cnd)
Let All the World, w. Dan Hyde (org) Symposium ▲ SYM 1181
Oakland Sym Chorus
M. Solomon (cnd)
Stravinsky, I.:Les Noces, w. E. Kujawsky (cnd), Redwood Sym Clarity ▲ CCD 1005
Svetoslav Obrenetov Bulgarian National Chorus
Music of Verdi, w. Verdi, Giuseppe, Sofia PO [cnd:Vassil Stefanov] Laserlight ♦ 90033 [DDD]
Puccini, G.:Madama Butterfly, w. Raina Kabaivanska (sop—Madama Butterfly), Alexandrina Milcheva (mez—Suzuki), Rossitza Troeva-Mircheva (cta—Kate Pinkerton), Nazzareno Antinori (ten—F.B. Pinkerton), Roumen Doikov (ten—Goro), Werther Vrachovski (ten—Il Principe Yamadori), Nelson Portella (bar—Sharpless), Kosta Dinkov (bass—Lo zio Bonzo), G. Bellini (cnd), Sofia PO *(rec Sophia, Bulgaria, Dec 1–13, 1982)* Arts Music 2-▲ 447161-2 [DDD]
Puccini, G.:Tosca, w. Raina Kabaivanska (sop—Floria Tosca), Nazzareno Antinori (ten—Mario Cavaradossi), Roumen Doikov (ten—Spoletta), Enzo Dara (bar—Casare Angelotti/Il sagrestano), Nelson Portella (bar—Il Barone Scarpia), Stoyan Balabanov (bass—Sciarrone/Un carceriere), Borislav Peev (sgr—Un Pastore), G. Bellini (cnd), Sofia PO, Bulgarian National Radio Children's Choir *(rec Sophia, Bulgaria, Nov 14–27, 1982)* Arts Music ▲ 47158-2 [DDD]
The Occasional Byrd
G. O'Reilly (cnd)
Gibbons, O.:Instrumental & Vocal Music, w. Andrew Lawrence King (org/hp), William Byrd Ensemble—The Eyes of All Wait upon Three; Do Not Repine, Fair Sun; Trust Not Too Much, Fair Youth; Blessed Are All They That Fear the Lord; O God, the King of Glory; In Nomine; The Cries of London; The Lord of Salisbury His Pavin; Sing unto the Lor, O Ye Saints of His; If Ye Be Risen Again with Christ; See, See, the Word is Incarnate; What is Our Life Adda ▲ ADD 581169 [DDD]
Occidental College Concert Choir
Brahms, J.:Alto Rhap, w. Mildred Miller (mez), B. Walter (cnd), Columbia SO *(rec Jan. 11, 1961)* Sony Classical ("Bruno Walter Edition, Vol. 2" series) ▲ SMK 64469 [ADD]
Occidental Collegiate Chorus
Wagner, R.:Tannhäuser (ov & venusberg), w. B. Walter (cnd), Columbia SO [G] CBS ▲ MK 42050
Okay Chorale
Schickele, P.:Music of, w. N. Wayland (cnd), Greater Hoople Area Off-Season Philharmonic—Oedipus Tex; Classical Rap; Knock, Knock; Birthday Ode to 'Big Daddy' Bach Telarc ▲ CD 80239 [DDD] ■ CS 30239 (D)
Oklahoma City Ambassors Choir
Gershwin, G.:Porgy & Bess (sels), w. D. Newman (sop), A. Woodley (bar), H. de la Fuente (cnd), Mineria SO, New Philharmonia Orch IMP Classics ▲ IMPPCD 1057 [DDD]
Olisipo Vocal Group
Brito, E. de:Officium defunctorum MP Classics ▲ 3-11037
John Oliver Chorale
Ives, C.:The Celestial Country, John Oliver Orch [E] Northeastern ▲ NR 226 CD [DDD]

CHORAL GROUPS

John Oliver Chorale (cont.)
Loeffler, C.M.:Psalm CXXXVII (By the rivers of Babylon), John Oliver Orch [E] Northeastern ▲ NR 226 CD [DDD]
Martino, D.:Seven Pious Pieces New World ▲ 80210-2
J. Oliver (cnd)
Amlin, M.:Choral Music Koch International Classics ▲ KIC 7178 [DDD]
Carter, E.:Choral Music Koch International Classics ▲ KIC 7178 [DDD]
McKinley, W.T.:Choral Music Koch International Classics ▲ KIC 7178 [DDD]
Sheng, B.:Choral Music Koch International Classics ▲ KIC 7178 [DDD]
Olsztyn Academy Chorus
Cimarosa, D.:Requiem pro defunctis, w. K. Rymarczyk (sop), B. Krahel (mez), I. Jakubowski (ten), A. Niemierowicz (bar), S. Frontalini (cnd), Warmia National Orch [L] Bongiovanni ▲ GB 2088 [DDD]
OMP Chorale
F. Kuyiyama (cnd)
Miyoshi, A.:Ballades Camerata ▲ 32CM-28
Omroep Chorus
Verdi, G.:Ernani (sels), w. Felicia Weathers (sop—Elvira), Delia Wallis (mez—Giovanna), Placido Domingo (ten—Ernani), Wynford Evans (ten—Don Riccardo), Piero Francia (bar—Don Carlo), Agostino Ferrin (bass—Don Ruy Gomex de Silva), Robert Holl (bass—Iago), E. Downes (cnd), Omroep Orch *(rec Amsterdam, Jan 15, 1972)* Bella Voce ▲ BLV 107.004 [AAD]
Michael O'Neal Singers
M. O'Neal (cnd)
Rutter, J.:Church Music—Te Deum [w. T. Alderman (org), J. Mautz (timp), M. delCampo (perc)]; Be Thou My Vision; All Things Bright and Beautiful [w. M. Woodall (pno)]; The Lord Bless You and Keep You [w. T. Alderman (org), M. Woodall (pno)] *(rec Roswell United Methodist Church, Atlanta GA, Mar 27, 1995)* ACA Digital Recording ▲ CM 20048 [DDD]
Rutter, J.:Requiem, w. Karyn List (sop), Kathy Farmer (fl), Barbara Cook (ob), Julie Albertson (hp), Mary Alice Swope (vc), Tom Alderman (org), Jennifer Mautz (timp), Mike Del Campo (perc) *(rec Roswell United Methodist Church, Atlanta, GA, Mar 27, 1995)* ACA Digital Recording ▲ CM 20048 [DDD]
Opera North Chorus
Tippett, M.:The Midsummer Marriage (dances), w. A. Hodgson (cta), M. Tippett (cnd), English Northern Philharmonia [E], Nimbus ▲ NI 5217 [DDD]
Walton, W.:Troilus & Cressida, w. Judith Howarth (sop—Cressida), Arthur Davies (ten—Troilus), Nigel Robson (ten—Pandarus), Brian Cookson (ten—3rd Watchman), Peter Bodenham (ten—Priest), Keith Mills (ten—Soldier), Alan Opie (bar—Diomede), James Thornton (bar—Antenor), Clive Bayley (bass—Calkas), David Owen-Lewis (bass—Horaste), R. Hickox (cnd), English Northern Philharmonia Chandos 2-▲ CHAN 9370/71 [DDD]
Operetta Chorus
Lehár, F.:Das Land des Lächelns (sels), w. I. Hallstein (sop), Renate Holm (sop), Heinz Hoppe (ten), Alexander (sgr), Marszalek (cnd), Operretta Orch [G] Acanta ▲ CD 43494 [DDD]
Lehár, F.:Die lustige Witwe (sels), w. I. Hallstein (sop), L. Popp (sop), H. Hoppe (ten), Alexander (bar), B. Kusche (bar), Marszalek (cnd), Operretta Orch [G] Acanta ▲ CD 43455 [DDD]
Oratorio Choir
Tobias, R.:Des Jonah Sendung, w. Pille Lill (sop), Urve Tauts (mez), Peter Svensson (ten), Raimo Laukka (bar), Mati Palm (bass), Ines Maidre (org), N. Järvi (cnd), Estonian State SO, Estonian Phil Chamber Choir, Tallinn Boys' Choir *(rec Estonia Concert Hall, Tallinn, Estonia, June 23-29, 1995)* BIS 2-▲ CD 731/732 [DDD]
Oregon Bach Festival Choir
Dvořák, A.:Stabat Mater, w. Marina Shaguch (sop), Ingeborg Danz (alt), James Taylor (ten), Thomas Quasthoff (bass), H. Rilling (cnd), Oregon Bach Festival Orch *(rec Silva Concert Hall, Hult Center for the Performing Arts, Eugene, Oregon, July 8-11, 1995)* Hänssler Classic ("Exclusive" series) 2-▲ CD 98.935 [DDD]
Oregon Repertory Singers
Harrison, L.:Mass to St. Anthony, Oregon Repertory Singers *(rec May, 1992)* Koch ▲ KIC 7177 [DDD]
Pärt, A.:Berliner Messe *(rec May, 1992)* Koch ▲ KIC 7177 [DDD]
G. Seeley (cnd)
Barber, S.:To Be Sung on the Water Koch International Classics ▲ KIC 7279 [DDD]
Barber, S.:12th Night Koch International Classics ▲ KIC 7279 [DDD]
Larsen, L.:Missa gaia Koch International Classics ▲ KIC 7279 [DDD]
Paulus, S.:Echoes between the Silent Peaks Koch International Classics ▲ KIC 7279 [DDD]
The Glory of Christmas Koch Schwann ▲ KIC CD 7362
Oregon State Univ Choir
R. Jeffers (cnd)
Make a Joyful Noise:Mainstreams & Backwaters of American Psalmody, 1770-1840 *(rec 1st Christian Church, Corvallis, OR)* New World ▲ 80255-2
Oriel College Choir Oxford
Oxford:Cathedrals of the World *(rec Keble College Chapel, Oxford, June 22-24, 1990)* Studio SM ▲ D 2447
Original Volga Cossacks
Lehár, F.:Der Zarewitsch (sels), w. D. Koller (sop), G. di Stefano (ten), H. Holecek (bar), E.-G. Scherzer (cnd), Vienna Operetta Orch Koch Schwann ▲ SCH 312732 [ADD]
Orlando Consort [R. H. Jones (ct), C. Daniels (ten), A. Smith (ten), D. Grieg (bar)]
Compère, L.:Music of—Omnium bonorum plena; Se j'ay parlé; Seray je vostre mieulx amée; Ave Maria; Alons fere nos barbes; Ne vous hastez pas; Asperges me, Domine; Che fa la ramancina; Scaramella; Missa in Nativitate Metronome ▲ MET 1002 [ADD]
Ormond College Choir Melbourne
Bach, J.S.:Motets, BWV 225-30—No. 5, Lobet den Herrn, alle Heiden, BWV 229 Move ▲ MD 3104 [DDD]
Britten, B.:A Ceremony of Carols Move ▲ MD 3104 [DDD]
Britten, B.:Flower Songs Move ▲ MD 3104 [DDD]
Byrd, W.:Mass in 4 Parts Move ▲ MD 3104 [DDD]
D. Lawrence (cnd)
I Can Tell the World Move ▲ MD 3109 [DDD]
ORTF Choir
Inghelbrecht, D.-E.:Vézelay, w. Christiane Ede-Pierre (sop), Bernard Kruyssen (bar), J. Fournet (cnd), ORTF Lyric Orch Studio SM ("Andre Charlin Collection" series) ▲ 2522
Ravel, M.:Daphnis et Chloé (suite 2), w. S. Celibidache (cnd), ORTF National Orch *(rec live, 1974)* Enterprise ("Documents" series) 2-▲ LV 946/47 (m/s) [ADD]
Verdi, G.:La battaglia di Legnano, w. K. Ricciarelli (sop), J. Carreras (ten), M. Manuguerra (bar), N. Ghiuselev (bass), L. Gardelli (cnd), ORF SO Philips 2-▲ 422435-2 [ADD]
ORTF Choirs
Ganne, L.:Hans, le joueur de flûte, w. J. Gressier (cnd), ORTF Lyric Orch Musidisc 2-▲ MUS 201512 [AAD]
Inghelbrecht, D.-E.:Requiem, w. Christiane Ede-Pierre (sop), Bernard Kruyssen (bar), J. Fournet (cnd), ORTF Lyric Orch Studio SM ("Andre Charlin Collection" series) ▲ 2522
ORTF Lyric Chorale
Audran, E.:Le grand mogol, w. M. Cariven (cnd), ORTF Lyric Orch Musidisc 2-▲ MUS 201702 [AAD]
Audran, E.:Miss Helyett, w. M. Cariven (cnd), ORTF Lyric Orch Musidisc 2-▲ MUS 202402 [AAD]
Bernicat, F.:François les bas-bleus, w. M. Cariven (cnd), ORTF Lyric Orch Musidisc 2-▲ MUS 202092 [AAD]
Boieldieu, F.-A.:Le Calife de Bagdad, w. Christiane Eda-Pierre (sop), Jane Berbié (mez), Jeannine Collard (mez), Jean Giraudeau (ten), Jean-Paul Vaquelin (sgr), L. Fourestier (cnd), ORTF Lyric Orch Musidisc ▲ MUS 201852 [AAD]
Donizetti, G.:Maria Stuarda, w. M. Caballé (sop—Maria Stuarda), R. Bezinian (mez—Anna), M. V. Menendez (mez—Elisabetta), J. Carreras (ten—Roberto), M. Mazzieri (bass—Giorgio Talbot), E. Serra (bass—Lord Gugliemo Cecil), N. Santi (cnd), ORTF Lyric Orch [I] *(rec live 3/26/72)* Memories 2-▲ HR4417/18 [ADD]

ORTF Lyric Chorale (cont.)
Lecocq, C.:Le Coeur et la main, w. M. Hamel (cnd), ORTF Lyric Orch Musidisc 2-▲ MUS 201962 [AAD]
Lecocq, C.:Giroflé-Girofla, w. M. Cariven (cnd), ORTF Lyric Orch Musidisc 2-▲ MUS 201842 [AAD]
Messager, A.:Coups de roulis, w. M. Cariven (cnd), ORTF Lyric Orch Musidisc 2-▲ MUS 202382 [AAD]
Offenbach, J.:Barbe-bleue, w. Henri Legay (ten), René Lenoty (ten), Aimé Doniat (bar), Rene Terrasson (sgr), J. Doussard (cnd), ORTF Lyric Orch *(rec 1967)* Memories 2-▲ MEM 4591 [ADD]
Offenbach, J.:Le Chanson de Fortunio, w. J.-C. Hartemann (cnd), ORTF Lyric Orch Musidisc 2-▲ MUS 201382 [AAD]
Offenbach, J.:Madame l'archiduc, w. J.-C. Hartemann (cnd), ORTF Lyric Orch Musidisc 2-▲ MUS 201382 [AAD]
Planquette, R.:Rip van Winkle, w. Claudine Collart (sop), Lina Dachary (sop), Freda Betti (cta), René Lenoty (ten), Joseph Peyron (ten), Charles Daguerressar (bar), Julien Giovannetti (bar), Jacques Pruvost (bar), Lucien Lovano (bass), Patrick Orladey (sgr), Joëlle Pierre (sgr), M. Cariven (cnd), ORTF Lyric Orch Musidisc ▲ MUS 201602 [AAD]
Terrasse, C.:Les Travaux d'Hercule, w. M. Cariven (cnd), ORTF Lyric Orch Musidisc 2-▲ MUS 201792 [AAD]
Orthodox Liturgical Choruses
Orthodox Liturgical Choruses Jade ▲ JAD C094
Orthodox Vocal Ensemble
V. Klochkov (cnd)
Hristov, Dobri:The Common Liturgy Gega ▲ GD 126 [DDD]
Oscar's Motet Choir
T. Nilsson (cnd)
Nilsson, T.:Out of Earthly Night, w. Gudrun Bruna (sop), Marianne Mellnäs (sop), Kaysa Hälldin (alt), Lars Sjögren (ten), Göran Swartz (bass), Sture Hedin (sgr), Ola Kyhlberg (sgr), Lars Ljungman (sgr), Nils Philipson (sgr), Ulrik Quale (sgr), Nils Spangenberg (sgr), Britta Therén (sgr), Karl-Erik Welin (org) *(rec Oscar's Church, Stockholm, Sweden, Apr 26-27, 1978)* BIS ▲ CD 138 [AAD]
Oslo Cathedral Choir
Beethoven, L. van:Missa Solemnis, w. M. Hirsti (sop), C. Watkinson (cta), A. Murgatroyd (ten), M. George (bass), T. Kvam (cnd), Hanover Band [period instrs] [L] Nimbus ▲ NI 5109 [DDD]
Beethoven, L. van:Sym 9, "Choral Sym", w. R. Goodman (cnd), Hanover Band [period instruments] [G] Nimbus ▲ NI 5134 [DDD]
T. Kvam (cnd)
Brahms, J.:Motets (misc)—Opp. 29/1, 30, 74/1, 109 & 110/1 [G] Victoria ▲ VCD 19009 [DDD]
Bruckner, A.:Motets—Ave Maria; Locus iste; Os Justi; Christus factus est; Virga Jesse [L] Victoria ▲ VCD 19009 [DDD]
Grieg, E.:Salmer, w. H. Hagegård (bar) Nimbus ▲ NI 5171 [DDD]
Mendelssohn, F.:Psalms, Op. 78, w. H. Hagegård (bar) Nimbus ▲ NI 5171 [DDD]
Oslo Phil Chorus
Grieg, E.:Landkjending, w. P. Dreier (cnd), London SO Unicorn-Kanchana ▲ UKCD 2056
Grieg, E.:Olav Trygvason, w. P. Dreier (cnd), London SO, Norwegian Soloists Unicorn-Kanchana ▲ UKCD 2056
Grieg, E.:Peer Gynt, w. P. Dreier (cnd), London SO—Choral scenes from Act 5 Unicorn-Kanchana ▲ UKCD 2056
Grieg, E.:Peer Gynt, w. C. Carlson (mez), V. Hanssen (mez), K. Bjørkøy (ten), A. Hansli (bar), P. Dreier (cnd), London SO [N] Unicorn-Kanchana 2-▲ UKCD 2003/04 [AAD]
Grieg, E.:Peer Gynt, w. B. Hendricks (sop), E.-P. Salonen (cnd), Oslo PO CBS ▲ MK 44528 [DDD] □ MM 44528
Habbestad, K.:Music of, w. *(soloists unknown)*, T. Mikkelsen (cnd), Lithuanian National SO—Moster Suite, Op. 15; 1st Mass on Norwegian Soil; Goat's Horn; Medieval Lyre; Song-Dance; Articles of Norwegian Christian Law Norway Music ▲ 2912
Mahler, G.:Sym 2, w. F. Lott (sop), J. Hamari (mez), M. Jansons (cnd), Oslo PO Chandos ("Collect" series) 2-▲ CHAN 6595/96 [DDD]
Oslo Phil Women's Chamber Choir
Habbestad, K.:Moster Suite, w. Kristin Kjølberg (sop), Njål Sparbo (bar), Odd Lund (goat's hn), T. Mikkelsen (cnd), Lithuanian National SO Norway Music ▲ 2912
Habbestad, K.:Song-Dance, w. Odd Lund (goat's hn), Åshild Watne (Medieval lyre), T. Mikkelsen (cnd), Scapoli Norway Music ▲ 2912
Osnabrück Youth Choir
Llibre Vermell de Montserrat [The Red Book of Montserrat]:Medieval Pilgrim Songs from Spain *(rec Osnabrück Cathedral, May 1993)* Mesa ▲ R2 79080
Ostankino Radio Chorus
L. Ermakova (cnd)
Scriabin, A.:Mysterium:Prefatory Act, w. Peter Izotov (pno), I. Golovshin (cnd), Russian State SO *(rec Large Hall of the Moscow Conservatory, 1995)* Triton ▲ 17001 [DDD]
Ostrava Female Chamber Chorus
Báchorek, M.:Hukvald Poem, w. Drahomíra Drobková (sop), Břetislav Vojkůvka (ten), Pavel Kamas (bar), Otakar Brousek (reciter), O. Trhlík (cnd), Prague SO, Permoník Children's Chorus *(rec Smetana Hall of Prague's Municipal House, Feb 10 & 11, 1988)* Panton ▲ 811338-2 [DDD]
Ostrava Janáček Chorus
Báchorek, M.:Lidice, w. Jana Stupárkova-Majtnerová (sop), Karel Průša (bar), Osvald Albín (speaker), Jan Vlasák (speaker), O. Trhlík (cnd), Ostrava Janáček PO *(rec Smetana Hall of Prague's Municipal House, Feb 10 & 11, 1988)* Panton ▲ 811338-2 [AAD]
Báchorek, M.:Music of, w. Osvald Albin (nar), Otakar Brousek (nar), Jan Vlassak (nar), Brigita Sulcová (sop), Drahomira Drobková (cta), Karel Průša (bass), Pavel Kamas (sgr), Jan Kyzlink (sgr), Jana Stuperkova-Majtnerova (sgr), Bretislav Vojkuvka (sgr), O. Trhlík (cnd), Ostrava Janáček PO, Prague SO, Ostrava Women's Chamber Chorus, Permoník Children's Chorus—Lidice; Stereofonietta; Hukvald Poem Panton ▲ PAN 811338 [AAD/DDD]
Ostrava Women's Chamber Chorus
Báchorek, M.:Music of, w. Osvald Albin (nar), Otakar Brousek (nar), Jan Vlassak (nar), Brigita Šulcová (sop), Drahomira Drobková (cta), Karel Průša (bass), Pavel Kamas (sgr), Jan Kyzlink (sgr), Jana Stuperkova-Majtnerova (sgr), Bretislav Vojkuvka (sgr), O. Trhlík (cnd), Ostrava Janáček PO, Prague SO, Ostrava Janáček Chorus, Permoník Children's Chorus—Lidice; Stereofonietta; Hukvald Poem Panton ▲ PAN 811338 [AAD/DDD]
Ottovoci Ensemble
M. Broussard (cnd)
Brahms, J.:Vocal Qts, w. K. Schul (pno)—Opp. 31, 64, 92, 112 [G] Partridge ▲ 1133-2 [DDD]
Brahms, J.:Zigeunerlieder, w. K. Schul (pno) [G] Partridge ▲ 1133-2 [DDD]
Our Lady of Lausanne Choir
Martin, F.:Requiem, w. E. Speiser (sop), R. Bollen (cta), E. Tappy (ten), P. Lagger (bass), A. Luy (org), F. Martin (cnd), Swiss-Italian Orch, Union Chorale, Ars Laeta Vocal Group *(rec live, May 4, 1973)* Jecklin-Disco ▲ JD 631-2 [ADD]
Oxford Camerata
J. Summerly (cnd)
Byrd, W.:Infelix ego *(rec Dec. 16-18, 1991)* Naxos ▲ 8.550574 [DDD]
Byrd, W.:Mass in 4 Parts *(rec Dec. 16-18, 1991)* Naxos ▲ 8.550574 [DDD]
Byrd, W.:Mass in 5 Parts *(rec Dec. 16-18, 1991)* Naxos ▲ 8.550574 [DDD]
Dufay, G.:Sacred Music—Kyrie; Gloria; Credo; Sanctus; Agnus Dei [all from Missa L'homme armé]; Veni Sancte Spiritus; Jubilate Deo; Illumina faciem tuam; Supremum est mortalibus bonum; L'homme armé [anon. song] *(rec Chapel of Hertford College, Oxford, Apr. 4-5, 1994)* Naxos ("Early Music" series) ▲ 8.553087 [DDD]
The Early Music Collection *(rec Chapel of New College, Oxford, July 23-25, 1991)* Naxos 4-▲ 8.504009 [DDD]
English Madrigals & Songs *(rec Chapel of Hertford College, Oxford, Mar 1994)* Naxos ▲ 8.553088 [DDD]
Fauré, G.:Cantique de Jean Racine, w. Oxford Schola Cantorum *(rec Hertford College Chapel, Oxford, May 17 & 18, 1993)* Naxos ▲ 8.550765 [DDD]

992 ▲ = CD ♦ = Enhanced CD Δ = MD ■ = Cassette Tape □ = DCC

Oxford Camerata (cont.)
J. Summerly (cnd) (cont.)
Fauré, G.:Messe basse (in 3 movts), w. Lisa Beckley (sop), Colm Carey (org), Oxford Schola Cantorum *(rec Hertford College Chapel, Oxford, May 17 & 18, 1993)* Naxos ▲ 8.550765 [DDD]
Fauré, G.:Requiem, w. Lisa Beckley (sop), Nicholas Gedge (b-bar), Colm Carey (org), Oxford Schola Cantorum *(rec Hertford College Chapel, Oxford, May 17 & 18, 1993)* Naxos ▲ 8.550765 [DDD]
Gesualdo, D.C.:Sacred Music—Illumina faciem tuam; Dues refugium et virtus; Exaudi Deus deprecationem meam; Tribulationem et delorem; Tribularer si nescirem; Precibus et meritus beatae Mariae; O Crux benedicta; O vos omnes; Dignare me laudare te; Maria mater gratiae; Laboravi in gemitu meo; Ave dulcisima Maria; Domine ne despicias; Peccantumme quotidie; Sancti Spiritus Domine; Hei mihi Domine; Venit lumen tuum Jerusalem; Reminiscere miscrationum tuarum; Ave regina coelorum *(rec Sept 1992)* Naxos ▲ 8.550742 [DDD]
Gibbons, O.:Choral Music—O clap your hands; Great Lord of Lords; Hosanna to the son of David; Out of the deep; See, see, the word is incarnate; Lift up your heads; Almighty and everlasting God; Magnificat (2nd Service); Nunc dimittis (2nd Service); Magnificat (Short Service); Nunc dimittis (Short Service); O God, the king of glory; O Lord, in thy wrath *(rec Chapel of Hertford College, Oxford, July 29-30, 1994)* Naxos ▲ 8.553130 [DDD]
Hildegard Of Bingen:Sacred Songs—O Euchari; Alleluia-O virga mediatrix; Ave generosa; Laus Trinitati; Kyrie; O presul vere; O ignis spiritus; Procession [from Ordo Virtutum]; O pastor animarum; O viridissima virga; O virga ac diadema *(rec Chapel of Hertford College, Oxford, Dec. 14-15, 1993)* Naxos ▲ 8.550998 [DDD]
Lamentations *(rec 1991)* Naxos ▲ 8.550572 [DDD]
Lassus, O. de:Sacred Music—Missa entre vous filles; Infelix ego; Missa Susanne un jour *(rec Apr. 1993)* Naxos ▲ 8.550842 [DDD]
Lobo, A.:Funeral motet [L] *(rec April 7-8, 1992)* Naxos ▲ 8.550575 [DDD]
Machaut, G. de:Ballades—Ballades 32, 33; Lai 13; Rondeaus 4, 17, 18 *(rec Maida Vale Studio 1, Feb 9-10, 1996)* Naxos ("Early Music" series) ▲ 8.553833 [DDD]
Machaut, G. de:Messe de Nostre Dame *(rec Reims Cathedral, Feb 20-21, 1996)* Naxos ("Early Music" series) ▲ 8.553833 [DDD]
Medieval Carols *(rec Dec. 15-17, 1992)* Naxos ▲ 8.5501751 [DDD]
Mundy, W.:Sacred Music—Kyrie; Magnificat *(rec Hertford College Chapel, Oxford, Sept. 13 & 14, 1993)* Naxos ▲ 8.550937 [DDD]
Purcell, H.:Anthems & Services, w. Laurence Cummings (org)—Jehova, quam multi sunt hostes mei, Z.135 [w. Andrew Carwood (ten), Michael McCarthy (bass)]; Remember not, Lord, our offences, Z.50; I will sing unto the Lord, as long as I live, Z.22; Voluntary in d, Z.718; O God, thou art my God, Z.35; O God, the King of glory, Z.34; Voluntary in G, Z.720; Lord, how long wilt thou be angry?, Z.25; Hear my prayer, O Lord, Z.15; Voluntary in C, Z.717; Blow up the trumpet in Sion, Z.10; O God, thou hast cast us out, Z.36 *(rec Chapel of Hertford College, Oxford, June 9-10, 1994)* Naxos ▲ 8.553129 [DDD]
Purcell, H.:Music for the Funeral of Queen Mary, w. Laurence Cummings (org)—March, Z.860a; Man that is born of a woman, Z.27; In the midst of life we are in death, Z.17a; Thou knowest, Lord, the secrets of our hearts, Z.58b; Incassum, Lesbia...The Queen's Epicedium, Z.383 [w. Carys-Anne Lane (sop)], Canzona, Z.860b; Thou knowest, Lord, the secrets of our hearts, Z.58c *(rec Chapel of Hertford College, Oxford, June 9-10, 1994)* Naxos ▲ 8.553129 [DDD]
Renaissance Masterpieces *(rec Apr. 19-20, 1993)* Naxos ▲ 8.550843 [DDD]
Schütz, H.:Cantiones sacrae *(rec Oxford, Aug 1995)* Naxos ▲ 8.553514 [DDD]
Schütz, H.:Deutsches Magnificat, w. Laurence Cummings (org) *(rec Hertford College Chapel, Oxford, Sept 5-6, 1994)* Naxos ▲ 8.553044 [DDD]
Schütz, H.:Motets (misc), w. Laurence Cummings (org)—Erhöre mich, wenn ich rufe (SWV.289); Ich liege und schlafe (SWV.310); Das ist je gewisslich wahr (SWV.277) *(rec Hertford College Chapel, Oxford, Sept 5-6, 1994)* Naxos ▲ 8.553044 [DDD]
Schütz, H.:Psalmen Davids, w. Laurence Cummings (org)—An den Wassern zu Babel [SWV 37]; Ach Herr, straf mich nicht mit deinem Zorn [SWV 24]; Singet dem Herrn ein neues Lied [SWV 35]; Wohl dem, der nicht wandelt im Rat der Gottlosen [SWV 28]; Wie lieblich sind deine Wohnungen [SWV 29]; Lobe den Herren, meine Seele [SWV 39] *(rec Hertford College Chapel, Oxford, Sept 5-6, 1994)* Naxos ▲ 8.553044 [DDD]
Schütz, H.:Psalms—Psalm 100 *(rec Oxford, Aug 1995)* Naxos ▲ 8.553514 [DDD]
Schütz, H.:Weihnachtshistorie, w. Anna Crookes (sop—Angel), Paul Agnew (ct—Evangelist), Michael McCarthy (bass—Herod) *(rec Oxford, Aug 1995)* Naxos ▲ 8.553514 [DDD]
Séverac, D. de:Tantum ergo, w. Colm Carey (org), Oxford Schola Cantorum, *(rec Hertford College Chapel, Oxford, May 17 & 18, 1993)* Naxos ▲ 8.550765 [DDD]
Tallis, T.:Church Music—Loquebantur variis linguis; Salvator mundi; O sacrum convivium; Audivi vocem; Sancte Deus; Videte miraculum; Te lucis ante terminum; In manus tuas Domine *(rec June 29-July 1, 1992)* Naxos ▲ 8.550576 [DDD]
Tallis, T.:Mass for 4 Voices *(rec June 29-July 1, 1992)* Naxos ▲ 8.550576 [DDD]
Tye, C.:Church Music—Omnes gentes, Missa Euge bone, Peccavimus *(rec Hertford College Chapel, Oxford, Sept. 13 & 14, 1993)* Naxos ▲ 8.550937 [DDD]
Victoria, T.L. de:Sacred Choral Music—Ave Maria; Miss O magnum mysterium; Missa O quam gloriosum [L] *(rec April 7-8, 1992)* Naxos ▲ 8.550575 [DDD]
Weelkes, T.:Anthems, w. Jeremy Summerly (org), Gary Cooper (org)—Hosanna to the son of David; Give ear, O Lord; All people clap your hands; What joy so true; O Lord, grant the king a long life; Lord, to thee I make my mooan; All laud and praise; Lachrimae Pavan (Morley); A remembrance of my friend Thomas Morley; Passymeasures Pavan (Morley); Gloria in excelsis Deo; When David hear; Give the king thy judgements; O Lord, arise; O how amiable are thy dwellings; Most mighty and all-knowing Lord; Alleluia, I heard a voice *(rec Chapel of Hertford College, Oxford, Jan 3-4, 1995)* Naxos ▲ 8.553209 [DDD]

Oxford Girls' Choir
Hildegard Of Bingen:Sacred Songs, w. Jocelyn West (sgr), Vivien Ellis (sgr), Stevie Wishart (sgr/h-g), Hester Briant (sgr), Fiona Cunningham (sgr), Tara Franks (sgr), Emily Levy (sgr), Lucy Steele (sgr), Vickie Couperim (sgr), Julie Murphy (sgr)—Honey & milk beneath her tongue; Ursula's virgins; The devil's virgins; Place of the ancient heart; Zeal of divinity; O fiery spirit; Red river falling; O orzchis ecclesia, Living-light angels; The clouds are grieving; The firstwoman; From their homeland; But the devil mocked; Song to Ecclesia *(rec Toddington, Gloucestershire, England, May 6-8, 1995)* Celestial Harmonies ▲ 13127-2

Oxford Schola Cantorum
Bach, J.S.:Magnificat, BWV 243, w. Anna Crookes (sop), Jayne Whitaker (sop), Caroline Trevor (alt), Timothy Robinson (ten), Nicholas Gedge (b-bar), N. Ward (cnd), Northern CO *(rec St. Peter's Church, Hale, Cheshire, Dec. 2, 1993)* Naxos ▲ 8.550763 [DDD]
Fauré, G.:Cantique de Jean Racine, w. J. Summerly (cnd), Oxford Camerata *(rec Hertford College Chapel, Oxford, May 17 & 18, 1993)* Naxos ▲ 8.550765 [DDD]
Fauré, G.:Messe basse (in 3 movts), w. Lisa Beckley (sop), Colm Carey (org), J. Summerly (cnd), Oxford Camerata *(rec Hertford College Chapel, Oxford, May 17 & 18, 1993)* Naxos ▲ 8.550765 [DDD]
Fauré, G.:Requiem, w. Lisa Beckley (sop), Nicholas Gedge (b-bar), Colm Carey (org), J. Summerly (cnd), Oxford Camerata *(rec Hertford College Chapel, Oxford, May 17 & 18, 1993)* Naxos ▲ 8.550765 [DDD]
Vivaldi, A.:Beatus vir, R.597, w. Carys-Anne Lane (sop), Jayne Whitaker (sop), Christine Swain (ob), Robert Glenton (vc), Christopher Stokes (org), N. Ward (cnd), Northern CO *(rec St. Peter's Church, Hale, Cheshire, Mar. 14, 1994)* Naxos ▲ 8.550767 [DDD]
Vivaldi, A.:Gloria, RV.589, w. Anna Crookes (sop), Jayne Whitaker (sop), Caroline Trevor (alt), Christine Swain (ob), Robert Glenton (vc), Christopher Stokes (org), N. Ward (cnd), Northern CO *(rec St. Peter's Church, Hale, Cheshire, Dec. 3, 1993)* Naxos ▲ 8.550767 [DDD]
J. Summerly (cnd)
Cardoso, M.:Sacred Music *(rec March 16-17, 1992)* Naxos ▲ 8.550682 [DDD]
Lassus, O. de:Bell'Amfitrit'altera *(rec Mar. 1993)* Naxos ▲ 8.550836 [DDD]
Lôbo, D.:Requiem, "Missa pro defunctis" *(rec March 16-17, 1992)* Naxos ▲ 8.550682 [DDD]
Palestrina, G.:Sacred Music—Missa Hodie Christus natus est; Motet:Hodie Christus natus est *(rec Mar. 1993)* Naxos ▲ 8.550836 [DDD]
Palestrina, G.:Stabat mater *(rec Mar. 1993)* Naxos ▲ 8.550836 [DDD]
Séverac, D. de:Tantum ergo, w. Colm Carey (org), Oxford Camerata *(rec Hertford College Chapel, Oxford, May 17 & 18, 1993)* Naxos ▲ 8.550765 [DDD]

D'Oyly Carte Opera Company Chorus
Sullivan, A.:The Gondoliers, w. W. Lawson (sop), A. Davies (ten), B. Lewis (cta), D. Oldham (ten), M. Bennett (sop), G. Baker (bar), L. Sheffield (bar), H. Lytton (bar), et al., H. Norris (cnd), D'Oyly Carte Opera Company Orch—dialogue omitted *(rec 1927)* Pearl 2-▲ PEAS 9961 (m) [AAD]
Sullivan, A.:The Mikado, w. R. Nash (cnd), Royal PO—highlights London ("Weekend Classics" series) ▲ 433684-2 [ADD] ■ 433684-4
Sullivan, A.:The Pirates of Penzance (sels), w. V. Masterson (sop), D. Adams (bass), I. Godfrey (cnd), Royal PO London ("Weekend Classics" series) ▲ 436292-2
Sullivan, A.:Trial by Jury, w. W. Lawson (sop), D. Oldham (ten), G. Baker (bar), L. Sheffield (bar), A. Hosking (bar), H. Norris (cnd), D'Oyly Carte Opera Company Orch *(rec 1928)* Pearl 2-▲ PEAS 9961 (m) [AAD]
Sullivan, A.:The Yeomen of the Guard, w. M. Sargent (cnd), D'Oyly Carte Opera Company Orch [E] *(rec 1928)* Pro Arte ▲ CDD 3417
Sullivan, A.:The Zoo, w. R. Nash (cnd), Royal PO London 2-▲ 436807-2 [ADD]

Pacific Chorale
Hopkins, J.:Songs of Eternity, w. J. Alexander (cnd), Pacific SO Albany ▲ TROY 182
Paulus, S.:Voices, w. Martha Jane Weaver (mez), Frank Kelley (ten), J. Alexander (cnd), Pacific SO Albany ▲ TROY 182

Pacific Northwest Chamber Chorus
J.C. Conlon (cnd)
Brahms, J.:Zigeunerlieder Ambassador ▲ ARC 1015
Castelnuovo-Tedesco, M.:Romancero gitano, w. Steven Novacek (gtr) Ambassador ▲ ARC 1015
Kodály, Z.:Choral Music—Turot eszik a cigany Ambassador ▲ ARC 1015
Schubert, Franz:Songs (misc)—Die Nacht, D.983c; Widerspruch, D.865; La Pastorella, D.513 Ambassador ▲ ARC 1015
Schumann, R.:Songs—Zigeunerleben, Op. 29/3 Ambassador ▲ ARC 1015
Viardot, P.G.:Songs—Choeur Bohemien Ambassador ▲ ARC 1015

Padua Bach Academy Chamber Chorus
Vivaldi, A.:Gloria, RV.589, w. R. Invernizzi (sop), P. Vaccari (sop), R. Balconi (ct), L. Gariboldi (ten), C. Gubert (cnd), Padua Bach Academy CO Rivoalto ▲ RIV 9301 [DDD]
Vivaldi, A.:Magnificat, RV.610, w. R. Invernizzi (sop), P. Vaccari (sop), R. Balconi (ct), L. Gariboldi (ten), C. Gubert (cnd), Padua Bach Academy CO Rivoalto ▲ RIV 9301 [DDD]

Les Pages de la Chapelle
Bouzignac, G.:Motets—Ecce festivitas; Ecce homo; Unus ex vobis; In pace, in ipsidium; Ha! Plange; Vulnerasti cor meum; Alleluia, venite amici; Flos in flores; Clamant clavi; Ecce Aurora; Dum silentium; Jubilate Deo; Salve, Jesu Piisime; Ave Maria; Tota pulchra est Harmonia Mundi France ▲ HMC 901471
Bouzignac, G.:Te Deum Harmonia Mundi France ▲ HMC 901471
Campra, A.:Messe de Requiem, w. D. Visse (ct), G. Ragon (ten), P. Harvey (bar), J. Malgoire (cnd), La Grande Ecurie et la Chambre du Roy *(rec Nov. 4-6, 1992)* FNAC Music ▲ 592223 [DDD]
Campra, A.:Misere, w. D. Visse (ct), G. Ragon (ten), P. Harvey (bar), J. Malgoire (cnd), La Grande Ecurie et la Chambre du Roy *(rec Nov. 4-6, 1992)* FNAC Music ▲ 592223 [DDD]
du Mont, H.:Motets pour la chapelle du roy, w. H. Crook (cta), H. Lamy (ten), P. Harvey (bar), O. Schneebeli (cnd), Musica Aeterna *(rec Sept. 1993)* FNAC Music ▲ 592054 [DDD]
Ockeghem, J.:Requiem, w. M. Pérès (cnd), Organum Ensemble Harmonia Mundi France ▲ HMC 901441

Palacio Bellas Artes Chorus
Bellini, V.:Norma, w. M. Callas (sop), G. Simionato (mez), K. Baum (ten), N. Moscona (bass), G. Picco (cnd), Palacio Bellas Artes Orch *(rec live, Mexico City 5/23/50)* Melodram 2-▲ MEL 26018
Bellini, V.:I Puritani, w. M. Callas (sop), G. di Stefano (ten), Campolonghi (sgr), R. Silva (bass), G. Picco (cnd), Palacio Bellas Artes Orch [I] *(rec live, Mexico City 5/29/52)* Melodram 2-▲ MEL 26027 (m) [AAD]
Donizetti, G.:La favorita, w. G. Simionato (mez), G. di Stefano (ten), E. Mascherini (bar), C. Siepi (bass-bar), Rodriguez (sgr), R. Cellini (cnd), Palacio Bellas Artes Orch [I] *(rec live, Mexico City, 7/12/49)* Standing Room Only 2-▲ SRO 816-2 [ADD]
Donizetti, G.:Lucia di Lammermoor, w. M. Callas (sop), G. di Stefano (ten), Campolonghi (sgr), G. Picco (cnd), Palacio Bellas Artes Orch [I] *(rec live, Mexico City 6/10/52)* Myto 2-▲ 2 MCD 91340 [ADD]
Puccini, G.:Tosca, w. M. Callas (sop), G. di Stefano (ten), Campolonghi (sgr), G. Picco (cnd), Palacio Bellas Artes Orch [I] *(rec live, Mexico City 1952)* Melodram 2-▲ 26028 (m) [AAD]
Puccini, G.:Tosca, w. M. Callas (sop), M. Filippeschi (ten), R. Weede (bar), U. Mugnai (cnd), Palacio Bellas Artes Orch [I] *(rec live, Mexico City, 6/8/50)* Standing Room Only 2-▲ SRO 820-2 [ADD]
Puccini, G.:Tosca, w. Maria Callas (sop), Mario Filippeschi (ten), Carlos Sagarminaga (ten), Robert Weede (bar), Ramon Alonso (bass), U. Mugnai (cnd), Palacio Bellas Artes Orch Melodram 3-▲ CDM 36032
Puccini, G.:Tosca (sels), w. M. Callas (sop), G. di Stefano (ten), G. Picco (cnd), Palacio Bellas Artes Orch—nine arias & duets [I] *(rec live, Mexico City, 7/1/52)* Standing Room Only 2-▲ SRO 820-2 [ADD]
Thomas, A.:Mignon (sels), w. G. Simionato (mez), G. Di Stefano (ten), C. Siepi (b-bar), G. Picco (cnd), Palacio Bellas Artes Orch *(rec live, Mexico City, 6/28/49)* Golden Age of Opera 2-▲ GAO 128/29 [ADD]
Verdi, G.:Aida, w. M. Callas (sop), G. Simionato (mez), K. Baum (ten), R. Weede (bar), G. Picco (cnd), Palacio Bellas Artes Orch *(rec live, Mexico City 5/30/50)* Melodram ▲ MLO 26009 [ADD]
Verdi, G.:Aida, w. M. Callas (sop), O. Dominguez (mez), M. Del Monaco (ten), G. Taddei (bar), O. de Fabritiis (cnd), Palacio Bellas Artes Orch *(rec live, Mexico City 7/3/51)* Melodram 2-▲ CDM 26015
Verdi, G.:Rigoletto, w. M. Callas (sop), G. Di Stefano (ten), Campolonghi (sgr), U. Mugnai (cnd), Palacio Bellas Artes Orch [I] *(rec live, Mexico City, 6/17/52)* Melodram 2-▲ CDM 26023
Verdi, G.:Rigoletto (sels), w. C. O'Connor (sop), O. Dominguez (mez), G. Di Stefano (ten), G. Valdengo (bar), I. Rufino (bass), R. Cellini (cnd), Palacio Bellas Artes Orch [abridged performance] *(rec live, Mexico City 6/22/48)* Golden Age of Opera 2-▲ GAO 128/29 [ADD]
Verdi, G.:La traviata, w. M. Callas (sop), G. Di Stefano (ten), Campolonghi (bar), U. Mugnai (cnd), Palacio Bellas Artes Orch [I] *(rec live, Mexico City, 6/3/52)* Melodram 2-▲ CDM 26021
Verdi, G.:La traviata, w. M. Callas (sop), Giron (sgr), C. Valletti (ten), G. Taddei (bar), O. de Fabritiis (cnd), Palacio Bellas Artes Orch [I] *(rec live, Mexico City, 7/17/51)* Melodram 2-▲ CDM 26019 [AAD]
Verdi, G.:Il trovatore, w. M. Callas (sop), G. Simionato (mez), K. Baum (ten), L. Warren (bar), G. Picco (cnd), Palacio Bellas Artes Orch *(rec live, Mexico City 6/20/50)* Melodram 2-▲ CDM 26017
Verdi, G.:Il trovatore (sels), w. M. Callas (sop), Feuss (sgr), C. Sagarminaga (ten), K. Baum (ten), L. Warren (bar), G. Picco (cnd), Palacio Bellas Artes Orch—ten selections from Acts 1 & 4 [I] *(rec live, Mexico City 6/20/50)* Myto 2-▲ 2 MCD 90213 (m) [ADD]

Palatine Kurrende
Draeseke, F.:Mysterium:Christus, w. C. Bischoff (sop), A. Vogel (sop), E. Dersen (alt), K. Markus (ten), H.J. Ritzerfeld (ten), P. Langshaw (bar), B. Kämpff (bass), J. Sonnenschmidt (org), U.-R. Follert (cnd), Breslau State PO, Evangelical Boys' Choir Palatine, Heilbronn Vocal Ensemble Bayer 5-▲ 100175/79

Palermo Teatro Massimo Chorus
Bellini, V.:La straniera, w. R. Scotto (sop), E. Zilio (mez), R. Cioni (ten), D. Trimarchi (bar), E. Campi (bass), N. Sanzogno (cnd), Palermo Teatro Massimo Orch [I] *(rec live, Palermo, 1968)* Verona 2-▲ 27097/98
Bellini, V.:La straniera, w. R. Scotto (sop), E. Zilio (mez), R. Cioni (ten), D. Trimarchi (bar), E. Campi (bass), N. Sanzogno (cnd), Palermo Teatro Massimo Orch [I] *(rec live, Palermo, 1968)* Melodram 2-▲ 27039
Donizetti, G.:Anna Bolena, w. Katia Ricciarelli (sop), Doris Soffel (cta), Pietro Ballo (ten), Nicolai Ghiuselev (bass), E. Pidò (cnd), Palermo Teatro Massimo Orch *(rec live, 1991)* Serenissima 3-▲ SER 360111

Palermo Teatro Massimo Chorus (cont.)

Rossini, G.:Elisabetta, regina d'Inghilterra, w. L. Gencer (sop), S. Geszty (sop), U. Grilli (ten), P. Bottazzo (ten), N. Sanzogno (cnd), Palermo Teatro Massimo Orch [I] *(rec live, 11/24/70)* Myto 2-▲ 2 MCD 90530 [ADD]

Verdi, G.:Macbeth, w. Leyla Gencer (sop), Mirto Picchi (ten), Giuseppe Taddei (bar), Ferruccio Mazzoli (bass), V. Gui (cnd), Palermo Teatro Massimo Orch *(rec Palermo, Jan. 14, 1960)* Pantheon 2-▲ PHE 6604 (m)

Verdi, G.:I vespri siciliani, w. A. Stella (sop—Elena), M. Filippeschi (ten—Arrigo), G. Taddei (bar—Monforte), B. Ladysz (bass—Procida), T. Serafin (cnd), Palermo Teatro Massimo Orch *(rec Jan. 18, 1957)* Golden Age of Opera 2-▲ GAO 145/46 [ADD]

Paris Chorus

Massenet, J.:Werther, w. V. De los Angeles (sop), M. Mesplé (sop), N. Gedda (ten), G. Prêtre (cnd), Orch de Paris [F] EMI Classics ("Studio" series) 2-▲ CDMB 63973

Paris Gregorian Choir

Tranquillity Erato ▲ 95771-2 ■ 95771-4

X. Chancerelle (cnd)

All Saints' Day Requiem, w. Schola Gregoriano Pragensis [cnd:David Eben] Jade ▲ JAD C 111

Paris Lyon Opera Chorus

Donizetti, G.:Don Pasquale, w. B. Hendricks (sop), L. Canonici (ten), G. Bacquier (bar), L. Quilico (bar), R. Schirrer (bar), G. Ferro (cnd), Paris Lyon Opera Orch [I] Erato 2-▲ 2292-45487-2-ZA [DDD]

Floyd, C.:Susannah, w. C. Studer (sop—Sussanah Polk), J. Hadley (ten—Sam Polk), S. Ramey (bass—Rev. Olin Blitch), K. Nagano (cnd), Paris Lyon Opera Orch Virgin Classics ▲ CDCB 45039

Gluck, C.W.:La Recontre imprévue, w. C. Le Coz (sop), L. Dawson (sop), C. Dubosc (sop), S. Marin-Degor (sop), G. Fletcher (sgr), F. Dudziak (ten), G. de Mey (ten), J.-L. Viala (ten), G. Cachémaille (bar), J.-P. Lafont (bass), J. E. Gardiner (cnd), Paris Lyon Opera Orch [F] Erato 2-▲ 2292-45516-2 [DDD]

Messager, A.:Fortunio, w. C. Alliot-Lugaz (sop), T. Dran (ten), G. Cachémaille (bar), R. Schirrer (bar), J. E. Gardiner (cnd), Paris Lyon Opera Orch Erato 2-▲ 45983-2

Prokofiev, S.:The Love for 3 Oranges (suite), w. C. Dubosc (sop), G. Gautier (ten), J.-L. Viala (ten), G. Bacquier (bar), J. Bastin (bass), K. Nagano (cnd), Paris Lyon Opera Orch [F] Virgin Classics ▲ 59566 [DDD]

Rameau, J.P.:Dardanus, w. C. Eda-Pierre (sop), F. von Stade (mez), G. Gautier (ten), R. Soyer (bar), J. Van Dam (b-bar), R. Leppard (cnd), Paris Lyon Opera Orch Erato 2-▲ 95312-2

Rossini, G.:Arias, w. K. Ricciarelli (sop), G. Ferro (cnd), Paris Lyon Opera Orch Virgin Classics ▲ CDC 59660

Strauss, R.:Salome, w. K. Huffstodt (sop), H. Jossoud (mez), J. Dupouy (ten), J.L. Viala (ten), J. van Dam (bar), K. Nagano (cnd), Paris Lyon Opera Orch Virgin Classics 2-▲ CDCB 59054

Paris Madrigal Choir

Les Trois Maries:A Liturgical Play from the Middle Ages from Origny-Sainte-Benoîte, w. B. Gagnepain (cnd), Academie Internationale de Sées Koch Schwann ▲ SCH 314252 [DDD]

Paris National Chorus

Mahler, G.:Sym 2, w. E. Selig (sop), E. Zareska (cta), C. Schuricht (cnd), Paris National Orch [G] *(rec live, Paris 2/20/58)* Melodram ("Connaisseur" series) 2-▲ CD 27504 (m) [AAD]

Paris Opera Children's Choir

Mozart, W.A.:Missa, K.427, w. C. Pozderec (sop), M. C. LeBlanc (sop), F. Bardot (ten), L. Peintre (bar), F. Bardot (cnd), Altaïr SO [L] Thésis ▲ THE11003

Paris Opera Chorus

Bellini, V.:Norma (sels), w. M. Callas (sop), F. Cossotto (mez), G. Cecchele (ten), I. Vinco (bass), G. Prêtre (cnd), Paris Opera Orch—sels. *(rec 1965)* Melodram ▲ MLO 16038 [ADD]

Berlioz, H.:La Damnation de Faust, w. Janet Baker (mez), Nicolai Gedda (ten), Gabriel Bacquier (bar), G. Prêtre (cnd), Orch de Paris EMI Classics 2-▲ CDFB 68583

Bizet, G.:Carmen, w. M. Freni (sop), G. Bumbry (mez), J. Vickers (ten), K. Paskalis (bar), R. Frühbeck de Burgos (cnd), Paris Opera Orch [opéra comique version] [F] EMI Classics ("Studio" series) 2-▲ CDMB 63643 [ADD]

Bizet, G.:Carmen, w. M. Callas (sop), A. Guiot (sop), N. Gedda (ten), R. Massard (bar), G. Prêtre (cnd), Paris Opera Orch [F] EMI Classics 2-▲ CDCB 54368

Bizet, G.:Carmen (sels), w. K. Ricciarelli (sop), A. Baltsa (mez), J. Carreras (ten), J. Van Dam (b-bar), H. von Karajan (cnd), Berlin PO [F] Deutsche Grammophon ▲ 413322-2 [DDD]

Bizet, G.:Les Pêcheurs de perles, w. I. Cotrubas (sop), A. Vanzo (ten), G. Sarabia (bar), R. Soyer (bass), G. Prêtre (cnd), Paris Opera Orch Classics for Pleasure ▲ CDCFP 4721 [ADD]

Charpentier, G.:Louise, w. B. Sills (sop—Louise), M. Dunn (mez—Louise's Mother), N. Gedda (ten—Julien), J. Van Dam (bass-bar—Louise's Father), J. Rudel (cnd), Paris Opera Orch EMI Classics ▲ CDMC 65299

Gounod, C.:Faust, w. M. Berthon (sop), M. Coiffier (sop), J. Montfort (mez), C. Vezzani (ten), L. Musy (b-bar), M. Cozette (bar), M. Journet (bass), H. Busser (cnd), Paris Opera Orch [F] *(rec 1930)* Pearl 2-▲ PEA 9987 [AAD]

Gounod, C.:Faust, w. M. Berthon (sop—Marguerite), C. Vezzani (ten—Faust), L. Musy (b-bar—Valentin), M. Journet (bass—Mephistofeles), H. Busser (cnd), Paris Opera Orch [F] *(rec 1930)* Music Memoria 2-▲ 30187

Gounod, C.:Faust (sels), w. M. Freni (sop), P. Domingo (ten), T. Allen (bar), N. Ghiaurov (bass), G. Prêtre (cnd), Paris Opera Orch, Orch de Paris EMI Classics ▲ ZDM 63090

Gounod, C.:Faust (sels), w. Liliane Berton (sop), Victoria de los Angeles (sop), Rita Gorr (mez), Nicolai Gedda (ten), Victor Autran (bar), Ernest Blanc (bar), Boris Christoff (bass), A. Cluytens (cnd), Paris Opera Orch Classics for Pleasure ("Eminence" series) ▲ CDEMX 2215 [DDD]

Gounod, C.:Roméo et Juliette, w. M. Freni (sop—Juliette), F. Corelli (ten—Roméo), H. Gui (bar—Mercutio), C. Câles (bar—Capulet), X. Depraz (bass—Frère Laurent), A. Lombard (cnd), Paris Opera Orch EMI Classics ▲ CDMB 65290

Massenet, J.:Amadis, w. A. Giorgi (cnd), Paris Opera Orch Forlane 2-▲ FRL 16578 [DDD]

Mozart, W.A.:Don Giovanni, w. E. Moser (sop), K. Te Kanawa (sop), T. Berganza (mez), K. Riegel (ten), G. Raimondi (ten), J. Van Dam (b-bar), J. Macurdy (bass), L. Maazel (cnd), Paris Opera Orch [I] CBS 3-▲ M3K 35192

Mozart, W.A.:Don Giovanni (sels), w. Kiri Te Kanawa (sop), Teresa Berganza (mez), José Van Dam (bass-bar), Ruggero Raimondi (bass), L. Maazel (cnd), Paris Opera Orch Sony Classical ("Essential Classics" series) ▲ SBK 62663 ■ SBT 62663

Mozart, W.A.:Nozze di Figaro, w. Mirella Freni (sop), Gundala Janowitz (sop), Jane Berbié (mez), Frederica von Stade (mez), Michel Sénéchal (ten), José Van Dam (b-bar), Kurt Moll (bass), G. Solti (cnd), Paris Opera Orch *(rec live, Paris, Apr 7, 1973)* Agorá ("Phoenix" series) 3-▲ 515

Mozart, W.A.:Requiem, w. K. Battle (sop), A. Murray (mez), D. Rendall (ten), M. Salminen (bass), D. Barenboim (cnd), Orch de Paris [L] EMI Classics ▲ CDC 47342 [DDD]

Puccini, G.:Tosca, w. M. Callas (sop), R. Cioni (ten), T. Gobbi (bar), N. Rescigno (cnd), Paris Opera Orch *(rec live, Paris March 3, 1965)* Melodram 2-▲ CDM 26033 [ADD]

Puccini, G.:Tosca, w. M. Callas (sop), C. Bergonzi (ten), T. Gobbi (bar), G. Prêtre (cnd), Paris Conservatory Societé des Concerts Orch [I] EMI Classics ("Studio" series) 2-▲ CDMB 69974 [ADD]

Satie, E.:Les Aventures de Mercure, w. P. Dervaux (cnd), Orch de Paris Virgin Classics 2-▲ CDZB 62877

Satie, E.:Geneviéve de Brabant, w. A. Guiot (sop), M. Mesplé (sop), D. Millet (sop), A. Esposito (sop), J.C. Benoit (bar), A. Ciccolini (pno), P. Dervaux (cnd), Orch de Paris Virgin Classics 2-▲ CDZB 62877

Satie, E.:Socrate, w. A. Guiot (sop), M. Mesplé (sop), D. Millet (sop), A. Esposito (sop), J. C. Benoit (bar), P. Dervaux (cnd), Orch de Paris Virgin Classics 2-▲ CDZB 62877

Paris Opéra-Comique Chorus

Bizet, G.:Carmen (sels), w. C. Supervia (mez), A. Vavon (sop), A. Bernadet (mez), G. Micheletti (ten), A. Endreze (bar), G. Cloëz (cnd), Paris Opéra-Comique Orch—8 arias & scenes *(rec Paris 1930)* Nimbus ("Prima Voce" series) 2-▲ NI 7836/7 [AAD]

Bizet, G.:Carmen (sels), w. C. Supervia (mez), A. Vavon (sop), A. Bernadet (mez), J.-F. Delmas (b-bar), G. Micheletti (ten), A. Endreze (bar), G. Cloëz (cnd), Paris Opéra-Comique Orch—14 arias & scenes [F] *(rec Paris, 1930)* The Classical Collector ▲ FDC 2002 (m) [AAD]

Paris Opéra-Comique Chorus (cont.)

Bizet, G.:Les Pêcheurs de perles, w. J. Micheau (sop), N. Gedda (ten), E. Blanc (bar), J. Mars (bar), P. Dervaux (cnd), Paris Opéra-Comique Orch [F] EMI Classics ("Studio" series) 2-▲ CDMB 69704 [ADD]

Delibes, L.:Lakmé, w. M. Mesplé (sop), D. Millet (sop), C. Burles (ten), R. Soyer (bass), A. Lombard (cnd), Paris Opéra-Comique Orch EMI Classics 2-▲ CDCB 49430

Delibes, L.:Lakmé (sels), w. M. Mesplé (sop), D. Millet (sop), C. Burles (ten), R. Soyer (bass), A. Lombard (cnd), Paris Opéra-Comique Orch EMI Classics ▲ ZDM 63447

Donizetti, G.:L'Esule di Roma, w. C. Gasdia (sop), E. Palacio (ten), A. Ariostini (bar), S. Alaimo (bass-bar), M. de Bernart (cnd), Piacenza SO *(rec live, 10/14/86)* Bongiovanni 2-▲ GB 2045/46 [DDD]

Gounod, C.:Roméo et Juliette, w. Yvonne Gall (sop—Juliette), Champell (sop—Stéphano), Jeanne Goulancourt (mez—Gertrude), Agustarello Affre (ten—Roméo), Edmond Tirmont (ten—Tybalt), Alexis Boyer (bar—Mercutio), Pierre Dupré (bar—Paris), Hypolite Belhomme (bar—Grégorio), Marcel Journet (bass—Frère Laurent), Henri Albers (bass—Capulet), Valermont (bass—The Duke), F. Rühlmann (cnd), Paris Opéra-Comique Orch *(rec 1912)* VAI Audio ▲ VAIA 1064-3 F

Massenet, J.:Manon, w. G. Féraldy (sop), J. Rogatchewsky (ten), L. Guénot (bass), E. Cohen (cnd), Paris Opéra-Comique Orch [F] *(rec 1928-29 for Columbia)* Classical Collector 2-▲ FDC 2 2001 (m) [AAD]

Massenet, J.:Manon, w. V. De los Angeles (sop), H. Legay (ten), M. Dens (bar), J. Borthayre (bass), P. Monteux (cnd), Paris Opéra-Comique Orch [F] EMI Classics 3-▲ CDMC 63549 (m) [ADD]

Puccini, G.:Tosca (sels), w. M.-C. Vallin (sop), E. di Mazzei (ten), P. Payen (bar), A. Endrèze (bar), G. Cloëz (cnd), Paris Opéra-Comique Orch [abridged version] [F] *(rec 1932)* Music Memoria ▲ 30376

Rossini, G.:Petite messe solennelle, w. E. Schmitt (sop), S. Gregoire (cta), R. Garin (ten), A. Golven (bass), F. Maciocchi (pno) J.-F. Hatton (harm) IMP Masters ▲ IMP MCD61

Paris Russian Orthodox Cathedral Choir

Russian Liturgical Chant, w. Nicolai Gedda (ten) Philips ("Collector" series) ▲ 434174-2 PM [ADD]

Paris Sorbonne Chorus

Caplet, A.:Myrrha, w. Sharon Coste (sop), Marc Duguay (ten), Jean-François Lapointe (bar), J. Grimbert (cnd), Paris Sorbonne Orch *(rec Grand Amphithéâtre of the Sorbonne, July 3-5, 1993 & May 8, 1)* Marco Polo ▲ 8.223755 [DDD]

Caplet, A.:Tout est lumière, w. J. Grimbert (cnd), Paris Sorbonne Orch *(rec Grand Amphithéâtre of the Sorbonne, July 3-5, 1993 & May 8, 1)* Marco Polo ▲ 8.223755 [DDD]

Debussy, C.:Le Printemps, w. J. Grimbert (cnd), Paris Sorbonne Orch *(rec Grand Amphithéâtre of the Sorbonne, July 3-5, 1993 & May 8, 1)* Marco Polo ▲ 8.223755 [DDD]

Ravel, M.:L'Aurore, w. J. Grimbert (cnd), Paris Sorbonne Orch *(rec Grand Amphithéâtre of the Sorbonne, July 3-5, 1993 & May 8, 1)* Marco Polo ▲ 8.223755 [DDD]

Ravel, M.:Les Bayadères, w. J. Grimbert (cnd), Paris Sorbonne Orch *(rec Grand Amphithéâtre of the Sorbonne, July 3-5, 1993 & May 8, 1)* Marco Polo ▲ 8.223755 [DDD]

Ravel, M.:Matinée de Provence, w. J. Grimbert (cnd), Paris Sorbonne Orch *(rec Grand Amphithéâtre of the Sorbonne, July 3-5, 1993 & May 8, 1)* Marco Polo ▲ 8.223755 [DDD]

Ravel, M.:La Nuit, w. Gaëlle Le Roi (sop), J. Grimbert (cnd), Paris Sorbonne Orch *(rec Grand Amphithéâtre of the Sorbonne, July 3-5, 1993 & May 8, 1)* Marco Polo ▲ 8.223755 [DDD]

Ravel, M.:Tout est lumière, w. Gaëlle Le Roi (sop), J. Grimbert (cnd), Paris Sorbonne Orch *(rec Grand Amphithéâtre of the Sorbonne, July 3-5, 1993 & May 8, 1)* Marco Polo ▲ 8.223755 [DDD]

Paris Sym Chorus

Boieldieu, F.-A.:La Dame blanche, w. Michel Sénéchal (ten—Georges Brown), Aimé Doniat (bar—Dikson), Pierre Héral (bass—Mac-Irton), Adrien Legros (bass—Gaveston), P. Stoll (cnd), Paris SO Accord 2-▲ ACD 220862 [AAD]

Parley of Instruments Chorus

Clarke, J.:Come, Come Along for a Dance & a Song, w. R. Holton (sop), C. Daniels (ten), S. Birchall (bass), R. Goodman (cnd), Parley of Instruments Hyperion ▲ CDA 66578 [DDD]

Hall, H.:Yes, My Aminta, 'tis True, w. R. Holton (sop), S. Birchall (bass), R. Goodman (cnd), Parley of Instruments Hyperion ▲ CDA 66578 [DDD]

Parma Teatro Regio Chorus

Verdi, G.:Luisa Miller, w. Cecilia Gasdia (sop), Mazzareno Antinori (ten), Simone Alaimo (b-bar), G. Gavazzeni (cnd), Parma Teatro Regio Orch *(rec live, 1981)* Serenissima 2-▲ SER 360143

Parthenia Vocal Ensemble

Bernhard, C.:Geistlicher Harmonien erster Theil, w. C. Brembeck (cnd), Parthenia Baroque Christophorus 2-▲ 77177

Keiser, R.:Passions Oratorium, w. T. d'Althann (sop), P. Geitner (sop), M. Paulsen (alt), J. Elbert (ten), H. Elbert (bass), C. Brembeck (cnd), Parthenia Baroque Christophorus ▲ 77143 [DDD]

Pasadena Boys' Choir

Kraft, William:Contextures II:The Final Beast, w. M. Rawcliffe (sop), J. Mack (ten), A. Previn (cnd), Los Angeles PO, New Albion Ensemble [E,G,Gr,L] Meet The Composer ▲ 79229-2 ■ 79229-4

Raphaël Passaquet Vocal Ensemble

Vivaldi, A.:Beatus vir (Psalm 111), w. M. Burgess (sop), J. Chamonin (sop), C. Watkinson (cta), J.-C. Malgoire (cnd), La Grande Écurie et la Chambre du Roy *(rec 1976)* Sony Classical ("Essential Classics" series) ▲ SBK 48280 [ADD] ■ SBT 48280

Vivaldi, A.:Gloria, RV.589, w. M. Burgess (sop), Jocelyne Chamonine (sop), Carolyn Watkinson (cta), J.-C. Malgoire (cnd), La Grande Écurie et la Chambre du Roy *(rec 1976)* Sony Classical ("Essential Classics" series) ▲ SBK 48280 [ADD] ■ SBT 48280

Patriarchal Cathedral of the Epiphany Choir

G. Kharitonov (cnd)

Hymns of the Russian Liturgy Russian Compact Disc ▲ RCD 15005 [AAD]

Pécs Chamber Choir

Haydn, J.:Die Schöpfung, w. Edith Mathis (sop), Christoph Prégardien (ten), Harald Stamm (bass), M. Atzmon (cnd), World SO, Berlin Academy of Arts Chamber Choir, Shin-Yuh Kai Choir [G] *(rec Basilica San Francesco in Assisi, as part of the IPPNW "Hiroshima Concert 1990")* BIS 2-▲ CD 493/94 [DDD]

Lickl, J.G.:Missa solemnis, w. Maria Zadori (sop), Judith Nemet (mez), Boldizsar Keönch (ten), Tamas Bator (bass), H. Williams (cnd), Pécs SO Koch Schwann ▲ SCH 312962

Lickl, J.G.:Requiem, w. Maria Zadori (sop), Judith Nemet (mez), Boldizsar Keönch (ten), Tamas Bator (bass), H. Williams (cnd), Pécs SO Koch Schwann ▲ SCH 312962

A. Tillai (cnd)

Kodály, Z.:Choral Music—18 works [Hun] Hungaroton ▲ HCD 31524 [DDD]

Perceval Ensemble

G. Robert (cnd)

Adams, J.:Le jeu de Robin et de Marion *(rec 1980)* Arion ▲ ARN 68162 [ADD]

The Art of the Lute in the Middle Ages, w. Guy Robert (lt) Arion ▲ ARN 60264

La Cour du Roi-René:Chansons et Danses Arion ▲ ARN 68104 [DDD]

Manuscrit du roi (vers 1250):Trouvères & troubadours Arion ▲ ARN 68225 [DDD]

The Songs of Kings & Princes of the Middle Ages Arion ▲ ARN 68031 [DDD]

Les Peres de Chevilly

Le Temps de Noël, w. En-Calcat Abbey Monks' Choir, Ligugé Abbey Monks' Choir, Timadeuc Abbey Monks' Choir, Bec-Hellouin Abbey Monks' Choir Studio SM 2-▲ 1219.10

Permoník Children's Chorus

Báchorek, M.:Hukvald Poem, w. Drahomíra Drobková (sop), Břetislav Vojkůvka (ten), Pavel Kamas (bar), Otakar Brousek (reciter), O. Trhlík (cnd), Prague SO, Ostrava Female Chamber Chorus *(rec Smetana Hall of Prague's Municipal House, Feb 10 & 11, 1988)* Panton ▲ 811338-2 [DDD]

Báchorek, M.:Music of, w. Osvald Albín (nar), Otakar Brousek (nar), Jan Vlassak (nar), Brigita Sulcová (sop), Drahomíra Drobková (cta), Karel Průša (bass), Pavel Kamas (sgr), Jan Kyzlink (sgr), Jana Stuperkova-Majtnerova (sgr), Bretislav Vojkuvka (sgr), O. Trhlík (cnd), Ostrava Janáček PO, Prague SO, Ostrava Janáček Chorus, Ostrava Women's Chamber Chorus—Lidice; Stereofonietta Panton ▲ PAN 811338 [AAD/DDD]

Pestalozzi School Children's Choir

German Opera Arias, w. Thomas Hampson (bar), Fabio Luisi (cnd), Munich RSO EMI Classics ▲ 55233-2

994 ▲ = CD ♦ = Enhanced CD Δ = MD ■ = Cassette Tape ◻ = DCC

Peterborough Cathedral Choir
S. Vann (cnd)
Stainer, J.:The Crucifixion, w. J. Griffett (ten), M. George (bass), A. Newberry (vc) ASV Quicksilva ▲ ASQ 6100 [ADD]
La Petite Bande Chorus
Bach, J.S.:Motets, BWV 225–30, w. S. Kuijken (cnd), La Petite Bande Accent ▲ 9287 [DDD]
Mozart, W.A.:Così fan tutte, w. S. Isokoski (sop—Fiordiligi), N. Argenta (sop—Despina), M. Groop (mez—Dorabella), M. Schäfer (ten—Ferrando), P. Vollestad (bar—Guglielmo), H. Claessens (b-bar—Don Alfonso)., S. Kuijken (cnd), La Petite Bande Accent 3-▲ ACC 9296/98
Petits Chanteurs de Monaco
Enescu, G.:Oedipe, w. B. Hendricks (sop), B. Fassbaender (mez), M. Lipovšek (mez), J. Taillon (mez), N. Gedda (ten), J. Aler (ten), G. Bacquier (bar), Quilico (bar), J. Van Dam (bass-bar), L. Foster (cnd), Monte Carlo PO, Orféon Donostiarra [F] EMI Classics 2-▲ CDCB 54011 [DDD]
Petits Chanteurs de Notre Dame de la Joie
Schubert, Ferdinand:Requiem, w. D. Degos (trb), K. Markus (ten), R. Soyer (bass), J. Galard (org), J.-P. Lore (cnd), French Oratorio Orch, J.-P. Lore Vocal Ensemble *(rec Nov. 9–11, 1980 & Jan. 25)* Esoldun ▲ MOS 1003 [ADD]
Schubert, Franz:Requiem, w. D. Degos (trb), K. Markus (ten), R. Soyer (bass), J. Galard (org), J.-P. Lore (cnd), French Oratorio Orch, J.-P. Lore Vocal Ensemble *(rec Nov. 9–11, 1980 & Jan. 25)* Esoldun ▲ MOS 1003 [ADD]
Petits Chanteurs de Paris
Lancino, T.:Aloni, w. P. Eötvös (cnd), Ensemble InterContemporain Wergo ▲ WER 2032-2
P. Piquemal, Marco (cnd)
Fauré, G.:Messe basse, w. B. Thomas (cnd), Bernard Thomas CO, Michel Piquemal Vocal Ensemble, Argenteuil Vittoria Choir Forlane ▲ FRL 16536 [DDD]
Fauré, G.:Requiem, w. B. Thomas (cnd), Bernard Thomas CO, Michel Piquemal Vocal Ensemble, Argenteuil Vittoria Choir Forlane ▲ FRL 16536 [DDD]
Petits Chanteurs du Mont-Royal
Nielsen, C.:Serenata in vano, w. O. Vänskä (cnd), Lahti Chamber Ensemble Ondine ▲ ODE 792-2 [DDD]
Poulenc, F.:Ave verum corpus Analekta ▲ AN 29302
Poulenc, F.:Exultate Deo Analekta ▲ AN 29302
Poulenc, F.:Mass Analekta ▲ AN 29302
Poulenc, F.:Motets (4) pour le temps de Noël Analekta ▲ AN 29302
Poulenc, F.:Quatre petites prières de Saint François d'Assise Analekta ▲ AN 29302
Poulenc, F.:Salve regina Analekta ▲ AN 29302
Prokofiev, S.:Winter Bonfire, w. M. Forrester (nar), A. Grossmann (cnd), Metropolitan Orch [E] CBC ("SM 5000" series) 2-▲ SMCD 5118-2 [DDD]
Philadelphia Choral Arts Society
Scriabin, A.:Sym 1, w. S. Toczyska (mez), M. Myers (ten), R. Muti (cnd), Philadelphia Orch EMI Classics 3-▲ CDC 54251
Philadelphia Festival Choir members
R.A.M. Ross (cnd)
Thompson, R.:Choral Music, w. Voces Novae et Antiquae—Cantata, "A Feast of Praise"; Frostiana; Glory to God in the Highest; Felices Ter; Mirror of St. Anne; Bitter-Sweet; Antiphon; Lord is My Sheperd; Alleluia; Pueri Hebraeorum Arkay ▲ AR 6110 [DDD]
Philadelphia Lyric Opera Chorus
Puccini, G.:La fanciulla del West, w. D. Kirsten (sop), F. Corelli (ten), A. Colzani (bar), A. Guadagno (cnd), Philadelphia Lyric Opera Orch [I] *(rec live, 11/10/64)* Melodram 2-▲ MEL 27081 [AAD]
Verdi, G.:La traviata, w. M. Caballé (sop), J. Carreras (ten), N. Mitic (bar), A. Guadagno (cnd), Philadelphia Lyric Opera Orch *(rec 1973)* Melodram 2-▲ MLO 270106 [ADD]
Philadelphia Opera Chorus
Puccini, G.:Tosca, w. B. Nilsson (sop), F. Tagliavini (ten), R. Vinay (ten), C. Maresco (cnd), Philadelphia Opera Orch *(rec Apr. 10, 1963)* Melodram 2-▲ MLO 270112 [ADD]
Philadelphia Orch Chorus
Beethoven, L. van:Sym 9, "Choral Sym", w. Agnes Davis (sop), Robert Betts (sgr), Ruth Cathcart (sgr), Eugene Lowenthal (sgr), L. Stokowski (cnd), Philadelphia Orch *(rec 1934)* Music & Arts ▲ CD 846 [ADD]
Brahms, J.:Alto Rhap, w. M. Anderson (cta), E. Ormandy (cnd), Philadelphia Orch [G] *(rec 1939 for HMV)* Pearl ▲ PEA 9405 (m) [AAD]
Philadelphia Singers
Respighi, O.:Lauda per la Natività del Signore, w. Valente (sop), M. Forrester (cta), Gordon (ten), M. Korn (cnd), Concerto Soloists Instrumental Ensemble RCA Red Seal ▲ 7787-2-RC [DDD] ■ 7787-4-RC (CrO2)
M. Korn (cnd)
Britten, B.:A Ceremony of Carols [E] RCA Red Seal ▲ 7787-2-RC [DDD] ■ 7787-4-RC (CrO2)
Poulenc, F.:Motets (4) pour le temps de Noël [L] RCA Red Seal ▲ 7787-2-RC [DDD] ■ 7787-4-RC (CrO2)
Philadelphia Voces Novae et Antiquae
B. Steinberg (cnd)
Shomeir Yisrael:A Musical Service for Friday Evening for Solo, Choir, Organ & Instruments, w. Richard Allen (cant) Arkay ▲ ARK 6126 [DDD] ■ ARK 4126
Philandros
Giteck, J.:Home (Revisited), Gamelan Pacifica New Albion ▲ NA 054
Philharmonia Chorus
Beethoven, L. van:Fidelio, w. I. Hallstein (sop), C. Ludwig (mez), J. Vickers (ten), G. Unger (ten), W. Berry (bass), G. Frick (bass), O. Klemperer (cnd), Philharmonia Orch [G]; w. minimal dialog EMI Classics ("Studio" series) 2-▲ CDMB 69324 [ADD]
Beethoven, L. van:Fidelio, w. Ingeborg Hallstein (sop—Marzelline), Christa Ludwig (mez—Leonore/Fidelio), Gerhard Unger (ten—Jaquino), Jon Vickers (ten—Florestan), Walter Berry (bass—Pizarro), Franz Crass (bass—Don Fernando), Gottlob Frick (bass—Rocco), O. Klemperer (cnd), Philharmonia Orch EMI Classics 2-▲ CDCB 55170
Brahms, J.:Alto Rhap, w. C. Ludwig (mez), O. Klemperer (cnd), Philharmonia Orch [G] EMI Classics ("Studio" series) ▲ CDM 69650 [ADD]
Brahms, J.:Ein Deutsches Requiem, w. E. Schwarzkopf (sop), D. Fischer-Dieskau (bar), O. Klemperer (cnd), Philharmonia Orch [G] EMI Classics 2-▲ CDC 47238
Cornelius, P.:Der Barbier von Bagdad, w. E. Schwarzkopf (sop), G. Hoffman (cta), N. Gedda (ten), G. Unger (ten), O. Czerwenka (bass), E. Leinsdorf (cnd), Philharmonia Orch EMI Classics ▲ CDMB 65284
Fauré, G.:Requiem, w. K. Battle (sop), A. Schmidt (bar), C. M. Giulini (cnd), Philharmonia Orch [L] Deutsche Grammophon ▲ 419243-2 [DDD]
Hadley, P.:The Trees So High, w. M. Bamert (cnd), Philharmonia Orch Chandos ▲ CHAN 9181 [DDD]
Handel, G.F.:Messiah, w. Elisabeth Schwarzkopf (sop), Grace Hoffman (cta), Nikolai Gedda (ten), Jerome Hines (bass), O. Klemperer (cnd), Philharmonia Orch EMI Classics 3-▲ ZDMC 63621
Legendary Three Tenors, w. Enrico Caruso (ten), Beniamino Gigli (ten), John McCormack (ten), Ruggiero Leoncavallo (pno), Edwin Schneider (pno), Metropolitan Opera Orch, Metropolitan Opera Chorus [cnd:Giulio Setti], Philharmonia Orch, Philharmonia Chorus [cnd:Stanford Robinson] *(rec 1904–1950)* RCA Gold Seal ▲ 09026-68534-2 [ADD] ■ 09026-68534-4
Lehár, F.:Die lustige Witwe, w. E. Schwarzkopf (sop), H. Steffek (sop), N. Gedda (ten), E. Wächter (bar), L. von Matačić (cnd), Philharmonia Orch [G] EMI Classics 2-▲ CDCB 47177
Lehár, F.:Die lustige Witwe, w. E. Schwarzkopf (sop), E. Loose (sop), N. Gedda (ten), E. Kunz (bar), A. Kraus (ten), O. Ackermann (cnd), Philharmonia Orch [G] EMI Classics ("Studio" series) ▲ CDH 69520 (m) [ADD]
Mahler, G.:Sym 2, w. E. Schwarzkopf (sop), H. Rössl-Majdan (mez), O. Klemperer (cnd), Philharmonia Orch [G] EMI Classics ("Studio" series) ▲ CDM 69662 [ADD]
Mahler, G.:Sym 2, w. R. Plowright (sop), B. Fassbaender (mez), G. Sinopoli (cnd), Philharmonia Orch [G] Deutsche Grammophon 2-▲ 415959-2 [DDD]

Philharmonia Chorus (cont.)
Mahler, G.:Sym 8, w. S. Jo (sop), C. Studer (sop), W. Meier (mez), K. Lewis (ten), T. Allen (bar), H. Sotin (bass), G. Sinopoli (cnd), Philharmonia Orch, Southend Boys' Choir [G] Deutsche Grammophon 2-▲ 435433-2
Mendelssohn, F.:A Midsummer Night's Dream (comp), w. H. Harper (sop), J. Baker (mez), O. Klemperer (cnd), Philharmonia Orch *(rec ca. 1961)* EMI Classics ▲ CDM 64144
Mendelssohn, F.:Sym 2, w. C. Haymon (sop), A. Hagley (sop), P. Straka (ten), W. Weller (cnd), Philharmonia Orch [G] Chandos ▲ CHAN 8995 [DDD]
Mozart, W.A.:Così fan tutte, w. E. Schwarzkopf (sop), H. Steffek (sop), C. Ludwig (mez), A. Kraus (ten), G. Taddei (bar), W. Berry (bass), K. Böhm (cnd), Philharmonia Orch [I] EMI Classics ("Studio" series) 3-▲ CDMC 69330 [ADD]
Mozart, W.A.:Così fan tutte, w. E. Schwarzkopf (sop), L. Otto (sop), N. Merriman (mez), L. Simoneau (ten), R. Panerai (bar), S. Bruscantini (bar), H. von Karajan (cnd), Philharmonia Orch [I] EMI Classics ("Studio" series) 3-▲ CDHC 69635 (m) [ADD]
Mozart, W.A.:Nozze di Figaro, w. A. Moffo (sop), E. Schwarzkopf (sop), F. Cossotto (mez), G. Taddei (bar), E. Wächter (bar), C. M. Giulini (cnd), Philharmonia Orch [I] EMI Classics ("Studio" series) 2-▲ CDMB 63266 [ADD]
Mozart, W.A.:Nozze di Figaro (sels), w. A. Moffo (sop), E. Schwarzkopf (sop), F. Cossotto (mez), G. Taddei (bar), E. Wächter (bar), C. M. Giulini (cnd), Philharmonia Orch—sels. EMI Classics ("Studio" series) ▲ CDM 63409
Mozart, W.A.:Ovs, w. C. Davis (cnd), Royal PO—(9) EMI Classics ▲ CDE 67777
Mozart, W.A.:Requiem, w. L. Dawson (sop), J. van Nes (cta), K. Lewis (ten), S. Estes (bass), C. M. Guilini (cnd), Philharmonia Orch [L] Sony Classical ▲ SK 45577 [DDD]
Mozart, W.A.:Zauberflöte, w. G. Janowitz (sop), L. Popp (sop), R. Pütz (sop), N. Gedda (ten), W. Berry (bass), G. Frick (bass), O. Klemperer (cnd), Philharmonia Orch [without dialog; G] EMI Classics ("Studio" series) 2-▲ CDMB 69971 [ADD]
Mozart, W.A.:Zauberflöte, w. Gundula Janowitz (sop—Pamina), Lucia Popp (sop—Queen of the Night), Nicolai Gedda (ten—Tamina), Walter Berry (bass—Papageno), Gottlob Frick (bass—Sarastro), O. Klemperer (cnd), Philharmonia Orch EMI Classics 2-▲ CDCB 55173
Orff, C.:Carmina burana, w. A. Augér (sop), J. Van Kesteren (ten), J. Summers (bar), R. Muti (cnd), Philharmonia Orch [G, L] EMI Classics ▲ CDC 47100
Orff, C.:Der Mond—Ein kleines Welttheater, w. R. Christ (ten), P. Kuén (ten), K. Schmitt-Walter (bar), H. Graml (bar), H. Hotter (b-bar), P. Lagger (bass), W. Sawallisch (cnd), Philharmonia Orch [G] EMI Classics ("Studio" series) 2-▲ CDMB 63712 [ADD]
Pärt, A.:Credo, w. B. Berman (pno), N. Järvi (cnd), Philharmonia Orch Chandos ▲ CHAN 9134 [DDD]
Prokofiev, S.:Cantata for the 20th Anniversary of the October Revolution, w. G. Rozhdestvensky (nar), N. Järvi (cnd), Philharmonia Orch Chandos ▲ CHAN 9095 [DDD]
Prokofiev, S.:Ivan the Terrible Cta, w. L. Finnie (mez), N. Storojev (bass), N. Järvi (cnd), Philharmonia Orch Chandos ▲ CHAN 8977 [DDD]
Sainton, P.:The Island, w. M. Bamert (cnd), Philharmonia Orch Chandos ▲ CHAN 9181 [DDD]
Sings Operetta, w. Elisabeth Schwarzkopf (sop), Philharmonia Orch, [cnd:O. Ackermann] EMI Classics ▲ CDC 47284
Strauss (II), Joh.:Die Fledermaus, w. E. Schwarzkopf (sop), R. Streich (sop), N. Gedda (ten), H. Krebs (ten), R. Christ (ten), E. Kunz (bar), K. Dönch (bar), H. von Karajan (cnd), Philharmonia Orch [G] EMI Classics ("Studio" series) 2-▲ CDHB 69531 (m) [ADD]
Strauss, R.:Der Rosenkavalier, w. Elisabeth Schwarzkopf (sop), Christa Ludwig (mez), Teresa Stich-Randall (mez), Otto Edelmann (b-bar), H. von Karajan (cnd), Philharmonia Orch *(rec 1956)* EMI Classics ▲ CDCC 56113 (m)
Strauss, R.:Der Rosenkavalier (sels), w. E. Schwarzkopf (sop), T. Stich-Randall (mez), C. Ludwig (mez), O. Edelmann (bass), H. von Karajan (cnd), Philharmonia Orch EMI Classics ▲ ZDM 63452
Vaughan Williams, R.:Sym 1, w. B. Valente (sop), T. Allen (bar), L. Slatkin (cnd), Philharmonia Orch RCA Red Seal ▲ 09026-61197-2
C.M. Giulini (cnd)
Mad About Angels, w. Cheryl Studer (sop), Christa Ludwig (mez), Anne Sofie von Otter (mez), José Carreras (ten), New York PO [cnd:Leonard Bernstein], English Baroque Soloists [cnd:John Eliot Gardiner], Philharmonia Orch, et al. Deutsche Grammophon ▲ 449113-2 ■ 449113-4
E. Kurtz (cnd)
Tchaikovsky, P.:Sleeping Beauty (sels) EMI Classics ▲ CDE 67790
Tchaikovsky, P.:Swan Lake (sels) EMI Classics ▲ CDE 67790
Philharmonia Women's Chorus
Debussy, C.:Nocturnes, w. G. Simon (cnd), Philharmonia Orch *(rec St. Jude-on-the-Hill, Hampstead, London, Jan 2–6, 1990)* Cala ▲ CACD 1002 [DDD]
Philippopolis
C. Arabadjiev (cnd)
Les voix de dieu:Russian Liturgical Orthodox Hymnal Songs Forlane ▲ FRL 16753 [DDD]
Phoenix Chamber Choir
C. Hultberg (cnd)
Ol Kosmos *(rec June 1994)* Skylark ▲ 9401 [DDD]
Piacenza Chorus
Bellini, V.:La sonnambula, w. M. Devia (sop), L. Canonici (ten), A. Verducci (bass), M. Viotti (cnd), Piacenza SO [I] *(rec live 11/88)* Nuova Era 2-▲ 6764/65 [DDD]
Donizetti, G.:Il furioso all'isola di Santo Domingo, w. P. Antonucci (sop), L. Serra (sop), E. Tandura (mez), L. Canonici (ten), R. Coviello (bar), Picconi (sgr), C. Rizzi (cnd), Piacenza SO [I] *(rec live, 11/10/87)* Bongiovanni 3-▲ GB 2056/58 [DDD]
Piacenza Polifonico Farnesiano Chorus
Traetta, T.:Stabat Mater, w. S. Krasteva (sop), I. Aramayo Sandivari (sgr), A. De Lucia (sgr), R. Gierlach (bar), I. Lo Vetere (cnd), Giovanile Ambrosiano Ensemble Bongiovanni ▲ GB 2127 [DDD]
Pioneer Choir
Bok, Skoraczewski (cnd)
Penderecki, K.:Utrenia, w. Delfina Ambroziak (sop), Stefania Woytowicz (sop), Krystyna Szczepanska (mez), Kazimierz Pustelak (ten), Boris Carmeli (bass), Wlodzimierz Denysenko (bass), A. Markowski (cnd), Warsaw PO, Warsaw National Phil Chorus *(rec Warsaw, 1973)* Polskie Nagrania ▲ PNCD 018
Michel Piquemal Vocal Ensemble
Debussy, C.:La Damoiselle élue, w. M. Delünsch (sop), S. Sullé (mez), J.-C. Casadesus (cnd), Lille National Orch Harmonia Mundi France ▲ HMC 901490
Debussy, C.:Nocturnes, w. J.-C. Casadesus (cnd), Lille National Orch Harmonia Mundi France ▲ HMC 901490
M. Piquemal (cnd)
Brahms, J.:Songs, Op. 104 *(rec 4/90)* Arion ▲ ARN 68132 [DDD]
Brahms, J.:Vocal Qts—Op. 112/1 & 2; Op. 64; Op. 17; Op. 92; Op. 30 *(rec 4/90)* Arion ▲ ARN 68132 [DDD]
Duruflé, M.:Mass, "Cum jubilo", w. Didier Henry (bar) *(rec Eglise Saint Antoine des Quinze-Vingts Paris, June & Oct. 1994)* Naxos ▲ 8.553197 [DDD]
Rossini, G.:Petite messe solennelle, w. Françoise Pollet (sop), Jacqueline Mayeur (mez), Jean-Luc Viala (ten), Michel Piquemal (bar), Raymond Alessandrini (pno), Emmanuel Mandrin (harm) Accord 2-▲ ACD 203562 [DDD]
Rossini, G.:Sacred Music, w. Evelyne Razimowsky (sop), Michel Piquemal (bar), Jean-Claude Pennetier (pno), Myriam Richardot (org)—La passegiata; Ave Marie; Inno Alla Pace; Ave Maria; Toast pour le nouvel an; Duetto Buffo di Due Batti; La fede; La speranza; La carita; Cantemus Domino; La notte del Santo Natalie; Preghiera; I Gondolieri Adès ▲ ADE 204192 [AAD]
Schubert, Franz:Kyrie [L] Gallo ▲ CD 584 [DDD]
Schubert, Franz:Mass 2, w. M. Pares-Reyna (sop), Fletcher (sgr), P. Fourcade (bass), Harmonia Nova Orch Ensemble [L] Gallo ▲ CD 584 [DDD]
Schubert, Franz:Mass 4, w. M. Pares-Reyna (sop), N. Stutzmann (alt), Fletcher (ten), P. Fourcade (bass), Harmonia Nova Orch Ensemble [L] Gallo ▲ CD 584 [DDD]
Schubert, Franz:Tantum ergo, D.739, w. Harmonia Nova Orch Ensemble [L] Gallo ▲ CD 584 [DDD]
P. Piquemal, Marco (cnd)
Fauré, G.:Messe basse, w. B. Thomas (cnd), Bernard Thomas CO, Petits Chanteurs de Paris, Argenteuil Vittoria Choir Forlane ▲ FRL 16536 [DDD]

CHORAL GROUPS

Michel Piquemal Vocal Ensemble (cont.)
P. Piquemal, Marco (cnd) (cont.)
Fauré, G.:Requiem, w. B. Thomas (cnd), Bernard Thomas CO, Petits Chanteurs de Paris, Argenteuil Vittoria Choir Forlane ▲ FRL 16536 [DDD]
Pittsburgh Mendelssohn Choir
R. Page (cnd)
Christmas!, w. D. Colwell (cnd), River City Brass Band *(rec Carnegie Library, July 1996)* RCBB ▲ BB 196 A [DDD]
Playford Consort
P. Holman (cnd)
Blow, J.:The Glorious Day Is Come, w. Suzie le Blanc (sop), Michael Chance (ct), Joseph Cornwell (ten), Richard Wistreich (bass), Parley of Instruments Hyperion ▲ CDA 66770
Draghi, G.B.:Song for St. Cecilia's Day Hyperion ▲ CDA 66770
Plifonia Choir
Pergolesi, G.B.:Mass in F, w. B. Retchitzka (sop), G. Ferracini (sop), M. Minetto (cta), V. Gohl (cta), C. Jauquier (ten), J. Loomis (bass), Milan Solisti *(rec 1967)* Rivoalto ▲ RIV 8922 [ADD]
Plovdiv Anghel Boukoreshtliev Choir
Samaras, S.:La Martyre, w. Luigi Illica (nar), B. Fidetzis (cnd), Pasardjik SO Orata ▲ ORAML 156
Plymouth Festival Chorus
Argento, D.:Te Deum [Verbi Domini cum verbus populi], w. P. Brunelle (cnd), Plymouth Festival Orch [L] Virgin Classics ▲ CDC 59009-2 [DDD]
Plymouth Music Series Chorus
Britten, B.:Paul Bunyan, w. *(soloists unknown)*, P. Brunelle (cnd), Plymouth Music Series Orch, Soloists [E] Virgin Classics 2-▲ 59126 [DDD]
Copland, A.:The Tender Land, w. P. Brunelle (cnd), Plymouth Music Series Orch Soloists [E] Virgin Classics 2-▲ 59207 [DDD]
Smyth, E.:The Boatswain's Mate, w. E. Harrhy (sop), J. Hardy (alt), D. Dressen (ten), J. Bohn (bass), P. Brunelle (cnd), Plymouth Music Series Orch—Mrs. Water's Aria Virgin Classics ▲ CDC 59022
Smyth, E.:The March of the Women, w. P. Brunelle (cnd), Plymouth Music Series Orch Virgin Classics ▲ CDC 59022
Smyth, E.:Mass in D, w. E. Harrhy (sop), J. Hardy (alt), D. Dressen (ten), J. Bohn (bass), P. Brunelle (cnd), Plymouth Music Series Orch Virgin Classics ▲ CDC 59022
Still, W.G.:Music of, w. William Warfield (nar), Yolanda Williams (sop), Hilda Harris (alt), P. Brunelle (cnd), Plymouth Music Series Orch, Leigh Morris Chorale—Wailing Woman; Swanee River; And They Lynched Him on a Tree; Miss Sally's Party Collins Classics ▲ COL 1454
Pochaev Lavra of the Dormiton Monks' Choir
D. Schemahegumen (cnd)
Thy Lavra is Joyful Today, Vol. 1 *(rec 1987)* Russian Compact Disc ▲ RCD 150061 [AAD]
A. Yary (cnd)
Thy Lavra is Joyful Today, Vol. 2 *(rec 1987)* Russian Compact Disc ▲ RCD 150062 [AAD]
Poliakin Chorale
Berlin, I.:Music of, w. R. Poliakin (cnd), Poliakin Orch—Easter Parade; With You; Let's Face the Music & Dance; I've Got My Love to Keep Me Warm; What'll I Do?; Say It Isn't So; How Deep Is the Ocean?; Now It Can Be Told; The Girl That I Marry; I'm Putting All My Eggs in One Basket; The Song Is Ended *(rec Syria Mosque, Pittsburgh; Belock Recording Studio, Bayside, NY)* Everest ▲ EVC 9027 [AAD]
Polifonica Ambrosiana Choir
G. Biella (cnd)
Spiritual Chants, w. J. Schabasser (cnd), Vienna Hofburg Chapel Choir Special Music 3-▲ S3D 5123
Polifonica Lucchese
Menichetti, D.:L'Epifania del Signore, w. K. Gamberucci (sop), F. Facini (bass), A. Palombi (sgr), A. Della Santa (sgr), F. Esposito (sgr), H. Handt (cnd), Toscana Accademia Strumentale Bongiovanni ▲ GB 5033 [DDD]
Polish Radio Chorus
Kievman, C.:Sym 2, w. D. D. Gier (cnd), Polish National RSO Katowice *(rec Katowice, Poland, June 29–July 3, 1995)* New Albion ▲ NA 081CD
Moniuszko, S.:Mass in E♭, w. H. Slonicka (sop), A. Malewicz (mez), W. Pilewski (bass), E. Kajdasz (cnd), Warsaw CO Olympia ▲ OLY 395 [ADD]
Moniuszko, S.:Sacred Music, w. H. Slonicka (sop), A. Malewicz (mez), W. Pilewski (bass), E. Kajdasz (cnd), Warsaw CO—Ne memineris; Vide humilitatem meam; Litanie Ostrobramskie, No. 1 Olympia ▲ OLY 395 [ADD]
Szymanowski, K.:Sym 2, w. J. Semkow (cnd), Polish National RSO Katowice EMI Classics ▲ CDM 65082
Szymanowski, K.:Sym 3, w. W. Ochman (ten), J. Semkow (cnd), Polish National RSO Katowice EMI Classics ▲ CDM 65082
Galonski, Kajdasz (cnd)
Gorczycki, G.G.:Sacred Choral Music, w. R. Stacewicz (sop), I. Tkaczyk (alt), A. Pagowska (alt), E. Sasiadek (ten), W. Brychcy (bass), Wroclaw Orch, Capella Bydgostiensis Pro Musica Antiqua, Madrigalists Choir—Completorium; In virtute tua; Iudica me deus; Laetatus sum; Missa paschalis [L] *(rec 1966)* Olympia ▲ OCD 320 [AAD]
E. Kajdasz (cnd)
Musica Antiqua Polonica:Choral Music from Poland, w. Polish Radio CO Olympia ▲ OLY 322 [ADD]
W. Lutoslawski (cnd)
Lutoslawski, W.:Poems of Henri Michaux, w. J. Krenz (cnd), Polish National RSO Katowice *(rec Katowice, 1964)* Polskie Nagrania ▲ PNCD 041 [AAD]
Polish Radio Women's Choir
Szymanowski, K.:Demeter, w. Krystyna Szostek-Radkowa (mez), Polish National RSO Katowice *(rec Concert Hall at the National PO, Warsaw, 1982)* Polskie Nagrania ▲ PLN 063 [ADD]
Polish Radio-TV Chorus
Kilar, W.:Angelus, w. D. Ambroziak (sop), *(orch unknown)* *(rec 1979 & 1985)* Olympia ▲ OCD 308 [AAD]
Kilar, W.:Exodus, *(orch unknown)* *(rec 1979 & 1985)* Olympia ▲ OCD 308 [AAD]
Penderecki, K.:Dies Irae, w. O. Szwajgier (sop), Z. Jankovski (ten), L. Mróz (bass), S. Kawalla (cnd), Polish Radio-TV SO [L] Vienna Modern Masters ▲ VMM 3015 [DDD]
Schoenberg, A.:A Survivor from Warsaw, w. D. Olbrychsk (nar), S. Kawalla (cnd), Polish Radio-TV SO [E] Vienna Modern Masters ▲ VMM 3015 [DDD]
Szymanowski, K.:Fragments from Poems by Jan Kasprowicz, w. Maksymiuk, Strugala, Wislocki (cnd), Polish Radio-TV SO—Tryptich Koch Schwann ▲ CD 312652 [DDD]
Szymanowski, K.:Stabat Mater, w. Maksymiuk, Strugala, Wislocki (cnd), Polish Radio-TV SO Koch Schwann ▲ CD 312652 [DDD]
Szymanowski, K.:Sym 3, w. Maksymiuk, Strugala, Wislocki (cnd), Polish Radio-TV SO Koch Schwann ▲ CD 312652 [DDD]
Van De Vate, N.:Katyn, w. S. Kawalla (cnd), Polish Radio-TV SO Vienna Modern Masters ▲ VMM 3015 [DDD]
Van De Vate, N.:Krakow Con, w. S. Kawalla (cnd), Polish Radio-TV SO Vienna Modern Masters ▲ VMM 3015 [DDD]
Polish State Phil Chorus
Szymanowski, K.:Demeter, w. A. Malewicz-Madej (cta), K. Stryja (cnd), Polish State PO Marco Polo ▲ 8.223293 [DDD]
Szymanowski, K.:King Roger, w. B. Zagòrzanka (sop), A. Malewicz-Madey (cta), H. Grychnik (ten), W. Ochman (ten), A. Hiolski (bar), L. A. Mròz (bass), K. Stryja (cnd), Polish State PO Katowice, Cracow Phil Boys' Chorus *(rec Apr. 7-9, 1990)* Marco Polo ("Opera Classics" series) 2-▲ 8.223339/40 [DDD]
Szymanowski, K.:Litany to the Virgin Mary, w. K. Stryja (cnd), Polish State PO Marco Polo ▲ 8.223293 [DDD]
Szymanowski, K.:Stabat Mater, w. J. Gadulanka (sop), K. Szostek-Radkowa (mez), A. Hlolski (bar), K. Stryja (cnd), Polish State PO Marco Polo ▲ 8.223293 [DDD]
Szymanowski, K.:Sym 3, w. W. Ochman (ten), K. Stryja (cnd), Polish State PO Marco Polo ▲ 8.223290 [DDD]
Szymanowski, K.:Veni Creator, w. B. Zagòrzanka (sop), K. Stryja (cnd), Polish State PO Marco Polo ▲ 8.223293 [DDD]

Polytech Choir
Schubert, Franz:Choral Part-Songs Ondine ▲ ODE 811 [DDD]
T. Länsiö (cnd)
Merikanto, A.:Choral Music—8 works for male chorus Ondine ▲ ODE 703-2
Polytech Men's Choir
Klami, U.:In the Belly of Vipunen, w. Petri Lindroos (bar), S. Oramo (cnd), Finnish RSO Ondine ▲ ODE 859 [DDD]
Pomerium Musices
Busnois, A.:Music of—In hydraulis; Anthony usqui lumina; Victim pascali; Regina celi; A que ville; Bel acueil; Je ne puis vivre Dorian ▲ DOR 90184 [DDD]
Busnois, A.:O crux lignum triumphale Dorian ▲ DOR 90184 [DDD]
Mass for St. Anthony of Padua Archiv ▲ 447722-2
A. Blachly (cnd)
Mannerist Revolution Dorian ▲ DOR 90154 [DDD]
Ponzan Boys' Choir
J. Kurczewski (cnd)
Górecki, H.-M.:Amen [Pol] *(rec 1976)* Olympia ▲ OCD 313 [AAD]
Portland Symphonic Choir
Flagello, N.:Passion of Martin Luther King, w. Raymond Bazemore (bass), Portland Symphonic Choir, J. DePreist (cnd), Oregon SO Koch International Classics ▲ KIC 7293-2 [DDD]
Poznan State PO Men & Boys' Choir
Polish Stars Sing the Carols, w. Zylis-Gara, Teresa (sop), Wieslaw Ochman (ten), Polish Radio-TV SO [cnd:Stefan Stuligrosz], Warsaw CO Polskie Nagrania Edition ▲ ECD 025
Prague Academie Muzichkych Umeni
Janácek, L.:Nursery Rhymes, w. T. Fischer (cnd), Netherlands Wind Ensemble Chandos ▲ CHAN 9399 [DDD]
Prague Chamber Choir
Abbesser, F.:Stabat Mater, w. J. Krček (cnd), Musica Bohemica Panton ▲ PAN 811180
Caldara, A.:Masses, w. J. Krček (cnd), Musica Bohemica—in F Panton ▲ PAN 811180
Dvořák, A.:Armida, w. Joanna Borowska (sop—Armida), Monika Brychtová (sgr—Siren), Wieslaw Ochman (ten—Rinald), Richard Sporka (ten—Dudo), Jan Markvart (bar—Sven), Pavel Daniluk (bass—King), George Fortune (bass—Ismen), Zdenek Harvánek (bass—Ubald), Miloslav Podskalský (bass—Peter), Milan Bürger (sgr—Gernand), Roman Janál (sgr—Muezzin/Hlasatel), Vratislav Kříz (sgr—Gottfried), Vladimír Nacházel (sgr—Roger), G. Albrecht (cnd), Czech PO *(rec 1995)* Orfeo 2-▲ 404962 [DDD]
Janácek, L.:Fate, w. Lívia Ághová (sop—Míla), Ludmila Nováková (sop—Frl. Stuhlá/Součková), Marta Benačková (cta—Mílas Mother), Štefan Margita (ten—Dr. Suda/Hrázda), Peter Straka (ten—Zivný), Ivan Kusnjer (bar—Konečný/Verva), Peter Mikuláš (bass—Lhotsky), G. Albrecht (cnd), Czech PO *(rec 1995)* Orfeo ▲ 384 951 [DDD]
Mahler, G.:Sym 3, w. Marta Benačková (alt), V. Neumann (cnd), Czech PO, Czech Phil Children's Choir *(rec House of Artists, Prague, Aug-Sept 1994)* Canyon Classics 2-▲ CD 256
Michna, A.V.:The Czech Lute, w. J. Krček (cnd), Musica Bohemica Panton ▲ PAN 811040
Mozart, W.A.:Missa, K.317, w. Ludmila Vernerova (sop), Marta Benackova (mez), Richard Sporka (ten), Ladislav Nezhyba (bass), G. Delogu (cnd), Prague Virtuosi *(rec Domovina Studio, Prague, June 4-6, 1994)* Discover International ▲ DI 920260 [DDD]
Mozart, W.A.:Vesperae solennes, w. Ludmila Vernerova (sop), Marta Benackova (mez), Richard Sporka (ten), Ladislav Nezhyba (bass), G. Delogu (cnd), Prague Virtuosi *(rec Domovina Studio, Prague, June 4-6, 1994)* Discover International ▲ DI 920260 [DDD]
Prustmann, I.:Miserere, w. J. Krček (cnd), Musica Bohemica Panton ▲ PAN 811180
Vanhal, J.B.:Missa Solemnis, w. Marta Filová (sop), Marta Benačková (mez), Jörg Dürmüller (ten), Jiří Sulzenko (bass), V. Neumann (cnd), Prague Virtuosi—Kyrie eleison, Adagio — Allegro; Christe eleison, Andante; Kyrie eleison, Allegro; Gloria, Allegro moderato; Laudamus te, Andante; Gratias agimus tibi, Allegro moderato; Domine Deus, Rex caelestis, andante; Domine Deus, Agnus Dei, Adagio; Quoniam tu solus sanctus, Allegro moderato, Cum sancto spiritu, Allegro; Credo, Allegro moderato, Et incarnatus est. Adagio; Et resurrexit, Allegro moderato; Sanctus, Adagio—Osanna, Allegro; Benedictus, Andante—Osanna, Allegro; Agnus Dei, Adagio; Dona nobis pacem, Allegro *(rec Evangelische Kirche der böhmischen Brüder, Prag, Sept 25-28, 1994)* Orfeo ▲ C 353 951 A [DDD]
R. Gandolfi (cnd)
Rossini, G.:Petite messe solennelle, w. Livia Aghova (sop), Marta Benackova (mez), Gil Manuel Beltran (ten), Peter Mikulas (bass), Raphaele Cortesi (pno), Peter Toperczer (pno), Josef Ksica (harm) *(rec Domovina Studios, Prague, Sept. 10-12, 1994)* Discover International 2-▲ DI 920324-5 [DDD]
Rossini, G.:Sacred Music—O Salutaris Hostia; Ave Maria; Cantemus Domino *(rec Domovina Studios, Prague, Sept. 10-12, 1994)* Discover International 2-▲ DI 920324-5 [DDD]
J. Pancik (cnd)
Bruckner, A.:Mass 3, w. Dagmar Masková (sgr), Vladimír Nacházel (sgr), Jiří Novotný (sgr), Jiří Seiler (sgr), Jiří Uherek (sgr), Eva Zbytovská (sgr), Jan Votava (trbn), Josef Kšica (org) Orfeo ▲ 327 951 [DDD]
Bruckner, A.:Motets, w. Dagmar Masková (sgr), Vladimír Nacházel (sgr), Jiří Novotný (sgr), Jiří Seiler (sgr), Jiří Uherek (sgr), Eva Zbytovská (sgr), Jan Votava (trbn), Josef Kšica (org)—Locus iste; Afferentur regi; Ave Maria (2); Pange lingua; Pange lingua (phrygisch); Tantum ergo (2); Libera me; Os iusti; Virga jesse; Vexilla regis; Christus factus est; Tota pulchra es Maria; Ecce sacerdos magnus Orfeo ▲ 327 951 [DDD]
Dvořák, A.:Mass, w. Dagmar Masková (sop), Marta Benacková (alt), Walter Coppola (ten), Peter Mikulás (bass), Josef Ksica (org) *(rec Dvořák Hall, Prague, Nov 1993)* ECM New Series ▲ 78118-21539-2 [DDD]
Dvořák, A.:Moravian Duets, Op. 32 Chandos ▲ CHAN 9257 [DDD]
Eben, Petr:Prague Te Deum, w. Josef Ksica (org) *(rec Dvořák Hall, Prague, Nov 1993)* ECM New Series ▲ 78118-21539-2 [DDD]
Eben, Petr:Prague Te Deum ECM ▲ 21539-2
Eben, Petr:Songs—5 Songs [from "About Swallows & Girls"] Chandos ▲ CHAN 9257 [DDD]
Janácek, L.:Our Father, w. Walter Coppola (ten), Josef Ksica (org) ECM ▲ 21539-2
Janácek, L.:Our Father, w. Lydie Härtelová (hp), Josef Ksica (org) [arr for hp, org & mixed chorus] *(rec Dvořák Hall, Prague, Nov 1993)* ECM New Series ▲ 78118-21539-2 [DDD]
Smetana, B.:Choruses Chandos ▲ CHAN 9257 [DDD]
Suk, J.:Songs, Op. 15, w. Daniel Buranovsky (pno), Marian Lapšanský (pno) Chandos ▲ CHAN 9257 [DDD]
Prague Chorus
Dvořák, A.:Armida, w. *(soloists unknown)*, V. Jiráček (cnd), Prague RSO *(rec Prague. 1956)* Multisonic ("Prague Opera Collection" series) 3-▲ 31 0246
Prague Festival Chorus
Orff, C.:Carmina burana, w. *(soloists unknown)*, P. Urbanek (cnd), Prague Festival Orch *(rec live)* LaserLight ▲ 14 020 [DDD]
Prague Madrigal Singers
M. Venhoda (cnd)
Dufay, G.:Masses—Missa Ecce ancilla Domini; Missa Ave Regina caelorum [L] Supraphon Collection ▲ 11 0637-2 [ADD]
Pascha, E.:Harmonia pastoralis—Christmas Mass in F Campion ▲ 1305 [AAD/DDD]
Prague National Theater Chorus
Blodek, V.:In the Well, w. J. Stych (cnd), Prague National Theater Orch Supraphon ▲ SUP 0033 [ADD]
Dvořák, A.:Rusalka, w. Milada Šubrtová (sop), Ivo Zídek (ten), Eduard Haken (bass), Z. Chalabala (cnd), Prague National Theater Orch Supraphon 2-▲ SUP 0013 [AAD]
Eduard Haken, w. Eduard Haken (bass), Prague National Theater Orch, Prague Smetana Theater Orch, Prague CO, Prague RSO Supraphon ▲ SUP 3186
Fibich, Z.:The Bride of Messina, w. G. Benackova (sop), L. Marova (mez), I. Zidek (ten), F. Jilek (cnd), Prague National Theater Orch Supraphon ▲ SUP 111492 [ADD]
Hába, A.:Quarter-Tone, w. J. Jirous (cnd), Prague National Theater Orch Supraphon ▲ SUP 108258 [ADD]

▲ = CD ♦ = Enhanced CD Δ = MD ■ = Cassette Tape ▯ = DCC

Prague National Theater Chorus (cont.)

Janácek, L.:The Cunning Little Vixen, w. Tattermuschova Helena (sop—Cunning Little Vixen), Eva Zikmundová (sop—The Fox), B. Gregor (cnd), Prague National Theater Orch *(rec 1970)* Supraphon 2-▲ SUP 3071

Janácek, L.:Jenůfa, w. Libuse Domininská (sop—Jenufa), Nadeshda Kniplová (sop—Kostelnicka), Vilém Príbyl (ten—Laca), Ivo Zidek (ten—Steva), B. Gregor (cnd), Prague National Theater Orch EMI Classics 2-▲ CDMB 65476

Janácek, L.:Kát'a Kabanová, w. D. Tikalová (sop), B. Blachut (ten), J. Krombholc (cnd), Prague National Theater Orch Supraphon 2-▲ SUP 108016 [ADD]

Janácek, L.:The Makropulos Affair, w. Libuse Prylova (sop), Helena Tattermuschová (sop), Rudolf Vanasek (ten), Ivo Zidek (ten), B. Gregor (cnd), Prague National Orch *(rec mid 1960's)* Supraphon 2-▲ SUP 108351 [AAD]

Martinů, B.:Julietta, w. M. Tauberová (sop), I. Zidek (ten), J. Krombholc (cnd), Prague National Theater Orch [Cz] *(rec 1964)* Supraphon 3-▲ 10 8176-2 [AAD]

Smetana, B.:The Bartered Bride, w. Drahomira Tikalová (sop), Ivo Zídek (ten), Eduard Haken (bass), Z. Chalabala (cnd), Prague National Theater Orch Supraphon 2-▲ SUP 0040 [AAD]

Smetana, B.:The Brandenbergers in Bohemia, w. V. Soukupova (sop), A. Vetava (ten), K. Kalas (bar), J.H. Tichy (cnd), Prague National Theater Orch [G] Supraphon 2-▲ SUP 111802 [AAD]

Smetana, B.:Dalibor, w. N. Kniplova (mez), V. Pribyl (ten), J. Jindrak (bar), J. Krombholc (cnd), Prague National Theater Orch [Cz] Supraphon 2-▲ 11 2185 [ADD]

Smetana, B.:Dalibor, w. Eva Urbanová (sgr), Leo Maria Vodička (ten), Iván Kusnjer (bar), Z. Košler (cnd), Prague National Theater Orch Supraphon 2-▲ SUP 0077 [DDD]

Smetana, B.:The Devil's Wall, w. Milada Šubrtová (sop), Ivana Mixová (mez), Václav Bednář (bass), Z. Chalabala (cnd), Prague National Theater Orch *(rec Prague, 1960)* Supraphon 2-▲ SUP 112201 [AAD]

Smetana, B.:Libuše, w. G. Benackova (sop), V. Soupukova (sop), V. Zitek (ten), Z. Košler (cnd), Prague National Theater Orch Supraphon 3-▲ SUP 111276 [DDD]

Smetana, B.:Libuše, w. Eva Urbanová (sop), Leo Marian Vodička (ten), O. Dohnányi (cnd), Prague National Theater Orch Supraphon 2-▲ SUP 3200

Smetana, B.:The 2 Widows, w. N. Sormova (sop), M. Machotková (sop), J. Zahradnicek (ten), F. Jílek (cnd), Prague National Theater Orch [Cz] *(rec 1975)* Supraphon 2-▲ SUP 11 2122 [AAD]

M. Maly (cnd)

Dvořák, A.:King & Charcoal Burner, w. Drahonira Drobkova (cta), Viktor Koci (ten), René Tucek (bar), Dalibor Jedlicka (bass), J. Chaloupka (cnd), Prague National Theater Orch [final version] *(rec 1989)* Supraphon ("Hidden Treasures from Prague" series) ▲ SUP CD 3078

Prague Phil Chorus

Dvořák, A.:Psalm 149, w. J. Bělohlávek (cnd), Czech PO [Cz] Chandos 2-▲ CHAN 8985/86 [DDD]

Dvořák, A.:Rusalka, w. G. Beňačkova (sop), V. Soukupová (mez), W. Ochman (ten), R. Novák (bass), V. Neumann (cnd), Czech PO [Cz] Supraphon Collection ▲ 11 0617-2 [DDD]

Dvořák, A.:Rusalka, w. G. Beňačkova (sop), V. Soukupová (mez), W. Ochman (ten), R. Novák (bass), V. Neumann (cnd), Czech PO [Cz] Supraphon 3-▲ 10 3641 [DDD]

Dvořák, A.:The Spectre's Bride, Op. 69, w. L. Aghova (sop), J. Protschka (ten), I. Kusnjer (bar), G. Albrecht (cnd), Hamburg State PO [Cz] *(rec live 1991)* Orfeo ▲ 259921 [DDD]

Dvořák, A.:Stabat Mater, w. L. Aghová (sop), M. Schiml (sop), A. Baldin (ten), L. Vele (bass), J. Bělohlávek (cnd), Czech PO [L] Chandos 2-▲ CHAN 8985/86 [DDD]

Górecki, H.-M.:Beatus Vir, w. N. Storjev (bass), J. Nelson (cnd), Czech PO Argo ▲ 436835-2 [DDD]

Górecki, H.-M.:Totus tuus Argo ▲ 436835-2 [DDD]

Havelka, S.:Music of, w. Brigita Sulcova (sop), Anna Barova (cta), Vladimir Dolezal (ten), Richard Novak (bass), V. Neumann (cnd), Czech PO—Epistola de M. Hieronymi De Praga Supplicio Panton ▲ PAN 810966

Kabeláč, M.:Sym 8, w. *(soloists unknown)*, V. Neumann (cnd), Prague Percussion Ensemble Panton ▲ PAN 811105

Liszt, F.:A Faust Sym, w. Peter Seiffert (ten), S. Rattle (cnd), Berlin PO EMI Classics ▲ CDC 55220

Mahler, G.:Sym 2, w. Nancy Gustafson (sop), Florence Quivar (mez), Z. Mehta (cnd), Israel PO *(rec Fredric R. Mann Auditorium, Tel Aviv, Jan-Feb. 1994)* Teldec ▲ 94545-2 [DDD]

Mahler, G.:Sym 8, w. Sylvia McNair (sop), Andrea Rost (sop), Cheryl Studer (sop), Anne Sofie von Otter (mez), Rosemarie Lang (cta), Peter Seiffert (ten), Bryn Terfel (bar), Jan-Hendrik Rootering (bass), C. Abbado (cnd), Berlin PO, Berlin Radio Chorus, Tölz Boys' Choir Deutsche Grammophon ("4D Audio" series) 2-▲ 445843-2

Mozart, W.A.:Masonic Music, w. P. Kühn (cnd), Prague CO—Masonic Cants. & Songs Supraphon ▲ SUP 112155 [DDD]

Rossini, G.:La donna del lago, w. K. Ricciarelli (sop), L. V. Terrani (mez), D. Raffanti (ten), S. Ramey (bass), M. Pollini (cnd), CO of Europe [I] CBS 2-▲ M2K 39311 [DDD]

Rossini, G.:Giovanna d'Arco, w. *(soloist unknown)*, E. Brizio (cnd), Prague PO Studio SM 3-▲ 12 23.27

Rossini, G.:L'italiana in Algeri, w. K. Battle (sop), M. Horne (mez), E. Palacio (ten), S. Ramey (bass), N. Zaccaria (bass), C. Scimone (cnd), Venice Solisti [I] Erato ("Libretto" series) 2-▲ 2292-45404-2

Rossini, G.:Sacred Music, w. E. Brizio (cnd), Prague PO—Kyrie; Credo; Gloria de Ravenne; Tantum Ergo; Kyrie; Pieces Liturgiques; Messe de Rimini; Miserere; Quoniam; Tantum Ergo Studio SM 3-▲ 12 23.27

Rossini, G.:The Siege of Corinth, w. L. Serra (sop), M. Comencini (ten), D. Raffanti (ten), A. Caforio (bass), M. Lippi (bass), P. Olmi (cnd), Genoa Teatro Carlo Felice Orch, Genoa Teatro Carlo Felice Chorus *(rec June 2 & 14, 1992)* Nuova Era 3-▲ 7140/42 [DDD]

Sarti, G.:Russian Oratorio, w. V. Smetáček (cnd), Bratislava SO Studio SM ▲ 2456

Veni Creator Supraphon ▲ SUP 111809

Verdi, G.:Messa per Rossini, w. G. Beňačková-Cápova (sop), F. Quivar (mez), J. Wagner (ten), A. Agache (bar), A. Haugland (bass), H. Rilling (cnd), Stuttgart RSO, Gächinger Kantorei [L] Hänssler Classic 2-▲ CD 98.949 [DDD] 2-■ MC 96.949 (D)

Wagner, R.:Lohengrin, w. A. Varnay (sop), I. Bjoner (sop), J. Thomas (ten), G. Neidlinger (b-bar), W. Sawallisch (cnd), La Scala Orch [G] *(rec live, Milan 1965)* Melodram 3-▲ MEL 37067 [AAD]

P. Kühn (cnd)

Dvořák, A.:The Spectre's Bride, Op. 110, w. Eva Urbanová (sop), Ludovit Ludha (ten), Ivan Kusnjer (b-bar), J. Bělohlávek (cnd), Prague SO *(rec live, 1995)* Supraphon ▲ SUP 3091

Shostakovich, D.:Sym 13, w. Peter Mikuláš (bass), M. Shostakovich (cnd), Prague SO Supraphon ▲ SUP 0160 [DDD]

L. Mátl (cnd)

Berlioz, H.:Requiem, "Grande Messe des Morts", w. Jean-Luc Viala (ten), A. Lombard (cnd), Bordeaux-Aquitaine National Orch, Slovak Phil Choir Forlane ▲ FRL 16639 [DDD]

J. Veselka (cnd)

Janácek, L.:Amarus, w. Vera Soukupová (mez), Vilém Přibyl (ten), F. Jílek (cnd), Czech PO *(rec Czech Raio Broadcast, 1974)* Praga ▲ PR 250100

Janácek, L.:Choruses Supraphon ▲ SUP 3022

Janácek, L.:Moravian Choruses Supraphon ▲ SUP 3022

Prague Phil Chorus members

Klein, G.:Czech & Russian Folk Songs *(rec Oct. 20 & 21, 1992)* Koch International Classics ▲ KIC 7230-2 [DDD]

Prague Radio Chorus

Dvořák, A.:The Cunning Peasant, w. Eva Depoltová (sop), Václav Zítek (bar), Karel Berman (bass), F. Vajnar (cnd), Prague RSO Supraphon 2-▲ SUP 0019 [DDD]

Fibich, Z.:At Twilight, w. F. Vajnar (cnd), Prague RSO Supraphon ▲ SUP 3197

Fibich, Z.:A Night at Karlstein, w. F. Vajnar (cnd), Prague RSO Supraphon ▲ SUP 3197

Fibich, Z.:The Romance of Spring, w. Nada Sormova (sop), Karel Prusa (bass), F. Vajnar (cnd), Prague RSO Supraphon ▲ SUP 3197

Fibich, Z.:Spring, w. F. Vajnar (cnd), Prague RSO Supraphon ▲ SUP 3197

Foerster, J.B.:Eva, w. Eva Depoltová (sop), Anna Barová (mez), Leo Marian Vodicka (ten), Jaroslav Soucek (bar), F. Vajnar (cnd), Prague RSO *(rec 1982)* Supraphon 2-▲ SUP 3001

Kozeluch, Joh. A.:Missa Pastoralis, w. S. Losová (sop), Y. Škvárová (cta), M. Švejda (ten), M. Podskalsky (bass), B. Kulínský (cnd), Prague PO Multisonic ▲ 31 0003-2 [ADD]

Martinů, B.:Hymn to St. James, w. N. Romanová (sop), D. Drobková (cta), R. Novák (ten), P. Haničinec (nar), P. Kühn (cnd), Prague SO members [Cz] *(rec 2-3/88)* Supraphon ▲ 11 0751-2 [DDD]

Prague Radio Chorus (cont.)

Martinů, B.:The Miracles of Mary, w. J. Bělohlávek (cnd), Prague SO Supraphon ▲ SUP 111802 [DDD]

Skroup, F.:Columbus (sels), w. M. Subrtová (sop), B. Blachut (ten), Z. Otava (bar), F. Dyk (cnd), Prague RSO *(rec 1962)* Multisonic ("Prague Opera Collection" series) ▲ 31 0153

Smetana, B.:The Bartered Bride, w. *(soloists unknown)*, K. Ančerl (cnd), Prague RSO *(rec 1947)* Multisonic ("Prague Opera Collection" series) ▲ 31 0185 [ADD]

Smetana, B.:Choral Music, w. Miroslav Švejda (ten), Vratislav Jahna (bar), Jaroslav Horáček (bass), Z. Košler (cnd), Prague SO, Czech Phil Chorus Supraphon ▲ SUP CD 3040

Smetana, B.:Dalibor, w. G. Abrahamová (sop), Vílém Přibyl (ten), J. Krombholc (cnd), Prague RSO [Cz] *(rec Sept. 1977)* Praga 2-▲ PR 250050/51

Vaughan Williams, R.:Flos Campi, w. Lubomír Malý (va), M. Konvalinka (cnd), Prague SO *(rec Smetana Hall, Prague, Dec. 15 & 21-22, 1987)* Panton ("Panorama" series) ▲ PAN 811306

J. Pinkas (cnd)

Dvořák, A.:Vanda, w. Drahomira Tikalova (sop), Stefa Petrova (mez), Beno Blachut (ten), Karel Kalas (bass), F. Dyk (cnd), Prague RSO *(rec 1951)* Supraphon ("Hidden Treasures from Prague" series) 2-▲ SUP CD 3007 (m)

Prague Radio Men's Chorus

Martinů, B.:Mount of 3 Lights, w. V. Dolezal (ten), R. Novák (bass), P. Haničinec (nar), J. Hora (org), P. Kühn (cnd), Kühn Chorus [Cz] *(rec 2-3/88)* Supraphon ▲ 11 0751-2 [DDD]

Martinů, B.:The Prophecy of Isaiah, w. N. Romanová (sop), D. Drobková (alto), R. Novák (bass), V. Kozderka (tpt), J. Peruška (va), I. Kiezlich (timp), S. Bogunia (pno), P. Kühn (cnd), Kühn Chorus [Cz] *(rec 2-3/88)* Supraphon ▲ 11 0751-2 [DDD]

Prague Radio Women's Chorus

Janácek, L.:The Diary of One Who Disappeared, w. Věra Soukupová (mez), Stepanka Stepanova (mez), Beno Blachut (ten), Nicolai Gedda (ten), Josef Paleníček (pno), Czech Chamber Singers Female Chorus—contains 2 complete performances *(rec 1984 & 1956)* Supraphon ▲ SUP 0022 [DDD/ADD]

Prague Soloists Choir

Ryba, J.J.:Church Music, w. J. Bělohlávek, New Czech CO—Mass in C; Mass in e; Mass in B♭ Multisonic ▲ 31 0200 [DDD]

Prague Sym Chorus

Massenet, J.:La Vierge, w. M. Command (sop), M. Castets (sop), M. Olmeda (sop), M. Keller (sop), P. Salmon (ten), M. Hacquard (bar), P. Fournillier (cnd), Prague SO Koch Schwann 2-▲ CD 313084 [DDD]

Paisiello, G.:Gloria Patri, w. E. Brizio (cnd), Prague SO *(rec June 1994)* Studio SM ▲ 12 23 89

Paisiello, G.:Missa in pastorale per il Natale per la cappella del Primo Consolo, w. E. Brizio (cnd), Prague SO *(rec June 1994)* Studio SM ▲ 12 23 89

Paisiello, G.:Tantum ergo, w. E. Brizio (cnd), Prague SO *(rec June 1994)* Studio SM ▲ 12 23 89

Paisiello, G.:Tecum principium, w. E. Brizio (cnd), Prague SO *(rec June 1994)* Studio SM ▲ 12 23 89

Stravinsky, I.:Les Noces, w. Z. Košler (cnd), Prague SO members Praga ▲ PR 250057

Prague Sym Youth Chorus

Krása, H.:Anna's Song, w. Group for New Music Koch International Classics ▲ KIC 7151

Krása, H.:Brundibár, w. Group for New Music Koch International Classics ▲ KIC 7151

Krása, H.:Songs, w. Group for New Music Koch International Classics ▲ KIC 7151

B. Kulinsky (cnd)

Ave Maria:Famous Sacred Choral Works, w. Bambini di Praga Multisonic ▲ MUL 310163 [DDD]

Prefontaine Montreal Choeur Classique

M. Lacasse (cnd)

Bach, J.S.:Motets, BWV 225-30, w. Yves-G. Préfontaine (org/hpd) Analekta Fleur de Lys ▲ FL 2 3001 [DDD]

Princeton Glee Club

Schoenberg, A.:Gurrelieder, w. R. Bampton (sop), P. Althouse (ten), L. Stokowski (cnd), Philadelphia Orch, Fortnightly Club, Mendelssohn Club Philadelphia *(rec live Apr. 9, 1932)* Pearl 2-▲ PEA 9066 [AAD]

Prinknash Abbey Monks' Choir

Latin Plainchant & English Chant Saydisc ■ C 330

O Give Thanks to the Lord, w. Stanbrook Abbey Nuns Choir Saydisc ■ CSDL 349 (D)

Pro Arte Chorale

Bach, J.S.:Masses, BWV 233-36, "Lutheran Masses", w. A. Giebel (sop), G. Litz (mez), H. Prey (bar), K. Redel (cnd), Pro Arte Orch—BWV 233 in F Philips 2-▲ 438739-2

Mozart, W.A.:Missa Solemnis, w. Christa Goetze (sop), Anna Schaffner (alt), Barnhard Gärtner (ten), Rudolf Rosen (bass), Philippe Laubscher (org), F. Pantillon (cnd), Bieler SO, Bern Vocal Ensemble Gallo ▲ CD 893 [DDD]

Pantillon, F.:Bethlehem, w. Christa Goetze (sop), Rudolf Rosen (nar), Philippe Laubscher (org), F. Pantillon (cnd), Bieler SO, Bern Vocal Ensemble Gallo ▲ CD 893 [DDD]

B. Folse (cnd)

Satoh, S.:Stabat mater, w. J. Thorngren (sop) New Albion ▲ NA 016 [DAD]

Pro Arte Lausanne

Mozart, W.A.:Zauberflöte, w. S. Jo (sop), L. Orgonasova (sop), Martina Bovet (sop), G. Winbergh (ten), H. Hagegard (bar), A. Jordan (cnd), Paris Orchestral Ensemble, Romande Chamber Choir Erato 2-▲ 2292-45469-2 [DDD]

Stravinsky, I.:Music of, w. N. Järvi (cnd), Swiss Romande Orch, Romande Chamber Choir—Oedipus Rex; Sym. In E♭, Op. 1; Con. for Violin [w. L. Mordkovitch]; Petruchka (1911 version); Apollon Musagète; Circus Polka; Le chant du Rossignol; Sym. in 3 Movements; Capriccio for Piano & Orch. [w. G. Tozer]; Sym. in C; Sym. of Psalms; Con. for Piano & Winds [w. B. Berman] Chandos 5-▲ CHAN 9240 [DDD]

Pro Arte Singers

T. Binkley (cnd)

Beyond Plainsong:Tropes & Polyphony in the Medieval Church Focus ▲ FOCUS 943

Dufay, G.:The Annunciation of the Blessed Mary Focus ▲ FOCUS 941

Pro Cantione Antiqua

M. Brown (cnd)

Allegri, G.:Miserere[L] IMP Classics ▲ PCD 806 [DDD]

Ars Britannica Teldec 2-▲ 46004-2

Brito, E. de:Sacred Music—Lamentationes Jeremiae Prophetae; Ego dilecto meo; Vidi Dominum; Agnus Dei & Communio Teldec ("Das Alte Werk" series) ▲ 93690-2 [ADD]

Byrd, W.:Mass in 4 Parts ASV Quicksilva ▲ ASQ 6132 [ADD]

Cardoso, M.:Sacred Music—Missa pro defunctis; Asperges me; Lamentationes Jeremiae Prophetae; Magnificat sexti toni Teldec ("Das Alte Werk" series) ▲ 93690-2 [ADD]

Hallelujah, w. [cnd:Andreas Kröper], Brnenský Academy Chorus Sbor, Prague Gioio della Musica IMP Classics ("Allegro" series) ▲ ALGPCD 1094 [DDD]

John IV:Crux fidelis Teldec ("Das Alte Werk" series) ▲ 93690-2 [ADD]

Lôbo, D.:Magnificat octavi toni Teldec ("Das Alte Werk" series) ▲ 93690-2 [ADD]

Magalhães, F. de:Sacred Music—Asperges me; Missa de Beata Virgine Maria Teldec ("Das Alte Werk" series) ▲ 93690-2 [ADD]

Medieval Christmas, w. Medieval Wind Ensemble IMP Classics ▲ PCD 844 [DDD]

Melgaz, D.D.:Motets, w. R. Aldwinckle (org), C. Harper (hp) Hyperion ▲ CDA 66715

Morago, E.L.:Motets, w. R. Aldwinckle (org), C. Harper (hp) Hyperion ▲ CDA 66715

Morago, E.L.:Sacred Music—Jesu Redemptor; Laudate pueri; Commissa mea; Magnificat octavi toni; Oculi mei Teldec ("Das Alte Werk" series) 3-▲ 93690-2 [ADD]

Palestrina, G.:Missa brevis IMP Masters ▲ ALGPCD 1076 [DDD]

Palestrina, G.:Missa "Lauda Sion" IMP Masters ▲ ALGPCD 1076 [DDD]

Palestrina, G.:Motets IMP Masters ▲ ALGPCD 1076 [DDD]

Purcell, H.:Music of, w. Collegium Aureum members—Incidental Music from Oedipus; Rounds & Catches [Christchurch Bells; I Gave Her Cakes & Ale; He That Drinks Is Immortal; Tom the Taylor; Sir Walter; My Lady's Coachman John; As Roger Last Night]; 'Tis Wine Was Made to Rule the Day; Arise Ye Subterranean Winds; Lost Is My Quiet Forever; When the Cock Begins to Crow; Hark, How the Wild Musicians; Not All My Torments; Laudate Ceciliam Ars Musici ▲ 1141 [ADD]

Tallis, T.:The Lamentations of Jeremiah [L] IMP Classics ▲ PCD 806 [DDD]

CHORAL GROUPS

Pro Cantione Antiqua (cont.)
M. Brown (cnd) (cont.)
Tallis, T.:Spem in alium [L] IMP Classics ▲ PCD 806 [DDD]
H. Hennig (cnd)
Monteverdi, C.:Vespro della Beata Vergine, w. Musica Fiata, Collegium Aureum, Hanover Boys' Choir Ars Musici 2-▲ 1000 [AAD]
J. O'Donnell (cnd)
The Essential Gregorian Chant, w. James Griffett (ten), Ian Partridge (ten), Michael George (b-bar), Stephen Roberts (b-bar), Gordon Jones (bass) United ▲ UNI 88035 [DDD]
J. O'Donnell (cnd)
The Essential Gregorian Chant, w. James Griffett (ten), Ian Partridge (ten), Stephen Roberts (bar), Michael George (bass), Gordon Jones (bass) Cala ▲ CAL CACD 88035 [DDD]
A Gregorian Feast Carlton ("Musick's Monument" series) ▲ MSK 6500012
Gregorian Lent & Easter, w. J. Griffett (ten), I. Partridge (ten), S. Roberts (bar), M. George (bass), G. Jones (bass) *(rec All Saints, East Finchley, Dec 7-9, 1993)* United ▲ UNI 88016 [DDD]
B. Turner (cnd)
Lassus, O. de:Lauda Sion salvatorem, w. B. Turner (cnd), Pro Cantione Antiqua Editio Classica ▲ 77083-2-RG [ADD]
Lassus, O. de:Magnificat, w. Collegium Aureum, Pro Cantione Antiqua Editio Classica ▲ 77066-2-RG [ADD]
Lassus, O. de:Missa Puisque j'ay perdu, w. B. Turner (cnd), Pro Cantione Antiqua Editio Classica ▲ 77083-2-RG [ADD]
Lassus, O. de:Motets, w. Collegium Aureum, Pro Cantione Antiqua Editio Classica ▲ 77066-2-RG [ADD]
Lassus, O. de:Musica Dei donum optimi, w. Pro Cantione Antiqua Editio Classica ▲ 77083-2-RG [ADD]
Lassus, O. de:Requiem, w. Collegium Aureum, Pro Cantione Antiqua Editio Classica ▲ 77066-2-RG [ADD]
Palestrina, G.:Missa de Beata Virgine, w. B. Turner (cnd), Pro Cantione Antiqua—Motets:Peccantem me quotidie; Dominus Jesus in qua nocte; Antiphon—Alma redemptoris mater [L] ASV Quicksilva ▲ QS 6086 [ADD]
Palestrina, G.:Missa "Papae marcelli", w. B. Turner (cnd), Pro Cantione Antiqua [L] ASV Quicksilva ▲ QS 6086 [ADD]
Palestrina, G.:The Song of Songs, w. Bruno Turner (cnd), Pro Cantione Antiqua Hyperion ▲ CDA 66733
Palestrina, G.:Stabat mater, w. B. Turner (cnd), Pro Cantione Antiqua [L] ASV Quicksilva ▲ QS 6086 [ADD]
Tavener, J.:Sacred Music, w. B. Turner (cnd), Pro Cantione Antiqua ASV Quicksilva ▲ ASQ 6132 [ADD]
Taverner, J.:Sacred Music, w. B. Turner (cnd), Pro Cantione Antiqua ASV Quicksilva ▲ ASQ 6132 [ADD]
Tears & Lamentations:Music from the Fairfax Manuscript & Henry VII's Book ASV ("Quicksilva" series) ▲ ASQ 6151 [DDD]
Victoria, T.L. de:Tenebrae Responsories, w. B. Turner (cnd), Pro Cantione Antiqua Editio Classica ▲ 77056-2-RG [ADD] ▀ 77056-4-RG

Pro Cantu
P. Rathje (cnd)
Aakjær Sange:Songs by Jeppe Aakjær *(rec Hall of the Sorø Academy)* Danica ▲ DCD 8174
Pro Christe Choir
Handel, G.F.:Messiah, w. Helen Kucharek (sop), Jennifer Smith (sop), Linda Finnie (mez), Niel Mackie (ten), Rodney Macann (b-bar), T. Dean (cnd), Pro Christe Orch *(rec St. Augustine's Church, Kilburn, London, 1986)* Guild 2-▲ GMDD 7112/3 [ADD]
Pro Civitate Christiana di Assisi Chorus
Rota, N.:Mysterium, w. A. Tuccari (sop), C. Vozza (mez), G. Sinimberghi (ten), U. Trama (bass), A. Renzi (cnd), Pro Civitate Christiana di Assisi Orch *(rec live 1962)* Claves ▲ CD 9323 [DDD]
Pro Musica Chamber Choir
Rosenberg, H.:Sym 4, w. Håkan Hagegård (bar), S. Ehrling (cnd), Gothenburg SO, Rilke Ensemble members, Swedish Radio Chorus Caprice ▲ CAP 21429 [DDD]
Where Love Reigns Swedish Society ▲ SCD 1050
Pro Musica Chorus
Musica para una boda Mexicana:Music for a Mexican Wedding, w. Lourdes Ambriz (sop), Grace Echauri (mez), Mexico CO Soloists Ensemble [cnd:Luis Sergio Hernandez] Spartacus ▲ 21015
Pro Musica Sacra Chorus
Schubert, Franz:Lazarus, or Die Feier der Auferstehung, w. Antonia Fahberg (sop), H. Banzhaf (cnd), Pro Musica Sacra Orch Studio SM ▲ 2498
Progetto Musica Vocal Ensemble
Ancina, G.:L'amorosa ero fatta spirituale, w. G. Monaco (cnd), Progetto Musica Instrumental Ensemble *(rec Santuario di Graglia, Mar. 1995)* Tactus ▲ TC 520001 [DDD]
Arascione, G.:Nuove laudi ariose della Beatissima Virgine scelte da diversi autori, w. G. Monaco (cnd), Progetto Musica Instrumental Ensemble *(rec Santuario di Graglia, Mar. 1995)* Tactus ▲ TC 520001 [DDD]
Palestrina, G.:Missa "In minoribus", w. G. Monaco (cnd), Progetto Musica Instrumental Ensemble *(rec Santuario di Graglia, Mar. 1995)* Tactus ▲ TC 520001 [DDD]
Razzi, G.:Laude spirituale, w. G. Monaco (cnd), Progetto Musica Instrumental Ensemble—Book 1 *(rec Santuario di Graglia, Mar. 1995)* Tactus ▲ TC 520001 [DDD]
Prohlis Church Choir Dresden
G. Schwarze (cnd)
Hell brennt ein Licht [Bright Burns a Light], w. Carl Maria von Weber School for Music Soloists, Dresden Church Choirs members, Dresden Wind Collegium members Christophorus ▲ 77165 [DDD]
Provence Camerata Chorus
Boieldieu, F.-A.:Le Calife de Bagdad, w. L. Mayo (sop), J. Michelini (sop), C. Cheriez (mez), L. Dale (ten), H. Rhys-Evans (ten), A. de Almeida (cnd), Camerata Provence Orch [F] Sonpact ▲ SPT 93007 [DDD]
Provence Vocal Ensemble
H. Guy (cnd)
Poulenc, F.:Figure humaine [F] Pierre Verany ▲ PV.788111 [ADD]
Poulenc, F.:Motets (4) pour le temps de Noël [F] Pierre Verany ▲ PV.788111 [ADD]
Poulenc, F.:Quatre petites prières de Saint François d'Assise [F] Pierre Verany ▲ PV.788111 [ADD]
Poulenc, F.:Salve regina [F] Pierre Verany ▲ PV.788111 [ADD]
Provence-Alpes-Côte d'Azur Regional Choir
Donizetti, G.:Messa di Gloria e Credo, w. Danielle Borst (sop), Hélène Jossoud (mez), Jean-Luc Viala (ten), Vincent Le Texier (bass-bar), M. Piquemal (cnd), Avignon-Provence Regional Lyric Orch, Accord ▲ ACD 212142 [DDD]
Psallette de Lorraine
Helfer, C. d':Missa pro defunctis, w. B. Fabre-Garrus (cnd), Toulouse Saqueboutiers, A Sei Voci Astrée ▲ E 8521
Psalmody
While Shepherds Watched:Christmas Music from English Parish Churches, 1740-1830, w. P. Holman (cnd), Parley of Instruments Hyperion ("English Orpheus" series) ▲ CDA 66924
P.S. 12 Boys' Choir
Mahler, G.:Sym 8, w. L. Stokowski (cnd), Philharmonic SO, Westminster Choir, Schola Cantorum *(rec 1950)* Music & Arts 2-▲ MUA 280 [AAD]
Giacomo Puccini Grosseto Chorale
F. Iannitti (cnd)
Tra classico e popolare Fonè ▲ 84F02 CD [ADD]
Pühtica Dormition Convent Choir
Sister Georgia (cnd)
There Is a Small Convent in the Far Land... RCD ▲ RCD 15011 [ADD]

Purcell Consort of Voices
Harrison, Dobson, Smithers (cnd)
Now Make We Merthe, w. London Brass Ensemble, All Saints Boys' Choir *(rec May 1965, Dec. 21-22, 196)* Boston Skyline ▲ BSD 121 [ADD]
Purcell Singers
Holst, G.:Psalms 86 & 148, w. I. Partridge (ten), R. Downes (org), I. Holst (cnd), English CO—Psalm 86 EMI Classics ▲ CDC 49784
Pythagore Vocal Ensemble
Lefébure-Wély, L.J.A.:Music of, w. Sylvie de May (sop), Sophie Fournier (sop), Catherine Ravenne (alt), Antoine Espagno (db), Vincent Genvrin (org), La Lyre Seraphique—Sainte cité, demeure permanente; Récit de Hautbois ou de Trompette harmonique; L'Encens divin; Offertoire [grand choeur]; Seigneur dès ma première enfance; Verset; Pleins de ferveur; Marche; Jour heureux, sainte allégresse; Esprit divin, Dieu de lumière; Andante, choeur de voix humaines; Afin d'être docile et sage; Mon fils, pour apprendre; Andante; Motet à la Sainte-Vierge; Andante; Du Roi des cieux tout célèbre la gloire; Scène pastorale; Andantino Media 7 ▲ 004 [DDD]
Pyuchtize Convent Choir
Russian Choirs Sing for the Children of Chernobyl, w. Moscow Patriarchate Children's Choir, Church of the Resurrection Choir Moscow, Korez Convent Choir, Zagorsk Monks' Choir, Moscow Religious Academy Choir, Moscow Religious Academy Choir, Dormition of the Virgin Church Choir Koch Schwann ▲ SCH 313322 [ADD/DDD]
Quattro Stagioni Vocal Quartet
Cantio:20th Century Norwegian Vocal Music Norway Music ▲ QCD 9303
Quink
Carols around the World Telarc ▲ CD 80202 [DDD] ▀ CS 30202 (D)
de Leeuw, T.:Music of—Missa Brevis (1953); Prière (1954); En begheeft my niet (1954); Egidius, waer bestu bleven? (1954); Het visschertje (1954) *(rec Commandery Room, Masonic Temple, Cleveland, OH, May 15-17, 1995)* Telarc ▲ CD 80384 [DDD]
English Madrigals *(rec Dec. 1991 & Jan. 1992)* Telarc ▲ CD 80328 [DDD]
Folk Songs of the World Telarc ▲ CD 80275 [DDD]
Heppener, R.:Canti carnascialeschi—Trionto di Bacco e d'Arianna (sel) *(rec Commandery Room, Masonic Temple, Cleveland, OH, May 15-17, 1995)* Telarc ▲ CD 80384 [DDD]
Kerstens, H.:Music of—Als ghy van de doodt sult zijn verbeten, Op. 38; Les mortels, Op. 19b *(rec Commandery Room, Masonic Temple, Cleveland, OH, May 15-17, 1995)* Telarc ▲ CD 80384 [DDD]
Manneke, D.:Choral Music—Madrigal:"Le città sottili" (1986); Psaume 121, "I Lift up Mine Eyes" (1960); Due Canti for Solo Voice & Chorus (1986) *(rec Commandery Room, Masonic Temple, Cleveland, OH, May 15-17, 1995)* Telarc ▲ CD 80384 [DDD]
Renaissance Madrigals Telarc ▲ CD 80209 [DDD]
Quodlibet
R. Morton (cnd)
Christmas Day, w. Queensland PO *(rec Thomas Dixon Centre, West End, Brisbane & the Great Hall of Brisbane Grammar School, 1992-93)* Tall Poppies ▲ TP 46 [DDD]
Radcliffe Choral Society
Berlioz, H.:La Damnation de Faust, w. Suzanne Danco (sop), David Poleri (ten), Martial Singher (bar), Donald Gramm (bass), McHenry Boatwright (bass), Joseph de Pasquale (va), Louis Speyer (hn), C. Munch (cnd), Boston SO, Harvard Glee Club *(rec Feb 1954)* RCA Victor Gold Seal 8-▲ 0902-668444-2 [ADD]
Berlioz, H.:Roméo et Juliette, w. Margaret Roggero (mez), Leslie Chabay (ten), Yi-Kwei Sze (bass), C. Munch (cnd), Boston SO, Harvard Glee Club *(rec Feb 1953)* RCA Victor Gold Seal 8-▲ 0902-668444-2 [ADD]
Berlioz, H.:Roméo et Juliette, w. M. Roggero (mez), L. Chabay (ten), Y. Sze (bass), C. Munch (cnd), Boston SO, Harvard Glee Club RCA Gold Seal 2-▲ 09026-60681-2
Debussy, C.:La Damoiselle élue, w. V. de los Angeles (sop), C. Smith (mez), C. Munch (cnd), Boston SO [F] RCA Gold Seal 2-▲ 7940-2-RG [ADD]
Radio City Music Hall Chorus
Charpentier, M.-A.:Louise (sels), w. Grace Moore (sop), Josef Schmidt (ten), Robert Weede (bar), E. Rapée (cnd), Radio City Music Hall Orch—Depuis le jour Enterprise ("The Radio Years" series) ▲ ENT RY 58
Leoncavallo, R.:Pagliacci (sels), w. Grace Moore (sop), Josef Schmidt (ten), Robert Weede (bar), E. Rapée (cnd), Radio City Music Hall Orch—Stridono lassù Enterprise ("The Radio Years" series) ▲ ENT RY 58
Massenet, J.:Manon (sels), w. Grace Moore (sop), Josef Schmidt (ten), Robert Weede (bar), E. Rapée (cnd), Radio City Music Hall Orch—Obéissons quand leur voix appelle [Gavotte] Enterprise ("The Radio Years" series) ▲ ENT RY 58
Puccini, G.:La Bohème (sels), w. Grace Moore (sop), Josef Schmidt (ten), Robert Weede (bar), E. Rapée (cnd), Radio City Music Hall Orch—Che Gelida Manina; Sì, Mi Chiamano Mimì; O Soave Fanciulla Enterprise ("The Radio Years" series) ▲ ENT RY 58
Puccini, G.:Madama Butterfly (sels), w. Grace Moore (sop), Josef Schmidt (ten), Robert Weede (bar), E. Rapée (cnd), Radio City Music Hall Orch—Vogliatemi Bene Enterprise ("The Radio Years" series) ▲ ENT RY 58
Puccini, G.:Tosca (sels), w. Grace Moore (sop), Josef Schmidt (ten), Robert Weede (bar), E. Rapée (cnd), Radio City Music Hall Orch—Recondita Armonia; Vissi d'Arte; E Lucevan le Stelle; Te Deum Enterprise ("The Radio Years" series) ▲ ENT RY 58
Ramsey Singers
M. Fenton (cnd)
Bax, A.:Choral Music—Epithalium; Gloria; Magnificat; Nunc Dimittis; Te Deum ASV ▲ ASV 941
Whitlock, P.:Choral Music—Communion Service in G; Evening Cantata; 3 Introits; Magnificat & Nunc Dimittis in D; Magnificat & Nunc Dimittis on plainsong; Solemn Te Deum ASV ▲ ASV 941
Randolph Singers
Randolph Singers CRI ▀ C 102
Raugel Chorus
Charpentier, G.:Louise, w. N. Vallin (sop—Louise), C. Gaudel (sop—Irma), A. Lecouvreur (mez—Mother), G. Thill (ten—Julien), A. Pernet (bass—Father), E. Bigot (cnd), Raugel Orch *(rec 1936)* Nimbus (Prima Voce) ▲ NI 7829 (m) [ADD]
RCA Italiana Opera Chorus
Puccini, G.:Madama Butterfly (sels), w. Leontyne Price (sop), Rosalind Elias (mez), Piero De Palma (ten), Richard Tucker (ten), Phillip Maero (bar), E. Leinsdorf (cnd), RCA Italian Opera Orch RCA Victor ▲ 09026-68089-2; ▀ 09026-68089-4
Verdi, G.:Falstaff, w. M. Freni (sop), I. Ligabue (sop), G. Simionato (mez), R. Elias (mez), R. Krause (ten), G. Evans (bar), R. Merrill (bar), G. Solti (cnd), RCA Italian Opera Orch [I] London 2-▲ 417168-2 [ADD]
Verdi, G.:Rigoletto, w. A. Moffo (sop), R. Elias (mez), A. Kraus (ten), R. Merrill (bar), G. Solti (cnd), RCA Italian Opera Orch [I] RCA Gold Seal 2-▲ 6506-2-RG [ADD]
Verdi, G.:Rigoletto, w. A. Moffo (sop), R. Elias (mez), A. Kraus (ten), R. Merrill (bar), G. Solti (cnd), RCA Italian Opera Orch [I] RCA Gold Seal ▲ 60203-2-RG ▀ 60203-4-RG
RCA Victor Chorus
Blitzstein, M.:The Airborne, w. W. Scheff (bar), R. Shaw (nar), L. Bernstein (cnd), New York City SO RCA Gold Seal ▲ 09026-62568-2
Gershwin, G.:Porgy & Bess (sels), w. H. Boatwright (sop), L. Price (sop), W. Warfield (bar), S. Henderson (cnd), RCA Victor SO [E] RCA Gold Seal ▲ 5234-2-RG [ADD]
The Voices of Living Stereo, Vol. 2, w. Farrell, Eileen (sop), Birgit Nilsson (sop), Roberta Peters (sop), Leontyne Price (sop), Galina Vishnevskaya (sop), Rosalind Elias (mez), Shirley Verrett (mez), Marian Anderson (cta), Maureen Forrester (cta), Sergio Franchi (ten), Mario Lanza (ten), Richard Lewis (ten), Jan Pee, Alexander Dedyukhin (pno), Franz Rupp (pno), Leo Taubman (pno), George Trovillo (pno), Charles Wadsworth (pno), Boston Pops Orch [cnd:Arthur Fiedler], Boston SO [cnd:Charles Munch], Chicago SO [cnd:Fritz Reiner], RCA Victor Orch, RCA Victor Chorus [cnd:Wa *(rec Boston & Chicago & New York & Rome, 1957-1964)* RCA Living Stereo ▲ 09026-68167-2 [ADD]

▲ = CD ♦ = Enhanced CD ∆ = MD ▀ = Cassette Tape □ = DCC

Red Byrd
Blow, J.:Music of, w. Parley of Instruments—Awake my lyre; Salvator mundi; Paratum cor meum; Son. in A; Poor Celadon, he sighs; Musik's the cordial of a troubled breast; Go, perjur'd man; Chloe found Amyntas lying all in tears; Ground in g; Septimnius and Acme; Gloria patri qui creavit; Diva quo tendis Hyperion ▲ CDA 66658
Byrd, W.:Consort Music, w. Rose Consort of Viols—Pavan; Galliard; Fantasia; Fantasia No. 2; Fantasia No. 3; In Nomine No. 2; In Nomine No. 5 *(rec Dorset, between Apr. & No)* Naxos ▲ 8.550604 [DDD]
Byrd, W.:Songs, w. T. Bonner (sop), Rose Consort of Viols—Susanna Fair; Rejoice unto the Lord; Have Mercy upon Me, O God; In Angel's Weed; Fair Britain Isle; Triumph with Pleasant Melody; Christ Rising Again *(rec Dorset, between Apr. & Nov. 1992)* Naxos ▲ 8.550604 [DDD]
Elizabethan Christmas Anthems, w. Rose Consort of Viols Amon Ra ▲ CDSAR 46 [DDD]
Gibbons, O.:The Cryes of London, w. P. Nicholson (org), Fretwork—Cries & Fancies; Fantasias, In Nomines Virgin Classics ▲ CDC 59191
Gibbons, O.:Instrumental & Vocal Music, w. Rose Consort of Viols—Behold, thou hast made my days for 5 Voices & 5 Viols; Pavan for 6 Viols; Galliard for 6 Viols; Fant. No. 1 for 2 Treble Viols; I weigh not Fortune's frown for Soprano & 4 Viols [w. Tessa Bonner]; I tremble not at noise of war; I see ambition never pleased; I feign not friendship where I hate; Go from my window for 6 Viols; Dainty fine bird for Soprano & 4 Viols [w. T. Bonner]; Fair is the Rose; Fant. No. 3 for 6 Viols; Fant. No. 5 for 6 viols; Lincoln's Inn Mask; Allmaine in G; Fantasia No. 1for the Great Double Bass for Organ & 3 Viols [w. Timothy Roberts]; Galliard for 3 Viols; The silver swan for Soprano & 5 Viols [w. T. Bonner]; In Nomine for 4 Viols; Glorious and powerful God for 5 Voices & 5 Viols *(rec Forde Abbey, Dorset, Apr. 27–28, May 11–13 & 2)* Naxos ▲ 8.550603 [DDD]
Monteverdi, C.:Altri canti d'amor, w. P. Holman (cnd), Parley of Instruments Hyperion ▲ CDA 66475 [DDD]
Monteverdi, C.:Ballo delle ingrate, w. P. Holman (cnd), Parley of Instruments Hyperion ▲ CDA 66475 [DDD]
Monteverdi, C.:Combattimento, w. P. Holman (cnd), Parley of Instruments Hyperion ▲ CDA 66475 [DDD]
Monteverdi, C.:Volgendo il ciel, w. P. Holman (cnd), Parley of Instruments Hyperion ▲ CDA 66475 [DDD]
Purcell, H.:Songs, w. P. Holman (cnd), Parley of Instruments—Hark Damon, hark; How pleasant is this flowery plain; We reap all the pleasures; Hark how wild musicians sing; See where she sits; Oh! what a scene does entertain my sight; Soft notes & gently raised; If ever I more riches did desire; Pavans in g, a, A & B♭ Hyperion ▲ CDA 66750
Songs of Love & Death
Szymanowski, K.:Mazurkas, w. Joanna Domanska (pno) Olympia ▲ OLY 344

Red Star Red Army Chorus
A.N. Bazhalkin (cnd)
Kalinka! Teldec ▲ 9031-77307-2
Moscow Nights Teldec ▲ 91786-2

Regensburg Cathedral Choir
Christmas Carols Editio Classica ▲ 77049-2-RG [DDD] ■ 77049-4-RG (CrO2)
Dittersdorf, K.D. von:Sacred Music, w. Hanna Farinelli (sop), Birgit Calm (alt), Heiner Hopfner (ten), Nikolaus Hillebrand (bass), G. Ratzinger (cnd), Munich Consortium Musicum—Requiem in c; Offertorium zu Ehren des Heiligen Johann von Nepomuk; Laurentanische Litanei Ars Musici ▲ AM 1158-2 [DDD]
Hassler, H.L.:Sacred Music, w. G. Ratzinger (cnd)—Litaniae lauretanae; Ecce quam bonum [motet & mass] Ars Musici ▲ 3011
Mozart, W.A.:Ave verum corpus Deutsche Grammophon ▲ 429820-2 [ADD]
Schubert, Franz:Duetsche Messe, w. G. Ratzinger (cnd), Augsburg PO, Munich RSO, Munich Radio Orch, Munich PO Soloists Ars Musici ▲ AM 0929 [DDD]

G. Ratzinger (cnd)
Brahms, J.:Marienlieder Ars Musici ▲ AM 0929 [DDD]
Lassus, O. de:Choral Music—Omnes de Saba; Lauda Jerusalem; Jubilate Deo omnis terra; Benedicam Dominum qui tribuit mihi; Missa super Bella Amfitrit' altera; Drei Kaiserchöre; Nunc gaudere licet; Audite nova; Baur Baur was tregst im Sacke; Ich waiss mir ein meidlein; So trincken wir alle; Wer frisch wil sein Ars Musici ▲ AM 1092 [DDD]
Rheinberger, J.:Choral Music, w. E. Kraus (org)—Morgenlied; Abendlied; Warum toben die Heiden; Es spricht der Tor in seinem Herzen; Adoramus te; Ave vivens hostia; Salve Regina; Dextera Domini; Eripe me Ars Musici ▲ 1063 [DDD]
Rheinberger, J.:Mass, Op. 117 Ars Musici ▲ 1063 [DDD]
Rheinberger, J.:Waldblumen, w. E. Kraus (org) Ars Musici ▲ 1063 [DDD]

Reggio Emilia Teatro Municipale Chorus
Puccini, G.:La Bohème (sels), w. Bianco Bellisia (sop—Musetta), Alberto Pellegrini (sop—Mimi), Luciano Pavarotti (ten—Rodolfo), Walter de Ambrosis (bar—Schaunard), Vito Mattioli (bar—Marcello), Dmitri Nabokov (bass—Colline), Reggio Emilia Teatro Municipale Orch Budget ("The Greatest Voice in Opera" series) ▲ SYP 105

Remembrance Florid Church Chorus
Bach, J.S.:Cant 88, w. I. Reichelt (sop), V. Gohl (mez), A. Kraus (ten), W. Schöne (bass), H. Rilling (cnd), Stuttgart Bach Collegium Hänssler Classic ▲ 98.804 [AAD]
Bach, J.S.:Cant 167, w. K. Graf (sop), H. Gardow (sop), A. Kraus (ten), N. Tüller (bass), H. Rilling (cnd), Stuttgart Bach Collegium Hänssler Classic ▲ 98.803 [AAD]

Renaissance Singers
Debussy, C.:Nocturnes, w. Y.P. Tortelier (cnd), Ulster Orch, Grosvenor High School Choir Chandos ▲ CHAN 8914 [DDD]
Fauré, G.:Pavane Orch, w. Y.P. Tortelier (cnd), Ulster Orch Chandos ▲ CHAN 8952 [DDD]
Moeran, E.J.:Nocturne, w. H. Mackey (bar), V. Handley (cnd), Ulster Orch [E] Chandos ▲ CHAN 8808 [DDD]
Ravel, M.:Daphins et Chloé, w. Y.P. Tortelier (cnd), Ulster Orch, Belfast Philharmonic Society Chorus Chandos ▲ CHAN 8893 [DDD]

Repertory Singers
Barber, S.:Music of, w. Alexa Still (fl), Chicago SO, San Diego CO, Atlantic Sinfonietta, New Zealand SO, Arioso Wind Quintet, Capricorn—Capricorn Con; Canzone; Fadograph of a Yestern Scene; Cave of the Heart; Adagio for Strs; Souvenirs; Hermit Songs; To Be Sung on Water; The Lovers; Summer Music Koch International Classics ▲ KIC 7361

Residentie Chamber Choir The Hague
Bach, J.S.:Cant 24, w. Baroque Orch Erasmus ▲ WVH 152
Bach, J.S.:Cant 182, w. Baroque Orch Erasmus ▲ WVH 152

Residentie Chorus The Hague
Van Der Horst, A.:Chorus II, w. A. Medveczky (cnd), Residentie Orch The Hague Olympia ▲ OCD 505 [AAD]

Reykjavik Men's Choir
Leifs, J.:Music of, w. P. Zukovsky (cnd), Iceland SO—Geysir; Ov for Orch; 3 Images; Hekla Music from Iceland ▲ ITM 604 [DDD]

Rhine Opera Chorus
Donizetti, G.:Roberto Devereux, w. Edita Gruberová (sop), Delores Ziegler (mez), Don Bernardini (sgr), Ettore Kim (sgr), F. Haider (cnd), Strasbourg PO Nightingale Classics 2-▲ NIG 70563
Mozart, W.A.:Così fan tutte, w. T. Stratas (sop), K. Te Kanawa (sop), F. von Stade (mez), A. Lombard (cnd), Strasbourg PO Erato 3-▲ 98494-2
Puccini, G.:Turandot, w. M. Caballé (sop—Turnadot), M. Freni (sop—Liu), J. Carreras (ten—Calaf), M. Sénéchal (ten—Emperor Altoum), V. Sardinero (bar—Ping), P. Plishka (bass—Timur), A. Lombard (cnd), Strasbourg PO, Maîtrise de la Cathédrale EMI Classics ▲ CDMB 65293
Puccini, G.:Turandot (sels), w. M. Caballé (sop), M. Freni (sop), J. Carreras (ten), M. Sénéchal (ten), A. Lombard (cnd), Strasbourg PO EMI Classics ("Studio" series) ▲ CDM 63410

Rhineland Kantorei
Bach, J.S.:St. Matthew Passion, w. Monika Frimmer (sop), Veronika Winter (sop), Lena Susanne Norin (alt), Wilfried Jochens (ten), Christoph Prégardien (ten), Klaus Mertens (bass), Hans-Georg Wimmer (bass), H. Max (cnd), Das Kliene Konzert Capriccio 2-▲ 60 046 [DDD]
Bach, W.F.:Cants (misc), w. B. Schlick (soprano), C. Schubert (contralto), W. Jochens (tenor), J. Schreckenberger (bass), Rheinische Kantorei, H. Max (cnd), Das Kleine Konzert—Dies ist der Tag; Erzittert und fallet Capriccio ▲ 10 426 [DDD]
Bach, W.F.:Cants (misc), w. B. Schlick (soprano), C. Schubert (contralto), W. Jochens (tenor), J. Schreckenberger (bass), Rheinische Kantorei, H. Max (cnd), Das Kleine Konzert—Lasset uns ablegen die Werke der Finsternis; Es ist eine Stimme eines Predigers in der Wüste Capriccio ▲ 10 425 [DDD]
Hasse, J.A.:Miserere in c Orch, w. H. Max (cnd), Das Kleine Konzert, Dormagen Boys' Choir Capriccio ▲ 10 557 [DDD]
Heinichen, J.D.:Sacred Music, w. H. Max (cnd), Das Kleine Konzert, Dormagen Boys' Choir—Magnificat in A Capriccio ▲ 10 557 [DDD]
Homilius, G.A.:Vocal Music, w. H. Max (cnd), Das Kleine Konzert, Dormagen Boys' Choir—Verwundrung, Mitleid, Furcht und Schrecken Capriccio ▲ 10 557 [DDD]
Telemann, G.P.:Auferstehung und Himmelfahrt Jesu, w. Monika Frimmer (sop), Veronika Winter (sop), Matthias Koch (alt), Nico Van der Meel (ten), Klaus Mertens (bass), H. Max (cnd), Das Kliene Konzert Capriccio ▲ CD 10596 [DDD]
Zelenka, J.D.:Miserere in c, w. H. Max (cnd), Das Kleine Konzert, Dormagen Boys' Choir Capriccio ▲ 10 557 [DDD]

Rhos Orpheus Male Voice Choir
The Voice of Wales, w. Tredegar Orpheus Chandos ("Collect" series) ▲ CHAN 6540 [ADD]

Ricercar Academy Chorus
Grétry, A.-E.-M.:La Caravane du Caire, w. I. Poulenard (sop), G. de Reyghere (sop), G. Ragon (ten), G. de Mey (ten), P. Huttenlocher (bar), V. Le Téxier (bar), J. Bastin (bass), M. Minkowski (cnd), Ricercar Academy [period instruments] [F] Ricercar 2-▲ RIC 100084/85 [DDD]

Riga Radio Chorus
Bach, J.S.:Motets, BWV 225–30, w. S. Klava (cnd), Riga Musicians Audiophile Classics ▲ 101.047
Mozart, W.A.:Alma Dei creatoris, w. Dita Paēgle (sop), Antra Bīgaca (mez), Martins Klisans (ten), S. Klava (cnd), Riga Musicians Audiophile Classics ▲ 101.048 [DDD]
Mozart, W.A.:Ave verum corpus, w. S. Klava (cnd), Riga Musicians Audiophile Classics ▲ 101.048 [DDD]
Mozart, W.A.:Litaniae Lauretanae, K.195, w. Dita Paēgle (sop), Antra Bīgaca (mez), Martins Klisans (ten), Janis Màrkovs (bass), S. Klava (cnd), Riga Musicians Audiophile Classics ▲ 101.048 [DDD]
Mozart, W.A.:Misericordias Domini, w. S. Klava (cnd), Riga Musicians Audiophile Classics ▲ 101.048 [DDD]
Mozart, W.A.:Regina coeli, K.276, w. Dita Paēgle (sop), Antra Bīgaca (mez), Martins Klisans (ten), Janis Màrkovs (bass), S. Klava (cnd), Riga Musicians Audiophile Classics ▲ 101.048 [DDD]
Mozart, W.A.:Sancta Maria, w. S. Klava (cnd), Riga Musicians Audiophile Classics ▲ 101.048 [DDD]
Mozart, W.A.:Te Deum, w. S. Klava (cnd), Riga Musicians Audiophile Classics ▲ 101.048 [DDD]
Mozart, W.A.:Venite populi, w. S. Klava (cnd), Riga Musicians Audiophile Classics ▲ 101.048 [DDD]

Rinat National Choir
Fleischer, T.:Scenes of Israel Opus One ▲ Cd 158 [DDD]

Rio de Janeiro Teatro Municipale Chorus
Verdi, G.:La forza del destino (sels), w. Barbato (sop), B. Gigli (ten), E. Mascherini (bar), G. Neri (bass), A. Votto (cnd), Rio de Janeiro Teatro Municipale Orch [I] *(rec live 8/16/51)* Standing Room Only ▲ SRO 807-1 (m) [ADD]
Verdi, G.:La traviata (sels), w. L. Gencer (sop), F. Labò (ten), P. Cappuccilli (bar), N. Rescigno (cnd), Rio de Janeiro Teatro Municipale Orch *(rec live 8/8/64)* Golden Age of Opera ▲ GAO 120 [ADD]

Riverside Choir New York
J. Walker (cnd)
Riverside Choir New York City Pro Organo ▲ POCD 7017

Riverside Church Choir
In the Spirit:Sacred Music for Christmas, w. Jessye Norman (sop), St. Luke's Orch [cnd:David Robertson], American Boys Choir, St. Barnabas Adult Choir, St. Thomas Men & Boys Choir Philips ▲ 454640-2 ■ 454640-4

Rochester Cathedral Choir
Te deum & Jubilate, Vol. 1 Priory ▲ PRI 433 [DDD]
B. Ferguson (cnd)
Hear My Voice, O God:Psalms of David, Vol. 9, w. Roger Sayer (org) Priory ▲ PRI 461 [DDD]
R. Sayer (cnd)
Magnificat & Nunc Dimittis, Vol. 6, w. William Whitehead (org) Priory ▲ PRI 529 [DDD]

Rochester Opera Theater Chorus
Stuart, P.:Kill Bear Comes Home, w. Elana Gizzi (sop—Hasty Girl), Mi-Kyung Huh (sop—Cold Feet), Therese Murray (sop—Song Bird), Cherie Pfeil (sop—1st Sister), Renia Shukis (sop—2nd Sister), Riki Connaughton (mez—4th Sister), Lucy Fee (mez—3rd Sister), David Averbach (ten—Song Leader), Mark Schmidt (ten—Kill Bear), Jason Smith (bar—Cheif Wife Hunter), P. Stuart (cnd), Rochester Opera Theater Orch VM ▲ DRK 154 [DDD]

Rodina Chorus
Schubert, Franz:Mass 2, w. E. Maksimova (sop), H. Kamenov (ten), I. Dobrev (bass), V. Kazandjiev (cnd), Sofia Soloists CO [L] Musique d'Abord ▲ HMA 190111 [AAD]

Rodiphus Choir
R. Allwood (cnd)
Bax, A.:Choral Music—Epithalamium; Magnificat [both w. Christopher Hughes (org)]; Lord, thou hast told us; I sing of a maiden; Mater, ora Filium; This worldes joie *(rec Eton College Chapel, Dec. 1993)* Herald ▲ HAVPCD 176 [DDD]
Grier, F.:Anthems, w. James Bowman (ct), Christopher Hughes (org)—Let us invoke Christ; Great is the Power of Thy Cross; God, Who Made the Earth & Sky; Proclaim His Triumph; Day After Day; Salve Regina; Corpus Christi Carol; O King of the Friday; Christ's Love-Song; The Voice of My Beloved; Dilectus Meus Mihi; Thou, O God, Art Praised in Sion *(rec Eton College Chapel, Dec 1994)* Herald ▲ HAVPCD 177 [DDD]
Grier, F.:Choral Music, w. Francis Grier (org)—A Sequence for the Ascension Herald ▲ HAVPCD 158
Villette, P.:Choral Music—Salve, Regina; O magnum mysterium; Attende, Domine; O sacrum convivium; Hymne à la Vierge *(rec Eton College Chapel, Dec. 1993)* Herald ▲ HAVPCD 176 [DDD]

Romande Chamber Choir
Mozart, W.A.:Zauberflöte, w. S. Jo (sop), L. Orgonasova (sop), Martina Bovet (sop), G. Winbergh (ten), H. Hagegard (bar), A. Jordan (cnd), Paris Orchestral Ensemble, Pro Arte Lausanne Erato 2-▲ 2292-45469-2 [DDD]
Stravinsky, I.:Music of, w. N. Järvi (cnd), Swiss Romande Orch, Pro Arte Lausanne—Oedipus Rex; Sym. In E♭, Op. 1; Con. for Violin [w. L. Mordkovitch]; Petruchka (1911 version); Apollon Musagète; Circus Polka; Le chant du Rossignol; Sym. in 3 Movements; Capriccio for Piano & Orch. [w. G. Tozer]; Sym. in C; Sym. of Psalms; Con. for Piano & Winds [w. B. Berman] Chandos 5-▲ CHAN 9240 [DDD]
Stravinsky, I.:Requiem Canticles, w. Irène Friedli (alt), Michel Brodard (bass), N. Järvi (cnd), Swiss Romande Orch, Lausanne Pro Arte Choir Chandos ▲ CHAN 9408 [DDD]
Stravinsky, I.:Sym of Psalms, w. N. Järvi (cnd), Swiss Romande Orch, Lausanne Pro Arte Choir Chandos ▲ CHAN 9239 [DDD]
A. Charlet (cnd)
Gounod, C.:Requiem, w. M. Veillon (db), C. Fleischmann (hp), F. Margot (org) *(rec 1992 & 1993)* Claves ▲ CD 9326 [DDD]

Romanian National Radio Chorus
Enescu, G.:Mélodies, Op. 4, w. Christina Anghelescu (vn), H. Andreescu (cnd), Romanian National RSO—No. 1 [arr for Vn & Orch] Olympia ▲ OLY 496
Enescu, G.:School Syms (4), w. H. Andreescu (cnd), Romanian National RSO—No. 1 in d Olympia ▲ OLY 496
Enescu, G.:Vox maris, w. Robert Nagy (ten), H. Andreescu (cnd), Romanian National RSO Olympia ▲ OLY 496

CHORAL GROUPS

Romanian Opera Chorus

Donizetti, G.:Lucia di Lammermoor, w. Silvia Voinea (sop—Lucia), Lucia Cicoara (mez—Alisa), Florin Georgescu (ten—Edgardo), Gabriel Nastase (ten—Arturo), Nicolae Herlea (bar—Lord Enrico), Pompei Harasteanu (bass—Raimondo), C. Petrovici (cnd), Romanian Opera Orch *(rec 1984)* Vox Box 2-▲ CDX 5164

Puccini, G.:La Bohème, w. Elvira Cirje-Druica (sop—Musetta), Eugenia Moldoveanu (sop—Mimi), Andrei Borsos (ten—Parpignol), Constantin Gabor (ten—Alcindoro), Ludovic Spiess (ten—Rodolfo), Lucian Marinescu (bar—Schaunard), David Ohanesian (bar—Marcello), Pompei Harasteanu (bass—Benoit), Dan Zancu (bass—Colline), C. Petrovici (cnd), Romanian Opera Orch *(rec 1982)* Vox Box 2-▲ CDX 5156

Puccini, G.:Tosca, w. Virginia Zeani (sop—Floria Tosca), Emilia Oprea (mez—Shepherd), Nicolae Andreescu (ten—Spoletta), Corneliu Fanateanu (ten—Mario Cavaradossi), Nicolae Herlea (bar—Baron Scarpia), Gheorghe Crasnaru (bass—Cesare Angelotti), Constantin Gabor (bass—Sacristan), Pompei Harasteanu (bass—Jailer), Adrian Stefanescu (bass—Sciarrone), C. Trailescu (cnd), Romanian Opera Orch *(rec Sept 1977)* Vox Box 2-▲ CDX 5153

Rossini, G.:Il barbiere di Siviglia, w. Magda Ianculescu (sop—Rosina), Maria Sandulescu (mez—Berta), Valentin Teodorian (ten—Count Almaviva), Nicolae Herlea (bar—Figaro), Stefan Petrescu (bar—Fiorello), Constantin Gabor (bass—Don Bartolo), Valentin Loghin (bass—Don Basilio), M. Brediceanu (cnd), Romanian Opera Orch *(rec 1960-61)* Vox Box 2-▲ CDX 5159

Verdi, G.:Rigoletto, w. Victoria Draganescu (sop—Countess Ceprano), Magda Ianculescu (sop—Gilda), Dorothea Palade (mez—Maddalena), Valeria Savu (mez—Giovanna), Ion Buzea (ten—Duke of Mantua), Dimitrie Scurtu (ten—Borsa), Nicolae Herlea (bar—Rigoletto), Stefan Petrescu (bar—Marullo), Jean Banescu (bass—Count Ceprano), Nicolae Florei (bass—Monterone), Nicolae Rafael (bass—Sparafucile), J. Bobescu (cnd), Romanian Opera Orch *(rec 1965)* Vox Box 2-▲ CDX 5162

Verdi, G.:Il trovatore, w. Elena Dima (sop—Leonora), Victoria Draganescu (sop—Ines), Zenaida Pally (mez—Azucena), Ion Buzea (ten—Duke of Mantua), Constantin Iliescu (ten—Ruiz), Cornel Stavru (ten—Manrico), Octav Enigarescu (bar—Count di Luna), Constantin Dumitru (bass—Ferrando), E. Massini (cnd), Romanian Opera Orch *(rec 1960-61)* Vox Box 2-▲ CDX 5163

S. Olariu (cnd)

Verdi, G.:La traviata, w. Elena Simionescu (sop—Annina), Virginia Zeani (sop—Violetta Valery), Elisabeta Neculce-Cartis (mez—Flora Bervoix), Ion Buzea (ten—Alfredo Germont), Vasile Moldoveanu (ten—Gastone/Viconte de Letorieres/Giuseppe), Teodor Panea (ten—Flora's Servant), Constantin Dumitru (bar—Commissioner/Baron Douphol), Nicolae Herlea (bar—Giorgio Germont), Valentin Loghin (bass—Marchese D'Obigny), Nicolae Rafael (bass—Doctor Grenvil), J. Bobescu (cnd), Romanian Opera Orch *(rec 1968)* Vox Box 2-▲ CDX 5154

Romanian Patriarchate Choir

I. Căstoiu (cnd)

Romanian Byzantine Hymns & Christmas Carols Electrecord ▲ ELC 101 [AAD]

Romanian Radio Chorus

Vieru, A.:Sym 5, w. L. Baci (cnd), Romanian National RSO Olympia ▲ OCD 409 [AAD]

Romanian Radio-TV Chorus

Enescu, G.:Romanian Poem, w. I. Conta (cnd), Romanian Radio-TV Orch Marco Polo ▲ 8.223146

Enescu, G.:Romanian Poem, w. I. Conta (cnd), Romanian Radio-TV Orch Stradivari Classics ▲ SCD 6038 [DDD] ■ SMC 6038 (D)

Puccini, G.:Turandot, w. Teodora Lucaciu (sop—Liù), Maria Slatinaru (sop—Princess Turandot), Corneliu Finateanu (ten—Pong), George Mircea (ten—Emperor Altoum), Ludovic Speiss (ten—Prince Calaf), Valentin Teodorian (ten—Pang), Octav Enigarescu (bar—Ping), Dionisie Konya (bar—A Mandarin), Mircea Stefanescu (bar—The Prince of Persia), Nicolae Florei (bass—Timur), C. Litvin (cnd), Romanian Radio-TV Orch *(rec Jan 1970)* Vox Box 2-▲ CDX 5160

Verdi, G.:La forza del destino, w. Maria Nistor-Slatinaru (sop—Donna Leonora), Mihaela Mariacineanu (mez—Curra), Zenaida Pally (mez—Preziosilla), Ludovic Speiss (ten—Don Alvaro), Ion Stoian (ten—Trabucco), Nicolae Herlea (bar—Don Carlo), Nicolae Florei (bass—Padre Guardiano) Constantin Gabor (bass—Fra Melitone), Dan Musetescu (bass—An Alcalde), Mihai Panghe (bass—Marquis of Calatrava), C. Litvin (cnd), Romanian Radio-TV Orch *(rec Jan 1970)* Vox Box 3-▲ CD3X 3038

Rome Opera Chorus

Bellini, V.:Norma (sels), w. M. Callas (sop), M. Pirazzini (mez), F. Corelli (ten), P. De Palma (ten), G. Santini (cnd), Rome Opera Orch [I] *(rec live 1/2/58)* Melodram ▲ MEL 16000 (m) [AAD]

Boito, A.:Mefistofele, w. Orietta Moscucci (sop—Margherita), Amalia Pini (mez—Martha), Piero de Palma (ten—Wagner), Giacinto Prandelli (ten—Faust), Boris Christoff (bass—Mefistofele), V. Gui (cnd), Rome Opera Orch EMI Classics 2-▲ CDMB 65655

Donizetti, G.:Lucia di Lammermoor, w. Roberta Peters (sop—Lucia), Mitì Truccato Pace (mez—Alisa), Jan Peerce (ten—Edgardo), Piero de Palma (ten—Lord Arturo Bucklaw), Mario Carlin (ten—Normanno), Philip Maero (bar—Lord Enrico Ashton), Giorgio Tozzi (bass—Raimondo), E. Leinsdorf (cnd), Rome Opera Orch *(rec Rome Opera House, Aug 5-14, 1957)* RCA Living Stereo 2-▲ 09026-68537-2 [ADD]

Donizetti, G.:Poliuto, w. E. Connell (sop), N. Martinucci (ten), R. Bruson (bar), J. Latham-König (cnd), Rome Opera Orch [I] *(rec live, 1988)* Nuova Era 2-▲ 6776/77 [DDD]

Giordano, U.:Andrea Chénier, w. A. Stella (sop—Maddalena), F. Corelli (ten—Andrea Chénier), M. Sereni (bar—Carlo Gerard), G. Santini (cnd), Rome Opera Orch EMI Classics ▲ CDMB 65287

Mascagni, P.:Cavalleria rusticana, w. V. De los Angeles (sop), F. Corelli (ten), G. Santini (cnd), Rome Opera Orch [I] EMI Classics ("Studio" series) 2-▲ CDMB 63967

Mascagni, P.:Cavalleria rusticana, w. E. Suliotis (sop), S. Malagu (mez), A. Di Stasio (mez), M. Del Monaco (ten), T. Gobbi (bar), S. Varviso (cnd), Rome Opera Orch [I] IMP Collectors Series ▲ IMPX 9018 [AAD]

Massenet, J.:Manon, w. V. De los Angeles (sop), F. Tagliavini (ten), A. Poli (bar), N. Annovazzi (cnd), Rome Opera Orch *(rec live 1957)* Melodram 2-▲ MEL 27082

Ponchielli, A.:La Gioconda, w. Leyla Gencer (sop), Anna di Stasio (mez), Gianni Raimondi (ten), Ruggero Raimondi (bass), B. Bartoletti (cnd), Rome Opera Orch Melodram 3-▲ CDM 37092

Puccini, G.:La Bohème, w. M. Freni (sop), N. Gedda (ten), M. Sereni (bar), T. Schippers (cnd), Rome Opera Orch [I] EMI Classics ("Studio" series) 2-▲ CDMB 69657

Puccini, G.:La Bohème, w. A. Moffo (sop), F. Costa (mez), G. Tucker (ten), R. Merrill (bar), G. Tozzi (bass), E. Leinsdorf (cnd), Rome Opera Orch [I] RCA Gold Seal 2-▲ 3969-2-RG [ADD] 2-■ 3969-4-RG (CrO2)

Puccini, G.:La Bohème, w. Schimenti (sop), Micheluzi (sgr), G. Lauri-Volpi (ten), G. Ciavola (bass), A. Paoletti (cnd), Rome Opera Orch *(rec 1952)* Bongiovanni 2-▲ GB 1057/58 [ADD]

Puccini, G.:La Bohème (sels), w. A. Moffo (sop), F. Costa (mez), G. Tucker (ten), R. Merrill (bar), G. Tozzi (bass), E. Leinsdorf (cnd), Rome Opera Orch RCA Gold Seal ▲ 60189-2-RG [ADD] ■ 60189-4-RG (CrO2)

Puccini, G.:La Bohème (sels), w. M. Freni (sop), N. Gedda (ten), M. Sereni (bar), T. Schippers (cnd), Rome Opera Orch EMI Classics ("Studio" series) ▲ CDM 63932 ■ EG 63932

Puccini, G.:La fanciulla del West (sels), w. Magda Olivero (sop—Minnie), Corinna Vozza (mez—Wowkle), Paolo Caroli (ten—Harry), Giacomo Lauri-Volpi (ten—Dick Johnson), Marco Rogani (ten—Pony Express Rider), Salvatore di Tommaso (ten—Trin), Adelio Zagonara (ten—Nick), Virgilio Ascorro (bar—Sid), Alfredo Colella (bar—Jake Wallace), Giuseppe Forgione (bar—Bello), Giancarlo Guelfi (bar—Jack Rance), Arturo la Porta (bar—Sonora), Gino Conti (bass—José Castro), Piere Passarotti (bass—Bill), Enzo Titta (bass—Larkens), Giulio Tomei (bass—Ashby), V. Bellezza (cnd), Rome Opera Orch—Minnie, dalla mia casa son partito; Laggiù nel Soledad; Chi c'è per farmi i ricci; Oh! Mister Johnson, siete rimasto; Non so ben neppur io; Io non son che una povera fanciulla; No, Minnie, non piangete; Vorrei mettermi queste; Hallo!; Oh, se sapeste; Credo che abbiate torto; Ma ti giuro ch'io non ti lascio più; Vieni fuori!; Una parola sola!...Or son sei mesi; Che c'è di nuovo Jack?; È là; Siete pronto; Ch'ella mi creda; È Minnie!...È Minnie! *(rec Rome, Mar. 30, 1957)* Golden Age of Opera ▲ GAO 180 [ADD]

Puccini, G.:Madama Butterfly, w. V. de los Angeles (sop), M. Pirazzini (mez), J. Bjoerling (ten), M. Sereni (bar), G. Santini (cnd), Rome Opera Orch [I] EMI Classics ("Studio" series) 2-▲ CDMB 63634 [ADD]

Puccini, G.:Madama Butterfly, w. R. Scotto (sop), C. Bergonzi (ten), R. Panerai (bar), J. Barbirolli (cnd), Rome Opera Orch EMI Classics 2-▲ CDMB 69654

Puccini, G.:Madama Butterfly, w. A. Moffo (sop), R. Elias (mez), C. Valletti (ten), R. Cesari (bar), E. Leinsdorf (cnd), Rome Opera Orch [I] RCA Gold Seal ▲ 60202-2-RG [ADD] ■ 60202-4-RG

Rome Opera Chorus (cont.)

Puccini, G.:Madama Butterfly, w. R. Scotto (sop), A. di Stasio (mez), C. Bergonzi (ten), R. Panerai (bar), J. Barbirolli (cnd), Rome Opera Orch [I] EMI Classics ("Studio" series) ▲ CDM 63411 ■ EG 63411

Puccini, G.:Madama Butterfly, w. A. Moffo (sop), R. Elias (mez), C. Valletti (ten), R. Cesari (bar), E. Leinsdorf (cnd), Rome Opera Orch [I] RCA Gold Seal 2-▲ 4145-2-RG [ADD]

Puccini, G.:Madama Butterfly (sels), w. R. Scotto (sop), C. Bergonzi (ten), J. Barbirolli (cnd), Rome Opera Orch EMI Classics ■ 4XS 36567

Puccini, G.:Manon Lescaut, w. L. Albanese (sop), J. Bjoerling (ten), R. Merrill (bar), J. Perlea (cnd), Rome Opera Orch [I] RCA Gold Seal 2-▲ 60573-2-RG [ADD]

Puccini, G.:Tosca, w. Z. Milanov (sop), J. Björling (ten), L. Warren (bar), E. Leinsdorf (cnd), Rome Opera Orch [I] RCA Gold Seal 2-▲ 4514-2-RG [ADD] 2-■ 4514-2-RG

Puccini, G.:Tosca, w. R. Kaibaivanska (sop—Floria), L. Pavarotti (ten—Mario), I. Wixell (bar—Scarpia), F. Federici (bass—Angelotti), D. Oren (cnd), Rome Opera Orch RCA Red Seal ▲ 09026-61807-2; ■ 09026-61807-4

Puccini, G.:Tosca, w. R. Kaibaivanska (sop—Floria), L. Pavarotti (ten—Mario), I. Wixell (bar—Scarpia), F. Federici (bass—Angelotti), D. Oren (cnd), Rome Opera Orch RCA Red Seal 2-▲ 09026-61806-2

Puccini, G.:Tosca (sels), w. Z. Milanov (sop), J. Björling (ten), L. Warren (bar), E. Leinsdorf (cnd), Rome Opera Orch RCA Gold Seal ▲ 60192-2-RG [ADD] ■ 60192-4-RG (CrO2)

Puccini, G.:Il trittico, w. V. de los Angeles (sop), F. Barbieri (mez), G. Prandelli (ten), T. Gobbi (bar), *(other soloists unknown),* Rome Opera Orch *(rec Rome, 1950s)* EMI Classics 3-▲ CDMC 64165 (m)

Puccini, G.:Turandot, w. Birgit Nilsson (sop—Turandot), Renata Tebaldi (sop—Liù), Jussi Björling (ten—Calaf), Alessio De Paolis (ten—Emperor Altoum), Piero de Palma (ten—Pang), Mario Sereni (bar—Ping), Adelio Zagonara (bar—Prince of Persia), Giorgio Tozzi (bass—Timur), Tommaso Frascati (bass—Pong), Leonardo Monreale (bass—Mandarin), E. Leinsdorf (cnd), Rome Opera Orch *(rec Rome Opera House, July 3-11, 1959)* RCA Living Stereo 2-▲ 09026-62687-2 [ADD]

Puccini, G.:Turandot, w. B. Nilsson (sop), R. Scotto (sop), F. Corelli (ten), B. Giaiotti (bass), F. Molinari-Pradelli (cnd), Rome Opera Orch [I] EMI Classics ("Studio" series) 2-▲ CDMB 69327 [ADD]

Puccini, G.:Turandot, w. B. Nilsson (sop), R. Tebaldi (sop), J. Bjoerling (ten), G. Tozzi (bass), E. Leinsdorf (cnd), Rome Opera Orch [I] RCA Red Seal 2-▲ 5932-2-RC 3-■ AGK3-3970

Three Tenors of the Golden Age, w. Jussi Björling (ten), Mario Lanza (ten), Jan Peerce (ten), John Corigliano (vn), Constantine Callinicos (pno), Frederick Schauwecker (pno), RCA Victor Orch [cnd:Renato Cellini, Constantine Callinicos, Erich Leinsdorf, Sylvan Levin, Maximilian Pilzer, Frieder Weissmann], Rome Opera Orch, et al. RCA Gold Seal ▲ 09026-68531-2 [ADD] ■ 09026-68531-4

Verdi, G.:Aida, w. Z. Milanov (sop), F. Barbieri (mez), J. Björling (ten), L. Warren (bar), B. Christoff (bass), J. Perlea (cnd), Rome Opera Orch [I] RCA Gold Seal 3-▲ 6652-2-RG (m) [ADD] 3-■ ALK3-5380 (m)

Verdi, G.:Aida, w. L. Price (sop), R. Gorr (mez), J. Vickers (ten), R. Merrill (bar), G. Tozzi (bass), G. Solti (cnd), Rome Opera Orch [I] London ▲ 421860-2 [ADD]

Verdi, G.:Aida, w. L. Price (sop), R. Gorr (mez), J. Vickers (ten), R. Merrill (bar), G. Tozzi (bass), G. Solti (cnd), Rome Opera Orch [I] London 3-▲ 417416-2 [ADD]

Verdi, G.:Aida, w. Z. Milanov (sop), F. Barbieri (mez), J. Björling (ten), L. Warren (bar), B. Christoff (bass), J. Perlea (cnd), Rome Opera Orch [I] RCA Gold Seal ▲ 60201-2-RG (m) ■ 60201-4-RG (m)

Verdi, G.:Alzira, w. V. Zeani (sop), G. Cecchele (ten), C. MacNeil (bar), C. Cava (bass), F. Capuana (cnd), Rome Opera Orch [I] *(rec live 3/16/67)* Melodram 2-▲ MEL 27013 (m) [AAD]

Verdi, G.:Alzira, w. V. Zeani (sop), G. Cecchele (ten), C. MacNeil (bar), C. Cava (bass), F. Capuana (cnd), Rome Opera Orch [I] *(rec live, 3/16/67)* Verona 2-▲ 27042/43 (m) [AAD]

Verdi, G.:Un ballo in maschera, w. Maria Caniglia (sop), Fedora Barbieri (cta), Beniamino Gigli (ten), Gino Bechi (bar), T. Serafin (cnd), Rome Opera Orch *(rec Rome, July, 1943)* Grammofono 2000 2-▲ GRM 78556

Verdi, G.:Don Carlos, w. L. Gencer (sop), F. Cossotto (mez), B. Prevedi (ten), S. Bruscantini (bar), N. Ghiaurov (bass), F. Previtali (cnd), Rome Opera Orch *(rec live)* Melodram 3-▲ MEL 37022

Verdi, G.:I lombardi alla prima crociata, w. R. Scotto (sop), L. Pavarotti (ten), R. Raimondi (bass), G. Gavazzeni (cnd), Rome Opera Orch [I] *(rec live, Rome, 11/20/69)* Memories 2-▲ HR 4337/38 [ADD]

Verdi, G.:I masnadieri, w. I. Ligabue (sop), G. Raimondi (ten), R. Bruson (bar), B. Christoff (bass), G. Gavazzeni (cnd), Rome Opera Orch [I] *(rec live, Rome, Nov. 25, 1972)* Golden Age of Opera 2-▲ GAO 135/36 [ADD]

Verdi, G.:Requiem Mass, w. Maria Caniglia (sop), Ebe Stignani (cta), Benjamino Gigli (ten), Ezio Pinza (bass), T. Serafin (cnd), Rome Opera Orch *(rec 1939)* Pearl ▲ PEA 9162 [ADD]

Verdi, G.:Rigoletto, w. R. Peters (sop), J. Björling (ten), R. Merrill (bar), G. Tozzi (bass), J. Perlea (cnd), Rome Opera Orch [I] RCA Gold Seal 2-▲ 60172-2-RG [ADD] 2-■ 60172-4-RG (CrO2)

Verdi, G.:Rigoletto (sels), w. Renata Scotto (sop—Gilda), Corinna Vozza (mez—Giovanna), Bianca Vortoluzzi (cta—Maddalena), Luciano Pavarotti (ten—Duke of Mantua), Kostas Paskalis (bar—Rigoletto), Paolo Washington (bass—Sparafucile), C. M. Guilini (cnd), Rome Opera Orch Budget ("The Greatest Voice in Opera" series) ▲ SYP 104

Verdi, G.:Stiffelio, w. Gulin-Dominguez (sop), G. Limarilli (ten), G. Guelfi (bar), G. Gavazzeni (cnd), Rome Opera Orch *(rec live, Rome 1964)* Melodram 2-▲ MEL 27033

Verdi, G.:Il trovatore, w. Fedora Barbieri (mez), Franco Corelli (ten), Ettore Bastianini (bar), Agostino Ferrin (bass), Mirella Parutto (sgr), O. de Fabritiis (cnd), Rome Opera Orch Stradivarius 2-▲ STV DTM 12313 [ADD]

Verdi, G.:I vespri siciliani, w. Leyla Gencer (sop), Giangiacomo Guelfi (bar), Nicola Rossi-Lemeni (bass), Gastone Limarilli (sgr), G. Gavazzeni (cnd), Rome Opera Orch *(rec Dec 5, 1964)* Pantheon 2-▲ PHE 6770

Verdi, G.:I vespri siciliani, w. L. Gencer (sop), G. Limarilli (ten), G. Guelfi (bar), N. Rossi-Lemeni (bass), G. Gavazzeni (cnd), Rome Opera Orch [I] *(rec live, Rome 1964)* Melodram 2-▲ MEL 27037 [ADD]

World's Greatest Choruses, w. Robert Shaw Chorale, et al. RCA Victor ▲ 09026-61241-2 ■ 09026-61241-4 (CrO2)

G. Conca (cnd)

Puccini, G.:Madama Butterfly, w. Toti dal Monte (sop—Madama Butterfly), Maria Huder (mez—Kate Pinkerton), Beniamino Gigli (ten—B.F. Pinkerton), Adelio Zagonara (ten—Goro), Mario Basiola (bar—Sharpless), Gino Conti (bass—Principe Yamadori), Ernesto Dominici (bass—Il Bonzo), Vittoria Paolombini (sgr—Suzuki), O. de Fabritiis (cnd), Rome Opera Orch *(rec Aug 1939)* Arkadia 2-▲ CD 78004 (m) [ADD]

Verdi, G.:Un ballo in maschera, w. Maria Caniglia (sop—Amelia), Fedora Barbieri (mez—Ulrica), Beniamino Gigli (ten—Riccardo), Gino Bechi (bar—Renato), Tancredi Pasero (bass—Samuel), Blando Giusti (sgr—Un Giudice), Nicola Niccolini (sgr—Silvano), Ugo Novelli (sgr—Tom), Elda Ribetti (sgr—Oscar), T. Serafin (cnd), Rome Opera Orch *(rec 1943)* Arkadia 2-▲ CD 78005 (m) [ADD]

Rome Phil Academy Chorus

Bernstein, L.:Chichester Psalms, w. G. D. Rodriguez (boy alto), G. Levine (cnd), Royal PO, St. Peter's Basilica Cappella Giulia Chorus Vatican City *(rec Apr. 7, 1994)* Justice ▲ JR 1801 [DDD]

Rome Radio-TV Chorus

Bellini, V.:Il pirata, w. M. Caballé (sop), F. Rafanelli (sop), B. Marti (ten), Baratti, P. Cappuccilli (bar), R. Raimondi (bass), G. Gavazzeni (cnd), Rome Radio-TV Orch [I] *(rec Rome, 1973)* EMI Classics 2-▲ CDMB 64169

Brahms, J.:Ein Deutsches Requiem, w. Rosanna Carteri (sop), Boris Christoff (bass), B. Walter (cnd), Rome Radio-TV SO Stradivarius 2-▲ STV DTM 12323 [ADD]

Wagner, R.:Parsifal, w. M. Callas (sop), Baldelli (sgr), R. Panerai (bar), D. Lopatto (bar), B. Christoff (bass), V. Gui (cnd), Rome Radio-TV SO [I] *(rec in concert, 11/20-21/50)* Verona 3-▲ 27085/87

Wagner, R.:Parsifal, w. M. Callas (sop), Baldelli (sgr), R. Panerai (bar), D. Lopatto (bar), B. Christoff (bass), V. Gui (cnd), Rome Radio-TV SO [I] *(rec 11/20-21/50)* Melodram 3-▲ MEL 36041 (m)

Rome RAI Chorus

Bellini, V.:I Capuleti e i Montecchi (sels), w. F. Cossotto (mez), R. Gavarini (ten), V. Tatozzi (bar), L. Maazel (cnd), Rome RAI Orch—2 solo tenor arias & 1 mezzo-bass duet [I] *(rec live 10/23/58)* Melodram ("Connaisseur" series) 2-▲ CDM 27509 [ADD]

Bellini, V.:I Puritani, w. M. Freni (sop), L. Pavarotti (ten), S. Bruscantini (bar), B. Giaotti (bass), R. Muti (cnd), Rome RAI SO [I] *(rec live, Rome 7/8/69)* Verona 3-▲ 27029/31

Bellini, V.:I Puritani, w. Mirella Freni (sop), Luciano Pavarotti (ten), Sesto Bruscantini (b-bar), R. Muti (cnd), Rome RAI SO *(rec Rome, 1969)* Enterprise ("Palladio" series) 3-▲ ENTPD 4205 [ADD]

1000 ▲ = CD ♦ = Enhanced CD Δ = MD ■ = Cassette Tape □ = DCC

Rome RAI Chorus (cont.)
Bellini, V.:I Puritani, w. Mirella Freni (sop), Mirelle Fiorentini (mez), Luciano Pavarotti (ten), Emilio Venturini (ten), Sesto Bruscantini (bar), Giovanni Antonini (bass), Bonaldo Giaiotti (bass), R. Muti (cnd), Rome RAI SO Melodram 2-▲ CDM 27062
Bellini, V.:I Puritani, w. Lina Pagliughi (sop), Mario Filippeschi (ten), Rolando Panerai (bar), Sesto Bruscantini (bass), F. Previtali (cnd), Rome RAI SO *(rec Rome, Jan. 4 & 5, 1952)* Pantheon 2-▲ PHE 6640 (m)
Bellini, V.:I Puritani (sels), w. Mirella Freni (sop), Luciano Pavarotti (ten), Giovanni Antonini (bass), Bonaldo Giaiotti (bass), R. Muti (cnd), Rome RAI SO—A te, o cara *(rec Rome, July 8, 1969)* Goldies ▲ GLD 63202 [ADD]
Berlioz, H.:La Damnation de Faust, w. M. Horne (mez—Marguerite), N. Gedda (ten—Faust), R. Soyer (bass—Mephistofeles), D. Petkov (bass—Brander), G. Prêtre (cnd), Rome RAI SO *(rec live 1/11/69)* Arkadia 4-▲ 461 [ADD]
Berlioz, H.:Les Troyens, w. M. Horne (mez), S. Verrett (mez), N. Gedda (ten), V. Luchetti (ten), R. Massard (bar), G. Prêtre (cnd), Rome RAI SO [F] *(rec live 5/30/69)* Melodram 3-▲ MEL 37060 [AAD]
Berlioz, H.:Les Troyens, w. M. Horne (mez), S. Verrett (mez), N. Gedda (ten), V. Luchetti (ten), R. Massard (bar), G. Prêtre (cnd), Rome RAI SO *(rec live 5/30/69)* Arkadia 4-▲ 461 [ADD]
Berlioz, H.:Les Troyens (sels), w. Shirley Verrett (sop—Didon), G. Prêtre (cnd), Rome RAI SO *(rec live, Rome, May 30, 1969)* Arkadia ▲ 619 [ADD]
Borodin, A.:Prince Igor, w. Kalmus (sgr), Infantino (sgr), G. Taddei (ten), B. Christoff (bass), O. Dominguez (mez), A. La Rosa Parodi (cnd), Rome RAI Orch *(rec live 9/19/64)* Melodram 2-▲ MEL 27028 (s)
Catalani, A.:La Wally, w. R. Tebaldi (sop), G. Prandelli (ten), S. Majonica (bass), G. Santini (cnd), Rome RAI SO *(rec 1960)* Enterprise (Palladio) 2-▲ ENTPD 4165 [ADD]
Debussy, C.:Pelléas et Mélisande, w. E. Schwarzkopf (sop), E. Haefliger (ten), M. Roux (bar), M. Petri (bass), H. von Karajan (cnd), Rome Radio Orch [F] *(rec live, 12/19/54)* Arkadia 2-▲ 218 (m) [ADD]
Donizetti, G.:L'elisir d'amore, w. A. Noni (sop), B. Rizzoli (sop), C. Valletti (ten), S. Bruscantini (bar), A. Poli (bar), G. Gavazzeni (cnd), Rome RAI SO *(rec 1952)* Cetra Classic ▲ CDO 5 [AAD]
Donizetti, G.:L'elisir d'amore, w. Alda Noni (sop), Cesare Valletti (ten), Sesto Bruscantini (bar), G. Gavazzeni (cnd), Rome RAI SO Fonit Cetra ("Classic Collection" series) 2-▲ FCT CDO 5
Donizetti, G.:Lucia di Lammermoor, w. Maria Callas (sop), Eugenio Fernandi (ten), Rolando Panerai (bar), Giuseppe Modesti (bass), T. Serafin (cnd), Rome RAI SO *(rec live, Rome, 1957)* Enterprise ("Documents" series) 2-▲ ENTLV 973 [ADD]
Elgar, E.:The Dream of Gerontius, w. C. Shacklock (mez), J. Vickers (ten), M. Nowkovski (bass), J. Barbirolli (cnd), Rome Radio Orch [E] *(rec live, Rome 11/20/57)* Arkadia 2-▲ 584 [ADD]
Mozart, W.A.:Don Giovanni, w. G. Janowitz (sop), S. Jurinac (sop), G. von Milivkovic (mez), A. Kraus (ten), N. Ghiaurov (bass), C. M. Giulini (cnd), Rome RAI Orch *(rec live, May 12, 1970)* Melodram 3-▲ MEL 37080
Mozart, W.A.:Zauberflöte, w. E. Schwarzkopf (sop), R. Streich (sop), A. Noni (sop), N. Gedda (ten), G. Taddei (bar), M. Petri (bass), H. von Karajan (cnd), Rome Radio Orch [I] *(rec live, Dec. 19, 1953)* Myto 2-▲ 2 MCD 89007 (m) [ADD]
Mussorgsky, M.:Khovanshchina, w. Irene Companez (cta), Herbert Handt (ten), Mirto Picchi (ten), Boris Christoff (bass), Armedeo Berdini (sgr), Giorgio Canello (sgr), Dmitri Lopatto (sgr), Michele Malaspina (sgr), Jolanda Mancini (sgr), Mario Petri (sgr), A. Rodzinski (cnd), Rome RAI Radio–TV SO Stradivarius 2-▲ STV DTM 12320 [ADD]
Mussorgsky, M.:Khovanshchina, w. Mietta Sighele (sop—Emma), Elena Souliotis (sop—Susanna), Fiorenza Cossotto (mez—Marfa), Herbert Handt (ten—Scribe), Veriano Luchetti (ten—Prince Andrey Khovansky), Ludovic Spiess (ten—Prince Vasily Golitsin), Claudio Strudthoff (ten—Streshnev), Angelo Marchiandi (bar—Kuz'ka), Teodoro Rovetta (bar—1st Strel'tsi), Siegmund Nimsgern (b-bar—Shaklovity), Cesare Siepi (b-bar—Dosifey), Carlo del Bosco (bass—2nd Strel'tsi), Ubaldo Carosi (bass—Varsonofiev), Nicolai Ghiaurov (bass—Prince Ivan Khovnasky), Giovanni Sciarpeletti (bass—Pastor), B. Leskovich (cnd), Rome RAI SO—also includes bonus Act V [w Boris Christoff] (Rome, 1958) *(rec Rome, 1973)* Bella Voce 3-▲ BLV 107.402 [AAD]
Nono, L.:Epitaffio 1, w. L. Marimpietri (sop), M. Boriello (bar), B. Maderna (cnd), Rome RAI Orch *(rec live, Rome 1/28/61)* Arkadia ▲ 027 [ADD]
Prokofiev, S.:Alexander Nevsky, w. Irene Compañez (cta), A. Rodzinski (cnd), Rome RAI Orch Stradivarius ▲ STV 10035 [ADD]
Rosanna Carteri, Antonietta Stella & Beniamino Gigli, w. Carteri, Rosanna (sop), Antonietta Stella (sop), Beniamino Gigli (ten), Rome RAI SO, Rome RAI Chorus [cnd:Nino Antonellini], Milan RAI SO [cnd:Nino Sanzogno] *(rec Milan & Sanremo, Feb. 9, 1953 & Dec. 21, 1)* Incontri memorabili ("Martini & Rossi Concert" series) ▲ CDMR 5005 [ADD]
Rossini, G.:Mosè in Egitto, w. Teresa Zylis-Gara (sop), Shirley Verrett (mez), Ottavio Garaventa (ten), Giampaolo Corradi (bass), Nicolai Ghiaurov (bass), Mario Petri (bass), W. Sawallisch (cnd), Rome RAI Orch *(rec live, Rome, 1968)* Italian Opera Rarities 2-▲ IOR 7724 [ADD]
Rossini, G.:Stabat Mater, w. Teresa Zylis-Gara (sop), Shirley Verrett (mez), Luciano Pavarotti (ten), Nicola Zaccaria (bass), C. M. Giulini (cnd), Rome RAI Orch *(rec Rome, Dec. 1967)* Emozioni ▲ ARCD 2041
Rossini, G.:Stabat Mater, w. T. Zylis-Gara (sop), S. Verrett (mez), L. Pavarotti (ten), N. Zaccaria (bass), C.M. Giulini (cnd), Rome Radio Orch [L] *(rec live 12/22/67)* Verona 2-▲ 27000/01 (m) [AAD]
Rossini, G.:Stabat Mater, w. T. Zylis-Gara (sop), S. Verrett (mez), L. Pavarotti (ten), N. Zaccaria (bass), C. M. Giulini (cnd), Rome RAI Orch [L] *(rec live 12/22/67)* Melodram 2-▲ MEL 28012
Spontini, G.:Agnes von Hohensauften, w. M. Caballé (sop), A. Stella (sop), B. Prevedi (ten), G. Guelfi (bar), R. Muti (cnd), Rome Radio Orch [I] *(rec live, 4/30/70)* Myto 2-▲ 2 MCD 90215 (m) [ADD]
Stravinsky, I.:Oedipus Rex, w. M. Laszlò (mez—Jocasta), N. Gedda (ten—Oedipus), A. Bertocci (ten—Shepherd), M. Petri (bar—Creon & Tireseus), N. Catalani (bar—Messenger), A. Foà (speaker), H. von Karajan (cnd), Rome RAI SO *(rec Dec. 20, 1952)* Stradivarius ▲ DAT 12311 [ADD]
Verdi, G.:Attila, w. Antonietta Stella (sop), Gianfranco Cecchele (ten), Giangiacomo Guelfi (bar), Ruggiero Raimondi (bass), R. Muti (cnd), Rome RAI Orch *(rec live 1970)* Memories 2-▲ HR 4178/79 (m)
Verdi, G.:Attila, w. Antonietta Stella (sop), Gianfranco Cecchele (ten), Giangiacomo Guelfi (bar), Ruggiero Raimondi (bass), R. Muti (cnd), Rome RAI SO *(rec Rome, Nov. 21, 1970)* Pantheon 2-▲ PHE 6642 (m)
Verdi, G.:La battaglia di Legnano, w. Caterina Mancini (sop), Amedeo Berdini (bar), Rolando Panerai (bar), Albino Gaggi (bass), Edmea Limberti (sgr), Manfredi Ponz de Leon (sgr), F. Previtali (cnd), Rome RAI SO *(rec 1951)* Cetra Classic 2-▲ CDON 40 [ADD]
Verdi, G.:Don Carlos, w. M. Caniglia (sop—Elisabeth de Valois), G. Sciutti (sop—Page), E. Stignani (mez—Princess Eboli), M. Picchi (ten—Don Carlos), M. Ponz de L. (ten—Count of Lerma), P. Silveri (bar—Rodrigue), N. Rossi Lemeni (bass—Philip II), G. Neri (bass—Grand Inquisitor), A. Gaggi (bass—Old Monk), F. Previtali (cnd), Rome RAI SO *(rec Rome, 1951)* Cetra Classic 3-▲ CDO 25 [ADD]
Verdi, G.:Ernani, w. Caterina Mancini (sop), Vittorio Pandano (ten), Gino Penno (ten), Giuseppe Taddei (bar), Giacomo Vaghi (bar), Ezio Achilli (sgr), Licia Rossini (sgr), F. Previtali (cnd), Rome RAI SO Cetra Classic 2-▲ CDON 39 [ADD]
Verdi, G.:La forza del destino (sels), w. G. Cigna (sop—Leonora), E. Ghirardini (bar—Melitone), G. Vaghi (bar—Guardiano), O. de Fabritiis (cnd), Rome RAI Orch *(rec Oct. 10, 1938)* Legato Classics 2-▲ LCD 173-2 [ADD]
Verdi, G.:Luisa Miller, w. L. Kelston (sop—Luisa), M.T. Pace (mez—Federica), G. Larui-Volpi (ten—Rodolfo), S. Colombo (bar—Miller), G. Vaghi (bar—Count Walter), D. Baronti (bass—Wurm), M. Rossi (cnd), Rome RAI Orch *(rec 1951)* Cetra Classic 2-▲ CDO 17 [AAD]
Verdi, G.:Nabucco, w. C. Mancini (sop—Abigaille), G. Gatti (sop—Fenena), B. Preziosa (sop—Anna), M. Binci (ten—Ismaele), L. Francardi (ten—Abdallo), P. Silveri (bar—Nabucodonosor), A. Cassinelli (bass—Zaccaria), A. Gaggi (bass—High Priest of Baal), F. Previtali (cnd), Rome RAI Orch *(rec Rome, 1951)* Cetra Classic 2-▲ CDO 26 [ADD]
Verdi, G.:Requiem Mass (sels), w. M. Caniglia (sop), E. Stignani (mez), B. Gigli (ten), T. Pasero (bass), V. de Sabata (cnd), Rome CO, Turin RAI Chorus—Dies irae; Sanctus; Libera me *(rec Dec. 14, 1940)* Legato Classics 2-▲ LCD 178-2
Verdi, G.:Rigoletto (sels), w. L. Pagliughi (sop), G. Lauri-Volpi (ten), T. Gobbi (bar), F. Previtali (cnd), Rome RAI Orch [highlights] *(rec 1947)* Melodram ▲ MEL 15008

Rome RAI Chorus (cont.)
Verdi, G.:Simon Boccanegra, w. A. Stella (sop—Maria), C. Bergonzi (ten—Gabriele), G. Giorgetti (bar—Pietro), W. Monachesi (bar—Paolo), M. Petri (bar—Jacopo), P. Silveri (bar—Simon), F. Molinari-Pradelli (cnd), Rome Radio Orch *(rec 1951)* Cetra Classic ▲ CDO 23 [ADD]
Wagner, R.:Tannhäuser, w. Gré Brouwestijn (sop), Murray Dickie (ten), Karl Liebl (ten), Eberhard Waechter (bar), Alois Pernerstorfer (b-bar), Deszö Ernster (bass), Walter Brunelli (sgr), Peter Harrower (sgr), Rosl Schweiger (sgr), Herta Wilfert (sgr), A. Rodzinski (cnd), Rome RAI Radio–TV SO Stradivarius 3-▲ STV 12318
Wagner, R.:Tannhäuser (sels), w. G. Brouwenstijn (sop), H. Wilfert (sgr), K. Liebl (ten), E. Wächter (bar), A. Rodzinski (cnd), Rome RAI Orch *(rec Nov. 21 1957)* Myto 3-▲ MCD 93277
Zandonai, R.:Francesca da Rimini, w. M. Caniglia (sop—Francesca), A. M. Canali (mez—Altichiara), A. Bertocci (ten—Ser Toldo Berardengo), M. Carlin (ten—Malatestino), G. Prandelli (ten—Paolo), C. Tagliabue (bar—Giovanni), E. Campi (bass—Il Giuliare/Il Torrigiano), A. Guarnieri (cnd), Rome RAI SO *(rec 1952)* Cetra Classic ▲ CDO 22 [ADD]

G. Piccillo (cnd)
Massenet, J.:Thérèse, w. Agnes Baltsa (mez—Thérèse), Francisco Araiza (ten—Armand), Gino Sinimberghi (ten—Officer), George Fortune (bass—André), Giancarlo Luccardi (bass—Morel), Eftimios Michalopoulos (sgr—Officer/Municipal Officer), G. Albrecht (cnd), Rome RAI SO Orfeo ▲ 387961 [DDD]

Rome Sym Chorus
Bellini, V.:I Puritani (sels), w. Mirella Freni (sop), Luciano Pavarotti (ten), Bonaldo Giaiotti (bass), R. Muti (cnd), Rome SO—A te, o cara, amor talora *(rec live, Oct. 7, 1969)* RCA Gold Seal ▲ 09026-68014-2 [ADD]

Rooke Chapel Choir

W. Payn (cnd)
An American Collage:Music for Solo Voice & Chorus, w. D. Fortunato (mez) Albany ▲ TROY 098 [ADD]
On This Day Earth Shall Ring!, w. Rooke Chapel Ringers, D'Anna Fortunato (mez), Elizabeth Etters-Asmus (hp), David Cover (org) *(rec Rooke Chapel, Bucknell Univ, Feb & May 1995)* Albany ▲ TROY 177 [DDD]

Rossendale Male Voice Choir

E. Tomlinson (cnd)
The Valley of Song TCC ("Collect" series) ▲ CHAN 6604 [ADD]

Rossini Teatro Comunale Chorus

G. Masini (cnd)
Lattuada, F.:Le Preziose ridicole, w. S. Valayre (sop—Madelon), A. Catarci (sop—Marotte), A. Cicogna (mez—Cathos), S. Tedesco (ten—La Grange), E. Di Cesare (ten—Mascarille), A. Veccia (bar—Croissy), R. Servile (bar—Jodelet), E. Fissore (bass—Gorgibus), E. Romagna (cnd), Toscanini SO [I] *(rec live, 1991)* Ermitage ▲ ERM 404 [DDD]

Rostock Motet Chorus
Bach, J.S.:Motets, BWV 225-30, w. C. Eschenburg (cnd), Capella Fidicinia Leipzig [G] Capriccio ▲ CDC 10030 [DDD]

Rotterdam Vocal Ensemble
Schnittke, A.:Life with an Idiot, w. T. Ringholz (sop), H. Haskin (ten), D. Duesing (bar), M. Rostropovich (cnd), Rotterdam PO *(rec Amsterdam, world premiere performance, April 13, 1992)* Sony Classical 2-▲ S2K 52495 [DDD]

Marielle Rousseau Vocal Ensemble
Kaufmann, S.:Et si un jour, w. Béatrice Barbary (sop), B. Calmel (cnd), Bernard Calmel Orch *(rec Feb 1996)* Pavane ▲ ADW 7362 [DDD]

Rovigo City Chorus

G. Mazzucato (cnd)
Scarlatti, A.:Répons du Vendredi Saint, w. Nadi Caristi (sop), Paola Serno (mez), Marco Scavazza (bar) Studio SM ▲ 2515 [DDD]

Royal Chapel European Vocal Ensemble

P. Herreweghe (cnd)
Palestrina, G.:Sacred Music, w. Organum Ensemble—Missa Viri Galilaei; Motet Viri Galilaei; Magnificat Primi Toni [L] Harmonia Mundi France ▲ HMC 901388

Royal Choral Society
Elgar, E.:The Dream of Gerontius (sels), w. M. Balfour (cta), S. Wilson (ten), H. Heyner (bar), E. Elgar (cnd), Royal Albert Hall Orch [E] *(rec 1927)* Opal ▲ CD 9810 (m) [AAD]
Elgar, E.:The Music Makers, w. M. Thomas (cta), M. Sargent (cnd), Leeds Philharmonic Society, London SO, Huddersfield Choral Society *(rec live, Royal Albert Hall April 29, 1965)* Intaglio ▲ INCD 7351 [ADD]
Handel, G.F.:Messiah, w. Yvonne Kenny (sop), Jean Rigby (cta), Thomas Randle (ten), Willard White (bass), O. A. Hughes (cnd), Royal PO IMP Classics 2-▲ IMPDPCD 1106 [DDD]

J. McCarthy (cnd)
Handel, G.F.:Messiah (sels), w. Jennifer Vyvyan (sop), Monica Sinclair (mez), Jon Vickers (ten), Giorgio Tozzi (bass), T. Beecham (cnd), Royal PO—Ov; Comfort Ye My People; Every Valley Shall Be Exalted; And the Glory of the Lord; And He Shall Purify; O Thou That Tellest Good Tidings; For unto Us a Child is Born; Pastoral Symphony; There Were Shepherds Abiding; And the Angel Said unto Them; And Suddenly There Was; Glory to God in the Highest; He Shall Feed His Flock; Come unto Him; Behold the Lamb of God; He Was Despised; All We Like Sheep Have Gone Astray; Hallelujah!; I Know That My Redeemer Liveth; The Trumpet Shall Sound *(rec Walthamstow Town Hall, London, June–Aug 1959)* RCA Victor ▲ 09026-68159-2 [ADD]

M. Sargent (cnd)
Coleridge-Taylor, S.:Scenes from *The Song of Hiawatha,* w. Richard Lewis (ten)—Hiawatha's Wedding Feast Theorema ▲ TH 121224
Sir Malcolm Sargent Conducts Favourite Choral Music, w. various London orchs *(rec 1926–1932)* Pearl ▲ PEA 9380 (m) [AAD]

Royal College of Music Chamber Choir

D. Willcocks (cnd)
Carols for Christmas, Vols. 1 & 2, w. Royal College of Music Brass Ensemble Rykodisk 2-▲ RCD 10004/5

Royal Conservatory Choir members
Wagemans, P.J.:Rosebud, w. J. van Steen (cnd), The Hague PO Donemus ▲ CV 28

Royal Liverpool Phil Choir
Beethoven, L. van:Sym 9, "Choral Sym", w. Joan Rodgers (sop), Della Jones (alt), Peter Bronder (ten), Bryn Terfel (bass), C. Mackerras (cnd), Royal Liverpool PO Classics for Pleasure ("Eminence" series) ▲ CFP 2186 [DDD]
Bizet, G.:Carmen (sels), w. M. Horne (sop), M. Molese (sgr), M. Pellegrini (sgr), G. Griffiths (bar), D. Bowman (bar), F. Egerton (ten), H. Lewis (cnd), Royal PO IMP Collectors Series ▲ IMPX 9016 [AAD]
Borodin, A.:Prince Igor (Polovtsian dances), w. L. Stokowski (cnd), Royal PO, Welsh National Opera Chorus *(rec Kingsway Hall, London, England, June 17, 1969)* London ("Phase 4 Stereo" series) ▲ 443896-2 [ADD]
Borodin, A.:Prince Igor (Polovtsian dances), w. L. Stokowski (cnd), Royal PO [R] London ▲ 417753-2 [ADD]
Delius, F.:Brigg Fair:An English Rhapsody, w. J. Shirley-Quirk (bar), C. Groves (cnd), Royal Liverpool PO EMI Classics ▲ ZDMB 64218
Delius, F.:Requiem, w. H. Harper (sop), T. Hemsley (bar), C. Groves (cnd), Royal Liverpool PO *(rec live, Liverpool 1965)* Intaglio 2-▲ INCD 702-2 [ADD]
Delius, F.:Songs of Sunset, w. J. Baker (mez), C. Groves (cnd), Royal Liverpool PO EMI Classics ▲ ZDMB 64218
Elgar, E.:The Light of Life, w. M. Marshall (sop), H. Watts (cta), J. Shirley-Quirk (bar), C. Groves (cnd), Royal Liverpool PO EMI Classics ▲ CDM 64732
Finzi, G.:Intimations of Immortality, w. P. Langridge (ten), R. Hickox (cnd), Royal Liverpool PO EMI Classics ▲ CDM 64720
Howells, H.:Hymnus Paradisi, w. J. Kennard (sop), J. M. Ainsley (ten), V. Handley (cnd), Royal Liverpool PO Hyperion ▲ CDA 66488

Royal Liverpool Phil Choir (cont.)

Ketèlbey, A.W.:Music of, w. E. Rogers (cnd), Royal PO—In a Monastery Garden; Wedgewood Blue; In the Mystic Land of Egypt; Bells across the Meadows; In a Chinese Temple Garden; Sanctuary of the Heart; 'Appy 'Ampstead; The Phantom Melody; In a Persian Market *(rec Kingsway Hall, London, Feb 1969)* London ("Phase 4 Stereo") ▲ 444786-2 [ADD]

McCartney, P.:Liverpool Oratorio, w. K. Te Kanawa (sop), S. Burgess (mez), J. Hadley (ten), W. White (bass), C. Davis (cnd), Royal Liverpool PO EMI Classics 2-▲ CDQB 54371 2-■ 4D2Q 54371

Tchaikovsky, P.:Ov 1812, w. L. Stokowski (cnd), Royal PO, Grenadier Guards Band, Welsh National Opera Chorus *(rec Kingsway Hall, London, England, June 16, 1969)* London ("Phase 4 Stereo" series) ▲ 443896-2 [ADD]

Vaughan Williams, R.:Flos Campi, w. Christopher Balmer (va), V. Handley (cnd), Royal Liverpool PO Classics for Pleasure ("Eminence" series) ▲ CDEMX 9512 [DDD]

Vaughan Williams, R.:Serenade to Music, w. V. Handley (cnd), Royal Liverpool PO Classics for Pleasure ("Eminence" series) ▲ CDEMX 2173 [DDD]

Vaughan Williams, R.:Sym 7, w. V. Handley (cnd), Royal Liverpool PO Classics for Pleasure ("Eminence" series) ▲ CDEMX 2173 [DDD]

V. Handley (cnd)

Howells, H.:An English Mass Hyperion ▲ CDA 66488

Royal Opera House Covent Garden Chorus

Beethoven, L. van:Fidelio, w. S. Jurinac (sop), J. Vickers (ten), H. Hotter (b-bar), G. Frick (bass), O. Klemperer (cnd), Royal Opera House Orch [G] *(rec live, Covent Garden, 3/7/61)* Melodram 2-▲ MEL 27076 (m) [AAD]

Bellini, V.:I Capuleti e i Montecchi, w. E. Guberova (sop—Giulietta), A. Baltsa (mez—Romeo), D. Raffanti (ten—Tebaldo), R. Muti (cnd), Royal Opera House Orch EMI Classics ▲ CDMB 64846

Bellini, V.:Norma, w. J. Sutherland (sop), M. Callas (sop), E. Stignani (mez), M. Picchi (ten), G. Vaghi (bass), V. Gui (cnd), Royal Opera House Orch [I] *(rec live, Covent Garden 11/52)* Melodram 2-▲ MEL 26025

Bellini, V.:Norma, w. M. Callas (sop), J. Sutherland (sop), E. Stignani (mez), M. Picchi (ten), G. Vaghi (bass), V. Gui (cnd), Royal Opera House Orch [I] *(rec live, Covent Garden 11/52)* Verona 3-▲ 27018/20 (m) [AAD]

Bellini, V.:Norma, w. M. Callas (sop), J. Sutherland (sop), E. Stignani (mez), M. Picchi (ten), G. Vaghi (bass), V. Gui (cnd), Royal Opera House Orch [I] *(rec live, Covent Garden 11/52)* Legato Classics 2-▲ LCD 130-2 (m) [AAD]

Bellini, V.:La sonnambula (sels), w. J. Sutherland (sop), T. Serafin (cnd), Royal Opera House Orch—seven arias & scenes [I] *(rec live, Covent Garden 1960)* Myto 2-▲ 2 MCD 90529 [ADD]

Bizet, G.:Carmen, w. Kiri Te Kanawa (sop), Shirley Verrett (mez), Placido Domingo (ten), José Van Dam (b-bar), G. Solti (cnd), Royal Opera House Orch *(rec live, London, 1973)* Arkadia 3-▲ 498

Britten, B.:Billy Budd, w. P. Pears (ten), T. Uppman (bar), H. Alan (bar), G. Evans (b-bar), F. Dalberg (bass), B. Britten (cnd), Royal Opera House Orch *(rec Dec. 1, 1951)* VAI Audio 3-▲ VAIA 1034-3 [ADD]

Britten, B.:Peter Grimes, w. C. Watson (sop), P. Pears (ten), G. Evans (bar), B. Britten (cnd), Royal Opera House Orch [E] London 3-▲ 414577-2 [ADD]

Britten, B.:Peter Grimes, w. F. Lott (soprano—Ellen Orford), T. Allen (tenor—Captain Balstrode), A. R. Johnson (tenor—Peter Grimes), Covent Garden, B. Haitink (cnd), Royal Opera House Orch EMI Classics ▲ CDCB 54832

Britten, B.:Peter Grimes, w. H. Harper (sop), J. Vickers (ten), J. Summers (bar), C. Davis (cnd), Royal Opera House Orch [E] Philips 2-▲ 432578-2 [ADD]

Cherubini, L.:Médée, w. M. Callas (sop), F. Cossotto (mez), J. Vickers (ten), N. Zaccaria (bass), N. Rescigno (cnd), Royal Opera House Orch [I] *(rec live, Covent Garden, 6/30/59)* Melodram 2-▲ MEL 26005

Christmas from Covent Garden, w. Royal Opera House Orch *(rec All Saints' Church, Tooting, London & All Saints' Church, Petersham, Surrey, May 1989 & May 1994)* Conifer Classics ▲ 75605-55011-2 [DDD]

Debussy, C.:Pelléas et Mélisande, w. E. Söderström (sop), Y. Minton (mez), G. Shirley (ten), D. McIntyre (bass-bar), D. Ward (bass), P. Boulez (cnd), Royal Opera House Orch Sony Classical (Pierre Boulez Edition) 3-▲ SM3K 47265

Donizetti, G.:L'elisir d'amore, w. I. Cotrubas (sop), L. Watson (sop), P. Domingo (ten), G. Evans (bar), I. Wixell (bar), J. Pritchard (cnd), Royal Opera House Orch *(rec 1977)* CBS 2-▲ M2K 34585 [ADD]

Donizetti, G.:Lucia di Lammermoor, w. J. McDonald (sop), J. Sutherland (sop), M. Elkins (mez), J. Bowman (alt), J. Gibin (ten), J. Rouleau (bass), Shaw (sgr), T. Serafin (cnd), Royal Opera House Orch—3 duets from Act 1, & 3 soprano solo arias from Act 2 [I] Myto ▲ 1 MCD 91545 [ADD]

Donizetti, G.:Lucia di Lammermoor (sels), w. J. Sutherland (sop), L. Pavarotti (ten), S. Milnes (bar), N. Ghiaurov (bass), R. Bonynge (cnd), Royal Opera House Orch [I] London ("Opera Gala" series) ▲ 421885-2 [ADD]

Gluck, C.W.:Orfeo ed Euridice, w. H. Donath (sop), P. Lorengar (sop), M. Horne (mez), G. Solti (cnd), Royal Opera House Orch London 2-▲ 417410-2 [ADD]

Janácek, L.:Jenůfa (sels), w. M. Collier (sop), A. Varnay (sop), R. Cassilly (ten), J. Lanigan (ten), R. Kubelik (cnd), Royal Opera House Orch—eight solo, duet & trio arias featuring Astrid Varnay [G] *(rec live at Covent Garden, Feb. 24, 1968)* Myto 2-▲ 2 MCD 90422 [ADD]

Live on Stage, w. Pavarotti, Luciano (ten), Rome Opera Orch [cnd.:Carlo Maria Giulini], Royal Opera House Covent Garden Orch, Royal Opera House Covent Garden Chorus [cnd:Carlo Felice Cillario], et al. LaserLight ▲ 15104

Mascagni, P.:L'amico Fritz, w. M. Freni (sop), L. Pavarotti (ten), V. Sardinero (bar), G. Gavazzeni (cnd), Royal Opera House Orch Covent Garden [I] EMI Classics 2-▲ CDCB 47905 [ADD]

Mascagni, P.:Cavalleria rusticana, w. A. Baltsa (mez), S. Mentzer (mez) P. Domingo (ten), J. Pons (bar), G. Sinopoli (cnd), Philharmonia Orch [I] Deutsche Grammophon 2-▲ 429568-2 [DDD]

Massenet, J.:Werther, w. F. von Stade (mez), J. Carreras (ten), T. Allen (bar), R. Lloyd (b-bar), C. Davis (cnd), Royal Opera House Orch Covent Garden [F] Philips 2-▲ 416654-2 [ADD]

Mozart, W.A.:Complete Mozart Edition, w. M. Caballé (sop), I. Cotrubas (sop), J. Baker (mez), N. Gedda (ten), C. Davis (cnd), Royal Opera House Orch Philips 3-▲ 422542-2 [ADD]

Mozart, W.A.:Complete Mozart Edition, w. L. Popp (sop), J. Baker (mez), Y. Minton (mez), F. von Stade (mez), S. Burrows (ten), R. Lloyd (b-bar), C. Davis (cnd), Royal Opera House Orch Philips 2-▲ 422544-2 [ADD]

Mozart, W.A.:Complete Mozart Edition, w. K. Te Kanawa (sop), M. Arroyo (sop), M. Freni (sop), S. Burrows (ten), I. Wixell (bar), C. Davis (cnd), Royal Opera House Orch Philips 3-▲ 422541-2 [ADD]

Opera Choruses, w. L. Gardelli (cnd), Royal Opera House Orch Covent Garden EMI Classics ▲ CDM 64356

Opera Spectacular 2, w. R. Stapleton (cnd), Royal PO RPO Records ▲ CDRPO 7009 [DDD]

Puccini, G.:Arias, w. Angela Gheorghiu (sop), Nina Rautio (sop), Johan Botha (ten), Anthony Michaels-Moore (bar), E. Downes (cnd), Royal Opera House Orch—Se come voi piccina io fossi [from Le villi]; Addio mio dolce amor [from Edgar]; Donna non vidi mai; Sola, perduta, abbandonata [both from Manon Lescaut]; Donde lieta usci [from La Bohème]; Act 1 Finale; E lucevan le stelle [both from Tosca]; Un tal baccano in chiesa; Or tutto è chiaro; Tre sbirri, una carrozza; Un bel dì [from Madama Butterfly]; Ch'ella mi creda [from La fanciulla del West]; Chi il bel sogno di Doretta [from La rondine]; Nulla, silenzio [from Il tabarro]; Senza mamma [from Suor Angelica]; O mio babbino caro [from Gianni Schicchi]; Act I Finale; Nessun dorma [both from Turandot]; Signore, ascolta; Non piangere, Liù *(rec Henry Wood Hall, London, Feb 12-27 & Mar 5, 1995)* Conifer Classics ("Royal Opera House" series) ▲ 75605-55013-2 [DDD]

Puccini, G.:La fanciulla del West, w. C. Neblett (sop), P. Domingo (ten), S. Milnes (bar), Z. Mehta (cnd), Royal Opera House Orch Covent Garden [I] Deutsche Grammophon 2-▲ 419640-2 [ADD]

Puccini, G.:Madama Butterfly, w. V. de los Angeles (sop—Madama Butterfly), B. Howitt (mez—Suzuki), J. Livingston (mez—Kate), J. Lanigan (ten—Pinkerton), D. Tree (ten—Goro), D. A. (ten—Yamadori), G. Evans (bar—Sharpless), M. Langdon (bass—Bonzo), R. Kempe (cnd), Royal Opera House Orch *(rec London, May 1957)* Ornamenti 2-▲ FE 112 [ADD]

Puccini, G.:Manon Lescaut, w. M. Freni (sop), P. Domingo (ten), R. Bruson (bar), G. Sinopoli (cnd), Philharmonia Orch [I] *(rec 1984)* Deutsche Grammophon 2-▲ 413893-2 [DDD]

Royal Opera House Covent Garden Chorus (cont.)

Puccini, G.:Tosca, w. Maria Callas (sop—Floria Tosca), Robert Bowman (ten—Spoletta), Renato Cioni (ten—Mario Cavaradossi), Eric Garrett (bar—Il Sagrestano), Tito Gobbi (bar—Scarpia), Victor Godfrey (bass—Casare Angelotti), Dennis Wicks (bass—Sciarrone), C. F. Cillario (cnd), Royal Opera House Orch *(rec London, 1964)* Melodram 2-▲ CDI 203003 [ADD]

Puccini, G.:Tosca, w. M. Callas (sop), R. Cioni (ten), T. Gobbi (bar), C. F. Cillario (cnd), Royal Opera House Orch [I] *(rec live, 1/21/64)* Verona 2-▲ 27027/28 (m) [AAD]

Puccini, G.:Tosca, w. M. Callas (sop), R. Cioni (ten), T. Gobbi (bar), C. F. Cillario (cnd), Royal Opera House Orch [I] *(rec live 1/21/64)* Melodram 2-▲ MEL 26011

Puccini, G.:Tosca, w. R. Tebaldi (sop), F. Tagliavini (ten), T. Gobbi (bar), F. Molinari-Pradelli (cnd), Royal Opera House Orch [I] *(rec live at Covent Garden, 6/30/55)* Legato Classics 2-▲ LCD 157-2 (m) [ADD]

Puccini, G.:Tosca, w. M. Freni (sop), P. Domingo (ten), S. Ramey (bass), G. Sinopoli (cnd), Philharmonia Orch [I] Deutsche Grammophon 2-▲ 431775-2 [DDD]

Smetana, B.:The Bartered Bride, w. H. Konetzni (sop), R. Tauber (ten), F. Krenn (bass), T. Beecham (cnd), Royal Opera House Orch [G] *(rec live, Covent Garden, 5/1/39)* Standing Room Only 2-▲ SRO 830-2 [ADD]

Tippett, M.:The Midsummer Marriage, w. Joan Carlyle (sop—Joan), Elizabeth Harwood (sop—Beth), Elizabeth Bainbridge (mez), Helen Watts (cta—Sosostris), Stuart Burrows (ten—Jack), Alberto Remedios (ten—Mark), Stafford Dean (bass), Raimund Herincx (bass—King Fisher), C. Davis (cnd), Royal Opera House Orch Lyrita 2-▲ SRCD 2217

Verdi, G.:Aida, w. Maria Callas (sop—Aida), Joan Sutherland (sop—Priestess), Giulietta Simionato (cta—Amneris), Kurt Baum (ten—Radames), Hector Thomas (ten—Messenger), Jess Walters (bar—Amonasro), Michael Langdon (bass—King), Giulio Neri (bass—Ramfis), J. Barbirolli (cnd), Royal Opera House Orch *(rec Covent Garden, London, June 10, 1953)* Legato Classics 2-▲ LCD 187-2

Verdi, G.:Aida, w. G. Jones (sop), J. Vickers (ten), Dourian (sgr), Shaw (sgr), E. Downes (cnd), Royal Opera House Orch [I] *(rec live, Covent Garden, 1/27/68)* Melodram 2-▲ MEL 27019

Verdi, G.:Aida, w. M. Caballé (sop), F. Cossotto (mez), P. Domingo (ten), P. Cappuccilli (bar), N. Ghiaurov (bass), R. Muti (cnd), New Philharmonia Orch [I] EMI Classics 3-▲ CDCC 47271 [ADD]

Verdi, G.:Un ballo in maschera, w. M. Arroyo (sop), R. Grist (sop), F. Cossotto (mez), P. Domingo (ten), P. Cappuccilli (bar), R. Muti (cnd), New Philharmonia Orch [I] EMI Classics (Studio) 2-▲ CDMB 69576 [ADD]

Verdi, G.:Un ballo in maschera, w. Reri Grist (sop), Katia Ricciarelli (sop), Elizabeth Bainbridge (mez), Plácido Domingo (ten), Piero Cappuccilli (bar), C. Abbado (cnd), Royal Opera House Orch *(rec 1975)* Arkadia 2-▲ 488

Verdi, G.:Don Carlos, w. R. Tebaldi (sop), G. Bumbry (mez), C. Bergonzi (ten), D. Fischer-Dieskau (bar), N. Ghiaurov (bass), G. Solti (cnd), Royal Opera House Orch Covent Garden [1886 5-act Italian version] [I] London 3-▲ 421114-2 [ADD]

Verdi, G.:Don Carlos, w. G. Brouwenstein (sop—Elisabeta di Valois), F. Barbieri (mez—Princess Eboli), J. Vickers (ten—Don Carlo), T. Gobbi (bar—Rodrigo), B. Christoff (bass—Fillipo), C. M. Giulini (cnd), Royal Opera House Orch *(rec 1958)* Myto 3-▲ MCD 94197

Verdi, G.:Macbeth, w. Amy Shuard (sop—Lady Macbeth), Noreen Berry (mez—Lady-in-waiting), John Dobson (ten—Malcolm), André Turp (ten—Macduff), Tito Gobbi (bar—Macbeth), Edgar Boniface (bass—Servant), Rydderch Davies (bass—Doctor), Forbes Robinson (bass—Banco), Jean Holmes (sgr—Apparition), Celia Penny (sgr—Apparition), Glynne Thomas (sgr—Apparition), Brian Wrigt (sgr—Araldo), F. Molinari-Pradelli (cnd), Royal Opera House Orch *(rec London, Apr 8, 1960)* Bella Voce 2-▲ 7203 [AAD]

Verdi, G.:Otello, w. Raina Kabaivanska (sop), Mario del Monaco (ten), Tito Gobbi (bar), G. Solti (cnd), Royal Opera House Orch Pantheon 2-▲ PHE 6608

Verdi, G.:Otello, w. Raina Kabaivanska (sop), Josephine Veasey (mez), John Lanigan (ten), Mario del Monaco (ten), Tito Gobbi (bar), G. Solti (cnd), Royal Opera House Orch *(rec June 30, 1962)* Memories ▲ MEM 4583 [AAD]

Verdi, G.:Otello (sels), w. Giovanni Zenatello (ten), Sabajno, Bellezza (cnd), La Scala Orch, Royal Opera House Orch Covent Garden Phonographe ("Great Voices" series) ▲ PHG 5048

Verdi, G.:La traviata, w. M. Callas (sop), C. Valletti (ten), A. Zanasi (bass), N. Rescigno (cnd), Royal Opera House Orch [I] *(rec live 6/20/58)* Melodram 2-▲ MEL 26007 (m)

Verdi, G.:La traviata, w. M. Callas (sop), C. Valletti (ten), A. Zanasi (bass), N. Rescigno (cnd), Royal Opera House Orch [I] *(rec live 6/20/58)* Verona 2-▲ 27054/55 (m) [AAD]

Verdi, G.:La traviata, w. Angela Gheorghiu (sop—Violetta), Leah-Marian Jones (mez—Flora Bervoix), Gillian Knight (mez—Annina), Robin Leggate (ten—Gastone), Frank Lopardo (ten—Alfredo Germont), Rodney Gibson (ten—Servo di Flora), Neil Griffiths (ten—Giuseppe), Mark Beesley (bar—Dottore Grenvile), Leo Nucci (bar—Giorgio Germont), Richard Van Allan (bass—Barone Douphol), Roderick Earle (bass—Marquese d'Obigny), Bryan Secombe (bass—Commissionario), G. Solti (cnd), Royal Opera House Orch *(rec live, Royal Opera House, Covent Garden, Dec. 1994)* London 2-▲ 448119-2

Verdi, G.:La traviata, w. R. Scotto (sop), L. Pavarotti (ten), P. Glossop (bar), C. F. Cillario (cnd), Royal Opera House Orch *(rec live 1965)* Memories 2-▲ HR 4404/05 (m)

Verdi, G.:La traviata (sels), w. R. Scotto (sop), L. Pavarotti (ten), C. F. Cillario (cnd), Royal Opera House Orch—2 scenes [I] *(rec live, Covent Garden 3/19/65)* Verona 2-▲ 27081/82

Verdi, G.:Il trovatore, w. G. Cigna (sop—Leonora), G. Wettergren (mez—Azucena), M. Huder (mez—Ines), J. Björling (ten—Manrico), O. Dua (ten—Ruiz), C. Zambelli (ten—Ferrando), M. Basiola (bar—Count di Luna), L. Horsman (bar—Old Gypsy), V. Gui (cnd), Royal Opera Orch *(rec May 12, 1939)* Legato Classics 2-▲ LCD 173-2 [ADD]

Verdi, G.:Il trovatore, w. Katia Ricciarelli (sop), Stefania Toczyska (mez), José Carreras (ten), Yuri Mazurok (bar), C. Davis (cnd), Royal Opera House Orch Philips ("Two-Fers" series) 2-▲ 446151-2

Verdi, G.:Il trovatore (sels), w. Hjördis Schymberg (sop), Kerstin Meyer (mez), Jussi Björling (ten), Olle Sivall (ten), Hugo Hasslo (bar), H. Sandberg (cnd), Royal Opera Orch—Non son tuo figlio?; Mal reggendo all'aspro assalto; Quale d'armi fragor; Ah! sì, ben mio, coll'essere; L'onda de' suoni mistici; Di quella pira l'orrendo foco; Miserere d'un'alma già vicina; Madre?...non dormi?; Se m'ami ancor; Ciell...non m'inganna; Ti scosta... *(rec Royal Opera, Stockholm, Mar 6, 1960)* Myto ▲ MCD 953130

Wagner, R.:Der fliegende Holländer, w. L. Rysanek (sop), K. Liebl (ten), G. London (bar), G. Tozzi (bass), A. Dorati (cnd), Royal Opera House Orch [G] London 2-▲ 417319-2 [ADD]

Wagner, R.:Der fliegende Holländer (sels), w. K. Flagstad (sop), M. Lorenz (ten), H. Janssen (bar), L. Weber (bass), F. Reiner (cnd), Royal Opera House Orch [G] *(rec live, Covent Garden, 6/11/37)* Standing Room Only ▲ SRO 808-1 (m) [ADD]

Wagner, R.:Der fliegende Holländer (sels), w. Kirsten Flagstad (sop), Tiana Lemnitz (sop), Torsten Ralf (ten), Rudolf Bockelmann (b-bar), Ludwig Weber (bass), T. Beecham (cnd), Royal Opera House Orch Memories ("Golden" series) ▲ MEM 3003

Wagner, R.:Götterdämmerung (sels), w. Frida Leider (sop), Kerstin Thorborg (mez), Lauritz Melchior (ten), Herbert Janssen (bar), Emanuel List (bass), Maria Nezadál (sgr), T. Beecham (cnd), London PO *(rec Covent Garden, London, 1936)* Preiser ▲ PRE 90266

Wagner, R.:Götterdämmerung (sels), w. F. Leider (sop), Nezadál (sop), K. Thorborg (mez), L. Melchior (ten), H. Janssen (bar), L. Weber (bass), T. Beecham (cnd), London PO [G] *(rec from 1925 Polydor & 1929)* Legato Classics 2-▲ LCD 146-2 (m) [ADD]

Wagner, R.:Götterdämmerung (sels), w. Kirsten Flagstad (sop), Tiana Lemnitz (sop), Torsten Ralf (ten), Rudolf Bockelmann (b-bar), Ludwig Weber (bass), T. Beecham (cnd), Royal Opera House Orch Memories ("Golden" series) ▲ MEM 3003

Wagner, R.:Lohengrin (sels), w. Kirsten Flagstad (sop), Tiana Lemnitz (sop), Torsten Ralf (ten), Rudolf Bockelmann (b-bar), Ludwig Weber (bass), T. Beecham (cnd), Royal Opera House Orch Memories ("Golden" series) ▲ MEM 3003

Wagner, R.:Die Meistersinger von Nürnberg (sels), w. Kirsten Flagstad (sop), Tiana Lemnitz (sop), Torsten Ralf (ten), Rudolf Bockelmann (b-bar), Ludwig Weber (bass), T. Beecham (cnd), Royal Opera House Orch Memories ("Golden" series) ▲ MEM 3003

Wagner, R.:Tannhäuser, w. C. Studer (sop), A. Baltsa (mez), P. Domingo (ten), A. Schmidt (bar), M. Salminen (bass), G. Sinopoli (cnd), Philharmonia Orch Deutsche Grammophon ▲ 435405-2 [DDD]

Wagner, R.:Tannhäuser, w. C. Studer (sop), A. Baltsa (mez), P. Domingo (ten), A. Schmidt (bar), M. Salminen (bass), G. Sinopoli (cnd), Philharmonia Orch [G] Deutsche Grammophon 3-▲ 427625-2 [DDD]

Royal Opera House Covent Garden Chorus (cont.)
Wagner, R.:Tristan und Isolde, w. K. Flagstad (sop), L. Melchior (ten), H. Janssen (bar), P. Schoeffler (b-bar), T. Beecham (cnd), Royal Opera House Orch *(rec live, Covent Garden, 6/18 & 22/37)* Melodram 3-▲ MEL 37029 (m) [AAD]
Wagner, R.:Tristan und Isolde, w. K. Flagstad (sop), S. Kalter (cta), L. Melchior (ten), H. Janssen (bar), E. List (bass), F. Reiner (cnd), Royal Opera House Orch [G] *(rec live, Covent Garden May/June 1936)* VAI Audio 3-▲ VAIA 1004-3 (m) [ADD]
Wagner, R.:Tristan und Isolde, w. Kirsten Flagstad (sop), Margarete Klose (mez), Lauritz Melchior (ten/bar), Herbert Janssen (bar), Sven Nilsson (bass), T. Beecham (cnd), Philharmonia Orch *(rec 1937)* Grammofono 2000 3-▲ GRM 78570 (m)
Wagner, R.:Tristan und Isolde (sels), w. Kirsten Flagstad (sop), Tiana Lemnitz (sop), Torsten Ralf (ten), Rudolf Bockelmann (b-bar), Ludwig Weber (bass), T. Beecham (cnd), Royal Opera House Orch Memories ("Golden" series) ▲ MEM 3003

Royal Opera House Covent Garden Women's Chorus
Mendelssohn, F.:A Midsummer Night's Dream (sels), w. Jennifer Vyvyan (sop), Marion Lowe (sop), P. Maag (cnd), London SO—Op. 21; Op. 61, Nos 1, 3, 5, 7, 9, 11, 12 Classic Records ▲ CSCD 6001

Royal Scottish Academy of Music & Drama St. Cecilia Choir
Elgar, E.:Partsongs, Op. 26, w. C. Groves (cnd), BBC Scottish SO IMP ("BBC Radio Classics" series) ▲ IMP 5691802

Royal Scottish National Chorus
Buechner, M.:The Liberty Bell, w. N. Mantle (cnd), Royal Scottish National Orch *(rec Henry Wood Hall, Glasgow, Sept. 1994)* Nord-Disc ▲ NORD 2034 [DDD] ■ NORDC 2035
The Holly & the Ivy, w. J. Currie (cnd), Royal Scottish Orch ASV ("White Line" series) ▲ ASV 2073
Leclair, J.-M.:Sons Vn (Books 1-4), w. A. Dubeau (vn), A. Tunis (pno) [arr for vn & pno]— Op. 9/3 *(rec 1988)* Analekta Fleur de Lys ▲ FL 2 3021 [DDD] ■ AN4-8702
Songs of Scotland ASV ▲ ASV 2087 [DDD]

Royal Swedish Opera Chorus
S. Ehrling (cnd)
The Most Beloved Opera Choruses, w. Carina Morling (mez), Ingrid Tobiasson (cta), Magnus Kyhle (ten), Anders Lorentzon (bass) Caprice ▲ CAP 21520

RTE Chamber Choir
:A Wedding Banquet, w. K. Alwyn (cnd), RTE Sinfonietta *(rec Taney Parish Ctr., Dublin, Feb 14 & 15, 1994)* Marco Polo ▲ 8.223716 [DDD]

RTE Phil Choir
Wallace, V.:Maritana, w. Majella Cullagh (sop), Lynda Lee (mez), Paul Charles Clarke (ten), Ian Caddy (bar), Damien Smith (bar), Quentin Hayes (bass), P. O. Duinn (cnd), RTE Concert Orch *(rec O'Reilly Hall, Dublin, Sept 1995)* Marco Polo 2-▲ 8.223406-7 [DDD]

Artur Rubinstein Phil Chorus
Orff, C.:Carmina burana, w. A. M. Dahl (sop), B. Grek (ten), J. Wolanski (bass), I. Stupel (cnd), Artur Rubinstein PO *(rec Apr. 1991)* Danacord ▲ DACOCD 400 [DDD]

Rudolfsheimer Children's Choir
Children's Songs of the World, w. Gruberova, Edita (sop), International Children's Choir Nightingale Classics ▲ NIG CD 70660

Rudolstadt Festival Chorus
Wagner, S.:Banadietrich, w. Beth Johanning (sop), Vivian Hanner (sgr), Volker Horn (ten), André Wenhold (bar), Andreas Schmidt (bar), Adalbert Walker (bass), V. Gailis (cnd), Thuringian SO *(rec Rudolstädt, June 1995)* Marco Polo 2-▲ 8.223895-6 [DDD]

Russian Academic Choir
Mahler, G.:Sym 3, w. Olga Alexandrova (mez), E. Svetlanov (cnd), Russian State SO, Moscow Boys' Cappella *(rec Large Hall of the Conservatory, Moscow, Dec. 1994)* Russian Season 2-▲ RUS 288111/12 [DDD]

Russian Chamber Choir
A. Roudenko (cnd)
Rachmaninoff, S.:All-Night Vigil, w. Voskreseniye Choir *(rec Moscow, Apr. 28-29, 1992)* Northeastern ▲ NR 256 [DDD]

Russian Monks Choir
Missa Russica, w. Moscow Cathedral Choir, Mainzer Cathedral Choir, Moscow Holy Synod Boys' Choir [cnd:Victor Popov] Koch Schwann ▲ SCH 312122 ■ SCH 212124

Russian Papel College Choir
Rachmaninoff, S.:All-Night Vigil, w. H. Czaja (cta), G. Schmitz (ten), E. Lohneisen (sgr), P. Blitznetzow (sgr), J. Stojaspal (sgr)—No. 2 Christophorus ▲ CHR 74609

Russian Patriarchate Choir
A. Grindenko (cnd)
Divine Liturgy for the Feast of St. Peter & St. Paul Opus 111 ▲ OPS 30161
Panikhida Opus 111 ▲ OPS 30-97
Romantic Choral Music from Russia Opus 111 ▲ OPS 30-112
Russian Medieval Chant Opus 111 ▲ OPS 30-120

Russian Phil Choir
Tchaikovsky, P.:Choral Music, w. V. Polianski (cnd), Russian PO—Legend Opus 111 ▲ OPS 57-9203 [DDD]

Russian Radio-TV Large Academic Choir
Mahler, G.:Sym 2, w. Natalia Guerassimova (sop), Olga Alexandrova (alt), E. Svetlanov (cnd), Russian State SO Russian Season 2-▲ 288136.37

Russian Republican Capelle
A. Yurlov (cnd)
Rachmaninoff, S.:The Bells, w. Yelizaveta Shumskaya (sop), Mikhail Dovenman (ten), Alexei Bolshakov (bar), K. Kondrashin (cnd), Moscow PO RCA Gold Seal ▲ 74321-32046-2 [ADD]

Russian Stars on Ice Chorus
Danova, R.:The Phantom of the Opera on Ice, w. Susannah Glanville (sop), Kathy Dooley (sop), Johnny Logan (ten), Stephen Lee Garden (ten), Mungo Jerry (bar), Nigel Paul (bar), P. Whitfield (cnd), Northern Light SO, Northern Light Choir Plaza ▲ PZA 008

Russian State Academy Chorus
Stravinsky, I.:Music of, w. Davis, Waart, Markevitch (cnd), London SO, Russian State SO, Netherlands Wind Ensemble—Sym. in C; Sym of Psalms; Con. for Violin & others Philips ("Duo" series) 2-▲ 442583-2
S. Gussev (cnd)
Haydn, J.:The Seven Last Words of Christ on the Cross, w. Elena Evseeva (sop), Margarita Maruna (mez), Arkady Mishenkin (ten), Boris Bezhko (bass), A. de Almeida (cnd), Moscow SO *(rec Mosfilm Studio, Moscow, Jan 27-28, 1995)* SOMM ▲ SOMMCD 203 [DDD]

Russian State Choir
Rachmaninoff, S.:Aleko, w. A. Tchistiakov (cnd), Bolshoi Theater SO Soloists Russian Season ("Russian Season" series) ▲ LDC 288079
Rachmaninoff, S.:Aleko, w. Natalia Erassova (sop), Galina Borissova (cta), Vitaly Tarastchenko (ten), Vladimir Matorin (bass), Viatcheslav Potchapski (bass), A. Tchistiakov (cnd), Bolshoi Theater Orch Russian Season 3-▲ CMX 388053
Rachmaninoff, S.:Francesca da Rimini, w. Maria Lapina (sop), Nikolaï Vassiliev (ten), Vitaly Tarastchenko (ten), Nikolaï Mechetniak (bar),Vladimir Matorin (bass), A. Tchistiakov (cnd), Bolshoi Theater Orch Russian Season 3-▲ CMX 388053
Rachmaninoff, S.:The Miserly Knight, w. Mikhail Krutikov (sgr), Vladimir Kudriashov (sgr), Alexander Arkhipov (sgr), Vladislav Verestnikov (sgr), Piotr Gluboky (sgr), A. Tchistiakov (cnd), Bolshoi Theater Orch Russian Season 3-▲ CMX 388053
Rimsky-Korsakov, N.:A May Night, w. Maria Lapina (sop), Natalia Erassova (mez), Elena Okolycheva (cta), Alexander Arkhipov (ten), Vitaly Tarastchenko (ten), Piotr Glouboky (bass), Viatcheslav Potchapski (bass), A. Tchistiakov (cnd), Bolshoi Theater Orch Russian Season 4-▲ CMX 388054
A. Tchistiakov (cnd)
Tchaikovsky, P.:The Snow Maiden, w. N. Erasova (mez) Russian Season (Russian Season) ▲ LDC 288090

Russian State Symphonic Cappella
Glazunov, A.:The King of the Jews, w. G. Rozhdestvensky (cnd), Russian State SO Chandos ▲ CHAN 9467
Gretchaninoff, A.:Liturgica Domestica for St. John Chrysostom, w. V. Polianski (cnd), Russian State SO—Great Litany; Antiphon I; Antiphon II; Glori & Unigenitus; Trisagion; Alleluia...After the Gospel; Litany of Supplication; Cherubic Hymn; After the Cherubic Hymn; Credo; Pax Hominibus; Hymn of the Blessed Virgin; Pater Noster; Laudate Deum; End of the Liturgy Chandos ▲ CHAN 9365 [DDD]
Gretchaninoff, A.:Missa Sancti Spiritus, w. Tatiana Jeranje (cta), V. Polianski (cnd), Russian State SO Chandos ▲ CHAN 9397 [DDD]
Schnittke, A.:Sacred Hymns, w. V. Polianski (cnd), Russian State SO Chandos ▲ CHAN 9463
Schnittke, A.:Schall und Hall Chandos ▲ CHAN 9466
Schnittke, A.:Sym 4, w. V. Polianski (cnd), Russian State SO Chandos ▲ CHAN 9463
Tchaikovsky, P.:Suite 2, w. G. Rozhdestvensky (cnd), Russian State Symphonic Cappella Erato ▲ 45970-2
V. Polianski (cnd)
Gretchaninoff, A.:Mass "Et in terra pax", w. Anatoly Obraztsov (bass), Ludmila Golub (org) Chandos ▲ CHAN 9486
Gretchaninoff, A.:The Seven Days of Passion Chandos ("New Direction" series) ▲ CHAN 9303 [DDD]
Rachmaninoff, S.:Liturgy of St John Chrysostom *(rec Oct. 1990)* Claves 2-▲ CD 9304/05 [DDD]

Russian State Yurlov Choir
Prokofiev, S.:Ivan the Terrible, w. M. Shostakovich (cnd), London PO *(rec live Nov. 26, 1972)* Intaglio ▲ INCD 7371 [ADD]

Russki Partes
Diletski, N.:In Front of Your Icon Pavane ▲ 7343 [DDD]
Lassus, O. de:Ecce Maria genuit Pavane ▲ 7343 [DDD]
Lassus, O. de:Timor et tremor Pavane ▲ 7343 [DDD]
Palestrina, G.:Alla riva del Tebro Pavane ▲ 7343 [DDD]
Palestrina, G.:Missa "L'Homme armé" Pavane ▲ 7343 [DDD]
Pekalitski, S.:The Divine Service Pavane ▲ 7343 [DDD]
Stepanov, F.:The Lord's Prayer Pavane ▲ 7343 [DDD]
Tolstiakov, N.:Priditie ka mnie Pavane ▲ 7343 [DDD]
Tretiakov, A.:Ave Maria, w. *(soloist unknown)* Pavane ▲ 7343 [DDD]

Rutgers Univ Choir
Orff, C.:Carmina burana, w. J. Harsanyi (sop), R. Petrak (ten), H. Presnell (bar), E. Ormandy (cnd), Philadelphia Orch Sony Classical ("Essential Classics" series) ▲ SBK 47668 ■ SBT 47668

Valery Rybin Choir
V. Novik (cnd)
Russian Religious Singing through the Age, Vol. 2, w. Ural Choir Russian Season 4-▲ CMX 388052

Rybin Choir Moscow
M. Popsavov (cnd)
Mystery of the East:Music from Russian Churches & Monasteries, w. Sofia Orthodox Ensemble, Bulgarian National Choir [cnd:Georgi Robev] Capriccio ▲ 10 597 [DDD]

Valery Rybin Male Choir
Historical Anthology of Russian Religious Chants, w. Drevnerousski Rospev Male Choir, Yourlov Academic Choir, Bolshoi Theater Children's Choir, St. Petersburg Cappella Russian Season ▲ LDC 288071
Serbian & Bulgarian Religious Chants Russian Season ▲ RUS 288087
20th Century Religious Singing in Moscow Russian Season ▲ LDC 288012 ■ KC 488012
V. Rybin (cnd)
Religious Singing in Moscow, Vol. 2 *(rec May 1992)* Russian Season ▲ LDC 288052 [DDD]

Sadler's Wells Opera Chorus
Lehár, F.:Die lustige Witwe (sels), w. W. Reid (cnd), Sadler's Wells Opera Orch Classics for Pleasure ▲ CDCFP 4485 [ADD]
Sullivan, A.:Iolanthe (sels), w. E. Harwood (sop), S. Bevin (ten), D. Dowling (bar), E. Shilling (bar), J. Holmes (bass), A. Faris (cnd), Sadler's Wells Opera Orch Classics for Pleasure 2-▲ CDCFP 4730 [ADD]
Sullivan, A.:The Mikado, w. M. Studholme (sop), J. Wakefield (ten), C. Revill (bar), D. Dowling (bar), J. Holmes (bass), A. Faris (cnd), Sadler's Wells Opera Orch Classics for Pleasure 2-▲ CDCFP 4730 [ADD]
Wagner, R.:Götterdämmerung (sels), w. M. Curphey (sop), R. Hunter (sop), A. Remedios (ten), N. Bailey (bar), C. Grant (bass), R. Goodall (cnd), Sadler's Wells Opera Orch—Act 3, Scenes 2 & 3 [E] Chandos ("Collect" series) ▲ CHAN 6593 [ADD]

Sagittarius Vocal Ensemble
Rameau, J.P.:Hippolyte et Aricie, w. Véronique Gens (sop), Bernarda Fink (cta), Jean-Paul Fouchécourt (ten), Laurent Naouri (bar), Russell Smythe (bar), M. Minkowski (cnd), Louvre Musicians Archiv 3-▲ 445853-2
Rameau, J.P.:Les Paladins, w. A. Michael (sop), G. Raphanel (sop), B. Brewer (ten), D. Nasrawi (ten), G. Reinhart (bar), N. Rivenq (bar), J. Malgoire (cnd), La Grande Ecurie et la Chambre du Roy [F] Pierre Verany 2-▲ PV.790121/22 [DDD]

St. Alban's Abbey Boys' Choir
D. Munrow (cnd)
Praetorius, M.:Motets [G, L] EMI Classics ("Studio" series) ▲ CDM 69024

St. Alban's Abbey Choir
S. Darlington (cnd)
Berkeley, L.:Look up, Sweet Babe Priory ("Celebration" series) ▲ PRI 4 [ADD]
Berkeley, L.:Lord, When the Sense of Thy Sweet Grace Priory ("Celebration" series) ▲ PRI 4 [ADD]
Berkeley, L.:Missa brevis Priory ("Celebration" series) ▲ PRI 4 [ADD]
Elgar, E.:O Hearken Thou Priory ("Celebration" series) ▲ PRI 4 [ADD]
Elgar, E.:Te Deum Priory ("Celebration" series) ▲ PRI 4 [ADD]

St. Alban's Cathedral Choristers
Orff, C.:Carmina burana, w. B. Hendricks (sop), M. Chance (ct), J. Black (bar), F. Welser-Möst (cnd), London PO, London Phil Chorus [G, L] EMI Classics ▲ CDC 54054 [DDD]

Saint Alexandre Nevski Church Choir Sofia
A. Konstantinov (cnd)
Bulgarian & Russian Orthodox Chant, w. Christoff, Boris (bass) Jade ▲ JAD C 059

St. Annae Girls' Choir
Danish Christmas Carols, w. Ketil Christensen (tpt), Flemming Dreisig (org), Erling Pedersen (org) Danica ▲ DCD 8103
E. Munk (cnd)
Brahms, J.:Choral Music, w. Niels Henrick Nielsen (org)—Es ist ein Ros' entsprungen; O Welt, ich muss dich lassen; O Welt, ich muss dich lassen [2nd version]; Herzlich tut mich verlangen; Fest- und Gedenksprüche, Op. 109 Canzone ▲ CAN 33007 [DDD]
Lange-Müller, P.E.:Tre Madonnasange, w. Niels Henrick Nielsen (org) *(rec 1991)* Canzone ▲ CAN 33007 [DDD]
Tchaikovsky, P.:Sacred Pieces, w. Niels Henrick Nielsen (org)—3 Pieces *(rec 1991)* Canzone ▲ CAN 33007 [DDD]
Wolf, H.:Geistliche Lieder *(rec 1991)* Canzone ▲ CAN 33007 [DDD]

St. Anne de Kergonan Abbey Monks' Choir
Initiation to Gregorian Chant Studio SM ▲ 12 16 66
Le Feuvre (cnd)
Gregorian Chant from the Abbey of Kergonan *(rec 1969-1974)* Arion 2-▲ ARN 268101

St. Anthony Singers
Handel, G.F.:Sosarme, Rè di Media, w. Margaret Ritchie (sop—Elmira), Alfred Deller (mez—Sosarme), Nancy Evans (mez—Erenice), Helen Watts (cta—Melo), John Kentish (ct—Argone), William Herbert (ten—King Haliate), Ian Wallace (bass—Altomaro), A. Lewis (cnd), St. Cecilia Academy Orch Rome Theorema 2-▲ TH 121194/195

CHORAL GROUPS

St. Anthony Singers (cont.)
Hill, Lewis (cnd)
Purcell, H.:Music of, w. Catherine Bott (sop), Emma Kirkby (sop), James Bowman (alt), Anthony Rooley (lt), Paula Chateauneuf (gtr), Monica Huggett (vn), Catherine Mackintosh (vn), Christophe Coin (vc), Hill, Hogwood (cnd), Academy of Ancient Music, Brandenburg Consort, Taverner Choir, Winchester Cathedral Choir—The Double Dealer; Come Ye Sons of Art; The Old Bachelor; Birthday Song for Queen Mary; Oedipus; King Arthur; Bonduca; The Fairy Queen; Son. No. 9 in F; Dido & Aeneas; Abdelazer; Bess of Bedlam; The Married Beau; Hear My Prayer, O Lord; Rejoice in the Lord Always London ("Editions de l'oiseau-lyre" series) ▲ 444620-2

St. Augustin Chorus
Dvořák, A.:Mass, w. G. Schmid (sop), J. Bernheimer (mez), J. Reinprecht (ten), A. Sramek (bar), F. Wolf (cnd), St. Augustin Orch [L] *(rec 1987)* Preiser ▲ 93378 [ADD]
Haydn, J.:Mass 5, "Missa Sancti Josephi", "Grosse Orgelmesse", w. F. Wolf (cnd), St. Augustin Orch Preiser ▲ PRE 93347 [ADD]
Haydn, J.:Mass 6, "Nikolai-messe", "6/4-Takt-Messe", w. F. Wolf (cnd), St. Augustin Orch Preiser ▲ PRE 93347 [ADD]
Mozart, W.A.:Ave verum corpus, w. F. Wolf (cnd), St. Augustin Orch Preiser ▲ 93325
Schubert, Franz:Duetsche Messe, w. R. Hansmann (sop), M. Lipovšek (mez), J. Reinprecht (ten), L. Spitzer (pno), F. Wolf (cnd), St. Augustin Orch Preiser ▲ 93325
Schubert, Franz:Mass 3, w. R. Hansmann (sop), M. Lipovšek (mez), J. Reinprecht (ten), Spitzer (bass), F. Wolf (cnd), St. Augustin Orch Preiser ▲ 93325

St. Barbara Roman Catholic Church Choir Brookfield IL
R. Batastini (cnd)
Taize:Wait for the Lord, w. Grace Lutheran Church Choir River Forest IL GIA ▲ GIA 173

St. Barnabas Adult Choir
In the Spirit:Sacred Music for Christmas, w. Jessye Norman (sop), St. Luke's Orch [cnd:David Robertson], American Boys Choir, Riverside Church Choir, St. Thomas Men & Boys Choir Philips ▲ 454640-2 ▮ 454640-4

St. Bavo Cathedral Boys' Choir
Tchaikovsky, P.:The Nutcracker, w. A. Dorati (cnd), Royal Concertgebouw Orch Philips ("Duo" series) 2-▲ 442562-2
Tchaikovsky, P.:Sleeping Beauty (sels), w. A. Dorati (cnd), Royal Concertgebouw Orch Philips ("Duo" series) 2-▲ 442562-2

St.-Benigne Cathedral Choir
Gregorien et Polyphonie...de Noel...a Paques at the Dijon Cathedral Studio SM ▲ 12 17.14

St. Benoît-du-Lac Abbey Monks' Choir
A. Saint-Cyr (cnd)
Cantus Mariales:Sacred Chants to the Virgin Mary from the Middle Ages *(rec Saint-Benoît-du-Lac Abbey, Feb. 1995)* Analekta ▲ AN 28101 [DDD]
Cantus Mariales:Sacred Chants to the Virgin Mary from the Middle Ages *(rec Saint-Benoît-du-Lac Abbey, Feb 1995)* Analekta ("Fleur de Lys" series) ▲ FL 2 3054 [DDD]
Gregorian Chants for Easter Forlane ▲ FOR 16684 [DDD]
Gregorian Chants in Honor of Our Lady Forlane ▲ FOR 16691 [DDD]
The Most Beautiful Gregorian Chants Forlane ▲ FOR 16690 [DDD]
Mysteries of Grief & Glory Forlane ▲ FRL 16750 [ADD]
Pax Analekta Fleur de Lys ▲ FL 23058 [DDD]

St. Cecilia Academy Chorus Rome
Boito, A.:Mefistofele, w. R. Tebaldi (sop), M. del Monaco (ten), C. Siepi (bass), T. Serafin (cnd), St. Cecilia Academy Orch Rome *(rec 1958)* London ▲ 440054-2
Cilea, F.:Adriana Lecouvreur, w. R. Tebaldi (sop), M. del Monaco (ten), F. Capuana (cnd), St. Cecilia Academy Orch Rome London 2-▲ 430256-2 [ADD]
Donizetti, G.:Lucia di Lammermoor, w. J. Sutherland (sop), R. Cioni (ten), R. Merrill (bar), C. Siepi (bass-bar), J. Pritchard (cnd), St. Cecilia Academy Orch Rome [I] London 2-▲ 411622-2 [ADD]
Leoncavallo, R.:Pagliacci, w. P. Lorengar (sop), R. Krause (ten), J. McCracken (ten), R. Merrill (bar), U. Benelli (bar), L. Gardelli (cnd), St. Cecilia Academy Orch Rome [I] IMP Collectors Series ▲ IMPX 9017 [AAD]
Ponchielli, A.:La Gioconda, w. R. Tebaldi (sop), C. Bergonzi (ten), *(other soloists unknown)*, L. Gardelli (cnd), St. Cecilia Academy Orch Rome London 3-▲ 430042-2 [ADD]
Ponchielli, A.:La Gioconda, w. Zinka Milanov (sop—La Gioconda), Rosalind Elias (mez—Laura), Belan Amparan (cta—La Cieca), Giacomo Cottino (ten—Isepo), Giuseppe Di Stefano (ten—Enzo Grimaldo), Fernando Valentini (bar—Zuane/Un Nocchiero), Leonard Warren (bar—Barnaba), Virgilio Carbonari (bass—Un Cantore), Plinio Clabassi (bass—Alvise Badoero), F. Previtali (cnd), St. Cecilia Academy Orch Rome Theorema 3-▲ TH 121182/184
Puccini, G.:La Bohème, w. R. Tebaldi (sop), H. Gueden (sop), G. Prandelli (ten), G. Inghilleri (bar), F. Corena (bass), Raphäel Arié (bass), A. Erede (cnd), St. Cecilia Academy Orch Rome London 2-▲ 440233-2 [ADD]
Puccini, G.:La Bohème, w. R. Tebaldi (sop), G. d'Angelo (sop), C. Bergonzi (ten), E. Bastianini (bar), C. Siepi (b-bar), T. Serafin (cnd), St. Cecilia Academy Orch Rome [I] London 2-▲ 425534-2 [ADD]
Puccini, G.:La Bohème (sels), w. R. Tebaldi (sop), C. Bergonzi (ten), E. Bastianini (bar), C. Siepi (b-bar), T. Serafin (cnd), St. Cecilia Academy Orch Rome—scenes & arias London ▲ 421301-2 [ADD]
Puccini, G.:La fanciulla del West, w. R. Tebaldi (sop), M. del Monaco (ten), C. MacNeil (bar), G. Tozzi (bass), F. Capuana (cnd), St. Cecilia Academy Orch Rome [I] London 2-▲ 421595-2 [ADD]
Puccini, G.:Madama Butterfly, w. R. Tebaldi (sop), F. Cossotto (mez), C. Bergonzi (ten), E. Sordello (bar), T. Serafin (cnd), St. Cecilia Academy Orch Rome [I] London 2-▲ 425531-2 [ADD]
Puccini, G.:Madama Butterfly (sels), w. R. Tebaldi (sop), F. Cossotto (mez), C. Bergonzi (ten), E. Sordello (bar), T. Serafin (cnd), St. Cecilia Academy Orch Rome [I] London ("Opera Gala" series) ▲ 421873-2 [ADD]
Puccini, G.:Madama Butterfly (sels), w. R. Tebaldi (sop), C. Bergonzi (ten), E. Sordello (bar), T. Serafin (cnd), St. Cecilia Academy Orch Rome London ▲ 417733-2 [ADD]
Puccini, G.:Manon Lescaut, w. R. Tebaldi (sop), M. del Monaco (ten), F. Molinari-Pradelli (cnd), St. Cecilia Academy Orch Rome London 2-▲ 430253-2 [ADD]
Puccini, G.:Tosca, w. R. Tebaldi (sop), M. del Monaco (ten), F. Molinari-Pradelli (cnd), St. Cecilia Academy Orch Rome London 2-▲ 411871-2 [ADD]
Puccini, G.:Tosca, w. R. Tebaldi (sop), G. Campora (ten), Enzo Mascherini (bar), F. Corena (bass), A. Erede (cnd), St. Cecilia Academy Orch Rome Enterprise 2-▲ ENTPD 4106 [ADD]
Puccini, G.:Tosca, w. R. Tebaldi (sop), G. Campora (ten), Enzo Mascherini (bar), F. Corena (bass), A. Erede (cnd), St. Cecilia Academy Orch Rome London 2-▲ 440236-2 [ADD]
Puccini, G.:Tosca, w. Ranata Tebaldi (sop), Gian Franco Volante (trb), Piero de Palma (ten), Giuseppe Campora (ten), Enzo Mascherini (bar), Fernando Corena (bass), Dario Caselli (bass), Antonio Sacchetti (bass), A. Erede (cnd), St. Cecilia Academy Orch Rome *(rec 1952)* Andromeda 2-▲ ANR 2539 [ADD]
Puccini, G.:Tosca, w. B. Nilsson (sop), F. Corelli (ten), D. Fischer-Dieskau (bar), L. Maazel (cnd), St. Cecilia Academy Orch Rome *(rec June 1966)* London ▲ 440051-2
Puccini, G.:Turandot, w. I. Borkh (sop), R. Tebaldi (sop), M. del Monaco (ten), A. Erede (cnd), St. Cecilia Academy Orch Rome London 2-▲ 433761-2 [ADD]
Verdi, G.:Aida, w. Renata Tebaldi (sop—Aida), Ebe Stignani (mez—Amneris), Mario Del Monaco (ten—Radamès), Piero de Palma (ten—Messenger), Aldo Protti (bar—Amonasro), Fernando Corena (bass—King), Dario Caselli (bass—Ramfis), A. Erede (cnd), St. Cecilia Academy Orch Rome *(rec 1952)* Theorema 2-▲ TH 121133/34
Verdi, G.:Aida, w. R. Tebaldi (sop), E. Stignani (mez), M. del Monaco (ten), A. Protti (bar), F. Corena (bass), A. Erede (cnd), St. Cecilia Academy Orch Rome London 2-▲ 440239-2 [ADD]
Verdi, G.:Un ballo in maschera, w. B. Nilsson (sop), G. Simionato (mez), C. Bergonzi (ten), C. MacNeil (bar), G. Solti (cnd), St. Cecilia Academy Orch Rome [I] London 2-▲ 425655-2 [ADD]
Verdi, G.:Un ballo in maschera, w. R. Tebaldi (sop), L. Pavarotti (ten), S. Milnes (bar), B. Bartoletti (cnd), St. Cecilia Academy Orch Rome London ▲ 440042-2
Verdi, G.:La forza del destino, w. R. Tebaldi (sop), G. Simionato (mez), M. del Monaco (ten), E. Bastianini (bar), C. Siepi (b-bar), F. Molinari-Pradelli (cnd), St. Cecilia Academy Orch Rome [I] London 3-▲ 421598-2 [ADD]

St. Cecilia Academy Chorus Rome (cont.)
Verdi, G.:La forza del destino, w. Zinka Milanov (sop), Rosalind Elias (mez), Giuseppe Di Stefano (ten), Leonard Warren (bar), Giorgio Tozzi (bass), Paolo Washington (bass), F. Previtali (cnd), St. Cecilia Academy Orch Rome *(rec 1959)* Theorema 3-▲ TH 121157/59
Verdi, G.:La forza del destino, w. Zinka Milanov (sop—Donna Leonora di Vargas), Rosalind Elias (mez—Preziosilla), Luisa Gioia (sgr—Curra), Angelo Mercuriali (ten—Trabuco), Giuseppe di Stefano (ten—Son Alvaro), Leonard Warren (bar—Don Carlos di Vargas), Giorgio Tozzi (b-bar—Padre guardiano), Dino Mantovani (bar—Fra Melitone), Paolo Washington (b-bar—Il marchese di Calatrava), Virgilio Carbonari (b-bar—un alcalde), Sergio Liviabella (sgr—un chirurgo), F. Previtali (cnd), St. Cecilia Academy Orch Rome [I] London ▲ 443678-2 [ADD]
Verdi, G.:Macbeth, w. B. Nilsson (sop), B. Prevedi (ten), G. Taddei (bar), T. Schippers (cnd), St. Cecilia Academy Orch Rome London ("Grand Opera" series) 2-▲ 433039-2 [ADD]
Verdi, G.:Otello, w. Renata Tebaldi (sop—Desdemona), Luisa Ribacchi (mez—Emilia), Angelo Mercuriali (ten—Roderigo), Mario del Monaco (ten—Otello), Piero de Palma (ten—Cassio), Aldo Protti (bar—Iago), Dario Caselli (bass—A Herald), Fernando Corena (bass—Lodovico), Pierluigi Martinucci (bass—Montano), A. Erede (cnd), St. Cecilia Academy Orch Rome Theorema ▲ TH 121141/142
Verdi, G.:Otello, w. H. Gueden (sop), G. Simionato (mez), M. del Monaco (ten), A. Protti (bar), C. Siepi (b-bar), A. Erede (cnd), St. Cecilia Academy Orch Rome London 2-▲ 440242-2 [ADD]
Verdi, G.:Rigoletto, w. Hilde Gueden (sop—Gilda), Piero de Palma (ten—Borsa), Luisa Ribacchi (mez—Giovanna), Giulietta Simionato (mez—Maddalena), Mario del Monaco (ten—Duca de Mantova), Aldo Protti (bar—Rigoletto), Fernando Corena (bass—Conte Monterone), Cesare Siepi (bass—Sparafucile), A. Erede (cnd), St. Cecilia Academy Orch Rome Theorema ▲ TH 121179/180
Verdi, G.:Rigoletto, w. E. Gruberova (sop), B. Fassbaender (mez), Schicoff (ten), R. Bruson (bar), R. Lloyd (b-bar), G. Sinopoli (cnd), St. Cecilia Academy Orch Rome [I] Philips 2-▲ 412592-2 [DDD]
Verdi, G.:Rigoletto, w. R. Tebaldi (sop), M. del Monaco (ten), A. Protti (bar), P. de Palma (bass), F. Corena (bass), A. Erede (cnd), St. Cecilia Academy Orch Rome London 2-▲ 440245-2 [ADD]
Verdi, G.:Rigoletto, w. Joan Sutherland (sop—Gilda), Renato Cioni (ten—Duke), Cornell MacNeil (bar—Rigoletto), N. Sanzogno (cnd), St. Cecilia Academy Orch Rome London ("Double Decca" series) 2-▲ 443853-2
Verdi, G.:La traviata, w. R. Tebaldi (sop), et al., F. Molinari-Pradelli (cnd), St. Cecilia Academy Orch Rome London 2-▲ 430250-2 [ADD]

St. Cecilia Cappella Musicale
Puccini, D.:Canticum simeonis, w. G. Cosmi (cnd), Lucca Teatro Comunale del Giglio Orch [L] Bongiovanni ▲ GB 2047 [DDD]
Puccini, M.:Kyrie, w. M. Frusoni (ten), G. Cosmi (cnd), Lucca Teatro Comunale del Giglio Orch [L] Bongiovanni ▲ GB 2047 [DDD]
Puccini, M.:Magnificat, w. M. Frusoni (ten), Nenci (ten), Di Benedetto (bass), G. Cosmi (cnd), Lucca Teatro Comunale del Giglio Orch [L] Bongiovanni ▲ GB 2047 [DDD]

St. Cecilia Vocal Ensemble
Werner, G.J.:Laetaniae de Venerabili Sacramento, w. J. Mezei (cnd), Vienna-Szász CO *(rec St. Columba's Presbyterian Church, Budapest, June 12-15, 1995)* Hungaroton ▲ HCD 31646 [DDD]

St. Cecilia's Abbey Ryde Nuns' Choir
Gregorian Chant Gaudete *(rec Mar. 1992)* Herald ▲ HAVPCD 157 [DDD]

St. Clement Danes Boys' Chorus
Orff, C.:Carmina burana, w. S. Armstrong (sop), G. English (ten), T. Allen (bar), A. Previn (cnd), London SO, London Sym Chorus [G, L] EMI Classics ▲ CDC 47411 ▮ 4AM 34770

St. Clement's Choir Philadelphia
P. Conte (cnd)
Brahms, J.:Geistliches Lied *(rec Daylesford Abbey, Paoli, PA, June 1994 & Jan 1995)* Dorian Discovery ▲ DIS 80137 [DDD]
Brahms, J.:Mass *(rec Daylesford Abbey, Paoli, PA, June 1994 & Jan 1995)* Dorian Discovery ▲ DIS 80137 [DDD]
Brahms, J.:Motets (misc)—Op. 110 *(rec Daylesford Abbey, Paoli, PA, June 1994 & Jan 1995)* Dorian Discovery ▲ DIS 80137 [DDD]
Rheinberger, J.:Geistliche Gesänge *(rec Daylesford Abbey, Paoli, PA, June 1994 & Jan 1995)* Dorian Discovery ▲ DIS 80137 [DDD]
Rheinberger, J.:Mass, Op. 109 *(rec Daylesford Abbey, Paoli, PA, June 1994 & Jan 1995)* Dorian Discovery ▲ DIS 80137 [DDD]
Rheinberger, J.:Mass, Op. 172—Ave Maria *(rec Daylesford Abbey, Paoli, PA, June 1994 & Jan 1995)* Dorian Discovery ▲ DIS 80137 [DDD]
Rheinberger, J.:Omnes de Saba *(rec Daylesford Abbey, Paoli, PA, June 1994 & Jan 1995)* Dorian Discovery ▲ DIS 80137 [DDD]
Victoria, T.L. de:Sacred Choral Music—Ave Maria; Vidi aquam; Mass "Laetatus sum"; Motet Laetatus sum; Mass "Ascehdens christus in altum"; Motet Ascendens christus in altum *(rec Daylesford Abbey, Paoli, PA, Oct 1995 & Feb 1996)* Dorian ▲ 80146 [DDD]

St. Esprit Univ Musicological Chorale
L. Hage (cnd)
Traditional Maronite Chants Studio SM ▲ 12 22 71 [AAD]

Saint-Etienne Nouvel Chorus
Massenet, J.:Cléopâtre, w. B. Harries (sop), Daniéle Streiff (sop), M. Olmeda (sop), J. Maurette (ten), D. Henry (bar), M. Hacquard (bar), P. Fournillier (cnd), St.-Etienne Nouvel Orch [F] *(rec live, Massenet Festival in Saint-Etienne 1990)* Koch Schwann 2-▲ 3-1032-2 [DDD]

St. Gayané Cathedral Choir
K. Keshishian (cnd)
Komitas, V.:Divine Liturgy [Armenian] New Albion ▲ NA 033 [DDD]

St. Gayanée Chapel Armenian Liturgical Choir
Komitas, V.:Armenian Mass ARB ▲ 1403
L. Chabanian (cnd)
Yekmalian, M.:Armenian Mass, w. Araxie Mansourian (sop), Vartan Haroutunian (bass) Arb ▲ 1416

St. George's Chapel Choristers
Mathias, W.:Ave Rex, w. Janet Price (sop), Kenneth Bowen (ten), Michael Rippon (bar), Geraint Evans (b-bar), Atherton, Willcocks (cnd), London SO, New Philharmonia Orch, Welsh National Opera Chorus, Windsor Bach Choir Lyrita ▲ SRCD .324
Mathias, W.:This Worlde's Joie, w. Janet Price (sop), Kenneth Bowen (ten), Michael Rippon (bar), Atherton, Willcocks (cnd), London SO, New Philharmonia Orch, Welsh National Opera Chorus, Windsor Bach Choir Lyrita ▲ SRCD .324

St. George's Singers
B. Smith (cnd)
Klatzow, P.:Mass, w. Rob Grishkoff (hn), Di Maris (mar) Claremont ▲ GSE 1524

St. Gervais Chorus
Berlioz, H.:La Damnation de Faust, w. M. Berthon (sop), J. de Trévi (ten), C. Panzéra (bar), P. Coppola (cnd), Pasdeloup Concerts Association Orch *(rec 1930)* Pearl ▲ PEA 9080 [ADD]
Berlioz, H.:La Damnation de Faust (sels), w. M. Berthon (sop), J. de Trévi (sgr), C. Panzéra (bar), L. Morturier (sgr), P. Coppola (cnd), Pasdeloup Concerts Association Orch [abridged vers] [F] *(rec 1931)* The Classical Collector 2-▲ FDC2 2006 [AAD]

St. Hedwig's Cathedral Children's Choir
Wolf-Ferrari, E.:La vita nuova, w. Celina Lindsley (sop), George Fortune (bar), R. Bader (cnd), Berlin RSO Koch Schwann ▲ SCH 312672 [DDD]

St. Hedwig's Cathedral Choir
Bach, J.S.:Cant 208, "Hunting Cant", w. Erika Köth (sop), Dietrich Fischer-Dieskau (bar), K. Forster (cnd), Berlin SO EMI Classics ("Baroque" series) ▲ CDK 65729
Beethoven, L. van:Missa Solemnis, w. M. Stader (sop), E. Cavalti (mez), E. Haefliger (ten), H. Rehfuss (bass), C. Schuricht (cnd), Hamburg SO *(rec Sept. 15, 1957)* Archipon 2-▲ ARCH 2.1CD (m) [ADD]
Brahms, J.:Ein Deutsches Requiem, w. E. Grümmer (sop), D. Fischer-Dieskau (bar), R. Kempe (cnd), Berlin PO [G] EMI Classics ▲ CDH 64705
David, Felicien:Le Désert, w. O. Pascalin (nar), B. Lazzaretti (ten), G.M. Guida (cnd), Berlin RSO Capriccio ▲ 10 379 [DDD]
Donizetti, G.:Messa di Gloria e Credo, w. H. Mané (sop), G. Vighi (mez), P. Maus (ten), M. Machi (bass), R. Bader (cnd), Berlin RSO [L] Koch Schwann ▲ CD 313031 [ADD]

St. Hedwig's Cathedral Choir (cont.)
Haydn, J.:Die Schöpfung, w. Irmgard Seefried (sop), Richard Holm (ten), Kim Borg (bass), I. Markevitch (cnd), Berlin PO — Deutsche Grammophon ("Double" series) 2–▲ 437380–2
Hoffmann, E.T.A.:Undine, w. Krisztina Láki (sop), R. Henry (sgr), Karl Ridderbusch (bass), R. Bader (cnd), Berlin RSO *(rec Feb. 1982)* — Koch Schwann 3–▲ SCH 310922 [DDD]
Kiel, F.:Der Stern von Bethlehem, w. M. Schiml (sop), H. Laubenthal (ten), R. Bader (cnd), Berlin RSO [G] — Koch Schwann ▲ CD 313032 [DDD]
Mahler, G.:Sym 3, w. L. West (alt), J. Barbirolli (cnd), Berlin PO [G] *(rec live, 3/8/69)* — Arkadia 3–▲ 719 [ADD]
Mozart, L.:Missa solemnis, w. A. Augér (sop), G. Schreckenbach (mez), H. Laubenthal (ten), B. McDaniel (bar), R. Bader (cnd), Berlin Domkapelle Instrumental Ensemble [L] — Koch Schwann ▲ CD 313028 [ADD]
Mozart, W.A.:Missa, K.317, w. Maria Stader (sop), Sieglinde Wagner (mez), Helmut Krebs (ten), Josef Griendl (bass), I. Markevitch (cnd), Berlin PO — Deutsche Grammophon 2–▲ 437383–2
Mozart, W.A.:Missa brevis, K.65, w. C. Malone (sop), G. Schreckenbach (mez), K. Markus (ten), W. Grönroos (bar), R. Bader (cnd), Berlin RSO [L] — Koch Schwann ▲ SCH 313021 [ADD/DDD]
Reyer, L.–E.–E.:Le Sélam, w. *(soloists unknown)*, G.M. Guida (cnd), Berlin RSO — Capriccio ▲ 10 380 [DDD]
Schmidt, F.:Notre Dame, w. G. Jones (sop), J. King (ten), R. Laubenthal (ten), K. Moll (bass), C. Perick (cnd), Berlin RSO, RIAS Chamber Chorus [G] — Capriccio 2–▲ 10248/9 [DDD]
Schoenberg, A.:Gurrelieder, w. S. Dunn (sop), B. Fassbaender (mez), S. Jerusalem (ten), P. Haage (ten), H. Becht (bass), H. Hotter (nar), R. Chailly (cnd), Berlin RSO, Düsseldorf Municipal Choral Society [G] — London 2–▲ 430321–2 [DDD]
Verdi, G.:Requiem Mass, w. Maria Stader (sop), Marjana Radev (mez), Helmut Krebs (ten), Kim Borg (bass), F. Fricsay (cnd), Berlin RIAS SO, Berlin RIAS Chamber Choir *(rec Jesus–Christus Church, Berlin, Sept 1953)* — Deutsche Grammophon ("The Originals" series) ▲ 447442–2 [ADD]

R. Bader (cnd)
Kiel, F.:Motets [G] — Koch Schwann ▲ CD 313032 [DDD]

St. Hildegard Rüdesheim–Eibingen Benedictine Abbey Choir
I. Ritscher (cnd)
Hildegard Of Bingen:Sacred Songs—Cum processit factura; Cum erubuerint infelices; O frondens virgo; Ave, generosa, gloriosa; O virga ac diadema purpurae regis; Caritas abundat; O pastor animarum; O quam pretiosa est; Kyrie; Patriarchae et Prophetae; Castitas; Virtutes; Antiphona ad Magnificat; In I Vesperis — Bayer ▲ 100116 [ADD]

St. Ignatius of Antioch Choir New York
H. Chaney (cnd)
Cum Jubilo! — Music & Arts ▲ MUA 798 [DDD]

St. Jacob Choir Stockholm
Mozart, W.A.:Requiem, Stockholm Conservatory Soloists — Prophone ▲ PCD 015

St. Jacob's Chamber Choir
Duruflé, M.:Mass, "Cum jubilo", w. P. Mattei (bar), M. Wager (org) *(rec Nov. 9–12, 1992)* — BIS ▲ CD 602 [DDD]
Duruflé, M.:Motets on Gregorian Chants, Op. 10 *(rec Dec. 2, 1992)* — BIS ▲ CD 602 [DDD]
Duruflé, M.:Requiem, w. P. Hofman (ten), P. Mattei (bar), E. Lavotha (vc), M. Wager (org) *(rec Nov. 9–12, 1992)* — BIS ▲ CD 602 [DDD]

St. James Cathedral Church Men & Boys' Choir Toronto
Vaughan Williams, R.:Mystical Songs, w. K. McMillan (bar) [E] — Marquis ▲ ERAD 127 [DDD]

St. John the Divine Cathedral Choir
R. Westenburg (cnd)
Christmas Eve at the Cathedral of St. John the Divine, New York City *(rec 1974)* — Vanguard Classics ▲ OVC 6013 [ADD]

St. John's College Choir Cambridge
G. Guest (cnd)
Allegri, G.:Miserere — EMI Classics (Classics for Pleasure) ▲ CDM 64115–2
Allegri, G.:Il Salmo Miserere mei Deus — Classics for Pleasure ("Eminence" series) ▲ CFP 2180 [DDD]
Bononcini, A.:Stabat Mater, w. Felicity Palmer (sop), Paul Esswood (ct), Philip Langridge (ten), Christopher Keyte (bass), John Scott (org), John Willison (vn), Chris Wellington (va), Don McVeigh (va), Philomusica Antiqua of London *(rec 1977)* — London 2–▲ 443868–2 [ADD]
Britten, B.:A Ceremony of Carols — London ("Jubilee" series) ▲ 430097–2 [ADD]
Britten, B.:Jubilate Deo — London ("Jubilee" series) ▲ 430097–2 [ADD]
Britten, B.:Missa brevis — London ("Jubilee" series) ▲ 430097–2 [ADD]
Britten, B.:Rejoice in the Lamb — London ("Jubilee" series) ▲ 430097–2 [ADD]
Britten, B.:Te Deum — London ("Jubilee" series) ▲ 430097–2 [ADD]
Christmas Carols From St. John's — Chandos ▲ CHAN 8485 [DDD]
Caldara, A.:Crucifixus, w. Felicity Palmer (sop), Paul Esswood (ct), Philip Langridge (ten), Christopher Keyte (bass), John Scott (org), John Willison (vn), Chris Wellington (va), Don McVeigh (va), Philomusica Antiqua of London *(rec 1977)* — London 2–▲ 443868–2 [ADD]
Charpentier, M.–A.:Messe de minuit pour Noël, w. City of London Sinfonia [L] — Chandos ▲ CHAN 8658 [DDD]
Duruflé, M.:Motets on Gregorian Chants, Op. 10, w. George Guest (org) — London ("Double Decca" series) 2–▲ 436486–2
Duruflé, M.:Requiem, w. George Guest (org) — London ("Double Decca" series) 2–▲ 436486–2
Fauré, G.:Cantique de Jean Racine, w. S. Cleobury (org) [F] — London ("Jubilee" series) ▲ 430360–2 [ADD]
Fauré, G.:Messe basse, w. George Guest (org) — London ("Double Decca" series) 2–▲ 436486–2
Fauré, G.:Requiem, w. J. Bond (trb), B. Luxon (bar), Academy of St. Martin in the Fields [L] — London ("Jubilee" series) ▲ 430360–2 [ADD]
Hear My Prayer:Choral Favourites — London ("Weekend Classics" series) ▲ 433685–2 LC
Lassus, O. de:Bell'Amfitrit'altera — Classics for Pleasure ("Eminence" series) ▲ CFP 2180 [DDD]
Lassus, O. de:Bell'Amfitrit'altera — EMI Classics ("Classics for Pleasure" series) ▲ CDM 64115
Lotti, A.:Crucifixus, w. Felicity Palmer (sop), Paul Esswood (ct), Philip Langridge (ten), Christopher Keyte (bass), John Scott (org), John Willison (vn), Chris Wellington (va), Don McVeigh (va), Philomusica Antiqua of London *(rec 1977)* — London 2–▲ 443868–2 [ADD]
Massenzio, D.:Completorium integrum cum Ave regina, Salve regina e motecta (sels) [L] — Meridian ▲ CDE 84121
Mozart, W.A.:Requiem, w. Y. Kenny (sop), S. Walker (mez), W. Kendall (ten), D. Wilson–Johnson (bar), English CO [L] — Chandos ▲ CHAN 8574 [DDD]
Palestrina, G.:Veni sponsa Christi — EMI Classics ("Classics for Pleasure" series) ▲ CDM 64115
Palestrina, G.:Veni sponsa Christi — Classics for Pleasure ("Eminence" series) ▲ CFP 2180 [DDD]
Pergolesi, G.B.:Stabat mater, w. Felicity Palmer (sop), Alfreda Hodgson (cta), David Hill (org), Argo CO *(rec 1978)* — London 2–▲ 443868–2 [ADD]
Poulenc, F.:Mass [L] — London ("Jubilee" series) ▲ 430360–2 [ADD]
Poulenc, F.:Motets (4) pour le temps de Noël, w. City of London Sinfonia [L] — Chandos ▲ CHAN 8658 [DDD]
Poulenc, F.:Motets (4) pour un temps de pénitence, w. City of London Sinfonia [L] — Chandos ▲ CHAN 8658 [DDD]
Poulenc, F.:Salve regina [L] — London ("Jubilee" series) ▲ 430360–2 [ADD]
Poulenc, F.:Salve regina, w. City of London Sinfonia [L] — Chandos ▲ CHAN 8658 [DDD]
Tallis, T.:Mass "Salve intemerata" — Classics for Pleasure ▲ CDCFP 4654 [DDD]
Taverner, J.:Western Wynde — Classics for Pleasure ▲ CDCFP 4654 [DDD]
Tippett, M.:Magnificat & Nunc dimittis *(rec St. John's College Chapel, Cambridge, July 25–27, 1991)* — Nimbus ▲ NI 7026 [DDD]
Vivaldi, A.:Beatus vir, RV. 597, w. S. Cleobury (cnd), King's College Choir Cambridge — London ("Double Decker" series) 2–▲ 443455–2
Vivaldi, A.:Dixit Dominus, w. S. Cleobury (cnd), King's College Choir Cambridge — London ("Double Decker" series) 2–▲ 443455–2
Vivaldi, A.:Gloria, RV.589, w. S. Cleobury (cnd), King's College Choir Cambridge — London ("Double Decker" series) 2–▲ 443455–2

St. John's College Choir Cambridge (cont.)
G. Guest (cnd) (cont.)
Vivaldi, A.:Gloria (& Intro), RV.588, w. S. Cleobury (cnd), King's College Choir Cambridge — London ("Double Decker" series) 2–▲ 443455–2
Vivaldi, A.:Magnificat, RV.611, w. S. Cleobury (cnd), King's College Choir Cambridge — London ("Double Decker" series) 2–▲ 443455–2

C. Robinson (cnd)
Advent Carols from St. John's *(rec St. John's College Chapel)* — Nimbus ▲ NI 5414 [DDD]
Tallis, T.:Church Music—Jesu salvator saeculi; Gloria tibi Trinitas [w. Robert Woolley (org)]; Iste confessor Domini sacratus [w. Woolley]; Salvator mundi; Jam lucis orto sidere [w. Woolley]; Ex more docti mistico [w. Woolley]; Videte miraculum; Ecce tempus idoneum I & II [w. Woolley]; Jam Christus astra ascenderat; Veni Redemptor gentium I & II [w. Woolley]; Quod chorus vatum; Clarifica me pater I–III [w. Woolley]; O nata lux de lumine; A Point [w. Woolley]; Natus est nobis hodie [w. Woolley]; Laudate Dominum *(rec Jesus College Chapel, Cambridge)* — Chandos ("Chaconne" series) ▲ CHAN 0588

R. Wooley (cnd)
Gibbons, O.:Org Music (comp), w. R. Wooley (org) [Dallam Organ, Ploujean]—Fant. No. 3 in d for Double Organ; Fant. No. 1 in d; Prelude No. 1 in a; Fant. No. 5 in g; Prelude No. 3 in d; Fant. No. 6 in a; Fant. No. 9 in C; Prelude No. 2 in G; Fant. No. 7 in a; Fant. No. 4 in d; Fant. No. 2 in d; Prelude No. 4 in a; Fant. No. 10 in C; Fant. No. 8 in a; If ye be risen again with Christ; Oh Lord, in thy wrath rebuke me not; Almighty God, who by thy son; O clap your hands; We praise thee, Oh Father; So God loved the world; O God the King of Glory — Chandos ("Chaconne" series) ▲ CHAN 0559 [DDD]

St. John's Episcopal Cathedral Boy & Girls' Choir
D. Pearson (cnd)
Hovhaness, A.:Sacred Music, w. Eric Plutz (org), St. John's Episcopal Cathedral Festival Orch, St. John's Episcopal Cathedral Choir—Magnificat, Op. 157; Psalm 23 [Cant from Sym No. 12, Op. 188]; A Rose Tree Blossoms, Op. 246/4; Jesus, Lover of My Soul, Op. 53b; Jesus Christ Is Risen Today, Op. 100/3b; The Lord's Prayer, Op. 35; Peace by Multiplied, Op. 259/1; O For a Shout of Sacred Joy, Op. 161; Out of the Depths, Op. 142/3; O God, Our Help in Ages Past, Op. 137 *(rec St. John's Episcopal Cathedral, Denver, Mar 6–8, 1995)* — Delos ▲ DE 3176 [DDD]
Sing We Merrily, w. Eric Plutz (org) — Delos ▲ DE 3125 [DDD]

St. John's Episcopal Cathedral Choir
Hovhaness, A.:Sacred Music, w. Eric Plutz (org), D. Pearson (cnd), St. John's Episcopal Cathedral Festival Orch, St. John's Episcopal Cathedral Boy & Girls' Choir—Magnificat, Op. 157; Psalm 23 [Cant from Sym No. 12, Op. 188]; A Rose Tree Blossoms, Op. 246/4; Jesus, Lover of My Soul, Op. 53b; Jesus Christ Is Risen Today, Op. 100/3b; The Lord's Prayer, Op. 35; Peace by Multiplied, Op. 259/1; O For a Shout of Sacred Joy, Op. 161; Out of the Depths, Op. 142/3; O God, Our Help in Ages Past, Op. 137 *(rec St. John's Episcopal Cathedral, Denver, Mar 6–8, 1995)* — Delos ▲ DE 3176 [DDD]

St. John's Episcopal Church Choir Lafayette Sq. Washington D.C.
S. Carabetta (cnd)
Anthems & Motets, w. Samuel Carabetta (org) *(rec 1991)* — Gothic ▲ GOT 49050

St. Julien Le Pauvre Byzantine Choir Paris
Chant Byzantin:Passion et Resurrection — Harmonia Mundi France ▲ HMC 901315

St. Klemens School Children's Choir
Nielsen, C.:Springtime, w. Inga Nielsen (sop), Kim von Binzer (ten), Jørgen Klint (bass), T. Vetö (cnd), Odense SO, Lille MUKO — Unicorn–Kanchana ▲ DKPCD 9054

St. Laurent Children's Choir
F. Rauber (cnd)
Children's Songs, w. St. Laurent Instrumental Ensemble, Maurice André (tpt), Jean–Pierre Rampal (fl) — CBS ▲ MK 39669

St. Louis Camerata Vocal Ensemble
G. Guillard (cnd)
Alain, J.:Music of, w. Delphine Collot (sop), Bruno Boterf (ten), Jacques Bona (bar), Françoise Gyps (fl), Laurent Decker (ob), Bruno Pazqueir (va), Philippe Muller (vc), Georges Guillard (org), Ludwig String Quartet—2 Melodies for Sop & Pno; Nuptial Song for Bar, Bass, Vc & Org; Post–Scriptum for 3 Female Voices & Pno; Canticle in Phrygian Mode for 4 Mixed–Voice, Sop & Strs; Invention for Fl, Ob & Cl; Monody for solo Fl; Prelude for Str Qnt; Adagio for Str Qnt; Funerals for Str Qnt; March of the Horiaces & the Curiaces for 2 Bugles, Drum & Org — Arion ▲ ARN 68321

St. Louis Sym Chorus
Beethoven, L. van:Elegischer Gesang, "Sanft wie du lebtest", w. J. Semkow (cnd), St. Louis SO [arr. for small 4–part chorus & string ensemble] — Vox Box 2–▲ CDX 5104 [ADD]
Beethoven, L. van:Fant Pno, Op. 80, "Choral Fant", w. W. Klien (pno), J. Semkow (cnd), St. Louis SO — Vox Box 2–▲ CDX 5104 [ADD]
Beethoven, L. van:Meeresstille und glückliche Fahrt, w. J. Semkow (cnd), St. Louis SO — Vox Box 2–▲ CDX 5104 [ADD]
Mahler, G.:Sym 2, w. K. Battle (sop), M. Forrester (cta), L. Slatkin (cnd), St. Louis SO — Telarc 2–▲ CD 80081/82 [DDD]
Paine, J.K.:Mass, Op. 10, w. C. Balthrop (sop), J. Blackett (cta), V. Cole (ten), J. Cheek (bass), J. Lange (org), G. Schuller (cnd), St. Louis SO [L] *(rec ca. mid–1970s)* — New World ▲ 80262–2 [AAD]
Prokofiev, S.:Alexander Nevsky, w. C. Carlson (mez), L. Slatkin (cnd), St. Louis SO [R] — Vox Box 2–▲ CDX 5021 [ADD]
Prokofiev, S.:Ivan the Terrible, w. C. Carlson (mez), S. Timberlake (bass), L. Slatkin (cnd), St. Louis SO [R] — Vox Box 2–▲ CDX 5021 [ADD]
Rachmaninoff, S.:The Bells, w. Christos (sop), Walter Planté (ten), Arnold Voketaitis (bar), L. Slatkin (cnd), St. Louis SO *(rec 1980)* — Vox Box 3–▲ CD3X 3002 [ADD]
Rachmaninoff, S.:Russian Songs, w. L. Slatkin (cnd), St. Louis SO *(rec 1980)* — Vox Box 3–▲ CD3X 3002 [ADD]
Rachmaninoff, S.:Spring, w. A. Voketaitis (bar), L. Slatkin (cnd), St. Louis SO *(rec 1980)* — Vox Box 3–▲ CD3X 3002 [ADD]
Wagner, R.:Ovs, Preludes & Orch Sels, w. J. Semkow (cnd), St. Louis SO—Rienzi:Ov.; Lohengrin:Preludes, Acts 1 & 3; Die Meistersinger von Nürnberg:Prelude; Parsifal:Good Friday Spell; Die Walküre:The Ride of the Valkyries — Vox Box 2–▲ CDX 5104 [ADD]

St. Marco Capella Musicale
Viadana, L. da:Vespri per l'Assunzione, w. S. Pozzer (sop), C. Calvino (alt), U. Müller Adam (ten), J. Clement (ten), S. Foresti (bass), L'Amaltea Ensemble, Vox Hesperia — Fonè ▲ FON 92F 08 [DDD]

St. Marie de Maumont Nuns Choir
Easter Dawn — Jade ▲ JAD C 134
Sing of the Convenant — Jade ▲ JAD C 115
M.D. Pacquetceau (cnd)
Cantate Domino — Milan ▲ 73138–35692–2 ■ 73138–35692–4

St. Mark's Cathedral Choir Minneapolis
H.D. Small (cnd)
Albright, W.:A Song to David, w. Melissa Semmes (nar), Charles Russell (nar), Deborah Carbaugh (sop), Susan Sacquitne–Druck (mez), Rick Penning (ten), James Bohn (bass), Dean Billmeyer (org) *(rec live, St. Mark's Cathedral, Minneapolis, MN, Apr. 28, 1991)* — Gothic ▲ G 49066 [DDD]

St Mary Magdalene Church Choir Toronto
R.H. Bell (cnd)
Willan, H.:Sacred Music—Missa brevis XI, "Sanctus Johannis Baptistae"; Missa Brevis IV, "Corde natus"; Motets in Honour of Our Lady; 12 Motets; St Basil (hymn); Stella Orientis (hymn); St. Osmund (hymn); Here Are We at Bethlehem (carol) — Virgin Classics ▲ CDC 45109

St. Mary's Cathedral Choir
Gounod, C.:Messe solennelle 3 de Pâques, w. D.R. Davies (cnd), Jubilee Orch, Conservatorium Choir — Walsingham Classics ▲ WAL 8011 [DDD]

St. Mary's Episcopal Cathedral Choir Edinburgh
D. Townhill (cnd)
Famous Hymns of Praise, w. Peter Backhouse (org) — Priory ▲ PRCD 376 [DDD]

CHORAL GROUPS

St. Mary's Monastery Monks Choir Petersham MA
A. Saint-Cyr (cnd)
Chants Clothed with the Rays of the Sun:Gregorian Chant in Honor of the Mother of God, w. St. Scholastica Priory Nuns' Choir Petersham MA *(rec Church of the Most Holy Rosary, Gardner, MA, 1989)* Vox ("Classics" series) ▲ VOX 7506 [DDD]

St. Maurice & St. Maur Abbey Monks' Choir
Gregorian Chant Philips 2-▲ 432506-2 [ADD]

St. Michael's Choir
Reger, M.:Orchestral Songs, w. D. Fischer-Dieskau (bar), G. Albrecht (cnd), Hamburg PO, Monteverdi Choir London—Der Einsiedler, Op. 144a; Hymnus der Liebe, Op. 136; Requiem, Op. 144b; An die Hoffnung, Op. 124 [G] Orfeo ▲ 209901 [DDD]
Weber, C.M. von:In die solemnitatis, w. M. Toborsky (sop), E. Ehret (cnd), St. Michael's Orch Koch Schwann ▲ CD 313 055 [ADD]

St. Michael's Chorus Munich
Weber, C.M. von:Gloria et honore, w. M. Toborsky, E. Ehret, St. Michael Orch Munich Koch Schwann ▲ CD 313 055 [ADD]
Weber, C.M. von:Missa sancta 1, w. Maria Taborsky (sop), Gerda Kink (cta), Hermann Pöllmann (ten), Hans Huber (bass), Gisela Schindler (org), E. Ehret (cnd), St. Michael Orch Munich Koch Schwann ▲ SCH CD 316372

St. Michael's de Laudes Monks' Choir
Gregorian Chants:The Best of the Benedictine Monks of St. Michael's Laserlight ▲ 14 164 [AAD]

St. Michael's Singers
Lambert, C.:The Rio Grande, w. A.H. Whitehead (alt), Hamilton Harty (pno), C. Lambert (cnd), Hallé Orch Claremont ▲ CDGSE 785065

St. Nicolas Russian Orthodox Choir
N. Spassky (cnd)
Russian Holiness:Orthodox Liturgical Chants Studio SM ▲ 2543 [DDD]

St. Ottilien Abbey Monks' Choir
The Oldest Marian Propers Calig ▲ CAL 50884 [DDD]
J.B. Göschl (cnd)
Gregorian Chants *(rec Sept. 5–8, 1988)* Calig ▲ CAL 50883 [DDD]

St. Ottilien Archabbey Schola
Easter Ascension Calig ▲ CAL 50919 [DDD]
Gregorianik Ergo Classics 2-▲ ERG 700971 [DDD]
Gregorianik, Vol. 1 Ergo Classics ▲ ERG 701003 [DDD]
Gregorianik, Vol. 2 Ergo Classics ▲ ERG 701011 [DDD]

St. Patrick's Cathedral Choir
Christmas with Renata Scotto at St. Patrick's Cathedral, w. Renata Scotto (sop), Lorenzo Anselmi (cnd), John Grady [org/cnd] *(rec St. Patrick's Cathedral, New York City, June 1981)* VAI Audio ▲ VAIA 1013 [AAD]

St. Paul Youth Choir Aachen
J. Hansen (cnd)
Berthier, J.:Songs—18 sels. Christophorus ▲ CHR 74518 [DDD]

St. Paul's Cathedral Choir
Berlioz, H.:L'Enfance du Christ, w. Jean Rigby (mez), John Aler (ten), Gerald Finley (ten), Alastair Miles (bar), Gwynne Howell (bass), M. Best (cnd), Cordon Orch, Corydon Singers Hyperion 2-▲ CDA 66991/2
British Music on Hyperion, w. Parley of Instruments, Roy Goodman (cnd), John Mark Ainsley (ten), Graham Johnson (pno), Salomon Quartet, BBC Scottish SO, Anthony Rolfe Johnson (ten), Royal PO, St. Paul's Cathedral Choir, Nash Ensemble, Martyn Hill (ten), Suasan Gritton (sop), et al. Hyperion ▲ HYP 15
Croft, W.:Musica sacra, w. P. Holman (cnd), Parley of Instruments—Te Deum in D; Rejoice in the Lord, O Ye Righteous (A Thanksgiving Anthem); The Burial Service; Jubilate in D *(rec Feb. 24–27, May 22, 1992)* Hyperion ▲ CDA 66606 [DDD]
Rosner, A.:Magnificat, w. D. Amos (cnd), Clarion Brass [L] Laurel ▲ LR 849CD [ADD/DDD]
T. Edwards (cnd)
Britten, B.:Hymn to St. Cecilia, w. S. Leonard (sop), N. Tibbels (sop), S. Bickley (mez), P. Hall (ten), G. Jess (bass), London Sinfonietta Chorus Virgin Classics ▲ CDC 59136
A. Lucas (cnd)
Psalms from St. Paul's, Vol. 3, w. John Scott (org) Hyperion ▲ CDP 11003
J. Scott (cnd)
The English Anthem, w. Andrew Lucas (org) Hyperion ▲ CDA 66519 [DDD] ■
The English Anthem, Vol. 4, w. Andrew Lucas (org) Hyperion ▲ CDA 66678 [DDD]
The English Anthem, Vol. 5, w. Andrew Lucas (org) Hyperion ▲ CDA 66758
Goss, J.:O Saviour of the World, w. Maldwyn Davies (ten), David Wilson-Johnson (bar), Andrew Lucas (org), St. Paul's Cathedral Special Choir Conifer Classics ▲ 75605-51193-2 [DDD]
Howells, H.:Choral Music—Magnificat & Nunc Dimittis for St. Paul's Cathedral; Te Deum and Jubilate; Like as the hart desireth the waterbrooks (anthem); Behold, O God, our defender; Take him, earth for cherishing [E,L] Hyperion ▲ CDA 66260 [DDD]
Psalms from St. Paul's, Vol. 5, w. Andrew Lucas (org) Hyperion ▲ 11005
Psalms from St. Paul's, Vol. 2, w. Andrew Lucas (org) Hyperion ▲ CDP 11002
Stainer, J.:The Crucifixion, w. Maldwyn Davies (ten), David Wilson-Johnson (bar), Andrew Lucas (org), St. Paul's Cathedral Special Choir Conifer Classics ▲ 75605-51193-2 [DDD]

St. Paul's Cathedral Choristers
Britten, B.:War Requiem, w. H. Harper (sop), P. Langridge (ten), J. Shirley-Quirk (bar), R. Elms (org), R. Hickox (cnd), London SO, London Sym Chorus [E,L] Chandos 2-▲ CHAN 8983/84 [DDD]
Vaughan Williams, R.:Dona nobis pacem, w. Y. Kenny (sop), B. Terfel (b-bar), R. Hickox (cnd), London SO, London Sym Chorus EMI Classics ▲ CDC 54788
Vaughan Williams, R.:Sancta civitas, w. P. Langridge (ten), B. Terfel (b-bar), R. Hickox (cnd), London SO, London Sym Chorus EMI Classics ▲ CDC 54788
T. Edwards (cnd)
Britten, B.:A Boy Was Born, w. S. Leonard (sop), N. Tibbels (sop), S. Bickley (mez), P. Hall (ten), G. Jess (bass), London Sinfonietta Chorus Virgin Classics ▲ CDC 59136
Britten, B.:Sonnets of Michelangelo, w. S. Leonard (sop), N. Tibbels (sop), S. Bickley (mez), P. Hall (ten), G. Jess (bass), London Sinfonietta Chorus Virgin Classics ▲ CDC 59136

St. Paul's Cathedral Special Choir
J. Scott (cnd)
Goss, J.:O Saviour of the World, w. Maldwyn Davies (ten), David Wilson-Johnson (bar), Andrew Lucas (org), St. Paul's Cathedral Choir Conifer Classics ▲ 75605-51193-2 [DDD]
Stainer, J.:The Crucifixion, w. Maldwyn Davies (ten), David Wilson-Johnson (bar), Andrew Lucas (org), St. Paul's Cathedral Choir Conifer Classics ▲ 75605-51193-2 [DDD]

St. Paul's Chorus
12 Ave Maria, w. St. Paul's PO Studio SM ▲ D 2442 [AAD]

St. Peter ad Vincula Choir within the Tower of London Chapel Royal
J. Williams (cnd)
Jubilate:Music for the Kings & Queens of England, w. Philip Jones Brass Ensemble Chandos ("Collect" series) ▲ CHAN 6560 [ADD]

St. Peter's Abbey of Solesmes Monastic Choir
Gregorian Chant Musketeer Classical ▲ MU 9516
J. Claire (cnd)
Apostles & Martyrs Paraclete ■ C 627
Apostles, Martyrs & Virgins Paraclete ▲ S 827
Bishops & Doctors Paraclete ■ C 628
Bishops, Doctors of the Church & Saints Paraclete ▲ S 828
Christ in Gethsemane Paraclete ▲ S 833 ■ C 633
Christmas Paraclete ▲ S 821 ■ C 621
Christmas Paraclete ▲ S 832 ■ C 632
The Classic, & Complete, 1930 HMV Recordings Pearl 2-▲ PEA 9152 [ADD]

St. Peter's Abbey of Solesmes Monastic Choir (cont.)
J. Claire (cnd) (cont.)
Easter Paraclete ▲ S 822 ■ C 622
Eastertide Paraclete ■ C 625
Feasts Of Our Lady Paraclete ▲ S 824 ■ C 624
Gregorian Sampler Paraclete ▲ PCL 829 ■ PCL 629
Gregorian Sampler I Paraclete ■ C 629-1
Gregorian Sampler II Paraclete ■ C 629-2
An Introduction to Chant Paraclete ▲ PCL 9502 [DDD] ■ PCL 9502
Maundy Thursday Paraclete ▲ S 831 ■ C 631
Pacques Accord ▲ ACD 221602 [AAD]
Requiem Mass & Office for the Dead Paraclete ▲ S 823 ■ C 623
Saint Benedict, w. Dom Claude Gay (org) Paraclete ▲ PCL 820 ■ PCL 620
Sunday Vespers & Compline Paraclete ▲ S 826 ■ C 626
Tenebrae of Good Friday Paraclete ▲ C 634 ■ C 634
A Very Solesmes Christmas Paraclete 2-▲ PCL 9501 [DDD] 2-■ PCL 9501
Vespers & Compline Paraclete ▲ PCL 826 ■ PCL 626
Virgins & Saints Paraclete ■ C 630
J. Gajard (cnd)
Anthologie Grégorienne Accord ▲ ACD 221662
Chant Gregorien Accord ▲ ACD 222012
Le dimanche des rameaux Accord ▲ ACD 201472 [AAD]
Gregorian Chant Rediscovered *(rec Choir of the Abbey Church of Saint Peter of Solesmes, Apr. 1930)* Solesmes ▲ S.835 [AAD]
Messes du Temps Pascal (Easter Masses) Accord ▲ ACD 201492 [AAD]
Messes du temps pascal, Vol. 2 Accord ▲ ACD 201502 [AAD]

St. Peter's Basilica Cappella Giulia Chorus Vatican City
Bernstein, L.:Chichester Psalms, w. G. D. Rodriguez (boy alto), G. Levine (cnd), Royal PO, Rome Phil Academy Chorus *(rec Apr. 7, 1994)* Justice ▲ JR 1801 [DDD]
Schubert, Franz:Psalm 92, w. Cantor H. Nevison (bar), P. Colino (cnd) *(rec Apr. 7, 1994)* Justice ▲ JR 1801 [DDD]

St. Peter's in the Great Valley Chamber Choir
Buxtehude, D.:Cants, w. Laura Heimes (sop), Tamara Crout Matthews (sop), Steven Richards (ct), James Russell (ten), John Alston (bass), M. N. Johnson (cnd), Sarum Consort—Wachet auf, ruft uns die Stimmel; Singet dem Herrn; Quemadmodum desiderat cervus; O fröhliche Stunden, o herrliche Zeit; Jubilate Domino omnis terra; Lobe den Herrn, meine Seele; Erfreue dich, Erdel *(rec St-Martin-in-the-Fields Church, Chestnut Hill, PA, Sept 7–9, 1994)* Pro gloria musicae ▲ PGM 102 [DDD]

St. Peter's in the Loop Schola Cantorum
The Chant of Christmas Midnight *(rec St Nicholas Ukrainian Catholic Cathedral, Chicago, IL, Aug 1995)* Imaginary Road ▲ 314 528 869-2 [DDD]
The Song of Angels Imaginary Road ▲ 314-534279-2 ■ 314-534279-4

St. Petersburg Capella Chorus
Historical Anthology of Russian Religious Chants, w. Drevnerousski Rospev Male Choir, Yourlov Academic Choir, Bolshoi Theater Children's Choir, Rybin Male Choir Russian Season ▲ LDC 288071
The Vespers Russian Season ▲ CMX 388050
V. Tchernushenko (cnd)
Le Sueur, J.-F.:Sacred Music, w. *(soloists unknown)*, St. Petersburg Cappella Orch, Guy Touvron Brass Ensemble—March; Unxerunt Salomonem; Tu es Petrus *(rec La Chaise-Dieu Abbey, Aug 22 & 23, 1995)* Koch Schwann ▲ SCH 312082
Paisiello, G.:Sacred Music, w. *(soloists unknown)*, St. Petersburg Cappella Orch, Guy Touvron Brass Ensemble, St. Petersburg Cappella—Mass; Te Deum *(rec La Chaise-Dieu Abbey, Aug 22 & 23, 1995)* Koch Schwann ▲ SCH 312082
Roze, N.:Vivat in aeternum—Vivat Rex, w. *(soloists unknown)*, St. Petersburg Cappella Orch *(rec La Chaise-Dieu Abbey, Aug 22 & 23, 1995)* Koch Schwann ▲ SCH 312082

St. Petersburg Chamber Choir
Suder, J.:Festival Mass, w. Natalia Kornewa (sop), Maria Neilau (alt), Vladimir Mostomoi (ten), Juri Dobrowolski (bass), Jessica Hartlieb (vn), Marlene Hinterberger (org), W.A. Albert (cnd), Bavarian State Youth Orch Calig ▲ CAL 50945 [DDD]
N. Korniev (cnd)
Rachmaninoff, S.:All-Night Vigil, w. O. Borodina (mez), V. Mostowoy (ten) *(rec St. Petersburg, Oct. 3–6, 1993)* Philips ▲ 442344-2
Rachmaninoff, S.:Liturgy of St John Chrysostom Philips ▲ 442776-2

St. Petersburg Conservatory Chamber Choir
Bach, J.S.:Christmas Oratorio (sels), w. A. Titov (cnd), St. Petersburg Conservatory CO—Jauchzet, frohlocket; Ach, mein herzliebes Jesulein!; Sinf; Brich an, o schönes Morgenlicht; Ich steh'an deiner Krippen hier Infinity Digital ▲ QK 69255 [DDD]
Handel, G.F.:Messiah (sels), w. A. Titov (cnd), St. Petersburg Conservatory CO—For Unto Us a Child is Born; Hallelujah! Infinity Digital ▲ QK 69255 [DDD]

St. Petersburg Conservatory Chorus
Bach, J.S.:Cant 122, w. A. Titov (cnd), St. Petersburg Conservatory CO Infinity Digital ▲ QK 57254 [DDD]
Bach, J.S.:Cant 191, w. A. Titov (cnd), St. Petersburg Conservatory CO Infinity Digital ▲ QK 57254 [DDD]
Bach, J.S.:Christmas Oratorio (sels), w. A. Titov (cnd), St. Petersburg Conservatory CO—Jauchzet, frohlocket; Ach, mein herzliebes Jesulein; Sinf.; Brich an, o schönes Morgenlicht; Ich steh' an deiner Krippen hier Infinity Digital ▲ QK 57254 [DDD]
Handel, G.F.:Messiah (sels), w. A. Titov (cnd), St. Petersburg Conservatory CO—Sinf.; For unto Us a Child Is Born; Pifa (pastoral sym.); He Shall Feed His Flock; Alleluia Chorus Infinity Digital ▲ QK 57254 [DDD]
Mozart, W.A.:Ave verum corpus, w. A. Titov (cnd), St. Petersburg Conservatory CO Infinity Digital ▲ QK 57254 [DDD]

St. Petersburg Russian Choir
N. Korniev (cnd)
Credo, w. Hvorostovsky (bar) Philips ▲ 446089-2

St. Petersburg Soglasie Men's Choir
A. Govorov (cnd)
Authentic Russian Sacred Music IMP ▲ IMP PCD 2030

St. Petersburg State Choir
V. Chernushenko (cnd)
Bortnyansky, D.:Sacred Choral Music—Con. No. 4, "Make a Joyful Noise unto God"; Cherubic Hymn No. 7; Con. No. 34, "Let God arise"; Con. No. 32, "Lord, Make Me Know Mine End"; Con. No. 6, "Glory to God in the Highest"; Con. No. 27, "I Cried unto God with My Voice"; Con. No. 15, "Come O Ye People"; Con. for Double Chorus, "We Praise Thee, O God" *(rec Walthamstow Assembly Hall, London, Oct. 1993)* Teldec ("Das alte Werke" series) ▲ 93856-2 [DDD]

St. Salvator Cathedral Bruges Schola Gregoriana
R. Deruwe (cnd)
Laudes Mariae:Cantiones ad honorem Beatae Mariae Virgine Talent ▲ DPM 2911010 [ADD]
Resurrexi:Gregorian chant for Easter, Ascension & Pentecost René Gailly ▲ 87102 [DDD]

St. Saviour's Cathedral Choir
Gregorian Chant, Vol. II *(rec St. Andrew Abbey, Zevenkerken)* Talent ▲ 291020 [DDD]

St. Scholastica Priory Nuns' Choir Petersham MA
A. Saint-Cyr (cnd)
Chants Clothed with the Rays of the Sun:Gregorian Chant in Honor of the Mother of God, w. St. Mary's Monastery Monks Choir Petersham MA *(rec Church of the Most Holy Rosary, Gardner, MA, 1989)* Vox ("Classics" series) ▲ VOX 7506 [DDD]

St. Thomas Aquinas Church Choir
P. Riedo (cnd)
Christmas at St. Thomas Aquinas Orchid ▲ PICORCD 11020 [DDD]

▲ = CD ♦ = Enhanced CD Δ = MD ■ = Cassette Tape □ = DCC

St. Thomas Choir
Bach, J.S.:Cant 31, w. Eberhard Büchner (ten), Siegfried Lorenz (bar), Hermann Christian Polster (bass), Lang (sgr), Termer (sgr), Weimann (sgr), H.-J. Rotzsch (cnd), Leipzig Gewandhaus Orch Berlin Classics ▲ BER 9025 [ADD]
Bach, J.S.:Cant 66, w. Eberhard Büchner (ten), Siegfried Lorenz (bar), Hermann Christian Polster (bass), Lang (sgr), Termer (sgr), Weimann (sgr), H.-J. Rotzsch (cnd), Leipzig Gewandhaus Orch Berlin Classics ▲ BER 9025 [ADD]
Bach, J.S.:Cant 106, "Actus tragicus", w. Eberhard Büchner (ten), Siegfried Lorenz (bar), Hermann Christian Polster (bass), Lang (sgr), Termer (sgr), Weimann (sgr), H.-J. Rotzsch (cnd), Leipzig Gewandhaus Orch Berlin Classics ▲ BER 9025 [ADD]
Bach, J.S.:St. Matthew Passion, w. A. Burmeister (mez), P. Schreier (ten), T. Adam (bass), R. & E. Mauersberger (cnd), Leipzig Gewandhaus Orch, Dresden Kreuz Choir *(rec 1970)* Berlin Classics 3-▲ BER 2144 [ADD]
Bach, J.S.:St. Matthew Passion, w. T. Lemnitz (sop), F. Beckmann (alt), K. Erb (ten), G. Hüsch (bar), S. Schulze (bass), G. Ramin (cnd), Leipzig Gewandhaus Orch, *(abridged performance)* [G] *(rec Mar 1941)* Calig 2-▲ CAL 50 859/60 (m) [AAD]

St. Thomas Church Choir New York
G. Hancock (cnd)
Praise the Lord Argo ▲ 425800-2 ZH [DDD]

St. Thomas Church Men & Boys' Choir New York
Evensong, w. Gerre Hancock (org) Koch International Classics ▲ KIC 7285 [DDD]
G. Hancock (cnd)
O God, My Heart Is Ready Koch International Classics ▲ KIC 7176 [DDD]

St. Thomas Men & Boys' Choir
In the Spirit:Sacred Music for Christmas, w. Jessye Norman (sop), St. Luke's Orch [cnd:David Robertson], American Boys Choir, Riverside Church Choir, St. Barnabas Adult Choir Philips ▲ 454640-2 ■ 454640-4
G. Hancock (cnd)
Bairstow, E.C.:Choral Music [E,L]—9 Anthems; Communion Service in D; Evening Service in D Koch International Classics ▲ KIC 7093-2 [DDD]
Britten, B.:A Hymn of St. Columba, "Regis regum rectissimi" [E] Koch International Classics ▲ KIC 7030-2 [DDD] ■ 3-7030-4 (D)
Britten, B.:Hymn to St. Cecilia [E] Koch International Classics ▲ KIC 7030-2 [DDD] ■ 3-7030-4 (D)
Britten, B.:Hymn to St. Peter [E] Koch International Classics ▲ KIC 7030-2 [DDD] ■ 3-7030-4 (D)
Britten, B.:A Hymn to the Virgin [E] Koch International Classics ▲ KIC 7030-2 [DDD] ■ 3-7030-4 (D)
Britten, B.:Jubilate Deo [E] Koch International Classics ▲ KIC 7030-2 [DDD] ■ 3-7030-4 (D)
Britten, B.:Rejoice in the Lamb [E] Koch International Classics ▲ KIC 7030-2 [DDD] ■ 3-7030-4 (D)
Britten, B.:Te Deum [E] Koch International Classics ▲ KIC 7030-2 [DDD] ■ 3-7030-4 (D)
Duruflé, M.:Motets on Gregorian Chants, Op. 10, w. Judith Hancock (org) Koch International Classics ▲ KIC 7228
Franck, C.:Psalm 150, w. Judith Hancock (org) Koch International Classics ▲ KIC 7228
Langlais, J.:Messe solenelle, w. Judith Hancock (org) Koch International Classics ▲ KIC 7228
Messiaen, O.:O sacrum convivium!, w. Judith Hancock (org) Koch International Classics ▲ KIC 7228
Poulenc, F.:Exultate Deo, w. Judith Hancock (org) Koch International Classics ▲ KIC 7228

St. Thomas Moore Cathedral Chorus
Mozart, W.A.:Missa brevis, K.194, w. M. Busching (mez), G. Tucker (ten), P. Fay (bar), C. Dill Smith (sgr), H. Mardirosian (cnd), St. Thomas Moore Cathedral Orch [L] Centaur ▲ CRC 2074 [DDD]
Mozart, W.A.:Tantum ergo, w. Carolyn Dill Smith (sop), Marianna Busching (mez), Gene Tucker (ten), Peter Fay (bar), H. Mardirosian (cnd), St. Thomas Moore Cathedral Orch [L] Centaur ▲ CRC 2074 [DDD]
Mozart, W.A.:Vesperae de Dominica, w. C. Dill Smith (sop), M. Busching (mez), G. Tucker (ten), P. Fay (bar), H. Mardirosian (cnd), St. Thomas Moore Cathedral Orch [L] Centaur ▲ CRC 2074 [DDD]

St. Wandrille Abbey Monks' Choir
Exsultate Deo:The Liturgy of St. Wandrille, w. Father Michèl Baumel (org) Studio SM ▲ 12 20.77
Feast Liturgies at St. Wandrille Studio SM ▲ 12 18.00
Sunday Mass at the Abbey of St. Wandrille Jade ▲ JAD C 113

St. Yves Choral Association
J.-P. Lore (cnd)
The Responsory of the Holy Week, w. Versailles Polyphonic Ensemble [cnd:S. Roger] *(rec May 24-26, 1980)* Esoldun ▲ MOS 1003 [ADD]

Salamanca Univ Chamber Chorus
B. Garcia-Bernalt (cnd)
Vasquez, J.:Agenda defunctorum RNE/Spanish National Radio ▲ 640036

Josquino Salepico Chorus
E. Velardi (cnd)
Glorias de España, 1492-1756, w. Alessandro Stradella Consort *(rec Oct. 8-10, 1992)* Bongiovanni ▲ GB 2161-2 [DDD]

Salisbury Cathedral Choir
Christmas Carols from Wells & Salisbury, w. Wells Cathedral Choir ASV ("Quicksilva" series) ▲ ASV 6077 [ADD/DDD]
Stanford, C.V.:For Lo, I Raise Up, w. R. Seal (org) [E] Meridian ▲ CDE 84140
Stanford, C.V.:A Song of Peace, w. R. Seal (org) [E] Meridian ▲ CDE 84140
Walmisley, T.A.:Remember, O Lord, What Is Come upon Us, w. R. Seal (org) [E] Meridian ▲ CDE 84140
Wesley, S.S.:Thou Wilt Keep Him in Perfect Peace [E] Meridian ▲ CDE 84140
R. Seal (cnd)
Anthems for America, w. David Hall (org) Meridian ▲ 84180
Anthems from Salisbury, w. Richard Seal (org) Meridian ▲ 84025
The Mighty Voice of Salisbury Cathedral Meridian ▲ 84140
Salisbury Cathedral Choir, w. Benjamin Dean (trb), Richarl Seal (org) Metronome ▲ MET CD 1016

Salt Lake Children's Choir
R.B. Woodward (cnd)
Beside Thy Cradle, w. Tamara B. Oswald (hp), Janet Peterson (hp), Kelly Parkinson (vn), Victoria Ferris (vn), Hadley Ferris (va), Ellen Bridger (vc) *(rec Maurice Abravanel Hall, Salt Lake City)* Cherbourne ▲ CH 121

Salt Lake City Symphonic Choir
Honegger, A.:Judith, w. Netania Davrath (sop), Blanche Christensen (sop), Madeleine Milhaud (nar), M. Abravanel (cnd), Utah SO [F] *(rec Dec. 1964)* Vanguard Classics ▲ OVC 8088 [ADD]

Salzburg Bach Choir
Biber, H. von:Vesperae longiores ac breviores una cum litaniis Laurentanis, w. Kym Amps (sop), Christopher Robson (alt), Anton Rosner (ten), Albert Hartinger (bass), H. Arman (cnd), Salzburg Baroque Ensemble, Innsbruck Woodwind Circle, Salzburg St. Benedict College Schola Ars Musici ("Essence" series) ▲ AME 3022-2 [DDD]
H. Arman (cnd)
Music at the Salzburg Court, Vol. 2:1587-1612, w. Innsbruck Wind Ensemble Deutsche Harmonia Mundi ▲ 77157-2-RC [DDD]

Salzburg Cathedral Choir
Mozart, W.A.:Grabmusik, w. Maria Seebach (sop), Otto Wiener (bass), J. Messner (cnd), Salzburg Mozarteum Orch *(rec Aug 24, 1952)* Orfeo d'or ("Festspiel Dokumente" series) ▲ 396951
Mozart, W.A.:Requiem, w. Hanna Seebach-Ziegler (sop), Jella von Braun (alt), Hermann Gallos (ten), Richard Mayr (bass), J. Messner (cnd), Cathedral Choral Society Orch *(rec Aug 9, 1931)* Orfeo d'or ("Festspiel Dokumente" series) ▲ 396951
Mozart, W.A.:Requiem, w. J. Messner (cnd), Cathedral Musician's Orch Orfeo d'or ▲ 409951

Salzburg Festival Chamber Choir
Gluck, C.W.:Iphigénie en Aulide, w. Inge Borkh (sop—Klytämnestra), Christa Ludwig (mez—Iphigenie), Elisabeth Steiner (mez—Artemis), James King (ten—Achilles), Otto Edelmann (b-bar), Alois Pernerstorfer (b-bar), Walter Berry (bass), K. Böhm (cnd), Vienna PO, Vienna State Opera Chorus *(rec Salzburg, Aug 3, 1962)* Orfeo d'or ("Festspiel Dikumente" series) 2-▲ C 428962 (m) [ADD]

Salzburg Mozarteum Chorus
Mozart, W.A.:Complete Mozart Edition, w. A. Augér (sop), E. Mathis (sop), H. Schwarz (mez), A. Rolfe Johnson (ten), L. Hager (cnd), Salzburg Mozarteum Orch Philips 2-▲ 422526-2 [ADD]
Mozart, W.A.:Don Giovanni, w. E. Rethberg (sop), L. Helletsgruber (sop), M. Bokor (mez), D. Borgioli (ten), A. Lazzari (ten), E. Pinza (bass), B. Walter (cnd), Salzburg Orch [I] *(rec live, Salzburg, Aug. 2, 1937)* Melodram ("Connaisseur" series) 3-▲ CD 37506 (m) [AAD]
Mozart, W.A.:Kyrie, K.322/296a, w. E. Hinreiner (cnd), Salzburg Mozarteum Camerata Academica Studio SM ▲ 2518
Mozart, W.A.:Missa, K.317, w. G. Fuchs (sop), Novak (alt), Sailer (ten), H. Müller (bass), E. Hinreiner (cnd), Salzburg Mozarteum Orch [L] Pro Arte ▲ CDD 471 [DDD]
Mozart, W.A.:Missa, K.427, w. Annelohre Cahnbley (sop), Maria Stader (sop), George Maran (ten), Walter Raninger (bass), B. Paumgartner (cnd), Salzburg Mozarteum Orch, Salzburg Radio Chorus *(rec Aug 16, 1958)* Orfeo d'or ("Festspiel Dokumente" series) ▲ 397951 (m)

Salzburg Radio Chorus
Haydn, J.:Mass 13, "Schöpfungsmesse", w. *(soloists unknown)*, E. Hinreiner (cnd), Salzburg Mozarteum CO Studio SM 2-▲ 2441
Mozart, W.A.:Missa, K.427, w. Annelohre Cahnbley (sop), Maria Stader (sop), George Maran (ten), Walter Raninger (bass), B. Paumgartner (cnd), Salzburg Mozarteum Orch, Salzburg Mozarteum Chorus *(rec Aug 16, 1958)* Orfeo d'or ("Festspiel Dokumente" series) ▲ 397951 (m)

Salzburg St. Benedict College Schola
Biber, H. von:Vesperae longiores ac breviores una cum litaniis Laurentanis, w. Kym Amps (sop), Christopher Robson (alt), Anton Rosner (ten), Albert Hartinger (bass), H. Arman (cnd), Salzburg Baroque Ensemble, Innsbruck Woodwind Circle, Salzburg Bach Choir Ars Musici ("Essence" series) ▲ AME 3022-2 [DDD]

Salzburg Univ Choral Group
R.G. Frieberger (cnd)
Missa et Officium de Beata Maria Virgine, w. I. Melchersson (org) Entrée ▲ 0056

San Diego Master Chorale
Berlioz, H.:Roméo et Juliette (sels), w. Y. Talmi (cnd), San Diego SO—Intro; Prologue [Ball at the Capulets]; Romeo Alone; Love Scene; Queen Mab Scherzo; Romeo at the tomb *(rec Copley Symphony Hall, San Diego, CA, Nov. 19-20, 1994)* Naxos ▲ 8.553195 [DDD]
Berlioz, H.:Les Troyens (sels), w. Y. Talmi (cnd), San Diego SO—Prelude; Royal Hunt & Storm *(rec Copley Symphony Hall, San Diego, CA, Nov. 19-20, 1994)* Naxos ▲ 8.553195 [DDD]
Wayditch, G. von:Jesus before Herod, w. Michael Best (ten—Jappeticus), Christopher Lindbloom (sgr—Philippo/Herod), Eileen Moss (sgr—Pabula), Vincent Russo (sgr—Pabo), Stephen A. Scot-Shepherd (sgr—Luke the Evangelist), Pauline Tweed (sgr—1st & 2nd girls), P. Erös (cnd), San Diego SO *(rec 1979)* VAI Audio 2-▲ VAIA 1095-2 [ADD]

San Francisco Boys' Chorus
Appling, Falletta (cnd)
Armer, E.:Music of, w. Ursula Le Guin (nar), Elinor Armer (nar), Women's Philharmonic, San Francisco Girls' Chorus, San Francisco Chamber Singers—The Great Instrument of the Geggerets; Anithaca; The Seasons of Oling; Eating with the Hoi; Open & Shut; Sailing Among the Pheromones; On the Antioriental Shores; Island Earth Koch International Classics 2-▲ KIC 7331 [DDD]

San Francisco Chamber Singers
Armer, E.:Music of, w. Ursula Le Guin (nar), Elinor Armer (nar), Women's Philharmonic, San Francisco Girls' Chorus, San Francisco Boys' Chorus—The Great Instrument of the Geggerets; Anithaca; The Seasons of Oling; Eating with the Hoi; Open & Shut; Sailing Among the Pheromones; On the Antioriental Shores; Island Earth Koch International Classics 2-▲ KIC 7331 [DDD]

San Francisco Girls' Chorus
Armer, E.:Music of, w. Ursula Le Guin (nar), Elinor Armer (nar), Women's Philharmonic, San Francisco Boys' Chorus, San Francisco Chamber Singers—The Great Instrument of the Geggerets; Anithaca; The Seasons of Oling; Eating with the Hoi; Open & Shut; Sailing Among the Pheromones; On the Antioriental Shores; Island Earth Koch International Classics 2-▲ KIC 7331 [DDD]

San Francisco Opera Chorus
Beethoven, L. van:Fidelio, w. Judith Blegen (sop), Leonie Rysanek (sop), Jon Vickers (ten), Walter Berry (bass), John Macurdy (bass), Giorgio Tozzi (bass), K. Böhm (cnd), San Francisco Opera Orch Melodram 2-▲ CDM 27086
Bellini, V.:I Puritani (sels), w. J. Sutherland (sop), D. Cole (sop), A. Kraus (ten), R. Wolansky (bar), N. Ghiuselev (bass), R. Bonynge (cnd), San Francisco Opera Orch *(rec live, San Francisco, 9/2/66)* Golden Age of Opera ▲ GAO 133 [ADD]
Massenet, J.:Hérodiade, w. Renée Fleming (sop—Salome), Dolora Zajick (mez—Hérodiade), Plácido Domingo (ten—Jean), Juan Pons (bar—Érode), Kenneth Cox (bass—Phanuel), V. Gergiev (cnd), San Francisco Opera Orch Sony Classical 2-▲ S2K 66847
Massenet, J.:Hérodiade (sels), w. Renée Fleming (sop—Salomé), Dolora Zajick (mez—Hérodiade), Plácido Domingo (ten—Jean), Juan Pons (bar—Hérode), Hector Vásquez (bar—Vitellius), Kenneth Cox (bass—Phanuel), V. Gergiev (cnd), San Francisco Opera Orch Sony Classical ▲ SK 61965
Massenet, J.:Hérodiade (sels), w. Renée Fleming (sop), Dolora Zajick (mez), Kristin Clayton (sgr), Plácido Domingo (ten), Kenneth Cox (bass), Juan Pons (bar), Hector Vásquez (sgr), V. Gergiev (cnd), San Francisco Opera Orch—highlights *(rec San Francisco Opera, Nov 1994)* Sony Classical ▲ SK 61965
Puccini, G.:Tosca, w. Leonie Rysanek (sop), Russell Christopher (ten), Andrea Velis (ten), Clifford Harvuot (bar), Cornell MacNeil (bar), Fernando Corena (bass), Paul Plishka (bass), F. Molinari-Pradelli (cnd), San Francisco Opera Orch Melodram 2-▲ CDM 27508

San Francisco Sym Chorus
Adams, J.:Harmonium, w. E. de Waart (cnd), San Francisco SO [E] ECM New Series ▲ 78118-21277-2
Brahms, J.:Alto Rhap, w. J. van Nes (mez), H. Blomstedt (cnd), San Francisco SO [G] London ▲ 430281-2 [DDD]
Brahms, J.:Begräbnisgesang, w. H. Blomstedt (cnd), San Francisco SO [G] London ▲ 430281-2 [DDD]
Brahms, J.:Gesang der Parzen, w. H. Blomstedt (cnd), San Francisco SO [G] London ▲ 430281-2 [DDD]
Brahms, J.:Nänie, w. H. Blomstedt (cnd), San Francisco SO [G] London ▲ 430281-2 [DDD]
Brahms, J.:Schicksalslied, w. H. Blomstedt (cnd), San Francisco SO [G] London ▲ 430281-2 [DDD]
Mahler, G.:Sym 2, w. R. Ziesak (sop), C. Hellekant (mez), H. Blomstedt (cnd), San Francisco SO London ▲ 443350-2
Orff, C.:Carmina burana, w. H. Blomstedt (cnd), San Francisco SO [G, L] London ▲ 430509-2 [DDD] □ 430509-5

San Francisco War Memorial Opera House Chorus
Donizetti, G.:L'elisir d'amore (sels), w. Reri Grist (sop), Luciano Pavarotti (ten), Sesto Bruscantini (bar), Ingvar Wixell (bar), Maria Ambrosio (sgr), G. Patanè (cnd), San Francisco War Memorial Opera House Orch *(rec live, San Francisco, 1969)* Budget ("The Greatest Voice in Opera" series) ▲ SYP 109

San Petronio Cappella Musicale Chorus
Colonna, G.P.:Magnificat, w. J. Feldman (sop), S. Vartolo (cnd), St. Petronio Cappella Musicale [L] Tactus 2-▲ TC 630390 [DDD]
Colonna, G.P.:Psalms, w. S. Vartolo (cnd), St. Petronio Cappella Musicale—Beatus vir; Dixit à 9; Laudate Dominum; Laudate pueri à 8 [L] Tactus 2-▲ TC 630390 [DDD]
S. Vartolo (cnd)
Monteverdi, C.:Sacred Vocal Music—Pianto della Madonna sopra il Lamento d'Arianna *(rec Music Room of the Magnagutti Palace, Sermide, Feb 1995)* Naxos ▲ 8.553318 [DDD]

San Petronio Cappella Musicale Soloists
Palestrina, G.:De Beata Marie, w. Liuwe Tamminga (org) *(rec Verona Cathedral, Jan 1995)* Bongiovanni 2-▲ GB 5556/57-2 [DDD]
Palestrina, G.:Masses, w. Liuwe Tamminga (org)—Missas in Duplicibus Minoribus I & II *(rec 1995)* Bongiovanni ▲ GB 5558 [DDD]
Rossi, L.:Laments—Lamento di Mustafà e Bajazet; Hor ch'in notturna pace *(rec Music Room of the Magnagutti Palace, Sermide, Feb 1995)* Naxos ▲ 8.553318 [DDD]
Sances, G.F.:Choral Music—Cantada sopra il Passacaglio *(rec Music Room of the Magnagutti Palace, Sermide, Feb 1995)* Naxos ▲ 8.553318 [DDD]

San Petronio Cappella Musicale Soloists (cont.)
Strozzi, B.:Arias & Cants—Le tre Grazie a Venere *(rec Music Room of the Magnagutti Palace, Sermide, Feb 1995)* Naxos ▲ 8.553318 [DDD]

San Petronio Voci Bianche Chorus
Barbieri, L.:Surgite pastores, w. S. Vartolo (cnd), St. Petronio Cappella Musicale, Tölz Boys' Choir, Avignon Vocal Ensemble *(rec Oct. 3–5, 1991)* Tactus ▲ TC 551801
Perti, G.A.:Messa e salmi concertati, w. S. Vartolo (cnd), San Petronio Cappella Musicale Orch, Avignon Vocal Ensemble, Tölz Boys' Choir *(rec Oct. 3–5, 1991)* Tactus ▲ TC 551801
Rota, A.:Missarum liber primus, w. S. Vartolo (cnd), San Petronio Cappella Musicale Orch, Avignon Vocal Ensemble, Tölz Boys' Choir *(rec Oct. 3–5, 1991)* Tactus ▲ TC 551801
Trombetti, A.:Il primo libro de motetti accomodati per cantare e far concerti, w. S. Vartolo (cnd), St. Petronio Cappella Musicale, Tölz Boys' Choir, Avignon Vocal Ensemble *(rec Oct. 3–5, 1991)* Tactus ▲ TC 551801

San Remo Sym Chorus
Ricci, L.:Crispino e la cornare, w. D. Lojarro (sop), A. Lazzarini (mez), Cossutta (ten), S. Alaimo (bar), R. Coviello (bar), A. Marani (bass), R. Ristori (bass), Benori (sgr), Siclari (sgr), P. Carignani (cnd), San Remo SO [l] *(rec live 11/89)* Bongiovanni 2–▲ GB 2095/96 [DDD]
Rossini, G.:Ciro in Babilonia, w. C. Calvi (cta), E. Palacio (ten), Dessy–Ceriani (sgr), C. Rizzi (cnd), San Remo SO [l] *(rec live 10/30/88)* Arkadia–Akademia 2–▲ 105 [DDD]

Santa Barbara Regional Choir
S.A. Pinner (cnd)
Ave Maria, w. organ VQR Digital ▲ VQR 2046 [DDD]

Santa Fe Sym Chamber Choir
McLaughlin, J.:The Flowers of Dawn, w. James Bustenid (bar), S. Robertson (cnd), Sante Fe SO Chamber Players *(rec St. Francis Auditorium, Sante Fe, NM, Mar 17, 1991)* Ludifichord ▲ LDCD 1001

Santiago Teatro Municipale Chorus
Bizet, G.:Carmen, w. Laura Bustamante (sop—Frasquita), Ximena Riveros (sop—Mercedes), Nancy Stokes (sop—Micaela), Regina Resnik (mez—Carmen), Plácido Domingo (ten—Don José), Ismildo Tedeschi (ten—Remendado), Ramon Vinay (ten—Escamillo), Juan Charles (ten/bar—Dancaire), Agustin Letelier (bar—Morles), Jorge Algorta (bass—Zuniga), A. Guadagno (cnd), Santiago Teatro Municipale Orch *(rec Santiago Municipal Theater, Sept. 4, 1967)* Legato Classics 2–▲ LCD 194–2 [ADD]

Santo Domingo de Silos Benedictine Monks' Choir
Gregorian Chants:Holy Week I EMI Classics ▲ CDZ 67195
The Mystery of Santo Domingo de Silos Deutsche Grammophon ▲ 445399–2 ■ 445399–4
The Soul of Chant Milan ▲ 73138–35703–2 ■ 73138–35703–4
J.L. Angulo (cnd)
Christmas Chants Milan ▲ 73138–35771–2
F. Lara (cnd)
Gregorian Chant at the Monastery of Silos EMI Classics ▲ CDZ 62735

Santo Spirito Academy Chorus
Stradella, A.:Cants, w. Cristina Miatello (sop), Gianpaolo Fagotto (ten), Antonio Abete (sgr), Roberto Balconi (sgr), Lavinia Bertotti (sgr), Roberta Giua (sgr), S. Balestracci (cnd), Santo Spirito Academy Orch—for 5 w. vns [For Holy Christmas]; for 5 w. instruments [For the Souls in Purgatory] Stradivarius ▲ STV 33392 [DDD]

São Paulo Teatro Municipale Chorus
Gomes, A.C.:Il Guarany, w. Niza De Castro Tank (sop—Cecilia), Roque Lotti (ten—Ruy Bento), Manrico Patassini (ten—Pery), Paschoal Raymundo (ten—Don Alvaro), Paulo Fortes (bar—Gonzales), Juan Carlos Ortiz (b–bar—Il Cacico), Waldomiro Furlan (bass—Alonso), Josè Perrotta (bass—Don Antonio De Mariz), A. Belardi (cnd), São Paulo Teatro Municipale Orch *(rec Studios of the Teatro Municipal, São Paulo, Brazil, 1959)* Arkadia 2–▲ HP 617.2 [ADD]

Saratov Phil Choir
Litsova, Berthelon (cnd)
Arkadiev, M.:Missa brevis, w. Louis Robilliard (org), Maîtrise de la Loire REM ▲ REM 311275 [DDD]
Bortnyansky, D.:Sacred Choral Music, w. Louis Robilliard (org), Maîtrise de la Loire—Cons Nos. 34 & 35 REM ▲ REM 311275 [DDD]
Duruflé, M.:Motets on Gregorian Chants, Op. 10, w. Louis Robilliard (org), Maîtrise de la Loire REM ▲ REM 311275 [DDD]
Mendelssohn, F.:Motets, Op. 39, w. Louis Robilliard (org), Maîtrise de la Loire REM ▲ REM 311275 [DDD]
Poulenc, F.:Litanies à la vierge noire, w. Louis Robilliard (org), Maîtrise de la Loire REM ▲ REM 311275 [DDD]
Tchesnokov, P.:Liturgie 6, w. Louis Robilliard (org), Maîtrise de la Loire REM ▲ REM 311275 [DDD]

Sarre Choir
Bach, J.S.:Cant 57, w. Jacob Staempfli (bass), K. Ristenpart (cnd), Sarre CO Accord ▲ ACD 202652 [AAD]
Bach, J.S.:Cant 82, w. Jacob Staempfli (bass), K. Ristenpart (cnd), Sarre CO Accord ▲ ACD 202652 [AAD]
Bach, J.S.:Cant 159, w. Jacob Staempfli (bass), K. Ristenpart (cnd), Sarre CO Accord ▲ ACD 202652 [AAD]

Sarrebrück Conservatory Choir
H. Schmolzi (cnd)
Mozart, W.A.:Missa, K.317, w. Teresa Stich–Randall (sop), Bianca Maria Casoni (alt), Pietro Bottazzo (ten), K. Ristenpart (cnd), Sarre CO Accord ▲ ACD 220252 [AAD]
Mozart, W.A.:Vesperae solennes, w. Teresa Stich–Randall (sop), Bianca Maria Casoni (alt), Pietro Bottazzo (ten), K. Ristenpart (cnd), Sarre CO Accord ▲ ACD 220252 [AAD]

Savaria Vocal Ensemble
Esterházy, P.:Harmonia caelestis, w. M. Fers (sop), M. Zádori (sop), K. Gémes (mez), K. Károlyi (cta), G. Kállay (ten), J. Moldvay (bass), P. Németh (cnd), Capella Savaria [period instruments] [L] Hungaroton 2–▲ HCD 31148/49 [DDD]
Vivaldi, A.:Juditha triumphans devicta Holofernes barbarie, w. M. Zádori (sop), J. Németh (mez), K. Gémes (mez), G. Banditelli (cta), A. Markert (cta), N. McGegan (cnd), Capella Savaria [L] Hungaroton 2–▲ HCD 31063/64 [DDD]

Savonlinna Opera Festival Chorus
Hindemith, P.:Das Marienleben, w. Karita Mattila (sop), U. Söderblom (cnd), Lahti SO *(rec Dec. 1987 & May 1988)* Finlandia ▲ 4509–95857–2 [DDD]
Kokkonen, J.:The Last Temptations, w. Ritva Auvinen (sop), Martti Talvela (bass), U. Söderblom (cnd), Savonlinna Opera Festival Orch Finlandia 2–▲ FIN 104 [AAD]
Kokkonen, J.:Requiem (in memoriam Maija Kokkonen), w. S. Isokoski (sop), W. Grönroos (bar), U. Söderblom (cnd), Lahti SO [L] BIS ▲ CD 508 [DDD]
Merikanto, A.:Genesis, w. Karita Mattila (sop), U. Söderblom (cnd), Lahti SO *(rec Dec. 1987 & May 1988)* Finlandia ▲ 4509–95857–2 [DDD]
Opera Scenes from Savonlinna, w. Haatanen (cnd), Savonlinna Opera Festival Orch BIS 2–▲ CD 373/74 [DDD]
Sallinen, A.:Dream Songs, w. K. Mattila (sop), U. Söderblom (cnd), Lahti SO *(rec Dec. 1987 & May 1988)* Finlandia ▲ 4509–95857–2 [DDD]

Saxon State Chorus
Wolf, H.:Der Corregidor, w. M. Teschemacher (sop), M. Fuchs (sop), K. Erb (ten), J. Herrmann (bar), K. Böhme (b–bar), G. Hann (bass), G. Frick (bass), K. Elmendorff (cnd), Saxon State Orch *(rec 1944)* Preiser 2–▲ PRE 90182 [AAD]

La Scala Chorus
Apollo Granforte, 1886–1975, w. Apollo Granforte (bar), La Scala Orch [cnd:Carlo Sabajno] *(rec HMV 1928–31)* Preiser ("Lebendige Vergangenheit" series) ▲ PRE 89048 (m) [AAD]
Beethoven, L. van:Fant Pno, Op. 80, "Choral Fant", w. D. Ciani (pno), R. Muti (cnd), La Scala Orch [G] *(rec live, Milan 11/5/70)* Arkadia ▲ 743 [ADD]
Bellini, V.:I Capuleti e i Montecchi, w. R. Scotto (sop), G. Aragall (ten), L. Pavarotti (ten), C. Abbado (cnd), La Scala Orch [l] *(rec live, La Scala, 1/8/68)* Arkadia 2–▲ 550 (m) [AAD]

La Scala Chorus (cont.)
Bellini, V.:I Capuleti e i Montecchi, w. R. Scotto (sop), G. Aragall (ten), L. Pavarotti (ten), A. Giacomotti (bass), A. Ferrin (bass), C. Abbado (cnd), La Scala Orch *(rec live 1967)* Butterfly Music 2–▲ BMC 12 [AAD]
Bellini, V.:I Capuleti e i Montecchi (sels), w. Luciano Pavarotti (ten), Gaetano Ferrin (bass), Alfredo Giacomotti (bass), C. Abbado (cnd), La Scala Orch—O di Cappelio generoso amici...E serbato a questo acciaro *(rec live, Nov. 20, 1969)* RCA Gold Seal ▲ 09026–68014–2 [ADD]
Bellini, V.:Norma, w. M. Callas (sop), E. Stignani (mez), M. Filippeschi (ten), N. Rossi–Lemeni (bass), T. Serafin (cnd), La Scala Orch [l] EMI Classics 3–▲ CDC 47303 (m)
Bellini, V.:Norma, w. Maria Callas (sop), Gabriella Carturan (mez), Giulietta Simionato (mez), Mario del Monaco (ten), Giuseppe Zampieri (ten), Nicola Zaccaria (bass), A. Votto (cnd), La Scala Orch Melodram 2–▲ CDM 26036
Bellini, V.:Norma, w. M. Callas (sop), C. Ludwig (mez), F. Corelli (ten), N. Zaccaria (bass), T. Serafin (cnd), La Scala Orch [l] EMI Classics ("Studio" series) 3–▲ CDMC 63000 [ADD]
Bellini, V.:Norma, w. M. Callas (sop), G. Simionato (mez), M. Del Monaco (ten), N. Zaccaria (bass), A. Votto (cnd), La Scala Orch *(rec 12/7/55)* HRE 2–▲ 1007–2
Bellini, V.:Norma (sels), w. M. Callas (sop), C. Ludwig (mez), F. Corelli (ten), N. Zaccaria (bass), T. Serafin (cnd), La Scala Orch EMI Classics ▲ ZDM 63091
Bellini, V.:I Puritani, w. M. Callas (sop), G. di Stefano (ten), R. Panerai (bar), N. Rossi–Lemeni (bass), T. Serafin (cnd), La Scala Orch [l] EMI Classics 2–▲ CDCB 47308 (m) [ADD]
Bellini, V.:La sonnambula, w. M. Callas (sop), F. Cossotto (mez), N. Monti (ten), N. Zaccaria (bass), A. Votto (cnd), La Scala Orch [l] *(rec live 1957)* Arkadia 2–▲ 503 (m) [AAD]
Bellini, V.:La sonnambula, w. M. Callas (sop), G. Carturan (mez), C. Valletti (ten), G. Modesti (bass), L. Bernstein (cnd), La Scala Orch [l] *(rec live, 3/5/55)* Myto 2–▲ 2 MCD 89006 (m) [ADD]
Bellini, V.:La sonnambula, w. Maria Callas (sop), Fiorenza Cossotto (mez), Nicola Monti (ten), Franco Ricciardi (ten), Dino Mantovani (bar), Nicola Zaccaria (bass), A. Votto (cnd), La Scala Orch Melodram 2–▲ CDM 26037
Bellini, V.:La sonnambula, w. M. Callas (sop), F. Cossotto (mez), N. Monti (ten), N. Zaccaria (bass), A. Votto (cnd), La Scala Orch [l] *(rec live 1957)* Melodram 2–▲ MEL 26003
Bellini, V.:La sonnambula, w. M. Callas (sop), F. Cossotto (mez), N. Monti (ten), N. Zaccaria (bass), A. Votto (cnd), La Scala Orch [l] *(rec live 1957)* Verona 2–▲ 2704/05 (m) [AAD]
Bellini, V.:La sonnambula, w. M. Callas (sop), F. Cossotto (mez), N. Monti (ten), N. Zaccaria (bass), A. Votto (cnd), La Scala Orch [l] EMI Classics 2–▲ CDCB 47377 (m)
Bellini, V.:La sonnambula (sels), w. M. Callas (sop), F. Cossotto (mez), N. Monti (ten), N. Zaccaria (bass), A. Votto (cnd), La Scala Orch, from Act 2—Oh! se una volta sola rivederio; Ah, non creda mirarti [l] *(rec live, 7/4/57)* Myto 2–▲ 2 MCD 89006 (m) [ADD]
Bizet, G.:Carmen, w. Ines Alfani Tellini (sop), Aurora d'Alessio Buades (cta), Aureliano Pertile (ten), Benvenuto Franci (bar), L. Molajoli (cnd), La Scala Orch *(rec Milan, 1933)* Phonographie 2–▲ PHG 5013 [ADD]
Bizet, G.:Carmen (sels), w. G. Simionato (mez), G. di Stefano (ten), H. von Karajan (cnd), La Scala Orch—14 arias [F] *(rec live, Milan, 1/18/55)* Arkadia 3–▲ 221 [ADD]
Boito, A.:Mefistofele, w. R. Noli (sop—Margherita), S. dall'Argine (sop—Elena), G. Poggi (ten—Faust), G. Neri (bass–Mefistofele), F. Capuana (cnd), La Scala Orch [l] *(rec 1952)* Preiser 2–▲ 90122 (m) [AAD]
Boito, A.:Mefistofele, w. Michèle Crider (sop—Margherita/Elena), Eleonora Jankovic (mez—Marta/Pantalis), Ernesto Gavazzi (ten—Wagner/Nereo), Vincenza La Scola (ten—Faust), Samuel Ramey (bass—Mefistofele), R. Muti (cnd), La Scala Orch *(rec live Mar 3,5 & 8, 1995, Milan)* RCA Victor 2–▲ 09026–68284–2 [DDD]
Boito, A.:Mefistofele, w. Giannina Arangi–Lombardi (sop), Mafalda Favero (sop), Antonio Melandri (ten), Giuseppe Nessi (ten), Nazzareno de Angelis (bass), L. Molajoli (cnd), La Scala Orch Grammofono 2000 2–▲ GRM 78606 (m)
Catalani, A.:Loreley, w. E. Suliotis (sop), G. Talarico (ten), P. Cappuccilli (bar), G. Gavazzeni (cnd), La Scala Orch *(rec 1968)* Memories 2–▲ MEM 4511 [ADD]
Catalani, A.:La Wally, w. R. Scotto (sop—Walter), R. Tebaldi (sop—Wally), J. Gardino (mez—Afra), M. Del Monaco (ten—Giuseppe Hagenbach), G.G. Guelfi (bar—Vincenzo Gellner), G. Tozzi (bass—Stromminger), C. M. Giulini (cnd), La Scala Orch *(rec Dec. 7, 1953)* Legato Classics 2–▲ LCD 177–2 [ADD]
Cherubini, L.:Ali Baba, ou Les Quarante voleurs, w. T. Stich–Randall (sop), A. Kraus (ten), V. Ganzarolli (bar), N. Sanzogno (cnd), La Scala Orch *(rec 1963)* Memories 2–▲ MEM 4513 [ADD]
Cherubini, L.:Lodoïska, w. M. Devia (sop), F. Pedaci (sgr), B. Lombardo (ten), T. Moser (ten), A. Corbelli (bar), W. Shimell (bar), R. Muti (cnd), La Scala Orch Sony Classical 2–▲ SM2K 47290
Cherubini, L.:Médée, w. M. Callas (sop), R. Scotto (sop), M. Pirazzini (mez), M. Picchi (ten), T. Serafin (cnd), La Scala Orch [l] *(rec live, 1953)* EMI Classics (Studio) 2–▲ CDMB 63625 [ADD]
Cherubini, L.:Médée, w. M. Callas (sop), F. Barbieri (mez), G. Penno (ten), G. Modesti (bass), Nache (sgr), L. Bernstein (cnd), La Scala Orch [l] *(rec live 12/10/53)* Melodram 2–▲ MEL 26022 (m) [AAD]
Cherubini, L.:Médée, w. M. Callas (sop), F. Barbieri (mez), G. Penno (ten), G. Modesti (bass), Nache (sgr), L. Bernstein (cnd), La Scala Orch [l] *(rec live, Milan 12/10/53)* Verona 2–▲ 27088/89
Donizetti, G.:Anna Bolena, w. M. Callas (sop—Anna Bolena), G. Simionato (mez—Giovanna), G. Raimondi (ten—Percy), N. Rossi–Lemeni (bass—King), G. Gavazzeni (cnd), La Scala Orch [l] *(rec live, Milan 4/14/57)* Verona 2–▲ 27090/91
Donizetti, G.:Anna Bolena, w. Maria Callas (sop), Gabriella Carturan (mez), Giulietta Simionato (mez), Gianni Raimondi (ten), Plinio Clabassi (bass), Nicola Rossi Lemmeni (sgr), Luigi Rumo (sgr), G. Gavazzeni (cnd), La Scala Orch Great Opera Performances 2–▲ GOP 768
Donizetti, G.:Anna Bolena, w. M. Callas (sop), G. Simionato (mez), G. Raimondi (ten), G. Gavazzeni (cnd), La Scala Orch [l] *(rec live, 4/17/57)* Melodram 2–▲ MEL 26010
Donizetti, G.:Don Pasquale, w. Adelaide Saraceni (sop), Tito Schipa (ten), Ernesto Badini (bar), Afro Poli (bar), C. Sabajno (cnd), La Scala Orch *(rec 1932)* Grammofono 2000 2–▲ GRM 78561 (m)
Donizetti, G.:Don Pasquale, w. Margherita Guglielmi (sop—Norina), Alfredo Kraus (ten—Ernesto), Rolando Panerai (bar—Malatesta), Paolo Montarsolo (bass—Don Pasquale), P. Bellugi (cnd), La Scala Orch *(rec Jan 13, 1974)* Golden Age of Opera 2–▲ GAO 202/203 [ADD]
Donizetti, G.:L'elisir d'amore, w. Rosanna Carteri (sop—Adina), Luigi Angela Vercelli (mez—Gianetta), Luigi Alva (ten—Nemorino), Rolando Panerai (bar—Belcore), Giuseppe Taddei (bar—Dulcamara), T. Serafin (cnd), La Scala Orch EMI Classics 2–▲ CDMB 65658
Donizetti, G.:La fille du régiment, w. M. Freni (sop), A. di Stasio (mez), L. Pavarotti (ten), W. Ganzarolli (bar), W. Monachesi (bar), N. Sanzogno (cnd), La Scala Orch [l] *(rec live, 2/11/69)* Melodram 2–▲ MEL 27045
Donizetti, G.:La fille du régiment, w. M. Freni (sop), A. di Stasio (mez), L. Pavarotti (ten), W. Ganzarolli (bar), W. Monachesi (bar), N. Sanzogno (cnd), La Scala Orch [l] *(rec live, 2/11/69)* Verona 2–▲ 27046/47 (m) [AAD]
Donizetti, G.:La fille du régiment, w. M. Freni (sop), L. Pavarotti (ten), W. Ganzarolli (bar), N. Sanzogno (cnd), La Scala Orch *(rec 1969)* Memories 2–▲ MEM 4507 [AAD]
Donizetti, G.:La fille du régiment (sels), w. Mirella Freni (sop), Anna di Stasio (mez), Angelo Mercuriali (ten), Luciano Pavarotti (ten), Wladimiro Ganzarolli (bar), Walter Monachesi (bar), Giuseppe Morresi (bass), V. Gullino (sgr), Luisa Rezzadore (sgr), N. Sanzogno (cnd), La Scala Orch Budget ("The Greatest Voice in Opera" series) ▲ SYP 108
Donizetti, G.:Lucia di Lammermoor, w. M. Callas (sop), G. di Stefano (ten), R. Panerai (bar), N. Zaccaria (bass), H. von Karajan (cnd), RIAS SO [l] *(rec live, 1955)* EMI Classics (Studio) 2–▲ CDMB 63631 [ADD]
Donizetti, G.:Lucia di Lammermoor, w. M. Capsir (sop—Lucia), E. de Muro Lomanto (ten—Sir Ravenswood), E. Venturini (ten—Lord Bucklaw), E. Molinari (bar—Lord Ashton), S. Baccaloni (bass—Bidebent), L. Molajoli (cnd), La Scala Orch *(rec 1933)* Myto 2–▲ 2MCD 94299
Donizetti, G.:Lucia di Lammermoor, w. M. Callas (sop), G. di Stefano (ten), R. Panerai (bar), N. Zaccaria (bass), H. von Karajan (cnd), RIAS SO [l] *(rec 9/29/55)* Melodram 2–▲ MEL 26004
Donizetti, G.:Lucia di Lammermoor, w. M. Callas (sop), G. di Stefano (ten), G. Zampieri (ten), R. Panerai (bar), G. Modesti (bass), H. von Karajan (cnd), La Scala Orch *(rec 1954)* Melodram 2–▲ MLO 26040 [DDD]

La Scala Chorus (cont.)

Donizetti, G.:Lucia di Lammermoor, w. M. Callas (sop), G. di Stefano (ten), R. Panerai (bar), H. von Karajan (cnd), La Scala Orch [I] *(rec live, Milan 1/18/54)* Standing Room Only 2-▲ SRO 831-2 [ADD]

Donizetti, G.:Lucia di Lammermoor, w. M. Callas (sop), G. di Stefano (ten), R. Panerai (bar), N. Zaccaria (bass), H. von Karajan (cnd), RIAS SO [I] *(rec 9/29/55)* Verona 2-▲ 2709/10 (m) [AAD]

Donizetti, G.:Lucia di Lammermoor, w. R. Scotto (sop), G. di Stefano (ten), E. Bastianini (bar), N. Sanzogno (cnd), La Scala Orch *(rec 1959)* Enterprise (Palladio) 2-▲ ENTPD 4117 [ADD]

Donizetti, G.:Lucia di Lammermoor, w. Mariella Devia (sop), Vencenzo La Scola (ten), Renato Bruson (bar), S. Ranzani (cnd), La Scala Orch Serenissima 2-▲ SER 360153 [DDD]

Donizetti, G.:Lucrezia Borgia, w. M. Caballé (sop), A. M. Rota (cta), G. Raimondi (ten), E. Flagello (bass), E. Gracis (cnd), La Scala Orch [I] *(rec live, 3/2/70)* Myto 2-▲ 2 MCD 90423 [ADD]

Donizetti, G.:Lucrezia Borgia (sels), w. L. Gencer (sop), G. Raimondi (ten), L. Roni (bass-bar), E. Gracis (cnd), La Scala Orch—8 scenes & arias [I] *(rec live, 3/12/70)* Myto 2-▲ 2 MCD 90423 [ADD]

Donizetti, G.:Maria Stuarda, w. M. Caballé (sop), S. Verrett (mez), O. Garaventa (ten), C.F. Cillario (cnd), La Scala Orch [I] *(rec live, Milan 4/20/71)* Myto 2-▲ 2 MCD 91137 [ADD]

Donizetti, G.:Poliuto, w. M. Callas (sop), F. Corelli (ten), E. Bastianini (bar), N. Zaccaria (bass), A. Votto (cnd), La Scala Orch [I] *(rec live, Milan 12/7/60)* Verona 2-▲ 28003/04

Donizetti, G.:Poliuto, w. Maria Callas (sop), Franco Corelli (ten), Ettore Bastianini (bar), A. Votto (cnd), La Scala Orch *(rec live, Milan, 1960)* Enterprise ("Documents" series) 2-▲ ENT LV 977 (m)

Donizetti, G.:Poliuto, w. M. Callas (sop), F. Corelli (ten), E. Bastianini (bar), N. Zaccaria (bass), A. Votto (cnd), La Scala Orch [I] *(rec live, 12/7/60)* Arkadia 2-▲ 520 (m) [AAD]

Donizetti, G.:Poliuto, w. M. Callas (sop), F. Corelli (ten), E. Bastianini (bar), N. Zaccaria (bass), A. Votto (cnd), La Scala Orch [I] *(rec live, 12/7/60)* Melodram 2-▲ MEL 26006

Falla, M. de:Atlántida, w. T. Stratas (sop), G. Simionato (mez), R. Browne (sgr), Halley (sgr), T. Schippers (cnd), La Scala Orch *(rec live, Milan 6/18/62)* Memories 2-▲ HR 4464/65 [ADD]

Giordano, U.:Andrea Chénier, w. M. Caniglia (sop), G. Simionato (mez), B. Gigli (ten), G. Bechi (bar), G. Taddei (bar), I. Tajo (bass), O. de Fabritiis (cnd), La Scala Orch [I] *(rec 1941, HMV DB 5423/35)* Angel ("Studio" series) 2-▲ CDHB 69996 (m) [ADD]

Giordano, U.:Andrea Chénier, w. Maria Caniglia (sop—Maddalena), Maria Huder (mez—Bersi), Vittoria Palombini (mez—Madelon), Giulietta Simionato (mez—Contessa), Beniamino Gigli (ten—Andrea), Adelio Zagonara (ten—Incroyable/Abbé), Gino Bechi (bar—Carlo), Leone Paci (bar—Mathieu), Giuseppe Taddei (b-bar—Pietro/Fouquier), Italo Tajo (b-bar—Roucher), Gino Conti (bass—Master/Schmidt), O. de Fabritiis (cnd), La Scala Orch *(rec Nov 1941)* Arkadia ("The 78's" series) 2-▲ 78012 [ADD]

Giordano, U.:Andrea Chénier, w. M. Callas (sop), M. del Monaco (ten), A. Protti (bar), A. Votto (cnd), La Scala Orch *(rec live, Milan, 1/8/55)* Melodram 2-▲ MEL 26002 [ADD]

Giordano, U.:Andrea Chénier, w. M. Callas (sop), M. del Monaco (ten), A. Protti (bar), A. Votto (cnd), La Scala Orch *(rec live)* Verona 2-▲ VER 28020

Giordano, U.:Andrea Chénier (sels), w. R. Tebaldi (sop), F. Barbieri (mez), M. del Monaco (ten), P. Silveri (bar), V. de Sabata (cnd), La Scala Orch—14 arias from Acts 1-3 [I] *(rec live, Milan, 3/6/49)* Myto ▲ 1 MCD 90634 [ADD]

Giordano, U.:Fedora, w. Mirella Freni (sop—Principessa Fedora), Adelina Scarabelli (sop—Contessa Olga), Silvia Mazzoni (mez—Dimitri), Monica Minarelli (sgr—Savoiardo), Placido Domingo (ten—Conte Loris), Ernesto Gavazzi (ten—Desiré), Aldo Bottion (ten—Barone Rouvel), Alessandro Corbelli (bar—Sìriex), Luigi Roni (bass—Cirillo), Silvestro Sammaritano (bass—Baroff), Alfredo Giacomotti (bass—Gretch), Ernesto Panariello (bass—Lorek), Vincenzo Alaimo (sgr—Nicola), Arnold Bosman (sgr—Boleslao), Bruno Capisani (sgr—Sergio), Renato Zanchetta (sgr—Michele), G. Gavazzeni (cnd), La Scala Orch *(rec La Scala, Apr 5, 1993)* Legato 2-▲ LCD 213-2 [ADD]

Gluck, C.W.:Alceste, w. M. Callas (sop), R. Gavarini (ten), R. Panerai (bar), S. Maionica (bass), C. M. Giulini (cnd), La Scala Orch—plus "Callas Sings Gluck & Rossini" [French version] *(rec live, La Scala, 4/4/54)* Melodram 2-▲ MEL 26026

Gluck, C.W.:Iphigénie en Tauride, w. M. Callas (sop), F. Cossotto (mez), Albanese (sgr), N. Sanzogno (cnd), La Scala Orch [I] *(rec live 6/1/57)* Melodram 2-▲ MEL 26012 (m)

Gluck, C.W.:Iphigénie en Tauride, w. C. Vaness (sop—Iphigénie), S. Brunet (sop—Diane), G. Winbergh (ten—Pylade), T. Allen (bar—Oreste), G. Surian (bass—Thoas), R. Muti (cnd), La Scala Orch *(rec Mar. 14-26, 1992)* Sony Classical 2-▲ S2K 52492 [DDD]

Gounod, C.:Faust, w. M. Freni (sop), G. Raimondi (ten), N. Ghiaurov (bass), G. Prêtre (cnd), La Scala Orch *(rec live 1967)* Melodram 3-▲ MEL 37005

Gounod, C.:Roméo et Juliette (sels), w. Renata Scotto (sop—Juliet), Giacomo Aragall (ten—Romeo), Luciano Pavarotti (ten—Tebaldo), Gaetano Ferrin (bass—Capellio), Alfredo Giacomotti (bass—Lorenzo), C. Abbado (cnd), La Scala Orch Budget ("The Greatest Voice in Opera" series) ▲ SYP 111

Janácek, L.:Jenůfa, w. Magda Olivero (sop—Kostelnicka), Bruna Baglioni (mez—La vecchia Buryja), Grace Bumbry (mez—Jenufa), Renato Cioni (ten—Steva Buryja), Robleto Merolla (bar—Laca Klemen), Carlo Meliciani (sgr—Vecchio compagno), J. Semkow (cnd), La Scala Orch *(rec Milan, Apr 2, 1974)* Myto 2-▲ MCD 961142

Leoncavallo, R.:Pagliacci, w. Rosetta Pampanini (sop), Francesco Merli (ten), Giuseppe Nessi (ten), Carlo Galeffi (bar), L. Molajoli (cnd), La Scala Orch *(rec Milan, 1930)* Phonographe 2-▲ PHG CD 5066

Leoncavallo, R.:Pagliacci, w. Adelaide Saraceni (sop—Nedda), Alessandro Valente (ten—Canio), Nello Palai (ten—Beppe), Apollo Granforte (bar—Tonio), Leonildo Basi (bass—Silvio), C. Sabajno (cnd), La Scala Orch *(rec Apr, Sept 1929 & Jan 1930)* VAI Audio 2-▲ VAIA 1082-2

Leoncavallo, R.:Pagliacci, w. I. Pacetti (sop—Nedda), B. Gigli (ten—Canio), G. Nessi (ten—Peppe), M. Basiola (bar—Tonio), F. Ghione (cnd), La Scala Orch [I] *(rec July 1934)* Nimbus 2-▲ NI 7843/44 [ADD]

Leoncavallo, R.:Pagliacci, w. Josefina Huguet (sop—Nedda), Antonio Paoli (ten), Gaetano Pini-Corsi (ten—Beppe), Ernesto Badini (bar—Silvio), Francesco Cigada (bar—Tonio), Giuseppe Rosci (sgr—Un contadino), C. Sabajno (cnd), La Scala Orch *(rec 1907)* Bongiovanni ▲ GB 1120-2 [ADD]

Leoncavallo, R.:Pagliacci, w. Lucine Amara (sop), France Corelli (ten), Tito Gobbi (bar), L. von Matačić (cnd), La Scala Orch [I] EMI Classics ("Studio" series) 2-▲ CDMB 63967

Leoncavallo, R.:Pagliacci, w. I. Pacetti (sop—Nedda), B. Gigli (ten—Canio), G. Nessi (ten—Peppe), M. Basiola (bar—Tonio), F. Ghione (cnd), La Scala Orch [I] *(rec 1934 for HMV)* Music Memoria ▲ 30275

Leoncavallo, R.:Pagliacci, w. T. Stratas (sop), P. Domingo (ten), J. Pons (bar), G. Prêtre (cnd), La Scala Orch [I] Philips 2-▲ 411484-2

Leoncavallo, R.:Pagliacci, w. Teresa Stratas (sop—Nedda), Placido Domingo (ten—Canio), Juan Pons (bar—Tonio), G. Prêtre (cnd), La Scala Orch Philips ("Duo" series) 2-▲ 454 265-2

Leoncavallo, R.:Pagliacci, w. Joan Carlyle (sop—Nedda/Colombina), Carlo Bergonzi (ten—Canio/Pagliaccio), Franco Ricciardi (ten—Villager), Ugo Benelli (bar—Peppe/Arlecchino), Rolando Panerai (bar—Silvio), Giuseppe Taddei (bar—Tonio/Taddeo), Giuseppe Morresi (bass—Villager), H. von Karajan (cnd), La Scala Orch *(rec La Scala, Milan, Oct 1965)* Deutsche Grammophon ("The Originals" series) ▲ 449727-2 [ADD]

Leoncavallo, R.:Pagliacci, w. I. Pacetti (sop—Nedda), B. Gigli (ten—Canio), G. Nessi (ten—Peppe), M. Basiola (bar—Tonio), F. Ghione (cnd), La Scala Orch [I] *(rec 1934)* EMI Classics ("Studio" series) ▲ CDH 63309 (m) [ADD]

Mascagni, P.:Cavalleria rusticana, w. Delia Sanzio (sop—Santuzza), Mimma Pantaleoni (mez—Lola), Olga de Franco (cta—Lucia), Giovanni Breviario (ten—Turiddu), Piero Biasini (bar—Alfio), C. Sabajno (cnd), La Scala Orch VAI Audio ▲ VAIA 1082-2

Mascagni, P.:Cavalleria rusticana, w. F. Cossotto (mez), C. Bergonzi (ten), G. Guelfi (bar), H. von Karajan (cnd), La Scala Orch [I] Deutsche Grammophon 3-▲ 419257-2 [ADD]

Mascagni, P.:Cavalleria rusticana, w. Elena Obraztsova (mez—Santuzza), Placido Domingo (ten—Turridu), G. Prêtre (cnd), La Scala Orch Philips ("Duo" series) 2-▲ 454 265-2

Mascagni, P.:Cavalleria rusticana, w. Lina Bruna-Rasa (sop), Giulietta Simionato (mez), Benia Gigli (ten), Giuseppe Nessi (ten), Gino Bechi (bar), Carlo Galeffi (bar), P. Mascagni (cnd), La Scala Orch *(rec Milan, 1940)* Phonographe 2-▲ PHG CD 5066

Mascagni, P.:Cavalleria rusticana, w. G. A. Lombardi (sop), I. Mannarini (mez), M. Castagna (mez), A. Melandri (ten), G. Lulli (bar), L. Molajoli (cnd), La Scala Orch *(rec 1930)* Preiser ▲ 90042 (m) [AAD]

Mascagni, P.:Cavalleria rusticana, w. G. Arangi-Lombardi (cta), A. Melandri (ten), G. Lulli (bar), L. Molajoli (cnd), Milan SO [I] *(rec 1930 for Columbia Records)* Standing Room Only ▲ SRO 806-1 (m) [ADD]

La Scala Chorus (cont.)

Mascagni, P.:Cavalleria rusticana, w. M. Callas (sop), E. Ticozzi (mez), G. di Stefano (ten), R. Panerai (bar), T. Serafin (cnd), La Scala Orch [I] EMI Classics 3-▲ CDCC 47981 [ADD]

Mascagni, P.:Cavalleria rusticana, w. L. Bruna Rasa (sop), G. Simionato (mez), B. Gigli (ten), G. Bechi (bar), P. Mascagni (cnd), La Scala Orch [I] *(rec 1940)* EMI Classics ("Studio" series) 2-▲ CDHB 69987 (m) [ADD]

Mascagni, P.:Cavalleria rusticana, w. L.B. Rasa (sop), M. Marucucci (mez), G. Simionato (mez), B. Gigli (ten), G. Bechi (bar), P. Mascagni (cnd), La Scala Orch *(rec 1940)* Nimbus 2-▲ NI 7843/44 [ADD]

Mascagni, P.:Cavalleria rusticana, w. E. Obraztsova (mez), F. Barbieri (mez), P. Domingo (ten), R. Bruson (bar), G. Prêtre (cnd), La Scala Orch [I] Philips ▲ 416137-2 [DDD]

Mascagni, P.:Cavalleria rusticana (sels), w. G. Simionato (mez), G. Di Stefano (ten), A. Votto (cnd), La Scala Orch—Tu qui Santuzza [I] *(rec live, Milan, 5/10/55)* Standing Room Only 2-▲ SRO 816-2 [ADD]

Massenet, J.:Manon, w. M. Freni (sop), L. Pavarotti (ten), R. Panerai (bar), P. Maag (cnd), La Scala Orch [I] *(rec live, 6/3/69)* Verona 2-▲ 27052/53 (m) [AAD]

Massenet, J.:Manon, w. M. Freni (sop), L. Pavarotti (ten), R. Panerai (bar), P. Maag (cnd), La Scala Orch [I] *(rec live, 6/3/69)* Melodram 2-▲ MEL 27046 [AAD]

Massenet, J.:Manon (sels), w. Mirella Freni (sop), Luciano Pavarotti (ten), Franco Ricciardi (ten), Wladimiro Ganzarolli (bar), Giuseppe Morresi (bass), Antonio Zerbini (bass), Ida Farina (sgr), P. Maag (cnd), La Scala Orch *(rec live, Milan, 1969)* Budget ("The Greatest Voice in Opera" series) ▲ SYP 110

Massenet, J.:Manon (sels), w. M. Favero (sop), G. Di Stefano (ten), M. Borriello (bar), M. Mainardi (bar), A. Guarnieri (cnd), La Scala Orch *(rec live, Milan, 3/15/47)* Myto ▲ 1 MCD 90526 [ADD]

Massenet, J.:Werther, w. D. Gatta (sop—Sofia), I. Ligabue (sop—Kaethlen), G. Simionato (mez—Charlotte), F. Tagliavini (ten—Werther), V. Pandano (ten—Schmidt), E. Campi (bass—Johann), S. Bruscantini (bass—Le Bailli), F. Capuana (cnd), La Scala Orch *(rec Apr. 21, 1951)* Bongiovanni 2-▲ GB 1101/02 [ADD]

Meyerbeer, G.:Les Huguenots, w. J. Sutherland (sop), F. Cossotto (mez), G. Simionato (mez), F. Corelli (ten), V. Ganzarolli (bar), N. Ghiaurov (bass), G. Tozzi (bass), G. Gavezzeni (cnd), La Scala Orch [I] *(rec live 5/28/62)* Melodram 3-▲ MEL 37026 (m) [AAD]

Mozart, W.A.:Così fan tutte, w. E. Schwarzkopf (sop—Fiordiligi), G. Sciurri (sop—Despina), N. Merriman (mez—Dorabella), L. Alva (ten—Ferrando), R. Panerai (bar—Guglielmo), F. Clabrese (b-bar—Don Alfonso), G. Cantelli (cnd), La Scala Orch *(rec Jan. 27, 1956)* Datum 2-▲ DAT 12304 [ADD]

Mozart, W.A.:Così fan tutte, w. Elisabeth Schwarzkopf (sop), Graziella Sciutti (sop), Nan Merriman (mez), Luigi Alva (ten), Rolando Panerai (bar), Franco Calabrese (bass), G. Cantelli (cnd), La Scala Orch Stradivarius 2-▲ STV DTM 12304 [ADD]

Mozart, W.A.:Entführung, w. Mariella Devia (sop), Uwe Peper (ten), Kurt Moss (sgr), W. Sawallisch (cnd), La Scala Orch *(rec live, 1994)* Serenissima 2-▲ SER 360161

Mozart, W.A.:Nozze di Figaro, w. E. Schwarzkopf (sop), I. Seefried (sop), S. Jurinac (sop), L. Villa (sop), R. Panerai (bar), H. von Karajan (cnd), La Scala Orch [I] *(rec live Feb. 4, 1954)* Melodram 3-▲ MEL 37075 [AAD]

Mozart, W.A.:Nozze di Figaro, w. Mirella Freni (sop), Daniela Mazzucato (sop), Teresa Berganza (mez), Mirto Picchi (ten), Hermann Prey (bar), José Van Dam (b-bar), Paolo Montarsolo (bass), C. Abbado (cnd), La Scala Orch *(rec live, Apr 22, 1974)* Arkadia 3-▲ 614

Pergolesi, G.B.:Lo frate 'nnamorato, w. N. Focile (sop), A. Felle (sop), B. Manca di Nissa (cta), A. Corbelli (bar), R. Muti (cnd), La Scala Orch EMI Classics 3-▲ CDCC 54240

Ponchielli, A.:La Gioconda, w. M. Callas (sop), F. Cossotto (mez), I. Companeez (cta), P. M. Ferraro (ten), P. Cappuccilli (bar), I. Vinco (bass), A. Votto (cnd), La Scala Orch EMI Classics ▲ CDCC 49518

Puccini, G.:La Bohème, w. M. Freni (sop), P. Dvorsky (ten), C. Kleiber (cnd), La Scala Orch Artists 2-▲ FED 15 [ADD]

Puccini, G.:La Bohème, w. L. Albanese (sop), T. Menotti (sop), B. Gigli (ten), A. Poli (bar), U. Berrettoni (cnd), La Scala Orch [I] *(rec 1937)* EMI Classics ("Studio" series) 2-▲ CDHB 63335 (m) [ADD]

Puccini, G.:La Bohème, w. Ileana Cotrubas (sop—Mimi), Margherita Guglielmi (sop—Musetta), José Carreras (ten—Rodolfo), Saverio Porzano (ten—Parpignol), Regolo Romani (ten—Vendor), Claudio Giombi (bar—Benoit), Gianni Maffeo (bar—Schaunard), Angelo Romero (bar—Marcello), Alfredo Giacomotti (bass—Alcindoro), Carlo Meliciani (bass—Customs Officer), Giuseppe Morresi (bass—Sergeant), Paolo Washington (bass—Colline), G. Prêtre (cnd), La Scala Orch *(rec Washington D.C., Sept 8, 1976)* Legato Classics 2-▲ LCD 201-2

Puccini, G.:La Bohème, w. Licia Albanese (sop), Tatiana Menotti (sop), Beniamino Gigli (ten), Afro Poli (bar), U. Berrettoni (cnd), La Scala Orch *(rec Milan, 1938)* Phonographe 2-▲ PHG CD 5071

Puccini, G.:La Bohème, w. Luba Mirella (sop—Musetta), Rosetta Pampanini (sop—Mimi), Luigi Marini (ten—Rodolfo), Giuseppe Nessi (ten—Alcindoro), Aristide Baracchi (bar—Schaunard), Gino Vanelli (bar—Marcello), Salvatore Baccaloni (bass—Benoit), Tancredi Pasero (bass—Colline), L. Molajoli (cnd), La Scala Orch Bongiovanni 2-▲ 1125/26 [ADD]

Puccini, G.:La Bohème, w. Rosina Torri (sop—Mimi), Thea Vitulli (sop—Musetta), Aristodemo Giorgini (ten—Rodolfo), Giuseppe Nessi (ten—Parpignol), Ernesto Badini (bar—Marcello), Aristide Baracchi (bar—Schaunard), Luigi Manfrini (bass—Colline), Salvatore Baccaloni (bass—Benoit/Alcindoro), C. Sabajno (cnd), La Scala Orch *(rec 1928)* VAI Audio 2-▲ VAIA 1078-2

Puccini, G.:La Bohème, w. M. Callas (sop), A. Moffo (sop), G. di Stefano (ten), R. Panerai (bar), A. Votto (cnd), La Scala Orch [I] *(rec 1956)* EMI Classics 2-▲ CDCB 47475 (m) [ADD]

Puccini, G.:La Bohème, w. L. Albanese (sop—Mimi), T. Menotti (sop—Musetta), B. Gigli (ten—Rodolfo), N. Palai (ten—Parpignol), A. Poli (bar—Marcello), A. Baracchi (bar—Schaunard), D. Baronti (bass—Colline), C. Scattola (bass—Benoit/Alcindoro), U. Berrettoni (cnd), La Scala Orch [I] *(rec Milan, May 1938)* Nimbus 2-▲ NI 7862/63 [ADD]

Puccini, G.:La Bohème (sels), w. M. Carosio (sop), A. Noni (sop), G. Poggi (ten), P. Silveri (bar), V. de Sabata (cnd), La Scala Orch—6 arias from Acts 3 & 4 [I] *(rec live, Milan, 12/7/49)* Myto ▲ 1 MCD 90634 [ADD]

Puccini, G.:La fanciulla del West, w. M. Zampieri (sop), P. Domingo (ten), J. Pons (bar), L. Maazel (cnd), La Scala Orch *(rec live 1991)* Sony Classical 2-▲ S2K 47189

Puccini, G.:La fanciulla del West, w. B. Nilsson (sop), J. Gibin (ten), A. Mongelli (bar), L. von Matačić (cnd), La Scala Orch [I] EMI Classics ("Studio" series) 2-▲ CDMB 63970

Puccini, G.:Madama Butterfly, w. M. Callas (sop), L. Danieli (mez), N. Gedda (ten), M. Borriello (bar), H. von Karajan (cnd), La Scala Orch [I] *(rec 1955)* EMI Classics 2-▲ CDCB 47959 (m) [ADD]

Puccini, G.:Madama Butterfly, w. Rosetta Pampanini (sop—Madama Butterfly), Conchita Velasquez (mez—Suzuki), Cesira Ferrari (mez—Kate Pinkerton), Alessandro Granda (ten—F. B. Pinkerton), Giuseppe Nessi (ten—Goro), Aristide Baracchi (bar—Il Principe Yamadori), Gino Vanelli (bar—Sharpless), Lino Bonardi (bass—Il Commissario Imperiale), Salvatore Baccaloni (bass—Lo zio Bonzo), L. Molajoli (cnd), La Scala Orch Bongiovanni 2-▲ 1123/24 [ADD]

Puccini, G.:Madama Butterfly, w. R. Pampanini (sop), A. Granda (ten), G. Nessi (ten), G. Vanelli (bar), S. Baccaloni (bass), L. Malajoli (cnd), La Scala Orch *(rec 1928)* Centaur 2-▲ CRC 2196/97

Puccini, G.:Manon Lescaut, w. Maria Zamboni (sop), Francesco Merli (ten), Lorenzo Conati (sgr), L. Molajoli (cnd), La Scala Orch *(rec Milan, 1930)* Phonographie 2-▲ PHG 5006 [ADD]

Puccini, G.:Manon Lescaut, w. Maria Zamboni (sop), Francesco Merli (ten), Lorenzo Conati (sgr), L. Molajoli (cnd), La Scala Orch *(rec Milan, 1930)* Melodram 2-▲ IMC 202001

Puccini, G.:Manon Lescaut, w. M. Callas (sop), G. di Stefano (ten), Fioravanti (sgr), T. Serafin (cnd), La Scala Orch [I] EMI Classics 2-▲ CDCB 47392 (m)

Puccini, G.:Manon Lescaut (sels), w. M. Favero (sop), R. Tebaldi (sop), J. Gardino (mez), G. Malipiero (ten), G. Nessi (ten), M. Stabile (bar), T. Pasero (b-bar), C. Forti (bass), A. Toscanini (cnd), La Scala Orch—Intermezzo; Act 3 *(rec live, Milan, May 18, 1946)* Arkadia ("Historical Performances" series) 2-▲ 604 (m)

Puccini, G.:Tosca, w. C. Melis (sop—Tosca), P. Pauloi (ten—Cavarodossi), N. Palai (ten—Spoletta), A. Granforte (bar—Scarpia), G. Azzimonti (bass—Sciarrone/Angelotti), A. Gelli (bass—Sacristan), C. Sabajno (cnd), La Scala Orch [I] *(rec Milan, Nov. 1929)* VAI Audio 2-▲ VAIA 1076-2 (m) [ADD]

Puccini, G.:Tosca, w. M. Callas (sop), G. di Stefano (ten), T. Gobbi (bar), V. de Sabata (cnd), La Scala Orch [I] *(rec 1953)* EMI Classics 2-▲ CDCB 47174 (m) [ADD] 2-▲ 4AV 34047 (m)

Puccini, G.:Tosca, w. Carmen Melis (sop—Tosca), Nello Palai (ten—Spoletta), Piero Pauli (ten—Cavaradossi), Apollo Granforte (bar—Scarpia), Giovanni Azzimonti (bass—Angelotti/Sciarrone), Antonio Gelli (bass—Sagrestano), C. Sabajno (cnd), La Scala Orch *(rec Nov 1929)* Arkadia 2-▲ CD 78002 (m) [ADD]

La Scala Chorus (cont.)

Puccini, G.:Turandot, w. M. Callas (sop), E. Schwarzkopf (sop), E. Fernandi (ten), N. Zaccaria (bass), T. Serafin (cnd), La Scala Orch [I] *(rec 1957)* EMI Classics 2-▲ CDCB 47971 (m) [ADD]
Rossini, G.:Il barbiere di Siviglia, w. D. Gatta (sop), C. Valletti (ten), G. Bechi (bar), N. Rossi-Lemeni (bass), V. de Sabata (cnd), La Scala Orch *(rec 1952)* Memories 2-▲ MEM 4525 [AAD]
Rossini, G.:Il barbiere di Siviglia, w. Cesira Ferrari (mez—Berta), Mercedes Capsir (cta—Rosina), Dino Borgioli (ten—Count), Salvatore Baccaloni (bar—Bortolo), Aristide Baracchi (bar—Officer), Riccardo Stracciari (bar—Figaro), Vincenzo Bettoni (bass—Don Basilio), Attilo Bordonali (bass—Fiorello), L. Molajoli (cnd), La Scala Orch *(rec 1930)* Arkadia ("The 78's" series) 2-▲ 78008 [ADD]
Rossini, G.:Il barbiere di Siviglia, w. M. Callas (sop), L. Alva (ten), T. Gobbi (bar), C. M. Giulini (cnd), La Scala Orch [I] *(rec live 1956)* Melodram 2-▲ MEL 26020
Rossini, G.:Il barbiere di Siviglia, w. M. Capsir (sop), D. Borgioli (ten), R. Stracciari (bar), S. Baccaloni (bass), V. Bettoni (bass), L. Molajoli (cnd), La Scala Orch *(rec 1929 for Columbia Records)* Music Memoria 2-▲ 30276/77
Rossini, G.:Il barbiere di Siviglia, w. M. Horne (mez), E. Dara (bar), L. Nucci (bar), S. Ramey (bass), R. Chailly (cnd), La Scala Orch [I] CBS 3-▲ M3K 37862 [DDD]
Rossini, G.:Il barbiere di Siviglia, w. Fiorenza Cossotto (mez), Luigi Alva (ten), Sesto Bruscantini (bar), Carlo Badioli (bass), Nicolai Ghiaurov (bass), G. Santini (cnd), La Scala Orch *(rec Jan 20, 1964)* Pantheon 2-▲ PHE 6644 (m)
Rossini, G.:Il barbiere di Siviglia (sels), w. M. Horne (mez), R. Pierotti (mez), P. Barbacini (ten), E. Dara (bar), L. Nucci (bar), S. Ramey (bass), S. Sammaritano (bass), R. Chailly (cnd), La Scala Orch *(rec Milan, Jan. 2-18, 1982)* Sony Classical ("Opera Highlights" series) ▲ SMK 53501 [DDD]
Rossini, G.:Guillaume Tell, w. C. Studer (sop), C. Merritt (ten), G. Zancanaro (bar), R. Muti (cnd), La Scala Orch [I] *(rec live, 12/7/88)* Philips 4-▲ 422391-2 [DDD]
Rossini, G.:Mosè in Egitto (sels), w. A. Toscanini (cnd), La Scala Orch—Prayer *(rec live, Milan, May 18, 1946)* Arkadia ("Historical Performances" series) 2-▲ 604 (m)
Rossini, G.:The Siege of Corinth, w. B. Sills (sop), M. Horne (mez), F. Bonisoli (ten), J. Diaz (bass), T. Schippers (cnd), La Scala Orch [I] *(rec live 1969)* Melodram 2-▲ MEL 27043 [AAD]
Spontini, G.:La vestale, w. Karen Huffstodt (sop—Julie), Denyce Graves (mez—La Grande Vestale), Patrick Raftery (ten—Cinna), Anthony Michaels-Moore (bar—Licinius), R. Muti (cnd), La Scala Orch Sony Classical 3-▲ S3K 66357
Spontini, G.:La vestale, w. M. Callas (sop), N. Rossi-Lemeni (bass), F. Corelli (ten), E. Sordello (bar), V. Tatozzi (bar), N. Zaccaria (bass), A. Votto (cnd), La Scala Orch Great Opera Performances ▲ GOP 741
Spontini, G.:La vestale, w. M. Callas (sop), F. Corelli (ten), E. Sordello (bar), A. Votto (cnd), La Scala Orch [I] *(rec live, Milan, 12/7/54)* Melodram 2-▲ MEL 26008
Spontini, G.:La vestale (sels), w. M. Callas (sop), A. Corelli (bar), E. Sordello (bar), A. Votto (cnd), La Scala Orch [I]—3 scenes *(rec live, Milan, 12/7/54)* Verona 2-▲ 28003/04
Strauss, R.:Der Rosenkavalier, w. Jarmila Barton (sop—Marianne), Lisa Della Casa (sop—Sophie), Sena Jurinac (sop—Octavian), Ilva Ligabue (sop—Orphan), Elisabeth Schwarzkopf (sop—Marschallin), Else Schürhoff (mez—Annina), Luisa Villa (mez—Milliner), Hugues Cuénod (ten—Marschallin's majordomo), Erich Majkut (ten—Valzacchi), Giuseppe Nessi (ten—Animal seller), Luciano Della Pergola (ten—Lackey/Faninal's majordomo), Antonio Pirino (ten—An Italian Singer), Gino Del Signore (ten—Lackey/Waiter), Erich Kunz (bar—Herr von Faninal), Paolo Pedani (bar—Lackey), Attilo Barbesi (bass—Lackey/Waiter), Enrico Campi (bass—Waiter), Otto Edelmann (bass—Baron Ochs), Bruno Fichtinger (bass—Notary), Franco Taino (bass—Waiter), Maria Amadini (sgr—Orphan), Pina Carrillo (sgr—Orphan), Joszi Trojan Regar (sgr—Innkeeper), H. von Karajan (cnd), La Scala Orch *(rec La Scala Theater, Milan, Jan. 26, 1952)* Legato Classics 3-▲ LCD 197-3
Vaughan Williams, R.:Sym 7, w. A. Boult (cnd), London PO EMI Classics (British Composers) ▲ CDM 64020
Verdi, G.:Aida, w. K. Ricciarelli (sop), E. Obraztsova (mez), P. Domingo (ten), L. Nucci (bar), N. Ghiaurov (bass), C. Abbado (cnd), La Scala Orch [I] Deutsche Grammophon ▲ 435410-2 [DDD]
Verdi, G.:Aida, w. K. Ricciarelli (sop), E. Obraztsova (mez), P. Domingo (ten), L. Nucci (bar), N. Ghiaurov (bass), C. Abbado (cnd), La Scala Orch [I] Deutsche Grammophon 3-▲ 410092-2 [DDD]
Verdi, G.:Aida, w. Dusolina Giannini (sop), Irene Minghini-Cattaneo (cta), Aureliano Pertile (ten), C. Sabajno (cnd), La Scala Orch *(rec Milan, 1928)* Phonographie 2-▲ PHG 5004 [ADD]
Verdi, G.:Aida, w. Antonietta Stella (sop—Aida), Mirella Parutto (sop—Priestess), Giulietta Simionato (mez—Amneris), Giuseppe DiStefano (ten—Radames), Giuseppe Zampiere (ten—Messenger), Giangiacomo Guelfi (bar—Amonasro), Silvio Maionica (bass—King of Egypt), Nicola Zaccaria (bass-Ramfis), A. Votto (cnd), La Scala Orch *(rec Milan, Dec 7, 1956)* Legato Classics 2-▲ LCD 204-2 [ADD]
Verdi, G.:Aida, w. M. Chiara (sop), G. Dimitrova (sop), L. Pavarotti (ten), L. Nucci (bar), P. Burchuladze (bass), L. Maazel (cnd), La Scala Orch [I] London □ 433162-5
Verdi, G.:Aida, w. M. Chiara (sop), G. Dimitrova (sop), L. Pavarotti (ten), L. Nucci (bar), P. Burchuladze (bass), L. Maazel (cnd), La Scala Orch [I] London 3-▲ 417439-2 [DDD] 2-■ 417439-4
Verdi, G.:Aida, w. M. Callas (sop), F. Barbieri (mez), G. Tucker (ten), T. Gobbi (bar), N. Zaccaria (bass), T. Serafin (cnd), La Scala Orch [I] EMI Classics 3-▲ CDCC 49030 [ADD]
Verdi, G.:Aida, w. Giannina Arangi-Lombardi (sop—Aida), Maria Capuana (mez—Amneris), Aroldo Lindi (ten—Radames), Giuseppe Nessi (ten—Messenger), Armando Borgioli (bar—Amonasro), Salvatore Baccaloni (bass—King), Tancredi Pasero (bass—Ramfis), L. Molajoli (cnd), La Scala Orch *(rec Nov 1928)* VAI Audio 2-▲ VAIA 1083-2
Verdi, G.:Aida, w. D. Giannini (sop), I. Minghini-Cattaneo (cta), A. Pertile (ten), G. Inghilleri (bar), L. Manfrini (bass), C. Sabajno (cnd), La Scala Orch [I] *(rec 1928 for HMV)* Pearl 2-▲ CDS 9402 (m) [AAD]
Verdi, G.:Attila, w. Rita Orlandi Malaspina (sop—Odabella), Veriano Luchetti (ten—Foresto), Piero de Palma (ten—Uldino), Piero Cappuccilli (bar—Ezio), Nicolai Ghiaurov (bass—Attila), Luigi Roni (bass—Leone), G. Patanè (cnd), La Scala Orch *(rec Milan, May 15, 1972)* Golden Age of Opera 2-▲ GAO 187/88 [ADD]
Verdi, G.:Attila, w. S. Studer (sop), N. Shicoff (ten), G. Zancanaro (bar), S. Ramey (bass), R. Muti (cnd), La Scala Orch [I] EMI Classics 2-▲ CDCB 49952 [DDD]
Verdi, G.:Attila, w. Rita Orlandi Malaspina (sop—Odabella), Veriano Luchetti (ten—Foresto), Piero De Palma (ten—Uldino), Piero Cappuccilli (bar—Ezio), Nicolai Ghiaurov (bass—Attila), Luigi Roni (bass—Leone), G. Patanè (cnd), La Scala Orch *(rec Milan, May 12, 1975)* Myto 2-▲ MCD 961140
Verdi, G.:Un ballo in maschera, w. M. Callas (sop), E. Ratti (sop), G. Simionato (mez), G. di Stefano (ten), E. Bastianini (bar), G. Gavazzeni (cnd), La Scala Orch *(rec 1957)* Melodram ▲ MLO 26039 [ADD]
Verdi, G.:Un ballo in maschera, w. M. Callas (sop), E. Ratti (sop), F. Barbieri (mez), G. Di Stefano (ten), T. Gobbi (bar), A. Votto (cnd), La Scala Orch [I] *(rec 1956)* EMI Classics 2-▲ CDCB 47498 (m)
Verdi, G.:Un ballo in maschera, w. M. Callas (sop), E. Ratti (sop), G. Simionato (mez), G. di Stefano (ten), E. Bastianini (bar), G. Gavazzeni (cnd), La Scala Orch [I] *(rec live 12/7/57)* Arkadia 2-▲ 519 (m) [AAD]
Verdi, G.:Un ballo in maschera (sels), w. Margherita Guglielmi (sop), José Carreras (ten), Frederico Davià (bass), Giovanni Foiani (bass), F. Molinari-Pradelli (cnd), La Scala Orch—S'avanza il Conte...La rivedrà nell'estasi; Ma se m'è forza perderti...Ah! dessa è là! *(rec Milan, Feb 13, 1975)* Goldies ▲ GLD 63203 [ADD]
Verdi, G.:La battaglia di Legnano, w. A. Stella (sop), F. Corelli (ten), E. Bastianini (bar), G. Gavazzeni (cnd), La Scala Orch [I] *(rec live 12/7/61)* Myto 2-▲ 2 MCD 89010 (m) [ADD]
Verdi, G.:Ernani, w. R. Kabaivanska (sop), P. Domingo (ten), N. Ghiaurov (bass), Meliciani (sgr), A. Votto (cnd), La Scala Orch *(rec live 12/7/69)* Melodram 2-▲ MEL 27064 (m) [AAD]
Verdi, G.:Ernani, w. M. Freni (sop), P. Domingo (ten), R. Bruson (bar), N. Ghiaurov (bass), R. Muti (cnd), La Scala Orch [I] EMI Classics 3-▲ CDC 47082 [DDD]
Verdi, G.:Falstaff, w. Maureen O'Flynn (sop), Daniela Dessi (sop), Bernadette Manca di Nissa (mez), Delores Ziegler (mez), Ramon Vargas (ten), Ernesto Gavazzi (ten), Paolo Barbacini (ten), Juan Pons (bar), Roberto Frontali (bar), Luigi Roni (bass), R. Muti (cnd), La Scala Orch *(rec Milan La Scala Theater, Italy, Mar. 29 & 31)* Sony Classical ▲ S2K 58961 [DDD]
Verdi, G.:Falstaff, w. Pia Tassinari (sop—Alice Ford), Ines Alfani Tellini (sop—Nannetta), Aurora Buades (mez—Quickly), Rita Monticone (mez—Meg Page), Roberto D'Alessio (ten—Fenton), Giuseppe Nessi (ten—Bardolfo), Emilio Venturini (ten—Dr. Caius), Emilio Ghirardini (bar—Ford), Giacomo Rimini (bar—Sir John Falstaff), Salvatore Baccaloni (bass—Pistola), L. Molajoli (cnd), Milan SO *(rec La Scala Theatre, Milan, Apr. 1932)* VAI Audio 2-▲ VAIA 1098-2

La Scala Chorus (cont.)

Verdi, G.:La forza del destino, w. Leyla Gencer (sop), Giuseppe di Stefano (ten), Aldo Protti (bar), Cesare Siepi (bass), A. Votto (cnd), La Scala Orch *(rec La Scala Theatre, Milan, July 5, 1957)* Pantheon 3-▲ PHE 6627 (m)
Verdi, G.:La forza del destino, w. Leyla Gencer (sop—Leonora), Gabriella Carturan (mez—Preziosilla), Giuseppe di Stefano (ten—Don Alvaro), Aldo Protti (bar—Don Carlo), Cesare Siepi (b-bar), Franco Calabrese (bass—Marchese di Calatrava), Enrico Campi (bass—Fra Melitone), A. Votto (cnd), La Scala Orch *(rec Bühnen der Stadt, Köln, July 5, 1957)* Agorá Music ("Phoenix" series) 3-▲ 510 [ADD]
Verdi, G.:La forza del destino (sels), w. I. Ligabue (sop), C. Bergonzi (ten), Meliciani (sgr), G. Gavazzeni (cnd), La Scala Orch [substantial highlights] *(rec live, Milan 12/7/65)* Myto 2-▲ 2 MCD 91750 [ADD]
Verdi, G.:Macbeth, w. Shirley Verrett (mez—Lady Macbeth), Plácido Domingo (ten—Macduff), Piero Cappuccilli (bar—Macbeth), Nicolai Ghiaurov (bass—Banco), C. Abbado (cnd), La Scala Orch Deutsche Grammophon ("The Originals" series) ▲ 449 732-2
Verdi, G.:Nabucco, w. Gloria Lane (mez), Gianni Raimondi (ten), Giangiacomo Guelfi (bar), Nicolai Ghiaurov (bass), Elena Saliotis (sgr), G. Gavazzeni (cnd), La Scala Orch *(rec La Scala Theater, Milan, Dec. 7, 1966)* Pantheon 2-▲ PHE 6757 (m)
Verdi, G.:Nabucco (sels), w. A. Toscanini (cnd), La Scala Orch—Ov.; Chorus of the Hebrew Slaves *(rec live, Milan, May 18, 1946)* Arkadia ("Historical Performances" series) 2-▲ 604 (m)
Verdi, G.:Otello, w. R. Tebaldi (sop), M. del Monaco (ten), L. Warren (bar), A. Votto (cnd), La Scala Orch *(rec July 1, 1954)* Melodram 2-▲ MLO 270101 [AAD]
Verdi, G.:Otello, w. Maria Carbone (sgr), Nicola Fusati (ten), Piero Girardi (ten), Corrado Zambelli (ten), Apollo Granforte (bar), Enrico Spada (sgr), C. Sabajno (cnd), La Scala Orch Grammofono 2000 2-▲ GRM 78651
Verdi, G.:Requiem Mass, w. Elizabeth Schwarzkopf (sop), Oralia Dominguez (mez), Giuseppe Di Stefano (ten), Cesare Siepi (b-bar), V. de Sabata (cnd), La Scala Orch Theorema 2-▲ TH 121123/24
Verdi, G.:Requiem Mass, w. L. Price (sop), F. Cossotto (mez), L. Pavarotti (ten), N. Ghiaurov (bass), H. von Karajan (cnd), La Scala Orch [L] *(rec live 1/16/67)* Melodram 2-▲ MEL 28012
Verdi, G.:Requiem Mass, w. Maria Luisa Fanelli (sop), Irene Minghini-Cattaneo (mez), Fracno Lo Giudice (ten), E. Pinza (bass), C. Sabajno (cnd), La Scala Orch *(rec 1927 for HMV)* Pearl ▲ GEMMCD 9374 (m) [AAD]
Verdi, G.:Requiem Mass, w. Maria Caniglia (sop), Ebe Stignani (cta), Beniamino Gigli (ten), Ezio Pinza (bass), T. Serafin (cnd), La Scala Orch *(rec 1939)* Phonographie ▲ PHG 5012 [ADD]
Verdi, G.:Requiem Mass, w. L. Price (sop), F. Cossotto (mez), L. Pavarotti (ten), N. Ghiaurov (bass), H. von Karajan (cnd), La Scala Orch [L] *(rec live 1/16/67)* Verona 2-▲ 27060/61 (m) [AAD]
Verdi, G.:Rigoletto, w. Mercedes Capsir (sop), Dino Borgioli (ten), Riccardo Stracciari (bar), Ernesto Dominici (bass), L. Molajoli (cnd), La Scala Orch Phonographe 2-▲ PHG 5036 [ADD]
Verdi, G.:Rigoletto, w. Lina Pagliughi (sop—Gilda), Linda Brambilla (mez—Contessa di Ceprano), Vera de Cristoff (cta—Maddalena), Tino Folgar (ten—Duca di Mantova), Giuseppe Nessi (ten—Borsa), Aristide Baracchi (bar—Conte di Monterone/Marullo), Luigi Piazza (bar—Rigoletto), Salvatore Baccaloni (bass—Sparafucile), Giuseppe Menni (bass—Conte di Ceprano), C. Sabajno (cnd), La Scala Orch *(rec 1927-28)* Arkadia 2-▲ CD 78003 (m) [ADD]
Verdi, G.:Rigoletto, w. Lina Pagliughi (sop), Salvatore Baccaloni (bass), Luigi Piazza (sgr), Tino Folgar (sgr), C. Sabajno (cnd), La Scala Orch Pearl 2-▲ PEA 9180 [ADD]
Verdi, G.:Rigoletto, w. Andrea Rost (sop—Gilda), Mariana Pentcheva (cta—Maddalena), Roberto Alagna (ten—Il Duca di Mantova), Renato Bruson (bar—Rigoletto), Dmitri Kavrakos (bass—Sparafucile), R. Muti (cnd), La Scala Orch Sony Classical 2-▲ S2K 66314
Verdi, G.:Rigoletto, w. Lina Pagliughi (sop—Gilda), Linda Brambilla (mez—Countess Ceprano), Vera De Cristoff (cta—Maddalena), Tino Folgar (ten—Duke of Mantua), Giuseppe Nessi (ten—Borsa), Luigi Piazza (bar—Rigoletto), Aristide Baracchi (b-bar—Monterone/Marullo), Salvatore Baccaloni (bass—Sparafucile), Giuseppe Menni (bass—Ceprano), C. Sabajno (cnd), La Scala Orch *(rec La Scala Theatre, Milan, Nov.-Dec. 1927 & Feb. 192)* VAI Audio 2-▲ VAIA 1097-2
Verdi, G.:Rigoletto (sels), w. Maria Callas (sop), T. Serafin (cnd), La Scala Orch—selected arias *(rec Milan, 1953)* Andromeda ▲ ANR 2541 [ADD]
Verdi, G.:Simon Boccanegra, w. K. Te Kanawa (sop), J. Aragall (ten), L. Nucci (bar), P. Burchuladze (bass), G. Solti (cnd), La Scala Orch [I] London 2-▲ 425628-2 [DDD]
Verdi, G.:Te Deum, w. A. Toscanini (cnd), La Scala Orch *(rec live, Milan, May 18, 1946)* Arkadia ("Historical Performances" series) 2-▲ 604 (m)
Verdi, G.:La traviata, w. Renata Scotto (sop—Violetta Valery), Giuliana Tavolaccini (sop—Flora Bervoix), Gianni Raimondi (ten—Alfredo Germont), Ettore Bastianini (bar—Giorgio Germont), A. Votto (cnd), La Scala Orch *(rec La Scala Theatre, Milan, 1963)* Deutsche Grammophon 2-▲ 439720-2 [ADD]
Verdi, G.:La traviata, w. M. Callas (sop), A. Zanolli (sop), L. Mandelli (sop), G. Raimondi (ten), E. Bastianini (bar), C. M. Giulini (cnd), La Scala Orch *(rec live 1/19/56)* Myto 2-▲ MCD 89003 (m) [ADD]
Verdi, G.:La traviata, w. T. Fabbricini (sop—Violetta), A. Trevisan (mez—Annina), N. Curiel (mez—Flora), R. Alagna (ten—Alfredo), E. Cossutta (ten—Gastone), E. Gavazzi (ten—Giuseppe), O. Mori (bar—Douphol), E. Capuano (bass—d'Obigny), F. Musinu (bass—Grenvil), R. Muti (cnd), La Scala Orch Sony Classical 2-▲ S2K 52486 [DDD]
Verdi, G.:La traviata, w. M. Callas (sop), G. Di Stefano (ten), E. Bastianini (bar), C. M. Giulini (cnd), La Scala Orch [I] *(rec live 5/28/55)* Arkadia 2-▲ 501 (m) [AAD]
Verdi, G.:La traviata, w. Olga de Franco (sop—Flora Bervoix/Annina), Anna Rosza (sop—Violetta Valéry), Giordano Callegari (ten—Gastone), Alessandro Ziliani (ten—Alfredo Germont), Luigi Borgonovo (bar—Giorgio Germont), Arnoldo Lenzi (bar—Baron Douphol), Antonio Gelli (bass—Marquis d'Obigny/Dr. Grenvil), C. Sabajno (cnd), La Scala Orch *(rec La Scala Theatre, Milan, Oct.-Nov. 1930)* VAI Audio 2-▲ VAIA 1108-2
Verdi, G.:La traviata, w. M. Callas (sop), G. Di Stefano (ten), E. Bastianini (bar), C. M. Giulini (cnd), La Scala Orch [I] *(rec 1955)* EMI Classics (Studio) 2-▲ CDMB 63628 (m) [ADD]
Verdi, G.:La traviata (sels), w. Elizabeth Schwarzkopf (sop), Oralia Dominguez (mez), Giuseppe DiStefano (ten), Cesare Siepi (b-bar), V. de Sabata (cnd), La Scala Orch—Preludes to Acts I & III Theorema 2-▲ TH 121123/24
Verdi, G.:La traviata (sels), w. R. Scotto (sop), G. Tavolccini (sop), A. Bonato (sop), G. Raimondi (ten), E. Bastianini (bar), A. Votto (cnd), La Scala Orch IMP Collectors Series ▲ IMPX 9025 [AAD]
Verdi, G.:Il trovatore, w. A. Stella (sop), M. Fiorentini (mez), F. Cossotto (mez), F. Corelli (ten), E. Bastianini (bar), I. Vinco (bass), G. Gavazzeni (cnd), La Scala Orch *(rec live, Milan, 12/7/62)* Melodram 2-▲ MEL 27068 (m) [AAD]
Verdi, G.:Il trovatore, w. Maria Caniglia (sop), Aureliano Pertile (ten), Apollo Granforte (bar), C. Sabajno (cnd), La Scala Orch *(rec Milan, Sept.-Oct. 1930)* Phonographie 2-▲ PHG 5002 [ADD]
Verdi, G.:Il trovatore, w. A. Stella (sop), M. Fiorentini (mez), F. Cossotto (mez), F. Corelli (ten), E. Bastianini (bar), I. Vinco (bass), G. Gavazzeni (cnd), La Scala Orch [I] *(rec live, Milan, 12/7/62)* Claque 2-▲ CLQ 2013 (m)
Verdi, G.:Il trovatore, w. Bianca Scacciati (sop), Giuseppina Zinetti (sop), Francesco Merli (ten), Enrico Molinari (bar), L. Molajoli (cnd), Milan SO *(rec live, 1930)* Melodram ▲ CDI 202002
Verdi, G.:Il trovatore, w. G. Tucci (sop), G. Simionato (mez), C. Bergonzi (ten), P. Cappuccilli (bar), G. Gavazzeni (cnd), La Scala Orch *(rec live, Moscow 1965)* Melodram 2-▲ MEL 27008
Verdi, G.:Il trovatore, w. M. Callas (sop), E. Stignani (mez), G. Penno (ten), C. Tagliabue (bar), A. Votto (cnd), La Scala Orch [I] *(rec live 2/23/53)* Myto 2-▲ 2 MCD 90213 (m) [ADD]
Verdi, G.:Il trovatore (sels), w. Maria Callas (sop), H. von Karajan (cnd), La Scala Orch—selected arias *(rec Milan, 1955)* Andromeda ▲ ANR 2541 [ADD]
Verdi, G.:I vespri siciliani, w. R. Scotto (sop), G. Raimondi (ten), P. Cappuccilli (bar), R. Raimondi (bass), G. Gavazzeni (cnd), La Scala Orch [I] *(rec live, 12/4/70 [Acts 1-3], 12/10)* Myto 2-▲ 2 MCD 90524 [ADD]
Verdi, G.:I vespri siciliani (sels), w. L. Gencer (sop), G. Casellato-Lamberti (ten), La Scala Orch—one solo soprano aria & three duets from Act 4 [I] Myto 2-▲ 2 MCD 90524 [ADD]
Wagner, R.:Der fliegende Holländer, w. L. Rysanek (sop), A.-M. Bessel (mez), C. Heater (ten), F. Crass (bass), K. Ridderbusch (bass), W. Sawallisch (cnd), La Scala Orch [G] *(rec live, Milan 2/2/66)* Memories 2-▲ HR 4281/82 (m) [ADD]
Wagner, R.:Der Ring des Nibelungen, w. K. Flagstad (sop), H. Konetzni (sop), E. Höngen (cta), G. Treptow (ten), S. Svanholm (ten), M. Lorenz (ten), F. Frantz (b-bar), L. Weber (bass), B. Herrmann (bass), W. Furtwängler (cnd), La Scala Orch *(rec live 1950)* Arkadia 12-▲ 351 [ADD]

▲ = CD ♦ = Enhanced CD Δ = MD ■ = Cassette Tape □ = DCC

La Scala Chorus (cont.)

Wagner, R.:Der Ring des Nibelungen, w. Kirsten Flagstad (sop), Hilde Konetzni (sop), Elisabeth Höngen (cta), Max Lorenz (ten), Set Svanholm (ten), Günther Treptow (ten), Josef Hermann (bar), Ludwig Weber (bass), Ferdinand Franz (sgr), W. Furtwängler (cnd), La Scala Orch *(rec Milan, 1950)* Music & Arts 12-▲ CD 914

Wagner, R.:Tannhäuser, w. S. Jurinac (sop), B. Martin (sop), H. Beirer (ten), H. Braun (bar), M. Talvela (bass), W. Sawallisch (cnd), La Scala Orch [G] *(rec live, Milan 4/13/67)* Melodram 3-▲ CDM 37091 [ADD]

Zandonai, R.:Francesca da Rimini, w. Lydia Marimpietri (sop—Biancofiore), Magda Olivero (sop—Francesca), Pinuccia Perotti (sop—Samaritana), Edda Vincenzi (sop—Garsenda), Gabriella Carturan (mez—Smaragdi), Biancamaria Casoni (mez—Altichiara), Anna Maria Rota (cta—Donella), Athos Cesarini (ten—Archer), Angelo Mercuriali (ten—Ser Toldo Berardengo), Mario del Monaco (ten—Paolo), Piero de Palma (ten—Malatestino), Rinaldo Pelizzoni (ten—Prisoner), Gianpiero Malaspina (bar—Gianciotto), Dino Mantovani (bar—Jester), Enrico Campi (bass—Ostasio), Giuseppe Morresi (bass—Tower warden), G. Gavazzeni (cnd), La Scala Orch *(rec La Scala Theatre, Milan, June 4, 1959)* Legato Classics 2-▲ LCD 186-2

V. Veneziani (cnd)

Puccini, G.:La Bohème, w. Licia Albanese (sop—Mimì), Tatiana Menotti (sop—Musetta), Beniamino Gigli (ten—Rodolfo), Nello Palai (ten—Parpignol), Aristide Baracchi (bar—Schaunard), Afro Poli (bar—Marcello), Duilio Baronti (bass—Colline), Carlo Scattola (bass—Benoit/Alcindoro), U. Berrettoni (cnd), La Scala Orch *(rec Feb-Mar 1938)* Arkadia ("The 78's" series) 2-▲ 78009 [ADD]

Puccini, G.:Manon Lescaut, w. Maria Zamboni (sop—Manon), Anna Masetti-Bassi (mez—Singer), Francesco Merli (ten—Chevalier), Giuseppe Nessi (ten—Edmondo/Dancing Master/ Lamplighter), Lorenzo Conati (bar—Lescaut), Aristide Baracchi (bass—Innkeeper/Sergeant), Attilio Bordonali (bass—Geronte), Natale Villa (bass—Naval Captain), L. Molajoli (cnd), La Scala Orch *(rec 1930)* Arkadia ("The 78's" series) 2-▲ 78014 [ADD]

Verdi, G.:Aida, w. Dusolina Giannini (sop—Aida), Irene Minghini-Cattaneo (mez—Amneris), Giuseppe Nessi (ten—Messenger), Aureliano Pertile (ten—Radames), Giovanni Inghilleri (bar—Amonasro), Luigi Manfrini (bass—Ramfis), Guglielmo Masini (bass—King), C. Sabajno (cnd), La Scala Orch *(rec 1928)* Arkadia ("The 78's" series) 2-▲ 78013 [ADD]

Verdi, G.:La traviata, w. Olga de Franco (sop—Flora Bervoix/Annina), Anna Rosza (sop—Violetta Valery), Giordano Callegari (ten—Gastone), Alessandro Ziliani (ten—Alfredo Germont), Luigi Borgonovo (bar—Giorgio Germont), Arnoldo Lenzi (bar—Barone Douphol), Antonio Gelli (bass—Marchese d'Obigny/Dottor Grenvil), C. Sabajno (cnd), La Scala Orch *(rec Oct-Nov 1930)* Arkadia 2-▲ CD 78001 (m) [ADD]

Verdi, G.:Il trovatore, w. Maria Carena (sop—Leonora), Olga De Franco (sop—Ines), Irene Minghini Cattaneo (mez—Azucena), Aureliano Pertile (ten—Manrico), Giordano Callegari (ten—Ruiz/Messenger), Apollo Granforte (bar—Count), Bruno Carmassi (bass—Ferrando), Antonio Gelli (bass—Old Gypsy), C. Sabajno (cnd), La Scala Orch *(rec 1930)* Arkadia ("The 78's" series) 2-▲ 78007 [ADD]

Arnold Schoenberg Choir

Bach, J.S.:Cant 208, "Hunting Cant", w. A. M. Blasi (sop), J. P. Kenny (alt), K. Equiluz (ten), R. Holl (bass), N. Harnoncourt (cnd), Vienna Concentus Musicus [G] Teldec ▲ 2292-46151-2 [DDD]

Bach, J.S.:Cant 212, "Peasant Cant", w. A. M. Blasi (sop), R. Holl (bass), N. Harnoncourt (cnd), Vienna Concentus Musicus [G] Teldec ▲ 2292-46151-2 [DDD]

Bach, J.S.:Magnificat, BWV 243, w. F. Palmer (sop), M. Lipovšek (mez), P. Langridge (ten), N. Harnoncourt (cnd), Vienna Concentus Musicus [L] Teldec ▲ 2292-42984-2

Bach, J.S.:Mass in b, BWV 232, w. A. M. Blasi (sop), D. Ziegler (mez), J. Rappé (cta), K. Equiluz (ten), R. Holl (bass), N. Harnoncourt (cnd), Vienna Concentus Musicus [L] Teldec 2-▲ 2292-42676-2 [DDD]

Bach, J.S.:Mass in b, BWV 232, w. M. Venuti (sop), C. Kallisch (cta), C. Prégardien (ten), A. Scharinger (bass), E. Ortner (cnd), Salzburg Baroque Ensemble Koch Schwann 2-▲ SCH 312512 [DDD]

Beethoven, L. van:Sym 9, "Choral Sym", w. N. Harnoncourt (cnd), CO of Europe Teldec ▲ 9031-75713-2-ZK

Brahms, J.:Alto Rhap, w. Anne Sofie von Otter (mez), J. Levine (cnd), Vienna PO Deutsche Grammophon ("4D Audio" series) ▲ 439887-2

Handel, G.F.:Choruses, w. N. Harnoncourt (cnd), Vienna Concentus Musicus, Stockholm Bach Choir, Stockholm Chamber Choir Teldec ▲ 95498-2

Handel, G.F.:Samson, w. Roberta Alexander (sop), Maria Venuti (sop), Jochen Kowalski (ct), Anthony Rolfe Johnson (ten), Aalstair Miles (bass), Anton Scharinger (bass), N. Harnoncourt (cnd), Vienna Concentus Musicus Teldec ▲ 74871-2

Handel, G.F.:Theodora, w. Roberta Alexander (sop), Jard van Nes (cta), Jochen Kowalski (ct), Hans-Peter Blochwitz (ten), Anton Scharinger (bass), N. Harnoncourt (cnd), Vienna Concentus Musicus [E] Teldec 2-▲ 2292-46447-2 [DDD]

Handel, G.F.:Utrecht Te Deum & Jubilate, w. Felicity Palmer (sop), Marjana Lipovšek (mez), Philip Langridge (ten), N. Harnoncourt (cnd), Vienna Concentus Musicus [L] Teldec ▲ 2292-42984-2

Haydn, J.:Die Jahreszeiten, w. Angela Marie Blasi (sop), Josef Protschka (ten), Robert Holl (bass), N. Harnoncourt (cnd), Vienna SO [G] Teldec 2-▲ 2292-42699-2

Haydn, J.:Die Schöpfung, w. Edita Gruberova (sop), Josef Protschka (ten), Robert Holl (bass), N. Harnoncourt (cnd), Vienna SO [G] Teldec 2-▲ 2292-42682-2

Haydn, J.:The Seven Last Words of Christ on the Cross, w. Inge Nielsen (sop), Margaretha Hintermeier (cta), Anthony Rolfe Johnson (ten), Robert Holl (bass), N. Harnoncourt (cnd), Vienna Concentus Musicus [oratorio version] Teldec ▲ 2292-46458-2 ZK

Mahler, G.:Sym 2, w. C. Studer (sop), W. Meier (mez), C. Abbado (cnd), Vienna PO Deutsche Grammophon ▲ 439953-2

Mozart, W.A.:Ave verum corpus, w. Barbara Bonney (sop), Charlotte Margiono (sop), Sylvia McNair (sop), Elisabeth von Magnus (cta), Christoph Pregardien (ten), Thomas Hampson (bass), N. Harnoncourt (cnd), Vienna Concentus Musicus Teldec ▲ 98928 2

Mozart, W.A.:Benedictus, w. Barbara Bonney (sop), N. Harnoncourt (cnd), Vienna Concentus Musicus *(rec Casino Zögernitz, Vienna, Dec. 1990)* Teldec ("Das alte Werke" series) ▲ 96147-2 [DDD]

Mozart, W.A.:Dixit Dominus et Magnificat, w. E. Mei (sop), E. von Magnus (cta), K. Azesberger (ten), G. Cachemaille (bass), N. Harnoncourt (cnd), Vienna Concentus Musicus Teldec ("Das alte Werke" series) ▲ 93025

Mozart, W.A.:Grabmusik, w. Barbara Bonney (sop), Charlotte Margiono (sop), Sylvia McNair (sop), Elisabeth von Magnus (cta), Christoph Pregardien (ten), Thomas Hampson (bass), N. Harnoncourt (cnd), Vienna Concentus Musicus Teldec ("Das alte Werk" series) ▲ 98928-2

Mozart, W.A.:Kyrie, K.341, w. N. Harnoncourt (cnd), Vienna Concentus Musicus Teldec ("Das alte Werke" series) ▲ 93025

Mozart, W.A.:Litaniae de venerabili, w. E. von Magnus (alt), A. Miles (bass), N. Harnoncourt (cnd), Vienna Concentus Musicus Teldec ▲ 72304-2

Mozart, W.A.:Litaniae Lauretanae, K.109, w. Eva Mei (sop), Elisabeth von Magnus (alt), Kurt Azesberger (ten), Gilles Cachemaille (bass), N. Harnoncourt (cnd), Vienna Concentus Musicus *(rec Casino Zögernitz, Vienna, Dec. 1992)* Teldec ("Das alte Werke" series) ▲ 96147-2 [DDD]

Mozart, W.A.:Litaniae Lauretanae, K.195, w. B. Bonney (sop), E. von Magnus (cta), U. Heilmann (tenor), G. Cachemaille (bass), N. Harnoncourt (cnd), Vienna Concentus Musicus Teldec ("Das alte Werke" series) ▲ 93025

Mozart, W.A.:Missa, K.257, w. E. von Magnus (alt), A. Miles (bass), N. Harnoncourt (cnd), Vienna Concentus Musicus Teldec ▲ 72304-2

Mozart, W.A.:Missa, K.317, w. J. Rodgers (sop), E. von Magnus (alt), J. Protschka (ten), L. Polgár (bass), N. Harnoncourt (cnd), Vienna Concentus Musicus [L] Teldec ▲ 2292-43354-2

Mozart, W.A.:Missa solemnis, K.139, w. B. Bonney (sop), J. Rappé (ten), J. Protschka (ten), H. Hagegard (bar), N. Harnoncourt (cnd), Vienna Concentus Musicus [L] Teldec ▲ 2292-44180-2 [DDD]

Mozart, W.A.:Missa brevis, K.275, w. E. Mei (sop), E. von Magnus (cta), K. Azesberger (teno, G. Cachemaille (bass), N. Harnoncourt (cnd), Vienna Concentus Musicus Teldec ("Das alte Werke" series) ▲ 93025

Mozart, W.A.:Regina coeli, K.108, w. Charlotte Margiono (sop), N. Harnoncourt (cnd), Vienna Concentus Musicus *(rec Casino Zögernitz, Vienna, Dec. 1991)* Teldec ("Das alte Werke" series) ▲ 96147-2 [DDD]

Arnold Schoenberg Choir (cont.)

Mozart, W.A.:Regina coeli, K.127, w. Barbara Bonney (sop), Charlotte Margiono (sop), Sylvia McNair (sop), Elisabeth von Magnus (cta), Christoph Pregardien (ten), Thomas Hampson (bass), N. Harnoncourt (cnd), Vienna Concentus Musicus Teldec ("Das alte Werk" series) ▲ 98928 2

Mozart, W.A.:Sacred Music, w. N. Harnoncourt (cnd), Vienna Concentus Musicus—Venite populi, K.260 [rec. Dec. 1991]; Inter natos mulierum, K.72 [rec. Feb. 1992]; Ergo interest, an quie—Quaere superna, K.143 [rec. Dec. 1990; w. Barbara Bonney (soprano)]; Te Deum laudamus, K.141 [rec. Dec. 1990]; Alma Dei creatoris, K.277 [rec. Dec. 1991; w. Charlotte Margiono (soprano), Elisabeth von Magnus (alto), Christoph Prégardien (tenor)]; Tantum ergo, K.197 [rec. Dec. 1990]; Sub tuum praesidium, K.198 [rec. Dec. 1990; w. Barbara Bonney (soprano), Elisabeth von Magnus (alto), Uwe Heilmann (tenor)]; Sancta Maria, mater Dei, K.273 [rec. Feb. 1992] Teldec ("Das alte Werke" series) ▲ 96147-2 [DDD]

Mozart, W.A.:Vesperae solennes, w. J. Rodgers (sop), E. von Magnus (alt), J. Protschka (ten), L. Polgár (bass), N. Harnoncourt (cnd), Vienna Concentus Musicus [L] Teldec ▲ 2292-43354-2

Orff, C.:Carmina burana, w. B. Bonney (sop), F. Lopardo (ten), A. Michaels-Moore (bar), A. Previn (cnd), Vienna PO, Vienna Boys' Choir Deutsche Grammophon ▲ 439950-2

Purcell, H.:Dido & Aeneas, w. R. Yakar (sop), A. Murray (mez), A. Scharinger (bass), N. Harnoncourt (cnd), Vienna Concentus Musicus Teldec ("Das alte Werke" series) ▲ 93686

Schubert, Franz:Fierrabras, w. K. Mattila (sop), C. Studer (sop), R. Gambill (ten), T. Hampson (bar), R. Holl (bass), L. Polgar (bass), C. Abbado (cnd), CO of Europe [G] *(rec live)* Deutsche Grammophon 2-▲ 427341-2 [DDD]

Strauss (II), Joh.:Der Zigeunerbaron, w. Pamela Coburn (sop), Christiane Oelze (sop), Julia Hamari (mez), Elisabeth von Magnus (alt), Herbert Lippert (ten), Rudolf Schasching (ten), Wolfgang Holzmair (bar), Jurgen Flimm (sgr), Robert Florianschutz (sgr), Hans-Jurgen Lazar (sgr), N. Harnoncourt (cnd), Vienna SO *(rec Vienna, 1994)* Teldec 2-▲ 94555-2

Thomas, A.:Hamlet, w. Alexandrina Pendachanska (sop), Viorica Cortez (mez), Boje Skovhus (bar), R. Giovanetti (cnd), ORF SO *(rec live, 1994)* Serenissima 3-▲ SER 360147

E. Ortner (cnd)

Beethoven, L. van:Missa Solemnis, w. M. Lipovsek (mez), R. Holl (bass), N. Harnoncourt (cnd), CO of Europe Teldec 2-▲ 9031-74884-2

Brahms, J.:Choral Music, w. A. Korondi (sop), G. Mossyrsch (hp), J. Keiding (hn), J. Widihofer (hn)—Lieder und Romanzen, Op. 93a; 3 Gesänge, Op. 42; 7 Lieder, Op. 62; 5 Gesänge, Op. 104; 4 Gesänge, Op. 17 Teldec ▲ 4509-92058-2 [DDD]

Arnold Schoenberg Male Choir

R. de Leeuw (cnd)

Vlijmen, J. van:Un Malheureux vêtu de noir, w. S. Kleindienst (sop), Guy de Mey (ten), Pittman-Jennings (bar) *(rec live, Flanders Opera, Antwerp, Dec 11, 1990)* Donemus ▲ CV 17/18

Schola Antiqua

J. Blackley (cnd)

German Plainchant & Polyphony Elektra/Nonesuch ■ 71312-4

Tenth Century Liturgical Chant in Proportional Rhythm Elektra/Nonesuch ■ 71348-4

Schola Cantorum

Bartók, B.:Village Scenes, w. P. Boulez (cnd), New York PO, Camerata Singers Sony Classical ("Pierre Boulez Edition" series) ▲ SMK 45837

Mahler, G.:Sym 8, w. L. Stokowski (cnd), Philharmonic SO, Westminster Choir, P.S. 12 Boys' Choir *(rec 1950)* Music & Arts 2-▲ MUA 280 [AAD]

Music & Chant from the Abbey of Einsiedeln/Music & Chant from the Cathedral of St. Gall Jade ▲ JAD C 009

Ravel, M.:Rapsodie espagnole, w. L. Bernstein (cnd), New York PO *(rec New York, Mar. 6, 1973)* Sony Classical ("Bernstein:The Royal Edition" series) △ SM 47603 [ADD]

B.J. Echenique (cnd)

Padilla, J.G. de:Maitines de Natividad, w. Angelicum de Puebla Urtext ▲ URT 2004 [DDD]

A. Mendoza (cnd)

Delgado, F.:Choral Music, w. Martha Molinar (sop), Luz Angélica Uribe (sop), Ana Paula Abitia (mez), Alfredo Mendoza (ten),Noé Colín (bass), B. J. Echenique (cnd), Mexico City CO—Te Deum al Sr. Felipe de Jesús Urtext ▲ URT 2001 [DDD]

Jerusalem, I.:Choral Music, w. Martha Molinar (sop), Luz Angélica Uribe (sop), Ana Paula Abitia (mez), Alfredo Mendoza (ten),Noé Colín (bass), B. J. Echenique (cnd), Mexico City CO—Magnificat a Dos Voces; Misa en Sol Mayor a 8 Voces Urtext ▲ URT 2001 [DDD]

Schola Cantorum Basiliensis

Adams, J.:Le jeu de Robin et de Marion *(rec live, May 1987)* Focus ▲ FOCUS 913 [AAD]

Caccini, G.:Le nuove musiche, w. Montserrat Figueras (sop), J. Savall (vl), R. Clancy (baroque gtr), H. Smith (baroque gtr), X. Schindler (hp) Editio Classica ▲ 77164-2-RG [ADD]

Cavalli, P.F.:Vespero della beata Vergine Maria, w. Barbara Borden (sop), Emily van Evera (sop), Markus Brutscher (ten), Mark Padmore (ten), Rodrigo del Pozo (ten), Gerd Türk (ten), Harry van der Kamp (bass), Peter Zimpel (sgr), Bruce Dickey (sackbut), Charles Toet (sackbut), Concerto Palatino Harmonia Mundi France ("Documenta" series) 2-▲ HMC 905219/20

Nova Cantica:Latin Songs of the High Middle Ages, w. Dominique Vellard (sgr), Emmanuel Bonnardot Deutsche Harmonia Mundi ▲ 77196-2-RC

William Byrd & His Age, w. A. Deller (cnd), Consort of Viols, August Wenzinger (cnd) *(rec Friends' Meeting House, Edgware Road, London, Feb 1956)* Vanguard Classics ▲ OVC 8101 [ADD]

Arlt, Vellard (cnd)

Codex Engelberg 314:Music of the Middle Ages Deutsche Harmonia Mundi ▲ 77185-2-RC [DDD]

R. Lutz (cnd)

Lamentationes, w. St. Gallen String Orch *(rec St. Mangen Church, St. Gallen, Switzerland)* Guild ▲ GMCD 7123 [DDD]

Schola Cantorum Coloniensis

Gregorian & Ambrosian Chant for Epiphany EMI Classics ▲ CDC 54318

Schola Cantorum Colonienses

Schola Cantorum Gedanensis

J. Lukaszewski (cnd)

Hakenberger, A.:Musique pour Sigismond III Vasa—Omni tempore; De sanctissimo; Beati omnes; In nativitate; Nigra sum; Ad te levavi; Vulnerasti; Vidi speciosam; De resurrectione; Salve regina; Ego flos campi; De beata virgine; Exultate justi; De sancto bernardo; In communi; In festo; Deus canticum novum; Gloria tibi Accord ▲ ACD 201042 [DDD]

Schola Cantorum of Boston

Lamentations, w. J. Cohen (cnd), Boston Camerata, Schola Cantorum of Boston [cnd:Frederick Jodry] *(rec Campion Center, Boston, Apr. 1994)* Erato ▲ 4509-98480-2 [DDD]

Nueva Espña:Close Encounters in the New World (1590-1690), w. J. Cohen (cnd), Boston Camerata, Boston Shawn and Sackbut Ensemble, Women's Choir of the Church Les Amis de la Sagesse Erato ▲ 45977-2

Schola Cantorum St. Godehard Hanover

Liturgy of the Presanctified Gifts in German, w. Niederaltaich Benedictine Chorus, Archimandrit Irenäus Tozzke (cnd) Christophorus ▲ 77175

Schola Cantorum Stuttgart

Cage, J.:Empty Words III, w. J. Cage (speaker) *(rec 1975)* Wergo ▲ WER 6074-2 [AAD]

Schola Discantus

French Sacred Music of the 14th Century, Vol. 1, w. Bradford Findell (ct), John Delorey (ct), Peter McCabe (ten), Arthur Rawding (ten), Paul Guttry (bar), Kevin Moll (cnd) *(rec Emmanuel Church, Boston, 1994)* Lyrichord ("Early Music" series) ▲ LYR 8012 [DDD]

K. Moll (cnd)

Libert, R.:Marian Mass Lyrichord ("Early Music" series) ▲ LYR CD 8025

Ockeghem, J.:Masses (2) for 3 Voices—Missa sine Nomine; Missa quinti Tone Lyrichord ▲ LYR 8010 [DDD]

Rue, P. de la:Lamentationes Hieremiae *(rec Memorial Church, Harvard Univ, Cambridge, MA)* Lyrichord ("Early Music" series) ▲ LEMS 8021

Rue, P. de la:Missa de Sancta Anna *(rec Memorial Church, Harvard Univ, Cambridge, MA)* Lyrichord ("Early Music" series) ▲ LEMS 8021

Schola Gregoriana
Ars Gregoriana 12:The Credo — Motette ▲ MOT 50511 [DDD]
Visitacio Sepulchri, — Supraphon ▲ SUP 111562 [DDD]
Acciai, Cristante (cnd)
Viadana, L. da:Responsoria ad lamentationes, w. Collegium Vocale Nova Ars Cantandi — Stradivarius 2-▲ STV 33444 [DDD]
M. Berry (cnd)
Dupré, M.:Les vêpres de la Vierge, w. David Hill (org), Philippe Lefebvre (org) — Herald ▲ HAVPCD 170
Schola Gregoriana Pragensis
Bohemian Saints — Supraphon ▲ SUP 0003 [DDD]
X. Chancerelle (cnd)
All Saints' Day Requiem, w. Paris Gregorian Choir, Schola Gregoriano Pragensis [cnd:D. Eben] — Jade ▲ JAD C 111
D. Eben (cnd)
In Pragensi Ecclesia — Supraphon ▲ SUP CD 3191
R.G. Frieberger (cnd)
Christus Natus Est Nobis — Christophorus ▲ 77179 [DDD]
Schola Hungarica
Dufay, G.:Hymns—15 hymns for Advent, Christmas, Epiphany, Lent, Passion-tide, Easter, Ascension Day, Pentecost, Trinity, Corpus Christi, Parish-feast, St John the Baptist, St Peter & Paul, & the B.V.M. (with introductory Gregorian chants from the Cambrai Antiphonal) [L] — Hungaroton ▲ HCD 12951 [DDD]
The Play of Daniel — Hungaroton ▲ HCD 12457 [DDD]
Azendrei, Dobszay (cnd)
Vohburg, A. von:The Regensburg Office in Honor of St. Emmeram *(rec June 1996)* — Calig ▲ CAL 50983 [DDD]
L. Dobszay (cnd)
Bartók, B.:Choruses (27) [Hun] — Hungaroton ▲ HCD 31080 [DDD]
Dobszay, Szendrei (cnd)
Ambrosian Liturgical Chants for Advent & Christmas — Hungaroton ▲ HCD 12889 [DDD]
Beneventan Chants — Hungaroton ▲ HCD 31168 [DDD]
Epiphany — Hungaroton ▲ HCD 12559
From Abraham to Moses:Gregorian Chants on Biblical Texts — Quintana ▲ QUI 903038 ■ QUI 403038
From Evening to Evening with Gregorian Chant — Hungaroton ▲ HCD 31086 [DDD]
Funeral Chants; Chants of the Blessed Mary — Hungaroton ▲ HCD 12170
Gregorian Chants for Advent, Christmas, Pentecost — Hungaroton ▲ HCD 12048
Gregorian Chants from Hungary, Vol. 3:Holy Week — Hungaroton ▲ HCD 12049
Gregorian Chants in a Village Church — Hungaroton ▲ HCD 12742 [DDD]
Greogorian Chant from Aquitaine *(rec 1990)* — Musique d'Abord ▲ HMA 1903031
Hungarian Saints — Hungaroton ▲ HCD 12169
Medieval Christmas Melodies — Hungaroton ▲ HCD 11477
Old Roman Liturgical Chants:Grand Vespers for Easter & Mass for the 2nd Sunday after Michelmas — Hungaroton ▲ HCD 12741 [DDD]
St. Elizabeth of Hungary:2 Medieval Offices *(rec Franciscan Church, Esztergom, 1995)* — Hungaroton ▲ HCD 31605 [DDD]

Schola Hungarica Boys' Chorus
Telemann, G.P.:Der Schulmeister, w. J. Gregor (bass), T. Pál (cnd), Corelli CO [G] — Hungaroton ▲ HCD 12573 [DDD]

Schola Saint Grégoire du Mans Chorus
Langlais, J.:Chant grégorien, w. Jacques Kauffman (org) [organ of the Dominican Church, Paris] — Skarbo ▲ SKR 1933 [DDD]
Langlais, J.:Missa in simplicitate, w. J. Kauffman (org) [organ of the Dominican Church, Paris] — Skarbo ▲ SKR 1933 [DDD]

Robert Schumann Hochschule Choralschola
Ars Gregoriana 13 — Motette ▲ MOT 50451 [ADD]
Heinrich Schütz Choir
Mozart, W.A.:Ave verum corpus, w. R. Norrington (cnd), London Classical Players — EMI Classics ▲ CDC 54525

Schütz Choir London
Beethoven, L. van:Sym 9, "Choral Sym", w. R. Norrington (cnd), London Classical Players [G] — EMI Classics ▲ CDC 49221 [DDD]
Mozart, W.A.:Don Giovanni, w. N. Argenta (sop), A. Halgrimson (sop), L. Dawson (sop), J. M. Ainsley (ten), G. Finley (ten), A. Miles (bar), A. Schmidt (bar), G. Yurisch (bar), R. Norrington (cnd), London Classical Players — EMI Classics ▲ CDCB 54859
Mozart, W.A.:Requiem, w. N. Argenta (sop), C. Robbin (mez), J.M. Ainsley (ten), A. Miles (bass), R. Norrington (cnd), London Classical Players [L] — EMI Classics ▲ CDC 54525
Purcell, H.:The Fairy Queen, w. Lorraine Hunt (sop), Susan Bickley (mez), Catherine Pierard (mez), Howard Crook (ten), Mark Padmore (ten), David Wilson-Johnson (bar), Richard Wistreich (bass), R. Norrington (cnd), London Classical Players — EMI Classics ▲ CDCB 55234
Scarlatti, A.:Domine refugium factus, w. Keith Majoram (bass), Marylin Sansom (vc), Charles Spinks (org), R. Norrington (cnd) *(rec 1973)* — London 2-▲ 443868-2 [ADD]
Scarlatti, D.:Stabat mater, w. Keith Majoram (bass), Marylin Sansom (vc), Charles Spinks (org), R. Norrington (cnd) *(rec 1973)* — London 2-▲ 443868-2 [ADD]
R. Norrington (cnd)
Scarlatti, A.:O magnum mysterium, w. Keith Majoram (bass), Marylin Sansom (vc), Charles Spinks (org) *(rec 1973)* — London 2-▲ 443868-2 [ADD]
Lee Scott Singers
K.L. Scott (cnd)
Scott, K.L.:The Wind of Heaven, w. S. M. Wallace (org), H. Rubin (vn) — VQR Digital ▲ QR 2051 [DDD]
Scottish Chamber Chorus
Bach, J.S.:Cant 56, w. O. Bär (bar), P. Schreier (cnd), Scottish CO [G] *(rec May 1991)* — EMI Classics ▲ CDC 54453-2 [DDD]
Bach, J.S.:Cant 82, w. O. Bär (bar), P. Schreier (cnd), Scottish CO *(rec May 1991)* — EMI Classics ▲ CDC 54453-2 [DDD]
Bach, J.S.:Cant 158, w. O. Bär (bar), P. Schreier (cnd), Scottish CO *(rec 5/91)* — EMI Classics ▲ CDC 54453-2 [DDD]
Mozart, W.A.:Don Giovanni, w. Christine Brewer (sop—Donna Anna), Nuccia Focile (sop—Zerlina), Felicity Lott (sop—Donna Elvira), Jerry Hadley (ten—Don Ottavio), Bo Skovhus (bar—Don Giovanni), Umberto Chiummo (bass—Masetto/Il Commendatore), Alessandro Corbelli (bass—Leporello), C. Mackerras (cnd), Scottish CO *(rec Usher Hall, Edinburgh, Scotland, July 31– Aug 11, 1995)* — Telarc 3-▲ CD 80420 [DDD]
Mozart, W.A.:Nozze di Figaro, w. Rebecca Evans (sop—Barbarina), Nuccia Focile (sop—Susanna), Suzanne Murphy (sop—Marcellina), Carol Vaness (sop—Countess Almaviva), Susanne Mentzer (mez—Cherubino), Ryland Davies (ten—Don Basilio/Don Curzio), Alessandro Corbelli (bar—Count Almaviva), Alfonso Antoniozzi (bass—Doctor Bartolo/Antonio), Alastair Miles (bass—Figaro), C. Mackerras (cnd), Scottish CO *(rec Usher Hall, Edingurgh, Scotland, July 31–Aug. 12, 1994)* — Telarc 3-▲ CD 80388 [DDD]
Mozart, W.A.:Zauberflöte, w. B. Hendricks (sop—Pamina), J. Anderson (sop—Queen of the Night), U. Steinsky (sop—Papagena), J. Hadley (ten—Tamino), T. Allen (bar—Papageno), R. Lloyd (bass—Sarastro), C. Mackerras (cnd), Scottish CO [G] — Telarc 2-▲ CD 80302 [DDD]
Rossini, G.:Arias, w. R. Giménez (ten), M. Veltri (cnd), Scottish CO — Nimbus ▲ NI 5106 [DDD]
Scottish National Chorus
Elgar, E.:Coronation Ode, w. T. Cahill (sop), A. Collins (cta), A. Rolfe Johnson (ten), G. Howell (bass), A. Gibson (cnd), Scottish National Orch [E] *(rec 1976)* — Chandos ("Collect" series) ▲ CHAN 6574 [ADD]
Elgar, E.:The Dream of Gerontius, w. Alfreda Hodgson (cta), Robert Tear (ten), Benjamin Luxon (bar), A. Gibson (cnd), Scottish National Orch — CRD 2-▲ 33267

Scottish National Chorus (cont.)
Elgar, E.:The Spirit of England, w. T. Cahill (sop), A. Gibson (cnd), Scottish National Orch [E] *(rec 1976)* — Chandos ("Collect" series) ▲ CHAN 6574 [ADD]
Haydn, J.:L'Anima del filosofo, or Orfeo ed Euridice, w. Joan Sutherland (sop), Nicolai Gedda (ten), R. Bonynge (cnd), Scottish National Orch *(rec live)* — Verona 2-▲ VER 28018
Prokofiev, S.:Alexander Nevsky, w. L. Finnie (mez), N. Järvi (cnd), Scottish National Orch — Chandos ▲ CHAN 8584 [DDD]
Rachmaninoff, S.:The Bells, w. S. Murphy (sop), K. Lewis (ten), D. Wilson-Johnson (bar), N. Järvi (cnd), Scottish National Orch [R] — Chandos ▲ CHAN 8476 [DDD]
Walton, W.:Belshazzar's Feast, w. S. Milnes (bar), A. Gibson (cnd), Scottish National Orch, Scottish Festival Brass Bands *(rec 1977)* — Chandos ("Collect" series) ▲ CHAN 6547 [ADD/DDD]
Walton, W.:Coronation Te Deum, w. A. Gibson (cnd), Scottish National Orch *(rec 1977)* — Chandos ("Collect" series) ▲ CHAN 6547 [ADD/DDD]
Scottish Opera Chorus
Blitzstein, M.:Regina, w. A. Réaux (sop), S. Greenawald (sop), K. Ciesinski (mez), S. Ramey (bass), J. Mauceri (cnd), Scottish Opera Orch [E] — London 2-▲ 433812-2 [DDD]
Maccunn, H.:The Dowie Dens o'Yarrow, w. Lisa Milne (sop), Janice Watson (sop), Jamie MacDougall (ten), Peter Sidhom (bar), Stephen Gadd (bass), M. Brabbins (cnd), BBC Scottish SO — Hyperion ▲ CDA 66815
Maccunn, H.:Jeanie Deans (sels), w. Lisa Milne (sop), Janice Watson (sop), Jamie MacDougall (ten), Peter Sidhom (bar), Stephen Gadd (bass), M. Brabbins (cnd), BBC Scottish SO — Hyperion ▲ CDA 66815
Maccunn, H.:Lay of Last Minstrel, w. Lisa Milne (sop), Janice Watson (sop), Jamie MacDougall (ten), Peter Sidhom (bar), Stephen Gadd (bass), M. Brabbins (cnd), BBC Scottish SO — Hyperion ▲ CDA 66815
Maccunn, H.:Ship o' the Fiend, w. Lisa Milne (sop), Janice Watson (sop), Jamie MacDougall (ten), Peter Sidhom (bar), Stephen Gadd (bass), M. Brabbins (cnd), BBC Scottish SO — Hyperion ▲ CDA 66815
Weill, K.:Street Scene, w. J. Barstow (sop), A. Réaux (sop), J. Hadley (ten), S. Ramey (bass), J. Mauceri (cnd), Scottish Opera Orch [E] — London 2-▲ 433371-2 [DDD]
Scottish Phil Singers
Elgar, E.:Caractacus, w. C. Groves (cnd), BBC Scottish SO — IMP ("BBC Radio Classics" series) ▲ IMP 5691802
Elgar, E.:Choral Songs (sels), w. C. Groves (cnd), BBC Scottish SO—Give Unto the Lord — IMP ("BBC Radio Classics" series) ▲ IMP 5691802
Handel, G.F.:Messiah (sels), w. Felicity Lott (sop), Linda Finnie (mez), Glenn Winslade (ten), Henry Herford (bar), G. Malcolm (cnd), Scottish CO — IMP ("Classic" series) ▲ IMP 2031
Mendelssohn, F.:A Midsummer Night's Dream (comp), w. J. Howarth (sop), E. James (mez), J. Laredo (cnd), Scottish CO [E] — Nimbus 2-▲ NI 5041/42 [DDD]
Scottish Sym Chorus
Mozart, W.A.:Zauberflöte (sels), w. B. Hendricks (sop), J. Hadley (sop), J. Anderson (sop), T. Allen (bar), R. Lloyd (b-bar), U. Steinsky (cnd), Scottish CO *(rec July 13–22, 1991)* — Telarc ▲ CD 80345 [DDD]
Norman Scribner Choir
Haydn, J.:Mass 10, "Kriegsmesse", "Paukenmesse", w. Patricia Wells (sop), Gwendoline Killebrew (mez), Michael Devlin (b-bar), Alan Titus (bar), L. Bernstein (cnd), *(orch unknown)* [L] *(rec 1973)* — Sony Classical ("Bernstein:The Royal Edition" series) 2-▲ SM2K 47563 [ADD]
Seattle Chorale
Bloch, E.:America, w. G. Schwarz (cnd), Seattle SO *(rec June 1–2, 1993)* — Delos ▲ DE 3135 [DDD]
Copland, A.:Canticle of Freedom, w. G. Schwarz (cnd), Seattle SO [E] — Delos ▲ DE 3140 [DDD]
Diamond, D.:This Sacred Ground, w. Erich Parce (bar), G. Schwarz (cnd), Seattle SO, Seattle Girls' Choir, Northwest Boychoir *(rec Feb. 13, 1994)* — Delos ▲ DE 3141 [DDD]
Handel, G.F.:Acis & Galatea, w. D. Kotoski (sop—Galatea), D. Gordon (ten—Acis), G. Siebert (ten—Damon), J. Opalach (bass—Polyphemus), G. Schwarz (cnd), Seattle SO [E] — Delos 2-▲ DE 3107 [DDD]
Hanson, H.:Lament for Beowulf, w. G. Schwarz (cnd), Seattle SO — Delos 4-▲ DE 3150 [DDD]
Hanson, H.:Lament for Beowulf, w. G. Schwarz (cnd), Seattle SO — Delos ▲ DE 3105 [DDD]
Hanson, H.:Lumen in Christo, w. G. Schwarz (cnd), Seattle SO *(rec June 6–7, 1994)* — Delos ▲ DE 3160 [DDD]
Hanson, H.:Lux Aeterna, w. G. Schwarz (cnd), Seattle SO *(rec June 6–7, 1994)* — Delos ▲ DE 3160 [DDD]
Hanson, H.:The Mystic Trumpeter, w. James Earl Jones (nar), G. Schwarz (cnd), Seattle SO *(rec June 6–7, 1994)* — Delos ▲ DE 3160 [DDD]
Hanson, H.:Sym 7, "A Sea Sym", w. G. Schwarz (cnd), Seattle SO — Delos ▲ DE 3130 [DDD]
Mendelssohn, F.:Sym 2, w. M. Chalker (sop), M. Rivera (sop), V. Cole (ten), G. Schwarz (cnd), Seattle SO *(rec Apr. 22–23, 1991)* — Delos ▲ DE 3112 [DDD]
Piston, W.:Psalm & Prayer of David, w. G. Schwarz (cnd), Seattle SO *(rec Jan. 27–28, 1992)* — Delos ▲ DE 3126 [DDD]
Ravel, M.:Daphins et Chloé, w. G. Schwarz (cnd), Seattle SO — Delos ▲ DE 3110 [DDD]
Seattle Girls' Choir
Diamond, D.:This Sacred Ground, w. Erich Parce (bar), G. Schwarz (cnd), Seattle SO, Seattle Chorale, Northwest Boychoir *(rec Feb. 13, 1994)* — Delos ▲ DE 3141 [DDD]
J. Wright (cnd)
Seattle Holiday *(rec ST. Thomas Center Chapel, Bothell, WA, 1991–94)* — SDG ▲ SDG 951 [DDD]
Sekundar School Children's Choir
T. Loosli (cnd)
Suter, H.:Le Laudi di San Francesco d'Assisi, w. A. Michael (sop), J. Winklet (alt), A. Baldin (ten), J. Will (bass), P. Laubschet (org), Bern SO, Bern Bach Choir — Ars Musici ▲ AM 1015-2 [DDD]
Seminarchor Wettingen
Schoeck, O.:Der Postillon, w. K. Grenacher (pno), E. Haefliger (ten), Wettinger CO, Wettinger Chamber Chorus [G] *(rec 1967)* — Jecklin-Disco ▲ JD 504-2 [ADD]
Schoeck, O.:Songs (misc), w. K. Grenacher (pno), E. Haefliger (ten), Wettinger CO, Wettinger Chamber Chorus [G] *(rec 1967)* — Jecklin-Disco ▲ JD 504-2 [ADD]
Il Seminario Musicale
Bononcini, G.:Cantate (12) e duetti, w. G. Lesne (ct)—Cants. for Alto Solo — EMI Classics ▲ CDC 45000
Bononcini, G.:Sons Vc — EMI Classics ▲ CDC 45000
Bononcini, G.:Sons for the Chamber — EMI Classics ▲ CDC 45000
Charpentier, M.-A.:Leçons de ténèbres (comp), w. G. Lesne (cnd) — Virgin Classics ▲ CDC 45075
Charpentier, M.-A.:Leçons de ténèbres (comp), w. G. Lesne (cnd) — Virgin Classics ▲ CDC 45107
Charpentier, M.-A.:Leçons de ténèbres, H. 96-110, w. G. Lesne (ct), A. Mellon (cnd)—3 du jeudi — Virgin Classics ▲ CDC 59295
Charpentier, M.-A.:Leçons de ténèbres, H. 96-110, w. A. Mellon (sop), G. Lesne (ct), I. Honeyman (cnd)—3 du jeudi — Virgin Classics ▲ CDC 59278
Galuppi, B.:Motets, w. G Lesne (male alt) — Virgin Classics ▲ CDC 45030
Handel, G.F.:Cants, w. G. Lesne (ct)—Carco sempre di gloria; La Lucrezia; Mi palpita il cor; Splenda l'alba in oriente [I] *(rec 10/90)* — Virgin Classics ▲ 59059 [DDD]
Handel, G.F.:Trio Sons, w. Gérard Lesne (alt)—Sonata in G, Op. 5/4 *(rec 10/90)* — Virgin Classics ▲ 59059 [DDD]
Monteverdi, C.:Motets, w. B. Lesne (mez), G. Lesne (ct), J. Benet (ten), J. Cabré (bar)—18 motets for 1, 2 & 3 voices [L] — Virgin Classics ("Veritas" series) ▲ 59602 [DDD]
Vivaldi, A.:Cants, w. Gérard Lesne (ct)—Cessate omai cessate in A, R.684; Perfidissimo cor! in A, R.674; Amor hai vinto in A, R.683; Qual per ignoto in A, R.677 — Adda ▲ ADD 241872 [ADD]
Vivaldi, A.:Sons Vn, Op. 2, w. Fabio Biondi (vn)—No. 3 — Adda ▲ ADD 241872 [ADD]
G. Lesne (cnd)
Vivaldi, A.:Cants—Cessate, Omai Cessate; Amor Hai Vinto; Qual Per Ignoto — Adda ▲ ADD 581053 [ADD]

Ernst Senff Chorus
Beethoven, L. van:Sym 9, "Choral Sym", w. C. M. Giulini (cnd), Berlin PO [soloists J. Varady, J. van Nes, K. Lewis, S. Estes] — Deutsche Grammophon ▲ 427655-2 [DDD]
Berlioz, H.:Requiem, "Grande Messe des Morts", w. L. Pavarotti (ten), J. Levine (cnd), Berlin PO — Deutsche Grammophon 2-▲ 429724-2 [DDD]

Ernst Senff Chorus (cont.)
Berlioz, H.:Rêverie et caprice, w. J. Wagner (vn), M. Schønwandt (cnd), Berlin SO, Berlin Radio Choir Kontrapunkt 2-▲ KPT 32143 [DDD]
Berlioz, H.:Roméo et Juliette, w. A. S. von Otter (sop), P. Langridge (ten), Morris (sgr), J. Levine (cnd), Berlin PO [F] Deutsche Grammophon 2-▲ 427665-2 [DDD]
Brahms, J.:Alto Rhap, w. M. Lipovšek (mez), C. Abbado (cnd), Berlin PO [G] Deutsche Grammophon ▲ 427643-2 [DDD]
Brahms, J.:Schicksalslied, w. C. Abbado (cnd), Berlin PO [G] Deutsche Grammophon ▲ 429765-2 [DDD]
Eisler, H.:Deutsche Sinfonie, w. Hendrikje Wangemann (sop), Annette Markert (alt), Matthias Görne (bar), Peter Lika (bass), Gert Gütschow (speaker), Volker Schwarz (speaker), L. Zagrosek (cnd), Leipzig Gewandhaus Orch *(rec Gewandhaus, Leipzig, May 1995)* London ("Entartet Musik" series) ▲ 448389-2 [DDD]
Mahler, G.:Sym 2, w. S. McNair (sop), J. van Nes (cta), B. Haitink (cnd), Berlin PO Philips ▲ 438935-2
Schubert, Franz:Rosamunde, w. A.-S. von Otter (mez), C. Abbado (cnd), CO of Europe Deutsche Grammophon ▲ 431655-2 [DDD]
Verdi, G.:Pezzi sacri, w. S. Sweet (sop), C. M. Giulini (cnd), Berlin PO Sony Classical ▲ SK 46491
Vivaldi, A.:Credo, RV. 591, w. C. M. Giulini (cnd), Berlin PO Sony Classical ▲ SK 46491

Ernst Senff Chorus Women's Voices
Mahler, G.:Sym 3, w. F. Quivar (cta), B. Haitink (cnd), Berlin PO, Tölz Boys' Choir Philips ▲ 432162-2
Mendelssohn, F.:Midsummer Night's Dream (ov & incidental), w. Kenneth Branagh (nar), Sylvia McNair (sop), Angelika Kirchschlager (mez), C. Abbado (cnd), Berlin PO Sony Classical ▲ SK 62826

Sept-fons Abbey Monks' Choir
Salve Regina, w. Citeaux Abbey Monks' Choir, Timadeuc Abbey Monks' Choir Studio SM ▲ 12 16 34

Sequentia
Aimeric De Peghuilhan:En amour tob alques en que'm refraing *(rec Abbaye de Fontevraud, France, Dec. 4-7, 1993)* Deutsche Harmonia Mundi ▲ 05472-77227-2 [DDD]
Ancient Music for a Modern Age RCA Red Seal ▲ 09026-61868-2 ■ 09026-61868-4
Bertran de Born:Rassa, tan creis e monta e poia *(rec Abbaye de Fontevraud, France, Dec. 4-7, 1993)* Deutsche Harmonia Mundi ▲ 05472-77227-2 [DDD]
Bordesholmer Marienklage:A Medieval Passionplay Deutsche Harmonia Mundi 2-▲ 05472-77280-2
Daniel, A.:Chanson do'ill mot son plan e prim *(rec Abbaye de Fontevraud, France, Dec. 4-7, 1993)* Deutsche Harmonia Mundi ▲ 05472-77227-2 [DDD]
Daniel, A.:Lo ferm voler qu'el cor m'intra *(rec Abbaye de Fontevraud, France, Dec. 4-7, 1993)* Deutsche Harmonia Mundi ▲ 05472-77227-2 [DDD]
Dante & the Troubadours *(rec Abbaye de Fontevraud, France, Dec. 4-7, 1993)* Deutsche Harmonia Mundi ▲ 05472-77227-2 [DDD]
English Songs of the Middle Ages Editio Classica ▲ 77019-2-RG [DDD] ■ 77019-4-RG (CrO2)
Folquet de Marseille:Tant m'abellis l'amoros pessamens *(rec Abbaye de Fontevraud, France, Dec. 4-7, 1993)* Deutsche Harmonia Mundi ▲ 05472-77227-2 [DDD]
Guiraut De Bornelh:No posc sifrir c'a la dolor *(rec Abbaye de Fontevraud, France, Dec. 4-7, 1993)* Deutsche Harmonia Mundi ▲ 05472-77227-2 [DDD]
Hildegard Of Bingen:Music of—O rubor sanguinis; Favus distillans; Laus Trinitati; In Matutinis Laudibus; O Ecclesia; Intrumental Piece; O aeterne Deus; O dulcissime amator; Rex noster promptus est; O cruor sanguinis; Cum vox sanguinis; Instrumental Piece; O virgo Ecclesia; Nunc gaudeant materna; O orzchis Ecclesia *(rec St Pantaleon, Cologne, Oct 30-Nov 3, 1994)* Deutsche Harmonia Mundi ▲ 05472-77346-2 [DDD]
Hildegard Of Bingen:Ordo virtutum, w. Margriet Tindemans (va da gamba), B. Thornton (cnd) Editio Classica 2-▲ 77051-2-RG [DDD] 2-■ 77051-4-RG (CrO2)
Hildegard Of Bingen:Sacred Music—O vis aternitatis Responsorium; Nunc aperuit nobis; Quia ergo femina morte instruxit; Cum processit factura digiti Dei; Alma Redemptoris Mater; Ave Maria, O auctrix vite; Spiritus sanctus vivificans vite; O ignis spiritus Paracliti; Caritas habundat in omnia; O virga mediatrix; O viridissima virga, Ave; Instrumental piece; O pastor animarum; O tu suavissima virga; O choruscans stellarum; O nobilissima viriditas Deutsche Harmonia Mundi ▲ 05472-77320-2 ■ 05472-77320-4
Hildegard Of Bingen:Sacred Songs [L] Editio Classica ▲ 77020-2-RG [ADD] ■ 77020-4-RG (CrO2)
Oswald von Wolkenstein:Songs Deutsche Harmonia Mundi ▲ 05472-77302-2
Peire d'Alvernhe:Dejosta'ls breus jorns e'ls loncs sers *(rec Abbaye de Fontevraud, France, Dec. 4-7, 1993)* Deutsche Harmonia Mundi ▲ 05472-77227-2 [DDD]
Shining Light *(rec Church of the Campion Center, Weston, MA, Feb 1996)* Deutsche Harmonia Mundi ▲ 77370-2 [DDD]
Trouvères:Courtly Love Songs from Northern France, ca. 1175-1300 Deutsche Harmonia Mundi 2-▲ 77155-2-RC [DDD]
Visions from the Book, w. Sons of Thunder *(rec Campion Center, Weston, MA, Nov 13-17, 1994)* Deutsche Harmonia Mundi ▲ 05472-77347-2 [DDD]
Vitry, P. de:Motets & Chansons Deutsche Harmonia Mundi ▲ 77095-2-RC [ADD]
Vox Iberica I:Sons of Thunder Deutsche Harmonia Mundi ▲ 05472-77199-2
Vox Iberica II:Music from the Royal Convent of Las Huelgas de Burgos Deutsche Harmonia Mundi ▲ 05472-77238-2

B. Bagby (cnd)
Shining Light Deutsche Harmonia Mundi ▲ 05472-77370-2 ■ 05472-77370-4

Severácek Children's Choir
M. Uherek (cnd)
Janácek, L.:Vocal Music, w. Eva Struplová (sop), Stanislav Predota (ten), Hanus Barton (pno), Adam Skoumal (pno), L. Cerny (cnd), *(ensemble unknown)*—Little Queens; Folk Poetry from Hukvaldy; Folk Nocturnes; Nursery Rhymes Studio Matous ▲ MAT 16 [DDD]

La Sfera Armoniosa
Kapsberger, G.G.:Villanelles (misc), w. Mike Fentross (lt)—Lasciavete Pastorelle; Avrilla Mia; Voi Che Dietro; Gia Risi del Mio Mal; Alla Caccia Pastore; Ite Sospiri Miei; Pieta di Chi Si Mora; Amor Non Piangere; Passacaglia; Tu Che Pallido e Sangue; Fuggi Fuggi l'Inganno; Figlio Dormi; Sussurat'aure; Spiega, Spiega; Canzona Prima; Tu Dormi Anima Mia; No No No Non Burlar; Che Fai Tu Carlton ("Musick's Monument" series) ▲ MSK 6500092

Shadyside Presbyterian Church Chancel Choir
To Behold the Fair Beauty, w. Dr. John Walker (org) Pro Organo ▲ POCD 7043 [DDD]

Robert Shaw Chamber Singers
Schubert, Franz:Choral Music, w. N. MacKenzie (pno), M. Ackerman (gtr), R. Shaw (cnd)—Die Nacht; Der Nachtigall [w. K. Dent (tenor)]; Wehmuth; Der Gondelfahrer; Mondenschein [w. Dent]; Nachthelle [w. Dent]; Das Dörfchen [w. Dent]; Die Einsiedelei; Sehnsucht; Grab und Mond; Frühlingsgesang [w. Dent & R. Clement (tenor)]; Liebe; Widerspruch; An den Frühling; La pastorella; Ständchen [w. M. Hart (mezzo-soprano)]; Der Entfernten *(rec Oct. 17-18, 1992)* Telarc ▲ CD 80340 [DDD]

Robert Shaw Chorale
Ave Maria, w. Plácido Domingo (ten), Mario Lanza (ten), Vienna Boys' Choir RCA Victor ▲ 09026-61838-2 ■ 09026-61838-4
The Battle Cry of Freedom, w. RCA Victor SO RCA Gold Seal ▲ 60814-2-RG [ADD] ■ 60814-4-RG
Beethoven, L. van:Missa Solemnis, w. M. Marshall (sop), N. Merriman (mez), E. Conley (ten), J. Hines (bass), A. Toscanini (cnd), NBC SO *(rec 1953)* RCA Gold Seal ▲ 60272-2-RG [ADD] ■ 60272-4-RG
The Best of Wagner, w. Philadelphia Orch [cnd:E. Ormandy], RCA Victor SO Victrola ("Victrola Best of" series) ▲ 60777-2-RV [ADD] ■ 60777-4-RV
Boito, A.:Mefistofele (sels), w. N. Moscona (bass), A. Toscanini (cnd), NBC SO, Columbus Boychoir—Prologue RCA Gold Seal ▲ 60276-2-RG [ADD] ■ 60276-4-RG
Brahms, J.:Gesang der Parzen, w. A. Toscanini (cnd), NBC SO [G] RCA Gold Seal ▲ 60260-2-RG [ADD] ■ 60260-4-RG (CrO2)
Brahms, J.:Gesang der Parzen, w. A. Toscanini (cnd), NBC SO [G] RCA Gold Seal 4-▲ 60325-2-RG (m) [ADD] 4-■ 60325-4-RG (CrO2)
Cherubini, L.:Requiem Mass in c, w. A. Toscanini (cnd), NBC SO RCA Gold Seal ▲ 60272-2-RG [ADD] ■ 60272-4-RG (CrO2)

Robert Shaw Chorale (cont.)
Christmas Treasures, w. Leontyne Price (sop), Marian Anderson (cta), Rosalind Elias (mez), Mario Lanza (ten), Giorgio Tozzi (bass), Arthur Fiedler (cnd), Leopold Stokowski (cnd) RCA Living Stereo ▲ 09026-61867-2 ■ 09026-61867-4
Classic Patriotic Choruses Victrola ■ ALK1-4987
A Festival of Carols RCA Gold Seal ▲ 6429-2-RG [ADD] ■ 6429-4 RG
Foster, S.C.:Songs—Beautiful Dreamer; My Old Kentucky Home; Oh! Susanna; Nelly Bly; Steal Away; Camptown Races *(rec 1958 & 1961)* RCA Living Stereo ▲ 09026-61253-2; ■ 09026-61253-4
Gluck, C.W.:Orfeo ed Euridice (sels), w. B. Gibson (sop), N. Merriman (mez), A. Toscanini (cnd), NBC SO—Act 2 RCA Gold Seal ▲ 60280-2-RG; ■ 60280-4-RG
Handel, G.F.:Messiah (choruses), w. R. Shaw (cnd), Robert Shaw Orch RCA Gold Seal ▲ 09026-61368-2; ■ 09026-61368-4
Leoncavallo, R.:Pagliacci, w. V. de los Angeles (sop), J. Björling (ten), R. Merrill (bar), L. Warren (bar), R. Cellini (cnd), Columbus Orch EMI Classics ▲ ZDC 49503
Mascagni, P.:Cavalleria rusticana, w. Z. Milanov (sop), Carol Smith (sop), J. Bjöerling (ten), R. Merrill (bar), R. Cellini (cnd), RCA Victor SO [I] RCA Gold Seal ▲ 6510-2-RG [ADD]
O Paradiso:Great Opera Arias, w. Jussi Björling (ten), Frederick Schauwecker (pno), RCA Victor Orch [cnd:Renato Cellini], Rome Opera Orch [cnd:Erich Leinsdorf, Jonel Perlea] *(rec 1951-1959)* RCA Gold Seal ▲ 09026-68429-2 [ADD]
Sacred Music for Deep Voices, w. Singphoniker Ambitus ▲ AMB 97876
Verdi, G.:Aida, w. H. Nelli (sop), E. Gustavson (mez), G. Tucker (ten), G. Valdengo (bar), A. Toscanini (cnd), NBC SO [I] RCA Gold Seal 7-▲ 60326-2-RG (m) [ADD] 6-■ 60326-4-RG (CrO2)
Verdi, G.:Aida, w. H. Nelli (sop), E. Gustavson (mez), G. Tucker (ten), G. Valdengo (bar), A. Toscanini (cnd), NBC SO [I] RCA Gold Seal 3-▲ 60251-2-RG (m) [ADD] 2-■ 60251-4-RG (CrO2)
Verdi, G.:Pezzi sacri, w. A. Toscanini (cnd), NBC SO—No. 4 "Te Deum" [L] RCA Gold Seal 7-▲ 60326-2-RG (m) [ADD] 6-■ 60326-4-RG (CrO2)
Verdi, G.:Pezzi sacri, w. A. Toscanini (cnd), NBC SO—No. 4 "Te Deum" [L] RCA Gold Seal 2-▲ 60299-2-RG (m) [ADD] 2-■ 60299-4-RG (CrO2)
Verdi, G.:Requiem Mass, w. H. Nelli (sop), F. Barbieri (mez), G. Di Stefano (Ten), C. Siepi (b-bar), A. Toscanini (cnd), NBC SO [L] RCA Gold Seal 2-▲ 60299-2-RG (m) [ADD] 2-■ 60299-4-RG (CrO2)
Verdi, G.:Il trovatore, w. Z. Milanov (sop), F. Barbieri (mez), J. Björling (ten), L. Warren (bar), R. Cellini (cnd), RCA Victor SO [I] RCA Gold Seal ▲ 60191-2-RG [ADD] ■ 60191-4-RG (CrO2)
Verdi, G.:Il trovatore, w. Z. Milanov (sop), F. Barbieri (mez), J. Björling (ten), L. Warren (bar), R. Cellini (cnd), RCA Victor SO [I] RCA Gold Seal 2-▲ 6643-2-RG (m) [ADD] 2-■ CLK2-5377 (m)
World's Greatest Choruses, w. Rome Opera Chorus, et al. RCA Victor ▲ 09026-61241-2 ■ 09026-61241-4 (CrO2)

Robert Shaw Festival Singers
Brahms, J.:Liebeslieder Waltzes SATB, w. N. Mackenzie (pno), J. Wustman (pno) [G] *(rec Aug. 6-7, 1992)* Telarc ▲ CD 80326 [DDD]
Brahms, J.:Neue Liebeslieder Waltzes, w. N. Mackenzie (pno), J. Wustman (pno) [G] *(rec Aug. 6-7, 1992)* Telarc ▲ CD 80326 [DDD]
Brahms, J.:Songs, w. N. Mackenzie (pno), J. Wustman (pno)—7 Abendlieder [G] *(rec Aug. 6-7, 1992)* Telarc ▲ CD 80326 [DDD]

R. Shaw (cnd)
Argento, D.:I Hate & I Love, w. Timothy Sivils (perc), Joe Pereira (perc) *(rec Church of St. Pierre, Gramat, France, July 26-28, 1994)* Telarc ▲ CD 80408 [DDD]
Badings, H.:Chansons bretonnes, w. Norman Mackenzie (pno) *(rec Church of St. Pierre, Gramat, France, July 26-28, 1994)* Telarc ▲ CD 80408 [DDD]
Barber, S.:Agnus Dei *(rec St. Pierre Church, Gramat, France, July 26-28, 1994)* Telarc ▲ CD 80406 [DDD]
Britten, B.:Hymn to St. Cecilia, w. Christine Goerke (sop), Nanette Soles (mez), Matthew Pittman (ten), Leonard Ratzlaff (bass) *(rec Church of St. Pierre, Gramat, France, July 26-28, 1994)* Telarc ▲ CD 80408 [DDD]
Debussy, C.:Chansons (3) de Charles d'Orléans, w. Julie McCoy (sop), Pam Elrod (mez), Nanette Soles (mez), Charles Bruffy (ten), Leonard Ratzlaff (bass) *(rec Church of St. Pierre, Gramat, France, July 26-28, 1994)* Telarc ▲ CD 80408 [DDD]
Górecki, H.-M.:Totus tuus *(rec St. Pierre Church, Gramat, France, July 26-28, 1994)* Telarc ▲ CD 80406 [DDD]
Martin, F.:Mass *(rec St. Pierre Church, Gramat, France, July 26-28, 1994)* Telarc ▲ CD 80406 [DDD]
Pärt, A.:Magnificat-Antiphones *(rec St. Pierre Church, Gramat, France, July 26-28, 1994)* Telarc ▲ CD 80406 [DDD]
Poulenc, F.:Mass, w. D. Carter (sop) [L] Telarc ▲ CD 80236 [DDD]
Poulenc, F.:Motets (4) pour le temps de Noël [L] Telarc ▲ CD 80236 [DDD]
Poulenc, F.:Motets (4) pour un temps de pénitence [L] Telarc ▲ CD 80236 [DDD]
Poulenc, F.:Quatre petites prières de Saint François d'Assise, w. C. Cock (ten) [F] Telarc ▲ CD 80236 [DDD]
Poulenc, F.:Un Soir de neige *(rec Church of St. Pierre, Gramat, France, July 26-28, 1994)* Telarc ▲ CD 80408 [DDD]
Rachmaninoff, S.:All-Night Vigil [R] Telarc ▲ CD 80172 [DDD]
Ravel, M.:Chansons, w. Mara Bonde (sop), Nannette Soles (mez), Charles Bruffy (ten), Bruce Tammen (bass) *(rec Church of St. Pierre, Gramat, France, July 26-28, 1994)* Telarc ▲ CD 80408 [DDD]
Schoenberg, A.:Friede auf Erden *(rec St. Pierre Church, Gramat, France, July 26-28, 1994)* Telarc ▲ CD 80406 [DDD]

Sheffield Cathedral Choir
P. Crowther (cnd)
Schubert, Franz:Mass 2, w. Martin Colton (org) Herald ▲ HAVPCD 130

Shin-Yuh Kai Choir
Haydn, J.:Die Schöpfung, w. Edith Mathis (sop), Christoph Prégardien (ten), Harald Stamm (bass), M. Atzmon (cnd), World SO, Pécs Chamber Choir, Berlin Academy of Arts Chamber Choir [G] *(rec Basilica San Francesco in Assisi, as part of the IPPNW "Hiroshima Concert 1990")* BIS 2-▲ CD 493/94 [DDD]
Mahler, G.:Das Klagende Lied, w. C. Studer (sop), W. Meier (mez), R. Goldberg (ten), T. Allen (bar), G. Sinopoli (cnd), Philharmonia Orch *(rec live, Japan 1990)* Deutsche Grammophon ▲ 435382-2 [DDD]
Orff, C.:Carmina burana, w. E. Gruberova (sop), J. Aler (ten), T. Hampson (bar), S. Ozawa (cnd), Berlin PO, Berlin Cathedral Boys' Choir [G, L] Philips ▲ 422363-2 [DDD] ☐ 422363-5

Silesian Univ Choir
Fortner, J.:Quadri, w. S. Kawalla (cnd), Koszalin State PO Vienna Modern Masters ▲ VMM 3022 [DDD]
Nakamura, H.:Litaniae, w. S. Kawalla (cnd), Koszalin State PO Vienna Modern Masters ▲ VMM 3022 [DDD]
Scott, D.:Arras:A Garden of Cinema, w. S. Girardi (mez), S. Kawalla (cnd), Koszalin State PO Vienna Modern Masters ▲ VMM 3022 [DDD]
Van De Vate, N.:How Fares the Night?, w. J. Kawalla (vn), S. Kawalla (cnd), Koszalin State PO Vienna Modern Masters ▲ VMM 3025 [DDD]
Van De Vate, N.:Voices for Women, w. S. Giraldi (mez), S. Kawalla (cnd), Koszalin State PO Vienna Modern Masters ▲ VMM 3022 [DDD]
Yu, J.J.-J.:Wu-Yu, w. S. Kawalla (cnd), Koszalin State PO Vienna Modern Masters ▲ VMM 3022 [DDD]

Sinfonia Chorus
Rózsa, M.:Julius Caesar, w. B. Broughton (cnd), Sinfonia of London Intrada ▲ ITDCD 7056

Singer Pur
Singer Pur:Vocal Soloists Ensemble Ars Musici ▲ 5035

Singers Of Imperial Russia
Vol. 1, w. Singers Of Imperial Russia Pearl 3-▲ PEA 9997 (m) [AAD]
Vol. 2, w. Singers Of Imperial Russia Pearl 3-▲ PEA 9001 (m) [AAD]
Vol. 3, w. Singers Of Imperial Russia Pearl 3-▲ PEA 9004 (m) [AAD]
Vol. 4, w. Singers Of Imperial Russia Pearl 3-▲ PEA 9007 (m) [AAD]
Vol. 5, w. Singers Of Imperial Russia *(rec 1901-14)* Pearl 3-▲ PEA 9111 [ADD]

CHORAL GROUPS

Singing City Choir
Beethoven, L. van:Missa Solemnis, w. M. Arroyo (sop), M. Forrester (cta), R. Lewis (ten), C. Siepi (b–bar), E. Ormandy (cnd), Philadelphia Orch *(rec Mar. 29–30, 1967)* Sony Classical ("Essential Classics" series) ▲ SBK 53517 [ADD] ■ SBT 53517

Singing Sergeants
An American Tribute, w. Mormon Tabernacle Choir, US Air Force Band CBS ▲ MK 42133 [DDD] ■ MT 42133 (D)

Singphoniker
Lassus, O. de:Choral Music—Deutsche Lieder; Französische Chansons; Italienische Madrigale und Villanellen Calig ▲ CAL 50915
Mendelssohn, F.:Choral Music—30 songs for male voices CPO ▲ CPO 999091 [DDD]
Sacred Music for Deep Voices, w. Robert Shaw Chorale Ambitus ▲ AMB 97876
Schubert, Franz:Choral Part-Songs—Der Entfernten; Zum Rudentanz; Sehnsucht; Dessen Fahne Donnerstüme walte; Grab und Mond; Liebe Wein und Liebe; Lied im freien; Die Nacht; Das stille Lied; Leise, leise, lasst uns singen; Nachtelle; Ständchen; Psalm 23; Gott ist mein Hirt; Das Dörfchen; Trinklied; Zur guten Nacht Calig ▲ CAL 50 899 [DDD]
Schubert, Franz:Songs (misc)—Naturhenuss, D.422; Das Dörfchen, D.598; Punschlied, D.277; Trinklied, D.148; Im Gegenwärtigen Vergangenes, D.267; Der Gondelfahrer, D.809; Trinklied, D.267; Bergknappenlied, D.269; Trinklied, D.75; Die Nachtigall, D.724; Frühlingsgesang, D.740; Geist der Liebe, D.747; Bootsgesang, D.835; Trinklied, D.356; Beitrag zur 50jährigen Jubelfeier, D.407; La Pastorella, D.513; Nachthelle, D.892; Widerspruch, D.865; Mondenschein, D.875; Zur guten Nacht, D.903 *(rec Nov 1995)* CPO ▲ 999397–2 [DDD]

G. Joppich (cnd)
Gregorian Chant from St. Gall CPO ▲ CPO 999267 [DDD]

Sion Vocal Octet
Poulenc, F.:Quatre petites prières de Saint François d'Assise Doron ▲ DRC 3022 [DDD]

Sipan–Komitas Choir Petit Chanteurs of Tebrotzassere School
Aprikian, G.:Naissance de David de Sassoun, w. Fabienne Chanoyan (sop—Angel), Anna Karakaya (mez—Queen Taline), Armand Arapian (bar—King Mehèr/Priest), H. Sakssian (cnd), Bell'Arte Orch *(rec Ivry-sur-Seine, Jan 17–18, 1995)* Studio SM ▲ D2514

Sirin Choir
Spiritual Chants of the Russian People Russian Season ▲ LCD 288073

The Sixteen
Bach, J.S.:Christmas Oratorio, w. H. Stephens (cnd), The Sixteen Orch Collins Classics 2–▲ COL 7028 [DDD]
Bach, J.S.:St. John Passion, w. P. Kwella (sop), D. James (ct), W. Kendall (ten), I. Partridge (ten), M. George (bar), D. Wilson-Johnson (b–bar), H. Christophers (cnd), The Sixteen Orch [G] Chandos ("Chaconne" series) 2–▲ CHAN 0507/08 [DDD]
Britten, B.:Choral Music—Missa brevis in D; Festival te deum; Jubilate deo; Hymn to St. Peter; Hymn to the Virgin; Hymn to St. Columba; Sweet Was the Song; A New Year Carol; A Shepherd's Carol; A Ceremony of Carols Collins Classics ▲ COL 1370 [DDD]
Caldara, A.:Stabat Mater, w. H. Christophers (cnd), The Sixteen Orch [L] *(rec 10/91)* Collins Classics ▲ 13202 [DDD]
Cardoso, M.:Missa Regina caeli, w. H. Christophers (cnd), The Sixteen Orch Collins Classics ▲ COL 1407 [DDD]
Cardoso, M.:Motets, w. H. Christophers (cnd), The Sixteen Orch—Sitivit anima mea; Tulerunt lapides ut iacerent in eum; Non mortui qui sunt in inferno Collins Classics ▲ COL 1407 [DDD]
Handel, G.F.:Alexander's Feast (ode), w. N. Argenta (sop), I. Partridge (ten), M. George (bass), H. Christophers (cnd), The Sixteen Orch Collins Classics 2–▲ COL 7016 [DDD]
Handel, G.F.:Chandos Anthems (11), w. L. Dawson (sop), P. Kwella (sop), J. Bowman (alt), I. Partridge (ten), M. George (bass), H. Christophers (cnd), The Sixteen Orch Chandos ("Chaconne" series) 4–▲ CHAN 0554 [DDD]
Handel, G.F.:Chandos Anthems (11), w. L. Dawson (sop), I. Partridge (ten), H. Christophers (cnd), The Sixteen Orch—Anthem Nos. 4–6 [E] Chandos ("Chaconne" series) ▲ CHAN 0504 [DDD]
Handel, G.F.:Chandos Anthems (11), w. P. Kwella (sop), J. Bowman (ct), I. Partridge (ten), M. George (bass), H. Christophers (cnd), The Sixteen Orch—Anthem Nos. 7–9 [E] Chandos ("Chaconne" series) ▲ CHAN 0505 [DDD]
Handel, G.F.:Chandos Anthems (11), w. L. Dawson (sop), I. Partridge (ten), H. Christophers (cnd), The Sixteen Orch—Anthem Nos. 10 & 11 [E] Chandos ("Chaconne" series) ▲ CHAN 0509 [DDD]
Handel, G.F.:Chandos Anthems (11), w. L. Dawson (sop), I. Partridge (ten), M. George (bass), H. Christophers (cnd), The Sixteen Orch—Nos. 1, 2 & 3 Chandos ("Chaconne" series) ▲ CHAN 0503 [DDD]
Handel, G.F.:Dixit Dominus, w. Lynn Dawson (sop), Linda Russell (alt), Charles Brett (ct), Ian Partridge (ten), Michael George (bass), H. Christophers (cnd), The Sixteen Orch [L] Chandos ("Chaconne" series) ▲ CHAN 0517 [DDD]
Handel, G.F.:Israel in Egypt, w. H. Christophers (cnd), The Sixteen Orch *(rec 1990)* Collins Classics ▲ COL 7035 [DDD]
Handel, G.F.:Messiah, w. Marjanne Kweksilber (sop), James Bowman (ct), Paul Elliot (ten), G. Reinhart (bar), T. Koopman (cnd), Amsterdam Baroque Orch Erato 3–▲ 2292–45960–2
Handel, G.F.:Messiah, w. Lynn Dawson (sop), Catherine Denley (mez), David James (alt), Arthur Davies (ten), Michael George (bass), H. Christophers (cnd), The Sixteen Orch [20–member orchestra, 19–member chorus] [E] *(rec 1986)* Hyperion 2–▲ CDA 66251/52 [DDD]
Handel, G.F.:Nisi Dominus, w. Charles Brett (ct), Ian Partridge (ten), Michael George (bass), H. Christophers (cnd), The Sixteen Orch [L] Chandos ("Chaconne" series) ▲ CHAN 0517 [DDD]
Handel, G.F.:Silete Venti, w. Lynne Dawson (sop), H. Christophers (cnd), The Sixteen Orch [L] Chandos ("Chaconne" series) ▲ CHAN 0517 [DDD]
Lôbo, D.:Sacred Music, w. H. Christophers (cnd), Sixteen Orch Collins Classics ▲ COL 1407 [DDD]
Lotti, A.:Crucifixus, w. H. Christophers (cnd), The Sixteen Orch [L] Collins Classics ▲ 50092 [DDD]
Poulenc, F.:Choral Music—8 Chansons Francaises (1945–46) Broadway Angel ▲ CDC 59311
Poulenc, F.:Figure humaine Broadway Angel ▲ CDC 59192
Poulenc, F.:Répons des ténèbres, w. H. Christophers (cnd), BBC PO Collins Classics ▲ COL 1446 [DDD]
Purcell, H.:The Fairy Queen, w. H. Christophers (cnd), The Sixteen Orch Collins Classics 2–▲ 7013
Purcell, H.:Music for the Funeral of Queen Mary, w. H. Christophers (cnd), The Sixteen Orch Collins Classics ▲ COL 1425 [DDD]
Purcell, H.:Music of, w. H. Christophers (cnd), The Sixteen Orch—Funeral Sentences; 2 Elegies on the Death of Queen Mary; 2 Latin Motets Collins Classics ▲ COL 1425 [DDD]
A Renaissance Anthology Collins Classics 2–▲ COL 7021 [DDD]
Tippett, M.:A Child Of Our Time, w. H. Christophers (cnd), BBC PO Collins Classics ▲ COL 1446 [DDD]
Vivaldi, A.:Gloria, RV.589, w. H. Christophers (cnd), The Sixteen Orch [L] Collins Classics ▲ 13202 [DDD]

H. Christophers (cnd)
Allegri, G.:Miserere [L] Collins Classics ▲ 50092 [DDD]
Bach, J.S.:Magnificat, BWV 243 [L] *(rec Oct 1991)* Collins Classics ▲ 13202 [DDD]
Bach, J.S.:Motets, BWV 225–30 [G] Hyperion ▲ CDA 66369 [DDD]
Barber, S.:Agnus Dei Collins Classics ▲ 12872 [DDD]
Barber, S.:Reincarnation Collins Classics ▲ 12872 [DDD]
Bernstein, L.:Choruses Collins Classics ▲ 12872 [DDD]
Britten, B.:A Boy Was Born *(rec 1 & 4/91)* Collins Classics ▲ 12862 [DDD]
Britten, B.:Flower Songs *(rec 1 & 4/91)* Collins Classics ▲ 12862 [DDD]
Britten, B.:Gloriana (choral dances), w. I. Partridge (ten), H. Tunstall (hp) *(rec 1 & 4/91)* Collins Classics ▲ 12862 [DDD]
Britten, B.:Hymn to St. Cecilia, w. N. Jenkin (sop), R. Dean (sop), C. Trevor (alt), P. Daggett (ten), S. Birchall (bass) *(rec 1 & 4/91)* Collins Classics ▲ 12862 [DDD]
Byrd, W.:Gradualia seu cantionum sacrarum, liber secundus—Feast of All Saints in 5 Parts [L] Veritas ▲ VC 7 90802–2 [DDD] ■ VC 7 90802–4 (D)
Byrd, W.:Motets—two eight-part motets—Diliges Dominum; Ad Dominum cum tribularer [L] Veritas ▲ VC 7 90802–2 [DDD] ■ VC 7 90802–4 (D)

The Sixteen (cont.)
H. Christophers (cnd) (cont.)
Christmas Music from Medieval & Renaissance Europe Hyperion ▲ CDA 66263
Copland, A.:Motets (4) Collins Classics ▲ 12872 [DDD]
Daniel-Lesur, D.J.Y.:Le cantique des cantiques Collins ▲ COL 1480
del Tredici, D.:Acrostic Song, w. S. Leonard (sop) Collins Classics ▲ 12872 [DDD]
Fayrfax, R.:Aeternae laudis lilium [L] Hyperion ▲ CDA 66073
Fayrfax, R.:Missa Albanus [L] Hyperion ▲ CDA 66073
Fine, I.:The Hour Glass Collins Classics ▲ 12872 [DDD]
In Celebration of Christmas Collins Classics 2–▲ COL 7011 [DDD]
Jolivet, A.:Epithalame Collins ▲ COL 1480
Melgaz, D.D.:Choral Music—Dies Irae; Popule Meus; Lamentations Collins Classics ▲ COL 1465
Messiaen, O.:Rechants Collins ▲ COL 1480
Music from the Eton Choirbook Meridian ▲ 84175
Music from the Eton Choirbook, Vol. 1:The Rose & the Ostrich Feather Collins Classics ▲ COL 1314 [DDD]
Music from the Eton Choirbook, Vol. 2:The Crown of Thorns Collins Classics ▲ COL 1316 [DDD]
Music from the Eton Choirbook, Vol. 3:The Pillars of Eternity Collins Classics ▲ COL 1342 [DDD]
Music from the Eton Choirbook, Vol. 4:The Flower of All Virginity *(rec 1992)* Collins Classics ▲ COL 1395 [DDD]
Palestrina, G.:Missa "Papae marcelli" [L] Collins Classics ▲ 50092 [DDD]
Palestrina, G.:Stabat mater [L] Collins Classics ▲ 50092 [DDD]
Rebelo, J.S.:Choral Music—In Te Domine Spervai; Ecce Nunc; Educes Me; Qui Habitat; Speraspidem Collins Classics ▲ COL 1465
Sacred Music from Venice & Rome Collins Classics ▲ COL 1360 [DDD]
Sheppard, J.:Church Music—Aeterne Rex altissime, Christe virgo dilectissima, Dum transisset sabbatum II, Hostes Herodes impie, In manus tuas III, Te Deum, Western Wynde Mass Hyperion ▲ CDA 66603
Sheppard, J.:Sacred Choral Music—Audivi vocem de caelo; Beata nobis gaudia; Dum transisset Sabbatum; Gaude, gaude, gaude Maria; Impetum fecerunt unanimes; Libera nos, salva nos; In manus tuas; Sacris solemniis; Sancte Dei pretiose; Spiritus Sanctus procedens II [L] Hyperion ▲ CDA 66570 [DDD]
Sheppard, J.:Sacred Choral Music—Verbum caro factum est; Laudem dicite Deo; Reges Tharsis et insulae; In manus tuas Domine; Filiae Hierusalem; In pace in idipsum; Paschal Kyrie; Haec dies quam fecit Dominus; Spiritus sanctus procedens; Justi in perpetuum vivent; Libera nos, salva nos [L] Hyperion ▲ CDA 66259 [DDD]
Sheppard, J.:Sacred Choral Music—Ave maria stella; Cantate Mass; Deus tuorum militum; Jesu salvator saeculi, redemptis; Jesu salvator saeculi, verbum; Salvator mundi, Domine [L] Hyperion ▲ CDA 66418 [DDD]
Tallis, T.:Church Music—Te lucis ante terminum; O nata lux; O sacrum convivium; Jesu salvator saeculi; Salvator mundi, salva nos; Loquebantur variis linguis [L] Chandos ("Chaconne" series) ▲ CHAN 0513 [DDD]
Tallis, T.:Gaude gloriosa Dei Mater [L] Chandos ("Chaconne" series) ▲ CHAN 0513 [DDD]
Tallis, T.:The Lamentations of Jeremiah [L] Chandos ("Chaconne" series) ▲ CHAN 0513 [DDD]
Tallis, T.:Spem in alium [L] Chandos ("Chaconne" series) ▲ CHAN 0513 [DDD]
Taverner, J.:Gloria tibi Trinitas [L] Hyperion ▲ CDA 66134 [DDD]
Taverner, J.:Motets—Audivi vocem [L] Hyperion ▲ CDA 66134 [DDD]
Taverner, J.:Motets—O splendor gloriae; Te Deum; Alleluia; Veni, electa mea Hyperion ▲ CDA 66507
Taverner, J.:Sacred Music—Missa, "O Michael"; Archangeli Michaelis interventione (respond); Leroy Kyrie; Dum transisset Sabbatum (Easter respond) [L] Hyperion ▲ CDA 66325 [DDD]
Taverner, J.:Sacred Music—Missa Mater Christi sanctissima; Hodie nobis caelorum rex; Mater Christi sactissima; Magnificat a 4; Auemadmodum x 6; In nomine a 4 Hyperion ▲ CDA 66639
Taverner, J.:Western Wynde [E,L] Hyperion ▲ CDA 66507
20th Century Christmas Collection, w. Margaret Philips (org) Collins Classics ▲ COL 1270 [DDD]
Victoria, T.L. de:Tenebrae Responsories [L] Virgin Classics ▲ 59042 [DDD]

Slaska–Katowice Phil Choir
Kopelent, M.:Legend, w. K. Stryja (cnd), Slaska PO Praga ▲ PR 255003

Slavonic Voices Male Chamber Choir
Stoyanov, L.:Liturgia Solemnis, w. A. Vassilev (bass), M. Mtakiev (cnd), Varna PO [Slavonic] Koch International Classics ▲ KIC 7033–2 [DDD] ■ 3–7033–4 (D)

Slavyanka Men's Chorus
A. Shipovalnikov (cnd)
Shvedov, K.:Liturgy of St. John Chrysostom Harmonia Mundi USA ▲ HMU 907105 ■

Slavyanka Men's Chorus San Francisco
P. Andrews (cnd)
Russian Church Music Harmonia Mundi ▲ HMU 907098

Slovak Chamber Choir
Nelson, M.:Song of the Goddesses MMC ("Chamber Music" series) ▲ MMC 2010

Slovak Opera Chorus
Miaskovsky, N.:Sym 6, w. R. Stankovsky (cnd), Czech–Slovak RSO Bratislava—4th movt. [L] Marco Polo ▲ 8.223301 [DDD]
Verdi, G.:La forza del destino (sels), w. Janez Lotrič (ten), Igor Morozov (bar), J. Wildner (cnd), Slovak RSO Bratislava—Invano, Alvaro; Nè gustare m'è dato *(rec Slovak Radio Concert Hall, Bratislava, Feb. 15–24, 1994)* Naxos ▲ 8.553030 [DDD]

Slovak Phil Chorus
Bartók, B.:Hungarian Folksongs Chorus Hungaroton ▲ HCD 31047 [ADD]
Bizet, G.:Carmen, w. D. Palade (sop), G. Alperyn (mez), G. Lamberti (ten), A. Titus (bar), et al., A. Rahbari (cnd), Czech–Slovak RSO Bratislava, Bratislava Children's Choir [F] Naxos 3–▲ 8.660005/07 [DDD]
Bizet, G.:Carmen (sels), w. D. Palade (sop—Micaëla), A. Liebeck (sop—Frasquita), G. Alperyn (mez—Carmen), D. Schaechter (mez—Mercédès), G. Lamberti (ten—Don José), M. Dvorsky (ten—Remandado), J. Durco (ten—Cancairo), A. Titus (bar—Escamillo), V. Chmelo (bar—Morales), D. Rigosa (bass—Zuniga), A. Rahbari (cnd), Czech–Slovak RSO Bratislava, Bratislava Children's Choir *(rec July 1990)* Naxos ▲ 8.550727 [DDD]
Bizet, G.:Les Pêcheurs de perles, w. A. Ruffini (sop), G. Morino (ten), B. Praticò (bar), C. Piantini (cnd), Italian International Orch [F] *(rec live 7/30–8/2/90)* Nuova Era 2–▲ 6944/45 [DDD]
Brahms, J.:Ein Deutsches Requiem, w. M. Gauci (sop), E. Tumagian (bar), A. Rahbari (cnd), Czech–Slovak RSO Bratislava *(rec June 1992)* Naxos ▲ 8.550213 [DDD]
Chabrier, E.:Gwendoline, w. Adriana Kohútková (sop—Gwendoline), Gérard Garino (ten—Armel), Didier Henry (bar—Harald), J.–P. Pepin (cnd), Slovak PO, Czech Phil Chorus L'Empreinte Digitale 2–▲ ED 13059
Donizetti, G.:Maria di Rohan (sels), w. M. Nicolesco (sop), G. Morino (ten), P. Coni (bar), M. de Bernart (cnd), Italian International Opera Orch [I] *(rec live)* Nuova Era 2–▲ 6732/33 [DDD]
Famous Tenor Arias, w. Thomas Harper (ten), M. Halász (cnd), Czech–Slovak RSO Bratislava Naxos ▲ 8.550497 [DDD] Δ 7.550497 [DDD]
Holbrooke, J.:Byron, w. A. Leaper (cnd), Czech–Slovak RSO Bratislava *(rec Jan. 6–13, 1992)* Marco Polo ▲ 8.223446 [DDD]
Ibert, J.:Chant de folie, w. M. Adriano (cnd), Slovak RSO Bratislava *(rec Feb. 8–13, 1993)* Marco Polo ▲ 8.223508 [DDD]
Ibert, J.:Suite élisabéthaine, w. D. Kubrická (sop), M. Adriano (cnd), Slovak RSO Bratislava *(rec Feb. 8–13, 1993)* Marco Polo ▲ 8.223508 [DDD]
Ketèlbey, A.W.:Music of, w. A. Leaper (cnd), Czech–Slovak RSO Bratislava—In a Monastery Garden; "The Adventurers" Ov.; Chal Romano; Suite Romantique; Caprice Pianistique; The Clock and the Dresden Figures; Cockney Suite; In the Moonlight; Wedgwood Blue; Bells across the Meadow; The Phantom Melody; In a Persian Market *(rec Jan. 13–18, 1992)* Marco Polo ▲ 8.223442 [DDD]
Marschner, H.A.:Hans Heiling, w. M. Hajóssyová (sop), E. Šeniglova (sop), M. Eklöf (mez), K. Markus (ten), T. Mohr (bar), L. Neshyba (bass), E. Körner (cnd), Slovak PO [G] Marco Polo ("Opera Rara" series) 2–▲ 8.223306/07 [DDD]
Martinů, B.:The Epic of Gilgamesh, w. *(soloists unknown)*, Z. Košler (cnd), Slovak PO Marco Polo ▲ 8.223316

1014 ▲ = CD ♦ = Enhanced CD Δ = MD ■ = Cassette Tape □ = DCC

Slovak Phil Chorus (cont.)
Mercadante, S.:Il bravo, w. J. Perry (sop), A. Tabiadon (mez), D. Di Domenico (ten), S. Bertocchi (ten), S. Antonucci (bar), B. Aprea (cnd), Italian International Orch [I] *(rec live 7/28–31/90)* Nuova Era 3-▲ 6971/73 [DDD]
Mozart, W.A.:Così fan tutte, w. J. Borowska (sop—Fiordiligi), P. Coles (sop—Despina), R. Yachmi (mez—Dorabella), J. Dickie (ten—Ferrando), A. Martin (bar—Guglielmo), P. Mikulas (b-bar—Don Alfonso), J. Wildner (cnd), Capella Istropolitana [I] *(rec Feb.–Mar. 1990)* Naxos 3-▲ 8.660008/10 [DDD]
Mozart, W.A.:Così fan tutte (sels), w. Joanna Borowska (sop—Fiordiligi), Priti Coles (sop—Despina), Rohangiz Yachmi (mez—Dorabella), John Dickie (ten—Ferrando), Andrea Martin (bar—Guglielmo), Peter Mikulaš (bass—Don Alfonso), Milada Synkova (hpd), J. Wildner (cnd), Capella Istropolitana—Ov.; [Act I] La mia Dorabella capace non è; E la fede della femmine; Una bella serenata; Ah guarda, sorella; Vorrei dir, e cor non ho; Sento, o Dio; Bella vita militar!; Soave sia il vento; Smanie implacabili; In uomini, in soldati; Alla bella Despinetta; Come Scoglio; Non siate ritrosi; Un'aura amorosa; [Act II] Una donna a quindici anni; Prenderò quel brunettino; La mano a me date; Ei parte...senti...ah no!; Donne mie la fate a tanti a tanti; Fra gle amplessi; Fortunato l'uom che prende *(rec Slovak Philharmonic Moyzes Hall, Bratislava, Feb.–Apr. 1990)* Naxos ▲ 8.553172 [DDD]
Mozart, W.A.:Requiem, w. M. Hajóssyová (sop), J. Horská (cta), J. Kundlák (ten), P. Mikuláš (bass), Z. Košler (cnd), Slovak PO Naxos ▲ 8.550235 [DDD] ∆ 7.550235 [DDD]
Mussorgsky, M.:Boris Godunov, w. V. Valente (sop—Xenia), E. Gorochovskaya (mez—Nurse), L. Nichiteanu (mez—Fyodor), E. Zarmeba (mez—Hostess), M. Lipovšek (cta—Marina), P. Langridge (ten—Prince Shuisky), H. Wildhaber (ten—Misail), A. Fedin (ten—Simpleton), S. Leiferkus (bar—Rangoni), A. Kotcherga (bass—B. Godounov), A. Shagidullin (bass—Shchelkalov), S. Ramey (bass—Pimen), S. Larin (bass—Girgory), G. Nikolsky (bass—Varlaam), C. Abbado (cnd), Berlin PO, Tölz Boys' Choir, Berlin Radio Chorus *(rec Nov. 7–30, 1993)* Sony Classical 3-▲ S3K 58977 [DDD]
Mussorgsky, M.:Khovanshchina, w. M. Lipovsek (mez), V. Atlantov (ten), P. Burchuladze (bass), A. Haugland (bass), C. Abbado (cnd), Vienna State Opera Orch [Shostakovich version] [R] Deutsche Grammophon 3-▲ 429758-2 [DDD]
Orff, C.:Carmina burana, w. E. Jenisová (sop), V. Dolezal (ten), I. Kusnjer (bar), S. Gunzenhauser (cnd), Czech–Slovak RSO Bratislava Naxos ▲ 8.550196 [DDD] ∆ 7.550196 [DDD]
Perry, W.:Film Music, w. Richard Hayman (hmc), W. Perry (cnd), Rome PO, Slovak PO, Vienna SO, Vienna Boys' Choir [scores for 6 Mark Twain films originally produced for PBS in the 1980s]—Adventures of Huckleberry Finn; The Innocents Abroad; Life on the Mississippi; The Mysterious Stranger; The Private History of a Campaign That Failed; Pudd'head Wilson Premier ▲ PRCD 1015 [DDD]
Puccini, G.:La Bohème (sels), w. Luba Orgonasova (sop—Mimi), Carmen Gonzales (sop—Musetta), Jonathan Welch (ten—Rudolfo), Fabio Previati (bar—Marcello), Boaz Senator (bar—Schaunard), Ivan Urbas (bass—Colline), Jiri Sulzenko (bass—Alcindoro), W. Humburg (cnd), Czech–Slovak RSO Bratislava, Bratislava Children's Choir *(rec Concert Hall, Czecho–Slovak Radio, Bratislava, Apr. 23–May 4, 1990)* Naxos ▲ 8.553151 [DDD]
Puccini, G.:Madama Butterfly, w. M. Gauci (sop), N. Boschkowá (mez), A. Michalková (mez), Y. Ramiro (ten), A. Rahbari (cnd), Czech–Slovak RSO Bratislava [I] Naxos 2-▲ 8.660015/16 [DDD]
Puccini, G.:Tosca, w. N. Miricioiu (sop), G. Lamberti (ten), S. Carroli (bar), A. Rahbari (cnd), Czech–Slovak RSO Bratislava [I] Naxos 2-▲ 8.660001/02 [DDD]
Puccini, G.:Tosca (sels), w. Nelly Miricioiu (sop—Tosca), Giorgio Lamberti (ten—Cavaradossi), Miroslav Dvorsky (ten—Spoletta), Silvano Carroli (bar—Baron Scarpia), Jozef Spaček (bass—Sacristan), Jan Durco (bass—Sciarrone), Stanislav Benačka (bass—Gaoler), A. Rahbari (cnd), Czech–Slovak RSO Bratislava *(rec Concert Hall of the Slovak Radio, Bratislava, Apr. 7–14, 1990)* Naxos ▲ 8.553153 [DDD]
Respighi, O.:La Primavera, w. Henrietta Lednárová (sop—Prima fanciulla), Jana Valásková (sop—Sirvard), Beata Geriová (mez—Seconda fanciulla), Miroslav Dvorský (ten—Il giovine), Richard Haan (bar—L'orante), Vladimír Kubovčík (bass—Il vecchio), Vera Rasková (fl), M. Adriano (cnd), Slovak RSO Bratislava *(rec Slovak Radio Concert Hall, Bratislava, Jan. 4–9, Feb. 19 & June)* Marco Polo ▲ 8.223595 [DDD]
Rossini, G.:Arias, w. E. Palacio (ten), C. Rizzi (cnd), Bratislava RSO—8 Cantata Arias (1808–1824)—Pianto di Armonia sulla morte di Orfeo; Dolci aurette che spirate; La mia pace io già perdei; Se ostinata ancor non cedi; Giusto cielo i voti miei; Guidò Marte i nostri passi; Il pianto delle Muse in morte di Lord Byron [I] Arkadia–Akademia ▲ 109 [DDD]
Shostakovich, D.:Sym 2, w. L. Slovák (cnd), Czech–Slovak RSO Bratislava *(rec Jan. 10, 1990)* Naxos ▲ 8.550624 [DDD]
Shostakovich, D.:Sym 3, w. L. Slovák (cnd), Czech–Slovak RSO Bratislava *(rec Nov. 20–26, 1990)* Naxos ▲ 8.550623 [DDD]
Shostakovich, D.:Sym 13, w. P. Mikulaš (bass), L. Slovák (cnd), Czech–Slovak RSO Bratislava Naxos ▲ 8.550630 [DDD]
Strauss (II), Joh.:Music of, w. J. Cohen (cnd), Slovak RSO Bratislava—Polka mazurka champêtre; Manhattan Waltzes; Centennial Waltzes; Enchantment Waltzes; Idylle 'Auf der Alm'; Engagement Waltzes; Farewell to America; Romance 2 Vc [w. Ivan Tvrdik (vc)]; Liebesbotschaft–Galopp; Tauben–walzer; Promenade–Abenteuer; Bauersleut'im Künstlerhaus; D'Hauptsach; Entr'acte from Fürstin Ninetta; An der schönen, blauen Donau *(rec Slovak Radio Concert Hall, Apr 1996)* Marco Polo ▲ 8.223279 [DDD]
Verdi, G.:Rigoletto, w. A. Ferrarini (sop), Y. Ramiro (ten), E. Tumagian (bar), J. Spaček (bar), A. Rahbari (cnd), Czech–Slovak RSO Bratislava [I] Naxos 2-▲ 8.660013/14 [DDD]
Verdi, G.:La traviata, w. R. Braga (mez), R. Krause (ten), Y. Ramiro (ten), A. Rahbari (cnd), Czech–Slovak RSO Bratislava [I] Naxos 2-▲ 8.660011/12 [DDD]

L. Mátl (cnd)
Berlioz, H.:Requiem, "Grande Messe des Morts", w. Jean–Luc Viala (ten), A. Lombard (cnd), Bordeaux–Aquitaine National Orch, Prague Phil Chorus Forlane ▲ FRL 16639 [DDD]

J. Rozehnal (cnd)
Respighi, O.:La bella dormente nel bosco, w. Ivana Czaková (sop—Old Woman/Green Fairy), Adriana Kohútková (sop—Blue Fairy/Nightingale), Henrietta Lednárová (sop—Frog/Spindle), Jana Valásková (sop—Princess), Dagmar Pecková (mez—Cuckoo/Cat), Denisa Šlepkovská (mez—Queen/Duchess), Karol Bernáth (ten—Doctor), Guillermo Dominguez (ten—Prince April), Igor Pasek (ten—Jester), Ján Durčo (bar—Ambassador), Richard Haan (bar—King/Woodcutter), Stanislav Benačka (bass—Doctor), Anton Kúrnava (bass—Doctor), Marián Smolárik (bass—Doctor), M. Adriano (nar—Mr. Dollar Chèques), M. Adriano (cnd), Slovak RSO Bratislava *(rec Concert Hall of the Slovak Radio, Bratislava, June 8–20, 1994)* Marco Polo ("Opera Classics" series) ▲ 8.223742 [DDD]
Verdi, G.:La traviata (sels), w. Monika Krause (sop), Ivica Neshybová (sop), Rannveig Braga (mez), Yordy Ramiro (ten), Gerog Tichy (bar), Ladislav Neshyba (bass), Jozef Spaček (bass), A. Rahbari (cnd), Czech–Slovak RSO Bratislava—Prelude act I; Libiam ne'lieti calici; Un dì, felice; E stranol Ah, fors'e lui; Follie!...sempre libera; Lunge da lei...de'miei bollenti spiriti; O Mio rimorosol; Pura si come un angelo...Dite alla giovine; Dammi tu forza; Di Provenza il mar; Noi siamo zingarelle; Prelude act III; Teneste la promessa...Addio del passato; Signora! Che t'accade?; Ah, Violettal *(rec Bratislava Concert Hall, Dec 1990)* Naxos ▲ 8.553041 [DDD]

Slovak Radio Chorus
Levy, F.E.:Sym 4, "Structures of the Mind", w. R. Stankovsky (cnd), Slovak RSO Bratislava *(rec Slovak Radio & Television Studios)* Master Musicians Collective ▲ MMC 2021 [DDD]
Packales, J.:I Was on the Sea, w. R. Stankovsky (cnd), Slovak RSO Bratislava *(rec Slovak Radio & Television Studios)* Master Musicians Collective ▲ MMC 2021 [DDD]
Vali, R.:Persian Folk Songs, w. Wendy Kallen (sop), R. Black (cnd), Slovak RSO Bratislava *(rec Slovak Radio & Television Studios)* Master Musicians Collective ▲ MMC 2021 [DDD]
Verdi, G.:Choruses, w. O. Dohnányi (cnd), Slovak RSO—from Aida, Battaglia di Legnano, Don Carlos, Ernani, Forza del destino, Macbeth, Nabucco, Otello, Traviata, Trovatore [I] Naxos ▲ 8.550241 [DDD] ∆ 7.550241 [DDD]

Sluk Chamber Chorus Bratislava
Cherubini, L.:Médée, w. Jano Tamar (sop), Patrizia Ciofi (sgr), Luca Lombardo (sgr), Magali Damonte (sgr), Jean–Philippe Courtis (bass), P. Fournillier (cnd), Italian International Opera Orch *(rec Martina Franca Festival, 1995)* Nuova Era 2-▲ NUO 7253

Sluk Chamber Chorus Bratislava (cont.)
Rossini, G.:La pietra del paragone, w. Tiziana Carraro (sop—Fulvia), Elisabetta Gutierrez (mez—Baronessa Aspasia), Sara Mingardo (cta—Clarice), William Matteuzzi (ten—Giocondo), Marco Camastra (bar—Pacuvio), Pietro Spagnoli (bar—Conte Asdrubale), Gioacchino Zarrelli (bar—Fabrizio), José Fardilha (bass—Macrobio), B. Aprea (cnd), Graz SO *(rec 1993)* Bongiovanni 2-▲ GB 2179/80 [DDD]

Gregg Smith Singers
America Sings:The Founding Years, Vol. 1 Vox Box 2-▲ CDX 5080 [ADD]
Barber, S.:A Hand of Bridge, w. C. Aks (sop), F. Kittelson (mez), W. Carney (ten), R. Muenz (bass), Adirondack CO [E] Premier ▲ PRCD 1009 [ADD]
Billings, W.:Anthems & Fuguing Tunes, w. G. Smith (cnd), Adirondack CO—Chester; Be Glad Then America; Hopkinton; When Jesus Wept; The Lord Is Risen; A Virgin Unspotted; Boston; The Shepherd's Carol; I Am the Rose of Sharon; David's Lamentation; The Bird; Kittery; Cobham; Morpheus; Swift as an Indian Arrow Flies; Connection; Consonance; Jargon; Modern Music Premier ▲ PRCD 1008 [ADD]
Blitzstein, M.:The Harpies, w. R. Rees (sop), T. Bogdan (ten), E. Najera (bar), et al., G. Smith (cnd), Adirondack CO [E] Premier ▲ PRCD 1009 [ADD]
Duckworth, W.E.:Southern Harmony, w. Bucknell Rooke Chapel Choir Lovely Music ▲ LCD 2033 [ADD]
Fine, I.:Choral Music, w. R. Beegle (cnd)—Alice In Wonderland, Series 1 & 2 (1942 & 1953); The Hour–Glass (1949); McCord's Menagerie (1957) [E] *(originally released on CRI SD 376)* CRI ▲ CD 630 [ADD]
Gabrieli, G.:Choral Music, w. E. P. Biggs (org), Texas Boys' Choir—7 Intonazioni d'organo; 7 Motets; 3 Mass Movements; Sonata in the 9th tone for 8 parts *(rec St. Mark's Basilica, Venice 1967)* CBS ▲ MK 42645 [ADD]
Gabrieli, G.:Sacred Music, w. E. P. Biggs (org), Edward Tarr Brass Ensemble, La Fenice Ensemble, Texas Boys' Choir—Deus, in nomine tuo; Beata es, virgo Maria; Juilemus singuli; Deus, Deus meus, ad te de luce vigilo; O quam suavis est; Kyrie; Sanctus; Benedictus; Cantate Domino; Domine, exuadi orationem meam; Hodie completi sunt; Magnificat; Surrexit Christus; Nunc dimittis; Jubilate Deo; Intonatio *(rec San Marco, Venice, Sept 14–22, 1967)* Sony Classical ("Essential Classics" series) ▲ SBK 62426 [ADD] ■ SBT 62426
The Great Sentimental Age, w. New York Vocal Arts Ensemble Vox Box 2-▲ CDX 5016 [ADD]
Ives, C.:Songs, w. L. Stokowski (cnd), American SO, Ithaca College Concert Choir—Election (It Strikes Me That); Lincoln, the Great Commoner; Majority (or The Masses); They are there! (A War Song March) [E] *(rec 1967)* Sony Masterworks ("Portrait" series) ▲ MPK 46726 [ADD]
Monteverdi, C.:Vespro della Beata Vergine, w. Gloria Prosper (sop), Adrienne Albert (mez), Melvin Brown (ten), Richard Levitt (ten), Archi Drake (bass), R. Craft (cnd), Columbia Baroque Ensemble, Texas Boys' Choir Sony Classical ("Essential Classics" series) 2-▲ SB2K 62656
Schuman, W.:The Mighty Casey, w. R. Rees (sop), T. Bogdan (ten), R. Muenz (b-bar), W. Schuman (cnd), Adirondack CO, Long Island Choral Association [E] Premier ▲ PRCD 1009 [ADD]
Smith, Gregg:The Continental Harmonist Ballet, w. G. Smith (cnd), Adirondack CO Premier ▲ PRCD 1008 [ADD]
Smith, Gregg:Magnificat, w. R. Rees (sop), G. Smith (cnd), Adirondack CO, Adirondack Festival Chorus Premier ("Composer" series) ▲ PRCD 1020 [ADD/DDD]
Smith, Gregg:Prayer for Peace, w. G. Smith (cnd), Adirondack CO, Adirondack Children's Choir, Adirondack Festival Chorus Premier ("Composer" series) ▲ PRCD 1020 [ADD/DDD]
Smith, Gregg:Vars on a Bach Chorale, w. G. Smith (cnd), Adirondack CO, Adirondack Festival Chorus Premier ("Composer" series) ▲ PRCD 1020 [ADD/DDD]
Songs of Humor & Satire:American Choral, Vol. 1 Premier ▲ PRCD 1030 [ADD/DDD]
Stravinsky, I.:Cant Sop, w. Catherine Ciesinski (mez), Jon Humphries (ten), R. Craft (cnd), Orch of St. Luke MusicMasters ▲ 01612-67158-2
Stravinsky, I.:Choral Music, w. R. Craft (cnd), Orch of St. Luke—Russian Peasant Choruses; Russian Sacred Choruses MusicMasters ▲ 01612-67086-2
Stravinsky, I.:L'Histoire du soldat, w. Catherine Ciesinski (mez), Jon Humphries (ten), David Evitts (bar), Mark Wait (pno), R. Craft (cnd), Orch of St. Luke MusicMasters ▲ 01612-67152-2
Stravinsky, I.:King of the Stars, w. R. Craft (cnd), Orch of St. Luke MusicMasters ▲ 01612-67103-2
Stravinsky, I.:Les Noces, w. R. Craft (cnd), Orch of St. Luke MusicMasters ▲ 01612-67086-2
Stravinsky, I.:Perséphone, w. I. Jacob (nar), J. Aler (ten), R. Craft (cnd), Orch of St. Luke, Newark Boys' Chorus MusicMasters ▲ 01612-67103-2
Talma, L.:Voices of Peace, w. Rosalind Rees (sop), Scott Whittaker (ten), Charles Robert Stevens (bar), G. Smith (cnd), Adirondack CO Vox Box ("The American Composers" series) 3-▲ CDX 3037

G. Bragg (cnd)
A Ceremony of Carols, w. Dorothy Shaw Hand Bell Choir, Fort Worth Chamber Ensemble, Texas Boys Choir Allegretto ▲ ACD 8407 [ADD]

E. London (cnd)
London, E.:Auricles Apertures Ventricles *(rec Church of the Holy Trinity, New York City)* New World ▲ 80477-2

G. Smith (cnd)
Garcia, O.J.:On the Eve of the 2nd Year Anniversary of Morton's Death, w. O.O. Discs ▲ OO 6 [DDD]
Gould, M.:Choral Music—Of Time & the River (1945); Quotations (1984); Tolling (1988); Solfegging (1988) Koch International Classics ▲ KIC 7026-2 [DDD] ■ 3-7026-4 (D)
Gould, M.:Of Time & the River Koch Schwann ▲ KIC CD 7380
Rorem, N.:Give All To Love, w. Ned Rorem (pno) Vox Box ("The American Composers" series) 3-▲ CDX 3037
Rorem, N.:In Time of Pestilence Vox Box ("The American Composers" series) 3-▲ CDX 3037
Rorem, N.:Letters from Paris, Adirondack CO Vox Box ("The American Composers" series) 3-▲ CDX 3037
Rorem, N.:Missa Brevis, w. Rosalind Rees (sop), Priscilla Magdamo (alt), Lin Garber (bar) Vox Box ("The American Composers" series) 3-▲ CDX 3037
Schnabel, A.:Dance & Secret & Joy & Peace, w. P. Zukovsky (cnd), New York City Free–Lance Orch *(rec BMG Studio A, New York City, Feb 1993)* CP² ▲ CP² 110 [DDD]
Schuman, W.:Carols of Death Vox Box ("The American Composers" series) 3-▲ CDX 3037
Schuman, W.:Esses:Short Suite for Singers on Words Beginning with S, w. Rosalind Rees (sop), Leslie Dorsey (bass) Vox Box ("The American Composers" series) 3-▲ CDX 3037
Schuman, W.:5 Rounds on Famous Words Vox Box ("The American Composers" series) 3-▲ CDX 3037
Schuman, W.:Mail Order Madrigals Vox Box ("The American Composers" series) 3-▲ CDX 3037
Schuman, W.:Orpheus & His Lute, w. Rosalind Rees (sop), Dwana Holroyd (pno) Vox Box ("The American Composers" series) 3-▲ CDX 3037
Schuman, W.:Perceptions, w. Rosalind Rees (sop) Vox Box ("The American Composers" series) 3-▲ CDX 3037
Schuman, W.:Prelude, w. Rosalind Rees (sop) Vox Box ("The American Composers" series) 3-▲ CDX 3037
Talma, L.:La Corona Vox Box ("The American Composers" series) 3-▲ CDX 3037
Talma, L.:The Leaden Echo & the Golden Echo, w. Eleanor Clark (sop), Jonathan Sherry (pno) Vox Box ("The American Composers" series) 3-▲ CDX 3037
Talma, L.:Let's Touch the Sky, w. Rebecka Troxler (fl), Gerard Reuter (ob), Peter Simmons (bn) Vox Box ("The American Composers" series) 3-▲ CDX 3037
Talma, L.:A Wreath of Blessings, w. Gina Scaggs (sop), April Lindevald (alt), Drew Martin (ten), Leslie Dorsey (bass) Vox Box ("The American Composers" series) 3-▲ CDX 3037
A World of Folksong, w. Texas Boys' Choir, Dorthy Shaw Bell Choir, Texas Little Sym *(rec Nov. 1981)* Premier ▲ PRCD 1031 [ADD]

Smithsonian Chamber Chorus
Bach, J.S.:St. John Passion, w. J. Baird (sop), J. Bryden (sop), J. Thomas (ten), D. Ripley (bar), J. Weaver (bass), K. Slowik (cnd), Smithsonian Chamber Players [period instruments] [G] *(Slowik performs the original 1724 version, & includes the two choruses & three arias added to Bach's 1725 revision as appended tracks at the end of the discs, allowing the listener to either ignore the end tracks & hear the standard version or program the discs to play the 1725 sequence)* Smithsonian Collection 5-▲ ND 0380 [DDD]

CHORAL GROUPS

Sofia Boys' Choir
Pergolesi, G.B.:Stabat mater, w. T. Gabrovska (sop), H. Angelakova (alt), A. Blagoeva (cnd), New CO — Gega ▲ GD 153 [DDD]
A. Blagoeva (cnd)
Britten, B.:Missa brevis, w. T. Atanassov (sop), M. Alexandrova (sop), A. Atanassov (org) [arr. A. Blagoeva for sopranos, organ & boy's chorus] — Gega ▲ GD 153 [DDD]
Sofia Choir of Priests
K. Popov (cnd)
Orthodox Chants for Lent & Easter, — Jade ▲ JAD C 086
Sofia Madrigal
S. Kralev (cnd)
Gesualdo, D.C.:Madrigals, w. V. Kissyova (sop), N. Pankova (sop), A. Bovarian (alt), V. Vassilev (ten), K. Mirinski (bass)—Io tacerò; Invan dunque o crudele; Moro lasso al mio duolo; Dolcissima mia vita — Gega ▲ GD 174 [DDD]
Nikolaev-Stroumsky, A.:Liturgy — Gega ▲ GD 178
Schütz, H.:Motets (misc), w. V. Kissyova (sop), A. Ivanova (sop), N. Pankova (sop), A. Bovarian (alt), V. Vassilev (ten), K. Mirinski (bass)—Christe Deus adjuva; Verbum caro factum est; Te Christe supplex invoco; Veni redemtor gentium; Veni sancte Spiritus — Gega ▲ GD 174 [DDD]
Sofia National Opera Chorus
Borodin, A.:Prince Igor, w. S. Evstatieva (sop), A. Milcheva (mez), B. Martinovich (b-bar), N. Ghiaurov (bass), N. Ghiuselev (bass), E. Tchakarov (cnd), Sofia Festival Orch [R] — Sony Classical 3-▲ S3K 44878 [DDD]
Glinka, M.:A Life for the Tsar, w. A. Pendachanska (sop), S. Toczyska (mez), C. Merritt (ten), B. Martinovich (bass), E. Tchakarov (cnd), Sofia Festival Orch [R] — Sony Classical 3-▲ S3K 46487 [DDD]
Mussorgsky, M.:Boris Godunov, w. S. Mineva (mez—Marina), M. Svetlev (ten—Gregory), N. Ghiaurov (bass—Boris), N. Ghiuselev (bass—Pimen), E. Tchakarov (cnd), Sofia Festival Orch [R] — Sony Classical ("Russian Opera" series) 3-▲ S3K 45763
Mussorgsky, M.:Khovanshchina, w. A. Miltcheva (mez), M. Popov (ten), K. Kaludov (ten), Z. Gadjev (bass), N. Ghiaurov (bass), N. Ghiuselev (bass), E. Tchakarov (cnd), Sofia National Opera Orch — Sony Classical 3-▲ S3K 45831
Rimsky-Korsakov, N.:Golden Cockerel, w. Yavora Stoilova (sop—Golden Cockerel), Elena Stoyanova (sop—Queen), Evgenia Babacheva (mez—Amelfa), Lyubomir Bodourov (ten—Prince), Lyubomir Dyakovski (ten—Astrologer), Emil Ugrinov (bar—Afron), Nikolai Stoilov (bass—Tsar), Kosta Videv (bass—Polkan), D. Manolov (cnd), Sofia National Opera Orch *(rec Sofia, 1985)* — Capriccio 2-▲ 10760/61 [DDD]
Tchaikovsky, P.:Eugene Onegin, w. A. Tomowa-Sintow (sop), R. Troava-Mircheva (cta), N. Gedda (ten), Y. Mazurok (bar), N. Ghiuselev (bass), E. Tchakarov (cnd), Sofia Festival Orch [R] — Sony Classical 2-▲ S2K 45539 [DDD]
Verdi, G.:Requiem Mass, w. Maria Belcheva (sop), Stefka Mineva (mez), Roumen Doykov (ten), Dimiter Petkov (bass), P. Tiboris (cnd), Sofia National Opera Orch *(rec Bulgarian National Radio Studio, Mar 14-17, 1994)* — Elysium ▲ GRK 708 [DDD]
Verdi, G.:Requiem Mass, w. Anna Tomowa-Sintow (sop), Agnes Baltsa (mez), José Carreras (ten), José Van Dam (bass-bar), H. von Karajan (cnd), Vienna PO, Vienna State Opera Chorus *(rec Great Hall, Musikverein, Vienna, June 1984)* — Deutsche Grammophon 2-▲ 439033-2 [DDD]
Sofia State Chorus
Beethoven, L. van:Mass, Op. 86, w. C. Iliev (cnd), Sofia State PO [L] — Vivace ▲ E 567 [ADD]
Beethoven, L. van:Mass, Op. 86, w. E. Markova (sop), L. Parachikova (cta), C. Kamenev (ten), I. Petrov (bass), C. Iliev (cnd), Sofia State PO [L] — Musique d'Abord ▲ HMA 190109 [AAD]
Verdi, G.:Requiem Mass, w. Wiener-Chenisheva (sop), A. Milcheva-Nonova (mez), L. Bodourov (ten), N. Ghiuselev (bass), I. Marinov (cnd), Sofia State PO [L] — Vivace 3-▲ E 326 [ADD]
Sofia Sym Chorus
Bach, J.S.:Christmas Oratorio (sels), w. E. Lanev (cnd), Sofia SO — RS Applausi ▲ 6367-220
Soli Deo Gloria Cantorum
Arvo:the Magnificat — Soli Deo Gloria ▲ SDG CD941
Berkey, J.:The Mountains & the Sea, w. Jackson Berkey (kbd) — SDG ▲ SDGCD 92
I Solisti del Madrigale
Monteverdi, C.:Madrigals, w. G. Acciai (cnd)—Madrigals à 5:Book Four, 1603 [I] — Nuova Era ("Ancient Music" series) ▲ 7006 [DDD]
G. Acciai (cnd)
Monteverdi, C.:Madrigals (book 6) — Nuova Era ("Ancient Music" series) ▲ NUO 7165 [DDD]
Solvguttene Boys' Choir
Norwegian Christmas Carols — Norway Music ▲ ACD 1923
Sønderborg St. Marie Church Motet Choir
Nielsen, C.:Cant for Centenary of Merchants, w. J. Frandsen (cnd), South Jutland SO—Danmark, i tusind år *(rec "Musikhuset", DK-Sønderborg, 1982)* — Paula ▲ PACD 18 [DAD]
Song Company
R. Peelman (cnd)
Bremner, A.:In the Shrubbery, w. Judy Glen (nar), David Miller (pno), Gerard Willems (pno), Philip South (perc) *(rec Studio 200, ABC Ultimo Centre, Apr 1993)* — Tall Poppies ▲ TP 064 [DDD]
Cronin, S.:Carmina Pul — Vox Australis ▲ VAST 016
Edwards, R.:Flower Songs *(rec Studio 200 ABC, Apr 1993)* — Tall Poppies ▲ TP 51 [DDD]
Edwards, R.:Flower Songs, w. David Hewitt (perc), Philip South (perc) *(rec Studio 200, ABC Ultimo Centre, Apr 1993)* — Tall Poppies ▲ TP 064 [DDD]
Ford, A.:The Laughter of Mermaids — Vox Australis ▲ VAST 016
Greenbaum, S.:Upon the Dark Water *(rec Studio 200, ABC Ultimo Centre, Apr 1993)* — Tall Poppies ▲ TP 064 [DDD]
Schultz, Andrew:The Song of Songs—Ekstasis — Vox Australis ▲ VAST 016
Wesley-Smith, M.:Who Killed Cock Robin? *(rec Studio 200, ABC Ultimo Centre, Apr 1993)* — Tall Poppies ▲ TP 064 [DDD]
Wesley-Smith, M.:Who Stopped the Rain? *(rec Studio 200, ABC Ultimo Centre, Apr 1993)* — Tall Poppies ▲ TP 064 [DDD]
Whitehead, Gillian:The Virgin & the Nightingale — Vox Australis ▲ VAST 016
Whiticker, M.:As Water Bears Salt — Vox Australis ▲ VAST 016
Sons of Thunder
Visions from the Book, w. Sequentia *(rec Campion Center, Weston, MA, Nov 13-17, 1994)* — Deutsche Harmonia Mundi ▲ 05472-77347-2 [DDD]
Sotto Voce Vocal Ensemble
Klein, G.:Original Sin, w. Julian Pike (ten) — Arion ▲ ARN 68272 [DDD]
South African Broadcasting Corp National Chamber Choir
Dijk, P.L. van:San Gloria, w. R. Cock (cnd), South African Broadcasting Corp National SO *(rec Radio Park, Johannesburg, Jan 1995)* — Marco Polo ▲ 8.223832 [DDD]
South German Madrigal Choir
Bach, J.S.:Magnificat, BWV 243, w. Helen Donath (sop), Gundula Bernát-Klein (sop), Birgit Finnilä (alt), Peter Schreier (ten), Barry McDaniel (bass), W. Gönnenwein (cnd), German Bach Soloists [E♭ version] *(rec Stuttgart Radio, 1966)* — Bayer ▲ 100081 [ADD]
Bach, J.S.:St. John Passion (sels), w. Brigitte Fassbaender (cta), W. Gönnenwein (cnd), Consortium Musicum—Es ist vollbracht; Ruht wohl, ihr heiligen Gebeine *(rec Eglise de Schwaigern, Oct. 1969)* — EMI Classics ▲ CDK 65334 [ADD]
Bach, J.S.:St. Matthew Passion (sels), w. Theo Altmeyer (ten), W. Gönnenwein (cnd), Consortium Musicum—Ich will bei meinem Jesu wachen; Kommt, ihr Töchter *(rec Eglise de Schwaigern, May & Jun. 1968)* — EMI Classics ▲ CDK 65334 [ADD]
Haydn, J.:Die Jahreszeiten, w. Helen Donath (sop), A. Kraus (ten), Kurt Widmer (bass), W. Gönnenwein (cnd), Ludwigsburg Festival Orch [G] — Vox Box 2-▲ CDX 5045 [ADD]
Haydn, J.:Die Schöpfung, w. Helen Donath (sop), Scherr (alt), Adalbert Kraus (ten),Kurt Widmer (bass), W. Gönnenwein (cnd), Ludwigsburg Festival Orch [G] — Vox Box 2-▲ CDX 5025 [ADD]
Verdi, G.:I masnadieri, w. M. Rowland (sgr), M. Malagnini (sgr), T. Migliorini (sgr), R. Bruson (bar), M. Lanskoy (bar), C. Colombara (bass), W. Gönnenwein (cnd), Ludwigsburg Festival Orch — Bayer 2-▲ BR 500 001/2 [DDD]

South German Radio Chorus
Ruzicka, P.:Sinf for 25, w. M. Gielen (cnd), Stuttgart RSO — CPO ▲ CPO 999053 [DDD]
Verdi, G.:Requiem Mass, w. M. Stader (sop), M. Höffgen (cta), F. Wunderlich (ten), G. Frick (bass), H. Müller-Kray (cnd), South German RSO *(rec live, Stuttgart, 11/2/60)* — Myto 2-▲ 2 MCD 91648 [ADD]
Zinsstag, G.:Trauma, w. M. Bair-Ivenz, M. Gerbert, G. Schatz, K. M. Ziegler *(rec April 14, 1981)* — Grammont ▲ CTSP 36-2 [ADD]
South Swiss Radio Chorus
Schubert, Franz:Fierrabras, w. H. Plümacher (cta), F. Wunderlich (ten), R. Wolansky (bar), O. von Rohr (bass), H. Müller-Kray (cnd), Bern State Orch, Berlin RIAS Chamber Choir—abridged performance *(rec 1959)* — Myto ▲ MCD 89001 [ADD]
South Westphalian Chorus
Cherubini, L.:Requiem Mass in c, w. H. Ermert (cnd), South Westphalian PO [L] — Koch Schwann ▲ 3-1346-2 [DDD]
Southend Boys' Choir
The Best of Richard Hickox, w. R. Hickox (cnd), London SO, London Sym Chorus, Penelope Walmsley-Clark (sop), John Graham-Hall (ten), D. Maxwell (bar), London Voices — IMP Classics 3-▲ TCD 1073 [DDD]
Britten, B.:Spring Sym, w. E. Gale (sop), A. Hodgson (cta), M. Hill (ten), R. Hickox (cnd), London SO, London Sym Chorus [E] — Chandos ▲ CHAN 8855 [DDD]
Britten, B.:Spring Sym, w. Eiddwen Harrhy (sop), Linda Finnie (cta), Robert Tear (ten), G. Rozhdestvensky (cnd), BBC SO, BBC Sym Chorus, London Voices — IMP ("BBC Radio Classics" series) ▲ IMP 5691752
Mahler, G.:Sym 8, w. S. Jo (sop), C. Studer (sop), W. Meier (mez), K. Lewis (ten), T. Allen (bar), H. Sotin (bass), G. Sinopoli (cnd), Philharmonia Orch, Philharmonia Chorus [G] — Deutsche Grammophon 2-▲ 435433-2
Orff, C.:Carmina burana, w. Norma Burrowes (sop), Louis Devos (ten), John Shirley-Quirk (bar), A. Dorati (cnd), Royal PO, Brighton Festival Chorus *(rec Kingsway Hall, London, Feb 1976)* — London ("Phase 4 Stereo" series) ▲ 444105-2 [ADD]
Orff, C.:Carmina burana, w. S. Jo (sop), J. Kowalski (alt), B. Skovhus (bar), Z. Mehta (cnd), London PO, London Phil Choir — Teldec ▲ 74886-2
Southern Baptist Theological Seminary Chorus
Barber, S.:Prayers of Kierkegaard, w. G. Capone (sop), J. Mester (cnd), Louisville Orch [E], 1977) — Albany ▲ TROY 021-2 [AAD]
Southwark Cathedral Choir
Great Cathedral Anthems, Vol. 3, w. Stephen Layton (org) — Priory ▲ PRI 435 [DDD]
Southwest German Radio Children's Choir
P. Holstein (cnd)
An Old World Christmas, w. Württemberg CO [cnd:Jrg Faerber] — Vox 90s ■ V9-9901
Southwest German Radio Chorus
Liszt, F.:A Faust Sym, w. F. Koch (ten), J. Horenstein (cnd), Southwest German RSO Baden-Baden *(rec 1950s)* — Vox Box ("Legends" series) 2-▲ CDX2 5504 [ADD]
Mozart, W.A.:Missa, K.427, w. Arleen Augér (sop), Heather Harper (sop), Horst Lubenthal (ten), Ulrik Cold (bass), S. Celibidache (cnd), Stuttgart RSO, Bavarian Radio Chorus *(rec live, 1980's)* — Topazio ▲ TOP 26045
Rossini, G.:Stabat Mater, w. Daniela Dessi (sop), Lucia Mazzaria (sop), Gloria Scalchi (mez), Pietro Ballo (ten), Chris Merritt (ten), Anatoli Kotscherga (bass), Roberto Scandiuzzi (bass), G. Gelmetti (cnd), Stuttgart RSO, North German Radio Chorus — Serenissima 2-▲ SER 360155 [DDD]
Verdi, G.:Requiem Mass, w. Lucia Mazzaria (sop), Daniela Dessi (sop), Gloria Scalchi (mez), Pietro Ballo (ten), Chris Merritt (ten), Anatoli Kotscherga (bass), Roberto Scandiuzzi (bass), G. Gelmetti (cnd), Stuttgart RSO, North German Radio Chorus — Serenissima 2-▲ SER 360155 [DDD]
Souvenirs de Venise [Felicity Lott, Ann Murray, Anthony Rolfe Johnson, Richard Jackson]
The Songmakers' Almanac, w. Graham Johnson (pno), et al. — Hyperion ▲ CDA 66112 [DDD]
Soviet Army Chorus
Soviet Army Chorus & Band, w. Soviet Army Band — EMI Classics ▲ CDC 47833
Soviet Cinema Chorus
Karetnikov, N.:Till Eulenspiegel, w. E. Mazo (sop), L. Mkrtchian (cta), A. Proujanski (ten), B. Koudriavtsev (bar), P. Glouboky (bass), A. Motchalov (bass), A. Martinov (sgr), Polianski (cnd), Soviet Cinema Orch *(rec Moscow, 1988)* — Russian Season ("Russian Season" Series) 2-▲ LDC 288029/30 [DDD]
Spain Schola Antiqua
L.S. de Buruaga (cnd)
Mozarabic Chant — Jade ▲ JAD C 122
Spandau Kantorei Berlin
M. Behrmann (cnd)
Dramatic Gospel Motets, w. Cappella Vocale Hamburg — Hänssler Classic ▲ CD 98.948 [DDD]
Spanish National Radio Chorus
Lehár, F.:Eva, w. J. Granados (sop—Prunelles), A. M. Olaria (sop—Eva), A. Kraus (ten—Octavio Flaubert), L. de Cordoba (sgr—Gipsy), S. Ramalle (sgr—Dagoberto), J. Peromingo (sgr—Voisin), E. Estella (cnd), Madrid CO [Sp] — Montilla ▲ CDFM 2036
Zarzuela Anthology, Vol. 2, w. Madrid CO — Montilla ▲ MNT 3023
Spratling Choir
Spratling, H.:Choral Music, w. Tracey Chadwell (sop), Susan Bullock (sop), Jeffery Dyball (hp), Helen Tunstall (hp), John Hatton (org), J. Rennert (cnd), Parnassus String Ensemble—Mass of the Holy Spirit; O Salutaris Hostia; Tantum Ergo; Sinf Str Orch; Son Hp; O Magnum Mysterium; In Paradisum *(rec St. Mary Magdelene, Paddington, May 15-17, 1988)* — SOMM ▲ SOMMCD 206 [ADD]
La Stagione Choir
Haydn, J.:L'Anima del filosofo, or Orfeo ed Euridice, w. Clara McFadden (sop), Marylin Schmiege (mez), Christoph Prégardien, Gotthold Schwarz (bass), M. Schneider (cnd), La Stagione — Deutsche Harmonia Mundi 2-▲ 05472-77229-2
Stanbrook Abbey Nuns Choir
O Give Thanks to the Lord, w. Prinknash Abbey Monks' Choir — Saydisc ■ CSDL 349 (D)
Wellsprings—Psalms from Stanbrook Abbey:Prayer in Song — Saydisc ■ SDLC 363 (D)
State Sym Cappella Choir
V. Poliansky (cnd)
Russian Musical Satire, w. Yakovenko, Sergei (bar), I. Scheps (pno) — Russian Season ▲ LDC 288075
Stavanger Sym Women's Choir
Debussy, C.:Nocturnes, w. A. Dmitriev (cnd), Stavanger SO *(rec June 1993)* — Victoria ▲ VCD 19081
Stockholm Bach Choir
Bach, J.S.:Motets, BWV 225-30, w. N. Harnoncourt (cnd), Vienna Concentus Musicus [G] — Teldec ▲ 2292-42881-2
Handel, G.F.:Choruses, w. N. Harnoncourt (cnd), Vienna Concentus Musicus, Stockholm Chamber Choir, Arnold Schoenberg Choir — Teldec ▲ 95498-2
Handel, G.F.:Dixit Dominus, w. Hillevi Martinpelto (sop), Anne Sofie von Otter (mez), A. Öhrwall (cnd), Drottningholm Baroque Ensemble [L] — BIS ▲ CD 322 [DDD]
Stockholm Boys' Choir
Nielsen, C.:Choral Music, w. Å. Bäverstam (sop), L. Ekdahl (girl sop), A. Thors (boy sop), K. M. Sandve (ten), P. Hoyer (bar), E.-P. Salonen (cnd), Swedish RSO, Swedish Radio Chorus—Springtime in Funen; The Blind Musician; The Old People; Dance Ballad *(rec Sept. 16-18, 1991)* — Sony Classical ▲ SK 53276 [DDD]
Stockholm Chamber Choir
Bach, J.S.:Mass in b, BWV 232 — Proprius ▲ PRCD 9062
Handel, G.F.:Choruses, w. N. Harnoncourt (cnd), Vienna Concentus Musicus, Stockholm Bach Choir, Arnold Schoenberg Choir — Teldec ▲ 95498-2
Handel, G.F.:Messiah (sels), w. Elizabeth Gale (sop), Marjana Lipovsek (mez), Werner Hollweg (ten), Roderick Kennedy (bass), N. Harnoncourt (cnd), Vienna Concentus Musicus [E] — Teldec ▲ 2292-42409-2
Haydn, J.:Die Schöpfung, w. Kathleen Battle (sop), Gösta Winbergh (ten), Kurt Moll (bass), J. Levine (cnd), Berlin PO, Stockholm Radio Chorus — Deutsche Grammophon 2-▲ 427629-2 [DDD]

▲ = CD ♦ = Enhanced CD Δ = MD ■ = Cassette Tape □ = DCC

Stockholm Chamber Choir (cont.)
Kraus, J.M.:Prosperin, w. Hillevi Martinpelto (sop), Susanne Rydén (sop), Anna Eklund-Tarantino (sgr), Peter Mattei (bar), Lars Arvidson (bass), Stephen Smith (sgr), M. Tatlow (cnd), Stockholm CO Musica Sveciae 2-▲ MSCD 422/23 [DDD]
Mozart, W.A.:Ave verum corpus, w. R. Muti (cnd), Berlin PO, Swedish Radio Chorus [L] EMI Classics ▲ CDC 49640
Purcell, H.:Anthems, Drottningholm Baroque Ensemble—O, Sing unto the Lord; Lord, How long wilt thou be angry?; O God, thou art my God; Blow up the trumpet in Sion; Praise the Lord, O Jerusalem; O god, thou hast cast us out; My heart is inditing Proprius ▲ PRCD 9062
Sandström, S.-D.:Mute the Bereaved Memories Speak, w. L. Segerstam (cnd), Swedish RSO, Swedish Radio Chorus, Stockholm Children's Choir Caprice 2-▲ CAP 22027 [AAD]
Bäck, Ericson (cnd)
Bäck, S.-E.:Motets, w. Swedish Radio Choir—Jag är livets bröd; Bedjen, och Eder skall varda givet; Och Ordet vart kött; Icke kommer var och en in I himmelriket; Den stund kommer; Vaken för den skull; Se, vi gå upp till Jerusalem; Han blev lydig intill döden; Jesus, tänk på mig; The Transfiguration; Natten är framskriden; Dessa äro de som komma ur den stora bedrövelsen; Behold, I Am Making All Things New; Herr, zu wem sollen wir gehen?; Utrannsaka mig Phono Suecia ▲ PHN 10 [AAD]
Stockholm Children's Choir
Sandström, S.-D.:Mute the Bereaved Memories Speak, w. L. Segerstam (cnd), Swedish RSO, Swedish Radio Chorus, Stockholm Chamber Choir Caprice 2-▲ CAP 22027 [AAD]
Stockholm Phil Chorus
Olsson, O.:Requiem, w. M. A. Häggander (sop), E. Paaske (cta), A. Andersson (ten), L. Wedin (bar), A. Öhrwall (cnd), Stockholm PO Caprice ▲ CAP 21368 [DDD]
Orff, C.:Carmina burana, w. E. Söderström (sop), G. Bäckelin (ten), S. Svanholm (ten), H. Schmidt-Isserstedt (cnd), Stockholm PO *(rec live, 11/26/54)* BIS 8-▲ CD 421/24 (m/s) [AAD]
Scriabin, A.:Sym 1, w. I. Blom (cta), L. Magnusson (ten), L. Segerstam (cnd), Stockholm PO [R] BIS ▲ CD 534 [DDD]
Scriabin, A.:Sym 5, w. L. Segerstam (cnd), Stockholm PO BIS ▲ CD 534 [DDD]
Stockholm Radio Chorus
Cherubini, L.:Les Deux journées, w. H. Hillebrecht (sop), F. Wunderlich (ten), M. Cordes (bar), R. Hoyem (sgr), H. Müller-Kray (cnd), Stockholm RSO *(rec live, Stockholm 1960)* Melodram ▲ CDM 19507 [ADD]
Haydn, J.:Die Schöpfung, w. Kathleen Battle (sop), Gösta Winbergh (ten), Kurt Moll (bass), J. Levine (cnd), Berlin PO, Stockholm Chamber Choir Deutsche Grammophon 2-▲ 427629-2 [DDD]
Stockholm Royal Conservatory Chamber Choir
E. Ericson (cnd)
Pergament, M.:Kol Nidre, w. L. Rosenblüth (bar), M. Thyresson (org) BIS ▲ CD 1 [AAD]
Rosenblüth, L.:Jewish Liturgical Music, w. L. Rosenblüth (cant), G. von Bahr (fl), A. Vitolius (org), M. Thyresson (org)—Psalms 93 & 155, plus 5 settings for High Holidays, Rosh Hashanah, Sabbath & Yom Kippur BIS ▲ CD 1 [AAD]
Stockholm Royal Opera Chorus
Mascagni, P.:Cavalleria rusticana, w. A. Nordmo-Lövberg (sop), A. Bjoerling (sop), M. Sehlmark (cta), J. Bjoerling (ten), G. Svedenbrandt (bass), K. Bendix (cnd), Stockholm Royal Opera House Orch [I, Sw] *(rec live, Stockholm, 12/8/54)* Legato Classics ▲ LCD 164-1 [ADD]
Naumann, J.G.:Gustaf Wasa, w. Anders Andersson (ten—Gustav Wasa), Nicolai Gedda (ten—Christjern), P. Brunelle (cnd), Royal Swedish Opera Orch Virgin Classics ▲ CDCB 45148
Penderecki, K.:Als Jakob erwachte, w. Jadwiga Gadulanka (sop), Zahos Terzakis (ten), Piotr Nowacki (bass), K. Penderecki (cnd), Royal Stockholm PO Chandos 2-▲ CHAN 9459
Penderecki, K.:Polish Requiem, w. Jadwiga Gadulanka (sop), Zahos Terzakis (ten), Piotr Nowacki (bass), K. Penderecki (cnd), Royal Stockholm PO Chandos 2-▲ CHAN 9459
Tchaikovsky, P.:Mazeppa, w. Galina Gorchakoova (sop), Larissa Dyadkova (mez), Sergei Larin (ten), Sergei Leiferkus (bar), Anatoly Kotscherga (bass), N. Järvi (cnd), Gothenburg SO Deutsche Grammophon 3-▲ 439906-2
Verdi, G.:Rigoletto, w. M. Hallin (sop), B. Nordin (sop), K. Meyer (mez), B. Ericson (mez), Kjellgren (mez), N. Gedda (ten), O. Sivall (ten), H. Hasslo (bar), I. Wixell (bar), B. Alstergård (bar), A. Tyrén (bass), S. Ehrling (cnd), Stockholm Royal Opera House Orch *(rec live Jan. 18, 1959)* BIS ▲ CD 296 [AAD]
Verdi, G.:La traviata, w. Hjördis Schymberg (sop), Jussi Björling (ten), Conni Molin (sgr), H. Sandberg (cnd), Stockholm Royal Opera House Orch Enterprise ("The 40's" series) 2-▲ ENT 331
Verdi, G.:La traviata, w. Hjördis Schymberg (sop), Jussi Björling (ten), Conny Molin (sgr), H. Sandberg (cnd), Stockholm Royal Opera House Orch Grammofono 2000 2-▲ GRM 78640
Stockholm State Academy of Music Chamber Choir
Stenhammar, W.:Sången, w. Iwa Sörenson (sop), Anne Sofie von Otter (mez), Stefan Dahlberg (ten), Per-Arne Wahlgren (bar), H. Blomstedt (cnd), Swedish RSO, Swedish Radio Chorus, Adolf Fredrik Music School Children's Choir Caprice ▲ CAP 21358
Stockholm Univ Chorus
E. Hemberg (cnd)
Pettersson, G.A.:Barefoot Songs Caprice ▲ CAP 21359 [AAD]
Stow Festival Chorus
Beach, A.M.C.:Mass, "Grand Mass", w. Margot Law (sop), Martha Remington (mez), Ray Bauwens (ten), Joel Schneider (bar), B. Jones (cnd), Stow Festival Orch *(rec Cathedral Church of St Paul, Tremont St, Boston, MA)* Albany ▲ TROY 179 [DDD]
Strasbourg Cathedral Choir
M. Wackenheim (cnd)
Les Quatre Saisons en Chant Gregorien, w. Clement Jacob (org) Studio SM ▲ 12 22 16 [AAD]
Strasbourg Opera Chorus
Wagner, R.:Der fliegende Holländer (sels), w. S. Jurinac (sop), N. Bailey (bar), A. Van Mill (bass), F. Adam (cnd), Strasbourg Opera Orch—Senta's ballad (Jo-ho-hoel...Traft ihr das Schiff) & Willst Du des Vaters Wahl [G] *(rec live, Strasbourg, 11/25/69)* Melodram 3-▲ CDM 37091 [ADD]
Strasbourg Univ Chorus
Xenakis, I.:Oresteïa, w. Spiros Sakkas (bar), Sylvio Gualda (perc)* Salabert ▲ SCD 8906
Strasbourg Univ Collegium Cantorum
Chailly, J.:Choral Music, Alsace Polyphonique Ensemble—Missa Solemnis; Salve Regina; Prière de Saint Françoise; Le cimetière marin Skarbo ▲ SKR 3912 [DDD]
Studium Chorale
E. Hermans (cnd)
Choral Music from the Portuguese Renaissance *(rec July 1993)* Globe ▲ GLO 5108 [DDD]
Stuttgart Chamber Choir
Adam, A.:Le Postillon de Lunjumeau, w. P. Coburn (sop), R. Swensen (ten), J. Linn (bar), P. Lika (bass), K. Arp (cnd), Kaiserslautern Radio Orch [G] Capriccio 2-▲ 60040-2 [DDD]
Bach, J.S.:Motets, BWV 225-30, w. F. Bernius (cnd), Stuttgart Baroque Orch—BWV 225-229 Sony Classical ("Vivarte" series) ▲ SK 45859
Bruckner, A.:Mass 2, w. F. Bernius (cnd), German Wind Phil Sony Classical ▲ SK 48037
Haydn, J.:Stabat Mater, w. Krisztina Láki (sop), Júlia Hamari (mez), Claes Hakan Ahnsjö (ten), Richard Anlauf (bass), F. Bernius (cnd), Württemberg CO *(rec 1978)* Vox Box 2-▲ CDX 5081 [ADD]
Schubert, Franz:Mass 6, w. F. Bernius (cnd), German Chamber PO Berlin Classics ▲ BER 1165
Schütz, H.:Easter Oratorio, w. F. Bernius (cnd), Stuttgart Baroque Orch, Musica Fiata Sony Classical ("Vivarte" series) ▲ SK 45943
Schütz, H.:Die Geburt unsers Herren Jesu Christi, w. F. Bernius (cnd), Stuttgart Baroque Orch, Musica Fiata Sony Classical ("Vivarte" series) ▲ SK 45943
Schütz, H.:Psalmen Davids, w. F. Bernius (cnd), Musica Fiata—complete 26 psalms [G] Sony Classical ("Vivarte" series) 2-▲ S2K 48042 [DDD]
F. Bernius (cnd)
Bach, J.S.:Cant 206 [G] Sony Classical ("Vivarte" series) ▲ SK 46492
Bach, J.S.:Cant 207a [G] Sony Classical ("Vivarte" series) ▲ SK 46492
Bruckner, A.:Motets—Ave Maria; Christus factus est; Locus iste; Virga Jesse Sony Classical ▲ SK 48037
Gluck, C.W.:Orfeo ed Euridice, w. N. Argenta (sop), M. Chance (ct), J. Lamon (cnd), Tafelmusik Sony Classical ("Vivarte" series) 2-▲ SX2K 48040
Stuttgart Gächinger Kantorei
Cherubini, L.:Requiem Mass 2, w. H. Rilling (cnd), Bach Collegium Chorus Hänssler Classic 2-▲ HAN 98981 [DDD]
Handel, G.F.:Messiah, w. Donna Brown (sop), Cornelia Kallisch (cta), R. Sacca (ten), Alastair Miles (bass), H. Rilling (cnd), Stuttgart Bach Collegium Hänssler Classic 2-▲ HAN 98975 [DDD]
H. Rilling (cnd)
Brahms, J.:Choral Music—6 Choruses, Op. 93a; 5 Choruses, Op. 104 [G] Acanta ▲ 43805
Stuttgart Gedächtnis Figural Choir
Bach, J.S.:Cant 40, w. V. Gohl (mez), A. Kraus (ten), S. Nimsgern (b-bar), H. Rilling (cnd), Stuttgart Bach Collegium [G] *(rec June-July 1970)* Hänssler Classic ▲ 98.824 [AAD]
H. Rilling (cnd)
Bach, J.S.:Das Orgelbüchlein, w. Helmuth Rilling (org)—BWV 599-609, 611-615 *(rec Walcker, Ludwigsburg, 1957)* Cantate ▲ C 57607 [AAD]
Bach, J.S.:Das Orgelbüchlein, w. Helmuth Rilling (org)—BWV 618-623, 625-630, 640, 641 *(rec Walcker, Ludwigsburg, 1957)* Cantate ▲ C 57608 [AAD]
Bach, J.S.:Das Orgelbüchlein, w. Helmuth Rilling (org)—Komm, Gott Schöpfer, Heiliger Geist, BWV 631; Herr Jesu Christ, dich zu uns wend, BWV 632; Liebster Jesu, wir sind hier, BWV 633; Dies sind die heilgen zehn Gebot, BWV 635; Vater unser im Himmelreich, BWV 636; Durch Adams Fall ist ganz verderbt, BWV 637; Es ist das Heil uns kommen her, BWV 638; Ich ruf zu dir, Herr Jesu Christ, BWV 639; Hilf Gott, dass mirs gelinge, BWV 624; Jesu, meine Freude, BWV 610; Mit Fried und Freud ich fahr dahin, BWV 616; Herr Gott, n. schleuss d. Himmel auf BWV 617; Wer nur den lieben Gott läss walten, BWV 642; Alle Menschen müssen sterben, BWV 643; Ach wie flüchtig, ach wie nichtig, BWV 644 *(rec Southwest Sound Studio, Stuttgart, May 1963 & Mar 1965)* Cantate ▲ C 57609 [AAD]
Stuttgart Hymnus Boys' Choir
Bach, J.S.:St. John Passion, w. C. Schäfer (sop), Y. Jänicke (mez), A. Kraus (ten), R. Hagen (bass), B. Possemeyer (bass), E. Weyand (cnd), Stuttgart Hymnus Orch [G] *(rec 1990)* Hänssler Classic 2-▲ 98.968
Stuttgart Memorial Church Figuralchor
Bach, J.S.:Cant 80, w. Antonia Fahberg (sop), Bargarete Bence (cta), Theophil Maier (ten), Ulrich Schaible (bass), H. Rilling (cnd), Württemberg CO *(rec 1964)* Vox Box 3-▲ CD3X 3039
Bach, J.S.:Cant 208, "Hunting Cant", w. Helen Donath (sop), Elisabeth Speiser (sop), Wilfrid Jochims (ten), Jakob Stämpfli (bass), H. Rilling (cnd), Stuttgart Bach Collegium *(rec Southwest Sound Studio, Stuttgart-Bottnang, May 1965)* Musicaphon ▲ 51351 [AAD]
Bach, J.S.:Cant 249a, w. Edith Mathis (sop), Hetty Plümacher (alt), Theo Altmeyer (ten), Jakob Stämpfli (bass), H. Rilling (cnd), Stuttgart Bach Collegium *(rec Gedächtniskirche Stuttgart, Mar 1967)* Musicaphon ▲ 51357 [AAD]
Stuttgart New Vocal Soloists
M. Schreier (cnd)
Fervers, A.:Worte (2) Accord ▲ ACD 205552 [DDD]
Stuttgart Phil Chorus
Lord's Prayer:Musical Settings from the 19th Century *(rec Feb. 29-Mar. 2, 1988)* Calig ▲ CAL 50873 [DDD]
Weber, C.M. von:Missa sancta 2, w. Gertrude Stoklassa (sop), Emmy Lisken (cta), Manfred Raucamp (ten), Hans Kagel (bass), R. Bader (cnd), Stuttgart PO Koch Schwann ▲ SCH CD 316372
Stuttgart Pro Musica Chorus
Vivaldi, A.:Stabat Mater Cta, w. M. Bence (cta), M. Couraud (cnd), Stuttgart Pro Musica Orch *(rec 1957)* Vox Box 2-▲ CDX 5081 [ADD]
Stuttgart Radio Chorus
Brahms, J.:Ein Deutsches Requiem, w. M. Stader (sop), H. Prey (bar), C. Schuricht (cnd), Stuttgart RSO, Frankfurt Radio Chorus *(rec Nov. 7, 1959)* Archipon ▲ ARCH 2.2CD (m) [ADD]
Debussy, C.:La Damoiselle élue, w. I. Cotrubas (sop), G. Maurice (mez), G. Bertini (cnd), Stuttgart RSO [F] Orfeo ▲ 012821 [DDD]
Debussy, C.:L'Enfant prodigue, w. J. Norman (sop), J. Carreras (ten), D. Fischer-Dieskau (bar), G. Bertini (cnd), Stuttgart RSO [F] Orfeo ▲ 012821
Haydn, J.:Die Schöpfung, w. Barbara Bonney (mez), Edith Wiens (sop), Hans-Peter Blochwitz (ten), Olaf Bär (bar), Jan-Herdrik Rootering (bass), N. Marriner (cnd), Stuttgart Radio Orch [G] EMI Classics 2-▲ CDCB 54038 [DDD]
Mahler, G.:Sym 2, w. H. Donath (sop), B. Finnilä (cta), J. Barbirolli (cnd), Stuttgart RSO [G] *(rec live 6/19/70)* Arkadia 3-▲ 719 [ADD]
Mozart, W.A.:Don Giovanni, w. Hedwig Jungkurth (sop—Elvira), Maria Reining (sop—Anna), Julius Patzak (ten—Ottavio), Karl Hammes (bar—Don Giovanni), Georg Hann (bass), Ludwig Weber (bass—Commandant), J. Keilberth (cnd), Stuttgart Reich RSO *(rec Mar, 1936)* Preiser 2-▲ PRE 90263
Schubert, Franz:Lazarus, or Die Feier der Auferstehung, w. E. Mathis (sop), C. Wulkopf (mez), H. Schwarz (mez), W. Hollweg (ten), H. Laubenthal (ten), H. Prey (bar), G. Chmura (cnd), Stuttgart RSO [G] Orfeo ▲ 011101 [DDD]
Schumann, R.:Manfred, w. C. Schuricht (cnd), Stuttgart RSO *(rec Mar. 25, 1952)* Archipon ▲ ARCH 2.3CD (m) [ADD]
Stravinsky, I.:Sym of Psalms, w. G. Bertini (cnd), Stuttgart RSO [L] Orfeo ▲ 015821 [DDD]
Wagner, R.:Tannhäuser, w. T. Eipperle (sop), F. Krauss (bar), K. Schmitt-Walter (bar), S. Nilsson (bass), C. Leonhardt (cnd), Stuttgart Radio Orch [G] *(rec Oct. 24, 1937, mat. 39695)* Preiser 3-▲ 90133 (m) [AAD]
Stuttgart Schola Cantorum
C. Gottwald (cnd)
Atelier Schola Cantorum, Vols. 1-8 Bayer 10-▲ CAD 800901
Penderecki, K.:Choral Music—Stabat Mater; Miserere *(rec Feb 1972)* Vox Box 2-▲ CDX 5142
Stuttgart State Opera Chorus
Glass, Philip:Akhnaten, w. D.R. Davies (cnd), Stuttgart State Opera Orch CBS 2-▲ M2K 42457 [DDD]
Stuttgart Teachers' Glee Club
Beethoven, L. van:Fant Pno, Op. 80, "Choral Fant", w. Alfred Brendel (pno), W. Boettcher (cnd), Stuttgart PO Vox Box ("Legends" series) 3-▲ CDX3 3502 [ADD]
Sulmona Phil Chorus
Carissimi, G.:Motets, w. F. Colusso (cnd), Strumenti Antichi, Gruppo di Voci—Vanitas Vanitatum I & II; Sponsa Canticorum; Tolle Sponsa [L] Bongiovanni ▲ GB 10003 [DDD]
Swedish Radio Choir
Beethoven, L. van:Sym 9, "Choral Sym", w. Jane Eaglen (sop), Waltraud Meier (cta), Ben Heppner (ten), Bryn Terfel (bar), C. Abbado (cnd), Berlin PO, Eric Ericson Chamber Choir *(rec Salzburg Easter Festival, 1996)* Sony Classical ▲ SK 62634 ∆ SM 62634
Blomdahl, K.-B.:In the Hall of Mirrors, w. *(soloists unknown)*, S. Ehrling (cnd), Stockholm PO Caprice ▲ CAP 21424 [AAD]
Dallapiccola, L.:Canti di prigionia, w. E.-P. Salonen (cnd), Swedish RSO members, Eric Ericson Chamber Choir Sony Classical ▲ SK 68323
Eliasson, A.:Canto del Vagabondo, w. H. Blomstedt (cnd), Swedish RSO, Eric Ericson Chamber Choir Caprice ▲ CAP 21402 [AAD]
Haeffner, J.C.F.:Electra, w. Hillevi Martinpelto (sop), Helle Hinz (sop), Peter Mattei (bar), Mikael Samuelson (bar), T. Schuback (cnd), Drottningholm Baroque Ensemble Caprice 2-▲ CAP 22030
Lidholm, I.:Nausikaa Alone, w. E. Söderström (sop), S. Westerberg (cnd), Swedish RSO Caprice ▲ CAP 21366 [AAD]
Mozart, W.A.:Ave verum corpus, w. R. Muti (cnd), Berlin PO, Stockholm Chamber Choir [L] EMI Classics ▲ CDC 49640
Mozart, W.A.:Requiem, w. P. Pace (sop), W. Meier (mez), F. Lopardo (ten), J. Morris (bass), R. Muti (cnd), Berlin PO [L] EMI Classics ▲ CDC 49640 [DDD]
Nielsen, C.:Aladdin, w. E.-P. Salonen (cnd), Swedish RSO CBS ▲ MK 44934 [DDD]
Nielsen, C.:Choral Music, w. A. Bäverstam (sop), L. Ekdahl (girl sop), A. Thors (boy sop), K. M. Sandve (ten), P. Hoyer (bar), E.-P. Salonen (cnd), Swedish RSO, Stockholm Boys' Choir—Springtime in Funen; The Blind Musician; The Old People; Dance Ballad *(rec Sept. 16-18, 1991)* Sony Classical ▲ SK 53276 [DDD]

CHORAL GROUPS

Swedish Radio Choir (cont.)
Nørgård, P.:Gilgamesh, w. T. Vetö (cnd), Swedish RSO, Swedish Radio Soloists *(rec Nov. 15, 1973)* Marco Polo ▲ DCCD 9001
Pettersson, G.A.:Vox Humana, w. Marianne Mellnäs (sop), Margot Rödin (alt), Sven-Erik Alexandersson (ten), Erland Hagegård (bar), S. Westerberg (cnd), Swedish RSO *(rec Royal Swedish Academy of Music, Stockholm, Sweden, Mar. 22 & May 24, 1976)* BIS ▲ CD 55 [AAD]
Rosenberg, H.:Sym 4, w. Håkan Hagegård (bar), S. Ehrling (cnd), Gothenburg SO, Rilke Ensemble members, Pro Musica Chamber Choir Caprice ▲ CAP 21429 [DDD]
Sandström, S.-D.:Mute the Bereaved Memories Speak, w. L. Segerstam (cnd), Swedish RSO, Stockholm Chamber Choir, Stockholm Children's Choir Caprice 2-▲ CAP 22027 [AAD]
Stenhammar, W.:Sången, w. Iwa Sörenson (sop), Anne Sofie von Otter (mez), Stefan Dahlberg (ten), Per-Arne Wahlgren (bar), H. Blomstedt (cnd), Swedish RSO, Stockholm State Academy of Music Chamber Choir, Adolf Fredrik Music School Children's Choir Caprice ▲ CAP 21358
Stravinsky, I.:Sym of Psalms, w. S. Ehrling (cnd), Swedish RSO BIS ▲ CD 400
Swedish Highlights, w. S. Westerberg (cnd), Swedish RSO Caprice ▲ CAP 21340 [DDD]
Bäck, Ericson (cnd)
Bäck, S.-E.:Motets, w. Stockholm Chamber Choir—Jag är livets bröd; Bedjen, och Eder skall varda givet; Och Ordet vart kött; Icke kommer var och en in I himmelriket; Den stund kommer; Vaken för den skull; Se, vi gå upp till Jerusalem; Han blev lydig intill döden; Jesus, tänk på mig; The Transfiguration; Natten är framskriden; Dessa äro de som komma ur den stora bedrövelsen; Behold, I Am Making All Things New; Herr, zu wem sollen wir gehen?; Utrannsaka mig Phono Suecia ▲ PHN 10 [AAD]
T. Kaljuste (cnd)
Górecki, H.-M.:Miserere, w. Eric Ericson Chamber Choir Caprice ▲ CAP 21515 [DDD]
Rachmaninoff, S.:All-Night Vigil Virgin Classics ▲ CDC 45124
Schnittke, A.:Requiem Caprice ▲ CAP 21515 [DDD]
Nilsson, Sjökvist (cnd)
Nilsson, T.:Music of, w. Ingmari Landin (alt), Lars Sjögren (ten), Lage Wedin (bass), Jerker Halldén (fl), Nils-Erik Sparf (vn), Hans-Ola Ericsson (org), Anders Loguin (perc)—Ordinarium Missae; Balthasar/Daniel; Drei Gedichte Phono Suecia ▲ PHN 40 [AAD]
Swedish Radio Soloists
Nørgård, P.:Gilgamesh, w. T. Vetö (cnd), Swedish RSO, Swedish Radio Chorus *(rec Nov. 15, 1973)* Marco Polo ▲ DCCD 9001
Swedish Royal Opera Chorus
Kraus, J.M.:Soliman II, w. L. Hoel (sop), B. Ortendahl-Corin (sop), B.-O. Morgny (ten), T. Wallstrom (bass), P. Brunelle (cnd), Royal Swedish Opera Orch Virgin Classics ▲ 59068 [DDD]
Swingle Singers
Bach, J.S.:Music of Philips ▲ 824703-2 ■ 824544-4
Mozart, W.A.:Music of—a cappella arrs. of selections from Sym. No. 40; Con. No. 21 for Piano; Eine kleine Nachtmusik; Così fan tutte; etc. Virgin Classics ▲ 59617 [DDD]
Swiss Romande Chorus
Massenet, J.:Don Quichotte, w. R. Crespin (sop), M. Command (sop), G. Bacquier (bar), N. Ghiaurov (bass), R. Bonynge (cnd), Swiss Romande Orch [F] London ("Grand Opera" series) 2-▲ 430636-2 [AAD]
Mozart, W.A.:Nozze di Figaro (sels), w. R. Pütz (sop), T. Stich-Randall (mez), T. Berganza (mez), A.-R. Johnson (ten), G. Bacquier (bar), F. Corena (bass), H. Wallberg (cnd), Swiss Romande Orch—Act IV Melodram 2-▲ CDM 27094 [ADD]
Swiss Romande Radio Choir
Schibler, A.:La Folie de Tristan, w. Audrey Michael (sop—Iseut), Arlette Chédel (mez—Brangien), Pierre-André Blaser (ten—Tristan), Philippe Huttenlocher (bar—Le roi Marc/Le pêcheur/Le portier), André Fauré (nar), William Jacques (nar), Snezana Zivojinovic (nar), J. Auberson (cnd), Lausanne CO, Romande Instrumental Group Rockband *(rec live, Festival de Montreux, Sept 15, 1980)* Jecklin ▲ JD 695
Swiss Romande Red Chorus
Falla, M. de:Atlántida, w. Montserrat Caballé (sop), Heinz Rehfuss (bar), E. Ansermet (cnd), Swiss Romande Orch, Lausanne Youth Chorus, Villamont College Little Chorus Cascavelle ▲ CVL 2005 [ADD]
Swiss-Italian Chorus
Respighi, O.:Christus, w. C. Gaifa (ten), R. Hermann (bar), G. Sarti (bar), M. Balderi (cnd), Swiss-Italian Orch [L] Claves ▲ CD 9203 [DDD]
Swiss-Italian Radio Chorus
Righini, V.:Alcide al Bivio, w. L. Serra (sop), S. Browne (cta), W. McKinney (ten), R. El Hage (bass), M. Barta (ob), P. Molinari (hpd), T. Gotti (cnd), Swiss-Italian RSO *(rec 1979)* Bongiovanni 2-▲ GB 2157/58 [ADD]
Zbinden, J.-F.:Impératifs, w. K. Rosat (sop), C. Miveloz (alt) [F] Grammont ▲ CTSP 3-2 [ADD]
A. Charlet (cnd)
Regamey, C.:Poèmes de Jean Tardieu [F] Grammont ▲ CTSP 5-2 [ADD]
E. Loehrer (cnd)
Cavalli, P.F.:Missa pro defunctis Accord ▲ ACD 201182 [AAD]
Swiss-Italian Radio-TV Chorus
Beethoven, L. van:Sym 9, "Choral Sym", w. Magda Laszlo (sop), Lucienne Devallier (cta), Petre Monteanu (ten), Raffaele Arié (bass), H. Scherchen (cnd), Swiss-Italian RSO Accord ▲ ACD 201002 [AAD]
Donizetti, G.:Imelda de' Lambertazzi, w. D. D'Auria (sop), F. Sovilla (sop), F. Tenzi (ten), A. Martin (bar), G. Sarti (bar), M. Andreae (cnd), Swiss-Italian Radio-TV Orch [I] *(rec live)* Nuova Era 2-▲ 6778/79 [DDD]
Mozart, W.A.:Litaniae de venerabili, w. E. Loehrer (cnd), Swiss-Italian Radio-TV Orch Accord ▲ ACD 201012 [AAD]
Mozart, W.A.:Litaniae Lauretanae, K.195, w. E. Loehrer (cnd), Swiss-Italian Radio-TV Orch Accord ▲ ACD 201012 [AAD]
Rossini, G.:Stabat Mater, w. Beatrice Haldas (sop), Lucia V. Terrani (mez), Antonio Savastano (ten), Raffaele Arié (bass), E. Loehrer (cnd), Swiss-Italian Radio-TV Orch Accord ▲ ACD 201752 [AAD]
Rossini, G.:Torvaldo e Dorliska, w. A. Buda (sop), F. Pediconi (sop), M. Ciliento (mez), E. Palacio (ten), S. Antonucci (bar), A. Marani (b-bar), M. de Bernart (cnd), Swiss-Italian Orch, Cantemus *(rec Jan. 11, 1992)* Arkadia-Akademia 2-▲ 123 [DDD]
Sydney Chamber Choir
N. Routley (cnd)
Josquin Desprez:Secular Songs—Illibata dei, Virgo nutrix; Ave, Christe; Missa, "Pange lingua"; Absalon, fili mi; Inviolata, integra, et casta es Maria *(rec Chapel of St. Scholastica's Convent, Aug. & Nov. 1993)* Tall Poppies ▲ TP 054 [DDD]
Maclean, C.:Choral Music—Et Misericordia; Hope There Is; A West Irish Ballad; Love was His Meaning; Rain; Christ the King Tall Poppies ▲ TP 73 [DDD]
Maclean, C.:Christ the King *(rec Chapel of St. Scholastica's Convent, Glebe, Sydney, Australia, Oct 1994 & Apr 1995)* Tall Poppies ▲ TP 073 [DDD]
Maclean, C.:Et Misercordia *(rec Chapel of St. Scholastica's Convent, Glebe, Sydney, Australia, Oct 1994 & Apr 1995)* Tall Poppies ▲ TP 073 [DDD]
Maclean, C.:Hope There Is *(rec Chapel of St. Scholastica's Convent, Glebe, Sydney, Australia, Oct 1994 & Apr 1995)* Tall Poppies ▲ TP 073 [DDD]
Maclean, C.:Love Was His Meaning *(rec Chapel of St. Scholastica's Convent, Glebe, Sydney, Australia, Oct 1994 & Apr 1995)* Tall Poppies ▲ TP 073 [DDD]
Maclean, C.:Rain *(rec Chapel of St. Scholastica's Convent, Glebe, Sydney, Australia, Oct 1994 & Apr 1995)* Tall Poppies ▲ TP 073 [DDD]
Maclean, C.:West Irish Ballad *(rec Chapel of St. Scholastica's Convent, Glebe, Sydney, Australia, Oct 1994 & Apr 1995)* Tall Poppies ▲ TP 073 [DDD]
Sydney Conservatorium Choir
Berlioz, H.:Requiem, "Grande Messe des Morts", w. D. Hamilton (ten), J. Hopkins (cnd), Sydney Conservatorium for Music Orch, Willoughby Sym Chorus Walsingham Classics ▲ WAL 8000 [DDD]

Sydney Philharmonia Motet Choir
J. Grundy (cnd)
Wesley-Smith, M.:Nonsense, Truth & Lewis Carroll, w. David Miller (kbd), Michael Askill (perc) Vox Australis 2-▲ VAST 010-2
Sydney Sym Chorus
Berlioz, H.:Marche funèbre, w. R. Pikler (cnd), Sydney SO Chandos ("Collect" series) ▲ CHAN 6587 [ADD]
Symbolon Ensemble Chorus
Bizet, G.:Don Procopio, w. Muscente (sgr), M. Gentile (sop), Carmona (sgr), Barry (sgr), A. Antoniozzi (bar), S. Sanna (cnd), Berlin Radio Youth Orch [I] *(rec live 5/25/86)* Bongiovanni 2-▲ GB 2043/44 [DDD]
Symposium Musicum
de Monte, P.:Cara la vita mia, w. P. Kühn (cnd), Kühn Chamber Soloists *(rec Martínek Studio, Prague, Jan 17, 19 & 20, 1995)* Panton ▲ 811401-2
de Monte, P.:Missa de Requiem, w. P. Kühn (cnd), Kühn Chamber Soloists *(rec Martínek Studio, Prague, Jan 17, 19 & 20, 1995)* Panton ▲ 811401-2
de Monte, P.:Motets, w. P. Kühn (cnd), Kühn Chamber Soloists—Domine Deus salutis meae; Ecce ego mitto vos; Quasi cedrus; Non turbetur cor vestrum; Advenit ignis divinus; Sancte Johannes Baptista *(rec Martínek Studio, Prague, Jan 17, 19 & 20, 1995)* Panton ▲ 811401-2
P. Kühn (cnd)
Rossi, S.:The Songs of Solomon, w. Kühn Chamber Soloists *(rec Martínek-Studio, Prague, Mar 24-26 & May 3-5, 1994)* Panton 2-▲ PAN 811271 [DDD]
Karol Szymanowski State Phil Choir
Orff, C.:Carmina burana, w. Venceslava Hruba-Freiberger (sop), Rolf Havenstein (sgr), Piotr Kusiewicz (sgr), K. Penderecki (cnd), Karol Szymanowski State PO *(rec Cracow, Poland, Jan 27-28, 1989)* Arts Music ▲ 47177-2 [DDD]
Täby Church Choir
Olsson, O.:Te Deum, w. K. Ek (cnd), Orpheus Chamber Ensemble [L] BIS ▲ CD 289 [DDD]
K. Ek (cnd)
Langlais, J.:Messe solenelle [L] BIS ▲ CD 289 [DDD]
Tafelmusik Chamber Choir
Purcell, H.:Dido & Aeneas, w. Meredith Hall (sop—2nd Witch/Spirit), Ann Monoyios (sop—Belinda), Shari Saunders (sop—2nd Woman/1st Woman), Jennifer Lane (mez—Dido/Sorceress), Benjamin Butterfield (ten—Sailor), Russell Braun (bar—Aeneas), J. Lamon (cnd), Tafelmusik *(rec Glenn Gould Studio, CBC Toronto, Apr 26-29, 1995)* CBC ▲ SM5 5147 [DDD]
Vivaldi, A.:Cants, w. E. Kirkby (sop), J. Lamon (cnd), Tafelmusik [period instruments]—Lungi dal vago volto, RV.680 [L] Hyperion ▲ CDA 66247 [DDD]
Vivaldi, A.:Magnificat, RV.610, w. S. LeBlanc (sop), D. Forget (sop), R. Cunningham (alt), H. Ingram (ten), J. Lamon (cnd), Tafelmusik [L] Hyperion ▲ CDA 66247 [DDD]
Vivaldi, A.:Motets, w. E. Kirkby (sop), J. Lamon (cnd), Tafelmusik—"In turbata mare irato," RV.627 [L] Hyperion ▲ CDA 66247 [DDD]
Talens Lyriques
C. Rousset (cnd)
Jommelli, N.:Armida abbandonata FNAC Music 3-▲ 592326
Tallinn Boys' Choir
Tobias, R.:Des Jonah Sendung, w. Pille Lill (sop), Urve Tauts (mez), Peter Svensson (ten), Raimo Laukka (bar), Mati Palm (bass), Ines Maidre (org), N. Järvi (cnd), Estonian State SO, Oratorio Choir, Estonian Phil Chamber Choir *(rec Estonia Concert Hall, Tallinn, Estonia, June 23-29, 1995)* BIS 2-▲ CD 731/732 [DDD]
Tallin Linnamussikud Vocal Ensemble
Zielenski, M.:Communiones totius anni, w. Kira Borescko (sop), Marcin Borus-Szczycinski (alt), Ryszard Minkiewicz (ten), Robert Hugo (org), M. Bornus-Szczycinski (cnd), Bornus Consort, Tallinn Linnamussikud Instrumental Ensemble Urtext ▲ ACD 202662 [DDD]
Zielenski, M.:Offertoria totius anni, w. Kira Borescko (sop), Marcin Borus-Szczycinski (alt), Ryszard Minkiewicz (ten), Robert Hugo (org), M. Bornus-Szczycinski (cnd), Bornus Consort, Tallinn Linnamussikud Instrumental Ensemble Urtext ▲ ACD 202662 [DDD]
Tallis Chamber Choir
Beethoven, L. van:Missa Solemnis, w. C. Vaness (sop), W. Meier (mez), H.-P. Blochwitz (ten), H. Tschammer (bass), J. Tate (cnd), English CO [L] EMI Classics ▲ CDC 49950 [DDD]
Beethoven, L. van:Sym 9, "Choral Sym", w. M. Tilson Thomas (cnd), English CO [G] CBS ▲ MDK 44646 [DDD]
Bellini, V.:Norma (sels), w. A. Baltsa (mez), J. Carreras (ten), P. Domingo (cnd), London SO—Eccola! Va, mi lascia; Va, crudele, al Dio spietato *(rec Jan.-Feb. 1991)* Sony Classical ▲ SK 53968 [DDD]
Bizet, G.:Carmen (sels), w. A. Baltsa (mez), J. Carreras (ten), P. Domingo (cnd), London SO—C'est toi? C'est moi; Mais moi, Carmen, je t'aime encore? *(rec Jan.-Feb. 1991)* Sony Classical ▲ SK 53968 [DDD]
Donizetti, G.:L'elisir d'amore, w. M. Devia (sop), B. Pratico (bar), P. Spagnoli (bar), M. Viotti (cnd), English CO Erato 2-▲ 4509-91701-2
Mascagni, P.:Cavalleria rusticana (sels), w. A. Baltsa (mez), J. Carreras (ten), P. Domingo (cnd), London SO—Tu qui, Santuzza?; La tua Santuzza [w. M. Hintermeier (mez)] *(rec Jan.-Feb. 1991)* Sony Classical ▲ SK 53968 [DDD]
Massenet, J.:Werther (sels), w. A. Baltsa (mez), J. Carreras (ten), P. Domingo (cnd), London SO—Orchestral Intro.; Il faut nous séparer; Mais vous ne savez rien de moi; Rêve! Extase! *(rec Jan.-Feb. 1991)* Sony Classical ▲ SK 53968 [DDD]
Mozart, W.A.:Ave verum corpus, w. B. Klee (cnd), English CO [L] Novalis ▲ 150064 [DDD]
Mozart, W.A.:Sacred Music, w. E. Mathis (sop), B. Klee (cnd), English CO—Inter natos mulierum, K.72; Regina coeli, K.276; Laudate dominus from Vesperae solennes de confessore, K.339; Laudamus te (soprano aria) from Missa in c, K.427; Benedictus (soprano aria) from Missa brevis in Bb, K.275 [L] Novalis ▲ 150064 [DDD]
Ringger, R.U.:Music of, w. W. Prossnitz (cnd), English CO—Gioia; Con Slancio; Cuando el Fuego Se Está Apagando...; Addio!; Odelette; Les Insaisissables; Dommage Que...; Mestizia Sospesa; A Moment of Sunrise Tudor ▲ TUD 7036 [DDD]
Verdi, G.:La traviata (sels), w. A. Baltsa (mez), J. Carreras (ten), P. Domingo (cnd), London SO—Libiamo, libiamo ne' lieti calici *(rec Jan.-Feb. 1991)* Sony Classical ▲ SK 53968 [DDD]
Verdi, G.:Il trovatore (sels), w. A. Baltsa (mez), J. Carreras (ten), P. Domingo (cnd), London SO—Soli or siamo; Non son tuo figlio; L'usato messo Ruiz m'invia [w. J. Howard (tenor)] *(rec Jan.-Feb. 1991)* Sony Classical ▲ SK 53968 [DDD]
Tallis Scholars
Byrd, W.:Songs—Anglican Music;The Great Service; O Lord, make thy; O God, the proud are risen; Sing joyfully unto God; Catholic Music; Mass for 5 voices; Mass for 4 voices; Ave venum corpus; Infelix ego Gimell 2-▲ CDGIM 343/44
Christmas Carols & Motets Gimell ▲ CDGIM 010
P. Phillips (cnd)
Allegri, G.:Miserere Gimell ▲ CDGIM 994 ■ MC 1585T-994
Allegri, G.:Miserere [L] Gimell ▲ CDGIM 339 [AAD] ■ 1585T-39
Barbingant:Au travail suis Gimell ▲ 454 935-2
Binchois, G. de B.D.:De plus en plus se renouvelle Gimell ▲ 454 935-2
Brumel, A.:Et ecce terrae motus, "Earthquake Mass" Gimell ▲ CDGIM 026 ■ 1585T-26
Brumel, A.:Lamentations & Magnificat secundi toni Gimell ▲ CDGIM 026 ■ 1585T-26
Byrd, W.:Anthems—O Lord, make thy servant Elizabeth; O God, the proud are risen; Sing joyfully unto God [E] Gimell ▲ CDGIM 011 [DDD] ■ 1585T-11
Byrd, W.:The Great Service [E] Gimell ▲ CDGIM 011 [DDD] ■ 1585T-11
Christmas Carols & Motets Gimell ▲ 454910-2
Clemens Non Papa, J.:Motets—Ego flos campi; Pater peccavi; Tribulationes civitatum [L] Gimell ▲ CDGIM 013 [DDD] ■ 1585T-13
Clemens Non Papa, J.:Pastores quidnam vidistis [L] Gimell ▲ CDGIM 013 [DDD] ■ 1585T-13

1018 ▲ = CD ♦ = Enhanced CD Δ = MD ■ = Cassette Tape □ = DCC

Tallis Scholars (cont.)
P. Phillips (cnd) (cont.)
Cornysh, W.:Sacred & Secular Choral Music—Stabat Mater; Salve regina; Magnificat; Gaude virgo mater Christi; Ave Maria, mater Dei; Woefully arrayed; Ah, Robin; Adieu, adieu, my heartes lust; Adieu, courage [E,L] Gimell ▲ CDGIM 014 [DDD] ■ 1585T-14
de Silva, A.:Nigra sum [L] Gimell ▲ CDGIM 003 [AAD] ■ 1585T-03
Josquin Desprez:Missa & Plainchant, "Pange lingua" [L] Gimell ▲ CDGIM 009 [DDD] ■ 1585T-09 (D)
Josquin Desprez:Missa, "L'homme armé' sexti toni" *(rec Church of St Peter & St Paul, Salle, Norfolk, England)* Gimell ▲ CDGIM 019 [DDD]
Josquin Desprez:Missa, "L'homme armé' super voces musicales" *(rec Church of St Peter & St Paul, Salle, Norfolk, England)* Gimell ▲ CDGIM 019 [DDD]
Josquin Desprez:Missa, "La sol fa re mi" [L] Gimell ▲ CDGIM 009 [DDD] ■ 1585T-09 (D)
Josquin Desprez:Motets—Praeter rerum seriem Gimell ▲ CDGIM 029 ■ 1585T-29
Lhéritier, J.:Motet & Plainchant, "Nigra sum" [L] Gimell ▲ CDGIM 003 [AAD] ■ 1585T-03
Lobo, A.:Funeral motet [L] Gimell ▲ CDGIM 012 [DDD] ■ 1585T-12
Lôbo, D.:Sacred Music—Requiem for Six Voices; Missa Vox clamantis [L] Gimell ▲ CDGIM 028 [DDD] ■ 1585T-28
Mundy, W.:Vox Patris [L] Gimell ▲ CDGIM 339 [AAD] ■ 1585T-39
Obrecht, J.:Missa "Maria zart" Gimell ▲ CD GIM 032 ■ 1585T-32
Ockeghem, J.:Missa "Au travail suis" Gimell ▲ 454 935-2
Ockeghem, J.:Missa "De plus en plus" Gimell ▲ 454 935-2
Palestrina, G.:Missa "Nigra sum" [L] Gimell ▲ CDGIM 003 [AAD] ■ 1585T-03
Palestrina, G.:Missa "Papae marcelli" Gimell ▲ CDGIM 994 ■ MC 1585T-994
Palestrina, G.:Missa "Papae marcelli" [L] *(rec 1980)* Gimell ▲ CDGIM 339 [AAD] ■ 1585T-39
Palestrina, G.:Sacred Music—Surge, illuminare; Alma redemptoris mater; Magnificat primi toni; Nunc dimittis Gimell ▲ CDGIM 994 ■ MC 1585T-994
Palestrina, G.:Sacred Music—Missa brevis; Missa, "Nasce la gioia mia" [L] Gimell ▲ CDGIM 008 [DDD] ■ 1585T-08
Palestrina, G.:Stabat mater Gimell ▲ CDGIM 994 ■ MC 1585T-994
Rore, C. de:Motets—Inflelix ego; Parce mihi; Ave Regina caelorum; Descendi in hortum meum Gimell ▲ CDGIM 029 ■ 1585T-29
Rore, C. de:Praeter rerum seriem Gimell ▲ CDGIM 029 ■ 1585T-29
Russian Orthodox Music Gimell ▲ CDGIM 002 [AAD]
Sheppard, J.:Sacred Choral Music—Media vita; Christe Redemptor omnium; Reges Tharsis; Sacris solemniis; In manus tuas I-III; Verbum caro [L] Gimell ▲ CDGIM 016 [DDD] ■ 1585T-16
Tallis, T.:Church Music—Salve Intermerata Virgo; Latin Motets Gimell ▲ CDGIM 025 ■ 1585T-25
Tallis, T.:Church Music—Sancte Deus; Salvator mundi, Nos. 1 & 2; Gaude gloriosa; Miserere nostri; Loquebantur variis linguis [L] Gimell ▲ CDGIM 006 [DDD]
Tallis, T.:English Anthems [E] Gimell ▲ CDGIM 007 [DDD]
Tallis, T.:The Lamentations of Jeremiah Gimell ▲ CDGIM 025 ■ 1585T-25
Tallis, T.:Spem in alium [L] Gimell ▲ CDGIM 006 [DDD]
Tavener, J.:Western Wind Masses Gimell ▲ CDGIM 027 [DDD] ■ 1585T-27
Taverner, J.:Gloria tibi Trinitas [L] Gimell ▲ CDGIM 004 [DDD] ■ 1585T-04
Taverner, J.:Kyrie 'Leroy' Gimell ▲ CDGIM 004 [DDD] ■ 1585T-04
Taverner, J.:Motets—Dum transisset Sabbatum Gimell ▲ CDGIM 004 [DDD] ■ 1585T-04
Tomkins, T.:Anthems—When David heard; Then David mourned; Almighty God, the fountain of all wisdom; Woe is me; Be strong and of a good courage; O sing unto the Lord a new song; O God, the proud are risen against me Gimell ▲ CDGIM 024 [DDD] ■ 1585T-24
Tomkins, T.:3rd or Great Service Gimell ▲ CDGIM 024 [DDD] ■ 1585T-24
Victoria, T.L. de:Officium defunctorum [L] Gimell ▲ CDGIM 012 [DDD] ■ 1585T-12
White, J.:Sacred Music—Magnificat; Portio mea; Regina caeli; Christe qui lux III; Christe qui lux es IV; Exaudiat te Dominus; Lamentations for 5 Voices Gimell ▲ CDGIM 030 ■ 1585T-30

Tanglewood Festival Chorus
Bartók, B.:The Miraculous Mandarin, w. S. Ozawa (cnd), Boston SO Philips ▲ 442783-2
Berlioz, H.:Requiem, "Grande Messe des Morts", w. Vincent Cole (ten), S. Ozawa (cnd), Boston SO RCA Red Seal ▲ 09026-62544-2
Bernstein, L.:Olympic Hymn, w. J. Williams (cnd), Boston Pops Orch *(rec Symphony Hall, Boston, MA, Jan 6, 10 & 13, 1996)* Sony Classical ▲ SK 62592 [DDD] ■ ST 62592
Brahms, J.:Alto Rhap, w. Jard van Nes (cta), Boston SO Philips ▲ 442130-2
Brahms, J.:Nänie, w. B. Haitink (cnd), Boston SO Philips ▲ 442 799-2
Holst, G.:The Planets, w. J. Williams (cnd), Boston Pops Orch Philips ▲ 420177-2 [DDD]
Ives, C.:Sym 4, w. S. Ozawa (cnd), Boston SO [E] Deutsche Grammophon ("20th Century Classics" series) ▲ 423243-2 [ADD]
Liszt, F.:A Faust Sym, w. Kenneth Riegel (ten), L. Bernstein (cnd), Boston SO *(rec Symphony Hall, Boston, July 1976)* Deutsche Grammophon ("The Originals" series) ▲ 447449-2 [ADD]
Mahler, G.:Sym 2, w. K. Te Kanawa (sop), M. Horne (mez), S. Ozawa (cnd), Boston SO [G] Philips 2-▲ 420824-2 [DDD]
Mahler, G.:Sym 3, w. Jessye Norman (sop), S. Ozawa (cnd), Boston SO, American Boychoir Philips ▲ 434909-2
Mendelssohn, F.:A Midsummer Night's Dream (comp), w. Kathleen Battle (sop), Frederica von Stade (mez), Judi Dench (nar), S. Ozawa (cnd), Boston SO Deutsche Grammophon ▲ 439897-2
Poulenc, F.:Gloria Sop, w. K. Battle (sop), S. Ozawa (cnd), Boston SO [L] Deutsche Grammophon ▲ 427304-2 [DDD]
Poulenc, F.:Stabat mater, w. K. Battle (sop), S. Ozawa (cnd), Boston SO [L] Deutsche Grammophon ▲ 427304-2 [DDD]
Schoenberg, A.:Gurrelieder, w. J. Norman (sop), T. Troyanos (mez), J. McCracken (ten), D. Arnold (bar), S. Ozawa (cnd), Boston SO Philips 2-▲ 412511-2
Sessions, R.:When Lilacs Last in the Dooryard Bloom'd, w. E. Hinds (sop), F. Quivar (mez), D. Cossa (bar), S. Ozawa (cnd), Boston SO [E] New World ▲ NW 296-2 [AAD]
Tchaikovsky, P.:Queen of Spades, w. M. Freni (sop), M. Forrester (cta), V. Atlantov (ten), D. Hvorostovsky (bar), S. Ozawa (cnd), Boston SO RCA Red Seal ▲ 09026-61227-2 [DDD] ▯ 09026-61227-5
Tchaikovsky, P.:Queen of Spades, w. M. Freni (sop), M. Forrester (cta), V. Atlantov (ten), D. Hvorostovsky (bar), S. Ozawa (cnd), Boston SO RCA Red Seal 3-▲ 09026-60992-2 [DDD]
Theodorakis, M.:Canto olympico, w. J. Williams (cnd), Boston Pops Orch *(rec Symphony Hall, Boston, MA, Jan 6, 10 & 13, 1996)* Sony Classical ▲ SK 62592 [DDD] ■ ST 62592

Tapiola Chamber Choir
Bergman, E.:The Singing Tree, w. K. Hannula (sop), C. Hellekant (cta), P. Lindroos (ten), P. Salomaa (bass), S. Tiilikainen (bar), M. Wallén (bass), U. Söderblom (cnd), Finnish National Opera Orch, Dominante Chamber Choir Ondine 2-▲ ODE 794-2D [DDD]
Heiniö, M.:Folk Songs [Fin] Ondine ▲ ODE 796 [DDD]
Kortekangas, O.:The Green Madonna [Fin] Ondine ▲ ODE 796 [DDD]
Kortekangas, O.:Parable [Fin] Ondine ▲ ODE 796 [DDD]
Kortekangas, O.:Verbum [E] Ondine ▲ ODE 796 [DDD]
Kyllönen, T.-J.:Cycle [Sp] Ondine ▲ ODE 796 [DDD]
Länsiö, T.:Chorales [Fin] Ondine ▲ ODE 796 [DDD]
Saariaho, K.:No & Not [Sw] Ondine ▲ ODE 796 [DDD]
Saariaho, K.:Piece [Fin] Ondine ▲ ODE 796 [DDD]

Tapiola Children's Choir
E. Pohjola (cnd)
Dreams, w. Tapiola Sinfonietta [cnd:O. Vänskä] Ondine ▲ ODE 786 [DDD]
Finland in Song, w. Tapiola Sinfonietta [cnd:O. Vänskä] Ondine ▲ ODE 785 [DDD]
Kortekangas, O.:Memoria, w. Timothy Ferchen (perc), Tapiola Choir [Fin] Ondine ▲ ODE 749-2 [ADD]
Rautavaara, E.:Children's Mass, w. P. Pohjola (cnd), Espoo CO *(rec Nov. 25, 1977)* BIS ▲ CD 66 [AAD]
Sounds of Finland *(rec German Church & Tapiola Church, Helsinki, Finland, Nov 25–26, 1977 & Jan 19–)* BIS ▲ CD 94 [AAD]

Tapiola Choir
Bergman, E.:Dreams Ondine ▲ ODE 786-2 [DDD]
Johansson, B.:Pater Noster Ondine ▲ ODE 786-2 [DDD]

Tapiola Choir (cont.)
Kortekangas, O.:A for Instruments & Choir, Tapiola Sinfonietta Ondine ▲ ODE 786-2 [DDD]
Kortekangas, O.:Grand Hotel, w. E.-L. Saarinen (mez), S. Tiilikainen (bar), K. Laurikainen (speaker), Pohjola, Söderström (cnd), Avanti! CO, Finnish Chamber Chorus [Fin] Ondine ▲ ODE 749-2 [ADD]
Rautavaara, E.:Children's Mass, Tapiola Sinfonietta Ondine ▲ ODE 786-2 [DDD]
Sallinen, A.:Suita grammaticale Ondine ▲ ODE 786-2 [DDD]
Sallinen, A.:Vinten var hard Ondine ▲ ODE 786-2 [DDD]
Tapiola Choir Christmas Album Finlandia ▲ FACD 566092
E. Pohjola (cnd)
Kortekangas, O.:Memoria, w. Timothy Ferchen (perc), Tapiola Children's Choir [Fin] Ondine ▲ ODE 749-2 [ADD]

Tarbes Midi-Pyrénées Régional Choir
Fauré, G.:Requiem, w. Antoine Brouquet (sop), Jean-Marie Fremeau (bar), J.-P. Salanne (cnd), Domaine Musical Orch Adès ▲ ADE 204782 [DDD]

Taverner Choir
Bach, J.S.:St. John Passion, w. A. Parrott (cnd), Taverner Consort Virgin Classics ▲ ZDCB 45096
The Carol Album:7 Centuries of Christmas Music, w. Taverner Consort, Taverner Players [cnd:A. Parrott] EMI Classics ▲ CDC 49809
The Carol Album 2, w. Taverner Consort, Taverner Players [cnd:A. Parrott] EMI Classics ▲ CDC 54902
Christmas Album, w. Taverner Consort, Taverner Players [cnd:A. Parrott] EMI Classics ▲ CDC 54529
DDD Christmas, w. Kathleen Battle (sop), Florence Quivar (mez), Taverner Consort, Taverner Players, New York Choral Artists, Toronto Mendelssohn Choir, King's Singers, Empire Brass Angel ▲ CDM 63666
Handel, G.F.:Carmelite Vespers, "Saeviat tellus inter vigores", w. A. Parrott (cnd), Taverner Players [L] EMI Classics 2-▲ CDCB 49749 [DDD]
Handel, G.F.:Israel in Egypt, w. Nancy Argenta (sop), Emily Van Evera (sop), Jan Wilson (mez), Anthony Rolfe Johnson (ten), Thomas (sgr), White (sgr), A. Parrott (cnd), Taverner Players [E] EMI Classics 2-▲ CDCB 54018 [DDD]
Handel, G.F.:Messiah, w. Emma Kirkby (sop), Emily Van Evera (sop), Margaret Cable (mez), James Bowman (ct), Joseph Cornwell (ten), David Thomas (bass), A. Parrott (cnd), Taverner Consort [E] EMI Classics 2-▲ CDCB 49801 [DDD]
Handel, G.F.:Messiah, w. Emily van Evera (sop), Emma Kirkby (sop), Margaret Cable (alt), James Bowman (ct), A. Parrott (cnd), Taverner Players Virgin Classics 2-▲ ZDMB 61330
Josquin Desprez:Chansons & Motets, w. A. Parrott (cnd), Taverner Consort EMI Classics ▲ CDC 54659
Josquin Desprez:Missa, "Ave Maris Stella", w. A. Parrott (cnd), Taverner Consort EMI Classics ▲ CDC 54659
Josquin Desprez:Motets, w. A. Parrott (cnd), Taverner Consort EMI Classics ▲ CDC 54659
Purcell, H.:Dido & Aeneas, w. E. Kirkby (sop), J. Nelson (mez), D. Thomas (bass), A. Parrott (cnd), Taverner Players [E] Chandos ("Chaconne" series) ▲ CHAN 0521 [DDD]
Purcell, H.:Te Deum & Jubilate, w. A. Parrott (cnd), Taverner Players Virgin Classics ▲ CDC 45061
Schütz, H.:Die Geburt unsers Herren Jesu Christi, w. A. Parrott (cnd), Taverner Players EMI Classics ▲ CDC 47633
Vivaldi, A.:Gloria, RV.589, w. A. Parrott (cnd), Taverner Players [period instruments] Virgin Classics ▲ CDC 59326

Hill, Lewis (cnd)
Purcell, H.:Music of, w. Catherine Bott (sop), Emma Kirkby (sop), James Bowman (alt), Anthony Rooley (lt), Paula Chateauneuf (gtr), Monica Huggett (vn), Catherine Mackintosh (vn), Christophe Coin (vc), Hill, Hogwood (cnd), Academy of Ancient Music, Brandenburg Consort, St. Anthony Singers, Winchester Cathedral Choir—The Double Dealer; Come Ye Sons of Art; The Old Bachelor; Birthday Song for Queen Mary; Oedipus; King Arthur; Bonduca; The Fairy Queen; Son. No. 9 in F; Dido & Aeneas; Abdelazer; Bess of Bedlam; The Married Beau; Hear My Prayer, O Lord; Rejoice in the Lord Always London ("Editions de l'oiseau-lyre" series) ▲ 444620-2

Taverner Consort
DDD Christmas, w. Kathleen Battle (sop), Florence Quivar (mez), Taverner Choir, Taverner Players, New York Choral Artists, Toronto Mendelssohn Choir, King's Singers, Empire Brass Angel ▲ CDM 63666
A. Parrott (cnd)
Bach, J.S.:Cant 4 Virgin Classics ▲ CDC 45011
Bach, J.S.:Easter Oratorio Virgin Classics ▲ CDC 45011
Bach, J.S.:Jesu Bleibet Meine Freude, w. Taverner Players Virgin Classics ▲ CDM 61304
Bach, J.S.:Magnificat, BWV 243, w. Taverner Players EMI Classics ▲ CDC 54926
Bach, J.S.:Mass in b, BWV 232, w. E. Kirkby (sop), E. Van Evera (sop), R. Covey-Crump (ct), D. Thomas (bass), Taverner Players, Tölz Boys' Choir [L] EMI Classics 2-▲ ZDCB 47292-2 [DDD]
Bach, J.S.:St. John Passion, w. Taverner Choir Virgin Classics ▲ ZDCB 45096
The Carol Album:7 Centuries of Christmas Music, w. Taverner Choir, Taverner Players EMI Classics ▲ CDC 49809
The Carol Album 2, w. Taverner Choir, Taverner Players EMI Classics ▲ CDC 54902
Christmas Album, w. Taverner Choir, Taverner Players EMI Classics ▲ CDC 54529
Gabrieli, G.:Music of, w. Taverner Players [period instruments]—canzoni, sonatas & motets EMI Classics ▲ CDC 54265
Handel, G.F.:Dixit Dominus, w. Taverner Players EMI Classics ▲ CDC 54926
Handel, G.F.:Messiah, w. Emma Kirkby (sop), Emily Van Evera (sop), Margaret Cable (mez), James Bowman (ct), Joseph Cornwell (ten), David Thomas (bass), Taverner Choir [E] EMI Classics 2-▲ CDCB 49801 [DDD]
Josquin Desprez:Chansons & Motets, w. Taverner Choir EMI Classics ▲ CDC 54659
Josquin Desprez:Missa, "Ave Maris Stella", w. Taverner Choir EMI Classics ▲ CDC 54659
Josquin Desprez:Motets, w. Taverner Choir EMI Classics ▲ CDC 54659
Monteverdi, C.:Madrigals, w. Taverner Players—Book Eight, 1638 EMI Classics ▲ CDC 54333
Praetorius, M.:Polyhymnia caduceatrix et panegyrica—4 Christmas Motets EMI Classics ▲ CDC 47633
Purcell, H.:Music for the Theater, w. Taverner Players Virgin Classics ▲ CDM 61304
Purcell, H.:Music of, w. Taverner Players Virgin Classics ▲ CDC 45116

Tbilisi Festival Choir
Debussy, C.:Nocturnes, w. J. Mardjani (cnd), Georgian Festival Orch Infinity Digital ▲ QK 66307 [DDD]

Te Deum Singers
R. Birney-Smith (cnd)
In Quires & Places Where They Sing, w. Karl Wilhelm (org) Te Deum ▲ TDR-CD004

Il Teatro Armonico Vocal Ensemble
Pasquini, B.:Cain & Abel, Il Teatro Armonico Instrumental Ensemble Symphonia ▲ SYM 90S01 [DDD]

Teatro La Gran Guardia Chorus
Mascagni, P.:Lodoletta, w. L. Saldari (ten), Beltrami (sgr), G. Mucci (cnd), Teatro La Gran Guardia Orch [I] *(rec live, 10/2/60)* Fonè 2-▲ 88 F 16-36 [ADD]
Mascagni, P.:Il piccolo Marat, w. Virginia Zeani (sop), Clara Betner (mez), Umberto Borso (ten), Nicola Rossi-Lemeni (bass), O. de Fabritiis (cnd), Teatro La Gran Guardia Orch [I] *(rec live, 10/26/61)* Fonè 2-▲ 88 F 17-37 [ADD]

Temple Univ Women's Choir
Debussy, C.:Nocturnes, w. E. Ormandy (cnd), Philadelphia Orch CBS 2-■ MGT 30950
Debussy, C.:Nocturnes, w. E. Ormandy (cnd), Philadelphia Orch *(rec Mar. 14, 1964)* Sony Classical ▲ SBK 53256 ■ SBT 53256

Juan D. Tercero Vocal Octet
Revueltas, S.:Music of, w. Lourdes Ambriz (sop), Jesús Suaste (bar), E. Diemecke (cnd), Camerata de las Américas, Latin American String Quartet—Troka; Cuauhnáhuac; The Owl; Frogs; Duet for Duck & Canary; Why Do You Believe?; Walking; Scenes from Childhood; 4 Little Pieces; The Knifesharpener; Market; Sensemayá *(rec Mexico City, Sept 1996)* Dorian ▲ 90244 [DDD]

Il Terzo Suono Vocal Ensemble
Giordani, G.:Lamentazioni e Miserere, w. Massimiliano Raschietti (org) Symphonia 2-▲ SYM 94D 31

Tewkesbury Abbey School Choir
P. Brough (cnd)
Weelkes, T.:Cathedral Music—Short Service (Magnificat & Nunc Dimittis); When David heard; Gloria in excelsis Deo; Christ rising again; Hosanna to the Son of David; Evening Service for "Trebles" (Magnificat & Nunc Dimittis); Give ear, O Lord; Alleluja, I heard a voice; Laboravi in gemitu meo; O how amiable; O Lord, arise; Evening Service for five voices (Magnificat & Nunc Dimittis) Duo ▲ 89011
A. Sackett (cnd)
Christmas Carols from Tewkesbury Abbey *(rec Tewkesbury Abbey, Jan. 31–Feb. 7, 1994)* Naxos ▲ 8.553077 [DDD]
Texas Boys' Choir
Gabrieli, G.:Choral Music, w. E. P. Biggs (org), Gregg Smith Singers—7 Intonazioni d'organo; 7 Motets; 3 Mass Movements; Sonata in the 9th tone for 8 parts *(rec St. Mark's Basilica, Venice 1967)* CBS ▲ MK 42645 [ADD]
Gabrieli, G.:Sacred Music, w. E. P. Biggs (org), Edward Tarr Brass Ensemble, La Fenice Ensemble, Gregg Smith Singers—Deus, in nomine tuo; Beata es, virgo Maria; Juilemus singuli; Deus, Deus meus, ad te de luce vigilo; O quam suavis est; Kyrie; Sanctus; Benedictus; Cantate Domino; Domine, exuadi orationem meam; Hodie completi sunt; Magnificat; Surrexit Christus; Nunc dimittis; Jubilate Deo; Intonatio *(rec San Marco, Venice, Sept 14–22, 1967)* Sony Classical ("Essential Classics" series) ▲ SBK 62426 [ADD] ■ SBT 62426
Monteverdi, C.:Vespro della Beata Vergine, w. Gloria Prosper (sop), Adrienne Albert (mez), Melvin Brown (ten), Richard Levitt (ten), Archi Drake (bass), R. Craft (cnd), Columbia Baroque Ensemble, Gregg Smith Singers Sony Classical ("Essential Classics" series) 2-▲ SB2K 62656
G. Bragg (cnd)
A Ceremony of Carols, w. Gregg Smith Singers, Dorothy Shaw Hand Bell Choir, Fort Worth Chamber Ensemble Allegretto ▲ ACD 8407 [ADD]
A. Buratto (cnd)
Christmas in the Great Hall Resmiranda ▲ RES 8015
G. Smith (cnd)
A World of Folksong, w. Gregg Smith Singers, Dorthy Shaw Bell Choir, Texas Little Sym *(rec Nov. 1981)* Premier ▲ PRCD 1031 [ADD]
J.N. White (cnd)
At Home in the Great Hall Resmiranda ▲ RES 8012
Texas Schola Cantorum
G. Ebensberger (cnd)
English Choral Music *(rec live, Irons Recital Hall, UTA, Arlington, TX, Oct. 17, 1994)* EPR ▲ EPR 9508 [DDD]
Theater of Voices
Byrd, W.:Mass in 4 Parts, w. C. Bowers-Broadbent (org) *(rec Feb. 1992)* ECM New Series ▲ 78118-21512-2 [DDD]
Byrd, W.:Motets *(rec Feb. 1992)* ECM New Series ▲ 78118-21512-2 [DDD]
Edwards, R.:Secular Songs, w. D. Minter (ct), P. Elliot (ten), P. Hillier (bar)]—In going to my naked bed *(rec Feb. 1992)* ECM New Series ▲ 78118-21512-2 [DDD]
Sheppard, J.:Secular Songs—Vaine, vaine, vaine *(rec Feb. 1992)* ECM New Series ▲ 78118-21512-2 [DDD]
Tallis, T.:Secular Partsongs—O ye tender babes *(rec Feb. 1992)* ECM New Series ▲ 78118-21512-2 [DDD]
P. Hillier (cnd)
The Age of Cathedrals, w. Paul Elliot (ten), Alan Bennett (ten), Paul Hillier (ten) Harmonia Mundi ▲ HMU 907157 ■ HMU 407157
Cantigas from the Court of Dom Dinis *(rec Skywalker Sound, Nicasio, CA, Feb. 14–16, 1994)* Harmonia Mundi France ▲ HMU 907129
Carols:From the Old & New Worlds *(rec Dec. 14–16, 1993)* Harmonia Mundi USA ▲ HMU 907079 ■
Josquin Desprez:Missa de Beata Virgine Harmonia Mundi France ▲ HMU 907136 ■
Lassus, O. de:Paschalis, w. P. Elliott (ten)—Exsultet Harmonia Mundi USA ▲ HMU 907076
Lassus, O. de:Passio Domini nostri Jesu Christi secundum Mathheum, w. P. Elliott (ten) Harmonia Mundi USA ▲ HMU 907076
Lassus, O. de:Sacred Music, w. P. Elliott (ten)—Visitatio [from *Easter Dialogue*] Harmonia Mundi USA ▲ HMU 907076
Mouton, J.:Motets Harmonia Mundi France ▲ HMU 907136
Thoronet Abbey Choir
Gregorian Chant, w. Abbé Damien Poisblaud Choir Pavane ▲ ADW 7239 [DDD]
3 Counter-Tenors [Pascal Bertin, Andreas Scholl, Dominique Visse]
The 3 Countertenors Harmonia Mundi France ▲ HMC 901552 ■ HMC 401552
Thüringian Academic Sing Circle
Hasse, J.A.:Mass for Dresden, "Terza messa", w. L. Güttler (cnd), Virtuosi Saxoniae Berlin Classics ▲ BER 1006 [DDD]
Mauersberger, R.:St. Luke, w. A. Bassenge (alt), H.-M. Uhle (ten) *(rec May 24–26, 1991)* Thorofon ▲ CTH 2127 [DDD]
Zelenka, J.D.:Confitebor, w. Burkhard Glaetzner (ob), L. Güttler (cnd), Virtuosi Saxoniae Berlin Classics 4-▲ BER 1150 [DDD]
Zelenka, J.D.:Laudate pueri, w. L. Güttler (cnd), Virtuosi Saxoniae Berlin Classics 4-▲ BER 1150 [DDD]
Zelenka, J.D.:Missa Dei Patris, w. L. Güttler (cnd), Virtuosi Saxoniae Berlin Classics ▲ BER 1078
Zelenka, J.D.:Missa Dei Patris, w. L. Güttler (cnd), Virtuosi Saxoniae Berlin Classics 4-▲ BER 1150 [DDD]
W. Unger (cnd)
Mauersberger, R.:Geh aus, mein Herz, und suche Freude, w. Sabine Dicke (sop), Dorothea Schmidt (sop), Friederike Urban (sop), Annette Bassenge (alt), Christiane Fischer (alt), Sabine Hering (alt), Johannes Unger (org) Thorofon ▲ CTH 2245 [DDD]
Thüringian Landestheater Rudolstadt Chorus
Wagner, S.:Schwarzschwanenreich, w. Beth Johanning (sop—Linda), Kerstin Quandt (cta—Ursula), Walter Raffeiner (ten—Ludwig), Lucian Chioreanu (ten—A Boy), André Wenhold (bar—Oswald), Roland Hartmann (sgr—Tempter/Priest), Jutta Maria Schmitz (sgr—Ash-Woman), Ksenija Lukie (sgr—A Girl), K. Bach (cnd), Thüringian Saalfeld-Rudolstadt SO *(rec Thüringer Landestheater, Rudolstadt, June 1994)* Marco Polo 2-▲ 8.223777-8 [DDD]
Thüringian State Theater Chorus
Wagner, S.:Der Bärenhäuter, w. B. Johanning (sop—Luise), K. Likic (sop—Lene), T. Koon (sop—Gunda), V. Horn (ten—Hans Kraft), A. Feilhaber (ten—Nikolaus Spitz), R. Hartmann (bar—Kaspar Wild), A. Wenhold (bar—Stranger), A. Waller (bass—Devil), H. Kiichli (bass—Melchior Fröhlich), K. Bach (cnd), Thüringian SO *(rec Rudolstadt, July 25–31, 1993)* Marco Polo ("Opera Classics" series) 2-▲ 8.223713/4 [DDD]
Tiffin Boys' School Choir
Mahler, G.:Sym 8, w. K. Tennstedt (cnd), London PO, London Phil Chorus [G,L] EMI Classics 2-▲ CDCB 47625 [DDD]
Stravinsky, I.:Perséphone, w. A. Fournet (nar), A. Rolfe-Johnson (ten), K. Nagano (cnd), London PO, London Phil Chorus [F] Virgin Classics 2-▲ 59077 [DDD]
Tilburgs Vocal Ensemble
M. van Woerkum (cnd)
Charpentier, M.-A.:Judicum Salomonis Erasmus ▲ WVH 174
Timadeuc Abbey Monks' Choir
Salve Regina, w. Citeaux Abbey Monks' Choir, Sept-fons Abbey Monks' Choir Studio SM ▲ 12 16 34
Le temps de Noël, w. Ligugé Abbey Monks' Choir Studio SM 2-▲ 121910
Le Temps de Noël, w. En-Calcat Abbey Monks' Choir, Ligugé Abbey Monks' Choir, Bec-Hellouin Abbey Monks' Choir, Les Peres de Chevilly Studio SM 2-▲ 1219.10
Veni Domine Studio SM ▲ 121700
Fabien (cnd)
Ubi Caritas:Chant Grégorian à l'Abbaye de Timadeuc *(rec Sept 1995)* Studio SM ▲ D2499 [DDD]

TimeChange
Caccini, F.:La liberazione di Ruggiero dall'isola d'Alcina, w. Linda De Rungs (sop—Alcian/Vistola), Cecilia Amorocho (sgr—Melissa/Nunzia), Laura Lea Duckworth (sgr—Siren/Harpy), Eric Friedlander (sgr—Monster), L. Ernest Gross (sgr—Enchanted Cypress), Phoebe Jevtovic (sgr—Siren), James Rittenhouse (sgr—Ruggiero/Neptune), Sharon Sim (sgr—Siren), R. Burchard (cnd), Ars Femina Ensemble *(rec Louisville, KY, 1993)* Nannerl ▲ NR-ARS 003; ■ NR-ARS 003
Timisoara Banatul Phil Chorus
Honegger, A.:Amphion, w. Olivier Lallouette (bar—Apollon), Laurent Manzoni (bar—Amphion), Iona Bentoiu (sgr—muse), Theodora Ciucur (sgr—muse), Lucia Kriska (sgr—muse), Adriana Mestes (sgr—muse), J.-F. Antonioli (cnd), Timisoara PO, Timisoara Children's Chorus *(rec Salle Ion Vidu, Timisoara, Romania, Oct 28 & Nov 1, 1995)* Timpani ▲ 1035 [DDD]
Timisoara Memorial, w. Timisoara Banatul PO, Timisoara Romanian Opera Orch, various cnds & soloists Electrecord ▲ ELC 109 [AAD]
D. Nicoara (cnd)
Cucu, G.:Orthodox Liturgy (sels) *(rec 6/90)* Electrecord ▲ ELCD 123 [AAD]
Timisoara Children's Chorus
Honegger, A.:Amphion, w. Olivier Lallouette (bar—Apollon), Laurent Manzoni (bar—Amphion), Iona Bentoiu (sgr—muse), Theodora Ciucur (sgr—muse), Lucia Kriska (sgr—muse), Adriana Mestes (sgr—muse), J.-F. Antonioli (cnd), Timisoara PO, Timisoara Banatul Phil Chorus *(rec Salle Ion Vidu, Timisoara, Romania, Oct 28 & Nov 1, 1995)* Timpani ▲ 1035 [DDD]
Timisoara Chorus
Landowski, M.:Adagio Cantabile, w. Steliana Calos (sop), Pompei Harasteanu (bass), Dominique de Williencourt (vc), Jacques Taddei (org), R. Georgescu (cnd), Timisoara PO *(rec Mar. 16–18, 1993)* Chamade ▲ 5611 [DDD]
Landowski, M.:Leçons de Ténèbres, w. Steliana Calos (sop), Pompei Harasteanu (bass), Dominique de Williencourt (vc), Jacques Taddei (org), R. Georgescu (cnd), Timisoara PO *(rec Mar. 16–18, 1993)* Chamade ▲ 5611 [DDD]
Tivoli Concert Choir
Gade, N.W.:Elverskud, w. Susanne Elmark (sop-Elf-King's Daughter), Kirsten Dolberg (cta-Mother), Guido Paëvatalu (bar-Oluf), M. Schønwandt (cnd), Tivoli SO *(rec Tivoli Concert Hall, Apr 29–30, May 4, 1996)* Marco Polo/Dacapo ▲ 8.224051 [DDD]
Tokyo Metropolitan Sym Chorus
Fauré, G.:Requiem, w. K. Ito (sop), Ohga, K. Yamada (cnd), Tokyo Metropolitan SO [L] *(rec 1973)* CBS ▲ MK 44738 [ADD]
Tokyo Phil Chorus
Mayuzumi, T.:Nirvana Sym, w. H. Iwaki (cnd), Tokyo Metropolitan SO Denon ▲ DEN 78839
Nishimura, A.:Mantra of the Light, w. K. Akiyama (cnd), Tokyo SO *(rec live Tokyo Metropolitan Theater, Large Hall, June 23, 1993)* Camerata ▲ 32CM 319 [DDD]
Suzuki, T.:Hymnos, w. T. Otaka (cnd), Tokyo PO *(rec Tokyo, June 2, 1990)* Camerata ▲ 32CM 190
Verdi, G.:La traviata, w. L. Aliberti (sop), M. Dvorsky (ten), R. Bruson (bar), R. Paternostro (cnd), Tokyo PO [I] *(rec live, Suntory Hall, Tokyo)* Capriccio 2-▲ 10274/75 [DDD]
Tölz Boys' Choir
Bach, J.S.:Cant 27, w. Markus Schäfer (ten), Harry van der Kamp (bass), G. Leonhardt (cnd), Baroque Orch Sony Classical ("Vivarte" series) ▲ SK 68265
Bach, J.S.:Cant 34, w. Markus Schäfer (ten), Harry van der Kamp (bass), G. Leonhardt (cnd), Baroque Orch Sony Classical ("Vivarte" series) ▲ SK 68265
Bach, J.S.:Cant 41, w. Markus Schäfer (ten), Harry van der Kamp (bass), G. Leonhardt (cnd), Baroque Orch Sony Classical ("Vivarte" series) ▲ SK 68265
Bach, J.S.:Cant 65, w. N. Harnoncourt (cnd), Vienna Concentus Musicus [G] Teldec 2-▲ 2292-42571-2 [AAD]
Bach, J.S.:Cant 68, w. N. Harnoncourt (cnd), Vienna Concentus Musicus [G] Teldec 2-▲ 2292-42571-2 [AAD]
Bach, J.S.:Cant 70, w. W. Wiedl (trb), P. Esswood (ct), K. Equiluz (ten), L. Visser (bass), N. Harnoncourt (cnd), Vienna Concentus Musicus [G] Teldec 2-▲ 2292-42572-2 [ADD]
Bach, J.S.:Cant 72, w. W. Wiedl (trb), P. Esswood (ct), R. van der Meer (bass), N. Harnoncourt (cnd), Vienna Concentus Musicus [G] Teldec 2-▲ 2292-42572-2 [ADD]
Bach, J.S.:Cant 84, w. W. Wiedl (trb), N. Harnoncourt (cnd), Vienna Concentus Musicus [G] Teldec 2-▲ 2292-42578-2 [ADD]
Bach, J.S.:Cant 104, w. K. Equiluz (ten), P. Huttenlocher (bar), N. Harnoncourt (cnd), Vienna Concentus Musicus [G] Teldec ▲ 2292-42602-2
Bach, J.S.:Cant 105, w. W. Wiedl (trb), P. Esswood (ct), K. Equiluz (ten), M. van Egmond (b-bar), N. Harnoncourt (cnd), Vienna Concentus Musicus [G] Teldec ▲ 2292-42602-2
Bach, J.S.:Cant 109, w. P. Esswood (ct), K. Equiluz (ten), N. Harnoncourt (cnd), Vienna Concentus Musicus [G] Teldec 2-▲ 2292-42603-2
Bach, J.S.:Cant 110, w. W. Wiedl (trb), S. Frangoulis (trb), P. Esswood (ct), Stumpf (sgr), K. Equiluz (ten), M. van Egmond (b-bar), S. Lorenz (b-bar), N. Harnoncourt (cnd), Vienna Concentus Musicus [G] Teldec 2-▲ 2292-42603-2
Bach, J.S.:Cant 153, w. S. Rampf (ct), K. Equiluz (ten), T. Hampson (b-bar), N. Harnoncourt (cnd), Vienna Concentus Musicus [G] Teldec 2-▲ 2292-42632-2 [DDD]
Bach, J.S.:Cant 154, w. P. Esswood (ct), K. Equiluz (ten), T. Hampson (b-bar), N. Harnoncourt (cnd), Vienna Concentus Musicus [G] Teldec 2-▲ 2292-42632-2 [DDD]
Bach, J.S.:Cant 155, w. A. Bergius (trb), P. Esswood (ct), K. Equiluz (ten), T. Hampson (b-bar), N. Harnoncourt (cnd), Vienna Concentus Musicus [G] Teldec 2-▲ 2292-42632-2 [DDD]
Bach, J.S.:Cant 156, w. P. Esswood (ct), K. Equiluz (ten), T. Hampson (b-bar), N. Harnoncourt (cnd), Vienna Concentus Musicus [G] Teldec 2-▲ 2292-42632-2 [DDD]
Bach, J.S.:Cant 185, w. H. Wittek (trb), P. Esswood (ct), K. Equiluz (ten), T. Hampson (b-bar), N. Harnoncourt (cnd), Vienna Concentus Musicus [G] Teldec 2-▲ 2292-44179-2 [DDD]
Bach, J.S.:Cant 186, w. R. Holl (bass), N. Harnoncourt (cnd), Vienna Concentus Musicus [G] Teldec 2-▲ 2292-44179-2 [DDD]
Bach, J.S.:Cant 188, w. R. Holl (bass), N. Harnoncourt (cnd), Vienna Concentus Musicus [G] Teldec 2-▲ 2292-44179-2 [DDD]
Bach, J.S.:Mass in b, BWV 232, w. E. Kirkby (sop), E. Van Evera (sop), R. Covey-Crump (ct), D. Thomas (bass), A. Parrott (cnd), Taverner Consort, Taverner Players [L] EMI Classics 2-▲ ZDCB 47292-2 [DDD]
Bach, J.S.:St. Matthew Passion, w. G. Leonhardt (cnd), La Petite Bande Editio Classica 3-▲ 7848-2-RC [DDD]
Barbieri, L.:Surgite pastores, w. S. Vartolo (cnd), St. Petronio Cappella Musicale, St. Petronio Voci Bianche Chorus, Avignon Vocal Ensemble *(rec Oct. 3–5, 1991)* Tactus ▲ TC 551801
Britten, B.:War Requiem, w. L. Orgonasova (sop), A. Rolfe-Johnson (ten), B. Skovhus (bar), J. E. Gardiner (cnd), North German RSO, Monteverdi Choir London, North German Radio Chorus Deutsche Grammophon 2-▲ 437801-2
Haydn, J.:Ave regina, w. Marie-Claude Vallin (sop), Bob Van Asperen (org), B. Weil (cnd), L'Archibudelli *(rec Bad Tolz, Germany, Jan. 2–4, 1993)* Sony Classical ("Vivarte" series) ▲ SK 53368 [DDD]
Haydn, J.:Lauda Sion, w. Ab Koster (nat hn), Knut Hasselmann (nat hn), Bob Van Asperen (org), B. Weil (cnd), L'Archibudelli *(rec Bad Tolz, Germany, Jan. 2–4, 1993)* Sony Classical ("Vivarte" series) ▲ SK 53368 [DDD]
Haydn, J.:Libera me, Domine, w. Bob Van Asperen (org), B. Weil (cnd), L'Archibudelli *(rec Bad Tolz, Germany, Jan. 2–4, 1993)* Sony Classical ("Vivarte" series) ▲ SK 53368 [DDD]
Haydn, J.:Mass 4, Missa 'Sunt bona mixta malis', w. Anner Bylsma (vc), Anthony Woodrow (db), Bob Van Asperen (org), B. Weil (cnd) *(rec Bad Tolz, Germany, June 6, 1992)* Sony Classical ("Vivarte" series) ▲ SK 53368 [DDD]
Haydn, J.:Mass 7, "Kleine Orgelmesse", w. Geoffery Lancaster (org), B. Weil (cnd), Tafelmusik *(rec Germany, Sept. 5, 1993)* Sony Classical ("Vivarte" series) ▲ SK 53368 [DDD]
Haydn, J.:Mass 9, "Heiligmesse", w. Matthias Ritter (sop), Simon Schnorr (alt), Jörg Hering (ten), Benedikt Schillo (ten), Panito Iconomou (bass), B. Weil (cnd) Sony Classical ("Vivarte" series) ▲ SK 66260

1020 ▲ = CD ♦ = Enhanced CD Δ = MD ■ = Cassette Tape □ = DCC

Tölz Boys' Choir (cont.)
Haydn, J.:Mass 10, "Kriegsmesse", "Paukenmesse", w. Ann Monoyios (sop), Monica Groop (mez), Jörg Hering (ten), Harry van der Kamp (bass), B. Weil (cnd), Tafelmusik
Sony Classical ("Vivarte" series) ▲ SK 68255
Haydn, J.:Non nobis, Domine, w. Anner Bylsma (vc), Anthony Woodrow (db), Bob Van Asperen (org), B. Weil (cnd) *(rec Bad Tolz, Germany, June 4, 1992)*
Sony Classical ("Vivarte" series) ▲ SK 53368 [DDD]
Haydn, J.:Sacred Music, w. Matthias Ritter (sop), Simon Schnorr (alt), Jörg Hering (ten), Benedikt Schillo (ten), Panito Iconomou (bass), B. Weil (cnd)—Mare clausum (oratorio fragment), H.XXI-Va:9; Motetto Insanae et vanae curae, H.XXI:1; Motetti de Venerabili Sacramento I-IV, H.XXIIIc:5a-d; Te Deum, H.XXIIIc:2
Sony Classical ("Vivarte" series) ▲ SK 66260
Haydn, J.:Salve regina, H.XXIIIb/1, w. Ann Monoyios (sop), B. Weil (cnd), Tafelmusik *(rec Bad Tolz, Germany, Sept. 5, 1993)* Sony Classical ("Vivarte" series) ▲ SK 53368 [DDD]
Haydn, J.:Die Schöpfung, w. Ann Monoyios (sop—Gabriel/Eva), Jörg Hering (ten—Uriel), Harry van der Kamp (bass—Raphael/Adam), B. Weil (cnd), Tafelmusik *(rec Bad Tolz, Germany, Aug. 31-Sept. 4, 1993)* Sony Classical ("Vivarte" series) 2-▲ SX2K 57965 [DDD]
Humperdinck, E.:Hänsel und Gretel, w. H. Behrens (sop—Gertrud, the Stepmother), R. Ziesak (sop—Gretel), R. Joshua (sop—Sandman), C. Schäfer (sop—Dew Fairy), J. Larmore (mez—Hänsel), H. Schwarz (cta—Nibblewitch), B. Weikl (bar—Peter, the Father), D. Runnicles (cnd), Bavarian RSO *(rec Munich, Feb. 1994)* Teldec 2-▲ 94549-2 [DDD]
Humperdinck, E.:Hänsel und Gretel, w. B. Bonney (sop), E. Lind (sop), B. Hendricks (sop), A.S. von Otter (mez), H. Schwarz (mez), M. Lipovšek (mez), Andreas Schmidt (bar), J. Tate (cnd), Bavarian RSO [G]
EMI Classics 2-▲ CDCB 54022 [DDD]
Mahler, G.:Sym 3, w. F. Quivar (cta), B. Haitink (cnd), Berlin PO, Ernst Senff Chorus Women's Voices
Philips ▲ 432162-2
Mahler, G.:Sym 8, w. Sylvia McNair (sop), Andrea Rost (sop), Cheryl Studer (sop), Anne Sofie von Otter (mez), Rosemarie Lang (cta), Peter Seiffert (ten), Bryn Terfel (bar), Jan-Hendrik Rootering (bass), C. Abbado (cnd), Berlin PO, Berlin Radio Chorus, Prague Phil Chorus
Deutsche Grammophon ("4D Audio" series) 2-▲ 445843-2
Mendelssohn, F.:Choral Music—Veni domine; Laudate pueri; Surrexit pastor bonus
Koch International ▲ KIC 340172
Missa Salisburgensis, w. F. Maier (cnd), Montserrat Escolania, Collegium Aureum
Deutsche Harmonia Mundi ▲ 77050-2-RC [DDD]
Mozart, W.A.:Ave verum corpus, w. G. Schmidt-Gaden (cnd), European Baroque Soloists [L]
Sony Classical ("Vivarte" series) ▲ SK 46493
Mozart, W.A.:Canons—K.553; K.554; K.555; K.557; K.562 Koch International ▲ KIC 340172
Mozart, W.A.:Inter natos mulierum, w. G. Schmidt-Gaden (cnd), European Baroque Soloists [L]
Sony Classical ("Vivarte" series) ▲ SK 46493
Mozart, W.A.:Missa [longa], K.262, w. G. Schmidt-Gaden (cnd), European Baroque Soloists [L]
Sony Classical ("Vivarte" series) ▲ SK 46493
Mozart, W.A.:Regina coeli, K.276, w. G. Schmidt-Gaden (cnd), European Baroque Soloists [L]
Sony Classical ("Vivarte" series) ▲ SK 46493
Mozart, W.A.:Te Deum, w. G. Schmidt-Gaden (cnd), European Baroque Soloists [L]
Sony Classical ("Vivarte" series) ▲ SK 46493
Mozart, W.A.:Venite populi, w. G. Schmidt-Gaden (cnd), European Baroque Soloists [L]
Sony Classical ("Vivarte" series) ▲ SK 46493
Mussorgsky, M.:Boris Godunov, w. V. Valente (sop—Xenia), E. Gorochovskaya (mez—Nurse), L. Nichiteanu (mez—Fyodor), E. Zarmeba (mez—Hostess), M. Lipovšek (cta—Marina), P. Langridge (ten—Prince Shuisky), H. Wildhaber (ten—Misail), A. Fedin (ten—Simpleton), S. Leiferkus (bar—Rangoni), A. Kotcherga (bass—B. Godounov), A. Shagidullin (bass—Shchelkalov), S. Ramey (bass—Pimen), S. Larin (bass—Girgory), G. Nikolsky (bass—Varlaam), C. Abbado (cnd), Berlin PO, Berlin Radio Chorus, Slovak Phil Chorus *(rec Nov. 7-30, 1993)* Sony Classical 3-▲ S3K 58977 [DDD]
Perti, G.A.:Messa e salmi concertati, w. S. Vartolo (cnd), San Petronio Cappella Musicale Orch, Avignon Vocal Ensemble, San Petronio Voci Bianche Chorus *(rec Oct. 3-5, 1991)* Tactus ▲ TC 551801
Purcell, H.:Anthems & Services, w. David Cordier (alt), John Elwes (ten), Harry van der Kamp (bass), Peter Kooy (bass), Gustav Leonhardt (org)—In thee, O Lord, do I put my trust; My beloved spake; O praise God in His holiness; Praise the Lord, O Jerusalem; Rejoice in the Lord always
Sony Classical ("Vivarte" series) ▲ SK 53981
Rota, A.:Missarum liber primus, w. S. Vartolo (cnd), San Petronio Cappella Musicale Orch, Avignon Vocal Ensemble, San Petroni Voci Bianche Chorus *(rec Oct. 3-5, 1991)* Tactus ▲ TC 551801
Schubert, Franz:Duetsche Messe, Schmidt-Gaden Orch [G] Acanta ▲ CD 42409
Trombetti, A.:Il primo libro de motetti accomodati per cantare e far concerti, w. S. Vartolo (cnd), St. Petronio Cappella Musicale, St. Petronio Voci Bianche Chorus, Avignon Vocal Ensemble *(rec Oct. 3-5, 1991)* Tactus ▲ TC 551801

G. Schmidt-Gaden (cnd)
Ihn Kinderlein kommet, w. Erich Ferstl (pno/gtr/perc/monochord) Capriccio ▲ 10491 [DDD]

Tomkins Vocal Ensemble
Bengraf, J.:Sacred Music, w. Ingrid Kertesi (sop), Katalin Gémes (mez), Gábor Kállay (ten), Ákos Ambrus (bar), István Ella (org), Zsolt Kovács (vc), Balázs Arnóth (bn), Vilmos Buza (db), J. Dobra (cnd), Vienna-Szász CO—Te Deum; O sacrum convivium; Libera me; Gloria [from Missa solemnis in D]
Hungaroton ▲ HCD 31609 [DDD]
Druschetzky, G.:Missa solemnis, w. Ingrid Kertesi (sop), Katalin Gémes (mez), Gábor Kállay (ten), Ákos Ambrus (bar), István Ella (org), Zsolt Kovács (vc), Balázs Arnóth (bn), Vilmos Buza (db), J. Dobra (cnd), Vienna-Szász CO Hungaroton ▲ HCD 31609 [DDD]
Fauré, G.:Requiem, w. D. Karasszon (org), E. Maros (hp), J. Dobra (cnd), Hungarian Virtuosi CO, Budapest SO Winds Hungaroton ▲ HCD 31424 [DDD]

J. Dobra (cnd)
Liszt, F.:Via Crucis, w. D. Várjon (pno), I. Prunyi (pno) [L] *(rec 2/91)*
Hungaroton ▲ HCD 31424 [DDD]

Z. Kocsis (cnd)
Rachmaninoff, S.:Liturgy of St John Chrysostom, w. Ida Szabó (sop), Tamás Bubnó (ten), Ákos Ambrus (bar) *(rec 1995)* Hungaroton 2-▲ HCD 31610/11 [DDD]

Toonkunst Chorus
Beethoven, L. van:Sym 9, "Choral Sym", w. To de Sluys (sop), Suze Luger (cta), Louis van Tulder (ten), Willem Ravelli (bass), W. Mengelberg (cnd), Royal Concertgebouw Orch *(rec 1938)*
Music & Arts ▲ CD 918
Mendelssohn, F.:A Midsummer Night's Dream (comp), w. L. Dawson (sop), S. Mentzer (mez), J. Tate (cnd), Rotterdam PO, Peter Hall Company EMI Classics 2-▲ CDCB 54348

Toronto Children's Chorus
Adeste Fideles, w. Louis Quilico (bar), Gino Quilico (bar), Judy Loman (hp), Toronto SO members [cnd:Jean Ashworth Bartle] CBC Records ("SM 5000" series) ▲ SMCD 5119 [DDD]
Christmas Dreams, w. Liona Boyd (gtr) A&M ▲ CD 9513 ■ CS 9513
Rutter, J.:Dancing Day, w. J. Loman (hp) Marquis ▲ ERAD 135 [DDD]

J. A. Bartle (cnd)
Christmas with MCA Classics ■ MCAC 15015
Dancing Day Marquis Classics ▲ ERAD 135 [DDD]

Toronto Festival Singers
Stravinsky, I.:Sym of Psalms, w. I. Stravinsky (cnd), CBC Vancouver SO [rev. ver.] [L] *(rec 1963)*
CBS ▲ MK 42434 [ADD]

Toronto Mendelssohn Choir
Beethoven, L. van:Fant Pno, Op. 80, "Choral Fant", w. Anton Kuerti (pno), A. Davis (cnd), Toronto SO *(rec Massey Hall, Toronto, 1986)* CBC ("SM 5000" series) ▲ SMCD 5155 [DDD]
DDD Christmas, w. Kathleen Battle (sop), Florence Quivar (mez), Taverner Consort, Taverner Choir, Taverner Players, New York Choral Artists, King's Singers, Empire Brass Angel ▲ CDM 63666

Toulouse Capitole Chorus
Bizet, G.:Les Pêcheurs de perles, w. B. Hendricks (sop), J. Aler (ten), G. Quilico (bar), M. Plasson (cnd), Toulouse Capitole Orch [F] EMI Classics 2-▲ CDCB 49837 [DDD]
Gounod, C.:Faust, w. C. Studer (sop), R. Leech (ten), T. Hampson (bar), J. Van Dam (b-bar), M. Plasson (cnd), Toulouse Capitole Orch, *(highlights from the above)* EMI Classics ▲ CDC 54358 [DDD]

Toulouse Capitole Chorus (cont.)
Gounod, C.:Faust, w. C. Studer (sop), R. Leech (ten), T. Hampson (bar), J. Van Dam (b-bar), M. Plasson (cnd), Toulouse Capitole Orch EMI Classics 3-▲ CDCC 54228 [DDD]
Gounod, C.:Roméo et Juliette, w. C. Malfitano (sop), A. Kraus (ten), L. Quilico (bar), J. Van Dam (b-bar), G. Bacquier (bar), M. Plasson (cnd), Toulouse Capitole Orch [F] EMI Classics 3-▲ CDCC 47365
Massenet, J.:Don Quichotte, w. T. Berganza (mez—La Belle Dulcinée), A. Fondary (bar—Sancho Pana), J. Van Dam (b-bar—Don Quichotte), M. Plasson (cnd), Toulouse Capitole Orch
EMI Classics ▲ CDCB 54767
Massenet, J.:Hérodiade, w. Cheryl Studer (sop—Salomé), Nadine Denize (mez—Hérodiade), Ben Heppner (ten—Jean), José Van Dam (b-bar—Phanuel), Thomas Hampson (bass—Hérode), M. Plasson (cnd), Toulouse Capitole Orch EMI Classics 3-▲ CDCC 55378

Toulouse Vocal Group
Dupuy, B.A.:Sacred Music, w. Isabelle Poulenard (sop), Jean-Louis Comorette (ct), Erik Gruchet (ten), Dominique Miraille (bar), Jean-Louis Bindi (bass), A. Bourbon (cnd), Baroque Instrumental Ensemble—Noël; Motet; Magnificat Arion ▲ ARN 68330 [DDD]

Tour de Peliz Union Chorus
Fauré, G.:Requiem, w. S. Danco (sop), G. Souzay (bar), E. Ansermet (cnd), Swiss Romande Orch
London ("Weekend Classics" series) ▲ 421026-2 [AAD]

Touraine Petits Chanteurs
Notre Dame de France:Chants de Pèlerinages pour la Sainte Vierge Studio SM ▲ 12 22 40 [DDD]

Trapp Family Singers
Best of MCA Classics 2-■ MCAC2-4048 (m)

Treble Chorus of New England

M. Stultz (cnd)
Angels Are Everywhere!, w. Tanya Kodinsk (pno/org), Richard Stultz (pno) AFKA ▲ SK 539
Stultz, M.:Suite on the Nativity AFKA ▲ SK 510

Tredegar Orpheus
The Voice of Wales, w. Rhos Orpheus Male Voice Choir
Chandos ("Collect" series) ▲ CHAN 6540 [ADD]

Trieste Teatro Comunale Giuseppe Verdi Chorus
Bellini, V.:Norma, w. M. Callas (sop), E. Nicolai (mez), F. Corelli (ten), B. Christoff (bass), A. Votto (cnd), Trieste Teatro Comunale Giuseppe Verdi Orch *(rec live 11/19/53)*
Melodram 2-▲ CDM 26031 [ADD]
Bellini, V.:Norma (sels), w. M. Callas (sop), E. Nicolai (mez), F. Corelli (ten), B. Christoff (bass), A. Votto (cnd), Trieste Teatro Comunale Giuseppe Verdi Orch—13 arias [I] *(rec live 11/19/53)*
Myto 2-▲ 2 MCD 91340 [ADD]
Donizetti, G.:Lucia di Lammermoor (sels), w. L. Gencer (sop), G. Prandelli (ten), N. Carta (bar), R. Botteghelli (bass), Hussu (sgr), Sabatucci (sgr), O. de Fabritiis (cnd), Trieste Teatro Comunale Giuseppe Verdi Orch *(rec live 12/13/57 & 2/10/58)* Melodram ▲ MEL 15003 (m) [AAD]
Mendelssohn, F.:Sym 2, w. Gemma Bertagnoli (sop), Milena Rudifera (sop), Wonjun Lee (ten), L. Jia (cnd), Trieste Teatro Comunale Giuseppe Verdi Orch RS Applausi ▲ 6367-91
Smareglia, A.:La falena, w. Leyla Gencer (sop—La Falena), Rita Lantieri (sop—Albina, sua figlia), Ruggero Bondino (ten—Re Stellio), Dario Zerial (ten—Il ladro), Mario D'Anna (bar—Il vecchio Uberto), Aurio Tomicich (bass—Morio), Giuseppe Botta (sgr—Un marinaio), G. Gavazzeni (cnd), Trieste Teatro Comunale Giuseppe Verdi Orch *(rec Trieste, Mar 18, 1876)* Bongiovanni 2-▲ GB 1131/32
Smareglia, A.:Nozze istriane, w. Maria Chiara (sop—Marussa), Eleonora Iancovich (cta—Luze), Ruggero Bondino (ten—Lorenzo), Alessandro Cassis (bar—Nicola), Alessandro Maddalena (bar—Biagio), Carlo Zardo (bass—Bara Menico), M. Wolf-Ferrari (cnd), Trieste Teatro Comunale Giuseppe Verdi Orch *(rec Trieste, Feb 17, 1973)* Bongiovanni ("Il Mito dell'Opera" series) 2-▲ 1133/34-2 [ADD]
Still, W.G.:Tristan und Isolde, w. C. Ligendza (sop), S. Anderson (cta), C. Heater (ten), A. Svorc (bass), M. Smith (bass), L. Toffolo (cnd), Trieste Teatro Comunale Giuseppe Verdi Orch [G] *(rec live, Trieste, 12/13/69)* Melodram 3-▲ MEL 37072 (m) [AAD]
Verdi, G.:La battaglia di Legnano (sels), w. L. Gencer (sop), J. Gibin (ten), U. Savarese (bar), F. Molinari-Pradelli (cnd), Trieste Teatro Comunale Giuseppe Verdi Orch—extensive selections from Acts 1,3 & 4 [I] *(rec live 3/8/63)* Myto 2-▲ 2 MCD 89010 (m) [ADD]
Verdi, G.:Rigoletto, w. Gianna D'Angelo (sop), Aldo Protti (bar), Vito Susca (bass), Giorgio Tadeo (bass), F. Molinari-Pradelli (cnd), Trieste Teatro Comunale Giuseppe Verdi Orch
Melodram 2-▲ CDM 27006
Zandonai, R.:Francesca da Rimini, w. L. Gencer (sop—Francesca), R. Cioni (ten—Paolo), M. Ferrara (ten—Malatesino), F. Capuana (cnd), Trieste Teatro Comunale Giuseppe Verdi Orch *(rec Mar. 19, 1961)* Arkadia 2-▲ 597 [ADD]

I. Meisters (cnd)
Mendelssohn, F.:Syms (comp), w. Gemma Bertagnolli (sop), Milena Rudiferia (mez), Wonjun Lee (ten), L. Jia (cnd), Trieste Teatro Comunale Giuseppe Verdi Orch RS Prestige 3-▲ 953-0090 [DDD]

Trinity Boys' Choir
Stravinsky, I.:Mass, w. L. Bernstein (cnd), English Bach Festival Orch, English Bach Fest Chorus [L]
Deutsche Grammophon ("20th Century Classics" series) ▲ 423251-2 [ADD]

Trinity Cathedral Choir
Bach, J.S.:St. John Passion, w. Tamara Matthews (sop), Jennifer Lane (alt), Mark Bleeke (ten—Evangelist), David Vanderwal (ten), Kevin Walsh (bar—Pilate), Nathaniel Watson (bass—Jesus), E. Milnes (cnd), Trinity Baroque Orch *(rec Trinity Cathedral, Portland, OR, Mar 31, 1996)*
PGM 2-▲ PGM 111

Trinity Choir

B. Jones (cnd)
With Heart & Voice, w. Ross Wood (org) *(rec Trinity Church, Boston, June 6, 7 & 9, 1994)*
Gothic ▲ GOT 49071 [DDD]

Trinity Chorale

G. Mitchell (cnd)
Green, P.:St. Patrick's Mass Alanna ▲ ALA 5552

Trinity Church Choir
Albright, W.:Chichester Mass Gothic ▲ G 78932 [DDD]
Felciano, R.:Words of Saint Peter Gothic ▲ G 78932 [DDD]
Kay, U.:A New Song Gothic ▲ G 78932 [DDD]
Rorem, N.:Motets on Poems of Gerard Manley Hopkins Gothic ▲ G 78932 [DDD]

J.A. Simms (cnd)
Hoiby, L.:Choral Music, w. R. Osborne (bar), L. King (org)—Ascension (Holy Sonnet No. 7); At the Round Earth's Imagined Corners; Hear Us, O Hear Us Lord; Hymn to the New Age; Inherit the Kingdom; Let This Mind Be In You; Magnificat & Nunc Dimittis; The Offering
Gothic ▲ G 49035 [DDD]

T. Smith (cnd)
King, L.:Org Music, w. L. King (org)—Fanfare to the Tongues of Fire; Introit for a Feast Day; Let Us Love in Deed & Truth; My Heart Is Ready, O God; The Lord's Prayer/And He Shall Reign as King; Benedictus es, Domine; O Gracious Light; Ressurection; The Prophet; The God-Fearing Woman Is Honoured; Revelations of St. John the Divine; The Transfiguration/The Song of Mary *(rec 1989-1990)* Gothic ▲ G 49056 [DDD]

Trinity Church Choir Broadway & Wall Street
Music from Trinity Church Wall Street, Vol. 1:Choral Music by 20th Century American Composers
Gothic ▲ GOT 78932 [DDD]
Sowerby, L.:Choral Music, w. L. King (org), L. King (cnd)—I Will Lift Up Mine Eyes; I was glad; O Light, from age to age; Benedicte Omnia Opera; Thy word is a lantern; Magnificat & Nunc Dimittis in D; And they drew nigh; Come, Holy Ghost; Eternal light; Organ Works—Arioso; Requiescat in Pace
Gothic ▲ G 49034 [DDD]

L. King (cnd)
Howells, H.:Choral Music—Requiem (1936); Te Deum & Benedictus (1952); Coventry Antiphon (1962); Thee Will I Love (1970); Come, My Soul and Antiphon (1978) Gothic ▲ G 49033 [DDD]

Trinity College Choir Cambridge
Duruflé, M.:Mass, "Cum jubilo", w. R. Marlow (cnd), London Musici
Conifer Classics ▲ 74321-2D15351-2D2

CHORAL GROUPS

Trinity College Choir Cambridge (cont.)
Duruflé, M.:Motets on Gregorian Chants, Op. 10, w. R. Marlow (cnd), London Musici Conifer Classics ▲ 74321-2D15351-2D2
Fauré, G.:Requiem, w. R. Marlow (cnd), London Musici Conifer Classics ▲ 74321-15351-2
Messiaen, O.:O sacrum convivium!, w. R. Marlow (cnd), London Musici Conifer Classics ▲ 74321 2D15351 2D2

R. Marlow (cnd)
Bach, J.S.:Motets, BWV 225-30 Conifer Classics ▲ 74321-15350-2
Carols from Trinity *(rec Trinity College Chapel, Cambridge, England, June 29-30, 1988 & July 9)* Conifer Classics 2-▲ 75605-51754-2 [DDD]
A Child Is Born:Carols from Trinity *(rec Trinity College Chapel, Cambridge, July 9-11, 1993)* Conifer Classics ▲ 75605-51517-2 [DDD]
The Choir of Trinity College Cambridge Conifer Classics ▲ 74321-16851-2 ■ 74321-16851-4
Gesualdo, D.C.:Responsoria et alia ad Officium Hebdomadae Sanctae spectantia Conifer Classics ▲ 75605-51232-2 [DDD]
Gibbons, O.:Instrumental & Vocal Music, Fretwork—Hosanna to the Son of David; O Lord, I lift my heart; O all true, faithful hearts; This is the Record of John; Lift up your heads; Almighty & everlasting God Conifer Classics ▲ 75605-51231-2 [DDD]
Glorious Trinity *(rec Trinity College Chapel, Cambridge, 1987-90)* Conifer Classics ▲ 74321-15355-2 [DDD]
Lassus, O. de:Motets—Seasonal motets Conifer Classics ▲ 75605-2130-2
Praetorius, M.:Motets—In dulci jubilo; Nun kommt der Heiden Heiland; Puer natus in Bethlehem; Resonet in laudibus; Vom Himmel hoch; Wachet auf!; Wie schön leuchtet *(rec Trinity College Chapel, Cambridge, England, Mar 21-23, 1995)* Conifer Classics ▲ 75605-51256-2 [ADD]
The Songs of Angels *(rec Trinity College Chapel, Cambridge)* Conifer Classics ▲ 75605-51261-2 [DDD]
Stairway to Heaven, w. Richard Pearce (org), Philip Rushforth (org), Silas Standage (org) *(rec Trinity College Chapel, Cambridge)* Conifer Classics ▲ 75605-51521-2 [DDD]
Stravinsky, I.:Choral Music—Pater Noster; Ave Maria; The Dove Descending; Tres sacrae cantiones di Gesualdo Conifer Classics ▲ 75605-51232-2 [DDD]
Tomkins, T.:Anthems Conifer Classics ▲ 74321-16071-2
Weelkes, T.:Anthems Conifer Classics ▲ 74321-16071-2

Trinity-St. Sergius Laura Monks' Choir
A. Matfei (cnd)
Hymns to the Mother of God at the Moleben, w. Moscow Theological Academy Choir, Nicolai Ivanov (cant), Nicolai Zabelich (cant) *(rec Cathedral of the Dormition, Trinity-St. Sergiy Lavra, June 1987)* Russian Compact Disc ▲ RCD 15002 [AAD]

Tritonus
Ellington, D.:Music of, w. Margareta Jalkéus (sop), Peder Pedersen's Big Band—Praise God [Introduction]; Heaven; Freedom-Suite; The Shepherd; The Majesty of God; Come Sunday; David Dances before the Lord; Almighty God; T.G.T.T.; Praise God & Dance [Final] *(rec Copenhagen, Jan 1996)* Classico ▲ CD 142

G. B. Trofello Schola Cantorum
Marcello, B.:Il pianto e il riso delle quattro stagioni, w. S. Piccollo (sop–Primavera), A. Carmignani (ct–Estate), M. Beasley (ten–Autunno), R. Franceschetto (bass–Inverno), F. Ghiglione (cnd), Don Milani Cultural Association Orch *(rec Mar. 29, 1992)* Bongiovanni 2-▲ GB 2159/60 [DDD]

Troitse-Sergeyev Monastery Chorus
A. Matfei (cnd)
Christmas Liturgy *(rec live, Upensky Cathedral of the Kremlin, Moscow, Jan 8, 1992)* Russian Disc ▲ RD CD 11036 [DDD]

Trondheim Sym Chorus
Jensen, L.I.:The Return, w. A. Bolstad (sop), R. Sterne (alt), H. Bjørkey (ten), I. Gilhuus (ten), P. Vollestad (bar), C. Stabell (bass), O.K. Ruud (cnd), Trondheim SO, Nidarso Cathedral Choir Simax 2-▲ PSC 3109

Truro Cathedral Choir
D. Briggs (cnd)
Choral Evensong from Truro Cathedral, w. Henry Doughty (org) Priory ▲ PRCD 322 [DDD]
Great Cathedral Anthems, Volume 5, w. Simon Morley (org) Priory ▲ PRI 429 [DDD]

Tudor Singers Montreal
Bach, J.S.:Cant 140, w. Rosemarie Landry (sop), Ben Heppner (ten), Mark Pedrotti (bass), W. Riddell (cnd), CBC Vancouver SO CBC ▲ 5163 [DDD]
Hétu, J.:Les Illusions fanées CBC ("Musica Viva" series) ▲ MVCD 1039 [DDD] ■ MVC 1039 (D)

Turin Cetra Chorus
Mascagni, P.:Cavalleria rusticana, w. G. Simionato (sop—Santuzza), F. Cadoni (mez—Lola), L. Pellogrino (cta—Lucia), A. Braschi (ten—Turiddu), C. Tagliabue (bar—Alfio), A. Basile (cnd), Italian Lyric Orch *(rec Turin, 1950)* Cetra Classic 2-▲ CDO 27 [ADD]

Turin EIAR Chorus
Bellini, V.:Norma, w. G. Cigna (sop), E. Stignani (mez), G. Breviario (ten), T. Pasero (bass), V. Gui (cnd), Turin EIAR SO *(rec 1937)* Memories 2-▲ MEM 4552 [ADD]
Bellini, V.:Norma, w. Gina Signa (sop), Ebe Stignani (mez), Giovanni Breviario (ten), Tancredi Pasero (bass), V. Gui (cnd), Turin EIAR SO *(rec 1937)* Grammofono 2000 2-▲ GRM 78583

Turin Lyric Chorus
Catalani, A.:La Wally, w. L. Marimpietri (sop), R. Tebaldi (sop), M. del Monaco (ten), P. Cappuccilli (bar), Justino Diaz (bass), F. Cleva (cnd), Monte Carlo Opera Orch [I] London 2-▲ 425417-2 [ADD]

Turin Polyphonic Chorus
Leo, L.:La Morte di Abele, w. Emilia Cundari (sop—Angelo), Giuliana Matteini (sop—Abele), Adriana Lazzarini (mez—Eva), Ferrando Ferrari (ten—Caino), Paolo Montarsolo (bass—Adamo), C. F. Cillario (cnd), Angelicum CO Dynamic 2-▲ CDL 144

Turin Radio Chorus
Bach, J.S.:Cant 106, "Actus tragicus", w. M. László (sop), H. Handt (ten), J. Loomis (bass), H. Scherchen (cnd), Turin Radio Orch [G] *(rec live, Jan 14, 1958)* Memories ▲ HR 4160 (m) [ADD]
Mascagni, P.:L'amico Fritz, w. P. Tassinari (sop—Suzel), A. Pini (mez—Beppe), F. Tagliavini (ten—Fritz), A. Giannotti (ten—Frederico), S. Meletti (bar—David), P. L. Latinucci (bass—Hanezò), P. Mascagni (cnd), Turin RSO *(rec 1941)* Cetra Classic 2-▲ CDO 18
Massenet, J.:Werther, w. M. Olivero (sop), A. Lazzari (ten), S. Meletti (bar), M. Rossi (cnd), Turin RSO *(rec live, 6/12/63)* Melodram 2-▲ MEL 27065 (m) [AAD]
Meyerbeer, G.:Le Prophète, w. M. Rinaldi (sop), M. Horne (mez), N. Gedda (ten), R. El Hage (bass), H. Lewis (cnd), Turin RSO [F] *(rec live 7/11/70)* Foyer 3-▲ FOY 2035 [AAD]
Verdi, G.:I vespri siciliani, w. A. Cerquetti (sop), Ortica (sgr), C. Tagliabue (bar), B. Christoff (bass), M. Rossi (cnd), Turin Radio Orch [I] *(rec live, Turin, 11/16/55)* Claque 2-▲ CLQ 2017 (m)

Turin RAI Chorus
Bellini, V.:Beatrice di Tenda, w. A. Gulin (sop), E. Zilio (mez), J. Carreras (ten), R. Bruson (bar), F. Mannino (cnd), Turin RAI Orch [I] *(rec live Oct. 9, 1973)* Golden Age of Opera 2-▲ GAO 158/59 [ADD]
Boito, A.:Nerone, w. I. Ligabue (sop), R. Baldani (mez), B. Prevedi (bar), A. Ferrin (bass), G. Gavazzeni (cnd), Turin RAI SO *(rec live 1975)* Italian Opera Rarities 2-▲ IOR 7704 [ADD]
Cilea, F.:Gloria, w. M. Roberti (sop), A. M. Rota (cta), F. Labò (ten), A. Albertini (bar), L. Testi (bar), E. Campi (bass), F. Mazzoli (bass), F. Previtali (cnd), Turin RAI Orch [I] *(rec live, Turin July 8, 1969)* Memories ▲ HR 4472 [ADD]
Donizetti, G.:Don Pasquale, w. A. Noni (sop—Norina), C. Valletti (ten—Ernesto), M. Borriello (bar—Dr. Malatesta), S. Bruscantini (bass-bar—Pasquale), M. Rossi (cnd), Turin RAI SO *(rec 1952)* Cetra Classic 2-▲ CDO 14 [AAD]
Donizetti, G.:La favorita, w. F. Cossotto (mez), J. Aragall (ten), A. Colzani (bar), E. Gracis (cnd), Turin RAI Orch *(rec live)* Melodram 2-▲ MEL 27020
Donizetti, G.:Lucia di Lammermoor, w. R. Scotto (sop—Lucia), L. Pavarotti (ten—Edgardo), P. Cappuccilli (bar—Enrico), F. Molinari-Pradelli (cnd), Turin RAI Orch [I] *(rec live, Turin 10/10/67)* Verona 2-▲ 27083/84

Turin RAI Chorus (cont.)
Flotow, F. von:Martha, w. E. Rizzieri (sop—Lady Enrichetta), P. Tassinari (sop—Nancy), F. Tagliavini (ten—Lionello), C. Tagliabue (bar—Plumkett), B. Carmassi (bass—Sir Tristano), F. Molinari-Pradelli (cnd), Turin RAI Orch *(rec 1953; Italian libretto)* Cetra Classic 2-▲ CDO 7 [AAD]
Giordano, U.:Fedora, w. Maria Caniglia (sop), Aldc Bertocci (ten), Giacinto Prandelli (ten), Scipio Colombo (bar), Andrea Piccinni (bass), Capozzi (sgr), M. Rossi (cnd), Turin RAI SO *(rec 1950)* Cetra Classic 2-▲ Don 35
Leoncavallo, R.:Pagliacci, w. C. Gavazzi (sop—Nedda), C. Bergonzi (ten—Canio), S. Di Tommaso (ten—Beppe), C. Tagliabue (bar—Tonio), M. Rossi (bar—Silvio), A. Simonetto (cnd), Turin RAI SO *(rec Turin, 1951)* Cetra Classic 2-▲ CDO 27 [ADD]
Mercadante, S.:Arias, w. M. Olivero (sop), R. Majone (cnd), Turin RAI Orch—single arias from Virginia & Pelagio; Aria (La sette parole di nostro signore); Sinfonia from Rossini's Stabat Mater *(rec live, Turin, 11/23/70)* Melodram 2-▲ MEL 27099 [ADD]
Ponchielli, A.:La Gioconda, w. M. Callas (sop), F. Barbieri (mez), G. Poggi (ten), P. Silveri (bar), G. Neri (bass), A. Votto (cnd), Turin RAI SO *(rec 1952)* Andromeda 3-▲ ANR 2528 [ADD]
Ponchielli, A.:La Gioconda, w. M. Callas (sop—Gioconda), F. Barbieri (mez—Laura), M. Amadini (sgr—La Cieca), G. Poggi (ten—Enzo), P. Silveri (bar—Barnaba), G. Neri (bass—Alvise), A. Votto (cnd), Turin RAI Orch *(rec 1952)* Cetra Classic 3-▲ CDO 8
Ponchielli, A.:La Gioconda, w. M. Callas (sop), F. Barbieri (mez), G. Poggi (ten), P. Silveri (bar), G. Neri (bass), A. Votto (cnd), Turin RAI SO *(rec 1952)* Enterprise ("Palladio" series) ▲ ENT PD 4152 [DDD]
Puccini, G.:Tosca, w. Magda Olivero (sop), Alvinio Misciano (ten), F. Vernizzi (cnd), Turin RAI Orch Melodram 2-▲ CDM 27025
Rossini, G.:La donna del lago, w. M. Caballé (sop), J. Hamari (mez), F. Bonisolli (ten), R. Bottazzo (ten), P. Bellugi (cnd), Turin RAI Orch [I] *(rec live 5/19/70)* Melodram 2-▲ MEL 27074 (m) [AAD]
Rossini, G.:La donna del lago, w. M. Caballé (sop), J. Hamari (mez), F. Bonisolli (ten), R. Bottazzo (ten), P. Bellugi (cnd), Turin Radio Orch [I] *(rec live 5/19/70)* Standing Room Only 2-▲ SRO 803-2 (m) [ADD]
Szymanowski, K.:Stabat Mater, w. A. Martino (sop), A. M. Rota (alt), R. Capecchi (bar), A. Rodzinski (cnd), Turin RAI SO *(rec 1955)* Stradivarius 2-▲ DAT 12306 [ADD]
Verdi, G.:Un ballo in maschera, w. M. Curtis Verna (sop—Amelia), M. Erato (sop—Oscar), P. Tassinari (cta—Ulrica), F. Tagliavini (ten—Riccardo), G. Valdengo (bar—Renato), A. Albertini (bar—Silvano), M. Stefanoni (bass—Samuel), V. Susca (bass—Tom), A. Questa (cnd), Turin RAI SO *(rec 1954)* Cetra Classic 2-▲ CDO 13 [AAD]
Verdi, G.:Jérusalem, w. K. Ricciarelli (sop), J. Carreras (ten), S. Nimsgern (b-bar), G. Gavazzeni (cnd), Turin RAI Orch [F] *(rec live 12/20/75)* Standing Room Only 2-▲ SRO 828-2 [ADD]
Verdi, G.:Oberto, Conte di San Bonifacio, w. Elena Nicolai (mez), Giuseppe Modesti (bass), Gino Bonelli (sgr), Lydia Roan (sgr), Maria Vitale (sgr), A. Simonetto (cnd), Turin RAI Orch Great Opera Performances 2-▲ GOP 774
Verdi, G.:Requiem Mass (sels), w. M. Caniglia (sop), E. Stignani (mez), B. Gigli (ten), T. Pasero (bass), V. de Sabata (cnd), Rome CO, Rome RAI Chorus—Dies irae; Sanctus; Libera me *(rec Dec. 14, 1940)* Legato Classics 2-▲ LCD 178-2
Wagner, R.:Die Meistersinger von Nürnberg, w. Bruna Rizzoli (sop), Fernanda Cadoni (mez), Luigi Infantino (ten), Vito Tatone (ten), Renato Capecchi (bar), Giuseppe Taddei (bar), Boris Christoff (bass), Giovanni Ciavola (bass), James Loomis (bass), Silvo Maionica (bass), Vito Susca (bass), Raimondo Botteghelli (sgr), Walter Brunelli (sgr), Carlo Franzini (sgr), Ezio de Giorgi (sgr), Renzo Gonzales (sgr), L. von Matačič (cnd), Turin RAI Radio-TV SO Stradivarius 4-▲ STV 12310

B. Erminero (cnd)
Rossini, G.:La Cenerentola, w. Ornella Rovero (sop), Miti Truccato Pace (mez), Giulietta Simionato (mez), Cesare Valletti (ten), Saturno Meletti (bar), Vito Susca (bass), Cristiano Dalamangas (sgr), M. Rossi (cnd), Turin RAI Orch Fonit Cetra ("Classic Collection" series) ▲ FCT CDON 34

Turin Sym Chorus
Donizetti, G.:Lucia di Lammermoor (sels), w. Luciano Pavarotti (ten), F. Molinari-Pradelli (cnd), Turin SO—Tombe degl'avi miei *(rec live, June 30, 1967)* RCA Gold Seal ▲ 09026-68014-2 [ADD]

Turin Teatro Regio Chorus
Boito, A.:Mefistofele, w. Marcella Pobbe (sop), Ebe Ticozzi (mez), Ferruccio Tagliavini (ten), Giulio Neri (bass), A. Questa (cnd), Turin RAI SO Fonit Cetra ("Classic Collection" series) 2-▲ FCT CDO 19
Boito, A.:Mefistofele, w. M. Pobbe (sop—Margherita), D. De Cecco (sop—Elena), E. Ticozzi (mez—Marta), F. Tagliavini (ten—Faust), G. Neri (bass—Mefistofele), A. Questa (cnd), Turin RSO *(rec 1954)* Cetra Classic ▲ CDO 19
Donizetti, G.:Don Pasquale, w. L. Serra (sop), E. Dara (bar), A. Corbelli (bar), Bartolo (sgr), B. Campanella (cnd), Turin Teatro Regio Orch [I] *(rec live)* Nuova Era ▲ 6766 [DDD]
Donizetti, G.:Don Pasquale, w. L. Serra (sop), E. Dara (bar), A. Corbelli (bar), Bartolo (sgr), B. Campanella (cnd), Turin Teatro Regio Orch [I] *(rec live)* Nuova Era 2-▲ 6715/16 [DDD]
Verdi, G.:Attila, w. Maria Chiara (sop), Silvano Carroli (bar), Nicolai Ghiuselev (bass), N. Santi (cnd), Turin Teatro Regio Orch *(rec live, 1980)* Serenissima 2-▲ SER 360138
Verdi, G.:Luisa Miller, w. K. Ricciarelli (sop—Luisa), M. G. Piolatto (mez—Laura), S. Silva (cta—Federica), J. Carreras (ten—Rodolfo), E. Pranod (ten—A Peasant), R. Bruson (bar—Miller), G. Casarini (bar—Wurm) M. Rinaudo (bass—Count Walter), F. Previtali (cnd), Turin Teatro Regio Orch *(rec May 9, 1976)* Legato Classics 2-▲ LCD 180 [ADD]

Turtle Creek Chorale
Bernstein, L.:Candide (sels), w. T. Seelig (cnd), Dallas Wind Sym—Make Our Garden Grow *(rec June 20-21, 1992)* Reference ▲ RR 49
Brahms, J.:Alto Rhap, w. Melanie Sonnenberg (mez), T. Seelig (cnd), Fort Worth CO *(rec Meyerson Symphony Center, Dallas, June 15-16, 1995)* Reference ▲ RR 67 [DDD]
Bruckner, A.:Choral Music, w. T. Seelig (cnd), Fort Worth CO, Fort Worth Sym Brass—Das deutsche Lied; Ave Maria; Abendzauber [w. Timothy Jenkins (ten)] *(rec Meyerson Symphony Center, Dallas, June 15-16, 1995)* Reference ▲ RR 67 [DDD]
Copland, A.:Old American Songs (set 1), w. T. Seelig (cnd), Dallas Wind Sym—Simple Gifts; The Promise of Living *(rec June 20-21, 1992)* Reference ▲ RR 49
Copland, A.:The Tender Land (sels), w. T. Seelig (cnd), Dallas Wind Sym—Simple Gifts; The Promise of Living *(rec June 20-21, 1992)* Reference ▲ RR 49
Hanson, H.:Song of Democracy, w. T. Seelig (cnd), Dallas Wind Sym *(rec June 20-21, 1992)* Reference ▲ RR 49
Mendelssohn, F.:An die Künstler, w. T. Seelig (cnd), Fort Worth Sym Brass *(rec Meyerson Symphony Center, Dallas, June 15-16, 1995)* Reference ▲ RR 67 [DDD]
Nelson, R.:Behold Man, w. T. Seelig (cnd), Dallas Wind Sym *(rec June 20-21, 1992)* Reference ▲ RR 49
Schubert, Franz:Choral Part-Songs, w. Melanie Sonnenberg (mez), T. Seelig (cnd), Fort Worth CO—Ständchen *(rec Meyerson Symphony Center, Dallas, June 15-16, 1995)* Reference ▲ RR 67 [DDD]
Strauss, R.:Die Tageszeiten, w. T. Seelig (cnd), Fort Worth CO *(rec Meyerson Symphony Center, Dallas, June 15-16, 1995)* Reference ▲ RR 67 [DDD]
Thompson, R.:Choral Music, w. T. Seelig (cnd), Dallas Wind Sym—Pasture & Stopping by Woods on a Snowy Evening (from *Frostiana*); Alleluja *(rec June 20-21, 1992)* Reference ▲ RR 49
Thompson, R.:The Testament of Freedom, w. T. Seelig (cnd), Dallas Wind Sym *(rec June 20-21, 1992)* Reference ▲ RR 49

T. Seelig (cnd)
Anthony, K.J.:When We No Longer Touch TCC ▲ 1030
Biebl, F.:Ave Maria *(rec Meyerson Symphony Center, Dallas, June 15-16, 1995)* Reference ▲ RR 67 [DDD]
From the Heart TCC ▲ 1010
Peace TCC ▲ 1020
A Roamin' Holiday TCC ▲ 1060
Rutter, J.:Church Music, w. J. Martinson (org), Dallas Women's Chorus—Praise Ye the Lord; The Lord Is My Light & My Salvation; All Things Bright & Beautiful; Lord, Make Me an Instrument of Thy Peace *(rec July 28-29, 1993)* Reference ▲ RR 57 CD [DDD]
Rutter, J.:Requiem, w. N. Keith (sop), J. Martinson (org), Dallas Women's Chorus *(rec July 28-29, 1993)* Reference ▲ RR 57 CD [DDD]

▲ = CD ♦ = Enhanced CD Δ = MD ■ = Cassette Tape □ = DCC

Turtle Creek Chorale (cont.)
T. Seelig (cnd) (cont.)
Simply Christmas, w. *(pianist unknown) (rec Morton H. Meyerson, Jan 1996)* TCC ▲ TCC 1100
Testament, w. Dallas Wind Sym Reference ▲ RR 49CD [DDD]
Tuscon Boys' Chorus
Maslanka, D.:Mass, w. Lydia Catherine Easley (sop), Charles Roe (bar), Jane Smith (org), G.I. Hanson (cnd), Univ of Arizona Wind Orch, Univ of Arizona Sym Choir, Arizona Chamber Choir *(rec St. Thomas the Apostle Church, Tuscon, Arizona, Apr 29–30, 1996)* Albany 2-▲ TROY 221–22 [DDD]
UCLA Madrigal Singers
D. Weiss (cnd)
Choral Music of 20th Century Americans Cambria ▲ CD 1068 [DDD]
Union Chorale
Martin, F.:Requiem, w. E. Speiser (sop), R. Bollen (cta), E. Tappy (ten), P. Lagger (bass), A. Luy (org), F. Martin (cnd), Swiss-Italian Orch, Choir of Our Lady of Lausanne, Ars Laeta Vocal Group *(rec live, May 4, 1973)* Jecklin–Disco ▲ JD 631-2 [ADD]
Univ Musical Society Choral Union
Tchaikovsky, P.:The Snow Maiden, w. Irina Mishura-Lekhtman (mez), Vladimir Grishko (ten), N. Järvi (cnd), Detroit SO Chandos ▲ CHAN 9324 [DDD]
Univ of Arizona Sym Choir
Maslanka, D.:Mass, w. Lydia Catherine Easley (sop), Charles Roe (bar), Jane Smith (org), G.I. Hanson (cnd), Univ of Arizona Wind Orch, Arizona Chamber Choir, Tuscon Boys' Chorus *(rec St. Thomas the Apostle Church, Tuscon, Arizona, Apr 29–30, 1996)* Albany 2-▲ TROY 221–22 [DDD]
Univ of Arkansas Schola Cantorum
J. Groh (cnd)
Still, W.G.:Choral Music—Lord I Looked Down the Road; Hard Trials; Holy Spirit Don't You Leave Me; I Feel Like My Time Ain't Long Cambria ▲ CD 1060 [ADD]
Univ of California at Berkeley Chamber Chorus
Handel, G.F.:Judas Maccabaeus, w. Linda Saffer (sop), Patricia Spence (mez), Brian Asawa (ct), Guy de Mey (ten), Leroy Kromm (b-bar), David Thomas (bass), N. McGegan (cnd), Philharmonia Baroque Orch [E] *(rec Nov. 15–18, 1992)* Harmonia Mundi USA 2-▲ HMU 907077/78
Handel, G.F.:Messiah, w. Lorraine Hunt (sop), Janet Williams (sop), Patricia Spence (mez), Drew Minter (alt), Jeffery Thomas (ten), William Parker (bar), N. McGegan (cnd), Philharmonia Baroque Orch—standard version of Messiah *occupies the first sections of each of the three CDs, one part per disc. Each part is followed, after a significant pause, by alternative versions of certain sections of the preceding material, 13 altogether.* [E] Harmonia Mundi USA 3-▲ HMU 907050/52
Handel, G.F.:Messiah (sels), w. Lorraine Hunt (sop), Janet Williams (sop), Patricia Spence (mez), Drew Minter (alt), Jeffery Thomas (ten), William Parker (bar), N. McGegan (cnd), Philharmonia Baroque Orch [E] Harmonia Mundi USA ("Nightingale" series) ▲ HMN 907601
Handel, G.F.:Messiah (sels), w. Lorraine Hunt (sop), Janet Williams (sop), Patricia Spence (mez), Drew Minter (alt), Jeffery Thomas (ten), William Parker (bar), N. McGegan (cnd), Philharmonia Baroque Orch Harmonia Mundi USA ▲ HMU 907120
Handel, G.F.:Susanna, w. Jill Feldman (sop), Lorraine Hunt (sop), Drew Minter (alt), Jeffery Thomas (ten), William Parker (bar), David Thomas (bass), N. McGegan (cnd), Philharmonia Baroque Orch [E] Harmonia Mundi USA 3-▲ HMU 907030/32
Handel, G.F.:Susanna (sels), w. Jill Feldman (sop), Lorraine Hunt (sop), Drew Minter (alt), Jeffery Thomas (ten), William Parker (bar), David Thomas (bass), N. McGegan (cnd), Philharmonia Baroque Orch [E] Harmonia Mundi USA ("Nightingale" series) ▲ HMN 907601
Handel, G.F.:Theodora, w. Lorraine Hunt (sop—Theodora), Jennifer Lane (mez—Irene), Drew Minter (alt—Didymus), Jeffery Thomas (ten—Septimius), David Thomas (bass—Valens), N. McGegan (cnd), Philharmonia Baroque Orch [period instruments] [E] *(rec 9/91)* Harmonia Mundi USA 3-▲ HMU 907060/62 [DDD]
Handel, G.F.:Theodora (sels), w. Lorraine Hunt (sop), Jennifer Lane (mez), Drew Minter (ct), Jeffrey Thomas (ten), David Thomas (bass), N. McGegan (cnd), Philharmonia Baroque Orch Harmonia Mundi France ▲ HMU 907188
Harrison, L.:La Koro Sutro, w. William Winant (gamelan cnd), Karen Gottlieb (hp), Agnes Sauerbeck (org), P. Brett (cnd) [Esperanto] New Albion ▲ NA 015 [ADD];
P. Brett (cnd)
Feldman, Morton:Rothko Chapel, w. D. Dietrich (sop), D. Abel (vn), K. Rosenak (pno), W. Winant (perc) *(rec 10/90)* New Albion ▲ NA 039 [DDD]
Univ of Connecticut Concert Choir
Hodkinson, S.:Missa brevis, w. P. Phillips (cnd), Eastern Connecticut SO [L] Centaur ▲ CRC 2073 [DDD]
Univ of Florida Choir
White, J.:But God's Own Descent, w. D. Waybright (cnd), Univ of Florida Wind Ensemble Opus One ▲ CD 167 [DDD]
Univ of Illinois Chorus
Partch, H.:The Bewitched (final scene), w. J. Garvey (cnd), Univ of Illinois New Music Ensemble *(rec 1957, mono)* CRI ▲ CD 7000 (m/s) [AAD]
Partch, H.:The Bewitched (final scene), w. J. Garvey (cnd), Univ of Illinois New Music Ensemble CRI ■ ACS 6001
Univ of Lausanne Chapelle Vocale
Monteverdi, C.:Madrigals (book 6) Gallo ▲ CD 733 [DDD]
Schütz, H.:Musicalische Exequien Gallo ▲ CD 733 [DDD]
Univ of Louisville Choir
Hovhaness, A.:Magnificat, w. Audrey Nossaman (sop), Elizabeth Johnson (cta), Thomas East (ten), Richard Dales (bar), R. Whitney (cnd), Louisville Orch Crystal ▲ CD 808
R. Spalding (cnd)
Balada, L.:Maria Sabina, w. América Dunham (nar—Maria Sabina), Burwell Hardy (nar—Town Crier), Guillermo Helguera (nar—Constable), Hector Cortés (nar—Executioner), J. Mester (cnd), Louisville Orch New World ▲ 804982
Univ of Louisville Concert Choir
Husa, K.:Apotheosis of this Earth, w. K. Husa (cnd), Louisville Orch Louisville ▲ LCD 005 [AAD]
Univ of Maryland Choral Society
Handel, G.F.:Messiah, w. Edith Mathis (sop), James Bowman (alt), Claes Hakan Ahnsjö (ten), Richard Krause (ten), A. Dorati (cnd), Smithsonian Concerto Grosso [E] Pro Arte 2-▲ CDD 232 [DDD]; ■ PCD 232
Univ of Maryland Chorus
Beethoven, L. van:Missa Solemnis, w. T. Kiberg (sop), R. Lang (cta), W. Cochran (ten), M. Krutikov (bass), A. Dorati (cnd), European SO [L] *(rec live, Berlin Philharmonie, 7/3/88)* BIS 2-▲ CD 406/07 [DDD]
Handel, G.F.:Music of, w. N. Simpson, A. Dorati (cnd), Royal Promenade CO, Smithsonian Concerto Grosso—Royal Fireworks Music; Water Music Suite; Messiah (sels.); etc. Pro Arte ▲ CDM 810; ■ PCD 810
Univ of Miami Chorale
Brahms, J.:Ein Deutsches Requiem, w. Marvis Martin (sop), Kieth Spencer (bar), T.M. Sleeper (cnd), Univ of Miami SO Cane ▲ CR 1003
J.-M. Scheibe (cnd)
Voices & Light, w. Robert Gower (pno) Albany ▲ TROY 215 [DDD]
Univ of Michigan Chamber Choir
T. Hilbish (cnd)
Carter, E.:To Music *(rec Hill Auditorium, Univ of Michigan, Ann Arbor)* New World ▲ 80219-2
Shifrin, S.:Odes of Shang, w. Univ of Michigan SO members *(rec Hill Auditorium, Univ of Michigan, Ann Arbor)* New World ▲ 80219-2
Thompson, R.:Americana, w. Univ of Michigan SO members *(rec Hill Auditorium, Univ of Michigan, Ann Arbor)* New World ▲ 80219-2
Univ of Texas Concert Chorale
Speller, F.:Choral Music, w. Frank Speller (org), P. Gardner (cnd)—Mass of Saint Louis [chorus & organ]; Gloria Patri [chorus & organ]; Hail Mary [Chorus a cappella] Albany ▲ TROY 049-2 [DDD]

Univ of Uppsala Choir
Pettersson, G.A.:Sym 12, w. C.R. Larsson (cnd), Stockholm PO, London Phil Choir Caprice ▲ CAP 21369 [AAD]
Univ of Utah Chorus
Milhaud, D.:L'Homme et son désir, w. F. Kopleff (cta), L. Quilico (bar), M. Abravanel (cnd), Utah SO *(rec 1968)* Vanguard Classics ▲ OVC 8067 [ADD]
Milhaud, D.:Pacem in terris, w. F. Kopleff (cta), L. Quilico (bar), M. Abravanel (cnd), Utah SO *(rec 1965)* Vanguard Classics ▲ OVC 8067 [ADD]
Univ of Utah Civic Chorale
Walton, W.:Belshazzar's Feast, w. R. Peterson (bar), M. Abravanel (cnd), Utah SO Allegretto ▲ ACD 8153 [ADD] ■ ACD 8153
Univ of Washington Chorale
J.C. Conlon (cnd)
Thome, D.:3 Psalms, w. J. Francis (ten) [E] Capstone ▲ CPS 8613
Univ of Wisconsin-Milwaukee Chorus
Downey, J.:What If?, Univ of Wisconsin-Milwaukee Orch Gasparo ▲ GS 276 ■ GS 276C
Uppsala Academic Chamber Choir
Schnittke, A.:Requiem, w. K. Salomonsson (sop), I. H. Sjöberg (sop), L. Lindholm (sop), A. F. Eker (cta), N. Högman (ten), S. Parkman (cnd), Stockholm Sinfonietta [L] BIS ▲ CD 497 [DDD]
Schnittke, A.:Sym 4, w. S. Parkman (ten), M. Bellini (alt), O. Kamu (cnd), Stockholm Sinfonietta [L] BIS ▲ CD 497 [DDD]
Uppsala Choir School Children's Chorus
C.R. Alin (cnd)
Orff, C.:Carmina burana, w. Lena Nordin (sop), Hans Dornbusch (ten), Peter Mattei (bar), Love Derwinger (pno), Roland Pöntinen (pno), Kroumata Percussion Ensemble, Allmänna Sången [chamber version] *(rec Uppsala Univ Hall, Uppsala, Sweden, June 9–11, 1995)* BIS ▲ CD 734 [DDD]
Uppsala Univ Chamber Choir
Kraus, J.M.:Funeral Music for Gustav III, w. C. Högman (sop), H. Martinpelto (sop), C.-H. Ahnsjö (ten), T. Lander (bass), S. Parkman (cnd), Drottningholm Baroque Ensemble Musica Sveciae ▲ MSCD 416 [DDD]
Uppsala Univ Choir
C. Rydinger-Alin (cnd)
A Swedish Bouquet, w. Anders Andersson (ten), Folke Alin (pno), Mats Nilsson (pno) BIS ▲ CD 591 [DDD]
Ural Choir
The Feasts of the Orthodox Liturgical Year, Vol. 1 Russian Season ▲ LDC 288076
The Office of Vespers in the Russian Church Russian Season 2-▲ LDC 288063/4
V. Novik (cnd)
Russian Religious Singing through the Age, Vol. 2, w. Valéry Rybin Choir Russian Season 4-▲ CMX 388052
Russian Religious Singing through the Ages, Vol 7:Orthodox Requiem Russian Season ▲ RUS 288099
Vol. 2 Russian Season ▲ LDC 288077
Ural Cossack Choir
Popular Russian Melodies, w. Russian Festival Ensemble [cnd:Marcel Verhoeff] Koch Schwann ▲ SCH 314048 [DDD]
Sacred Hymns of Old Russia Koch Schwann ▲ SCH 313033 [DDD]
USSR Ministry of Culture Chamber Choir
V. Polianski (cnd)
Rachmaninoff, S.:All-Night Vigil Melodiya ("Russian Choral Music" series) ▲ 74321-25188-2 [DDD]
Tchaikovsky, P.:Liturgy of St. John Chrysostom Melodiya ("Russian Choral Music" series) ▲ 74321-25186-2 [DDD]
USSR Radio Chorus
Scriabin, A.:Sym 1, w. N. Gaponova (sop), Andrei Salynikov (ten), E. Svetlanov (cnd), USSR SO *(rec live, Moscow, April 14, 1990)* Russian Disc ▲ RC CD 11 056 [ADD]
USSR Radio-TV Large Sym Chorus
Khachaturian, A.:Ode to Joy, w. E. Obraztsova (mez), A. Khachaturian (cnd), USSR Radio-TV Large SO Russian Disc ▲ RUS 11 014 [AAD]
USSR State Academic Choir
A. Sveshnikov (cnd)
Tchaikovsky, P.:Choral Music—Hymn to Sts. Cyril & Methodius; As Sleep Approaches; Evening; Song for the Golden Jubilee of the Imperial School of Jurisprudence; Blessed is He Who Smiles; The Golden Cloud was Slumbering *(rec 1966)* Consonance ▲ 815003 [AAD]
Utah Choral
Liszt, F.:Dante Sym, w. V. Kojian (cnd), Utah SO Citadel ▲ CTD 88102 [DDD]
Utah State Univ Chamber Singers
W. Kesling (cnd)
Gawthrop, D.:Choral Music—Sing Me to Heaven; The Bridgewater Motets; Night, Sleep, Death & the Stars; Bright Journeys, Songs of Love & Light; God That Madest Earth & Heaven *(rec Tippetts Art Gallery, USU Chase Fine Arts Center, Logan, UT, Feb. 4–5, 1995)* Integra Classic ▲ IMCD 951 [DDD]
Gawthrop, D.:This Child, This King, w. Rebecca Parkinson (org), Tamara Bischoff-Oswald (hp), Dennis Griffin (timp) *(rec Kent Concert Hall, USU Chase Fine Arts Center, Logan, UT, Feb. 4–5, 1995)* Integra Classic ▲ IMCD 951 [DDD]
Utah Sym Chorus
Handel, G.F.:Judas Maccabaeus, w. Martina Arroyo (sop), Grace Bumbry (mez), J. McCollum (ten), Marvin Sorensen (ten), D. Watts (bass), M. Abravanel (cnd), Utah SO [E] *(rec ca. 1959; originally rele)* MCA Classics 3-▲ MCAD3-10515 [ADD]
Mahler, G.:Sym 3, w. C. Krooskos (cta), M. Abravanel (cnd), Utah SO [G] *(rec 1969)* Vanguard Classics 2-▲ OVC 4005/06 [ADD]
Johanna Uys Melodic Choir
Mendelssohn, F.:Elijah, w. A. Coates (cnd), Cape Town SO *(rec live, 1952)* GSE Claremont ▲ GSE 78 50 54
Valaam Singing Culture Institute Male Choir
I. Ushakov (cnd)
The Kirillo-Belozersk Monastery *(rec Classical Music Studio, 1995)* Russian Compact Disc ("Orthodox Shrines of the Russian North" series) ▲ RCD 29007 [DDD]
The Konev Monastery *(rec Classical Music Studio, 1995)* Russian Compact Disc ("Orthodox Shrines of the Russian North" series) ▲ RCD 29008 [DDD]
The Solovki Monastery, Part 1 *(rec Classical Music Studio, Oct 1994)* Russian Compact Disc ("Orthodox Shrines of the Russian North" series) ▲ RCD 29005 [DDD]
The Valaam Monastery of the Transfiguration of the Lord *(rec Classical Music Studio, Oct 1994)* Russian Compact Disc ("Orthodox Shrines of the Russian North" series) ▲ RCD 29004 [DDD]
Valle de los Caídos Monastery School Children's Choir
Alfonso El Sabio:Cantigas de Santa Maria, w. E. Paniagua (cnd), Ancient Music Group—Star of the Day; Prologue to the 5 Feasts; Dawn of All Dawns; Nativity of Holy Mary; Virginity; Trinity of Holy Mary; Mother of Jesus Christ; Mother of God; Old Woman & Child; Humanity of Holy Mary; Flower of All Flowers; Annunciation; Ave Maria; The Angels' Greeting; Purification-Candlemas; 7 Gifts; Nun & Gentleman; Assumption; Procession; Day of Judgment; Sybil-Judgement Sony Classical 2-▲ S2K 62284
Valley Choral Society
Bach, J.S.:Cant 118, w. E. Flath (org), E. Flath (cnd), California Bach Society CO, California Bach Society Chorus [G] Bainbridge ▲ BCD 2502 [DDD]
Kobialka, D.:Antiphony Across..., w. E. Flath (org), E. Flath (cnd), California Bach Society CO, California Bach Society Chorus Bainbridge ▲ BCD 2502 [DDD]
Vancouver Bach Choir
B. Pullan (cnd)
Serenade to Music, w. Vancouver SO CBC Records ("SM 5000" series) ▲ SMCD 5121 [DDD]

Vancouver Cantata Singers
J. Frankhauser (cnd)
Venetian Vespers of 1640 Skylark ▲ 9301 [DDD]
Vancouver Chamber Choir
Fauré, G.:Messe basse, w. Henriette Schellenberg (sop), Laverne G' Froerer (mez), Keith Boldt (ten), George Roberts (bar), J. Washburn (cnd), CBC Vancouver SO [orchd J. Washburn] *(rec Ryerson United Church & The Orpheum, Vancouver, May 4–7, 1992)* CBC ▲ 5160 [DDD]
Glick, S.I.:Canticle for Peace Centrediscs ▲ CMCCD 4893 [DDD]
Haydn, J.:Mass 7, "Kleine Orgelmesse", w. Henriette Schellenberg (sop), Laverne G' Froerer (mez), Keith Boldt (ten), George Roberts (bar), J. Washburn (cnd), CBC Vancouver SO *(rec Ryerson United Church & The Orpheum, Vancouver, May 4–7, 1992)* CBC ▲ 5160 [DDD]
Louie, A.:Love Songs for a Small Planet, w. E. Goodman (hp), S. Ferreras (perc) Centrediscs ▲ CMCCD 4893 [DDD]
Raminsh, I.:Choral Music, w. J. Washburn (cnd), CBC Vancouver SO—And I think over again; Ave Maria; Ave, verum corpus; Come, My Light; The Great Sea; Magnificat; Songs of the Lights [E,L] CBC ("SM 5000" series) ▲ SMCD 5116 [DDD]
Schafer, R.M.:Magic Song Centrediscs ▲ CMCCD 4893 [DDD]
Sweet Was the Song, w. Catherine Robbin (mez) Marquis Classics ▲ MAR 107
Weber, C.M. von:Missa sancta 2, w. Henriette Schellenberg (sop), Laverne G' Froerer (mez), Keith Boldt (ten), George Roberts (bar), J. Washburn (cnd), CBC Vancouver SO *(rec Ryerson United Church & The Orpheum, Vancouver, May 4–7, 1992)* CBC ▲ 5160 [DDD]
Weisgarber, E.:Night, w. B. Pullan (bar), W. Fawcett (db), J. Washburn (cnd), Purcell Quartet [E] Centrediscs ▲ CMCCD 3790 [DDD]
J. Washburn (cnd)
Beckwith, J.:Harp of David [E] Centrediscs ▲ CMC CD 3790 [DDD]
Chatman, S.:Love & Shapes High Fantastical Centrediscs ▲ CMC CD 3388
Simple Gifts CBC Records ("SM 5000" series) ▲ SMCD 5097 [DDD] ■ SMC 5097 (D)
Varna Phil Chorus
Shostakovich, D.:The Execution of Stepan Razin, w. A. Vassilev (bass), A. Andreev (cnd), Varna PO [R] Koch International Classics ▲ KIC 7017-2 [DDD] ■ 3-7017-4 (D)
Sviridov, G.:Oratorio pathétique, w. A. Vassilev (bass), A. Andreev (cnd), Varna PO [R] Koch International Classics ▲ KIC 7017-2 [DDD] ■ 3-7017-4 (D)
Vasari Singers
J. Backhouse (cnd)
Clucas, H.:Sacred Music—Requiem; Mater Dei; My God, My God; Lux Hominum United ▲ UNI 88020 [DDD]
Górecki, H.-M.:Totus tuus EMI Classics ▲ CDM 65903
Howells, H.:Choral Music—Take him, earth, for cherishing [Motet on the Death of President Kennedy] *(rec All Hallows, Gospel Oak, Feb 18–20, 1994)* United ▲ CAL 88033 [DDD]
Howells, H.:Requiem, w. Sally Barber (sop), Julia Field (alt), Mark Johnstone (ten), Andrew Angus (bar) *(rec All Hallows, Gospel Oak, Feb 18–20, 1994)* United ▲ CAL 88033 [DDD]
Martin, F.:Mass *(rec All Hallows, Gospel Oak, Feb 18–20, 1994)* United ▲ CAL 88033 [DDD]
Pärt, A.:The Beatitudes EMI Classics ▲ CDM 65903
Pärt, A.:Magnificat-Antiphones EMI Classics ▲ CDM 65903
Pärt, A.:Summa [choral version] EMI Classics ▲ CDM 65903
Ridout, A.:Litany EMI Classics ▲ CDM 65903
Tavener, J.:Funeral Ikos EMI Classics ▲ CDM 65903
Tavener, J.:Hymns to the Mother of God EMI Classics ▲ CDM 65903
Tavener, J.:The Lamb EMI Classics ▲ CDM 65903
Tavener, J.:Magnificat & Nunc dimittis EMI Classics ▲ CDM 65903
Venance Fortunat
A.-M. Deschamps (cnd)
Water & Baptism L'Empreinte Digitale ▲ ED 13060
Venice Teatro La Fenice Chorus
Beethoven, L. van:Christus am Ölberg, w. C. Deutekom (sop), L. Kozma (ten), F. Lindauer (sgr), R. Muti (cnd), Venice Teatro La Fenice Orch [G] *(rec live, Venice 7/4/70)* Arkadia ▲ 743 [ADD]
Bellini, V.:Beatrice di Tenda, w. L. Gencer (sop), J. Oncina (ten), M. Zanasi (bar), V. Gui (cnd), Venice Teatro La Fenice Orch *(rec 1964)* Memories 2-▲ MEM 4543 [ADD]
Bellini, V.:I Capuleti e i Montecchi, w. K. Ricciarelli (sop), D. Montague (mez), D. Raffanti (ten), M. Lippi (bass), B. Campanella (cnd), Venice Teatro La Fenice Orch [I] *(rec 1991)* Nuova Era 2-▲ 7020/21 [DDD]
Bellini, V.:I Capuleti e i Montecchi (sels), w. Katia Ricciarelli (sop), Diana Montague (mez), Dano Raffanati (ten), B. Campanella (cnd), Venice Teatro La Fenice Orch Nuova Era ▲ NUO 7183 [DDD]
Bellini, V.:La sonnambula, w. R. Scotto (sop), A. Kraus (ten), I. Vinco (bass), N. Santi (cnd), Venice Teatro La Fenice Orch [I] *(rec live, Venice 5/26/61)* Golden Age of Opera 2-▲ GAO 111/12 [ADD]
Bizet, G.:Carmen, w. M. Chiara (sop—Micaela), A. Caminada (mez—Mercedes), F. Cossotto (mez—Carmen), F. Andreoli (ten—Il Remendado), P. M. Ferraro (ten—Don José), R. Bruson (bar—Escamillo), G. Zancanaro (bar—Morales), A. Carusi (bass—Il Dancairo), P. Maag (cnd), Venice Teatro La Fenice Orch *(rec 1971)* Myto 2-▲ MCD 93487
Donizetti, G.:Belisario, w. L. Gencer (sop), M. Pecile (cta), U. Grilli (ten), G. Taddei (bar), N. Zaccaria (bass), G. Gavazzeni (cnd), Venice Teatro La Fenice Orch [I] *(rec live in Venice, 5/14/69)* Verona 2-▲ 27048/49 (m) [AAD]
Donizetti, G.:Belisario, w. L. Gencer (sop), M. Pecile (cta), U. Grilli (ten), G. Taddei (bar), N. Zaccaria (bass), G. Gavazzeni (cnd), Venice Teatro La Fenice Orch [I] *(rec live, Venice 5/14/69)* Melodram 2-▲ MEL 27051 [AAD]
Donizetti, G.:Maria di Rohan, w. R. Scotto (sop—Maria), E. Zilio (mez—Armando di Gondi), U. Grilli (ten—Riccardo), R. Bruson (bar—Enrico), G. Gavazzeni (cnd), Venice Teatro La Fenice Orch *(rec live Mar. 26, 1974)* Golden Age of Opera 2-▲ GAO 156/57 [ADD]
Donizetti, G.:Les Martyrs, w. L. Gencer (sop), R. Bruson (bar), O. Garaventa (bar), F. Furlanetto (bass), G. Gelmetti (cnd), Venice Teatro La Fenice Orch *(rec 1978)* Italian Opera Rarities ▲ IOR 7178 [ADD]
Leoncavallo, R.:La Bohème, w. L. Mazzaria (sop), M. Senn (mez), B. Praticò (sgr), M. Malagnini (sgr), J. Summers (bar), J. Latham-König (cnd), Venice Teatro La Fenice Orch *(rec live, 1990)* Nuova Era 3-▲ 6917/19 [DDD]
Puccini, G.:La fanciulla del West, w. E. Steber (sop), M. del Monaco (ten), G. Guelfi (bar), D. Mitropoulos (cnd), Venice Teatro La Fenice Orch *(rec live, 6/15/54)* Arkadia 2-▲ 565 (m)
Rossini, G.:Arias, w. C. Bartoli (mez), I. Marin (cnd), Venice Teatro La Fenice Orch—8 scenes from Donna del Lago, Elisabetta, Maometto II, Nozze di Teti e di Peleo, Semiramide, Zelmira [I] London ▲ 436075-2 [DDD] ■ 436075-4 ☐ 436075-5
Rossini, G.:Armida, w. C. Deutekom (sop), P. Bottazzo (ten), O. Garaventa (ten), E. Gimenez (ten), B. Trotta (sgr), A. Maddalena (bass), G. Antonini (bass), C. Franci (cnd), Venice Teatro La Fenice Orch *(rec live, Venice, 1970)* Foyer 2-▲ FOY 2030 [AAD]
Rossini, G.:Armida, w. C. Deutekom (sop), P. Bottazzo (ten), O. Garaventa (ten), E. Gimenez (ten), C. Franci (cnd), Venice Teatro La Fenice Orch [I] *(rec live, 4/3/70)* Memories 2-▲ HR 4152/53 (m) [ADD]
Rossini, G.:Maometto II (sels), w. Cecilia Bartoli (mez), I. Marin (cnd), Venice Teatro La Fenice Orch—Giusto ciel, in tal periglio *(rec 1991)* London ▲ 448300-2 [DDD]; ■ 448300-4
Rossini, G.:Semiramide (sels), w. Cecilia Bartoli (mez), I. Marin (cnd), Venice Teatro La Fenice Orch—Bel raggio lusinghier *(rec 1991)* London ▲ 448300-2 [DDD]; ■ 448300-4
Verdi, G.:Jérusalem, w. Leyla Gencer (sop), Giacomo Aragall (ten), Giancarlo Guelfi (bar), G. Gavazzeni (cnd), Venice Teatro La Fenice Orch [I] *(rec live 9/24/63)* Melodram 2-▲ MEL 27004
Verdi, G.:Jérusalem, w. Leyla Gencer (sop), Giacomo Aragall (ten), Giancarlo Guelfi (bar), G. Gavazzeni (cnd), Venice Teatro La Fenice Orch *(rec Venice, Sept 24, 1963)* Agorá Music ("Phoenix" series) 2-▲ 506
Verdi, G.:Macbeth (sels), w. L. Gencer (sop), G. Lamberti (ten), G. Guelfi (bar), G. Gavazzeni (cnd), Venice Teatro La Fenice Orch [I] [highlights] *(rec live 4/9/68)* Melodram ▲ MEL 15002
Vereinigung Favres Soloists
Mozart, W.A.:Zauberflöte, w. E. Berger (sop), T. Lemnitz (sop), I. Beilke (sop), H. Roswaenge (ten), G. Hüsch (bar), W. Strienz (bass), T. Beecham (cnd), Berlin PO [G] *(rec Nov. 1937 & Feb.–Mar. 193)* Nimbus ("Prima Voce" series) 2-▲ NI 7827/8 (m) [ADD]
Vermont Sym Chorus members
Ullmann, V.:Kaiser von Atlantis, w. R. Decormier (cnd), Vermont SO members *(rec Ira Allen Chapel, Univ of Vermont, Burlington, VT, Jan 28, 1996)* Arabesque ▲ ARA 6681 [DDD]
C. Price (cnd)
Krása, H.:Brundibár, w. R. Decormier (cnd), Vermont SO members, Essex Children's Choir *(rec Ira Allen Chapel, Univ of Vermont, Burlington, VT, Jan 28, 1996)* Arabesque ▲ ARA 6680 [DDD]
Verona Cathedral Cappella Musicale
Salieri, A.:La passione di Gesù Cristo, w. Daniela Citino (sop), Maria Teresa Toso (alt), Nikola Yovanovitch (ten), Mario Scardoni (bass), Giovanna Scardoni (voc), A. Turco (cnd) *(rec Verona Cathedral, Italy, Mar 30, 1995)* Bongiovanni ▲ GB 2190 [DDD]
A. Turco (cnd)
Caldara, A.:Stabat Mater [L] Bongiovanni ▲ GB 5023 [DDD]
Dal Barba, D.:Gloria *(rec Mar. 14, 1993)* Bongiovanni ▲ GB 5536 [DDD]
Dal Barba, D.:Kyrie *(rec Mar. 14, 1993)* Bongiovanni ▲ GB 5536 [DDD]
Gazzaniga, G.:Dies Irae [L] *(rec 3/91)* Bongiovanni ▲ GB 5513 [DDD]
Gazzaniga, G.:Salve Regina [L] *(rec 3/91)* Bongiovanni ▲ GB 5513 [DDD]
Gazzaniga, G.:Stabat Mater & Gloria [L] Bongiovanni ▲ GB 5518 [DDD]
Gazzaniga, G.:Te Deum [L] *(rec 3/91)* Bongiovanni ▲ GB 5513 [DDD]
Giacometti, B.:Sacred Music—Ave Maria Stella; Te Deum *(rec Mar. 14, 1993)* Bongiovanni ▲ GB 5536 [DDD]
Perazzini, B.:Sacred Music—Plange Quasi Virgo; Spulto Domino *(rec Mar. 14, 1993)* Bongiovanni ▲ GB 5536 [DDD]
The Stabat Mater by Antonio Caldara (1725) Bongiovanni ▲ GB 5023-2 [DDD]
Versailles Boys' Choir
Campra, A.:Mass for Christmas Day, w. M. Pérès (org), M. Pérès (cnd), Organum Ensemble Harmonia Mundi France ▲ HMC 901480
Versailles National Masters
Motets en espace, w. Gervais (cnd), New College Choir Oxford [cnd:Edward Higginbottom], Gary Cooper (org) K617 ▲ 7010 [DDD]
Vesna Moscow Children's Choir
Songs of the World Opus 111 ▲ OPS 30157
Vézelay Abbey Choir
I. Reznikoff (cnd)
Le Chant de Vézelay:Marie Magdalen Entombed Studio SM ▲ 12 21 62 [DDD]
Victorian State Opera Chorus
Conyngham, B.:Fly, w. J. Hopkins (cnd), Victorian State Opera Orch Move ▲ MD 3076 [DDD]
Vienna Academy Chamber Choir
Beethoven, L. van:Cant on the Death of the Emperor Joseph II, w. Ilona Steingruber (sop), Alfred Poell (b-bar), C. Krauss (cnd), Vienna SO *(rec live, 1953)* Originals ▲ ORISH 825 [ADD]
Haydn, J.:Mass 6, "Nikolai–messe", "6/4–Takt–Messe", w. Elisabeth Thoman (sop), Rose Bahl (cta), Kurt Equiluz (ten), G. Barati (cnd), Vienna State Opera Orch *(rec 1964)* Tuxedo ▲ TUXCD 1055 [ADD]
Haydn, J.:Mass 14, "Harmoniemesse", w. Christiane Sorell (sop), Elisabeth Thoman (sop), Rose Bahl (cta), Maura Moreira (cta), Kurt Equiluz (ten), Gerhard Eder (bass), P. Wimburger (bass), G. Barati (cnd), Vienna State Opera Orch *(rec 1964)* Tuxedo ▲ TUXCD 1055 [ADD]
Schubert, Franz:Mass 1, w. Laurence Dutoit (sop), Rose Bahl (alt), Kurt Equiluz (ten), Kunikazu Ohashi (bass), Xaver Mayer (org), G. Barati (cnd), Vienna State Opera Orch *(rec 1960)* Tuxedo ▲ TUXCD 1040 [ADD]
Schubert, Franz:Mass 4, w. Laurence Dutoit (sop), Rose Bahl (alt), Kurt Equiluz (ten), Kunikazu Ohashi (bass), Xaver Mayer (org), G. Barati (cnd), Vienna State Opera Orch *(rec 1960)* Tuxedo ▲ TUXCD 1040 [ADD]
Schubert, Franz:Die Verschworenen, w. Ilona Steingruber (sop—Countess), Elizabeth Roon (mez—Helene), Laurence Dutoit (trb—Isella), Walter Anton (ten—Udolin), Walter Berry (bar—Count), Rudolf Kreutzberger (sgr—Astolf), F. Grossmann (cnd), Vienna SO Theorema ▲ TH 121178
Vienna Academy Chorus
Bach, J.S.:Magnificat, BWV 243, w. E. Ameling (sop), H. van Bork (sop), H. Watts (cta), W. Krenn (ten), T. Krause (bass), K. Münchinger (cnd), Stuttgart CO London ("Serenata" series) ▲ 433175-2 [ADD]
Bach, J.S.:Mass in b, BWV 232, w. P. Alarie (sop), N. Merriman (cta), L. Simoneau (ten), G. Neidlinger (bass), H. Scherchen (cnd), Vienna State Opera Orch [L] MCA Classics 2-▲ MCAD2-9821 [AAD]
Bach, J.S.:St. John Passion, w. P. Curtin (sop), E. Thomann (sop), E. Alberts (cta), W. Kmentt, J. Van Kesteren (ten), R. Springer (bar), O. Wiener (bar), D. Smith (b-bar), F. Guthrie (bass), F. Lukasowsky (bass), H. Scherchen (cnd), Vienna State Opera Orch [G] *(rec ca 1960)* MCA Classics 2-▲ MCAD2-9804
Bach, J.S.:St. John Passion, w. P. Curtin (sop), E. Alberts (cta), W. Kmentt (ten), O. Weiner (bar), H. Scherchen (cnd), Vienna State Opera Orch *(rec 1962)* Enterprise ("Documents" series) ▲ ENT LV 925
Handel, G.F.:Judas Maccabaeus, w. Martina Arroyo (sop), Mary Davenport (mez), Lawrence Avery (ten), Jan Peerce (ten), David Smith (bar), T. Scherman (cnd), Vienna State Opera Orch Vox Box 2-▲ CDX 5125 [ADD]
Mahler, G.:Lieder eines fahrenden Gesellen, w. Lucretia West (alt), H. Scherchen (cnd), Vienna State Opera Orch Theorema ▲ TH 121203/04
Mahler, G.:Sym 2, w. M. Coertse (sop), L. West (alt), H. Scherchen (cnd), London Phil SO MCA Classics ("Double Decker" series) 2-▲ MCAD2-99833 [AAD]
Vienna Boys' Choir
Ave Maria, w. Plácido Domingo (ten), Vienna SO [cnd:Helmuth Froschauer] RCA Gold Seal ▲ 07863-53835-2
Ave Maria, w. Plácido Domingo (ten), Mario Lanza (ten), Robert Shaw Chorale RCA Victor ▲ 09026-61838-2 ■ 09026-61838-4
Bach, J.S.:Cant 1, w. P. Esswood (ct), K. Equiluz (ten), M. van Egmond (b-bar), N. Harnoncourt (cnd), Vienna Concentus Musicus [G] Teldec 2-▲ 2292-42497-2 [AAD]
Bach, J.S.:Cant 2, w. P. Esswood (ct), K. Equiluz (ten), M. van Egmond (b-bar), N. Harnoncourt (cnd), Vienna Concentus Musicus [G] Teldec 2-▲ 2292-42497-2 [AAD]
Bach, J.S.:Cant 3, w. P. Esswood (ct), K. Equiluz (ten), M. van Egmond (b-bar), N. Harnoncourt (cnd), Vienna Concentus Musicus [G] Teldec 2-▲ 2292-42497-2 [AAD]
Bach, J.S.:Cant 4, w. P. Esswood (ct), K. Equiluz (ten), M. van Egmond (b-bar), N. Harnoncourt (cnd), Vienna Concentus Musicus [G] Teldec 2-▲ 2292-42497-2 [AAD]
Bach, J.S.:Cant 5, w. P. Esswood (ct), K. Equiluz (ten), M. van Egmond (b-bar), N. Harnoncourt (cnd), Vienna Concentus Musicus Teldec 2-▲ 2292-42498-2 [AAD]
Bach, J.S.:Cant 6, w. P. Esswood (ct), K. Equiluz (ten), M. van Egmond (b-bar), N. Harnoncourt (cnd), Vienna Concentus Musicus Teldec 2-▲ 2292-42498-2 [AAD]
Bach, J.S.:Cant 21, w. P. Esswood (ct), K. Equiluz (ten), W. Wyatt (bass), N. Harnoncourt (cnd), Vienna Concentus Musicus, Chorus Viennensis [G] Teldec 2-▲ 2292-42502-2 [AAD]
Bach, J.S.:Cant 47, w. R. van der Meer (bass), N. Harnoncourt (cnd), Vienna Concentus Musicus, Chorus Viennensis [G] Teldec 2-▲ 2292-42560-2 [AAD]
Bach, J.S.:Cant 49, w. R. van der Meer (bass), N. Harnoncourt (cnd), Vienna Concentus Musicus, Chorus Viennensis [G] Teldec 2-▲ 2292-42560-2 [AAD]
Bach, J.S.:Cant 50, w. N. Harnoncourt (cnd), Vienna Concentus Musicus, Chorus Viennensis [G] Teldec 2-▲ 2292-42560-2 [AAD]
Bach, J.S.:Cant 57, w. N. Harnoncourt (cnd), Vienna Concentus Musicus [G] Teldec 2-▲ 2292-42423-2 [AAD]
Bach, J.S.:Cant 58, w. N. Harnoncourt (cnd), Vienna Concentus Musicus [G] Teldec 2-▲ 2292-42423-2 [AAD]
Bach, J.S.:Cant 59, w. N. Harnoncourt (cnd), Vienna Concentus Musicus [G] Teldec 2-▲ 2292-42423-2 [AAD]

Vienna Boys' Choir (cont.)
Bach, J.S.:Cant 60, w. N. Harnoncourt (cnd), Vienna Concentus Musicus Teldec 2-▲ 2292-42423-2 [AAD]
Bach, J.S.:Cant 61, w. S. Kronwitter (trb), K. Equiluz (ten), R. van der Meer (bass), N. Harnoncourt (cnd), Vienna Concentus Musicus [G] Teldec 2-▲ 2292-42565-2 [AAD]
Bach, J.S.:Cant 64, w. P. Esswood (ct), P. Jelosits (ten), R. van der Meer (bass), N. Harnoncourt (cnd), Vienna Concentus Musicus [G] Teldec 2-▲ 2292-42565-2 [AAD]
Bach, J.S.:Christmas Oratorio, w. P. Esswood (ct), K. Equiluz (ten), S. Nimsgern (b-bar), N. Harnoncourt (cnd), Vienna Concentus Musicus [G] Teldec ▲ 9031-74893-2
Berg, A.:Wozzeck, w. H. Behrens (sop), P. Langridge (ten), H. Zednik (ten), F. Grundheber (bar), A. Haugland (bass), C. Abbado (cnd), Vienna PO, Vienna State Opera Chorus [G] *(rec live, 6/88)* Deutsche Grammophon 2-▲ 423587-2 [DDD]
Berg, A.:Wozzeck (sels), w. D. Vejzovic (sop), C. Kleiber (cnd), Vienna PO *(rec Feb. 28, 1982)* Exclusive ▲ EXL 47 [ADD]
Bernstein, L.:Chichester Psalms, w. L. Bernstein (cnd), Israel PO [He] Deutsche Grammophon ▲ 415965-2 [ADD]
Christmas Angels, w. Uwe Christian Harrer (cnd), Hans Gillesberger (cnd), Helmuth Froschauer (cnd) RCA Gold Seal ▲ 09026-68150-2 [ADD]
Christmas Sampler, w. Plácido Domingo (ten), James Galway (fl), Boston Pops Orch [cnd:Arthur Fiedler] RCA Victor ▲ 09026-61840-2 ■ 09026-61840-4
Christmas with the Vienna Boys' Choir, w. Placido Domingo (ten), Hermann Prey (bar) RCA Gold Seal ▲ 7930-2-RG [ADD] ■ 7930-4-RG
Exsultate Jubilate Philips ▲ 426307-2 PH [DDD]
Haydn, J.:Mass 6, "Nikolai-messe", "6/4-Takt-Messe", w. Agnes Giebel (sop), Waldemar Kmentt (ten), Gottlob Frick (bass), E. Jochum (cnd), Bavarian RSO, Vienna Cathedral Choir Philips ("Two-Fers" series) 2-▲ 446175-2
Haydn, J.:Mass 7, "Kleine Orgelmesse", w. Agnes Giebel (sop), Waldemar Kmentt (ten), Gottlob Frick (bass), E. Jochum (cnd), Bavarian RSO, Vienna Cathedral Choir Philips ("Two-Fers" series) 2-▲ 446175-2
Haydn, J.:Die Schöpfung, w. Agnes Giebel (sop), Waldemar Kmentt (ten), Gottlob Frick (bass), E. Jochum (cnd), Bavarian RSO, Vienna Cathedral Choir Philips ("Two-Fers" series) 2-▲ 446175-2
Haydn, J.:Te Deum, w. H. Gillesberger (cnd) RCA Gold Seal ("Papillon Collection" series) ▲ 6535-2-RG [ADD] ■ 6535-4-RG
High Mass at the Viennese Court Philips ▲ 422997-2 PH [DDD]
Humperdinck, E.:Hänsel und Gretel, w. Lislotte Maikl (sop—Sandman/Dew Fairy), Anneliese Rothenberger (sop—Gretel), Irmgard Seefried (sop—Hänsel), Grace Hoffman (mez—Gertrude), Elisabeth Höngen (cta—Witch), Walter Berry (bass—Peter), A. Cluytens (cnd), Vienna PO EMI Classics 2-▲ CDMB 65661
Mahler, G.:Syms, w. J. Blegen (sop), B. Hendricks (sop), M. Price (sop), G. Zeumer (sop), H. Wittek (trb), A. Baltsa (mez), C. Ludwig (mez), K. Riegel (ten), H. Prey (bar), A. Schmidt (bar), J. Van Dam (b-bar), L. Bernstein (cnd), New York PO, Royal Concertgebouw Orch, Vienna PO, Westminster Choir, New York Choral Artists, Brooklyn Boys' Choir, Vienna State Opera Chorus, Vienna Singverein Deutsche Grammophon 13-▲ 435162-2 [DDD]
Mahler, G.:Sym 3, w. J. Norman (sop), C. Abbado (cnd), Vienna PO, Vienna State Opera Chorus [G] Deutsche Grammophon 2-▲ 410715-2 [DDD]
Mahler, G.:Sym 8, w. A. Augér (sop), H. Harper (sop), L. Popp (sop), Y. Minton (mez), H. Watts (cta), A. Kollo (ten), J. Shirley-Quirk (bar), M. Talvela (bass), G. Solti (cnd), Chicago SO, Vienna State Opera Chorus, Vienna Singverein [G,L] London 2-▲ 414493-2 [ADD]
Mahler, G.:Sym 8, w. J. Blegen (sop), M. Price (sop), G. Zeumer (sop), A. Baltsa (mez), K. Riegel (ten), H. Prey (bar), A. Schmidt (bar), J. Van Dam (b-bar), L. Bernstein (cnd), Vienna PO, Vienna State Opera Chorus *(rec Salzburg Festival, 1975)* Deutsche Grammophon 2-▲ 435102-2 [ADD]
Merry Christmas from the Vienna Boys' Choir Philips ▲ 412551-2 PH
Monteverdi, C.:Vespro della Beata Vergine, w. L. Marshall (sop), F. Palmer (sop), P. Langridge (ten), K. Equiluz (ten), T. Hampson (bar), A. Korn (bass), N. Harnoncourt (cnd), Vienna Concentus Musicus, Hamburg Monteverdi Chorus [L] Teldec 2-▲ 2292-42671-2
Monteverdi, C.:Vespro della Beata Vergine, w. M. Marshall (sop), F. Palmer (sop), P. Langridge (ten), K. Equiluz (ten), T. Hampson (bar), A. Korn (bass), N. Harnoncourt (cnd), Vienna Concentus Musicus, Hamburg Monteverdi Chorus Teldec 2-▲ 92629-2
Mozart, W.A.:Ave verum corpus, w. H. Gillesberger (cnd), Vienna Orch [L] RCA Gold Seal ("Papillon Collection" series) ▲ 6535-2-RG [ADD] ■ 6535-4-RG
Mozart, W.A.:Complete Mozart Edition, w. U.C. Harrer (cnd) Philips ▲ 422527-2 [ADD]
Mozart, W.A.:Requiem, w. H. Gillesberger (cnd), Vienna Orch [L] RCA Red Seal ("Papillon Collection" series) ▲ 6535-2 [ADD] ■ 6535-4
Nono, L.:Liebeslied, w. C. Abbado (cnd), Vienna PO Deutsche Grammophon ▲ 429260-2 [DDD]
Orff, C.:Carmina burana, w. B. Bonney (sop), F. Lopardo (ten), A. Michaels-Moore (bar), A. Previn (cnd), Vienna PO, Arnold Schoenberg Choir Deutsche Grammophon ▲ 439950-2
Perry, W.:Film Music, w. Richard Hayman (hmc), W. Perry (cnd), Rome PO, Slovak PO, Vienna SO, Slovak Phil Chorus [scores for 6 Mark Twain films originally produced for PBS in the 1980s]—Adventures of Huckleberry Finn; The Innocents Abroad; Life on the Mississippi; The Mysterious Stranger; The Private History of a Campaign That Failed; Pudd'nhead Wilson Premier ▲ PRCD 1015 [DDD]
Plácido Domingo, w. Plácido Domingo (ten), Vienna SO [cnd:H. Froschauer] RCA Gold Seal ▲ 07863-53835 ■ ARK1-3835
Schubert, Franz:Deutsche Messe, w. B. Weil (cnd), Orch of the Age of Enlightenment *(rec Austria, May 16-19, 1993)* Sony Classical ▲ SK 53984 [DDD]
Schubert, Franz:Mass 1, w. Alexander Nader (sop), Thomas Puchegger (sop), Georg Leskovich (alto), Jörg Hering (ten), Kurt Azesberger (ten), Harry van der Kamp (bass), Arno Hartmann (org), B. Weil (cnd), Orch of the Age of Enlightenment *(rec Vienna, Austria, Sept 1995)* Sony Classical ("Vivarte" series) ▲ SK 68247 [DDD]
Schubert, Franz:Mass 1, w. B. Weil (cnd), Orch of the Age of Enlightenment, Chorus Viennensis Sony Classical ▲ SK 68247
Schubert, Franz:Mass 2, w. B. Weil (cnd), Orch of the Age of Enlightenment, Chorus Viennensis Sony Classical ▲ SK 68247
Schubert, Franz:Mass 2, w. Thomas Puchegger (sop), Jörg Hering (ten), Harry van der Kamp (bass), Arno Hartmann (org), B. Weil (cnd), Orch of the Age of Enlightenment *(rec Vienna, Austria, Sept 1995)* Sony Classical ("Vivarte" series) ▲ SK 68247 [DDD]
Schubert, Franz:Mass 3, w. Alexander Nader (sop), Thomas Puchegger (sop), Belá Fischer (alt), Georg Leskovich (alt), Jörg Hering (ten), Harry Van der Kamp (bass), Arno Hartmann (org), B. Weil (cnd), Orch of the Age of Enlightenment, Chorus Viennensis Sony Classical ("Vivarte" series) ▲ SK 68248
Schubert, Franz:Mass 4, w. Alexander Nader (sop), Thomas Puchegger (sop), Belá Fischer (alt), Georg Leskovich (alt), Jörg Hering (ten), Harry Van der Kamp (bass), Arno Hartmann (org), B. Weil (cnd), Orch of the Age of Enlightenment, Chorus Viennensis Sony Classical ("Vivarte" series) ▲ SK 68248
Schubert, Franz:Mass 5, w. B. Weil (cnd), Orch of the Age of Enlightenment *(rec Austria, May 16-19, 1993)* Sony Classical ▲ SK 53984 [DDD]
Schubert, Franz:Mass 6, w. Benjamin Schmidinger (sop), Albin Lenzer (alt), Kurt Azesberger (ten), Jörg Hering (ten), Harry van der Kamp (bass), B. Weil (cnd), Orch of the Age of Enlightenment Sony Classical ▲ SK 66255
Shostakovich, D.:Sym 3, w. E. Inbal (cnd), Vienna SO Denon/PCM Digital ▲ CO 75444 [DDD]
Wagner, R.:Parsifal, w. C. Ludwig (mez), A. Kollo (ten), D. Fischer-Dieskau (bar), Z. Kelemen (bar), G. Frick (bass), G. Solti (cnd), Vienna PO, Vienna State Opera Chorus [G] London 4-▲ 417143-2 [ADD]

H. Gillesberger (cnd)
Bruckner, A.:Motets, w. Chorus Viennensis—Locus iste; Jesse floruit; Os iusti; Christus factus est; Ave Maria Acanta ▲ CD 41232 [DDD]
Gallus-Messe Acanta ▲ 41303
Gallus, J.:Missa ad imitationem Pater noster, w. Chorus Viennensis [L] Acanta ▲ 41303
Gallus, J.:Motets, w. Chorus Viennensis—Puer concinite; Repleti sunt [L] Acanta ▲ 41303
Mozart, W.A.:Missa, K.167 RCA Gold Seal ▲ 6724-2 [ADD] ■ 6724-4 (CrO2)
Mozart, W.A.:Missa, K.317 RCA Gold Seal ▲ 6724-2 [ADD] ■ 6724-4 (CrO2)

Vienna Boys' Choir (cont.)
H. Gillesberger (cnd) (cont.)
Mozart, W.A.:Notturnos Sops—K.346, 437 & 439 RCA Gold Seal ▲ 6724-2 [ADD] ■ 6724-4 (CrO2)
Mozart, W.A.:Più non si trovano RCA Gold Seal ▲ 6724-2 [ADD] ■ 6724-4 (CrO2)

U.C. Harrer (cnd)
Britten, B.:A Ceremony of Carols, w. Osian Ellis (hp) RCA Gold Seal ▲ 09026-68150-2 [ADD]

N. Neyder (cnd)
Britten, B.:A Ceremony of Carols Acanta ▲ CD 41232 [DDD]

M. Schebesta (cnd)
Handel, G.F.:Messiah, w. Max Emanuel Cencic (sop), Charles Humphries (ct), Ivan Sharpe (ten), Robert Torday (b-bar), P. Marschik (cnd), Academy of London Orch *(rec Symphony Hall, Birmingham & Barbican Center, London, Nov 17 & 19, 1994)* Capriccio 2-▲ 60068-2 [DDD]

Vienna Boys' Choir soloists
Bach, J.S.:St. John Passion, w. K. Equiluz (ten), M. Van Egmond (b-bar), J. Villisech (bass), N. Harnoncourt (cnd), Vienna Concentus Musicus Teldec ▲ 2292-42492-2

Vienna Cathedral Choir
Haydn, J.:Mass 6, "Nikolai-messe", "6/4-Takt-Messe", w. Agnes Giebel (sop), Waldemar Kmentt (ten), Gottlob Frick (bass), E. Jochum (cnd), Bavarian RSO, Vienna Boys' Choir Philips ("Two-Fers" series) 2-▲ 446175-2
Haydn, J.:Mass 7, "Kleine Orgelmesse", w. Agnes Giebel (sop), Waldemar Kmentt (ten), Gottlob Frick (bass), E. Jochum (cnd), Bavarian RSO, Vienna Boys' Choir Philips ("Two-Fers" series) 2-▲ 446175-2
Haydn, J.:Die Schöpfung, w. Agnes Giebel (sop), Waldemar Kmentt (ten), Gottlob Frick (bass), E. Jochum (cnd), Bavarian RSO, Vienna Boys' Choir Philips ("Two-Fers" series) 2-▲ 446175-2

Vienna Chamber Choir
Bach, J.S.:Cant 4, w. L. Dutoit (trb), K. Equiluz (ten), H. Braun (bar), F. Prohaska (cnd), Vienna State Opera Orch [G] *(rec 1959)* Vanguard Classics ("The Bach Guild" series) ▲ OVC 2001 [ADD]
Haydn, J.:Mass 7, "Kleine Orgelmesse", w. Eiko Katonosaka (sop), Elfriede Jahn (alt), Kurt Equiluz (ten), Leo Heppe (bass), H. Gillesberger (cnd), Vienna State Opera Orch *(rec 1965)* Tuxedo ▲ TUXCD 1025
Haydn, J.:Mass 10, "Kriegsmesse", "Paukenmesse", w. Elisabeth Thomann (sop), Elfriede Jahn (alt), Stafford Wing (ten), Eishi Kawamura (bass), H. Gillesberger (cnd), Vienna State Opera Orch *(rec 1965)* Tuxedo ▲ TUXCD 1025
Schubert, Franz:Deutsche Messe, w. Elisabeth Thomann (sop), Gertrude Jahn (alt), Stafford Wing (ten), Kunikazu Ohashi (bass), H. Gillesberger (cnd), Vienna SO Tuxedo ▲ TUXCD 1074 [ADD]
Schubert, Franz:Mass 3, w. Elisabeth Thomann (sop), Gertrude Jahn (alt), Stafford Wing (ten), Kunikazu Ohashi (bass), H. Gillesberger (cnd), Vienna SO Tuxedo ▲ TUXCD 1074 [ADD]

Vienna Children's Choir
Christmas Songs, w. Carlo Bergonzi (ten), Austrian RSO [cnd:Paul Angerer] Orfeo ▲ 030821

Vienna Choral Academy
Bach, J.S.:Mass in b, BWV 232, w. Gundula Janowitz (sop), Christa Ludwig (mez), Peter Schreier (ten), Karl Ridderbusch (bass), Vienna Choral Academy, H. von Karajan (cnd), Berlin PO Deutsche Grammophon ("Double" series) 2-▲ 439696-2

Vienna Chorus
Donizetti, G.:Poliuto, w. K. Ricciarelli (sop), J. Carreras (ten), J. Pons (bar), O. Caetani (cnd), Vienna SO CBS 2-▲ M2K 44821

Vienna Concentus Musicus Chorus
Bach, J.S.:Cant 11, "Ascension Oratorio", w. P. Esswood (ct), K. Equiluz (ten), M. van Egmond (b-bar), N. Harnoncourt (cnd), Vienna Concentus Musicus [G] Teldec 2-▲ 2292-42499-2 [AAD]
Bach, J.S.:Cant 41, w. P. Esswood (ct), K. Equiluz (ten), R. van der Meer (bass), N. Harnoncourt (cnd), Vienna Concentus Musicus [G] Teldec 2-▲ 2292-42556-2 [AAD]
Bach, J.S.:Cant 42, w. P. Esswood (ct), K. Equiluz (ten), R. van der Meer (bass), N. Harnoncourt (cnd), Vienna Concentus Musicus [G] Teldec 2-▲ 2292-42556-2 [AAD]
Bach, J.S.:Cant 43, w. P. Esswood (ct), K. Equiluz (ten), R. van der Meer (bass), N. Harnoncourt (cnd), Vienna Concentus Musicus [G] Teldec 2-▲ 2292-42559-2 [AAD]
Bach, J.S.:Cant 44, w. P. Esswood (ct), K. Equiluz (ten), R. van der Meer (bass), N. Harnoncourt (cnd), Vienna Concentus Musicus [G] Teldec 2-▲ 2292-42559-2 [AAD]
Bach, J.S.:Cant 48, w. P. Esswood (ct), K. Equiluz (ten), Vienna Concentus Musicus [G] Teldec 2-▲ 2292-42560-2 ZL [AAD]
Bach, J.S.:Cant 62, w. P. Esswood (ct), P. Jelosits (ten), K. Equiluz (ten), R. van der Meer (bass), N. Harnoncourt (cnd), Vienna Concentus Musicus [G] Teldec 2-▲ 2292-42565-2 [AAD]
Bach, J.S.:Cant 63, w. P. Esswood (ct), P. Jelosits (ten), K. Equiluz (ten), R. van der Meer (bass), N. Harnoncourt (cnd), Vienna Concentus Musicus [G] Teldec 2-▲ 2292-42565-2 [AAD]
Bach, J.S.:Cant 69, w. W. Wiedl (trb), P. Esswood (ct), K. Equiluz (ten), R. van der Meer (bass), N. Harnoncourt (cnd), Vienna Concentus Musicus [G] Teldec 2-▲ 2292-42572-2 [AAD]
Bach, J.S.:Cant 71, w. W. Wiedl (trb), P. Esswood (ct), K. Equiluz (ten), R. van der Meer (bass), N. Harnoncourt (cnd), Vienna Concentus Musicus [G] Teldec 2-▲ 2292-42572-2 [ADD]
Bach, J.S.:Cant 76, w. P. Esswood (ct), K. Equiluz (ten), R. van der Meer (bass), N. Harnoncourt (cnd), Vienna Concentus Musicus [G] Teldec 2-▲ 2292-42576-2 [ADD]
Bach, J.S.:Cant 78, w. P. Esswood (ct), K. Equiluz (ten), R. van der Meer (bass), N. Harnoncourt (cnd), Vienna Concentus Musicus [G] Teldec 2-▲ 2292-42576-2 [AAD]
Bach, J.S.:Cant 85, w. W. Wiedl (trb), P. Esswood (ct), K. Equiluz (ten), N. Harnoncourt (cnd), Vienna Concentus Musicus [G] Teldec 2-▲ 2292-42578-2 [AAD]
Bach, J.S.:Cant 86, w. W. Wiedl (trb), P. Esswood (ct), K. Equiluz (ten), N. Harnoncourt (cnd), Vienna Concentus Musicus [G] Teldec 2-▲ 2292-42578-2 [AAD]
Bach, J.S.:Cant 87, w. P. Esswood (ct), K. Equiluz (ten), N. Harnoncourt (cnd), Vienna Concentus Musicus [G] Teldec 2-▲ 2292-42578-2 [AAD]

Vienna Concert House Chorus
Mozart, W.A.:Requiem, w. F. Grossmann (cnd), Vienna Concert House Orch [L] Vivace 3-▲ E 326 [ADD]

Vienna Hofburg Chapel Choir
Biber, H. von:Missa alleluja, w. K. Junghänel (cnd), Gradus ad Parnassum, Concerto Palatino Choir Deutsche Harmonia Mundi ▲ 05472-77326-2 [DDD]
Gregorian Chants Allegretto ▲ ACD 8156 [ADD] ■ ACS 8156
Mozart:Missa Solemnis & Salieri:Te Deum (The Coronation Mass for Leopold II in Prague, September 1791), w. Vienna Academy, Ruth Ziesak (sop), E. von Magnus (mez), H. Wildahaber (ten), G. Hornik (bass), Hugo Distler Chorus Novalis ▲ 150087 [DDD]
Mozart, W.A.:Missa solemnis, K.337, w. R. Ziesak (sop), E. von Magnus (alt), H. Wildhaber (ten), G. Hornik (bar), H. Hüttler (cant), M. Jankowitsch (cant), P. Jelosits (cant), I. Rainer (org), M. Haselböck (cnd), Vienna Academy [L] *(rec Apr. 1992)* Novalis ▲ 150087 [DDD]
Schmelzer, J.H.:Vesperae solennes, w. K. Junghänel (cnd), Concerto Palatino Choir, Gradus ad Parnassum Deutsche Harmonia Mundi ▲ 05472-77326-2 [DDD]
Vienna Hofburg Chapel Schola Philips ▲ 411140-2 ■ 411140-4□

P.H. Dopf (cnd)
Gregorian Chant Philips ▲ 432089-2 □ 432089-5

J. Schabasser (cnd)
Gregorian Chants for all Seasons Vox Box 2-▲ CDX 5010 [ADD]
Gregorian Chants for the Christmas Season Allegretto ▲ ACD 8404
Mystical Chants Special Music ▲ SCD 5118
A Sacred Christmas, w. W. Kraft (org), Jean Claude Raynaud (org) Vox 90s ■ V9-9904
Spiritual Chants, w. Polifonica Ambrosiana Choir [cnd:Monsignor Giuseppe Biella] Special Music 3-▲ S3D 5123

Vienna Landstrasse Church Choir
Mozart, W.A.:Arias, w. A. Raunig (ct), K. F. Schmid (cl), M. Dostal (org), W. Kobera (cnd), Vienna Amadeus Ensemble—Il padre adorato [from Idomneo]; Cara, lontano ancora [from Ascanio in Alba]; Parto, ma tu ben mio [from La clemenza di Tito] Divertimento ▲ DIV 31013 [DDD]
Mozart, W.A.:Exsultate, w. A. Raunig (ct), K. F. Schmid (cl), M. Dostal (org), W. Kobera (cnd), Vienna Amadeus Ensemble Divertimento ▲ DIV 31013 [DDD]

Vienna Landstrasse Church Choir (cont.)
Salieri, A.:Arias, w. A. Raunig (ct), K. F. Schmid (cl), M. Dostal (org), W. Kobera (cnd), Vienna Amadeus Ensemble—Perdermi? [from Axur, Re d'ormus]; Lungi da te [from Armida]; A fulminas m'invita [from Anibale] Divertimento ▲ DIV 31013 [DDD]
Salieri, A.:Songs, w. A. Raunig (ct), K. F. Schmid (cl), M. Dostal (org), W. Kobera (cnd), Vienna Amadeus Ensemble—Fremat Thyrannus (motet) Divertimento ▲ DIV 31013 [DDD]
Vienna Men's Choral Association
Strauss (II), Joh.:Choral Music, w. J. Wildner (cnd), Czech-Slovak RSO Bratislava—An der schönen, blauen Donau Waltz, Op. 314; Aufs Korn March, Op. 478; Bei uns z'Haus Waltz, Op. 361; Burschenwanderung Polka, Op. 389; Gross Wien Waltz, Op. 440; Hoch Osterreich! March, Op. 371; Myrthenblüten Waltz, Op. 395; Neu Wien Waltz, Op. 342; 's gibt nur a Kaiserstadt Polka, Op. 291; Sängerlust Polka, Op. 328; Wein, Weib und Gesang Waltz, Op. 333 [G] Marco Polo ▲ 8.223250 [DDD]
Strauss (II), Joh.:Music of, w. H. Gueden (sop), H. von Karajan (cnd), Vienna PO—5 waltzes & polkas—Blue Danube; Annen-Polka; Pizzicato Polka; Voices of Spring; Imperial Waltz [G] Arkadia 3-▲ 215 (m) [ADD]
Vienna Motet Choir
B. Klebel (cnd)
Palestrina, G.:Missa "Papae marcelli" [L] Christophorus ▲ CD 74512
Palestrina, G.:The Song of Songs [L] Christophorus ▲ CD 74512
Vienna Opera Chorus
Janácek, L.:From the House of the Dead, w. I. Zítek (sgr), V. Zítek (ten), D. Jedlička (bass), C. Mackerras (cnd), Vienna PO London 2-▲ 430375-2 [DDD]
Janácek, L.:The Makropulos Affair, w. E. Söderström (sop), V. Krejčík (ten), Z. Švehla (ten), V. Zítek (ten), D. Jedlička (bass), C. Mackerras (cnd), Vienna PO London 2-▲ 430372-2 [ADD]
Lehár, F.:Giuditta (sels), w. F. Lehár (cnd), Vienna RSO Bel Age 2-▲ BLA 103.352
Vienna Oratorio Chorus
Mozart, W.A.:Missa, K.427, w. W. Lipp (sop), C. Ludwig (sop), M. Dickie (ten), W. Berry (bass), F. Grossmann (cnd), Pro Musica Orch [L] *(rec stereo, 1958)* Preiser ▲ 90053 [AAD]
Vienna Phil Chorus
Mahler, G.:Sym 2, w. Galina Vishnevskaya (sop), Hilde Rössl-Majdan (alt), O. Klemperer (cnd), Vienna PO Music & Arts ▲ CD 881 [ADD]
Mahler, G.:Sym 3, w. A. Baltsa (mez), L. Maazel (cnd), Vienna PO [G] CBS 2-▲ M2K 42403 [DDD]
Mahler, G.:Sym 8, w. *(soloists unknown)*, D. Mitropoulos (cnd), Vienna PO Enterprise 2-▲ ENT LV 1000
Mozart, W.A.:Requiem, w. A. Augér (sop), C. Bartoli (mez), V. Cole (ten), R. Pape (bass), G. Solti (cnd), Vienna PO [L] *(rec live 12/5/91)* London ▲ 433688-2 [DDD] ▯ 433688-5
Mozart, W.A.:Zauberflöte, w. D. Komarek (sop), J. Novotna (sop), J. Osvath (sop), H. Roswaenge (ten), W. Domgraf-Fassbaender (bar), A. Kipnis (bass), A. Toscanini (cnd), Vienna PO [G] *(rec live, Salzburg, July 30, 1937)* Melodram 3-▲ MEL 37040 (m) [AAD]
Vienna Radio Chorus
Lehár, F.:Paganini (sels), w. F. Lehár (cnd), Vienna RSO Bel Age 2-▲ BLA 103.351
Lehár, F.:Wo die Lerche singt (sels), w. F. Lehár (cnd), Vienna RSO Bel Age 2-▲ BLA 103.352
Marschner, H.A.:Der Vampyr, w. L. Synek (sop), L. Heppe (ten), G. Oeggl (bar), Rathauscher (sgr), Skladal (sgr), Sperlbauer (sgr), Weise (sgr), K. Tenner (cnd), Vienna RSO [G] *(rec live, Vienna, 4/9/51)* Memories 2-▲ HR 4466/67 [ADD]
Vienna Singakademie
Beethoven, L. van:Sym 9, "Choral Sym", w. M. László (sop), P.-L. Munteanu (ten), H. Scherchen (cnd), Vienna State Opera Orch *(rec 1954)* Andromeda ▲ ANR 2533 [ADD]
Beethoven, L. van:Sym 9, "Choral Sym", w. E. Inbal (cnd), Vienna SO, Chorus Viennensis [G] *(rec live, Konzerthaus, 12/30/89 & 1/1/90)* Denon ▲ CO 76646 [DDD]
Vienna Singverein
Bach, J.S.:Mass in b, BWV 232, w. E. Schwarzkopf (sop), C. Ludwig (mez), K. Ferrier (cta), A. Poell (b-bar), Schöffler (bass), H. von Karajan (cnd), Vienna SO—6 arias excerpted from the above rec'g Verona ▲ 27076 (m) [AAD]
Bach, J.S.:St. Matthew Passion, w. G. Janowitz (sop), C. Ludwig (mez), H. Laubenthal (ten), P. Schreier (ten), W. Berry (bar), D. Fischer-Dieskau (bar), H. von Karajan (cnd), Berlin PO, German Opera Chorus [G] Deutsche Grammophon 3-▲ 419789-2 [ADD]
Bach, J.S.:St. Matthew Passion, w. I. Seefried (sop), C. Ludwig (mez), K. Ferrier (cta), O. Edelmann (b-bar), P. Schoeffler (bass), H. von Karajan (cnd), Vienna SO [G] *(rec live June 9, 1950)* Verona 3-▲ 27070/72 (m) [AAD]
Bach, J.S.:St. Matthew Passion (sels), w. I. Seefried (sop), C. Ludwig (mez), K. Ferrier (cta), O. Edelmann (b-bar), P. Schöffler (bass), H. von Karajan (cnd), Vienna SO Verona ▲ 27076 (m) [AAD]
Beethoven, L. van:Missa Solemnis, w. G. Janowitz (sop), C. Ludwig (mez), F. Wunderlich (ten), W. Berry (bass), H. von Karajan (cnd), Berlin PO [L] Deutsche Grammophon ("Galleria" series) 2-▲ 423913-2 [ADD]
Beethoven, L. van:Sym 9, "Choral Sym", w. G. Janowitz (sop), H. Rössel-Majdan (alt), W. Kmentt (ten), W. Berry (bass), H. von Karajan (cnd), Berlin PO Deutsche Grammophon ("The Originals" series) ▲ 447401-2
Beethoven, L. van:Sym 9, "Choral Sym", w. W. Lipp (sop), F. Wunderlich (ten), F. Crass (bass), O. Klemperer (cnd), Philharmonia Orch Arkadia ▲ 759
Beethoven, L. van:Sym 9, "Choral Sym", w. H. von Karajan (cnd), Berlin PO [G] *(rec 1976)* Deutsche Grammophon ("Galleria" series) ▲ 415832-2 [ADD] ■ 415832-4
Bizet, G.:Carmen, w. H. Gueden (sop), G. Simionato (mez), N. Gedda (ten), H. von Karajan (cnd), Vienna SO *(rec live, Vienna Oct. 1954)* Melodram 2-▲ MEL 27012
Brahms, J.:Choral Music, w. Wilma Lipp (sop), Aafje Heynis (cta), Franz Crass (bar), W. Sawallisch (cnd), Vienna SO—Ein deutsches Requiem, Op. 45; Academic Festival Ov., Op. 80; Tragic Ov., Op. 81; Schicksalslied, Op. 54; Alto Rhap., Op. 53; Var. on a Theme of Haydn, Op. 56a Philips ▲ 438760-2
Brahms, J.:Ein Deutsches Requiem, w. A. Tomowa-Sintow (sop), J. van Dam (b-bar), H. von Karajan (cnd), Berlin PO [G] *(rec 1976)* EMI Classics ▲ CDM 69229 [ADD]
Brahms, J.:Ein Deutsches Requiem, w. E. Schwarzkopf (sop), H. Hotter (bar), H. von Karajan (cnd), Vienna PO [G] *(rec 10/47)* EMI Classics ("Great Recordings of the Century" series) ▲ CDH 61010 (m) [ADD]
Brahms, J.:Ein Deutsches Requiem, w. G. Janowitz (sop), E. Wächter (bar), H. von Karajan (cnd), Berlin PO [G] Deutsche Grammophon ("Galleria" series) ▲ 427252-2 [ADD]
Brahms, J.:Ein Deutsches Requiem, w. B. Hendricks (sop), J. Van Dam (bar), H. von Karajan (cnd), Vienna PO [G] *(rec 1986)* Deutsche Grammophon ▲ 431651-2 [DDD]
Haydn, J.:Die Schöpfung, w. Gunalda Janowitz (sop), Fritz Wunderlich (ten), Dietrich Fischer-Dieskau (bass), H. von Karajan (cnd), Berlin PO *(rec 1966 & 1968)* Deutsche Grammophon ("Galleria" series) 2-▲ 435077-2 [ADD]
Haydn, J.:Die Schöpfung, w. Gundula Janowitz (sop—Gabriel), Fritz Wünderlich (ten—Uriel), Kim Borg (bass—Raphael), H. von Karajan (cnd), Vienna PO *(rec Salzburg, Aug 29, 1965)* Bella Voce 2-▲ 7204 [AAD]
Kalomiris, M.:Sym 1, w. M. Caridis (cnd), Vienna RSO *(rec live, 10/31/86)* Koch Schwann ▲ CD 311110 [ADD]
Mahler, G.:Syms, w. J. Blegen (sop), B. Hendricks (sop), M. Price (sop), G. Zeumer (sop), H. Wittek (trb), A. Baltsa (mez), C. Ludwig (mez), K. Riegel (ten), H. Prey (bar), A. Schmidt (bar), J. Van Dam (b-bar), L. Bernstein (cnd), New York PO, Royal Concertgebouw Orch, Vienna PO, Westminster Choir, New York Choral Artists, Brooklyn Boys' Choir, Vienna Boys' Choir, Vienna State Opera Chorus Deutsche Grammophon 13-▲ 435162-2 [DDD]
Mahler, G.:Sym 8, w. A. Augér (sop), H. Harper (sop), L. Popp (sop), Y. Minton (mez), H. Watts (cta), A. Kollo (ten), J. Shirley-Quirk (bar), M. Talvela (bass), G. Solti (cnd), Chicago SO, Vienna State Opera Chorus, Vienna Boys' Choir [G,L] London 2-▲ 414493-2 [ADD]
Mozart, W.A.:Missa, K.317, w. A. Tomowa-Sintow (sop), A. Baltsa (mez), W. Krenn (ten), J. van Dam (b-bar), H. von Karajan (cnd), Berlin PO [L] Deutsche Grammophon ("Galleria" series) 2-▲ 423913-2 [ADD]
Mozart, W.A.:Missa, K.317, w. A. Tomowa-Sintow (sop), A. Baltsa (mez), W. Krenn (ten), J. van Dam (b-bar), H. von Karajan (cnd), Berlin PO Deutsche Grammophon ▲ 429820-2 [ADD]

Vienna Singverein (cont.)
Mozart, W.A.:Requiem, w. L. Price (sop), H. Rössl-Majdan (mez), F. Wunderlich (ten), W. Berry (bass), H. von Karajan (cnd), Vienna PO [L] *(rec live, Salzburg Festival, Aug. 24, 1960)* Melodram ▲ MEL 18003
Mozart, W.A.:Requiem, w. A. Tomowa-Sintow (sop), A. Baltsa (mez), W. Krenn (ten), J. van Dam (b-bar), H. von Karajan (cnd), Berlin PO Deutsche Grammophon ▲ 429821-2 [ADD] ■ 429821-4
Mozart, W.A.:Requiem, w. A. Tomowa-Sintow (sop), A. Baltsa (mez), W. Krenn (ten), J. van Dam (b-bar), H. von Karajan (cnd), Berlin PO [L] Deutsche Grammophon ("Galleria" series) ▲ 419867-2 [ADD] ■ 419867-4
Mozart, W.A.:Requiem, w. A. Tomowa-Sintow (sop), H. Müller Molinari (cta), V. Cole (ten), P. Burchuladze (bass), H. von Karajan (cnd), Vienna PO [L] Deutsche Grammophon ("Karajan Gold" series) ▲ 439023-2 [DDD]
Mozart, W.A.:Requiem, w. W. Lipp (sop), H. Rössl-Majdan (mez), A. Dermota (ten), W. Berry (bass), H. von Karajan (cnd), Berlin PO [L] *(rec 1961)* Deutsche Grammophon ("Resonance" series) ▲ 429160-2 [ADD] ■ 429160-4
Mozart, W.A.:Zauberflöte (sels), w. H. von Karajan (cnd), Vienna PO Classics for Pleasure ("Eminence" series) ▲ CDEMX 2220 [ADD]
Schmidt, F.:Das Buch mit sieben Siegeln, w. H. Gueden (sop), I. Malaniuk (cta), A. Dermota (ten), F. Wunderlich (ten), W. Berry (bass), D. Mitropoulos (cnd), Vienna PO *(rec live, Salzburg Festival 1959)* Melodram 2-▲ MEL 27078
Verdi, G.:Requiem Mass, w. Hilde Zadek (sop), Margarete Klose (cta), Helge Roswaenge (ten), Boris Christoff (bass), H. von Karajan (cnd), Vienna PO Stradivarius 2-▲ STV DTM 12323 [ADD]
Verdi, G.:Requiem Mass, w. L. Price (sop), R. Elias (mez), J. Björling (ten), G. Tozzi (bass), F. Reiner (cnd), Vienna PO [L] London 2-▲ 421608-2 [ADD]
Verdi, G.:Requiem Mass, w. O. Rovero (sop), J. Madeira (mez), J. Lambert (sgr), G. Neri (bass), E. Kleiber (cnd), Vienna SO *(rec live, Vienna 11/23/55)* Melodram 2-▲ CDM 28044 [ADD]
Vienna Singverein Women's Chorus
Shostakovich, D.:Sym 2, w. E. Inbal (cnd), Vienna SO *(rec Oct. 16-18, 1992)* Denon/PCM Digital ▲ DEN 75719 [DDD]
Vienna State Opera Chorus
Bach, J.S.:Cant 50, w. F. Prohaska (cnd), Vienna State Opera Orch [G] *(rec June 1957)* Vanguard Classics ("The Bach Guild" series) ▲ OVC 2010 [ADD]
Bach, J.S.:Cant 70, w. A. Felbermayer (sop), E. Wiens (sop), H. M. Welfing (ten), N. Foster (bass), F. Prohaska (cnd), Vienna State Opera Orch [G] *(rec June 1957)* Vanguard Classics ("The Bach Guild" series) ▲ OVC 2010 [ADD]
Bach, J.S.:Cant 140, w. L. Dutoit (trb), K. Equiluz (ten), H. Braun (bar), F. Prohaska (cnd), Vienna State Opera Orch [G] *(rec 1959)* Vanguard Classics ("The Bach Guild" series) ▲ OVC 2001 [ADD]
Bach, J.S.:Magnificat, BWV 243, w. M. Coertse (sop), M. Sjöstedt (sop), H. Rössl-Majdan (mez), A. Dermota (ten), F. Guthrie (bass), F. Prohaska (cnd), Vienna State Opera Orch [L] *(rec June 1957)* Vanguard Classics ("The Bach Guild" series) ▲ OVC 2010 [ADD]
Beethoven, L. van:Fant Pno, Op. 80, "Choral Fant", w. M. Pollini (pno), C. Abbado (cnd), Vienna PO [G] Deutsche Grammophon ▲ 419779-2 [DDD]
Beethoven, L. van:Fidelio, w. K. Flagstad (sop), J. Patzak (ten), P. Schöffler (b-bar), J. Greindl (bass), W. Furtwängler (cnd), Vienna PO [G] *(rec live 1950)* Arkadia 2-▲ 354
Beethoven, L. van:Fidelio, w. H. Konetzni (sop), I. Seefried (sop), P. Klein (ten), T. Ralf (ten), P. Schöffler (b-bar), H. Alsen (bass), K. Böhm (cnd), Vienna State Opera Orch *(rec Feb. 1944)* Preiser 2-▲ PRE 90195 [AAD]
Beethoven, L. van:Fidelio, w. K. Flagstad (sop), J. Patzak (ten), P. Schöffler (b-bar), J. Greindl (bass), W. Furtwängler (cnd), Vienna PO [G] *(rec live, Salzburg 8/5/50)* Verona 2-▲ 27044/45 (m) [AAD]
Beethoven, L. van:Fidelio, w. C. Goltz (sop), S. Jurinac (sop), G. Zampieri (ten), P. Schöffler (b-bar), O. Edelmann (bass), H. von Karajan (cnd), Vienna PO [G] *(rec live, Salzburg Festival 7/27/57)* Claque 2-▲ CLQ 2007 (m)
Beethoven, L. van:Fidelio, w. G. Janowitz (sop), L. Popp (sop), R. Kollo (ten), H. Sotin (bass), D. Fischer-Dieskau (bar), L. Bernstein (cnd), Vienna PO [G] Deutsche Grammophon 2-▲ 419436-2 [ADD]
Beethoven, L. van:Fidelio, w. K. Flagstad (sop), J. Patzak (ten), J. Griendl (bass), W. Furtwängler (cnd), Vienna PO EMI Classics 2-▲ CDC 64901
Beethoven, L. van:Fidelio (sels), w. E. Schlüte (sop), L. della Casa (sop), J. Patzak (ten), R. Schock (ten), F. Frantz (b-bar), H. Alsen (bass), W. Furtwängler (cnd), Vienna State Opera Orch—Overture, 16 arias & choruses *(rec live, Salzburg Festspielhaus Aug. 3, 1948)* Melodram 2-▲ CDM 25009 [ADD]
Beethoven, L. van:Leonore (opera), w. H. Zadek (sop), A. Dermota (ten), P. Schöffler (b-bar), O. von Rohr (bass), F. Leitner (cnd), Vienna SO [G] *(rec live, Bregenz 1960)* Melodram 2-▲ CDM 27085 [AAD]
Beethoven, L. van:Meeresstille und glückliche Fahrt, w. C. Abbado (cnd), Vienna PO [G] Deutsche Grammophon 6-▲ 427306-2 [DDD]
Beethoven, L. van:Missa Solemnis, w. Margaret Price (sop), Christa Ludwig (mez), Wieslaw Ochman (ten), Martti Talvela (bass), K. Böhm (cnd), Vienna PO *(rec 1957)* Deutsche Grammophon ("Double" series) 2-▲ 437386-2 [ADD]
Beethoven, L. van:Syms (comp), w. C. Abbado (cnd), Vienna PO Deutsche Grammophon 6-▲ 427306-2 [DDD]
Beethoven, L. van:Sym 9, "Choral Sym", w. K. Böhm (cnd), Vienna PO [G] Deutsche Grammophon ("Resonance" series) ■ 427196-4
Beethoven, L. van:Sym 9, "Choral Sym", w. F. von Weingartner (cnd), Vienna PO [G] *(rec 1935)* Pearl ▲ PEA 9407 (m) [AAD]
Beethoven, L. van:Sym 9, "Choral Sym", w. Jessye Norman (sop), Brigitte Fassbaender (mez), Plácido Domingo (ten), Walter Berry (bass), K. Böhm (cnd), Vienna PO Deutsche Grammophon ("Masters" series) ▲ 445503-2 [DDD]
Beethoven, L. van:Sym 9, "Choral Sym", w. Gwyneth Jones (sop), Tatiana Troyanos (mez), Jess Thomas (ten), Karl Ridderbusch (bass), K. Böhm (cnd), Vienna PO Deutsche Grammophon ("Double" series) 2-▲ 437368-2
Beethoven, L. van:Sym 9, "Choral Sym", w. C. Abbado (cnd), Vienna PO [G] Deutsche Grammophon ▲ 419598-2 [DDD] ▯ 419598-5
Beethoven, L. van:Sym 9, "Choral Sym", w. Luise Helletsgruber (sop), Rosette Anday (cta), Georg Maikl (ten), Richard Mayr (bass), F. von Weingartner (cnd), Vienna PO *(rec Feb. 2-5, 1935)* Preiser ▲ PRE 90193 [ADD]
Beethoven, L. van:Sym 9, "Choral Sym", w. K. Böhm (cnd), Vienna PO [G] Deutsche Grammophon ("3D Classics" series) ▲ 427802-2 [DDD]
Berg, A.:Wozzeck, w. H. Behrens (sop), P. Langridge (ten), H. Zednik (ten), F. Grundheber (bar), A. Haugland (bass), C. Abbado (cnd), Vienna PO, Vienna Boys' Choir [G] *(rec live, 6/88)* Deutsche Grammophon 2-▲ 423587-2 [DDD]
Berlioz, H.:Roméo et Juliette, w. B. Fassbaender (mez), N. Gedda (ten), J. Shirley-Quirk (bar), L. Gardelli (cnd), ORF SO [F] Orfeo 2-▲ 087842 [DDD]
Bizet, G.:Carmen, w. L. Price (sop), M. Freni (sop), F. Corelli (ten), R. Merrill (bar), H. von Karajan (cnd), Vienna PO [F] RCA Gold Seal 3-▲ 6199-2-RG [ADD] 2-■ 6199-4-RG
Bizet, G.:Carmen, w. G. Bumbry (sop), M. Freni (sop), J. Vickers (ten), J. Diaz (bass), H. von Karajan (cnd), Vienna PO [F] *(rec live, Salzburg 1967)* Arkadia 3-▲ 221 [ADD]
Bizet, G.:Carmen, w. L. Price (sop), M. Freni (sop), F. Corelli (ten), R. Merrill (bar), H. von Karajan (cnd), Vienna PO [F] RCA Gold Seal ▲ 60190-2-RG [ADD] ■ 60190-4-RG
Bizet, G.:Carmen, w. E. Obraztsova (mez), P. Domingo (ten), J. Mazurok (bar), C. Kleiber (cnd), Vienna State Opera Orch Exclusive 2-▲ EXL 11 [ADD]
Bizet, G.:Carmen (sels), w. Mirella Freni (sop), Leontyne Price (sop), Franco Corelli (ten), H. von Karajan (cnd), Vienna PO RCA Victor ▲ 09026-68021-2; ■ 09026-68021-4
Bruckner, A.:Te Deum, w. Hilde Güden (sop), Hilde Zadeck (cta), Erich Majkut (ten), Gottlob Frick (bass), B. Walter (cnd), Vienna PO *(rec live, 1955)* Enterprise ("Palladio" series) ▲ ENTPD 4209 [ADD]
Cherubini, L.:Médée, w. L. Popp (sop), L. Rysanek (sop), M. Lilowa (mez), B. Prevedi (ten), N. Ghiuselev (bass), H. Stein (cnd), Vienna State Opera Orch *(rec live, Vienna 1/31/72)* Melodram 2-▲ CDM 27087 [ADD]

 ▲ = CD ♦ = Enhanced CD Δ = MD ■ = Cassette Tape ▯ = DCC

Vienna State Opera Chorus (cont.)

Debussy, C.:Pelléas et Mélisande, w. M. Ewing (sop), C. Ludwig (mez), F. Le Roux (bar), J. Van Dam (bass-bar), J.-P. Courtis (bass), C. Abbado (cnd), Vienna PO
Deutsche Grammophon 2-▲ 435344-2 [DDD]

Donizetti, G.:Don Pasquale, w. E. Ravaglia (sop), P. Bottazzo (ten), A. Frati (ten), R. Panerai (bar), F. Corena (bass), R. Muti (cnd), Vienna PO [I] *(rec live, Salzburg, 8/11/71)*
Melodram 2-▲ CDM 27094 [ADD]

Einem, G. von:Dantons Tod, w. M. Cebotari (sop—Lucille Desmoulins), R. Anday (cta—Frau des Simon), P. Klein (ten—de Séchelles), J. Patzak (ten—Camille Desmoulins), J. Witt (ten—Robspierre), P. Schöffler (bar—Danton), L. Weber (bass—Saint Just), F. Fricsay (cnd), Vienna PO *(rec Aug. 6, 1947)*
Stradivarius 2-▲ STR 10067 [ADD]

Einem, G. von:Der Prozess, w. Lisa Della Casa (sop—Frl. Bürstner/Die Frau des Gerichtsdieners/Leni), Peter Klein (ten—Der Direktorstellvertreter/Der Student), Max Lorenz (ten—Josef K.), Erich Majkut (ten—Ein Bursche), László Szemere (ten—Titorelli), Alois Pernerstorfer (b-bar—Willem/Der Gerichtsdiener), Alfred Poell (b-bar—Der Advokat), Walter Berry (bass—Franz/Kanzleidirektor), Oskar Czerwenka (bass—Der Untersuchungsrichter/Der Prügler), Ludwig Hofmann (bass—Der Aufseher/Ein Passant/Der Geistliche/Der Fabrikant), Polly Batic (sgr—Frau Grubach), Endreh Koreh (sgr—Albert K.), Luise Leitner (sgr—Ein buckliges Mädchen), K. Böhm (cnd), Vienna PO *(rec Aug 17, 1953)*
Orfeo d'or ("Festspiel Dokumente" series) 2-▲ 392952 (m)

Gluck, C.W.:Iphigénie en Aulide, w. Inge Borkh (sop—Klytämnestra), Christa Ludwig (mez—Iphigenie), Elisabeth Steiner (mez—Artemis), James King (ten—Achilles), Otto Edelmann (b-bar), Alois Pernerstorfer (b-bar), Walter Berry (bass), K. Böhm (cnd), Vienna PO, Salzburg Festival Chamber Choir *(rec Salzburg, Aug 3, 1962)* Orfeo d'or ("Festspiel Dikumente" series) 2-▲ C 428962 (m) [ADD]

Gluck, C.W.:Orfeo ed Euridice, w. S. Jurinac (sop), G. Sciutti (sop), G. Simionato (mez), H. von Karajan (cnd), Vienna PO *(rec live 1959)* Memories 2-▲ HR 4382/83 (m)

Gluck, C.W.:Orfeo ed Euridice, w. H. Steffek (sop—Amore), T. Stich-Randall (mez—Euridice), M. Forrester (cta—Orfeo), C. Mackerras (cnd), Vienna State Opera Orch [Italian version w. additions composed for the French production] *(rec 6/66)* Vanguard Classics 2-▲ OVC 4039/40 [ADD]

Haydn, J.:Die Jahreszeiten, w. Trude Eipperle (sop), Julius Patzak (ten), Georg Hann (bass), C. Krauss (cnd), Vienna PO [G] *(rec live, June 1942)* Preiser 2-▲ PRE 93053 [AAD]

Haydn, J.:Mass 10, "Kriegsmesse", "Paukenmesse", w. Netania Davrath (sop), Hilde Rössl-Majdan (alt), Anton Dermota (ten), W. Bery (bass), Anton Heiller (org), R. Harand (vc), M. Wöldike (cnd), Vienna State Opera Orch *(rec May 14-16, 1960)*
Vanguard Classics ("The Bach Guild" series) ▲ OVC 2518 [ADD]

Haydn, J.:Die Schöpfung, w. Anny Felbermayer (sop—Eve), Teresa Stich-Randall (sop—Gabriel), Anton Dermota (ten—Uriel), Paul Schöffler (b-bar—Adam), Frederick Guthrie (bass—Raphael), Franz Holletschek (cembalo), M. Wöldike (cnd), Vienna State Opera Orch *(rec Musikverein, Vienna, Austria, May 1955)* Vanguard Classics 2-▲ SVC 34/35 [AAD]

Haydn, J.:Die Schöpfung, w. Trude Eipperle (sop), Julius Patzak (ten), Georg Hann (bass), C. Krauss (cnd), Vienna PO *(rec early 1940's)* Preiser 2-▲ PRE 90104 [AAD]

Haydn, J.:The Seven Last Words of Christ on the Cross, w. Albert (sop), John Van Kesteren (ten), Otto Wiener (bar), Anatoli Babikian (bass), H. Scherchen (cnd), Vienna State Opera Orch [oratorio version] [G] *(rec 1962)* MCA Classics 2-▲ MCAD2-9816 [AAD]

Hindemith, P.:When Lilacs Last In The Dooryard Bloom'd, w. Elisabeth Höngen (mez), Hans Braun (bar), P. Hindemith (cnd), Vienna SO *(rec 1956)* Tuxedo ▲ TUXCD 1061

Hindemith, P.:When Lilacs Last In The Dooryard Bloom'd, w. B. Fassbaender (mez), D.Fischer-Dieskau (bar), W. Sawallisch (cnd), Vienna SO [E] *(rec live, 11/1/83)* Orfeo ▲ 112851 [DDD]

Mahler, G.:Syms, w. J. Blegen (sop), B. Hendricks (sop), M. Price (sop), G. Zeumer (sop), H. Wittek (trb), A. Baltsa (mez), C. Ludwig (mez), K. Riegel (ten), H. Prey (bar), A. Schmidt (bar), J. Van Dam (b-bar), L. Bernstein (cnd), New York PO, Royal Concertgebouw Orch, Vienna PO, Westminster Choir, New York Choral Artists, Brooklyn Boys' Choir, Vienna Boys' Choir, Vienna Singverein
Deutsche Grammophon 13-▲ 435162-2 [DDD]

Mahler, G.:Sym 2, w. E. Marton (sop), J. Norman (sop), L. Maazel (cnd), Vienna PO [G]
CBS 2-▲ M2K 38667 [DDD]

Mahler, G.:Sym 2, w. Ileana Cotrubas (sop), Christa Ludwig (cta), Z. Mehta (cnd), Vienna PO *(rec 1975)*
London ("Double Decker" series) 2-▲ 440615-2 [ADD]

Mahler, G.:Sym 2, w. M. Coertse (sop), L. West (alt), H. Scherchen (cnd), Vienna State Opera Orch *(rec 1958)* Enterprise ("Palladio" series) ▲ ENTPD 4180 [ADD]

Mahler, G.:Sym 3, w. J. Norman (sop), C. Abbado (cnd), Vienna PO, Vienna Boys' Choir [G]
Deutsche Grammophon 2-▲ 410715-2 [DDD]

Mahler, G.:Sym 8, w. J. Blegen (sop), M. Price (sop), G. Zeumer (sop), A. Baltsa (mez), K. Riegel (ten), H. Prey (bar), A. Schmidt (bar), J. Van Dam (b-bar), L. Bernstein (cnd), Vienna PO, Vienna Boys' Choir *(rec Salzburg Festival, 1975)* Deutsche Grammophon 2-▲ 435102-2 [ADD]

Mahler, G.:Sym 8, w. A. Augér (sop), H. Harper (sop), L. Popp (sop), Y. Minton (mez), H. Watts (cta), A. Kollo (ten), J. Shirley-Quirk (bar), M. Talvela (bass), G. Solti (cnd), Chicago SO, Vienna Boys' Choir, Vienna Singverein [G,L] London 2-▲ 414493-2 [ADD]

Mozart, W.A.:Ave verum corpus, w. R. Leibowitz (cnd), Vienna State Opera Orch [L] *(rec 1958)*
MCA Classics 2-▲ MCAD2-9816 [AAD]

Mozart, W.A.:Clemenza, w. Christine Barbaux (sop—Servilia), Carol Vaness (sop—Viellia), Martha Senn (mez—Annio), Delores Ziegler (mez—Sesto), Gösta Winbergh (ten—Tito), László Polgár (bass—Publio), R. Muti (cnd), Vienna PO *(rec live, Salzburg Festival, 1988)* EMI Classics 2-▲ CDCB 55489

Mozart, W.A.:Clemenza, w. M. Casula (sop), L. Popp (sop), T. Berganza (mez), B. Fassbaender (mez), T. Franc (bass), F. Krenn (bass), I. Kertész (cnd), Vienna State Opera Orch
London ("Grand Opera" series) 2-▲ 430105-2 [ADD]

Mozart, W.A.:Così fan tutte, w. Kiri Te Kanawa (sop), Marie McLaughlin (sop), Ann Murray (mez), Hans-Peter Blochwitz (ten), Thomas Hampson (bar), G. Furlanetto (bar), J. Levine (cnd), Vienna PO [I]
Deutsche Grammophon 3-▲ 423897-2 [DDD]

Mozart, W.A.:Così fan tutte, w. E. Schwarzkopf (sop—Fiordiligi), C. Ludwig (sop—Dorabella), G. Sciutti (sop—Despina), W. Kmentt (ten—Ferrando), H. Prey (bar—Gugliemo), K. Dönch (bar—D. Alfonso), K. Böhm (cnd), Vienna PO [I] *(rec live, Salzburg, Aug. 8, 1962)* Arkadia 2-▲ 455 [ADD]

Mozart, W.A.:Così fan tutte (sels), w. G. Janowitz (sop), R. Grist (sop), B. Fassbaender (mez), P. Schreier (ten), H. Prey (bar), R. Panerai (bar), K. Böhm (cnd), Vienna PO—scenes & arias
Deutsche Grammophon ▲ 429824-2 [ADD]

Mozart, W.A.:Don Giovanni, w. Birgit Nilsson (sop—Donna Anna), Leontyne Price (sop—Donna Elvira), Eugenia Ratti (sop—Zerlina), Cesare Valletti (ten—Don Ottavio), Heinz Blankenburg (bar—Masetto), Fernando Corena (b-bar—Leporello), Arnold van Mill (b-bar—Il Commendatore), Cesare Siepi (b-bar—Don Giovanni), E. Leinsdorf (cnd), Vienna PO [I] London 3-▲ 444594-2 [ADD]

Mozart, W.A.:Don Giovanni, w. E. Schwarzkopf (sop), E. Grümmer (sop), E. Berger (sop), A. Dermota (ten), C. Siepi (b-bar), O. Edelmann (b-bar), W. Berry (bass), W. Furtwängler (cnd), Vienna PO *(rec 1953)* Arkadia 3-▲ 509 (m) [AAD]

Mozart, W.A.:Don Giovanni, w. L. Helletsgruber (sop), E. Rethberg (sop), M. Bokor (mez), D. Borgioli (ten), K. Ettl (bass), E. Pinza (bass), B. Walter (cnd), Vienna PO *(rec Salzburg, Aug. 2, 1937)*
Melodram 3-▲ MLO 37506 [ADD]

Mozart, W.A.:Don Giovanni, w. E. Grümmer (sop—D. Anna), R. Streich (sop—Zerlina), L. Della Casa (sop—D. Elvira), L. Simoneau (ten—Don Ottavio), C. Siepi (bass-baritone—Don Giovanni), W. Berry (bass—Masetto), G. Frick (bass—Il Commendatore), F. Corena (bass—Leporello), D. Mitropoulos (cnd), Vienna PO *(rec Salzburg, July 24, 1956)* Sony Classical 3-▲ SM3K 64263 [ADD]

Mozart, W.A.:Don Giovanni, w. E. Schwarzkopf (sop), E. Grümmer (sop), E. Berger (sop), A. Dermota (ten), C. Siepi (b-bar), O. Edelmann (b-bar), W. Berry (bass), W. Furtwängler (cnd), Vienna PO *(rec Salzburg, Aug. 3, 1953)* EMI Classics ("Great Recordings of the Century" series) 2-▲ CDHB 63860

Mozart, W.A.:Don Giovanni, w. S. Danco (sop), L. della Casa (sop), A. Dermota (ten), C. Siepi (b-bar), F. Corena (bass), J. Krips (cnd), Vienna PO London 3-▲ 411626-2 [ADD]

Mozart, W.A.:Don Giovanni, w. G. Janowitz (sop), T. Zylis-Gara (sop), M. Freni (sop), A. Kraus (ten), R. Panerai (bar), V. von Halem (bass), N. Ghiaurov (bass), H. von Karajan (cnd), Vienna PO [I] *(rec live, Salzburg, Aug. 1, 1969)* Memories 3-▲ HR 4362/64 (m) [ADD]

Mozart, W.A.:Don Giovanni, w. L. Price (sop), H. Gueden (sop), G. Sciurri (sop), F. Wunderlich (ten), E. Wächter (bar), W. Berry (bass), H. von Karajan (cnd), Vienna PO [I] *(rec live, 1963)*
Verona 3-▲ 27065/67 (m) [AAD]

Vienna State Opera Chorus (cont.)

Mozart, W.A.:Don Giovanni, w. E. Grümmer (sop), L. Della Casa (sop), R. Streich (sop), L. Simoneau (ten), C. Siepi (b-bar), G. Frick (bass), W. Berry (bass), F. Corena (bass), D. Mitropoulos (cnd), Vienna PO [I] *(rec live, Salzburg, July 24, 1956)* Arkadia 3-▲ 552 (m) [ADD]

Mozart, W.A.:Don Giovanni, w. G. Grob-Prandl (sop), H. Konetzni (sop), M. Stabile (bar), A. Pernerstorfer (b-bar), O. Czerwenka (bass), H. Swarowsky (cnd), Vienna SO *(rec 1950)*
Preiser 2-▲ PRE 90166 [AAD]

Mozart, W.A.:Don Giovanni (sels), w. A. Tomowa-Sintow (sop), T. Zylis-Gara (sop), E. Mathis (sop), S. Milnes (bar), W. Berry (bass), K. Böhm (cnd), Vienna PO—Scenes & Arias
Deutsche Grammophon ▲ 429823-2 [ADD]

Mozart, W.A.:Entführung, w. C. Studer (sop), E. Szmytka (sop), K. Streit (ten), R. Gambill (ten), G. Missenhardt (bar), M. Heltau (nar), B. Weil (cnd), Vienna SO Sony Classical 2-▲ S2K 48053

Mozart, W.A.:Entführung, w. Reri Grist (sop—Blondchen), Anneliese Rothenberger (sop—Konstanze), Gerhard Unger (ten—Pedrillo), Fritz Wunderlich (ten—Belmonte), Fernando Corena (bass—Osmin), Michael Heltau (nar—Selim), Z. Mehta (cnd), Vienna PO *(rec July 28, 1965)*
Orfeo d'or ("Festspiel Dokumente" series) 2-▲ 392952 (m)

Mozart, W.A.:Entführung (sels), w. C. Studer (sop), E. Szmytka (sop), K. Streit (ten), R. Gambill (ten), Gunter Missenhardt (bar), B. Weil (cnd), Vienna SO *(rec Vienna, Apr. 2-10, 1991)*
Sony Classical ("Opera Highlights" series) ▲ SMK 53500 [DDD]

Mozart, W.A.:Idomeneo, w. L. Popp (sop), E. Gruberova (sop), A. Baltsa (mez), L. Pavarotti (ten), L. Nucci (bar), J. Pritchard (cnd), Vienna PO [I] London 3-▲ 411805-2 [DDD]

Mozart, W.A.:Idomeneo (sels), w. E. Réthy (sop—Idamante), A. Konetzni (sop—Ismene), J. Sabel (ten—Idomeneo), E. Kunz (bar—Arbace), R. Strauss (cnd), Vienna State Opera Orch *(rec Dec. 3, 1941)*
Koch Schwann 2-▲ SCH 314532 [ADD]

Mozart, W.A.:Missa, K.427, w. K. Láki (sop), Z. Dénes (sop), K. Equiluz (ten), R. Holl (bass), N. Harnoncourt (cnd), Vienna Concentus Musicus [L] Teldec ▲ 2292-43070-2

Mozart, W.A.:Missa, K.427, w. K. Battle (sop), L. Cuberli (sop), P. Seiffert (ten), K. Moll (bass), J. Levine (cnd), Vienna PO Deutsche Grammophon ▲ 423664-2 [DDD]

Mozart, W.A.:Nozze di Figaro, w. M. Price (sop), K. Battle (sop), M. Nicolesco (sop), A. Murray (mez), J. Hynninen (bar), K. Rydl (bass), R. Muti (cnd), Vienna PO [I] EMI Classics 3-▲ CDCC 47978 [DDD]

Mozart, W.A.:Nozze di Figaro, w. Elisabeth Schwarzkopf (sop—Countess), Irmgard Seefried (sop—Susanna), Hilde Güden (mez—Cherubino), Paul Schöffler (bar—Almaviva), Erich Kunz (bass—Figaro), W. Furtwängler (cnd), Vienna PO *(rec Salzburg Festival, Aug 8, 1953)*
EMI Classics 3-▲ CDHC 66080

Mozart, W.A.:Nozze di Figaro, w. Jarmila Novotna (sop), Aulikki Rautawaara (sop), Esther Réthy (sop), Agostino Lazzari (ten), Mariano Stabile (bar), Ezio Pinza (bass), B. Walter (cnd), Vienna PO *(rec live, 1937)* Melodram ▲ CDI 205003

Mozart, W.A.:Nozze di Figaro, w. E. Schwarzkopf (sop), I. Seefried (sop), S. Jurinac (sop), E. Höngen (cta), G. London (bar), E. Kunz (bar), H. von Karajan (cnd), Vienna PO—omitting recitatives [I] *(rec 1950)* EMI Classics ("Studio" series) 2-▲ CDMB 69639 (m) [ADD]

Mozart, W.A.:Nozze di Figaro, w. Irma Beilke (sop), Helena Braun (sop), Gerda Sommerschuh (sop), Josef Witt (ten), Hans Hotter (bar), Erich Kunz (bar), Gustav Neidlinger (b-bar), C. Krauss (cnd), Vienna PO *(rec live, Salzburg Festival, Aug. 1942)* Preiser 3-▲ PRE 90203 [ADD]

Mozart, W.A.:Nozze di Figaro, w. Cecilia Bartoli (sop—Cherubino), Sylvia McNair (sop—Susanna), Cheryl Studer (sop—Countess Almaviva), Lucio Gallo (bar—Figaro), Boje Skovhus (bar—Count Almaviva), C. Abbado (cnd), Vienna PO Deutsche Grammophon 3-▲ 445903-2

Mozart, W.A.:Nozze di Figaro (sels), w. M. Price (sop), K. Battle (sop), M. Nicolesco (sop), A. Murray (mez), J. Hynninen (bar), K. Rydl (bass), R. Muti (cnd), Vienna PO [I] EMI Classics ▲ CDC 54321

Mozart, W.A.:Regina coeli, K.108, w. R. Leibowitz (cnd), Vienna State Opera Orch [L] *(rec 1958)*
MCA Classics 2-▲ MCAD2 9816 [AAD]

Mozart, W.A.:Requiem, w. E. Mathis (sop), J. Hamari (mez), W. Ochman (ten), K. Ridderbusch (bass), K. Böhm (cnd), Vienna PO [L] Deutsche Grammophon ▲ 413553-2 [ADD]

Mozart, W.A.:Requiem, w. Lisa della Casa (sop), Ira Malaniuk (cta), Anton Dermota (ten), Cesare Siepi (b-bar), B. Walter (cnd), Vienna PO *(rec Salzburg, July 26, 1956)*
Orfeo d'or ("Festspiel Dikumente" series) ▲ C 430961 (m) [ADD]

Mozart, W.A.:Requiem, w. Rachel Yakar (sop), Ortrun Wenkel (cta), Kurt Equiluz (ten), Robert Holl (bass), N. Harnoncourt (cnd), Vienna Concentus Musicus [L] Teldec ▲ 2292-42911-2

Mozart, W.A.:Requiem, w. S. Jurinac (sop), L. West (alt), H. Loeffler (ten), F. Gutherie (bass), R. Leibowitz (cnd), Vienna State Opera Orch [L] *(rec 1958)* MCA Classics 2-▲ MCAD2 9816 [AAD]

Mozart, W.A.:Requiem, w. E. Schumann (sop), K. Thorborg (mez), A. Dermota (ten), A. Kipnis (bass), B. Walter (cnd), Vienna PO EMI Classics ("Great Recordings of the Century" series) 3-▲ CDHC 63912

Mozart, W.A.:Requiem, w. E. Ameling (sop), M. Horne (mez), U. Benelli (bar), T. Franc (bass), I. Kertész (cnd), Vienna PO London ("Weekend Classics" series) ▲ 417681-2 [ADD] ■ 417681-4

Mozart, W.A.:Requiem, w. S. Jurinac (sop), L. West (alt), H. Loeffler (ten), F. Gutherie (bass), H. Scherchen (cnd), Vienna State Opera Orch *(rec 1958)* Andromeda ▲ ANR 2525 [ADD]

Mozart, W.A.:Sancta Maria, w. R. Leibowitz (cnd), Vienna State Opera Orch [L] *(rec 1958)*
MCA Classics 2-▲ MCAD2 9816 [AAD]

Mozart, W.A.:Te Deum, w. R. Leibowitz (cnd), Vienna State Opera Orch [L] *(rec 1958)*
MCA Classics 2-▲ MCAD2-9816 [AAD]

Mozart, W.A.:Zauberflöte, w. I. Seefried (sop-Pamina), W. Lipp (sop—Queen of the Night), A. Dermota (ten—Tamino), E. Kunz (bar—Papageno), J. Greindl (bass—Sarastro), W. Furtwängler (cnd), Vienna PO *(rec live 1951)* EMI Classics ▲ CDMC 65356

Mozart, W.A.:Zauberflöte, w. H. Gueden (sop), W. Lipp (sop), L. Simoneau (ten), W. Berry (bass), K. Bohme (bass), K. Böhm (cnd), Vienna PO London ("Grand Opera" series) 2-▲ 414362-2 [ADD]

Mozart, W.A.:Zauberflöte, w. Jarmila Novotna (sop), Helge Roswaenge (ten), Alexander Kipnis (bass), Julie Osvath (sgr), A. Toscanini (cnd), Vienna PO Enterprise ("The 40's" series) 2-▲ ENT 321

Mozart, W.A.:Zauberflöte, w. Reri Grist (sop), Edita Gruberová (sop), Edith Mathis (sop), Rene Kollo (ten), Gerhard Unger (ten), Hermann Prey (bar), José Van Dam (b-bar), Peter Meven (bass), H. von Karajan (cnd), Vienna PO *(rec live, Salzburg, July 26, 1974)* Arkadia 2-▲ 233

Mozart, W.A.:Zauberflöte, w. I. Seefried (sop-Pamina), W. Lipp (sop—Queen of the Night), A. Dermota (ten—Tamino), E. Kunz (bar—Papageno), J. Greindl (bass—Sarastro), W. Furtwängler (cnd), Vienna PO [G] *(rec live, Salzburg, Aug. 6, 1951)* Arkadia 3-▲ 361 [ADD]

Mozart, W.A.:Zauberflöte, w. S. Jo (sop), R. Ziesak (sop), U. Heilmann (ten), A. Kraus (ten), K. Moll (bass), G. Solti (cnd), Vienna PO London 2-▲ 433210-2 [DDD]

Mozart, W.A.:Zauberflöte, w. L. Della Casa (sop), E. Köth (sop), G. Sciurri (sop), L. Simoneau (ten), W. Berry (bass), K. Böhme (bass), G. Szell (cnd), Vienna PO [G] *(rec live at the Salzburg Festival, July 27, 1959)* Melodram ("Connaisseur" series) 2-▲ MEL 27505 (m) [AAD]

Mozart, W.A.:Zauberflöte, w. Wilma Lipp (sop), Irmgard Seefried (sop), Peter Klein (ten), Walther Ludwig (ten), Karl Schmitt-Walter (bar), Josef Greindl (bass), Paul Schöffler (sgr), W. Furtwängler (cnd), Vienna PO *(rec 1949)* Music & Arts 3-▲ CD 882 [AAD]

Mozart, W.A.:Zauberflöte (sels), w. I. Seefried (sop), W. Lipp (sop), W. Ludwig (ten), K. Schmitt-Walter (bar), J. Greindl (bass), W. Furtwängler (cnd), Vienna PO—Ov. & 11 arias *(rec live, Salzburg, July, 27, 1949)* Arkadia 3-▲ 361 [ADD]

Mozart, W.A.:Zauberflöte (sels), w. S. Jo (sop), R. Ziesak (sop), U. Heilmann (ten), A. Kraus (ten), K. Moll (bass), G. Solti (cnd), Vienna PO London ▲ 433667-2 [DDD]

Mussorgsky, M.:Boris Godunov, w. N. Dobrianova (sop), S. Jurinac (sop), D. Usunow (ten), N. Ghiaurov (bass), N. Ghiuselev (bass), A. Diakov (bass), H. von Karajan (cnd), Vienna PO [R] *(rec live in Salzburg, 7/26/64)* Arkadia 2-▲ 210 (m) [ADD]

Pfitzner, H.:Palestrina, w. S. Jurinac (sop), C. Ludwig (mez), F. Wunderlich (ten), G. Stolze (ten), O. Wiener (bar), G. Frick (bass), W. Berry (bass), R. Heger (cnd), Vienna State Opera Orch *(rec live, Vienna 12/16/64)* Myto 3-▲ 3 MCD 92259 [ADD]

Pfitzner, H.:Von deutscher Seele, w. Trude Eipperle (sop), Luise Willer (mez), Julius Patzak (ten), Ludwig Weber (bass), C. Krauss (cnd), Vienna PO *(rec Jan 1945)* Preiser 2-▲ PRE 90255 [ADD]

Puccini, G.:La Bohème, w. M. Freni (sop), H. Gueden (sop), G. Raimondi (ten), G. Taddei (bar), H. von Karajan (cnd), Vienna State Opera Orch [I] *(rec live 11/30/63)* Melodram 2-▲ MELCD 27007

Puccini, G.:Tosca, w. L. Price (sop), G. di Stefano (ten), G. Taddei (bar), H. von Karajan (cnd), Vienna PO [I] London 2-▲ 421670-2 [ADD]

Vienna State Opera Chorus (cont.)

Puccini, G.:Turandot, w. B. Nilsson (sop), L. Price (sop), G. di Stefano (ten), T. Gobbi (bar), F. Molinari-Pradelli (cnd), Vienna State Opera Orch [I] *(rec live, 6/22/61)* Legato Classics 2-▲ LCD 153-2 (m) [ADD]

Puccini, G.:Turandot, w. K. Ricciarelli (sop), B. Hendricks (sop), P. Domingo (ten), R. Raimondi (bass), H. von Karajan (cnd), Vienna PO [I] Deutsche Grammophon 2-▲ 423855-2 [DDD]

Puccini, G.:Turandot (sels), w. E. Martón (sop), K. Ricciarelli (sop), J. Carreras (ten), L. Maazel (cnd), Vienna State Opera Orch [I] CBS ▲ MK 42168 [DDD] ■ MT 42168 (D)

Puccini, G.:Turandot (sels), w. K. Ricciarelli (sop), B. Hendricks (sop), P. Domingo (ten), R. Raimondi (bass), H. von Karajan (cnd), Vienna PO [I] Deutsche Grammophon ▲ 435409-2 [DDD]

Rossini, G.:Arias, w. A. Baltsa (mez), I. Marin (cnd), Vienna SO—arias from Barbiere di Siviglia, Cenerentola, Donna del lago, Italiana in Algeri, Maometto II, Semiramide, Tancredi [I] Sony Classical ▲ SK 45964

Rossini, G.:Il barbiere di Siviglia, w. R. Grist (sop), F. Wunderlich (ten), E. Wächter (bar), O. Czerwenka (bass), Kunz (sgr), K. Böhm (cnd), Vienna State Opera Orch *(rec live, Vienna 4/28/66)* Myto 2-▲ 2 MCD 91752 [ADD]

Rossini, G.:L'italiana in Algeri, w. A. Baltsa (mez), F. Lopardo (ten), E. Dara (bar), R. Raimondi (bass), C. Abbado (cnd), Vienna PO [I] Deutsche Grammophon 2-▲ 427331-2 [DDD]

Rossini, G.:Stabat Mater, w. Luba Orgonasova (sop), Cecilia Bartoli (mez), Raul Gimenez (ten), Roberto Scandiuzzi (bass), M.-W. Chung (cnd), Vienna PO Deutsche Grammophon ▲ 449 178-2

Schmidt, F.:Das Buch mit sieben Siegeln, w. Sylvia Greenberg (sop), Carolyn Watkinson (cta), Peter Schreier (ten), Thomas Moser (ten), Robert Holl (bass), Kurt Rydl (bass), L. Zagrosek (cnd), Austrian RSO [G] Orfeo 2-▲ 143862 [DDD]

Schoenberg, A.:A Survivor from Warsaw, w. G. Hornik (nar), C. Abbado (cnd), Vienna PO Deutsche Grammophon ▲ 431774-2 [DDD]

Sibelius, J.:Sym 5, w. J. Horenstein (cnd), BBC Northern SO *(rec live, Sheffield, 1970)* Intaglio ▲ INCD 7331 [ADD]

Smetana, B.:Dalibor, w. L. Rysanek (sop), L. Spiess (ten), E. Wächter (bar), J. Krips (cnd), Vienna State Opera Orch *(rec live, Vienna, 10/19/69)* Myto 2-▲ 2 MCD 92465 [ADD]

Still, W.G.:Tristan und Isolde, w. Catarina Ligendza (sop), Ruša Baldani (mez), Hans Hopf (ten), Hans Sotin (bass), C. Kleiber (cnd), Vienna PO *(rec Vienna, Oct. 7, 1973)* Pantheon 3-▲ PHE 6601 (m)

Still, W.G.:Tristan und Isolde, w. C. Ligendza (sop), R. Baldani (mez), H. Hopf (ten), A. Dermota (ten), H. Sotin (bass), G. Neidlinger (bass), C. Kleiber (cnd), Vienna State Opera Orch *(rec Oct. 7, 1973)* Exclusive 3-▲ EXL 18 [ADD]

Strauss (II), Joh.:Die Fledermaus, w. K. Te Kanawa (sop), E. Gruberová (sop), B. Fassbaender (mez), W. Brendel (bar), R. Leech (ten), O. Bär (bar), T. Krause (bar), A. Previn (cnd), Vienna PO [G] Philips 2-▲ 432157-2 [DDD]

Strauss (II), Joh.:Die Fledermaus, w. H. Gueden (sop), R. Streich (sop), G. Di Stefano (ten), G. Stolze (ten), G. Zampieri (ten), E. Wächter (bar), W. Berry (bass), E. Kunz (bar), H. von Karajan (cnd), Vienna State Opera Orch [G] Arkadia 3-▲ 215 (m) [ADD]

Strauss (II), Joh.:Die Fledermaus, w. H. Gueden (sop), E. Köth (sop), R. Resnik (mez), W. Kmentt (ten), G. Zampieri (ten), E. Wächter (bar), W. Berry (bass), E. Kunz (bar), H. von Karajan (cnd), Vienna PO, with Gala Sequence [G] London 2-▲ 421046-2 [ADD]

Strauss (II), Joh.:Der Zigeunerbaron, w. Emmy Loose (sop—Arsena), Gerda Scheyrer (sop—Saffi), Elisabeth Fez (cta—Mirabella), Hilde Rössl-Majdan (cta—Czipra), Waldemar Kmentt (ten—Barinkay), Paul Spani (ten—Ottokar), Erich Kunz (bar—Homonay), Kurt Preger (bar—Zsupan), Eberhard Wächter (bass—Carnero), A. Paulik (cnd), Vienna State Opera Orch *(rec Brahmssaal, Vienna, Austria, June 1956)* Vanguard Classics 2-▲ OVC 8082/83 [ADD]

Strauss (II), Joh.:Der Zigeunerbaron, w. Emmy Loose (sop), Hilde Zadek (sop), Rosette Anday (cta), Julius Patzak (ten), Karl Dönch (bar), Alfred Poell (bar), Steffi Leverenz (sgr), C. Krauss (cnd), Vienna PO Phonographe 2-▲ PHG 5020 [AAD]

Strauss, R.:Die ägyptische Helena (sels), w. V. Ursuleac (sop—Helena), F. Völker (ten—Menelas), H. Roswaenge (ten—Da-Ud), E. Kunz (bar—Arbace), C. Krauss (cnd), Vienna State Opera Orch *(rec Sept. 20, 1933)* Koch Schwann 2-▲ SCH 314552 [ADD]

Strauss, R.:Arabella, w. L. Della Casa (sop), M. Reining (sop), R. Anday (cta), H. Hotter (b-bar), G. Hann (bass), J. Patzak (ten), K. Böhm (cnd), Vienna PO *(rec live, Salzburg Festival, 8/12/47)* Melodram 3-▲ MEL 37077

Strauss, R.:Ariadne auf Naxos, w. Erna Berger (sop), Miliza Korjus (sop), Viorica Ursuleac (sop), Helge Rosvaenge (ten), *(other soloists unknown),* C. Krauss (cnd), Vienna State Opera Orch *(rec 1935)* Arlecchino 3- ARL

Strauss, R.:Ariadne auf Naxos, w. L. Rysanek (sop), J. Scovotti (sop), T. Troyanos (mez), J. King (ten), P. Schöffler (b-bar), K. Böhm (cnd), Vienna State Opera Orch *(rec 1967)* Melodram 2-▲ MLO 270105 [ADD]

Strauss, R.:Daphne, w. H. Gueden (sop), F. Wunderlich (ten), J. King (ten), P. Schöffler (bass), K. Böhm (cnd), Vienna SO *(rec live 1963)* Deutsche Grammophon 2-▲ 445322-2

Strauss, R.:Daphne (sels), w. M. Reining (sop—Daphne), A. Dermota (ten—Leukippos), R. Moralt (cnd), Vienna State Opera Orch *(rec May 8, 1942)* Koch Schwann 2-▲ SCH 314552 [ADD]

Strauss, R.:Elektra, w. A. Varnay (sop/mez), M. Mödl (sop/mez), H. Hillebrecht (sop), J. King (ten), E. Wächter (bar), H. von Karajan (cnd), Vienna PO [G] *(rec 1964)* Melodram 2-▲ MEL 27044 [ADD]

Strauss, R.:Elektra (sels), w. A. Varnay (sop/mez), H. Hillebrecht (sop), J. King (ten), H. von Karajan (cnd), Vienna PO [G] *(rec live in Salzburg, 8/11/64)* Arkadia 3-▲ 213 (m) [ADD]

Strauss, R.:Die Frau ohne Schatten, w. L. Rysanek (sop), Hoffman (sgr), Thomas (sgr), H. von Karajan (cnd), Vienna State Opera Orch [G] *(rec live, Vienna, 6/11/64)* Arkadia 3-▲ 207 (m) [ADD]

Strauss, R.:Die Frau ohne Schatten (sels), w. H. Konetzni (sop—Die Kaiserin), E. Schulz (sop—Die Färberin), T. RA. (ten—Der Kaiser), J. Herrmann (bar—Barak), K. Böhm (cnd), Vienna State Opera Orch *(rec Nov. 23, 1943)* Koch Schwann 2-▲ SCH 314552 [ADD]

Strauss, R.:Die Liebe der Danae, w. A. Kupper (sop), J. Traxel (ten), L. Szemere (ten), P. Schöffler (b-bar), C. Krauss (cnd), Vienna PO [G] *(rec live, Salzburg, 8/14/52)* Melodram 3-▲ MEL 37061 (m) [AAD]

Strauss, R.:Der Rosenkavalier, w. A. Tomowa-Sintow (sop), J. Perry (sop), A. Baltsa (mez), K. Moll (bass), H. von Karajan (cnd), Vienna PO [G] Deutsche Grammophon 3-▲ 423850-2 [DDD]

Strauss, R.:Der Rosenkavalier, w. L. Della Casa (sop), H. Gueden (sop), S. Jurinac (sop), E. Kunz (bar), O. Edelmann (b-bar), H. von Karajan (cnd), Vienna PO [G] *(rec live in Salzburg, 7/26/60)* Arkadia 3-▲ 213 [ADD]

Strauss, R.:Der Rosenkavalier, w. L. Lehmann (sop), E. Schumann (sop), M. Olczewska (mez), R. Mayr (bass), R. Heger (cnd), Vienna PO—abridged performance [G] *(rec 1933 for HMV)* Pearl 2-▲ GEMMCDS 9365 (m) [AAD]

Strauss, R.:Der Rosenkavalier, w. M. Reining (sop), H. Gueden (sop), S. Jurinac (sop), L. Weber (bass), E. Kleiber (cnd), Vienna PO [G] London ("Historic" series) ▲ 425950-2 [ADD]

Strauss, R.:Salome, w. Maria Cebotari (sop—Salome), Elisabeth Höngen (mez—Herodias), Karl Friedrich (ten—Narraboth), Julius Patzak (ten—Herod), Marko Rothmüller (bar—Jokanaan), C. Krauss (cnd), Vienna State Opera Orch *(rec Covent Garden, London, Sept 30, 1947)* Legato 2-▲ LCD 211-2 [ADD]

Strauss, R.:Salome (sels), w. E. Schulz (sop—Salome), A. Dermota (ten—Narraboth), J. Witt (ten—Herodes), H. Hotter (bar—Jochanaan), P. Schöffler (b-bar—Jochanaan), R. Strauss (cnd), Vienna State Opera Orch *(rec Feb. 15 & May 6, 1942)* Koch Schwann 2-▲ SCH 314532 [ADD]

Strauss, R.:Die Schweigsame Frau, w. G. von Milinkovic (mez), F. Wunderlich (ten), H. Hotter (b-bar), H. Prey (bar), K. Böhm (cnd), Vienna PO *(rec live, Salzburg Festival, 8/8/59)* Melodram 2-▲ MEL 27071 (m) [AAD]

Tchaikovsky, P.:Ov 1812, w. L. Maazel (cnd), Vienna PO CBS ▲ MDK 44786 [DDD]

Verdi, G.:Aida, w. R. Tebaldi, (sop) G. Simionato (mez), C. Bergonzi (ten), C. MacNeil (bar), A. van Mill (bass), H. von Karajan (cnd), Vienna PO [I] London ("Jubilee" series) ▲ 417763-2 [ADD]

Verdi, G.:Aida, w. R. Tebaldi, (sop) G. Simionato (mez), C. Bergonzi (ten), C. MacNeil (bar), A. van Mill (bass), H. von Karajan (cnd), Vienna PO [I] London 3-▲ 414087-2 [ADD]

Verdi, G.:Aida, w. L. Freni (sop), K. Ricciarelli (sop), A. Baltsa (mez), J. Carreras (ten), P. Cappuccilli (bar), G. Raimondi (ten), J. Van Dam (b-bar), H. von Karajan (cnd), Vienna PO [I] EMI Classics (Studio) 3-▲ CDMC 69300 [ADD]

Verdi, G.:Aida (sels), w. D. Illitsch (sop—Aida), E. Nikolaidi (cta), M. Lorenz (ten), L. Ludwig (cnd), Vienna State Opera Orch *(rec Sept. 22, 1942)* Koch Schwann 2-▲ SCH 314562 [ADD]

Vienna State Opera Chorus (cont.)

Verdi, G.:Un ballo in maschera, w. J. Barstow (sop), S. Jo (sop), F. Quivar (mez), P. Domingo (ten), L. Nucci (bar), H. von Karajan (cnd), Vienna PO [I] Deutsche Grammophon 2-▲ 427635-2 [DDD]

Verdi, G.:Un ballo in maschera, w. Gabriele Lechner (sop), Luciano Pavarotti (ten), Piero Cappuccilli (bar), C. Abbado (cnd), Vienna PO *(rec live, 1986)* Serenissima 2-▲ SER 360118

Verdi, G.:Don Carlos, w. S. Jurinac (sop), G. Simionato (mez), E. Fernandi (ten), E. Bastianini (bar), C. Siepi (b-bar), H. von Karajan (cnd), Vienna PO [I] *(rec live, Salzburg 7/26/58)* Arkadia 2-▲ 220 [ADD]

Verdi, G.:Don Carlos, w. S. Jurinac (sop—Elisabetta), L. Rysanek (sop—Celestial Voice), F. Cossotto (mez—Princess Eboli), L. Dutoit (boy sop—Tebaldo), P. Domingo (ten—Don Carlo), E. Majkut (ten—Count of Lerma), M. Sereni (bar—Rodrigo), C. Siepi (bass—Philip II), I. Vinco (bass—Grand Inquisitor), T. Franc (bass—Friar), S. Varviso (cnd), Vienna State Opera Orch Standing Room Only 2-▲ SRO 850 [ADD]

Verdi, G.:Don Carlos, w. Gundula Janowitz (sop), Shirley Verrett (mez), Franco Corelli (ten), Eberhard Waechter (bar), Nicolai Ghiaurov (bass), Martti Talvela (bass), H. Stein (cnd), Vienna PO *(rec Vienna, Oct. 25, 1970)* Pantheon 2-▲ PHE 6614

Verdi, G.:Don Carlos (sels), w. H. Konetzni (sop—Elisabetta), F. Völker (ten—Don Carlos), A. Kipnis (bass—Filippo), B. Walter (cnd), Vienna State Opera Orch *(rec Dec. 16, 1936)* Koch Schwann 2-▲ SCH 314602

Verdi, G.:Falstaff, w. Augusta Ottrabella (sop—Nannetta), Franca Somigli (sop—Alice), Angelica Cravcenko (mez—Mrs. Quickly), Mita Vasari (mez—Meg), Dino Borgioli (ten—Fenton), Giuseppe Nessi (ten—Bardolfo), Alfredo Tedeschi (ten—Dr. Cajus), Piero Biasini (bar—Ford), Mariano Stabile (bar—Falstaff), Virgilio Lazzari (bass—Pistola), A. Toscanini (cnd), Vienna PO *(rec Salzburg, Aug 23, 1937)* Minerva 2-▲ MN A36/37 (m) [ADD]

Verdi, G.:Falstaff, w. Dino Borgioli (ten), Ismildo Tedeschi (ten), Mariano Stabile (bar), A. Toscanini (cnd), Vienna PO *(rec live, Salzburg Festival, 1936)* Arkadia 2-▲ 625

Verdi, G.:Macbeth, w. C. Ludwig (mez), C. Cossutta (ten), K. Ridderbusch (bass), S. Milnes (bass), K. Böhm (cnd), Vienna State Opera Orch *(rec live 1970)* Legato Classics 2-▲ LCD 143-2 [ADD]

Verdi, G.:Macbeth, w. E. Höngen (cta), J. Witt (ten), M. Ahlersmeyer (bar), H. Alsen (bass), K. Böhm (cnd), Vienna State Opera Orch *(rec 1943)* Preiser 2-▲ PRE 90175 [AAD]

Verdi, G.:Nabucco, w. E. Suliotis (sop), B. Prevedi (ten), T. Gobbi (ten), C. Cava (bass), L. Gardelli (cnd), Vienna State Opera Orch [I] London 2-▲ 417407-2 [ADD]

Verdi, G.:Otello, w. Hilde Konetzni (sop), Elena Nikolaidi (cta), Torsten Ralf (ten), Paul Schöffler (b-bar), K. Böhm (cnd), Vienna State Opera Orch *(rec live, Aug. 1944)* Preiser 2-▲ PRE 90230 [ADD]

Verdi, G.:Otello, w. Carla Martinis (sop—Desdemona), Sieglinde Wagner (mez—Emilia), Anton Dermota (ten—Cassio), Paul Schöffler (ten—Iago), Ramon Vinay (ten—Otello), Josef Greindl (bass—Lodovico), W. Furtwängler (cnd), Vienna PO *(rec live, Salzburg Festival, Aug 7, 1951)* EMI Classics ▲ CDMB 65751

Verdi, G.:Requiem Mass, w. Anna Tomowa-Sintow (sop), Agnes Baltsa (mez), José Carreras (ten), José Van Dam (bass-bar), H. von Karajan (cnd), Vienna PO, Sofia National Opera Chorus *(rec Great Hall, Musikverein, Vienna, June 1984)* Deutsche Grammophon 2-▲ 439033-2 [DDD]

Verdi, G.:Requiem Mass, w. J. Sutherland (sop), M. Horne (mez), L. Pavarotti (ten), M. Talvela (bass), G. Solti (cnd), Vienna PO [L] London 2-▲ 411944-2 [ADD]

Verdi, G.:Requiem Mass, w. C. Studer (sop), M. Lopivšek (cta), J. Carreras (ten), R. Riamondi (bass), C. Abbado (cnd), Vienna PO Deutsche Grammophon 2-▲ 435884-2

Verdi, G.:quattro pezzi sacri, w. C. Studer (sop), M. Lopivšek (cta), J. Carreras (ten), R. Riamondi (bass), C. Abbado (cnd), Vienna PO Deutsche Grammophon 2-▲ 435884-2

Verdi, G.:La traviata, w. A. Moffo (sop), G. Janowitz (sop), G. Zampieri (ten), E. Bastianini (bar), B. Klobucar (cnd), Vienna State Opera Orch [I] *(rec live, Vienna, 1964)* Melodram (Connaisseur) 2-▲ CDM 27510 [ADD]

Wagner, R.:Der fliegende Holländer, w. H. Beherns (sop—Senta), I. Vermillion (mez—Mary), U. Heilmann (ten—Helmsman), J. Protschka (ten—Erik), R. Hale (bar—The Dutchman), K. Rydl (bass—Daland), C. von Dohnányi (cnd), Vienna PO London 2-▲ 436418-2 [DDD]

Wagner, R.:Götterdämmerung (sels), w. G. Kappel (sop—Brünhilde), J. Kalenberg (ten—Siegfried), J. von Manowarda (bass—Mime), R. Heger (cnd), Vienna State Opera Orch *(rec June 15, 1933)* Koch Schwann 2-▲ SCH 314592

Wagner, R.:Götterdämmerung (sels), w. M. Lorenz (ten—Siegfried), P. Schöffler (b-bar—Gunther), J. von Manowarda (bass—Hagen), L. Reichwein (cnd), Vienna State Opera Orch *(rec Sept. 10, 1942)* Koch Schwann 2-▲ SCH 314562 [ADD]

Wagner, R.:Lohengrin, w. Leonore Kirchstein (sop—Elsa von Brabant), Ruth Hesse (mez—Ortrud), Herbert Schachtschneider (ten—Lohengrin), Hans Helm (bar—Der Heerrufer des Königs), Otto von Rohr (bass—Heinrich der Vogler), Heinz Imdahl (sgr—Friedrich von Telramund), H. Swarowsky (cnd), Czech PO, Prague National Theater Orch *(rec Aug 1968)* Weltbild Classics 3-▲ 703835 [ADD]

Wagner, R.:Lohengrin, w. J. Norman (sop), E. Randová (mez), P. Domingo (ten), D. Fischer-Dieskau (bar), S. Nimsgern (b-bar), H. Sotin (bass), G. Solti (cnd), Vienna PO [G] London 4-▲ 421053-2 [DDD]

Wagner, R.:Lohengrin, w. J. Norman (sop), E. Randová (mez), P. Domingo (ten), D. Fischer-Dieskau (bar), S. Nimsgern (b-bar), H. Sotin (bass), G. Solti (cnd), Vienna PO [G] London ▲ 425530-2 [DDD]

Wagner, R.:Lohengrin, w. E. Grümmer (sop), C. Ludwig (mez), J. Thomas (ten), D. Fischer-Dieskau (bar), G. Frick (bass), R. Kempe (cnd), Vienna PO [G] EMI Classics 3-▲ CDCC 49017 [ADD]

Wagner, R.:Die Meistersinger von Nürnberg, w. I. Seefried (sop), H. Beirer (ten), P. Schoeffler (b-bar), F. Reiner (cnd), Vienna PO *(rec live, Vienna, 1955)* Melodram 4-▲ MEL 47083

Wagner, R.:Die Meistersinger von Nürnberg, w. Irmgard Seefried (sop—Eva), Else Schürhoff (mez—Magdelene), Peter Klein (ten—David), August Seider (ten—Walther), Erich Kunz (bar—Beckmesser), Paul Schoeffler (b-bar—Hans Sachs), Herbert Alsen (bass—Pogner), K. Böhm (cnd), Vienna PO *(rec Vienna, Nov. & Dec. 1944)* Preiser 4-▲ PRE 90234 [ADD]

Wagner, R.:Die Meistersinger von Nürnberg, w. H. Bode (sop), J. Hamari (mez), A. Kollo (ten), N. Bailey (bar), B. Weikl (bar), K. Moll (bass), G. Solti (cnd), Vienna PO [G] London 4-▲ 417497-2 [ADD]

Wagner, R.:Die Meistersinger von Nürnberg (sels), w. V. Ursuleac (sop—Eva), F. Völker (ten—Walther), A. Jerger (b-bar—Hans Sachs), C. Krauss (cnd), Vienna State Opera Orch *(rec Apr. 13, 1934)* Koch Schwann 2-▲ SCH 314602

Wagner, R.:Die Meistersinger von Nürnberg (sels), w. V. Ursuleac (sop—Eva), M. Lorenz (ten—Walther), E. Zimmermann (ten—David), A. Jerger (b-bar—Hans Sachs), C. Krauss (cnd), Vienna State Opera Orch *(rec Feb. 26, 1933)* Koch Schwann 2-▲ SCH 314552 [ADD]

Wagner, R.:Die Meistersinger von Nürnberg (sels), w. T. Lemnitz (sop), E. Laholm (ten), R. Bockelmann (bar), E. Fuchs (bar), W. Furtwängler (cnd), Vienna State Opera Orch *(rec Sept. 5, 1938)* Koch Schwann 2-▲ SCH 314522 [ADD]

Wagner, R.:Die Meistersinger von Nürnberg (sels), w. Lotte Lehmann (sop—Eva), Eyvind Laholm (ten—Walther), Ludwig Hofmann (bass—Hans Sachs), F. von Weingartner (cnd), Vienna State Opera Orch *(rec Vienna, Sept. 20, 1935)* Koch Schwann 2-▲ SCH 314622 [ADD]

Wagner, R.:Die Meistersinger von Nürnberg (sels), w. Viorica Ursuleac (sop—Eva), Rudolf Bockelmann (ten—Hans Sachs), Josef Kalenberg (ten—Walther), Hermann Wiedemann (bar—Beckmesser), C. Krauss (cnd), Vienna State Opera Orch *(rec Jan. 20, 1933)* Koch Schwann 2-▲ SCH 314642 [ADD]

Wagner, R.:Parsifal, w. Anny Konetzni (sop—Kundry), Günther Treptow (ten—Parsifal), Paul Schöffler (bar—Amfortas), Hans Braun (bass—Titurel), Adolf Vogel (bass—Klingsor), Ludwig Weber (bass—Gurnemanz), R. Moralt (cnd), Vienna SO *(rec Vienna)* Myto 4-▲ 4 MCD 954.136

Wagner, R.:Parsifal, w. C. Ludwig (mez), E. Höngen (cta), H.-M. Uhle (ten), H. Hotter (b-bar), T. Franc (bass), W. Berry (bass), H. von Karajan (cnd), Vienna State Opera Orch [G] *(rec live 4/1/61)* Arkadia 3-▲ 219 (m) [ADD]

Wagner, R.:Parsifal, w. C. Ludwig (mez), A. Kollo (ten), D. Fischer-Dieskau (bar), Z. Kelemen (bar), G. Frick (bass), G. Solti (cnd), Vienna PO, Vienna Boys' Choir [G] London 4-▲ 417143-2 [ADD]

Wagner, R.:Parsifal (sels), w. A. Konetzni (sop), H. Grahl (ten), H. Weidemann (bar), H. Alsen (bass), H. Knappertsbusch (cnd), Vienna State Opera Orch *(rec Apr. 6, 1939)* Koch Schwann 2-▲ SCH 314522 [ADD]

Wagner, R.:Parsifal (sels), w. H. Braun (sop—Kundry), M. Lorenz (ten—Parsifal), P. Schöffler (b-bar—Amfortas), Reichwein, Knappertsbusch (cnd), Vienna State Opera Orch *(rec Apr. 4, 1942 & Nov. 10, 1)* Koch Schwann 2-▲ SCH 314562 [ADD]

Vienna State Opera Chorus (cont.)
Wagner, R.:Das Rheingold (sels), w. A. Konetzni (sop—Fricka), J. Prohaska (bar—Wotan), N. Zec (b-bar—Fasolt), H. Alsen (bass—Fafner), J. Krips (cnd), Vienna State Opera Orch *(rec Jan. 18, 1937)* Koch Schwann 2-▲ SCH 314592
Wagner, R.:Siegfried (sels), w. E. Szantho (cta—Erda), M. Lorenz (ten—Siegfried), W. Wernigk (ten—Mime), L. Hoffmann (bass—Wanderer), H. Knappertsbusch (cnd), Vienna State Opera Orch *(rec June 16, 1937)* Koch Schwann 2-▲ SCH 314602
Wagner, R.:Siegfried (sels), w. A. Konetzni (sop—Brünhilde), J. Kalenberg (ten—Siegfried), H. Knappertsbusch (cnd), Vienna State Opera Orch *(rec Apr. 18, 1936)* Koch Schwann 2-▲ SCH 314562 [ADD]
Wagner, R.:Siegfried (sels), w. G. Kappel (sop—Brünhilde), R. Schubert (ten—Siegfried), E. Zimmermann (ten—Mime), R. Heger (cnd), Vienna State Opera Orch *(rec June 13, 1933)* Koch Schwann 2-▲ SCH 314592
Wagner, R.:Tristan und Isolde (sels), w. A. Konetzni (sop—Isolde), M. Klose (cta—Brangäne), M. Lorenz (ten—Tristan), W. Furtwängler (cnd), Vienna State Opera Orch *(rec Dec. 25, 1941)* Koch Schwann 2-▲ SCH 314562 [ADD]
Wagner, R.:Tristan und Isolde (sels), w. Anny Konetzni (sop—Isolde), Margarete Klose (cta—Brangäne), Max Lorenz (ten—Tristan), Paul Schöffler (b-bar—Kurwenal), Herbert Alsen (bass—King Marke), W. Furtwängler (cnd), Vienna State Opera Orch—extended excerpts from Acts 1 & 2; Act 3 (comp.) *(rec Vienna, Jan. 2, 1943 & Dec. 25, 1)* Koch Schwann 2-▲ SCH 314612 [ADD]
Wagner, R.:Die Walküre (sels), w. H. Konetzni (sop—Sieglinde), R. Merker (sop—Brünhilde), F. Völker (ten—Sigmund), L. Hofmann (bass—Wotan), B. Walter (cnd), Vienna State Opera Orch *(rec Oct. 19, 1936)* Koch Schwann 2-▲ SCH 314592
Wagner, R.:Die Walküre (sels), w. A. Konetzni (sop—Brünhilde), L. Hofmann (bass—Wotan), H. Knappertsbusch (cnd), Vienna State Opera Orch *(rec Oct. 28, 1942)* Koch Schwann 2-▲ SCH 314562 [ADD]
Webern, A.:Bach Transcription, w. C. Abbado (cnd), Vienna PO Deutsche Grammophon ▲ 431774-2 [DDD]
Webern, A.:Passacaglia, w. C. Abbado (cnd), Vienna PO Deutsche Grammophon ▲ 431774-2 [DDD]
Webern, A.:Pieces Orch, Op. 6, w. C. Abbado (cnd), Vienna PO Deutsche Grammophon ▲ 431774-2 [DDD]
Webern, A.:Pieces Orch, Op. 10, w. C. Abbado (cnd), Vienna PO Deutsche Grammophon ▲ 431774-2 [DDD]
Webern, A.:Vars Orch, w. C. Abbado (cnd), Vienna PO Deutsche Grammophon ▲ 431774-2 [DDD]
G. Solti (cnd)
Wagner, R.:Choruses, w. Chicago Sym Chorus London ▲ 421865-2 [ADD/DDD]
Vienna State Opera Concert Association Chorus
Beethoven, L. van:Fidelio, w. Birgit Nilsson (sop—Leonore), Graziella Sciutti (sop—Marzelline), Kurt Equiluz (ten—Erster Gefangener), Donald Grobe (ten—Jacquino), James McCracken (ten—Florestan), Tom Krause (bar—Don Pizarro), Hermann Prey (bar—Don Fernando), Kurt Böhme (bass—Rocco), Günther Adam (sgr—Zweiter Gefangener), L. Maazel (cnd), Vienna PO *(rec Sofiensaal, Vienna, Mar 1964)* London 2-▲ 448104-2 [ADD]
Vienna State Opera Men's Chorus
German University Songs, w. F. Litschauer (cnd), Vienna State Opera Orch, Erich Kunz (bar) Vanguard Classics ▲ OVC 6009 [ADD]
German University Songs, Vol. 2, w. Erich Kunz (bar), Vienna State Opera Orch [cnd:Anton Paulik] *(rec Brahmssaal, Musikverein, Vienna, June 1956)* Vanguard Classics ▲ OVC 6010 [ADD]
Vienna Sym Chorus
Schmidt, F.:Das Buch mit sieben Siegeln, w. Gabriele Fontana (sop), Margareta Hintermeier (alt), Kurt Azesberger (ten), Eberhard Büchner (ten—Johannes), Robert Holl (bass—Voice of the Lord), Robert Holzer (bass), Martin Haselböck (org), H. Stein (cnd), Vienna SO *(rec live, Vienna Music Hall, May 1996)* Calig 2-▲ CAL 50978/9 [DDD]
Vienna Volksoper Chorus
Benatzky, R.:Im weissen Rössl (sels), w. F. Loor (sop), H. Brauner (cta), K. Equiluz (ten), K. Terkal (ten), F. Bauer-Theussl (cnd), Vienna Volksoper Orch [G] Koch Präsent ▲ CD 399225 [AAD]
Golden Operetta, Vol. 1, w. F. Bauer-Theussl (cnd), Vienna Volksoper Orch, various soloists Koch Präsent ▲ 399 223 [AAD]
Golden Operetta, Vol. 2:Operetta Melodies, w. F. Bauer-Theussl (cnd), Vienna Volksoper Orch, Renate Holm (sop), Lotte Rysanek (sop), Dagmar Hermann (mez), Kurt Equiluz (ten), Horst Winter (ten), et al. Koch Präsent ▲ 399 224 [AAD]
Golden Operetta, Vol. 3, w. F. Bauer-Theussl (cnd), Vienna Volksoper Orch Koch Präsent ▲ 399 225 [AAD]
Golden Operetta, Vol. 4, w. F. Bauer-Theussl (cnd), Vienna Volksoper Orch Koch Präsent ▲ 399 226 [AAD]
Kálmán, I.:Die Csárdásfürstin (sels), w. E. Liebesberg (sop), L. Rysanek (sop), R. Christ (ten), H. Prikopa (bar), F. Bauer-Theussl (cnd), Vienna Volksoper Orch [G] Koch Präsent ▲ CD 399226 [AAD]
Lehár, F.:Der Graf von Luxemburg (sels), w. Renate Holm (sop), Else Liebesberg (sop), Hilde Brauner (cta), Dagmar Hermann (mez), Rudolf Christ (ten), Herbert Prikopa (bar), F. Bauer-Theussl (cnd), Vienna Volksoper Orch [G] Koch Präsent ▲ CD 399223 [AAD]
Lehár, F.:Paganini (sels), w. E. Liebesberg (sop), E. Mechera (sop), Rudolf Christ (ten), K. Equiluz (ten), F. Bauer-Theussl (cnd), Vienna Volksoper Orch [G] Koch Präsent ▲ CD 399226 [AAD]
Millöcker, C.:Bettelstudent, w. Wilma Lipp (sop—Laura), Esther Rethy (sop—Bronislava), Rosette Anday (cta—Palmatica), Rudolf Christ (ten—Symon), Kurt Preger (ten—Ollendorf), Eberhard Waechter (bar—Jan), A. Paulik (cnd), Vienna Volksoper Orch *(rec Brahmssaal, Vienna, June 1995)* Omega 2-▲ OCD 1018/19 [AAD]
Mozart, W.A.:Masonic Music, w. K. Equiluz (ten), K. Rapf (pno/org), P. Maag (cnd), Vienna Volksoper Orch—Adagios, K.410 & 411; Adagio & Fugue, K.546; Adagio & Rondo, K.617; Anhang zum Schluss der Freimaurerloge, K.623a; Cants, K.429, 471, 619 & 623; Graduale, K.273; Lieder, K.148, 468, 483 & 484; Maurerische; Motet, K.618; Psalm 129, K.93 *(rec 1966)* Vox Box 2-▲ CDX 5055 [ADD]
Straus, O.:Ein Walzertraum (sels), w. H. Brauner (cta), R. Holm (sop), E. Liebesberg (sop), D. Hermann (mez), R. Christ (ten), H. Prikopa (bar), F. Bauer-Theussl (cnd), Vienna Volksoper Orch [G] Koch Präsent ▲ CD 399223 [AAD]
Strauss (II), Joh.:Wiener Blut, w. H. Papouschek (sop), S. Martikke (sop), E. Kales (sop), A. Dallapozza (ten), K. Ruzicka (ten), E. Kuchar (ten), W. Kandutsch (bar), K. Dönch (bar), O. Kolmann (bass), R. Bibl (cnd), Vienna Volksoper Orch Denon 2-▲ CO 8105 [DDD]
Vienna W. U. Choir
J. Prinz (cnd)
Britten, B.:Rejoice in the Lamb [E] Koch Schwann ▲ 3-1043-2 [DDD]
Fauré, G.:Cantique de Jean Racine [F] Koch Schwann ▲ 3-1043-2 [DDD]
Kodály, Z.:Laudes Organi [L] Koch Schwann ▲ 3-1043-2 [DDD]
Mendelssohn, F.:Hear my prayer [G] Koch Schwann ▲ 3-1043-2 [DDD]
Villamont College Little Chorus
Falla, M. de:Atlántida, w. Montserrat Caballé (sop), Heinz Rehfuss (bar), E. Ansermet (cnd), Swiss Romande Orch, Lausanne Youth Chorus, Swiss Romande Red Chorus Cascavelle ▲ CVL 2005 [ADD]
Vittoria d'Ile Choir
Poulenc, F.:Gloria Sop, w. Danielle Borst (sop), M. Piquemal (cnd), Orch de la Cité *(rec Paris, Oct 1992)* Naxos ▲ 8.553176 [DDD]
Poulenc, F.:Litanies à la vierge noire, w. M. Piquemal (cnd), Orch de la Cité *(rec Paris, Oct 1992)* Naxos ▲ 8.553176 [DDD]
Poulenc, F.:Stabat mater, w. Danielle Borst (sop), M. Piquemal (cnd), Orch de la Cité *(rec Paris, Oct 1992)* Naxos ▲ 8.553176 [DDD]
Vittoria French Regional Choir
Bruneau, A.:Lazare, w. Françoise Pollet (sop), Mary Saint-Palais (sop), Sylvie Sullé (mez), Jean-Luc Viala (ten), Laurent Naouri (b-bar), J. Mercier (cnd), French National Orch, Maîtrise de Paris Adès ▲ ADE 204512
Bruneau, A.:Requiem, w. Françoise Pollet (sop), Mary Saint-Palais (sop), Sylvie Sullé (mez), Jean-Luc Viala (ten), Laurent Naouri (b-bar), J. Mercier (cnd), French National Orch, Maîtrise de Paris Adès ▲ ADE 204512

Vittoria French Regional Choir (cont.)
Ropartz, G.:Choral Music, w. Christian Papis (nar), Didier Henry (bar), Vincent Le Texier (b-bar), Christine Lajarrige (pno), Irène Brissot (hp), Eric Lebrun (org), M. Piquemal (cnd), Nancy SO, French Radio Chorus Soloists—Psaume 136; Dimanche; Nocturne; Les Vêpres sonnent; Le Miracle de Saint Nicolas *(rec Salle Poirel, Nancy, Apr. 22-24, 1994)* Marco Polo ▲ 8.223774 [DDD]
Viva Voce
J. Rosser (cnd)
Hamilton, D.:Choral Music—Caliban's Song; Carol of the Mother & Child; Didn't it Rain?; From Age to Age Endure; Lullaby Carol; Lux Aeterna; Nunc Dimittis; Poem About the Sun Slinking Off & Pinning Up a Notice; Song for a Young Country; Three Songs from Othello; Transatlantic; Tydynges, Tydynges [E] *(rec 1990-91)* Ode/New Zealand ▲ 1308
Vivente Voce Choir
Gotkovsky, I.:Chant de la forêt, w. N. Nozy (cnd), Belgian Guides Symphonic Band, Vocal Ensemble ex Tempore René Gailly ▲ CD 87058 [DDD]
P. Benoit (cnd)
Haydn, M.:Missa Pro Defuncto Archiepiscopo Sigismundo, w. Lena Lootens (sop), Cornelia Salje (alt), Bernard Loonens (ten), Dirk Snellings (b-bar) *(rec Steurbaut Sound Recording Centre)* René Gailly ▲ CD 87125 [DDD]
Haydn, M.:Motets, w. Lena Lootens (sop), Cornelia Salje (alt), Bernard Loonens (ten), Dirk Snellings (b-bar)—Aria de Passione Domini *(rec Steurbaut Sound Recording Centre)* René Gailly ▲ CD 87125 [DDD]
Vocal Audite Nova Ensemble
J. Sourisse (cnd)
Saint-Saëns, C.:Choral Music, w. D. Collot (sop), B. Vinson (mez), J. Bouillat (ten), G. Wieclaw (bass), E. Strosser (pno), C. Desert (pno), Jean Sourisse Ensemble—Calme des nuits, Op. 68/1; Les fleurs et les arbres, Op. 68/2; Salterelle, Op. 74 FNAC Music ▲ 592224 [DDD]
Vocal Contrepoint Ensemble
Charpentier, M.-A.:Psaumes de David, w. O. Schneebeli (cnd), Marais SO Adda ▲ ADD 241972 [ADD]
Vocal Ensemble
J.-P. Gipon (cnd)
Victoria, T.L. de:Officium Hebdomadae Sanctae—Palm Sunday; Maundy Thursday [Matins; Lauds]; Good Friday [Passion of St. John; Adoration of the Cross]; Holy Saturday [Matins; Lauds] Jade 3-▲ JAD C 332
G. Sporken (cnd)
Pousseur, H.:Traverser la forêt, w. Christian Crahay (nar), Marianne Pousseur (sop), Peter Harvey (bar), J.-P. Peuvion (cnd), Liège New Music Ensemble Adda ▲ ADD 581295 [DDD]
Vocal Ensemble ex Tempore
Gotkovsky, I.:Chant de la forêt, w. N. Nozy (cnd), Belgian Guides Symphonic Band, Vivente Voce Choir René Gailly ▲ CD 87058 [DDD]
Vocal Majority
The Chorus, w. Mormon Tabernacle Choir, New York Choral Society, Westminster Choir, Chicago Sym Chorus members, et al. Sony Classical ("Greatest Hits" series) ▲ MLK 62684 ■ MLT 62684
Voices in Harmony, w. Mormon Tabernacle Choir CBS ▲ MK 42380 [DDD] ■ FMT 42380 (D)
E Voce di U Cumune Ensemble
Corsican Traditional Polyphonic Chants Harmonia Mundi ▲ HMC 90.1256 [DDD]
Voces Novae et Antiquae
The Gregorian Heritage:Gregorian Based Choral Masterworks Arkay ▲ ARK 6145
R.A.M. Ross (cnd)
Thompson, R.:Choral Music, w. Philadelphia Festival Choir members—Cantata, "A Feast of Praise"; Frostiana; Glory to God in the Highest; Felices Ter; Mirror of St. Anne; Bitter-Sweet; Antiphon; Lord is My Sheperd; Alleluia; Pueri Hebraeorum Arkay ▲ AR 6110 [DDD]
Voci Angeli
Handel, G.F.:Messiah (sels), w. M. J. Newman (cnd), New York Musica Antiqua—Worthy Is the Lamb *(rec Presbyterian Church, Mt. Kisco, NY, Aug 26-27, 1995)* Helicon ▲ HE 1006 [DDD]
Voices of Ascension Chorus
Duruflé, M.:Mass, "Cum jubilo", w. François le Roux (bar), D. Keene (cnd), Voices of Ascension Orch *(rec Church of the Ascension, New York City, May 13, 17 & 18 (1995))* Delos ▲ DE 3169 [DDD]
Duruflé, M.:Requiem, w. Patricia Spence (mez), François le Roux (bar), D. Keene (cnd), Voices of Ascension Orch *(rec Church of the Ascension, New York City, June 5-6, 1994)* Delos ▲ DE 3169 [DDD]
D. Keene (cnd)
Beyond Chant:Mysteries of the Renaissance *(rec Mar. 4, 7, 9 & 10, 1994)* Delos ▲ DE 3165 [DDD]
From Chant to Renaissance *(rec Church of the Ascension)* Delos ▲ DE 3174 [DDD]
Mysteries Beyond:Songs & Chants in Praise of Mary, w. V. Cole (ten), Kathleen Bride (hp), Patrick Stephens (pno), M. Kruczek (org) *(rec Apr. 17, 28-30, 1993)* Delos ▲ DE 3138 [DDD]
Voices of Change
Erb, D.:Music of—The Devil's Quickstep for Flute, Clarinet, Violin, Cello, Piano, Harp & Percussion (1988); Quintet for Flute/Harmonica, Clarinet, Violin, Cello, Piano/Electric Piano (1976); The Last Quintet for Flute, Oboe, Clarinet, Horn & Bassoon (1982); The Rainbow Snake for Trombone, Percussion & Piano (1984); Sonata for Clarinet & Percussion (1980) CRI ▲ CD 593 [ADD/DDD]
Kraft, William:Melange, w. W. Kraft (cnd) Crystal ▲ CD 740
Rodriguez, R.X.:Chronies Crystal ▲ CD 740
Rodriguez, R.X.:Meditation Fl Crystal ▲ CD 740
Rodriguez, R.X.:Sonatina d'Estate Crystal ▲ CD 740
Smith, L.A.:The Scrolls Crystal ▲ CD 740
D. Welcher (cnd)
Welcher, D.:Evening Scenes, w. P. Sperry (ten) Crystal ▲ CD 740
Voices of the Azusa Pacific Univ
G. Bonner (cnd)
Adoration, w. London Concertante Ensemble [cnd:R. Mosley] Resmiranda ▲ RES 8000
Adoration II, w. London Concertante Ensemble [cnd:R. Mosley] Resmiranda ▲ RES 8001
Adoration III, w. London Concertante Ensemble [cnd:R. Mosley] Resmiranda ▲ RES 8002
Gloria, w. London Concertante Ensemble [cnd:R. Mosley] Resmiranda ▲ RES 8006
How Excellent Thy Name, w. London Concertante Ensemble [cnd:R. Mosley] Resmiranda ▲ RES 8016
Voix Nouvelles Ensemble
Klein, G.:Madrigals, w. Patricia Schacher Garnier (sop), Zehava Gal (mez), Julian Pike (ten), Nicholas Isherwood (bass)] Arion ▲ ARN 68272 [DDD]
Voronezh Chamber Choir
O. Shepel (cnd)
Rachmaninoff, S.:All-Night Vigil, w. Y. Necheporenko (ten), A. Zlobin (ten), R. Sevostyanov (ten) Globe ▲ GLO 5077 [DDD]
J. Wood (cnd)
Stravinsky, I.:Choral Music, w. New London Chamber Ensemble, New London Chamber Choir—Ave Maria [1934 Slavonic version]; Pater Noster [1926 Slavonic version]; Credo [1964 Slavonic version]; The dove descending breaks the air (1962); Introitus:T.S. Eliot in memoriam (1965) Hyperion ▲ CDA 66410 [DDD]
Stravinsky, I.:Les Noces, w. New London Chamber Ensemble, New London Chamber Choir [R] Hyperion ▲ CDA 66410 [DDD]
Stravinsky, I.:Russian Peasant Songs, w. New London Chamber Choir [performing both the original & revised versions] [R] Hyperion ▲ CDA 66410 [DDD]
Voskreseniye Choir
A. Roudenko (cnd)
Rachmaninoff, S.:All-Night Vigil, w. Russian Chamber Choir *(rec Moscow, Apr. 28-29, 1992)* Northeastern ▲ NR 256 [DDD]
Vox
Hildegard Of Bingen:Sacred Music—O pulchrae facies; O lucidissima apostolorum turba; O Euchari; O virga ac diadema; O successores fortissimi leonis; Spiritui sancto; Cum vox sanguinis *(rec Down Town Studio, Munich)* Real Music ▲ RM 8999

Vox (cont.)
V. Ivanoff (cnd)
Hildegard Of Bingen:Sacred Songs—O Euchari *(rec Down Town Studio, Munich, 1990)*
Catalyst ▲ 09026-68331-2 [DDD/ADD]

Vox Danica Chamber Choir
E. Munk (cnd)
Cour, N. la:Choral Music—4 Salmi; De Profundis; The Prayer of St. Francis of Assisi; Peace Reigns in Country & Town *(rec Vangede Church, Mar–Apr 1989)* Danica ▲ DCD 8130
Duruflé, M.:Requiem, w. Bo Grønbech (org) *(rec Jesus Church, Copenhagen, Spring 1990)*
Danica ▲ DCD 8140
Gounod, C.:Sacred Music, w. Bo Grønbech (org)—Te Deum *(rec Jesus Church, Copenhagen, Spring 1990)* Danica ▲ DCD 8140
Jersild, J.:Choral Music—3 Danish Love Songs; Fant for Hp; 3 Madrigals for Chorus
Danica ▲ DCD 8130
Songs of the Danish Summer Danica ▲ DCD 8155

Vox Hesperia
Kerle, J. de:Preces speciales pro salubri generalis Concili successu, w. Academy of Ancient Music Chamber Ensemble *(rec Santa Maria Maggiore Church, Oct. 28–31, 1994)*
Bongiovanni ▲ GB 5570 [DDD]
Kerle, J. de:Preces speciales pro salubri generalis Concili successu, w. R. Vettori (cnd), Academy of Ancient Music Instumental Ensemble—Pro Concilio; Pro Populi Christiane unione; Contra Ecclesiae hostium furorem; contra eosdem hostes *(rec Church of S. Maria del Carmine, Rovereto)*
Bongiovanni ▲ GB 5571 [DDD]
Viadana, L. da:Vespri per l'Assunzione, w. S. Pozzer (sop), C. Calvino (alt), U. Müller Adam (ten), J. Clement (ten), S. Foresti (bass), L'Amaltea Ensemble, St. Marco Capella Musicale
Fonè ▲ FON 92F 08 [DDD]

Roger Wagner Chorale
Christmas with Roger Wagner Delos ▲ DCD 3072 [DDD]
Holst, G.:The Planets, w. L. Stokowski (cnd), Los Angeles PO
EMI Classics ("Full Dimensional Sound" series) ▲ CDM 65423
Lazarof, H.:Canti [E] CRI ▲ CD 588 [ADD]
Roger Wagner Chorale:Gregorian Chants GIA ■ CS 23
Vivaldi, A.:Gloria, RV.589, w. Andrée Esposito (sop), Solange Michel (sop), Janine Collard (cta), R. Wagner (cnd), Paris Conservatory Societé des Concerts Orch
EMI Classics ("Baroque" series) ▲ CDK 65737

Wakefield Cathedral Choir
J. Bielby (cnd)
Heaven & Earth Are Full of Thy Glory, w. Keith Wright (org) Priory ▲ PRCD 341 [DDD]

Wandsworth School Boys' Choir
Berlioz, H.:Te Deum, w. F. Tagliavini (ten), C. Davis (cnd), London SO, London Sym Chorus [L]
Philips ▲ 416660-2 [ADD]
Britten, B.:Owen Wingrave, w. S. Fisher (Miss Wingrave), J. Vyvyan (Mrs. Julian), H. Harper (Mrs. Coyle), J. Baker (Kate), P. Pears (Sir P. Wingrave; Narrator), B. Luxon (Owen Wingrave), J. Shirley-Quirk (Coyle), B. Britten, English CO London 2-▲ 433200-2
Mahler, G.:Sym 3, w. H. Watts (cta), G. Solti (cnd), London SO, Ambrosian Chorus [G]
London 2-▲ 414254-2 [ADD]
Mahler, G.:Sym 3, w. N. Procter (cta), J. Horenstein (cnd), London SO, Ambrosian Singers [G]
Unicorn-Kanchana ("Souvenir" series) 2-▲ UKCD 2006/07 [ADD]
Mendelssohn, F.:Elijah, w. Gwyneth Jones (sop), Janet Baker (mez), Simon Woolf (trb), Nicolai Gedda (ten), Dietrich Fischer-Dieskau (bar), R. Frühbeck de Burgos (cnd), New Philharmonia Orch, New Philharmonia Chorus *(rec 1968)* EMI Classics ("Doublefforte" series) 2-▲ CDFB 68601

Warsaw Cathedral Choir
A. Filaber (cnd)
Gloria Tibi Trinitas:Sacred Music of Slav Composers 18th-20th Centuries, w. Jolanta Kaufman (sop), Anna Lubanska (alt), Ryszard Wróblewski (ten), Czeslaw Galka (bass), Maciej Piwowarski (org)
Polskie Nagrania Edition ▲ ECD 057 [DDD]

Warsaw Chamber Opera Chorus
Bach, J.S.:St. Mark Passion, w. K. Myrlak (ten), B. Jaszkowski (bar), et al., J. Bok (cnd), Warsaw SO [G]
Bongiovanni 2-▲ GB 2024/25 [ADD]

Warsaw National Chorus
MMC Warsaw Series, Vol. 2, w. R. Black (cnd), Warsaw National PO, Victoria Griswold
Master Musicians Collective ▲ MMC 2004 [DDD]

Warsaw National Opera Chorus
Moniuszko, S.:Halka, w. Barbara Nieman (sop), Halina Sloniowska (sop), Jan Góralski (ten), Bogdan Paprocki (ten), Leslaw Pawluk (ten), Kazimierz Pustelak (ten), Andrzej Hiolski (bar), Edmund Kossowski (bass), Edward Pawlak (bass), Z. Gorzynski (cnd), Warsaw State Opera House Orch *(rec Warsaw, 1965)*
Polskie Nagrania ▲ PNCD 092 [AAD]
Moniuszko, S.:Haunted Manor, w. Halina Slonicka (sop), Bozena Brun-Baranska (mez), Barbara Lawcewicz (mez), Krystyna Szczepanska (mez), Zdzislaw Nikodem (ten), Bogdan Paprocki (ten), Andrzej Hiolski (bar), Edmund Kossowski (bass), Bernard Ladysz (bass), W. Rowicki (cnd), Warsaw State Opera House Orch *(rec Warsaw, 1965)* Polskie Nagrania ▲ PNCD 093 [AAD]
Szymanowski, K.:Harnasie, w. J. Stepien (ten), R. Satanowski (cnd), Warsaw Opera Orch
Koch Schwann ▲ CD 311064 [DDD]
Szymanowski, K.:Mandragora, w. P. Raptis (ten), R. Satanowski (cnd), Warsaw Opera Orch
Koch Schwann ▲ CD 311064 [DDD]

Warsaw National Phil Chorus
Bizet, G.:Carmen (sels), w. Krystyna Szczepanska (alt—Carmen), Bogdan Paprocki (ten—Don José), Andrzej Hiolski (bar—Escamillo), Alina Bolechowska (sgr—Micaela), J. Semkow (cnd), Warsaw PO
Polskie Nagrania ▲ PNCD 213 [AAD]
Elsner, J.:Passio Domini Nostri Jesu Christi, w. B. Harasimowicz (sop), K. Szmyt (ten), C. Galka (bar), P. Nowacki (bass), K. Kord (cnd), Warsaw National Philharmonic SO *(rec 1990)*
Muza ▲ PNCD 078 [DDD]
Penderecki, K.:Choral Music, w. K. Penderecki (cnd), Sinfonia Varsovia—Benedicamus Domino; Song of Cherubin; Lacrimosa *(rec National Philharmonic Hall, Warsaw, Poland, Nov. 23, 1993)*
Sony Classical ▲ SK 66284 [DDD]
Penderecki, K.:Dimensions, w. A. Markowski (cnd), Warsaw PO Polskie Nagrania 2-▲ PNCD 017 A/B
Penderecki, K.:Psalms, w. A. Markowski (cnd), Warsaw PO Polskie Nagrania 2-▲ PNCD 017 A/B
Penderecki, K.:St. Luke Passion, w. S. van Osten (sop), S. Roberts (bar), K. Rydl (bass), E. Lubaszenko (narr), K. Penderecki (cnd), Polish National RSO Katowice, Cracow Boys Choir
Argo ▲ 430328-2 [DDD]
Szymanowski, K.:Litany to the Virgin Mary, w. Stefania Woytowicz (sop), W. Rowicki (cnd), Warsaw PO—12-note Zither; Like a Dwarf Bush *(rec Concert Hall at the National PO, Warsaw, 1961)*
Polskie Nagrania ▲ PLN 063 [ADD]
Szymanowski, K.:Stabat Mater, w. Stefania Woytowicz (sop), Krystyna Szczepanska (alt), Andrzej Hiolski (bar), W. Rowicki (cnd), Warsaw PO *(rec Concert Hall at the National PO, Warsaw, 1961)*
Polskie Nagrania ▲ PLN 063 [ADD]
Szymanowski, K.:Sym 3, w. Stefania Woytowicz (sop), W. Rowicki (cnd), Warsaw PO *(rec Concert Hall at the National PO, Warsaw, 1961)* Polskie Nagrania ▲ PLN 063 [ADD]

Bok, Skoraczewski (cnd)
Penderecki, K.:Utrenia, w. Delfina Ambroziak (sop), Stefania Woytowicz (sop), Krystyna Szczepanska (mez), Kazimierz Pustelak (ten), Boris Carmeli (bass), Wlodzimierz Denysenko (bass), A. Markowski (cnd), Warsaw PO, Pioneer Choir *(rec Warsaw, 1973)* Polskie Nagrania ▲ PNCD 018

A. Szalinski (cnd)
Szymanowski, K.:Harnasie, w. Kazimierz Pustelak (ten), W. Rowicki (cnd), Warsaw PO
Polskie Nagrania ▲ PNCD 242 [AAD]

H. Wojnarowski (cnd)
Maciejewski, R.:Missa pro defunctis, w. Zdzislawa Donat (sop), Jadwiga Rappé (alt), Jerzy Knetig (ten), Janusz Niziolek (bass), T. Strugala (cnd), Warsaw PO *(rec National Philharmonic, Warsaw, May 2–15, 1989)* Polskie Nagrania 2-▲ PNCD 039 A/B

Warsaw National Phil Chorus (cont.)
H. Wojnarowski (cnd) (cont.)
Mozart, W.A.:Requiem, w. Barbara Nieman (sop), Krystyna Szostek-Radkowa (mez), Wieslaw Ochman (ten), Leonard Mróz (bass), K. Kord (cnd), Warsaw PO *(rec Warsaw, 1979)*
Polskie Nagrania ▲ PNCD 135 [ADD]
Penderecki, K.:Choral Music—Aus den Psalmen Davids (1958); Stabat Mater und Psalmen (1962–66); Sicut locutus est (1973–74); Agnus Dei (1981); Veni creator spiritus (1987); Hymn of the Cherubim (1986) Wergo ▲ WER 6261-2

Wojnarowski, Marchwicka (cnd)
Elsner, J.:Passio Domini Nostri Jesu Christi, w. Bozena Harasimowicz (sop), Krzysztof Szmyt (ten), Czeslaw Galka (bar), Bogdan Sliwa (bar), Piotr Nowacki (bass), K. Kord (cnd), Warsaw PO, E. Mlynarski State School of Music Children's Choir *(rec National Philharmonic, Warsaw, 1990)*
Polskie Nagrania ▲ PNCD 078 [DDD]

Warsaw Radio Chorus
Liszt, F.:Legend of Saint Elizabeth, w. Maria Szechowska (sop), Doreen Millmann (mez), Klaus Lapins (bar), István Bercewy (bass), S. Heinrich (cnd), Warsaw RSO [G] *(rec 1983)*
Koch Schwann 2-▲ 3-1291-2 [ADD]

Warsaw Teatr Wielki Chorus
Moniuszko, S.:Halka, w. B. Zagòrzanka (sop), R. Racewicz (mez), W. Ochman (ten), A. Hiolski (bar), J. Ostapuik (bass), R. Satanowski (cnd), Warsaw Teatr Wielki Orch *(rec live, 10/14/86)*
CPO 2-▲ CPO 999032-2 [DDD]
Szymanowski, K.:King Roger, w. B. Zagórzanka (sop—Roger), S. Kowalski (ten—Shepherd), Z. Nikodem (ten—Edrisi), F. Skulski (bar—Roger II), R. Satanowski (cnd), Warsaw Teatr Wielki Orch [Polish]
Koch Schwann 2-▲ CD 314 014 [DDD]
Verdi, G.:Il trovatore (sels), w. Z. Gorzynski (cnd), Warsaw Teatr Wielki Orch—Introdukcja I Cavatina Ferranda; Cavatina Leonory; Tercet Leonory, Manrica I Di Luny; Chór Cyganów; Canzona Azuceny; Duet Manrica I Azuceny; Aria Di Luny; Introdukcja I Chór Zolierzy; Scena I Aria Manrica; Scena I Aria Leonory-Miserere; Duet Leonory I Di Luny; Tercet Manrica, Leonory I Azuceny
Polskie Nagrania ▲ PNCD 228 [AAD]

Washington Bach Consort
J.R. Lewis (cnd)
Bach, J.S.:Motets, BWV 225–30 [G] Pro Organo ▲ CD 7020

Washington Camerata Chorus
Foster, S.C.:Songs, w. Jan DeGaetani (mez), L. Guinn (bar), G. Kalish (pno)
Elektra/Nonesuch ■ 71333-4

Washington Choral Arts Society
Christmas Music, w. National SO members Empire Music ▲ CA 10102

Washington National Cathedral Choral Society
J.R. Lewis (cnd)
Berlioz, H.:Messe solennelle Bar, w. Gene Tucker (ten), Terry Cook (bass), Rosa Lamoreaux (sgr)
Koch International Classics ▲ KIC 7204 [DDD]
Millennium:Russian Choral Music Centaur ▲ CRC 2038 [DAD]

Washington National Cathedral Men & Boys' Choir
P. Callaway (cnd)
Barber, S.:Let down the Bars, O Death! [E] *(rec ca. 1959)* Vanguard Classics ▲ OVC 4016 [ADD]

Washington Oratorio Society
Mussorgsky, M.:Boris Godunov, w. G. Vishnevskaya (sop), N. Gedda (ten), G. Raimondi (ten), M. Rostropovich (cnd), National SO Washington D.C., Choral Arts Society [R]
Erato 3-▲ 2292-45418-2 ZB [DDD]

Washington Oratorio Society Men's Chorus
Corigliano, J.:Of Rage & Remembrance, w. Michelle DeYoung (mez), Michael Accinno (boy sop), Robert Baker (ten), Michael Forest (ten), Jason Stearns (bar), James Shaffran (bar), L. Slatkin (cnd), National SO Washington D.C. *(rec J. F. K. Center for the Performing Arts, Washington, D. C., Nov 9–11, 1995 & Apr 19 &)* RCA Red Seal ▲ 09026-68450-2 [DDD]

Waterland Music School
W. Maczewski (cnd)
Schoenberg, A.:Moses und Aaron, w. David Pittman-Jennings (nar), Gabriele Fontana (sop—Young Girl), Yvonne Naef (cta—Sick Woman), John Graham-Hall (ten—Young Man/Naked Youth), Pår Lindskog (ten—Youth), Chris Merritt (ten—Aaron), Siegfried Lorenz (bar—Another Man), Michael Devlin (b-bar—Ephraimite), László Polgár (bass—Priest), P. Boulez (cnd), Royal Concertgebouw Orch, Netherlands Opera Chorus, Zaans Youth Choir *(rec Concertgebouw, Amsterdam, Oct 1995)*
Deutsche Grammophon 2-▲ 449 174-2 [DDD]

George Watson's College Boys' Chorus
McCarthy, Criswell (cnd)
Bizet, G.:Carmen (sels), w. Teresa Berganza (mez—Carmen), Plácido Domingo (ten—Don José), C. Abbado (cnd), London SO, Ambrosian Singers—C'est toi? C'est moi
Deutsche Grammophon ▲ 447270-2 [ADD] ■ 447 270-4

Waynflete Singers
Finzi, G.:In terra pax, w. Libby Crabtree (sop), Donald Sweeney (bass), D. Hill (cnd), Bournemouth SO, Winchester Cathedral Choir *(rec Winchester Cathedral, Jan 10–13, 1994)*
London ▲ 444130-2 [DDD]
Mahler, G.:Das Klagende Lied, w. J. Rodgers (sop), L. Finnie (cta), H. P. Blochwitz (ten), R. Hickox (cnd), Bournemouth SO, Bath Festival Chorus Chandos ▲ CHAN 9247 [DDD]
Vaughan Williams, R.:Fant on Christmas Carols, w. Donald Sweeney (bass), David Dunnett (org), D. Hill (cnd), Bournemouth SO, Winchester Cathedral Choir *(rec Winchester Cathedral, Jan 10–13, 1994)*
London ▲ 444130-2 [DDD]
Walton, W.:Belshazzar's Feast, w. Bryn Terfel (b-bar), A. Litton (cnd), Bournemouth SO, Bournemouth Sym Chorus, L'Inviti *(rec Winchester Cathedral, Feb 1995)* London ▲ 448134-2 [DDD]

D. Hill (cnd)
Jerusalem, w. Winchester Cathedral Choir, Bournemouth SO Argo ▲ 430836-2 ZH [DDD]
Walton, W.:Jubilate Deo, w. T. Byram-Wigfield (org), Winchester Cathedral Choir
Argo ▲ 436120-2 [DDD]

Carl Maria von Weber School for Music Soloists
G. Schwarze (cnd)
Hell brennt ein Licht [Bright Burns a Light], w. Prohlis Church Choir Dresden, Dresden Church Choirs members, Dresden Wind Collegium members Christophorus ▲ 77165 [DDD]

Anton Webern Choir Freiburg
H.M. Beuerle (cnd)
Brahms, J.:Qts SATB, Op. 112 Ars Musici ▲ 1136 [DDD]
Brahms, J.:Songs, w. T.A. Körber (pno)—In stiller Nacht; Die Wollust in den Maien; Von edler Art; Mit Lust tät ich ausreiten; Abschiedslied Ars Musici ▲ 1136 [DDD]
Brahms, J.:Songs, Op. 104 Ars Musici ▲ 1136 [DDD]
Brahms, J.:Zigeunerlieder Ars Musici ▲ 1136 [DDD]

Wellington Cathedral Choir
P. Walsh (cnd)
A Sound Came From Heaven, w. Andrew Macmillan (org) Herald ▲ HAPVCD 191 [DDD]

Wells Cathedral Choir
Christmas Carols from Wells & Salisbury, w. Salisbury Cathedral Chorus
ASV ("Quicksilva" series) ▲ ASV 6077 [ADD/DDD]
Music for Passiontide & Easter Priory ▲ PRI 362 [DDD]

A. Crossland (cnd)
The Psalms of David, Vol. 2:O Praise the Lord of Heaven, w. Anthony Crossland (org)
Priory ▲ PRCD 337 [DDD]

Welsh National Opera Chorus
Bellini, V.:Norma, w. J. Sutherland (sop), M. Caballé (sop), L. Pavarotti (sop), S. Ramey (bass), R. Bonynge (cnd), Welsh National Opera Orch [I] London 3-▲ 414476-2 [DDD]
Borodin, A.:Prince Igor (Polovtsian dances), w. L. Stokowski (cnd), Royal PO, Royal Liverpool Phil Choir *(rec Kingsway Hall, London, England, June 17, 1969)*
London ("Phase 4 Stereo" series) ▲ 443896-2 [ADD]

Welsh National Opera Chorus (cont.)

Britten, B.:Gloriana, w. J. Barstow (sop—Queen Elizabeth I), D. Jones (mez—Lady Essex), P. Langridge (ten—Earl of Essex), J. M. Ainsley (ten—Spirit of the Masque), J. Summers (bar—Lord Mountjoy), J. Shirley-Quirk (bar—Recorder of Norwich), B. Terfel (b-bar—Henry Cuffe), C. Mackerras (cnd), Welsh National Opera Orch Argo 2-▲ 440213-2 [DDD]

Cilea, F.:Adriana Lecouvreur, w. J. Sutherland (sop), C. Bergonzi (ten), L. Nucci (bar), R. Bonynge (cnd), Welsh National Opera Orch London 2-▲ 425815-2 [DDD]

Delius, F.:Sea Drift, w. T. Hampson (bar), C. Mackerras (cnd), Welsh National Opera Orch Argo ▲ 430206-2 [DDD]

Gilbert, W.S.:Trial by Jury, w. Rebecca Evans (sop—Plaintiff), Barry Banks (ten—Defendant), Gareth Rhys-Davies (bar—Foreman of the Jury), Peter Savidge (bar—Counsel for the Plaintiff), Donald Adams (bass—Usher), Richard Suart (bass—The Learned Judge), C. Mackerras (cnd), Welsh National Opera Orch *(rec Brangwyn Hall, Swasea, Wales, Apr 18-30 & May 1, 1995)* Telarc 2-▲ CD 80404 [DDD]

Gilbert, W.S.:The Yeomen of the Guard, w. Felicity Palmer (sop—Dame Carruthers), Pamela Helen Stephens (mez—Phoebe Meryll), Alwyn Mellor (sgr—Elsie Maynard), Clare O'Neill (sgr—Kate), Neill Archer (ten—Col Fairfax), Peter Hoare (ten—Leonard Meryll), Ralph Mason (ten—1st Yeoman), Donald Maxwell (bar—Wilfred Shadbolt), Peter Savidge (bar—Lieutenant Sir Richard Cholmondely), Donald Adams (bass—Sergeant Meryll), Richard Suart (bass—Jack Point), Peter Lloyd Evans (sgr—2nd Yeoman), C. Mackerras (cnd), Welsh National Opera Orch *(rec Brangwyn Hall, Swasea, Wales, Apr 18-30 & May 1, 1995)* Telarc 2-▲ CD 80404 [DDD]

Gounod, C.:Faust, w. C. Gasdia (sop), B. Fassbaender (mez), S. Mentzer (mez), J. Hadley (ten), A. Agache (bar), P. Fourcade (bass), C. Rizzi (cnd), Welsh National Opera Orch Teldec 3-▲ 90872

The Incomparable Alfredo Kraus, w. Alfredo Kraus (ten), Welsh National Opera Orch [cnd:Carlo Rizzi] Philips ▲ 442785-2

Jones, D.:The Country Behind the Stars, *(orch unknown)* Lyrita ▲ 326

Lloyd, G.:The Vigil of Venus, w. Carolyn James (sop), Thomas Booth (ten), G. Lloyd (cnd), Welsh National Opera Orch Albany ▲ TROY 170 [DDD]

Mathias, W.:Ave Rex, w. Janet Price (sop), Kenneth Bowen (ten), Michael Rippon (bar), Geraint Evans (b-bar), Atherton, Willcocks (cnd), London SO, New Philharmonia Orch, Windsor Bach Choir, St. George's Chapel Choristers Lyrita ▲ SRCD .324

Mathias, W.:This Worlde's Joie, w. Janet Price (sop), Kenneth Bowen (ten), Michael Rippon (bar), Atherton, Willcocks (cnd), London SO, New Philharmonia Orch, Windsor Bach Choir, St. George's Chapel Choristers Lyrita ▲ SRCD .324

Puccini, G.:Tosca (sels), w. K. Te Kanawa (sop), J. Aragall (ten), L. Nucci (bar), G. Solti (cnd), National PO London London ▲ 421611-2 [DDD]

Sullivan, A.:HMS Pinafore, w. F. Palmer (sop—Little Buttercup), R. Evans (mez—Josephine), M. Schade (ten—Ralph Rackstraw), T. Allen (bar—Capt. Corcoran), R. Suart (bass—Rt. Hon. Sir Joseph Porter, K.C.B.), D. Adams (bass—Dick Deadeye), R. Van A. (bass—Bill Bobstay), C. Mackerras (cnd), Welsh National Opera Orch *(rec Swansea, Wales, June 5-8, 1994)* Telarc ▲ CD 80374 [DDD]

Sullivan, A.:The Mikado, w. M. McLaughlin (sop), A. Howells (mez), J. Watson (sop), F. Palmer (sop/mez), D. Adams (bass), A. Rolfe Johnson (ten), R. Stuart (bar), R. Van Allan (bass), N. Folwell (bar), C. Mackerras (cnd), Welsh National Opera Orch—Ov & dialogue omitted [E] Telarc ▲ CD 80284 [DDD]; ■ CS 30284 (D)

Sullivan, A.:The Pirates of Penzance, w. R. Evans (sop—Mabel), G. Knight (mez—Ruth), J. Gossage (mez—Edith), J. M. Ainsley (ten—Frederic), R. Suart (bar—Maj.-Gen. Stanley), N. Folwell (bar—Samuel), D. Adams (b-bar—Pirate King), R. Van Allan (bass—Sergeant of Police), C. Mackerras (cnd), Welsh National Opera Orch *(rec May 4-6, 1993)* Telarc ▲ CD 80353 [DDD]; ■ CS 30353

Sullivan, A.:Trial by Jury, w. Rebecca Evans (sop—Plaintiff), Barry Banks (ten—Defendant), Gareth Rhys-Davies (bar—Foreman of the Jury), Peter Savidge (bar—Counsel for the Plaintiff), Donald Adams (bass—Usher), Richard Suart (bass—The Learned Judge), C. Mackerras (cnd), Welsh National Opera Orch *(rec Brangwyn Hall, Swasea, Wales, Apr 18-30 & May 1, 1995)* Telarc 2-▲ CD 80404 [DDD]

Sullivan, A.:The Yeomen of the Guard, w. Felicity Palmer (sop—Dame Carruthers), Pamela Helen Stephens (mez—Phoebe Meryll), Neill Archer (ten—Col Fairfax), Peter Hoare (ten—Leonard Meryll), Ralph Mason (ten—1st Yeoman), Donald Maxwell (bar—Wilfred Shadbolt), Peter Savidge (bar—Lieutenant Sir Richard Cholmondely), Donald Adams (bass—Sergeant Meryll), Richard Suart (bass—Jack Point), Peter Lloyd Evans (sgr—2nd Yeoman), Alwyn Mellor (sgr—Elsie Maynard), Clare O'Neill (sgr—Kate), C. Mackerras (cnd), Welsh National Opera Orch *(rec Brangwyn Hall, Swasea, Wales, Apr 18-30 & May 1, 1995)* Telarc 2-▲ CD 80404 [DDD]

Tchaikovsky, P.:Eugene Onegin, w. K. Te Kanawa (sop—Tatiana), P. Bardon (mez—Olga), N. Rosenshein (ten—Lensky), T. Hampson (b-bar—Eugene Onegin), J. Connell (bass—Prince Gremin), C. Mackerras (cnd), Welsh National Opera Orch [E] EMI Classics ▲ CDCB 55004

Tchaikovsky, P.:Ov 1812, w. L. Stokowski (cnd), Royal PO, Grenadier Guards Band, Royal Liverpool Phil Choir *(rec Kingsway Hall, London, England, June 16, 1969)* London ("Phase 4 Stereo" series) ▲ 443896-2 [ADD]

Thomas, A.:Hamlet, w. J. Sutherland (sop), S. Milnes (bar), R. Bonynge (cnd), Welsh National Opera Orch London ("Grand Opera" series) 3-▲ 433857-2 [DDD]

Verdi, G.:I masnadieri, w. J. Sutherland (sop), F. Bonisolli (ten), M. Manuguerra (bar), S. Ramey (bass), R. Bonynge (cnd), Welsh National Opera Orch London ("Grand Opera" series) 2-▲ 433854-2 [DDD]

Wagner, R.:Parsifal, w. Waltraud Meier (mez—Kundry), Warren Ellsworth (ten—Parsifal), Nicholas Folwell (bar—Klingsor), Philip Joll (b-bar—Amfortas), Donald McIntyre (b-bar—Gurnemanz), R. Goodall (cnd), Welsh National Opera Orch EMI Classics 2-▲ CDMD 65665

Wesleyan College Chorale

Mozart, W.A.:Missa, K.317, w. C. Bogard (sop), J. de Gaetani (mez), R. White (ten), T. Paul (bass), D. Zinman (cnd), Rochester PO *(rec 1978)* Allegretto ▲ ACD 8164 [ADD] ■ ACS 8164

R. Shewan (cnd)

Bruckner, A.:Choral Music, w. T.J. Stuart (org), Roberts Wesleyan College Brass Ensemble—Ave Maria I [w. E. Stedman (soprano), J. Richardson (mezzo-soprano)]; Ave Maria II; Aequale; Afferentur regi; Aequale II; Germanenzug [w. J. Richardson (tenor), B. Clicker (tenor)]; Inveni David; Trösterin Musik; Tota pulchra es Maria [w. C. Jones (tenor)]; Or justi meditabitur; Ave Maria III [w. A. Mosher (baritone)]; Christus factus est pro nobis; Ecce sacerdos magnus; Ave Regina coelorum; Virga Jesse floruit; Vexilla regis prodeunt; Das deutsche Lied *(rec Apr. 19-21, 1991)* Albany ▲ TROY 063 [DDD]

Hanson, H.:Pieces (4) Bar, w. T. Sipes (bar), Barbara Harbach (org) Albany ▲ TROY 129 [ADD]

Harris, R.:Easter Cant, w. Ann Honeywell (org), Roberts Wesleyan College Brass Ensemble—Alleluia *(rec St. Louis Roman Catholic Church, Pittsford, NY)* Albany ▲ TROY 164 [DDD]

Harris, R.:Freedom -Toleration *(rec 1st Lutheran Church, Lyons, NY)* Albany ▲ TROY 164 [ADD]

Harris, R.:Madrigal, w. Daryl Scott (pno) *(rec Parmenter Chapel, Roberts Wesleyan College, Rochester, NY)* Albany ▲ TROY 164 [DDD]

Harris, R.:Mass, w. Ann Honeywell (org) (cnd) *(rec St. Louis Roman Catholic Church, Pittsford, NY)* Albany ▲ TROY 164 [DDD]

Harris, R.:To Thee, O Cause (cnd) *(rec 1st Lutheran Church, Lyons, NY)* Albany ▲ TROY 164 [ADD]

Harris, R.:When Johnny Comes Marching Home Chorus *(rec 1st Lutheran Church, Lyons, NY)* Albany ▲ TROY 164 [ADD]

Harris, R.:Whitman Triptych *(rec St. Louis Roman Catholic Church, Pittsford, NY)* Albany ▲ TROY 164 [DDD]

Harris, R.:Year That Trembled *(rec 1st Lutheran Church, Lyons, NY)* Albany ▲ TROY 164 [ADD]

S. Shewan (cnd)

Shewan, S.:A Feast of Carols, w. Jill Richardson (sop), Alexander Burgess (bar), Roberts Wesleyan College Brass Ensemble Albany ▲ TROY 149 [DDD]

Shewan, S.:Of Animals & Insects:A Musical Zoo, w. Roberts Wesleyan College Wind Ensemble Albany ▲ TROY 149 [DDD]

West German Chorus

Verdi, G.:Macbeth, w. Astrid Varnay (sop—Lady Macbeth), Trude Roesler (mez—Lady-in-waiting), Hasso Eschert (ten—Malcolm), Walter Geisler (ten—Macduff), Joseph Metternich (bar—Macbeth), Ludwig Weber (bass—Banquo), R. Kraus (cnd), West German Orch *(rec Cologne, 1954)* Myto 2-▲ 952128

West German Radio Chorus

Puccini, G.:Mass, w. K. Lövaas (sop), W. Hollweg (ten), B. McDaniel (bar), E. Inbal (cnd), Frankfurt RSO Philips ("Collector" series) ▲ 434170-2 [ADD]

Verdi, G.:Requiem Mass, w. Gré Brouwenstijn (sop), Oralia Dominguez (mez), Giuseppe Zampieri (ten), Nicola Zaccaria (bass), G. Solti (cnd), West German Radio Orch Globe 2-▲ GLO 5141 [ADD]

West German Radio Men's Chorus

Wagner, R.:Lohengrin, w. Maud Cunitz (sop—Elsa), Margarete Klose (mez—Ortrud), Rudolf Schock (ten—Lohengrin), Josef Metternich (bar—Friedrich von Telramund), Gottlob Frick (bass—King Henry), W. Schüchter (cnd), North German RSO, North German Radio Chorus *(rec 1953)* EMI Classics 2-▲ CDHC 65517

Erik Westberg Vocal Ensemble

E. Westberg (cnd)

Bach, J.S.:Chorale Settings (misc)—BWV 478 [arr Knut Nystedt/Gunnar Eriksson for chorus], BWV 659 [w Mattias Wagner (org)] Opus 3 ▲ 19506 [AAD]

Jansson, L.:Sacred Music—To the Mothers of Brazil [w Anders Paulsson (sax), Tomas Isaksson (perc)]; Den signade dag; Stilla sköna aftontimma; Kristallen den fina Opus 3 ▲ 19506 [AAD]

Morales, C. de:Sacred Music, w. Anders Paulsson (s sax)—Parce mihi domine Opus 3 ▲ 19506 [AAD]

Olsson, O.:Sacred Music—Jesu dulcis memoria; Ave maris stella Opus 3 ▲ 19506 [AAD]

Sandström, J.:Sanctus Opus 3 ▲ 19506 [AAD]

Westchester Choral Society

Verdi, G.:Aroldo, w. M. Caballé (sop), G. Cecchele (ten), J. Pons (bar), E. Queler (cnd), New York Opera Orch, New York Oratorio Society [I] *(rec live, Carnegie Hall 4/8/79)* CBS 2-▲ M2K 35906 [ADD]

Western Wind Chamber Chorus

The Chanukkah Story, w. Theodore Bikel (nar) Western Wind ▲ 1818 CD [DDD] ■ 1818 CT (D)

Early American Vocal Music, Vol. 1 Elektra/Nonesuch ■ 71276-4

Léon, T.:Batéy, w. D. Ponce (conga), E. Charlston (perc), J. Passaro (perc), T. Léon (cnd) CRI ▲ CD 662 [DDD]

Morrow, C.:Canticle [E] Laurel ▲ LR 840CD [DDD]

Morrow, C.:Cloud [E] Laurel ▲ LR 840CD [DDD]

O Western Wind:An (Almost) a capella Songbook Western Wind ▲ WW 2002

Pärt, A.:Miserere, w. Hilliard Ensemble ECM New Series ▲ 78118-21430-2 [DDD]; ■ 78118-21430-4

The Passover Story, w. Theodore Bikel (nar) Western Wind ▲ 1800 CD [DDD] ■ 1800 CT (D)

A Portrait in Song of the Spanish Jews, w. Tovah Feldshuh (nar) Western Wind ▲ 1836 CD [DDD] ■ 1836 CT (D)

Western Wind Vocal Ensemble:Vol. 1—Sacred Resmiranda ▲ Resmiranda 8003

P. Hillier (cnd)

Pärt, A.:Passio Domini nostri Jesu Christi secundum Joannem, w. L. Dawson (sop), D. James (alt), R. Covey-Crump (ten), J. Potter (ten), G. Jones (bass), M. George (bass), Hilliard Ensemble [L] ECM New Series ▲ 78118-21370-2 [DDD]; ■ 78118-21370-4 (D)

M. Lazar (cnd)

The Birthday of the World:Music & Traditions of the High Holy Days, Part 1 [Rosh Hashanah], w. Leonard Nimoy (nar) *(rec West End Theater, NYC)* Western Wind ▲ 1854

Westminster Abbey Choir

Handel, G.F.:Coronation Anthems (4) for George II, w. T. Pinnock (cnd), English CO Deutsche Grammophon ▲ 447280-2

Music for Ceremonial Occasions, w. London SO, D. Hill (org), Francis Jackson (org) Pickwick ("The Orchid" series) ▲ PICORCD 11016

O for the Wings of a Dove, w. Ely Cathedral Choir, Worcester Cathedral Choir Chandos ("Collect" series) ▲ CHAN 6519 [ADD]

D. Guest (cnd)

A Choral Festival, w. T. Farrell (org) Chandos ("Collect" series) ▲ CHAN 6603 [ADD]

M. Neary (cnd)

Adeste Fideles! Christmas Down the Ages, w. Emma Kirkby (sop), English CO, Westminster Abbey Consort, Westminster Abbey Ensemble Sony Classical ▲ SK 62688 ■ ST 62688

Blow, J.:Songs, w. Emma Kirby (sop), Michael Chance (ct), New London Consort—Whilst sullen years are past; The sullen years are past Sony Classical ▲ SK 66243

Psalms Vol. I, Psalms from the first half of the Psalter, w. Lumsden, Andrew (org) Virgin Classics ▲ CDC 59632

Purcell, H.:Songs, w. Emma Kirkby (sop), Michael Chance (ct), New London Consort—I was glad; Praise the Lord, O Jerusalem; Script for their green our groves appear; Ode for Queen Mary's Birthday; Elegy on the death of Queen Mary; The Queen's Epicedium; March; The Burial Service [composed w. Thomas Morley] Sony Classical ▲ SK 66243

Tavener, J.:Akathist of Thanksgiving, w. J. Bowman (ct), T. Wilson (ten), M. Baker (org), BBC SO, BBC Singers *(rec Jan. 21, 1994)* Sony Classical ▲ SK 64446 [DDD]

Tavener, J.:Annunciation *(rec Westminster Abbey, July 19-22, 1994)* Sony Classical ▲ SK 66613 [DDD]

Tavener, J.:Hymns to the Mother of God *(rec Westminster Abbey, May 1-5, 1995)* Sony Classical ▲ SK 66613 [DDD]

Tavener, J.:Innocence, w. Patricia Rozario (sop), Leigh Nixon (ten), Graham Titus (bass), Alice Neary (vc), Charles Fullbrook (bells), Martin Baker (org) *(rec Westminster Abbey, May 1-5, 1995)* Sony Classical ▲ SK 66613 [DDD]

Tavener, J.:The Lamb *(rec Westminster Abbey, May 1-5, 1995)* Sony Classical ▲ SK 66613 [DDD]

Tavener, J.:Little Requiem for Father Malachy Lynch, w. English CO *(rec Westminster Abbey, Oct 6, 1994)* Sony Classical ▲ SK 66613 [DDD]

Tavener, J.:Song for Athene *(rec Westminster Abbey, July 19-22, 1994)* Sony Classical ▲ SK 66613 [DDD]

Tavener, J.:The Tyger *(rec Westminster Abbey, May 1-5, 1995)* Sony Classical ▲ SK 66613 [DDD]

Tollett, T.:Music of, w. Emma Kirby (sop), Michael Chance (ct), New London Consort—The Queen's Farewell (march) Sony Classical ▲ SK 66243

S. Preston (cnd)

Allegri, G.:Miserere Archiv ▲ 415517-2 [DDD]

Coronation Music for King James II (1685) Archiv ▲ 419613-2 AH [DDD]

Handel, G.F.:Dixit Dominus, w. Arleen Augér (sop), Lynne Dawson (sop), Diana Montague (mez), Leigh Nixon (ten), Simon Birchall (bass), Westminster Abbey Orch [L] Archiv ▲ 423594-2 [DDD]

Handel, G.F.:Nisi Dominus, w. Diana Montague (mez), John Mark Ainsley (ten), Simon Birchall (bass), Westminster Abbey Orch [L] Archiv ▲ 423594-2 [DDD]

Sacred Works Archiv ▲ 415517-2 AH [DDD]

Westminster Cathedral Boys' Choir

Mozart, W.A.:Exsultate, w. Emma Kirkby (sop), C. Hogwood (cnd), Academy of Ancient Music [L] L'Oiseau-Lyre ▲ 411832-2 [DDD]

Mozart, W.A.:Sacred Music, w. E. Kirkby (sop), C. Hogwood (cnd), Academy of Ancient Music—Regina coeli, K.108; Ergo interest, K.143; Regina coeli, K.127 [L] L'Oiseau-Lyre ▲ 411832-2 [DDD]

Westminster Cathedral Choir

Brahms, J.:Ein Deutsches Requiem, w. Irmgard Seefried (sop), George London (bass), B. Walter (cnd), New York PO *(rec New York City, Dec. 20-29, 1954)* Sony Classical ("Bruno Walter Edition, Vol. 2" series) ▲ SMK 64469 [ADD]

Franco, H.:Salve Regina [L] Hyperion ▲ CDA 66330 [DDD];

López Capillas, F.:Alleluia, "Dic nobis, Maria"; Magnificat Quarti Toni [L] Hyperion ▲ CDA 66330 [DDD]

Morales, C. de:Sacred Music, w. J. O'Donnell (org)—Missa Quaeramus cum pastoribus; Andreas Christi famulus; Clamabat autem mulier Chananea; O sacrum convivium; Regina caeli; Sancta Maria, succurre miseris; O magnum mysterium; Lamentebatur Jacob Hyperion ▲ CDA 66635 [DDD]

Mouton, J.:Quaeramus cum pastoribus Hyperion ▲ CDA 66635

Padilla, J.G. de:Sacred Music—Lamentation for Maundy Thursday; Salve Regina; Psalm for None, "Mirabilia testimonium"; Versicle & Response, "Deus in adiutorium"[L] Hyperion ▲ CDA 66330 [DDD]

CHORAL GROUPS

Westminster Cathedral Choir (cont.)

Peñalosa, F. de:Sacred Music—Missa Ave Maria; Sacris Solemniis; Missa Nunc Fué; Pena Mayor Hyperion ▲ CDA 66629
Salazar, A. de:O sacrum convivium [L] Hyperion ▲ CDA 66330 [DDD]
Stravinsky, I.:Motets—Ave Maria, Credo, Pater Noster (1949) Hyperion ▲ CDA 66437
Victoria, T.L. de:Masses, w. James O'Donnell (org)—Dum complerentur Hyperion ▲ CDA 66886
Victoria, T.L. de:Sacred Choral Music, w. James O'Donnell (org)—Populе meus & 5 other hymns Hyperion ▲ CDA 66886

D. Hill (cnd)

Britten, B.:A Ceremony of Carols [E] Hyperion ▲ CDA 66220 [DDD]
Britten, B.:Deus in adjutorium meum [L] Hyperion ▲ CDA 66220 [DDD]
Britten, B.:Hymn to St. Peter [E] Hyperion ▲ CDA 66220 [DDD]
Britten, B.:A Hymn to the Virgin [E] Hyperion ▲ CDA 66220 [DDD]
Britten, B.:Jubilate Deo [L] Hyperion ▲ CDA 66220 [DDD]
Britten, B.:Missa brevis [L] Hyperion ▲ CDA 66220 [DDD]
Christmas Music by Michael Praetorius, w. Parley of Instruments Hyperion ▲ CDA 66200
Fauré, G.:Maria Mater gratiae IMP ▲ PCD 2015
Fauré, G.:Messe basse (in 3 movts), w. *(soloist unknown)* IMP ▲ PCD 2015
Fauré, G.:Requiem, w. Harry Escott (trb), David Wilson-Johnson (bar), City of London Sinfonia IMP ▲ PCD 2015
Praetorius, M.:Music of, w. Parley of Instruments [G, L] Hyperion ▲ CDA 66200 [DDD]
Victoria, T.L. de:Masses—Vidi speciosam (also a motet) [L] Hyperion ▲ CDA 66129 [DDD]
Victoria, T.L. de:Officium defunctorum [L] Hyperion ▲ CDA 66250 [DDD]
Victoria, T.L. de:Tenebrae Responsories, Hyperion ▲ CDA 66304 ■

J. O'Donnell (cnd)

Duruflé, M.:Mass, "Cum jubilo", w. Aaron Webber (trb), Simon Keenlyside (bar), Natalie Clein (vc), Iain Simcock (org) Hyperion ▲ CDA 66757
Duruflé, M.:Motets on Gregorian Chants, Op. 10, w. Aaron Webber (trb), Simon Keenlyside (bar), Natalie Clein (vc), Iain Simcock (org) Hyperion ▲ CDA 66757
Duruflé, M.:Notre Père, w. Aaron Webber (trb), Simon Keenlyside (bar), Natalie Clein (vc), Iain Simcock (org) Hyperion ▲ CDA 66757
Duruflé, M.:Requiem, w. Aaron Webber (trb), Simon Keenlyside (bar), Natalie Clein (vc), Iain Simcock (org) Hyperion ▲ CDA 66757
Josquin Desprez:Missa & Plainchant, "Pange lingua" [L] Hyperion ▲ CDA 66614
Josquin Desprez:Motets—Planxit autem David; Vultum [L] Hyperion ▲ CDA 66614
Masterpieces of Mexican Polyphony, w. Andrew Watts (dulcian), Andrew Lawrence-King (hp), Iain Simcock (org) Hyperion ▲ CDA 66330 [DDD] ■
Masterpieces of Portuguese Polyphony, Vol. 1 Hyperion ▲ CDA 66218
Masterpieces of Portuguese Polyphony, Vol. 2 Hyperion ▲ CDA 66512 ■
Palestrina, G.:Missa de Beata Virgine Hyperion ▲ CDA 66364
Palestrina, G.:Sacred Music—Missa, "Aeterna Christi Munera"; Magnificat Primi Toni; Three Motets [Sicut cervus desiderat; Super flumina Babylonis; Vidi turbam magnum]; Fourt Motets from Canticum Canticorum [Quae est ista; Duo ubera tua; Nigra sum, sed formosa; Surge, amica mea] [L] Hyperion ▲ CDA 66490 [DDD]
Palestrina, G.:Sacred Music—Motet & Mass, "O Rex Gloriae"; Motet & Mass, "Viri Galilaei" [L] Hyperion ▲ CDA 66316
Palestrina, G.:Sacred Music—Missa Ave Maria Hyperion ▲ CDA 66364
Poulenc, F.:Choral Music, w. I. Simcock (org)—Quatre petites prières de St. Francois d'Assise; Quatre motets pour un temps de pénitence; Quatre motets pour le temps de Noël; Salve Regina; Exultate Deo; Litanies à la Vierge Noire Hyperion ▲ CDA 66664
Poulenc, F.:Mass, w. I. Simcock (org) Hyperion ▲ CDA 66664
Stravinsky, I.:Canticum sacrum, w. J. M. Ainsley (ten), S. Roberts (bar), City of London Sinfonia Hyperion ▲ CDA 66437
Stravinsky, I.:Mass, w. City of London Sinfonia Hyperion ▲ CDA 66437
Stravinsky, I.:Sym of Psalms, w. City of London Sinfonia Hyperion ▲ CDA 66437
Victoria, T.L. de:Trahe me post te Hyperion ▲ CDA 66738

J. Poole (cnd)

Britten, B.:A Boy Was Born IMP ("BBC Radio" series) ▲ IMP 5691482

J. West (cnd)

Erbach, C.:Sacred Music, w. J. O'Donnell (org), His Majesties Sagbutts & Cornetts—Sacredotes Dei; Canzona decundi toni; Alleluia, Hic est sacredos; Fantasia sub elevatione; Toccata octavi toni [frag.]; Post-communion; Posuisti Domine; La Paglia Hyperion ▲ CDA 66688
Hassler, H.L.:Sacred Music, w. J. O'Donnell (org), His Majesties Sagbutts & Cornetts—Canzon duodecimi toni; Cantate Dominio canticum novum; Toccata in G; Canzon noni toni; O sacrum convivium; Domine Dominus noster Hyperion ▲ CDA 66688
Lassus, O. de:Bell'Amfitrit'altera, w. J. O'Donnell (cnd), His Majesties Sagbutts & Cornetts Hyperion ▲ CDA 66688

Westminster Cathedral Choristers

M. Best (cnd)

Britten, B.:A Boy Was Born, w. Corydon Singers [E] Hyperion ▲ CDA 66126

Westminster Choir

Bach, J.S.:Motets, BWV 225-30, w. Daniel Beckwith (org), W. Ehmann (cnd), Westminster CO [G]—final chorales of BWV 226 & 229 are omitted Gothic ▲ G 49052
Barber, S.:Antony & Cleopatra, w. E. Hinds (sop), J. Wells (bass), C. Badea (cnd), Spoleto Festival Orch [E] *(rec live, Spoleto Festival, Spoleto, Italy, June 1983)* New World 2-▲ 322/24-2 [AAD]
Beethoven, L. van:Fant Pno, Op. 80, "Choral Fant", w. Ania Dorfmann (pno), A. Toscanini (cnd), NBC SO *(rec New York City, 1939)* Grammofono 2000 ▲ GRM 78524 (m)
Beethoven, L. van:Fant Pno, Op. 80, "Choral Fant", w. A. Dorfmann (pno), A. Toscanini (cnd), NBC SO [G] *(rec live 12/2/39)* Melodram 2-▲ MEL 28031 (m) [AAD]
Beethoven, L. van:Fant Pno, Op. 80, "Choral Fant", w. R. Serkin (pno), L. Bernstein (cnd), New York PO Sony Classical 2-▲ SM2K 47522 [ADD]
Beethoven, L. van:Fant Pno, Op. 80, "Choral Fant", w. R. Serkin (pno), L. Bernstein (cnd), New York PO [G] CBS ▲ MYK 38526 [ADD] ■ MYT 38526
Beethoven, L. van:Missa Solemnis, w. E. Rethberg (sop), M. Telva (mez), G. Martinelli (ten), E. Pinza (bass), A. Toscanini (cnd), New York PO [L] *(rec live, New York 4/28/35)* Melodram 2-▲ CDM 28036 [ADD]
Beethoven, L. van:Missa Solemnis, w. Z. Milanov (sop), B. Castagna (mez), J. Björling, A. Kipnis (bass), A. Toscanini (cnd), NBC SO [L] *(rec live 12/28/40)* Melodram 3-▲ MEL 38006
Beethoven, L. van:Missa Solemnis, w. Zinka Milanov (sop), Bruna Castagna (cta), Jussi Björling (ten), Alexander Kipnis (bass), A. Toscanini (cnd), NBC SO *(rec 1940)* Grammofono 2000 ▲ GRM 78626
Beethoven, L. van:Missa Solemnis, w. E. Farrell (sop), C. Smith (mez), R. Lewis (ten), K. Borg (bass), L. Bernstein (cnd), New York PO [L] Sony Classical 2-▲ SM2K 47522 [ADD]
Beethoven, L. van:Sym 9, "Choral Sym", w. A. Toscanini (cnd), NBC SO [soloists J. Novotna, K. Thorborg, J. Peerce, N. Moscona] *(rec Carnegie Hall, 1944)* Legato Classics ▲ LCD 136-1 (m) [ADD]
Beethoven, L. van:Sym 9, "Choral Sym", w. A. Toscanini (cnd), NBC SO [soloists Bovy, Thorborg, Peerce, Pinza] *(rec 1938)* Music & Arts ▲ CD 3007
Beethoven, L. van:Sym 9, "Choral Sym", w. Jarmila Novotna (sop), Kerstin Thorborg (mez), Jan Pierce (ten), Nicola Moscona (bass), A. Toscanini (cnd), NBC SO *(rec 1939)* LYS ▲ LYS 128
Beethoven, L. van:Sym 9, "Choral Sym", w. R. Muti (cnd), Philadelphia Orch [G] EMI Classics ▲ CDC 49493 [DDD] ■ 4DS 49493 (D)
Beethoven, L. van:Sym 9, "Choral Sym", w. Jarmila Novotná (sop), Kerstin Thorborg (mez), Jan Peerce (ten), Nicola Moscona (bass), A. Toscanini (cnd), NBC SO *(rec New York City, 1939)* Grammofono 2000 ▲ GRM 78524 (m)
Brahms, J.:Alto Rhap, w. Martha Lipton (alt), G. Cantelli (cnd), New York PO *(rec live, 1956)* Legend ▲ LGD 121
Bruckner, A.:Te Deum, w. B. Walter (cnd), New York PO Sony Classical ("Bruno Walter:The Edition" series) ▲ SMK 64480

Westminster Choir (cont.)

The Chorus, w. Mormon Tabernacle Choir, New York Choral Society, Vocal Majority, Chicago Sym Chorus members, et al. Sony Classical ("Greatest Hits" series) ▲ MLK 62684 ■ MLT 62684
Handel, G.F.:Messiah (sels), w. Adele Addison (sop), Russell Oberlin (ct), Edward Lloyd (ten), William Warfield (bar), L. Bernstein (cnd), New York PO [E] CBS ▲ MYK 38481 ■ MYT 38481
Haydn, J.:Mass 11, "Nelsonmesse", "Imperial Mass", "Coronation Mass", w. Judith Blegen (sop), Gwendolen Killebrew (mez), Kenneth Riegel (ten), Simon Estes (bass), L. Bernstein (cnd), New York PO [L] *(rec 1976)* Sony Classical ("Bernstein:The Royal Edition" series) 2-▲ SM2K 47563 [ADD]
Haydn, J.:Mass 14, "Harmoniemesse", w. Judith Blegen (sop), Fredrica von Stade (mez), Kenneth Riegel (ten), Simon Estes (bass), L. Bernstein (cnd), New York PO [L] *(rec 1966)* Sony Classical 2-▲ SM2K 47560 [ADD]
Janácek, L.:Slavonic Mass, w. H. Pilarczyk (sop), J. Martin (mez), N. Gedda (ten), G. Gaynes (sgr), L. Bernstein (cnd), New York PO *(rec 1963)* Sony Classical ("Bernstein:The Royal Edition" series) ▲ SMK 47569 [ADD]
Mahler, G.:Syms, w. J. Blegen (sop), B. Hendricks (sop), M. Price (sop), G. Zeumer (sop), H. Wittek (trb), A. Baltsa (mez), C. Ludwig (mez), K. Riegel (ten), H. Prey (bar), A. Schmidt (bar), J. Van Dam (b-bar), L. Bernstein (cnd), New York PO, Royal Concertgebouw Orch, Vienna PO, New York Choral Artists, Brooklyn Boys' Choir, Vienna Boys' Choir, Vienna State Opera Chorus, Vienna Singverein Deutsche Grammophon 13-▲ 435162-2 [DDD]
Mahler, G.:Sym 2, w. E. Cundari (sop), M. Forrester (cta), B. Walter (cnd), New York PO [G] Odyssey ■ YT 30848
Mahler, G.:Sym 8, w. L. Stokowski (cnd), Philharmonic SO *(rec live, Carnegie Hall, New York, 4/6/50)* Arkadia ▲ 761 [ADD]
Mahler, G.:Sym 8, w. L. Stokowski (cnd), Philharmonic SO, P.S. 12 Boys' Choir, Schola Cantorum *(rec 1950)* Music & Arts 2-▲ MUA 280 [AAD]
Menotti, G.C.:Goya, w. Josie de Guzman (sgr), Daner (sgr), Hernandez (sgr), Wentzel (sgr), S. Mercurio (cnd), Spoleto Festival Orch [I] *(rec live 1991)* Nuova Era 2-▲ 7060/61 [DDD]
Mozart, W.A.:Requiem, w. B. Walter (cnd), New York PO Sony Classical ("Bruno Walter:The Edition" series) ▲ SMK 64480
Poulenc, F.:Gloria Sop, w. J. Blegen (sop), L. Bernstein (cnd), New York PO *(rec 1976)* Sony Classical ("Bernstein:The Royal Edition" series) ▲ SMK 47569 [ADD]
Poulenc, F.:Gloria Sop, w. J. Blegen (sop), L. Bernstein (cnd), New York PO [L] CBS ▲ MK 44710 [ADD]
Prokofiev, S.:Alexander Nevsky, w. T. Schippers (cnd), New York PO—Song about Alexander Nevsky *(rec New York City, Feb 18, 1961)* Sony Classical ("Greatest Hits" series) ▲ MLK 69249 [ADD] ■ LT 69
Verdi, G.:Arias, w. J. Peerce (ten), A. Toscanini (cnd), NBC SO—arias from Luisa Miller *(Oh! fede negar potessi; Quando le sere al placido)* & chorus from Nabucco *(Va pensiero sull'ali dorate)* [I] RCA Gold Seal 2-▲ 60299-2-RG (m) [ADD] 2-■ 60299-4-RG (CrO2)
Verdi, G.:Arias, w. J. Peerce (ten), A. Toscanini (cnd), NBC SO—arias from Luisa Miller *(Oh! fede negar potessi; Quando le sere al placido)* & chorus from Nabucco *(Va pensiero sull'ali dorate)* [I] RCA Gold Seal 7-▲ 60326-2-RG (m) [ADD] 6-■ 60326-4-RG (CrO2)
Verdi, G.:Inno delle nazioni, w. J. Peerce (ten), A. Toscanini (cnd), NBC SO RCA Gold Seal 7-▲ 60326-2-RG (m) [ADD] 6-■ 60326-4-RG (CrO2)
Verdi, G.:Inno delle nazioni, w. J. Peerce (ten), A. Toscanini (cnd), NBC SO RCA Gold Seal 2-▲ 60299-2-RG (m) [ADD] 2-■ 60299-4-RG (CrO2)
Verdi, G.:Requiem Mass, w. Z. Milanov (sop), B. Castagna (cta), J. Björling (ten), N. Moscona (bass), A. Toscanini (cnd), NBC SO [L] *(rec 11/23/40)* Melodram 3-▲ MEL 38006
Verdi, G.:Requiem Mass, w. L. Amara (sop), M. Forrester (cta), R. Tucker (ten), G. London (bar), E. Ormandy (cnd), Philadelphia Orch Sony Classical ▲ SB2K 53252
Verdi, G.:Requiem Mass, w. Z. Milanov (sop), B. Castagna (cta), J. Björling (ten), N. Moscona (bass), A. Toscanini (cnd), NBC SO *(rec Mar. 4, 1938)* Legato Classics 2-▲ LCD 178-2
Verdi, G.:Requiem Mass, w. L. Amara (sop), M. Forrester (cta), R. Tucker (ten), G. London (bar), E. Ormandy (cnd), Philadelphia Orch [L] Odyssey ■ YT 35230
Verdi, G.:Requiem Mass, w. Zinka Milanov (sop), Bruna Castagna (mez), Jussi Björling (ten), Nicola Moscona (bass), A. Toscanini (cnd), NBC SO *(rec Nov 23, 1940)* Music & Arts 2-▲ CD 240
Verdi, G.:Te Deum, w. A. Toscanini (cnd), NBC SO *(rec Nov 23, 1940)* Music & Arts 2-▲ CD 240
Verdi, G.:Te Deum, w. A. Toscanini (cnd), NBC SO [L] *(rec live, New York, 12/2/45)* Melodram 2-▲ MEL 28022 (m) [AAD]
Wagner, R.:Das Liebesmahl der Apostel, w. Y. Minton (mez), P. Boulez (cnd), *(orch unknown)* Sony Classical ("Pierre Boulez Edition" series) ▲ SMK 68330
Walton, W.:Film Music, w. N. Marriner (cnd), Academy of St. Martin in the Fields Chandos ▲ CHAN 8892 ■ CHAAB 1503

J. Flummerfeldt (cnd)

Brahms, J.:Deutsche Volkslieder—Nos. 8, 9 & 11 *(rec Bristol Chapel, Westminster Choir College of Rider Univ., Princeton, NJ, May 14-16, 1995)* Delos ▲ DE 3193 [DDD]
Brahms, J.:Liebeslieder Waltzes SATB, w. Glenn Parker (pno), Nancianne Parrella (pno)—Nos. 8-16 *(rec Bristol Chapel, Westminster Choir College of Rider Univ., Princeton, NJ, May 14-16, 1995)* Delos ▲ DE 3193 [DDD]
Brahms, J.:Motets Op. 74—No. 2 *(rec Bristol Chapel, Westminster Choir College of Rider Univ., Princeton, NJ, May 14-16, 1995)* Delos ▲ DE 3193 [DDD]
Brahms, J.:Neue Liebeslieder Waltzes, w. Glenn Parker (pno), Nancianne Parrella (pno)—No. 15 *(rec Bristol Chapel, Westminster Choir College of Rider Univ., Princeton, NJ, May 14-16, 1995)* Delos ▲ DE 3193
Brahms, J.:Qts SATB, Op. 64, w. Glenn Parker (pno), Nancianne Parrella (pno)—Nos. 1 & 2 *(rec Bristol Chapel, Westminster Choir College of Rider Univ., Princeton, NJ, May 14-16, 1995)* Delos ▲ DE 3193 [DDD]
Brahms, J.:Qts SATB, Op. 92, w. Glenn Parker (pno), Nancianne Parrella (pno)—Nos. 2 & 3 *(rec Bristol Chapel, Westminster Choir College of Rider Univ., Princeton, NJ, May 14-16, 1995)* Delos ▲ DE 3193 [DDD]
Brahms, J.:Zigeunerlieder, w. Glenn Parker (pno), Nancianne Parrella (pno)—Nos 5-9 *(rec Bristol Chapel, Westminster Choir College of Rider Univ., Princeton, NJ, May 14-16, 1995)* Delos ▲ DE 3193 [DDD]
Christmas Masterpieces & Familiar Carols, w. New Jersey SO, Philadelphia Concerto Soloists members Gothic ▲ GOT 47931 ■ MC 47931
Favorite Hymns & Anthems Gothic ▲ GOT 49044 [DDD]
Folk Songs Gothic ▲ GOT 38130
O Magnum Mysterium Chesky ▲ CD 83 [DDD]
Westminster Choir at Spoleto Festival USA *(rec Spoleto Festival, Charleston, SC, 1995)* Gothic ("Westminster Choir" series) ▲ GOT 49078 [DDD]

Westminster Oratorio Choir

Hummel, J.N.:Mass in B♭, Op. 77, w. J. E. Floreen (cnd), New Brunswick CO [L] Koch International Classics ▲ KIC 7117-2 [DDD]
Hummel, J.N.:Tantum ergo, w. J. E. Floreen (cnd), New Brunswick CO [L] Koch International Classics ▲ KIC 7117-2 [DDD]

Westminster Singers

Bush, G.:A Summer Serenade, w. A. Thompson (ten), R. Hickox (cnd), City of London Sinfonia [E] Chandos ▲ CHAN 8864 [DDD]
Poulenc, F.:Gloria Sop, w. C. Dubosc (sop), R. Hickox (cnd), London Sinfonietta Virgin Classics ▲ CDC 59286
Poulenc, F.:Litanies à la vierge noire, w. R. Hickox (cnd), London Sinfonietta Virgin Classics ▲ CDC 59286
Poulenc, F.:Stabat mater, w. C. Dubosc (sop), R. Hickox (cnd), London Sinfonietta Virgin Classics ▲ CDC 59286
Walton, W.:Christopher Columbus (suite), w. L. Finnie (mez), A. Davies (ten), R. Hickox (cnd), City of London Sinfonia [E] Chandos ▲ CHAN 8824 [DDD]

R. Hickox (cnd)

Bush, G.:A Menagerie [E] Chandos ▲ CHAN 8864 [DDD]

Westminster Sym Choir
Beethoven, L. van:Sym 9, "Choral Sym", w. Emilia Cundari (sop), Nell Rankin (mez), Albert Da Costa (ten), William Wilderman (bass), B. Walter (cnd), Columbia SO *(rec American Legion Hall, Los Angeles, CA, Apr. 6, 1954)* Sony Classical ("Bruno Walter Edition, Vol. 2" series) ▲ SMK 64464 [ADD]

J. Flummerfeldt (cnd)
Dvořák, A.:Stabat Mater, w. K. Erickson (sop), C. Carlson (mez), J. Aler (ten), J. Cheek (bass), Z. Macal (cnd), New Jersey SO *(rec Feb. 8–11, 1994)* Delos 2-▲ DE 3161 [DDD]

Westphalia Kantorei
Caldara, A.:Stabat Mater, w. Monika Frimmer (sop), Gloria Banditelli (mez), Gerd Türk (ten), Peter Frank (bass), L. Rovatkay (cnd), Capella Agostino Steffani EMI Classics ▲ CDC 54845
Pergolesi, G.B.:Stabat mater, w. Monika Frimmer (sop), Gloria Banditelli (mez), Gerd Türk (ten), Peter Frank (bass), L. Rovatkay (cnd), Capella Agostino Steffani EMI Classics ▲ CDC 54845
Schütz, H.:St. John Passion, w. Herta Flebbe (sop), Johannes Hoeflin (ten—Evangelist), Rolf Bössow (ten—Pilate), Gert Spierting (ten), Jakob Stämpfli (bass—Jesus), Teinhard Tuge (bass—soliloquies), W. Ehmann (cnd) *(rec Münster zu Herfor, Sept. 1961)* Cantate ▲ 57602 [ADD]
Vivaldi, A.:Son al St. Sepolcro, w. Monika Frimmer (sop), Gloria Banditelli (mez), Gerd Türk (ten), Peter Frank (bass), L. Rovatkay (cnd), Capella Agostino Steffani EMI Classics ▲ CDC 54845
Weill, K.:Down in the Valley, w. I. Davidson (sop), M. Acito (ten), D. Collup (bar), J. Mabry (sgr), D. P. Lang (sgr), W. Gundlach (cnd), Westphalia CO Capriccio ▲ 60 020–1 [DDD]
Weill, K.:Der Jasager, w. H. Helling (cta), T. Schmeisser (treb), T. Bräutigam (ten), T. Fischer (ten), U. Schütte (bar), M. Knöppel (bass), W. Gundlach (cnd), Westphalia CO Capriccio ▲ 60 020–1 [DDD]

W. Ehmann (cnd)
Schütz, H.:Kleine geistliche Konzerte (sels)—[Part I] Ein Kind ist uns geboren, SWV 302 (No. 21); Wir gläuben all an einen Gott, SWV 303 (No. 22); Siehe, mein Fürsprecher, SWV 304 (No. 23); Ich hab mein Sach Gott Heimgestellt, SWV 305 (No. 24); [Part II] Ich will den Herren loben allezeit, SWV 306 (No. 1); Was hast du verwirket, SWV 307 (No. 2); O Jesu, nomen dulce, SWV 308 (No. 3); O misericordissime Jesu, SWV 309 (No. 4); Ich liege und schlafe, SWV 310 (No. 5); Habe deine Lust an dem Herren, SWV 311 (No. 6); Herr, ich hoffe darauf, SWV 312 (No. 7) *(rec Petrikirche, Herford, Sept. 1963 & June 1965)* Cantate ▲ 57604 [ADD]
Schütz, H.:Musicalische Exequien *(rec Münster zu Herfor, Sept. 1960)* Cantate ▲ 57602 [ADD]

Westphalian Ensemble
Praetorius, M.:Polyhymnia caduceatrix et panegyrica [G, L] Elektra/Nonesuch ■ 71242–4

Westvlaams Vocal Ensemble
Fiocco, J.–H.:Libera me Domine, w. P. Peire (cnd), Collegium Instrumentale Brugense Eufoda ▲ 1133 [DDD]
Fiocco, J.–H.:Tandem fulget, w. P. Peire (cnd), Collegium Instrumentale Brugense Eufoda ▲ 1133 [DDD]

Wettinger Chamber Chorus
Schoeck, O.:Der Postillon, w. K. Grenacher (pno), E. Haefliger (ten), Wettinger CO, Seminarchor Wettingen [G] *(rec 1967)* Jecklin-Disco ▲ JD 504–2 [ADD]
Schoeck, O.:Songs (misc), w. K. Grenacher (pno), E. Haefliger (ten), Wettinger CO, Seminarchor Wettingen [G] *(rec 1967)* Jecklin-Disco ▲ JD 504–2 [ADD]

Wexford Festival Opera Chorus
L. Mátl (cnd)
Pacini, G.:Saffo, w. Francesca Pedaci (sop—Saffo), Gemma Bertagnolli (sop—Dirce), Mariana Pentcheva (mez—Climene), Carlo Ventre (ten—Faone), Aled Hall (ten—Ippia), Roberto de Candia (bar—Alcandro), Davide Baronchelli (bass—Lisimaco), M. Benini (cnd), Irish National SO *(rec Wexford, Oct & Nov 1995)* Marco Polo 2-▲ 8.223883–4 [DDD]

G. Rose (cnd)
Rubinstein, A.:The Demon, w. Ludmilla Andrew (sop—Nanny), Marina Mescheriakova (sop—Tamara), Alison Browner (mez—Angel), Anatoly Lochak (sgr—Demon), Richard Robson (sgr—Old Servant), Valery Serkin (sgr—Prince Sinodal), Wjacheslav Weinorowski (sgr—Messenger), Leonid Zimnenko (sgr—Prince Gudal), A. Anissimov (cnd), Irish National SO *(rec Wexford, Oct & Nov, 1994)* Marco Polo 2-▲ 8.223781–2 [DDD]

Wilhelmshaven Vocal Ensemble
R. Popken (cnd)
Handel, G.F.:Ariodante, w. J. Gondek (sop), L. Saffer (sop), L. Hunt (mez), Jennifer Lane (mez), J. Lindemann (ten), R. Müller (ten), N. Cavallier (bass), N. McGegan (cnd), Freiburg Baroque Orch [172-page libretto w. production photos] Harmonia Mundi France 3-▲ HMC 907146.48

Willoughby Sym Chorus
Berlioz, H.:Requiem, "Grande Messe des Morts", w. D. Hamilton (ten), J. Hopkins (cnd), Sydney Conservatorium for Music Orch, Sydney Conservatorium Choir Walsingham Classics ▲ WAL 8000 [DDD]

Winchester Cathedral Choir
Blow, J.:Anthems, w. Joseph Cornwell (ten), Stephen Varcoe (bar), Robin Blaze (sgr), D. Hill (cnd), Parley of Instruments Hyperion 2-▲ CDA 67031/32
Finzi, G.:In terra pax, w. Libby Crabtree (sop), Donald Sweeney (bass), D. Hill (cnd), Bournemouth SO, Waynflete Singers *(rec Winchester Cathedral, Jan 10–13, 1994)* London ▲ 444130 2 [DDD]
Handel, G.F.:Messiah (sels), w. M. Neary (cnd), London Handel Orch [F] ASV Quicksilva ▲ QS 6001 [DDD]
Haydn, J.:Mass 7, "Kleine Orgelmesse", w. Linda Russell (alto), Catherine Wyn-Rogers (alt), William Kendall (ten), Michael George (bass), D. Hill (cnd), Brandenburg Orch Hyperion ▲ CDA 66508 [DDD]
Haydn, J.:Mass 14, "Harmoniemesse", w. Linda Russell (alto), Catherine Wyn-Rogers (alt), William Kendall (ten), Michael George (bass), D. Hill (cnd), Brandenburg Orch Hyperion ▲ CDA 66508 [DDD]
Holst, G.:Choral Music, w. David Dunnett (org)—Christmas Song [Personent hodie] *(rec Winchester Cathedral, Jan 10–13, 1994)* London ▲ 444130–2 [DDD]
Howells, H.:Choral Music—A Spotless Rose [w. Donald Sweeney (bass)]; Sing Lullaby *(rec Winchester Cathedral, Jan 10–13, 1994)* London ▲ 444130–2 [DDD]
Lloyd Webber, A.:Requiem for Soloists, Orch & Chorus, w. Sarah Brightman (sop), Paul Miles-Kingston (trb), Placido Domingo (ten), L. Maazel (cnd), English CO *(rec Studio 1, Abbey Road, London, Dec 20–22, 1984)* London ▲ 448616–2 ■ 48616
Lloyd Webber, A.:Requiem for Soloists, Orch & Chorus, w. Sarah Brightman (sop), Paul Miles-Kingston (trb), Placido Domingo (ten), L. Maazel (cnd), English CO [L] EMI Classics ▲ CDC 47146 [DDD] ■ 4DS 38218 (D)
Mozart, W.A.:Missa, K.317, w. E. Kirkby (sop), C. Robbin (mez), J.M. Ainsley (ten), M. George (bass), C. Hogwood (cnd), Academy of Ancient Music Argo ▲ 436585–2 [DDD]
Philips, P.:Motets, w. D. Hill (cnd), Parley of Instruments Hyperion ▲ CDA 66643
Purcell, H.:Anthems, w. D. Dunnett (org), D. Hill (cnd), Brandenburg Consort, London Baroque Brass—Funeral Sentences; Rejoice in the Lord Always; Jehova, Quam Multi Sunt Hostes; O God, Thou Art My God; Remember Not, Lord, Our Offences; Give Sentence with Me, O God; Hear My Prayer, O Lord; Voluntary in C; A Double Verse in G; O, I'm Sick of Life Argo ▲ 436833–2 [DDD]
Purcell, H.:Music for the Funeral of Queen Mary, w. D. Dunnett (org), D. Hill (cnd), Brandenburg Consort, London Baroque Brass Argo ▲ 436833–2 [DDD]
Purcell, H.:My Beloved Spake, w. D. Dunnett (org), D. Hill (cnd), Brandenburg Consort, London Baroque Brass Argo ▲ 436833–2 [DDD]
Vaughan Williams, R.:Choral Music—Wassail Song [arr of trad song]; The Blessed Son of God *(rec Winchester Cathedral, Jan 10–13, 1994)* London ▲ 444130–2 [DDD]
Vaughan Williams, R.:Fant on Christmas Carols, w. Donald Sweeney (bass), David Dunnett (org), D. Hill (cnd), Bournemouth SO, Waynflete Singers *(rec Winchester Cathedral, Jan 10–13, 1994)* London ▲ 444130–2 [DDD]
Vaughan Williams, R.:Let Us Now Praise Famous Men, w. D. Hill (cnd), Bournemouth SO Argo ▲ 436120–2 [DDD]
Vaughan Williams, R.:O Clap Your Hands, w. D. Hill (cnd), Bournemouth SO Argo ▲ 436120–2 [DDD]
Vaughan Williams, R.:The Old 100th Psalm Tune, w. D. Hill (cnd), Bournemouth SO Argo ▲ 436120–2 [DDD]

Winchester Cathedral Choir (cont.)
Vaughan Williams, R.:Toward the Unknown, w. D. Hill (cnd), Bournemouth SO Argo ▲ 436120–2 [DDD]
Walton, W.:Coronation Te Deum, w. T. Byram-Wigfield (org), D. Hill (cnd), Bournemouth SO Argo ▲ 436120–2 [DDD]
Warlock, P.:Choral Music—Lullaby my Jesus; Balulalow [w. David Dunnett (org)]; Benedicamus Domino; Bethlehem Down *(rec Winchester Cathedral, Jan 10–13, 1994)* London ▲ 444130–2 [DDD]

M. Berry (cnd)
Abelard, P.:Sacred Music—Hymns & Sequences for Heloise Herald ▲ HAVPCD 168
12th Century Chant, w. Cambridge Schola Gregoriana Herald ▲ HAVPCD 168

D. Hill (cnd)
Byrd, W.:Church Music—Ego sum panis vivus; Introit Cibavit eos; Kyrie; Gloria; Gradual Oculi omnium; Sequence Lauda Sion; Credo; Offertory Sacerdotes Domini; Sanctus; Benedictus; Agnus Dei; Communion Quotiescunque manducabitis; Processional Pange lingua; Ab ortu solis; Alleluia, cognoverunt discipuli; O sacrum convivium; O salutaris hostia; Ave verum corpus Hyperion ▲ CDA 66837
Byrd, W.:Mass in 3 Parts Argo ▲ 430164–2 [DDD]
Byrd, W.:Mass in 4 Parts Argo ▲ 430164–2 [DDD]
Byrd, W.:Mass in 5 Parts Argo ▲ 430164–2 [DDD]
Byrd, W.:Mass in 5 Parts Hyperion ▲ CDA 66837
Jerusalem, w. Waynflete Singers, Bournemouth SO Argo ▲ 430836–2 ZH [DDD]
Tavener, J.:Music of, w. S. Kringelborn (sop)—Thunder Entered Her; Angels; The Annunciation; Lament of the Mother of God; Hymns of Paradise; God Is with Us Virgin Classics ▲ CDC 45035
Vaughan Williams, R.:O Taste & See, w. T. Byram-Wigfield (org) Argo ▲ 436120–2 [DDD]
Walton, W.:Jubilate Deo, w. T. Byram-Wigfield (org), Waynflete Singers Argo ▲ 436120–2 [DDD]
Walton, W.:A Litany Argo ▲ 436120–2 [DDD]
Walton, W.:Set Me as a Seal upon Thine Heart Argo ▲ 436120–2 [DDD]
Weelkes, T.:Cathedral Music, w. T. Byram-Wigfield (org)—All Laud and Praise; Alleluia, I Heard a Voice; Give Ear, O Lord; Give the King Thy Judgements; Gloria in excelsis Deo; Hosanna to the Son of David; If King Manasses; Laboravi in gemitu meo; Magnificat; Nunc dimittis; O How Amiable; O Jonathan; O Lord Arise; When David Heard [E,L] Hyperion ▲ CDA 66477

D. Hill, A. Lewis (cnd)
Purcell, H.:Music of, w. Catherine Bott (sop), Emma Kirkby (sop), James Bowman (alt), Anthony Rooley (lt), Paula Chateauneuf (gtr), Monica Huggett (vn), Catherine Mackintosh (vn), Christophe Coin (vc), Academy of Ancient Music, Brandenburg Consort, St. Anthony Singers, Taverner Choir—The Double Dealer; Come Ye Sons of Art; The Old Bachelor; Birthday Song for Queen Mary; Oedipus; King Arthur; Bonduca; The Fairy Queen; Son. No. 9 in F; Dido & Aeneas; Abdelazer; Bess of Bedlam; The Married Beau; Hear My Prayer, O Lord; Rejoice in the Lord Always London ("Editions de l'oiseau-lyre" series) ▲ 444620–2

Windsbach Boys' Choir
K.-F. Beringer (cnd)
Brahms, J.:Alto Rhap, w. Lioba Braun (alt), Austro-Hungarian PO *(rec Ansbach, July 1996)* Hänssler Classic 2-▲ CD 98.134 [DDD]
Brahms, J.:Fest- und Gedenksprüche *(rec Ansbach, July 1996)* Hänssler Classic 2-▲ CD 98.134 [DDD]
Mendelssohn, F.:Motets—Jauchzet dem Herrn, alle Welt (Psalm 100), Op. 69/2; Richte mich Gott (Psalm 43), Op. 78/2; Denn er hat seinen Englen befohlen (Psalm 91) *(rec Ansbach, July 1996)* Hänssler Classic 2-▲ CD 98.134 [DDD]

H. Thamm (cnd)
Schütz, H.:Die Geburt unsers Herren Jesu Christi, w. Edith Mathis (sop), Georg Jelden (ten), Claus Ocker (bass), *(ensemble unknown)* EMI Classics ("Baroque" series) ▲ CDK 65736

Windsor Bach Choir
Mathias, W.:Ave Rex, w. Janet Price (sop), Kenneth Bowen (ten), Michael Rippon (bar), Geraint Evans (b-bar), Atherton, Willcocks (cnd), London SO, New Philharmonia Orch, Welsh National Opera Chorus, St. George's Chapel Choristers Lyrita ▲ SRCD .324
Mathias, W.:This Worlde's Joie, w. Janet Price (sop), Kenneth Bowen (ten), Michael Rippon (bar), Atherton, Willcocks (cnd), London SO, New Philharmonia Orch, Welsh National Opera Chorus, St. George's Chapel Choristers Lyrita ▲ SRCD .324

Winterthur Vocal Ensemble
Fröhlich, F.T.:Choral Music, w. E. Speiser (sop), P. Steiner (ten), J. Krattiger (bass), B. Billeter (pno), C. Spring (pno) [G] *(rec 1988)* Jecklin-Disco ▲ JD 627–2 [ADD]

Worcester Cathedral Choir
Celestial Christmas 4, w. Robert Stringer (trb), Raymond Johnston (org) Celestial Harmonies ▲ 13077–2
Elgar, E.:Choral Songs (comp), w. D. Hunt (cnd), Donald Hunt Singers [E] Hyperion 2-▲ CDA 66271/72 [DDD]
Elgar, E.:Choral Songs (sels)—From the Bavarian Highlands, Op. 27; O salutaris Hostia, Nos. 1–3; Tantum ergo, Ecce sacerdos magnus; Doubt Not Thy Father's Care; Light of the World Chandos ("Collect" series) ▲ CHAN 6601
Handel, G.F.:Messiah (sels), w. J. Malgoire (cnd), La Grande Écurie et la Chambre du Roy—choruses [E] CBS ▲ MDK 44787 [DDD]; ■ MDT 44787 (D)
O for the Wings of a Dove, w. Westminster Abbey Choir, Ely Cathedral Choir Chandos ("Collect" series) ▲ CHAN 6519 [ADD]

D. Hunt (cnd)
Howells-Britten-Gibbons, w. Adrian Partington (org) IMP ("Classics" series) ▲ IMP 6700422
Stanford, C.V.:Church Music, w. Paul Trepte (org)—Magnificat & Nunc dimittis in A, Op. 12; Motets, Op. 38, Nos. 1–3 & Op. 135, Nos. 1 & 3; Motet, "O living will"; Anthems, Op. 123 & Op. 145; Anthem, "The Lord is my shepherd" [E,L] Hyperion ▲ CDA 66030 [DDD]
Wesley, S.S.:Anthems, w. A. Partington (org)—selections include Ascribe unto the Lord; Blessed be the God and Father; Cast me not away; Let us lift up our heart with our hands; Thou wilt keep him in perfect peace; The Wilderness Hyperion ▲ CDA 66446
Wesley, S.S.:Anthems, w. A. Partington (org)—selections include The face of the Lord; I will exalt Thee; Man that is born of a woman; O Give thanks unto the Lord; O Lord, my God; O Lord, thou art my God; Praise the Lord, o my soul; Wash me thoroughly from my wickedness Hyperion ▲ CDA 66449

C. Robinson (cnd)
Vaughan Williams, R.:Choral Music—Come down, o love divine; For all the saints (Sine nomine); O Taste and see; Prayer to the Father of heaven; Te Deum; Three Choral Hymns (Easter, Christmas & Whitsunday Hymns); Valiant - for - truth; We've been awhile (children's Christmas song); Wither's rocking hymn; Choir of Westminster Abbey [dir.:Douglas Guest]—Festival Te Deum; Sanctus (from Communion Service in g) Chandos ("Collect" series) ▲ CHAN 6550 [ADD]

Worcester Cathedral Choristers
Walton, W.:Gloria, w. B. Robotham (sop), A. Rolfe Johnson (ten), B. Rayner Cook, L. Frémaux (cnd), City of Birmingham SO EMI Classics ▲ CDM 64201

Word of Mouth Chorus
Rivers of Delight Elektra/Nonesuch ▲ 71360–2 ■ 71360–4

World Choir
10,000 Voices, w. G. Jones (bar), D. O'Neill (ten), A. Sammons (vn), Massed Guards Bands [cnd:O. Arwel Hughes] *(rec live May 23, 1992)* EMI Classics ▲ CDC 54628–2 [DDD]

Wroclaw Choir
Mielczewski, M.:Vesperae Dominicales, w. E. Kajdasz (cnd), Polish Radio CO [L] *(rec 1966)* Olympia ▲ OCD 317 [AAD]

Württemburg Choir
Mozart, W.A.:Davidde penitente, w. E. Csapo (sop), G. Koban (sop), A. Baldin (ten), D. Kurz (cnd), Württemberg CO *(rec 1978)* Allegretto ▲ ACD 8164 [ADD] ■ ACS 8164
Wolf, H.:Choral Music, w. Alison Browner (sop), D. Kurz (cnd), Stuttgart Ensemble—Elfenlied; Der Feuerreiter; Dem Vaterland; Morgenhymnus; Frühlingschor *(rec live, Stuttgart, Feb 18, 1996)* Claves ▲ CD 509622 [DDD]

CHORAL GROUPS

Württemburg Choir

Württemburg Choir (cont.)
Wolf, H.:Christnacht, w. Alison Browner (sop—Engel der Verkündigung), Katherin Koch (alt—Hirte), Christian Beller (ten), D. Kurz (cnd), Stuttgart Ensemble *(rec live, Stuttgart, Feb 18, 1996)*
    Claves ▲ CD 509622 [DDD]

Würzburg Vocal Soloists
Christmas Carols, w. Instrumental Ensemble [cnd:Herbert Roth]
    Christophorus ▲ CHR 74578 [DDD]

Yale Russian Chorus
M. Bailey (cnd)
Chants & Carols *(rec Dwight Chapel, Yale Univ, Mar 19-20, 1996)*
    Epiphany (Limited Edition) ▲ EP 9 [DDD]

Yekaterinburg Children's Chorus
Senator, R.:Holocaust Requiem Kaddish, w. B. Kaufman (nar), J. Spiegelman (cnd), Moscow PO, Yurlof State Choir *(rec live Oct., 1992)*
    Delos ▲ DE 1032 [DDD]

Yorkminster Park Baptist Church Choir Toronto
C. Palmer (cnd)
The Joy of God:Great Hymns Across the Ages, w. Ronald Jordan (org)
    Marquis ▲ MAR 175 [DDD]

Yurlov Academic Choir
Historical Anthology of Russian Religious Chants, w. Drevnerousski Rospev Male Choir, Bolshoi Theater Children's Choir, Rybin Male Choir, St. Petersburg Cappella
    Russian Season ▲ LDC 288071
Rimsky-Korsakov, N.:Christmas Eve, w. Ekaterina Koudriavtchenko (sop), Elena Zaremba (mez), Vladimir Bogtatchov (ten), Alexei Maslennikov (ten), Viatcheslav Voinarovski (ten), Viatcheslav Verestnikov (bar), Maxime Mikhailov (bass), Stanislav Souleimanov (bass), M. Yurovski (cnd), Moscow Forum Theater Orch
    Russian Season 4-▲ CMX 388054

S. Gussev (cnd)
18th Century Russian Religious Choruses   Russian Season ▲ LDC 288041 ■ KC 488041

Yurlov Russian Choir
Miaskovsky, N.:Sym 6, w. K. Kondrashin (cnd), USSR SO   Russian Disc ▲ RUS 15 008 [ADD]
Rimsky-Korsakov, N.:Kaschei the Immortal, w. I. Jourina (sop), N. Terentieva (mez), A. Arkhipov (ten), V. Verestnikov (bar), V. Matorin (bass), A. Tchistiakov (cnd), Bolshoi Theater Orch [Russian]
    Russian Season ("Russian Season" series) ▲ LDC 288046 [DDD]
Shostakovich, D.:Song of the Forest, w. V. Ivanovsky (ten), I. Petrov (bass), A. Yulov (cnd), Moscow PO, Moscow State Boys' Choir   Russian Disc ▲ RUS 11 048 [AAD]
Shostakovich, D.:The Sun Shines on Our Motherland, w. K. Ivanov (cnd), USSR SO, Moscow State Boys' Choir   Russian Disc ▲ RUS 11 048 [AAD]

Yurlov State Choir
Senator, R.:Holocaust Requiem Kaddish, w. B. Kaufman (nar), J. Spiegelman (cnd), Moscow PO, Yekaterinburg Children's Chorus *(rec live Oct., 1992)*   Delos ▲ DE 1032 [DDD]
Sviridov, G.:Cants, w. V. Fedoseyev (cnd), Ostankino SO—Snow Is Falling   Olympia ▲ OLY 520 [ADD]
Sviridov, G.:Choruses, w. V. Fedoseyev (cnd), Ostankino SO   Olympia ▲ OLY 520 [ADD]
Taneyev, S.:At the Reading of a Psalm, w. Yuri Antonov (sgr), Yuri Belokrynkin (sgr), Ralsa Kotova (sgr), Adelina Kozlova (sgr), E. Svetlanov (cnd), USSR SO   Russian Disc ▲ RUS 10044 [AAD]

Zaans Youth Choir
W. Maczewski (cnd)
Schoenberg, A.:Moses und Aaron, w. David Pittman-Jennings (nar), Gabriele Fontana (sop—Young Girl), Yvonne Naef (cta—Sick Woman), John Graham-Hall (ten—Young Man/Naked Youth), Pär Lindskog (ten—Youth), Chris Merritt (ten—Aaron), Siegfried Lorenz (bar—Another Man), Michael Devlin (b-bar—Ephraimite), László Polgár (bass—Priest), P. Boulez (cnd), Royal Concertgebouw Orch, Netherlands Opera Chorus, Waterland Music School *(rec Concertgebouw, Amsterdam, Oct 1995)*
    Deutsche Grammophon 2-▲ 449 174-2 [DDD]

Zaanstad Opera Chorus
Donizetti, G.:Il borgomastro di Saardam, w. Philipp Langridge (ten), Renato Capecchi (bar), Let Kiel (sgr), J. Schaap (cnd), Zaanstad Opera Orch *(rec 1973)*   Pantheon 2-▲ PHE 6630 (m)

Zagorsk Monastery Monks' Choir
Gott in Russland [God in Russia]   Koch Schwann ▲ SCH 313003 [ADD]
Gott in Russland, Vol. 2   Koch Schwann ▲ SCH 313019 [ADD]
The Monks of Zagorsk in Paris   Pierre Verany ▲ 789031 [DDD]
1000 Years of Russian Monastery Music   Koch Schwann ▲ SCH 313079 [DDD]
Religious & Liturgical Chants   ARB ▲ 1402
Russian Choirs Sing for the Children of Chernobyl, w. Moscow Patriarchate Children's Choir, Church of the Resurrection Choir Moscow, Korez Convent Choir, Pyuchtize Convent Choir, Moscow Religious Academy Choir, Moscow Religious Academy Choir, Dormition of the Virgin Church Choir
    Koch Schwann ▲ SCH 313322 [ADD/DDD]

A. Matwej (cnd)
The Monks from Zagorsk   Koch Schwann ▲ SCH 317732

Zemel Choir
R. Max (cnd)
Lewandowksi, L.L.:Choral Music, w. Sandra Lee (sop), Ann Sadan (alt), Don Carter (ten), Adam Cohn (b-bar), Michael Morris (bass), Carys Hughes (org)—Ma Towu in F; Ma Towu in B♭; L'cho Dodi; Tow L'hodoss; Adoshem Moloch; W'hogen Ba'adenu [Uw'tsel]; W'schomru; L'icho Adoshem; J'Halahu [Hodo Al Erez]; Ladoshem Ho'orets; Uw'nucho Jomar; Adon Olom; Ki K'schimcho; Hajom Harass Olom; Kol Nidre; Schuwi Nafschi; Enosch, K'chozir Jomow; Halalujoh; Preise, Meine Seele
    Olympia ▲ OLY 347 [DDD]

Zimrat Women's Chorus
Fleischer, T.:Lamentation, w. C. Grossmeyer (sop), A. Haroz (hp), E. Lavry (hp), D. Kovalsky (perc)
    Opus One ▲ Cd 158 [DDD]

Zion Evangelical Church Choir Wooster OH
With Pipes & Voices, w. Tidwell, Burton (org), Beverly Hoch (sop)   Arkay ▲ ARK 6150 [DDD]

Zurich Ad Hoc Chorus
K. Scheuber (cnd)
Schneider, U.P.:Chorbuch [G] *(rec. Dec. 14, 1985)*   Grammont ▲ CTSP 34-2 [ADD]

Zurich Bach Kantorei
H. Reichel (cnd)
Bruckner, A.:Motets—Os justi; Afferentur regi; Christus factus est; Tota pulchra; Pange lingua; Ave Maria; Ecce sacerdos; Vexilla regis; Virge Jesse; Locus iste [L]   FSM-Adagio ▲ FCD 91 229 [ADD]

Zurich Boys' Choir
Haydn, M.:Missa Sancti Leopoldi in festo Innocentium, w. R. Zela, A. Schram (sop), O. Messerli (alto), A. von Aarburg (cnd), Capella Concertante [L] *(rec 12/89)*   Tudor ▲ 754 [DDD]
Haydn, M.:Vesperae pro festo Sanctorum Innocentium, w. L. Tsimitselis (sop), A. Schram (sop), O. Messerli (alt), A. von Aarburg (cnd), Capella Concertante [L] *(rec 12/89)*   Tudor ▲ 754 [DDD]

A. von Aarburg (cnd)
Ave Maria, w. Daniel Perret (trb), Frieder Lang (ten), Alain Clément (bass), Praxedis Rütti (hp), Daniel Winiger (org), Andrej Lütschg (vn)   Tudor ▲ TUD 7029 [DDD]

Zurich Mozart Opera Chorus
Mozart, W.A.:Entführung, w. Yvonne Kenny (sop), Carolyn Watson (cta), Peter Schreier (ten), Wilfried Gamlich (ten), Matti Salminen (bass), Wolfgang Reichmann (nar), N. Harnoncourt (cnd), Zurich Mozart Opera Orch [G]   Teldec 2-▲ 2292-42643-2

Zurich Opera Chorus
Mozart, W.A.:Clemenza, w. L. Popp (sop), R. Ziesack (sop), A. Murray (mez), D. Ziegler (mez), P. Langridge (ten), L. Polgar (bass), T. Grabowski (hpd), C. Hermann (vc), N. Harnoncourt (cnd), Zurich Opera Orch   Teldec 2-▲ 90857-2
Mozart, W.A.:Zauberflöte, w. E. Gruberova (sop), B. Bonney (sop), G. Schmid (sop), H.-P. Blochwitz (ten), T. Hampson (bar), M. Salminen (bass), A. Scharinger (bass), N. Harnoncourt (cnd), Zurich Opera Orch [G]   Teldec 2-▲ 2292-42716-2
Zemlinsky, A. von:Kleider machen Leute, w. E. Mathis (sop), H. Winkler (ten), V. Vogel (ten), C. Otelli (bar), H. Franzen (bass), R. Scholze (bass), W. Slabbert (sgr), R. Weikert (cnd), Zurich Opera Orch [G] *(rec live, Zurich Opera House, 6/29/90)*   Koch Schwann 2-▲ CD 314 069 [DDD]

Zurich Sprechchor
Ruzicka, P.:Feedback, w. E. Bour (cnd), Southwest German RSO Baden-Baden
    CPO ▲ CPO 999053 [DDD]

Zurich Sprechchor (cont.)
Erne, Merz (cnd)
Ringger, R.U.:Chari-Vari-études [F/G]   Grammont ▲ CTSP 29-2 [ADD]
Ringger, R.U.:Variétudes [G]   Grammont ▲ CTSP 29-2 [ADD]

▲ = CD   ♦ = Enhanced CD   △ = MD   ■ = Cassette Tape   □ = DCC

VOCALISTS

Aalbers, Dieuwke (sop)
Schubert, Franz:Der Hirt auf dem Felsen, w. F. van den Brink (cl), S. Hoogland (pno) [G] Partridge ▲ 1132-2 [DDD]
Schubert, Franz:Songs (misc), w. S. Hoogland (pno)—10 songs (D.118, 136 [w. van den Brink (cl)], 342, 367, 433, 564, 762, 787 [w. van den Brink (cl)], 800, 828) [G] Partridge ▲ 1132-2 [DDD]

Aambo, Marit Osnes (mez)
Delius, F.:Songs, w. Graham Johnson (pno)—Slumber Song (5 Norw. Songs no. 1); Evening Mood (Evening Voices) (7 Norw. Songs no. 3); Young Venevil (Sweet Venevil) (7 NS no. 4); Hidden Love (Love Concealed) (7 NS no. 6); Softly the Forest; I Once had a Newly Cut Willow Pipe; Sing, Sing (The Nightingale) (5 NS no. 2); Longing (5 NS no. 4); Sunset (5 NS no. 5); Summer Eve (5 NS no. 3); At Rondane (The Homeward Journey) (7 NS no. 2); Fiddlers (The Minstrel) (7 NS no. 5); Cradle Song (7 NS no 1); A Birdsong (The Bird's Story) (7 NS no. 7) *(rec Eidsvoll Church, Nov 3-5, 1994)* Simax ▲ PSC 1120 [DDD]
Grainger, P.:Songs, w. Graham Johnson (pno)—The Spring of Thyme; Six Dukes Went A Fishin'; Willow, Willow, Died for Love; Power of Love *(rec Eidsvoll Church, Nov 3-5, 1994)* Simax ▲ PSC 1120 [DDD]
Grieg, E.:Songs, w. Graham Johnson (pno)—The Orphan; Morning Dew; Parting; Hunting Song; The Old Song; Where Have They Gone? [all Op. 4]; The Maid of the Mill; Closely Wrapped in Misty Billows; I Stood Before Her Portrait; What shall I say? [all Op. 2] *(rec Eidsvoll Church, Nov 3-5, 1994)* Simax ▲ PSC 1120 [DDD]

Abarello, Stefano (alt)
Caldara, A.:La costanza vince il rigore, w. Sylva Pozzer (sop), Ensemble Barocco Padua Sans Souci *(rec Carrara Santo Stefano Church, Padua, May 3-7, 1996)* Dynamic ▲ CD 166 [DDD]
Caldara, A.:La lode premiata, w. Sylva Pozzer (sop), Ensemble Barocco Padua Sans Souci *(rec Carrara Santo Stefano Church, Padua, May 3-7, 1996)* Dynamic ▲ CD 166 [DDD]

Abbondanza, Roberto (bass)
Carissimi, G.:Oratorio della Santissima Vergine, w. P. Borri (sop), A. M. Ferrante (sop), P. Pace (sop), A. Christofellis (alt), L. Petroni (ten), F. Sclaverano (ten), M. Mondelli (bass), P. Spagnoli (bass), F. Colusso (cnd), Seicentonovecento Ensemble [I] Bongiovanni ▲ GB 10011 [DDD]
Carissimi, G.:Oratorio di Daniele Profeta, w. P. Borri (sop), A. M. Ferrante (sop), P. Pace (sop), A. Christofellis (alt), L. Petroni (ten), F. Sclaverano (ten), M. Mondelli (bass), P. Spagnoli (bass), F. Colusso (cnd), Seicentonovecento Ensemble [I] Bongiovanni ▲ GB 10011 [DDD]

Abdoun, Georges (bar)
Charpentier, M.-A.:Magnificat, w. Martha Angelici (sop), Jocelyn Chamonin (sop), André Mallabrera (ct), Rémy Corazza (ten), Jacques Mars (bass), Maurice André (tpt), Marie-Claire Alain (org), L. Martini (cnd), Jean-François Paillard CO, French Jeunesses Musicales Chorale *(rec Paris, Mar 15, 1963)* Vanguard Classics ▲ OVC 8075 [ADD]
Charpentier, M.-A.:Te Deum, H. 146, w. Martha Angelici (sop), Jocelyn Chamonin (sop), André Mallabrera (ct), Rémy Corazza (ten), Jacques Mars (bass), Maurice André (tpt), Marie-Claire Alain (org), L. Martini (cnd), Jean-François Paillard CO, French Jeunesses Musicales Chorale *(rec Paris, Mar 15, 1963)* Vanguard Classics ▲ OVC 8075 [ADD]

Abel, Josef (ten)
Puccini, G.:Madama Butterfly (sels), w. Miriam Gauci (sop—Madama Butterfly), Nelly Boschkowa (mez—Suzuki), Yordi Ramiro (ten—F.B. Pinkerton), Jozef Abel (ten—Goro), Georg Tichy (bass—Sharpless), Anna Tomkovicová (sgr), Mária Stahelová (sgr), Elena Hanzelová (sgr) *(rec Concert Hall of the Czecho-Slovak Radio, Bratislava, May 2-10, 1991)* Naxos ▲ 8.553152 [DDD]

Abelson, R. (bar)
Gottlieb, J.:Sacred Music, w. M. Stone (sop), H. Reps (mez), D. Lefkowitz (ten), H. Stahl (ten), R. Botton (bar), P. Newman (reader), S. Sturk (cnd), Metropolitan Brass Ensemble, New York Motet Choir Premier ("Composer" series) ▲ PRCD 1018 [DDD]

Abete, Antonio (bass)
Cavalieri, E. de:Rappresentatione di Anima et di Corpo, w. G. Bertagnolli (sop), C. Cavina (alt), B. Rossetti (sgr), G. Maletto (ten), R. Mattei (bar), M. Longhini (cnd), Verona Istitutioni Harmoniche Stradivarius ▲ STR 33339 [DDD]
Monteverdi, C.:Vespro della Beata Vergine, w. Barbara Borden (sop), Maria Cristina Kiehr (sop), Andreas Scholl (alt), John Bowen (ten), Andrew Murgatroyd (ten), Victor Torres (bar), Jelle Draijer (bass), René Jacobs (cnd), Concerto Vocale, Netherlands Chamber Choir Harmonia Mundi 2-▲ 901566.67
Stradella, A.:Cants, w. Cristina Miatello (sop), Gianpaolo Fagotto (ten), Roberto Balconi (sgr), Lavinia Bertotti (sgr), Roberta Giua (sgr), S. Balestracci (cnd), Santo Spirito Academy Orch, Santo Spirito Academy Chorus—for 5 w. vns [For Holy Christmas]; for 5 w. instruments [For the Souls in Purgatory] Stradivarius ▲ STV 33392 [DDD]
Wolf-Ferrari, E.:I quatro rusteghi, w. A. P (Margarita), D. Lombardi (Lucieta), G. Merrino (Marina), M. Fratarcangeli (Felice) L. Belluso (Servant), A. Abete (Lunardo), M. Nicolini (Maurizio), G. Sorrentino (Fillipeto), M. Peirone (Simon), D. Baronchelli (Cancian), A. Lemmo (Count Riccard) Arkadia-Akademia 2-▲ 139 [DDD]

Abgottspon, Franziskus (nar)
Holliger, H.:Alb-Chehr, w. Oswald Brumann (bass), Sabine Gertschen (dlc), Edmund Volken (dlc), Elmar Schmid (cl), Klaus Schmid (cl), Markus Tenisch (Swiss org), Marcel Volken (Swiss org), Paul Locher (vn) ECM New Series ▲ 78118-21540-2 [DDD]

Abitia, Ana Paula (mez)
Delgado, F.:Choral Music, w. Martha Molinar (sop), Luz Angélica Uribe (sop), Alfredo Mendoza (ten), Noé Colín (bass), B. J. Echenique (cnd), Mexico City CO, Alfredo Mendoza (cnd), Schola Cantorum—Te Deum al Sr. Felipe de Jesús Urtext ▲ URT 2001 [DDD]
Jerusalem, I.:Choral Music, w. Martha Molinar (sop), Luz Angélica Uribe (sop), Alfredo Mendoza (ten), Noé Colín (bass), B. J. Echenique (cnd), Mexico City CO, Alfredo Mendoza (cnd), Schola Cantorum—Magnificat a Dos Voces; Misa en Sol Mayor a 8 Voces Urtext ▲ URT 2001 [DDD]

Ablaberdyeva, A. (sop)
Shostakovich, D.:Songs Sop, Op. 127, w. Munich Piano Trio [R] MD + G ▲ L 3334 [DDD]

Abrahamová, G. (sop)
Smetana, B.:Dalibor, w. Vilém Přibyl (ten), J. Krombholc (cnd), Prague RSO, Prague Radio Chorus [Cz] *(rec Sept. 1977)* Praga 2-▲ PR 250050/51

Abrahamson, G. (sop)
Fleischer, T.:Girl-Butterfly-Girl, w. N. Rogel (rcr), M. Meckier (hpd) Opus One ▲ Cd 158 [DDD]

Accinno, Michael (boy sop)
Corigliano, J.:Of Rage & Remembrance, w. Michelle DeYoung (mez), Robert Baker (ten), Michael Forest (ten), Jason Stearns (bar), James Shaffran (bar), L. Slatkin (cnd), National SO Washington D.C., Washington Oratorio Society Men's Chorus *(rec J. F. K. Center for the Performing Arts, Washington, D. C.)* RCA Red Seal ▲ 09026-68450-2 [DDD]

Achilli, Ezio (sgr)
Verdi, G.:Ernani, w. Caterina Mancini (sop), Vittorio Pandano (ten), Gino Penno (ten), Giuseppe Taddei (bar), Giacomo Vaghi (bar), Licia Rossini (sgr), F. Previtali (cnd), Rome RAI SO, Rome RAI Chorus Cetra Classic 2-▲ CDON 39 [ADD]

Acito, Marc (ten)
Weill, K.:Down in the Valley, w. I. Davidson (sop), D. Collup (bar), J. Mabry (sgr), D. P. Lang (sgr), W. Gundlach (cnd), Westphalia CO, Westphalia Kantorei Capriccio ▲ 60 020-1 [DDD]

Ackté, Aino (sop)
Collected Recordings (1902-1913) Ondine ▲ ODE 883

Adám (sop)
Bartók, B.:Village Scenes, w. Faragó (sop), A. Dorati (cnd), Budapest Chamber Ensemble, Györ Girls' Choir [Slovak] Hungaroton ▲ HCD 31047 [ADD]

Adam, Günther (sgr)
Beethoven, L. van:Fidelio, w. Birgit Nilsson (sop—Leonore), Graziella Sciutti (sop—Marzelline), Kurt Equiluz (ten—Erster Gefangener), Donald Grobe (ten—Jacquino), James McCracken (ten—Florestan), Tom Krause (bar—Don Pizarro), Hermann Prey (bar—Don Fernando), Kurt Böhme (bass—Rocco), Günther Adam (sgr—Zweiter Gefangener), L. Maazel (cnd), Vienna PO, Vienna State Opera Concert Association Chorus *(rec Sofiensaal, Vienna, Mar 1964)* London 2-▲ 448104-2 [ADD]

Adam, Theo (b-bar)
Bach, J.S.:Cants (misc), w. Edith Mathis (sop), Carolyn Watkinson (cta), Eberhard Büchner (ten), Peter Schreier (ten), Siegfried Lorenz (bar), P. Schreier (cnd), Berlin CO, Berlin Soloists Berlin Classics ▲ BER 9221
Bach, J.S.:Cant 21, w. Arleen Augér (sop), Ortrun Wenkel (cta), Siegfried Jerusalem (ten), Peter Schreier (ten), H.-J. Rotzsch (cnd), New Bach Collegium Musicum, Leipzig St. Thomas Church Choir Berlin Classics ▲ BER 2175 [ADD]
Bach, J.S.:Cant 50, w. Arleen Auger (sop), Ortrun Wenkel (cta), Peter Schreier (ten), H.-J. Rotzsch (cnd), New Bach Collegium Musicum, Leipzig St. Thomas Church Choir Berlin Classics ▲ BER 2176 [ADD]
Bach, J.S.:Cant 79, w. Arleen Augér (sop), Ortrun Wenkel (cta), Peter Schreier (ten), H.-J. Rotzsch (cnd), New Bach Collegium Musicum, Leipzig St. Thomas Church Choir Berlin Classics ▲ BER 2176 [ADD]
Bach, J.S.:Cant 80, w. Arleen Augér (sop), Ortrun Wenkel (cta), Peter Schreier (ten), H.-J. Rotzsch (cnd), New Bach Collegium Musicum, Leipzig St. Thomas Church Choir Berlin Classics ▲ BER 2176 [ADD]
Bach, J.S.:Cant 137, w. Arleen Augér (sop), Ortrun Wenkel (cta), Peter Schreier (ten), Siegfried Jerusalem (ten), H.-J. Rotzsch (cnd), New Bach Collegium Musicum, Leipzig St. Thomas Church Choir Berlin Classics ▲ BER 2175 [ADD]
Bach, J.S.:Cant 192, w. Arleen Auger (sop), Ortrun Wenkel (cta), Peter Schreier (ten), H.-J. Rotzsch (cnd), New Bach Collegium Musicum, Leipzig St. Thomas Church Choir Berlin Classics ▲ BER 2176 [ADD]
Bach, J.S.:Cant 211, "Coffee Cant", w. Edith Mathis (sop), Peter Schreier (ten), P. Schreier (cnd), Berlin CO Berlin Classics ▲ BER 9226
Bach, J.S.:Cant 212, "Peasant Cant", w. Edith Mathis (sop), Peter Schreier (ten), P. Schreier (cnd), Berlin CO Berlin Classics ▲ BER 9226
Bach, J.S.:Mass in b, BWV 232, w. Maria Stader (sop), Sieglinde Wagner (mez), Ernst Haefliger (ten), R. Mauersberger (cnd), Dresden State Orch, Dresden Kreuz Choir *(rec 1958)* Berlin Classics ▲ BER 9171
Bach, J.S.:Masses, BWV 233-36, "Lutheran Masses", w. Renate Krahmer (sop), Annelies Burmeister (alt), Peter Schreier (ten), M. Flämig (cnd), Dresden PO Berlin Classics 2-▲ BER 9130
Bach, J.S.:St. Matthew Passion, w. A. Burmeister (mez), P. Schreier (ten), R. & E. Mauersberger (cnd), Leipzig Gewandhaus Orch, Dresden Kreuz Choir, St. Thomas Chorus *(rec 1970)* Berlin Classics 3-▲ BER 2144 [ADD]
Beethoven, L. van:Fidelio, w. H. Behrens (sop), S. Ghazarian (sop), P. Hofmann (ten), H. Sotin (bass), G. Solti (cnd), Chicago SO, Chicago Sym Chorus [G] London 2-▲ 410227-2 [DDD]
Beethoven, L. van:Leonore (opera), w. Helen Donath (sop), Edda Moser (sop), Eberhard Büchner (ten), Richard Cassilly (ten), Hermann Christian Polster (bass), Karl Ridderbusch (bass), H. Blomstedt (cnd), Dresden Staatskapelle, Leipzig Radio Chorus Berlin Classics ▲ BER 1140
Beethoven, L. van:Syms (comp), w. Marga Schiml (sop), Peter Schreier (ten), Helena Doese (sgr), H. Blomstedt (cnd), Dresden Staatskapelle, Dresden State Opera Chorus *(rec late 1970's-early 1980's)* Berlin Classics 5-▲ BER 2194 [DDD]
Beethoven, L. van:Syms (comp), w. Helena Doese (sop), Marga Schiml (alt), Peter Schreier (ten), H. Blomstedt (cnd), Dresden Staatskapelle, Dresden State Opera Chorus, Leipzig Radio Choir *(rec Lukaskirche, Dresden, 1975-80)* Berlin Classics 5-▲ 0021942BC [ADD]
Beethoven, L. van:Syms (comp), w. I. Wenglor (sop), U. Zollenkopf (cta), Hans Joachim Rotzsch (ten), F. Konwitschny (cnd), Leipzig Gewandhaus Orch, Leipzig Radio Chorus *(rec 1959-1961)* Berlin Classics ("Eterna" series) 6-▲ BER 2005 [ADD]
Beethoven, L. van:Sym 9, "Choral Sym", w. Ingeborg Wenglor (sop), Ursula Zollenkopf (alt), Hans Jochim Rotzsch (ten), F. Konwitschny (cnd), Leipzig Gewandhaus Orch, Leipzig Radio Chorus Polskie Nagrania Edition ▲ ECD 028
Berg, A.:Wozzeck, w. G. Schröter (mez), R. Goldberg (ten), H. Hiestermann (ten), H. Kegel (cnd), Leipzig RSO *(rec Apr. 9, 1973)* Berlin Classics ("Eterna" series) 2-▲ BER 2068 [ADD]
Cerha, F.:Baal Gesänge, w. K. Masur (cnd), Leipzig Gewandhaus Orch *(rec 1984)* Berlin Classics ▲ BER 2072 [ADD]
Dessau, P.:Einstein, w. Peter Schreier (ten), Reiner Suss (bass), O. Suitner (cnd), Berlin Staatskapelle, Berlin State Opera Chorus Berlin Classics 2-▲ BER CD 9109
Dvořák, A.:Biblical Songs, Op. 99, w. H. Kegel (cnd), Dresden PO Berlin Classics ▲ BER 9168
Dvořák, A.:Requiem Mass, w. Elisabeth Rose (sop), Gertraud Prenzlow (cta), Peter Schreier (ten), K. Ančerl (cnd), Berlin RSO, Berlin Radio Chorus Forlane 2-▲ FRL 16636 [AAD]
Dvořák, A.:Rusalka (sels), w. A. Burmeister (mez), E. Mitzewa (mez), A. Apelt (cnd), Berlin Staatskapelle Berlin Classics ("Eterna" series) ▲ BER 2033 [ADD]
Einem, G. von:Dantons Tod, w. K. Laki (sop), I. Mayr (mez), H. Hiestermann (ten), W. Hollweg (ten), K. Rydl (bass), L. Zagrosek (cnd), Austrian RSO, Austrian Radio Chorus [G] *(rec live, Salzburg, 8/13/83)* Orfeo 2-▲ 102842 [ADD]
Handel, G.F.:Judas Maccabaeus, w. Gundula Janowitz (sop), Hertha Töpper (alt), Peter Schreier (ten), Ernest Haefliger (ten), Siegfried Vogel (bass), H. Koch (cnd), Berlin RSO, Berlin Radio Chorus Berlin Classics 2-▲ BER 9112
Haydn, J.:Die Schöpfung, w. Regina Werner (sop), Peter Schreier (ten), H. Koch (cnd), Berlin RSO, Berlin Radio Chorus Berlin Classics 2-▲ BER CD 9115
Haydn, J.:Die Schöpfung, w. Jeannette van Dijck (sop), Peter Schreier (ten), Hans Plumacher (vc), Heinz Detering (db), Fritz Lehan (hpd), G. Wand (cnd), Cologne Gürzenich Orch, Cologne Gürzenich Chorus Accord 2-▲ ACD 200422 [AAD]
Humperdinck, E.:Hänsel und Gretel, w. G. Schöter (sop), I. Springer (mez), P. Schrier (ten), O. Suitner (cnd), Dresden Staatskapelle, Dresden Kreuz Choir Berlin Classics ("Eterna" series) 2-▲ BER 2007 [ADD]
Martin, F.:Monologe (6) aus "Jedermann", w. H. Kegel (cnd), Dresden PO Berlin Classics ▲ BER 9168
Mendelssohn, F.:Elijah, w. E. Ameling (sop), A. Burmeister (mez), P. Schreier (ten), W. Sawallisch (cnd), Leipzig Gewandhaus Orch, Leipzig Radio Chorus Philips 2-▲ 438368-2
Mendelssohn, F.:Elijah, w. E. Ameling (sop), A. Burmeister (mez), P. Schreier (ten), W. Sawallisch (cnd), Leipzig Gewandhaus Orch, Leipzig Radio Chorus [G] Philips 2-▲ 420106-2 [AAD]
Mozart, W.A.:Bastien und Bastienne, w. Adele Stolte (sop), Peter Schreier (ten), H. Koch (cnd), Berlin CO Berlin Classics ▲ BER 9129
Mozart, W.A.:Complete Mozart Edition, w. M. Price (sop), L. Serra (sop), R. Tear (ten), P. Schreier (ten), K. Moll (bass), C. Davis (cnd), Dresden Staatskapelle, Dresden State Chorus Philips 3-▲ 422543-2 [ADD]
Mozart, W.A.:Idomeneo, w. A. Rothenberger (sop), E. Moser (sop), N. Gedda (ten), A. Dallapozza (ten), P. Schreier (ten), H. Schmidt-Isserstedt (cnd), Dresden Staatskapelle, Leipzig Radio Chorus EMI Classics ("Studio" series) 3-▲ CDMC 63990
Mozart, W.A.:Thamos, w. T. Stich-Randall (mez), A. Deloire (mez), J. Traxel (ten), M. Rossi (cnd), Cologne RSO, Cologne Radio Chorus [G] *(rec live, Cologne May 20, 1956)* Melodram 3-▲ CDM 37084 [AAD]
Mozart, W.A.:Zauberflöte, w. H. Donath (sop), S. Geszty (sop), P. Schreier (ten), G. Leib (bass), O. Suitner (cnd), Dresden Staatskapelle [I] RCA Gold Seal 3-▲ 6511-2 [ADD]
Mussorgsky, M.:Boris Godunov (sels), w. Hanne-Lore Kuhse (sop), Peter Schreier (ten), Martin Ritzmann (ten), H. Kegel (cnd), Dresden State Orch, Leipzig Radio Chorus Berlin Classics ▲ BER 2032 [ADD]
Rimsky-Korsakov, N.:Mozart & Salieri, w. P. Schreier (ten), M. Janowski (cnd), Dresden Staatskapelle [G] Berlin Classics ("Eterna" series) ▲ BER 2089 [ADD]

Adam, Theo (b–bar) (cont.)

Schubert, Franz:Alfonso und Estrella, w. E. Mathis (sop), M. Falewicz (sop), P. Schreier (ten), H. Prey (bar), D. Fischer-Dieskau (bar), O. Suitner (cnd), Berlin Staatskapelle, Berlin Radio Chorus
Berlin Classics 3–▲ BER 2156 [ADD]

Schubert, Franz:Schwanngesang, w. Rudolf Dunckel (pno), Jorg Demus (pno)
Berlin Classics 2–▲ BER CD 9216

Schubert, Franz:Winterreise, w. Rudolf Dunckel (pno), Jorg Demus (pno)
Berlin Classics 2–▲ BER CD 9216

Schumann, R.:Dichterliebe, w. Rudolf Dunckel (pno), Jorg Demus (pno)
Berlin Classics 2–▲ BER CD 9216

Strauss, R.:Der Rosenkavalier, w. E. Mathis (sop), C. Ludwig (mez), T. Troyanos (mez), O. Wiener (bar), K. Böhm (cnd), Vienna PO *(rec Salzburg Festival, 1969)*
Deutsche Grammophon 3–▲ 445338–2 [ADD]

Strauss, R.:Der Rosenkavalier (sels), w. A. Pusar-Jeric (sop), M. Stejskal (sop), A. Jahns (mez), U. Walther (cta), R. Haunstein (bar), H. Vonk (cnd), Dresden Staatskapelle, Dresden State Chorus [G] *(rec live 2/85)*
Denon ▲ CO 8010 [DDD]

Strauss, R.:Songs, w. O. Suitner (cnd), Berlin Staatskapelle
Berlin Classics ▲ BER 9215

Wagner, R.:Der fliegende Holländer, w. A. Silja (sop), E. Kozub (ten), M. Talvela (bass), O. Klemperer (cnd), New Philharmonia Orch, BBC Sym Chorus [G]
EMI Classics ("Studio" series) 3–▲ CDMC 63344 [ADD]

Wagner, R.:Der fliegende Holländer, w. Anja Silja (sop—Senta), Anneliese Burmeister (mez—Mary), Ernst Kozub (ten—Erik), Gerhard Unger (ten—Steersman), Theo Adam (bass—Dutchman), Martti Talvela (bass—Daland), O. Klemperer (cnd), New Philharmonia Orch, BBC Sym Chorus
EMI Classics 3–▲ CDCC 55179

Wagner, R.:Die Meistersinger von Nürnberg, w. H. Donath (sop), R. Hesse (mez), A. Kollo (ten), P. Schreier (ten), R. Evans (bass), K. Ridderbusch (bass), H. von Karajan (cnd), Dresden Staatskapelle, Dresden State Chorus, Leipzig Radio Chorus [G]
EMI Classics 4–▲ CDCD 49683 [ADD]

Wagner, R.:Die Meistersinger von Nürnberg, w. E. Grümmer (sop), W. Windgassen (ten), J. Greindl (bass), H. Knappertsbusch (cnd), Bayreuth Festival Orch, Bayreuth Festival Chorus [G] *(rec live, Bayreuth, 1960)*
Melodram 4–▲ MEL 46103

Wagner, R.:Das Rheingold, w. E. Grümmer (sop), R. Gorr (mez), A. Andersson (ten), S. Konya (ten), H. Hotter (b–bar), J. Greindl (bass), H. Knappertsbusch (cnd), Bayreuth Festival Orch, Bayreuth Festival Chorus [G] *(rec live 1958)*
Arkadia 2–▲ 441 [AAD]

Wagner, R.:Das Rheingold, w. M. Lipovšek (mez), J. Rappé (ten), H. Zednik (ten), P. Haage (ten), A. Schmidt (bar), H. Tschammer (bass), K. Rydl (bass), J. Morris (bass), B. Haitink (cnd), Bavarian RSO [G]
EMI Classics 2–▲ CDCB 49853 [DDD]

Wagner, R.:Rienzi, der Letzte der Tribunen, w. S. Wennberg (sop), Martin (sop), A. Kollo (ten), P. Schreier (ten), H. Hollreiser (cnd), Dresden State Opera Orch, Dresden State Opera Chorus [G]
EMI Classics ("Studio" series) 3–▲ CDMB 63980

Wagner, R.:Der Ring des Nibelungen, w. B. Nilsson (sop), L. Rysanek (sop), K. Dvořaková (sop), M. Mödl (sop), A. Burmeister (mez), V. Soukupova (mez), E. Wohlfahrt (ten), W. Windgassen (ten), T. Stewart (bar), G. Neidlinger (b–bar), K. Böhme (bass), G. Nienstedt (bass), K. Böhm (cnd), Bayreuth Festival Orch, Bayreuth Festival Chorus [G] *(rec live, 1966–67)*
Philips 14–▲ 420325–2 [ADD]

Wagner, R.:Der Ring des Nibelungen (sels), w. Birgit Nilsson (sop—Brünnhilde), Leonie Rysanek (sop—Sieglinde), James King (ten—Siegmund), Wolfgang Windgassen (ten), Theo Adam (b–bar—Wotan), Gustav Neidlinger (b–bar), Josef Greindl (bass), K. Böhm (cnd), Bayreuth Festival Orch *(rec Bayreuth, 1967)*
Philips 2–▲ 454020–2

Wagner, R.:Siegfried, w. B. Nilsson (sop), W. Windgassen (ten), E. Wohlfahrt (ten), G. Neidlinger (b–bar), K. Böhm (cnd), Bayreuth Festival Orch, Bayreuth Festival Chorus [G]
Philips 4–▲ 412483–2 [ADD]

Wagner, R.:Songs, w. O. Suitner (cnd), Berlin Staatskapelle
Berlin Classics ▲ BER 9215

Wagner, R.:Tannhäuser, w. V. de Los Angeles (sop), G. Bumbry (mez), W. Windgassen (ten), G. Stolze (ten), D. Fischer-Dieskau (bar), J. Greindl (bass), F. Crass (bass), W. Sawallisch (cnd), Bayreuth Festival Orch, Bayreuth Festival Chorus [G] *(rec 1961)*
Myto 3–▲ MCD 93277

Wolf, H.:Michelangelo-Lieder, w. Rudolf Dunckel (pno), Jorg Demus (pno)
Berlin Classics 2–▲ BER CD 9216

Adam, Ulrich Müller (ten)

Viadana, L. da:Vespri per l'Assunzione, w. S. Pozzer (sop), C. Calvino (alt), J. Clement (ten), S. Foresti (bass), L'Amaltea Ensemble, Vox Hesperia, St. Marco Capella Musicale
Fonè ▲ FON 92F 08 [DDD]

Adams, Bryan (sgr)

Pavarotti & Friends 2, w. L. Pavarotti (ten), Nancy Gustafson (sop), Andreas Vollenweider (kbd), Michael Kamen (cnd), Leone Mageira (cnd), Bologna Community Theater Orch
London ▲ 444460–2 ■ 444460–4

Adams, Donald (bass)

Sullivan, A.:HMS Pinafore, w. F. Palmer (sop—Little Buttercup), R. Evans (mez—Josephine), M. Schade (ten—Ralph Rackstraw), T. Allen (bar—Capt. Corcoran), R. Suart (bass—Rt. Hon. Sir Joseph Porter, K.C.B.), D. Adams (bass—Dick Deadeye), R. Van A. (bass—Bill Bobstay), C. Mackerras (cnd), Welsh National Opera Orch, Welsh National Opera Chorus *(rec Swansea, Wales, June 5–8, 1994)*
Telarc ▲ CD 80374 [DDD]

Sullivan, A.:The Mikado, w. M. McLaughlin (sop), A. Howells (mez), J. Watson (sop), F. Palmer (sop/mez), A. Rolfe Johnson (ten), R. Stuart (bar), R. Van Allan (bass), N. Folwell (bar), C. Mackerras (cnd), Welsh National Opera Orch, Welsh National Opera Chorus—Ov & dialogue omitted [E]
Telarc ▲ CD 80284 [DDD]; ■ CS 30284 (D)

Sullivan, A.:The Pirates of Penzance, w. R. Evans (sop—Mabel), G. Knight (mez—Ruth), J. Gossage (mez—Edith), J. M. Ainsley (ten—Frederic), R. Suart (bar—Maj.-Gen. Stanley), N. Folwell (bar—Samuel), D. Adams (b–bar—Pirate King), R. Van Allan (bass—Sergeant of Police), C. Mackerras (cnd), Welsh National Opera Orch, Welsh National Opera Chorus *(rec May 4–6, 1993)*
Telarc ▲ CD 80353 [DDD]; ■ CS 30353

Sullivan, A.:The Pirates of Penzance (sels), w. V. Masterson (sop), I. Godfrey (cnd), Royal PO, D'Oyly Carte Opera Chorus
London ("Weekend Classics" series) ▲ 436292–2

Sullivan, A.:Trial by Jury, w. Rebecca Evans (sop—Plaintiff), Barry Banks (ten—Defendant), Gareth Rhys-Davies (bar—Foreman of the Jury), Peter Savidge (bar—Counsel for the Plaintiff), Donald Adams (bass—Usher), Richard Suart (bass—The Learned Judge), C. Mackerras (cnd), Welsh National Opera Orch, Welsh National Opera Chorus *(rec Brangwyn Hall, Swasea, Wales, Apr 18–30 & May 1, 1995)*
Telarc 2–▲ CD 80404 [DDD]

Sullivan, A.:The Yeomen of the Guard, w. Felicity Palmer (sop—Dame Carruthers), Pamela Helen Stephens (mez—Phoebe Meryll), Neill Archer (ten—Col Fairfax), Peter Hoare (ten—Leonard Meryll), Ralph Mason (ten—1st Yeoman), Donald Maxwell (bar—Wilfred Shadbolt), Peter Savidge (bar—Lieutenant Sir Richard Cholmondely), Donald Adams (bass—Sergeant Meryll), Richard Suart (bass—Jack Point), Peter Lloyd Evans (sgr—2nd Yeoman), Alwyn Mellor (sgr—Elsie Maynard), Clare O'Neill (sgr—Kate), C. Mackerras (cnd), Welsh National Opera Orch, Welsh National Opera Chorus *(rec Brangwyn Hall, Swasea, Wales, Apr 18–30 & May 1, 1995)*
Telarc 2–▲ CD 80404 [DDD]

Adani, Mariella (sop)

Cherubini, L.:Pimmalione, w. I. Ligabue (sop), G. Carturan (mez), U. Borghi (sgr), E. Gerelli (cnd), Milan RAI Orch, Milan RAI Chorus [I] *(rec live 1955)*
Melodram ▲ CDM 19501 [AAD]

Cherubini, L.:Pimmalione, w. Ilva Ligabue (sop), Gabriella Carturan (mez), Umberto Borghi (sgr), E. Gerelli (cnd), Milan RAI SO, Milan RAI Chorus
Melodram 2–▲ CDM 29501

Mozart, W.A.:Così fan tutte, w. T. Stich-Randall (mez), T. Berganza (mez), L. Alva (ten), A. Cortis (ten), R. Panerai (bar), H. Rosbaud (cnd), Paris Conservatory Societé des Concerts Orch, Aix-en-Provence Festival Chorus [I] *(rec live, Aix-en-Provence, July 26, 1957)*
Melodram 3–▲ MEL 37084 [AAD]

Puccini, G.:La Bohème, w. M. Freni (sop), L. Pavarotti (ten), L. Saccomani (bar), M. Wolf-Ferrari (cnd), Genoa Teatro Comunale Orch, Genoa Teatro Comunale Chorus [I] *(rec live 4/12/69)*
Verona 2–▲ 27079/80

Puccini, G.:La Bohème, w. M. Freni (sop), L. Pavarotti (ten), L. Saccomani (bar), M. Wolf-Ferrari (cnd), Genoa Teatro Comunale Orch, Genoa Teatro Comunale Chorus *(rec live, Apr 12, 1969)*
Melodram 2–▲ MEL 27031 [AAD]

Addison, Adele (sop)

Handel, G.F.:Messiah (sels), w. Russell Oberlin (ct), Edward Lloyd (ten), William Warfield (bar), L. Bernstein (cnd), New York PO, Westminster Choir [E]
CBS ▲ MYK 38481 ■ MYT 38481

Ade-Jesemann, Ingrid (sop)

Nono, L.:Prometeo, w. M. Bair-Ivenz (sop), S. Otto (alt), P. Hall (ten), U. Krumbiegel (nar), M. Schadock (nar), C. Abbado (cnd), Berlin PO, Freiburg Soloists Choir *(rec May 23–25, 1993)*
Sony Classical ▲ SK 53978 [DDD]

Adler, Stephen (bar)

Bach, J.S.:Cant 211, "Coffee Cant", w. L. Dawson (sop), N. Robertson (ten), Friends of Apollo [G]
Meridian ▲ ECD 84110

Bach, J.S.:Cant 212, "Peasant Cant", w. L. Dawson (sop), Friends of Apollo [G]
Meridian ▲ ECD 84110

Adorf, Mario (sgr)

Weill, K.:The Threepenny Opera, w. U. Lemper (sop), Milva (sgr), S. Tremper (sgr), H. Dernesch (mez), R. Kollo (ten), W. Reichmann (sgr), J. Mauceri (cnd), Berlin RIAS Sinfonietta, Berlin RIAS Chamber Choir [G]
London ▲ 430075–2 [DDD]

Adrian, Max (sgr)

Bernstein, L.:Candide, w. Barbara Cook (sop), Robert Rounseville (ten), et al.
Sony Broadway ▲ SK 48017 ■ ST 48017

Adriano, M. (nar)

Respighi, O.:La bella dormente nel bosco, w. Ivana Czaková (sop—Old Woman/Green Fairy), Adriana Kohútková (sop—Blue Fairy/Nightingale), Henrietta Lednárová (sop—Frog/Spindle), Jana Valášková (sop—Princess), Dagmar Pecková (mez—Cuckoo/Cat), Denisa Šlepkovská (mez—Queen/Duchess), Karol Bernáth (ten—Doctor), Guillermo Dominguez (ten—Prince April), Igor Pasek (ten—Jester), Ján Durčo (bar—Ambassador), Richard Haan (bar—King/Woodcutter), Stanislav Benačka (bass—Doctor), Anton Kúrnava (bass—Doctor), Marián Smolárik (bass—Doctor), M. Adriano (nar—Mr. Dollar Chèques), M. Adriano (cnd), Slovak RSO Bratislava, Ján Rozehnal (cnd), Slovak Phil Chorus *(rec Concert Hall of the Slovak Radio, Bratislava, June 8–20, 1994)*
Marco Polo ("Opera Classics" series) ▲ 8.223742 [DDD]

Aebi, Irene (sgr)

Beck, Julian:Songs, w. Steve Lacy (sax), Frederic Rzewski (pno)—Theatre [w. lyrics by Julian Beck]; Joy; The Hour Is Late; 1st & Last Pain; Love & Politics; I Heard the Indian Sage; Do Not Judge Me Lightly; The True & the Contrary; The Melancholy Life of Woman; Do Not Judge Me Lightly No. 2 [all w. lyrics by Judith Malina] *(rec Studio Acousti, Paris, Mar 16–17, 1995)*
New Albion ▲ NA 080

Affre, Agustarello (ten)

Gounod, C.:Roméo et Juliette, w. Yvonne Gall (sop—Juliette), Champell (sop—Stéphano), Jeanne Goulancourt (mez—Gertrude), Agustarello Affre (ten—Roméo), Edmond Tirmont (ten—Tybalt), Alexis Boyer (bar—Mercutio), Pierre Dupré (bar—Paris), Hypolite Belhomme (bar—Grégorio), Marcel Journet (bass—Frère Laurent), Henri Albers (bass—Capulet), Valermont (bass—The Duke), F. Rühlmann (cnd), Paris Opéra-Comique Orch, Paris Opéra-Comique Chorus *(rec 1912)*
VAI Audio ▲ VAIA 1064–3 F

Agache, Alexander (bar)

Donizetti, G.:Lucia di Lammermoor (sels), w. E. Gruberova (sop), A. Miles (bass), R. Bonynge (cnd), London SO, Ambrosian Singers—Oh giusto cielo...Il dolce suono; Ohimè! sorge il tremendo fantasma; S'avanza Enrico; Spargi d'amore pianto
Teldec ▲ 4509–93691–2 [DDD]

Gounod, C.:Faust, w. C. Gasdia (sop), B. Fassbaender (mez), S. Mentzer (mez), J. Hadley (ten), P. Fourcade (bass), C. Rizzi (cnd), Welsh National Opera Orch, Welsh National Opera Chorus
Teldec 3–▲ 90872

Verdi, G.:Messa per Rossini, w. G. Benačková-Cápova (sop), F. Quivar (mez), J. Wagner (ten), A. Haugland (bass), H. Rilling (cnd), Stuttgart RSO, Gächinger Kantorei, Prague Phil Chorus [L]
Hänssler Classic 2–▲ CD 98.949 [DDD] 2–■ MC 96.949 (D)

Verdi, G.:Rigoletto, w. L. Vaduva (sop), J. Larmore (mez), R. Leech (ten), S. Ramey (bass), C. Rizzi (cnd), Welsh National Opera Orch
Teldec ▲ 90851–2

Agachi, Mihaela (mez)

Puccini, G.:Madama Butterfly, w. Eugenia Moldoveanu (sop—Madama Butterfly), Mihaela Agachi (mez—Suzuki), Corina Circa (mez—Kate Pinkerton), Emil Gherman (ten—B.F. Pinkerton), Stefan Popescu (ten—Goro), Ioan Soanea (bar—The Bonze/Yakuside), Eduard Tumageanian (bar—Sharpless), Alexandru Kopeczi (bass—Prince Yamadori), Mircea Moisa (bass—Commissioner), P. Popescu (cnd), Satu Mare PO, Cluj-Napoca Phil Chorus *(rec 1979)*
Vox Box 2–▲ CDX 5155

Agay, Karola (sop)

Erkel, F.:Bánk Bán, w. E. Komlóssy (cta), J. Réti (ten), J. Simándy (ten), S. Sólyom-Nagy (bar), J. Ferencsik (cnd), Budapest PO, Hungarian State Opera Chorus [Hun] *(rec 1969)*
Hungaroton 2–▲ HCD 11376/77 [ADD]

Ághová, Lívia (sop)

Dvořák, A.:The Spectre's Bride, Op. 69, w. J. Protschka (ten), I. Kusnjer (bar), G. Albrecht (cnd), Hamburg State PO, Prague Phil Chorus [Cz] *(rec live 1991)*
Orfeo ▲ 259921 [DDD]

Dvořák, A.:Stabat Mater, w. M. Schiml (sop), A. Baldin (ten), L. Vele (bass), J. Bělohlávek (cnd), Czech PO, Prague Phil Chorus [L]
Chandos 2–▲ CHAN 8985/86 [DDD]

Janácek, L.:Fate, w. Lívia Ághová (sop—Míla), Ludmila Nováková (sop—Frl. Stuhlá/Součková), Marta Benačková (cta—Mílas Mother), Štefan Margita (ten—Dr. Suda/Hrázda), Peter Straka (ten—Zivny), Ivan Kusnjer (bar—Konečny/Verva), Peter Mikuláš (bass—Lhotsky), G. Albrecht (cnd), Czech PO, Prague Chamber Choir *(rec 1995)*
Orfeo ▲ 384 951 [DDD]

Rossini, G.:Petite messe solennelle, w. Marta Benackova (mez), Gil Manuel Beltran (ten), Peter Mikulas (bass), Raphaele Cortesi (pno), Peter Toperczer (pno), Josef Ksica (harm), Romano Gandolfi (cnd), Prague Chamber Choir *(rec Domovina Studios, Prague, Sept. 10–12, 1994)*
Discover International 2–▲ DI 920324–5 [DDD]

Agnew, Paul (ct)

Monteverdi, C.:Combattimento, w. E. Kirkby (sop), J. King (ten), A. Rooley (cnd), Consort of Musicke [I]
Virgin Classics ▲ 59606 [DDD]

Monteverdi, C.:Volgendo il ciel, w. E. Kirkby (sop), S. LeBlanc (sop), M. Nichols (mez), Alan Ewing (bass), A. Rooley (cnd), Consort of Musicke [I]
Virgin Classics ▲ 59606 [DDD]

Rameau, J.P.:Motets, w. S. Daneman (sop), N. Rime (sop), N. Rivenq (bar), N. Cavallier (bass), W. Christie (cnd), Les Arts Florissants—In convertendo, Quam dilecta, Deus noster refugium *(rec June 8–12, 1994)*
Erato ▲ 96967–2 [DDD]

Schütz, H.:Weihnachtshistorie, w. Anna Crookes (sop—Angel), Paul Agnew (ct—Evangelist), Michael McCarthy (bass—Herod), Jeremy Summerly (cnd), Oxford Camerata *(rec Oxford, Aug 1995)*
Naxos ▲ 8.553514 [DDD]

Agnew, Paul (ten)

Dowland, J.:The First Booke of Songs or Ayres, w. Christopher Wilson (lt)—Awake sweet love thou art returnd; Goe crystall teares; If my complaints could passions move; Come again:sweet love doth now invite; Can she excuse my wrongs with vertues cloak?; Deare, if you change, ile never chuse again; All ye whom love or fortune hath betraid; Sleep wayward thoughts
Metronome ▲ MET CD 1010 [DDD]

Dowland, J.:The Second Booke of Songs or Ayres, w. Christopher Wilson (lt)—Flow my teares fall from your springs; If fluds of teares could cleanse my follies past; Fine knacks for Ladies, cheape, choise, brave and new; I saw my Lady weepe; Tymes eldest sonne, old age the heire of ease; Then sit thee downe, & say thy Nunc demittis; When others sings Venite exultemus; Come ye heavie states of night; Shall I sue, shall I seeke for grace; Sorrow sorrow stay, lend true repentant teares
Metronome ▲ MET CD 1010 [DDD]

Aguilar, Silvia (nar)

Falla, M. de:El amor brujo, w. A.B. Egea (nar), A. Nafe (nar), J. López-Cobos (cnd), Lausanne CO *(rec Mar. 25–27, 1992)*
Denon ▲ CO 75339 [DDD]

Ahlersmeyer, Mathieu (bar)

Mozart, W.A.:Don Giovanni, w. M. Schech (sop), M. Teschemacher (sop), H. Hopf (ten), K. Böhme (bass), G. Frick (bass), K. Elmendorff (cnd), Saxon State Orch, Dresden State Opera Chorus [G] *(rec 1943)*
Berlin Classics ("Dokumente" series) 3–▲ BER 2048 [ADD]

Mozart, W.A.:Nozze di Figaro (sels), w. M. Reining (sop—Countess), M. Cebotari (sop—Susanna), M. Ahlersmeyer (bar—Count Almaviva), K. Böhm (cnd), Vienna State Opera Orch *(rec Nov. 7, 1941)*
Koch Schwann 2–▲ SCH 314602

Puccini, G.:La Bohème, w. H. Ranczak (sop), P. A. (ten), C. Krauss (cnd), Stuttgart RSO *(rec 1938)*
Preiser 2–▲ PRE 90210 [ADD]

Verdi, G.:Macbeth, w. E. Höngen (cta), J. Witt (ten), H. Alsen (bass), K. Böhm (cnd), Vienna State Opera Orch, Vienna State Opera Chorus *(rec 1943)*
Preiser 2–▲ PRE 90175 [AAD]

Ahlstedt, Douglas (ten)
Huber, K.:Soliloquia, w. H. Lukomska (sop), S. Klare (mez), B. McDaniel (bar), H. G. Ahrens (b-bar), H. Zender (cnd), Munich Bavarian RSO, Munich Bavarian Radio Chorus [L] *(rec Dec. 17, 1979)* Grammont ▲ CTSP 24-2 [ADD]
Huber, K.:Soliloquia, Part II:Cuius legibus rotantur poli, w. H. Lukomska (sop), S. Klare (mez), B. McDaniel (bar), H. G. Ahrens (b-bar), H. Zender (cnd), Munich Bavarian RSO, Munich Bavarian Radio Chorus [L] *(rec Dec. 17, 1979)* Grammont ▲ CTSP 24-2 [ADD]
Mysliveček, J.:Belerofonte, w. C. Lindsleyová (sop), G. Mayová (sop), K. Lakiová (sop), R. Gimenéz (ten), S. Margita (ten), Z. Peskó (cnd), Prague CO, Czech Phil Chorus [l] *(rec 1987)* Supraphon 3-▲ 11 0006-2 [DDD]

Ahnsjö, Claes Hakon (ten)
Alfvén, H.:Choral Music, w. F. Alin (pno), R. Sund (cnd), Orphei Drängar—Hör I Orphei Drängar; Dawn at Sea; Papillon; Gustaf Frödings Funeral; Berceuse; Spring in Roslagen; Sweden's Flag; My Sweetheart; Serenade; Night; Evening; Lullaby; So Take My Heart; Quiet Hours; Scents of Summer; You Are Peaceful Calm; I Long for You; The Forest Sleeps; The Trial; Flowers of Joy; Värmlandsvisan; Oxberg March; Swedish Dance; Fatheads; Herdboy's Song; Andrew Was a Lively Lad; And the Maiden Joins the Ring; In Our Meadow; Mood [Sw] *(rec Feb 6-7 & Sept 4-5, 1993)* BIS ▲ CD 633 [DDD]
Alfvén, H.:Sym 4, "Fran havsbandet [From the Seaward Skerries]", w. C. Hogman (sop), N. Järvi (cnd), Stockholm PO BIS ▲ CD 505 [DDD]
Bach, J.S.:Mass in b, BWV 232, w. Helen Donath (sop), Brigitte Fassbaender (cta), Roland Hermann (bar), Robert Holl (bass), E. Jochum (cnd), Bavarian RSO, Bavarian Radio Chorus EMI Classics ("Doublefforte" series) 2-▲ CDFB 68640
Donizetti, G.:Lucia di Lammermoor, w. M. Caballé (sop), A. Murray (mez), V. Bello (ten), J. Carreras (ten), V. Sardinero (bar), S. Ramey (bass), J. López-Cobos (cnd), New Philharmonia Orch, Ambrosian Opera Chorus Philips 2-▲ 426563-2
Gluck, C.W.:La Recontre imprévue, w. J. Kaufmann (sop—Rezia), A. Stumphius (sop—Dardané), A.-M. Rodde (sop—Amine), I. Vermillion (mez—Balkis), R. Gambill (ten—Ali), C. H. Ahnsjö (ten—Osmin), J.-H. Rootering (bass—Un Calender), L. Hager (cnd), Munich RSO Orfeo 2-▲ 242912 [DDD]
Handel, G.F.:Messiah, w. Edith Mathis (sop), James Bowman (alt), Richard Krause (ten), A. Dorati (cnd), Smithsonian Concerto Grosso, Univ of Maryland Choral Society [E] Pro Arte 2-▲ CDD 232 [DDD]; ■ PCD 232
Haydn, J.:Mass 10, "Kriegsmesse", "Paukenmesse", w. Judith Blegen (sop), Brigette Fassbaender (mez), Hans Sotin (bass), L. Bernstein (cnd), Bavarian RSO, Bavarian Radio Chorus [L] Philips ▲ 412734-2 [DDD]
Haydn, J.:Stabat Mater, w. Krisztina Láki (sop), Júlia Hamari (mez), Richard Anlauf (bass), F. Bernius (cnd), Württemberg CO, Stuttgart Chamber Choir *(rec 1978)* Vox Box 2-▲ CDX 5081 [ADD]
Kraus, J.M.:Funeral Music for Gustav III, w. C. Högman (sop), H. Martinpelto (sop), T. Lander (bass), S. Parkman (cnd), Drottningholm Baroque Ensemble, Uppsala Univ Chamber Choir Musica Sveciae ▲ MSCD 416 [DDD]
Mozart, W.A.:Complete Mozart Edition, w. A. M. Blasi (sop), S. McNair (sop), I. Vermillion (mez), J. Hadley (ten), N. Marriner (cnd), Academy of St. Martin in the Fields Philips 2-▲ 422535-2 [DDD]
Mozart, W.A.:Schuldigkeit, w. A. Augér (sop), K. Láki (sop), S. Geszty (sop), W. Hollweg (ten), R. Bader (cnd), Berlin Cathedral Choir [G] *(rec 1980)* Koch Schwann 2-▲ CD 313065 [ADD]
Norman, L.:Songs, w. A. Kontarsky (pno)—Waldlieder (song cycle—1867); Ahasverus; Blomstring; Höst; Fran sol och stjärnor; Manestralar; Pagens visa; Själens frid; Stille Sicherheit; Ungt mod [G,Sw] Musica Sveciae ▲ MSCD 525 [DDD]
Söderman, A.:Choral Music, w. F. Alin (pno), Orphei Drängar [arr. Alfvén]—In the Gleam of the Moon BIS ▲ CD 633 [DDD]

Ahrens, H. G. (b-bar)
Huber, K.:Soliloquia, w. H. Lukomska (sop), S. Klare (mez), D. Ahlstedt (ten), B. McDaniel (bar), H. Zender (cnd), Munich Bavarian RSO, Munich Bavarian Radio Chorus [L] *(rec Dec. 17, 1979)* Grammont ▲ CTSP 24-2 [ADD]
Huber, K.:Soliloquia, Part II:Cuius legibus rotantur poli, w. H. Lukomska (sop), S. Klare (mez), D. Ahlstedt (ten), B. McDaniel (bar), H. Zender (cnd), Munich Bavarian RSO, Munich Bavarian Radio Chorus [L] *(rec Dec. 17, 1979)* Grammont ▲ CTSP 24-2 [ADD]

Aikawa, Yumi (sop)
Hayashi, H.:Pieces Sop & Fl, w. Masami Nakagawa (fl) *(rec Niiza City Auditorium, May 1, 1985)* Camerata ▲ 32CM 118 [DDD]

Ainsley, John Mark (ten)
Arne, T.:Songs, w. Miles Golding (vn), Roy Goodman (vn), Anthony Robson (sop rcr), Jane Coe (vc), Robert King (hpd/org)—Under the Greenwood Tree; Come Away Death; Where the Bee Sucks *(rec St Jude-on-the-Hill, London, Dec 20-21, 1968)* United ▲ CAL 88002 [DDD]
Bach, J.S.:Magnificat, BWV 243, w. T. Bonner (sop), E. Kirkby (sop), M. Chance (ct), S. Varcoe (b-bar), R. Hickox (cnd), Collegium Musicum 90 Chandos ("Chaconne" series) ▲ CHAN 0518 [DDD]
Beethoven, L. van:Mass, Op. 86, w. Janice Watson (sop), Jean Rigby (mez), Gwynne Howell (bass), M. Best (cnd), Corydon Orch, Corydon Singers Hyperion ▲ CDA 66830
Beethoven, L. van:Ne' giorni tuoi felici, w. Janice Watson (sop), M. Best (cnd), Corydon Orch Hyperion ▲ CDA 66830
Berlioz, H.:Les Troyens, w. F. Pollet (sop—Dido), D. Voigt (sop—Cassandre), C. Dubosc (sop—Ascagne), H. Perraguin (cta—Anna), G. Lakes (ten—Aeneas), J.-L. Maurette (ten—Iopas), J. M. Ainsley (ten—Hylas), M. P. (ten—Panthee), G. Cross (ten—Sinon), G. Quilico (bar—Chorebe), J.-P. Courtis (b-bar—Narbal), M. Belleau (bass—Ghost of Hector), R. Schirrer (bass—Priam), C. Dutoit (cnd), Montreal SO, Montreal Sym Chorus London 4-▲ 443693-2 [DDD]
Blow, J.:Songs, w. T. Roberts (spinet/hpd/chamber org), P. Chateauneuf (gtr/thb)—No More, the Dear, Lovely Nymph's No More; Lovely Selina, Innocent & Free; O Turn Not Those Fine Eyes away; Fairest Work of Happy Nature; Flavia Grown Old; Oh! That Mine Eyes Would Melt into a Flood; O Might God, Who Sit'st on High; Sabina Has a Thousand Charms; Of All the Torments, All the Cares; No, Lesbia, You Ask in Vain *(rec Jan. 25-27, 1993)* Hyperion ▲ CDA 66646 [DDD]
Blow, J.:Songs, w. James Bowman (ct), Michael George (bass), Charles Pott (bass), R. King (cnd), King's Consort—Sing unto the Lord, Oh ye Saints *(rec St Jude-on-the-Hill, London, Dec 20-21, 1968)* United ▲ CAL 88002 [DDD]
Britten, H.:Cant misericordium, w. S. Varcoe (bar), R. Hickox (cnd), City of London Sinfonia, Britten Singers [L] Chandos ▲ CHAN 8997 [DDD]
Britten, H.:Gloriana, w. J. Barstow (sop—Queen Elizabeth I), D. Jones (mez—Lady Essex), P. Langridge (ten—Earl of Essex), J. M. Ainsley (ten—Spirit of the Masque), J. Summers (bar—Lord Mountjoy), J. Shirley-Quirk (bar—Recorder of Norwich), B. Terfel (b-bar—Henry Cuffe), C. Mackerras (cnd), Welsh National Opera Orch, Welsh National Opera Chorus Argo 2-▲ 440213-2 [DDD]
Britten, H.:Les Illuminations, w. N. Cleobury (cnd), Britten Sinfonia EMI Classics ▲ CDM 65899
Britten, H.:Nocturne, w. N. Cleobury (cnd), Britten Sinfonia EMI Classics ▲ CDM 65899
Britten, H.:Purcell Realizations, w. Susan Gritton (sop), Felicity Lott (sop), Sarah Walker (mez), James Bowman (alto), Anthony Rolfe Johnson (ten), Richard Jackson (bass), Simon Keenlyside (bass), Ian Bostridge (sgr), Graham Johnson (pno) Hyperion 2-▲ CDA 67061/62
Britten, H.:Serenade, Op. 31, w. N. Cleobury (cnd), Britten Sinfonia EMI Classics ▲ CDM 65899
British Music on Hyperion, w. Parley of Instruments, Roy Goodman (cnd), Graham Johnson (pno), Salomon Quartet, BBC Scottish SO, Anthony Rolfe Johnson (ten), Royal PO, St. Paul's Cathedral Choir, Nash Ensemble, Martyn Hill (ten), Suasan Gritton (sop), et al. Hyperion ▲ HYP 15
Finzi, G.:Dies natalis, w. M. Best (cnd), Corydon Orch Hyperion ▲ CDA 66876
Finzi, G.:Intimations of Immortality, w. M. Best (cnd), Corydon Orch, Corydon Singers Hyperion ▲ CDA 66876
Grainger, P.:Jungle Book (comp), w. David Wilson-Johnson (bar), S. Layton (cnd), Polyphony Hyperion ▲ CDA 66863
Handel, G.F.:Jephtha, w. Julia Gooding (sop), Christiane Oelze (sop), Catherine Denley (mez), Axel Köhler (ct), Michael George (bass), M. Creed (cnd), Berlin Academy for Early Music *(rec June 1992)* Berlin Classics 2-▲ BER 1057-2 [DDD]
Handel, G.F.:Joseph & His Brethren, w. Yvonne Kenney (sop), Catherine Denley (mez), Connor Burrowes (trb), James Bowman (ct), Michael George (bass), R. King (cnd), King's Consort, New College Choir Oxford, King's Consort Choir Hyperion 3-▲ CDA 67171/3

Ainsley, John Mark (ten) (cont.)
Handel, G.F.:Messiah, w. Lynne Dawson (sop), Hilary Summers (cta), Alastair Miles (bass), R. Goodman (cnd), Brandenburg Consort, Stephen Cleobury (cnd), King's College Choir Cambridge [1752 version] Argo 2-▲ 440672-2 [DDD]
Handel, G.F.:Messiah (sels), w. Patrizia Kwella (sop), Catherine Denley (mez), Bryn Terfel (b-bar), M. Stephenson (cnd), London Musici, London Chamber Choir Conifer Classics ▲ 74321-15354-2
Handel, G.F.:Nisi Dominus, w. Diana Montague (mez), Simon Birchall (bass), S. Preston (cnd), Westminster Abbey Orch, Westminster Abbey Choir [L] Archiv ▲ 423594-2 [DDD]
Handel, G.F.:Occasional Oratorio, w. Susan Gritton (sop), Lisa Milne (sop), James Brown (ct), Michael George (bass), R. King (cnd), King's Consort, New College Choir Oxford Hyperion 2-▲ CDA 66961/62
Handel, G.F.:Saul, w. D. Brown (sop), L. Dawson (sop), D. L. Ragin (ct), A. Miles (bar), J. E. Gardiner (cnd), English Baroque Soloists, Monteverdi Choir London Philips 3-▲ 426265-2 3PH [DDD]
Howells, H.:Hymnus Paradisi, w. J. Kennard (sop), V. Handley (cnd), Royal Liverpool PO, Royal Liverpool Phil Choir Hyperion ▲ CDA 66488
Howells, H.:Songs, w. L. Dawson (sop), C. Pierard (mez), B. Luxon (bar), J. Drake (pno)—7 various songs; 2 South African Settings; 3 Folksongs; A Garland for De la Mare; Peacock Pie, Op. 33; 4 French Chansons, Op. 29; In Green Ways, Op. 43; 12 various songs; 3 Children's Songs; 4 Songs, Op. 22 Chandos 2-▲ CHAN 9185/86 [DDD]
Monteverdi, C.:Orfeo, w. P. Pickett (cnd), New London Consort L'Oiseau-Lyre 2-▲ 433545-2 [DDD]
Mozart, W.A.:Don Giovanni, w. N. Argenta (sop), A. Halgrimson (sop), L. Dawson (sop), G. Finley (ten), A. Miles (bar), A. Schmidt (bar), G. Yurisch (bar), R. Norrington (cnd), London Classical Players, Schütz Choir London EMI Classics ▲ CDCB 54859
Mozart, W.A.:Missa, K.317, w. E. Kirkby (sop), C. Robbin (mez), M. George (bass), C. Hogwood (cnd), Academy of Ancient Music, Winchester Cathedral Choir Argo ▲ 436585-2 [DDD]
Mozart, W.A.:Requiem, w. N. Argenta (sop), C. Robbin (mez), A. Miles (bass), R. Norrington (cnd), London Classical Players, Schütz Choir London [L] EMI Classics ▲ CDC 54525
Purcell, H.:Anthems & Services, w. Tom Seligman (trb), James Bowman (ct), Ashley Stafford (ct), Andrew Gant (ten), Michael George (bass), Charles Pott (bass), R. King (cnd), King's Consort, King's Consort—O Sing unto the Lord; My beloved spake *(rec St Jude-on-the-Hill, London, Dec 20-21, 1968)* United ▲ CAL 88002 [DDD]
Purcell, H.:Dido & Aeneas, w. Catherine Bott (sop—Dido), Emma Kirkby (sop—Belinda), Michael Chance (alt—Spirit), John Mark Ainsley (bar—Aeneas), David Thomas (bar—Sorceress), C. Hogwood (cnd), Academy of Ancient Music L'Oiseau-Lyre ▲ 436992-2 [DDD]
Purcell, H.:The Indian Queen, w. Catherine Bott (sop—Orazia/Married Woman), Emma Kirkby (sop—Indian Girl/Zempoalla/Cupid), John Mark Ainsley (ten—Indian Boy/Fame/Follower of Cupid/Aerial Spirits), Julian Podger (ten—Follower of Envy/Aerial Spirit), Gerald Finley (bar—Conjurer/Hymen/Follower of Cupid), Helen Parker (sgr—Aerial Spirits), David Thomas (bass—Envy/High Priest/Married Man/Follower of Cupid), Simon Berridge (sgr—Follower of Envy), Libby Crabtree (sgr—Follower of Hymen/Aerial Spirit), Tommy Williams (sgr—God of Dreams), C. Hogwood (cnd), Academy of Ancient Music *(rec Walthamstow Assembly Hall, London, July 1994)* L'Oiseau-Lyre ▲ 444339-2 [DDD]
Purcell, H.:Odes & Welcome Songs (misc), w. J. Smith (sop), E. Priday (sop), K. Amps (sop), M. Chance (ct), Wilson (sgr), S. Richardson (bar), T. Pinnock (cnd), English Concert, *(chorus unknown)*—Come ye Sons of Art; Welcome to All the Pleasures; Of Old, When Heroes Thought it Base Archiv ▲ 427663-2 [DDD]
Purcell, H.:The Prophetess, or The History of Dioclesian, w. Catherine Pierard (sop), James Bowman (alt), Michael George (bass), R. Hickox (cnd), Collegium Musicum 90 Chandos ▲ CHAN 0569/70 [DDD]
Purcell, H.:The Prophetess, or The History of Dioclesian, w. C. Pierard (sop), J. Bowman (alt), I. Bostridge (ten), M. George (bass), R. Hickox (cnd), Collegium Musicum 90—Masque Chandos ("Chaconne" series) ▲ CHAN 0558 [DDD]
Purcell, H.:Timon of Athens, w. I. Davies (trb), C. de la Hoyde (trb), J. Bowman (alt), M. George (bass), R. Hickox (cnd), Collegium Musicum 90—Masque Chandos ("Chaconne" series) ▲ CHAN 0558 [DDD]
Quilter, R.:Songs, w. Malcolm Martineau (pno)—Now Sleeps the Crimson Petal; Go, Lovely Rose; plus others Hyperion ▲ CDA 66878
Schubert, Franz:Songs (comp), w. P. Rozario (sop), I. Bostridge (ten), M. George (bass), G. Johnson (pno), S. Layton (cnd), London Schubert Chorale—Winterlied; Ossians Lied nach dem Falle Nathos; Das Mädchen von Inistore; Als ich sie erröten; Schwangesang; Totenkranz für ein Kind; Die Fröhlichkeit; Der Zufriedene; Alles um Liebe; Geist der Liebe; Dei erste Liebe; Die Täuschung; Liebesrausch; Huldigung; Heidenröslein; Nachtgesang; Der Morgenstern; Der Knappenlied; Trinklied vor der Schlacht; Schwertlied; Begräbnislied; Grablied; Osterlied; Hoffnung; Punschlied; Klage um Ali Bey; Abendständchen; Tische'rlied; Wiegenlied; Die Macht der Liebe; Trinklied, D.183; Trinklied, D.267 Hyperion ▲ CDJ 33020
Schubert, Franz:Songs (comp), w. Michael George (bass), Simon Keenlyside (bass), Graham Schäfer (sgr), Graham Johnson (cnd), London Schubert Chorale—settings of Goethe's poetry Hyperion ▲ CDJ 33024
Schubert, Franz:Songs (comp), w. Academy of Ancient Music Chamber Ensemble—Die Forelle, D.550; Am Strome, D.539; Auf dem See, D.543; Erlafsee, D.586; An eine Quelle, D.530, Der Jüngling am Bache, D.192; Der Schiffer, D.536 [G] L'Oiseau-Lyre ▲ 433848-2 [DDD]
Schubert, Franz:Songs (comp), w. Christine Schäfer (sop), Richard Jackson (bar), Graham Johnson (pno), Stephen Layton (cnd), London Schubert Chorale—Der Einsame; Des Sängers Habe; Zwei Szenen aus dem Schauspiel Lacrimas (Lied der Delphine; Lied des Florio); Mondenschien (chorale); Gesänge Aus Wilhwlm Meister (Nur wer die Sehnsucht kennt; Hwiss mich nicht reden; So lasst mich scheinen); Totengräberweise; Das Echo; An Silvia; Horch, horch die Lerch'; Trinklied; Wiegenlied; Widerspruch; Der Wanderer an den Mond; Grab und Mond (chorale); Nachthelle; Abschied von der Erde Hyperion ▲ CDJ 33026
Stravinsky, I.:Canticum sacrum, w. S. Roberts (bar), J. O'Donnell (cnd), City of London Sinfonia, Westminster Cathedral Choir Hyperion ▲ CDA 66437
Sullivan, A.:The Pirates of Penzance, w. R. Evans (sop—Mabel), G. Knight (mez—Ruth), J. Gossage (mez—Edith), J. M. Ainsley (ten—Frederic), R. Suart (bar—Maj.-Gen. Stanley), N. Folwell (bar—Samuel), D. Adams (b-bar—Pirate King), R. Van Allan (bass—Sergeant of Police), C. Mackerras (cnd), Welsh National Opera Orch, Welsh National Opera Chorus *(rec May 4-6, 1993)* Telarc ▲ CD 80353 [DDD]; ■ CS 30353
Tavener, J.:We Shall See Him As He Is, w. P. Rozario (sop), A. Murgatroyd (ten), R. Hickox (cnd), BBC Welsh National SO, BBC Welsh National Chorus [E] Chandos ▲ CHAN 9128 [DDD]
Tippett, M.:The Heart's Assurance, w. R. Hickox (cnd), City of London Sinfonia Chandos ▲ CHAN 9409 [DDD]
Vaughan Williams, R.:Sacred Songs, w. J. Howarth (sop), T. Allen (bar), M. Best (cnd), Corydon Orch, Corydon Singers—Towards the Unknown Region; Dona nobis pacem; O Clap your hands; Lord, Thou hast been our refuge; 4 Hymns Hyperion ▲ CDA 66655 [DDD]
Vaughan Williams, R.:The Shepherds of the Delectable Mountains, w. L. Kitchen (sop), A. Thompson (ten), A. Opie (bar), B. Terfel (b-bar), J. Best (bass), M. Best (cnd), City of London Sinfonia [E] Hyperion ▲ CDA 66569 [DDD]
Warlock, P.:Songs, w. Rodger Vignoles (pno)—The Wind from the West; To the Memory of a Great Singer; Take, O Take Those Lips away; As Ever I Saw; The Bayley Berith the Bell away; There is a Lady Sweet & Kind; Lullaby; Sweet Content; Late Summer; The Singer; Rest, Sweet Nymphs; Sleep; A Sad Song; In an Arbour Green; Autumn Twilight; I Held Love's Head; Thou Gav'st Me Leave to Kiss; Yarmouth Fair; Pretty Ring Time; A Prayer to St. Anthony; The Sick Heart; Robin Good-Fellow; Jillian of Berry; Fair & True; Ha'nacker Mill; My Own Country; The First Mercy; The Lover's Maze; Cradle Song; Sing No More Ladies; Passing by; The Contended Lover; The Fox Hyperion ▲ CDA 66736

Åkerlund, Lina (sop)
Feo, F.:Salve regina, w. C. Chiarappa (cnd), Accademia Bizantina Denon ▲ CO 78904 [DDD]
Fux, J.J.:Dafne in Lauro, w. S. Piccollo (sop), M. van der Sluis (sop), G. Lesne (alt), M. Klietmann (ten), R. Clemencic (cnd), Clemencic Consort, La Cappella Vocal Ensemble [I] Nuova Era ("Ancient Music" series) 2-▲ 6930/31 [DDD]
Handel, G.F.:Cants, w. August Wenzinger Ensemble—Qual ti riveggio; No se Emenderá Jamás; Clori, mia bella Clori Accord ▲ ACD 201102 [DDD]

Åkerlund, Lina (sop) (cont.)
Pergolesi, G.B.:Salve regina in a, w. C. Chiarappa (cnd), Accademia Bizantina
Denon ▲ CO 78904 [DDD]
Pergolesi, G.B.:Stabat mater, w. Giuseppe Zambon (ct), C. Chiarappa (cnd), Accademia Bizantina
Denon ▲ CO 78904 [DDD]
Perti, G.A.:Gesù al sepolcro, w. M. Zanetti (sop), C. Cavina (alt), M. Cecchetti (ten), A. W. Schultze (bass), S. Vartolo (cnd), San Petronio Cappella Musicale Orch [I] Tactus ▲ TC 661601
Ringger, R.U.:Memories 2, w. M. Ziegler (fl), P. Zaugg (hp), U. Walker (vn), D. Pezzoti (vc), F. Mohr, R.U. Ringger [G] Grammont ▲ CTSP 29-2 [ADD]
Ringger, R.U.:Memories of Tomorrow, w. M. Ziegler (fl), P. Zaugg (hp), U. Walker (vn), D. Pezzoti (vc), F. Mohr, R.U. Ringger [G] Grammont ▲ CTSP 29-2 [ADD]
Wyttenbach, J.:Lamentoroso, w. H. Bissegger (cl), N. Calame (cl), M. Maurer (cl), E. Molinari (cl), M. Weber (cl), H. Zwahlen (cl) *(rec May 19-20, 1990)* Grammont ▲ CTSP 37-2 [ADD]

Aks, Catherine (sop)
Barber, S.:A Hand of Bridge, w. F. Kittelson (mez), W. Carney (ten), R. Muenz (bass), Adirondack CO, Gregg Smith Singers [E] Premier ▲ PRCD 1009 [ADD]
Xenakis, I.:N'shima, w. April Lindevald (mez), C. Z. Bornstein (cnd), ST-X Ensemble *(rec live, Thread Waxing Space, New York, June 21, 1995)* Mode ▲ mode 53

Alagna, Roberto (ten)
James Levine's 25th Anniversary Metropolitan Opera Gala, w. J. Levine (cnd), Metropolitan Opera Orch, Ileana Cotrubas (sop), Renée Fleming (sop), Hei-Kyung Hong (sop), Karita Mattila (sop), Birgit Nilsson (sop), Ruth Ann Swenson (sop), Kiri Te Kanawa (sop), Deborah Voigt (sop), Grace Bumbry (mez), Heidi Grant Murphy (mez), Anne Sofie von Otter (mez) *(rec live, Metropolitan Opera House, New York, Apr 27, 1996)* Deutsche Grammophon ▲ 449177-2 [DDD]
Operatic Arias, w. London PO [cnd:Richard Armstrong] *(rec Studio 1, Abbey Road, London, Jan., Mar. & Apr. 1995)* EMI Classics ▲ CDC 55477 [DDD]
Our Christmas Songs for You, w. K. Te Kanawa (sop), Thomas Hampson (bar), Jonathan Tunick (cnd), *(orch unknown)* EMI Classics ▲ CDC 56176
Puccini, G.:La Bohème, w. Leontina Vaduva (sop—Mimi), Ruth Ann Swenson (sop—Musetta), Roberto Alagna (ten—Rodolfo), Simon Keenlyside (bar—Schaunard), Thomas Hampson (bar—Marcello), Samuel Ramey (bass—Colline), Enrico Fissore (bass—Benoit), A. Pappano (cnd), Philharmonia Orch
EMI Classics 2-♦ CDCB 56120
Puccini, G.:Il trittico, w. M. Freni (sop), E. Souljois (sop), G. Giacomini (ten), J. Pons (bar), L. Nucci (bar), B. Bartoletti (cnd), Florence Maggio Musicale Orch, Florence Maggio Musicale Chorus
London 3-▲ 436261-2 [DDD]
Verdi, G.:Rigoletto, w. Andrea Rost (sop—Gilda), Mariana Pentcheva (cta—Maddalena), Roberto Alagna (ten—Il Duca di Mantova), Renato Bruson (bar—Rigoletto), Dmitri Kavrakos (bass—Sparafucile), R. Muti (cnd), La Scala Orch, La Scala Chorus Sony Classical 2-▲ S2K 66314
Verdi, G.:Rigoletto (sels), w. Andrea Rost (sop), Renato Bruson (bar), R. Muti (cnd), La Scala Orch
Sony Classical ▲ SK 61966
Verdi, G.:La traviata, w. T. Fabbricini (sop—Violetta), A. Trevisan (mez—Annina), N. Curiel (mez—Flora), R. Alagna (ten—Alfredo), E. Cossutta (ten—Gastone), E. Gavazzi (ten—Giuseppe), O. Mori (bar—Douphol), E. Capuano (bass—d'Obigny), F. Musinu (bass—Grenvil), R. Muti (cnd), La Scala Orch, La Scala Chorus Sony Classical 2-▲ S2K 52486 [DDD]

Alaimo, S. (ten)
Bellini, V.:Zaira, w. K. Ricciarelli (sop), A. Papadjakou (cta), R. Vargas (ten), P. Olmi (cnd), Catania Teatro Massimo Bellini Orch, Catania Teatro Massimo Bellini Chorus [I] *(rec live 1990)*
Nuova Era 2-▲ 6982/83 [DDD]

Alaimo, Simone (b-bar)
Donizetti, G.:L'Esule di Roma, w. C. Gasdia (sop), E. Palacio (ten), A. Ariostini (bar), M. de Bernart (cnd), Piacenza SO, Paris Opéra-Comique Chorus *(rec live, 10/14/86)*
Bongiovanni 2-▲ GB 2045/46 [DDD]
Donizetti, G.:Torquato Tasso, w. A. D'Auria (sop), L. Serra (sop), N. Ciliento (mez), E. Palacio (ten), R. Coviello (bar), A. Riva (bass), M.. Bernart (cnd), Genoa Teatro Comunale Orch, Genoa Teatro Comunale Chorus [I] *(rec live 10/16/85)* Bongiovanni 3-▲ GB 2028/30 [DDD]
Mozart, W.A.:Don Giovanni, w. S. Sweet (sop), K. Mattila (sop), M. McLaughlin (sop), F. Araiza (ten), T. Allen (bar), R. Lloyd (bass), N. Marriner (cnd), Academy of St. Martin in the Fields, Ambrosian Opera Chorus Philips 3-▲ 432129-2 [DDD]
Verdi, G.:Luisa Miller, w. Cecilia Gasdia (sop), Mazzareno Antinori (ten), G. Gavazzeni (cnd), Parma Teatro Regio Orch, Parma Teatro Regio Chorus *(rec live, 1981)* Serenissima 2-▲ SER 360143
Zingarelli, N.A.:La passione di Gesù Cristo, w. Ernesto Palacio (ten), Juan Diego Florez (sgr), P. Pelucchi (cnd), Bergamo Collegium Musicum *(rec S. Martino Church, Tirano, June 30, 1995)*
Agorá ▲ 018 [DDD]

Alaimo, Simone (bar)
Donizetti, G.:L'elisir d'amore, w. Alessandra Ruffini (sop—Adina), Mariangela Spotorno (sop—Gianetta), Vincenzo La Scola (ten—Nemorino), Simone Alaimo (bar—Dulcamara), Roberto Frontali (bar—Belcore), P.G. Morandi (cnd), Hungarian State Opera Orch, Anikó Katona (cnd), Hungarian State Opera Chorus *(rec Budapest, July 1995)* Naxos 2-▲ 8.60045-6 [DDD]
Ricci, L.:Crispino e la cornare, w. D. Lojarro (sop), A. Lazzarini (mez), Cossutta (ten), R. Coviello (bar), A. Marani (bass), R. Ristori (bass), Benori (sgr), Siclari (sgr), P. Carignani (cnd), San Remo SO, San Remo Sym Chorus [I] *(rec live 11/89)* Bongiovanni 2-▲ GB 2095/96 [DDD]
Rossini, G.:La Cenerentola, w. C. Malone (sop), F. Palmer (sop), A. Baltsa (mez), F. Araiza (ten), J. del Carlo (bass), R. Raimondi (bass), N. Marriner (cnd), Academy of St. Martin in the Fields, Ambrosian Chorus Philips ("Digital Classics" series) 3-▲ 420468-2 [DDD]

Alaimo, Vincenzo (sgr)
Giordano, U.:Fedora, w. Mirella Freni (sop—Principessa Fedora), Adelina Scarabelli (sop—Contessa Olga), Silvia Mazzoni (mez—Dimitri), Monica Minarelli (sgr—Savoiardo), Placido Domingo (ten—Conte Loris), Ernesto Gavazzi (ten—Desiré), Aldo Bottion (ten—Barone Rouvel), Alessandro Corbelli (bar—Siriex), Luigi Roni (bass—Cirillo), Silvestro Sammaritano (bass—Baroff), Alfredo Giacomotti (bass—Gretch), Ernesto Panariello (bass—Lorek), Vincenzo Alaimo (sgr—Nicola), Arnold Bosman (sgr—Boleslao), Bruno Capisani (sgr—Sergio), Renato Zanchetta (sgr—Michele), G. Gavazzeni (cnd), La Scala Orch, La Scala Chorus *(rec La Scala, Apr 5, 1993)* Legato 2-▲ LCD 213-2 [ADD]

Alan, Hervey (bass)
Britten, H.:Billy Budd, w. P. Pears (ten), T. Uppman (bar), G. Evans (b-bar), F. Dalberg (bass), B. Britten (cnd), Royal Opera House Orch, Royal Opera House Chorus Covent Garden *(rec Dec. 1, 1951)*
VAI Audio 3-▲ VAIA 1034-3 [ADD]
Donizetti, G.:Emilia di Liverpool (sels), w. A. Cantelo (sop), J. Sutherland (sop), W. McAlpine (ten), D. Dowling (bar), J. Pritchard (cnd), Royal Liverpool PO, Liverpool Music Group Singers—13 arias from Act 1, & 4 from Act 2 [I] *(rec live, Liverpool Sept. 1957)* Myto ▲ 1 MCD 91545 [ADD]
Rossini, G.:La Cenerentola, w. A. Noni (sop), F. Cadoni (mez), M. de Gabarain (mez), V. Gui (cnd), Glyndebourne Festival Orch, Glyndebourne Festival Chorus *(rec 1955)*
EMI Classics 2-▲ CDMB 64183

Alard (sgr)
Verdi, G.:La traviata, w. H. Schymberg (sop), J. Björling (ten), Molin (sgr), H. Sandberg (cnd), *(orch unknown) (rec live 8/29/39)* Standing Room Only 2-▲ SRO 832-2 [ADD]

Alarie, Pierrette (sop)
Bach, J.S.:Mass in b, BWV 232, w. N. Merriman (cta), L. Simoneau (ten), G. Neidlinger (bass), H. Scherchen (cnd), Vienna State Opera Orch, Vienna Academy Chorus [L]
MCA Classics 2-▲ MCAD2-9821 [AAD]

Albanese, Cecilia Nunez (sop)
Verdi, G.:Rigoletto, w. Cecilia Nunez Albanese (sop—Gilda), Wilma Borrelli (cta—Maddalena), Jaime Aragall (ten—Duke of Mantua), Renato Bruson (bar—Rigoletto), Loris Gambelli (bass—Sparafucile), G. Campanino (cnd), Naples Teatro San Carlo Orch, Naples Teatro San Carlo Chorus *(rec San Carlo Theatre, Naples, Feb. 1973)* Golden Age of Opera 2-▲ GAO 177-78 [ADD]
Verdi, G.:La traviata, w. J. Peerce (ten), R. Merrill (bar), A. Toscanini (cnd), NBC SO
Music & Arts 2-▲ CD 271
Verdi, G.:La traviata, w. J. Peerce (ten), R. Merrill (bar), A. Toscanini (cnd), NBC SO [I]
RCA Gold Seal 2-▲ 60303-2-RG [ADD] 2-■ 60303-4-RG (CrO2)

Albanese, Francesco (ten)
Verdi, G.:La traviata, w. Maria Callas (sop), Ugo Savarese (bar), G. Santini (cnd), Turin RAI SO, Coro Cetra *(rec 1953)* Enterprise ("Documents" series) 2-▲ ENT 1002 (m)

Albanese, Licia (sop)
Gluck, C.W.:Iphigénie en Tauride, w. M. Callas (sop), F. Cossotto (mez), N. Sanzogno (cnd), La Scala Orch, La Scala Chorus [I] *(rec live 6/1/57)* Melodram 2-▲ MEL 26012 (m)
Licia Albanese RCA Gold Seal ▲ 60384-2-RG (m) [ADD]
Operatic Duets, w. J. Björling (ten), Zinka Milanov (sop), Renata Tebaldi (sop), Robert Merrill (bar)
RCA Gold Seal ▲ 7799-2-RG (m) [ADD] ■ 7799-4-RG (CrO2)
Puccini, G.:La Bohème, w. L. Albanese (sop—Mimi), T. Menotti (sop—Musetta), B. Gigli (ten—Rodolfo), N. Palai (ten—Parpignol), A. Poli (bar—Marcello), A. Baracchi (bar—Schaunard), D. Baronti (bass—Colline), C. Scattola (bass—Benoit/Alcindoro), U. Berrettoni (cnd), La Scala Orch, La Scala Chorus [I] *(rec Milan, May 1938)* Nimbus 2-▲ NI 7862/63 [ADD]
Puccini, G.:La Bohème, w. Licia Albanese (sop—Mimi), Audrey Schuh (sop—Musetta), Giuseppe di Stefano (ten—Rodolfo), Arthur Cosenza (bar—Schaunard), Giuseppe Valdengo (bar—Marcello), Norman Treigle (bass—Colline), Warren Gadpaille (bass—Benoît/Alcindoro), Thomas Carter (sgr—Parpignol), Harold Crane (sgr—Custom House Official), Steve Harun (sgr—Sergeant), R. Cellini (cnd), New Orleans Opera Orch, New Orleans Opera Chorus *(rec Nov 1959)* VAI Audio 2-▲ VAIA 1119-2 [ADD]
Puccini, G.:La Bohème, w. Licia Albanese (sop—Mimi), Tatiana Menotti (sop—Musetta), Beniamino Gigli (ten—Rodolfo), Nello Palai (ten—Parpignol), Aristide Baracchi (bar—Schaunard), Afro Poli (bar—Marcello), Duilio Baronti (bass—Colline), Carlo Scattola (bass—Benoit/Alcindoro), U. Berrettoni (cnd), La Scala Orch, Vittore Veneziani (cnd), La Scala Chorus *(rec Feb-Mar 1938)*
Arkadia ("The 78's" series) 2-▲ 78009 [ADD]
Puccini, G.:La Bohème, w. T. Menotti (sop), B. Gigli (ten), A. Poli (bar), U. Berrettoni (cnd), La Scala Orch, La Scala Chorus [I] *(rec 1937)* EMI Classics ("Studio" series) 2-▲ CDHB 63335 (m) [ADD]
Puccini, G.:La Bohème, w. Tatiana Menotti (sop), Beniamino Gigli (ten), Afro Poli (bar), U. Berrettoni (cnd), La Scala Orch, La Scala Chorus *(rec Milan, 1938)* Phonographe 2-▲ PHG CD 5071
Puccini, G.:La Bohème, w. L. Hurley (sop), C. Bergonzi (ten), C. Harvuot (bar), M. Sereni (bar), N. Scott (bass), E. Flagello (bass), T. Schippers (cnd), New York Metropolitan Opera Orch, New York Metropolitan Opera Chorus *(rec Feb. 15, 1958)* Golden Age of Opera 2-▲ GAO 139/40 [ADD]
Puccini, G.:La Bohème, w. A. McKnight (sop), J. Peerce (ten), F. Valentino (bar), A. Toscanini (cnd), NBC SO, NBC Sym Chorus [I] RCA Gold Seal 2-▲ 60288-2-RG [ADD] 2-■ 60288-4-RG (CrO2)
Puccini, G.:Manon Lescaut, w. J. Bjoerling (ten), R. Merrill (bar), J. Perlea (cnd), Rome Opera Orch, Rome Opera Chorus [I] RCA Gold Seal 2-▲ 60573-2-RG [ADD]
Rossini, G.:Armida, w. M. Callas (sop), M. Filippeschi (ten), G. Raimondi (ten), T. Serafin (cnd), Florence Teatro Comunale Orch, Florence Teatro Comunale Chorus [I] *(rec live, Florence, 4/26/52)*
Melodram 2-▲ MEL 26024

Albani, Carlo (ten)
The World of Singing, Vol 4:The Italian School Part 1:Tenors before World War I, Book 2, w. Edoardo Garbin (ten), Fiorello Giraud (ten), Florencio Costantino (ten), Antonio Paoli (ten), Giuseppe Borgatti (ten), Enrico Caruso (ten), Amedeo Bassi (ten), Piero Schivazzi (ten), Elvino Ventura (ten), Giovanni Zenatello (ten) Enterprise ("Vocal Archives" series) 3-▲ ENT VA 2107

Alberghini, Simone (bar)
Liszt, F.:Via Crucis, w. Elisa Savani Zamballi (sop), Allesandra Mazzanti (org), Bonifacio Manduchi (cnd), Fabio de Bologne Polyphonic Chorus [orig version] Studio SM 2-▲ 2515 [DDD]

Albers, Henri (bass)
Gounod, C.:Roméo et Juliette, w. Yvonne Gall (sop—Juliette), Champell (sop—Stéphano), Jeanne Goulancourt (mez—Gertrude), Agustarello Affre (ten—Roméo), Edmond Tirmont (ten—Tybalt), Alexis Boyer (bar—Mercutio), Pierre Dupré (bar—Paris), Hypolite Belhomme (bar—Grégorio), Marcel Journet (bass—Frère Laurent), Henri Albers (bass—Capulet), Valermont (bass—The Duke), F. Rühlmann (cnd), Paris Opéra-Comique Orch, Paris Opéra-Comique Chorus *(rec 1912)* VAI Audio ▲ VAIA 1064-3 F

Albert (sop)
Haydn, J.:The Seven Last Words of Christ on the Cross, w. John Van Kesteren (ten), Otto Wiener (bar), Anatoli Babikian (bass), H. Scherchen (cnd), Vienna State Opera Orch, Vienna State Opera Chorus [oratorio version] [G] *(rec 1962)* MCA Classics 2-▲ MCAD2-9816 [AAD]

Albert, Adrienne (mez)
Monteverdi, C.:Vespro della Beata Vergine, w. Gloria Prosper (sop), Melvin Brown (ten), Richard Levitt (ten), Archi Drake (bass), R. Craft (cnd), Columbia Baroque Ensemble, Gregg Smith Singers, Texas Boys' Choir Sony Classical ("Essential Classics" series) 2-▲ SB2K 62656

Albert, E. (sgr)
Berlin, I.:Miss Liberty, w. A. McLerie (sgr), M. McCarty (sgr), E. Griffies (sgr) [1949 Broadway cast]
Sony Broadway ▲ SK 48015 ■ ST 48015

Albert, Laurence (bass)
Handel, G.F.:Messiah, w. Ruth Holton (sop), Vanessa Williamson (mez), James Griffett (ten), U. Walser (tpt), M. Brown (cnd), Gioia della Musica, Bmensky Akademicky Sbor
Allegro 2-▲ ALGDPCD 1068 [DDD]
Handel, G.F.:Messiah (sels), w. Ruth Holton (sop), Vanessa Williamson (mez), James Griffett (ten), M. Brown (cnd), Gioia della Musica, Bmensky Akademicky Sbor Allegro ▲ ALG PCD 1078 [DDD]

Albert, Michael (bass)
Hoffmann, E.T.A.:Undine, w. Barbara Baier (sop—Berthalda), Heidrun Plesch (sop—Undine), Corinna Tippe (sop—Die Herzogin), Maria Hiefinger (mez—Fisherman's Wife), Achim Schamberger (ten—Der Herzog), Johannes Beck (bar—Ritter Huldbrand von Ringstetten), Michael Albert (bass—Fisherman), Ulrich Bosch (bass—Heilmann), Bernd Hofmann (bass—Kühleborn), H. Dechant (cnd), Bamberg Youth Orch Bayer 3-▲ 100256/58 [DDD]

Alberti, Walter (bar)
Donizetti, G.:Don Pasquale, w. R. Scotto (sop), L. Alva (ten), F. Corena (bass), B. Rigacci (cnd), Florence Maggio Musicale Orch, Florence Maggio Musicale Chorus [I] *(rec live, Florence 3/1/67)*
Claque 2-▲ CLQ 2011 (m)
Donizetti, G.:Roberto Devereux, w. Montserrat Caballé (sop), Beverly Wolff (mez), Guido Fabbris (ten), Gianni Raimondi (ten), Paolo Badoer (sgr), Carlo Micalucci (sgr), Carlo Padoan (sgr), B. Bartoletti (cnd), Venice Teatro La Fenice Orch, Venice Teatro La Fenice Chorus
Great Opera Performances 2-▲ GOP 764
Donizetti, G.:Roberto Devereux (sels), w. M. Caballé (sop), L. Chookasian (mez), J. Oncina (ten), C.F. Cillario (cnd), *(orch & chorus unknown)*—9 arias from Acts 1 & 2 [I] *(rec live in Carnegie Hall, 12/16/65)* Standing Room Only 2-▲ SRO 801-2 (m) [ADD]
Leoncavallo, R.:Pagliacci, w. Mietta Sighele (sop), Richard Tucker (ten), Kari Murmela (bar), R. Muti (cnd), Florence Maggio Musicale Orch, Florence Maggio Musicale Chorus *(rec Florence , 1971)*
Memories ▲ MEM 4576 [ADD]
Verdi, G.:Aida, w. Jessye Norman (sop), Yannula Pappas (mez), Luigi Roni (b-bar), N. Sanzogno (cnd), Belgian Radio-TV Orch, Belgian Radio-TV Chorus *(rec live, Paris, May 4, 1973)*
Agorá ("Phoenix" series) 2-▲ 507

Albertini, Alberto (bar)
Cilea, F.:Gloria, w. M. Roberti (sop), A. M. Rota (cta), F. Labò (ten), L. Testi (bar), E. Campi (bass), F. Mazzoli (bass), F. Previtali (cnd), Turin RAI Orch, Turin RAI Chorus [I] *(rec live, Turin July 8, 1969)*
Memories ▲ HR 4472 [ADD]
Puccini, G.:Madama Butterfly, w. C. Petrella (sop—Madama Butterfly), M. Masini (mez—Suzuki), M. C. Foscale (sgr—Kate Pinkerton), F. Tagliavini (ten—Pinkerton), M. Caruso (ten—Goro), G. Taddei (bar—Sharpless), A. Albertini (bar—Yamadori), A. Biancardo (bass—Bonze), A. Questa (cnd), Turin RAI Orch, Cetra Chorus *(rec 1953)* Cetra Classic 2-▲ CDO 10 [AAD]
Verdi, G.:Un ballo in maschera, w. M. Curtis Verna (sop—Amelia), M. Erato (sop—Oscar), P. Tassinari (cta—Ulrica), F. Tagliavini (ten—Riccardo), G. Valdengo (bar—Renato), A. Albertini (bar—Silvano), M. Stefanoni (bass—Samuel), V. Susca (bass—Tom), A. Questa (cnd), Turin RAI SO, Turin RAI Chorus *(rec 1954)* Cetra Classic 2-▲ CDO 13 [AAD]
Verdi, G.:Rigoletto, w. L. Pagliughi (sop—Gilda), I. Colasanti (mez—Maddalena), F. Tagliavini (ten—Duca), A. Albertini (bar—Il Cavaliere Marullo), G. Taddei (bar—Rigoletto), G. Neri (bass—Sparafucile), A. Zerbini (bass—Conte di Monterone), A. Questa (cnd), Turin RSO, Turin Radio Chorus *(rec 1953)* Cetra Classics 2-▲ CDO 11 [AAD]

Alberts, Eunice (cta)
Bach, J.S.:St. John Passion, w. P. Curtin (sop), E. Thomann (sop), W. Kmentt, J. Van Kesteren (ten), R. Springer (bar), O. Wiener (bar), D. Smith (b-bar), F. Guthrie (bass), F. Lukasowsky (bass), H. Scherchen (cnd), Vienna State Opera Orch, Vienna Academy Chorus [G] *(rec ca 1960)* MCA Classics 2-▲ MCAD2-9804
Bach, J.S.:St. John Passion, w. P. Curtin (sop), W. Kmentt (ten), O. Weiner (ten), H. Scherchen (cnd), Vienna State Opera Orch, Vienna Academy Chorus *(rec 1962)* Enterprise ("Documents" series) ▲ ENT LV 925
Barber, S.:A Hand of Bridge, w. P. Neway (sop), W. Lewis (ten), P. Maero (bass), V. Golschmann (cnd), Symphony of the Air [E] *(rec ca. 1960)* Vanguard Classics ▲ OVC 4016 [ADD]
Fine, I.:Mutability, w. I. Fine (pno) [E] CRI ▲ CD 630 [ADD]

Albín, Osvald (nar)
Báchorek, M.:Lidice, w. Jana Stupárkova-Majtnerová (sop), Karel Průša (bar), Jan Vlasák (speaker), O. Trhlík (cnd), Ostrava Janáček PO, Ostrava Janáček Mixed Chorus *(rec Smetana Hall of Prague's Municipal House, Feb 10 & 11, 1988)* Panton ▲ 811338-2 [AAD]
Báchorek, M.:Music of, w. Otakar Brousek (nar), Jan Vlassak (nar), Brigita Šulcová (sop), Drahomira Drobková (cta), Karel Průša (bass), Pavel Kamas (sgr), Jan Kyzlink (sgr), Jana Stuperkova-Majtnerova (sgr), Bretislav Vojkuvka (sgr), O. Trhlík (cnd), Ostrava Janáček PO, Prague SO, Ostrava Janáček Chorus, Ostrava Women's Chamber Chorus, Permoník Children's Chorus—Lidice; Stereofonietta; Hukvald Poem Panton ▲ PAN 811338 [AAD/DDD]

Albrecht, Johanna (mez)
Berio, L.:Surabaya Johnny, w. J. Thome (cnd), Orch of Our Time Vox Box 2-▲ CDX 5144

Albright, L. (sgr)
Mancini, H.:Film Music, w. A. Williams (sgr), J. Mathis (sgr), B. Hackett (sgr), B. Greco (sgr), C. Byrd (sgr), P. Page (sgr), Mancini (cnd), Costa Orch, Conniff Orch, Mancini Orch—sels from Breakfast at Tiffany's; Peter Gunn; Mr. Lucky & others Columbia/Legacy ▲ CK 66505

Alda, R. (sgr)
Loesser, F.:Guys and Dolls, w. V. Blaine (sgr), S. Levene (sgr) [1950 Broadway cast] MCA Classics ▲ MCAD 10301 [AAD] ■ MCAC 10301

Aldenhoff, Bernd (ten)
Strauss, R.:Die ägyptische Helena, w. Annelies Kupper (sop—Aithra), Leonie Rysanek (sop—Helena), Ira Malaniuk (cta—Omniscient Seashell), Bernd Aldenhoff (ten—Menelas), Richard Holm (ten—Da-ud), Hermann Uhde (bar—Altair), J. Keilberth (cnd), Bavarian State Opera Orch, Bavarian State Opera Chorus *(rec Munich Opera Festival, Prince Regent Theater, Aug 10, 1956)* Orfeo d'or 2-▲ 424962
Strauss, R.:Die ägyptische Helena, w. L. Rysanek (sop), A. Kupper (sop), H. Uhde (bar), J. Keilberth (cnd), Bavarian State Opera Orch, Bavarian State Opera Chorus [G] *(rec live, Munich, 8/27/56)* Melodram 2-▲ MEL 27066 (m) [AAD]
Wagner, R.:Götterdämmerung, w. Birgit Nilsson (sop—Brünnhilde), Leonie Rysanek (sop—Gutrune), Gerda Sommerschuh (sop—Woglinde), Elisabeth Lindermeier (sop—Wellgunde), Ruth Michaelis (sop—Flohilde), Marianne Schech (sop—Dritte Norne), Ira Malaniuk (mez—Waltraute), Irmgarth Barth (mez—Erste Norne), Hertha Töpper (mez—Zweite Norne), Bernd Aldenhoff (ten—Siegfried), Hermann Uhde (bar—Gunther), Gottlob Frick (bass—Hagen), H. Knappertsbusch (cnd), Bavarian State Opera Orch, Bavarian State Opera Chorus *(rec live, Prinzregententheater, Sept. 1, 1955)* Orfeo 4-▲ 356944 (m)
Wagner, R.:Götterdämmerung (sels), w. A. Varnay (sop), E. Grümmer (sop), H. Uhde (bar), G. Frick (bass), J. Greindl (bass), H. Knappertsbusch (cnd), Bavarian State Opera Orch, Bayreuth Festival Orch, Bavarian State Opera Chorus, Bayreuth Festival Chorus [G] *(rec live 1955 & 1957)* Melodram 4-▲ MEL 46106 (m) [AAD]
Wagner, R.:Die Meistersinger von Nürnberg, w. Tiana Lemnitz (sop—Eva), Bernd Aldenhoff (ten—Walther von Stolzing), Gerhard Unger (ten—David), Ferdinand Frantz (b-bar—Hans Sachs), Kurt Boehme (bass—Veit Pogner), Heinrich Pflanzl (bass—Sixtus Beckmesser), R. Kempe (cnd), Saxon State Orch *(rec Dresden, 1951)* Myto 4-▲ MCD 961138
Wagner, R.:Siegfried, w. A. Varnay (sop), R. Siewert (cta), P. Kuen (ten), S. Björling (bar), H. Pflanzl (bass), F. Dalberg (bass), H. von Karajan (cnd), Bayreuth Festival Orch, Bayreuth Festival Chorus [G] *(rec live 1951)* Melodram 4-▲ MEL 46106 (m) [AAD]
Wagner, R.:Siegfried (sels), w. A. Varnay (sop), H. Knappertsbusch (cnd), Bayreuth Festival Orch, Bayreuth Festival Chorus—Act 3 Scene 3 [G] *(rec live 1957)* Arkadia 4-▲ 443 [AAD]

Alderson, Ann (sgr)
Catholic Classics, Vol. 1, w. Richard Alderson (sgr), Stacy Kowalczyk (sgr), Carey Lovett (sgr) Gia ▲ GIA 375

Alderson, Richard (sgr)
Catholic Classics, Vol. 1, w. A. Alderson (sgr), Stacy Kowalczyk (sgr), Carey Lovett (sgr) Gia ▲ GIA 375
Rapchak, L.:The Lifework of Juan Diaz, w. C. Loverde (sop), R. Hovencamp (sgr), D. Rowader (sgr), L. Rapchak (cnd), Chicago Chamber Opera Albany ▲ TROY 091 [DDD]

Aleksashkin, Sergei (bass)
Shostakovich, D.:Sym 14, w. Elena Prokina (sop), Wilfried Rehm (vc), E. Inbal (cnd), Vienna SO *(rec Konzerthaus, Vienna, Apr 26-29, 1993)* Denon ▲ CO 78821 [DDD]

Aler, John (ten)
Bach, J.S.:Mass in b, BWV 232, w. S. McNair (sop), G. Simpson (mez), D. Ziegler (mez), W. Stone (bar), T. Paul (bass), R. Shaw (cnd), Atlanta SO, Atlanta Chamber Chorus [L] Telarc 2-▲ CD 80233 [DDD]
Bartók, B.:Cant Profana, "The Giant Stags", w. J. Tomlinson (bass), P. Boulez (cnd), Chicago SO, Chicago Sym Chorus Deutsche Grammophon ▲ 435863-2 [DDD]
Basic 100, Vol. 60, w. Barbara Hendricks (sop), Håkan Hagegård (bar), London SO [cnd:Eduardo Mata] RCA Victor ▲ 09026-68085-2 ■ 09026-68085-4
Beethoven, L. van:Missa Solemnis, w. S. McNair (sop), Janice Taylor (mez), T. Krause (bar), R. Shaw (cnd), Atlanta SO, Atlanta Sym Chorus [L] Telarc 2-▲ CD 80150 [DDD]
Berlioz, H.:L'Enfance du Christ, w. Jean Rigby (mez), Gerald Finley (ten), Alastair Miles (bar), Gwynne Howell (bass), M. Best (cnd), Cordon Orch, Corydon Singers, St. Paul's Cathedral Choir Hyperion 2-▲ CDA 66991/2
Berlioz, H.:L'Enfance du Christ, w. M. Zimmermann (mez), E. Wilm Schulte (bass), S. Dean (bass), P. Kang (bass), E. Inbal (cnd), Frankfurt RSO, Cologne Radio Chorus [F] Denon 2-▲ CO 76863/4 [DDD]
Berlioz, H.:Requiem, "Grande Messe des Morts", w. R. Shaw (cnd), Atlanta SO, Atlanta Sym Chorus [L] Telarc 2-▲ CD 80109-2 [DDD]
Berlioz, H.:Songs, w. F. Pollet (sop), A. S. von Otter (mez), T. Allen (bar), C. Garben (cnd), *(orch unknown)* Deutsche Grammophon 2-▲ 435860-2
Bizet, G.:Les Pêcheurs de perles, w. B. Hendricks (sop), G. Quilico (bar), M. Plasson (cnd), Toulouse Capitole Orch, Toulouse Capitole Chorus [F] EMI Classics 2-▲ CDCB 49837 [DDD]
Charpentier, M.-A.:Magnificat, w. D. Upshaw (sop), A. Murray (mez), E. Robinson (mez), K. Moll (bass), N. Marriner (cnd), Academy of St. Martin in the Fields, Academy of St. Martin in the Fields Chorus EMI Classics ▲ CDC 54284
Charpentier, M.-A.:Te Deum in C, w. D. Upshaw (sop), A. Murray (mez), E. Robinson (mez), K. Moll (bass), N. Marriner (cnd), Academy of St. Martin in the Fields, Academy of St. Martin in the Fields Chorus EMI Classics ▲ CDC 54284
Dvořák, A.:Stabat Mater, w. K. Erickson (sop), C. Carlson (mez), J. Cheek (bass), Z. Macal (cnd), New Jersey SO, J. Flummerfeldt (cnd), Westminster Sym Choir *(rec Feb. 8-11, 1994)* Delos 2-▲ DE 3161 [DDD]
Enescu, G.:Oedipe, w. B. Hendricks (sop), B. Fassbaender (mez), M. Lipovšek (mez), J. Taillon (mez), N. Gedda (ten), G. Bacquier (bar), Quilico (bar), J. Van Dam (bass-bar), L. Foster (cnd), Monte Carlo PO, Orféon Donostiarra, Petits Chanteurs de Monaco [F] EMI Classics 2-▲ CDCB 54011 [DDD]
Gazzaniga, G.:Don Giovanni, w. P. Coburn (sop), J. Kaufmann (sop), R. Swensen (ten), J.-L. Chaignaud (bar), G. von Kannen (bass), A. Scharinger (bass), S. Soltesz (cnd), Munich RSO, Munich Radio Chorus [I] Orfeo 2-▲ 214902 [DDD]
Gluck, C.W.:Iphigénie en Aulide, w. L. Dawson (sop), A. S. von Otter (mez), J. Van Dam (b-bar), Lyon Opera Orch, J. E. Gardiner (cnd), Monteverdi Choir London Erato ("Musifrance" series) 2-▲ 2292-45003-2-ZA [DDD]

Aler, John (ten) (cont.)
Gluck, C.W.:Iphigénie en Tauride, w. D. Montague (mez), T. Allen (bar), R. Massis (bar), J.E. Gardiner (cnd), Lyon Opera Orch [F] Philips 2-▲ 416148-2 [DDD]
Gounod, C.:Mors et vita, w. B. Hendricks (sop), N. Denize (mez), J. Van Dam (b-bar), M. Plasson (cnd), Toulouse Capitole Orch, Orféon Donostiarra [F] *(rec 1/92)* EMI Classics 2-▲ CDCB 54459
Handel, G.F.:Joshua, w. Julianne Baird (sop), D'Anna Fortunato (mez), John Ostendorf (b-bar), R. Palmer (cnd), Brewer CO, Brewer Chorus [period instrs] Newport Classic 2-▲ NPD 85515/1-2 [DDD]
Handel, G.F.:Messiah, w. Kathleen Battle (sop), Florence Quivar (mez), Samuel Ramey (bass), A. Davis (cnd), Toronto SO, Mendelssohn Club Chorus Philadelphia [E] EMI Classics ▲ CDC 49407 [DDD]; ■ 4DS 49407 (D)
Handel, G.F.:Messiah, w. Kathleen Battle (sop), Florence Quivar (mez), Samuel Ramey (bass), A. Davis (cnd), Toronto SO, Mendelssohn Club Chorus Philadelphia [E] EMI Classics 2-▲ CDCB 49027 [DDD]; ■ 4D2S 49027 (D)
Handel, G.F.:Messiah (sels), w. Judith Blegen (sop), Katherine Ciesinski (mez), John Cheek (bass), R. Westenburg (cnd), Musica Sacra, Musica Sacra Chorus RCA Silver Seal ▲ 60481-2-RV [DDD]; ■ 60481-4-RV (CrO2)
Handel, G.F.:Semele, w. Kathleen Battle (sop), Sylvia McNair (sop), Marylin Horne (mez), Michael Chance (ct), Samuel Ramey (bass), J. Nelson (cnd), English CO, Ambrosian Opera Chorus Deutsche Grammophon 3-▲ 435782-2 -
Handel, G.F.:Sosarme, Rè di Media, w. Julinne Baird (sop—Elmira), D'Anna Fortunato (mez—Sosarme), Jennifer Lane (mez—Erenice), Drew Minter (ct—Melo), Rarmond Pellerin (ct—Argone), John Aler (ten—King Haliate), Nathaniel Watson (bass—Varo), Edward Brewer (hpd) Newport Classic 2-▲ NPT 85575 [DDD]
Haydn, J.:Die Jahreszeiten, w. Arleen Auger (sop), Håkan Hågegard (bar), J. Revzen (cnd), St. Paul CO, Minnesota Chorale [G] Koch International Classics 2-▲ KIC 7065-2 [DDD]
Lehár, F.:Die lustige Witwe, w. F. Lott (sop), E. Szmytka (sop), T. Hampson (b-bar), D. Bogarde (nar), F. Welser-Möst (cnd), London PO, Glyndebourne Festival Chorus EMI Classics ▲ CDCB 55152
Mozart, W.A.:Così fan tutte, w. Carol Vaness (sop), Delores Ziegler (mez), C. Watson (cta), D. Duesing (bar), C. Desderi (bar), B. Haitink (cnd), London PO, Glyndebourne Festival Chorus EMI Classics 3-▲ CDCC 47727
Mozart, W.A.:Missa, K.427, w. Edith Wiens (sop), Delores Ziegler (mez), William Stone (bar), R. Shaw (cnd), Atlanta SO, Atlanta Sym Chorus [L] Telarc 2-▲ CD 80150 [DDD]
Orff, C.:Carmina burana, w. Barbara Hendricks (sop), Håakan Hagegård (bar), E. Mata (cnd), London SO, London Sym Chorus RCA Victor ▲ 09026-68085-2; ■ 09026-68085-4
Orff, C.:Carmina burana, w. E. Gruberova (sop), T. Hampson (bar), S. Ozawa (cnd), Berlin PO, Berlin Cathedral Boys' Choir, Shin-Yuh Kai Chorus [G, L] Philips ▲ 422363-2 [DDD] □ 422363-5
Orff, C.:Carmina burana, w. S. McNair (sop), Håkan Hagegård (bar), L. Slatkin (cnd), St. Louis SO RCA Red Seal ▲ 09026-61673-2; ■ 09026-61673-4
Rossini, G.:Péchés de vieillesse (sels), w. A. Auger (sop), J. Larmore (mez), S. Kimbrough (bar), D. Baldwin (pno)—Les Amants de Séville; Chanson de Zora; L'Esule; La Fioraia Fiorentina; La Lontananza; Musique Anodine; L'Orpheline du Tyrol; La Passegiata Quartettino; L'Ultimo Ricordo; Un Sou Complainte [I,F] Arabesque ▲ Z 6623 [ADD]
Stravinsky, I.:Cant Sop, w. Y. Kenny (sop), E.-P. Salonen (cnd), London Sinfonietta, London Sinfonietta Chorus Sony Classical ▲ SK 46667
Stravinsky, I.:Perséphone, w. I. Jacob (nar), R. Craft (cnd), Orch of St. Luke, Gregg Smith Singers, Newark Boys' Chorus MusicMasters ▲ 01612-67103-2
Stravinsky, I.:Pulcinella, w. Y. Kenny (sop), J. Tomlinson (bass), E.-P. Salonen (cnd), London Sinfonietta Sony Classical ▲ SK 45965
Stravinsky, I.:Renard, w. N. Robson (ten), D. Wilson-Johnson (bar), J. Tomlinson (bass), E.-P. Salonen (cnd), London Sinfonietta Sony Classical ▲ SK 45965

Alerie, P. (sgr)
Bizet, G.:Les Pêcheurs de perles, w. L. Simoneau (ten), X. Depraz (bass), J. Fournet (cnd), Lamoureux Orch *(rec 1953)* Philips 2-▲ 434782-2

Alessio, Roberto d' (ten)
Verdi, G.:Falstaff, w. Pia Tassinari (sop—Alice Ford), Ines Alfani Tellini (sop—Nannetta), Aurora Buades (mez—Quickly), Rita Monticone (mez—Meg Page), Roberto D'Alessio (ten—Fenton), Giuseppe Nessi (ten—Bardolfo), Emilio Venturini (ten—Dr. Caius), Emilio Ghirardini (bar—Ford), Giacomo Rimini (bar—Sir John Falstaff), Salvatore Baccaloni (bass—Pistola), L. Molajoli (cnd), Milan SO, La Scala Chorus *(rec La Scala Theatre, Milan, Apr. 1932)* VAI Audio 2-▲ VAIA 1098-2

Alessio, Ugo d' (ten)
Donizetti, G.:Don Pasquale, w. Gianna D'Angelo (sop), Alfredo Kraus (ten), Renato Capecchi (bar), Fernando Corena (bass), A. Erede (cnd), Naples Teatro San Carlo Orch, Naples Teatro San Carlo Chorus Great Opera Performances 2-▲ GOP 763
Donizetti, G.:Don Pasquale, w. G. D'Angelo (sop), A. Kraus (ten), R. Capecchi (bar), F. Corena (bass), A. Erede (cnd), Naples Teatro San Carlo Orch, Naples Teatro San Carlo Chorus [I] *(rec live in Edinburgh, 9/7/63)* Verona 2-▲ 27023/24 (m) [AAD]

Alexander (bar)
Lehár, F.:Die lustige Witwe (sels), w. I. Hallstein (sop), L. Popp (sop), H. Hoppe (ten), B. Kusche (bar), Marszalek (cnd), Operretta Orch, Operetta Chorus [G] Acanta ▲ CD 43455 [DDD]

Alexander (sgr)
Lehár, F.:Das Land des Lächelns (sels), w. I. Hallstein (sop), Renate Holm (sop), Heinz Hoppe (ten), Marszalek (cnd), Operretta Orch, Operetta Chorus [G] Acanta ▲ CD 43494 [DDD]

Alexander, John (ten)
Bellini, V.:Norma, w. J. Sutherland (sop), M. Horne (mez), R. Cross (bass), R. Bonynge (cnd), London SO, London Sym Chorus [I] London 3-▲ 425488-2 [ADD]
Bellini, V.:Norma (sels), w. J. Sutherland (sop), M. Horne (mez), R. Cross (bass), R. Bonynge (cnd), London SO, London Sym Chorus [I] London ("Opera Gala" series) ▲ 421886-2 [ADD]

Alexander, Pamela (sop)
Weill, K.:Songs, w. Dale Wolford (sax/syn), Ivan Rosenblum (kbd)—Complainte de la Seine; Le Roi d'Aquitaine; Youkali; Je ne t'aime pas; Le train du Ciel; Scène au Dancing; Es regnet; Der Abschiedsbrief; Pirate Jenny; Barbara Song; Die Muschel von Margate; Nanna's Lied; What Did She Get, That Soldier's Wife?; Surabaya Johnny *(rec Bay View Studios, Richmond, CA)* Laurel ▲ LR 855

Alexander, Roberta (sop)
Andriessen, H.:Music of, w. Paul Verhey (fl), Ernestine Stoop (hp), D. Porcelijn (cnd), Netherlands Radio CO—Miroir de Peine; Magna res est amor; Fiat Domine; Vars & Fugue on a Theme by Kuhnau; Vars on a Theme by Couperin; Chromatic Vars NM Classics ▲ NM 92023
Beethoven, L. van:Sym 9, "Choral Sym", w. Florence Quivar (cta), Gary Lakes (ten), Paul Plishka (bass), A. Previn (cnd), Royal PO RCA Red Seal ▲ 09026-60363-2
Diepenbrock, A.:Songs, w. Christa Pfeiler (mez), Jard Van Ness (mez), Robert Holl (bass), Daniel Esser (vc), Rudolf Jansen (pno)—Berceuse; Clair de lune; Mandoline; L'Invitation au voyage; Les Chats; Receuillement; Puisque l'aube grandit; Incantation; En Sourdine; La Chanson de l'hypertrophique NM Classics ▲ NM 92051
Gershwin, G.:Porgy & Bess (sels), w. G. Baker (bar), Z. Mehta (cnd), New York PO, New York Choral Artists—Introduction & Summertime; A woman is a sometime thing; Overflow; Since I lose my man; The promise' lan'; I got plenty o' nuttin'; Bess, you is my woman now; O, I can't sit down; It ain't necesssarily so; There's a boat dat's leavin' soon for New York; O, Lawd I'm on my way [E] Teldec ▲ 2292-46318-2 [DDD]
Gershwin, G.:Porgy & Bess (sels), w. S. Estes (bass), L. Slatkin (cnd), Berlin RSO, Berlin Radio Chorus [E] Philips ▲ 412720-2 [DDD]
Goldschmidt, B.:Der gewaltige Hahnrei, w. M. Posselt (sop), H. Lawrence (sop), R. Wörle (ten), M. Kraus (ten), M. Petzold (ten), C. Otelli (bar), L. Zagrosek (cnd), German SO, Berlin Radio Chorus London ▲ 440850-2 [DDD]
Goldschmidt, B.:Mediterranean Songs, w. M. Posselt (sop), H. Lawrence (sop), R. Wörle (ten), M. Kraus (ten), M. Petzold (ten), C. Otelli (bar), L. Zagrosek (cnd), German SO, Berlin Radio Chorus London ▲ 440850-2 [DDD]
Handel, G.F.:Apollo e Dafne, w. T. Hampson (bass), N. Harnoncourt (cnd), Vienna Concentus Musicus Teldec ("Das alte Werk" series) ▲ 98645-2

Alexander, Roberta (sop) (cont.)
Handel, G.F.:Giulio Cesare in Egitto (sels), w. Thomas Hampson (bass), N. Harnoncourt (cnd), Vienna Concentus Musicus Teldec ("Das alte Werk" series) ▲ 98645-2
Handel, G.F.:Samson, w. Maria Venuti (sop), Jochen Kowalski (ct), Anthony Rolfe Johnson (ten), Aalstair Miles (bass), Anton Scharinger (bass), N. Harnoncourt (cnd), Vienna Concentus Musicus, Arnold Schoenberg Choir Teldec ▲ 74871-2
Handel, G.F.:Theodora, w. Jard van Nes (cta), Jochen Kowalski (ct), Hans-Peter Blochwitz (ten), Anton Scharinger (bass), N. Harnoncourt (cnd), Vienna Concentus Musicus, Arnold Schoenberg Choir [E] Teldec 2-▲ 2292-46447-2 [DDD]
Mahler, G.:Sym 4, w. B. Haitink (cnd), Royal Concertgebouw Orch [G] Philips ▲ 412119-2 [DDD]
Mozart, W.A.:Don Giovanni, w. E. Gruberova (sop), B. Bonney (sop), T. Hampson (bar), N. Harnoncourt (cnd), Royal Concertgebouw Orch [I] Teldec 3-▲ 2292-44184-2 [DDD]
Telemann, G.P.:Der Tag des Gerichts, w. K. Equiliz (ten), M. Van Egmond (bass), N. Harnoncourt (cnd), Vienna Concentus Musicus, Monteverdi Choir Hamburg Teldec 2-▲ 77621-2
Telemann, G.P.:Ino, w. K. Equiliz (ten), M. Van Egmond (bar), N. Harnoncourt (cnd), Vienna Concentus Musicus, Monteverdi Choir London Teldec 2-▲ 9031-77621-2
Wagner, R.:Die Feen, w. L. E. Gray (sop), K. Lövaas (sop), K. Láki (sop), Anderson (sop), R. Hermann (bar), K. Moll (bass), W. Sawallisch (cnd), Bavarian RSO, Bavarian Radio Chorus [G] *(rec live, Munich Opera Fest. 1983)* Orfeo 3-▲ 062833 [DDD]

Alexander, Van (sgr)
Romberg, S.:Music of (operetta sels), w. D. Kirsten (sop), MacRae (sgr), *(orch & chorus unknown)* —selections from *Desert Song, New Moon, Student Prince* EMI Classics ("Studio" series) ▲ CDM 69052

Alexandersson, Sven-Erik (ten)
Dallapiccola, L.:Il Prigioniero, w. Phyllis Bryn-Julson (sop), Howard Haskin (ten), Jorma Hynninen (bar), Lage Wedin (bar), E.-P. Salonen (cnd), Swedish RSO, Eric Ericson Chamber Choir Sony Classical ▲ SK 68323
Pettersson, G.A.:Vox Humana, w. Marianne Mellnäs (sop), Margot Rödin (alt), Erland Hagegård (bar), S. Westerberg (cnd), Swedish RSO, Swedish Radio Chorus *(rec Royal Swedish Academy of Music, Stockholm, Sweden, Mar. 22 & May 24, 1976)* BIS ▲ CD 55 [AAD]

Alexandrova, Mariela (sop)
Britten, H.:Missa brevis, w. T. Atanassov (sop), A. Atanassov (org), A. Blagoeva (cnd), Sofia Boys' Choir [arr. A. Blagoeva for sopranos, organ & boy's chorus] Gega ▲ GD 153 [DDD]

Alexandrova, Olga (mez)
Mahler, G.:Sym 2, w. Natalia Guerassimova (sop), E. Svetlanov (cnd), Russian State SO, Russian Radio-TV Large Academic Choir Russian Season 2-▲ 288136.37
Mahler, G.:Sym 3, w. E. Svetlanov (cnd), Russian State SO, Russian Academic Choir, Moscow Boys' Cappella *(rec Large Hall of the Conservatory, Moscow, Dec. 1994)* Russian Season 2-▲ RUS 288111/12 [DDD]

Alexashkin, Sergei (bass)
Tchaikovsky, P.:Iolanta, w. Galina Gorchakova (sop), Nikolai Gassiev (ten), Gegam Grigorian (ten), Dmitri Hvorostovsky (bar), Nikolai Putilin (bar), Gennady Bezzubenkov (bass), Larissa Diadkova (sgr), Olga Korzhenskaya (sgr), Tatyana Kravtsova (sgr), V. Gergiev (cnd), Kirov Opera Orch, Kirov Opera Chorus *(rec Mariinsky Theatre, St. Petersburg)* Philips 2-▲ 442796-2

Alexiou, Haris (sgr)
Hadjidakis, M.:Film Music—Topkapi; Zorba the Greek; Blade Runner; Missing; Z; Never on Sunday; Phaedra Silva America ▲ SSD 1052
Hatzinassios, G.:Film Music—Topkapi; Zorba the Greek; Blade Runner; Missing; Z; Never on Sunday; Phaedra Silva America ▲ SSD 1052
Theodorakis, M.:Film Music—Topkapi; Zorba the Greek; Blade Runner; Missing; Z; Never on Sunday; Phaedra Silva America ▲ SSD 1052
Vangelis:Film Music—Topkapi; Zorba the Greek; Blade Runner; Missing; Z; Never on Sunday; Phaedra Silva America ▲ SSD 1052
Yanni:Film Music—Topkapi; Zorba the Greek; Blade Runner; Missing; Z; Never on Sunday; Phaedra Silva America ▲ SSD 1052

Alfonso, H. (sop)
Luzzaschi, L.:Madrigali, w. C. Miatello (sop), M. Pennichi (sop), S. Vartolo (hpd) Musique d'Abord ▲ HMA 1901136

Algorta, Jorge (bass)
Bizet, G.:Carmen, w. Laura Bustamante (sop—Frasquita), Ximena Riveros (sop—Mercedes), Nancy Stokes (sop—Micaela), Regina Resnik (mez—Carmen), Plácido Domingo (ten—Don José), Ismildo Tedeschi (ten—Remendado), Ramon Vinay (ten—Escamillo), Juan Charles (ten/bar—Dancaire), Agustin Letelier (bar—Morles), Jorge Algorta (bass—Zuniga), A. Guadagno (cnd), Santiago Teatro Municipale Orch, Santiago Teatro Municipale Chorus *(rec Santiago Municipal Theater, Sept. 4, 1967)* Legato Classics 2-▲ LCD 194-2 [ADD]

Aliberti, Lucia (sop)
Bellini, V.:Arias, w. L. Gardelli (cnd), Munich RSO—Il Pirata—Oh! s'io potessi...Col sorriso d'innocenza; I Puritani—Qui la voce sua soave; La Sonnambula—Ah! non credea mirarti [I] Orfeo ▲ 119841
Bellini, V.:Beatrice di Tenda, w. C. Capasso (treble), M. Thompson (ten), P. Gavanelli (bass), F. Luisi (cnd), Berlin German Opera Orch, Berlin German Opera Chorus Berlin Classics 2-▲ BER 1042 [DDD]
Bellini, V.:Il pirata, w. Roberto Frontali (sgr), Stuart Neill (sgr), José Guadalupe Reyes (sgr), M. Viotti (cnd), Berlin German Opera Orch, Berlin German Opera Chorus Berlin Classics 2-▲ BER 1115 [DDD]
Bellini, V.:I Puritani (sels), w. Giuseppe Sabbatini (ten), Carlos Alvarez (bass), Michele Pertusi (bass)—All'erta! All'erta!; A te, o cara, amor talora; Son vergin vezzosa; Ah..Dolor! Ah Terror!; Cinta di fiori e col ben crin disciolto; O Rendetemi la speme—Vien, Diletto; Il Rival salvar tu dei—Suoni la tromba Laserlight ▲ 14208 [DDD]
Bellini, V.:La straniera, w. L. Alberti (sop—Alaide), S. Mingardo (mez—Isoletta), V. Bello (ten—Arturo), R. Frontale (bar—Il Barone di Valdeburgo), V. Sagona (bass—Il signore di Montalino), P. Zizich (bass—Osburgo), G. Masini (cnd), Trieste Teatro Comunale Giuseppe Verdi Orch, Trieste Teatro Comunale G. Verdi Chorus *(rec Dec. 1990)* Ricordi ▲ RFCD 2015 [DDD]
Donizetti, G.:Arias, w. L. Gardelli (cnd), Munich RSO [I] Orfeo ▲ 119841
Famous Opera Arias, w. Munich Radio Orch [cnd:L. Gardelli] Orfeo ▲ C 119841 [DDD] ■ M 119841 (D)
Piccinni, N.:La cecchina, ossia la buona figliola, w. Lucia Alberti (sop—Il Cavaliere Armidoro), Emilia Ravaglia (sop—La Marchesa), Margherita Rinaldi (sop—Cecchina), Elena Zilio (mez—Paoluccia), Ugo Benelli (bar—Il Marchese della Conchiglia), Alessandro Corbelli (bar—Mengotto), Enzo Dara (bar—Tagliaferro), Renata Baldisseri (sgr—Sandrina), G. Gelmetti (cnd), Rome Opera Orch, Rome Opera Chorus *(rec Rome, Feb 4, 1981)* Italia 2-▲ CDC 95 [ADD]
Verdi, G.:La traviata, w. M. Dvorsky (ten), R. Bruson (bar), R. Paternostro (cnd), Tokyo PO, Tokyo Phil Chorus [I] *(rec live, Suntory Hall, Tokyo)* Capriccio 2-▲ 10274/75 [DDD]

Allam, Roger (nar)
Vaughan Williams, R.:Sym 7, w. D. Labelle (sop), R. Leppard (cnd), Indianapolis SO, Indianapolis Symphonic Women's Choir Koss Classics ▲ KC 2214 [DDD]

Allan, Richard Van (bass)
Mozart, W.A.:Don Giovanni, w. C. Vaness (sop), M. Ewing (sop), E. Gale (sop), K. Lewis (ten), T. Allen (bar), B. Haitink (cnd), London PO, Glyndebourne Festival Chorus [I] EMI Classics 3-▲ CDCC 47036 [DDD]
Sullivan, A.:The Mikado, w. M. McLaughlin (sop), A. Howells (mez), J. Watson (sop), F. Palmer (sop/mez), D. Adams (bass), A. Rolfe Johnson (ten), R. Stuart (bar), N. Folwell (bar), C. Mackerras (cnd), Welsh National Opera Orch, Welsh National Opera Chorus—Ov & dialogue omitted [E] Telarc ▲ CD 80284 [DDD]; ■ CS 30284 (D)
Sullivan, A.:The Mikado, w. L. Garrett (sop), J. Rigby (mez), S. Bullock (sop), F. Palmer (sop/mez), B. Bottone (ten), R. Angas (bass), E. Idle (bar), M. Richardson (bar), P. Robinson (cnd), English National Opera Orch, English Opera Group Chorus—sels [E] MCA Classics ▲ MCAD 6215 [DDD]; ■ MCAC 6215 (D)

Allan, Richard Van (bass) (cont.)
Sullivan, A.:The Pirates of Penzance, w. R. Evans (sop—Mabel), G. Knight (mez—Ruth), J. Gossage (mez—Edith), J. M. Ainsley (ten—Frederic), R. Suart (bar—Maj.-Gen. Stanley), N. Folwell (bar—Samuel), D. Adams (b-bar—Pirate King), R. Van Allan (bass—Sergeant of Police), C. Mackerras (cnd), Welsh National Opera Orch, Welsh National Opera Chorus *(rec May 4-6, 1993)* Telarc ▲ CD 80353 [DDD]; ■ CS 30353
Vaughan Williams, R.:Hugh the Dover, w. R. Evans (sop), S. Walker (mez), B. Bottone (ter), N. Jenkins (ten), A. Opie (bar), M. Best (cnd), Corydon Orch, Corydon Singers, New London Children's Choir Hyperion 2-▲ CDA 66901/02
Verdi, G.:La traviata, w. Angela Gheorghiu (sop—Violetta), Leah-Marian Jones (mez—Flora Bervoix), Gillian Knight (mez—Annina), Robin Leggate (ten—Gastone), Frank Lopardo (ten—Alfredo Germont), Rodney Gibson (ten—Servo di Flora), Neil Griffiths (ten—Giuseppe), Mark Beesley (bar—Dottore Grenvile), Leo Nucci (bar—Giorgio Germont), Richard Van Allan (bass—Barone Douphol), Roderick Earle (bass—Marquese d'Obigny), Bryan Secombe (bass—Commissionario), G. Solti (cnd), Royal Opera House Orch, Royal Opera House Chorus Covent Garden *(rec live, Royal Opera House, Covent Garden, Dec. 1994)* London 2-▲ 448119-2

Allanson, Peter (bar)
An Album of Victorian Song, Vol. 1, w. Stephen Betteridge (pno) Symposium ▲ SYM 1074
Harrison, M.:The May Song, w. Stephen Betteridge (pno) *(rec 1989)* Symposium ▲ 1075
Horder, M.:Songs (40), w. Winifred Soutter (sop), Carl Murray (bar), Stephen Betteridge (pno), Gordon Kirkwood (pno) Symposium ▲ 1039

Allemano, Carlo (ten)
Mascagni, P.:Messa di Gloria, w. Domenico Colaianni (bar), M. Letonja (cnd), Italian International Opera Orch, Bratislava Camera Chorus Nuova Era ▲ NUO CD 7270

Allen, Jo Harvey (nar)
Allen, T.:Bleeder, w. Jo Harvey Allen (nar—The Woman), Panhandle Mystery Band ¿What Next? ▲ WN 0013 F

Allen, Richard (cant)
Shomeir Yisrael:A Musical Service for Friday Evening for Solo, Choir, Organ & Instruments, w. Allen, Richard (cant), Philadelphia Voces Novae et Antiquae [cnd:Ben Steinberg] Arkay ▲ ARK 6126 [DDD] ■ ARK 4126

Allen, Richard Van (bass)
Verdi, G.:La traviata (sels), w. Ileana Cotrubas (sop—Violetta), Elizabeth Bainbridge (mez—Annina), José Carreras (ten—Alfredo), Richard Creeger (ten—Gastone), Victor Braun (bar—Germont), Richard Van Allen (bass—Grenvil), J. Pritchard (cnd), *(orch unknown)*—Libiamo ne' lietialici; Oh, qual pallor!...Un di felice; Ebben? Che diavol fate?...Amor, dunque non piu; E strano!...Ah, fors'e lui; Follie! Follie!...Sempre libera; Lunge da lei...De' miei bollenti spiriti; Che fai?...Amami, Alfredo; Invitato a qui seguirmi...Ogni suo aver tal femmina; Signora...Parigi, o cara; Ah, non piu...Ah, gran Dio, morir si giovine; E strano! Cessarono gli spasimi del dolore *(rec Apr 15, 1974)* Legato Classics 2-▲ LCD 201-2

Allen, Stiles (sop)
Vaughan Williams, R.:Serenade to Music, w. I. Baillie (sop), E. Suddaby (sop), E. Turner (sop), M. Balfour (cta), A. Desmond (cta), M. Brunskill (cta), M. Jarred (cta), H. Nash (ten), W. Widdop (ten), P. Jones (ten), F. Titterton (ten), R. Henderson (bass), R. Easton (bass), H. Williams (bass), N. Allin (bass), H. J. Wood (cnd), BBC SO Dutton Laboratories ▲ CDAX 8004 [ADD]
Vaughan Williams, R.:Serenade to Music, w. I. Baillie (sop), E. Suddaby (sop), S. Allen (sop), E. Turner (sop), M. Balfour (cta), A. Desmond (cta), M. Brunskill (cta), M. Jarred (cta), H. Nash (ten), W. Widdop (ten), P. Jones (ten), F. Titterton (ten), R. Henderson (bass), R. Easton (bass), H. Williams (bass), N. Allin (bass), H. Wood (cnd), BBC SO [E] *(rec 10/15/38)* Pearl ▲ GEMMCD 9342 (m) [AAD]

Allen, T. (ten)
Britten, H.:Peter Grimes, w. F. Lott (soprano—Ellen Orford), T. Allen (tenor—Captain Balstrode), A. R. Johnson (tenor—Peter Grimes), Covent Garden, B. Haitink (cnd), Royal Opera House Orch, Royal Opera House Chorus Covent Garden EMI Classics ▲ CDCB 54832

Allen, Thomas (bar)
Barber, S.:Dover Beach, w. Endellion String Quartet Virgin Classics ▲ CDC 45033
Barber, S.:Songs, w. Roger Vignoles (pno)—3 Songs [The Daisies; With Rue My Heart Is Laden; Bessie Bobtail], Op. 2; 3 Songs [Rain Has Fallen; Sleep Now; I Hear an Army], Op. 10; Sure on This Shining Night; Nocturne [both from 4 Songs, Op. 13]; Solitary Hotel [from Despite & Still, Op. 41]; 3 Songs [Now I Have Fed & Eaten up the Rose; A Green Lowland of Pianos; O Boundless, Boundless Evening], Op. 45 Virgin Classics ▲ CDC 45033
Berlioz, H.:Songs, w. F. Pollet (sop), A. S. von Otter (mez), J. Aler (ten), C. Garben (cnd), *(orch unknown)* Deutsche Grammophon 2-▲ 435860-2
Brahms, J.:Ein Deutsches Requiem, w. M. Price (sop), W. Sawallisch (cnd), Bavarian RSO, Bavarian Radio Chorus [G] Orfeo ▲ 039101
Britten, H.:War Requiem, w. E. Söderström (sop), R. Tear (ten), S. Rattle (cnd), City of Birmingham SO, City of Birmingham Sym Chorus, Christ Church Boys' Chorus [E,L] EMI Classics 2-▲ CDC 47033
Butterworth, G.:Bredon Hill & Other Songs, w. G. Parsons (pno) [E] Virgin Classics ▲ 59581 [DDD]
Butterworth, G.:Songs (3) Voc & Strs, w. R. Tear (ten), Rattle, Handley (cnd), City of Birmingham SO EMI Classics ▲ CDM 64731
Butterworth, G.:Songs (6) from *A Shropshire Lad*, w. G. Parsons (pno) [E] Virgin Classics ▲ 59581 [DDD]
Delius, F.:An Arabesk, w. Royal PO, Ambrosian Singers Unicorn-Kanchana ▲ UK 2076
Delius, F.:Cynara, w. E. Fenby (cnd), Royal PO Unicorn-Kanchana ▲ UK 2076
Donizetti, G.:Don Pasquale, w. E. Mei (sop), R. Abbado (cnd), Munich RSO, Bavarian Radio Chorus RCA Red Seal 2-▲ 09026-61924-2
Elgar, E.:Songs, w. R. Tear (ten), Rattle, Handley (cnd), City of Birmingham SO EMI Classics ▲ CDM 64731
Fauré, G.:L'Horizon chimérique [F] Hyperion ▲ CDA 66165
Gluck, C.W.:Iphigénie en Tauride, w. C. Vaness (sop—Iphigénie), S. Brunet (sop—Diane), G. Winbergh (ten—Pylade), T. Allen (bar—Oreste), G. Surian (bass—Thoas), R. Muti (cnd), La Scala Orch, La Scala Chorus *(rec Mar. 14-26, 1992)* Sony Classical 2-▲ S2K 52492 [DDD]
Gluck, C.W.:Iphigénie en Tauride, w. D. Montague (mez), J. Aler (ten), R. Massis (bar), J.E. Gardiner (cnd), Lyon Opera Orch [F] Philips 2-▲ 416148-2 [DDD]
Gounod, C.:Faust, w. M. Freni (sop), P. Domingo (ten), N. Ghiaurov (bass), G. Prêtre (cnd), Paris Opera Orch [F] EMI Classics 3-▲ CDCC 47493 [ADD]
Gounod, C.:Faust (sels), w. M. Freni (sop), P. Domingo (ten), N. Ghiaurov (bass), G. Prêtre (cnd), Paris Opera Orch, Orch de Paris, Paris Opera Chorus EMI Classics ▲ ZDM 63090
Handel, G.F.:Serse, w. L. Atkinson (trb), D. Cole (sop), A. Terzian (mez), A. Andersson (ten), Schumann-Halley (sgr), J. Teal (sgr), A. Duczmal (cnd), Amadeus CO [I] *(rec live recording produced by "Studios Classique Berlin")* Koch Schwann 3-▲ CD SC 100 300 [DDD]
Janácek, L.:The Cunning Little Vixen, w. L. Watson (sop), E. Bainbridge (mez), G. Knight (mez), D. Montague (mez), J. Dobson (ten), R. Tear (ten), G. Howell (bass), S. Rattle (cnd), Royal Opera House Orch [E] EMI Classics 2-▲ CDCB 54212
Leoncavallo, R.:Pagliacci, w. M. Caballé (sop), R. Scotto (sop), A. Varnay (mez), J. Hamari (mez), J. Carreras (ten), M. Manuguerra (bar), K. Nurmela (bar), U. Benelli (bar), R. Muti (cnd), Philharmonia Orch, Ambrosian Opera Chorus EMI Classics 2-▲ CDMB 63650
Love Songs & Lullabies, w. S. Isbin (gtr), Benita Valente (sop), Guadencio Thiago de Mello (perc), Julia Bogorad (fl) Virgin Classics ▲ 59226
Mahler, G.:Das Klagende Lied, w. C. Studer (sop), W. Meier (mez), R. Goldberg (ten), G. Sinopoli (cnd), Philharmonia Orch, Shin-Yuh Kai Chorus *(rec live, Japan 1990)* Deutsche Grammophon ▲ 435382-2 [DDD]
Mahler, G.:Des Knaben Wunderhorn, w. A. Murray (mez), C. Mackerras (cnd), London PO Virgin Classics ▲ CDC 59037
Mahler, G.:Des Knaben Wunderhorn, w. Ann Murray (mez), C. Mackerras (cnd), London PO Virgin Classics ("Ultraviolet" series) ▲ CUV 61202
Mahler, G.:Sym 8, w. S. Jo (sop), C. Studer (sop), W. Meier (mez), K. Lewis (ten), H. Sotin (bass), G. Sinopoli (cnd), Philharmonia Orch, Philharmonia Chorus, Southend Boys' Choir [G] Deutsche Grammophon 2-▲ 435433-2

▲ = CD ♦ = Enhanced CD Δ = MD ■ = Cassette Tape □ = DCC

Allen, Thomas (bar) (cont.)

Massenet, J.:Werther, w. F. von Stade (mez), J. Carreras (ten), R. Lloyd (b–bar), C. Davis (cnd), Royal Opera House Orch Covent Garden, Royal Opera House Chorus Covent Garden [F] Philips 2–▲ 416654–2 [ADD]

Mendelssohn, F.:Elijah, w. Y. Kenny (sop), A.S. von Otter (mez), A. Rolfe Johnson (ten), N. Marriner (cnd), Academy of St. Martin in the Fields Philips 2–▲ 432984–2 [DDD]

Mozart, W.A.:Complete Mozart Edition, w. B. Hendricks (sop), J. Varady (sop), S. Mentzer (mez), F. Araiza (ten), C. Davis (cnd), Bavarian RSO Philips 3–▲ 422537–2 [ADD]

Mozart, W.A.:Così fan tutte, w. K. Mattila (sop), E. Szmytka (sop), A. S. von Otter (mez), F. Araiza (ten), J. van Dam (b–bar), N. Marriner (cnd), Academy of St. Martin in the Fields, Ambrosian Opera Chorus [I] Philips 3–▲ 422381–2 [DDD]

Mozart, W.A.:Don Giovanni, w. C. Vaness (sop), M. Ewing (sop), E. Gale (sop), K. Lewis (ten), R. Van Allan (bass), B. Haitink (cnd), London PO, Glyndebourne Festival Chorus [I] EMI Classics 3–▲ CDCC 47036 [DDD]

Mozart, W.A.:Don Giovanni, w. S. Sweet (sop), K. Mattila (sop), M. McLaughlin (sop), F. Araiza (ten), S. Alaimo (b–bar), R. Lloyd (bass), N. Marriner (cnd), Academy of St. Martin in the Fields, Ambrosian Opera Chorus Philips 3–▲ 432129–2 [DDD]

Mozart, W.A.:Don Giovanni (sels), w. K. Mattila (sop), F. Araiza (ten), R. Lloyd (bass), N. Marriner (cnd), Academy of St. Martin in the Fields Philips ▲ 438494–2

Mozart, W.A.:Nozze di Figaro, w. K. Te Kanawa (sop), L. Popp (sop), F. von Stade (mez), S. Ramey (bass), K. Moll (bass), G. Solti (cnd), London PO [I] London 3–▲ 410150–2 [DDD]

Mozart, W.A.:Nozze di Figaro (sels), w. K. Te Kanawa (sop), L. Popp (sop), F. von Stade (mez), S. Ramey (bass), K. Moll (bass), G. Solti (cnd), London PO [I] London ▲ 417395–2 [DDD] □ 417395–5

Mozart, W.A.:Zauberflöte, w. B. Hendricks (sop—Pamina), J. Anderson (sop—Queen of the Night), U. Steinsky (sop—Papagena), J. Hadley (ten—Tamino), T. Allen (bar—Papageno), R. Lloyd (bass—Sarastro), C. Mackerras (cnd), Scottish CO, Scottish Chamber Chorus [G] Telarc 2–▲ CD 80302 [DDD]

Mozart, W.A.:Zauberflöte (sels), w. B. Hendricks (sop), J. Hadley (sop), J. Anderson (sop), R. Lloyd (b–bar), U. Steinsky (cnd), Scottish CO, Scottish Sym Chorus *(rec July 13–22, 1991)* Telarc ▲ CD 80345 [DDD]

Orff, C.:Carmina burana, w. S. Armstrong (sop), G. English (ten), A. Previn (cnd), London SO, London Sym Chorus, St. Clement Danes Boys' Chorus [G, L] EMI Classics ▲ CDC 47411 ■ 4AM 34770

Peel, G.:In Summertime on Bredon, w. G. Parsons (pno) [E] Virgin Classics ▲ 59581 [DDD]

Poulenc, F.:Le Bal masqué, w. Nash Ensemble [F] CRD ▲ 3437 [DDD]

Poulenc, F.:Le Bestiarire, w. Nash Ensemble [F] CRD ▲ 3437 [DDD]

Purcell, H.:Dido & Aeneas, w. J. Norman (sop), M. McLaughlin (sop), R. Leppard (cnd), English CO, Ambrosian Singers [E] Philips ▲ 416299–2 [DDD]

Quilter, R.:Elizabethan Lyrics, w. G. Parsons (pno) [E] Virgin Classics ▲ 59581 [DDD]

Quilter, R.:Now Sleeps the Crimson Petal, w. G. Parsons (pno) [E] Virgin Classics ▲ 59581 [DDD]

Rossini, G.:Il barbiere di Siviglia (sels), w. A. Baltsa (mez), S. Burgess (mez), F. Araiza (ten), D. Trimarchi (bar), R. Lloyd (bass), N. Marriner (cnd), Academy of St. Martin in the Fields Philips ▲ 438498–2

Schubert, Franz:Winterreise, w. R. Vignoles (pno) Virgin Classics ▲ CDC 59036

The Sea, w. Sarah Walker (mez), R. Vignoles (pno) Hyperion ▲ CDA 66165

Sullivan, A.:HMS Pinafore, w. F. Palmer (sop—Little Buttercup), R. Evans (mez—Josephine), M. Schade (ten—Ralph Rackstraw), T. Allen (bar—Capt. Corcoran), R. Suart (bass—Rt. Hon. Sir Joseph Porter, K.C.B.), D. Adams (bass—Dick Deadeye), R. Van A. (bass—Bill Bobstay), C. Mackerras (cnd), Welsh National Opera Orch, Welsh National Opera Chorus *(rec Swansea, Wales, June 5–8, 1994)* Telarc ▲ CD 80374 [DDD]

Tippett, M.:King Priam, w. Heather Harper (sop—Hecuba), Linda Hirst (sop—Serving Woman), Felicity Palmer (sop—Andromache), Julian Saipe (sop—Paris), Yvonne Minton (mez—Helen), Ann Murray (mez—Nurse), Kenneth Bowen (ten—Hermes), Peter Hall (ten—Young Guard), Philip Langridge (ten—Paris), Robert Tear (ten—Achilles), Thomas Allen (bar—Hector), Norman Bailey (bar—Priam), Stephen Roberts (bar—Patroclus), David Wilson–Johnson (bar—Old Man), D. Atherton (cnd), London Sinfonietta, London Sinfonietta Chorus Chandos ▲ CHAN 9406/7 [DDD]

Vaughan Williams, R.:Fant on Christmas Carols, w. M. Best (cnd), English CO, Corydon Singers [E] Hyperion ▲ CDA 66420 [DDD]

Vaughan Williams, R.:The House of Life, w. G. Parsons (pno) [E] Virgin Classics ▲ 59581 [DDD]

Vaughan Williams, R.:Mystical Songs, w. M. Best (cnd), English CO, Corydon Singers [E] Hyperion ▲ CDA 66420 [DDD]

Vaughan Williams, R.:Sacred Songs, w. J. Howarth (sop), J.M. Ainsley (ten), M. Best (cnd), Corydon Orch, Corydon Singers—Towards the Unknown Region; Dona nobis pacem; O Clap your hands; Lord, Thou hast been our refuge; 4 Hymns Hyperion ▲ CDA 66655 [DDD]

Vaughan Williams, R.:Songs, w. G. Parsons (pno)—Linden Lea, a Dorset Song (1902) [E] Virgin Classics ▲ 59581 [DDD]

Vaughan Williams, R.:Songs of Travel, w. Rattle, Handley (cnd), City of Birmingham SO [orch. version] EMI Classics ▲ CDM 64731

Vaughan Williams, R.:Sym 1, w. B. Valente (sop), L. Slatkin (cnd), Philharmonia Orch, Philharmonia Chorus RCA Red Seal ▲ 09026–61197–2

Walton, W.:Belshazzar's Feast, w. L Slatkin (cnd), St. Louis SO RCA Red Seal ▲ 09026–60813–2

Wolf, H.:Songs (misc), w. G. Parsons (pno) [G] Virgin Classics ▲ CDC 59221

Alley, Kirstie (nar)

Prokofiev, S.:Peter & the Wolf, w. Lloyd Bridges (nar), Ross Malinger (nar), G. Daugherty (cnd), RCA Victor SO—2 versions:1 with narration & 1 without *(rec Studio 1 & LA Studios East, Salt Lake City, Utah)* RCA Gold Seal ▲ 74321–31869–2 [DDD]

Allin, Norman (bass)

Mozart, W.A.:Nozze di Figaro (sels), w. Luise Helletsgrüber (sop), Audrey Mildmay (sop), Aulikki Rautawaara (sop), Constance Willis (mez), John Heddle Nash (ten), Willi Domgraf–Fassbaender (bar), Roy Henderson (bar), F. Busch (cnd), Glyndebourne Festival Orch Pearl ▲ PEA CD 9230

Vaughan Williams, R.:Serenade to Music, w. I. Baillie (sop), E. Suddaby (sop), S. Allen (sop), E. Turner (sop), M. Balfour (cta), A. Desmond (cta), M. Brunskill (cta), M. Jarred (cta), H. Nash (ten), W. Widdop (ten), P. Jones (ten), F. Titterton (ten), R. Henderson (bass), R. Easton (bass), H. Williams (bass), H. J. Wood (cnd), BBC SO Dutton Laboratories ▲ CDAX 8004 [ADD]

Vaughan Williams, R.:Serenade to Music, w. I. Baillie (sop), E. Suddaby (sop), S. Allen (sop), E. Turner (sop), M. Balfour (cta), A. Desmond (cta), M. Brunskill (cta), M. Jarred (cta), H. Nash (ten), W. Widdop (ten), P. Jones (ten), F. Titterton (ten), R. Henderson (bass), R. Easton (bass), H. Williams (bass), H. Wood (cnd), BBC SO [E] *(rec 10/15/38)* Pearl ▲ GEMMCD 9342 (m) [AAD]

Vaughan Williams, R.:Serenade to Music, w. Isobel Baillie (sop), Lilian Stiles–Allen (sop), Elsie Suddaby (sop), Eva Turner (sop), Margaret Balfour (cta), Muriel Brunskill (cta), Astra Desmond (cta), Mary Jarred (cta), Parry Jones (ten), Heddle Nash (ten), Frank Titterton (ten), Walter Widdop (ten), Roy Henderson (bar), Harold Williams (bar), Robert Easton (bass), H. Wood (cnd), BBC SO *(rec Abbey Road, Oct 15, 1938)* Claremont ▲ CDGSE 785066

Alliot–Lugaz, Colette (sop)

Campra, A.:Tancrède, w. D. Evangelatos (cta), G. Reinhart (bar), F. le Roux (bar), P.–Y. le Maigat (bass–bar), Dubose (sgr), J. Malgoire (cnd), La Grande Écurie et la Chambre du Roy Erato (Musifrance) 2–▲ 2292–45001–2 ZA [DDD]

Debussy, C.:Pelléas et Mélisande, w. F. Golfier (sop), C. Carlson (mez), D. Henry (ten), G. Cachemaille (bar), P. Thau (bass), C. Dutoit (cnd), Montreal SO, Montreal Sym Chorus [F] London 2–▲ 430502–2 [DDD]

Mélodies Françaises en duo, w. François Le Roux (bar), Jeff Cohen (pno) *(rec 9/88)* REM ▲ 311086 [DDD]

Messager, A.:Fortunio, w. T. Dran (ten), G. Cachémaille (bar), R. Schirrer (bar), J. E. Gardiner (cnd), Paris Lyon Opera Orch, Paris Lyon Opera Chorus Erato 2–▲ 45983–2

Mozart, W.A.:Requiem, w. Dominique Vissé (ct), Martyn Hill (ten), G. Reinhart (bar), J. Malgoire (cnd), La Grande Écurie et la Chambre du Roy, Nord–Pas–de–Calais Choir [L] CBS ▲ MDK 44904 [DDD]

Allister, Jean (cta)

Sullivan, A.:Music of, w. M. Studholme (sop), E. Bohan (ten), I. Wallace (bar), M. Dods (cnd), London Concert Orch, English Chorale—sels. from Gondoliers; H.M.S. Pinafore; Mikado; Pirates of Penzance PWK Classics ▲ PWK 1157 [AAD]

Allouche, Roselyne (mez)

Caplet, A.:Le miroir de Jésus, w. P. Bender (cnd), Cannes–Provençe Alpes–Côte d'Azur Regional Orch, Maîtrise Gabriel Fauré Sonpact ▲ SPT 94010 [DDD]

Almajano, Maria (sop)

Barroco Español, Vol. 1, w. Al Ayre Enspañol [cnd:Eduardo Lopez Banzo] Conifer Classics ▲ 75605–77325–2 [DDD]

Boccherini, L.:Aria accademica 14, w. C. Coin (cnd), Baroque Ensemble Limoges Astrée ▲ E 8517 [DDD]

Almquist, N. (sgr)

For Citizens & Peasants:Popular Tunes from Old Norwegian Music Books, w. J. Arnold, T. Chancey, E. Bulkely Folger Consort ▲ BDCD1 9003 [DDD]

Alonso, Ramon (bass)

Carrion, M.R.:La Tempestad, w. L. Huarte (sop), D. Perez (sop), A. Kraus (ten), F. Kraus (bar), S. Ramalle (bass), E. Estella (cnd), Concierto Montilla Orch, Concierto Montilla Chorus Montilla ▲ MON 3011 [ADD]

Puccini, G.:Tosca, w. Maria Callas (sop), Mario Filippeschi (ten), Carlos Sagarminaga (ten), Robert Weede (bar), U. Mugnai (cnd), Palacio Bellas Artes Orch, Palacio Bellas Artes Chorus Melodram 3–▲ CDM 36032

Alpar, Gitta (sop)

Gitta Alpar *(rec 1928–31)* Preiser ("Lebendige Vergangenheit" series) ▲ PRE CD 89128

The Legendary Singers at Lindenoper Berlin (1927–1945), w. Erna Berger (sop), Tiana Lemnitz (sop), Maria Müller (sop), Margarete Klose (cta), Peter Anders (ten), Max Lorenz (ten), Walter Ludwig (ten), Lauritz Melchior (ten), Rudolf Schock (ten), Franz Völker (ten), Willi Domgraf–Fassb *(rec 1927; 1937; 1941–45)* Minerva ▲ MN A21 [ADD]

Alperyn, Graciela (mez)

Bizet, G.:Carmen, w. D. Palade (sop), G. Lamberti (ten), A. Titus (bar), et al., A. Rahbari (cnd), Czech–Slovak RSO Bratislava, Slovak Phil Chorus, Bratislava Children's Choir [F] Naxos 3–▲ 8.660005/07 [DDD]

Bizet, G.:Carmen (sels), w. D. Palade (sop—Micaëla), A. Liebeck (sop—Frasquita), G. Alperyn (mez—Carmen), D. Schaechter (mez—Mercédès), G. Lamberti (ten—Don José), M. Dvorsky (ten—Remandado), J. Durco (ten—Cancairo), A. Titus (bar—Escamillo), V. Chmelo (bar—Morales), D. Rigosa (bass—Zuniga), A. Rahbari (cnd), Czech–Slovak RSO Bratislava, Slovak Phil Chorus, Bratislava Children's Choir *(rec July 1990)* Naxos ▲ 8.550727 [DDD]

Alsen, Herbert (bass)

Beethoven, L. van:Fidelio, w. H. Konetzni (sop), I. Seefried (sop), P. Klein (ten), T. Ralf (ten), P. Schöffler (b–bar), K. Böhm (cnd), Vienna State Opera Orch, Vienna State Opera Chorus *(rec Feb. 1944)* Preiser 2–▲ PRE 90195 [AAD]

Beethoven, L. van:Fidelio (sels), w. E. Schlüte (sop), L. della Casa (sop), J. Patzak (ten), R. Schock (ten), F. Frantz (b–bar), W. Furtwängler (cnd), Vienna State Opera Orch, Vienna State Opera Chorus—Overture, 16 arias & choruses *(rec live, Salzburg Festspielhaus Aug. 3, 1948)* Melodram 2–▲ CDM 25009 [ADD]

Mozart, W.A.:Don Giovanni (sels), w. Hilde Konetzni (sop), Emmy Loose (sop), Irmgard Seefried (sop), Anton Dermota (ten), Erich Kunz (bar), Paul Schöffler (b–bar), Böhm, Moralt (cnd), Vienna PO *(rec 1944)* Preiser ▲ PRE 90249 [ADD]

Mozart, W.A.:Entführung (sels), w. Hilde Konetzni (sop), Emmy Loose (sop), Irmgard Seefried (sop), Anton Dermota (ten), Erich Kunz (bar), Paul Schöffler (b–bar), Böhm, Moralt (cnd), Vienna PO *(rec 1944)* Preiser ▲ PRE 90249 [ADD]

Mozart, W.A.:Zauberflöte (sels), w. Hilde Konetzni (sop), Emmy Loose (sop), Irmgard Seefried (sop), Anton Dermota (ten), Erich Kunz (bar), Paul Schöffler (b–bar), Böhm, Moralt (cnd), Vienna PO *(rec 1944)* Preiser ▲ PRE 90249 [ADD]

Strauss, R.:Friedenstag, w. Viorica Ursuleac (sop—Maria), Anton Dermota (ten—Ein Piemonteser), Hans Hotter (b–bar—Kommandant), Herbert Alsen (bass—Wachtmeister), C. Krauss (cnd), Vienna State Opera Orch *(rec Vienna, Oct. 16, 1941)* Koch Schwann 2–▲ SCH 314625 [ADD]

Verdi, G.:Macbeth, w. E. Höngen (cta), J. Witt (ten), M. Ahlersmeyer (bar), K. Böhm (cnd), Vienna State Opera Orch, Vienna State Opera Chorus *(rec 1943)* Preiser 2–▲ PRE 90175 [AAD]

Wagner, R.:Götterdämmerung (sels), w. Set Svanholm (ten—Siegfried), Paul Schöffler (b–bar—Gunther), Herbert Alsen (bass—Hagen), H. Knappertsbusch (cnd), Vienna State Opera Orch *(rec Vienna, June 27, 1941)* Koch Schwann ▲ SCH 314692 [ADD]

Wagner, R.:Die Meistersinger von Nürnberg, w. M. Reining (sop), H. Noort (ten), A. Dermota (ten), H. H. Nissen (bar), A. Toscanini (cnd), Vienna PO *(rec live, Salzburg, 1937)* Melodram 4–▲ MEL 47041

Wagner, R.:Die Meistersinger von Nürnberg, w. Irmgard Seefried (sop—Eva), Else Schürhoff (mez—Magdelene), Peter Klein (ten—David), August Seider (ten—Walther), Erich Kunz (bar—Beckmesser), Paul Schoeffler (b–bar—Hans Sachs), Herbert Alsen (bass—Pogner), K. Böhm (cnd), Vienna PO, Vienna State Opera Chorus *(rec Vienna, Nov. & Dec. 1944)* Preiser 4–▲ PRE 90234 [ADD]

Wagner, R.:Parsifal (sels), w. A. Konetzni (sop), H. Grahl (ten), H. Weidemann (bar), H. Knappertsbusch (cnd), Vienna State Opera Orch, Vienna State Opera Chorus *(rec Apr. 6, 1939)* Koch Schwann 2–▲ SCH 314522 [ADD]

Wagner, R.:Parsifal (sels), w. Fred Destal (bar—Amfortas), Herbert Alsen (bass—Gurnemanz), Nikolaus Zec (bass–Titurel), H. Knappertsbusch (cnd), Vienna State Opera Orch *(rec Nov. 1, 1937)* Koch Schwann 2–▲ SCH 314632 [ADD]

Wagner, R.:Das Rheingold (sels), w. A. Konetzni (sop—Fricka), J. Prohaska (bar—Wotan), N. Zec (b–bar—Fasolt), H. Alsen (bass—Fafner), J. Krips (cnd), Vienna State Opera Orch, Vienna State Opera Chorus *(rec Jan. 18, 1937)* Koch Schwann 2–▲ SCH 314592

Wagner, R.:Tristan und Isolde (sels), w. Anny Konetzni (sop—Isolde), Margarete Klose (cta—Brangäne), Max Lorenz (ten—Tristan), Paul Schöffler (b–bar—Kurwenal), Herbert Alsen (bass—King Marke), W. Furtwängler (cnd), Vienna State Opera Orch, Vienna State Opera Chorus—extended excerpts from Acts 1 & 2; Act 3 (comp.) Koch Schwann 2–▲ SCH 314612 [ADD]

Wagner, R.:Die Walküre (sels), w. Hilde Konetzni (sop—Sieglinde), Günther Treptow (ten—Siegmund), Herbert Alsen (bass—Hunding), R. Moralt (cnd), Vienna SO—Act 1 Myto 4–▲ 4 MCD 954.136

Weber, C.M. von:Der Freischütz (sels), w. Maria Reining (sop—Agathe), Elisabeth Rutgers (mez—Ännchen), Julius Pölzer (ten—Max), Herbert Alsen (bass—Kaspar), R. Moralt (cnd), Vienna State Opera Orch *(rec Jan. 1, 1939)* Koch Schwann 2–▲ SCH 314632 [ADD]

Alstergård, Bertil (bar)

Verdi, G.:Rigoletto, w. M. Hallin (sop), B. Nordin (sop), K. Meyer (mez), B. Ericson (mez), Kjellgren (mez), N. Gedda (ten), O. Sivall (ten), H. Hasslo (bar), I. Wixell (bar), A. Tyrén (bass), S. Ehrling (cnd), Stockholm Royal Opera House Orch, Stockholm Royal Opera Chorus *(rec live Jan. 18, 1959)* BIS ▲ CD 296 [AAD]

Alston, John (bass)

Buxtehude, D.:Cants, w. Laura Heimes (sop), Tamara Crout Matthews (sop), Steven Richards (ct), James Russell (ten), M. N. Johnson (cnd), Sarum Consort, St. Peter's in the Great Valley Chamber Choir—Wachet auf, ruft uns die Stimme!; Singet dem Herrn; Quemadmodum desiderat cervus; O fröhliche Stunden, o herrliche Zeit; Jubilate Domino omnis terra; Lobe den Herrn, meine Seele; Erfreue dich, Erde! *(rec St–Martin–in–the–Fields Church, Chestnut Hill, PA, Sept 7–9, 1994)* Pro gloria musicae ▲ PGM 102 [DDD]

Altena, Marius van (ten)

Bach, J.S.:Cant 14, w. M. van Egmond (b–bar), Leonhardt Consort, King's College Choir Cambridge [G] Teldec 2–▲ 2292–42500–2 [AAD]

Bach, J.S.:Cant 23, w. W. Gampert (trb), P. Esswood (ct), M. van Egmond (b–bar), Leonhardt Consort, King's College Choir Cambridge [G] Teldec 2–▲ 2292–42502–2 [AAD]

Bach, J.S.:Cant 33, w. R. Jacobs (ct), G. Leonhardt (cnd), Leonhardt Consort, Hanover Boys' Choir [G] Teldec 2–▲ 2292–42505–2 [AAD]

Bach, J.S.:Cant 40, w. R. Jacobs (ct), M. van Egmond (b–bar), Leonhardt Consort, Hanover Boys' Choir [G] Teldec 2–▲ 2292–42556–2 [AAD]

Bach, J.S.:Cant 106, "Actus tragicus", w. M. Klein (trb), R. Harten (alt), M. van Egmond (b–bar), Leonhardt Consort, Collegium Vocale, Hanover Boys' Chorus [G] Teldec ▲ 2292–42602–2

Althann, Tanja d' (sop)
Keiser, R.:Passions Oratorium, w. P. Geitner (sop), M. Paulsen (alt), J. Elbert (ten), H. Elbert (bass), C. Brembeck (cnd), Parthenia Baroque, Parthenia Vocal Christophorus ▲ 77143 [DDD]

Althouse, Paul (ten)
Schoenberg, A.:Gurrelieder, w. R. Bampton (sop), L. Stokowski (cnd), Philadelphia Orch, Fortnightly Club, Princeton Glee Club, Mendelssohn Club Philadelphia *(rec live Apr. 9, 1932)* Pearl 2-▲ PEA 9066 [AAD]

Altman, M. (sgr)
Handel, G.F.:Messiah (reorchd Mozart), w. Andrew Murphy (b–bar), J. Davidson (sgr), Peter Elvin (sgr), P. Price (sgr), L. Woodside (cnd), Sinfonia Rubinstein, New York Oratorio Society [Sinfonia Rubinstein is made up from musicians from the Lodz Philharmonic Orchestra and the Lodz Opera of Poland] [E] Koch Schwann 2-▲ SC 100308 [DDD]

Altmeyer, Jeannine (sop)
Britten, H.:War Requiem, w. Douglas Lawrence (ten), Michael Sells (bar), Ladd Thomas (org), W. Hall (cnd), William Hall Orch, William Hall Chorale, Columbus Boys' Choir Klavier ▲ KCD 11017 [ADD]

Altmeyer, Theo (ten)
Bach, J.S.:Cant 20, w. V. Gohl (mez), M. Kessler (mez), A. Kraus (ten), W. Schöne (bass), H. Rilling (cnd), Stuttgart Bach Collegium, Frankfurt Kantorei Hänssler Classic ▲ 98.801 [AAD]
Bach, J.S.:Cant 213, w. Sheila Armstrong (sop), Hertha Töpper (alt), Jakob Stämpfli (bass), H. Rilling (cnd), Stuttgart Bach Collegium *(rec 1967)* Musicaphon ▲ 51356 [AAD]
Bach, J.S.:Cant 249a, w. Edith Mathis (sop), Hetty Plümacher (alt), Jakob Stämpfli (bass), H. Rilling (cnd), Stuttgart Bach Collegium, Stuttgart Memorial Church Figuralchor *(rec Gedächtniskirche Stuttgart, Mar 1967)* Musicaphon ▲ 51357 [AAD]
Bach, J.S.:St. Matthew Passion (sels), w. W. Gönnenwein (cnd), Consortium Musicum, South German Madrigal Choir—Ich will bei meinem Jesu wachen; Kommt, ihr Töchter *(rec Église de Schwaigern, May & Jun. 1968)* EMI Classics ▲ CDK 65334 [ADD]
Mendelssohn, F.:St. Paul, w. A. Giebel (sop), O. Dominguez (mez), S. Nimsgern (b–bar), R. A. El Hage (bass), R. Muti (cnd), Milan RAI Orch, Milan RAI Chorus [G] *(rec live, Milan, 12/15/70)* Memories 2-▲ HR 4267/68 (m) [ADD]
Wagner, R.:Der Ring des Nibelungen, w. G. Jones (sop), H. Schwarz (mez), L. Hofmann (bass), D. McIntyre (b–bar), P. Boulez (cnd), Bayreuth Festival Orch, Bayreuth Festival Chorus Philips 32-▲ 434420–2 [ADD/DDD]

Altorjay, Tamás (bar)
Górecki, H.–M.:Beatus Vir, w. T. Pál (cnd), Fricsay SO, Bartók Chorus Stradivarius ▲ STR 33324 [DDD]
Górecki, H.–M.:Beatus Vir, w. T. Pál (cnd), Fricsay SO, Bartók Chorus Stradivarius ▲ STV 33324 [DDD]
Górecki, H.–M.:Sym 2, "Copernican Sym", w. E. Soós (sop), T. Pál (cnd), Fricsay SO, Bartók Chorus Stradivarius ▲ STR 33324 [DDD]
Górecki, H.–M.:Sym 2, "Copernican Sym", w. Emese Soós (sop), T. Pál (cnd), Fricsay SO Stradivarius ▲ STV 33324 [DDD]

Alva, Luigi (ten)
Donizetti, G.:Don Pasquale, w. R. Scotto (sop), W. Alberti (bar), F. Corena (bass), B. Rigacci (cnd), Florence Maggio Musicale Orch, Florence Maggio Musicale Chorus [I] *(rec live, Florence 3/1/67)* Claque 2-▲ CLQ 2011 (m)
Donizetti, G.:L'elisir d'amore, w. Rosanna Carteri (sop—Adina), Luigi Angela Vercelli (mez—Gianetta), Luigi Alva (ten—Nemorino), Rolando Panerai (bar—Belcore), Giuseppe Taddei (bar—Dulcamara), T. Serafin (cnd), La Scala Orch, La Scala Chorus EMI Classics 2-▲ CDMB 65658
Mozart, W.A.:Così fan tutte, w. E. Schwarzkopf (sop—Fiordiligi), G. Sciurri (sop—Despina), N. Merriman (mez—Dorabella), L. Alva (ten—Ferrando), R. Panerai (bar—Guglielmo), F. Clabrese (b–bar—Don Alfonso)., G. Cantelli (cnd), La Scala Orch, La Scala Chorus *(rec Jan. 27, 1956)* Datum 2-▲ DAT 12304 [ADD]
Mozart, W.A.:Così fan tutte, w. Elisabeth Schwarzkopf (sop), Graziella Sciutti (sop), Nan Merriman (mez), Rolando Panerai (bar), Franco Calabrese (bass), G. Cantelli (cnd), La Scala Orch, La Scala Chorus Stradivarius 2-▲ STV DTM 12304 [ADD]
Mozart, W.A.:Così fan tutte, w. M. Price (sop), L. Popp (sop), Y. Minton (mez), G. Evans (bar), H. Sotin (bass), O. Klemperer (cnd), New Philharmonia Orch, John Alldis Choir EMI Classics 3-▲ CDMC 63845
Mozart, W.A.:Così fan tutte, w. M. Adani (sop), T. Stich–Randall (mez), T. Berganza (mez), A. Cortis (ten), R. Panerai (bar), H. Rosbaud (cnd), Paris Conservatory Societé des Concerts Orch, Aix–en–Provence Festival Chorus [I] *(rec live, Aix–en–Provence, July 26, 1957)* Melodram 3-▲ MEL 37084 [AAD]
Mozart, W.A.:Don Giovanni (sels), w. E. Schwarzkopf (sop), G. Sciutti (sop), J. Sutherland (sop), E. Wächter (bar), C. M. Giulini (cnd), Philharmonia Orch EMI Classics ▲ ZDM 63078
Rossini, G.:Il barbiere di Siviglia, w. M. Callas (sop), T. Gobbi (bar), C. M. Giulini (cnd), La Scala Orch, La Scala Chorus [I] *(rec live 1956)* Melodram 2-▲ MEL 26020
Rossini, G.:Il barbiere di Siviglia, w. Fiorenza Cossotto (mez), Sesto Bruscantini (bar), Carlo Badioli (bass), Nicolai Ghiaurov (bass), G. Santini (cnd), La Scala Orch, La Scala Chorus *(rec Jan 20, 1964)* Pantheon 2-▲ PHE 6644 (m)
Rossini, G.:Il barbiere di Siviglia, w. T. Berganza (mez), H. Prey (bar), P. Montarsolo (bass), C. Abbado (cnd), London SO, London Sym Chorus [I] Deutsche Grammophon 2-▲ 415695–2 [ADD]
Rossini, G.:Il barbiere di Siviglia, w. V. de los Angeles (sop), C. Cava (bass), I. Wallace (bass), V. Gui (cnd), Royal PO, Glyndebourne Festival Chorus *(rec 1962)* EMI Classics 2-▲ CDMB 64162
Rossini, G.:Il barbiere di Siviglia, w. M. Callas (sop), T. Gobbi (bar), A. Galliera (cnd), Philharmonia Orch [I] *(rec 1957)* EMI Classics 2-▲ CDCB 47634 [ADD]
Rossini, G.:Il barbiere di Siviglia, w. M. Callas (sop), T. Gobbi (bar), N. Zaccaria (bass), F. Ollendorf (bass), A. Galliera (cnd), Philharmonia Orch EMI Classics ▲ ZDM 63076
Rossini, G.:La Cenerentola, w. Teresa Berganza (mez), Renato Capecchi (bar), Paolo Montarsolo (bass), C. Abbado (cnd), Florence Maggio Musicale Orch, Florence Maggio Musicale Chorus *(rec Florence, May 1971)* Memories 2-▲ MEM 4283 [ADD]
Rossini, G.:La Cenerentola, w. T. Berganza (mez), R. Capecchi (bar), U. Trama (bass), C. Abbado (cnd), London SO, London Sym Chorus [I] Deutsche Grammophon 2-▲ 423861–2 [ADD]
Scarlatti, A.:La Griselda, w. M. Freni (sop), V. Luchetti (ten), R. Panerai (bar), S. Bruscantini (bar), N. Sanzogno (cnd), Naples Alessandro Scarlatti RAI Orch, Naples Scarlatti Chorus [I] *(rec live 10/29/70)* Memories 2-▲ HR 4154/55 (m) [ADD]
Verdi, G.:Falstaff, w. M. Freni (sop), I. Ligabue (sop), R. Capecchi (bar), F. Corena (bass), C. M. Giulini (cnd), Royal Concertgebouw Orch, Netherlands Chamber Choir [I] *(rec live, The Hague 6/20/63)* Verona 2-▲ 27095/96
Verdi, G.:Falstaff, w. Ilva Ligabue (sop), Oralia Dominguez (mez), Geraint Evans (bar), Eberhardt Wächter (bar), F. Previtali (cnd), *(orch unknown)* *(rec Teatro Colon, Buenos Aires, Aug. 30, 1963)* Ornamenti ("Gala Evenings, Teatro Colon") 2-▲ 119

Alvarado, William (bar)
Estévez, A.:Florentino, el que cantó con el diablo, w. I. Alvarez (ten), E. Mata (cnd), Simón Bolívar SO, Simón Bolívar Orfeón Univ Schola Cantorum [L] *(rec 2 & 6/90)* Dorian Discovery ▲ DIS 80101 [DDD]
Falla, M. de:El retablo de maese Pedro, w. Lourdes Ambriz (sop), Julianne Baird (sop), Miguel Cortez (ten), Rafael Puyana (hpd), E. Mata (cnd), Mexican Soloists *(rec Sala Nezahualcóyotl, Universidad Nacional Autónoma de Mexico, Mexico City, Oct. 1994)* Dorian ▲ DOR 90214 [DDD]

Alvarez, Carlos (bass)
Bellini, V.:I Puritani (sels), w. Lucia Albert (sgr), Giuseppe Sabbatini (ten), Michele Pertusi (bass)—All'erta! All'erta!; A te, o cara, amor talora; Son vergin vezzosa; Ah..Dolor! Ah Terror!; Cinta di fiori e col ben crin disciolto; O Rendetemi la speme—Vien, Diletto; Il Rival salvar tu dei—Suoni la tromba Laserlight ▲ 14208 [DDD]
Vives, A.:Bohemios, w. M. Bayo (sop), L. Lima (ten), A. R. Marbà (cnd), Tenerife SO Valois ▲ V 4711

Alvarez, Idwer (ten)
Estévez, A.:Florentino, el que cantó con el diablo, w. W. Alvarado (bar), E. Mata (cnd), Simón Bolívar SO, Simón Bolívar Orfeón Univ Schola Cantorum [L] *(rec 2 & 6/90)* Dorian Discovery ▲ DIS 80101 [DDD]

Alvary, Lorenzo (bass)
Bach, J.S.:St. Matthew Passion, w. Nadine Conner (sop), Jean Watson (cta), William Hain (ten), Mack Harrell (bar), Herbert Janssen (bar), B. Walter (cnd), New York PO, New York Phil Chorus—Part I Minerva ▲ 20
Her First Recordings, w. Steber, Eleanor (sop), Armand Tokatyan (ten), Lucielle Browning (mez), Pino Bontempi (sgr), Annamary Dickey (sgr), George Cehanovsky (bar), Lorenzo Alvary ((bass), A. Kent (bar), Raoul Jobin (ten), Norman Cordon (bass) VAI Audio ▲ VAIA 1023 (m) [ADD]

Amade, Raymond (ten)
Adam, A.:Le toréador, ou l'accord parfait, w. Mady Mesplé (sop), Charles Clavensy (b–bar), E. Bigot (cnd), ORTF Lyric Orch Musidisc ▲ MUS 201672 [AAD]
Boulanger, L.:Du fond de l'abîme, w. Oralia Dominguez (ct), J. J. Grunenwald (org), I. Markevitch (cnd), Lamoureux Orch, Elisabeth Brasseur Chorale *(rec Salle Pleyel, Paris)* Everest ▲ EVC 9034 [AAD]

Amadini, Maria (sgr)
Ponchielli, A.:La Gioconda, w. M. Callas (sop—Gioconda), F. Barbieri (mez—Laura), M. Amadini (sgr—La Cieca), G. Poggi (ten—Enzo), P. Silveri (bar—Barnaba), G. Neri (bass—Alvise), A. Votto (cnd), Turin RAI Orch, Turin RAI Chorus *(rec 1952)* Cetra Classic 3-▲ CDO 8
Strauss, R.:Der Rosenkavalier, w. Jarmila Barton (sop—Marianne), Lisa Della Casa (sop—Sophie), Sena Jurinac (sop—Octavian), Ilva Ligabue (sop—Orphan), Elisabeth Schwarzkopf (sop—Marschallin), Else Schürhoff (mez—Annina), Luisa Villa (mez—Milliner), Hugues Cuénod (ten—Marschallin's majordomo), Erich Majkut (ten—Valzacchi), Giuseppe Nessi (ten—Animal seller), Luciano Della Pergola (ten—Lackey/Faninal's majordomo), Antonio Pirino (ten—An Italian Singer), Gino Del Signore (ten—Lackey/Waiter), Erich Kunz (bar—Herr von Faninal), Paolo Pedani (bar—Lackey), Attilo Barbesi (bass—Lackey/Waiter), Enrico Campi (bass—Waiter), Otto Edelmann (bass—Baron Ochs), Bruno Fichtinger (bass—Notary), Franco Taino (bass—Waiter), Maria Amadini (sgr—Orphan), Pina Carrillo (sgr—Orphan), Joszi Trojan Regar (sgr—Innkeeper), H. von Karajan (cnd), La Scala Orch, La Scala Chorus *(rec La Scala Theater, Milan, Jan. 26, 1952)* Legato Classics 3-▲ LCD 197–3

Amara, Lucine (sop)
Leoncavallo, R.:Pagliacci, w. France Corelli (ten), Tito Gobbi (bar), L. von Matačič (cnd), La Scala Orch, La Scala Chorus [I] EMI Classics ("Studio" series) 2-▲ CDMB 63967
Offenbach, J.:Les Contes d'Hoffmann, w. R. Peters (sop), R. Stevens (mez), R. Tucker (ten), M. Singher (bar), P. Monteux (cnd), Metropolitan Opera Orch, New York Metropolitan Opera Chorus Stradivarius 2-▲ DAT 12302
Verdi, G.:Requiem Mass, w. M. Forrester (cta), R. Tucker (ten), G. London (bar), E. Ormandy (cnd), Philadelphia Orch, Westminster Choir [L] Odyssey ■ YT 35230
Verdi, G.:Requiem Mass, w. M. Forrester (cta), R. Tucker (ten), G. London (bar), E. Ormandy (cnd), Philadelphia Orch, Westminster Choir Sony Classical ▲ SB2K 53252

Amato, Pasquale (bar)
Le Amato *(rec 1910–14* Pearl ▲ PEA 9104 [ADD]
Bizet, G.:Carmen (sels), w. Geraldine Farrar (sop—Carmen), Giovanni Martinelli (ten—Don José), Pasquale Amato (bar—Escamillo), W. Rogers (cnd), *(orch unknown)*—L'amour est un oiseau rebelle; Près des remparts; Les tringles des sistres; Couplets du Toréador; Halte là! Qui va là?; Au quartier! pour l'appell; La fleur que tu m'avais jetée; Non, tu ne m'aimes pas...Là-bas, dans la montagne; Voyons que j'essaie; Je dis que rien ne m'épouvante; Aragonaise [Prelude to Act 4; w. Arturo Toscanini (cnd), La Scala Orch]; Si tu m'aimes, Carmen; C'est toi! C'est moi!; Mais moi, Carmen, je t'aime encore Nimbus ▲ NI 7872 [ADD]
Il mito dell'opera Bongiovanni ▲ GB 10732 [ADD]
Pasquale Amato, w. Margarete Matzenauer (mez), Frieda Hempel (sop) *(rec by Victor & Fonotipia 1909–1914)* Preiser ("Lebendige Vergangenheit" series) ▲ PRE 89064 (m) [ADD]
Verdi, G.:La forza del destino (sels), w. Enrico Caruso (ten), *(orch unknown)* Forlane ▲ FRL 16718 [ADD]

Ambriz, Lourdes (sop)
Falla, M. de:El retablo de maese Pedro, w. Julianne Baird (sop), Miguel Cortez (ten), William Alvarado (bar), Rafael Puyana (hpd), E. Mata (cnd), Mexican Soloists *(rec Sala Nezahualcóyotl, Universidad Nacional Autónoma de Mexico, Mexico City, Oct. 1994)* Dorian ▲ DOR 90214 [DDD]
Falla, M. de:El sombrero de tres picos (sels), w. E. Mata (cnd), Dallas SO Pro Arte ▲ CDS 581 [DDD]
Musica para una boda Mexicana:Music for a Mexican Wedding, w. Grace Echauri (mez), Pro Musica Chorus, Mexico CO Soloists Ensemble [cnd:Luis Sergio Hernandez] Spartacus ▲ 21015
Revueltas, S.:Music of, w. Jesús Suaste (bar), E. Diemecke (cnd), Camerata de las Américas, Latin American String Quartet, Juan D. Tercero Vocal Octet—Troka; Cuauhnáhuac; The Owl; Frogs; Duet for Duck & Canary; Why Do You Believe?; Walking; Scenes from Childhood; 4 Little Pieces; The Knifesharpener; Market; Sensemayá *(rec Mexico City, Sept 1996)* Dorian ▲ 90244 [DDD]

Ambrosio, Maria (sgr)
Donizetti, G.:L'elisir d'amore (sels), w. Reri Grist (sop), Luciano Pavarotti (ten), Sesto Bruscantini (bar), Ingvar Wixell (bar), G. Patanè (cnd), San Francisco War Memorial Opera House Orch, San Francisco War Memorial Opera House Chorus *(rec live, San Francisco, 1969)* Budget ("The Greatest Voice in Opera" series) ▲ SYP 109

Ambrosis, Walter de (bar)
Puccini, G.:La Bohème (sels), w. Bianco Bellisia (sop—Musetta), Alberto Pellegrini (sop—Mimi), Luciano Pavarotti (ten—Rodolfo), Walter de Ambrosis (bar—Schaunard), Vito Mattioli (bar—Marcello), Dmitri Nabokov (bass—Colline), Reggio Emilia Teatro Municipale Orch, Reggio Emilia Teatro Municipale Chorus Budget ("The Greatest Voice in Opera" series) ▲ SYP 105

Ambroziak, Delfina (sop)
Kilar, W.:Angelus, w. *(orch unknown)*, Polish Radio–TV Chorus *(rec 1979 & 1985)* Olympia ▲ OCD 308 [AAD]
Penderecki, K.:Utrenia, w. Stefania Woytowicz (sop), Krystyna Szczepanska (mez), Kazimierz Pustelak (ten), Boris Carmeli (bass), Wlodzimierz Denysenko (bass), A. Markowski (cnd), Warsaw PO, Józef Bok (cnd), Stanislaw Skoraczewski (cnd), Warsaw National Phil Chorus, Pioneer Choir *(rec Warsaw, 1973)* Polskie Nagrania ▲ PNCD 018

Ambrus, Ákos (bar)
Bengraf, J.:Sacred Music, w. Ingrid Kertesi (sop), Katalin Gémes (mez), Gábor Kállay (ten), István Ella (org), Zsolt Kovács (vc), Balázs Árnóth (bn), Vilmos Buza (db), J. Dobra (cnd), Vienna–Szász CO, Tomkins Vocal Ensemble—Te Deum; O sacrum convivium; Libera me; Gloria [from Missa solemnis in D] Hungaroton ▲ HCD 31609 [DDD]
Druschetzky, G.:Missa solemnis, w. Ingrid Kertesi (sop), Katalin Gémes (mez), Gábor Kállay (ten), István Ella (org), Zsolt Kovács (vc), Balázs Árnóth (bn), Vilmos Buza (db), J. Dobra (cnd), Vienna–Szász CO, Tomkins Vocal Ensemble Hungaroton ▲ HCD 31609 [DDD]
Rachmaninoff, S.:Liturgy of St John Chrysostom, w. Ida Szabó (sop), Tamás Bubnó (ten), Zoltán Kocsis (cnd), Tomkins Vocal Ensemble *(rec 1995)* Hungaroton 2-▲ HCD 31610/11 [DDD]

Ameche, D. (sgr)
Porter, C.:Silk Stockings, w. H. Neff (sgr) [1955 Broadway cast] RCA ▲ 1102 RG [ADD] ■ 1102–4 RG

Ameling, Elly (sop)
Bach, C.P.E.:Magnificat, Collegium Aureum—Quia Respexit Deutsche Harmonia Mundi ▲ 74321–26613–2
Bach, C.P.E.:Songs, w. *(accompianists unknown)*—Quia respexit Deutsche Harmonia Mundi ▲ 74321–26617–2 [ADD]
Bach, J.S.:Anna Magdalena Bach Notebook, w. H.–M. Linde (bar), G. Leonhardt (hpd), J. Koch (va), A. May (vc)—sels. Editio Classica ▲ 77150–2–RG [DDD]
Bach, J.S.:Arias, w. *(accompianists unknown)*—Bist du bei mir; Ich habe genug; Schlummert ein, ihr matten Augen Deutsche Harmonia Mundi ▲ 74321–26617–2 [ADD]
Bach, J.S.:Cant 130, w. H. Watts (cta), W. Krenn (ten), T. Krause (bass), E. Ansermet (cnd), Swiss Romande Orch, Lausanne Pro Arte Choir London ("Serenata" series) ▲ 433175–2 [ADD]
Bach, J.S.:Cant 202, "Wedding Cant", Collegium Aureum Editio Classica 2-▲ 77151–2–RG [ADD]
Bach, J.S.:Cant 202, "Wedding Cant", w. F.–J. Maier (cnd), Collegium Aureum Deutsche Harmonia Mundi ▲ 74321–26614–2
Bach, J.S.:Cant 202, "Wedding Cant", w. *(accompianists unknown)* Deutsche Harmonia Mundi ▲ 74321–26617–2 [ADD]
Bach, J.S.:Cant 209, w. *(accompianists unknown)* Deutsche Harmonia Mundi ▲ 74321–26617–2 [ADD]

1042 ▲ = CD ♦ = Enhanced CD ∆ = MD ■ = Cassette Tape □ = DCC

Ameling, Elly (sop) (cont.)
Bach, J.S.:Cant 209, Collegium Aureum Editio Classica 2-▲ 77151-2-RG [ADD]
Bach, J.S.:Cant 211, "Coffee Cant", w. G. English (ten), S. Nimsgern (b-bar), Collegium Aureum Editio Classica 2-▲ 77151-2-RG [ADD]
Bach, J.S.:Cant 211, "Coffee Cant", w. *(accompianists unknown)* Deutsche Harmonia Mundi ▲ 74321-26617-2 [ADD]
Bach, J.S.:Cant 211, "Coffee Cant", w. F.-J. Maier (cnd), Collegium Aureum—Ei, wie schmeckt der Coffee susse Heute noch, heute noch Deutsche Harmonia Mundi ▲ 74321-26614-2
Bach, J.S.:Cant 212, "Peasant Cant", w. G. English (ten), S. Nimsgern (b-bar), Collegium Aureum Editio Classica 2-▲ 77151-2-RG [ADD]
Bach, J.S.:Cant 212, "Peasant Cant", w. *(accompianists unknown)* Deutsche Harmonia Mundi ▲ 74321-26617-2 [ADD]
Bach, J.S.:Cant 212, "Peasant Cant", w. F.-J. Maier (cnd), Collegium Aureum—Klein Zschocher Deutsche Harmonia Mundi ▲ 74321-26614-2
Bach, J.S.:Christmas Oratorio, w. B. Fassbaender (mez), H. Laubenthal (ten), H. Prey (bar), E. Jochum (cnd), Tölz SO, Bavarian Radio Boys' Chorus—highlights Philips ("Silver Line" series) ▲ 422252-2 [ADD]
Bach, J.S.:Christmas Oratorio, w. Janet Baker (mez), Robert Tear (ten), Dietrich Fischer-Dieskau (bar), P. Ledger (cnd), Academy of St. Martin in the Fields, King's College Choir Cambridge *(rec 1976)* EMI Classics ("Doubleforte" series) 2-▲ CDFB 69503
Bach, J.S.:Magnificat, BWV 243, w. H. van Bork (sop), H. Watts (cta), W. Krenn (ten), T. Krause (bass), K. Münchinger (cnd), Stuttgart CO, Vienna Academy Chorus London ("Serenata" series) ▲ 433175-2 [ADD]
Bach, J.S.:St. Matthew Passion, w. B. Finnilä (cta), E. Haefliger (ten), S. McCoy (ten), B. Luxon (bar), B. McDaniel (bar), J. Somary (cnd), English CO, Ambrosian Singers *(rec 1977)* Vanguard Classics 3-▲ OVC 4060/62 [ADD]
Bach, J.S.:St. Matthew Passion (sels), w. B. Finnilä (cta), E. Haefliger (ten), S. McCoy (ten), B. Luxon (bar), B. McDaniel (bar), J. Somary (cnd), English CO, Ambrosian Singers Vanguard Classics ▲ OVC 4063 [ADD]
Bach, J.S.:Songs—Bist du bei mir; Ich habe genug - Schlummert ein, ihr matten Augen Deutsche Harmonia Mundi ▲ 74321-26613-2
Berlioz, H.:Les Nuits d'été, w. R. Shaw (cnd), Atlanta SO [F] Telarc ▲ CD 80084 [DDD]
Brahms, J.:Songs, w. *(accompianists unknown)*—18 songs Deutsche Harmonia Mundi ▲ 74321-26617-2 [ADD]
Fauré, G.:Requiem, w. B. Kruysen (bar), J. Fournet (cnd), Rotterdam PO [L] Philips ▲ 420707-2 [ADD]
Fauré, G.:Songs, w. G. Souzay (bar), D. Baldwin (pno) [complete edition of Fauré's songs] EMI Classics 4-▲ CDMD 64079
Handel, G.F.:Arias, w. *(accompianists unknown)*—Pensiero notturni di filli; Ah che troppo inegall Deutsche Harmonia Mundi ▲ 74321-26617-2 [ADD]
Handel, G.F.:Cants—Pensiero notturni di Filli "Nel dolce dell'oblio"; Ah, che troppo inegal Deutsche Harmonia Mundi ▲ 74321-26613-2
Handel, G.F.:Messiah, w. Anna Reynolds (mez), Philip Langridge (ten), Gwynne Howell (bass), N. Marriner (cnd), Academy of St. Martin in the Fields, Academy of St. Martin in the Fields Chorus [E] Argo ▮ 421234-4
Handel, G.F.:Messiah, w. Anna Reynolds (alt), Philip Langridge (ten), Gwynne Howell (bass), N. Marriner (cnd), Academy of St. Martin in the Fields, Academy of St. Martin in the Fields Chorus *(rec St John's, Smith Square, London, Jan & July 1976)* London ("Double Decker" series) 2-▲ 444824-2 [ADD]
Mahler, G.:Syms, w. H. Harper (mez), M. Forrester (cta), H. Prey (bar), B. Haitink (cnd), Royal Concertgebouw Orch Philips 10-▲ 442050-2
Mahler, G.:Sym 4, w. B. Haitink (cnd), Royal Concertgebouw Orch Philips ("Solo" series) ▲ 442394-2
Mahler, G.:Sym 4, w. A. Previn (cnd), Pittsburgh SO EMI Classics ▲ CDM 65179
Martin, F.:Chants de Noël, w. P. Odé (fl), F. Martin (pno) [F] Jecklin-Disco ▲ JD 563-2 [ADD]
Martin, F.:Le Mystère de la Nativité, w. Aafje Heynis (cta), Hugues Cuénod (ten), Louis Devos (ten), Eric Tappy (ten), Pierre Bollet (bar), Derrik Olsen (bar), Charles Clavensy (b-bar), André Vessières (bass), E. Ansermet (cnd), Swiss Romande Orch, Jeunes de l'Eglise Chorus, Geneva Motet Chorus Cascavelle 2-▲ CVL 2006 [ADD]
Martin, F.:Songs, w. F. Martin (pno), P. Odé (fl)—Drey Minnelieder:Ach Herzeliep; Es stuont ein frouwe alleine; Under der linden [G] Jecklin-Disco ▲ JD 563-2 [ADD]
Mendelssohn, F.:Elijah, w. A. Burmeister (mez), P. Schreier (ten), T. Adam (b-bar), W. Sawallisch (cnd), Leipzig Gewandhaus Orch, Leipzig Radio Chorus [G] Philips 2-▲ 420106-2 [AAD]
Mendelssohn, F.:Elijah, w. A. Burmeister (mez), P. Schreier (ten), T. Adam (b-bar), W. Sawallisch (cnd), Leipzig Gewandhaus Orch, Leipzig Radio Chorus Philips 2-▲ 438368-2
Monteverdi, C.:Vespro della Beata Vergine, w. Norma Burrowes (sop), Charles Brett (ct), Martyn Hill (ten), Anthony Rolfe-Johnson (ten), Robert Tear (ten), Peter Knapp (bass), John Noble (bass), Francis Grier (org/hpd), James Lancelot (org/hpd), Andrew Leach (org/hpd), P. Ledger (cnd), London Early Music Consort, King's College Choir Cambridge—Nigra sum [con.]; Laudate pueri [psalm]; Sancta Maria [son. sopra]; Magnificat *(rec Chapel of King's College, Cambridge, July & Aug. 1975)* EMI Classics ▲ CDK 65330 [ADD]
Monteverdi, C.:Vespro della Beata Vergine, w. Norma Burrowes (sop), Charles Brett (ct), Robert Tear (ten), Anthony Rolfe Johnson (ten), Martyn Hill (ten), Peter Knapp (bass), John Noble (bass), Munrow, Ledger (cnd), London Early Music Consort EMI Classics ("Doubleforte" series) 2-▲ CDFB 68631
Mozart, W.A.:Complete Mozart Edition, w. Dalton Baldwin (pno), Netherlands Wind Ensemble Philips 2-▲ 422524-2 [ADD]
Mozart, W.A.:Requiem, w. M. Horne (mez), U. Benelli (bar), T. Franc (bass), I. Kertész (cnd), Vienna PO, Vienna State Opera Chorus London ("Weekend Classics" series) ▲ 417681-2 [ADD] ▮ 417681-4
Poulenc, F.:Songs, w. G. Souzay (bar), D. Baldwin (pno)—complete EMI Classics 4-▲ CDMD 64087
Schubert, Franz:Der Hirt auf dem Felsen, w. I. Gage (pno), J. Demus (pno) EMI Classics ▲ CDM 65179
Schubert, Franz:Rosamunde, w. K. Masur (cnd), Leipzig Gewandhaus Orch, Leipzig Radio Chorus [G] Philips ▲ 412432-2 [DDD]
Schubert, Franz:Songs (comp), w. G. Johnson (pno)—23 songs [G] Hyperion ▲ CDJ 33007 [DDD]
Schubert, Franz:Songs (misc), w. A. Previn (cnd), Pittsburgh SO—An die Musik; Ständchen EMI Classics ▲ CDM 65179
Schubert, Franz:Songs (misc), w. D. Baldwin (pno)—13 songs [G] Philips ("Silver Line" series) ▲ 420870-2 [ADD]
Schubert, Franz:Songs (misc), w. J. Demus (pno), H. Deinzer (cl) Editio Classica ▲ 77085-2-RG [ADD]
Schubert, Franz:Songs (misc), w. R. Jansen (pno)—18 songs [G] *(rec live, Tanglewood Theatre-Concert Hall, 7/2/87)* Omega ▲ OCD 1001 [DDD]
Schubert, Franz:Songs (misc), w. Elly Ameling (sop) *(accompianists unknown)*—9 songs Deutsche Harmonia Mundi ▲ 74321-26617-2 [ADD]
Schubert, Franz:Songs (misc), w. Judith Blegen (sop), Judith Raskin (sop), Kiri Te Kanawa (sop)—Rastlose Liebe; Gretchen am Spinnrade; Trockne Blumen; Nur wer die Sehnsucht kennt Sony Classical ("Essential Classics" series) ▲ SBK 62422 ▮ SBT 62422
Schumann, R.:Lieder-Album (sels), w. *(accompianists unknown)*—5 sels Deutsche Harmonia Mundi ▲ 74321-26617-2 [ADD]
Schumann, R.:Myrthen, w. *(accompianists unknown)* Deutsche Harmonia Mundi ▲ 74321-26617-2 [ADD]
Schumann, R.:Songs, w. J. Demus (pno) Editio Classica ▲ 77085-2-RG [ADD]
Telemann, G.P.:Cants—Mit sehnenden verlangen [from Trauerkantate]; Richt ihr muede Augen nieder Deutsche Harmonia Mundi ▲ 74321-26613-2
Telemann, G.P.:Songs—Mit sehnenden Verlangen; Richt ihr müde Augen nieder Deutsche Harmonia Mundi ▲ 74321-26617-2 [ADD]
Wolf, H.:Songs (misc), w. Rudolf Jansen (pno)—Die ihr schwebet; Komm, o Tod; Mögen alle bösen Zungen; Sagt, seid ihr es; Tief im Herzen trag ich Pein; In dem Schatten meiner Locken; Wer tat deinem Füsslein weh?; Ach, des Knaben Augen; Ob auch finstre Blicken glitten; Alle gingen, Herz, zur Ruh'; Bedeckt mich mit Blumen; Müh voll komm ich; Sie blasen zum Abmarsch; Geh, Geliebter; Auf ein altes Bild; Im Frühling; Elfenlied; Verborgenheit; Das verlassene Mägdlein; Lied von Winde; Nimmersatte Liebe Hyperion ▲ CDA 66788

Ames, Donna (alt)
Purcell, H.:Dido & Aeneas, w. Nancy Maultsby (sop—Dido), Susannah Waters (sop—Belinda), Margaret O'Keefe (sop—1st Witch), Sharon Baker (sop—2nd Woman), Laura Tucker (mez—Sorceress), Donna Ames (alt—Spirit), Richard Clement (ten—Sailor), Russell Braun (bar—Aeneas), M. Pearlman (cnd), Boston Baroque Orch Telarc ▲ CD 80424 [DDD]

Amihai, Y. (sgr)
Avni, T.:Collage, w. E. Talmi (fl), Milo [Leon Malloy] (perc) Symposium ▲ 1110

Amis, John (nar)
Poulenc, F.:L'Histoire de Babar, w. L. Howard (pno) [recited in English] Nimbus ▲ NI 5342 [DDD]

Amis, John (ten)
Herrmann, B.:Moby Dick, w. Robert Bowman (ten), David Kelly (bass), Michael Rippon (bass), London PO, Aeolian Singers [E] Unicorn-Kanchana ▲ UKCD 2061
John Amis:A Miscellany Nimbus ▲ NI 5342 [DDD]

Amit, Sheila (nar)
Gorb, A.:Hymns Uproarious, w. B. Luxon (nar), P. Gilbert-Dyson (cnd), Belmont Ensemble London Symposium ▲ SYM 1180
Walton, W.:Façade, w. B. Luxon (nar), P. Gilbert-Dyson (cnd), Belmont Ensemble London Symposium ▲ SYM 1180
Watson, T.:Dick Whittington & His Cat, w. B. Luxon (nar), P. Gilbert-Dyson (cnd), Belmont Ensemble London Symposium ▲ SYM 1180

Amorocho, Cecilia (sgr)
Caccini, F.:La liberazione di Ruggiero dall'isola d'Alcina, w. Linda De Rungs (sop—Alcian/Vistola), Cecilia Amorocho (sgr—Melissa/Nunzia), Laura Lea Duckworth (sgr—Siren/Harpy), Eric Friedlander (sgr—Monster), L. Ernest Gross (sgr—Enchanted Cypress), Phoebe Jevtovic (sgr—Siren), James Rittenhouse (sgr—Ruggiero/Neptune), Sharon Sim (sgr—Siren), R. Burchard (cnd), Ars Femina Ensemble, TimeChange *(rec Louisville, KY, 1993)* Nannerl ▲ NR-ARS 003; ▮ NR-ARS 003

Amos, Diana (sop)
Krenek, E.:Der Sprung über den Schatten, w. L. Kemeny (sop), S. MacLean (mez), J. Dürmüller (ten), U. Neuweiler (ten), J. Pflieger (bar), T. Brüning (sgr), D. de Villiers (cnd), Bielefeld PO, Bielefeld Phil Chorus [G] *(rec live, May 1989)* CPO 2-▲ CPO 999082-2 [DDD]

Amparan, Belan (cta)
Ponchielli, A.:La Gioconda, w. Zinka Milanov (sop—La Gioconda), Rosalind Elias (mez—Laura), Belan Amparan (cta—La Cieca), Giacomo Cottino (ten—Isepo), Giuseppe Di Stefano (ten—Enzo Grimaldo), Fernando Valentini (bar—Zuane/Un Nocchiero), Leonard Warren (bar—Barnaba), Virgilio Carbonari (bass—Un Cantore), Plinio Clabassi (bass—Alvise Badoero), F. Previtali (cnd), St. Cecilia Academy Orch Rome, St. Cecilia Academy Chorus Rome Theorema 3-▲ TH 121182/184

Amps, Kym (sop)
Adams, J.:Grand Pianola Music, w. Ruth Holton (sop), Lyndsay Wagstaff (sop), Ellen Corver (pno), Sepp Grotenhuis (pno), S. Mosko (cnd), Netherlands Wind Ensemble Chandos ▲ CHAN 9363 [DDD]
Biber, H. von:Vesperae longiores ac breviores una cum litaniis Laurentanis, w. Christopher Robson (alt), Anton Rosner (ten), Albert Hartinger (bass), H. Arman (cnd), Salzburg Baroque Ensemble, Innsbruck Woodwind Circle, Salzburg Bach Choir, Salzburg St. Benedict College Schola Ars Musici ("Essence" series) ▲ AME 3022-2 [DDD]
Purcell, H.:Odes & Welcome Songs (misc), w. J. Smith (sop), E. Priday (sop), M. Chance (ct), Wilson (sgr), J. M. Ainsley (ten), S. Richardson (bar), T. Pinnock (cnd), English Concert, *(chorus unknown)* —Come ye Sons of Art; Welcome to All the Pleasures; Of Old, When Heroes Thought it Base Archiv ▲ 427663-2 [DDD]

Amsler, Ruth (sop)
Wehrli, W.:Ein weltliches Requiem, w. D. Labusch (cta), B. Hunziker (ten), R. Strebel (bass), K. Girod (cnd), Aargauer CO, Aargauer Chamber Choir *(rec live Jan. 12, 1992)* Jecklin ▲ JS 276-2 [DDD]

Ancona, Mario (bar)
Caruso in Arias, Duets & Songs, w. E. Caruso (ten), Louise Homer (cta), Titta Ruffo (bar), Antonio Scotti (bar) Supraphon Collection ▲ SUP 110618 (m) [ADD]

Anday, Rosette (cta)
Beethoven, L. van:Sym 9, "Choral Sym", w. Luise Helletsgruber (sop), Georg Maikl (ten), Richard Mayr (bass), F. von Weingartner (cnd), Vienna PO, Vienna State Opera Chorus *(rec Feb. 2-5, 1935)* Preiser ▲ PRE 90193 [ADD]
Einem, G. von:Dantons Tod, w. M. Cebotari (sop—Lucille Desmoulins), R. Anday (cta—Frau des Simon), P. Klein (ten—de Séchelles), J. Patzak (ten—Camille Desmoulins), J. Witt (ten—Robspierre), P. Schöffler (bar—Danton), L. Weber (bass—Saint Just), F. Fricsay (cnd), Vienna PO, Vienna State Opera Chorus *(rec Aug. 6, 1947)* Stradivarius 2-▲ STR 10067 [ADD]
Millöcker, C.:Bettelstudent, w. Wilma Lipp (sop—Laura), Esther Rethy (sop—Bronislava), Rosette Anday (cta—Palmatica), Rudolf Christ (ten—Symon), Kurt Preger (ten—Ollendorf), Eberhard Waechter (bar—Jan), A. Paulik (cnd), Vienna Volksoper Orch, Vienna Volksoper Chorus *(rec Brahmssaal, Vienna, June 1995)* Omega 2-▲ OCD 1018/19 [ADD]
Rosette Anday, w. Vienna State Opera Orch [cnd:Carl Alwin], Berlin State Opera Orch [cnd:Julius Prüwer], London SO [cnd:Robert Heger] Preiser ("Lebendige Vergangenheit" series) ▲ PRE 89016 (m) [AAD]
Strauss (II), Joh.:Der Zigeunerbaron, w. Emmy Loose (sop), Hilde Zadek (sop), Julius Patzak (ten), Karl Dönch (bar), Alfred Poell (bar), Steffi Leverenz (sgr), C. Krauss (cnd), Vienna PO, Vienna State Opera Chorus Phonographe 2-▲ PHG 5020 [AAD]
Strauss, R.:Arabella, w. L. Della Casa (sop), M. Reining (sop), H. Hotter (b-bar), G. Hann (bass), J. Patzak (ten), K. Böhm (cnd), Vienna PO, Vienna State Opera Chorus *(rec live, Salzburg Festival, 8/12/47)* Melodram 3-▲ MEL 37077
Verdi, G.:Aida (sels), w. Maria Nemeth (sop—Aida), Rosette Anday (cta—Amneris), Benjamino Gigli (ten—Radames), Alexander Kipnis (bass—Ramfis), K. Alwin (cnd), Vienna State Opera Orch *(rec May 23, 1937)* Koch Schwann 2-▲ SCH 314632 [ADD]
Weill, K.:The Threepenny Opera, w. Liane (sop—Polly Peachum), A. Felbermayer (sop—Lucy), H. Fassler (sop—Jenny), R. Anday (cta—Mrs. Peachum), K. Preger (ten—Macheath), H. Roswaenge (ten—Street Crier), A. Jerger (bar—Peachum), F. Gutherie (bar), *(cnd & orch unknown)* Vanguard Classics ▲ OVC 8057 [ADD]

Anders, C. (spkr)
Goebbels, H.:Befreiung, w. P. Rundel (cnd), Ensemble Modern *(rec May 1992)* ECM New Series ("New" series) ▲ 78118-21483-2 [DDD]

Anders, Peter (ten)
Beethoven, L. van:Songs, w. Michael Raucheisen (pno)—Adelaide Berlin Classics ▲ BER 2167 [ADD]
Beethoven, L. van:Sym 9, "Choral Sym", w. Tilla Briem (sop), Elisabeth Höngen (cta), Rudolf Watzke (bass), W. Furtwängler (cnd), Berlin PO, Bruno Kittel Choir *(rec 1942)* Grammofono 2000 ▲ GRM 78581
Beethoven, L. van:Sym 9, "Choral Sym", w. Tilla Briem (sop), Elisabeth Höngen (cta), Rudolf Watzke (bass), W. Furtwängler (cnd), Berlin PO, Bruno Kittel Choir *(rec Mar 22, 1942)* Iron Needle 3-▲ IN 1348/50 [ADD]
Brahms, J.:Songs, w. Michael Raucheisen (pno)—Sehnsucht Berlin Classics ▲ BER 2167 [ADD]
Flotow, F. von:Martha, w. E. Berger (sop), E. Fuchs (bar), J. Greindl (bass), J. Schüler (cnd), Berlin State Opera Orch *(rec 1944)* Berlin Classics 2-▲ BER 2163 [ADD]
Flotow, F. von:Martha, w. Erna Berger (sop), Eugene Fuchs (bar), Josef Greindl (bass), J. Schüler (cnd), Berlin German Opera Orch, Berlin German Opera Chorus Phonographe 2-▲ PHG 5050
The Legendary Singers at Lindenoper Berlin (1927-1945)—, w. Gitta Alpar (sop), Erna Berger (sop), Tiana Lemnitz (sop), Maria Müller (sop), Margarete Klose (cta), Max Lorenz (ten), Walter Ludwig (ten), Lauritz Melchior (ten), Rudolf Schock (ten), Franz Völker (ten), Willi Domgraf-Fassbaender *(rec 1927; 1937; 1941-45)* Minerva ▲ MN A21 [ADD]
Lehár, F.:Paganini (sels), w. A. Schlemm (mez), Lisolette Losch (sop), Gehly (sgr), Hofmann (sgr), Schneider (sgr), Marszalek (cnd), Cologne RSO, Cologne Radio Chorus [G] Acanta ▲ CD 43810 [DDD]
Mozart, W.A.:Entführung (sels), *(cnd & orch unknown)* Berlin Classics ▲ BER 2168 [ADD]
Mozart, W.A.:Zauberflöte (sels), w. *(other artists unknown)* Berlin Classics ▲ BER 2168 [ADD]
Nicolai, O.:Lustigen Weiber (sels), w. *(other artists unknown)* Berlin Classics ▲ BER 2168 [ADD]

Anders, Peter (ten) (cont.)
Offenbach, J.:Les Contes d'Hoffmann (sels), w. *(other artists unknown)* Berlin Classics ▲ BER 2168 [ADD]
Opera & Operetta Arias Acanta ▲ 43268
Opera Arias, w. Anders, Peter (ten), Berlin German Opera House Orch Teldec ▲ 95512-2 [ADD]
Schillings, M. von:Glockenlieder, w. R. Heger (cnd), Berlin Staatskapelle [G] *(rec 5/20/43)* Acanta ▲ 43275 (m)
Schillings, M. von:Glockenlieder, w. *(other artists unknown)* Berlin Classics ▲ BER 2168 [ADD]
Schoeck, O.:Das Schloss Dürande (sels), w. Maria Cebotari (sop—Gabriele), Marta Fuchs (sop—Gräfin Morvaille), Brigitte Fassbaender (mez—Renald Willi Domgraf), Rut Berglund (cta—Priorin), Peter Anders (ten—Armand), Benno Arnold (ten—Jäger), Josef Greindl (bass—Nicole), Hans Wrana (bass—Jäger), Vasso Argyris (sgr—Volksredner), Otto Hüsch (sgr—Wildhüter), Leo Laschet (sgr—Jäger), Fritz Marcks (sgr—Jäger), Felix Schneider (sgr—Jäger), R. Heger (cnd)—Text; Ich kann es nicht glauben [from Act 1]; Text; Heil dir, du Feuerquelle [from Act 2]; Text; Gesucht und nicht gefunden [from Act 3]; Text; Der Jäger ist frei! [Act 3 Finale]; Text; Sie kommen mit Flinten und Stangen [Act 4]; Text; Du Narr des vermeintlichen Rechts [Act 4 finale]; Text *(rec live, Apr 1943)* Jecklin ▲ JD 692
Schubert, Franz:Songs (misc), w. Michael Raucheisen (pno) *(rec 1942–44)* Berlin Classics ▲ BER 2166 [ADD]
Schubert, Franz:Winterreise, w. G. Weissenborn (pno) [G] Acanta ▲ CD 43806 [DDD]
Schumann, R.:Songs, w. Michael Raucheisen (pno) Berlin Classics ▲ BER 2167 [ADD]
Strauss (II), Joh.:Die Fledermaus, w. R. Streich (sop), A. Schlemm (mez), H. Krebs (ten), F. Fricsay (cnd), Berlin RSO, Berlin Radio Chorus [G] *(rec live, Berlin, 11/8/49)* Melodram 2-▲ MEL 29001 (m) [AAD]
Strauss (II), Joh.:Der Zigeunerbaron (sels), w. S. Jurinac (sop), W. Hollweg (ten), K. Schmitt-Walter (bar), Schneider (sgr), G. Hann (bass), Marszalek (cnd), Cologne RSO, Cologne Radio Chorus [G] Acanta ▲ CD 43807 [DDD]
Strauss, R.:Songs, w. Michael Raucheisen (pno)—Allerseelen Berlin Classics ▲ BER 2167 [ADD]
Strauss, R.:Songs, w. W. Furtwängler (cnd), Berlin PO *(rec 2/42)* Arabesque ▲ Z 6082 (m)
Strauss, R.:Songs, w. W. Furtwängler (cnd), Berlin PO—4 Songs *(rec Feb. 15–17, 1942)* Music & Arts ▲ CD 829 [AAD]
Wagner, R.:Lohengrin, w. H. Braun (sop—Ortrud), T. Epperle (sop—Elsa von Brabant), P. Anders (ten—Lohengrin), C. Kronenberg (bar—Frederich von Telramund), J. Greindl (bass—Heinrich der Vogler), R. Kraus (cnd), Cologne RSO, Cologne Radio Chorus *(rec Nov. 1951)* Myto 3-▲ MCD 93485
Wie wir ihn niemals vergessen Acanta ▲ 43812
Wolf, H.:Songs (misc), w. Michael Raucheisen (pno) Berlin Classics ▲ BER 2167 [ADD]

Andersen, B. (bass)
Milesi, P.:Modi 2, w. L. M. Pickova (sop), Françoise Goddard (alt), M. Ferradini (ten), D. Cassamagnaghi (fl), S. Scanziani (ob), A. Bianchi (cl/b cl), E. Crisafulli (bn), C. Gazzola (hn), F. Gualandris (tuba), A. Girardi (celtic hp), R. Anedda (vn), E. Groppo (vn), M. Pagani (vn), M. Ravasio (va), S. Righini (vc), P. Rizzi (db), J. Scully (perc), P. Milesi (cnd) Cuneiform ▲ RUNE 63

Andersen, Duane (b-bar)
Parker, H.:Hora novissima, w. A. Soranno (sop), J. Simson (mez), K. Hall (b-bar), J. Levick (cnd), Nebraska CO, Abendmusik Chorus, Nebraska Wesleyan Univ Choir Albany 2-▲ TROY 124/25

Andersen, Hanne (sop)
Klit, L.:The Last Virtuoso, w. Edith Guillaume (mez), Jan Lund (ten), Jesper Buhl (bar), Jørgen Ole Børch (bass), S. A. Johansen (cnd), *(ensemble unknown)* Kontrapunkt ▲ KPT 32221
Musiana 95:Electroacoustic Music from Denmark & Japan, w. Ensemble from the East, Trio Sparnaay/Kooistra/Abe, Sofia Asunción Claro, Mari Kimura (hp/vn), Thomas Sandberg, Harry Sparnaay (b cl) Classico ▲ CLASSCD 139 [DDD]

Andersen, Hans Christian (bass)
Liszt, F.:Missa choralis, w. Irene Graaner (sop), Else Paaske (alt), Kai Hansen (ten), Michael Hansen (bar), Niels Henrik Nielsen (org), Tamás Vető (cnd), Copenhagen Univ Choir Point ▲ PCD 5075 [ADD]

Andersen, Stig (ten)
Beethoven, L. van:Fidelio (sels), w. Evelyn Herlitzius (sop—Leonore), Ruth Ziesak (sop—Marzelline), Stig Andersen (ten—Florestan), Herbert Lippert (ten—Jaquino), Albert Dohmen (bar—Don Pizarro), Andreas Kohn (bass—Don Fernando), Hans Tschammer (bass—Rocco), G. Solti (cnd), World Orch for Peace, London Voices—Finale Act II *(rec Victoria Hall, Geneva, July 5, 1995)* London ▲ 448901-2 [DDD]

Anderson, Douglas (bar)
Telemann, G.P.:Der Tag des Gerichts, w. Patrice Michaels Bell (sop), Sandra Walker (mez), Karen Brunssen (mez), Bruce Fowler (ten), Kurt R. Hansen (ten), William Stone (bar), T. Wikman (cnd), Music of the Baroque Orch, Baroque Music Chorus *(rec live, St. Paul's United Church of Christ, Feb 23, 1992)* Music of the Baroque 2-▲ MB 107

Anderson, June (sop)
Albinoni, T.:Il Nascimento de l'Aurora, w. Susanne Klare (sop), Margarita Zimmermann (sop), Sandra Browne (alt), Yoshihisa Yamaj (ten), C. Scimone (cnd), Venice Solisti Erato 2-▲ ERA SEL 96374 [DDD]
Beethoven, L. van:Christus am Ölberg, w. M. Pick-Hieronimi (sop), V. von Halem (bass), S. Baudo (cnd), Lyon National Orch, Lyon National Chorus [G] Harmonia Mundi France ▲ HMC 905181
Bellini, V.:Arias, w. N. Rescigno (cnd), Monte Carlo PO—I puritani—Son vergin vezzosa; Ah! rendetemi la speme...Qui la voce...Vien diletto; I Capuleti e i Montecchi—Eccomi in lieta vesta...Oh! quante volte; La sonnambula—Oh! se una volta...Ah! non credea mirarti...Ah! non giunge; Beatrice di Tenda—Oh! miei fideli...Ma la sola...Ah! la pena [I] EMI Classics ▲ CDC 47561 [DDD]
Bernstein, L.:Candide (restored), w. C. Ludwig (mez), D. Jones (mez), J. Hadley (ten), N. Gedda (ten), A. Green (sgr), K. Ollmann (bar), L. Bernstein (cnd), London SO, London Sym Chorus *(rec 1989)* Deutsche Grammophon ▲ 429734-2 [DDD] ■ 429734-4
Bernstein, L.:Candide (restored), w. C. Ludwig (mez), D. Jones (mez), J. Hadley (ten), N. Gedda (ten), A. Green (sgr), K. Ollmann (bar), L. Bernstein (cnd), London SO, London Sym Chorus Deutsche Grammophon ■ 437328-4
Bernstein, L.:Music of, w. J. Norman (sop), K. Te Kanawa (sop), F. von Stade (mez), C. Ludwig (mez), T. Troyanos (mez), J. Carreras (ten), D. Garrison (ten), J. Hadley (ten), T. Hampson (bar), T. Daly (sgr), G. Kremer (vn), M. Rostropovich (vc), M.T. Thomas (vc), L. Bernstein (cnd), *(orch unknown)*—various popular works Deutsche Grammophon ▲ 439251-2 ■ 439251-4
Live at the Paris Opera, w. Alfredo Kraus (ten), Paris Opera Orch [cnd:Michelangelo Veltri] EMI Classics ▲ CDC 49067 [DDD]
Live in Concert, w. Emilia Romagna Toscanini SO *(rec 11/24/84)* Bongiovanni ▲ GB 2504-2
Mozart, W.A.:Zauberflöte, w. B. Hendricks (sop—Pamina), J. Anderson (sop—Queen of the Night), U. Steinsky (sop—Papagena), J. Hadley (ten—Tamino), T. Allen (bar—Papageno), R. Lloyd (bass—Sarastro), C. Mackerras (cnd), Scottish CO, Scottish Chamber Chorus [G] Telarc 2-▲ CD 80302 [DDD]
Mozart, W.A.:Zauberflöte (sels), w. B. Hendricks (sop), J. Hadley (sop), T. Allen (bar), R. Lloyd (b-bar), U. Steinsky (sop), Scottish CO, Scottish Sym Chorus *(rec July 13–22, 1991)* Telarc ▲ CD 80345 [DDD]
Orff, C.:Carmina burana, w. P. Creech (ten), B. Weikl (bar), J. Levine (cnd), Chicago SO, Chicago Sym Chorus [G,L] Deutsche Grammophon ▲ 415136-2 [DDD] ■ 415136-4
Pergolesi, G.B.:Salve regina in a, w. C. Dutoit (cnd), Montreal Sinfonietta London ▲ 436209-2 [DDD]
Pergolesi, G.B.:Stabat mater, w. C. Bartoli (mez), *(organist unknown)*, C. Dutoit (cnd), Montreal Sinfonietta London ▲ 436209-2 [DDD]
Rossini, G.:Arias, w. Montserrat Caballé (sop), Maria Callas (sop), Edita Gruberova (sop), Pilar Lorengar (sop), Mady Mesplé (sop), Nicolai Gedda (ten), Tito Gobbi (bar), Samuel Ramey (bass), *(orchs unknown)* —from Barbiere di Siviglia; La Cenerentola; La Gazza ladra; Petite messe solennelle; Semiramide; Stabat Mater *(rec 1958–89)* EMI Classics 2-▲ CZS 67440-2 [ADD/DDD]
Rossini, G.:Arias, w. D. Gatti (cnd), Bologna Teatro Comunale Orch, Bologna Teatro Comunale Chorus—arias from La Donna Del Lago, Semiramide, Otello, Guillaume Tell, Ermione, Il viaggio a Reims [I] London ▲ 436377-2 [DDD]
Rossini, G.:Mosè in Egitto, w. S. Nimsgern (b-bar), R. Raimondi (bass), C. Scimone (cnd), Philharmonia Orch, Ambrosian Opera Chorus [I] Philips 2-▲ 420109-2 [ADD]
Rossini, G.:Les Soirées musicales, w. K. Bouleyn (sop), R. Giménez (ten), A. Corbelli (bar), N. Walker (pno) [I] Nimbus ▲ NI 5132 [DDD]

Anderson, June (sop) (cont.)
Scarlatti, A.:Salve regina, w. C. Bartoli (mez), C. Dutoit (cnd), Montreal Sinfonietta London ▲ 436209-2 [DDD]
Thomas, A.:Hamlet, w. J. Anderson (sop—Ophelie), D. Graves (mez—Gertrude), G. Kunde (ten—Laerte), T. Hampson (bar—Hamlet), S. Ramey (bass—Claudius), A. de Almeida (cnd), London PO, Ambrosian Singers EMI Classics 3-▲ CDCC 54820
Verdi, G.:Arias, w. K. Battle (sop), J. Sutherland (sop), M. Price (sop), L. Pavarotti (ten), L. Nucci (bar)—includes favorite arias from Aida, Ballo in maschera, Don Carlos, Nabucco, Rigoletto, Traviata, Trovatore London ("Ovation" series) ▲ 430748-2 [DDD]
Verdi, G.:Rigoletto (sels), w. S. Verrett (mez), L. Pavarotti (ten), L. Nucci (bar), N. Ghiaurov (bass), R. Chailly (cnd), Bologna Teatro Comunale Orch, Bologna Teatro Comunale Chorus London ▲ 436097-2 [DDD]
Wagner, R.:Die Feen, w. L. E. Gray (sop), K. Lövaas (sop), K. Láki (sop), R. Alexander (sop), R. Hermann (bar), K. Moll (bass), W. Sawallisch (cnd), Bavarian RSO, Bavarian Radio Chorus [G] *(rec live, Munich Opera Fest. 1983)* Orfeo 3-▲ 062833 [DDD]

Anderson, Kevin (ten)
Weisgall, H.:Six Characters in Search of an Author, w. E. Byrne (sop—Stepdaughter), S. Foster (sop—Prompter), E. Furtal (sop—Coloratura), J. King (mez—Mezzo), N. Maultsby (mez—Mother), P. LoVerne (cta—Madame Pace), D. Pritchett (alt—Wardrobe Mistress), B. Fowler (ten—Tenore Boffo), K. Anderson (ten—Director), A. Schroeder (bar—Accompanist), P. Zawisza (bar—Stage Manager), R. Orth (bar—Father), G. Lehman (bar—Son), M. Wadsworth (b-bar—Basso Cantante), L. Schaenen (cnd), Chicago Lyric Opera Orch, Lyric Opera Center Chorus *(rec Chicago, June 14 & 16, 1990)* New World 2-▲ 80454-2

Anderson, Lorna (sop)
Schubert, Franz:Songs (misc), w. Catherine Wyn-Rogers (alt), Jamie McDougall (ten) Simon Keenlyside (bar), Graham Johnson (pno), London Schubert Chorale—Das Leben ist ein Traum; Das Grab; Trinklied; Punschlied; Vaterlandslied; Selma und Selmar; Morgenlied; An die Sonne; Hermann und Thusnelda; Cora und die Sonne; Lorna; Genugsamkeit; Der Abend; Das Mädchen aus der Fremde; Am Rosa (I); Am Rosa (II); An Sie; Gebet während der Schlacht; Das Abendroth; Die drei Sänger; Die Sterne; Cronnan; Furcht der Geliebten; Die Erscheinung; Stolie; Das Bild; Lob des Tokayers Hyperion ▲ CDJ 33022

Anderson, Marian (cta)
Brahms, J.:Alto Rhap, w. E. Ormandy (cnd), Philadelphia Orch, Philadelphia Orch Chorus [G] *(rec 1939 for HMV)* Pearl ▲ PEA 9405 (m) [AAD]
Brahms, J.:Schicksalslied, w. P. Monteux (cnd), San Francisco SO [arr for voc & orch] RCA Gold Seal ("Pierre Monteux Edition" series) ▲ 09026-61891-2
Brahms, J.:Songs, w. E. Ormandy (cnd), Philadelphia Orch—Der Schmied, Op. 19/4; Dein blaues Auge, Op. 59/8; Immer leiser wird mein Schlummer, Op. 105/2 [G] *(rec 1939 for HMV)* Pearl ▲ PEA 9405 (m) [AAD]
Christmas Treasures, w. L. Price (sop), Rosalind Elias (mez), Mario Lanza (ten), Giorgio Tozzi (bass), Arthur Fiedler (cnd), Leopold Stokowski (cnd), Robert Shaw Chorale RCA Living Stereo ▲ 09026-61867-2 ■ 09026-61867-4
The Lady from Philadelphia *(rec between 1938 & 1941)* Pearl ▲ PEA 9069 [AAD]
Mahler, G.:Kindertotenlieder, w. P. Monteux (cnd), San Francisco SO RCA Gold Seal ("Pierre Monteux Edition" series) ▲ 09026-61891-2
Marian Anderson RCA Gold Seal ▲ 7911-2-RG (m) [ADD] ■ 7911-4-RG
Marian Anderson *(rec 1928–1939)* Pearl ▲ PEA 9405 (m) [AAD]
Marian Anderson Memoir Classics ▲ 432 [ADD]
Marian Anderson *(rec 1927–1937)* Pearl ▲ PEA 9318 (m) [AAD]
Massenet, J.:Chérubin, w. D. Upshaw (sop), F. von Stade (mez), S. Ramey (bass), P. Steinberg (cnd), Munich RSO, Bavarian State Opera Chorus RCA Red Seal 2-▲ 09026-60593-2 [DDD]
Sibelius, J.:Songs, w. K. Vehanen (pno)—Come away, death; Säv, säv susa, Op. 36/4; Flickan kom ifran sin, Op. 37/5; Aus banger Brust, Op. 50/4; Langsamt som Kvällaskyn, Op. 61/1 [E,G,Sw] *(rec 1936–37)* Pearl ▲ PEA 9405 (m) [AAD]
Spirituals *(rec 1930–43)* Pearl ▲ PEA 7073 [ADD]
The Voices of Living Stereo, Vol. 2, w. E. Farrell (sop), Birgit Nilsson (sop), Roberta Peters (sop), Leontyne Price (sop), Galina Vishnevskaya (sop), Rosalind Elias (mez), Shirley Verrett (mez), Maureen Forrester (cta), Sergio Franchi (ten), Mario Lanza (ten), Richard Lewis (ten), Jan Pee, Alexander Dedyukhin (pno), Franz Rupp (pno), Leo Taubman (pno), George Trovillo (pno), Charles Wadsworth (pno), Boston Pops Orch [cnd:Arthur Fiedler], Boston SO [cnd:Charles Munch], Chicago SO [cnd:Fritz Reiner], RCA Victor Orch, RCA Victor Chorus [cnd:Wa *(rec Boston & Chicago & New York & Rome, 1957–1964)* RCA Living Stereo ▲ 09026-68167-2 [ADD]

Anderson, Philip (ten)
Jane's Hand:The Jane Austen Songbooks, w. J. Baird (sop), Elizabeth Henreckson-Farnum (sop), Lorie Gratis (mez), Daniel Pincus (ten), Martil Dillon (ten), Nancy Wilson (bar vn), Peter Segal (bar gtr), Mary Jane Newman (pno/hpd), Anthony Newman (pno) Vox Classics ▲ VOX 7537 [DDD]

Anderson, Richard (bar)
Flowering of Vocal Music in America, 1767–1823, w. Susan Belling (sop), Cynthia Clarey (sop), Barbara Wallace (sop), Debra Vanderlinde (sop), D'Anna Fortunato (mez), Evelyn Petros (mez), Charles Bressler (ten), James Tyeska (bar), Joseph McKee (bass), Cynthia Otis (hp), Leonard Rav New World ▲ 80467-2

Anderson, Roberta (sop)
Harbison, J.:The Flight into Egypt, w. Sanford Sylvan (bar), D. Hoose (cnd), Cantata Ensemble, Cantata Singers [E] New World ▲ 80395-2 [DDD]

Anderson, Sylvia (cta)
Still, W.G.:Tristan und Isolde, w. C. Ligendza (sop), C. Heater (ten), A. Švorc (bass), M. Smith (bass), L. Toffolo (cnd), Trieste Teatro Comunale Giuseppe Verdi Orch, Trieste Teatro Comunale G. Verdi Chorus [G] *(rec live, Trieste, 12/13/69)* Melodram 3-▲ MEL 37072 (m) [AAD]

Anderson, Valdine (sop)
Lutoslawski, W.:Chantefleurs et Chantefables, w. T. Otaka (cnd), BBC Welsh National SO *(rec Brangwyn Hall, Swansea, Wales, July 27–28, 1995)* BIS ▲ CD 743 [DDD]
Lutoslawski, W.:Sym 3, w. T. Otaka (cnd), BBC Welsh National SO *(rec Brangwyn Hall, Swansea, Wales, July 27–28, 1995)* BIS ▲ CD 743 [DDD]

Andersson, Anders (ten)
Handel, G.F.:Alessandro, w. L. Atkinson (trb), Watson (sop), A. Terzian (mez), B. J. Rieders (cta), T. Poole (ten), D. Price (ten), M. Nowakowski (cnd), Sinfonia Varsovia [I] *(rec live)* Koch Schwann 3-▲ CD SC 100 303 [DDD]
Handel, G.F.:Serse, w. L. Atkinson (trb), D. Cole (sop), A. Terzian (mez), T. Allen (bar), Schumann-Halley (sgr), J. Teal (sgr), A. Duczmal (cnd), Amadeus CO [I] *(rec live recording produced by "Studios Classique Berlin")* Koch Schwann 3-▲ CD SC 100 300 [DDD]
Naumann, J.G.:Gustaf Wasa, w. Anders Andersson (ten—Gustav Wasa), Nicolai Gedda (ten—Christjern), P. Brunelle (cnd), Royal Swedish Opera Orch, Stockholm Royal Theater Opera Chorus Virgin Classics ▲ CDCB 45148
Olsson, O.:Requiem, w. M. A. Häggander (sop), E. Paaske (cta), L. Wedin (bar), A. Öhrwall (cnd), Stockholm PO, Stockholm Phil Chorus Caprice ▲ CAP 21368 [DDD]
A Swedish Bouquet, w. Folke Alin (pno), Mats Nilsson (pno), Uppsala Univ Choir [cnd:Cecilia Rydinger-Alin] BIS ▲ CD 591 [DDD]
Wagner, R.:Das Rheingold, w. E. Grümmer (sop), R. Gorr (mez), S. Konya (ten), T. Adam (b-bar), H. Hotter (b-bar), J. Greindl (bass), H. Knappertsbusch (cnd), Bayreuth Festival Orch, Bayreuth Festival Chorus [G] *(rec live 1958)* Arkadia 2-▲ 441 [AAD]
Wagner, R.:Siegfried, w. A. Varnay (sop), W. Windgassen (ten), G. Stoltze (ten), H. Hotter (b-bar), J. Greindl (bass), H. Knappertsbusch (cnd), Bayreuth Festival Orch, Bayreuth Festival Chorus [G] *(rec live 1958)* Arkadia 4-▲ 443 [AAD]

Andersson, Karl-Gustav (ten)
Schnittke, A.:Penitential Psalms, w. Eva Bruun Hansen (sop), Elisabeth Rehling (sop), Annette Simonsen (alt), Maria Streijffert (alt), Poul Vejbo (ten), Stefan Parkman (cnd), Danish National Radio Choir Chandos ▲ CHAN 9480

▲ = CD ♦ = Enhanced CD △ = MD ■ = Cassette Tape □ = DCC

Andor, Éva (sop)

Beethoven, L. van:Syms (comp), w. Márta Szirmay (cta), György Korondi (ten), Sándor Sólyom–Nagy (bar), J. Ferencsik (cnd), Hungarian State Orch, Miklós Forrai (cnd), Budapest Chorus *(rec 1969, 1971, 1974–76)* Classical Diamonds 6–▲ 4013–18 [ADD]

Beethoven, L. van:Sym 9, "Choral Sym", w. H. Szirmay (cta), G. Korondy (ten), S. Solyom–Nagy (bar), J. Ferencsik (cnd), Hungarian PO, Budapest Phil Chorus Laserlight ▲ 15 905

Schumann, R.:Requiem, Op. 148, w. Barlay (sgr), Korondy (sgr), J. Gregor (bass), M. Forrai (cnd), Hungarian State Orch, Budapest Chorus [L] Hungaroton ▲ HCD 11809

Schumann, R.:Requiem Mignon, w. Barlay (sgr), Korondy (sgr), J. Gregor (bass), M. Forrai (cnd), Hungarian State Orch, Budapest Chorus [L] Hungaroton ▲ HCD 11809

Andrade, Rosario (sgr)

Moniuszko, S.:Halka (sels)—Aria Halki z II aktu Polskie Nagrania ▲ PNCD 080 [AAD]

Andrassy, Anni (mez)

Strauss, R.:Der Rosenkavalier (sels), w. Richard May (bass), B. Walter (cnd), *(orch unknown)*—Finale from Act 2 *(rec May 18, 1929)* Iron Needle ▲ IN 1312 [ADD]

Andreani, A. (sgr)

Pugnani, G.:Werther, w. M. Cei (sgr), A. Flint (sgr), T. Yamashita (sgr), M. Andreae (cnd), Swiss–Italian Radio–TV Orch *(rec Dec. 14, 1989)* Bongiovanni 2–▲ GB 5028/29 [DDD]

Andreas (sgr)

Rodgers, R.:Oklahoma!, w. Guittard (sgr), *(other artists unknown)* [1979 Broadway revival cast] RCA ▲ RCD 13572 ■ CBK 13572

Andreescu, Nicolae (ten)

Puccini, G.:Tosca, w. Virginia Zeani (sop—Floria Tosca), Emilia Oprea (mez—Shepherd), Nicolae Andreescu (ten—Spoletta), Corneliu Fanateanu (ten—Mario Cavaradossi), Nicolae Herlea (bar—Baron Scarpia), Gheorghe Crasnaru (bass—Cesare Angelotti), Constantin Gabor (bass—Sacristan), Pompei Harasteanu (bass—Jailer), Adrian Stefanescu (bass—Sciarrone), C. Trailescu (cnd), Romanian Opera Orch, Romanian Opera Chorus *(rec Sept 1977)* Vox Box 2–▲ CDX 5153

Andreev, Avram (ten)

Rimsky–Korsakov, N.:Snow Maiden, w. Stefka Evstatieva (sop—Kupava), Elena Zemenkova (sop—Snow Maiden), Alexandrina Milcheva (mez—Spring Fairy), Vessela Zorova (mez—wife), Stefka Mineva (alt—Lehl), Avram Andreev (ten—Tsar), Lyubomir Dyakovski (ten—Cottager, Sprite), Lyubomir Videnov (bar—Misgir), Nicola Ghiuselev (bass—King), S. Angelov (cnd), Bulgarian RSO, Bulgarian National Chorus *(rec Sofia, 1985)* Capriccio 3–▲ 10749–51 [DDD]

Andreoli, Florindo (ten)

Bizet, G.:Carmen, w. M. Chiara (sop—Micaela), A. Caminada (mez—Mercedes), F. Cossotto (mez—Carmen), F. Andreoli (ten—Il Remendado), P. M. Ferraro (ten—Don José), R. Bruson (bar—Escamillo), G. Zancanaro (bar—Morales), A. Carusi (bass—Il Dancairo), P. Maag (cnd), Venice Teatro La Fenice Orch, Venice Teatro La Fenice Chorus *(rec 1971)* Myto 2–▲ MCD 93487

Andreozzi, Robert (ten)

Massenet, J.:Werther, w. Mady Mesplé (sop—Sophie), Rita Gorr (mez—Charlotte), Robert Andreozzi (ten—Schmidt), Albert Lance (ten—Werther), Gabriel Bacquier (bar—Albert), Julien Giovannetti (bar—Le Bailli), Jacques Mars (bar—Johann), J. Etcheverry (cnd), *(orch unknown)* Adès 2–▲ ADE 140832 [AAD]

Andrésen, Ivar (bass)

Ivar Andresen *(rec 1926–29)* Preiser ("Lebendige Vergangenheit" series) ▲ PRE CD 89125

Opera Arias, w. Berlin State Opera Orch [var. cnds] *(rec 1927–29)* Preiser ("Lebendige Vergangenheit" series) ▲ PRE 89028 (m) [AAD]

Wagner, R.:Der Ring des Nibelungen (sels), w. Florence Austral (sop), Frieda Leider (sop), Elsie Suddaby (sop), Göta Ljunberg (sop), Walter Widdop (ten), Horst Laubenthal (ten), Lauritz Melchoir (ten), Friedrich Schorr (bar), Rudolf Bockelmann (b–bar), Ivar Andresen (bass), Emmanuel List (bass), Collingwood, Blech, Coates, Barbirolli, Heger, Alwin, Muck (cnd), London SO—scenes from Siegriend & Götterdämmerung; 90 Motives from Der Ring [w. Collingwood & LSO] Pearl 7–▲ PEA 9137 [ADD]

Andreva, Stella (sop)

Verdi, G.:Un ballo in maschera, w. Stella Andreva (sop—Oscar), Zinka Milanov (sop—Amelia), Bruna Castagna (cta—Ulrica), Jussi Björling (ten—Riccardo), Lodovico Oliviero (ten—Un Servo D'Amelia), John Cartet (bar—Un Giudice), Alexander Sved (bar—Renato), Normann Cordon (bass—Samuel), Arthur Kent (bass—Silvano), Nicola Moscona (bass—Tom), E. Panizza (cnd), *(orch unknown)* *(rec live, New York, Dec. 14, 1940)* The Fourties 2–▲ ENT FT 1515

Andrew, Ludmilla (sop)

Donizetti, G.:Rosmonda d'Inghilterra, w. Yvonne Kenny (sop), Enid Hartle (mez), Richard Greager (ten), Christian du Plessis (bar), A. Francis (cnd), Ulster Orch, Opera Rara Chorus *(rec live, 1970's)* Italian Opera Rarities 2–▲ IOR 7730

Massenet, J.:Sapho, w. Jenny Hill (sop), Laura Sarti (mez), Bernard Dickerson (ten), Alexander Oliver (ten), Neilson Taylor (bar), George Macpherson (bass), B. Keefe (cnd), BBC SO, BBC Sym Chorus *(rec live, 1973)* Memories 2–▲ MEM 4601 [AAD]

Rubinstein, A.:The Demon, w. Ludmilla Andrew (sop—Nanny), Marina Mescheriakova (sop—Tamara), Alison Browner (mez—Angel), Anatoly Lochak (sgr—Demon), Richard Robson (sgr—Old Servant), Valery Serkin (sgr—Prince Sinodal), Wjacheslav Weinorowski (sgr—Messenger), Leonid Zimnenko (sgr—Prince Gudal), A. Anissimov (cnd), Irish National SO, Gregory Rose (cnd), Wexford Festival Opera Chorus *(rec Wexford, Oct & Nov, 1994)* Marco Polo 2–▲ 8.223781–2 [DDD]

Andrews, Julie (sop)

Julie Andrews Broadway Philips ▲ 446219–2 ■ 446219–4

Lerner, A.J.:My Fair Lady, w. R. Harrison (sgr), S. Holloway (sgr), *(other artists unknown)* [1956 Broadway original cast] Columbia ▲ CK 05090 ■ JST 05090

Lerner, A.J.:My Fair Lady, w. R. Harrison (sgr), *(other artists unknown)* [1959 London cast] Columbia ▲ CK 02015 ■ JST 02015

Lerner, A.J.:My Fair Lady, w. R. Harrison (sgr), *(other artists unknown)* [1956 Broadway original cast] Legacy ("Mastersound" series) ▲ SK 66128

Mancini, H.:Victor/Victoria, w. R. Preston (sgr), L. Ann Warren (sgr) GNP Crescendo ▲ GNPD 8038

Rodgers, R.:Cinderella, w. *(other artists unknown)*—from the 1957 television soundtrack Columbia ▲ CK 02005 ■ JST 02005

Rodgers, R.:The King & I, w. J. Andrews (sgr—Anna Leonowens), L. Salonga (sgr—Tuptim), B. Kingsley (sgr—The King), P. Bryson (sgr—Lun Tha), M. Horne (mez—Lady Thiang), M. Liufau (sgr—Prince Chulalongkorn), E. Kingsley (sgr—Louis Leonowens), R. Moore (sgr—Sir Edward Ramsay), M. Sheen (sgr—The Kralahome), J. Mauceri (cnd), Hollywood Bowl Orch, Los Angeles Master Chorale *(rec Culver City, CA, Apr 1992)* Philips ▲ 438007–2 [DDD]

Rodgers, R.:Music of, w. S. Bass (sgr), P. Como (sgr), D. Reese (sgr), J. Jones (sgr), N. Luboff (sgr), M. Gold (sgr), N. Walker (sgr), H. Bowen (sgr), V. Damone (sgr), P. Nero (pno), J. P. Morgan (sgr), E. Fisher (sgr), B. Goodman (cl), Ann–Margaret (sgr), Shorty Rogers (sgr), D. Shore (sgr), T. Martin (sgr), M. King (sgr), A. Newley (sgr) RCA ▲ 8590–2 R ■ 8590–4 R

Rodgers, R.:The Sound of Music, w. C. Plummer (sgr), *(other artists unknown)* *(rec 1965)* RCA ▲ PCD 12005 ■ 2005–4 R

Andsy, Rosette (cta)

Wagner, R.:Rienzi, der Letzte der Tribunen (sels), w. Rosette Andsy (cta—Adriano), Hermann Gallos (ten—Baroncelli), Franz Völker (tenor–Rienzi), Karl Ettl (bass—Cecco), J. Krips (cnd), Vienna State Opera Orch *(rec Vienna, May 15, 1933)* Koch Schwann 2–▲ SCH 314662 [ADD]

Anelli, Anna Maria (mez/sop)

Bellini, V.:La sonnambula, w. Lina Pagliughi (sop), Ferruccio Tagliavini (ten), Cesare Siepi (b–bar), F. Capuana (cnd), Turin RAI SO Fonit Cetra ("Classic Collection" series) 2–▲ FCT CDO 16

Bellini, V.:La sonnambula, w. L. Pagliughi (sop—Amina), W. Ruggeri (sop—Lisa), A. M. Anelli (mez—Teresa), F. Tagliavini (ten—Elvino), P. L. Latinucci (bass—Alessio), C. Siepi (bass—Conte Rodolfo), F. Capuana (cnd), Turin RSO, Turin Radio Chorus *(rec 1952)* Cetra Classics 2–▲ CDO 16 [AAD]

Angas, Richard (bass)

Sullivan, A.:The Mikado, w. L. Garrett (sop), J. Rigby (mez), S. Bullock (sop), F. Palmer (sop/mez), B. Bottone (ten), E. Idle (bar), R. Van Allan (bass), M. Richardson (bar), P. Robinson (cnd), English National Opera Orch, English Opera Group Chorus—sels [E] MCA Classics ▲ MCAD 6215 [DDD]; ■ MCAC 6215 (D)

Angel, Michael (ten)

Nyman, M.:Prospero's Books, w. S. Leonard (sop), U. Lemper (sop), D. Conway (sgr), Michael Nyman Band London ▲ 425224–2 [DDD]

Angelakova, Hristina (alt)

Pergolesi, G.B.:Stabat mater, w. T. Gabrovska (sop), A. Blagoeva (cnd), New CO, Sofia Boys' Choir Gega ▲ GD 153 [DDD]

Angeles, Victoria de los (sop)

Baroque & Religious Arias *(rec 1950–59)* Testament ▲ SBT 1088

Berlioz, H.:L'Enfance du Christ, w. Nicolai Gedda (ten), Roger Soyer (bar), Ernest Blanc (bar), A. Cluytens (cnd), Paris Conservatory Societé des Concerts Orch, René DuClos Chorus EMI Classics ("Doublefforte" series) 2–▲ CDFB 68586

Berlioz, H.:Les Nuits d'été, w. M. Roggero (mez), L. Chabay (ten), Y. Sze (bass), C. Munch (cnd), Boston SO RCA Gold Seal 2–▲ 09026–60681–2

Berlioz, H.:Les Nuits d'été, w. C. Munch (cnd), Boston SO *(rec Apr 1955)* RCA Victor Gold Seal 8–▲ 0902–668444–2 [ADD]

Bizet, G.:Carmen, w. J. Micheau (sop), N. Gedda (ten), E. Blanc (bar), T. Beecham (cnd), *(orch unknown)* [F] EMI Classics 3–▲ CDCC 49240 [ADD]

Canteloube, J.:Songs of Auvergne, w. J.–P. Jacquillat (cnd), Lamoureux Orch EMI Classics (Studio) ▲ CDM 63178 [ADD]

Chausson, E.:Poème de l'amour et de la mer, w. J.–P. Jacquillat (cnd), Lamoureux Concerts Orch EMI Classics ▲ CDM 64365

Debussy, C.:La Damoiselle élue, w. C. Smith (mez), C. Munch (cnd), Boston SO, Radcliffe Choral Society [F] RCA Gold Seal 2–▲ 7940–2–RG [ADD]

The Early Recordings, 1942–1953, w. Gerald Moore (pno), Ivor Newton (pno), Agrupación de Cámara Barcelona, Ars Musicae Barcelona Testament ▲ SBT 1087

An Evening with Victoria de Los Angeles, w. Geoffrey Parsons (pno) *(rec Wigmore Hall Recital, 5/3/90)* Collins Classics ▲ COL 1247 [DDD]

The Fabulous Victoria de los Angeles EMI Classics 4–▲ ZDMD 65061

Falla, M. de:El amor brujo, w. C. M. Giulini (cnd), Philharmonia Orch [Sp] EMI Classics ▲ CDM 64746 CDM 64746

Falla, M. de:El amor brujo (sels), w. R. Frühbeck de Burgos (cnd), New Philharmonia Orch EMI Classics ▲ CDM 64746

Falla, M. de:Canciones populares españolas (7), w. G. Moore (pno) [Sp] *(rec 9/12/51)* EMI Classics ▲ CDH 64028–2 (m) [ADD]

Falla, M. de:Canciones populares españolas (7), w. J. Pons (cnd), Barcelona Teatro Lliure CO Harmonia Mundi France ▲ HMC 901432

Falla, M. de:Psyché, w. J. Pons (cnd), Barcelona Teatro Lliure CO Harmonia Mundi France ▲ HMC 901432

Falla, M. de:El sombrero de tres picos, w. C. M. Giulini (cnd), New Philharmonia Orch EMI Classics ▲ CDM 64746

Falla, M. de:La vida breve, w. F. Cossutta (mez), I. Rivadeneyra (mez), R. Burgos (cnd), Spanish National Orch, Orféon Donostiarra [Sp] EMI Classics ▲ CDM 69590 [ADD]

Falla, M. de:La vida breve, w. S. Robinson (cnd), Philharmonia Orch—"Vivan los que rien!"; & "Alli está! Riyendo" [Sp] *(rec 3/14/48)* EMI Classics ▲ CDH 64028–2 (m) [ADD]

Fauré, G.:Requiem, w. D. Fischer–Dieskau (bar), A. Cluytens (cnd), Paris Conservatory Societé des Concerts Orch, Brasseur Choir [L] EMI Classics ▲ CDC 47836

Gounod, C.:Faust, w. L. Berton (sop), R. Gorr (mez), N. Gedda (ten), E. Blanc (bar), B. Christoff (bass), A. Cluytens (cnd), Paris Opera Orch [F] Angel ("Studio" series) 3–▲ CDMC 69983 [ADD]

Gounod, C.:Faust, w. C. Ward (sgr), M. Mayhoff (sgr), R. Tucker (ten), H. Noel (sgr), N. Moscona (bass), D. Bernard (sgr), W. Herbert (cnd), New Orleans Opera Orch [F] *(rec Feb. 26, 1953)* Legato Classics 2–▲ LCD 167–2 [AAD]

Gounod, C.:Faust (sels), w. Liliane Berton (sop), Rita Gorr (mez), Nicolai Gedda (ten), Victor Autran (bar), Ernest Blanc (bar), Boris Christoff (bass), A. Cluytens (cnd), Paris Opera Orch, Paris Opera Chorus Classics for Pleasure ("Eminence" series) ▲ CDEMX 2215 [DDD]

Granados, E.:Goyescas (sels), w. A. Fistoulari (cnd), Philharmonia Orch—La maja y el ruiseñor [Sp] *(rec 3/7/50)* EMI Classics ▲ CDH 64028–2 (m) [ADD]

Great Sopranos of Our Time, w. Maria Callas (sop), Joan Sutherland (sop), Renata Scotto (sop), Montserrat Caballé (sop), Elisabeth Schwarzkopf (sop), Mirella Freni (sop), Ileana Cotrubas (sop), Edita Gruberova (sop) Classics for Pleasure ▲ CDEMX 9519 [ADD]

Leoncavallo, R.:Pagliacci, w. J. Björling (ten), R. Merrill (bar), L. Warren (bar), R. Cellini (cnd), Columbus Orch, Robert Shaw Chorale EMI Classics ▲ ZDC 49503

Mascagni, P.:Cavalleria rusticana, w. F. Corelli (ten), G. Santini (cnd), Rome Opera Orch, Rome Opera Chorus [I] EMI Classics ("Studio" series) 2–▲ CDMB 63967

Massenet, J.:Manon, w. F. Tagliavini (ten), A. Poli (bar), N. Annovazzi (cnd), Rome Opera Orch, Rome Opera Chorus *(rec live 1957)* Melodram 2–▲ MEL 27082

Massenet, J.:Manon, w. H. Legay (ten), M. Dens (bar), J. Borthayre (bass), P. Monteux (cnd), Paris Opéra–Comique Orch, Paris Opéra–Comique Chorus [F] EMI Classics 3–▲ CDMC 63549 (m) [ADD]

Massenet, J.:Werther, w. M. Mesplé (sop), N. Gedda (ten), G. Prêtre (cnd), Orch de Paris, Paris Chorus [F] EMI Classics ("Studio" series) 2–▲ CDMB 63973

Mozart, W.A.:Arias, w. P. Casals (cnd), Collegium Musicum—aria from Idomeneo *(rec live July 9, 1959)* Music & Arts 4–▲ CD 689 (m) [AAD]

Offenbach, J.:Les Contes d'Hoffmann, w. E. Schwarzkopf (sop), G. d'Angelo (sop), N. Gedda (ten), G. London (bar), E. Blanc (bar), A. Cluytens (cnd), Paris Conservatory Societé des Concerts Orch, René DuClos Chorus [F] EMI Classics ("Studio" series) 2–▲ CDMB 63222 [ADD]

On Wings of Song, w. Paris Conservatory Orch [cnd:R. Frühbeck de Burgos] EMI Classics ▲ CDM 69502

Opera Arias Serphim ■ 4XG 60262

Operatic Arias & Scenes EMI Classics ("Great Recordings of the Century" series) ▲ CDH 63495 (m) [ADD]

Puccini, G.:La Bohème, w. J. Bjoerling (ten), R. Merrill (bar), T. Beecham (cnd), RCA Victor SO [I] EMI Classics 2–▲ CDCB 47235 (m) [ADD] 2–■ 4X2G 47235

Puccini, G.:Madama Butterfly, w. V. de los Angeles (sop—Madama Butterfly), B. Howitt (mez—Suzuki), J. Livingston (mez—Kate), J. Lanigan (ten—Pinkerton), D. Tree (ten—Goro), D. A. (ten—Yamadori), G. Evans (bar—Sharpless), M. Langdon (bass—Bonzo), R. Kempe (cnd), Royal Opera House Orch, Royal Opera House Chorus Covent Garden *(rec London, May 1957)* Ornamenti 2–▲ FE 112 [ADD]

Puccini, G.:Madama Butterfly, w. M. Pirazzini (mez), J. Bjoerling (ten), M. Sereni (bar), G. Santini (cnd), Rome Opera Orch, Rome Opera Chorus [I] EMI Classics ("Studio" series) 2–▲ CDMB 63634 [ADD]

Puccini, G.:Madama Butterfly, w. R. Nadell (mez), B. Faulkner (sgr), W. Fredericks (sgr), J. Thresh (sgr), D. Bernard (sgr), R. Torigi (sgr), A. Cosenza (bar), W. Herbert (cnd), New Orleans Opera Orch, New Orleans Opera Chorus *(rec live March 18, 1954)* Legato Classics 2–▲ LCD 168–2 [ADD]

Puccini, G.:Il trittico, w. F. Barbieri (mez), G. Prandelli (ten), T. Gobbi (bar), *(other soloists unknown)*, Rome Opera Orch, Rome Opera Chorus *(rec Rome, 1950s)* EMI Classics 3–▲ CDMC 64165 (m)

Purcell, H.:Dido & Aeneas, w. Victoria de los Angeles (sop—Dido), Heather Harper (sop—Belinda), Patricia Johnson (mez—Sorceress), Peter Glossup (bar—Aeneas), J. Barbirolli (cnd), English CO, Ambrosian Singers EMI Classics 2–▲ ZDM 65664

Purcell, H.:Dido & Aeneas (sels), w. Victoria de los Angeles (sop—Dido), Heather Harper (sop—Belinda), Sibyl Michelow (sop), Elizabeth Robson (sop), Derek Simpson (vc), Colin Tilney (hpd), J. Barbirolli (cnd), English CO, Ambrosian Singers—Ov.; Shake the Cloud; Ah! Ah! Belinda; When Monarchs Unite; But Ere We This Perform; But Death, Alas! I Cannot Shun...When I am Laid in Earth; With Drooping Wings *(rec Abbey Road Studio 1, London, Aug. 1965)* EMI Classics ▲ CDK 65341 [ADD]

Ravel, M.:Shéhérazade Mez, w. P. Monteux (cnd), Royal Concertgebouw Orch *(rec Nov. 20, 1953)* Music & Arts ▲ CD 812 [AAD]

Rossini, G.:Il barbiere di Siviglia, w. L. Alva (ten), C. Cava (bass), I. Wallace (bass), V. Gui (cnd), Royal PO, Glyndebourne Festival Chorus *(rec 1962)* EMI Classics 2–▲ CDMB 64162

A Seventieth Birthday Tribute *(rec between 1944–1993)* Legato Classics ▲ LCD 172–1 [ADD]

Traditional Catalan Songs, w. Geoffrey Parsons (pno) Collins Classics ▲ COL 1318 [DDD]

Turina, J.:Canto a Sevilla, w. A. Fistoulari (cnd), Philharmonia Orch [Sp] *(rec 10/52 & 10/53)* EMI Classics ▲ CDH 64028–2 (m) [ADD]

Angeles, Victoria de los (sop) (cont.)
Turina, J.:Poema en forma de canciones, w. W. Susskind (cnd), Philharmonia Orch—Cantares [Sp] *(rec 1949)* EMI Classics ▲ CDH 64028-2 (m) [ADD]
Turina, J.:Saeta en forma de Salve a la Virgen de la Esperanza, w. W. Susskind (cnd), Philharmonia Orch [Sp] *(rec 1949)* EMI Classics ▲ CDH 64028-2 (m) [ADD]
Victoria de los Angeles EMI Classics ("Diva" series) ▲ CDM 65579
Victoria de los Angeles Live in Concert, w. Pablo Casals (pno), P. Berl (pno) *(rec 1952-60)* VAI Audio 2-▲ VAIA 1025 (m) [ADD]
Villa-Lobos, H.:Bachiana brasileira 5, w. H. Villa-Lobos (cnd), French National Orch EMI Classics ("Great Recordings of the Century" series) ▲ CDH 61015 (m)
Vivaldi, A.:Orlando Furioso, w. M. Horne (mez), L. Valentini-Terrani (mez), C. Gonzales (mez), Kosma (sgr), S. Bruscantini (bar), N. Zaccaria (bass), C. Scimone (cnd), Venice Solisti Erato 3-▲ 2292-45147-2 ZB
Wagner, R.:Tannhäuser, w. G. Bumbry (mez), W. Windgassen (ten), G. Stolze (ten), D. Fischer-Dieskau (bar), T. Adam (b-bar), J. Greindl (bass), F. Crass (bass), W. Sawallisch (cnd), Bayreuth Festival Orch, Bayreuth Festival Chorus [G] *(rec 1961)* Myto 3-▲ MCD 93277
Wagner, R.:Tannhäuser (sels), w. W. Sawallisch (cnd), *(orch unknown)*—Dich teure Halle!; Allmacht'ge Jungfrau [G] *(rec July 23, 1961)* Legato Classics 2-▲ LCD 168-2 [ADD]
Zarzuela Arias, w. Spanish National Orch [cnd:R. Frühbeck de Burgos] EMI Classics ("Studio" series) ▲ CDM 69078

Angelici, Martha (sop)
Charpentier, M.-A.:Magnificat, w. Jocelyn Chamonin (sop), André Mallabrera (ct), Rémy Corazza (ten), Georges Abdoun (bar), Jacques Mars (bass), Maurice André (tpt), Marie-Claire Alain (org), L. Martini (cnd), Jean-François Paillard CO, French Jeunesses Musicales Chorale *(rec Paris, Mar 15, 1963)* Vanguard Classics ▲ OVC 8075 [ADD]
Charpentier, M.-A.:Te Deum, H. 146, w. Jocelyn Chamonin (sop), André Mallabrera (ct), Rémy Corazza (ten), Georges Abdoun (bar), Jacques Mars (bass), Maurice André (tpt), Marie-Claire Alain (org), L. Martini (cnd), Jean-François Paillard CO, French Jeunesses Musicales Chorale *(rec Paris, Mar 15, 1963)* Vanguard Classics ▲ OVC 8075 [ADD]

Angelis, Nazzareno de (bass)
Boito, A.:Mefistofele, w. Giannina Arangi-Lombardi (sop), Mafalda Favero (sop), Antonio Melandri (ten), Giuseppe Nessi (ten), L. Molajoli (cnd), La Scala Orch, La Scala Chorus Grammofono 2000 2-▲ GRM 78606 (m)
The Italian Vocal Tradition, Vol. 1:The Voices of Toscanini, w. Toti dal Monte (sop), Claudio Muzio (sop), Rosetta Pampanini (sop), Biata Scacciati (sop), Giacomo Lauri-Volpi (ten), Francesco Merli (ten), Aureliano Pertile (ten), Carlo Galeffi (bar), Mariano Stabile (bar), Riccardo Stracciari (bar), *(rec 1921-35)* Iron Needle ▲ 1304
Nazzareno de Angelis, w. Angelis, Nazzareno de (bass) *(rec 1927-1929)* Preiser ("Lebendige Vergangenheit" series) ▲ PRE 89042 (m) [AAD]
Verdi, G.:Simon Boccanegra, w. M. Nicolesco (sop), G. Sabbatini (ten), R. Bruson (bar), S. Rinaldi-Miliani (bar), R. Scandiuzzi (bass), R. Paternostro (cnd), Tokyo SO, Nikikai Chorus *(rec live 2/90)* Capriccio 2-▲ 60018-2 [DDD]

Angell, Cecilia (mez)
Falla, M. de:La vida breve, w. M. Senn (mez), F. de la Mora (ten), E. Mata (cnd), Simón Bolívar SO [Sp] *(rec July 1993)* Dorian ▲ DOR 90192 [DDD]

Angelo, Gianna d' (sop)
D'Angelo & Christoff, w. Boris Christoff (bass), Rome RAI SO [cnd:Alfredo Simonetto] *(rec Martini & Rossi Concert, 1961)* Incontri Memorabili ▲ CDMR 5034
Donizetti, G.:Don Pasquale, w. A. Kraus (ten), R. Capecchi (bar), F. Corena (bass), U. d'Alessio (sgr), A. Erede (cnd), Naples Teatro San Carlo Orch, Naples Teatro San Carlo Chorus [I] *(rec live in Edinburgh, 9/7/63)* Verona 2-▲ 27023/24 (m) [AAD]
Donizetti, G.:Don Pasquale, w. Alfredo Kraus (ten), Renato Capecchi (bar), Fernando Corena (bass), Ugo D'Alessio (sgr), A. Erede (cnd), Naples Teatro San Carlo Orch, Naples Teatro San Carlo Chorus Great Opera Performances 2-▲ GOP 763
Famous Love Duets, Vol. 2, w. Montserrat Caballé (sop), Maria Callas (sop), Renata Scotto (sop), Beverly Sills (sop), Renata Tebaldi (sop), José Carreras (ten), Mario Del Monaco (ten), Giuseppe Di Stefano (ten), Plácido Domingo (ten), Luciano Pava Enterprise ("Documents" series) ▲ ENTLV 999
Gounod, C.:Roméo et Juliette, w. G. d'Angelo (sop—Juliette), F. Corelli (ten—Romeo), A. Ferrin (bar—Friar Lawrence), P. Gottlieb (bass—Mercutio), A. Guadagno (cnd), *(orch unknown) (rec live, Philadelphia, 4/14/64)* HRE 2-▲ 1011-2 [ADD]
Offenbach, J.:Les Contes d'Hoffmann, w. E. Schwarzkopf (sop), V. de los Angeles (sop), N. Gedda (ten), G. London (bar), E. Blanc (bar), A. Cluytens (cnd), Paris Conservatory Societé des Concerts Orch, René DuClos Chorus [F] EMI Classics ("Studio" series) 2-▲ CDMB 63222 [ADD]
Puccini, G.:La Bohème, w. R. Tebaldi (sop), C. Bergonzi (ten), E. Bastianini (bar), C. Siepi (b-bar), T. Serafin (cnd), St. Cecilia Academy Orch Rome, St. Cecilia Academy Chorus Rome [I] London 2-▲ 425534-2 [ADD]
Rossini, G.:Il barbiere di Siviglia (sels), w. G. Carturan (mez), N. Monti (ten), R. Capecchi (bar), G. Giorgetti (bar), C. Cava (bass), G. Tadeo (bass), B. Bartoletti (cnd), Bavarian RSO IMP Collectors Series ▲ IMPX 9022 [AAD]
Verdi, G.:Rigoletto, w. Aldo Protti (bar), Vito Susca (bass), Giorgio Tadeo (bass), F. Molinari-Pradelli (cnd), Trieste Teatro Comunale Giuseppe Verdi Orch, Trieste Teatro Comunale G. Verdi Chorus Melodram 2-▲ CDM 27006

Angeloni, Katia (mez)
Vivaldi, A.:Il Farnace, w. M. Dupuy (mez), P. Malakova (mez), D. Dessy (mez), L. Rizzi (cta), R. Garazioti (sgr), M. de Bernart (cnd), San Remo SO [I] *(rec live 12/1/82)* Arkadia-Akademia 2-▲ 110 [ADD]

Angervo, Heljä (alt)
Strauss, R.:Salome, w. H. Behrens (sop), A. Baltsa (mez), K.W. Böhm (ten), W. Ochman (ten), J. van Dam (bar), H. von Karajan (cnd), Vienna PO EMI Classics 2-▲ CDCB 49358

Angus, Andrew (bar)
Howells, H.:Requiem, w. Sally Barber (sop), Julia Field (alt), Mark Johnstone (ten), Jeremy Backhouse (cnd), Vasari Singers *(rec All Hallows, Gospel Oak, Feb 18-20, 1994)* United ▲ CAL 88033 [DDD]

Anhorn, Carmen (sop)
Wagner, R.:Rienzi, der Letzte der Tribunen, w. Cheryl Studer (sop—Irene), René Kollo (ten—Rienzi), Friedrich Lenz (ten—Gesandte), Norbert Orth (ten—Baroncelli), Bodo Brinkmann (bar—Paolo Orsini), Keith Engen (bass—Cecco del Vecchio), Raimund Grumbach (bass—Gesandte), Jan-Hendrik Rootering (bass—Steffano Colonna), Carmen Anhorn (sgr—Ein Friedensbote), Karl Helm (sgr—Kardinal Orvieto), John Janssen (sgr—Adriano), Alfred Kuhn (sgr—Gesandte), Hans Wilbrink (sgr—Gesandte), W. Sawallisch (cnd), Bavarian State Opera Orch, Bavarian State Opera Chorus *(rec live, July 6, 1983)* Orfeo d'or 3-▲ 346953

Anlauf, Richard (bass)
Haydn, J.:Stabat Mater, w. Krisztina Láki (sop), Júlia Hamari (mez), Claes Hakan Ahnsjö (ten), F. Bernius (cnd), Württemberg CO, Stuttgart Chamber Choir *(rec 1978)* Vox Box 2-▲ CDX 5081 [ADD]

Anna, Mario d' (bar)
Donizetti, G.:Don Pasquale, w. Edoardo Gimenez (ten), Geraint Evans (bar), Carol Webber (sgr), H. Holt (cnd), *(orch unknown) (rec Seattle, 1981)* Ornamenti ("Gala Evenings, Teatro Colon" series) 2-▲ 121
Puccini, G.:Manon Lescaut, w. R. Kabaivanska (sop—Manon), R. Pallini (mez—Singer), P. Domingo (ten—des Grieux), E. Lorenzi (ten—Edmondo), F. Ricciardi (ten—Dancing Master), M. D'Anna (bar—Lescaut), A. Mariotti (bass—Geronte), F. Federici (bass—Innkeeper) Golden Age of Opera 2-▲ GAO 162/63 [ADD]
Smareglia, A.:La falena, w. Leyla Gencer (sop—La Falena), Rita Lantieri (sop—Albina, sua figlia), Ruggero Bondino (ten—Re Stellio), Dario Zerial (ten—Il ladro), Mario D'Anna (bar—Il vecchio Uberto), Aurio Tomicich (bass—Morio), Giuseppe Botta (sgr—Un marinaio), G. Gavazzeni (cnd), Trieste Teatro Comunale Giuseppe Verdi Orch, Trieste Teatro Comunale G. Verdi Chorus *(rec Trieste, Mar 18, 1876)* Bongiovanni 2-▲ GB 1131/32

Annaloro, Antonio (ten)
Tchaikovsky, P.:Queen of Spades (sels), w. L. Gencer (sop—Liza), A. Annaloro (ten—Hermann), N. Sanzogno (cnd), La Scala Orch [I] *(rec Feb. 2, 1960)* Arkadia 2-▲ 599 [ADD]

Ann-Margaret (sgr)
Rodgers, R.:Music of, w. S. Bass (sgr), J. Andrews (sgr), P. Como (sgr), D. Reese (sgr), J. Jones (sgr), N. Luboff (sgr), M. Gold (sgr), N. Walker (sgr), H. Bowen (sgr), V. Damone (sgr), P. Nero (pno), J. P. Morgan (sgr), E. Fisher (sgr), B. Goodman (cl), Shorty Rogers (sgr), D. Shore (sgr), T. Martin (sgr), M. King (sgr), A. Newley (sgr) RCA ▲ 8590-2 R ■ 8590-4 R

Anselmi, Giuseppe (ten)
The Great Tenor Aria & Song Recordings of 1907-1913 Pearl ▲ PEA CD 9227
The Harold Wayne Collection, Vol. 20 Symposium ▲ SYM 1170
Il mito dell'opera Bongiovanni 2-▲ GB 1074/75 [ADD]

Anselmi, Susanna (cta)
Scarlatti, A.:Concerti sacri, motetti, w. Ilaria Galgani (sop), Luca Casalin (ten), Daniele Tonini (bass), Il Ruggiero—Nos. 6-10 Tactus ▲ TC 661904 [DDD]
Scarlatti, A.:Concerti sacri, motetti, w. Ilaria Galgani (sop), Luca Casalin (ten), Daniele Tonini (bass), Il Ruggiero—Nos. 1-5 Tactus ▲ TC 661903 [DDD]

Anselmi, Susanna (sop)
Mayr, S.:La rosa bianca e la rosa rossa, w. Anna Caterina Antonacci (sop), Silvia Mazzoni (mez), Luca Canonici (ten), Francesco Facini (bass), Danilo Serraiocco (bass), T. Briccetti (cnd), Bergamo Stabile Orch Fonit Cetra ("Ricordi" series) 2-▲ FCT RFCD 2007
Pergolesi, G.B.:Adriano in Siria, w. D. Dessi (sop), J. Omilian (sop), L. Mazzaria (sop), G. Banditelli (cta), E. di Cesare (ten), M. Panni (cnd), Rome Opera CO [I] *(rec live 12/20/86)* Bongiovanni 3-▲ GB 2078/80 [DDD]

Ansseau, Fernand (ten)
Leoncavallo, R.:Pagliacci (sels), w. Enrico Caruso (ten), Antonio Paoli (ten), Giovanni Zenatello (ten), Amedeo Bassi (ten), Hermann Jadlowker (ten), Hipolito Lazaro (ten), Nino (Filippo) Piccaluga (ten), Mario Chamlee (ten), Giacomo Lauri-Volpi (ten), Miguel Fleta (ten), Giovanni Martinelli (ten), Aureliano Pertile (ten), Georges Thill (ten), Alessandro Valente (ten), Francesco Merli (ten), Lauritz Melchior (ten), Marcel Wittrisch (ten), Joseph Schmidt (ten), Beniamino Gigli (ten), Giuseppe Lugo (ten), Helge Roswaenge (ten), Jussi Bjoerling (ten)—23 versions of the tenor aria "Vesti la giubba" *(rec 1907-1944)* Bongiovanni ▲ GB 1071 [ADD]
Opera Arias *(rec 1923-29)* Preiser ("Lebendige Vergangenheit" series) ▲ PRE 89022 [AAD]
The Art of Fernand Ansseau Pearl ▲ PEA CD 9240

Anthoni, Greetje (sop)
Telemann, G.P.:Cants, w. Yves Saelens (ten), Stefan Geyer (bar), F. Heyerick (cnd), Le Mercure Galant Baroque Orch, Ex Tempore Vocal Ensemble—Der Tod Jesu *(rec Studio Steurbaut, Gent, June 1995)* René Gailly ▲ 92025 [DDD]

Anthony, Charles (ten)
Puccini, G.:Turandot, w. B. Nilsson (sop—Turnadot), A. Moffo (sop—Liù), F. Corelli (ten—Calaf), C. Anthony (ten—Pong), R. Nagy (ten—Pang), F. Guarrera (bar—Ping), B. Giaiotti (bass—Timur), L. Stokowski (cnd), Metropolitan Opera Orch, New York Metropolitan Opera Chorus *(rec Mar. 4, 1961)* Datum 2-▲ DAT 12301 [ADD]
Verdi, G.:Ernani, w. L. Price (sop), C. Ordassy (sop), F. Corelli (ten), M. Sereni (bar), C. Siepi (bass), C. Russel (bass), T. Schippers (cnd), *(orch unknown) (rec 1965)* Great Opera Performances ▲ GOP 702

Anthony, Grace (sop)
Verdi, G.:Ernani (sels), w. Alfio Tedesco (ten), Giuseppe De Luca (bar)—O sommo Carlo *(rec 1928)* Minerva ▲ MN-A23 [ADD]

Anthony, Susan (sop)
Buechner, M.:Elizabeth, w. J. McLean (ten), G. Schmöhe (cnd), Nuremberg SO [G] Nord-Disc 2-▲ NORD 2026 [DDD]

Anthony, Trevor (bass)
Sullivan, A.:Patience, w. J. Shaw (bar), A. Young (ten), G. Baker (bar), M. Sargent (cnd), Pro Arte Orch, Glyndebourne Festival Chorus EMI Classics 2-▲ CDMB 64406

Antinori, Nazzareno (ten)
Puccini, G.:Madama Butterfly, w. Raina Kabaivanska (sop—Madama Butterfly), Alexandrina Milcheva (mez—Suzuki), Rossitza Troeva-Mircheva (cta—Kate Pinkerton), Nazzareno Antinori (ten—F.B. Pinkerton), Roumen Doikov (ten—Goro), Werther Vrachovski (ten—Il Principe Yamadori), Nelson Portella (bar—Sharpless), Kosta Dinkov (bass—Lo zio Bonzo), G. Bellini (cnd), Sofia PO, Svetoslav Obrenetov Bulgarian National Chorus *(rec Sophia, Bulgaria, Dec 1-13, 1982)* Arts Music 2-▲ 447161-2 [DDD]
Puccini, G.:Tosca, w. Raina Kabaivanska (sop—Floria Tosca), Nazzareno Antinori (ten—Mario Cavaradossi), Roumen Doikov (ten—Spoletta), Enzo Dara (bar—Casare Angelotti/Il sagrestano), Nelson Portella (bar—Il Barone Scarpia), Stoyan Balabanov (bass—Sciarrone/Un carceriere), Borislav Peev (sgr—Un Pastore), G. Bellini (cnd), Sofia PO, Bulgarian National Radio Children's Choir, Svetoslav Obrenetov Bulgarian National Chorus *(rec Sophia, Bulgaria, Nov 14-27, 1982)* Arts Music ▲ 47158-2 [DDD]
Verdi, G.:Luisa Miller, w. Cecilia Gasdia (sop), Simone Alaimo (b-bar), G. Gavazzeni (cnd), Parma Teatro Regio Orch, Parma Teatro Regio Chorus *(rec live, 1981)* Serenissima 2-▲ SER 360143

Antioli, D. (sgr)
Concerti, w. M. Olivero (sop), U. Trama (bass), A. Protti (bar), K. Ostar (sgr), Fulvio Vernizzi (cnd) Great Opera Performances 2-▲ GOP 709

Anton, Walter (ten)
Schubert, Franz:Die Verschworenen, w. Ilona Steingruber (sop—Countess), Elizabeth Roon (mez—Helene), Laurence Dutoit (trb—Isella), Walter Anton (ten—Udolin), Walter Berry (bar—Count), Rudolf Kreutzberger (sgr—Astolf), F. Grossmann (cnd), Vienna SO, Vienna Academy Chamber Choir Theorema ▲ TH 121178

Antonacci, Anna Caterina (sop)
Manfroce, N.A.:Ecuba, w. D. di Domenico (ten), F. Piccoli (ten), G. De Bellida (sgr), M. de Bernart (cnd), Italian PO, Italian Phil Chorus [I] *(rec live 1990)* Bongiovanni 2-▲ GB 2119/20 [DDD]
Mayr, S.:La rosa bianca e la rosa rossa, w. Susanna Anselmi (sop), Silvia Mazzoni (mez), Luca Canonici (ten), Francesco Facini (bass), Danilo Serraiocco (bass), T. Briccetti (cnd), Bergamo Stabile Orch Fonit Cetra ("Ricordi" series) 2-▲ FCT RFCD 2007
Mozart, W.A.:Così fan tutte, w. A. C. Antonacci (sop—Fiordiligi), M. Bacelli (sop—Dorabella), L. Cherici (sop—Despina), R. Decker (ten—Ferrando), A. Dohmen (bar—Gugliemo), S. Bruscantini (bar—Don Alfonso), G. Kuhn (cnd), Marchigiana PO, Marchigiana Phil Chorus [I] *(rec live, Teatro Lauro Rossi at the Festival di Macerata, Aug. 3, 1990)* Orfeo 3-▲ 243913 [DDD]
Rossini, G.:Messa di gloria, w. B. Manca Di Nissa (cta), F. Araiza (ten), R. Gambill (ten), P. Spagnoli (bar), S. Accardo (cnd), St. Cecilia Academy Orch Rome, St. Cecilia Academy Chorus Rome *(rec Mar. 1-2, 1992)* Ricordi ▲ RFCD 2012 [DDD]

Antoni, C. de (sgr)
Cimarosa, D.:Giannina e Bernardone, w. D. De Cecco (sop), S. Jurinac (sop), G. Sciutti (sop), M. Carlin (ten), M. Boriello (bar), S. Bruscantini (bar), N. Sanzogno (cnd), Milan RAI SO, Milan RAI Chorus [I] *(rec live, Milan July 26, 1953)* Melodram 2-▲ CDM 29505 [ADD]

Antoniak, Mieczyslaw (ten)
Verdi, G.:I due Foscari, w. K. Ricciarelli (sop), E. Connell (sop), J. Carreras (ten), V. Bello (ten), P. Cappuccilli (bar), S. Ramey (bass), F. Handlos (bass), L. Gardelli (cnd), Austrian RSO, Austrian Radio Chorus Philips 2-▲ 422426-2 [ADD]

Antonicelli, Catherine (sop)
Sauguet, H.:Mélodies sur les poèmes symbolistes, w. D. Abramovitz (pno) Sonpact ▲ SPT 93008 [DDD]

Antonini, Giovanni (bass)
Bellini, V.:I Puritani, w. Mirella Freni (sop), Mirelle Fiorentini (mez), Luciano Pavarotti (ten), Emilio Venturini (ten), Sesto Bruscantini (bar), Bonaldo Giaiotti (bass), R. Muti (cnd), Rome RAI SO, Rome RAI Chorus Melodram 2-▲ CDM 27062
Bellini, V.:I Puritani (sels), w. Mirella Freni (sop), Luciano Pavarotti (ten), Bonaldo Giaiotti (bass), R. Muti (cnd), Rome RAI SO, Rome RAI Chorus—A te, o cara *(rec Rome, July 8, 1969)* Goldies ▲ GLD 63202 [ADD]

Antonini, Giovanni (bass) (cont.)
Rossini, G.:Armida, w. C. Deutekom (sop), P. Bottazzo (ten), O. Garaventa (ten), E. Gimenez (ten), B. Trotta (sgr), A. Maddalena (bass), C. Franci (cnd), Venice Teatro La Fenice Orch, Venice Teatro La Fenice Chorus *(rec live, Venice, 1970)* Foyer 2-▲ FOY 2030 [AAD]

Antonioli (ten)
Verdi, G.:Rigoletto (sels), w. A. Pastori (sop), C. Tagliabue (bar), U. Rapalo (cnd), Naples Teatro San Carlo Orch, Naples Teatro San Carlo Chorus [I] *(rec live, Naples, 1/20/56)* The Golden Age of Opera ▲ GAO 115 [ADD]

Antoniozzi, Alfonso (bass)
Bizet, G.:Don Procopio, w. Muscente (sgr), M. Gentile (sop), Carmona (sgr), Barry (sgr), S. Sanna (cnd), Berlin Radio Youth Orch, Symbolon Ensemble Chorus [I] *(rec live 5/25/86)* Bongiovanni 2-▲ GB 2043/44 [DDD]
Cimarosa, D.:Il Matrimonio segreto, w. Susan Patterson (sop—Carolina), Janet Williams (mez—Elisseta), Gloria Banditelli (cta—Fidalma), William Matteuzzi (ten—Paolino), Alfonso Antoniozzi (bass—Geronimo), Petteri Salomaa (bass—Count Robinson), Hans Ludwig Hirsch (pno), G. Bellini (cnd), Eastern Netherlands Orch *(rec Muziekcentrum Enschede, Holland, Aug 26–Sept 8, 1991)* Arts 3-▲ 471172 [DDD]
Donizetti, G.:Linda di Chamounix, w. Mariella Devia (sop—Linda), Sonia Ganassi (mez—Pierotto), Francesca Provvisionato (mez—Maddalena), Luca Canonici (ten—Carlo), Alfonso Antoniozzi (bass—Il Marchese di Boisfleury), Petteri Salomaa (bass—Antonio), Boguslaw Fiksinski (sgr—L'intendente), Donato Di Stefano (sgr—Il Prefetto), G. Bellini (cnd), Eastern Netherlands Orch, Andrew Wise (cnd), National Reisopera Choir *(rec Muziekcentrum Enschede, Holland, June 24–July 2, 1992)* Arts Music 3-▲ 47151-2 [DDD]
Ferrero, L.:Mare nostro, w. A. Felle (sop—Candeggina), E. Jankovic (mez—Astradiva), C. Di Segni (ten—Rimestino), D. Serraiocco (bass-bar—Marchingello), A. Antoniozzi (bass-bar—Pigliatutto), G. Maisni (cnd), Venezze di Rovigo Conservatory of Music Orch, Venezze di Rovigo Conservatory of Music Chorus *(rec Oct. 21–24, 1991)* Ricordi 2-▲ RFCD 2016 [DDD]
Mozart, W.A.:Nozze di Figaro, w. Rebecca Evans (sop—Barbarina), Nuccia Focile (sop—Susanna), Suzanne Murphy (sop—Marcellina), Carol Vaness (sop—Countess Almaviva), Susanne Mentzer (mez—Cherubino), Ryland Davies (ten—Don Basilio/Don Curzio), Alessandro Corbelli (bar—Count Almaviva), Alfonso Antoniozzi (bass—Doctor Bartolo/Antonio), Alastair Miles (bass—Figaro), C. Mackerras (cnd), Scottish CO, Scottish Chamber Chorus *(rec Usher Hall, Edingurgh, Scotland, July 31–Aug. 12, 1994)* Telarc 3-▲ CD 80388 [DDD]

Antonov, Yuri (sgr)
Taneyev, S.:At the Reading of a Psalm, w. Yuri Belokrynkin (sgr), Raisa Kotova (sgr), Adelina Kozlova (sgr), E. Svetlanov (cnd), USSR SO, Yurloff State Choir Russian Disc ▲ RUS 10044 [AAD]

Antonucci, Paola (sop)
Donizetti, G.:Il furioso all'isola di Santo Domingo, w. L. Serra (sop), E. Tandura (mez), L. Canonici (ten), R. Coviello (bar), Picconi (sgr), C. Rizzi (cnd), Piacenza SO, Piacenza Chorus [I] *(rec live, 11/10/87)* Bongiovanni 3-▲ GB 2056/58 [DDD]

Antonucci, Stefano (bar)
Coccia, C.:Caterina di Guisa, w. C. Apollonio (sop), N. Ciliento (mez), M. Leonardi (ten), M. de Bernart (cnd), Italian PO, Calabria Francesca Cilea Chorus *(rec Oct. 30 & Nov. 3, 1990)* Bongiovanni 2-▲ GB 2117/18 [DDD]
Mercadante, S.:Il bravo, w. J. Perry (sop), A. Tabiadon (mez), D. Di Domenico (ten), S. Bertocchi (ten), B. Aprea (cnd), Italian International Orch, Slovak Phil Chorus [I] *(rec live 7/28–31/90)* Nuova Era 3-▲ 6971/73 [DDD]
Puccini, G.:La Bohème, w. Katia Ricciarelli (sop), Francisco Araiza (ten), Angelo Casertano (ten), Claudio Giombi (bar), Paata Burchuladze (bass), Alfredo Mariotti (bass), Alberto Noli (bass), Andrea Piccinni (bass), Lauren Broglia (sgr), A. Guadagno (cnd), Arena di Verona Orch, Limburg Cathedral Boys' Chorus Koch Schwann 2-▲ SCH 315922
Puccini, G.:Le Villi, w. José Cura (sgr), Nana Gordaze (sgr), B. Aprea (cnd), Italian International Orch Nuova Era ▲ NUO 7218 [DDD]
Rossini, G.:Torvaldo e Dorliska, w. A. Buda (sop), F. Pediconi (sop), M. Ciliento (mez), E. Palacio (ten), A. Marani (b-bar), M. de Bernart (cnd), Swiss-Italian Orch, Cantemus, Swiss-Italian Radio-TV Chorus *(rec Jan 11, 1992)* Arkadia-Akademia 2-▲ 123 [DDD]

Aoyama, M..oko (cta)
Mozart, W.A.:Missa, K.66, w. P. Wise (sop), P. Baillie (ten), H. Müller (bass), E. Hinreiner (cnd), Salzburg Camerata Academica, Salzburg RSO, Mozart Choir [L] *(rec May 1974)* Koch Treasure ▲ 316182 [ADD]

Aparici, Montserrat (sop)
Verdi, G.:I lombardi alla prima crociata, w. C. Deutekom (sop), D. Malvisi (sop), P. Domingo (ten), G. Raimondi (ten), M. Lo Monaco (ten), M. Dean (b-bar), C. Grant (bass), L. Gardelli (cnd), Royal PO, Ambrosian Singers Philips 2-▲ 422420-2 [ADD]

Apollonio, Carmela (sop)
Coccia, C.:Caterina di Guisa, w. N. Ciliento (mez), M. Leonardi (ten), S. Antonucci (bar), M. de Bernart (cnd), Italian PO, Calabria Francesca Cilea Chorus *(rec Oct. 30 & Nov. 3, 1990)* Bongiovanni 2-▲ GB 2117/18 [DDD]

Appelman, Tine (mez)
Puccini, G.:Manon Lescaut, w. Magda Olivero (sop—Manon), Tine Appelman (mez—Singer), Umberto Borso (ten—Chevalier), Mario Carlin (ten—Edmondo/Dancing Master/Lamplighter), Ferdinando Lidonni (bar—Lescaut), Giovanni Foiani (bass—Geronte/Sergeant/Captain), Joop Ruivenkamp (bass—Innkeeper), F. Vernizzi (cnd), Groot Omroep Orch, Groot Omroep Choir *(rec Amsterdam, Oct 31, 1964)* Bella Voce 2-▲ BLV 107.221 [AAD]

Applebaum, Jody Karin (sop)
Bolcom, W.:Cabaret Songs, w. M.-A. Hamelin (pno) Music & Arts ▲ CD 729-1 [DDD]
Britten, H.:Cabaret Songs, w. M.-A. Hamelin (pno) Music & Arts ▲ CD 729-1 [DDD]
Schoenberg, A.:The Cabaret Songs, w. M.-A. Hamelin (pno) Music & Arts ▲ CD 729-1 [DDD]
Wright, M.:Night Watch, w. M.-A. Hamelin (pno) CRI ▲ CD 660 [DDD]

Apreck, Rolf (ten)
Mozart, W.A.:Entführung, w. Rosemarie Ronisch (sop), Jutta Vulpius (sop), Jurgen Forster (ten), Arnold van Mill (bass), O. Suitner (cnd), Dresden State Opera Orch, Dresden State Opera Chorus Berlin Classics 2-▲ BER 9116

Aragall, Giacomo (ten)
Bellini, V.:I Capuleti e i Montecchi, w. M. Rinaldi (sop—Giulietta), G. Aragall (ten—Romeo), L. Pavarotti (ten—Tebaldo), N. Zaccaria (bass—Capellio), C. Abbado (cnd), Residentie Orch The Hague, Bologna Chorus [I] *(rec live, Amsterdam 6/30/66)* Verona 2-▲ 28001/2
Bellini, V.:I Capuleti e i Montecchi, w. R. Scotto (sop), L. Pavarotti (ten), A. Giacomotti (bass), A. Ferrin (bass), C. Abbado (cnd), La Scala Orch, La Scala Chorus *(rec live 1967)* Butterfly Music 2-▲ BMC 12 [AAD]
Bellini, V.:I Capuleti e i Montecchi, w. R. Scotto (sop), L. Pavarotti (ten), C. Abbado (cnd), La Scala Orch, La Scala Chorus [I] *(rec live, La Scala, 1/8/68)* Arkadia 2-▲ 550 (m) [AAD]
Bellini, V.:I Capuleti e i Montecchi, w. M. Rinaldi (sop), L. Pavarotti (ten), N. Zaccaria (bass), C. Abbado (cnd), Residentie Orch The Hague, Bologna Chorus *(rec live, Amsterdam 6/30/66)* Melodram 2-▲ MEL 27001
Donizetti, G.:Caterina Cornaro, w. L. Gencer (sop), R. Bruson (bar), L. Risani (sgr), C.F. Cillario (cnd), Naples Teatro San Carlo Orch, Naples Teatro San Carlo Chorus *(rec live, 5/28/72)* Myto 2-▲ 2 MCD 92153 [ADD]
Donizetti, G.:Caterina Cornaro, w. L. Gencer (sop), R. Bruson (bar), C.F. Cillario (cnd), Naples Teatro San Carlo Orch, Naples Teatro San Carlo Chorus [I] *(rec live, Naples 5/28/72)* Memories 2-▲ HR 4448/49 (m) [ADD]
Donizetti, G.:Caterina Cornaro, w. Montserrat Caballé (sop), Gwynne Howell (bass), Ryan Edwards (sgr), G.-F. Masini (cnd), ORTF Orch *(rec Paris, Nov 25, 1973)* Agorá Music ("Phoenix" series) 2-▲ 505
Donizetti, G.:Lucrezia Borgia, w. J. Sutherland (sop), M. Horne (mez), I. Wixell (bar), R. Bonynge (cnd), National PO London [I] London 2-▲ 421497-2 [ADD]
Duets & Arias from Italian Operas, w. E. Tumagian (bar), A. Rahbari (cnd), Czech-Slovak RSO Bratislava Naxos ▲ 8.550684 [DDD]

Aragall, Giacomo (ten) (cont.)
From the Official Barcelona Games Ceremony, w. P. Domingo (ten), José Carreras (ten), Montserrat Caballé (sop), Teresa Berganza (mez), Juan Pons (bar) RCA Red Seal ▲ 09026-61204-2 ■ 09026-61204-4 □ 09026-61204-5
Gounod, C.:Roméo et Juliette (sels), w. Renata Scotto (sop—Juliet), Giacomo Aragall (ten—Romeo), Luciano Pavarotti (ten—Tebaldo), Gaetano Ferrin (bass—Capellio), Alfredo Giacomotti (bass—Lorenzo), C. Abbado (cnd), La Scala Orch, La Scala Chorus Budget ("The Greatest Voice in Opera" series) ▲ SYP 111
Verdi, G.:Jérusalem, w. Leyla Gencer (sop), Giancarlo Guelfi (bar), G. Gavazzeni (cnd), Venice Teatro La Fenice Orch, Venice Teatro La Fenice Chorus *(rec Venice, Sept 24, 1963)* Agorá Music ("Phoenix" series) 2-▲ 506
Verdi, G.:Jérusalem, w. Leyla Gencer (sop), Giancarlo Guelfi (bar), G. Gavazzeni (cnd), Venice Teatro La Fenice Orch, Venice Teatro La Fenice Chorus [I] *(rec live 9/24/63)* Melodram 2-▲ MEL 27004
Verdi, G.:Jérusalem, w. Leyla Gencer (sop), Giancarlo Guelfi (bar), G. Gavazzeni (cnd), Venice Teatro La Fenice Orch [I] *(rec live 9/24/63)* Verona 2-▲ 27040/41 (m) [AAD]
Verdi, G.:La traviata, w. I. Cotrubas (sop), R. Bruson (bar), C. Kleiber (cnd), Bavarian State Orch [I] *(rec 1978)* Artists 2-▲ FED 45 [ADD]
Verdi, G.:La traviata, w. P. Lorengar (sop), S. Malagu (mez), D. Fischer-Dieskau (bar), L. Maazel (cnd), Berlin German Opera Orch, Berlin German Opera Chorus London ("Double Decker" series) 2-▲ 443000-2

Aragall, Jaime (ten)
Donizetti, G.:La favorita, w. F. Cossotto (mez), A. Colzani (bar), E. Gracis (cnd), Turin RAI Orch, Turin RAI Chorus *(rec live)* Melodram 2-▲ MEL 27020
Donizetti, G.:La favorita (sels), w. *(orch unknown) (rec 1968–73)* Golden Age of Opera 2-▲ GAO 195/196
Donizetti, G.:Lucia di Lammermoor (sels), w. *(orch unknown) (rec 1968–73)* Golden Age of Opera 2-▲ GAO 195/196
Mascagni, P.:L'amico Fritz (sels), w. *(orch unknown) (rec 1968–73)* Golden Age of Opera 2-▲ GAO 195/196
Massenet, J.:Werther (sels) *(rec 1968–73)* Golden Age of Opera 2-▲ GAO 195/196
Puccini, G.:La Bohème (sels), w. *(orch unknown) (rec 1968–73)* Golden Age of Opera 2-▲ GAO 195/196
Puccini, G.:Tosca (sels), w. K. Te Kanawa (sop), L. Nucci (bar), G. Solti (cnd), National PO London, Welsh National Opera Chorus London ▲ 421611-2 [DDD]
Verdi, G.:Don Carlos, w. M. Caballé (sop—Elisabeth de Valois), G. Bumbry (mez—Princess Eboli), J. Aragall (ten—Don Carlos), R. Bruson (bar—Rodrigue), S. Estes (bass—Philip II), T. Fulton (cnd), *(orch unknown) (rec Orange, France, 1979)* Ornamenti 2-▲ FE 110 [ADD]
Verdi, G.:Rigoletto, w. Cecilia Nunez Albanese (sop—Gilda), Wilma Borrelli (cta—Maddalena), Jaime Aragall (ten—Duke of Mantua), Renato Bruson (bar—Rigoletto), Loris Gambelli (bass—Sparafucile), G. Campanino (cnd), Naples Teatro San Carlo Orch, Naples Teatro San Carlo Chorus *(rec San Carlo Theatre, Naples, Feb. 1973)* Golden Age of Opera 2-▲ GAO 177–78 [ADD]
Verdi, G.:Simon Boccanegra, w. K. Te Kanawa (sop), L. Nucci (bar), P. Burchuladze (bass), G. Solti (cnd), La Scala Orch, La Scala Chorus [I] London 2-▲ 425628-2 [DDD]
Verdi, G.:La traviata (sels) *(rec 1968–73)* Golden Age of Opera 2-▲ GAO 195/196

Araiza, Francisco (ten)
Catalani, A.:La Wally, w. E. Marton (sop), A. Titus (bar), F. Ellero d'Artegna (bass), P. Steinberg (cnd), Munich RSO, Bavarian Radio Chorus [I] Eurodisc 2-▲ 69073-2-RC [DDD] ■ 69073-4-RC (CrO2)
Gounod, C.:Faust, w. K. Te Kanawa (sop), E. Nesterenko (bass), C. Davis (cnd), Bavarian RSO, Bavarian Radio Chorus [F] Philips 3-▲ 420164-2 [DDD]
Mahler, G.:Das Lied von der Erde, w. B. Fassbaender (mez), C. M. Giulini (cnd), Berlin PO [G] Deutsche Grammophon ▲ 413459-2 [DDD]
Massenet, J.:Thérèse, w. Agnes Baltsa (mez—Thérèse), Francisco Araiza (ten—Armand), Gino Sinimberghi (ten—Officer), George Fortune (bass—André), Giancarlo Luccardi (bass—Morel), Eftimios Michalopoulos (sgr—Officer/Municipal Officer), G. Albrecht (cnd), Rome RAI SO, Giuseppe Piccillo (cnd), Rome RAI Chorus Orfeo ▲ 387961 [DDD]
Mozart, W.A.:Arias, w. I. Cotrubas (sop), E. Gruberova (sop), L. Price (sop), J. Varady (sop), L. Popp (mez), P. Domingo (ten), P. de Palma (ten), P. Schreier (ten), F. Wunderlich (ten), S. Milnes (bar), A. Titus (bar), M. Talvela (bass)—sels. from Entführung aus dem Serail, Così fan tutte, Don Giovanni, Idomeneo, Die Zauberflöte, Le nozze di Figaro Eurodisc ▲ 69256-2-RG
Mozart, W.A.:Arias, w. Arleen Augér (sop), Kathleen Battle (sop), Irma Beilke (sop), Helena Braun (sop), Lisa Della Casa (sop), Maria Cebotari (sop), Ileana Cotrubas (sop), Helen Donath (sop), Mirella Freni (sop), Reri Grist (sop), Edita Gruberova (sop), Elisabeth Grümmer (sop), Hilde Güden (sop), Ingeborg Hallstein (sop), Luise Helletsgruber (sop), Gundula Janowitz (sop), Sena Jurinac (sop), Erika Köth (sop), Evelyn Lear (sop), Wilma Lipp (sop), Margaret Marshall (sop), Edith Mathis (sop), Jarmila Novotna (sop), Margherita Perras (sop), Lucia Popp (sop), Elisabeth Rethberg (sop), Anneliese Rothenberger (sop), Elisabeth Schumann (sop), Elisabeth Schwarzkopf (sop), Graziella Sciutti (sop), Irmgard Seefried (sop), Graziella Sciutti (sop), Julia Varady (sop), Agnes Baltsa (mez), Margit Bokor (mez), Brigitte Fassbaender (mez), Christa Ludwig (mez), Ann Murray (mez), Anton Dermota (ten), Helge Rosvaenge (ten), Rudolf Schock (ten), Peter Schreier (ten), Leopold Simoneau (ten), Eric Tappy (ten), Richard Tauber (ten), Gösta Winbergh (ten), Josef Witt (ten), Fritz Wunderlich (ten), Christian Boesch (bar), Willy Domgraf-Fassbaender (bar), Karl Dönch (bar), Dietrich Fischer-Dieskau (bar), Erich Kunz (bar), Eberhard Wächter (bar), Hans Hotter (b-bar), Paul Schöffler (b-bar), Cesare Siepi (b-bar), José Van Dam (b-bar), Walter Berry (bass), Geraint Evans (bass), Nicolai Ghiaurov (bass), Alexander Kipnis (bass), Richard Mayr (bass), Kurt Moll (bass), James Morris (bass), Ezio Pinza (bass), Martti Talvela (bass), Giorgio Tozzi (bass), Hans Duhan (sgr), Res Fischer (sgr), Marie Gerhart (sgr), *(various orchs & cnds)*—sels from Idomeneo, Die Entführung aus der Serail, Le nozze di Figaro, Don Giovanni, Così fan tutte, Die Zauberflöte & various arias Orfeo d'or ("Festspiel Dokumente" series) 5-▲ 408955
Mozart, W.A.:Complete Mozart Edition, w. B. Hendricks (sop), J. Varady (sop), S. Mentzer (mez), T. Allen (bar), C. Davis (cnd), Bavarian RSO Philips 3-▲ 422537-2 [ADD]
Mozart, W.A.:Complete Mozart Edition, w. E. Gruberova (sop), E. Mathis (sop), L. Popp (mez), P. Schreier (ten), W. Berry (bass), Salzburg Mozarteum Orch Philips 8-▲ 422523-2 [ADD]
Mozart, W.A.:Così fan tutte, w. K. Mattila (sop), E. Szmytka (sop), A. S. von Otter (mez), T. Allen (bar), J. van Dam (b-bar), N. Marriner (cnd), Academy of St. Martin in the Fields, Ambrosian Opera Chorus [I] Philips 3-▲ 422381-2 [DDD]
Mozart, W.A.:Don Giovanni, w. S. Sweet (sop), K. Mattila (sop), M. McLaughlin (sop), T. Allen (bar), S. Alaimo (b-bar), R. Lloyd (bass), N. Marriner (cnd), Academy of St. Martin in the Fields, Ambrosian Opera Chorus Philips 3-▲ 432129-2 [DDD]
Mozart, W.A.:Don Giovanni (sels), w. K. Mattila (sop), T. Allen (bar), R. Lloyd (bass), N. Marriner (cnd), Academy of St. Martin in the Fields Philips ▲ 438494-2
Mozart, W.A.:Entführung, w. E. Gruberova (sop), R. Orth (bar), R. Bracht (bass), H. Wallberg (cnd), Munich RSO Eurodisc 2-▲ 7792-2 [ADD]
Mozart, W.A.:Requiem, w. S. McNair (sop), C. Watkinson (cta), R. Lloyd (b-bar), N. Marriner (cnd), Academy of St. Martin in the Fields, Academy Chorus [L] Philips ▲ 432087-2 [DDD]
Mozart, W.A.:Zauberflöte, w. K. Te Kanawa (sop), C. Studer (sop), E. Lind (sop), O. Bär (bar), S. Ramey (bass), N. Marriner (cnd), Academy of St. Martin in the Fields, Ambrosian Opera Chorus [G] Philips 2-▲ 426276-2 [DDD]
Mozart, W.A.:Zauberflöte, w. Edith Mathis (sop), Karin Ott (sop), Janet Perry (sop), Anna Tomowa-Sintow (sop), Agnes Baltsa (mez), Hannah Schwarz (mez), Gottfried Hornik (bar), José Van Dam (b-bar), H. von Karajan (cnd), Berlin PO, German Opera Chorus [G] Deutsche Grammophon 3-▲ 410967-2 [DDD]
Mozart, W.A.:Zauberflöte (sels), w. Edith Mathis (sop), Karin Ott (sop), Janet Perry (sop), Anna Tomowa-Sintow (sop), Agnes Baltsa (mez), Hannah Schwarz (mez), Gottfried Hornik (bar), José Van Dam (b-bar), H. von Karajan (cnd), Berlin PO, German Opera Chorus [G] Deutsche Grammophon ▲ 415287-2 [DDD]
Mozart, W.A.:Zauberflöte (sels), w. K. Te Kanawa (sop), C. Studer (sop), E. Lind (sop), O. Bär (bar), S. Ramey (bass), N. Marriner (cnd), Academy of St. Martin in the Fields Philips ▲ 438495-2
Offenbach, J.:Les Contes d'Hoffmann, w. J. Norman (sop), E. Lind (sop), C. Studer (sop), A. Sofie von Otter (mez), S. Ramey (bass), J. Tate (cnd), Dresden Staatskapelle Philips ▲ 438502-2

Araiza, Francisco (ten) (cont.)

Offenbach, J.:Les Contes d'Hoffmann, w. J. Norman (sop), C. Studer (sop), E. Lind (sop), A. S. von Otter (mez), S. Ramey (bass), J. Tate (cnd), Dresden Staatskapelle Philips 3-▲ 422374-2 [DDD]

Puccini, G.:La Bohème, w. Katia Ricciarelli (sop), Angelo Casertano (ten), Stefano Antonucci (bar), Claudio Giombi (bar), Paata Burchuladze (bass), Alfredo Mariotti (bass), Alberto Noli (bass), Andrea Piccinni (bass), Lauren Broglia (sgr), A. Guadagno (cnd), Arena di Verona Orch, Limburg Cathedral Boys' Chorus Koch Schwann 2-▲ SCH 315922

The Romantic Tenor, w. Munich Radio Orch [cnd:Ralf Weikert] RCA Red Seal ▲ 09026-61163-2

Rossini, G.:Il barbiere di Siviglia (sels), w. A. Baltsa (mez), S. Burgess (mez), T. Allen (bar), D. Trimarchi (bar), R. Lloyd (bass), N. Marriner (cnd), Academy of St. Martin in the Fields Philips ▲ 438498-2

Rossini, G.:La Cenerentola, w. E. Ravaglia (sop), L. V. Terrani (mez), E. Dara (bar), G. Ferro (cnd), Cappella Coloniensis, Cologne Radio Chorus [I] Sony Classical 2-▲ S2K 46433 [ADD]

Rossini, G.:La Cenerentola, w. C. Malone (sop), F. Palmer (sop), A. Baltsa (mez), S. Alaimo (bar), J. del Carlo (bass), R. Raimondi (bass), N. Marriner (cnd), Academy of St. Martin in the Fields, Ambrosian Chorus Philips ("Digital Classics" series) 3-▲ 420468-2 [DDD]

Rossini, G.:Messa di gloria, w. A. C. Antonacci (sop), B. Manca Di Nissa (cta), R. Gambill (ten), P. Spagnoli (bar), S. Accardo (cnd), St. Cecilia Academy Orch Rome, St. Cecilia Academy Chorus Rome *(rec Mar. 1-2, 1992)* Ricordi ▲ RFCD 2012 [DDD]

Rossini, G.:Semiramide, w. M. Caballé (sop), M. Horne (mez), S. Ramey (bass), J. López-Cobos (cnd), *(orch unknown) (rec live, France, 1980)* HRE 2-▲ 1002-2 [ADD]

Schubert, Franz:Mass 4, w. H. Donath (sop), B. Fassbaender (mez), D. Fischer-Dieskau (bar), W. Sawallisch (cnd), Bavarian RSO, Bavarian Radio Chorus [L] EMI Classics ("Studio" series) ▲ CDM 69222

Schubert, Franz:Mass 6, w. H. Donath (sop), B. Fassbaender (mez), D. Fischer-Dieskau (bar), W. Sawallisch (cnd), Bavarian RSO, Bavarian Radio Chorus [L] EMI Classics ("Studio" series) ▲ CDM 69223

Spontini, G.:La vestale, w. R. Plowright (sop), G. Pasino (mez), P. Lefèbvre (ten), A. Cauli (bar), F. de Grandis (bass), G. Kuhn (cnd), Munich RSO, Munich Radio Chorus [F] Orfeo 2-▲ 256922 [DDD]

Verdi, G.:Alzira, w. M. Cotrubas (sop), R. Bruson (bar), L. Gardelli (cnd), Munich RSO, Bavarian Radio Chorus [I] Orfeo 2-▲ 057832 [DDD]

Weber, C.M. von:Der Freischütz (sels), w. K. Mattila (sop), E. Lind (sop), K. Moll (bass), C. Davis (cnd), Dresden Staatskapelle Philips ▲ 438497-2

Aramburo, Antonio (ten)

The World of Singing, Vol. 3:The Italian School, Part 1:The Italian Tenors Before World War I (1902-13), w. Alessandro Bonci (ten), Giuseppe Borgatti (ten), Enrico Caruso (ten), Edoardo Garbin (ten), Fiorello Giraud (ten), Fernando de Lucia (ten), Francesco Marconi (ten), Giovanni Battista de Negri (ten), Antonio Paoli (ten), Francesco T Enterprise ("Vocal Archives" series) 3-▲ ENT VA 2104

Arangi-Lombardi, Giannina (cta)

Mascagni, P.:Cavalleria rusticana, w. A. Melandri (ten), G. Lulli (bar), L. Molajoli (cnd), Milan SO, La Scala Chorus [I] *(rec 1930 for Columbia Records)* Standing Room Only ▲ SRO 806-1 (m) [ADD]

Arangi-Lombardi, Giannina (sop)

Boito, A.:Mefistofele, w. Mafalda Favero (sop), Antonio Melandri (ten), Giuseppe Nessi (ten), Nazzareno de Angelis (bass), L. Molajoli (cnd), La Scala Orch, La Scala Chorus Grammofono 2000 2-▲ GRM 78606 (m)

Opera Arias, w. La Scala Orch [cnd:Lorenzo Molajoli] *(rec 1928-33)* Preiser ("Lebendige Vergangenheit" series) ▲ PRE 89013 [AAD]

Verdi, G.:Aida, w. Giannina Arangi-Lombardi (sop—Aida), Maria Capuana (mez—Amneris), Aroldo Lindi (ten—Radames), Giuseppe Nessi (ten—Messenger), Armando Borgioli (bar—Amonasro), Salvatore Baccaloni (bass—King), Tancredi Pasero (bass—Ramfis), L. Molajoli (cnd), La Scala Orch, La Scala Chorus *(rec Nov 1928)* VAI Audio 2-▲ VAIA 1083-2

Arapian, Armand (bar)

Aprikian, G.:Naissance de David de Sassoun, w. Fabienne Chanoyan (sop—Angel), Anna Karakaya (mez—Queen Taline), Armand Arapian (bar—King Mehèr/Priest), H. Sakssian (cnd), Bell'Arte Orch, Sipan-Komitas Choir Petit Chanteurs of Tebrotzassere School *(rec Ivry-sur-Seine, Jan 17-18, 1995)* Studio SM ▲ D2514

Arapian, Armand (ten)

Campra, A.:Tancrède, w. C. Dussaut (sop—Herminie), A. Arapian (ten—Argant), J. Bona (bar—Tancrède), C. Zaffini (cnd), Provence Instrumental Ensemble, Avignon Vocal Ensemble—highlights *(rec 1986)* Pierre Verany ▲ PV.786111 [ADD]

Handel, G.F.:Rinaldo, w. Sophie Boulin (sop—Donna), Ileana Cotrubas (sop—Almirena), Marie-Françoise Jacquelin (sop—Sirene), Nicole Leport (sop—Sirene), Jeanette Scovotti (sop—Armida), Carolyn Watkinson (cta—Rinaldo), Charles Brett (ct—Eustazio), Paul Esswood (ct—Goffredo), Armand Arapian (ten—Mago Christiano/Araldo), Ulrik Cold (bass—Argante), J. Malgoire (cnd), La Grande Écurie et la Chambre du Roy *(rec Paris, 1977)* Sony Classical 3-▲ SM3K 34592

Arcangelo, Ildebrando d' (bass)

Haydn, J.:L'Anima del filosofo, or Orfeo ed Euridice, w. Cecilia Bartoli (mez), Uwe Heilmann (ten), C. Hogwood (cnd), Academy of Ancient Music, Academy of Ancient Music Chorus L'oiseau Lyre ▲ 452 668-2

Mozart, W.A.:Don Giovanni, w. Charlotte Margiono (sop—Donna Elvira), Luba Orgonasova (sop—Donna Anna), Eirian James (mez—Zerlina), Julian Clarkson (alt—Masetto), Christoph Prégardien (ten—Don Ottavio), Rodney Gilfry (bar—Don Giovanni), Ildebrando d'Arcangelo (bass—Leporello), Andrea Silvestrelli (bass—Il Commendatore), J. E. Gardiner (cnd), English Baroque Soloists, Monteverdi Choir London Deutsche Grammophon ("4D Audio" series) 3-▲ 445870-2

Rossini, G.:Armida, w. R. Fleming (sop), C. Bosi (ten), B. Fowler (ten), J. Francis (ten), D. Kaasch (ten), G. Kunde (ten), I. Zennaro (ten), S. Zadvorny (bass), D. Gatti (cnd), Bologna Teatro Comunale Orch, Bologna Teatro Comunale Chorus *(rec Pesaro, Italy, Aug. 6-17, 1993)* Sony Classical 3-▲ S3K 58968 [DDD]

Wolf-Ferrari, E.:Il campiello, w. D. Mazzucato (Gasparina), G. Devinu (Lucieta), M. Bolgan (Gnese), C. de Mola (Orsola), U. Benelli (Dona Cate Panciana), M. Rene Cosotti (Dona Pasqua Polegana), M. Comencini (Zorozeto), M. Biscotti (Astolfi), I. D'Arcangelo (Anzoleto), C. Striuli (Fabrizio dei Ritorti), N. Bareza (cnd), Trieste Teatro Comunale Giuseppe Verdi Orch, Trieste Teatro Comunale G. Verdi Chorus *(rec Feb. 1992)* Ricordi 2-▲ RFCD 2014 [DDD]

Archer, Neill (ten)

Howells, H.:Stabat mater, w. G. Rozhdestvensky (cnd), London SO, London Sym Chorus Chandos ▲ CHAN 9314 [DDD]

Sullivan, A.:The Yeomen of the Guard, w. Felicity Palmer (sop—Dame Carruthers), Pamela Helen Stephens (mez—Phoebe Meryll), Neill Archer (ten—Col Fairfax), Peter Hoare (ten—Leonard Meryll), Ralph Mason (ten—1st Yeoman), Donald Maxwell (bar—Wilfred Shadbolt), Peter Savidge (bar—Lieutenant Sir Richard Cholmondely), Donald Adams (bass—Sergeant Meryll), Richard Suart (bass—Jack Point), Peter Lloyd Evans (sgr—2nd Yeoman), Alwyn Mellor (sgr—Elsie Maynard), Clare O'Neill (sgr—Kate), C. Mackerras (cnd), Welsh National Opera Orch, Welsh National Opera Chorus *(rec Brangwyn Hall, Swasea, Wales, Apr 18-30 & May 1, 1995)* Telarc 2-▲ CD 80404 [DDD]

Argenta, Nancy (sop)

Bach, J.S.:Cant 36, w. R. Lang (mez), A. Rolfe Johnson (ten), O. Bär (bar), J. E. Gardiner (cnd), English Baroque Soloists, Monteverdi Choir London Archiv ▲ 437327-2

Bach, J.S.:Cant 49, w. K. Mertens (bass), M. Ponseele (ob), S. Kuijken (vn), H. Suzuki (vc), P. Hantaï (org), La Petite Bande Accent ▲ ACC 9395 D [DDD]

Bach, J.S.:Cant 51, w. M. Hugget (vn), M. Huggett (cnd), Sonnerie Ensemble Virgin Classics ▲ CDC 45038

Bach, J.S.:Cant 58, w. K. Mertens (bass), M. Ponseele (ob), S. Kuijken (vn), H. Suzuki (vc), P. Hantaï (org), La Petite Bande Accent ▲ ACC 9395 D [DDD]

Bach, J.S.:Cant 61, w. R. Lang (mez), A. Rolfe Johnson (ten), O. Bär (bar), J. E. Gardiner (cnd), English Baroque Soloists, Monteverdi Choir London Archiv ▲ 437327-2 [DDD]

Bach, J.S.:Cant 62, w. R. Lang (mez), A. Rolfe Johnson (ten), O. Bär (bar), J. E. Gardiner (cnd), English Baroque Soloists, Monteverdi Choir London Archiv ▲ 437327-2 [DDD]

Bach, J.S.:Cant 82, w. M. Hugget (vn), M. Huggett (cnd), Sonnerie Ensemble Virgin Classics ▲ CDC 45038

Bach, J.S.:Cant 82, w. K. Mertens (bass), M. Ponseele (ob), S. Kuijken (vn), H. Suzuki (vc), P. Hantaï (org), La Petite Bande Accent ▲ ACC 9395 D [DDD]

Argenta, Nancy (sop) (cont.)

Bach, J.S.:Cant 84, w. Sonnerie Ensemble Virgin Classics ▲ CDC 45059

Bach, J.S.:Cant 106, "Actus tragicus", w. M. Chance (ct), A. Rolfe Johnson (ten), S. Varcoe (b-bar), J. E. Gardiner (cnd), English Baroque Soloists, Monteverdi Choir London [G] Archiv ▲ 429782-2 [DDD]

Bach, J.S.:Cant 198, w. M. Chance (ct), A. Rolfe Johnson (ten), S. Varcoe (b-bar), J. E. Gardiner (cnd), English Baroque Soloists, Monteverdi Choir London [G] Archiv ▲ 429782-2 [DDD]

Bach, J.S.:Cant 199, w. M. Hugget (vn), M. Huggett (cnd), Sonnerie Ensemble Virgin Classics ▲ CDC 45038

Bach, J.S.:Cant 202, "Wedding Cant", w. Sonnerie Ensemble Virgin Classics ▲ CDC 45059

Bach, J.S.:Cant 209, w. Sonnerie Ensemble Virgin Classics ▲ CDC 45059

Bach, J.S.:Christmas Oratorio, w. A. S. von Otter (mez), H.-P. Blochwitz (ten), O. Bär (bar), J. E. Gardiner (cnd), English Baroque Soloists, Monteverdi Choir London [G] Archiv 2-▲ 423232-2 [DDD]

Bach, J.S.:Christmas Oratorio (sels), w. A. S. von Otter (mez), H.-P. Blochwitz (ten), O. Bär (bar), J. E. Gardiner (cnd), English Baroque Soloists, Monteverdi Choir London [G] Archiv ▲ 427653-2 [DDD]

Bach, J.S.:Mass in b, BWV 232, w. C. Denley (mez), M. Tucker (ten), S. Varcoe (b-bar), R. Hickox (cnd), Collegium Musicum 90 Chandos ("Chaconne" series) 2-▲ CHAN 0533/34 [DDD]

Bach, J.S.:St. Matthew Passion, w. L. Lee (mez), J. Kenny (alt), J. MacDougall (ten), R. Müller (ten), R. Jackson (bar), S. Varcoe (b-bar), P. Goodwin (cnd), *(orch & chorus unknown)* United 2-▲ UNI 89301 [DDD]

Bach, J.S.:St. Matthew Passion (sels), w. L. Lee (mez), J. Kenny (alt), J. MacDougall (ten), R. Müller (ten), R. Jackson (bar), S. Varcoe (b-bar), P. Goodwin (cnd), *(orch & chorus unknown) (rec St. George's Theater, London, Feb 24-27, 1994)* United ▲ UNI 88030 [DDD]

Gluck, C.W.:Orfeo ed Euridice, w. M. Chance (ct), J. Lamon (cnd), Tafelmusik, F. Bernius (cnd), Stuttgart Chamber Choir Sony Classical ("Vivarte" series) 2-▲ SX2K 48040

Handel, G.F.:The Alchymist, w. M. Huggett (cnd), CBC Vancouver SO [I] CBC ("SM 5000" series) ▲ SMCD 5091 [DDD]; ■ SMC 5091 (D)

Handel, G.F.:Alcina (sels), w. M. Huggett (cnd), CBC Vancouver SO—2 arias & several orchestral sels. [I] CBC ("SM 5000" series) ▲ SMCD 5091 [DDD]; ■ SMC 5091 (D)

Handel, G.F.:Alexander's Feast (ode), w. I. Partridge (ten), M. George (bass), H. Christophers (cnd), The Sixteen Orch, The Sixteen Chorus Collins Classics 2-▲ COL 7016 [DDD]

Handel, G.F.:Apollo e Dafne, w. M. George (bass), S. Standage (cnd), Collegium Musicum 90 Chandos ("Early Music" series) ▲ CHAN 0583 [DDD]

Handel, G.F.:Cants, w. M. Chance (ct), G. von der Goltz (cnd), Freiburg Baroque Orch—Il duello amoroso, HWV 82 *(rec Jan 1993)* Deutsche Harmonia Mundi ▲ 05472-77295-2 [DDD]

Handel, G.F.:Crudel tiranno amor, w. S. Standage (cnd), Collegium Musicum 90 Chandos ("Early Music" series) ▲ CHAN 0583 [DDD]

Handel, G.F.:Floridante (sels), w. Nancy Argenta (sop—Rossane), Ingrid Attrot (sop—Timante), Linda Maguire (mez—Elmira), Catherine Robbin (mez—Floridante), Mel Braun (bar—Coralbo/Orontes), A. Curtis (cnd), Tafelmusik [I] CBC ("SM 5000" series) ▲ SMCD 5110 [DDD]

Handel, G.F.:Israel in Egypt, w. Emily Van Evera (sop), Jan Wilson (mez), Anthony Rolfe Johnson (ten), Thomas (sgr), White (sgr), A. Parrott (cnd), Taverner Players, Taverner Choir [E] EMI Classics 2-▲ CDCB 54018 [DDD]

Handel, G.F.:La Rezurrezione, w. Barbara Schlick (sop), Guillemette Laurens (mez), Guy de Mey (ten), Klaus Mertens (bar), T. Koopman (cnd), Amsterdam Baroque Orch [I] Erato 2-▲ 2292-45617-2 [DDD]

Handel, G.F.:Solomon, w. Barbara Hendricks (sop), Carolyn Watkinson (cta), Anthony Rolfe Johnson (ct), J. E. Gardiner (cnd), English Baroque Soloists, Monteverdi Choir London [E] Philips 2-▲ 412612-2 [DDD]

Mozart, W.A.:Così fan tutte, w. S. Isokoski (sop—Fiordiligi), N. Argenta (sop—Despina), M. Groop (mez—Dorabella), M. Schäfer (ten—Ferrando), P. Vollestad (bar—Guglielmo), H. Claessens (b-bar—Don Alfonso)., S. Kuijken (cnd), La Petite Bande, La Petite Bande Chorus Accent 3-▲ ACC 9296/98

Mozart, W.A.:Don Giovanni, w. A. Halgrimson (sop), L. Dawson (sop), J. M. Ainsley (ten), G. Finley (ten), A. Miles (bar), A. Schmidt (bar), G. Yurisch (bar), R. Norrington (cnd), London Classical Players, Schütz Choir London EMI Classics ▲ CDCB 54859

Mozart, W.A.:Requiem, w. C. Robbin (mez), J.M. Ainsley (ten), A. Miles (bass), R. Norrington (cnd), London Classical Players, Schütz Choir London [L] EMI Classics ▲ CDC 54525

Purcell, H.:King Arthur, w. J. Gooding (sop), L. Perillo (sop), J. MacDougall (ten), M. Tucker (ten), G. Finley (bar), B. Bannatyne-Scott (bass), T. Pinnock (cnd), English Concert, *(chorus unknown)* Archiv 2-▲ 435490-2 [DDD]

Purcell, H.:Music for the Theater, w. M. Huggett (cnd), CBC Vancouver SO—sels. from *The Fairy Queen* (2 arias), *King Arthur* (overture & 5 sels.), & *The Married Beau* (overture & 9 sels.) [E] CBC ("SM 5000" series) ▲ SMCD 5091 [DDD] ■ SMC 5091 (D)

Purcell, H.:The Prophetess (sels), w. Michael Chance (ct), G. von der Goltz (cnd), Freiburg Baroque Orch—Ov; Dance; If Music Be the Food (song); Dance of the Bacchanals; Tpt tune; Prelude; Oh How Happy (song); Hornpipe; Dance of the Furies; 1st Music; Lost es My Quiet (duet); Prelude; Let the Soldiers Rejoice (song); Act Tune; Chaconne; 2nd Music; Paspe; Chair Dance *(rec Jan 1993)* Deutsche Harmonia Mundi ▲ 05472-77295-2 [DDD]

Scarlatti, A.:Dixit Dominus, w. I. Attrot (sop), C. Denley (mez), T. Pinnock (cnd), English Concert, English Chorale Archiv ▲ 423386-2 [DDD]

Vivaldi, A.:Gloria, RV.589, w. I. Attrot (sop), C. Denley (mez), T. Pinnock (cnd), English CO, English Concert Choir Archiv ▲ 423386-2 [DDD]

Argyris, Vasso (sgr)

Schoeck, O.:Das Schloss Dürande (sels), w. Maria Cebotari (sop—Gabriele), Marta Fuchs (sop—Gräfin Morvaille), Brigitte Fassbaender (mez—Renald Willi Domgraf), Rut Berglund (cta—Priorin), Peter Anders (ten—Armand), Benno Arnold (ten—Jäger), Josef Greindl (bass—Nicole), Hans Wrana (bass—Jäger), Vasso Argyris (sgr—Volksredner), Otto Hüsch (sgr—Wildhüter), Leo Laschet (sgr—Jäger), Fritz Marcks (sgr—Jäger), Felix Schneider (sgr—Jäger), R. Heger (cnd)—Text; Ich kann es nicht glauben [from Act 1]; Text; Heil dir, du Feuerquelle [from Act 2]; Text; Gesucht und nicht gefunden [from Act 3]; Text; Der Jäger ist frei! [Act 3 Finale]; Text; Sie kommen mit Flinten und Stangen [Act 4]; Text; Du Narr des vermeintlichen Rechts [Act 4 finale]; Text *(rec live, Apr 1943)* Jecklin ▲ JD 692

Arié, Raffaele (bass)

Beethoven, L. van:Sym 9, "Choral Sym", w. Magda Laszlo (sop), Lucienne Devallier (cta), Petre Monteanu (ten), H. Scherchen (cnd), Swiss-Italian RSO, Swiss-Italian Radio-TV Chorus Accord ▲ ACD 201002 [AAD]

Bellini, V.:I Puritani, w. Mirella Freni (sop—Elvira), Rita Bezzi (mez—Enrichetta), Alfredo Kraus (ten—Arturo Talbot), Augusto Pedroni (ten—Sir Bruno Robertson), Attilio d'Orazi (bar—Sir Riccardo Forth), Raffaele Arié (bass—Sir Giorgio), Bruno Cioni (bass—Lord Gualtiero Walton), N. Verchi (cnd), Modena Teatro Comunale Orch, Modeno Teatro Comunale Chorus *(rec Modena Teatro Comunale, Dec. 26, 1962)* Legato Classics 2-▲ LCD 195-2 [ADD]

Donizetti, G.:Lucia di Lammermoor, w. M. Callas (sop), G. di Stefano (ten), T. Gobbi (bar), T. Serafin (cnd), Florence Maggio Musicale Orch [I] EMI Classics (Studio) 2-▲ CDMB 69980 (m) [ADD]

Puccini, G.:La Bohème, w. R. Tebaldi (sop), H. Gueden (sop), G. Prandelli (ten), G. Inghilleri (bar), F. Corena (bass), A. Erede (cnd), St. Cecilia Academy Orch Rome, St. Cecilia Academy Chorus Rome London 2-▲ 440233-2 [ADD]

Rossini, G.:Stabat Mater, w. Beatrice Haldas (sop), Lucia V. Terrani (mez), Antonio Savastano (ten), E. Loehrer (cnd), Swiss-Italian Radio-TV Orch, Swiss-Italian Radio-TV Chorus Accord ▲ ACD 201752 [AAD]

Ariostini, Armando (bar)

Donizetti, G.:L'Esule di Roma, w. C. Gasdia (sop), E. Palacio (ten), S. Alaimo (bass-bar), M. de Bernart (cnd), Piacenza SO, Paris Opéra-Comique Chorus *(rec live, 10/14/86)* Bongiovanni 2-▲ GB 2045/46 [DDD]

Arista, Guiseppina (mez)

Bellini, V.:Norma, w. Margherita Rinaldi (sop—Adalgisa), Renata Scotto (sop—Norma), Giuseppina Arista (mez—Clotilde), Ermanno Mauro (ten—Pollione), Giancarlo Turati (ten—Flavio), Agostino Ferrin (bass—Oroveso), R. Muti (cnd), Florence Teatro Comunale Orch, Florence Teatro Comunale Chorus *(rec Florence, Dec 19, 1978)* Legato Classics 2-▲ LCD 203-2

Mascagni, P.:Zanetto, w. P. Malgarini (mez), T. Petralia (cnd), Milan RAI SO *(rec 1969)* Memories 2-▲ MEM 4519 [AAD]

Arkhipov, Alexander (ten)
Rachmaninoff, S.:The Miserly Knight, w. Mikhail Krutikov (sgr), Vladimir Kudriashov (sgr), Vladislav Verestnikov (sgr), Piotr Gluboky (sgr), A. Tchistiakov (cnd), Bolshoi Theater Orch, Russian State Choir Russian Season 3-▲ CMX 388053
Rimsky-Korsakov, N.:Kaschei the Immortal, w. I. Jourina (sop), N. Terentieva (mez), V. Verestnikov (bar), V. Matorin (bass), A. Tchistiakov (cnd), Bolshoi Theater Orch, Yurloff Russian Choir [Russian] Russian Season ("Russian Season" series) ▲ LDC 288046 [DDD]
Rimsky-Korsakov, N.:A May Night, w. Maria Lapina (sop), Natalia Erassova (mez), Elena Okolycheva (cta), Vitaly Tarastchenko (ten), Piotr Glouboky (bass), Viatcheslav Potchapski (bass), A. Tchistiakov (cnd), Bolshoi Theater Orch, Russian State Choir Russian Season 4-▲ CMX 388054

Arkhipova, Irina (mez)
Mussorgsky, M.:Boris Godunov, w. Irina Arkhipova (mez—Marina Mnishek), Evgenya Verbitskaya (mez—Nurse to Xenia), Valentina Klepatskaya (sgr—Fyodor), Tamara Sorokina (sgr—Xenia), Anton Grigoryev (ten—Simpleton), Vladimir Ivanovsky (ten—Grigory, the Pretender), Gyorgy Shulpin (bar—Prince Shuisky), Alexey Geleva (bass—Varlaam), Ivan Petrov (bass—Boris Godounov), Mark Reshetin (bass—Pimen), Alexi Ivanov (sgr—Andrei Shchelkalov), Evgeny Kibkalo (sgr—Rangoni), A. Melik-Pashayev (cnd), Bolshoi Theater Orch, Bolshoi Theater Chorus *(rec Moscow, 1962)* Melodiya ("The Russian Opera" series) 3-▲ 74321-29349-2 [ADD]
Prokofiev, S.:War & Peace, w. Galina Vishnevskaya (sop—Natasha Rostovoa), Irina Arkhipova (mez—Hélène Bezukhova), Evgenya Verbitskaya (mez—Marya Akhrosimova), Alexi Maslennikov (ten—Anatole Kuragin), Vladimir Petrov (ten—Pierre Bezukhov), Pavel Lisitsian (bar—Napoleon), Alexi Krivchenya (bass—Field-Marshall Kutuzov), Evgeny Kibkalo (sgr—Prince Andrei Bolkonsky), A. Melik-Pashayev (cnd), Bolshoi Theater Orch, Bolshoi Theater Chorus *(rec Moscow, 1961)* Melodiya ("The Russian Opera" series) 3-▲ 74321-29350-2 [ADD]
Tchaikovsky, P.:Eugene Onegin, w. N. Focile (sop), S. Walker (mez), F. Egerton (ten), D. Hvorostovsky (bar)., S. Bychkov (cnd), Orch de Paris Philips 2-▲ 438235-2

Arkin, Adam (sgr)
Gershwin, G.:Oh, Kay!, w. Dawn Upshaw (sop—Kay), Kurt Ollmann (bar—Jimmy Winter), Adam Arkin (sgr—Shory McGee), E. Stern (cnd), *(orch unknown)* Elektra/Nonesuch ▲ 79361-2 ■ 79361-4

Armer, Elinor (nar)
Armer, E.:Music of, w. Ursula Le Guin (nar), Women's Philharmonic, Elizabeth Appling (cnd), JoAnn Falletta (cnd), San Francisco Girls' Chorus, San Francisco Boys' Chorus, San Francisco Chamber Singers—The Great Instrument of the Geggerets; Anithaca; The Seasons of Oling; Eating with the Hoi; Open & Shut; Sailing Among the Pheromones; On the Antioriental Shores; Island Earth Koch International Classics 2-▲ KIC 7331 [DDD]

Armiliato, Fabio (ten)
Giordano, U.:La Cena delle beffe, w. R. Lantieri (sop), M. Chingari (bar), N. Sanzogno (cnd), Piacenza SO [I] *(rec live, 12/14/88)* Bongiovanni 2-▲ GB 2068/69 [DDD]
Mascagni, P.:Amica, w. Katia Ricciarelli (sop), Monica Minarelli (sgr), Elia Padovan (sgr), Walter Donati (sgr), M. Pace (cnd), Hungarian Radio-TV SO, Hungarian Radio-TV Chorus *(rec Budapest, Nov 1995)* Kicco Classic 2-▲ KC 00296 [DDD]

Armstrong, Karen (sop)
Zemlinsky, A. von:Lyric Sym, w. I. Kusnjer (bar), B. Gregor (cnd), Czech PO Supraphon ▲ 11 0395-2 [DDD]

Armstrong, Nancy (sop)
Mozart, W.A.:Missa, K.427, w. Dominique Labelle (sop), Jeffery Thomas (ten), Richard Morrison (bass), A. Parrott (cnd), Boston Early Music Festival Orch, Handel & Haydn Society Chorus [L] Denon ▲ CO 79573 [DDD]
Tippett, M.:A Child Of Our Time, w. F. Palmer (sop), P. Langridge (ten), J. Shirley-Quirk (bar), A. Previn (cnd), Royal PO, Brighton Festival Chorus [E] RPO ▲ RPO 7012 [DDD]
Vaughan Williams, R.:Sym 1, w. J. C. Case (bar), A. Boult (cnd), London PO, London Phil Chorus EMI Classics ▲ CDM 64016
Vaughan Williams, R.:Sym 7, w. B. Haitink (cnd), London PO EMI Classics ▲ CDC 47516 [DDD]
Wagner, R.:Lohengrin, w. E. Connell (sop), P. Hofmann (ten), L. Roar (bass), B. Weikl (bass), S. Vogel (bass), W. Nelsson (cnd), Bayreuth Festival Orch, Bayreuth Festival Chorus CBS 3-▲ M3K 38594
York, W.:Native Songs, w. S. Sylvan (bar), S. Downey (sgr), R. Woodhouse (sgr), P. Friedland (fl), J. Fischer (pno), J. Russell Smith (perc) *(rec May 1987)* New World ▲ 80439-2

Armstrong, Sheila (sop)
Bach, J.S.:Cant 213, w. Hertha Töpper (alt), Theo Altmeyer (ten), Jakob Stämpfli (bass), H. Rilling (cnd), Stuttgart Bach Collegium *(rec 1967)* Musicaphon ▲ 51356 [AAD]
Britten, H.:Spring Sym, w. J. Baker (mez), R. Tear (ten), A. Previn (cnd), London SO, London Sym Chorus EMI Classics ▲ CDM 64736
Elgar, E.:The Apostles, w. H. Watts (cta), R. Tear (ten), J. C. Case (bar), B. Luxon (bar), C. Grant (bass), A. Boult (cnd), London PO, London Phil Chorus, Downe House School Choir [E] EMI Classics ▲ CDMB 64206
Fauré, G.:Pavane Orch, w. D. Fischer-Dieskau (bar), Orch de Paris, Edinburgh Festival Chorus EMI Classics ▲ CDM 64634
Fauré, G.:Requiem, w. D. Fischer Dieskau (bar), Orch de Paris, Edinburgh Festival Chorus EMI Classics ▲ CDM 64634
Handel, G.F.:Messiah (sels), w. Norma Proctor (cta), Kenneth Bowen (ten), John Cameron (bar), L. Stokowski (cnd), London SO, London Sym Chorus [E] London ("Weekend Classics" series) ▲ 433874-2 [ADD] ■ 433874-4
Mahler, G.:Sym 2, w. J. Baker (mez), L. Bernstein (cnd), London SO, Edinburgh Festival Chorus *(rec 1974)* Sony Classical ("Bernstein:The Royal Edition" series) 2-▲ SM2K 47573 [ADD]
Orff, C.:Carmina burana, w. P. Hall (ten), B. Rayner Cook (bar), M. Handford (cnd), Hallé Orch, Hallé State Chorus Classics for Pleasure ▲ CDCFP 9005 [ADD]
Orff, C.:Carmina burana, w. G. English (ten), T. Allen (bar), A. Previn (cnd), London SO, London Sym Chorus, St. Clement Danes Boys' Chorus [G, L] EMI Classics ▲ CDC 47411 ■ 4AM 34770
Sullivan, A.:Music of, w. V. Masterson (sop), R. Tear (ten), B. Luxon (bar), Alwyn, Hickox (cnd), Bournemouth Sinfonietta, Northern Sinfonietta of England—sels. from all operettas of Gilbert & Sullivan EMI Classics ▲ CDM 64393

Arnaud, Etienne (bar)
Offenbach, J.:Le Fille du tambour-major, w. Christiane Harbell (sop—Stella), Monique de Pondeau (sop—Claudine), Germaine Light (mez—Duchess Della Volta), Marcelle Ranson-Hervé (ten—Duke Della Volta), André Mallabrera (ten—Griolet), Etienne Arnaud (bar—Robert), Louis Musy (bar—Monthabor), *(orch unknown)* Accord ▲ ACD 220692 [AAD]

Arnesen, Bodil (sop)
Alnaes, E.:Songs, w. E. R. Eriksen (pno)—The Skogsråo, Op. 38/4; Out There in the World, Op. 12/4; A Little Tune about Spring, Op. 38/2; Narcissus, Op. 28/2; The Last Voyage, Op. 17/2; February Morning by the Gulf, Op. 28/5; Longings of Spring, Op. 17/3; I Was Lying by the Sea, Op. 2/3; Northern Lights, Op. 14/3; Sun, Op. 15/1; In the Season of Lilacs, Op. 30/2; Early Summer Morning, Op. 30/3; Promenade, Op. 31/1; Rocking Song, Op. 1/4; Gone!, Op. 1/1; The Mind Young and Full of Sweetness, Op. 14/2; Old Spinster, Op. 22/3; A Summer Melody, Op. 35/4; The Hundred Violins, Op. 42/2; See, the Sun Is Setting, Op. 42/1; Happiness between Two People, Op. 26/1; Where You Lead the Way, Op. 17/1; Poet, Op. 31/3; Little Kirsten, Op. 2/4; Living , Op. 42/3; The Dress, Op. 29/3; Rain, Op. 45/3; Anne Knutsdotter, Norwegian Traditional Melody [N] Simax ▲ PSC 1110
Beethoven, L. van:Cant on the Death of the Emperor Joseph II, w. Markus Schäfer (ten), Alan Titus (bar), K.A. Rickenbacher (cnd), Berlin RSO, Berlin Radio Chorus Koch Schwann ▲ SCH 314352 [DDD]
Beethoven, L. van:Di Flamme lodert, Op. 121, w. K.A. Rickenbacher (cnd), Berlin RSO, Berlin Radio Chorus Koch Schwann ▲ SCH 314852
Beethoven, L. van:Di Flamme lodert, Op. 121b, w. K.A. Rickenbacher (cnd), Berlin RSO, Berlin Radio Chorus Koch Schwann ▲ SCH 314852
Beethoven, L. van:In allen guten Stunden, w. K.A. Rickenbacher (cnd), Berlin RSO, Berlin Radio Chorus Koch Schwann ▲ SCH 314852

Arno, Franciszek (ten)
Moniuszko, S.:Halka (sels), w. Maria Foltyn (sop), Rezler, Latoszewski (cnd), Polish National RSO Katowice, Warsaw Opera Orch—Gdyby rannym slonkiem; O mój malenki Polskie Nagrania ▲ PNCD 275
Puccini, G.:Arias, w. Maria Foltyn (sop), Latoszewski, Rezler (cnd), Polish National RSO Katowice, Warsaw Opera Orch—Mi chiamano Mimi [from Cyganeria]; Ah! que gli ochi; Vissi d'arte [both from Tosca] Polskie Nagrania ▲ PNCD 275
Verdi, G.:Arias, w. Maria Foltyn (sop), Rezler, Latoszewski (cnd), Polish National RSO Katowice, Warsaw Opera Orch—O Patria mia [from Aida]; Ma dall'arido stelo [from Bal Maskowy]; Pace, pace, mio Dio [from Moc Przeznaczenia] Polskie Nagrania ▲ PNCD 275
Wagner, R.:Lohengrin (sels), w. Maria Foltyn (sop), Rezler, Latoszewski (cnd), Polish National RSO Katowice, Warsaw Opera Orch—Einsam in truben Tagen Polskie Nagrania ▲ PNCD 275

Arnold, Benno (ten)
Schoeck, O.:Das Schloss Dürande (sels), w. Maria Cebotari (sop—Gabriele), Marta Fuchs (sop—Gräfin Morvaille), Brigitte Fassbaender (mez—Renald Willi Domgraf), Rut Berglund (cta—Priorin), Peter Anders (ten—Armand), Benno Arnold (ten—Jäger), Josef Greindl (bass—Nicole), Hans Wrana (bass—Jäger), Vasso Argyris (sgr—Volksredner), Otto Hüsch (sgr—Wildhüter), Leo Laschet (sgr—Jäger), Fritz Marcks (sgr—Jäger), Felix Schneider (sgr—Jäger), R. Heger (cnd)—Text; Ich kann es nicht glauben [from Act 1]; Text; Heil dir, du Feuerquelle [from Act 2]; Text; Gesucht und nicht gefunden [from Act 3]; Text; Der Jäger ist frei! [Act 3 Finale]; Text; Sie kommen mit Flinten und Stangen [Act 4]; Text; Du Narr des vermeintlichen Rechts [Act 4 finale]; Text *(rec live, Apr 1943)* Jecklin ▲ JD 692

Arnold, David (bar)
Mozart, W.A.:Requiem, w. Ruth Ziesak (sop), Nancy Maultsby (mez), Richard Croft (ten), M. Pearlman (cnd), Boston Baroque Orch [completion by Robert Levin; performed on period instruments] *(rec Campion Center, Weston, MA, Nov 2-3, 1994)* Telarc ▲ CD 80410 [DDD]
Schoenberg, A.:Gurrelieder, w. J. Norman (sop), T. Troyanos (mez), J. McCracken (ten), S. Ozawa (cnd), Boston SO, Tanglewood Festival Chorus Philips 2-▲ 412511-2

Arnold, Elizabeth (sop)
Britten, H.:Te Deum, w. Alfred Calabrese (cnd), Britten Singers ACA Digital Recording ▲ CM 20039

Arnold, John (sgr)
For Citizens & Peasants:Popular Tunes from Old Norwegian Music Books, w. N. Almquist (sgr), J. Arnold, T. Chancey, E. Bulkely Folger Consort ▲ BDCD1 9003 [DDD]

Arnold, Jonathan (bass)
Purcell, H.:Dido & Aeneas, w. Véronique Gens (sop—Dido), Sophie Marin-Degor (sop—Belinda), Sophie Daneman (sop—2nd woman/1st witch), Gaëlle Mechaly (sop—2nd witch), Claire Brua (mez—Sorceress), Steve Dugardin (alt—Chorus), Jean-Paul Fouchécourt (ten—Spirit/Sailor), Nathan Berg (b-bar—Aeneas), Jonathan Arnold (bass—Chorus), William Christie (hpd), W. Christie (cnd), Les Arts Florissants *(rec Massy Opera Theatre, Nov. 8-11, 1994)* Erato ▲ 98477-2 [DDD]

Arnot, David (ten)
Caldara, A.:Vaticini di pace, w. Mary Enid Hains (sop), Linda Dayiantis-Straub (sop), Jennifer Lane (mez), K. Mallon (cnd), Aradia Baroque Ensemble *(rec Toronto, Canada, Jan 1996)* Naxos ▲ 8.553772 [DDD]

Arnoult, Louis (ten)
Ravel, M.:L'Heure espagnole, w. Jeanne Krieger (sop—Concepcion), Louis Arnoult (ten—Gonzalve), Raoul Gilles (ten—Torquemada), J. Aubert (bar—Ramiro), Hector Dufranne (bass—Don Inigo Gomez), G. Truc (cnd), *(orch unknown) (rec premiere recording, supervised by Ravel, 1929)* VAI Audio ▲ VAIA 1073

Arroyo, Martina (sop)
Barber, S.:Andromache's Farewell, w. T. Schippers (cnd), New York PO [E] *(rec 1963)* Sony Masterworks ("Portrait" series) ▲ MPK 46727 [ADD]
Barber, S.:Andromache's Farewell, w. T. Schippers (cnd), New York PO Sony Classical ("Masterworks Heritage" series) ▲ MHK 62837
Beethoven, L. van:Missa Solemnis, w. M. Forrester (cta), R. Lewis (ten), C. Siepi (b-bar), E. Ormandy (cnd), Philadelphia Orch, Singing City Choir *(rec Mar. 29-30, 1967)* Sony Classical ("Essential Classics" series) ▲ SBK 53517 [ADD] ■ SBT 53517
Beethoven, L. van:Sym 9, "Choral Sym", w. R. Sarfaty (mez), N. di Virgilio (ten), N. Scott (bass), L. Bernstein (cnd), New York PO, Juilliard Chorus *(rec New York, May 18, 1964)* Sony Classical ("Bernstein:The Royal Edition" series) △ SM 47513 [ADD]
Handel, G.F.:Judas Maccabaeus, w. Grace Bumbry (mez), J. McCollum (ten), Marvin Sorensen (ten), D. Watts (bass), M. Abravanel (cnd), Utah SO, Utah Sym Chorus [E] *(rec ca. 1959; originally rele)* MCA Classics 3-▲ MCAD3-10515 [ADD]
Handel, G.F.:Judas Maccabaeus, w. Mary Davenport (mez), Lawrence Avery (ten), Jan Peerce (ten), David Smith (bar), T. Scherman (cnd), Vienna State Opera Orch, Vienna Academy Chorus Vox Box 2-▲ CDX 5125 [ADD]
Meyerbeer, G.:Les Huguenots, w. J. Sutherland (sop), H. Tourangeau (mez), A. Vrenios (ten), D. Cossa (bar), G. Bacquier (bar), N. Ghiuselev (bass), R. Bonynge (cnd), New Philharmonia Orch, Ambrosian Opera Chorus London ("Grand Opera" series) 4-▲ 430549-2 [AAD]
Mozart, W.A.:Complete Mozart Edition, w. K. Te Kanawa (sop), M. Freni (sop), S. Burrows (ten), I. Wixell (bar), C. Davis (cnd), Royal Opera House Orch, Royal Opera House Chorus Covent Garden Philips 3-▲ 422541-2 [ADD]
Mozart, W.A.:Don Giovanni (sels), w. R. Grist (sop), B. Nilsson (sop), P. Schreier (ten), D. Fischer-Dieskau (bar), M. Talvela (bass), K. Böhm (cnd), Prague National Theater Orch IMP Collectors Series ▲ IMPX 9023 [AAD]
Rossini, G.:Stabat Mater, w. B. Wolff (mez), T. del Bianco (ten), J. Diaz (bass), T. Schippers (cnd), New York PO, Camerata Singers Sony Classical ▲ SB2K 53252
Spirituals, w. Henri Venanzi (pno) Centaur ▲ CRC 2060 [DDD]
Verdi, G.:Un ballo in maschera, w. R. Grist (sop), F. Cossotto (mez), P. Domingo (ten), P. Cappuccilli (bar), R. Muti (cnd), New Philharmonia Orch, Royal Opera House Chorus Covent Garden [I] EMI Classics (Studio) 2-▲ CDMB 69576 [ADD]
Verdi, G.:Un ballo in maschera (sels), w. L. Pavarotti (ten), C. Mackerras (cnd), San Francisco Opera Orch—Ma dall'arido stelo...Teco io sto *(rec Nov. 5, 1971)* Golden Age of Opera 2-▲ GAO 164/65 [ADD]
Verdi, G.:La forza del destino, w. Martina Arroyo (sop—Donna Leonora), Janet Coster (mez—Preziosilla), Kenneth Bowen (ten—Trabuco), Kenneth Collins (ten—Don Alvaro), Peter Glossop (bar—Don Carlo), Roderick Kennedy (bass—Marquis), J. Matheson (cnd), BBC Concert Orch, BBC Concert Chorus *(rec live, early 1980's)* Exclusive 2-▲ EXL 80 [ADD]

Arruabarrena, Maite (sop)
Nebra, J.:Viento, w. Marta Almajano (sop), Raquel Pierotti (sop), Pilar Jurado (sgr), Maria del Mar Doval (sgr), C. Coin (cnd), Limoges Baroque Ensemble Valois ▲ V 4752

Artegna, Francesco Ellero d' (bass)
Bellini, V.:I Puritani, w. Edita Gruberova (sop), Katia Lytting (mez), Justin Lavender (ten), Carlo Tuand (ten), Ettore Kim (bar), Dankwart Siegele (bass), F. Luisi (cnd), Munich RSO, Bavarian Radio Chorus Nightingale Classics 3-▲ NIG 70562
Catalani, A.:La Wally, w. E. Marton (sop), F. Araiza (ten), A. Titus (bar), P. Steinberg (cnd), Munich RSO, Bavarian Radio Chorus [I] Eurodisc 2-▲ 69073-2-RC [DDD] ■ 69073-4-RC (CrO2)
Monteverdi, C.:Incoronazione, w. Constanze Backes (sop—Valletto), Catherine Bott (sop—Drusilla/Pallade/La Virtù), Dana Hanchard (sop—Nerone), Sylvia McNair (sop—Poppea), Marinella Pennicchi (sop—Amore/Damigella), Annie Sofie von Otter (mez—Ottavia/Venere/La Fortuna), Julian Clarkson (alt—Littore/Mercurio), Bernarda Fink (cta—Arnalta), Roberto Balconi (ct—Nutrice), Michael Chance (ct—Ottone), Nigel Robson (ten—Liberto/Soldato Secondo), Mark Tucker (ten—Lucano/Soldato Primo), Francesco Ellero d'Artegna (bass—Seneca), J. E. Gardiner (cnd), English Baroque Soloists *(rec Queen Elizabeth Hall, South Bank Ctr, London, Dec 1993)* Archiv 3-▲ 447088-2

Artegna, Francesco Ellero d' (bass) (cont.)
Verdi, G.:Il trovatore, w. Antonella Banaudi (sop—Leonora), Barbara Frittoli (sop—Ines), Shirley Verrett (mez—Azucena), Enrico Facini (ten—Un messo), Piero de Palma (ten—Ruiz), Luciano Pavarotti (ten—Marico), Leo Nucci (bar—Il Conte di Luna), Roberto Scaltriti (bar—Un vecchio zingaro), Francesco Ellero d'Artegna (bass—Ferrando), Z. Mehta (cnd), Florence Maggio Musicale Orch, Florence Maggio Musicale Chorus *(rec Maggio Musicale Fiorentino Community Theater, June 18–July 2, 1990)* London 2-▲ 430694-2

Arthur, B. (sgr)
Weill, K.:The Threepenny Opera, w. L. Lenya (sop), C. Rae (sgr), *(orch unknown)* [E] Polydor ▲ 820260-2 ■ 820260-4E

Arthur, Maurice (ten)
Donizetti, G.:Ugo, conte di Parigi, w. E. Harrhy (sop), Y. Kenny (sop), J. Price (sop), D. Jones (mez), C. du Plessis (bar), A. Francis (cnd), New Philharmonia Orch, Geoffrey Mitchell Choir Opera Rara 3-▲ ORC 1

Artioli, Walter (ten)
Verdi, G.:Il trovatore, w. Leyla Gencer (sop—Leonora), Laura Londi (sop—Ines), Fedora Barbieri (mez—Azucena), Mario del Monaco (ten—Manrico), Athos cesarini (ten—Ruiz), Walter Artioli (ten—Messanger) Ettore Bastianini (bar—Count Luna), Plinio Clabassi (bass—Ferrando), Sergio Liliani (bass—Gypsy), F. Previtali (cnd), Milan RAI SO, Milan RAI Chorus *(rec live, Milan, May 29, 1957)* Arkadia 2-▲ 483 [ADD]

Artmann, H. C. (spkr)
Cerha, F.:Eine Art Chanson, w. HK Gruber (reader), J. Holland (reader), M. Jones (reader), R. McGee (reader), G. Rühm (reader) *(rec live Apr. 30, 1993)* Largo ▲ 5126 [DDD]

Artysz, Jerzy (bar)
Baird, T.:Tomorrow, w. K. Szostek-Radkowa (mez), E. Pawlak (bass), J. Ostrowski (nar), R. Czajkowski (cnd), Poznan Philharmonic SO [Pol] Olympia ▲ OCD 326 [AAD]

Aruhn, Britt Marie (sop)
Strauss, R.:4 Last Songs, w. Viktor Åslund (pno), S. Köhler (cnd), Royal Stockholm Orch Bluebell ▲ BLU 062 [DDD]
Strauss, R.:Songs, w. Viktor Åslund (pno), S. Köhler (cnd), Royal Stockholm Orch—Begegnung, AV.72; Die Nacht, Op. 10; Allerseelen, Op. 10; Wie sollten wir geheim sie halten, Op. 19; Du meines herzens Krönelein, Op. 21; Cäcilie, Op. 27; Morgen, Op. 27; Befreit, Op. 39; Wiegenlied, Op. 41; Freundliche Vision, Op. 48; Sie wissen's nicht, Op. 49; Frühlingsfeier, Op. 56; Ich wolt' ein Sträusslein binden, Op. 68; Säusle, liebe Myrthe, Op. 68; Malven, AV.304 Bluebell ▲ BLU 062 [DDD]

Arvidson, Lars (bass)
Kraus, J.M.:Prosperin, w. Hillevi Martinpelto (sop), Susanne Rydén (sop), Anna Eklund-Tarantino (sgr), Peter Mattei (bar), Stephen Smith (sgr), M. Tatlow (cnd), Stockholm CO, Stockholm Chamber Choir Musica Sveciae 2-▲ MSCD 422/23 [DDD]
The Royal Court of the Vasa Kings, 1523-1611, w. M. Bellini (ct), Lennart Löwgren (ct), Carl Unander-Scharin (ten), Sven-Anders Benktsson (bass), Sven Aberg (six-course Renaissance lt), Hortus Musicus, Tallinn [cnd:Andres Mustonen] Musica Sveciae ▲ MSV 202 [DDD]

Asawa, Brian (ct)
Britten, H.:A Midsummer Night's Dream, w. Sylvia McNair (sop—Tytania), Brian Asawa (ct—Oberon), Robert Lloyd (bass), C. Davis (cnd), London SO Philips 2-▲ 454 122-2
Handel, G.F.:Judas Maccabaeus, w. Linda Saffer (sop), Patricia Spence (mez), Guy de Mey (ten), Leroy Kromm (b-bar), David Thomas (bass), N. McGegan (cnd), Philharmonia Baroque Orch, Univ of California at Berkeley Chamber Chorus [E] *(rec Nov. 15–18, 1992)* Harmonia Mundi USA 2-▲ HMU 907077/78

Ascher, Christina (mez)
Alcalay, L.:fluchtpunktzeile, w. M. Hemm (b-bar), C. Kalmar (cnd), Vienna SO Vienna Modern Masters ▲ VMM 3020 [AAD]
Asmus, B.:Lieder (3), w. Volker Höh (gtr) *(rec Altensteig, July 18-20, 1996)* Signum ▲ X 74-00 [DDD]
Brandmüller, T.:Despedida, w. Volker Höh (gtr), Christina Ascher (perc) *(rec Altensteig, July 18-20, 1996)* Signum ▲ X 74-00 [DDD]
Heyn, V.:I(–na), w. Volker Höh (gtr), Christina Ascher (perc) *(rec Altensteig, July 18-20, 1996)* Signum ▲ X 74-00 [DDD]
Jung, H.:Lieder, w. Volker Höh (gtr) *(rec Altensteig, July 18-20, 1996)* Signum ▲ X 74-00 [DDD]
Liberda, B.:Berenice, w. Volker Höh (gtr) *(rec Altensteig, July 18-20, 1996)* Signum ▲ X 74-00 [DDD]
Rosenfeld, G.:Quasi un madrigale, w. Volker Höh (gtr) *(rec Altensteig, July 18-20, 1996)* Signum ▲ X 74-00 [DDD]
Spassov, B.:Calliope, w. Volker Höh (gtr), Christina Ascher (perc) *(rec Altensteig, July 18-20, 1996)* Signum ▲ X 74-00 [DDD]

Asciak, Paul (sgr)
Bellini, V.:Norma, w. Maria Callas (sop), Joan Sutherland (sop), Ebe Stignani (cta), Mirto Picchi (ten), V. Gui (cnd), Royal Opera House Orch, Royal Opera House Chorus Covent Garden *(rec live, London, 1952)* Enterprise ("Documents" series) 3-▲ ENTLV 968 [ADD]

Ascorro, Virgilio (bar)
Puccini, G.:La fanciulla del West (sels), w. Magda Olivero (sop—Minnie), Corinna Vozza (mez—Wowkle), Paolo Caroli (ten—Harry), Giacomo Lauri-Volpi (ten—Dick Johnson), Marco Rogani (ten—Pony Express Rider), Salvatore di Tommaso (ten—Trin), Adelio Zagonara (ten—Nick), Virgilio Ascorro (bar—Sid), Alfredo Colella (bar—Jake Wallace), Giuseppe Forgione (bar—Bello), Giancarlo Guelfi (bar—Jack Rance), Arturo la Porta (bar—Sonora), Gino Conti (bass—José Castro), Piere Passarotti (bass—Bill), Enzo Titta (bass—Larkens), Giulio Tomei (bass—Ashby), V. Bellezza (cnd), Rome Opera Orch, Rome Opera Chorus—Minnie, dalla mia casa son partito; Laggiù nel Soledad; Chi c'è per farmi i ricci; Oh! Mister Johnson, siete rimasto; Non so ben neppur io; Io non son che una povera fanciulla; No, Minnie, non piangete; Vorrei mettermi queste; Credo che abbiate torto; Ma ti giuro ch'io non ti lascio più; Vieni fuori!; Una parola sola!...Or son sei mesi; Che c'è di nuovo Jack?; È là; Siete pronto; Ch'ella mi creda; È Minnie!...È Minnie! *(rec Rome, Mar. 30, 1957)* Golden Age of Opera ▲ GAO 180 [ADD]

Ashe, Susan (sop)
Britten, H.:Rejoice in the Lamb, w. Cynthia Calabrese (alt), Victor Floyd (ten), Charles Sprawls (bass), Alfred Calabrese (cnd), Britten Singers ACA Digital Recording ▲ CM 20039

Ashley, Mary (sgr)
Ashley, R.:Purposeful Lady Slow Afternoon, w. Cynthia Liddell (nar), Barbara Lloyd (sgr), Mary Lucier (sgr) Lovely Music ▲ LCD 1002 [AAD]

Ashley, Robert (voc)
Ashley, R.:Private Parts (The Record), w. "Blue" Gene Tyranny (pno/polymoog/other instrs) Lovely Music ▲ LCD 1001 [ADD]
Radigue, E.:Mila's Journey Inspired By A Dream, w. Lama Kunga Rinpoche (sgr), Eliane Radigue (syn) Lovely Music ▲ LCD 2002 [AAD]

Ashley, Robert (voc/elec/syn)
Ashley, R.:Automatic Writing, w. Mimi Johnson (nar) Lovely Music ▲ LCD 1002 [AAD]

Ashley, Russell (bar)
Splendor of the High Holydays, w. Lowe, Stacey (sop), Lisa Rautenberg (vn), Mary Jane Newman (org/cnd) *(rec SUNY, Purchase, 1995)* Vox Classics ▲ VOX 7510 [DDD]

Ashley, Sam (sgr)
Ashley, R.:eL/Aficionado, w. J. Humbert (sgr—Interrogator No. 2), T. Buckner (sgr—Agent), R. Ashley (sgr—Interrogator No. 1), S. Ashley (sgr—Interrogator No. 3), *(orch unknown)* Lovely Music ▲ LCD 1004 [DDD]
Ashley, R.:Improvement, w. J. Humbert (sgr—Linda), J. La Barbara (sop—Now Eleanor), A. X. Neuburg (sgr—Mr. Payne's Mother), T. Buckner (sgr—Don/Mr. Payne/Linda's Companion), S. Ashley (sgr—Junior, Jr.), A. Klein (sgr—Doctor), R. Ashley (sgr—Narrator), *(cnd & orch unknown)* [E] Elektra/Nonesuch 2-▲ 79289-2

Ashton, Caroline (sop)
Fauré, G.:Requiem, w. S. Varcoe (bar), J. Rutter (cnd), City of London Sinfonia members, Cambridge Singers [1893 ver.] [L] Collegium ▲ COLCD 109 [DDD] ■ COLC 109 (D)

Ashton, Caroline (sop) (cont.)
Rutter, J.:Requiem, w. D. Deam (sop), J. Rutter (cnd), City of London Sinfonia, Cambridge Singers [E,L] Collegium ▲ COLCD 103 [DDD] ■ COLC 103 (D)

Asker, B. (bar)
Wagner, R.:Songs, w. L. Koppel (sop), J. E. Frederiksen (pno), Hymnia Chamber Choir—Seven Faust-Lieder (1832); Der Tannenbaum; Geburtsangrüss an Cosima; Kraft-lied; Adieux de Marie Stuart; Dors mon enfant; Attente; Mignonne; Tout n'est qu'images fugitives; Les deux grenadiers *(rec 1988)* Classico ▲ CLASSCD 102

Assandri, Virginio (ten)
Verdi, G.:Falstaff, w. Vivian Della Chiesa (sop—Alice), Audrey Schuh (sop—Nannetta), Lizabeth Pritchett (mez—Quickly), Evelyn Sachs (mez—Meg), André Turp (ten—Fenton), Virginio Assandri (ten—Caius), Luigi Vellucci (ten—Bardolfo), Leonard Warren (bar—Falstaff), Richard Torigi (bar—Ford), R. Cellini (cnd), New Orleans Opera Orch, New Orleans Opera Chorus *(rec live, May 5, 1956)* VAI Audio 2-▲ VAIA 1056-2

Astaire, Adele (sgr)
Gershwin, G.:Music of, w. F. Astaire (sgr), G. Gershwin (pno)—Hang on to me; Fascinatin' rhythm; The half of it dearie blues; I'd rather Charleston; solo piano rec'gs by Gershwin—Sweet & low down; That certain feeling; Looking for a boy; Then do we dance?; Do-do-do; Someone to watch over me; Clap yo' hands; Maybe; My one & only; Andante from Rhapsody in Ble; S' wonderful/Funny face *(rec 1926 & 1928 Columbia rec')* Pearl 2-▲ PEAS 9483 (m) [AAD]

Astaire, Fred (sgr)
Berlin, I.:Blue Skies, w. B. Crosby (sgr), *(other artists unknown)*—sels from the 1946 soundtrack Sandy Hook ▲ CDSH 2095 ■ CSH 2095
Berlin, I.:Blue Skies, w. B. Crosby (sgr), *(other artists unknown)* *(rec Hollywood, CA, 1946)* VJC ▲ VJC 1012-2
Berlin, I.:Holiday Inn, w. B. Crosby (sgr) *(rec Hollywood, CA, 1942)* VJC ▲ VJC 1012-2
Gershwin, G.:Music of, w. A. Astaire (sgr), G. Gershwin (pno)—Hang on to me; Fascinatin' rhythm; The half of it dearie blues; I'd rather Charleston; solo piano rec'gs by Gershwin—Sweet & low down; That certain feeling; Looking for a boy; Then do we dance?; Do-do-do; Someone to watch over me; Clap yo' hands; Maybe; My one & only; Andante from Rhapsody in Ble; S' wonderful/Funny face *(rec 1926 & 1928 Columbia rec')* Pearl 2-▲ PEAS 9483 (m) [AAD]
Kern, J.:You Were Never Lovelier, w. N. Wynn (sgr) *(rec 1942)* Curtain Calls ▲ CC 100/24
Kern, J.:You Were Never Lovelier, w. N. Wynn (sgr), L. Romay (sgr) *(rec 1942)* Hollywood Soundstage ▲ HSCD 4005

Astrup, Margaret (sop)
Still, W.G.:Music of, w. R.A. Clark (cnd), Manhattan CO—American Scene:The Southwest; From the Hearts of Women; Mother & Child; American Scene:The Far West; Citadel; Phantom Chapel; Golden Days; Serenade; American Scene:The East Newport Classics ▲ NPD 85596 [DDD]

Atanassov, Theodora (sop)
Britten, H.:Missa brevis, w. M. Alexandrova (sop), A. Atanassov (org), A. Blagoeva (cnd), Sofia Boys' Choir [arr. A. Blagoeva for sopranos, organ & boy's chorus] Gega ▲ GD 153 [DDD]

Atkinson (sgr)
Bernstein, L.:Trouble in Tahiti, w. Wolff (sgr), A. Winograd (cnd), MGM Studio SO [E] Polydor ▲ 827845-2 (m) ■ 827845-4 (m)

Atkinson, Lynton (ten)
Lehár, F.:Das Land des Lächelns, w. Nancy Gustafson (sop—Lisa), Naomi Itami (sop—Mi), Lynton Atkinson (ten—Gustl), Jerry Hadley (ten—Prince Sou Chong), R. Bonynge (cnd), English CO *(rec EMI Abbey Road, Studio One, London, England; Aug 2-25, 1995)* Telarc ▲ CD-80419 [DDD]
Lehár, F.:Der Zarewitsch, w. Nancy Gustafson (sop—Sonia), Naomi Itami (sop—Mascha), Lynton Atkinson (ten—Ivan), Jerry Hadley (ten—the Czarevitch), Jeffrey Carl (bar—Grand Duke/Soldier), R. Bonynge (cnd), English CO *(rec EMI Abbey Road, Studio One, London, England; Aug 25-27, 1995)* Telarc ▲ CD-80395 [DDD]

Atkinson, Lynton (trb)
Handel, G.F.:Alessandro, w. Watson (sop), A. Terzian (mez), B. J. Rieders (cta), T. Poole (ten), D. Price (ten), Andersson (sgr), M. Nowakowski (cnd), Sinfonia Varsovia [I] *(rec live)* Koch Schwann 3-▲ CD SC 100 303 [DDD]
Handel, G.F.:Serse, w. D. Cole (sop), A. Terzian (mez), A. Andersson (ten), T. Allen (bar), Schumann-Halley (sgr), J. Teal (sgr), A. Duczmal (cnd), Amadeus CO [I] *(rec live recording produced by "Studios Classique Berlin")* Koch Schwann 3-▲ CD SC 100 300 [DDD]
Vivaldi, A.:Sacred Choral Music, w. Susan Gritton (sop), Catherine Denley (mez), David Wilson-Johnson (bar), Lisa Milne (sgr), R. King (cnd), King's Consort—Magnificat; Lauda, Jerusalem; Kyrie eleison; Credo in unum Deum; Dixit Dominus Hyperion ▲ CDA 66769

Atlan, Franoise (mez)
Musica Humana, w. John Fleagle (ten/hp), Crawford Young (lt), Anonymous 4, Ensemble Discantus, Ensemble Gilles Binchois, Ensemble Organum, Gothic Voices, Greece Byzantine Choir, Hilliard Ensemble, Musica Nova, et al. L'Empreinte Digitale ▲ ED 13047
Ohana, M.:Cantigas, w. M. Quercia (sop), R. Conil (pno), R. Hayrabedian (cnd), Strasbourg Percussion Ensemble, Choeur Contemporain [Sp] Pierre Verany ▲ PV 787032 [DDD]

Atlantov, Vladimir (ten)
Borodin, A.:Prince Igor, w. Elana Obraztsova (mez—Konchakovna), Tatiana Tugarinova (mez—Yaroslavna), Vladimir Atlantov (ten—Vladimir Igoryevich), Artur Eisen (bass—Vladimir Galitsky), Ivan Petrov (bass—Igor Svyatoslavich), Alexander Vedernikov (bass—Konchak), M. Ermler (cnd), Bolshoi Theater Orch, Bolshoi Theater Chorus *(rec Moscow, 1969)* Melodiya ("The Russian Opera" series) 3-▲ 74321-29346-2 [ADD]
Mussorgsky, M.:Khovanshchina, w. M. Lipovsek (mez), P. Burchuladze (bass), A. Haugland (bass), C. Abbado (cnd), Vienna State Opera Orch, Slovak Phil Chorus [Shostakovich version] [R] Deutsche Grammophon 3-▲ 429758-2 [DDD]
Tchaikovsky, P.:Queen of Spades, w. M. Freni (sop), M. Forrester (cta), D. Hvorostovsky (bar), S. Ozawa (cnd), Boston SO, Tanglewood Festival Chorus RCA Red Seal 3-▲ 09026-60992-2 [DDD]
Tchaikovsky, P.:Queen of Spades, w. T. Milachkina (sop), V. Levko (mez), M. Ermler (cnd), Bolshoi Theater Orch, Bolshoi Theater Chorus [R] Philips 3-▲ 420375-2 [ADD]
Tchaikovsky, P.:Queen of Spades, w. M. Freni (sop), M. Forrester (cta), D. Hvorostovsky (bar), S. Ozawa (cnd), Boston SO, Tanglewood Festival Chorus RCA Red Seal ▲ 09026-61227-2 [DDD] ▯ 09026-61227-5

Attrot, Ingrid (sop)
Handel, G.F.:Floridante (sels), w. Nancy Argenta (sop—Rossane), Ingrid Attrot (sop—Timante), Linda Maguire (mez—Elmira), Catherine Robbin (mez—Floridante), Mel Braun (bar—Coralbo/Orontes), A. Curtis (cnd), Tafelmusik [I] CBC ("SM 5000" series) ▲ SMCD 5110 [DDD]
Respighi, O.:Deità silvana, w. R. Hickox (cnd), BBC PO [arr for voc & orch] Chandos ▲ CHAN 9453
Respighi, O.:Nebbie, w. R. Hickox (cnd), BBC PO [arr for voc & orch] Chandos ▲ CHAN 9453
Scarlatti, A.:Dixit Dominus, w. N. Argenta (sop), C. Denley (mez), T. Pinnock (cnd), English Concert, English Chorale Archiv ▲ 423386-2 [DDD]
Vaughan Williams, R.:Riders to the Sea, w. Ingrid Attrot (sop—Nora), Lynn Dawson (sop—Cathleen), Linda Finnie (mez—Maurya), Karl Daymond (bar—Bartley), R. Hickox (cnd), Northern Sinfonia of England Chandos ▲ CHAN 9392 [DDD]
Vivaldi, A.:Gloria, RV.589, w. N. Argenta (sop), C. Denley (mez), T. Pinnock (cnd), English CO, English Concert Choir Archiv ▲ 423386-2 [DDD]

Aubert, J. (bar)
Ravel, M.:L'Heure espagnole, w. Jeanne Krieger (sop—Concepcion), Louis Arnoult (ten—Gonzalve), Raoul Gilles (ten—Torquemada), J. Aubert (bar—Ramiro), Hector Dufranne (bass—Don Inigo Gomez), G. Truc (cnd), *(orch unknown)* *(rec premiere recording, supervised by Ravel, 1929)* VAI Audio ▲ VAIA 1073

Aubin, Alain (ct)
Fratris Solis, w. Aubin, Alain (ct) Sonpact ▲ SPT 95014
Scarlatti, A.:Cants, w. J. Nicolas (sop)—Diana & Endimione; Ero & Leandro; Correa nel sen Amato [I; w. strs & hpd ensemble] Pierre Verany ▲ PV.790013 [DDD]

Auer, Erich (spkr)
Kaufmann, D.:Der Tod des Trompeters Kirilenko, w. S. Palm (vc), I. Karabtchevsky (cnd), Lower Austria Tonkünst Orch Vienna Modern Masters ▲ VMM 3020 [AAD]

Auez, I. (sop)
Verdi, G.:Requiem Mass, w. L. Fischer (cta), L. van Tulder (ten), H. Schey (bar), C. Schuricht (cnd), Royal Concertgebouw Orch, Amsterdam Toonkunst Choir *(rec live, Amsterdam, Nov. 2, 1939)* Archipon 2–▲ ARC 3.2/3 (m) [ADD]

Augér, Arleen (mez)
Bach, J.S.:Cant 86, w. H. Watts (cta), A. Kraus (ten), W. Heldwein (bass), H. Rilling (cnd), Stuttgart Bach Collegium, Gächinger Kantorei [G] *(rec 1979)* Hänssler Classic ▲ 98.885 [AAD]
Mahler, G.:Sym 2, w. J. Baker (mez), S. Rattle (cnd), City of Birmingham SO, City of Birmingham Sym Chorus [G] EMI Classics 2–▲ CDCB 47962 [DDD]

Augér, Arleen (sop)
The Art of Arleen Augér, w. J. Rezven (pno) Koch International Classics ▲ KIC 7248 [DDD]
Bach, J.S.:Arias, w. G. Schwarz (cnd), Mostly Mozart Festival Orch Delos ▲ DCD 3026 [DDD]
Bach, J.S.:Cant 5, w. C. Watkinson (alt), A. Baldin (ten), W. Schöne (bass), H. Rilling (cnd), Stuttgart Bach Collegium, Gächinger Kantorei [G] *(rec Feb & Oct 1979)* Hänssler Classic ▲ 98.816 [AAD]
Bach, J.S.:Cant 8, w. H. Watts (cta), A. Kraus (ten), P. Huttenlocher (bar), H. Rilling (cnd), Stuttgart Bach Collegium, Gächinger Kantorei [G] *(rec 1979)* Hänssler Classic ▲ 98.813 [AAD]
Bach, J.S.:Cant 21, w. Ortrun Wenkel (cta), Siegfried Jerusalem (ten), Peter Schreier (ten), Theo Adam (b-bar), H.-J. Rotzsch (cnd), New Bach Collegium Musicum, Leipzig St. Thomas Church Choir Berlin Classics ▲ BER 2175 [ADD]
Bach, J.S.:Cant 23, w. H. Watts (cta), A. Baldin (ten), N. Tütler (bass), H. Rilling (cnd), Stuttgart Bach Collegium, Gächinger Kantorei [G] *(rec 1977)* Hänssler Classic ▲ 98.879 [AAD]
Bach, J.S.:Cant 24, w. H. Watts (cta), K. Pugh (cta), A. Kraus (ten), W. Heldwein (bass), W. Schöne (bass), H. Rilling (cnd), Stuttgart Bach Collegium, Gächinger Kantorei Hänssler Classic ▲ 98.803 [AAD]
Bach, J.S.:Cant 25, w. A. Kraus (ten), P. Huttenlocher (bar), H. Rilling (cnd), Stuttgart Bach Collegium, Gächinger Kantorei Hänssler Classic ▲ 98.810 [ADD]
Bach, J.S.:Cant 26, w. D. Soffel (sop), A. Kraus (ten), P. Huttenlocher (bar), H. Rilling (cnd), Stuttgart Bach Collegium, Gächinger Kantorei [G] *(rec 1979 & 1980)* Hänssler Classic ▲ 98.821 [AAD]
Bach, J.S.:Cant 28, w. G. Schreckenbach (cta), A. Kraus (ten), W. Heldwein (bass), H. Rilling (cnd), Stuttgart Bach Collegium, Gächinger Kantorei [G] *(rec Nov 1981 & Feb 1982)* Hänssler Classic ▲ 98.827 [AAD]
Bach, J.S.:Cant 36, w. G. Schreckenbach (cta), P. Schreier (ten), W. Heldwein (bass), H. Rilling (cnd), Stuttgart Bach Collegium, Gächinger Kantorei [G] Hänssler Classic ▲ 98.823 [AAD]
Bach, J.S.:Cant 37, w. C. Watkinson (mez), A. Kraus (ten), P. Huttenlocher (bar), H. Rilling (cnd), Stuttgart Bach Collegium, Gächinger Kantorei [G] *(rec 1979)* Hänssler Classic ▲ 98.886 [AAD]
Bach, J.S.:Cant 38, w. H. Watts (cta), L.-M. Harder (ten), P. Huttenlocher (bar), H. Rilling (cnd), Stuttgart Bach Collegium, Gächinger Kantorei [G] *(rec Feb & Apr 1980)* Hänssler Classic ▲ 98.818 [AAD]
Bach, J.S.:Cant 39, w. G. Schreckenbach (cta), F. Gerishen (bar), H. Rilling (cnd), Stuttgart Bach Collegium, Gächinger Kantorei Hänssler Classic ▲ 98.802 [AAD]
Bach, J.S.:Cant 43, w. J. Hamari (cta), L.-M. Harder (ten), P. Huttenlocher (bar), H. Rilling (cnd), Stuttgart Bach Collegium, Gächinger Kantorei [G] *(rec 1981–82)* Hänssler Classic ▲ 98.885 [AAD]
Bach, J.S.:Cant 44, w. H. Watts (cta), A. Baldin (ten), W. Schöne (bass), H. Rilling (cnd), Stuttgart Bach Collegium, Gächinger Kantorei [G] *(rec 1979)* Hänssler Classic ▲ 98.886 [AAD]
Bach, J.S.:Cant 47, w. P. Huttenlocher (bar), H. Rilling (cnd), Stuttgart Bach Collegium, Gächinger Kantorei [G] *(rec 1982)* Hänssler Classic ▲ 98.815 [AAD]
Bach, J.S.:Cant 49, w. P. Huttenlocher (bar), H. Rilling (cnd), Stuttgart Bach Collegium [G] *(rec Oct 1982)* Hänssler Classic ▲ 98.817 [AAD]
Bach, J.S.:Cant 50, w. Ortrun Wenkel (cta), Peter Schreier (ten), Theo Adam (b-bar), H.-J. Rotzsch (cnd), New Bach Collegium Musicum, Leipzig St. Thomas Church Choir Berlin Classics ▲ BER 2176 [ADD]
Bach, J.S.:Cant 51, w. H. Rilling (cnd), Stuttgart Bach Collegium, Gächinger Kantorei [G] Novalis ▲ 150029 [DDD]
Bach, J.S.:Cant 52, w. H. Rilling (cnd), Stuttgart Bach Collegium, Gächinger Kantorei [G] *(rec 1982 & 1983)* Hänssler Classic ▲ 98.821 [AAD]
Bach, J.S.:Cant 57, w. W. Heldwein (bass), H. Rilling (cnd), Stuttgart Bach Collegium, Gächinger Kantorei [G] *(rec Nov 1981 & Feb 1982)* Hänssler Classic ▲ 98.825 [AAD]
Bach, J.S.:Cant 59, w. N. Tüller (bass), H. Rilling (cnd), Stuttgart Bach Collegium, Gächinger Kantorei [G] *(rec 1976–77)* Hänssler Classic ▲ 98.886 [AAD]
Bach, J.S.:Cant 63, w. J. Hamarī (mez), H. Laurich (cta), A. Kraus (ten), W. Heldwein (bass), W. Schöne (bass), H. Rilling (cnd), Stuttgart Bach Collegium, Gächinger Kantorei [G] *(rec Feb 1971 & Feb 1981)* Hänssler Classic ▲ 98.823 [AAD]
Bach, J.S.:Cant 64, w. A. Murray (mez), P. Huttenlocher (bar), H. Rilling (cnd), Stuttgart Bach Collegium, Gächinger Kantorei [G] *(rec Jan 1978 & Mar 1981)* Hänssler Classic ▲ 98.825 [AAD]
Bach, J.S.:Cant 68, w. P. Huttenlocher (bass), H. Rilling (cnd), Stuttgart Bach Collegium, Gächinger Kantorei [G] *(rec 1980–81)* Hänssler Classic ▲ 98.890 [AAD]
Bach, J.S.:Cant 72, w. H. Laurich (cta), W. Schöne (bass), H. Rilling (cnd), Bach Ensemble [G] *(rec 1983)* Hänssler Classic ▲ 98.875 [AAD]
Bach, J.S.:Cant 79, w. Ortrun Wenkel (cta), Peter Schreier (ten), Theo Adam (b-bar), H.-J. Rotzsch (cnd), New Bach Collegium Musicum, Leipzig St. Thomas Church Choir Berlin Classics ▲ BER 2176 [ADD]
Bach, J.S.:Cant 80, w. G. Schreckenbach (cta), L.-M. Harder (ten), P. Huttenlocher (bar), H. Rilling (cnd), Württemberg CO, Gächinger Kantorei [G] *(rec 1976 & 1983)* Hänssler Classic ▲ 98.819 [AAD]
Bach, J.S.:Cant 80, w. Ortrun Wenkel (cta), Peter Schreier (ten), Theo Adam (b-bar), H.-J. Rotzsch (cnd), New Bach Collegium Musicum, Leipzig St. Thomas Church Choir Berlin Classics ▲ BER 2176 [ADD]
Bach, J.S.:Cant 84, w. H. Rilling (cnd), Bach Ensemble [G] *(rec 1983)* Hänssler Classic ▲ 98.877 [AAD]
Bach, J.S.:Cant 89, w. H. Watts (cta), P. Huttenlocher (bar), H. Rilling (cnd), Stuttgart Bach Collegium, Gächinger Kantorei [G] *(rec Sept & Dec 1977)* Hänssler Classic ▲ 98.818 [AAD]
Bach, J.S.:Cant 92, w. G. Schreckenbach (cta), H. Watts (cta), A. Baldin (ten), P. Huttenlocher (bar), H. Rilling (cnd), Bach Ensemble [G] *(rec 1980)* Hänssler Classic ▲ 98.877 [AAD]
Bach, J.S.:Cant 95, w. A. Kraus (ten), W. Heldwein (bass), H. Rilling (cnd), Stuttgart Bach Collegium, Württemberg CO, Gächinger Kantorei Hänssler Classic ▲ 98.812 [AAD]
Bach, J.S.:Cant 98, w. J. Hamari (cta), L.-M. Harder (ten), W. Heldwein (bass), H. Rilling (cnd), Stuttgart Bach Collegium, Gächinger Kantorei [G] *(rec Oct 1982 & July 1983)* Hänssler Classic ▲ 98.817 [AAD]
Bach, J.S.:Cant 99, w. H. Watts (cta), L.-M. Harder (ten), J. Bröcheler (bar), H. Rilling (cnd), Stuttgart Bach Collegium, Gächinger Kantorei [G] *(rec 1979)* Hänssler Classic ▲ 98.813 [AAD]
Bach, J.S.:Cant 100, w. J. Hamari (cta), A. Kraus (ten), P. Huttenlocher (bar), H. Rilling (cnd), Württemberg CO, Gächinger Kantorei [G] *(rec 1983–84)* Hänssler Classic 5–▲ 98.976
Bach, J.S.:Cant 101, w. H. Watts (cta), A. Baldin (ten), J. Bröcheler (bar), H. Rilling (cnd), Stuttgart Bach Collegium, Gächinger Kantorei Hänssler Classic ▲ 98.809 [AAD]
Bach, J.S.:Cant 107, w. A. Baldin (ten), J. Bröcheler (bar), H. Rilling (cnd), Stuttgart Bach Collegium, Gächinger Kantorei Hänssler Classic ▲ 98.805 [AAD]
Bach, J.S.:Cant 113, w. G. Schreckenbach (cta), A. Kraus (ten), N. Tüller (bass), H. Rilling (cnd), Stuttgart Bach Collegium, Gächinger Kantorei Hänssler Classic ▲ 98.810 [ADD]
Bach, J.S.:Cant 115, w. H. Watts (cta), L.-M. Harder (ten), W. Schöne (bass), H. Rilling (cnd), Stuttgart Bach Collegium, Gächinger Kantorei [G] *(rec 1980)* Hänssler Classic ▲ 98.819 [AAD]
Bach, J.S.:Cant 116, w. H. Watts (cta), L.-M. Harder (ten), P. Huttenlocher (bar), H. Rilling (cnd), Stuttgart Bach Collegium, Gächinger Kantorei [G] *(rec 1980)* Hänssler Classic ▲ 98.820 [AAD]
Bach, J.S.:Cant 119, w. A. Murray (mez), A. Kraus (ten), W. Schöne (bass), H. Rilling (cnd), Bach Ensemble Hänssler Classic ▲ 98.828 [AAD]
Bach, J.S.:Cant 121, w. D. Soffel (cta), A. Kraus (ten), W. Schöne (bass), H. Rilling (cnd), Stuttgart Bach Collegium, Gächinger Kantorei [G] *(rec Feb & Apr 1980)* Hänssler Classic ▲ 98.824 [AAD]
Bach, J.S.:Cant 122, w. G. Schreckenbach (cta), A. Kraus (ten), N. Tüller (bass), H. Rilling (cnd), Stuttgart Bach Collegium, Frankfurt Kantorei [G] *(rec Feb 1972)* Hänssler Classic ▲ 98.826 [AAD]

Augér, Arleen (sop) (cont.)
Bach, J.S.:Cant 127, w. L.-M. Harder (ten), W. Schöne (bass), H. Rilling (cnd), Stuttgart Bach Collegium, Gächinger Kantorei [G] *(rec 1980)* Hänssler Classic ▲ 98.878 [AAD]
Bach, J.S.:Cant 132, w. H. Watts (cta), K. Equiluz (ten), W. Schöne (bass), H. Rilling (cnd), Stuttgart Bach Collegium, Gächinger Kantorei [G] *(rec Sept 1976 & Jan & Apr 197)* Hänssler Classic ▲ 98.822 [AAD]
Bach, J.S.:Cant 133, w. D. Soffel (cta), A. Baldin (ten), P. Huttenlocher (bar), H. Rilling (cnd), Stuttgart Bach Collegium, Gächinger Kantorei [G] *(rec Feb–Mar 1980)* Hänssler Classic ▲ 98.826 [AAD]
Bach, J.S.:Cant 137, w. Ortrun Wenkel (cta), Peter Schreier (ten), Siegfried Jerusalem (ten), Theo Adam (b-bar), H.-J. Rotzsch (cnd), New Bach Collegium Musicum, Leipzig St. Thomas Church Choir Berlin Classics ▲ BER 2175 [ADD]
Bach, J.S.:Cant 138, w. R. Bollen (cta), A. Baldin (ten), P. Huttenlocher (bar), H. Rilling (cnd), Stuttgart Bach Collegium, Gächinger Kantorei Hänssler Classic ▲ 98.812 [AAD]
Bach, J.S.:Cant 140, w. A. Baldin (ten), P. Huttenlocher (bar), H. Rilling (cnd), Stuttgart Bach Collegium, Gächinger Kantorei [G] Novalis ▲ 150029 [DDD]
Bach, J.S.:Cant 144, w. H. Watts (cta), A. Kraus (ten), H. Rilling (cnd), Bach Ensemble [G] *(rec 1978)* Hänssler Classic ▲ 98.876 [AAD]
Bach, J.S.:Cant 149, w. M. Georg (mez), A. Baldin (ten), P. Huttenlocher (bar), H. Rilling (cnd), Stuttgart Bach Collegium, Gächinger Kantorei [G] *(rec 1984)* Hänssler Classic ▲ 98.815 [AAD]
Bach, J.S.:Cant 152, w. W. Schöne (bass), H. Rilling (hpd), et al. [G] *(rec Mar–Apr 1976)* Hänssler Classic ▲ 98.826 [AAD]
Bach, J.S.:Cant 162, w. A. Rogers (mez), K. Equiluz (ten), W. Schöne (bass), H. Rilling (cnd), Stuttgart Bach Collegium, Frankfurt Kantorei [G] *(rec Dec 1975 & Mar 1976)* Hänssler Classic ▲ 98.816 [AAD]
Bach, J.S.:Cant 163, w. H. Watts (cta), A. Kraus (ten), N. Tüller (bass), H. Rilling (cnd), Stuttgart Bach Collegium, Gächinger Kantorei [G] *(rec 1976 & 1977)* Hänssler Classic ▲ 98.820 [AAD]
Bach, J.S.:Cant 171, w. J. Hamari (cta), A. Badin (ten), W. Heldwein (bass), H. Rilling (cnd), Württemberg CO, Gächinger Kantorei [G] Hänssler Classic ▲ 98.871 [AAD]
Bach, J.S.:Cant 177, w. J. Hamari (cta), P. Schreier (ten), H. Rilling (cnd), Stuttgart Bach Collegium, Gächinger Kantorei Hänssler Classic ▲ 98.803 [AAD]
Bach, J.S.:Cant 179, w. K. Equiluz (ten), W. Schöne (bass), H. Rilling (cnd), Stuttgart Bach Collegium, Gächinger Kantorei Hänssler Classic ▲ 98.808 [AAD]
Bach, J.S.:Cant 180, w. C. Watkinson (cta), A. Kraus (ten), W. Heldwein (sop), H. Rilling (cnd), Stuttgart Bach Collegium, Gächinger Kantorei [G] *(rec Feb & Oct 1979)* Hänssler Classic ▲ 98.816 [AAD]
Bach, J.S.:Cant 181, w. G. Schnaut (mez), G. Schreckenbach (cta), K. Equiluz (ten), N. Tütler (bass), H. Rilling (cnd), Stuttgart Bach Collegium, Gächinger Kantorei [G] *(rec 1981)* Hänssler Classic ▲ 98.878 [AAD]
Bach, J.S.:Cant 183, w. J. Hamari (cta), P. Schreier (ten), W. Heldwein (bass), H. Rilling (cnd), Stuttgart Bach Collegium, Gächinger Kantorei Hänssler Classic ▲ 98.801 [AAD]
Bach, J.S.:Cant 185, w. H. Laurich (mez), A. Baldin (ten), P. Huttenlocher (bar), H. Rilling (cnd), Stuttgart Bach Collegium, Frankfurt Kantorei Hänssler Classic ▲ 98.804 [AAD]
Bach, J.S.:Cant 186, w. H. Watts (cta), K. Equiluz (ten), H. Rilling (cnd), Stuttgart Bach Collegium, Gächinger Kantorei Hänssler Classic ▲ 98.805 [AAD]
Bach, J.S.:Cant 188, w. J. Hamari (cta), A. Baldin (ten), W. Heldwein (bass), H. Rilling (cnd), Württemberg CO, Gächinger Kantorei [G] *(rec June & Sept 1983)* Hänssler Classic ▲ 98.817 [AAD]
Bach, J.S.:Cant 192, w. Ortrun Wenkel (cta), Peter Schreier (ten), Theo Adam (b-bar), H.-J. Rotzsch (cnd), New Bach Collegium Musicum, Leipzig St. Thomas Church Choir Berlin Classics ▲ BER 2176 [ADD]
Bach, J.S.:Cant 193, w. J. Hamari (cta), H. Rilling (cnd), Bach Ensemble *(rec July 1983)* Hänssler Classic ▲ 98.829 [AAD]
Bach, J.S.:Cant 198, w. G. Schreckenbach (cta), A. Baldin (ten), P. Huttenlocher (bar), H. Rilling (cnd), Bach Ensemble *(rec Sept 1983)* Hänssler Classic ▲ 98.830 [AAD]
Bach, J.S.:Cant 199, w. H. Rilling (cnd), Stuttgart Bach Collegium Hänssler Classic ▲ 98.810 [ADD]
Bach, J.S.:Christmas Oratorio, w. J. Hamari (cta), P. Schreier (ten), W. Schöne (bass), H. Rilling (cnd), Stuttgart Bach Collegium, Gächinger Kantorei [G] *(rec 1984)* Hänssler Classic 5–▲ 98.976
Bach, J.S.:Christmas Oratorio, w. J. Hamari (cta), P. Schreier (ten), W. Schöne (bass), H. Rilling (cnd), Stuttgart Bach Collegium Hänssler Classic 3–▲ 98.854 [DDD]
Bach, J.S.:Easter Oratorio, w. J. Hamari (cta), A. Kraus (ten), P. Huttenlocher (bar), H. Rilling (cnd), Stuttgart Bach Collegium, Gächinger Kantorei [G] *(rec 1980–81)* Hänssler Classic 5–▲ 98.976
Bach, J.S.:Magnificat, BWV 243, w. A. Murray (mez), H. Watts (cta), A. Kraus (ten), P. Huttenlocher (bar), W. Schöne (bass), H. Rilling (cnd), Stuttgart Bach Collegium, Gächinger Kantorei *(rec 1979)* Sony Classical ("Essential Classics" series) ▲ SBK 48280 [ADD] ■ SBT 48280
Berg, A.:Lulu (suite), w. S. Rattle (cnd), City of Birmingham SO EMI ▲ CDC 49857
Brahms, J.:Ein Deutsches Requiem, w. R. Stilwell (bar), R. Shaw (cnd), Atlanta SO, Atlanta Sym Chorus [G] Telarc 2–▲ CD 80092 [DDD]
Canteloube, J.:Songs of Auvergne, w. Y.P. Tortelier (cnd), English CO Virgin Classics ("Ultraviolet" series) ▲ CUV 61120
Diepenbrock, A.:Hymnen an die Nacht (2), w. R. Chailly (cnd), Royal Concertgebouw Orch—Gehoben ist der Stein *(rec live, Concertgebouw Amsterdam, Oct 18, 1990)* Donemus ▲ CV 50 [DDD]
Fauré, G.:Messe basse (in 3 movts), w. John Butt (org), King's College Choir Cambridge Classics for Pleasure ("Eminence" series) ▲ CDEMX 2166 [DDD]
Fauré, G.:Requiem, w. Benjamin Luxon (bar), John Butt (org), English CO, King's College Choir Cambridge Classics for Pleasure ("Eminence" series) ▲ CDEMX 2166 [DDD]
Handel, G.F.:Arias, w. G. Schwarz (cnd), Mostly Mozart Festival Orch Delos ▲ DCD 3026
Handel, G.F.:Arias Berlin Classics ▲ BER 9050 [DDD]
Handel, G.F.:The Choice of Hercules, w. Venceslava Hruba-Freiberger (sop), Eberhard Büchner (ten), Zäppfel (sgr), M. Pommer (cnd), Leipzig New Bach Collegium Musicum, Leipzig Univ Choir [E] Capriccio ▲ CDC 10019 [DDD]
Handel, G.F.:Dixit Dominus, w. Lynne Dawson (sop), Diana Montague (mez), Leigh Nixon (ten), Simon Birchall (bass), S. Preston (cnd), Westminster Abbey Orch, Westminster Abbey Choir [L] Archiv ▲ 423594-2 [DDD]
Handel, G.F.:Messiah, w. Anne Sofie von Otter (mez), Michael Chance (ct), Howard Crook (ten), John Tomlinson (bass), T. Pinnock (cnd), English CO, English Concert Choir [E] Archiv 2–▲ 423630-2 [DDD]
Handel, G.F.:Messiah (sels), w. Anne Sofia von Otter (mez), Michael Chance (ct), Paul Crook (ten), John Tomlinson (bass), T. Pinnock (cnd), English CO, English Concert Choir [E] Archiv ▲ 427664-2 [DDD] ■ 427664-4
Handel, G.F.:Orlando, w. Emma Kirkby (sop), Catherine Robbin (mez), James Bowman (ct), David Thomas (bass), C. Hogwood (cnd), Academy of Ancient Music L'Oiseau-Lyre 3–▲ 430845-2 [DDD]
Haydn, J.:Arias—Erenice, che fai? [from Scene di Berenice]; Son pietosa, son bonina [from Aria per la Circe]; Arianna a Naxos; Solo e pensoso [from Aria da Il Canzoniere]; Miseri noi misera patria London ("Grande voici" series) ▲ 440414-2
Haydn, J.:Die Jahreszeiten, w. John Aler (ten), Håkan Hågegard (bar), J. Revzen (cnd), St. Paul CO, Minnesota Chorale [G] Koch International Classics 2–▲ KIC 7065-2 [DDD]
Haydn, J.:Salve regina, H.XXIIIb/2, w. Alfreda Hodgson (cta), Anthony Rolfe Johnson (ten), Gwynne Howell (bass), John Birch (db), L. Heltay (cnd), Argo CO, London Chamber Choir *(rec St. Jude's, London, Feb 1979)* London 2–▲ 443027-2 [ADD]
Haydn, J.:Die Schöpfung, w. Philip Langridge (ten), David Thomas (bass), S. Rattle (cnd), City of Birmingham SO, City of Birmingham Sym Chorus [E] EMI Classics 2–▲ CDCB 54159 [DDD]
Love Songs, w. Dalton Baldwin (pno) Delos ▲ DCD 3029 [DDD]
Mahler, G.:Sym 8, w. H. Harper (sop), L. Popp (sop), Y. Minton (mez), H. Watts (cta), A. Kollo (ten), J. Shirley-Quirk (bar), M. Talvela (bass), G. Solti (cnd), Chicago SO, Vienna State Opera Chorus, Vienna Boys' Choir, Vienna Singverein [G,L] London 2–▲ 414493-2 [ADD]
Marschner, H.A.:Der Vampyr, w. Donald Grobe (ten), Roland Hermann (bar), Nikolas Hillebrand (bass), F. Rieger (cnd), Bavarian RSO, Bavarian Radio Chorus *(rec live, Munich, 1974)* Enterprise ("Documents" series) 2–▲ ENT 1009
Mendelssohn, F.:A Midsummer Night's Dream (comp), w. A. Murray (mez), N. Marriner (cnd), Philharmonia Orch, Ambrosian Singers [E] Philips ▲ 411106-2 [DDD]

Augér, Arleen (sop) (cont.)
Monteverdi, C.:Incoronazione, w. A. Augér (soprano—Poppea), D. Jones (mez—Nerone), L. Hirst (mez—Ottavia), J. Bowman (ct—Ottone), R. Hickox (cnd), City of London Baroque Sinfonia
Virgin Classics ▲ CDCC 45082
Monteverdi, C.:Incoronazione, w. S. Leonard (sop), D. Jones (mez), L. Hirst (mez), J. Bowman (ct), G. Reinhart (bass)., R. Hickox (cnd), City of London Baroque Sinfonia Virgin Classics 3–▲ CDCC 59524
Mozart, L.:Missa solemnis, w. G. Schreckenbach (mez), H. Laubenthal (ten), B. McDaniel (bar), R. Bader (cnd), Berlin Domkapelle Instrumental Ensemble, St. Hedwig's Cathedral Choir [L]
Koch Schwann ▲ CD 313028 [ADD]
Mozart, W.A.:Arias, w. Kathleen Battle (sop), Irma Beilke (sop), Helena Braun (sop), Lisa Della Casa (sop), Maria Cebotari (sop), Ileana Cotrubas (sop), Helen Donath (sop), Mirella Freni (sop), Reri Grist (sop), Edita Gruberova (sop), Elisabeth Grümmer (sop), Hilde Güden (sop), Ingeborg Hallstein (sop), Luise Helletsgruber (sop), Gundula Janowitz (sop), Sena Jurinac (sop), Erika Köth (sop), Evelyn Lear (sop), Wilma Lipp (sop), Margaret Marshall (sop), Edith Mathis (sop), Jarmila Novotna (sop), Margherita Perras (sop), Lucia Popp (sop), Elisabeth Rethberg (sop), Anneliese Rothenberger (sop), Elisabeth Schumann (sop), Elisabeth Schwarzkopf (sop), Graziella Sciutti (sop), Irmgard Seefried (sop), Graziella Sciutti (sop), Julia Varady (sop), Agnes Baltsa (mez), Margit Bokor (mez), Brigitte Fassbaender (mez), Christa Ludwig (mez), Ann Murray (mez), Francisco Araiza (ten), Anton Dermota (ten), Helge Rosvaenge (ten), Rudolf Schock (ten), Peter Schreier (ten), Leopold Simoneau (ten), Eric Tappy (ten), Richard Tauber (ten), Gösta Winbergh (ten), Josef Witt (ten), Fritz Wunderlich (ten), Christian Boesch (bar), Willy Domgraf-Fassbaender (bar), Karl Dönch (bar), Dietrich Fischer-Dieskau (bar), Erich Kunz (bar), Eberhard Wächter (bar), Hans Hotter (b-bar), Paul Schöffler (b-bar), Cesare Siepi (b-bar), José Van Dam (b-bar), Walter Berry (bass), Geraint Evans (bass), Nicolai Ghiaurov (bass), Alexander Kipnis (bass), Richard Mayr (bass), Kurt Moll (bass), James Morris (bass), Ezio Pinza (bass), Martti Talvela (bass), Giorgio Tozzi (bass), Hans Duhan (sgr), Res Fischer (sgr), Marie Gerhart (sgr), *(various orchs & cnds)* —sels from Idomeneo, Die Entführung aus der Serail, Le nozze di Figaro, Don Giovanni, Così fan tutte, Die Zauberflöte & various arias Orfeo d'or ("Festspiel Dokumente" series) 5–▲ 408955
Mozart, W.A.:Arias—Porgi amor; E Susanna non vien!...Dove sono [both from Le nozze di Figaro]; Non mi dir [from Don Giovanni]; Et incarnatus est [from Mass in c, K.427]
London ("Grande voici" series) ▲ 440414–2
Mozart, W.A.:Complete Mozart Edition, w. E. Mathis (sop), J. Varady (sop), H. Donath (sop), P. Schreier (ten), L. Hager (cnd), Salzburg Mozarteum Orch Philips 3–▲ 422532–2 [ADD]
Mozart, W.A.:Complete Mozart Edition, w. E. Mathis (sop), A. Baltsa (mez), P. Schreier (ten), L. Hager (cnd), Salzburg Mozarteum Orch Philips 3–▲ 422530–2 [ADD]
Mozart, W.A.:Complete Mozart Edition, w. E. Gruberova (sop), I. Cotrubas (sop), A. Baltsa (mez), W. Hollweg (ten), L. Hager (cnd), Salzburg Mozarteum Orch Philips 3–▲ 422529–2 [ADD]
Mozart, W.A.:Complete Mozart Edition, w. E. Mathis (sop), H. Schwarz (mez), A. Rolfe Johnson (ten), L. Hager (cnd), Salzburg Mozarteum Orch, Salzburg Mozarteum Chorus Philips 2–▲ 422526–2 [ADD]
Mozart, W.A.:Don Giovanni, w. J. Varady (sop), E. Mathis (sop), T. Moser (ten), A. Titus (bar), R. Panerai (bar), R. Scholze (bass), J.-H. Rootering (bass), R. Kubelik (cnd), Bavarian RSO, Bavarian Radio Chorus [I] Eurodisc 3–▲ 7798–2 [DDD]
Mozart, W.A.:Exsultate, w. L. Bernstein (cnd), Bavarian RSO, Bavarian Radio Chorus *(rec live April 1990)*
Deutsche Grammophon ▲ 431791–2 [DDD] ▯ 431791–5
Mozart, W.A.:Missa, K.427, w. B. Bonney (sop), H.-P. Blochwitz (ten), Robert Holl (bass), C. Abbado (cnd), Berlin PO, Berlin Radio Chorus [L] Sony Classical ▲ SK 46671 [DDD]
Mozart, W.A.:Missa, K.427, w. F. von Stade (mez), F. Lopardo (ten), C. Hauptmann (bass), L. Bernstein (cnd), Bavarian RSO, Bavarian Radio Chorus *(rec live April 1990)*
Deutsche Grammophon ▲ 431791–2 [DDD] ▯ 431791–5
Mozart, W.A.:Missa, K.427, w. Heather Harper (sop), Horst Lubenthal (ten), Ulrik Cold (bass), S. Celibidache (cnd), Stuttgart RSO, Bavarian Radio Chorus, Southwest German Radio Chorus *(rec live, 1980's)* Topazio ▲ TOP 26045
Mozart, W.A.:Nozze di Figaro, w. B. Bonney (sop), A. Nafé (mez), H. Hagegard (bar), P. Salomaa (bass), A. Östman (cnd), Drottningholm Court Theater Orch, Drottingholm Court Thea Chorus [I]
L'Oiseau-Lyre 3–▲ 421333–2 [DDD]
Mozart, W.A.:Requiem, w. C. Watkinson (cta), S. Jerusalem (ten), S. Nimsgern (b-bar), H. Rilling (cnd), Stuttgart Bach Ensemble, Gächinger Kantorei [L] Odyssey ▲ MBK 42614 ■ YT 42614
Mozart, W.A.:Requiem, w. C. Bartoli (mez), V. Cole (ten), R. Pape (bass), G. Solti (cnd), Vienna PO, Vienna Phil Chorus [L] *(rec live 12/5/91)* London ▲ 433688–2 [DDD] ▯ 433688–5
Mozart, W.A.:Requiem, w. D. Ziegler (mez), J. Hadley (ten), T. Krause (bar), R. Shaw (cnd), Atlanta SO, Atlanta Sym Chorus [L] Telarc ▲ CD 80128 [DDD]
Mozart, W.A.:Schuldigkeit, w. K. Láki (sop), S. Geszty (sop), W. Hollweg (ten), C. H. Ahnsjö (ten), R. Bader (cnd), Berlin Cathedral Choir [G] *(rec 1980)* Koch Schwann 2–▲ CD 313065 [ADD]
Orff, C.:Carmina burana, w. J. Van Kesteren (ten), J. Summers (bar), R. Muti (cnd), Philharmonia Orch, Philharmonia Chorus [G, L] EMI Classics ▲ CDC 47100
Ravel, M.:L'Enfant et les sortilèges, w. Marilyn Richardson (sop), Jane Berbié (mez), Linda Finnie (mez), Jocelyne Taillon (mez), Davenny Wyner (mez), Philip Langridge (ten), Philippe Huttenlocher (bar), Jules Bastin (bass), A. Previn (cnd), London SO, Ambrosian Opera Chorus
Classics for Pleasure ("Eminence" series) ▲ CFP 2241
Ravel, M.:Shéhérazade Mez, w. L. Pešek (cnd), Philharmonia Orch Virgin Classics ▲ CDC 59235
Rossini, G.:Arias, w. J. Larmore (mez), M. Kimbrough (bar), D. Baldwin (pno)—La Pesca (duet); Il Trovatore Arabesque ▲ Z 6623 [ADD]
Rossini, G.:Péchés de vieillesse (sels), w. J. Larmore (mez), J. Aler (ten), S. Kimbrough (bar), D. Baldwin (pno)—Les Amants de Séville; Chanson de Zora; L'Esule; La Fioraia Fiorentina; La Lontananza; Musique Anodine; L'Orpheline du Tyrol; La Passegiata Quartettino; L'Ultimo Ricordo; Un Sou Complainte [I,F]
Arabesque ▲ Z 6623 [ADD]
Schubert, Franz:Songs (comp), w. G. Johnson (pno), Thea King (cl)—D.273, 301, 510, 528, 588, 595, 631, 857, 965 (Der Hirt auf dem Felsen), etc. [G] Hyperion ▲ CDJ 33009
Schubert, Franz:Songs (misc), w. Walter Olbertz (pno)—songs after Goethe
Berlin Classics ▲ BER 2185 [ADD]
Schubert, Franz:Songs (misc), w. L. Orkis (pno)—23 songs [G] Virgin Classics ▲ 59630 [DDD]
Schumann, R.:Songs, w. Walter Olbertz (pno) Berlin Classics ▲ BER 2186 [ADD]
Strauss, R.:4 Last Songs, w. A. Previn (cnd), Vienna PO [G] Telarc ▲ CD 80180 [DDD]
Villa-Lobos, H.:Bachiana brasileira 5, w. Parisot (cnd), Yale Cellos Delos ▲ DCD 3041
Vocal Music Sampler, w. English CO [cnd:L. Pesek], et al. Virgin Classics 2–▲ CDC 59098
Weber, C.M. von:Oberon, w. B. Nilsson (sop), J. Hamari (mez), P. Domingo (ten), H. Prey (bar), R. Kubelik (cnd), Bavarian RSO Deutsche Grammophon ("Domingo Edition" series) ▲ 435406–2 [ADD]
Weber, C.M. von:Oberon, w. B. Nilsson (sop), J. Hamari (mez), P. Domingo (ten), H. Prey (bar), R. Kubelik (cnd), Bavarian RSO Deutsche Grammophon 2–▲ 419038–2 [ADD]
Wolf, H.:Goethe-Lieder (sels), w. I. Gage (pno)—Agnes; An eine Äolsharfe; Auf ein altes Bild; Er ist's; Erstes Liebeslied eines Mädchens; Im Frühling; In der Frühe; Lied vom Winde; Neue Liebe; Schlafendes Jesuskind; Das verlassene Mägdlein; Wo find' ich Trost?; Zitronenfalter im April [G]
Hyperion ▲ CDA 66590 [DDD]
Wolf, H.:Mörike-Lieder (sels), w. I. Gage (pno)—Die Bekehrte; Frühling übers Jahr; Ganymed; Heiss mich nicht reden; Nur wer die Sehnsucht kennt; Phänomen; Die Spröde [G]
Hyperion ▲ CDA 66590 [DDD]

August, Joan (sop/mez)
Puccini, G.:Suor angelica, w. Elisabeth Carron (sop—Angelica), Joan Summers (sop—Genovieffa), Donna Owen (sop—Dolcina), Lou Ann Wyckoff (sop—Alms collector), Hanna Owen (sop—novice), Anthea De Forest (sop—novice), Charlotte Povia (mez—Abbess), Beverly Evans (mez—Monitress), Kay Creed (mez—Mistress), La Vergne Monette (sop/mez—lay sister), Joan August (sop/mez—lay sister), Pearle Goldsmith (sop/mez—other sister), Lila Herbert (sop/mez—other sister), Jodell Kenting (sop/mez—other sister), Ann Pretzat (sop/mez—other sister), Evelyn Sachs (cta—Princess), F. Patanè (cnd), *(orch unknown)* *(rec New York, Feb 23, 1967)* Legato Classics ▲ LCD 212–1 [ADD]

Augustin, Fritz (sgr)
Verdi, G.:Un ballo in maschera, w. Martha Mödl (sop—Ulrica), Walburga Wegner (sop—Amelia), Anny Schlemm (mez—Oscar), Lorenz Fehenberger (ten—Ricardo), Dietrich Fischer-Dieskau (bar—Renato), Wilhelm Schirp (bass—Samuel), Willy Schoneweib (bass—Tom), Gunther Wilhelms (bass—Silvan), Fritz Augustin (sgr—Ein Richter), Friedrich Himmelmann (sgr—Ein Diener Amelia), F. Busch (cnd), Cologne RSO, Bernhard Alois Zimmermann (cnd), Cologne Radio Chorus Calig 2–▲ 50946/47 (m) [ADD]

Aumonier, Paul (bass)
The French Tradition, Vol. 1 (1897–1909), w. Bontoux (sop) *(rec 1897–1909)*
Minerva ▲ MN A39 [ADD]

Aumont, Jean-Pierre (nar)
Milhaud, D.:Les Mariés de la tour eiffel, w. Raymond Gérome (nar), B. Desgraupes (cnd), Erwartung Ensemble *(rec L'Opéra Comique, Paris, Dec 1989 & May 1990)* Marco Polo ▲ 8.223788 [DDD]
Stravinsky, I.:L'Histoire du soldat, w. M. Milhaud (nar), M. Singher (the Devil), L. Stokowski (cnd), *(orch unknown)* [F] *(rec 1967)* Vanguard Classics ▲ OVC 8004 [ADD]

Auria, A. d' (sop)
Donizetti, G.:Torquato Tasso, w. L. Serra (sop), N. Ciliento (mez), E. Palacio (ten), R. Coviello (bar), S. Alaimo (bass-bar), A. Riva (bass), M.. Bernart (cnd), Genoa Teatro Comunale Orch, Genoa Teatro Comunale Chorus [I] *(rec live 10/16/85)* Bongiovanni 3–▲ GB 2028/30 [DDD]

Auria, D. d' (sop)
Donizetti, G.:Imelda de' Lambertazzi, w. F. Sovilla (sop), F. Tenzi (ten), A. Martin (bar), G. Sarti (bar), M. Andreae (cnd), Swiss-Italian Radio-TV Orch, Swiss-Italian Radio-TV Chorus [I] *(rec live)*
Nuova Era 2–▲ 6778/79 [DDD]

Aurich, Frieder (ten)
Helmschrott, R.:Cross & Freedom, w. Helmut Schatz, Nancy Gibson (sop), Frieder Aurich (ten), Matthias Weichert (bass), Manfred Ball (nar), Anett Baumann (vn), Frank Phillipstch, Linda Robbins, Gerhard Wolf, Martin Homann (perc), Robert M. Helmschrott (org), H.-C. Rademann (cnd), Munich Trombone Quartet, Dresden Chamber Choir Vienna Modern Masters ▲ VMM 3027 [DDD]

Ausensi, Manuel (bar)
Puccini, G.:Madama Butterfly, w. Montserrat Caballé (sop—Cio-Cio-San), Carmen Rigai (mez—Suzuki), Bernabé Martí (ten—Pinkerton), Diego Monjo (ten—Goro), Juan Rico (ten—Yamadori), Manuel Ausensi (bar—Sharpless), Jose Lemar (bass—Bonze), Antonio Leval (bass—Imperial Commissioner), Alejandro Chiara (bass—Registrar), G. Rivoli (cnd), Madrid Radio-TV Orch, Madrid Radio-TV Chorus *(rec Madrid, June 12, 1968)* Legato Classics 2–▲ LCD 210–2 [ADD]

Austin, Patti (sgr)
The Gershwins in Hollywood, w. J. Mauceri (cnd), Hollywood Bowl SO, Gregory Hines, Patti Austin
Philips ▲ 434274–2 [DDD]

Austin, Sumner (bar)
Warlock, P.:Songs Bar, w. M. Harrison (vn), H. Gaskell (ob), C. Lynch (pno)—(2) Ha'Nacker Mill; Away to Twiver *(rec live 2/3/36)* Symposium ▲ 1075

Austral, Florence (sop)
Florence Austral:Great Recordings *(rec 1923–27)* Pearl ▲ PEA 9146 [ADD]
Wagner, R.:Der Ring des Nibelungen (sels), w. Frieda Leider (sop), Elsie Suddaby (sop), Göta Ljunberg (sop), Walter Widdop (ten), Horst Laubenthal (ten), Lauritz Melchior (ten), Friedrich Schorr (bar), Rudolf Bockelmann (b-bar), Ivar Andresen (bass), Emmanuel List (bass), Collingwood, Blech, Coates, Barbirolli, Heger, Alwin, Muck (cnd), London SO—scenes from Siegriend & Götterdämmerung; 90 Motives from Der Ring [w. Collingwood & LSO] Pearl 7–▲ PEA 9137 [ADD]

Autran, Victor (bar)
Gounod, C.:Faust (sels), w. Liliane Berton (sop), Victoria de los Angeles (sop), Rita Gorr (mez), Nicolai Gedda (ten), Ernest Blanc (bar), Boris Christoff (bass), A. Cluytens (cnd), Paris Opera Orch, Paris Opera Chorus Classics for Pleasure ("Eminence" series) ▲ CDEMX 2215 [DDD]

Auvinen, Ritva (sop)
Kokkonen, J.:The Last Temptations, w. Martti Talvela (bass), U. Söderblom (cnd), Savonlinna Opera Festival Orch, Savonlinna Opera Festival Chorus Finlandia 2–▲ FIN 104 [AAD]
Sibelius, J.:Songs, w. G. Djupsjöbacka (pno)—27 songs [Fin,Sw] Ondine ▲ ODE 728–2 [DDD]

Auyanet, Yolanda (sop)
Falla, M. de:Songs, w. Jorge Romero (pno)—7 songs Kicco Classic ▲ 1595
Granados, E.:Songs, w. Jorge Romero (pno)—La Maja Dolorosa Kicco Classic ▲ 1595
Toldrá, E.:Songs, w. Jorge Romero (pno)—Marinereo en Tierra Kicco Classic ▲ 1595
Turina, J.:Songs, w. Jorge Romero (pno)—3 songs Kicco Classic ▲ 1595

Avdeyeva, Larissa (mez)
Shchedrin, R.:Dead Souls, w. Larisa Avdeyeva (mez—Korobochka), Galina Borisova (mez—Plyushkin), Alexi Maslennikov (ten—Selifan), Vladislav Piavko (ten—Nozdryov), Vitali Vlasov (ten—Manilov), Boris Morozov (bass—Sobakevich), Alexander Voroshilo (sgr—Chichikov), Y. Temirkanov (cnd), Bolshoi Theater Orch, Bolshoi Theater Chorus, Moscow Chamber Choir *(rec Moscow, 1982)*
Melodiya ("The Russian Opera" series) 2–▲ 74321-29347-2 [ADD]
Tchaikovsky, P.:Eugene Onegin, w. G. Vishnevskaya (sop), S. Lemeshev (ten), Belov (sgr), Petrov (sgr), B. Khaikin (cnd), Bolshoi Theater Orch, Bolshoi Theater Chorus [R] *(rec ca. early '60s for Melodi)*
Legato Classics 2–▲ LCD 163–2 (m) [ADD]

Averbach, David (ten)
Stuart, P.:Kill Bear Comes Home, w. Elana Gizzi (sop—Hasty Girl), Mi-Kyung Huh (sop—Cold Feet), Therese Murray (sop—Song Bird), Cherie Pfeil (sop—1st Sister), Renia Shukis (sop—2nd Sister), Riki Connaughton (mez—4th Sister), Lucy Fee (mez—3rd Sister), David Averbach (ten—Song Leader), Mark Schmidt (ten—Kill Bear), Jason Smith (bar—Cheif Wife Hunter), P. Stuart (cnd), Rochester Opera Theater Orch, Rochester Opera Theater Chorus VM ▲ DRK 154 [DDD]

Avery, Lawrence (ten)
Handel, G.F.:Judas Maccabaeus, w. Martina Arroyo (sop), Mary Davenport (mez), Jan Peerce (ten), David Smith (bar), T. Scherman (cnd), Vienna State Opera Orch, Vienna Academy Chorus
Vox Box 2–▲ CDX 5125 [ADD]

Avocat, Jean-Marc (sgr)
Mendelssohn, F.:Athalie, w. Danielle Borst (sop), Brigitte Desnoues (sop), Carolyn Watkinson (cta), Souad Natech (sgr), B. Tetu (cnd), Lorraine PO, Lyon National Chorus
Koch Schwann ▲ SCH 314282 [DDD]

Avolanti, Enrico (ten)
Puccini, G.:La Bohème, w. R. Tebaldi (sop), E. Ribetti (mez), G. Lauri Volpi (ten), T. Gobbi (bar), S. Meletti (bar), C. Badioli (bass), G. Neri (bass), G. Santini (cnd), *(orch unknown)* *(rec 1951)*
Great Opera Performances ▲ GOP 743

Ayars, Ann (sop)
Gluck, C.W.:Orfeo ed Euridice (sels), w. Z. Vlachopoulos (sop), K. Ferrier (cta), F. Stiedry (cnd), Southern PO, Glyndebourne Festival Chorus *(rec 1947)* Enterprise ("Palladio" series) ▲ ENTPD 4171 [ADD]

Ayers, Vanessa (mez)
Black Christmas:Sprituals in the African-American Tradition, w. Thomas Young (ten), Robert Mosley (bar), Dinard Smith (pno), Ronald Isaac (cnd) ESS.A.Y ▲ ESS 1011 [DDD]

Azeberger, Kurt (ten)
Bach, J.S.:Cant 201, w. Maria Cristina Kiehr (sop), Andreas Scholl (ct), James Taylor (ten), Roman Trekel (bar), Peter Lika (bass), R. Jacobs (cnd), Berlin Academy for Early Music, Berlin Chamber Chorus
Harmonia Mundi France 2–▲ HMC 901544.45

Azéma, Anne (sop)
Gilles, J.:Mess des morts, w. J. Nirouët (alt), W. Hite (ten), P. Mason (bar), J. Cohen (cnd), Boston Camerata, Ensemble de Tambours Provençaux, Aix-en-Provence Festival Chorus
Erato ▲ 2292–45989–2
Lo Gai Saber:Troubadours and Minstrels, 1100–1300, w. J. Cohen (cnd), Camerata Mediterranea, François Harismendy (voc), Jean-Luc Madier (voc), Cheryl Ann Fulton (hp), Joel Cohen (instr), Shira Kammen (instr) Erato ▲ 2292–45647–2 [DDD]
Machover, T.:Valis, w. J. Felty (mez), T. Edwards (ten), P. Mason (bar), T. Machover (elec), T. Machover (cnd), *(ensemble unknown)* [E] Bridge ▲ BCD 9007 [DDD] ■ BCS 7007 (D)
Tristan et Iseult:A Medieval Romance in Music & Poetry, w. Ellen Hargis (sop), Henri Ledroit (alt), William Hite (ten), Richard Morrison (bass), Andrea von Ramm (sgr), Boston Camerata [cnd:Joel Cohen]
Erato ▲ 98482–2
The Unicorn:Myth & Miracle in Medieval France (1200–1300), w. C. Ann Fulton (hps), Shira Kammen (rebec/vielle/hp), Jesse Lepkoff (fl) Erato ▲ 94380 [DDD]

▲ = CD ♦ = Enhanced CD Δ = MD ■ = Cassette Tape ▯ = DCC

Azesberger, Kurt (bar)

Schoenberg, A.:Die Jakobsleiter, w. Barbara Kilduff (sop—Seele 1), Jadwiga Rappé (cta—Sterbende), Wilfried Gahmlich (ten—Aufrührerischer), Cornelius Hauptmann (ten—Gabriel), Keith Lewis (ten—Berfener), Kurt Azesberger (bar—Mönch), Barbara Fuchs (sgr—Seele 2), Matteo de Monti (sgr—Ringender), Bjorn Waag (sgr—Auserwählter), E. Inbal (cnd), Frankfurt RSO, Robin Gritton (cnd), Berlin Radio Chorus *(rec Alte Oper, Frankfurt, Sept 6–9, 1994)* Denon ▲ CO 78977 [DDD]

Azesberger, Kurt (ten)

Mozart, W.A.:Dixit Dominus et Magnificat, w. E. Mei (sop), E. von Magnus (cta), G. Cachemaille (bass), N. Harnoncourt (cnd), Vienna Concentus Musicus, Arnold Schoenberg Choir Teldec ("Das alte Werke" series) ▲ 93025

Mozart, W.A.:Litaniae Lauretanae, K.109, w. Eva Mei (sop), Elisabeth von Magnus (alt), Gilles Cachemaille (bass), N. Harnoncourt (cnd), Vienna Concentus Musicus, Arnold Schoenberg Choir *(rec Casino Zögernitz, Vienna, Dec. 1992)* Teldec ("Das alte Werke" series) ▲ 96147-2 [DDD]

Mozart, W.A.:Missa brevis, K.275, w. E. Mei (sop), E. von Magnus (cta), G. Cachemaille (bass), N. Harnoncourt (cnd), Vienna Concentus Musicus, Arnold Schoenberg Choir Teldec ("Das alte Werke" series) ▲ 93025

Schmidt, F.:Das Buch mit sieben Siegeln, w. Gabriele Fontana (sop), Margareta Hintermeier (alt), Eberhard Büchner (ten—Johannes), Robert Holl (bass—Voice of the Lord), Robert Holzer (bass), Martin Haselböck (org), H. Stein (cnd), Vienna SO, Vienna Sym Chorus *(rec live, Vienna Music Hall, May 1996)* Calig 2-▲ CAL 50978/9 [DDD]

Schubert, Franz:Mass 1, w. Alexander Nader (sop), Thomas Puchegger (sop), Georg Leskovich (alto), Jörg Hering (ten), Harry van der Kamp (bass), Arno Hartmann (org), B. Weil (cnd), Orch of the Age of Enlightenment, Vienna Boys' Choir *(rec Vienna, Austria, Sept 1995)* Sony Classical ("Vivarte" series) ▲ SK 68247 [DDD]

Schubert, Franz:Mass 6, w. Benjamin Schmidinger (sop), Albin Lenzer (alt), Jörg Hering (ten), Harry van der Kamp (bass), B. Weil (cnd), Orch of the Age of Enlightenment, Vienna Boys' Choir Sony Classical ▲ SK 66255

Aznavour, Charles (sgr)

The Best of Christmas in Vienna, w. P. Domingo (ten), Vienna SO, José Carreras (ten), Sissel Kyrkjebø (sgr), Dionne Warwick (sgr) *(rec Vienna)* Sony Classical ▲ SK 62696 ■ ST 62696

Plácido Domingo:The Best of Christmas in Vienna, w. P. Domingo (ten), José Carreras (ten), Dionne Warwick (sgr), Charles Aznavour, Sissel Kyrkjebø, Vienna SO [cnd:Vjekoslav Šutej] Sony Classical ▲ SK 62696 ■ ST 62696

Azzimonti, Giovanni (bass)

Puccini, G.:Tosca, w. Carmen Melis (sop—Tosca), Nello Palai (ten—Spoletta), Piero Pauli (ten—Cavaradossi), Apollo Granforte (bar—Scarpia), Giovanni Azzimonti (bass—Angelotti/Sciarrone), Antonio Gelli (bass—Sagrestano), C. Sabajno (cnd), La Scala Orch, La Scala Chorus *(rec Nov 1929)* Arkadia 2-▲ CD 78002 (m) [ADD]

Puccini, G.:Tosca, w. C. Melis (sop—Tosca), P. Pauloi (ten—Cavarodossi), N. Palai (ten—Spoletta), A. Granforte (bar—Scarpia), G. Azzimonti (bass—Sciarrone/Angelotti), A. Gelli (bass—Sacristan), C. Sabajno (cnd), La Scala Orch, La Scala Chorus [I] *(rec Milan, Nov. 1929)* VAI Audio 2-▲ VAIA 1076-2 (m) [ADD]

Babacheva, Evgenia (mez)

Rimsky-Korsakov, N.:Golden Cockerel, w. Yavora Stoilova (sop—Golden Cockerel), Elena Stoyanova (sop—Queen), Evgenia Babacheva (mez—Amelfa), Lyubomir Bodourov (ten—Prince), Lyubomir Dyakovski (ten—Astrologer), Emil Ugrinov (bar—Afron), Nikolai Stoilov (bass—Tsar), Kosta Videv (bass—Polkan), D. Manolov (cnd), Sofia National Opera Orch, Sofia National Opera Chorus *(rec Sofia, 1985)* Capriccio 2-▲ 10760/61 [DDD]

Babatunde, O. (sgr)

Partch, H.:Revelation in the Courthouse Park, w. S. Costallos (sgr—Mom & Agave), C. Durham (ten—Sonny & Pentheus), M. Kimbrough (bar—Vendor & Herdsman), E. Earle (b-bar—Hobo & Tiresias), O. Babatunde (sgr—Dion & Dionysus), C. Roos (sgr—Mayor & Cadmus), O. Williams (sgr—Korypheus), R. Young (sgr—Cop & Guard), D. Mitchell (cnd), Partch Instrumentalists, marching band, *(chorus unknown)* [E] *(rec 10/87)* Tomato 2-▲ R2 70390 [DDD]

Babikian, Anatoli (bass)

Haydn, J.:The Seven Last Words of Christ on the Cross, w. Albert (sop), John Van Kesteren (ten), Otto Wiener (bar), H. Scherchen (cnd), Vienna State Opera Orch, Vienna State Opera Chorus [oratorio version] [G] *(rec 1962)* MCA Classics 2-▲ MCAD2-9816 [AAD]

Babikian, Virginia (sop)

Milhaud, D.:Choëphores, w. Vera Zorina (nar), Irene Jordan (sop), McHenry Boatwright (bar), L. Bernstein (cnd), New York PO, New York Schola Cantorum Sony Classical ("Masterworks Heritage" series) ▲ MHK 62352

Baccaloni, Salvatore (bar)

Rossini, G.:Il barbiere di Siviglia, w. Cesira Ferrari (mez—Berta), Mercedes Capsir (cta—Rosina), Dino Borgioli (ten—Count), Salvatore Baccaloni (bar—Bortolo), Aristide Baracchi (bar—Officer), Riccardo Stracciari (bar—Figaro), Vincenzo Bettoni (bass—Don Basilio), Attilo Bordonali (bass—Fiorello), L. Molajoli (cnd), La Scala Orch, La Scala Chorus *(rec 1930)* Arkadia ("The 78's" series) 2-▲ 78008 [ADD]

Baccaloni, Salvatore (bass)

Donizetti, G.:Lucia di Lammermoor, w. M. Capsir (sop—Lucia), E. de Muro Lomanto (ten—Sir Ravenswood), E. Venturini (ten—Lord Bucklaw), E. Molinari (bar—Lord Ashton), S. Baccaloni (bass—Bidebent), L. Molajoli (cnd), La Scala Orch, La Scala Chorus *(rec 1933)* Myto 2-▲ 2MCD 94299

Mozart, W.A.:Don Giovanni, w. I. Souez (sop), L. Helletsgrüber (sop), A. Mildmay (sop), K. von Pataky (ten), J. Brownlee (bar), R. Henderson (bar), T. Franklin (bar), F. Busch (cnd), Glyndebourne Festival Orch, Glyndebourne Festival Chorus [I] *(rec 1936, orig. issued by HMV)* Pearl 3-▲ PEAS 9369 (m) [AAD]

Mozart, W.A.:Nozze di Figaro, w. Bidu Sayao (sop—Susanna), Eleanor Steber (sop—Countess Almaviva), Jarmila Novotna (sop—Cherubino), Ira Petina (sop—Marcellina), John Brownlee (bar—Count Almaviva), Salvatore Baccaloni (bass—Bartolo), Ezio Pinza (bass—Figaro), B. Walter (cnd), *(orch unknown)* The Fourties 2-▲ ENT FT 1509

Puccini, G.:La Bohème, w. Luba Mirella (sop—Musetta), Rosetta Pampanini (sop—Mimì), Luigi Marini (ten—Rodolfo), Giuseppe Nessi (ten—Alcindoro), Aristide Baracchi (bar—Schaunard), Gino Vanelli (bar—Marcello), Salvatore Baccaloni (bass—Benoit), Tancredi Pasero (bass—Colline), L. Molajoli (cnd), La Scala Orch, La Scala Chorus Bongiovanni 2-▲ 1125/26 [ADD]

Puccini, G.:La Bohème, w. Rosina Torri (sop—Mimi), Thea Vitulli (sop—Musetta), Aristodemo Giorgini (ten—Rodolfo), Giuseppe Nessi (ten—Parpignol), Ernesto Badini (bar—Marcello), Aristide Baracchi (bar—Schaunard), Luigi Manfrini (bass—Colline), Salvatore Baccaloni (bass—Benoit/Alcindoro), C. Sabajno (cnd), La Scala Orch, La Scala Chorus *(rec 1928)* VAI Audio 2-▲ VAIA 1078-2

Puccini, G.:Madama Butterfly, w. R. Pampanini (sop), A. Granda (ten), G. Nessi (ten), G. Vanelli (bar), L. Malajoli (cnd), La Scala Orch, La Scala Chorus *(rec 1928)* Centaur 2-▲ CRC 2196/97

Puccini, G.:Madama Butterfly, w. Rosetta Pampanini (sop—Madama Butterfly), Conchita Velasquez (mez—Suzuki), Cesira Ferrari (mez—Kate Pinkerton), Alessandro Granda (ten—F. B. Pinkerton), Giuseppe Nessi (ten—Goro), Aristide Baracchi (bar—Il Principe Yamadori), Gino Vanelli (bar—Sharpless), Lino Bonardi (bass—Il Commissario Imperiale), Salvatore Baccaloni (bass—Lo zio Bonzo), L. Molajoli (cnd), La Scala Orch, La Scala Chorus Bongiovanni 2-▲ 1123/24 [ADD]

Rossini, G.:Il barbiere di Siviglia, w. Ira Petina (sop), Bidú Sayão (sop), John Brownlee (bar), Ezio Pinza (bass), Nino Martini (sgr), F. St. Leger (cnd), *(orch unknown)* *(rec Oct 4, 1943)* Enterprise ("The Fourties" series) 2-▲ ENT 307

Rossini, G.:Il barbiere di Siviglia, w. M. Capsir (sop), D. Borgioli (ten), R. Stracciari (bar), V. Bettoni (bass), L. Molajoli (cnd), La Scala Orch, La Scala Chorus *(rec 1929 for Columbia Records)* Music Memoria 2-▲ 30276/77

Verdi, G.:Aida, w. Giannina Arangi-Lombardi (sop—Aida), Maria Capuana (mez—Amneris), Aroldo Lindi (ten—Radames), Giuseppe Nessi (ten—Messenger), Armando Borgioli (bar—Amonasro), Salvatore Baccaloni (bass—King), Tancredi Pasero (bass—Ramfis), L. Molajoli (cnd), La Scala Orch, La Scala Chorus *(rec Nov 1928)* VAI Audio 2-▲ VAIA 1083-2

Baccaloni, Salvatore (bass) (cont.)

Verdi, G.:Falstaff, w. Pia Tassinari (sop—Alice Ford), Ines Alfani Tellini (sop—Nannetta), Aurora Buades (mez—Quickly), Rita Monticone (mez—Meg Page), Roberto D'Alessio (ten—Fenton), Giuseppe Nessi (ten—Bardolfo), Emilio Venturini (ten—Dr. Caius), Emilio Ghirardini (bar—Ford), Giacomo Rimini (bar—Sir John Falstaff), Salvatore Baccaloni (bass—Pistola), L. Molajoli (cnd), Milan SO, La Scala Chorus *(rec La Scala Theatre, Milan, Apr. 1932)* VAI Audio 2-▲ VAIA 1098-2

Verdi, G.:La forza del destino, w. Stella Roman (sop), Frederick Jagel (ten), Lawrence Tibbett (bar), Ezio Pinza (bass), B. Walter (cnd), New York Metropolitan Opera Orch *(rec live, Jan 23, 1943)* The Fourties 2-▲ ENT 1503

Verdi, G.:Rigoletto, w. Lina Pagliughi (sop—Gilda), Linda Brambilla (mez—Contessa di Ceprano), Vera de Cristoff (cta—Maddalena), Tino Folgar (ten—Duca di Mantova), Giuseppe Nessi (ten—Borsa), Aristide Baracchi (bar—Conte di Monterone/Marullo), Luigi Piazza (bar—Rigoletto), Salvatore Baccaloni (bass—Sparafucile), Giuseppe Menni (bass—Conte di Ceprano), C. Sabajno (cnd), La Scala Orch, La Scala Chorus *(rec 1927–28)* Arkadia 2-▲ CD 78003 (m) [ADD]

Verdi, G.:Rigoletto, w. Lina Pagliughi (sop—Gilda), Linda Brambilla (mez—Countess Ceprano), Vera De Cristoff (cta—Maddalena), Tino Folgar (ten—Duke of Mantua), Giuseppe Nessi (ten—Borsa), Luigi Piazza (bar—Rigoletto), Aristide Baracchi (b-bar—Monterone/Marullo), Salvatore Baccaloni (bass—Sparafucile), Giuseppe Menni (bass—Ceprano), C. Sabajno (cnd), La Scala Orch, La Scala Chorus *(rec La Scala Theatre, Milan, Nov.–Dec. 1927 & Feb. 192)* VAI Audio 2-▲ VAIA 1097-2

Verdi, G.:Rigoletto, w. Lina Pagliughi (sop), Luigi Piazza (sgr), Tino Folgar (sgr), C. Sabajno (cnd), La Scala Orch, La Scala Chorus Pearl 2-▲ PEA 9180 [ADD]

Bacchetta, L. (sop)

Scarlatti, A.:Abramo, il tuo sembiante, w. S. Piccolo (sop), M. Lazzara (alt), M. Nuvoli (ten), G. Dagnino (bass), E. Velardi (cnd), Alessandro Stradella Consort [period instrs] [I] Nuova Era ("Ancient Music" series) ▲ 7117 [DDD]

Bacelli, Monica (mez)

Mozart, W.A.:Nozze di Figaro, w. L. Cherici (sop), K. Mattila (sop), M. McLaughlin (sop), N. Curiel (mez), U. Benelli (ten), L. Gallo (bar), A. Nosotti (bass), M. Pertusi (bass), G. Tadeo (bass), Z. Mehta (cnd), Florence Maggio Musicale Orch, Florence Maggio Musicale Chorus Sony Classical ▲ SK 53286

Bacelli, Monica (sop)

Cherubini, L.:Il Giuocatore, w. Giorgio Gatti (bar), G. Bernasconi (cnd), Italian Instrumental Academy *(rec Parma, Mar 20–22, 1989)* Agorá Music ("Phoenix" series) ▲ 504

Mozart, W.A.:Così fan tutte, w. A. C. Antonacci (sop—Fiordiligi), M. Bacelli (sop—Dorabella), L. Cherici (sop—Despina), R. Decker (ten—Ferrando), A. Dohmen (bar—Gugliemo), S. Bruscantini (bar—Don Alfonso), G. Kuhn (cnd), Marchigiana PO, Marchigiana Phil Chorus [I] *(rec live, Teatro Lauro Rossi at the Festival di Macerata, Aug. 3, 1990)* Orfeo 3-▲ 243913 [DDD]

Mozart, W.A.:Finta giardiniera, w. E. Gruberova (sop), C. Margiono (sop), D. Upshaw (sop), U. Heilmann (ten), A. Scharinger (bass), N. Harnoncourt (cnd), Vienna Concentus Musicus Teldec 3-▲ 72309-2

Bach, Mechthild (mez)

Jommelli, N.:Didone abbandonata, w. Dorothea Röschmann (sop), Martina Borst (mez), William Kendall (ct), Daniel Taylor (ct), Arno Raunig (ten), F. Bernius (cnd), Stuttgart CO—Didone; Enea; Iarba; Selene; Araspe; Osmida Orfeo 3-▲ CD 381953 [DDD]

Bach, Mechthild (sop)

Durante, F.:Lamentationes Jeremiae Prophetae, w. Monika Frimmer (sop), Margarete Joswig (sgr), P. Neumann (cnd), Collegium Cartusianum, Cologne Chamber Choir CPO ▲ CPO 999325

Haydn, M.:Missa in honorem Sanctae Ursulae, w. Gabriele Binder (cta), Karl-Heinz Lampe (ten), Joachim Gebhardt (bass), H.R. Zöbeley (cnd), Munich Residenz Orch, Munich Motet Choir Calig ▲ CAL 50901 [DDD]

Mendelssohn, F.:Sym 2, w. S. Isokoski (sop), F. Lang (ten), C. Spering (cnd), Das Neue Orch, Cologne Chorus Musicus [period instrs] Opus 111 ▲ OPS 30-98

Orff, C.:Songs & Hymns, w. Gerd Rürk (ten), Michael Schopper (bar), Wolfgang Brunner (pno) Wergo ▲ WER 6279-2

Scarlatti, A.:Passion Oratorio, w. P. Geitner (sop), K. Wessel (alt), M. Schneider (cnd), La Stagione, Frankfurt Vocal Ensemble Capriccio 2-▲ CD 10 411/12

Bachleda, Andrzej (ten)

Chopin, F.:Songs Sop (comp), w. Stefania Woytowicz (sop), Wanda Klimowicz (pno) *(rec Warsaw, 1960)* Polskie Nagrania ▲ PNCD 315

Bäckelin, Gösta (ten)

Beethoven, L. van:Sym 9, "Choral Sym", w. H. Schymberg (sop), L. Tunell (cta), S. Björling (bar), W. Furtwängler (cnd), Stockholm Concert Society Orch *(rec Dec. 1, 1943)* Music & Arts ▲ CD 774 [AAD]

Orff, C.:Carmina burana, w. E. Söderström (sop), S. Svanholm (ten), H. Schmidt-Isserstedt (cnd), Stockholm PO, Stockholm Phil Chorus *(rec live, 11/26/54)* BIS 8-▲ CD 421/24 (m/s) [AAD]

Backes, Constanze (sop)

Monteverdi, C.:Incoronazione, w. Constanze Backes (sop—Valletto), Catherine Bott (sop—Drusilla/Pallade/La Virtù), Dana Hanchard (sop—Nerone), Sylvia McNair (sop—Poppea), Marinella Pennicchi (sop—Amore/Damigella), Annie Sofie von Otter (mez—Ottavia/Venere/La Fortuna), Julian Clarkson (alt—Littore/Mercurio), Bernarda Fink (cta—Arnalta), Roberto Balconi (ct—Nutrice), Michael Chance (ct—Ottone), Nigel Robson (ten—Liberto/Soldato Secondo), Mark Tucker (ten—Lucano/Soldato Primo), Francesco Ellero d'Artegna (bass—Seneca), J. E. Gardiner (cnd), English Baroque Soloists *(rec Queen Elizabeth Hall, South Bank Ctr, London, Dec 1993)* Archiv 3-▲ 447088-2

Mozart, W.A.:Zauberflöte, w. Constanze Backes (sop—Papagena), Christiane Oelze (sop—Pamina), Susan Roberts (sop—First Lady), Cyndia Sieden (sop—Queen of the Night), Carola Guber (cta—Second Lady), Maria Jonas (cta—Third Lady), Andreas Dieterich (trb—First Boy), Jan Andreas Mendel (trb—Second Boy), Florian Wöller (trb—Third Boy), Uwe Peper (ten—Monostatos), Nicolas Robertson (ten—First Man in Armor), Michael Schade (ten—Tamino), Gerald Finley (bar—Papageno), Noel Mann (bass—Second Man in Armour), Harry Peeters (bass—Sarastro), Detlef Roth (bass—Speaker/First Priest), Robert Burt (speaker—Third Priest), Robert Johnston (speaker—Second Priest), Wolfgang Knauer (speaker—Fourth Priest), Douglas Welbat (speaker—Second Priest), J. E. Gardiner (cnd), English Baroque Soloists, Monteverdi Choir London *(rec Forum am Schlosspark, Ludwigsburg, July 1995)* Archiv 2-▲ 449166-2

Telemann, G.P.:Cants, w. Mechthild Georg (mez), Klaus Mertens (bar), Andreas Post (sgr), L. Rémy (cnd), Telemann CO, Helko Siede (cnd), Michaelstein Chamber Choir—Christmas cantatas, "Siehe, ich verkündige Euch" (1761) & "Der Herr hat offenbaret" (1762) *(rec Apr 28–May 2, 1996)* CPO ▲ CPO 999419-2 [DDD]

Telemann, G.P.:Hirten an der Krippe zu Bethlehem, w. Mechthild Georg (mez), Klaus Mertens (bar), Andreas Post (sgr), L. Rémy (cnd), Telemann CO, Helko Siede (cnd), Michaelstein Chamber Choir *(rec Apr 28–May 2, 1996)* CPO ▲ CPO 999419-2 [DDD]

Bacon, Thomas (nar)

Plog, A.:Music of, w. Summit Brass, St. Louis Brass Quintet—Animal Ditties [poetry by Ogden Nash] for Narrator & Brass Ensemble (1989); Concerto for Trumpet, Brass Ensemble & Percussion (1989); Four Sketches for Brass Quintet (1989); Mini-Variations on Amazing Grace for Brass Ensemble (1987); Music for Brass Octet (1981) Summit ▲ DCD 116 [DDD]

Bacquier, Gabriel (b-bar)

Mozart, W.A.:Arias, w. R. Dunand (cnd), Collegium Academicum Orch—Der Schausspieldirektor; Airs de concert italiens pour basse; Grand airs d'opéras Gallo ▲ CD 816

Bacquier, Gabriel (bar)

Berlioz, H.:La Damnation de Faust, w. Janet Baker (mez), Nicolai Gedda (ten), G. Prêtre (cnd), Orch de Paris, Paris Opera Chorus EMI Classics 2-▲ CDFB 68583

Charpentier, G.:Louise, w. I. Cotrubas (sop), J. Berbié (mez), P. Domingo (ten), M. Sénéchal (ten), G. Prêtre (cnd), New Philharmonia Orch, Ambrosian Opera Chorus [F] Sony Classical 3-▲ S3K 46429 [ADD]

Debussy, C.:Pelléas et Mélisande, w. A. Martino (soprano), A. Reynolds (mez), T. Rovetta (bar), N. Zaccaria (bass), L. Maazel (cnd), *(orch unknown)* *(rec 1969* Great Opera Performances 3-▲ GOP 711

Delibes, L.:Lakmé, w. J. Sutherland (sop), A. Vanzo (ten), R. Bonynge (cnd), Monte Carlo Opera Orch [F] London 2-▲ 425485-2 [ADD]

Bacquier, Gabriel (bar) (cont.)
Donizetti, G.:Don Pasquale, w. B. Hendricks (sop), L. Canonici (ten), L. Quilico (bar), R. Schirrer (bar), G. Ferro (cnd), Paris Lyon Opera Orch, Paris Lyon Opera Chorus [I] Erato 2-▲ 2292-45487-2-ZA [DDD]
Donizetti, G.:La favorita, w. F. Cossotto (mez), L. Pavarotti (ten), N. Ghiaurov (bass), R. Bonynge (cnd), Bologna Teatro Comunale Orch, Bologna Teatro Comunale Chorus London 3-▲ 430038-2 [ADD]
Enescu, G.:Oedipe, w. B. Hendricks (sop), B. Fassbaender (mez), M. Lipovšek (mez), J. Taillon (mez), N. Gedda (ten), J. Aler (ten), Quilico (bar), J. Van Dam (bass-bar), L. Foster (cnd), Monte Carlo PO, Orféon Donostiarra, Petits Chanteurs de Monaco [F] EMI Classics 2-▲ CDCB 54011 [DDD]
Gounod, C.:Roméo et Juliette, w. C. Malfitano (sop), A. Kraus (ten), L. Quilico (bar), J. Van Dam (b-bar), M. Plasson (cnd), Toulouse Capitole Orch, Toulouse Capitole Chorus [F] EMI Classics 3-▲ CDCC 47365
Massenet, J.:Don Quichotte, w. R. Crespin (sop), M. Command (sop), N. Ghiaurov (bass), R. Bonynge (cnd), Swiss Romande Orch, Swiss Romande Chorus [F] London ("Grand Opera" series) 2-▲ 430636-2 [AAD]
Massenet, J.:Manon, w. B. Sills (sop), N. Gedda (ten), G. Souzay (bar), J. Rudel (cnd), New Philharmonia Orch, Ambrosian Opera Chorus [F] EMI Classics ("Studio" series) 3-▲ CDMC 69831 [ADD]
Massenet, J.:Werther, w. Mady Mesplé (sop—Sophie), Rita Gorr (mez—Charlotte), Robert Andreozzi (ten—Schmidt), Albert Lance (ten—Werther), Gabriel Bacquier (bar—Albert), Julien Giovannetti (bar—Le Bailli), Jacques Mars (bar—Johann), J. Etcheverry (cnd), *(orch unknown)* Adès 2-▲ ADE 140832 [AAD]
Meyerbeer, G.:Les Huguenots, w. J. Sutherland (sop), M. Arroyo (sop), H. Tourangeau (mez), A. Vrenios (ten), D. Cossa (bar), N. Ghiuselev (bass), R. Bonynge (cnd), New Philharmonia Orch, Ambrosian Opera Chorus London ("Grand Opera" series) 4-▲ 430549-2 [AAD]
Mozart, W.A.:Don Giovanni, w. L. Price (sop), L. Popp (sop), S. Sass (sop), S. Burrows (ten), B. Weikl (bar), A. Sramek (bar), K. Moll (bass), G. Solti (cnd), London PO, London Opera Chorus London ("Grand Opera" series) 3-▲ 425169-2 [ADD]
Mozart, W.A.:Nozze di Figaro (sels), w. R. Pütz (sop), T. Stich-Randall (mez), T. Berganza (mez), A.-R. Johnson (ten), F. Corena (bass), H. Wallberg (cnd), Swiss Romande Orch, Swiss Romande Chorus—Act IV Melodram 2-▲ CDM 27094 [ADD]
Offenbach, J.:Les Contes d'Hoffmann, w. J. Sutherland (sop), H. Tourangeau (mez), P. Domingo (ten), H. Cuénod (ten), R. Bonynge (cnd), Swiss Romande Orch London 2-▲ 417363-2 [ADD]
Offenbach, J.:Les Contes d'Hoffmann, w. H. Harper (sop), Bakocevic (sgr), M. Mesplé (sop), S. Kónya (ten), P. Maag (cnd), Buenos Aires Teatro Colón Orch, Buenos Aires Teatro Colón Chorus [F] *(rec live, Buenos Aires 8/3/70)* Melodram 2-▲ MEL 27090 [ADD]
Offenbach, J.:Les Contes d'Hoffmann, w. E. Gruberova (sop), C. Eder (mez), P. Domingo (ten), M. Sénéchal (ten), Schmidt (sgr), J. Morris (bass), J. Diaz (bass), S. Ozawa (cnd), French National Orch, French Radio Chorus [F] Deutsche Grammophon 2-▲ 427682-2 [DDD]
Offenbach, J.:Les Contes d'Hoffmann (sels), w. Andréa Guiot (sop—Antonia), Mady Mesplé (sop—Olympia), Suzanne Sarroca (sop—Giulietta), Albert Lance (ten—Hoffmann), Gabriel Bacquier (bar—Docteur Miracle), Robert Massard (bar—Dapertutto), J. Etcheverry (cnd), *(orch unknown)* —Prologue; Dans les rôles d'amoureux...; Il était une fois...; Allons! Courage et confiance...; C'est moi, coppélius!...; Les oiseaux dans la charmille; Barcarolle; Scintille, diamant...; Malheureux, tu ne comprends donc pas...; Hélas! Mon coeur s'égare encore...; Elle a fui, la tourterelle...; Eh bien! Quoi! Toujours en colère!...; Tu ne chanteras plus?... Adès ▲ ADE 202702 [AAD]
Prokofiev, S.:The Love for 3 Oranges (suite), w. C. Dubosc (sop), G. Gautier (ten), J.-L. Viala (ten), J. Bastin (bass), K. Nagano (cnd), Paris Lyon Opera Orch, Paris Lyon Opera Chorus [F] Virgin Classics ▲ 59566 [DDD]
Rossini, G.:Guillaume Tell, w. M. Caballé (sop), M. Mesplé (sop), C. Burles (ten), N. Gedda (ten), G. Howell (bass), L. Gardelli (cnd), Royal PO, Ambrosian Opera Chorus EMI Classics 4-▲ CDMD 69951
Varney, L.:Les Mousquetaires au couvent, w. Gabrielle Ristori (mez), Camille Rouquetty (ten), Louis Musy (b-bar), Pierre Blanc (sgr), Pauline Carton (sgr), Jacqueline Cauchard (sgr), Mireille Lacoste (sgr), Colette Riedinger (sgr), R. Benedetti (cnd) Musidisc 2-▲ MUS 202262 [AAD]

Baddeley, John (nar)
Lumsdaine, D.:Aria for Edward John Eyre, w. J. Manning (sop), J. Rye (nar), E. Howarth (cnd), Gemini Ensemble NM Classics ▲ NMCD 007 [DDD]

Badin, A. (ten)
Bach, J.S.:Cant 171, w. A. Augér (sop), J. Hamari (cta), W. Heldwein (bass), H. Rilling (cnd), Württemberg CO, Gächinger Kantorei [G] Hänssler Classic ▲ 98.871 [AAD]

Badini, Ernesto (bar)
Donizetti, G.:Don Pasquale, w. Adelaide Saraceni (sop), Tito Schipa (ten), Afro Poli (bar), C. Sabajno (cnd), La Scala Orch, La Scala Chorus *(rec 1932)* Grammofono 2000 2-▲ GRM 78561 (m)
Fernando de Lucia, w. F. de Lucia (ten), Antonio Pini-Corsi (bar), Josefina Huguet (sop), Maria Galvany (sop), Celestina Boninsegna (sop) Symposium ▲ SYM 1149
Leoncavallo, R.:Pagliacci, w. Josefina Huguet (sop—Nedda), Antonio Paoli (ten), Gaetano Pini-Corsi (ten—Beppe), Ernesto Badini (bar—Silvio), Francesco Cigada (bar—Tonio), Giuseppe Rosci (sgr—Un contadino), C. Sabajno (cnd), La Scala Orch, La Scala Chorus *(rec 1907)* Bongiovanni ▲ GB 1120-2 [ADD]
Puccini, G.:La Bohème, w. R. Torri (sop), T. Vitulli (sop), A. Giorgini (ten), L. Manfrini (bass), C. Sabajno (cnd), La Scala Orch [I] *(rec 1927)* InSync 2-■ C 4131/2 (m)
Puccini, G.:La Bohème, w. Rosina Torri (sop—Mimi), Thea Vitulli (sop—Musetta), Aristodemo Giorgini (ten—Rodolfo), Giuseppe Nessi (ten—Parpignol), Ernesto Badini (bar—Marcello), Aristide Baracchi (bar—Schaunard), Luigi Manfrini (bass—Colline), Salvatore Baccaloni (bass—Benoit/Alcindoro), C. Sabajno (cnd), La Scala Orch, La Scala Chorus *(rec 1928)* VAI Audio 2-▲ VAIA 1078-2

Badioli, Carlo (bass)
Massenet, J.:Don Quichotte, w. Teresa Berganza (mez), Pina Malgarini (mez), Tommaso Frascati (ten), Boris Christoff (bass), A. Simonetto (cnd), Milan RAI SO, Milan RAI Chorus Melodram 2-▲ CDM 27027
Puccini, G.:La Bohème, w. R. Tebaldi (sop), E. Ribetti (mez), E. Avolanti (ten), G. Lauri Volpi (ten), T. Gobbi (bar), S. Meletti (bar), G. Neri (bass), G. Santini (cnd), *(orch unknown)* *(rec 1951)* Great Opera Performances ▲ GOP 743
Puccini, G.:Tosca, w. Renata Tebaldi (sop—Floria Tosca), Guiseppe di Stefano (ten—Mario Cavardossi), Rinaldo Pelizzoni (ten—Spoletta), Ettore Bastianini (bar—Baron Scarpia), Carlo Badioli (bass—Sacristan), Guiseppe Moresi (bass—Sciarrone), Franco Piva (bass—Jailer), Nicola Zaccaria (bass—Cesare Angelotti), G. Gavazzeni (cnd) *(rec Great Auditorium, Brussels World Fair, 1958)* Legato Classics 2-▲ LCD 2092 [ADD]
Rossini, G.:Il barbiere di Siviglia, w. R. Broilo (sop—Berta), G. Simionato (mez—Rosina), L. Infantino (ten—Almaviva), G. Taddei (bar—Figaro), C. Badioli (bass—Bartolo), A. Cassinelli (bass—Basilio), F. Previtali (cnd), Milan RAI SO, Milan RAI Chorus *(rec 1950)* Cetra Classic 2-▲ CDO 6 [AAD]
Rossini, G.:Il barbiere di Siviglia, w. Fiorenza Cossotto (mez), Luigi Alva (ten), Sesto Bruscantini (bar), Nicolai Ghiaurov (bass), G. Santini (cnd), La Scala Orch, La Scala Chorus *(rec Jan 20, 1964)* Pantheon 2-▲ PHE 6644 (m)
Rossini, G.:Il barbiere di Siviglia (sels), w. R. Scotto (sop), A. di Stasio (mez), A. Kraus (ten), A. Protti (bar), E. Campi (bass), V. Bellezza (cnd), Naples Teatro San Carlo Orch, Naples Teatro San Carlo Chorus *(rec July 26, 1958)* Golden Age of Opera 2-▲ GAO 137/38 [ADD]

Badoer, Paolo (sgr)
Donizetti, G.:Roberto Devereux, w. Montserrat Caballé (sop), Beverly Wolff (mez), Guido Fabbris (ten), Gianni Raimondi (ten), Walter Alberti (bar), Carlo Micalucci (sgr), Carlo Padoan (sgr), B. Bartoletti (cnd), Venice Teatro La Fenice Orch, Venice Teatro La Fenice Chorus Great Opera Performances 2-▲ GOP 764

Baggiore, Elena (sgr)
Cherubini, L.:Médée, w. M. Olivero (sop), L. Ganbelli (bass), A. Lo Forese (sgr), N. Rescigno (cnd), Mantova Teatro Sociale Orch, Mantova Teatro Sociale Chorus [I] *(rec live, Mantova 1/23/71)* Myto 2-▲ 2 MCD 91136 [ADD]
Giordano, U.:Fedora (sels), w. Magda Olivero (sop), Giuseppe Giacomini (ten), Franco Piva (ten), M. Braggio (cnd), *(orch unknown)*—Amor ti vieta; Loris Ipanoff, oggi la Zar; Muta è mia madre, muto il fratello *(rec Piacenza, Jan. 9, 1972)* Golden Age of Opera 2-▲ GAO 189/90 [ADD]

Baglioni, Bruna (mez)
Janácek, L.:Jenůfa, w. Magda Olivero (sop—Kostelnicka), Bruna Baglioni (mez—La vecchia Buryja), Grace Bumbry (mez—Jenufa), Renato Cioni (ten—Steva Buryja), Robleto Merolla (bar—Laca Klemen), Carlo Meliciani (sgr—Vecchio compagno), J. Semkow (cnd), La Scala Orch, La Scala Chorus *(rec Milan, Apr 2, 1974)* Myto 2-▲ MCD 961142

Bagnoli, Lucia (alt)
Perti, G.A.:Liturgy for Good Friday, w. Patrizia Vaccari (sop), Maura Pederzoli (sop), Cristina Calzolari (sop), Alida Oliva (sop), Claudia Bugli (sop), Cinzia Meneghel (alt), Renzo Bez (alt), Alessandro Carmignani (alt), Michel van Goethem (alt), Mauro Collina (ten), Vincenzo Di Donato (ten), Paolo Fanciullacci (ten), Giovanni Caccamo (ten), Paolo Da Col (ten), Sergio Foresti (bass), Marco Scavazza (bass), Luca Ferracin (bass), Paride Montanari (bass), Liuwe Tamminga (org), Sergio Vartolo (org), S. Vartolo (cnd), Bologna San Petronio Capella Musicale Orch—Omnes amici mei; De lamentatione Jeremiae Prophetae:Heth. Cogitavit; Velum templi; Vinea mea; De lamentatione Jeremiae Prophetae:Lamed. Matribus suis; Tamquam ad latronem; Tenebrae factae sunt; Animam meam; Tradiderunt me; Jesum tradidit; De lamentatione Jeremiae Prophetae:Aleph. Ego vir; Caligaverunt *(rec St. Petronio Basilica, Bologna, Mar 28-31, 1995)* Naxos ▲ 8.553321 [DDD]

Bahl, Rose (alt)
Schubert, Franz:Mass 1, w. Laurence Dutoit (sop), Kurt Equiluz (ten), Kunikazu Ohashi (bass), Xaver Mayer (org), G. Barati (cnd), Vienna State Opera Orch, Vienna Academy Chamber Choir *(rec 1960)* Tuxedo ▲ TUXCD 1040 [ADD]
Schubert, Franz:Mass 4, w. Laurence Dutoit (sop), Kurt Equiluz (ten), Kunikazu Ohashi (bass), Xaver Mayer (org), G. Barati (cnd), Vienna State Opera Orch, Vienna Academy Chamber Choir *(rec 1960)* Tuxedo ▲ TUXCD 1040 [ADD]

Bahl, Rose (cta)
Haydn, J.:Mass 6, "Nikolai-messe", "6/4-Takt-Messe", w. Elisabeth Thoman (sop), Kurt Equiluz (ten), G. Barati (cnd), Vienna State Opera Orch, Vienna Academy Chamber Choir *(rec 1964)* Tuxedo ▲ TUXCD 1055 [ADD]
Haydn, J.:Mass 14, "Harmoniemesse", w. Christiane Sorell (sop), Elisabeth Thoman (sop), Maura Moreira (cta), Kurt Equiluz (ten), Gerhard Eder (bass), P. Wimburger (bass), G. Barati (cnd), Vienna State Opera Orch, Vienna Academy Chamber Choir *(rec 1964)* Tuxedo ▲ TUXCD 1055 [ADD]

Baiano, Valeria (bass)
Pergolesi, G.B.:Il flaminio, w. D. Dessi (sop—Flaminio), F. Pediconi (sop—Agata), E. Zilio (mez—Giustina), M. Ferrugia (ten—Fernando), G. Sica (ten—Polidoro), S. Pagliuca (bass—Bastiano), M. Panni (cnd), Naples Teatro San Carlo Orch *(rec Nov. 12, 1983)* Fonit Cetra 3-▲ CDC 39 [ADD]
Rossini, G.:La cambiale di matrimonio, w. Alessandra Rossi (sop), Maurizio Comencini (ten), Bruno Praticò (bar), Bruno De Simone (bar), Francesco Facini (bass), M. Viotti (cnd), English CO Claves ▲ 50-9101

Baier, Barbara (sop)
Hoffmann, E.T.A.:Undine, w. Barbara Baier (sop—Berthalda), Heidrun Plesch (sop—Undine), Corinna Tippe (sop—Die Herzogin), Maria Hiefinger (mez—Fisherman's Wife), Achim Schamberger (ten—Der Herzog), Johannes Beck (bar—Ritter Huldbrand von Ringstetten), Michael Albert (bass—Fisherman), Ulrich Bosch (bass—Heilmann), Bernd Hofmann (bass—Kühleborn), H. Dechant (cnd), Bamberg Youth Orch Bayer 3-▲ 100256/58 [DDD]

Bailey, Norman (bar)
Britten, H.:A Midsummer Night's Dream, w. J. Gomez (sop), D. Jones (sop), J. Bowman (ct), H. Herford (bar), R. Hickox (cnd), City of London Sinfonia Virgin Classics ▲ CDCB 59305
Tippett, M.:King Priam, w. Heather Harper (sop—Hecuba), Linda Hirst (sop—Serving Woman), Felicity Palmer (sop—Andromache), Julian Saipe (sop—Paris), Yvonne Minton (mez—Helen), Ann Murray (mez—Nurse), Kenneth Bowen (ten—Hermes), Peter Hall (ten—Young Guard), Philip Langridge (ten—Paris), Robert Tear (ten—Achilles), Thomas Allen (bar—Hector), Norman Bailey (bar—Priam), Stephen Roberts (bar—Patroclus), David Wilson-Johnson (bar—Old Man), D. Atherton (cnd), London Sinfonietta, London Sinfonietta Chorus Chandos ▲ CHAN 9406/7 [DDD]
Wagner, R.:Der fliegende Holländer, w. Martin (sop), A. Kollo (ten), M. Talvela (bass), G. Solti (cnd), Chicago SO, Chicago Sym Chorus [G] London 2-▲ 414551-2 [ADD]
Wagner, R.:Der fliegende Holländer (sels), w. S. Jurinac (sop), A. Van Mill (bass), F. Adam (cnd), Strasbourg Opera Orch, Strasbourg Opera Chorus—Senta's ballad (Jo-ho-hoe!...Traft ihr das Schiff) & Willst Du des Vaters Wahl [G] *(rec live, Strasbourg, 11/25/69)* Melodram 3-▲ CDM 37091 [ADD]
Wagner, R.:Götterdämmerung (sels), w. M. Curphey (sop), R. Hunter (sop), A. Remedios (ten), C. Grant (bass), R. Goodall (cnd), Sadler's Wells Opera Orch, Sadler's Wells Opera Chorus—Act 3, Scenes 2 & 3 [E] Chandos ("Collect" series) ▲ CHAN 6593 [ADD]
Wagner, R.:Die Meistersinger von Nürnberg, w. H. Bode (sop), J. Hamari (cta), A. Kollo (ten), B. Weikl (bar), K. Moll (bass), G. Solti (cnd), Vienna PO, Vienna State Opera Chorus [G] London 4-▲ 417497-2 [ADD]

Baileys, B. (mez)
Mendelssohn, F.:St. Paul, w. R. Yakar (sop), M. Schäfer (ten), T. Hampson (bar), M. Corboz (cnd), Lisbon Gulbenkian Foundation Orch, Lisbon Gulbenkian Foundation Chorus Erato 2-▲ 45279-2

Baillie, Isobel (sop)
The Art of Kathleen Ferrier, w. K. Ferrier (cta), Gerald Moore (pno), Netherlands Opera Orch [cnd:Charles Bruck] EMI Classics ("Great Recordings of the Century" series) ▲ CDH 61003 (m)
Dame Isobel Baillie, w. various orchs & pno accompaniment *(rec 1927-1941)* Pearl ▲ PEA 9934 (m) [AAD]
Mendelssohn, F.:Elijah, w. Gladys Ripley (cta), James Johnston (ten), Harold Williams (b-bar), M. Sargent (cnd), Liverpool PO, Huddersfield Choral Society Dutton Laboratories 2-▲ DUT 2004 [ADD]
The Unforgettable Isobel Baillie Dutton Laboratories ▲ DUT 7013 [ADD]
Vaughan Williams, R.:Serenade to Music, w. E. Suddaby (sop), S. Allen (sop), E. Turner (sop), M. Balfour (cta), A. Desmond (cta), M. Brunskill (cta), M. Jarred (cta), H. Nash (ten), W. Widdop (ten), P. Jones (ten), F. Titterton (ten), R. Henderson (bass), R. Easton (bass), H. Williams (bass), N. Allin (bass), H. J. Wood (cnd), BBC SO Dutton Laboratories ▲ CDAX 8004 [ADD]
Vaughan Williams, R.:Serenade to Music, w. E. Suddaby (sop), S. Allen (sop), E. Turner (sop), M. Balfour (cta), A. Desmond (cta), M. Brunskill (cta), M. Jarred (cta), H. Nash (ten), W. Widdop (ten), P. Jones (ten), F. Titterton (ten), R. Henderson (bass), R. Easton (bass), H. Williams (bass), N. Allin (bass), H. Wood (cnd), BBC SO [E] *(rec 10/15/38)* Pearl ▲ GEMMCD 9342 (m) [AAD]
Vaughan Williams, R.:Serenade to Music, w. Lilian Stiles-Allen (sop), Elsie Suddaby (sop), Eva Turner (sop), Margaret Balfour (cta), Muriel Brunskill (cta), Astra Desmond (cta), Mary Jarred (cta), Parry Jones (ten), Heddle Nash (ten), Frank Titterton (ten), Walter Widdop (ten), Roy Henderson (bar), Harold Williams (bar), Norman Allin (bass), Robert Easton (bass), H. Wood (cnd), BBC SO *(rec Abbey Road, Oct 15, 1938)* Claremont ▲ CDGSE 785066

Baillie, Peter (ten)
Mozart, W.A.:Missa, K.66, w. P. Wise (sop), M. Aoyama (cta), H. Müller (bass), E. Hinreiner (cnd), Salzburg Camerata Academica, Salzburg RSO, Mozart Choir [L] *(rec May 1974)* Koch Treasure ▲ 316182 [ADD]

Bainbridge, Elizabeth (mez)
Herrmann, B.:Wuthering Heights, w. M. Beaton (sop—Catherine), P. Bowden (mez—Isabella), E. Bainbridge (mez—Nelly), M. Snashall (trb—Hareton), D. Bell (bar—Heathcliff), J. Kitchiner (bar—Hindley), J. Ward (bar—Edgar), M. Rippon (bass—Joseph), D. Kelly (bass—Mr. Lockwood), B. Herrmann (cnd), Pro Arte Orch *(rec 1965-66)* Unicorn-Kanchana 3-▲ UKCD 2050/51/52 [ADD]
Janácek, L.:The Cunning Little Vixen, w. L. Watson (sop), G. Knight (mez), D. Montague (mez), J. Dobson (ten), R. Tear (ten), T. Allen (bar), G. Howell (bass), S. Rattle (cnd), Royal Opera House Orch [E] EMI Classics 2-▲ CDCB 54212
Mozart, W.A.:Kyrie, K.341, w. K. Te Kanawa (sop), A. Davies (ten), G. Howell (bass), C. Davis (cnd), London SO, London Sym Chorus [L] Philips ▲ 412873-2
Mozart, W.A.:Vesperae solennes, w. K. Te Kanawa (sop), A. Davies (ten), G. Howell (bass), C. Davis (cnd), London SO, London Sym Chorus [L] Philips ▲ 412873-2 [ADD]
Tippett, M.:The Midsummer Marriage, w. Joan Carlyle (sop—Joan), Elizabeth Harwood (sop—Beth), Helen Watts (cta—Sosostris), Stuart Burrows (ten—Jack), Alberto Remedios (ten—Mark), Stafford Dean (bass), Raimund Herincx (bass—King Fisher), C. Davis (cnd), Royal Opera House Orch, Royal Opera House Chorus Covent Garden Lyrita 2-▲ SRCD 2217

Bainbridge, Elizabeth (mez) (cont.)
Verdi, G.:Un ballo in maschera, w. Reri Grist (sop), Katia Ricciarelli (sop), Plácido Domingo (ten), Piero Cappuccilli (bar), C. Abbado (cnd), Royal Opera House Orch, Royal Opera House Chorus Covent Garden *(rec 1975)* Arkadia 2-▲ 488
Verdi, G.:La traviata (sels), w. Ileana Cotrubas (sop—Violetta), Elizabeth Bainbridge (mez—Annina), José Carreras (ten—Alfredo), Richard Creeger (ten—Gastone), Victor Braun (bar—Germont), Richard Van Allen (bass—Grenvil), J. Pritchard (cnd), *(orch unknown)*—Libiamo ne' lietialici; Oh, qual pallor!...Un di felice; Ebben? Che diavol fate?...Amor, dunque non piu; E strano!...Ah, fors'e lui; Follie! Follie!...Sempre libera; Lunge da lei...De' miei bollenti spiriti; Che fai?...Amami, Alfredo; Invitato a qui seguirmi...Ogni suo aver tal femmina; Signora...Parigi, o cara; Ah, non piu...Ah, gran Dio, morir si giovine; E strano! Cessarono gli spasimi del dolore *(rec Apr 15, 1974)* Legato Classics 2-▲ LCD 201-2

Baird, Julianne (sop)
Bach, J.S.:Cant 8, w. S. Rickards (alt), J. Thomas (ten), J. Weaver (bass), J. Thomas (cnd), American Bach Soloists [G] Koch International Classics ▲ KIC 7163-2 [DDD]
Bach, J.S.:Cant 51, w. J. Thomas (cnd), American Bach Soloists [G] *(rec Apr & Oct 1990)* Koch International Classics ▲ KIC 7138-2 [DDD]
Bach, J.S.:Magnificat, BWV 243, w. Lorie Gratis (mez), David Price (ten), Kevin Deas (bass-bar), Bronwyn Fix-Keller (hpd), V. Radu (cnd), Ama Deus Ensemble Vox Classics ▲ VOX 7531
Bach, J.S.:Magnificat, BWV 243, w. J. Bryden (sop), J Gall (ct), F. Hoffmeister (ten), J. Opalach (bass), J. Rifkin (cnd), Bach Ensemble [L] Pro Arte ▲ CDD 185 [DDD]
Bach, J.S.:Mass in b, BWV 232, w. J. Nelson (sop), J. Dooley (ct), F. Hoffmeister (ten), J. Opalach (bass), J. Rifkin (cnd), Bach Ensemble [L] Elektra/Nonesuch 2-▲ 79036-2 [DDD] 2-■ 79036-4 (D)
Bach, J.S.:Mass in b, BWV 232, w. J. Nelson (sop), N. Zylstra, J. Lane, Z. Muñoz, S. Rickards, P. Romano, W. Sharp, J. Weaver (bass), J. Thomas (cnd), American Bach Soloists Koch International Classics 2-▲ KIC 7194-2 [DDD]
Bach, J.S.:St. John Passion, w. J. Bryden (sop), J. Thomas (ten), D. Ripley (bar), J. Weaver (bass), K. Slowik (cnd), Smithsonian Chamber Players, Smithsonian Chamber Chorus [period instrs] [G] *(Slowik performs the original 1724 version, & includes the two choruses & three arias added to Bach's 1725 revision as appended tracks at the end of the discs, allowing the listener to either ignore the end tracks & hear the standard version or program the discs to play the 1725 sequence)* Smithsonian Collection 5-▲ ND 0380 [DDD]
A Baroque Christmas from the Metropolitan Museum of Art Concerts, w. Aulos Ensemble MusicMasters ▲ 01612-67119-2 ■ 01612-67119-4
Bartók, B.:Music of, w. Croft Consort, Boston Univ Women's Chorus—various works based upon Rumanian, Ruthenian, Bulgarian & Hungarian folksongs, lullabies, & dances Albany ▲ TROY 046 [DDD]
Clérambault, L.N.:Cants, w. Music's Re-Creation—Léandre et Héro; Orphée; Zephire et Flore [F] Meridian ▲ CDE 84182
The English Lute Song, w. Ronn McFarlane (lt) Dorian ▲ DOR 90109 [DDD]
Falla, M. de:El retablo de maese Pedro, w. Lourdes Ambriz (sop), Miguel Cortez (ten), William Alvarado (bar), Rafael Puyana (hpd), E. Mata (cnd), Mexican Soloists *(rec Sala Nezahualcóyotl, Universidad Nacional Autónoma de Mexico, Mexico City, Oct. 1994)* Dorian ▲ DOR 90214 [DDD]
Foster, S.C.:Songs, w. L. Russell (alt/mountain dulcimer), F. Urrey (ten), J. Van Buskirk (pno), R. Enslow (fid)—The Glendy Burke; Nelly Was a Lady; Melinda May; The Soirée Polka; The Moustache Song; O Willie, Is It You, Dear?; Mr. & Mr Albany ▲ TROY 119
Greensleeves:A Collection of English Lute Songs, w. Ronn McFarlane (lts) Dorian ▲ DOR 90126 [DDD]
Handel, G.F.:Acis & Galatea, w. L. Hirst (mez), S. Oosting (ten), J. Ostendorf (b-bar), J. Somary (cnd), Amor Artis Orch, Amor Artis Chorale [E] Newport Classic 2-▲ NC 60045 [DDD]
Handel, G.F.:Arias, Philomel Baroque CO—"Tra le fiamme", "Pensieri notturni di Filli," "Alpestre monte" Dorian ▲ DOR 90147 [DDD]
Handel, G.F.:Arias, w. R. Palmer (cnd), Brewer CO—Oh had I Jubal's Lyre [from *Joshua]; O Sleep why dost thou leave me [from Semele]*; Falsa immagine [from *Ottone]*; Lascia ch'io pianga [from *Rinaldo]*; Dopo notte [from *Ariodante]* Newport Classic ▲ NPD 85568
Handel, G.F.:Berenice, w. Julianne Baird (sop—Berenice), Andrea Matthews (sop—Alessandro), D'Anna Fortunato (mez—Selene), Jennifer Lane (mez—Demetrio), Drew Minter (alt—Arsace), John McMaster (ten—Fabio), Jan Opalach (bass—Aristobolo), R. Palmer (cnd), Brewer CO Newport Classic 3-▲ NPD 85620/3 [DDD]
Handel, G.F.:Cants, w. J. Dornenburg (vl), M. Proud (hpd)—Occhi miei, che faceste?; Quel fior che all'alba ride; Solitudini care, amata liberata; Udite il mil consiglio [I] *(rec 6/90)* Meridian ▲ CDE 84189
Handel, G.F.:Cants, Philomel Baroque CO—3 Italian Cantatas—"Tra le fiamme"; "Nel dolce dell'oblio"; Alpestre monte" [I] Dorian ▲ DOR 90147 [DDD]
Handel, G.F.:Ezio, w. Julianne Baird (sop—Fulvia), Jennifer Lane (mez—Onoria), D'Anna Fortunato (cta—Ezio), Raymond Pellerin (alt—Emperor), Frederick Urrey (ten—Massimo), Nathaniel Watson (bar—Varo), Johannes Somary (org), R.A. Clark (cnd), Manhattan CO *(rec St. Jean Baptiste Church, New York, Mar. 1994)* Vox Classics 2-▲ VOX 27503 [DDD]
Handel, G.F.:Faramondo, w. Julianne Baird (sop—Clotilde), Mary Ellen Callahan (sop—Adolfo), D'Anna Fortunado (mez—Faramondo), Jennifer Lane (mez—Rosimonda), Drew Minter (alt—Gernando), Peter Castaldi (bar—Gustavo), Mark Singer (bar—Tebaldo), Edward Brewer (hpd), R. Palmer (cnd), Brewer CO [period instrs] Vox Classics 3-▲ VOX3 7536 [DDD]
Handel, G.F.:Imeneo, w. Julianne Baird (sop—Rosmene), Beverly Hoch (sop—Clomiri), D'Anna Fortunato (mez—Tirinto), Jan Opalach (bass—Argenio), John Ostendorf (bass—Imeneo), Edward Brewer (hpd), R. Palmer (cnd), Brewer CO Vox Box 2-▲ CDX 5135 [DDD]
Handel, G.F.:Joshua, w. D'Anna Fortunato (mez), John Aler (ten), John Ostendorf (b-bar), R. Palmer (cnd), Brewer CO, Brewer Chorus [period instrs] Newport Classic 2-▲ NPD 85515/1-2 [DDD]
Handel, G.F.:Messiah, w. Jennifer Lane (mez), David Price (ten), Kevin Deas (b-bar), V. Radu (cnd), Ama Deus Ensemble, Ama Deus Ensemble Chorus [period instruments; 1749 Covent Garden version] Vox Classics 2-▲ VOX2 7502 [DDD]
Handel, G.F.:Messiah (sels), w. Jennifer Lane (mez), David Price (ten), Kevin Deas (b-bar), V. Radu (cnd), Ama Deus Ensemble—[Part 1] Sinf.; Comfort Ye My People; Every Valley Shall Be Exalted; And the Glory of the Lord; O Thou That Tellest Good Tidings to Zion; For Unto Us a Child is Born; Pifa; Rejoice Greatly o Daughter of Zion; He Shall Feed His Flock by Night; [Part 2] He was Despised and Rejected of Men; All We Like Sheep Have Gone Astray; Lift Up Your Heads, O Ye Gates; Why do the Nations So Furiously Rage Together; [Part 3] I Know That My Redeemer Liveth; Behold, I Tell You a Mystery; The Trumpet Shall Sound; Hallelujah Vox Classics ▲ VOX 7508 [DDD]
Handel, G.F.:Muzio Scevola, w. Julianne Baird (sop—Clelia), Andrea Matthews (sop—Fidalma), Erie Mills (sop—Orazio), D'Anna Fortunato (mez—Muzio), Jennifer Lane (mez—Irene), Frederick Urrey (ten—Tarquino), John Ostendorf (b-bar—Porsenna), R. Palmer (cnd), Brewer Baroque CO [period instrs] [I] *(rec 10/91)* Newport Classic 2-▲ NPD 85540/2 [DDD]
Handel, G.F.:Siroe, Rè di Persia, w. Andrea Matthews (sop), D'Anna Fortunato (mez), Steven Rickards (ct), Frederick Urrey (ten), John Ostendorf (b-bar), R. Palmer (cnd), Brewer Baroque CO [period instrs] [I] Newport Classic 3-▲ NCD 60125 [DDD]
Handel, G.F.:Sosarme, Rè di Media, w. Julinne Baird (sop—Elmira), D'Anna Fortunato (mez—Sosarme), Jennifer Lane (mez—Erenice), Drew Minter (ct—Melo), Rarmond Pellerin (ct—Argone), John Aler (ten—King Haliate), Nathaniel Watson (bass—Varo), Edward Brewer (hpd) Newport Classic 2-▲ NPT 85575 [DDD]
Hasse, J.A.:Cants, w. Erin Headley (vl), Malcolm Proud (hpd)—Quel vago seno, O Fille; Fille dolce, mio bene *(rec May 30-June 1, 1991)* CRD ▲ CRD 3488 [DDD]
Hasse, J.A.:Songs, Airs & Solfeggi, w. Malcolm Proud (hpd)—Quelle agli inganni tuoi; No ste' a condanarme; Cosa e' sta Cossa?; Si', la gondola avere', no crie' *(rec May 30-June 1, 1991)* CRD ▲ CRD 3488 [DDD]
The Italian Lute Song, w. Ronn McFarlane (lt) *(rec Troy Savings Bank Music Hall, Troy, NY, Oct 1995 & Feb 1996)* Dorian ▲ DOR 90236 [DDD]
Jane's Hand:The Jane Austen Songbooks, w. Elizabeth Henreckson-Farnum (sop), Lorie Gratis (mez), Daniel Pincus (ten), Philip Anderson (ten), Martil Dillon (ten), Nancy Wilson (bar vn), Peter Segal (bar gtr), Mary Jane Newman (pno/hpd), Anthony Newman (pno) Vox Classics ▲ VOX 7537 [DDD]
Kodály, Z.:Songs, w. Croft Consort, Boston Univ Women's Chorus—Ave Maria; The Gypsy; Evening Song Albany ▲ TROY 046 [DDD]

Baird, Julianne (sop) (cont.)
Mozart, W.A.:Songs, w. C. Tilney (pno)—Als Luise die Briefe, K.520; An Chloe, K.524; Lied zur Gesellenreise, K.468; Oiseaux, si tous les ans, K.307; Dans un bois solitaire, K.308; Ridente la calma, K.152; Sei du mein Trost, K.391; Ich würd' auf meinem Pfad, K.390; Der Zauberer, K.472; Die Alte, K.517 Dorian ▲ DOR 90173 [DDD]
Musica Dolce, w. Colin Tilney (hpd) Dorian ▲ DOR 90123 [DDD]
Pergolesi, G.B.:La serva padrona, w. J. Ostendorf (b-bar), R. Palmer (cnd), Philomel Baroque CO [I] Omega ▲ OCD 1016 [DDD]
Songs of Love & War:Italian Dramatic Songs of the 17th & 18th Centuries, w. Colin Tilney (hpd), Myron Lutzke (vc) Dorian ▲ DOR 90104 [DDD]
Teasin':Turn of the Century Parlor Songs & Rags, w. Rudolph Palmer (pno), Magic Circle Ensemble *(rec Mallory Room, Rutger's University, Camden, NJ, June 1995)* Helicon ▲ HE 1001
Telemann, G.P.:Cants, w. J. Bowman (ct), Music's Re-creation—Ihr Völker, hört; Ergeuss dich zur Salbung; Erscheine, Gott, in deinem Tempel; Packe dich, gelähmter Drache Meridian ▲ CDE 84159
Telemann, G.P.:Pimpinone, w. Julianne Baird (sop—Vespetta), John Ostendorf (bass—Pimpinone), R. Palmer (cnd), St. Luke's Baroque Orch Newport Classics ▲ NCD 60117 [DDD]
Vivaldi, A.:Cants, Philomel—"All'ombra di sospetto," RV.678 [I] Dorian ▲ DOR 90147 [DDD]

Bair-Ivenz, Monika (sop)
Nono, L.:Prometeo, w. I. Ade-Jesemann (sop), S. Otto (alt), P. Hall (ten), U. Krumbiegel (nar), M. Schadock (nar), C. Abbado (cnd), Berlin PO, Freiburg Soloists Choir *(rec May 23-25, 1993)* Sony Classical ▲ SK 53978 [DDD]
Zinsstag, G.:Trauma, w. M. Gerbert, G. Schatz, K. M. Ziegler, South German Radio Chorus *(rec April 14, 1981)* Grammont ▲ CTSP 36-2 [ADD]

Bajew (sgr)
Künneke, E.:Die grosse Sünderin (sels), w. M. Cunitz (sop), R. Schock (ten), Gehly (sgr), Rau (sgr), Schröder (sgr), Weigelt (sgr), Marszalek (cnd), Cologne RSO, Cologne Radio Chorus [G] Acanta ▲ CD 42483 [DDD]

Baker, George (bar)
Gershwin, G.:Porgy & Bess, w. C. Haymon (sop—Bess), C. Clarey (sop—Serena), M. Simpson (sop—Maria), D. Evans (ten—Sporting Life), G. Baker (bar—Crown), W. White (bar—Porgy), S. Rattle (cnd), London PO, Glyndebourne Festival Chorus EMI Classics 3-▲ CDCC 49568
Gershwin, G.:Porgy & Bess (sels), w. R. Alexander (sop), Z. Mehta (cnd), New York PO, New York Choral Artists—Introduction & Summertime; A woman is a sometime thing; Overflow; Since I lose my man; The promise' lan'; I got plenty o' nuttin'; Bess, you is my woman now; O, I can't sit down; It ain't necesssarily so; There's a boat dat's leavin' soon for New York; O, Lawd I'm on my way [E] Teldec ▲ 2292-46318-2 [DDD]
Sullivan, A.:The Gondoliers, w. W. Lawson (sop), A. Davies (ten), B. Lewis (cta), D. Oldham (ten), M. Bennett (sop), L. Sheffield (bar), H. Lytton (bar), et al., H. Norris (cnd), D'Oyly Carte Opera Company Orch, D'Oyly Carte Opera Chorus—dialogue omitted *(rec 1927)* Pearl 2-▲ PEAS 9961 (m) [AAD]
Sullivan, A.:HMS Pinafore, w. J. Cameron (bar), R. Lewis (ten), M. Sargent (cnd), Pro Arte Orch, Glyndebourne Festival Chorus EMI Classics 2-▲ CDMB 64397
Sullivan, A.:Patience, w. J. Shaw (bar), T. Anthony (bass), A. Young (ten), M. Sargent (cnd), Pro Arte Orch, Glyndebourne Festival Chorus EMI Classics 2-▲ CDMB 64406
Sullivan, A.:The Pirates of Penzance, w. J. Milligan (b-bar), J. Cameron (bar), R. Lewis (ten), M. Sargent (cnd), Pro Arte Orch, Glyndebourne Festival Chorus EMI Classics 2-▲ CDMB 64409
Sullivan, A.:The Sorcerer (sels), w. E. Morison (sop), J. Cameron (bar), R. Lewis (ten), M. Sargent (cnd), Pro Arte Orch, Glyndebourne Festival Chorus EMI Classics 2-▲ CDMB 64397
Sullivan, A.:Trial by Jury, w. W. Lawson (sop), D. Oldham (ten), L. Sheffield (bar), A. Hosking (bar), H. Norris (cnd), D'Oyly Carte Opera Company Orch, D'Oyly Carte Opera Chorus *(rec 1928)* Pearl 2-▲ PEAS 9961 (m) [AAD]

Baker, Janet (mez)
An Anthology of English Songs, w. Martin Isepp (pno) Saga Classics ▲ EC 3340
Arie Amorose, w. Academy of St. Martin in the Fields [cnd:Neville Marriner] Philips ("Collector" series) ▲ 434173-2 [ADD]
Bach, J.S.:Cant 82, w. R. Tear (ten), J. Shirley-Quirk (bar), N. Marriner (cnd), Academy of St. Martin in the Fields London ("Jubilee" series) ▲ 430260-2 [ADD]
Bach, J.S.:Cant 159, w. R. Tear (ten), J. Shirley-Quirk (bar), N. Marriner (cnd), Academy of St. Martin in the Fields London ("Jubilee" series) ▲ 430260-2 [ADD]
Bach, J.S.:Cant 170, w. R. Tear (ten), J. Shirley-Quirk (bar), N. Marriner (cnd), Academy of St. Martin in the Fields London ("Jubilee" series) ▲ 430260-2 [ADD]
Bach, J.S.:Christmas Oratorio, w. Elly Ameling (sop), Robert Tear (ten), Dietrich Fischer-Dieskau (bar), P. Ledger (cnd), Academy of St. Martin in the Fields, King's College Choir Cambridge *(rec 1976)* EMI Classics ("Doublefforte" series) 2-▲ CDFB 69503
Bach, J.S.:Magnificat, BWV 243, w. L. Popp (sop), A. Pashley (sop), R. Tear (ten), D. Barenboim (cnd), New Philharmonia Orch, New Philharmonia Chorus EMI Classics ▲ CDM 64634-2
Bach, J.S.:Magnificat, BWV 243, w. Anne Pashley (sop), Lucia Popp (sop), Robert Tear (ten), Thomas Hemsley (bar), D. Barenboim (cnd), New Philharmonia Orch, New Philharmonia Chorus *(rec All Saints, Tooting, London, May 1968)* EMI Classics ▲ CDK 65334 [ADD]
Bach, J.S.:Mass in b, BWV 232, w. A. Giobol (sop), N. Gedda (ten), H. Prey (bar), F. Crass (bass), O. Klemperer (cnd), New Philharmonia Orch, BBC Sym Chorus [L] EMI Classics ("Studio" series) 2-▲ ZDMB 63364-2 [ADD]
Bach, J.S.:Mass in b, BWV 232, w. M. Marshall (sop), R. Tear (ten), S. Ramey (bass), N. Marriner (cnd), Academy of St. Martin in the Fields, *(chorus unknown)* [L] Philips 2-▲ 416415-2 [ADD]
Berlioz, H.:La Damnation de Faust, w. Nicolai Gedda (ten), Gabriel Bacquier (bar), G. Prêtre (cnd), Orch de Paris, Paris Opera Chorus EMI Classics 2-▲ CDFB 68583
Berlioz, H.:La Mort de Cléopâtre, w. A. Gibson (cnd), London SO EMI Classics ("Studio" series) ▲ CDM 69544
Berlioz, H.:La Mort de Cléopâtre, w. A. Gibson (cnd), London SO EMI Classics 2-▲ CDFB 68583
Berlioz, H.:Les Nuits d'été, w. J. Barbirolli (cnd), New Philharmonia Orch EMI Classics ("Studio" series) ▲ CDM 69544
Berlioz, H.:Les Nuits d'été, w. R. Hickox (cnd), City of London Sinfonia Virgin Classics ("Ultraviolet" series) ▲ CUV 61118
Berlioz, H.:Songs, w. R. Hickox (cnd), City of London Sinfonia—Zaïde, Op. 19/1; La belle voyageuse, Op. 2/4; La captive, Op. 12; Les nuits d'été, Op. 7 Virgin Classics ▲ CDC 59622
Berlioz, H.:Les Troyens (sels), w. A. Gibson (cnd), London SO—final scenes EMI Classics ("Studio" series) ▲ CDM 69544
Brahms, J.:Alto Rhap, w. A. Boult (cnd), London PO, John Alldis Choir Male Voices EMI Classics ("Doublefforte" series) 2-▲ CDFB 68655
Brahms, J.:Alto Rhap, w. R. Hickox (cnd), City of London Sinfonia, London Sym Chorus Virgin Classics ▲ CDC 59589
Brahms, J.:Duets, Op. 28, w. Dietrich Fischer-Dieskau (bar), Daniel Barenboim (pno) EMI Classics ("Doublefforte" series) 2-▲ CDFB 68667
Brahms, J.:Ernste Gesänge, w. André Previn (pno) EMI Classics ("Doublefforte" series) 2-▲ CDFB 68667
Brahms, J.:Songs, Op. 91, w. Cecil Aronowitz (va), André Previn (pno) EMI Classics ("Doublefforte" series) 2-▲ CDFB 68667
Britten, H.:Owen Wingrave, w. S. Fisher (Miss Wingrave), J. Vyvyan (Mrs. Julian), H. Harper (Mrs. Coyle), P. Pears (Sir P. Wingrave; Narrator), B. Luxon (Owen Wingrave), J. Shirley-Quirk (Coyle), B. Britten, Wandworth School Boys' Choir, English CO London 2-▲ 433200-2
Britten, H.:Phaedra, w. B. Britten (cnd), English CO London 2-▲ 425666-2 [ADD]
Britten, H.:The Rape of Lucretia, w. H. Harper (sop), P. Pears (ten), B. Drake (bar), B. Luxon (bar), J. Shirley-Quirk (bar), B. Britten (cnd), English CO London 2-▲ 425666-2 [ADD]
Britten, H.:Spring Sym, w. S. Armstrong (sop), R. Tear (ten), A. Previn (cnd), London SO, London Sym Chorus EMI Classics ▲ CDM 64736
Chausson, E.:Poème de l'amour et de la mer, w. A. Previn (cnd), London SO EMI Classics ("Doublefforte" series) 2-▲ CDFB 68667
Chausson, E.:Poème de l'amour et de la mer, w. E. Svetlanov (cnd), London SO IMP ("BBC Radio Classics" series) ▲ IMP 5691742

Baker, Janet (mez) (cont.)

Delius, F.:Songs of Sunset, w. C. Groves (cnd), Royal Liverpool PO, Royal Liverpool Phil Choir EMI Classics ▲ ZDMB 64218

Duparc, H.:Songs, w. A. Previn (cnd), London SO—5 songs EMI Classics ("Doublefforte" series) 2–▲ CDFB 68667

Elgar, E.:Sea Pictures, w. J. Barbirolli (cnd), London SO EMI Classics ▲ CDC 47329

Elgar, E.:Sea Pictures, w. J. Loughran (cnd), BBC SO IMP ("BBC Radio Classics" series) ▲ IMP 5691672

Fauré, G.:Après un rêve, w. L. Emenheiser Logan (pno) [flute & piano trans. Julius Baker] *(rec 1982)* VAI Audio ▲ VAIA 1022 [ADD]

Gluck, C.W.:Orfeo ed Euridice, w. E. Gale (sop), E. Speiser (sop), R. Leppard (cnd), London PO Erato 2–▲ 2292–45864–2

Gurney, I.:Songs, w. M. Isepp (pno)—I Will Go with My Father A-ploughing Saga Classics ▲ 3353 [ADD]

Handel, G.F.:Dixit Dominus (sels), w. Teresa Zylis-Gara (sop), Robert Tear (ten), D. Willcocks (cnd), King's College Choir Cambridge—Dixit Dominus [chorus w. solos]; Gloria [chorus] *(rec King's College Chapel, Cambridge, Aug. 1965)* EMI Classics ▲ CDK 65336 [ADD]

Handel, G.F.:Messiah, w. Elisabeth Harwood (sop), Paul Esswood (ct), Robert Tear (ten), Raimund Herincx (bass), C. Mackerras (cnd), English CO, Ambrosian Singers [E] Angel ("Studio" series) 2–▲ CDMB 62748 [ADD]

Handel, G.F.:Messiah, w. Elisabeth Harwood (sop), Paul Esswood (ct), Robert Tear (ten), Raimund Herincx (bass), C. Mackerras (cnd), English CO, Ambrosian Singers [E] Angel ("Studio" series) ▲ CDM 69040

Handel, G.F.:Rodelinda, Regina de' Longobardi, w. Joan Sutherland (sop), Raimund Herincx (bar), C. Farncombe (cnd), Philomusica Orch, Chandos Choir *(rec 1959)* Memories 2–▲ MEM 4577 [ADD]

Handel, G.F.:Salve Regina, w. Helen Watts (cta), Robert Tear (ten), Benjamin Luxon (bar), John Shirley-Quirk (bar), R. Leppard (cnd), English CO, London Voices Erato 3–▲ 2292–45994–2

Haydn, J.:Mass 11, "Nelsonmesse", "Imperial Mass", "Coronation Mass", w. Pamela Dellal (mez), Jeffery Thomas (ten), James Maddalena (bar), M. Pearlman (cnd), Banchetto Musicale [L] Arabesque ▲ Z 6560 [DDD]

Haydn, J.:Mass 11, "Nelsonmesse", "Imperial Mass", "Coronation Mass", w. Elizabeth Vaughan (sop), N. Marriner (cnd), Academy of St. Martin in the Fields, King's College Choir Cambridge London ("Jubilee" series) ▲ 421146–2 [ADD]

Mahler, G.:Kindertotenlieder, w. J. Barbirolli (cnd), Hallé Orch EMI Classics ▲ CDZB 62707

Mahler, G.:Kindertotenlieder, w. J. Barbirolli (cnd), Hallé Orch [G] EMI Classics ▲ CDC 47793 [ADD]

Mahler, G.:Das Klagende Lied, w. Teresa Cahill (sop), Robert Tear (ten), Gwynne Howell (bass), G. Rozhdestvensky (cnd), BBC SO, BBC Sym Chorus IMP ("BBC Radio" series) ▲ IMP 5691412

Mahler, G.:Des Knaben Wunderhorn, w. Geraint Evans (bar), Roland Hermann (bar), W. Morris (cnd), London PO, London Symphonica IMP ▲ PCD 2020

Mahler, G.:Des Knaben Wunderhorn, w. G. Evans (ten), W. Morris (cnd), London PO [G] *(rec 1966)* Nimbus ▲ NI 5084 [AAD]

Mahler, G.:Des Knaben Wunderhorn, w. L. Popp (sop), M. Dickie (ten), D. Fischer-Dieskau (bar), B. Weikl (bar), K. Tennstedt (cnd), London PO EMI Classics ▲ CDZB 62707

Mahler, G.:Das Lied von der Erde, w. L. Popp (sop), M. Dickie (ten), D. Fischer-Dieskau (bar), B. Weikl (bar), P. Kletzki (cnd), Philharmonia Orch EMI Classics ▲ CDZB 62707

Mahler, G.:Das Lied von der Erde, w. W. Kmentt (ten), R. Kubelik (cnd), Bavarian RSO *(rec 1975)* Originals ▲ ORISH 806 [ADD]

Mahler, G.:Das Lied von der Erde, w. J. King (ten), B. Haitink (cnd), Royal Concertgebouw Orch Philips ("Silver Line" series) ▲ 432279–2 [ADD]

Mahler, G.:Lieder eines fahrenden Gesellen, w. J. Barbirolli (cnd), Hallé Orch EMI Classics ▲ CDZB 62707

Mahler, G.:Lieder eines fahrenden Gesellen, w. J. Barbirolli (cnd), Hallé Orch [G] EMI Classics ▲ CDC 47793 [ADD]

Mahler, G.:Lieder eines fahrenden Gesellen, w. Geraint Evans (bar), Roland Hermann (bar), W. Morris (cnd), London PO, London Symphonica IMP ▲ PCD 2020

Mahler, G.:Lieder eines fahrenden Gesellen, w. G. Parsons (pno) [G] Hyperion ▲ CDA 66100

Mahler, G.:Songs, w. G. Parsons (pno)—Im Lenz; Winterlied [G] Hyperion ▲ CDA 66100

Mahler, G.:Songs from Rückert, w. J. Barbirolli (cnd), New Philharmonia Orch EMI Classics ▲ CDZB 62707

Mahler, G.:Songs from Rückert, w. J. Barbirolli (cnd), New Philharmonia Orch [G] EMI Classics ▲ CDC 47793 [ADD]

Mahler, G.:Songs from Rückert, w. M. Tilson Thomas (cnd), London SO, London Sym Chorus [G] CBS 2–▲ M2K 44553 [DDD]

Mahler, G.:Sym 2, w. H. Harper (sop), O. Klemperer (cnd), Bavarian RSO *(rec 1965)* Enterprise ("Document" series) ▲ ENT LV 937 [DDD]

Mahler, G.:Sym 2, w. S. Armstrong (sop), L. Bernstein (cnd), London SO, Edinburgh Festival Chorus *(rec 1974)* Sony Classical ("Bernstein:The Royal Edition" series) 2–▲ SM2K 47573 [ADD]

Mahler, G.:Sym 2, w. A. Augér (mez), S. Rattle (cnd), City of Birmingham SO, City of Birmingham Sym Chorus [G] EMI Classics 2–▲ CDCB 47962 [DDD]

Mahler, G.:Sym 2, w. Rae Woodland (sop), L. Stokowski (cnd), London SO, BBC Chorus, BBC Choral Society, Goldsmith's Choral Union, Harrow Choral Society *(rec 1963)* Music & Arts ▲ CD 885 [AAD]

Mahler, G.:Sym 3, w. M. Tilson Thomas (cnd), London SO, London Sym Chorus [G] CBS 2–▲ M2K 44553 [DDD]

Mahler, G.:Sym 9, w. W. Kmentt (ten), R. Kubelik (cnd), Bavarian RSO *(rec 1975)* Originals ▲ ORISH 806 [ADD]

Mendelssohn, F.:Elijah, w. Gwyneth Jones (sop), Simon Woolf (trb), Nicolai Gedda (ten), Dietrich Fischer-Dieskau (bar), R. Frühbeck de Burgos (cnd), New Philharmonia Orch, New Philharmonia Chorus, Wandsworth School Boys' Choir *(rec 1968)* EMI Classics ("Doublefforte" series) 2–▲ CDFB 68601

Mendelssohn, F.:Hear my prayer, w. R. Hickox (cnd), City of London Sinfonia Virgin Classics ▲ CDC 59589

Mendelssohn, F.:A Midsummer Night's Dream (comp), w. H. Harper (sop), O. Klemperer (cnd), Philharmonia Orch, Philharmonia Chorus *(rec ca. 1961)* EMI Classics ▲ CDM 64144

Mendelssohn, F.:Psalm 42, w. R. Hickox (cnd), City of London Sinfonia, London Sym Chorus Virgin Classics ▲ CDC 59589

Mendelssohn, F.:Songs (4) (1830), w. F. Lloyd (hn), R. Masters (hp), R. Hickox (cnd), City of London Sinfonia, London Sym Chorus Virgin Classics ▲ CDC 59589

Mozart, W.A.:Arias, w. R. Leppard (cnd), Scottish CO—Arias di Madama Lucilla, K.582 & 583; Aria di Sesto, K.624; Recitativo & Rondo di Idamante, K.505; others Erato ("Recital" series) ▲ 98497–2

Mozart, W.A.:Complete Mozart Edition, w. M. Caballé (sop), I. Cotrubas (sop), N. Gedda (ten), C. Davis (cnd), Royal Opera House Orch, Royal Opera House Chorus Covent Garden Philips 3–▲ 422542–2 [ADD]

Mozart, W.A.:Complete Mozart Edition, w. L. Popp (sop), Y. Minton (mez), F. von Stade (mez), S. Burrows (ten), R. Lloyd (b-bar), C. Davis (cnd), Royal Opera House Orch, Royal Opera House Chorus Covent Garden Philips 2–▲ 422544–2 [ADD]

Pergolesi, G.B.:Magnificat in C, w. Elizabeth Vaughan (sop), Ian Partridge (ten), Christopher Keyte (bass), D. Willcocks (cnd), Academy of St. Martin in the Fields, King's College Choir Cambridge *(rec 1966)* London 2–▲ 443868–2 [ADD]

Ravel, M.:Shéhérazade Mez, w. J. Barbirolli (cnd), New Philharmonia Orch EMI Classics ("Doublefforte" series) 2–▲ CDFB 68667

Respighi, O.:La Sensitiva, w. R. Hickox (cnd), City of London Sinfonia Virgin Classics ("Ultraviolet" series) ▲ CUV 61118

Scarlatti, A.:Non so qual più m'ingombra, w. R. Leppard (cnd), English CO EMI Classics ("Baroque" series) ▲ CDK 65735

Scarlatti, D.:Salve regina Sop, w. R. Leppard (cnd), English CO EMI Classics ("Baroque" series) ▲ CDK 65735

Schubert, Franz:Songs (comp), w. G. Johnson (pno)—19 songs—D.30, 73, 121, 159, 162, 195, 216, 224, 225, 226, 250, 260, 284, 296, 402, 587, 588, 636, 794 [G] Hyperion ▲ CDJ 33001 [DDD]

Baker, Janet (mez) (cont.)

Schubert, Franz:Songs (misc)—Gretchen am Spinnrade; Suleika I & II; Schwestergruss Schlummerlied; An die untergehende Sonne; Mignon I, II & III; Kennst du das Land; Berta's Lied in der Nacht; Herrn Josef Spaun; Ellens Gesang I & II; Ave Maria; Hin und wieder; Liebe schwärmt; An die Nachtigall; Schlafe, schlafe; Delphine; Wiegenlied; Die Männer sind méchant; Abendstern; Die Götter Griechlands; Gondelfahrer Auflösung [all w. Gerald Moore (pno)]; Die Forelle; Rastlose Liebe; Auf dem Wasser zu singen; Der Tod und das Mädchen; An die Musik; Frülingsglaube; Der Musensohn; An Sylvia; Litenei; Heidenröslein; Nacht und Träume; Du bist die Ruh' [all w. Geoffery Parsons (pno)] EMI Classics 2–▲ CDFB 69389

Schumann, R.:Frauenliebe und -leben, w. Daniel Barenboim (pno) EMI Classics ("Doublefforte" series) 2–▲ CDFB 68667

Verdi, G.:quattro pezzi sacri, w. C. M. Giulini (cnd), Philharmonia Orch, London Phil Choir [I,L] EMI Classics 2–▲ CDCB 47257 [ADD]

Vivaldi, A.:Gloria, RV.589, w. E. Vaughan (sop), N. Marriner (cnd), Academy of St. Martin in the Fields, King's College Choir Cambridge London ("Jubilee" series) ▲ 421146–2 [ADD]

Baker, Polly Jo (sop)

La Montaine, J.:Lessons of Christmas, w. David Griffith (ten), Carol Baum (hp), Scott Shepherd (perc), J. Montaine (cnd), Fredonia Singers Fredonia Discs ▲ FDCD 14

Baker, Richard (nar)

Prokofiev, S.:Peter & the Wolf, w. R. Leppard (cnd), New Philharmonia Orch Classics for Pleasure ▲ CDCFP 185

Walton, W.:Façade, w. S. Walton (nar), R. Hickox (cnd), City of London Sinfonia members [E] Chandos ▲ CHAN 8869 [DDD]

Baker, Robert (ten)

Corigliano, J.:Of Rage & Remembrance, w. Michelle DeYoung (mez), Michael Accinno (boy sop), Michael Forest (ten), Jason Stearns (bar), James Shaffran (bar), L. Slatkin (cnd), National SO Washington D.C., Washington Oratorio Society Men's Chorus RCA Red Seal ▲ 09026–68450–2 [DDD]

Baker, Sharon (sop)

Mozart, W.A.:Missa, K.317, w. J. Malafronte (mez), F. Kelley (ten), J. Maddalena (bar), M. Pearlman (cnd), Banchetto Musicale Harmonia Mundi USA ▲ HMU 907021

Mozart, W.A.:Vesperae solennes, w. J. Malafronte (mez), F. Kelley (ten), J. Maddalena (bar), M. Pearlman (cnd), Banchetto Musicale Harmonia Mundi USA ▲ HMU 907021

Purcell, H.:Dido & Aeneas, w. Nancy Maultsby (sop—Dido), Susannah Waters (sop—Belinda), Margaret O'Keefe (sop—1st Witch), Sharon Baker (sop—2nd Woman), Laura Tucker (mez—Sorceress), Donna Ames (alt—Spirit), Richard Clement (ten—Sailor), Russell Braun (bar—Aeneas), M. Pearlman (cnd), Boston Baroque Orch Telarc ▲ CD 80424 [DDD]

Bakocevic (sgr)

Offenbach, J.:Les Contes d'Hoffmann, w. H. Harper (sop), M. Mesplé (sop), S. Kónya (ten), G. Bacquier (bar), P. Maag (cnd), Buenos Aires Teatro Colón Orch, Buenos Aires Teatro Colón Chorus [F] *(rec live, Buenos Aires 8/3/70)* Melodram 2–▲ MEL 27090 [ADD]

Tchaikovsky, P.:Mazeppa, w. Cakarevic (sgr), Cangalovic (sgr), N. Mitic (bar), O. Danon (cnd), Belgrade National Opera Orch, Belgrade National Opera Chorus [R] *(rec live, Berlin, 9/27/69)* Myto 2–▲ 2 MCD 90527 [ADD]

Balabanov, Stoyan (bass)

Puccini, G.:Tosca, w. Raina Kabaivanska (sop—Floria Tosca), Nazzareno Antinori (ten—Mario Cavaradossi), Roumen Doikov (ten—Spoletta), Enzo Dara (bar—Casare Angelotti/Il sagrestano), Nelson Portella (bar—Il Barone Scarpia), Stoyan Balabanov (bass—Sciarrone/Un carceriere), Borislav Peev (sgr—Un Pastore), G. Bellini (cnd), Sofia PO, Bulgarian National Radio Children's Choir, Svetoslav Obrenetov Bulgarian National Chorus *(rec Sophia, Bulgaria, Nov 14–27, 1982)* Arts Music ▲ 47158–2 [DDD]

Balach, Nancy Maria (mez)

Balada, L.:Escenas borrascosas, w. Katy Shackelton-Williams (sop—Isabel), Nancy Maria Balach (mez—Beatriz), Matthew Walley (ten—Colón), J.P. Izquierdo (cnd), Carnegie Mellon PO, Robert Page (cnd), Carnegie Mellon Concert Choir, Carnegie Mellon Repertory Chorus New World ▲ 804982

Balada, L.:Escenas borrascosas, w. Kay Shackleton-Williams (sop—Isabel), Nancy Maria Balach (mez—Beatriz), Matthew Walley (ten—Colón), J.P. Izquierdo (cnd), Carnegie Mellon PO, Robert Page (cnd), Carnegie Mellon Concert Choir, Carnegie Mellon Repertory Chorus *(rec Carnegie Music Hall, Pittsburgh, PA, Apr 7–8, 1994)* New World ▲ 80498–2

Balboni, Annamaria (sop)

Rossini, G.:La donna del lago, w. M. Caballé (sop), J. Hamari (mez), F. Bonisolli (ten), R. Bottazzo (ten), G. Sinimberghi (ten), P. Washington (bass), P. Bellugi (cnd), Turin RAI Orch, Turin RAI Chorus *(rec live, Torino, 1970)* Foyer 2–▲ FOY 2028 [AAD]

Balconi, Roberto (ct)

De Vitae Fugacitate:Lamentos, Cantatas & Arias, w. R. Bertini (sop), R. Gini (cnd), Concerto delle Viole *(rec Aug. 1992)* Glossa ▲ GCD 920901 [DDD]

Gesualdo, D.C.:Madrigals, w. Elena Cecchi Fedi (sop), Roberta Invernizzi (sop), Daniela Del Monaco (cta), Gian Paolo Fagotto (ten), Giuseppe Zambon (ten), Giovanni Dagnino (bass), A. Curtis (cnd), I Fegi Armonici—Book 6 [Se la Mia Morte Brami; Beltà Poi Che T'Assenti; Tu Piangi O Fille Mia; Resta di Darmi Noia; Chiaro Risplender Suole; others] Symphonia ▲ SYM 94133

Monteverdi, C.:Incoronazione, w. Constanze Backes (sop—Valletto), Catherine Bott (sop—Drusilla/Pallade/La Virtù), Dana Hanchard (sop—Nerone), Sylvia McNair (sop—Poppea), Marinella Pennicchi (sop—Amore/Damigella), Annie Sofie von Otter (mez—Ottavia/Venere/La Fortuna), Julian Clarkson (alt—Littore/Mercurio), Bernarda Fink (cta—Arnalta), Roberto Balconi (ct—Nutrice), Michael Chance (ct—Ottone), Nigel Robson (ten—Liberto/Soldato Secondo), Mark Tucker (ten—Lucano/Soldato Primo), Francesco Ellero d'Artegna (bass—Seneca), J. E. Gardiner (cnd), English Baroque Soloists *(rec Queen Elizabeth Hall, South Bank Ctr, London, Dec 1993)* Archiv 3–▲ 447088–2

Scarlatti, A.:Cants, w. S. Picollo (sop), S. Bagliano (rcr), Collegium Pro Musica—includes Clori mia, Clori bella; Filli che esprime la sua fede a Fileno; Ardo e ver per te d'amore; Tu sei quella che al nime sembri giusta, plus others Nuova Era ("Ancient Music" series) ▲ NUO 7162 [DDD]

Stradella, A.:Cants, w. Cristina Miatello (sop), Gianpaolo Fagotto (ten), Antonio Abete (sgr), Lavinia Bertotti (sgr), Roberta Giua (sgr), S. Balestracci (cnd), Santo Spirito Academy Orch, Santo Spirito Academy Chorus—for 5 w. vns [For Holy Christmas]; for 5 w. instruments [For the Souls in Purgatory] Stradivarius ▲ STV 33392 [DDD]

Stradella, A.:Vocal Music, w. E. Smith (hpd), G. Dagnino (bass), S. Picollo (sop), M. Mazzara (alt), E. Velardi (cnd), Alessandro Stradella Consort—Sinfonia in E from the Cantata "Crudo Mar"; Toccata in a for Harpsichord; Exultate in Deo Fideles, Motet for Bass Solo & Violins; Si Apra al Riso Ogni Labbro, Cantata for 3 Voices & Strings [I,L] Bongiovanni ▲ GB 2123 [DDD]

Vivaldi, A.:Gloria, RV.589, w. R. Invernizzi (sop), P. Vaccari (sop), L. Gariboldi (cnd), C. Gubert (cnd), Padua Bach Academy CO, Padua Bach Academy Chamber Chorus Rivoalto ▲ RIV 9301 [DDD]

Vivaldi, A.:Magnificat, RV.610, w. R. Invernizzi (sop), P. Vaccari (sop), L. Gariboldi (cnd), C. Gubert (cnd), Padua Bach Academy CO, Padua Bach Academy Chamber Chorus Rivoalto ▲ RIV 9301 [DDD]

Baldani, Rusa (mez)

Boito, A.:Nerone, w. I. Ligabue (sop), B. Prevedi (bar), A. Ferrin (bass), G. Gavazzeni (cnd), Turin RAI SO, Turin RAI Chorus *(rec live 1975)* Italian Opera Rarities 2–▲ IOR 7704 [ADD]

Still, W.G.:Tristan und Isolde, w. C. Ligendza (sop), H. Hopf (ten), A. Dermota (ten), H. Sotin (bass), G. Neidlinger (bass), C. Kleiber (cnd), Vienna State Opera Orch, Vienna State Opera Chorus *(rec Oct. 7, 1973)* Exclusive 3–▲ EXL 18 [ADD]

Still, W.G.:Tristan und Isolde, w. Catarina Ligendza (sop), Hans Hopf (ten), Hans Sotin (bass), C. Kleiber (cnd), Vienna PO, Vienna State Opera Chorus *(rec Vienna, Oct. 7, 1973)* Pantheon 3–▲ PHE 6601 (m)

Verdi, G.:Oberto, Conte di San Bonifacio, w. G. Dimitrova (sop), A. Browner (mez), C. Bergonzi (ten), R. Panerai (bar), L. Gardelli (cnd), Munich RSO, Munich Radio Chorus [I] Orfeo 2–▲ 105842 [DDD] 3–■ A 105843 F

Verdi, G.:Oberto, Conte di San Bonifacio, w. G. Dimitrova (sop), A. Browner (mez), C. Bergonzi (ten), R. Panerai (bar), L. Gardelli (cnd), Munich RSO, Munich Radio Chorus [I] Orfeo ▲ 175881 [DDD]

Wagner, R.:Tristan und Isolde (sels), w. Catarina Ligendza (sop), Hans Hopf (ten), C. Kleiber (cnd), Vienna State Opera Orch *(rec live, 1973)* AS Disc ▲ ASD 2510

Baldelli (sgr)

Wagner, R.:Parsifal, w. M. Callas (sop), R. Panerai (bar), D. Lopatto (bar), B. Christoff (bass), V. Gui (cnd), Rome Radio–TV SO, Rome Radio–TV Chorus [I] *(rec in concert, 11/20–21/50)* Verona 3–▲ 27085/87

Wagner, R.:Parsifal, w. M. Callas (sop), R. Panerai (bar), D. Lopatto (bar), B. Christoff (bass), V. Gui (cnd), Rome Radio–TV SO, Rome Radio–TV Chorus [I] *(rec 11/20–21/50)* Melodram 3–▲ MEL 36041 (m)

Baldin, Aldo (ten)

Bach, J.S.:Cant 2, w. H. Watts (cta), W. Heldwein (bass), H. Rilling (cnd), Stuttgart Bach Collegium, Gächinger Kantorei Hänssler Classic ▲ 98.801 [AAD]

Bach, J.S.:Cant 5, w. A. Augér (sop), C. Watkinson (alt), W. Schöne (bass), H. Rilling (cnd), Stuttgart Bach Collegium, Gächinger Kantorei [G] *(rec Feb & Oct 1979)* Hänssler Classic ▲ 98.816 [AAD]

Bach, J.S.:Cant 23, w. A. Augér (sop), H. Watts (cta), N. Tütler (bass), H. Rilling (cnd), Stuttgart Bach Collegium, Gächinger Kantorei [G] *(rec 1977)* Hänssler Classic ▲ 98.879 [AAD]

Bach, J.S.:Cant 44, w. A. Augér (sop), H. Watts (cta), W. Schöne (bass), H. Rilling (cnd), Stuttgart Bach Collegium, Gächinger Kantorei [G] *(rec 1979)* Hänssler Classic ▲ 98.886 [AAD]

Bach, J.S.:Cant 48, w. M. Hoffgen (mez), H. Rilling (cnd), Stuttgart Bach Collegium, Gächinger Kantorei [G] *(rec 1973)* Hänssler Classic ▲ 98.813 [AAD]

Bach, J.S.:Cant 62, w. I. Nielsen (sop), H. Watts (cta), P. Huttenlocher (bar), H. Rilling (cnd), Stuttgart Bach Collegium, Gächinger Kantorei [G] *(rec Feb & Apr 1980)* Hänssler Classic ▲ 98.822 [AAD]

Bach, J.S.:Cant 75, w. I. Reichelt, V. Gohl (mez), J. Hamari (cta), A. Kraus (ten), H.–F. Kunz (bass), H. Rilling (cnd), Stuttgart Bach Collegium, Frankfurt Kantorei [G] *(rec 1970)* Hänssler Classic ▲ 98.891 [AAD]

Bach, J.S.:Cant 87, w. J. Hamari (cta), W. Heldwein (bass), H. Rilling (cnd), Stuttgart Bach Collegium, Gächinger Kantorei [G] *(rec 1980–81)* Hänssler Classic ▲ 98.885 [AAD]

Bach, J.S.:Cant 92, w. A. Augér (sop), G. Schreckenbach (cta), H. Watts (cta), P. Huttenlocher (bar), H. Rilling (cnd), Bach Ensemble [G] *(rec 1980)* Hänssler Classic ▲ 98.877 [AAD]

Bach, J.S.:Cant 94, w. H. Donath (sop), E. Paaske (cta), H.–F. Kunz (bass), W. Schöne (bass), H. Rilling (cnd), Stuttgart Bach Collegium, Württemberg CO, Gächinger Kantorei Hänssler Classic ▲ 98.808 [AAD]

Bach, J.S.:Cant 101, w. A. Augér (sop), H. Watts (cta), J. Bröcheler (bar), H. Rilling (cnd), Stuttgart Bach Collegium, Gächinger Kantorei Hänssler Classic ▲ 98.809 [AAD]

Bach, J.S.:Cant 107, w. A. Augér (sop), J. Bröcheler (bar), H. Rilling (cnd), Stuttgart Bach Collegium, Gächinger Kantorei Hänssler Classic ▲ 98.805 [AAD]

Bach, J.S.:Cant 110, w. K. Graf (sop), H. Gardow (sop), W. Schöne (bass), H. Rilling (cnd), Stuttgart Bach Collegium, Gächinger Kantorei [G] *(rec Jan–Feb 1974)* Hänssler Classic ▲ 98.824 [AAD]

Bach, J.S.:Cant 128, w. G. Schreckenbach (cta), W. Schöne (bass), H. Rilling (cnd), Stuttgart Bach Collegium, Gächinger Kantorei [G] *(rec 1980–81)* Hänssler Classic ▲ 98.886 [AAD]

Bach, J.S.:Cant 133, w. A. Augér (sop), D. Soffel (cta), P. Huttenlocher (bar), H. Rilling (cnd), Stuttgart Bach Collegium, Gächinger Kantorei [G] *(rec Feb–Mar 1980)* Hänssler Classic ▲ 98.826 [AAD]

Bach, J.S.:Cant 138, w. A. Augér (sop), R. Bollen (cta), P. Huttenlocher (bar), H. Rilling (cnd), Stuttgart Bach Collegium, Gächinger Kantorei Hänssler Classic ▲ 98.812 [AAD]

Bach, J.S.:Cant 140, w. A. Augér (sop), P. Huttenlocher (bar), H. Rilling (cnd), Stuttgart Bach Collegium, Gächinger Kantorei [G] Novalis ▲ 150029 [DDD]

Bach, J.S.:Cant 149, w. A. Augér (sop), M. Georg (mez), P. Huttenlocher (bar), H. Rilling (cnd), Stuttgart Bach Collegium, Gächinger Kantorei [G] *(rec 1984)* Hänssler Classic ▲ 98.815 [AAD]

Bach, J.S.:Cant 159, w. J. Hamari (cta), P. Huttenlocher (bar), H. Rilling (cnd), Stuttgart Bach Collegium, Gächinger Kantorei [G] *(rec 1983)* Hänssler Classic ▲ 98.879 [AAD]

Bach, J.S.:Cant 178, w. G. Schreckenbach (cta), K. Equiluz (ten), W. Schöne (bass), H. Rilling (cnd), Stuttgart Bach Collegium, Gächinger Kantorei Hänssler Classic ▲ 98.806 [AAD]

Bach, J.S.:Cant 182, w. D. Soffel (cta), P. Huttenlocher (bar), H. Rilling (cnd), Stuttgart Bach Collegium, Gächinger Kantorei [G] *(rec 1975)* Hänssler Classic ▲ 98.880 [AAD]

Bach, J.S.:Cant 185, w. A. Augér (sop), H. Laurich (mez), P. Huttenlocher (bar), H. Rilling (cnd), Stuttgart Bach Collegium, Frankfurt Kantorei Hänssler Classic ▲ 98.804 [AAD]

Bach, J.S.:Cant 188, w. A. Augér (sop), J. Hamari (cta), W. Heldwein (bass), H. Rilling (cnd), Württemberg CO, Gächinger Kantorei [G] *(rec June & Sept 1983)* Hänssler Classic ▲ 98.817 [AAD]

Bach, J.S.:Cant 196, w. D. Soffel (cta), N. Tüller (b–bar), H. Rilling (cnd), Bach Ensemble *(rec Jan 1975)* Hänssler Classic ▲ 98.828 [AAD]

Bach, J.S.:Cant 198, w. A. Augér (sop), G. Schreckenbach (cta), P. Huttenlocher (bar), H. Rilling (cnd), Bach Ensemble *(rec Sept 1983)* Hänssler Classic ▲ 98.830 [AAD]

Beethoven, L. van:Missa Solemnis, w. P. Coburn (sop), F. Quivar (cta), A. Schmidt (bar), H. Rilling (cnd), Stuttgart Bach Collegium, Gächinger Kantorei [L] Hänssler Classic 2–▲ CD 98.956 [DDD] 2–■ MC 98.956 (D)

Donizetti, G.:Requiem Mass, w. C. Studer (sop), H. Müller–Molinari (mez), J. P. Bogart (bass), J.–H. Rootering (bass), M. A. G. Martínez (cnd), Bamberg SO, Bamberg Sym Chorus [L] Orfeo ▲ 172881 [DDD]

Dvořák, A.:Stabat Mater, w. L. Aghová (sop), M. Schiml (sop), L. Vele (bass), J. Belohlávek (cnd), Czech PO, Prague Phil Chorus [L] Chandos 2–▲ CHAN 8985/86 [DDD]

Mozart, W.A.:Davidde penitente, w. E. Csapo (sop), G. Koban (sop), D. Kurz (cnd), Württemberg CO, Württemburg Choir *(rec 1978)* Allegretto ▲ ACD 8164 [ADD] ■ ACS 8164

Mozart, W.A.:Requiem, w. Edith Wiens (sop), Gabriele Schreckenbach (mez), Gerhard Faulstich (bar), U. Gronostay (cnd), Berlin RSO, Berlin RIAS Chamber Choir [L] LaserLight ▲ 15 882 [DDD]

Suter, H.:Le Laudi di San Francesco d'Assisi, w. A. Michael (sop), J. Winklet (alt), J. Will (bass), P. Laubschet (org), Bern SO, T. Loosli (cnd), Bern Bach Choir, Sekundar School Children's Choir Ars Musici ▲ AM 1015–2 [DDD]

Baldisseri, Renata (sgr)

Piccinni, N.:La cecchina, ossia la buona figliola, w. Lucia Alberti (sop—Il Cavaliere Armidoro), Emilia Ravaglia (sop—La Marchesa), Margherita Rinaldi (sop—Cecchina), Elena Zilio (mez—Paoluccia), Ugo Benelli (bar—Il Marchese della Conchiglia), Alessandro Corbelli (bar—Mengotto), Enzo Dara (bar—Tagliaferro), Renata Baldisseri (sgr—Sandrina), G. Gelmetti (cnd), Rome Opera Orch, Rome Opera Chorus *(rec Rome, Feb 4, 1981)* Italia 2–▲ CDC 95 [ADD]

Balfour, Margaret (cta)

Bach, J.S.:Mass in b, BWV 232, w. E. Schumann (sop), W. Widdop (ten), F. Schorr (bar), A. Coates (cnd), London SO, London Phil Chorus [L] *(rec Kingsway Hall, London Mar–Apr 1929)* Pearl 2–▲ PEAS 9900 (m) [AAD]

Elgar, E.:The Dream of Gerontius (sels), w. S. Wilson (ten), H. Heyner (bar), E. Elgar (cnd), Royal Albert Hall Orch, Royal Choral Society [E] *(rec 1927)* Opal ▲ CD 9810 (m) [AAD]

Vaughan Williams, R.:Serenade to Music, w. I. Baillie (sop), E. Suddaby (sop), S. Allen (sop), E. Turner (sop), A. Desmond (cta), M. Brunskill (cta), M. Jarred (cta), H. Nash (ten), W. Widdop (ten), P. Jones (ten), F. Titterton (ten), R. Henderson (bass), R. Easton (bass), H. Williams (bass), N. Allin (bass), H. Wood (cnd), BBC SO [E] *(rec 10/15/38)* Pearl ▲ GEMMCD 9342 (m) [AAD]

Vaughan Williams, R.:Serenade to Music, w. Isobel Baillie (sop), Lilian Stiles–Allen (sop), Elsie Suddaby (sop), Eva Turner (sop), Margaret Balfour (cta), Muriel Brunskill (cta), Astra Desmond (cta), Mary Jarred (cta), Parry Jones (ten), Heddle Nash (ten), Frank Titterton (ten), Walter Widdop (ten), Roy Henderson (bar), Harold Williams (bar), Norman Allin (bass), Robert Easton (bass), H. Wood (cnd), BBC SO *(rec Abbey Road, Oct 15, 1938)* Claremont ▲ CDGSE 785066

Vaughan Williams, R.:Serenade to Music, w. I. Baillie (sop), E. Suddaby (sop), S. Allen (sop), E. Turner (sop), M. Balfour (cta), A. Desmond (cta), M. Brunskill (cta), M. Jarred (cta), H. Nash (ten), W. Widdop (ten), P. Jones (ten), F. Titterton (ten), R. Henderson (bass), R. Easton (bass), H. Williams (bass), N. Allin (bass), H. J. Wood (cnd), BBC SO Dutton Laboratories ▲ CDAX 8004 [ADD]

Balkov, Sergei (bar)

Prokofiev, S.:Hamlet, w. Elena Def–donskaya (sop), E. Khachaturian (cnd), USSR Ministry of Culture SO *(rec 1989)* Consonance ▲ 81–5005 [AAD]

Ball, Manfred (nar)

Helmschrott, R.:Cross & Freedom, w. Helmut Schatz, Nancy Gibson (sop), Frieder Aurich (ten), Matthias Weichert (bass), Anett Baumann (vn), Frank Phillipsch, Linda Robbins, Gerhard Wolf, Martin Homann (perc), Robert M. Helmschrott (org), H.–C. Rademann (cnd), Munich Trombone Quartet, Dresden Chamber Choir Vienna Modern Masters ▲ VMM 3027 [DDD]

Ballard, Kay (sgr)

Porter, C.:Nymph Errant, w. E. Belcourt (sgr), *(other sgrs unknown),* D. Pippin (cnd), Stephen Hill Orch, Stephen Hill Singers Angel ▲ CDC 54079

Balleys, Brigitte (mez)

Berg, A.:Early Songs, w. V. Ashkenazy (cnd), Berlin German SO London ▲ 436567–2 [DDD]

Berg, A.:Orchesterlieder (5) nach Ansichtskartentexten von Peter Altenberg, w. V. Ashkenazy (cnd), Berlin German SO London ▲ 436567–2 [DDD]

Berlioz, H.:Les Nuits d'été, w. P. Herreweghe (cnd), Champs Élysées Theater Orch Harmonia Mundi France ▲ HMC 90152

Chausson, E.:Mélodies (comp), w. Sandrine Piau (sop), Jean François Gardeil (bar), Billy Eidi (pno), Ludwig String Quartet Timpani 2–▲ 2C 2028

Honegger, A.:Songs, w. Jean–François Gardeil (bar), Billy Eidi (pno)—Mimaamaquim; Nature morte; O Salutaris; O Temps suspends ton Vol; Panis Angelicus; Petit Cours de Morale; Quatre Chansons pour voix grave; Quatre Poèms; Saluste du Bartas; Six Poésie de Jean Cocteau; Trois Poèmes de Claudel; Trois Poèmes de Paul Fort; Trois Psaumes; Vocalise–Etude [F,L,Heb] *(rec Aug. 1992)* Timpani ▲ 1C1015 [DDD]

Balliett, Julie Lyon (voc)

Deep Listening Band:Troglodyte's Delight, w. Pauline Oliveros (acc/voc/whistles), Stuart Dempster (trbn), Panaiotis (voc), Fritz Hauser (perc) *(rec Tarpaper Cave, Rosendale, NY, June 1989)* ¿What Next? ▲ WN 003 ■ WN 0003

Ballo, Pietro (ten)

Donizetti, G.:Anna Bolena, w. Katia Ricciarelli (sop), Doris Soffel (cta), Nicolai Ghiuselev (bass), E. Pidò (cnd), Palermo Teatro Massimo Orch, Palermo Teatro Massimo Chorus *(rec live, 1991)* Serenissima 3–▲ SER 360111

Donizetti, G.:Rita, or Le mari battu, w. A. Scarabelli (sop), A. Corbelli (bar), F. Amendola (cnd), Sicilian CO [I] *(rec live, Palermo 6/19–20/91)* Nuova Era ▲ 7045 [DDD]

Rossini, G.:Stabat Mater, w. Daniela Dessi (sop), Lucia Mazzaria (sop), Gloria Scalchi (mez), Chris Merritt (ten), Anatoli Kotscherga (bass), Roberto Scandiuzzi (bass), G. Gelmetti (cnd), Stuttgart RSO, North German Radio Chorus, Southwest German Radio Chorus Serenissima 2–▲ SER 360155 [DDD]

Verdi, G.:Requiem Mass, w. Lucia Mazzaria (sop), Daniela Dessi (sop), Gloria Scalchi (mez), Chris Merritt (ten), Anatoli Kotscherga (bass), Roberto Scandiuzzi (bass), G. Gelmetti (cnd), Stuttgart RSO, North German Radio Chorus, Southwest German Radio Chorus Serenissima 2–▲ SER 360155 [DDD]

Balslev, Lisbeth (sop)

Gade, N.W.:Elverskud, w. E. Guillaume (mez), M. Melbye (bar), F. Rasmussen (cnd), Collegium Musicum, Canzone Choir [Da] Kontrapunkt ▲ 32070 [DDD]

Wagner, R.:Der fliegende Holländer, w. R. Schunk (ten), S. Estes (bass), M. Salminen (bass), W. Nelsson (cnd), Bayreuth Festival Orch, Bayreuth Festival Chorus [G] Philips 2–▲ 434599–2 [DDD]

Balthrop, Carmen (sop)

Con Amores:Spanish & Portuguese Songs, w. Robert McCoy (pno) Elan ▲ CD 2208 [DDD]

Paine, J.K.:Mass, Op. 10, w. J. Blackett (cta), V. Cole (ten), J. Cheek (bass), J. Lange (org), G. Schuller (cnd), St. Louis SO, St. Louis Sym Chorus [L] *(rec ca. mid–1970s)* New World ▲ 80262–2 [AAD]

Baltsa, Agnes (mez)

Bellini, V.:I Capuleti e i Montecchi, w. E. Guberova (sop—Giulietta), A. Baltsa (mez—Romeo), D. Raffanti (ten—Tebaldo), R. Muti (cnd), Royal Opera House Orch, Royal Opera House Chorus Covent Garden EMI Classics ▲ CDMB 64846

Bellini, V.:Norma (sels), w. J. Carreras (ten), P. Domingo (cnd), London SO, Tallis Chamber Choir—Eccola! Va, mi lascia; Va, crudele, al Dio spietato *(rec Jan.–Feb. 1991)* Sony Classical ▲ SK 53968 [DDD]

Bizet, G.:Carmen (sels), w. J. Carreras (ten), P. Domingo (cnd), London SO, Tallis Chamber Choir—C'est toi? C'est moi; Mais moi, Carmen, je t'aime encore? *(rec Jan.–Feb. 1991)* Sony Classical ▲ SK 53968 [DDD]

Bizet, G.:Carmen (sels), w. K. Ricciarelli (sop), J. Carreras (ten), J. Van Dam (b–bar), H. von Karajan (cnd), Berlin PO, Paris Opera Chorus [F] Deutsche Grammophon ▲ 413322–2 [DDD]

Gluck, C.W.:Orfeo ed Euridice, w. E. Gruberova (sop), Marshall (sop), R. Muti (cnd), Philharmonia Orch, Ambrosian Opera Chorus Angel ("Studio" series) 2–▲ CDMB 63637 [DDD]

Mahler, G.:Kindertotenlieder, w. L. Maazel (cnd), Vienna PO [G] CBS 2–▲ M2K 42403 [DDD]

Mahler, G.:Das Lied von der Erde, w. K. König (ten), K. Tennstedt (cnd), London PO EMI Classics ▲ CDC 54603

Mahler, G.:Syms, w. J. Blegen (sop), B. Hendricks (sop), M. Price (sop), G. Zeumer (sop), H. Wittek (trb), C. Ludwig (mez), K. Riegel (ten), H. Prey (bar), A. Schmidt (bar), J. Van Dam (b–bar), L. Bernstein (cnd), New York PO, Royal Concertgebouw Orch, Vienna PO, Westminster Choir, New York Choral Artists, Brooklyn Boys' Choir, Vienna Boys' Choir, Vienna State Opera Chorus, Vienna Singverein Deutsche Grammophon 13–▲ 435162–2 [DDD]

Mahler, G.:Sym 3, w. L. Maazel (cnd), Vienna PO, Vienna Phil Chorus [G] CBS 2–▲ M2K 42403 [DDD]

Mahler, G.:Sym 8, w. J. Blegen (sop), M. Price (sop), G. Zeumer (sop), K. Riegel (ten), H. Prey (bar), A. Schmidt (bar), J. Van Dam (b–bar), L. Bernstein (cnd), Vienna PO, Vienna State Opera Chorus, Vienna Boys' Choir *(rec Salzburg Festival, 1975)* Deutsche Grammophon 2–▲ 435102–2 [ADD]

Mascagni, P.:Cavalleria rusticana, w. S. Mentzer (mez) P. Domingo (ten), J. Pons (bar), G. Sinopoli (cnd), Philharmonia Orch, Royal Opera House Chorus Covent Garden [I] Deutsche Grammophon ▲ 429568–2 [DDD]

Mascagni, P.:Cavalleria rusticana (sels), w. J. Carreras (ten), P. Domingo (cnd), London SO, Tallis Chamber Choir—Tu qui, Santuzza?; La tua Santuzza [w. M. Hintermeier (mez)] *(rec Jan.–Feb. 1991)* Sony Classical ▲ SK 53968 [DDD]

Mascagni, P.:Cavalleria rusticana (sels), w. Agnes Baltsa (mez—Santuzza), Plácido Domingo (ten—Turiddu), G. Sinopoli (cnd), Philharmonia Orch—No, no, Turiddu Deutsche Grammophon ▲ 447270–2 [DDD] ■ 447 270–4

Massenet, J.:Thérèse, w. Agnes Baltsa (mez—Thèrése), Francisco Araiza (ten—Armand), Gino Sinimberghi (ten—Officer), George Fortune (bass—André), Giancarlo Luccardi (bass—Morel), Eftimios Michalopoulos (sgr—Officer/Municipal Officer), G. Albrecht (cnd), Rome RAI SO, Giuseppe Piccillo (cnd), Rome RAI Chorus Orfeo ▲ 387961 [DDD]

Massenet, J.:Werther (sels), w. J. Carreras (ten), P. Domingo (cnd), London SO, Tallis Chamber Choir—Orchestral Intro.; Il faut nous séparer; Mais vous ne savez rien de moi; Rêve! Extase! *(rec Jan.–Feb. 1991)* Sony Classical ▲ SK 53968 [DDD]

Mozart, W.A.:Arias, w. Arleen Augér (sop), Kathleen Battle (sop), Irma Beilke (sop), Helena Braun (sop), Lisa Della Casa (sop), Maria Cebotari (sop), Ileana Cotrubas (sop), Helen Donath (sop), Mirella Freni (sop), Reri Grist (sop), Edita Gruberova (sop), Elisabeth Grümmer (sop), Hilde Güden (sop), Ingeborg Hallstein (sop), Luise Helletsgruber (sop), Gundula Janowitz (sop), Sena Jurinac (sop), Erika Köth (sop), Evelyn Lear (sop), Wilma Lipp (sop), Margaret Marshall (sop), Edith Mathis (sop), Jarmila Novotna (sop), Margherita Perras (sop), Lucia Popp (sop), Elisabeth Rethberg (sop), Anneliese Rothenberger (sop), Elisabeth Schumann (sop), Elisabeth Schwarzkopf (sop), Graziella Sciutti (sop), Irmgard Seefried (sop), Graziella Sciutti (sop), Julia Varady (sop), Margit Bokor (mez), Brigitte Fassbaender (mez), Christa Ludwig (mez), Ann Murray (mez), Francisco Araiza (ten), Anton Dermota (ten), Helge Rosvaenge (ten), Rudolf Schock (ten), Peter Schreier (ten), Leopold Simoneau (ten), Eric Tappy (ten), Richard Tauber (ten), Gösta Winbergh (ten), Josef Witt (ten), Fritz Wunderlich (ten), Christian Boesch (bar), Willy Domgraf–Fassbaender (bar), Karl Dönch (bar), Dietrich Fischer–Dieskau (bar), Erich Kunz (bar), Eberhard Wächter (bar), Hans Hotter (b–bar), Paul Schöffler (b–bar), Cesare Siepi (b–bar), José Van Dam (b–bar), Walter Berry (bass), Geraint Evans (bass), Nicolai Ghiaurov (bass), Alexander Kipnis (bass), Richard Mayr (bass), Kurt Moll (bass), James Morris (bass), Ezio Pinza (bass), Martti Talvela (bass), Giorgio Tozzi (bass), Hans Duhan (sgr), Res Fischer (sgr), Marie Gerhart (sgr), *(various orchs & cnds)*—sels from Idomeneo, Die Entführung aus der Serail, Le nozze di Figaro, Don Giovanni, Così fan tutte, Die Zauberflöte & various arias Orfeo d'or ("Festspiel Dokumente" series) 5–▲ 408955

Mozart, W.A.:Complete Mozart Edition, w. A. Augér (sop), E. Gruberova (sop), I. Cotrubas (sop), W. Hollweg (ten), L. Hager (cnd), Salzburg Mozarteum Orch Philips 3–▲ 422529–2 [ADD]

Baltsa, Agnes (mez) (cont.)
Mozart, W.A.:Complete Mozart Edition, w. A. Augér (sop), E. Mathis (sop), P. Schreier (ten), L. Hager (cnd), Salzburg Mozarteum Orch Philips 3–▲ 422530–2 [ADD]
Mozart, W.A.:Don Giovanni, w. A. Tomowa-Sintow (sop), K. Battle (sop), G. Winbergh (ten), S. Ramey (bass), F. Furlanetto (bass), P. Burchuladze (bass), H. von Karajan (cnd), Berlin PO, German Opera Chorus [I] Deutsche Grammophon 3–▲ 419179–2 [DDD]
Mozart, W.A.:Don Giovanni (sels), w. A. Tomowa-Sintow (sop), K. Battle (sop), G. Winbergh (ten), S. Ramey (bass), F. Furlanetto (bass), P. Burchuladze (bass), H. von Karajan (cnd), Berlin PO, German Opera Chorus [I] Deutsche Grammophon ▲ 419635–2 [DDD]
Mozart, W.A.:Idomeneo, w. L. Popp (sop), E. Gruberova (sop), L. Pavarotti (ten), L. Nucci (bar), J. Pritchard (cnd), Vienna PO, Vienna State Opera Chorus [I] London 3–▲ 411805–2 [DDD]
Mozart, W.A.:Missa, K.317, w. A. Tomowa-Sintow (sop), W. Krenn (ten), J. van Dam (b–bar), H. von Karajan (cnd), Berlin PO, Vienna Singverein Deutsche Grammophon ▲ 429820–2 [ADD]
Mozart, W.A.:Missa, K.317, w. A. Tomowa-Sintow (sop), W. Krenn (ten), J. van Dam (b–bar), H. von Karajan (cnd), Berlin PO, Vienna Singverein [L] Deutsche Grammophon ("Galleria" series) 2–▲ 423913–2 [ADD]
Mozart, W.A.:Nozze di Figaro, w. L. Popp (sop), B. Hendricks (sop), G. Raimondi (ten), J. Van Dam (bar), N. Marriner (cnd), Academy of St. Martin in the Fields, Ambrosian Opera Chorus [I] Philips 3–▲ 416370–2 [DDD]
Mozart, W.A.:Nozze di Figaro (sels), w. L. Popp (sop), B. Hendricks (sop), G. Raimondi (ten), J. van Dam (b–bar), N. Marriner (cnd), Academy of St. Martin in the Fields, Ambrosian Opera Chorus [I] Philips ▲ 416870–2 [DDD]
Mozart, W.A.:Requiem, w. A. Tomowa-Sintow (sop), W. Krenn (ten), J. van Dam (b–bar), H. von Karajan (cnd), Berlin PO, Vienna Singverein [L] Deutsche Grammophon ("Galleria" series) ▲ 419867–2 [ADD] ■ 419867–4
Mozart, W.A.:Requiem, w. A. Tomowa-Sintow (sop), W. Krenn (ten), J. van Dam (b–bar), H. von Karajan (cnd), Berlin PO, Vienna Singverein Deutsche Grammophon ▲ 429821–2 [ADD] ■ 429821–4
Mozart, W.A.:Zauberflöte, w. Edith Mathis (sop), Karin Ott (sop), Janet Perry (sop), Anna Tomowa-Sintow (sop), Hannah Schwarz (mez), Francisco Araiza (ten), Gottfried Hornik (bar), José Van Dam (b–bar), H. von Karajan (cnd), Berlin PO, German Opera Chorus [G] Deutsche Grammophon 3–▲ 410967–2 [DDD]
Mozart, W.A.:Zauberflöte (sels), w. Edith Mathis (sop), Karin Ott (sop), Janet Perry (sop), Anna Tomowa-Sintow (sop), Hannah Schwarz (mez), Francisco Araiza (ten), Gottfried Hornik (bar), José Van Dam (b–bar), H. von Karajan (cnd), Berlin PO, German Opera Chorus [G] Deutsche Grammophon ▲ 415287–2 [DDD]
Opera Arias, w. Munich Radio Orch [cnd:Heinz Wallberg] Orfeo ▲ 171881 [DDD]
Ponchielli, A.:La Gioconda, w. M. Caballé (sop), L. Pavarotti (ten), S. Milnes (bar), N. Ghiaurov (bass), B. Bartoletti (cnd), National PO [I] London 3–▲ 414349–2 [DDD]
Rossini, G.:Arias, w. I. Marin (cnd), Vienna SO, Vienna State Opera Chorus—arias from Barbiere di Siviglia, Cenerentola, Donna del lago, Italiana in Algeri, Maometto II, Semiramide, Tancredi [I] Sony Classical ▲ SK 45964
Rossini, G.:Il barbiere di Siviglia (sels), w. S. Burgess (mez), F. Araiza (ten), T. Allen (bar), D. Trimarchi (bar), R. Lloyd (bass), N. Marriner (cnd), Academy of St. Martin in the Fields Philips ▲ 438498–2
Rossini, G.:La Cenerentola, w. C. Malone (sop), F. Palmer (sop), F. Araiza (ten), S. Alaimo (bar), J. del Carlo (bass), R. Raimondi (bass), N. Marriner (cnd), Academy of St. Martin in the Fields, Ambrosian Chorus Philips ("Digital Classics" series) 3–▲ 420468–2 [DDD]
Rossini, G.:L'italiana in Algeri, w. F. Lopardo (ten), E. Dara (bar), R. Raimondi (bass), C. Abbado (cnd), Vienna PO, Vienna State Opera Chorus [I] Deutsche Grammophon 2–▲ 427331–2 [DDD]
Saint-Saëns, C.:Samson et Dalila, w. J. Carreras (ten), Summers (bar), Estes (bass), Burchuladze (bass), C. Davis (cnd), Bavarian RSO, Bavarian Radio Chorus Philips 2–▲ 426243–2 [DDD]
Saint-Saëns, C.:Samson et Dalila (sels), w. J. Carreras (ten), D. George (ten), J. Summers (bar), S. Estes (bass), P. Burchuladze (bass), C. Davis (cnd), Bavarian RSO Philips ▲ 438504–2
Strauss (II), Joh.:Die Fledermaus, w. L. Popp (sop), E. Lind (sop), P. Domingo (ten), W. Brendel (bar), K. Rydl (bass), P. Domingo (cnd), Munich RSO, Bavarian Radio Chorus [G] EMI Classics 2–▲ CDCB 47480
Strauss, R.:Ariadne auf Naxos, w. A. Tomowa-Sintow (sop), K. Battle (sop), G. Lakes (ten), H. Prey (bar), J. Levine (cnd), Vienna PO Deutsche Grammophon 2–▲ 419225–2 [DDD]
Strauss, R.:Der Rosenkavalier, w. A. Tomowa-Sintow (sop), J. Perry (sop), K. Moll (bass), H. von Karajan (cnd), Vienna PO, Vienna State Opera Chorus [G] Deutsche Grammophon 3–▲ 423850–2 [DDD]
Strauss, R.:Salome, w. H. Behrens (sop), H. Angervo (alt), K.W. Böhm (ten), W. Ochman (ten), J. van Dam (bar), H. von Karajan (cnd), Vienna PO EMI Classics 2–▲ CDCB 49358
Verdi, G.:Aida, w. L. Freni (sop), K. Ricciarelli (sop), J. Carreras (ten), P. Cappuccilli (bar), G. Raimondi (ten), J. Van Dam (b–bar), H. von Karajan (cnd), Vienna PO, Vienna State Opera Chorus [I] EMI Classics (Studio) 3–▲ CDMC 69300 [ADD]
Verdi, G.:Requiem Mass, w. Anna Tomowa-Sintow (sop), José Carreras (ten), José Van Dam (bass-bar), H. von Karajan (cnd), Vienna PO, Vienna State Opera Chorus, Sofia National Opera Chorus *(rec Great Hall, Musikverein, Vienna, June 1984)* Deutsche Grammophon 2–▲ 439033–2 [DDD]
Verdi, G.:Requiem Mass, w. Renata Scotto (sop), Veriano Luchetti (ten), Evgeny Nesterenko (bass), R. Muti (cnd), Philharmonia Orch, Ambrosian Chorus EMI Classics 2–▲ CDFB 68613
Verdi, G.:La traviata (sels), w. J. Carreras (ten), P. Domingo (cnd), London SO, Tallis Chamber Choir—Libiamo, libiamo ne' lieti calici *(rec Jan.-Feb. 1991)* Sony Classical ▲ SK 53968 [DDD]
Verdi, G.:Il trovatore (sels), w. J. Carreras (ten), P. Domingo (cnd), London SO, Tallis Chamber Choir—Soli or siamo; Non son tuo figlio; L'usato messo Ruiz m'invia [w. J. Howard (tenor)] *(rec Jan.-Feb. 1991)* Sony Classical ▲ SK 53968 [DDD]
Wagner, R.:Tannhäuser, w. C. Studer (sop), P. Domingo (ten), A. Schmidt (bar), M. Salminen (bass), G. Sinopoli (cnd), Philharmonia Orch, Royal Opera House Chorus Covent Garden Deutsche Grammophon ▲ 435405–2 [DDD]
Wagner, R.:Tannhäuser, w. C. Studer (sop), P. Domingo (ten), A. Schmidt (bar), M. Salminen (bass), G. Sinopoli (cnd), Philharmonia Orch, Royal Opera House Chorus Covent Garden [G] Deutsche Grammophon 3–▲ 427625–2 [DDD]

Bampton, Rose (sop)
Beethoven, L. van:Fidelio (sels), w. A. Toscanini (cnd), NBC SO—Act 1 aria, "Abscheulicher! Wo eilst du hin?" ("The Toscanini Collection, Vol. 46") RCA Gold Seal ▲ 60280–2–RG ■ 60280–4–RG
Mozart, W.A.:Don Giovanni, w. Jarmila Novotna (sop), Bidú Sayão (sop), Charles Kullman (ten), Alexander Kipnis (bass), Ezio Pinza (bass), B. Walter (cnd), *(orch unknown) (rec Mar 7, 1942)* Enterprise ("The Fourties" series) 3–▲ ENT 301
Schoenberg, A.:Gurrelieder, w. P. Althouse (ten), L. Stokowski (cnd), Philadelphia Orch, Fortnightly Club, Princeton Glee Club, Mendelssohn Club Philadelphia *(rec live Apr. 9, 1932)* Pearl 2–▲ PEA 9066 [AAD]
Verdi, G.:Aida (sels), w. Lydia Summers (mez), Arthur Carron (ten), Leonard Warren (bar), W. Pelletier (cnd), Philadelphia studio musicians, New York studio musicians—Ritorna vincitor!; Rivedrai le foreste imbalsamate; Odimi, Aida; La fatal pietra...O terra, addio! *(rec Academy of Music, Philadelphia & Town Hall, New York, May 30 & June 17, 1940)* VAI Audio ▲ VAIA 1084
Wagner, R.:Lohengrin (sels), w. Arthur Carron (ten), Norman Cordon (bass), W. Steinberg (cnd), Philadelphia studio musicians, New York studio musicians—Einsam in trüben Tagen; Das süsse Lied verhallt *(rec Academy of Music, Philadelphia & Town Hall, New York, May 27 & 28, 1940)* VAI Audio ▲ VAIA 1084
Wagner, R.:Tannhäuser (sels), w. W. Steinberg (cnd), Philadelphia studio musicians, New York studio musicians—Dich, teure Halle *(rec Academy of Music, Philadelphia, May 27, 1940)* VAI Audio ▲ VAIA 1084
Wagner, R.:Tristan und Isolde (sels), w. Lydia Summers (mez), Arthur Carron (ten), W. Steinberg (cnd), Philadelphia studio musicians, New York studio musicians—Wohl kenn' ich Irlands Königin; O sink' hernieder; Wohin nun Tristan scheidet; Mild und leise *(rec Academy of Music, Philadelphia & Town Hall, New York, May 26 & 27, 1940)* VAI Audio ▲ VAIA 1084
Wagner, R.:Die Walküre (act 1/scene 3), w. Set Svanholm (ten), A. Toscanini (cnd), NBC SO, NBC Sym Chorus [G] *(rec rehearsals & performance, New York, 4/4–6/47)* Myto 2–▲ 2 MCD 90316 (m) [ADD]

Banaudi, Antonella (sop)
Verdi, G.:Il trovatore, w. Antonella Banaudi (sop—Leonora), Barbara Frittoli (sop—Ines), Shirley Verrett (mez—Azucena), Enrico Facini (ten—Un messo), Piero de Palma (ten—Ruiz), Luciano Pavarotti (ten—Marico), Leo Nucci (bar—Il Conte di Luna), Roberto Scaltriti (bar—Un vecchio zingaro), Francesco Ellero d'Artegna (bass—Ferrando), Z. Mehta (cnd), Florence Maggio Musicale Orch, Florence Maggio Musicale Chorus *(rec Maggio Musicale Fiorentino Community Theater, June 18–July 2, 1990)* London 2–▲ 430694–2

Bandera, Claudia Nicole (alt)
Rossini, G.:Petite messe solennelle, w. M. Musacchio (sop), G. Dominguez (ten), J. Mannov (bass), U. Koella (pno), N. Clayton (pno), F. Näf (cnd), *(chorus unknown)* Ars Musici ▲ AM 1091 [DDD]

Bándi, Janos (ten)
Handel, G.F.:Brockes-Passion, w. K. Farkas (sop), M. Zádori (sop), D. Minter (alt), M. Klietmann (ten), G. de Mey (ten), I. Gáti (bar), N. McGegan (cnd), Capella Savaria, Hallé State Chorus [period instrs] [G] Hungaroton 3–▲ HCD 12734/36 [DDD]
Liszt, F.:Septam sacramenta, w. T. Takács (mez), G. Kallay (ten), K. Kaváts (bar), Zsuzsa Elekes (org), I. Zámbó (cnd), Hungarian State Orch, Hungarian People's Army Male Chorus, Jeunesses Musicales Women's Chorus [L] Hungaroton ▲ HCD 12748 [DDD]
Mahler, G.:Sym 8, w. Lyudmila Hadzhieva (sop), Maria Temeshi (sop), Darina Takova (sop), Tamara Takac (alt), Boryana Tabakova (alt), Pal Kovacs (bar), Tamash Syule (bass), E. Tabakov (cnd), Sofia PO, Bulgarian National Chorus, Bulgarian National Radio Chorus, Bulgarian National Radio Children's Choir *(rec National Palace of Culture, Sofia, June 1991)* Capriccio 15–▲ 49043 [DDD]

Banditelli, Gloria (cta)
Caldara, A.:Stabat Mater, w. Monika Frimmer (sop), Gerd Türk (ten), Peter Frank (bass), L. Rovatkay (cnd), Capella Agostino Steffani, Westphalia Kantorei EMI Classics ▲ CDC 54845
Cimarosa, D.:Il Matrimonio segreto, w. Susan Patterson (sop—Carolina), Janet Williams (mez—Elisseta), Gloria Banditelli (cta—Fidalma), William Matteuzzi (ten—Paolino), Alfonso Antoniozzi (bass—Geronimo), Petteri Salomaa (bass—Count Robinson), Hans Ludwig Hirsch (pno), G. Bellini (cnd), Eastern Netherlands Orch *(rec Muziekcentrum Enschede, Holland, Aug 26–Sept 8, 1991)* Arts 3–▲ 471172 [DDD]
Frescobaldi, G.:Arie musicali per cantarsi, w. R. Bertini (sop), C. Cavina (alt), G. Maletto (ten), S. Naglia (ten), S. Foresti (bass), R. Alessandrini (cnd), Concerto Italiano Opus 111 2–▲ OPS 30–105/106
Gluck, C.W.:Le Cinesi, w. I. Poulenard (sop), A. S. von Otter (mez), G. de Mey (ten), R. Jacobs (cnd), Schola Cantorum Basiliensis Instrumental Ensemble Editio Classica ▲ 77174–2–RG [DDD]
Handel, G.F.:Agrippina, w. S. Bradshaw (sop), W. Hill (sop), L. Saffer (sop), D. Minter (alt), R. Popken (alt), B. Szilágyi (bar), M. Dean (b–bar), N. Isherwood (bass), N. McGegan (cnd), Capella Savaria [period instrs] [I] Harmonia Mundi USA 3–▲ HMU 907063/65 ■ HMU 407063/65
Handel, G.F.:Poro, Rè dell'Indie, w. Rossana Bertini (sop), Bernarda Fink (cta), Gérard Lesne (ct), F. Biondi (cnd), Europa Galante Opus 111 3–▲ OPS 30–113/15
Monteverdi, C.:Ritorno d'Ulisse, w. Villanueva (sgr), Tucker (sgr), A. Curtis (cnd), Sonatori de la Gioiosa Marca [I] Nuova Era ("Ancient Music" series) 3–▲ 7103/05 [DDD]
Pergolesi, G.B.:Adriano in Siria, w. D. Dessi (sop), J. Omilian (sop), L. Mazzaria (sop), S. Anselmi (sop), E. di Cesare (ten), M. Panni (cnd), Rome Opera CO [I] *(rec live 12/20/86)* Bongiovanni 3–▲ GB 2078/80 [DDD]
Pergolesi, G.B.:Stabat mater, w. Monika Frimmer (sop), Gerd Türk (ten), Peter Frank (bass), L. Rovatkay (cnd), Capella Agostino Steffani, Westphalia Kantorei EMI Classics ▲ CDC 54845
Peri, J.:Euridice, w. Monica Benvenuti (sop—Ninfa I/Venere), Rossana Bertini (sop—Dafne/Ninfa II), Gloria Banditelli (cta—Euridice/Ninfa III/Tragedia/Proserpina), Mario Cecchetti (ten—Aminta/Radamanto), Paolo Da Col (ten—Tirsi), Gianpaolo Fagotto (ten—Orfeo), Giuseppe Zambon (ct—Arcetro), Sergio Foresti (bass—Caronte/Pastore), Furio Zanasi (bass—Plutone), R. de Caro (cnd), Arpeggione Ensemble *(rec Bologna, Italy, Nov 1992)* Arts Music 2–▲ 47276–2 [DDD]
Rossini, G.:La Cenerentola, w. C. Bartoli (mez—Cenerentola), F. Costa (mez—Clorinda), G. Banditelli (cta—Tisbe), W. Matteuzzi (ten—Don Ramiro), A. Corbelli (bar—Dandini), E. Dara (bar—Don Magnifico), M. Pertusi (bass—Alidoro), R. Chailly (cnd), Bologna Teatro Comunale Orch, Bologna Teatro Comunale Chorus *(rec June 22–July 2, 1992)* London 2–▲ 436902–2 [DDD]
Scarlatti, A.:Santa Maria Maddalena de'pazzi, w. R. Bertini (sop), Sylvia Piccollo (sop), F. Biondi (cnd), Europa Galante Opus 111 ▲ OPS 30–96
Vivaldi, A.:Juditha triumphans devicta Holofernes barbarie, w. M. Zádori (sop), J. Németh (mez), K. Gémes (mez), A. Markert (cta), N. McGegan (cnd), Capella Savaria, Savaria Vocal Ensemble [L] Hungaroton 2–▲ HCD 31063/64 [DDD]
Vivaldi, A.:Son al St. Sepolcro, w. Monika Frimmer (sop), Gerd Türk (ten), Peter Frank (bass), L. Rovatkay (cnd), Capella Agostino Steffani, Westphalia Kantorei EMI Classics ▲ CDC 54845
Werner, G.J.:Debora, w. W. Hill (sop), M. Klietmann (ten), K. Mertens (b–bar), P. Németh (cnd), Capella Savaria Quintana ▲ QUI 903062

Banescu, Jean (bass)
Verdi, G.:Rigoletto, w. Victoria Draganescu (sop—Countess Ceprano), Magda Ianculescu (sop—Gilda), Dorothea Palade (mez—Maddalena), Valeria Savu (mez—Giovanna), Ion Buzea (ten—Duke of Mantua), Dimitrie Scurtu (ten—Borsa), Nicolae Herlea (bar—Rigoletto), Stefan Petrescu (bar—Marullo), Jean Banescu (bass—Count Ceprano), Nicolae Florei (bass—Monterone), Nicolae Rafael (bass—Sparafucile), J. Bobescu (cnd), Romanian Opera Orch, Romanian Opera Chorus *(rec 1965)* Vox Box 2–▲ CDX 5162

Baniewicz, Wiera (mez)
Moniuszko, S.:Haunted Manor, w. Bozena Betley-Siradzka (sop—Hanna), Anna Witkowska (sop—Marta/Stara Niewiasta), Wiera Baniewicz (mez—Jadwiga), Aleksandra Imalska (mez—Czesnikowa), Kazimierz Dluha (Grzes), Zdzislaw Nikodem (ten—Damazy), Wieslaw Ochman (ten—Stefan), Andrzej Hiolski (bar—Miecznik), Florian Skulski (bar—Maciej), Leonard Mróz (bass—Zbigniew), Andrzej Saciuk (bass—Skoluba), J. Krenz (cnd), Cracow Polish Radio-TV Orch, Cracow Polish Radio-TV Chorus *(rec Cracovia, 1978)* Agorá Music ("Phoenix" series) 3–▲ 509 [ADD]

Banks, Anna Victoria (mez)
Menotti, G.C.:Canti della lontananza, w. S. Costanzo (pno) [I] Nuova Era ▲ 7122 [DDD]
Menotti, G.C.:The Telephone, w. G. L. Ricci (bar), P. Vaglieri (cnd), Milan CO [E] Nuova Era ▲ 7122 [DDD]
Paisiello, G.:La Serva padrona, w. A. V. Banks (mez—Serpina), G. L. Ricci (bar—Umberto), P. Vaglieri (cnd), Milan CO [I] Nuova Era ▲ 7043 [DDD]

Banks, Barry (ten)
Sullivan, A.:Trial by Jury, w. Rebecca Evans (sop—Plaintiff), Barry Banks (ten—Defendant), Gareth Rhys-Davies (bar—Foreman of the Jury), Peter Savidge (bar—Counsel for the Plaintiff), Donald Adams (bass—Usher), Richard Suart (bass—The Learned Judge), C. Mackerras (cnd), Welsh National Opera Orch, Welsh National Opera Chorus *(rec Brangwyn Hall, Swasea, Wales, Apr 18–30 & May 1, 1995)* Telarc 2–▲ CD 80404 [DDD]

Bannatyne-Scott, Brian (bass)
Purcell, H.:King Arthur, w. N. Argenta (sop), J. Gooding (sop), L. Perillo (sop), J. MacDougall (ten), M. Tucker (ten), G. Finley (bar), T. Pinnock (cnd), English Concert, *(chorus unknown)* Archiv 2–▲ 435490–2 [DDD]
Smyth, E.:The Wreckers, w. Judith Howarth (sop), Anne-Marie Owens (mez), Annemarie Sand (mez), Justin Lavender (ten), Anthony Roden (ten), Peter Sidhom (bar), David Wilson-Johnson (bar), O. de la Martinez (cnd), BBC PO, Huddersfield Choral Society *(rec live, Royal Albert Hall, London, July 31, 1994)* Conifer Classics 2–▲ 75605–51250–2

Banse, Juliane (sop)
Hindemith, P.:Songs, w. Axel Bauni (pno)—34 sels including Lieder mit Klavier, Op. 18; Gesang; Vier Lieder nach Texten des Angelus Silesius; Abendständchen; Singet leise; Wer wusste je das Leben; Der Einsiedler; Du bist mein; Zum Abscheid meiner Tochter; Ich will Trauern lassen stehn; Abendwolke Orfeo ▲ 413961 [DDD]
Mozart, W.A.:Regina coeli, K.276, w. H.R. Zöbeley (cnd), Munich Residenz Orch, Munich Motet Choir Calig ▲ CAL 50901 [DDD]
Schoeck, O.:Songs (comp), w. D. Henschel (ten), W. Rieger (pno)—Wandsbecker Liederbuch, Op. 52; Im Nebel, Op. 45; 6 Lieder, Op. 51; 3 Lieder, Op. 35 *(rec May 1991)* Jecklin ▲ JD 677–2 [DDD]

1058 ▲ = CD ♦ = Enhanced CD Δ = MD ■ = Cassette Tape □ = DCC

Banse, Juliane (sop) (cont.)
Schoeck, O.:Songs (comp), w. Dietrich Henschel (bar), Wolfram Rieger (pno)—3 Songs, Op. 4; 4 Songs, Op. 8; Vorwurf, Op. 27; 3 Songs, Op. 10; 3 Songs, Op. 13; Lieder nach Gedichten von Goethe, Op. 19a; Lieder aus dem "Westöstlichen Divan" von Goethe, Op. 19b *(rec Feb 1994)* Jecklin ▲ JD 675

Bantzer, C. (nar)
Mendelssohn, F.:A Midsummer Night's Dream (comp), w. P. Coburn (sop), E. von Magnus (alt/nar), N. Harnoncourt (cnd), CO of Europe Teldec ▲ 74882-2
Zimmermann, B.A.:Ich wandte mich und sah an alles Unrecht, das geschah unter der Sonne, w. W. Quadflieg (nar), S. Nimsgem (b-bar), W. Humburg (cnd), Münster SO Stradivarius ▲ STR 33340

Banuelas, Roberto (bar)
Beethoven, L. van:Sym 9, "Choral Sym", w. Irma Gonzalez (sop), Oralia Dominguez (cta), Flavio Becerra (ten), F. Lozano (cnd), Mexico City PO, Mexico City Chorus Forlane ▲ FRL 18 [AAD]

Banzet, M.-L. (bar)
Haik-Vantoura, S.:The Song of Songs, w. S. Haik-Vantoura (mez), R. Boschiero (hp), S. Chefson (fl), E. Dutrieux (cnd), *(chorus unknown)* [He] *(rec 1986)* Alienor ▲ AL 1045 [DDD]

Baquerizo, Enrique (sgr)
Bretón, T.:La Verbena de la paloma, w. Maria Bayo (sop), Raquel Pierotti (sop), Plácido Domingo (ten), Rafael Castejon (sgr), Milagros Martin (sgr), Silva Tro (sgr), A. Ros-Marbá (cnd), Madrid SO Valois ("Zarauela" series) ▲ V 4725

Bär, Olaf (bar)
Bach, C.P.E.:Magnificat, w. V. Hruba-Freiberger (sop), B. Bornemann (alt), P. Schreier (ten), H. Haenchen (cnd), C.P.E. Bach CO, Berlin Radio Chorus Berlin Classics ▲ BER 1011 [DDD]
Bach, J.S.:Cant 36, w. N. Argenta (sop), R. Lang (mez), A. Rolfe Johnson (ten), J. E. Gardiner (cnd), English Baroque Soloists, Monteverdi Choir London Archiv ▲ 437327-2
Bach, J.S.:Cant 56, w. P. Schreier (cnd), Scottish CO, Scottish Chamber Chorus [G] *(rec May 1991)* EMI Classics ▲ CDC 54453-2 [DDD]
Bach, J.S.:Cant 61, w. N. Argenta (sop), R. Lang (mez), A. Rolfe Johnson (ten), J. E. Gardiner (cnd), English Baroque Soloists, Monteverdi Choir London Archiv ▲ 437327-2 [DDD]
Bach, J.S.:Cant 62, w. N. Argenta (sop), R. Lang (mez), A. Rolfe Johnson (ten), J. E. Gardiner (cnd), English Baroque Soloists, Monteverdi Choir London Archiv ▲ 437327-2 [DDD]
Bach, J.S.:Cant 82, w. P. Schreier (cnd), Scottish CO, Scottish Chamber Chorus *(rec May 1991)* EMI Classics ▲ CDC 54453-2 [DDD]
Bach, J.S.:Cant 158, w. P. Schreier (cnd), Scottish CO, Scottish Chamber Chorus *(rec 5/91)* EMI Classics ▲ CDC 54453-2 [DDD]
Bach, J.S.:Christmas Oratorio, w. N. Argenta (sop), A. S. von Otter (mez), H.-P. Blochwitz (ten), J. E. Gardiner (cnd), English Baroque Soloists, Monteverdi Choir London [G] Archiv 2-▲ 423232-2 [DDD]
Bach, J.S.:Christmas Oratorio (sels), w. N. Argenta (sop), A. S. von Otter (mez), H.-P. Blochwitz (ten), J. E. Gardiner (cnd), English Baroque Soloists, Monteverdi Choir London [G] Archiv ▲ 427653-2 [DDD]
Bach, J.S.:St. Matthew Passion, w. B. Bonney (sop), A. Monoyios (sop), A. S. von Otter (mez), M. Chance (ct), H. Crook (ten), A. Rolfe Johnson (ten), A. Schmidt (bar), C. Hauptmann (bass), J. E. Gardiner (cnd), English Baroque Soloists, Monteverdi Choir London [G] Archiv 3-▲ 427648-2 [DDD]
Bach, J.S.:St. Matthew Passion, w. K. Te Kanawa (sop), A. S. von Otter (mez), H. P. Blochwitz (ten), A. Rolfe Johnson (ten), T. Krause (bass), G. Solti (cnd), Chicago SO, Chicago Sym Chorus, Glen Ellyn Children's Chorus [G] London 3-▲ 421177-2 [DDD]
Bach, J.S.:St. Matthew Passion (sels), w. K. Te Kanawa (sop), A. S. von Otter (mez), H. P. Blochwitz (ten), A. Rolfe Johnson (ten), T. Krause (bass), G. Solti (cnd), Chicago SO, Chicago Sym Chorus, Glen Ellyn Children's Chorus [G] London ▲ 425691-2 [DDD]
Beethoven, L. van:Songs, w. G. Parsons (pno) EMI Classics ▲ CDC 54879
Brahms, J.:Liebeslieder Waltzes SATB, w. Barbara Bonney (sop), Anne Sofie von Otter (mez), Kurt Streit (ten), Bengt Forsberg (pno), Helmut Deutsch (pno) EMI Classics ▲ CDC 55430
Brahms, J.:Neue Liebeslieder Waltzes, w. Barbara Bonney (sop), Anne Sofie von Otter (mez), Kurt Streit (ten), Bengt Forsberg (pno), Helmut Deutsch (pno) EMI Classics ▲ CDC 55430
Fauré, G.:Requiem, w. A. Murray (mez), S. Cleobury (cnd), English CO, King's College Choir Cambridge EMI Classics ▲ CDC 49880
Haydn, J.:Die Schöpfung, w. Barbara Bonney (mez), Edith Wiens (sop), Hans-Peter Blochwitz (ten), Jan-Herdrik Rootering (bass), N. Marriner (cnd), Stuttgart Radio Orch, Stuttgart Radio Chorus [G] EMI Classics 2-▲ CDCB 54038 [DDD]
Lieder, w. Geoffrey Parsons (pno) EMI Classics ▲ ZDHB 64292 [DDD]
Mozart, W.A.:Così fan tutte, w. Renée Fleming (sop—Fiordiligi), Adelina Scarabelli (sop—Despina), Anne Sofie Von Otter (mez—Dorabella), Frank Lopardo (ten—Ferrando), Olaf Bar (bar—Guglielmo), Michele Pertusi (bass—Don Alfonso), G. Solti (cnd), CO of Europe London 3-▲ 444174-2
Mozart, W.A.:Zauberflöte, w. K. Te Kanawa (sop), C. Studer (sop), E. Lind (sop), F. Araiza (ten), S. Ramey (bass), N. Marriner (cnd), Academy of St. Martin in the Fields, Ambrosian Opera Chorus [G] Philips 2-▲ 426276-2 [DDD]
Mozart, W.A.:Zauberflöte (sels), w. K. Te Kanawa (sop), C. Studer (sop), E. Lind (sop), F. Araiza (ten), S. Ramey (bass), N. Marriner (cnd), Academy of St. Martin in the Fields Philips ▲ 430495-2
Schumann, R.:Spanisches Liederspiel, w. Barbara Bonney (sop), Anne Sofie von Otter (mez), Kurt Streit (ten) Olaf Bär (bar), Bengt Forsberg (pno), Helmut Deutsch (pno) EMI Classics ▲ CDC 55430
Strauss (II), Joh.:Die Fledermaus, w. K. Te Kanawa (sop), E. Gruberová (sop), B. Fassbaender (mez), W. Brendel (bar), R. Leech (ten), T. Krause (bar), A. Previn (cnd), Vienna PO, Vienna State Opera Chorus [G] Philips 2-▲ 432157-2 [DDD]
Strauss (II), Joh.:Die Fledermaus (sels), w. K. Te Kanawa (sop), E. Gruberova (sop), B. Fassbaender (mez), R. Leech (ten), W. Brendel (bar), A. Previn (cnd), Vienna PO Philips ▲ 438503-2
Strauss, R.:Ariadne auf Naxos, w. J. Norman (sop), J. Varady (sop), E. Gruberova (sop), P. Frey (ten), D. Fischer-Dieskau (bar), K. Masur (cnd), Leipzig Gewandhaus Orch [G] Philips 2-▲ 422084-2 [DDD]
Strauss, R.:Capriccio, w. Kiri Te Kanawa (sop—Gräfin), Brigitte Fassbaender (mez—Clairon), Uwe Heilmann (ten—Flamand), Werner Hollweg (ten—Taupe), Olaf Bär (bar—Olivier), Håkan Hagegård (bar—Graf), Victor von Halem (b-bar—La Roche), U. Schirmer (cnd), Vienna PO [G] *(rec Vienna, Dec 1993)* London 2-▲ 444405-2 [DDD]
Wolf, H.:Italienische Liederbücher (comp), w. Dawn Upshaw (sop), Helmut Deutsch (pno) EMI Classics ▲ CDC 55618
Wolf, H.:Spanisches Liederbuch, w. Anne Sofie von Otter (mez), Geoffrey Parsons (pno) EMI Classics ▲ CDC 55325

Barabas, Sari (sop)
Dostal, N.:Clivia (sels), w. Heinz Hoppe (ten), W. Schubert (cnd), Graunke SO, Bavarian Radio Chorus Emperor Operetta ▲ KO 86352
Fall, L.:Die Dollarprinzessin (sels), w. Christine Gorner (sop), Harry Friedauer (ten), Heinz Hoppe (ten), C. Michalski (cnd), Graunke SO, Botho Lucas Chorus Emperor Operetta ▲ KO 86353
Fall, L.:Der liebe Augustin (sels), w. Christine Gorner (sop), Heinz Hoppe (ten), Benno Kusche (b-bar), C. Michalski (cnd), Graunke SO, Rudolf Lamy Singers Emperor Operetta ▲ KO 86352
Lehár, F.:Zigeunerliebe (sels), w. Christine Gorner (sop), Harry Friedauer (ten), Heinz Hoppe (ten), C. Michalski (cnd), Graunke SO, Rudolf Lamy Singers Emperor Operetta ▲ KO 86342
Mozart, W.A.:Entführung, w. R. Streich (sop), A. Dermota (ten), H. Krebs (ten), J. Greindl (bass), F. Fricsay (cnd), Berlin RSO, Berlin Radio Chorus [G] *(rec Jesus-Christuskirche, Berlin-Dahlem, Dec. 19-21, 1949)* Myto 2-▲ 2 MCD 92361 [ADD]

Baracchi, Aristide (bar)
Puccini, G.:La Bohème, w. Luba Mirella (sop—Musetta), Rosetta Pampanini (sop—Mimì), Luigi Marini (ten—Rodolfo), Giuseppe Nessi (ten—Alcindoro), Aristide Baracchi (bar—Schaunard), Gino Vanelli (bar—Marcello), Salvatore Baccaloni (bass—Benoit), Tancredi Pasero (bass—Colline), L. Molajoli (cnd), La Scala Orch, La Scala Chorus Bongiovanni 2-▲ 1125/26 [ADD]
Puccini, G.:La Bohème, w. Licia Albanese (sop—Mimì), Tatiana Menotti (sop—Musetta), Beniamino Gigli (ten—Rodolfo), Nello Palai (ten—Parpignol), Aristide Baracchi (bar—Schaunard), Afro Poli (bar—Marcello), Duilio Baronti (bass—Colline), Carlo Scattola (bass—Benoit/Alcindoro), U. Berrettoni (cnd), La Scala Orch, Vittore Veneziani (cnd), La Scala Chorus *(rec Feb-Mar 1938)* Arkadia ("The 78's" series) 2-▲ 78009 [ADD]

Baracchi, Aristide (bar) (cont.)
Puccini, G.:La Bohème, w. L. Albanese (sop—Mimì), T. Menotti (sop—Musetta), B. Gigli (ten—Rodolfo), N. Palai (ten—Parpignol), A. Poli (bar—Marcello), A. Baracchi (bar—Schaunard), D. Baronti (bass—Colline), C. Scattola (bass—Benoit/Alcindoro), U. Berrettoni (cnd), La Scala Orch, La Scala Chorus [I] *(rec Milan, May 1938)* Nimbus 2-▲ NI 7862/63 [ADD]
Puccini, G.:La Bohème, w. Rosina Torri (sop—Mimì), Thea Vitulli (sop—Musetta), Aristodemo Giorgini (ten—Rodolfo), Giuseppe Nessi (ten—Parpignol), Ernesto Badini (bar—Marcello), Aristide Baracchi (bar—Schaunard), Luigi Manfrini (bass—Colline), Salvatore Baccaloni (bass—Benoit/Alcindoro), C. Sabajno (cnd), La Scala Orch, La Scala Chorus *(rec 1928)* VAI Audio 2-▲ VAIA 1078-2
Puccini, G.:Madama Butterfly, w. Rosetta Pampanini (sop—Madama Butterfly), Conchita Velasquez (mez—Suzuki), Cesira Ferrari (mez—Kate Pinkerton), Alessandro Granda (ten—F. B. Pinkerton), Giuseppe Nessi (ten—Goro), Aristide Baracchi (bar—Il Principe Yamadori), Gino Vanelli (bar—Sharpless), Lino Bonardi (bass—Il Commissario Imperiale), Salvatore Baccaloni (bass—Lo zio Bonzo), L. Molajoli (cnd), La Scala Orch, La Scala Chorus Bongiovanni 2-▲ 1123/24 [ADD]
Rossini, G.:Il barbiere di Siviglia, w. Cesira Ferrari (mez—Berta), Mercedes Capsir (cta—Rosina), Dino Borgioli (ten—Count), Salvatore Baccaloni (bar—Bortolo), Aristide Baracchi (bar—Officer), Riccardo Stracciari (bar—Figaro), Vincenzo Bettoni (bass—Don Basilio), Attilo Bordonali (bass—Fiorello), L. Molajoli (cnd), La Scala Orch, La Scala Chorus *(rec 1930)* Arkadia ("The 78's" series) 2-▲ 78008 [ADD]
Verdi, G.:Rigoletto, w. Lina Pagliughi (sop—Gilda), Linda Brambilla (mez—Contessa di Ceprano), Vera de Cristoff (cta—Maddalena), Tino Folgar (ten—Duca di Mantova), Giuseppe Nessi (ten—Borsa), Aristide Baracchi (bar—Conte di Monterone/Marullo), Luigi Piazza (bar—Rigoletto), Salvatore Baccaloni (bass—Sparafucile), Giuseppe Menni (bass—Conte di Ceprano), C. Sabajno (cnd), La Scala Orch, La Scala Chorus *(rec 1927-28)* Arkadia 2-▲ CD 78003 (m) [ADD]
Verdi, G.:Rigoletto, w. Lina Pagliughi (sop—Gilda), Linda Brambilla (mez—Countess Ceprano), Vera De Cristoff (cta—Maddalena), Tino Folgar (ten—Duke of Mantua), Giuseppe Nessi (ten—Borsa), Luigi Piazza (bar—Rigoletto), Aristide Baracchi (b-bar—Monterone/Marullo), Salvatore Baccaloni (bass—Sparafucile), Giuseppe Menni (bass—Ceprano), C. Sabajno (cnd), La Scala Orch, La Scala Chorus VAI Audio 2-▲ VAIA 1097-2
Verdi, G.:La traviata, w. Maria Caniglia (sop—Violetta), Maria Huder (mez—Flora), Gladys Palmer (cta—Annina), Octave Dua (ten—Giuseppe), Beniamino Gigli (ten—Alfredo), Booth Hitchen (ten—D'Obigny), Adelio Zagonara (bar—Gastone), Aristide Baracchi (bar—Douphol), Mario Basiola (bar—Germont), Norman Walker (bass—Dr. Grenville), V. Gui (cnd), London PO, London Phil Chorus *(rec Royal Opera House, Covent Garden, May 22, 1939)* Minerva 2-▲ MN A28/29 (m) [ADD]

Baracchi, Aristide (bass)
Puccini, G.:Manon Lescaut, w. Maria Zamboni (sop—Manon), Anna Masetti-Bassi (mez—Singer), Francesco Merli (ten—Chevalier), Giuseppe Nessi (ten—Edmondo/Dancing Master/ Lamplighter), Lorenzo Conati (bar—Lescaut), Aristide Baracchi (bass—Innkeeper/Sergeant), Attilio Bordonali (bass—Geronte), Natale Villa (bass—Naval Captain), L. Molajoli (cnd), La Scala Orch, Vittore Veneziani (cnd), La Scala Chorus *(rec 1930)* Arkadia ("The 78's" series) 2-▲ 78014 [ADD]

Barainsky, Claudia (sop)
Reimann, A.:Lady Lazarus *(rec Studio II, Radio Free Berlin, Jan 1995)* Orfeo ▲ C 412 961 [DDD]

Baran (sgr)
Verdi, G.:I vespri siciliani, w. J. Brumaire (sop), P. Bowden (mez), Bonhomme (sgr), Taylor (sgr), M. Rossi (cnd), BBC Concert Orch, BBC Concert Chorus [original French version] *(rec live, London, 5/10/69)* Arkadia 3-▲ 456 [ADD]

Baranska, Aleksandra (sop)
Suppé, F. von:Requiem, w. Katarzyna Suska (cta), Jerzy Knetig (ten), Andrjez Hiolski (bass), R. Bader (cnd), Cracow PO, Cracow Phil Chorus Koch Schwann ▲ SCH CD 312482

Baratti, Giuseppe (ten)
Bellini, V.:Il pirata, w. M. Caballé (sop), F. Rafanelli (sop), B. Marti (ten), P. Cappuccilli (bar), R. Raimondi (bass), G. Gavazzeni (cnd), Rome Radio-TV Orch, Rome Radio-TV Chorus [I] *(rec Rome, 1973)* EMI Classics 2-▲ CDMB 64169
Bellini, V.:Il pirata, w. Montserrat Caballé (sop—Imogene), Flora Raffanelli (sop—Adele), Flaviano Labó (ten—Gualtiero), Giuseppe Baratti (ten—Itulbo), Piero Cappuccilli (bar—Ernesto), E. Ghiglia (cnd), Florence Teatro Comunale Orch, Florence Teatro Comunale Chorus *(rec live, Florence, 1967)* Melodram 2-▲ IMC 205002 [ADD]
Bellini, V.:Il pirata, w. M. Caballè (sop), F. Raffanelli (sop), F. Labò (ten), P. Cappuccilli (bar), U. Trama (bass), E. Ghiglia (cnd), *(orch unknown)* *(rec Florence, 1967)* Great Opera Performances ▲ GOP 729
Rossini, G.:L'equivoco Stravagante, w. M. Guglielmi (sop), R. Panerai (bar), S. Bruscantini (b-bar), B. Rigacci (cnd), *(orch unknown)* [I] *(rec Naples, 1974)* Golden Age of Opera 2-▲ GAO 154/55

Barbacini, Paolo (ten)
Rossini, G.:Il barbiere di Siviglia (sels), w. M. Horne (mez), R. Pierotti (mez), E. Dara (bar), L. Nucci (bar), S. Ramey (bass), S. Sammaritano (bass), R. Chailly (cnd), La Scala Orch, La Scala Chorus *(rec Milan, Jan. 2-18, 1982)* Sony Classical ("Opera Highlights" series) ▲ SMK 53501 [DDD]
Rossini, G.:La pietra del paragone, w. M. C. Nocentini (sop), A. Trovarelli (mez), H. M. Molinari (cta), V. Di Matteo (bar), R. Scaltriti (bar), A. Svab (bar), P. Rumetz (bass), C. Desderi (cnd), Camerata Musicale Orch, Modeno Teatro Comunale Chorus [I] *(rec 1992)* Nuova Era 2-▲ 7132/33 [DDD]
Verdi, G.:Falstaff, w. Maureen O'Flynn (sop), Daniela Dessi (sop), Bernadette Manca di Nissa (mez), Delores Ziegler (mez), Ramon Vargas (ten), Ernesto Gavazzi (ten), Juan Pons (bar), Roberto Frontali (bar), Luigi Roni (bass), R. Muti (cnd), La Scala Orch, La Scala Chorus *(rec Milan La Scala Theater, Italy, Mar. 29 & 31)* Sony Classical ▲ S2K 58961 [DDD]

Barbary, Béatrice (sop)
Kaufmann, S.:Et si un jour, w. B. Calmel (cnd), Bernard Calmel Orch, Marielle Rousseau Vocal Ensemble *(rec Feb 1996)* Pavane ▲ ADW 7362 [DDD]
Kaufmann, S.:Un Matin à varsovie, w. Philippe Pennanguer (vc), Serge Kaufmann (nar), B. Calmel (cnd), Bernard Calmel Orch *(rec Feb 1996)* Pavane ▲ ADW 7362 [DDD]

Barbato, Elisabetta (sop)
Cilea, F.:Adriana Lecouvreur (sels), w. A. Simonetto (cnd), Turin Radio-TV SO—Io Son l'Umile Ancella Fonit Cetra ("Martini & Rossi" series) ▲ FCT CDMR 5009
Puccini, G.:Tosca (sels), w. A. Simonetto (cnd), Turin Radio-TV SO—Vissi d'Arte Fonit Cetra ("Martini & Rossi" series) ▲ FCT CDMR 5009
Verdi, G.:Aida (sels), w. A. Simonetto (cnd), Turin Radio-TV SO Fonit Cetra ("Martini & Rossi" series) ▲ FCT CDMR 5009
Verdi, G.:La forza del destino (sels), w. A. Simonetto (cnd), Turin Radio-TV SO—Pace, Mio Dio Fonit Cetra ("Martini & Rossi" series) ▲ FCT CDMR 5009
Verdi, G.:La forza del destino (sels), w. B. Gigli (ten), E. Mascherini (bar), G. Neri (bass), A. Votto (cnd), Rio de Janeiro Teatro Municipale Orch, Rio de Janeiro Teatro Municipale Chorus [I] *(rec live 8/16/51)* Standing Room Only ▲ SRO 807-1 (m) [ADD]

Barbaux, Christina (sop)
Debussy, C.:La Chute de la maison Usher, w. J.P. Lafont (bass), G. Prêtre (cnd), Monte Carlo PO EMI Classics ▲ CDM 64687
Mozart, W.A.:Clemenza, w. Christine Barbaux (sop—Servilia), Carol Vaness (sop—Viellia), Martha Senn (mez—Annio), Delores Ziegler (mez—Sesto), Gösta Winbergh (ten—Tito), László Polgár (bass—Publio), R. Muti (cnd), Vienna PO, Vienna State Opera Chorus *(rec live, Salzburg Festival, 1988)* EMI Classics 2-▲ CDCB 55489
Schmitt, F.:Le palais hanté, w. J.P. Lafont (bass), G. Prêtre (cnd), Monte Carlo PO EMI Classics ▲ CDM 64687

Barber, Kim (mez)
Kernis, A.J.:America(n) (Day) Dreams, w. Mary Rowell (vn), Leslie Tomkins (va), Tonya Tomkins (vc), Robert Black (db), Kathleen Nester (fl), Larry Guy (cl/b cl), John Dent (tpt), Anthony Cecere (hn), Leslie Stifelman (pno), Susan Jolles (hp), Jeffrey Milarsky (perc), M. Barrett (cnd)—A Navajo Blanket; Wednesday at the Waldorf; The Pregnant Dream; The Blue Bottle; "So Long" to the Moon from the Men of Apollo; Epilogue:The Pure Suit of Happiness *(rec Manhattan Center Studios, New York, May 31-June 3, 1995)* New Albion ♦ NA 083CD

Barber, Sally (sop)
Howells, H.:Requiem, w. Julia Field (alt), Mark Johnstone (ten), Andrew Angus (bar), Jeremy Backhouse (cnd), Vasari Singers *(rec All Hallows, Gospel Oak, Feb 18-20, 1994)* United ▲ CAL 88033 [DDD]

Barbesi, Attilo (bass)
Strauss, R.:Der Rosenkavalier, w. Jarmila Barton (sop—Marianne), Lisa Della Casa (sop—Sophie), Sena Jurinac (sop—Octavian), Ilva Ligabue (sop—Orphan), Elisabeth Schwarzkopf (sop—Marschallin), Else Schürhoff (mez—Annina), Luisa Villa (mez—Milliner), Hugues Cuénod (ten—Marschallin's majordomo), Erich Majkut (ten—Valzacchi), Giuseppe Nessi (ten—Animal seller), Luciano Della Pergola (ten—Lackey/Faninal's majordomo), Antonio Pirino (ten—An Italian Singer), Gino Del Signore (ten—Lackey/Waiter), Erich Kunz (bar—Herr von Faninal), Paolo Pedani (bar—Lackey), Attilo Barbesi (bass—Lackey/Waiter), Enrico Campi (bass—Waiter), Otto Edelmann (bass—Baron Ochs), Bruno Fichtinger (bass—Notary), Franco Taino (bass—Waiter), Maria Amadini (sgr—Orphan), Pina Carrillo (sgr—Orphan), Joszi Trojan Regar (sgr—Innkeeper), H. von Karajan (cnd), La Scala Orch, La Scala Chorus *(rec La Scala Theater, Milan, Jan. 26, 1952)* Legato Classics 3-▲ LCD 197-3

Barbieri, Fedora (cta)
Verdi, G.:Un ballo in maschera, w. Maria Caniglia (sop), Beniamino Gigli (ten), Gino Bechi (bar), T. Serafin (cnd), Rome Opera Orch, Rome Opera Chorus *(rec Rome, July, 1943)* Grammofono 2000 2-▲ GRM 78556

Barbieri, Fedora (mez)
Cherubini, L.:Médée, w. M. Callas (sop), G. Penno (ten), G. Modesti (bass), Nache (sgr), L. Bernstein (cnd), La Scala Orch, La Scala Chorus [I] *(rec live, Milan 12/10/53)* Verona 2-▲ 27088/89
Cherubini, L.:Médée, w. M. Callas (sop), G. Penno (ten), G. Modesti (bass), Nache (sgr), L. Bernstein (cnd), La Scala Orch, La Scala Chorus [I] *(rec live 12/10/53)* Melodram 2-▲ MEL 26022 (m) [AAD]
Cherubini, L.:Médée, w. M. Callas (sop), M. Petri (bar), V. Gui (cnd), Florence Maggio Musicale Orch, Florence Maggio Musicale Chorus [I] *(rec 1953)* Arkadia 2-▲ 516 (m) [AAD]
Cimarosa, D.:Il Matrimonio segreto (sels), w. H. Gueden (sop), A. Noni (sop), T. Schipa (ten), S. Bruscantini (bar), B. Christoff (bass), M. Rossi (cnd), La Scala Orch—Act I highlights [I] *(rec live, Milan March 22, 1949)* Melodram 2-▲ CDM 29505 [ADD]
Giordano, U.:Andrea Chénier (sels), w. R. Tebaldi (sop), M. del Monaco (ten), P. Silveri (bar), V. de Sabata (cnd), La Scala Orch, La Scala Chorus—14 arias from Acts 1-3 [I] *(rec live, Milan, 3/6/49)* Myto ▲ 1 MCD 90634 [ADD]
Mascagni, P.:Cavalleria rusticana, w. E. Obraztsova (mez), P. Domingo (ten), R. Bruson (bar), G. Prêtre (cnd), La Scala Orch, La Scala Chorus [I] Philips ▲ 416137-2 [DDD]
Ponchielli, A.:La Gioconda, w. M. Callas (sop), G. Poggi (ten), P. Silveri (bar), G. Neri (bass), A. Votto (cnd), Turin RAI SO, Turin RAI Chorus *(rec 1952)* Andromeda 3-▲ ANR 2528 [ADD]
Ponchielli, A.:La Gioconda, w. M. Callas (sop), G. Poggi (ten), P. Silveri (bar), G. Neri (bass), A. Votto (cnd), Turin RAI SO, Turin RAI Chorus *(rec 1952)* Enterprise ("Palladio" series) ▲ ENT PD 4152 [DDD]
Ponchielli, A.:La Gioconda, w. M. Callas (sop—Gioconda), F. Barbieri (mez—Laura), M. Amadini (sgr—La Cieca), G. Poggi (ten—Enzo), P. Silveri (bar—Barnaba), G. Neri (bass—Alvise), A. Votto (cnd), Turin RAI Orch, Turin RAI Chorus *(rec 1952)* Cetra Classic 3-▲ CDO 8
Puccini, G.:Il trittico, w. V. de los Angeles (sop), G. Prandelli (ten), T. Gobbi (bar), *(other soloists unknown)*, Rome Opera Orch, Rome Opera Chorus *(rec Rome, 1950s)* EMI Classics 3-▲ CDMC 64165 (m)
Rossini, G.:Il barbiere di Siviglia, w. Beverly Sills (sop), Nicolai Gedda (ten), Renato Capecchi (bar), Sherill Milnes (bar), Ruggero Raimondi (bass), J. Levine (cnd), London SO, John Alldis Choir EMI Classics 2-▲ CDMB 66040
Tebaldi, Barbieri & Valletti, w. R. Tebaldi (sop), Cesare Valletti (ten), Fighera, Nino Sanzogno (cnd), Turin RAI SO, Milan RAI SO *(rec Martini & Rossi Concert, 1951 & 1953)* Incontri Memorabili ▲ CDMR 5012
Verdi, G.:Aida, w. Z. Milanov (sop), J. Björling (ten), L. Warren (bar), B. Christoff (bass), J. Perlea (cnd), Rome Opera Orch, Rome Opera Chorus [I] RCA Gold Seal ▲ 60201-2-RG (m) [ADD] ■ 60201-4-RG (m)
Verdi, G.:Aida, w. Z. Milanov (sop), J. Björling (ten), L. Warren (bar), B. Christoff (bass), J. Perlea (cnd), Rome Opera Orch, Rome Opera Chorus [I] RCA Gold Seal 3-▲ 6652-2-RG (m) [ADD] 3-■ ALK3-5380 (m)
Verdi, G.:Aida, w. A. Stella (sop), F. Corelli (ten), A. Colzani (bar), M. Petri (bar), V. Gui (cnd), Naples Teatro San Carlo Orch, Naples Teatro San Carlo Chorus [I] *(rec live, Naples 11/2/55)* Golden Age of Opera 2-▲ GAO 116/17 [ADD]
Verdi, G.:Aida, w. M. Callas (sop), G. Tucker (ten), T. Gobbi (ten), N. Zaccaria (bass), T. Serafin (cnd), La Scala Orch, La Scala Chorus [I] EMI Classics 3-▲ CDCC 49030 [ADD]
Verdi, G.:Un ballo in maschera, w. M. Callas (sop), E. Ratti (sop), G. Di Stefano (ten), T. Gobbi (bar), A. Votto (cnd), La Scala Orch, La Scala Chorus [I] *(rec 1956)* EMI Classics 2-▲ CDCB 47498 (m)
Verdi, G.:Un ballo in maschera, w. Maria Caniglia (sop—Amelia), Fedora Barbieri (mez—Ulrica), Beniamino Gigli (ten—Riccardo), Gino Bechi (bar—Renato), Tancredi Pasero (bass—Samuel), Blando Giusti (sgr—Un Giudice), Nicola Niccolini (sgr—Silvano), Ugo Novelli (sgr—Tom), Elda Ribetti (sgr—Oscar), T. Serafin (cnd), Rome Opera Orch, Giuseppe Conca (cnd), Rome Opera Chorus *(rec 1943)* Arkadia 2-▲ CD 78005 (m) [ADD]
Verdi, G.:Un ballo in maschera (sels), w. Maria Caniglia (sop), Gina Cigna (sop), Enrico Carusa (ten), Beniamino Gigli (ten), Giovanni Zenatello (ten), Carlo Galeffi (bar), Lawrence Tibbett (bar), *(various orchs & cnds) (rec 1911-43)* Grammofono 2000 ▲ GRM 78527 (m)
Verdi, G.:Don Carlos, w. A. Cerquetti (sop), A. LoForese (ten), E. Bastianini (bar), C. Siepi (b-bar), G. Neri (bass), A. Votto (cnd), Florence Maggio Musicale Orch, Florence Maggio Musicale Chorus *(rec July 16, 1956)* Melodram 3-▲ MLO 670104 [ADD]
Verdi, G.:Don Carlos, w. G. Brouwenstein (sop—Elisabeta di Valois), F. Barbieri (mez—Princess Eboli), J. Vickers (ten—Don Carlo), T. Gobbi (bar—Rodrigo), B. Christoff (bass—Fillipo), C. M. Giulini (cnd), Royal Opera House Orch, Royal Opera House Chorus Covent Garden *(rec 1958)* Myto 3-▲ MCD 94197
Verdi, G.:Requiem Mass, w. H. Nelli (sop), G. Di Stefano (Ten), C. Siepi (b-bar), A. Toscanini (cnd), NBC SO, Robert Shaw Chorale [L] RCA Gold Seal 2-▲ 60299-2-RG (m) [ADD] 2-■ 60299-4-RG (CrO2)
Verdi, G.:Il trovatore, w. Leyla Gencer (sop—Leonora), Laura Londi (sop—Ines), Fedora Barbieri (mez—Azucena), Mario del Monaco (ten—Manrico), Athos cesarini (ten—Ruiz), Walter Artioli (ten—Messanger) Ettore Bastianini (bar—Count Luna), Plinio Clabassi (bass—Ferrando), Sergio Liliani (bass—Gypsy), F. Previtali (cnd), Milan RAI SO, Milan RAI Chorus *(rec live, Milan, May 29, 1957)* Arkadia 2-▲ 483 [ADD]
Verdi, G.:Il trovatore, w. Franco Corelli (ten), Ettore Bastianini (bar), Agostino Ferrin (bass), Mirella Parutto (sgr), O. de Fabritiis (cnd), Rome Opera Orch, Rome Opera Chorus Stradivarius 2-▲ STV DTM 12313 [ADD]
Verdi, G.:Il trovatore, w. Z. Milanov (sop), J. Björling (ten), L. Warren (bar), R. Cellini (cnd), RCA Victor SO, Robert Shaw Chorale [I] RCA Gold Seal 2-▲ 6643-2-RG (m) [ADD] 2-■ CLK2-5377 (m)
Verdi, G.:Il trovatore, w. Z. Milanov (sop), J. Björling (ten), L. Warren (bar), R. Cellini (cnd), RCA Victor SO, Robert Shaw Chorale [I] RCA Gold Seal ▲ 60191-2-RG [ADD] ■ 60191-4-RG (CrO2)

Barbieri, Gianni (bass)
Verdi, G.:Don Carlos, w. Anita Cerquetti (sop), Cesare Siepi (b-bar), Ettore Bastianini (bar), A. Votto (cnd), Florence Maggio Musicale Orch, Florence Maggio Musicale Chorus Melodram 3-▲ CDM 370104

Barcellona, Daniela (sgr)
Monteverdi, C.:Ballo delle ingrate, w. Carlo Lepore (bass), Daniela Ciliberti (sgr), Andrea Concetti (sgr), Hans van Dijk (sgr), Remo Guerrini (sgr), Nadia Mantelli (sgr), Elena Marazzi (sgr), Humberto Orellana (sgr), Claudia Pallini (sgr), Luigi Polsini (sgr), Rosa Ricciotti (sgr), Alberto Rota (sgr), Ludovica Scoppola (sgr), *(orch unknown)* Nuova Era ▲ NUO 7224

Barcoe, S. (sgr)
Bach, C.P.E.:Die Israeliten in der Wüste, w. L. Lootens (sop), B. Schlick (sop), H. Meens (ten), W. Christie (cnd), Cappella Coloniensis, Corona Musique d'Abord ▲ HMA 1901321

Bardelli, Cesare (bar)
Ponchielli, A.:La Gioconda (sels), w. Z. Milanov (sop), C. Turner (mez), R. Turrini (sgr), W. Herbert (cnd), *(orch & chorus unknown)*—abridged:the part of Goiconda [Milanov] is presented complete [I] *(rec live, New Orleans, 11/5/53)* Standing Room Only ▲ SRO 814-1 [ADD]

Bardi, Giorgio Kokolios (ten)
Verdi, G.:I vespri siciliani, w. Maria Callas (sop—Duchess), Giorgio Kokolios Bardi (ten—Arrigo), Gino Sarri (ten—Danieli), Enzo Mascherini (bar—Guido di Monforte), Boris Christoff (bass—Giovanni da Procida), Mario Forsini (bass—Count Vaudemont), Bruneo Carmassi (bass—Bethune), E. Kleiber (cnd), Florence Teatro Comunale Orch, Florence Teatro Comunale Chorus *(rec live, Florence, 1951)* Melodram 3-▲ IMC 303016 [ADD]

Bardolet, Sebastiá (trb)
Britten, H.:A Ceremony of Carols, w. X. Canadell (trb), J. Pieres (alt), F. Gasa (alt), M. L. Ibañez (hp), G. Estrada (org), Escolania de Montserrat, I. Segarra (cnd) *(rec 1978?)* Koch Treasure ▲ 31624-2 [ADD]
Mendelssohn, F.:Motets, Op. 39, w. X. Canadell (trb), J. Pieres (alt), F. Gasa (alt), M. L. Ibañez (hp), G. Estrada (org), I. Segarra (cnd), Montserrat Escolania *(rec 1978?)* Koch Treasure ▲ 31624-2 [ADD]

Bardon, Patricia (mez)
Tchaikovsky, P.:Eugene Onegin, w. K. Te Kanawa (sop—Tatiana), P. Bardon (mez—Olga), N. Rosenshein (ten—Lensky), T. Hampson (b-bar—Eugene Onegin), J. Connell (bass—Prince Gremin), C. Mackerras (cnd), Welsh National Opera Orch, Welsh National Opera Chorus [E] EMI Classics ▲ CDCB 55004

Bardot, Francis (ten)
Mozart, W.A.:Missa, K.427, w. C. Pozderec (sop), M. C. LeBlanc (sop), L. Peintre (bar), F. Bardot (cnd), Altaïr SO, Paris Opera Children's Choir [L] Thésis ▲ THE11003

Barés, Equidad (sgr)
Poder a Santa Maria, w. S. Wishart (cnd), Sinfonye, Vivien Ellis (sgr), Paula Chateauneuf (sgr), Jim Denley (sgr) *(rec Cartuja de Santa María de Cazalla de la Sierra, Seville, Oct. 1993)* Almaviva ▲ 0105 [DDD]

Bareva, Rumiana (sop)
Orff, C.:Carmina burana, w. H. Kamenov (ten), Yanukov (bar), G. Robev (cnd), Sofia PO, Bulgarian choirs [G, L] Forlane ▲ FOR 16556 [DDD]

Barha, Edmund (ten)
Rule Britannia, w. J. Wallace (tpt), Wallace Collection, Leeds Festival Chorus, English String Orch [cnd:William Boughton] Nimbus ▲ NI 5155 [DDD]

Barham, Edmund (ten)
Golden Melodies from Opera, w. R. Hickox (cnd), London SO, Royal PO [cnd:R. Stapelton], S. McCulloch (sop), Josephine Barstow (sop), J. Oakman (ten) Pickwick ("The Orchid" series) ▲ PICORCD 11005

Barick, David (bar)
Andriessen, L.:Mausoleum, w. Charles van Tassel (bar), R. de Leeuw (cnd), Asko Ensemble, Schoenberg Ensemble Donemus ▲ CV 20
Purcell, H.:Dido & Aeneas, w. C. Van Lunen (sop), R. A. Morgan (mez), R. Shaw (cnd), Academy of the Begynhof Amsterdam [E] Globe ▲ GLO 5020 [DDD]

Barioni, Daniele (ten)
Il mito dell'opera, w. Barioni, Daniele (ten), various orchs *(rec between 1962-68)* Bongiovanni ▲ GB 1077 [ADD]
Puccini, G.:Madama Butterfly, w. Dorothy Kirsten (sop—Madama Butterfly), Rosalind Nadell (mez—Suzuki), Eileen Ireland (mez—Kate), Daniele Barioni (ten—Pinkerton), Thomas Carter (ten—Goro), Arthur Cosenza (ten—Yamadori), Richard Torigi (bar—Sharpless), Rodney Hall (bass—The Bronze), Harold Crane (bass—Commissioner), R. Cellini (cnd), New Orleans Opera Orch, New Orleans Opera Chorus *(rec live, Mar 1960)* VAI Audio 2-▲ VAIA 1054-2

Barker, Edwin (bass)
In The Family, w. R. Barron (trbn), Marianne Gedigian (fl), Ann Hobson Pilot (hp), Douglas Yeo (trbn), Thomas Gauger (perc) *(rec Morse Auditorium, Boston Univ, Dec 1995)* Boston Brass ▲ BB 1004

Barlay, Zsuzsa (cta)
Puccini, G.:Suor angelica, w. I. Tokody (sop), B. Póka (bar), L. Gardelli (cnd), Hungarian State Opera Orch, Hungarian State Opera Chorus [I] Hungaroton ▲ HCD 12490
Schumann, R.:Requiem, Op. 148, w. E. Andor (sop), Korondy (sgr), J. Gregor (bass), M. Forrai (cnd), Hungarian State Orch, Budapest Chorus [L] Hungaroton ▲ HCD 11809
Schumann, R.:Requiem Mignon, w. E. Andor (sop), Korondy (sgr), J. Gregor (bass), M. Forrai (cnd), Hungarian State Orch, Budapest Chorus [L] Hungaroton ▲ HCD 11809
Vivaldi, A.:Juditha triumphans devicta Holofernes barbarie, w. Margit László (sop—Abra), Zsuzsa Barlay (cta—Juditha), József Réti (ten—Servo), Zsolt Bende (bar—Holofernes), József Dene (bar—Ozias), F. Szekeres (cnd), Hungarian State Orch, György Czigány (cnd), Budapest Madrigal Choir, 1968 Classical Diamonds ▲ CLD 4022-23 [ADD]

Baronchelli, Davide (bass)
Pacini, G.:Saffo, w. Francesca Pedaci (sop—Saffo), Gemma Bertagnolli (sop—Dirce), Mariana Pentcheva (mez—Climene), Carlo Ventre (ten—Faone), Aled Hall (ten—Ippia), Roberto de Candia (bar—Alcandro), Davide Baronchelli (bass—Lisimaco), M. Benini (cnd), Irish National SO, Lubomír Mátl (cnd), Wexford Festival Opera Chorus *(rec Wexford, Oct & Nov 1995)* Marco Polo 2-▲ 8.223883-4 [DDD]
Wolf-Ferrari, E.:I quatro rusteghi, w. A P (Margarita), D. Lombardi (Lucieta), G. Merrino (Marina), M. Fratarcangeli (Felice) L. Belluso (Servant), A. Abete (Lunardo), M. Nicolini (Maurizio), G. Sorrentino (Filipeto), M. Peirone (Simon), D. Baronchelli (Cancian), A. Lemmo (Count Riccard) Arkadia-Akademia 2-▲ 139 [DDD]

Baronti, Duilio (bass)
Puccini, G.:La Bohème, w. L. Albanese (sop—Mimi), T. Menotti (sop—Musetta), B. Gigli (ten—Rodolfo), N. Palai (ten—Parpignol), A. Poli (bar—Marcello), A. Baracchi (bar—Schaunard), D. Baronti (bass—Colline), C. Scattola (bass—Benoit/Alcindoro), U. Berrettoni (cnd), La Scala Orch, La Scala Chorus [I] *(rec Milan, May 1938)* Nimbus 2-▲ NI 7862/63 [ADD]
Puccini, G.:La Bohème, w. Licia Albanese (sop—Mimi), Tatiana Menotti (sop—Musetta), Beniamino Gigli (ten—Rodolfo), Nello Palai (ten—Parpignol), Aristide Baracchi (bar—Schaunard), Afro Poli (bar—Marcello), Duilio Baronti (bass—Colline), Carlo Scattola (bass—Benoit/Alcindoro), U. Berrettoni (cnd), La Scala Orch, Vittore Veneziani (cnd), La Scala Chorus *(rec Feb-Mar 1938)* Arkadia ("The 78's" series) 2-▲ 78009 [ADD]
Verdi, G.:Luisa Miller, w. L. Kelston (sop—Luisa), M.T. Pace (mez—Federica), G. Larui-Volpi (ten—Rodolfo), S. Colombo (bar—Miller), G. Vaghi (bar—Count Walter), D. Baronti (bass—Wurm), M. Rossi (cnd), Rome RAI Orch, Rome RAI Chorus *(rec 1951)* Cetra Classic 2-▲ CDO 17 [AAD]
Verdi, G.:Rigoletto, w. Mercedes Capsir (sop), Dino Borgioli (ten), Riccardo Stracciari (bar), Ernesto Dominici (bass), Anna Masetti Bassi (sgr) *(rec 1930)* Grammofono 2000 2-▲ GRM 78632

Barová, Anna (cta)
Blacher, B.:A Jewish Chronicle, w. Vladimir Bauer (sgr), H. Kegel (cnd), Leipzig RSO, Leipzig Radio Chorus Berlin Classics ▲ BER 9016 [ADD]
Havelka, S.:Music of, w. Brigita Sulcova (sop), Vladimir Dolezal (ten), Richard Novak (bass), V. Neumann (cnd), Czech PO, Prague Phil Chorus—Epistola de M. Hieronymi De Praga Supplicio Panton ▲ PAN 810966

Barová, Anna (mez)
Foerster, J.B.:Eva, w. Eva Depoltová (sop), Leo Marian Vodicka (ten), Jaroslav Soucek (bar), F. Vajnar (cnd), Prague RSO, Prague Radio Chorus *(rec 1982)* Supraphon 2-▲ SUP 3001
Martinů, B.:Alexandre bis, w. J. Krátká (sop), R. Novák (ten), R. Tuček (bar), F. Jílek (cnd), Brno Janáček Opera Orch Supraphon ▲ SUP 11 2140 [AAD]
Martinů, B.:Comedy on the Bridge, w. J. Krátká (sop), R. Novák (ten), R. Tuček (bar), F. Jílek (cnd), Brno Janáček Opera Orch Supraphon ▲ SUP 11 2140 [AAD]
Martinů, B.:Echec au roi, w. V. Nosek (cnd), Brno State PO members *(rec Studio Dukla Brno, Aug 27, 1976)* Panton ("Protokol XX" series) ▲ PAN 811417 [ADD]
Reicha, A.:Der neue Psalm, w. Magdaléna Hajóssyová (sop), Andreas Schmidt (bar), Karel Průša (bass), L. Mátl (cnd), Dvořák CO, Czech Phil Chorus Panton ▲ PAN 810758 [DDD]
Reicha, A.:Requiem, w. V. Hrubá-Freiberger (sop), V. Dolezal (ten), L. Vele (bass), L. Mátl (cnd), Dvořák CO, Czech Phil Chorus [L] Supraphon ▲ 11 0332-2 [DDD]

Barrard, Marc (bar)
Ravel, M.:L'Enfant et les sortilèges, w. M. Lagrange (sop), E. Vidal (sop), M. Damonte (mez), M. Mahé (mez), A. Chedel (cta), L. Pezzino (ten), V. le Texier (b-bar), A. Lombard (cnd), Bordeaux-Aquitaine National Orch, Bordeaux Grand Théâtre Municipal Chorus [F] Valois ▲ V 4670

Barraud, Dany (sop)
Jolivet, A.:Hymne à St. André, w. Daniel Roth (org) Arion ▲ ARN 68299 [AAD]

Barreto-Ramos, Jonathan (sgr)
Schnittke, A.:Historia von D. Johann Fausten, w. Hanna Schwarz (mez—Fair Helen), Arno Raunig (alt—Mephostophiles), Eberhard Büchner (ten—Old Man), Jürgen Freier (bar—Dr. Johann Faustus), Jonathan Barreto-Ramos (sgr—Student), Jürgen Fersch (sgr—Student), Eberhard Lorenz (sgr—Erzähler), Christoph Johannes Wendel (sgr—Student), G. Albrecht (cnd), Hamburg State PO, Hamburg State Opera Chorus RCA Red Seal 2-▲ 09026-68413-2

Barrett, Brent (sgr)
Gershwin, G.:Strike up the Band, w. D. Chastain (sgr), R. Luker (sgr), J. Mauceri (cnd), *(orch unknown)* [based on original Gershwin manuscripts] Elektra/Nonesuch 2-▲ 79273-2 2-■ 79273-4

Barrett, David (bar)
Beethoven, L. van:Cant on the Death of the Emperor Joseph II, w. K. Te Kanawa (sop), Y. Newman (mez), M. Langdon (bass), C. Davis (cnd), BBC SO, BBC Chorus, BBC Choral Society [G] *(rec live Oct. 7, 1970)* Intaglio ▲ INCD 7361 [ADD]

Barrett, David (ten)
Milhaud, D.:L'Homme et son désir, w. Marion Davies (sop), Yvonne Newman (mez), Anthony Holt (bass), D. Milhaud (cnd), BBC SO IMP ("BBC Radio Classics" series) ▲ IMP 5691512

Barrientos, Maria (sop)
Falla, M. de:Canciones populares españolas (7), w. M. de Falla (pno) *(rec 1928)* Opal ▲ CD 9852 (m) [AAD]
Falla, M. de:Songs, w. M. de Falla (pno)—Canción del fuego fatuo from *Amor brujo*; Soneto a Cordoba *(rec 1928)* Opal ▲ CD 9852 (m) [AAD]
Maria Barrientos Opal ▲ CD 9852 (m) [AAD]

Barringer, Heather (voc)
Spasm, w. M. Lowenstern, Mark Gibbons (voc), Jay Johnson (voc), Jerome Kitzke (voc), Matt Lambiase (voc), Tom Linker (voc), Ed Lowenstern (voc), Michael Lowenstern (voc) *(rec Creation Audio, Minneapolis, NYU Studios, New York City & Studio A, Stony Brook, Aug 1994–July 1996)* New World ▲ 80468-2

Barrow, John (bar)
Vaughan Williams, R.:Fant on Christmas Carols, w. B. Rose (cnd), Guildford String Orch, Guildford Cathedral Choir [2 Christmas Carol choral arr. Vaughan Williams]—And all in the morning & Wassail Song EMI Classics (Studio) ▲ CDM 64131 2 [ADD]

Barrowman, John (sgr)
Lloyd Webber, A.:Music of, w. M. Friedman (sgr), C. Carter (sgr), C. Moore (sgr), L. Robertson (sgr), J. Diedrich (sgr), Grania Renihan (sgr), J.O. Edwards (cnd), Munich SO—Cats; Joseph & the Amazing Technicolor Dreamcoat; Phantom of the Opera; Evita; Jesus Christ Superstar; Starlight Express; Song & Dance; Aspects of Love Koch International ▲ CD 340022 [DDD] ■ MC 340022

Barrow-Theofanidis, Darla (sop)
Thofanidis, C.:Voices, w. C. Theofanidis (cnd), Barrow CO Albany ▲ TROY 158 [DDD]

Barry (sgr)
Bizet, G.:Don Procopio, w. Muscente (sgr), M. Gentile (sop), Carmona (sgr), A. Antoniozzi (bar), S. Sanna (cnd), Berlin Radio Youth Orch, Symbolon Ensemble Chorus [I] *(rec live 5/25/86)* Bongiovanni 2-▲ GB 2043/44 [DDD]

Barry, Jonathan (bar)
Beach, A.M.C.:Songs, w. Alan Mandel (pno)—The Year's at the Spring; Villanelle *(rec Harmony Hall, Hyattsville, MD, Nov 17–20, 1994)* Premier ▲ PRCD 1047 [DDD]
Carpenter, J.A.:Songs, w. Alan Mandel (pno)—In Spring; May, the Maiden; Sicilian Lullaby; To 1 Unknown *(rec Harmony Hall, Hyattsville, MD, Nov 17–20, 1994)* Premier ▲ PRCD 1047 [DDD]
Chadwick, G.W.:Songs, w. Alan Mandel (pno)—In Bygone Days; Sweet Wind; Sweetheart, Thy Lips Are Touched with Flame; Before the Dawn; The Bobolink; The Northern Days; O Love & Joy *(rec Harmony Hall, Hyattsville, MD, Nov 17–20, 1994)* Premier ▲ PRCD 1047 [DDD]
Foote, A.:Songs, w. Alan Mandel (pno)—The Wanderer to His Heart's Desire; A Song of 4 Seasons; The Nightingale Has a Lyre of Gold; The Rose & the Gardener; If Love Were What the Rose Is; Before Sunrise; Constancy; The Hawthorne Wins the Damask Rose; Love Me, If I Live!; A Song of Summer; Love in Her Cold Grave Lies *(rec Harmony Hall, Hyattsville, MD, Nov 17–20, 1994)* Premier ▲ PRCD 1047 [DDD]
Paine, J.K.:Songs, w. Alan Mandel (pno)—A Bird Upon a Rosy Bough; Matin Song; I Wore Your Roses Yesterday *(rec Harmony Hall, Hyattsville, MD, Nov 17–20, 1994)* Premier ▲ PRCD 1047 [DDD]
Parker, H.:Songs, w. Alan Mandel (pno)—The Complacent Lover; Pack, Clouds Away!; Come, O Come My Life's Delight; Slumber Song; Once I Loved a Maiden Fair *(rec Harmony Hall, Hyattsville, MD, Nov 17–20, 1994)* Premier ▲ PRCD 1047 [DDD]
Whiting, A.B.:Songs, w. Alan Mandel (pno)—O Love, Stay By & Sing *(rec Harmony Hall, Hyattsville, MD, Nov 17–20, 1994)* Premier ▲ PRCD 1047 [DDD]

Barstow, Josephine (sop)
Britten, H.:Gloriana, w. J. Barstow (sop—Queen Elizabeth I), D. Jones (mez—Lady Essex), P. Langridge (ten—Earl of Essex), J. M. Ainsley (ten—Spirit of the Masque), J. Summers (bar—Lord Mountjoy), J. Shirley-Quirk (bar—Recorder of Norwich), B. Terfel (b-bar—Henry Cuffe), C. Mackerras (cnd), Welsh National Opera Orch, Welsh National Opera Chorus Argo 2-▲ 440213-2 [DDD]
Dvořák, A.:Rusalka (sels), w. R. Stapleton (cnd), Royal PO—O Silver Moon IMP ("Concert Classics" series) ▲ IMP PCD 1103
Golden Melodies from Opera, w. R. Hickox (cnd), London SO, Royal PO [cnd:R. Stapelton], S. McCulloch (sop), J. Oakman (ten), Edmund Barham (ten) Pickwick ("The Orchid" series) ▲ PICORCD 11005
Tippett, M.:Sym 3, w. R. Leppard (cnd), BBC SO IMP ("BBC Radio Classics" series) ▲ IMP 9140
Verdi, G.:Un ballo in maschera, w. S. Jo (sop), F. Quivar (mez), P. Domingo (ten), L. Nucci (bar), H. von Karajan (cnd), Vienna PO, Vienna State Opera Chorus [I] Deutsche Grammophon 2-▲ 427635-2 [DDD]
Weill, K.:Street Scene, w. A. Réaux (sop), J. Hadley (ten), S. Ramey (bass), J. Mauceri (cnd), Scottish Opera Orch, Scottish Opera Chorus [E] London 2-▲ 433371-2 [DDD]

Bartelloni, Anne (mez)
Barraqué, J.:Le temps restitué, w. P. Méfano (cnd), Ensemble 2E2M Musique d'Abord ▲ HMA 1905199

Bartelme, Reid (trb)
Mendelssohn, F.:Elijah, w. Barbara Bonney (sop), Henriette Schellenberg (sop), Florence Quivar (mez), Marietta Simpson (mez), Jerry Hadley (ten), Richard Clement (ten), Thomas Hampson (bar), Thomas Paul (bar), R. Shaw (cnd), Atlanta SO, Atlanta Sym Chorus [E] *(rec Symphony Hall, Woodruff Arts Center, Atlanta, GA, Nov. 5–7, 1994)* Telarc 2-▲ CD 80389 [DDD]

Barth, Irmgard (mez)
Strauss, R.:Feuersnot, w. Maud Cunitz (sop—Diemut), Antonia Fahberg (sop—Elsbeth), Irmgard Barth (mez—Wigelis), Liselotte Nölser (sgr—Margret), Karl Ostertag (ten—Schweiker), Marcel Cordes (bar—Kunrad), Kieth Engen (bass—Kofel), Karl Hoppe (bass—Hämerlein), Max Proebstl (bass—Ortolf), Georg Wieter (bass—Jörg), R. Kempe (cnd), Bavarian State Opera Orch, Bavarian State Opera Chorus *(rec Munich Opera Festival, Prince Regent Theater, Aug 14, 1958)* Orfeo d'or 2-▲ 423962
Wagner, R.:Götterdämmerung, w. Birgit Nilsson (sop—Brünnhilde), Leonie Rysanek (sop—Gutrune), Gerda Sommerschuh (sop—Woglinde), Elisabeth Lindermeier (sop—Wellgunde), Ruth Michaelis (sop—Flohilde), Marianne Schech (sop—Dritte Norne), Ira Malaniuk (mez—Waltraute), Irmgarth Barth (mez—Erste Norne), Hertha Töpper (mez—Zweite Norne), Bernd Aldenhoff (ten—Siegfried), Hermann Uhde (bar—Gunther), Gottlob Frick (bass—Hagen), H. Knappertsbusch (cnd), Bavarian State Opera Orch, Bavarian State Opera Chorus *(rec live, Prinzregententheater, Sept. 1, 1955)* Orfeo 4-▲ 356944 (m)

Barth, Ned (bar)
Orff, C.:Antigonae, w. Christel Goltz (sop), Paul Kuen (ten), Karl Ostertag (ten), Benno Kusche (bar), Hermann Uhde (bar), G. Solti (cnd), Bavarian State Opera Orch, Bavarian State Opera Chorus *(rec Prinzregententheater, Jan. 12, 1951)* Orfeo d'or 2-▲ 407952
Rihm, W.:O Notte, w. B. Neuhold, G. Neuhold (cnd), *(orch unknown)* Bayer ▲ CAD 800886

Barth, Ned (bar) (cont.)
Verdi, G.:Simon Boccanegra, w. Alberto Cupido (ten), José Van Dam (b-bar), Manfred Schenk (bass), Daniela Longhi (sgr), Dino Musio (sgr), M. Veltri (cnd), Marseille Opera Orch, Marseille Opera Chorus Lyrinx 3-▲ LYX 127 [DDD]

Bartha, Alfonz (ten)
Liszt, F.:Requiem, w. Sándor Palcsó (ten), Zsolt Bende (bar), Pál Kovács (bar), A. Ferencsik (cnd), Hungarian State Orch, Hungarian People's Army Male Chorus [L] Hungaroton ▲ HCD 11267

Bartoli, Cecilia (mez)
Beethoven, L. van:Songs, w. A. Schiff (pno)—Ecco quel fiero istante!, WoO 124; Che fa il mio bene?, Op. 82/3; Che fa il mio bene?, Op. 82/4; T'intendo, si, mio cor, Op.82/1; Dimmi, ben mio, Op. 82/1; In questa tomba oscura, WoO 133 *(rec Aug. 5–8, 1992)* London ▲ 440297-2 [DDD]
Berlioz, H.:Songs, w. Myung-Whun Chung (pno)—La Mort d'Ophelie; Zaide London ▲ 452667-2 ■ 452667-4
Bizet, G.:Songs, w. Myung-Whun Chung (pno)—Chant d'amour; Oeuvre ton coeur; Adieux de l'hotesse arabe; Tarantelle; La Coccinelle London ▲ 452667-2 ■ 452667-4
Caccini, G.:Amarilli mia bella, w. György Fischer (pno) *(rec 1990)* London ▲ 448300-2 [DDD]; ■ 448300-4
Delibes, L.:Les Filles de Cadix, w. Myung-Whun Chung (pno) London ▲ 452667-2 ■ 452667-4
Giordano, U.:Arias, w. György Fischer (pno)—Caro mio ben *(rec 1990)* London ▲ 448300-2 [DDD] ■ 448300-4
Haydn, J.:L'Anima del filosofo, or Orfeo ed Euridice, w. Uwe Heilmann (ten), Ildebrando d'Arcangelo (bass), C. Hogwood (cnd), Academy of Ancient Music, Academy of Ancient Music Chorus L'oiseau Lyre ▲ 452 668-2
Haydn, J.:Arianna a Naxos, w. András Schiff (pno) *(rec Aug. 5–8, 1992)* London ▲ 440297-2 [DDD]
Mozart, W.A.:Arias, w. G. Fischer (cnd), Vienna CO—Ch'io mi scordi di te? *(rec 1989)* London ▲ 448300-2 [DDD]; ■ 448300-4
Mozart, W.A.:Arias, w. A. Schiff (pno), A. Fischer (cnd), Vienna CO—arias from Clemenza di Tito, Così fan tutte, Don Giovanni & Le nozze di Figaro; & three concert arias [I] London ▲ 430513-2 [DDD]
Mozart, W.A.:Arias, w. G. Fischer (cnd), Vienna CO—Temerai...Come Scoglio; Ei Parte...per pieta; In nomini [all from Così fan tutte]; E Susanne non vien...Dove Sono [from Le nozze di Figaro]; Batti, batti; In quali eccessi...mi tradi [both from Don Giovanni] London ▲ 443452-2 ■ 443452-4 ◻ 443452-5
Mozart, W.A.:Clemenza, w. Barbara Bonney (sop—Servilia), Cecilia Bartoli (mez—Sesto), Della Jones (mez—Vitellia), Diana Montague (mez—Annio), Uwe Heilman (ten—Tito), Giles Cachemaille (bar—Publio), C. Hogwood (cnd), Academy of Ancient Music, Academy of Ancient Music Chorus London ("Editions de l'oiseau-lyre" series) 2-▲ 444131-2 [DDD]
Mozart, W.A.:Così fan tutte (sels), w. G. Fischer (cnd), Vienna CO—Temerari!...Come scoglio; In uomini, in soldati *(rec 1993)* London ▲ 448300-2 [DDD]; ■ 448300-4
Mozart, W.A.:Così fan tutte (sels), w. L. Cuberli (sop), J. Rodgers (sop), J. Tomlinson (bass), D. Barenboim (cnd), Berlin PO, Berlin RIAS Chamber Choir Erato ▲ 94821
Mozart, W.A.:Davidde penitente, w. G. Fischer (cnd), Vienna CO—Lungi le cive ingrate London ▲ 443452-2 ■ 443452-4 ◻ 443452-5
Mozart, W.A.:Don Giovanni (sels), w. G. Fischer (cnd), Vienna CO—Batti, batti, o bel Masetto *(rec 1993)* London ▲ 448300-2 [DDD]; ■ 448300-4
Mozart, W.A.:Exsultate, w. G. Fischer (cnd), Vienna CO London ▲ 443452-2 ■ 443452-4 ◻ 443452-5
Mozart, W.A.:Idomeneo, w. Carol Vaness (sop—Elettra), Cecilia Bartoli (mez—Idamante), Heidi Grant Murphy (mez—Ilia), Plácido Domingo (ten— Idomeneo), Thomas Hampson (bar—Arbace), Bryn Terfel (bass-bar—La Voce), J. Levine (cnd), Metropolitan Opera Orch, New York Metropolitan Opera Chorus Deutsche Grammophon ▲ 447737-2
Mozart, W.A.:Idomeneo, w. Heidi Grant-Murphy (sop—Ilia), Carol Vaness (sop—Elettra), Cecilia Bartoli (mez—Idamante), Plácido Domingo (ten—Idomeneo), Frank Lopardo (ten—High Priest), Thomas Hampson (bar—Arbace), Bryn Terfel (b-bar—The Voice), J. Levine (cnd), Metropolitan Opera Orch, Raymond Hughes (cnd), New York Metropolitan Opera Chorus *(rec Manhattan Center Studios, New York, Mar & Apr 1994)* Deutsche Grammophon 3-▲ 447 737-2
Mozart, W.A.:Nozze di Figaro (sels), w. G. Fischer (cnd), Vienna CO—Voi che sapete; Giunse alfin il momento...Deh vieni *(rec 1989)* London ▲ 448300-2 [DDD]; ■ 448300-4
Mozart, W.A.:Nozze di Figaro (sels), w. L. Cuberli (sop), J. Rodgers (sop), A. Schmidt (bar), D. Barenboim (cnd), Berlin PO, Berlin RIAS Chamber Choir Erato ▲ 94822
Mozart, W.A.:Requiem, w. A. Augér (sop), V. Cole (ten), R. Pape (bass), G. Solti (cnd), Vienna PO, Vienna Phil Chorus [L] *(rec live 12/5/91)* London ▲ 433688-2 [DDD] ◻ 433688-5
Mozart, W.A.:Songs, w. A. Schiff (pno)—Ridente la calma, K.152 *(rec Aug. 5–8, 1992)* London ▲ 440297-2 [DDD]
Parisotti, A.:Se tu m'ami, w. György Fischer (pno) *(rec 1990)* London ▲ 448300-2 [DDD]; ■ 448300-4
Pergolesi, G.B.:Stabat mater, w. J. Anderson (sop), *(organist unknown)*, C. Dutoit (cnd), Montreal Sinfonietta London ▲ 436209-2 [DDD]
Puccini, G.:Manon Lescaut, w. M. Freni (sop—Manon), C. Bartoli (mez—Musici I), L. Pavarotti (ten—Des Grieux), R. Vargas (ten—Edmondo), D. Croft (ten—Lescaut), G. Taddei (bar—Geronte), J. Levine (cnd), Metropolitan Opera Orch, New York Metropolitan Opera Chorus [I] *(rec 1992)* London ▲ 440200-2 [DDD]
Ravel, M.:Songs, w. Myung-Whun Chung (pno)—Chanson française; Chanson espagnole; Chanson italienne; Chanson hébraïque; Vocalise-Etude; Kaddisch; L'Enigme eternelle; Tripatos London ▲ 452667-2 ■ 452667-4
Rossini, G.:Arias, w. G. Patanè (cnd), Vienna Volksoper Orch—arias from L'italiana in Algeri, La donna del lago, Tancredi, Otello, Stabat Mater, La pietra del paragone, Cenerentola London ▲ 425430-2 [DDD]
Rossini, G.:Arias, w. Charles Spencer (pno)—Beltà crudele *(rec 1990)* London ▲ 448300-2 [DDD]; ■ 448300-4
Rossini, G.:Arias, w. I. Marin (cnd), Venice Teatro La Fenice Orch, Venice Teatro La Fenice Chorus—8 scenes from Donna del Lago, Elisabetta, Maometto II, Nozze di Teti e di Peleo, Semiramide, Zelmira [I] London ▲ 436075-2 [DDD] ■ 436075-4 ◻ 436075-5
Rossini, G.:Il barbiere di Siviglia, w. W. Matteuzzi (ten), L. Nucci (bar), P. Burchuladze (bass), G. Patanè (cnd), Bologna Teatro Comunale Orch, Bologna Teatro Comunale Chorus [I] London 3-▲ 425520-2 [DDD]
Rossini, G.:Il barbiere di Siviglia (sels), w. W. Matteuzzi (ten), L. Nucci (bar), P. Burchuladze (bass), G. Patanè (cnd), Bologna Teatro Comunale Orch, Bologna Teatro Comunale Chorus London ▲ 440289-2 [DDD]
Rossini, G.:La Cenerentola, w. C. Bartoli (mez—Cenerentola), F. Costa (mez—Clorinda), G. Banditelli (cta—Tisbe), W. Matteuzzi (ten—Don Ramiro), A. Corbelli (bar—Dandini), E. Dara (bar—Don Magnifico), M. Pertusi (bass—Alidoro), R. Chailly (cnd), Bologna Teatro Comunale Orch, Bologna Teatro Comunale Chorus *(rec June 22–July 2, 1992)* London 2-▲ 436902-2 [DDD]
Rossini, G.:La Cenerentola (sels), w. R. Chailly (cnd), Bologna Teatro Comunale Orch, Bologna Teatro Comunale Chorus—Nacqui all'affanno...Non più mesta *(rec 1992)* London ▲ 448300-2 [DDD]; ■ 448300-4
Rossini, G.:Maometto II (sels), w. I. Marin (cnd), Venice Teatro La Fenice Orch, Venice Teatro La Fenice Chorus—Giusto ciel, in tal periglio *(rec 1991)* London ▲ 448300-2 [DDD]; ■ 448300-4
Rossini, G.:Semiramide (sels), w. I. Marin (cnd), Venice Teatro La Fenice Orch, Venice Teatro La Fenice Chorus—Bel raggio lusinghier *(rec 1991)* London ▲ 448300-2 [DDD]; ■ 448300-4
Rossini, G.:Songs, w. C. Spencer (pno) [I] London ▲ 430518-2 [DDD]
Rossini, G.:Stabat Mater, w. Luba Orgonasova (sop), Raul Gimenez (ten), Roberto Scandiuzzi (bass), M.-W. Chung (cnd), Vienna PO, Vienna State Opera Chorus Deutsche Grammophon ▲ 449 178-2
Scarlatti, A.:Salve regina, w. J. Anderson (sop), C. Dutoit (cnd), Montreal Sinfonietta London ▲ 436209-2 [DDD]
Schubert, Franz:Songs (misc), w. A. Schiff (pno)—Vedi quanto adoro, D.510; Se dall'Etra, D.738; Io vuo' cantar di Cadmo, D.737; La pastorella, D.528; Non t'accostar all'urna, D.688/1; Guarda, che bianca luna, D.688/2; Da quel sembiante appresi, D.688/3; Mio ben ricordati, D.688/4; Pensa, che questo istante, D.76; Mi batte 'l cor, D.767 *(rec Aug. 5–8, 1992)* London ▲ 440297-2 [DDD]

VOCALISTS

Bartoli, Cecilia (mez) (cont.)
Schubert, Franz:Songs (misc), w. András Schiff (pno)—La pastorella; Vedi quanto adoro ancora ingrato! *(rec 1991 & 1992)* London ▲ 448300-2 [DDD]; ■ 448300-4
Se tu m'ami [If You Love Me]:18th Century Italian Songs, w. György Fischer (pno) London ▲ 436267-2 [DDD] ■ 436267-4
Viardot-Garcia, P.:Songs, w. Myung-Whun Chung (pno)—Hai luli; Havanaise; Les Filles de Cadix London ▲ 452667-2 ■ 452667-4

Bartoli, Cecilia (sop)
Mozart, W.A.:Nozze di Figaro, w. Cecilia Bartoli (sop—Cherubino), Sylvia McNair (sop—Susanna), Cheryl Studer (sop—Countess Almaviva), Lucio Gallo (bar—Figaro), Boje Skovhus (bar—Count Almaviva), C. Abbado (cnd), Vienna PO, Vienna State Opera Chorus Deutsche Grammophon 3-▲ 445903-2

Bartolini, Lando (ten)
Lando Live!, w. Bartolini, Lando (ten) *(rec U.S., Germany, Hungary & France, live, 1980–92)* Legato Classics ▲ LCD 165-1 [ADD]
Respighi, O.:Semirama, w. E. Marton (sop), V. Kincses (sop), L Miller (bar), L. Polgaar (bass), T. Clementis (bass), L. Gardelli (cnd), Hungarian State Orch, Hungarian Radio-TV Chorus [I] Hungaroton 2-▲ HCD 31197/98
Zandonai, R.:I cavalieri di Ekebù, w. Fiorenza Cossotto (sop), Gina Longobardo Fiordaliso (sgr), G. Gavazzeni (cnd), Milan RAI SO, Milan RAI Chorus Fonit Cetra ("Italia" series) 2-▲ FCT CDC 93

Bartolo (sgr)
Donizetti, G.:Don Pasquale, w. L. Serra (sop), E. Dara (bar), A. Corbelli (bar), B. Campanella (cnd), Turin Teatro Regio Orch, Turin Teatro Regio Chorus [I] *(rec live)* Nuova Era 2-▲ 6715/16 [DDD]
Donizetti, G.:Don Pasquale, w. L. Serra (sop), E. Dara (bar), A. Corbelli (bar), B. Campanella (cnd), Turin Teatro Regio Orch, Turin Teatro Regio Chorus [I] *(rec live)* Nuova Era ▲ 6766 [DDD]

Barton, J. (sgr)
Lerner, A.J.:Paint Your Wagon, w. O. San Juan (sgr) [1951 Broadway original cast] RCA ▲ 60243-2 RG [ADD] ■ 60243-4 RG

Barton, J. (trb)
Howells, H.:Requiem, w. P. Flight (ct), D. Honoré (ten), T. Woody (bar), F. Burgomeister (cnd), Indianapolis Festival Orch, Christ Church Cathedral Men & Boys Choir Oxford Gothic ▲ G 49062 [DDD]

Barton, Jarmila (sop)
Strauss, R.:Der Rosenkavalier, w. Jarmila Barton (sop—Marianne), Lisa Della Casa (sop—Sophie), Sena Jurinac (sop—Octavian), Ilva Ligabue (sop—Orphan), Elisabeth Schwarzkopf (sop—Marschallin), Else Schürhoff (mez—Annina), Luisa Villa (mez—Milliner), Hugues Cuénod (ten—Marschallin's majordomo), Erich Majkut (ten—Valzacchi), Giuseppe Nessi (ten—Animal seller), Luciano Della Pergola (ten—Lackey/Faninal's majordomo), Antonio Pirino (ten—An Italian Singer), Gino Del Signore (ten—Lackey/Waiter), Erich Kunz (bar—Herr von Faninal), Paolo Pedani (bar—Lackey), Attilo Barbesi (bass—Lackey/Waiter), Enrico Campi (bass—Waiter), Otto Edelmann (bass—Baron Ochs), Bruno Fichtinger (bass—Notary), Franco Taino (bass—Waiter), Maria Amadini (sgr—Orphan), Pina Carrillo (sgr—Orphan), Joszi Trojan Regar (sgr—Innkeeper), H. von Karajan (cnd), La Scala Orch, La Scala Chorus *(rec La Scala Theater, Milan, Jan. 26, 1952)* Legato Classics 3-▲ LCD 197-3

Bartos, Anna (sop)
Cantares, w. Gregg Nestor (gtr) *(rec The Place, NYC)* Town Hall ▲ THCD 44

Basa, Sibrand (ten)
Weber, C.M. von:Peter Schmoll und seine Nachbarn, w. A. Pfeffer (sop—Minnette), J. Schmidt (ten—Martin Schmoll), S. Basa (ten—Karl Pirkner), H.-J. Schöpflin (ten—Niklas), R. Busching (bar—Peter Schmoll), H.J. Porcher (bass—Hans Bast), G. Markson (cnd), Hagen PO [G] *(rec Feb. 1–5, 1993)* Marco Polo 2-▲ 8.223592/93 [DDD]

Bashkirova, Elena (nar)
Ridout, A.:Little Sad Sound, w. G. Kremer (nar), A. Posch (db) Philips ("Digital Classics" series) ▲ 416841-2 [DDD]

Basi, Leonildo (bass)
Leoncavallo, R.:Pagliacci, w. Adelaide Saraceni (sop—Nedda), Alessandro Valente (ten—Canio), Nello Palai (ten—Beppe), Apollo Granforte (bar—Tonio), Leonildo Basi (bass—Silvio), C. Sabajno (cnd), La Scala Orch, La Scala Chorus *(rec Apr, Sept 1929 & Jan 1930)* VAI Audio 2-▲ VAIA 1082-2

Basile, Sal (voc)
Hays, S.:Dreaming the World, w. Thomas Bruckner (bar), Jennifer López (voc), John Schaffer (voc), Sorrel Hays (voc), Joseph Kubera (pno), John Kennedy (perc), Charles Wood (perc), Maya Gunji (perc), Eric Kivnick (perc), Jai Smith (perc) New World ▲ 805202 [DDD]

Basilides, Maria (mez)
Bartók, B.:Pno Music, w. B. Bartók (pno), V. Medgyaszay (sop), F. Székelyhidy (ten), J. Szigeti (vn), B. Goodman (cl), D. Bartók Pásztory (pno), H. J. Baker, E. J. Rubsam (perc)—studio, broadcast & piano roll recordings of music by Bartók, Kodály, Beethoven, Debussy, Liszt & Scarlatti, chronologically arranged from ca. 1920 through 1945—Sonatina; 6 Romanian Folk Dances; Evening in Transylvania; 8 sels. from 15 Hungarian Peasant Songs; Suite, Op. 14 (both the issued & test recordings); Allegro barbaro; 5 sels. from 2 Romanian Dances, 3 Burlesques, 10 Easy Pieces & 14 Bagatelles; & 4 Sons. by D. Scarlatti (test recordings); 8 sels. from 15 Hungarian Peasant Songs; 4 sels. from 9 Little Piano Pieces, Petite Suite & 3 Rondos on Folk Melodies; & "Sursum corda" from Liszt's Années de pèlerinage; 20 Hungarian Folk Songs; 5 Hungarian Folk Tunes; 8 Hungarian Folksongs; Hungarian Folk Tunes; 6 Romanian Folk Dances; Rhap. 1 Violin & Piano; Contrasts for Clarinet, Violin & Piano; 2 sels. from Mikrokosmos; 32 sels. from Mikrokosmos; Rhap. 1; Son. No. 2; Beethoven's "Kreutzer" Son.; Debussy's Son. 3; Son. 2 Pianos & Percussion; Petite Suite; 3 Hungarian Folk Tunes; 11 sels. from Improvs. on Hungarian Peasant Songs; Mikrokosmos; 3 Rondos on Folk Melodies; 9 Little Piano Pieces; 14 Bagatelles; 15 sels. from For Children & 2 sels. from 10 Easy Pieces Hungaroton 6-▲ HCD 12326/31 (m) [ADD]
Kodály, Z.:Hungarian Folk Music, w. V. Medgyaszay (sop), F. Székelyhidy (ten), B. Bartók (pno) [arr. by Kodály for solo voice & piano]—20 Hungarian folk songs *(rec Budapest, 1928)* Hungaroton 6-▲ HCD 12326/31 (m) [ADD]

Basiola, Mario (bar)
Iva Pacetti, w. I. Pacetti (sop), Beniamino Gigli (ten), Benvenuto Franci (bar) *(rec 1928–40)* Preiser ("Lebendige Vergangenheit" series) ▲ PRE 89124
Leoncavallo, R.:Pagliacci, w. I. Pacetti (sop—Nedda), B. Gigli (ten—Canio), G. Nessi (ten—Peppe), M. Basiola (bar—Tonio), F. Ghione (cnd), La Scala Orch, La Scala Chorus [I] *(rec 1934 for HMV)* Music Memoria ▲ 30275
Leoncavallo, R.:Pagliacci, w. I. Pacetti (sop—Nedda), B. Gigli (ten—Canio), G. Nessi (ten—Peppe), M. Basiola (bar—Tonio), F. Ghione (cnd), La Scala Orch, La Scala Chorus [I] *(rec July 1934)* Nimbus 2-▲ NI 7843/44 [ADD]
Leoncavallo, R.:Pagliacci, w. I. Pacetti (sop—Nedda), B. Gigli (ten—Canio), G. Nessi (ten—Peppe), M. Basiola (bar—Tonio), F. Ghione (cnd), La Scala Orch, La Scala Chorus [I] *(rec 1934)* EMI Classics ("Studio" series) ▲ CDH 63309 (m) [ADD]
Mascagni, P.:Iris (sels), w. M. Olivero (sop—Iris), G. Gismondo (ten—Osaka), M. Basiola II (bar—Kyoto), O. de Fabritiis (cnd), *(orch unknown)*—scenes from Acts II & III *(rec live, June 3, 1966)* VAI Audio 2-▲ VAIA 1062 (m) [ADD]
Massenet, J.:Werther, w. V. Zeani (sop), A. Kraus (ten), D. Trimarchi (bar), A. Votto (cnd), *(orch unknown) (rec Palermo, 1971)* Great Opera Performances 2-▲ GOP 749
Puccini, G.:Madama Butterfly, w. Toti dal Monte (sop—Madama Butterfly), Maria Huder (mez—Kate Pinkerton), Beniamino Gigli (ten—B.F. Pinkerton), Adelio Zagonara (ten—Goro), Mario Basiola (bar—Sharpless), Gino Conti (bass—Principe Yamadori), Ernesto Dominici (bass—Il Bonzo), Vittoria Paolombini (sgr—Suzuki), O. de Fabritiis (cnd), Rome Opera Orch, Giuseppe Conca (cnd), Rome Opera Chorus *(rec Aug 1939)* Arkadia 2-▲ CD 78004 (m) [ADD]
Verdi, G.:La traviata, w. Maria Caniglia (sop), Beniamino Gigli (ten), V. Gui (cnd), London PO, London Phil Chorus *(rec Royal Opera House, Covent Garden, May 22, 1939)* Enterprise ("The Fourties" series) 2-▲ ENT 313
Verdi, G.:La traviata, w. Maria Caniglia (sop—Violetta), Maria Huder (mez—Flora), Gladys Palmer (cta—Annina), Octave Dua (ten—Giuseppe), Beniamino Gigli (ten—Alfredo), Booth Hitchen (ten—D'Obigny), Adelio Zagonara (bar—Gastone), Aristide Baracchi (bar—Douphol), Mario Basiola (bar—Germont), Norman Walker (bass—Dr. Grenville), V. Gui (cnd), London PO, London Phil Chorus *(rec Royal Opera House, Covent Garden, May 22, 1939)* Minerva 2-▲ MN A28/29 (m) [ADD]

Basiola, Mario (bar) (cont.)
Verdi, G.:La traviata, w. Maria Caniglia (sop—Violetta), Baniamino Gigli (ten—Alfredo), Mario Basiola (bar—Germont), V. Gui (cnd), London SO, London Sym Chorus Enterprise ("The Radio Years" series) 2-▲ ENT RY 64
Verdi, G.:Il trovatore, w. G. Cigna (sop—Leonora), G. Wettergren (mez—Azucena), M. Huder (mez—Ines), J. Björling (ten—Manrico), O. Dua (ten—Ruiz), C. Zambelli (ten—Ferrando), M. Basiola (bar—Count di Luna), L. Horsman (bar—Old Gypsy), V. Gui (cnd), Royal Opera Orch, Royal Opera House Chorus Covent Garden *(rec May 12, 1939)* Legato Classics 2-▲ LCD 173-2 [ADD]

Baskerville, Priscilla (sop)
Davis, A.:X, The Life & Times of Malcolm X, w. Hilda Harris (mez), Thomas J. Young (ten), Eugene Perry (bar—Malcolm), Herbert Perry (bass), W. H. Curry (cnd), Orch of St. Luke, Episteme [E] Gramavision 2-▲ R2-79470 [DDD]

Bass, S. (sgr)
Rodgers, R.:Music of, w. J. Andrews (sgr), P. Como (sgr), D. Reese (sgr), J. Jones (sgr), N. Luboff (sgr), M. Gold (sgr), N. Walker (sgr), H. Bowen (sgr), V. Damone (sgr), P. Nero (pno), J. P. Morgan (sgr), E. Fisher (sgr), B. Goodman (cl), Ann-Margaret (sgr), Shorty Rogers (sgr), D. Shore (sgr), T. Martin (sgr), M. King (sgr), A. Newley (sgr) RCA ▲ 8590-2 R ■ 8590-4 R

Bassenge, Annette (alt)
Mauersberger, R.:Geh aus, mein Herz, und suche Freude, w. Sabine Dicke (sop), Dorothea Schmidt (sop), Friederike Urban (sop), Christiane Fischer (alt), Sabine Hering (alt), Johannes Unger (org), Wolfgang Unger (dir), Thüringian Academic Sing Circle Thorofon ▲ CTH 2245 [DDD]
Mauersberger, R.:St. Luke, w. H.-M. Uhle (ten), Thüringian Academic Sing Circle *(rec May 24–26, 1991)* Thorofon ▲ CTH 2127 [DDD]

Bassermann, Alex (sgr)
Austin, E.:An Die Nachgeborenen, w. Kirsten Grünenpült (sgr), Veronika Winter (sgr), Sibylle Dotzauer (pno), Gerald Kegelmann (cnd), Heidelberg-Mannheim State Univ Chamber Choir Capstone ▲ CPS 8625

Bassett, Ralph (bar)
Nielsen, C.:Sym 3, w. S. Burghardt (sop), S. Ehrling (cnd), Danish National Orch *(rec live, Kennedy Center, 5/19/84)* Audiofon ▲ CD 72025

Bassi, Amedeo (ten)
Leoncavallo, R.:Pagliacci (sels), w. Enrico Caruso (ten), Antonio Paoli (ten), Giovanni Zenatello (ten), Hermann Jadlowker (ten), Fernand Ansseau (ten), Hipolito Lazaro (ten), Nino (Filippo) Piccaluga (ten), Mario Chamlee (ten), Giacomo Lauri-Volpi (ten), Miguel Fleta (ten), Giovanni Martinelli (ten), Aureliano Pertile (ten), Georges Thill (ten), Alessandro Valente (ten), Francesco Merli (ten), Lauritz Melchior (ten), Marcel Wittrisch (ten), Joseph Schmidt (ten), Beniamino Gigli (ten), Giuseppe Lugo (ten), Helge Roswaenge (ten), Jussi Bjoerling (ten)—23 versions of the tenor aria "Vesti la giubba" *(rec 1907–1944)* Bongiovanni ▲ GB 1071 [ADD]
The World of Singing, Vol 4:The Italian School Part 1:Tenors before World War I, Book 2, w. Edoardo Garbin (ten), Fiorello Giraud (ten), Florencio Costantino (ten), Antonio Paoli (ten), Giuseppe Borgatti (ten), Carlo Albani (ten), Enrico Caruso (ten), Piero Schivazzi (ten), Elvino Ventura (ten), Giovanni Zenatello (ten) Enterprise ("Vocal Archives" series) 3-▲ ENT VA 2107

Bassi, Anna Masetti (sgr)
Verdi, G.:Rigoletto, w. Mercedes Capsir (sop), Dino Borgioli (ten), Riccardo Stracciari (bar), Duilio Baronti (bass), Ernesto Dominici (bass) *(rec 1930)* Grammofono 2000 2-▲ GRM 78632

Bastian, William (ten)
Mozart, W.A.:Laut verkünde unsre Freude, w. W. Hite (ten), W. Sharp (bar), A. Parrott (cnd), Boston Early Music Festival Orch, Boston Early Music Festival Chorus [G] Denon ▲ CO 77152 [DDD]

Bastianini, Ettore (bar)
Berlioz, H.:La Damnation de Faust, w. Giulietta Simionato (mez), Plinio Clabassi (bass), Ruggero Bondino (sgr), P. Maag (cnd), *(orch unknown)* Great Opera Performances 2-▲ GOP 776
Cilea, F.:Adriana Lecouvreur, w. M. Olivero (sop), G. Simionato (mez), F. Corelli (ten), M. Rossi (cnd), Naples Teatro San Carlo Orch, Naples Teatro San Carlo Chorus [I] *(rec live 11/28/59)* Melodram 2-▲ MEL 27009 (m) [AAD]
Cilea, F.:Adriana Lecouvreur, w. Magda Olivero (sop), Giulletta Simionato (mez), Franco Corelli (ten), M. Rossi (cnd), Naples Teatro San Carlo Orch, Naples Teatro San Carlo Chorus *(rec Naples, Nov 28, 1959)* Agorá Music ("Phoenix" series) 2-▲ 502
Donizetti, G.:Lucia di Lammermoor, w. R. Scotto (sop), G. di Stefano (ten), N. Sanzogno (cnd), La Scala Orch, La Scala Chorus *(rec 1959)* Enterprise (Palladio) 2-▲ ENTPD 4117 [ADD]
Donizetti, G.:Poliuto, w. M. Callas (sop), F. Corelli (ten), N. Zaccaria (bass), A. Votto (cnd), La Scala Orch, La Scala Chorus [I] *(rec live, 12/7/60)* Melodram 2-▲ MEL 26006
Donizetti, G.:Poliuto, w. M. Callas (sop), F. Corelli (ten), N. Zaccaria (bass), A. Votto (cnd), La Scala Orch, La Scala Chorus [I] *(rec live, 12/7/60)* Arkadia 2-▲ 520 (m) [AAD]
Donizetti, G.:Poliuto, w. M. Callas (sop), F. Corelli (ten), N. Zaccaria (bass), A. Votto (cnd), La Scala Orch, La Scala Chorus [I] *(rec live, Milan 12/7/60)* Verona 2-▲ 28003/04
Donizetti, G.:Poliuto, w. Maria Callas (sop), Franco Corelli (ten), A. Votto (cnd), La Scala Orch, La Scala Chorus *(rec live, Milan, 1960)* Enterprise ("Documents" series) 2-▲ ENT LV 977 (m)
Ettore Bastianini *(rec live, 1955–1965)* Memories ("Great Voices" series) 2-▲ HR 4400/01 (m)
Ettore Bastianini:A Portrait of the Artist *(rec live, 1955–1962)* Legato Classics ▲ LCD 151-1 (m) [AAD]
Giordano, U.:Andrea Chénier, w. R. Tebaldi (sop), F. Corelli (ten), L. von Matačič (cnd), *(orch unknown)* —eleven arias [I] *(rec live, Vienna, 6/26/60)* Standing Room Only 2-▲ SRO 821-2 [ADD]
Giordano, U.:Andrea Chénier, w. H. Konetzni (sop—Madelon), M. Sjöstedt (sop—Bersi), R. Tebaldi (sop—Maddalena de Coigny), E. Höngen (cta—La Contessa de Coigny), F. Corelli (ten—Andrea Chénier), E. Bastianini (bar—C. Gérard), K. Paskalis (bar—Pietro Fléville), L. Welter (bar—Fouquier Tinville), A. Pernerstorfer (b-bar—Mathieu), L. von Matačič (cnd), Vienna State Opera Orch, Vienna State Opera Chorus *(rec Vienna, June 26, 1960)* Fortissimo 2-▲ CDE 3003 [ADD]
In Recital, 1965, w. Yoichi Miura (pno) *(rec Tokyo, June 9, 1965)* Legendary ▲ CD 1002
Puccini, G.:La Bohème, w. R. Tebaldi (sop), G. d'Angelo (sop), C. Bergonzi (ten), C. Siepi (b-bar), T. Serafin (cnd), St. Cecilia Academy Orch Rome, St. Cecilia Academy Chorus Rome [I] London 2-▲ 425534-2 [ADD]
Puccini, G.:La Bohème, w. R. Tebaldi (sop), C. Bergonzi (ten), C. Siepi (b-bar), T. Serafin (cnd), St. Cecilia Academy Orch Rome, St. Cecilia Academy Chorus Rome Enterprise ("Flowers" series) 2-▲ ENTBL 15 [ADD]
Puccini, G.:La Bohème (sels), w. R. Tebaldi (sop), C. Bergonzi (ten), C. Siepi (b-bar), T. Serafin (cnd), St. Cecilia Academy Orch Rome, St. Cecilia Academy Chorus Rome—scenes & arias London ▲ 421301-2 [ADD]
Puccini, G.:Il tabarro, w. N. De Rosa (sop—Giorgietta), S. Puma (ten—Luigi), E. Bastianini (bar—Michèle), M. Cordone (cnd), *(orch & chorus unknown)* [I] *(rec live, Hamburg Radio 1954)* Standing Room Only ▲ SRO 827-1
Puccini, G.:Tosca, w. Renata Tebaldi (sop—Floria Tosca), Guiseppe di Stefano (ten—Mario Cavardossi), Rinaldo Pelizzoni (ten—Spoletta), Ettore Bastianini (bar—Baron Scarpia), Carlo Badioli (bass—Sacristan), Guiseppe Moresi (bass—Sciarrone), Franco Piva (bass—Jailer), Nicola Zaccaria (bass—Cesare Angelotti), G. Gavazzeni (cnd) *(rec Great Auditorium, Brussels World Fair, 1958)* Legato Classics 2-▲ LCD 2092 [ADD]
Tchaikovsky, P.:Mazeppa, w. M. Olivero (sop), M. Radev (mez), D. Poleri (ten), B. Christoff (bass), J. Perlea (cnd), Florence Maggio Musicale Orch, Florence Maggio Musicale Chorus [I] *(rec live 6/6/54)* Melodram 2-▲ MEL 27070 (m) [AAD]
Verdi, G.:Un ballo in maschera, w. M. Callas (sop), E. Ratti (sop), G. Simionato (mez), G. di Stefano (ten), G. Gavazzeni (cnd), La Scala Orch, La Scala Chorus *(rec 1957)* Melodram ▲ MLO 26039 [ADD]
Verdi, G.:Un ballo in maschera, w. M. Callas (sop), E. Ratti (sop), G. Simionato (mez), G. di Stefano (ten), G. Gavazzeni (cnd), La Scala Orch, La Scala Chorus [I] *(rec live 12/7/57)* Arkadia 2-▲ 519 (m) [AAD]
Verdi, G.:Un ballo in maschera, w. A. Cerquetti (sop), E. Stignani (mez), G. Poggi (ten), E. Tieri (cnd), Florence Teatro Comunale Orch, Florence Teatro Comunale Chorus [I] *(rec live 1/6/57)* Standing Room Only 2-▲ SRO 804-2 (m) [ADD]
Verdi, G.:La battaglia di Legnano, w. A. Stella (sop), F. Corelli (ten), G. Gavazzeni (cnd), La Scala Orch, La Scala Chorus [I] *(rec live 12/7/61)* Myto 2-▲ 2 MCD 89010 (m) [ADD]

1062 ▲ = CD ♦ = Enhanced CD Δ = MD ■ = Cassette Tape □ = DCC

Bastianini, Ettore (bar) (cont.)
Verdi, G.:Don Carlos, w. S. Jurinac (sop), G. Simionato (mez), E. Fernandi (ten), C. Siepi (b-bar), H. von Karajan (cnd), Vienna PO, Vienna State Opera Chorus [l] *(rec live, Salzburg 7/26/58)* Arkadia 2-▲ 220 [ADD]
Verdi, G.:Don Carlos, w. Anita Cerquetti (sop), Cesare Siepi (b-bar), Gianni Barbieri (bass), A. Votto (cnd), Florence Maggio Musicale Orch, Florence Maggio Musicale Chorus Melodram 3-▲ CDM 370104
Verdi, G.:Don Carlos, w. A. Cerquetti (sop), F. Barbieri (mez), A. LoForese (ten), C. Siepi (b-bar), G. Neri (bass), A. Votto (cnd), Florence Maggio Musicale Orch, Florence Maggio Musicale Chorus *(rec July 16, 1956)* Melodram 3-▲ MLO 670104 [ADD]
Verdi, G.:Ernani, w. Margherita Roberti (sop), Anna di Stasio (mez), Athos Cesarini (ten), Mario del Monaco (ten), Mario Rinaudo (bass), Nicola Rossi-Lemeni (bass), F. Previtali (cnd), Naples Teatro San Carlo Orch, Naples Teatro San Carlo Chorus Melodram 2-▲ CDM 270100
Verdi, G.:Ernani, w. A. Cerquetti (sop), M. Del Monaco (ten), B. Christoff (bass), D. Mitropoulos (cnd), Florence Maggio Musicale Orch [l] *(rec live 6/14/57)* Melodram 2-▲ MEL 27016
Verdi, G.:La forza del destino, w. R. Tebaldi (sop), G. Simionato (mez), M. del Monaco (ten), C. Siepi (b-bar), F. Molinari-Pradelli (cnd), St. Cecilia Academy Orch Rome, St. Cecilia Academy Chorus Rome [l] London 3-▲ 421598-2 [ADD]
Verdi, G.:La forza del destino, w. R. Tebaldi (sop), O. Dominguez (mez), F. Corelli (ten), R. Capecchi (bar), B. Christoff (bass), F. Molinari-Pradelli (cnd), Naples Teatro San Carlo Orch, Naples Teatro San Carlo Chorus *(rec Oct. 1 1958)* Melodram 3-▲ MLO 370102 [AAD]
Verdi, G.:La forza del destino (sels), w. F. Corelli (ten), F. Molinari-Pradelli (cnd), *(orch unknown)*—Act III, Scene 2 Duet, "Sleale! Il segreto fu dunque violato" [l] *(rec live, Naples 1958)* Standing Room Only 2-▲ SRO 826-2 [ADD]
Verdi, G.:Nabucco, w. Mirella Parutto (sgr), Ivo Vinco (bass), B. Bartoletti (cnd), *(orch unknown)*, *(orch & chorus unknown) (rec live, Florence, Aug. 26, 1961)* Great Opera Performances 2-▲ GOP 751
Verdi, G.:La traviata, w. Renata Scotto (sop—Violetta Valery), Giuliana Tavolaccini (sop—Flora Bervoix), Gianni Raimondi (ten—Alfredo Germont), Ettore Bastianini (bar—Giorgio Germont), A. Votto (cnd), La Scala Orch, La Scala Chorus *(rec La Scala Theatre, Milan, 1963)* Deutsche Grammophon 2-▲ 439720-2 [ADD]
Verdi, G.:La traviata, w. A. Moffo (sop), G. Janowitz (sop), G. Zampieri (ten), B. Klobucar (cnd), Vienna State Opera Orch, Vienna State Opera Chorus [l] *(rec live, Vienna, 1964)* Melodram (Connaisseur) 2-▲ CDM 27510 [ADD]
Verdi, G.:La traviata, w. M. Callas (sop), G. Di Stefano (ten), C. M. Giulini (cnd), La Scala Orch, La Scala Chorus [l] *(rec live 5/28/55)* Arkadia 2-▲ 501 (m) [AAD]
Verdi, G.:La traviata, w. M. Callas (sop), G. Di Stefano (ten), C. M. Giulini (cnd), La Scala Orch, La Scala Chorus [l] *(rec 1955)* EMI Classics (Studio) 2-▲ CDMB 63628 (m) [ADD]
Verdi, G.:La traviata, w. M. Callas (sop), A. Zanolli (sop), L. Mandelli (sop), G. Raimondi (ten), C. M. Giulini (cnd), La Scala Orch, La Scala Chorus *(rec live 1/19/56)* Myto 2-▲ MCD 89003 (m) [ADD]
Verdi, G.:La traviata (sels), w. R. Scotto (sop), G. Tavolccini (sop), A. Bonato (sop), G. Raimondi (ten), A. Votto (cnd), La Scala Orch, La Scala Chorus IMP Collectors Series ▲ IMPX 9025 [AAD]
Verdi, G.:Il trovatore, w. A. Stella (sop), M. Fiorentini (mez), F. Cossotto (mez), F. Corelli (ten), I. Vinco (bass), G. Gavazzeni (cnd), La Scala Orch, La Scala Chorus *(rec live, Milan, 12/7/62)* Melodram 2-▲ MEL 27068 (m) [AAD]
Verdi, G.:Il trovatore, w. A. Stella (sop), M. Fiorentini (mez), F. Cossotto (mez), F. Corelli (ten), I. Vinco (bass), G. Gavazzeni (cnd), La Scala Orch, La Scala Chorus [l] *(rec live, Milan, 12/7/62)* Claque 2-▲ CLQ 2013 (m)
Verdi, G.:Il trovatore, w. Fedora Barbieri (mez), Franco Corelli (ten), Agostino Ferrin (bass), Mirella Parutto (sgr), O. de Fabritiis (cnd), Rome Opera Orch, Rome Opera Chorus Stradivarius 2-▲ STV DTM 12313 [ADD]
Verdi, G.:Il trovatore, w. Leyla Gencer (sop—Leonora), Laura Londi (sop—Ines), Fedora Barbieri (mez—Azucena), Mario del Monaco (ten—Manrico), Athos cesarini (ten—Ruiz), Walter Artioli (ten—Messanger) Ettore Bastianini (bar—Count Luna), Plinio Clabassi (bass—Ferrando), Sergio Liliani (bass—Gypsy), F. Previtali (cnd), Milan RAI SO, Milan RAI Chorus *(rec live, Milan, May 29, 1957)* Arkadia 2-▲ 483 [ADD]
Verdi, G.:Il trovatore (sels), w. Leyla Gencer (sop—Leonora), Laura Londi (sop—Ines), Athos Cesarini (ten—Ruiz), Mario del Monaco (ten—Manrico), F. Previtali (cnd), Milan RAI SO, Milan RAI Chorus *(rec Milan, May 18, 1957)* Agorá Music ("Phoenix" series) 3-▲ 510 [ADD]

Bastin, G. (bar)
Berlioz, H.:La Damnation de Faust, w. J. Veasey (mez), N. Gedda (ten), C. Davis (cnd), London SO, London Sym Chorus, Ambrosian Singers [F] Philips 2-▲ 416395-2 [ADD]

Bastin, Jules (bass)
Auber, D.-F.:Le Domino noir, w. Sumi Jo (sop), Doris Lamprecht (sop), Martine Olmeda (sop), Isabelle Vernet (sop), Jocelyne Taillon (mez), Bruce Ford (ten), Patrick Power (ten), Gilles Cachemaille (bar), R. Bonynge (cnd), English CO, London Voices London 2-▲ 440646-2
Auber, D.-F.:Fra Diavolo, w. M. Mesplé (sop—Zerline), J. Berbié (mez—Lady Pamela), N. Gedda (ten—Fra Diavolo), R. Corazza (ten—Lord Cockburn), T. Dran (ten—Lorenzo), J. Bastin (bass—Matheo), M. Soustrot (cnd), Monte Carlo PO, Jean LaForge Ensemble Choir EMI Classics ▲ CDCB 54810
Berlioz, H.:L'Enfance du Christ, w. A. S. von Otter (mez), Johnson (sgr), G. Cachemaille (bar), J. Van Dam (b-bar), J.E. Gardiner (cnd), Lyon Opera Orch, Monteverdi Choir London [F] Erato 2-▲ 2292-45275-2 [DDD]
Grétry, A.-E.-M.:La Caravane du Caire, w. I. Poulenard (sop), G. de Reyghere (sop), G. Ragon (ten), G. de Mey (ten), P. Huttenlocher (bar), V. Le Téxier (bar), M. Minkowski (cnd), Ricercar Academy, Ricercar Academy Chorus [period instrs] [F] Ricercar 2-▲ RIC 100084/85 [DDD]
Massenet, J.:Cendrillon, w. R. Welting (sop), F. von Stade (mez), N. Gedda (ten), J. Rudel (cnd), Philharmonia Orch, Ambrosian Opera Chorus [F] CBS 2-▲ M2K 35194 [ADD]
Prokofiev, S.:The Love for 3 Oranges (suite), w. C. Dubosc (sop), G. Gautier (ten), J.-L. Viala (ten), G. Bacquier (bar), K. Nagano (cnd), Paris Lyon Opera Orch, Paris Lyon Opera Chorus [F] Virgin Classics ▲ 59566 [DDD]
Ravel, M.:L'Enfant et les sortilèges, w. Arleen Augér (sop), Marilyn Richardson (sop), Jane Berbié (mez), Linda Finnie (mez), Jocelyne Taillon (mez), Davenny Wyner (mez), Philip Langridge (ten), Philippe Huttenlocher (bar), A. Previn (cnd), London SO, Ambrosian Opera Chorus Classics for Pleasure ("Eminence" series) ▲ CFP 2241
Stravinsky, I.:Oedipus Rex, w. F. Quivar (mez), P. Langridge (ten), D. Kaasch (ten), J. Morris, J.-H. Rootering (bass), J. Levine (cnd), Chicago SO, Chicago Sym Chorus Deutsche Grammophon ▲ 435872-2

Basto, Carla (sop)
Catalani, A.:Dejanice, w. M. L. Garbato (sop), O. Garaventa (ten), R. Massis (bar), C. Zardo (bass), J. Latham-König (cnd), Lucca Teatro Comunale del Giglio Orch, Lucca Teatro Comunale del Giglio Chorus [l] *(rec 9/6/85)* Bongiovanni 2-▲ GB 2031/32 [DDD]
Catalani, A.:Mass, w. A. Cipriani (cta), M. Frusoni (ten), P. Janowski (bass), G. Cosmi (cnd), Lucca Teatro Comunale Giglio Orch [L] *(rec 1985)* Bongiovanni ▲ GB 2027 [DDD]

Bater, Glenn (bass)
Verdi, G.:Il trovatore, w. A. Millo (sop), D. Zajick (mez), S. Kelly (cta), P. Domingo (ten), T. Willson (ten), A. Laciura (ten), J. Morris (bass), J. Levine (cnd), Metropolitan Opera Orch, New York Metropolitan Opera Chorus *(rec June 18, 1991)* Sony Classical 2-▲ S2K 48070 [DDD]

Bates, Jennifer (sop)
Schubert, Franz:Der Hirt auf dem Felsen, w. N. Westlake (cl), D. Bollard (pno), Australia Ensemble [G] *(rec July 1991)* Tall Poppies ▲ TP 011 [DDD]

Báthy, Anna (sop)
Wagner, R.:Tannhäuser (sels), w. Maria Müller (sop), Max Lorenz (ten), W. Furtwängler (cnd), Vienna State Opera Orch Koch Schwann 2-▲ SCH 314702 [ADD]

Batic, Polly (sgr)
Einem, G. von:Der Prozess, w. Lisa Della Casa (sop—Frl. Bürstner/Die Frau des Gerichtsdieners/Leni), Peter Klein (ten—Der Direktorstellvertreter/Der Student), Max Lorenz (ten—Josef K.), Erich Majkut (ten—Ein Bursche), László Szemere (ten—Titorelli), Alois Pernerstorfer (b-bar—Willem/Der Gerichtsdiener), Alfred Poell (b-bar—Der Advokat), Walter Berry (bass—Franz/Kanzleidirektor), Oskar Czerwenka (bass—Der Untersuchungsrichter/Der Prügler), Ludwig Hofmann (bass—Der Aufseher/Ein Passant/Der Geistliche/Der Fabrikant), Polly Batic (sgr—Frau Grubach), Endreh Koreh (sgr—Albert K.), Luise Leitner (sgr—Ein buckliges Mädchen), K. Böhm (cnd), Vienna PO, Vienna State Opera Chorus *(rec Aug 17, 1953)* Orfeo d'or ("Festspiel Dokumente" series) 2-▲ 392952 (m)

Bátor, Tamás (bass)
Caldara, A.:Magnificat, w. M. Szücs (sop), K. Takács (cta), D. Gulyás (ten), F. Szekeres (cnd), Budapest Strings, Budapest Madrigal Choir [L] Hungaroton ▲ HCD 31259 [DDD]
Lickl, J.G.:Missa solemnis, w. Maria Zadori (sop), Judith Nemet (mez), Boldizsar Keönch (ten), H. Williams (cnd), Pécs SO, Pécs Chamber Choir Koch Schwann ▲ SCH 312962
Lickl, J.G.:Requiem, w. Maria Zadori (sop), Judith Nemet (mez), Boldizsar Keönch (ten), H. Williams (cnd), Pécs SO, Pécs Chamber Choir Koch Schwann ▲ SCH 312962
Sammartini, G.B.:Magnificat in B♭, w. Szücs (sop), Takács (alt), Gulyás (ten), F. Szekeres (cnd), Budapest Strings, Budapest Madrigal Choir [L] Hungaroton ▲ HCD 31259 [DDD]
Vivaldi, A.:Magnificat, RV.610, w. T. Takács (mez), D. Gulyás (ten), R. Szücs (bass), F. Szekeres (cnd), Budapest Strings, Budapest Madrigal Choir [L] Hungaroton ▲ HCD 31259 [DDD]

Bátori (sgr)
Vivaldi, A.:Magnificat, RV.611, w. T. Takács (mez), J. Németh (mez), Kovács (sgr), Szökefalvi-Nagy (sgr), F. Szekeres (cnd), Budapest Strings, Budapest Madrigal Choir [L] Hungaroton ▲ HCD 31259 [DDD]

Battaglia, Elio (bar)
Busoni, F.:Songs, w. Erik Werba (pno)—2 Songs [text Byron], Op. 15; Old German Song, Op. 18/1; 2 Songs, Op. 31; 2 Songs, Op. 24; Ave Maria, Op. 1; 5 Songs [text Goethe] Fonit Cetra ("Italia" series) ▲ FCT CDC 84

Battaglia, Elisabetta (sop)
Astorga, E. d':E pur Cesare ha vinto, w. Concentus Musicae Antiqua Nuova Era ("Ancient Music" series) ▲ NUO 7198 [DDD]
Astorga, E. d':Stabat Mater, w. Mapelli (sgr), Narita (sgr), Zaramella (sgr), Concentus Musicae Antiqua Nuova Era ("Ancient Music" series) ▲ NUO 7198 [DDD]

Battiato, Franco (voc)
Battiato, F.:Haiku, w. Pouran Ghaffarpour (voc), Antonio Ballista (pno), Marco Boni (vc), Guido Corti (cnt), Filippo Destrieri (kbd/computer), John Giblin (bass), Gavin Harrison (dr/perc), Jakko Jakszyk (gtr), Roberto Mazza (ob), Fabrizio Merlini (va), Angelo Privitera (kbd/computer), Mino Bordignon (cnd), Milan Chamber Music Choir Hemisphere ▲ 837234-2
Battiato, F.:Messa Arcaica, w. Akemi Sakamoto (mez), Filippo Destrieri (kbd/cmpt), Carlo Guaitoli (pno), Angelo Privitera (kbd/cmpt), A. Ballista (cnd), Italian Virtuosi, Filippo Maria Bressan (cnd), Athestis Chorus Hemisphere ▲ 837234-2
Battiato, F.:L'Ombra della Luce, w. Antonio Ballista (pno), Roger Chase (va), Filippo Destrieri (kbd/computer), Anthony Pleeth (vc), Gavin Wright (vn), G. Pio (cnd), London Astarte Orch Hemisphere ▲ 837234-2
Battiato, F.:Povera Patria, w. Antonio Ballista (pno), Roger Chase (va), Filippo Destrieri (kbd/computer), Anthony Pleeth (vc), Gavin Wright (vn), G. Pio (cnd), London Astarte Orch Hemisphere ▲ 837234-2
Battiato, F.:Ricerca sul Terzo, w. Alessio Alba (tamboura), Antonio Ballista (pno), Marco Boni (vc), Debendra Kanti Chakraborty (tabla), Guido Corti (cnt), Filippo Destrieri (kbd/computer), John Giblin (bass), Buddhadeu Das Gupta (sarod), Gavin Harrison (dr/perc), Jakko Jakszyk (gtr), Roberto Mazza (ob), Fabrizio Merlini (va), Angelo Privitera (kbd/computer), Mino Bordignon (cnd), Milan Chamber Music Choir Hemisphere ▲ 837234-2
Battiato, F.:Le Sacre Sinfonie del Tiempo, w. Antonio Ballista (pno), Roger Chase (va), Filippo Destrieri (kbd/computer), Anthony Pleeth (vc), Gavin Wright (vn), G. Pio (cnd), London Astarte Orch Hemisphere ▲ 837234-2

Battistini, Mattia (bar)
Mattia Battistini *(rec 1902-1913)* Nimbus ("Prima Voce" series) ▲ NI 7831 [ADD]
Mattia Battistini *(rec 1906 & 1911)* Preiser ("Lebendige Vergangenheit" series) ▲ PRE 89045 [AAD]
Mattia Battistini, Vol. 1 *(rec 1902-1921)* Pearl ▲ PEA 9936 (m) [AAD]
Mattia Battistini, Vol. 3 *(rec 1903-24)* Pearl ▲ PEA 9016 [ADD]
Mozart, W.A.:Don Giovanni (sels), w. Emilia Corsi (sop), Adelina Patti (sop), John McCormack (ten), Ezio Pinza (bass), Landon Ronald (pno), C. Sabajno (cnd)—Alfin Siam liberati...Là ci darem la mano; Finch'han del vino; Batti, batti, o bel Masetto; Il mio tesoro; L'amerò, sarò costante *(rec 1905 - 1944)* Minerva ▲ MN A14 [ADD]
Opera Arias Phonographe ▲ PHG CD 5024
Il Re di baritoni, Vol. 2 *(rec 1907-23)* Pearl ▲ PEA 9946 [AAD]
Verdi, G.:Arias, w. *(other artists unknown)*—Da quel dì che ti ho veduta; Lo vedremo; O de' verd' anni miei; Vieni meco sol di rose; O sommo Carlo [all from Ernani]; Perfidi, all'Anglo contro... [from Macbeth]; Qual voce...Mira d'acerbe...Vivrà! [from Il Trovatore]; Madamigella Valery?...Pura siccome un angelo; Di Provenza il mar [both from La traviata]; Alla vita che l'arride; Eri tu che macchiavi [both from Un ballo in maschera]; Urna fatale [from La forza del destino]; O Carlo ascolta; Felice ancor io son...Per me giunto [both from Don Carlo] Minerva ▲ MN A25 (m) [ADD]

Battle, Kathleen (sop)
Angels' Glory, w. Christopher Parkening (gtr) Sony Classical ▲ SK 62723 ■ ST 62723
At Carnegie Hall, w. Margo Garrett (pno) *(rec Carnegie Hall debut concert, 1991)* Deutsche Grammophon ▲ 435440-2 GH [DDD]
The Bach Album, w. I. Perlman (vn)
The Bach Album, w. Itzhak Perlman (vn) Deutsche Grammophon ▲ 429737-2 GH [DDD] ■ 429737-4 GH (D) □ 429737-5
Bach, J.S.:Arias, w. I. Perlman (vn) Deutsche Grammophon ▲ 429737-2 [DDD] □ 429737-5
Bach, J.S.:Cant 202, "Wedding Cant", w. J. Levine (cnd), Ravinia Festival Ensemble [G] RCA Gold Seal ▲ 09026-61365-2 [ADD] ■ 09026-61365-4-RG
Barber, S.:Knoxville:Summer of 1915, w. A. Previn (cnd), Orch of St. Luke's Deutsche Grammophon ▲ 437787-2 ■ 437 787-4
Baroque Duet, w. Wynton Marsalis (tpt), Anthony Newman (hpd/org), Orch of St. Luke [cnd:John Nelson] Sony Classical ▲ SK 46672 △ SM 46672 ■ ST 46672
Bel Canto, w. Benno Campanella (cnd), London PO, Ambrosian Opera Chorus Deutsche Grammophon ▲ 435866-2 ■ 435866-4
Berg, A.:Lulu (suite), w. M. Gielen (cnd), Cincinnati SO *(rec 1981)* Vox Box 2-▲ CDX 5136 [DDD]
Berlioz, H.:Béatrice et Bénédict (sels), w. M.-W. Chung (cnd), Bastille Opera Orch, Bastille Opera Chorus—Je vais le voir *(rec Salle Gounod, Bastille Opera, Paris, Nov 1993 & June 1994)* Deutsche Grammophon ▲ 447114-2 [DDD]
Brahms, J.:Ein Deutsches Requiem, w. H. Hagegard (bar), J. Levine (cnd), Chicago SO, Chicago Sym Chorus [G] *(rec ca. 1984)* RCA Gold Seal ▲ 09026-61349-2 ■ 09026-61349-4
Charpentier, G.:Louise (sels), w. M.-W. Chung (cnd), Bastille Opera Orch—Depuis le jour *(rec Salle Gounod, Bastille Opera, Paris, Nov 1993 & June 1994)* Deutsche Grammophon ▲ 447114-2 [DDD]
A Christmas Celebration, w. Leonard Slatkin (cnd), Orch of St. Luke, New York Choral Artists, Harlem Boys Choir EMI Classics ▲ CDC 47587
DDD Christmas, w. Florence Quivar (mez), Taverner Consort, Taverner Choir, Taverner Players, New York Choral Artists, Toronto Mendelssohn Choir, King's Singers, Empire Brass Angel ▲ CDM 63666
Donizetti, G.:L'elisir d'amore, w. D. Upshaw (sop), L. Pavarotti (ten), E. Dara (bar), L. Nucci (bar), J. Levine (cnd), Metropolitan Orch, New York Metropolitan Opera Chorus Deutsche Grammophon 2-▲ 429744-2 [DDD]
Donizetti, G.:La fille du régiment (sels), w. M.-W. Chung (cnd), Bastille Opera Orch—C'en est donc fait/Salut à la France! *(rec Salle Gounod, Bastille Opera, Paris, Nov 1993 & June 1994)* Deutsche Grammophon ▲ 447114-2 [DDD]
Fauré, G.:Requiem, w. A. Schmidt (bar), C. M. Giulini (cnd), Philharmonia Orch, Philharmonia Chorus [L] Deutsche Grammophon ▲ 419243-2 [DDD]

Battle, Kathleen (sop) (cont.)

Gershwin, G.:Porgy & Bess (sels), w. A. Previn (cnd), Orch of St. Luke—Summertime; I Loves You, Porgy Deutsche Grammophon ▲ 437787–2 ■ 437 787–4

Gounod, C.:Roméo et Juliette (sels), w. M.–W. Chung (cnd), Bastille Opera Orch—Je veux vivre; Dieu! quel frisson/Amour, ranime mon courage *(rec Salle Gounod, Bastille Opera, Paris, Nov 1993 & June 1994)* Deutsche Grammophon ▲ 447114–2 [DDD]

Great American Spirituals, w. Barbara Hendricks (sop), Florence Quivar (mez) Angel ▲ CDM 64669

Handel, G.F.:Arias, w. N. Marriner (cnd), Academy of St. Martin in the Fields—Acis & Galatea—Oh, didst thou know...As when the dove; Giulio Cesare—E pur così in un giorno...Piangerò la sorte mia; Joshua—Oh! had I Jubal's lyre; L'Allegro, il Penseroso ed il Moderato—Sweet bird; Messiah—Rejoice greatly, o daughter of Zion; Solomon—Ev'ry sight these eyes behold; May peace in Salem...Will the sun forget to streak; Alcina—Ah! mio cor!; Tornami a vagheggiar [E,I] EMI Classics ▲ CDC 49179 [DDD]

Handel, G.F.:Messiah, w. Florence Quivar (mez), John Aler (ten), Samuel Ramey (bass), A. Davis (cnd), Toronto SO, Mendelssohn Club Chorus Philadelphia [E] EMI Classics ▲ CDC 49407 [DDD]; ■ 4DS 49407 (D)

Handel, G.F.:Messiah, w. Florence Quivar (mez), John Aler (ten), Samuel Ramey (bass), A. Davis (cnd), Toronto SO, Mendelssohn Club Chorus Philadelphia [E] EMI Classics 2–▲ CDCB 49027 [DDD]; ■ 4D2S 49027 (D)

Handel, G.F.:Semele, w. Sylvia McNair (sop), Marylin Horne (mez), Michael Chance (ct), John Aler (ten), Samuel Ramey (bass), J. Nelson (cnd), English CO, Ambrosian Opera Chorus Deutsche Grammophon 3–▲ 435782–2 –

Haydn, J.:Die Schöpfung, w. Gösta Winbergh (ten), Kurt Moll (bass), J. Levine (cnd), Berlin PO, Stockholm Radio Chorus, Stockholm Chamber Choir Deutsche Grammophon 2–▲ 427629–2 [DDD]

In Concert, w. Jean–Pierre Rampal (fl), Anthony Newman (hpd), Myron Lutzke (vc), Margo Garrett (pno), John Steel Ritter (pno) *(rec Feb. 24, 1991)* Sony Classical ▲ SK 53106 [ADD] ■ ST 53106

In Concert, w. J.–P. Rampal (fl) Sony Classical ▲ SK 53106 [ADD] ■ ST 53106

Kathleen Battle in Concert, w. James Levine (pno) Deutsche Grammophon ("Masters" series) ▲ 445524–2 [DDD]

Live in Tokyo 1988, w. Plácido Domingo (ten), Metropolitan Opera Orch [cnd:James Levine] Deutsche Grammophon ▲ 427686–2 GH [DDD] ■ 427686–4

Mahler, G.:Sym 2, w. M. Forrester (cta), L. Slatkin (cnd), St. Louis SO, St. Louis Sym Chorus Telarc 2–▲ CD 80081/82 [DDD]

Mahler, G.:Sym 4, w. L. Maazel (cnd), Vienna PO CBS ▲ MDK 44908 [DDD] ■ MDT 44908 (D)

Massenet, J.:Manon (sels), w. M.–W. Chung (cnd), Bastille Opera Orch—Allons! il le faut!/Adieu, notre petite table; Suis–je gentille ainsi?/Obéissons, quand leur voix appelle *(rec Salle Gounod, Bastille Opera, Paris, Nov 1993 & June 1994)* Deutsche Grammophon ▲ 447114–2 [DDD]

Mendelssohn, F.:A Midsummer Night's Dream (comp), w. Frederica von Stade (mez), Judi Dench (nar), S. Ozawa (cnd), Boston SO, Tanglewood Festival Chorus Deutsche Grammophon ▲ 439897–2

Mozart, W.A.:Arias, w. Arleen Auger (sop), Irma Beilke (sop), Helena Braun (sop), Lisa Della Casa (sop), Maria Cebotari (sop), Ileana Cotrubas (sop), Helen Donath (sop), Mirella Freni (sop), Reri Grist (sop), Edita Gruberova (sop), Elisabeth Grümmer (sop), Hilde Güden (sop), Ingeborg Hallstein (sop), Luise Helletsgruber (sop), Gundula Janowitz (sop), Sena Jurinac (sop), Erika Köth (sop), Evelyn Lear (sop), Wilma Lipp (sop), Margaret Marshall (sop), Edith Mathis (sop), Jarmila Novotna (sop), Margherita Perras (sop), Lucia Popp (sop), Elisabeth Rethberg (sop), Anneliese Rothenberger (sop), Elisabeth Schumann (sop), Elisabeth Schwarzkopf (sop), Graziella Sciutti (sop), Irmgard Seefried (sop), Graziella Sciutti (sop), Julia Varady (sop), Agnes Baltsa (mez), Margit Bokor (mez), Brigitte Fassbaender (mez), Christa Ludwig (mez), Ann Murray (mez), Francisco Araiza (ten), Anton Dermota (ten), Helge Rosvaenge (ten), Rudolf Schock (ten), Peter Schreier (ten), Leopold Simoneau (ten), Eric Tappy (ten), Richard Tauber (ten), Gösta Winbergh (ten), Josef Witt (ten), Fritz Wunderlich (ten), Christian Boesch (bar), Willy Domgraf–Fassbaender (bar), Karl Dönch (bar), Dietrich Fischer–Dieskau (bar), Erich Kunz (bar), Eberhard Wächter (bar), Hans Hotter (b–bar), Paul Schöffler (b–bar), Cesare Siepi (b–bar), José Van Dam (b–bar), Walter Berry (bass), Geraint Evans (bass), Nicolai Ghiaurov (bass), Alexander Kipnis (bass), Richard Mayr (bass), Kurt Moll (bass), James Morris (bass), Ezio Pinza (bass), Martti Talvela (bass), Giorgio Tozzi (bass), Hans Duhan (sgr), Res Fischer (sgr), Marie Gerhart (sgr), *(various orchs & cnds)*—sels from Idomeneo, Die Entführung aus der Serail, Le nozze di Figaro, Don Giovanni, Così fan tutte, Die Zauberflöte & various arias Orfeo d'or ("Festspiel Dokumente" series) 5–▲ 408955

Mozart, W.A.:Arias, w. A. Previn (cnd), Royal PO [I] EMI Classics ▲ CDC 47355 [DDD] ■ 4DS 38297 (D)

Mozart, W.A.:Don Giovanni, w. A. Tomowa–Sintow (sop), A. Baltsa (mez), G. Winbergh (ten), S. Ramey (bass), F. Furlanetto (bass), P. Burchuladze (bass), H. von Karajan (cnd), Berlin PO, German Opera Chorus [I] Deutsche Grammophon 3–▲ 419179–2 [DDD]

Mozart, W.A.:Don Giovanni (sels), w. A. Tomowa–Sintow (sop), A. Baltsa (mez), G. Winbergh (ten), S. Ramey (bass), F. Furlanetto (bass), P. Burchuladze (bass), H. von Karajan (cnd), Berlin PO, German Opera Chorus [I] Deutsche Grammophon ▲ 419635–2 [DDD]

Mozart, W.A.:Entführung, w. E. Gruberova (sop), G. Winbergh (ten), H. Zednik (ten), M. Talvela (bass), Will Quadflieg (nar), G. Solti (cnd), Vienna PO [G] London 2–▲ 417402–2 [DDD]

Mozart, W.A.:Exsultate, w. A. Previn (cnd), Royal PO [L] EMI Classics ▲ CDC 47355 [DDD] ■ 4DS 38297 (D)

Mozart, W.A.:Missa, K.427, w. L. Cuberli (sop), P. Seiffert (ten), K. Moll (bass), J. Levine (cnd), Vienna PO, Vienna State Opera Chorus Deutsche Grammophon ▲ 423664–2 [DDD]

Mozart, W.A.:Nozze di Figaro, w. M. Price (sop), M. Nicolesco (sop), A. Murray (mez), J. Hynninen (bar), K. Rydl (bass), R. Muti (cnd), Vienna PO, Vienna State Opera Chorus [I] EMI Classics 3–▲ CDCC 47978 [DDD]

Mozart, W.A.:Nozze di Figaro (sels), w. M. Price (sop), M. Nicolesco (sop), A. Murray (mez), J. Hynninen (bar), K. Rydl (bass), R. Muti (cnd), Vienna PO, Vienna State Opera Chorus [I] EMI Classics ▲ CDC 54321

Mozart, W.A.:Requiem, w. A. Murray (mez), D. Rendall (ten), M. Salminen (bass), D. Barenboim (cnd), Orch de Paris, Paris Opera Chorus [L] EMI Classics ▲ CDC 47342 [DDD]

Offenbach, J.:Belle Lurette (sels), w. M.–W. Chung (cnd), Bastille Opera Orch—On s'amuse, on applaudit *(rec Salle Gounod, Bastille Opera, Paris, Nov 1993 & June 1994)* Deutsche Grammophon ▲ 447114–2 [DDD]

Pleasures of Their Company, w. Christopher Parkening (gtr) EMI Classics ▲ CDC 47196 [DDD] ■ 4DS 37351 (D)

Poulenc, F.:Gloria Sop, w. S. Ozawa (cnd), Boston SO, Tanglewood Festival Chorus [L] Deutsche Grammophon ▲ 427304–2 [DDD]

Poulenc, F.:Stabat mater, w. S. Ozawa (cnd), Boston SO, Tanglewood Festival Chorus [L] Deutsche Grammophon ▲ 427304–2 [DDD]

Previn, A.:Honey & Rue, w. Chris Gekker (tpt), James Pugh (trbn), Rufus Reid (bass), Grady Tate (dr), A. Previn (cnd), Orch of St. Luke's Deutsche Grammophon ▲ 437787–2 ■ 437 787–4

Rossini, G.:Il barbiere di Siviglia, w. P. Domingo (ten), F. Lopardo (ten), L. Gallo (bar), R. Raimondi (bass), C. Abbado (cnd), CO of Europe [I] Deutsche Grammophon 2–▲ 435763–2

Rossini, G.:L'italiana in Algeri, w. M. Horne (mez), E. Palacio (ten), S. Ramey (bass), N. Zaccaria (bass), C. Scimone (cnd), Venice Solisti, Prague Phil Chorus [I] Erato ("Libretto" series) 2–▲ 2292–45404–2

Rossini, G.:Il Signor Bruschino, w. F. Lopardo (ten), C. Desderi (bar), S. Ramey (bass), I. Marin (cnd), English CO Deutsche Grammophon ▲ 435865–2

Schubert, Franz:Songs (misc), w. J. Levine (pno) [G] Deutsche Grammophon ▲ 419237–2 [DDD]

So Many Stars, w. Antonio Hart (sax), Grover Washington Jr (sax), Tom Harrell (flgl), James Carter (b cl), Cyrus Chestnut (pno), Jon Herrington (gtr), Romero Lubambo (gtr), Ira Coleman (elec bass), Christian McBride (elec bass), Cyro Baptista (perc), Steven Berrios (perc) *(rec Hit Factory, Clinton Recording Studios, R.P.M. Sound Studios, Unique Recording Studios, Power Station)* Sony Classical ▲ SK 68473 [DDD]

Spirituals in Concert, w. J. Norman (sop), James Levine (cnd) *(rec in Carnegie Hall)* Deutsche Grammophon ▲ 429790–2 GH [DDD] ■ 429790–4 GH (D) ☐ 429790–5

Strauss, R.:Ariadne auf Naxos, w. A. Tomowa–Sintow (sop), A. Baltsa (mez), G. Lakes (ten), H. Prey (bar), J. Levine (cnd), Vienna PO Deutsche Grammophon 2–▲ 419225–2 [DDD]

Strauss, R.:Der Rosenkavalier (sels), w. R. Fleming (sop), F. von Stade (mez), A. Schmidt (bar), C. Abbado (cnd), Berlin PO *(rec Dec. 31, 1992)* Sony Classical ▲ SK 52565

Battle, Kathleen (sop) (cont.)

Thomas, A.:Hamlet (sels), w. M.–W. Chung (cnd), Bastille Opera Orch—Mais quelle est cette belle/Pâle et blonde *(rec Salle Gounod, Bastille Opera, Paris, Nov 1993 & June 1994)* Deutsche Grammophon ▲ 447114–2 [DDD]

Thomas, A.:Mignon (sels), w. M.–W. Chung (cnd), Bastille Opera Orch—Oui, pour ce soir/Je suis Titania la blonde *(rec Salle Gounod, Bastille Opera, Paris, Nov 1993 & June 1994)* Deutsche Grammophon ▲ 447114–2 [DDD]

Verdi, G.:Arias, w. J. Sutherland (sop), J. Anderson (sop), M. Price (sop), L. Pavarotti (ten), L. Nucci (bar)—includes favorite arias from Aida, Ballo in maschera, Don Carlos, Nabucco, Rigoletto, Traviata, Trovatore London ("Ovation" series) ▲ 430748–2 [DDD]

Verdi, G.:Un ballo in maschera, w. M. Price (sop), C. Ludwig (mez), L. Pavarotti (ten), R. Bruson (bar), G. Solti (cnd), National PO London, National Phil London Chorus [I] London 2–▲ 410210–2 [DDD]

Verdi, G.:Un ballo in maschera, w. M. Price (sop), C. Ludwig (mez), L. Pavarotti (ten), R. Bruson (bar), G. Solti (cnd), National PO London, National Phil London Chorus [I] London ▲ 425529–2 [DDD]

Wagner, R.:Der Ring des Nibelungen (sels), w. J. Norman (sop), H. Behrens (sop), J. Morris (mez), C. Ludwig (mez), R. Goldberg (ten), S. Jerusalem (ten), E. Wlaschiha (bar), M. Salminen (bass), J. Levine (cnd), Metropolitan Opera Orch—The Compact Ring—Ride of the Valkyries Wotan's Farewell & Magic Fire Music, Forest Murmurs, Brünnhilde's Awakening, Siegfried's Funeral Music, Brünnhilde's Immolation, & others Deutsche Grammophon ▲ 437825–2

Battles, J. (sgr)

Rodgers, R.:Allegro, w. L. Kirby (sgr) [1947 Broadway cast] RCA ▲ 07863–52758–2 ■ 07863–52758–4

Batty, Christine (mez)

Mozart, W.A.:Ave verum corpus, w. Noemi Rime (sop), Stuart Patterson (ten), Bernard Deletre (bass), G. Vashegyi (cnd), Budapest Orfeo Orch, Patrick Marco (cnd), Maitrise de Paris Pierre Verany ▲ PVY 730058 [DDD]

Mozart, W.A.:Missa, K.317, w. Noemi Rime (sop), Stuart Patterson (ten), Bernard Deletre (bass), G. Vashegyi (cnd), Budapest Orfeo Orch, Patrick Marco (cnd), Maitrise de Paris Pierre Verany ▲ PVY 730058 [DDD]

Mozart, W.A.:Vesperae solennes, w. Noemi Rime (sop), Stuart Patterson (ten), Bernard Deletre (bass), G. Vashegyi (cnd), Budapest Orfeo Orch, Patrick Marco (cnd), Maitrise de Paris Pierre Verany ▲ PVY 730058 [DDD]

Baucomont, Janette (sop)

Berio, L.:Laborintus II, w. Sanguineti (nar), C. Legrand (sop), C. Meunier (cta), L. Berio (cnd), Musique Vivante Ensemble, Chorale Experimentale [E,I] Musique d'Abord ▲ HMA 190764

Baudoin, Jean–Luc (ten)

Palestrina, G.:Sacred Music, w. Catherine Greuillet (sop), Thierry Gregoire (alt), Pierre Sciema (alt), Bruno Boterf (ten), Joel Suhubiette (ten), Jean–Claude Sarragosse (bass), Laurent Stewart (org), Françoise Lasserre (cnd), Champagne–Ardenne Akademia Regional Vocal Ensemble—Ave maria; Salve regina; Vergine bella; Vergine saggia; Virgine pura; Virgine santa; Vergine sola; Vergine chiara; Vergine, quante lagrime; Vergine, tale è terra; Ave mundi spes; Ave regina coelorum; Alma redemptoris mater; Regina coeli laetare; Salve regina; Magnificat; others *(rec Convent of the Annunciation Dominican Church, Paris, Jan., 1994)* Pierre Verany ▲ PVY 794041 [DDD]

Baudry, Elisabeth (sop)

Campra, A.:Messe de Requiem, w. M. Zanetti (sop), J. Benet (ten), J. Elwes (ten), S. Varcoe (bar), P. Herreweghe (cnd), La Chapelle Royale Orch [L] Harmonia Mundi France ▲ HMC 901251

Charpentier, M.–A.:In honorem Sancti Xaverii canticum, w. C. Dune (sop), G. Ragon (ten), P. Colléaux (cnd), Stradivaria Ensemble, Nantes Vocal Ensemble [L] Arion ▲ ARN 68037 [DDD]

Bauer, Vladimir (sgr)

Blacher, B.:A Jewish Chronicle, w. Anna Barová (cta), H. Kegel (cnd), Leipzig RSO, Leipzig Radio Chorus Berlin Classics ▲ BER 9016 [ADD]

Baum, Kurt (ten)

Bellini, V.:Norma, w. M. Callas (sop), G. Simionato (mez), N. Moscona (bass), G. Picco (cnd), Palacio Bellas Artes Orch, Palacio Bellas Artes Chorus *(rec live, Mexico City 5/23/50)* Melodram 2–▲ MEL 26018

Verdi, G.:Aida, w. M. Callas (sop), G. Simionato (mez), R. Weede (bar), G. Picco (cnd), Palacio Bellas Artes Orch, Palacio Bellas Artes Chorus *(rec live, Mexico City 5/30/50)* Melodram ▲ MLO 26009 [ADD]

Verdi, G.:Aida, w. Maria Callas (sop—Aida), Joan Sutherland (sop—Priestess), Giulietta Simionato (cta—Amneris), Kurt Baum (ten—Radames), Hector Thomas (ten—Messenger), Jess Walters (bar—Amonasro), Michael Langdon (bass—King), Giulio Neri (bass—Ramfis), J. Barbirolli (cnd), Royal Opera House Orch, Royal Opera House Chorus Covent Garden *(rec Covent Garden, London, June 10, 1953)* Legato Classics 2–▲ LCD 187–2

Verdi, G.:Il trovatore, w. M. Callas (sop), G. Simionato (mez), L. Warren (bar), G. Picco (cnd), Palacio Bellas Artes Orch, Palacio Bellas Artes Chorus *(rec live, Mexico City 6/20/50)* Melodram 2–▲ CDM 26017

Verdi, G.:Il trovatore (sels), w. M. Callas (sop), Feuss (sgr), C. Sagarminaga (ten), L. Warren (bar), G. Picco (cnd), Palacio Bellas Artes Orch, Palacio Bellas Artes Chorus—ten selections from Acts 1 & 4 [I] *(rec live, Mexico City 6/20/50)* Myto 2–▲ 2 MCD 90213 (m) [ADD]

Bauman, M. (sgr)

Ives, C.:Songs, w. A. Hirsch (pno)—6 songs *(rec 1938)* CRI ■ ACS 6014

Baumann, Christiane (sop)

Hindemith, P.:Motets, w. M. Baumann (pno)—Exiit edictum; Pastores loquebantur; Dicebat Jesus scribis et pharisaeis; Dixit Jesus Petro; Angelus Domini apparuit; Erat Joseph et Maria; Defuncto Herode; Cum natus esset; Cum factus esset Jesus; Vidit Joannes Jesum; Nuptiae factae sunt; Cum descendisset Jesus; Ascendente Jesu in naviculam Christophorus ▲ CD 74546 [DDD]

Bauwens, Ray (ten)

Beach, A.M.C.:Mass, "Grand Mass", w. Margot Law (sop), Martha Remington (mez), Joel Schneider (bar), B. Jones (cnd), Stow Festival Orch, Stow Festival Chorus *(rec Cathedral Church of St Paul, Tremont St, Boston, MA)* Albany ▲ TROY 179 [DDD]

Bäverstam, Åsa (sop)

Nielsen, C.:Choral Music, w. L. Ekdahl (girl sop), A. Thors (boy sop), K. M. Sandve (ten), P. Hoyer (bar), E.–P. Salonen (cnd), Swedish RSO, Stockholm Boys' Choir, Swedish Radio Chorus—Springtime in Funen; The Blind Musician; The Old People; Dance Ballad *(rec Sept. 16–18, 1991)* Sony Classical ▲ SK 53276 [DDD]

Sørensen, B.:The Echoing Garden, w. Martyn Hill (ten), L. Segerstam (cnd), Danish National RSO, Danish National Radio Choir *(rec live, Danish Radio Concert Hall, 1992 & 1994)* Marco Polo/Dacapo ▲ 8.224039 [DDD]

Baxter, C. (sgr)

Rodgers, R.:Carousel, w. J. Raitt (sgr), J. Clayton (sgr), J. Darling (sgr), C. Johnson (sgr), E. Mattson (sgr), M. Vye (sgr), J. Littau (cnd) [1945 cast] MCA Classics ▲ MCAD 10048 [AAD] ■ MCAC 10048

Bayer, M. (alt)

Haydn, J.:Mass 1a, Missa 'Rorate coeli desuper', w. G. Öhlinger (sop), M. Klietmann (ten), A. Lebeda (bass), D. de Rooij an der Reil (org), Collegium Musicum Pragense Christophorus ▲ CD 74541 [DDD]

Haydn, J.:Mass 7, "Kleine Orgelmesse", w. G. Öhlinger (sop), M. Klietmann (ten), A. Lebeda (bass), Collegium Musicum Pragense Christophorus ▲ CD 74541 [DDD]

Bayley, Clive (bass)

Walton, W.:Troilus & Cressida, w. Judith Howarth (sop—Cressida), Arthur Davies (ten—Troilus), Nigel Robson (ten—Pandarus), Brian Cookson (ten—3rd Watchman), Peter Bodenham (ten—Priest), Keith Mills (ten—Soldier), Alan Opie (bar—Diomede), James Thornton (bar—Antenor), Clive Bayley (bass—Calkas), David Owen–Lewis (bass—Horaste), R. Hickox (cnd), English Northern Philharmonia, Opera North Chorus Chandos 2–▲ CHAN 9370/71 [DDD]

Bayo, Maria (sop)

Arie Antiche, w. Irsula Duetschler (hpd) Claves ▲ CD 9023 [DDD]

Bretón, T.:La Verbena de la paloma, w. Raquel Pierotti (sop), Plácido Domingo (ten), Enrique Baquerizo (sgr), Rafael Castejon (sgr), Milagros Martin (sgr), Silva Tro (sgr), A. Ros–Marbá (cnd), Madrid SO Valois ("Zarauela" series) ▲ V 4725

Bayo, Maria (sop) (cont.)

Canciones Españolas, w. Juan Antonio Alvarez-Parejo (pno) Claves ▲ CD 9205 [DDD]

Cavalli, P.F.:Calisto, w. Graham Pushee (ct), Simon Keenlyside (bar), Marcello Lippi (bar), René Jacobs (cnd), Concerto Vocale Harmonia Mundi France 3-▲ HMC 901515/17

Falla, M. de:Atlántida, w. T. Berganza (mez), S. Estes (bass), E. Colomer (cnd), Spanish National Youth Orch Valois 2-▲ V 4685

Rossini, G.:L'occassione fa il ladro, w. Francesca Provvisionato (mez), Fulvio Massa (ten), Iorio Zennaro (ten), Fabio Previati (bar), Natale de Carolis (b-bar), M. Viotti (cnd), English CO Claves 2-▲ 50-9208/9

Rossini, G.:L'occassione fa il ladro, w. F. Provvisionato (mez), F. Massa (ten), I. Zennaro (ten), F. Previati (bar), N. de Carolis (b-bar), M. Viotti (cnd), English CO [I] Claves 8-▲ CD 9200 [DDD]

Sorozábal, P.:La Tabernera del Puerto, w. Plácido Domingo (ten), Juan Pons (bar), V.P. Pérez (cnd), Galicia SO Auvidis Valois ("Zarzuela Collection" series) ▲ V 4766

Turina, J.:Las musas de Andalucía, w. R. Requeno (pno), Sine Nomine String Quartet *(rec Apr. 1992)* Claves ▲ CD 9320 [DDD]

Turina, J.:Qt Strs, w. R. Requeno (pno), Sine Nomine String Quartet *(rec Apr. 1992)* Claves ▲ CD 9320 [DDD]

Vives, A.:Bohemios, w. L. Lima (ten), C. Alvarez (bass), A. R. Marbà (cnd), Tenerife SO Valois ▲ V 4711

Bazemore, Raymond (bass)

Flagello, N.:Passion of Martin Luther King, w. Portland Symphonic Choir, J. DePreist (cnd), Oregon SO Koch International Classics ▲ KIC 7293-2 [DDD]

Bazemore, Raymond (nar)

Schwantner, J.:New Morning for the World, w. J. DePreist (cnd), Oregon SO Koch International Classics ▲ KIC 7293-2 [DDD]

Bazola, François (bar)

Charpentier, M.-A.:Médée, w. Isabelle Desrochers (sop—Cleone), Lorraine Hunt (sop—Medee), Noemi Rime (sop—Nerine), Monique Zanetti (sop—Creuse), Mark Padmore (ten—Jason), François Bazola (bar—Arcas), Jean-Marc Salzmann (bar—Oronte), Bernard Deletre (bass-Creon), W. Christie (cnd), Les Arts Florissants Erato 3-▲ 96558-2

Bazzini, Amelia (sgr)

Mascagni, P.:Isabeau, w. Marcella Pobbe (sop—Isabeau), Licia Galvano (mez—Giglietta), Pier Miranda Ferraro (ten—Folco), Orazio Gualtiero (bar—Cornelius), Rinaldo Rola (bass—Re Raimondo), Amelia Bazzini (sgr—Ermyngarde), Piero Benzi (sgr—L'araldo), Renata Davini (sgr—Ermynthrude), Piero Francia (sgr—Il Cavaliere), T. Serafin (cnd), San Remo SO *(rec Sanremo, Jan 13, 1962)* Bongiovanni ("Il Mito dell'Opera" series) 2-▲ GB 1135/36-2 [ADD]

Beardslee, Bethany (sop)

Babbitt, M.:Philomel Sop & 4-Track Tape *(rec General Theological Seminary Chapel, NYC)* New World ▲ 80466-2

Babbitt, M.:Vision & Prayer [E] CRI ▲ CD 521

But Yesterday Is Not Today:The American Art Song 1927-1972, w. Robert Helps (pno) *(rec Columbia Recording Studios, 30th St, New York)* New World ▲ 80243-2

Debussy, C.:Ariettes oubliées, w. Robert Helps (pno) [F] GM ▲ GM2029CD [DDD]

Debussy, C.:Proses lyriques, w. Robert Helps (pno) [F] GM ▲ GM2029CD [DDD]

Helps, R.:Gossamer Noons, w. G. Schuller (cnd), American Composers Orch *(rec Church of Holy Trinity, Mar 1978)* CRI ("American Masters" series) ▲ CD 717 [ADD]

Lerdahl, F.:Wake, w. D. Epstein (cnd), Boston Sym Chamber Players [E] CRI ▲ CD 580 [ADD/DDD]

Perle, G.:Dickinson Songs, w. M. Ritt (pno) [E] CRI ■ ACS 6015

Perle, G.:Rilke Songs, w. Perle (pno) [E] CRI ■ ACS 6015

Ravel, M.:Histoires naturelles, w. Robert Helps (pno) [F] GM ▲ GM2029CD [DDD]

Shapey, R.:Incantations, w. R. Shapey (cnd), Univ of Chicago Contemporary Chamber Players CRI ▲ CD 690 [ADD]

Beasley, Marco (ten)

Marcello, B.:Il pianto e il riso delle quattro stagioni, w. S. Piccollo (sop-Primavera), A. Carmignani (ct-Estate), R. Franceschetto (bass-Inverno), F. Ghiglione (cnd), Don Milani Cultural Association Orch, G. B. Trofello Schola Cantorum *(rec Mar. 29, 1992)* Bongiovanni 2-▲ GB 2159/60 [DDD]

Stradella, A.:Il moro per amore, w. R. Invernizzi (sop—Eurinda), S. Piccollo (sop—Lucinda), M. Grazia Liguori (sop—Fiorino), M. Lazzara (cta—Lindora), V. Matacchini (cta—Feraspe/Floridoro), M. Beasley (ten—Filandro), R. Ristori (bass—Rodrigo), E. Velardi (cnd), Alessandro Stradella Consort [I] *(rec Oct. 31-Nov. 3, 1992)* Bongiovanni 3-▲ GB 2153/55

Beasom, Samela Aird (sop)

Jacob, G.:Songs Sop & Cl, w. Daniel Geeting (cl) *(rec Memorial Chapel, Univ. of Redlands, Redlands, CA, Mar. 5, Apr. 30 & June 30)* PROdigital ▲ PRO 9226 [DDD]

Beaton, Morag (sop)

Herrmann, B.:Wuthering Heights, w. M. Beaton (sop—Catherine), P. Bowden (mez—Isabella), E. Bainbridge (mez—Nelly), M. Snashall (trb—Hareton), D. Bell (bar—Heathcliff), J. Kitchiner (bar—Hindley), J. Ward (bar—Edgar), M. Rippon (bass—Joseph), D. Kelly (bass—Mr. Lockwood), B. Herrmann (cnd), Pro Arte Orch *(rec 1965-66)* Unicorn-Kanchana 3-▲ UKCD 2050/51/52 [ADD]

Beaudoin, Lee (mez)

Eastman, D.K.:Just Us, w. Linda Eagleston (fl) Capstone ▲ CPS 8032

Beavan, Nigel (bass)

Purcell, H.:King Arthur, w. R. Hardy (sop), H. Sheppard (sop), J. Knibbs (cta), A. Deller (ct), M. Deller (alt), P. Elliott (ten), L. Nixon (ten), M. Bevan (bar), A. Deller (cnd), Deller Consort, King's Musick [E] Harmonia Mundi France 2-▲ HMC 90252/53

Beavon, Constance (mez)

Cordero, R.:Dodecaconcerto, w. A. M. Ketchum (sop), M. Lifchitz (cnd), North/South Consonance Ensemble North/South Recordings ▲ NS 1003 [DDD]

Levinson, G.:Black Magic/White Magic, w. J. Freeman (cnd), Orch 2001 CRI ▲ CD 642 [DDD]

Rands, B.:...in the receding mist Sop, w. A. M. Ketchum (sop), M. Lifchitz (cnd), North/South Consonance Ensemble North/South Recordings ▲ NS 1003 [DDD]

Saylor, B.:See You in the Morning, w. A. M. Ketchum (sop), M. Lifchitz (cnd), North/South Consonance Ensemble North/South Recordings ▲ NS 1003 [DDD]

Saylor, B.:Songs from Water St, w. M. Hoffman (va), D. Abramowitz (pno) [E] CRI ▲ CD 578 [DDD]

Vega, A. de la:Testimonial, w. A. M. Ketchum (sop), M. Lifchitz (cnd), North/South Consonance Ensemble North/South Recordings ▲ NS 1003 [DDD]

Becerra, Flavio (ten)

Beethoven, L. van:Sym 9, "Choral Sym", w. Irma Gonzalez (sop), Oralia Dominguez (cta), Roberto Banuelas (bar), F. Lozano (cnd), Mexico City PO, Mexico City Chorus Forlane ▲ FRL 18 [AAD]

Bechi, Gino (bar)

Giordano, U.:Andrea Chénier, w. M. Caniglia (sop), G. Simionato (mez), B. Gigli (ten), G. Taddei (bar), I. Tajo (bass), O. de Fabritiis (cnd), La Scala Orch, La Scala Chorus [I] *(rec 1941, HMV DB 5423/35)* Angel ("Studio" series) 2-▲ CDHB 69996 (m) [ADD]

Giordano, U.:Andrea Chénier, w. Maria Caniglia (sop—Maddalena), Maria Huder (mez—Bersi), Vittoria Palombini (mez—Madelon), Giulietta Simionato (mez—Contessa), Beniamino Gigli (ten—Andrea), Adelio Zagonara (ten—Incroyable/Abbé), Gino Bechi (bar—Carlo), Leone Paci (bar—Mathieu), Giuseppe Taddei (b-bar—Pietro/Fouquier), Italo Tajo (b-bar—Roucher), Gino Conti (bass—Master/Schmidt), O. de Fabritiis (cnd), La Scala Orch, La Scala Chorus *(rec Nov 1941)* Arkadia ("The 78's" series) 2-▲ 78012 [ADD]

Mascagni, P.:Cavalleria rusticana, w. L.B. Rasa (sop), M. Marucucci (mez), G. Simionato (mez), B. Gigli (ten), P. Mascagni (cnd), La Scala Orch, La Scala Chorus *(rec 1940)* Nimbus 2-▲ NI 7843/44 [ADD]

Mascagni, P.:Cavalliera rusticana, w. Lina Bruna-Rasa (sop), Giulietta Simionato (mez), Benia Gigli (ten), Giuseppe Nessi (ten), Carlo Galeffi (bar), P. Mascagni (cnd), La Scala Orch, La Scala Chorus *(rec Milan, 1940)* Phonographe 2-▲ PHG CD 5066

Mascagni, P.:Cavalleria rusticana, w. L. Bruna Rasa (sop), G. Simionato (mez), B. Gigli (ten), P. Mascagni (cnd), La Scala Orch, La Scala Chorus [I] *(rec 1940)* EMI Classics ("Studio" series) 2-▲ CDHB 69987 (m) [ADD]

Opera Arias & Scenes, w. various Italian orchs *(rec 1941-1951)* Preiser ("Lebendige Vergangenheit" series) ▲ PRE 89009 (m) [AAD]

Bechi, Gino (bar) (cont.)

Rossini, G.:Il barbiere di Siviglia, w. D. Gatta (sop), C. Valletti (ten), N. Rossi-Lemeni (bass), V. de Sabata (cnd), La Scala Orch, La Scala Chorus *(rec 1952)* Memories 2-▲ MEM 4525 [AAD]

Verdi, G.:Un ballo in maschera, w. Maria Caniglia (sop), Fedora Barbieri (cta), Beniamino Gigli (ten), T. Serafin (cnd), Rome Opera Orch, Rome Opera Chorus *(rec Rome, July, 1943)* Grammofono 2000 2-▲ GRM 78556

Verdi, G.:Un ballo in maschera, w. Maria Caniglia (sop—Amelia), Fedora Barbieri (mez—Ulrica), Beniamino Gigli (ten—Riccardo), Gino Bechi (bar—Renato), Tancredi Pasero (bass—Samuel), Blando Giusti (sgr—Un Giudice), Nicola Niccolini (sgr—Silvano), Ugo Novelli (sgr—Tom), Elda Ribetti (sgr—Oscar), T. Serafin (cnd), Rome Opera Orch, Giuseppe Conca (cnd), Rome Opera Chorus *(rec 1943)* Arkadia 2-▲ CD 78005 (m) [ADD]

Verdi, G.:Nabucco, w. M. Callas (sop), L. Neroni (bass), V. Gui (cnd), Naples Teatro San Carlo Orch, Naples Teatro San Carlo Chorus [I] *(rec live 12/20/49)* Melodram 2-▲ MEL 26029 (m) [AAD]

Becht, H. (bass)

Schoenberg, A.:Gurrelieder, w. S. Dunn (sop), B. Fassbaender (mez), S. Jerusalem (ten), P. Haage (ten), H. Hotter (nar), R. Chailly (cnd), Berlin RSO, St. Hedwig's Cathedral Choir, Düsseldorf Municipal Choral Society [G] London 2-▲ 430321-2 [DDD]

Becht, Hermann (bar)

Wagner, R.:Götterdämmerung, w. G. Jones (sop), H. Jung (mez), F. Mazura (bar), P. Boulez (cnd), Bayreuth Festival Orch, Bayreuth Festival Chorus [G] Philips 4-▲ 434424-2 [DDD]

Wagner, R.:Das Rheingold, w. H. Schwarz (mez), H. Zednik (ten), D. McIntyre (b-bar), P. Boulez (cnd), Bayreuth Festival Orch, Bayreuth Festival Chorus [G] Philips 2-▲ 434421-2 [DDD]

Wagner, R.:Siegfried, w. G. Jones (sop), H. Zednik (ten), D. McIntyre (b-bar), P. Boulez (cnd), Bayreuth Festival Orch, Bayreuth Festival Chorus [G] Philips 3-▲ 434423-2 [DDD]

Beck, Johannes (bar)

Hoffmann, E.T.A.:Undine, w. Barbara Baier (sop—Berthalda), Heidrun Plesch (sop—Undine), Corinna Tippe (sop—Die Herzogin), Maria Hiefinger (mez—Fisherman's Wife), Achim Schamberger (ten—Der Herzog), Johannes Beck (bar—Ritter Huldbrand von Ringstetten), Michael Albert (bass—Fisherman), Ulrich Bosch (bass—Heilmann), Bernd Hofmann (bass—Kühleborn), H. Dechant (cnd), Bamberg Youth Orch Bayer 3-▲ 100256/58 [DDD]

Becker, Josef (bass)

Mendelssohn, F.:Die Hochzeit des Camacho, w. R. Schudel (sop—Quiteria), C. Swanson (sop—Lucinda), C. Bieber (ten—Basilio), W. Mok (ten—Vivaldo), V. Horn (ten—Camacho), R. Lukas (bar—Carrasco), J. Becker (bass—Sancho Panza), W. Murray (bass—Don Quixote), B. Klee (cnd), Berlin RSO, Berlin Radio Chorus [G] Koch Schwann 2-▲ 314042 [DDD]

Spontini, G.:Olympia, w. J. Varady (sop), S. Toczyska (mez), F. Tagliavini (ten), D. Fischer-Dieskau (bar), G. Fortune (bass), G. Albrecht (cnd), Berlin RSO, Berlin Radio Chorus [Paris version] Orfeo 2-▲ 137862 [DDD]

Becker-Egner, Liselotte (sop)

Wagner, R.:Der Ring des Nibelungen, w. Liselotte Becker-Egner (sop—Woglinde/Ortlinde/Wellgunde), Angelika Berger (sop—Wellgunde/Waltraute), Siw Ericsdotter (sop—Norn 3), Heidemaria Ferch (sop—Freia/Gerhilde), Bella Jasper (sop—Helmwige/Waldvogel/Woglinde), Ditha Sommer (sop—Sieglinde/Gutrune), Ursula Boese (mez—Erda), Ruth Hesse (mez—Fricka), Nadezda Kniplová (mez—Brünnhilde), Margit Kobeck (mez—Schwertleite/Norn 2), Hilde Rosner (mez—Flosshilde/Siegrunde), Erica Schubert (mez—Grimgerde/Flosshilde), Ingrid Göritz (cta—Rossweisse/Norn 1), Herbert Doussant (ten—Froh), Herold Kraus (ten—Mime), Gerald McKee (ten—Siegmund/Siegfried), Fritz Uhl (ten—Loge), Rudolf Knoll (bar—Gunther/Donner), Rolf Polke (bass-bar—Wotan/Wanderer), Rolf Kühne (bass—Alberich), Takao Okamura (bass—Fafner), Otto von Rohr (bass—Hagen/Fasolt/Hunding), H. Swarowsky (cnd), Czech PO, Prague National Theater Orch *(rec June 3 & 5, July 26-31, A)* Weltbild Classics 14-▲ 703769 [ADD]

Beckley, Lisa (sop)

Fauré, G.:Messe basse (in 3 movts), w. Colm Carey (org), J. Summerly (cnd), Oxford Camerata, Oxford Schola Cantorum *(rec Hertford College Chapel, Oxford, May 17 & 18, 1993)* Naxos ▲ 8.550765 [DDD]

Fauré, G.:Requiem, w. Nicholas Gedge (b-bar), Colm Carey (org), J. Summerly (cnd), Oxford Camerata, Oxford Schola Cantorum *(rec Hertford College Chapel, Oxford, May 17 & 18, 1993)* Naxos ▲ 8.550765 [DDD]

Beckmann, Friedel (alt)

Bach, J.S.:St. Matthew Passion, w. T. Lemnitz (sop), K. Erb (ten), G. Hüsch (bar), S. Schulze (bass), G. Ramin (cnd), Leipzig Gewandhaus Orch, St. Thomas Choir, *(abridged performance)* [G] *(rec Mar 1941)* Calig 2-▲ CAL 50 859/60 (m) [AAD]

Beckmann, Judith (sop)

Bach, J.S.:Cant 198, w. A. Kraus (ten), W. Heldwein (bass), H. Rilling (cnd), Stuttgart Bach Collegium, Gächinger Kantorei [G] *(rec Sept 1976 & Jan 1977)* Hänssler Classic ▲ 98.827 [AAD]

Beddall, Kate (voc)

Ziporyn, E.:Aneh Tapi Nyata, Sekar Jaya Gamelan Orch New World ▲ 804302

Bedi, Patrice Michaels (sop)

Argento, D.:Elizabethan Songs (6), w. Rembrandt Chamber Players Cedille ▲ CDR 90000 011 [DDD]

Argento, D.:Letters from Composers, w. Jeffrey Kust (gtr) *(rec Mandel Hall, Univ of Chicago, June 17-21, 1996)* Cedille ▲ CDR 90000029 [DDD]

Argento, D.:Songs About Spring, w. Elizabeth Buccheri (pno) *(rec Mandel Hall, Univ of Chicago, June 17-21, 1996)* Cedille ▲ CDR 90000029 [DDD]

Argento, D.:To Be Sung Upon The Water, w. Larry Combs (cl), Elizabeth Buccheri (pno) *(rec Mandel Hall, Univ of Chicago, June 17-21, 1996)* Cedille ▲ CDR 90000029 [DDD]

Songs of the Romantic Age, w. Patrice Michaels Bedi (sop), D. Sobol (pno) *(rec Chicago, June 20-22 & 27, 1994)* Cedille ▲ CDR 90000 019 [DDD]

Vaughan Williams, R.:Along The Field, w. Elliot Golub (vn)—Along the Field; Goodbye; Fancy's Knell; With Rue My Heart is Laden *(rec Mandel Hall, Univ of Chicago, June 17-21, 1996)* Cedille ▲ CDR 90000029 [DDD]

Vaughan Williams, R.:Vocalises, w. Larry Combs (cl) *(rec Mandel Hall, Univ of Chicago, June 17-21, 1996)* Cedille ▲ CDR 90000029 [DDD]

Vivaldi, A.:Cants, w. Chicago Baroque Ensemble—All'ombra di sospetto, R.178; Lungi dal vago volto, R.680 *(rec St. Luke's Church, Evanston, IL, May-Aug 1995)* Cedille ▲ CDR 90000 025 [DDD]

Vivaldi, A.:Motets, w. Chicago Baroque Ensemble—Nulla in mundo pax sincera, R.630; Londe mala, umbrae, terrores, R.629 *(rec St. Luke's Church, Evanston, IL, May-Aug 1995)* Cedille ▲ CDR 90000 025 [DDD]

Bednář, Vaclav (bass)

Smetana, B.:The Devil's Wall, w. Milada Šubrtová (sop), Ivana Mixová (mez), Z. Chalabala (cnd), Prague National Theater Orch, Prague National Theater Chorus *(rec Prague, 1960)* Supraphon 2-▲ SUP 112201 [AAD]

Beek, Andrea van (sop)

Meijering, Chiel:St. Louis Blues, w. Francine van der Heijden (sop), Jeanette Huizinga (mez), Rein Kolpa (ten), Willem-Jan van Deuveren (ten), John Vredeveldt (ten), Gérard Bernts (bar), W. Megens (cnd), De Ereprijs Orch [I] *(rec Schouwburg Arnhem, Mar 10, 1995)* Donemus 2-▲ neos 01-02

Been, Birgit (sop)

Mozart, W.A.:Zauberflöte, w. Birgit Been (sop), Nathalie Boissy (sop), Marianne Seibel (sop), Renate Springer (sop), Elizabeth Vidal (sop), Eleanor James (mez), Salvador Guzman (ten), Herbert Hechenberger (ten), Wolfgang Newmann (ten), Klaus Häger (bass), Philip Langshaw (bass), Hans-Georg Moser (bass), P. Kuentz (cnd), Paul Kuentz Orch, Francis Bardot (cnd), Maitrise des Hauts-de-Seine members, Paul Kuentz Choirs Pierre Verany 2-▲ PVY 730055 [DDD]

Beesley, Mark (bar)

Verdi, G.:La traviata, w. Angela Gheorghiu (sop—Violetta), Leah-Marian Jones (mez—Flora Bervoix), Gillian Knight (mez—Annina), Robin Leggate (ten—Gastone), Frank Lopardo (ten—Alfredo Germont), Rodney Gibson (ten—Servo di Flora), Neil Griffiths (ten—Giuseppe), Mark Beesley (bar—Dottore Grenvile), Leo Nucci (bar—Giorgio Germont), Richard Van Allan (bass—Barone Douphol), Roderick Earle (bass—Marquese d'Obigny), Bryan Secombe (bass—Commissionario), G. Solti (cnd), Royal Opera House Orch, Royal Opera House Chorus Covent Garden *(rec live, Royal Opera House, Covent Garden, Dec. 1994)* London 2-▲ 448119-2

Beesley, Shauna (sop)
Purcell, H.:Dido & Aeneas, w. Ruth Holton (sop—Belinda), Elisabeth Priday (sop—2nd Woman), Donna Deam (sop—1st Witch), Shauna Beesley (sop—2nd Witch), Teresa Shaw (mez—Sorceress), Carolyn Watkinson (cta—Dido), Jonathan Peter Kenny (alt—Spirit), Paul Tindall (ten—Sailor), George Mosley (bass—Aeneas), J.E. Gardiner (cnd), English Baroque Soloists, Monteverdi Choir London *(rec Saint George's, Bristol, UK, July 12-14, 1990)* Philips ▲ 432114-2

Beggiato, Ortensia (sop)
Paisiello, G.:Fedra, w. R. Mattioli (sop), A. Tuccari (sop), L. Udovick (sop), A. Lazzari (ten), A. Questa (cnd), Milan RAI SO, Milan RAI Chorus *(rec 1958)* Memories 2-▲ MEM 4502 [AAD]

Begley, Kim (ten)
Verdi, G.:Falstaff, w. E. Norberg-Schulz (sop—Nannetta), L. Serra (sop—Alice), S. Graham (mez—Meg Page), M. Lipovsek (cta—Miss Quickly), K. Begley (ten—Dr. Caius), P. Conti (ten—Ford), M. Luperi (ten—Pistol), J. Van Dam (b-bar—Falstaff), P. LeFebvre (bass—Bardolph), G. Solti (cnd), Berlin PO, Berlin Radio Chorus London ▲ 440650-2 [DDD]
Wagner, R.:Das Rheingold, w. Gabriele Fontana (sop—Woglinde), Nancy Gustafson (sop—Freia), Ildiko Komlosi (mez—Wellgunde), Hanna Schwarz (mez—Fricka), Elena Zaremba (mez—Erda), Margareta Hintermeier (cta—Flosshilde), Kim Begley (ten—Loge), Peter Schreier (ten—Mime), Thomas Sunnegardh (ten—Froh), Robert Hale (bass-bar—Wotan), Walter Fink (bass—Fafner), Franz-Josef Kapellmann (bass—Alberich), Jan-Hendrik Rootering (bass—Fasolt), Eike Wilm Schulte (bass—Donner), C. von Dohnányi (cnd), Cleveland Orch *(rec Severance Hall, Cleveland, Ohio, Dec 1993)* London 2-▲ 443690-2

Behle, Renate (sop)
Rihm, W.:Die Eroberung von Mexico, w. R. Salter (bar), I. Metzmacher (cnd), Hamburg State PO, Hamburg State Opera Chorus [G] *(rec live Feb. 9, 1992)* CPO 2-▲ CPO 999185-2 [DDD]
Schumann, R.:Genoveva, w. J. Faulkner (sop—Genoveva), R. Behle (sop—Margaretha), K. Lewis (ten—Golo), A. Titus (bar—Siegfried), H. Stamm (bass—Hidulfus, Caspar), J. Tilli (bass—Balthasar), G. Albrecht (cnd), Hamburg State PO, Hamburg State Opera Chorus [G] *(rec 1992)* Orfeo 2-▲ 289932 [DDD]
Spohr, L.:Jessonda, w. J. Varady (sop), T. Moser (ten), D. Fischer-Dieskau (bar), K. Moll (bass), G. Albrecht (cnd), Hamburg State PO, Hamburg State Opera Chorus [G] Orfeo 2-▲ 240912 [DDD]

Behm, Gisela (sop)
Puccini, G.:Tosca (sels), w. G. Behms (sop—Tosca), *(other soloists unknown)*, H. Löwlein (cnd), Berlin State Opera Orch—6 arias [G] *(rec live, Berlin, 3/3/57)* Preiser ▲ 90103 (m) [ADD]

Behrens, Hildegard (sop)
Beethoven, L. van:Fidelio, w. S. Ghazarian (sop), P. Hofmann (ten), T. Adam (b-bar), H. Sotin (bass), G. Solti (cnd), Chicago SO, Chicago Sym Chorus [G] London 2-▲ 410227-2 [DDD]
Berg, A.:Wozzeck, w. P. Langridge (ten), H. Zednik (ten), F. Grundheber (bar), A. Haugland (bass), C. Abbado (cnd), Vienna PO, Vienna State Opera Chorus, Vienna Boys' Choir [G] *(rec live, 6/88)* Deutsche Grammophon 2-▲ 423587-2 [DDD]
Humperdinck, E.:Hänsel und Gretel, w. H. Behrens (sop—Gertrud, the Stepmother), R. Ziesak (sop—Gretel), R. Joshua (sop—Sandman), C. Schäfer (sop—Dew Fairy), J. Larmore (mez—Hänsel), H. Schwarz (cta—Nibblewitch), B. Weikl (bar—Peter, the Father), D. Runnicles (cnd), Bavarian RSO, Tölz Boys' Choir *(rec Munich, Feb. 1994)* Teldec 2-▲ 94549-2 [DDD]
Strauss, R.:Die Frau ohne Schatten, w. J. Varady (sop), P. Domingo (ten), J. Van Dam (b-bar), G. Solti (cnd), Vienna PO, Vienna State Opera Chorus [G] London 3-▲ 436243-2
Strauss, R.:Salome, w. A. Baltsa (mez), H. Angervo (alt), K.W. Böhm (ten), W. Ochman (ten), J. van Dam (bar), H. von Karajan (cnd), Vienna PO EMI Classics 2-▲ CDCB 49358
Wagner, R.:Der fliegende Holländer, w. H. Beherns (sop—Senta), I. Vermillion (mez—Mary), U. Heilmann (ten—Helmsman), J. Protschka (ten—Erik), R. Hale (bar—The Dutchman), K. Rydl (bass—Daland), C. von Dohnányi (cnd), Vienna PO, Vienna State Opera Chorus London 2-▲ 436418-2 [DDD]
Wagner, R.:Götterdämmerung, w. C. Studer (sop), H. Schwarz (mez), R. Goldberg (ten), B. Weikl (bar), E. Wlaschiha (bar), M. Salminen (bass), J. Levine (cnd), Metropolitan Opera Orch, New York Metropolitan Opera Chorus Deutsche Grammophon 4-▲ 429385-2 [DDD]
Wagner, R.:Der Ring des Nibelungen (sels), w. J. Norman (sop), K. Battle (sop), J. Morris (mez), C. Ludwig (mez), R. Goldberg (ten), S. Jerusalem (ten), E. Wlaschiha (bar), M. Salminen (bass), J. Levine (cnd), Metropolitan Opera Orch—The Compact Ring—Ride of the Valkyries Wotan's Farewell & Magic Fire Music, Forest Murmurs, Brünnhilde's Awakening, Siegfried's Funeral Music, Brünnhilde's Immolation, & others Deutsche Grammophon ▲ 437825-2
Wagner, R.:Siegfried, w. B. Svenden (sop), R. Goldberg (ten), J. Morris (bass), J. Levine (cnd), Metropolitan Opera Orch, New York Metropolitan Opera Chorus [G] Deutsche Grammophon 4-▲ 429407-2 [DDD]
Wagner, R.:Tristan und Isolde (sels), w. Y. Minton (mez), P. Hofmann (ten), B. Weikl (bass), L. Bernstein (cnd), Bavarian RSO, Bavarian Radio Chorus Philips ▲ 438501-2

Beidler, Katharina (sop)
Burkhard, W.:Mass, Op. 85, w. M. Brodard (bass), H. Gafner (cnd), Bern SO, Bern Gabrieli Chorus Jecklin ▲ JD 687

Beilke, Irma (sop)
Mozart, W.A.:Arias, w. Arleen Augér (sop), Kathleen Battle (sop), Helena Braun (sop), Lisa Della Casa (sop), Maria Cebotari (sop), Ileana Cotrubas (sop), Helen Donath (sop), Mirella Freni (sop), Reri Grist (sop), Edita Gruberova (sop), Elisabeth Grümmer (sop), Hilde Güden (sop), Ingeborg Hallstein (sop), Luise Helletsgruber (sop), Gundula Janowitz (sop), Sena Jurinac (sop), Erika Köth (sop), Evelyn Lear (sop), Wilma Lipp (sop), Margaret Marshall (sop), Edith Mathis (sop), Jarmila Novotna (sop), Margherita Perras (sop), Lucia Popp (sop), Elisabeth Rethberg (sop), Anneliese Rothenberger (sop), Elisabeth Schumann (sop), Elisabeth Schwarzkopf (sop), Graziella Sciutti (sop), Irmgard Seefried (sop), Graziella Sciutti (sop), Julia Varady (sop), Agnes Baltsa (mez), Margit Bokor (mez), Brigitte Fassbaender (mez), Christa Ludwig (mez), Ann Murray (mez), Francisco Araiza (ten), Anton Dermota (ten), Helge Rosvaenge (ten), Rudolf Schock (ten), Peter Schreier (ten), Leopold Simoneau (ten), Eric Tappy (ten), Richard Tauber (ten), Gösta Winbergh (ten), Josef Witt (ten), Fritz Wunderlich (ten), Christian Boesch (bar), Willy Domgraf-Fassbaender (bar), Karl Dönch (bar), Dietrich Fischer-Dieskau (bar), Erich Kunz (bar), Eberhard Wächter (bar), Hans Hotter (b-bar), Paul Schöffler (b-bar), Cesare Siepi (b-bar), José Van Dam (b-bar), Walter Berry (bass), Geraint Evans (bass), Nicolai Ghiaurov (bass), Alexander Kipnis (bass), Richard Mayr (bass), Kurt Moll (bass), James Morris (bass), Ezio Pinza (bass), Martti Talvela (bass), Giorgio Tozzi (bass), Hans Duhan (sgr), Res Fischer (sgr), Marie Gerhart (sgr), *(various orchs & cnds)* —sels from Idomeneo, Die Entführung aus der Serail, Le nozze di Figaro, Don Giovanni, Così fan tutte, Die Zauberflöte & various arias Orfeo d'or ("Festspiel Dokumente" series) 5-▲ 408955
Mozart, W.A.:Nozze di Figaro, w. Helena Braun (sop), Gerda Sommerschuh (sop), Josef Witt (ten), Hans Hotter (bar), Erich Kunz (bar), Gustav Neidlinger (b-bar), C. Krauss (cnd), Vienna PO, Vienna State Opera Chorus *(rec live, Salzburg Festival, Aug. 1942)* Preiser 3-▲ PRE 90203 [ADD]
Mozart, W.A.:Zauberflöte, w. T. Lemnitz (sop), E. Berger (sop), H. Roswaenge (ten), H. Tessmer (ten), G. Hüsch (bar), W. Strienz (bass), T. Beecham (cnd), Berlin PO, Favre Chorus [without dialog; G] *(rec 1937-38 for HMV)* EMI Classics ("Great Recordings of the Century" series) 2-▲ CDHB 61034 (m) [ADD]
Mozart, W.A.:Zauberflöte, w. E. Berger (sop), T. Lemnitz (sop), H. Roswaenge (ten), G. Hüsch (bar), W. Strienz (bass), T. Beecham (cnd), Berlin PO, Vereinigung Favres Soloists [G] *(rec Nov. 1937 & Feb.-Mar. 1938)* Nimbus ("Prima Voce" series) 2-▲ NI 7827/8 (m) [ADD]
Mozart, W.A.:Zauberflöte, w. T. Lemnitz (sop), E. Berger (sop), H. Roswaenge (tên), H. Tessmer (ten), G. Hüsch (bar), W. Strienz (bass), T. Beecham (cnd), Berlin PO, Favre Chorus [without dialog; G] *(rec 1937-38 for HMV)* Pearl 2-▲ PEAS 9371 (m) [AAD]
Mozart, W.A.:Zauberflöte, w. T. Lemnitz (sop), E. Berger (sop), H. Roswaenge (ten), H. Tessmer (ten), G. Hüsch (bar), W. Strienz (bass), T. Beecham (cnd), Berlin PO, Favre Chorus [without dialog; G] *(rec 1937-38 for HMV)* Melodram 2-▲ MEL 27056 (m) [AAD]

Beirer, Hans (ten)
Wagner, R.:Die Meistersinger von Nürnberg, w. I. Seefried (sop), P. Schoeffler (b-bar), F. Reiner (cnd), Vienna PO, Vienna State Opera Chorus *(rec live, Vienna, 1955)* Melodram 4-▲ MEL 47083
Wagner, R.:Tannhäuser, w. S. Jurinac (sop), B. Martin (sop), H. Braun (bar), M. Talvela (bass), W. Sawallisch (cnd), La Scala Orch, La Scala Chorus [G] *(rec live, Milan 4/13/67)* Melodram 3-▲ CDM 37091 [ADD]

Beirer, Hans (ten) (cont.)
Wagner, R.:Tannhäuser (sels), w. R. Tebaldi (sop), C. Tagliabue (bar), B. Christoff (bass), K. Böhm (cnd), Naples Teatro San Carlo Orch, Naples Teatro San Carlo Chorus—10 soprano solo, duet & ensemble arias Acts 2 & 3 [I; Hans Beirer (Tannhäuser) sings in German] *(rec live, Naples, 3/12/50)* Standing Room Only ▲ SRO 834-1 [ADD]

Belamaric, Neven (sgr)
Schreker, F.:Irrelohe, w. Eva Randová (mez—Old Lola), Michael Pabst (ten—Count Heinrich), Monte Pederson (bar—Peter), Neven Belamaric (sgr—The Parson), Luana Devol (sgr—Eva), Sebastian Holecek (sgr—The Miller), Goran Smimic (sgr—The Forester) Sony Classical 2-▲ S2K 66850

Belaza-Leoz, Fernando (bar)
Martin Y Soler, V.:Una Cosa rara, w. M. A. Peters (sop), M. Figueras (sop), G. Fabuel (sop), E. Palacio (ten), S. Palatchi (bass), F. Garrigosa (bass), I. Fresán (sgr), J. Savall (cnd), Concert des Nations, La Capella Reial de Catalunya [I] *(rec 1991)* Astrée 3-▲ E 8760 [DDD]

Belcheva, Maria (sop)
Verdi, G.:Requiem Mass, w. Stefka Mineva (mez), Roumen Doykov (ten), Dimiter Petkov (bass), P. Tiboris (cnd), Sofia National Opera Orch, Sofia National Opera Chorus *(rec Bulgarian National Radio Studio, Mar 14-17, 1994)* Elysium ▲ GRK 708 [DDD]

Belcourt, Emile (ten)
Porter, C.:Nymph Errant, w. K. Ballard (sgr), *(other sgrs unknown)*, D. Pippin (cnd), Stephen Hill Orch, Stephen Hill Singers Angel ▲ CDC 54079

Belden, S. D. (cta)
Belden, G.:Gilgamesh, w. M. Stratman (pno), T. Heavner (perc) [E] Capstone ▲ CPS 8613

Belhomme, Hypolite (bar)
Gounod, C.:Roméo et Juliette, w. Yvonne Gall (sop—Juliette), Champell (sop—Stéphano), Jeanne Goulancourt (mez—Gertrude), Agustarello Affre (ten—Roméo), Edmond Tirmont (ten—Tybalt), Alexis Boyer (bar—Mercutio), Pierre Dupré (bar—Paris), Hypolite Belhomme (bar—Grégorio), Marcel Journet (bass—Frère Laurent), Henri Albers (bass—Capulet), Valermont (bass—The Duke), F. Rühlmann (cnd), Paris Opéra-Comique Orch, Paris Opéra-Comique Chorus *(rec 1912)* VAI Audio ▲ VAIA 1064-3 F

Bell, D. (bar)
Beckwith, J.:Love Songs (4), w. C. Foreman (pno) Unical ▲ UCCD 9101
Johnston, B.:Folk Love, Canadian Style, w. C. Foreman (pno) Unical ▲ UCCD 9101
Kálmán, I.:Folk Love, Canadian Style, w. C. Foreman (pno) Unical ▲ UCCD 9101
Schumann, R.:Dichterliebe, w. C. Foreman (pno) Unical ▲ UCCD 9101

Bell, Donaldson (bar)
Herrmann, B.:Wuthering Heights, w. M. Beaton (sop—Catherine), P. Bowden (mez—Isabella), E. Bainbridge (mez—Nelly), M. Snashall (trb—Hareton), D. Bell (bar—Heathcliff), J. Kitchiner (bar—Hindley), J. Ward (bar—Edgar), M. Rippon (bass—Joseph), D. Kelly (bass—Mr. Lockwood), B. Herrmann (cnd), Pro Arte Orch *(rec 1965-66)* Unicorn-Kanchana 3-▲ UKCD 2050/51/52 [ADD]

Bell, Kevin (bass)
Cage, J.:Europera 3, w. Suzan Hanson (sop), Ruby Hinds (mez), Patricia McAfee (mez), Michael Lyon (ten), Richard Powell (ten), Kevin Bell (bass), Brian Pezzone (pno), Vicki Ray (pno), Hannes Geiger (record players), Joseph Giri (record players), William Houston (record players), Dren McDonald (record players), Ronda Rindone (record players), Clarice Ross (record players), Scott Fraser (tape), A. Culver (cnd), Long Beach Opera Orch *(rec Center Theater, Long Beach, CA, Nov. 13, 1993)* Mode 2-▲ MODE 38/39

Bell, M. (sgr)
Lerner, A.J.:Brigadoon, w. D. Brooks (sgr), P. Britton (sgr), L. Sullivan (sgr) [1947 Broadway original cast] RCA ▲ 1001-2 RG [ADD] ■ 1001-4 RG

Bell, Patrice Michaels (sop)
Telemann, G.P.:Der Tag des Gerichts, w. Sandra Walker (mez), Karen Brunssen (mez), Bruce Fowler (ten), Kurt R. Hansen (ten), William Stone (bar), Douglas Anderson (bar), T. Wikman (cnd), Music of the Baroque Orch, Baroque Music Chorus *(rec live, St. Paul's United Church of Christ, Feb 23, 1992)* Music of the Baroque 2-▲ MB 107

Bella, Benito di (bar)
Mascagni, P.:Cavalleria rusticana, w. Ruth Falcon (sop—Lola), Leonie Rysanek (sop—Santuzza), Astrid Varnay (sop—Mamma Lucia), Plácido Domingo (ten—Turiddu), Benito di Bella (bar—Alfio), N. Santi (cnd), Munich National Theater Orch, Munich National Theater Chorus *(rec Munich, Dec 25, 1978)* Legato Classics ▲ LCD 202-1

Belleau, M. (bass)
Berlioz, H.:Les Troyens, w. F. Pollet (sop—Dido), D. Voigt (sop—Cassandre), C. Dubosc (sop—Ascagne), H. Perraguin (cta—Anna), G. Lakes (ten—Aeneas), J.-L. Maurette (ten—Iopas), J. M. Ainsley (ten—Hylas), M. P. (ten—Panthee), G. Cross (ten—Sinon), G. Quilico (bar—Chorebe), J.-P. Courtis (b-bar—Narbal), M. Belleau (bass—Ghost of Hector), R. Schirrer (bass—Priam), C. Dutoit (cnd), Montreal SO, Montreal Sym Chorus London 4-▲ 443693-2 [DDD]

Beller, Christian (ten)
Wolf, H.:Christnacht, w. Alison Browner (sop—Engel der Verkündigung), Katherin Koch (alt—Hirte), D. Kurz (cnd), Stuttgart Ensemble, Württemburg Choir *(rec live, Stuttgart, Feb 18, 1996)* Claves ▲ CD 509622 [DDD]

Bellesia (sgr)
Puccini, G.:La Bohème (sels), w. R. Mattioli (sop), P. Pellegrini (sgr), L. Pavarotti (ten), F. Molinari-Pradelli (cnd), Reggio Emilia Teatro Municipale Orch—sels from Pavarotti's debut performance *(rec live, Apr 29, 1961)* Melodram 2-▲ MEL 27031 [AAD]

Belliard, Jean (ten)
Satie, E.:Socrate, w. B. Eidi (pno) *(rec Aug. 26-27, 1993)* Timpani ▲ 1020 [DDD]

Bellida, G. de (sgr)
Manfroce, N.A.:Ecuba, w. A. C. Antonacci (sop), D. di Domenico (ten), F. Piccoli (ten), M. de Bernart (cnd), Italian PO, Italian Phil Chorus [I] *(rec live 1990)* Bongiovanni 2-▲ GB 2119/20 [DDD]

Belling, Susan (sop)
Flowering of Vocal Music in America, 1767-1823, w. Cynthia Clarey (sop), Barbara Wallace (sop), Debra Vanderlinde (sop), D'Anna Fortunato (mez), Evelyn Petros (mez), Charles Bressler (ten), Richard Anderson (bar), James Tyeska (bar), Joseph McKee (bass), Cynthia Otis (hp), Leonard Rav New World ▲ 80467-2

Bellini, Mikael (alt)
Schnittke, A.:Faust Cant, w. Inger Blom (cta), Louis Devos (ten), Urik Cold (bass), J. DePreist (cnd), Malmö SO, Malmö Sym Chorus BIS ("BIS Twins" series) 2-▲ CD 437/507
Schnittke, A.:Sym 4, w. S. Parkman (ten), O. Kamu (cnd), Stockholm Sinfonietta, Uppsala Academic Chamber Choir [L] BIS ▲ CD 497 [DDD]

Bellini, Mikael (ct)
The Royal Court of the Vasa Kings, 1523-1611, w. Lennart Löwgren (ct), Carl Unander-Scharin (ten), Lars Arvidson (bass), Sven-Anders Benktsson (bass), Sven Aberg (six-course Renaissance lt), Hortus Musicus, Tallinn [cnd:Andres Mustonen] Musica Sveciae ▲ MSV 202 [DDD]
Schnittke, A.:Sym 2, w. Malena Ernman (alt), Göran Eliasson (ten), Torkel Borelius (bass), L. Segerstam (cnd), Royal Stockholm PO, Anders Eby (cnd), Mikaeli Chamber Choir *(rec Stockholm Concert Hall, Sweden, Feb. 24-25, 1994)* BIS ▲ CD 667 [DDD]

Bellisia, Bianco (sop)
Puccini, G.:La Bohème (sels), w. Bianco Bellisia (sop—Musetta), Alberto Pellegrini (sop—Mimi), Luciano Pavarotti (ten—Rodolfo), Walter de Ambrosis (bar—Schaunard), Vito Mattioli (bar—Marcello), Dmitri Nabokov (bass—Colline), Reggio Emilia Teatro Municipale Orch, Reggio Emilia Teatro Municipale Chorus Budget ("The Greatest Voice in Opera" series) ▲ SYP 105

Bello, Vincenzo (ten)
Bellini, V.:La straniera, w. L. Alberti (sop—Alaide), S. Mingardo (mez—Isoletta), V. Bello (ten—Arturo), R. Frontale (bar—Il Barone di Valdeburgo), V. Sagona (bass—Il signore di Montalino), P. Zizich (bass—Osburgo), G. Masini (cnd), Trieste Teatro Comunale Giuseppe Verdi Orch, Trieste Teatro Comunale G. Verdi Chorus *(rec Dec. 1990)* Ricordi ▲ RFCD 2015 [DDD]
Donizetti, G.:Lucia di Lammermoor, w. M. Caballé (sop), A. Murray (mez), C. H. Ahnsjö (ten), J. Carreras (ten), V. Sardinero (bar), S. Ramey (bass), J. López-Cobos (cnd), New Philharmonia Orch, Ambrosian Opera Chorus Philips 2-▲ 426563-2

▲ = CD ♦ = Enhanced CD ∆ = MD ■ = Cassette Tape □ = DCC

Bello, Vincenzo (ten) (cont.)

Verdi, G.:I due Foscari, w. K. Ricciarelli (sop), E. Connell (sop), J. Carreras (ten), M. Antoniak (ten), P. Cappuccilli (bar), S. Ramey (bass), F. Handlos (bass), L. Gardelli (cnd), Austrian RSO, Austrian Radio Chorus Philips 2-▲ 422426-2 [ADD]

Bellsolà, Gisela (sgr)

Tensons e partimens de Trobairitz, Vol. 3, w. G. Zuchetto (sgr), Katia Caré (sgr), Patrice Brient (voc/h-g/rebeck), Guy Robert (medieval lt/oud/hp) Gallo ▲ CD 769 [DDD]

Belluso, Lucia (sgr)

Wolf-Ferrari, E.:I quatro rusteghi, w. A. P (Margarita), D. Lombardi (Lucieta), G. Merrino (Marina), M. Fratarcangeli (Felice) L. Belluso (Servant), A. Abete (Lunardo), M. Nicolini (Maurizio), G. Sorrentino (Filipeto), M. Peirone (Simon), D. Baronchelli (Cancian), A. Lemmo (Count Riccard) Arkadia-Akademia 2-▲ 139 [DDD]

Belmas, Xenia (sop)

Lebendige Vergangenheit:Xenia Belmas *(rec 1927-29)* Preiser ▲ PRE 89047 [ADD]

Belobragina, Ludmilla (sop)

Schoenberg, A.:Qt 2 Strs, w. Borodin String Quartet MK ▲ MKA 418019 [AAD]

Belokrynkin, Yuri (sgr)

Taneyev, S.:At the Reading of a Psalm, w. Yuri Antonov (sgr), Ralsa Kotova (sgr), Adelina Kozlova (sgr), E. Svetlanov (cnd), USSR SO, Yurloff State Choir Russian Disc ▲ RUS 10044 [AAD]

Beloni, G. (bass)

Puccini, G.:Tosca, w. R. Tebaldi (sop—Tosca), F. Corelli (ten—Cavaradossi), A. Colzani (bar—Scarpia), P. L. Latinucci (b-bar—Sacristan), G. Beloni (bass—Angelotti), M. Parenti (cnd), Livorno Teatro La Gran Guardia Orch, Livorno Teatro La Gran Guardia Chorus *(rec live Sept. 21, 1959)* Legato Classics 2-▲ LCD 171-2 [ADD]

Belor, Jaromir (bar)

Klein, G.:Madrigals, w. M. Čejková (sop), J. Suchánková (sop), H. Pracnové (alt), K. Kozunik (ten) *(rec Oct. 20 & 21, 1992)* Koch International Classics ▲ KIC 7230-2 [DDD]

Belov (sgr)

Tchaikovsky, P.:Eugene Onegin, w. G. Vishnevskaya (sop), L. Avdeyeva (mez), S. Lemeshev (ten), Petrov (sgr), B. Khaikin (cnd), Bolshoi Theater Orch, Bolshoi Theater Chorus [R] *(rec ca. early '60s for Melodi)* Legato Classics 2-▲ LCD 163-2 (m) [ADD]

Beltrami (sgr)

Mascagni, P.:Lodoletta, w. L. Saldari (ten), G. Mucci (cnd), Teatro La Gran Guardia Orch, Teatro La Gran Guardia Chorus [I] *(rec live, 10/2/60)* Fonè 2-▲ 88 F 16-36 [ADD]

Beltran, Gil Manuel (ten)

Boccherini, L.:Credo, w. Svetla Krasteva (sop), Fernanda Piccini (cta), Duccio Dal Monte (bass), G. Cosmi (cnd), Lucca Teatro Comunale Giglio Orch *(rec Dec 18, 1993)* Bongiovanni ▲ GB 2178 [DDD]

Boccherini, L.:Kyrie & Gloria, w. Svetla Krasteva (sop), Fernanda Piccini (cta), Duccio Dal Monte (bass), G. Cosmi (cnd), Lucca Teatro Comunale Giglio Orch *(rec Dec 18, 1993)* Bongiovanni ▲ GB 2178 [DDD]

Haydn, J.:Lo Speziale, w. Gil Manuel Beltran (ten—Sempronio), Daniela Broganelli (sgr—Volpino), Cinzia Forte (sgr—Grilletta), Paolo Pellegrini (sgr—Mengone), Maurizio Gambini (vc), Marco Tinarelli (db), Gabriele Catalucci (hpd), F. Maestri (cnd), In Canto CO *(rec 1993)* Bongiovanni 2-▲ GB 2171/72 [DDD]

Rossini, G.:Petite messe solennelle, w. Livia Aghova (sop), Marta Benackova (mez), Peter Mikulas (bass), Raphaele Cortesi (pno), Peter Toperczer (pno), Josef Ksica (harm), Romano Gandolfi (cnd), Prague Chamber Choir *(rec Domovina Studios, Prague, Sept. 10-12, 1994)* Discover International 2-▲ DI 920324-5 [DDD]

Beltran, Tito (ten)

Tito Beltran, w. Royal PO [cnd:Robin Stapleton] Silva Classics ▲ SIL 6005 [DDD] ■ SIL 6005

Ben, Alexander (bar)

Tchaikovsky, P.:Iolanta, w. Michaela Gurevich (sop—Iolanta), Jaqueline Miura (sop—Brigitta), Tatjana Tabachuk (mez—Martha), Annette Kuhn (mez—Laura), Ian Denolfo (ten—Godefroy), Keith Alexander Bolves (ten—Alméric), Alexander Ben (bar—Robert), Georg Lehner (bar—Ibn-Hakia), Arutiun Kotchinian (bass—René), Kurt Geysen (bass—Bertrand), H. Rotman (cnd), Warsaw PO, ECOV Ensemble Members *(rec Vooruit Center of the Arts, Ghent, Belgium, Aug 28-29, 1993)* CPO 2-▲ CPO 999456-2 [DDD]

Benačka, Stanislav (bass)

Puccini, G.:La Bohème, w. Veronika Kinsces (sop—Mimi), Sidonia Haljakova (sop—Musette), Peter Dvorsky (ten—Rodolfo), Vijtech Scherenkel (ten—Parpingol), Ian Konsulov (bar—Marcello), Balazs Poka (bar—Schaunard), Stanislav Benacka (bass—Benoit), Dariusz Niemirowicz (bass—Colline), Stefan Janci (bass—Alcindoro), *(cnd & orch unknown)* Griffin ▲ GCD 2942

Puccini, G.:Tosca (sels), w. Nelly Miricioiu (sop—Tosca), Giorgio Lamberti (ten—Cavaradossi), Miroslav Dvorsky (ten—Spoletta), Silvano Carroli (bar—Baron Scarpia), Jozef Spaček (bar—Sacristan), Jan Durco (bass—Sciarrone), Stanislav Benačka (bass—Gaoler), A. Rahbari (cnd), Czech-Slovak RSO Bratislava, Slovak Phil Chorus *(rec Concert Hall of the Slovak Radio, Bratislava, Apr. 7-14, 1990)* Naxos ▲ 8.553153 [DDD]

Respighi, O.:La bella dormente nel bosco, w. Ivana Czaková (sop—Old Woman/Green Fairy), Adriana Kohútková (sop—Blue Fairy/Nightingale), Henrietta Lednárová (sop—Frog/Spindle), Jana Valásková (sop—Princess), Dagmar Pecková (mez—Cuckoo/Cat), Denisa Slepkovská (mez—Queen/Duchess), Karol Bernáth (ten—Doctor), Guillermo Dominguez (ten—Prince April), Igor Pasek (ten—Jester), Ján Durčo (bar—Ambassador), Richard Haan (bar—King/Woodcutter), Stanislav Benačka (bass—Doctor), Anton Kúrnava (bass—Doctor), Marián Smolárik (bass—Doctor), M. Adriano (nar—Mr. Dollar Chèques), M. Adriano (cnd), Slovak RSO Bratislava, Ján Rozehnal (cnd), Slovak Phil Chorus *(rec Concert Hall of the Slovak Radio, Bratislava, June 8-20, 1994)* Marco Polo ("Opera Classics" series) ▲ 8.223742 [DDD]

Benačková, Gabriela (sop)

Beethoven, L. van:Sym 9, "Choral Sym", w. Vera Soukupova (alt), Vilem Pribyl (ten), Karel Prusa (bass), L. von Matačič (cnd), Czech PO Praga ▲ PR 250076

Caccini, G.:Music of, w. Ronald Schneider (pno) *(rec live, Prague, Oct. 8, 1995)* Supraphon ▲ SUP 3027

Carolling, w. Lubomír Vraspír (ten), Bambini di Praga [cnd:Jaroslav Krček], Tuma (org), Prague Brass Quintet Supraphon ▲ SUP 111417 [DDD]

Dvořák, A.:Requiem Mass, w. B. Fassbaender (mez), T. Moser (ten), J.-H. Rootering (bass), W. Sawallisch (cnd), Czech PO, Czech Chorus [L] Supraphon 2-▲ 10 4241 [DDD]

Dvořák, A.:Rusalka, w. V. Soukupová (mez), W. Ochman (ten), R. Novák (bass), V. Neumann (cnd), Czech PO, Prague Phil Chorus [Cz] Supraphon Collection ▲ 11 0617-2 [DDD]

Dvořák, A.:Rusalka, w. V. Soukupová (mez), W. Ochman (ten), R. Novák (bass), V. Neumann (cnd), Czech PO, Prague Phil Chorus [Cz] Supraphon 3-▲ 10 3641 [DDD]

Dvořák, A.:Rusalka (sels), w. Vera Soukupová (mez), Richard Novák (bass), V. Neumann (cnd), Czech PO, Czech Chorus Supraphon ▲ SUP 112252 [DDD]

Dvořák, A.:Songs, w. R. Firkušný (pno)—Love Songs, Op. 83; Gypsy Songs, Op. 55; In Folk Style, Op. 73; Biblical Songs, Op. 99 RCA Red Seal ▲ 09026-60823-2

Dvořák, A.:Stabat Mater, w. O. Wenkel (cta), P. Dvorský (ten), J.-H. Rootering (bass), W. Sawallisch (cnd), Czech PO, Czech Phil Chorus [L] Supraphon 2-▲ 10 3561-2 [DDD]

Fibich, Z.:The Bride of Messina, w. L. Marova (mez), I. Zidek (ten), F. Jílek (cnd), Prague National Theater Orch, Prague National Theater Chorus Supraphon ▲ SUP 111492 [ADD]

Gabriela Benačková:Soprano Supraphon ▲ SUP 112239 [DDD]

Janácek, L.:The Cunning Little Vixen, w. G. Benačková (sop—Goldskin), M. Hajóssyová (sop—Cunning Little Vixen), R. Novák (bass—Forester), V. Neumann (cnd), Czech PO, Czech Phil Chorus, Kühn Children's Chorus [Cz] *(rec 1979-80)* Supraphon 2-▲ 10 3471-2 [AAD]

Janácek, L.:Jenůfa, w. L. Rysanek (sop), P. Kazaras (ten), W. Ochman (ten), E. Queler (cnd), New York City Opera Orch [Cz] *(rec live at Carnegie Hall, Mar. 30, 1988)* BIS 2-▲ CD 449/50 [DDD]

Janácek, L.:Jenůfa, w. G. Benačková (sop—Jenufa), N. Kniplová (mez—Kostelnička Buryja), V. Krejčík (ten—Steva Buryja), V. Přibyl (ten—Laca Klemen), F. Jílek (cnd), Brno Janáček Opera Orch, Brno Janáček Opera Chorus [Cz] *(rec 1977-8)* Supraphon 2-▲ 10 2751-2 [AAD]

Janácek, L.:Moravian Folk Poetry, w. R. Firkušný (pno) RCA Red Seal ▲ 09026-60823-2

Janácek, L.:Slavonic Mass, w. Eva Randova (cta), Vilem Pribyl (ten), Sergej Kopack (bass), F. Jílek (cnd), Brno State PO, Josef Veselka (cnd), Czech Phil Chorus *(rec 1979)* Supraphon ▲ SUP CD 3045

Benačková, Gabriela (sop) (cont.)

Janácek, L.:Slavonic Mass, w. Vera Soukupová (cta), Frantisek Livora (ten), Karel Pruss (bass), V. Neumann (cnd), Czech PO, Czech Phil Chorus Panton ▲ PAN 811217

Janácek, L.:Slavonic Mass, w. F. Palmer (sop), G. Lakes (ten), A. Kotcherga (bass), M. Tilson Thomas (cnd), London SO, London Sym Chorus Sony Classical ▲ SK 47182

Mahler, G.:Sym 2, w. E. Randova (mez), V. Neumann (cnd), Czech PO, Czech Phil Chorus *(rec June 11-16, 1980)* Supraphon ▲ 11 1971-2 [AAD]

Mozart, W.A.:Music of, w. Ronald Schneider (pno) *(rec live, Prague, Oct 8, 1995)* Supraphon ▲ SUP 3027

Smetana, B.:The Bartered Bride, w. P. Dvorsky (ten), R. Novak (bass), Z. Košler (cnd), Czech PO, Czech Phil Chorus [Cz] Supraphon 3-▲ 10 3511-2 [DDD]

Smetana, B.:The Bartered Bride (orch sels), w. Peter Dvorský (ten), Miroslav Kopp (ten), Z. Košler (cnd), Czech PO, Czech Phil Chorus Supraphon ▲ SUP 112251 [DDD]

Smetana, B.:Libuše, w. V. Soupukova (sop), V. Zitek (ten), Z. Košler (cnd), Prague National Theater Orch, Prague National Theater Chorus Supraphon 3-▲ SUP 111276 [DDD]

Suchon, E.:The Whirlpool, w. P. Dvorsky (ten), O. Malachovsky (bass), O. Lenárd (cnd), Bratislava RSO Campion 2-▲ 1311/12 [DDD]

Verdi, G.:Messa per Rossini, w. F. Quivar (mez), J. Wagner (ten), A. Agache (bar), A. Haugland (bass), H. Rilling (cnd), Stuttgart RSO, Gächinger Kantorei, Prague Phil Chorus [L] Hänssler Classic 2-▲ CD 98.949 [DDD] 2-■ MC 96.949 (D)

Benačková, Marta (mez)

Dvořák, A.:Mass, w. Dagmar Masková (sop), Walter Coppola (ten), Peter Mikulás (bass), Josef Ksica (org), Josef Pancík (cnd), Prague Chamber Choir *(rec Dvořák Hall, Prague, Nov 1993)* ECM New Series ▲ 78118-21539-2 [DDD]

Janácek, L.:Fate, w. Lívia Ághová (sop—Míla), Ludmila Nováková (sop—Frl. Stuhlá/Součková), Marta Benačková (cta—Mílas Mother), Stefan Margita (ten—Dr. Suda/Hrázda), Peter Straka (ten—Zivný), Ivan Kusnjer (bar—Konečný/Verva), Peter Mikuláš (bass—Lhotský), G. Albrecht (cnd), Czech PO, Prague Chamber Choir *(rec 1995)* Orfeo ▲ 384 951 [DDD]

Mozart, W.A.:Missa, K.317, w. Ludmila Vernerova (sop), Richard Sporka (ten), Ladislav Nezhyba (bass), G. Delogu (cnd), Prague Virtuosi, Prague Chamber Choir *(rec Domovina Studio, Prague, June 4-6, 1994)* Discover International ▲ DI 920260 [DDD]

Mozart, W.A.:Vesperae solennes, w. Ludmila Vernerova (sop), Richard Sporka (ten), Ladislav Nezhyba (bass), G. Delogu (cnd), Prague Virtuosi, Prague Chamber Choir *(rec Domovina Studio, Prague, June 4-6, 1994)* Discover International ▲ DI 920260 [DDD]

Rossini, G.:Petite messe solennelle, w. Livia Aghova (sop), Gil Manuel Beltran (ten), Peter Mikulas (bass), Raphaele Cortesi (pno), Peter Toperczer (pno), Josef Ksica (harm), Romano Gandolfi (cnd), Prague Chamber Choir *(rec Domovina Studios, Prague, Sept. 10-12, 1994)* Discover International 2-▲ DI 920324-5 [DDD]

Vanhal, J.B.:Missa Solemnis, w. Marta Filová (sop), Jörg Dürmüller (ten), Jiří Sulzenko (bass), V. Neumann (cnd), Prague Virtuosi, Prague Chamber Choir—Kyrie eleison, Adagio— Allegro; Christe eleison, Andante; Kyrie eleison, Allegro; Gloria, Allegro moderato; Laudamus te, Andante; Gratias agimus tibi, Allegro moderato; Domine Deus, Rex caelestis, andante; Domine Deus, Agnus Dei, Adagio; Quoniam tu solus sanctus, Allegro moderato, Cum sancto spiritu, Allegro; Credo, Allegro moderato, Et incarnatus est. Adagio; Et resurrexit, Allegro moderato; Sanctus, Adagio—Osanna, Allegro; Benedictus, Andante—Osanna, Allegro; Agnus Dei, Adagio; Dona nobis pacem, Allegro *(rec Evangelische Kirche der böhmischen Brüder, Prag, Sept 25-28, 1994)* Orfeo ▲ C 353 951 A [DDD]

Bence, Margaret (alt)

Vivaldi, A.:Gloria, RV.589, w. Friederike Sailer (sop), M. Couraud (cnd), Stuttgart Pro Musica Orch *(rec 1964)* Tuxedo ▲ TUXCD 1032 [ADD]

Vivaldi, A.:Stabat Mater Cta, w. M. Couraud (cnd), Stuttgart Pro Musica Orch *(rec 1964)* Tuxedo ▲ TUXCD 1032 [ADD]

Bence, Margaret (cta)

Bach, J.S.:Cant 80, w. Antonia Fahberg (sop), Theophil Maier (ten), Ulrich Schaible (bass), H. Rilling (cnd), Württemberg CO, Stuttgart Memorial Church Figuralchor *(rec 1964)* Vox Box 3-▲ CD3X 3039

Mozart, W.A.:Requiem, w. U. Buckel (sop), H.-U. Mielsch (ten), E. Wollitz (bass), R. Bader (cnd), Stuttgart PO, Böblingen Bach Choir Allegretto ▲ ACD 8060 [ADD] ■ ACS 8060

Reger, M.:An die Hoffnung, w. H. Scherchen (cnd), Northwest German PO *(rec 1960)* CPO 2-▲ CPO 999143-2 (m) [ADD]

Strauss, R.:Der Rosenkavalier, w. Claire Watson (sop—Feldmarschallin), Lucia Popp (sop—Sophie), Annelie Waas (sop—Marianne), Brigitte Fassbaender (mez—Octavian), Margaretthe Bence (ct—Annina), David Thaw (ten—Valzacchi), Karl Ridderbusch (bass—Baron Ochs), Benno Kusche (bass—Herr von Faninal), Albrecht Peter (bass—Police Inspector), C. Kleiber (cnd), Bavarian State Orch, Bavarian State Chorus *(rec live, Münchner Festspiele, July 20, 1974)* Arkadia 3-▲ 486 [ADD]

Vivaldi, A.:Stabat Mater Cta, w. M. Couraud (cnd), Stuttgart Pro Musica Orch, Stuttgart Pro Musica Chorus *(rec 1957)* Vox Box 2-▲ CDX 5081 [ADD]

Bencivenga, Roberto (ten)

Generali, P.:Sacred Music, w. Leila Bersiani (sop), Valentina di Cola (sop), Emanuela Deffai (mez), Sella Salvati (cta), Paolo Macedonio (ton), Carlo Lepore (bass), E. Brizio (cnd), Czech Radio-TV Orch, Czech Radio TV Chorus—Magnificat; Domine ad Adjuvandum; Virgam Virtutis; Ecce Virgo; Ave Maria Messe Pastorale; Te Deum *(rec FHS Studios, Prague, 1995)* Studio SM ▲ 2517 [DDD]

Bende, Zoltan (bar)

Lehár, F.:Das Land des Lächelns (sels), w. Házy (sop), Magda Kalmár (sop), Szimándy (sgr), G. Oberfrank (cnd), Budapest SO, Hungarian Radio-TV Chorus [Hun] Hungaroton ▲ HCD 16809 [ADD]

Liszt, F.:Requiem, w. Alfonz Bartha (ten), Sándor Palcsó (ten), Pál Kovács (bar), A. Ferencsik (cnd), Hungarian State Orch, Hungarian People's Army Male Chorus [L] Hungaroton ▲ HCD 11267

Vivaldi, A.:Juditha triumphans devicta Holofernes barbarie, w. Margit László (sop—Abra), Zsuzsa Barlay (cta—Juditha), József Réti (ten—Servo), Zsolt Bende (bar—Holofernes), József Dene (bar—Ozias), F. Szekeres (cnd), Hungarian State Orch, György Czigány (cnd), Budapest Madrigal Choir, 1968 Classical Diamonds ▲ CLD 4022-23 [ADD]

Wayditch, G. von:The Caliph's Magician, w. Júlia Pászthi (sop—Eunuch), Sándor Palcso (ten—The Emir), István Rozsos (ten—Nawab), Zsolt Bende (bar—The Magician), Arpád Kishegyi (sgr—Djinn), András Nagy-Soljom (sgr—The Caliph), Csaba Ötvös (sgr—Djinn), Csilla Ötvös (sgr—Odalisk), A. Kórodi (cnd), Budapest National Opera Orch, Budapest National Opera Chorus *(rec 1975)* VAI Audio 2-▲ VAIA 1095-2 [ADD]

Bender, Fritz Richard (bar)

Wagner, R.:Tristan und Isolde, w. Helena Braun (sop—Isolde), Margarete Klose (mez—Brangäne), Günther Treptow (ten—Tristan), Paul Kuen (ten—Ein Hirte), Albrecht Peter (bar—Melot), Fritz Richard Bender (bar—Ein Steuermann), Ferdinand Frantz (b-bar—König Marke), Paul Schöffler (b-bar—Kurwenal), H. Knappertsbusch (cnd), Bavarian State Opera Orch, Bavarian State Opera Chorus *(rec live, Prinzregententheater, July 23, 1950)* Orfeo 3-▲ 355

Benedetto, di (bass)

Puccini, M.:Magnificat, w. M. Frusoni (ten), Nenci (ten), G. Cosmi (cnd), Lucca Teatro Comunale del Giglio Orch, St. Cecilia Cappella Musicale [L] Bongiovanni ▲ GB 2047 [DDD]

Benelli, Ugo (bar)

Donizetti, G.:Il giovedì grasso, w. J. Gomez (sop), J. Hughes (mez), J. Peters (mez), B. Donlan (bar), F. Davià (bass), E. Esparza (sgr), M. Williams (sgr), D. Atherton (cnd), Eireann Radio-TV SO [I] *(rec live, 1970)* Memories ▲ HR 4482 [ADD]

Donizetti, G.:Il giovedì grasso, w. J. Gomez (sop), J. Peters (mez), J. Hughes (mez), B. Donlan (bar), F. Davià (bass), E. Esparza (sgr), D. Atherton (cnd), Eireann Radio-TV SO [I] *(rec live, 1970)* Foyer ▲ FOY 2036 [AAD]

Donizetti, G.:Rita, or Le mari battu, w. S. Figacci (sgr), R. Franceschetto (sgr), G. Manini (sgr), F. Maestri (cnd), In Canto CO *(rec Sept. 1990)* Bongiovanni 2-▲ GB 2109/10 [DDD]

Gluck, C.W.:L'Innocenza giustificata, w. B. Lucarini (sop—Flaminia), A. Ruffini (sop—Claudia), A. R. de Simone (sop—Flavio), U. Benelli (bar—Valerio), G. Catalucci (cnd), In Canto di Terni Youth Orch [I] *(rec live 9/90)* Bongiovanni 2-▲ GB 2111/12 [DDD]

Leoncavallo, R.:Pagliacci, w. P. Lorengar (sop), R. Krause (ten), J. McCracken (ten), R. Merrill (bar), L. Gardelli (cnd), St. Cecilia Academy Orch Rome, St. Cecilia Academy Chorus Rome [I] IMP Collectors Series ▲ IMPX 9017 [AAD]

Benelli, Ugo (bar) (cont.)

Leoncavallo, R.:Pagliacci, w. J. Carlyle (sop), C. Bergonzi (ten), R. Panerai (bar), G. Taddei (bar), H. von Karajan (cnd), La Scala Orch [I] Deutsche Grammophon 3-▲ 419257-2 [ADD]

Leoncavallo, R.:Pagliacci, w. M. Caballé (sop), R. Scotto (sop), A. Varnay (mez), J. Hamari (mez), J. Carreras (ten), M. Manuguerra (bar), T. Allen (bar), K. Nurmela (bar), R. Muti (cnd), Philharmonia Orch, Ambrosian Opera Chorus EMI Classics 2-▲ CDMB 63650

Leoncavallo, R.:Pagliacci, w. Joan Carlyle (sop—Nedda/Colombina), Carlo Bergonzi (ten—Canio/Pagliaccio), Franco Ricciardi (ten—Villager), Ugo Benelli (bar—Peppe/Arlecchino), Rolando Panerai (bar—Silvio), Giuseppe Taddei (bar—Tonio/Taddeo), Giuseppe Morresi (bass—Villager), H. von Karajan (cnd), La Scala Orch, La Scala Chorus *(rec La Scala, Milan, Oct 1965)* Deutsche Grammophon ("The Originals" series) ▲ 449727-2 [ADD]

Meyerbeer, G.:Il crociato, w. Linda Kitchen (sop), Y. Kenny (sop), R. Platt (sop), D. Montague (mez), D. Jones (mez), B. Ford (ten), D. Parry (cnd), Royal PO, Geoffrey Mitchell Choir [I] *(rec CTS Studios, Wembley, London, Dec. 1990–June 1991)* Opera Rara 4-▲ OR 10

Mozart, W.A.:Requiem, w. E. Ameling (sop), M. Horne (mez), T. Franc (bass), I. Kertész (cnd), Vienna PO, Vienna State Opera Chorus London ("Weekend Classics" series) ▲ 417681-2 [ADD] ▮ 417681-4

Piccinni, N.:La cecchina, ossia la buona figliola, w. Lucia Alberti (sop—Il Cavaliere Armidoro), Emilia Ravaglia (sop—La Marchesa), Margherita Rinaldi (sop—Cecchina), Elena Zilio (mez—Paoluccia), Ugo Benelli (bar—Il Marchese della Conchiglia), Alessandro Corbelli (bar—Mengotto), Enzo Dara (bar—Tagliaferro), Renata Baldisseri (sgr—Sandrina), G. Gelmetti (cnd), Rome Opera Orch, Rome Opera Chorus *(rec Rome, Feb 4, 1981)* Italia 2-▲ CDC 95 [ADD]

Salieri, A.:Arlecchinata, w. P. Pellegrini (sgr), G. Gatti (bar), G. Catalucci (cnd), In Canto di Terni Youth Orch [I] *(rec live 9/90)* Bongiovanni 2-▲ GB 2111/12 [DDD]

Wolf-Ferrari, E.:Il campiello, w. D. Mazzucato (Gasparina), G. Devinu (Lucieta), M. Bolgan (Gnese), C. de Mola (Orsola), U. Benelli (Dona Cate Panciana), M. Rene Cosotti (Dona Pasqua Polegana), M. Comencini (Zorozeto), M. Biscotti (Astolfi), I. D'Arcangelo (Anzoleto), C. Striuli (Fabrizio del Ritorti), N. Bareza (cnd), Trieste Teatro Comunale Giuseppe Verdi Orch, Trieste Teatro Comunale G. Verdi Chorus *(rec Feb. 1992)* Ricordi 2-▲ RFCD 2014 [DDD]

Benelli, Ugo (ten)

Mozart, W.A.:Nozze di Figaro, w. L. Cherici (sop), K. Mattila (sop), M. McLaughlin (sop), M. Bacelli (mez), N. Curiel (mez), U. Benelli (ten), L. Gallo (bar), A. Nosotti (bass), M. Pertusi (bass), G. Tadeo (bass), Z. Mehta (cnd), Florence Maggio Musicale Orch, Florence Maggio Musicale Chorus Sony Classical ▲ SK 53286

Rossini, G.:La Cenerentola, w. B. Casoni (mez), S. Bruscantini (bar), A. Mariotti (bass), P. Bellugi (cnd), Berlin RSO, Berlin Radio Chorus [I] Acanta 2-▲ CD 43271 [DDD]

Rossini, G.:L'italiana in Algeri, w. T. Berganza (sop), L. Zannini (mez), E. Dara (bar), A. Romero (bar), P. Montarsolo (bass), C. Abbado (cnd), Florence Teatro Comunale Orch, Florence Teatro Comunale Chorus *(rec 1973)* Great Opera Performances ▲ GOP 740

Rossini, G.:L'italiana in Algeri, w. L. V. Terrani (mez), S. Bruscantini (bar), A. Mariotti (bass), G. Bertini (cnd), Dresden State Orch [I] Acanta 2-▲ CD 42308 [DDD]

Benet, Josep (ten)

Campra, A.:Messe de Requiem, w. E. Baudry (sop), M. Zanetti (sop), J. Elwes (ten), S. Varcoe (bar), P. Herreweghe (cnd), La Chapelle Royale Orch [L] Harmonia Mundi France ▲ HMC 901251

Charpentier, M.-A.:Judicum Salomonis, w. A. Zaepffel (ct), Elwes (ten), G. Ragon (ten), J. Cabré (bar), G. Reinhart (bar), P. Colléaux (cnd), Stradivaria Ensemble, Nantes Vocal Ensemble [L] Arion ▲ ARN 68037 [DDD]

Monteverdi, C.:Motets, w. B. Lesne (mez), G. Lesne (ct), J. Cabré (bar), Il Seminario Musicale—18 motets for 1, 2 & 3 voices [L] Virgin Classics ("Veritas" series) ▲ 59602 [DDD]

Torrejón Y Velasco, T. de:La purpura de la rosa, w. M. van der Sluis (sop), P. Mildenhall (sop), A. Martin (bar), R. Clemencic (cnd), Clemencic Consort, La Cappella Vocal Ensemble [Sp] Nuova Era ("Ancient Music" series) ▲ 6936 [DDD]

Benetti, Margherita (sop)

Bizet, G.:Carmen (sels), w. Margherita Benetti (sop—Micaela), Pia Tassinari (sop—Carmen), Franco Corelli (ten—Don José), Giangiacomo Guelfi (bar—Escamillo), A. Basile (cnd), Turin RAI Orch—[Act. 1] È l'amore uno strano augello; José!...Micaela!...Ah! mi parla di lei; Mia madre io vedo ancor, sì, sì; Presso il bastion di Siviglia; Tacer, dì, non vuoi tu?; [Act 2] Con voi ber; Alto là! Chi va là ; Il fior che avevi a me tu dato; [Act 3] Andiam, nostra sorte sappiam!; [Act 4] Largo! Largo! L'Alcade; Sei tu?...Son io; Più non m'ama il tuo cor? *(rec Torino Dec. 15, 1961)* Myto ▲ MCD 953132

Benktsson, Sven-Anders (bass)

The Royal Court of the Vasa Kings, 1523-1611, w. Lennart Löwgren (ct), Carl Unander-Scharin (ten), Lars Arvidson (bass), Sven Aberg (six-course Renaissance lt), Hortus Musicus, Tallinn [cnd:Andres Mustonen] Musica Sveciae ▲ MSV 202 [DDD]

Bennert, Karl Hermann (sgr)

Mussorgsky, M.:Boris Godunov, w. Martha Mödl (sop—Marina Mniszek), Lotte Schädle (sop—Xenia), Dorothea Siebert (mez—Fyodor), Hertha Töpper (mez—Xenia's wet-nurs), Karl Hermann Bennert (Boyer Khrushchyov), Lorenz Fehenberger (ten—Prince Shuysky), Hans Hopf (ten—Grigory), Karl Ostertag (ten—Missail), Hans Hotter (b-bar—Boris Godunov), Hermann Uhde (bar—Andrey Shchelkalov), Kurt Böhme (bass—Varlaam), Kim Borg (bass—Pimen), Kieth Engen (bass—Lewicki), Adolf Keil (bass—Nikitich), Benno Kusche (bar—Rangoni), Heinz Maria Linz (bass—Czernikowski), E. Jochum (cnd), Bavarian RSO, Bavarian Radio Chorus *(rec Munich, May 1957)* Myto 3-▲ MCD 953131

Bennett, Alan (ten)

The Age of Cathedrals, w. [cnd:Paul Hillier], Theater of Voices, Paul Elliot (ten), Paul Hillier (ten) Harmonia Mundi ▲ HMU 907157 ▮ HMU 407157

Bennett, Donna (sop)

Lullabies for Benjamin, w. Brian Finley (pno) Marquis Classics ▲ MAR 155

Bennett, Karol (sop)

Harbison, J.:Simple Daylight, w. John McDonald (pno) *(rec Kresge Auditorium, between 1988 & 1994)* Archetype ▲ 60104 [DDD]

Harvey, J.:From Silence, w. et al., B. Vercoe (cnd) [E] Bridge ▲ BCD 9031 [DDD]

Bennett, Lawrence (ten)

Camilo, M.:Batéy, w. P. E. Clark (sop), C.B. Rowe (sop), W. Zukof (ct), W. L. Lee (ten), E. Levine (bar), Puntilla (sgr), New Generation Western Wind ▲ WW 2001

Darling, D.:Blessings:A Prayer for the Planet, w. P.E. Clark (sop), C.B. Rowe (sop), W. Zukof (ct), W.L. Lee (ten), E. Levine (bar), D. Darling (acoustic & electric vc/syn/voice) Western Wind ▲ WW 2001

Darling, D.:Blessings (sels), w. P.E. Clark (sop), C.B. Rowe (sop), W. Zukof (ct), W.L. Lee (ten), E. Levine (bar), D. Darling (acoustic & electric vc/syn/voice) Western Wind ▲ WW 2001

Bennett, Mavis (sop)

Sullivan, A.:The Gondoliers, w. W. Lawson (sop), A. Davies (ten), B. Lewis (cta), D. Oldham (ten), G. Baker (bar), L. Sheffield (bar), H. Lytton (bar), et al., H. Norris (cnd), D'Oyly Carte Opera Company Orch, D'Oyly Carte Opera Chorus—dialogue omitted *(rec 1927)* Pearl 2-▲ PEAS 9961 (m) [AAD]

Benningsen, Lilian (cta)

Janáček, L.:The Excursions of Mr. Brouček, w. Antonie Fahberg (sop—Piccolo), Wilma Lipp (sop—Málinka), Lilian Benningsen (cta—Fanny Nowak), Paul Kuen (ten—Trambahn-Kondukteur), Karl Ostertag (ten—Vorsitzender des Hausbesitzerverbandes), Fritz Wunderlich (ten—Mazal), Kurt Böhme (b-bar—Sakristan von St. Veit), Kieth Engen (bass—Würfl), J. Keilberth (cnd), Bavarian SO *(rec live, Prinzregententheater, Nov. 19, 1959)* Orfeo 2-▲ 354942 (m)

Ben-Nun, Efrat (sop)

Bach, J.S.:Cant 205, w. Katharina Kammerloher (alt), Christoph Prégardien (ten), Klaus Häger (bass), R. Jacobs (cnd), Berlin Academy for Early Music, Berlin Chamber Chorus Harmonia Mundi France 2-▲ HMC 901544.45

Bach, J.S.:Cant 213, w. Andreas Scholl (ct), James Taylor (ten), Klaus Häger (bass), R. Jacobs (cnd), Berlin Academy for Early Music, Berlin Chamber Chorus Harmonia Mundi France 2-▲ HMC 901544.45

Benoit, Christophe (bar)

Gounod, C.:Le Médecin malgré lui, w. Lina Dachary (sop), Monique Stiot (mez), Michel Hamel (ten), Joseph Peyron (ten), Janine Capderou (sgr), Jean-Louis Soumagnas (sgr), J.-C. Hartemann (cnd), ORTF Lyric Orch Musidisc ▲ MUS 202322 [AAD]

Benoit, Jean-Christoph (bar)

Hahn, R.:Songs, w. Bernard Ringeissen (pno)—3 jours de vendange; Si mes vers avaient des ailes!; Les cygnes; Dans la nuit; Néère [Etudes latines No. 2]; Le printemps; Séraphine; Quand je fus pris au pavillon; Nocturne; Mai; L'heure exquise [Chansons grises No. 5]; Paysage; Sur l'eau; Tyndares [Etudes latines No. 7]; La nuit; Cantique sur le bonheur des justes et sur le malheur des réprouvés; Infidélité; A Chloris; D'une prison Adès ▲ ADE 203432 [AAD]

Kosma, J.:Songs, w. Bernard Ringeissen (pno)—Les Enfants qui s'aiment; Il Pleut; La Pêche a la aleine; La Dame pavot nouvelle épousée; Page d'écriture; La Belle jambe; Le Jardin; Les Feuilles mortes; Chanson de l'oiseleur; Le Chat qui ne ressemble a rien; Dans ma maison; La Petite chèvre; Paris at Night; Art poétique; Chansons pour les enfants l'Hiver; Barbara; Baptiste, suite d'orchestre Adès ▲ ADE 132922 [AAD]

Landowski, M.:Music of, w. Nadine Sautereau (sop), Xavier Depraz (bass), Michel Bouquet (spkr), Gilbert Audin (bn), Evelyne Aïello, Didier Bouture, Ludovic Chevalier, Laurent Decker, Françoise Deslogères, Landowski, Tzipine (cnd), Colonne Association des Concerts Orch, Boulogne-Billancourt Orch Conservatory, Paris Conservatory Société des Concerts Orch, L'Itinéraire Ensemble, Harmonia Nova Orch Ensemble—Con Bn; Con pour ondes Martenot; Femme sans passé; Hauts de Hurlevent; Horologe; Mouvement; Notes de Nuit; Souvenir d'un jardin d'enfance; Ventriloque Chamade 3-▲ 5639/40/41 [AAD/DDD]

Martin, F.:Pilate, w. Ariette Chedel (cta), Eugenia Zareska (mez), Eric Tappy (ten), Derrik Olsen (bar), E. Ansermet (cnd), Swiss Romande Orch, Lausanne Pro Arte Choir Cascavelle 2-▲ CVL 2006 [ADD]

Satie, E.:Geneviève de Brabant, w. A. Guiot (sop), M. Mesplé (sop), D. Millet (sop), A. Esposito (sop), A. Ciccolini (pno), P. Dervaux (cnd), Orch de Paris, Paris Opera Chorus Virgin Classics 2-▲ CDZB 62877

Satie, E.:Socrate, w. A. Guiot (sop), M. Mesplé (sop), D. Millet (sop), A. Esposito (sop), P. Dervaux (cnd), Orch de Paris, Paris Opera Chorus Virgin Classics 2-▲ CDZB 62877

Benori (sgr)

Ricci, L.:Crispino e la cornare, w. D. Lojarro (sop), A. Lazzarini (mez), Cossutta (ten), S. Alaimo (bar), R. Coviello (bar), A. Marani (bass), R. Ristori (bass), Siclari (sgr), P. Carignani (cnd), San Remo SO, San Remo Sym Chorus [I] *(rec live 11/89)* Bongiovanni 2-▲ GB 2095/96 [DDD]

Bensman Rowe, Cheryl (sop)

Camilo, M.:Batéy, w. P. E. Clark (sop), W. Zukof (ct), L. Bennett (ten), W. L. Lee (ten), E. Levine (bar), Puntilla (sgr), New Generation Western Wind ▲ WW 2001

Darling, D.:Blessings:A Prayer for the Planet, w. P.E. Clark (sop), W. Zukof (ct), L. Bennett (ten), W.L. Lee (ten), E. Levine (bar), D. Darling (acoustic & electric vc/syn/voice) Western Wind ▲ WW 2001

Darling, D.:Blessings (sels), w. P.E. Clark (sop), W. Zukof (ct), L. Bennett (ten), W.L. Lee (ten), E. Levine (bar), D. Darling (acoustic & electric vc/syn/voice) Western Wind ▲ WW 2001

Ghezzo, D.:Prayers (2), w. Dinu Ghezzo (elec) *(rec Aaron Copland School of Music, Queens College, NYC)* Capstone ▲ CPS 8616 [ADD]

Mayer, William:Two News Items, w. Weisberg Ensemble CRI ▮ C 291

Benson, J. (sgr)

Gershwin, G.:Crazy for You, w. H. Groener (sgr) [1992 Broadway cast] Broadway Angel ▲ CDQ 54618 ▮ 4DQ 54618

Bentoiu, Iona (sop)

Honegger, A.:Amphion, w. Olivier Lallouette (bar—Apollon), Laurent Manzoni (bar—Amphion), Iona Bentoiu (sgr—muse), Theodora Ciucur (sgr—muse), Lucia Kriska (sgr—muse), Adriana Mestes (sgr—muse), J.-F. Antonioli (cnd), Timisoara PO, Timisoara Banatul Phil Chorus, Timisoara Children's Chorus *(rec Salle Ion Vidu, Timisoara, Romania, Oct 28 & Nov 1, 1995)* Timpani ▲ 1035 [DDD]

Benton, Jeffrey (bar)

Quilter, R.:The Arnold Book of Old Songs, w. Rona Lowe (pno) Symposium ▲ 1159

Quilter, R.:Shakespeare Songs (misc), w. Rona Lowe (pno), Graham Kirkland (pno)—Orpheus with His Lute, Op. 32/1; When Icicles Hang by the Wall, Op. 32/2; Come away, Death, Op. 6/1; Oh Mistress Mine, Op. 6/2; Blow, Blow, Thou Winter Wind, Op. 6/3; Who Is Sylvia?, Op. 30/1; When Daffodils Begin to Peer, Op. 30/2; How Should I Your True Love Know?, Op. 30/3; Sigh No More, Ladies, Op. 30/4; Fear No More the Heat of the Sun, Op. 23/1; Under the Greenwood Tree, Op. 23/2; It Was a Lover & His Lass, Op. 23/3; Take, O Take Those Lips away, Op. 23/4; Hey, Ho, the Wind & the Rain, Op. 23/5 Symposium ▲ SYM 1184

Quilter, R.:Songs, w. Rona Lowe (pno)—Fairy Lullaby; songs set to the poems of Heywood *(Morning Song)*, Ben Jonson *(Drink to me only with thine eyes)*, Percy *(Over the Mountains)*, John Irvine *(My Lady Greensleeves; Wind from the South)*, Thomas Moore *(Believe me, if all those endearing young charms...; Oh, tis sweet to think)*, Burns *(Ye Banks and Braes; Ca the yowes to the knowes)*, Rodney Bennett *(The man behind the plow...; The ash grove)*, Tennyson *(Now sleeps the Crimson petal)*, Mary Coleridge *(The valley and the hill...)*, William Blake *(Dream Valley)*, Edmund Waler *(Go lovely rose)*, Thomas Dekker *(O, the month of May)*, Shelley *(Love's Philosophy)*, a Manx ballad *(The Fuchsia tree)* Symposium ▲ 1159

Quilter, R.:Songs, w. Rona Lowe (pno), Graham Kirkland (pno)—To Julia [Prelude/The Bracelet/The Maiden Blush/To Daisies/The Night Piece/Julia's Hair/Cherry Ripe; poems by Herrick], Op. 8; Weep You No More; My Life's Delight [Campion]; Damask Roses; The Faithless Shepherdess [Byrd]; Browen Is My Love; By a Fountainside [Ben Johnson]; Fair House of Joy Symposium ▲ SYM 1184

Schubert, Franz:Winterreise, w. R. Lowe (pno) [E] Symposium ▲ SYM 1118

Benvenuti, Monica (sop)

Peri, J.:Euridice, w. Monica Benvenuti (sop—Ninfa I/Venere), Rossana Bertini (sop—Dafne/Ninfa II), Gloria Banditelli (cta—Euridice/Ninfa III/Tragedia/Proserpina), Mario Cecchetti (ten—Aminta/Radamanto), Paolo Da Col (ten—Tirsi), Gianpaolo Fagotto (ten—Orfeo), Giuseppe Zambon (ct—Arcetro), Sergio Foresti (bass—Caronte/Pastore), Furio Zanasi (bass—Plutone), R. de Caro (cnd), Arpeggione Ensemble *(rec Bologna, Italy, Nov 1992)* Arts Music 2-▲ 47276-2 [DDD]

Benzi, Piero (sgr)

Mascagni, P.:Isabeau, w. Marcella Pobbe (sop—Isabeau), Licia Galvano (mez—Giglietta), Pier Miranda Ferraro (ten—Folco), Orazio Gualtiero (bar—Cornelius), Rinaldo Rola (bass—Re Raimondo), Amelia Bazzini (sgr—Ermyngarde), Piero Benzi (sgr—L'araldo), Renata Davini (sgr—Ermynthrude), Piero Francia (sgr—Il Cavaliere), T. Serafin (cnd), San Remo SO *(rec Sanremo, Jan 13, 1962)* Bongiovanni ("Il Mito dell'Opera" series) 2-▲ GB 1135/36-2 [ADD]

Berberian (sgr)

Debussy, C.:Chansons de Bilitis Wergo ▲ WER 60054-50

Berberian, Ara (bass)

Hovhaness, A.:Flute Player of the Armenian Mountains, w. S. Arzruni (pno) [Armenian] *(rec 1985)* Positively Armenian ▮ PA 104C

Hovhaness, A.:Songs, w. S. Arzruni (pno)—4 songs [Armenian] *(rec 1985)* Positively Armenian ▮ PA 104C

Saint-Saëns, C.:Samson et Dalila, w. Risë Stevens (mez—Dalila), Ramón Vinay (ten—Samson), Thomas Carter (ten—1st Philistine), Tony Lopez (ten—Philistine Messenger), Joseph Mordino (bar—High Priest), Arthur Cosenza (bass—Abimélech), Joseph Knight (bass—2nd Philistine), Ara Berberian (bass—Old Hebrew), R. Cellini (cnd), New Orleans Opera Orch, New Orleans Opera Chorus *(rec live, Apr 2, 1960)* VAI Audio 2-▲ VAIA 1055-2 [ADD]

Verdi, G.:Simon Boccanegra, w. Renata Tebaldi (sop—Maria Boccanegra), Penelope Jensen (mez—Maria's Maidservant), Richard Tucker (ten—Gabriele Adorno), Rod MacWerter (ten—Paolo), Cornell MacNeil (bar—Simon Boccanegra), Ara Berberian (bar—Pietro), Ezio Flagello (bass—Jacopo Fiesco), Franco Iglesias (bass—Paolo), J. Levine (cnd), *(orch unknown)* *(rec live, Miami, 1970)* Legato Classics 2-▲ LCD 189-2 [ADD]

Berberian, Cathy (mez)

Berberian, C.:Stripsody Wergo ▲ WER 60054-50

Berio, L.:Circles, w. F. Pierre (hp), J.-P. Drouet (perc), J.-C. Casadesus (perc) *(rec 1967)* Wergo ▲ WER 6021-2 [AAD]

Berio, L.:Folk Songs Mez, w. L. Berio (cnd), London Sinfonietta, Juilliard Ensemble RCA Gold Seal ▲ 09026-62540-2

Berio, L.:Sequenza III *(rec 1967)* Wergo ▲ WER 6021-2 [AAD]

Bussotti, S.:O, w. Bruno Canino (pno) Wergo ▲ WER 60054-50

Cage, J.:Songs, w. Bruno Canino (pno)—A Flower; The Wonderful Widow of Eighteen Springs Wergo ▲ WER 60054-50

Berberian, Cathy (mez) (cont.)

Maderna, B.:Dimensioni 2, w. B. Maderna (elec), M. Zuccheri (elec) Stradivarius ▲ STR 33349

"MagnifiCathy":The Many Voices of Cathy Berberian, w. Bruno Canino (pno/hpd) Wergo ▲ WER 60054-50

Monteverdi, C.:Incoronazione, w. H. Donath (sop), E. Söderström (sop), P. Esswood (ct), N. Harnoncourt (cnd), Vienna Concentus Musicus [I] Teldec 4-▲ 2292-42547-2

Monteverdi, C.:Orfeo, w. R. Hansmann (sop), L. Kozma (ten), K. Equiluz (bar), M. Van Egmond (bass), N. Harnoncourt (cnd), Vienna Concentus Musicus, Capella Antiqua München Teldec 2-▲ 42494-2

Weill, K.:Songs, w. L. Berio (cnd), London Sinfonietta, Juilliard Ensemble—3 songs [arr. Berio] RCA Gold Seal ▲ 09026-62540-2

Berbié, Jane (mez)

Auber, D.-F.:Fra Diavolo, w. M. Mesplé (sop—Zerline), J. Berbié (mez—Lady Pamela), N. Gedda (ten—Fra Diavolo), R. Corazza (ten—Lord Cockburn), T. Dran (ten—Lorenzo), J. Bastin (bass—Matheo), M. Soustrot (cnd), Monte Carlo PO, Jean LaForge Ensemble Choir EMI Classics ▲ CDCB 54810

Boieldieu, F.-A.:Le Calife de Bagdad, w. Christiane Eda-Pierre (sop), Jeannine Collard (mez), Jean Giraudeau (ten), Jean-Paul Vaquelin (sgr), L. Fourestier (cnd), ORTF Lyric Orch, ORTF Lyric Chorale Musidisc ▲ MUS 201852 [AAD]

Charpentier, G.:Louise, w. I. Cotrubas (sop), P. Domingo (ten), M. Sénéchal (ten), G. Bacqier (bar), G. Prêtre (cnd), New Philharmonia Orch, Ambrosian Opera Chorus [F] Sony Classical 3-▲ S3K 46429 [ADD]

Donizetti, G.:Lucrezia Borgia, w. Montserrat Caballé (sop), Alain Vanzo (ten), Kostas Paskalis (bar), Arnold Voketaitis (bass-bar), L. D. Clements (sgr), Adib Fazah (sgr), Mauro Lampi (sgr), Vern Shinall (sgr), Jerold Siena (sgr), William Wiederanders (sgr), J. Perlea (cnd), New York City Opera Orch, New York City Chorus Great Opera Performances 2-▲ GOP 769

Donizetti, G.:Lucrezia Borgia, w. M. Caballé (sop), A. Vanzo (ten), K. Paskalis (bar), J. Perlea (cnd), *(orch & chorus unknown)* [I] *(rec live in New York, 4/20/65)* Standing Room Only 2-▲ SRO 801-2 (m) [ADD]

Mozart, W.A.:Nozze di Figaro, w. Mirella Freni (sop), Gundala Janowitz (sop), Frederica von Stade (mez), Michel Sénéchal (ten), José Van Dam (b-bar), Kurt Moll (bass), G. Solti (cnd), Paris Opera Orch, Paris Opera Chorus *(rec live, Paris, Apr 7, 1973)* Agorá ("Phoenix" series) 3-▲ 515

Ravel, M.:L'Enfant et les sortilèges, w. Arleen Augér (sop), Marilyn Richardson (sop), Linda Finnie (mez), Jocelyne Taillon (mez), Davenny Wyner (mez), Philip Langridge (ten), Philippe Huttenlocher (bar), Jules Bastin (bass), A. Previn (cnd), London SO, Ambrosian Opera Chorus Classics for Pleasure ("Eminence" series) ▲ CFP 2241

Bercewy, István (bass)

Liszt, F.:Legend of Saint Elizabeth, w. Maria Szechowska (sop), Doreen Millmann (mez), Klaus Lapins (bar), S. Heinrich (cnd), Warsaw RSO, Warsaw Radio Chorus [G] *(rec 1983)* Koch Schwann 2-▲ 3-1291-2 [ADD]

Berdini, Amadeo (bar)

Mercadante, S.:Il giuramento (sels), w. M. Vitale (sop), M. Pirazzini (mez), R. Panerai (bar), A. Simonetto (cnd), Milan RAI Orch, Milan RAI Chorus [I]—14 scenes & arias *(rec live, Milan, 4/5/51)* Myto 2-▲ 2 MCD 90632 [ADD]

Verdi, G.:La battaglia di Legnano, w. Caterina Mancini (sop), Rolando Panerai (bar), Albino Gaggi (bass), Edmea Limberti (sgr), Manfredi Ponz de Leon (sgr), F. Previtali (cnd), Rome RAI SO, Rome RAI Chorus *(rec 1951)* Cetra Classic 2-▲ CDON 40 [ADD]

Berdini, Amedeo (bar)

Mussorgsky, M.:Khovanshchina, w. Jolanda Mancini (sop—Emma), Irene Companez (mez), Amedeo Berdini (ten—Prince Andrei Khovanski), Mirto Picchi (ten—Prince Vasili Golitsin), Herbert Handt (ten—Scribe), Andrea Mineo (bar—Kuzka), Giampiero Malaspina (bar—Shaklovity), Boris Christoff (bass—Dosifei), Mario Petri (bass—Prince Ivan Khovanski), Dimitri Lopatto (Varsonofiev/First Strelyets), Giorgio Conello (Second Strelyets), A. Rodzinski (cnd), *(orch unknown)* [I] *(rec Rome, 1958)* VAI Audio 2-▲ VAIA 1052-2

Mussorgsky, M.:Khovanshchina, w. Irene Companez (cta), Herbert Handt (ten), Mirto Picchi (ten), Boris Christoff (bass), Giorgio Canello (sgr), Dmitri Lopatto (sgr), Michele Malaspina (sgr), Jolanda Mancini (sgr), Mario Petri (sgr), A. Rodzinski (cnd), Rome RAI Radio-TV SO, Rome RAI Chorus Stradivarius 2-▲ STV DTM 12320 [ADD]

Berendsen, E. (sgr)

Avni, T.:Beside the Depths of a River, w. D. Bloch (pno) Symposium ▲ 1110

Avni, T.:Leda & the Swan, w. E. Heifetz (cl) Symposium ▲ 1110

Avni, T.:Love under a Different Sun, w. M. Meltzer (fl), E. Zaltsman (vn), S. Magen (vc) Symposium ▲ 1110

Berg, Lori (nar)

Van Appledorn, M.J.:Freedom of Youth, w. Mary Jeanne Van Appledorn (syn) Capstone ▲ CPS 8618

Berg, Nathan (bass)

Handel, G.F.:Messiah, w. Sandrine Piau (sop), Barbara Schlick (sop), Andreas Scholl (alt), Mark Padmore (ten), W. Christie (cnd), Les Arts Florissants [1742 Dublin version] Harmonia Mundi France 2-▲ HMC 901498/99

Purcell, H.:Dido & Aeneas, w. Véronique Gens (sop—Dido), Sophie Marin-Degor (sop—Belinda), Sophie Daneman (sop—2nd woman/1st witch), Gaëlle Mechaly (sop—2nd witch), Claire Brua (mez—Sorceress), Steve Dugardin (alt—Chorus), Jean-Paul Fouchécourt (ten—Spirit/Sailor), Nathan Berg (b-bar—Aeneas), Jonathan Arnold (bass—Chorus), William Christie (hpd), W. Christie (cnd), Les Arts Florissants *(rec Massy Opera Theatre, Nov. 8-11, 1994)* Erato ▲ 98477-2 [DDD]

Schoeck, O.:Songs (comp), w. Julius Drake (pno), Oskar Birchmeier (org)—3 geistliche Gesänge, Op. 11; 3 Lieder, Op. 7; 2 Gesänge, Op. 9; 5 Lieder, Op. 31; 12 Eichendorff-Lieder, Op. 30 *(rec Sept 1995)* Jecklin ▲ JD 672

Berg, Pieter van der (bass)

Donizetti, G.:Betly, w. P. Langridge (ten), R. Capecchi (bar), J. Schaap (cnd), Zaanstad Opera Orch *(rec live, 1973)* Italian Opera Rarities ▲ IOR 7721 [ADD]

Handel, G.F.:Rodelinda, Regina de' Longobardi, w. Joan Sutherland (sop—Rodelinda), Margaretha Elkins (mez—Bertarido's sister), Huguette Tourangeau (mez—Bertarido), Cora Canne-Meijer (alt—Unulfo), Eric Tappy (ten—Grimoaldo), Pieter van der Berg (bass—Garibaldo), R. Bonynge (cnd), Netherlands CO *(rec Amsterdam, June 30, 1973)* Bella Voce 2-▲ BLV 107.206 [AAD]

Bergamaschi, Ettore (ten)

Carlo Tagliabue, w. C. Tagliabue (bar), Margherita Carosio (sop), Zinka Milanov (sop), Bruna Castagna (cta), Frederick Jagel (ten), Norman Cordon (bass), Renata Tebaldi (sop), Alfredo Colella (bass) *(rec in studio and live, 1928-1951)* Bongiovanni ▲ GB 1070-2 [ADD]

Verdi, G.:Il trovatore (sels), w. J. Biel (ten), F. Tamagno (ten), L.-A. Escalaïs (ten), M. Gilion (ten), E. Caruso (ten), A. Paoli (ten), G. Zenatello (ten), J. Sembach (ten), L. Slezak (ten), F. Constantino (ten), G. Martinelli (ten), B. De Muro (ten), N. Fusati (ten), N. Piccaluga (ten), G. Lauri-Volpi (ten), A. Pertile (ten), R. Tauber (ten), J. O'Sullivan (ten), H. Roswaenge (ten), G. Taccani (ten), V. Lois (ten), H. Lazaro (ten), A. Lindi (ten), A. Cortis (ten), F. Merli (ten), F. Völker (ten), J. Kiepura (ten), J. Schmidt (ten), J. Bjoerling (ten), B. Gigli (ten), A. Salvarezza (ten), J. Soler (ten), M. Filippeschi (ten)—34 performances of the Act III tenor aria "Di quella pira!," *(rec from 1903-1956)* Bongiovanni ▲ GB 1051 [AAD]

Berganza, Teresa (mez)

The Art of Teresa Berganza Replay ("Butterfly" series) ▲ BMCD 034 [AAD]

Bizet, G.:Carmen, w. I. Cotrubas (sop), P. Domingo (ten), S. Milnes (bar), C. Abbado (cnd), London SO, Ambrosian Opera Chorus [F] Deutsche Grammophon 3-▲ 419636-2 [ADD]

Bizet, G.:Carmen (sels), w. Teresa Berganza (mez—Carmen), Plácido Domingo (ten—Don José), C. Abbado (cnd), London SO, John McCarthy (cnd), Patrick Criswell (cnd), Ambrosian Singers, George Watson's College Boys' Chorus—C'est toi? C'est moi Deutsche Grammophon ▲ 447270-2 [ADD] ■ 447 270-4

Bizet, G.:Carmen (sels), w. I. Cotrubas (sop), P. Domingo (ten), S. Milnes (bar), C. Abbado (cnd), London SO, Ambrosian Opera Chorus [F] Deutsche Grammophon ▲ 435401-2 [ADD]

Braga, E.:Songs, w. Alvarez Parejo (pno)—6 songs [Port] Claves ▲ CD 8401 [DDD]

Cherubini, L.:Médée, w. M. Callas (sop), J. Vickers (ten), N. Zaccaria (bass), N. Rescigno (cnd), Dallas SO *(rec live, Dallas Civic Opera, State Fair Music Hall 11/6/58)* Melodram 2-▲ MEL 26016

Falla, M. de:El amor brujo (sels), w. P. Argento (cnd), French National Orch *(rec live, Paris 2/21/57)* Memories 2-▲ HR 4464/65 [ADD]

Berganza, Teresa (mez) (cont.)

Falla, M. de:Atlántida, w. M. Bayo (sop), S. Estes (bass), E. Colomer (cnd), Spanish National Youth Orch Valois 2-▲ V 4685

Falla, M. de:Canciones populares españolas (7), w. J. López-Cobos (cnd), Lausanne CO [Sp] Claves ▲ CD 8405

Falla, M. de:Canciones populares españolas (7), w. Juan Antonio Alvarez-Parejo (pno) Claves ▲ 50-8405

Falla, M. de:El corregidor y la molinera, w. J. López-Cobos (cnd), Lausanne CO Claves ▲ 50-8405

Falla, M. de:El sombrero de tres picos, w. J. López-Cobos (cnd), Lausanne CO [Sp] Claves ▲ CD 8405

From the Official Barcelona Games Ceremony, w. P. Domingo, José Carreras (ten), Montserrat Caballé (sop), Giacomo Aragall (ten), Juan Pons (bar) RCA Red Seal ▲ 09026-61204-2 ■ 09026-61204-4 □ 09026-61204-5

Granados, E.:Songs, w. Juan Antonio Alvarez-Parejo (pno) (6) Claves ▲ 50-8704

Guastavino, C.:Songs, w. Alvarez Parejo (pno)—9 songs [Sp] Claves ▲ CD 8401 [DDD]

Guridi, J.:Canciones Castellanas (6), w. Juan Antonio Alvarez-Parejo (pno) Claves ▲ 50-8704

Handel, G.F.:Alcina, w. M. Freni (sop), J. Sutherland (sop), R. Bonynge (cnd), London SO London ("Grand Opera" series) 3-▲ 433723-2 [ADD]

Haydn, J.:Arianna a Naxos, w. M. Viotti (cnd), English CO [18th cent. orchestral arr. by Sigismund Ritter von Neukomm] [I] Claves ▲ CD 9016 [DDD]

Haydn, J.:Arias, w. R. Leppard (cnd), Scottish CO—Aria di Giannina; Aria di Agatina; Aria di Errisena; Cantilena Pro Adventu; Cant Miseri Noi!, Misera Patria; Cavatina di Alcina; Aria di Merlina; Aria di Lindora Erato ("Recital" series) ▲ 98498-2

Massenet, J.:Don Quichotte, w. Pina Malgarini (mez), Tommaso Frascati (ten), Carlo Badioli (bass), Boris Christoff (bass), A. Simonetto (cnd), Milan RAI SO, Milan RAI Chorus Melodram 2-▲ CDM 27027

Massenet, J.:Don Quichotte, w. T. Berganza (mez—La Belle Dulcinée), A. Fondary (bar—Sancho Pana), J. Van Dam (b-bar—Don Quichotte), M. Plasson (cnd), Toulouse Capitole Orch, Toulouse Capitole Chorus EMI Classics ▲ CDCB 54767

Monteverdi, C.:Lamento d'Arianna, w. M. Viotti (cnd), English CO [orchestral arr. by Claudio Gallico] [I] Claves ▲ CD 9016 [DDD]

Monteverdi, C.:Lamento d'Arianna, w. M. Viotti (cnd), English CO Claves ▲ 50-9016

Mozart, W.A.:Clemenza, w. M. Casula (sop), L. Popp (sop), B. Fassbaender (mez), T. Franc (bass), F. Krenn (bass), I. Kertész (cnd), Vienna State Opera Orch, Vienna State Opera Chorus London ("Grand Opera" series) 2-▲ 430105-2 [ADD]

Mozart, W.A.:Così fan tutte, w. M. Adani (sop), T. Stich-Randall (mez), L. Alva (ten), A. Cortis (ten), R. Panerai (bar), H. Rosbaud (cnd), Paris Conservatory Societé des Concerts Orch, Aix-en-Provence Festival Chorus [I] *(rec live, Aix-en-Provence, July 26, 1957)* Melodram 3-▲ MEL 37084 [AAD]

Mozart, W.A.:Don Giovanni, w. E. Moser (sop), K. Te Kanawa (sop), K. Riegel (ten), G. Raimondi (ten), J. Van Dam (b-bar), J. Macurdy (bass), L. Maazel (cnd), Paris Opera Orch, Paris Opera Chorus [I] CBS 3-▲ M3K 35192

Mozart, W.A.:Don Giovanni (sels), w. Kiri Te Kanawa (sop), José Van Dam (bass-bar), Ruggero Raimondi (bass), L. Maazel (cnd), Paris Opera Orch, Paris Opera Chorus Sony Classical ("Essential Classics" series) ▲ SBK 62663 ■ SBT 62663

Mozart, W.A.:Don Giovanni (sels), w. E. Moser (sop), K. Te Kanawa (sop), K. Riegel (ten), G. Raimondi (ten), J. Van Dam (b-bar), J. Macurdy (bass), L. Maazel (cnd), Paris Opera Orch CBS ■ MT 35859

Mozart, W.A.:Finta semplice, w. Helen Donath (sop), Jutta-Renate Ihloff (sop), A. Rolfe Johnson (ten), Thomas Moser (ten), Robert Lloyd (b-bar), Robert Holl (bass), L. Hager (cnd), Salzburg Mozarteum Orch [I] Orfeo 3-▲ 085843 [DDD]

Mozart, W.A.:Nozze di Figaro, w. Mirella Freni (sop), Daniela Mazzucato (sop), Mirto Picchi (ten), Hermann Prey (bar), José Van Dam (b-bar), Paolo Montarsolo (bass), C. Abbado (cnd), La Scala Orch, La Scala Chorus *(rec live, Apr 22, 1974)* Arkadia 3-▲ 614

Mozart, W.A.:Nozze di Figaro, w. H. Harper (sop), J. Blegen (sop), D. Fischer-Dieskau (bar), G. Evans (bar), D. Barenboim (cnd), English CO, John Alldis Choir [I] EMI Classics ("Studio" series) 3-▲ CDMC 63646 [ADD]

Mozart, W.A.:Nozze di Figaro, w. E. Söderström (sop), R. Grist (sop), G. Evans (bar), O. Klemperer (cnd), New Philharmonia Orch, John Alldis Choir EMI Classics 3-▲ CDMC 63849

Mozart, W.A.:Nozze di Figaro, w. S. Jurinac (sop), T. Stratas (sop), N. Condò (mez), A. Lazzari (ten), S. Bruscantini (bar), M. Petri (bass), G. Tadeo (bass), A. Mariotti (bass), Z. Mehta (cnd), *(orch unknown)* *(rec 1968)* Great Opera Performances 3-▲ GOP 712

Mozart, W.A.:Nozze di Figaro (sels), w. R. Pütz (sop), T. Stich-Randall (mez), A.-R. Johnson (ten), G. Bacquier (bar), F. Corena (bass), H. Wallberg (cnd), Swiss Romande Orch, Swiss Romande Chorus—Act IV Melodram 2-▲ CDM 27094 [ADD]

Musiche Veneziene per Voce e Strumenti, w. Yasunori Imamura (lt/thb/gtr), Pere Ros (vl), Lynn Dickinson (vl), Carol Lewis (vl), Silvie Mocquet (vl), Jörg Ewald Dähler (pno), Jörg Ewald Dähler (cnd) *(rec Kirche Saanen, Feb 1982)* Claves ▲ CD 508206 [DDD]

Mussorgsky, M.:Nursery, w. Ricardo Requejo (pno) *(rec Kirche Seon, June 1982)* Claves ▲ CD 508204 [DDD]

Mussorgsky, M.:Songs (misc), w. Ricardo Requejo (pno)—Kinderstube Claves ▲ 50-8204

Penella, M.:El gato montés, w. V. Villarroel (sop), P. Domingo (ten), J. Pons (bar), M. Roa (cnd), Madrid SO [Sp] Deutsche Grammophon 2-▲ 435776-2 [DDD]

Puccini, G.:Madama Butterfly, w. M. Freni (sop), J. Carreras (ten), J. Pons (bar), G. Sinopoli (cnd), Philharmonia Orch, Ambrosian Opera Chorus [I] Deutsche Grammophon 3-▲ 423567-2 [DDD]

Rossini, G.:Il barbiere di Siviglia, w. L. Alva (ten), H. Prey (bar), P. Montarsolo (bass), C. Abbado (cnd), London SO, London Sym Chorus [I] Deutsche Grammophon 2-▲ 415695-2 [ADD]

Rossini, G.:Il barbiere di Siviglia, w. R. Casellato (ten), S. Bruscantini (bar), G. Tozzi (bass), B. Bartoletti (cnd), Buenos Aires Teatro Colón Orch, Buenos Aires Teatro Colón Chorus [I] *(rec 1969)* Golden Age of Opera 2-▲ GAO 149/50

Rossini, G.:La Cenerentola, w. Luigi Alva (ten), Renato Capecchi (bar), Paolo Montarsolo (bass), C. Abbado (cnd), Florence Maggio Musicale Orch, Florence Maggio Musicale Chorus *(rec Florence, May 1971)* Memories 2-▲ MEM 4283 [ADD]

Rossini, G.:La Cenerentola, w. L. Alva (ten), R. Capecchi (bar), U. Trama (bass), C. Abbado (cnd), London SO, London Sym Chorus [I] Deutsche Grammophon 2-▲ 423861-2 [ADD]

Rossini, G.:La Cenerentola, w. Nicola Monti (ten), Sesto Bruscantini (bar), Mario Petri (bar), Leonardo Monreale (sgr), M. Rossi (cnd), Naples RAI SO, Naples Teatro San Carlo Chorus *(rec Oct 8, 1958)* Pantheon 2-▲ PHE 6656 (m)

Rossini, G.:Giovanna d'Arco, w. M. Viotti (cnd), English CO Claves ▲ 50-9016

Rossini, G.:L'italiana in Algeri, w. L. Zannini (mez), U. Benelli (ten), E. Dara (bar), A. Romero (bar), P. Montarsolo (bass), C. Abbado (cnd), Florence Teatro Comunale Orch, Florence Teatro Comunale Chorus *(rec 1973)* Great Opera Performances ▲ GOP 740

Rossini, G.:L'italiana in Algeri, w. Alvino Misciano (ten), Sesto Bruscantini (bar), Mario Petri (sgr), N. Sanzogno (cnd), Milan RAI SO, Milan RAI Chorus *(rec June 28, 1957)* Pantheon 2-▲ PHE 6646 (m)

Schumann, R.:Frauenliebe und -leben, w. Ricardo Requejo (pno) *(rec Kirche Seon, June 1982)* Claves ▲ CD 508204 [DDD]

Schumann, R.:Frauenliebe und -leben, w. Ricardo Requejo (pno) Claves ▲ 50-8204

Solo Cantatas Claves ▲ CD 9016 [DDD]

Spanish Songs Claves ▲ CD 8704 [DDD]

Teresa Berganza, Giuseppe Taddei, w. Giuseppe Taddei (bar), Milan RAI SO [cnd:Frieder Weissman] *(rec Dec. 16, 1957)* Incontri Memorabili ("Martini & Rossi Concerts" series) ▲ 5025

Toldrá, E.:Songs, w. Juan Antonio Alvarez-Parejo (pno)—6 sels Claves ▲ 50-8704

Turina, J.:Poema en forma de canciones, w. Juan Antonio Alvarez-Parejo (pno) Claves ▲ 50-8704

Venetian Music for Voice & Instruments Claves ▲ 50-8206

Villa-Lobos, H.:Songs, w. A. Parejo (pno)—6 songs [Port] Claves ▲ CD 8401 [DDD]

Vivaldi, A.:Cants, w. M. Viotti (cnd), English CO—"Piango, gemo, sospiro", RV.675 Claves ▲ 50-9016 [DDD]

Vivaldi, A.:Gloria, RV.589, w. L. Valentini-Terrani (mez), R. Muti (cnd), New Philharmonia Orch, New Philharmonia Chorus [L] EMI Classics ▲ CDC 47990 [ADD]

Vivaldi, A.:Magnificat, RV.611, w. L. Valentini-Terrani (mez), R. Muti (cnd), New Philharmonia Orch, New Philharmonia Chorus [L] EMI Classics ▲ CDC 47990 [ADD]

Zarzuelas y Canciones, w. Felix Lavilla (pno), various orchs Acanta ▲ 49403

Berger, Angelika (sop)
Wagner, R.:Der Ring des Nibelungen, w. Liselotte Becker-Egner (sop—Woglinde/Ortlinde/Wellgunde), Angelika Berger (sop—Wellgunde/Waltraute), Siw Ericsdotter (sop—Norn 3), Heidemaria Ferch (sop—Freia/Gerhilde), Bella Jasper (sop—Helmwige/Waldvogel/Woglinde), Ditha Sommer (sop—Sieglinde/Gutrune), Ursula Boese (mez—Erda), Ruth Hesse (mez—Fricka), Nadezda Kniplová (mez—Brünnhilde), Margit Kobeck (mez—Schwertleite/Norn 2), Hilde Rosner (mez—Flosshilde/Siegrunde), Erica Schubert (mez—Grimgerde/Flosshilde), Ingrid Göritz (cta—Rossweisse/Norn 1), Herbert Doussant (ten—Froh), Herold Kraus (ten—Mime), Gerald McKee (ten—Siegmund/Siegfried), Fritz Uhl (ten—Loge), Rudolf Knoll (bar—Gunther/Donner), Rolf Polke (bass-bar—Wotan/Wanderer), Rolf Kühne (bass—Alberich), Takao Okamura (bass—Fafner), Otto von Rohr (bass—Hagen/Fasolt/Hunding), H. Swarowsky (cnd), Czech PO, Prague National Theater Orch *(rec June 3 & 5, July 26–31, A)* Weltbild Classics 14-▲ 703769 [ADD]

Berger, Erna (sop)
Beethoven, L. van:Sym 9, "Choral Sym", w. Gertrude Pitzinger (cta), Walther Ludwig (ten), Rudolf Watzke (bass), W. Furtwängler (cnd), Berlin PO, Bruno Kittel Choir *(rec Queens Hall, London, May 1, 1937)* Music & Arts ▲ CD 818 [ADD]
Brahms, J.:Liebeslieder Waltzes SATB, w. G. Pfitzinger (alt), W. Ludwig (ten), E. Wenk (bass), E.-G. Scherzer (pno), G. Falbe (pno) *(rec 1959)* FNAC Music ▲ 642313
Brahms, J.:Neue Liebeslieder Waltzes, w. G. Pfitzinger (alt), W. Ludwig (ten), E. Wenk (bass), E.-G. Scherzer (pno), G. Falbe (pno) *(rec 1959)* FNAC Music ▲ 642313
Erna Berger Koch Schwann 3-▲ SCH 310582 [ADD]
Erna Berger, Vol. 2 *(rec 1935–40)* Preiser ("Lebendige Vergangenheit" series) ▲ PRE 89092 [AAD]
Flotow, F. von:Martha, w. Peter Anders (ten), Eugene Fuchs (bar), Josef Greindl (bass), J. Schüler (cnd), Berlin German Opera Orch, Berlin German Opera Chorus Phonographe 2-▲ PHG 5050
Flotow, F. von:Martha, w. P. Anders (ten), E. Fuchs (bar), J. Greindl (bass), J. Schüler (cnd), Berlin State Opera Orch *(rec 1944)* Berlin Classics 2-▲ BER 2163 [ADD]
Great Love Duets, w. Miliza Korjus (sop), Lotte Lehmann (sop), Frida Leider (sop), Charles Kullman (ten), Lauritz Melchior (ten), Helge Roswaenge (ten), Tito Schipa (ten), Richard Tauber (ten), et al. Pearl ▲ PEA 9217
The Legendary Singers at Lindenoper Berlin (1927–1945)—, w. Gitta Alpar (sop), Erna Berger (sop), Tiana Lemnitz (sop), Maria Müller (sop), Margarete Klose (cta), Peter Anders (ten), Max Lorenz (ten), Walter Ludwig (ten), Lauritz Melchior (ten), Rudolf Schock (ten), Franz Völker (ten), Willi Domgraf-Fassb *(rec 1927; 1937; 1941–45)* Minerva ▲ MN A21 [ADD]
Mozart, W.A.:Don Giovanni, w. E. Schwarzkopf (sop), E. Grümmer (sop), A. Dermota (ten), C. Siepi (b-bar), O. Edelmann (b-bar), W. Berry (bass), W. Furtwängler (cnd), Vienna PO, Vienna State Opera Chorus *(rec 1953)* Arkadia 3-▲ 509 (m) [AAD]
Mozart, W.A.:Don Giovanni, w. E. Schwarzkopf (sop), E. Grümmer (sop), A. Dermota (ten), C. Siepi (b-bar), O. Edelmann (b-bar), W. Berry (bass), W. Furtwängler (cnd), Vienna PO, Vienna State Opera Chorus *(rec Salzburg, Aug. 3, 1953)* EMI Classics ("Great Recordings of the Century" series) 2-▲ CDHB 63860
Mozart, W.A.:Songs, w. M. Callas (sop), E. Grümmer (sop), E. Schwarzkopf (sop), R. Scotto (sop), T. Lemnitz (sop), S. Jurinac (sop), E. Schumann (sop), I. Souez (sop), E. Rethberg (sop), L. Lehmann (sop), N. Gedda (ten), J. McCormack (ten), H. Roswenge (ten), H. Nash (ten), T. Gobbi (bar), G. Hüsch (bar), E. Kunz (bar), G. Frick (bass), E. Pinza (bass), A. Kipnis (bass) EMI Classics 4-▲ CDMD 63750
Mozart, W.A.:Zauberflöte, w. T. Lemnitz (sop), I. Beilke (sop), H. Roswaenge (ten), H. Tessmer (ten), G. Hüsch (bar), W. Strienz (bass), T. Beecham (cnd), Berlin PO, Favre Chorus [without dialog; G] *(rec 1937–38 for HMV)* Melodram 2-▲ MEL 27056 (m) [AAD]
Mozart, W.A.:Zauberflöte, w. T. Lemnitz (sop), I. Beilke (sop), H. Roswaenge (ten), H. Tessmer (ten), G. Hüsch (bar), W. Strienz (bass), T. Beecham (cnd), Berlin PO, Favre Chorus [without dialog; G] *(rec 1937–38 for HMV)* EMI Classics ("Great Recordings of the Century" series) 2-▲ CDHB 61034 (m) [ADD]
Mozart, W.A.:Zauberflöte, w. T. Lemnitz (sop), I. Beilke (sop), H. Roswaenge (ten), H. Tessmer (ten), G. Hüsch (bar), W. Strienz (bass), T. Beecham (cnd), Berlin PO, Favre Chorus [without dialog; G] *(rec 1937–38 for HMV)* Pearl 2-▲ PEAS 9371 (m) [AAD]
Mozart, W.A.:Zauberflöte, w. T. Lemnitz (sop), I. Beilke (sop), H. Roswaenge (ten), G. Hüsch (bar), W. Strienz (bass), T. Beecham (cnd), Berlin PO, Vereinigung Favres Soloists [G] *(rec Nov. 1937 & Feb.–Mar. 193)* Nimbus ("Prima Voce" series) 2-▲ NI 7827/8 (m) [ADD]
Mozart, W.A.:Zauberflöte (sels), w. Erna Berger (sop—Queen of the Night), Maria Reining (sop—Pamina), Josef von Manowarda (bass—Sarastro), H. Knappertsbusch (cnd), Vienna State Opera Orch *(rec Vienna, Dec. 4, 1941)* Koch Schwann 2-▲ SCH 314672 [ADD]
Opera Arias *(rec 1932–37 from Grammophon)* Preiser ("Lebendige Vergangenheit" series) ▲ PRE 89035 (m) [AAD]
Schubert, H.:Hymnisches Konzert, w. Walther Ludwig (ten), *(organist unknown),* W. Furtwängler (cnd), Berlin PO Arkadia 2-▲ 365
Strauss, R.:Ariadne auf Naxos, w. Viorica Ursuleac (sop), Helge Roswaenge (ten), Karl Hammes (bar), C. Krauss (cnd), Berlin Reich RSO *(rec Berlin, 1935)* Preiser ▲ PRE 90259
Strauss, R.:Ariadne auf Naxos, w. Miliza Korjus (sop), Viorica Ursuleac (sop), Helge Rosvaenge (ten), *(other soloists unknown),* C. Krauss (cnd), Vienna State Opera Orch, Vienna State Opera Chorus *(rec 1935)* Arlecchino 3- ARL
Verdi, G.:Rigoletto, w. R. Jacobs (alt), H. Roswaenge (ten), H. Schlusnus (bass), J. Greindl (bass), R. Heger (cnd), Berlin State Opera Orch, Berlin State Opera Chorus [G] *(rec 11/20–22/44)* Preiser 2-▲ 90036 (m) [AAD]

Berger, Mark (nar)
Monk, M.:Key, w. Meredith Monk (sgr/elec org/jews hp), Daniel Sverdlik (sgr), Dick Higgins (sgr), Collin Walcott (sgr/mrdingam), Lanny Harrison (nar) *(rec live, Gary Weis' loft, Santa Monica, CA, Ace Gallery, Los Angeles, CA, The House, New York City, The Farm, Los Angeles, CA, July 1970–Jan 1971)* Lovely Music ▲ LCD 1051 [ADD]

Berger-Tuna, Helmut (bass)
Strauss, R.:Feuersnot, w. J. Varady (sop), B. Weikl (bar), H. Fricke (cnd), Munich RSO, Bavarian Radio Chorus [G] Acanta 2-▲ 43530-1-2 [DDD]

Berggold, Christiane (alt)
Schulhoff, E.:The Flames, w. Jane Eaglen (sop—Donna Anna, Nun, Woman, Marguerite), Carola Höhn (sop—Shadow), Celina Lindsley (sop—Shadow), Regina Schudel (sop—Shadow), Iris Vermillion (mez—La Morte), Christiane Berggold (alt—Shadow), Kaja Borris (alt—Shadow), Elvira Dressen (alt—Shadow), Kurt Westi (ten—Don Juan), Johann-Werner Prein (bass—Commendatore), Gerd Wolf (bass—Harlequin), J. Mauceri (cnd), Berlin German SO, Berlin RIAS Chamber Choir *(rec Jesus-Christus Church, Berlin Dahlem, Oct 1993/Apr 1994)* London 2-▲ 444630-2 [DDD]

Bergius, Allan (trb)
Bach, J.S.:Cant 155, w. P. Esswood (ct), K. Equiluz (ten), T. Hampson (b-bar), N. Harnoncourt (cnd), Vienna Concentus Musicus, Tölz Boys' Choir [G] Teldec 2-▲ 2292-42632-2 [DDD]

Berglund, Joel (bar)
Gounod, C.:Faust (sels), w. Luise Helletsgruber (sop—Marguerite), Helge Roswaenge (ten—Faust), Joel Berglund (ten—Mephistopheles), J. Krips (cnd), Vienna State Opera Orch *(rec Vienna, Nov. 10, 1936)* Koch Schwann 2-▲ SCH 314622 [ADD]
Wagner, R.:Der fliegende Holländer, w. Maria Müller (sop), Franz Völker (ten), Ludwig Hoffmann (bass), R. Kraus (cnd), Bayreuth Festival Orch, Bayreuth Festival Chorus *(rec live, Bayreuth, July 18, 1942)* Preiser 2-▲ PRE 90232 [ADD]
Wagner, R.:Der fliegende Holländer (sels), w. Maria Nemeth (sop—Senta), Set Svanholm (ten—Erik), Joel Berglund (bar—Holländer), L. Reichwein (cnd), Vienna State Opera Orch *(rec Vienna, Sept. 28, 1942)* Koch Schwann ▲ SCH 314692 [ADD]

Berglund, Rut (cta)
Schoeck, O.:Das Schloss Dürande (sels), w. Maria Cebotari (sop—Gabriele), Marta Fuchs (sop—Gräfin Morvaille), Brigitte Fassbaender (mez—Renald Willi Domgraf), Rut Berglund (cta—Priorin), Peter Anders (ten—Armand), Benno Arnold (ten—Jäger), Josef Greindl (bass—Nicole), Hans Wrana (bass—Jäger), Vasso Argyris (sgr—Volksredner), Otto Hüsch (sgr—Wildhüter), Leo Laschet (sgr—Jäger), Fritz Marcks (sgr—Jäger), Felix Schneider (sgr—Jäger), R. Heger (cnd)—Text; Ich kann es nicht glauben [from Act 1]; Text; Heil dir, du Feuerquelle [from Act 2]; Text; Gesucht und nicht gefunden [from Act 3]; Text; Der Jäger ist frei! [Act 3 Finale]; Text; Sie kommen mit Flinten und Stangen [Act 4]; Text; Du Narr des vermeintlichen Rechts [Act 4 finale]; Text *(rec live, Apr 1943)* Jecklin ▲ JD 692

Bergonzi, Carlo (ten)
Boito, A.:Mefistofele, w. R. Tebaldi (sop), N. Ghiaurov (bass), L. Gardelli (cnd), *(orch unknown) (rec live, New York 1/25/66)* Standing Room Only 2-▲ SRO 824-2 [ADD]
Carlo Bergonzi London ("Grandi Voici" series) ▲ 440417-2
Carlo Bergonzi Bongiovanni ▲ GB 1100-2 [ADD]
Catalani, A.:La Wally, w. R. Tebaldi (sop), P. Glossop (bar), F. Corena (bass), F. Cleva (cnd), American Opera Society Orch, American Opera Society Chorus *(rec Mar. 13, 1968)* Intaglio 2-▲ ING 764 [ADD]
Catalani, A.:La Wally (sels), w. R. Tebaldi (sop), *(sels unknown) (rec Carnegie Hall, 1968)* Great Opera Performances 2-▲ GOP 734
Christmas Songs, w. Austrian RSO [cnd:Paul Angerer], Vienna Children's Choir Orfeo ▲ 030821
Cilea, F.:Adriana Lecouvreur, w. J. Sutherland (sop), L. Nucci (bar), R. Bonynge (cnd), Welsh National Opera Orch, Welsh National Opera Chorus London 2-▲ 425815-2 [DDD]
Donizetti, G.:L'elisir d'amore, w. Renata Scotto (sop), Giuseppe Taddei (bar), Carlo Cava (bass), G. Gavazzeni (cnd), Florence Teatro Comunale Orch, Florence Teatro Comunale Chorus *(rec June 1967)* Pantheon 2-▲ PHE 6612 (m)
Donizetti, G.:L'elisir d'amore, w. R. Scotto (sop), P. Cava (ten), G. Taddei (bar), G. Gavazzeni (cnd), Florence Maggio Musicale Orch, Florence Maggio Musicale Chorus *(rec live 1967)* Memories 2-▲ HR 4129/30 (s)
Donizetti, G.:Lucia di Lammermoor, w. A. Moffo (sop), M. Sereni (bar), E. Flagello (bass), G. Prêtre (cnd), RCA Italian Opera Orch [I] RCA Gold Seal 2-▲ 6504-2-RG [ADD]
Duets, w. Bergonzi, Carlo (ten), Dietrich Fischer-Dieskau (ten) Orfeo ▲ C 028821 [DDD]
Giordano, U.:Andrea Chénier, w. A. Gulin (sop—Maddalena), C. Bergonzi (ten—Andrea Chenier), S. Milnes (bar—Gérard), A. Guadagno (cnd), New Philharmonia Orch, Ambrosian Chorus *(rec live, London, 2/8/70)* Myto 2-▲ 2 MCD 91750 [ADD]
In Concert, w. Vincent Scalera (pno) *(rec live, 3/30/84)* Bongiovanni ▲ GB 2502-2 [ADD]
Leoncavallo, R.:Pagliacci, w. J. Carlyle (sop), U. Benelli (bar), R. Panerai (bar), G. Taddei (bar), H. von Karajan (cnd), La Scala Orch [I] Deutsche Grammophon 3-▲ 419257-2 [ADD]
Leoncavallo, R.:Pagliacci, w. C. Gavazzi (sop—Nedda), C. Bergonzi (ten—Canio), S. Di Tommaso (ten—Beppe), C. Tagliabue (bar—Tonio), M. Rossi (bar—Silvio), A. Simonetto (cnd), Turin RAI SO, Turin RAI Chorus *(rec Turin, 1951)* Cetra Classic 2-▲ CDO 27 [ADD]
Leoncavallo, R.:Pagliacci, w. Joan Carlyle (sop—Nedda/Colombina), Carlo Bergonzi (ten—Canio/Pagliaccio), Franco Ricciardi (ten—Villager), Ugo Benelli (bar—Peppe/Arlecchino), Rolando Panerai (bar—Silvio), Giuseppe Taddei (bar—Tonio/Taddeo), Giuseppe Morresi (bass—Villager), H. von Karajan (cnd), La Scala Orch, La Scala Chorus *(rec La Scala, Milan, Oct 1965)* Deutsche Grammophon ("The Originals" series) ▲ 449727-2 [ADD]
Mascagni, P.:Cavalleria rusticana, w. F. Cossotto (mez), G. Guelfi (bar), H. von Karajan (cnd), La Scala Orch, La Scala Chorus [I] Deutsche Grammophon 3-▲ 419257-2 [ADD]
Massenet, J.:Werther, w. E. Ravaglia (sop), B. Casoni (mez), D. Trimarchi (bar), O. de Fabritiis (cnd), Naples Teatro San Carlo Orch, Naples Teatro San Carlo Chorus [I] *(rec live, Naples, 2/13/69)* Melodram 2-▲ 27058 [AAD]
Ponchielli, A.:La Gioconda, w. R. Tebaldi (sop), *(other soloists unknown),* L. Gardelli (cnd), St. Cecilia Academy Orch Rome, St. Cecilia Academy Chorus Rome London 3-▲ 430042-2 [ADD]
Puccini, G.:La Bohème, w. R. Tebaldi (sop), E. Bastianini (bar), C. Siepi (b-bar), T. Serafin (cnd), St. Cecilia Academy Orch Rome, St. Cecilia Academy Chorus Rome Enterprise ("Flowers" series) 2-▲ ENTBL 15 [ADD]
Puccini, G.:La Bohème, w. L. Albanese (sop), L. Hurley (sop), C. Harvuot (bar), M. Sereni (bar), N. Scott (bass), E. Flagello (bass), T. Schippers (cnd), New York Metropolitan Opera Orch, New York Metropolitan Opera Chorus *(rec Feb. 15, 1958)* Golden Age of Opera 2-▲ GAO 139/40 [ADD]
Puccini, G.:La Bohème, w. R. Tebaldi (sop), G. d'Angelo (sop), E. Bastianini (bar), C. Siepi (b-bar), T. Serafin (cnd), St. Cecilia Academy Orch Rome, St. Cecilia Academy Chorus Rome [I] London 2-▲ 425534-2 [ADD]
Puccini, G.:La Bohème (sels), w. R. Tebaldi (sop), E. Bastianini (bar), C. Siepi (b-bar), T. Serafin (cnd), St. Cecilia Academy Orch Rome, St. Cecilia Academy Chorus Rome—scenes & arias London ▲ 421301-2 [ADD]
Puccini, G.:Edgar, w. R. Scotto (sop), G. Killebrew (mez), V. Sardinero (bar), E. Queler (cnd), New York City Opera Orch, New York Schola Cantorum *(rec in concert at Carnegie Hall, 4/13/77)* CBS 2-▲ M2K 34584
Puccini, G.:Madama Butterfly, w. R. Tebaldi (sop), F. Cossotto (mez), E. Sordello (bar), T. Serafin (cnd), St. Cecilia Academy Orch Rome, St. Cecilia Academy Chorus Rome [I] London 2-▲ 425531-2 [ADD]
Puccini, G.:Madama Butterfly, w. R. Scotto (sop), A. di Stasio (mez), R. Panerai (bar), J. Barbirolli (cnd), Rome Opera Orch, Rome Opera Chorus [I] EMI Classics ("Studio" series) ▲ CDM 63411 ∎ EG 63411
Puccini, G.:Madama Butterfly, w. R. Scotto (sop), R. Panerai (bar), J. Barbirolli (cnd), Rome Opera Orch, Rome Opera Chorus EMI Classics 2-▲ CDMB 69654
Puccini, G.:Madama Butterfly (sels), w. R. Scotto (sop), J. Barbirolli (cnd), Rome Opera Orch, Rome Opera Chorus EMI Classics ∎ 4XS 36567
Puccini, G.:Madama Butterfly (sels), w. R. Tebaldi (sop), F. Cossotto (mez), E. Sordello (bar), T. Serafin (cnd), St. Cecilia Academy Orch Rome, St. Cecilia Academy Chorus Rome [I] London ("Opera Gala" series) ▲ 421873-2 [ADD]
Puccini, G.:Madama Butterfly (sels), w. R. Tebaldi (sop), E. Sordello (bar), T. Serafin (cnd), St. Cecilia Academy Orch Rome, St. Cecilia Academy Chorus Rome London ▲ 417733-2 [ADD]
Puccini, G.:Tosca, w. M. Callas (sop), T. Gobbi (bar), G. Prêtre (cnd), Paris Conservatory Societé des Concerts Orch, Paris Opera Chorus [I] EMI Classics ("Studio" series) 2-▲ CDMB 69974 [ADD]
Puccini, G.:Tosca (sels), w. Luisa Maragliano (sop), F. Scaglia (cnd), *(orch unknown)*—Mario... son qui *(rec Naples, 1965)* Golden Age of Opera ▲ GAO 204 [ADD]
Puccini, G.:Tosca (sels), w. M. Callas (sop), R. Scotto (sop), A. Kraus (ten), T. Gobbi (bar), G. Prêtre (cnd), Orch de Paris EMI Classics ▲ ZDM 63087
Rosanna Carteri, Carlo Bergonzi, w. R. Carteri (sop), Turin RAI SO [cnd:F. M. Pradelli] *(rec Jan. 30, 1960)* Incontri Memorabili ("Martini & Rossi Concerts" series) ▲ 5026
Tosti, P.F.:Songs, w. E. Müller (cnd), Rome CO [I] Orfeo ▲ 073831 [DDD]
Verdi, G.:Aida, w. R. Tebaldi (sop) G. Simionato (mez), C. MacNeil (bar), A. van Mill (bass), H. von Karajan (cnd), Vienna PO, Vienna State Opera Chorus [I] London 3-▲ 414087-2 [ADD]
Verdi, G.:Aida, w. R. Tebaldi (sop) G. Simionato (mez), C. MacNeil (bar), A. van Mill (bass), H. von Karajan (cnd), Vienna PO, Vienna State Opera Chorus [I] London ("Jubilee" series) ▲ 417763-2 [ADD]
Verdi, G.:Attila, w. C. Deutekom (sop), G. Raimondi (ten), S. Milnes (bar), L. Gardelli (cnd), Royal PO, Ambrosian Singers Philips 2-▲ 426115-2
Verdi, G.:Un ballo in maschera, w. Leyla Gencer (sop), Adriana Lazzarini (mez), Mario Zanasi (bar), O. de Fabritiis (cnd), Bologna Teatro Comunale Orch, Bologna Teatro Comunale Chorus *(rec live, Nov 28, 1961)* Arkadia 2-▲ 622
Verdi, G.:Un ballo in maschera, w. L. Price (sop), R. Merrill (bar), E. Leinsdorf (cnd), RCA Italian Opera Orch [I] RCA Gold Seal 2-▲ 6645-2-RG [ADD]
Verdi, G.:Un ballo in maschera, w. B. Nilsson (sop), G. Simionato (mez), C. MacNeil (bar), G. Solti (cnd), St. Cecilia Academy Orch Rome, St. Cecilia Academy Chorus Rome [I] London 2-▲ 425655-2 [ADD]

Bergonzi, Carlo (ten) (cont.)
Verdi, G.:Don Carlos, w. R. Tebaldi (sop), G. Bumbry (mez), D. Fischer-Dieskau (bar), N. Ghiaurov (bass), G. Solti (cnd), Royal Opera House Orch Covent Garden, Royal Opera House Chorus Covent Garden [1886 5-act Italian version] [I] London 3-▲ 421114-2 [ADD]
Verdi, G.:Ernani, w. L. Price (sop), M. Sereni (bar), E. Flagello (bass), T. Schippers (cnd), RCA Italian Opera Orch [I] RCA Gold Seal 2-▲ 6503-2-RG [ADD]
Verdi, G.:Ernani, w. Licia Galvano (sop—Giovanna), Leyla Gencer (sop—Elvira), Carlo Bergonzi (ten—Ernani), Nino Valori (ten—Don Riccardo), Piero Cappuccilli (bar—Don Carlo), Alessandro Cassis (bar—Jago), Ruggero Raimondi (bass—Don Ruy Gomez de Silva), G. Gavazzeni (cnd), Catania Teatro Massimo Bellini Orch, Catania Teatro Massimo Bellini Chorus *(rec live, Catania, Jan 15, 1972)* Arkadia 2-▲ 621 [ADD]
Verdi, G.:La forza del destino (sels), w. Raina Kabalvanska (sop), I. Savini (cnd), Barcelona Teatro Liceo Orch, Barcelona Gran Teatro de Liceo Chorus *(rec live, Nov 13, 1972)* Arkadia ▲ 499
Verdi, G.:La forza del destino (sels), w. I. Ligabue (sop), Meliciani (sgr), G. Gavazzeni (cnd), La Scala Orch, La Scala Chorus [substantial highlights] *(rec live, Milan 12/7/65)* Myto 2-▲ 2 MCD 91750 [ADD]
Verdi, G.:La forza del destino (sels), w. Meliciani (sgr), A. Votto (cnd), La Scala Orch—La vita è inferno all'infelice; O tu che in seno; Invano, Alvaro [I] *(rec live 12/7/65)* Melodram 2-▲ 27058 [AAD]
Verdi, G.:Giovanna d'Arco, w. Renata Tebaldi (sop), Rolando Panerai (bar), A. Simonetto (cnd), Milan RAI SO, Milan RAI Chorus *(rec Milan, May 26, 1951)* Pantheon 2-▲ PHE 6610 (m)
Verdi, G.:Giovanna d'Arco, w. R. Tebaldi (sop), R. Panerai (bar), A. Simonetto (cnd), Milan RAI Orch, Milan RAI Chorus [I] *(rec live)* Melodram 2-▲ 27021
Verdi, G.:I lombardi alla prima crociata (sels), w. A. Millo (sop—Giselda), C. Bergonzi (ten—Oronte), P. Plishka (bass—Pagano), E. Queler (cnd), *(orch unknown)*—4 acts abridged *(rec live 1986)* Legato Classics ▲ LCD 105-1 [ADD]
Verdi, G.:Luisa Miller, w. A. Moffo (sop), S. Verrett (mez), C. MacNeil (bar), G. Tozzi (bass), F. Cleva (cnd), RCA Italian Opera Orch [I] RCA Gold Seal 2-▲ 6646-2-RG [ADD]
Verdi, G.:Macbeth, w. L. Rysanek (sop), L. Warren (bar), J. Hines (bass), E. Leinsdorf (cnd), Metropolitan Opera Orch, New York Metropolitan Opera Chorus [I] RCA Gold Seal 2-▲ 4516-2-RG [ADD]
Verdi, G.:Oberto, Conte di San Bonifacio, w. G. Dimitrova (sop), R. Baldani (mez), A. Browner (mez), R. Panerai (bar), L. Gardelli (cnd), Munich RSO, Munich Radio Chorus [I] Orfeo ▲ 175881 [DDD]
Verdi, G.:Oberto, Conte di San Bonifacio, w. G. Dimitrova (sop), R. Baldani (mez), A. Browner (mez), R. Panerai (bar), L. Gardelli (cnd), Munich RSO, Munich Radio Chorus [I] Orfeo 2-▲ 105842 [DDD] 3-■ A 105843 F
Verdi, G.:Simon Boccanegra, w. A. Stella (sop—Maria), C. Bergonzi (ten—Gabriele), G. Giorgetti (bar—Pietro), W. Monachesi (bar—Paolo), M. Petri (bar—Jacopo), P. Silveri (bar—Simon), F. Molinari-Pradelli (cnd), Rome Radio Orch, Rome RAI Chorus *(rec 1951)* Cetra Classic ▲ CDO 23 [ADD]
Verdi, G.:La traviata, w. M. Caballé (sop), S. Milnes (bar), G. Prêtre (cnd), RCA Italian Opera Orch RCA Gold Seal 2-▲ 6180-2 RC [ADD]
Verdi, G.:La traviata, w. J. Sutherland (sop), R. Merrill (bar), J. Pritchard (cnd), Florence Maggio Musicale Orch, Florence Maggio Musicale Chorus [I] London 2-▲ 411877-2 [ADD]
Verdi, G.:La traviata (sels), w. J. Sutherland (sop), R. Merrill (bar), J. Pritchard (cnd), Florence Maggio Musicale Orch London ▲ 421325-2 [ADD]
Verdi, G.:Il trovatore, w. G. Tucci (sop), G. Simionato (mez), P. Cappuccilli (bar), G. Gavazzeni (cnd), La Scala Orch, La Scala Chorus *(rec live, Moscow 1965)* Melodram 2-▲ MEL 27008

Bergström, Anders (bar)
Donizetti, G.:Maria Stuarda (sels), w. Lena Nordin (sop), Carina Morling (mez), Ingus Petterssons (ten), Tord Wallström (bar), Maria Wieslander (org), Sven Åberg (chit), Chrichan Larsson (vc), Nanette Nowels-Stenholm (pno), M. Guidarini (cnd), *(orch unknown)* Swedish Society ▲ SCD 1076

Berkes, János (ten)
Kálmán, I.:Gräfin Mariza (sels), w. Ingrid Kirtesi (sop), Zsuzsa Csonka (sop), L. Kovács (cnd), Hungarian Operetta Orch—Komm mit nach Varasadin *(rec Budapest, Oct 1995)* Naxos ▲ 8.550941 [DDD]
Kálmán, I.:Gräfin Mariza (sels), w. Ingrid Kirtesi (sop), Zsuzsa Csonka (sop), L. Kovács (cnd), Hungarian Operetta Orch—Auftrittsleid Mariza; Komm Zigány; Grüss mir die süssen *(rec Budapest, Jan 1996)* Naxos ▲ 8.550943 [DDD]
Lehár, F.:Operetta Arias, w. Ingrid Kirtesi (sop), Zsuzsa Csonka (sop), L. Kovács (cnd), Hungarian Operetta Orch—Freunde, das Leben ist lebenswert!; Meine Lippen, sie küssen si heiss [both from Giuditta]; O Mädchen, mein Mädchen [from Friedericke]; Dein ist mein ganzes Herz; Wer hat die Liebe uns ins Herz gesenkt?; Immer nur lächeln; Von Apfelblüten einen Kranz [all from Das Land des Lächlens]; Lippen schweigen [from Die lustige Witwe] *(rec Budapest, Oct 1995)* Naxos ▲ 8.550941 [DDD]
Lehár, F.:Paganini (sels), w. Ingrid Kirtesi (sop), Zsuzsa Csonka (sop), L. Kovács (cnd), Hungarian Operetta Orch—Liebe, du Himmel auf Erden *(rec Budapest, Jan 1996)* Naxos ▲ 8.550943 [DDD]
Stolz, R.:Arias, w. Ingrid Kirtesi (sop), Zsuzsa Csonka (sop), L. Kovács (cnd), Hungarian Operetta Orch—Ich liebe dich! [from Zauber der Bohème]; Zwei gerzen im Dreiviertaltakt; Du sollst der Kaiser meiner Seele sein [both from Der Favorit]; Adieu, mein kleiner Gardeoffizer [from Das Lied ist aus] *(rec Budapest, Jan 1996)* Naxos ▲ 8.550943 [DDD]
Strauss (II), Joh.:Arias, w. Ingrid Kirtesi (sop), Zsuzsa Csonka (sop), L. Kovács (cnd), Hungarian Operetta Orch—Óv; Klänge der Heimat; Trinke Liebchen! Trinke schnell!; Mein Herr Marquis [all from Die Fledermaus]; Laguenwaltzer [from Eine Nacht in Venedig] *(rec Budapest, Jan 1996)* Naxos ▲ 8.550943 [DDD]
Strauss (II), Joh.:Arias, w. Ingrid Kirtesi (sop), Zsuzsa Csonka (sop), L. Kovács (cnd), Hungarian Operetta Orch—Óv; Wer uns getraut; Als flotter Geist [both from Der Zigeunerbaron]; Frühlingstimmen (waltz); Komm in die Gondel [from Eine Nacht in Venedig] *(rec Budapest, Oct 1995)* Naxos ▲ 8.550941 [DDD]
Zeller, C.A.:Vogelhändler (sels), w. Ingrid Kirtesi (sop), Zsuzsa Csonka (sop), L. Kovács (cnd), Hungarian Operetta Orch—Wie mein Ahn'l zwanzig Jahr' *(rec Budapest, Jan 1996)* Naxos ▲ 8.550943 [DDD]

Berkman, Louis (bar)
Beethoven, L. van:An die ferne Geliebte, w. G. Johnson (pno) [G] Duo ▲ 89010
Beethoven, L. van:Songs, w. G. Johnson (pno)—Gellert-Lieder, Op. 48, Nos. 1-6; Six Goethe-Lieder (Opp. 52/4 & 7, 75/2 & 3, 83/1 & 2); Six Italian Love Songs (Op. 82/2-4; Op. 88; WoO 124; WoO 133) [G,I] Duo ▲ 89010

Berlin, P. (mez)
Crawford, R.:Songs (3), w. J. Ostryniec (ob), D.C. Armstrong (perc), P. Hoffman (pno) CRI ▲ CD 658 [ADD]

Berman, Karel (bass)
Berman, K.:Songs (4), "Poupata", w. P. Charvát (pno) [Czech] *(rec 2-3/85)* Channel Classics ▲ CCS 3191 [ADD]
Dvořák, A.:The Cunning Peasant, w. Eva Depoltová (sop), Václav Zítek (bar), F. Vajnar (cnd), Prague RSO, Prague Radio Chorus Supraphon 2-▲ SUP 0019 [DDD]
Dvořák, A.:The Jacobin, w. D. Šounová-Broukov (sop), V. Přybl (ten), J. Pinkas (cnd), Brno State PO, Kühn Chorus Supraphon 2-▲ SUP 11 2190 [AAD]
Haas, P.:Songs (4) to the Texts of Chinese Poetry, w. A. Holoček (pno) [Cz] *(rec 2-3/85)* Channel Classics ▲ CCS 3191 [ADD]
Mahler, G.:Songs from Rückert, w. V. Neumann (cnd), Czech PO—3 songs [G] *(rec Oct. 10-12, 1977)* Supraphon 2-▲ 11 1978-2

Bern, Jeni (sop)
Purcell, H.:Odes & Welcome Songs (misc), w. Susan Bisatt (sop), William Purefoy (ct), Christopher Robson (ct), Ian Honeyman (ten), Thomas Guthrie (bass), R. Glenton (cnd), Orch of the Golden Age, Golden Age Choir—The noise of foreign wars (fragment) [ed. by Bruce Wood] *(rec Manchester Grammar School, England, May 13 & 14, 1995)* Naxos ▲ 8.553444 [DDD]
Purcell, H.:Raise, Raise the Voice, w. Susan Bisatt (sop), William Purefoy (ct), Christopher Robson (ct), Ian Honeyman (ten), Thomas Guthrie (bass), R. Glenton (cnd), Orch of the Golden Age, Golden Age Choir *(rec Manchester Grammar School, England, May 13 & 14, 1995)* Naxos ▲ 8.553444 [DDD]

Bern, Jeni (sop) (cont.)
Purcell, H.:Te Deum & Jubilate, w. Susan Bisatt (sop), William Purefoy (ct), Christopher Robson (ct), Ian Honeyman (ten), Thomas Guthrie (bass), David Staff (tpt), R. Glenton (cnd), Orch of the Golden Age, Golden Age Choir *(rec Manchester Grammar School, England, May 13 & 14, 1995)* Naxos ▲ 8.553444 [DDD]
Purcell, H.:Welcome to All the Pleasures, w. Susan Bisatt (sop), William Purefoy (ct), Christopher Robson (ct), Ian Honeyman (ten), Thomas Guthrie (bass), R. Glenton (cnd), Orch of the Golden Age, Golden Age Choir *(rec Manchester Grammar School, England, May 13 & 14, 1995)* Naxos ▲ 8.553444 [DDD]

Bernac, Pierre (bar)
Chabrier, E.:Songs, w. F. Poulenc (pno)—L'île heureuse; Villanelle des petits canards [F] *(rec 1950)* Sony Masterworks (Portrait) ▲ MPK 47684 [ADD]
Poulenc, F.:Le Bal masqué, w. Francis Poulenc (pno), L. Frémaux (cnd), Paris Opera Orch Soloists Adès ▲ ADE 202522 [AAD]
Poulenc, F.:Songs, w. Francis Poulenc (pno)—Tel jour, telle nuit; Dans le jardin d'Anna; Reine des mouttes; C'est ainsi que tu es; Paganini; "C"; Ftes galantes; Montparnasse EMI Classics ▲ CDC 54605

Bernadet, Andrée (mez)
Bizet, G.:Carmen (sels), w. C. Supervia (mez), A. Vavon (sop), G. Micheletti (ten), A. Endreze (bar), G. Cloëz (cnd), Paris Opéra-Comique Orch, Paris Opéra-Comique Chorus—8 arias & scenes *(rec Paris 1930)* Nimbus ("Prima Voce" series) 2-▲ NI 7836/7 [ADD]
Bizet, G.:Carmen (sels), w. C. Supervia (mez), A. Vavon (sop), J.-F. Delmas (b-bar), G. Micheletti (ten), A. Endreze (bar), G. Cloëz (cnd), Paris Opéra-Comique Orch, Paris Opéra-Comique Chorus—14 arias & scenes [F] *(rec Paris, 1930)* The Classical Collector ▲ FDC 2002 (m) [AAD]

Bernard, Annabelle (sgr)
Dallapiccola, L.:Ulisse, w. C. Gayer (sop), E. Saedén (bar), V. von Halem (bass), L. Maazel (cnd), Berlin German Opera Orch, Berlin German Opera Chorus *(rec live, Berlin 9/28/68)* Stradivarius 2-▲ STR 10063 [ADD]

Bernard, D. (sgr)
Gounod, C.:Faust, w. V. de los Angeles (sop), C. Ward (sgr), M. Mayhoff (sgr), R. Tucker (ten), H. Noel (sgr), N. Moscona (bass), W. Herbert (cnd), New Orleans Opera Orch [F] *(rec Feb. 26, 1953)* Legato Classics 2-▲ LCD 167-2 [AAD]
Puccini, G.:Madama Butterfly, w. V. de los Angeles (sop), R. Nadell (mez), B. Faulkner (sgr), W. Fredericks (sgr), J. Thresh (sgr), R. Torigi (sgr), A. Cosenza (bar), W. Herbert (cnd), New Orleans Opera Orch, New Orleans Opera Chorus *(rec live March 18, 1954)* Legato Classics 2-▲ LCD 168-2 [ADD]

Bernard, Donald (bar)
Offenbach, J.:Les Contes d'Hoffmann, w. Beverly Sills (sop—Olympia/Giulietta/Antonia/Stella), Edith Evans (mez—Nicklausse/Mother's Voice), Michael Devlin (ten—Spalanzani), André Turp (ten—Hoffmann), Luigi Vellucci (ten—Andrès/Cochenille/Pitichinaccio/Frantz), Donald Bernard (bar—Luther/Schlemil), Norman Treigle (bass—Lindorf/Coppélius/Dapertutto/Dr. Miracle), John West (bass—Crespel), Alton Brim (sgr—Nathanaël), Rodney Hall (sgr—Hermann), K. Andersson (cnd), New Orleans Opera Orch, New Orleans Opera Chorus *(rec Feb 27, 1964)* VAI Audio 2-▲ VAIA 1121-2 [ADD]

Bernard, Marie Stéphane (sop)
Shostakovich, D.:Sym 14, w. Lionel Peintre (bass), R. Hayrabedian (cnd), Musicatreize Opus 111 ▲ OPS 30165

Bernardini, Don (ten)
Bellini, V.:Beatrice di Tenda, w. E. Gruberová (sop—Beatrice), V. Kasarova (mez—Agnese), D. Bernardini (ten—Orombello), B. Robinšak (ten—Anichino), I. Morosov (ten—Filippo Maria Visconti), D. Sumegi (bass—Rizzardo), P. Steinberg (cnd), Austrian RSO, Austrian Radio Chorus [I] *(rec live, Vienna Concert House 1/30 & 2/1/92)* Nightingale Classics 2-▲ NC 070560-2 [DDD]
Donizetti, G.:Linda di Chamounix, w. Edita Gruberová (sop), Monica Groop (mez), Ettore Kim (sgr), F. Haider (cnd), Swedish RSO, Mikaeli Chamber Choir Nightingale Classics 3-▲ NIG 70561
Donizetti, G.:Roberto Devereux, w. Edita Gruberová (sop), Delores Ziegler (mez), Ettore Kim (sgr), F. Haider (cnd), Strasbourg PO, Rhine Opera Chorus Nightingale Classics 2-▲ NIG 70563
Paisiello, G.:Nina, o sia La pazza per amore, w. M. Bolgan (sop), F. Pediconi (sop), F. Musinu (bass), G. Surian (bass), R. Bonynge (cnd), Catania Teatro Massimo Bellini Orch, Catania Teatro Massimo Bellini Chorus [I] *(rec live 1989)* Nuova Era 2-▲ 6872/73 [DDD]

Bernáth, Karol (ten)
Respighi, O.:La bella dormente nel bosco, w. Ivana Czaková (sop—Old Woman/Green Fairy), Adriana Kohútková (sop—Blue Fairy/Nightingale), Henrietta Lednárová (sop—Frog/Spindle), Jana Valásková (sop—Princess), Dagmar Pecková (mez—Cuckoo/Cat), Denisa Slepkovská (mez—Queen/Duchess), Karol Bernáth (ten—Doctor), Guillermo Dominguez (ten—Prince April), Igor Pasek (ten—Jester), Ján Durco (bar—Ambassador), Richard Haan (bar—King/Woodcutter), Stanislav Benacka (bass—Doctor), Anton Kúrnava (bass—Doctor), Marián Smolárik (bass—Doctor), M. Adriano (nar—Mr. Dollar Chèques), M. Adriano (cnd), Slovak RSO Bratislava, Ján Rozehnal (cnd), Slovak Phil Chorus *(rec Concert Hall of the Slovak Radio, Bratislava, June 8-20, 1994)* Marco Polo ("Opera Classics" series) ▲ 8.223742 [DDD]

Bernát-Klein, Gundula (sop)
Bach, J.S.:Magnificat, BWV 243, w. Helen Donath (sop), Birgit Finnilä (alt), Peter Schreier (ten), Barry McDaniel (bass), W. Gönnenwein (cnd), German Bach Soloists, South German Madrigal Choir [E♭ version] *(rec Stuttgart Radio, 1966)* Bayer ▲ 100081 [ADD]

Bernheimer, Julia (mez)
Dvořák, A.:Mass, w. G. Schmid (sop), J. Reinprecht (ten), A. Sramek (bar), F. Wolf (cnd), St. Augustin Orch, St. Augustin Chorus [L] *(rec 1987)* Preiser ▲ 93378 [ADD]
Mozart, W.A.:Music of, w. Gundula Janowitz (sop), Martyn Hill (ten), David Thomas (bass), Anthony Halstead (hn), Colin Lawson (b cl), Christopher Kite (pno), R. Goodman (cnd), Hanover Band—Cons for Hn, K.412, 417, 447, 494a & 495; Sym No. 40; Con for Cl; Eine kleine Nachtmusik; Requiem; Sym No. 41; Con No. 20 for Pno; Serenata Notturna Nimbus 4-▲ NI 1791 [DDD]
Mozart, W.A.:Requiem, w. G. Janowitz (sop), M. Hill (ten), D. Thomas (bass), R. Goodman (cnd), Hanover Band, Hanover Chorus [period instruments; H.C. Robbins Landon edition] Nimbus 4-▲ NI 1791 [DDD]
Mozart, W.A.:Requiem, w. G. Janowitz (sop), M. Hill (ten), D. Thomas (bass), R. Goodman (cnd), Hanover Band, Hanover Chorus [period instruments; H.C. Robbins Landon's edition; L] Nimbus ▲ NI 5241-2 [DDD]

Bernhofen, Helmut (sgr)
Henze, H.-W.:Elegy for Young Lovers, w. Regina Schudel (sop), Richard Lloyd Morgan (bass), Lawrence Richard (bass), Bruno Fath (sgr), Aurelia Hajek (sgr), Silvia Weiss (sgr), B. Jones (cnd), Berlin Chamber Opera Orch *(rec Berlin)* Deutsche Schallplatten 2-▲ DS 1050

Bernstein, Leonard (nar)
Prokofiev, S.:Peter & the Wolf, w. L. Bernstein (cnd), New York PO *(rec Symphony Hall, Boston, Feb 14-15, 1992)* Sony Classical ("Greatest Hits" series) ▲ MLK 69249 [ADD] ■ LT 69
Prokofiev, S.:Peter & the Wolf, w. L. Bernstein (cnd), New York PO CBS ▲ MYK 37765 ■ MYT 37765
Saint-Saëns, C.:Carnival of the Animals, w. L. Bernstein (cnd), New York PO CBS ▲ MYK 37765 ■ MYT 37765

Bernstein, Richard (bass)
Axelrod, L.:Songs, w. Louisa Ann Parks (sop), Michael Horton (ten), Nmon Ford-Livene (ten), Malcolm Mackenzie (bar), M. Beltrami (cnd)—sels w. lyrics by Burns, Browning, Keats, Morris, Poe, Rossetti, Shelley, Wordsworth & Yeats Marquis ▲ MAR 171

Bernts, Gérard (bar)
Meijering, Chiel:St. Louis Blues, w. Andrea van Beek (sop), Francine van der Heijden (sop), Jeanette Huizinga (mez), Rein Kolpa (ten), Willem-Jan van Deuveren (ten), John Vredeveldt (ten), W. Megens (cnd), De Ereprijs Orch [I] *(rec Schouwburg Arnhem, Mar 10, 1995)* Donemus 2-▲ neos 01-02

Berntsen, Anne-Lise (nar)
Schoenberg, A.:Pierrot lunaire, w. C. Eggen (cnd), Borealis Ensemble Victoria ▲ VCD 19088

Berntsen, Anne-Lise (sop)
Engleskyts:Angels' Arrows, w. Nils Henrik Asheim (pno) Norway Music ▲ FXCD 136

Berntsen, Anne-Lise (sop) (cont.)
Kvandal, J.:Music of, w. H. Blomstedt (cnd), Oslo PO—Symphonic Epos, Op. 21; Con for Fl & Strs, Op. 22; Qt No. 2 for Strs, Op. 27; Qt for Fl, Vn, Va & Vc, Op. 42; Duo for Vn & Vc, Op. 19; Son for Vn, Op. 45; Da Lontano for Alto Fl & Pno, Op. 32; Intro & Allegro for Hn & Pno, Op. 30; Aria Cadenza e Finale, Op. 24; Stevtoner, Op. 40 Norway Music 2-▲ CD 4986
Schoenberg, A.:Qt 2 Strs, w. C. Eggen (cnd), Borealis Ensemble Victoria ▲ VCD 19088

Beronesi, Debora (sop)
Graun, K.H.:Cesare e Cleopatra, w. Janet Williams (sop), Lynne Dawson (sop), Curtis Rayam (ten), R. Jacobs (cnd), Concerto Cologne, Berlin State Opera Chorus members Serenissima 3-▲ SER 360171 [DDD]
Jommelli, N.:La Passione di Gesù Cristo, w. Anke Herrmann (sgr), Jeffrey Francis (ten), Maurizio Picconi (sgr), A. de Marchi (cnd), Berlin Baroque Academy, Eufonia, Sigismondo D'India *(rec Mar 31–Apr 4, 1996)* K617 2-▲ 7063 [DDD]

Berridge, Simon (sgr)
Purcell, H.:The Indian Queen, w. Catherine Bott (sop—Orazia/Married Woman), Emma Kirkby (sop—Indian Girl/Zempoalla/Cupid), John Mark Ainsley (ten—Indian Boy/Fame/Follower of Cupid/Aerial Spirits), Julian Podger (ten—Follower of Envy/Aerial Spirit), Gerald Finley (bar—Conjurer/Hymen/Follower of Cupid), Helen Parker (sgr—Aerial Spirits), David Thomas (bass—Envy/High Priest/Married Man/Follower of Cupid), Simon Berridge (sgr—Follower of Envy), Libby Crabtree (sgr—Follower of Hymen/Aerial Spirit), Tommy Williams (sgr—God of Dreams), C. Hogwood (cnd), Academy of Ancient Music *(rec Walthamstow Assembly Hall, London, July 1994)* L'Oiseau-Lyre ▲ 444339-2 [DDD]

Berry, Noreen (mez)
Verdi, G.:Macbeth, w. Amy Shuard (sop—Lady Macbeth), Noreen Berry (mez—Lady-in-waiting), John Dobson (ten—Malcolm), André Turp (ten—Macduff), Tito Gobbi (bar—Macbeth), Edgar Boniface (bass—Servant), Rydderch Davies (bass—Doctor), Forbes Robinson (bass—Banco), Jean Holmes (sgr—Apparition), Celia Penny (sgr—Apparition), Glynne Thomas (sgr—Apparition), Brian Wrigt (sgr—Araldo), F. Molinari-Pradelli (cnd), Royal Opera House Orch, Royal Opera House Chorus Covent Garden *(rec London, Apr 8, 1960)* Bella Voce 2-▲ 7203 [AAD]

Berry, Walter (bar)
Bach, J.S.:St. Matthew Passion, w. G. Janowitz (sop), C. Ludwig (mez), H. Laubenthal (ten), P. Schreier (ten), D. Fischer-Dieskau (bar), H. von Karajan (cnd), Berlin PO, Vienna Singverein, German Opera Chorus [G] Deutsche Grammophon 3-▲ 419789-2 [ADD]
Haydn, J.:Mass 10, "Kriegsmesse", "Paukenmesse", w. Netania Davrath (sop), Hilde Rössl-Majdan (alt), Anton Dermota (ten), Anton Heiller (org), R. Harand (vc), M. Wöldike (cnd), Vienna State Opera Orch, Vienna State Opera Chorus *(rec May 14–16, 1960)* Vanguard Classics ("The Bach Guild" series) ▲ OVC 2518 [ADD]
Mozart, W.A.:Nozze di Figaro, w. Anneliese Rothenberger (sop), Hilde Gueden (sop), Edith Mathis (sop), Peter Schreier (ten), Hermann Prey (bar), O. Suitner (cnd), Dresden Staatskapelle Berlin Classics 3-▲ BER 2096 [ADD]
Schubert, Franz:Die Verschworenen, w. Ilona Steingruber (sop—Countess), Elizabeth Roon (mez—Helene), Laurence Dutoit (trb—Isella), Walter Anton (ten—Udolin), Walter Berry (bar—Count), Rudolf Kreutzberger (sgr—Astolf), F. Grossmann (cnd), Vienna SO, Vienna Academy Chamber Choir Theorema ▲ TH 121178
Strauss (II), Joh.:Die Fledermaus (sels), w. Wilma Lipp (sop), Gerda Scheyer (sop), Christa Ludwig (mez), Anton Dermota (ten), Erich Kunz (bar), Eberhard Wachter (bar), O. Ackermann (cnd), Philharmonia Orch, London Phil Chorus Emperor Operetta ▲ KO 86340

Berry, William (bass)
Akademie Chamber Choir & Vienna SO, w. [cnd:Ferdinand Grossmann], Akademie Chamber Choir, Vienna SO, Elisabeth Roon (sop), Laurence Dutoit (sop), Daagmar Herrmann-Braun (cta), Erich Majkut (ten) Vox 90s ■ V9-9903
Bach, J.S.:Christmas Oratorio, w. E. Roon (sop), D.H. Braun (mez), E. Majkut (ten), L. Dutoit (echo), B. Seidlhofer (hpd), J. Nebois (org), F. Grossmann (cnd), Vienna SO, Akademie Chamber Choir Vox Box 2-▲ CDX 5096 [ADD]
Bach, J.S.:St. Matthew Passion, w. E. Schwarzkopf (sop), C. Ludwig (mez), N. Gedda (ten), S. Fischer-Dieskau (bar), O. Klemperer (cnd), Philharmonia Orch EMI Classics 3-▲ ZDMC 63058
Beethoven, L. van:Fidelio, w. Ingeborg Hallstein (sop—Marzelline), Christa Ludwig (mez—Leonore/Fidelio), Gerhard Unger (ten—Jaquino), Jon Vickers (ten—Florestan), Walter Berry (bass—Pizarro), Franz Crass (bass—Don Fernando), Gottlob Frick (bass—Rocco), O. Klemperer (cnd), Philharmonia Orch, Philharmonia Chorus EMI Classics 2-▲ CDCB 55170
Beethoven, L. van:Fidelio, w. Judith Blegen (sop), Leonie Rysanek (sop), Jon Vickers (ten), John Macurdy (bass), Giorgio Tozzi (bass), K. Böhm (cnd), San Francisco Opera Orch, San Francisco Opera Chorus Melodram 2-▲ CDM 27086
Beethoven, L. van:Fidelio, w. I. Hallstein (sop), C. Ludwig (mez), J. Vickers (ten), G. Unger (ten), G. Frick (bass), O. Klemperer (cnd), Philharmonia Orch, Philharmonia Chorus [G]; w. minimal dialog EMI Classics ("Studio" series) 2-▲ CDMB 69324 [ADD]
Beethoven, L. van:Missa Solemnis, w. G. Janowitz (sop), C. Ludwig (mez), F. Wunderlich (ten), H. von Karajan (cnd), Berlin PO, Vienna Singverein [L] Deutsche Grammophon ("Galleria" series) 2-▲ 423913-2 [ADD]
Beethoven, L. van:Sym 9, "Choral Sym", w. Jessye Norman (sop), Brigitte Fassbaender (mez), Plácido Domingo (ten), K. Böhm (cnd), Vienna PO, Vienna State Opera Chorus Deutsche Grammophon ("Masters" series) ▲ 445503-2 [DDD]
Beethoven, L. van:Sym 9, "Choral Sym", w. G. Janowitz (sop), H. Rössel-Majdan (alt), W. Kmentt (ten), H. von Karajan (cnd), Berlin PO, Vienna Singverein Deutsche Grammophon ("The Originals" series) ▲ 447401-2
Berg, A.:Lulu, w. A. Silja (sop), B. Fassbaender (mez), K. Moll (bass), H. Hotter (b-bar), A. Szramek (sgr), C. von Dohnányi (cnd), Vienna PO London 2-▲ 430415-2 [ADD]
Einem, G. von:Der Prozess, w. Lisa Della Casa (sop—Frl. Bürstner/Die Frau des Gerichtsdieners/Leni), Peter Klein (ten—Der Direktorstellvertreter/Der Student), Max Lorenz (ten—Josef K.), Erich Majkut (ten—Ein Bursche), László Szemere (ten—Titorelli), Alois Pernerstorfer (b-bar—Willem/Der Gerichtsdiener), Alfred Poell (b-bar—Der Advokat), Walter Berry (bass—Franz/Kanzleidirektor), Oskar Czerwenka (bass—Der Untersuchungsrichter/Der Prügler), Ludwig Hofmann (bass—Der Aufseher/Ein Passant/Der Geistliche/Der Fabrikant), Polly Batic (sgr—Frau Grubach), Endreh Koreh (sgr—Albert K.), Luise Leitner (sgr—Ein buckliges Mädchen), K. Böhm (cnd), Vienna PO, Vienna State Opera Chorus *(rec Aug 17, 1953)* Orfeo d'or ("Festspiel Dokumente" series) 2-▲ 392952 (m)
Gluck, C.W.:Iphigénie en Aulide, w. Inge Borkh (sop—Klytämnestra), Christa Ludwig (mez—Iphigenie), Elisabeth Steiner (mez—Artemis), James King (ten—Achilles), Otto Edelmann (b-bar), Alois Pernerstorfer (b-bar), K. Böhm (cnd), Vienna PO, Salzburg Festival Chamber Choir, Vienna State Opera Chorus *(rec Salzburg, Aug 3, 1962)* Orfeo d'or ("Festspiel Dikumente" series) 2-▲ C 428962 (m) [ADD]
Handel, G.F.:Giulio Cesare in Egitto, w. Lucia Popp (sop), Christa Ludwig (mez), Fritz Wunderlich (ten), F. Leitner (cnd), Munich PO, Bavarian Radio Chorus [G] *(rec live, Munich 7/1–5/65)* Verona 3-▲ 27035/37 [AAD]
Handel, G.F.:Giulio Cesare in Egitto, w. Lucia Popp (sop), Christa Ludwig (mez), Fritz Wunderlich (ten), F. Leitner (cnd), Munich PO, Bavarian Radio Chorus Melodram 3-▲ MEL 37059 [AAD]
Humperdinck, E.:Hänsel und Gretel, w. Lislotte Maikl (sop—Sandman/Dew Fairy), Anneliese Rothenberger (sop—Gretel), Irmgard Seefried (sop—Hänsel), Grace Hoffman (mez—Gertrude), Elisabeth Höngen (cta—Witch), Walter Berry (bass—Peter), A. Cluytens (cnd), Vienna PO, Vienna Boys' Choir EMI Classics 2-▲ CDMB 65661
Humperdinck, E.:Hänsel und Gretel, w. L. Popp (sop), B. Fassbaender (mez), J. Hamari (mez), A. Schlemm (mez), G. Solti (cnd), Vienna PO London 2-▲ 421111-2 [ADD]
Korngold, E.W.:Violanta, w. E. Martón (sop), S. Jerusalem (ten), M. Janowski (cnd), Munich RSO, Bavarian Radio Chorus [G] CBS ▲ MK 35909 [ADD]
Liebermann, R.:Die Schule der Frauen, w. Anneliese Rothenberger (sop—Agnes), Christa Ludwig (mez—Georgette), Nicolai Gedda (ten—Horace), Alois Pernerstorfer (b-bar—Gronte), Walter Berry (bass—Poquelin), Kurt Böhme (bass—Arnolphe), G. Szell (cnd), Vienna PO *(rec Salzburg, Aug 17, 1957)* Orfeo d'or ("Festspiel Dikumente" series) 2-▲ C 429962 (m) [ADD]
Mozart, W.A.:Complete Mozart Edition, w. E. Gruberova (sop), E. Mathis (sop), L. Popp (mez), F. Araiza (ten), P. Schreier (ten), Salzburg Mozarteum Orch Philips 8-▲ 422523-2 [ADD]

Berry, William (bass) (cont.)
Mozart, W.A.:Così fan tutte, w. E. Schwarzkopf (sop), H. Steffek (sop), C. Ludwig (mez), A. Kraus (ten), G. Taddei (bar), K. Böhm (cnd), Philharmonia Orch, Philharmonia Chorus [I] EMI Classics ("Studio" series) 3-▲ CDMC 69330 [ADD]
Mozart, W.A.:Don Giovanni, w. L. Price (sop), H. Gueden (sop), G. Sciurri (sop), F. Wunderlich (ten), E. Wächter (bar), H. von Karajan (cnd), Vienna PO, Vienna State Opera Chorus [I] *(rec live, 1963)* Verona 3-▲ 27065/67 (m) [AAD]
Mozart, W.A.:Don Giovanni, w. E. Grümmer (sop—D. Anna), R. Streich (sop—Zerlina), L. Della Casa (sop—D. Elvira), L. Simoneau (ten—Don Ottavio), C. Siepi (bass-baritone—Don Giovanni), W. Berry (bass—Masetto), G. Frick (bass—Il Commendatore), F. Corena (bass—Leporello), D. Mitropoulos (cnd), Vienna PO, Vienna State Opera Chorus *(rec Salzburg, July 24, 1956)* Sony Classical 3-▲ SM3K 64263 [ADD]
Mozart, W.A.:Don Giovanni, w. E. Schwarzkopf (sop), E. Grümmer (sop), E. Berger (sop), A. Dermota (ten), C. Siepi (b-bar), O. Edelmann (b-bar), W. Furtwängler (cnd), Vienna PO, Vienna State Opera Chorus *(rec 1953)* Arkadia 3-▲ 509 (m) [AAD]
Mozart, W.A.:Don Giovanni, w. E. Schwarzkopf (sop), E. Grümmer (sop), E. Berger (sop), A. Dermota (ten), C. Siepi (b-bar), O. Edelmann (b-bar), W. Furtwängler (cnd), Vienna PO, Vienna State Opera Chorus *(rec Salzburg, Aug. 3, 1953)* EMI Classics ("Great Recordings of the Century" series) 2-▲ CDHB 63860
Mozart, W.A.:Don Giovanni, w. E. Grümmer (sop), L. Della Casa (sop), R. Streich (sop), L. Simoneau (ten), C. Siepi (b-bar), G. Frick (bass), F. Corena (bass), D. Mitropoulos (cnd), Vienna PO, Vienna State Opera Chorus [I] *(rec live, Salzburg, July 24, 1956)* Arkadia 3-▲ 552 (m) [ADD]
Mozart, W.A.:Don Giovanni (sels), w. A. Tomowa-Sintow (sop), T. Zylis-Gara (sop), E. Mathis (sop), S. Milnes (bar), K. Böhm (cnd), Vienna PO, Vienna State Opera Chorus—Scenes & Arias Deutsche Grammophon ▲ 429823-2 [ADD]
Mozart, W.A.:Missa, K.317, w. Wilma Lipp (sop), Christa Ludwig (alt), Murray Dickie (ten), J. Horenstein (cnd), Vienna SO Vox Legends 2-▲ CDX 5524
Mozart, W.A.:Missa, K.427, w. W. Lipp (sop), C. Ludwig (mez), M. Dickie (ten), F. Grossmann (cnd), Pro Musica Orch, Vienna Oratorio Chorus [L] *(rec stereo, 1958)* Preiser ▲ 90053 [AAD]
Mozart, W.A.:Nozze di Figaro (sels), w. Hilde Gueden (sop), Anneliese Rothenberger (sop), Hermann Prey (bar), O. Suitner (cnd), Dresden Staatskapelle Berlin Classics ▲ BER 9079 [ADD]
Mozart, W.A.:Requiem, w. L. Price (sop), H. Rössl-Majdan (mez), F. Wunderlich (ten), H. von Karajan (cnd), Vienna PO, Vienna Singverein [L] *(rec live, Salzburg Festival, Aug. 24, 1960)* Melodram ▲ MEL 18003
Mozart, W.A.:Requiem, w. W. Lipp (sop), H. Rössl-Majdan (mez), A. Dermota (ten), H. von Karajan (cnd), Berlin PO, Vienna Singverein [L] *(rec 1961)* Deutsche Grammophon ("Resonance" series) ▲ 429160-2 [ADD] ■ 429160-4
Mozart, W.A.:Vesperae solennes, w. Wilma Lipp (sop), Christa Ludwig (alt), Murray Dickie (ten), J. Horenstein (cnd), Vienna SO Vox Legends 2-▲ CDX 5524
Mozart, W.A.:Zauberflöte, w. L. Della Casa (sop), E. Köth (sop), G. Sciurri (sop), L. Simoneau (ten), K. Böhme (bass), G. Szell (cnd), Vienna PO, Vienna State Opera Chorus [G] *(rec live at the Salzburg Festival, July 27, 1959)* Melodram ("Connaisseur" series) 2-▲ MEL 27505 (m) [AAD]
Mozart, W.A.:Zauberflöte, w. H. Gueden (sop), W. Lipp (sop), L. Simoneau (ten), K. Bohme (bass), K. Böhm (cnd), Vienna PO, Vienna State Opera Chorus London ("Grand Opera" series) 2-▲ 414362-2 [ADD]
Mozart, W.A.:Zauberflöte, w. Gundula Janowitz (sop—Pamina), Lucia Popp (sop—Queen of the Night), Nicolai Gedda (ten-Tamina), Walter Berry (bass—Papageno), Gottlob Frick (bass—Sarastro), O. Klemperer (cnd), Philharmonia Orch, Philharmonia Chorus EMI Classics 2-▲ CDCB 55173
Mozart, W.A.:Zauberflöte, w. G. Janowitz (sop), L. Popp (sop), R. Pütz (sop), N. Gedda (ten), G. Frick (bass), O. Klemperer (cnd), Philharmonia Orch, Philharmonia Chorus [without dialog; G] EMI Classics ("Studio" series) 2-▲ CDMB 69971 [ADD]
Pfitzner, H.:Palestrina, w. S. Jurinac (sop), C. Ludwig (mez), F. Wunderlich (ten), G. Stolze (ten), O. Wiener (bar), G. Frick (bass), R. Heger (cnd), Vienna State Opera Orch, Vienna State Opera Chorus *(rec live, Vienna 12/16/64)* Myto 3-▲ 3 MCD 92259 [ADD]
Schmidt, F.:Das Buch mit sieben Siegeln, w. H. Gueden (sop), I. Malaniuk (cta), A. Dermota (ten), F. Wunderlich (ten), D. Mitropoulos (cnd), Vienna PO, Vienna Singverein *(rec live, Salzburg Festival 1959)* Melodram 2-▲ MEL 27078
Schmidt, F.:Das Buch mit sieben Siegeln, w. Hilde Gueden (sop), Ira Malaniuk (cta), Anton Dermota (ten), Fritz Wunderlich (ten), D. Mitropoulos (cnd), Vienna PO, Vienna Singverein Sony Classical ("Festspiel Dokumente:Salzburger Festspiele" series) 2-▲ SM2K 68442
Smetana, B.:The Bartered Bride, w. T. Stratas (sop), R. Kollo (ten), A. Malta (bass), J. Krombholc (cnd), Munich RSO Eurodisc 2-▲ 7795-2-RG [ADD]
Strauss (II), Joh.:Die Fledermaus, w. H. Gueden (sop), E. Köth (sop), R. Resnik (mez), W. Kmentt (ten), G. Zampieri (ten), E. Wächter (bar), E. Kunz (bar), H. von Karajan (cnd), Vienna PO, Vienna State Opera Chorus, with Gala Sequence [G] London 2-▲ 421046-2 [ADD]
Strauss (II), Joh.:Die Fledermaus, w. H. Gueden (sop), R. Streich (sop), G. Di Stefano (ten), G. Stolze (ten), G. Zampieri (ten), E. Wächter (bar), E. Kunz (bar), H. von Karajan (cnd), Vienna State Opera Orch, Vienna State Opera Chorus [G] Arkadia 3-▲ 215 (m) [ADD]
Strauss (II), Joh.:Die Fledermaus (sels), w. W. Lipp (sop), R. Schock (ten), O. Schenck (nar), R. Stolz (cnd), Vienna SO [G] Eurodisc ▲ 25-8369 [ADD]
Strauss, R.:Arabella, w. H. Donath (sop), J. Varady (sop), D. Fischer-Dieskau (bar), A. Schmidt (bar), W. Sawallisch (cnd), Bavarian State Orch Orfeo 2-▲ 169882 [DDD]
Strauss, R.:Arias, w. C. Ludwig (mez), H. Hollreiser (cnd), German Opera Orch, German Opera Chorus—two of Ariadne's solo arias from Ariadne auf Naxos, duets from Elektra, Frau ohne Schatten, Rosenkavalier [G] *(rec Berlin, 1963–64)* Tessitura ▲ 0049-2 [ADD]
Strauss, R.:Die Frau ohne Schatten, w. B. Nilsson (sop), L. Rysanek (sop), R. Hesse (mez), J. King (ten), K. Böhm (cnd), Vienna SO Deutsche Grammophon 3-▲ 445325-2
Strauss, R.:Der Rosenkavalier, w. G. Jones (sop), L. Popp (sop), C. Ludwig (mez), P. Domingo (ten), L. Bernstein (cnd), Vienna PO [G] CBS 3-▲ M3K 42564 [ADD]
Ullmann, V.:Kaiser von Atlantis, w. C. Oelze (sop—Bubikopf), I. Vermillion (mez—The Drummer), M. Petzold (ten—A Soldier), M. Kraus (ten—Kaiser Overall), H. Lippert (ten—Harlekin), F. Mazura (bar—The Loudspeaker), W. Berry (bass—Death), L. Zagrosek (cnd), Leipzig Gewandhaus Orch London ▲ 440854-2 [DDD]
Wagner, R.:Parsifal, w. C. Ludwig (mez), E. Höngen (cta), H.-M. Uhle (ten), H. Hotter (b-bar), T. Franc (bass), H. von Karajan (cnd), Vienna State Opera Orch, Vienna State Opera Chorus [G] *(rec live 4/1/61)* Arkadia 3-▲ 219 (m) [ADD]
Wagner, R.:Tristan und Isolde, w. H. Dernesch (sop), C. Ludwig (mez), J. Vickers (ten), P. Schreier (ten), B. Weikl (bar), K. Ridderbusch (bass), H. von Karajan (cnd), Berlin PO, German Opera Chorus [G] EMI Classics ("Studio" series) 4-▲ CDMD 69319 [ADD]

Bersanetti, M. Rosa (sop)
Catalani, A.:Songs, w. G. Cocozza (pno)—La viola; Ad una stella; Fior di collina; O rea Gomorra, o Sodoma perversa; Sognal; Chanson groenlandaise; L'odalisque; In riva al mare; Il m'aimait tant; Le gondolier; Senza baci; La pescatrice Ducale ▲ DUC 17 [DDD]
Martucci, G.:Songs, w. G. Cocozza (pno)—Alma gentile; Sogno di morte; Sogno d'amore; 6 liriche, Op. 68; Ballando; 3 liriche, Op. 84 *(rec July 7–9, 1993)* Ducale ▲ DUC 17 [DDD]

Bersiani, Leila (sop)
Bellini, V.:Mass in a, w. Valentina di Cola (sop), Stella Salvati (cta), José Antonio Campo (ten), Carlo Lepore (bass), E. Brizio (cnd), Prague SO, Czech Radio-TV Chorus *(rec Prague, June 1994)* Studio SM ▲ D 2444
Generali, P.:Sacred Music, w. Valentina di Cola (sop), Emanuela Deffai (mez), Sella Salvati (cta), Paolo Macedonio (ten), Roberto Bencivenga (ten), Carlo Lepore (bass), E. Brizio (cnd), Czech Radio-TV Orch, Czech Radio-TV Chorus—Magnificat; Domine ad Adjuvandum; Virgam Virtutis; Ecce Virgo; Ave Maria Messe Pastorale; Te Deum *(rec FHS Studios, Prague, 1995)* Studio SM ▲ 2517 [DDD]

Bertagnoli, Gemma (sop)
Mendelssohn, F.:Sym 2, w. Milena Rudifera (sop), Wonjun Lee (ten), L. Jia (cnd), Trieste Teatro Comunale Giuseppe Verdi Orch, Trieste Teatro Comunale G. Verdi Chorus RS Applausi ▲ 6367-91

Bertagnolli, Gemma (sop)
Cavalieri, E. de:Rappresentatione di Anima et di Corpo, w. C. Cavina (alt), B. Rossetti (sgr), G. Maletto (ten), R. Mattei (bar), A. Abete (sgr), M. Longhini (cnd), Verona Istitutioni Harmoniche · Stradivarius ▲ STR 33339 [DDD]
Cimarosa, D.:Amor rende sagace, w. D. Bruera (sop), C. Mantese (sop), M. Dalena (ten), E. Dara (bar), M. Nicolini (sgr), F. Neri (cnd), Bolzano Claudio Monteverdi Conservatory Youth Orch [I] *(rec live, Bolzano 7/25–27/91)* Bongiovanni 2–▲ GB 2126/27 [DDD]
Mendelssohn, F.:Syms (comp), w. Milena Rudiferia (mez), Wonjun Lee (ten), L. Jia (cnd), Trieste Teatro Comunale Giuseppe Verdi Orch, Ine Meisters (cnd), Trieste Teatro Comunale G. Verdi Chorus RS Prestige 3–▲ 953–0090 [DDD]
Pacini, G.:Saffo, w. Francesca Pedaci (sop—Saffo), Gemma Bertagnolli (sop—Dirce), Mariana Pentcheva (mez—Climene), Carlo Ventre (ten—Faone), Aled Hall (ten—Ippia), Roberto de Candia (bar—Alcandro), Davide Baronchelli (bass—Lisimaco), M. Benini (cnd), Irish National SO, Lubomír Mátl (cnd), Wexford Festival Opera Chorus *(rec Wexford, Oct & Nov 1995)* Marco Polo 2–▲ 8.223883–4 [DDD]
Paisiello, G.:Il mondo della luna, w. Gemma Bertagnolli (sop—Clarice), Enzo Dara (bar—Buonafede), Riccardo Ristori (bass—Cecco), Carla Di Censo (sgr—Flaminia), Daniele Gaspari (sgr—Ecclittico), Mattia Nicolini (sgr—Ernesto), F. Neri (cnd), Bolzano Monteverdi Orch *(rec Aug 4–6, 1993)* Bongiovanni 2–▲ GB 2173/74 [DDD]

Bertelsen, Lars Thodberg (bar)
Nielsen, C.:Songs, w. Eva Hess Thaysen (sop), Mette Ejsing (alt), John Laursen (ten), Frode Stengaard (org), Tove Lønskov (pno)—Little Helle; Sir Oluf's Song; Dance–Song; Dawn [all from the play Sir Oluf He Rides]; The Storm Wages over the Dark Waters; My Girl Is as Fair as Amber; The Day the Eagle was Ready to Fly; A Mother was Told at the Feast; The Thistle Crop Looks Promising; Once When Death was Awaited; So Bitter was My Heart; Like a Venturous Fleet at Anchor [all from the play The Mother]; The Sign & the Word of the Cross; Of All the Flowers that Grow on Earth; As the Golden Sun Breaks Through; There is a Path; It Is No Great Struggle; Daffodil, Why Are You Here? [all from Hymns & Sacred Songs]; The Sun Springs Out Like a Rose [from the play Cosmus]; The Great Master Comes; See My Fragile Web; Our Eyes May Rejoice; When Summer's Song is Sung; Earth in Whose Embrace [all from 20 Popular Melodies]; Of What are You Singing? [The Lark]; Teach Me, O Stars of Night [both from 4 Popular Melodies]; Italian Shepherd's Song; We Love You, Our Lofty North!; Vocalise; The Power that Gave Me My Little Song [all from Amor & the Poet]; May Song [Merrily, with Joyful Song!] Rondo Grammofon ▲ RCD 8329
Nielsen, C.:Songs, w. Tove Lønskov (pno)—Bjarke's Lay [When Odin Waves...]; You Are Setting Out on Life's Journey; If Luck Should Abandon You... [Comfort in Adversity]; I Praise Our World a Thousandfold; The Rose Now Blooms in Dana's Garden [Denmark, My Joy]; Out of the Mist Emerges My Native Soil [Jutland] [all from 20 Danish Songs]; Old Anders the Cowherd's Song [There Stands a Stunted Tree]; Are You Coming Soon, You Cottagers! [The Shout Rises...] [both from the play Son of Wolf]; The Merchant's Song; Hymn to Denmark [Denmark for a Thousand Years] [both from the Cant for the Merchant Society's Centenary]; Gone Are the Days of Old; On the Ground...; That Tiny Lark on the Moors; The Noble Nature–Lover; A Fisherman Sat So Pensive; I Only Looked Back; Like the Deepest Well...; Freedom is the Purest Gold; The Barques Meet...; Heavy, Sombre Clouds of Night [all from 20 Popular Melodies]; O Danish Man [Patriotic Song]; Halloge's Song [My Helmet is Too Shiny & Heavy for Me; from the play Hagbarth & Signe]; The Bard's Lay [The Days Inscribe the Runes of Fortune; from the play The Liar]; Now Shall It Be Revealed; The Song Casts Light; Christmas Song [all from 4 Popular Melodies]; Heaven Darkens, Great & Silent; In Praise of Bjørnson [We Mention a Name]; Breezy Morning [The Wind Is With Us]; King David [I Was a Lad Keeping Watch O'er the Sheep]; Sign of Light [We Gaze Out Where Ever We Are]; Do You Notice, It is Brightening...; There Is a Lovely Land Rondo Grammofon ▲ RCD 8325
Nielsen, C.:Songs, w. Frode Stengaard (org)—I Drive Forth Through Joyful Radiance; O For a Thousand Voices; The Great White Flock We See; This Is the Day Which the Lord Has Made; I Will Love You, Who Are My Strength; Draw Me Towards You, Jesus; Deeply the Year Draws to a Close; Peace Be with You, One & All!; Be of Good Cheer! Once Again; Peace & Happiness; The Peace of God is More than Guardian Angels; If You Have Put Your Hand to the Plough of the Lord; The Lord Says Are You Weary; I Know a Little Heaven; When I Consider the Time & Hour; Christians, Open Your Eyes!; O Christianity!; Whichever Way You Go; Let the Heavens Resound; Undaunted, However My Fortune; Jesus, Let My Heart Receive; Our Lord is a Mighty King; Are You Down–Hearted, Dear Friend; Like Dew on Mown Fields; Strange to Say Rondo Grammofon ▲ RCD 8335
Nielsen, C.:Sym 3, w. Eva Hess Thaysen (sop), E. Serov (cnd), Odense SO Kontrapunkt ▲ KPT 32203
Schoenberg, A.:Songs, w. S. Lange (mez), T. Lonskov (pno)—Seven Early Songs; Two Songs, Op. 1; Four Songs, Op. 2; Six Songs, Op. 3; Gruss in die Ferne; Eight Songs, Op. 6; Two Ballads, Op. 12; Two Songs, Op. 14; The Book of the Hanging Gardens, Op. 15; Two Songs (Gedenken; Am Strande); Four Deutsche Volkslieder; Three Songs, Op. 48 [G] Kontrapunkt 3–▲ 32028/30 [DDD]

Berthon, Mireille (sop)
Berlioz, H.:La Damnation de Faust, w. J. de Trévi (ten), C. Panzéra (bar), P. Coppola (cnd), Pasdeloup Concerts Association Orch, St. Gervais Chorus *(rec 1930)* Pearl ▲ PEA 9080 [ADD]
Berlioz, H.:La Damnation de Faust (sels), w. J. de Trévi (sgr), C. Panzéra (bar), L. Morturier (sgr), P. Coppola (cnd), Pasdeloup Orch, St. Gervais Chorus [abridged vers] [F] *(rec 1931)* The Classical Collector 2–▲ FDC2 2006 [AAD]
Gounod, C.:Faust, w. M. Berthon (sop—Marguerite), C. Vezzani (ten—Faust), L. Musy (b–bar—Valentin), M. Journet (bass—Mephistofeles), H. Busser (cnd), Paris Opera Orch, Paris Opera Chorus [F] *(rec 1930)* Music Memoria 2–▲ 30187
Gounod, C.:Faust, w. M. Coiffier (sop), J. Montfort (mez), C. Vezzani (ten), L. Musy (b–bar), M. Cozette (bar), M. Journet (bass), H. Busser (cnd), Paris Opera Orch, Paris Opera Chorus [F] *(rec 1930)* Pearl 2–▲ PEA 9987 [AAD]

Berti, Marco (ten)
Franchetti, A.:Cristoforo Colombo, w. R. Ragatzu (sop—Isabella), G. Pasino (mez—Annacoana), M. Berti (ten—Ferdinand), R. Bruson (bar—Cristoforo Colombo), R. Scandiuzzi (bass—Don Roldano Ximenes), M. Viotti (cnd), Frankfurt RSO, Frankfurt Radio Chorus [I] *(rec live, Alte Oper Frankfurt, 8/30 & 9/2 1991)* Koch Schwann 3–▲ CD 3–1030–2 [DDD]

Berti, Renato (sgr)
Giordano, U.:Madame Sans–Gêne, w. Magda László (sop—Caterina), Carlo Tagliabue (bar—Napoleone), Renato Berti (sgr—Despréaux), Irene Callaway (sgr—Toniotta/Carolina), Danilo Cestari (sgr—Neipperg/Vinaigre), Maria Luisa Malacchi (sgr—Giulia/Principessa Elisa), Carlo Perucci (sgr—Fouché), Danilo Vega (sgr—Lefebvre), Enzo Viaro (sgr—De Brigode/Gelsomino), A. Basile (cnd), Milan RAI SO, Milan RAI Chorus *(rec Milan, Aug 10, 1957)* Bongiovanni 2–▲ GB 1129/30

Bertin, Pascal (alt)
Handel, G.F.:Amadigi di Gaula, w. E. Harrhy (sop—Melissa), J. Smith (sop—Oriana), P. Bertin (mez—Orgando), B. Fink (cta—Dardano), N. Stutzmann (cta—Amadigi), M. Minkowski (cnd), Louvre Musicians, Louvre Choir [I] Erato 2–▲ 2292–45490–2 [DDD]
Handel, G.F.:Riccardo Primo, w. Claire Brua (sop—Pulcheria), Sandrine Piau (sop—Costanza), Sara Mingardo (cta—Riccardo), Pascal Bertin (alt—Oronte), Roberto Scaltriti (bar—Isacio), Olivier Lallouette (bass—Berardo), C. Rousset (cnd), Les Talens Lyriques L'oiseau Lyre ▲ 452 201–2

Bertini, Rossana (sop)
De Vitae Fugacitate:Lamentos, Cantatas & Arias, w. Cavina, Claudio (ct/alt), R. Balconi (ct), R. Gini (cnd), Concerto delle Viole *(rec Aug. 1992)* Glossa ▲ GCD 920901 [DDD]
Frescobaldi, G.:Arie musicali per cantarsi, w. G. Banditelli (mez), C. Cavina (alt), G. Maletto (ten), S. Naglia (ten), S. Foresti (bass), R. Alessandrini (cnd), Concerto Italiano Opus 111 2–▲ OPS 30–105/106
Handel, G.F.:Poro, Rè dell'Indie, w. Gloria Banditelli (cta), Bernarda Fink (cta), Gérard Lesne (ct), F. Biondi (cnd), Europa Galante Opus 111 3–▲ OPS 30–113/15
Marcello, B.:Cants & Duets, w. Claudio Cavina (alt), La Venexiana—Andromaca; Cassandra; La Lucrezia; La Stravaganza; plus others & duets Opus 111 ▲ OPS 30–149
Peri, J.:Euridice, w. Monica Benvenuti (sop—Ninfa I/Venere), Rossana Bertini (sop—Dafne/Ninfa II), Gloria Banditelli (cta—Euridice/Ninfa III/Tragedia/Proserpina), Mario Cecchetti (ten—Aminta/Radamanto), Paolo Da Col (ten—Tirsi), Gianpaolo Fagotto (ten—Orfeo), Giuseppe Zambon (ct—Arcetro), Sergio Foresti (bass—Caronte/Pastore), Furio Zanasi (bass—Plutone), R. de Caro (cnd), Arpeggione Ensemble *(rec Bologna, Italy, Nov 1992)* Arts Music 2–▲ 47276–2 [DDD]

Bertini, Rossana (sop) (cont.)
Scarlatti, A.:Humanità e Lucifero, w. Massimo Crispi (ten), F. Biondi (cnd), Europa Galante Opus 111 ▲ OPS 30–129
Scarlatti, A.:Santa Maria Maddalena de'pazzi, w. Sylvia Piccollo (sop), G. Banditelli (mez), F. Biondi (cnd), Europa Galante Opus 111 ▲ OPS 30–96

Bertocchi, Sergio (ten)
Mercadante, S.:Il bravo, w. J. Perry (sop), A. Tabiadon (mez), D. Di Domenico (ten), S. Antonucci (bar), B. Aprea (cnd), Italian International Orch, Slovak Phil Chorus [I] *(rec live 7/28–31/90)* Nuova Era 3–▲ 6971/73 [DDD]

Bertocci, Aldo (ten)
Donizetti, G.:Anna Bolena, w. L. Gencer (sop), G. Simionato (mez), P. Clabassi (bass), G. Gavazzeni (cnd), Milan RAI SO, Milan RAI Chorus *(rec 1958)* Memories 2–▲ MEM 4517 [AAD]
Donizetti, G.:Anna Bolena, w. Leyla Gencer (sop), Giulieta Simionato (mez), Plinio Clabassi (bass), G. Gavazzeni (cnd), Milan RAI SO, Milan RAI Chorus *(rec July 11, 1958)* Agorá Music ("Phoenix" series) 2–▲ 503
Giordano, U.:Fedora, w. Maria Caniglia (sop), Giacinto Prandelli (ten), Scipio Colombo (bar), Andrea Piccinni (bass), Capozzi (sgr), M. Rossi (cnd), Turin RAI SO, Turin RAI Chorus *(rec 1950)* Cetra Classic 2–▲ Don 35
Petrassi, G.:Inni sacri, w. Renato Cesari (bar), G. Petrassi (cnd), Turin RAI Radio–TV SO Stradivarius ▲ STV DTM 90001 [ADD]
Rimsky–Korsakov, N.:The Maid of Pskov, w. N. Panni (sop), F. Cadoni (mez), B. Christoff (bass), T. Schippers (cnd), *(orch unknown) (rec 1969)* Great Opera Performances 2–▲ GOP 720
Stravinsky, I.:Oedipus Rex, w. M. Laszlò (mez—Jocasta), N. Gedda (ten—Oedipus), A. Bertocci (ten—Shepherd), M. Petri (bar—Creon & Tireseus), N. Catalani (bar—Messenger), A. Foà (speaker), H. von Karajan (cnd), Rome RAI SO, Rome RAI Chorus *(rec Dec. 20, 1952)* Stradivarius ▲ DAT 12311 [ADD]
Verdi, G.:I lombardi alla prima crociata, w. Renata Broilo (sop), Maria Vitale (sop), Miriam Pirazzini (mez), Mario Frosini (sgr), Mario Petri (bass), Bruno Franchi (sgr), Gustavo Gallo (sgr), Renato Pasquali (sgr), M. Wolf–Ferrari (cnd), Milan RAI Lyric Orch, Milan RAI Chorus *(rec 1954)* Cetra Classic 2–▲ CDON 41 [ADD]
Zandonai, R.:Francesca da Rimini, w. M. Caniglia (sop—Francesca), A. M. Canali (mez—Altichiara), A. Bertocci (ten—Ser Toldo Berardengo), M. Carlin (ten—Malatestino), G. Prandelli (ten—Paolo), C. Tagliabue (bar—Giovanni), E. Campi (bass—Il Giuliare/Il Torrigiano), A. Guarnieri (cnd), Rome RAI SO, Rome RAI Chorus *(rec 1952)* Cetra Classic ▲ CDO 22 [ADD]

Berton, Liliane (sop)
Gounod, C.:Faust, w. V. de los Angeles (sop), R. Gorr (mez), N. Gedda (ten), E. Blanc (bar), B. Christoff (bass), A. Cluytens (cnd), Paris Opera Orch [F] Angel ("Studio" series) 3–▲ CDMC 69983 [ADD]
Gounod, C.:Faust (sels), w. Victoria de los Angeles (sop), Rita Gorr (mez), Nicolai Gedda (ten), Victor Autran (bar), Ernest Blanc (bar), Boris Christoff (bass), A. Cluytens (cnd), Paris Opera Orch, Paris Opera Chorus Classics for Pleasure ("Eminence" series) ▲ CDEMX 2215 [DDD]
Poulenc, F.:Dialogues des Carmélites, w. D. Duval (sop), R. Crespin (sop), D. Scharley (mez), R. Gorr (mez), P. Finel (ten), X. Depraz (bass), P. Dervaux (cnd), Paris Opera Orch [F] EMI Classics 2–▲ CDCB 49331 (m) [ADD]

Bertotti, Lavinia (sop)
Stradella, A.:Cants, w. Cristina Miatello (sop), Gianpaolo Fagotto (ten), Antonio Abete (sgr), Roberto Balconi (sgr), Roberta Giua (sgr), S. Balestracci (cnd), Santo Spirito Academy Orch, Santo Spirito Academy Chorus—for 5 w. vns [For Holy Christmas]; for 5 w. instruments [For the Souls in Purgatory] Stradivarius ▲ STV 33392 [DDD]
Stradella, A.:Susanna, w. S. Piccollo (sop), M. Lazzara (cta), M. Nuvoli (ten), M. Perrella (bass), E. Velardi (cnd), Camerata Ligure [period instrs] [I] Bongiovanni 2–▲ GB 2121/22 [DDD]

Bessel, Anne Marie (mez)
Wagner, R.:Der fliegende Holländer, w. L. Rysanek (sop), C. Heater (ten), F. Crass (bass), K. Ridderbusch (bass), W. Sawallisch (cnd), La Scala Orch, La Scala Chorus [G] *(rec live, Milan 2/2/66)* Memories 2–▲ HR 4281/82 (m) [ADD]

Bessis, Sandra (sgr)
Judeo–Spanish Songs, w. Joyhn McLean (instrs) ARB ▲ 1413

Best (sgr)
Duruflé, M.:Requiem, w. Murray, Allen, Corydon Singers, English CO [L] Hyperion ▲ CDA 66191 [DDD]

Best, Jonathan (bass)
Vaughan Williams, R.:The Shepherds of the Delectable Mountains, w. L. Kitchen (sop), J.–M. Ainsley (ten), A. Thompson (ten), A. Opie (bar), B. Terfel (b–bar), M. Best (cnd), City of London Sinfonia [E] Hyperion ▲ CDA 66569 [DDD]

Best, M. (sgr/cittern/gtr)
Bellman, C.M.:Songs Nimbus ▲ NI 5174 [DDD]

Best, Martin (ten)
Wayditch, G. von:Jesus before Herod, w. Michael Best (ten—Jappeticus), Christopher Lindbloom (sgr—Philippo/Herod), Eileen Moss (sgr—Pabula), Vincent Russo (sgr—Pabo), Stephen A. Scot–Shepherd (sgr—Luke the Evangelist), Pauline Tweed (sgr—1st & 2nd girls), P. Erös (cnd), San Diego SO, San Diego Master Chorale *(rec 1979)* VAI Audio 2–▲ VAIA 1095–2 [ADD]

Bethea, David (ten)
Thomson, V.:4 Saints in 3 Acts, w. Inez Matthews (sop—St Settlement), Beatrice Robinson–Wayne (sop—St Teresa I), Altonell Hines (mez—Commère), Ruby Greene (alt—St Teresa II), David Bethea (ten—St Stephen), Charles Holland (ten—St Chavez), Edward Matthews (bar—St Ignatius), Randolph Robinson (bar—St Plan), Abner Dorsey (bass—Compère), V. Thomson (cnd), *(orch unknown)* [abridged by Thompson] *(rec June 25, 1947)* RCA Gold Seal ▲ 09026–68163–2 [ADD]

Betley–Siradzka, Bozena (sop)
Ave Maria, w. Wieslaw Ochman (ten), Leonard Mróz (bass), Marian Sawa (org) Polskie Nagrania Edition ▲ ECD 049 [DDD]
Moniuszko, S.:Haunted Manor, w. Bozena Betley–Siradzka (sop—Hanna), Anna Witkowska (sop—Marta/Stara Niewiasta), Wiera Baniewicz (mez—Jadwiga), Aleksandra Imalska (mez—Czesnikowa), Kazimierz Dluha (Grzes), Zdzislaw Nikodem (ten—Damazy), Wieslaw Ochman (ten—Stefan), Andrzej Hiolski (bar—Miecznik), Florian Skulski (bar—Maciej), Leonard Mróz (bass—Zbigniew), Andrzej Saciuk (bass—Skoluba), J. Krenz (cnd), Cracow Polish Radio–TV Orch, Cracow Polish Radio–TV Chorus *(rec Cracovia, 1978)* Agorá Music ("Phoenix" series) 3–▲ 509 [ADD]
Nicolai, O.:Te Deum, w. Zofie Kilanowicz (sop), Katarztna Suska (cta), Henryk Grychnik (ten), Czeslaw Galka (bar), Jerzy Gruszczynski (bass), R. Bader (cnd), Cracow PO, Cracow Phil Chorus Koch Schwann ▲ SCH CD 310872

Betner, Clara (mez)
Mascagni, P.:Il piccolo Marat, w. Virginia Zeani (sop), Umberto Borso (ten), Nicola Rossi–Lemeni (bass), O. de Fabritiis (cnd), Teatro La Gran Guardia Orch, Teatro La Gran Guardia Chorus [I] *(rec live, 10/26/61)* Fonè 2–▲ 88 F 17–37 [ADD]

Betti, Freda (cta)
Planquette, R.:Rip van Winkle, w. Claudine Collart (sop), Lina Dachary (sop), René Lenoty (ten), Joseph Peyron (ten), Charles Daguerressar (bar), Julien Giovannetti (bar), Jacques Pruvost (bar), Lucien Lovano (bass), Patrick Orladey (sgr), Joëlle Pierre (sgr), M. Cariven (cnd), ORTF Lyric Orch, ORTF Lyric Chorale Musidisc ▲ MUS 201602 [AAD]

Bettina, Judith (sop)
Babbitt, M.:The Head of the Bed, w. A. Korf (cnd), Parnassus [E] New World ▲ 80346–2 [DDD]
Babbitt, M.:Philomel Sop, Recorded Sop & Elecs Neuma ▲ 45074 [ADD/DDD]
Babbitt, M.:Phonemena Sop & Elecs Neuma ▲ 45074 [ADD/DDD]
Biscardi, C.:The Gift of Life, w. James Goldsworthy (pno) *(rec SUNY Purchase Recital Hall, Feb. 12, 1993)* CRI ▲ CD 686 [DDD]
Olan, D.:After Great Pain CRI ▲ CD 565 [AAD/DDD]

Bettini, F. (sgr)
Rossini, G.:Songs, w. M. A. Peters (sop), A. Cicogna (mez), E. Palacio (ten), M. Carraro (cnd), *(orch unknown)*—Il carnevale di Venezia; L'Asia in Faville; Egle ed Irene; Un sou; Laus Deo; Dalle quete e pallid'ombre; Nella stagion di maggio; Hai la sottana; Ridiamo cantiamo; Les amants de Seville; La passeggiata; Le depart; Gli animali parlanti del giorno [I] Bongiovanni ▲ GB 2125 [DDD]

Bettoni, Vincenzo (bass)
Rossini, G.:Il barbiere di Siviglia, w. M. Capsir (sop), D. Borgioli (ten), R. Stracciari (bar), S. Baccaloni (bass), L. Molajoli (cnd), La Scala Orch, La Scala Chorus *(rec 1929 for Columbia Records)* Music Memoria 2-▲ 30276/77
Rossini, G.:Il barbiere di Siviglia, w. Cesira Ferrari (mez—Berta), Mercedes Capsir (cta—Rosina), Dino Borgioli (ten—Count), Salvatore Baccaloni (bar—Bortolo), Aristide Baracchi (bar—Officer), Riccardo Stracciari (bar—Figaro), Vincenzo Bettoni (bass—Don Basilio), Attilio Bordonali (bass—Fiorello), L. Molajoli (cnd), La Scala Orch, La Scala Chorus *(rec 1930)* Arkadia ("The 78's" series) 2-▲ 78008 [ADD]

Betts, Robert (sgr)
Beethoven, L. van:Sym 9, "Choral Sym", w. Agnes Davis (sop), Ruth Cathcart (sgr), Eugene Lowenthal (sgr), L. Stokowski (cnd), Philadelphia Orch, Philadelphia Orch Chorus *(rec 1934)* Music & Arts ▲ CD 846 [ADD]
Beethoven, L. van:Sym 9, "Choral Sym", w. Agnes Davis (sop), Ruth Cathcart (sgr), Eugene Lowenthal (sgr), L. Stokowski (cnd), Philadelphia Orch Grammofono 2000 ▲ GRM 78577 (m)

Bevan, Maurice (bar)
Byrd, W.:Mass in 3 Parts, w. A. Deller (ct), N. Jenkins (ten), Deller Consort [L] Musique d'Abord ▲ HMA 190211
Byrd, W.:Mass in 4 Parts, w. H. Sheppard (sop), A. Deller (ct), N. Jenkins (ten), Deller Consort [L] Musique d'Abord ▲ HMA 190211
Byrd, W.:Mass in 5 Parts, w. H. Sheppard (sop), A. Deller (ct), J. Buttrey (ten), N. Jenkins (ten), Deller Consort [L] Musique d'Abord ▲ HMA 190211
La Musique de Notre Dame, w. A. Deller (ct), Wilfred Brown (ten), Gerald English (ten) *(rec Jan. 1961 & May 1964)* Vanguard Classics ▲ SVC 36 [AAD]
Purcell, H.:Hail. Bright Cecilia, w. April Cantelo (sop), Alfred Deller (alt), Wilfred Brown (ten), M. Tippett (cnd), Kalmar CO, Ambrosian Singers Vanguard Classics ▲ OVC 8020 [ADD]
Purcell, H.:King Arthur, w. R. Hardy (sop), H. Sheppard (sop), J. Knibbs (cta), A. Deller (ct), M. Deller (alt), P. Elliott (ten), L. Nixon (ten), N. Beavan (bass), A. Deller (cnd), Deller Consort, King's Musick [E] Harmonia Mundi France 2-▲ HMC 90252/53
Purcell, H.:Music of, w. April Cantelo (sop), Alfred Deller (ct), Neville Marriner (vn), Peter Gibbs (vn), Granville Jones (vn), Desmond Dupré (vl), George Malcolm (hpd), Walter Bergmann (hpd)—15 Songs & Airs; Fantasia upon a Ground in d for 3 Violins & Continuo, Z.731; Fantasia upon One Note in F for 5 Viols, Z.745; Hornpipe in e (from The Old Bachelor); Music Lessons 1-12 from Musick's Hand-Maid, Part II; A New Irish Tune, "Lilliburlero," Z.646; Pavan in g for 3 Violins & Bass Viol, Z.752; Sonata in g for Violin & Continuo, Z.780; Sonata No. 9 in F, "Golden Sonata," Z.810 (from Ten Sonatas in Four Parts); Suite in D for Harpsichord, Z.667 Vanguard Classics ("The Bach Guild" series) 2-▲ OVC 2002/03 [ADD]
Purcell, H.:The Prophetess, or The History of Dioclesian, w. H. Sheppard (sop), S. Le Sage (sop), A. Deller (ct), M. Worthley (ten), P. Todd (ten), A. Deller (cnd), Vienna Concentus Musicus—also includes incidental music from the play *(rec June 1965)* Vanguard Classics ("The Bach Guild" series) ▲ OVC 2517 [ADD]
Tallis, T.:The Lamentations of Jeremiah, w. Alfred Deller (ct), Wilfred Brown (ten), Gerald English (ten), John Frost (bass) *(rec Walthamstow Hall, London, 1960)* Vanguard Classics ("The Bach Guild" series) ▲ OVC 2525 [ADD]

Bevin, Stanley (ten)
Sullivan, A.:Iolanthe (sels), w. E. Harwood (sop), D. Dowling (bar), E. Shilling (bar), J. Holmes (bass), A. Faris (cnd), Sadler's Wells Opera Orch, Sadler's Wells Opera Chorus Classics for Pleasure 2-▲ CDCFP 4730 [ADD]

Bez, Renzo (alt)
Perti, G.A.:Liturgy for Good Friday, w. Patrizia Vaccari (sop), Maura Pederzoli (sop), Cristina Calzolari (sop), Alida Oliva (sop), Claudia Bugli (sop), Lucia Bagnoli (alt), Cinzia Meneghel (alt), Renzo Bez (alt), Alessandro Carmignani (alt), Michel van Goethem (alt), Mauro Collina (ten), Vincenzo Di Donato (ten), Paolo Fanciullacci (ten), Giovanni Caccamo (ten), Paolo Da Col (ten), Sergio Foresti (bass), Marco Scavazza (bass), Luca Ferracin (bass), Paride Montanari (bass), Liuwe Tamminga (org), Sergio Vartolo (org), S. Vartolo (cnd), Bologna San Petronio Capella Musicale Orch—Omnes amici mei; De lamentatione Jeremiae Prophetae:Heth. Cogitavit; Velum templi; Vinea mea; De lamentatione Jeremiae Prophetae:Lamed. Matribus suis; Tamquam ad latronem; Tenebrae factae sunt; Animam meam; Tradiderunt me; Jesum tradidit; De lamentatione Jeremiae Prophetae:Aleph. Ego vir; Caligaverunt *(rec St. Petronio Basilica, Bologna, Mar 28-31, 1995)* Naxos ▲ 8.553321 [DDD]

Bezhko, Boris (bass)
Haydn, J.:The Seven Last Words of Christ on the Cross, w. Elena Evseeva (sop), Margarita Maruna (mez), Arkady Mishenkin (ten), A. de Almeida (cnd), Moscow SO, Stanislav Gussev (cnd), Russian State Academy Chorus *(rec Mosfilm Studio, Moscow, Jan 27-28, 1995)* SOMM ▲ SOMMCD 203 [DDD]

Bezinian, Ruth (mez)
Donizetti, G.:Maria Stuarda, w. M. Caballé (sop—Maria Stuarda), R. Bezinian (mez—Anna), M. V. Menendez (mez—Elisabetta), J. Carreras (ten—Roberto), M. Mazzieri (bass—Giorgio Talbot), E. Serra (bass—Lord Gugliemo Cecil), N. Santi (cnd), ORTF Lyric Orch, ORTF Lyric Chorale [I] *(rec live 3/26/72)* Memories 2-▲ HR4417/18 [ADD]

Bezzi, Rita (mez)
Bellini, V.:I Puritani, w. Mirella Freni (sop—Elvira), Rita Bezzi (mez—Enrichetta), Alfredo Kraus (ten—Arturo Talbot), Augusto Pedroni (ten—Sir Bruno Robertson), Attilio d'Orazi (bar—Sir Riccardo Forth), Raffaele Arié (bass—Sir Giorgio), Bruno Cioni (bass—Lord Gualtiero Walton), N. Verchi (cnd), Modena Teatro Comunale Orch, Modeno Teatro Comunale Chorus *(rec Modena Teatro Comunale, Dec. 26, 1962)* Legato Classics 2-▲ LCD 195-2 [ADD]

Bezzubenkov, Gennadi (bass)
Glinka, M.:Russian & Ludmilla, w. Galina Gorchakova (sop), Larissa Diadkova (cta), Irinia Bogachova (sgr), Anna Netrebko (sgr), Yuri Masurin (ten), Konstantin Pluzhnikov (ten), Mikhail Kit (bar), Vladimir Ognovenko (bass), V. Gergiev (cnd), Kirov Opera Orch, Kirov Opera Chorus Philips ▲ 456 248-2
Mozart, W.A.:Requiem, w. Jitka Pavlová (sop), Polovecova (mez), Vorapajev (ten), M. Glinka (cnd), Ljubljana SO, Leningrad Chorus [L] Stradivari Classics ▲ SCD 6003 [DDD] ■ SMC 6003 (D)
Tchaikovsky, P.:Iolanta, w. Galina Gorchakova (sop), Nikolai Gassiev (ten), Gegam Grigorian (ten), Dmitri Hvorostovsky (bar), Nikolai Putilin (bar), Sergei Alexashkin (bass), Larissa Diadkova (sgr), Olga Korzhenskaya (sgr), Tatyana Kravtsova (sgr), V. Gergiev (cnd), Kirov Opera Orch, Kirov Opera Chorus *(rec Mariinsky Theatre, St. Petersburg)* Philips 2-▲ 442796-2

Biancardo, A. (bass)
Puccini, G.:Madama Butterfly, w. C. Petrella (sop—Madama Butterfly), M. Masini (mez—Suzuki), M. C. Foscale (sgr—Kate Pinkerton), F. Tagliavini (ten—Pinkerton), M. Caruso (ten—Goro), G. Taddei (bar—Sharpless), A. Albertini (bar—Yamadori), A. Biancardo (bass—Bonze), A. Questa (cnd), Turin RAI Orch, Cetra Chorus *(rec 1953)* Cetra Classic 2-▲ CDO 10 [AAD]

Bianco, Tito del (ten)
Pacini, G.:Saffo, w. L. Gencer (sop), F. Mattiucci (mez), L. Quilico (bar), F. Capuana (cnd), Naples Teatro San Carlo Orch, Naples Teatro San Carlo Chorus [I] *(rec live, 4/7/67)* Arkadia 2-▲ 541 (m) [AAD]
Rossini, G.:Stabat Mater, w. M. Arroyo (sop), B. Wolff (mez), J. Diaz (bass), T. Schippers (cnd), New York PO, Camerata Singers Sony Classical ▲ SB2K 53252

Biasini, Piero (bar)
Mascagni, P.:Cavalleria rusticana, w. Delia Sanzio (sop—Santuzza), Mimma Pantaleoni (mez—Lola), Olga de Franco (cta—Lucia), Giovanni Breviario (ten—Turiddu), Piero Biasini (bar—Alfio), C. Sabajno (cnd), La Scala Orch, La Scala Chorus VAI Audio ▲ VAIA 1082-2
Verdi, G.:Falstaff, w. Augusta Ottrabella (sop—Nannetta), Franca Somigli (sop—Alice), Angelica Cravcenko (mez—Mrs. Quickly), Mita Vasari (mez—Meg), Dino Borgioli (ten—Fenton), Giuseppe Nessi (ten—Bardolfo), Alfredo Tedeschi (ten—Dr. Cajus), Piero Biasini (bar—Ford), Mariano Stabile (bar—Falstaff), Virgilio Lazzari (bass—Pistola), A. Toscanini (cnd), Vienna PO, Vienna State Opera Chorus *(rec Salzburg, Aug 23, 1937)* Minerva 2-▲ MN A36/37 (m) [ADD]

Bibb, Leon (sgr)
Berlin, I.:Annie Get Your Gun, w. E. Merman (sgr), R. Middleton (sgr), K. Carnes (sgr), J. Garth (sgr), R. Lenn (sgr), C. Turner (sgr), J. Blackton (cnd) [1946 cast] MCA Classics ▲ MCAD 10047 [AAD] ■ MCAC 10047
Rosenstock, M.:The Legend of John Henry, w. *(ensemble unknown)* Premier ▲ PRCD 1017 [ADD]

Bible, Frances (mez)
Ward, R.:The Crucible, w. P. Brooks (sop), C. Ludgin (bar), E. Buckley (cnd), New York City Opera Orch, New York City Opera Chorus [E] Albany 2-▲ TROY 025/26-2 [ADD]

Bickhardt, Johanan (bar)
Handel, G.F.:Music of, w. Sheldon Rosenbaum (pno)—Arm, Arm Ye Brave; Father of Heaven; Dank Sei Dir Herr; See, the Raging Flames Arise [all are sels. from oratorios] *(rec StudioMedia, Evanston, IL)* ZC Music ■ 010893T
Mendelssohn, F.:Elijah (sels), w. Sheldon Rosenbaum (pno)—Draw Near All Ye People; Is Not His Word; What Have I to Do With Thee [w. Theresa Ludden (sop)] *(rec StudioMedia, Evanston, IL)* ZC Music ■ 010893T

Bickley, Susan (mez)
Britten, H.:A Boy Was Born, w. S. Leonard (sop), N. Tibbels (sop), P. Hall (ten), G. Jess (bass), T. Edwards (cnd), London Sinfonietta Chorus, St. Paul's Cathedral Choristers Virgin Classics ▲ CDC 59136
Britten, H.:Hymn to St. Cecilia, w. S. Leonard (sop), N. Tibbels (sop), P. Hall (ten), G. Jess (bass), T. Edwards (cnd), London Sinfonietta Chorus, St. Paul's Cathedral Choir Virgin Classics ▲ CDC 59136
Britten, H.:Sonnets of Michelangelo, w. S. Leonard (sop), N. Tibbels (sop), P. Hall (ten), G. Jess (bass), T. Edwards (cnd), London Sinfonietta Chorus, Choristers of St. Paul's Cathedral Virgin Classics ▲ CDC 59136
Hahn, R.:Songs, w. Felicity Lott (sop), Ian Bostridge (ten), Stephen Varcoe (bar), Graham Johnson (pno), Stephen Layton (cnd), London Choral Society—[CD 1] Si mes vers avaient des ailes; Paysage; Rêverie; Offrande; Mai; Infidelité; Seule; Les Cygnes; Nocturne; 3 jours de vendange; D'une prison; Séraphine; L'Heure exquise; Fêtes galantes; 12 Rondels; [CD 2] Quand la nuit n'est pas étoilée; Le Plus beau présent; Sur l'eau; Le Rossignol des lilas; A Chloris; Ma jeunesse; Puisque j'ai mis ma lèvre; Etudes Latines; La Nymphe de la Source; Au Rossignol; Je me souviens; Air de la lettre; C'est très vilain d'être infidèle; C'est sa banlieue; Nous avons fait un beau voyage; La Dernière Valse Hyperion ("The Hyperion French Song Edition" series) 2-▲ CDA 67141/42
Purcell, H.:The Fairy Queen, w. Lorraine Hunt (sop), Catherine Pierard (mez), Howard Crook (ten), Mark Padmore (ten), David Wilson-Johnson (bar), Richard Wistreich (bass), R. Norrington (cnd), London Classical Players, Schütz Choir London EMI Classics ▲ CDCB 55234

Bickly, Graham (sgr)
Lloyd Webber, A.:Music of, w. C. Burt (sgr), J. Kelly (sgr), C. D. Carroll (sgr), Yates (cnd), National SO, Munich SO—Song & Dance; The Phantom of the Opera; Starlight Express; Jeeves; Jesus Christ Superstar; Aspects of Love; Cats; The Requiem Mass Koch International ▲ KOCCD 340132 ■ KOCC 340134

Bieber, Clemens (ten)
Mendelssohn, F.:Die Hochzeit des Camacho, w. R. Schudel (sop—Quiteria), C. Swanson (sop—Lucinda), C. Bieber (ten—Basilio), W. Mok (ten—Vivaldo), V. Horn (ten—Camacho), R. Lukas (bar—Carrasco), J. Becker (bass—Sancho Panza), W. Murray (bass—Don Quixote), B. Klee (cnd), Berlin RSO, Berlin Radio Chorus [G] Koch Schwann 2-▲ 314042 [DDD]

Biel, J. (ten)
Verdi, G.:Il trovatore (sels), w. F. Tamagno (ten), L.-A. Escalaïs (ten), M. Gilion (ten), E. Caruso (ten), A. Paoli (ten), G. Zenatello (ten), J. Sembach (ten), L. Slezak (ten), F. Constantino (ten), G. Martinelli (ten), B. De Muro (ten), N. Fusati (ten), N. Piccaluga (ten), G. Lauri-Volpi (ten), A. Pertile (ten), E. Bergamaschi (ten), R. Tauber (ten), J. O'Sullivan (ten), H. Roswaenge (ten), G. Taccani (ten), V. Lois (ten), H. Lazaro (ten), A. Lindi (ten), A. Cortis (ten), F. Merli (ten), F. Völker (ten), J. Kiepura (ten), J. Schmidt (ten), J. Bjoerling (ten), B. Gigli (ten), A. Salvarezza (ten), J. Soler (ten), M. Filippeschi (ten)—34 performances of the Act III tenor aria "Di quella pira!," *(rec from 1903-1956)* Bongiovanni ▲ GB 1051 [AAD]

Bielke, I. (sop)
Nicolai, O.:Lustigen Weiber, w. M. L. Schilp (mez), W. Ludwig (ten), G. Hann (bass), W. Streinz (bass), A. Rother (cnd), Berlin RSO, Berlin State Opera Chorus *(rec May 2, 1943)* Preiser 2-▲ PRE 90208 [ADD]

Bierett, Doris (sop)
Weill, K.:The Seven Deadly Sins, w. D. Ellenbeck (ten), L. Zagrosek (cnd), Cologne RSO Capriccio ▲ 60028 [DDD]

Bierschenk, Jerry (bar)
Ito, Y.:Gloriosa, w. D. W. Fisher (cnd), North Texas College of Music Wind Sym Klavier ▲ KCD 11077 [DDD]

Bieshu, Maria (sop)
Russian Vocal School:Maria Bieshu Russian Compact Disc ("Talents of Russia" series) ▲ RCD 16023 [ADD]

Bigaca, Antra (mez)
Mozart, W.A.:Alma Dei creatoris, w. Dita Paēgle (sop), Martins Klisans (ten), S. Klava (cnd), Riga Musicians, Riga Radio Chorus Audiophile Classics ▲ 101.048 [DDD]
Mozart, W.A.:Litaniae Lauretanae, K.195, w. Dita Paēgle (sop), Martins Klisans (ten), Janis Màrkovs (bass), S. Klava (cnd), Riga Musicians, Riga Radio Chorus Audiophile Classics ▲ 101.048 [DDD]
Mozart, W.A.:Regina coeli, K.276, w. Dita Paēgle (sop), Martins Klisans (ten), Janis Màrkovs (bass), S. Klava (cnd), Riga Musicians, Riga Radio Chorus Audiophile Classics ▲ 101.048 [DDD]

Biggs, Elizabeth (sop)
The Lyric Trumpet, w. S. Friedman (tpt), Bruce Greenfield (pno), Judith McDonald (pno), et al. Ode/New Zealand ▲ ODE 1327 [DDD]

Bigley, I. (sgr)
Rodgers, R.:Me & Juliet, w. R. Walston (sgr), B. Hayes (sgr), J. McCracken (sgr) [1953 Broadway cast] RCA ▲ 09026-61480-2 ■ 09026-61480-4

Bikel, Theodore (nar)
The Chanukkah Story, w. Western Wind Western Wind ▲ 1818 CD [DDD] ■ 1818 CT (D)
The Passover Story, w. Western Wind Western Wind ▲ 1800 CD [DDD] ■ 1800 CT (D)

Bilandzija, Beate (sop)
Korngold, E.W.:Der Ring des Polykrates, w. Beate Bilandzija (sop—Laura), Kirsten Blanck (sop—Lieschen), Endrik Wottrich (ten—Wilhelm), Jürgen Sacher (ten—Florian), Dietrich Henschel (bar—Peter), K. Seibel (cnd), German SO *(rec Jesus Christ Church, Dahlem, Sept 19-25, 1995)* CPO ▲ CPO 999402-2 [DDD]
Schillings, M. von:Mona Lisa, w. Albert Bonnema (sgr), Klaus Wallprecht (sgr), K. Seibel (cnd), Kiel PO CPO 2-▲ CPO 999303 [DDD]

Bilicsi, Tivadar (sgr)
Kacsóh, P.:János Vitéz, w. Mária Gyurkovics (sop), Anna Zentai (sop—Iluska), Hilda Gobbi (sgr), Sándor Pethes (sgr—Bartolo), Róbert Ilosfalvy (ten—Kukorica), György Melis (bar—Bagó), György Radnai (bar—Strázsamester), László Domahidy (bass—Csősz), E. Lukács (cnd), Hungarian State Opera Orch, Hungarian Radio-TV Chorus *(rec Budapest, 1961)* Classical Diamonds 2-▲ CLD 4011-12 [AAD]

Billings, James (bar)
Puccini, G.:Tosca, w. Birgit Nilsson (sop—Floria Tosca), Puli Toro (mez—Shepherd), Jose Carreras (ten—Mario Cavaradossi), Joaquin Romaguera (ten—Spoleta), James Billings (bar—Sacristan), Richard Fredricks (bar—Baron Scarpa), Samuel Ramey (bass—Cesare Angelotti), William Ledbetter (sgr—Sciarrone), Richard Park (sgr—Cardinal), Don Yule (sgr—Jailer), J. Rudel (cnd), *(orch & chorus unknown) (rec Nov 13, 1974)* Legato Classics 2-▲ LCD-200-2

Bilt, Peter van der (bass)
Berlioz, H.:La Damnation de Faust, w. Régine Crespin (sop—Marguerite), Guy Fouché (ten—Faust), Michel Roux (bar—Méphistophélès), Peter van der Bilt (bass—Brander), J. Fournet (cnd), Amsterdam Radio PO, Groot Omroepkoor *(rec Amsterdam, Mar 23, 1963)* Bella Voce 2-▲ BLV 107.202 [AAD]

Bima, Jeanne Marie (sop)
Berecuse Lullaby Wiegenlied, w. Georg Mönch (vn), Massimiliano Damerini (pno) *(rec Roma, Italy, Feb 1987)* Arts ▲ 447282-2 [DDD]
Haydn, J.:Arianna a Naxos, w. Hans Ludwig Hirsch (hpd) *(rec Venice, Italy, June 1990)* Arts ▲ 47286-2 [DDD]
Haydn, J.:Canzonettas, w. Hans Ludwig Hirsch (hpd)—6 sels *(rec Venice, Italy, June 1990)* Arts ▲ 47286-2 [DDD]

Bima, Jeanne Marie (sop) (cont.)
Pergolesi, G.B.:La serva padrona, w. Jeanne Marie Bima (sop—Serpina); Petteri Salomaa (b–bar—Uberto);, H.L. Hirsch (cnd), Musica Poetica Freiberg *(rec Waldkirch, Germany, Nov 14-18, 1990)* Arts ▲ 47119-2 [DDD]

Binci, M. (ten)
Verdi, G.:Nabucco, w. C. Mancini (sop—Abigaille), G. Gatti (sop—Fenena), B. Preziosa (sop—Anna), M. Binci (ten—Ismaele), L. Francardi (ten—Abdallo), P. Silveri (bar—Nabucodonosor), A. Cassinelli (bass—Zaccaria), A. Gaggi (bass—High Priest of Baal), F. Previtali (cnd), Rome RAI Orch, Rome RAI Chorus *(rec Rome, 1951)* Cetra Classic 2-▲ CDO 26 [ADD]

Binder, Gabriele (cta)
Haydn, M.:Missa in honorem Sanctae Ursulae, w. Mechthild Bach (sop), Karl-Heinz Lampe (ten), Joachim Gebhardt (bass), H.R. Zöbeley (cnd), Munich Residenz Orch, Munich Motet Choir Calig ▲ CAL 50901 [DDD]

Binder, Peter (bar)
Bach, J.S.:Cant 198, w. Marnie Nixon (sop), Elaine Bonazzi (mez), Nico Castel (ten), R. Craft (cnd), Columbia SO, American Concert Choir Sony Classical ("Essential Classics" series) 2-▲ SB2K 62656
Orff, C.:Carmina burana, w. J. Blegen (sop), K. Riegel (ten), M. Tilson Thomas (cnd), Cleveland Orch, Cleveland Orch Chorus [G, L] CBS ▲ MK 33172 [ADD]

Bindernagel, G. (sop)
Mahler, G.:Sym 2, w. E. Leisner (cta), O. Fried (cnd), Berlin State Opera Orch, Berlin Cathedral Choir *(rec 1923 for Polydor)* Pearl 2-▲ PEAS 9929 (m) [AAD]

Bindi, Jean-Louis (bass)
Charpentier, M.-A.:In nativitatem Domini canticum, w. P. Colléaux (cnd), Nantes Instrumental Ensemble, Nantes Vocal Ensemble [L] Arion ▲ ARN 68015 [AAD]
Charpentier, M.-A.:Messe de minuit pour Noël, w. E. Lestringant (ten), G. Ragon (ten), Piniec (sgr), P. Colléaux (cnd), Nantes Instrumental Ensemble [L] Arion ▲ ARN 68015 [AAD]
Dupuy, B.A.:Sacred Music, w. Isabelle Poulenard (sop), Jean-Louis Comorette (ct), Erik Gruchet (ten), Dominique Miraille (bar), A. Bourbon (cnd), Baroque Instrumental Ensemble, Toulouse Vocal Group—Noël; Motet; Magnificat Arion ▲ ARN 68330 [DDD]
Handel, G.F.:Cants, w. G. Delvaux (cnd), Artificii Musicali—Cuopre Talvolta il Cielo, H.98; Dalla Guerra Amorosa, H.102a; Spande Ancor a Mio Dispetto, H.165; Dal Fatale Momento, H.101b; Nell'Africane Selve, H.136a Stradivarius ▲ STV 33425 [DDD]

Bini, Carlo (ten)
Strauss (II), Joh.:Eine Nacht in Venedig (sels), w. J. Scovotti (sop), E. Schary (mez), E. Steiner (mez), F. Stricker (ten), W. Brendel (bar), E. Märzendorfer (cnd), Hungarian State Orch, Hungarian State Chorus [G] Acanta ▲ CD 43809 [DDD]

Binzer, Kim von (ten)
Kuhlau, F.:Lulu, w. T. Kiberg (sop), A. Frellesvig (sgr), R. Saarman (ten), U. Cold (bass), E. Harbo (sgr), M. Schønwandt (cnd), Danish National RSO, Danish National Radio Choir [Da] Kontrapunkt 3-▲ 32009/11 [DDD]
Nielsen, C.:Springtime, w. Inga Nielsen (sop), Jørgen Klint (bass), T. Vetö (cnd), Odense SO, Lille MUKO, St. Klemens School Children's Choir Unicorn-Kanchana ▲ DKPCD 9054

Birch, C. (sgr)
Mozart, W.A.:Songs, w. J. Edwards (cta), P. Sharpe (sgr), D. Russell (sgr), D. Hamilton (ten), M. Glasgow (sgr), P. Hooper (sgr), G. Lancaster (pno) *(rec July 1991)* Tall Poppies ▲ TP009 [DDD]

Birch, Clive (nar)
Whiticker, M.:Man, Skin Cancer of the Earth, w. Jane Edwards (nar), Matthew Glasgow (nar), Roger Frampton (sax), David Hewitt (perc), R. Peelman (cnd) *(rec Studio 200, ABC Ultimo Centre, Apr 1993)* Tall Poppies ▲ TP 064 [DDD]

Birch, Karen (sgr)
Brooke, N.:Obomobile, w. Brandon Adrien, Jennifer Baker, Daniel Cate, Judy Christy, Richard Cochran, Jessica Cooper, Leslie Dominguez, Erin Hannigan, Dorothy Knight, Jason Lichtenwalter, Jay Moore, Hwa-Ling Russell, Toyin Spellman, Sarah Weiner, Jay Weinland Opus One ▲ CD 160

Birchall, Simon (bass)
Britten, H.:Hymn to St. Cecilia, w. N. Jenkin (sop), R. Dean (sop), C. Trevor (alt), P. Daggett (ten), H. Christophers (cnd), The Sixteen *(rec 1 & 4/91)* Collins Classics ▲ 12862 [DDD]
Clarke, J.:Come, Come Along for a Dance & a Song, w. R. Holton (sop), C. Daniels (ten), R. Goodman (cnd), Parley of Instruments, Parley of Instruments Chorus Hyperion ▲ CDA 66578 [DDD]
Hall, H.:Yes, My Aminta, 'tis True, w. R. Holton (sop), R. Goodman (cnd), Parley of Instruments, Parley of Instruments Chorus Hyperion ▲ CDA 66578 [DDD]
Handel, G.F.:Dixit Dominus, w. Arleen Augér (sop), Lynne Dawson (sop), Diana Montague (mez), Leigh Nixon (ten), S. Preston (cnd), Westminster Abbey Orch, Westminster Abbey Choir [L] Archiv ▲ 423594-2 [DDD]
Handel, G.F.:Nisi Dominus, w. Diana Montague (mez), John Mark Ainsley (ten), S. Preston (cnd), Westminster Abbey Orch, Westminster Abbey Choir [L] Archiv ▲ 423594-2 [DDD]
Odes on the Death of Henry Purcell, w. G. Holman (cnd), Parley of Instruments, Baroque Orch, Baroque Choir, R. Holton (sop), R. Covey-Crump (ten), C. Daniels (ten) Hyperion ▲ CDA 66578 [DDD]

Birnbaum, K. (sop)
Wallach, J.:Mourning Madrigals, w. F. Urrey (ten), C. Abraham (fl), A. Tarantiles (hp) [E] Capstone ▲ CPS 8613

Bisatt, Susan (sop)
Lampe, J.F.:Pyramus & Thisbe, w. Mark Padmore (ten), P. Holman (cnd), Opera Restor'd Hyperion ▲ CDA 66759
Purcell, H.:Odes & Welcome Songs (misc), w. Jeni Bern (sop), William Purefoy (ct), Christopher Robson (ct), Ian Honeyman (ten), Thomas Guthrie (bass), R. Glenton (cnd), Orch of the Golden Age, Golden Age Choir—The noise of foreign wars (fragment) [ed. by Bruce Wood] *(rec Manchester Grammar School, England, May 13 & 14, 1995)* Naxos ▲ 8.553444 [DDD]
Purcell, H.:Raise, Raise the Voice, w. Jeni Bern (sop), William Purefoy (ct), Christopher Robson (ct), Ian Honeyman (ten), Thomas Guthrie (bass), R. Glenton (cnd), Orch of the Golden Age, Golden Age Choir *(rec Manchester Grammar School, England, May 13 & 14, 1995)* Naxos ▲ 8.553444 [DDD]
Purcell, H.:Te Deum & Jubilate, w. Jeni Bern (sop), William Purefoy (ct), Christopher Robson (ct), Ian Honeyman (ten), Thomas Guthrie (bass), David Staff (tpt), R. Glenton (cnd), Orch of the Golden Age, Golden Age Choir *(rec Manchester Grammar School, England, May 13 & 14, 1995)* Naxos ▲ 8.553444 [DDD]
Purcell, H.:Welcome to All the Pleasures, w. Jeni Bern (sop), William Purefoy (ct), Christopher Robson (ct), Ian Honeyman (ten), Thomas Guthrie (bass), R. Glenton (cnd), Orch of the Golden Age, Golden Age Choir *(rec Manchester Grammar School, England, May 13 & 14, 1995)* Naxos ▲ 8.553444 [DDD]
Verdi, G.:Il trovatore, w. G. Quinn (bar), D. Hinnells (cnd), European Chamber Opera Orch, European Chamber Chorus ASV 2-▲ ASV 225 [DDD]

Bischoff, C. (sop)
Draeseke, F.:Mysterium:Christus, w. A. Vogel (sop), E. Dersen (alt), K. Markus (ten), H.J. Ritzerfeld (ten), P. Langshaw (bar), B. Kämpff (bass), J. Sonnenschmidt (org), U.-R. Follert (cnd), Breslau State PO, Evangelical Boys' Choir Palatine, Heilbronn Vocal Ensemble, Palatine Kurrende Bayer 5-▲ 100175/79

Biscotti, M. (sgr)
Wolf-Ferrari, E.:Il campiello, w. D. Mazzucato (Gasparina), G. Devinu (Lucieta), M. Bolgan (Gnese), C. de Mola (Orsola), U. Benelli (Dona Cate Panciana), M. Rene Cosotti (Dona Pasqua Polegana), M. Comencini (Zorzeto), M. Biscotti (Astolfi), I. D'Arcangelo (Anzoleto), C. Striuli (Fabrizio del Ritorti), N. Bareza (cnd), Trieste Teatro Comunale Giuseppe Verdi Orch, Trieste Teatro Comunale G. Verdi Chorus *(rec Feb. 1992)* Ricordi 2-▲ RFCD 2014 [DDD]

Bise, Julietta (sop)
Keiser, R.:Passions Oratorium, w. M. Conrad (cta), G. Jelden (ten), U. Gilgen (bass), J.E. Dähler (cnd), Bernese Orch, Bernese Chorus [G] *(rec Feb. 1971)* Claves 2-▲ CD 9223/24 [ADD]

Bishop, Margaret (sop)
Moore, D.:Gallantry, w. Margaret Bishop (sop—Lola Markham), Julia Parks (mez—Announcer), Carl Halvorson (ten—Donald Hopewell), Richard Holmes (bar—Doctor Gregg), S. R. Radcliffe (cnd), New York Chamber Ensemble *(rec LeFrak Concert Hall, Queens College, Flushing, NY, May 30 & 31, 1994)* Albany ▲ TROY 173 [DDD]

Bizineche-Eisinger, Liliana (mez)
Beethoven, L. van:Mass, Op. 86, w. A. Michael (sop), M. Schaeffer (ten), M. Brodard (bar), M. Corboz (cnd), Lisbon Gulbenkian Foundation Orch, Lisbon Gulbenkian Foundation Chorus [L] Erato ▲ 2292-45461-2 ZK [DDD]
Bomtempo, J.D.:Messe de requiem consacrée à...Camões, w. Angela Maria Blasi (sop), Reinaldo Macias (ten), Michel Brodard (bass), M. Corboz (cnd), Lisbon Gulbenkian Foundation Orch, Lisbon Gulbenkian Foundation Chorus *(rec Gulbenkian Foundation Grand Auditorium, June 14-16, 1994)* FNAC Music ▲ 592302 [DDD]

Bjerno, Majken (sop)
Heise, P.:Dyveke's Songs, w. T. Lonskov (pno) Kontrapunkt ▲ KPT 32170 [DDD]
Mahler, G.:Sym 8, w. Henriette Bonde-Hansen (sop), Inga Nielsen (sop), Kirsten Dolberg (alt), Anne Gjevang (alt), Raimo Sirkiä (ten), Jorma Hynninen (bar), Carsten Stabell (bass), L. Segerstam (cnd), Danish National RSO, Copenhagen Boys' Choir, Berlin Phil Choir, Danish National Radio Choir Chandos 2-▲ CHAN 9305/06 [DDD]
Roussel, A.:Chamber Music, w. Toke Lund Christiansen (fl), Bjørn Carl Nielsen (ob), Niels Thomsen (cl), Per Jacobsen (hn), Asger Svendsen (bn), Ketil Christensen (tpt), Anne Søe Hansen (vn), Zwi Carmelli (va), Piotr Zelazny (va), Niels Ullner (vc), Michael Dabelsteen (db), Tine Rehling (hp), Morten Mogensen (pno), Per Salo (pno), Per Jensen (perc)—Divertissement, Op. 6; Trio, Op. 40; Joueurs de Flute, Op. 27; Serenade, Op. 30; Le marchand de sable qui passe, Op. 13; Andante et scherzo, Op. 13; 2 poèmes de ronsard, Op. 26; Aria; Elpenor, Op. 59; Pipe Kontrapunkt 2-▲ KPT 32218 [DDD]

Bjoner, Ingrid (sop)
Wagner, R.:Arias & Scenes, *(orchs unknown)*—arias from Fliegende Holländer, Meistersinger, Tannhäuser, Walküre [G] *(rec 1961-1969)* Melodram 3-▲ MEL 37067 [AAD]
Wagner, R.:Lohengrin, w. A. Varnay (sop), J. Thomas (ten), G. Neidlinger (b–bar), W. Sawallisch (cnd), La Scala Orch, Prague Phil Chorus [G] *(rec live, Milan 1965)* Melodram 3-▲ MEL 37067 [AAD]

Bjørkey, Haral (ten)
Jensen, L.I.:The Return, w. A. Bolstad (sop), R. Sterne (alt), I. Gilhuus (ten), P. Vollestad (bar), C. Stabell (bass), O.K. Ruud (cnd), Trondheim SO, Trondheim Sym Chorus, Nidarso Cathedral Choir Simax 2-▲ PSC 3109

Bjørkøy, Kåre (ten)
Grieg, E.:Peer Gynt, w. C. Carlson (mez), V. Hanssen (mez), A. Hansli (bar), P. Dreier (cnd), London SO, Oslo Phil Chorus [N] Unicorn-Kanchana 2-▲ UKCD 2003/04 [AAD]

Björling, Anna-Lisa (sop)
At the Hollywood Bowl, w. J. Björling (ten) *(rec Aug. 23, 1949 & Oct. 3, 1)* Standing Room Only ▲ SRO 8451 [ADD]
Mascagni, P.:Cavalleria rusticana, w. A. Nordmo-Lövberg (sop), M. Sehlmark (cta), J. Bjoerling (ten), G. Svedenbrandt (bass), K. Bendix (cnd), Stockholm Royal Opera House Orch, Stockholm Royal Opera Chorus [I, Sw] *(rec live, Stockholm, 12/8/54)* Legato Classics ▲ LCD 164-1 [ADD]

Björling, Jussi (ten)
Alfvén, H.:Songs, w. N. Grevillius (cnd), Göteborg SO—Skogen sover; Jag längtar dig *(rec Concert Hall, Göteborg, Aug 5, 1960)* Myto ▲ MCD 953130
At Carnegie Hall, w. Frederick Schauwecker (pno) *(rec Mar 2, 1958)* RCA Gold Seal ▲ 60520-2-RG [ADD] ■ 60520-4-RG
At the Hollywood Bowl, w. Anna-Lisa Björling (sop) *(rec Aug. 23, 1949 & Oct. 3, 1)* Standing Room Only ▲ SRO 8451 [ADD]
Beethoven, L. van:Missa Solemnis, w. Z. Milanov (sop), B. Castagna (mez), J. Björling, A. Kipnis (bass), A. Toscanini (cnd), NBC SO, Westminster Choir [L] *(rec live 12/28/40)* Melodram 3-▲ MEL 38006
Beethoven, L. van:Missa Solemnis, w. Zinka Milanov (sop), Bruna Castagna (cta), Alexander Kipnis (bass), A. Toscanini (cnd), NBC SO, Westminster Choir *(rec 1940)* Grammofono 2000 ▲ GRM 78626
Bizet, G.:Carmen (sels)—La fleur que tu m'avais jetée RCA Gold Seal ▲ 09026-68429-2
Björling Sings Operatic Arias, Duets & Songs, Vol. 2 *(rec 1936-49)* EMI Classics ▲ CDH 64707
Donizetti, G.:L'elisir d'amore (sels), *(cnd & orch unknown)* Enterprise ("Vocal Archives" series) ▲ ENT 1115
The Early Recordings, 1929-36 Minerva ▲ MN A27 (m) [ADD]
The Essential Björling Mastersound ▲ MST 114 [ADD]
The First 10 Years Nimbus ▲ NI 7835 [ADD]
In Opera & Song:Recordings from 1930-1941 Nimbus ("Prima Voce" series) 3-▲ NI 1776
Jussi Björling:A Discographic Career, 1933-1957 *(rec between 1933-1957)* Enterprise ("Documents" series) 2-▲ ENTLV 909 [ADD]
Jussi Björling:The Golden Years, Vol. 1, w. Stockholm Royal Orch [cnd:Nils Grevillius] *(rec 1933-45)* Iron Needle ▲ 1301 (m) [ADD]
Jussi Björling in Concert, w. Frederick Schauwecker (pno) *(rec Glenn Memorial Auditorium, Atlanta, Georgia, 4/13/59)* Myto ▲ MCD 912.39 [ADD]
Jussi Björling:In Song & Ballad, w. Harry Ebert (pno), Bertil Bokstedt (pno), Swedish Radio Orch [cnd:Sixten Ehrling], New York PO [cnd:Martti Similä] *(rec 1940, 1942 & 1957)* Bluebell ▲ BLU 050 [ADD]
Jussi Björling on Radio, Vol. 2, w. various orchs *(rec 1936-44)* Enterprise ("The Radio Years" series) ▲ ENTRY 15
Jussi Bjorling:Recital, w. Hjordis Schymberg (bar) *(rec 1941-51)* Myto ▲ MCD 934.86
Jussi Björling:The Swedish Caruso, w. *(rec live performances, 1937-1960)* Legato Classics ("Biographies in Music" series) 2-▲ BIM 708-2 (m)
Jussi Björling, Vol. 2, w. Harry Ebert (pno), Nils Grevillius (cnd) *(rec New York and Stockholm 1936-1941 for HMV/Victor)* Nimbus ("Prima Voce" series) ▲ NI 7842 [ADD]
Leoncavallo, R.:Pagliacci, w. V. de los Angeles (sop), R. Merrill (bar), L. Warren (bar), R. Cellini (cnd), Columbus Orch, Robert Shaw Chorale EMI Classics ▲ ZDC 49503
Leoncavallo, R.:Pagliacci, w. R. Moberg [sop—Nedda], J. Björling [ten—Canio], E. Sundquist [bar—Tonio], L. Gardelli (cnd), Milan RAI SO, Milan RAI Chorus [Sw] *(rec live, Stockholm, 12/8/54)* Legato Classics ▲ LCD 155-1 [ADD]
Leoncavallo, R.:Pagliacci (sels), w. Enrico Caruso (ten), Antonio Paoli (ten), Giovanni Zenatello (ten), Amedeo Bassi (ten), Hermann Jadlowker (ten), Fernand Ansseau (ten), Hipolito Lazaro (ten), Nino (Filippo) Piccaluga (ten), Mario Chamlee (ten), Giacomo Lauri-Volpi (ten), Miguel Fleta (ten), Giovanni Martinelli (ten), Aureliano Pertile (ten), Georges Thill (ten), Alessandro Valente (ten), Francesco Merli (ten), Lauritz Melchior (ten), Marcel Wittrisch (ten), Joseph Schmidt (ten), Beniamino Gigli (ten), Giuseppe Lugo (ten), Helge Roswaenge (ten)—23 versions of the tenor aria "Vesti la giubba" *(rec 1907-1944)* Bongiovanni ▲ GB 1071 [ADD]
Leoncavallo, R.:Pagliacci (sels), w. M. Bokor [sop—Nedda], Bjoerling [ten—Canio], K. Alwin (cnd), *(orch unknown)*—A ventitre ore/Recitar!...Vesti la giubba [Act 1]; No, Pagliacco non son through e il nome del tuo ganzo [Act 2] [Bjoerling sings in Swedish, Bokor in German] *(rec live, Vienna State Opera, 3/12/37)* Legato Classics ▲ LCD 155-1
Leoncavallo, R.:Pagliacci (sels), w. L. Gardelli (cnd), *(orch unknown)*—Recitar!; Vesti la giubba *(rec Dec 8, 1954)* Myto ▲ MCD 953130
Live Recordings *(rec 1929-60)* Legato Classics ▲ LCD 103-1 (m) [AAD]
The Magnificent Björling IMP Classics ▲ GLRS 103 [ADD]
Mascagni, P.:Cavalleria rusticana, w. Z. Milanov (sop), Carol Smith (sop), R. Merrill (bar), R. Cellini (cnd), RCA Victor SO, Robert Shaw Chorale [I] RCA Gold Seal ▲ 6510-2-RG [ADD]
Mascagni, P.:Cavalleria rusticana, w. A. Nordmo-Lövberg (sop), A. Björling (sop), M. Sehlmark (cta), G. Svedenbrandt (bass), K. Bendix (cnd), Stockholm Royal Opera House Orch, Stockholm Royal Opera Chorus [I, Sw] *(rec live, Stockholm, 12/8/54)* Legato Classics ▲ LCD 164-1 [ADD]
Mascagni, P.:Cavalleria rusticana, w. R. Tebaldi (sop), A. Erede (cnd), Florence Maggio Musicale Orch, Florence Maggio Musicale Chorus *(rec Sept. 1957)* London ("Historic" series) ▲ 425985-2 [ADD]
Mascagni, P.:Cavalleria rusticana (sels), w. *(cnd & orch unknown)*—Turiddu, ascolta; Intanto, amici (Brindisi); Addio alla madre; Fedora Amor ti vieta RCA Gold Seal ▲ 09026-68429-2
Mascagni, P.:Cavalleria rusticana (sels), *(cnd & orch unknown)* Enterprise ("Vocal Archives" series) ▲ ENT 1115
Massenet, J.:Manon (sels)—Instant charmant; En fermant les yeux (Le rêve) RCA Gold Seal ▲ 09026-68429-2

VOCALISTS

Björling, Jussi (ten) (cont.)
Meyerbeer, G.:L'Africaine (sels)—O paradiso RCA Gold Seal ▲ 09026-68429-2
Mozart, W.A.:Don Giovanni (sels)—Il mio tesero RCA Gold Seal ▲ 09026-68429-2
O Paradiso:Great Opera Arias, w. Frederick Schauwecker (pno), RCA Victor Orch [cnd:Renato Cellini], Rome Opera Orch [cnd:Erich Leinsdorf, Jonel Perlea], Robert Shaw Chorale [cnd:Robert Shaw] *(rec 1951-1959)* RCA Gold Seal ▲ 09026-68429-2 [ADD]
Omaggio a Jussi Björling Great Opera Performances 2-▲ GOP 786
Opera Arias, w. Nils Grevillius (cnd) *(rec Stockholm 1936-47 from HMV 78 rpms)* EMI Classics ("Great Recordings of the Century" series) ▲ CDH 61053 (m) [ADD]
Opera Gala London ▲ 421316-2 LA [ADD]
Opera, Lieder & Song, w. Nils Grevillius (cnd) Happy Days ▲ CDHD 214 [ADD]
Operatic Arias RCA Red Seal ▲ 5934-2-RC [ADD]
Operatic Duets, w. Licia Albanese (sop), Zinka Milanov (sop), Renata Tebaldi (sop), Robert Merrill (bar) RCA Gold Seal ▲ 7799-2-RG (m) [ADD] ■ 7799-4-RG (CrO2)
Operetta & Song, Vol. 2 *(rec 1929-38)* Pearl ▲ PEA 9042 [AAD]
Ponchielli, A.:La Gioconda (sels), *(cnd & orch unknown)* Enterprise ("Vocal Archives" series) ▲ ENT 1115
Puccini, G.:Arias, *(cnd & orch unknown)*—sels from La Bohème, Tosca & La fanciulla del West Enterprise ("Vocal Archives" series) ▲ ENT 1115
Puccini, G.:La Bohème, w. V. de los Angeles (sop), R. Merrill (bar), T. Beecham (cnd), RCA Victor SO [I] EMI Classics 2-▲ CDCB 47235 (m) [ADD] 2-■ 4X2G 47235
Puccini, G.:La Bohème (sels)—Che gelida manina RCA Gold Seal ▲ 09026-68429-2
Puccini, G.:Madama Butterfly, w. V. de los Angeles (sop), M. Pirazzini (mez), M. Sereni (bar), G. Santini (cnd), Rome Opera Orch, Rome Opera Chorus [I] EMI Classics ("Studio" series) 2-▲ CDMB 63634 [ADD]
Puccini, G.:Manon Lescaut, w. L. Albanese (sop), R. Merrill (bar), J. Perlea (cnd), Rome Opera Orch, Rome Opera Chorus [I] RCA Gold Seal 2-▲ 60573-2-RG [ADD]
Puccini, G.:Manon Lescaut (sels)—Ah, Manon, mi tradisce; No! no! pazzo son! RCA Gold Seal ▲ 09026-68429-2
Puccini, G.:Manon Lescaut (sels), w. N. Grevillius (cnd), Göteborg SO—Donna non vidi mai *(rec Concert Hall, Göteborg, Aug 5, 1960)* Myto ▲ MCD 953130
Puccini, G.:Tosca, w. Z. Milanov (sop), L. Warren (bar), E. Leinsdorf (cnd), Rome Opera Orch, Rome Opera Chorus [I] RCA Gold Seal 2-▲ 4514-2-RG [ADD] 2-■ 4514-2-RG
Puccini, G.:Tosca (sels)—E lucevan le stelle, Amaro sol per te RCA Gold Seal ▲ 09026-68429-2
Puccini, G.:Tosca (sels), w. Z. Milanov (sop), L. Warren (bar), E. Leinsdorf (cnd), Rome Opera Orch, Rome Opera Chorus RCA Gold Seal ▲ 60192-2-RG [ADD] ■ 60192-4-RG (CrO2)
Puccini, G.:Turandot, w. Birgit Nilsson (sop—Turandot), Renata Tebaldi (sop—Liù), Jussi Björling (ten—Calaf), Alessio De Paolis (ten—Emperor Altoum), Piero de Palma (ten—Pang), Mario Sereni (bar—Ping), Adelio Zagonara (bar—Prince of Persia), Giorgio Tozzi (bass—Timur), Tommaso Frascati (bass—Pong), Leonardo Monreale (bass—Mandarin), E. Leinsdorf (cnd), Rome Opera Orch, Rome Opera Chorus *(rec Rome Opera House, July 3-11, 1959)* RCA Living Stereo 2-▲ 09026-62687-2 [ADD]
Puccini, G.:Turandot, w. B. Nilsson (sop), R. Tebaldi (sop), G. Tozzi (bass), E. Leinsdorf (cnd), Rome Opera Orch, Rome Opera Chorus [I] RCA Red Seal 2-▲ 5932-2-RC 3-■ AGK3-3970
Puccini, G.:Turandot (sels)—Nessun dorma RCA Gold Seal ▲ 09026-68429-2
The Rare Repertoire, 1930-45 Enterprise ("Vocal Archives" series) ▲ ENT VA 1124
Recital, Vol. 1 *(rec live, 1939, 1951 & 1952)* Verona ▲ 27022 (m) [AAD]
Recital, Vol. 2 *(rec live)* Verona ▲ 27068 (m) [AAD]
The Records & the Beginning of a Legend (1930-1945) *(rec 1930-45)* Grammofono 2000 ▲ GRM 78664
Rossini, G.:Stabat Mater, *(cnd & orch unknown)* Enterprise ("Vocal Archives" series) ▲ ENT 1115
Scandinavian Songs & German Lieder, Vol. 1 *(rec between 1920-1940)* Pearl ▲ PEA 9041 [AAD]
Sibelius, J.:Songs, w. N. Grevillius (cnd), Göteborg SO—Säv, säv, susa; Svarta rosor *(rec Concert Hall, Göteborg, Aug 5, 1960)* Myto ▲ MCD 953130
Songs & Arias, Vol. 3 *(rec 1929-1939)* Pearl ▲ PEA 9043 [AAD]
Tchaikovsky, P.:Eugene Onegin (sels), w. N. Grevillius (cnd), Göteborg SO—Kuda, kuda *(rec Concert Hall, Göteborg, Aug 5, 1960)* Myto ▲ MCD 953130
Three Legendary Tenors:In Opera & Song, w. Enrico Caruso (ten), Beniamino Gigli (ten), Giuseppe de Luca (bar) Nimbus ▲ NI 1434 [ADD]
Three Tenors of the Golden Age, w. Mario Lanza (ten), Jan Peerce (ten), John Corigliano (vn), Constantine Callinicos (pno), Frederick Schauwecker (pno), RCA Victor Orch [cnd:Renato Cellini, Constantine Callinicos, Erich Leinsdorf, Sylvan Levin, Maximilian Pilzer, Frieder Weissmann], Rome Opera Orch, Rome Opera Chorus [cnd:Eri RCA Gold Seal ▲ 09026-68531-2 [ADD] ■ 09026-68531-4
Verdi, G.:Aida, w. Z. Milanov (sop), F. Barbieri (mez), L. Warren (bar), B. Christoff (bass), J. Perlea (cnd), Rome Opera Orch, Rome Opera Chorus [I] RCA Gold Seal 3-▲ 6652-2-RG (m) [ADD] 3-■ ALK3-5380 (m)
Verdi, G.:Aida, w. Z. Milanov (sop), F. Barbieri (mez), L. Warren (bar), B. Christoff (bass), J. Perlea (cnd), Rome Opera Orch, Rome Opera Chorus [I] RCA Gold Seal ▲ 60201-2-RG (m) [ADD] ■ 60201-4-RG (m)
Verdi, G.:Aida (sels)—Fuggiam gli ardori inospiti, Misero appien mi festi RCA Gold Seal ▲ 09026-68429-2
Verdi, G.:Arias, *(cnd & orch unknown)*—sels from Rigoletto, Il Trovatore, Un ballo in maschera, Aida & Requiem Mass Enterprise ("Vocal Archives" series) ▲ ENT 1115
Verdi, G.:Un ballo in maschera, w. Stella Andreva (sop—Oscar), Zinka Milanov (sop—Amelia), Bruna Castagna (cta—Ulrica), Jussi Björling (ten—Riccardo), Lodovico Oliviero (ten—Un Servo D'Amelia), John Cartet (bar—Un Giudice), Alexander Sved (bar—Renato), Normann Cordon (bass—Samuel), Arthur Kent (bass—Silvano), Nicola Moscona (bass—Tom), E. Panizza (cnd), *(orch unknown) (rec live, New York, Dec. 14, 1940)* The Fourties 2-▲ ENT FT 1515
Verdi, G.:Un ballo in maschera (sels), w. A. Schuh (sgr), Larrimore (sgr), M. Rothmüller (bar), N. Treigle (bass), J. Morris (bass), Feux (sgr), W. Herbert (cnd), *(orch unknown)* [I] *(rec live, New Orleans, 4/22/50)* Legato Classics ▲ LCD 154-1 (m) [ADD]
Verdi, G.:Requiem Mass, w. Z. Milanov (sop), B. Castagna (cta), N. Moscona (bass), A. Toscanini (cnd), NBC SO, Westminster Choir [L] *(rec 11/23/40)* Melodram 3-▲ MEL 38006
Verdi, G.:Requiem Mass, w. Zinka Milanov (sop), Bruna Castagna (mez), Nicola Moscona (bass), A. Toscanini (cnd), NBC SO, Westminster Choir *(rec Nov 23, 1940)* Music & Arts 2-▲ CD 240
Verdi, G.:Requiem Mass, w. Z. Milanov (sop), B. Castagna (cta), N. Moscona (bass), A. Toscanini (cnd), NBC SO, Westminster Choir *(rec Mar. 4, 1938)* Legato Classics 2-▲ LCD 178-2
Verdi, G.:Requiem Mass, w. L. Price (sop), R. Elias (mez), G. Tozzi (bass), F. Reiner (cnd), Vienna PO, Vienna Singverein [L] London 2-▲ 421608-2 [ADD]
Verdi, G.:Requiem Mass, w. Leontyne Price (sop), Rosalind Elias (mez), Giorgio Tozzi (bass), F. Reiner (cnd), Vienna PO, French Musical Society Vocal Group *(rec 1959)* London ("Double Decker" series) 2-▲ 444833-2 [ADD]
Verdi, G.:Rigoletto, w. R. Peters (sop), R. Merrill (bar), G. Tozzi (bass), J. Perlea (cnd), Rome Opera Orch, Rome Opera Chorus [I] RCA Gold Seal 2-▲ 60172-2-RG [ADD] 2-■ 60172-4-RG (CrO2)
Verdi, G.:Rigoletto (sels), w. K. Bendix (cnd), *(orch unknown)*—Ella mi fu rapita; Parmi veder le lagrime; La donna è mobile *(rec Royal Opera, Stockholm, Mar 5, 1957)* Myto ▲ MCD 953130
Verdi, G.:Rigoletto (sels)—Questa o quella, È il sol dell'anima, Bella figlia dell'amore RCA Gold Seal ▲ 09026-68429-2
Verdi, G.:La traviata, w. Hjördis Schymberg (sop), Conny Molin (sgr), H. Sandberg (cnd), Stockholm Royal Opera House Orch, Stockholm Royal Opera Chorus Grammofono 2000 2-▲ GRM 78640
Verdi, G.:La traviata, w. H. Schymberg (sop), Alard (sgr), Molin (sgr), H. Sandberg (cnd), *(orch unknown) (rec live 8/29/39)* Standing Room Only 2-▲ SRO 832-2 [ADD]
Verdi, G.:La traviata, w. Hjördis Schymberg (sop), Conni Molin (sgr), H. Sandberg (cnd), Stockholm Royal Opera House Orch, Stockholm Royal Theater Opera Chorus Enterprise ("The 40's" series) 2-▲ ENT 331
Verdi, G.:Il trovatore, w. Norina Greco (sop—Leonora), Bruna Castagna (cta—Azucena), Jussi Björling (ten—Manrico), Francesco Valentino (bar—Count di Luna), Nicola Moscona (bass—Ferrando), F. Calusio (cnd), *(orch unknown) (rec live, New York, Jan. 11, 1941)* The Fourties 2-▲ ENT FT 1507

Björling, Jussi (ten) (cont.)
Verdi, G.:Il trovatore, w. G. Cigna (sop—Leonora), G. Wettergren (mez—Azucena), M. Huder (mez—Ines), J. Björling (ten—Manrico), O. Dua (ten—Ruiz), C. Zambelli (ten—Ferrando), M. Basiola (bar—Count di Luna), L. Horsman (bar—Old Gypsy), V. Gui (cnd), Royal Opera Orch, Royal Opera House Chorus Covent Garden *(rec May 12, 1939)* Legato Classics 2-▲ LCD 173-2 [ADD]
Verdi, G.:Il trovatore, w. Z. Milanov (sop), F. Barbieri (mez), L. Warren (bar), R. Cellini (cnd), RCA Victor SO, Robert Shaw Chorale [I] RCA Gold Seal ▲ 60191-2-RG [ADD] ■ 60191-4-RG (CrO2)
Verdi, G.:Il trovatore, w. Z. Milanov (sop), F. Barbieri (mez), L. Warren (bar), R. Cellini (cnd), RCA Victor SO, Robert Shaw Chorale [I] RCA Gold Seal 2-▲ 6643-2-RG (m) [ADD] 2-■ CLK2-5377 (m)
Verdi, G.:Il trovatore, w. Norina Greco (sop), Bruna Castagna (mez), Nicola Moscona (bass), Francesco Valentino (sgr), F. Calusio (cnd), *(orch & chorus unknown)* Enterprise ("The Radio Years" series) 2-▲ ENT 44 (m)
Verdi, G.:Il trovatore (sels), w. Hjördis Schymberg (sop), Kerstin Meyer (mez), Olle Sivall (ten), Hugo Hasslo (bar), H. Sandberg (cnd), Royal Opera Orch, Royal Opera House Chorus Covent Garden—Non son tuo figlio?; Mal reggendo all'aspro assalto; Quale d'armi fragor; Ah! sì, ben mio, coll'essere; L'onda de' suoni mistici; Di quella pira l'orrendo foco; Miserere d'un'alma già vicina; Madre?...non dormi?; Se m'ami ancor; Ciel!...non m'inganna; Ti scosta... *(rec Royal Opera, Stockholm, Mar 6, 1960)* Myto ▲ MCD 953130
Verdi, G.:Il trovatore (sels)—Deserto sulla terra, Mai reggendo, Ah si ben mio; Di quella pira RCA Gold Seal ▲ 09026-68429-2
Verdi, G.:Il trovatore (sels), w. J. Biel (ten), F. Tamagno (ten), L.-A. Escalaïs (ten), M. Gilion (ten), E. Caruso (ten), A. Paoli (ten), G. Zenatello (ten), J. Sembach (ten), L. Slezak (ten), F. Constantino (ten), G. Martinelli (ten), B. De Muro (ten), N. Fusati (ten), N. Piccaluga (ten), G. Lauri-Volpi (ten), A. Pertile (ten), E. Bergamaschi (ten), R. Tauber (ten), J. O'Sullivan (ten), H. Roswaenge (ten), G. Taccani (ten), V. Lois (ten), H. Lazaro (ten), A. Lindi (ten), A. Cortis (ten), F. Merli (ten), F. Völker (ten), J. Kiepura (ten), J. Schmidt (ten), B. Gigli (ten), A. Salvarezza (ten), J. Soler (ten), M. Filippeschi (ten)—34 performances of the Act III tenor aria "Di quella pira!," *(rec from 1903-1956)* Bongiovanni ▲ GB 1051 [AAD]
Wagner, R.:Lohengrin (sels), w. N. Grevillius (cnd), Göteborg SO—In fernem Land *(rec Concert Hall, Göteborg, Aug 5, 1960)* Myto ▲ MCD 953130

Björling, Sigurd (bar)
Beethoven, L. van:Sym 9, "Choral Sym", w. L. Tunell (alto), G. Bckelin (ten), W. Furtwängler (cnd), Stockholm PO *(rec Dec. 1, 1943)* Music & Arts ▲ CD 2002 [AAD]
Beethoven, L. van:Sym 9, "Choral Sym", w. H. Schymberg (sop), L. Tunell (cta), G. Bäckelin (ten), W. Furtwängler (cnd), Stockholm Concert Society Orch *(rec Dec. 1, 1943)* Music & Arts ▲ CD 774 [AAD]
Rossini, G.:Il barbiere di Siviglia (sels), w. Birgit Nilsson (sop), Set Svanholm (ten), Ehrling, Grevillius, Larsson, Mann, Sandberg (cnd), Royal Stockholm PO, Swedish RSO—Largo al factotum Bluebell ▲ BLU 058 [ADD]
Strauss, R.:Ariadne auf Naxos (sels), w. Birgit Nilsson (sop), Set Svanholm (ten), *(orch unknown)*—Circe, Circe kannst du mich hören? Bluebell ▲ BLU 058 [ADD]
Verdi, G.:Otello (sels), w. Birgit Nilsson (sop), Set Svanholm (ten), Ehrling, Grevillius, Larsson, Mann, Sandberg (cnd), Royal Stockholm PO, Swedish RSO—Desdemona rea!...Ora e per sempre adio...Si, pel ciel marmoreo giuro! Bluebell ▲ BLU 058 [ADD]
Wagner, R.:Arias & Scenes, w. Birgit Nilsson (sop), Set Svanholm (ten), Ehrling, Grevillius, Larsson, Mann, Sandberg (cnd), Royal Stockholm PO, Swedish RSO—Morgenlich leuchtend [from Die Meistersinger von Nürnberg]; Ein Schwert verhiess mir der Vater [from Die Walküre]; Mime hiess ein mürrischer Zwerg...Brünnhilde, heilige Braut [from Götterdämmerung] Bluebell ▲ BLU 058 [ADD]
Wagner, R.:Das Rheingold, w. E. Schwarzkopf (sop), I. Malaniuk (cta), W. Windgassen (ten), Pflanzl (sgr), H. von Karajan (cnd), Bayreuth Festival Orch, Bayreuth Festival Chorus [G] *(rec live, 1951)* Arkadia 2-▲ 216 (m) [ADD]
Wagner, R.:Das Rheingold, w. P. Brivkalne (sop), I. Malaniuk (cta), R. Siewert (cta), Fritz (sgr), Pflanzl (ten), W. Faulhaber (bass), L. Weber (bass), F. Dalberg (bass), H. von Karajan (cnd), Bayreuth Festival Orch, Bayreuth Festival Chorus [G] *(rec live 8/1/51)* Melodram 2-▲ MEL 26107 (m) [AAD]
Wagner, R.:Siegfried, w. A. Varnay (sop), R. Siewert (cta), B. Aldenhoff (ten), P. Kuen (ten), H. Pflanzl (bass), F. Dalberg (bass), H. von Karajan (cnd), Bayreuth Festival Orch, Bayreuth Festival Chorus [G] *(rec live 1951)* Melodram 4-▲ MEL 46106 (m) [AAD]
Wagner, R.:Die Walküre (act 3), w. A. Varnay (sop—Brünnhilde), L. Rysanek (sop—Sieglinde), S. Björling (bar—Wotan), H. von Karajan (cnd), Bayreuth Festival Orch *(rec Aug. 12, 1951)* EMI Classics ▲ ZDH 64704
Weber, C.M. von:Der Freischütz (sels), w. Birgit Nilsson (sop), Set Svanholm (ten), Ehrling, Grevillius, Larsson, Mann, Sandberg (cnd), Royal Stockholm PO, Swedish RSO—Durch die Wälder, durch die Auen Bluebell ▲ BLU 058 [ADD]

Bjørnhaug, Ståle (nar)
Habbestad, K.:The Articles of Norwegian Christian Law, w. Adomas Kontautas (lure), Zigmas Kazlauskas (lure), Rimantas Valanctus (lure), Marius Balcytis (lure) Norway Music ▲ 2912

Blachut, Beno (ten)
Dvořák, A.:Evening Songs, Op. 3, w. Ferdinand Pohlreich (pno) Supraphon ▲ SUP 0206 [AAD]
Dvořák, A.:The Jacobin (sels), w. Marcela Machotková (sop), Vilém Přibyl (ten), J. Pinkas (cnd), Brno State PO Supraphon ▲ SUP 112250 [AAD]
Dvořák, A.:St Ludmilla, w. Vera Soukupová (mez), Eva Zikmundová (mez), Richard Novák (bass), V. Smetáček (cnd), Prague SO, Czech Phil Chorus *(rec 1963)* Supraphon 2-▲ SUP 112141 [AAD]
Dvořák, A.:Stabat Mater, w. Drahomira Tikalova (sop), Marta Krasova (cta), Karel Kalas (bass), V. Talich (cnd), Czech PO, Czech Phil Chorus *(rec 1952)* Supraphon 2-▲ SUP 111902 [AAD]
Dvořák, A.:Vanda, w. Drahomira Tikalova (sop), Stefa Petrova (mez), Karel Kalas (bass), F. Dyk (cnd), Prague RSO, Jiri Pinkas (cnd), Prague Radio Chorus *(rec 1951)* Supraphon ("Hidden Treasures from Prague" series) 2-▲ SUP CD 3007 (m)
Janácek, L.:The Diary of One Who Disappeared, w. Věra Soukupová (mez), Stepanka Stepanova (mez), Nicolai Gedda (ten), Josef Paleníček (pno), Prague Radio Women's Chorus, Czech Chamber Singers Female Chorus—contains 2 complete performances *(rec 1984 & 1956)* Supraphon ▲ SUP 0022 [DDD/ADD]
Janácek, L.:Kát'a Kabanová, w. D. Tikalová (sop), J. Krombholc (cnd), Prague National Theater Orch, Prague National Theater Chorus Supraphon 2-▲ SUP 108016 [ADD]
Novák, V.:Storm, w. Maria Tauberová (sop), Drahomíra Tikalová (sop), Ladislav Mráz (bar), J. Krombholc (cnd), Czech PO, Czech Phil Chorus *(rec 1956)* Supraphon 2-▲ SUP 111982 (m) [DDD]
Skroup, F.:Columbus (sels), w. M. Subrtová (sop), Z. Otava (bar), F. Dyk (cnd), Prague RSO, Prague Radio Chorus *(rec 1962)* Multisonic ("Prague Opera Collection" series) ▲ 31 0153

Black, Andrew (bass)
Sullivan, A.:Henry VIII, w. A. Black, *(orch unknown)*—King Henry's song Symposium ▲ 1123

Black, Jeffrey (bar)
Orff, C.:Carmina burana, w. B. Hendricks (sop), M. Chance (ct), F. Welser-Möst (cnd), London PO, London Phil Chorus, St. Alban's Cathedral Choristers [G, L] EMI Classics ▲ CDC 54054 [DDD]

Blackburn, David (sgr)
Rorem, N.:Miss Julie, w. Theodora Fried (sgr—Miss Julie), Heather Sarris (sgr—Christine, the cook), Laurelyn Watson (sgr—Young Girl), David Blackburn (sgr—Mr. Niels), Mark Mulligan (sgr—Young Boy), Philip Torre (sgr—John, the valet), Judd Ernster (bass), D. Gilbert (cnd), Manhattan School of Music Opera Orch, Manhattan School of Music Opera Chorus Newport Classic 2-▲ NPT 85605 [DDD]

Blackburn, Olivia (sop)
Ginastera, A.:Qts Strs (comp), w. Lyric String Quartet ASV ▲ ASV 944
Ginastera, A.:Songs, w. A. Portugheis (pno)—2 canciones, Op. 3; 5 canciones, Op. 5; Las horas de una estancia, Op. 11 ASV ▲ ASV 902 [DDD]

Blackburn, Philip (voc)
Partch, H.:While My Heart Keeps Beating Time, w. Liz Schmidt (pno) [orig published under alias Paul Pirate] *(rec 1995)* Innova 4-▲ 401

Blackett, Joy (cta)
Paine, J.K.:Mass, Op. 10, w. C. Balthrop (sop), V. Cole (ten), J. Cheek (bass), J. Lange (org), G. Schuller (cnd), St. Louis SO, St. Louis Sym Chorus [L] *(rec ca. mid-1970s)* New World ▲ 80262-2 [AAD]

▲ = CD ◆ = Enhanced CD Δ = MD ■ = Cassette Tape □ = DCC

Blackwell, Harolyn (sop)

Bernstein, L.:Songs & Duets, w. D. Troob (cnd)—A Simple Song [from Mass; w. John Miller (bass), Scott Kuney (gtr), Brian Koonin (nylon-str gtr), Bill Hayes (perc), Melanie Feld (ob)]; A Little Bit In Love[from Wonderful Town; w. Danny Troob (syn), John Miller (bass), Scott Kuney (gtr), John Redsecker (dr/bell tree), Glenn Drewes (tpt/flgl), Lou Marini (sax/fl)]; I Hate Music; Jupiter Has 7 Moons; My Name Is Barbara; A Big Indian & a Little Indian; I'm a Person Too [all from I Hate Music; w. Bill Hicks (pno), Bill Hayes (perc)]; Glitter & Be Gay [from Candide; w. Bill Hicks (pno/cel), John Beal (bass), Scott Kuney (gtr), Gordon Gottlieb (perc), Dick Clark (trbn), Neil Balm (tpts), Kathy Fink (fl/pic), Melanie Feld (ob/E hn), Al Ragni (sax/cl/fl/pic), Jeff Lang (hn), Tony Cecere (hn), Diminick Cortese (acc), Sanford Allen (vn), Dale Stuckenbruck (vn), Bleinda Whitney (vn), Robert Chausow (vn), Richard Locker (vc), Caryl Paisner (vc)]; Who Am I; Peter, Peter; My House [all from Peter Pan; w. Kathy Sommer (pno), Danny Troob (syn), John Miller (bass), Scott Kuney (gtr), John Redsecker (dr/bell tree), Geln Drewes (tpt/flgl), Lou Marini (sax/fl)]; Dream with Me [from Peter Pan; w. Bill Hicks (pno/cel), John Miller (bass), Scott Kuney (gtrs), Kathy Fink (fl), Richard Locker (vc)]; A Julia de Burgos [from Songfest; w. Bill Hicks (pno/cel), John Beal (bass), Scott Kuney (gtr), Gordon Gottlieb (perc), Dick Clark (trbn), Neil Balm (tpts), Kathy Fink (fl/pic), Melanie Feld (ob/E hn), Al Ragni (sax/cl/fl/pic), Jeff Lang (hn), Tony Cecere (hn), Dominick Cortese (acc), Sanford Allen (vn), Dale Stuckenbruck (vn), Belinda Whitney (vn), Robert Chausow (vn), Richard Locker (vc), Caryl Paisner (vc)]; America; A Boy Like That; I Have a Love; Somewhere [all from West Side Story; w. Vanessa Williams (sgr), Judy Sugarman (bass), Scott Kuney (gtr), Jim Saporito (dr), Bill Hayes (perc), Joe Passaro (perc), Jim Pugh (trbn), Paul Faulise (trbn), Rich Kelley (tpt), Glen Drewes (tpt), Dave Gale (tpt), Les Scott (fl/pic/cl/E♭ cl), Dennis Anderson (fl/ob/cl/bass cl), Kathy Fink (fl/pic), John Campo (bn), Tony Cecere (hn), Glen Estrin (hn), Sanford Allen (vn), Charlie Libove (vn), Belinda Whitney (vn), Susan Orenstein (vn), Joyce Hammon (vn), Cenovia Cummins (vn), Richard Locker (vc), Caryl Paisner (vc)]; Sean Song; A Simple Song (reprise) [w. Kathy Sommer (pno), John Miller (bass), Scott Kuney (gtr), Brian Koonin (nylon-str gtr), Bill Hayes (perc), Melanie Feld (ob)] *(rec Manhattan Center's 7th Floor Ballroom & Clinton Studios, NYC, Nov 14–18, 1994)* RCA ▲ 09026-68321-2 [DDD]

Noël, w. Canadian Brass, Canadian Brass Jazz All-Stars, Angel Romero (gtr), *(children's choir unknown),* Richard Stoltzman (cl), Jerry Hadley (ten), King's Singers, James Galway (fl) *(rec Apr. 17–20, 1994)* RCA Victor ▲ 09026-62683-2 ■ 09026-62683-4

Blades, Christopher (bar)

Pacini, G.:Maria Tudor, w. M. Hill Smith (sop), P. Walker (sop), K. Lewis (ten), D. Parry (cnd), English SO *(rec 1983)* Italian Opera Rarities ▲ IOR 7714 [ADD]

Blaine, V. (sgr)

Loesser, F.:Guys and Dolls, w. R. Alda (sgr), S. Levene (sgr) [1950 Broadway cast] MCA Classics ▲ MCAD 10301 [AAD] ■ MCAC 10301

Blake, J. (sgr)

Hamelin, C.:Archangelus Gabriel, w. C. Hamelin Horizon ▲ HOCD 7003

Blake, Rockwell (ten)

French Opera Arias for Tenor, w. R. Blake (ten), Monte Carlo PO, Monte Carlo Phil Chorus [cnd:Patrick Fournillier] EMI Classics ▲ CDC 55058

Mozart, W.A.:Arias, w. N. McGegan (cnd), London SO— from Clemenza di Tito *(Se all'impero);* Così fan tutte *(Un aura amorosa);* Don Giovanni *(Dalla sua pace; Il mio tesoro);* Entführung aus dem Serail *(Ich baue ganze);* Idomeneo *(Fuor del mar);* Mitridate, Rè di Ponto *(Vado incontro; Se di lauri);* Concert Aria, "Misero! O Sogno!," K.431 [G,I] Arabesque ▲ Z 6598

Rossini, G.:Arias, w. J. McCarthy (cnd), London SO, Ambrosian Singers [I] Arabesque ▲ Z 6582

Rossini, G.:Arias, w. M. Valdes (cnd), London SO, Ambrosian Singers—8 arias from Armida, Ermione, Gazza ladra, Otello, Ricciardo e Zoraide, Semiramide, Zelmira [I] Arabesque ▲ Z 6612

Rossini, G.:Music of, w. M. Fortuna (sop), M. Lerner (sop), D. Voigt (sop), M. Horne (mez), K. Kuhlmann (mez), F. von Stade (mez), C. Estep (ten), C. Merritt (ten), T. Hampson (b-bar), H. Runey (b-bar), J. Opalach (bass), S. Ramey (bass), R. Norrington (cnd), Orch of St. Luke's, New York Concert Chorale EMI Classics ▲ CDC 54643

Rossini, G.:Songs, w. Antonio Pappano (pno)—La promessa; La gita in gondola; L'orgia; Il rimprovero; La danza; La partenza; Le dodo des enfants; Romeó; Le sylvain; Le Lazzarone; Ariette à l'ancienne; Au chevet d'un mourant; La dichiarazione; Il fanciullo smarito; La lontanza; L'esule; Nizza; Mi lagnero tacendo (9 versions); La duo des chats [w Gérard Lesne (ct)] EMI Classics ▲ CDC 55614

Blanc, Ernst (bar)

Bellini, V.:I Puritani, w. J. Sutherland (sop—Elvira), N. Gedda (ten—Arturo), E. Blanc (bar—Riccardo), J. Diaz (bass—Giorgio), R. Bonynge (cnd), *(orch unknown)* [I] *(rec live, Philadelphia 4/18/63)* Standing Room Only 2-▲ SRO 838-2 [ADD]

Bellini, V.:I Puritani (sels), w. J. Sutherland (sop), N. Filacuridi (sgr), G. Modesti (bass), *(orch unknown) (rec live, Edinburgh, Sept. 8, 1960)* Standing Room Only 2-▲ SRO 841-2 [ADD]

Berlioz, H.:L'Enfance du Christ, w. Victoria de los Angeles (sop), Nicolai Gedda (ten), Roger Soyer (bar), A. Cluytens (cnd), Paris Conservatory Societé des Concerts Orch, René DuClos Chorus EMI Classics ("Doublefforte" series) 2-▲ CDFB 68586

Bizet, G.:Carmen, w. J. Micheau (sop), V. de los Angeles (sop), N. Gedda (ten), T. Beecham (cnd), *(orch unknown)* [F] EMI Classics 3-▲ CDCC 49240 [ADD]

Bizet, G.:Les Pêcheurs de perles, w. J. Micheau (sop), N. Gedda (ten), J. Mars (bar), P. Dervaux (cnd), Paris Opéra-Comique Orch, Paris Opéra-Comique Chorus [F] EMI Classics ("Studio" series) 2-▲ CDMB 69704 [ADD]

Gounod, C.:Faust, w. V. de los Angeles (sop), L. Berton (sop), R. Gorr (mez), N. Gedda (ten), B. Christoff (bass), A. Cluytens (cnd), Paris Opera Orch [F] Angel ("Studio" series) 3-▲ CDMC 69983 [ADD]

Gounod, C.:Faust (sels), w. Liliane Berton (sop), Victoria de los Angeles (sop), Rita Gorr (mez), Nicolai Gedda (ten), Victor Autran (bar), Boris Christoff (bass), A. Cluytens (cnd), Paris Opera Orch, Paris Opera Chorus Classics for Pleasure ("Eminence" series) ▲ CDEMX 2215 [DDD]

Massenet, J.:Hérodiade, w. Nadine Denize (mez), D. Lloyd-Jones (cnd), French Radio Lyric Orch, French Radio Chorus *(rec Paris, Dec 5, 1974)* Agorá ("Phoenix" series) 2-▲ 514

Offenbach, J.:Les Contes d'Hoffmann, w. E. Schwarzkopf (sop), G. d'Angelo (sop), V. de los Angeles (sop), N. Gedda (ten), G. London (bar), A. Cluytens (cnd), Paris Conservatory Societé des Concerts Orch, René DuClos Chorus [F] EMI Classics ("Studio" series) 2-▲ CDMB 63222 [ADD]

Saint-Saëns, C.:Samson et Dalila, w. R. Gorr (mez), J. Vickers (ten), G. Prêtre (cnd), Paris Opera Orch, René DuClos Chorus [F] EMI Classics 2-▲ CDCB 47895

Saint-Saëns, C.:Samson et Dalila (sels), w. R. Gorr (mez), J. Vickers (ten), G. Prêtre (cnd), Paris Opera Orch EMI Classics ▲ ZDM 63935

Wagner, R.:Lohengrin, w. L. Rysanek (sop), A. Varnay (sop), S. Kónya (ten), A. Cluytens (cnd), Bayreuth Festival Orch, Bayreuth Festival Chorus [G] *(rec live, 7/23/58)* Myto 3-▲ MCD 89002 (m) [ADD]

Blanc, Pierre (sgr)

Varney, L.:Les Mousquetaires au couvent, w. Gabrielle Ristori (mez), Camille Rouquetty (ten), Gabriel Bacquier (bar), Louis Musy (b-bar), Pauline Carton (sgr), Jacqueline Cauchard (sgr), Mireille Lacoste (sgr), Colette Riedinger (sgr), R. Benedetti (cnd) Musidisc 2-▲ MUS 202262 [AAD]

Blanck, Kirsten (sop)

Korngold, E.W.:Der Ring des Polykrates, w. Beate Bilandzija (sop—Laura), Kirsten Blanck (sop—Lieschen), Endrik Wottrich (ten—Wilhelm), Jürgen Sacher (ten—Florian), Dietrich Henschel (bar—Peter), K. Seibel (cnd), German SO *(rec Jesus Christ Church, Dahlem, Sept 19–25, 1995)* CPO ▲ CPO 999402-2 [DDD]

Blankenburg, Heinz (bar)

Mozart, W.A.:Don Giovanni, w. Birgit Nilsson (sop—Donna Anna), Leontyne Price (sop—Donna Elvira), Eugenia Ratti (sop—Zerlina), Cesare Valletti (ten—Don Ottavio), Heinz Blankenburg (bar—Masetto), Fernando Corena (b-bar—Leporello), Arnold van Mill (b-bar—Il Commendatore), Cesare Siepi (b-bar—Don Giovanni), E. Leinsdorf (cnd), Vienna PO, Vienna State Opera Chorus [I] London 3-▲ 444594-2 [ADD]

Blankenship, William (ten)

Krenek, E.:Jonny spielt auf, w. E. Lear (sop—Anita), L. Popp (sop—Yvonne), W. Blankenship (ten—Max), K. Equiluz (ten—Station Announcer), L. Heppe (ten—Manager), T. Stewart (bar—Daniello), G. Feldhof (bass—Jonny), H. Hollreiser (cnd), Vienna State Opera Orch [G] Vanguard Classics ▲ OVC 8048 [ADD]

Blaser, Pierre-André (ten)

Schibler, A.:La Folie de Tristan, w. Audrey Michael (sop—Iseut), Arlette Chédel (mez—Brangien), Pierre-André Blaser (ten—Tristan), Philippe Huttenlocher (bar—Le roi Marc/Le pêcheur/Le portier), André Fauré (nar), William Jacques (nar), Snezana Zivojinovic (nar), J. Auberson (cnd), Lausanne CO, Romande Instrumental Group Rockband, Swiss Romande Radio Choir *(rec live, Festival de Montreux, Sept 15, 1980)* Jecklin ▲ JD 695

Blasi, Angela Maria (sop)

Bach, J.S.:Cant 208, "Hunting Cant", w. J. P. Kenny (alt), K. Equiluz (ten), R. Holl (bass), N. Harnoncourt (cnd), Vienna Concentus Musicus, Arnold Schoenberg Choir [G] Teldec ▲ 2292-46151-2 [DDD]

Bach, J.S.:Cant 212, "Peasant Cant", w. R. Holl (bass), N. Harnoncourt (cnd), Vienna Concentus Musicus, Arnold Schoenberg Choir [G] Teldec ▲ 2292-46151-2 [DDD]

Bach, J.S.:Mass in b, BWV 232, w. D. Ziegler (mez), J. Rappé (cta), K. Equiluz (ten), R. Holl (bass), N. Harnoncourt (cnd), Vienna Concentus Musicus, Arnold Schoenberg Choir [L] Teldec 2-▲ 2292-42676-2 [DDD]

Bizet, G.:Te Deum, w. Christian Elsner (ten), H.R. Zöbeley (cnd), Munich SO, Munich Motet Choir *(rec live, Herkulessaal, Munich, Mar 13 & 17, 1996)* Calig ▲ CAL 50956 [DDD]

Bomtempo, J.D.:Messe de requiem consacrée à...Camões, w. Liliana Bizineche-Eisinger (mez), Reinaldo Macias (ten), Michel Brodard (bass), M. Corboz (cnd), Lisbon Gulbenkian Foundation Orch, Lisbon Gulbenkian Foundation Chorus *(rec Gulbenkian Foundation Grand Auditorium, June 14–16, 1994)* FNAC Music ▲ 592302 [DDD]

Brahms, J.:Ein Deutsches Requiem, w. B. Terfel (b-bar), E. Schloter (org), C. Davis (cnd), Bavarian RSO, Bavarian Radio Chorus [G] RCA Red Seal ▲ 09026-60868-2

Gounod, C.:Messe solennelle de St. Cécile, w. Christian Elsner (ten), Dietrich Henschel (bar), H.R. Zöbeley (cnd), Munich SO, Munich Motet Choir *(rec live, Herkulessaal, Munich, Mar 13 & 17, 1996)* Calig ▲ CAL 50956 [DDD]

Haydn, J.:Die Jahreszeiten, w. Josef Protschka (ten), Robert Holl (bass), N. Harnoncourt (cnd), Vienna SO, Arnold Schoenberg Choir [G] Teldec 2-▲ 2292-42699-2

Mahler, G.:Sym 4, w. C. Davis (cnd), Bavarian RSO *(rec Munich, Germany, Oct 13 & 14, 1993)* RCA Red Seal ▲ 09026-62521-2 [DDD]

Mozart, W.A.:Complete Mozart Edition, w. S. McNair (sop), I. Vermillion (mez), J. Hadley (ten), C. H. Ahnsjö (ten), N. Marriner (cnd), Academy of St. Martin in the Fields Philips 2-▲ 422535-2 [ADD]

Mozart, W.A.:Requiem, w. M. Lipovšek (mez), U. Heilmann (ten), J.-H. Rootering (bass), C. Davis (cnd), Bavarian RSO, Bavarian Radio Chorus [L] RCA Red Seal ▲ 09026-60599-2 [DDD] ■ 09026-60599-4 (CrO2) □ 09026-60599-5

Blasius, Martin (bass)

Zemlinsky, A. von:Der Traumgörge, w. P. Coburn (sop), J. Martin (sop), G. M. Ronge (sop), B. Calm (mez), P. Haage (ten), H. Kruse (ten), J. Protschka (ten), H. Welker (bar), V. von Halem (bass), G. Albrecht (cnd), Frankfurt RSO [G] Capriccio 2-▲ CD 10241/2 [DDD]

Blatter, Johanna (mez)

Wagner, R.:Das Rheingold, w. L. Otto (sop), M. Muszely (sop), R. Stewart (mez), S. Wagner (mez), R. Schock (ten), H. Melchert (ten), F. Frantz (bass), B. Kusche (bass), J. Metternich (bass), R. Kempe (cnd), Berlin Staatskapelle *(rec Mar. 1959)* Berlin Classics ("Eterna" series) ▲ BER 2035 [ADD]

Wagner, R.:Tristan und Isolde (sels), w. Martha Mödl (sop—Isolde), Johanna Blatter (mez—Brangäne), Wolfgang Windgassen (ten—Tristan), A. Rother (cnd), Berlin City Opera Orch—Weh, ach wehe! dies zu dulden [rec. Nov 24., 1954]; Isolde!— Tristan! Geliebter! [rec. Oct. 24, 1954]; Lausch', Geliebter!— Lass mich sterben! [rec. Oct 24., 1954]; Mild und leise wie er lächelt [rec. Oct 22., 1952] Teldec ("Historic" series) ▲ 95516-2 [ADD]

Blaze, Robin (sgr)

Blow, J.:Anthems, w. Joseph Cornwell (ten), Stephen Varcoe (bar), D. Hill (cnd), Parley of Instruments, Winchester Cathedral Choir Hyperion 2-▲ CDA 67031/32

Blazer, Judith (sop)

Gershwin, G.:Girl Crazy, w. L. Luft (sgr), D. Carroll (sgr), J. Mauceri (cnd), *(orch unknown)* Elektra/Nonesuch ▲ 9 79250-2

Bledsoe, J. (sgr)

Kern, J.:Show Boat (sels), w. P. Robeson (b-bar), M. Burke (sgr), E. Day (sgr), *(other artists unknown)* [original cast] Pearl ("Flapper" series) ▲ PEA CD 9105 [ADD]

Bleeke, Mark (ten)

Bach, J.S.:St. John Passion, w. Tamara Matthews (sop), Jennifer Lane (alt), Mark Bleeke (ten—Evangelist), David Vanderwal (ten), Kevin Walsh (bar—Pilate), Nathaniel Watson (bass—Jesus), E. Milnes (cnd), Trinity Baroque Orch, Trinity Cathedral Choir *(rec Trinity Cathedral, Portland, OR, Mar 31, 1996)* PGM 2-▲ PGM 111

Brubeck, D.:To Hope!:A Celebration, w. Shelley Waite (sop), Kevin Deas (b-bar), R. Gloyd (cnd), Cathedral Choral Society Orch, Dave Brubeck Quartet, Cathedral Choral Society Chorus *(rec Washington National Cathedral, Washington, D.C., June 12, 1995)* Telarc ▲ CD 80430 [DDD]

Carmina Burana & Other Spirited Songs from the German Middle Ages, w. Folger Consort, T. Chancey Folger Consort ▲ BDCD1 8901 [DAD]

Dance Songs of Renaissance England, w. Folger Consort, T. Chancey, W. Gillespie, M. Springfels, B. Wissick *(rec Jan. 24, 1988)* Folger Consort ▲ BDCD1 9004 [DDD]

Imbrie, A.W.:Campion Songs, w. Joan Peterson (sop), Nancy Wertsch (alt), Nathaniel Watson (bar), A. Korf (cnd), Parnassus *(rec Sept. 29, 1993)* New World ▲ 80441-2

Blegen, Judith (sop)

Bach, J.S.:Anna Magdalena Bach Notebook, w. Luxon (bar), Kipnis (hpd/clvd), Meinis (vl) [G] Elektra/Nonesuch 2-▲ 79020-2 [DDD]

Basic 100, Vol. 63, w. Frederica von Stade (mez), Philadelphia Orch [cnd:Eugene Ormandy] RCA Victor ▲ 09026-68088-2 ■ 09026-68088-4

Beethoven, L. van:Fidelio, w. Leonie Rysanek (sop), Jon Vickers (ten), Walter Berry (bass), John Macurdy (bass), Giorgio Tozzi (bass), K. Böhm (cnd), San Francisco Opera Orch, San Francisco Opera Chorus Melodram 2-▲ CDM 27086

Berg, A.:Der Wein, w. P. Boulez (cnd), New York PO Sony Classical ▲ SMK 45838 [DDD]

Duruflé, M.:Requiem, w. Morris, Shaw, Atlanta SO, Atlanta Sym Chorus [L] Telarc ▲ CD 80135 [DDD]

Fauré, G.:Requiem, w. J. Morris (bass), R. Shaw (cnd), Atlanta SO, Atlanta Sym Chorus [L] Telarc ▲ CD 80135 [DDD]

Handel, G.F.:Alessandro (sels), w. G. Schwarz (cnd), Mostly Mozart Festival Orch—Lusinghe più care Sony Classical ("Essential Classics" series) ▲ SBK 62646 ■ SBT 62646

Handel, G.F.:Cants, w. G. Schwarz (cnd), Mostly Mozart Festival Orch—Eternal Source of Light Divine; Let the Bright Seraphim Sony Classical ("Essential Classics" series) ▲ SBK 62646 ■ SBT 62646

Handel, G.F.:Messiah (sels), w. Katherine Ciesinski (mez), John Aler (ten), John Cheek (bass), R. Westenburg (cnd), Musica Sacra, Musica Sacra Chorus RCA Silver Seal ▲ 60481-2-RV [DDD]; ■ 60481-4-RV (CrO2)

Haydn, J.:Mass 10, "Kriegsmesse", "Paukenmesse", w. Brigette Fassbaender (mez), Claes Hakan Ahnsjö (ten), Hans Sotin (bass), L. Bernstein (cnd), Bavarian RSO, Bavarian Radio Chorus [L] Philips ▲ 412734-2 [DDD]

Haydn, J.:Mass 11, "Nelsonmesse", "Imperial Mass", "Coronation Mass", w. Gwendolen Killebrew (mez), Kenneth Riegel (ten), Simon Estes (bass), L. Bernstein (cnd), New York PO, Westminster Choir [L] *(rec 1976)* Sony Classical ("Bernstein:The Royal Edition" series) 2-▲ SM2K 47563 [ADD]

Haydn, J.:Mass 14, "Harmoniemesse", w. Fredrica von Stade (mez), Kenneth Riegel (ten), Simon Estes (bass), L. Bernstein (cnd), New York PO, Westminster Choir [L] *(rec 1966)* Sony Classical 2-▲ SM2K 47560 [ADD]

Mahler, G.:Syms, w. B. Hendricks (sop), M. Price (sop), G. Zeumer (sop), H. Wittek (trb), A. Baltsa (mez), C. Ludwig (mez), K. Riegel (ten), H. Prey (bar), A. Schmidt (bar), J. Van Dam (b-bar), L. Bernstein (cnd), New York PO, Royal Concertgebouw Orch, Vienna PO, Westminster Choir, New York Choral Artists, Brooklyn Boys' Choir, Vienna Boys' Choir, Vienna State Opera Chorus, Vienna Singverein Deutsche Grammophon 13-▲ 435162-2 [DDD]

Mahler, G.:Sym 8, w. M. Price (sop), G. Zeumer (sop), A. Baltsa (mez), K. Riegel (ten), H. Prey (bar), A. Schmidt (bar), J. Van Dam (b-bar), L. Bernstein (cnd), Vienna PO, Vienna State Opera Chorus, Vienna Boys' Choir *(rec Salzburg Festival, 1975)* Deutsche Grammophon 2-▲ 435102-2 [ADD]

Mendelssohn, F.:A Midsummer Night's Dream (comp), w. F. von Stade (mez), E. Ormandy (cnd), Mendelssohn Club Chorus Philadelphia [G] RCA Red Seal ▲ RCD1-2084

Blegen, Judith (sop) (cont.)
Mozart, W.A.:Exsultate, w. P. Zukerman (cnd), Mostly Mozart Festival Orch
Sony Classical ("Essential Classics" series) ▲ SBK 62646 ■ SBT 62646
Mozart, W.A.:Idomeneo (sels), w. P. Zukerman (cnd), Mostly Mozart Festival Orch—Non temer, amato bene
Sony Classical ("Essential Classics" series) ▲ SBK 62646 ■ SBT 62646
Mozart, W.A.:Nozze di Figaro, w. H. Harper (sop), T. Berganza (mez), D. Fischer-Dieskau (bar), G. Evans (bar), D. Barenboim (cnd), English CO, John Alldis Choir [I]
EMI Classics ("Studio" series) 3-▲ CDMC 63646 [ADD]
Mozart, W.A.:Rè pastore (sels), w. P. Zukerman (cnd), Mostly Mozart Festival Orch—L'amerò, sarò costante
Sony Classical ("Essential Classics" series) ▲ SBK 62646 ■ SBT 62646
Mozart, W.A.:Vorrei spiegarvi, w. P. Zukerman (cnd), Mostly Mozart Festival Orch
Sony Classical ("Essential Classics" series) ▲ SBK 62646 ■ SBT 62646
Mozart, W.A.:Zaide, w. I. Hollweg (sop), T. Moser (ten), W. Schöne (bass), R. Holl (bass), L. Hager (cnd), Salzburg Mozarteum Orch [G]
Orfeo 2-▲ 055832 [DDD]
Orff, C.:Carmina burana, w. W. Brown (ten), H. Hagegård (bar), R. Shaw (cnd), Atlanta SO, Atlanta Sym Chorus [G, L]
Telarc ▲ CD 80056 [DDD]
Orff, C.:Carmina burana, w. K. Riegel (ten), P. Binder (bar), M. Tilson Thomas (cnd), Cleveland Orch, Cleveland Orch Chorus [G, L]
CBS ▲ MK 33172 [ADD]
Poulenc, F.:Gloria Sop, w. L. Bernstein (cnd), New York PO, Westminster Choir [L]
CBS ▲ MK 44710 [ADD]
Poulenc, F.:Gloria Sop, w. L. Bernstein (cnd), New York PO, Westminster Choir *(rec 1976)*
Sony Classical ("Bernstein:The Royal Edition" series) ▲ SMK 47569 [ADD]
Puccini, G.:La Bohème, w. M. Caballé (sop), P. Domingo (ten), S. Milnes (bar), R. Raimondi (bass), G. Solti (cnd), London PO, John Alldis Choir [I]
RCA Red Seal 2-▲ RCD2-0371 2-■ ARK2-0371
Puccini, G.:La Bohème (sels), w. M. Cabballé (sop), P. Domingo (ten), S. Milnes (bar), G. Solti (cnd), London PO
RCA Victor ▲ 09026-61725-2; ■ 09026-61725-4 (CrO2)
Scarlatti, A.:Su le sponde del Tebro, w. P. Zukerman (cnd), Mostly Mozart Festival Orch
Sony Classical ("Essential Classics" series) ▲ SBK 62646 ■ SBT 62646
Schubert, Franz:Songs (misc), w. Elly Ameling (sop), Judith Raskin (sop), Kiri Te Kanawa (sop)—Rastlose Liebe; Gretchen am Spinnrade; Trockne Blumen; Nur wer die Sehnsucht kennt
Sony Classical ("Essential Classics" series) ▲ SBK 62422 ■ SBT 62422

Bleidorn, Matthias (ten)
Bruch, M.:Das Lied von der Glocke, w. Ute Selbig (sop), Elisabeth Graf (alt), André Eckert (, Dresden PO *(rec Kreuzkirche Dresden, Jun 24, 1995)*
Thorofon 2-▲ DCTH 2291/2 [DDD]

Blessed, Brian (nar)
Bliss, A.:Morning Heroes, w. M. Kibblewhite (cnd), London PO, East London Chorus, Harlow Chorus, Hertfordshire Chorus *(rec All Hallows Church, London, Nov. 16-17, 1991 & Jan 26)*
Cala ▲ CACD 1010 [DDD]

Bliese, J. (nar)
Tal, J.:Else-Hommage, w. C. Gayer (sop), H. Ganz (va), G. Teutsch (vc), N. Hauptmann (hn), K. Helwig (pno), J. Tal (cnd)
Academy ▲ ACA 8506 [ADD]

Blighton, Elaine (sop)
Vaughan Williams, R.:Sym 1, w. John Cameron (bar), M. Sargent (cnd), BBC SO, BBC Chorus, BBC Choral Society, Christchurch Harmonic Choir New Zealand *(rec 1965)*
IMP ("BBC Radio" series) ▲ IMP 5691502

Blochwitz, Hans-Peter (ten)
Bach, J.S.:Christmas Oratorio, w. N. Argenta (sop), A. S. von Otter (mez), O. Bär (bar), J. E. Gardiner (cnd), English Baroque Soloists, Monteverdi Choir London [G]
Archiv 2-▲ 423232-2 [DDD]
Bach, J.S.:Christmas Oratorio (sels), w. N. Argenta (sop), A. S. von Otter (mez), O. Bär (bar), J. E. Gardiner (cnd), English Baroque Soloists, Monteverdi Choir London [G]
Archiv ▲ 427653-2 [DDD]
Bach, J.S.:Mass in b, BWV 232, w. F. Lott (sop), A. S. von Otter (mez), W. Shimell (bar), G. Howell (b-bar), G. Solti (cnd), Chicago SO, Chicago Sym Chorus
London 2-▲ 430353-2 [DDD]
Bach, J.S.:St. Matthew Passion, w. B. Schlick (sop), R. Jacobs (ct), H. Crook (ten), U. Cold (bass), P. Kooy (bass), P. Herreweghe (cnd), La Chapelle Royale Orch, Ghent Collegium Vocale [G]
Harmonia Mundi France 3-▲ HMC 901155/57
Bach, J.S.:St. Matthew Passion, w. K. Te Kanawa (sop), A. S. von Otter (mez), A. Rolfe Johnson (ten), O. Bär (bar), T. Krause (bass), G. Solti (cnd), Chicago SO, Chicago Sym Chorus, Glen Ellyn Children's Chorus [G]
London 3-▲ 421177-2 [DDD]
Bach, J.S.:St. Matthew Passion (sels), w. K. Te Kanawa (sop), A. S. von Otter (mez), A. Rolfe Johnson (ten), O. Bär (bar), T. Krause (bass), G. Solti (cnd), Chicago SO, Chicago Sym Chorus, Glen Ellyn Children's Chorus [G]
London ▲ 425691-2 [DDD]
Beethoven, L. van:Fidelio, w. J. Norman (sop), P. Coburn (sop), R. Goldberg (ten), K. Möll (bass), B. Haitink (cnd), Dresden Staatskapelle, Dresden State Chorus
Philips ▲ 438496-2
Beethoven, L. van:Fidelio, w. J. Norman (sop), P. Coburn (sop), R. Goldberg (ten), A. Schmidt (bar), E. Wlaschiha (bass), K. Moll (bass), B. Haitink (cnd), Dresden Staatskapelle, Dresden State Chorus [G]
Philips 2-▲ 426308-2 [DDD]
Beethoven, L. van:Missa Solemnis, w. C. Vaness (sop), W. Meier (mez), H. Tschammer (bass), J. Tate (cnd), English CO, Tallis Chamber Choir [L]
EMI Classics ▲ CDC 49950 [DDD]
Brahms, J.:Romanzen aus Tieck's *Magelone*, w. Cornelia Froboess (nar), Eric Schneider (pno)
Berlin Classics ▲ BER 1125 [DDD]
Bruckner, A.:Motets, w. H. Skarba (trbn), H. Breika (trbn), H. Weimer (trbn), S. Rommelspacher (org), Freiburg Vocal Ensemble—Os justi; Afferentur regi; Christus factus est; Tota pulchra es Maria; Vexilla regis prodeunt; Ecce sacerdos magnus; Pange lingua; Locus iste; Ave Maria; Virga Jesse floruit
Entrée ▲ 0039 [ADD]
Handel, G.F.:Messiah (reorchd Mozart), w. Audrey Michael (sop), Jard van Nes (cta), Marcus Fink (bass), M. Corboz (cnd), Lausanne Instrumental Ensemble, Lausanne Vocal Ensemble [G]
Erato 2-▲ 2292-45497-2 [DDD]
Handel, G.F.:Theodora, w. Roberta Alexander (sop), Jard van Nes (cta), Jochen Kowalski (ct), Anton Scharinger (bass), N. Harnoncourt (cnd), Vienna Concentus Musicus, Arnold Schoenberg Choir [E]
Teldec 2-▲ 2292-46447-2 [DDD]
Haydn, J.:Mass 10, "Kriegsmesse", "Paukenmesse", w. Sylvia McNair (sop), Delores Ziegler (mez), Andreas Schmidt (bar), J. Levine (cnd), Berlin SO, Berlin RIAS Chamber Choir
Deutsche Grammophon ▲ 435853-2
Haydn, J.:Die Schöpfung, w. Barbara Bonney (mez), Edith Wiens (sop), Olaf Bär (bar), Jan-Herdrik Rootering (bass), N. Marriner (cnd), Stuttgart Radio Orch, Stuttgart Radio Chorus [G]
EMI Classics 2-▲ CDCB 54038 [DDD]
Kagel, M.:Sankt-Bach-Passion, w. Anne Sofie von Otter (mez), Roland Hermann (bar), Peter Roggisch (narr), Gerd Zacher (org), M. Kagel (cnd), South German RSO, Limburg Cathedral Boys' Chorus, Hamburg North German Choir
Montaigne ▲ MO 782044
Mahler, G.:Das Klagende Lied, w. J. Rodgers (sop), L. Finnie (cta), R. Hickox (cnd), Bournemouth SO, Bath Festival Chorus, Waynflete Singers
Chandos ▲ CHAN 9247 [DDD]
Mahler, G.:Das Lied von der Erde, w. B. Remmert (cta), P. Herreweghe (cnd), Musique Oblique Ensemble [arr. Schoenberg & Riehn for chamber orch.]
Harmonia Mundi France ▲ HMC 901477
Mozart, W.A.:Complete Mozart Edition, w. Barbara Hendricks (sop), P. Schreier (cnd), C.P.E. Bach CO
Philips 2-▲ 422528-2 [DDD]
Mozart, W.A.:Così fan tutte, w. Kiri Te Kanawa (sop), Marie McLaughlin (sop), Ann Murray (mez), Thomas Hampson (bar), G. Furlanetto (bar), J. Levine (cnd), Vienna PO, Vienna State Opera Chorus [I]
Deutsche Grammophon 3-▲ 423897-2 [DDD]
Mozart, W.A.:Missa, K.317, w. E. Mathis (sop), J. Rappé (ten), T. Quasthoff (bar), P. Schreier (cnd), Dresden Staatskapelle, Leipzig Radio Chorus
Philips ▲ 426275-2
Mozart, W.A.:Missa, K.317, w. S. McNair (sop), D. Ziegler (mez), A. Schmidt (bar), J. Levine (cnd), Berlin SO, Berlin RIAS Chamber Choir
Deutsche Grammophon ▲ 435853-2
Mozart, W.A.:Missa, K.427, w. A. Augér (sop), B. Bonney (sop), Robert Holl (bass), C. Abbado (cnd), Berlin PO, Berlin Radio Chorus [L]
Sony Classical ▲ SK 46671 [DDD]
Mozart, W.A.:Requiem, w. Barbara Bonney (sop), Anne Sophie von Otter (mez), Willard White (bass), J. E. Gardiner (cnd), English Baroque Soloists, Monteverdi Choir London [L]
Philips ▲ 420197-2 [DDD]

Blochwitz, Hans-Peter (ten) (cont.)
Mozart, W.A.:Zauberflöte, w. Natalie Dessay (sop—Queen of the Night), Linda Kitchen (sop—Papagena), Rosa Mannion (sop—Pamina), Anna-Maria Panzarella (sop—First Lady), Doris Lamprecht (mez—Second Lady), Delphine Haidan (cta—Third Lady), Hans Peter Blochwitz (ten—Tamino), Steven Cole (ten—Monostatos), Chrisopher Josey (ten—First Priest/First Armed Man), Anton Scharinger (bar—Papageno), Reinhard Hagen (bass—Sarastro), Laurent Naouri (bass—Second Priest/Second Armed Man), Willard White (bass—Speaker), W. Christie (cnd), Les Arts Florissants *(rec Paris Oct 2-9 1995)*
Erato 2-▲ 12705-2 [DDD]
Mozart, W.A.:Zauberflöte, w. E. Gruberova (sop), B. Bonney (sop), G. Schmid (sop), T. Hampson (bar), M. Salminen (bass), A. Scharinger (bass), N. Harnoncourt (cnd), Zurich Opera Orch, Zurich Opera House Chorus [G]
Teldec 2-▲ 2292-42716-2
Schubert, Franz:Winterreise, w. H. Zender (cnd), Ensemble Modern [arr. Zender] *(rec Hessian Radio, Aug. 1-5, 1994)*
RCA Red Seal ▲ 09026-68067-2 [DDD]
Telemann, G.P.:St. Matthew Passion, w. M. Zedelius (sop), A. Browner (alt), W. Schmidt (bar), A. Scharinger (bass), W. Seeliger (cnd), Darmstadt CO, Darmstadt Concert Choir
Christophorus ▲ 77149 [DDD]
Zemlinsky, A. von:Songs (misc), w. Ruth Ziesak (sop), Iris Vermillion (mez), Andreas Schmidt (bar), Cord Garben (pno)—Die schlanke Wasserlilie; Gute Nacht; Liebe und Frühling; Ich sah mein eigen Angesicht; In der Ferne; Waldgespräch; Der Rosenband; Abendstern; Des Mädchens Klage; Der Morgenstern; Wandl' ich im Wald des Abends; Orientalisches Sonett; Süsse, süsse Sommernacht; Herbsten; Nun schwillt der See so bang; In der Sonnengasse; Herr Bombardil; Es war ein alter König; Über eine Wiege; Mädel, kommst du mit zum Tanz?; Jane Grey; Der verlorene Haufen; Vorspiel; Ansturm; Auf See; Noch spür ich ihren Atem; Hörtest du denn nicht hinein; Die Beiden; Harmonie des Abends; Und einmal gehst du *(rec Stuttgart & Berlin, Germany, Mar. 30-June 8, 1993)*
Sony Classical ▲ SK 57960
Zemlinsky, A. von:Songs (misc), w. B. Bonney (sop), A.-S. von Otter (mez), A. Schmidt (bar), C. Garben (pno)—Lieder, Op. 2; Gesänge, Op. 5; Walzer-Gesänge nach toskanischen Volksliedern, Op. 6; Irmelin Rose und andere Gesänge, Op. 7; Turmwächterlied und andere Gesänge, Op. 8; Ehetanzlied und andere Gesänge, Op. 10; Schlummerlied; 6 Gesänge, Op. 13; 6 Lieder, Op. 22; Ahnung Beatricens; 12 Lieder, Op. 27 [G]
Deutsche Grammophon 2-▲ 427348-2 [DDD]

Blom, Inger (cta)
Schnittke, A.:Faust Cant, w. Mikael Bellini (alt), Louis Devos (ten), Urik Cold (bass), J. DePreist (cnd), Malmö SO, Malmö Sym Chorus
BIS ("BIS Twins" series) 2-▲ CD 437/507
Scriabin, A.:Sym 1, w. L. Magnusson (ten), L. Segerstam (cnd), Stockholm PO, Stockholm Phil Chorus [R]
BIS ▲ CD 534 [DDD]

Bloom, Claire (nar)
del Tredici, D.:Haddocks' Eyes, w. S. Narucki (sop), Z. Mehta (cnd), New York PO Ensemble
New World ▲ 80390-2 [DDD]

Blum, Eberhard (sgr)
Cage, J.:Sixty-Two Mesostics Re Merce Cunningham *(rec Hessen Radio, Frankfurt, Aug. 14, 1991)*
Hat Hut ("NOW." series) 2-▲ hat ART CD 2-60951/2

Blum, Mina (sop)
Verdi, G.:Nabucco, w. Monica Pick-Hieronimi (sop), Anna Schiatti (sop), Angelo Casertano (ten), Gilberto Maffezzoni (ten), Paolo Gavanelli (bass), Paata Burchuladze (bass), Franco Federici (bass), A. Guadagno (cnd), Arena di Verona Orch, Arena di Verona Chorus *(rec Berlin, Spring 1996)*
Koch Schwann 2-▲ SCH CD 364272

Boatwright, Helen (sop)
Bacon, E.:Songs from Dickenson, w. John Kirkpatrick (pno), Ernst Bacon (pno)—It's All I Have to Bring; Eden; I'm Nobody; As Well as Jesus?; A Word; Weeping and Sighing; O Friend; She Went; A Threadless Way; The Imperial Hear; Summer's Lapse; Is There Such a Thing as Day?; To Make a Prairie; A Spider; The Grass So Little Has to Do; The Snake; So Bashful; Alabaster Wool; Eternity; Sunset; The Simple Days; On this Wondrous Sea *(rec 1954 & 1964)*
CRI ▲ CD 675 [ADD]
Gershwin, G.:Porgy & Bess (sels), w. L. Price (sop), W. Warfield (bar), S. Henderson (cnd), RCA Victor SO, RCA Victor Chorus [E]
RCA Gold Seal ▲ 5234-2-RG [ADD]
Ives, C.:Songs, w. Ernst Bacon (pno), John Kirkpatrick (pno)—Abide with Me; Walking; Where the Eagle; Disclosure; The White Gulls; Two Little Flowers; The Greatest Man; The Children's Hour; Berceuse; Ann Street; General William Booth Enters into Heaven; Autumn; Swimmers; Evening; Harpalus; Tarrant Moss; Serenity; At the River; The See'r; Maple Leaves; "1, 2, 3"; Tom Sails away; He Is There!; In Flanders Fields *(rec 1954 & 1964)*
CRI ▲ CD 675 [ADD]

Boatwright, McHenry (bar)
Milhaud, D.:Choëphores, w. Vera Zorina (nar), Virginia Babikian (sop), Irene Jordan (sop), L. Bernstein (cnd), New York PO, New York Schola Cantorum
Sony Classical ("Masterworks Heritage" series) ▲ MHK 62352

Boatwright, McHenry (bass)
Berlioz, H.:La Damnation de Faust, w. Suzanne Danco (sop), David Poleri (ten), Martial Singher (bar), Donald Gramm (bass), Joseph de Pasquale (va), Louis Speyer (hn), C. Munch (cnd), Boston SO, Harvard Glee Club, Radcliffe Choral Society *(rec Feb 1954)*
RCA Victor Gold Seal 8-▲ 0902-668444-2 [ADD]

Bock, Claus (ten)
Hindemith, P.:Hin und zurück, w. Barbara Miller (sop), Ulrich Schaible (bar), Helmut Kühnle (bass), A. Grüber (cnd), Berlin SO members *(rec 1971)*
Allegretto ▲ ACD 8191

Böckelin, G. (ten)
Beethoven, L. van:Sym 9, "Choral Sym", w. L. Tunell (alto), S. Björling (bass), W. Furtwängler (cnd), Stockholm PO *(rec Dec. 1, 1943)*
Music & Arts ▲ CD 2002 [AAD]

Bockelmann, Rudolf (b-bar)
Loewe, C.:Arias *(rec 1928-38)*
Preiser ("Lebendige Vergangenheit" series) ▲ PRE 89121
Wagner, R.:Arias & Scenes *(rec 1928-38)*
Preiser ("Lebendige Vergangenheit" series) ▲ PRE 89121
Wagner, R.:Der fliegende Holländer (sels), w. Kirsten Flagstad (sop), Tiana Lemnitz (sop), Torsten Ralf (ten), Ludwig Weber (bass), T. Beecham (cnd), Royal Opera House Orch, Royal Opera House Chorus Covent Garden
Memories ("Golden" series) ▲ MEM 3003
Wagner, R.:Götterdämmerung (sels), w. Kirsten Flagstad (sop), Tiana Lemnitz (sop), Torsten Ralf (ten), Ludwig Weber (bass), T. Beecham (cnd), Royal Opera House Orch, Royal Opera House Chorus Covent Garden
Memories ("Golden" series) ▲ MEM 3003
Wagner, R.:Lohengrin (sels), w. Kirsten Flagstad (sop), Tiana Lemnitz (sop), Torsten Ralf (ten), Ludwig Weber (bass), T. Beecham (cnd), Royal Opera House Orch, Royal Opera House Chorus Covent Garden
Memories ("Golden" series) ▲ MEM 3003
Wagner, R.:Die Meistersinger von Nürnberg (sels), w. Kirsten Flagstad (sop), Tiana Lemnitz (sop), Torsten Ralf (ten), Ludwig Weber (bass), T. Beecham (cnd), Royal Opera House Orch, Royal Opera House Chorus Covent Garden
Memories ("Golden" series) ▲ MEM 3003
Wagner, R.:Die Meistersinger von Nürnberg (sels), w. Viorica Ursuleac (sop—Eva), Rudolf Bockelmann (ten—Hans Sachs), Josef Kalenberg (ten—Walther), Hermann Wiedemann (bar—Beckmesser), C. Krauss (cnd), Vienna State Opera Orch, Vienna State Opera Chorus *(rec Jan. 20, 1933)*
Koch Schwann 2-▲ SCH 314642 [ADD]
Wagner, R.:Der Ring des Nibelungen (sels), w. Florence Austral (sop), Frieda Leider (sop), Elsie Suddaby (sop), Göta Ljunberg (sop), Walter Widdop (ten), Horst Laubenthal (ten), Lauritz Melchoir (ten), Friedrich Schorr (bar), Ivar Andresen (bass), Emmanuel List (bass), Collingwood, Blech, Coates, Barbirolli, Heger, Alwin, Muck (cnd), London SO—scenes from Siegriend & Götterdämmerung; 90 Motives from Der Ring [w. Collingwood & LSO]
Pearl 7-▲ PEA 9137 [ADD]
Wagner, R.:Tristan und Isolde (sels), w. Kirsten Flagstad (sop), Tiana Lemnitz (sop), Torsten Ralf (ten), Ludwig Weber (bass), T. Beecham (cnd), Royal Opera House Orch, Royal Opera House Chorus Covent Garden
Memories ("Golden" series) ▲ MEM 3003

Bode, Hannelore (sop)
Wagner, R.:Die Meistersinger von Nürnberg, w. J. Hamari (mez), A. Kollo (ten), N. Bailey (bar), B. Weikl (bar), K. Moll (bass), G. Solti (cnd), Vienna PO, Vienna State Opera Chorus [G]
London 4-▲ 417497-2 [ADD]
Wagner, R.:Die Meistersinger von Nürnberg, w. Jean Cox (ten), Klaus Hirte (bar), Karl Ridderbusch (bass), Hans Sotin (bass), S. Varviso (cnd), Bayreuth Festival Orch, Bayreuth Festival Chorus [1974]
Philips 32-▲ 434420-2 [ADD/DDD]

Bode, Hannelore (sop) (cont.)

Wagner, R.:Die Meistersinger von Nürnberg, w. Jean Cox (ten), Klaus Hirte (bar), Karl Ridderbusch (bass), Hans Sotin (bass), S. Varviso (cnd), Bayreuth Festival Orch, Bayreuth Festival Chorus [1974] [G] Philips 4-▲ 434611-2 [ADD]

Bodenham, Peter (ten)

Walton, W.:Troilus & Cressida, w. Judith Howarth (sop—Cressida), Arthur Davies (ten—Troilus), Nigel Robson (ten—Pandarus), Brian Cookson (ten—3rd Watchman), Peter Bodenham (ten—Priest), Keith Mills (ten—Soldier), Alan Opie (bar—Diomede), James Thornton (bar—Antenor), Clive Bayley (bass—Calkas), David Owen-Lewis (bass—Horaste), R. Hickox (cnd), English Northern Philharmonia, Opera North Chorus Chandos 2-▲ CHAN 9370/71 [DDD]

Bódi, Mariann (sop)

Franck, C.:Choral Music, w. Attila Wendler (ten), Istvan Rácz (bass), Salomon Kamp (cnd), Debrecen Kodaly Choir—Quae est ista; Dextera Domini Hungaroton ▲ HCD 31579 [DDD]

Bodrogi, Éva (sop)

Werner, G.J.:Vesperae de Confessoris, w. Regina Fülöp (cta), Kornél Pechan (ten), Péter Cser (bass), János Mezei (org), J. Mezei (cnd), Vienna-Szász CO, Budapest Schola Cantorum *(rec St. Columba's Presbyterian Church, Budapest, June 12-15, 1995)* Hungaroton ▲ HCD 31646 [DDD]

Bodurov, Lyubomir (ten)

Rimsky-Korsakov, N.:Golden Cockerel, w. Yavora Stoilova (sop—Golden Cockerel), Elena Stoyanova (sop—Queen), Evgenia Babacheva (mez—Amelfa), Lyubomir Bodourov (ten—Prince), Lyubomir Dyakovski (ten—Astrologer), Emil Ugrinov (bar—Afron), Nikolai Stoilov (bass—Tsar), Kosta Videv (bass—Polkan), D. Manolov (cnd), Sofia National Opera Orch, Sofia National Opera Chorus *(rec Sofia, 1985)* Capriccio 2-▲ 10760/61 [DDD]

Verdi, G.:Requiem Mass, w. Wiener-Chenisheva (sop), A. Milcheva-Nonova (mez), N. Ghiuselev (bass), I. Marinov (cnd), Sofia State PO, Sofia State Chorus [L] Vivace 3-▲ E 326 [ADD]

Bódy, József (bass)

Verdi, G.:Rigoletto (sels), w. Mária Gyurkovics (sop), Olga Szönyi (mez), Ernö Kenéz (ten), János Fodor (bar), Alexander Svéd (bar), Kórodi, Molinari-Pradelli (cnd), Hungarian State Opera Orch—Pari siamo!; Figlia! Mio padre! A te dappresso; Cortigiani! Vil' razza dannata; Tutte le feste al tempio...Ah! solo per me!; Chi è mai... *(rec 1955-56)* Hungaroton ("Great Hungarian Voices" series) ▲ HCD 31614 [ADD]

Boehme, Kurt (bass)

Wagner, R.:Die Meistersinger von Nürnberg, w. Tiana Lemnitz (sop—Eva), Bernd Aldenhoff (ten—Walther von Stolzing), Gerhard Unger (ten—David), Ferdinand Frantz (b-bar—Hans Sachs), Kurt Boehme (bass—Veit Pogner), Heinrich Pflanzl (bass—Sixtus Beckmesser), R. Kempe (cnd), Saxon State Orch *(rec Dresden, 1951)* Myto 4-▲ MCD 961138

Boelens, Reina (sop)

Vries, K. de:Diafonia, w. G. de Vries (sop), D. Porcelijn (cnd), Asko Ensemble Donemus ▲ CV 34

Boerner, Charlotte (sop)

Halévy, F.:La Juive (sels), w. C. Boerner (sop—Eudoxie), E. Rethberg (sop—Rachel), G. Martinelli (ten—Éléazar), H. Clemens (ten—Léopold), Heller, Merola (cnd), *(orch unknown)*—Act 2 & Act 4 (sels.) *(rec Oct. 30, 1936 & 1926-27)* Standing Room Only ▲ SRO 848-1 [ADD]

Boesch, Christian (bar)

Strauss (II), Joh.:Die Fledermaus (sels), w. E. Gruberova (sop), B. Bonney (sop), M. Lipovšek (mez), W. Kmentt (ten), W. Hollweg (ten), J. Protschka (ten), A. Scharinger (bass), N. Harnoncourt (cnd), Royal Concertgebouw Orch, Netherlands Opera Chorus Teldec ▲ 42427-2

Boesch, R. (bar)

Strauss (II), Joh.:Eine Nacht in Venedig, w. E. Réthy (sop), M. Schober (sop), K. Friedrich (ten), A. Jerger (b-bar), K. Preger (ten), A. Paulik (cnd), Vienna SO, Bregenz Festival Choir [G] *(rec 1951)* Koch Schwann ▲ 3-1272-2 [ADD]

Boese, Ursula (mez)

Wagner, R.:Der Ring des Nibelungen, w. Liselotte Becker-Egner (sop—Woglinde/Ortlinde/Wellgunde), Angelika Berger (sop—Wellgunde/Waltraute), Siw Ericsdotter (sop—Norn 3), Heidemaria Ferch (sop—Freia/Gerhilde), Bella Jasper (sop—Helmwige/Waldvogel/Woglinde), Ditha Sommer (sop—Sieglinde/Gutrune), Ursula Boese (mez—Erda), Ruth Hesse (mez—Fricka), Nadezda Kniplová (mez—Brünnhilde), Margit Kobeck (mez—Schwertleite/Norn 2), Hilde Rosner (mez—Flosshilde/Siegrunde), Erica Schubert (mez—Grimgerde/Flosshilde), Ingrid Göritz (cta—Rossweisse/Norn 1), Herbert Doussant (ten—Froh), Herold Kraus (ten—Mime), Gerald McKee (ten—Siegmund/Siegfried), Fritz Uhl (ten—Loge), Rudolf Knoll (bar—Gunther/Donner), Rolf Polke (bass-bar—Wotan/Wanderer), Rolf Kühne (bass—Alberich), Takao Okamura (bass—Fafner), Otto von Rohr (bass—Hagen/Fasolt/Hunding), H. Swarowsky (cnd), Czech PO, Prague National Theater Orch *(rec June 3 & 5, July 26-31, A)* Weltbild Classics 14-▲ 703769 [ADD]

Bogachev, Vladimir (ten)

Glinka, M.:Songs, w. M. Storojev (sgr), Montreal Musici Chandos ▲ CHAN 9149 [DDD]

Rimsky-Korsakov, N.:Mozart & Salieri, w. M. Storojev (cnd), Montreal Musici Chandos ▲ CHAN 9149 [DDD]

Rimsky-Korsakov, N.:Songs, w. M. Storojev (cnd), Montreal Musici—The Clouds Begin to Scatter, Op. 42/3; On the Hills of Georgia, Op. 3/4 Chandos ▲ CHAN 9149 [DDD]

Bogachova, Irinia (sgr)

Glinka, M.:Russlan & Ludmilla, w. Galina Gorchakova (sop), Larissa Diadkova (cta), Anna Netrebko (sgr), Yuri Masurin (ten), Konstantin Pluzhnikov (ten), Mikhail Kit (bar), Gennady Bezzubenkov (bass), Vladimir Ognovenko (bass), V. Gergiev (cnd), Kirov Opera Orch, Kirov Opera Chorus Philips ▲ 456 248-2

Bogard, Carole (sop)

Mozart, W.A.:Missa, K.317, w. J. de Gaetani (mez), R. White (ten), T. Paul (bass), D. Zinman (cnd), Rochester PO, Roberts Wesleyan College Chorale *(rec 1978)* Allegretto ▲ ACD 8164 [ADD] ▮ ACS 8164

Bogarde, D. (nar)

Lehár, F.:Die lustige Witwe, w. F. Lott (sop), E. Szmytka (sop), J. Aler (ten), T. Hampson (b-bar), F. Welser-Möst (cnd), London PO, Glyndebourne Festival Chorus EMI Classics ▲ CDCB 55152

Bogart, John Paul (bass)

Donizetti, G.:Requiem Mass, w. C. Studer (sop), H. Müller-Molinari (mez), A. Baldin (ten), J.-H. Rootering (bass), M. A. G. Martínez (cnd), Bamberg SO, Bamberg Sym Chorus [L] Orfeo ▲ 172881 [DDD]

Bogdan, Thomas (ten)

Blitzstein, M.:The Harpies, w. R. Rees (sop), E. Najera (bar), et al., G. Smith (cnd), Adirondack CO, Gregg Smith Singers [E] Premier ▲ PRCD 1009 [ADD]

Purcell, H.:Dido & Aeneas, w. Cassandra Hoffman (sop—Belinda), Arlene Travis (sop—2nd Witch), Desirée Halac (mez—Sorceress/Spirit), Jennifer Lane (mez—Dido), Elizabeth Norman (alt), Thomas Bogdan (ten—A Sailor), Michael Brown (bar—Aeneas), Curtis Streetman (bar), Caitriona O'Leary (sgr—2nd Woman), Sarah Pillow (sgr—1st Witch), B. Brookshire (cnd), San Cassiano Musici *(rec St. Ignatius of Antioch Episcopal Church, New York City, Spring 1995)* Vox Classics ▲ VOX 7518

Schuman, W.:The Mighty Casey, w. R. Rees (sop), R. Muenz (b-bar), W. Schuman (cnd), Adirondack CO, Gregg Smith Singers, Long Island Choral Association [E] Premier ▲ PRCD 1009 [ADD]

Bogtatchov, Vladimir (ten)

Rimsky-Korsakov, N.:Christmas Eve, w. Ekaterina Koudriavtchenko (sop), Elena Zaremba (mez), Alexei Maslennikov (ten), Viatcheslav Voinarovski (ten), Viatcheslav Verestnikov (bar), Maxime Mikhailov (bass), Stanislav Souleimanov (bass), M. Yurovski (cnd), Moscow Forum Theater Orch, Yurloff Academic Choir Russian Season 4-▲ CMX 388054

Boháčová, Marta (sop)

Reicha, A.:Te Deum, w. Oldřich Lindauer (ten), Karel Průša (bass), Ladislav Vachulka (org), V. Smetáček (cnd), Prague SO, Kühn Chorus *(rec Cathedral of the Ascension of the Virgin, Karlov, Prague, 1970)* Panton ▲ PAN 800242 [AAD]

Bohan, Edmund (ten)

Sullivan, A.:Music of, w. M. Studholme (sop), J. Allister (cta), I. Wallace (bar), M. Dods (cnd), London Concert Orch, English Chorale—sels. from Gondoliers; H.M.S. Pinafore; Mikado; Pirates of Penzance PWK Classics ▲ PWK 1157 [AAD]

Böhm, Karl-Walter (ten)

Strauss, R.:Salome, w. H. Behrens (sop), A. Baltsa (mez), H. Angervo (alt), W. Ochman (ten), J. van Dam (bar), H. von Karajan (cnd), Vienna PO EMI Classics 2-▲ CDCB 49358

Bohman, Gunnel (sop)

Mozart, W.A.:Arias, w. J.-O. Wedin (cnd), Kalmar Läns CO—K.272, K.369, K.374 & K.528 [I] BIS ▲ CD 299 [DDD]

Mozart, W.A.:Exsultate, w. J.-O. Wedin (cnd), Kalmar Läns CO [L] BIS ▲ CD 299 [DDD]

Peterson-Berger, W.:Songs, w. Thomas Lander (bar), Anders Kilström (pno) Musica Sveciae ▲ MSV 619 [DDD]

Böhme, Kurt (bass)

Beethoven, L. van:Fidelio, w. Birgit Nilsson (sop—Leonore), Graziella Sciutti (sop—Marzelline), Kurt Equiluz (ten—Erster Gefangener), Donald Grobe (ten—Jacquino), James McCracken (ten—Florestan), Tom Krause (bar—Don Pizarro), Hermann Prey (bar—Don Fernando), Kurt Böhme (bass—Rocco), Günther Adam (sgr—Zweiter Gefangener), L. Maazel (cnd), Vienna PO, Vienna State Opera Concert Association Chorus *(rec Sofiensaal, Vienna, Mar 1964)* London 2-▲ 448104-2 [ADD]

Bizet, G.:Carmen, w. E. Weidlich (sop), E. Höngen (cta), T. Ralf (ten), J. Herrmann (bar), K. Böhm (cnd), Dresden State Opera Orch, Dresden State Opera Chorus *(rec Dec. 4 & 5, 1942)* Preiser 2-▲ 90152 (m)

Janácek, L.:The Excursions of Mr. Brouček, w. Antonie Fahberg (sop—Piccolo), Wilma Lipp (sop—Málinka), Lilian Benningsen (cta—Fanny Nowak), Paul Kuen (ten—Trambahn-Kondukteur), Karl Ostertag (ten—Vorsitzender des Hausbesitzerverbandes), Fritz Wunderlich (ten—Mazal), Kurt Böhme (b-bar—Sakristan von St. Veit), Kieth Engen (bass—Würfl), J. Keilberth (cnd), Bavarian SO *(rec live, Prinzregententheater, Nov. 19, 1959)* Orfeo 2-▲ 354942 (m)

Liebermann, R.:Die Schule der Frauen, w. Anneliese Rothenberger (sop—Agnes), Christa Ludwig (mez—Georgette), Nicolai Gedda (ten—Horace), Alois Pernerstorfer (b-bar—Gronte), Walter Berry (bass—Poquelin), Kurt Böhme (bass—Arnolphe), G. Szell (cnd), Vienna PO *(rec Salzburg, Aug 17, 1957)* Orfeo d'or ("Festspiel Dikumente" series) 2-▲ C 429962 (m) [ADD]

Mozart, W.A.:Don Giovanni, w. M. Schech (sop), M. Teschemacher (sop), H. Hopf (ten), M. Ahlersmeyer (bar), G. Frick (bass), K. Elmendorff (cnd), Saxon State Orch, Dresden State Opera Chorus [G] *(rec 1943)* Berlin Classics ("Dokumente" series) 3-▲ BER 2048 [ADD]

Mozart, W.A.:Zauberflöte, w. L. Della Casa (sop), E. Köth (sop), G. Sciurri (sop), L. Simoneau (ten), W. Berry (bass), G. Szell (cnd), Vienna PO, Vienna State Opera Chorus [G] *(rec live at the Salzburg Festival, July 27, 1959)* Melodram ("Connaisseur" series) 2-▲ MEL 27505 (m) [AAD]

Mozart, W.A.:Zauberflöte, w. H. Gueden (sop), W. Lipp (sop), L. Simoneau (ten), W. Berry (bass), K. Böhm (cnd), Vienna PO, Vienna State Opera Chorus London ("Grand Opera" series) 2-▲ 414362-2 [ADD]

Mussorgsky, M.:Boris Godunov, w. Martha Mödl (sop—Marina Mniszek), Lotte Schädle (sop—Xenia), Dorothea Siebert (mez—Fyodor), Hertha Töpper (mez—Xenia's wet-nurs), Karl Hermann Bennert (Boyer Khrushchyov), Lorenz Fehenberger (ten—Prince Shuysky), Hans Hopf (ten—Grigory), Karl Ostertag (ten—Missail), Hans Hotter (b-bar—Boris Godunov), Hermann Uhde (bar—Andrey Shchelkalov), Kurt Böhme (bass—Varlaam), Kim Borg (bass—Pimen), Kieth Engen (bass—Lewicki), Adolf Keil (bass—Nikitich), Benno Kusche (bar—Rangoni), Heinz Maria Linz (bass—Czernikowski), E. Jochum (cnd), Bavarian RSO, Bavarian Radio Chorus *(rec Munich, May 1957)* Myto 3-▲ MCD 953131

Smetana, B.:The Bartered Bride, w. Dorothea Siebert (sop), Dagmar Hermann (mez), Maria von Ilosvay (mez), Hans Braun (bar), J. Keilberth (cnd), Bavarian RSO, Bavarian Radio Chorus *(rec 1958)* Pantheon 2-▲ PHE 6652 (m)

Strauss (II), Joh.:Der Zigeunerbaron (sels), w. Rita Streich (sop), Grace Bumbry (mez), Biserka Cvejic (mez), Gisela Litz (alt), Nicolai Gedda (ten), Hermann Prey (bar), F. Allers (cnd), Munich Bavarian State Opera Orch, Munich Bavarian State Opera Chorus Emperor Operetta ▲ KO 86346

Strauss, R.:Der Rosenkavalier, w. Erika Köth (sop—Sophie), Annelie Waas (sop—Marianne), Claire Watson (sop—Marschallin), Hertha Töpper (mez—Octavian), Brigitte Fassbaender (cta—Annina), Gerhard Stolze (ten—Valzacchi), Fritz Wunderlich (ten—Singer), Otto Wiener (bar—Faninal), Kurt Böhme (bass—Baron), J. Keilberth (cnd), Bavarian State Opera Orch, Bavarian State Opera Chorus *(rec Munich Opera Festival, National Theater, May 21, 1965)* Orfeo d'or 3-▲ 425963

Wagner, R.:Arias & Scenes, w. Kathe Heidersbach (sop), Maria Reining (sop), Hilde Scheppan (sop), Margarete Teschemacher (sop), Margarete Klose (mez), Max Lorenz (ten), Jaro Prohaska (bar), Karl Schmitt-Walter (bar), *(orch unknown)*—selections from Rienzi; Der Fliegende Holländer; Tannhäuser; Lohengrin; Tristan und Isolde; Die Meistersinger von Nürnberg; Die Walküre & Götterdämmerung *(rec 1927-1944)* Phonographe 2-▲ PHG 5016 [AAD]

Wagner, R.:Die Meistersinger von Nürnberg, w. L. Della Casa (sop), I. Malaniuk (cta), H. Hopf (ten), O. Edelmann (b-bar), H. Knappertsbusch (cnd), Bayreuth Festival Orch, Bayreuth Festival Chorus [G] *(rec live, 1952)* Arkadia 4-▲ 440 (m) [AAD]

Wagner, R.:Die Meistersinger von Nürnberg (sels), w. Maria Reining (sop—Eva), Torsten Ralf (ten—Walther), Josef Herrman (bar—Hans Sachs), Erich Kunz (bar—Beckmesser), Kurt Böhme (bass—Pogner), K. Böhm (cnd), Vienna State Opera Orch *(rec Vienna, 1944)* Koch Schwann 2-▲ SCH 314682 [ADD]

Wagner, R.:Das Rheingold, w. K. Flagstad (sop), J. Madeira (mez), S. Svanholm (ten), G. London (bar), G. Neidlinger (b-bar), G. Solti (cnd), Vienna PO [G] London 3-▲ 414101-2 [ADD]

Wagner, R.:Der Ring des Nibelungen, w. B. Nilsson (sop), L. Rysanek (sop), K. Dvořaková (sop), M. Mödl (sop), A. Burmeister (mez), V. Soukupova (mez), E. Wohlfahrt (ten), W. Windgassen (ten), T. Stewart (bar), T. Adam (b-bar), G. Neidlinger (b-bar), G. Nienstedt (bass), K. Böhm (cnd), Bayreuth Festival Orch, Bayreuth Festival Chorus [G] *(rec live, 1966-67)* Philips 14-▲ 420325-2 [ADD]

Wagner, R.:Die Walküre (act 1), w. M. Teschemacher (sop), M. Lorenz (ten), K. Elmendorff (cnd), Saxon State Orch [G] *(rec 9/21/44)* Preiser ▲ 90015 (m) [AAD]

Weber, C.M. von:Der Freischütz, w. Irmgard Seefried (sop), Rita Streich (sop), Richard Holm (ten), Eberhard Wächter (bar), E. Jochum (cnd), Bavarian RSO, Bavarian Radio Chorus Deutsche Grammophon 2-▲ 439717-2 [ADD]

Wolf, H.:Der Corregidor, w. M. Teschemacher (sop), M. Fuchs (sop), K. Erb (ten), J. Herrmann (bar), G. Hann (bass), G. Frick (bass), K. Elmendorff (cnd), Saxon State Orch, Saxon State Chorus *(rec 1944)* Preiser 2-▲ PRE 90182 [AAD]

Bohn, James (bass)

Albright, W.:A Song to David, w. Melissa Semmes (nar), Charles Russell (nar), Deborah Carbaugh (sop), Susan Sacquitne-Druck (mez), Rick Penning (ten), Dean Billmeyer (org), Howard Don Small (cnd), St. Mark's Cathedral Choir Minneapolis *(rec live, St. Mark's Cathedral, Minneapolis, MN, Apr. 28, 1991)* Gothic ▲ G 49066 [DDD]

Smyth, E.:The Boatswain's Mate, w. E. Harrhy (sop), J. Hardy (alt), D. Dressen (ten), P. Brunelle (cnd), Plymouth Music Series Orch, Plymouth Music Series Chorus—Mrs. Water's Aria Virgin Classics ▲ CDC 59022

Smyth, E.:Mass in D, w. E. Harrhy (sop), J. Hardy (alt), D. Dressen (ten), P. Brunelle (cnd), Plymouth Music Series Orch, Plymouth Music Series Chorus Virgin Classics ▲ CDC 59022

Böhnen, Michael (bass)

Gounod, C.:Faust, w. H. Singstreu (sop—Margarete), H. Rosvaenge (ten—Faust), M. Bohnen (bass—Mephistopheles), H. Steiner (cnd), Berlin RSO, Berlin Radio Chorus *(rec 1938)* Myto 2-▲ MCD 94196

The Great Michael Bohnen *(rec 1914-30)* Preiser 2-▲ PRE 89215 [ADD]

The Voice of Tino Pattiera:Arias, Duets & Songs, w. T. Pattiera (ten), Anka Horvath (sgr), Meta Seinmeyer (sop) *(rec 1916-30)* Preiser 2-▲ PRE CD 89222

Wagner, R.:Arias & Scenes, w. Emmy Destinn (sop), Lilly Hafgren (sop), Frida Leider (sop), Emmi Leisner (cta), Ernst Kraus (ten), Lauritz Melchoir (ten), Leopold Demuth (bar), Friedrich Schorr (b-bar), Paul Knupfer (bass), Richard Mayr (bass), Heinrich Hensel (sgr), Walter Soomer (sgr) Iron Needle ▲ 1307 (m)

Weber, C.M. von:Abu Hassan, w. E. Schwarzkopf (sop), E. Witte (ten), L. Ludwig (cnd), Berlin RSO, Berlin Radio Chorus [G] *(rec Germany 1941)* Forlane ▲ FOR 16572 (m) [AAD]

Weber, C.M. von:Abu Hassan, w. Elisabeth Schwarzkopf (sop), Erich Witte (ten), L. Ludwig (cnd), Berlin RSO, Berlin Radio Chorus Grammofono 2000 ▲ GRM 78650

Weber, C.M. von:Der Freischütz (sels), w. Tiana Lemnitz (sop—Agathe), Michael Bohnen (b-bar—Kaspar), H. Knappertsbusch (cnd), Vienna State Opera Orch *(rec Salzburg, Aug. 3, 1939)* Koch Schwann 2-▲ SCH 314672 [ADD]

The Young Lotte Lehmann, w. Robert Hutt (ten), Heinrich Schlusnus (bar) Preiser ("Lebendige Vergangenheit" series) 3-▲ PRE 89302 (m) [AAD]

Boissy, Nathalie (sop)
Mozart, W.A.:Zauberflöte, w. Birgit Been (sop), Marianne Seibel (sop), Renate Springer (sop), Elizabeth Vidal (sop), Eleanor James (mez), Salvador Guzman (ten), Herbert Hechenberger (ten), Wolfgang Newmann (ten), Klaus Häger (bass), Philip Langshaw (bass), Hans-Georg Moser (bass), P. Kuentz (cnd), Paul Kuentz Orch, Francis Bardot (cnd), Maitrise des Hauts-de-Seine members, Paul Kuentz Choirs Pierre Verany 2-▲ PVY 730055 [DDD]

Bokhour, Ray (nar)
Bokhour, R.:Angel Butcher, w. J. Swoboda (cnd), Warsaw PO MMC ▲ MMC 2027 [DDD]

Bokor, Margit (mez)
Leoncavallo, R.:Pagliacci (sels), w. M. Bokor [sop—Nedda], Bjoerling [ten—Canio], K. Alwin (cnd), *(orch unknown)*—A ventitre ore/Recitar!...Vesti la giubba [Act 1]; No, Pagliacco non son through e il nome del tuo ganzo [Act 2] [Bjoerling sings in Swedish, Bokor in German] *(rec live, Vienna State Opera, 3/12/37)* Legato Classics ▲ LCD 155-1
Mendelssohn, F.:A Midsummer Night's Dream (comp), w. Magda Kalmár (sop), A. Fischer (cnd), Hungarian State Orch [G] White Label ▲ HRC 049 [DDD]
Mozart, W.A.:Arias, w. Arleen Augér (sop), Kathleen Battle (sop), Irma Beilke (sop), Helena Braun (sop), Lisa Della Casa (sop), Maria Cebotari (sop), Ileana Cotrubas (sop), Helen Donath (sop), Mirella Freni (sop), Reri Grist (sop), Edita Gruberova (sop), Elisabeth Grümmer (sop), Hilde Güden (sop), Ingeborg Hallstein (sop), Luise Helletsgruber (sop), Gundula Janowitz (sop), Sena Jurinac (sop), Erika Köth (sop), Evelyn Lear (sop), Wilma Lipp (sop), Margaret Marshall (sop), Edith Mathis (sop), Jarmila Novotna (sop), Margherita Perras (sop), Lucia Popp (sop), Elisabeth Rethberg (sop), Anneliese Rothenberger (sop), Elisabeth Schumann (sop), Elisabeth Schwarzkopf (sop), Graziella Sciutti (sop), Irmgard Seefried (sop), Graziella Sciutti (sop), Julia Varady (sop), Agnes Baltsa (mez), Brigitte Fassbaender (mez), Christa Ludwig (mez), Ann Murray (mez), Francisco Araiza (ten), Anton Dermota (ten), Helge Rosvaenge (ten), Rudolf Schock (ten), Peter Schreier (ten), Leopold Simoneau (ten), Eric Tappy (ten), Richard Tauber (ten), Gösta Winbergh (ten), Josef Witt (ten), Fritz Wunderlich (ten), Christian Boesch (bar), Willy Domgraf-Fassbaender (bar), Karl Dönch (bar), Dietrich Fischer-Dieskau (bar), Erich Kunz (bar), Eberhard Wächter (bar), Hans Hotter (b-bar), Paul Schöffler (b-bar), Cesare Siepi (b-bar), José Van Dam (b-bar), Walter Berry (bass), Geraint Evans (bass), Nicolai Ghiaurov (bass), Alexander Kipnis (bass), Richard Mayr (bass), Kurt Moll (bass), James Morris (bass), Ezio Pinza (bass), Martti Talvela (bass), Giorgio Tozzi (bass), Hans Duhan (sgr), Res Fischer (sgr), Marie Gerhart (sgr), *(various orchs & cnds)*—sels from Idomeneo, Die Entführung aus der Serail, Le nozze di Figaro, Don Giovanni, Così fan tutte, Die Zauberflöte & various arias Orfeo d'or ("Festspiel Dokumente" series) 5-▲ 408955
Mozart, W.A.:Don Giovanni, w. E. Rethberg (sop), L. Helletsgruber (sop), D. Borgioli (ten), A. Lazzari (ten), E. Pinza (bass), B. Walter (cnd), Salzburg Orch, Salzburg Mozarteum Chorus [I] *(rec live, Salzburg, Aug. 2, 1937)* Melodram ("Connaisseur" series) 3-▲ CD 37506 (m) [AAD]
Mozart, W.A.:Don Giovanni, w. L. Helletsgruber (sop), E. Rethberg (sop), D. Borgioli (ten), K. Ettl (bass), E. Pinza (bass), B. Walter (cnd), Vienna PO, Vienna State Opera Chorus *(rec Salzburg, Aug. 2, 1937)* Melodram 3-▲ MLO 37506 [ADD]

Bokor, Margit (sop)
Strauss, R.:Arabella (sels), w. Margit Bokor (sop—Zdenka), Viorica Ursuleac (sop—Arabella), Alfred Jerger (bar—Mandryka), Richard Mayr (bass—Waldner), C. Krauss (cnd), Vienna State Opera Orch *(rec Vienna, Oct. 29, 1933)* Koch Schwann 2-▲ SCH 314625 [ADD]
Strauss, R.:Der Rosenkavalier (sels), w. Margit Bokor (sop—Octavian), Hilde Konetzni (sop—Marschallin), Elisabeth Schumann (sop—Sophie), H. Knappertsbusch (cnd), Vienna State Opera Orch *(rec Salzburg, June 13, 1937)* Koch Schwann 2-▲ SCH 314672 [ADD]

Boldin, Leonid (bar)
Kabalevsky, D.:Colas Breugnon (ov), w. N. Isakova (sop), V. Kayevchenko (sop), N. Gutorovich (bar), G. Dudarev (bass), E. Maksimenko (sgr), G. Zhemchuzhin (cnd), Dantchenko Moscow Stanislavsky Music Theater Orch, Dantchenko Moscow Stanislavsky Music Theater Chorus Olympia 2-▲ OLY 291 [ADD]

Boldrini, Giancarlo (bass)
Mercadante, S.:La Vestale, w. G. Dimitrova (sop), D. Vejzovic (sop), G. Cecchele (ten), Romanò (sgr), Cepreaga (sgr), Kliskic (sgr), Sioli (sgr), V. Sutej (cnd), Spalato National Theater Orch, Spalato National Theater Chorus [I] *(rec 4/9/87)* Bongiovanni 2-▲ GB 2065/66 [DDD]

Boldt, Keith (ten)
Bernhard, C.:Missa "Durch Adams Fall", w. Henriette Schellenberg (sop), Laverne G' Froerer (mez), George Roberts (bar), J. Washburn (cnd), CBC Vancouver SO, Vancouver Chamber Choir *(rec Ryerson United Church & The Orpheum, Vancouver, May 4–7, 1992)* CBC ▲ 5160 [DDD]
Fauré, G.:Messe basse, w. Henriette Schellenberg (sop), Laverne G' Froerer (mez), George Roberts (bar), J. Washburn (cnd), CBC Vancouver SO, Vancouver Chamber Choir [orchd J. Washburn] *(rec Ryerson United Church & The Orpheum, Vancouver, May 4–7, 1992)* CBC ▲ 5160 [DDD]
Haydn, J.:Mass 7, "Kleine Orgelmesse", w. Henriette Schellenberg (sop), Laverne G' Froerer (mez), George Roberts (bar), J. Washburn (cnd), CBC Vancouver SO, Vancouver Chamber Choir *(rec Ryerson United Church & The Orpheum, Vancouver, May 4–7, 1992)* CBC ▲ 5160 [DDD]
Weber, C.M. von:Missa sancta 2, w. Henriette Schellenberg (sop), Laverne G' Froerer (mez), George Roberts (bar), J. Washburn (cnd), CBC Vancouver SO, Vancouver Chamber Choir *(rec Ryerson United Church & The Orpheum, Vancouver, May 4–7, 1992)* CBC ▲ 5160 [DDD]

Bolechowska, Alina (sgr)
Bizet, G.:Carmen (sels), w. Krystyna Szczepanska (alt—Carmen), Bogdan Paprocki (ten—Don José), Andrzej Hiolski (bar—Escamillo), Alina Bolechowska (sgr—Micaela), J. Semkow (cnd), Warsaw PO, Warsaw National Phil Chorus Polskie Nagrania ▲ PNCD 213 [AAD]

Bolgan, Marina (sop)
Paisiello, G.:Nina, o sia La pazza per amore, w. F. Pediconi (sop), D. Bernardini (ten), F. Musinu (bass), G. Surian (bass), R. Bonynge (cnd), Catania Teatro Massimo Bellini Orch, Catania Teatro Massimo Bellini Chorus [I] *(rec live 1989)* Nuova Era 2-▲ 6872/73 [DDD]
Wolf-Ferrari, E.:Il campiello, w. D. Mazzucato (Gasparina), G. Devinu (Lucieta), M. Bolgan (Gnese), C. de Mola (Orsola), U. Benelli (Dona Cate Panciana), M. Rene Cosotti (Dona Pasqua Polegana), M. Comencini (Zorzeto), M. Biscotti (Astolfi), I. D'Arcangelo (Anzoleto), C. Striuli (Fabrizio del Ritorti), N. Bareza (cnd), Trieste Teatro Comunale Giuseppe Verdi Orch, Trieste Teatro Comunale G. Verdi Chorus *(rec Feb. 1992)* Ricordi 2-▲ RFCD 2014 [DDD]

Bolkestein, Els (sop)
Theodorakis, M.:Sym 3, w. H. Rögner (cnd), Berlin Comic Opera Orch, Berlin Radio Chorus Berlin Classics 2-▲ BER 1128 [ADD]

Bollen, Ria (alt)
Haydn, J.:Mass 14, "Harmoniemesse", w. Barbara Martig-Tüller (sop), Adalbert Kraus (ten), Kurt Widmer (bass), Melitta Veits (org), D. Hellmann (cnd), Southwest German RSO Baden-Baden Calig ▲ CAL 50490
Vivaldi, A.:Gloria, RV.589, w. Ana-Maria Miranda (sop), J. E. Dähler (cnd), Southwest German CO Pforzheim, Bern Chamber Choir *(rec Berner Münster, Dec 1977)* Claves ▲ CD 50801 [ADD]

Bollen, Ria (cta)
Bach, J.S.:Cant 138, w. A. Augér (sop), A. Baldin (ten), P. Huttenlocher (bar), H. Rilling (cnd), Stuttgart Bach Collegium, Gächinger Kantorei Hänssler Classic ▲ 98.812 [AAD]
Martin, F.:Requiem, w. E. Speiser (sop), E. Tappy (ten), P. Lagger (bass), A. Luy (org), F. Martin (cnd), Swiss-Italian Orch, Union Chorale, Choir of Our Lady of Lausanne, Ars Laeta Vocal Group *(rec live, May 4, 1973)* Jecklin-Disco ▲ JD 631-2 [ADD]

Bollet, Pierre (bar)
Martin, F.:Le Mystère de la Nativité, w. Elly Ameling (sop), Aafje Heynis (cta), Hugues Cuénod (ten), Louis Devos (ten), Eric Tappy (ten), Derrik Olsen (bar), Charles Clavensy (b-bar), André Vessières (bass), E. Ansermet (cnd), Swiss Romande Orch, Jeunes de l'Eglise Chorus, Ceneva Motet Chorus Cascavelle 2-▲ CVL 2006 [ADD]

Bolshakov, Alexei (bar)
Rachmaninoff, S.:The Bells, w. Yelizaveta Shumskaya (sop), Mikhail Dovenman (ten), K. Kondrashin (cnd), Moscow PO, Alexander Yurlov (cnd), Russian Republican Capelle RCA Gold Seal ▲ 74321-32046-2 [ADD]

Bolstad, Anne (sop)
Jensen, L.I.:The Return, w. R. Sterne (alt), H. Bjørkey (ten), I. Gilhuus (ten), P. Vollestad (bar), C. Stabell (bass), O.K. Ruud (cnd), Trondheim SO, Trondheim Sym Chorus, Nidarso Cathedral Choir Simax 2-▲ PSC 3109

Bolves, Keith Alexander (ten)
Tchaikovsky, P.:Iolanta, w. Michaela Gurevich (sop—Iolanta), Jaqueline Miura (sop—Brigitta), Tatjana Tabachuk (mez—Martha), Annette Kuhn (mez—Laura), Ian Denolfo (ten—Godefroy), Keith Alexander Bolves (ten—Alméric), Alexander Ben (bar—Robert), Georg Lehner (bar—Ibn-Hakia), Arutiun Kotchinian (bass—René), Kurt Geysen (bass—Bertrand), H. Rotman (cnd), Warsaw PO, ECOV Ensemble Members *(rec Vooruit Center of the Arts, Ghent, Belgium, Aug 28–29, 1993)* CPO 2-▲ CPO 999456-2 [DDD]

Bömches, Helge (bass)
Constantinescu, P.:The Nativity, w. E. Petrescu (sop), M. Kessler (mez), V. Teodorian (ten), M. Basarab (cnd), Bucharest George Enescu PO, Bucharest George Enescu Phil Chorus *(rec 1977)* Olympia ▲ OCD 402 [AAD]

Bona, Jacques (bar)
Alain, J.:Music of, w. Delphine Collot (sop), Bruno Boterf (ten), Françoise Gyps (fl), Laurent Decker (ob), Bruno Pazqueir (va), Philippe Muller (vc), Georges Guillard (org), Ludwig String Quartet, Georges Guillard (cnd), St. Louis Camerata Vocal Ensemble—2 Melodies for Sop & Pno; Nuptial Song for Bar, Bass, Vc & Org; Post-Scriptum for 3 Female Voices & Pno; Canticle in Phrygian Mode for 4 Mixed-Voice, Sop & Strs; Invention for Fl, Ob & Cl; Monody for solo Fl; Prelude for Str Qnt; Adagio for Str Qnt; Funerals for Str Qnt; March of the Horiaces & the Curiaces for 2 Bugles, Drum & Org Arion ▲ ARN 68321
Campra, A.:Tancrède, w. C. Dussaut (sop—Herminie), A. Arapian (ten—Argant), J. Bona (bar—Tancrède), C. Zaffini (cnd), Provence Instrumental Ensemble, Avignon Vocal Ensemble—highlights *(rec 1986)* Pierre Verany ▲ PV.786111 [ADD]

Bonardi, Lino (bass)
Puccini, G.:Madama Butterfly, w. Rosetta Pampanini (sop—Madama Butterfly), Conchita Velasquez (mez—Suzuki), Cesira Ferrari (mez—Kate Pinkerton), Alessandro Granda (ten—F. B. Pinkerton), Giuseppe Nessi (ten—Goro), Aristide Baracchi (bar—Il Principe Yamadori), Gino Vanelli (bar—Sharpless), Lino Bonardi (bass—Il Commissario Imperiale), Salvatore Baccaloni (bass—Lo zio Bonzo), L. Molajoli (cnd), La Scala Orch, La Scala Chorus Bongiovanni 2-▲ 1123/24 [ADD]

Bonato, Armanda (sop)
Verdi, G.:La traviata (sels), w. R. Scotto (sop), G. Tavolccini (sop), G. Raimondi (ten), E. Bastianini (bar), A. Votto (cnd), La Scala Orch, La Scala Chorus IMP Collectors Series ▲ IMPX 9025 [AAD]

Bonazzi, Elaine (mez)
Bach, J.S.:Cant 198, w. Marnie Nixon (sop), Nico Castel (ten), Peter Binder (bar), R. Craft (cnd), Columbia SO, American Concert Choir Sony Classical ("Essential Classics" series) 2-▲ SB2K 62656
Rossini, G.:La pietra del paragone, w. A. Elgar (sop), B. Wolff (mez), J. Carreras (ten), J. Reardon (bar), R. Murcell (bar), A. Foldi (b-bar), J. Diaz (bass), N. Jenkins (cnd), Clarion Concerts Orch, Clarion Concerts Chorus [I] *(rec. ca. 1972)* Vanguard Classics 3-▲ OVC 8043/45 [ADD]

Bonci, Alessandro (ten)
Alessandro Bonci Bongiovanni 2-▲ GB 1062/63-2 [ADD]
The Great Recordings of 1912-1913 Pearl ▲ PEA 9168 [ADD]
The World of Singing, Vol. 3:The Italian School, Part 1:The Italian Tenors Before World War I (1902–13), w. Antonio Aramburo (ten), Giuseppe Borgatti (ten), Enrico Caruso (ten), Edoardo Garbin (ten), Fiorello Giraud (ten), Fernando de Lucia (ten), Francesco Marconi (ten), Giovanni Battista de Negri (ten), Antonio Paoli (ten), Francesco T Enterprise ("Vocal Archives" series) 3-▲ ENT VA 2104

Bond, Jonathon (trb)
Fauré, G.:Requiem, w. B. Luxon (bar), G. Guest (cnd), Academy of St. Martin in the Fields, St. John's College Choir Cambridge [L] London ("Jubilee" series) ▲ 430360-2 [ADD]

Bonde, Mara (sop)
Ravel, M.:Chansons, w. Nannette Soles (mez), Charles Bruffy (ten), Bruce Tammen (bass), Robert Shaw (cnd), Robert Shaw Festival Singers *(rec Church of St. Pierre, Gramat, France, July 26–28, 1994)* Telarc ▲ CD 80408 [DDD]

Bonde-Hansen, Henriette (sop)
Mahler, G.:Sym 8, w. Majken Bjerno (sop), Inga Nielsen (sop), Kirsten Dolberg (alt), Anne Gjevang (alt), Raimo Sirkiä (ten), Jorma Hynninen (bar), Carsten Stabell (bass), L. Segerstam (cnd), Danish National RSO, Copenhagen Boys' Choir, Berlin Phil Choir, Danish National Radio Choir Chandos 2-▲ CHAN 9305/06 [DDD]
Schierbeck, P.:Songs, w. Christen Stubbe Teglbjærg (pno)—I Danmark; Alverden går omkring; Sommerklange og Vintertoner; Fjerne Melodier; Fem Sange; Nakjælen *(rec Copenhagen, June 1995)* Marco Polo/Dacapo ▲ 8.224017 [DDD]

Bondi, F. (sgr)
Scarlatti, A.:Cain, the First Murder, w. R. Alessandrini (cnd), Concerto Italiano, L'Europa Galante Opus 111 2-▲ OPS 30-75/76

Bondino, Ruggiero (ten)
Berlioz, H.:La Damnation de Faust, w. Giulietta Simionato (mez), Ettore Bastianini (bar), Plinio Clabassi (bass), P. Maag (cnd), *(orch unknown)* Great Opera Performances 2-▲ GOP 776
Smareglia, A.:La falena, w. Leyla Gencer (sop—La Falena), Rita Lantieri (sop—Albina, sua figlia), Ruggero Bondino (ten—Re Stellio), Dario Zerial (ten—Il ladro), Mario D'Anna (bar—Il vecchio Uberto), Aurio Tomicich (bass—Morio), Giuseppe Botta (sgr—Un marinaio), G. Gavazzeni (cnd), Trieste Teatro Comunale Giuseppe Verdi Orch, Trieste Teatro Comunale G. Verdi Chorus *(rec Trieste, Mar 18, 1876)* Bongiovanni 2-▲ GB 1131/32
Smareglia, A.:Nozze istrane, w. Maria Chiara (sop—Marussa), Eleonora Iancovich (cta—Luze), Ruggero Bondino (ten—Lorenzo), Alessandro Cassis (bar—Nicola), Alessandro Maddalena (bar—Biagio), Carlo Zardo (bass—Bara Menico), M. Wolf-Ferrari (cnd), Trieste Teatro Comunale Giuseppe Verdi Orch, Trieste Teatro Comunale G. Verdi Chorus *(rec Trieste, Feb 17, 1973)* Bongiovanni ("Il Mito dell'Opera" series) 2-▲ 1133/34-2 [ADD]

Bone, Jacques (bass)
Boësset, A.:Music of, w. Marcel Bozonnet (nar), Véronique Dietschy (sop), Alain Zaepffel (ct), Christophe Le Paludier (ten), Claire Antonini (lt), Marianne Muller (vl)—Madame de la fayette; Airs de cour; La princesse de cleves (sels) Adès ▲ ADE 204722

Bonelli, Gino (sgr)
Verdi, G.:Oberto, Conte di San Bonifacio, w. Elena Nicolai (mez), Giuseppe Modesti (bass), Lydia Roan (sgr), Maria Vitale (sgr), A. Simonetto (cnd), Turin RAI Orch, Turin RAI Chorus Great Opera Performances 2-▲ GOP 774

Bonfatti, Gregory (sgr)
Mercadante, S.:Caritea, regina di Spagna, w. Nana Gordaze (sgr), Sonia Lee (sgr), Jacek Laszczkowski (sgr), Nicolas Rivenq (bar), Ayhan Ustuk (sgr), G. Carella (cnd), Italian International Opera Orch, Bratislava Camera Chorus *(rec Italy, 1995)* Nuova Era 3-▲ NUO 7258

Bongers, Benjamin (ten)
Moore, D.:Devil & Daniel Webster, w. Joyce Guyer (sop—Mary Stone), Benjamin Bongers (ten—Walter Butler), Michael Philip Davis (ten—Simon Girty), Matthew Foerschler (ten—Miser Stephens), Darren Keith Woods (ten—Mr. Scratch), Michael Lanman (bass—Blackbeard Teach), David Soxman (bass—Clerk), Brian Steele (bass—Daniel Webster), John Stephens (bass—Jabez Stone), Andrew Stuckey (bass—King Philip), Robert Gibby Brand (actor), Cary Miller (actor), R. Patterson (cnd), Kansas City SO, Kansas City Lyric Opera Chorus *(rec Sept 1995)* Newport Classic ▲ NPD 85585 [DDD]

Bongers, Els (sop)
Biber, H. von:Requiem à 15, w. A. Grimm (sop), K. Wessel (alt), P. de Groot (alt), M. Reyans (ten), S. Davies (ten), R. Steur (bass), K.-J. de Koning (bass), T. Koopman (cnd), Amsterdam Baroque Orch, Amsterdam Baroque Choir Erato ▲ 91725
Biber, H. von:Vesperae longiores ac breviores una cum litaniis Laurentanis, w. A. Grimm (sop), K. Wessel (alt), P. de Groot (alt), M. Reyans (ten), S. Davies (ten), R. Steur (bass), K.-J. de Koning (bass), T. Koopman (cnd), Amsterdam Baroque Orch, Amsterdam Baroque Choir Erato ▲ 91725

▲ = CD ♦ = Enhanced CD Δ = MD ■ = Cassette Tape □ = DCC

Bonhomme (sgr)
Verdi, G.:I vespri siciliani, w. J. Brumaire (sop), P. Bowden (mez), Taylor (sgr), Baran (sgr), M. Rossi (cnd), BBC Concert Orch, BBC Concert Chorus [original French version] *(rec live, London, 5/10/69)* Arkadia 3-▲ 456 [ADD]

Bonifaccio, Maddalena (sop)
Pergolesi, G.B.:La serva padrona, w. S. Nimsgern (b–bar), Collegium Aureum [I] Deutsche Harmonia Mundi ▲ 77184-2-RC [DDD]

Boniface, Edgar (bass)
Verdi, G.:Macbeth, w. Amy Shuard (sop—Lady Macbeth), Noreen Berry (mez—Lady-in-waiting), John Dobson (ten—Malcolm), André Turp (ten—Macduff), Tito Gobbi (bar—Macbeth), Edgar Boniface (bass—Servant), Rydderch Davies (bass—Doctor), Forbes Robinson (bass—Banco), Jean Holmes (sgr—Apparition), Celia Penny (sgr—Apparition), Glynne Thomas (sgr—Apparition), Brian Wrigt (sgr—Araldo), F. Molinari-Pradelli (cnd), Royal Opera House Orch, Royal Opera House Chorus Covent Garden *(rec London, Apr 8, 1960)* Bella Voce 2-▲ 7203 [AAD]

Boninsegna, Celestina (sop)
Arias Pearl ▲ PEA CD 9219
Boninsegna (sop) *(rec 1904–09)* Pearl ▲ PEA 9980 [AAD]
Fernando de Lucia, w. F. de Lucia (ten), Antonio Pini–Corsi (bar), Josefina Huguet (sop), Maria Galvany (sop), Ernesto Badini (bar) Symposium ▲ SYM 1149

Bonisolli, Franco (ten)
Bizet, G.:Djamileh, w. L. Popp (sop), L. Gardelli (cnd), Munich RSO [F] Orfeo ▲ 174881 [DDD]
Cosi si Canta...! (ten) *(rec Liceo, Barcelona, Spain)* Ornamenti ▲ 123
Gluck, C.W.:Iphigénie en Tauride, w. P. Lorengar (sop), D. Fischer-Dieskau (bar), W. Grönroos (bar), L. Gardelli (cnd), Bavarian RSO, Bavarian Radio Chorus [F] Orfeo 2-▲ 052832 [DDD]
Gluck, C.W.:Paride ed Elena, w. I. Cotrubas (sop), S. Greenberg (sop), Fontana (sgr), L. Zagrosek (cnd), Austrian RSO, Austrian Radio Chorus [I] *(rec 1983)* Orfeo 2-▲ 118842 [DDD]
Leoncavallo, R.:La Bohème, w. Lucia Popp (sop), Alexandrina Milcheva (mez), Bernd Weikl (bar), H. Wallberg (cnd), Munich RSO, Bavarian Radio Chorus [I] Orfeo 2-▲ 023822 [DDD]
Neapolitan Songs, Vol. 1 Orfeo ▲ C 075101-A ■ M 075101-A
Vol. 2 Orfeo ▲ C 075201-A ■ M 075201-A
Rossini, G.:La donna del lago, w. M. Caballé (sop), J. Hamari (mez), R. Bottazzo (ten), P. Bellugi (cnd), Turin Radio Orch, Turin RAI Chorus [I] *(rec live 5/19/70)* Standing Room Only 2-▲ SRO 803-2 (m) [ADD]
Rossini, G.:La donna del lago, w. M. Caballé (sop), J. Hamari (mez), R. Bottazzo (ten), P. Bellugi (cnd), Turin RAI Orch, Turin RAI Chorus [I] *(rec live 5/19/70)* Melodram 2-▲ MEL 27074 (m) [AAD]
Rossini, G.:La donna del lago, w. A. Balboni (sop), M. Caballé (sop), J. Hamari (mez), R. Bottazzo (ten), G. Sinimberghi (ten), P. Washington (bass), P. Bellugi (cnd), Turin RAI Orch, Turin RAI Chorus *(rec live, Torino, 1970)* Foyer 2-▲ FOY 2028 [AAD]
Rossini, G.:The Siege of Corinth, w. B. Sills (sop), M. Horne (mez), J. Diaz (bass), T. Schippers (cnd), La Scala Orch, La Scala Chorus [I] *(rec live 1969)* Melodram 2-▲ MEL 27043 [AAD]
Verdi, G.:Arias, *(various cnds & orchs)*—13 arias from Aida, Luisa Miller, Otello, Rigoletto, Traviata, Trovatore [I] Acanta ▲ 43317
Verdi, G.:I masnadieri, w. J. Sutherland (sop), M. Manugerra (bar), S. Ramey (bass), R. Bonynge (cnd), Welsh National Opera Orch, Welsh National Opera Chorus London ("Grand Opera" series) 2-▲ 433854-2 [DDD]
Verdi, G.:Rigoletto, w. M. Rinaldi (sop), V. Cortez (mez), R. Panerai (bar), B. Rundgren (b–bar), F. Molinari–Pradelli (cnd), Dresden State Orch, Dresden State Chorus [I] Acanta 2-▲ CD 41474 [DDD]
Verdi, G.:La traviata, w. M. Freni (sop), S. Bruscantini (bar), L. Gardelli (cnd), Berlin State Opera Orch, Berlin State Opera Chorus [I] Acanta 2-▲ CD 41644 [DDD]
Verdi, G.:Il trovatore, w. R. Kabaivanska (sop), M. Cortez (ten), G. Zancanaro (bar), B. Bartoletti (cnd), Berlin State Opera Orch, Berlin State Opera Chorus [I] Acanta 2-▲ CD 43301 [DDD]

Bonitatibus (sgr)
Vivaldi, A.:Beatus vir, R.795, w. Caterina Calvi (sop), Susanna Moncayo Von Hase (cta), Vincenzo Manno (ten), Trogu (sgr) Agora Music ▲ 001
Vivaldi, A.:Gloria (& Intro), RV.588, w. Caterina Calvi (sop), Susanna Moncayo Von Hase (cta), Vincenzo Manno (ten), Trogu (sgr) Agora Music ▲ 001

Bonnema, Albert (sgr)
Schillings, M. von:Mona Lisa, w. Beate Bilandzija (sgr), Klaus Wallprecht (sgr), K. Seibel (cnd), Kiel PO CPO 2-▲ CPO 999303 [DDD]

Bonner, Tessa (sop)
Bach, J.S.:Magnificat, BWV 243, w. E. Kirkby (sop), M. Chance (ct), J. M. Ainsley (ten), S. Varcoe (b–bar), R. Hickox (cnd), Collegium Musicum 90 Chandos ("Chaconne" series) ▲ CHAN 0518 [DDD]
Byrd, W.:Songs, w. Rose Consort of Viols, Red Byrd—Susanna Fair; Rejoice unto the Lord; Have Mercy upon Me, O God; In Angel's Weed; Fair Britain Isle; Triumph with Pleasant Melody; Christ Rising Again *(rec Dorset, between Apr. & Nov. 1992)* Naxos ▲ 8.550604 [DDD]
Purcell, H.:The Indian Queen, w. Sally Bruce–Payne (alt), Steven Liley (ten), Edward Caswell (bass), C. Mackintosh (cnd), Purcell Sinfony *(rec St. Bartholomew's Church, Orford, Suffolk, Sept 21–23, 1994)* Linn ▲ CKD 035
Vivaldi, A.:Gloria, RV.589, w. E. Kirkby (sop), M. Chance (ct), R. Hickox (cnd), Collegium Musicum 90 Chandos ("Chaconne" series) ▲ CHAN 0518 [DDD]

Bonnet, Cécile (sop)
Essyad, A.:Le Collier des ruses, w. F. Gonzalez (sop), V. Reinbold (mez), P. Nahon (cnd), Ensemble Instrumental K617 2-▲ 7051

Bonney, Barbara (mez)
Haydn, J.:Die Schöpfung, w. Edith Wiens (sop), Hans–Peter Blochwitz (ten), Olaf Bär (bar), Jan–Herdrik Rootering (bass), N. Marriner (cnd), Stuttgart Radio Orch, Stuttgart Radio Chorus [G] EMI Classics 2-▲ CDCB 54038 [DDD]

Bonney, Barbara (sop)
Bach, J.S.:Mass in b, BWV 232, w. C. Wulkopf (mez), P. Schrier (ten), A. Scharinger (bass), S. Celibidache (cnd), Munich PO, Munich Bach Choir Exclusive ▲ EXL 33 [ADD]
Bach, J.S.:St. Matthew Passion, w. A. Monoyios (sop), A. S. von Otter (mez), M. Chance (ct), H. Crook (ten), A. Rolfe Johnson (ten), O. Bär (bar), A. Schmidt (bar), C. Hauptmann (bass), J. E. Gardiner (cnd), English Baroque Soloists, Monteverdi Choir London [G] Archiv 3-▲ 427648-2 [DDD]
Brahms, J.:Liebeslieder Waltzes SATB, w. Anne Sofie von Otter (mez), Kurt Streit (ten) Olaf Bär (bar), Bengt Forsberg (pno), Helmut Deutsch (pno) EMI Classics ▲ CDC 55430
Brahms, J.:Neue Liebeslieder Waltzes, w. Anne Sofie von Otter (mez), Kurt Streit (ten) Olaf Bär (bar), Bengt Forsberg (pno), Helmut Deutsch (pno) EMI Classics ▲ CDC 55430
Duruflé, M.:Requiem, w. J. Larmore (mezzo-soprano), T. Hampson (bass-baritone), Ambrosian Singers, M. Legrand (cnd), Philharmonia Orch Teldec ▲ 90879-2
Fauré, G.:Requiem, w. J. Larmore (mez), T. Hampson (bass–bar), M. Legrand (cnd), Philharmonia Orch, Ambrosian Singers Teldec ▲ 90879-2
Grieg, E.:Peer Gynt, w. M. Eklöf (mez), K. M. Sandve (ten), U. Malmberg (bar), N. Järvi (cnd), Gothenburg SO, Gothenburg Sym Chorus [N] Deutsche Grammophon 2-▲ 423079-2 [DDD]
Grieg, E.:Sigurd Jorsalfar, w. M. Eklöf (mez), K. M. Sandve (ten), U. Malmberg (bar), N. Järvi (cnd), Gothenburg SO, Gothenburg Sym Chorus [N] Deutsche Grammophon 2-▲ 423079-2 [DDD]
Handel, G.F.:Acis & Galatea [arr Mozart], w. J. MacDougall (ten), M. Schäfer (ten), J. Tomlinson (bass), T. Pinnock (cnd), English Concert, English Concert Choir London 2-▲ 425792-2
Haydn, J.:Die Jahreszeiten, w. Anthony Rolfe Johnson (ct), Andreas Schmidt (bar), J. E. Gardiner (cnd), English Baroque Soloists, Monteverdi Choir London [period instrs] Archiv 2-▲ 431818-2 [DDD]
Haydn, J.:Die Jahreszeiten (sels), w. Anthony Rolfe Johnson (ten), Andreas Schmidt (bar), J. E. Gardiner (cnd), English Baroque Soloists, Monteverdi Choir London—arias & choruses Archiv ▲ 447282-2
Humperdinck, E.:Hänsel und Gretel, w. E. Lind (sop), B. Hendricks (sop), A.S. von Otter (mez), H. Schwarz (mez), M. Lipovšek (mez), Andreas Schmidt (bar), J. Tate (cnd), Bavarian RSO, Tölz Boys' Choir [G] EMI Classics 2-▲ CDCB 54022 [DDD]
Humperdinck, E.:Hänsel und Gretel, w. E. Gruberova (sop), G. Jones (sop), C. Oelze (sop), A. Murray (mez), C. Ludwig (mez), F. Grundheber (bar), C. Davis (cnd), Dresden Staatskapelle Philips 2-▲ 438013-2

Bonney, Barbara (sop) (cont.)
Lehár, F.:Die lustige Witwe, w. Cheryl Studer (sop), Boje Skovhus (bar), Bryn Terfel (b–bar), J.E. Gardiner (cnd), Vienna PO, Monteverdi Choir London Deutsche Grammophon ▲ 439911-2
Mendelssohn, F.:Elijah, w. Henriette Schellenberg (sop), Florence Quivar (mez), Marietta Simpson (mez), Reid Bartelme (trb), Jerry Hadley (ten), Richard Clement (ten), Thomas Hampson (bar), Thomas Paul (bar), R. Shaw (cnd), Atlanta SO, Atlanta Sym Chorus [E] *(rec Symphony Hall, Woodruff Arts Center, Atlanta, GA, Nov. 5–7, 1994)* Telarc 2-▲ CD 80389 [DDD]
Mendelssohn, F.:Songs, w. G. Parsons (pno) Teldec ▲ 2292-44946-2 ZK
Mendelssohn, F.:Sym 2, w. E. Wiens (sop), P. Schreier (ten), K. Masur (cnd), Leipzig Gewandhaus Orch, Leipzig Gewandhaus Chorus [G] Teldec ▲ 2292-44178-2 ZK [DDD]
Mozart, W.A.:Ave verum corpus, w. Charlotte Margiono (sop), Sylvia McNair (sop), Elisabeth von Magnus (cta), Christoph Pregardien (ten), Thomas Hampson (bass), N. Harnoncourt (cnd), Vienna Concentus Musicus, Arnold Schoenberg Choir Teldec ▲ 98928 2
Mozart, W.A.:Benedictus, w. N. Harnoncourt (cnd), Vienna Concentus Musicus, Arnold Schoenberg Choir *(rec Casino Zögernitz, Vienna, Dec. 1990)* Teldec ("Das alte Werke" series) ▲ 96147-2 [DDD]
Mozart, W.A.:Clemenza, w. Barbara Bonney (sop—Servilia), Cecilia Bartoli (mez—Sesto), Della Jones (mez—Vitellia), Diana Montague (mez—Annio), Uwe Heilman (ten—Tito), Giles Cachemaille (bar—Publio), C. Hogwood (cnd), Academy of Ancient Music, Academy of Ancient Music Chorus London ("Editions de l'oiseau–lyre" series) 2-▲ 444131-2 [DDD]
Mozart, W.A.:Don Giovanni, w. E. Gruberova (sop), R. Alexander (sop), T. Hampson (bar), N. Harnoncourt (cnd), Royal Concertgebouw Orch [I] Teldec 3-▲ 2292-44184-2 [DDD]
Mozart, W.A.:Exsultate, w. T. Pinnock (cnd), English CO, English Concert Choir Archive ▲ 445353-2
Mozart, W.A.:Exsultate, w. N. Harnoncourt (cnd), Vienna Concentus Musicus [L] Teldec ▲ 2292-44180-2 [DDD]
Mozart, W.A.:Grabmusik, w. Charlotte Margiono (sop), Sylvia McNair (sop), Elisabeth von Magnus (cta), Christoph Pregardien (ten), Thomas Hampson (bass), N. Harnoncourt (cnd), Vienna Concentus Musicus, Arnold Schoenberg Choir Teldec ("Das alte Werk" series) ▲ 98928-2
Mozart, W.A.:Litaniae Lauretanae, K.195, w. E. von Magnus (cta), U. Heilmann (tenor), G. Cachemaille (bass), N. Harnoncourt (cnd), Vienna Concentus Musicus, Arnold Schoenberg Choir Teldec ("Das alte Werke" series) ▲ 93025
Mozart, W.A.:Missa, K.317, w. Catherine Wyn–Rogers (cta), Jamie MacDougall (ten), Stephen Gadd (bass), T. Pinnock (cnd), English CO, English Concert Choir Archive ▲ 445353-2
Mozart, W.A.:Missa, K.427, w. A. Augér (sop), H.–P. Blochwitz (ten), Robert Holl (bass), C. Abbado (cnd), Berlin PO, Berlin Radio Chorus [L] Sony Classical ▲ SK 46671 [DDD]
Mozart, W.A.:Missa solemnis, K.139, w. J. Rappé (ten), J. Protschka (ten), H. Hagegard (bar), N. Harnoncourt (cnd), Vienna Concentus Musicus, Arnold Schoenberg Choir [L] Teldec ▲ 2292-44180-2 [DDD]
Mozart, W.A.:Nozze di Figaro, w. C. Margiono (sop), I. Rey (sop), A. Murray (mez, P.–L. Lang (mez), P. Langridge (ten), C. Späth (ten), T. Hampson (bar), K. Moll (bass), A. Scharinger (bass), K. Langan (bass), N. Harnoncourt (cnd), Royal Concertgebouw Orch, Netherlands Opera Chorus *(rec Amsterdam, May 1993)* Teldec 3-▲ 90861-2 [DDD]
Mozart, W.A.:Nozze di Figaro, w. A. Augér (sop), A. Nafé (mez), H. Hagegard (bar), P. Salomaa (bass), A. Östman (cnd), Drottningholm Court Theater Orch, Drottingholm Court Thea Chorus [I] L'Oiseau–Lyre 3-▲ 421333-2 [DDD]
Mozart, W.A.:Regina coeli, K.127, w. Charlotte Margiono (sop), Sylvia McNair (sop), Elisabeth von Magnus (cta), Christoph Pregardien (ten), Thomas Hampson (bass), N. Harnoncourt (cnd), Vienna Concentus Musicus, Arnold Schoenberg Choir Teldec ("Das alte Werk" series) ▲ 98928 2
Mozart, W.A.:Requiem, w. Anne Sophie von Otter (mez), Hans–Peter Blochwitz (ten), Willard White (bass), J. E. Gardiner (cnd), English Baroque Soloists, Monteverdi Choir London [L] Philips ▲ 420197-2 [DDD]
Mozart, W.A.:Songs, w. G. Parsons (pno) Teldec ▲ 2292-46334-2
Mozart, W.A.:Vesperae solennes, w. Catherine Wyn–Rogers (cta), Jamie MacDougall (ten), Stephen Gadd (bass), T. Pinnock (cnd), English CO, English Concert Choir Archive ▲ 445353-2
Mozart, W.A.:Zauberflöte, w. B. Bonney (sop—Pamina), S. Jo (sop—Queen of the Night), K. Streit (ten—Tamino), G. Cachemaille (b–bar—Papageno), K. Sigmundsson (bass—Sarastro), A. Östman (cnd), Drottningholm Court Theater Orch, Drottingholm Court Thea Chorus L'Oiseau–Lyre 2-▲ 440085-2 [DDD]
Mozart, W.A.:Zauberflöte, w. E. Gruberova (sop), G. Schmid (sop), H.–P. Blochwitz (ten), T. Hampson (bar), M. Salminen (bass), A. Scharinger (bass), N. Harnoncourt (cnd), Zurich Opera Orch, Zurich Opera House Chorus [G] Teldec 2-▲ 2292-42716-2
Nono, L.:Canto sospeso, w. S. Otto (alt), M. Torzewski (ten), S. Lothar (nar), B. Ganz (nar), Berlin Radio Chorus *(rec Dec. 9–11, 1992)* Sony Classical ▲ SK 53360 [DDD]
Orff, C.:Carmina burana, w. F. Lopardo (ten), A. Michaels–Moore (bar), A. Previn (cnd), Vienna PO, Arnold Schoenberg Choir, Vienna Boys' Choir Deutsche Grammophon ▲ 439950-2
Purcell, H.:Songs, w. S. Gritton (sop), J. Bowman (ct), R. Covoy Crump (ton), C. Daniels (ten), M. George (bass), D. Miller (archlt/thb/baroque gtr), M. Caudle (b vl), R. King (org/hpd), King's Consort—Incassum Lesbia; Gentle Shepherds, you that know the charms; I love and I must; Through mournful shades and solitary groves; The Knotting Song Hyperion ▲ CDA 66720 [DDD]
Purcell, H.:Songs, w. S. Gritton (sop), J. Bowman (ct), R. Covey–Crump (ten), C. Daniels (ten), M. George (bass), D. Miller (archlt/thb/baroque gtr), M. Caudle (b vl), R. King (chamber org)—Draw near, you lovers; While Thyrsis, wrapt in downy sleep; Love, thou canst hear, I lov'd fair Celia; What hope for us remains now he is gone; Pastora's beauties, when unblown; A thousand sev'ral ways I tried; Urge me no more; Farewell all joys; If music be the food of love [1st setting]; Amidst the shades and cool refreshing streams; They say you're angry; Let each gallant heart; This poet sings the Trojan wars; Ah, how pleasant 'tis to love; My heart whenever you appear; On the brow of Richard Hill; Rashly I swore I would disown; Since the pox or the plague; Beneath a dark and melancholy grove; Musing on cares of human fate; Whilst Cynthia sung, all angry winds lay still Hyperion ▲ CDA 66710
Purcell, H.:Songs, w. S. Gritton (sop), J. Bowman (ct), R. Covey–Crump (ten), C. Daniels (ten), M. George (bass), R. King (cnd), King's Consort—When Strephon Found; Let Us, Kind Lesbia; Corinna Is Divinely Fair; Olinda in the Shades; If Music Be the Food of Love [3rd setting]; Lovely Albina; I Came, I Saw; No, to What Purpose; Young Thrysis' Fate; She Loves Me and Confesses Too; From Silent Shade (Bess of Bedlam); O Solitude; If Pray'rs and Tears; The Fatal Hour; Sylvia, 'Tis True You're Fair; Amintor, Heedless of His Flocks; Love is Now Become a Trade; Phyllis, I Can Never Forgive It; Who Can Behold?; He Himself Courts His Own Ruin; Let Formal Lovers Still Pursue; Ask Me to Love No More; In Cloris All Soft Charms; Spite of the Godhead Hyperion ▲ CDA 66730
Schoenberg, A.:Moses und Aaron, w. M. Zakai (cta), P. Langridge (ten), F. Mazura (bar), A. Haugland (bass), G. Solti (cnd), Chicago SO, Chicago Sym Chorus, Glen Ellyn Children's Chorus [G] London 2-▲ 414264-2 [DDD]
Schubert, Franz:Mass 2, w. B. Poschner (ten), M. Hintermeier (cta), J. A. Pita (ten), A. Schmidt (bar), C. Abbado (cnd), CO of Europe Deutsche Grammophon ▲ 435486-2
Schubert, Franz:Songs (misc), w. Geoffrey Parsons (pno)—Gretchen am Spinnrade; Gretchens Bitte; Heidenröslein; Auf dem Wasser zu Singen; Horch, horch die Lerch im Ätherblau; Nähe des Geliebten; Ganymed; Die Forelle; Du bist die Ruth; Mignon Lieder [Kennst du das Land; Heiss mich nicht reden; So lasst mich scheinen; Nur wer die Sehnsucht kennt]; Liebhaber in allen Gestalten; Im Abenrot; Ave Maria; Der Hirt auf dem Felsen [w. Sharon Kam (clarinet)]; Liebe Schwärmt auf allen Wegen; An die Nachtigall *(rec Apr. 1994)* Teldec ▲ 90873-2 [DDD]
Schumann, R.:Requiem Mignon, w. B. Poschner (ten), M. Hintermeier (cta), J. A. Pita (ten), A. Schmidt (bar), C. Abbado (cnd), CO of Europe Deutsche Grammophon ▲ 435486-2
Schumann, R.:Spanisches Liederspiel, w. Anne Sofie von Otter (mez), Kurt Streit (ten) Olaf Bär (bar), Bengt Forsberg (pno), Helmut Deutsch (pno) EMI Classics ▲ CDC 55430
Strauss (II), Joh.:Die Fledermaus (sels), w. E. Gruberova (sop), M. Lipovšek (mez), W. Kmentt (ten), W. Hollweg (ten), J. Protschka (ten), C. Boesch (bar), A. Scharinger (bass), N. Harnoncourt (cnd), Royal Concertgebouw Orch, Netherlands Opera Chorus Teldec ▲ 42427-2
Wolf, H.:Italienische Liederbücher (comp), w. H. Hageġuard (bar), G. Parsons (pno) Teldec ▲ 72301

Bonney, Barbara (sop) (cont.)
Zemlinsky, A. von:Songs (misc), w. A.-S. von Otter (mez), H.-P. Blochwitz (ten), A. Schmidt (bar), C. Garben (pno)—Lieder, Op. 2; Gesänge, Op. 5; Walzer-Gesänge nach toskanischen Volksliedern, Op. 6; Irmelin Rose und andere Gesänge, Op. 7; Turmwächterlied und andere Gesänge, Op. 8; Ehetanzlied und andere Gesänge, Op. 10; Schlummerlied; 6 Gesänge, Op. 13; 6 Lieder, Op. 22; Ahnung Beatricens; 12 Lieder, Op. 27 [G] Deutsche Grammophon 2-▲ 427348-2 [DDD]

Bontempi, Pino (sgr)
Her First Recordings, w. Steber, Eleanor (sop), Armand Tokatyan (ten), Lucielle Browning (mez), Annamary Dickey (sgr), George Cehanovsky (bar), Lorenzo Alvary ((bass), A. Kent (bar), Raoul Jobin (ten), Norman Cordon (bass) VAI Audio ▲ VAIA 1023 (m) [ADD]

Bontoux (sop)
The French Tradition, Vol. 1 (1897-1909), w. P. Aumonier (bass) *(rec 1897-1909)* Minerva ▲ MN A39 [ADD]

Bontoux, Bertrand (bass)
Liszt, F.:Requiem, w. Jacques Maresch (ten), Daniel Galvez-Vallejo (ten), Lionel Peintre (bar), Francois-Henri Houbart (org), Y. Parmentier (cnd), Republican Guard Brass & Percussion, French Army Chorus Adès ▲ ADE 203032

Bookspan, Janet (nar)
Paulus, S.:Voices from the Gallery, w. T. Russell (cnd), Pro Musica CO—The Winged Victory of Samothrace; American Gothic; The Garden of Earthly Delights; Infanta Margarita; She-Goat; Nude Descending a Staircase; The Birth of Venus; Mona Lisa; The Beggars; Cristina's World; Dance at Bougival *(rec Weigel Hall, Ohio State Univ.; Magee Audio Engineering, Los Angeles, CA)* d'Note Classics ▲ DND 1010 [DDD]
Walton, W.:Façade, w. S. Baron (fl), C. Russon (cl), H. Estrin (sax), M. Broiles (tpt), K. Moore (vc), H. Harris (perc), D. Epstein (cnd) Allegretto ▲ ACD 8153 [ADD] ■ ACD 8153

Boom, Peter (sgr)
Marschner, H.A.:Der Vampyr, w. Carole Farley (sop—Malwina), Nucci Condò (mez—Suse), Oslavio Di Credico (ten—George Dibdin), Josef Protschka (ten—Edgar Aubry), Romano Truffelli (ten—Richard Scrop), Martin Egel (bar—Sir Humphrey Davenaut), Andrea Snarski (bar—Toms Blunt), Siegmund Nimsgern (b-bar—Lord Ruthven), Armando Caforio (bass—Robert Green), Peter Boom (sgr—Il capo dei Vampiri), Carlo Di Giacomo (sgr—James Gadshill), Wolfgang Lenz (sgr—Sir Berkley), Galina Pisarenko (sgr—Janthe), Renzo Scorsoni (sgr—Un servitore di Berkley), Anastasia Tomaszewska Schepis (sgr—Emmy), G. Neuhold (cnd), Rome RAI SO, Rome RAI Chorus *(rec Rome, Jan 26, 1980)* Italia 2-▲ CDC 99 [ADD]

Booth, Thomas (ten)
Lloyd, G.:John Socman (sels), w. J. Watson (sop), D. Montague (mez), D. Wilson-Johnson (bar), M. Rivers (bar), M. George (bass), G. Lloyd (cnd), Philharmonia Orch, London Voices Albany ▲ TROY 131 [DDD]
Lloyd, G.:The Vigil of Venus, w. Carolyn James (sop), G. Lloyd (cnd), Welsh National Opera Orch, Welsh National Opera Chorus Albany ▲ TROY 170 [DDD]

Booth, Webster (ten)
German, E.:Music of, w. P. Dawson (b-bar), Sargent (cnd), *(orchs unknown)*—Nell Gwyn:Overture; Pavane from Romeo & Juliet; Glorious Devon; Henry VIII:Overture; Gipsy Suite; Tom Jones (sels.); The English Rose from Merrie England; Theme & 6 Diversions; Rolling Down to Rio; Valse Gracieuse from Leeds Suite; Berceuse from The Tempter; March Rhapsody on Original Themes *(rec 1920-1939)* Pearl ▲ PEA 9024 [AAD]

Booth-Jones, Christopher (bar)
Puccini, G.:Tosca, w. Jane Eaglen (sop—Floria Tosca), Charbel Michael (alt—Shepherd Boy), John Daszak (ten—Spoletta), Dennis O'Neill (ten—Mario Cavaradossi), Christopher Booth-Jones (bar—Sciarrone), Ashley Holland (bar—Jailor), Gregory Yurisich (bar—Baron Scarpia), Peter Rose (bass—Cesare Angelotti), Andrew Shore (bass—Sacristan), D. Parry (cnd), Philharmonia Orch, Geoffrey Mitchell Choir, Peter Kay Children's Chorus Chandos ("Opera in English" series) 2-▲ CHAN 3000

Boothman, Donald (bar)
Duke, J.:Songs, w. J. Duke (pno)—22 songs [E] AFKA ▲ SK 505

Boraly (sgr)
Nivers, G.G.:Motets, w. Fanjat (sop), J. Nicolas (sop), Malardenti (sgr), Maréchal (sgr), Houbart (org)—Motet a la Sainte Vierge pour le temps de Paques; Motet pour L'Elévation; Motet pour le Saint Sacrement; Motet du temps de carême pour le Saint Sacrement; Motet du temps de Noël pour le Saint Sacrement; Motet final du tout office pour le Roy [L] Pierre Verany ▲ PV.791101 [DDD]

Børch, Jørgen Ole (bar)
Kayser, L.:Psalms Bar & Org, w. Kristian Olesen (org) Point ▲ PCD 5097
Klit, L.:The Last Virtuoso, w. Hanne Andersen (sop), Edith Guillaume (mez), Jan Lund (ten), Jesper Buhl (bar), S. A. Johansen (cnd), *(ensemble unknown)* Kontrapunkt ▲ KPT 32221

Borchers, Christel (cta)
Brixi, F.X.:Missa Interga, w. I. Verebics (sop), S. Weir (ten), Genhardt (bass), H. Rilling (cnd), Prague CO, Kühn Chorus Supraphon ▲ 11 0092-2 [DDD]
Brixi, F.X.:Opus Patheticum de Septem Doloribus Beatae Mariae Virginis, w. I. Verebics (sop), S. Weir (ten), Genhardt (bass), H. Rilling (cnd), Prague CO, Kühn Chorus Supraphon ▲ 11 0092-2 [DDD]

Borden, Barbara (sop)
Blow, J.:No, Lesbia, no, you ask in vain, w. R. Shaw (hpd) [E] Globe ▲ GLO 5029 [DDD]
Cavalli, P.F.:Vespero della beata Vergine Maria, w. Emily van Evera (sop), Markus Brutscher (ten), Mark Padmore (ten), Rodrigo del Pozo (ten), Gerd Türk (ten), Harry van der Kamp (bass), Peter Zimpel (sgr), Bruce Dickey (sackbut), Charles Toet (sackbut), Concerto Palatino, Schola Cantorum Basiliensis Harmonia Mundi France ("Documenta" series) 2-▲ HMC 905219/20
Monteverdi, C.:Vespro della Beata Vergine, w. Maria Cristina Kiehr (sop), Andreas Scholl (alt), John Bowen (ten), Andrew Murgatroyd (ten), Victor Torres (bar), Antonio Abete (bass), Jelle Draijer (bass), René Jacobs (cnd), Concerto Vocale, Netherlands Chamber Choir Harmonia Mundi 2-▲ 901566.67
Schütz, H.:Symphoniae sacrae 1, w. Nele Gramss (sop), Rogers Covey-Crump (ten), John Potter (ten), Douglas Nasrawi (ten), Harry van der Kamp (bass), Concerto Palatino Choir Accent 2-▲ 9178/79 [DDD]

Bordonali, Attilio (bass)
Puccini, G.:Manon Lescaut, w. Maria Zamboni (sop—Manon), Anna Masetti-Bassi (mez—Singer), Francesco Merli (ten—Chevalier), Giuseppe Nessi (ten—Edmondo/Dancing Master/ Lamplighter), Lorenzo Conati (bar—Lescaut), Aristide Baracchi (bass—Innkeeper/Sergeant), Attilio Bordonali (bass—Geronte), Natale Villa (bass—Naval Captain), L. Molajoli (cnd), La Scala Orch, Vittore Veneziani (cnd), La Scala Chorus *(rec 1930)* Arkadia ("The 78's" series) 2-▲ 78014 [ADD]
Rossini, G.:Il barbiere di Siviglia, w. Cesira Ferrari (mez—Berta), Mercedes Capsir (cta—Rosina), Dino Borgioli (ten—Count), Salvatore Baccaloni (bar—Bortolo), Aristide Baracchi (bar—Officer), Riccardo Stracciari (bar—Figaro), Vincenzo Bettoni (bass—Don Basilio), Attilo Bordonali (bass—Fiorello), L. Molajoli (cnd), La Scala Orch, La Scala Chorus *(rec 1930)* Arkadia ("The 78's" series) 2-▲ 78008 [ADD]

Bordoni, Franco (bar)
Bizet, G.:Carmen, w. Giovanna di Rocco (sop—Frasquita), Grace Bumbry (mez—Carmen), Anita Caminada (mez—Mercedes), Franco Corelli (ten—Don José), Mario Ferrara (ten—Dancario), Franco Bordoni (bar—Escamillo), Carlo Scaravelli (bar—Morales), Giuseppe Morresi (bass—Remendado), Francesco Signor (bass—Zuniga), O. de Fabritiis (cnd), *(orch unknown)* *(rec Macerata, July 21, 1974)* Golden Age of Opera 2-▲ GAO 181/82 [ADD]
Verdi, G.:I vespri siciliani, w. M. Caballé (sop), P. Domingo (ten), J. Diaz (bass), E. Queler (cnd), *(orch unknown)* *(rec live, Barcelona, 1974)* Standing Room Only 2-▲ SRO 837-2 [ADD]

Borelius, Torkel (bass)
Schnittke, A.:Sym 2, w. Malena Ernman (alt), Mikael Bellini (ct), Göran Eliasson (ten), L. Segerstam (cnd), Royal Stockholm PO, Anders Eby (cnd), Mikaeli Chamber Choir *(rec Stockholm Concert Hall, Sweden, Feb. 24-25, 1994)* BIS ▲ CD 667 [DDD]

Borelli, Giannella (mez)
Bellini, V.:Norma, w. A. Cerquetti (sop), G. Borelli, M. Pirazzini (mez), F. Corelli (ten), P. de Palma (ten), G. Neri (bass), G. Santini (cnd), *(orch unknown)* *(rec Rome, 1958)* Great Opera Performances 2-▲ GOP 722

Borelli, Giannella (mez) (cont.)
Verdi, G.:La traviata, w. B. Sills (sop), M. Zotti (sop), A. Kraus (ten), M. Zanasi (bar), A. Ceccato (cnd), Naples Teatro San Carlo Orch, Naples Teatro San Carlo Chorus *(rec live 1/17/70)* Melodram 2-▲ MEL 27063 (m) [AAD]

Borescko, Kira (sop)
Zielenski, M.:Communiones totius anni, w. Marcin Borus-Szczycinski (alt), Ryszard Minkiewicz (ten), Robert Hugo (org), M. Bornus-Szczycinski (cnd), Bornus Consort, Tallinn Linnamussikud Instrumental Ensemble, Tallin Linnamussikud Vocal Ensemble Urtext ▲ ACD 202662 [DDD]
Zielenski, M.:Offertoria totius anni, w. Marcin Borus-Szczycinski (alt), Ryszard Minkiewicz (ten), Robert Hugo (org), M. Bornus-Szczycinski (cnd), Bornus Consort, Tallinn Linnamussikud Instrumental Ensemble, Tallin Linnamussikud Vocal Ensemble Urtext ▲ ACD 202662 [DDD]

Borg, Kim (bass)
Bach, J.S.:Mass in b, BWV 232, w. L. Marshall (sop), H. Töpper (mez), P. Pears (ten), E. Jochum (cnd), Bavarian RSO, Bavarian Radio Chorus Philips 2-▲ 438739-2
Beethoven, L. van:Missa Solemnis, w. E. Farrell (sop), C. Smith (mez), R. Lewis (ten), L. Bernstein (cnd), New York PO, Westminster Choir [L] Sony Classical 2-▲ SM2K 47522 [ADD]
Bruckner, A.:Mass 3, w. M. Stader (sop), A. Hellmann (alt), E. Haefliger (ten), E. Jochum (cnd), Bavarian RSO, Bavarian Radio Chorus [L] Deutsche Grammophon 4-▲ 423127-2 [ADD]
Bruckner, A.:Mass 3, w. M. Stader (sop), C. Hellmann (mez), E. Haefliger (ten), E. Jochum (cnd), Bavarian RSO, Bavarian Radio Chorus Deutsche Grammophon ("The Originals" series) 2-▲ 447409-2
Dvořák, A.:Requiem Mass, w. Maria Stader (sop), Sieglinde Wagner (cta), Ernst Haefliger (ten), K. Ancerl (cnd), Czech PO, Czech Chorus Deutsche Grammophon ("Double" series) 2-▲ 437377-2
Haydn, J.:Die Schöpfung, w. Irmgard Seefried (sop), Richard Holm (ten), I. Markevitch (cnd), Berlin PO, St. Hedwig's Cathedral Choir Deutsche Grammophon ("Double" series) 2-▲ 437380-2
Haydn, J.:Die Schöpfung, w. Gundula Janowitz (sop—Gabriel), Fritz Wünderlich (ten—Uriel), Kim Borg (bass—Raphael), H. von Karajan (cnd), Vienna PO, Vienna Singverein *(rec Salzburg, Aug 29, 1965)* Bella Voce 2-▲ 7204 [AAD]
Mussorgsky, M.:Boris Godunov, w. Martha Mödl (sop—Marina Mniszek), Lotte Schädle (sop—Xenia), Dorothea Siebert (mez—Fyodor), Hertha Töpper (mez—Xenia's wet-nurs), Karl Hermann Bennert (Boyer Khrushchyov), Lorenz Fehenberger (ten—Prince Shuysky), Hans Hopf (ten—Grigory), Karl Ostertag (ten—Missail), Hans Hotter (b-bar—Boris Godunov), Hermann Uhde (bar—Andrey Shchelkalov), Kurt Böhme (bass—Varlaam), Kim Borg (bass—Pimen), Kieth Engen (bass—Lewicki), Adolf Keil (bass—Nikitich), Benno Kusche (bar—Rangoni), Heinz Maria Linz (bass—Czernikowski), E. Jochum (cnd), Bavarian RSO, Bavarian Radio Chorus *(rec Munich, May 1957)* Myto 3-▲ MCD 953131
Nicolai, O.:Lustigen Weiber, w. Erika Köth (sop), Hertha Töpper (mez), Maria Rogner (sgr), Hans Günter Nöcker (b-bar), Naan Pödl (sgr), F. Rieger (cnd), Bavarian RSO, Bavarian Chorus *(rec 1960's)* Pantheon 2-▲ PHE 6660 (m)
Verdi, G.:Requiem Mass, w. Maria Stader (sop), Marjana Radev (mez), Helmut Krebs (ten), F. Fricsay (cnd), Berlin RIAS SO, Berlin RIAS Chamber Choir, St. Hedwig Cathedral Choir *(rec Jesus-Christus Church, Berlin, Sept 1953)* Deutsche Grammophon ("The Originals" series) ▲ 447442-2 [ADD]

Borgatti, Giuseppe (ten)
The World of Singing, Vol. 3:The Italian School, Part 1:The Italian Tenors Before World War I (1902-13), w. Antonio Aramburo (ten), Alessandro Bonci (ten), Enrico Caruso (ten), Edoardo Garbin (ten), Fiorello Giraud (ten), Fernando de Lucia (ten), Francesco Marconi (ten), Giovanni Battista de Negri (ten), Antonio Paoli (ten), Francesco T Enterprise ("Vocal Archives" series) 3-▲ ENT VA 2104
The World of Singing, Vol 4:The Italian School Part 1:Tenors before World War I, Book 2, w. Edoardo Garbin (ten), Fiorello Giraud (ten), Florencio Costantino (ten), Antonio Paoli (ten), Carlo Albani (ten), Enrico Caruso (ten), Amedeo Bassi (ten), Piero Schivazzi (ten), Elvino Ventura (ten), Giovanni Zenatello (ten) Enterprise ("Vocal Archives" series) 3-▲ ENT VA 2107

Borghi, Umberto (sgr)
Cherubini, L.:Pimmalione, w. M. Adani (sop), I. Ligabue (sop), G. Carturan (mez), E. Gerelli (cnd), Milan RAI Orch, Milan RAI Chorus [I] *(rec live 1955)* Melodram ▲ CDM 19501 [AAD]
Cherubini, L.:Pimmalione, w. Mariella Adani (sop), Ilva Ligabue (sop), Gabriella Carturan (mez), E. Gerelli (cnd), Milan RAI SO, Milan RAI Chorus Melodram 2-▲ CDM 29501

Borgioli, Armando (bar)
Puccini, G.:Tosca, w. Maria Caniglia (sop), Beniamino Gigli (ten), O. de Fabritiis (cnd), Rome Teatro Reale Opera Orch, Reale Theater Chorus *(rec 1938)* Grammofono 2000 2-▲ GRM 78591 (m)
Verdi, G.:Aida, w. Maria Caniglia (sop—Aida), Ebe Stignani (mez—Amneris), Beniamino Gigli (ten—Radamés), Armando Borgioli (bar—Amonasro), T. Beecham (cnd), London SO, London Sym Chorus *(rec Royal Opera House, Covent Garden, May 24, 1939)* Enterprise ("The Radio Years" series) 2-▲ ENT RY 62
Verdi, G.:Aida, w. Giannina Arangi-Lombardi (sop—Aida), Maria Capuana (mez—Amneris), Aroldo Lindi (ten—Radames), Giuseppe Nessi (ten—Messenger), Armando Borgioli (bar—Amonasro), Salvatore Baccaloni (bass—King), Tancredi Pasero (bass—Ramfis), L. Molajoli (cnd), La Scala Orch, La Scala Chorus *(rec Nov 1928)* VAI Audio 2-▲ VAIA 1083-2

Borgioli, Dino (ten)
Dino Borgioli *(rec 1921-42)* Pearl ▲ PEA 9091 [ADD]
Mozart, W.A.:Don Giovanni, w. E. Rethberg (sop), L. Helletsgruber (sop), M. Bokor (mez), A. Lazzari (ten), E. Pinza (bass), B. Walter (cnd), Salzburg Orch, Salzburg Mozarteum Chorus [I] *(rec live, Salzburg, Aug. 2, 1937)* Melodram ("Connaisseur" series) 3-▲ CD 37506 (m) [AAD]
Mozart, W.A.:Don Giovanni, w. L. Helletsgruber (sop), E. Rethberg (sop), M. Bokor (mez), K. Ettl (bass), E. Pinza (bass), B. Walter (cnd), Vienna PO, Vienna State Opera Chorus *(rec Salzburg, Aug. 2, 1937)* Melodram 3-▲ MLO 37506 [ADD]
Rossini, G.:Il barbiere di Siviglia, w. Cesira Ferrari (mez—Berta), Mercedes Capsir (cta—Rosina), Dino Borgioli (ten—Count), Salvatore Baccaloni (bar—Bortolo), Aristide Baracchi (bar—Officer), Riccardo Stracciari (bar—Figaro), Vincenzo Bettoni (bass—Don Basilio), Attilio Bordonali (bass—Fiorello), L. Molajoli (cnd), La Scala Orch, La Scala Chorus *(rec 1930)* Arkadia ("The 78's" series) 2-▲ 78008 [ADD]
Rossini, G.:Il barbiere di Siviglia, w. M. Capsir (sop), R. Stracciari (bar), S. Baccaloni (bass), V. Bettoni (bass), L. Molajoli (cnd), La Scala Orch, La Scala Chorus *(rec 1929 for Columbia Records)* Music Memoria 2-▲ 30276/77
Verdi, G.:Falstaff, w. Ismildo Tedeschi (ten), Mariano Stabile (bar), A. Toscanini (cnd), Vienna PO, Vienna State Opera Chorus *(rec live, Salzburg Festival, 1936)* Arkadia 2-▲ 625
Verdi, G.:Falstaff, w. Augusta Ottrabella (sop—Nannetta), Franca Somigli (sop—Alice), Angelica Cravcenko (mez—Mrs. Quickly), Mita Vasari (mez—Meg), Dino Borgioli (ten—Fenton), Giuseppe Nessi (ten—Bardolfo), Alfredo Tedeschi (ten—Dr. Cajus), Piero Biasini (bar—Ford), Mariano Stabile (bar—Falstaff), Virgilio Lazzari (bass—Pistola), A. Toscanini (cnd), Vienna PO, Vienna State Opera Chorus *(rec Salzburg, Aug 23, 1937)* Minerva 2-▲ MN A36/37 (m) [ADD]
Verdi, G.:Rigoletto, w. Mercedes Capsir (sop), Riccardo Stracciari (bar), Duilio Baronti (bass), Ernesto Dominici (bass), Anna Masetti Bassi (sgr) *(rec 1930)* Grammofono 2000 2-▲ GRM 78632
Verdi, G.:Rigoletto, w. Mercedes Capsir (sop), Riccardo Stracciari (bar), Ernesto Dominici (bass), L. Molajoli (cnd), La Scala Orch, La Scala Chorus Phonographe 2-▲ PHG 5036 [ADD]

Borgonovo, Luigi (bar)
Verdi, G.:La traviata, w. Olga de Franco (sop—Flora Bervoix/Annina), Anna Rosza (sop—Violetta Valéry), Giordano Callegari (ten—Gastone), Alessandro Ziliani (ten—Alfredo Germont), Luigi Borgonovo (bar—Giorgio Germont), Arnoldo Lenzi (bar—Baron Douphol), Antonio Gelli (bass—Marquis d'Obigny/Dr. Grenvil), C. Sabajno (cnd), La Scala Orch, La Scala Chorus *(rec La Scala Theatre, Milan, Oct.-Nov. 1930)* VAI Audio 2-▲ VAIA 1108-2
Verdi, G.:La traviata, w. Olga de Franco (sop—Flora Bervoix/Annina), Anna Rosza (sop—Violetta Valery), Giordano Callegari (ten—Gastone), Alessandro Ziliani (ten—Alfredo Germont), Luigi Borgonovo (bar—Giorgio Germont), Arnoldo Lenzi (bar—Barone Douphol), Antonio Gelli (bass—Marchese d'Obigny/Dottor Grenvil), C. Sabajno (cnd), La Scala Orch, Vittore Veneziani (cnd), La Scala Chorus *(rec Oct-Nov 1930)* Arkadia 2-▲ CD 78001 (m) [ADD]

Bori, Lucrezia (sop)
Donizetti, G.:Don Pasquale (sels), w. Giuseppe De Luca (bar)—Pronta io son *(rec 1921)* Minerva ▲ MN-A23 [ADD]
The Electric Recordings (sop) *(rec 1925-37)* Pearl ▲ PEA CD 9246

▲ = CD ♦ = Enhanced CD Δ = MD ■ = Cassette Tape □ = DCC

Bori, Lucrezia (sop) (cont.)
Leider Singer, w. J. McCormack (ten), E. Schneider (sgr), Grace Moore (sop), F. Kreisler (vn), V. O'Brien (pno), L. Kennedy (vc) Symposium ▲ 1164
Lucrezia Bori *(rec 1921–1937)* Pearl ▲ PEA 9458 (m) [AAD]

Boriello, Mario (bar)
Cimarosa, D.:Giannina e Bernardone, w. D. De Cecco (sop), S. Jurinac (sop), G. Sciutti (sop), M. Carlin (ten), S. Bruscantini (bar), C. De Antoni (sgr), N. Sanzogno (cnd), Milan RAI SO, Milan RAI Chorus [I] *(rec live, Milan July 26, 1953)* Melodram 2–▲ CDM 29505 [ADD]
Nono, L.:Epitaffio 1, w. L. Marimpietri (sop), B. Maderna (cnd), Rome RAI Orch, Rome RAI Chorus *(rec live, Rome 1/28/61)* Arkadia ▲ 027 [ADD]

Borisova, Galina (mez)
Rachmaninoff, S.:Aleko, w. Natalia Erassova (sop), Vitaly Tarastchenko (ten), Vladimir Matorin (bass), Viatcheslav Potchapski (bass), A. Tchistiakov (cnd), Bolshoi Theater Orch, Russian State Choir Russian Season 3–▲ CMX 388053
Shchedrin, R.:Dead Souls, w. Larisa Avdeyeva (mez—Korobochka), Galina Borisova (mez—Plyushkin), Alexi Maslennikov (ten—Selifan), Vladislav Piavko (ten—Nozdryov), Vitali Vlasov (ten—Manilov), Boris Morozov (bass—Sobakevich), Alexander Voroshilo (sgr—Chichikov), Y. Temirkanov (cnd), Bolshoi Theater Orch, Bolshoi Theater Chorus, Moscow Chamber Choir *(rec Moscow, 1982)* Melodiya ("The Russian Opera" series) 2–▲ 74321–29347–2 [ADD]

Bork, Hanneke van (sop)
Bach, J.S.:Magnificat, BWV 243, w. E. Ameling (sop), H. Watts (cta), W. Krenn (ten), T. Krause (bass), K. Münchinger (cnd), Stuttgart CO, Vienna Academy Chorus London ("Serenata" series) ▲ 433175–2 [ADD]
Mahler, G.:Sym 8, w. Ileana Cotrubas (sop), Heather Harper (sop), Brigit Finnila (mez), Marianne Dieleman (cta), William Cochran (ten), Hermann Prey (bar), Hans Sotin (bass), B. Haitink (cnd), Royal Concertgebouw Orch Philips ("Solo" series) ▲ 446195–2

Borkh, Inge (sop)
Beethoven, L. van:Sym 9, "Choral Sym", w. R. Siewert (cta), R. Lewis (ten), L. Weber (bass), R. Leibowitz (cnd), Royal PO, Beecham Choral Society [G] *(rec 6/61)* Chesky ▲ CD66 [ADD]
Cherubini, L.:Médée (sels), w. I. Borkh (sop—Medea), L. Suthaus (ten—Giasone), V. Gui (cnd), Berlin State Opera Orch, Berlin State Opera Chorus—3 soprano arias & 3 duets *(rec live, Berlin 1958)* Melodram 2–▲ CDM 27087 [ADD]
Gluck, C.W.:Iphigénie en Aulide, w. Inge Borkh (sop—Klytämnestra), Christa Ludwig (mez—Iphigenie), Elisabeth Steiner (mez—Artemis), James King (ten—Achilles), Otto Edelmann (b-bar), Alois Pernerstorfer (b-bar), Walter Berry (bass), K. Böhm (cnd), Vienna PO, Salzburg Festival Chamber Choir, Vienna State Opera Chorus *(rec Salzburg, Aug 3, 1962)* Orfeo d'or ("Festspiel Dikumente" series) 2–▲ C 428962 (m) [ADD]
Inge Borkh *(rec 1956–58)* Preiser ▲ PRE CD 90302
Puccini, G.:Turandot, w. R. Tebaldi (sop), M. del Monaco (ten), A. Erede (cnd), St. Cecilia Academy Orch Rome, St. Cecilia Academy Chorus Rome London 2–▲ 433761–2 [ADD]
Schoenberg, A.:Gurrelieder, w. H. Schachtschneider (ten), H. Töpper (mez), L. Fehenberger (ten), K. Engen (bass), R. Kubelik (cnd), Bavarian RSO—also includes songs by Berg, Schoenberg & Webern Deutsche Grammophon ("20th Century Classics" series) ▲ 431744–2 [ADD]
Strauss, R.:Elektra, w. M. Schech (sop), J. Madeira (mez), D. Fischer-Dieskau (bar), K. Böhm (cnd), Dresden Staatskapelle [G] *(rec 1961)* Deutsche Grammophon 2–▲ 445329–2
Strauss, R.:Elektra (sels), w. F. Reiner (cnd), Chicago SO—Elektra's Soliloquy, Recognition Scene, & Finale RCA Gold Seal ▲ 09026–60874–2 [ADD] ■ 09026–60874–4
Strauss, R.:Salome, w. I. Borkh (sop—Salome), M. Klose (mez—Herodias), C. Ludwig (mez—Page), M. Lorenz (ten—Herodes), F. Fehringer (ten—Narraboth), F. Frantz (bar—Jokanaan), K. Schröder (cnd), Hessian RSO *(rec 1952)* Myto 2–▲ 93592
Strauss, R.:Salome (sels), w. F. Reiner (cnd), Chicago SO—Dance of the Seven Veils & Final Scene RCA Gold Seal ▲ 09026–60874–2 [ADD] ■ 09026–60874–4

Bornemann, Barbara (alt)
Bach, C.P.E.:Magnificat, w. V. Hruba-Freiberger (sop), P. Schreier (ten), O. Bär (bar), H. Haenchen (cnd), C.P.E. Bach CO, Berlin Radio Chorus Berlin Classics ▲ BER 1011 [DDD]

Bornus-Szczycinski, Marcin (alt)
Zielenski, M.:Communiones totius anni, w. Kira Borescko (sop), Ryszard Minkiewicz (ten), Robert Hugo (org), M. Bornus-Szczycinski (cnd), Bornus Consort, Tallinn Linnamussikud Instrumental Ensemble, Tallin Linnamussikud Vocal Ensemble Urtext ▲ ACD 202662 [DDD]
Zielenski, M.:Offertoria totius anni, w. Kira Borescko (sop), Ryszard Minkiewicz (ten), Robert Hugo (org), M. Bornus-Szczycinski (cnd), Bornus Consort, Tallinn Linnamussikud Instrumental Ensemble, Tallin Linnamussikud Vocal Ensemble Urtext ▲ ACD 202662 [DDD]

Bornus-Szczycinski, Marcin (sgr)
Michna, A.V.:Sacred Music, w. M. Cechalová (sgr), J. Lewitová (sgr), M. Pospí il (sgr), M. Predota (sgr), R. Hugo (cnd), Capella Regis Musicalis—Missa V à 5 et à 7 si placet; Cantiones pro Defunctis; Missa VI pro Defunctis à 6 et à 10; Requiem Studio Matou ▲ MAT 1 [DDD]

Borodina, Olga (mez)
Balakirev, M.:Songs, w. Larissa Gergieva (pno)—When I but Hear Your Voice; The Pleasure You Bring Is Enthralling; The Crescent Moon; Over the Lake; My Restless Heart; Selim's Song; Spanish Song; I Loved Him Philips ▲ 442780–2
Berlioz, H.:Roméo et Juliette, w. Thomas Moser (ten), Alastair Miles (bass), C. Davis (cnd), Vienna PO, Bavarian Radio Chorus Philips ▲ 442134–2
Borodin, A.:Songs, w. Larissa Gergieva (pno)—A Note of Insincerity; The Princess of the Sea Philips ▲ 442780–2
Cui, C.:Songs, w. Larissa Gergieva (pno)—I Remember an Evening; You & Thou; A Statue in Tsarskoye; My Desire; Here the Lilac Blossom Fades So Quickly; I Touched the Bloom Lightly; It's Over Philips ▲ 442780–2
Mussorgsky, M.:Khovanshchina, w. V. Galusin (ten), B. Minjelkiev (bass), Ohotnikav (sgr), V. Gergiev (cnd), Kirov Opera Orch, Kirov Opera Chorus [R] Philips 3–▲ 432147–2 [DDD]
Mussorgsky, M.:Songs (misc), w. Larissa Gergieva (pno)—What Are Love's Words to You?; In the Night Philips ▲ 442780–2
Prokofiev, S.:War & Peace, w. Y. Prokina (sop), G. Gregoriam (ten), A. Gergalov (bar), V. Gergiev (cnd), Kirov Orch, Kirov Opera Chorus [R] Philips 3–▲ 434097–2
Rachmaninoff, S.:All-Night Vigil, w. V. Mostowoy (ten), N. Korniev (cnd), St. Petersburg Chamber Choir *(rec St. Petersburg, Oct. 3–6, 1993)* Philips ▲ 442344–2
Rimsky-Korsakov, N.:Songs, w. Larissa Gergieva (pno)—The Octave; The Swift Parade of Clouds; My Dreams; The Nightingale; 'Twas Not the Wind; The Lark's Song Philips ▲ 442780–2
Tchaikovsky, P.:Queen of Spades, w. M. Gulegina (sop), G. Grigorian (ten), V. Gergiev (cnd), Kirov Opera Orch, Kirov Opera Chorus Philips ▲ 438141–2
Tchaikovsky, P.:Songs, w. L. Gergieva (pnoo)—None but the Lonely Heart; Night; Once Again, Alone; The Frightening Moment; Gypsy Girl's Song; Serenade; Lullaby; Heed Not, My Love; Spirit My Heart away; This, Our First Reunion; Indoors, the Light Philips ▲ 442013–2

Borowska, Joanna (sop)
Dvořák, A.:Armida, w. Joanna Borowska (sop—Armida), Monika Brychtová (sgr—Siren), Wieslaw Ochman (ten—Rinald), Richard Sporka (ten—Dudo), Jan Markvart (bar—Sven), Pavel Daniluk (bass—King), George Fortune (bass—Ismen), Zdenek Harvánek (bass—Ubald), Miloslav Podskalský (bass—Peter), Milan Bürger (sgr—Gernand), Roman Janál (sgr—Muezzin/Hlasatel), Vratislav Kříz (sgr—Gottfried), Vladimír Nacházel (sgr—Roger), G. Albrecht (cnd), Czech PO, Prague Chamber Choir *(rec 1995)* Orfeo 2–▲ 404962 [DDD]
Mozart, W.A.:Così fan tutte, w. J. Borowska (sop—Fiordiligi), P. Coles (sop—Despina), R. Yachmi (mez—Dorabella), J. Dickie (ten—Ferrando), A. Martin (bar—Guglielmo), P. Mikulaš (b-bar—Don Alfonso), J. Wildner (cnd), Capella Istropolitana, Slovak Phil Chorus [I] *(rec Feb.–Mar. 1990)* Naxos 3–▲ 8.660008/10 [DDD]

Borowska, Joanna (sop) (cont.)
Mozart, W.A.:Così fan tutte (sels), w. Joanna Borowska (sop—Fiordiligi), Priti Coles (sop—Despina), Rohangiz Yachmi (mez—Dorabella), John Dickie (ten—Ferrando), Andrea Martin (bar—Guglielmo), Peter Mikulaš (bass—Don Alfonso), Milada Synkova (hpd), J. Wildner (cnd), Capella Istropolitana, Slovak Phil Chorus—Ov.; [Act I] La mia Dorabella capace non è; È la fede della femmine; Una bella serenata; Ah guarda, sorella; Vorrei dir, e cor non ho; Sento, o Dio; Bella vita militar!; Soave sia il vento; Smanie implacabili; In uomini, in soldati; Alla bella Despinetta; Come Scoglio; Non siate ritrosi; Un'aura amorosa; [Act II] Una donna a quindici anni; Prenderò quel brunettino; La mano a me date; Ei parte...senti...ah no!; Donne mie la fate a tanti a tanti; Fra gle amplessi; Fortunato l'uom che prende *(rec Slovak Philharmonic Moyzes Hall, Bratislava, Feb.–Apr. 1990)* Naxos ▲ 8.553172 [DDD]
Strauss, R.:4 Last Songs, w. F. Haider (cnd), Polish National RSO Cracow Nightingale Classics ▲ NIG 161864

Borrelli, Gloria Guida (sop)
Music in Neapolitan Theaters in the 1700's, w. Borrelli, Gloria Guida (sop), Piccolo Ensemble, Quintetto da Camera Kicco Classics ▲ 496 [DDD]

Borrelli, Wilma (cta)
Verdi, G.:Rigoletto, w. Cecilia Nunez Albanese (sop—Gilda), Wilma Borrelli (cta—Maddalena), Jaime Aragall (ten—Duke of Mantua), Renato Bruson (bar—Rigoletto), Loris Gambelli (bass—Sparafucile), G. Campanino (cnd), Naples Teatro San Carlo Orch, Naples Teatro San Carlo Chorus *(rec San Carlo Theatre, Naples, Feb. 1973)* Golden Age of Opera 2–▲ GAO 177–78 [ADD]

Borri, Pamela (sop)
Carissimi, G.:Oratorio della Santissima Vergine, w. A. M. Ferrante (sop), P. Pace (sop), A. Christofellis (alt), L. Petroni (ten), F. Sclaverano (ten), R. Abbondanza (bass), M. Mondelli (bass), P. Spagnoli (bass), F. Colusso (cnd), Seicentonovecento Ensemble [I] Bongiovanni ▲ GB 10011 [DDD]
Carissimi, G.:Oratorio di Daniele Profeta, w. A. M. Ferrante (sop), P. Pace (sop), A. Christofellis (alt), L. Petroni (ten), F. Sclaverano (ten), R. Abbondanza (bass), M. Mondelli (bass), P. Spagnoli (bass), F. Colusso (cnd), Seicentonovecento Ensemble [I] Bongiovanni ▲ GB 10011 [DDD]

Borriello, Mario (bar)
Donizetti, G.:Don Pasquale, w. A. Noni (sop—Norina), C. Valletti (ten—Ernesto), M. Borriello (bar—Dr. Malatesta), S. Bruscantini (bass-bar—Pasquale), M. Rossi (cnd), Turin RAI SO, Turin RAI Chorus *(rec 1952)* Cetra Classic 2–▲ CDO 14 [AAD]
Massenet, J.:Manon (sels), w. M. Favero (sop), G. Di Stefano (ten), M. Mainardi (bar), A. Guarnieri (cnd), La Scala Orch, La Scala Chorus *(rec live, Milan, 3/15/47)* Myto ▲ 1 MCD 90526 [ADD]
Massenet, J.:Werther, w. L. Gencer (sop—Carlotta), G. Tavolaccini (sop—Sofia), F. Tagliavini (ten—Werther), M. Borriello (bar—Alberto), E. Mocchiutti (bar—Johann), V. Susca (bass—Il Podestà), R. Botteghelli (bass—Schmidt), C.F. Cillario (cnd), *(orch unknown)* Arkadia 2–▲ 599 [ADD]
Mozart, W.A.:Così fan tutte (sels), w. S. Jurinac (sop), A. Noni (sop), B. Thebom (mez), R. Lewis (ten), E. Kunz (bar), F. Busch (cnd), Glyndebourne Festival Orch *(rec Glyndebourne Festival, 1950)* Testament ▲ TES SBT 1040 [ADD]
Puccini, G.:Madama Butterfly, w. M. Callas (sop), L. Danieli (mez), N. Gedda (ten), H. von Karajan (cnd), La Scala Orch, La Scala Chorus [I] *(rec 1955)* EMI Classics 2–▲ CDCB 47959 (m) [ADD]
Puccini, G.:Manon Lescaut (sels), w. B. Guerrini (mez), B. Gigli (ten), *(orch unknown) (rec Milan, 1950)* Melodram ▲ CD 15005 (m)

Borris, Kaja (alt)
Schulhoff, E.:The Flames, w. Jane Eaglen (sop—Donna Anna, Nun, Woman, Marguerite), Carola Höhn (sop—Shadow), Celina Lindsley (sop—Shadow), Regina Schudel (sop—Shadow), Iris Vermillion (mez—La Morte), Christiane Berggold (alt—Shadow), Kaja Borris (alt—Shadow), Elvira Dressen (alt—Shadow), Kurt Westi (ten—Don Juan), Johann-Werner Prein (bass—Commendatore), Gerd Wolf (bass—Harlequin), J. Mauceri (cnd), Berlin German SO, Berlin RIAS Chamber Choir *(rec Jesus-Christus Church, Berlin Dahlem, Oct 1993/Apr 1994)* London 2–▲ 444630–2 [DDD]

Borso, Umberto (ten)
Mascagni, P.:Il piccolo Marat, w. Virginia Zeani (sop), Clara Betner (mez), Nicola Rossi-Lemeni (bass), O. de Fabritiis (cnd), Teatro La Gran Guardia Orch, Teatro La Gran Guardia Chorus [I] *(rec live, 10/26/61)* Fonè 2–▲ 88 F 17–37 [ADD]
Puccini, G.:Manon Lescaut, w. Magda Olivero (sop—Manon), Tine Appelman (mez—Singer), Umberto Borso (ten—Chevalier), Mario Carlin (ten—Edmondo/Dancing Master/Lamplighter), Ferdinando Lidonni (bar—Lescaut), Giovanni Foiani (bass—Geronte/Sergeant/Captain), Joop Ruivenkamp (bass—Innkeeper), F. Vernizzi (cnd), Groot Omroep Orch, Groot Omroep Choir *(rec Amsterdam, Oct 31, 1964)* Bella Voce 2–▲ BLV 107.221 [AAD]

Borsos, Andrei (ten)
Puccini, G.:La Bohème, w. Elvira Cirje-Druica (sop—Musetta), Eugenia Moldoveanu (sop—Mimi), Andrei Borsos (ten—Parpignol), Constantin Gabor (ten—Alcindoro), Ludovic Spiess (ten—Rodolfo), Lucian Marinescu (bar—Schaunard), David Ohanesian (bar—Marcello), Pompei Harasteanu (bass—Benoit), Dan Zancu (bass—Colline), C. Petrovici (cnd), Romanian Opera Orch, Romanian Opera Chorus *(rec 1982)* Vox Box 2–▲ CDX 5156

Borst, Danielle (sop)
Cornelius, P.:Stabat Mater, w. J. Mayeur (cta), J.-L. Viala (ten), F. Vassar (bass-bar), M. Piquemal (cnd), Cannes-Provençe Alpes-Côte d'Azur Regional Orch, Cannes Regional Chorus Musique d'Abord ▲ HMA 1905206
Donizetti, G.:Messa di Gloria e Credo, w. Hélène Jossoud (mez), Jean-Luc Viala (ten), Vincent Le Texier (bass-bar), M. Piquemal (cnd), Avignon-Provence Regional Lyric Orch, Provence-Alpes-Côte d'Azur Regional Choir Accord ▲ ACD 212142 [DDD]
Mendelssohn, F.:Athalie, w. Brigitte Desnoues (sop), Carolyn Watkinson (cta), Jean-Marc Avocat (sgr), Souad Natech (sgr), B. Tetu (cnd), Lorraine PO, Lyon National Chorus Koch Schwann ▲ SCH 314282 [DDD]
Monteverdi, C.:Incoronazione, w. Lootens (sop), G. Laurens (mez), J. Larmore (mez), A. Köhler (alt), M. Schopper (bass), R. Jacobs (cnd), Concerto Vocale [direction & new musical realization by René Jacobs] [I] Harmonia Mundi France 3–▲ HMC 901330/32
Mozart, W.A.:Don Giovanni, w. Danielle Borst (sop—Donna Anna), Véronique Gens (sop—Donna Elvira), Sophie Marin-Degor (sop—Zerlina), Huub Claessens (bar—Leporello), Nicolas Revenq (bar—Don Giovanni), Patrick Donnelly (bass—Commendatore), Simon Edwards (sgr—Don Ottavio), J. Malgoire (cnd), La Grande Écurie et la Chambre du Roy Astrée 8–▲ E 8606
Mozart, W.A.:Nozze di Figaro, w. Danielle Borst (sop—Countess Almaviva), Claudine Le Coz (sop—Marcellina), Sophie Marin-Degor (sop—Suzanna), Laura Polverelli (mez—Cherubino), Valérie Lecoq (sgr—Barberina), Philippe Cantor (ten—Antonio), Stuart Patterson (ten—Dons Basile & Curzio), Huub Claessens (bar—Figaro), Nicolas Revenq (bar—Count Almaviva), Patrick Donnelly (bass—Bartolo), J. Malgoire (cnd), La Grande Écurie et la Chambre du Roy Astrée 8–▲ E 8606
Poulenc, F.:Gloria Sop, w. M. Piquemal (cnd), Orch de la Cité, Vittoria d'Ile Choir *(rec Paris, Oct 1992)* Naxos ▲ 8.553176 [DDD]
Poulenc, F.:Stabat mater, w. M. Piquemal (cnd), Orch de la Cité, Vittoria d'Ile Choir *(rec Paris, Oct 1992)* Naxos ▲ 8.553176 [DDD]

Borst, Martina (mez)
Jommelli, N.:Didone abbandonata, w. Dorothea Röschmann (sop), Mechthild Bach (mez), William Kendall (ct), Daniel Taylor (ct), Arno Raunig (ten), F. Bernius (cnd), Stuttgart CO—Didone; Enea; Iarba; Selene; Araspe; Osmida Orfeo 3–▲ CD 381953 [DDD]
Strauss, R.:Arabella (sels), w. P. Coburn (sop), R. Klepper (sop), B. Skovhus (bar), F. Hawlata (bass), M. Honeck (cnd), Munich RSO Capriccio ▲ 10481 [DDD]
Strauss, R.:Ariadne auf Naxos, w. P. Coburn (sop), R. Klepper (sop), B. Skovhus (bar), F. Hawlata (bass), M. Honeck (cnd), Munich RSO Capriccio ▲ 10481 [DDD]
Strauss, R.:Capriccio (sels), w. P. Coburn (sop), R. Klepper (sop), B. Skovhus (bar), F. Hawlata (bass), M. Honeck (cnd), Munich RSO Capriccio ▲ 10481 [DDD]
Strauss, R.:Der Rosenkavalier (sels), w. P. Coburn (sop), R. Klepper (sop), B. Skovhus (bar), F. Hawlata (bass), M. Honeck (cnd), Munich RSO Capriccio ▲ 10481 [DDD]

Borthayre, Jean (bass)
Massenet, J.:Manon, w. V. De los Angeles (sop), H. Legay (ten), M. Dens (bar), P. Monteux (cnd), Paris Opéra-Comique Orch, Paris Opéra-Comique Chorus [F] EMI Classics 3–▲ CDMC 63549 (m) [ADD]

Bosch, Betty van den (sop)
Schubert, Franz:Rosamunde (sels), w. W. Mengelberg (cnd), Royal Concertgebouw Orch—Lieder & Arias Archive Documents ("The Mengelberg Edition" series) ▲ ADCD 109

Bosch, Ulrich (bass)
Hoffmann, E.T.A.:Undine, w. Barbara Baier (sop—Berthalda), Heidrun Plesch (sop—Undine), Corinna Tippe (sop—Die Herzogin), Maria Hiefinger (mez—Fisherman's Wife), Achim Schamberger (ten—Der Herzog), Johannes Beck (bar—Ritter Huldbrand von Ringstetten), Michael Albert (bass—Fisherman), Ulrich Bosch (bass—Heilmann), Bernd Hofmann (bass—Kühleborn), H. Dechant (cnd), Bamberg Youth Orch Bayer 3-▲ 100256/58 [DDD]

Boschetti, Guerrino (bass)
Verdi, G.:Rigoletto, w. Renata Scotto (sop—Gilda), Stella Maris Silva (sop—Giovanna), Martha Carrizo (mez—Page), Carmen de la Mata (mez—Countess Ceprano), Noemi Souza (cta—Maddalena), Horacio Mastrango (ten—Borso), Richard Tucker (ten—Duke of Mantua), Cornell MacNeil (bar—Rigoletto), Riccardo Yost (bar—Marullo), Guerrino Boschetti (bass—Usher), Tulio Gagliardo (bass—Count Ceprano), Victor de Narké (bass—Monterone), William Wilderman (bass—Sparafucile), F. Previtali (cnd), Buenos Aires Teatro Colón Orch, Buenos Aires Teatro Colón Chorus *(rec Colon Theater, Buenos Aires, Aug. 22, 1967)* Legato Classics 2-▲ LCD 198-2

Boschková, Nelly (mez)
Puccini, G.:Madama Butterfly, w. M. Gauci (sop), A. Michalková (mez), Y. Ramiro (ten), A. Rahbari (cnd), Czech-Slovak RSO Bratislava, Slovak Phil Chorus [I] Naxos 2-▲ 8.660015/16 [DDD]
Puccini, G.:Madama Butterfly (sels), w. Miriam Gauci (sop—Madama Butterfly), Nelly Boschkowa (mez—Suzuki), Yordi Ramiro (ten—F.B. Pinkerton), Jozef Abel (ten—Goro), Georg Tichy (bass—Sharpless), Anna Tomkovicová (sgr), Mária Stahelová (sgr), Elena Hanzelová (sgr) *(rec Concert Hall of the Czecho-Slovak Radio, Bratislava, May 2-10, 1991)* Naxos ▲ 8.553152 [DDD]

Bosco, Carlo del (bass)
Mussorgsky, M.:Khovanshchina, w. Mietta Sighele (sop—Emma), Elena Souliotis (sop—Susanna), Fiorenza Cossotto (mez—Marfa), Herbert Handt (ten—Scribe), Veriano Luchetti (ten—Prince Andrey Khovansky), Ludovic Spiess (ten—Prince Vasily Golitsin), Claudio Strudthoff (ten—Streshnev), Angelo Marchiandi (bar—Kuz'ka), Teodoro Rovetta (bar—1st Strel'tsi), Siegmund Nimsgern (b-bar—Shaklovity), Cesare Siepi (b-bar—Dosifey), Carlo del Bosco (bass—2nd Strel'tsi), Ubaldo Carosi (bass—Varsonofiev), Nicolai Ghiaurov (bass—Prince Ivan Khovnasky), Giovanni Sciarpeletti (bass—Pastor), B. Leskovich (cnd), Rome RAI SO, Rome RAI Chorus—also includes bonus Act V [w Boris Christoff] (Rome, 1958) *(rec Rome, 1973)* Bella Voce 3-▲ BLV 107.402 [AAD]
Verdi, G.:Un ballo in maschera, w. M. Caballé (sop—Amelia), T. Paniagua (sop—Oscar), L. Chookasian (cta—Ulrica), P. Domingo (ten—Riccardo), C. MacNeil (bar—Renato), J. Pons (bar—Tom), C. del Bosco (bass—Samuel), G. Patanè (cnd), *(orch unknown)* Ornamenti 2-▲ FE 103

Bosi, Carlo (ten)
Rossini, G.:Armida, w. R. Fleming (sop), B. Fowler (ten), J. Francis (ten), D. Kaasch (ten), G. Kunde (ten), I. Zennaro (ten), I. D'Arcangelo (bass), S. Zadvorny (bass), D. Gatti (cnd), Bologna Teatro Comunale Orch, Bologna Teatro Comunale Chorus *(rec Pesaro, Italy, Aug. 6-17, 1993)* Sony Classical 3-▲ S3K 58968 [DDD]

Bosman, Arnold (sgr)
Giordano, U.:Fedora, w. Mirella Freni (sop—Principessa Fedora), Adelina Scarabelli (sop—Contessa Olga), Silvia Mazzoni (mez—Dimitri), Monica Minarelli (sgr—Savoiardo), Placido Domingo (ten—Conte Loris), Ernesto Gavazzi (ten—Desirè), Aldo Bottion (ten—Barone Rouvel), Alessandro Corbelli (bar—Siriex), Luigi Roni (bass—Cirillo), Silvestro Sammaritano (bass—Baroff), Alfredo Giacomotti (bass—Gretch), Ernesto Panariello (bass—Lorek), Vincenzo Alaimo (sgr—Nicola), Arnold Bosman (sgr—Boleslao), Bruno Capisani (sgr—Sergio), Renato Zanchetta (sgr—Michele), G. Gavazzeni (cnd), La Scala Orch, La Scala Chorus *(rec La Scala, Apr 5, 1993)* Legato 2-▲ LCD 213-2 [ADD]

Bössow, Rolf (ten)
Schütz, H.:St. John Passion, w. Herta Flebbe (sop), Johannes Hoeflin (ten—Evangelist), Rolf Bössow (ten—Pilate), Gert Spierting (ten), Jakob Stämpfli (bass—Jesus), Teinhard Tuge (bass—soliloquies), W. Ehmann (cnd), Westphalia Kantorei *(rec Münster zu Herfor, Sept. 1961)* Cantate ▲ 57602 [ADD]

Bostridge, Ian (ten)
Britten, H.:The Holy Sonnets of John Donne, w. Graham Johnson (pno) Hyperion ▲ CDA 66823
Britten, H.:Purcell Realizations, w. Susan Gritton (sop), Felicity Lott (sop), Sarah Walker (mez), James Bowman (alto), John Mark Ainsley (ten), Anthony Rolfe Johnson (ten), Richard Jackson (bass), Simon Keenlyside (bass), Graham Johnson (pno) Hyperion 2-▲ CDA 67061/62
Britten, H.:Songs, w. Graham Johnson (pno)—The Red Cockatoo; other songs Hyperion ▲ CDA 66823
Hahn, R.:Songs, w. Felicity Lott (sop), Susan Bickley (mez), Stephen Varcoe (bar), Graham Johnson (pno), Stephen Layton (cnd), London Choral Society—[CD 1] Si mes vers avaient des ailes; Paysage; Rêverie; Offrande; Mai; Infidelité; Seule; Les Cygnes; Nocturne; 3 jours de vendange; D'une prison; Séraphine; L'Heure exquise; Fêtes galantes; 12 Rondels; [CD 2] Quand la nuit n'est pas étoilée; Le Plus beau présent; Sur l'eau; Le Rossignol des lilas; A Chloris; Ma jeunesse; Puisque j'ai mis ma lèvre; Etudes Latines; La Nymphe de la Source; Au Rossignol; Je me souviens; Air de la lettre; C'est très vilain d'être infidèle; C'est sa banlieue; Nous avons fait un beau voyage; La Dernière Valse Hyperion ("The Hyperion French Song Edition" series) 2-▲ CDA 67141/42
Nyman, M.:Noises, w. Catherine Bott (sop), Hilary Summers (alt), Andrew Findon (sax), David Roach (sax), D. Debart (cnd), Basse Normandie Instrumental Ensemble *(rec Caen, June 1991 & Abbey Road Studios, London, June 1993)* Argo ▲ 440842-2 [DDD]
Purcell, H.:The Prophetess, or The History of Dioclesian, w. C. Pierard (sop), J. Bowman (alt), J. M. Ainsley (ten), M. George (bass), R. Hickox (cnd), Collegium Musicum 90—Masque Chandos ("Chaconne" series) ▲ CHAN 0558 [DDD]
Schubert, Franz:Die Schöne Müllerin, w. Dietrich Fischer-Dieskau (reader), Graham Johnson (pno)—5 additional poems read by Fischer-Dieskau Hyperion ▲ CDJ 33025
Schubert, Franz:Songs (comp), w. P. Rozario (sop), J.M. Ainsley (ten), M. George (bass), G. Johnson (pno), S. Layton (cnd), London Schubert Chorale—Winterlied; Ossians Lied nach dem Falle Nathos; Das Mädchen von Inistore; Als ich sie erröten; Schwangesang; Totenkranz für ein Kind; Die Fröhlichkeit; Der Zufriedene; Alles um Liebe; Geist der Liebe; Dei erste Liebe; Die Täuschung; Liebesrausch; Huldigung; Heidenröslein; Nachtgesang; Der Morgenstern; Der Knappenlied; Trinklied vor der Schlacht; Schwertlied; Begräbnislied; Grablied; Osterlied; Hoffnung; Punschlied; Klage um Ali Bey; Abendständchen; Tische'rlied; Wiegenlied; Die Macht der Liebe; Trinklied, D.183; Trinklied, D.267 Hyperion ▲ CDJ 33020
Vaughan Williams, R.:Songs, w. Michael George (bass), Stephen Layton (cnd), Holst Singers—Loch Lomond; 3 Shakespeare Songs; Alister McAlpine's Lament; An Acre of Land; The Seeds of Love; Ca' the yowes; 5 English Folksongs; The Winter Is Gone; Mannin Veen; Bushes & Briars; Down among the Dead Men; 3 Elizabethan Songs; Greensleeves; Rest; Heart's Music; Come away, Death; The Turtle Dove Hyperion ▲ CDA 66777

Boswinkel, Job (bass)
Hollander, H.:Sacred Music, w. S. van Grootel (sop), K. van der Poel (mez), P. Rikkers (vn), J. van der Meer (db), T. van Eijk (org), Cappella Breda—Cantabant sancti; Domine Jesu Christe; Domine Deus; Ecce vicit leo; O nomen Jesu; Recipe me; Quem vidistis pastores; Sanctus Jacobus; Quid est hoc; O vos omnes; Ecce clamo; Ave Maria; O'Beatum Virum; O bone Jesu; Te gloriosus Erasmus ▲ WVH 047 [DDD]

Boterf, Bruno (ten)
Alain, J.:Music of, w. Delphine Collot (sop), Jacques Bona (bar), Françoise Gyps (fl), Laurent Decker (ob), Bruno Pazqueir (va), Philippe Muller (vc), Georges Guillard (org), Ludwig String Quartet, Georges Guillard (cnd), St. Louis Camerata Vocal Ensemble—2 Melodies for Sop & Pno; Nuptial Song for Bar, Bass, Vc & Org; Post-Scriptum for 3 Female Voices & Pno; Canticle in Phrygian Mode for 4 Mixed-Voice, Sop & Strs; Invention for Fl, Ob & Cl; Monody for solo Fl; Prelude for Str Qnt; Adagio for Str Qnt; Funerals for Str Qnt; March of the Horiaces & the Curiaces for 2 Bugles, Drum & Org Arion ▲ ARN 68321
Palestrina, G.:Sacred Music, w. Catherine Greuillet (sop), Thierry Gregoire (alt), Pierre Sciema (alt), Joel Suhubiette (ten), Jean-Luc Baudoin (ten), Jean-Claude Sarragosse (bass), Laurent Stewart (org), Françoise Lasserre (cnd), Champagne-Ardenne Akademia Regional Vocal Ensemble—Ave maria; Salve regina; Vergine bella; Vergine saggia; Virgine pura; Virgine santa; Vergine sola; Vergine chiara; Vergine, quante lagrime; Vergine, tale è terra; Ave mundi spes; Ave regina coelorum; Alma redemptoris mater; Regina coieli laetare; Salve regina; Magnificat; others *(rec Convent of the Annunciation Dominican Church, Paris, Jan., 1994)* Pierre Verany ▲ PVY 794041 [DDD]

Botha, Johan (ten)
Puccini, G.:Arias, w. Angela Gheorghiu (sop), Nina Rautio (sop), Anthony Michaels-Moore (bar), E. Downes (cnd), Royal Opera House Orch, Royal Opera House Chorus Covent Garden—Se come voi piccina io fossi [from Le villi]; Addio mio dolce amor [from Edgar]; Donna non vidi mai; Sola, perduta, abbandonata [both from Manon Lescaut]; Donde lieta usci [from La Bohème]; Act 1 Finale; E lucevan le stelle [both from Tosca]; Un tal baccano in chiesa; Or tutto è chiaro; Tre sbirri, una carrozza; Un bel dì [from Madama Butterfly]; Ch'ella mi creda [from La fanciulla del West]; Chi il bel sogno di Doretta [from La rondine]; Nulla, silenzio [from Il tabarro]; Senza mamma [from Suor Angelica]; O mio babbino caro [from Gianni Schicchi]; Act I Finale; Nessun dorma [both from Turandot]; Signore, acolta; Non piangere, Liù *(rec Henry Wood Hall, London, Feb 12-27 & Mar 5, 1995)* Conifer Classics ("Royal Opera House" series) ▲ 75605-55013-2 [DDD]

Bott, Catherine (sop)
Arne, T.:Artaxerxes, w. Patricia Spence (mez), Philippa Hyde (sgr), Christopher Robson (alt), Richard Edgar-Wilson (ten), Ian Partridge (ten), R. Goodman (cnd), Parley of Instruments Hyperion ("The English Orpheus" series) 2-▲ CDA 67051/2
Handel, G.F.:Messiah (sels), w. Clare Henry (cta), Gareth Roberts (ten), David Stephenson (bass), D. Jackson (cnd), London SO—Comfort Ye, My People, Saith Your God; Every Valley Shall Be Exalted; And the Glory of the Lord Shall Be Revealed; And He Shall Purify the Sons of Levi; For unto Us a Child Is Born; Pifa; Rejoice Greatly, O Daughter of Zion; Air:He Shall Feed His Flock Like a Shepherd; Behold the Lamb of God; He Was Despised and Rejected of Men; All We Like Sheep Have Gone Astray; The Trumpet Shall Sound; Chorus:Hallelujah! For the Lord God Omnipotent Reigneth Special Music Co. 2-▲ S2D 5110 [DDD]
Handel, G.F.:Messiah (sels), w. Clare Henry (cta), Gareth Roberts (ten), David Stephenson (bass), D. Jackson (cnd), London SO—Comfort Ye, My People, Saith Your God; Every Valley Shall Be Exalted; And the Glory of the Lord Shall Be Revealed; And He Shall Purify the Sons of Levi; For unto Us a Child Is Born; Pifa; Rejoice Greatly, O Daughter of Zion; Air:He Shall Feed His Flock Like a Shepherd; Behold the Lamb of God; He Was Despised and Rejected of Men; All We Like Sheep Have Gone Astray; The Trumpet Shall Sound; Chorus:Hallelujah! For the Lord God Omnipotent Reigneth Special Music Co. ▲ SCD 5102 [DDD]
Mad Songs, w. New London Consort members L'Oiseau-Lyre ▲ 433187-2 OH [DDD]
Monteverdi, C.:Incoronazione, w. Constanze Backes (sop—Valletto), Catherine Bott (sop—Drusilla/Pallade/La Virtù), Dana Hanchard (sop—Nerone), Sylvia McNair (sop—Poppea), Marinella Pennicchi (sop—Amore/Damigella), Annie Sofie von Otter (mez—Ottavia/Venere/La Fortuna), Julian Clarkson (alt—Littore/Mercurio), Bernarda Fink (cta—Arnalta), Roberto Balconi (ct—Nutrice), Michael Chance (ct—Ottone), Nigel Robson (ten—Liberto/Soldato Secondo), Mark Tucker (ten—Lucano/Soldato Primo), Francesco Ellero d'Artegna (bass—Seneca), J. E. Gardiner (cnd), English Baroque Soloists *(rec Queen Elizabeth Hall, South Bank Ctr, London, Dec 1993)* Archiv 3-▲ 447088-2
Nyman, M.:Noises, w. Hilary Summers (alt), Ian Bostridge (ten), Andrew Findon (sax), David Roach (sax), D. Debart (cnd), Basse Normandie Instrumental Ensemble *(rec Caen, June 1991 & Abbey Road Studios, London, June 1993)* Argo ▲ 440842-2 [DDD]
Purcell, H.:Dido & Aeneas, w. Catherine Bott (sop—Dido), Emma Kirkby (sop—Belinda), Michael Chance (alt—Spirit), John Mark Ainsley (bar—Aeneas), David Thomas (bar—Sorceress), C. Hogwood (cnd), Academy of Ancient Music L'Oiseau-Lyre ▲ 436992-2 [DDD]
Purcell, H.:The Fairy Queen, w. J. Thomas (ten), M. Schopper (bass), T. Koopman (cnd), Amsterdam Baroque Orch, Amsterdam Baroque Choir Erato 2-▲ 98507-2
Purcell, H.:The Indian Queen, w. Catherine Bott (sop—Orazia/Married Woman), Emma Kirkby (sop—Indian Girl/Zempoalla/Cupid), John Mark Ainsley (ten—Indian Boy/Fame/Follower of Cupid/Aerial Spirits), Julian Podger (ten—Follower of Envy/Aerial Spirit), Gerald Finley (bar—Conjurer/Hymen/Follower of Cupid), Helen Parker (sgr—Aerial Spirits), David Thomas (bass—Envy/High Priest/Married Man/Follower of Cupid), Simon Berridge (sgr—Follower of Envy), Libby Crabtree (sgr—Follower of Hymen/Aerial Spirit), Tommy Williams (sgr—God of Dreams), C. Hogwood (cnd), Academy of Ancient Music *(rec Walthamstow Assembly Hall, London, July 1994)* L'Oiseau-Lyre ▲ 444339-2 [DDD]
Purcell, H.:Music of, w. Emma Kirkby (sop), James Bowman (alt), Anthony Rooley (lt), Monica Huggett (vn), Catherine Mackintosh (vn), Christophe Coin (vc), Paula Chateauneuf (gtr), Hill, Hogwood (cnd), Brandenburg Consort, Academy of Ancient Music, Anthony Lewis (cnd), David Hill (cnd), St. Anthony Singers, Taverner Choir, Winchester Cathedral Choir—The Double Dealer; Come Ye Sons of Art; The Old Bachelor; Birthday Song for Queen Mary; Oedipus; King Arthur; Bonduca; The Fairy Queen; Son. No. 9 in F; Dido & Aeneas; Abdelazer; Bess of Bedlam; The Married Beau; Hear My Prayer, O Lord; Rejoice in the Lord Always L'Oiseau-Lyre ▲ 444620-2
Purcell, H.:Music of, w. Emma Kirkby (sop), James Bowman (alt), Anthony Rooley (lt), Paula Chateauneuf (gtr), Monica Huggett (vn), Catherine Mackintosh (vn), Christophe Coin (vc), Hill, Hogwood (cnd), Academy of Ancient Music, Brandenburg Consort, David Hill (cnd), Anthony Lewis (cnd), St. Anthony Singers, Taverner Choir, Winchester Cathedral Choir—The Double Dealer; Come Ye Sons of Art; The Old Bachelor; Birthday Song for Queen Mary; Oedipus; King Arthur; Bonduca; The Fairy Queen; Son. No. 9 in F; Dido & Aeneas; Abdelazer; Bess of Bedlam; The Married Beau; Hear My Prayer, O Lord; Rejoice in the Lord Always London ("Editions de l'oiseau-lyre" series) ▲ 444620-2
Purcell, H.:Songs, w. Purcell Quartet—Hark how all things; If Music be the food of love; If love's a sweet passion; See, even Night herself is here; Thus the ever grateful Spring; Lord, what is man?, Z.192 Chandos ("Chaconne" series) ▲ CHAN 0571 [DDD]
Vaughan Williams, R.:Sym 7, w. B. Thomson (cnd), London SO [E] Chandos ▲ CHAN 8796 [DDD]
Walton, W.:As You Like It, w. N. Marriner (cnd), Academy of St. Martin in the Fields Chandos ▲ CHAN 8842 [DDD]

Bott, Paula (sop)
Ireland, J.:Greater Love Hath No Man, w. B. Terfel (bass-bar), R. Hickox (cnd), London SO, London Sym Chorus [E] Chandos ▲ CHAN 8879 [DDD]
Ireland, J.:Vexilla Regis, w. T. Shaw (mez), J. Oxley (ten), B. Terfel (bass-bar), R. Hickox (cnd), London SO, London Sym Chorus [L] Chandos ▲ CHAN 8879 [DDD]

Botta, Giuseppe (sgr)
Smareglia, A.:La falena, w. Leyla Gencer (sop—La Falena), Rita Lantieri (sop—Albina, sua figlia), Ruggero Bondino (ten—Re Stellio), Dario Zerial (ten—Il ladro), Mario D'Anna (bar—Il vecchio Uberto), Aurio Tomicich (bass—Morino), Giuseppe Botta (sgr—Un marinaio), G. Gavazzeni (cnd), Trieste Teatro Comunale Giuseppe Verdi Orch, Trieste Teatro Comunale G. Verdi Chorus *(rec Trieste, Mar 18, 1876)* Bongiovanni 2-▲ GB 1131/32

Bottazzo, Pietro (ten)
Donizetti, G.:Don Pasquale, w. E. Ravaglia (sop), A. Frati (ten), R. Panerai (bar), F. Corena (bass), R. Muti (cnd), Vienna PO, Vienna State Opera Chorus [I] *(rec live, Salzburg, 8/11/71)* Melodram 2-▲ CDM 27094 [ADD]
Mozart, W.A.:Missa, K.317, w. Teresa Stich-Randall (sop), Bianca Maria Casoni (alt), K. Ristenpart (cnd), Sarre CO, Herbert Schmolzi (cnd), Sarrebrück Conservatory Choir Accord ▲ ACD 220252 [AAD]
Mozart, W.A.:Vesperae solennes, w. Teresa Stich-Randall (sop), Bianca Maria Casoni (alt), K. Ristenpart (cnd), Sarre CO, Herbert Schmolzi (cnd), Sarrebrück Conservatory Choir Accord ▲ ACD 220252 [AAD]
Rossini, G.:Armida, w. C. Deutekom (sop), O. Garaventa (ten), E. Gimenez (ten), B. Trotta (sgr), A. Maddalena (bass), G. Antonini (bass), C. Franci (cnd), Venice Teatro La Fenice Orch, Venice Teatro La Fenice Chorus *(rec live, Venice, 1970)* Foyer 2-▲ FOY 2030 [AAD]
Rossini, G.:Armida, w. C. Deutekom (sop), O. Garaventa (ten), E. Gimenez (ten), C. Franci (cnd), Venice Teatro La Fenice Orch, Venice Teatro La Fenice Chorus [I] *(rec live, 4/3/70)* Memories 2-▲ HR 4152/53 (m) [ADD]
Rossini, G.:La donna del lago, w. M. Caballé (sop), J. Hamari (mez), F. Bonisolli (ten), P. Bellugi (cnd), Turin RAI Orch, Turin RAI Chorus [I] *(rec live 5/19/70)* Melodram 2-▲ MEL 27074 (m) [AAD]
Rossini, G.:La donna del lago, w. M. Caballé (sop), J. Hamari (mez), F. Bonisolli (ten), P. Bellugi (cnd), Turin Radio Orch, Turin RAI Chorus [I] *(rec live 5/19/70)* Standing Room Only 2-▲ SRO 803-2 (m) [ADD]
Rossini, G.:La donna del lago, w. A. Balboni (sop), M. Caballé (sop), J. Hamari (mez), F. Bonisolli (ten), G. Sinimberghi (ten), P. Washington (bass), P. Bellugi (cnd), Turin RAI Orch, Turin RAI Chorus *(rec live, Torino, 1970)* Foyer 2-▲ FOY 2028 [AAD]

Bottazzo, Pietro (ten) (cont.)
Rossini, G.:Elisabetta, regina d'Inghilterra, w. L. Gencer (sop), S. Geszty (sop), U. Grilli (ten), N. Sanzogno (cnd), Palermo Teatro Massimo Orch, Palermo Teatro Massimo Chorus [I] *(rec live, 11/24/70)* Myto 2-▲ 2 MCD 90530 [ADD]

Botteghelli, Raimondo (bass)
Donizetti, G.:Lucia di Lammermoor (sels), w. L. Gencer (sop), G. Prandelli (ten), N. Carta (bar), Hussu (sgr), Sabatucci (sgr), O. de Fabritiis (cnd), Trieste Teatro Comunale Giuseppe Verdi Orch, Trieste Teatro Comunale G. Verdi Chorus *(rec live 12/13/57 & 2/10/58)* Melodram ▲ MEL 15003 (m) [AAD]
Massenet, J.:Werther, w. L. Gencer (sop—Carlotta), G. Tavolaccini (sop—Sofia), F. Tagliavini (ten—Werther), M. Borriello (bar—Alberto), E. Mocchiutti (bar—Johann), V. Susca (bass—Il Podestà), R. Botteghelli (bass—Schmidt), C.F. Cillario (cnd), *(orch unknown)* Arkadia 2-▲ 599 [ADD]
Wagner, R.:Die Meistersinger von Nürnberg, w. Bruna Rizzoli (sop), Fernanda Cadoni (mez), Luigi Infantino (ten), Vito Tatone (ten), Renato Capecchi (bar), Giuseppe Taddei (bar), Boris Christoff (bass), Giovanni Ciavola (bass), James Loomis (bass), Silvo Maionica (bass), Vito Susca (bass), Walter Brunelli (sgr), Carlo Franzini (sgr), Ezio de Giorgi (sgr), Renzo Gonzales (sgr), L. von Matačić (cnd), Turin RAI Radio-TV SO, Turin RAI Chorus Stradivarius 4-▲ STV 12310

Botti, S. (sop)
Dun, T.:Silk Road, w. P. Guerguerian (perc) *(rec June 4, 1992)* CRI ▲ CD 655 [DDD]
York, W.:My Heart Is Different, w. D. Buechner (pno) *(rec Feb. 1989)* New World ▲ 80439-2
York, W.:Songs from Levertov Scores, w. Marimolin *(rec May 1987)* New World ▲ 80439-2

Bottion, Aldo (ten)
Giordano, U.:Fedora, w. Mirella Freni (sop—Principessa Fedora), Adelina Scarabelli (sop—Contessa Olga), Silvia Mazzoni (mez—Dimitri), Monica Minarelli (sgr—Savoiardo), Placido Domingo (ten—Conte Loris), Ernesto Gavazzi (ten—Desiré), Aldo Bottion (ten—Barone Rouvel), Alessandro Corbelli (bar—Siriex), Luigi Roni (bass—Cirillo), Silvestro Sammaritano (bass—Baroff), Alfredo Giacomotti (bass—Gretch), Ernesto Panariello (bass—Lorek), Vincenzo Alaimo (sgr—Nicola), Arnold Bosman (sgr—Boleslao), Bruno Capisani (sgr—Sergio), Renato Zanchetta (sgr—Michele), G. Gavazzeni (cnd), La Scala Orch, La Scala Chorus *(rec La Scala, Apr 5, 1993)* Legato 2-▲ LCD 213-2 [ADD]
Leoncavallo, R.:Zingari, w. Gianna Galli (sgr), Renzo Scarsoni (sgr), Guido Guarneri (sgr), E. Boncompagni (cnd), Turin RAI Orch, Turin RAI Chorus *(rec live, 1975)* Italian Opera Rarities ▲ IOR 7729 [ADD]

Botton, R. (bar)
Gottlieb, J.:Sacred Music, w. M. Stone (sop), H. Reps (mez), D. Lefkowitz (ten), H. Stahl (ten), R. Abelson (bar), P. Newman (reader), S. Sturk (cnd), Metropolitan Brass Ensemble, New York Motet Choir Premier ("Composer" series) ▲ PRCD 1018 [DDD]

Bottone, Bonaventura (ten)
Sullivan, A.:The Mikado, w. L. Garrett (sop), J. Rigby (mez), S. Bullock (sop), F. Palmer (sop/mez), R. Angas (bass), E. Idle (bar), R. Van Allan (bass), M. Richardson (bar), P. Robinson (cnd), English National Opera Orch, English Opera Group Chorus—sels [E] MCA Classics ▲ MCAD 6215 [DDD]; ■ MCAC 6215 (D)
Vaughan Williams, R.:Hugh the Drover, w. R. Evans (sop), S. Walker (mez), N. Jenkins (ten), A. Opie (bar), R. Van Allan (bass), M. Best (cnd), Corydon Orch, Corydon Singers, New London Children's Choir Hyperion 2-▲ CDA 66901/02

Boucher, Gene (bar)
Verdi, G.:La traviata (sels), w. Loretta di Franco (sop), Joan Sutherland (sop), Frederica von Stade (mez), Leo Goeke (ten), Lou Marcella (ten), Luciano Pavarotti (ten), Gene Boucher (bar), Raymond Gibbs (bar), Sherrill Milnes (bar), Louis Sgarro (bar), John Trehy (bar) Budget ("The Greatest Voice in Opera" series) ▲ SYP 112

Boucher, Leslie (nar)
Schoenberg, A.:Pierrot lunaire, w. Julie Stone (fl/pic), Tod Kerstetter (cl/b cl), Andrew Carlson (vn), Philip Singleton (va), Juanita Karpf (vc), F. Joseph Lozier (pno) *(rec Roswell United Methodist Church, Roswell, GA, July 20, Aug. 2 & Sept. 1)* ACA Digital ▲ CM 20027

Boucher, Leslie (sop)
Kálmán, I.:Gräfin Mariza, w. M. Dubois (ten), R. Armenian (cnd), Kitchener-Waterloo SO CBC ("SM 5000" series) ▲ SMCD 5045 [DDD]
Lehár, F.:Das Land des Lächelns (sels), w. M. Dubois (ten), R. Armenian (cnd), Kitchener-Waterloo SO CBC ("SM 5000" series) ▲ SMCD 5045 [DDD]
Lehár, F.:Die lustige Witwe (sels), w. M. Dubois (ten), R. Armenian (cnd), Kitchener-Waterloo SO CBC ("SM 5000" series) ▲ SMCD 5045 [DDD]
Strauss (II), Joh.:Music of, w. Dubois (ten), R. Armenian (cnd), Kitchener-Waterloo SO—selections from Die Fledermaus & Gypsy Baron CBC ("SM 5000" series) ▲ SMCD 5045 [DDD]
Zwilich, E.T.:Passages, w. Julie Stone (fl/pic), Tod Kerstetter (cl/b cl), Andrew Carlson (vn), Philip Singleton (va), Juanita Karpf (vc), F. Joseph Lozier (pno), Joanna Parks (perc), Shannon O'Kelley (perc) *(rec Roswell United Methodist Church, Roswell, GA, July 20, Aug. 2 & Sept. 1)* ACA Digital ▲ CM 20027

Boughton, Ian (ten)
Stokowski, L.:Transcriptions Orch, w. G. Simon (cnd), Philharmonia Orch, BBC Sym Men's Chorus—Borodin:Requiem *(rec All Hallows Church, Gospel Oak, London)* Cala ▲ CAL 1011 [DDD]

Bouillat, J. (ten)
Chausson, E.:Duos, "La nuit" & "Le réveil", w. D. Collot (sop), B. Vinson (mez), G. Wieclaw (bass), E. Strosser (pno), C. Desert (pno), J. Sourisse (cnd), Jean Sourisse Ensemble, Audite Nova Vocal Ensemble FNAC Music ▲ 592224 [DDD]
Debussy, C.:Songs, w. D. Collot (sop), B. Vinson (mez), G. Wieclaw (bass), C. Desert (pno), E. Strosser (pno), J. Sourisse (cnd), Jean Sourisse Ensemble, Audite Nova Vocal Ensemble—3 chansons de Chateau D'Orleans FNAC Music ▲ 592224 [DDD]
Fauré, G.:Madrigal, w. D. Collot (sop), B. Vinson (mez), G. Wieclaw (bass), C. Desert (pno), E. Strosser (pno) FNAC Music ▲ 592224 [DDD]
Fauré, G.:Pavane Orch, w. D. Collot (sop), B. Vinson (mez), G. Wieclaw (bass), C. Desert (pno), E. Strosser (pno), J. Sourisse (cnd), Jean Sourisse Ensemble, Audite Nova Vocal Ensemble FNAC Music ▲ 592224 [DDD]
Fauré, G.:Songs, w. D. Collot (sop), B. Vinson (mez), G. Wieclaw (bass), C. Desert (pno), E. Strosser (pno), J. Sourisse (cnd), Jean Sourisse Ensemble, Audite Nova Vocal Ensemble—Le Ruisseau, Op. 22; Puisqu'ici bas, Op. 10/1, Les Djinns, Op. 12 FNAC Music ▲ 592224 [DDD]
Ravel, M.:Songs, w. D. Collot (sop), B. Vinson (mez), G. Wieclaw (bass), E. Strosser (pno), C. Desert (pno), J. Sourisse (cnd), Jean Sourisse Ensemble, Audite Nova Vocal Ensemble—3 a capella songs FNAC Music ▲ 592224 [DDD]
Saint-Saëns, C.:Choral Music, w. D. Collot (sop), B. Vinson (mez), G. Wieclaw (bass), E. Strosser (pno), C. Desert (pno), J. Sourisse (cnd), Jean Sourisse Ensemble , Vocal Audite Nova Ensemble—Calme des nuits, Op. 68/1; Les fleurs et les arbres, Op. 68/2; Salterelle, Op. 74 FNAC Music ▲ 592224 [DDD]

Bouleyn, Kathryn (sop)
Rossini, G.:Les Soirées musicales, w. J. Anderson (sop), R. Giménez (ten), A. Corbelli (bar), N. Walker (pno) [I] Nimbus ▲ NI 5132 [DDD]

Boulin, Sophie (sop)
Dao, N.-T.:Les Enfants d'Izieu, w. Eric Trémolières (ten), Christian Tréguier (bass), S. Gualda (cnd), Radio France PO Musique Francaise d'Aujourd'hui ("Collection MFA-Radio France" series) ▲ MFA 216003
Handel, G.F.:Rinaldo, w. Sophie Boulin (sop—Donna), Ileana Cotrubas (sop—Almirena), Marie-Françoise Jacquelin (sop—Sirene), Nicole Leport (sop—Sirene), Jeanette Scovotti (sop—Armida), Carolyn Watkinson (cta—Rinaldo), Charles Brett (ct—Eustazio), Paul Esswood (ct—Goffredo), Armand Arapian (ten—Mago Christiano/Araldo), Ulrik Cold (bass—Argante), J. Malgoire (cnd), La Grande Écurie et la Chambre du Roy *(rec Paris, 1977)* Sony Classical 3-▲ SM3K 34592

Boult, W. (nar)
Britten, B.:The Young Person's Guide to the Orchestra, w. A. Boult (cnd), London PO EMI Classics ("Studio" series) ▲ CDM 63777 [ADD]

Bouman, H. (sop)
Morin, J.-B.:Motet pour le Saint-Sacrement, w. Haydn-Héritage Ensemble [L] REM ▲ 311110 XCD [DDD]

Bouquet, Michel (spkr)
Landowski, M.:Music of, w. Nadine Sautereau (sop), Jean-Christophe Benoit (bar), Xavier Depraz (bass), Gilbert Audin (bn), Evelyne Aïello, Didier Bouture, Ludovic Chevalier, Laurent Decker, Françoise Deslogères, Landowski, Tzipine (cnd), Colonne Association des Concerts Orch, Boulogne-Billancourt Orch Conservatory, Paris Conservatory Société des Concerts Orch, L'Itinéraire Ensemble, Harmonia Nova Orch Ensemble—Con Bn; Con pour ondes Martenot; Femme sans passé; Hauts de Hurlevent; Horologe; Mouvement; Notes de Nuit; Souvenir d'un jardin d'enfance; Ventriloque Chamade 3-▲ 5639/40/41 [AAD/DDD]

Bourgault, Pierre (nar)
Normandeau, R.:Petit Prince, w. Michel Dumont (nar—Aviator), Martin Pensa (nar—Little Prince), Christine Séguin (nar—Rose), Jean Marchand (nar—King), Luc Durand (nar—Conceited Man), Gilles Dupuis (nar—Drunkard), Guy Nadon (nar—Businessman), Jacques Languirand (nar—Lamplighter), Pierre Bourgault (nar—Geographer), Cynthia Dubois (nar—Snake), Monique Giroux (nar—Flower), Françoise Davoine (nar—Rose Garden), Jean-Louis Millette (nar—Fox), Gérard Poirier (nar—Railway Switchman), Claude Préfontaine (nar—Water Pill Salesman) *(rec Montreal, Aug 1994)* CBC 2-▲ 1091 [DDD]

Boursin, Denise (sop)
Adam, A.:Le Chalet, w. Joseph Peyron (ten), Stanislas Staskiewicz (sgr), A. Wolff (cnd), ORTF Lyric Orch Musidisc ▲ MUS 201942 [AAD]
Adam, A.:Le Farfadet, w. Joseph Peyron (ten), Stanislas Staskiewicz (sgr), A. Wolff (cnd), ORTF Lyric Orch Musidisc ▲ MUS 201942 [AAD]

Boutet, René (ten)
Chaynes, C.:Jocaste, w. Jean-Marie Frémeau (bar), André Cognet (b-bar), F. Chaslin (cnd), Rouen SO, Théâtre des Arts Chorus *(rec Rouen Theater, Rouen, France, 1993)* Chamade 2-▲ 5633/34

Bouwenstijn, Greé (sop)
Greé Bouwenstijn Philips ("Legendary Classics" series) ▲
Verdi, G.:Un ballo in maschera, w. E. Ratti (sop), A. Delori (cta), G. Zampieri (ten), F. Molinari-Pradelli (cnd), Netherlands Opera Orch, Netherlands Opera Chorus *(rec live 1958)* Globe 2-▲ GLO 5109

Bovarian, Alis (alt)
Gesualdo, D.C.:Madrigals, w. V. Kissyova (sop), N. Pankova (sop), V. Vassilev (ten), K. Mirinski (bass), S. Kralev (cnd), Sofia Madrigal—Io tacerò; Invan dunque o crudele; Moro lasso al mio duolo; Dolcissima mia vita Gega ▲ GD 174 [DDD]
Monteverdi, C.:Madrigals, w. V. Kissyova (sop), N. Pankova (sop), V. Vassilev (ten), K. Mirinski (bass), S. Kralev (cnd), Sofia Madrigal Ensemble—Psalmus 121, "Laetatus sum"; Batto qui pianse; Chiome d'oro; Amor che deggio far?; O come sei gentile; Psalmus 147, "Lauda Jerusalem" Gega ▲ GD 174 [DDD]
Schütz, H.:Motets (misc), w. V. Kissyova (sop), A. Ivanova (sop), N. Pankova (sop), V. Vassilev (ten), K. Mirinski (bass), S. Kralev (cnd), Sofia Madrigal—Christe Deus adjuva; Verbum caro factum est; Te Christe supplex invoco; Veni redemtor gentium; Veni sancte Spiritus Gega ▲ GD 174 [DDD]

Bovet, Martina (sop)
Keller, M.:Gesänge IV, w. J. Henneberger (cnd), Opera Nova Ensemble *(rec June 1994–Apr 1995)* Jecklin ▲ JEC 310 [DDD]
Mozart, W.A.:Zauberflöte, w. S. Jo (sop), L. Orgonasova (sop), G. Winbergh (ten), H. Hagegard (bar), A. Jordan (cnd), Paris Orchestral Ensemble, Romande Chamber Choir, Pro Arte Lausanne Erato 2-▲ 2292-45469-2 [DDD]

Bowden, Pamela (mez)
Delius, F.:A Mass of Life, w. K. Te Kanawa (sop), R. Dowd (ten), J. Shirley-Quirk (bar), N. del Mar (cnd), BBC SO, BBC Sym Chorus *(rec live, London 5/3/71)* Intaglio 2-▲ INCD 702-2 [ADD]
Herrmann, B.:Wuthering Heights, w. M. Beaton (sop—Catherine), P. Bowden (mez—Isabella), E. Bainbridge (mez—Nelly), M. Snashall (trb—Hareton), D. Bell (bar—Heathcliff), J. Kitchiner (bar—Hindley), J. Ward (bar—Edgar), M. Rippon (bass—Joseph), D. Kelly (bass—Mr. Lockwood), B. Herrmann (cnd), Pro Arte Orch *(rec 1965-66)* Unicorn-Kanchana 3-▲ UKCD 2050/51/52 [ADD]
Verdi, G.:I vespri siciliani, w. J. Brumaire (sop), Bonhomme (sgr), Taylor (sgr), Baran (sgr), M. Rossi (cnd), BBC Concert Orch, BBC Concert Chorus [original French version] *(rec live, London, 5/10/69)* Arkadia 3-▲ 456 [ADD]

Bowen, H. (sgr)
Rodgers, R.:Music of, w. S. Bass (sgr), J. Andrews (sgr), P. Como (sgr), D. Reese (sgr), J. Jones (sgr), N. Luboff (sgr), M. Gold (sgr), N. Walker (sgr), H. Bowen (sgr), V. Damone (sgr), P. Nero (pno), J. P. Morgan (sgr), E. Fisher (sgr), B. Goodman (cl), Ann-Margaret (sgr), Shorty Rogers (sgr), D. Shore (sgr), T. Martin (sgr), M. King (sgr), A. Newley (sgr) RCA ▲ 8590-2 R ■ 8590-4 R

Bowen, John (ten)
Monteverdi, C.:Vespro della Beata Vergine, w. Barbara Borden (sop), Maria Cristina Kiehr (sop), Andreas Scholl (alt), Andrew Murgatroyd (ten), Victor Torres (bar), Antonio Abete (bass), Jelle Draijer (bass), René Jacobs (cnd), Concerto Vocale, Netherlands Chamber Choir Harmonia Mundi 2-▲ 901566.67
Vaughan Williams, R.:Choral Hymns, w. M. Best (cnd), City of London Sinfonia, Corydon Singers [E] Hyperion ▲ CDA 66569 [DDD]

Bowen, Kenneth (ten)
Handel, G.F.:Messiah (sels), w. Sheila. Armstrong (sop), Norma Proctor (cta), John Cameron (bar), L. Stokowski (cnd), London SO, London Sym Chorus [E] London ("Weekend Classics" series) ▲ 433874-2 [ADD] ■ 433874-4
Mathias, W.:Ave Rex, w. Janet Price (sop), Michael Rippon (bar), Geraint Evans (b-bar), Atherton, Willcocks (cnd), London SO, New Philharmonia Orch, Welsh National Opera Chorus, Windsor Bach Choir, St. George's Chapel Choristers Lyrita ▲ SRCD .324
Mathias, W.:This Worlde's Joie, w. Janet Price (sop), Michael Rippon (bar), Atherton, Willcocks (cnd), London SO, New Philharmonia Orch, Welsh National Opera Chorus, Windsor Bach Choir, St. George's Chapel Choristers Lyrita ▲ SRCD .324
Tippett, M.:King Priam, w. Heather Harper (sop—Hecuba), Linda Hirst (sop—Serving Woman), Felicity Palmer (sop—Andromache), Julian Saipe (sop—Paris), Yvonne Minton (mez—Helen), Ann Murray (mez—Nurse), Kenneth Bowen (ten—Hermes), Peter Hall (ten—Young Guard), Philip Langridge (ten—Paris), Robert Tear (ten—Achilles), Thomas Allen (bar—Hector), Norman Bailey (bar—Priam), Stephen Roberts (bar—Patroclus), David Wilson-Johnson (bar—Old Man), D. Atherton (cnd), London Sinfonietta, London Sinfonietta Chorus Chandos ▲ CHAN 9406/7 [DDD]
Verdi, G.:La forza del destino, w. Martina Arroyo (sop—Donna Leonora), Janet Coster (mez—Preziosilla), Kenneth Bowen (ten—Trabuco), Kenneth Collins (ten—Don Alvaro), Peter Glossop (bar—Don Carlo), Roderick Kennedy (bass—Marquis), J. Matheson (cnd), BBC Concert Orch, BBC Concert Chorus *(rec live, early 1980's)* Exclusive 2-▲ EXL 80 [ADD]

Bowie, David (nar)
Basic 100, Vol. 43, w. Eugene Ormandy (cnd), Arthur Fiedler (cnd) RCA Victor ▲ 09026-62563-2 ■ 09026-62563-4
Peter & the Wolf [Prokofiev], w. E. Ormandy (cnd), Philadelphia Orch RCA Victor ▲ 09026-60878-2 [ADD] ■ 09026-60878-4 (CrO2)

Bowman, David (bar)
Bizet, G.:Carmen (sels), w. M. Horne (sop), M. Molese (sgr), M. Pellegrini (sgr), G. Griffiths (bar), F. Egerton (ten), H. Lewis (cnd), Royal PO, Royal Liverpool Phil Choir IMP Collectors Series ▲ IMPX 9016 [AAD]

Bowman, James (ct)
The Art of James Bowman, w. Crispian Steel-Perkins (nat tpt), Downshire Players of London, King's Consort, Music's Re-creation Meridian ▲ MER 84332
Bach, J.S.:Arias, w. R. King (cnd), King's Consort—Erbarme dich; Stirb in mir Hyperion ▲ KING 3
Bach, J.S.:Cant 54, w. R. King (cnd), King's Consort [G] Meridian ▲ CDE 84138
Bach, J.S.:Cant 54, w. R. King (cnd), King's Consort [G] Hyperion ▲ CDA 66326 [DDD]
Bach, J.S.:Cant 169, w. R. King (cnd), King's Consort [G] Hyperion ▲ CDA 66326 [DDD]
Bach, J.S.:Cant 170, w. R. King (cnd), King's Consort [G] Hyperion ▲ CDA 66326 [DDD]
Bach, J.S.:St. Matthew Passion, w. P. Esswood (ct), T. Sutcliffe (ct), K. Equiluz (ten), M. van Egmond (b-bar), N. Harnoncourt (cnd), Vienna Concentus Musicus [G] Teldec 3-▲ 2292-42509-2 [AAD]
Baroque Beauties, w. J. Laredo (cnd), Scottish CO, City of London Sinfonia [cnd:R. Hickox], E. Ritchie (sop), J. Purvis (pno) Pickwick ("The Orchid" series) ▲ PICORCD 11010
Biber, H. von:Requiem à 15, w. G. de Reyghere (sop), J. Feldman (sop), I. Honeyman (ten), M. van Egmond (bass), Ricercar Consort, Erik Van Nevel (cnd), Capella Sancti Michaelis [L] *(rec 5/90)* Ricercar ▲ RIC 81063 [DDD]

VOCALISTS

Bowman, James (ct) (cont.)

Blow, J.:Ah, Heaven! What Is't I Hear?, w. M. Chance (ct), R. King (cnd), King's Consort [E] Hyperion ▲ CDA 66253 [DDD]

Blow, J.:Ode on the Death of Mr. Henry Purcell, w. M. Chance (ct), R. King (cnd), King's Consort [E] Hyperion ▲ CDA 66253 [DDD]

Blow, J.:Songs, w. John Mark Ainsley (ten), Michael George (bass), Charles Pott (bass), R. King (cnd), King's Consort—Sing unto the Lord, Oh ye Saints *(rec St Jude-on-the-Hill, London, Dec 20-21, 1968)* United ▲ CAL 88002 [DDD]

Britten, H.:Death in Venice, w. P. Pears (ten), J. Shirley-Quirk (bar), S. Bedford (cnd), English CO, English Opera Group Chorus [E] London 2-▲ 425669-2 [ADD]

Britten, H.:A Midsummer Night's Dream, w. J. Gomez (sop), D. Jones (sop), N. Bailey (bar), H. Herford (bar), R. Hickox (cnd), City of London Sinfonia Virgin Classics ▲ CDCB 59305

Britten, H.:Purcell Realizations, w. Susan Gritton (sop), Felicity Lott (sop), Sarah Walker (mez), John Mark Ainsley (ten), Anthony Rolfe Johnson (ten), Richard Jackson (bass), Simon Keenlyside (bass), Ian Bostridge (sgr), Graham Johnson (pno) Hyperion 2-▲ CDA 67061/62

Bruhns, N.:Cants, w. Jill Feldman (sop), Greta de Reyghere (sop), Ian Honeyman (ten), Guy de Mey (ten), Max Van Egmond (bass), Ricercar Consort—Hemmt eure Tränenflut; Jauchzet dem Herren alle Welt; Wohl dem, der den Herren fürchtet; De profundis; Paratum cor meum; O werter heil'ger Geis; Zeit meines Abschieds; Erstanden ist der heilige Christ; Herr hat seinem Stuhl im Himmel bereitet; Ich liege und schlafe; Mein Herz ist bereit; Muss nicht der Mensch auf dieser Erden in Stetem Streite sein Ricercar In Ecco 2-▲ REC8001/2

Burgon, G.:The Fall of Lucifer, w. R. Covey-Crump (ten), D. Thomas (bass), G. Burgon (cnd), Endymion Ensemble, M. Greenall (cnd), Elysian Singers London Silva Classics ▲ SIL 6002 [DDD]

Burgon, G.:Naring the Upper Air, w. G. Burgon (cnd), Endymion Ensemble Silva Classics ▲ SIL 6002 [DDD]

Buxtehude, D.:Jesu, meine Freud und Lust, w. R. King (cnd), King's Consort [G] Meridian ▲ CDE 84126

Buxtehude, D.:Jubilate Domino, omnis terra, w. R. King (cnd), King's Consort [G] Meridian ▲ CDE 84126

Couperin, F.:Leçons de ténèbres (for Ash Wednesday), w. M. Chance (ct), R. King (trb), M. Caudle (bass vl) Hyperion ▲ CDA 66474

Couperin, F.:Motets, w. R. King (cnd), King's Consort—Jerusalem, convertere Hyperion ▲ KING 3

Donizetti, G.:Lucia di Lammermoor, w. J. McDonald (sop), J. Sutherland (sop), M. Elkins (mez), J. Gibin (ten), J. Rouleau (bass), Shaw (sgr), T. Serafin (cnd), Royal Opera House Orch, Royal Opera House Chorus Covent Garden—3 duets from Act 1, & 3 soprano solo arias from Act 2 [I] Myto ▲ 1 MCD 91545 [ADD]

Eternal Source of Light, w. King's Consort Meridian ▲ 84126

Ford, T.:Since First I Saw Your Face, w. R. King (cnd), King's Consort Hyperion ▲ KING 3

Gabrieli, G.:O magnum mysterium, w. R. King (cnd), King's Consort Hyperion ▲ KING 3

Gottschalk, L.M.:Orfeo ed Euridice (sels), w. J. Malgoire (cnd), La Grande Écurie et la Chambre du Roy—Act 2, scene 2, "Les Champs-Elysées" [w. Namur Chamber Choir]; Act 3, scene 1, "Che farò senza Euridice? Astrée ▲ E 8552 [DDD]

Grier, F.:Anthems, w. Christopher Hughes (org), Ralph Allwood (cnd), Rodolfus Choir—Let us invoke Christ; Great is the Power of Thy Cross; God, Who Made the Earth & Sky; Proclaim His Triumph; Day After Day; Salve Regina; Corpus Christi Carol; O King of the Friday; Christ's Love-Song; The Voice of My Beloved; Dilectus Meus Mihi; Thou, O God, Art Praised in Sion *(rec Eton College Chapel, Dec 1994)* Herald ▲ HAVPCD 177 [DDD]

Handel, G.F.:Arias, w. R. King (cnd), King's Consort—sels. from Alcina, Amadigi, Ariodante, Giulio Cesare, Giustino, Ottone, Rinaldo Hyperion ▲ CDA 66483

Handel, G.F.:Arias, w. S. Gritton (sop), R. King (cnd), King's Consort—Yet can I hear that dulcet lay; How can I stay, when love invites; O fairest of 10 thousand fair; Great God! Who yet but darkly known; The raptur'd soul; Father of Heaven; Ov to Esther; O Lord, whose mercies numberless; What though I trace each herb; Martial Sym & Destructive War; Welcome as the dawn of day; Kind Heaven if virtue be thy care; Almighty pow'r; Tune your harps Hyperion ▲ CDA 66797

Handel, G.F.:Chandos Anthems (11), w. P. Kwella (sop), I. Partridge (ten), M. George (bass), H. Christophers (cnd), The Sixteen Orch, The Sixteen—Anthem Nos. 7-9 [E] Chandos ("Chaconne" series) ▲ CHAN 0505 [DDD]

Handel, G.F.:Chandos Anthems (11), w. L. Dawson (sop), P. Kwella (sop), I. Partridge (ten), M. George (bass), H. Christophers (cnd), The Sixteen Orch, The Sixteen Chandos ("Chaconne" series) 4-▲ CHAN 0554 [DDD]

Handel, G.F.:Deborah, w. S. Gritton (sop), Y. Kenny (sop), C. Denley (mez), M. George (bass), R. King (cnd), King's Consort, Oxford New College Choir Hyperion 2-▲ CDA 66841 [DDD]

Handel, G.F.:Giulio Cesare in Egitto, w. Lynne Dawson (sop), Eirian James (mez), Guillemette Laurens (mez), Dominique Visse (alt), Nicolas Rivenq (bar), J. Malgoire (cnd), La Grande Écurie et la Chambre du Roy Astrée 3-▲ E 8558

Handel, G.F.:Israel in Egypt, w. Elizabeth Gale (sop), Lillian Watson (sop), Ian Partridge (ten), Tom McDonnell (bass), Alan Watt (bass), S. Preston (cnd), English CO, Christ Church Cathedral Choir Oxford *(rec Chapel of Merton College, Oxford, 1975)* London 2-▲ 443470-2 [ADD]

Handel, G.F.:Israel in Egypt, w. Elizabeth Gale (sop), Ian Partridge (ten), Tom McDonnell (bar), Alan Watt (bass), Watson (sgr), S. Preston (cnd), English CO, Christ Church Cathedral Choir Oxford London ("Jubilee" series) 2-▲ 421602-2 [ADD]

Handel, G.F.:Joseph & His Brethren, w. Yvonne Kenney (sop), Catherine Denley (mez), Connor Burrowes (trb), John Mark Ainsley (ten), Michael George (bass), R. King (cnd), King's Consort, New College Choir Oxford, King's Consort Choir Hyperion 3-▲ CDA 67171/3

Handel, G.F.:Messiah, w. Marjanne Kweksilber (sop), Paul Elliot (ten), G. Reinhart (bar), T. Koopman (cnd), Amsterdam Baroque Orch, The Sixteen Erato 3-▲ 2292-45960-2

Handel, G.F.:Messiah, w. Emma Kirkby (sop), Emily Van Evera (sop), Margaret Cable (mez), Joseph Cornwell (ten), David Thomas (bass), A. Parrott (cnd), Taverner Consort, Taverner Choir [E] EMI Classics 2-▲ CDCB 49801 [DDD]

Handel, G.F.:Messiah, w. Edith Mathis (sop), Claes Hakan Ahnsjö (ten), Richard Krause (ten), A. Dorati (cnd), Smithsonian Concerto Grosso, Univ of Maryland Choral Society [E] Pro Arte 2-▲ CDD 232 [DDD]; ■ PCD 232

Handel, G.F.:Messiah, w. Emily van Evera (sop), Emma Kirkby (sop), Margaret Cable (alt), A. Parrott (cnd), Taverner Players, Taverner Choir Virgin Classics 2-▲ ZDMB 61330

Handel, G.F.:Music of, w. R. King (cnd), King's Consort—Almighty Power; Or la tromba; Eternal Source of Light; Thou Shalt Bring Them In; Tune Your Harps; Welcome As the Dawn of Day; Impious Mortal; Yet Can I Hear That Dulcet Lay; Crudeltà né lontananza Hyperion ▲ KING 3

Handel, G.F.:Music of, w. Pauline Tinsley (sop), Anthony Rolfe-Johnson (ten), David Wilson-Johnson (ten), Simon Preston (org), R. Leppard (cnd), English CO, London Phil Chorus—Zadok the Priest; Eternal Source of Light Divine; Tamerlano Ov; Dead March [from Saul]; When the Ear Heard Her; She Delivered the Poor That Cried; Their Bodies Are Buried in Peace; Glory Be to the Father; As It Was in the Beginning; Con a Due Cori in B♭; Waft Her Angels to the Skies; Con in g for Org, Op. 7/5; Hallelujah Chorus [from The Messiah] IMP ("BBC Radio Classics" series) ▲ IMP 5691522

Handel, G.F.:Orlando, w. Arleen Augér (sop), Emma Kirkby (sop), Catherine Robbin (mez), David Thomas (bass), C. Hogwood (cnd), Academy of Ancient Music L'Oiseau-Lyre 3-▲ 430845-2 [DDD]

Handel, G.F.:Ottone, Rè di Germania, w. Jennifer Smith (sop—Gismonda), Catherine Denley (mez—Matilda), James Bowman (ct—Ottone), Dominique Visse (ct—Adelberto), Michael George (bass—Emireno), R. King (cnd), King's Consort Hyperion 3-▲ CDA 66751/53

Handel, G.F.:Theodora (sels), w. R. King (cnd), King's Consort—As with rosy steps the morn advancing *(rec St Jude-on-the-Hill, London, Dec 20-21, 1968)* United ▲ CAL 88002 [DDD]

Hasse, J.A.:Salve Regina, w. Deborah York (sop), R. King (cnd), King's Consort Hyperion ▲ CDA 66875

Howells, H.:Songs, w. P. Ash (cnd), Downshire Players of London—2 songs—Full Moon; O my deir hert [E] *(rec 1988)* Meridian ▲ CDE 84158

Humfrey, P.:Anthems, w. Jane Coe (vc), Robert King (org), R. King (cnd), King's Consort—A Hymn to God the Father *(rec St Jude-on-the-Hill, London, Dec 20-21, 1968)* United ▲ CAL 88002 [DDD]

Italian Arias & Cantatas, w. Skip Sempé (org), Jay Bernfeld (va da gamba) *(rec 10/87)* Arion ▲ ARN 68046 [DDD]

Bowman, James (ct) (cont.)

Kerll, J.C.:Missa pro defunctis, w. G. de Reyghere (sop), I. Honeyman (ten), G. de Mey (ten), M. van Egmond (bass), E. van Nevel (cnd), Capella Sancti Michaelis, Ricercar Consort [L] *(rec 5/90)* Ricercar ▲ RIC 81063 [DDD]

Loussier, J.:Lumières, w. Déborah Rees (sop), André Arpino (perc), J.-P. Wallez (cnd), Harmonia Nova Orch, Patrick Marco Vocal Ensemble *(rec Studio de Miraval, 1957)* Media 7 ▲ CD 707 [DDD]

Monteverdi, C.:Incoronazione, w. A. Augér (sop), S. Leonard (sop), D. Jones (mez), L. Hirst (mez), G. Reinhart (bass)., R. Hickox (cnd), City of London Baroque Sinfonia Virgin Classics 3-▲ CDCC 59524

Monteverdi, C.:Incoronazione, w. A. Augér (soprano—Poppea), D. Jones (mez—Nerone), L. Hirst (mez—Ottavia), J. Bowman (ct—Ottone), R. Hickox (cnd), City of London Baroque Sinfonia Virgin Classics ▲ CDCC 45082

Pergolesi, G.B.:Salve regina in f, w. E. Kirkby (sop), C. Hogwood (cnd), Academy of Ancient Music L'Oiseau-Lyre ▲ 425692-2 [DDD]

Pergolesi, G.B.:Salve regina in f, w. R. King (cnd), King's Consort [L] Meridian ▲ CDE 84138

Pergolesi, G.B.:Salve regina in f, w. J.-W. Audoli (cnd), Audoli Instrumental Ensemble [L] Arion ▲ ARN 68026 [DDD]

Pergolesi, G.B.:Stabat mater, w. E. Kirkby (sop), C. Hogwood (cnd), Academy of Ancient Music L'Oiseau-Lyre ▲ 425692-2 [DDD]

Purcell, H.:Anthems, w. R. Covey-Crump (ten), C. Daniels (ten), M. George (b-bar), King's Consort, New College Choir Oxford Hyperion ▲ CDA 66656

Purcell, H.:Anthems & Services, w. S. Gritton (sop), M. Kennedy (sop), E. O'Dwyer (trb), J. Goodman (trb), J. Bowman (ct), N. Short (ct), Rogers Covey-Crump (ten), C. Daniels (ten), M. Milhofer (ten), M. George (bass), R. Evans (bass), R. King (cnd), King's Consort—I Was Glad When They Said unto Me (coronation & verse anthem); O Consider My Adversity; Beati omnes qui timent Dominum; In the Black Dismal Dungeon of Dispair; Save Me, O God; Te Deum in B♭; Jubilant in B♭; Thy Way, O God, Is Holy Hyperion ▲ CDA 66677 [DDD]

Purcell, H.:Anthems & Services, w. R. Covey-Crump (ten), C. Daniels (ten), S. Varcoe (bar), M. George (bass), R. King (cnd), King's Consort, New College Choir Oxford—My heart is inditing; The way of God is an undefiled way; Sing unto God; Behold, I bring you glad tidings; Since God so tender a regard; Early, O Lord, my fainting soul; Sleep, Adam, sleep and take thy rest; Awake, ye dead; The earth trembled; Lord not to us but to thy name; O all ye people, clap your hands Hyperion ▲ CDA 66644

Purcell, H.:Anthems & Services, w. Roger Covey-Crump (ten), Michael George (bass), R. King (cnd), King's Consort, New College Choir Oxford—Behold, now praise the Lord; Blessed are they that fear the Lord; I will give thanks unto Thee, O Lord; My song shall be always Hyperion ▲ CDA 66609

Purcell, H.:Anthems & Services, w. Charles Daniels (ten), Michael George (bass), Robert Evans (bass), R. King (cnd), King's Consort, New College Choir Oxford—O sing unto the Lord; O praise God in His holiness; Praise the Lord, O Jerusalem; It is a good thing to give thanks; O give thanks unto the Lord; Let mine eyes run down with tears; My beloved spake Hyperion ▲ CDA 66585

Purcell, H.:Anthems & Services, w. Tom Seligman (trb), Ashley Stafford (ct), John Mark Ainsley (ten), Andrew Gant (ten), Michael George (bass), Charles Pott (bass), R. King (cnd), King's Consort, King's Consort—O Sing unto the Lord; My beloved spake *(rec St Jude-on-the-Hill, London, Dec 20-21, 1968)* United ▲ CAL 88002 [DDD]

Purcell, H.:Dido & Aeneas, w. Rebecca Evans (sop—Belinda), Maria Ewing (sop—Dido), Mary Plazas (sop—1st witch), Patricia Rozario (sop—2nd woman), Sally Burgess (mez—Sorceress), Pamela Helen Stephens (mez—2nd witch), James Bowman (ct—Spirit), Jamie MacDougal (ten—Sailor), Karl Daymond (bar—Aeneas), R. Hickox (cnd), Collegium Musicum 90 Chandos ("Early Music" series) ▲ CHAN 0586 [DDD]

Purcell, H.:Music for the Funeral of Queen Mary, w. S. Gritton (sop), M. Kennedy (sop), E. O'Dwyer (trb), J. Goodman (trb), N. Short (ct), Rogers Covey-Crump (ten), C. Daniels (ten), M. Milhofer (ten), M. George (bass), R. Evans (bass), R. King (cnd), King's Consort Hyperion ▲ CDA 66677 [DDD]

Purcell, H.:Music for the Theater, w. E. Kirkby (sop), J. Nelson (sop), M. Hill (ten), R. Covey-Crump (ten), C. Keyte (bass), D. Thomas (bass), C. Hogwood (cnd), Academy of Ancient Music L'Oiseau-Lyre 6-▲ 425893-2 [ADD]

Purcell, H.:Music of, w. Catherine Bott (sop), Emma Kirkby (sop), Anthony Rooley (lt), Monica Huggett (vn), Catherine Mackintosh (vn), Christophe Coin (vc), Paula Chateauneuf (gtr), Hill, Hogwood (cnd), Brandenburg Consort, Academy of Ancient Music, Anthony Lewis (cnd), David Hill (cnd), St. Anthony Singers, Taverner Choir, Winchester Cathedral Choir—The Double Dealer; Come Ye Sons of Art; The Old Bachelor; Birthday Song for Queen Mary; Oedipus; King Arthur; Bonduca; The Fairy Queen; Son. No. 9 in F; Dido & Aeneas; Abdelazer; Bess of Bedlam; The Married Beau; Hear My Prayer, O Lord; Rejoice in the Lord Always L'Oiseau-Lyre ▲ 444620-2

Purcell, H.:Music of, w. Catherine Bott (sop), Emma Kirkby (sop), Anthony Rooley (lt), Paula Chateauneuf (gtr), Monica Huggett (vn), Catherine Mackintosh (vn), Christophe Coin (vc), Hill, Hogwood (cnd), Academy of Ancient Music, Brandenburg Consort, David Hill (cnd), Anthony Lewis (cnd), St. Anthony Singers, Taverner Choir, Winchester Cathedral Choir—The Double Dealer; Come Ye Sons of Art; The Old Bachelor; Birthday Song for Queen Mary; Oedipus; King Arthur; Bonduca; The Fairy Queen; Son. No. 9 in F; Dido & Aeneas; Abdelazer; Bess of Bedlam; The Married Beau; Hear My Prayer, O Lord; Rejoice in the Lord Always London ("Editions de l'oiseau-lyre" series) ▲ 444620-2

Purcell, H.:Odes & Welcome Songs (misc), w. H. Cook (ten), C. Robson (ct), D. Wilson-Johnson (bar), G. Leonhardt (hpd), G. Leonhardt (cnd), Orch of the Age of Enlightenment Virgin Classics ▲ CDC 59243

Purcell, H.:The Prophetess, or The History of Dioclesian, w. C. Pierard (sop), J. M. Ainsley (ten), I. Bostridge (ten), M. George (bass), R. Hickox (cnd), Collegium Musicum 90—Masque Chandos ("Chaconne" series) ▲ CHAN 0558 [DDD]

Purcell, H.:The Prophetess, or The History of Dioclesian, w. Catherine Pierard (sop), John Mark Ainsley (ten), Michael George (bass), R. Hickox (cnd), Collegium Musicum 90 Chandos ▲ CHAN 0569/70 [DDD]

Purcell, H.:Songs, w. B. Bonney (sop), S. Gritton (sop), R. Covey-Crump (ten), C. Daniels (ten), M. George (bass), D. Miller (archlt/thb/baroque gtr), M. Caudle (b vl), R. King (org/hpd), King's Consort—Incassum Lesbia; Gentle Shepherds, you that know the charms; I love and I must; Through mournful shades and solitary groves; The Knotting Song Hyperion ▲ CDA 66720 [DDD]

Purcell, H.:Songs, w. M. Chance (ct), R. King (cnd), King's Consort [E, L] Hyperion ▲ CDA 66253 [DDD]

Purcell, H.:Songs, w. B. Bonney (sop), S. Gritton (sop), R. Covey-Crump (ten), C. Daniels (ten), M. George (bass), R. King (cnd), King's Consort—When Strephon Found; Let Us, Kind Lesbia; Corinna Is Divinely Fair; Olinda in the Shades; If Music Be the Food of Love [3rd setting]; Lovely Albina; I Came, I Saw; No, to What Purpose; Young Thrysis' Fate; She Loves Me and Confesses Too; From Silent Shade (Bess of Bedlam); O Solitude; If Pray'rs and Tears; The Fatal Hour; Sylvia, 'Tis True You're Fair; Amintor, Heedless of His Flocks; Love is Now Become a Trade; Phyllis, I Can Never Forgive It; Who Can Behold?; He Himself Courts His Own Ruin; Let Formal Lovers Still Pursue; Ask Me to Love No More; In Cloris All Soft Charms; Spite of the Godhead Hyperion ▲ CDA 66730

Purcell, H.:Songs, w. B. Bonney (sop), S. Gritton (sop), R. Covey-Crump (ten), C. Daniels (ten), M. George (bass), D. Miller (archlt/thb/baroque gtr), M. Caudle (b vl), R. King (chamber org)—Draw near, you lovers; While Thyrsis, wrapt in downy sleep; Love, thou canst hear, I lov'd fair Celia; What hope for us remains now he is gone; Pastora's beauties, when unblown; A thousand sev'ral ways I tried; Urge me no more; Farewell all joys; If music be the food of love [1st setting]; Amidst the shades and cool refreshing streams; They say you're angry; Let each gallant heart; This poet sings the Trojan wars; Ah, how pleasant 'tis to love; My heart whenever you appear; On the brow of Richard Hill; Rashly I swore I would disown; Since the pox or the plague; Beneath a dark and melancholy grove; Musing on cares of human fate; Whilst Cynthia sung, all angry winds lay still Hyperion ▲ CDA 66710

Purcell, H.:Songs, w. R. King (cnd), King's Consort—Britain, Thou Now Art Great; O Solitude; By Beauteous Softness Mixed; An Evening Hymn; On the Brow of Richmond Hill; Vouchsafe, O Lord Hyperion ▲ KING 3

Purcell, H.:Timon of Athens, w. I. Davies (trb), C. de la Hoyde (trb), J. M. Ainsley (ten), M. George (bass), R. Hickox (cnd), Collegium Musicum 90—Masque Chandos ("Chaconne" series) ▲ CHAN 0558 [DDD]

Ridout, A.:Songs Ct, w. P. Ash (cnd), Downshire Players of London [E]—5 songs—Epitaph for Amy; For Infants, Time is Like a Humming Shell; Our Youth-Time Passes Down a Colonnade; Prism of Life; To Travel Like a Bird Meridian ▲ CDE 84158

Bowman, James (ct) (cont.)
Scarlatti, A.:Cants, w. Deborah York (sop), Crispian Steele-Perkins (tpt), R. King (cnd), King's Consort—3 cants Hyperion ▲ CDA 66875
Scarlatti, D.:Salve Regina, w. Deborah York (sop), R. King (cnd), King's Consort Hyperion ▲ CDA 66875
Steptoe, R.:Elegy on the Death of Cock Robin, w. P. Ash (cnd), Downshire Players of London [E] Meridian ▲ CDE 84158
Tavener, J.:Akathist of Thanksgiving, w. T. Wilson (ten), M. Baker (org), M. Neary (cnd), BBC SO, Westminster Abbey Choir, BBC Singers *(rec Jan. 21, 1994)* Sony Classical ▲ SK 64446 [DDD]
Telemann, G.P.:Cants, w. J. Baird (sop), Music's Re-creation—Ihr Völker, hört; Ergeuss dich zur Salbung; Erscheine, Gott, in deinem Tempel; Packe dich, gelähmter Drache Meridian ▲ CDE 84159
Telemann, G.P.:Cants, w. R. King (cnd), King's Consort—Easter cantata, "Weg mit Sodoms gift'gen Früchten" [G] Meridian ▲ CDE 84138
Vaughan Williams, R.:Songs, w. P. Ash (cnd), Downshire Players of London—Ah! Sunflower; Cruelty Has a Human Heart; Divine Image; Eternity; How Can the Tree But Wither; Infant Joy; The Lamb; The Lawyer; Linden Lea; London; Piper; Poison Tree; Searching for Lambs; Sheperd; Sky Above the Roof [E] *(rec 1988)* Meridian ▲ CDE 84158
Vivaldi, A.:Dixit Dominus, w. J.-C. Malgoire (cnd), La Grande Écurie et la Chambre du Roy—De torrente Astrée ▲ E 8552 [DDD]
Vivaldi, A.:Nisi Dominus, w. J.-C. Malgoire (cnd), La Grande Écurie et la Chambre du Roy—Sicut erat, Amen Astrée ▲ E 8552 [DDD]
Vivaldi, A.:Nisi Dominus, w. C. Hogwood (cnd), Academy of Ancient Music [L] L'Oiseau-Lyre ▲ 414329-2 [ADD]
Vivaldi, A.:Sacred Choral Music, w. Catherine Denley (sop), Deborah York (sop), R. King (cnd), King's Consort Hyperion ▲ CDA 66779
Vivaldi, A.:Salve regina, RV.616, w. J.-W. Audoli (cnd), Audoli Instrumental Ensemble [L] Arion ▲ ARN 68026 [DDD]
Vivaldi, A.:Salve regina, RV.619, w. R. King (cnd), King's Consort [L] Meridian ▲ CDE 84138
Vivaldi, A.:Stabat Mater Cta, w. C. Hogwood (cnd), Academy of Ancient Music L'Oiseau-Lyre ▲ 414329-2 [ADD]
Warlock, P.:Songs Ct, w. P. Ash (cnd), Downshire Players of London—(3) Love for Love; My Own Country; Sleep [E] Meridian ▲ CDE 84158

Bowman, K. (sgr)
Schoenberg, A.:Gurrelieder, w. M. Napier (sop), Y. Minton (mez), J. Thomas (ten), G. Reich (nar), S. Nimsgern (b-bar), P. Boulez (cnd), BBC SO *(rec Oct. 26–Dec. 06, 1974)* Sony Classical 2-▲ SM2K 48459 [ADD]

Bowman, Robert (ten)
Herrmann, B.:Moby Dick, w. John Amis (ten), David Kelly (bass), Michael Rippon (bass), London PO, Aeolian Singers [E] Unicorn-Kanchana ▲ UKCD 2061
Puccini, G.:Tosca, w. Maria Callas (sop—Floria Tosca), Robert Bowman (ten—Spoletta), Renato Cioni (ten—Mario Cavaradossi), Eric Garrett (bar—Il Sagrestano), Tito Gobbi (bar—Scarpia), Victor Godfrey (bass—Casare Angelotti), Dennis Wicks (bass—Sciarrone), C. F. Cillario (cnd), Royal Opera House Orch, Royal Opera House Chorus Covent Garden *(rec London, 1964)* Melodram 2-▲ CDI 203003 [ADD]

Boyce, Bruce (bar)
Delius, F.:Sea Drift, w. T. Beecham (cnd), Royal PO, BBC Sym Chorus *(rec 1954)* Sony Masterworks (Portrait) ▲ MPK 47680 [ADD]

Boyer, Antonio (bar)
Alfano, F.:Risurrezione, w. M. Olivero (Katiusha), A. Di Stasio (Matrena), Gismondo (Prince Dmitri), E. Boncompagni (cnd), Turin RAI Orch [I] *(rec live, Oct 22, 1971)* Standing Room Only 2-▲ SRO 839-2 [ADD]
Gounod, C.:Roméo et Juliette, w. Yvonne Gall (sop—Juliette), Champell (sop—Stéphano), Jeanne Goulancourt (mez—Gertrude), Agustarello Affre (ten—Roméo), Edmond Tirmont (ten—Tybalt), Alexis Boyer (bar—Mercutio), Pierre Dupré (bar—Paris), Hypolite Belhomme (bar—Grégorio), Marcel Journet (bass—Frère Laurent), Henri Albers (bass—Capulet), Valermont (bass—The Duke), F. Rühlmann (cnd), Paris Opéra-Comique Orch, Paris Opéra-Comique Chorus *(rec 1912)* VAI Audio ▲ VAIA 1064-3 F

Boylan, Patricia (sop)
Cresswell, L.:A Modern Ecstacy, w. N. Leeson-Williams (bass-bar), R. Bernas (cnd), CSR Bratislava SO *(rec 4/91)* Continuum ▲ CCD 1033

Bozhkova (sgr)
Pergolesi, G.B.:Stabat mater, w. T. Genova (sop), V. Kazandjiev (cnd), Bulgarian PO, Bulgarian Phil Chorus [L] Vivace 2-▲ 140141 [ADD/DDD]

Bozonnet, Marcel (nar)
Boësset, A.:Music of, w. Véronique Dietschy (sop), Alain Zaepffel (ct), Christophe Le Paludier (ten), Jacques Bone (bass), Claire Antonini (lt), Marianne Muller (vl)—Madame de la fayette; Airs de cour; La princesse de cleves (sels) Adès ▲ ADE 204722

Brachet, Huguette (mez)
Honegger, A.:Jeanne d'Arc au bûcher, w. C. Château (sop), A.M. Rodde (sop), P. Proenza (ten), Z. Jankovsky (ten), F. Loup (bass), S. Baudo (cnd), Czech PO, Czech Chorus *(rec 1974)* Supraphon 2-▲ 11 0557-2 [AAD]

Bracht, Roland (bass)
Mozart, W.A.:Entführung, w. E. Gruberova (sop), F. Araiza (ten), R. Orth (bar), H. Wallberg (cnd), Munich RSO Eurodisc 2-▲ 7792-2 [ADD]
Mozart, W.A.:Zauberflöte, w. L. Popp (sop), E. Gruberova (sop), S. Jerusalem (ten), W. Brendel (bar), B. Haitink (cnd), Bavarian RSO, Bavarian Radio Chorus [G] EMI Classics 3-▲ CDCC 47951 [DDD]
Mozart, W.A.:Zauberflöte (sels), w. L. Popp (sop), E. Gruberova (sop), S. Jerusalem (ten), W. Brendel (bar), B. Haitink (cnd), Bavarian RSO, Bavarian Radio Chorus [G] EMI Classics ▲ CDC 47008 [DDD]
Stravinsky, I.:Oedipus Rex, w. J. Norman (sop), T. Moser (ten), S. Nimsgern (b-bar), C. Davis (cnd), Bavarian RSO, Bavarian Radio Chorus [L] Orfeo ▲ 071831 [DDD] ▮ 071831 (D)

Bradshaw, Sally (sop)
Handel, G.F.:Agrippina, w. W. Hill (sop), L. Saffer (sop), G. Banditelli (cta), D. Minter (alt), R. Popken (alt), B. Szilágyi (bar), M. Dean (b-bar), N. Isherwood (bass), N. McGegan (cnd), Capella Savaria [period instrs] [I] Harmonia Mundi USA 3-▲ HMU 907063/65 ▮ HMU 407063/65

Bragadóttir, Rannveig Fríoa (mez)
Pálsson, P.P.:Music of, w. S. Saemundsdóttir (sop), Reykjavik CO—Gudis-Mana-Hasi; Crystals; Tomorrow; August Sonnet; September Sonnet; Lantao; 6 Thoughtful Songs Music from Iceland ▲ ITM 807
Verdi, G.:La traviata, w. R. Krause (ten), Y. Ramiro (ten), A. Rahbari (cnd), Czech-Slovak RSO Bratislava, Slovak Phil Chorus [I] Naxos 2-▲ 8.660011/12 [DDD]
Verdi, G.:La traviata (sels), w. Monika Krause (sop), Ivica Neshybová (sop), Yordy Ramiro (ten), Gerog Tichy (bar), Ladislav Neshyba (bass), Jozef Špaček (bass), A. Rahbari (cnd), Czech-Slovak RSO Bratislava, Jan Rozehnal (cnd), Slovak Phil Chorus—Prelude act I; Libiam ne'lieti calici; Un dì, felice; È strano! Ah, fors'e lui; Follie!...sempre libera; Lunge da lei...de'miei bollenti spiriti; O Mio rimorosol; Pura si come un angelo...Dite alla giovine; Dammi tu forza; Di Provenza il mar; Noi siamo zingarelle; Prelude act III; Teneste la promessa...Addio del passato; Signoral Che t'accade?; Ah, Violettal *(rec Bratislava Concert Hall, Dec 1990)* Naxos ▲ 8.553041 [DDD]

Brahaspati, Sulochana (voc)
Leçons de ténèbres et raga de la nuit avancée, w. V. Dietschy (sop), Alain Zaepffel (ct), Ensemble Gradiva K617 ▲ 7017 [DDD]

Bramante, Aldo (bar)
Puccini, G.:Turandot, w. Montserrat Caballé (sop—Turandot), Leona Mitchell (sop—Liu), Remy Corazza (ten—Pang), Joseph Franck (ten—Pong), Robert Johnson (ten—Prince of Persia), Raymond Manton (ten—Altoum), Luciano Pavarotti (ten—Calaf), Aldo Bramante (bar—a mandarin), Dale Duesing (bar—Ping), Giorgio Tozzi (bass—Timur), R. Chailly (cnd), *(orch unknown) (rec San Francisco, Nov. 4, 1977)* Legato Classics 2-▲ LCD 188-2

Brambilla, Linda (mez)
Verdi, G.:Rigoletto, w. Lina Pagliughi (sop—Gilda), Linda Brambilla (mez—Countess Ceprano), Vera De Cristoff (cta—Maddalena), Tino Folgar (ten—Duke of Mantua), Giuseppe Nessi (ten—Borsa), Luigi Piazza (bar—Rigoletto), Aristide Baracchi (b-bar—Monterone/Marullo), Salvatore Baccaloni (bass—Sparafucile), Giuseppe Menni (bass—Ceprano), C. Sabajno (cnd), La Scala Orch, La Scala Chorus *(rec La Scala Theatre, Milan, 1927–28)* VAI Audio 2-▲ VAIA 1097-2

Brambilla, Linda (mez) (cont.)
Verdi, G.:Rigoletto, w. Lina Pagliughi (sop—Gilda), Linda Brambilla (mez—Contessa di Ceprano), Vera de Cristoff (cta—Maddalena), Tino Folgar (ten—Duca di Mantova), Giuseppe Nessi (ten—Borsa), Aristide Baracchi (bar—Conte di Monterone/Marullo), Luigi Piazza (bar—Rigoletto), Salvatore Baccaloni (bass—Sparafucile), Giuseppe Menni (bass—Conte di Ceprano), C. Sabajno (cnd), La Scala Orch, La Scala Chorus *(rec 1927–28)* Arkadia 2-▲ CD 78003 (m) [ADD]

Branagh, Kenneth (nar)
Mendelssohn, F.:Midsummer Night's Dream (ov & incidental), w. Sylvia McNair (sop), Angelika Kirchschlager (mez), C. Abbado (cnd), Berlin PO, Ernst Senff Chorus Women's Voices Sony Classical ▲ SK 62826

Brand, Adrian (ten)
Bach, J.S.:Mass in b, BWV 232, w. Hélène Obadia (sop), Madeleine Jalbert (alt), Paul Gay (bass), Eric Aubier (tpt), P. Kuentz (cnd), Paul Kuentz Orch, Paul Kuentz Choir Pierre Verany ▲ PVY 730060 [DDD]
Bach, J.S.:St. John Passion, w. Barbara Schlick (sop), Ingeborg Most (alt), Alexander Stevenson (ten), Philip Langshaw (bass), Peter Lika (bass), P. Kuentz (cnd), Paul Kuentz Orch, Paul Kuentz Choir Pierre Verany 2-▲ PVY 730051 [DDD]

Brandes, Christine (sop)
Bach, J.S.:Cant 106, "Actus tragicus", w. D. Minter (alt), W. Sharp (bar), American Bach Soloists Koch International Classics ▲ KIC 7164 [DDD]
Blow, J.:Songs, w. N. McGegan (cnd), Arcadian Academy—The Self Banished; It Grieves Me; Welcome, Welcome [prologue] *(rec Sept 18–21, 1994)* Harmonia Mundi France ▲ HMU 907167
Blow, J.:Songs, w. Mary Springfels (va), N. McGegan (cnd), Arcadian Academy Harmonia Mundi USA ▲ HMU 907167
Purcell, H.:Dido & Aeneas, w. L. Hunt (sop), L. Saffer (sop), D. Deam (sop), R. Rainero (sop), E. Rabiner (mez), P. Elliot (ten), M. Dean (bar), N. McGegan (cnd), Philharmonia Baroque Orch, Clare College Choir Cambridge Harmonia Mundi USA ▲ HMU 907110
Purcell, H.:Music of, w. Mary Springfels (va), N. McGegan (cnd), Arcadian Academy Harmonia Mundi France ▲ HMU 907167
Purcell, H.:Songs, w. N. McGegan (cnd), Arcadian Academy—The Bashful Thames; So When the Glitt'ring Queen; Lord, What Is Man; Cupid, the Slyest Rogue Alive; Oh Lead Me to Some Peaceful Gloom; Dry Those Eyes; O Solitude; Amidst the Shades; When First Amintas; The Blessed Virgin's Expostulation; Fly Swift, Ye Hours; 'Twas within a Furlong *(rec Sept 18–21, 1994)* Harmonia Mundi France ▲ HMU 907167
Rameau, J.P.:Le Berger fidèle, w. Ann Monoyios (sop), Howard Crook (ten), Nat Wilson (b-bar), Concert Royal Newport Classic ▲ NPT 85555

Brandt, B. (sgr)
Argento, D.:Postcard from Morocco, w. S. Roche, J. Hardy, Y. Marshall, V. Sutton, B. Busse, M. Foreman, P. Brunelle (cnd), Minnesota Opera Orch CRI 2-▲ CD 614 [ADD]

Brandt, Karl-Heinz (ten)
Weill, K.:The Seven Deadly Sins, w. B. Fassbaender (mez), H. Sojer (ten), H. Komatsu (bass), I. Urbas (bass), C. Garben (cnd), North German Radio PO Harmonia Mundi France ▲ HMC 901420

Brannigan, Owen (bass)
Britten, H.:Albert Herring, w. S. Fisher (sop), A. Cantelo (sop), S. Rex (mez), P. Pears (ten), J. Noble (bar), B. Britten (cnd), English CO [E] London 2-▲ 421849-2 [ADD]
Britten, H.:Billy Budd, w. P. Pears (ten), P. Glossop (bar), J. Shirley-Quirk (bar), B. Luxon (bar), M. Langdon (bass), B. Britten (cnd), London SO, Ambrosian Singers [E] London 3-▲ 417428-2 [ADD]
Sullivan, A.:The Gondoliers, w. G. Evans (bar), A. Young (ten), R. Lewis (ten), M. Sargent (cnd), Pro Arte Orch, Glyndebourne Festival Chorus EMI Classics 2-▲ CDMB 64394
Sullivan, A.:The Mikado, w. R. Lewis (ten), G. Evans (bar), I. Wallace (bass), M. Sargent (cnd), Pro Arte Orch, Glyndebourne Festival Chorus EMI Classics 2-▲ CDMB 64403

Branzell, Karin (mez)
Opera Arias *(rec 1927–28 from 78 rpm discs)* Preiser ("Legendary Classics" series) ▲ PRE 89039 (m) [AAD]

Braschi, A. (ten)
Mascagni, P.:Cavalleria rusticana, w. G. Simionato (sop—Santuzza), F. Cadoni (mez—Lola), L. Pellogrino (cta—Lucia), A. Braschi (ten—Turiddu), C. Tagliabue (bar—Alfio), A. Basile (cnd), Italian Lyric Orch, Turin Cetra Chorus *(rec Turin, 1950)* Cetra Classic 2-▲ CDO 27 [ADD]

Bratschke, Detlef (trb)
Bach, J.S.:Cant 100, w. P. Esswood (ct), K. Equiluz (ten), M. van Egmond (b-bar), G. Leonhardt (cnd), Leonhardt Consort [G] Teldec ▲ 2292-42584-2
Bach, J.S.:Cant 113, w. S. Hennig (trb), R. Jacobs (ct), K. Equiluz (ten), M. van Egmond (b-bar), Leonhardt Consort, Collegium Vocale, Hanover Boys' Chorus [G] Teldec 2-▲ 2292-42606-2

Bratschke, Detlef (alt)
Monteverdi, C.:Vespers, w. Susanne Ryden (sop), Irena Troupova-Wilke (sop), Erich Mentzel (ten), Hermann Oswald (ten), Manuel Warwitz (ten), Thomas Herberich (bass), Günther Schmidt (bass), H. Arman (cnd), Schütz Academy Capriccio ▲ CD 10521 [DDD]

Braun, D.H. (mez)
Bach, J.S.:Christmas Oratorio, w. E. Roon (sop), E. Majkut (ten), W. Berry (bass), L. Dutoit (echo), B. Seidlhofer (hpd), J. Nebois (org), F. Grossmann (cnd), Vienna SO, Akademie Chamber Choir Vox Box 2-▲ CDX 5096 [ADD]

Braun, Hans (bar)
Bach, J.S.:Cant 4, w. L. Dutoit (trb), K. Equiluz (ten), F. Prohaska (cnd), Vienna State Opera Orch, Vienna Chamber Choir [G] *(rec 1959)* Vanguard Classics ("The Bach Guild" series) ▲ OVC 2001 [ADD]
Bach, J.S.:Cant 78, w. T. Stich-Randall (sop), D. Hermann (sop), A. Dermota (ten), F. Prohaska (cnd), Bach Guild Orch, Bach Guild Chorus [G] *(rec May 1954)* Vanguard Classics ("The Bach Guild" series) ▲ OVC 2009 [ADD]
Bach, J.S.:Cant 106, "Actus tragicus", w. T. Stich-Randall (sop), D. Hermann (sop), A. Dermota (ten), F. Prohaska (cnd), Bach Guild Orch, Bach Guild Chorus [G] *(rec May 1954)* Vanguard Classics ("The Bach Guild" series) ▲ OVC 2009 [ADD]
Bach, J.S.:Cant 140, w. L. Dutoit (trb), K. Equiluz (ten), F. Prohaska (cnd), Vienna State Opera Orch, Vienna State Opera Chorus [G] *(rec 1959)* Vanguard Classics ("The Bach Guild" series) ▲ OVC 2001 [ADD]
Hindemith, P.:When Lilacs Last In The Dooryard Bloom'd, w. Elisabeth Höngen (mez), P. Hindemith (cnd), Vienna SO, Vienna State Opera Chorus *(rec 1956)* Tuxedo ▲ TUXCD 1061
Smetana, B.:The Bartered Bride, w. Dorothea Siebert (sop), Dagmar Hermann (mez), Maria von Ilosvay (mez), Kurt Böhme (bass), J. Keilberth (cnd), Bavarian RSO, Bavarian Radio Chorus *(rec 1958)* Pantheon 2-▲ PHE 6652 (m)
Strauss, R.:Salome, w. Astrid Varnay (sop—Salome), Hertha Töpper (mez—Der Page der Herodias), Margarete Klose (cta—Herodias), Hans Hopf (ten—Narraboth), Karl Hoppe (ten—1st Nazarene), Karl Ostertag (ten—1st Jew), Julius Patzak (ten—Herodes), Hans Braun (bar—Jochanaan), Benno Kusche (bar—2nd Soldier), Adolf Keil (bass—1st Soldier), Hans Hermann Nissen (bass—Ein Kappadozier), Max Proebstl (bass—2nd Nazarene), Walter Carnotch (sgr—4th Jew), Emil Graf (sgr—3rd Jew), Paul Kaussen (sgr—2nd Jew), Hildegard Limmer (sgr—A slave), Georg Witter (sgr—5th Jew), H. Weigert (cnd), Bavarian RSO *(rec June 21–25, 1953)* Bella Voce 2-▲ BLV 7210 [AAD]
Wagner, R.:Parsifal, w. Anny Konetzni (sop—Kundry), Günther Treptow (ten—Parsifal), Paul Schöffler (bar—Amfortas), Hans Braun (bass—Titurel), Adolf Vogel (bass—Klingsor), Ludwig Weber (bass—Gurnemanz), R. Moralt (cnd), Vienna SO, Vienna State Opera Chorus *(rec Vienna)* Myto 4-▲ 4 MCD 954.136
Wagner, R.:Tannhäuser, w. S. Jurinac (sop), B. Martin (sop), H. Beirer (ten), M. Talvela (bass), W. Sawallisch (cnd), La Scala Orch, La Scala Chorus [G] *(rec live, Milan 4/13/67)* Melodram 3-▲ CDM 37091 [ADD]
Wagner, R.:Tannhäuser, w. H. Dernesch (sop), C. Ludwig (mez), A. Kollo (ten), H. Sotin (bass), G. Solti (cnd), Vienna PO [Paris version] [G] London 3-▲ 414581-2 [ADD]

Braun, Helena (sop)
Gluck, C.W.:Iphigénie en Aulide (sels), w. Helena Braun (sop—Klytämnestra), Hilde Konetzni (sop—Iphigenie), Set Svanholm (ten—Achilles), Paul Schöffler (b-bar—Agamemnon), L. Ludwig (cnd), Vienna State Opera Orch *(rec Vienna, Oct. 29, 1942)* Koch Schwann ▲ SCH 314692 [ADD]

VOCALISTS

Braun, Helena (sop) (cont.)

Mozart, W.A.:Arias, w. Arleen Augér (sop), Kathleen Battle (sop), Irma Beilke (sop), Lisa Della Casa (sop), Maria Cebotari (sop), Ileana Cotrubas (sop), Helen Donath (sop), Mirella Freni (sop), Reri Grist (sop), Edita Gruberova (sop), Elisabeth Grümmer (sop), Hilde Güden (sop), Ingeborg Hallstein (sop), Luise Helletsgruber (sop), Gundula Janowitz (sop), Sena Jurinac (sop), Erika Köth (sop), Evelyn Lear (sop), Wilma Lipp (sop), Margaret Marshall (sop), Edith Mathis (sop), Jarmila Novotna (sop), Margherita Perras (sop), Lucia Popp (sop), Elisabeth Rethberg (sop), Anneliese Rothenberger (sop), Elisabeth Schumann (sop), Elisabeth Schwarzkopf (sop), Graziella Sciutti (sop), Irmgard Seefried (sop), Graziella Sciutti (sop), Julia Varady (sop), Agnes Baltsa (mez), Margit Bokor (mez), Brigitte Fassbaender (mez), Christa Ludwig (mez), Ann Murray (mez), Francisco Araiza (ten), Anton Dermota (ten), Helge Rosvaenge (ten), Rudolf Schock (ten), Peter Schreier (ten), Leopold Simoneau (ten), Eric Tappy (ten), Richard Tauber (ten), Gösta Winbergh (ten), Josef Witt (ten), Fritz Wunderlich (ten), Christian Boesch (bar), Willy Domgraf-Fassbaender (bar), Karl Dönch (bar), Dietrich Fischer-Dieskau (bar), Erich Kunz (bar), Eberhard Wächter (bar), Hans Hotter (b-bar), Paul Schöffler (b-bar), Cesare Siepi (b-bar), José Van Dam (b-bar), Walter Berry (bass), Geraint Evans (bass), Nicolai Ghiaurov (bass), Alexander Kipnis (bass), Richard Mayr (bass), Kurt Moll (bass), James Morris (bass), Ezio Pinza (bass), Martti Talvela (bass), Giorgio Tozzi (bass), Hans Duhan (sgr), Res Fischer (sgr), Marie Gerhart (sgr), *(various orchs & cnds)* —sels from Idomeneo, Die Entführung aus der Serail, Le nozze di Figaro, Don Giovanni, Così fan tutte, Die Zauberflöte & various arias Orfeo d'or ("Festspiel Dokumente" series) 5-▲ 408955

Mozart, W.A.:Nozze di Figaro, w. Irma Beilke (sop), Gerda Sommerschuh (sop), Josef Witt (ten), Hans Hotter (bar), Erich Kunz (bar), Gustav Neidlinger (b-bar), C. Krauss (cnd), Vienna PO, Vienna State Opera Chorus *(rec live, Salzburg Festival, Aug. 1942)* Preiser 3-▲ PRE 90203 [ADD]

Wagner, R.:Lohengrin, w. H. Braun (sop—Ortrud), T. Epperle (sop—Elsa von Brabant), P. Anders (ten—Lohengrin), C. Kronenberg (bar—Frederich von Telramund), J. Greindl (bass—Heinrich der Vogler), R. Kraus (cnd), Cologne RSO, Cologne Radio Chorus *(rec Nov. 1951)* Myto 3-▲ MCD 93485

Wagner, R.:Parsifal (sels), w. H. Braun (sop—Kundry), M. Lorenz (ten—Parsifal), P. Schöffler (b-bar—Amfortas), Reichwein, Knappertsbusch (cnd), Vienna State Opera Orch, Vienna State Opera Chorus Koch Schwann 2-▲ SCH 314562 [ADD]

Wagner, R.:Tristan und Isolde, w. Helena Braun (sop—Isolde), Margarete Klose (mez—Brangäne), Günther Treptow (ten—Tristan), Paul Kuen (ten—Ein Hirte), Albrecht Peter (bar—Melot), Fritz Richard Bender (bar—Ein Steuermann), Ferdinand Frantz (b-bar—König Marke), Paul Schöffler (b-bar—Kurwenal), H. Knappertsbusch (cnd), Bavarian State Opera Orch, Bavarian State Opera Chorus *(rec live, Prinzregententheater, July 23, 1950)* Orfeo 3-▲ 355

Braun, Jella von (alt)

Mozart, W.A.:Requiem, w. Hanna Seebach-Ziegler (sop), Hermann Gallos (ten), Richard Mayr (bass), J. Messner (cnd), Cathedral Choral Society Orch, Salzburg Cathedral Choir *(rec Aug 9, 1931)* Orfeo d'or ("Festspiel Dokumente" series) ▲ 396951

Braun, Lioba (alt)

Brahms, J.:Alto Rhap, w. K.-F. Beringer (cnd), Austro-Hungarian PO, Windsbach Boys' Choir *(rec Ansbach, July 1996)* Hänssler Classic 2-▲ CD 98.134 [DDD]

Mendelssohn, F.:Sym 2, w. Pamela Coburn (sop), Deon van der Walt (ten), K.-F. Beringer (cnd), Austro-Hungarian PO *(rec Ansbach, July 1996)* Hänssler Classic 2-▲ CD 98.134 [DDD]

Braun, Mel (bar)

Handel, G.F.:Floridante (sels), w. Nancy Argenta (sop—Rossane), Ingrid Attrot (sop—Timante), Linda Maguire (mez—Elmira), Catherine Robbin (mez—Floridante), Mel Braun (bar—Coralbo/Orontes), A. Curtis (cnd), Tafelmusik [I] CBC ("SM 5000" series) ▲ SMCD 5110 [DDD]

Braun, Russell (bar)

Brahms, J.:Liebeslieder Waltzes SATB, w. Kathleen Brett (sop), Catherine Robbin (mez), Benjamin Butterfield (ten), Stephen Ralls (pno), Bruce Ubukata (pno) *(rec Glenn Gould Studio, CBC Toronto, Dec. 7-9, 1993)* CBC ("Musica Viva" series) ▲ MVCD 1077 [DDD]

Greer, J.:All Around the Circle, w. Kathleen Brett (sop), Catherine Robbin (mez), Benjamin Butterfield (ten), Stephen Ralls (pno), Bruce Ubukata (pno) *(rec Glenn Gould Studio, CBC Toronto, Dec. 7-9, 1993)* CBC ("Musica Viva" series) ▲ MVCD 1077 [DDD]

Purcell, H.:Dido & Aeneas, w. Meredith Hall (sop—2nd Witch/Spirit), Ann Monoyios (sop—Belinda), Shari Saunders (sop—2nd Woman/1st Woman), Jennifer Lane (mez—Dido/Sorceress), Benjamin Butterfield (ten—Sailor), Russell Braun (bar—Aeneas), J. Lamon (cnd), Tafelmusik, Tafelmusik Chamber Choir *(rec Glenn Gould Studio, CBC Toronto, Apr 26-29, 1995)* CBC ▲ SM5 5147 [DDD]

Purcell, H.:Dido & Aeneas, w. Nancy Maultsby (sop—Dido), Susannah Waters (sop—Belinda), Margaret O'Keefe (sop—1st Witch), Sharon Baker (sop—2nd Woman), Laura Tucker (mez—Sorceress), Donna Ames (alt—Spirit), Richard Clement (ten—Sailor), Russell Braun (bar—Aeneas), M. Pearlman (cnd), Boston Baroque Orch Telarc ▲ CD 80424 [DDD]

Schumann, R.:Spanische Liebeslieder, w. Kathleen Brett (sop), Catherine Robbin (mez), Benjamin Butterfield (ten), Stephen Ralls (pno), Bruce Ubukata (pno) CBC ("Musica Viva" series) ▲ MVCD 1077 [DDD]

Le Souvenir, w. S. Dibblee (sop), Carolyn Maule (pno) Centrediscs ("Lacalée" series) ▲ CMC CD 5696 [DDD]

Braun, Victor (bar)

Brahms, J.:Ernste Gesänge, w. A. Kubalek (pno) [G] Dorian ▲ DOR 90132 [DDD]

Schubert, Franz:Winterreise, w. A. Kubalek (pno) [G] Dorian ▲ DOR 90145 [DDD]

Schumann, R.:Liederkreis, Op. 24, w. A. Kubalek (pno) [G] Dorian ▲ DOR 90132 [DDD]

Schumann, R.:Liederkreis, Op. 39, w. A. Kubalek (pno) [G] Dorian ▲ DOR 90132 [DDD]

Verdi, G.:La traviata (sels), w. Ileana Cotrubas (sop—Violetta), Elizabeth Bainbridge (mez—Annina), José Carreras (ten—Alfredo), Richard Creeger (ten—Gastone), Victor Braun (bar—Germont), Richard Van Allen (bass—Grenvil), J. Pritchard (cnd), *(orch unknown)*—Libiamo ne' lietialici; Oh, qual pallor!...Un di felice; Ebben? Che diavol fate?...Amor, dunque non piu; E strano!...Ah, fors'e lui; Follie! Follie!...Sempre libera; Lunge da lei...De' miei bollenti spiriti; Che fai?...Amami, Alfredo; Invitato a qui seguirmi...Ogni suo aver tal femmina; Signora...Parigi, o cara; Ah, non piu...Ah, gran Dio, morir si giovine; E strano! Cessarono gli spasimi del dolore *(rec Apr 15, 1974)* Legato Classics 2-▲ LCD 201-2

Brauner, Hilde (cta)

Benatzky, R.:Im weissen Rössl (sels), w. F. Loor (sop), K. Equiluz (ten), K. Terkal (ten), F. Bauer-Theussl (cnd), Vienna Volksoper Orch, Vienna Volksoper Chorus [G] Koch Präsent ▲ CD 399225 [AAD]

Lehár, F.:Der Graf von Luxemburg (sels), w. Renate Holm (sop), Else Liebesberg (sop), Dagmar Hermann (mez), Rudolf Christ (ten), Herbert Prikopa (bar), F. Bauer-Theussl (cnd), Vienna Volksoper Orch, Vienna Volksoper Chorus [G] Koch Präsent ▲ CD 399223 [AAD]

Straus, O.:Ein Walzertraum (sels), w. R. Holm (sop), E. Liebesberg (sop), D. Hermann (mez), R. Christ (ten), H. Prikopa (bar), F. Bauer-Theussl (cnd), Vienna Volksoper Orch, Vienna Volksoper Chorus [G] Koch Präsent ▲ CD 399223 [AAD]

Bräutigam, Thomas (ten)

Weill, K.:Der Jasager, w. H. Helling (cta), T. Schmeisser (treb), T. Fischer (ten), U. Schütte (bar), M. Knöppel (bass), W. Gundlach (cnd), Westphalia CO, Westphalia Kantorei Capriccio ▲ 60 020-1 [DDD]

Brechbüller, Peter (bar)

Sauguet, H.:L'Espace du dedans Sonpact ▲ SPT 93008 [DDD]

Sauguet, H.:Visions infernales, w. D. Abramovitz (pno) Sonpact ▲ SPT 93008 [DDD]

Breck (sgr)

Künneke, E.:Der Vetter aus Dingsda (sels), w. G. Van Jüten (sop), Kollo (ten), B. Kusche (bar), Wolff (sgr), Geese, Künneke (cnd), Cologne RSO, Cologne Radio Chorus [G] Acanta ▲ CD 43460 [DDD]

Brecknock, John (ten)

Elgar, E.:Songs, w. V. Morris (pno), D. Temple (cnd), London Phil Chamber Choir—20 songs—O Happy Eyes; Love; To Her Beneath Whose Stedfast Star; Is She Not Passing Fair?; Sheperd's Song; Weary Wind of the West; Evening Scene; Windlass Song; Poet's Life; Song of Autumn; Death on the Hills; Serenade; Credo in e; Was it Some Golden Star?; Speak, Music; Lo! Christ the Lord is Risen; O Mightiest of the Mighty; The River; How Calmly the Evening; Good Morrow [E] Meridian ▲ CDE 84173

Brégan, Antonieta de (sop)

Villa-Lobos, H.:Songs, w. Y. Storms (gtr)—Canção do Poeta; Duas Paisagens; Canção de Cristal Xangô; Samba Clássico; Jardim Fanado; Vôo; Dinga-Donga; Canção do Carreiro; Bachianas Brasileiras No. 5; Canide Ioune [Port] Pavane ▲ ADW 7256 [DDD]

Brehu, T. (ten)

Josquin Desprez:Missa, "Ave Maris Stella", w. D. Collot (sop), R. Holton (sop), J.-L. Comoretto (ct), R. Le Chenadec (ct), H. Lamy (ten), B. Fabre-Garrus (bar), J. Gowings (bar) *(rec Jan. 1993)* Astrée ▲ E 8507 [DDD]

Josquin Desprez:Motets, w. D. Collot (sop), R. Holton (sop), J.-L. Comoretto (ct), R. Le Chenadec (ct), H. Lamy (ten), B. Fabre-Garrus (bar), J. Gowings (bar)—Motets à la vierge *(rec Jan. 1993)* Astrée ▲ E 8507 [DDD]

Brekke, Ingeborg Marie (alt)

Braein, E.F.:Anne Pedersdotter, w. K. Ekeberg (sop—Anne Pedersdotter), V. Hanssen (mez—Merete Beyer), R. Eriksen (alt—Herlofs-Marte), I. M. Brekke (alt—Bente), K. M. Sandve (ten—Martin Beyer), C. Ehrstedt (ten—Master Olaus), A. Helleland (ten—David), T. Gilje (ten—Jørund), S. A. Thorsen (bar—Master Johannes), S. Carlsen (bass—Absalon Pedersøn Beyer), T. Stensvold (bass—Master Laurentius), G. Oskarsson (bass—Jens Schelderup), P. Andersson (cnd), Norwegian National Opera Orch, Norwegian National Opera Chorus Simax 2-▲ PSC 3121

Brendel, Wolfgang (bar)

Mozart, W.A.:Zauberflöte, w. L. Popp (sop), E. Gruberova (sop), S. Jerusalem (ten), R. Bracht (bass), B. Haitink (cnd), Bavarian RSO, Bavarian Radio Chorus [G] EMI Classics 3-▲ CDCC 47951 [DDD]

Mozart, W.A.:Zauberflöte (sels), w. L. Popp (sop), E. Gruberova (sop), S. Jerusalem (ten), R. Bracht (bass), B. Haitink (cnd), Bavarian RSO, Bavarian Radio Chorus [G] EMI Classics ▲ CDC 47008 [DDD]

Strauss (II), Joh.:Die Fledermaus, w. K. Te Kanawa (sop), E. Gruberová (sop), B. Fassbaender (mez), R. Leech (ten), O. Bär (bar), T. Krause (bar), A. Previn (cnd), Vienna PO, Vienna State Opera Chorus [G] Philips 2-▲ 432157-2 [DDD]

Strauss (II), Joh.:Die Fledermaus, w. L. Popp (sop), E. Lind (sop), A. Baltsa (mez), P. Domingo (ten), K. Rydl (bass), P. Domingo (cnd), Munich RSO, Bavarian Radio Chorus [G] EMI Classics 2-▲ CDCB 47480

Strauss (II), Joh.:Die Fledermaus (sels), w. K. Te Kanawa (sop), E. Gruberova (sop), B. Fassbaender (mez), R. Leech (ten), O. Bär (bar), A. Previn (cnd), Vienna PO Philips ▲ 438503-2

Strauss (II), Joh.:Eine Nacht in Venedig (sels), w. J. Scovotti (sop), E. Schary (mez), E. Steiner (mez), C. Bini (ten), F. Stricker (ten), E. Märzendorfer (cnd), Hungarian State Orch, Hungarian State Chorus [G] Acanta ▲ CD 43809 [DDD]

Bressler, Charles (ten)

Flowering of Vocal Music in America, 1767-1823, w. Susan Belling (sop), Cynthia Clarey (sop), Barbara Wallace (sop), Debra Vanderlinde (sop), D'Anna Fortunato (mez), Evelyn Petros (mez), Richard Anderson (bar), James Tyeska (bar), Joseph McKee (bass), Cynthia Otis (hp), et al. New World ▲ 80467-2

Liszt, F.:A Faust Sym, w. L. Bernstein (cnd), New York PO, Choral Arts Society *(rec 1960)* Sony Classical ("Bernstein:The Royal Edition" series) ▲ SMK 47570 [ADD]

Music of the Middle Ages, Vol. 4:English Polyphony of the 13th & Early 14th Centuries, w. R. Oberlin (ct), D. Perry (ten), S. Barab (vl), M. Blackman (vl) Lyrichord ▲ LYR 8004 [ADD]

Music of the Middle Ages, Vol. 6:English Polyphony of the 14th & Early 15th Centuries, w. R. Oberlin (ct), R. Price (ten), G. Meyers (bar), M. Blackman (vl) Lyrichord ▲ LYR 8006 [ADD]

Music of the Middle Ages, Vol. 7, w. French Ars Antiqua, Russell Oberlin (ct), R. Price (ten), G. Meyers (bar), M. Blackman (vl), P. Wolfe (org) Lyrichord ▲ LYR 8007 [ADD]

Notre Dame Organa Leonius & Perotinus Magister, w. R. Oberlin (ct), D. Perry (ten), S. Barab (vl) Lyrichord ▲ LYR 8002 [ADD]

Weisgall, H.:End of Summer, w. New York Chamber Soloists CRI ■ C 343

Brett, Charles (ct)

Bach, J.S.:Mass in b, BWV 232, w. B. Schlick (sop), C. Patriasz (cta), H. Crook (ten), P. Kooy (bass), P. Herreweghe (cnd), Collegium Vocale Orch, Collegium Vocale [L] Virgin Classics ("Veritas" series) 2-▲ CDCB 59517-2 [DDD]

Handel, G.F.:Dixit Dominus, w. Lynn Dawson (sop), Linda Russell (alt), Ian Partridge (ten), Michael George (bass), H. Christophers (cnd), The Sixteen Orch, The Sixteen [L] Chandos ("Chaconne" series) ▲ CHAN 0517 [DDD]

Handel, G.F.:Israel in Egypt, w. Norma Burrowes (sop), Paul Elliot (sgr), J.E. Gardiner (cnd), Monteverdi Orch, Monteverdi Choir London Erato 2-▲ 2292-45399-2 ZA

Handel, G.F.:Messiah, w. Saul Quirke (trb), Margaret Marshall (sop), Catherine Robbin (mez), Anthony Rolfe Johnson (ten), Robert Hale (b-bar), J. E. Gardiner (cnd), English Baroque Soloists, Monteverdi Choir London [E] Philips 3-▲ 411041-2 [DDD]

Handel, G.F.:Messiah, w. Saul Quirke (trb), Margaret Marshall (sop), Catherine Robbin (mez), Anthony Rolfe Johnson (ten), Robert Hale (b-bar), J. E. Gardiner (cnd), English Baroque Soloists, Monteverdi Choir London [E] Philips ▲ 412267-2 [DDD]

Handel, G.F.:Nisi Dominus, w. Ian Partridge (ten), Michael George (bass), H. Christophers (cnd), The Sixteen Orch, The Sixteen [L] Chandos ("Chaconne" series) ▲ CHAN 0517 [DDD]

Handel, G.F.:Rinaldo, w. Sophie Boulin (sop—Donna), Ileana Cotrubas (sop—Almirena), Marie-Françoise Jacquelin (sop—Sirene), Nicole Leport (sop—Sirene), Jeanette Scovotti (sop—Armida), Carolyn Watkinson (cta—Rinaldo), Charles Brett (ct—Eustazio), Paul Esswood (ct—Goffredo), Armand Arapian (ten—Mago Christiano/Araldo), Ulrik Cold (bass—Argante), J. Malgoire (cnd), La Grande Écurie et la Chambre du Roy *(rec Paris, 1977)* Sony Classical 3-▲ SM3K 34592

Handel, G.F.:St. John Passion, w. Mária Zádori (sop), Judit Németh (mez), Martin Klietmann (ten), Jósef Moldvay (bass), G. Németh (cnd), Capella Savaria, Capella Savaria Hungaroton ▲ HCD 12908 [DDD]

Handel, G.F.:The Triumph of Time & Truth, w. James Goodman (trb), Fisher (sop), Emma Kirkby (sop), Ian Partridge (ten), Stephen Varcoe (bar), D. Darlow (cnd), London Handel Orch, London Handel Chorus [E] Hyperion 2-▲ CDA 66071/72

Handel, G.F.:The Ways of Zion Do Mourn, w. Norma Burrowes (sop), Paul Elliot (ten), J.E. Gardiner (cnd), Monteverdi Orch, Monteverdi Choir London Erato 2-▲ 2292-45399-2 ZA

Holloway, R.:Sea Surface Full of Clouds, w. P. Walmsley-Clark (sop), M. Cable (mez), M. Hill (ten), R. Hickox (cnd), City of London Sinfonia Chandos ▲ CHAN 9228 [DDD]

Monteverdi, C.:Vespro della Beata Vergine, w. Elly Ameling (sop), Norma Burrowes (sop), Robert Tear (ten), Anthony Rolfe Johnson (ten), Martyn Hill (ten), Peter Knapp (bass), John Noble (bass), Munrow, Ledger (cnd), London Early Music Consort EMI Classics ("Doublefforte" series) 2-▲ CDFB 68631

Monteverdi, C.:Vespro della Beata Vergine, w. Elly Ameling (sop), Norma Burrowes (sop), Martyn Hill (ten), Anthony Rolfe-Johnson (ten), Robert Tear (ten), Peter Knapp (bass), John Noble (bass), Francis Grier (org/hpd), James Lancelot (org/hpd), Andrew Leach (org/hpd), P. Ledger (cnd), London Early Music Consort, King's College Choir Cambridge—Nigra sum [con.]; Laudate pueri [psalm]; Sancta Maria [son. sopra]; Magnificat *(rec Chapel of King's College, Cambridge, July & Aug. 1975)* EMI Classics ▲ CDK 65339 [ADD]

Brett, Kathleen (sop)

Brahms, J.:Liebeslieder Waltzes SATB, w. Catherine Robbin (mez), Benjamin Butterfield (ten), Russell Braun (bar), Stephen Ralls (pno), Bruce Ubukata (pno) *(rec Glenn Gould Studio, CBC Toronto, Dec. 7-9, 1993)* CBC ("Musica Viva" series) ▲ MVCD 1077 [DDD]

Greer, J.:All Around the Circle, w. Catherine Robbin (mez), Benjamin Butterfield (ten), Russell Braun (bar), Stephen Ralls (pno), Bruce Ubukata (pno) *(rec Glenn Gould Studio, CBC Toronto, Dec. 7-9, 1993)* CBC ("Musica Viva" series) ▲ MVCD 1077 [DDD]

Greer, J.:All Around the Circle, w. Catherine Robbin (mez), Benjamin Butterfield (ten), Russell Braun (bar), Stephen Ralls (pno), Bruce Ubukata (pno) CBC ▲ MVV 1077 [DDD]

Schumann, R.:Spanische Liebeslieder, w. Catherine Robbin (mez), Benjamin Butterfield (ten), Russell Braun (bar), Stephen Ralls (pno), Bruce Ubukata (pno) CBC ("Musica Viva" series) ▲ MVCD 1077 [DDD]

Breul, Elisabeth (sop)

Beethoven, L. van:Egmont (incidental music), w. Horst Schulze (spkr), H. Bongartz (cnd), Berlin State Orch Berlin Classics ▲ BER 9106

Breviario, Giovanni (ten)

Bellini, V.:Norma, w. G. Cigna (sop), E. Stignani (mez), V. Gui (cnd), EIAR Orch, EIAR Chorus [I] *(rec 1936 for Cetra)* Pearl 2-▲ PEAS 9422 (m) [AAD]

Bellini, V.:Norma, w. G. Cigna (sop), E. Stignani (mez), T. Pasero (bass), V. Gui (cnd), Turin EIAR SO, Turin EIAR Chorus *(rec 1937)* Memories 2-▲ MEM 4552 [ADD]

Bellini, V.:Norma, w. Gina Signa (sop), Ebe Stignani (mez), Tancredi Pasero (bass), V. Gui (cnd), Turin EIAR SO, Turin EIAR Chorus *(rec 1937)* Grammofono 2000 2-▲ GRM 78583

Breviario, Giovanni (ten) (cont.)

Bellini, V.:Norma, w. Gina Cigna (sop—Norma), Ebe Stignani (sop—Adalgisa), Adriana Perris (mez—Clotilde), Giovanni Breviario (ten—Pollione), Emilio Renzi (ten—Flavio), Tancredi Pasero (bass—Oroveso), V. Gui (cnd), EIAR Orch, Achille Consoli (cnd), EIAR Chorus *(rec Aug/Sept 1937)* Arkadia ("The 78's" series) 2–▲ 78010 [ADD]

Mascagni, P.:Cavalleria rusticana, w. Delia Sanzio (sop—Santuzza), Mimma Pantaleoni (mez—Lola), Olga de Franco (cta—Lucia), Giovanni Breviario (ten—Turiddu), Piero Biasini (bar—Alfio), C. Sabajno (cnd), La Scala Orch, La Scala Chorus VAI Audio ▲ VAIA 1082–2

Brewer, Bruce (ten)

Rameau, J.P.:Les Paladins, w. A. Michael (sop), G. Raphanel (sop), D. Nasrawi (ten), G. Reinhart (bar), N. Rivenq (bar), J. Malgoire (cnd), La Grande Écurie et la Chambre du Roy, Sagittarius Vocal Ensemble [F] Pierre Verany 2–▲ PV.790121/22 [DDD]

Brewer, Christine (sop)

Janácek, L.:Slavonic Mass, w. M. Simpson (mez), K. Dent (ten), R. Roloff (bass), R. Shaw (cnd), Atlanta SO, Atlanta Sym Chorus [Sla] Telarc ▲ CD 80287 [DDD]

Mozart, W.A.:Don Giovanni, w. Christine Brewer (sop—Donna Anna), Nuccia Focile (sop—Zerlina), Felicity Lott (sop—Donna Elvira), Jerry Hadley (ten—Don Ottavio), Bo Skovhus (bar—Don Giovanni), Umberto Chiummo (bass—Masetto/Il Commendatore), Alessandro Corbelli (bass—Leporello), C. Mackerras (cnd), Scottish CO, Scottish Chamber Chorus *(rec Usher Hall, Edinburgh, Scotland, July 31–Aug 11, 1995)* Telarc 3–▲ CD 80420 [DDD]

Briant, Hester (sgr)

Hildegard Of Bingen:Sacred Songs, w. Jocelyn West (sgr), Vivien Ellis (sgr), Stevie Wishart (sgr/h–g), Fiona Cunningham (sgr), Tara Franks (sgr), Emily Levy (sgr), Lucy Steele (sgr), Vickie Couperim (sgr), Julie Murphy (sgr), Oxford Girls' Choir—Honey & milk beneath her tongue; Ursula's virgins; The devil's virgins; Place of the ancient heart; Zeal of divinity; O fiery spirit; Red river falling; O orzchis ecclesia, Living–light angels; The clouds are grieving; The firstwoman; From their homeland; But the devil mocked; Song to Ecclesia *(rec Toddington, Gloucestershire, England, May 6–8, 1995)*. Celestial Harmonies ▲ 13127–2

Bridge, T. W. (ten)

Pinkham, D.:Wedding Cant, w. C. Swistro (sop), B. Bruns (pno), Boston Cecilia *(rec Dec. 1992)* Koch International Classics ▲ KIC 7180 [DDD]

Bridges, Lloyd (nar)

Prokofiev, S.:Peter & the Wolf, w. Kirstie Alley (nar), Ross Malinger (nar), G. Daugherty (cnd), RCA Victor SO—2 versions:1 with narration & 1 without *(rec Studio 1 & LA Studios East, Salt Lake City, Utah)* RCA Gold Seal ▲ 74321–31869–2 [DDD]

Briem, Tilla (sop)

Beethoven, L. van:Sym 9, "Choral Sym", w. Elisabeth Höngen (cta), Peter Anders (ten), Rudolf Watzke (bass), W. Furtwängler (cnd), Berlin PO, Bruno Kittel Choir *(rec 1942)* Grammofono 2000 ▲ GRM 78581

Beethoven, L. van:Sym 9, "Choral Sym", w. Elisabeth Höngen (cta), Peter Anders (ten), Rudolf Watzke (bass), W. Furtwängler (cnd), Berlin PO, Bruno Kittel Choir *(rec Mar 22, 1942)* Iron Needle 3–▲ IN 1348/50 [ADD]

Brightman, Sarah (sop)

Britten, H.:Folksong Arrs, w. G. Parsons (pno)—Early One Morning; Come You Not from Newcastle?; Sweet Polly Oliver; The Trees They Grow So High; The Ash Grove; O Waly, Waly; How Sweet the Answer; The Plough Boy; Voici le printemps; The Last Rose of Summer; La belle est au jardin d'amour; Fileuse; Dear Harp of My Country; Little Sir William; O Can Ye Sew Cushions?; Oft in the Silly Night; Quand j'etais chez mon père; There's None to Soothe; Oliver Cromwell Classics for Pleasure ▲ CDCFP 4636 [DDD]

Lloyd Webber, A.:Music of, w. J. Carreras (ten), P. Domingo (ten), M. Crawford (sgr), Royal PO—Cats; Joseph & the Amazing Technicolor Dreamcoat; Requiem; Jesus Christ Superstar; Phantom of the Opera; Aspects of Love; Starlight Express; Evita Polydor ▲ 314 517336–2 ■ 314 517336–4

Lloyd Webber, A.:The Phantom of the Opera, w. M. Crawford (sgr) [1986 London cast] Polydor 2–▲ 831273–2 2 ■ 831273–4

Lloyd Webber, A.:Requiem for Soloists, Orch & Chorus, w. Paul Miles–Kingston (trb), Placido Domingo (ten), L. Maazel (cnd), English CO, Winchester Cathedral Choir [L] EMI Classics ▲ CDC 47146 [DDD] ■ 4DS 38218 (D)

Lloyd Webber, A.:Requiem for Soloists, Orch & Chorus, w. Paul Miles–Kingston (trb), Placido Domingo (ten), L. Maazel (cnd), English CO, Winchester Cathedral Choir *(rec Studio 1, Abbey Road, London, Dec 20–22, 1984)* London ▲ 448616–2 ■ 48616

Rodgers, R.:Carousel, w. B. Cook (sop), S. Ramey (bass), M. Forrester (cta), et al., P. Geminiani (cnd), Royal PO, Ambrosian Singers [1987 studio cast] MCA Classics ▲ MCAD 6209 [DDD] ■ MCAC 6209

Brilioth, Helge (ten)

Wagner, R.:Tristan und Isolde, w. C. Ligendza (sop—Isolde), Y. Minton (mez—Brangäne), H. Brilioth (ten—Tristan), K. Moll (bass—King Mark), C. Kleiber (cnd), Bayreuth Festival Orch, Bayreuth Festival Chorus *(rec Bayreuth Festival, 1975)* Exclusive 3–▲ EXL 54 [ADD]

Brim, Alton (sgr)

Floyd, C.:Susannah, w. Phyllis Curtin (sop—Susannah Polk), Richard Cassilly (ten—Sam Polk), Norman Treigle (bass—Olin Blitch), Marietta Muhs Cosenza (sgr—Mrs. McLean), Marilyn Davidson (sgr—Mrs. Gleaton), Kay Long (sgr—Mrs. Hayes), Jean Young (sgr—Mrs. Ott), Alton Brim (sgr—Elder Hayes), Thomas Carter (sgr—Elder Gleaton), Jack Davis (sgr—Elder McLean), Keith Kaldenberg (sgr—Little Bat McLean), Burton Parker (sgr—Elder Ott), K. Andersson (cnd), New Orleans Opera Orch, New Orleans Opera Chorus *(rec Mar 31, 1962)* VAI Audio 2–▲ VAIA 1115–2 [ADD]

Offenbach, J.:Les Contes d'Hoffmann, w. Beverly Sills (sop—Olympia/Giulietta/Antonia/Stella), Edith Evans (mez—Nicklausse/Mother's Voice), Michael Devlin (ten—Spalanzani), André Turp (ten—Hoffmann), Luigi Vellucci (ten—Andrès/Cochenille/Pitichinaccio/Frantz), Donald Bernard (bar—Luther/Schlemil), Norman Treigle (bass—Lindorf/Coppélius/Dapertutto/Dr. Miracle), John West (bass—Crespel), Alton Brim (sgr—Nathanaël), Rodney Hall (sgr—Hermann), K. Andersson (cnd), New Orleans Opera Orch, New Orleans Opera Chorus *(rec Feb 27, 1964)* VAI Audio 2–▲ VAIA 1121–2 [ADD]

Brinkmann, Bodo (bar)

Wagner, R.:Das Rheingold, w. L. Finnie (mez—Fricka), G. Clark (ten—Loge), J. Tomlinson (bar—Wotan), B. Brinkmann (bar—Donner), D. Barenboim (cnd), Bayreuth Festival Orch, Bayreuth Festival Chorus [G] Teldec 2–▲ 4509–91185–2

Wagner, R.:Rienzi, der Letzte der Tribunen, w. Cheryl Studer (sop—Irene), René Kollo (ten—Rienzi), Friedrich Lenz (ten—Gesandte), Norbert Orth (ten—Baroncelli), Bodo Brinkmann (bar—Paolo Orsini), Keith Engen (bass—Cecco del Vecchio), Raimund Grumbach (bass—Gesandte), Jan–Hendrik Rootering (bass—Steffano Colonna), Carmen Anhorn (sgr—Ein Friedensbote), Karl Helm (sgr—Kardinal Orvieto), John Janssen (sgr—Adriano), Alfred Kuhn (sgr—Gesandte), Hans Wilbrink (sgr—Gesandte), W. Sawallisch (cnd), Bavarian State Opera Orch, Bavarian State Opera Chorus *(rec live, July 6, 1983)* Orfeo d'or 3–▲ 346953

Britton, P. (sgr)

Lerner, A.J.:Brigadoon, w. D. Brooks (sgr), M. Bell (sgr), L. Sullivan (sgr) [1947 Broadway original cast] RCA ▲ 1001–2 RG [ADD] ■ 1001–4 RG

Brivkalne, Paula (sop)

Wagner, R.:Das Rheingold, w. I. Malaniuk (cta), R. Siewert (cta), Fritz (sgr), Pflanzl (ten), S. Björling (bar), W. Faulhaber (bass), L. Weber (bass), F. Dalberg (bass), H. von Karajan (cnd), Bayreuth Festival Orch, Bayreuth Festival Chorus [G] *(rec live 8/1/51)* Melodram 2–▲ MEL 26107 (m) [AAD]

Bröcheler, John (bass)

Bach, J.S.:Cant 99, w. A. Augér (sop), H. Watts (cta), L.–M. Harder (ten), H. Rilling (cnd), Stuttgart Bach Collegium, Gächinger Kantorei [G] *(rec 1979)* Hänssler Classic ▲ 98.813 [AAD]

Bach, J.S.:Cant 101, w. A. Augér (sop), H. Watts (cta), A. Baldin (ten), H. Rilling (cnd), Stuttgart Bach Collegium, Gächinger Kantorei Hänssler Classic ▲ 98.809 [AAD]

Bach, J.S.:Cant 107, w. A. Augér (sop), A. Baldin (ten), H. Rilling (cnd), Stuttgart Bach Collegium, Gächinger Kantorei Hänssler Classic ▲ 98.805 [AAD]

Busoni, F.:Berceuse élégiaque, w. J. van Nes (alt), Schoenberg Ensemble Koch Schwann ▲ SCH 312632 [DDD]

Bröcheler, John (bass) (cont.)

Mahler, G.:Kindertotenlieder, w. J. Van Nes (alt), Schoenberg Ensemble Koch Schwann ▲ SCH 312632 [DDD]

Mahler, G.:Des Knaben Wunderhorn, w. J. Van Ness (cta), R. Benzi (cnd), Arnheim PO Ottavo ▲ OTT 79238 [DDD]

Mahler, G.:Lieder eines fahrenden Gesellen, w. J. Van Nes (alt), Schoenberg Ensemble Koch Schwann ▲ SCH 312632 [DDD]

Brockenbrough, Mary (sop)

Lovenstein, J.:Music of, w. Laura Sanders (sop), Barton Green (ten), Rockland Osgood (ten), David Murray (bar), Benjamin Sears (bar), Jonathan Lovenstein (pno), Heather O'Donnell (pno), James Silvers (pno), Rocy Reider (fl), Jason Horowitz (vn), Adrianna Hulscher (vn), James Johnston (vn), Mimi Ragson (vn), Peter Landeen (vc), Reinmar Seidler (vc)—Blake Songs; other works Titanic ▲ Ti 221 [DDD]

Brodalka, F. (nar)

Bolleter, R.:Labyrinth, w. R. Bolleter (acc/ruined pno/nar) Tall Poppies ▲ TP 45 [DDD]

Brodalka, L. (nar)

Bolleter, R.:Labyrinth, w. R. Bolleter (acc/ruined pno/nar), F. Brodalka (nar) Tall Poppies ▲ TP 45 [DDD]

Brodard, Michel (bar)

Bach, J.S.:Christmas Oratorio, w. B. Schlick (sop), C. Watkinson (cta), K. Equiluz (ten), M. Corboz (cnd), Lausanne CO Erato ▲ 2292–45865–2

Beethoven, L. van:Mass, Op. 86, w. A. Michael (sop), L. Bizimeche–Eisinger (mez), M. Schaeffer (ten), M. Corboz (cnd), Lisbon Gulbenkian Foundation Orch, Lisbon Gulbenkian Foundation Chorus [L] Erato ▲ 2292–45461–2 ZK [DDD]

Bomtempo, J.D.:Messe de requiem consacrée à...Camões, w. Angela Maria Blasi (sop), Liliana Bizineche–Eisinger (mez), Reinaldo Macias (ten), M. Corboz (cnd), Lisbon Gulbenkian Foundation Orch, Lisbon Gulbenkian Foundation Chorus *(rec Gulbenkian Foundation Grand Auditorium, June 14–16, 1994)* FNAC Music ▲ 592302 [DDD]

Burkhard, W.:Mass, Op. 85, w. K. Beidler (sop), H. Gafner (cnd), Bern SO, Bern Gabrieli Chorus Jecklin ▲ JD 687

Carvalho, J. de S.:Te Deum, w. Brigitte Fournier (sop), Naoko Okada (sop), Elisabeth Graf (cta), John Elwes (ten), M. Corboz (cnd), Lisbon Gulbenkian Foundation Orch, Lisbon Gulbenkian Foundation Chorus Cascavelle ▲ CVL 1016 [DDD]

Marescotti, A.–F.:Insomnies, w. Jean–Claude Charrez (pno) [arr for Bass & Pno] Grammont ▲ CTSP 13–2

Orff, C.:Carmina burana, w. Brigitte Fournier (sop), Peter Sigrist (ten), Jean–Jacques Balet (pno), Mayumi Kameda (pno), Geneva Percussion Ensemble [version for 2 pnos & perc] Cascavelle ▲ CVL 1009 [DDD]

Rossini, G.:Péchés de vieillesse (sels), w. M. Castets (sop), M. Georg (mez), J.–L. Maurette (ten), R. Nolte (bass), E. Kalvelage (pno), C. Spering (org), M. Jorand (perc), Cologne Chorus Musicus—Toast pour le nouvel an, Roméo, La Grande Coquette, Un sou, Chanson de Zora, La Nuit de Noël, Le Dodo des enfants, Le Lazzarone, Adieux à la vie!, Soupirs et sourire, L'Orpheline du Tyrol, Choeur de chasseurs démocrates; *Morceaux réservés*—Ave Maria, Les Amants de Séville, Le Chant des Titans, Chant funèbre [F] *(rec Aug. 1992)* Opus 111 ▲ OPS 30–70 [DDD]

Stravinsky, I.:Requiem Canticles, w. Irène Friedli (alt), N. Järvi (cnd), Swiss Romande Orch, Lausanne Pro Arte Choir, Romande Chamber Choir Chandos ▲ CHAN 9408 [DDD]

Broderick, Matthew (sgr)

Loesser, F.:How to Succeed in Business without Really Trying, w. *(other artists unknown)* [Broadway cast] RCA ▲ 09026–68197–2 ■ 09026–68197–4

Broganelli, Daniela (cta)

Donizetti, G.:Olimpiade, w. S. Rigacci (sop), F. Maestri (cnd), In Canto CO *(rec May 1991)* Bongiovanni 2–▲ GB 2109/10 [DDD]

Haydn, J.:Lo Speziale, w. Gil Manuel Beltran (ten—Sempronio), Daniela Broganelli (sgr—Volpino), Cinzia Forte (sgr—Grilletta), Paolo Pellegrini (sgr—Mengone), Maurizio Gambini (vc), Marco Tinarelli (db), Gabriele Catalucci (hpd), F. Maestri (cnd), In Canto CO *(rec 1993)* Bongiovanni 2–▲ GB 2171/72 [DDD]

Broglia, Lauren (sop)

Puccini, G.:La Bohème, w. Katia Ricciarelli (sop), Francisco Araiza (ten), Angelo Casertano (ten), Stefano Antonucci (bar), Claudio Giombi (bar), Paata Burchuladze (bass), Alfredo Mariotti (bass), Alberto Noli (bass), Andrea Piccinni (bass), A. Guadagno (cnd), Arena di Verona Orch, Limburg Cathedral Boys' Chorus Koch Schwann 2–▲ SCH 315922

Broilo, R. (sop)

Rossini, G.:Il barbiere di Siviglia, w. R. Broilo (sop—Berta), G. Simionato (mez—Rosina), L. Infantino (ten—Almaviva), G. Taddei (bar—Figaro), C. Badioli (bass—Bartolo), A. Cassinelli (bass—Basilio), F. Previtali (cnd), Milan RAI SO, Milan RAI Chorus *(rec 1950)* Cetra Classic 2–▲ CDO 6 [AAD]

Verdi, G.:I lombardi alla prima crociata, w. Maria Vitale (sop), Miriam Pirazzini (mez), Aldo Bertocci (ten), Mario Frosini (sgr), Mario Petri (bass), Bruno Franchi (sgr), Gustavo Gallo (sgr), Renato Pasquali (sgr), M. Wolf–Ferrari (cnd), Milan RAI Lyric Orch, Milan RAI Chorus *(rec 1954)* Cetra Classic 2–▲ CDON 41 [ADD]

Brokmeier, Willi (ten)

Lincke, P.:Frau Luna (sels), w. Ingeborg Hallstein (sop), Renata Tebaldi (sop), W. Schmidt–Boelcke (cnd), Bavarian RSO, Bavarian Radio Chorus [G] Acanta ▲ CD 42484 [DDD]

Bron, A. (sgr)

Recital, w. I. Kozlovsky (ten), USSR SO [cnd:S. Samosud, A. Orlov, A. Bron] Myto ▲ MCD 921.55 [ADD]

Vol. 2, w. I. Kozlovsky (ten), USSR SO [cnd:S. Samosud, A. Orlov, A. Bron] Myto ▲ MCD 925.68 [ADD]

Bronder, Peter (ten)

Beethoven, L. van:Sym 9, "Choral Sym", w. Joan Rodgers (sop), Della Jones (alt), Bryn Terfel (bass), C. Mackerras (cnd), Royal Liverpool PO, Royal Liverpool Phil Choir Classics for Pleasure ("Eminence" series) ▲ CFP 2186 [DDD]

Bronsgeest, Cornelius (bar)

Wagner, R.:Parsifal, w. Gotthelf Pistor (ten), Ludwig Hofmann (bass), K. Muck (cnd), Berlin German Opera Orch, Berlin German Opera Chorus Preiser ▲ PRE 90270

Brooks, D. (sgr)

Lerner, A.J.:Brigadoon, w. M. Bell (sgr), P. Britton (sgr), L. Sullivan (sgr) [1947 Broadway original cast] RCA ▲ 1001–2 RG [ADD] ■ 1001–4 RG

Brooks, Patricia (sop)

Dittersdorf, K.D. von:Arcifanfano, King of Fools, or It's Always Too Late to Learn, w. A. Russell (sop), E. Steber (sop), J. McCollum (ten), J. Sopher (ten), H. Rehfuss (bar), D. Smith (bar), N. Jenkins (cnd), Clarion Music Society Orch, Clarion Music Society Chorus [E] *(rec live, New York 1965)* VAI Audio 2–▲ VAIA 1010–2 (m) [ADD]

Ward, R.:The Crucible, w. F. Bible (mez), C. Ludgin (bar), E. Buckley (cnd), New York City Opera Orch, New York City Opera Chorus [E] Albany 2–▲ TROY 025/26–2 [ADD]

Brouquet, Antoine (sop)

Boulanger, L.:Pie Jesu, w. J.–P. Salanne (cnd), Domaine Musical Orch Adès ▲ ADE 204782 [DDD]

Fauré, G.:Requiem, w. Jean–Marie Fremeau (bar), J.–P. Salanne (cnd), Domaine Musical Orch, Tarbes Midi–Pyrénées Régional Choir Adès ▲ ADE 204782 [DDD]

Brousek, Otakar (nar)

Báchorek, M.:Hukvald Poem, w. Drahomíra Drobková (sop), Břetislav Vojkůvka (ten), Pavel Kamas (bar), O. Trhlík (cnd), Prague SO, Ostrava Female Chamber Chorus, Permoník Children's Chorus *(rec Smetana Hall of Prague's Municipal House, Feb 10 & 11, 1988)* Panton ▲ 811338–2 [DDD]

Báchorek, M.:Music of, w. Osvald Albin (nar), Jan Vlassak (nar), Brigita Šulcová (sop), Drahomira Drobková (cta), Karel Průša (bass), Pavel Kamas (sgr), Jan Kyzlink (sgr), Jana Stuperkova–Majtnerova (sgr), Bretislav Vojkuvka (sgr), O. Trhlík (cnd), Ostrava Janáček PO, Prague SO, Ostrava Janáček Chorus, Ostrava Women's Chamber Chorus, Permoník Children's Chorus—Lidice; Stereofonietta; Hukvald Poem Panton ▲ PAN 811338 [AAD/DDD]

Brouwenstijn, Gré (sop)

Albert, E. d':Tiefland, w. G. Brouwenstijn, H. Hopf, W. Kmentt, E. Wächter, P. Schöffler, O. Czerwenka, R. Moralt (cnd), Vienna SO *(rec 1957)* Philips 2–▲ 434781–2

Brouwenstijn, Gré (sop) (cont.)
Beethoven, L. van:Ah, perfido!, w. O. Klemperer (cnd), Royal Concertgebouw Orch *(rec live April 26, 1951)* Music & Arts ▲ CD 752-1 (m) [AAD]
Beethoven, L. van:Ah, perfido!, w. O. Klemperer (cnd), Royal Concertgebouw Orch *(rec Amsterdam, Apr 26, 1951)* Bella Voce 2-▲ 107.201 [AAD]
Verdi, G.:Arias, *(various cnds & orchs)*—arias & scenes from Aida, Ballo in maschera, Forza del destino, Otello, Trovatore *(rec live, 1952–1958)* Verona ▲ 27056 (m) [AAD]
Verdi, G.:Don Carlos, w. G. Brouwenstein (sop—Elisabeta di Valois), F. Barbieri (mez—Princess Eboli), J. Vickers (ten—Don Carlo), T. Gobbi (bar—Rodrigo), B. Christoff (bass—Fillipo), C. M. Giulini (cnd), Royal Opera House Orch, Royal Opera House Chorus Covent Garden *(rec 1958)* Myto 3-▲ MCD 94197
Verdi, G.:Requiem Mass, w. Oralia Dominguez (mez), Giuseppe Zampieri (ten), Nicola Zaccaria (bass), G. Solti (cnd), Cologne RSO, Cologne Radio Chorus *(rec Nov 17, 1958)* Bella Voce 2-▲ 107.201 [AAD]
Verdi, G.:Requiem Mass, w. Oralia Dominguez (mez), Giuseppe Zampieri (ten), Nicola Zaccaria (bass), G. Solti (cnd), West German Radio Orch, West German Radio Chorus Globe 2-▲ GLO 5141 [ADD]
Wagner, R.:Der Ring des Nibelungen, w. Gré Brouwenstein (sop—Freia/Sieglinde), Ilse Hollweg (sop—Waldvogel), Gerda Lammers (sop—Ortlinde), Paula Lenchner (sop—Wellgunde/Gerhilde), Hilde Scheppan (sop—Helmwige), Astrid Varnay (sop—Brünnilde/3rd Norn), Lore Wissmann (sop—Woglinde), Maria von Ilosvay (mez—Flosshilde/Schwertleite/2nd Norn), Louise Charlotte Kamps (mez—Siegrune), Jean Madeira (mez—Erda/Rossweisse/1st Norn), Georgine van Milinkovic (mez—Fricka/Grimgerde), Elisabeth Schärtel (mez—Waltraute), Paul Kuën (ten—Mime), Ludwig Suthaus (ten—Loge), Josef Traxel (ten—Froh), Wolfgang Windgassen (ten—Siegmund/Siegfried), Alfons Herwig (bar—Donner), Hermann Uhde (bar—Gunther), Hans Hotter (b-bar—Wotan), Gustav Neidlinger (b-bar—Alberich), Josef Griendl (bass—Fasolt/Hunding/Hagen), Arnold van Mill (bass—Fafner), H. Knappertsbusch (cnd), Bayreuth Festival Orch, Bayreuth Festival Chorus *(rec live, Bayreuth, Aug 13–17, 1956)* Golden Melodram 14-▲ GM 1.001 [ADD]
Wagner, R.:Tannhäuser, w. R. Vinay (ten), D. Fischer-Dieskau (bar), J. Greindl (bass), J. Keilberth (cnd), Bayreuth Festival Orch, Bayreuth Festival Chorus *(rec live, Bayreuth, 1954)* Melodram 3-▲ MEL 36105
Wagner, R.:Tannhäuser, w. Murray Dickie (ten), Karl Liebl (ten), Eberhard Waechter (bar), Alois Pernerstorfer (b-bar), Deszö Ernster (bass), Walter Brunelli (sgr), Peter Harrower (sgr), Rosl Schweiger (sgr), Herta Wilfert (sgr), A. Rodzinski (cnd), Rome RAI Radio-TV SO, Rome RAI Chorus Stradivarius 3-▲ STV 12318
Wagner, R.:Tannhäuser (sels), w. H. Wilfert (sgr), K. Liebl (ten), E. Wächter (bar), A. Rodzinski (cnd), Rome RAI Orch, Rome RAI Chorus *(rec Nov. 21 1957)* Myto 3-▲ MCD 93277

Brown, A. (sgr)
Gershwin, G.:Porgy & Bess, w. E. Matthews (sgr), H. Jackson (sgr), Todd Duncan (sgr), H. Dowdy (sgr), A. Long (sgr), Eva Jessye Choir [1940–1942 original cast] MCA Classics ("Broadway Gold" series) ▲ MCAD 10520 ▮ MCAC 10520

Brown, Antonia E. (sop)
Carulli, F.:Ariettes (3) et romances italiennes (3), w. Adriano Sebastiani (gtr)—Frena le belle lagrime; Amo te sola; Ombre amene; Ecco quel fiero istante; Parlami pur sincero; Solitario bosc'ombroso *(rec Florence, Sept 11–12, 1994)* Dynamic ▲ CDS 124 [DDD]
Carulli, F.:Ariettes italiennes (3), w. Adriano Sebastiani (gtr)—Che fa il mio bene; Deh con me non vi sdegnate; Tornate sereni begl'astri *(rec Florence, Sept 11–12, 1994)* Dynamic ▲ CDS 124 [DDD]
Carulli, F.:Ariettes italiennes (12) sur motifs de Rossini, w. Adriano Sebastiani (gtr)—Ecco quel fiero istante; Sognai mia fillide; O bella fillide; Tornate sereni begl'astri; Ha negli occhi; Se son lontana; Già la notte s'avvicina; Amene selve, amiche piante; Conservati fedele; Amo te sola; Son lungi; Già pronta là t'aspetta *(rec Florence, Sept 11–12, 1994)* Dynamic ▲ CDS 124 [DDD]
Carulli, F.:Grand air italien, w. Adriano Sebastiani (gtr)—Senti mio bene *(rec Florence, Sept 11–12, 1994)* Dynamic ▲ CDS 124 [DDD]
Carulli, F.:Nocturnes (6) for 2 Voices & Gtr, w. Lucia Sciannimanico (mez), Adriano Sebastiani (gtr)—Dal di ch'io vi mirai; Di me chi vide mai; Quel cor che mi prometti; Io rivedrò sovente; V'è com'è bello il mar; Selve ombrose *(rec Florence, Sept 11–12, 1994)* Dynamic ▲ CDS 124 [DDD]

Brown, Donna (sop)
Berlioz, H.:Messe solennelle Sop, w. Jean-Luc Viala (ten), Gilles Cachemaille (bar), J. E. Gardiner (cnd), Orch Révolutionnaire et Romantique, Monteverdi Choir London Philips ▲ 442137-2 ▮ 442137-4 ◻ 442137-5
Brahms, J.:Ein Deutsches Requiem, w. G. Cachemaille (bar), H. Rilling (cnd), Stuttgart Bach Collegium, Gächinger Kantorei [G] Hänssler Classic ▲ 98.966 [DDD]
Gershwin, G.:Porgy & Bess (sels), w. A. Matthews (sop), Jackson (sgr), Duncan (sgr), A. Smallens (cnd), *(orch unknown) (rec 1942 Broadway revival cast)* MCA ▮ MCAC 1631 (m)
Handel, G.F.:Messiah, w. Cornelia Kallisch (cta), R. Sacca (ten), Alastair Miles (bass), H. Rilling (cnd), Stuttgart Bach Collegium, Stuttgart Gächinger Kantorei Hänssler Classic 2-▲ HAN 98975 [DDD]
Handel, G.F.:Messiah (reorchd Mozart), w. Cornelia Kallisch (cta), R. Saccà (ten), Alastair Miles (bass), H. Rilling (cnd), Stuttgart Bach Collegium, Gächinger Kantorei [G] Hänssler Classic 2-▲ 98.975 [DDD]
Handel, G.F.:Saul, w. L. Dawson (sop), D. L. Ragin (ct), J. M. Ainsley (ten), A. Miles (bar), J. E. Gardiner (cnd), English Baroque Soloists, Monteverdi Choir London Philips 3-▲ 426265-2 3PH [DDD]
Haydn, J.:Die Schöpfung, w. Sylvia McNair (sop), Michael Schade (ten), Gerald Finley (bar), Rodney Gilfry (bar), J. E. Gardiner (cnd), English Baroque Soloists, Monteverdi Choir London Archiv ▲ 449 217-2
Verdi, G.:Requiem Mass, w. Luba Orgonasova (sop), Anne Sofie von Otter (mez), Luca Canonici (ten), Alastair Miles (bass), J. E. Gardiner (cnd), Orch Révolutionnaire et Romantique, Monteverdi Choir London Philips 2-▲ 442142-2

Brown, James (ct)
Handel, G.F.:Occasional Oratorio, w. Susan Gritton (sop), Lisa Milne (sop), John Mark Ainsley (ten), Michael George (bass), R. King (cnd), King's Consort, New College Choir Oxford Hyperion 2-▲ CDA 66961/62

Brown, Melvin (ten)
Monteverdi, C.:Vespro della Beata Vergine, w. Gloria Prosper (sop), Adrienne Albert (mez), Richard Levitt (ten), Archi Drake (bass), R. Craft (cnd), Columbia Baroque Ensemble, Gregg Smith Singers, Texas Boys' Choir Sony Classical ("Essential Classics" series) 2-▲ SB2K 62656

Brown, Michael (bar)
Monteverdi, C.:Orfeo, w. Jennifer Lane (mez), Jeffrey Thomas (ten), Dana Hanchard (sgr), Timothy Leigh Evans (sgr), Paul Shipper (sgr), G. Toth (cnd), ARTEK Lyrichord 2-▲ LYR 9002 [DDD]
Purcell, H.:Dido & Aeneas, w. Cassandra Hoffman (sop—Belinda), Arlene Travis (sop—2nd Witch), Desirée Halac (mez—Sorceress/Spirit), Jennifer Lane (mez—Dido), Elizabeth Norman (alt), Thomas Bogdan (ten—A Sailor), Michael Brown (bar—Aeneas), Curtis Streetman (bar), Caitriona O'Leary (sgr—2nd Woman), Sarah Pillow (sgr—1st Witch), B. Brookshire (cnd), San Cassiano Musici *(rec St. Ignatius of Antioch Episcopal Church, New York City, Spring 1995)* Vox Classics ▲ VOX 7518

Brown, Ray (bass)
Dring, M.:Pastel Panche, w. Bud Shank (fl), Bill Perkins (sax/fl), Leigh Kaplan (pno), Shelley Manne (perc)Shank Perkins Brown—Teal for Two; Muave Mood; Lime Clash Cambria ▲ CD 1084 [ADD]
Dring, M.:Shades of Dring, w. Bud Shank (fl), Bill Perkins (sax/fl), Leigh Kaplan (pno), Shelley Manne (perc)—In the Pink; Hallelujah Red; Brown and Out; Hello Yellow; Saxy Blue Cambria ▲ CD 1084 [ADD]

Brown, Wilfred (ten)
Bach, C.P.E.:Magnificat, w. Jennifer Vyvyan (sop), Helen Watts (cta), Thomas Hemsley (bass), G. Jones (cnd), Geraint Jones Orch, Geraint Jones Singers EMI Classics ("Baroque" series) ▲ CDK 65737
Couperin, F.:Leçons de ténèbres (for Good Friday), w. Alfred Deller (ct), Desmond Dupré (vl), Harry Gabb (org) Vanguard Classics ("The Bach Guild" series) ▲ OVC 2525 [ADD]
Gruenberg, L.:The Creation, w. G. Schuller (cnd), Collage New Music Ensemble [E] GM ▲ GM 2015CD
La Musique de Notre Dame, w. Gerald English (ten), Maurice Bevan (bar) *(rec Jan. 1961 & May 1964)* Vanguard Classics ▲ SVC 36 [AAD]
Orff, C.:Carmina burana, w. J. Blegen (sop), H. Hagegård (bar), R. Shaw (cnd), Atlanta SO, Atlanta Sym Chorus [G, L] Telarc ▲ CD 80056 [DDD]
Purcell, H.:Hail, Bright Cecilia, w. April Cantelo (sop), Alfred Deller (alt), Maurice Bevan (bar), M. Tippett (cnd), Kalmar CO, Ambrosian Singers Vanguard Classics ▲ OVC 8020 [ADD]

Brown, Wilfred (ten) (cont.)
Tallis, T.:The Lamentations of Jeremiah, w. Alfred Deller (ct), Gerald English (ten), Maurice Bevan (bar), John Frost (bass) *(rec Walthamstow Hall, London, 1960)* Vanguard Classics ("The Bach Guild" series) ▲ OVC 2525 [ADD]

Browne, R. (sgr)
Falla, M. de:Atlántida, w. T. Stratas (sop), G. Simionato (mez), Halley (sgr), T. Schippers (cnd), La Scala Orch, La Scala Chorus *(rec live, Milan 6/18/62)* Memories 2-▲ HR 4464/65 [ADD]

Browne, Sandra (cta)
Albinoni, T.:Il Nascimento de l'Aurora, w. June Anderson (sop), Susanne Klare (sop), Margarita Zimmermann (sop), Yoshihisa Yamaj (ten), C. Scimone (cnd), Venice Solisti Erato 2-▲ ERA SEL 96374 [DDD]
Righini, V.:Alcide al Bivio, w. L. Serra (sop), W. McKinney (ten), R. El Hage (bass), M. Barta (ob), P. Molinari (hpd), T. Gotti (cnd), Swiss-Italian RSO, Swiss-Italian Radio Chorus *(rec 1979)* Bongiovanni 2-▲ GB 2157/58 [ADD]

Browner, Alison (mez)
Rubinstein, A.:The Demon, w. Ludmilla Andrew (sop—Nanny), Marina Mescheriakova (sop—Tamara), Alison Browner (mez—Angel), Anatoly Lochak (sgr—Demon), Richard Robson (sgr—Old Servant), Valery Serkin (sgr—Prince Sinodal), Wjacheslav Weinorowski (sgr—Messenger), Leonid Zimnenko (sgr—Prince Gudal), A. Anissimov (cnd), Irish National SO, Gregory Rose (cnd), Wexford Festival Opera Chorus *(rec Wexford, Oct & Nov, 1994)* Marco Polo 2-▲ 8.223781-2 [DDD]
Telemann, G.P.:St. Matthew Passion, w. M. Zedelius (sop), H.P. Blochwitz (ten), W. Schmidt (bar), A. Scharinger (bass), W. Seeliger (cnd), Darmstadt CO, Darmstadt Concert Choir Christophorus ▲ 77149 [DDD]
Verdi, G.:Oberto, Conte di San Bonifacio, w. G. Dimitrova (sop), R. Baldani (mez), C. Bergonzi (ten), R. Panerai (bar), L. Gardelli (cnd), Munich RSO, Munich Radio Chorus [I] Orfeo 2-▲ 105842 [DDD] 3-▮ A 105843 F
Verdi, G.:Oberto, Conte di San Bonifacio, w. G. Dimitrova (sop), R. Baldani (mez), C. Bergonzi (ten), R. Panerai (bar), L. Gardelli (cnd), Munich RSO, Munich Radio Chorus [I] Orfeo ▲ 175881 [DDD]
Wolf, H.:Choral Music, w. D. Kurz (cnd), Stuttgart Ensemble, Württemburg Choir—Elfenlied; Der Feuerreiter; Dem Vaterland; Morgenhymnus; Frühlingschor *(rec live, Stuttgart, Feb 18, 1996)* Claves ▲ CD 509622 [DDD]
Wolf, H.:Christnacht, w. Alison Browner (sop—Engel der Verkündigung), Katherin Koch (alt—Hirte), Christian Beller (ten), D. Kurz (cnd), Stuttgart Ensemble, Württemburg Choir *(rec live, Stuttgart, Feb 18, 1996)* Claves ▲ CD 509622 [DDD]

Browning, A. (sop)
Nielsen, C.:Sym 3, w. C. Wheatley (sgr), J. Horenstein (cnd), BBC Northern SO Intaglio ▲ ING 738 [ADD]

Browning, Lucielle (mez)
Her First Recordings, w. Steber, Eleanor (sop), Armand Tokatyan (ten), Pino Bontempi (sgr), Annamary Dickey (sgr), George Cehanovsky (bar), Lorenzo Alvary ((bass), A. Kent (bar), Raoul Jobin (ten), Norman Cordon (bass) VAI Audio ▲ VAIA 1023 (m) [ADD]

Brownlee, John (bar)
Donizetti, G.:Lucia di Lammermoor, w. Lily Pons (sop—Lucia), Thelma Votipka (mez—Alisa), Frederick Jagel (ten—Edgardo), John Brownlee (bar—Enrico), Ezio Pinza (bass—Raimondo), G. Papi (cnd), *(orch unknown)* The Fourties 2-▲ ENT FT 1511
Mozart, W.A.:Così fan tutte, w. I. Souez (sop), L. Helletsgrüber (sop), I. Eisinger (sop), H. Nash (ten), W. Domgraf-Fassbänder (bar), F. Busch (cnd), Glyndebourne Festival Orch, Glyndebourne Festival Chorus [I] *(rec 1935)* Pearl 3-▲ PEAS 9406 (m) [AAD]
Mozart, W.A.:Don Giovanni, w. I. Souez (sop), L. Helletsgrüber (sop), A. Mildmay (sop), K. von Pataky (ten), R. Henderson (bar), T. Franklin (bar), S. Baccaloni (bass), F. Busch (cnd), Glyndebourne Festival Orch, Glyndebourne Festival Chorus [I] *(rec 1936, orig. issued by HMV)* Pearl 3-▲ PEAS 9369 (m) [AAD]
Mozart, W.A.:Nozze di Figaro, w. Bidu Sayao (sop—Susanna), Eleanor Steber (sop—Countess Almaviva), Jarmila Novotna (sop—Cherubino), Ira Petina (sop—Marcellina), John Brownlee (bar—Count Almaviva), Salvatore Baccaloni (bass—Bartolo), Ezio Pinza (bass—Figaro), B. Walter (cnd), *(orch unknown)* The Fourties 2-▲ ENT FT 1509
Rossini, G.:Il barbiere di Siviglia, w. Ira Petina (sop), Bidú Sayão (sop), Salvatore Baccaloni (bass), Ezio Pinza (bass), Nino Martini (sgr), F. St. Leger (cnd), *(orch unknown) (rec Oct 4, 1943)* Enterprise ("The Fourties" series) 2-▲ ENT 307

Brownlee, John (bass)
Mozart, W.A.:Così fan tutte, w. Irene Eisinger (sop—Despina), Luise Helletsgruber (sop—Dorabella), Ina Souez (sop—Fiordiligi), Heddle Nash (ten—Ferrando), John Brownlee (bass—Don Alfonso), Willi Domgraf-Fassbaender (bass—Guglielmo), F. Busch (cnd), Glyndebourne Festival Orch, Glyndebourne Festival Chorus *(rec June 25–28, 1935)* Arkadia ("The 78's" series) 2-▲ 78011 [ADD]

Brua, Claire (sop)
Berlioz, H.:L'Enfance du Christ (sels), w. Mariette Kemmer (sop), Gilles Ragon (ten), Nicolas Cavallier (bass), F. Quattrocchi (cnd), Lorraine PO—Toujours ce rêve *(rec June 1994)* Maguelone ▲ 350.509 [DDD]
Charpentier, M.-A.:Le Malade imaginaire, w. N. Rime (sop), M. Zanetti (sop), D. Visse (ct), H. Crook (ten), J.-F. Gardeil (bar), W. Christie (cnd), Les Arts Florissants [F] Harmonia Mundi France ▲ HMC 901336
Gluck, C.W.:Alceste (sels), w. Mariette Kemmer (sop), Gilles Ragon (ten), Nicolas Cavallier (bass), F. Quattrocchi (cnd), Lorraine PO—Vivre sans toi *(rec June 1994)* Maguelone ▲ 350.509 [DDD]
Gounod, C.:Faust (sels), w. Mariette Kemmer (sop), Gilles Ragon (ten), Nicolas Cavallier (bass), F. Quattrocchi (cnd), Lorraine PO—Faites lui mes aveux; La coupe du Roi de Thulé; Air des Bijoux *(rec June 1994)* Maguelone ▲ 350.509 [DDD]
Handel, G.F.:Riccardo Primo, w. Claire Brua (sop—Pulcheria), Sandrine Piau (sop—Costanza), Sara Mingardo (cta—Riccardo), Pascal Bertin (alt—Oronte), Roberto Scaltriti (bar—Isacio), Olivier Lallouette (bass—Berardo), C. Rousset (cnd), Les Talens Lyriques L'oiseau Lyre ▲ 452 201-2
Mozart, W.A.:Così fan tutte (sels), w. Mariette Kemmer (sop), Gilles Ragon (ten), Nicolas Cavallier (bass), F. Quattrocchi (cnd), Lorraine PO—Come scoglio *(rec June 1994)* Maguelone ▲ 350.509 [DDD]
Mozart, W.A.:Nozze di Figaro (sels), w. Mariette Kemmer (sop), Gilles Ragon (ten), Nicolas Cavallier (bass), F. Quattrocchi (cnd), Lorraine PO—Ov; Voi che Sapete *(rec June 1994)* Maguelone ▲ 350.509 [DDD]
Purcell, H.:Dido & Aeneas, w. Véronique Gens (sop—Dido), Sophie Marin-Degor (sop—Belinda), Sophie Daneman (sop—2nd woman/1st witch), Gaëlle Mechaly (sop—2nd witch), Claire Brua (mez—Sorceress), Steve Dugardin (alt—Chorus), Jean-Paul Fouchécourt (ten—Spirit/Sailor), Nathan Berg (b-bar—Aeneas), Jonathan Arnold (bass—Chorus), William Christie (hpd), W. Christie (cnd), Les Arts Florissants *(rec Massy Opera Theatre, Nov. 8–11, 1994)* Erato ▲ 98477-2 [DDD]
Rossini, G.:Le Comte Ory (sels), w. Mariette Kemmer (sop), Gilles Ragon (ten), Nicolas Cavallier (bass), F. Quattrocchi (cnd), Lorraine PO—Ov; Que les destins prospères *(rec June 1994)* Maguelone ▲ 350.509 [DDD]

Bruce-Payne, Sally (alt)
Purcell, H.:The Indian Queen, w. Tessa Bonner (sop), Steven Liley (ten), Edward Caswell (bass), C. Mackintosh (cnd), Purcell Sinfony *(rec St. Bartholomew's Church, Orford, Suffolk, Sept 21–23, 1994)* Linn ▲ CKD 035

Bruckner, Thomas (bar)
Ashley, R.:Tract, w. Robert Ashley (cmpt/syn), Nathaniel Reichman (cmpt/syn), Tom Hamilton (syn) *(rec 10 Beach St, NYC)* New World ▲ 80460-2
Hays, S.:Dreaming the World, w. Sal Basile (voc), Jennifer López (voc), John Schaffer (voc), Sorrel Hays (voc), Joseph Kubera (pno), John Kennedy (perc), Charles Wood (perc), Maya Gunji (perc), Eric Kivnick (perc), Jai Smith (perc) New World ▲ 805202 [DDD]

Bruera, Daniela (sop)
Cimarosa, D.:Amor rende sagace, w. G. Bertagnolli (sop), C. Mantese (sop), M. Dalena (ten), E. Dara (bar), M. Nicolini (sgr), F. Neri (cnd), Bolzano Claudio Monteverdi Conservatory Youth Orch [I] *(rec live, Bolzano 7/25–27/91)* Bongiovanni 2-▲ GB 2126/27 [DDD]

Bruffy, Charles (ten)

Debussy, C.:Chansons (3) de Charles d'Orléans, w. Julie McCoy (sop), Pam Elrod (mez), Nanette Soles (mez), Leonard Ratzlaff (bass), Robert Shaw (cnd), Robert Shaw Festival Singers *(rec Church of St. Pierre, Gramat, France, July 26–28, 1994)* Telarc ▲ CD 80408 [DDD]

Ravel, M.:Chansons, w. Mara Bonde (sop), Nannette Soles (mez), Bruce Tammen (bass), Robert Shaw (cnd), Robert Shaw Festival Singers *(rec Church of St. Pierre, Gramat, France, July 26–28, 1994)* Telarc ▲ CD 80408 [DDD]

Brumaire, Jacqueline (sop)

Honegger, A.:Le Roi David, w. Henri Doublier (nar), Denise Scharley (alt), Jacques Pottier (ten), S. Baudo (cnd), Paris Opera Orch, Elisabeth Brasseur Chorale Accord ▲ ACD 200822 [AAD]

Milhaud, D.:Les Malheurs d'Orphée (sels), w. Jean Giraudeau (ten), D. Milhaud (cnd), Paris Opera Orch Adès ▲ ADE 203452 [AAD]

Milhaud, D.:Pauvre matelot (sels), w. Jean Giraudeau (ten), D. Milhaud (cnd), Paris Opera Orch Adès ▲ ADE 203452 [AAD]

Verdi, G.:I vespri siciliani, w. P. Bowden (mez), Bonhomme (sgr), Taylor (sgr), Baran (sgr), M. Rossi (cnd), BBC Concert Orch, BBC Concert Chorus [original French version] *(rec live, London, 5/10/69)* Arkadia 3–▲ 456 [ADD]

Brumann, Oswald (bass)

Holliger, H.:Alb–Chehr, w. Sabine Gertschen (dlc), Edmund Volken (dlc), Elmar Schmid (cl), Klaus Schmid (cl), Markus Tenisch (Swiss org), Marcel Volken (Swiss org), Paul Locher (vn), Franziskus Abgottspon (nar) ECM New Series ▲ 78118–21540–2 [DDD]

Brumeister, Annelies (mez)

Dessau, P.:Puntila, w. Annelies Brumeister (mez—Lsins), Erich Witte (ten—Fredrick), Reiner Süss (bar—Johannes Puntila), P. Dessau (cnd), Berlin State Opera Orch, Berlin State Chorus *(rec Berlin, May 1988)* Berlin Classics 2–▲ BER 2184 [ADD]

Brun, Johanne (sop)

Vilhelm Herold, w. Herold, Vilhelm (ten), Emilie Ulrich (sop), Helge Nissen (b–bar) Nimbus ("Prima Voce" series) ▲ NI 7880 [ADD]

Bruna, Gudrun (sop)

Nilsson, T.:Out of Earthly Night, w. Marianne Mellnäs (sop), Kaysa Hälldin (alt), Lars Sjögren (ten), Göran Swartz (bass), Sture Hedin (sgr), Ola Kyhlberg (sgr), Lars Ljungman (sgr), Nils Philipson (sgr), Ulrik Quale (sgr), Nils Spangenberg (sgr), Britta Therén (sgr), Karl–Erik Welin (org), Torsten Nilsson (cnd), Oscar's Motet Choir *(rec Oscar's Church, Stockholm, Sweden, Apr 26–27, 1978)* BIS ▲ CD 138 [AAD]

Bruna–Rasa, Lina (sop)

Mascagni, P.:Cavalliera rusticana, w. Giulietta Simionato (mez), Benia Gigli (ten), Giuseppe Nessi (ten), Gino Bechi (bar), Carlo Galeffi (bar), P. Mascagni (cnd), La Scala Orch, La Scala Chorus *(rec Milan, 1940)* Phonographe 2–▲ PHG CD 5066

Brun–Baranska, Bozena (mez)

Moniuszko, S.:Haunted Manor, w. Halina Slonicka (sop), Barbara Lawcewicz (mez), Krystyna Szczepanska (mez), Zdzislaw Nikodem (ten), Bogdan Paprocki (ten), Andrzej Hiolski (bar), Edmund Kossowski (bass), Bernard Ladysz (bass), W. Rowicki (cnd), Warsaw State Opera House Orch, Warsaw National Opera Chorus *(rec Warsaw, 1965)* Polskie Nagrania ▲ PNCD 093 [AAD]

Brunelli, Walter (sgr)

Wagner, R.:Die Meistersinger von Nürnberg, w. Bruna Rizzoli (sop), Fernanda Cadoni (mez), Luigi Infantino (ten), Vito Tatone (ten), Renato Capecchi (bar), Giuseppe Taddei (bar), Boris Christoff (bass), Giovanni Ciavola (bass), James Loomis (bass), Silvo Maionica (bass), Vito Susca (bass), Raimondo Botteghelli (sgr), Carlo Franzini (sgr), Ezio de Giorgi (sgr), Renzo Gonzales (sgr), L. von Matačič (cnd), Turin RAI Radio–TV SO, Turin RAI Chorus Stradivarius 4–▲ STV 12310

Wagner, R.:Tannhäuser, w. Gré Brouwestijn (sop), Murray Dickie (ten), Karl Liebl (ten), Eberhard Waechter (bar), Alois Pernerstorfer (b–bar), Deszö Ernster (bass), Walter Brunelli (sgr), Peter Harrower (sgr), Rosl Schweiger (sgr), Herta Wilfert (sgr), A. Rodzinski (cnd), Rome RAI Radio–TV SO, Rome RAI Chorus Stradivarius 3–▲ STV 12318

Brunet, Sylvie (sop)

Gluck, C.W.:Iphigénie en Tauride, w. C. Vaness (sop—Iphigénie), S. Brunet (sop—Diane), G. Winbergh (ten—Pylade), T. Allen (bar—Oreste), G. Surian (bass—Thoas), R. Muti (cnd), La Scala Orch, La Scala Chorus *(rec Mar. 14–26, 1992)* Sony Classical 2–▲ S2K 52492 [DDD]

Brunetti, Vita Maria (bass)

Donizetti, G.:I pazzi per progetto, w. S. Rigacci (sop), A. Cicogna (mez), G. Polidori (bar), G. Sarti (bar), E. Fissore (bass), L. Monreale (bass), G. Micheli (cnd), Emilia Romagna Arturo Toscanini SO [I] *(rec live, 12/88)* Bongiovanni ▲ GB 2070 [DDD]

Brüning, Thomas (sgr)

Krenek, E.:Der Sprüng über den Schatten, w. D. Amos (sop), L. Kemeny (sop), S. MacLean (mez), J. Dürmüller (ten), U. Neuweiler (ten), J. Pflieger (bar), D. de Villiers (cnd), Bielefeld PO, Bielefeld Phil Chorus [G] *(rec live, May 1989)* CPO 2–▲ CPO 999082–2 [DDD]

Brunskill, Muriel (cta)

Gounod, C.:Faust, w. M. Licette (sop—Margarita), D. Vane (sop—Siebel), M. Brunskill (cta—Martha), H. Nash (ten—Faust), H. Williams (b–bar—Valentine), R. Easton (bass—Mephistopheles), R. Carr (bass—Wagner), T. Beecham (cnd), BBC SO, BBC Sym Chorus Dutton Laboratories 2–▲ CDAX 2001 [ADD]

Handel, G.F.:Messiah, w. Dora Labbette (sop), Hubert Eisdell (ten), Harold Williams (bar), T. Beecham (cnd), BBC SO, BBC Choir *(rec 1927)* Pearl 2–▲ PEA 9456 [DDD]

Vaughan Williams, R.:Serenade to Music, w. I. Baillie (sop), E. Suddaby (sop), S. Allen (sop), E. Turner (sop), M. Balfour (cta), A. Desmond (cta), M. Jarred (cta), H. Nash (ten), W. Widdop (ten), P. Jones (ten), F. Titterton (ten), R. Henderson (bass), R. Easton (bass), H. Williams (bass), N. Allin (bass), H. J. Wood (cnd), BBC SO Dutton Laboratories ▲ CDAX 8004 [ADD]

Vaughan Williams, R.:Serenade to Music, w. Isobel Baillie (sop), Lilian Stiles–Allen (sop), Elsie Suddaby (sop), Eva Turner (sop), Margaret Balfour (cta), Astra Desmond (cta), Mary Jarred (cta), Parry Jones (ten), Heddle Nash (ten), Frank Titterton (ten), Walter Widdop (ten), Roy Henderson (bar), Harold Williams (bar), Norman Allin (bass), Robert Easton (bass), H. Wood (cnd), BBC SO *(rec Abbey Road, Oct 15, 1938)* Claremont ▲ CDGSE 785066

Vaughan Williams, R.:Serenade to Music, w. I. Baillie (sop), E. Suddaby (sop), S. Allen (sop), E. Turner (sop), M. Balfour (cta), A. Desmond (cta), M. Jarred (cta), H. Nash (ten), W. Widdop (ten), P. Jones (ten), F. Titterton (ten), R. Henderson (bass), R. Easton (bass), H. Williams (bass), N. Allin (bass), H. Wood (cnd), BBC SO [E] *(rec 10/15/38)* Pearl ▲ GEMMCD 9342 (m) [AAD]

Brunssen, Karen (mez)

Telemann, G.P.:Der Tag des Gerichts, w. Patrice Michaels Bell (sop), Sandra Walker (mez), Bruce Fowler (ten), Kurt R. Hansen (ten), William Stone (bar), Douglas Anderson (bar), T. Wikman (cnd), Music of the Baroque Orch, Baroque Music Chorus *(rec live, St. Paul's United Church of Christ, Feb 23, 1992)* Music of the Baroque 2–▲ MB 107

Bruscantini, Sesto (b–bar)

Alda Noni, Sesto Bruscantini, w. A. Noni (sop), Turin RAI Orch [cnd:Nino Sanzogno] *(rec Dec. 3, 1951)* Incontri Memorabili ("Martini & Rossi Concerts" series) ▲ 5016

Bellini, V.:I Puritani, w. Lina Pagliughi (sop), Mario Filippeschi (ten), Rolando Panerai (bar), F. Previtali (cnd), Rome RAI SO, Rome RAI Chorus *(rec Rome, Jan. 4 & 5, 1952)* Pantheon 2–▲ PHE 6640 (m)

Bellini, V.:I Puritani, w. M. Freni (sop), L. Pavarotti (ten), B. Giaotti (bass), R. Muti (cnd), Rome RAI SO, Rome RAI Chorus [I] *(rec live, Rome 7/8/69)* Verona 3–▲ 27029/31

Bellini, V.:I Puritani, w. Mirella Freni (sop), Mirelle Fiorentini (mez), Luciano Pavarotti (ten), Emilio Venturini (ten), Giovanni Antonini (bass), Bonaldo Giaiotti (bass), R. Muti (cnd), Rome RAI SO, Rome RAI Chorus Melodram 2–▲ CDM 27062

Bellini, V.:I Puritani, w. C. Deutekom (sop), F. Raffanelli (sop), N. Gedda (ten), A. Ferrin (bass), G. del Vivo (bass), R. Muti (cnd), *(orch unknown)* *(rec 1970)* Great Opera Performances ▲ GOP 735

Bellini, V.:I Puritani, w. Mirella Freni (sop), Luciano Pavarotti (ten), R. Muti (cnd), Rome RAI SO, Rome RAI Chorus *(rec Rome, 1969)* Enterprise ("Palladio" series) 3–▲ ENTPD 4205 [ADD]

Bizet, G.:Les Pêcheurs de perles, w. A. Maliponte (sop—Leila), A. Kraus (ten—Nadir), S. Bruscantini (bar—Zurga), C. F. Cillario (cnd), Barcelona Teatro Liceo Orch, Barcelona Gran Teatro de Liceo Chorus Bongiovanni 2–▲ GB 516/17 [ADD]

Bruscantini, Sesto (b–bar) (cont.)

Cimarosa, D.:Les Astuzie femminili (sels), w. Teresa Stich Randall (sop), M. Rossi (cnd), Turin RAI SO—Le figliole che so' de vent'anni *(rec Concerto Martini & Rossi, Torino, Nov 9, 1959)* Incontri Memorabili ▲ 5027 [ADD]

Cimarosa, D.:Giannina e Bernardone, w. D. De Cecco (sop), S. Jurinac (sop), G. Sciutti (sop), M. Carlin (ten), M. Boriello (bar), C. De Antoni (sgr), N. Sanzogno (cnd), Milan RAI SO, Milan RAI Chorus [I] *(rec live, Milan July 26, 1953)* Melodram 2–▲ CDM 29505 [ADD]

Cimarosa, D.:Il Matrimonio segreto, w. Alda Noni (sop), Giulietta Simionato (mez), Riccardo Cassinelli (ten), Cesare Valletti (ten), Rovero (sgr), M. Wolf–Ferrari (cnd), Florence Maggio Musicale Orch *(rec 1950)* Cetra Classic 2–▲ CDO 32

Cimarosa, D.:Il Matrimonio segreto (sels), w. H. Gueden (sop), A. Noni (sop), F. Barbieri (mez), T. Schipa (ten), B. Christoff (bass), M. Rossi (cnd), La Scala Orch—Act I highlights [I] *(rec live, Milan March 22, 1949)* Melodram 2–▲ CDM 29505 [ADD]

Donizetti, G.:Don Pasquale, w. A. Noni (sop—Norina), C. Valletti (ten—Ernesto), M. Borriello (bar—Dr. Malatesta), S. Bruscantini (bass–bar—Pasquale), M. Rossi (cnd), Turin RAI SO, Turin RAI Chorus *(rec 1952)* Cetra Classic 2–▲ CDO 14 [AAD]

Donizetti, G.:Don Pasquale, w. M. Freni (sop), G. Winbergh (ten), L. Nucci (bar), R. Muti (cnd), Philharmonia Orch, Ambrosian Opera Chorus EMI Classics 2–▲ CDCB 47068

Donizetti, G.:Don Pasquale (sels), w. M. Freni (sop), G. Winbergh (ten), L. Nucci (bar), R. Muti (cnd), Philharmonia Orch, Ambrosian Opera Chorus EMI Classics ▲ CDC 54490

Donizetti, G.:L'elisir d'amore, w. Alda Noni (sop), Cesare Valletti (ten), G. Gavazzeni (cnd), Rome RAI SO, Rome RAI Chorus Fonit Cetra ("Classic Collection" series) 2–▲ FCT CDO 5

Donizetti, G.:L'elisir d'amore, w. A. Noni (sop), B. Rizzoli (sop), C. Valletti (ten), A. Poli (bar), G. Gavazzeni (cnd), Rome RAI SO, Rome RAI Chorus *(rec 1952)* Cetra Classic ▲ CDO 5 [AAD]

Donizetti, G.:L'elisir d'amore (sels), w. Reri Grist (sop), Luciano Pavarotti (ten), Ingvar Wixell (bar), Maria Ambrosio (sgr), G. Patanè (cnd), San Francisco War Memorial Opera House Orch, San Francisco War Memorial Opera House Chorus *(rec live, San Francisco, 1969)* Budget ("The Greatest Voice in Opera" series) ▲ SYP 109

Donizetti, G.:Emilia di Liverpool, w. Y. Kenny (sop), A. Mason (sop), B. Mills (sop), C. Merritt (ten), G. Dolton (bar), C. Thornton–Holmes (bar), D. Parry (cnd), Philharmonia Orch, Geoffrey Mitchell Choir—complete opera, without dialogue Opera Rara 3–▲ OR 8

Donizetti, G.:L'Eremitaggio di Liverpool, w. Y. Kenny (sop), A. Mason (sop), B. Mills (sop), C. Merritt (ten), G. Dolton (bar), C. Thornton–Holmes (bar), D. Parry (cnd), Philharmonia Orch, Geoffrey Mitchell Choir—complete opera, without dialogue Opera Rara 3–▲ OR 8

Donizetti, G.:La fille du régiment, w. Lina Pagliughi (sop), Rina Corsi (mez), Cesare Valletti (ten), Eraldo Coda (bar), M. Rossi (cnd), Milan RAI Lyric Orch, Milan RAI Chorus *(rec 1950)* Cetra Classic 2–▲ CDON 38 [ADD]

Donizetti, G.:Lucia di Lammermoor, w. R. Scotto (sop), A. Kraus (ten), P. Washington (bar), B. Rigacci (cnd), *(orch unknown)* *(rec 1963)* Great Opera Performances 2–▲ GOP 747

Massenet, J.:Thaïs, w. R. Kabaivanska (sop), O. de Fabritiis (cnd), Catania Teatro Massimo Bellini Orch, Catania Teatro Massimo Bellini Chorus [I] *(rec live, 4/3/69)* Golden Age of Opera 2–▲ GAO 121/122 [ADD]

Massenet, J.:Werther, w. D. Gatta (sop—Sofia), I. Ligabue (sop—Kaethlen), G. Simionato (mez—Charlotte), F. Tagliavini (ten—Werther), V. Pandano (ten—Schmidt), E. Campi (bass—Johann), S. Bruscantini (bass—Le Bailli), F. Capuana (cnd), La Scala Orch, La Scala Chorus *(rec Apr. 21, 1951)* Bongiovanni 2–▲ GB 1101/02 [ADD]

Mozart, W.A.:Arias, w. Teresa Stich Randall (sop), M. Rossi (cnd), Turin RAI SO—Martern aller Arten [from Entführung aus dem Serail]; Tutto è disposto; E Susanna non vien! [both from Le nozze di Figaro]; Ei parte... Per pietá, ben mio perdona [from Così fan tutte]; Crudele?... Non mi dir, bell'idol mio [from Don Giovanni] *(rec Concerto Martini & Rossi, Torino, Nov 9, 1959)* Incontri Memorabili ▲ 5027 [ADD]

Mozart, W.A.:Così fan tutte, w. A. C. Antonacci (sop—Fiordiligi), M. Bacelli (sop—Dorabella), L. Cherici (sop—Despina), R. Decker (ten—Ferrando), A. Dohmen (bar—Gugliemo), S. Bruscantini (bar—Don Alfonso), G. Kuhn (cnd), Marchigiana PO, Marchigiana Phil Chorus [I] *(rec live, Teatro Lauro Rossi at the Festival di Macerata, Aug. 3, 1990)* Orfeo 3–▲ 243913 [DDD]

Mozart, W.A.:Così fan tutte, w. E. Schwarzkopf (sop), L. Otto (sop), N. Merriman (mez), L. Simoneau (ten), R. Panerai (bar), H. von Karajan (cnd), Philharmonia Orch, Philharmonia Chorus [I] EMI Classics ("Studio" series) 3–▲ CDHC 69635 (m) [ADD]

Mozart, W.A.:Così fan tutte (sels), w. Lisa Otto (sop), Elizabeth Schwarzkopf (sop), Nan Merriman (mez), Rolando Panerai (bar), Leopold Simoneau (ten), H. von Karajan (cnd), Philharmonia Orch Classics for Pleasure ("Eminence" series) ▲ CDEMX 2211 [DDD]

Mozart, W.A.:Don Giovanni, w. Leyla Gencer (sop—Donn'Elvra), Teresa Stich–Randall (mez—Donn'Anna), Sesto Bruscantini (bar—Leporello), Mario Petri (bar—Don Giovanni), F. Molinari–Pradelli (cnd), Milan RAI SO, Milan RAI Chorus Stradivarius 3–▲ STV DTM 12321 [ADD]

Mozart, W.A.:Nozze di Figaro, w. S. Jurinac (sop), T. Stratas (sop), T. Berganza (mez), N. Condò (mez), A. Lazzari (ten), M. Petri (bass), G. Tadeo (bass), A. Mariotti (bass), Z. Mehta (cnd), *(orch unknown)* *(rec 1968)* Great Opera Performances 3–▲ GOP 712

Mozart, W.A.:Nozze di Figaro, w. G. Gatti (sop), A. Noni (sop), G. Sciurri (sop), J. Gardino (mez), M.T. Pace (mez), A. Mercuriali (ten), I. Tajo (bass), F. Corena (bass), F. Previtali (cnd), Rome RAI Orch [I] *(rec 1951)* Cetra Classic 2–▲ CDO 12

Mozart, W.A.:Nozze di Figaro, w. S. Jurinac (sop), G. Sciutti (sop), R. Stevens (mez), M. Sinclair (cta), D. McCoshan (ten), H. Counod (ten), G. Griffith (bar), F. Calabrese (bass), V. Gui (cnd), Glyndebourne Festival Orch, Glyndebourne Festival Chorus Classics for Pleasure ▲ CDCFP 4724 [ADD]

Paisiello, G.:La Molinara, w. Graziella Sciutti (sop), Agostino Lazzari (ten), Alvinio Misciano (ten), Franco Calabrese (bass), Leonardo Monreale (bass), F. Caracciolo (cnd), Alessandro Scarlatti CO Melodram 2–▲ CDM 29502

Pergolesi, G.B.:La serva padrona, w. Angelica Tuccari (sop), Milan RAI Lyric Orch Cetra Classic ▲ CDO 33

Piccinni, N.:La cecchina (sels), w. M. Freni (sop), I. Hollweg (sop), R. Panerai (bar), F. Caracciolo (cnd), Naples RAI Orch—13 arias *(rec live 11/25/69)* Arkadia 2–▲ 596 [ADD]

Rossini, G.:Il barbiere di Siviglia, w. T. Berganza (mez), R. Casellato (ten), G. Tozzi (bass), B. Bartoletti (cnd), Buenos Aires Teatro Colón Orch, Buenos Aires Teatro Colón Chorus [I] *(rec 1969)* Golden Age of Opera 2–▲ GAO 149/50

Rossini, G.:Il barbiere di Siviglia, w. Fiorenza Cossotto (mez), Luigi Alva (ten), Carlo Badioli (bass), Nicolai Ghiaurov (bass), G. Santini (cnd), La Scala Orch, La Scala Chorus *(rec Jan 20, 1964)* Pantheon 2–▲ PHE 6644 (m)

Rossini, G.:Il barbiere di Siviglia (sels), w. Teresa Stich Randall (sop), M. Rossi (cnd), Turin RAI SO—Largo al factotum *(rec Concerto Martini & Rossi, Torino, Nov 9, 1959)* Incontri Memorabili ▲ 5027 [ADD]

Rossini, G.:La Cenerentola, w. B. Casoni (mez), U. Benelli (ten), A. Mariotti (bass), P. Bellugi (cnd), Berlin RSO, Berlin Radio Chorus [I] Acanta 2–▲ CD 43271 [DDD]

Rossini, G.:La Cenerentola, w. Teresa Berganza (mez), Nicola Monti (ten), Mario Petri (bar), Leonardo Monreale (sgr), M. Rossi (cnd), Naples RAI SO, Naples Teatro San Carlo Chorus *(rec Oct 8, 1958)* Pantheon 2–▲ PHE 6656 (m)

Rossini, G.:L'equivoco Stravagante, w. M. Guglielmi (sop), G. Baratti (ten), R. Panerai (bar), B. Rigacci (cnd), *(orch unknown)* [I] *(rec Naples, 1974)* Golden Age of Opera 2–▲ GAO 154/55

Rossini, G.:L'italiana in Algeri, w. L. V. Terrani (mez), U. Benelli (ten), A. Mariotti (bass), G. Bertini (cnd), Dresden State Orch [I] Acanta 2–▲ CD 42308 [DDD]

Rossini, G.:L'italiana in Algeri, w. Teresa Berganza (mez), Alvino Misciano (ten), Mario Petri (sgr), N. Sanzogno (cnd), Milan RAI SO, Milan RAI Chorus *(rec June 28, 1957)* Pantheon 2–▲ PHE 6646 (m)

Rossini, G.:Il turco in Italia, w. Graziella Sciurri (sop), Agostino Lazzari (ten), Scipio Colombo (bar), N. Sanzogno (cnd), *(orch & chorus unknown)* *(rec Milan, Feb 25, 1958)* Pantheon 2–▲ PHE 6654 (m)

Scarlatti, A.:La Griselda, w. M. Freni (sop), L. Alva (ten), V. Luchetti (ten), R. Panerai (bar), N. Sanzogno (cnd), Naples Alessandro Scarlatti RAI Orch, Naples Scarlatti Chorus [I] *(rec live 10/29/70)* Memories 2–▲ HR 4154/55 (m) [ADD]

Verdi, G.:Don Carlos, w. L. Gencer (sop), F. Cossotto (mez), B. Prevedi (ten), N. Ghiaurov (bass), F. Previtali (cnd), Rome Opera Orch, Rome Opera Chorus *(rec live)* Melodram 3–▲ MEL 37022

VOCALISTS 1091

VOCALISTS

Bruscantini, Sesto (b–bar) (cont.)
Verdi, G.:Ernani (sels), w. Teresa Stich Randall (sop), M. Rossi (cnd), Turin RAI SO—Gran Dio!... Ohe de' verd'anni miei *(rec Concerto Martini & Rossi, Torino, Nov 9, 1959)*
Incontri Memorabili ▲ 5027 [ADD]
Verdi, G.:Un giorno di regno, w. Lina Pagliughi (sop), Mario Carlin (ten), Juan Oncina (ten), Renato Capecchi (bar), Laura Cozzi (sgr), Cristiano Dalamangas (sgr), A. Simonetto (cnd), Milan RAI Lyric Orch, Milan RAI Chorus *(rec 1951)* Cetra Classic 2-▲ CDON 37 [ADD]
Verdi, G.:La traviata, w. M. Freni (sop), F. Bonisolli (ten), L. Gardelli (cnd), Berlin State Opera Orch, Berlin State Opera Chorus [I] Acanta 2-▲ CD 41644 [DDD]
Vivaldi, A.:Orlando Furioso, w. V. de los Angeles (sop), M. Horne (mez), L. Valentini-Terrani (mez), C. Gonzales (mez), Kosma (sgr), N. Zaccaria (bass), C. Scimone (cnd), Venice Solisti
Erato 3-▲ 2292-45147-2 ZB

Bruson, Renato (bar)
Arie Antiche, w. Berlin Radio Sinfonietta [cnd:Roberto Paternostro] Acanta ▲ 43310
Bellini, V.:Beatrice di Tenda, w. A. Gulin (sop), E. Zilio (mez), J. Carreras (ten), F. Mannino (cnd), Turin RAI Orch, Turin RAI Chorus [I] *(rec live Oct. 9, 1973)*
Golden Age of Opera 2-▲ GAO 158/59 [ADD]
Bizet, G.:Carmen, w. M. Chiara (sop—Micaela), A. Caminada (mez—Mercedes), F. Cossotto (mez—Carmen), F. Andreoli (ten—Il Remendado), P. M. Ferraro (ten—Don José), R. Bruson (bar—Escamillo), G. Zancanaro (bar—Morales), A. Carusi (bass—Il Dancairo), P. Maag (cnd), Venice Teatro La Fenice Orch, Venice Teatro La Fenice Chorus *(rec 1971)* Myto 2-▲ MCD 93487
Donizetti, G.:Caterina Cornaro, w. L. Gencer (sop), G. Aragall (ten), L. Risani (sgr), C.F. Cillario (cnd), Naples Teatro San Carlo Orch, Naples Teatro San Carlo Chorus *(rec live, 5/28/72)*
Myto 2-▲ 2 MCD 92153 [ADD]
Donizetti, G.:Caterina Cornaro, w. L. Gencer (sop), G. Aragall (ten), C.F. Cillario (cnd), Naples Teatro San Carlo Orch, Naples Teatro San Carlo Chorus [I] *(rec live, Naples 5/28/72)*
Memories 2-▲ HR 4448/49 (m) [ADD]
Donizetti, G.:Fausta, w. R. Kabaiwanska (sop), G. Giacomini (ten), D. Oren (cnd), Rome Opera Orch, Rome Opera Chorus *(rec live, 1981)* Italian Opera Rarities 3-▲ IOR 7701 [ADD]
Donizetti, G.:Gemma di Vergy, w. Montserrat Caballé (sop—Gemma di Vergy), Biancamaria Casoni (mez—Ida di Greville), Giorgio Lamberti (ten—Tamas), Renato Bruson (bar—Conte di Vergy), Mario Machì (bass—Rolando), Mario Rinaudo (bass—Guido), A. Gatto (cnd), Naples Teatro San Carlo Orch, Naples Teatro San Carlo Chorus *(rec Naples, Dec. 12, 1975)* Myto 2-▲ 952124
Donizetti, G.:Lucia di Lammermoor, w. E. Gruberová (sop), A. Kraus (ten), D. Lloyd (ten), Royal PO, Ambrosian Opera Chorus *(rec 1983)* EMI Classics ▲ CDMB 64622
Donizetti, G.:Lucia di Lammermoor, w. Mariella Devia (sop), Vencenzo La Scola (ten), S. Ranzani (cnd), La Scala Orch, La Scala Chorus Serenissima 2-▲ SER 360153 [DDD]
Donizetti, G.:Maria di Rohan, w. R. Scotto (sop—Maria), E. Zilio (mez—Armando di Gondi), U. Grilli (ten—Riccardo), R. Bruson (bar—Enrico), G. Gavazzeni (cnd), Venice Teatro La Fenice Orch, Venice Teatro La Fenice Chorus *(rec live Mar. 26, 1974)* Golden Age of Opera 2-▲ GAO 156/57 [ADD]
Donizetti, G.:Les Martyrs, w. L. Gencer (sop), O. Garaventa (bar), F. Furlanetto (bass), G. Gelmetti (cnd), Venice Teatro La Fenice Orch, Venice Teatro La Fenice Chorus *(rec 1978)*
Italian Opera Rarities ▲ IOR 7716 [ADD]
Donizetti, G.:Poliuto, w. E. Connell (sop), N. Martinucci (ten), J. Latham-König (cnd), Rome Opera Orch, Rome Opera Chorus [I] *(rec live, 1988)* Nuova Era 2-▲ 6776/77 [DDD]
Donizetti, G.:Requiem Mass, w. L. Pavarotti (ten), M. Cortez (ten), P. Washington (bass), G. Fackler (cnd), Arena di Verona Orch, Arena di Verona Chorus London ("Ovation" series) ▲ 425043-2 [ADD]
Favorite Songs, w. Craig Sheppard (pno) *(rec live, Wigmore Hall, London)*
Chandos ("Collect" series) ▲ CHAN 6551 [ADD]
Franchetti, A.:Cristoforo Colombo, w. R. Ragatzu (sop—Isabella), G. Pasino (mez—Annacoana), M. Berti (ten—Ferdinand), R. Bruson (bar—Cristoforo Colombo), R. Scandiuzzi (bass—Don Roldano Ximenes), M. Viotti (cnd), Frankfurt RSO, Frankfurt Radio Chorus [I] *(rec live, Alte Oper Frankfurt, 8/30 & 9/2 1991)* Koch Schwann 3-▲ CD 3-1030-2 [DDD]
Mascagni, P.:Cavalleria rusticana, w. E. Obraztsova (mez), F. Barbieri (mez), P. Domingo (ten), G. Prêtre (cnd), La Scala Orch, La Scala Chorus [I] Philips ▲ 416137-2 [DDD]
Mozart, W.A.:Don Giovanni, w. S. Ghazarian (sop), G. Ottenthal (sop), P. Pace (sop), G. Sabbatini (ten), A> Rinaldi-Miliani (bar), F. De Grandis (bass), N. Ghiuselev (bass), N. Järvi (cnd), Cologne RSO, Cologne Radio Chorus [I] Chandos 3-▲ CHAN 8920/22 [DDD]
Puccini, G.:Manon Lescaut, w. M. Freni (sop), P. Domingo (ten), G. Sinopoli (cnd), Philharmonia Orch, Royal Opera House Chorus Covent Garden [I] *(rec 1984)*
Deutsche Grammophon 2-▲ 413893-2 [DDD]
Puccini, G.:Tosca, w. R. Scotto (sop), P. Domingo (ten), J. Levine (cnd), Philharmonia Orch, Ambrosian Opera Chorus [I] EMI Classics 2-▲ CDCB 49364 [DDD]
Puccini, G.:Tosca (sels), w. R. Scotto (sop), P. Domingo (ten), J. Levine (cnd), Philharmonia Orch, Ambrosian Opera Chorus EMI Classics ▲ CDC 54324
Saint-Saëns, C.:Samson et Dalila, w. E. Obraztsova (mez), P. Domingo (ten), R. Lloyd (b-bar), D. Barenboim (cnd), Orch de Paris Deutsche Grammophon 2-▲ 413297-2 [DDD]
Tosti, P.F.:Romanzas on Italian Texts, w. Robert Kettelson (pno) Nuova Era ▲ NUO 7233 [DDD]
Tosti, P.F.:Songs, w. V. Antonellini (cnd), I Solisti Aquilani [string orch. trans. Giuseppe Piccinino]—Sogno; Malia; Ideale; Ridonami la calma; 'A Vucchella; La serenata; L'ultima canzone; Tristezza; La chanson de l'adieu; E morto Pulcinella; Vorrei morire; Non t'amo più [F,I] *(rec live, 9/19-21/86)* Bongiovanni ▲ GB 2505 [DDD]
Tosti, P.F.:Songs, w. R. Cognazzo (pno), 33 songs, w. lyrics by Gabriele D'Annunzio [I] *(rec Nov. 30 & Dec. 8, 1991)* Nuova Era 2-▲ 7090/91
Verdi, G.:Alzira, w. M. Cotrubas (sop), F. Araiza (ten), L. Gardelli (cnd), Munich RSO, Bavarian Radio Chorus [I] Orfeo 2-▲ 057832 [DDD]
Verdi, G.:Un ballo in maschera, w. C. Deutekom (sop), G. Tucker (ten), R. Muti (cnd), Florence Teatro Comunale Orch, Florence Teatro Comunale Chorus *(rec live, Florence 1972)*
Foyer 2-▲ FOY 2047 [AAD]
Verdi, G.:Un ballo in maschera, w. M. Price (sop), K. Battle (sop), C. Ludwig (mez), L. Pavarotti (ten), G. Solti (cnd), National PO London, National Phil London Chorus [I] London 4-▲ 425529-2 [DDD]
Verdi, G.:Un ballo in maschera, w. M. Price (sop), K. Battle (sop), C. Ludwig (mez), L. Pavarotti (ten), G. Solti (cnd), National PO London, National Phil London Chorus [I] London 2-▲ 410210-2 [DDD]
Verdi, G.:Don Carlos, w. M. Caballé (sop—Elisabeth de Valois), G. Bumbry (mez—Princess Eboli), J. Aragall (ten—Don Carlos), R. Bruson (bar—Rodrigue), S. Estes (bass—Philip II), T. Fulton (cnd), *(orch unknown)* *(rec Orange, France, 1979)* Ornamenti 2-▲ FE 110 [ADD]
Verdi, G.:Ernani, w. M. Freni (sop), P. Domingo (ten), N. Ghiaurov (bass), R. Muti (cnd), La Scala Orch, La Scala Chorus [I] EMI Classics 3-▲ CDC 47082 [DDD]
Verdi, G.:Luisa Miller, w. K. Ricciarelli (sop—Luisa), M. G. Piolatto (mez—Laura), S. Silva (cta—Federica), J. Carreras (ten—Rodolfo), E. Pranod (ten—A Peasant), R. Bruson (bar—Miller), G. Casarini (bar—Wurm) M. Rinaudo (bass—Count Walter), F. Previtali (cnd), Turin Teatro Regio Orch, Turin Teatro Regio Chorus *(rec May 9, 1976)* Legato Classics 2-▲ LCD 180 [ADD]
Verdi, G.:Macbeth, w. Grace Bumbry (mez—Lady Macbeth), Luciano Saldari (ten—Macduff), Paride Venturi (ten—Malcolm), Renato Bruson (bar—Macbeth), Agostino Ferrin (bass—Banquo), A. Gatto (cnd), Bologna Teatro Comunale Orch, Bologna Teatro Comunale Chorus *(rec Bologna, Mar. 18, 1975)*
Golden Age of Opera 2-▲ GAO 185/86 [ADD]
Verdi, G.:I masnadieri, w. I. Ligabue (sop), G. Raimondi (ten), B. Christoff (bass), G. Gavazzeni (cnd), Rome Opera Orch, Rome Opera Chorus [I] *(rec live, Rome, Nov. 25, 1972)*
Golden Age of Opera 2-▲ GAO 135/36 [ADD]
Verdi, G.:I masnadieri, w. M. Rowland (sgr), M. Malagnini (sgr), T. Migliorini (sgr), M. Lanskoy (bar), C. Colombara (bass), W. Gönnenwein (cnd), Ludwigsburg Festival Orch, South German Madrigal Choir
Bayer 2-▲ BR 500 001/2 [DDD]
Verdi, G.:Rigoletto, w. Andrea Rost (sop—Gilda), Mariana Pentcheva (cta—Maddalena), Roberto Alagna (ten—Il Duca di Mantova), Renato Bruson (bar—Rigoletto), Dmitri Kavrakos (bass—Sparafucile), R. Muti (cnd), La Scala Orch, La Scala Chorus Sony Classical 2-▲ S2K 66314
Verdi, G.:Rigoletto, w. Cecilia Nunez Albanese (sop—Gilda), Wilma Borrelli (cta—Maddalena), Jaime Aragall (ten—Duke of Mantua), Renato Bruson (bar—Rigoletto), Loris Gambelli (bass—Sparafucile), G. Campanino (cnd), Naples Teatro San Carlo Orch, Naples Teatro San Carlo Chorus *(rec San Carlo Theatre, Naples, Feb. 1973)* Golden Age of Opera 2-▲ GAO 177-78 [ADD]

Bruson, Renato (bar) (cont.)
Verdi, G.:Rigoletto, w. E. Gruberova (sop), B. Fassbaender (mez), Schicoff (ten), R. Lloyd (b-bar), G. Sinopoli (cnd), St. Cecilia Academy Orch Rome, St. Cecilia Academy Chorus Rome [I]
Philips 2-▲ 412592-2 [DDD]
Verdi, G.:Rigoletto (sels), w. Andrea Rost (sop), Roberto Alagna (ten), R. Muti (cnd), La Scala Orch
Sony Classical ▲ SK 61966
Verdi, G.:Simon Boccanegra, w. M. Nicolesco (sop), G. Sabbatini (ten), S. Rinaldi-Miliani (bar), R. Scandiuzzi (bass), N. de Angelis (bass), R. Paternostro (cnd), Tokyo SO, Nikikai Chorus *(rec live 2/90)*
Capriccio 2-▲ 60018-2 [DDD]
Verdi, G.:La traviata, w. I. Cotrubas (sop), G. Aragall (ten), C. Kleiber (cnd), Bavarian State Orch [I] *(rec 1978)* Artists 2-▲ FED 45 [ADD]
Verdi, G.:La traviata, w. L. Aliberti (sop), M. Dvorsky (ten), R. Paternostro (cnd), Tokyo PO, Tokyo Phil Chorus [I] *(rec live, Suntory Hall, Tokyo)* Capriccio 2-▲ 10274/75 [DDD]
Verdi, G.:Il trovatore, w. Katia Ricciarelli (sop), Richard Tucker (ten), Zanibelli (sgr), A. Erede (cnd), Parma Teatro Regio Orch *(rec Parma, 1971)* Golden Age of Opera 2-▲ GAO 193/194

Brutscher, Markus (ten)
Cavalli, P.F.:Vespero della beata Vergine Maria, w. Barbara Borden (sop), Emily van Evera (sop), Mark Padmore (ten), Rodrigo del Pozo (ten), Gerd Türk (ten), Harry van der Kamp (bass), Peter Zimpel (sgr), Bruce Dickey (sackbut), Charles Toet (sackbut), Concerto Palatino, Schola Cantorum Basiliensis
Harmonia Mundi France ("Documenta" series) 2-▲ HMC 905219/20
Zelenka, J.D.:Missa sanctissimae trinitatis, w. Monika Frimmer (sop), Elisabeth Graf (cta), W. Wehnert (cnd), Marburg Bach Choir Thorofon ▲ CTH 2265

Bryant, Dinah (sop)
Uy, P.:Choral pour la Paix, w. Zeger Vandersteene (ten), Philippe Huttenlocher (bar), Alain Carré (nar), Dominique Cornil (pno), G. Octors (cnd), Wallonie Royal CO, Denis Menier (cnd), Namur Chamber Choir *(rec Aulne, Belgium, 1995)* Cypres ▲ 2611 [DDD]
Wolf, H.:Mörike-Lieder (sels), w. Daniel Blumenthal (pno)—Auf einer Wanderung; Eine Stündlein wohl vor Tag; Erstes Liebeslied eine Mädchens; Das Verlassene Mägdlein; Nixe Binsefuss; Gesang Weylas; Fussreise; Schlafendes Jesuskind; Lied vom Winde; Im Frühling; Verborgenheit; Elfenlied; Zitronenfalter im April; Heimweh; Er ist's; Abschied Pavane ▲ ADW 7323 [DDD]

Brychcy, W. (bass)
Gorczycki, G.G.:Sacred Choral Music, w. R. Stacewicz (sop), I. Tkaczyk (alt), A. Pagowska (alt), E. Sasiadek (ten), Wroclaw Orch, S. Galonski (cnd), Edmund Kajdasz (cnd), Capella Bydgostiensis Pro Musica Antiqua, Madrigalists Choir, Polish Radio Chorus—Completorium; In virtute tua; Iudica me deus; Laetatus sum; Missa paschalis [L] *(rec 1966)* Olympia ▲ OCD 320 [AAD]

Brychtová, Monika (sgr)
Dvořák, A.:Armida, w. Joanna Borowska (sop—Armida), Monika Brychtová (sgr—Siren), Wieslaw Ochman (ten—Rinald), Richard Sporka (ten—Dudo), Jan Markvart (bar—Sven), Pavel Daniluk (bass—King), George Fortune (bass—Ismen), Zdenek Harvánek (bass—Ubald), Miloslav Podskalský (bass—Peter), Milan Bürger (sgr—Gernand), Roman Janál (sgr—Muezzin/Hlasatel), Vratislav Kříž (sgr—Gottfried), Vladimír Nacházel (sgr—Roger), G. Albrecht (cnd), Czech PO, Prague Chamber Choir *(rec 1995)* Orfeo 2-▲ 404962 [DDD]

Bryden, Jane (sop)
Bach, J.S.:Magnificat, BWV 243, w. J. Baird (sop), J Gall (ct), F. Hoffmeister (ten), J. Opalach (bass), J. Rifkin (cnd), Bach Ensemble [L] Pro Arte ▲ CDD 185 [DDD]
Bach, J.S.:St. John Passion, w. J. Baird (sop), J. Thomas (ten), D. Ripley (bar), J. Weaver (bass), K. Slowik (cnd), Smithsonian Chamber Players, Smithsonian Chamber Chorus [period instrs] [G] *(Slowik performs the original 1724 version, & includes the two choruses & three arias added to Bach's 1725 revision as appended tracks at the end of the discs, allowing the listener to either ignore the end tracks & hear the standard version or program the discs to play the 1725 sequence)*
Smithsonian Collection 5-▲ ND 0380 [DDD]
Hoffmann, M.:German Magnificat, w. J. Rifkin (cnd), Bach Ensemble [G] Pro Arte ▲ CDD 185 [DDD]
Mozart, W.A.:Requiem, w. M. Westbrook-Geha (mez), W. Hite (ten), S. Richardson (bar), A. Parrott (cnd), Boston Early Music Festival Orch, Boston Early Music Festival Chorus [L]
Denon ▲ CO 77152 [DDD]

Bryn-Julson, Phyllis (sop)
Beethoven, L. van:Meeresstille und glückliche Fahrt, w. S. Skrowaczewski (cnd), Minnesota Orch, Minnesota Bach Society Vox Box 2-▲ CDX 5099 [ADD]
Boulez, P.:Le Soleil des eaux, w. P. Boulez (cnd), BBC SO, BBC Singers [F]
Erato ▲ 2292-45494-2 [DDD]
Boulez, P.:Le Visage Nuptial, w. E. Laurence (alt), P. Boulez (cnd), BBC SO, BBC Singers [F]
Erato ▲ 2292-45494-2 [DDD]
Britten, H.:Our Hunting Fathers, w. S. Bedford, English CO [E] *(rec 1990)*
Collins Classics ▲ 11922 [DDD]
Carter, E.:Poems (3) of Robert Frost, w. Mark Markham (pno) [arr for sop & pno]
Music & Arts ▲ CD 900 [DDD]
Carter, E.:Songs, w. Mark Markham (pno)—Voyage; Warble for Lilac Time
Music & Arts ▲ CD 900 [DDD]
Dallapiccola, L.:Il Prigioniero, w. Sven-Erik Alexandersson (ten), Howard Haskin (ten), Jorma Hynninen (bar), Lage Wedin (bar), E.-P. Salonen (cnd), Swedish RSO, Eric Ericson Chamber Choir
Sony Classical ▲ SK 68323
Dallapiccola, L.:Songs, w. Mark Markham (pno) Music & Arts ▲ CD 912
del Tredici, D.:An Alice Sym, w. O. Knussen (cnd), Tanglewood Music Center Orch *(rec Theatre-Concert Hall, Tanglewood, Lenox, MA, Aug. 7, 1991)* CRI ▲ CD 688 [DDD]
del Tredici, D.:I Hear an Army, w. Composers String Quartet [E] CRI ■ ACS 6004
del Tredici, D.:I Hear an Army, w. Composers String Quartet
CRI ("American Masters" series) ▲ CD 689 [DDD]
del Tredici, D.:In Memory of a Summer Day, w. L. Slatkin (cnd), St. Louis SO [E]
Elektra/Nonesuch ▲ 79043-2 [DDD]
del Tredici, D.:Syzygy, w. R. Dufallo (cnd), Festival CO [E] CRI ■ ACS 6004
del Tredici, D.:Syzygy, w. R. Dufallo (cnd), Festival CO
CRI ("American Masters" series) ▲ CD 689 [DDD]
Gideon, M.:The Condemned Playground, w. C. Cassolas (ten), Jahoda, *(ensemble unknown)*
CRI ■ C 343
Griffes, C.T.:Poems (3) of Fiona McLeod, w. S. Ozawa (cnd), Boston SO [E]
New World ▲ NW 273-2 [ADD]
Ligeti, G.:The Ligeti Edition, w. Rosemary Hardy (sop), Christiane Oelze (sop), Rose Taylor (mez), Sibylle Ehlert (sgr), Omar Ebrahim (bar), Pierre-Laurent Aimard (pno), E.-P. Salonen (cnd), Philharmonia Orch, King's Singers—Vocal Works; Madrigals; Mysteries; Adventures; Songs; Nonsense Madrigals
Sony Classical ▲ SK 62311
Mamlok, U.:Stray Birds, w. H. Sollberger (fl), F. Sherry (vc) CRI ■ C 301
Messiaen, O.:Poèmes pour Mi, w. Mark Markham (pno) Music & Arts ▲ CD 912
Rhodes, P.:Autumn Setting, w. Speculum Musicae String Quartet CRI ■ C 301
Rorem, N.:Nantucket Songs, w. N. Rorem (pno) [E] *(rec Library of Congress, world premiere performance, 10/30/79)* CRI ■ ACS 6007
Rorem, N.:Nantucket Songs, w. N. Rorem (pno) CRI ▲ CD 657 [ADD]
Schoenberg, A.:Book of the Hanging Gardens, w. U. Oppens (pno) [G] Music & Arts ▲ CD 650 [DDD]
Schoenberg, A.:The Cabaret Songs, w. U. Oppens (pno) [G] Music & Arts ▲ CD 650 [DDD]
Schoenberg, A.:Erwartung, w. S. Rattle (cnd), Birmingham Contemporary Music Group
EMI Classics ▲ CDC 55212
Schoenberg, A.:Songs, Op. 2, w. U. Oppens (pno) [G] Music & Arts ▲ CD 650 [DDD]
Schuller, G.:Early Songs, w. Mark Markham (pno) Music & Arts ▲ CD 900 [DDD]
Starer, R.:Anna Margarita's Will, w. K. Kraber (fl), S. Kates (vc), P. Ingraham (hn), D. Sutherland (pno) *(rec 1980)* CRI ▲ CD 612 [ADD]
Wuorinen, C.:Songs, w. Mark Markham (pno) Music & Arts ▲ CD 912
Wuorinen, C.:A Winter's Tale, w. Mark Markham (pno) Music & Arts ▲ CD 900 [DDD]
Wuorinen, C.:A Winter's Tale, w. C. Wuorinen (cnd), Lincoln Center Chamber Music Society
Koch International Classics ▲ KIC 7272 [DDD]

Bryn-Julson, Phyllis (spkr)
Schoenberg, A.:Pierrot lunaire, w. R. Black (cnd), New York New Music Ensemble [G] *(rec Sep. 1991)* GM ▲ GM 2030

Brynner, Yul (sgr)
Rodgers, R.:The King & I, w. M. Nixon (sgr), R. Moreno (sgr), *(artists unknown) (rec 1956)* Broadway Angel ▲ ZDM 64693 ■ EG 64693
Rodgers, R.:The King & I, w. C. Towers (sgr), *(other artists unknown)* [1977 Broadway revival cast] RCA ▲ RCD 12610 ■ ABK 12610
Rodgers, R.:The King & I, w. Gertrude Lawrence (sgr), *(other artists unknown)* [1951 Broadway cast] MCA Classics ▲ MCAD 10049 [AAD] ■ MCAC 10049
Rodgers, R.:Music of, w. J. Raitt (sgr)—The Sound of Music; Oklahoma!; The King & I; Carousel RCA 4-▲ 60569-2 RG 4-■ 60569-4 RG

Bryson, Peabo (sgr)
Rodgers, R.:The King & I, w. J. Andrews (sgr—Anna Leonowens), L. Salonga (sgr—Tuptim), B. Kingsley (sgr—The King), P. Bryson (sgr—Lun Tha), M. Horne (mez—Lady Thiang), M. Liufau (sgr—Prince Chulalongkorn), E. Kingsley (sgr—Louis Leonowens), R. Moore (sgr—Sir Edward Ramsay), M. Sheen (sgr—The Kralahome), J. Mauceri (cnd), Hollywood Bowl Orch, Los Angeles Master Chorale *(rec Culver City, CA, Apr 1992)* Philips ▲ 438007-2 [DDD]

Buades, Aurora (mez)
Bizet, G.:Carmen, w. Ines Alfani Tellini (sop), Aureliano Pertile (ten), Benvenuto Franci (bar), L. Molajoli (cnd), La Scala Orch, La Scala Chorus *(rec Milan, 1933)* Phonographie 2-▲ PHG 5013 [ADD]
Verdi, G.:Falstaff, w. Pia Tassinari (sop—Alice Ford), Ines Alfani Tellini (sop—Nannetta), Aurora Buades (mez—Quickly), Rita Monticone (mez—Meg Page), Roberto D'Alessio (ten—Fenton), Giuseppe Nessi (ten—Bardolfo), Emilio Venturini (ten—Dr. Caius), Emilio Ghirardini (bar—Ford), Giacomo Rimini (bar—Sir John Falstaff), Salvatore Baccaloni (bass—Pistola), L. Molajoli (cnd), Milan SO, La Scala Chorus *(rec La Scala Theatre, Milan, Apr. 1932)* VAI Audio 2-▲ VAIA 1098-2

Bubnó, Tamás (ten)
Rachmaninoff, S.:Liturgy of St John Chrysostom, w. Ida Szabó (sop), Ákos Ambrus (bar), Zoltán Kocsis (cnd), Tomkins Vocal Ensemble *(rec 1995)* Hungaroton 2-▲ HCD 31610/11 [DDD]
Werner, G.J.:Vesperae de Apostolis, w. Ágnes Dobszay (sop), Péter Patay (cta), Péter Cser (bass), J. Mezei (cnd), Vienna-Szász CO, Budapest Schola Cantorum *(rec St. Columba's Presbyterian Church, Budapest, June 12-15, 1995)* Hungaroton ▲ HCD 31646 [DDD]

Buchanan, Isobel (sop)
Mahler, G.:Sym 2, w. M. Zakai (cta), G. Solti (cnd), Chicago SO, Chicago Sym Chorus [G] London 2-▲ 410202-2 [DDD]

Buchanan, Jack (sgr)
Kern, J.:Sunny (sels), w. B. Hale (sgr), C. Hulbert (sgr), *(other artists unknown)* Pearl ("Flapper" series) ▲ PEA CD 9105 [ADD]

Buchin, Werner (alt)
Luneburg 1647, w. Ensemble Lanterly, Mona Spagele (sop), Albrecht Pohl (bass) MD + G ▲ MDG CD 6050647

Büchner, Eberhard (ten)
Auber, D.-F.:Fra Diavolo, w. H. Termer (sop), G. Neumann (ten), W.-D. Hauschild (cnd), Berlin RSO Berlin Classics ▲ BER 2140 [ADD]
Bach, J.S.:Cants (misc), w. Edith Mathis (sop), Carolyn Watkinson (cta), Peter Schreier (ten), Siegfried Lorenz (bar), Theo Adam (b-bar), P. Schreier (cnd), Berlin CO, Berlin Soloists Berlin Classics ▲ BER 9221
Bach, J.S.:Cant 4, w. Helga Terner (sop), Ortrun Wenkel (cta), Peter Schreier (ten), H.-J. Rotzsch (cnd), Leipzig Gewandhaus Orch, Leipzig St. Thomas Church Choir, Leipzig New Bach Collegium Musicum Berlin Classics ▲ BER 2067 [ADD]
Bach, J.S.:Cant 14, w. M. Frimmer (sop), A. Scheibner (bar), M. Pommer (cnd), Leipzig New Bach Collegium Musicum, Leipzig St. Thomas Church Choir [G] Capriccio ▲ CDC 10027
Bach, J.S.:Cant 31, w. Helga Terner (sop), Ortrun Wenkel (cta), Peter Schreier (ten), H.-J. Rotzsch (cnd), Leipzig Gewandhaus Orch, Leipzig St. Thomas Church Choir, Leipzig New Bach Collegium Musicum Berlin Classics ▲ BER 2067 [ADD]
Bach, J.S.:Cant 31, w. Siegfried Lorenz (bar), Hermann Christian Polster (bass), Lang (sgr), Termer (sgr), Weimann (sgr), H.-J. Rotzsch (cnd), Leipzig Gewandhaus Orch, St. Thomas Choir Berlin Classics ▲ BER 9025 [ADD]
Bach, J.S.:Cant 66, w. Siegfried Lorenz (bar), Hermann Christian Polster (bass), Lang (sgr), Termer (sgr), Weimann (sgr), H.-J. Rotzsch (cnd), Leipzig Gewandhaus Orch, St. Thomas Choir Berlin Classics ▲ BER 9025 [ADD]
Bach, J.S.:Cant 106, "Actus tragicus", w. Siegfried Lorenz (bar), Hermann Christian Polster (bass), Lang (sgr), Termer (sgr), Weimann (sgr), H.-J. Rotzsch (cnd), Leipzig Gewandhaus Orch, St. Thomas Choir Berlin Classics ▲ BER 9025 [ADD]
Bach, J.S.:Cant 134, w. Helga Terner (sop), Ortrun Wenkel (cta), Peter Schreier (ten), H.-J. Rotzsch (cnd), Leipzig Gewandhaus Orch, Leipzig New Bach Collegium Musicum, Leipzig St. Thomas Church Choir Berlin Classics ▲ BER 2067 [ADD]
Bach, J.S.:Cant 143, w. M. Frimmer (sop), A. Scheibner (bar), M. Pommer (cnd), Leipzig New Bach Collegium Musicum, Leipzig St. Thomas Church Choir [G] Capriccio ▲ CDC 10027 [DDD]
Beethoven, L. van:Leonore (opera), w. Helen Donath (sop), Edda Moser (sop), Richard Cassilly (ten), Theo Adam (b-bar), Hermann Christian Polster (bass), Karl Ridderbusch (bass), H. Blomstedt (cnd), Dresden Staatskapelle, Leipzig Radio Chorus Berlin Classics ▲ BER 1140
Beethoven, L. van:Sym 9, "Choral Sym", w. A. Hargan (sop), U. Walther (cta), K. Kováts (bass), H. Kegel (cnd), Dresden PO Capriccio ▲ 10 453 [DDD]
Dessau, P.:Leonce & Lena, w. C. Nossek (sop), R. Süss (bar), O. Suitner (cnd), Berlin Staatskapelle Berlin Classics ▲ BER 1074 [ADD]
Handel, G.F.:The Choice of Hercules, w. Arleen Augér (sop), Venceslava Hruba-Freiberger (sop), Zäpffel (sgr), M. Pommer (cnd), Leipzig New Bach Collegium Musicum, Leipzig Univ Choir [E] Capriccio ▲ CDC 10019 [DDD]
Mendelssohn, F.:Die erste Walpurgisnacht, w. A. Burmeister (mez), S. Lorenz (bar), K. Masur (cnd), Leipzig Gewandhaus Orch Berlin Classics ("Eterna" series) ▲ BER 2057 [ADD]
Mendelssohn, F.:Ov, Op. 101, w. A. Burmeister (mez), S. Lorenz (bar), K. Masur (cnd), Leipzig Gewandhaus Orch Berlin Classics ("Eterna" series) ▲ BER 2057 [ADD]
Prokofiev, S.:Betrothal in a Monastery (sels), w. A. Burmeister (mez), R. Süss (bar), H. Kegel (cnd), Leipzig RSO [G] Berlin Classics ▲ BER 2081 [ADD]
Schmidt, F.:Das Buch mit sieben Siegeln, w. Gabriele Fontana (sop), Margareta Hintermeier (alt), Kurt Azesberger (ten), Eberhard Büchner (ten—Johannes), Robert Holl (bass—Voice of the Lord), Robert Holzer (bass), Martin Haselböck (org), H. Stein (cnd), Vienna SO, Vienna Sym Chorus *(rec live, Vienna Music Hall, May 1996)* Calig 2-▲ CAL 50978/9 [DDD]
Schnittke, A.:Historia von D. Johann Fausten, w. Hanna Schwarz (mez—Fair Helen), Arno Raunig (alt—Mephostophiles), Eberhard Büchner (ten—Old Man), Jürgen Freier (bar—Dr. Johann Faustus), Jonathan Barreto-Ramos (sgr—Student), Jürgen Fersch (sgr—Student), Eberhard Lorenz (sgr—Erzähler), Christoph Johannes Wendel (sgr—Student), G. Albrecht (cnd), Hamburg State PO, Hamburg State Opera Chorus RCA Red Seal 2-▲ 09026-68413-2

Buchner, Paula (sop)
Strauss, R.:Feuersnot (sels), w. Maria Cebotari (sop), Tiana Lemnitz (sop), Karl Schmitt-Walter (bar), A. Rother (cnd), Berlin Radio Orch *(rec 1943-44)* Preiser ▲ PRE 90222 [ADD]
Strauss, R.:Der Rosenkavalier (sels), w. Maria Cebotari (sop), Tiana Lemnitz (sop), Karl Schmitt-Walter (bar), A. Rother (cnd), Berlin Radio Orch *(rec 1943-44)* Preiser ▲ PRE 90222 [ADD]
Strauss, R.:Salome (sels), w. Maria Cebotari (sop), Tiana Lemnitz (sop), Karl Schmitt-Walter (bar), A. Rother (cnd), Berlin Radio Orch—Final Scene *(rec 1943-44)* Preiser ▲ PRE 90222 [ADD]

Buchta, Hubert (ten)
Lortzing, A.:Zar und Zimmermann, w. M. Gripekoven (sop—Marie), E. Mayer (cta—Widow Browe), H. Buchta (ten—Peter Ivonov), H. Schmid-Berikoven (ten—Marquis de Chateauneuf), G. Hann (b-bar—Tsar Peter I), W. Strienz (b-bar—Van Bett), B. Müller (bass) Myto 2-▲ MCD 943103

Buck, D. (sgr)
Sousa, J.P.:Songs, w. J. Guyer (sop), M. Wilson (sgr)—(6 soprano solos, 7 baritone solos, & 5 duets) I've made my plans for the summer (1907); The love that lives forever (1917); Valse song [The Crystal lute - from *The American Maid*, 1909]; Oh, ye lilies white (1887); Girls who have loved [or The Mystery of History - from *The Free Lance*, 1905]; There's a mery brown thrush (1926); The fighting race (1919); A Serenade in Seville (1924); My own, my Geraldine (1887); Sweet Miss Industry (1887); I wonder (1888); You can hold how old they are by looking at their skirts (1923); Forever and a day (1927); Sweetheart, I'm waiting (1895); Blue Ridge, I'm coming back to you (1917); Love's radiant hour (1928); A rare old fellow (1881); The Stars and Stripes forever (1898) [E] Premier ▲ PRCD 1011 [DDD]

Buckel, Ursula (sop)
Bach, J.S.:Cant 202, "Wedding Cant", w. Willy Schnell (ob), Werner Keltsch (vn), Peter Buck (vc), Martin Galling (hpd), R. Ewerhart (cnd), Württemberg CO *(rec 1965)* Vox Box 3-▲ CD3X 3039
Bach, J.S.:Cant 212, "Peasant Cant", w. Claus Ocker (bass), Gabriele Zimmerman (fl), Peter Buck (vc), Martin Galling (hpd), R. Ewerhart (cnd), Württemberg CO *(rec 1965)* Vox Box 3-▲ CD3X 3039
Mozart, W.A.:Requiem, w. M. Bence (cta), H.-U. Mielsch (ten), E. Wollitz (bass), R. Bader (cnd), Stuttgart PO, Böblingen Bach Choir Allegretto ▲ ACD 8060 [ADD] ■ ACS 8060

Buckingham, Walter (sgr)
Cage, J.:Apartment House 1776, w. Walter Buckingham (sgr—Protestant), Darrell Dunn (sgr—Native American), Semenya McCord (sgr—African American), Chiam Parchi (sgr—Sephardi), New England Conservatory Philharmonia *(rec New England Conservatory of Music, Boston, MA, Mar. 4 & 6, 1991)* Mode ▲ MODE 41

Buckner, Thomas (bar)
Ashley, R.:eL/Aficionado, w. J. Humbert (sgr—Interrogator No. 2), T. Buckner (sgr—Agent), R. Ashley (sgr—Interrogator No. 1), S. Ashley (sgr—Interrogator No. 3), *(orch unknown)* Lovely Music ▲ LCD 1004 [DDD]
Ashley, R.:Improvement, w. J. Humbert (sgr—Linda), J. La Barbara (sop—Now Eleanor), A. X. Neuburg (sgr—Mr. Payne's Mother), T. Buckner (sgr—Don/Mr. Payne/Linda's Companion), S. Ashley (sgr—Junior, Jr.), A. Klein (sgr—Doctor), R. Ashley (sgr—Narrator), *(cnd & orch unknown)* [E] Elektra/Nonesuch 2-▲ 79289-2
Ashley, R.:The Producer Speaks, w. J. Kubera (pno) Lovely Music ▲ LCD 3022 [DDD]
Full Spectrum Voice Lovely Music ▲ LCD 3021 [DDD]
Gibson, Jon:Running Commentary, w. J. Gibson (sax), J. Kubera (pno), Bill Ruyle (perc) Lovely Music ▲ LCD 3022 [DDD]
Hamilton, T.:Off-Hour Wait State, w. Roscoe Mitchell (a sax), Ralph Samuelson (shak), Peter Zummo (trbn), Tom Hamilton (syn/elec), Jonathan Haas (perc) O.O. Discs ▲ OO 26 [DDD]
Jenkins, L.:Dream of Dreams of Home, w. S. Starin (fl), L. Jenkins (va) Lovely Music ▲ LCD 3022 [DDD]
Kim, J.H.:Yoeum, w. Whang Kyu-Nam (kagok) O. O. Discs ▲ OO24
Lockwood, A.:The Angel of Repose, w. S. Starin (fl/khaen) Lovely Music ▲ LCD 3022 [DDD]
Smith, B.:The Panther, w. J. Kubera (pno) Lovely Music ▲ LCD 3022 [DDD]

Buda, Adriana (sop)
Rossini, G.:Torvaldo e Dorliska, w. F. Pediconi (sop), M. Ciliento (mez), E. Palacio (ten), S. Antonucci (bar), A. Marani (b-bar), M. de Bernart (cnd), Swiss-Italian Orch, Cantemus, Swiss-Italian Radio-TV Chorus *(rec Jan. 11, 1992)* Arkadia-Akademia 2-▲ 123 [DDD]

Budd, Harold (voc/pno)
Budd, H.:In Delius' Sleep, w. Zeitgeist *(rec Westminster Church, Minneapolis, MN, Nov. 20, 1993)* New Albion ▲ NA066
Budd, H.:She Is a Phantom, w. Zeitgeist *(rec Westminster Church, Minneapolis, MN, Nov. 20, 1993)* New Albion ▲ NA066

Budd, Jeremy (trb)
Mendelssohn, F.:Elijah, w. R. Plowright (sop), L. Finnie (mez), A. Davies (ten), J. White (bass), R. Hickox (cnd), London SO, London Sym Chorus [E] Chandos 2-▲ CHAN 8774/75 [DDD]

Budoiu, Marius (ten)
Bretan, N.:The Evening Star, w. Adriana Croitoru (sop—King's Daughter), Elena Casian (mez—Lady-in-Waiting), Marius Budoiu (ten—Mariner), Ioan Pojar (ten—Page), Ionel Voineag (ten—Evening Star), Bálint Szabó (bass—Michael the Archangel), B. Hary (cnd), Transylvania PO Cluj *(rec Cluj, Sept 1994)* Nimbus ▲ NI 5463 [DDD]

Budwig, Monty (bass)
Saxophone Quartet, w. H. Pittel (sax), Shelly Manne (drums) Crystal ■ C 155

Bugli, Claudia (sop)
Perti, G.A.:Liturgy for Good Friday, w. Patrizia Vaccari (sop), Maura Pederzoli (sop), Cristina Calzolari (sop), Alida Oliva (sop), Lucia Bagnoli (alt), Cinzia Meneghel (alt), Renzo Bez (alt), Alessandro Carmignani (alt), Michel van Goethem (alt), Mauro Collina (ten), Vincenzo Di Donato (ten), Paolo Fanciullacci (ten), Giovanni Caccamo (ten), Paolo Da Col (ten), Sergio Foresti (bass), Marco Scavazza (bass), Luca Ferracin (bass), Paride Montanari (bass), Liuwe Tamminga (org), Sergio Vartolo (org), S. Vartolo (cnd), Bologna San Petronio Capella Musicale Orch—Omnes amici mei; De lamentatione Jeremiae Prophetae:Heth. Cogitavit; Velum templi; Vinea mea; De lamentatione Jeremiae Prophetae:Lamed. Matribus suis; Tamquam ad latronem; Tenebrae factae sunt; Animam meam; Trадiderunt me; Jesum tradidit; De lamentatione Jeremiae Prophetae:Aleph. Ego vir; Caligaverunt *(rec St. Petronio Basilica, Bologna, Mar 28-31, 1995)* Naxos ▲ 8.553321 [DDD]

Buhl, Jesper (bar)
Klit, L.:The Last Virtuoso, w. Hanne Andersen (sop), Edith Guillaume (mez), Jan Lund (ten), Jørgen Ole Børch (bass), S. A. Johansen (cnd), *(ensemble unknown)* Kontrapunkt ▲ KPT 32221

Bullock, Susan (sop)
Spratling, H.:Choral Music, w. Tracey Chadwell (sop), Jeffery Dyball (hp), Helen Tunstall (hp), John Hatton (org), J. Rennert (cnd), Parnassus String Ensemble, Spratling Choir—Mass of the Holy Spirit; O Salutaris Hostia; Tantum Ergo; Sinf Str Orch; Son Hp; O Magnum Mysterium; In Paradisum *(rec St. Mary Magdelene, Paddington, May 15-17, 1988)* SOMM ▲ SOMMCD 206 [ADD]
Sullivan, A.:The Mikado, w. L. Garrett (sop), J. Rigby (mez), F. Palmer (sop/mez), B. Bottone (ten), R. Angas (bass), E. Idle (bar), R. Van Allan (bass), M. Richardson (bar), P. Robinson (cnd), English National Opera Orch, English Opera Group Chorus—sels [E] MCA Classics ▲ MCAD 6215 [DDD]; ■ MCAC 6215 (D)

Bumbry, Grace (mez)
Bizet, G.:Carmen, w. Giovanna di Rocco (sop—Frasquita), Grace Bumbry (mez—Carmen), Anita Caminada (mez—Mercedes), Franco Corelli (ten—Don José), Mario Ferrara (ten—Dancario), Franco Bordoni (bar—Escamillo), Carlo Scaravelli (bar—Morales), Giuseppe Morresi (bass—Remendado), Francesco Signor (bass—Zuniga), O. de Fabritiis (cnd), *(orch unknown) (rec Macerata, July 21, 1974)* Golden Age of Opera 2-▲ GAO 181/82 [ADD]
Bizet, G.:Carmen, w. M. Freni (sop), J. Vickers (ten), K. Paskalis (bar), R. Frühbeck de Burgos (cnd), Paris Opera Orch, Paris Opera Chorus [opéra comique version] [F] EMI Classics ("Studio" series) 2-▲ CDMB 63643 [ADD]
Bizet, G.:Carmen (sels), w. Mirella Freni (sop), Jon Vickers (ten), H. von Karajan (cnd), Vienna PO *(rec Salzburg, 1967)* Arkadia 3-▲ 498
Falla, M. de:El amor brujo, w. L. Maazel (cnd), Berlin RSO Deutsche Grammophon ("The Originals" series) ▲ 447414-2
Famous Opera Arias, w. Stuttgart Radio SO [cnd:S. Soltesz] Orfeo ▲ C 081841 A [DDD] ■ M 081841 A (D)
Gluck, C.W.:Orfeo ed Euridice, w. Ruth-Margaret Pütz (sop), Anneliese Rothenberger (sop), V. Neumann (cnd), Leipzig Opera Orch, Leipzig Radio Chorus *(rec Leipzig, 1967)* Berlin Classics 2-▲ BER 9033 [ADD]
Handel, G.F.:Judas Maccabaeus, w. Martina Arroyo (sop), J. McCollum (ten), Marvin Sorensen (ten), D. Watts (bass), M. Abravanel (cnd), Utah SO, Utah Sym Chorus [E] *(rec ca. 1959)lite* MCA Classics 3-▲ MCAD3-10515 [ADD]
Handel, G.F.:Messiah, w. Joan Sutherland (sop), Kenneth McKeller (ten), Joseph Ward (bar), A. Boult (cnd), London PO London 3-▲ 433003-2 [DDD]

Bumbry, Grace (mez) (cont.)
Handel, G.F.:Messiah (sels), w. Joan Sutherland (sop), Kenneth McKellar (ten), Joseph Ward (bar), A. Boult (cnd), London SO, London Sym Chorus—arias & choruses
London ("Weekend Classics" series) ▲ 417879-2 [AAD] ■ 417879-4
James Levine's 25th Anniversary Metropolitan Opera Gala, w. J. Levine (cnd), Metropolitan Opera Orch, Ileana Cotrubas (sop), Renée Fleming (sop), Hei-Kyung Hong (sop), Karita Mattila (sop), Birgit Nilsson (sop), Ruth Ann Swenson (sop), Kiri Te Kanawa (sop), Deborah Voigt (sop), Heidi Grant Murphy (mez), Anne Sofie von Otter (mez) *(rec live, Metropolitan Opera House, New York, Apr 27, 1996)*
Deutsche Grammophon ▲ 449177-2 [DDD]
Janácek, L.:Jenůfa, w. Magda Olivero (sop—Kostelnicka), Bruna Baglioni (mez—La vecchia Buryja), Grace Bumbry (mez—Jenufa), Renato Cioni (ten—Steva Buryja), Robleto Merolla (bar—Laca Klemen), Carlo Meliciani (sgr—Vecchio compagno), J. Semkow (cnd), La Scala Orch, La Scala Chorus *(rec Milan, Apr 2, 1974)*
Myto 2-▲ MCD 961142
Massenet, J.:Le Cid, w. P. Domingo (ten), P. Plishka (bass), E. Queler (cnd), New York Opera Orch *(rec 1976)*
CBS 2-▲ M2K 34211 [ADD]
Mozart, W.A.:Requiem, w. E. Mathis (sop), G. Shirley (ten), M. Rintzler (bass), R. Frühbeck de Burgos (cnd), New Philharmonia Orch, New Philharmonia Chorus
Classics for Pleasure ▲ CDCFP 4399 [ADD]
Strauss (II), Joh.:Der Zigeunerbaron (sels), w. Rita Streich (sop), Biserka Cvejic (mez), Gisela Litz (alt), Nicolai Gedda (ten), Hermann Prey (bar), Kurt Bohme (bass), F. Allers (cnd), Munich Bavarian State Opera Orch, Munich Bavarian State Opera Chorus
Emperor Operetta ▲ KO 86346
Verdi, G.:Aida, w. L. Price (sop), P. Domingo (ten), S. Milnes (bar), R. Raimondi (bass), E. Leinsdorf (cnd), London SO [I]
RCA ■ RK 1237
Verdi, G.:Aida, w. L. Price (sop), P. Domingo (ten), S. Milnes (bar), R. Raimondi (bass), E. Leinsdorf (cnd), London SO [I]
RCA Red Seal 3-▲ 6198-2-RC [ADD] 3-■ ARK3-2541
Verdi, G.:Aida (sels), w. L. Price (sop), P. Domingo (ten), S. Milnes (bar), E. Leinsdorf (cnd), London SO
RCA Victor ▲ 09026-62676-2 ■ 09026-62676-4
Verdi, G.:Aida (sels), w. B. Nilsson (sop), F. Corelli (ten), Z. Mehta (cnd), Rome Opera Orch [I] [highlights]
EMI Classics (Classics for Pleasure) ▲ CDM 64035
Verdi, G.:Don Carlos, w. M. Caballé (sop—Elisabeth de Valois), G. Bumbry (mez—Princess Eboli), J. Aragall (ten—Don Carlos), R. Bruson (bar—Rodrigue), S. Estes (bass—Philip II), T. Fulton (cnd), *(orch unknown) (rec Orange, France, 1979)*
Ornamenti 2-▲ FE 110 [ADD]
Verdi, G.:Don Carlos, w. R. Tebaldi (sop), C. Bergonzi (ten), D. Fischer-Dieskau (bar), N. Ghiaurov (bass), G. Solti (cnd), Royal Opera House Orch Covent Garden, Royal Opera House Chorus Covent Garden [1886 5-act Italian version] [I]
London 3-▲ 421114-2 [ADD]
Verdi, G.:Macbeth, w. Grace Bumbry (mez—Lady Macbeth), Luciano Saldari (ten—Macduff), Paride Venturi (ten—Malcolm), Renato Bruson (bar—Macbeth), Agostino Ferrin (bass—Banquo), A. Gatto (cnd), Bologna Teatro Comunale Orch, Bologna Teatro Comunale Chorus *(rec Bologna, Mar. 18, 1975)*
Golden Age of Opera 2-▲ GAO 185/86 [ADD]
Wagner, R.:Tannhäuser, w. A. Silja (sop), W. Windgassen (ten), E. Wächter (bar), J. Greindl (bass), W. Sawallisch (cnd), Bayreuth Festival Orch, Bayreuth Festival Chorus [Dresden version with Paris Venusberg music] [G]
Philips 3-▲ 434607-2 [ADD]
Wagner, R.:Tannhäuser, w. V. de Los Angeles (sop), W. Windgassen (ten), G. Stolze (ten), D. Fischer-Dieskau (bar), T. Adam (b-bar), J. Greindl (bass), F. Crass (bass), W. Sawallisch (cnd), Bayreuth Festival Orch, Bayreuth Festival Chorus [G] *(rec 1961)*
Myto 3-▲ MCD 93277

Bumbry, Grace (sop)
Bizet, G.:Carmen, w. M. Freni (sop), J. Vickers (ten), J. Diaz (bass), H. von Karajan (cnd), Vienna PO, Vienna State Opera Chorus [F] *(rec live, Salzburg 1967)*
Arkadia 3-▲ 221 [ADD]
Verdi, G.:La forza del destino, w. G. Bumbry (sop—Leonora), H. Dernesch (sop—Preziosilla), N. Gedda (ten—Alvaro), H. Prey (bar—Don Carlos), G. Frick (bass—Pater Guardian), S. Vogel (bass—Marchese), G. Patanè (cnd), Dresden State Orch, Dresden State Opera Chorus *(rec Aug. 1965)*
Berlin Classics ("Eterna" series) ▲ BER 2025-2 [ADD]

Bundschuh, Eva-Maria (sop)
Wagner, R.:Götterdämmerung, w. A. Evans (sop—Brünnhilde), E.-M. Bundschuh (sop—Gutrune), H. Leidland (sop—Woglinde), A. Küttenbaum (sop—Wellgunde), W. Meier (mez—Waltraute), B. Svendén (mez—1st Norn), J. Turner (mez), *(cnd & orch unknown)*
Teldec 4-▲ 4509-94194-2 [DDD]

Bunnell, Jane (mez)
Bernstein, L.:Arias & Barcarolles, w. Dale Duesing (bar), G. Schwarz (cnd), Seattle SO [E]
Delos ▲ DE 3078 [DDD]

Bunnell, Jane (sop)
Verdi, G.:Don Carlos (sels), w. A. Millo (sop), D. Zajick (mez), M. Sylvester (ten), V. Chernov (bar), F. Furlanetto (bass), P. Plishka (bass), J. Levine (cnd), Metropolitan Opera Orch, New York Metropolitan Opera Chorus *(rec New York, Apr. 20–May 14, 1992)*
Sony Classical ("Opera Highlights" series) ▲ SMK 53507 [DDD]

Buntschu, Christiane (sgr)
Mendelssohn, F.:Psalms, Op. 78, w. Natacha Casagrande (sgr), Kurt Kempf (sgr), Pablo Pavon (sgr), M. Corboz (cnd), Lausanne Vocal Ensemble *(rec Lausanne Cathedral, Jan. 29–31, 1994)*
FNAC Music ▲ 592298 [DDD]

Burchuladze, Paata (bass)
Mozart, W.A.:Don Giovanni, w. A. Tomowa-Sintow (sop), K. Battle (sop), A. Baltsa (mez), G. Winbergh (ten), S. Ramey (bass), F. Furlanetto (bass), H. von Karajan (cnd), Berlin PO, German Opera Chorus [I]
Deutsche Grammophon 3-▲ 419179-2 [DDD]
Mozart, W.A.:Don Giovanni (sels), w. A. Tomowa-Sintow (sop), K. Battle (sop), A. Baltsa (mez), G. Winbergh (ten), S. Ramey (bass), F. Furlanetto (bass), H. von Karajan (cnd), Berlin PO, German Opera Chorus [I]
Deutsche Grammophon ▲ 419635-2 [DDD]
Mozart, W.A.:Requiem, w. A. Tomowa-Sintow (sop), H. Müller Molinari (cta), V. Cole (ten), H. von Karajan (cnd), Vienna PO, Vienna Singverein [L]
Deutsche Grammophon ("Karajan Gold" series) ▲ 439023-2 [DDD]
Mussorgsky, M.:Khovanshchina, w. M. Lipovsek (mez), V. Atlantov (ten), A. Haugland (bass), C. Abbado (cnd), Vienna State Opera Orch, Slovak Phil Chorus [Shostakovich version] [R]
Deutsche Grammophon 3-▲ 429758-2 [DDD]
Puccini, G.:La Bohème, w. Katia Ricciarelli (sop), Francisco Araiza (ten), Angelo Casertano (ten), Stefano Antonucci (bar), Claudio Giombi (bar), Alfredo Mariotti (bass), Alberto Noli (bass), Andrea Piccinni (bass), Lauren Broglia (sgr), A. Guadagno (cnd), Arena di Verona Orch, Limburg Cathedral Boys' Chorus
Koch Schwann 2-▲ SCH 315922
Rossini, G.:Il barbiere di Siviglia, w. C. Bartoli (mez), W. Matteuzzi (ten), L. Nucci (bar), G. Patanè (cnd), Bologna Teatro Comunale Orch, Bologna Teatro Comunale Chorus [I]
London 3-▲ 425520-2 [DDD]
Rossini, G.:Il barbiere di Siviglia (sels), w. C. Bartoli (mez), W. Matteuzzi (ten), L. Nucci (bar), G. Patanè (cnd), Bologna Teatro Comunale Orch, Bologna Teatro Comunale Chorus
London ▲ 440289-2 [DDD]
Saint-Saëns, C.:Samson et Dalila, w. J. Carreras (ten), A. Baltsa (mez), Summers (bar), Estes (bass), C. Davis (cnd), Bavarian RSO, Bavarian Radio Chorus
Philips 2-▲ 426243-2 [DDD]
Saint-Saëns, C.:Samson et Dalila (sels), w. A. Baltsa (mez), J. Carreras (ten), D. George (ten), J. Summers (bar), S. Estes (bass), C. Davis (cnd), Bavarian RSO
Philips ▲ 438504-2
Verdi, G.:Aida, w. M. Chiara (sop), G. Dimitrova (sop), L. Pavarotti (ten), L. Nucci (bar), L. Maazel (cnd), La Scala Orch, La Scala Chorus [I]
London 3-▲ 417439-2 [DDD] 2-■ 417439-4
Verdi, G.:Aida, w. M. Chiara (sop), G. Dimitrova (sop), L. Pavarotti (ten), L. Nucci (bar), L. Maazel (cnd), La Scala Orch, La Scala Chorus [I]
London □ 433162-5
Verdi, G.:Nabucco, w. Monica Pick-Hieronimi (sop), Anna Schiatti (sop), Mina Blum (sop), Angelo Casertano (ten), Gilberto Maffezzoni (ten), Paolo Gavanelli (bass), Franco Federici (bass), A. Guadagno (cnd), Arena di Verona Orch, Arena di Verona Chorus *(rec Berlin, Spring 1996)*
Koch Schwann 2-▲ SCH CD 364272
Verdi, G.:Simon Boccanegra, w. K. Te Kanawa (sop), J. Aragall (ten), L. Nucci (bar), G. Solti (cnd), La Scala Orch, La Scala Chorus [I]
London 2-▲ 425628-2 [DDD]

Burg, Robert (bar)
Wagner, R.:Götterdämmerung, w. M. Fuchs (sop), H. Scheppan (sop), S. Svanholm (ten), F. Dalberg (bass), K. Elmendorff (cnd), Bayreuth Festival Orch, Bayreuth Festival Chorus *(rec July 21, 1942)*
Preiser 4-▲ PRE 90164 [AAD]

Burg, Susanna von der (sop)
Corghi, A.:Divara—Wasser und Blut, w. Susanna von der Burg (sop—Divara), Suzanne McLeod (mez—Else Windscherer), Eva Lillian Thingboe (mez—Hille Feiken), Robert Schwarts (ten—Lame Man), Heinz Fitz (spkr—Bernd Knipperdollinck), Hanslutz Hildmann (spkr—Jan Matthys), Michael Holm (spkr—Bernhard Rothmann), Christopher Krieg (spkr—Jan van Leiden), W. Humburg (cnd), Münster SO, Münster City Theater Chorus [G] *(rec Grosses Haus, Münster State Theater, Nov. 27–29, 1993)*
Marco Polo 2-▲ 8.223706/07 [DDD]

Bürger, Milan (sgr)
Dvořák, A.:Armida, w. Joanna Borowska (sop—Armida), Monika Brychtová (sgr—Siren), Wieslaw Ochman (ten—Rinald), Richard Sporka (ten—Dudo), Jan Markvart (bar—Sven), Pavel Daniluk (bass—King), George Fortune (bass—Ismen), Zdenek Harvánek (bass—Ubald), Miloslav Podskalský (bass—Peter), Milan Bürger (sgr—Gernand), Roman Janál (sgr—Muezzin/Hlasatel), Vratislav Kříž (sgr—Gottfried), Vladimír Nacházel (sgr—Roger), G. Albrecht (cnd), Czech PO, Prague Chamber Choir *(rec 1995)*
Orfeo 2-▲ 404962 [DDD]

Burgess, Alexander (bar)
Shewan, S.:A Feast of Carols, w. Jill Richardson (sop), S. Shewan (cnd), Roberts Wesleyan College Brass Ensemble, Roberts Wesleyan College Chorale
Albany ▲ TROY 149 [DDD]
Shewan, S.:Magnificat, w. Erin Stedman (sop), Kimberly Higgins (alt), Robert Dingman (ten), Paul Shewan (tpt), Barbara Hull (tpt), Nanita Wilson (hn), Scott Emmons (trbn), Kirk Kettinger (tuba), Ann Musser Honeywell (org)
Albany ▲ TROY 149 [DDD]
Shewan, S.:The Voice of the Lord in the Storm, w. Erin Stedman (sop), Kimberly Higgins (alt), Robert Dingman (ten), Paul Shewan (tpt), Barbara Hull (tpt), Nanita Wilson (hn), Scott Emmons (trbn), Kirk Kettinger (tuba), Ann Musser Honeywell (org)
Albany ▲ TROY 149 [DDD]

Burgess, Gary (ten)
Cage, J.:Europera 5, w. M. Herr (sop), Y. Mikhashoff (pno), J. Wiliams (victrola [78 rpm]), D. Metz (tape) *(rec Apr. 12, 1991)*
Mode ▲ MOD 36 [DDD]

Burgess, Mary (sop)
del Tredici, D.:Night Conjure-Verse, w. Benita Valente (sop), D. del Tredici (cnd), Marlboro Festival Players
CRI ("American Masters" series) ▲ CD 689 [DDD]
del Tredici, D.:Night Conjure-Verse, w. A. Valente (ten), D. del Tredici (cnd), Marlboro Festival Ensemble [E]
CRI ■ ACS 6004
Vivaldi, A.:Beatus vir (Psalm 111), w. J. Chamonin (sop), C. Watkinson (cta), J.-C. Malgoire (cnd), La Grande Écurie et la Chambre du Roy, Raphaël Passaquet Vocal Ensemble *(rec 1976)*
Sony Classical ("Essential Classics" series) ▲ SBK 48280 [ADD] ■ SBT 48280
Vivaldi, A.:Gloria, RV.589, w. Jocelyne Chamonine (sop), Carolyn Watkinson (cta), J.-C. Malgoire (cnd), La Grande Écurie et la Chambre du Roy, Raphaël Passaquet Vocal Ensemble *(rec 1976)*
Sony Classical ("Essential Classics" series) ▲ SBK 48280 [ADD] ■ SBT 48280

Burgess, Sally (mez)
Delius, F.:Songs of Sunset, w. B. Terfel (bass-bar), R. Hickox (cnd), Bournemouth SO, Bournemouth Chorus
Chandos ▲ CHAN 9214 [DDD]
Lambert, C.:The Rio Grande, w. J. Gibbons (pno), D. Lloyd-Jones (cnd), English Northern Philharmonia [E]
Hyperion ▲ CDA 66565 [DDD]
McCartney, P.:Liverpool Oratorio, w. K. Te Kanawa (sop), J. Hadley (ten), W. White (bass), C. Davis (cnd), Royal Liverpool PO, Royal Liverpool Phil Choir
EMI Classics 2-▲ CDQB 54371 2-■ 4D2Q 54371
Purcell, H.:Dido & Aeneas, w. Rebecca Evans (sop—Belinda), Maria Ewing (sop—Dido), Mary Plazas (sop—1st witch), Patricia Rozario (sop—2nd woman), Sally Burgess (mez—Sorceress), Pamela Helen Stephens (mez—2nd witch), James Bowman (ct—Spirit), Jamie MacDougal (ten—Sailor), Karl Daymond (bar—Aeneas), R. Hickox (cnd), Collegium Musicum 90
Chandos ("Early Music" series) ▲ CHAN 0586 [DDD]
Ravel, M.:Mélodies populaires grecques, w. G. Simon (cnd), Philharmonia Orch [F] *(rec St. Jude-on-the-Hill, Hampstead, London, Feb 8–12, 1991)*
Cala ▲ CACD 1004 [DDD]
Rossini, G.:Il barbiere di Siviglia (sels), w. A. Baltsa (mez), F. Araiza (ten), T. Allen (bar), D. Trimarchi (bar), R. Lloyd (bass), N. Marriner (cnd), Academy of St. Martin in the Fields
Philips ▲ 438498-2

Burghardt, Susan (sop)
Nielsen, C.:Sym 3, w. R. Bassett (bar), S. Ehrling (cnd), Danish National Orch *(rec live, Kennedy Center, 5/19/84)*
Audiofon ▲ CD 72025

Burke, M. (sgr)
Kern, J.:Show Boat (sels), w. P. Robeson (b-bar), J. Bledsoe (sgr), E. Day (sgr), *(other artists unknown)* [original cast]
Pearl ("Flapper" series) ▲ PEA CD 9105 [ADD]

Burke, Tom (ten)
Tom Burke *(rec 1920–1934)*
Pearl ▲ PEA 9411 (m) [AAD]

Burles, Charles (ten)
Delibes, L.:Lakmé, w. M. Mesplé (sop), D. Millet (sop), R. Soyer (bass), A. Lombard (cnd), Paris Opéra-Comique Orch, Paris Opéra-Comique Chorus
EMI Classics 2-▲ CDCB 49430
Delibes, L.:Lakmé (sels), w. M. Mesplé (sop), D. Millet (sop), R. Soyer (bass), A. Lombard (cnd), Paris Opéra-Comique Orch, Paris Opéra-Comique Chorus
EMI Classics ▲ ZDM 63447
Rossini, G.:Guillaume Tell, w. M. Caballé (sop), M. Mesplé (sop), N. Gedda (ten), G. Bacquier (bar), G. Howell (bass), L. Gardelli (cnd), Royal PO, Ambrosian Opera Chorus
EMI Classics 4-▲ CDMD 69951

Burmeister, Annelies (mez)
Bach, J.S.:Masses, BWV 233–36, "Lutheran Masses", w. Renate Krahmer (sop), Peter Schreier (ten), Theo Adam (bass), M. Flämig (cnd), Dresden PO
Berlin Classics 2-▲ BER 9130
Bach, J.S.:St. Matthew Passion, w. P. Schreier (ten), T. Adam (bass), R. & E. Mauersberger (cnd), Leipzig Gewandhaus Orch, Dresden Kreuz Choir, St. Thomas Chorus *(rec 1970)*
Berlin Classics 3-▲ BER 2144 [ADD]
Beethoven, L. van:Missa Solemnis, w. Anna Tomowa-Sintow (sop), Peter Schreier (ten), Hermann Christian Polster (bass), Gerhard Bosse (vn), Hannes Kastner (org), K. Masur (cnd), Leipzig Gewandhaus Orch, Leipzig Radio Chorus
Berlin Classics ("Masur Edition" series) ▲ BER 9160
Dessau, P.:Die Verurteilung des Lukullus, w. Annelies Burmeister (mez—Das Fischweib), Helmut Melchert (ten—Lukullus), Hans-Joachim Rotzsch (ten—Der Kirschbaumträger), Peter Schreier (ten—Lukullus' Cook), Boris Carmeli (bass—King), H. Kegel (cnd), Leipzig RSO, Leipzig Radio Chorus
Berlin Classics 2-▲ BER 1073 [ADD]
Dvořák, A.:Rusalka (sels), w. E. Mitzewa (mez), T. Adam (bass-bar), A. Apelt (cnd), Berlin Staatskapelle
Berlin Classics ("Eterna" series) ▲ BER 2033 [ADD]
Mendelssohn, F.:Elijah, w. E. Ameling (sop), P. Schreier (ten), T. Adam (b-bar), W. Sawallisch (cnd), Leipzig Gewandhaus Orch, Leipzig Radio Chorus [G]
Philips 2-▲ 420106-2 [AAD]
Mendelssohn, F.:Elijah, w. E. Ameling (sop), P. Schreier (ten), T. Adam (b-bar), W. Sawallisch (cnd), Leipzig Gewandhaus Orch, Leipzig Radio Chorus
Philips 2-▲ 438368-2
Mendelssohn, F.:Die erste Walpurgisnacht, w. E. Büchner (ten), S. Lorenz (bar), K. Masur (cnd), Leipzig Gewandhaus Orch
Berlin Classics ("Eterna" series) ▲ BER 2057 [ADD]
Mendelssohn, F.:Infelice, w. K. Masur (cnd), Leipzig Gewandhaus Orch
Berlin Classics ("Eterna" series) ▲ BER 2057 [ADD]
Mendelssohn, F.:Ov, Op. 101, w. E. Büchner (ten), S. Lorenz (bar), K. Masur (cnd), Leipzig Gewandhaus Orch
Berlin Classics ("Eterna" series) ▲ BER 2057 [ADD]
Prokofiev, S.:Betrothal in a Monastery (sels), w. E. Büchner (bar), R. Süss (bar), H. Kegel (cnd), Leipzig RSO [G]
Berlin Classics ▲ BER 2081 [ADD]
Reger, M.:An die Hoffnung, w. H. Bongartz (cnd), *(orch unknown)*
Berlin Classics ▲ BER 9122
Reger, M.:Hymnus der Liebe, w. H. Bongartz (cnd), *(orch unknown)*
Berlin Classics ▲ BER 9122
Rossini, G.:Il barbiere di Siviglia, w. Ruth-Margaret Pütz (sop), Peter Schreier (ten), Hermann Prey (bar), Franz Crass (bass), Fritz Ollendorff (bass), O. Suitner (cnd), Berlin State Opera Orch
Berlin Classics 2-▲ BER 9021 [ADD]
Shostakovich, D.:From Jewish Folk Poetry, w. Maria Croonen (sgr), Peter Schreier (ten), K. Sanderling (cnd), Berlin SO
Berlin Classics ▲ BER 9016 [ADD]
Wagner, R.:Der fliegende Holländer, w. Anja Silja (sop—Senta), Anneliese Burmeister (mez—Mary), Ernst Kozub (ten—Erik), Gerhard Unger (ten—Steersman), Theo Adam (bass—Dutchman), Martti Talvela (bass—Daland), O. Klemperer (cnd), New Philharmonia Orch, BBC Sym Chorus
EMI Classics 3-▲ CDCC 55179

Burmeister, Annelies (mez) (cont.)
Wagner, R.:Der Ring des Nibelungen, w. B. Nilsson (sop), L. Rysanek (sop), K. Dvořáková (sop), M. Mödl (sop), V. Soukupova (mez), E. Wohlfahrt (ten), W. Windgassen (ten), T. Stewart (bar), T. Adam (b-bar), G. Neidlinger (b-bar), K. Böhme (bass), G. Nienstedt (bass), K. Böhm (cnd), Bayreuth Festival Orch, Bayreuth Festival Chorus [G] *(rec live, 1966–67)* Philips 14-▲ 420325-2 [ADD]

Burns, Karla (mez)
Kern, J.:Show Boat, w. P. O'Hara (sop), T. Stratas (sop), F. von Stade (mez), D. Garrison (ten), J. Hadley (ten), B. Hubbard (bar), J. McGlinn (cnd), London Sinfonietta, Ambrosian Opera Chorus EMI Classics ▲ ZDC 49847
Kern, J.:Show Boat, w. F. von Stade (mez), T. Stratas (sop), J. Hadley (ten), B. Hubbard (bar), P. O'Hara (sgr), N. Kulp (sgr), J. McGlinn (cnd), London Sinfonietta, Ambrosian Chorus [original orchd Robert Russell Bennett]—also includes 45 minutes of music intended for the original performance but never included, plus music from revivals and films [1988 studio cast] Angel 3-▲ A23 49108 [DDD]
Kern, J.:Show Boat, w. P. O'Hara (sop), T. Stratas (sop), F. von Stade (mez), D. Garrison (ten), J. Hadley (ten), B. Hubbard (bar), J. McGlinn (cnd), London Sinfonietta, Ambrosian Opera Chorus, Ambrosian Singers EMI Classics 3-▲ A23 49108

Burrowes, Connor (trb)
Consort Songs, w. Amsterdam Loeki Stardust Quartet, David Miller (lt/gtr) Channel Classics ▲ CCS 9196
Handel, G.F.:Joseph & His Brethren, w. Yvonne Kenney (sop), Catherine Denley (mez), James Bowman (ct), John Mark Ainsley (ten), Michael George (bass), R. King (cnd), King's Consort, New College Choir Oxford, King's Consort Choir Hyperion 3-▲ CDA 67171/3

Burrowes, Norma (sop)
Handel, G.F.:Acis & Galatea, w. M. Hill (ten), A. R. Johnson (ten), W. White (bass), J. E. Gardiner (cnd), English Baroque Soloists [E] Archiv ▲ 423406-2 [ADD]
Handel, G.F.:Israel in Egypt, w. Charles Brett (ct), Paul Elliot (sgr), J.E. Gardiner (cnd), Monteverdi Orch, Monteverdi Choir London Erato 2-▲ 2292-45399-2 ZA
Handel, G.F.:Semele, w. Patrizia Kwella (sop), Elizabeth Priday (sop), Catherine Denley (mez), Della Jones (mez), Timothy Penrose (alt), Anthony Rolfe-Johnson (ct), Maldwyn Davies (ten), Robert Lloyd (b-bar), David Thomas (bass), J. E. Gardiner (cnd), English Baroque Soloists, Monteverdi Choir London Erato 2-▲ 2292-45982-2
Handel, G.F.:The Ways of Zion Do Mourn, w. Charles Brett (ct), Paul Elliot (ten), J.E. Gardiner (cnd), Monteverdi Orch, Monteverdi Choir London Erato 2-▲ 2292-45399-2 ZA
Haydn, J.:Die Schöpfung, w. Rüdger Wohlers (ten), James Morris (bass), G. Solti (cnd), Chicago SO, Chicago Sym Chorus—sels. London ("Jubilee" series) ▲ 430739-2 [DDD]
Monteverdi, C.:Vespro della Beata Vergine, w. Elly Ameling (sop), Charles Brett (ct), Martyn Hill (ten), Anthony Rolfe-Johnson (ten), Robert Tear (ten), Peter Knapp (bass), John Noble (bass), Francis Grier (org/hpd), James Lancelot (org/hpd), Andrew Leach (org/hpd), P. Ledger (cnd), London Early Music Consort, King's College Choir Cambridge—Nigra sum [con.]; Laudate pueri [psalm]; Sancta Maria [son. sopra]; Magnificat *(rec Chapel of King's College, Cambridge, July & Aug. 1975)* EMI Classics ▲ CDK 65339 [ADD]
Monteverdi, C.:Vespro della Beata Vergine, w. Elly Ameling (sop), Charles Brett (ct), Robert Tear (ten), Anthony Rolfe Johnson (ten), Martyn Hill (ten), Peter Knapp (bass), John Noble (bass), Munrow, Ledger (cnd), London Early Music Consort EMI Classics ("Doublefforte" series) 2-▲ CDFB 68631
Mozart, W.A.:Complete Mozart Edition, w. C. Eda-Pierre (sop), R. Tear (ten), S. Burrows (ten), C. Davis (cnd), Academy of St. Martin in the Fields, John Alldis Choir Philips 2-▲ 422538-2 [ADD]
Orff, C.:Carmina burana, w. L. Devos (ten), J. Shirley-Quirk (bar), A. Dorati (cnd), Royal PO, Brighton Festival Chorus [G,L] London ▲ 417714-2 [ADD]
Orff, C.:Carmina burana, w. Louis Devos (ten), John Shirley-Quirk (bar), A. Dorati (cnd), Royal PO, Brighton Festival Chorus, Southend Boys' Choir *(rec Kingsway Hall, London, Feb 1976)* London ("Phase 4 Stereo" series) ▲ 444105-2 [ADD]

Burrows, Stuart (ten)
Berlioz, H.:Requiem, "Grande Messe des Morts", w. L. Bernstein (cnd), French National Orch [L] Sony Classical 2-▲ SM2K 47526 [ADD]
Mahler, G.:Das Klagende Lied, w. E. Lear (sop), E. Söderström (sop), G. Hoffman (mez), E. Haefliger (ten), G. Nienstedt (bass), P. Boulez (cnd), London SO, London Sym Chorus Sony Classical ("Pierre Boulez Edition" series) ▲ SK 45841
Mozart, W.A.:Complete Mozart Edition, w. L. Popp (sop), J. Baker (mez), Y. Minton (mez), F. von Stade (mez), R. Lloyd (b-bar), C. Davis (cnd), Royal Opera House Orch, Royal Opera House Chorus Covent Garden Philips 2-▲ 422544-2 [ADD]
Mozart, W.A.:Complete Mozart Edition, w. K. Te Kanawa (sop), M. Arroyo (sop), M. Freni (sop), I. Wixell (bar), C. Davis (cnd), Royal Opera House Orch, Royal Opera House Chorus Covent Garden Philips 3-▲ 422541-2 [ADD]
Mozart, W.A.:Complete Mozart Edition, w. C. Eda-Pierre (sop), N. Burrowes (sop), R. Tear (ten), C. Davis (cnd), Academy of St. Martin in the Fields, John Alldis Choir Philips 2-▲ 422538-2 [ADD]
Mozart, W.A.:Don Giovanni, w. L. Price (sop), L. Popp (sop), S. Sass (sop), G. Bacquier (bar), B. Weikl (bar), A. Sramek (bar), K. Moll (bass), G. Solti (cnd), London PO, London Opera Chorus London ("Grand Opera" series) 3-▲ 425169-2 [ADD]
Mozart, W.A.:Zauberflöte, w. P. Lorengar (sop), C. Deutekom (sop), H. Prey (bar), D. Fischer-Dieskau (bar), M. Talvela (bass), G. Solti (cnd), Vienna PO [G] London 3-▲ 414568-2
Mozart, W.A.:Zauberflöte (sels), w. Pilar Lorengar (sop), Cristina Deutekom (sop), Hermann Prey (bar), Martti Talvela (bass), G. Solti (cnd), Vienna PO London ▲ 421302-2 [ADD]
Tippett, M.:The Midsummer Marriage, w. Joan Carlyle (sop—Joan), Elizabeth Harwood (sop—Beth), Elizabeth Bainbridge (mez), Helen Watts (cta—Sosostris), Stuart Burrows (ten—Jack), Alberto Remedios (ten—Mark), Stafford Dean (bass), Raimund Herincx (bass—King Fisher), C. Davis (cnd), Royal Opera House Orch, Royal Opera House Chorus Covent Garden Lyrita 2-▲ SRCD 2217

Burt, Clare (sgr)
Lloyd Webber, A.:Music of, w. Graham Bickly (sgr), J. Kelly (sgr), C. D. Carroll (sgr), Yates (cnd), National SO, Munich SO—Song & Dance; The Phantom of the Opera; Starlight Express; Jeeves; Jesus Christ Superstar; Aspects of Love; Cats; The Requiem Mass Koch International ▲ KOCCD 340132 ■ KOCC 340134

Burt, Robert (nar)
Mozart, W.A.:Zauberflöte, w. Constanze Backes (sop—Papagena), Christiane Oelze (sop—Pamina), Susan Roberts (sop—First Lady), Cyndia Sieden (sop—Queen of the Night), Carola Guber (cta—Second Lady), Maria Jonas (cta—Third Lady), Andreas Dieterich (trb—First Boy), Jan Andreas Mendel (trb—Second Boy), Florian Wöller (trb—Third Boy), Uwe Peper (ten—Monostatos), Nicolas Robertson (ten—First Man in Armor), Michael Schade (ten—Tamino), Gerald Finley (bar—Papageno), Noel Mann (bass—Second Man in Armour), Harry Peeters (bass—Sarastro), Detlef Roth (bass—Speaker/First Priest), Robert Burt (speaker—Third Priest), Robert Johnston (speaker—Second Priest), Wolfgang Knauer (speaker—Fourth Priest), Douglas Welbat (speaker—Second Priest), J. E. Gardiner (cnd), English Baroque Soloists, Monteverdi Choir London *(rec Forum am Schlosspark, Ludwigsburg, July 1995)* Archiv 2-▲ 449166-2

Burt, Warren (voc)
Partch, H.:Bitter Music, w. Sheila Guymer (pno) [prepared by Warren Burt] *(rec Melbourne, Australia, Jan 24, 1992)* Innova 4-▲ 401

Burton, Amy (sop)
Gershwin, G.:Blue Monday Blues, w. G. Hopkins (ten), W. Sharp (bar), A. Woodley (b-bar), J. J. Offenbach (b-bar), M. Alsop (cnd), Concordia Orch EMI Classics ▲ CDC 54851
Wilson, R.:Persuasions, w. B. Uribe (pno), J. Solum (alt fl), M. Schachman (ob/E hn), G. Dejean (bn/ctbn) Albany ▲ TROY 074 [DDD]

Busch, Michael (bar)
Platz, R.H.:Dunkles Haus, w. Maria Husmann (sop—Woman), Michael Busch (bar—Man), Udo Zickwolf (nar—Child/Bird/Man), Carin Levine (a fl/b fl), R. Platz (cnd), Marstall Ensemble of the Bavarian State Opera *(rec 1991)* Thorofon ▲ CTH 2170

Busching, Marianna (mez)
Mozart, W.A.:Missa brevis, K.194, w. G. Tucker (ten), P. Fay (bar), C. Dill Smith (sgr), H. Mardirosian (cnd), St. Thomas Moore Cathedral Orch, St. Thomas Moore Cathedral Chorus [L] Centaur ▲ CRC 2074 [DDD]

Busching, Marianna (mez) (cont.)
Mozart, W.A.:Tantum ergo, w. Carolyn Dill Smith (sop), Gene Tucker (ten), Peter Fay (bar), H. Mardirosian (cnd), St. Thomas Moore Cathedral Orch, St. Thomas Moore Cathedral Chorus [L] Centaur ▲ CRC 2074 [DDD]
Mozart, W.A.:Vesperae de Dominica, w. C. Dill Smith (sop), G. Tucker (ten), P. Fay (bar), H. Mardirosian (cnd), St. Thomas Moore Cathedral Orch, St. Thomas Moore Cathedral Chorus [L] Centaur ▲ CRC 2074 [DDD]
Pfitzner, H.:Songs, w. M. Cordovana (pno)—24 songs [G] Centaur ▲ CRC 2136

Busching, Rupert (bar)
Weber, C.M. von:Peter Schmoll und seine Nachbarn, w. A. Pfeffer (sop—Minnette), J. Schmidt (ten—Martin Schmoll), S. Basa (ten—Karl Pirkner), H.-J. Schöpflin (ten—Niklas), R. Busching (bar—Peter Schmoll), H.J. Porcher (bass—Hans Bast), G. Markson (cnd), Hagen PO [G] *(rec Feb. 1–5, 1993)* Marco Polo 2-▲ 8.223592/93 [DDD]

Buschmann, K. (ten)
Wagner, R.:Die Walküre (sels), w. G. Rünger (sop), E. Friedrich (sop), W. Rode (bar), W. Brückner-Rüggeberg (cnd), Reich Radio Königsberg Large Orch—Act II, Scenes 2,3 & 4 & Act III, Scenes 1,2 & 3 [G] *(rec live 2/17 & 5/1 1938)* Preiser 2-▲ 90075 (m) [AAD]

Bushby (sgr)
Berlioz, H.:Benvenuto Cellini, w. J. Carlyle (sop), J. Veasey (mez), K. Lewis (ten), Kentish, Cameron, Garrard, Ward, A. Dorati (cnd), BBC SO, BBC Sym Chorus [E] *(rec live, Royal Festival Hall, 1964)* Music & Arts 2-▲ CD 618 (m) [AAD]

Bushkin, Isser (bass)
Shostakovich, D.:Sym 14, w. T. Kubiak (sop), L. Bernstein (cnd), New York PO [R] *(rec Dec. 8, 1976)* Sony Classical ▲ SMK 47617 [ADD]

Busse, B. (sgr)
Argento, D.:Postcard from Morocco, w. S. Roche, B. Brandt, J. Hardy, Y. Marshall, V. Sutton, M. Foreman, P. Brunelle (cnd), Minnesota Opera Orch CRI 2-▲ CD 614 [ADD]

Bustamante, Carmen (sop)
Mompou, F.:Songs Sop, w. C. Cebro (pno)—(22) Becquerianas (set of 6 songs); Cinq Mélodies [P. Valery]; Combat del Somni (set of 3 songs); etc. Arcobaleno ▲ SBCD 1502 [DDD]

Bustamante, Laura (sop)
Bizet, G.:Carmen, w. Laura Bustamante (sop—Frasquita), Ximena Riveros (sop—Mercedes), Nancy Stokes (sop—Micaela), Regina Resnik (mez—Carmen), Plácido Domingo (ten—Don José), Ismildo Tedeschi (ten—Remendado), Ramon Vinay (ten—Escamillo), Juan Charles (ten/bar—Dancaire), Agustin Letelier (bar—Morles), Jorge Algorta (bass—Zuniga), A. Guadagno (cnd), Santiago Teatro Municipale Orch, Santiago Teatro Municipale Chorus *(rec Santiago Municipal Theater, Sept. 4, 1967)* Legato Classics 2-▲ LCD 194-2 [ADD]

Bustenid, James (bar)
McLaughlin, J.:The Flowers of Dawn, w. S. Robertson (cnd), Sante Fe SO Chamber Players, Santa Fe Sym Chamber Choir *(rec St. Francis Auditorium, Sante Fe, NM, Mar 17, 1991)* Ludifichord ▲ LDCD 1001

Butler, James (bass)
Puccini, G.:Madama Butterfly, w. Maria Spacagna (sop), Sharon Grahm (mez), Vivica Genaux (mez), Richard di Renzi (ten), Richard Markley (ten), Erich Parce (bar), C. Rosenkrans (cnd), Hungarian State Opera Orch, Anikó Katona (cnd), Hungarian State Opera Chorus—3 versions *(rec Italian Institute, Budapest, Sept 5–21, 1995)* Vox Classics 4-▲ VOX4 7525 [DDD]

Butterfield, Benjamin (ten)
Brahms, J.:Liebeslieder Waltzes SATB, w. Kathleen Brett (sop), Catherine Robbin (mez), Russell Braun (bar), Stephen Ralls (pno), Bruce Ubukata (pno) *(rec Glenn Gould Studio, CBC Toronto, Dec. 7–9, 1993)* CBC ("Musica Viva" series) ▲ MVCD 1077 [DDD]
Greer, J.:All Around the Circle, w. Kathleen Brett (sop), Catherine Robbin (mez), Russell Braun (bar), Stephen Ralls (pno), Bruce Ubukata (pno) CBC ▲ MVV 1077 [DDD]
Greer, J.:All Around the Circle, w. Kathleen Brett (sop), Catherine Robbin (mez), Russell Braun (bar), Stephen Ralls (pno), Bruce Ubukata (pno) *(rec Glenn Gould Studio, CBC Toronto, Dec. 7–9, 1993)* CBC ("Musica Viva" series) ▲ MVCD 1077 [DDD]
Purcell, H.:Dido & Aeneas, w. Meredith Hall (sop—2nd Witch/Spirit), Ann Monoyios (sop—Belinda), Shari Saunders (sop—2nd Woman/1st Woman), Jennifer Lane (mez—Dido/Sorceress), Benjamin Butterfield (ten—Sailor), Russell Braun (bar—Aeneas), J. Lamon (cnd), Tafelmusik, Tafelmusik Chamber Choir *(rec Glenn Gould Studio, CBC Toronto, Apr 26–29, 1995)* CBC ▲ SM5 5147 [DDD]
Schumann, R.:Spanische Liebeslieder, w. Kathleen Brett (sop), Catherine Robbin (mez), Russell Braun (bar), Stephen Ralls (pno), Bruce Ubukata (pno) CBC ("Musica Viva" series) ▲ MVCD 1077 [DDD]

Buttrey, John (ten)
Byrd, W.:Mass in 5 Parts, w. H. Sheppard (sop), A. Deller (ct), N. Jenkins (ten), M. Bevan (bar), Deller Consort [L] Musique d'Abord ▲ HMA 190211

Buzea, Ion (ten)
Verdi, G.:Rigoletto, w. Victoria Draganescu (sop—Countess Ceprano), Magda Ianculescu (sop—Gilda), Dorothea Palade (mez—Maddalena), Valeria Savu (mez—Giovanna), Ion Buzea (ten—Duko of Mantua), Dimitrie Scurtu (ten—Borsa), Nicolae Herlea (bar—Rigoletto), Stefan Petrescu (bar—Marullo), Jean Banescu (bass—Count Ceprano), Nicolae Florei (bass—Monterone), Nicolae Rafael (bass—Sparafucile), J. Bobescu (cnd), Romanian Opera Orch, Romanian Opera Chorus *(rec 1965)* Vox Box 2-▲ CDX 5162
Verdi, G.:La traviata, w. Elena Simionescu (sop—Annina), Virginia Zeani (sop—Violetta Valery), Elisabeta Neculce-Cartis (mez—Flora Bervoix), Ion Buzea (ten—Alfredo Germont), Vasile Moldoveanu (ten—Gastone/Viconte de Letorieres/Giuseppe), Teodor Panea (ten—Flora's Servant), Constantin Dumitru (bar—Commissioner/Baron Douphol), Nicolae Herlea (bar—Giorgio Germont), Valentin Loghin (bass—Marchese D'Obigny), Nicolae Rafael (bass—Doctor Grenvil), J. Bobescu (cnd), Romanian Opera Orch, Stelian Olariu (cnd), Romanian Opera Chorus *(rec 1968)* Vox Box 2-▲ CDX 5154
Verdi, G.:La traviata (sels), w. V. Zeani (sop), Herlea (sgr), J. Bobescu (cnd), Bucharest State Opera Orch [I] Allegretto ▲ ACD 8084 [ADD] ■ ACS 8084
Verdi, G.:Il trovatore, w. Elena Dima (sop—Leonora), Victoria Draganescu (sop—Ines), Zenaida Pally (mez—Azucena), Ion Buzea (ten—Duke of Mantua), Constantin Iliescu (ten—Ruiz), Cornel Stavru (ten—Manrico), Octav Enigarescu (bar—Count di Luna), Constantin Dumitru (bass—Ferrando), E. Massini (cnd), Romanian Opera Orch, Romanian Opera Chorus *(rec 1960–61)* Vox Box 2-▲ CDX 5163

Bybee, Ariel (sop)
Varèse, E.:Nocturnal, w. M. Abravanel (cnd), Utah SO Vanguard Classics ▲ OVC 4031 [ADD]

Byrd, C. (sgr)
Mancini, H.:Film Music, w. A. Williams (sgr), J. Mathis (sgr), L. Albright (sgr), B. Hackett (sgr), B. Greco (sgr), P. Page (sgr), Mancini (cnd), Costa Orch, Conniff Orch, Mancini Orch—sels from Breakfast at Tiffany's; Peter Gunn; Mr. Lucky & others Columbia/Legacy ▲ CK 66505

Byrding, Holger (bar)
Beethoven, L. van:Sym 9, "Choral Sym", w. Kerstin Lindberg-Torlind (sop), Else Jena (mez), Erik Sjöberg (ten), F. Busch (cnd), Danish National RSO, Danish National Radio Choir Arlecchino ARL

Byriel, Sten (b-bar)
Gade, N.W.:Frühlings Fant, w. Anne Margrethe Dahl (sop), Kirsten Dolberg (cta), Gert Hennig-Jensen (ten), Elisabeth Westenholz (pno), M. Schønwandt (cnd), Tivoli SO *(rec Tivoli Concert Hall, Apr 29–30, May 4, 1996)* Marco Polo/Dacapo ▲ 8.224051 [DDD]
Nielsen, C.:Springtime, w. I. Nielsen (sop), P. Gronlund (ten), L. Segerstam (cnd), Danish National RSO, Danish National Radio Choir, Danish National Radio Children's Choir [Da] Chandos ▲ CHAN 8853 [DDD]

Byrne, Desmond (bass)
Haydn, J.:Applausus:Jubilaeum virtutis Palatium, w. Rosemary Musoleno (sop—Temperantia), Kirsten Dolberg (mez—Prudentia), Douglas Johnson (ten—Justitia), Desmond Byrne (bass—Fortitudo), Jean-Philippe Courtis (bass—Theologia), P. Fournillier (cnd), Picardie Orch, Haydn Vocal Ensemble [L] *(rec 9/91)* Opus 111 2-▲ OPS 61-9207/8 [DDD]

Byrne, Elisabeth (sop)
Weisgall, H.:Six Characters in Search of an Author, w. E. Byrne (sop—Stepdaughter), S. Foster (sop—Prompter), E. Furtal (sop—Coloratura), J. King (mez—Mezzo), N. Maultsby (mez—Mother), P. LoVerne (cta—Madame Pace), D. Pritchett (alt—Wardrobe Mistress), B. Fowler (ten—Tenore Boffo), K. Anderson (ten—Director), A. Schroeder (bar—Accompanist), P. Zawisza (bar—Stage Manager), R. Orth (bar—Father), G. Lehman (bar—Son), M. Wadsworth (b-bar—Basso Cantante), L. Schaenen (cnd), Chicago Lyric Opera Orch, Lyric Opera Center Chorus *(rec Chicago, June 14 & 16, 1990)* New World 2-▲ 80454-2

Caals, Jan (ten)
Charpentier, M.-A.:Leçons de ténèbres, H. 96–110, w. Harry Ruyl (ten), Howard Crook (ct), Luc de Meulenaere (ct), Michel Verschaeve (bar), Kurt Widmer (bass), L. Devos (cnd), Musica Polyphonica Erato 2-▲ ERA 96376 [DDD]

Caballé, Montserrat (sop)
Bellini & Verdi Opera Arias EMI Classics ▲ CDM 69500
Bellini, V.:Arias—arias from Norma, Il pirata [I] RCA Gold Seal ▲ 09026-61458-2 ■ 09026-61458-4
Bellini, V.:Norma, w. Caballé (soprano—Norma), F. Cossotto (mez), B. Prevedi (ten), J. Carreras (ten), I. Vinco (bass), C. F. Cillario (cnd), Barcelona Teatro Liceo Orch, Barcelona Gran Teatro de Liceo Chorus [I] *(rec live, Barcelona 1/11/70)* Melodram 2-▲ CDM 27089 [ADD]
Bellini, V.:Norma, w. J. Sutherland (sop), L. Pavarotti (sop), S. Ramey (bass), R. Bonynge (cnd), Welsh National Opera Orch, Welsh National Opera Chorus [I] London 3-▲ 414476-2 [DDD]
Bellini, V.:Norma, w. F. Cossotto (mez), P. Domingo (ten), R. Raimondi (bass), C.F. Cillario (cnd), London PO, Ambrosian Opera Chorus [I] RCA Gold Seal 3-▲ 6502-2-RG [ADD]
Bellini, V.:Norma (sels)—Casta diva Replay ("Butterfly" series) ▲ BMCD 031 [AAD]
Bellini, V.:Il pirata, w. F. Raffanelli (sop), G. Baratti (ten), F. Labò (ten), P. Cappuccilli (bar), U. Trama (bass), E. Ghiglia (cnd), *(orch unknown)* *(rec Florence, 1967)* Great Opera Performances ▲ GOP 729
Bellini, V.:Il pirata, w. Montserrat Caballé (sop—Imogene), Flora Raffanelli (sop—Adele), Flaviano Labò (ten—Gualtiero), Giuseppe Baratti (ten—Itulbo), Piero Cappuccilli (bar—Ernesto), E. Ghiglia (cnd), Florence Teatro Comunale Orch, Florence Teatro Comunale Chorus *(rec live, Florence, 1967)* Melodram 2-▲ IMC 205002 [ADD]
Bellini, V.:Il pirata, w. F. Rafanelli (sop), B. Marti (ten), Baratti, P. Cappuccilli (bar), R. Raimondi (bass), G. Gavazzeni (cnd), Rome Radio-TV Orch, Rome Radio-TV Chorus [I] *(rec Rome, 1973)* EMI Classics 2-▲ CDMB 64169
Bellini, V.:Il pirata, w. F. Labò (ten), P. Cappuccilli (bar), F. Capuana (cnd), Florence Maggio Musicale Orch, Florence Maggio Musicale Chorus [I] *(rec live, Florence 1967)* Memories 2-▲ HR 4186/87 [ADD]
Bellini, V.:Il pirata, w. F. Labò (ten), P. Cappuccilli (bar), F. Capuana (cnd), Florence Maggio Musicale Orch, Florence Maggio Musicale Chorus [I] *(rec live, Florence 1967)* Melodram 2-▲ MEL 27015
Bellini, V.:Il pirata (sels)—Oh, s'io potessi ("The Art of Montserrat Caballé") Replay ("Butterfly" series) ▲ BMCD 031 [AAD]
Bellini, V.:La straniera, w. B. M. Casoni (cta), A. Zambon (ten), A. Guadagno (cnd), American Opera Society Orch, American Opera Society Chorus *(rec 1969)* Melodram 2-▲ MLO 270111 [DDD]
Bellini, V.:La straniera (sels), w. A. Zambon (ten), A. Guadagno (cnd), *(orch unknown)*— 5 arias [I] *(rec live, Carnegie Hall, 3/22/69)* Verona 2-▲ 27097/98
Bernstein, L.:Sym 3, "Kaddish", w. M. Wager (nar), L. Bernstein (cnd), Israel PO, *(chorus unknown)* Deutsche Grammophon 2-▲ 445245-2 [ADD]
Boito, A.:Mefistofele, w. P. Domingo (ten), N. Treigle (bass), J. Rudel (cnd), London SO, Ambrosian Opera Chorus [I] EMI Classics 2-▲ CDCB 49522 [ADD]
Boito, A.:Mefistofele, w. M. Freni (sop), L. Pavarotti (ten), N. Ghiaurov (bass), O. de Fabritiis (cnd), National PO London [I] London 3-▲ 410175-2 [DDD]
Casta Diva RCA Gold Seal ▲ 09026-23675-2
Chausson, E.:Poème de l'amour et de la mer, w. W. Morris (cnd), Symphonica of London [F] IMP Classics ▲ IMP PCD 1037 [DDD]
Cilea, F.:Adriana Lecouvreur, w. F. Cossotto (mez), J. Carreras (ten), A. D'Orazi (bar), G.-F. Masini (cnd), *(orch unknown)* [I] *(rec 1976)* Legato Classics 2-▲ LCD 111-2 [AAD]
Debussy, C.:La Damoiselle élue, w. W. Morris (cnd), London Symphonica [F] IMP Classics ▲ IMP PCD 1037 [DDD]
Divas in Song: Marylin Horne, a 60th Birthday Celebration, w. H. Donath (sop), R. A. Swenson (sop), F. von Stade (mez), R. Fleming (mez), S. Ramey (bass), J. Levine (cnd), M. Katz (pno), W. Jones (pno), K. Donath (pno), Manuel Burgueras (pno) RCA Red Seal ▲ 09026-62547-2
Donizetti, G.:Arias—includes arias from Belisario, Gemma di Vergy, Parisina d'Este, Torquato Tasso RCA Gold Seal 2-▲ 09026-60941-2
Donizetti, G.:Arias—arias from Roberto Devereux, Lucrezia Borgia, Maria di Rohan, Anna Bolena [I] RCA Gold Seal ▲ 09026-61458-2 ■ 09026-61458-4
Donizetti, G.:Caterina Cornaro, w. Giacomo Aragall (ten), Gwynne Howell (bass), Ryan Edwards (sgr), G.-F. Masini (cnd), ORTF Orch *(rec Paris, Nov 25, 1973)* Agorá Music ("Phoenix" series) 2-▲ 505
Donizetti, G.:Gemma di Vergy, w. Montserrat Caballé (sop—Gemma di Vergy), Biancamaria Casoni (mez—Ida di Greville), Giorgio Lamberti (ten—Tamas), Renato Bruson (bar—Conte di Vergy), Mario Machì (bass—Rolando), Mario Rinaudo (bass—Guido), A. Gatto (cnd), Naples Teatro San Carlo Orch, Naples Teatro San Carlo Chorus *(rec Naples, Dec. 12, 1975)* Myto 2-▲ 952124
Donizetti, G.:Gemma di Vergy, w. Montserrat Caballe (sop—Gemma), Anna Ringart (mez—Ida), Luis Lima (ten—Tamas), Vicente Sardinero (bar—Il Conte), Juan Pons (bar—Guido), Francois Loup (b—Rolando), A. Gatto (cnd), Nouvel PO, Jean-Paul Kreder (cnd), French Radio Chorus *(rec live, Salle Pleyel, Paris, Apr 20, 1976)* Agorá Music ("Phoenix" series) 2-▲ 501 [ADD]
Donizetti, G.:Lucia di Lammermoor, w. A. Murray (mez), C. H. Ahnsjö (ten), V. Bello (ten), J. Carreras (ten), V. Sardinero (bar), S. Ramey (bass), J. López-Cobos (cnd), New Philharmonia Orch, Ambrosian Opera Chorus Philips 2-▲ 426563-2
Donizetti, G.:Lucrezia Borgia, w. Jane Berbié (mez), Alain Vanzo (ten), Kostas Paskalis (bar), Arnold Voketaitis (bass-bar), L. D. Clements (sgr), Adib Fazah (sgr), Mauro Lampi (sgr), Vern Shinall (sgr), Jerold Siena (sgr), William Wiederanders (sgr), J. Perlea (cnd), New York City Opera Orch, New York City Chorus Great Opera Performances 2-▲ GOP 769
Donizetti, G.:Lucrezia Borgia, w. A. M. Rota (cta), G. Raimondi (ten), E. Flagello (bass), E. Gracis (cnd), La Scala Orch, La Scala Chorus [I] *(rec live, 3/2/70)* Myto 2-▲ 2 MCD 90423 [ADD]
Donizetti, G.:Lucrezia Borgia, w. J. Berbié (mez), A. Vanzo (ten), K. Paskalis (bar), J. Perlea (cnd), *(orch & chorus unknown)* [I] *(rec live in New York, 4/20/65)* Standing Room Only 2-▲ SRO 801-2 (m) [ADD]
Donizetti, G.:Lucrezia Borgia (sels)—Come è bello! Quale incanto! Replay ("Butterfly" series) ▲ BMCD 031 [AAD]
Donizetti, G.:Maria Stuarda, w. S. Verrett (mez), O. Garaventa (ten), C.F. Cillario (cnd), La Scala Orch, La Scala Chorus [I] *(rec live, Milan 4/20/71)* Myto 2-▲ 2 MCD 91137 [ADD]
Donizetti, G.:Maria Stuarda, w. M. Caballé (sop—Maria Stuarda), R. Bezinian (mez—Anna), M. V. Menendez (mez—Elisabetta), J. Carreras (ten—Roberto), M. Mazzieri (bass—Giorgio Talbot), E. Serra (bass—Lord Gugliemo Cecil), N. Santi (cnd), ORTF Lyric Orch, ORTF Lyric Chorale [I] *(rec live 3/26/72)* Memories 2-▲ HR4417/18 [ADD]
Donizetti, G.:Parisina, w. Jérôme Pruett (ten), Louis Quilico (bar), James Morris (bass), E. Queler (cnd), New York City Opera Orch, New York Opera Chorus *(rec live, New York 1974)* Standing Room Only 2-▲ SRO 836-2 [ADD]
Donizetti, G.:Parisina, w. Jérôme Pruett (ten), Louis Quilico (bar), James Morris (bass), E. Queler (cnd), New York City Opera Orch, New York Opera Chorus Pantheon 2-▲ PHE 6638
Donizetti, G.:Roberto Devereux, w. Beverly Wolff (mez), Guido Fabbris (ten), Gianni Raimondi (ten), Walter Alberti (bar), Paolo Badoer (sgr), Carlo Micalucci (sgr), Carlo Padoan (sgr), B. Bartoletti (cnd), Venice Teatro La Fenice Orch, Venice Teatro La Fenice Chorus Great Opera Performances 2-▲ GOP 764
Donizetti, G.:Roberto Devereux, w. S. Marsee (mez), J. Carreras (ten), V. Sardinero (bar), J. Rudel (cnd), *(orch & chorus unknown)* [I] *(rec live, France 1977)* HRE 2-▲ 1004-2 [ADD]
Donizetti, G.:Roberto Devereux (sels), w. S. Marsee (mez), J. Carreras (ten), V. Sardinero (bar), J. Rudel (cnd), *(orch & chorus unknown)* [I] *(rec live, 1977)* Legato Classics ▲ LCD 108-1 [AAD]

Caballé, Montserrat (sop) (cont.)
Donizetti, G.:Roberto Devereux (sels), w. L. Chookasian (mez), J. Oncina (ten), W. Alberti (bar), C.F. Cillario (cnd), *(orch & chorus unknown)*—9 arias from Acts 1 & 2 [I] *(rec live in Carnegie Hall, 12/16/65)* Standing Room Only 2-▲ SRO 801-2 (m) [ADD]
Eternal Caballé RCA Red Seal ▲ 09026-60865-2
Falla, M. de:Atlántida, w. Heinz Rehfuss (bar), E. Ansermet (cnd), Swiss Romande Orch, Lausanne Youth Chorus, Swiss Romande Red Chorus, Villamont College Little Chorus Cascavelle ▲ CVL 2005 [ADD]
Famous Love Duets, Vol. 2, w. Gianna d'Angelo (sop), Maria Callas (sop), Renata Scotto (sop), Beverly Sills (sop), Renata Tebaldi (sop), José Carreras (ten), Mario Del Monaco (ten), Giuseppe Di Stefano (ten), Plácido Domingo (ten), Luciano Pava Enterprise ("Documents" series) ▲ ENTLV 999
From the Official Barcelona Games Ceremony, w. P. Domingo (ten), José Carreras (ten), Giacomo Aragall (ten), Teresa Berganza (mez), Juan Pons (bar) RCA Red Seal ▲ 09026-61204-2 ■ 09026-61204-4 □ 09026-61204-5
Gala Operatic Concert, w. Franco Corelli (ten), Bonaldi Giaiotti (bass) *(rec live, 1968)* Legato Classics ▲ LCD 101-1 [AAD]
Giordano, U.:Andrea Chénier, w. L. Pavarotti (ten), L. Nucci (bar), R. Chailly (cnd), National PO London [I] London 2-▲ 410117-2 [DDD]
Giordano, U.:Andrea Chénier, w. Franco Corelli (ten), R. de Carlo (sgr), D. Dondi (sgr), G. Ellsworth (sgr), J. Fair (sgr), R. Falk (sgr), S. Felter (sgr), E. Green (sgr), H. Hicks (sgr), H. Krauss (sgr), L. Miller (sgr), N. Riggins (sgr), H. Salerno (sgr), A. Guadagno (cnd), Academy of Music Orch, Academy of Music Chorus Great Opera Performances 2-▲ GOP 766
Gounod, C.:Faust (sels), w. A. Lombard (cnd), Strasbourg PO Erato ("Recital" series) ▲ 98499-2
Granados, E.:Songs—Descúbrase el Pensamiento de Mi Secreto Duiado; Llorad; Corazon; Razon; Mira Que Soy Niña; Amor; Déjame; No Lloreis; Ojuelos; Iban al Pinar; Gracia Mia; La maja; Dolorosa Nosa. 1–3; El Tra la la y el Panteado; El Mirar de la Maja; Callejeo; Amor e Odio; El Majo Discreto; El Majo Timido; La Maja de Goya; Elegia eterna; La maja y el ruisenor; Canco d'amor; L'Ocell profeta RCA Gold Seal ▲ 09026-62539-2
Great Operatic Duets, w. Shirley Verrett (mez), Anton Guadagno (cnd), New Philharmonia Orch, Ambrosian Opera Chorus RCA Gold Seal ▲ 60818-2-RG [ADD]
Great Sopranos of Our Time, w. Maria Callas (sop), Joan Sutherland (sop), Renata Scotto (sop), Elisabeth Schwarzkopf (sop), Victoria de los Angeles (sop), Mirella Freni (sop), Ileana Cotrubas (sop), Edita Gruberova (sop) Classics for Pleasure ▲ CDEMX 9519 [ADD]
Leoncavallo, R.:Pagliacci, w. R. Scotto (sop), A. Varnay (mez), J. Hamari (mez), J. Carreras (ten), M. Manuguerra (bar), T. Allen (bar), K. Nurmela (bar), U. Benelli (bar), R. Muti (cnd), Philharmonia Orch, Ambrosian Opera Chorus EMI Classics 2-▲ CDMB 63650
Leoncavallo, R.:Pagliacci, w. P. Domingo (ten), S. Milnes (bar), N. Santi (cnd), London SO, John Alldis Choir RCA Gold Seal 2-▲ 09026-60865-2 [ADD]
Mascagni, P.:Cavalleria rusticana (sels), w. J. Carreras (ten), R. Muti (cnd), Philharmonia Orch, Ambrosian Opera Chorus EMI Classics ("Studio" series) ▲ CDM 63933 ■ EG 63933
Massenet, J.:Hérodiade, w. M. Caballé (sop—Salomé), D. Vejzovic (mez—Hérodiade), J. Carreras (ten—Jean), J. Pons (bar—Hérode), E. Serra (bar—Vitellius), V. Esteve (bar—High Priest), R. Kennedy (bass—Phanuel), J. Delacôte (cnd), Barcelona Teatro Liceo Orch, Barcelona Gran Teatro de Liceo Chorus *(rec Jan. 6, 1984)* Legato Classics 2-▲ LCD 182 [ADD]
Meyerbeer, G.:L'Africiane, w. Montserrat Caballe (sop—Selika), Christine Weidinger (sop—Inez), Miriam Ucelay (mez—Anna), Placido Domingo (ten—Vasco de Gama), Guillermo Sarabia (bar—Nelusko), Juan Thomas (b-bar—High Priest of Brahma), Dimiter Petkov (bass—Don Pedro), Juan Pons (bass—Don Diego), Eduardo Soto (bass—Grand Inquisitor), A. de Almeida (cnd), Barcelona Teatro Liceo Orch, Barcelona Gran Teatro de Liceo Chorus *(rec Barcelona, Nov 27, 1977)* Legato Classics 2-▲ LCD 208-2 [ADD]
Montserrat Caballé EMI Classics ("Diva" series) ▲ CDM 65575
Mozart, W.A.:Complete Mozart Edition, w. I. Cotrubas (sop), J. Baker (mez), N. Gedda (ten), C. Davis (cnd), Royal Opera House Orch, Royal Opera House Chorus Covent Garden Philips 3-▲ 422542-2 [ADD]
Mozart, W.A.:Don Giovanni, w. T. Stich-Randall (mez), E. Wächter (bar), E. Kunz (bar), M. Gielen (cnd), Naples Teatro San Carlo Orch, Naples Teatro San Carlo Chorus [I] *(rec live, Lisbon, 1960)* Standing Room Only 2-▲ SRO 813-2 [ADD]
Ponchielli, A.:La Gioconda, w. M. Caballé (sop—Gioconda), M. L. Nave (mez—Laura), P. Payne (mez—La Cieca), J. Carreras (ten—Enzo), M. Manuguerra (bar—Barnaba), B. Giaiotti (bass—Alvise), J. López-Cobos (cnd), *(orch unknown)* *(rec Dec. 6, 1979)* Legato Classics ▲ LCD 170-2 [ADD]
Ponchielli, A.:La Gioconda, w. A. Baltsa (mez), L. Pavarotti (ten), S. Milnes (bar), N. Ghiaurov (bass), B. Bartoletti (cnd), National PO [I] London 3-▲ 414349-2 [DDD]
Public Performances 1967–1970 *(rec 1967–70)* Memories ("Great Voices" series) 2-▲ MEM 4279 (m) [ADD]
Puccini, G.:Arias, w. M. Chiara (sop), M. Freni (sop), B. Nilsson (sop), J. Sutherland (sop), R. Tebaldi (sop), F. Corelli (ten), L. Pavarotti (ten), S. Milnes (bar) London ▲ 421315-2 [ADD]
Puccini, G.:Arias, w. F. Corelli (ten), P. Domingo (ten), *(orch unknown)* EMI Classics ▲ CDE 67782
Puccini, G.:Arias—11 arias [I] EMI Classics ▲ CDC 47841
Puccini, G.:La Bohème, w. J. Blegen (sop), P. Domingo (ten), S. Milnes (bar), R. Raimondi (bass), G. Solti (cnd), London PO, John Alldis Choir [I] RCA Red Seal 2-▲ RCD2-0371 2-■ ARK2-0371
Puccini, G.:La Bohème, w. J. Blegen (sop), P. Domingo (ten), S. Milnes (bar), G. Solti (cnd), London PO RCA Victor ▲ 09026-61725-2; ■ 09026-61725-4 (CrO2)
Puccini, G.:Madama Butterfly, w. Montserrat Caballé (sop—Cio-Cio-San), Carmen Rigai (mez—Suzuki), Bernabé Martí (ten—Pinkerton), Diego Monjo (ten—Goro), Juan Rico (ten—Yamadori), Manuel Ausensi (bar—Sharpless), Jose Lemar (bass—Bonze), Antonio Leval (bass—Imperial Commissioner), Alejandro Chiara (bass—Registrar), G. Rivoli (cnd), Madrid Radio-TV Orch, Madrid Radio-TV Chorus *(rec Madrid, June 12, 1968)* Legato Classics 2-▲ LCD 210-2 [ADD]
Puccini, G.:Manon Lescaut, w. M. Caballé (sop—Manon Lescaut), P. Domingo (ten—Des Grieux), R. Tear (ten—Edmondo), V. Sardinero (bar—Lescaut), N. Mangin (bass—Geronte), B. Bartoletti (cnd), New Philharmonia Orch, Ambrosian Opera Chorus EMI Classics ▲ CDMB 64852
Puccini, G.:Manon Lescaut (sels), w. Montserrat Caballé (sop—Manon), Plácido Domingo (ten—Des Grieux), J. Levine (cnd), Metropolitan Opera Orch—Tu, tu, amore? Tu? [Act II] Deutsche Grammophon ▲ 447270-2 [ADD] ■ 447270-4
Puccini, G.:Tosca, w. J. Carreras (ten), I. Wixell (bar), C. Davis (cnd), Royal Opera House Orch Covent Garden [I] Philips 2-▲ 412885-2 [ADD]
Puccini, G.:Tosca, w. J. Carreras (ten), C. Davis (cnd), Royal Opera House Orch Covent Garden Philips 2-▲ 438359-2
Puccini, G.:Turandot, w. M. Caballé (sop—Turnadot), M. Freni (sop—Liu), J. Carreras (ten—Calaf), M. Sénéchal (ten—Emperor Altoum), V. Sardinero (bar—Ping), P. Plishka (bass—Timur), A. Lombard (cnd), Strasbourg PO, Maîtrise de la Cathédrale, Rhine Opera Chorus EMI Classics 2-▲ CDMB 65293
Puccini, G.:Turandot, w. Montserrat Caballé (sop—Turandot), Leona Mitchell (sop—Liu), Remy Corazza (ten—Pang), Joseph Franck (ten—Pong), Robert Johnson (ten—Prince of Persia), Raymond Manton (ten—Altoum), Luciano Pavarotti (ten—Calaf), Aldo Bramante (bar—a mandarin), Dale Duesing (bar—Ping), Giorgio Tozzi (bass—Timur), R. Chailly (cnd), *(orch unknown)* *(rec San Francisco, Nov. 4, 1977)* Legato Classics 2-▲ LCD 188-2
Puccini, G.:Turandot, w. J. Sutherland (sop), L. Pavarotti (ten), N. Ghiaurov (bass), Z. Mehta (cnd), London PO, John Alldis Choir [I] London 2-▲ 414274-2 [ADD]
Puccini, G.:Turandot (sels), w. M. Freni (sop), J. Carreras (ten), M. Sénéchal (ten), A. Lombard (cnd), Strasbourg PO, Rhine Opera Chorus EMI Classics ("Studio" series) ▲ CDM 63410
Puccini, G.:Turandot (sels), w. J. Sutherland (sop), L. Pavarotti (ten), N. Ghiaurov (bass), Z. Mehta (cnd), London PO London ▲ 421320-2 [ADD] ■ 421320-4
Rossini, G.:Arias, *(orch unknown)*—includes arias from Donna del lago, Otello, Siege of Corinth, Stabat Mater, Tancredi RCA Gold Seal 2-▲ 09026-60941-2
Rossini, G.:Arias, w. June Anderson (sop), Maria Callas (sop), Edita Gruberova (sop), Pilar Lorengar (sop), Mady Mesplé (sop), Nicolai Gedda (ten), Tito Gobbi (bar), Samuel Ramey (bass), *(orchs unknown)*—from Barbiere di Siviglia; La Cenerentola; La Gazza ladra; Petite messe solennelle; Semiramide; Stabat Mater *(rec 1958–89)* EMI Classics 2-▲ CZS 67440-2 [ADD/DDD]
Rossini, G.:La donna del lago, w. J. Hamari (mez), F. Bonisolli (ten), R. Bottazzo (ten), P. Bellugi (cnd), Turin Radio Orch, Turin RAI Chorus [I] *(rec live 5/19/70)* Standing Room Only 2-▲ SRO 803-2 (m) [ADD]

Caballé, Montserrat (sop) (cont.)

Rossini, G.:La donna del lago, w. J. Hamari (mez), F. Bonisolli (ten), R. Bottazzo (ten), P. Bellugi (cnd), Turin RAI Orch, Turin RAI Chorus [I] *(rec live 5/19/70)* Melodram 2–▲ MEL 27074 (m) [AAD]

Rossini, G.:La donna del lago, w. A. Balboni (sop), J. Hamari (mez), F. Bonisolli (ten), R. Bottazzo (ten), G. Sinimberghi (ten), P. Washington (bass), P. Bellugi (cnd), Turin RAI Orch, Turin RAI Chorus *(rec live, Torino, 1970)* Foyer 2–▲ FOY 2028 [AAD]

Rossini, G.:La donna del lago (sels), *(orch unknown)*—Tanti affetti in tal momento Replay ("Butterfly" series) ▲ BMCD 031 [AAD]

Rossini, G.:Guillaume Tell, w. M. Mesplé (sop), C. Burles (ten), N. Gedda (ten), G. Bacquier (bar), G. Howell (bass), L. Gardelli (cnd), Royal PO, Ambrosian Opera Chorus EMI Classics 4–▲ CDMD 69951

Rossini, G.:Semiramide, w. M. Horne (mez), F. Araiza (ten), S. Ramey (bass), J. López–Cobos (cnd), *(orch unknown) (rec live, France, 1980)* HRE 2–▲ 1002–2 [ADD]

Rossini, G.:Il turco in Italia, w. E. Dara (bar), L. Nucci (bar), S. Ramey (bass), R. Chailly (cnd), National PO London, Ambrosian Opera Chorus [I] CBS 2–▲ M2K 37859 [DDD]

Souvenirs Sony Classical ▲ SMK 48155 ■ SMT 48155

Spontini, G.:Agnes von Hohensauften, w. A. Stella (sop), B. Prevedi (ten), G. Guelfi (bar), R. Muti (cnd), Rome Radio Orch, Rome RAI Chorus [I] *(rec live, 4/30/70)* Myto 2–▲ 2 MCD 90215 (m) [ADD]

Strauss, R.:4 Last Songs, w. A. Lombard (cnd), Strasbourg PO Erato ("Recital" series) ▲ 98499–2

Strauss, R.:Salome, w. R. Resnik (mez), R. Lewis (ten), S. Milnes (bar), E. Leinsdorf (cnd), London SO RCA Gold Seal 2–▲ 6644–2–RG [ADD]

Verdi, G.:Aida, w. F. Cossotto (mez), P. Domingo (ten), P. Cappuccilli (bar), N. Ghiaurov (bass), R. Muti (cnd), New Philharmonia Orch, Royal Opera House Chorus Covent Garden [I] EMI Classics 3–▲ CDCC 47271 [ADD]

Verdi, G.:Arias, w. G.–F. Masini (cnd), Barcelona SO—7 arias & scenes from Ballo in maschera, Macbeth, Rigoletto, Trovatore, Vespri siciliani [I] Acanta ▲ 49395

Verdi, G.:Arias—includes arias from Alzira, Aroldo, Attila, Il corsaro, Due foscari RCA Gold Seal 2–▲ 09026–60941–2

Verdi, G.:Arias—Il trovatore:Tacea la notte placida; Timor di me? D'amor sull'ali rosee; Un ballo in maschera:Ecco l'orrido campo; Morrò, ma prima in grazia Gaspare Spontini; Luisa Miller:Tu, puniscimi, o Signore; Ernani:Surta è la notte Replay ("Butterfly" series) ▲ BMCD 031 [AAD]

Verdi, G.:Aroldo, w. G. Cecchele (ten), J. Pons (bar), E. Queler (cnd), New York Opera Orch, Westchester Choral Society, New York Oratorio Society [I] *(rec live, Carnegie Hall 4/8/79)* CBS 2–▲ M2K 35906 [ADD]

Verdi, G.:Un ballo in maschera, w. M. Caballé (sop—Amelia), T. Paniagua (sop—Oscar), L. Chookasian (cta—Ulrica), P. Domingo (ten—Riccardo), C. MacNeil (bar—Renato), J. Pons (bar—Tom), C. del Bosco (bass—Samuel), G. Patanè (cnd), *(orch unknown)* Ornamenti 2–▲ FE 103

Verdi, G.:Il corsaro, w. J. Norman (sop), J. Carreras (ten), L. Gardelli (cnd), New Philharmonia Orch, Ambrosian Singers [I] Philips 2–▲ 426118–2 [ADD]

Verdi, G.:Don Carlos, w. F. Cossotto (mez), P. Domingo (ten), P. Cappuccilli (bar), G. Petkov (bar), E. Inbal (cnd), Arena di Verona Orch, Arena di Verona Chorus [I] *(rec live 7/2/69)* Melodram 3–▲ MEL 37057 (m) [AAD]

Verdi, G.:Don Carlos, w. M. Caballé (sop—Elisabeth de Valois), G. Bumbry (mez—Princess Eboli), J. Aragall (ten—Don Carlos), R. Bruson (bar—Rodrigue), S. Estes (bass—Philip II), T. Fulton (cnd), *(orch unknown) (rec Orange, France, 1979)* Ornamenti 2–▲ FE 110 [ADD]

Verdi, G.:Ernani, w. Bruno Prevedi (ten), Peter Glossop (bar), Boris Christoff (bass), G. Gavazzeni (cnd), Milan RAI SO, Milan RAI Chorus *(rec Milan, Mar. 25, 1969)* Pantheon 2–▲ PHE 6634 (m)

Verdi, G.:La traviata, w. J. Carreras (ten), N. Mitic (bar), A. Guadagno (cnd), Philadelphia Lyric Opera Orch, Philadelphia Lyric Opera Chorus *(rec 1973)* Melodram 2–▲ MLO 270106 [ADD]

Verdi, G.:La traviata, w. C. Bergonzi (ten), S. Milnes (bar), G. Prêtre (cnd), RCA Italian Opera Orch RCA Gold Seal 2–▲ 6180–2 RC [ADD]

Verdi, G.:La traviata (sels), w. N. Rescigno (cnd), Dallas Civic Opera Orch—4 arias from Acts 1 & 3 [I] *(rec live 11/13/65)* Melodram 2–▲ MEL 27047 [AAD]

Verdi, G.:Il trovatore, w. P. Domingo (ten), E. Sordello (bar), K. Andersson (cnd), New Orleans Opera Orch, New Orleans Opera Chorus [I] *(rec live 3/14/68)* Melodram 2–▲ MEL 27047 [AAD]

Verdi, G.:Il trovatore, w. G. Tucker (ten), M. Zanasi (bar), T. Schippers (cnd), Florence Maggio Musicale Orch, Florence Maggio Musicale Chorus [I] *(rec live 1968)* Melodram 2–▲ MEL 27035

Verdi, G.:Il trovatore, w. G. Tucker (ten), M. Zanasi (bar), T. Schippers (cnd), Florence Maggio Musicale Orch, Florence Maggio Musicale Chorus *(rec 1968)* Memories ▲ MEM 4521 [ADD]

Verdi, G.:I vespri siciliani, w. P. Domingo (ten), F. Bordoni (bar), J. Diaz (bass), E. Queler (cnd), *(orch unknown) (rec live, Barcelona, 1974)* Standing Room Only 2–▲ SRO 837–2 [ADD]

Wagner, R.:Arias & Scenes, w. Z. Mehta (cnd), New York PO [G] CBS ▲ MK 37294

Wagner, R.:Götterdämmerung (immolation scene), w. Z. Mehta (cnd), New York PO [G] CBS ▲ MK 37294

Wagner, R.:Der Ring des Nibelungen (sels), w. P. Wimberger (b–bar), Z. Mehta (cnd), New York PO—Rheingold *(Entry of the Gods)*, Walküre *(Ride of the Valkyries; Magic Fire Music)* Siegfried *(Waldweben)*, Götterdämmerung *(Rhine Journey & Funeral Music; Immolation Scene)* CBS ▲ MDK 44657 [DDD] ■ MDT 44657 (D)

Wagner, R.:Tannhäuser (sels), w. A. Lombard (cnd), Strasbourg PO Erato ("Recital" series) ▲ 98499–2

Wagner, R.:Tristan und Isolde (sels), w. A. Lombard (cnd), Strasbourg PO Erato ("Recital" series) ▲ 98499–2

Wagner, R.:Tristan und Isolde (prelude & liebestod), w. Z. Mehta (cnd), New York PO [G] CBS ▲ MK 37294

Zarzuela Arias & Duets, w. Eugenio Marco (cnd) *(rec 1965 & 1967 [duets])* RCA Gold Seal ▲ 09026–68148–2 [ADD]

Cabero, Joan (ten)

Halffter, E.:Dominus pastor meus, w. Susan Chilcott (sop), Claire Powell (mez), José Antonio Carril (bass), V. P. Pérez (cnd), Tenerife SO, La Laguna Univ Choir Discobi ▲ DIS 2009 [DDD]

Cable, Jennifer (sop)

Brings, A.:Madrigali concertati (3), w. M. Ingolfsson (vc), U. Ingolfsson (hpd) CRS ▲ CD 9153

Pleskow, R.:From Holy Week in Genoa, w. K. Merrill (pno) CRS ▲ CD 9153

Pleskow, R.:Songs (2) on Latin Fragments, w. K. Merrill (pno) CRS ▲ CD 9153

Cable, Margaret (mez)

Gay, J.:The Beggar's Opera (sels), w. P. Clark (sop), A. Jenkins (sop), E. Lane (mez), S. Minty (mez), E. Fleet (sgr), P. Hall (ten), V. Midgley (ten), N. Rogers (ten), J. Noble (bar), D. Stevens (cnd), Accademia Monteverdiana Orch, Accademia Monteverdiana Chorus—59 songs *(rec Aug. 1978)* Koch Treasure ▲ 31621–2 [ADD]

Handel, G.F.:Messiah, w. Emma Kirkby (sop), Emily Van Evera (sop), James Bowman (ct), Joseph Cornwell (ten), David Thomas (bass), A. Parrott (cnd), Taverner Consort, Taverner Choir [E] EMI Classics 2–▲ CDCB 49801 [DDD]

Handel, G.F.:Messiah, w. Emily van Evera (sop), Emma Kirkby (sop), James Bowman (ct), A. Parrott (cnd), Taverner Players, Taverner Choir Virgin Classics 2–▲ ZDMB 61330

Holloway, R.:Sea Surface Full of Clouds, w. P. Walmsley–Clark (sop), C. Brett (alt), M. Hill (ten), R. Hickox (cnd), City of London Sinfonia Chandos ▲ CHAN 9228 [DDD]

Hommages, w. Fingerhut, Margaret (pno), William Bennett (fl), Kenneth Sillito (vn), Clifford Benson (pno) Chandos ▲ CHAN 8578 [DDD]

Cabre, Josep (bar)

Charpentier, M.–A.:Judicum Salomonis, w. A. Zaepffel (ct), J. Benet (ten), Elwes (ten), G. Ragon (ten), G. Reinhart (bar), P. Colléaux (cnd), Stradivaria Ensemble, Nantes Vocal Ensemble [L] Arion ▲ ARN 68037 [DDD]

Charpentier, M.–A.:Salve regina à 3 voix pareilles, w. Gérard Lesne (ct), John Elves (ten), J. Savall (cnd), Concert des Nations Astrée ▲ E 8552 [DDD]

Monteverdi, C.:Motets, w. B. Lesne (mez), G. Lesne (ct), J. Benet (ten), Il Seminario Musicale—18 motets for 1, 2 & 3 voices [L] Virgin Classics ("Veritas" series) ▲ 59602 [DDD]

Caccamo, Giovanni (bar)

Perti, G.A.:Liturgy for Good Friday, w. Patrizia Vaccari (sop), Maura Pederzoli (sop), Cristina Calzolari (sop), Alida Oliva (sop), Claudia Bugli (sop), Lucia Bagnoli (alt), Cinzia Meneghel (alt), Renzo Bez (alt), Alessandro Carmignani (alt), Michel van Goethem (alt), Mauro Collina (ten), Vincenzo Di Donato (ten), Paolo Fanciullacci (ten), Paolo Da Col (ten), Sergio Foresti (bass), Marco Scavazza (bass), Luca Ferracin (bass), Paride Montanari (bass), Liuwe Tamminga (org), Sergio Vartolo (org), S. Vartolo (cnd), Bologna San Petronio Capella Musicale Orch—Omnes amici mei; De lamentatione Jeremiae Prophetae:Heth. Cogitavit; Velum templi; Vinea mea; De lamentatione Jeremiae Prophetae:Lamed. Matribus suis; Tamquam ad latronem; Tenebrae factae sunt; Animam meam; Tradiderunt me; Jesum tradidit; De lamentatione Jeremiae Prophetae:Aleph. Ego vir; Caligaverunt *(rec St. Petronio Basilica, Bologna, Mar 28–31, 1995)* Naxos ▲ 8.553321 [DDD]

Cachemaille, Gilles (bar)

Auber, D.–F.:Le Domino noir, w. Sumi Jo (sop), Doris Lamprecht (sop), Martine Olmeda (sop), Isabelle Vernet (sop), Jocelyne Taillon (mez), Bruce Ford (ten), Patrick Power (ten), Jules Bastin (bass), R. Bonynge (cnd), English CO, London Voices London 2–▲ 440646–2

Beethoven, L. van:Sym 9, "Choral Sym", w. Luba Orgonasova (sop), Anne Sofie von Otter (mez), Anthony Rolfe Johnson (ten), J. E. Gardiner (cnd), Orch Révolutionnaire et Romantique [period instrs] *(rec All Saints' Church, London, Oct 1992)* Archiv ▲ 447074–2 [DDD]

Berlioz, H.:L'Enfance du Christ, w. A. S. von Otter (mez), Johnson (sgr), J. Van Dam (b–bar), J. Bastin (bass), J.E. Gardiner (cnd), Lyon Opera Orch, Monteverdi Choir London [F] Erato 2–▲ 2292–45275–2 [DDD]

Berlioz, H.:Messe solennelle Sop, w. Donna Brown (sop), Jean–Luc Viala (ten), J. E. Gardiner (cnd), Orch Révolutionnaire et Romantique, Monteverdi Choir London Philips ▲ 442137–2 ■ 442137–4 □ 442137–5

Berlioz, H.:Les Nuits d'été, w. D. Montague (mez), C. Robbin (mez), H. Crook (ten), J.E. Gardiner (cnd), Lyon Opera Orch [F] Erato ("Musifrance" series) ▲ 2292–45517–2 [DDD]

Berlioz, H.:Songs, w. B. Fournier (sop), D. Montague (mez), C. Robbin (mez), H. Crook (ten), J.E. Gardiner (cnd), Lyon Opera Orch—Zaïde [Fournier]; La belle voyageuse [Montague]; La Captive [Robbin]; La mort d'Ophélie [Robbin]; Le jeune pâtre breton [Crook]; Aubade [Crook]; Le Chasseur danois [Cachémaille] [F] Erato ("Musifrance" series) ▲ 2292–45517–2 [DDD]

Brahms, J.:Ein Deutsches Requiem, w. D. Brown (sop), H. Rilling (cnd), Stuttgart Bach Collegium, Gächinger Kantorei [G] Hänssler Classic ▲ 98.966 [DDD]

Debussy, C.:Pelléas et Mélisande, w. C. Alliot–Lugaz (sop), F. Golfier (sop), C. Carlson (mez), D. Henry (ten), P. Thau (bass), C. Dutoit (cnd), Montreal SO, Montreal Sym Chorus [F] London 2–▲ 430502–2 [DDD]

Dutilleux, H.:Sonnets (2) de Jean Cassou, w. G. Joy (pno) Erato 2–▲ 91721

Franck, C.:Les Béatitudes, w. D. Montague (mez), K. Lewis (ten), J. Cheek (bass), H. Rilling (cnd), Stuttgart RSO, Gächinger Kantorei [F] Hänssler Classic 2–▲ 98.964 [DDD]

Gluck, C.W.:La Recontre imprévue, w. C. Le Coz (sop), L. Dawson (sop), C. Dubosc (sop), S. Marin–Degor (sop), G. Fletcher (sgr), F. Dudziak (ten), G. de Mey (ten), J.–L. Viala (ten), J.–P. Lafont (bass), J. E. Gardiner (cnd), Paris Lyon Opera Orch, Paris Lyon Opera Chorus [F] Erato 2–▲ 2292–45516–2 [DDD]

Mangold, C.A.:Abraham, w. Monika Frimmer (sop), Georg Mechthild (mez), B Gärtner (ten), Gerd Türk (ten), Philadelphia Orch, Darmstadt Concert Choir Christophorus 2–▲ 77172

Martin, F.:Monologe (6) aus "Jedermann", w. A. Jordan (cnd), Swiss Romande Orch Erato ▲ 2292–45694–2 [DDD]

Mendelssohn, F.:O Haupt voll Blut und Wunden, w. M. Corboz (cnd), Lausanne Vocal & Instrumental Ensemble [G] Erato ▲ 2292–45462–2 [DDD]

Messager, A.:Fortunio, w. C. Alliot–Lugaz (sop), T. Dran (ten), R. Schirrer (bar), J. E. Gardiner (cnd), Paris Lyon Opera Orch, Paris Lyon Opera Chorus Erato 2–▲ 45983–2

Mozart, W.A.:Clemenza, w. Barbara Bonney (sop—Servilia), Cecilia Bartoli (mez—Sesto), Della Jones (mez—Vitellia), Diana Montague (mez—Annio), Uwe Heilman (ten—Tito), Giles Cachemaille (bar—Publio), C. Hogwood (cnd), Academy of Ancient Music, Academy of Ancient Music Chorus London ("Editions de l'oiseau–lyre" series) 2–▲ 444131–2 [DDD]

Mozart, W.A.:Così fan tutte (sels), w. Felicity Lott (sop), Marie McLaughlin (sop), Nuccia Focile (sop), Jerry Hadley (ten), Alessandro Corbelli (bass) *(rec Usher Hall, Edinburgh, Scotland)* Telarc ▲ CD 80399 [DDD]

Mozart, W.A.:Così fan tutte (sels), w. C. Margiono (sop), van der Walt (sop), D. Ziegler (mez), N. Harnoncourt (cnd), Royal Concertgebouw Orch—sels. Teldec ▲ 9031–76455–2

Mozart, W.A.:Dixit Dominus et Magnificat, w. E. Mei (sop), E. von Magnus (cta), K. Azesberger (ten), N. Harnoncourt (cnd), Vienna Concentus Musicus, Arnold Schoenberg Choir Teldec ("Das alte Werke" series) ▲ 93025

Mozart, W.A.:Litaniae Lauretanae, K.109, w. Eva Mei (sop), Elisabeth von Magnus (alt), Kurt Azesberger (ten), N. Harnoncourt (cnd), Vienna Concentus Musicus, Arnold Schoenberg Choir *(rec Casino Zögernitz, Vienna, Dec. 1992)* Teldec ("Das alte Werke" series) ▲ 96147–2 [DDD]

Mozart, W.A.:Litaniae Lauretanae, K.195, w. B. Bonney (sop), E. von Magnus (cta), U. Heilmann (tenor), N. Harnoncourt (cnd), Vienna Concentus Musicus, Arnold Schoenberg Choir Teldec ("Das alte Werke" series) ▲ 93025

Mozart, W.A.:Missa brevis, K.275, w. E. Mei (sop), E. von Magnus (cta), K. Azesberger (teno, N. Harnoncourt (cnd), Vienna Concentus Musicus, Arnold Schoenberg Choir Teldec ("Das alte Werke" series) ▲ 93025

Mozart, W.A.:Zauberflöte, w. B. Bonney (sop—Pamina), S. Jo (sop—Queen of the Night), K. Streit (ten—Tamino), G. Cachemaille (b–bar—Papageno), K. Sigmundsson (bass—Sarastro), A. Östman (cnd), Drottningholm Court Theater Orch, Drottingholm Court Thea Chorus L'Oiseau–Lyre 2–▲ 440085–2 [DDD]

Cadan, Timothy (bass)

Somers, H.:Kyrie, w. Roxolana Roslak (sop), Susan Cooper (mez), Robert Missen (ten), Nelson Lohnes (bass), E. Iseler (cnd), *(orch unknown)*, Elmer Iseler Singers *(rec Flora McRae Eaton Memorial Auditorium & St. Anne's Anglican Church, Toronto)* Centrediscs ▲ CMC 5495 [DDD]

Caddy, Ian (b–bar)

Donizetti, G.:Songs, w. A. Halstead (hn), S. Comberti (vc), M. Tan (pno)—Canto d'Ugolino; L'amor funesto; Trovatore in caricatura; Spirito di Dio; Viva il matrimonio; Le renégat; Noé—scène du Déluge; Le départ pour la chasse; On coeur pour abri; La hart [I, F] *(rec 8/84 & 12/85)* Meridian ▲ CDE 84183

Gay, J.:The Beggar's Opera, w. S. Walker (mez), B. Hoskins (sgr), A. Thompson (ten), C. Daniels (ten), J. Barlow (cnd), Broadside Band [E] Hyperion 2–▲ CDA 66591/92

Wallace, V.:Maritana, w. Majella Cullagh (sop), Lynda Lee (mez), Paul Charles Clarke (ten), Damien Smith (bar), Quentin Hayes (bass), P. Ó. Duinn (cnd), RTE Concert Orch, RTE Phil Choir *(rec O'Reilly Hall, Dublin, Sept 1995)* Marco Polo 2–▲ 8.223406–7 [DDD]

Cadelo, Cettina (sop)

Cimarosa, D.:I Finti nobili (sels), w. M.G. Ferracini (sop), R. Cassinelli (ten), R. Malacarne (ten), G. Sarti (bar), B. Marinotti (cnd), RTSI Orch—Li sposi per accidente (Act 3) *(rec 1970)* Foyer ▲ FOY 2057 [AAD]

Cadoni, Fernanda (mez)

Gounod, C.:Faust (sels), w. R. Tebaldi (sop), M. Filippeschi (ten), R. Panerai (bar), I. Tajo (bass), F. Patanè (cnd), Naples Teatro San Carlo Orch, Naples Teatro San Carlo Chorus—Act IV, Scenes 1 & 2 & Act V, Scene 2 *(rec live, 4/26/51)* Standing Room Only 2–▲ SRO 810–2 [ADD]

Mascagni, P.:Cavalleria rusticana, w. G. Simionato (sop—Santuzza), F. Cadoni (mez—Lola), L. Pellogrino (cta—Lucia), A. Braschi (ten—Turiddu), C. Tagliabue (bar—Alfio), A. Basile (cnd), Italian Lyric Orch, Turin Cetra Chorus *(rec Turin, 1950)* Cetra Classic 2–▲ CDO 27 [ADD]

Rimsky–Korsakov, N.:The Maid of Pskov, w. N. Panni (sop), A. Bertocci (ten), B. Christoff (bass), T. Schippers (cnd), *(orch unknown) (rec 1969)* Great Opera Performances 2–▲ GOP 720

Rossini, G.:La Cenerentola, w. A. Noni (sop), M. de Gabarain (mez), H. Alan (bass), V. Gui (cnd), Glyndebourne Festival Orch, Glyndebourne Festival Chorus *(rec 1955)* EMI Classics 2–▲ CDMB 64183

Cadoni, Fernanda (mez) (cont.)
Wagner, R.:Die Meistersinger von Nürnberg, w. Bruna Rizzoli (sop), Fernanda Cadoni (mez), Luigi Infantino (ten), Vito Tatone (ten), Renato Capecchi (bar), Giuseppe Taddei (bar), Boris Christoff (bass), Giovanni Ciavola (bass), James Loomis (bass), Silvo Maionica (bass), Vito Susca (bass), Raimondo Botteghelli (sgr), Walter Brunelli (sgr), Carlo Franzini (sgr), Ezio de Giorgi (sgr), Renzo Gonzales (sgr), L. von Matačić (cnd), Turin RAI Radio-TV SO, Turin RAI Chorus Stradivarius 4-▲ STV 12310

Caforio, Armando (bass)
Marschner, H.A.:Der Vampyr, w. Carole Farley (sop—Malwina), Nucci Condò (mez—Suse), Oslavio Di Credico (ten—George Dibdin), Josef Protschka (ten—Edgar Aubry), Romano Truffelli (ten—Richard Scrop), Martin Egel (bar—Sir Humphrey Davenaut), Andrea Snarski (bar—Toms Blunt), Siegmund Nimsgern (b-bar—Lord Ruthven), Armando Caforio (bass—Robert Green), Peter Boom (sgr—Il capo dei Vampiri), Carlo Di Giacomo (sgr—James Gadshill), Wolfgang Lenz (sgr—Sir Berkley), Galina Pisarenko (sgr—Janthe), Renzo Scorsoni (sgr—Un servitore di Berkley), Anastasia Tomaszewska Schepis (sgr—Emmy), G. Neuhold (cnd), Rome RAI SO, Rome RAI Chorus *(rec Rome, Jan 26, 1980)* Italia 2-▲ CDC 99 [ADD]
Rossini, G.:The Siege of Corinth, w. L. Serra (sop), M. Comencini (ten), D. Raffanti (ten), M. Lippi (bass), P. Olmi (cnd), Genoa Teatro Carlo Felice Orch, Genoa Teatro Carlo Felice Chorus, Prague Phil Choir *(rec June 2 & 14, 1992)* Nuova Era 3-▲ 7140/42 [DDD]

Cage, John (voc)
Cage, J.:Diary—How to Improve the World (You Will Only Make Matters Worse) *(rec June 1991)* Wergo 8-▲ WER 6231-2 [DDD]
Cage, J.:Empty Words III, w. Schola Cantorum Stuttgart *(rec 1975)* Wergo ▲ WER 6074-2 [AAD]
Cage, J.:Indeterminacy, w. D. Tudor (insts/elec) Smithsonian/Folkways 2-▲ SF 40804/5 [AAD]
Cage, J.:Roaratorio:An Irish Circus on Finnegans Wake, w. J. Heaney (sgr), P. Glackin (fid), M. Mercier (bodhran), P. Mercier (bodhran), M. Mallory (fl), S. Ellis (uillean pipes) Wergo ▲ WER 6303-2
Cage, J.:Roaratorio:An Irish Circus on Finnegans Wake, w. J. Heaney (sgr), P. Glackin (fid), M. Mercier (bodhran), P. Mercier (bodhran), M. Mallory (fl), S. Ellis (uillean pipes) Mode 2-▲ mode 28/29

Cage, John (voc/perc)
Cage, J.:Four [6], w. Joan La Barbara (sop/perc), Leonard Stein (pno/perc), William Winant (perc) *(rec Central Park Summerstage, New York City, July 23, 1992)* Music & Arts ▲ CD 875 [DDD]

Cahill, Teresa (sop)
Elgar, E.:Coronation Ode, w. A. Collins (cta), A. Rolfe Johnson (ten), G. Howell (bass), A. Gibson (cnd), Scottish National Orch, Scottish National Chorus [E] *(rec 1976)* Chandos ("Collect" series) ▲ CHAN 6574 [ADD]
Elgar, E.:The Spirit of England, w. A. Gibson (cnd), Scottish National Orch, Scottish National Chorus [E] *(rec 1976)* Chandos ("Collect" series) ▲ CHAN 6574 [ADD]
Lutyens, E.:Music of, w. C. Austin (cnd), Brunel Ensemble—Bagatelles; O saisons, o chateaux Cala ▲ CAL CACD 77005
McCabe, J.:Red Leaves, w. C. Austin (cnd), Brunel Ensemble Cala ▲ CAL CACD 77005
Mahler, G.:Das Klagende Lied, w. Janet Baker (mez), Robert Tear (ten), Gwynne Howell (bass), G. Rozhdestvensky (cnd), BBC SO, BBC Sym Chorus IMP ("BBC Radio" series) ▲ IMP 5691412
Williamson, M.:Sym 7, w. C. Austin (cnd), Brunel Ensemble Cala ▲ CAL CACD 77005

Cahn (sgr)
Ligeti, G.:Aventures, w. Charlent (sgr), Pearson (sgr), B. Maderna (cnd), Darmstadt International Chamber Ensemble Wergo ▲ WER 60045-50 [ADD]
Ligeti, G.:Nouvelles aventures, w. Charlent (sgr), Pearson (sgr), B. Maderna (cnd), Darmstadt International Chamber Ensemble Wergo ▲ WER 60045-50 [ADD]

Cahnbley, Annelohre (sop)
Mozart, W.A.:Missa, K.427, w. Maria Stader (sop), George Maran (ten), Walter Raninger (bass), B. Paumgartner (cnd), Salzburg Mozarteum Orch, Salzburg Radio Chorus, Salzburg Mozarteum Chorus *(rec Aug 16, 1958)* Orfeo d'or ("Festspiel Dokumente" series) ▲ 397951 (m)

Cairns, Christine (mez)
Prokofiev, S.:Alexander Nevsky, w. A. Previn (cnd), Los Angeles PO, Master Chorale of Orange County [R] Telarc ▲ CD 80143 [DDD]

Cakarevic (sgr)
Tchaikovsky, P.:Mazeppa, w. Bakocevic (sgr), Cangalovic (sgr), N. Mitic (bar), O. Danon (cnd), Belgrade National Opera Orch, Belgrade National Opera Chorus [R] *(rec live, Berlin, 9/27/69)* Myto 2-▲ 2 MCD 90527 [ADD]

Calabrese, Cynthia (alt)
Britten, H.:Rejoice in the Lamb, w. Susan Ashe (sop), Victor Floyd (ten), Charles Sprawls (bass), Alfred Calabrese (cnd), Britten Singers ACA Digital Recording ▲ CM 20039

Calabrese, Franco (bass)
Mozart, W.A.:Così fan tutte, w. Elisabeth Schwarzkopf (sop), Graziella Sciutti (sop), Nan Merriman (mez), Luigi Alva (ten), Rolando Panerai (bar), G. Cantelli (cnd), La Scala Orch, La Scala Chorus Stradivarius 2-▲ STV DTM 12304 [ADD]
Mozart, W.A.:Così fan tutte, w. E. Schwarzkopf (sop—Fiordiligi), G. Sciurri (sop—Despina), N. Merriman (mez—Dorabella), L. Alva (ten—Ferrando), R. Panerai (bar—Guglielmo), F. Clabrese (b-bar—Don Alfonso)., G. Cantelli (cnd), La Scala Orch, La Scala Chorus *(rec Jan. 27, 1956)* Datum 2-▲ DAT 12304 [ADD]
Mozart, W.A.:Nozze di Figaro, w. S. Jurinac (sop), G. Sciutti (sop), R. Stevens (mez), M. Sinclair (cta), D. McCoshan (ten), H. Counod (ten), G. Griffith (bar), S. Bruscantini (b-bar), V. Gui (cnd), Glyndebourne Festival Orch, Glyndebourne Festival Chorus Classics for Pleasure ▲ CDCFP 4724 [ADD]
Paisiello, G.:La Molinara, w. Graziella Sciutti (sop), Agostino Lazzari (ten), Alvinio Misciano (ten), Sesto Bruscantini (bar), Leonardo Monreale (bass), F. Caracciolo (cnd), Alessandro Scarlatti CO Melodram 2-▲ CDM 29502
Verdi, G.:La forza del destino, w. Leyla Gencer (sop—Leonora), Gabriella Carturan (mez—Preziosilla), Giuseppe di Stefano (ten—Don Alvaro), Aldo Protti (bar—Don Carlo), Cesare Siepi (b-bar), Franco Calabrese (bass—Marchese di Calatrava), Enrico Campi (bass—Fra Melitone), A. Votto (cnd), La Scala Orch, La Scala Chorus *(rec Bühnen der Stadt, Köln, July 5, 1957)* Agorá Music ("Phoenix" series) 3-▲ 510 [ADD]

Calaminus, Joachim (ten)
Fux, J.J.:La Fede sacrilega nella morte del Precursor San Giovanni Battista, "Johannes der Täufer", w. J. Koslowsky (sop), M. Lins (sop), H. Helling (cta), G. Schwarz (bass), T. Reuber (cnd), Capella Piccola Neuss [period instrs] [I] Thorofon 2-▲ CTH 2071/72 [DDD]

Calazans, Teca (sgr)
Chevalier, C.:Music of, w. Ze-Luis (sgr), Regina Machado (sgr), Nigel Scragg (fl/a sax), Rosihna de Valenca (gtr), Jean-Yves Candela (pno), Wilson das Neves (perc), Regina Machado (perc), Silvano Michelino (perc)—Comme d'habitude; Couleur café; Une histoire d'amour; Les feuilles mortes; Les moulins de mon coeur; Syracuse; Je t'aimerai; Ces petits rien; La valse des lilas; L'absent; Que reste-il de nos amours; Un homme et une femme *(rec Studio Bastille)* Iris ▲ 010 [DDD]

Caldini (sgr)
Pergolesi, G.B.:San Guglielmo Duca d'Aquitania, w. K. Gamberucci (sop), B. Lucarini (sop), R. Girolami (bass), G. Gatti (bar), Herron (sgr), F. Maestri (cnd), Terni CO [I] *(rec live, 12/18/86)* Bongiovanni 2-▲ GB 2060/61 [DDD]

Calès, Claude (bar)
Gounod, C.:Roméo et Juliette, w. M. Freni (sop—Juliette), F. Corelli (ten—Roméo), H. Gui (bar—Mercutio), C. Câles (bar—Capulet), X. Depraz (bass—Frère Laurent), A. Lombard (cnd), Paris Opera Orch, Paris Opera Chorus EMI Classics ▲ CDMB 65290

Caley, Ian (ten)
Weill, K.:The Seven Deadly Sins, w. E. Ross (sop), A. R. Johnson (ten), M. Rippon (bass), J. Tomlinson (bass), S. Rattle (cnd), City of Birmingham SO EMI Classics ▲ CDM 64739

Calix, Ariane (sop)
Strauss (II), Joh.:Die Fledermaus (sels), w. Ariane Calix (sop—Ida), Gabriele Fontana (sop—Rosalinde), Brigitte Karwautz (sop—Adele), Rohangiz Yachmi-Caucig (cta—Orlofsky), John Dickie (ten—Eisenstein), Josef Hopferwieser (ten—Alfred), Erich Wessner (ten—Dr. Blind), Andrea Martin (bar—Falke), Alfred Werner (bar—Frank), J. Wildner (cnd), Czech-Slovak RSO Bratislava, Bratislava City Chorus—Ov.; [Act I] Täubchen, das entflattert ist...; Ach, ich darf nicht hin zu dir; Nein, mit solchen Advokaten; Komm mit mir zum Souper; So muss allein ich bleiben; Trinke, Liebchen, trinke schnell; [Act II] Ein Souper heut' uns winkt; Ich lade gern mir Gäste ein; Mein Herr Marquis, ein Mann wie Sie; Dieser Anstand, so manierlich; Klänge der Heimat; Im Feuerstrom der Reben; Marianka komm und tanz me hier; [Act III] Entr'acte; Spiel' ich die Unschuld vom Lande; O Fledermaus, o Fledermaus *(rec Slovak Radio Concert Hall, Bratislava)* Naxos ▲ 8.553171 [DDD]

Callahan, Mary Ellen (sop)
Handel, G.F.:Faramondo, w. Julianne Baird (sop—Clotilde), Mary Ellen Callahan (sop—Adolfo), D'Anna Fortunado (mez—Faramondo), Jennifer Lane (mez—Rosimonda), Drew Minter (alt—Gernando), Peter Castaldi (bar—Gustavo), Mark Singer (bar—Tebaldo), Edward Brewer (hpd), R. Palmer (cnd), Brewer CO [period instrs] Vox Classics 3-▲ VOX3 7536 [DDD]
Yukechev, Y.:Sacred Choral Music, w. Nikolai Kachanov (cnd), New York Russian Chamber Chorus—My Heart Is Ready; O, Beauty; Chant; By Candlelight Helicon Classics ▲ HE 1005

Callas, Maria (sop)
Arias, w. Turin RAI SO, Rome RAI SO, Milan RAI SO, Royal Opera House Orch Covent Garden *(rec 1949-1962)* Verona 2-▲ 27058/59 (m) [AAD]
The Art of Maria Callas EMI Classics ▲ CDMD 63244
At the Concertgebouw Amsterdam, w. Concertgebouw Orch [cnd:Nicola Rescigno] *(rec July 1950)* Verona ▲ 2706 [AAD]
Beethoven, L. van:Ah, perfido!, w. N. Rescigno (cnd), Paris Conservatory Societé des Concerts Orch [I] EMI Classics ("Studio" series) 2-▲ CDMB 63625 [ADD]
Bellini, V.:Arias, w. T. Serafin (cnd), La Scala Orch—La sonnambula—Compagne, teneri amici...Come per me sereno; Oh, se una volta sola...Ah, non credea mirarti [I] *(rec 1955)* EMI Classics ▲ CDC 47966 [ADD]
Bellini, V.:Norma, w. J. Sutherland (sop), E. Stignani (mez), M. Picchi (ten), G. Vaghi (bass), V. Gui (cnd), Royal Opera House Orch, Royal Opera House Chorus Covent Garden [I] *(rec live, Covent Garden 11/52)* Legato Classics 2-▲ LCD 130-2 (m) [AAD]
Bellini, V.:Norma, w. Gabriella Carturan (mez), Giulietta Simionato (mez), Mario del Monaco (ten), Giuseppe Zampieri (ten), Nicola Zaccaria (bass), A. Votto (cnd), La Scala Orch, La Scala Chorus Melodram 2-▲ CDM 26036
Bellini, V.:Norma, w. E. Nicolai (mez), F. Corelli (ten), B. Christoff (bass), A. Votto (cnd), Trieste Teatro Comunale Giuseppe Verdi Orch, Trieste Teatro Comunale G. Verdi Chorus *(rec live 11/19/53)* Melodram 2-▲ CDM 26031 [ADD]
Bellini, V.:Norma, w. G. Simionato (mez), M. Del Monaco (ten), N. Zaccaria (bass), A. Votto (cnd), La Scala Orch, La Scala Chorus *(rec 12/7/55)* HRE 2-▲ 1007-2
Bellini, V.:Norma, w. J. Sutherland (sop), E. Stignani (mez), M. Picchi (ten), G. Vaghi (bass), V. Gui (cnd), Royal Opera House Orch, Royal Opera House Chorus Covent Garden [I] *(rec live, Covent Garden 11/52)* Verona 3-▲ 27018/20 (m) [AAD]
Bellini, V.:Norma, w. C. Ludwig (mez), F. Corelli (ten), N. Zaccaria (bass), T. Serafin (cnd), La Scala Orch, La Scala Chorus [I] EMI Classics ("Studio" series) 3-▲ CDMC 63000 [ADD]
Bellini, V.:Norma, w. J. Sutherland (sop), E. Stignani (mez), M. Picchi (ten), G. Vaghi (bass), V. Gui (cnd), Royal Opera House Orch, Royal Opera House Chorus Covent Garden [I] *(rec live, Covent Garden 11/52)* Melodram 2-▲ MEL 26025
Bellini, V.:Norma, w. Joan Sutherland (sop), Ebe Stignani (cta), Mirto Picchi (ten), Paul Asciak (sgr), V. Gui (cnd), Royal Opera House Orch, Royal Opera House Chorus Covent Garden *(rec live, London, 1952)* Enterprise ("Documents" series) 3-▲ ENTLV 968 [ADD]
Bellini, V.:Norma, w. G. Simionato (mez), K. Baum (ten), N. Moscona (bass), G. Picco (cnd), Palacio Bellas Artes Orch, Palacio Bellas Artes Chorus *(rec live, Mexico City 5/23/50)* Melodram 2-▲ MEL 26018
Bellini, V.:Norma, w. E. Stignani (mez), M. Filippeschi (ten), N. Rossi-Lemeni (bass), T. Serafin (cnd), La Scala Orch, La Scala Chorus [I] EMI Classics 3-▲ CDC 47303 (m)
Bellini, V.:Norma (sels), w. C. Ludwig (mez), F. Corelli (ten), N. Zaccaria (bass), T. Serafin (cnd), La Scala Orch, La Scala Chorus EMI Classics ▲ ZDM 63091
Bellini, V.:Norma (sels), w. M. Pirazzini (mez), F. Corelli (ten), P. De Palma (ten), G. Santini (cnd), Rome Opera Orch, Rome Opera Chorus [I] *(rec live 1/2/58)* Melodram ▲ MEL 16000 (m) [ADD]
Bellini, V.:Norma (sels), w. E. Nicolai (mez), F. Corelli (ten), B. Christoff (bass), A. Votto (cnd), Trieste Teatro Comunale Giuseppe Verdi Orch, Trieste Teatro Comunale G. Verdi Chorus—13 arias [I] *(rec live 11/19/53)* Myto 2-▲ 2 MCD 91340 [ADD]
Bellini, V.:Norma (sels), w. F. Cossotto (mez), G. Cecchele (ten), I. Vinco (bass), G. Prêtre (cnd), Paris Opera Orch, Paris Opera Chorus—sels. *(rec 1965)* Melodram ▲ MLO 16038 [ADD]
Bellini, V.:Norma (sels), w. *(other artists unknown)* EMI Classics ▲ CDC 56341
Bellini, V.:Il pirata, w. P. M. Ferraro (ten), C. Ego (bar), N. Rescigno (cnd), American Opera Society Orch, American Opera Society Chorus [I] *(rec live, New York 1/27/59)* Melodram 2-▲ MEL 26013
Bellini, V.:Il pirata, w. M. Callas (sop—Imogene), P. M. Ferraro (ten—Gualterio), Constantine Ego (bar—Ernesto), N. Rescigno (cnd), American Opera Society Orch, American Opera Society Chorus *(rec 1959)* EMI Classics ▲ CDMB 64938
Bellini, V.:Il pirata (sels), w. N. Rescigno (cnd), Stuttgart RSO *(rec Stuttgart, May 19, 1959)* Originals ▲ ORISH 850
Bellini, V.:Il pirata (sels), w. N. Rescigno (cnd), Stuttgart RSO *(rec May 19, 1959)* Enterprise ("Palladio" series) ▲ ENT PD 4188
Bellini, V.:Il pirata (sels), w. *(other artists unknown)* EMI Classics ▲ CDC 56341
Bellini, V.:I Puritani, w. G. di Stefano (ten), Campolonghi (sgr), R. Silva (bass), G. Picco (cnd), Palacio Bellas Artes Orch, Palacio Bellas Artes Chorus [I] *(rec live, Mexico City 5/29/52)* Melodram 2-▲ MEL 26027 (m) [AAD]
Bellini, V.:I Puritani, w. G. di Stefano (ten), R. Panerai (bar), N. Rossi-Lemeni (bass), T. Serafin (cnd), La Scala Orch, La Scala Chorus [I] EMI Classics 2-▲ CDCB 47308 (m) [ADD]
Bellini, V.:I Puritani (sels), w. A. Simonetto (cnd), Milan Italian Radio-TV Orch, Milan Italian Radio-TV Chorus—Ah! Vieni al Tempio Fonit Cetra ("Martini & Rossi" series) ▲ FCT CDMR 5007
Bellini, V.:La sonnambula, w. F. Cossotto (mez), N. Monti (ten), N. Zaccaria (bass), A. Votto (cnd), La Scala Orch, La Scala Chorus [I] *(rec live 1957)* Arkadia 2-▲ 503 (m) [AAD]
Bellini, V.:La sonnambula, w. F. Cossotto (mez), N. Monti (ten), N. Zaccaria (bass), A. Votto (cnd), La Scala Orch, La Scala Chorus [I] *(rec live 1957)* Verona 2-▲ 2704/05 (m) [AAD]
Bellini, V.:La sonnambula, w. F. Cossotto (mez), N. Monti (ten), N. Zaccaria (bass), A. Votto (cnd), La Scala Orch, La Scala Chorus [I] EMI Classics 2-▲ CDCB 47377 (m)
Bellini, V.:La sonnambula, w. F. Cossotto (mez), N. Monti (ten), N. Zaccaria (bass), A. Votto (cnd), La Scala Orch, La Scala Chorus [I] *(rec live 1957)* Melodram 2-▲ MEL 26003
Bellini, V.:La sonnambula, w. Fiorenza Cossotto (mez), Nicola Monti (ten), Franco Ricciardi (ten), Dino Mantovani (bar), Nicola Zaccaria (bass), A. Votto (cnd), La Scala Orch, La Scala Chorus Melodram 2-▲ CDM 26037
Bellini, V.:La sonnambula, w. G. Carturan (mez), C. Valletti (ten), G. Modesti (bass), L. Bernstein (cnd), La Scala Orch, La Scala Chorus [I] *(rec live, 3/5/55)* Myto 2-▲ 2 MCD 89006 (m) [ADD]
Bellini, V.:La sonnambula (sels), w. F. Cossotto (mez), N. Monti (ten), N. Zaccaria (bass), A. Votto (cnd), La Scala Orch, La Scala Chorus, from Act 2—Oh! se una volta sola rivederio; Ah, non creda mirarti [I] *(rec live, 7/4/57)* Myto 2-▲ 2 MCD 89006 (m) [ADD]
Bellini, V.:La sonnambula (sels), w. *(other artists unknown)* EMI Classics ▲ CDC 56341
Bizet, G.:Carmen, w. A. Guiot (sop), N. Gedda (ten), R. Massard (bar), G. Prêtre (cnd), Paris Opera Orch, Paris Opera Chorus [F] EMI Classics 2-▲ CDCB 54368
Bizet, G.:Carmen (sels), w. A. Guiot (sop), N. Gedda (ten), R. Massard (bar), G. Prêtre (cnd), Paris Opera Orch [F] EMI Classics ▲ CDM 63075 ■ EG 63075
Callas à Paris:Great Arias from French Opera EMI Classics ▲ CDC 49059 [ADD]
Callas & Tebaldi:The Early Recordings, w. Renata Tebaldi (sop) Andromeda 2-▲ ANR 2518/19
Callas-Dallas *(rec 11/57)* Legato Classics ▲ LCD 131-1 (m) [AAD]

1098 ▲ = CD ♦ = Enhanced CD Δ = MD ■ = Cassette Tape ◻ = DCC

Callas, Maria (sop) (cont.)

Callas, Gigli, w. Beniamino Gigli (ten), Milan RAI SO [cnd:Alfredo Simonetto] *(rec Casino Municipale Opera Theatre, Sanremo, Dec. 27, 1954)* Incontri Memorabili ▲ CDMR 5002
Casa Sonzogno, w. Enrico Caruso (ten), et al. Arkadia 2-▲ 626
Cherubini, L.:Médée, w. F. Barbieri (mez), M. Petri (bar), V. Gui (cnd), Florence Maggio Musicale Orch, Florence Maggio Musicale Chorus [I] *(rec 1953)* Arkadia 2-▲ 516 (m) [AAD]
Cherubini, L.:Médée, w. F. Barbieri (mez), G. Penno (ten), G. Modesti (bass), Nache (sgr), L. Bernstein (cnd), La Scala Orch, La Scala Chorus [I] *(rec live 12/10/53)* Melodram 2-▲ MEL 26022 (m) [AAD]
Cherubini, L.:Médée, w. T. Berganza (mez), J. Vickers (ten), N. Zaccaria (bass), N. Rescigno (cnd), Dallas SO *(rec live, Dallas Civic Opera, State Fair Music Hall 11/6/58)* Melodram 2-▲ MEL 26016
Cherubini, L.:Médée, w. F. Cossotto (mez), J. Vickers (ten), N. Zaccaria (bass), N. Rescigno (cnd), Royal Opera House Orch, Royal Opera House Chorus Covent Garden [I] *(rec live, Covent Garden, 6/30/59)* Melodram 2-▲ MEL 26005
Cherubini, L.:Médée, w. R. Scotto (sop), M. Pirazzini (mez), M. Picchi (ten), T. Serafin (cnd), La Scala Orch, La Scala Chorus [I] *(rec live, 1953)* EMI Classics (Studio) 2-▲ CDMB 63625 [ADD]
Cherubini, L.:Médée, w. F. Barbieri (mez), G. Penno (ten), G. Modesti (bass), Nache (sgr), L. Bernstein (cnd), La Scala Orch, La Scala Chorus [I] *(rec live, Milan 12/10/53)* Verona 2-▲ 27088/89
Cherubini, L.:Médée (sels)—three versions of Medea's Act 1 aria "Dei tuoi figli la madre" [I] Verona 2-▲ 27088/89
I Concerti "Live" di Maria Callas 3 Great Opera Performances 2-▲ GOP 748
D'Art et d'Amour EMI Classics 2-▲ ZDCB 54103
La Davina 1 EMI Classics ■ 4DS 54702
La Divina 2 EMI Classics ▲ CDC 55016 ■ 4DS 55016
La Divina 3 EMI Classics ▲ CDC 55216 ■ 4DS 55216
Donizetti, G.:Anna Bolena, w. Gabriella Carturan (mez), Giulietta Simionato (mez), Gianni Raimondi (ten), Plinio Clabassi (bass), Nicola Rossi Lemmeni (sgr), Luigi Rumo (sgr), G. Gavazzeni (cnd), La Scala Orch, La Scala Chorus Great Opera Performances 2-▲ GOP 768
Donizetti, G.:Anna Bolena, w. G. Simionato (mez), G. Raimondi (ten), G. Gavazzeni (cnd), La Scala Orch, La Scala Chorus [I] *(rec live, 4/17/57)* Melodram 2-▲ MEL 26010
Donizetti, G.:Anna Bolena, w. M. Callas (sop—Anna Bolena), G. Simionato (mez—Giovanna Seymour), N. Rossi-Lemeni (bass—Enrico VIII), G. Gavazzeni (cnd), Milan RAI SO, Milan RAI Chorus *(rec May 14, 1957)* EMI Classics ▲ CDMB 64941
Donizetti, G.:Anna Bolena, w. M. Callas (sop—Anna Bolena), G. Simionato (mez—Giovanna), G. Raimondi (ten—Percy), N. Rossi-Lemeni (bass—King), G. Gavazzeni (cnd), La Scala Orch, La Scala Chorus [I] *(rec live, Milan 4/14/57)* Verona 2-▲ 27090/91
Donizetti, G.:Lucia di Lammermoor, w. G. di Stefano (ten), R. Panerai (bar), N. Zaccaria (bass), H. von Karajan (cnd), RIAS SO, La Scala Chorus [I] *(rec 9/29/55)* Melodram 2-▲ MEL 26004
Donizetti, G.:Lucia di Lammermoor, w. G. di Stefano (ten), R. Panerai (bar), N. Zaccaria (bass), H. von Karajan (cnd), RIAS SO, La Scala Chorus [I] *(rec 9/29/55)* Verona 2-▲ 2709/10 (m) [AAD]
Donizetti, G.:Lucia di Lammermoor, w. Eugenio Fernandi (ten), Rolando Panerai (bar), Giuseppe Modesti (bass), T. Serafin (cnd), Rome RAI SO, Rome RAI Chorus *(rec live, Rome, 1957)* Enterprise ("Documents" series) 2-▲ ENTLV 973 [ADD]
Donizetti, G.:Lucia di Lammermoor, w. F. Tagliavini (ten), P. Cappuccilli (bar), B. Ladysz (bass), T. Serafin (cnd), Philharmonia Orch [I] EMI Classics 2-▲ CDCB 47440
Donizetti, G.:Lucia di Lammermoor, w. G. di Stefano (ten), T. Gobbi (bar), R. Arie (bass), T. Serafin (cnd), Florence Maggio Musicale Orch [I] EMI Classics (Studio) 2-▲ CDMB 69980 (m) [ADD]
Donizetti, G.:Lucia di Lammermoor, w. G. di Stefano (ten), Campolonghi (sgr), G. Picco (cnd), Palacio Bellas Artes Orch, Palacio Bellas Artes Chorus [I] *(rec live, Mexico City 6/10/52)* Myto 2-▲ 2 MCD 91340 [ADD]
Donizetti, G.:Lucia di Lammermoor, w. G. di Stefano (ten), R. Panerai (bar), N. Zaccaria (bass), H. von Karajan (cnd), RIAS SO, La Scala Chorus [I] *(rec live, 1955)* EMI Classics (Studio) 2-▲ CDMB 63631 [ADD]
Donizetti, G.:Lucia di Lammermoor, w. G. Raimondi (ten), R. Panerai (bar), A. Zerbini (bass), F. Molinari-Pradelli (cnd), Naples Teatro San Carlo Orch, Naples Teatro San Carlo Chorus [I] *(rec live, 3/22/56)* Myto ▲ 2 MCD 90319 (m) [ADD]
Donizetti, G.:Lucia di Lammermoor, w. G. di Stefano (ten), R. Panerai (bar), H. von Karajan (cnd), La Scala Orch, La Scala Chorus [I] *(rec live, Milan 1/18/54)* Standing Room Only 2-▲ SRO 831-2 [ADD]
Donizetti, G.:Lucia di Lammermoor, w. G. di Stefano (ten), G. Zampieri (ten), R. Panerai (bar), G. Modesti (bass), H. von Karajan (cnd), La Scala Orch, La Scala Chorus *(rec 1954)* Melodram 2-▲ MLO 26040 [DDD]
Donizetti, G.:Lucia di Lammermoor (sels), w. *(other artists unknown)* EMI Classics ▲ CDC 56341
Donizetti, G.:Lucia di Lammermoor (sels), w. G. Raimondi (ten), *(orch unknown)* [I] *(rec live, 3/24/56)* Myto ▲ 2 MCD 90319 (m) [ADD]
Donizetti, G.:Lucia di Lammermoor (sels), w. G. Picco (cnd), Palacio Bellas Artes Orch—Mad Scene *(rec Mexico City, June 10, 14 & 26, 1952)* Memories ▲ MEM 4581 [AAD]
Donizetti, G.:Lucia di Lammermoor (sels), w. R. Casellato (ten), P. Cappuccilli (bar), T. Serafin (cnd), Philharmonia Orch—highlights *(rec live, London 3/16-21/59)* EMI Classics (Studio) ▲ CDM 63934 ■ EG 63934
Donizetti, G.:Poliuto, w. Franco Corelli (ten), Ettore Bastianini (bar), A. Votto (cnd), La Scala Orch, La Scala Chorus *(rec live, Milan, 1960)* Enterprise ("Documents" series) 2-▲ ENT LV 977 (m)
Donizetti, G.:Poliuto, w. F. Corelli (ten), E. Bastianini (bar), N. Zaccaria (bass), A. Votto (cnd), La Scala Orch, La Scala Chorus [I] *(rec live, 12/7/60)* Arkadia 2-▲ 520 (m) [AAD]
Donizetti, G.:Poliuto, w. F. Corelli (ten), E. Bastianini (bar), N. Zaccaria (bass), A. Votto (cnd), La Scala Orch, La Scala Chorus [I] *(rec live, 12/7/60)* Melodram 2-▲ MEL 26006
Donizetti, G.:Poliuto, w. F. Corelli (ten), E. Bastianini (bar), N. Zaccaria (bass), A. Votto (cnd), La Scala Orch, La Scala Chorus [I] *(rec live, Milan 12/7/60)* Verona 2-▲ 28003/04
Duets, w. Giuseppe Di Stefano (ten), Guido Picco (cnd) *(rec live, Mexico City, 1952)* Melodram 2-▲ CDM 26028 (m) [AAD]
Famous Love Duets, Vol. 2, w. Gianna d'Angelo (sop), Montserrat Caballé (sop), Renata Scotto (sop), Beverly Sills (sop), Renata Tebaldi (sop), José Carreras (ten), Mario Del Monaco (ten), Giuseppe Di Stefano (ten), Plácido Domingo (ten), Luciano Pava Enterprise ("Documents" series) ▲ ENTLV 999
The Farewell Recitals, w. Callas, Maria (sop), Giusepe Di Stefano (ten), Ivor Newton (pno) *(rec Philadelphia & Miami & Cincinnati)* Ornamenti 2-▲ FE 124
Five Heroines, w. La Scala Orch, T. Serafin (cnd), H. von Karajan (cnd), V. de Sabata (cnd), C. M. Giulini (cnd) EMI Classics 5-▲ CDME 64418
Giordano, U.:Andrea Chénier, w. M. del Monaco (ten), A. Protti (bar), A. Votto (cnd), La Scala Orch, La Scala Chorus *(rec live, Milan, 1/8/55)* Melodram 2-▲ MEL 26002 [ADD]
Giordano, U.:Andrea Chénier, w. M. del Monaco (ten), A. Protti (bar), A. Votto (cnd), La Scala Orch, La Scala Chorus *(rec live)* Verona 2-▲ VER 28020
Gluck, C.W.:Alceste, w. R. Gavarini (ten), R. Panerai (bar), S. Maionica (bass), C. M. Giulini (cnd), La Scala Orch, La Scala Chorus—plus "Callas Sings Gluck & Rossini" [French version] *(rec live, La Scala, 4/4/54)* Melodram 2-▲ MEL 26026
Gluck, C.W.:Iphigénie en Tauride, w. F. Cossotto (mez), Albanese (sgr), N. Sanzogno (cnd), La Scala Orch, La Scala Chorus [I] *(rec live 6/1/57)* Melodram 2-▲ MEL 26012 (m)
Great Sopranos of Our Time, w. Joan Sutherland (sop), Renata Scotto (sop), Montserrat Caballé (sop), Elisabeth Schwarzkopf (sop), Victoria de los Angeles (sop), Mirella Freni (sop), Ileana Cotrubas (sop), Edita Gruberova (sop) Classics for Pleasure ▲ CDEMX 9519 [ADD]
The Incomparable Callas EMI Classics ▲ CDM 63182
Leoncavallo, R.:Pagliacci, w. G. di Stefano (ten), T. Gobbi (bar), R. Panerai (bar), T. Serafin (cnd), La Scala Orch [I] EMI Classics 3-▲ CDCC 47981 [ADD]
Live Recordings, Vol. 1 *(rec 1957-63)* LaserLight ▲ 15223
Live Recordings, Vol. 2 *(rec 1953-62)* LaserLight ▲ 15224
Mad Scenes & Other Arias EMI Classics ▲ CDC 47283
Maria Callas & Gianni Raimondi, w. Gianni Raimondi (ten), Milan RAI SO, Milan RAI Chorus [cnd:A. Simonetto] *(rec Milan, Nov. 19, 1956)* Incontri memorabili ("Martini & Rossi Concert" series) ▲ CDMR 5007 [ADD]
Maria Callas & Giuseppe di Stefano, Opera Duets EMI Classics ▲ CDM 69543

Callas, Maria (sop) (cont.)

Maria Callas & Nicola Filacuridi, w. Nicola Filacuridi (ten), Turin RAI SO [cnd:Oliviero De Fabritiis] *(rec Milan, Feb. 18, 1952)* Incontri memorabili ("Martini & Rossi Concert" series) ▲ CDMR 5001 [ADD]
Maria Callas:Great Performances *(rec 1977-87)* Fortissimo ▲ CDE 3001 [ADD]
Maria Callas:Her First Recordings in Italy *(rec 1952)* Enterprise ("Palladio" series) ▲ ENTPD 4137 [ADD]
Maria Callas:Intimate Portrait *(rec 1935-1976)* Ornamenti ▲ FE 109 [ADD]
A Maria Callas Recital Melodram ▲ CDM 16502
Maria Callas Sings Opera Arias EMI Classics ▲ CDM 63259
Maria Callas Sings Operatic Arias Classics for Pleasure ("Eminence" series) ▲ CDEMX 2123 [ADD]
Mascagni, P.:Cavalleria rusticana, w. E. Ticozzi (mez), G. di Stefano (ten), R. Panerai (bar), T. Serafin (cnd), La Scala Orch, La Scala Chorus [I] EMI Classics 3-▲ CDCC 47981 [ADD]
Il Mito *(rec 1958-63)* Foyer ▲ FOY 4004
Mozart, W.A.:Songs, w. E. Grümmer (sop), E. Schwarzkopf (sop), R. Scotto (sop), T. Lemnitz (sop), E. Berger (sop), S. Jurinac (sop), E. Schumann (sop), I. Souez (sop), E. Rethberg (sop), L. Lehmann (sop), N. Gedda (ten), J. McCormack (ten), H. Roswenge (ten), H. Nash (ten), T. Gobbi (bar), G. Hüsch (bar), E. Kunz (bar), G. Frick (bass), E. Pinza (bass), A. Kipnis (bass) EMI Classics 4-▲ CDMD 63750
Opera Arias EMI Classics ▲ CDC 47282 (m)
Ponchielli, A.:La Gioconda, w. M. Callas (sop—Gioconda), F. Barbieri (mez—Laura), M. Amadini (sgr—La Cieca), G. Poggi (ten—Enzo), P. Silveri (bar—Barnaba), G. Neri (bass—Alvise), A. Votto (cnd), Turin RAI Orch, Turin RAI Chorus *(rec 1952)* Cetra Classic 3-▲ CDO 8
Ponchielli, A.:La Gioconda, w. F. Cossotto (mez), I. Companeez (cta), P. M. Ferraro (ten), P. Cappuccilli (bar), I. Vinco (bass), A. Votto (cnd), La Scala Orch, La Scala Chorus EMI Classics ▲ CDCC 49518
Ponchielli, A.:La Gioconda, w. F. Barbieri (mez), G. Poggi (ten), P. Silveri (bar), G. Neri (bass), A. Votto (cnd), Turin RAI SO, Turin RAI Chorus *(rec 1952)* Andromeda 3-▲ ANR 2528 [ADD]
Ponchielli, A.:La Gioconda, w. F. Barbieri (mez), G. Poggi (ten), P. Silveri (bar), G. Neri (bass), A. Votto (cnd), Turin RAI SO, Turin RAI Chorus *(rec 1952)* Enterprise ("Palladio" series) ▲ ENT PD 4152 [DDD]
Puccini, G.:Arias, w. T. Serafin (cnd), Philharmonia Orch—11 arias [I] *(rec 1954)* EMI Classics ▲ CDC 47966 [ADD]
Puccini, G.:Arias, w. Renata Tebaldi (sop), *(orch unknown)*—sels from La Bohème, Tosca & Madama Butterfly *(rec 1953-64)* Andromeda ▲ ANR 2546 [ADD]
Puccini, G.:La Bohème, w. A. Moffo (sop), G. di Stefano (ten), R. Panerai (bar), A. Votto (cnd), La Scala Orch, La Scala Chorus [I] *(rec 1956)* EMI Classics 2-▲ CDCB 47475 (m) [ADD]
Puccini, G.:La Bohème (sels), w. *(other artists unknown)* EMI Classics ▲ CDC 56341
Puccini, G.:Madama Butterfly, w. L. Danieli (mez), N. Gedda (ten), M. Borriello (bar), H. von Karajan (cnd), La Scala Orch, La Scala Chorus [I] *(rec 1955)* EMI Classics 2-▲ CDCB 47959 (m) [ADD]
Puccini, G.:Manon Lescaut, w. G. di Stefano (ten), Fioravanti (sgr), T. Serafin (cnd), La Scala Orch, La Scala Chorus [I] EMI Classics 2-▲ CDCB 47392 (m)
Puccini, G.:Tosca, w. R. Cioni (ten), T. Gobbi (bar), C. F. Cillario (cnd), Royal Opera House Orch, Royal Opera House Chorus Covent Garden [I] *(rec live 1/21/64)* Melodram 2-▲ MEL 26011
Puccini, G.:Tosca, w. M. Filippeschi (ten), R. Weede (bar), U. Mugnai (cnd), Palacio Bellas Artes Orch, Palacio Bellas Artes Chorus [I] *(rec live, Mexico City, 6/8/50)* Standing Room Only 2-▲ SRO 820-2 [ADD]
Puccini, G.:Tosca, w. Mario Filippeschi (ten), Carlos Sagarminaga (ten), Robert Weede (bar), Ramon Alonso (bass), U. Mugnai (cnd), Palacio Bellas Artes Orch, Palacio Bellas Artes Chorus Melodram 3-▲ CDM 36032
Puccini, G.:Tosca, w. G. di Stefano (ten), Campolonghi (sgr), G. Picco (cnd), Palacio Bellas Artes Orch, Palacio Bellas Artes Chorus [I] *(rec live, Mexico City 1952)* Melodram 2-▲ 26028 (m) [AAD]
Puccini, G.:Tosca, w. Maria Callas (sop—Floria Tosca), Robert Bowman (ten—Spoletta), Renato Cioni (ten—Mario Cavaradossi), Eric Garrett (bar—Il Sagrestano), Tito Gobbi (bar—Scarpia), Victor Godfrey (bass—Casare Angelotti), Dennis Wicks (bass—Sciarrone), C. F. Cillario (cnd), Royal Opera House Orch, Royal Opera House Chorus Covent Garden *(rec London, 1964)* Melodram 2-▲ CDI 203003 [ADD]
Puccini, G.:Tosca, w. R. Cioni (ten), T. Gobbi (bar), N. Rescigno (cnd), Paris Opera Orch, Paris Opera Chorus *(rec live, Paris March 3, 1965)* Melodram 2-▲ CDM 26033 [ADD]
Puccini, G.:Tosca, w. G. di Stefano (ten), T. Gobbi (bar), V. de Sabata (cnd), La Scala Orch, La Scala Chorus [I] *(rec 1953)* EMI Classics 2-▲ CDCB 47174 (m) 2-■ 4AV 34047 (m)
Puccini, G.:Tosca, w. C. Bergonzi (ten), T. Gobbi (bar), G. Prêtre (cnd), Paris Conservatory Societé des Concerts Orch, Paris Opera Chorus [I] EMI Classics ("Studio" series) 2-▲ CDMB 69974 [ADD]
Puccini, G.:Tosca, w. R. Cioni (ten), T. Gobbi (bar), C. F. Cillario (cnd), Royal Opera House Orch, Royal Opera House Chorus Covent Garden [I] *(rec live, 1/21/64)* Verona 2-▲ 27027/28 (m) [AAD]
Puccini, G.:Tosca (sels), w. *(other artists unknown)* EMI Classics ▲ CDC 56341
Puccini, G.:Tosca (sels), w. G. di Stefano (ten), G. Picco (cnd), Palacio Bellas Artes Orch, Palacio Bellas Artes Chorus—nine arias & duets [I] *(rec live, Mexico City, 7/1/52)* Standing Room Only 2-▲ SRO 820-2 [ADD]
Puccini, G.:Tosca (sels), w. R. Scotto (sop), C. Bergonzi (ten), A. Kraus (ten), T. Gobbi (bar), G. Prêtre (cnd), Orch de Paris EMI Classics ▲ ZDM 63087
Puccini, G.:Turandot, w. E. Schwarzkopf (sop), E. Fernandi (ten), N. Zaccaria (bass), T. Serafin (cnd), La Scala Orch, La Scala Chorus [I] *(rec 1957)* EMI Classics 2-▲ CDCB 47971 (m) [ADD]
Rarities EMI Classics ▲ CDC 54437
Rarities:Interviews, Rehearsal, Arias Verona 3-▲ 28007/9
Recitals, Volume 2 *(rec live, Amsterdam & Paris, 1959 & 1963)* Verona ▲ 27069 [AAD]
Rossini, G.:Arias, w. June Anderson (sop), Montserrat Caballé (sop), Edita Gruberova (sop), Pilar Lorengar (sop), Mady Mesplé (sop), Nicolai Gedda (ten), Tito Gobbi (bar), Samuel Ramey (bass), *(orchs unknown)*—from Barbiere di Siviglia; La Cenerentola; La Gazza ladra; Petite messe solennelle; Semiramide; Stabat Mater *(rec 1958-89)* EMI Classics 2-▲ CZS 67440-2 [ADD/DDD]
Rossini, G.:Arias, *(orch unknown)* Melodram 2-▲ MEL 26024
Rossini, G.:Armida, w. L. Albanese (sop), M. Filippeschi (ten), G. Raimondi (ten), T. Serafin (cnd), Florence Teatro Comunale Orch, Florence Teatro Comunale Chorus [I] *(rec live, Florence, 4/26/52)* Melodram 2-▲ MEL 26024
Rossini, G.:Il barbiere di Siviglia, w. L. Alva (ten), T. Gobbi (bar), N. Zaccaria (bass), F. Ollendorf (bass), A. Galliera (cnd), Philharmonia Orch EMI Classics ▲ ZDM 63076
Rossini, G.:Il barbiere di Siviglia, w. L. Alva (ten), T. Gobbi (bar), A. Galliera (cnd), Philharmonia Orch [I] *(rec 1957)* EMI Classics 2-▲ CDCB 47634 [ADD]
Rossini, G.:Il barbiere di Siviglia, w. L. Alva (ten), T. Gobbi (bar), C. M. Giulini (cnd), La Scala Orch, La Scala Chorus [I] *(rec live 1956)* Melodram 2-▲ MEL 26020
Rossini, G.:Il barbiere di Siviglia (sels), w. N. Rescigno (cnd), Stuttgart RSO *(rec Stuttgart, May 19, 1959)* Originals ▲ ORISH 850
Rossini, G.:Il barbiere di Siviglia (sels), w. N. Rescigno (cnd), Stuttgart RSO *(rec May 19, 1959)* Enterprise ("Palladio" series) ▲ ENT PD 4188
Rossini, G.:Semiramide (sels), w. A. Simonetto (cnd), Milan Italian Radio-TV Orch, Milan Italian Radio-TV Chorus—Bel Raggio Lusinghiero Fonit Cetra ("Martini & Rossi" series) ▲ FCT CDMR 5007
Spontini, G.:La vestale, w. N. Rossi-Lemeni (bass), F. Corelli (ten), E. Sordello (bar), V. Tatozzi (bar), N. Zaccaria (bass), A. Votto (cnd), La Scala Orch, La Scala Chorus Great Opera Performances ▲ GOP 741
Spontini, G.:La vestale, w. F. Corelli (ten), E. Sordello (bar), A. Votto (cnd), La Scala Orch, La Scala Chorus [I] *(rec live, Milan, 12/7/54)* Melodram 2-▲ MEL 26008
Spontini, G.:La vestale (sels), w. N. Rescigno (cnd), Stuttgart RSO *(rec May 19, 1959)* Enterprise ("Palladio" series) ▲ ENT PD 4188
Spontini, G.:La vestale (sels), w. N. Rescigno (cnd), Stuttgart RSO *(rec Stuttgart, May 19, 1959)* Originals ▲ ORISH 850
Spontini, G.:La vestale (sels), w. A. Simonetto (cnd), Milan Italian Radio-TV Orch, Milan Italian Radio-TV Chorus—Tu Che Invoco con Orrore Fonit Cetra ("Martini & Rossi" series) ▲ FCT CDMR 5007
Spontini, G.:La vestale (sels), w. A. Corelli (bar), E. Sordello (bar), A. Votto (cnd), La Scala Orch, La Scala Chorus [I]—3 scenes *(rec live, Milan, 12/7/54)* Verona 2-▲ 28003/04
Thomas, A.:Hamlet (sels), w. A. Simonetto (cnd), Milan Italian Radio-TV Orch, Milan Italian Radio-TV Chorus—Vi Voglio Offrire i Fiori Fonit Cetra ("Martini & Rossi" series) ▲ FCT CDMR 5007
The Unknown Recordings *(rec 1957-69)* EMI Classics ▲ CDC 49428 [ADD]

Callas, Maria (sop) (cont.)

Verdi, G.:Aida, w. G. Simionato (mez), K. Baum (ten), R. Weede (bar), G. Picco (cnd), Palacio Bellas Artes Orch, Palacio Bellas Artes Chorus *(rec live, Mexico City 5/30/50)* Melodram ▲ MLO 26009 [ADD]

Verdi, G.:Aida, w. Maria Callas (sop—Aida), Joan Sutherland (sop—Priestess), Giulietta Simionato (cta—Amneris), Kurt Baum (ten—Radames), Hector Thomas (ten—Messenger), Jess Walters (bar—Amonasro), Michael Langdon (bass—King), Giulio Neri (bass—Ramfis), J. Barbirolli (cnd), Royal Opera House Orch, Royal Opera House Chorus Covent Garden *(rec Covent Garden, London, June 10, 1953)* Legato Classics 2-▲ LCD 187-2

Verdi, G.:Aida, w. F. Barbieri (mez), G. Tucker (ten), T. Gobbi (ten), N. Zaccaria (bass), T. Serafin (cnd), La Scala Orch, La Scala Chorus [I] EMI Classics 3-▲ CDCC 49030 [ADD]

Verdi, G.:Aida, w. O. Dominguez (mez), M. Del Monaco (ten), G. Taddei (bar), O. de Fabritiis (cnd), Palacio Bellas Artes Orch, Palacio Bellas Artes Chorus *(rec live, Mexico City 7/3/51)* Melodram 2-▲ CDM 26015

Verdi, G.:Aida (sels), w. *(other artists unknown)* EMI Classics ▲ CDC 56341

Verdi, G.:Aida (sels), w. E. Stignani (mez), M. Picchi (ten), R. De Falchi (bar), G. Neri (bass), V. Bellezza (cnd), Rome Opera Orch—five arias with Callas (solo, three duets & quintet) *(rec live 10/2/50)* Melodram 2-▲ CDM 26019 [AAD]

Verdi, G.:Arias, w. N. Rescigno (cnd), Paris Conservatory Societé des Concerts Orch—arias from Aroldo, Attila, Ballo in maschera, Il corsaro, Don Carlos, Otello, Trovatore [I] EMI Classics ▲ CDC 47943

Verdi, G.:Arias, w. G. Prêtre (cnd), North German RSO—Tu che la vanità..., from Don Carlos [I] *(rec live 3/16/62)* Melodram 2-▲ MEL 26029 (m) [AAD]

Verdi, G.:Arias, w. M. Gavazzeni (ten), G. Di Stefano (ten), C.M. Giulini (cnd), La Scala Orch—E strano...Sempre libera;—Ecco l'orrido campo...Ma dall' arido stelo Myto 2-▲ MCD 89003 (m) [ADD]

Verdi, G.:Arias, w. N. Rescigno (cnd), Philharmonia Orch, Paris Conservatory Société des Concerts Orch—arias from Aida, Attila, Ballo in maschera, Don Carlos, Ernani, I Lombardi, Macbeth, Nabucco, Vespri siciliani [I] EMI Classics ▲ CDC 47730 [ADD]

Verdi, G.:Arias, w. Renata Tebaldi (sop), *(orchs & choruses unknown)*—sels from La traviata, Il Trovatore & Un ballo in maschera *(rec 1953–64)* Andromeda ▲ ANR 2546 [ADD]

Verdi, G.:Un ballo in maschera, w. E. Ratti (sop), G. Simionato (mez), G. di Stefano (ten), E. Bastianini (bar), G. Gavazzeni (cnd), La Scala Orch, La Scala Chorus *(rec 1957)* Melodram ▲ MLO 26039 [ADD]

Verdi, G.:Un ballo in maschera, w. E. Ratti (sop), G. Simionato (mez), G. di Stefano (ten), E. Bastianini (bar), G. Gavazzeni (cnd), La Scala Orch, La Scala Chorus [I] *(rec live 12/7/57)* Arkadia 2-▲ 519 (m) [AAD]

Verdi, G.:Un ballo in maschera, w. E. Ratti (sop), F. Barbieri (mez), G. Di Stefano (ten), T. Gobbi (bar), A. Votto (cnd), La Scala Orch, La Scala Chorus [I] *(rec 1956)* EMI Classics 2-▲ CDCB 47498 (m)

Verdi, G.:Don Carlos (sels), w. N. Rescigno (cnd), Stuttgart RSO *(rec Stuttgart, May 19, 1959)* Originals ▲ ORISH 850

Verdi, G.:Don Carlos (sels), w. N. Rescigno (cnd), Stuttgart RSO *(rec May 19, 1959)* Enterprise ("Palladio") ▲ ENT PD 4188

Verdi, G.:Macbeth, w. G. Penno (ten), E. Mascherini (bar), I. Tajo (bass), V. de Sabata (cnd), *(orch unknown)* *(rec Milan, 1952)* Great Opera Performances 2-▲ GOP 750

Verdi, G.:Macbeth (sels), w. N. Rescigno (cnd), Stuttgart RSO *(rec Stuttgart, May 19, 1959)* Originals ▲ ORISH 850

Verdi, G.:Macbeth (sels), w. N. Rescigno (cnd), Stuttgart RSO *(rec May 19, 1959)* Enterprise ("Palladio") ▲ ENT PD 4188

Verdi, G.:Nabucco, w. G. Bechi (bar), L. Neroni (bass), V. Gui (cnd), Naples Teatro San Carlo Orch, Naples Teatro San Carlo Chorus [I] *(rec live 12/20/49)* Melodram 2-▲ MEL 26029 (m) [AAD]

Verdi, G.:Rigoletto, w. G. Di Stefano (ten), Campolonghi (sgr), U. Mugnai (cnd), Palacio Bellas Artes Orch, Palacio Bellas Artes Chorus [I] *(rec live, Mexico City, 6/17/52)* Melodram 2-▲ CDM 26023

Verdi, G.:Rigoletto (sels), w. T. Serafin (cnd), La Scala Orch, La Scala Chorus—selected arias *(rec Milan, 1953)* Andromeda ▲ ANR 2541 [ADD]

Verdi, G.:La traviata, w. G. Di Stefano (ten), Campolonghi (bar), U. Mugnai (cnd), Palacio Bellas Artes Orch, Palacio Bellas Artes Chorus [I] *(rec live, Mexico City, 6/3/52)* Melodram 2-▲ CDM 26021

Verdi, G.:La traviata, w. A. Zanolli (sop), L. Mandelli (sop), G. Raimondi (ten), E. Bastianini (bar), C. M. Giulini (cnd), La Scala Orch, La Scala Chorus *(rec live 1/19/56)* Myto 2-▲ MCD 89003 (m) [ADD]

Verdi, G.:La traviata, w. G. Di Stefano (ten), E. Bastianini (bar), C. M. Giulini (cnd), La Scala Orch, La Scala Chorus [I] *(rec 1955)* EMI Classics (Studio) 2-▲ CDMB 63628 (m) [ADD]

Verdi, G.:La traviata, w. G. Di Stefano (ten), E. Bastianini (bar), C. M. Giulini (cnd), La Scala Orch, La Scala Chorus [I] *(rec live 5/28/55)* Arkadia 2-▲ 501 (m) [AAD]

Verdi, G.:La traviata, w. A. Kraus (ten), M. Sereni (bar), F. Ghione (cnd), Lisbon Teatro São Carlos Orch [I] *(rec live, Lisbon 3/27/58)* EMI Classics 2-▲ CDCB 49187

Verdi, G.:La traviata, w. C. Valletti (ten), A. Zanasi (bass), N. Rescigno (cnd), Royal Opera House Orch, Royal Opera House Chorus Covent Garden [I] *(rec live 6/20/58)* Verona 2-▲ 27054/55 (m) [AAD]

Verdi, G.:La traviata, w. Giron (sgr), C. Valletti (ten), G. Taddei (bar), O. de Fabritiis (cnd), Palacio Bellas Artes Orch, Palacio Bellas Artes Chorus [I] *(rec live, Mexico City, 7/17/51)* Melodram 2-▲ CDM 26019 [AAD]

Verdi, G.:La traviata, w. C. Valletti (ten), A. Zanasi (bass), N. Rescigno (cnd), Royal Opera House Orch, Royal Opera House Chorus Covent Garden [I] *(rec live 6/20/58)* Melodram 2-▲ MEL 26007 (m)

Verdi, G.:La traviata, w. Francesco Albansese (ten), Ugo Savarese (bar), G. Santini (cnd), Turin RAI SO, Coro Cetra *(rec 1953)* Enterprise ("Documents" series) 2-▲ ENT 1002 (m)

Verdi, G.:La traviata (sels), w. G. Santini (cnd), Turin RAI Orch—selected arias *(rec Milan, 1956)* Andromeda ▲ ANR 2541 [ADD]

Verdi, G.:La traviata (sels), w. *(other artists unknown)* EMI Classics ▲ CDC 56341

Verdi, G.:Il trovatore, w. C. Elmo (mez), G. Lauri-Volpi (ten), P. Silveri (bar), T. Serafin (cnd), Naples Teatro San Carlo Orch, Naples Teatro San Carlo Chorus [I] *(rec live, Naples, 1/27/51)* Melodram 2-▲ MEL 26001 (m) [AAD]

Verdi, G.:Il trovatore, w. Cloe Elmo (cta), Giacomo Lauri-Volpi (ten), Paolo Siveri (sgr), T. Serafin (cnd), Naples Teatro San Carlo Orch, Naples Teatro San Carlo Chorus *(rec Theatre of San Carlo, Naples, Jan. 27, 1951)* Pantheon 2-▲ PHE 6636 (m)

Verdi, G.:Il trovatore, w. G. Simionato (mez), K. Baum (ten), L. Warren (bar), G. Picco (cnd), Palacio Bellas Artes Orch, Palacio Bellas Artes Chorus *(rec live, Mexico City 6/20/50)* Melodram 2-▲ CDM 26017

Verdi, G.:Il trovatore, w. E. Stignani (mez), G. Penno (ten), C. Tagliabue (bar), A. Votto (cnd), La Scala Orch, La Scala Chorus [I] *(rec live 2/23/53)* Myto 2-▲ 2 MCD 90213 (m) [ADD]

Verdi, G.:Il trovatore (sels), w. Feuss (sgr), C. Sagarminaga (ten), K. Baum (ten), L. Warren (bar), G. Picco (cnd), Palacio Bellas Artes Orch, Palacio Bellas Artes Chorus—ten selections from Acts 1 & 4 [I] *(rec live, Mexico City 6/20/50)* Myto 2-▲ 2 MCD 90213 (m) [ADD]

Verdi, G.:Il trovatore (sels), w. H. von Karajan (cnd), La Scala Orch, La Scala Chorus—selected arias *(rec Milan, 1955)* Andromeda ▲ ANR 2541 [ADD]

Verdi, G.:Il trovatore (sels), w. G. Sébastian (cnd), Paris Opera Orch—3 arias [I] *(rec live, Paris, 12/19/58)* Melodram 2-▲ MEL 26001 (m) [AAD]

Verdi, G.:I vespri siciliani, w. Maria Callas (sop—Duchess), Giorgio Kokolios Bardi (ten—Arrigo), Gino Sarri (ten—Danieli), Enzo Mascherini (bar—Guido di Monforte), Boris Christoff (bass—Giovanni da Procida), Mario Forsini (bass—Count Vaudemont), Bruneo Carmassi (bass—Bethune), E. Kleiber (cnd), Florence Teatro Comunale Orch, Florence Teatro Comunale Chorus *(rec live, Florence, 1951)* Melodram 3-▲ IMC 303016 [ADD]

Verdi, G.:I vespri siciliani, w. Boris Christoff (bass), Giorgio Kokolios (sgr), E. Kleiber (cnd), Florence Maggio Musicale Orch, Florence Maggio Musicale Chorus *(rec live, Florence, May 26, 1951)* Enterprise ("Documents" series) 3-▲ ENT LV 996

Verdi, G.:I vespri siciliani, w. Kokolios-Bardi (sgr), E. Mascherini (bar), E. Kleiber (cnd), Florence Teatro Comunale Orch, Florence Teatro Comunale Chorus [I] *(rec live 5/26/51)* Melodram 3-▲ MEL 36020 (m)

The Very Best of Maria Callas:Public Performances *(rec 1953–63)* Memories ("Great Voices" series) 2-▲ MEM 4293 (m) [ADD]

La Voix du Siècle EMI Classics ▲ CDC 49502

Callas, Maria (sop) (cont.)

Wagner, R.:Parsifal, w. Baldelli (sgr), R. Panerai (bar), D. Lopatto (bar), B. Christoff (bass), V. Gui (cnd), Rome Radio-TV SO, Rome Radio-TV Chorus [I] *(rec in concert, 11/20–21/50)* Verona 3-▲ 27085/87

Wagner, R.:Parsifal, w. Baldelli (sgr), R. Panerai (bar), D. Lopatto (bar), B. Christoff (bass), V. Gui (cnd), Rome Radio-TV SO, Rome Radio-TV Chorus [I] *(rec 11/20–21/50)* Melodram 3-▲ MEL 36041 (m)

Callataÿ, Marie-Noelle de (sop)

Gluck, C.W.:Orfeo ed Euridice, w. E. Podles (mez), P. Peire (cnd), Collegium Instrumentale Brugensè, Capella Brugensis [original instruments] Forlane 2-▲ FOR 16720 [DDD]

Marc Grauwels & Friends, w. M. Grauwels (fl), Hiroko Masaki (sop), Dennis James (glass hmc), Ingrid Procureur (hp), Yves Storms (gtr), Yvietta Matison (va), Mark Drobinsky (vc), Alain De Rijckere (bn), Daniel Blumenthal (pno), Frank Michiels (perc), Belgian RSO, W Syrinx 2-▲ 96101 [DDD]

Callaway, Irene (sop)

Giordano, U.:Madame Sans-Gêne, w. Magda László (sop—Caterina), Carlo Tagliabue (bar—Napoleone), Renato Berti (sgr—Despréaux), Irene Callaway (sgr—Toniotta/Carolina), Danilo Cestari (sgr—Neipperg/Vinaigre), Maria Luisa Malacchi (sgr—Giulia/Principessa Elisa), Carlo Perucci (sgr—Fouché), Danilo Vega (sgr—Lefebvre), Enzo Viaro (sgr—De Brigode/Gelsomino), A. Basile (cnd), Milan RAI SO, Milan RAI Chorus *(rec Milan, Aug 10, 1957)* Bongiovanni 2-▲ GB 1129/30

Callegari, Giordano (ten)

Verdi, G.:La traviata, w. Olga de Franco (sop—Flora Bervoix/Annina), Anna Rosza (sop—Violetta Valéry), Giordano Callegari (ten—Gastone), Alessandro Ziliani (ten—Alfredo Germont), Luigi Borgonovo (bar—Giorgio Germont), Arnoldo Lenzi (bar—Baron Douphol), Antonio Gelli (bass—Marquis d'Obigny/Dr. Grenvil), C. Sabajno (cnd), La Scala Orch, La Scala Chorus *(rec La Scala Theatre, Milan, Oct.–Nov. 1930)* VAI Audio 2-▲ VAIA 1108-2

Verdi, G.:La traviata, w. Olga de Franco (sop—Flora Bervoix/Annina), Anna Rosza (sop—Violetta Valery), Giordano Callegari (ten—Gastone), Alessandro Ziliani (ten—Alfredo Germont), Luigi Borgonovo (bar—Giorgio Germont), Arnoldo Lenzi (bar—Barone Douphol), Antonio Gelli (bass—Marchese d'Obigny/Dottor Grenvil), C. Sabajno (cnd), La Scala Orch, Vittore Veneziani (cnd), La Scala Chorus *(rec Oct–Nov 1930)* Arkadia 2-▲ CD 78001 (m) [ADD]

Verdi, G.:Il trovatore, w. Maria Carena (sop—Leonora), Olga De Franco (sop—Ines), Irene Minghini Cattaneo (mez—Azucena), Aureliano Pertile (ten—Manrico), Giordano Callegari (ten—Ruiz/Messenger), Apollo Granforte (bar—Count), Bruno Carmassi (bass—Ferrando), Antonio Gelli (bass—Old Gypsy), C. Sabajno (cnd), La Scala Orch, Vittore Veneziani (cnd), La Scala Chorus *(rec 1930)* Arkadia ("The 78's" series) 2-▲ 78007 [ADD]

Callow, Simon (nar)

Schoenberg, A.:A Survivor from Warsaw, w. R. Craft (cnd), London SO Koch International Classics ▲ KIC 7263-2 [DDD]

Calm, Birgit (alt)

Dittersdorf, K.D. von:Sacred Music, w. Hanna Farinelli (sop), Heiner Hopfner (ten), Nikolaus Hillebrand (bass), G. Ratzinger (cnd), Munich Consortium Musicum, Regensburg Cathedral Choir—Requiem in c; Offertorium zu Ehren des Heiligen Johann von Nepomuk; Laurentanische Litanei Ars Musici ▲ AM 1158-2 [DDD]

Calm, Birgit (mez)

Zemlinsky, A. von:Der Traumgörge, w. P. Coburn (sop), J. Martin (sop), G. M. Ronge (sop), P. Haage (ten), H. Kruse (ten), J. Protschka (ten), H. Welker (bar), M. Blasius (bass), V. von Halem (bass), G. Albrecht (cnd), Frankfurt RSO [G] Capriccio 2-▲ CD 10241/2 [DDD]

Calos, Steliana (sop)

Landowski, M.:Adagio Cantabile, w. Pompei Harasteanu (bass), Dominique de Williencourt (vc), Jacques Taddei (org), R. Georgescu (cnd), Timisoara PO, Timisoara Chorus *(rec Mar. 16–18, 1993)* Chamade ▲ 5611 [DDD]

Landowski, M.:Leçons de Ténèbres, w. Pompei Harasteanu (bass), Dominique de Williencourt (vc), Jacques Taddei (org), R. Georgescu (cnd), Timisoara PO, Timisoara Chorus *(rec Mar. 16–18, 1993)* Chamade ▲ 5611 [DDD]

Calvé, Emma (sop)

The Complete Known Issued Recordings Pearl 2-▲ PEA 9482 (m) [AAD]

Diva de la Belle Epoque *(rec 1906–1919 & 1942)* Music Memoria ▲ 30365 [AAD]

Calvi, Caterina (sop)

Frescobaldi, G.:Sonetto spirituale:Maddalena all Croce, w. R. Gini (vc) [I] *(rec 5/91)* Nuova Era ("Ancient Music" series) ▲ 7030 [DDD]

Ricci, F.P.:Lezione terza per il Mercoldi Santo, w. Fernando Ferrari (ten) Nuova Era ▲ NUO 7244

Rossini, G.:Ciro in Babilonia, w. E. Palacio (ten), Dessy-Ceriani (sgr), C. Rizzi (cnd), San Remo SO, San Remo Sym Chorus [I] *(rec live 10/30/88)* Arkadia-Akademia 2-▲ 105 [DDD]

Sammartini, G.B.:Cants for the Fridays in Lent, w. Silvia Mapelli (sop), Vito Martino (ten), D. Ferrari (cnd), Capriccio Italiano Ensemble—Il pianto delle pie Donne; Pianto di Maddalena al Sepolcro Nuova Era ▲ NUO CD 7269

Sammartini, G.B.:Cants for the Fridays in Lent, w. Silvia Mapelli (sop), Vito Martino (ten), D. Ferrari (cnd), Capriccio Italiano Ensemble—Il Pianto Delle Pie Donne, J.118; Pianto di Maddalena al Sepolcro, J.120 Enterprise ("Tiziano" series) ▲ ENT TZ 96007 [DDD]

Sances, G.F.:Stabat mater dolorosa, w. R. Gini (vc) [L] *(rec 5/91)* Nuova Era ("Ancient Music" series) ▲ 7030 [DDD]

Vivaldi, A.:Beatus vir, R.795, w. Susanna Moncayo Von Hase (cta), Vincenzo Manno (ten), Bonitatibus (sgr), Trogu (sgr) Agora Music ▲ 001

Vivaldi, A.:Cants, w. R. Gini (cnd), Camera Concerto—2 Cantatas—"Amor hai vinto," R.683; "Cessate, omai cessate," RV.684 [I] Nuova Era ("Ancient Music" series) ▲ 6877 [DDD]

Vivaldi, A.:Cants, w. A. Ruffini (sop), R. Gini (cnd), Concerto Ensemble—(5 Cantatas) "Fonte del pianto," RV.656; "Sorge vermiglia in ciel," RV.667; "Lungi dal vago volto," RV.680; "Perfidissimo cor, iniquo fato," RV.674; "Piango, gemo, sospiro e peno," RV.675 [I] Nuova Era ("Ancient Music" series) ▲ 6859 [DDD]

Vivaldi, A.:Gloria (& Intro), RV.588, w. Susanna Moncayo Von Hase (cta), Vincenzo Manno (ten), Bonitatibus (sgr), Trogu (sgr) Agora Music ▲ 001

Vivaldi, A.:Stabat Mater Cta, w. R. Gini (cnd), Camera Concerto [L] Nuova Era ("Ancient Music" series) ▲ 6877 [DDD]

Calvino, Claudio (alt)

Viadana, L. da:Vespri per l'Assunzione, w. S. Pozzer (sop), U. Müller Adam (ten), J. Clement (ten), S. Foresti (bass), L'Amaltea Ensemble, Vox Hesperia, St. Marco Capella Musicale Fonè ▲ FON 92F 08 [DDD]

Calzolari, Cristina (sop)

Perti, G.A.:Liturgy for Good Friday, w. Patrizia Vaccari (sop), Maura Pederzoli (sop), Alida Oliva (sop), Claudia Bugli (sop), Lucia Bagnoli (alt), Cinzia Meneghel (alt), Renzo Bez (alt), Alessandro Carmignani (alt), Michel van Goethem (alt), Mauro Collina (ten), Vincenzo Di Donato (ten), Paolo Fanciullacci (ten), Giovanni Caccamo (ten), Paolo Da Col (ten), Sergio Foresti (bass), Marco Scavazza (bass), Luca Ferracin (bass), Paride Montanari (bass), Liuwe Tamminga (org), Sergio Vartolo (org), S. Vartolo (cnd), Bologna San Petronio Capella Musicale Orch—Omnes amici mei; De lamentatione Jeremiae Prophetae:Heth. Cogitavit; Velum templi; Vinea mea; De lamentatione Jeremiae Prophetae:Lamed. Matribus suis; Tamquam ad latronem; Tenebrae factae sunt; Animam meam; Tradiderunt me; Jesum tradidit; De lamentatione Jeremiae Prophetae:Aleph. Ego vir; Caligaverunt *(rec St. Petronio Basilica, Bologna, Mar 28–31, 1995)* Naxos ▲ 8.553321 [DDD]

Camastra, Marco (bar)

Rossini, G.:La pietra del paragone, w. Tiziana Carraro (sop—Fulvia), Elisabetta Gutierrez (mez—Baronessa Aspasia), Sara Mingardo (cta—Clarice), William Matteuzzi (ten—Giocondo), Marco Camastra (bar—Pacuvio), Pietro Spagnoli (bar—Conte Asdrubale), Gioacchino Zarrelli (bar—Fabrizio), Josè Fardilha (bass—Macrobio), B. Aprea (cnd), Graz SO, Sluk Chamber Chorus Bratislava *(rec 1993)* Bongiovanni 2-▲ GB 2179/80 [DDD]

Cameron (sgr)

Berlioz, H.:Benvenuto Cellini, w. J. Carlyle (sop), J. Veasey (mez), K. Lewis (ten), Kentish, Bushby, Garrard, Ward, A. Dorati (cnd), BBC SO, BBC Sym Chorus [E] *(rec live, Royal Festival Hall, 1964)* Music & Arts 2-▲ CD 618 (m) [AAD]

Cameron, John (bar)

Handel, G.F.:Messiah (sels), w. Sheila. Armstrong (sop), Norma Proctor (cta), Kenneth Bowen (ten), L. Stokowski (cnd), London SO, London Sym Chorus [E] London ("Weekend Classics" series) ▲ 433874-2 [ADD] ■ 433874-4

Ravel, M.:L'Heure espagnole, w. S. Danco (mez—Concepcion), J. Giraudeau (ten—Gonzalve), M. Hamel (ten—Torquemada), J. Cameron (bar—Ramiro), A. Vessières (bass—Gomez), B. Maderna (cnd), BBC SO *(rec Nov. 1960)* Stradivarius ▲ STR 10062 [ADD]

Sullivan, A.:HMS Pinafore, w. G. Baker (bar), R. Lewis (ten), M. Sargent (cnd), Pro Arte Orch, Glyndebourne Festival Chorus EMI Classics 2-▲ CDMB 64397

Sullivan, A.:The Pirates of Penzance, w. G. Baker (bar), J. Milligan (b-bar), R. Lewis (ten), M. Sargent (cnd), Pro Arte Orch, Glyndebourne Festival Chorus EMI Classics 2-▲ CDMB 64409

Sullivan, A.:The Sorcerer (sels), w. G. Baker (bar), E. Morison (sop), R. Lewis (ten), M. Sargent (cnd), Pro Arte Orch, Glyndebourne Festival Chorus EMI Classics 2-▲ CDMB 64397

Sullivan, A.:The Yeomen of the Guard, w. R. Lewis (ten), A. Young (ten), M. Sargent (cnd), Pro Arte Orch, Glyndebourne Festival Chorus EMI Classics 2-▲ CDMB 64415

Vaughan Williams, R.:Sym 1, w. Elaine Blighton (sop), M. Sargent (cnd), BBC SO, BBC Chorus, BBC Choral Society, Christchurch Harmonic Choir New Zealand *(rec 1965)* IMP ("BBC Radio" series) ▲ IMP 5691502

Caminada, Anita (mez)

Bizet, G.:Carmen, w. M. Chiara (sop—Micaela), A. Caminada (mez—Mercedes), F. Cossotto (mez—Carmen), F. Andreoli (ten—Il Remendado), P. M. Ferraro (ten—Don José), R. Bruson (bar—Escamillo), G. Zancanaro (bar—Morales), A. Carusi (bass—Il Dancairo), P. Maag (cnd), Venice Teatro La Fenice Orch, Venice Teatro La Fenice Chorus *(rec 1971)* Myto 2-▲ MCD 93487

Bizet, G.:Carmen, w. Giovanna di Rocco (sop—Frasquita), Grace Bumbry (mez—Carmen), Anita Caminada (mez—Mercedes), Franco Corelli (ten—Don José), Mario Ferrara (ten—Dancario), Franco Bordoni (bar—Escamillo), Carlo Scaravelli (bar—Morales), Giuseppe Morresi (bass—Remendado), Francesco Signor (bass—Zuniga), O. de Fabritiis (cnd), *(orch unknown)* *(rec Macerata, July 21, 1974)* Golden Age of Opera 2-▲ GAO 181/82 [ADD]

Campbell, Alan (sgr)

Lloyd Webber, A.:Sunset Boulevard, w. Glenn Close (sgr), George Hearn (sgr), J. Kuhn (sgr)—highlights Polydor ▲ 31452-7241-2 ■ 31452-7241-4

Lloyd Webber, A.:Sunset Boulevard, w. Glenn Close (sgr), George Hearn (sgr), J. Kuhn (sgr) [1994 cast] A&M ▲ 31452 3507-2 ■ 31452 3507-4

Campbell, Sharon (sgr)

Lloyd Webber, A.:Music of, w. L. Garrett (sgr), Dave Willets (sgr), C. Corcoran (sgr), Gerard Casey (sgr), Royal PO, Royal PO Pops Orch, Royal PO Concert Orch—sels from The Phantom of the Opera; Evita; Cats; Joseph & the Amazing Technicolor Dreamcoat; Jesus Christ Superstar; Tell Me on a Sunday; Song & Dance; Starlight Express; Sunset Boulevard Silva America 2-▲ SILCD 1044 [DDD] ■ SILMC 1044

Lloyd Webber, A.:Music of, w. L. Garrett (sgr), Dave Willets (sgr), C. Corcoran (sgr), *(other artists unknown)*—The Phantom of the Opera; Aspects of Love; Cats; Evita; Jesus Christ Superstar; Starlight Express Silva America ▲ SILCD 1022 [DDD] ■ SILMC 1022

Taylor, B.J.:Wuthering Heights, w. Dave Willets (sgr), L. Garrett (sop), C. Carter (sgr), J. Sladdon (sgr), Philharmonia Orch, Contorum Choir Silva America ▲ SSD 1008 ■ SSC 1008

Campi, Enrico (bass)

Bellini, V.:La straniera, w. R. Scotto (sop), E. Zilio (mez), R. Cioni (ten), D. Trimarchi (bar), N. Sanzogno (cnd), Palermo Teatro Massimo Orch, Palermo Teatro Massimo Chorus [I] *(rec live, Palermo, 1968)* Verona 2-▲ 27097/98

Bellini, V.:La straniera, w. R. Scotto (sop), E. Zilio (mez), R. Cioni (ten), D. Trimarchi (bar), N. Sanzogno (cnd), Palermo Teatro Massimo Orch, Palermo Teatro Massimo Chorus [I] *(rec live, Palermo, 1968)* Melodram 2-▲ 27039

Cilea, F.:Gloria, w. M. Roberti (sop), A. M. Rota (cta), F. Labò (ten), A. Albertini (bar), L. Testi (bar), F. Mazzoli (bass), F. Previtali (cnd), Turin RAI Orch, Turin RAI Chorus [I] *(rec live, Turin July 8, 1969)* Memories ▲ HR 4472 [ADD]

Massenet, J.:Werther, w. D. Gatta (sop—Sofia), I. Ligabue (sop—Kaethlen), G. Simionato (mez—Charlotte), F. Tagliavini (ten—Werther), V. Pandano (ten—Schmidt), E. Campi (bass—Johann), S. Bruscantini (bass—Le Bailli), F. Capuana (cnd), La Scala Orch, La Scala Chorus *(rec Apr. 21, 1951)* Bongiovanni 2-▲ GB 1101/02 [ADD]

Rossini, G.:Il barbiere di Siviglia (sels), w. R. Scotto (sop), A. di Stasio (mez), A. Kraus (ten), A. Protti (bar), C. Badioli (bass), V. Bellezza (cnd), Naples Teatro San Carlo Orch, Naples Teatro San Carlo Chorus *(rec July 26, 1958)* Golden Age of Opera 2-▲ GAO 137/38 [ADD]

Rossini, G.:Zelmira, w. Virginia Zeani (sop), Anna Maria Rota (cta), Guido Mazzini (bass), Paolo Washington (bass), Gastone Limarilli (sgr), Giuseppe Moretti (sgr), Nicola Tagger (sgr), C. Franci (cnd), *(orch unknown)* Great Opera Performances 2-▲ GOP 780

Strauss, R.:Der Rosenkavalier, w. Jarmila Barton (sop—Marianne), Lisa Della Casa (sop—Sophie), Sena Jurinac (sop—Octavian), Ilva Ligabue (sop—Orphan), Elisabeth Schwarzkopf (sop—Marschallin), Else Schürhoff (mez—Annina), Luisa Villa (mez—Milliner), Hugues Cuénod (ten—Marschallin's majordomo), Erich Majkut (ten—Valzacchi), Giuseppe Nessi (ten—Animal seller), Luciano Della Pergola (ten—Lackey/Faninal's majordomo), Antonio Pirino (ten—An Italian Singer), Gino Del Signore (ten—Lackey/Waiter), Erich Kunz (bar—Herr von Faninal), Paolo Pedani (bar—Lackey), Attilo Barbesi (bass—Lackey/Waiter), Enrico Campi (bass—Waiter), Otto Edelmann (bass—Baron Ochs), Bruno Fichtinger (bass—Notary), Franco Taino (bass—Waiter), Maria Amadini (sgr—Orphan), Pina Carrillo (sgr—Orphan), Joszi Trojan Regar (sgr—Innkeeper), H. von Karajan (cnd), La Scala Orch, La Scala Chorus *(rec La Scala Theater, Milan, Jan. 26, 1952)* Legato Classics 3-▲ LCD 197-3

Verdi, G.:La forza del destino, w. Leyla Gencer (sop—Leonora), Gabriella Carturan (mez—Preziosilla), Giuseppe di Stefano (ten—Don Alvaro), Aldo Protti (bar—Don Carlo), Cesare Siepi (b-bar), Franco Calabrese (bass—Marchese di Calatrava), Enrico Campi (bass—Fra Melitone), A. Votto (cnd), La Scala Orch, La Scala Chorus *(rec Bühnen der Stadt, Köln, July 5, 1957)* Agorá Music ("Phoenix" series) 3-▲ 510 [ADD]

Zandonai, R.:Francesca da Rimini, w. M. Caniglia (sop—Francesca), A. M. Canali (mez—Altichiara), A. Bertocci (ten—Ser Toldo Berardengo), M. Carlin (ten—Malatestino), G. Prandelli (ten—Paolo), C. Tagliabue (bar—Giovanni), E. Campi (bass—Il Giuliare/Il Torrigiano), A. Guarnieri (cnd), Rome RAI SO, Rome RAI Chorus *(rec 1952)* Cetra Classic ▲ CDO 22 [ADD]

Zandonai, R.:Francesca da Rimini, w. Lydia Marimpietri (sop—Biancofiore), Magda Olivero (sop—Francesca), Pinuccia Perotti (sop—Samaritana), Edda Vincenzi (sop—Garsenda), Gabriella Carturan (mez—Smaragdi), Biancamaria Casoni (mez—Altichiara), Anna Maria Rota (cta—Donella), Athos Cesarini (ten—Archer), Angelo Mercuriali (ten—Ser Toldo Berardengo), Mario del Monaco (ten—Paolo), Piero de Palma (ten—Malatestino), Rinaldo Pelizzoni (ten—Prisoner), Gianpiero Malaspina (bar—Gianciotto), Dino Mantovani (bar—Jester), Enrico Campi (bass—Ostasio), Giuseppe Morresi (bass—Tower warden), G. Gavazzeni (cnd), La Scala Orch, La Scala Chorus *(rec La Scala Theatre, Milan, June 4, 1959)* Legato Classics 2-▲ LCD 186-2

Campo, José Antonio (ten)

Bellini, V.:Mass in a, w. Leila Bersiani (sop), Valentina di Cola (sop), Stella Salvati (cta), Carlo Lepore (bass), E. Brizio (cnd), Prague SO, Czech Radio-TV Chorus *(rec Prague, June 1994)* Studio SM ▲ D 2444

Campolonghi (bar)

Bellini, V.:I Puritani, w. M. Callas (sop), G. di Stefano (ten), R. Silva (bass), G. Picco (cnd), Palacio Bellas Artes Orch, Palacio Bellas Artes Chorus [I] *(rec live, Mexico City 5/29/52)* Melodram 2-▲ MEL 26027 (m) [AAD]

Donizetti, G.:Lucia di Lammermoor, w. M. Callas (sop), G. di Stefano (ten), G. Picco (cnd), Palacio Bellas Artes Orch, Palacio Bellas Artes Chorus [I] *(rec live, Mexico City 6/10/52)* Myto 2-▲ 2 MCD 91340 [ADD]

Puccini, G.:Tosca, w. M. Callas (sop), G. di Stefano (ten), G. Picco (cnd), Palacio Bellas Artes Orch, Palacio Bellas Artes Chorus [I] *(rec live, Mexico City 1952)* Melodram 2-▲ 26028 (m) [AAD]

Verdi, G.:Rigoletto, w. M. Callas (sop), G. Di Stefano (ten), U. Mugnai (cnd), Palacio Bellas Artes Orch, Palacio Bellas Artes Chorus [I] *(rec live, Mexico City, 6/17/52)* Melodram 2-▲ CDM 26023

Verdi, G.:La traviata, w. M. Callas (sop), G. Di Stefano (ten), U. Mugnai (cnd), Palacio Bellas Artes Orch, Palacio Bellas Artes Chorus [I] *(rec live, Mexico City, 6/3/52)* Melodram 2-▲ CDM 26021

Campora, Giuseppe (ten)

Donizetti, G.:La fille du régiment, w. A. Moffo (sop), J. Gardino (mez), G. Fioravanti (bar), F. Mannino (cnd), Milan RAI Orch, Milan RAI Chorus *(rec live Dec 2, 1960)* Melodram 2-▲ MEL 27018 [ADD]

Leoncavallo, R.:Zazà, w. C. Petrella (sop), E. Parker (mez), A. Silipigni (cnd), Turin RAI SO *(rec 1969)* Memories 2-▲ MEM 4519 [AAD]

Puccini, G.:Tosca, w. R. Tebaldi (sop), Enzo Mascherini (bar), F. Corena (bass), A. Erede (cnd), St. Cecilia Academy Orch Rome, St. Cecilia Academy Chorus Rome Enterprise 2-▲ ENTPD 4106 [ADD]

Puccini, G.:Tosca, w. Ranata Tebaldi (sop), Gian Franco Volante (trb), Piero de Palma (ten), Enzo Mascherini (bar), Fernando Corena (bass), Dario Caselli (bass), Antonio Sacchetti (bass), A. Erede (cnd), St. Cecilia Academy Orch Rome, St. Cecilia Academy Chorus Rome *(rec 1952)* Andromeda 2-▲ ANR 2539 [ADD]

Puccini, G.:Tosca, w. R. Tebaldi (sop), Enzo Mascherini (bar), F. Corena (bass), A. Erede (cnd), St. Cecilia Academy Orch Rome, St. Cecilia Academy Chorus Rome London 2-▲ 440236-2 [ADD]

Rossini, G.:Elisabetta, regina d'Inghilterra (sels), w. M. Vitale (sop), L. Pagliughi (sop), Pinno (sgr), A. Simonetto (cnd), Milan RAI SO, Milan RAI Chorus—six arias [I] *(rec live, 4/27/53)* Myto 2-▲ 2 MCD 90530 [ADD]

Verdi, G.:La traviata (sels), w. Anna de Santis (sop—Annina), Renata Tebaldi (sop—Violetta), Giuseppe Campora (ten—Alfredo), Gerardo Gaudioso (bar—Douphol), Giuseppe Taddei (bar—Germont), Antonio Picillo (bass—Grenvil), G. Santini (cnd), Naples Teatro San Carlo Orch, Naples Teatro San Carlo Chorus—E strano...Ah, fors'e lui; Follie!...Sempre libera; Pero l'attendo...Amami, Alfredo; Invitato a qui seguirmi; Alfredo, Alfredo, di questo core; Teneste la promessa...Addio del passato; Ma se tornando...Ah! Gran Dio! Morir si giovine; Se una pudica vergine *(rec San Carlo Theater, Naples, Jan. 17, 1952)* Legato Classics 2-▲ LCD 193-2 [ADD]

Campos, Maria Dolores (sop)

Esplá, O.:Canciones playeras, w. Katharine Durran (pno) *(rec West Road Concert Hall, Univ of Cambridge, Jan 17-19, 1995)* Herald ▲ HAVPCD 184 [DDD]

Falla, M. de:Canciones populares españolas (7), w. Katharine Durran (pno) *(rec West Road Concert Hall, Univ of Cambridge, Jan 17-19, 1995)* Herald ▲ HAVPCD 184 [DDD]

Granados, E.:Colección de Tonadillas escritas en estilo antiguo, w. Katharine Durran (pno)—La maja de Goya; El tra-la-I y el punteado; El majo tímido; El mirar de la maja; La maja dolorosa no. 2; Callejeo; El majo discreto; Las currutacas modestas *(rec West Road Concert Hall, Univ of Cambridge, Jan 17-19, 1995)* Herald ▲ HAVPCD 184 [DDD]

Mompou, F.:Combat del somni, w. Katharine Durran (pno) *(rec West Road Concert Hall, Univ of Cambridge, Jan 17-19, 1995)* Herald ▲ HAVPCD 184 [DDD]

Obradors, F.:Canciones clásicas españolas, w. Katharine Durran (pno) *(rec West Road Concert Hall, Univ of Cambridge, Jan 17-19, 1995)* Herald ▲ HAVPCD 184 [DDD]

Turina, J.:Poema en forma de canciones, w. Katharine Durran (pno) *(rec West Road Concert Hall, Univ of Cambridge, Jan 17-19, 1995)* Herald ▲ HAVPCD 184 [DDD]

Canadell, Xavier (trb)

Britten, H.:A Ceremony of Carols, w. S. Bardolet (trb), J. Pieres (alt), F. Gasa (alt), M. L. Ibañez (hp), G. Estrada (org), Escolania de Montserrat, I. Segarra (cnd) *(rec 1978?)* Koch Treasure ▲ 31624-2 [ADD]

Mendelssohn, F.:Motets, Op. 39, w. S. Bardolet (trb), J. Pieres (alt), F. Gasa (alt), M. L. Ibañez (hp), G. Estrada (org), I. Segarra (cnd), Montserrat Escolania *(rec 1978?)* Koch Treasure ▲ 31624-2 [ADD]

Canali, Anna Maria (mez)

Verdi, G.:Falstaff, w. Anna Moffo (sop—Nannetta), Renata Tebaldi (sop—Alice Ford), Anna Maria Canali (mez—Meg Page), Giulietta Simionato (mez—Dame Quickly), Mariano Caruso (ten—Doctor Caius), Alvinio Misciano (ten—Fenton), Luigi Vellucci (ten—Bardolfo), Tito Gobi (bar—Falstaff), Carnell MacNeil (bar—Ford), Kenneth Smith (bass-Pistola), T. Serafin (cnd), *(orch unknown)* *(rec Chicago, 1958)* Legato Classics 2-▲ LCD 206-2 [ADD]

Zandonai, R.:Francesca da Rimini, w. M. Caniglia (sop—Francesca), A. M. Canali (mez—Altichiara), A. Bertocci (ten—Ser Toldo Berardengo), M. Carlin (ten—Malatestino), G. Prandelli (ten—Paolo), C. Tagliabue (bar—Giovanni), E. Campi (bass—Il Giuliare/Il Torrigiano), A. Guarnieri (cnd), Rome RAI SO, Rome RAI Chorus *(rec 1952)* Cetra Classic ▲ CDO 22 [ADD]

Candia, Roberto de (bar)

Pacini, G.:Saffo, w. Francesca Pedaci (sop—Saffo), Gemma Bertagnolli (sop—Dirce), Mariana Pentcheva (mez—Climene), Carlo Ventre (ten—Faone), Aled Hall (ten—Ippia), Roberto de Candia (bar—Alcandro), Davide Baronchelli (bass—Lisimaco), M. Benini (cnd), Irish National SO, Lubomír Mátl (cnd), Wexford Festival Opera Chorus *(rec Wexford, Oct & Nov 1995)* Marco Polo 2-▲ 8.223883-4 [DDD]

Canello, Giorgio (sgr)

Mussorgsky, M.:Khovanshchina, w. Irene Companez (cta), Herbert Handt (ten), Mirto Picchi (ten), Boris Christoff (bass), Armedeo Berdini (sgr), Dmitri Lopatto (sgr), Michele Malaspina (sgr), Jolanda Mancini (sgr), Mario Petri (sgr), A. Rodzinski (cnd), Rome RAI Radio-TV SO, Rome RAI Chorus Stradivarius 2-▲ STV DTM 12320 [ADD]

Cangalovic (sgr)

Mussorgsky, M.:Boris Godunov, w. Djokic (sgr), Milosevic (sgr), Petrovic (sgr), D. Miladinovic (cnd), Belgrade National Opera Orch, Belgrade National Opera Chorus *(rec live, La Fenice Theater, Venice, Jan. 3, 1967)* Arkadia 3-▲ 492

Tchaikovsky, P.:Mazeppa, w. Bakocevic (sgr), Cakarevic (sgr), N. Mitic (bar), O. Danon (cnd), Belgrade National Opera Orch, Belgrade National Opera Chorus [R] *(rec live, Berlin, 9/27/69)* Myto 2-▲ 2 MCD 90527 [ADD]

Cangemi, Veronica (sop)

Rossini, G.:Tancredi, w. Veronica Cangemi (sop—Roggiero), Eva Mei (sop—Amenaide), Vasselina Kasarova (mez—Tancredi), Melinda Paulsen (cta—Isaura), Ramón Vargas (ten—Argirio), Harry Peeters (bass—Orbazzano), Janos Maté (vn), Gottfried Greiner (vc), Ingo Nawra (db), David Syrus (hpd), R. Abbado (cnd), Munich RSO, Bavarian Radio Chorus *(rec Studio 1, Munich, July 17-30, 1995)* RCA Red Seal 3-▲ 09026-68349-2 [DDD]

Caniglia, Flavia (mez)

Handel, G.F.:Cants, w. M. Peca (cnd), Rome Stradivari Ensemble—"Il Pianto di Maria al Sepolcro di Cristo" [I] Bongiovanni ▲ GB 2100 [DDD]

Caniglia, Maria (sop)

Gigli:Arias, Duets & Songs, w. G. Gigli (ten), Dusolina Giannini (sop), Titta Ruffo (bar), John Barbirolli (cnd), Eugene Goossens (cnd), Carlo Sabajno (cnd), et al. *(rec 1926-37)* Pearl 2-▲ PEA 9176 [ADD]

Giordano, U.:Andrea Chénier, w. Maria Caniglia (sop—Maddalena), Maria Huder (mez—Bersi), Vittoria Palombini (mez—Madelon), Giulietta Simionato (mez—Contessa), Beniamino Gigli (ten—Andrea), Adelio Zagonara (ten—Incroyable/Abbé), Gino Bechi (bar—Carlo), Leone Paci (bar—Mathieu), Giuseppe Taddei (b-bar—Pietro/Fouquier), Italo Tajo (b-bar—Roucher), Gino Conti (bass—Master/Schmidt), O. de Fabritiis (cnd), La Scala Orch, La Scala Chorus *(rec Nov 1941)* Arkadia ("The 78's" series) 2-▲ 78012 [ADD]

Giordano, U.:Andrea Chénier, w. G. Simionato (mez), B. Gigli (ten), G. Bechi (bar), G. Taddei (bar), I. Tajo (bass), O. de Fabritiis (cnd), La Scala Orch, La Scala Chorus [I] *(rec 1941, HMV DB 5423/35)* Angel ("Studio" series) 2-▲ CDHB 69996 (m) [ADD]

Giordano, U.:Fedora, w. Aldo Bertocci (ten), Giacinto Prandelli (ten), Scipio Colombo (bar), Andrea Piccinni (bass), Capozzi (sgr), M. Rossi (cnd), Turin RAI SO, Turin RAI Chorus *(rec 1950)* Cetra Classic 2-▲ Don 35

Maria Caniglia *(rec 1930-46)* Preiser ▲ PRE CD 89131

Puccini, G.:La Bohème (sels), w. Beniamino Gigli (ten), *(orch unknown)* Forlane ▲ FRL 16718 [ADD]

Puccini, G.:Tosca, w. Beniamino Gigli (ten), Armando Borgioli (bar), O. de Fabritiis (cnd), Rome Teatro Reale Opera Orch, Reale Theater Chorus *(rec 1938)* Grammofono 2000 2-▲ GRM 78591 (m)

Verdi, G.:Aida, w. Maria Caniglia (sop—Aida), Ebe Stignani (mez—Amneris), Beniamino Gigli (ten—Radamés), Armando Borgioli (bar—Amonasro), T. Beecham (cnd), London SO, London Sym Chorus *(rec Royal Opera House, Covent Garden, May 24, 1939)* Enterprise ("The Radio Years" series) 2-▲ ENT RY 62

Caniglia, Maria (sop) (cont.)

Verdi, G.:Un ballo in maschera, w. Maria Caniglia (sop—Amelia), Fedora Barbieri (mez—Ulrica), Beniamino Gigli (ten—Riccardo), Gino Bechi (bar—Renato), Tancredi Pasero (bass—Samuel), Blando Giusti (sgr—Un Giudice), Nicola Niccolini (sgr—Silvano), Ugo Novelli (sgr—Tom), Elda Ribetti (sgr—Oscar), T. Serafin (cnd), Rome Opera Orch, Giuseppe Conca (cnd), Rome Opera Chorus *(rec 1943)* Arkadia 2-▲ CD 78005 (m) [ADD]

Verdi, G.:Un ballo in maschera, w. Fedora Barbieri (cta), Beniamino Gigli (ten), Gino Bechi (bar), T. Serafin (cnd), Rome Opera Orch, Rome Opera Chorus *(rec Rome, July, 1943)* Grammofono 2000 2-▲ GRM 78556

Verdi, G.:Un ballo in maschera (sels), w. Gina Cigna (sop), Fedora Barbieri (mez), Enrico Carusa (ten), Beniamino Gigli (ten), Giovanni Zenatello (ten), Carlo Galeffi (bar), Lawrence Tibbett (bar), *(various orchs & cnds) (rec 1911–43)* Grammofono 2000 ▲ GRM 78527 (m)

Verdi, G.:Don Carlos, w. M. Caniglia (sop—Elisabeth de Valois), G. Sciutti (sop—Page), E. Stignani (mez—Princess Eboli), M. Picchi (ten—Don Carlos), M. Ponz de L. (ten—Count of Lerma), P. Silveri (bar—Rodrigue), N. Rossi Lemeni (bass—Philip II), G. Neri (bass—Grand Inquisitor), A. Gaggi (bass—Old Monk), F. Previtali (cnd), Rome RAI SO, Rome RAI Chorus *(rec Rome, 1951)* Cetra Classic 3-▲ CDO 25 [ADD]

Verdi, G.:La forza del destino, w. Ebe Stignani (mez), Galliano Masini (ten), Carlo Tagliabue (bar), Tancredi Pasero (bass), G. Marinuzzi (cnd), EIAR Orch, EIAR Chorus *(rec 1941)* Grammofono 2000 ▲ GRM 78567 (m)

Verdi, G.:Requiem Mass, w. Ebe Stignani (cta), Benjamino Gigli (ten), Ezio Pinza (bass), T. Serafin (cnd), Rome Opera Orch, Rome Opera Chorus *(rec 1939)* Pearl ▲ PEA 9162 [ADD]

Verdi, G.:Requiem Mass, w. Ebe Stignani (cta), Beniamino Gigli (ten), Ezio Pinza (bass), T. Serafin (cnd), La Scala Orch, La Scala Chorus *(rec 1939)* Phonographie ▲ PHG 5012 [ADD]

Verdi, G.:Requiem Mass (sels), w. E. Stignani (mez), B. Gigli (ten), T. Pasero (bass), V. de Sabata (cnd), Rome CO, Rome RAI Chorus, Turin RAI Chorus—Dies irae; Sanctus; Libera me *(rec Dec. 14, 1940)* Legato Classics 2-▲ LCD 178-2

Verdi, G.:La traviata, w. Maria Caniglia (sop—Violetta), Baniamino Gigli (ten—Alfredo), Mario Basiola (bar—Germont), V. Gui (cnd), London SO, London Sym Chorus Enterprise ("The Radio Years" series) 2-▲ ENT RY 64

Verdi, G.:La traviata, w. Maria Caniglia (sop—Violetta), Maria Huder (mez—Flora), Gladys Palmer (cta—Annina), Octave Dua (ten—Giuseppe), Beniamino Gigli (ten—Alfredo), Booth Hitchen (ten—D'Obigny), Adelio Zagonara (bar—Gastone), Aristide Baracchi (bar—Douphol), Mario Basiola (bar—Germont), Norman Walker (bass—Dr. Grenville), V. Gui (cnd), London PO, London Phil Chorus *(rec Royal Opera House, Covent Garden, May 22, 1939)* Minerva 2-▲ MN A28/29 (m) [ADD]

Verdi, G.:La traviata, w. Beniamino Gigli (ten), Mario Basiola (bar), V. Gui (cnd), London PO, London Phil Chorus *(rec Royal Opera House, Covent Garden, May 22, 1939)* Enterprise ("The Fourties" series) 2-▲ ENT 313

Verdi, G.:Il trovatore, w. Aureliano Pertile (ten), Apollo Granforte (bar), C. Sabajno (cnd), La Scala Orch, La Scala Chorus *(rec Milan, Sept.-Oct. 1930)* Phonographie 2-▲ PHG 5002 [ADD]

Zandonai, R.:Francesca da Rimini, w. M. Caniglia (sop—Francesca), A. M. Canali (mez—Altichiara), A. Bertocci (ten—Ser Toldo Berardengo), M. Carlin (ten—Malatestino), G. Prandelli (ten—Paolo), C. Tagliabue (bar—Giovanni), E. Campi (bass—Il Giuliare/Il Torrigiano), A. Guarnieri (cnd), Rome RAI SO, Rome RAI Chorus *(rec 1952)* Cetra Classic ▲ CDO 22 [ADD]

Cannan, Phyllis (mez)

Britten, H.:The Turn of the Screw, w. F. Lott (sop), N. Secunde (sop), E. Hulse (sop), P. Langridge (ten), S. Pay (bar), S. Bedford (cnd), Aldeburgh Festival Ensemble Collins Classics ▲ COL 7030 [DDD]

Canne-Meijer, Cora (alt)

Handel, G.F.:Rodelinda, Regina de' Longobardi, w. Joan Sutherland (sop—Rodelinda), Margaretha Elkins (mez—Bertarido's sister), Huguette Tourangeau (mez—Bertarido), Cora Canne-Meijer (alt—Unulfo), Eric Tappy (ten—Grimoaldo), Pieter van der Berg (bass—Garibaldo), R. Bonynge (cnd), Netherlands CO *(rec Amsterdam, June 30, 1973)* Bella Voce 2-▲ BLV 107.206 [AAD]

Canonici, Luca (ten)

Bellini, V.:La sonnambula, w. M. Devia (sop), A. Verducci (bass), M. Viotti (cnd), Piacenza SO, Piacenza Chorus [I] *(rec live 11/88)* Nuova Era 2-▲ 6764/65 [DDD]

Donizetti, G.:Don Pasquale, w. B. Hendricks (sop), G. Bacquier (bar), L. Quilico (bar), R. Schirrer (bar), G. Ferro (cnd), Paris Lyon Opera Orch, Paris Lyon Opera Chorus [I] Erato 2-▲ 2292-45487-2-ZA [DDD]

Donizetti, G.:La favorita, w. Gloria Scalchi (mez), René Massis (bar), Giorgio Surjan (bass), D. Renzetti (cnd), Milan RAI SO, Milan RAI Chorus Fonit Cetra ("Ricordi" series) 3-▲ FCT RFCD 2015

Donizetti, G.:Il furioso all'isola di Santo Domingo, w. P. Antonucci (sop), L. Serra (sop), E. Tandura (mez), R. Coviello (bar), Picconi (sgr), C. Rizzi (cnd), Piacenza SO, Piacenza Chorus [I] *(rec live, 11/10/87)* Bongiovanni 3-▲ GB 2056/58 [DDD]

Donizetti, G.:Linda di Chamounix, w. Mariella Devia (sop—Linda), Sonia Ganassi (mez—Pierotto), Francesca Provvisionato (mez—Maddalena), Luca Canonici (ten—Carlo), Alfonso Antoniozzi (bass—Il Marchese di Boisfleury), Petteri Salomaa (bass—Antonio), Boguslaw Fiksinski (sgr—L'intendente), Donato Di Stefano (sgr—Il Prefetto), G. Bellini (cnd), Eastern Netherlands Orch, Andrew Wise (cnd), National Reisopera Choir *(rec Muziekcentrum Enschede, Holland, June 24-July 2, 1992)* Arts Music 3-▲ 47151-2 [DDD]

Mayr, S.:La rosa bianca e la rosa rossa, w. Susanna Anselmi (sop), Anna Caterina Antonacci (sop), Silvia Mazzoni (mez), Francesco Facini (bass), Danilo Serraiocco (bass), T. Briccetti (cnd), Bergamo Stabile Orch Fonit Cetra ("Ricordi" series) 2-▲ FCT RFCD 2007

Rossini, G.:La cambiale di matrimonio, w. S. Jeun (sop—Fanny), M. Laurenza (sop—Clarina), L. Canonici (ten—Edoardo Milfort), R. Frontali (bar—Slook), E. Dara (bar—Tobia Mill), D. Renzetti (cnd), Turin RAI Orch *(rec Aug. 1991)* Ricordi ▲ RFCD 2011 [DDD]

Rossini, G.:Il Signor Bruschino, w. P. Orciani (sop), K. Lytting (mez), F. Massa (ten), B. Praticò (bar), P. Spagnoli (bar), N. de Carolis (b-bar), M. Viotti (cnd), Turin PO [I] Claves 8-▲ CD 9200 [DDD]

Rossini, G.:Il Signor Bruschino, w. Patrizia Orciani (sop), Katia Lytting (mez), Fulvio Massa (ten), Bruno Praticò (bar), Pietro Spagnoli (bar), Natale de Carolis (b-bar), M. Viotti (cnd), Turin PO Claves 2-▲ 50-8904/5

Verdi, G.:Requiem Mass, w. Donna Brown (sop), Luba Orgonasova (sop), Anne Sofie von Otter (mez), Alastair Miles (bass), J. E. Gardiner (cnd), Orch Révolutionnaire et Romantique, Monteverdi Choir London Philips 2-▲ 442142-2

Cantelo, April (sop)

Britten, H.:Albert Herring, w. S. Fisher (sop), S. Rex (mez), P. Pears (ten), J. Noble (bar), O. Brannigan (bass), B. Britten (cnd), English CO [E] London 2-▲ 421849-2 [ADD]

Donizetti, G.:Emilia di Liverpool (sels), w. J. Sutherland (sop), W. McAlpine (ten), D. Dowling (bar), H. Alan (bass), J. Pritchard (cnd), Royal Liverpool PO, Liverpool Music Group Singers—13 arias from Act 1, & 4 from Act 2 [I] *(rec live, Liverpool Sept. 1957)* Myto ▲ 1 MCD 91545 [ADD]

Handel, G.F.:Chandos Anthems (11), w. Ian Partridge (ten), Andrew Davis (org), D. Willcocks (cnd), Academy of St. Martin in the Fields, King's College Choir Cambridge—No. 10 only *(rec Chapel of King's College, Cambridge, 1967)* London 2-▲ 443470-2 [ADD]

Monteverdi, C.:Ballo delle ingrate, w. April Cantelo (sop—Una dell' Ingrate), Eileen McLoughlin (sop—Amore), Alfred Deller (alt—Venere), David Ward (bass—Plutone), Julian Bream (lt), Desmond Dupre (vl), A. Deller (cnd), London Chamber Players *(rec Walthamstow Hall, London)* Vanguard Classics ▲ OVC 8100 [ADD]

Purcell, H.:Hail. Bright Cecilia, w. Alfred Deller (alt), Wilfred Brown (ten), Maurice Bevan (bar), M. Tippett (cnd), Kalmar CO, Ambrosian Singers Vanguard Classics ▲ OVC 8020 [ADD]

Purcell, H.:Music of, w. Alfred Deller (ct), Maurice Bevan (bar), Neville Marriner (vn), Peter Gibbs (vn), Granville Jones (vn), Desmond Dupré (vl), George Malcolm (hpd), Walter Bergmann (hpd)—15 Songs & Airs; Fantasia upon a Ground in d for 3 Violins & Continuo, Z.731; Fantasia upon One Note in F for 5 Viols, Z.745; Hornpipe in e (from The Old Bachelor); Music Lessons 1–12 from Musick's Hand-Maid, Part II; A New Irish Tune, "Lilliburlero," Z.646; Pavan in g for 3 Violins & Bass Viol, Z.752; Sonata in g for Violin & Continuo, Z.780; Sonata No. 9 in F, "Golden Sonata," Z.810 (from Ten Sonatas in Four Parts); Suite in D for Harpsichord, Z.667 Vanguard Classics ("The Bach Guild" series) 2-▲ OVC 2002/03 [ADD]

Cantor, Philippe (ten)

Bach, J.C.F:Die Auferweckung Lazarus, w. Véronique Dietschy (sop), Consuelo Caroli (mez), John Elwes (ten), G. Bezzina (cnd), Nice Baroque Ensemble, Nicole Blanchi Vocal Ensemble Adda ▲ ADD 581182 [DDD]

Charpentier, M.-A.:Les Arts florissants, w. C. Dussaut (sop), J. Feldman (sop), A. Mellon (sop), G. Laurens (mez), D. Visse (ct), G. Reinhart (bar), W. Christie (cnd), Les Arts Florissants [F] Musique d'Abord ▲ HMA 1901083

Mozart, W.A.:Nozze di Figaro, w. Danielle Borst (sop—Countess Almaviva), Claudine Le Coz (sop—Marcellina), Sophie Marin-Degor (sop—Susanna), Laura Polverelli (mez—Cherubino), Valérie Lecoq (sgr—Barberina), Philippe Cantor (ten—Antonio), Stuart Patterson (ten—Dons Basile & Curzio), Huub Claessens (bar—Figaro), Nicolas Revenq (bar—Count Almaviva), Patrick Donnelly (bass—Bartolo), J. Malgoire (cnd), La Grande Écurie et la Chambre du Roy Astrée 8-▲ E 8606

Pergolesi, G.B.:La serva padrona, w. Isabelle Poulenard (sop), G. Bezzina (cnd), Nice Baroque Ensemble Pierre Verany ▲ PVY 795111

Purcell, H.:Dido & Aeneas, w. J. Feldman (sop), G. Laurens (mez), W. Christie (cnd), Les Arts Florissants [E] Harmonia Mundi France ▲ HMC 905173

Capasso, Camille (trb)

Bellini, V.:Beatrice di Tenda, w. L. Aliberti (sop), M. Thompson (ten), P. Gavanelli (bass), F. Luisi (cnd), Berlin German Opera Orch, Berlin German Opera Chorus Berlin Classics 2-▲ BER 1042 [DDD]

Capderou, Janine (sgr)

Gounod, C.:Le Médecin malgré lui, w. Lina Dachary (sop), Monique Stiot (mez), Michel Hamel (ten), Joseph Peyron (ten), Christophe Benoit (bar), Jean-Louis Soumagnas (sgr), J.-C. Hartemann (cnd), ORTF Lyric Orch Musidisc ▲ MUS 202322 [AAD]

Capecchi, Renato (bar)

Cilea, F.:Adriana Lecouvreur, w. M. Olivero (sop—Adriana), F. Ferrari (ten—Maurizio), R. Capecchi (bar—Michonnet), F. Vernizzi (cnd), *(orch unknown)* [I] *(rec live, Amsterdam 11/6/65)* Verona 2-▲ 27077/78

Donizetti, G.:Betly, w. P. Langridge (ten), P. Van den Berg (bass), J. Schaap (cnd), Zaanstad Opera Orch *(rec live, 1973)* Italian Opera Rarities ▲ IOR 7721 [ADD]

Donizetti, G.:Il borgomastro di Saardam, w. Philipp Langridge (ten), Let Kiel (sgr), J. Schaap (cnd), Zaanstad Opera Orch, Zaanstad Opera Chorus *(rec 1973)* Pantheon 2-▲ PHE 6630 (m)

Donizetti, G.:Don Pasquale, w. G. D'Angelo (sop), A. Kraus (ten), F. Corena (bass), U. d'Alessio (sgr), A. Erede (cnd), Naples Teatro San Carlo Orch, Naples Teatro San Carlo Chorus [I] *(rec live in Edinburgh, 9/7/63)* Verona 2-▲ 27023/24 (m) [AAD]

Donizetti, G.:Don Pasquale, w. Gianna D'Angelo (sop), Alfredo Kraus (ten), Fernando Corena (bass), Ugo D'Alessio (sgr), A. Erede (cnd), Naples Teatro San Carlo Orch, Naples Teatro San Carlo Chorus Great Opera Performances 2-▲ GOP 763

Donizetti, G.:L'elisir d'amore, w. M. Freni (sop), N. Gedda (ten), M. Sereni (bar), F. Molinari-Pradelli (cnd), Rome Opera Orch [I] EMI Classics (Studio) 2-▲ CDMB 69897 [ADD]

Donizetti, G.:Linda di Chamounix, w. A. Stella (sop), C. Valletti (ten), G. Taddei (bar), T. Serafin (cnd), Naples Teatro San Carlo Orch, Naples Teatro San Carlo Chorus *(rec 1959)* Andromeda ▲ ANR 2509 [ADD]

Mascagni, P.:Iris, w. M. Olivero (sop), L. Ottolini (ten), P. Clabassi (bass), F. Vernizzi (cnd), Netherlands Radio Orch, Netherlands Radio Chorus *(rec live, 1963)* Verona 2-▲ 27014/15 [AAD]

Mascagni, P.:Iris, w. M. Olivero (sop), L. Ottolini (ten), P. Clabassi (bass), F. Vernizzi (cnd), Netherlands Radio Orch, Netherlands Radio Chorus *(rec Amsterdam, 1963)* Great Opera Performances ▲ GPO 708

Mozart, W.A.:Nozze di Figaro, w. M. Stader (sop), I. Seefried (sop), H. Töpper (mez), D. Fischer-Dieskau (bar), I. Sardi (bass), F. Fricsay (cnd), Berlin RSO [G] *(rec 1960)* Deutsche Grammophon 3-▲ 437671-2

Rossini, G.:Il barbiere di Siviglia, w. Beverly Sills (sop), Fedora Barbieri (mez), Nicolai Gedda (ten), Sherill Milnes (bar), Ruggero Raimondi (bass), J. Levine (cnd), London SO, John Alldis Choir EMI Classics 2-▲ CDMB 66040

Rossini, G.:Il barbiere di Siviglia (sels), w. G. d' Angelo (sop), G. Carturan (mez), N. Monti (ten), G. Giorgetti (bar), C. Cava (bass), G. Tadeo (bass), B. Bartoletti (cnd), Bavarian RSO IMP Collectors Series ▲ IMPX 9022 [AAD]

Rossini, G.:La Cenerentola, w. T. Berganza (mez), L. Alva (ten), U. Trama (bass), C. Abbado (cnd), London SO, London Sym Chorus [I] Deutsche Grammophon 2-▲ 423861-2 [ADD]

Rossini, G.:La Cenerentola, w. Teresa Berganza (mez), Luigi Alva (ten), Paolo Montarsolo (bass), C. Abbado (cnd), Florence Maggio Musicale Orch, Florence Maggio Musicale Chorus *(rec Florence, May 1971)* Memories 2-▲ MEM 4283 [ADD]

Szymanowski, K.:Stabat Mater, w. A. Martino (sop), A. M. Rota (alt), A. Rodzinski (cnd), Turin RAI SO, Turin RAI Chorus *(rec 1955)* Stradivarius 2-▲ DAT 12306 [ADD]

Verdi, G.:Falstaff, w. M. Freni (sop), I. Ligabue (sop), L. Alva (ten), F. Corena (bass), C. M. Giulini (cnd), Royal Concertgebouw Orch, Netherlands Chamber Choir [I] *(rec live, The Hague 6/20/63)* Verona 2-▲ 27095/96

Verdi, G.:La forza del destino, w. R. Tebaldi (sop), O. Dominguez (mez), F. Corelli (ten), E. Bastianini (bar), B. Christoff (bass), F. Molinari-Pradelli (cnd), Naples Teatro San Carlo Orch, Naples Teatro San Carlo Chorus *(rec Oct. 1 1958)* Melodram 3-▲ MLO 370102 [AAD]

Verdi, G.:Un giorno di regno, w. Lina Pagliughi (sop), Mario Carlin (ten), Juan Oncina (ten), Sesto Bruscantini (bar), Laura Cozzi (sgr), Cristiano Dalamangas (sgr), A. Simonetto (cnd), Milan RAI Lyric Orch, Milan RAI Chorus *(rec 1951)* Cetra Classic 2-▲ CDON 37 [ADD]

Wagner, R.:Die Meistersinger von Nürnberg, w. Bruna Rizzoli (sop), Fernanda Cadoni (mez), Luigi Infantino (ten), Vito Tatone (ten), Renato Capecchi (bar), Giuseppe Taddei (bar), Boris Christoff (bass), Giovanni Ciavola (bass), James Loomis (bass), Silvo Maionica (bass), Vito Susca (bass), Raimondo Botteghelli (sgr), Walter Brunelli (sgr), Carlo Franzini (sgr), Ezio de Giorgi (sgr), Renzo Gonzales (sgr), L. von Matačić (cnd), Turin RAI Radio-TV SO, Turin RAI Chorus Stradivarius 4-▲ STV 12310

Capelle, Pierre (ten)

Stravinsky, I.:Les Noces, w. M. Quercia (sop), S. Cooper (mez), P. Marinov (bass), Vieuxtemps (pno), R. Conil (pno), Arzoumanian (pno), Raynaut (pno), R. Hayrabedian (cnd), Strasbourg Percussion Ensemble, Contemporary Choir Pierre Verany ▲ PV 787032 [DDD]

Capisani, Bruno (sgr)

Giordano, U.:Fedora, w. Mirella Freni (sop—Principessa Fedora), Adelina Scarabelli (sop—Contessa Olga), Silvia Mazzoni (mez—Dimitri), Monica Minarelli (sgr—Savoiardo), Placido Domingo (ten—Conte Loris), Ernesto Gavazzi (ten—Desiré), Aldo Bottion (ten—Barone Rouvel), Alessandro Corbelli (bar—Siriex), Luigi Roni (bass—Cirillo), Silvestro Sammaritano (bass—Baroff), Alfredo Giacomotti (bass—Gretch), Ernesto Panariello (bass—Lorek), Vincenzo Alaimo (sgr—Nicola), Arnold Bosman (sgr—Boleslao), Bruno Capisani (sgr—Sergio), Renato Zanchetta (sgr—Michele), G. Gavazzeni (cnd), La Scala Orch, La Scala Chorus *(rec La Scala, Apr 5, 1993)* Legato 2-▲ LCD 213-2 [ADD]

Capone, Gloria (sop)

Barber, S.:Prayers of Kierkegaard, w. J. Mester (cnd), Louisville Orch, Southern Baptist Theological Seminary Chorus [E] 1977 Albany ▲ TROY 021-2 [AAD]

Capozzi, Gilda (sgr)

Giordano, U.:Fedora, w. Maria Caniglia (sop), Aldo Bertocci (ten), Giacinto Prandelli (ten), Scipio Colombo (bar), Andrea Piccinni (bass), M. Rossi (cnd), Turin RAI SO, Turin RAI Chorus *(rec 1950)* Cetra Classic 2-▲ Don 35

Puccini, G.:Suor angelica, w. Miti Truccato Pace (mez), Rosanna Certeri (sgr), F. Previtali (cnd), *(orch & chorus unknown)* Cetra Classic 3-▲ 36

Cappuccilli, Piero (bar)

Bellini, V.:Il pirata, w. M. Caballé (sop), F. Rafanelli (sop), B. Marti (ten), Baratti, R. Raimondi (bass), G. Gavazzeni (cnd), Rome Radio-TV Orch, Rome Radio-TV Chorus [I] *(rec Rome, 1973)* EMI Classics 2-▲ CDMB 64169

Bellini, V.:Il pirata, w. M. Caballè (sop), F. Raffanelli (sop), G. Baratti (ten), F. Labò (ten), U. Trama (bass), E. Ghiglia (cnd), *(orch unknown) (rec Florence, 1967)* Great Opera Performances ▲ GOP 729

Bellini, V.:Il pirata, w. M. Caballé (sop), F. Labò (ten), F. Capuana (cnd), Florence Maggio Musicale Orch, Florence Maggio Musicale Chorus [I] *(rec live, Florence 1967)* Memories 2-▲ HR 4186/87 [ADD]

▲ = CD ♦ = Enhanced CD Δ = MD ▮ = Cassette Tape ▯ = DCC

Cappuccilli, Piero (bar) (cont.)

Bellini, V.:Il pirata, w. Montserrat Caballé (sop—Imogene), Flora Raffanelli (sop—Adele), Flaviano Labó (ten—Gualtiero), Giuseppe Baratti (ten—Itulbo), Piero Cappuccilli (bar—Ernesto), E. Ghiglia (cnd), Florence Teatro Comunale Orch, Florence Teatro Comunale Chorus *(rec live, Florence, 1967)* Melodram 2-▲ IMC 205002 [ADD]

Bellini, V.:Il pirata, w. M. Caballé (sop), F. Labò (ten), F. Capuana (cnd), Florence Maggio Musicale Orch, Florence Maggio Musicale Chorus [l] *(rec live, Florence 1967)* Melodram 2-▲ MEL 27015

Bellini, V.:I Puritani, w. J. Sutherland (sop), L. Pavarotti (ten), N. Ghiaurov (bass), R. Bonynge (cnd), London SO [l] London 3-▲ 417588-2 [ADD]

Bellini, V.:I Puritani, w. A. Maliponte (sop—Elvira), A. di Stasio (sop—Enrichetta di Francia), A. Kraus (ten—Lord Arturo Talbo), A. Pedroni (ten—Bruno Roberton), P. Cappuccilli (bar—Sir Riccardo Forth), R. Raimondi (bass—Sir Giorgio), G. Gavazzeni (cnd), Catania Teatro Massimo Bellini Orch, Catania Teatro Massimo Bellini Chorus *(rec Feb. 6, 1972)* Ornamenti 2-▲ FE 107 [ADD]

Catalani, A.:Loreley, w. E. Suliotis (sop), G. Talarico (ten), G. Gavazzeni (cnd), La Scala Orch, La Scala Chorus *(rec 1968)* Memories 2-▲ MEM 4511 [ADD]

Catalani, A.:La Wally, w. L. Marimpietri (sop), R. Tebaldi (sop), M. del Monaco (ten), Justino Diaz (bass), F. Cleva (cnd), Monte Carlo Opera Orch, Turin Lyric Chorus [l] London 2-▲ 425417-2 [ADD]

Donizetti, G.:Lucia di Lammermoor, w. M. Callas (sop), F. Tagliavini (ten), B. Ladysz (bass), T. Serafin (cnd), Philharmonia Orch [l] EMI Classics 2-▲ CDCB 47440

Donizetti, G.:Lucia di Lammermoor, w. R. Scotto (sop—Lucia), L. Pavarotti (ten—Edgardo), P. Cappuccilli (bar—Enrico), F. Molinari-Pradelli (cnd), Turin RAI Orch, Turin RAI Chorus [l] *(rec live, Turin 10/10/67)* Verona 2-▲ 27083/84

Donizetti, G.:Lucia di Lammermoor (sels), w. M. Callas (sop), R. Casellato (ten), T. Serafin (cnd), Philharmonia Orch—highlights *(rec live, London 3/16–21/59)* EMI Classics (Studio) ▲ CDM 63934 ■ EG 63934

Gounod, C.:Faust, w. Renata Scotto (sop—Margherita), Anna di Stasio (mez—Marta), Flaviano Labò (ten—Faust), Edoardo Gimenez (ten—Siebel), Piero Cappuccilli (bar—Valentino), Bruno Grella (bar—Wagner), Ruggero Raimondi (bass—Mefistofele), M. Gusella (cnd), Margherita Theater Orch, Margherita Theater Chorus *(rec Genova, 1970)* Golden Age of Opera 2-▲ GAO 170/71 [ADD]

Great Baritone Arias Melodram ▲ CDM 16505

Leoncavallo, R.:Pagliacci (sels), w. J. Varady (sop), M. Freni (sop), L. Pavoratti (ten), I. Wixell (bar), G. Gavazzeni (cnd), National PO London London ▲ 421870-2 [ADD]

Live in Concert, w. Leone Magiera (pno) *(rec aria & song recital, 5/15/84)* Bongiovanni ▲ GB 2501-2 [ADD]

Live Recordings 1960–1969 Melodram 2-▲ CDM 26528 [ADD]

Mascagni, P.:Cavalleria rusticana, w. J. Varady (sop), L. Pavarotti (ten), G. Gacazzeni (cnd), National PO London, National Phil London Chorus [l] London 2-▲ 414590-2 [ADD]

Mascagni, P.:Cavalleria rusticana (sels), w. Julia Varady (sop), Mirella Freni (sop), Luciano Pavoratti (ten), Ingvar Wixel (bar), G. Gavazzeni (cnd), National PO London London ▲ 421870-2 [ADD]

Piero Cappuccilli *(rec live, 1964–1971)* Memories ("Great Voices" series) 2-▲ MEM 4273 (m)

Ponchielli, A.:La Gioconda, w. M. Callas (sop), F. Cossotto (mez), I. Companeez (cta), P. M. Ferraro (ten), I. Vinco (bass), A. Votto (cnd), La Scala Orch, La Scala Chorus EMI Classics ▲ CDCC 49518

Verdi, G.:Aida, w. M. Caballé (sop), F. Cossotto (mez), P. Domingo (ten), N. Ghiaurov (bass), R. Muti (cnd), New Philharmonia Orch, Royal Opera House Chorus Covent Garden [l] EMI Classics 3-▲ CDCC 47271 [ADD]

Verdi, G.:Aida, w. L. Freni (sop), K. Ricciarelli (sop), A. Baltsa (mez), J. Carreras (ten), G. Raimondi (ten), J. Van Dam (b-bar), H. von Karajan (cnd), Vienna PO, Vienna State Opera Chorus [l] EMI Classics (Studio) 3-▲ CDMC 69300 [ADD]

Verdi, G.:Attila, w. Rita Orlandi Malaspina (sop—Odabella), Veriano Luchetti (ten—Foresto), Piero de Palma (ten—Uldino), Piero Cappuccilli (bar—Ezio), Nicolai Ghiaurov (bass—Attila), Luigi Roni (bass—Leone), G. Patanè (cnd), La Scala Orch, La Scala Chorus *(rec Milan, May 15, 1972)* Golden Age of Opera 2-▲ GAO 187/88 [ADD]

Verdi, G.:Attila, w. Rita Orlandi Malaspina (sop—Odabella), Veriano Luchetti (ten—Foresto), Piero De Palma (ten—Uldino), Piero Cappuccilli (bar—Ezio), Nicolai Ghiaurov (bass—Attila), Luigi Roni (bass—Leone), G. Patanè (cnd), La Scala Orch, La Scala Chorus *(rec Milan, May 12, 1975)* Myto 2-▲ MCD 961140

Verdi, G.:Un ballo in maschera, w. Reri Grist (sop), Katia Ricciarelli (sop), Elizabeth Bainbridge (mez), Plácido Domingo (ten), C. Abbado (cnd), Royal Opera House Orch, Royal Opera House Chorus Covent Garden *(rec 1975)* Arkadia 2-▲ 488

Verdi, G.:Un ballo in maschera, w. Ghena Dimitrova (sop—Amelia), Isabella Stramaglia (sop—Oscar), Mirna Pecile (cta—Ulrica), Mario Carlin (ten—Un giudice), José Carreras (ten—Riccardo), Piero Cappuccilli (bar—Renato), Massimiliano Malaspina (bass—Samuel), Americo de Santis (bass—Silvano), Francesco Signor (bass—Tom), Ivan Del Manto (sgr—Un servo), G. Patanè (cnd), Parma Teatro Regio Orch *(rec Teatro Regio, Dec. 26, 1972)* Golden Age of Opera 2-▲ GAO 183/84

Verdi, G.:Un ballo in maschera, w. Gabriele Lechner (sop), Luciano Pavarotti (ten), C. Abbado (cnd), Vienna PO, Vienna State Opera Chorus *(rec live, 1986)* Serenissima 2-▲ SER 360118

Verdi, G.:Un ballo in maschera, w. M. Arroyo (sop), R. Grist (sop), F. Cossotto (mez), P. Domingo (ten), R. Muti (cnd), New Philharmonia Orch, Royal Opera House Chorus Covent Garden [l] EMI Classics (Studio) 2-▲ CDMB 69576 [ADD]

Verdi, G.:Un ballo in maschera (sels), w. Luisa Maragliano (sop), F. Mannino (cnd)—Morrò, ma prima in grazia *(rec Naples, 1964)* Golden Age of Opera ▲ GAO 204 [ADD]

Verdi, G.:Don Carlos, w. M. Caballé (sop), F. Cossotto (mez), P. Domingo (ten), G. Petkov (bar), E. Inbal (cnd), Arena di Verona Orch, Arena di Verona Chorus [l] *(rec live 7/2/69)* Melodram 3-▲ MEL 37057 (m) [AAD]

Verdi, G.:Don Carlos, w. Katia Ricciarelli (sop), Fiorenza Cossotto (mez), Guido Fabbris (ten), Veriano Luchetti (ten), Gianfranco Casarini (bass), Nicolai Ghiaurov (bass), Alessandro Maddalena (bass), Aracelly Haengel (sgr), Marisa Salimbeni (sgr), Giorgio Zoranca (sgr), G. Prêtre (cnd), *(orch unknown)* Great Opera Performances 3-▲ GOP 777

Verdi, G.:I due Foscari, w. K. Ricciarelli (sop), E. Connell (sop), J. Carreras (ten), V. Bello (ten), M. Antoniak (ten), S. Ramey (bass), F. Handlos (bass), L. Gardelli (cnd), Austrian RSO, Austrian Radio Chorus Philips 2-▲ 422426-2 [ADD]

Verdi, G.:Ernani, w. Licia Galvano (sop—Giovanna), Leyla Gencer (sop—Elvira), Carlo Bergonzi (ten—Ernani), Nino Valori (ten—Don Riccardo), Piero Cappuccilli (bar—Don Carlo), Alessandro Cassis (bar—Jago), Ruggero Raimondi (bass—Don Ruy Gomez de Silva), G. Gavazzeni (cnd), Catania Teatro Massimo Bellini Orch, Catania Teatro Massimo Bellini Chorus *(rec live, Catania, Jan 15, 1972)* Arkadia 2-▲ 621 [ADD]

Verdi, G.:Ernani, w. I. Ligabue (sop), F. Corelli (ten), R. Raimondi (bass), O. de Fabritiis (cnd), Arena di Verona Orch, Arena di Verona Chorus *(rec live, Verona 7/15/72)* Golden Age of Opera 2-▲ GAO 131/32 [ADD]

Verdi, G.:Macbeth, w. Shirley Verrett (mez—Lady Macbeth), Plácido Domingo (ten—Macduff), Piero Cappuccilli (bar—Macbeth), Nicolai Ghiaurov (bass—Banco), C. Abbado (cnd), La Scala Orch, La Scala Chorus Deutsche Grammophon ("The Originals" series) ▲ 449 732-2

Verdi, G.:Nabucco, w. G. Dimitrova (sop), L. V. Terrani (mez), P. Domingo (ten), E. Nesterenko (bass), G. Sinopoli (cnd), German Opera Orch, German Opera Chorus [l] Deutsche Grammophon 2-▲ 410512-2 [DDD]

Verdi, G.:Simon Boccanegra (sels), w. Luisa Maragliano (sop), M. Rossi (cnd), *(orch unknown)*—Non sono una Grimaldi...; Figlia a tal nome io palpito' *(rec Naples, 1970)* Golden Age of Opera ▲ GAO 204 [ADD]

Verdi, G.:La traviata (sels), w. L. Gencer (sop), F. Labò (ten), N. Rescigno (cnd), Rio de Janeiro Teatro Municipale Orch, Rio de Janeiro Teatro Municipale Chorus *(rec live 8/8/64)* Golden Age of Opera ▲ GAO 120 [ADD]

Verdi, G.:Il trovatore, w. G. Tucci (sop), G. Simionato (mez), C. Bergonzi (ten), G. Gavazzeni (cnd), La Scala Orch, La Scala Chorus *(rec live, Moscow 1965)* Melodram 2-▲ MEL 27008

Verdi, G.:I vespri siciliani, w. R. Scotto (sop), G. Raimondi (ten), R. Raimondi (bass), G. Gavazzeni (cnd), La Scala Orch, La Scala Chorus [l] *(rec live, 12/4/70 [Acts 1–3], 12/10)* Myto 2-▲ 2 MCD 90524 [ADD]

Capsir, Mercedes (sop)

Donizetti, G.:Lucia di Lammermoor, w. M. Capsir (sop—Lucia), E. de Muro Lomanto (ten—Sir Ravenswood), E. Venturini (ten—Lord Bucklaw), E. Molinari (bar—Lord Ashton), S. Baccaloni (bass—Bidebent), L. Molajoli (cnd), La Scala Orch, La Scala Chorus *(rec 1933)* Myto 2-▲ 2MCD 94299

Rossini, G.:Il barbiere di Siviglia, w. D. Borgioli (ten), R. Stracciari (bar), S. Baccaloni (bass), V. Bettoni (bass), L. Molajoli (cnd), La Scala Orch, La Scala Chorus *(rec 1929 for Columbia Records)* Music Memoria 2-▲ 30276/77

Rossini, G.:Il barbiere di Siviglia, w. Cesira Ferrari (mez—Berta), Mercedes Capsir (cta—Rosina), Dino Borgioli (ten—Count), Salvatore Baccaloni (bar—Bortolo), Aristide Baracchi (bar—Officer), Riccardo Stracciari (bar—Figaro), Vincenzo Bettoni (bass—Don Basilio), Attilo Bordonali (bass—Fiorello), L. Molajoli (cnd), La Scala Orch, La Scala Chorus *(rec 1930)* Arkadia ("The 78's" series) 2-▲ 78008 [ADD]

Verdi, G.:Rigoletto, w. Dino Borgioli (ten), Riccardo Stracciari (bar), Ernesto Dominici (bass), L. Molajoli (cnd), La Scala Orch, La Scala Chorus Phonographe 2-▲ PHG 5036 [ADD]

Verdi, G.:Rigoletto, w. Dino Borgioli (ten), Riccardo Stracciari (bar), Duilio Baronti (bass), Ernesto Dominici (bass), Anna Masetti Bassi (sgr) *(rec 1930)* Grammofono 2000 2-▲ GRM 78632

Capuana, Maria (mez)

Verdi, G.:Aida, w. Giannina Arangi-Lombardi (sop—Aida), Maria Capuana (mez—Amneris), Aroldo Lindi (ten—Radames), Giuseppe Nessi (ten—Messenger), Armando Borgioli (bar—Amonasro), Salvatore Baccaloni (bass—King), Tancredi Pasero (bass—Ramfis), L. Molajoli (cnd), La Scala Orch, La Scala Chorus *(rec Nov 1928)* VAI Audio 2-▲ VAIA 1083-2

Capuano, Enzo (bass)

Verdi, G.:La traviata, w. T. Fabbricini (sop—Violetta), A. Trevisan (mez—Annina), N. Curiel (mez—Flora), R. Alagna (ten—Alfredo), E. Cossutta (ten—Gastone), E. Gavazzi (ten—Giuseppe), O. Mori (bar—Douphol), E. Capuano (bass—d'Obigny), F. Musinu (bass—Grenvil), R. Muti (cnd), La Scala Orch, La Scala Chorus Sony Classical 2-▲ S2K 52486 [DDD]

Carbaugh, Deborah (sop)

Albright, W.:A Song to David, w. Melissa Semmes (nar), Charles Russell (nar), Susan Sacquitne-Druck (mez), Rick Penning (ten), James Bohn (bass), Dean Billmeyer (org), Howard Don Small (cnd), St. Mark's Cathedral Choir Minneapolis *(rec live, St. Mark's Cathedral, Minneapolis, MN, Apr. 28, 1991)* Gothic ▲ G 49066 [DDD]

Carbonari, Virgilio (bass)

Ponchielli, A.:La Gioconda, w. Zinka Milanov (sop—La Gioconda), Rosalind Elias (mez—Laura), Belan Amparan (cta—La Cieca), Giacomo Cottino (ten—Isepo), Giuseppe Di Stefano (ten—Enzo Grimaldo), Fernando Valentini (bar—Zuane/Un Nocchiero), Leonard Warren (bar—Barnaba), Virgilio Carbonari (bass—Un Cantore), Plinio Clabassi (bass—Alvise Badoero), F. Previtali (cnd), St. Cecilia Academy Orch Rome, St. Cecilia Academy Chorus Rome Theorema 3-▲ TH 121182/184

Verdi, G.:La forza del destino, w. Zinka Milanov (sop—Donna Leonora di Vargas), Rosalind Elias (mez—Preziosilla), Luisa Gioia (sgr—Curra), Angelo Mercuriali (ten—Trabuco), Giuseppe di Stefano (ten—Son Alvaro), Leonard Warren (bar—Don Carlos di Vargas), Giorgio Tozzi (b-bar—Padre guardiano), Dino Mantovani (bar—Fra Melitone), Paolo Washington (b-bar—Il marchese di Calatrava), Virgilio Carbonari (b-bar—un alcalde), Sergio Liviabella (sgr—un chirurgo), F. Previtali (cnd), St. Cecilia Academy Orch Rome, St. Cecilia Academy Chorus Rome [l] London ▲ 443678-2 [ADD]

Zandonai, R.:Francesca da Rimini (sels), w. M. Olivero (sop), A. Gasparini (mez), A. Cesarini (ten), M. del Monaco (ten), N. Rescigno (cnd), Monte Carlo Opera Orch London ("Grand Opera" series) 2-▲ 433033-2 [ADD]

Carbone, Maria (sgr)

Verdi, G.:Otello, w. Nicola Fusati (ten), Piero Girardi (ten), Corrado Zambelli (ten), Apollo Granforte (bar), Enrico Spada (sgr), C. Sabajno (cnd), La Scala Orch, La Scala Chorus Grammofono 2000 2-▲ GRM 78651

Carden, Joan (sop)

Butterly, N.:The Owl, w. S. Challender (cnd), Seymour Group Vox Australis ▲ VAST 011

Caré, Katia (sgr)

Tensons e partimens de Trobairitz, Vol. 3, w. G. Zuchetto, Gisela Bellsolà (sgr), Patrice Brient (voc/h-g/rebeck), Guy Robert (medieval lt/oud/hp) Gallo ▲ CD 769 [DDD]

Carena, Maria (sop)

Verdi, G.:Il trovatore, w. Maria Carena (sop—Leonora), Olga De Franco (sop—Ines), Irene Minghini Cattaneo (mez—Azucena), Aureliano Pertile (ten—Manrico), Giordano Callegari (ten—Ruiz/Messenger), Apollo Granforte (bar—Count), Bruno Carmassi (bass—Ferrando), Antonio Gelli (bass—Old Gypsy), C. Sabajno (cnd), La Scala Orch, Vittore Veneziani (cnd), La Scala Chorus *(rec 1930)* Arkadia ("The 78's" series) 2-▲ 78007 [ADD]

Carerras, José (ten)

Tenors Greatest Hits, w. Luciano Pavarotti (ten), Placido Domingo (ten) RCA Victor ▲ 09026-62709-2 ■ 09026-62709-4

Carey, Michel (bar)

Grigny, N. de:Premier livre d'orgue, w. R. Saorgin (org)—5 Hymns [L] REM ▲ 311077 XCD [DDD]

Caristi, Nadi (sop)

Scarlatti, A.:Répons du Vendredi Saint, w. Paola Serno (mez), Marco Scavazza (bar), Giorgi Mazzucato (cnd), Rovigo City Chorus Studio SM ▲ 2515 [DDD]

Carl, Jeffrey (bar)

Lehár, F.:Der Zarewitsch, w. Nancy Gustafson (sop—Sonia), Naomi Itami (sop—Mascha), Lynton Atkinson (ten—Ivan), Jerry Hadley (ten—the Czarevitch), Jeffrey Carl (bar—Grand Duke/Soldier), R. Bonynge (cnd), English CO *(rec EMI Abbey Road, Studio One, London, England; Aug 25–27, 1995)* Telarc ▲ CD-80395 [DDD]

Carlin, Mario (ten)

Cimarosa, D.:Giannina e Bernardone, w. D. De Cecco (sop), S. Jurinac (sop), G. Sciutti (sop), M. Boriello (bar), S. Bruscantini (bar), C. De Antoni (sgr), N. Sanzogno (cnd), Milan RAI SO, Milan RAI Chorus [l] *(rec live, Milan July 26, 1953)* Melodram 2-▲ CDM 29505 [ADD]

Donizetti, G.:Lucia di Lammermoor, w. Roberta Peters (sop—Lucia), Mitì Truccato Pace (mez—Alisa), Jan Peerce (ten—Edgardo), Piero de Palma (ten—Lord Arturo Bucklaw), Mario Carlin (ten—Normanno), Philip Maero (bar—Lord Enrico Ashton), Giorgio Tozzi (bass—Raimondo), E. Leinsdorf (cnd), Rome Opera Orch, Rome Opera Chorus *(rec Rome Opera House, Aug 5–14, 1957)* RCA Living Stereo 2-▲ 09026-68537-2 [ADD]

Leoncavallo, R.:Pagliacci, w. M. Micheluzzi (sop), F. Corelli (ten), T. Gobbi (bar), L. Puglisi (bar), A. Simonetto (cnd), Milan RAI Orch, Milan RAI Chorus *(rec live 9/26/54 from RAI Milan)* HRE ▲ 1001-1 [ADD]

Puccini, G.:Manon Lescaut, w. Magda Olivero (sop—Manon), Tine Appelman (mez—Singer), Umberto Borso (ten—Chevalier), Mario Carlin (ten—Edmondo/Dancing Master/Lamplighter), Ferdinando Lidonni (bar—Lescaut), Giovanni Foiani (bass—Geronte/Sergeant/Captain), Joop Ruivenkamp (bass—Innkeeper), F. Vernizzi (cnd), Groot Omroep Orch, Groot Omroep Choir *(rec Amsterdam, Oct 31, 1964)* Bella Voce 2-▲ BLV 107.221 [AAD]

Verdi, G.:Un ballo in maschera, w. Ghena Dimitrova (sop—Amelia), Isabella Stramaglia (sop—Oscar), Mirna Pecile (cta—Ulrica), Mario Carlin (ten—Un giudice), José Carreras (ten—Riccardo), Piero Cappuccilli (bar—Renato), Massimiliano Malaspina (bass—Samuel), Americo de Santis (bass—Silvano), Francesco Signor (bass—Tom), Ivan Del Manto (sgr—Un servo), G. Patanè (cnd), Parma Teatro Regio Orch *(rec Teatro Regio, Dec. 26, 1972)* Golden Age of Opera 2-▲ GAO 183/84

Verdi, G.:Un giorno di regno, w. Lina Pagliughi (sop), Juan Oncina (ten), Sesto Bruscantini (bar), Renato Capecchi (bar), Laura Cozzi (sgr), Cristiano Dalamangas (sgr), A. Simonetto (cnd), Milan RAI Lyric Orch, Milan RAI Chorus *(rec 1951)* Cetra Classic 2-▲ CDON 37 [ADD]

Zandonai, R.:Francesca da Rimini, w. M. Caniglia (sop—Francesca), A. M. Canali (mez—Altichiara), A. Bertocci (ten—Ser Toldo Berardengo), M. Carlin (ten—Malatestino), G. Prandelli (ten—Paolo), C. Tagliabue (bar—Giovanni), E. Campi (bass—Il Giuliare/Il Torrigiano), A. Guarnieri (cnd), Rome RAI SO, Rome RAI Chorus *(rec 1952)* Cetra Classic ▲ CDO 22 [ADD]

Carlo, John del (bass)

Rossini, G.:La Cenerentola, w. C. Malone (sop), F. Palmer (sop), A. Baltsa (mez), F. Araiza (ten), S. Alaimo (bar), R. Raimondi (bass), N. Marriner (cnd), Academy of St. Martin in the Fields, Ambrosian Chorus Philips ("Digital Classics" series) 3-▲ 420468-2 [DDD]

Carlo, R. de (sgr)
Giordano, U.:Andrea Chénier, w. Montserrat Caballé (sop), Franco Corelli (ten), D. Dondi (sgr), G. Ellsworth (sgr), J. Fair (sgr), R. Falk (sgr), S. Felter (sgr), E. Green (sgr), H. Hicks (sgr), H. Krauss (sgr), L. Miller (sgr), N. Riggins (sgr), H. Salerno (sgr), A. Guadagno (cnd), Academy of Music Orch, Academy of Music Chorus Great Opera Performances 2-▲ GOP 766

Carlos, Wendy (nar)
Secrets of Synthesis CBS ▲ MK 42333

Carlos, Wendy (sgr)
Beethoven, L. van:Music of, w. *(other artists unknown)* Warner Bros. ▲ 2573-2 ■ M5 2573-4
Elgar, E.:Music of, w. *(other artists unknown)* Warner Bros. ▲ 2573-2 ■ M5 2573-4
Purcell, H.:Music of, w. *(other artists unknown)* Warner Bros. ▲ 2573-2 ■ M5 2573-4
Rossini, G.:Music of, w. *(other artists unknown)* Warner Bros. ▲ 2573-2 ■ M5 2573-4

Carlsen, Svein (b-bar)
Brahms, J.:Songs, w. E. Steen-Nokleberg (pno) Victoria ▲ VCD 19073
Mussorgsky, M.:Songs (misc), w. E. Steen-Nokleberg (pno) Victoria ▲ VCD 19073
Schubert, Franz:Songs (misc), w. E. Steen-Nokleberg (pno) Victoria ▲ VCD 19073
Schumann, R.:Songs, w. E. Steen-Nokleberg (pno) Victoria ▲ VCD 19073

Carlsen, Svein (bass)
Braein, E.F.:Anne Pedersdotter, w. K. Ekeberg (sop—Anne Pedersdotter), V. Hanssen (mez—Merete Beyer), R. Eriksen (alt—Herlofs-Marte), I. M. Brekke (alt—Bente), K. M. Sandve (ten—Martin Beyer), C. Ehrstedt (ten—Master Olaus), A. Helleland (ten—David), T. Gilje (ten—Jørund), S. A. Thorsen (bar—Master Johannes), S. Carlsen (bass—Absalon Pedersøn Beyer), T. Stensvold (bass—Master Laurentius), G. Oskarsson (bass—Jens Schelderup), P. Andersson (cnd), Norwegian National Opera Orch, Norwegian National Opera Chorus Simax 2-▲ PSC 3121

Carlson, Claudine (mez)
Debussy, C.:Pelléas et Mélisande, w. C. Alliot-Lugaz (sop), F. Golfier (sop), D. Henry (ten), G. Cachemaille (bar), P. Thau (bass), C. Dutoit (cnd), Montreal SO, Montreal Sym Chorus [F] London 2-▲ 430502-2 [DDD]
Dvořák, A.:Stabat Mater, w. K. Erickson (sop), J. Aler (ten), J. Cheek (bass), Z. Macal (cnd), New Jersey SO, J. Flummerfeldt (cnd), Westminster Sym Choir *(rec Feb. 8-11, 1994)* Delos 2-▲ DE 3161 [DDD]
Grieg, E.:Peer Gynt, w. V. Hanssen (mez), K. Bjørkøy (ten), A. Hansli (bar), P. Dreier (cnd), London SO, Oslo Phil Chorus [N] Unicorn-Kanchana 2-▲ UKCD 2003/04 [AAD]
Mahler, G.:Songs, w. Y. Kenny (sop), G. Mahler (pno) [from 4 rolls for automatic piano Mahler created from his own music in 1905]—Ging heut' morgen übers Feld; Ich ging mit Lust durch einen grünen Wald IMP Classics ▲ IMPGLRS 101 [DDD]
Prokofiev, S.:Alexander Nevsky, w. L. Slatkin (cnd), St. Louis SO, St. Louis Sym Chorus [R] Vox Box 2-▲ CDX 5021 [ADD]
Prokofiev, S.:Ivan the Terrible, w. S. Timberlake (bass), L. Slatkin (cnd), St. Louis SO, St. Louis Sym Chorus [R] Vox Box 2-▲ CDX 5021 [ADD]

Carlyle, Joan (sop)
Berlioz, H.:Benvenuto Cellini, w. J. Veasey (mez), K. Lewis (ten), Kentish, Cameron, Bushby, Garrard, Ward, A. Dorati (cnd), BBC SO, BBC Sym Chorus [E] *(rec live, Royal Festival Hall, 1964)* Music & Arts 2-▲ CD 618 (m) [AAD]
Leoncavallo, R.:Pagliacci, w. Joan Carlyle (sop—Nedda/Colombina), Carlo Bergonzi (ten—Canio/Pagliaccio), Franco Ricciardi (ten—Villager), Ugo Benelli (bar—Peppe/Arlecchino), Rolando Panerai (bar—Silvio), Giuseppe Taddei (bar—Tonio/Taddeo), Giuseppe Morresi (bass—Villager), H. von Karajan (cnd), La Scala Orch, La Scala Chorus *(rec La Scala, Milan, Oct 1965)* Deutsche Grammophon ("The Originals" series) ▲ 449727-2 [ADD]
Leoncavallo, R.:Pagliacci, w. Joan Carlyle (sop—Nedda), Jon Vickers (ten—Canio), José Noit (ten—Beppe), Cornell MacNeil (bar—Tonio), Bruno Tornasaetti (bar—Silvio), B. Bartoletti (cnd), *(orch unknown) (rec live, Buenos Aires, 1968)* VAI Audio ▲ VAIA 1014 [ADD]
Leoncavallo, R.:Pagliacci, w. C. Bergonzi (ten), U. Benelli (bar), R. Panerai (bar), G. Taddei (bar), H. von Karajan (cnd), La Scala Orch [I] Deutsche Grammophon 3-▲ 419257-2 [ADD]
Purcell, H.:The Fairy Queen (sels), w. Yehudi Menuhin (vn), Y. Menuhin (cnd), Bath Festival Orch—Entry of Phoebus; Syms. [Acts 4 & 5]; Dance for the Haymakers; 1st Music; Dance for the Fairies; Prelude; 2nd Music; 1st Act Tune *(rec Abbey Road Studio 1, London, July 1965)* EMI Classics ▲ CDK 65341 [ADD]
Purcell, H.:The Indian Queen (sels), w. Yehudi Menuhin (vn), Y. Menuhin (cnd), Bath Festival Orch—Tpt Tune; 4th Act Tune; I Attempt from Love's Sickness to Fly in Vain; Syms. [Acts 2 & 3]; 1st Music; Air *(rec Abbey Road Studio 1, London, July 1965)* EMI Classics ▲ CDK 65341 [ADD]
Purcell, H.:King Arthur (sels), w. Yehudi Menuhin (vn), Y. Menuhin (cnd), Bath Festival Orch—Tpt Tune; 2nd Music; Sym.; Passacaglia; Aria of Venus; 2nd Act Tune *(rec Abbey Road Studio 1, London, July 1965)* EMI Classics ▲ CDK 65341 [ADD]
Purcell, H.:Music for the Theater, w. Yehudi Menuhin (vn), Y. Menuhin (cnd), Bath Festival Orch—Bonduca [ov.]; The Old Bachelor [ov.]; Abdelazar [rondeau]; Bonduca [air]; Pausanias [air of Pandora:Sweeter than Roses or Cool Evening Breeze]; The Married Beau [jig]; Distressed Innocence [air]; Amphitryon [sarabande]; The Double Dealer [air] *(rec Abbey Road Studio 1, London, July 1965)* EMI Classics ▲ CDK 65341 [ADD]
Tippett, M.:The Midsummer Marriage, w. Joan Carlyle (sop—Joan), Elizabeth Harwood (sop—Bella), Elizabeth Bainbridge (mez), Helen Watts (cta—Sosostris), Stuart Burrows (ten—Jack), Alberto Remedios (ten—Mark), Stafford Dean (bass), Raimund Herincx (bass—King Fisher), C. Davis (cnd), Royal Opera House Orch, Royal Opera House Chorus Covent Garden Lyrita 2-▲ SRCD 2217

Carmassi, Bruno (bass)
Cilea, F.:L'Arlesiana, w. L. di Lelio (sop), P. Tassinari (sop), F. Tagliavini (ten), G. Galli (bar), P. Silveri (bar), A. Zerbini (bass), A. Basile (cnd), Turin RAI Orch, Turin RAI Chorus *(rec 1951)* Cetra Classics ▲ CDO 21 [AAD]
Flotow, F. von:Martha, w. E. Rizzieri (sop—Lady Enrichetta), P. Tassinari (sop—Nancy), F. Tagliavini (ten—Lionello), C. Tagliabue (bar—Plumkett), B. Carmassi (bass—Sir Tristano), F. Molinari-Pradelli (cnd), Turin RAI Orch, Turin RAI Chorus *(rec 1953; Italian libretto)* Cetra Classic 2-▲ CDO 7 [AAD]
Verdi, G.:Il trovatore, w. Maria Carena (sop—Leonora), Olga De Franco (sop—Ines), Irene Minghini Cattaneo (mez—Azucena), Aureliano Pertile (ten—Manrico), Giordano Callegari (ten—Ruiz/Messenger), Apollo Granforte (bar—Count), Bruno Carmassi (bass—Ferrando), Antonio Gelli (bass—Old Gypsy), C. Sabajno (cnd), La Scala Orch, Vittore Veneziani (cnd), La Scala Chorus *(rec 1930)* Arkadia ("The 78's" series) 2-▲ 78007 [ADD]
Verdi, G.:I vespri siciliani, w. Maria Callas (sop—Duchess), Giorgio Kokolios Bardi (ten—Arrigo), Gino Sarri (ten—Danieli), Enzo Mascherini (bar—Guido di Monforte), Boris Christoff (bass—Giovanni da Procida), Mario Forsini (bass—Count Vaudemont), Bruneo Carmassi (bass—Bethune), E. Kleiber (cnd), Florence Teatro Comunale Orch, Florence Teatro Comunale Chorus *(rec live, Florence, 1951)* Melodram 3-▲ IMC 303016 [ADD]

Carmeli, Boris (bass)
Bach, J.S.:Magnificat, BWV 243, w. L. Marimpietri (sop), N. Panni (sop), A. Reynolds (mez), P. Munteanu (ten), H. Scherchen (cnd), Milan RAI SO, Milan RAI Chorus [L] *(rec live, Apr 5, 1963)* Memories ▲ HR 4160 (m) [ADD]
Dessau, P.:Die Verurteilung des Lukullus, w. Annelies Burmeister (mez—Das Fischweib), Helmut Melchert (ten—Lukullus), Hans-Joachim Rotzsch (ten—Der Kirschbaumträger), Peter Schreier (ten—Lukullus' Cook), Boris Carmeli (bass—King), H. Kegel (cnd), Leipzig RSO, Leipzig Radio Chorus Berlin Classics 2-▲ BER 1073 [ADD]
Penderecki, K.:Utrenia, w. Delfina Ambroziak (sop), Stefania Woytowicz (sop), Krystyna Szczepanska (mez), Kazimierz Pustelak (ten), Wlodzimierz Denysenko (bass), A. Markowski (cnd), Warsaw PO, Józef Bok (cnd), Stanislaw Skoraczewski (cnd), Warsaw National Phil Chorus, Pioneer Choir *(rec Warsaw, 1973)* Polskie Nagrania ▲ PNCD 018

Carmignani, Alessandro (ct)
Marcello, B.:Il pianto e il riso delle quattro stagioni, w. S. Piccollo (sop—Primavera), M. Beasley (ten—Autunno), R. Franceschetto (bass—Inverno), F. Ghiglione (cnd), Don Milani Cultural Association Orch, G. B. Trofello Schola Cantorum *(rec Mar. 29, 1992)* Bongiovanni 2-▲ GB 2159/60 [DDD]

Carmignani, Alessandro (ct) (cont.)
Perti, G.A.:Liturgy for Good Friday, w. Patrizia Vaccari (sop), Maura Pederzoli (sop), Cristina Calzolari (sop), Alida Oliva (sop), Claudia Bugli (sop), Lucia Bagnoli (alt), Cinzia Meneghel (alt), Renzo Bez (alt), Michel van Goethem (alt), Mauro Collina (ten), Vincenzo Di Donato (ten), Paolo Fanciullacci (ten), Giovanni Caccamo (ten), Paolo Da Col (ten), Sergio Foresti (bass), Marco Scavazza (bass), Luca Ferracin (bass), Paride Montanari (bass), Liuwe Tamminga (org), Sergio Vartolo (org), S. Vartolo (cnd), Bologna San Petronio Capella Musicale Orch—Omnes amici mei; De lamentatione Jeremiae Prophetae:Heth. Cogitavit; Velum templi; Vinea mea; De lamentatione Jeremiae Prophetae:Lamed. Matribus suis; Tamquam ad latronem; Tenebrae factae sunt; Animam meam; Tradiderunt me; Jesum tradidit; De lamentatione Jeremiae Prophetae:Aleph. Ego vir; Caligaverunt *(rec St. Petronio Basilica, Bologna, Mar 28-31, 1995)* Naxos ▲ 8.553321 [DDD]

Carmona, Juan Luque (ten)
Bellini, V.:I Puritani, w. Katia Ricciarelli (sop), Eleonora Jankovic (mez), Carlo Gaifa (ten), Chris Merritt (ten), Roberto Scandiuzzi (bass), G. Ferro (cnd), Sicilian SO, Bari Teatro Petruzzelli Chorus Fonit Cetra ("Digital Operas" series) 3-▲ FCT CDC 20
Bizet, G.:Don Procopio, w. Muscente (sgr), M. Gentile (sop), Barry (sgr), A. Antoniozzi (bar), S. Sanna (cnd), Berlin Radio Youth Orch, Symbolon Ensemble Chorus [I] *(rec live 5/25/86)* Bongiovanni 2-▲ GB 2043/44 [DDD]

Carnes, K. (sgr)
Berlin, I.:Annie Get Your Gun, w. E. Merman (sgr), R. Middleton (sgr), L. Bibb (sgr), J. Garth (sgr), R. Lenn (sgr), C. Turner (sgr), J. Blackton (cnd) [1946 cast] MCA Classics ▲ MCAD 10047 [AAD] ■ MCAC 10047

Carney, William (ten)
Barber, S.:A Hand of Bridge, w. C. Aks (sop), F. Kittelson (mez), R. Muenz (bass), Adirondack CO, Gregg Smith Singers [E] Premier ▲ PRCD 1009 [ADD]

Carnotch, Walter (sgr)
Strauss, R.:Salome, w. Astrid Varnay (sop—Salome), Hertha Töpper (mez—Der Page der Herodias), Margarete Klose (cta—Herodias), Hans Hopf (ten—Narraboth), Karl Hoppe (ten—1st Nazarene), Karl Ostertag (ten—1st Jew), Julius Patzak (ten—Herodes), Hans Braun (bar—Jochanaan), Benno Kusche (bar—2nd Soldier), Adolf Keil (bass—1st Soldier), Hans Hermann Nissen (bass—Ein Kappadozier), Max Proebstl (bass—2nd Nazarene), Walter Carnotch (sgr—4th Jew), Emil Graf (sgr—3rd Jew), Paul Kaussen (sgr—2nd Jew), Hildegard Limmer (sgr—A slave), Georg Witter (sgr—5th Jew), H. Weigert (cnd), Bavarian RSO *(rec June 21-25, 1953)* Bella Voce 2-▲ BLV 7210 [AAD]

Caroli, Consuelo (mez)
Bach, J.C.F:Die Auferweckung Lazarus, w. Véronique Dietschy (sop), John Elwes (ten), Philippe Cantor (bar), G. Bezzina (cnd), Nice Baroque Ensemble, Nicole Blanchi Vocal Ensemble Adda ▲ ADD 581182 [DDD]

Caroli, Paolo (ten)
Puccini, G.:La fanciulla del West (sels), w. Magda Olivero (sop—Minnie), Corinna Vozza (mez—Wowkle), Paolo Caroli (ten—Harry), Giacomo Lauri-Volpi (ten—Dick Johnson), Marco Rogani (ten—Pony Express Rider), Salvatore di Tommaso (ten—Trin), Adelio Zagonara (ten—Nick), Virgilio Ascorro (bar—Sid), Alfredo Colella (bar—Jake Wallace), Giuseppe Forgione (bar—Bello), Giancarlo Guelfi (bar—Jack Rance), Arturo la Porta (bar—Sonora), Gino Conti (bass—José Castro), Piere Passarotti (bass—Bill), Enzo Titta (bass—Larkens), Giulio Tomei (bass—Ashby), V. Bellezza (cnd), Rome Opera Orch, Rome Opera Chorus—Minnie, dalla mia casa son partito; Laggiù nel Soledad; Chi c'è per farmi i ricci; Oh! Mister Johnson, siete rimasto; Non so ben neppur io; Io non son che una povera fanciulla; No, Minnie, non piangete; Vorrei mettermi queste; Hallo!; Oh, se sapeste; Credo che abbiate torto; Ma ti giuro ch'io non ti lascio più; Vieni fuori!; Una parola sola!...Or son sei mesi; Che c'è di nuovo Jack?; È là; Siete pronto; Ch'ella mi creda; È Minnie!...È Minnie! *(rec Rome, Mar. 30, 1957)* Golden Age of Opera ▲ GAO 180 [ADD]

Carolis, Natale de (b-bar)
Mozart, W.A.:Arias, w. B. Giuranna (cnd), Padua & Venice CO—includes Un bacio di mano; Per questa bella mano; arias from Don Giovanni; Le nozze di Figaro; Così fan tutte; La finta semplice Claves ▲ 50-9120
Rossini, G.:L'inganno felice, w. A. Felle (sop), I. Zennaro (ten), F. Previati (bar), D. Serraiocco (b-bar), M. Viotti (cnd), English CO [I] Claves 8-▲ CD 9200 [DDD]
Rossini, G.:L'inganno felice, w. Amelia Felle (sop), Iorio Zennaro (ten), Fabio Previati (bar), Danilo Serraiocco (bass), M. Viotti (cnd), English CO Claves ▲ 50-9211
Rossini, G.:L'occassione fa il ladro, w. M. Bayo (sop), F. Provvisionato (mez), F. Massa (ten), I. Zennaro (ten), F. Previati (bar), M. Viotti (cnd), English CO [I] Claves 8-▲ CD 9200 [DDD]
Rossini, G.:L'occassione fa il ladro, w. Maria Bayo (sop), Francesca Provvisionato (mez), Fulvio Massa (ten), Iorio Zennaro (ten), Fabio Previati (bar), M. Viotti (cnd), English CO Claves 2-▲ 50-9208/9
Rossini, G.:La scala di seta, w. Teresa Ringholz (sop), Francesca Provvisionata (mez), Fulvio Massa (ten), Ramon Vargas (ten), Alessandro Corbelli (bar), M. Viotti (cnd), English CO Claves 2-▲ 9219/20
Rossini, G.:La scala di seta, w. Luciana Serra (sop), Oslavio di Credico (ten), William Matteuzzi (ten), Roberto Coviello (bar), G. Ferro (cnd), Bologna Teatro Comunale Orch Fonit Cetra ("Ricordi" series) 2-▲ FCT RFCD 2003
Rossini, G.:Il Signor Bruschino, w. Patrizia Orciani (sop), Katia Lytting (mez), Luca Canonici (ten), Fulvio Massa (ten), Bruno Praticò (bar), Pietro Spagnoli (bar), M. Viotti (cnd), Turin PO Claves 2-▲ 50-8904/5
Rossini, G.:Il Signor Bruschino, w. P. Orciani (sop), K. Lytting (mez), L. Canonici (ten), F. Massa (ten), B. Praticò (bar), P. Spagnoli (bar), M. Viotti (cnd), Turin PO [I] Claves 8-▲ CD 9200 [DDD]

Caron, Elise (sop)
Rebotier, J.:Terre et son ombre Adès ▲ ADE 204472 [DDD/AAD]

Carosi, Ubaldo (bass)
Mussorgsky, M.:Khovanshchina, w. Mietta Sighele (sop—Emma), Elena Souliotis (sop—Susanna), Fiorenza Cossotto (mez—Marfa), Herbert Handt (ten—Scribe), Veriano Luchetti (ten—Prince Andrey Khovansky), Ludovic Spiess (ten—Prince Vasily Golitsin), Claudio Strudthoff (ten—Streshnev), Angelo Marchiandi (bar—Kuz'ka), Teodoro Rovetta (bar—1st Strel'tsi), Siegmund Nimsgern (b-bar—Shaklovity), Cesare Siepi (b-bar—Dosifey), Carlo del Bosco (bass—2nd Strel'tsi), Ubaldo Carosi (bass—Varsonofiev), Nicolai Ghiaurov (bass—Prince Ivan Khovnasky), Giovanni Sciarpeletti (bass—Pastor), B. Leskovich (cnd), Rome RAI SO, Rome RAI Chorus—also includes bonus Act V [w Boris Christoff] (Rome, 1958) *(rec Rome, 1973)* Bella Voce 3-▲ BLV 107.402 [AAD]

Carosio, Margherita (sop)
Carlo Tagliabue, w. C. Tagliabue (bar), Ettore Bergamaschi (ten), Zinka Milanov (sop), Bruna Castagna (cta), Frederick Jagel (ten), Norman Cordon (bass), Renata Tebaldi (sop), Alfredo Colella (bass) *(rec in studio and live, 1928-1951)* Bongiovanni ▲ GB 1070-2 [ADD]
Cilea, F.:Adriana Lecouvreur (sels), w. Agostino Lazzari (ten), E. Piazza (cnd), Milan RAI SO, Milan RAI Chorus Fonit Cetra ("Martini & Rossi" series) ▲ FCT CDMR 5010
Cilea, F.:L'Arlesiana (sels), w. Agostino Lazzari (ten), E. Piazza (cnd), Milan RAI SO, Milan RAI Chorus Fonit Cetra ("Martini & Rossi" series) ▲ FCT CDMR 5010
Donizetti, G.:Don Pasquale (sels), w. Agostino Lazzari (ten), E. Piazza (cnd), Milan RAI SO, Milan RAI Chorus Fonit Cetra ("Martini & Rossi" series) ▲ FCT CDMR 5010
Donizetti, G.:Lucia di Lammermoor (sels), w. Agostino Lazzari (ten), E. Piazza (cnd), Milan RAI SO, Milan RAI Chorus Fonit Cetra ("Martini & Rossi" series) ▲ FCT CDMR 5010
Giordano, U.:Il re (sels), w. Agostino Lazzari (ten), E. Piazza (cnd), Milan RAI SO, Milan RAI Chorus Fonit Cetra ("Martini & Rossi" series) ▲ FCT CDMR 5010
The Martini & Rossi Concerts, Vol. 3, w. Giuseppe Di Stefano (ten), Turin RAI Orch [cnd:Oliviero de Fabritiis] Fonit Cetra ("Martini & Rossi" series) ▲ FCT CDMR 5003
Mascagni, P.:Nerone (sels), w. Agostino Lazzari (ten), E. Piazza (cnd), Milan RAI SO, Milan RAI Chorus Fonit Cetra ("Martini & Rossi" series) ▲ FCT CDMR 5010
Pannain, G.:Beatrice Cenci (sels), w. Agostino Lazzari (ten), E. Piazza (cnd), Milan RAI SO, Milan RAI Chorus Fonit Cetra ("Martini & Rossi" series) ▲ FCT CDMR 5010
Puccini, G.:La Bohème (sels), w. A. Noni (sop), G. Poggi (ten), P. Silveri (bar), V. de Sabata (cnd), La Scala Orch, La Scala Chorus—6 arias from Acts 3 & 4 [I] *(rec live, Milan, 12/7/49)* Myto ▲ 1 MCD 90634 [ADD]
Verdi, G.:Nabucco (sels), w. Agostino Lazzari (ten), E. Piazza (cnd), Milan RAI SO, Milan RAI Chorus Fonit Cetra ("Martini & Rossi" series) ▲ FCT CDMR 5010

Carosio, Margherita (sop) (cont.)

Wagner, R.:Tannhäuser (sels), w. Agostino Lazzari (ten), E. Piazza (cnd), Milan RAI SO, Milan RAI Chorus — Fonit Cetra ("Martini & Rossi" series) ▲ FCT CDMR 5010

Carr, Robert (bass)

Gounod, C.:Faust, w. M. Licette (sop—Margarita), D. Vane (sop—Siebel), M. Brunskill (cta—Martha), H. Nash (ten—Faust), H. Williams (b-bar—Valentine), R. Easton (bass—Mephistopheles), R. Carr (bass—Wagner), T. Beecham (cnd), BBC SO, BBC Sym Chorus — Dutton Laboratories 2-▲ CDAX 2001 [ADD]

Carradine, John (nar)

Kosins, M.S.:Songs of the Seeker, w. A. Kavafian (vn), R. Williams (bn), T. D. Barna (pno) *(rec 1980)* — Centaur ▲ CRC 2105 [ADD]

Carraro, Tiziana (sop)

Rossini, G.:La pietra del paragone, w. Tiziana Carraro (sop—Fulvia), Elisabetta Gutierrez (mez—Baronessa Aspasia), Sara Mingardo (cta—Clarice), William Matteuzzi (ten—Giocondo), Marco Camastra (bar—Pacuvio), Pietro Spagnoli (bar—Conte Asdrubale), Gioacchino Zarrelli (bar—Fabrizio), Josè Fardilha (bass—Macrobio), B. Aprea (cnd), Graz SO, Sluk Chamber Chorus Bratislava *(rec 1993)* — Bongiovanni 2-▲ GB 2179/80 [DDD]

Carré, Alain (nar)

Uy, P.:Choral pour la Paix, w. Dinah Bryant (sop), Zeger Vandersteene (ten), Philippe Huttenlocher (bar), Dominique Cornil (pno), G. Octors (cnd), Wallonie Royal CO, Denis Menier (cnd), Namur Chamber Choir *(rec Aulne, Belgium, 1995)* — Cypres ▲ 2611 [DDD]

Carreras, José (ten)

The Album — EMI Classics ▲ CDC 54524

Amigos para Siempre:Friends for Life — Atlantic ▲ 82413-2 ■ 82413-4

An Enchanted Evening with José Carreras *(rec 1983-1990)* — Sony Classical ▲ SMK 53296 [DDD] ■ SMT 53296 (D)

The Art of José Carreras — Replay ▲ BMCD 027 [AAD]

Bellini, V.:Beatrice di Tenda, w. A. Gulin (sop), E. Zilio (mez), R. Bruson (bar), F. Mannino (cnd), Turin RAI Orch, Turin RAI Chorus [I] *(rec live Oct. 9, 1973)* — Golden Age of Opera 2-▲ GAO 158/59 [ADD]

Bellini, V.:Norma, w. Caballé (soprano—Norma), F. Cossotto (mez), B. Prevedi (ten), I. Vinco (bass), C. F. Cillario (cnd), Barcelona Teatro Liceo Orch, Barcelona Gran Teatro de Liceo Chorus [I] *(rec live, Barcelona 1/11/70)* — Melodram 2-▲ CDM 27089 [ADD]

Bellini, V.:Norma (sels), w. A. Baltsa (mez), P. Domingo (cnd), London SO, Tallis Chamber Choir—Eccola! Va, mi lascia; Va, crudele, al Dio spietato *(rec Jan.-Feb. 1991)* — Sony Classical ▲ SK 53968 [DDD]

Bernstein, L.:Music of, w. J. Norman (sop), K. Te Kanawa (sop), J. Anderson (sop), F. von Stade (mez), C. Ludwig (mez), T. Troyanos (mez), D. Garrison (ten), J. Hadley (ten), T. Hampson (bar), T. Daly (sgr), G. Kremer (vn), M. Rostropovich (vc), M.T. Thomas (va), L. Bernstein (cnd), *(orch unknown)*—various popular works — Deutsche Grammophon ▲ 439251-2 ■ 439251-4

Bernstein, L.:West Side Story, w. K. Te Kanawa (sop), T. Troyanos (mez), K. Ollmann (bass), L. Bernstein (cnd), *(orch unknown)* [E] — Deutsche Grammophon ▲ 415963-2 [DDD] ■ 415963-4 □ 415963-5

The Best of Christmas in Vienna, w. P. Domingo (ten), Vienna SO, Charles Aznavour (sgr), Sissel Kyrkjebø (sgr), Dionne Warwick (sgr) *(rec Vienna)* — Sony Classical ▲ SK 62696 ■ ST 62696

The Best of José Carreras — Philips 2-▲ 422570-2

Bizet, G.:Carmen (sels), w. A. Baltsa (mez), P. Domingo (cnd), London SO, Tallis Chamber Choir—C'est toi? C'est moi; Mais moi, Carmen, je t'aime encore? *(rec Jan.-Feb. 1991)* — Sony Classical ▲ SK 53968 [DDD]

Bizet, G.:Carmen (sels), w. K. Ricciarelli (sop), A. Baltsa (mez), J. Van Dam (b-bar), H. von Karajan (cnd), Berlin PO, Paris Opera Chorus [F] — Deutsche Grammophon ▲ 413322-2 [DDD]

Canciones Españoles, w. Martin Katz (pno), English CO — Philips ("Spanish" series) ▲ 432825-2 FM [ADD]

Cilea, F.:Adriana Lecouvreur, w. M. Caballé (sop), F. Cossotto (mez), A. D'Orazi (bar), G.-F. Masini (cnd), *(orch unknown)* [I] *(rec 1976)* — Legato Classics 2-▲ LCD 111-2 [AAD]

Debussy, C.:L'Enfant prodigue, w. J. Norman (sop), D. Fischer-Dieskau (bar), G. Bertini (cnd), Stuttgart RSO, Stuttgart Radio Chorus [F] — Orfeo ▲ 012821

Donizetti, G.:Lucia di Lammermoor, w. M. Caballé (sop), A. Murray (mez), C. H. Ahnsjö (ten), V. Bello (ten), V. Sardinero (bar), S. Ramey (bass), J. López-Cobos (cnd), New Philharmonia Orch, Ambrosian Opera Chorus — Philips 2-▲ 426563-2

Donizetti, G.:Lucia di Lammermoor, w. C. Deutekom (sop), G. Fioravanti (bar), C. Cava (bass), A. Gatto (cnd), *(orch unknown)* [I] *(rec live in Madrid, 1975)* — Standing Room Only 2-▲ SRO 809-2 [ADD]

Donizetti, G.:Lucrezia Borgia, w. L. Gencer (sop), T. Troyanos (mez), N. Rescigno (cnd), Dallas Civic Opera Orch, Dallas Civic Opera Chorus *(rec 1973)* — Melodram 2-▲ MLO 270109 [ADD]

Donizetti, G.:Maria Stuarda, w. M. Caballé (sop—Maria Stuarda), R. Bezinian (mez—Anna), M. V. Menendez (mez—Elisabetta), J. Carreras (ten—Roberto), M. Mazzieri (bass—Giorgio Talbot), E. Serra (bass—Lord Gugliemo Cecil), N. Santi (cnd), ORTF Lyric Orch, ORTF Lyric Chorale [I] *(rec live 3/26/72)* — Memories 2-▲ HR4417/18 [ADD]

Donizetti, G.:Maria Stuarda (sels), w. Maurizio Mazzieri (bass), N. Santi (cnd), ORTF Lyric Orch—Ah!, rimiro il bel sembiante *(rec Paris, Mar 26, 1972)* — Goldies ▲ GLD 63203 [ADD]

Donizetti, G.:Poliuto, w. K. Ricciarelli (sop), J. Pons (bar), O. Caetani (cnd), Vienna SO, Vienna Chorus — CBS 2-▲ M2K 44821

Donizetti, G.:Roberto Devereux, w. M. Caballé (sop), S. Marsee (mez), V. Sardinero (bar), J. Rudel (cnd), *(orch & chorus unknown)* [I] *(rec live, France 1977)* — HRE 2-▲ 1004-2 [ADD]

Donizetti, G.:Roberto Devereux (sels), w. M. Caballé (sop), S. Marsee (mez), V. Sardinero (bar), J. Rudel (cnd), *(orch & chorus unknown)* [I] *(rec live, 1977)* — Legato Classics ▲ LCD 108-1 [AAD]

Early Live Recordings *(rec 1972-1976)* — Legato Classics ▲ LCD 110-1 [AAD]

The Essential 3 Tenors, w. Plácido Domingo (ten), Luciano Pavarotti (ten) — RCA Gold Seal ▲ 74321-21273-2 [ADD]

Famous Love Duets, Vol. 2, w. Gianna d'Angelo (sop), Montserrat Caballé (sop), Maria Callas (sop), Renata Scotto (sop), Beverly Sills (sop), Renata Tebaldi (sop), Mario Del Monaco (ten), Giuseppe Di Stefano (ten), Plácido Domingo (ten), et al. — Enterprise ("Documents" series) ▲ ENTLV 999

Favorite Arias — Laserlight ▲ 14296

First American Recital *(rec live, Carmel, California, 14 October 1975)* — Legato Classics ▲ LCD 166-1 [ADD]

From the Official Barcelona Games Ceremony, w. P. Domingo, Montserrat Caballé (sop), Giacomo Aragall (ten), Teresa Berganza (mez), Juan Pons (bar) — RCA Red Seal ▲ 09026-61204-2 ■ 09026-61204-4 □ 09026-61204-5

Giordano, U.:Andrea Chénier, w. E. Martón (sop), G. Zancanaro (bar), G. Patanè (cnd), Hungarian State Orch, Hungarian State Chorus [I] — CBS 2-▲ M2K 42369 [DDD]

Giordano, U.:Fedora, w. V. Kincses (sop), E. Martón (sop), J. Gregor (bass), G. Patanè (cnd), Hungarian Radio-TV SO, Hungarian Radio-TV Chorus [I] — CBS 2-▲ M2K 42181 [DDD]

Great Operatic Scenes, w. R. Scotto (sop) (rec. live 1973 & 1974) — Legato Classics ▲ LCD 150-1 (m) [AAD]

Hollywood Golden Classics — Atlantic ▲ 82257-2

Italian Opera Composers' Songs, w. Martin Katz (pno) — Sony Classical ▲ SK 45863 [DDD]

José Carreras in Recital, w. Lorenzo Bavaj (pno) *(rec Seattle, 5/4/89)* — Legato Classics ▲ LCD 156-1 [AAD]

José Carreras:La Mia letizia infondere *(rec live, between 1972 & 1973)* — Foyer ▲ FOY 14001 [ADD]

Leoncavallo, R.:Pagliacci, w. M. Caballé (sop), R. Scotto (sop), A. Varnay (mez), J. Hamari (mez), M. Manuguerra (bar), T. Allen (bar), K. Nurmela (bar), U. Benelli (bar), R. Muti (cnd), Philharmonia Orch, Ambrosian Opera Chorus — EMI Classics 2-▲ CDMB 63650

Leoncavallo, R.:Pagliacci (sels), w. R. Scotto (sop), K. Nurmela (bar), R. Muti (cnd), Philharmonia Orch, Ambrosian Opera Chorus — EMI Classics ("Studio" series) ▲ CDM 63933 ■ EG 63933

Lieder Recital, w. Carreras, José (ten), Ronald Schneider (pno) — Acanta ▲ CD 43578

Liszt, F.:Sonetti di Petrarca Voice & Pno, w. Alexander Schneider (pno) [I] — Acanta ▲ CD 43578

Lloyd Webber, A.:Music of, w. S. Brightman (sop), P. Domingo (ten), M. Crawford (sgr), Royal PO—Cats; Joseph & the Amazing Technicolor Dreamcoat; Requiem; Jesus Christ Superstar; Phantom of the Opera; Aspects of Love; Starlight Express; Evita — Polydor ▲ 314 517336-2 ■ 314 517336-4

Love Is..., w. Carreras, José (ten), Robert Farnon Orch — Philips ▲ 412270-2 [DDD]

Carreras, José (ten) (cont.)

Mad About Angels, w. Cheryl Studer (sop), Christa Ludwig (mez), Anne Sofie von Otter (mez), New York PO [cnd:Leonard Bernstein], English Baroque Soloists [cnd:John Eliot Gardiner], Philharmonia Orch, Philharmonia Chorus [cnd:Carlo Maria Giulini], Orp — Deutsche Grammophon ▲ 449113-2 ■ 449113-4

Mad About Love, w. Cheryl Studer (sop), Kiri Te Kanawa (sop), Jerry Hadley (ten), Philharmonia Orch [cnd:Giuseppe Sinopoli], Bastille Opera Orch [cnd:Myung-Whun Chung], Boston SO [cnd:Seiji Ozawa], Vienna PO [cnd:John Eliot Gardiner, James Levine] — Deutsche Grammophon ▲ 449112-2 ■ 449112-4

Mascagni, P.:Cavalleria rusticana (sels), w. A. Baltsa (mez), P. Domingo (cnd), London SO, Tallis Chamber Choir—Tu qui, Santuzza?; La tua Santuzza [w. M. Hintermeier (mez)] *(rec Jan.-Feb. 1991)* — Sony Classical ▲ SK 53968 [DDD]

Mascagni, P.:Cavalleria rusticana (sels), w. M. Caballé (sop), R. Muti (cnd), Philharmonia Orch, Ambrosian Opera Chorus — EMI Classics ("Studio" series) ▲ CDM 63933 ■ EG 63933

Massenet, J.:Hérodiade, w. M. Caballé (sop—Salomé), D. Vejzovic (mez—Hérodiade), J. Carreras (ten—Jean), J. Pons (bar—Hérode), E. Serra (bar—Vitellius), V. Esteve (bar—High Priest), R. Kennedy (bass—Phanuel), J. Delacôte (cnd), Barcelona Teatro Liceo Orch, Barcelona Gran Teatro de Liceo Chorus *(rec Jan. 6, 1984)* — Legato Classics 2-▲ LCD 182 [ADD]

Massenet, J.:Werther, w. F. von Stade (mez), T. Allen (bar), R. Lloyd (b-bar), C. Davis (cnd), Royal Opera House Orch Covent Garden, Royal Opera House Chorus Covent Garden [F] — Philips 2-▲ 416654-2 [ADD]

Massenet, J.:Werther (sels), w. A. Baltsa (mez), P. Domingo (cnd), London SO, Tallis Chamber Choir—Orchestral Intro.; Il faut nous séparer; Mais vous ne savez rien de moi; Rêve! Extase! *(rec Jan.-Feb. 1991)* — Sony Classical ▲ SK 53968 [DDD]

Plácido Domingo:The Best of Christmas in Vienna, w. P. Domingo (ten), Dionne Warwick (sgr), Charles Aznavour, Sissel Kyrkjebø, Vienna SO [cnd:Vjekoslav Šutej] — Sony Classical ▲ SK 62696 ■ ST 62696

The Pleasure of Love, w. English CO [cnd:Vjekoslav Sutej] — Philips ▲ 434926-2

Ponchielli, A.:La Gioconda, w. M. Caballé (sop—Gioconda), M. L. Nave (mez—Laura), P. Payne (mez—La Cieca), J. Carreras (ten—Enzo), M. Manuguerra (bar—Barnaba), B. Giaiotti (bass—Alvise), J. López-Cobos (cnd), *(orch unknown)* *(rec Dec. 6, 1979)* — Legato Classics ▲ LCD 170-2 [ADD]

Puccini, G.:La Bohème, w. K. Ricciarelli (sop), A. Putnam (sop), I. Wixell (bar), C. Davis (cnd), Royal Opera House Orch [I] — Philips 2-▲ 416492-2 [ADD]

Puccini, G.:La Bohème, w. K. Ricciarelli (sop), C. Davis (cnd), Royal Opera House Orch — Philips 2-▲ 442260-2

Puccini, G.:La Bohème, w. Ileana Cotrubas (sop—Mimi), Margherita Guglielmi (sop—Musetta), José Carreras (ten—Rodolfo), Saverio Porzano (ten—Parpignol), Regolo Romani (ten—Vendor), Claudio Giombi (bar—Benoit), Gianni Maffeo (bar—Schaunard), Angelo Romero (bar—Marcello), Alfredo Giacomotti (bass—Alcindoro), Carlo Meliciani (bass—Customs Officer), Giuseppe Morresi (bass—Sergeant), Paolo Washington (bass—Colline), G. Prêtre (cnd), La Scala Orch, La Scala Chorus *(rec Washington D.C., Sept 8, 1976)* — Legato Classics 2-▲ LCD 201-2

Puccini, G.:Madama Butterfly, w. M. Freni (sop), T. Berganza (mez), J. Pons (bar), G. Sinopoli (cnd), Philharmonia Orch, Ambrosian Opera Chorus [I] — Deutsche Grammophon 3-▲ 423567-2 [DDD]

Puccini, G.:Madame Butterfly (sels), w. *(other artists unknown)*—Ancora Un Passo Or Via; Bimba, Bimba Non Piangere — Laserlight ▲ 14 296

Puccini, G.:Manon Lescaut, w. K. Te Kanawa (sop), P. Coni (bar), I. Tajo (bass), R. Chailly (cnd), Bologna Teatro Comunale Orch [I] — London 2-▲ 421426-2 [DDD]

Puccini, G.:Mass, w. H. Prey (bar), C. Scimone (cnd), *(orch unknown),* Ambrosian Singers — Erato ▲ 96367-2

Puccini, G.:Music of, w. Kiri Te Kanawa (sop), Eva Marton (sop), Luciano Pavarotti (ten), Richard Tucker (ten), *(other artists unknown)*—19 arias & duets from La bohème, Gianni Schicchi, Madama Butterfly, La Rondine, Tosca & Turandot *(six mono & 13 stereo recordings)* — CBS ▲ MLK 45809 [AAD/ADD/D ■ MLT 45809

Puccini, G.:Tosca, w. E. Marton (sop), J. Pons (bar), M. Tilson Thomas (cnd), Hungarian State Orch, Hungarian State Chorus — Sony Classical 2-▲ S2K 45847

Puccini, G.:Tosca, w. M. Caballé (sop), I. Wixell (bar), C. Davis (cnd), Royal Opera House Orch Covent Garden [I] — Philips 2-▲ 412885-2 [ADD]

Puccini, G.:Tosca, w. K. Ricciarelli (sop), R. Raimondi (bass), H. von Karajan (cnd), Berlin PO, German Opera Chorus [I] — Deutsche Grammophon 2-▲ 413815-2 [ADD]

Puccini, G.:Tosca, w. M. Caballé (sop), C. Davis (cnd), Royal Opera House Orch Covent Garden — Philips 2-▲ 438359-2

Puccini, G.:Tosca, w. Birgit Nilsson (sop—Floria Tosca), Puli Toro (mez—Shepherd), Jose Carreras (ten—Mario Cavaradossi), Joaquin Romaguera (ten—Spoleta), James Billings (bar—Sacristan), Richard Fredricks (bar—Baron Scarpa), Samuel Ramey (bass—Cesare Angelotti), William Ledbetter (sgr—Sciarrone), Richard Park (sgr—Cardinal), Don Yule (sgr—Jailer), J. Rudel (cnd), *(orch & chorus unknown)* *(rec Nov 13, 1974)* — Legato Classics 2-▲ LCD-200-2

Puccini, G.:Tosca (sels), w. E. Marton (sop), B. Heja (trb), F. Gerdesits (ten), J. Pons (bar), J. Nemeth (bar), J. Gregor (bass), M. Tilson Thomas (cnd), Hungarian State Orch, Hungarian Radio-TV Chorus *(rec Budapest, Dec. 14-22, 1988)* — Sony Classical ("Opera Highlights" series) ▲ SMK 53500 [DDD]

Puccini, G.:Turandot, w. M. Caballé (sop—Turnadot), M. Freni (sop—Liu), J. Carreras (ten—Calaf), M. Sénéchal (ten—Emperor Altoum), V. Sardinero (bar—Ping), P. Plishka (bass—Timur), A. Lombard (cnd), Strasbourg PO, Maîtrise de la Cathédrale, Rhine Opera Chorus — EMI Classics ▲ CDMB 65293

Puccini, G.:Turandot (sels), w. M. Caballé (sop), M. Freni (sop), M. Sénéchal (ten), A. Lombard (cnd), Strasbourg PO, Rhine Opera Chorus — EMI Classics ("Studio" series) ▲ CDM 63410

Puccini, G.:Turandot (sels), w. E. Martón (sop), K. Ricciarelli (sop), L. Maazel (cnd), Vienna State Opera Orch, Vienna State Opera Chorus [I] — CBS ▲ MK 42168 [DDD] ■ MT 42168 (D)

Ramirez, A.:Misa Criolla, w. A. Ramirez (kbd), Laredo Instrumental Ensemble, J. L. Ocejo (cnd), Bilbao Choral Society, Laredo Choral Salvé — Philips ("Digital Classics" series) ▲ 420955-2 [DDD] □ 420955-5

Ramirez, A.:Navidad en Verano, w. A. Ramirez (kbd), Laredo Instrumental Ensemble, J. L. Ocejo (cnd), Bilbao Choral Society, Laredo Choral Salvé — Philips ("Digital Classics" series) ▲ 420955-2 [DDD] □ 420955-5

Ramirez, A.:Navidad nuestra, w. A. Ramirez (kbd), Laredo Instrumental Ensemble, J. L. Ocejo (cnd), Bilbao Choral Society, Laredo Choral Salvé — Philips ("Digital Classics" series) ▲ 420955-2 [DDD] □ 420955-5

The Romantic Carreras — Philips ▲ 446822-2; ■ 446822-4

Rossini, G.:Otello, w. F. von Stade (mez), S. Fisichella (ten), S. Ramey (bass), J. López-Cobos (cnd), Philharmonia Orch, Ambrosian Opera Chorus [I] — Philips 2-▲ 432456-2 [ADD]

Rossini, G.:La pietra del paragone, w. A. Elgar (sop), B. Wolff (mez), E. Bonazzi (mez), J. Reardon (bar), R. Murcell (bar), A. Foldi (b-bar), J. Diaz (bass), N. Jenkins (cnd), Clarion Concerts Orch, Clarion Concerts Chorus [I] *(rec. ca. 1972)* — Vanguard Classics 3-▲ OVC 8043/45 [ADD]

Saint-Saëns, C.:Samson et Dalila, w. A. Baltsa (mez), Summers (bar), Estes (bass), Burchuladze (bass), C. Davis (cnd), Bavarian RSO, Bavarian Radio Chorus — Philips 2-▲ 426243-2 [DDD]

Saint-Saëns, C.:Samson et Dalila (sels), w. A. Baltsa (mez), D. George (ten), J. Summers (bar), S. Estes (bass), P. Burchuladze (bass), C. Davis (cnd), Bavarian RSO — Philips ▲ 438504-2

Sings Catalan Songs, w. Joan Casa, Barcelona Liceu Theater SO — Sony Classical ▲ SK 47177

Sings "Memory" from *Cats* & 15 Other Great Love Songs — Philips ▲ 416973-2 PM [DDD/ADD] ■ 416973-4 PM

Sings Zarzuelas, w. English CO [cnd:Antonio Ros-Marbá] — Koch International ▲ KOC 321948 [AAD]

Souvenirs — Sony Classical ▲ SMK 48155 ■ SMT 48155

Tenorissimi, Mondiale 90, w. Plácido Domingo (ten), Luciano Pavarotti (ten) — EMI Classics ▲ CDC 54109

The Three Tenors In Concert, w. P. Domingo (ten), L. Pavarotti (ten), Zubin Mehta (cnd) *(rec Rome, July 7, 1990)* — London ▲ 430433-2 ■ 430433-4 □ 430433-5

Tosti, P.F.:Songs, w. *(pianist unknown)*—Ideale; Malia; L'alba separa dalla luce lombra *(rec Carmel, CA, Oct 14, 1975)* — Goldies ▲ GLD 63203 [ADD]

Verdi, G.:Aida, w. L. Freni (sop), K. Ricciarelli (sop), A. Baltsa (mez), P. Cappuccilli (bar), G. Raimondi (ten), J. Van Dam (b-bar), H. von Karajan (cnd), Vienna PO, Vienna State Opera Chorus [I] — EMI Classics (Studio) 3-▲ CDMC 69300 [ADD]

Carreras, José (ten) (cont.)
Verdi, G.:Un ballo in maschera, w. Ghena Dimitrova (sop—Amelia), Isabella Stramaglia (sop—Oscar), Mirna Pecile (cta—Ulrica), Mario Carlin (ten—Un giudice), José Carreras (ten—Riccardo), Piero Cappuccilli (bar—Renato), Massimiliano Malaspina (bass—Samuel), Americo de Santis (bass—Silvano), Francesco Signor (bass—Tom), Ivan Del Manto (sgr—Un servo), G. Patanè (cnd), Parma Teatro Regio Orch *(rec Teatro Regio, Dec. 26, 1972)* Golden Age of Opera 2-▲ GAO 183/84
Verdi, G.:Un ballo in maschera (sels), w. Margherita Guglielmi (sop), Frederico Davià (bass), Giovanni Foiani (bass), F. Molinari-Pradelli (cnd), La Scala Orch, La Scala Chorus—S'avanza il Conte...La rivedrà nell'estasi; Ma se m'è forza perderti...Ah! dessa è là! *(rec Milan, Feb 13, 1975)* Goldies ▲ GLD 63203 [ADD]
Verdi, G.:Un ballo in maschera (sels), w. S. Sass (sop), C. Mackerras (cnd), *(orch unknown)*—Act 2 duet, "Teco io sto" & Act 3 tenor aria, "Forse la soglia attinse...Ma se m'è forza perderti" [I] *(rec live, London, 1978)* Standing Room Only 2-▲ SRO 829-2 [ADD]
Verdi, G.:La battaglia di Legnano, w. K. Ricciarelli (sop), M. Manuguerra (bar), N. Ghiuselev (bass), L. Gardelli (cnd), ORF SO, ORTF Choir Philips 2-▲ 422435-2 [ADD]
Verdi, G.:Il corsaro, w. M. Caballé (sop), J. Norman (sop), L. Gardelli (cnd), New Philharmonia Orch, Ambrosian Singers [I] Philips 2-▲ 426118-2 [ADD]
Verdi, G.:I due Foscari, w. K. Ricciarelli (sop), E. Connell (sop), V. Bello (ten), M. Antoniak (ten), P. Cappuccilli (bar), S. Ramey (bass), F. Handlos (bass), L. Gardelli (cnd), Austrian RSO, Austrian Radio Chorus Philips 2-▲ 422426-2 [ADD]
Verdi, G.:Un giorno di regno, w. J. Norman (sop), F. Cossotto (mez), I. Wixell (bar), V. Sardinero (bar), W. Ganzarolli (bar), P. Elvin (bass), A. Cassinelli (bass), L. Gardelli (cnd), Royal PO, Ambrosian Singers Philips 2-▲ 422429-2 [ADD]
Verdi, G.:Jérusalem, w. K. Ricciarelli (sop), S. Nimsgern (b-bar), G. Gavazzeni (cnd), Turin RAI Orch, Turin RAI Chorus [F] *(rec live 12/20/75)* Standing Room Only 2-▲ SRO 828-2 [ADD]
Verdi, G.:I lombardi alla prima crociata, w. S. Sass (sop), N. Ghiuselev (bass), L. Gardelli (cnd), *(orch unknown)* [I] *(rec live, London, 1976)* Standing Room Only 2-▲ SRO 829-2 [ADD]
Verdi, G.:I lombardi alla prima crociata (sels), w. Renata Scotto (sop), E. Queler (cnd), *(orch unknown)*—La mia letizia infondere; Oh belle a questa misera; Al'armi!...Che ascolto! *(rec New York, Dec 7, 1972)* Goldies ▲ GLD 63203 [ADD]
Verdi, G.:I lombardi alla prima crociata (sels)—Al Siloe! Al Siloe!...Guerra!; Che Vid Io Mai?; La Mia Letizia Infondere Come Poteva Un Angelo; Mostro D'Averno Orribile; No! No! Giusta Causa Non e D'Iddio; Or S'Ascolti; Parriciada!; Qui Nel Luogo Laserlight ▲ 14 296
Verdi, G.:I lombardi alla prima crociata (sels), w. K. Ricciarelli (sop), *(pianist unknown)*—Act 3 duet, "Dove sola m'inoltro...Per dirupi e per foreste" *(rec live, New York, 1975)* Standing Room Only 2-▲ SRO 828-2 [ADD]
Verdi, G.:Luisa Miller, w. K. Ricciarelli (sop—Luisa), M. G. Piolatto (mez—Laura), S. Silva (cta—Federica), J. Carreras (ten—Rodolfo), E. Pranod (ten—A Peasant), R. Bruson (bar—Miller), G. Casarini (bar—Wurm) M. Rinaudo (bass—Count Walter), F. Previtali (cnd), Turin Teatro Regio Orch, Turin Teatro Regio Chorus *(rec May 9, 1976)* Legato Classics 2-▲ LCD 180 [ADD]
Verdi, G.:Requiem Mass, w. Anna Tomowa-Sintow (sop), Agnes Baltsa (mez), José Van Dam (bass-bar), H. von Karajan (cnd), Vienna PO, Vienna State Opera Chorus, Sofia National Opera Chorus *(rec Great Hall, Musikverein, Vienna, June 1984)* Deutsche Grammophon 2-▲ 439033-2 [DDD]
Verdi, G.:Requiem Mass, w. C. Studer (sop), M. Lopivšek (cta), R. Riamondi (bass), C. Abbado (cnd), Vienna PO, Vienna State Opera Chorus Deutsche Grammophon 2-▲ 435884-2
Verdi, G.:Rigoletto, w. P. Wise (sop—Gilda), B. Evans (sop—Giovanna), M. Yauger (mez—Maddalena), J. Carreras (ten—Duke), L. Quilico (bar—Rigoletto), J. Rudel (cnd), *(orch unknown)* *(rec Apr. 22, 1973)* Standing Room Only 2-▲ SRO 843 [ADD]
Verdi, G.:Rigoletto (sels), w. J. Rudel (cnd), New York City Opera Orch, New York City Opera Chorus—Questa o quella; Ella mi fu rapital...Parmi veder le lagrime; La donna è mobile *(rec New York, Apr 26, 1973)* Goldies ▲ GLD 63203 [ADD]
Verdi, G.:quattro pezzi sacri, w. C. Studer (sop), M. Lopivšek (cta), R. Riamondi (bass), C. Abbado (cnd), Vienna PO, Vienna State Opera Chorus Deutsche Grammophon 2-▲ 435884-2
Verdi, G.:La traviata, w. M. Caballé (sop), N. Mitic (bar), A. Guadagno (cnd), Philadelphia Lyric Opera Orch, Philadelphia Lyric Opera Chorus *(rec 1973)* Melodram 2-▲ MLO 270106 [ADD]
Verdi, G.:La traviata (sels), w. A. Baltsa (mez), P. Domingo (cnd), London SO, Tallis Chamber Choir—Libiamo, libiamo ne' lieti calici *(rec Jan.-Feb. 1991)* Sony Classical ▲ SK 53968 [DDD]
Verdi, G.:La traviata (sels), w. N. Verchi (cnd), *(orch & chorus unknown)*—Libiamo ne'lieti calici; Lunge da lei...De' miei bollenti spiriti *(rec Tokyo, Sept 18, 1973)* Goldies ▲ GLD 63203 [ADD]
Verdi, G.:La traviata (sels), w. Ileana Cotrubas (sop—Violetta), Elizabeth Bainbridge (mez—Annina), José Carreras (ten—Alfredo), Richard Creeger (ten—Gastone), Victor Braun (bar—Germont), Richard Van Allen (bass—Grenvil), J. Pritchard (cnd), *(orch unknown)*—Libiamo ne' lietialici; Oh, qual pallor!...Un di felice; Ebben? Che diavol fate?...Amor, dunque non piu; E strano!...Ah, fors'e lui; Follie! Follie!...Sempre libera; Lunge da lei...De' miei bollenti spiriti; Che fai?...Amami, Alfredo; Invitato a qui seguirmi...Ogni suo aver tal femmina; Signora...Parigi, o cara; Ah, non piu...Ah, gran Dio, morir si giovine; E strano! Cessarono gli spasimi del dolore *(rec Apr 15, 1974)* Legato Classics 2-▲ LCD 201-2
Verdi, G.:Il trovatore, w. Katia Ricciarelli (sop), Stefania Toczyska (mez), Yuri Mazurok (bar), C. Davis (cnd), Royal Opera House Orch, Royal Opera House Chorus Covent Garden Philips ("Two-Fers" series) 2-▲ 446151-2
Verdi, G.:Il trovatore (sels), w. A. Baltsa (mez), P. Domingo (cnd), London SO, Tallis Chamber Choir—Soli or siamo; Non son tuo figlio; L'usato messo Ruiz m'invia [w. J. Howard (tenor)] *(rec Jan.-Feb. 1991)* Sony Classical ▲ SK 53968 [DDD]
With a Song in My Heart:A Tribute to Mario Lanza, w. London Studio Orch [cnd:Marcello Viotti] Teldec ▲ 92369-2 ■ 92369-4
World Stars Sing Operetta, w. A. Moffo (sop), Lucia Popp (sop), Ants Kollo (ten), Thomas Moser (ten), Giuseppe Di Stefano (ten), Hermann Prey (bar), Karl Ridderbusch (bass), et al., various orchs *(rec 1968-1985)* Acanta ▲ 42941
Zarzuelas, w. I. Rey (sop), English CO [cnd:E. Ricci] Erato ▲ 95789-2 ■ 95789-4

Carril, José Antonio (bass)
Halffter, E.:Dominus pastor meus, w. Susan Chilcott (sop), Claire Powell (mez), Joan Cabero (ten), V. P. Pérez (cnd), Tenerife SO, La Laguna Univ Choir Discobi ▲ DIS 2009 [DDD]

Carrillo, Pina (sgr)
Strauss, R.:Der Rosenkavalier, w. Jarmila Barton (sop—Marianne), Lisa Della Casa (sop—Sophie), Sena Jurinac (sop—Octavian), Ilva Ligabue (sop—Orphan), Elisabeth Schwarzkopf (sop—Marschallin), Else Schürhoff (mez—Annina), Luisa Villa (mez—Milliner), Hugues Cuénod (ten—Marschallin's majordomo), Erich Majkut (ten—Valzacchi), Giuseppe Nessi (ten—Animal seller), Luciano Della Pergola (ten—Lackey/Faninal's majordomo), Antonio Pirino (ten—An Italian Singer), Gino Del Signore (ten—Lackey/Waiter), Erich Kunz (bar—Herr von Faninal), Paolo Pedani (bar—Lackey), Attilo Barbesi (bass—Lackey/Waiter), Enrico Campi (bass—Waiter), Otto Edelmann (bass—Baron Ochs), Bruno Fichtinger (bass—Notary), Franco Taino (bass—Waiter), Maria Amadini (sgr—Orphan), Pina Carrillo (sgr—Orphan), Joszi Trojan Regar (sgr—Innkeeper), H. von Karajan (cnd), La Scala Orch, La Scala Chorus *(rec La Scala Theater, Milan, Jan. 26, 1952)* Legato Classics 3-▲ LCD 197-3

Carrizo, Martha (mez)
Verdi, G.:Rigoletto, w. Renata Scotto (sop—Gilda), Stella Maris Silva (sop—Giovanna), Martha Carrizo (mez—Page), Carmen de la Mata (mez—Countess Ceprano), Noemi Souza (cta—Maddalena), Horacio Mastrango (ten—Borso), Richard Tucker (ten—Duke of Mantua), Cornell MacNeil (bar—Rigoletto), Riccardo Yost (bar—Marullo), Guerrino Boschetti (bass—Usher), Tulio Gagliardo (bass—Count Ceprano), Victor de Narké (bass—Monterone), William Wilderman (bass—Sparafucile), F. Previtali (cnd), Buenos Aires Teatro Colón Orch, Buenos Aires Teatro Colón Chorus *(rec Colon Theater, Buenos Aires, Aug. 22, 1967)* Legato Classics 2-▲ LCD 198-2

Carroli, Silvano (bar)
Puccini, G.:Tosca, w. N. Miricioiu (sop), G. Lamberti (ten), A. Rahbari (cnd), Czech-Slovak RSO Bratislava, Slovak Phil Chorus [I] Naxos 2-▲ 8.660001/02 [DDD]
Puccini, G.:Tosca (sels), w. Nelly Miricioiu (sop—Tosca), Giorgio Lamberti (ten—Cavaradossi), Miroslav Dvorsky (ten—Spoletta), Silvano Carroli (bar—Baron Scarpia), Jozef Spaček (bar—Sacristan), Jan Durco (bass—Sciarrone), Stanislav Benačka (bass—Gaoler), A. Rahbari (cnd), Czech-Slovak RSO Bratislava, Slovak Phil Chorus *(rec Concert Hall of the Slovak Radio, Bratislava, Apr. 7-14, 1990)* Naxos ▲ 8.553153 [DDD]

Carroli, Silvano (bar) (cont.)
Verdi, G.:Attila, w. Maria Chiara (sop), Nicolai Ghiuselev (bass), N. Santi (cnd), Turin Teatro Regio Orch, Turin Teatro Regio Chorus *(rec live, 1980)* Serenissima 2-▲ SER 360138

Carroll, C. D. (sgr)
Lloyd Webber, A.:Music of, w. C. Burt (sgr), Graham Bickly (sgr), J. Kelly (sgr), Yates (cnd), National SO, Munich SO—Song & Dance; The Phantom of the Opera; Starlight Express; Jeeves; Jesus Christ Superstar; Aspects of Love; Cats; The Requiem Mass Koch International ▲ KOCCD 340132 ■ KOCC 340134

Carroll, David (sgr)
Gershwin, G.:Girl Crazy, w. L. Luft (sgr), J. Blazer (sop), J. Mauceri (cnd), *(orch unknown)* Elektra/Nonesuch ▲ 9 79250-2
Rodgers, R.:No Strings, w. R. Kiley (sgr), *(artists unknown)* [1962 cast] Broadway Angel ▲ ZDM 64694 ■ EG 64694

Carron, Arthur (ten)
Verdi, G.:Aida (sels), w. Rose Bampton (sop), Lydia Summers (mez), Leonard Warren (bar), W. Pelletier (cnd), Philadelphia studio musicians, New York studio musicians—Ritorna vincitor!; Rivedrai le foreste imbalsamate; Odimi, Aida; La fatal pietra...O terra, addio! *(rec Academy of Music, Philadelphia & Town Hall, New York, May 30 & June 17, 1940)* VAI Audio ▲ VAIA 1084
Wagner, R.:Lohengrin (sels), w. Rose Bampton (sop), Norman Cordon (bass), W. Steinberg (cnd), Philadelphia studio musicians, New York studio musicians—Einsam in trüben Tagen; Das süsse Lied verhallt *(rec Academy of Music, Philadelphia & Town Hall, New York, May 27 & 28, 1940)* VAI Audio ▲ VAIA 1084
Wagner, R.:Tristan und Isolde (sels), w. Rose Bampton (sop), Lydia Summers (mez), W. Steinberg (cnd), Philadelphia studio musicians, New York studio musicians—Wohl kenn' ich Irlands Königin; O sink' hernieder; Wohin nun Tristan scheidet; Mild und leise *(rec Academy of Music, Philadelphia & Town Hall, New York, May 26 & 27, 1940)* VAI Audio ▲ VAIA 1084

Carron, Elisabeth (sop)
Puccini, G.:Madama Butterfly (sels), w. Elisabeth Carron (sop—Cio-Cio-San), Deborah Kieffer (mez—Suzuki), Herman Malamood (ten—Pinkerton), David Clatworthy (bar—Sharpless), G. Morelli (cnd), *(orch unknown)*—Ancora un passo or via; Ieri son salita...Io seguo il mio destino; Adesso voi siete per me...Vogliatemi bene; Ti sero palpitante...Ah! Quanti occhi fisi, attenti!; Egli, col cuore grosso...Un bel di, vedremo; Ebbene, che fareste Madama Butterfly...Due cose potrei far; Sai cos'ebbe cuore di pensare...Che tua madre; Troppa luce e di fuor; Con onor muore...Tu? Tu? Piccolo Iddio *(rec New York, Oct 23, 1973)* Legato Classics ▲ LCD 212-1 [ADD]
Puccini, G.:Suor angelica, w. Elisabeth Carron (sop—Angelica), Joan Summers (sop—Genovieffa), Donna Owen (sop—Dolcina), Lou Ann Wyckoff (sop—Alms collector), Hanna Owen (sop—novice), Anthea De Forest (sop—novice), Charlotte Povia (mez—Abbess), Beverly Evans (mez—Monitress), Kay Creed (mez—Mistress), La Vergne Monette (sop/mez—lay sister), Joan August (sop/mez—lay sister), Pearle Goldsmith (sop/mez—other sister), Lila Herbert (sop/mez—other sister), Jodell Kenting (sop/mez—other sister), Ann Pretzat (sop/mez—other sister), Evelyn Sachs (cta—Princess), F. Patanè (cnd), *(orch unknown)* *(rec New York, Feb 23, 1967)* Legato Classics ▲ LCD 212-1 [ADD]

Carron, Ruth (mez)
Donizetti, G.:Lucia di Lammermoor (sels), w. Renata Scotto (sop—Lucia), Ruth Carron (mez—Alisa), Richard Tucker (ten—Edgardo), Matteo Manuguerra (bar—Enrico), Robert Hale (bass-bar—Raimondo), A. Guadagno (cnd), *(orch & chorus unknown)*—Lucia, perdona...Verranno a te; Sconsigliato! In queste porte; Il dolce suono; Non mi guardar si fiero...Spargi d'amaro pianto; Tombe degli avi miei...Fra poco a me ricovero; Tu che a Dio spiegasti l'ali *(rec Philadelphia, 1973)* Legato Classics 2-▲ LCD 198-2

Carta, Nino (bar)
Donizetti, G.:Lucia di Lammermoor (sels), w. L. Gencer (sop), G. Prandelli (ten), R. Botteghelli (bass), Hussu (sgr), Sabatucci (sgr), O. de Fabritiis (cnd), Trieste Teatro Comunale Giuseppe Verdi Orch, Trieste Teatro Comunale G. Verdi Chorus *(rec live 12/13/57 & 2/10/58)* Melodram ▲ MEL 15003 (m) [AAD]

Carter, Clive (sgr)
Lloyd Webber, A.:Music of, w. M. Friedman (sgr), C. Moore (sgr), J. Barrowman (sgr), L. Robertson (sgr), J. Diedrich (sgr), Grania Renihan (sgr), J.O. Edwards (cnd), Munich SO—Cats; Joseph & the Amazing Technicolor Dreamcoat; Phantom of the Opera; Evita; Jesus Christ Superstar; Starlight Express; Song & Dance; Aspects of Love Koch International ▲ CD 340022 [DDD] ■ MC 340022
Taylor, B.J.:Wuthering Heights, w. Dave Willets (sgr), L. Garrett (sop), J. Sladdon (sgr), S. Campbell (sgr), Philharmonia Orch, Contorum Choir Silva America ▲ SSD 1008 ■ SSC 1008

Carter, Don (ten)
Lewandowksi, L.L.:Choral Music, w. Sandra Lee (sop), Ann Sadan (alt), Adam Cohn (b-bar), Michael Morris (bass), Carys Hughes (org), Robert Max (cnd), Zemel Choir—Ma Towu in F; Ma Towu in B♭; L'cho Dodi; Tow L'hodoss; Adoshem Moloch; W'hogen Ba'adenu [Uw'tsel]; W'schomru; L'icho Adoshem; J'Halahu [Hodo Al Erez]; Ladoshem Ho'orets; Uw'nucho Jomar; Adon Olom; Ki K'schimcho; Hajom Harass Olom; Kol Nidre; Schuwi Nafschi; Enosch, K'chozir Jomow; Halalujoh; Preise, Meine Seele Olympia ▲ OLY 347 [DDD]

Carter, Donna (sop)
Poulenc, F.:Mass, w. R. Shaw (cnd), Robert Shaw Festival Singers [L] Telarc ▲ CD 80236 [DDD]

Carter, Elizabeth (sgr)
Verdi, G.:Rigoletto (sels), w. Daniella Lojarro (sop), Roberto Serville (bar), Boiko Zvetanov (sgr)—Ov; Questa o quella; Pari siamo! Io la lingua—Figlia! Mio Padre; Giovanna, ho Dei rimorsi; Gualtier Maldé - Caro nome; Ella mi fu rapital; Scorrendo uniti remota via; Cortigiani, vil razza danata; plus others Laserlight ▲ 14207 [DDD]

Carter, John (bar)
Verdi, G.:Un ballo in maschera, w. Stella Andreva (sop—Oscar), Zinka Milanov (sop—Amelia), Bruna Castagna (cta—Ulrica), Jussi Björling (ten—Riccardo), Lodovico Oliviero (ten—Un Servo D'Amelia), John Cartet (bar—Un Giudice), Alexander Sved (bar—Renato), Normann Cordon (bass—Samuel), Arthur Kent (bass—Silvano), Nicola Moscona (bass—Tom), E. Panizza (cnd), *(orch unknown)* *(rec live, New York, Dec. 14, 1940)* The Fourties 2-▲ ENT FT 1515

Carter, Thomas (ten)
Floyd, C.:Susannah, w. Phyllis Curtin (sop—Susannah Polk), Richard Cassilly (ten—Sam Polk), Norman Treigle (bass—Olin Blitch), Marietta Muhs Cosenza (sgr—Mrs. McLean), Marilyn Davidson (sgr—Mrs. Gleaton), Kay Long (sgr—Mrs. Hayes), Jean Young (sgr—Mrs. Ott), Alton Brim (sgr—Elder Hayes), Thomas Carter (sgr—Elder Gleaton), Jack Davis (sgr—Elder McLean), Keith Kaldenberg (sgr—Little Bat McLean), Burton Parker (sgr—Elder Ott), K. Andersson (cnd), New Orleans Opera Orch, New Orleans Opera Chorus *(rec Mar 31, 1962)* VAI Audio 2-▲ VAIA 1115-2 [ADD]
Puccini, G.:La Bohème, w. Licia Albanese (sop—Mimì), Audrey Schuh (sop—Musetta), Giuseppe di Stefano (ten—Rodolfo), Arthur Cosenza (bar—Schaunard), Giuseppe Valdengo (bar—Marcello), Norman Treigle (bass—Colline), Warren Gadpaille (bass—Benoît/Alcindoro), Thomas Carter (sgr—Parpignol), Harold Crane (sgr—Custom House Official), Steve Harun (sgr—Sergeant), R. Cellini (cnd), New Orleans Opera Orch, New Orleans Opera Chorus *(rec Nov 1959)* VAI Audio 2-▲ VAIA 1119-2 [ADD]
Puccini, G.:Madama Butterfly, w. Dorothy Kirsten (sgr—Madama Butterfly), Rosalind Nadell (mez—Suzuki), Eileen Ireland (mez—Kate), Daniele Barioni (ten—Pinkerton), Thomas Carter (ten—Goro), Arthur Cosenza (ten—Yamadori), Richard Torigi (bar—Sharpless), Rodney Hall (bass—The Bronze), Harold Crane (bass—Commissioner), R. Cellini (cnd), New Orleans Opera Orch, New Orleans Opera Chorus *(rec live, Mar 1960)* VAI Audio 2-▲ VAIA 1054-2
Saint-Saëns, C.:Samson et Dalila, w. Risë Stevens (mez—Dalila), Ramón Vinay (ten—Samson), Thomas Carter (ten—1st Philistine), Tony Lopez (ten—Philistine Messenger), Joseph Mordino (bar—High Priest), Arthur Cosenza (bass—Abimélech), Joseph Knight (bass—2nd Philistine), Ara Berberian (bass—Old Hebrew), R. Cellini (cnd), New Orleans Opera Orch, New Orleans Opera Chorus *(rec live, Apr 2, 1960)* VAI Audio 2-▲ VAIA 1055-2 [ADD]

Carteri, Rosanna (sop)
Brahms, J.:Ein Deutsches Requiem, w. Boris Christoff (bass), B. Walter (cnd), Rome Radio-TV SO, Rome Radio-TV Chorus *(rec live, Turin RAI Auditorium, Apr. 16, 1952)* Emozioni ▲ CDAR 2029 [ADD]
Brahms, J.:Ein Deutsches Requiem, w. Boris Christoff (bass), B. Walter (cnd), Rome Radio-TV SO, Rome Radio-TV Chorus Stradivarius 2-▲ STV DTM 12323 [ADD]
Donizetti, G.:Don Pasquale (sels), w. A. Simonetto (cnd), Milan Italian Radio-TV Orch—Quel Guardo il Cavaliere...So Anch'io la Virtù Magica Fonit Cetra ("Martini & Rossi" series) ▲ FCT CDMR 5008

Carteri, Rosanna (sop) (cont.)

Donizetti, G.:L'elisir d'amore, w. Rosanna Carteri (sop—Adina), Luigi Angela Vercelli (mez—Gianetta), Luigi Alva (ten—Nemorino), Rolando Panerai (bar—Belcore), Giuseppe Taddei (bar—Dulcamara), T. Serafin (cnd), La Scala Orch, La Scala Chorus EMI Classics 2-▲ CDMB 65658

Mascagni, P.:L'amico Fritz, w. R. Carteri (sop—Suzel), R. Corsi (mez—Beppe), C. Valletti (ten—Fritz), C. Tagliabue (bar—David), V. Gui (cnd), Milan RAI SO, Milan RAI Chorus *(rec live, Apr. 25, 1953)* Bongiovanni 2-▲ GB 1098/99 [ADD]

Mascagni, P.:Lodoletta (sels), w. A. Simonetto (cnd), Milan Italian Radio-TV Orch—Ah! Il Suo Nome...Flammen Perdonami Fonit Cetra ("Martini & Rossi" series) ▲ FCT CDMR 5008

Poulenc, F.:Gloria Sop, w. G. Prêtre (cnd), French National RSO, French National Radio Chorus [L] EMI Classics ▲ CDC 47723 [ADD]

Rosanna Carteri, Carlo Bergonzi, w. Carlo Bergonzi (ten), Turin RAI SO [cnd:F. M. Pradelli] *(rec Jan. 30, 1960)* Incontri Memorabili ("Martini & Rossi Concerts" series) ▲ 5026

Rosanna Carteri, Tito Gobbi, w. Tito Gobbi (bar), Milan RAI SO [cnd:Alfredo Simonetto] *(rec Dec. 24, 1956)* Incontri Memorabili ("Martini & Rossi Concerts" series) ▲ 5008

Rosanna Carteri, Antonietta Stella & Beniamino Gigli, w. Antonietta Stella (sop), Beniamino Gigli (ten), Rome RAI SO, Rome RAI Chorus [cnd:Nino Antonellini], Milan RAI SO [cnd:Nino Sanzogno] *(rec Milan & Sanremo)* Incontri memorabili ("Martini & Rossi Concert" series) ▲ CDMR 5005 [ADD]

Verdi, G.:Otello (sels), w. A. Simonetto (cnd), Milan Italian Radio-TV Orch—Mia Madre Aveva...Canzone del Salice Fonit Cetra ("Martini & Rossi" series) ▲ FCT CDMR 5008

Carton, Pauline (sgr)

Varney, L.:Les Mousquetaires au couvent, w. Gabrielle Ristori (mez), Camille Rouquetty (ten), Gabriel Bacquier (bar), Louis Musy (b-bar), Pierre Blanc (sgr), Jacqueline Cauchard (sgr), Mireille Lacoste (sgr), Colette Riedinger (sgr), R. Benedetti (cnd) Musidisc 2-▲ MUS 202262 [AAD]

Carturan, Gabriella (mez)

Bellini, V.:Norma, w. Maria Callas (sop), Giulietta Simionato (mez), Mario del Monaco (ten), Giuseppe Zampieri (ten), Nicola Zaccaria (bass), A. Votto (cnd), La Scala Orch, La Scala Chorus Melodram 2-▲ CDM 26036

Bellini, V.:La sonnambula, w. M. Callas (sop), C. Valletti (ten), G. Modesti (bass), L. Bernstein (cnd), La Scala Orch, La Scala Chorus [I] *(rec live, 3/5/55)* Myto 2-▲ 2 MCD 89006 (m) [ADD]

Cherubini, L.:Pimmalione, w. M. Adani (sop), I. Ligabue (sop), U. Borghi (sgr), E. Gerelli (cnd), Milan RAI Orch, Milan RAI Chorus [I] *(rec live 1955)* Melodram ▲ CDM 19501 [AAD]

Cherubini, L.:Pimmalione, w. Mariella Adani (sop), Ilva Ligabue (sop), Umberto Borghi (sgr), E. Gerelli (cnd), Milan RAI SO, Milan RAI Chorus Melodram 2-▲ CDM 29501

Donizetti, G.:Anna Bolena, w. Maria Callas (sop), Giulietta Simionato (mez), Gianni Raimondi (ten), Plinio Clabassi (bass), Nicola Rossi Lemmeni (sgr), Luigi Rumo (sgr), G. Gavazzeni (cnd), La Scala Orch, La Scala Chorus Great Opera Performances 2-▲ GOP 768

Rossini, G.:Il barbiere di Siviglia (sels), w. G. d' Angelo (sop), N. Monti (ten), R. Capecchi (bar), G. Giorgetti (bar), C. Cava (bass), G. Tadeo (bass), B. Bartoletti (cnd), Bavarian RSO IMP Collectors Series ▲ IMPX 9022 [AAD]

Verdi, G.:La forza del destino, w. L. Gencer (sop), G. Di Stefano (ten), A. Priotti (bar), C. Siepi (b-bar), A. Votto (cnd), *(orch unknown)* *(rec live, Cologne 1957)* Melodram 3-▲ MEL 37010

Verdi, G.:La forza del destino, w. Leyla Gencer (sop—Leonora), Gabriella Carturan (mez—Preziosilla), Giuseppe di Stefano (ten—Don Alvaro), Aldo Protti (bar—Don Carlo), Cesare Siepi (b-bar), Franco Calabrese (bass—Marchese di Calatrava), Enrico Campi (bass—Fra Melitone), A. Votto (cnd), La Scala Orch, La Scala Chorus *(rec Bühnen der Stadt, Köln, July 5, 1957)* Agorá Music ("Phoenix" series) 3-▲ 510 [ADD]

Zandonai, R.:Francesca da Rimini, w. Lydia Marimpietri (sop—Biancofiore), Magda Olivero (sop—Francesca), Pinuccia Perotti (sop—Samaritana), Edda Vincenzi (sop—Garsenda), Gabriella Carturan (mez—Smaragdi), Biancamaria Casoni (mez—Altichiara), Anna Maria Rota (cta—Donella), Athos Cesarini (ten—Archer), Angelo Mercuriali (ten—Ser Toldo Berardengo), Mario del Monaco (ten—Paolo), Piero de Palma (ten—Malatestino), Rinaldo Pelizzoni (ten—Prisoner), Gianpiero Malaspina (bar—Gianciotto), Dino Mantovani (bar—Jester), Enrico Campi (bass—Ostasio), Giuseppe Morresi (bass—Tower warden), G. Gavazzeni (cnd), La Scala Orch, La Scala Chorus *(rec La Scala Theatre, Milan, June 4, 1959)* Legato Classics 2-▲ LCD 186-2

Cartwright, G. (voc)

Lebaron, A.:Con for Active Frogs, w. D. Shea (voc), J. Staley (voc), W. Trigg (perc), A. LeBaron (cnd), New Music Consort [E] Mode ▲ 30

Carusi, Alberto (bass)

Bizet, G.:Carmen, w. M. Chiara (sop—Micaela), A. Caminada (mez—Mercedes), F. Cossotto (mez—Carmen), F. Andreoli (ten—Il Remendado), P. M. Ferraro (ten—Don José), R. Bruson (bar—Escamillo), G. Zancanaro (bar—Morales), A. Carusi (bass—Il Dancairo), P. Maag (cnd), Venice Teatro La Fenice Orch, Venice Teatro La Fenice Chorus *(rec 1971)* Myto 2-▲ MCD 93487

Caruso, Enrico (ten)

Addio mia bella Napoli Replay ▲ 4026

Arias & Songs *(rec 1902–04)* EMI Classics ("Great Recordings of the Century" series) ▲ CDH 61046 (m)

Caruso Duets & Ensembles RCA Gold Seal ▲ 09026-61638-2 [ADD]

The Caruso Edition, Vol. 1 *(rec 1902–08)* Pearl 3-▲ PEA EVC 1 (m) [AAD]

The Caruso Edition, Vol. 2 *(rec 1908–12)* Pearl 3-▲ PEA EVC 2 (m) [AAD]

The Caruso Edition, Vol. 3 *(rec 1912–16)* Pearl 3-▲ PEA EVC 3 (m) [AAD]

The Caruso Edition, Vol. 4 *(rec 1916–21)* Pearl 3-▲ PEA EVC 4 (m) [AAD]

Caruso, Ferrar & Journet:Highlights from Faust & French Opera, w. Geraldine Farrar (sop), Marcel Journet (bass) Nimbus ▲ NI 7859 [ADD]

Caruso in Arias, Duets & Songs, w. Louise Homer (cta), Mario Ancona (bar), Titta Ruffo (bar), Antonio Scotti (bar) Supraphon Collection ▲ SUP 110618 (m) [ADD]

Caruso in Ensemble, w. *(rec 1906–14)* Nimbus ("Prima Voce" series) ▲ NI 7834 [ADD]

Caruso in Love RCA Gold Seal ▲ 09026-61639-2

Caruso in Opera *(rec 1904–20)* Nimbus ("Prima Voce" series) ▲ NI 7803 (m) [ADD]

Caruso in Song Nimbus ("Prima Voce" series) ▲ NI 7809-2 (m) [ADD]

Casa Sonzogno, w. Maria Callas (sop), et al. Arkadia 2-▲ 626

Chante en Français *(rec 1908–20)* Music Memoria ▲ 30182 [AAD]

The Complete Caruso RCA Gold Seal 12-▲ 60495-2-RG [ADD]

The Complete Destinn, w. E. Destinn (sop), J. McCormack (ten), K. Jörn (ten), G. Martinelli (ten), G. Zenatello (ten), et al. Supraphon 12-▲ SUP 112136 [ADD]

The Complete Electrical Re-Creations Pearl 2-▲ PEA 9030 [AAD]

Dodge, C.:Any Resemblance Is Purely Coincidental, w. A. Feinberg (pno) New Albion ▲ NA 043

Duets *(rec 1906–14)* Memoir Classics ▲ CDMOIR 414 [AAD]

Enrico Caruso RCA Gold Seal ▲ 09026-61244-2

Enrico Caruso, Vol. 1 Pearl ▲ PEA 9309 (m) [AAD]

Enrico Caruso, Vol. 2 *(rec 1902–20)* Pearl ▲ PEA 9361 (m) [AAD]

Gounod, C.:Faust (sels) RCA Gold Seal ▲ 09026-61244-2

Legendary Three Tenors, w. Beniamino Gigli (ten), John McCormack (ten), Ruggiero Leoncavallo (pno), Edwin Schneider (pno), Metropolitan Opera Orch, Metropolitan Opera Chorus [cnd:Giulio Setti], Philharmonia Orch, Philharmonia Chorus [cnd:Stanford Robinson] *(rec 1904–1950)* RCA Gold Seal ▲ 09026-68534-2 [ADD] ■ 09026-68534-4

Leoncavallo, R.:Pagliacci (sels), w. Antonio Paoli (ten), Giovanni Zenatello (ten), Amedeo Bassi (ten), Hermann Jadlowker (ten), Fernand Ansseau (ten), Hipolito Lazaro (ten), Nino (Filippo) Piccaluga (ten), Mario Chamlee (ten), Giacomo Lauri-Volpi (ten), Miguel Fleta (ten), Giovanni Martinelli (ten), Aureliano Pertile (ten), Georges Thill (ten), Alessandro Valente (ten), Francesco Merli (ten), Lauritz Melchior (ten), Marcel Wittrisch (ten), Joseph Schmidt (ten), Beniamino Gigli (ten), Giuseppe Lugo (ten), Helge Roswaenge (ten), Jussi Bjoerling (ten)—23 versions of the tenor aria "Vesti la giubba" *(rec 1907–1944)* Bongiovanni ▲ GB 1071 [ADD]

Puccini, G.:Tosca (sels), *(orch unknown)* Forlane ▲ FRL 16718 [ADD]

A Selection from the Universally Acclaimed Caruso Edition, Vol. 1:Caruso Sings Italian Opera *(rec 1906–20)* Pearl ▲ PEA 9046 [AAD]

Vol. 2:Caruso Sings Pearl ▲ PEA 9047 [DDD]

Vol. 3:Caruso Sings French Opera Pearl ▲ PEA 9048 [AAD]

Caruso, Enrico (ten) (cont.)

Three Legendary Tenors:In Opera & Song, w. J. Björling, Beniamino Gigli (ten), Giuseppe de Luca (bar) Nimbus ▲ NI 1434 [ADD]

21 Favorite Arias *(rec 1906–1920)* RCA Red Seal ▲ 5911-2-RC (m)

Verdi, G.:Arias—arias from Aida, Ballo in maschera, Don Carlos, Forza del destino, I Lombardi, Macbeth, Otello, Rigoletto, Traviata, Trovatore RCA Gold Seal ▲ 09026-61242-2

Verdi, G.:Un ballo in maschera (sels), w. Maria Caniglia (sop), Gina Cigna (sop), Fedora Barbieri (mez), Beniamino Gigli (ten), Giovanni Zenatello (ten), Carlo Galeffi (bar), Lawrence Tibbett (bar), *(various orchs & cnds)* *(rec 1911–43)* Grammofono 2000 ▲ GRM 78527 (m)

Verdi, G.:La forza del destino (sels), w. Pasquale Amato (bar), *(orch unknown)* Forlane ▲ FRL 16718 [ADD]

Verdi, G.:Otello (sels), w. C. Muzio (sop), R. Ponselle (sop), H. Spani (sop), N. Fusati (ten), L. Melchior (ten), F. Merli (ten), F. Tamagno (ten), B. Franci (bar), V. Maurel (bar), R. Stracciari (bar), T. Ruffo (bar) *(rec 1906–1933)* Music Memoria ▲ 30219

Verdi, G.:Il trovatore (sels), w. J. Biel (ten), F. Tamagno (ten), L.-A. Escalaïs (ten), M. Gilion (ten), A. Paoli (ten), G. Zenatello (ten), J. Sembach (ten), L. Slezak (ten), F. Constantino (ten), G. Martinelli (ten), B. De Muro (ten), N. Fusati (ten), N. Piccaluga (ten), G. Lauri-Volpi (ten), A. Pertile (ten), E. Bergamaschi (ten), R. Tauber (ten), J. O'Sullivan (ten), H. Roswaenge (ten), G. Taccani (ten), V. Lois (ten), H. Lazaro (ten), A. Lindi (ten), A. Cortis (ten), F. Merli (ten), F. Völker (ten), J. Kiepura (ten), J. Schmidt (ten), J. Bjoerling (ten), B. Gigli (ten), A. Salvarezza (ten), J. Soler (ten), M. Filippeschi (ten)—34 performances of the Act III tenor aria "Di quella pira!," *(rec from 1903–1956)* Bongiovanni ▲ GB 1051 [AAD]

Verismo Arias RCA Gold Seal ▲ 09026-61243-2

The World of Singing, Vol. 3:The Italian School, Part 1:The Italian Tenors Before World War I (1902–13), w. Antonio Aramburo (ten), Alessandro Bonci (ten), Giuseppe Borgatti (ten), Edoardo Garbin (ten), Fiorello Giraud (ten), Fernando de Lucia (ten), Francesco Marconi (ten), Giovanni Battista de Negri (ten), Antonio Paoli (ten), et al. Enterprise ("Vocal Archives" series) 3-▲ ENT VA 2104

The World of Singing, Vol 4:The Italian School Part 1:Tenors before World War I, Book 2, w. Edoardo Garbin (ten), Fiorello Giraud (ten), Florencio Costantino (ten), Antonio Paoli (ten), Giuseppe Borgatti (ten), Carlo Albani (ten), Amedeo Bassi (ten), Piero Schivazzi (ten), Elvino Ventura (ten), Giovanni Zenatello (ten) Enterprise ("Vocal Archives" series) 3-▲ ENT VA 2107

Caruso, Mariano (ten)

Puccini, G.:Madama Butterfly, w. C. Petrella (sop—Madama Butterfly), M. Masini (mez—Suzuki), M. C. Foscale (sgr—Kate Pinkerton), F. Tagliavini (ten—Pinkerton), M. Caruso (ten—Goro), G. Taddei (bar—Sharpless), A. Albertini (bar—Yamadori), A. Biancardo (bass—Bonze), A. Questa (cnd), Turin RAI Orch, Cetra Chorus *(rec 1953)* Cetra Classic 2-▲ CDO 10 [AAD]

Verdi, G.:Falstaff, w. Anna Moffo (sop—Nannetta), Renata Tebaldi (sop—Alice Ford), Anna Maria Canali (mez—Meg Page), Giulietta Simionato (mez—Dame Quickly), Mariano Caruso (ten—Doctor Caius), Alvinio Misciano (ten—Fenton), Luigi Vellucci (ten—Bardolfo), Tito Gobi (bar—Falstaff), Carnell MacNeil (bar—Ford), Kenneth Smith (bass—Pistola), T. Serafin (cnd), *(orch unknown)* *(rec Chicago, 1958)* Legato Classics 2-▲ LCD 206-2 [ADD]

Carwood, Andrew (ten)

Vivaldi, A.:Gloria, RV.589, w. P. Kwella (sop), E. Priday (sop), C. Wyn-Rogers (alt), S. Darlington (cnd), Hanover Band, Christ Church Cathedral Choir Oxford Nimbus ▲ NI 5278 [DDD]

Vivaldi, A.:Gloria (& Intro), RV.588, w. P. Kwella (sop), E. Priday (sop), C. Wyn-Rogers (alt), S. Darlington (cnd), Hanover Band, Christ Church Cathedral Choir Oxford Nimbus ▲ NI 5278 [DDD]

Casa, Joan (sgr)

Sings Catalan Songs, w. J. Carreras, José (ten), Barcelona Liceu Theater SO Sony Classical ▲ SK 47177

Casa, Lisa della (sop)

Beethoven, L. van:Fidelio (sels), w. E. Schlüte (sop), J. Patzak (ten), R. Schock (ten), F. Frantz (b-bar), H. Alsen (bass), W. Furtwängler (cnd), Vienna State Opera Orch, Vienna State Opera Chorus—Overture, 16 arias & choruses *(rec live, Salzburg Festspielhaus Aug. 3, 1948)* Melodram 2-▲ CDM 25009 [ADD]

Einem, G. von:Der Prozess, w. Lisa Della Casa (sop—Frl. Bürstner/Die Frau des Gerichtsdieners/Leni), Peter Klein (ten—Der Direktorstellvertreter/Der Student), Max Lorenz (ten—Josef K.), Erich Majkut (ten—Ein Bursche), László Szemere (ten—Titorelli), Alois Pernerstorfer (b-bar—Willem/Der Gerichtsdiener), Alfred Poell (b-bar—Der Advokat), Walter Berry (bass—Franz/Kanzleidirektor), Oskar Czerwenka (bass—Der Untersuchungsrichter/Der Prügler), Ludwig Hofmann (bass—Der Aufseher/Ein Passant/Der Geistliche/Der Fabrikant), Polly Batic (sgr—Frau Grubach), Endreh Koreh (sgr—Albert K.), Luise Leitner (sgr—Ein buckliges Mädchen), K. Böhm (cnd), Vienna PO, Vienna State Opera Chorus *(rec Aug 17, 1953)* Orfeo d'or ("Festspiel Dokumente" series) 2-▲ 392952 (m)

Mozart, W.A.:Arias, w. Arleen Augér (sop), Kathleen Battle (sop), Irma Beilke (sop), Helena Braun (sop), Maria Cebotari (sop), Ileana Cotrubas (sop), Helen Donath (sop), Mirella Freni (sop), Reri Grist (sop), Edita Gruberova (sop), Elisabeth Grümmer (sop), Hilde Güden (sop), Ingeborg Hallstein (sop), Luise Helletsgruber (sop), Gundula Janowitz (sop), Sena Jurinac (sop), Erika Köth (sop), Evelyn Lear (sop), Wilma Lipp (sop), Margaret Marshall (sop), Edith Mathis (sop), Jarmila Novotna (sop), Margherita Perras (sop), Lucia Popp (sop), Elisabeth Rethberg (sop), Anneliese Rothenberger (sop), Elisabeth Schumann (sop), Elisabeth Schwarzkopf (sop), Graziolla Sciutti (sop), Irmgard Seefried (sop), Graziella Sciutti (sop), Julia Varady (sop), Agnes Baltsa (mez), Margit Bokor (mez), Brigitte Fassbaender (mez), Christa Ludwig (mez), Ann Murray (mez), Francisco Araiza (ten), Anton Dermota (ten), Helge Rosvaenge (ten), Rudolf Schock (ten), Peter Schreier (ten), Leopold Simoneau (ten), Eric Tappy (ten), Richard Tauber (ten), Gösta Winbergh (ten), Josef Witt (ten), Fritz Wunderlich (ten), Christian Boesch (bar), Willy Domgraf-Fassbaender (bar), Karl Dönch (bar), Dietrich Fischer-Dieskau (bar), Erich Kunz (bar), Eberhard Wächter (bar), Hans Hotter (b-bar), Paul Schöffler (b-bar), Cesare Siepi (b-bar), José Van Dam (b-bar), Walter Berry (bass), Geraint Evans (bass), Nicolai Ghiaurov (bass), Alexander Kipnis (bass), Richard Mayr (bass), Kurt Moll (bass), James Morris (bass), Ezio Pinza (bass), Martti Talvela (bass), Giorgio Tozzi (bass), Hans Duhan (sgr), Res Fischer (sgr), Marie Gerhart (sgr), *(various orchs & cnds)*—sels from Idomeneo, Die Entführung aus der Serail, Le nozze di Figaro, Don Giovanni, Così fan tutte, Die Zauberflöte & various arias Orfeo d'or ("Festspiel Dokumente" series) 5-▲ 408955

Mozart, W.A.:Così fan tutte, w. E. Loose (sop), C. Ludwig (mez), A. Dermota (ten), E. Kunz (bar), P. Schoeffler (bass) London 2-▲ 417185-2 [ADD]

Mozart, W.A.:Don Giovanni, w. E. Grümmer (sop—D. Anna), R. Streich (sop—Zerlina), L. Della Casa (sop—D. Elvira), L. Simoneau (ten—Don Ottavio), C. Siepi (bass-baritone—Don Giovanni), W. Berry (bass—Masetto), G. Frick (bass—Il Commendatore), F. Corena (bass—Leporello), D. Mitropoulos (cnd), Vienna PO, Vienna State Opera Chorus *(rec Salzburg, July 24, 1956)* Sony Classical 3-▲ SM3K 64263 [ADD]

Mozart, W.A.:Don Giovanni, w. S. Danco (sop), A. Dermota (ten), C. Siepi (b-bar), F. Corena (bass), J. Krips (cnd), Vienna PO, Vienna State Opera Chorus London 3-▲ 411626-2 [ADD]

Mozart, W.A.:Don Giovanni, w. E. Grümmer (sop), R. Streich (sop), L. Simoneau (ten), C. Siepi (b-bar), G. Frick (bass), W. Berry (bass), F. Corena (bass), D. Mitropoulos (cnd), Vienna PO, Vienna State Opera Chorus [I] *(rec live, Salzburg, July 24, 1956)* Arkadia 3-▲ 552 (m) [ADD]

Mozart, W.A.:Requiem, w. Ira Malaniuk (cta), Anton Dermota (ten), Cesare Siepi (b-bar), B. Walter (cnd), Vienna PO, Vienna State Opera Chorus *(rec Salzburg, July 26, 1956)* Orfeo d'or ("Festspiel Dikumente" series) ▲ C 430961 (m) [ADD]

Mozart, W.A.:Zauberflöte, w. E. Köth (sop), G. Sciurri (sop), L. Simoneau (ten), W. Berry (bass), K. Böhme (bass), G. Szell (cnd), Vienna PO, Vienna State Opera Chorus [G] *(rec live at the Salzburg Festival, July 27, 1959)* Melodram ("Connaisseur" series) 2-▲ MEL 27505 (m) [AAD]

Recital *(rec live, 1948–67)* Melodram 2-▲ CDM 26526 [ADD]

Strauss, R.:Arabella, w. M. Reining (sop), R. Anday (cta), H. Hotter (b-bar), G. Hann (bass), J. Patzak (ten), K. Böhm (cnd), Vienna PO, Vienna State Opera Chorus *(rec live, Salzburg Festival, 8/12/47)* Melodram 3-▲ MEL 37077

Strauss, R.:Arabella, w. M. Reining (sop), H. Taubmann (ten), H. Hotter (b-bar), K. Böhm (cnd), Vienna PO *(rec Salzburg Festival, 1947)* Deutsche Grammophon 3-▲ 445342-2 (m) [ADD]

Strauss, R.:Arabella, w. H. Gueden (sop), I. Malaniuk (cta), A. Dermota (ten), W. Kmentt (ten), G. London (bar), O. Edelmann (bass), G. Solti (cnd), Vienna PO [G] London ("Grand Opera" series) 2-▲ 430387-2 [ADD]

Casa, Lisa della (sop) (cont.)
Strauss, R.:Ariadne auf Naxos, w. H. Güden (sop), I. Seefried (sop), R. Schock (ten), P. Schöffler (bass), K. Böhm (cnd), Vienna PO *(rec Salzburg Festival, 1954)* Deutsche Grammophon 2-▲ 445332-2 (m) [ADD]
Strauss, R.:Ariadne auf Naxos, w. Lisa Della Casa (sop—Ariadne), Lisa Otto (sop—Najade), Rudolf Schock (ten—Bacchus), Leonore Kirschstein (sgr—Echo), Nada Puttar (sgr—Dryade), A. Erede (cnd), Berlin PO Testament ▲ SBT 1036 [ADD]
Strauss, R.:Der Rosenkavalier, w. Jarmila Barton (sop—Marianne), Lisa Della Casa (sop—Sophie), Sena Jurinac (sop—Octavian), Ilva Ligabue (sop—Orphan), Elisabeth Schwarzkopf (sop—Marschallin), Else Schürhoff (mez—Annina), Luisa Villa (mez—Milliner), Hugues Cuénod (ten—Marschallin's majordomo), Erich Majkut (ten—Valzacchi), Giuseppe Nessi (ten—Animal seller), Luciano Della Pergola (ten—Lackey/Faninal's majordomo), Antonio Pirino (ten—An Italian Singer), Gino Del Signore (ten—Lackey/Waiter), Erich Kunz (bar—Herr von Faninal), Paolo Pedani (bar—Lackey), Attilo Barbesi (bass—Lackey/Waiter), Enrico Campi (bass—Waiter), Otto Edelmann (bass—Baron Ochs), Bruno Fichtinger (bass—Notary), Franco Taino (bass—Waiter), Maria Amadini (sgr—Orphan), Pina Carrillo (sgr—Orphan), Joszi Trojan Regar (sgr—Innkeeper), H. von Karajan (cnd), La Scala Orch, La Scala Chorus *(rec La Scala Theater, Milan, Jan. 26, 1952)* Legato Classics 3-▲ LCD 197-3
Strauss, R.:Der Rosenkavalier, w. H. Gueden (sop), S. Jurinac (sop), E. Kunz (bar), O. Edelmann (b-bar), H. von Karajan (cnd), Vienna PO, Vienna State Opera Chorus [G] *(rec live in Salzburg, 7/26/60)* Arkadia 3-▲ 213 [ADD]
Strauss, R.:Der Rosenkavalier (sels), w. L. Della Casa (sop—Feldmarschallin), S. Jurinac (sop—Octavian), H. von Karajan (cnd), Vienna PO *(rec live, Salzburg, 7/26/60)* Arkadia 3-▲ 227 [ADD]
Strauss, R.:songs, w. Sebastian Peschko (pno)—Morgen!, Op. 27/4; Einerlei, Op. 69/3; Waldseligkeit, Op. 49/1; Hat gesagt...bleibt's nicht dabei, Op. 36/3; Seitdem dein Aug' in meines schaute, Op. 17/1; Schlechtes Wetter, Op. 69/5; Begreit, Op. 39/4 Testament ▲ SBT 1036 [ADD]
Wagner, R.:Die Meistersinger von Nürnberg, w. I. Malaniuk (cta), H. Hopf (ten), O. Edelmann (b-bar), K. Böhme (bass), H. Knappertsbusch (cnd), Bayreuth Festival Orch, Bayreuth Festival Chorus [G] *(rec live, 1952)* Arkadia 4-▲ 440 (m) [AAD]

Casagrande, Natacha (sgr)
Mendelssohn, F.:Psalms, Op. 78, w. Christiane Buntschu (sgr), Kurt Kempf (sgr), Pablo Pavon (sgr), M. Corboz (cnd), Lausanne Vocal Ensemble *(rec Lausanne Cathedral, Jan. 29-31, 1994)* FNAC Music ▲ 592298 [DDD]

Casali, G. (bass)
Rossini, G.:L'inganno felice, w. S. Rigacci (sop—Isabella), E. Palacio (ten—Duke Bertrando), G. Gatti (bar—Batone), R. Ripesi (bass—Tarabotto), G. Casali (bass—Ormondo), F. Maestri (cnd), In Canto CO *(rec Dec. 1992)* Bongiovanni 2-▲ GB 2133/34 [DDD]

Casalin, Luca (ten)
Scarlatti, A.:Concerti sacri, motetti, w. Ilaria Galgani (sop), Susanna Anselmi (cta), Daniele Tonini (bass), Il Ruggiero—Nos. 1-5 Tactus ▲ TC 661903 [DDD]
Scarlatti, A.:Concerti sacri, motetti, w. Ilaria Galgani (sop), Susanna Anselmi (cta), Daniele Tonini (bass), Il Ruggiero—Nos. 6-10 Tactus ▲ TC 661904 [DDD]

Casarini, Gianfranco (bass)
Verdi, G.:Un ballo in maschera, w. R. Orlandi Malaspina (sop—Ameilia), D. Mazzuccato (sop—Oscar), A. Lazzarini (mez—Ulrica), L. Pavarotti (ten—Riccardo), M. Zanasi (bar—Renato), A. Zerbini (bass—Samuel), G. Casarini (bass—Tom), G. Zecchillo (bass—Sil) Golden Age of Opera 2-▲ GAO 164/65 [ADD]
Verdi, G.:Don Carlos, w. Katia Ricciarelli (sop), Fiorenza Cossotto (mez), Guido Fabbris (ten), Veriano Luchetti (ten), Piero Cappuccilli (bar), Nicolai Ghiaurov (bass), Alessandro Maddalena (bass), Aracelly Haengel (sgr), Marisa Salimbeni (sgr), Giorgio Zoranca (sgr), G. Prêtre (cnd), *(orch unknown)* Great Opera Performances 3-▲ GOP 777
Verdi, G.:Luisa Miller, w. K. Ricciarelli (sop—Luisa), M. G. Piolatto (mez—Laura), S. Silva (cta—Federica), J. Carreras (ten—Rodolfo), E. Pranod (ten—A Peasant), R. Bruson (bar—Miller), G. Casarini (bar—Wurm) M. Rinaudo (bass—Count Walter), F. Previtali (cnd), Turin Teatro Regio Orch, Turin Teatro Regio Chorus *(rec May 9, 1976)* Legato Classics 2-▲ LCD 180 [ADD]

Case, Anna (sop)
Phonograph Society of New South Wales Presents Anna Case *(rec 1920-30)* Claremont ▲ GSE 785068 [AAD]

Case, J. Carol (bar)
Elgar, E.:The Apostles, w. S. Armstrong (sop), H. Watts (cta); R. Tear (ten), B. Luxon (bar), C. Grant (bass), A. Boult (cnd), London PO, London Phil Chorus, Downe House School Choir [E] EMI Classics ▲ CDMB 64206
Elgar, E.:The Shepherd's Song, w. D. Ibbott (pno) Saga Classics ▲ 3353 [ADD]
Fauré, G.:Pavane Orch, w. R. Chilcott (trb), D. Willcocks (cnd), New Philharmonia Orch, King's College Choir Cambridge [choral ver.] EMI ▲ CDM 64715
Fauré, G.:Requiem, w. J. Price (sop), N. Boulanger (cnd), BBC SO, BBC Sym Chorus *(rec live, London Nov. 1968)* Intaglio ▲ INCD 703-1 [ADD]
Fauré, G.:Requiem, w. R. Chilcott (trb), D. Willcocks (cnd), New Philharmonia Orch, King's College Choir Cambridge EMI Classics ▲ CDM 64715
Vaughan Williams, R.:Sym 1, w. N. Armstrong (sop), A. Boult (cnd), London PO, London Phil Chorus EMI Classics ▲ CDM 64016

Casellato, Renato (ten)
Bellini, V.:Beatrice di Tenda, w. M. Freni (sop), C. Gonzales (mez), C. Desderi (bar), M. Arena (cnd), *(orch unknown) (rec live, Bologna 1976)* Legato Classics 2-▲ LCD 152-2 [ADD]
Donizetti, G.:Lucia di Lammermoor (sels), w. M. Callas (sop), P. Cappuccilli (bar), T. Serafin (cnd), Philharmonia Orch—highlights *(rec live, London 3/16-21/59)* EMI Classics (Studio) ▲ CDM 63934 ■ EG 63934
Rossini, G.:Il barbiere di Siviglia, w. T. Berganza (mez), S. Bruscantini (bar), G. Tozzi (bass), B. Bartoletti (cnd), Buenos Aires Teatro Colón Orch, Buenos Aires Teatro Colón Chorus [I] *(rec 1969)* Golden Age of Opera 2-▲ GAO 149/50

Casellato-Lamberti, G. (ten)
Verdi, G.:I vespri siciliani (sels), w. L. Gencer (sop), La Scala Orch, La Scala Chorus—one solo soprano aria & three duets from Act 4 [I] Myto 2-▲ 2 MCD 90524 [ADD]

Caselli, Dario (bass)
Puccini, G.:Tosca, w. Ranata Tebaldi (sop), Gian Franco Volante (trb), Piero de Palma (ten), Giuseppe Campora (ten), Enzo Mascherini (bar), Fernando Corena (bass), Antonio Sacchetti (bass), A. Erede (cnd), St. Cecilia Academy Orch Rome, St. Cecilia Academy Chorus Rome *(rec 1952)* Andromeda 2-▲ ANR 2539 [ADD]
Verdi, G.:Aida, w. Renata Tebaldi (sop—Aida), Ebe Stignani (mez—Amneris), Mario Del Monaco (ten—Radamès), Piero de Palma (ten—Messenger), Aldo Protti (bar—Amonasro), Fernando Corena (bass—King), Dario Caselli (bass—Ramfis), A. Erede (cnd), St. Cecilia Academy Orch Rome, St. Cecilia Academy Chorus Rome *(rec 1952)* Theorema 2-▲ TH 121133/34
Verdi, G.:Otello, w. Renata Tebaldi (sop—Desdemona), Luisa Ribacchi (mez—Emilia), Angelo Mercuriali (ten—Roderigo), Mario del Monaco (ten—Otello), Piero de Palma (ten—Cassio), Aldo Protti (bar—Iago), Dario Caselli (bass—A Herald), Fernando Corena (bass—Lodovico), Pierluigi Martinucci (bass—Montano), A. Erede (cnd), St. Cecilia Academy Orch Rome, St. Cecilia Academy Chorus Rome Theorema ▲ TH 121141/142

Casertano, Angelo (ten)
Puccini, G.:La Bohème, w. Katia Ricciarelli (sop), Francisco Araiza (ten), Stefano Antonucci (bar), Claudio Giombi (bar), Paata Burchuladze (bass), Alfredo Mariotti (bass), Alberto Noli (bass), Andrea Piccinni (bass), Lauren Broglia (sgr), A. Guadagno (cnd), Arena di Verona Orch, Limburg Cathedral Boys' Chorus Koch Schwann 2-▲ SCH 315922
Verdi, G.:Nabucco, w. Monica Pick-Hieronimi (sop), Anna Schiatti (sop), Mina Blum (sop), Gilberto Maffezzoni (ten), Paolo Gavanelli (bass), Paata Burchuladze (bass), Franco Federici (bass), A. Guadagno (cnd), Arena di Verona Orch, Arena di Verona Chorus *(rec Berlin, Spring 1996)* Koch Schwann 2-▲ SCH CD 364272

Casey, Gerard (sgr)
Lloyd Webber, A.:Music of, w. L. Garrett (sgr), Dave Willets (sgr), C. Corcoran (sgr), S. Campbell (sgr), Royal PO, Royal PO Pops Orch, Royal PO Concert Orch—sels from The Phantom of the Opera; Evita; Cats; Joseph & the Amazing Technicolor Dreamcoat; Jesus Christ Superstar; Tell Me on a Sunday; Song & Dance; Starlight Express; Sunset Boulevard Silva America 2-▲ SILCD 1044 [DDD] ■ SILMC 1044

Casian, Elena (mez)
Bretan, N.:The Evening Star, w. Adriana Croitoru (sop—King's Daughter), Elena Casian (mez—Lady-in-Waiting), Marius Budoiu (ten—Mariner), Ioan Pojar (ten—Page), Ionel Voineag (ten—Evening Star), Bálint Szabó (bass—Michael the Archangel), B. Hary (cnd), Transylvania PO Cluj *(rec Cluj, Sept 1994)* Nimbus ▲ NI 5463 [DDD]

Casoni, Biancamaria (mez)
Bellini, V.:La straniera, w. M. Caballé (sop), A. Zambon (ten), A. Guadagno (cnd), American Opera Society Orch, American Opera Society Chorus *(rec 1969)* Melodram 2-▲ MLO 270111 [DDD]
Donizetti, G.:Gemma di Vergy, w. Montserrat Caballé (sop—Gemma di Vergy), Biancamaria Casoni (mez—Ida di Greville), Giorgio Lamberti (ten—Tamas), Renato Bruson (bar—Conte di Vergy), Mario Machì (bass—Rolando), Mario Rinaudo (bass—Guido), A. Gatto (cnd), Naples Teatro San Carlo Orch, Naples Teatro San Carlo Chorus *(rec Naples, Dec. 12, 1975)* Myto 2-▲ 952124
Massenet, J.:Werther, w. E. Ravaglia (sop), C. Bergonzi (ten), D. Trimarchi (bar), O. de Fabritiis (cnd), Naples Teatro San Carlo Orch, Naples Teatro San Carlo Chorus [I] *(rec live, Naples, 2/13/69)* Melodram 2-▲ 27058 [AAD]
Mozart, W.A.:Missa, K.317, w. Teresa Stich-Randall (sop), Pietro Bottazzo (ten), K. Ristenpart (cnd), Sarre CO, Herbert Schmolzi (cnd), Sarrebrück Conservatory Choir Accord ▲ ACD 220252 [AAD]
Mozart, W.A.:Vesperae solennes, w. Teresa Stich-Randall (sop), Pietro Bottazzo (ten), K. Ristenpart (cnd), Sarre CO, Herbert Schmolzi (cnd), Sarrebrück Conservatory Choir Accord ▲ ACD 220252 [AAD]
Rossini, G.:La Cenerentola, w. U. Benelli (ten), S. Bruscantini (bar), A. Mariotti (bass), P. Bellugi (cnd), Berlin RSO, Berlin Radio Chorus [I] Acanta 2-▲ CD 43271 [DDD]
Zandonai, R.:Francesca da Rimini, w. Lydia Marimpietri (sop—Biancofiore), Magda Olivero (sop—Francesca), Pinuccia Perotti (sop—Samaritana), Edda Vincenzi (sop—Garsenda), Gabriella Carturan (mez—Smaragdi), Biancamaria Casoni (mez—Altichiara), Anna Maria Rota (cta—Donella), Athos Cesarini (ten—Archer), Angelo Mercuriali (ten—Ser Toldo Berardengo), Mario del Monaco (ten—Paolo), Piero de Palma (ten—Malatestino), Rinaldo Pelizzoni (ten—Prisoner), Gianpiero Malaspina (bar—Gianciotto), Dino Mantovani (bar—Jester), Enrico Campi (bass—Ostasio), Giuseppe Morresi (bass—Tower warden), G. Gavazzeni (cnd), La Scala Orch, La Scala Chorus *(rec La Scala Theatre, Milan, June 4, 1959)* Legato Classics 2-▲ LCD 186-2

Cass, P. (sgr)
Porter, C.:Fifty Million Frenchmen, w. H. McGillin (sgr), K. Criswell (sop), K. McClelland (sgr), S. Powell (sgr), K. Ziemba (sgr), J. Graae (sgr), J. Harder (sgr), S. Waara (sgr), J. LeClerc (sgr) [1991 studio cast] New World ▲ 80417-2 [DDD]

Cassidy, Geraldine (sgr)
Míča, F.A.:L'origine di Jaromeriz in Moravia, w. Manfred Equiluz (sgr), Geraldine Geister (sgr), Michael Nowak (sgr), Le Monde Classique [Cz] Supraphon 2-▲ SUP 112192 [DDD]

Cassilly, Richard (ten)
Beethoven, L. van:Leonore (opera), w. Helen Donath (sop), Edda Moser (sop), Eberhard Büchner (ten), Theo Adam (b-bar), Hermann Christian Polster (bass), Karl Ridderbusch (bass), H. Blomstedt (cnd), Dresden Staatskapelle, Leipzig Radio Chorus Berlin Classics ▲ BER 1140
Bellini, V.:I Capuleti e i Montecchi, w. L. Hurley (sop), G. Simionato (mez), E. Flagello (bass), A. Gamson (cnd), American Opera Society Orch, American Opera Society Chorus [I] *(rec live, New York 10/14/58)* Melodram ("Connaisseur" series) 2-▲ CDM 27509 [ADD]
Berlioz, H.:Les Troyens, w. R. Resnik (mez—Dido), E. Steber (sop—Cassandra), R. Cassily (ten—Aeneas), R. Lawrence (cnd), American Opera Society Orch, American Opera Society Chorus *(rec live, Carnegie Hall, 12/29/59 & 1/12/60)* VAI Audio 3-▲ VAIA 1006-3 [ADD]
Floyd, C.:Susannah, w. Phyllis Curtin (sop—Susannah Polk), Richard Cassilly (ten—Sam Polk), Norman Treigle (bass—Olin Blitch), Marietta Muhs Cosenza (sgr—Mrs. McLean), Marilyn Davidson (sgr—Mrs. Gleaton), Kay Long (sgr—Mrs. Hayes), Jean Young (sgr—Mrs. Ott), Alton Brim (sgr—Elder Hayes), Thomas Carter (sgr—Elder Gleaton), Jack Davis (sgr—Elder McLean), Keith Kaldenberg (sgr—Little Bat McLean), Burton Parker (sgr—Elder Ott), K. Andersson (cnd), New Orleans Opera Orch, New Orleans Opera Chorus *(rec Mar 31, 1962)* VAI Audio 2-▲ VAIA 1115-2 [ADD]
Janácek, L.:Jenůfa (sels), w. M. Collier (sop), A. Varnay (sop), J. Lanigan (ten), R. Kubelik (cnd), Royal Opera House Orch, Royal Opera House Chorus Covent Garden—eight solo, duet & trio arias featuring Astrid Varnay [G] *(rec live at Covent Garden, Feb. 24, 1968)* Myto 2-▲ 2 MCD 90422 [ADD]
Mahler, G.:Das Lied von der Erde, w. Lili Chookasian (cta), W. Susskind (cnd), Cincinnati SO *(rec 1978)* Vox Box 2-▲ CDX 5138 [ADD]
Saint-Saëns, C.:Samson et Dalila, w. Shirley Verrett (mez), Robert Massard (bar), G. Prêtre (cnd), La Scala Orch *(rec La Scala Theatre, May 30, 1969)* Arkadia ("Historical Performances" series) 2-▲ 495
Schoenberg, A.:Moses und Aaron, w. G. Reich (nar), P. Boulez (cnd), BBC SO, Ensemble InterContemporain, BBC Singers *(rec Nov. 30-Dec. 06, 1974)* Sony Classical 2-▲ SM2K 48456 [ADD]

Cassinelli, Antonio (bass)
Rossini, G.:Il barbiere di Siviglia, w. R. Broilo (sop—Berta), G. Simionato (mez—Rosina), L. Infantino (ten—Almaviva), G. Taddei (bar—Figaro), C. Badioli (bass—Bartolo), A. Cassinelli (bass—Basilio), F. Previtali (cnd), Milan RAI SO, Milan RAI Chorus *(rec 1950)* Cetra Classic 2-▲ CDO 6 [AAD]
Verdi, G.:Un giorno di regno, w. J. Norman (sop), F. Cossotto (mez), J. Carreras (ten), I. Wixell (bar), V. Sardinero (bar), W. Ganzarolli (bar), P. Elvin (bass), L. Gardelli (cnd), Royal PO, Ambrosian Singers Philips 2-▲ 422429-2 [ADD]
Verdi, G.:Nabucco, w. C. Mancini (sop—Abigaille), G. Gatti (sop—Fenena), B. Preziosa (sop—Anna), M. Binci (ten—Ismaele), L. Francardi (ten—Abdallo), P. Silveri (bar—Nabucodonosor), A. Cassinelli (bass—Zaccaria), A. Gaggi (bass—High Priest of Baal), F. Previtali (cnd), Rome RAI Orch, Rome RAI Chorus *(rec Rome, 1951)* Cetra Classic 2-▲ CDO 26 [ADD]

Cassinelli, Riccardo (ten)
Cimarosa, D.:I Finti nobili (sels), w. C. Cadelo (sop), M.G. Ferracini (sop), R. Malacarne (ten), G. Sarti (bar), B. Marinotti (cnd), RTSI Orch—Li sposi per accidente (Act 3) *(rec 1970)* Foyer ▲ FOY 2057 [AAD]
Cimarosa, D.:Il Matrimonio segreto, w. Alda Noni (sop), Giulietta Simionato (mez), Cesare Valletti (ten), Sesto Bruscantini (bar), Rovero (sgr), M. Wolf-Ferrari (cnd), Florence Maggio Musicale Orch *(rec 1950)* Cetra Classic 2-▲ CDO 32

Cassis, Alessandro (bar)
Catalani, A.:Loreley, w. M. Colalillo (sop), M. L. Garbato (sop), P. Visconti (ten), N. Annovazzi (cnd), Lucca Teatro Comunale del Giglio Orch, Lucca Teatro Comunale del Giglio Chorus *(rec live 9/19/82)* Bongiovanni 2-▲ GB 2015/16 [ADD]
Smareglia, A.:Nozze istrane, w. Maria Chiara (sop—Marussa), Eleonora Iancovich (cta—Luze), Ruggero Bondino (ten—Lorenzo), Alessandro Cassis (bar—Nicola), Alessandro Maddalena (bar—Biagio), Carlo Zardo (bass—Bara Menico), M. Wolf-Ferrari (cnd), Trieste Teatro Comunale Giuseppe Verdi Orch, Trieste Teatro Comunale G. Verdi Chorus *(rec Trieste, Feb 17, 1973)* Bongiovanni ("Il Mito dell'Opera" series) 2-▲ 1133/34-2 [ADD]
Verdi, G.:Ernani, w. Licia Galvano (sop—Giovanna), Leyla Gencer (sop—Elvira), Carlo Bergonzi (ten—Ernani), Nino Valori (ten—Don Riccardo), Piero Cappuccilli (bar—Don Carlo), Alessandro Cassis (bar—Jago), Ruggero Raimondi (bass—Don Ruy Gomez de Silva), G. Gavazzeni (cnd), Catania Teatro Massimo Bellini Orch, Catania Teatro Massimo Bellini Chorus *(rec live, Catania, Jan 15, 1972)* Arkadia 2-▲ 621 [ADD]

Cassolas, Constantine (ten)
Alfonso El Sabio:Cantigas de Santa Maria, w. J. DeGaetani (sop), N. Kepros (troubadour), M. Jaffee (cnd), Waverly Consort [Port] *(rec 1972)* Vanguard Classics ("The Bach Guild" series) ▲ OVC 2013 [ADD]
Gideon, M.:The Condemned Playground, w. P. Bryn-Julson (sop), Jahoda, *(ensemble unknown)* CRI ■ C 343

Castagna, Bruna (mez)
Beethoven, L. van:Missa Solemnis, w. Zinka Milanov (sop), Jussi Björling (ten), Alexander Kipnis (bass), A. Toscanini (cnd), NBC SO, Westminster Choir *(rec 1940)* Grammofono 2000 ▲ GRM 78626
Beethoven, L. van:Missa Solemnis, w. Z. Milanov (sop), J. Björling, A. Kipnis (bass), A. Toscanini (cnd), NBC SO, Westminster Choir [L] *(rec live 12/28/40)* Melodram 3-▲ MEL 38006
Bellini, V.:Norma, w. Gina Cigna (sop—Norma), Thelma Votipka (mez—Clotilde), Bruna Castagna (cta—Adalgisa), Giovanni Martinelli (ten—Pollione), Giodano Paltrinieri (ten—Flavio), Ezio Pinza (bass—Oroveso), E. Panizza (cnd), *(orch unknown) (rec live, New York, Feb. 20, 1937)* The Fourties 2-▲ ENT FT 1517
Carlo Tagliabue, w. C. Tagliabue (bar), Margherita Carosio (sop), Ettore Bergamaschi (ten), Zinka Milanov (sop), Frederick Jagel (ten), Norman Cordon (bass), Renata Tebaldi (sop), Alfredo Colella (bass) *(rec in studio and live, 1928-1951)* Bongiovanni ▲ GB 1070-2 [ADD]
Verdi, G.:Aida, w. Gina Cigna (sop), Giovanni Martinelli (ten), Ezio Pinza (bass), E. Panizza (cnd), New York Metropolitan Opera Orch, New York Metropolitan Opera Chorus *(rec live, Feb 6, 1937)* The Fourties 2-▲ ENT 1501
Verdi, G.:Un ballo in maschera, w. Stella Andreva (sop—Oscar), Zinka Milanov (sop—Amelia), Bruna Castagna (cta—Ulrica), Jussi Björling (ten—Riccardo), Lodovico Oliviero (ten—Un Servo D'Amelia), John Cartet (bar—Un Giudice), Alexander Sved (bar—Renato), Normann Cordon (bass—Samuel), Arthur Kent (bass—Silvano), Nicola Moscona (bass—Tom), E. Panizza (cnd), *(orch unknown) (rec live, New York, Dec. 14, 1940)* The Fourties 2-▲ ENT FT 1515
Verdi, G.:Requiem Mass, w. Z. Milanov (sop), J. Björling (ten), N. Moscona (bass), A. Toscanini (cnd), NBC SO, Westminster Choir [L] *(rec 11/23/40)* Melodram 3-▲ MEL 38006
Verdi, G.:Requiem Mass, w. Z. Milanov (sop), J. Björling (ten), N. Moscona (bass), A. Toscanini (cnd), NBC SO, Westminster Choir *(rec Mar. 4, 1938)* Legato Classics 2-▲ LCD 178-2
Verdi, G.:Requiem Mass, w. Zinka Milanov (sop), Jussi Björling (ten), Nicola Moscona (bass), A. Toscanini (cnd), NBC SO, Westminster Choir *(rec Nov 23, 1940)* Music & Arts 2-▲ CD 240
Verdi, G.:Il trovatore, w. Norina Greco (sop), Jussi Björling (ten), Nicola Moscona (bass), Francesco Valentino (sgr), F. Calusio (cnd), *(orch & chorus unknown)* Enterprise ("The Radio Years" series) 2-▲ ENT 44 (m)
Verdi, G.:Il trovatore, w. Norina Greco (sop—Leonora), Bruna Castagna (cta—Azucena), Jussi Björling (ten—Manrico), Francesco Valentino (bar—Count di Luna), Nicola Moscona (bass—Ferrando), F. Calusio (cnd), *(orch unknown) (rec live, New York, Jan. 11, 1941)* The Fourties 2-▲ ENT FT 1507

Castagna, Maria (mez)
Mascagni, P.:Cavalleria rusticana, w. G. A. Lombardi (sop), I. Mannarini (mez), A. Melandri (ten), G. Lulli (bar), L. Molajoli (cnd), La Scala Orch, La Scala Chorus *(rec 1930)* Preiser ▲ 90042 (m) [AAD]

Castaldi, Peter (bar)
Handel, G.F.:Faramondo, w. Julianne Baird (sop—Clotilde), Mary Ellen Callahan (sop—Adolfo), D'Anna Fortunado (mez—Faramondo), Jennifer Lane (mez—Rosimonda), Drew Minter (alt—Gernando), Peter Castaldi (bar—Gustavo), Mark Singer (bar—Tebaldo), Edward Brewer (hpd), R. Palmer (cnd), Brewer CO [period instrs] Vox Classics 3-▲ VOX3 7536 [DDD]
Handel, G.F.:Tolomeo, Rè di Egitto, w. Brenda Harris (sop—Seleuce), Andrea Matthews (sop—Elisa), Mary Ann Hart (mez—Alessandro), Jennifer Lane (mez—Tolomeo), Peter Castaldi (bar—King Araspe), Bradley Brookshire (hpd), R.A. Clark (cnd), Manhattan CO *(rec St. Jean Baptiste Church, NY, Mar 1995)* Vox Classics 3-▲ VOX 7530
Rorem, N.:A Childhood Miracle, w. Michele Couture (sop—Peony), Darcy Dunn (sgr—Violet), Madeline Tsingopoulos (sgr—Mother), Mary Cidoni (sgr—Emma), Patrick Greene (sgr—Snowman), Peter Castaldi (sgr—Father), R. E. Harrell (cnd), Magic Circle CO Newport Classic ▲ NPT 85594 [DDD]

Castejon, Rafael (sgr)
Bretón, T.:La Verbena de la paloma, w. Maria Bayo (sop), Raquel Pierotti (sop), Plácido Domingo (ten), Enrique Baquerizo (sgr), Milagros Martin (sgr), Silva Tro (sgr), A. Ros-Marbá (cnd), Madrid SO Valois ("Zarauela" series) ▲ V 4725

Castel, François (sgr)
Donizetti, G.:La fille du régiment, w. Edita Gruberová (sop), Rosa Laghezza (mez), Deon van der Walt (sgr), Philippe Fourcade (bass), M. Panni (cnd), Munich RSO, Bavarian Radio Chorus Nightingale Classics 2-▲ NIG 70566

Castel, Nico (ten)
Bach, J.S.:Cant 198, w. Marnie Nixon (sop), Elaine Bonazzi (mez), Peter Binder (bar), R. Craft (cnd), Columbia SO, American Concert Choir Sony Classical ("Essential Classics" series) 2-▲ SB2K 62656
Massenet, J.:Manon, w. Beverly Sills (sop—Manon), Plácido Domingo (ten—Des Grieux), Nico Castel (ten—Guillot), Richard Fredricks (bar—Lescaut), Robert Hale (bar—De Brétigny), Malcom Smith (bass—Count de Grieux), J. Rudel (cnd), New York City Opera Orch, New York City Opera Chorus *(rec live, New York, 1969)* Melodram 2-▲ IMC 205008 [ADD]

Castellani, Luisa (sop)
Donatoni, F.:L'Ultima sera, w. A. Molino (cnd), Gruppo Musica Insieme Stradivarius ▲ STR 33315 [DDD]
Górecki, H.-M.:Sym 3, "Sym of Sorrowful Songs", w. A. Nanut (cnd), Slovenian SO Audiophile Classics ▲ 101.040 [DDD]
Pablo, L. de:Tarde de Poetas, w. Jorge Chaminé (bar), J. Pons (cnd), Barcelona Teatro Lliure CO Harmonia Mundi France 2-▲ HMC 901568
Savinio, A.:Album 1914, w. A. Jona (sgr), B. Canino (pno/cel), D. Zaffaroni (bn) Stradivarius ▲ STR 33309 [DDD]

Castets, Maryse (sop)
Massenet, J.:La Vierge, w. M. Command (sop), M. Olmeda (sop), M. Keller (sop), P. Salmon (ten), M. Hacquard (bar), P. Fournillier (cnd), Prague SO, Prague Sym Chorus Koch Schwann 2-▲ CD 313084 [DDD]
Rossini, G.:Péchés de vieillesse (sels), w. M. Georg (mez), J.-L. Maurette (ten), M. Brodard (bar), R. Nolte (bass), E. Kalvelage (pno), C. Spering (org), M. Jorand (perc), Cologne Chorus Musicus—Toast pour le nouvel an, Roméo, La Grande Coquette, Un sou, Chanson de Zora, La Nuit de Noël, Le Dodo des enfants, Le Lazzarone, Adieux à la vie!, Soupirs et sourire, L'Orpheline du Tyrol, Choeur de chasseurs démocrates; *Morceaux réservés*—Ave Maria, Les Amants de Séville, Le Chant des Titans, Chant funèbre [F] *(rec Aug. 1992)* Opus 111 ▲ OPS 30-70 [DDD]

Castle, Joyce (mez)
Fennimore, J.:Berlitz:Introduction to French, w. J. Fennimore (pno) [F] Albany ▲ TROY 023-2 [ADD]
Fennimore, J.:Inscape, w. J. Fennimore (pno) [E] Albany ▲ TROY 023-2 [ADD]
Wolpe, S.:Music of, w. A. Korf (cnd), Parnassus—Musik für Hamlet for Flute, Clarinet & Cello (1929); To the Dancemaster for Mezzo, Clarinet & Piano (1938); Drei Lieder von Bertolt Brecht for Mezzo & Piano (1943); Quartet No. 1 for Trumpet, Tenor Sax, Percussion & Piano (1950); Piece in Two Parts for Six Players (1962); Piece for Two Instrumental Units (1962); Solo Piece for Trumpet (1966); Piece for Trumpet & 7 Instruments (1971) Koch International Classics ▲ KIC 7141-2 [DDD]

Castro Tank, Niza de (sop)
Gomes, A.C.:Il Guarany, w. Niza De Castro Tank (sop—Cecilia), Roque Lotti (ten—Ruy Bento), Manrico Patassini (ten—Pery), Paschoal Raymundo (ten—Don Alvaro), Paulo Fortes (bar—Gonzales), Juan Carlos Ortiz (b-bar—Il Cacico), Waldomiro Furlan (bass—Alonso), José Perrotta (bass—Don Antonio De Mariz), A. Belardi (cnd), São Paulo Teatro Municipale Orch, São Paulo Teatro Municipale Chorus *(rec Studios of the Teatro Municipal, São Paulo, Brazil, 1959)* Arkadia 2-▲ HP 617.2 [AAD]

Casula, Maria (sop)
Mozart, W.A.:Clemenza, w. L. Popp (sop), T. Berganza (mez), B. Fassbaender (mez), T. Franc (bass), F. Krenn (bass), I. Kertész (cnd), Vienna State Opera Orch, Vienna State Opera Chorus London ("Grand Opera" series) 2-▲ 430105-2 [ADD]
Verdi, G.:Un giorno di regno, w. Angelo Romero (bar), Enrico Fissore (bass), Franca Fabbri (sgr), Michele Guento (sgr), Islen Moubayed (sgr), Ruggero Rado (sgr), Bernardino Trotta (sgr), A. Zedda (cnd), *(orch unknown)* Great Opera Performances 2-▲ GOP 782

Caswell, Edward (bass)
Purcell, H.:The Indian Queen, w. Tessa Bonner (sop), Sally Bruce-Payne (alt), Steven Liley (ten), C. Mackintosh (cnd), Purcell Sinfony *(rec St. Bartholomew's Church, Orford, Suffolk, Sept 21-23, 1994)* Linn ▲ CKD 035

Catalani, Nestore (bar)
Stravinsky, I.:Oedipus Rex, w. M. Laszlò (mez—Jocasta), N. Gedda (ten—Oedipus), A. Bertocci (ten—Shepherd), M. Petri (bar—Creon & Tiresias), N. Catalani (bar—Messenger), A. Foà (speaker), H. von Karajan (cnd), Rome RAI SO, Rome RAI Chorus *(rec Dec. 20, 1952)* Stradivarius ▲ DAT 12311 [ADD]

Catarci, Anna (sop)
Lattuada, F.:Le Preziose ridicole, w. S. Valayre (sop—Madelon), A. Catarci (sop—Marotte), A. Cicogna (mez—Cathos), S. Tedesco (ten—La Grange), E. Di Cesare (ten—Mascarille), A. Veccia (bar—Croissy), R. Servile (bar—Jodelet), E. Fissore (bass—Gorgibus), E. Romagna (cnd), Toscanini SO, G. Masini (cnd), Rossini Teatro Comunale Chorus [I] *(rec live, 1991)* Ermitage ▲ ERM 404 [DDD]

Cathcart, Ruth (sgr)
Beethoven, L. van:Sym 9, "Choral Sym", w. Agnes Davis (sop), Robert Betts (sgr), Eugene Lowenthal (sgr), L. Stokowski (cnd), Philadelphia Orch Grammofono 2000 ▲ GRM 78577 (m)
Beethoven, L. van:Sym 9, "Choral Sym", w. Agnes Davis (sop), Robert Betts (sgr), Eugene Lowenthal (sgr), L. Stokowski (cnd), Philadelphia Orch, Philadelphia Orch Chorus *(rec 1934)* Music & Arts ▲ CD 846 [ADD]

Catlin, Wendy (sgr)
Myers, G.:God's Trbn, w. Christine Helfrich (sop), Gordon Myers (bar), Richard Cragg (sgr), Matthew Gillis (sgr), Timothy Pehta (sgr), Paul Norman (sgr), Katherine Mary Hamilton (sgr), Sharon Hunter (sgr), Gloriae Dei Brass Ensemble Paraclete ▲ CDGD 017 [DDD]; ■ GDC 017

Cattaneo, Irene Minghini (mez)
Irene Minghini Cattaneo, w. J. Barbiroll (cnd), La Scala Orch [cnd:C. Sabagno] *(rec for HMV 1928-1930)* Preiser ("Lebendige Vergangenheit" series) ▲ PRE 89008 (m) [AAD]
Verdi, G.:Il trovatore, w. Maria Carena (sop—Leonora), Olga De Franco (sop—Ines), Irene Minghini Cattaneo (mez—Azucena), Aureliano Pertile (ten—Manrico), Giordano Callegari (ten—Ruiz/Messenger), Apollo Granforte (bar—Count), Bruno Carmassi (bass—Ferrando), Antonio Gelli (bass—Old Gypsy), C. Sabajno (cnd), La Scala Orch, Vittore Veneziani (cnd), La Scala Chorus *(rec 1930)* Arkadia ("The 78's" series) 2-▲ 78007 [ADD]

Cauchard, Jacqueline (sgr)
Varney, L.:Les Mousquetaires au couvent, w. Gabrielle Ristori (mez), Camille Rouquetty (ten), Gabriel Bacquier (bar), Louis Musy (b-bar), Pierre Blanc (sgr), Pauline Carton (sgr), Mireille Lacoste (sgr), Colette Riedinger (sgr), R. Benedetti (cnd) Musidisc 2-▲ MUS 202262 [AAD]

Cauli, Arturo (bar)
Spontini, G.:La vestale, w. R. Plowright (sop), G. Pasino (mez), F. Araiza (ten), P. Lefèbvre (ten), F. de Grandis (bass), G. Kuhn (cnd), Munich RSO, Munich Radio Chorus [F] Orfeo 2-▲ 256922 [DDD]

Cava, Carlo (bass)
Bizet, G.:Les Pêcheurs de perles, w. M. Pobbe (sop), F. Tagliavini (ten), U. Savarese (bar), O. de Fabritiis (cnd), Naples Teatro San Carlo Orch, Naples Teatro San Carlo Chorus [I] *(rec live 1/4/59)* Melodram 2-▲ MEL 27069 (m) [AAD]
Donizetti, G.:L'elisir d'amore, w. Renata Scotto (sop), Carlo Bergonzi (ten), Giuseppe Taddei (bar), G. Gavazzeni (cnd), Florence Teatro Comunale Orch, Florence Teatro Comunale Chorus *(rec June 1967)* Pantheon 2-▲ PHE 6612 (m)
Donizetti, G.:Lucia di Lammermoor, w. C. Deutekom (sop), J. Carreras (ten), G. Fioravanti (bar), A. Gatto (cnd), *(orch unknown)* [I] *(rec live in Madrid, 1975)* Standing Room Only 2-▲ SRO 809-2 [ADD]
Rossini, G.:Il barbiere di Siviglia, w. V. de los Angeles (sop), L. Alva (ten), I. Wallace (bass), V. Gui (cnd), Royal PO, Glyndebourne Festival Chorus *(rec 1962)* EMI Classics 2-▲ CDMB 64162
Rossini, G.:Il barbiere di Siviglia (sels), w. G. d' Angelo (sop), G. Carturan (mez), N. Monti (ten), R. Capecchi (bar), G. Giorgetti (bar), G. Tadeo (bass), B. Bartoletti (cnd), Bavarian RSO IMP Collectors Series ▲ IMPX 9022 [AAD]
Verdi, G.:Aida (sels), w. O. Rovere (sop), E. Stignani (mez), M. Filippeschi (ten), B. McFerrin (sgr), V. Bellezza (cnd), Naples Teatro San Carlo Orch, Naples Teatro San Carlo Chorus [I] [highlights] *(rec live, Arena Fregna, Naples, 7/15/56)* Golden Age of Opera ▲ GAO 130 [ADD]
Verdi, G.:Alzira, w. V. Zeani (sop), G. Cecchele (ten), C. MacNeil (bar), F. Capuana (cnd), Rome Opera Orch, Rome Opera Chorus [I] *(rec live, 3/16/67)* Verona 2-▲ 27042/43 (m) [AAD]
Verdi, G.:Alzira, w. V. Zeani (sop), G. Cecchele (ten), C. MacNeil (bar), F. Capuana (cnd), Rome Opera Orch, Rome Opera Chorus [I] *(rec live 3/16/67)* Melodram 2-▲ MEL 27013 (m) [AAD]
Verdi, G.:Nabucco, w. E. Suliotis (sop), B. Prevedi (ten), T. Gobbi (ten), L. Gardelli (cnd), Vienna State Opera Orch, Vienna State Opera Chorus [I] London 2-▲ 417407-2 [ADD]

Cava, P. (ten)
Donizetti, G.:L'elisir d'amore, w. R. Scotto (sop), C. Bergonzi (ten), G. Taddei (bar), G. Gavazzeni (cnd), Florence Maggio Musicale Orch, Florence Maggio Musicale Chorus *(rec live 1967)* Memories 2-▲ HR 4129/30 (s)

Cavalieri, Anna de (sop/mez)
De Cavalieri, Fineschi, Olivero, Stignani, Tassinari, w. Cavalieri, Anna de (sop), Ornella Fineschi (sop), Magda Olivero (sop), Ebe Stignani (mez), Pia Tassinari (mez), Rome RAI SO, Milan RAI SO *(rec 1953-58)* Incontri Memorabili ("Martini & Rossi Concerts" series) ▲ 5020
Meyerbeer, G.:Les Huguenots, w. A. Pastori (sop), G. Lauri-Volpi (ten), G. Taddei (bar), G. Tozzi (bass), N. Zaccaria (bass), T. Serafin (cnd), Milan RAI SO, Milan RAI Chorus *(rec 1956)* Memories 3-▲ MEM 4566 [ADD]

Cavallier, Nicolas (bass)
Berlioz, H.:L'Enfance du Christ (sels), w. Mariette Kemmer (sop), Claire Brua (mez), Gilles Ragon (ten), F. Quattrocchi (cnd), Lorraine PO—Toujours ce rêve *(rec June 1994)* Maguelone ▲ 350.509 [DDD]
Gluck, C.W.:Alceste (sels), w. Mariette Kemmer (sop), Claire Brua (mez), Gilles Ragon (ten), F. Quattrocchi (cnd), Lorraine PO—Vivre sans toi *(rec June 1994)* Maguelone ▲ 350.509 [DDD]
Gounod, C.:Faust (sels), w. Mariette Kemmer (sop), Claire Brua (mez), Gilles Ragon (ten), F. Quattrocchi (cnd), Lorraine PO—Faites lui mes aveux; La coupe du Roi de Thulé; Air des Bijoux *(rec June 1994)* Maguelone ▲ 350.509 [DDD]
Handel, G.F.:Ariodante, w. J. Gondek (sop), L. Saffer (sop), L. Hunt (mez), Jennifer Lane (mez), J. Lindemann (ten), R. Müller (ten), N. McGegan (cnd), Freiburg Baroque Orch, Ralf Popken (cnd), Wilhelmshaven Vocal Ensemble [172-page libretto w. production photos] Harmonia Mundi France 3-▲ HMC 907146.48
Handel, G.F.:Radamisto, w. Monika Frimmer (sop), Juliana Gondek (sop), Dana Hanchard (sop), Lisa Saffer (sop), R. Popken (cta), Michael Dean (b-bar), N. McGegan (cnd), Freiburg Baroque Orch Harmonia Mundi USA 3-▲ HMU 907111/13
Mozart, W.A.:Così fan tutte (sels), w. Mariette Kemmer (sop), Claire Brua (mez), Gilles Ragon (ten), F. Quattrocchi (cnd), Lorraine PO—Come scoglio *(rec June 1994)* Maguelone ▲ 350.509 [DDD]
Mozart, W.A.:Nozze di Figaro (sels), w. Mariette Kemmer (sop), Claire Brua (mez), Gilles Ragon (ten), F. Quattrocchi (cnd), Lorraine PO—Ov; Voi che Sapete *(rec June 1994)* Maguelone ▲ 350.509 [DDD]
Rameau, J.P.:Motets, w. S. Daneman (sop), N. Rime (sop), P. Agnew (ct), N. Rivenq (bar), W. Christie (cnd), Les Arts Florissants—In convertendo, Quam dilecta, Deus noster refugium *(rec June 8-12, 1994)* Erato ▲ 96967-2 [DDD]
Rossini, G.:Le Comte Ory (sels), w. Mariette Kemmer (sop), Claire Brua (mez), Gilles Ragon (ten), F. Quattrocchi (cnd), Lorraine PO—Ov; Que les destins prospères *(rec June 1994)* Maguelone ▲ 350.509 [DDD]

Cavalti, Elsa (mez)
Beethoven, L. van:Missa Solemnis, w. M. Stader (sop), E. Haefliger (ten), H. Rehfuss (bass), C. Schuricht (cnd), Hamburg SO, St. Hedwig's Cathedral Choir *(rec Sept. 15, 1957)* Archipon 2-▲ ARCH 2.1CD (m) [ADD]

Cavazzini, Pietrina (sgr)
Distel, H.:Die Reise, w. Felix Hochuli (gtr/Afr pno) *(rec Bern, Switzerland & Toscana, Italy, 1984-85)* Hat Hut ("NOW." series) ▲ hat ART CD 6001 [ADD]

Cave, Philip (ten)
Dvořák, A.:Mass, w. Coupe (trb), S. Taylor (ct), S. Foulkes (bass), A. Pinel (org), M. Archer (cnd), Bristol Cathedral Choir [L] Meridian ▲ CDE 84188

Cavelti, Elsa (mez)
Beethoven, L. van:Sym 9, "Choral Sym", w. Elisabeth Schwarzkopf (sop), Ernst Haefliger (ten), Otto Edelmann (bass), W. Furtwängler (cnd), Philharmonia Orch, Lucerne Festival Chorus *(rec Aug 22, 1954)* Music & Arts ▲ CD 790 [ADD]
Mahler, G.:Lied von der Erde, w. Anton Dermota (ten), O. Klemperer (cnd), Vienna SO *(rec 1957)* Tuxedo ▲ TUXCD 1036 [ADD]

Cavicchioli, Rosina (sgr)
Purcell, H.:Dido & Aeneas, w. Helen Donath (sop—Belinda), Shirley Verrett (sop—Dido), Oralia Dominguez (mez—Sorceress), Carmen Lavani (alt—A Spirit), Margaret Lensky (cta—2nd Witch), Carlo Gaifa (ten—A Sailor), Dan Jordacescu (bar—Aeneas), Rosina Cavicchioli (sgr—A Woman), Lilia Teresita Reyes (sgr—1st Witch), R. Leppard (cnd), Turin RAI SO, Ambrosian Chorus *(rec Torino, May 20, 1971)* Arkadia ▲ 619 [ADD]

Cavina, Claudio (alt)
Cavalieri, E. de:Rappresentatione di Anima et di Corpo, w. G. Bertagnolli (sop), B. Rossetti (sgr), G. Maletto (ten), R. Mattei (bar), A. Abete (sgr), M. Longhini (cnd), Verona Istitutioni Harmoniche Stradivarius ▲ STR 33339 [DDD]
De Vitae Fugacitate:Lamentos, Cantatas & Arias, w. R. Bertini (sop), R. Balconi (ct), R. Gini (cnd), Concerto delle Viole *(rec Aug. 1992)* Glossa ▲ GCD 920901 [DDD]
Frescobaldi, G.:Arie musicali per cantarsi, w. G. Banditelli (mez), R. Bertini (sop), G. Maletto (ten), S. Naglia (ten), S. Foresti (bass), R. Alessandrini (cnd), Concerto Italiano Opus 111 2-▲ OPS 30-105/106
Love Songs & Dances:Consort Music for Lute & Voices from "Pratum Musicum", w. Kirchhof, Lutz (lt), Marie-Claude Vallin (sop), Max van Egmond (bar), Sabine Dreier (trns fl), Petra Manz (vl) *(rec Evangelische Kirche, St Osdag, Mandelsloh, Germany, Nov 21-24, 1994)* Sony Classical ("Vivarte" series) ▲ SK 66263 [DDD]
Marcello, B.:Cants & Duets, w. Rossana Bertini (sop), La Venexiana—Andromaca; Cassandra; La Lucrezia; La Stravaganza; plus others & duets Opus 111 ▲ OPS 30-149
Perti, G.A.:Gesù al sepolcro, w. L. M. Åkerlund (sop), M. Zanetti (sop), M. Cecchetti (ten), A. W. Schultze (bass), S. Vartolo (cnd), San Petronio Cappella Musicale Orch [I] Tactus ▲ TC 661601
Scarlatti, A.:Cants & Duets, w. C. Miatello (sop), G. Fagotto (ten), L. Scoppola (sgr), P. Pandolfo (ctb), R. Sensi (sgr), R. Alessandrini (cnd)—Clori mia, Clori bella (cantata for soprano, flute & bass continuo); Dimmi crudele, e quando (duet for soprano, alto & bass continuo); Son pur care le catene (duet for soprano, alto & bass continuo); Sovente Amor mi chiama (cantata for alto & bass continuo); Ammore, brutto figlio de pottana (cantata for tenor & bass continuo) [I] Tactus ▲ TC 661901

Cawelti, Andrea (sop)
Ekizian, M.:Octoechos, w. H. Sollberger (cnd), Group for Contemporary Music [E] New World ▲ 80425-2 [DDD]
Karchin, L.:Songs of John Keats, w. H. Sollberger (cnd), Group for Contemporary Music [E] New World ▲ 80425-2 [DDD]

Cebotari, Maria (sop)
Einem, G. von:Dantons Tod, w. M. Cebotari (sop—Lucille Desmoulins), R. Anday (cta—Frau des Simon), P. Klein (ten—de Séchelles), J. Patzak (ten—Camille Desmoulins), J. Witt (ten—Robspierre), P. Schöffler (bar—Danton), L. Weber (bass—Saint Just), F. Fricsay (cnd), Vienna PO, Vienna State Opera Chorus *(rec Aug. 6, 1947)* Stradivarius 2-▲ STR 10067 [ADD]
Mozart, W.A.:Arias, w. Arleen Augér (sop), Kathleen Battle (sop), Irma Beilke (sop), Helena Braun (sop), Lisa Della Casa (sop), Ileana Cotrubas (sop), Helen Donath (sop), Mirella Freni (sop), Reri Grist (sop), Edita Gruberova (sop), Elisabeth Grümmer (sop), Hilde Güden (sop), Ingeborg Hallstein (sop), Luise Helletsgruber (sop), Gundula Janowitz (sop), Sena Jurinac (sop), Erika Köth (sop), Evelyn Lear (sop), Wilma Lipp (sop), Margaret Marshall (sop), Edith Mathis (sop), Jarmila Novotna (sop), Margherita Perras (sop), Lucia Popp (sop), Elisabeth Rethberg (sop), Anneliese Rothenberger (sop), Elisabeth Schumann (sop), Elisabeth Schwarzkopf (sop), Graziella Sciutti (sop), Irmgard Seefried (sop), Graziella Sciutti (sop), Julia Varady (sop), Agnes Baltsa (mez), Margit Bokor (mez), Brigitte Fassbaender (mez), Christa Ludwig (mez), Ann Murray (mez), Francisco Araiza (ten), Anton Dermota (ten), Helge Rosvaenge (ten), Rudolf Schock (ten), Peter Schreier (ten), Leopold Simoneau (ten), Eric Tappy (ten), Richard Tauber (ten), Gösta Winbergh (ten), Josef Witt (ten), Fritz Wunderlich (ten), Christian Boesch (bar), Willy Domgraf-Fassbaender (bar), Karl Dönch (bar), Dietrich Fischer-Dieskau (bar), Erich Kunz (bar), Eberhard Wächter (bar), Hans Hotter (b-bar), Paul Schöffler (b-bar), Cesare Siepi (b-bar), José Van Dam (b-bar), Walter Berry (bass), Geraint Evans (bass), Nicolai Ghiaurov (bass), Alexander Kipnis (bass), Richard Mayr (bass), Kurt Moll (bass), James Morris (bass), Ezio Pinza (bass), Martti Talvela (bass), Giorgio Tozzi (bass), Hans Duhan (sgr), Res Fischer (sgr), Marie Gerhart (sgr), *(various orchs & cnds)*—sels from Idomeneo, Die Entführung aus der Serail, Le nozze di Figaro, Don Giovanni, Così fan tutte, Die Zauberflöte & various arias Orfeo d'or ("Festspiel Dokumente" series) 5-▲ 408955
Mozart, W.A.:Nozze di Figaro (sels), w. M. Reining (sop—Countess), M. Cebotari (sop—Susanna), M. Ahlersmeyer (bar—Count Almaviva), K. Böhm (cnd), Vienna State Opera Orch *(rec Nov. 7, 1941)* Koch Schwann 2-▲ SCH 314602
Opera Arias, w. Vienna PO [cnd:Karajan], Vienna PO [cnd:Prohaska[, Philharmonia Orch [cnd:Krips], et al. *(rec ca. 1934-1949)* Preiser ▲ PRE 90034 (m) [AAD]
Schoeck, O.:Das Schloss Dürande (sels), w. Maria Cebotari (sop—Gabriele), Marta Fuchs (sop—Gräfin Morvaille), Brigitte Fassbaender (mez—Renald Willi Domgraf), Rut Berglund (cta—Priorin), Peter Anders (ten—Armand), Benno Arnold (ten—Jäger), Josef Greindl (bass—Nicole), Hans Wrana (bass—Jäger), Vasso Argyris (sgr—Volksredner), Otto Hüsch (sgr—Wildhüter), Leo Laschet (sgr—Jäger), Fritz Marcks (sgr—Jäger), Felix Schneider (sgr—Jäger), R. Heger (cnd)—Text; Ich kann es nicht glauben [from Act 1]; Text; Heil dir, du Feuerquelle [from Act 2]; Text; Gesucht und nicht gefunden [from Act 3]; Text; Der Jäger ist frei! [Act 3 Finale]; Text; Sie kommen mit Flinten und Stangen [Act 4]; Text; Du Narr des vermeintlichen Rechts [Act 4 finale]; Text *(rec live, Apr 1943)* Jecklin ▲ JD 692
Strauss, R.:Feuersnot (sels), w. Paula Buchner (sop), Tiana Lemnitz (sop), Karl Schmitt-Walter (bar), A. Rother (cnd), Berlin Radio Orch *(rec 1943-44)* Preiser ▲ PRE 90222 [ADD]
Strauss, R.:Der Rosenkavalier (sels), w. Paula Buchner (sop), Tiana Lemnitz (sop), Karl Schmitt-Walter (bar), A. Rother (cnd), Berlin Radio Orch *(rec 1943-44)* Preiser ▲ PRE 90222 [ADD]
Strauss, R.:Salome, w. Maria Cebotari (sop—Salome), Elisabeth Höngen (mez—Herodias), Karl Friedrich (ten—Narraboth), Julius Patzak (ten—Herod), Marko Rothmüller (bar—Jokanaan), C. Krauss (cnd), Vienna State Opera Orch, Vienna State Opera Chorus *(rec Covent Garden, London, Sept 30, 1947)* Legato 2-▲ LCD 211-2 [ADD]
Strauss, R.:Salome (sels), w. Paula Buchner (sop), Tiana Lemnitz (sop), Karl Schmitt-Walter (bar), A. Rother (cnd), Berlin Radio Orch—Final Scene *(rec 1943-44)* Preiser ▲ PRE 90222 [ADD]
Strauss, R.:Taillefer, w. Walter Ludwig (ten), Hans Hotter (bar), *(orch & chorus unknown)* *(rec 1943-44)* Preiser ▲ PRE 90222 [ADD]

Cecchele, Gianfranco (ten)
Bellini, V.:Norma (sels), w. M. Callas (sop), F. Cossotto (mez), I. Vinco (bass), G. Prêtre (cnd), Paris Opera Orch, Paris Opera Chorus—sels. *(rec 1965)* Melodram ▲ MLO 16038 [ADD]
Mercadante, S.:La Vestale, w. G. Dimitrova (sop), D. Vejzovic (sop), Romanò (sgr), Cepreaga (sgr), Kliskic (sgr), Sioli (sgr), Boldrini (sgr), V. Sutej (cnd), Spalato National Theater Orch, Spalato National Theater Chorus [I] *(rec 4/9/87)* Bongiovanni 2-▲ GB 2065/66 [DDD]
Verdi, G.:Alzira, w. V. Zeani (sop), C. MacNeil (bar), C. Cava (bass), F. Capuana (cnd), Rome Opera Orch, Rome Opera Chorus [I] *(rec live 3/16/67)* Melodram 2-▲ MEL 27013 (m) [AAD]
Verdi, G.:Alzira, w. V. Zeani (sop), C. MacNeil (bar), C. Cava (bass), F. Capuana (cnd), Rome Opera Orch, Rome Opera Chorus [I] *(rec live, 3/16/67)* Verona 2-▲ 27042/43 (m) [AAD]
Verdi, G.:Aroldo, w. M. Caballé (sop), J. Pons (bar), E. Queler (cnd), New York Opera Orch, Westchester Choral Society, New York Oratorio Society [I] *(rec live, Carnegie Hall 4/8/79)* CBS 2-▲ M2K 35906 [ADD]
Verdi, G.:Attila, w. Antonietta Stella (sop), Giangiacomo Guelfi (bar), Ruggiero Raimondi (bass), R. Muti (cnd), Rome RAI Orch, Rome RAI Chorus *(rec live 1970)* Memories 2-▲ HR 4178/79 (m)
Verdi, G.:Attila, w. Antonietta Stella (sop), Giangiacomo Guelfi (bar), Ruggiero Raimondi (bass), R. Muti (cnd), Rome RAI SO, Rome RAI Chorus *(rec Rome, Nov. 21, 1970)* Pantheon 2-▲ PHE 6642 (m)

Cecchetti, Mario (ten)
Peri, J.:Euridice, w. Monica Benvenuti (sop—Ninfa I/Venere), Rossana Bertini (sop—Dafne/Ninfa II), Gloria Banditelli (cta—Euridice/Ninfa III/Tragedia/Proserpina), Mario Cecchetti (ten—Aminta/Radamanto), Paolo Da Col (ten—Tirsi), Gianpaolo Fagotto (ten—Orfeo), Giuseppe Zambon (ct—Arcetro), Sergio Foresti (bass—Caronte/Pastore), Furio Zanasi (bass—Plutone), R. de Caro (cnd), Arpeggione Ensemble *(rec Bologna, Italy, Nov 1992)* Arts Music 2-▲ 47276-2 [DDD]
Perti, G.A.:Gesù al sepolcro, w. L. M. Åkerlund (sop), M. Zanetti (sop), C. Cavina (alt), A. W. Schultze (bass), S. Vartolo (cnd), San Petronio Cappella Musicale Orch [I] Tactus ▲ TC 661601

Cecco, Disma de (sop)
Boito, A.:Mefistofele, w. M. Pobbe (sop—Margherita), D. De Cecco (sop—Elena), E. Ticozzi (mez—Marta), F. Tagliavini (ten—Faust), G. Neri (bass—Mefistofele), A. Questa (cnd), Turin RSO, Turin Teatro Regio Chorus *(rec 1954)* Cetra Classic ▲ CDO 19
Cimarosa, D.:Giannina e Bernardone, w. S. Jurinac (sop), G. Sciutti (sop), M. Carlin (ten), M. Boriello (bar), S. Bruscantini (bar), C. De Antoni (sgr), N. Sanzogno (cnd), Milan RAI SO, Milan RAI Chorus [I] *(rec live, Milan July 26, 1953)* Melodram 2-▲ CDM 29505 [ADD]

Cechalová, Milada (sop)
Dvořák, A.:Songs, w. Stanislav Predota (ten), Adam Skoumal (pno)—Evening Songs, Opp. 3, 9 & 31; Songs, Op. 2; The Orphan, Op. 5; Rosemary; 2 Songs on Folk Poems, Op. posth.; 4 Songs, Op. 6; 3 Modern Greek Poems, Op. 50; 4 Songs, Op. 82 Studio Matous ▲ MAT 24 [DDD]
Michna, A.V.:Sacred Music, w. M. Bornus-Szczycinski (sgr), J. Lewitová (sgr), M. Pospí il (sgr), M. Predota (sgr), R. Hugo (cnd), Capella Regis Musicalis—Missa V à 5 et à 7 si placet; Cantiones pro Defunctis; Missa VI pro Defunctis à 6 et à 10; Requiem Studio Matou ▲ MAT 1 [DDD]

Cecil, Lionello (ten)
Puccini, G.:Madama Butterfly (sels), w. Margaret Sheridan (sop), Ida Mannarini (mez), Vittorio Wenberg (sgr), Carlo Sabajno (pno) *(rec La Scala, 1929-30)* Romophone ("Opera Magna" series) 2-▲ 89001-2

Cehanovsky, George (bar)
Her First Recordings, w. Steber, Eleanor (sop), Armand Tokatyan (ten), Lucielle Browning (mez), Pino Bontempi (sgr), Annamary Dickey (sgr), Lorenzo Alvary ((bass), A. Kent (bar), Raoul Jobin (ten), Norman Cordon (bass) VAI Audio ▲ VAIA 1023 (m) [ADD]

Cei, M. (sgr)
Pugnani, G.:Werther, w. A. Andreani (sgr), A. Flint (sgr), T. Yamashita (sgr), M. Andreae (cnd), Swiss-Italian Radio-TV Orch *(rec Dec. 14, 1989)* Bongiovanni 2-▲ GB 5028/29 [DDD]

Čejková, Milada (sop)
Klein, G.:Madrigals, w. J. Suchánková (sop), H. Pracnové (alt), K. Kozunik (ten), J. Belor (bar) *(rec Oct. 20 & 21, 1992)* Koch International Classics ▲ KIC 7230-2 [DDD]
Martinů, B.:Dandelion Romance, w. P. Kühn (cnd), Kühn Chorus [Cz] Supraphon 2-▲ 11 0752-2 [DDD]

Cencic, Max Emanuel (sop)
Handel, G.F.:Messiah, w. Charles Humphries (ct), Ivan Sharpe (ten), Robert Torday (b-bar), P. Marschik (cnd), Academy of London Orch, Martin Schebesta (cnd), Vienna Boys' Choir *(rec Symphony Hall, Birmingham & Barbican Center, London, Nov 17 & 19, 1994)* Capriccio 2-▲ 60068-2 [DDD]

Censo, Carla Di (sop)
Paisiello, G.:Il mondo della luna, w. Gemma Bertagnolli (sop—Clarice), Enzo Dara (bar—Buonafede), Riccardo Ristori (bass—Cecco), Carla Di Censo (sgr—Flaminia), Daniele Gaspari (sgr—Ecclittico), Mattia Nicolini (sgr—Ernesto), F. Neri (cnd), Bolzano Monteverdi Orch *(rec Aug 4-6, 1993)* Bongiovanni 2-▲ GB 2173/74 [DDD]
Tosti, P.F.:Canti populari e romanze abruzzesi, w. M. Gentile (mez), W. Omaggio (ten), P. Speca (sgr), I. Crissante (pno) Nuova Era ▲ NUO 7166 [DDD]

Cepreaga (sgr)
Mercadante, S.:La Vestale, w. G. Dimitrova (sop), D. Vejzovic (sop), G. Cecchele (ten), Romanò (sgr), Kliskic (sgr), Sioli (sgr), Boldrini (sgr), V. Sutej (cnd), Spalato National Theater Orch, Spalato National Theater Chorus [I] *(rec 4/9/87)* Bongiovanni 2-▲ GB 2065/66 [DDD]

Černá, Olga (mez)
Schulhoff, E.:Folk Songs & Dances from the Tesin Region, w. František Kůda (pno) Supraphon ▲ SUP 3196
Schulhoff, E.:Mood Pictures, w. František Kůda (pno) Supraphon ▲ SUP 3196
Schulhoff, E.:Songs, w. František Kůda (pno)—Songs (3), Op. 14; Songs (3), "Das Lied vom Kinde"; Songs, "Die Garbe" Supraphon ▲ SUP 3196

Cerno, Marcela (sop)
Wien, Wien, Schönes Wien, w. Miroslav Dvorsky (ten), Bratislava RSO [cnd:Jan Pospíchal] Supraphon ▲ SUP CD 3193

Cerquetti, Anita (sop)
Bellini, V.:Norma, w. G. Borelli, M. Pirazzini (mez), F. Corelli (ten), P. de Palma (ten), G. Neri (bass), G. Santini (cnd), *(orch unknown)* *(rec Rome, 1958)* Great Opera Performances 2-▲ GOP 722
Portrait of the Artist *(rec live, 1954-1958)* Legato Classics ▲ LCD 109-1 (m) [AAD]
Verdi, G.:Aida (sels), w. E. Nicolai (mez), G. Penno (ten), G. Guelfi (bar), B. Christoff (bass), G. Santini (cnd), Naples Teatro San Carlo Orch, Naples Teatro San Carlo Chorus [I] [highlights] *(rec live, Naples, July 24, 1954)* Golden Age of Opera ▲ GAO 134 [ADD]
Verdi, G.:Un ballo in maschera, w. E. Stignani (mez), G. Poggi (ten), E. Bastianini (bar), E. Tieri (cnd), Florence Teatro Comunale Orch, Florence Teatro Comunale Chorus [I] *(rec live 1/6/57)* Standing Room Only 2-▲ SRO 804-2 (m) [ADD]
Verdi, G.:Don Carlos, w. Cesare Siepi (b-bar), Ettore Bastianini (bar), Gianni Barbieri (bass), A. Votto (cnd), Florence Maggio Musicale Orch, Florence Maggio Musicale Chorus Melodram 3-▲ CDM 370104
Verdi, G.:Don Carlos, w. F. Barbieri (mez), A. LoForese (ten), E. Bastianini (bar), C. Siepi (b-bar), G. Neri (bass), A. Votto (cnd), Florence Maggio Musicale Orch, Florence Maggio Musicale Chorus *(rec July 16, 1956)* Melodram 3-▲ MLO 670104 [ADD]
Verdi, G.:Ernani, w. M. Del Monaco (ten), E. Bastianni (bar), B. Christoff (bass), D. Mitropoulos (cnd), Florence Maggio Musicale Orch [I] *(rec live 6/14/57)* Melodram 2-▲ MEL 27016
Verdi, G.:I vespri siciliani, w. Ortica (sgr), C. Tagliabue (bar), B. Christoff (bass), M. Rossi (cnd), Turin Radio Orch, Turin Radio Chorus [I] *(rec live, Turin, 11/16/55)* Claque 2-▲ CLQ 2017 (m)

Certeri, Rosanna (sgr)
Puccini, G.:Suor angelica, w. Miti Truccato Pace (mez), Gilda Capozzi (sgr), F. Previtali (cnd), *(orch & chorus unknown)* Cetra Classic 3-▲ 36

Červená, Soňa (alt)
Martinů, B.:Bouquet, w. Libuše Domanínská (sop), Lubomír Havlák (ten), Ladislav Mráz (bass), K. Ančerl (cnd), Czech PO, Czech Phil Chorus *(rec 1967)* Praga ("Karel Ančerl Edition" series) ▲ PR 254061
Waits, T.:The Black Rider:The Casting of Magic Bullets, w. Angelika Thomas (sgr—Anne), Annette Paulmann (sgr—Kätchen), Sona Cervena (sgr—Bird/Messenger/Spoonwoman), Monika Tahal (sgr—Witness/Bird/Shrink/Wilhelm's Double/Skeleton), Susi Eisenkolb (sgr—Bridesmaid/Pegleg's Double), Heinz Vossbrink (sgr—Kuno), Dominique Horwitz (sgr—Pegleg), Gerd Kunath (sgr—Bertram), Stefan Kurt (sgr—Wilhelm), Klaus Schreiber (sgr—Robert/Man on Stag/Georg Schmid), Jörg Holm (Old Uncle/Duke), Jan Moritz Steffen (sgr—Young Kuno/Bird/Shrink/Skeleton), Tom Waits (vocals/coliope/organ/chamberlain/mar/emax/guitar/train whistle), Ralph Carney (saxophone/bass clarinet/baritone horn), Bill Douglas (bass instrument), Kenny Wollesen (perc) Island ▲ 314518559-2

Cesare, Ezio de (ten)
Lattuada, F.:Le Preziose ridicole, w. S. Valayre (sop—Madelon), A. Catarci (sop—Marotte), A. Cicogna (mez—Cathos), S. Tedesco (ten—La Grange), E. Di Cesare (ten—Mascarille), A. Veccia (bar—Croissy), R. Servile (bar—Jodelet), E. Fissore (bass—Gorgibus), E. Romagna (cnd), Toscanini SO, G. Masini (cnd), Rossini Teatro Comunale Chorus [I] *(rec live, 1991)* Ermitage ▲ ERM 404 [DDD]
Pergolesi, G.B.:Adriano in Siria, w. D. Dessi (sop), J. Omilian (sop), L. Mazzaria (sop), S. Anselmi (sop), G. Banditelli (cta), M. Panni (cnd), Rome Opera CO [I] *(rec live 12/20/86)* Bongiovanni 3-▲ GB 2078/80 [DDD]
Rossini, G.:Aureliano in Palmira, w. L. d' Intino (sop), N. Ciliento (mez), Mazzola (sgr), G. Zani (cnd), Lucca Teatro Comunale Giglio Orch [I] *(rec live, Lucca, 10/28-11/2 1991)* Nuova Era 2-▲ 7069/70 [DDD]

▲ = CD ♦ = Enhanced CD Δ = MD ▮ = Cassette Tape ▯ = DCC

Cesari, Renato (bar)
Falla, M. de:El retablo de maese Pedro, w. T. Tourne (sop), P. Lavigren (ten), P. de Freitas Branco (cnd), Madrid Concert Orch EMI Classics 2-▲ ZDMB 64555
Petrassi, G.:Inni sacri, w. Aldo Bertocci (ten), G. Petrassi (cnd), Turin RAI Radio–TV SO Stradivarius ▲ STV DTM 90001 [ADD]
Puccini, G.:Madama Butterfly, w. A. Moffo (sop), R. Elias (mez), C. Valletti (ten), E. Leinsdorf (cnd), Rome Opera Orch, Rome Opera Chorus [I] RCA Gold Seal 2-▲ 4145-2-RG [ADD]
Puccini, G.:Madama Butterfly, w. A. Moffo (sop), R. Elias (mez), C. Valletti (ten), E. Leinsdorf (cnd), Rome Opera Orch, Rome Opera Chorus [I] RCA Gold Seal ▲ 60202-2-RG [ADD] ■ 60202-4-RG

Cesarini, Athos (ten)
Bellini, V.:Norma (sels), w. Mario del Monaco (ten), T. Serafin (cnd), Rome RAI SO—Svanir le voci; Meco all'altar di Venere; Me protegge, me difende *(rec Rome, June 29, 1955)* Melodram ▲ CDI 104006 [ADD]
Verdi, G.:Ernani, w. Margherita Roberti (sop), Anna di Stasio (mez), Mario del Monaco (ten), Ettore Bastianini (bar), Mario Rinaudo (bass), Nicola Rossi-Lemeni (bass), F. Previtali (cnd), Naples Teatro San Carlo Orch, Naples Teatro San Carlo Chorus Melodram 2-▲ CDM 270100
Verdi, G.:Il trovatore, w. Leyla Gencer (sop—Leonora), Laura Londi (sop—Ines), Fedora Barbieri (mez—Azucena), Mario del Monaco (ten—Manrico), Athos cesarini (ten—Ruiz), Walter Artioli (ten—Messanger) Ettore Bastianini (bar—Count Luna), Plinio Clabassi (bass—Ferrando), Sergio Liliani (bass—Gypsy), F. Previtali (cnd), Milan RAI SO, Milan RAI Chorus *(rec live, Milan, May 29, 1957)* Arkadia 2-▲ 483 [ADD]
Verdi, G.:Il trovatore, w. Leyla Gencer (sop—Leonora), Laura Londi (sop—Ines), Athos Cesarini (ten—Ruiz), Mario del Monaco (ten—Manrico), Ettore Bastianini (bar), F. Previtali (cnd), Milan RAI SO, Milan RAI Chorus *(rec Milan, May 18, 1957)* Agorá Music ("Phoenix" series) 3-▲ 510 [ADD]
Zandonai, R.:Francesca da Rimini, w. Lydia Marimpietri (sop—Biancofiore), Magda Olivero (sop—Francesca), Pinuccia Perotti (sop—Samaritana), Edda Vincenzi (sop—Garsenda), Gabriella Carturan (mez—Smaragdi), Biancamaria Casoni (mez—Altichiara), Anna Maria Rota (cta—Donella), Athos Cesarini (ten—Archer), Angelo Mercuriali (ten—Ser Toldo Berardengo), Mario del Monaco (ten—Paolo), Piero de Palma (ten—Malatestino), Rinaldo Pelizzoni (ten—Prisoner), Gianpiero Malaspina (bar—Gianciotto), Dino Mantovani (bar—Jester), Enrico Campi (bass—Ostasio), Giuseppe Morresi (bass—Tower warden), G. Gavazzeni (cnd), La Scala Orch, La Scala Chorus *(rec La Scala Theatre, Milan, June 4, 1959)* Legato Classics 2-▲ LCD 186-2
Zandonai, R.:Francesca da Rimini (sels), w. M. Olivero (sop), A. Gasparini (mez), M. del Monaco (ten), V. Carbonari (bass), N. Rescigno (cnd), Monte Carlo Opera Orch London ("Grand Opera" series) 2-▲ 433033-2 [ADD]

Cestari, Danilo (sgr)
Giordano, U.:Madame Sans-Gêne, w. Magda László (sop—Caterina), Carlo Tagliabue (bar—Napoleone), Renato Berti (sgr—Despréaux), Irene Callaway (sgr—Toniotta/Carolina), Danilo Cestari (sgr—Neipperg/Vinaigre), Maria Luisa Malacchi (sgr—Giulia/Principessa Elisa), Carlo Perucci (sgr—Fouché), Danilo Vega (sgr—Lefebvre), Enzo Viaro (sgr—De Brigode/Gelsomino), A. Basile (cnd), Milan RAI SO, Milan RAI Chorus *(rec Milan, Aug 10, 1957)* Bongiovanni 2-▲ GB 1129/30

Chabay, Leslie (ten)
Berlioz, H.:Les Nuits d'été, w. V. de los Angeles (sop), M. Roggero (mez), Y. Sze (bass), C. Munch (cnd), Boston SO RCA Gold Seal 2-▲ 09026-60681-2
Berlioz, H.:Roméo et Juliette, w. Margaret Roggero (mez), Yi-Kwei Sze (bass), C. Munch (cnd), Boston SO, Harvard Glee Club, Radcliffe Choral Society *(rec Feb 1953)* RCA Victor Gold Seal 8-▲ 0902-668444-2 [ADD]
Berlioz, H.:Roméo et Juliette, w. M. Roggero (mez), Y. Sze (bass), C. Munch (cnd), Boston SO, Harvard Glee Club, Radcliffe Choral Society RCA Gold Seal 2-▲ 09026-60681-2

Chabros, Monika (sgr)
Bizet, G.:Carmen (sels), w. Krystyna Szostek-Radkowa (mez), Ryszard Karczykowski (ten) *(other artists unknown)*—Habanera z I aktu; Aris Don Jose z II aktu; Aria Micaeli z III aktu Polskie Nagrania ▲ PNCD 080 [AAD]

Chadwell, Tracey (sop)
Rawsthorne, A.:Sym 2, w. N. Braithwaite (cnd), London PO Lyrita ▲ SRCD 291
Spratling, H.:Choral Music, w. Susan Bullock (sop), Jeffery Dyball (hp), Helen Tunstall (hp), John Hatton (org), J. Rennert (cnd), Parnassus String Ensemble, Spratling Choir—Mass of the Holy Spirit; O Salutaris Hostia; Tantum Ergo; Sinf Str Orch; Son Hp; O Magnum Mysterium; In Paradisum *(rec St. Mary Magdelene, Paddington, May 15–17, 1988)* SOMM ▲ SOMMCD 206 [ADD]

Chafin, Robert (ten)
Stravinsky, I.:In memoriam Dylan Thomas, w. Datura Trombone Quartet, Robin Gritton (cnd), North German Radio Chorus Ars Musici ▲ AM 1154 [DDD]

Chaignaud, Jean-Luc (bar)
Gazzaniga, G.:Don Giovanni, w. P. Coburn (sop), J. Kaufmann (sop), J. Aler (ten), R. Swensen (ten), G. von Kannen (bass), A. Scharinger (bass), S. Soltesz (cnd), Munich RSO, Munich Radio Chorus [I] Orfeo 2-▲ 214902 [DDD]

Chakoyan, Ellada (sop)
Ave Maria, w. Rouben Aivazian (org) Leonarda ▲ LE 341 [DDD]

Chaliapin, Feodor (bass)
Bass of the Century *(rec Hayes, Middlesex; Kingsway Hall, London; Salle Pleyel, Paris; Royal Opera House, Covent Garden, London; Small Queen's Hall, London; Salle Chopin, Paris)* Happy Days ▲ CDHD 226 [ADD]
Boito, A.:Mefistofele (sels) *(other artists unknown)* *(rec Covent Garden, 1926–28)* Phonographe ("Great Voices" series) ▲ PHG 5047 [ADD]
Chant l'âme slave Music Memoria ▲ MMA 30909 (m) [AAD]
Feodor Chaliapin *(rec live, rec. 1911–1936)* Nimbus ("Prima Voce" series) 2-▲ NI 7823/24 [ADD]
Feodor Chaliapin Pearl ▲ PEA 9182
Feodor Chaliapin Song Book *(rec 1926–1933 HMV electrical)* Preiser ("Lebendige Vergangenheit" series) 2-▲ PRE 89207 (m) [AAD]
Feodor Chaliapin *(rec 1907–1912)* Preiser ("Lebendige Vergangenheit" series) ▲ PRE 89030 (m) [AAD]
Lebendige Vergangenheit:Feodor Chaliapin, Vol. 2 *(rec 1925–1931)* Preiser ("Lebendige Vergangenheit" series) ▲ PRE 89087 [AAD]
Gounod, C.:Faust (sels), w. *(orch unknown)* Forlane ▲ FRL 16718 [ADD]
Gounod, C.:Faust (sels), w. *(other artists unknown)* *(rec Covent Garden, 1926–28)* Phonographe ("Great Voices" series) ▲ PHG 5047 [ADD]
The Great Chaliapin Pearl 2-▲ PEA 9208
Mussorgsky, M.:Boris Godunov (sels) *(rec Covent Garden, 1926–28)* Phonographe ("Great Voices" series) ▲ PHG 5047 [ADD]
Russian Opera Arias EMI Classics ("Great Recordings of the Century" series) ▲ CDH 61009 (m)
Sings Russian Music, Vol. 1 *(rec 1910–1936 HMV recordings)* Pearl 2-▲ PEA 9920 (m) [AAD]
Sings Russian Music, Vol. 2 *(rec 1911–1936 for HMVordings)* Pearl ▲ PEA 9921 (m) [AAD]
The World of Singing, Vol. 2: Singers of Imperial Russia, w. Nina Koshetz (sop), Evgenia Zbrueva (cta), Nicolai Figner (ten), Nina Friede (sgr), Maria Kouznetsova (sgr), Anastasia Vialtzeva (sgr) Enterprise ("Vocal Archives" series) 2-▲ ENT VA 2102

Chalker, Margaret (sop)
Mendelssohn, F.:Sym 2, w. M. Rivera (sop), V. Cole (ten), G. Schwarz (cnd), Seattle SO, Seattle Chorale *(rec Apr. 22–23, 1991)* Delos ▲ DE 3112 [DDD]

Chamberlain, Richard (nar)
Welcher, D.:Haleakala:How Maui Snared the Sun, w. A. McCutchan (nar), D. Johanos (cnd), Honolulu SO *(rec Jan. 10, 1992)* Marco Polo ▲ 8.223457 [DDD]

Chaminé, Jorge (bar)
Pablo, L. de:Tarde de Poetas, w. Luisa Castellani (sop), J. Pons (cnd), Barcelona Teatro Lliure CO Harmonia Mundi France 2-▲ HMC 901568

Chamlee, Mario (ten)
Leoncavallo, R.:Pagliacci (sels), w. Enrico Caruso (ten), Antonio Paoli (ten), Giovanni Zenatello (ten), Amedeo Bassi (ten), Hermann Jadlowker (ten), Fernand Ansseau (ten), Hipolito Lazaro (ten), Nino (Filippo) Piccaluga (ten), Giacomo Lauri-Volpi (ten), Miguel Fleta (ten), Giovanni Martinelli (ten), Aureliano Pertile (ten), Georges Thill (ten), Alessandro Valente (ten), Francesco Merli (ten), Lauritz Melchior (ten), Marcel Wittrisch (ten), Joseph Schmidt (ten), Beniamino Gigli (ten), Giuseppe Lugo (ten), Helge Roswaenge (ten), Jussi Bjoerling (ten)—23 versions of the tenor aria "Vesti la giubba" *(rec 1907–1944)* Bongiovanni ▲ GB 1071 [ADD]

Chamonin, Jocelyne (sop)
Charpentier, M.-A.:Magnificat, w. Martha Angelici (sop), André Mallabrera (ct), Rémy Corazza (ten), Georges Abdoun (bar), Jacques Mars (bass), Maurice André (tpt), Marie-Claire Alain (org), L. Martini (cnd), Jean-François Paillard CO, French Jeunesses Musicales Chorale *(rec Paris, Mar 15, 1963)* Vanguard Classics ▲ OVC 8075 [ADD]
Charpentier, M.-A.:Te Deum, H. 146, w. Martha Angelici (sop), André Mallabrera (ct), Rémy Corazza (ten), Georges Abdoun (bar), Jacques Mars (bass), Maurice André (tpt), Marie-Claire Alain (org), L. Martini (cnd), Jean-François Paillard CO, French Jeunesses Musicales Chorale *(rec Paris, Mar 15, 1963)* Vanguard Classics ▲ OVC 8075 [ADD]
Vivaldi, A.:Beatus vir (Psalm 111), w. M. Burgess (sop), C. Watkinson (cta), J.-C. Malgoire (cnd), La Grande Écurie et la Chambre du Roy, Raphaël Passaquet Vocal Ensemble *(rec 1976)* Sony Classical ("Essential Classics" series) ▲ SBK 48280 [ADD] ■ SBT 48280
Vivaldi, A.:Gloria, RV.589, w. M. Burgess (sop), Carolyn Watkinson (cta), J.-C. Malgoire (cnd), La Grande Écurie et la Chambre du Roy, Raphaël Passaquet Vocal Ensemble *(rec 1976)* Sony Classical ("Essential Classics" series) ▲ SBK 48280 [ADD] ■ SBT 48280

Champell (sop)
Gounod, C.:Roméo et Juliette, w. Yvonne Gall (sop—Juliette), Champell (sop—Stéphano), Jeanne Goulancourt (mez—Gertrude), Agustarello Affre (ten—Roméo), Edmond Tirmont (ten—Tybalt), Alexis Boyer (bar—Mercutio), Pierre Dupré (bar—Paris), Hypolite Belhomme (bar—Grégorio), Marcel Journet (bass—Frère Laurent), Henri Albers (bass—Capulet), Valermont (bass—The Duke), F. Rühlmann (cnd), Paris Opéra-Comique Orch, Paris Opéra-Comique Chorus *(rec 1912)* VAI Audio ▲ VAIA 1064-3 F

Chance, Michael (ct)
Bach, J.S.:Cant 106, "Actus tragicus", w. N. Argenta (sop), A. Rolfe Johnson (ten), S. Varcoe (b-bar), J. E. Gardiner (cnd), English Baroque Soloists, Monteverdi Choir London [G] Archiv ▲ 429782-2 [DDD]
Bach, J.S.:Cant 147, w. R. Holton (sop), A. Rolfe Johnson (ten), S. Varcoe (b-bar), J. E. Gardiner (cnd), English Baroque Soloists, Monteverdi Choir London [G] Archiv ▲ 431809-2 [DDD]
Bach, J.S.:Cant 198, w. N. Argenta (sop), A. Rolfe Johnson (ten), S. Varcoe (b-bar), J. E. Gardiner (cnd), English Baroque Soloists, Monteverdi Choir London [G] Archiv ▲ 429782-2 [DDD]
Bach, J.S.:Christmas Oratorio, w. B. Schlick (sop), H. Crook (ten), P. Kooy (bass), P. Herreweghe (cnd), Ghent Collegium Vocale Orch, Ghent Collegium Vocale [G] Virgin Classics (Veritas) 2-▲ ZDCB 59530-2 [DDD]
Bach, J.S.:Magnificat, BWV 243, w. T. Bonner (sop), E. Kirkby (sop), J. M. Ainsley (ten), S. Varcoe (b-bar), R. Hickox (cnd), Collegium Musicum 90 Chandos ("Chaconne" series) ▲ CHAN 0518 [DDD]
Bach, J.S.:Mass in b, BWV 232, w. J. Smith (sop), N. van der Meel (ten), H. van der Kamp (bass), F. Brüggen (cnd), Orch of the 18th Century, Netherlands Chamber Choir [L] *(rec live)* Philips ("Digital Classics" series) 2-▲ 426238-2 [DDD]
Bach, J.S.:St. Matthew Passion, w. B. Bonney (sop), A. Monoyios (sop), A. S. von Otter (mez), H. Crook (ten), A. Rolfe Johnson (ten), O. Bär (bar), A. Schmidt (bar), C. Hauptmann (bass), J. E. Gardiner (cnd), English Baroque Soloists, Monteverdi Choir London [G] Archiv 3-▲ 427648-2 [DDD]
Blow, J.:Ah, Heaven! What Is't I Hear?, w. J. Bowman (ct), R. King (cnd), King's Consort [E] Hyperion ▲ CDA 66253 [DDD]
Blow, J.:The Glorious Day Is Come, w. Suzie le Blanc (sop), Joseph Cornwell (ten), Richard Wistreich (bass), P. Holman (cnd), Parley of Instruments, Playford Consort Hyperion ▲ CDA 66770
Blow, J.:Ode on the Death of Mr. Henry Purcell, w. J. Bowman (ct), R. King (cnd), King's Consort [E] Hyperion ▲ CDA 66253 [DDD]
Blow, J.:Songs, w. Emma Kirby (sop), M. Neary (cnd), New London Consort, Westminster Abbey Choir—Whilst sullen years are past; The sullen years are past Sony Classical ▲ SK 66243
Britten, H.:Canticles I–V, w. A. Rolfe-Johnson (ten), A. Opie (bar), R. Vignoles (pno), S. Williams (hp), M. Thompson (hn) Hyperion ▲ CDA 66498
Britten, H.:Purcell Realizations, w. A. Rolfe-Johnson (ten), A. Opie (bar), R. Vignoles (pno)—3 Realizations (An evening hymn; Let the dreadful engines; In the black dismal dungeon of despair) Hyperion ▲ CDA 66498
Byrd, W.:Songs, w. Christopher Wilson (lt), Fretwork—If women could be fair; Lullaby, my sweet little baby; Ah silly soul; Ye sacred muses Virgin Classics ▲ 59586 [DDD]
Couperin, F.:Leçons de ténèbres (for Ash Wednesday), w. J. Bowman (ct), R. King (trb), M. Caudle (bass vl) Hyperion ▲ CDA 66474
Dowland, J.:Songs, w. Christopher Wilson (lt), Fretwork—Goe nightly cares, the enemy to rest; Lasso vita mia, mi fu morire Virgin Classics ▲ 59586 [DDD]
Gluck, C.W.:Orfeo ed Euridice, w. N. Argenta (sop), J. Lamon (cnd), Tafelmusik, F. Bernius (cnd), Stuttgart Chamber Choir Sony Classical ("Vivarte" series) 2-▲ SX2K 48040
Handel, G.F.:Cants, w. N. Argenta (sop), G. von der Goltz (cnd), Freiburg Baroque Orch—Il duello amoroso, HWV 82 *(rec Jan 1993)* Deutsche Harmonia Mundi ▲ 05472-77295-2 [DDD]
Handel, G.F.:Giustino, w. Juliana Gondek (sop), Dawn Kotoski (sop), Dorothea Röschmann (sop), Jennifer Lane (mez), Drew Minter (alt), Mark Padmore (ten), Dean Ely (sgr), N. McGegan (cnd), Freiburg Baroque Orch Harmonia Mundi France 3-▲ HMU 907130.32
Handel, G.F.:Israel in Egypt, w. Ruth Holton (sop), Elisabeth Friday (sgr), Philip Salmon (ten), Paul Tindall (sgr), J. E. Gardiner (cnd), English Baroque Soloists, Monteverdi Choir London Philips ▲ 432110-2
Handel, G.F.:Messiah, w. Sylvia McNair (sop), Anne Sofie von Otter (mez), Jerry Hadley (ten), Robert Lloyd (b-bar), N. Marriner (cnd), Academy of St. Martin in the Fields [E] *(rec live, Dublin 4/13/92)* Philips 2-▲ 434695-2 [DDD]
Handel, G.F.:Messiah, w. Arleen Augér (sop), Anne Sofie von Otter (mez), Howard Crook (ten), John Tomlinson (bass), T. Pinnock (cnd), English CO, English Concert Choir [E] Archiv 2-▲ 423630-2 [DDD]
Handel, G.F.:Messiah (sels), w. Arleen Augér (sop), Anne Sofia von Otter (mez), Paul Crook (ten), John Tomlinson (bass), T. Pinnock (cnd), English CO, English Concert Choir [E] Archiv ▲ 427664-2 [DDD] ■ 427664-4
Handel, G.F.:Semele, w. Kathleen Battle (sop), Sylvia McNair (sop), Marylin Horne (mez), John Aler (ten), Samuel Ramey (bass), J. Nelson (cnd), English CO, Ambrosian Opera Chorus Deutsche Grammophon 3-▲ 435782-2 -
Jones, Robert:Duets for 2 Cts, w. D. Cordier (ct), Tragicomedia—eleven duets by Jones, coupled with two duets by John Coprario & Angelo Notari, a solo song by John Dowland, & eight instrumental pieces by Dowland, Giles Farnaby & Tobias Hume Hyperion ▲ CDA 66335 [DDD]
Monteverdi, C.:Incoronazione, w. Constanze Backes (sop—Valletto), Catherine Bott (sop—Drusilla/Pallade/La Virtù), Dana Hanchard (sop—Nerone), Sylvia McNair (sop—Poppea), Marinella Pennicchi (sop—Amore/Damigella), Annie Sofie von Otter (mez—Ottavia/Venere/La Fortuna), Julian Clarkson (alt—Littore/Mercurio), Bernarda Fink (cta—Arnalta), Roberto Balconi (ct—Nutrice), Michael Chance (ct—Ottone), Nigel Robson (ten—Liberto/Soldato Secondo), Mark Tucker (ten—Lucano/Soldato Primo), Francesco Ellero d'Artegna (bass—Seneca), J. E. Gardiner (cnd), English Baroque Soloists *(rec Queen Elizabeth Hall, South Bank Ctr, London, Dec 1993)* Archiv 3-▲ 447088-2
Monteverdi, C.:Vespro della Beata Vergine, w. A. Monoyios (sop), M. Pennicchi (sop), G. Tucker (ten), N. Robson (ten), S. Naglia (ten), B. Terfel (b-bar), A. Miles (bass), J. E. Gardiner (cnd), English Baroque Soloists, His Majesties Sagbutts & Cornetts, London Monteverdi Choir Archiv 2-▲ 429565-2 [DDD]
Music for Viols, w. Fretwork, C. Wilson (lt), P. Nicholson (kbd) Virgin Classics ▲ CDZ 59691
A Musicall Dreame, w. Chance, Michael (ct), David Cordier (ct), Tragicomedia Hyperion ▲ CDA 66335 [DDD]
Orff, C.:Carmina burana, w. B. Hendricks (sop), J. Black (bar), F. Welser-Möst (cnd), London PO, London Phil Chorus, St. Alban's Cathedral Choristers [G, L] EMI Classics ▲ CDC 54054 [DDD]

Chance, Michael (ct) (cont.)
Purcell, H.:Dido & Aeneas, w. Catherine Bott (sop—Dido), Emma Kirkby (sop—Belinda), Michael Chance (alt—Spirit), John Mark Ainsley (bar—Aeneas), David Thomas (bar—Sorceress), C. Hogwood (cnd), Academy of Ancient Music L'Oiseau-Lyre ▲ 436992-2 [DDD]
Purcell, H.:Odes & Welcome Songs (misc), w. J. Smith (sop), E. Priday (sop), K. Amps (sop), Wilson (sgr), J. M. Ainsley (ten), S. Richardson (bar), T. Pinnock (cnd), English Concert, *(chorus unknown)* —Come ye Sons of Art; Welcome to All the Pleasures; Of Old, When Heroes Thought it Base Archiv ▲ 427663-2 [DDD]
Purcell, H.:The Prophetess (sels), w. Nancy Argenta (sop), G. von der Goltz (cnd), Freiburg Baroque Orch—Ov; Dance; If Music Be the Food (song); Dance of the Bacchanals; Tpt tune; Prelude; Oh How Happy (song); Hornpipe; Dance of the Furies; 1st Music; Lost es My Quiet (duet); Prelude; Let the Soldiers Rejoice (song); Act Tune; Chaconne; 2nd Music; Paspe; Chair Dance *(rec Jan 1993)* Deutsche Harmonia Mundi ▲ 05472-77295-2 [DDD]
Purcell, H.:Songs, w. J. Bowman (ct), R. King (cnd), King's Consort [E, L] Hyperion ▲ CDA 66253 [DDD]
Purcell, H.:Songs, w. Emma Kirkby (sop), M. Neary (cnd), New London Consort, Westminster Abbey Choir—I was glad; Praise the Lord, O Jerusalem; Script for their green our groves appear; Ode for Queen Mary's Birthday; Elegy on the death of Queen Mary; The Queen's Epicedium; March; The Burial Service [composed w. Thomas Morley] Sony Classical ▲ SK 66243
Purcell, H.:Welcome to All the Pleasures, w. Ruth Holton (sop), Nicola Jenkin (sop), Paul Tindall (ten), George Mosly (bass), J.E. Gardiner (cnd), English Baroque Soloists, Monteverdi Choir London *(rec Saint George's, Bristol, UK, July 12-14, 1990)* Philips ▲ 432114-2
Tollett, T.:Music of, w. Emma Kirby (sop), M. Neary (cnd), New London Consort, Westminster Abbey Choir—The Queen's Farewell (march) Sony Classical ▲ SK 66243
Vivaldi, A.:Gloria, RV.589, w. E. Kirkby (sop), T. Bonner (sop), R. Hickox (cnd), Collegium Musicum 90 Chandos ("Chaconne" series) ▲ CHAN 0518 [DDD]

Chanoyan, Fabienne (sop)
Aprikian, G.:Naissance de David de Sassoun, w. Fabienne Chanoyan (sop—Angel), Anna Karakaya (mez—Queen Taline), Armand Arapian (bar—King Meher/Priest), H. Sakssian (cnd), Bell'Arte Orch, Sipan-Komitas Choir Petit Chanteurs of Tebrotzassere School *(rec Ivry-sur-Seine, Jan 17-18, 1995)* Studio SM ▲ D2514

Chaplin, Sydney (sgr)
Bernstein, L.:Wonderful Town, w. R. Russell (sgr), J. McKeever (sgr), et al. Sony Broadway ▲ SK 48021 ■ ST 48021

Charisse, Cyd (sgr)
Lerner, A.J.:Brigadoon, w. Gene Kelly (sgr), V. Johnson (sgr) *(rec 1954)* Sony Music Special Products ▲ AK 45440 ■ AT 45440

Charlent, Gertie (sop)
Ligeti, G.:Aventures, w. Cahn (sgr), Pearson (sgr), B. Maderna (cnd), Darmstadt International Chamber Ensemble Wergo ▲ WER 60045-50 [ADD]
Ligeti, G.:Nouvelles aventures, w. Cahn (sgr), Pearson (sgr), B. Maderna (cnd), Darmstadt International Chamber Ensemble Wergo ▲ WER 60045-50 [ADD]
Varèse, E.:Offrandes, w. F. Cerha (cnd), Reihe Ensemble *(rec Nov 1968-Mar 1969)* Vox Box 2-▲ CDX 5142

Charles, Juan (ten/bar)
Bizet, G.:Carmen, w. Laura Bustamante (sop—Frasquita), Ximena Riveros (sop—Mercedes), Nancy Stokes (sop—Micaela), Regina Resnik (mez—Carmen), Plácido Domingo (ten—Don José), Ismildo Tedeschi (ten—Remendado), Ramon Vinay (ten—Escamillo), Juan Charles (ten/bar—Dancaire), Agustin Letelier (bar—Morles), Jorge Algorta (bass—Zuniga), A. Guadagno (cnd), Santiago Teatro Municipale Orch, Santiago Teatro Municipale Chorus *(rec Santiago Municipal Theater, Sept. 4, 1967)* Legato Classics 2-▲ LCD 194-2 [ADD]

Charles-Cahier, S. (sgr)
Mahler, G.:Songs, w. S. Meyrowitz (cnd), Berlin State Opera Orch—Urlicht (from Knaben Wunderhorn) & Ich bin der Welt (from Rückert-Lieder) [G] *(rec 1930 for Ultraphon)* Pearl 2-▲ PEAS 9929 (m) [AAD]

Charlston, Elsa (sop)
Eaton, J.:A Greek Vision, w. Carole Morgan (fl) *(rec Musical Arts Ctr, Bloomington, IN, Aug 28, 1986)* Indiana Univ School of Music ▲ 0-253-31842-4
Shapey, R.:The Covenant, w. R. Shapey (cnd), Univ of Chicago Contemporary Chamber Players CRI ▲ CD 690 [ADD]

Charon, G. (sgr)
"Le Patron" of the Saxophone, w. Mule, Marcel (sax), Guy Chauvet (ten), F. l'Homme (sgr), P. Romby (sgr), Eugène Bozza (cnd), Francis Çebron (cnd), Phillipe Gaubert (cnd), *(orchs unknown)*, Joseph Benvenutti (pno), Marcel Gaveau (pno), Marthe Pellas-Lenom (pno), François Combelle (sax) *(rec 1930-1940)* Clarinet Classics ▲ CC 0013 [AAD]

Chastain, Don (sgr)
Gershwin, G.:Strike up the Band, w. B. Barrett (sgr), R. Luker (sgr), J. Mauceri (cnd), *(orch unknown)* [based on original Gershwin manuscripts] Elektra/Nonesuch 2-▲ 79273-2 2-■ 79273-4

Château, Christiane (sop)
Hahn, R.:O mon del inconnul, w. Lina Dachary (sop), Monique Stiot (mez), Michel Hamel (ten), Joseph Peyron (ten), Aimé Doniat (bar), Dominique Tirmont (bar), Philippe Gaudin (sgr), Jacques Provins (sgr), J. Brebion (cnd), ORTF Lyric Orch Musidisc 2-▲ MUS 202562 [AAD]
Honegger, A.:Jeanne d'Arc au bûcher, w. A.M. Rodde (sop), H. Brachet (mez), P. Proenza (ten), Z. Jankovsky (ten), F. Loup (bass), S. Baudo (cnd), Czech PO, Czech Chorus *(rec 1974)* Supraphon 2-▲ 11 0557-2 [AAD]

Chateauneuf, Paula (sgr)
Poder á Santa Maria, w. S. Wishart (cnd), Sinfonye, Equidad Barés (sgr), Vivien Ellis (sgr), Jim Denley (sgr) *(rec Cartuja de Santa María de Cazalla de la Sierra, Seville, Oct. 1993)* Almaviva ▲ 0105 [DDD]

Chauvet, Guy (ten)
Massenet, J.:Hérodiade (sels), w. Michele Le Bris (sop—Salomé), Denise Scharley (cta—Hérodiade), Guy Chauvet (ten—Jean), Robert Massard (bar—Hérode), J. Etcheverry (cnd), Paris Lyric Orch—Il est doux, Il est bon; Hérode, Ne me refuse pas; Jean, je le revois; Vision fugitive; Astres etincelants; Charme des jours passés; Salomé, laisse-moi t'aimer; Ne pouvant réprimer les élans de la foi; Quand nos jours s'éteindront...; Ballet Accord ▲ ACD 204272 [AAD]
"Le Patron" of the Saxophone, w. Mule, Marcel (sax), G. Charon (sgr), F. l'Homme (sgr), P. Romby (sgr), Eugène Bozza (cnd), Francis Çebron (cnd), Phillipe Gaubert (cnd), *(orchs unknown)*, Joseph Benvenutti (pno), Marcel Gaveau (pno), Marthe Pellas-Lenom (pno), François Combelle (sax) *(rec 1930-1940)* Clarinet Classics ▲ CC 0013 [AAD]

Chédel, Ariette (cta)
Martin, F.:Pilate, w. Eugenia Zareska (mez), Eric Tappy (ten), Derrik Olsen (bar), Jean-Christoph Benoit (bar), E. Ansermet (cnd), Swiss Romande Orch, Lausanne Pro Arte Choir Cascavelle 2-▲ CVL 2006 [ADD]
Ravel, M.:L'Enfant et les sortilèges, w. M. Lagrange (sop), E. Vidal (sop), M. Damonte (mez), M. Mahé (mez), L. Pezzino (ten), M. Barrard (bar), V. le Texier (b-bar), A. Lombard (cnd), Bordeaux-Aquitaine National Orch, Bordeaux Grand Théâtre Municipal Chorus [F] Valois ▲ V 4670

Chédel, Arlette (cta)
Derbès, J.:Music of, w. D. Duport (pno), V. Desarzens (cnd), Lausanne CO—Chant d'amour et de mort; Con for Pno; 7 mélodies; Adagio for Large Orch Grammont ▲ CTSP 46
Schibler, A.:La Folie de Tristan, w. Audrey Michael (sop—Iseut), Arlette Chédel (mez—Brangien), Pierre-André Blaser (ten—Tristan), Philippe Huttenlocher (bar—Le roi Marc/Le pêcheur/Le portier), André Fauré (nar), William Jacques (nar), Snezana Zivojinovic (nar), J. Auberson (cnd), Lausanne CO, Romande Instrumental Group Rockband, Swiss Romande Radio Choir *(rec live, Festival de Montreux, Sept 15, 1980)* Jecklin ▲ JD 695

Cheek, John (bass)
Beethoven, L. van:Sym 9, "Choral Sym", w. B. Valente (sop), F. Kopleff (cta), J. Hadley (ten), R. Shaw (cnd), Atlanta SO, Atlanta Sym Chorus Pro Arte ▲ CDD 245 [DDD]
Bernstein, L.:Songfest, w. Linda Hohenfeld (sop), Wendy White (mez), Patricia Spence (mez), Walter Plante (ten), Vernon Hartman (bar), L. Slatkin (cnd), St. Louis SO RCA Red Seal ▲ 09026-61581-2

Cheek, John (bass) (cont.)
Boito, A.:Mefistofele (sels), w. R. Shaw (cnd), Atlanta SO, Atlanta Sym Chorus—Prologue [I] Telarc 2-▲ CD 80109-2 [DDD]
Dvořák, A.:Stabat Mater, w. K. Erickson (sop), C. Carlson (mez), J. Aler (ten), Z. Macal (cnd), New Jersey SO, J. Flummerfeldt (cnd), Westminster Sym Choir *(rec Feb. 8-11, 1994)* Delos 2-▲ DE 3161 [DDD]
Franck, C.:Les Béatitudes, w. D. Montague (mez), K. Lewis (ten), G. Cachemaille (bar), H. Rilling (cnd), Stuttgart RSO, Gächinger Kantorei [F] Hänssler Classic 2-▲ 98.964 [DDD]
Handel, G.F.:Messiah (sels), w. Judith Blegen (sop), Katherine Ciesinski (mez), John Aler (ten), R. Westenburg (cnd), Musica Sacra, Musica Sacra Chorus RCA Silver Seal ▲ 60481-2-RV [DDD]; ■ 60481-4-RV (CrO2)
Haydn, J.:Die Schöpfung, w. Dawn Upshaw (sop), Jon Humphrey (ten), R. Shaw (cnd), Atlanta SO, Atlanta Chamber Chorus [E] Telarc 2-▲ CD 80298 [DDD]
Haydn, J.:Die Schöpfung, w. Lynn Dawson (sop), Neil Rosenshein (ten), J. Revzen (cnd), St. Paul CO, Minnesota Chorale Albany 2-▲ AR 005-6-2
Mozart, W.A.:Requiem, w. Lorna Haywood (sop), D'Anna Fortunado (mez), Partick Romero (ten), J. Sommary (cnd), Amor Artis Orch, Amor Artis Chorale [period instrs] *(rec St. Jean Baptiste Church, New York City, Mar 1996)* Vox Classics ▲ VOX 7534 [DDD]
Paine, J.K.:Mass, Op. 10, w. C. Balthrop (sop), J. Blackett (cta), V. Cole (ten), J. Lange (org), G. Schuller (cnd), St. Louis SO, St. Louis Sym Chorus [L] *(rec ca. mid-1970s)* New World ▲ 80262-2 [AAD]
Tippett, M.:The Mask of Time, w. F. Robinson (sop), S. Walker (mez), R. Tear (ten), A. Davis (cnd), BBC SO, BBC Sym Chorus EMI Classics ▲ ZDMB 64111

Chen, Elsa (sop)
Dai, V.:Illustrations, w. J.-J. Werner (cnd), Jeune PO Quantum ▲ QM 6917 [DDD]

Chen, Qilian (sop)
Puccini, G.:Arias, w. G. Notev (cnd), Pleven PO—Intermezzo [orch solo]; In quelle trine morbide; Sola, perduta, abbandonata [all from Manon Lescaut]; O mio babbino caro [from Gianni Schicchi]; Un bel dì vedremo; Che tua madre; Con onor muore [all from Madame Butterfly]; Signore, ascolta; Tu che di gel sei cinta [both from Turandot]; Senza mamma [from Suor Angelica]; Sì, mi chiamano; Donde lieta usci; Quando men vo [all from La bohème]; Chi il bel sogno di Doretta [from La rondine] *(rec Sofia, 1996)* Pavane ▲ ADW 7366 [DDD]

Chen, Shi-Zheng (sgr)
Monk, M.:Atlas, w. D. Hanchard (sop), R. Een (sgr), S. Kalm (bar), M. Monk (cnd), *(orch unknown) (rec June 1992)* ECM New Series ▲ 78118-21491-2 [DDD]

Chéreau, Patrice (nar)
Stravinsky, I.:Oedipus Rex, w. A. S. von Otter (mez/sop), V. Cole (ten), N. Gedda (ten), S. Estes (bass), H. Sotin (bass), E.-P. Salonen (cnd), Swedish RSO, *(chorus unknown)* Sony Classical ▲ SK 48057

Cherici, Laura (sop)
Mozart, W.A.:Così fan tutte, w. A. C. Antonacci (sop—Fiordiligi), M. Bacelli (sop—Dorabella), L. Cherici (sop—Despina), R. Decker (ten—Ferrando), A. Dohmen (bar—Gugliemo), S. Bruscantini (bar—Don Alfonso), G. Kuhn (cnd), Marchigiana PO, Marchigiana Phil Chorus [I] *(rec live, Teatro Lauro Rossi at the Festival di Macerata, Aug. 3, 1990)* Orfeo 3-▲ 243913 [DDD]
Mozart, W.A.:Nozze di Figaro, w. K. Mattila (sop), M. McLaughlin (sop), M. Bacelli (mez), N. Curiel (mez), U. Benelli (ten), L. Gallo (bar), A. Nosotti (bass), M. Pertusi (bass), G. Tadeo (bass), Z. Mehta (cnd), Florence Maggio Musicale Orch, Florence Maggio Musicale Chorus Sony Classical ▲ SK 53286

Cheriez, Claudine (mez)
Boieldieu, F.-A.:Le Calife de Bagdad, w. L. Mayo (sop), J. Michelini (sop), L. Dale (ten), H. Rhys-Evans (ten), A. de Almeida (cnd), Camerata Provence Orch, Provence Camerata Chorus [F] Sonpact ▲ SPT 93007 [DDD]

Chernikh, Lidiya (sop)
Tchaikovsky, P.:Eugene Onegin, w. Tamara Sinyavskaya (mez), Alexander Vedernikov (bass), Alexander Fedin (sgr), Yuri Mazurok (sgr), V. Fedoseyev (cnd), USSR SO, Moscow SO, Fernseh SO Audiophile Classics ("Legacy Collection" series) 2-▲ 101.751

Chernov, Vladimir (bar)
Verdi, G.:Don Carlos (sels), w. J. Bunnell (sop), A. Millo (sop), D. Zajick (mez), M. Sylvester (ten), F. Furlanetto (bass), P. Plishka (bass), J. Levine (cnd), Metropolitan Opera Orch, New York Metropolitan Opera Chorus *(rec New York, Apr. 20-May 14, 1992)* Sony Classical ("Opera Highlights" series) ▲ SMK 53507 [DDD]
Verdi, G.:Luisa Miller, w. A. Millo (sop), F. Quivar (mez), P. Domingo (ten), J. Levine (cnd), Metropolitan Opera Orch, New York Metropolitan Opera Chorus Sony Classical 2-▲ S2K 48073
Verdi, G.:Luisa Miller (sels), w. A. Millo (sop), W. White (mez), F. Quivar (cta), P. Domingo (ten), J.-H. Rootering (bass), P. Plishka (bass), J. Levine (cnd), Metropolitan Opera Orch, New York Metropolitan Opera Chorus *(rec New York, May 2-18, 1991)* Sony Classical ("Opera Highlights" series) ▲ SMK 53508 [DDD]

Chevalier, Ludovic (sgr)
Landowski, M.:Music of, w. Nadine Sautereau (sop), Jean-Christophe Benoit (bar), Xavier Depraz (bass), Michel Bouquet (spkr), Gilbert Audin (bn), Evelyne Aïello, Didier Bouture, Laurent Decker, Françoise Deslogères, Landowski, Tzipine (cnd), Colonne Association des Concerts Orch, Boulogne-Billancourt Orch Conservatory, Paris Conservatory Société des Concerts Orch, L'Itinéraire Ensemble, Harmonia Nova Orch Ensemble—Con Bn; Con pour ondes Martenot; Femme sans passé; Hauts de Hurlevent; Horologe; Mouvement; Notes de Nuit; Souvenir d'un jardin d'enfance; Ventrilogue Chamade 3-▲ 5639/40/41 [AAD/DDD]

Chiara, Alejandro (bass)
Puccini, G.:Madama Butterfly, w. Montserrat Caballé (sop—Cio-Cio-San), Carmen Rigai (mez—Suzuki), Bernabé Martí (ten—Pinkerton), Diego Monjo (ten—Goro), Juan Rico (ten—Yamadori), Manuel Ausensi (bar—Sharpless), Jose Lemar (bass—Bonze), Antonio Leval (bass—Imperial Commissioner), Alejandro Chiara (bass—Registrar), G. Rivoli (cnd), Madrid Radio-TV Orch, Madrid Radio-TV Chorus *(rec Madrid, June 12, 1968)* Legato Classics 2-▲ LCD 210-2 [ADD]

Chiara, Maria (sop)
Bizet, G.:Carmen, w. M. Chiara (sop—Micaela), A. Caminada (mez—Mercedes), F. Cossotto (mez—Carmen), F. Andreoli (ten—Il Remendado), P. M. Ferraro (ten—Don José), R. Bruson (bar—Escamillo), G. Zancanaro (bar—Morales), A. Carusi (bass—Il Dancairo), P. Maag (cnd), Venice Teatro La Fenice Orch, Venice Teatro La Fenice Chorus *(rec 1971)* Myto 2-▲ MCD 93487
Puccini, G.:Arias, w. M. Caballé (sop), M. Freni (sop), B. Nilsson (sop), J. Sutherland (sop), R. Tebaldi (sop), F. Corelli (ten), L. Pavarotti (ten), S. Milnes (bar) London ▲ 421315-2 [ADD]
Smareglia, A.:Nozze istrane, w. Maria Chiara (sop—Marussa), Eleonora Iancovich (cta—Luze), Ruggero Bondino (ten—Lorenzo), Alessandro Cassis (bar—Nicola), Alessandro Maddalena (bar—Biagio), Carlo Zardo (bass—Bara Menico), M. Wolf-Ferrari (cnd), Trieste Teatro Comunale Giuseppe Verdi Orch, Trieste Teatro Comunale G. Verdi Chorus *(rec Trieste, Feb 17, 1973)* Bongiovanni ("Il Mito dell'Opera" series) 2-▲ 1133/34-2 [ADD]
Verdi, G.:Aida, w. G. Dimitrova (sop), L. Pavarotti (ten), L. Nucci (bar), P. Burchuladze (bass), L. Maazel (cnd), La Scala Orch, La Scala Chorus [I] London □ 433162-5
Verdi, G.:Aida, w. G. Dimitrova (sop), L. Pavarotti (ten), L. Nucci (bar), P. Burchuladze (bass), L. Maazel (cnd), La Scala Orch, La Scala Chorus [I] London 3-▲ 417439-2 [DDD] 2-■ 417439-4
Verdi, G.:Attila, w. Silvano Carroli (bar), Nicolai Ghiuselev (bass), N. Santi (cnd), Turin Teatro Regio Orch, Turin Teatro Regio Chorus *(rec live, 1980)* Serenissima 2-▲ SER 360138

Chiesa, Vivian della (sop)
Verdi, G.:Falstaff, w. Vivian Della Chiesa (sop—Alice), Audrey Schuh (sop—Nannetta), Lizabeth Pritchett (mez—Quickly), Evelyn Sachs (mez—Meg), André Turp (ten—Fenton), Virginio Assandri (ten—Caius), Luigi Vellucci (ten—Bardolfo), Leonard Warren (bar—Falstaff), Richard Torigi (bar—Ford), R. Cellini (cnd), New Orleans Opera Orch, New Orleans Opera Chorus *(rec live, May 5, 1956)* VAI Audio 2-▲ VAIA 1056-2
Verdi, G.:I lombardi alla prima crociata (sels), w. J. Peerce (ten), N. Moscona (bass), A. Toscanini (cnd), NBC SO—Act 3 Trio RCA Gold Seal ▲ 60276-2-RG [ADD] ■ 60276-4-RG (CrO2)

Chilcott, Robert (trb)
Fauré, G.:Pavane Orch, w. J.C. Case (bar), D. Willcocks (cnd), New Philharmonia Orch, King's College Choir Cambridge [choral ver.] EMI ▲ CDM 64715

▲ = CD ♦ = Enhanced CD Δ = MD ■ = Cassette Tape □ = DCC

Chilcott, Robert (trb) (cont.)
Fauré, G.:Requiem, w. J.C. Case (bar), D. Willcocks (cnd), New Philharmonia Orch, King's College Choir Cambridge EMI Classics ▲ CDM 64715

Chilcott, Susan (sop)
Albéniz, I.:Pepita Jiménez (suite), w. Francesc Garrigosa (ten), Barcelona Children's Choir, J. Pons (cnd), Barcelona's Free Theater CO Harmonia Mundi France ▲ HMC 901537
Halffter, E.:Dominus pastor meus, w. Claire Powell (mez), Joan Cabero (ten), José Antonio Carril (bass), V. P. Pérez (cnd), Tenerife SO, La Laguna Univ Choir Discobi ▲ DIS 2009 [DDD]
Schubert, Franz:Mass 5, w. R. Cyrille (alt), Vonk (ten), G. Schwarz (bass), R. Delcroix (cnd), Basque Bayonne-Côte Orch, Ametsa D'Irun Choir [L] Forlane ▲ FOR 16649 [DDD]

Childs, Linda (mez)
Demars, J.:An American Requiem, w. Joni Killian (sop), George Killian (ten), Robert La France (b-bar), James DeMars (cnd), Arizona State Univ Choirs *(rec Phoenix Symphony Hall, Jan 17, 1994)* Renaissance ▲ 94001 [DDD]

Childs, Linda (nar)
Glass, Philip:Songs from the Trilogy, w. M. Vargas (sop), P. Esswood, D. Perry (ten), Philip Glass Ensemble CBS ▲ MK 45580 ■ FMT 45580

Chingari, Mario (bar)
Catalani, A.:Edmea, w. M. Sokolinska Noto (sop), M. Frusoni (ten), P. Lefebvre (bass), A. Nosotti (bass), G. Pasella (bass), G. del Vivo (bass), M. de Bernart (cnd), Lucca Teatro Comunale Giglio Orch, Lucca Teatro Comunale del Giglio Chorus [I] *(rec live 9/89)* Bongiovanni 2-▲ GB 2093/94 [DDD]
Giordano, U.:La Cena delle beffe, w. R. Lantieri (sop), Armiliato (sgr), N. Sanzogno (cnd), Piacenza SO [I] *(rec live, 12/14/88)* Bongiovanni 2-▲ GB 2068/69 [DDD]

Chioreanu, Lucian (ten)
Wagner, S.:Schwarzschwanenreich, w. Beth Johanning (sop—Linda), Kerstin Quandt (cta—Ursula), Walter Raffeiner (ten—Ludwig), Lucian Chioreanu (ten—A Boy), André Wenhold (bar—Oswald), Roland Hartmann (sgr—Tempter/Priest), Jutta Maria Schmitz (sgr—Ash-Woman), Ksenija Lukie (sgr—A Girl), K. Bach (cnd), Thüringian Saalfeld-Rudolstadt SO, Thüringian Landestheater Rudolstadt Chorus *(rec Thüringer Landestheater, Rudolstadt, June 1994)* Marco Polo 2-▲ 8.223777-8 [DDD]

Chiti, Patricia Adkins (mez)
Desolation & Despair:Italian Drawing Room Music of the Romantic Era (1800's), w. Hiroko Sato (pno) Kicco Classics ▲ 1195 [DDD]

Chiummo, Umberto (bass)
Mozart, W.A.:Don Giovanni, w. Christine Brewer (sop—Donna Anna), Nuccia Focile (sop—Zerlina), Felicity Lott (sop—Donna Elvira), Jerry Hadley (ten—Don Ottavio), Bo Skovhus (bar—Don Giovanni), Umberto Chiummo (bass—Masetto/Il Commendatore), Alessandro Corbelli (bass—Leporello), C. Mackerras (cnd), Scottish CO, Scottish Chamber Chorus *(rec Usher Hall, Edinburgh, Scotland, July 31–Aug 11, 1995)* Telarc 3-▲ CD 80420 [DDD]

Chmelo, Vladimir (bar)
Bizet, G.:Carmen (sels), w. D. Palade (sop—Micaëla), A. Liebeck (sop—Frasquita), G. Alperyn (mez—Carmen), D. Schaechter (mez—Mercédès), G. Lamberti (ten—Don José), M. Dvorsky (ten—Remandado), J. Durco (ten—Cancairo), A. Titus (bar—Escamillo), V. Chmelo (bar—Morales), D. Rigosa (bass—Zuniga), A. Rahbari (cnd), Czech-Slovak RSO Bratislava, Slovak Phil Chorus, Bratislava Children's Choir *(rec July 1990)* Naxos ▲ 8.550727 [DDD]

Choi, Y.-H. (sop)
Chopin, F.:Songs Sop (comp), w. C. Grasser (pno) [Pol] Quantum ▲ QM 6900 [DDD] ■ QM 1995 (D)

Chookasian, Lili (mez)
Mahler, G.:Das Lied von der Erde, w. Richard Cassilly (ten), W. Susskind (cnd), Cincinnati SO *(rec 1978)* Vox Box 2-▲ CDX 5138 [ADD]
Verdi, G.:Un ballo in maschera, w. M. Caballé (sop—Amelia), T. Paniagua (sop—Oscar), L. Chookasian (cta—Ulrica), P. Domingo (ten—Riccardo), C. MacNeil (bar—Renato), J. Pons (bar—Tom), C. del Bosco (bass—Samuel), G. Patanè (cnd), *(orch unknown)* Ornamenti 2-▲ FE 103

Chookasian, Lilli (mez)
Donizetti, G.:Roberto Devereux (sels), w. M. Caballé (sop), J. Oncina (ten), W. Alberti (bar), C.F. Cillario (cnd), *(orch & chorus unknown)*—9 arias from Acts 1 & 2 [I] *(rec live in Carnegie Hall, 12/16/65)* Standing Room Only 2-▲ SRO 801-2 (m) [ADD]
Mahler, G.:Das Lied von der Erde, w. R. Lewis (ten), E. Ormandy (cnd), Philadelphia Orch *(rec Feb. 9, 1966)* Sony Classical ("Essential Classics" series) ▲ SBK 53518 [ADD] ■ SBT 53518

Choquette, Natalie (sop)
La Diva, w. Montreal La Scala Orch [cnd:Eric Lagacé] Isba ▲ ISCD 2070

Choy (sgr)
Mozart, W.A.:Bastien und Bastienne, w. Kirchner (sgr), Müller De Vries (sgr), R. Clemencic (cnd), Alpe Adria Ensemble [G] Nuova Era 2-▲ 7106/07 [DDD]
Rousseau, J.-J.:Le Devin du village, w. Kirchner (sgr), Müller de Vries (sgr), R. Clemencic (cnd), Alpe Adria Ensemble, Alpe Adria Chorus [F] Nuova Era 2-▲ 7106/07 [DDD]

Christ, Rudolf (ten)
Kálmán, I.:Die Csárdásfürstin (sels), w. E. Liebesberg (sop), L. Rysanek (sop), H. Prikopa (bar), F. Bauer-Theussl (cnd), Vienna Volksoper Orch, Vienna Volksoper Chorus [G] Koch Präsent ▲ CD 399226 [AAD]
Lehár, F.:Der Graf von Luxemburg (sels), w. Renate Holm (sop), Else Liebesberg (sop), Hilde Brauner (cta), Dagmar Hermann (mez), Herbert Prikopa (bar), F. Bauer-Theussl (cnd), Vienna Volksoper Orch, Vienna Volksoper Chorus [G] Koch Präsent ▲ CD 399223 [AAD]
Lehár, F.:Paganini (sels), w. E. Liebesberg (sop), E. Mechera (sop), K. Equiluz (ten), F. Bauer-Theussl (cnd), Vienna Volksoper Orch, Vienna Volksoper Chorus [G] Koch Präsent ▲ CD 399226 [AAD]
Millöcker, C.:Bettelstudent, w. Wilma Lipp (sop—Laura), Esther Rethy (sop—Bronislava), Rosette Anday (cta—Palmatica), Rudolf Christ (ten—Symon), Kurt Preger (ten—Ollendorf), Eberhard Waechter (bar—Jan), A. Paulik (cnd), Vienna Volksoper Orch, Vienna Volksoper Chorus *(rec Brahmssaal, Vienna, June 1995)* Omega 2-▲ OCD 1018/19 [ADD]
Orff, C.:Die Kluge, w. E. Schwarzkopf (sop), P. Kuén (ten), M. Cordes (bar), B. Kusche (bar), H. Prey (bar), G. Frick (bass), G. Wieter (bass), W. Sawallisch (cnd), Philharmonia Orch [G] EMI Classics ("Studio" series) 2-▲ CDMB 63712 [ADD]
Orff, C.:Der Mond—Ein kleines Welttheater, w. P. Kuén (ten), K. Schmitt-Walter (bar), H. Graml (bar), H. Hotter (b-bar), P. Lagger (bass), W. Sawallisch (cnd), Philharmonia Orch, Philharmonia Chorus [G] EMI Classics ("Studio" series) 2-▲ CDMB 63712 [ADD]
Straus, O.:Ein Walzertraum (sels), w. H. Brauner (cta), R. Holm (sop), E. Liebesberg (sop), D. Hermann (mez), H. Prikopa (bar), F. Bauer-Theussl (cnd), Vienna Volksoper Orch, Vienna Volksoper Chorus [G] Koch Präsent ▲ CD 399223 [AAD]
Strauss (II), Joh.:Die Fledermaus, w. E. Schwarzkopf (sop), R. Streich (sop), N. Gedda (ten), H. Krebs (ten), E. Kunz (bar), K. Dönch (bar), H. von Karajan (cnd), Philharmonia Orch, Philharmonia Chorus [G] EMI Classics ("Studio" series) 2-▲ CDHB 69531 (m) [ADD]

Christensen, Blanche (sop)
Honegger, A.:Judith, w. Netania Davrath (sop), Madeleine Milhaud (nar), M. Abravanel (cnd), Utah SO, Salt Lake City Symphonic Choir [F] *(rec Dec. 1964)* Vanguard Classics ▲ OVC 8088 [ADD]
Vaughan Williams, R.:Dona nobis pacem, w. William Metcalf (bar), M. Abravanel (cnd), Utah SO Vanguard Classics ▲ SVC 7 [ADD]

Christiansen, Christian (bass)
Heise, P.:King & Marshall, w. P. Elming (ten), A. Haugland (bass), M. Schønwandt (cnd), Danish National RSO, Danish National Choir Chandos 3-▲ CHAN 9143 [DDD]
Koppel, H.D.:Moses, w. Elisabeth Meyer-Topsøe (sop), Kirsten Dolberg (mez), Kurt Westi (ten), Michael Kristensen (ten), Per Høyer (bar), O.A. Hughes (cnd), Danish National RSO, Jesper Grovw Jørgensen (cnd), Danish National Radio Choir *(rec Danish Radio Concert Hall, Mar 1996)* Marco Polo/Dacapo ▲ 8.224046 [DDD]
Nielsen, C.:Saul & David, w. T. Kiberg (sop), A. Gjevang (mez), P. Lindroos (ten), K. Westi (ten), A. Haugland (bass), J. Klint (bass), N. Järvi (cnd), Danish National RSO, Danish National Radio Choir [Da] Chandos 2-▲ CHAN 8911/12 [DDD]

Christofellis, Aris (alt)
Carissimi, G.:Oratorio della Santissima Vergine, w. P. Borri (sop), A. M. Ferrante (sop), P. Pace (sop), L. Petroni (ten), F. Sclaverano (ten), R. Abbondanza (bass), M. Mondelli (bass), P. Spagnoli (bass), F. Colusso (cnd), Seicentonovecento Ensemble [I] Bongiovanni ▲ GB 10011 [DDD]

Christofellis, Aris (alt) (cont.)
Carissimi, G.:Oratorio di Daniele Profeta, w. P. Borri (sop), A. M. Ferrante (sop), P. Pace (sop), L. Petroni (ten), F. Sclaverano (ten), R. Abbondanza (bass), M. Mondelli (bass), P. Spagnoli (bass), F. Colusso (cnd), Seicentonovecento Ensemble [I] Bongiovanni ▲ GB 10011 [DDD]
Vivaldi, A.:L'Olimpiade, w. L. Meeuwsen (sop), M. van der Sluis (sop), E. von Magnus (alt), G. Lesne (alt), W. Oberholtzer (bar), A. Walker Schultze (bass), R. Clemencic (cnd), Clemencic Consort, La Cappella Vocal Ensemble [I] *(rec live, Paris, 2/8–10/90)* Nuova Era ("Ancient Music" series) 2-▲ 6932/33 [DDD]

Christoff, Boris (bass)
Beethoven, L. van:Fidelio (sels), w. E. Gracis (cnd), Bulgarian RSO, Bulgarian National Chorus—Aria of Piazarro Forlane ▲ FRL 16651 [AAD]
Bellini, V.:Norma, w. M. Callas (sop), E. Nicolai (mez), F. Corelli (ten), A. Votto (cnd), Trieste Teatro Comunale Giuseppe Verdi Orch, Trieste Teatro Comunale G. Verdi Chorus *(rec live 11/19/53)* Melodram 2-▲ CDM 26031 [ADD]
Bellini, V.:Norma (sels), w. M. Callas (sop), E. Nicolai (mez), F. Corelli (ten), A. Votto (cnd), Trieste Teatro Comunale Giuseppe Verdi Orch, Trieste Teatro Comunale G. Verdi Chorus—13 arias [I] *(rec live 11/19/53)* Myto 2-▲ 2 MCD 91340 [ADD]
Boito, A.:Mefistofele, w. Orietta Moscucci (sop—Margherita), Amalia Pini (mez—Martha), Piero de Palma (ten—Wagner), Giacinto Prandelli (ten—Faust), Boris Christoff (bass—Mefistofele), V. Gui (cnd), Rome Opera Orch, Rome Opera Chorus EMI Classics 2-▲ CDMB 65655
Boris Christoff in Concert *(rec 1961)* Arkadia 3-▲ 549 (m) [ADD]
Borodin, A.:Prince Igor, w. Kalmus (sgr), Infantino (sgr), G. Taddei (ten), O. Dominguez (mez), A. La Rosa Parodi (cnd), Rome RAI Orch, Rome RAI Chorus *(rec live 9/19/64)* Melodram 2-▲ MEL 27028 (s)
Brahms, J.:Ein Deutsches Requiem, w. Rosanna Carteri (sop), B. Walter (cnd), Rome Radio-TV SO, Rome Radio-TV Chorus Stradivarius 2-▲ STV DTM 12323 [ADD]
Brahms, J.:Ein Deutsches Requiem, w. Rosanna Carteri (sop), B. Walter (cnd), Rome Radio-TV SO, Rome Radio-TV Chorus *(rec live, Turin RAI Auditorium, Apr. 16, 1952)* Emozioni ▲ CDAR 2029 [ADD]
Bulgarian & Russian Orthodox Chant, w. Saint Alexandre Nevski Church Choir Sofia [cnd:Angel Konstantinov] Jade ▲ JAD C 059
Cimarosa, D.:Il Matrimonio segreto (sels), w. H. Gueden (sop), A. Noni (sop), F. Barbieri (mez), T. Schipa (ten), S. Bruscantini (bar), M. Rossi (cnd), La Scala Orch—Act I highlights [I] *(rec live, Milan March 22, 1949)* Melodram 2-▲ CDM 29505 [ADD]
D'Angelo & Christoff, w. G. D'Angelo (sop), Rome RAI SO [cnd:Alfredo Simonetto] *(rec Martini & Rossi Concert, 1961)* Incontri Memorabili ▲ CDMR 5034
Gatta, Moffo, Rizzieri, Christoff & Mazzoli, w. D. Gatta (sop), Anna Moffo (sop), Elena Rizzieri (sop), Ferruccio Mazzoli (bass), Rome RAI SO, Turin RAI SO *(rec Martini & Rossi Concert)* Incontri Memorabili ▲ CDMR 5033
Glinka, M.:A Life for the Tsar (sels), w. A. Simonetto (cnd), Turin Radio-TV SO—Monologo di Ivan Fonit Cetra ("Martini & Rossi" series) ▲ FCT CDMR 5009
Gluck, C.W.:Iphigénie en Aulide (sels), w. E. Gràcis (cnd), Bulgarian RSO, Bulgarian National Chorus—Récitatif & Aria of Agamemnon Forlane ▲ FRL 16651 [AAD]
Gounod, C.:Faust, w. V. de los Angeles (sop), L. Berton (sop), R. Gorr (mez), N. Gedda (ten), E. Blanc (bar), A. Cluytens (cnd), Paris Opera Orch [F] Angel ("Studio" series) 3-▲ CDMC 69983 [ADD]
Gounod, C.:Faust (sels), w. Liliane Berton (sop), Victoria de los Angeles (sop), Rita Gorr (mez), Nicolai Gedda (ten), Victor Autran (bar), Ernest Blanc (bar), A. Cluytens (cnd), Paris Opera Orch, Paris Opera Chorus Classics for Pleasure ("Eminence" series) ▲ CDEMX 2215 [DDD]
Gretchaninoff, A.:Liturgica Domestica for St. John Chrysostom, w. Bulgarian National Chorus Jade ▲ JAD C062
Live Recordings *(rec 1953–80)* Legato Classics ▲ LCD 107-1 (m) [AAD]
Massenet, J.:Don Quichotte, w. Teresa Berganza (mez), Pina Malgarini (mez), Tommaso Frascati (ten), Carlo Badioli (bass), A. Simonetto (cnd), Milan RAI SO, Milan RAI Chorus Melodram 2-▲ CDM 27027
Mélodies Russes [Russian Songs] EMI Classics 5-▲ CDZE 67496
Meyerbeer, G.:Le Prophète (sels), w. A. Simonetto (cnd), Turin Radio-TV SO Fonit Cetra ("Martini & Rossi" series) ▲ FCT CDMR 5009
Meyerbeer, G.:Roberto il Diavolo, w. R. Scotto (sop), G. Merighi (sgr), N. Sanzogno (cnd), Florence Maggio Musicale Orch, Florence Maggio Musicale Chorus [I] *(rec live 4/7/68)* Melodram 3-▲ MEL 37024
Meyerbeer, G.:Roberto il Diavolo, w. R. Scotto (sop), G. Merighi (sgr), N. Sanzogno (cnd), Florence Maggio Musicale Orch, Florence Maggio Musicale Chorus [I] *(rec live, 4/7/68)* Arkadia 3-▲ 549 (m) [ADD]
Monteverdi, C.:Arias & Duets, w. E. Gracis (cnd), Bulgarian RSO, Bulgarian National Chorus—Aria of Seneca [from The Coronation of Poppea] Forlane ▲ FRL 16651 [AAD]
Mozart, W.A.:Arias, w. E. Gracis (cnd), Bulgarian RSO, Bulgarian National Chorus—Così dunque tradisci Forlane ▲ FRL 16651 [AAD]
Mozart, W.A.:Don Giovanni (sels), w. A. Simonetto (cnd), Turin Radio-TV SO—Madamina il Catalogo è Questo Fonit Cetra ("Martini & Rossi" series) ▲ FCT CDMR 5009
Mussorgsky, M.:Khovanshchina, w. Irene Companez (cta), Herbert Handt (ten), Mirto Picchi (ten), Armedeo Berdini (sgr), Giorgio Canello (sgr), Dmitri Lopatto (sgr), Michele Malaspina (sgr), Jolanda Mancini (sgr), Mario Petri (sgr), A. Rodzinski (cnd), Rome RAI Radio-TV SO, Rome RAI Chorus Stradivarius 2-▲ STV DTM 12320 [ADD]
Mussorgsky, M.:Khovanshchina, w. Jolanda Mancini (sop—Emma), Irene Companez (mez), Amedeo Berdini (ten—Prince Andrei Khovanski), Mirto Picchi (ten—Prince Vasili Golitsin), Herbert Handt (ten—Scribe), Andrea Mineo (bar—Kuzka), Giampiero Malaspina (bar—Shaklovity), Boris Christoff (bass—Dosifei), Mario Petri (bass—Prince Ivan Khovanski), Dimitri Lopatto (Varsonofiev/First Strelyets), Giorgio Conello (Second Strelyets), A. Rodzinski (cnd), *(orch unknown)* [I] *(rec Rome, 1958)* VAI Audio 2-▲ VAIA 1052-2
Mussorgsky, M.:Songs (comp), w. Alexandre Labinsky (pno), Gerald Moore (pno), French National Radio Orch EMI Classics ("Great Recordings of the Century" series) 3-▲ CHS 63025 (m) [ADD]
Rameau, J.P.:Dardanus (sels), w. E. Gracis (cnd), Bulgarian RSO, Bulgarian National Chorus—Aria of Antenor Forlane ▲ FRL 16651 [AAD]
Recital, w. Ettore Gracis (cnd), Bulgarian RSO, Bulgarian Radio Sym Chorus Forlane ▲ FOR 16651 [AAD]
Recital, w. various orchs *(rec live, Milan, Turin & Rome, 1954–1965)* Melodram ▲ CDM 16508 (m) [AAD]
Rimsky-Korsakov, N.:The Maid of Pskov, w. N. Panni (sop), F. Cadoni (mez), A. Bertocci (ten), T. Schippers (cnd), *(orch unknown)* *(rec 1969)* Great Opera Performances 2-▲ GOP 720
Russian Opera Arias & Songs EMI Classics ▲ CDH 64252
Tchaikovsky, P.:Mazeppa, w. M. Olivero (sop), M. Radev (mez), D. Poleri (ten), E. Bastianini (bar), J. Perlea (cnd), Florence Maggio Musicale Orch, Florence Maggio Musicale Chorus [I] *(rec live 6/6/54)* Melodram 2-▲ MEL 27070 (m) [AAD]
Verdi, G.:Aida, w. Z. Milanov (sop), F. Barbieri (mez), J. Björling (ten), L. Warren (bar), J. Perlea (cnd), Rome Opera Orch, Rome Opera Chorus [I] RCA Gold Seal ▲ 60201-2-RG (m) [ADD] ■ 60201-4-RG (m)
Verdi, G.:Aida, w. Z. Milanov (sop), F. Barbieri (mez), J. Björling (ten), L. Warren (bar), J. Perlea (cnd), Rome Opera Orch, Rome Opera Chorus [I] RCA Gold Seal 3-▲ 6652-2-RG (m) [ADD] 3-■ ALK3-5380 (m)
Verdi, G.:Aida (sels), w. A. Cerquetti (sop), E. Nicolai (mez), G. Penno (ten), G. Guelfi (bar), G. Santini (cnd), Naples Teatro San Carlo Orch, Naples Teatro San Carlo Chorus [I] [highlights] *(rec live, Naples, July 24, 1954)* Golden Age of Opera ▲ GAO 134 [ADD]
Verdi, G.:Attila, w. M. Roberti (sop—Odabella), G. Limarilli (tenor—Foresto), G. Guelfi (baritone—Ezio), B. Christoff (bass—Attila), B. Bartoletti (cnd), Florence Teatro Comunale Orch, Florence Teatro Comunale Chorus *(rec Jan. 12, 1962)* Myto 2-▲ MCD 93589 [DDD]
Verdi, G.:Don Carlos, w. G. Brouwenstein (sop—Elisabetta di Valois), F. Barbieri (mez—Princess Eboli), J. Vickers (ten—Don Carlo), T. Gobbi (bar—Rodrigo), B. Christoff (bass—Fillipo), C. M. Giulini (cnd), Royal Opera House Orch, Royal Opera House Chorus Covent Garden *(rec 1958)* Myto 3-▲ MCD 94197

VOCALISTS

Christoff, Boris (bass) (cont.)

Verdi, G.:Ernani, w. Montserrat Caballè (sop), Bruno Prevedi (ten), Peter Glossop (bar), G. Gavazzeni (cnd), Milan RAI SO, Milan RAI Chorus *(rec Milan, Mar. 25, 1969)* Pantheon 2-▲ PHE 6634 (m)

Verdi, G.:Ernani, w. A. Cerquetti (sop), M. Del Monaco (ten), E. Bastianni (bar), D. Mitropoulos (cnd), Florence Maggio Musicale Orch [I] *(rec live 6/14/57)* Melodram 2-▲ MEL 27016

Verdi, G.:La forza del destino, w. R. Tebaldi (sop), O. Dominguez (mez), F. Corelli (ten), R. Capecchi (bar), E. Bastianini (bar), F. Molinari-Pradelli (cnd), Naples Teatro San Carlo Orch, Naples Teatro San Carlo Chorus *(rec Oct. 1 1958)* Melodram 3-▲ MLO 370102 [AAD]

Verdi, G.:Macbeth (sels), w. E. Gracis (cnd), Bulgarian RSO, Bulgarian National Chorus—Recitative & Aria of Banco Forlane ▲ FRL 16651 [AAD]

Verdi, G.:I masnadieri, w. I. Ligabue (sop), G. Raimondi (ten), R. Bruson (bar), G. Gavazzeni (cnd), Rome Opera Orch, Rome Opera Chorus [I] *(rec live, Rome, Nov. 25, 1972)* Golden Age of Opera 2-▲ GAO 135/36 [ADD]

Verdi, G.:Requiem Mass, w. Hilde Zadek (sop), Margarete Klose (cta), Helge Roswaenge (ten), H. von Karajan (cnd), Vienna PO, Vienna Singverein Stradivarius 2-▲ STV DTM 12323 [ADD]

Verdi, G.:I vespri siciliani, w. Maria Callas (sop), Giorgio Kokolios (sgr), E. Kleiber (cnd), Florence Maggio Musicale Orch, Florence Maggio Musicale Chorus *(rec live, Florence, May 26, 1951)* Enterprise ("Documents" series) 3-▲ ENT LV 996

Verdi, G.:I vespri siciliani, w. A. Cerquetti (sop), Ortica (sgr), C. Tagliabue (bar), M. Rossi (cnd), Turin Radio Orch, Turin Radio Chorus [I] *(rec live, Turin, 11/16/55)* Claque 2-▲ CLQ 2017 (m)

Verdi, G.:I vespri siciliani, w. Maria Callas (sop—Duchess), Giorgio Kokolios Bardi (ten—Arrigo), Gino Sarri (ten—Danieli), Enzo Mascherini (bar—Guido di Monforte), Boris Christoff (bass—Giovanni da Procida), Mario Forsini (bass—Count Vaudemont), Bruneo Carmassi (bass—Bethune), E. Kleiber (cnd), Florence Teatro Comunale Orch, Florence Teatro Comunale Chorus *(rec live, Florence, 1951)* Melodram 3-▲ IMC 303016 [ADD]

Wagner, R.:Die Meistersinger von Nürnberg, w. Bruna Rizzoli (sop), Fernanda Cadoni (mez), Luigi Infantino (ten), Vito Tatone (ten), Renato Capecchi (bar), Giuseppe Taddei (bar), Giovanni Ciavola (bass), James Loomis (bass), Silvo Maionica (bass), Vito Susca (bass), Raimondo Botteghelli (sgr), Walter Brunelli (sgr), Carlo Franzini (sgr), Ezio de Giorgi (sgr), Renzo Gonzales (sgr), L. von Matačič (cnd), Turin RAI Radio-TV SO, Turin RAI Chorus Stradivarius 4-▲ STV 12310

Wagner, R.:Parsifal, w. M. Callas (sop), Baldelli (sgr), R. Panerai (bar), D. Lopatto (bar), V. Gui (cnd), Rome Radio-TV SO, Rome Radio-TV Chorus [I] *(rec in concert, 11/20-21/50)* Verona 3-▲ 27085/87

Wagner, R.:Parsifal, w. M. Callas (sop), Baldelli (sgr), R. Panerai (bar), D. Lopatto (bar), V. Gui (cnd), Rome Radio-TV SO, Rome Radio-TV Chorus [I] *(rec 11/20-21/50)* Melodram 3-▲ MEL 36041 (m)

Wagner, R.:Tannhäuser (sels), w. R. Tebaldi (sop), H. Beirer (ten), C. Tagliabue (bar), K. Böhm (cnd), Naples Teatro San Carlo Orch, Naples Teatro San Carlo Chorus—10 soprano solo, duet & ensemble arias Acts 2 & 3 [I; Hans Beirer (Tannhäuser) sings in German] *(rec live, Naples, 3/12/50)* Standing Room Only ▲ SRO 834-1 [ADD]

Christopher, Russell (ten)

Puccini, G.:Tosca, w. Leonie Rysanek (sop), Andrea Velis (ten), Clifford Harvuot (bar), Cornell MacNeil (bar), Fernando Corena (bass), Paul Plishka (bass), F. Molinari-Pradelli (cnd), San Francisco Opera Orch, San Francisco Opera Chorus Melodram 2-▲ CDM 27508

Christos (sop)

Rachmaninoff, S.:The Bells, w. Walter Planté (ten), Arnold Voketaitis (bar), L. Slatkin (cnd), St. Louis SO, St. Louis Sym Chorus *(rec 1980)* Vox Box 3-▲ CD3X 3002 [ADD]

Chuen, Ah (voc)

Sung, L.C.:Music of, w. Li Chin Sung (voc/gtr/syn/perc)—Grandfather 1; Garden; Point of Death; Dream On; Give Up; Known; Treasure; Speed Game; Buddha; Mad Birds; East. West; Silence; Suffocation; Shame; Wake up & Death; Jump; Grandfather 3; Run; Ear Games; Grandfather 4; Yin 1; Grandfather 2; Muzzy; and others *(rec 1992-95)* Tzadik ("Composer" series) ▲ TZA 7014 [DDD]

Chung, Locky (bar)

Wolf, H.:Goethe-Lieder (sels), w. Markus Hadulla (pno), Stephan Genz (bar), Claar Ter Horst (pno)—24 sels Claves ▲ 50-9517

Ciavola, Giovanni (bass)

Puccini, G.:La Bohème, w. Schimenti (sop), Micheluzi (sgr), G. Lauri-Volpi (ten), A. Paoletti (cnd), Rome Opera Orch, Rome Opera Chorus *(rec 1952)* Bongiovanni 2-▲ GB 1057/58 [ADD]

Wagner, R.:Die Meistersinger von Nürnberg, w. Bruna Rizzoli (sop), Fernanda Cadoni (mez), Luigi Infantino (ten), Vito Tatone (ten), Renato Capecchi (bar), Giuseppe Taddei (bar), Boris Christoff (bass), James Loomis (bass), Silvo Maionica (bass), Vito Susca (bass), Raimondo Botteghelli (sgr), Walter Brunelli (sgr), Carlo Franzini (sgr), Ezio de Giorgi (sgr), Renzo Gonzales (sgr), L. von Matačič (cnd), Turin RAI Radio-TV SO, Turin RAI Chorus Stradivarius 4-▲ STV 12310

Cicoara, Lucia (mez)

Donizetti, G.:Lucia di Lammermoor, w. Silvia Voinea (sop—Lucia), Lucia Cicoara (mez—Alisa), Florin Georgescu (ten—Edgardo), Gabriel Nastase (ten—Arturo), Nicolae Herlea (bar—Lord Enrico), Pompei Harasteanu (bass—Raimondo), C. Petrovici (cnd), Romanian Opera Orch, Romanian Opera Chorus *(rec 1984)* Vox Box 2-▲ CDX 5164

Cicogna, Adriana (mez)

Donizetti, G.:Le Convenienze Teatrali, w. M.A. Peters (sop), S. Tedesco (ten), R. Scaltriti (bar), B. Rigacci (cnd), Emilia Romagna Arturo Toscanini SO, Lugo Teatro Comunale Rossini Chorus [I] *(rec live, 6/90)* Bongiovanni 2-▲ GB 2091/92 [DDD]

Donizetti, G.:I pazzi per progetto, w. S. Rigacci (sop), G. Polidori (bar), G. Sarti (bar), V. M. Brunetti (bass), E. Fissore (bass), L. Monreale (bass), G. Micheli (cnd), Emilia Romagna Arturo Toscanini SO [I] *(rec live, 12/88)* Bongiovanni ▲ GB 2070 [DDD]

Lattuada, F.:Le Preziose ridicole, w. S. Valayre (sop—Madelon), A. Catarci (sop—Marotte), A. Cicogna (mez—Cathos), S. Tedesco (ten—La Grange), E. Di Cesare (ten—Mascarille), A. Veccia (bar—Croissy), R. Servile (bar—Jodelet), E. Fissore (bass—Gorgibus), E. Romagna (cnd), Toscanini SO, G. Masini (cnd), Rossini Teatro Comunale Chorus [I] *(rec live, 1991)* Ermitage ▲ ERM 404 [DDD]

Rossini, G.:Songs, w. M. A. Peters (sop), E. Palacio (ten), F. Bettini (sgr), M. Carraro (cnd), *(orch unknown)* —Il carnevale di Venezia; L'Asia in Faville; Egle ed Irene; Un sou; Laus Deo; Dalle quete e pallid'ombre; Nella stagion di maggio; Hai la sottana; Ridiamo cantiamo; Les amants de Seville; La passeggiata; Le depart; Gli animali parlanti del giorno [I] Bongiovanni ▲ GB 2125 [DDD]

Cidoni, Mary (sgr)

Rorem, N.:A Childhood Miracle, w. Michele Couture (sop—Peony), Darcy Dunn (sgr—Violet), Madeline Tsingopoulos (sgr—Mother), Mary Cidoni (sgr—Emma), Patrick Greene (sgr—Snowman), Peter Castaldi (sgr—Father), R. E. Harrell (cnd), Magic Circle CO Newport Classic ▲ NPT 85594 [DDD]

Ciecla, Ryczard (bar)

Reichardt, J.F.:Stiller Friede, w. S. Kawalla (cnd), Polish Radio-TV SO [G] Vienna Modern Masters ▲ VMM 3003 [DDD]

Ciesinşki, Catherine (mez)

Dvořák, A.:Songs, w. G. Hirst (ten), J. Ostendorf (bass-bar), R. Palmer (pno)—Serbian Songs, Op. 6; Folk Tunes, Op. 73; 4 Lieder, Op. 82; Love Songs, Op. 83; Russian Folk Duets Erasmus ▲ WVH 084

Stravinsky, I.:Cant Sop, w. Jon Humphries (ten), R. Craft (cnd), Orch of St. Luke, Gregg Smith Singers MusicMasters ▲ 01612-67158-2

Stravinsky, I.:L'Histoire du soldat, w. Jon Humphries (ten), David Evitts (bar), Mark Wajt (pno), R. Craft (cnd), Orch of St. Luke, Gregg Smith Singers MusicMasters ▲ 01612-67152-2

Ciesinski, Katherine (mez)

Blitzstein, M.:Regina, w. A. Réaux (sop), S. Greenawald (sop), S. Ramey (bass), J. Mauceri (cnd), Scottish Opera Orch, Scottish Opera Chorus [E] London 2-▲ 433812-2 [DDD]

Carter, E.:Syringa, w. J. Opalach (bass), W. Purvis (cnd), Speculum Musicae Bridge ▲ BCD 9014 [DDD]

Donizetti, G.:Anna Bolena, w. R. Scotto (sop—Anna Bolena), K. Ciesinski (mez—Smeton), S. Marsee (mez—Giovanna Seymour), S. Kolk (ten—Riccardo Percy), S. Ramey (bass—Enrico VIII), J. Rudel (cnd), Philadelphia Opera Orch *(rec live, Dec. 16, 1975)* Legato Classics 2-▲ LCD 175 [ADD]

Handel, G.F.:Messiah (sels), w. Judith Blegen (sop), John Aler (ten), John Cheek (bass), R. Westenburg (cnd), Musica Sacra, Musica Sacra Chorus RCA Silver Seal ▲ 60481-2-RV [DDD]; ■ 60481-4-RV (CrO2)

Rorem, N.:Women's Voices, w. N. Rorem (pno) CRI ▲ CD 657 [ADD]

Cigada, Francesco (bar)

Leoncavallo, R.:Pagliacci, w. Josefina Huguet (sop—Nedda), Antonio Paoli (ten), Gaetano Pini-Corsi (ten—Beppe), Ernesto Badini (bar—Silvio), Francesco Cigada (bar—Tonio), Giuseppe Rosci (sgr—Un contadino), C. Sabajno (cnd), La Scala Orch, La Scala Chorus *(rec 1907)* Bongiovanni ▲ GB 1120-2 [ADD]

Cigna, Gina (sop)

Bellini, V.:Norma, w. E. Stignani (mez), G. Breviario (ten), V. Gui (cnd), EIAR Orch, EIAR Chorus [I] *(rec 1936 for Cetra)* Pearl 2-▲ PEAS 9422 (m) [AAD]

Bellini, V.:Norma, w. E. Stignani (mez), G. Breviario (ten), T. Pasero (bass), V. Gui (cnd), Turin EIAR SO, Turin EIAR Chorus *(rec 1937)* Memories 2-▲ MEM 4552 [ADD]

Bellini, V.:Norma, w. Gina Cigna (sop—Norma), Thelma Votipka (mez—Clotilde), Bruna Castagna (cta—Adalgisa), Giovanni Martinelli (ten—Pollione), Giodano Paltrinieri (ten—Flavio), Ezio Pinza (bass—Oroveso), E. Panizza (cnd), *(orch unknown)* *(rec live, New York, Feb. 20, 1937)* The Fourties 2-▲ ENT FT 1517

Bellini, V.:Norma, w. Gina Cigna (sop—Norma), Ebe Stignani (sop—Adalgisa), Adriana Perris (mez—Clotilde), Giovanni Breviario (ten—Pollione), Emilio Renzi (ten—Flavio), Tancredi Pasero (bass—Oroveso), V. Gui (cnd), EIAR Orch, Achille Consoli (cnd), EIAR Chorus *(rec Aug/Sept 1937)* Arkadia ("The 78's" series) 2-▲ 78010 [ADD]

Gina Cigna & Toti Dal Monte, w. Toti Dal Monte (sop) Phonographe ("Great Voices" series) ▲ PHG 5057

Gina Cigna:A 90th Birthday Celebration Standing Room Only ▲ SRO 805-1 (m) [ADD]

Gina Cigna:Opera Arias *(rec 1930-41)* Preiser ("Lebendige Vergangenheit" series) ▲ PRE 89016 (m) [AAD]

Puccini, G.:Turandot, w. Magda Olivero (sop), Francesco Merli (ten), F. Ghione (cnd), Turin RAI SO *(rec 1938)* Phonographe 2-▲ PHG 5053

Verdi, G.:Aida, w. Bruna Castagna (mez), Giovanni Martinelli (ten), Ezio Pinza (bass), E. Panizza (cnd), New York Metropolitan Opera Orch, New York Metropolitan Opera Chorus *(rec live, Feb 6, 1937)* The Fourties 2-▲ ENT 1501

Verdi, G.:Un ballo in maschera (sels), w. Maria Caniglia (sop), Fedora Barbieri (mez), Enrico Carusa (ten), Beniamino Gigli (ten), Giovanni Zenatello (ten), Carlo Galeffi (bar), Lawrence Tibbett (bar), *(various orchs & cnds)* *(rec 1911-43)* Grammofono 2000 ▲ GRM 78527 (m)

Verdi, G.:La forza del destino (sels), w. G. Cigna (sop—Leonora), E. Ghirardini (bar—Melitone), G. Vaghi (bar—Guardiano), O. de Fabritiis (cnd), Rome RAI Orch, Rome RAI Chorus *(rec Oct. 10, 1938)* Legato Classics 2-▲ LCD 173-2 [ADD]

Verdi, G.:Il trovatore, w. G. Cigna (sop—Leonora), G. Wettergren (mez—Azucena), M. Huder (mez—Ines), J. Björling (ten—Manrico), O. Dua (ten—Ruiz), C. Zambelli (ten—Ferrando), M. Basiola (bar—Count di Luna), L. Horsman (bar—Old Gypsy), V. Gui (cnd), Royal Opera Orch, Royal Opera House Chorus Covent Garden *(rec May 12, 1939)* Legato Classics 2-▲ LCD 173-2 [ADD]

Ciliberti, Daniela (sgr)

Monteverdi, C.:Ballo delle ingrate, w. Carlo Lepore (bass), Daniela Barcellona (sgr), Daniela Ciliberti (sgr), Andrea Concetti (sgr), Hans van Dijk (sgr), Remo Guerrini (sgr), Nadia Mantelli (sgr), Elena Marazzi (sgr), Humberto Orellana (sgr), Claudia Pallini (sgr), Luigi Polsini (sgr), Rosa Ricciotti (sgr), Alberto Rota (sgr), Ludovica Scoppola (sgr), *(orch unknown)* Nuova Era ▲ NUO 7224

Ciliento, Nicoletta (mez)

Coccia, C.:Caterina di Guisa, w. C. Apollonio (sop), M. Leonardi (ten), S. Antonucci (bar), M. de Bernart (cnd), Italian PO, Calabria Francesca Cilea Chorus *(rec Oct. 30 & Nov. 3, 1990)* Bongiovanni 2-▲ GB 2117/18 [DDD]

Donizetti, G.:Torquato Tasso, w. A. D'Auria (sop), L. Serra (sop), E. Palacio (ten), R. Coviello (bar), S. Alaimo (bass-bar), A. Riva (bass), M.. Bernart (cnd), Genoa Teatro Comunale Orch, Genoa Teatro Comunale Chorus [I] *(rec live 10/16/85)* Bongiovanni 3-▲ GB 2028/30 [DDD]

Rossini, G.:Aureliano in Palmira, w. L. d' Intino (sop), E. di Cesare (ten), Mazzola (sgr), G. Zani (cnd), Lucca Teatro Comunale Giglio Orch [I] *(rec live, Lucca, 10/28-11/2 1991)* Nuova Era 2-▲ 7069/70 [DDD]

Rossini, G.:Torvaldo e Dorliska, w. A. Buda (sop), F. Pediconi (sop), E. Palacio (ten), S. Antonucci (bar), A. Marani (b-bar), M. de Bernart (cnd), Swiss-Italian Orch, Cantemus, Swiss-Italian Radio-TV Chorus *(rec Jan. 11, 1992)* Arkadia-Akademia 2-▲ 123 [DDD]

Ciniselli, Ferdinando (ten)

The Art of Ferdinando Ciniselli *(rec 1924-28)* Preiser ▲ PRE 89994

Ciofi, Patrizia (sgr)

Bellini, V.:La sonnambula, w. Maria Costanza Nocentini (sop), Vitalba Mosca (mez), Giuseppe Morino (ten), Giovanni Furlanetto (bar), Etienne Ligot (sgr), Walter Mikus (sgr), G. Carella (cnd), Italian International Orch Nuova Era 2-▲ NUO 7215 [DDD]

Cherubini, L.:Médée, w. Jano Tamar (sop), Luca Lombardo (sgr), Magali Damonte (sgr), Jean-Philippe Courtis (bass), P. Fournillier (cnd), Italian International Opera Orch, Sluk Chamber Chorus Bratislava *(rec Martina Franca Festival, 1995)* Nuova Era 2-▲ NUO 7253

Cioni, Bruno (bass)

Bellini, V.:I Puritani, w. Mirella Freni (sop—Elvira), Rita Bezzi (mez—Enrichetta), Alfredo Kraus (ten—Arturo Talbot), Augusto Pedroni (ten—Sir Bruno Robertson), Attilio d'Orazi (bar—Sir Riccardo Forth), Raffaele Arié (bass—Sir Giorgio), Bruno Cioni (bass—Lord Gualtiero Walton), N. Verchi (cnd), Modena Teatro Comunale Orch, Modeno Teatro Comunale Chorus *(rec Modena Teatro Comunale, Dec. 26, 1962)* Legato Classics 2-▲ LCD 195-2 [ADD]

Cioni, Renato (ten)

Bellini, V.:La sonnambula, w. J. Sutherland (sop), E. Flagello (bass), *(cnd & orch unknown)* *(rec live Dec. 5, 1961)* Standing Room Only 2-▲ SRO 841-2 [ADD]

Bellini, V.:La straniera, w. R. Scotto (sop), E. Zilio (mez), D. Trimarchi (bar), E. Campi (bass), N. Sanzogno (cnd), Palermo Teatro Massimo Orch, Palermo Teatro Massimo Chorus [I] *(rec live, Palermo, 1968)* Melodram 2-▲ 27039

Bellini, V.:La straniera, w. R. Scotto (sop), E. Zilio (mez), D. Trimarchi (bar), E. Campi (bass), N. Sanzogno (cnd), Palermo Teatro Massimo Orch, Palermo Teatro Massimo Chorus [I] *(rec live, Palermo, 1968)* Verona 2-▲ 27097/98

Donizetti, G.:Il Duca d'Alba, w. Wladimiro Ganzarolli (bar), Franco Ventriglia (bass), T. Schippers (cnd), Trieste PO Melodram ▲ CDM 27036

Donizetti, G.:Lucia di Lammermoor, w. J. Sutherland (sop), R. Merrill (bar), C. Siepi (bass-bar), J. Pritchard (cnd), St. Cecilia Academy Orch Rome, St. Cecilia Academy Chorus Rome [I] London 2-▲ 411622-2 [ADD]

Janácek, L.:Jenůfa, w. Magda Olivero (sop—Kostelnicka), Bruna Baglioni (mez—La vecchia Buryja), Grace Bumbry (mez—Jenufa), Renato Cioni (ten—Steva Buryja), Robleto Merolla (bar—Laca Klemen), Carlo Meliciani (sgr—Vecchio compagno), J. Semkow (cnd), La Scala Orch, La Scala Chorus *(rec Milan, Apr 2, 1974)* Myto 2-▲ MCD 961142

Puccini, G.:Tosca, w. M. Callas (sop), T. Gobbi (bar), N. Rescigno (cnd), Paris Opera Orch, Paris Opera Chorus *(rec live, Paris March 3, 1965)* Melodram 2-▲ CDM 26033 [ADD]

Puccini, G.:Tosca, w. M. Callas (sop), T. Gobbi (bar), C. F. Cillario (cnd), Royal Opera House Orch, Royal Opera House Chorus Covent Garden [I] *(rec live, 1/21/64)* Verona 2-▲ 27027/28 (m) [AAD]

Puccini, G.:Tosca, w. Maria Callas (sop—Floria Tosca), Robert Bowman (ten—Spoletta), Renato Cioni (ten—Mario Cavaradossi), Eric Garrett (bar—Il Sagrestano), Tito Gobbi (bar—Scarpia), Victor Godfrey (bass—Casare Angelotti), Dennis Wicks (bass—Sciarrone), C. F. Cillario (cnd), Royal Opera House Orch, Royal Opera House Chorus Covent Garden *(rec London, 1964)* Melodram 2-▲ CDI 203003 [ADD]

Puccini, G.:Tosca, w. M. Callas (sop), T. Gobbi (bar), C. F. Cillario (cnd), Royal Opera House Orch, Royal Opera House Chorus Covent Garden [I] *(rec live 1/21/64)* Melodram 2-▲ MEL 26011

Verdi, G.:Rigoletto, w. Joan Sutherland (sop—Gilda), Renato Cioni (ten—Duke), Cornell MacNeil (bar—Rigoletto), N. Sanzogno (cnd), St. Cecilia Academy Orch Rome, St. Cecilia Academy Chorus Rome London ("Double Decca" series) 2-▲ 443853-2

Verdi, G.:La traviata, w. M. Freni (sop), R. Righetti (mez), M. Sereni (bar), H. von Karajan (cnd), La Scala Orch, La Scala Chorus *(rec Milan, 1964)* Legend 2-▲ LGD 125 [ADD]

Zandonai, R.:Francesca da Rimini, w. L. Gencer (sop—Francesca), R. Cioni (ten—Paolo), M. Ferrara (ten—Malatesino), F. Capuana (cnd), Trieste Teatro Comunale Giuseppe Verdi Orch, Trieste Teatro Comunale G. Verdi Chorus *(rec Mar. 19. 1961)* Arkadia 2-▲ 597 [ADD]

Cipriani, Aurora (cta)
Catalani, A.:Mass, w. C. Basto (sop), M. Frusoni (ten), P. Janowski (bass), G. Cosmi (cnd), Lucca Teatro Comunale Giglio Orch [L] *(rec 1985)* Bongiovanni ▲ GB 2027 [DDD]

Circa, Corina (mez)
Puccini, G.:Madama Butterfly, w. Eugenia Moldoveanu (sop—Madama Butterfly), Mihaela Agachi (mez—Suzuki), Corina Circa (mez—Kate Pinkerton), Emil Gherman (ten—B.F. Pinkerton), Stefan Popescu (ten—Goro), Ioan Soanea (bar—The Bonze/Yakuside), Eduard Tumageanian (bar—Sharpless), Alexandru Kopeczi (bass—Prince Yamadori), Mircea Moisa (bass—Commissioner), P. Popescu (cnd), Satu Mare PO, Cluj-Napoca Phil Chorus *(rec 1979)* Vox Box 2-▲ CDX 5155

Cirje-Druica, Elvira (sop)
Puccini, G.:La Bohème, w. Elvira Cirje-Druica (sop—Musetta), Eugenia Moldoveanu (sop—Mimi), Andrei Borsos (ten—Parpignol), Constantin Gabor (ten—Alcindoro), Ludovic Spiess (ten—Rodolfo), Lucian Marinescu (bar—Schaunard), David Ohanesian (bar—Marcello), Pompei Harasteanu (bass—Benoit), Dan Zancu (bass—Colline), C. Petrovici (cnd), Romanian Opera Orch, Romanian Opera Chorus *(rec 1982)* Vox Box 2-▲ CDX 5156

Cisternino, Tiziana (sop)
Respighi, E.O.S.:Songs, w. Massimo Palumbo (pno)—3 Spanish Songs; 4 Rubaiyat Songs; 2 Songs Nuova Era ("Icarus" series) ▲ NUO 7182 [DDD]
Respighi, O.:Songs, w. Massimo Palumbo (pno)—5 unpublished songs; Miranda, Ballata alla luna; Voici Noel; Il pleut, gentil berger; Canzone sarda, La funtanelle Nuova Era ("Icarus" series) ▲ NUO 7182 [DDD]

Citino, Daniela (sop)
Salieri, A.:La passione di Gesù Cristo, w. Maria Teresa Toso (alt), Nikola Yovanovitch (ten), Mario Scardoni (bass), Giovanna Scardoni (voc), A. Turco (cnd), Verona Cathedral Cappella Musicale *(rec Verona Cathedral, Italy, Mar 30, 1995)* Bongiovanni ▲ GB 2190 [DDD]

Ciucur, Theodora (sgr)
Honegger, A.:Amphion, w. Olivier Lallouette (bar—Apollon), Laurent Manzoni (bar—Amphion), Iona Bentoiu (sgr—muse), Theodora Ciucur (sgr—muse), Lucia Kriska (sgr—muse), Adriana Mestes (sgr—muse), J.-F. Antonioli (cnd), Timisoara PO, Timisoara Banatul Phil Chorus, Timisoara Children's Chorus *(rec Salle Ion Vidu, Timisoara, Romania, Oct 28 & Nov 1, 1995)* Timpani ▲ 1035 [DDD]

Clabassi, Plinio (bass)
Berlioz, H.:La Damnation de Faust, w. Giulietta Simionato (mez), Ettore Bastianini (bar), Ruggero Bondino (sgr), P. Maag (cnd), *(orch unknown)* Great Opera Performances 2-▲ GOP 776
Donizetti, G.:Anna Bolena, w. L. Gencer (sop), G. Simionato (mez), A. Bertocci (ten), G. Gavazzeni (cnd), Milan RAI SO, Milan RAI Chorus *(rec 1958)* Memories 2-▲ MEM 4517 [AAD]
Donizetti, G.:Anna Bolena, w. Maria Callas (sop), Gabriella Carturan (mez), Giulietta Simionato (mez), Gianni Raimondi (ten), Nicola Rossi Lemmeni (sgr), Luigi Rumo (sgr), G. Gavazzeni (cnd), La Scala Orch, La Scala Chorus Great Opera Performances 2-▲ GOP 768
Donizetti, G.:Anna Bolena, w. Leyla Gencer (sop), Giulieta Simionato (mez), Aldo Bertocci (ten), G. Gavazzeni (cnd), Milan RAI SO, Milan RAI Chorus *(rec July 11, 1958)* Agorá Music ("Phoenix" series) 2-▲ 503
Mascagni, P.:Iris, w. M. Olivero (sop), L. Ottolini (ten), R. Capecchi (bar), F. Vernizzi (cnd), Netherlands Radio Orch, Netherlands Radio Chorus *(rec Amsterdam, 1963)* Great Opera Performances ▲ GPO 708
Mascagni, P.:Iris, w. M. Olivero (sop), L. Ottolini (ten), R. Capecchi (bar), F. Vernizzi (cnd), Netherlands Radio Orch, Netherlands Radio Chorus *(rec live, 1963)* Verona 2-▲ 27014/15 [AAD]
Ponchielli, A.:La Gioconda, w. Zinka Milanov (sop—La Gioconda), Rosalind Elias (mez—Laura), Belan Amparan (cta—La Cieca), Giacomo Cottino (ten—Isepo), Giuseppe Di Stefano (ten—Enzo Grimaldo), Fernando Valentini (bar—Zuane/Un Nocchiero), Leonard Warren (bar—Barnaba), Virgilio Carbonari (bass—Un Cantore), Plinio Clabassi (bass—Alvise Badoero), F. Previtali (cnd), St. Cecilia Academy Orch Rome, St. Cecilia Academy Chorus Rome Theorema 3-▲ TH 121182/184
Verdi, G.:Il trovatore, w. Leyla Gencer (sop—Leonora), Laura Londi (sop—Ines), Fedora Barbieri (mez—Azucena), Mario del Monaco (ten—Manrico), Athos cesarini (ten—Ruiz), Walter Artioli (ten—Messanger) Ettore Bastianini (bar—Count Luna), Plinio Clabassi (bass—Ferrando), Sergio Liliani (bass—Gypsy), F. Previtali (cnd), Milan RAI SO, Milan RAI Chorus *(rec live, Milan, May 29, 1957)* Arkadia 2-▲ 483 [ADD]

Claessens, Huub (bar)
Berlioz, H.:La Damnation de Faust, w. J. Larmor (mez—Marguerite), K. Olsen (ten—Faust), D. Wilson-Johnson (bar—Méphistophélès), H. Claessens (bar—Brander), G. Neuhold (cnd), Flanders Royal PO, Düsseldorf Municipal Choral Society Bayer 2-▲ 500017/18 [DDD]
Mozart, W.A.:Don Giovanni, w. Danielle Borst (sop—Donna Anna), Véronique Gens (sop—Donna Elvira), Sophie Marin-Degor (sop—Zerlina), Huub Claessens (bar—Leporello), Nicolas Reveng (bar—Don Giovanni), Patrick Donnelly (bass—Commendatore), Simon Edwards (sgr—Don Ottavio), J. Malgoire (cnd), La Grande Écurie et la Chambre du Roy Astrée 8-▲ E 8606
Mozart, W.A.:Nozze di Figaro, w. Danielle Borst (sop—Countess Almaviva), Claudine Le Coz (sop—Marcellina), Sophie Marin-Degor (sop—Susanna), Laura Polverelli (mez—Cherubino), Valérie Lecoq (sgr—Barberina), Philippe Cantor (ten—Antonio), Stuart Patterson (ten—Dons Basile & Curzio), Huub Claessens (bar—Figaro), Nicolas Reveng (bar—Count Almaviva), Patrick Donnelly (bass—Bartolo), J. Malgoire (cnd), La Grande Écurie et la Chambre du Roy Astrée 8-▲ E 8606

Claessens, Huub (bass)
Brahms, J.:Liebeslieder Waltzes SATB, w. Greta De Reyghere (sop), Lucienne Van Deyck (mez), Guy De Mey (ten), Jean-Claude Vanden Eynden (pno), Luc Devos (pno) *(rec Consevatoire Royal, Liège, 1994)* Ricercar ▲ 153138
Brahms, J.:Neue Liebeslieder Waltzes, w. Greta De Reyghere (sop), Lucienne Van Deyck (mez), Guy De Mey (ten), Jean-Claude Vanden Eynden (pno), Luc Devos (pno) *(rec Consevatoire Royal, Liège, 1994)* Ricercar ▲ 153138
Mascagni, P.:Il piccolo Marat, w. S. Neves (sop—Mariella), C. Pfeiler (mez—Principessa di Fleury), D. Galvez-Vallejo (ten—Marat), S. Cowan (bar—Soldier), M. Dirks (bar—Il Ladro), F. Vassar (bass—L'Orco), H. Claessens (bass—Spy), K. Bakels (cnd), Netherlands RSO, Netherlands Radio Chorus *(rec Feb. 9, 1992)* Bongiovanni 2-▲ GB 2168/69 [DDD]
Mozart, W.A.:Così fan tutte, w. S. Isokoski (sop—Fiordiligi), N. Argenta (sop—Despina), M. Groop (mez—Dorabella), M. Schäfer (ten—Ferrando), P. Vollestad (bar—Guglielmo), H. Claessens (b-bar—Don Alfonso)., S. Kuijken (cnd), La Petite Bande, La Petite Bande Chorus Accent 3-▲ ACC 9296/98
Ryelandt, J.:Agnus Dei, w. Ingrid Kapelle (sop), Lucienne van Deyck (mez), Joseph Cornwell (ten), Stephan Macleod (bass), G. Llewellyn (cnd), Royal Flanders PO, Altra Voce, Audite Nova *(rec live, Elisabeth Hall, Antwerp, Holland, Dec 9, 1994)* Marco Polo 2-▲ 8.223785/86 [DDD]

Clapton, Eric (sgr)
Pavarotti & Friends for War Child, w. L. Pavarotti (ten), Sheryl Crow (sgr), Elton John (sgr), Liza Minelli (sgr), Joan Osborne (sgr), Jon Secada (sgr), Eric Clapton (gtr), John McLaughlin (gtr), Marco Armiliato, Edoardo Bennato, José Molina, Al DiMeola, Kelly Family, Ligabue, Litfiba, P *(rec Modena, Italy, 1996)* London ▲ 452900-2 ▮ 452900-4

Clapton, Nicholas (alt)
Scarlatti, D.:Salve regina, w. C. Harris (trb), Bryam-Wigfield (org) Hyperion ▲ CDA 66182 [DDD]

Clarey, Cynthia (sop)
Duffy, J.:A Time for Remembrance:A Peace Cant, w. James Earl Jones (nar), Z. Macal (cnd), Milwaukee SO *(rec Uihlein Hall, Milwaukee, WI, Nov. 22, 1993)* Koss Classics ▲ KC 1022 [DDD]
Flowering of Vocal Music in America, 1767–1823, w. Susan Belling (sop), Barbara Wallace (sop), Debra Vanderlinde (sop), D'Anna Fortunato (mez), Evelyn Petros (mez), Charles Bressler (ten), Richard Anderson (bar), James Tyeska (bar), Joseph McKee (bass), Cynthia Otis (hp), Leonard Rav New World ▲ 80467-2
Gershwin, G.:Porgy & Bess, w. C. Haymon (sop—Bess), C. Clarey (sop—Serena), M. Simpson (sop—Maria), D. Evans (ten—Sporting Life), G. Baker (bar—Crown), W. White (bar—Porgy), S. Rattle (cnd), London PO, Glyndebourne Festival Chorus EMI Classics 3-▲ CDCC 49568

Clarey, Cynthia (sop) (cont.)
Gershwin, G.:Porgy & Bess (sels), w. Cynthia Clarey (sop—Serena), Cynthia Haymon (sop—Bess), Damon Evans (ten—Sportin' Life), Gordon Hawkins (bar—Porgy), Andrew Litton (pno), A. Litton (cnd), Dallas SO, Dallas Sym Chorus—Intro/Jasbo Brown; Summertime; A Woman Is a Sometime Thing; Gone, Gone, Gone; My Man's Gone Now; Leavin' for the Promise' Lan'; Oh I Got Plenty O' Nuttin'; Bess, You Is My Woman Now; Oh, I Can't Sit Down; I Ain't Got No Shame; It Ain't Necessarily So; Shame on All You Sinners; I Loves You, Porgy; Hurricane; There's a Boat Dat's Leavin' Soon for New York; Act 3, Scene 3 Orchestral Intro; Good Mornin', Sistuh; Oh Lawd, I'm on My Way! [concert suite arr A. Litton] *(rec Eugene McDermott Hall, Dallas, May 1995)* Dorian ▲ DOR 90223 [DDD]

Clarich, Claudia (mez)
Monteverdi, C.:Orfeo, w. Nuccia Focile (sop), Enrico Facini (ten), Paolo Coni (bar), James Loomis (bass), H. Handt (cnd), Lucchese CO [orchd Respighi, 1934–35] *(rec live, VII Festival Internazionale di Marlia, 1984)* Claves ▲ CD 9419 [ADD]

Clark, Alicia (sop)
Sowerby, L.:Forsaken of Man, w. Judith Compton (alt), Thomas Potter (bass), Paul Grizzell (bass), Matthew Greenberg (bass), Bruce Hall (sgr), John Vorassi (sgr), Thomas Weisflog (org), William Ferris (cnd), William Ferris Chorale *(rec St. Thomas the Apostle Church, Chicago, June 1990)* New World ▲ 803942 [AAD]

Clark, Eleanor (sop)
Talma, L.:The Leaden Echo & the Golden Echo, w. Jonathan Sherry (pno), Gregg Smith (cnd), Gregg Smith Singers Vox Box ("The American Composers" series) 3-▲ CDX 3037

Clark, Graham (ten)
Donizetti, G.:Maria Padilla, w. L. McDonall (sop—Maria Padilla), D. Jones (mez—Ines Padilla), G. Clark (ten—Don Ruiz), C. du Plessis (bar—Don Pedro), A. Francis (cnd), London SO, Geoffrey Mitchell Choir [I] *(rec at Henry Wood Hall, London June 1980)* Opera Rara 3-▲ ORC 6
Wagner, R.:Das Rheingold, w. L. Finnie (mez—Fricka), G. Clark (ten—Loge), J. Tomlinson (bar—Wotan), B. Brinkmann (bar—Donner), D. Barenboim (cnd), Bayreuth Festival Orch, Bayreuth Festival Chorus [G] Teldec 2-▲ 4509-91185-2
Wagner, R.:Siegfried, w. A. Evans (sop—Brünnhilde), H. Leidland (sop—Waldvogel), B. Svendén (mez—Erda), S. Jerusalem (ten—Siegfried), G. Clark (ten—Mime), J. Tomlinson (bass—Der Wanderer), G. von Kannen (bass—Alberich), P. Kang (bass), *(cnd & orch unknown)* Teldec 4-▲ 4509-94193-2 [DDD]

Clark, James (ten)
Mahler, G.:Beethoven's Sym 9, w. Leah Anne Myers (sop), Ilene Sameth (mez), Richard Conant (bass), P. Tiboris (cnd), Brno State PO, Janáček Opera Chorus Bridge ▲ BCD 9033 [DDD]

Clark, Karen (alt)
Wheldon, R.:Music of, w. American Baroque—I Was 16; Fugue State No. 1; I Was at a New Year's Eve Dance; Like a Passing River; The Graffiti on the Subway Cars; White Light Cant., New York 1980 [Sinf.; Right on 42nd Street; A Sudden Pang Seizes My Heart; On the Street It's Still Light; We're Out in the Boat]; Fugue State No. 2; Rucker Songs; So What's the Point; Adagio; What's the Point; Into the Light *(rec St. Stephen's Church, Belvedere, CA)* New Albion ▲ NA 072

Clark, P. E. (sop)
Camilo, M.:Batey, w. C.B. Rowe (sop), W. Zukof (ct), L. Bennett (ten), W. L. Lee (ten), E. Levine (bar), Puntilla (sgr), New Generation Western Wind ▲ WW 2001

Clark, Patricia (sop)
Darling, D.:Blessings:A Prayer for the Planet, w. C.B. Rowe (sop), W. Zukof (ct), L. Bennett (ten), W.L. Lee (ten), E. Levine (bar), D. Darling (acoustic & electric vc/syn/voice) Western Wind ▲ WW 2001
Darling, D.:Blessings (sels), w. C.B. Rowe (sop), W. Zukof (ct), L. Bennett (ten), W.L. Lee (ten), E. Levine (bar), D. Darling (acoustic & electric vc/syn/voice) Western Wind ▲ WW 2001
Gay, J.:The Beggar's Opera (sels), w. A. Jenkins (sop), M. Cable (mez), E. Lane (mez), S. Minty (mez), E. Fleet (sgr), P. Hall (ten), V. Midgley (ten), N. Rogers (ten), J. Noble (bar), D. Stevens (cnd), Accademia Monteverdiana Orch, Accademia Monteverdiana Chorus—59 songs *(rec Aug. 1978)* Koch Treasure ▲ 31621-2 [ADD]
Hovhaness, A.:Lady of Light, w. Leslie Fyson (bar), A. Hovhaness (cnd), Royal PO, Ambrosian Chorus Crystal ▲ CD 806

Clark, V. (sgr)
Rodgers, R.:Music of, w. Gregg Edelman (sgr), J. Graae (sgr), A. Reed (sgr), L. Wintersteller (sgr)—Oklahoma; Carousel; The Sound of Music; South Pacific; Flower Drum Song; Cinderella & others Varèse Sarabande ▲ VSD 5516 ▮ VSC 5516

Clarke, Adrian (bar)
Casken, J.:Golem, w. P. Rozario (sop), C. Robson (ct), J. Hall (bar), R. Bernas (cnd), Music Projects London Virgin Classics 2-▲ CDC 59028

Clarke, Paul Charles (ten)
Gounod, C.:Roméo et Juliette, w. Susan Graham (sop—Stephano), Ruth Ann Swenson (sop—Juliette), Sarah Walker (mez—Gertrude), Paul Charles Clarke (ten—Tybalt), Placido Domingo (ten—Roméo), Kurt Ollmann (bar—Mercutio), Alastair Miles (bass—Frère Laurent), David Pittman-Jennings (bass—Le Duc), Alain Vernhes (bass—Capulet), L. Slatkin (cnd), Munich RSO, Munich Radio Chorus *(rec Studio 1, Bavarian Radio, Munich, Nov 29 - Dec 10, 1995)* RCA Red Seal 2-▲ 09026-68440-2 [DDD]
Wallace, V.:Maritana, w. Majella Cullagh (sop), Lynda Lee (mez), Ian Caddy (bar), Damien Smith (bar), Quentin Hayes (bass), P. O. Duinn (cnd), RTE Concert Orch, RTE Phil Choir *(rec O'Reilly Hall, Dublin, Sept 1995)* Marco Polo 2-▲ 8.223406-7 [DDD]

Clarke, Stanley (bass)
Duke, G.:Muir Woods Suite, w. George Duke (pno), Chester Thompson (dr), Paulinho Dacosta (perc), E. Stratta (cnd), Lille National Orch *(rec live, Montreaux Music Festival, Montreaux, Switzerland, July 12, 1993)* Warner Bros ▲ 9 46132-2 [DDD]

Clarkson, Julian (alt)
Monteverdi, C.:Incoronazione, w. Constanze Backes (sop—Valletto), Catherine Bott (sop—Drusilla/Pallade/La Virtù), Dana Hanchard (sop—Nerone), Sylvia McNair (sop—Poppea), Marinella Pennicchi (sop—Amore/Damigella), Annie Sofie von Otter (mez—Ottavia/Venere/La Fortuna), Julian Clarkson (alt—Littore/Mercurio), Bernarda Fink (cta—Arnalta), Roberto Balconi (ct—Nutrice), Michael Chance (ct—Ottone), Nigel Robson (ten—Liberto/Soldato Secondo), Mark Tucker (ten—Lucano/Soldato Primo), Francesco Ellero d'Artegna (bass—Seneca), J. E. Gardiner (cnd), English Baroque Soloists *(rec Queen Elizabeth Hall, South Bank Ctr, London, Dec 1993)* Archiv 3-▲ 447088-2
Mozart, W.A.:Don Giovanni, w. Charlotte Margiono (sop—Donna Elvira), Luba Orgonasova (sop—Donna Anna), Eirian James (mez—Zerlina), Julian Clarkson (alt—Masetto), Christoph Prégardien (ten—Don Ottavio), Rodney Gilfry (bar—Don Giovanni), Ildebrando d'Arcangelo (bass—Leporello), Andrea Silvestrelli (bass—Il Commendatore), J. E. Gardiner (cnd), English Baroque Soloists, Monteverdi Choir London Deutsche Grammophon ("4D Audio" series) 3-▲ 445870-2

Clasen, D. (bar)
Insalata, w. I Fagiolini, E. Kenny (theorbo), D. Burchell (hpd/org), Riona D.(baroque vn), T. Cronin (baroque vn) Metronome ▲ METCD 1004

Clatworthy, David (bar)
Puccini, G.:Madama Butterfly (sels), w. Elisabeth Carron (sop—Cio-Cio-San), Deborah Kieffer (mez—Suzuki), Herman Malamood (ten—Pinkerton), David Clatworthy (bar—Sharpless), G. Morelli (cnd), *(orch unknown)*—Ancora un passo or via; Ieri son salita...Io seguo il mio destino; Adesso voi siete per me...Vogliatemi bene; Ti sero palpitante...Ah! Quanti occhi fisi, attenti!; Egli, col cuore grosso...Un bel dì, vedremo; Ebbene, che fareste Madama Butterfly...Due cose potrei far; Sai cos'ebbe cuore di pensare...Che tua madre; Troppa luce e di fuor; Con onor muore...Tu? Tu? Piccolo Iddio *(rec New York, Oct 23, 1973)* Legato Classics ▲ LCD 212-1 [ADD]

Clavensy, Charles (b-bar)
Adam, A.:Le toréador, ou l'accord parfait, w. Mady Mesplé (sop), Raymond Amade (ten), E. Bigot (cnd), ORTF Lyric Orch Musidisc ▲ MUS 201672 [AAD]
Martin, F.:Le Mystère de la Nativité, w. Elly Ameling (sop), Aafje Heynis (cta), Hugues Cuénod (ten), Louis Devos (ten), Eric Tappy (ten), Pierre Bollet (bar), Derrik Olsen (bar), André Vessières (bass), E. Ansermet (cnd), Swiss Romande Orch, Jeunes de l'Eglise Chorus, Geneva Motet Chorus Cascavelle 2-▲ CVL 2006 [ADD]

Clayton, Desmond (ten)
Diabelli, A.:Pastoralmesse, w. C. Degler (sop), S. Linden (sop), S. Rauschkolb (cta), H. Müller (bass), E. Ehret (cnd), Munich St. Michael's Orch, Munich St. Michael Choir [L] Koch Schwann ▲ CD 313015 [ADD]
Mozart, W.A.:Vesperae, w. Christa Degler (sop), Margarete Kissel (alt), Hartmut Müller (bass), E. Hinreiner (cnd), Salzburg Mozarteum Camerata Academica Studio SM ▲ 2518
Clayton, Jay (sgr)
Cage, J.:Four Walls, w. R. Burger (pno) Tomato ▲ R2-70696
Rodgers, R.:Carousel, w. J. Raitt (sgr), J. Darling (sgr), C. Johnson (sgr), E. Mattson (sgr), M. Vye (sgr), C. Baxter (sgr), J. Littau (cnd) [1945 cast] MCA Classics ▲ MCAD 10048 [AAD] ■ MCAC 10048
Clayton, Kristin (sgr)
Massenet, J.:Hérodiade (sels), w. Renée Fleming (sop), Dolora Zajick (mez), Plácido Domingo (ten), Kenneth Cox (bass), Juan Pons (bar), Hector Vásquez (sgr), V. Gergiev (cnd), San Francisco Opera Orch, San Francisco Opera Chorus—highlights *(rec San Francisco Opera, Nov 1994)* Sony Classical ▲ SK 61965
Clemens, H. (ten)
Halévy, F.:La Juive (sels), w. C. Boerner (sop—Eudoxie), E. Rethberg (sop—Rachel), G. Martinelli (ten—Éléazar), H. Clemens (ten—Léopold), Heller, Merola (cnd), *(orch unknown)*—Act 2 & Act 4 (sels.) *(rec Oct. 30, 1936 & 1926–27)* Standing Room Only ▲ SRO 848-1 [ADD]
Clément, Alain (bass)
Ave Maria, w. [cnd:Alphons von Aarburg], Zurich Boys' Choir, Daniel Perret (trb), Frieder Lang (ten), Praxedis Rütti (hp), Daniel Winiger (org), Andrej Lütschg (vn) Tudor ▲ TUD 7029 [DDD]
Clément, Edmond (ten)
The Complete Odeon & Victor Recordings, w. Geraldine Farrar (sop), Marcel Journet (bass), Frank La Forge (pno), Rosario Bourdon (cnd) *(rec Odeon 1905; Victor 1911–1)* Romophone ▲ 82002-2
French Opera & Mélodies, Traditional Chansons *(rec 1911–16)* Pearl ▲ PEA 9161 [ADD]
Clement, Joël (ten)
Viadana, L. da:Vespri per l'Assunzione, w. S. Pozzer (sop), C. Calvino (alt), U. Müller Adam (ten), S. Foresti (bass), L'Amaltea Ensemble, Vox Hesperia, St. Marco Capella Musicale Fonè ▲ FON 92F 08 [DDD]
Clement, Richard (ten)
Mendelssohn, F.:Elijah, w. Barbara Bonney (sop), Henriette Schellenberg (sop), Florence Quivar (mez), Marietta Simpson (mez), Reid Bartelme (trb), Jerry Hadley (ten), Thomas Hampson (bar), Thomas Paul (bar), R. Shaw (cnd), Atlanta SO, Atlanta Sym Chorus [E] *(rec Symphony Hall, Woodruff Arts Center, Atlanta, GA, Nov. 5–7, 1994)* Telarc 2-▲ CD 80389 [DDD]
Purcell, H.:Dido & Aeneas, w. Nancy Maultsby (sop—Dido), Susannah Waters (sop—Belinda), Margaret O'Keefe (sop—1st Witch), Sharon Baker (sop—2nd Woman), Laura Tucker (mez—Sorceress), Donna Ames (alt—Spirit), Richard Clement (ten—Sailor), Russell Braun (bar—Aeneas), M. Pearlman (cnd), Boston Baroque Orch Telarc ▲ CD 80424 [DDD]
Clementis, Tamás (bass)
Cilea, F.:L'Arlesiana, w. M. Spacagna (sop), E. Zilio (mez), P. Kelen (ten), B. Póka (bar), C. Rosekrans (cnd), Hungarian State Orch, Hungarian State Chorus Quintana 2-▲ QUI 903067/68
Respighi, O.:Semirama, w. E. Marton (sop), V. Kincses (sop), L. Bartolini (ten), L. Miller (bar), L. Polgaar (bass), L. Gardelli (cnd), Hungarian State Orch, Hungarian Radio–TV Chorus [I] Hungaroton 2-▲ HCD 31197/98
Clements, L. D. (sgr)
Donizetti, G.:Lucrezia Borgia, w. Montserrat Caballé (sop), Jane Berbié (mez), Alain Vanzo (ten), Kostas Paskalis (bar), Arnold Voketaitis (bass–bar), Adib Fazah (sgr), Mauro Lampi (sgr), Vern Shinall (sgr), Jerold Siena (sgr), William Wiederanders (sgr), J. Perlea (cnd), New York City Opera Orch, New York City Chorus Great Opera Performances 2-▲ GOP 769
Clift, Karen (sop)
Handel, G.F.:Messiah, w. Catherine Robbin (mez), Bruce Fowler (ten), Victor Ledbetter (bar), M. Pearlman (cnd), Boston Baroque Orch, Boston Baroque Chorus [E] Telarc 2-▲ CD 80322 [DDD]
Handel, G.F.:Messiah (sels), w. Catherine Robbin (mez), Bruce Fowler (ten), Victor Ledbetter (bar), M. Pearlman (cnd), Boston Baroque Orch, Boston Baroque Chorus—Sinfonia; Comfort ye, my people; Every valley shall be exalted; And the glory of the Lord; And He shall purify; Behold, a virgin shall conceive; O thou that tellest good tidings to Zion; For unto us a Child is born; Rejoice greatly, O daughter of Zion; His yoke is easy; All we like sheep; Lift up your heads; The Lord gave the word; Their sound is gone out; Why do the nations?; Let us break their bonds asunder; He that dwelleth in heaven; Thou shalt break them; Hallelujah; I know that my Redeemer liveth; Since by man came death; Behold, I tell you a mystery; The trumpet shall sound; Then shall be brought to pass; O death, where is thy sting?; But thanks be to God; Worthy is the Lamb...Amen *(rec May 18–22, 1992)* Telarc ▲ CD 80348 [DDD]
Clooney, Rosemary (sgr)
Romberg, S.:Deep in My Heart, w. H. Traubel (sgr), J. Ferrer (sgr), Gene Kelly (sgr), F. Kelly (sgr), V. Damone (sgr), J. Powell (sgr), A. Miller (sgr), W. Olvis (sgr), C. Richards (sgr), H. Keel (sgr), T. Martin (sgr), J. Weldon (sgr) Sony Music Special Products ▲ AK 47703
Close, Glenn (sgr)
Lloyd Webber, A.:Sunset Boulevard, w. A. Campbell (sgr), George Hearn (sgr), J. Kuhn (sgr)—highlights Polydor ▲ 31452-7241-2 ■ 31452-7241-4
Lloyd Webber, A.:Sunset Boulevard, w. A. Campbell (sgr), George Hearn (sgr), J. Kuhn (sgr) [1994 cast] A&M ▲ 31452 3507-2 ■ 31452 3507-4
Cloutier, Louise (mez)
Lebaron, A.:The E. & O. Line (sels), w. Louise Cloutier (mez—Eurydice/Vendors), Hugh Panero (ten—Hermes), Lawrence Hamilton (bar—Orpheus/Men), Frank London (tpt), Marcus Rojas (tuba), Myra Melford (pno/kbd), Davey Williams (gtr), Fred Hopkins (elec bass), Thurman Barker (dr), A. LeBaron (cnd)—Juke Joint Jam Session; Eurydice Meets Hermes; Eurydice's Death [Funeral Band]; Eurydice's River Journey; Orpheus Laments [Looked Away] *(rec Coolidge Auditorium, Library of Congress, 1987)* Mode ▲ Mode 42
Clunes (nar)
Britten, H.:The Young Person's Guide to the Orchestra, w. L. Maazel (cnd), French National Orch [E] Deutsche Grammophon ("Musikfest" series) ▲ 415921-2 [ADD] ■ 415921-4
Coburn, Pamela (sop)
Adam, A.:Le Postillon de Lonjumeau, w. R. Swensen (ten), J. Linn (bar), P. Lika (bass), K. Arp (cnd), Kaiserslautern Radio Orch, Stuttgart Chamber Choir [G] Capriccio 2-▲ 60040-2 [DDD]
Beethoven, L. van:Fidelio, w. J. Norman (sop), R. Goldberg (ten), H.-P. Blochwitz (ten), K. Möll (bass), B. Haitink (cnd), Dresden Staatskapelle, Dresden State Chorus Philips ▲ 438496-2
Beethoven, L. van:Fidelio, w. J. Norman (sop), R. Goldberg (ten), H.-P. Blochwitz (ten), A. Schmidt (bar), E. Wlaschiha (bass), K. Moll (bass), B. Haitink (cnd), Dresden Staatskapelle, Dresden State Chorus [G] Philips 2-▲ 426308-2 [DDD]
Beethoven, L. van:Missa Solemnis, w. F. Quivar (cta), A. Baldin (ten), A. Schmidt (bar), H. Rilling (cnd), Stuttgart Bach Collegium, Gächinger Kantorei [L] Hänssler Classic 2-▲ CD 98.956 [DDD] 2-■ MC 98.956 (D)
Gazzaniga, G.:Don Giovanni, w. J. Kaufmann (sop), J. Aler (ten), R. Swensen (ten), J.-L. Chaignaud (bar), G. von Kannen (bass), A. Scharinger (bass), S. Soltesz (cnd), Munich RSO, Munich Radio Chorus [I] Orfeo 2-▲ 214902 [DDD]
Haydn, J.:The Seven Last Words of Christ on the Cross, w. Ingeborg Danz (mez), Uwe Heilmann (ten), Andreas Schmidt (bar), H. Rilling (cnd), Stuttgart Bach Collegium, Gächinger Kantorei [oratorio version] [G] Hänssler Classic ▲ 98.977 [DDD]
Haydn, M.:Requiem in B♭, w. Ingeborg Danz (mez), Andreas Schmidt (bar), H. Rilling (cnd), Stuttgart Bach Collegium, Gächinger Kantorei [L] Hänssler Classic ▲ 98.977 [DDD]
Mahler, G.:Sym 4, w. V. Neumann (cnd), Czech PO *(rec House of Artists, Prague, Nov 22–27, 1993)* Canyon Classics ▲ CD 240
Mendelssohn, F.:A Midsummer Night's Dream (comp), w. E. von Magnus (alt/nar), C. Bantzer (nar), N. Harnoncourt (cnd), CO of Europe Teldec ▲ 74882-2
Mendelssohn, F.:Sym 2, w. Lioba Braun (alt), Deon van der Walt (ten), K.-F. Beringer (cnd), Austro-Hungarian PO *(rec Ansbach, July 1996)* Hänssler Classic 2-▲ CD 98.134 [DDD]

Coburn, Pamela (sop) (cont.)
Strauss (II), Joh.:Der Zigeunerbaron, w. Christiane Oelze (sop), Julia Hamari (mez), Elisabeth von Magnus (alt), Herbert Lippert (ten), Rudolf Schasching (ten), Wolfgang Holzmair (bar), Jurgen Flimm (sgr), Robert Florianschutz (sgr), Hans-Jurgen Lazar (sgr), N. Harnoncourt (cnd), Vienna SO, Arnold Schoenberg Choir *(rec Vienna, 1994)* Teldec 2-▲ 94555-2
Strauss, R.:Arabella (sels), w. R. Klepper (sop), M. Borst (mez), B. Skovhus (bar), F. Hawlata (bass), M. Honeck (cnd), Munich RSO Capriccio ▲ 10481 [DDD]
Strauss, R.:Ariadne auf Naxos, w. R. Klepper (sop), M. Borst (mez), B. Skovhus (bar), F. Hawlata (bass), M. Honeck (cnd), Munich RSO Capriccio ▲ 10481 [DDD]
Strauss, R.:Capriccio (sels), w. R. Klepper (sop), M. Borst (mez), B. Skovhus (bar), F. Hawlata (bass), M. Honeck (cnd), Munich RSO Capriccio ▲ 10481 [DDD]
Strauss, R.:Der Rosenkavalier (sels), w. R. Klepper (sop), M. Borst (mez), B. Skovhus (bar), F. Hawlata (bass), M. Honeck (cnd), Munich RSO Capriccio ▲ 10481 [DDD]
Suder, J.:Leider machen Leute, w. K. König (ten), M. Morgan (bar), W. Probst (bar), U. Mund (cnd), Bamberg SO, Bavarian Radio Chorus [G] Orfeo 2-▲ 124862 [DDD]
Wagner, R.:Das Liebesverbot, w. Pamela Coburn (sop—Mariana), Friedrich Lenz (ten—Antonio), Hermann Prey (bar—Friedrich), Keith Engen (bass—Angelo), Raimund Grumbach (bass—Danieli/Wirt), Wolfgang Fassler (sgr—Luzio), Sabine Haas (sgr—Isabella/Claudios Schwester), Alfred Kuhn (sgr—Brighella/Chef der Sbirren), Hermann Sapell (sgr—Pontio Pilato), Robert Schunk (sgr—Claudio), Marianne Seibel (sgr—Dorella), W. Sawallisch (cnd), Bavarian State Orch, Bavarian State Chorus *(rec July 9, 1983)* Orfeo d'or 3-▲ 345953
Zemlinsky, A. von:Der Traumgörge, w. J. Martin (sop), G. M. Ronge (sop), B. Calm (mez), P. Haage (ten), H. Kruse (ten), J. Protschka (ten), H. Welker (bar), M. Blasius (bass), V. von Halem (bass), G. Albrecht (cnd), Frankfurt RSO [G] Capriccio 2-▲ CD 10241/2 [DDD]
Cochran, William (ten)
Beethoven, L. van:Missa Solemnis, w. T. Kiberg (sop), R. Lang (cta), M. Krutikov (bass), A. Dorati (cnd), European SO, Univ of Maryland Chorus [L] *(rec live, Berlin Philharmonie, 7/3/88)* BIS 2-▲ CD 406/07 [DDD]
Busoni, F.:Doktor Faust, w. H. Hillebrecht (sop), D. Fischer-Dieskau (bar), K. C. Kohn (bass), F. Leitner (cnd), Bavarian RSO, Bavarian Radio Sym Chorus [G] Deutsche Grammophon ("20th Century Classics" series) 3-▲ 427413-2 [ADD]
Hindemith, P.:Mathis der Maler, w. Urszula Koszut (sop), Trudeliese Schmidt (mez), Rose Wagemann (mez), Donald Grobe (ten), James King (ten), Manfred Schmidt (ten), Dietrich Fischer-Dieskau (bar), Gerd Feldhoff (bass), Alexander Malta (bass), Peter Meven (bass), Karl Kreile (sgr), R. Kubelik (cnd), Bavarian RSO, Bavarian Radio Chorus EMI Classics 2-▲ CDCC 55237
Janácek, L.:Jenůfa, w. H. Hillebrecht (sop), A. Varnay (sop), Cox (sgr), R. Kubelik (cnd), Bavarian State Opera Orch, Bavarian State Opera Chorus [G] *(rec live in Munich, Mar. 17, 1970)* Myto 2-▲ 2 MCD 90422 [ADD]
Mahler, G.:Sym 8, w. Hanneke van Bork (sop), Ileana Cotrubas (sop), Heather Harper (sop), Brigit Finnila (mez), Marianne Dieleman (cta), Hermann Prey (bar), Hans Sotin (bass), B. Haitink (cnd), Royal Concertgebouw Orch Philips ("Solo" series) ▲ 446195-2
Schreker, F.:Die Gezeichneten, w. M. Schmiege (mez), S. Cowan (bar), W. Oosterkamp (bass), E. de Waart (cnd), Dutch Radio PO, Dutch Radio Phil Chorus Marco Polo 3-▲ 8.223328/30
Cock, C. (ten)
Poulenc, F.:Quatre petites prières de Saint François d'Assise, w. R. Shaw (cnd), Robert Shaw Festival Singers [F] Telarc ▲ CD 80236 [DDD]
Coda, Eraldo (bar)
Donizetti, G.:La fille du régiment, w. Lina Pagliughi (sop), Rina Corsi (mez), Cesare Valletti (ten), Sesto Bruscantini (bar), M. Rossi (cnd), Milan RAI Lyric Orch, Milan RAI Chorus *(rec 1950)* Cetra Classic 2-▲ CDON 38 [ADD]
Coertse, Mimi (sop)
Bach, J.S.:Magnificat, BWV 243, w. M. Sjöstedt (sop), H. Rössl-Majdan (mez), A. Dermota (ten), F. Guthrie (bass), F. Prohaska (cnd), Vienna State Opera Orch, Vienna State Opera Chorus [L] *(rec June 1957)* Vanguard Classics ("The Bach Guild" series) ▲ OVC 2010 [ADD]
Mahler, G.:Sym 2, w. L. West (alt), H. Scherchen (cnd), Vienna State Opera Orch, Vienna State Opera Chorus *(rec 1958)* Enterprise ("Palladio" series) ▲ ENTPD 4180 [ADD]
Mahler, G.:Sym 2, w. Lucretia West (alt), H. Scherchen (cnd), Vienna State Opera Orch Theorema 2-▲ TH 121203/04
Mahler, G.:Sym 2, w. L. West (alt), H. Scherchen (cnd), London Phil SO, Vienna Academy Chorus MCA Classics ("Double Decker" series) 2-▲ MCAD2-99833 [AAD]
Cognet, André (b-bar)
Chaynes, C.:Jocaste, w. René Boutet (ten), Jean-Marie Frémeau (bar), F. Chaslin (cnd), Rouen SO, Théâtre des Arts Chorus *(rec Rouen Theater, Rouen, France, 1993)* Chamade 2-▲ 5633/34
Cognet, André (bass)
Orff, C.:Carmina burana, w. Elisabeth Vidal (sop), Alexander Stevensen (ten), P. Kuentz (cnd), Paul Kuentz Orch, Paul Kuentz Choir, Mouez Armor Chorale, Lorient Conservatory Chorus, Notre Dame College Chorus Pierre Verany ▲ PVY 730044
Cohn, Adam (b-bar)
Lewandowksi, L.L.:Choral Music, w. Sandra Lee (sop), Ann Sadan (alt), Don Carter (ten), Michael Morris (bass), Carys Hughes (org), Robert Max (cnd), Zemel Choir—Ma Towu in F; Ma Towu in B♭; L'cho Dodi; Tow L'hodoss; Adoshem Moloch; W'hogen Ba'adenu [Uw'tsel]; W'schomru; L'icho Adoshem; J'Halahu [Hodo Al Erez]; Ladoshem Ho'orets; Uw'nucho Jomar; Adon Olom; Ki K'schimcho; Hajom Harass Olom; Kol Nidre; Schuwi Nafschi; Enosch, K'chozir Jomow; Halalujoh; Preise, Meine Seele Olympia ▲ OLY 347 [DDD]
Coiffier, Marthe (sop)
Gounod, C.:Faust, w. M. Berthon (sop), J. Montfort (mez), C. Vezzani (ten), L. Musy (b-bar), M. Cozette (bar), M. Journet (bass), H. Busser (cnd), Paris Opera Orch, Paris Opera Chorus [F] *(rec 1930)* Pearl 2-▲ PEA 9987 [AAD]
Col, Paolo da (ten)
Peri, J.:Euridice, w. Monica Benvenuti (sop—Ninfa I/Venere), Rossana Bertini (sop—Dafne/Ninfa II), Gloria Banditelli (cta—Euridice/Ninfa III/Tragedia/Proserpina), Mario Cecchetti (ten—Aminta/Radamanto), Paolo Da Col (ten—Tirsi), Gianpaolo Fagotto (ten—Orfeo), Giuseppe Zambon (ct—Arcetro), Sergio Foresti (bass—Caronte/Pastore), Furio Zanasi (bass—Plutone), R. de Caro (cnd), Arpeggione Ensemble *(rec Bologna, Italy, Nov 1992)* Arts Music 2-▲ 47276-2 [DDD]
Perti, G.A.:Liturgy for Good Friday, w. Patrizia Vaccari (sop), Maura Pederzoli (sop), Cristina Calzolari (sop), Alida Oliva (sop), Claudia Bugli (sop), Lucia Bagnoli (alt), Cinzia Meneghel (alt), Renzo Bez (alt), Alessandro Carmignani (alt), Michel van Goethem (alt), Mauro Collina (ten), Vincenzo Di Donato (ten), Paolo Fanciullacci (ten), Giovanni Caccamo (ten), Sergio Foresti (bass), Marco Scavazza (bass), Luca Ferracin (bass), Paride Montanari (bass), Liuwe Tamminga (org), Sergio Vartolo (org), S. Vartolo (cnd), Bologna San Petronio Capella Musicale Orch—Omnes amici mei; De lamentatione Jeremiae Prophetae:Heth. Cogitavit; Velum templi; Vinea mea; De lamentatione Jeremiae Prophetae:Lamed. Matribus suis; Tamquam ad latronem; Tenebrae factae sunt; Animam meam; Tradiderunt me; Jesum tradidit; De lamentatione Jeremiae Prophetae:Aleph. Ego vir; Caligaverunt *(rec St. Petronio Basilica, Bologna, Mar 28–31, 1995)* Naxos ▲ 8.553321 [DDD]
Cola, Valentina di (sop)
Bellini, V.:Mass in a, w. Leila Bersiani (sop), Stella Salvati (cta), José Antonio Campo (ten), Carlo Lepore (bass), E. Brizio (cnd), Prague SO, Czech Radio-TV Chorus *(rec Prague, June 1994)* Studio SM ▲ D 2444
Generali, P.:Sacred Music, w. Leila Bersiani (sop), Emanuela Deffai (mez), Sella Salvati (cta), Paolo Macedonio (ten), Roberto Bencivenga (ten), Carlo Lepore (bass), E. Brizio (cnd), Czech Radio–TV Orch, Czech Radio–TV Chorus—Magnificat; Domine ad Adjuvandum; Virgam Virtutis; Ecce Virgo; Ave Maria Messe Pastorale; Te Deum *(rec FHS Studios, Prague, 1995)* Studio SM ▲ 2517 [DDD]
Colaianni, Domenico (bar)
Leo, L.:Amor vuol sofferenze, w. Marilena Laurenza (sop), Vitalba Mosca (mez), Piero Guarnera (bar), Giovanna Donadini (sgr), Marilyne Fallot (sgr), Hyun Lee (sgr), D. Moles (cnd), Naples New Scarlatti Orch *(rec Martinafranca Festival, 1994)* Nuova Era 3-▲ NUO 7221
Mascagni, P.:Messa di Gloria, w. Carlo Allemano (ten), M. Letonja (cnd), Italian International Opera Orch, Bratislava Camera Chorus Nuova Era ▲ NUO CD 7270

Colaiillo, Martha (sop)
Catalani, A.:Loreley, w. M. L. Garbato (sop), P. Visconti (ten), A. Cassis (bar), N. Annovazzi (cnd), Lucca Teatro Comunale del Giglio Orch, Lucca Teatro Comunale del Giglio Chorus *(rec live 9/19/82)* Bongiovanni 2-▲ GB 2015/16 [ADD]

Colasanti, I. (mez)
Verdi, G.:Rigoletto, w. L. Pagliughi (sop—Gilda), I. Colasanti (mez—Maddalena), F. Tagliavini (ten—Duca), A. Albertini (bar—Il Cavaliere Marullo), G. Taddei (bar—Rigoletto), G. Neri (bass—Sparafucile), A. Zerbini (bass—Conte di Monterone), A. Questa (cnd), Turin RSO, Turin Radio Chorus *(rec 1953)* Cetra Classics 2-▲ CDO 11 [AAD]

Cold, Ulrik (bass)
Bach, J.S.:St. Matthew Passion, w. B. Schlick (sop), R. Jacobs (ct), H. P. Blochwitz (ten), H. Crook (ten), P. Kooy (bass), P. Herreweghe (cnd), La Chapelle Royale Orch, Ghent Collegium Vocale [G] Harmonia Mundi France 3-▲ HMC 901155/57

Cavalli, P.F.:Ercole amante, w. Felicity Palmer (sop—Jole), Yvonne Minton (mez—Giunone), Patricia Miller (sgr—Dejanira), M. Corboz (cnd), English Bach Baroque Orch, English Bach Festival Chorus Erato 3-▲ ERA SEL 12980 [ADD]

Gade, N.W.:Korsfarerne, w. Rorholm (mez), Westi (ten), F. Rasmussen (cnd), Aarhus SO, Aarhus Sym Chorus [Da] BIS ▲ CD 465 [DDD]

Handel, G.F.:Rinaldo, w. Sophie Boulin (sop—Donna), Ileana Cotrubas (sop—Almirena), Marie-Françoise Jacquelin (sop—Sirene), Nicole Leport (sop—Sirene), Jeanette Scovotti (sop—Armida), Carolyn Watkinson (cta—Rinaldo), Charles Brett (ct—Eustazio), Paul Esswood (ct—Goffredo), Armand Arapian (ten—Mago Christiano/Araldo), Ulrik Cold (bass—Argante), J. Malgoire (cnd), La Grande Ecurie et la Chambre du Roy *(rec Paris, 1977)* Sony Classical 3-▲ SM3K 34592

Handel, G.F.:Serse, w. Barbara Hendricks (sop—Romilda), Anne-Marie Rodde (sop—Atalanta), Carolyn Watkinson (cta—Xerxes), Otrun Wenkel (cta—Amastre), Paul Esswood (ct—Arsamene), Ulrich Studer (bar—Elviro), Ulrik Cold (bass—Ariodate), J. Malgoire (cnd), La Grande Ecurie et la Chambre du Roy *(rec Paris, 1979)* Sony Classical 3-▲ SM3K 36941

Janácek, L.:Slavonic Mass, w. T. Kiberg (sop), R. Stene (cta), P. Svensson (ten), C. Mackerras (cnd), Danish National RSO, Danish National Radio Choir, Copenhagen Boys' Choir Chandos ▲ CHAN 9310 [DDD]

Kuhlau, F.:Lulu, w. T. Kiberg (sop), A. Frellesvig (sgr), K. von Binzer (ten), R. Saarman (ten), E. Harbo (sgr), M. Schønwandt (cnd), Danish National RSO, Danish National Radio Choir [Da] Kontrapunkt 3-▲ 32009/11 [DDD]

Mendelssohn, F.:Die Hochzeit des Camacho, w. R. Hofman (sop—Quiteria), A. Ulbrich (mez—Lucinda), S. Weir (ten—Basilio), H. Rhys-Evans (ten—Vivaldo), N. van der Meel (ten—Camacho), W. Wild (bar—Carrasco), U. Malmberg (bass—Sancho Panza), U. Cold (bass—Don Quixote), J. van Immerseel (cnd), Anima Eterna Orch, Aachen Boys Choir, Chor Modus Novus [G] *(rec Sept. 19–22, 1992)* Channel Classics 2-▲ CCS 5593 [DDD]

Mozart, W.A.:Missa, K.427, w. Arleen Augér (sop), Heather Harper (sop), Horst Lubenthal (ten), S. Celibidache (cnd), Stuttgart RSO, Bavarian Radio Chorus, Southwest German Radio Chorus *(rec live, 1980's)* Topazio ▲ TOP 26045

Schnittke, A.:Faust Cant, w. Mikael Bellini (alt), Inger Blom (cta), Louis Devos (ten), J. DePreist (cnd), Malmö SO, Malmö Sym Chorus BIS ("BIS Twins" series) 2-▲ CD 437/507

Ulrik Cold, w. Kristian Buhl Mortensen (lt) Danacord ▲ DACOCD 376 [DDD]

Cole, Deborah (sop)
Bellini, V.:I Puritani (sels), w. J. Sutherland (sop), A. Kraus (ten), R. Wolansky (bar), N. Ghiuselev (bass), R. Bonynge (cnd), San Francisco Opera Orch, San Francisco Opera Chorus *(rec live, San Francisco, 9/2/66)* Golden Age of Opera ▲ GAO 133 [ADD]

Handel, G.F.:Serse, w. L. Atkinson (trb), A. Terzian (mez), A. Andersson (ten), T. Allen (bar), Schumann-Halley (sgr), J. Teal (sgr), A. Duczmal (cnd), Amadeus CO [I] *(rec live recording produced by "Studios Classique Berlin")* Koch Schwann 3-▲ CD SC 100 300 [DDD]

Cole, Steven (ten)
Burleigh, H.T.:Songs, w. Hilda Harris (mez), Philip Creech (ten), Arthur Woodley (bass), Joseph Smith (pno)—Now Sleeps the Crimson Petal; Promis' Lan'; Ethiopia Saluting the Colors; Lovely Dark & Lonely One; Love Watches; Almona; O, Night of Dream & Wonder; His Helmet's Blaze; I Hear His Footsteps, Music Sweet; Thou Art Weary; This is Nirvana; Ahmed's Song of Farewell; Through Moanin' Pines; The Frolic; In de Col' Moonlight; A Jubilee; On Bended Knees; A New Hiding-Place; Worth While; The Jungle Flower; Kashmiri Song; Among the Fuchsias; Till I Wake; By an' By; Ev'ry Time I Feel de Spirit; Deep River; Oh, Didn't it Rain; Swing Low, Sweet Chariot; Wade in de Water; Heav'n, Heav'n Premier ▲ PRCD 1041 [DDD]

Mozart, W.A.:Zauberflöte, w. Natalie Dessay (sop—Queen of the Night), Linda Kitchen (sop—Papagena), Rosa Mannion (sop—Pamina), Anna-Maria Panzarella (sop—First Lady), Doris Lamprecht (mez—Second Lady), Delphine Haidan (cta—Third Lady), Hans Peter Blochwitz (ten—Tamino), Steven Cole (ten—Monostatos), Chrisopher Josey (ten—First Priest/First Armed Man), Anton Scharinger (bar—Papageno), Reinhard Hagen (bass—Sarastro), Laurent Naouri (bass—Second Priest/Second Armed Man), Willard White (bass—Speaker), W. Christie (cnd), Les Arts Florissants *(rec Paris Oct 2–9 1995)* Erato 2-▲ 12705-2 [DDD]

Cole, Vinson (ten)
Beethoven, L. van:Missa Solemnis, w. Julia Varady (sop), Iris Vermillion (mez), Rene Pape (bass), Kolja Blacher (vn), G. Solti (cnd), Berlin PO, Berlin Radio Chorus London ▲ 444337-2 [DDD]

Berlioz, H.:Requiem, "Grande Messe des Morts", w. S. Ozawa (cnd), Boston SO, Tanglewood Festival Chorus RCA Red Seal ▲ 09026-62544-2

Berlioz, H.:Roméo et Juliette, w. N. Denize (mez), R. Lloyd (bass), E. Inbal (cnd), Frankfurt RSO, Frankfurt Radio Chorus Denon 2-▲ CO 73210/11 [DDD]

Bizet, G.:Songs, w. P. Stephens (pno)—J'aime l'amour!; Chanson d'avril; Absence; La chanson du fou [F] *(rec Apr. 8–10, 1993)* Delos ▲ DE 3131 [DDD]

Hahn, R.:Songs, w. P. Stephens (pno)—Le rossignol des lilas; A Chloris; Si mes vers avaient des ailes; L'Heure exquise; Cantique; D'Une prison; Infidelité; Paysage; Le souvenir d'avoir chanté [F] *(rec Apr. 8–10, 1993)* Delos ▲ DE 3131 [DDD]

Haydn, J.:Die Schöpfung, w. Margaret Marshall (sop), Lucia Popp (sop), Bernd Weikl (bar), Gwynne Howell (bass), R. Kubelik (cnd), Bavarian RSO, Bavarian Radio Chorus Orfeo 2-▲ 150852 [DDD] 2-■ 150852 (D)

Massenet, J.:Songs, w. P. Stephens (pno)—Ouvre tes yeux bleus; Elégie; Berceuse; Sonnet; Nuit d'espagne; Stances; Vous aimerez demain *(rec Apr. 8–10, 1993)* Delos ▲ DE 3131 [DDD]

Mendelssohn, F.:Sym 2, w. M. Chalker (sop), M. Rivera (sop), G. Schwarz (cnd), Seattle SO, Seattle Chorale *(rec Apr. 22–23, 1991)* Delos ▲ DE 3112 [DDD]

Mozart, W.A.:Bastien und Bastienne, w. E. Gruberova (sop), L. Polgár (bass), R. Leppard (cnd), Franz Liszt CO Sony Classical ▲ SK 45855

Mozart, W.A.:Requiem, w. A. Tomowa-Sintow (sop), H. Müller Molinari (cta), P. Burchuladze (bass), H. von Karajan (cnd), Vienna PO, Vienna Singverein [L] Deutsche Grammophon ("Karajan Gold" series) ▲ 439023-2 [DDD]

Mozart, W.A.:Requiem, w. A. Augér (sop), C. Bartoli (mez), R. Pape (bass), G. Solti (cnd), Vienna PO, Vienna Phil Chorus [L] *(rec live 12/5/91)* London ▲ 433688-2 [DDD] □ 433688-5

Mysteries Beyond:Songs & Chants in Praise of Mary, w. [cnd:Dennis Keene], Voices of Ascension, Kathleen Bride (hp), Patrick Stephens (pno), M. Kruczek (org) *(rec Apr. 17, 28–30, 1993)* Delos ▲ DE 3138 [DDD]

Paine, J.K.:Mass, Op. 10, w. C. Balthrop (sop), J. Blackett (cta), J. Cheek (bass), J. Lange (org), G. Schuller (cnd), St. Louis SO, St. Louis Sym Chorus [L] *(rec ca. mid-1970s)* New World ▲ 80262-2 [AAD]

Stravinsky, I.:Oedipus Rex, w. A. S. von Otter (mez/sop), N. Gedda (ten), S. Estes (bass), H. Sotin (bass), P. Chéreau (nar), E.-P. Salonen (cnd), Swedish RSO, *(chorus unknown)* Sony Classical ▲ SK 48057

Vinson Cole, w. Patrick Stephens (pno) Connoisseur Society ▲ CD 4184 [DDD]

Colella, Alfredo (bar)
Puccini, G.:La fanciulla del West (sels), w. Magda Olivero (sop—Minnie), Corinna Vozza (mez—Wowkle), Paolo Caroli (ten—Harry), Giacomo Lauri-Volpi (ten—Dick Johnson), Marco Rogani (ten—Pony Express Rider), Salvatore di Tommaso (ten—Trin), Adelio Zagonara (ten—Nick), Virgilio Ascorro (bar—Sid), Alfredo Colella (bar—Jake Wallace), Giuseppe Forgione (bar—Bello), Giancarlo Guelfi (bar—Jack Rance), Arturo la Porta (bar—Sonora), Gino Conti (bass—José Castro), Piere Passarotti (bass—Bill), Enzo Titta (bass—Larkens), Giulio Tomei (bass—Ashby), V. Bellezza (cnd), Rome Opera Orch, Rome Opera Chorus—Minnie, dalla mia casa son partito; Laggiù nel Soledad; Chi c'è per farmi i ricci; Oh! Mister Johnson, siete rimasto; Non so ben neppur io; Io non son che una povera fanciulla; No, Minnie, non piangete; Vorrei mettermi queste; Hallo!; Oh, se sapeste; Credo che abbiate torto; Ma ti giuro ch'io non ti lascio più; Vieni fuori!; Una parola sola!...Or son sei mesi; Che c'è di nuovo Jack?; E là; Siete pronto; Ch'ella mi creda; E Minnie!...E Minnie! *(rec Rome, Mar. 30, 1957)* Golden Age of Opera ▲ GAO 180 [ADD]

Colella, Alfredo (bass)
Carlo Tagliabue, w. C. Tagliabue (bar), Margherita Carosio (sop), Ettore Bergamaschi (ten), Zinka Milanov (sop), Bruna Castagna (cta), Frederick Jagel (ten), Norman Cordon (bass), Renata Tebaldi (sop) *(rec in studio and live, 1928–1951)* Bongiovanni ▲ GB 1070-2 [ADD]

Coleman, Gwendolyn (sop)
Schubert, Franz:Der Graf von Gleichen, w. Karen Driscoll (sop), Tracy Thomas (sop), Brad Diamond (ten), John M. Koch (bar), G. Samuel (cnd), Cincinnati PO, CCM Chamber Choir *(rec Corbett Auditorium, Univ of Cincinnati, Mar 12–13, 1994)* Centaur 2-▲ 2281/2282 [DDD]

Coles, Priti (sop)
Mozart, W.A.:Così fan tutte, w. J. Borowska (sop—Fiordiligi), P. Coles (sop—Despina), R. Yachmi (mez—Dorabella), J. Dickie (ten—Ferrando), A. Martin (bar—Guglielmo), P. Mikuláš (b-bar—Don Alfonso), J. Wildner (cnd), Capella Istropolitana, Slovak Phil Chorus [I] *(rec Feb.–Mar. 1990)* Naxos 3-▲ 8.660008/10 [DDD]

Mozart, W.A.:Così fan tutte (sels), w. Joanna Borowska (sop—Fiordiligi), Priti Coles (sop—Despina), Rohangiz Yachmi (mez—Dorabella), John Dickie (ten—Ferrando), Andrea Martin (bar—Guglielmo), Peter Mikuláš (bass—Don Alfonso), Milada Synkova (hpd), J. Wildner (cnd), Capella Istropolitana, Slovak Phil Chorus—Ov.; [Act I] La mia Dorabella capace non è; È la fede della femmine; Una bella serenata; Ah guarda, sorella; Vorrei dir, e cor non ho; Sento, o Dio; Bella vita militar!; Soave sia il vento; Smanie implacabili; In uomini, in soldati; Alla bella Despinetta; Come Scoglio; Non siate ritrosi; Un'aura amorosa; [Act II] Una donna a quindici anni; Prenderò quel brunettino; La mano a me date; Ei parte...senti...ah no!; Donne mie la fate a tanti a tanti; Fra gle amplessi; Fortunato l'uom che prende *(rec Slovak Philharmonic Moyzes Hall, Bratislava, Feb.–Apr. 1990)* Naxos ▲ 8.553172 [DDD]

Coletti, Antonio Magini (bar)
Antonio Magini Coletti Bongiovanni ▲ GB 1089-2 [ADD]

Coleva, Maria (sop)
Maria Coleva, Cesare Valletti, w. Cesare Valletti (ten), Rome RAI SO [cnd:Rigacci] *(rec Dec. 4, 1961)* Incontri Memorabili ("Martini & Rossi Concerts" series) ▲ 5030

Colín, Noé (bass)
Delgado, F.:Choral Music, w. Martha Molinar (sop), Luz Angélica Uribe (sop), Ana Paula Abitia (mez), Alfredo Mendoza (ten), B. J. Echenique (cnd), Mexico City CO, Alfredo Mendoza (cnd), Schola Cantorum—Te Deum al Sr. Felipe de Jesús Urtext ▲ URT 2001 [DDD]

Jerusalem, I.:Choral Music, w. Martha Molinar (sop), Luz Angélica Uribe (sop), Ana Paula Abitia (mez), Alfredo Mendoza (ten), B. J. Echenique (cnd), Mexico City CO, Alfredo Mendoza (cnd), Schola Cantorum—Magnificat a Dos Voces; Misa en Sol Mayor a 8 Voces Urtext ▲ URT 2001 [DDD]

Collard, Jeannine (mez)
Boieldieu, F.-A.:Le Calife de Bagdad, w. Christiane Eda-Pierre (sop), Jane Berbié (mez), Jean Giraudeau (ten), Jean-Paul Vaquelin (sgr), L. Fourestier (cnd), ORTF Lyric Orch, ORTF Lyric Chorale Musidisc ▲ MUS 201852 [AAD]

Vivaldi, A.:Gloria, RV.589, w. Andrée Esposito (sop), Solange Michel (sop), R. Wagner (cnd), Paris Conservatory Societé des Concerts Orch, Roger Wagner Chorale EMI Classics ("Baroque" series) ▲ CDK 65737

Collart, Claudine (sop)
Planquette, R.:Rip van Winkle, w. Lina Dachary (sop), Freda Betti (cta), René Lenoty (ten), Joseph Peyron (ten), Charles Daguerressar (bar), Julien Giovannetti (bar), Jacques Pruvost (bar), Lucien Lovano (bass), Patrick Orladey (sgr), Joëlle Pierre (sgr), M. Cariven (cnd), ORTF Lyric Orch, ORTF Lyric Chorale Musidisc ▲ MUS 201602 [AAD]

Collier, Marie (sop)
Janácek, L.:Jenůfa (sels), w. A. Varnay (sop), R. Cassilly (ten), J. Lanigan (ten), R. Kubelik (cnd), Royal Opera House Orch, Royal Opera House Chorus Covent Garden—eight solo, duet & trio arias featuring Astrid Varnay [G] *(rec live at Covent Garden, Feb. 24, 1968)* Myto 2-▲ 2 MCD 90422 [ADD]

Strauss, R.:Elektra, w. B. Nilsson (sop), R. Resnik (mez), G. Stolze (ten), T. Krause (bar), G. Solti (cnd), Vienna PO [G] London 2-▲ 417345-2 [DDD]

Collina, Mauro (ten)
Perti, G.A.:Liturgy for Good Friday, w. Patrizia Vaccari (sop), Maura Pederzoli (sop), Cristina Calzolari (sop), Alida Oliva (sop), Claudia Bugli (sop), Lucia Bagnoli (alt), Cinzia Meneghel (alt), Renzo Bez (alt), Alessandro Carmignani (alt), Michel van Goethem (alt), Vincenzo Di Donato (ten), Paolo Fanciullacci (ten), Giovanni Caccamo (ten), Paolo Da Col (ten), Sergio Foresti (bass), Marco Scavazza (bass), Luca Ferracin (bass), Paride Montanari (bass), Liuwe Tamminga (org), Sergio Vartolo (org), S. Vartolo (cnd), Bologna San Petronio Capella Musicale Orch—Omnes amici mei; De lamentatione Jeremiae Prophetae:Heth. Cogitavit; Velum templi; Vinea mea; De lamentatione Jeremiae Prophetae:Lamed. Matribus suis; Tamquam ad latronem; Tenebrae factae sunt; Animam meam; Tradiderunt me; Jesum tradidit; De lamentatione Jeremiae Prophetae:Aleph. Ego vir; Caligaverunt *(rec St. Petronio Basilica, Bologna, Mar 28–31, 1995)* Naxos ▲ 8.553321 [DDD]

Collingsworth, Jean (sop)
Byrd, W.:Songs, w. Elizabethan Consort of Viols Duo ▲ 89027 [DDD]

Collins, Anne (cta)
Britten, H.:The Beggar's Opera, w. A. Collins (sop—Mrs. Peachum), A. Murray (mez—Polly Peachum), P. Langridge (ten—MacHeath), R. Lloyd (b-bar—Peachum), *(not advised of orchestra & chorus)*, S. Bedford (cnd) Argo 2-▲ 436850-2 [DDD]

Elgar, E.:Coronation Ode, w. T. Cahill (sop), A. Rolfe Johnson (ten), G. Howell (bass), A. Gibson (cnd), Scottish National Orch, Scottish National Chorus [E] *(rec 1976)* Chandos ("Collect" series) ▲ CHAN 6574 [ADD]

Rule Brittania, w. C. Groves (cnd), Royal Liverpool PO, Liverpool Philharmonic Choir Classics for Pleasure ▲ CDCFP 4567 [ADD]

Collins, Judy (sgr)
Innervoices RCA Victor ▲ 7888-2-RC [DDD]

Collins, Kenneth (ten)
Verdi, G.:La forza del destino, w. Martina Arroyo (sop—Donna Leonora), Janet Coster (mez—Preziosilla), Kenneth Bowen (ten—Trabuco), Kenneth Collins (ten—Don Alvaro), Peter Glossop (bar—Don Carlo), Roderick Kennedy (bass—Marquis), J. Matheson (cnd), BBC Concert Orch, BBC Concert Chorus *(rec live, early 1980's)* Exclusive 2-▲ EXL 80 [ADD]

Collis, Andrew (sgr)
Zemlinsky, A. von:Der Geburtstag der Infantin, w. Soile Isokoski (sop), Iride Martinez (sgr), David Kuebler (ten), Juanita Lascarro (sgr), Machiko Obata (sgr), Anne Schwanewilms (sgr), Natalie Karl (sgr), Martina Rüping (sgr), Franfurter Kantorei (sgr), J. Conlon (cnd), Gürzenich Orch, Cologne PO *(rec Cologne, Feb 1996)* EMI Classics 2-▲ CDCB 56208

Collot, Delphine (sop)
Alain, J.:Music of, w. Bruno Boterf (ten), Jacques Bona (bar), Françoise Gyps (fl), Laurent Decker (ob), Bruno Pazqueir (va), Philippe Muller (vc), Georges Guillard (org), Ludwig String Quartet, Georges Guillard (cnd), St. Louis Camerata Vocal Ensemble—2 Melodies for Sop & Pno; Nuptial Song for Bar, Bass, Vc & Org; Post-Scriptum for 3 Female Voices & Pno; Canticle in Phrygian Mode for 4 Mixed-Voice, Sop & Strs; Invention for Fl, Ob & Cl; Monody for solo Fl; Prelude for Str Qnt; Adagio for Str Qnt; Funerals for Str Qnt; March of the Horiaces & the Curiaces for 2 Bugles, Drum & Org Arion ▲ ARN 68321

Collot, Delphine (sop) (cont.)
Capricornus, S.F.:Theatrum musicum quod per duodecim scenas seu sacras cantiones aperuit, w. L. S. Norin (mez), K. Wessel (alt), I. Honeyman (ten), S. Schreckenberger (bass), M. Gester (cnd), Parlement de Musique Opus 111 ▲ OPS 30-99
Chausson, E.:Duos, "La nuit" & "Le réveil", w. B. Vinson (mez), J. Bouillat (ten), G. Wieclaw (bass), E. Strosser (pno), C. Desert (pno), J. Sourisse (cnd), Jean Sourisse Ensemble, Audite Nova Vocal Ensemble FNAC Music ▲ 592224 [DDD]
Dalla Casa, G.:Music of, w. Ricercar Consort—Susane un jour Ricercar ▲ 154149
Debussy, C.:Songs, w. B. Vinson (mez), J. Bouillat (ten), G. Wieclaw (bass), C. Desert (pno), E. Strosser (pno), J. Sourisse (cnd), Jean Sourisse Ensemble, Audite Nova Vocal Ensemble—3 chansons de Chateau D'Orleans FNAC Music ▲ 592224 [DDD]
Fauré, G.:Madrigal, w. B. Vinson (mez), J. Bouillat (ten), G. Wieclaw (bass), C. Desert (pno), E. Strosser (pno) FNAC Music ▲ 592224 [DDD]
Fauré, G.:Pavane Orch, w. B. Vinson (mez), J. Bouillat (ten), G. Wieclaw (bass), C. Desert (pno), E. Strosser (pno), J. Sourisse (cnd), Jean Sourisse Ensemble, Audite Nova Vocal Ensemble FNAC Music ▲ 592224 [DDD]
Fauré, G.:Songs, w. B. Vinson (mez), J. Bouillat (ten), G. Wieclaw (bass), C. Desert (pno), E. Strosser (pno), J. Sourisse (cnd), Jean Sourisse Ensemble, Audite Nova Vocal Ensemble—Le Ruisseau, Op. 22; Puisqu'ici bas, Op. 10/1, Les Djinns, Op. 12 FNAC Music ▲ 592224 [DDD]
Jarzebski, A.:Music of, w. Ricercar Consort—Susanna Videns Ricercar ▲ 154149
Josquin Desprez:Missa, "Ave Maris Stella", w. R. Holton (sop), J.-L. Comoretto (ct), R. Le Chenadec (ct), T. Brehu (ten), H. Lamy (ten), B. Fabre-Garrus (bar), J. Gowings (bar) *(rec Jan. 1993)* Astrée ▲ E 8507 [DDD]
Josquin Desprez:Motets, w. R. Holton (sop), J.-L. Comoretto (ct), R. Le Chenadec (ct), T. Brehu (ten), H. Lamy (ten), B. Fabre-Garrus (bar), J. Gowings (bar)—Motets à la vierge *(rec Jan. 1993)* Astrée ▲ E 8507 [DDD]
Lassus, O. de:Chansons & Moresche, w. Ricercar Consort—Chanter je veux; Je ne veux plus que chanter; Ton nom que mon vers dira; Et d'où venez-vous, Madame Lucette; Du fond de ma pensée; Vivre sera et toujours perdurable; Il estoit une religieuse; etc. Ricercar ▲ 154149
Mendelssohn, F.:A Midsummer Night's Dream (comp), w. Sandrine Piau (sop), P. Herreweghe (cnd), Champs Elysées Theater Orch Harmonia Mundi France ▲ HMC 901502
Philips, P.:Kbd Music, w. Ricercar Consort—Le Rossignuol [after Lassus] (1595); Margott laborez [after Lassus] (1605) Ricercar ▲ 154149
Ravel, M.:Songs, w. B. Vinson (mez), J. Bouillat (ten), G. Wieclaw (bass), E. Strosser (pno), C. Desert (pno), J. Sourisse (cnd), Jean Sourisse Ensemble, Audite Nova Vocal Ensemble—3 a capella songs FNAC Music ▲ 592224 [DDD]
Saint-Saëns, C.:Choral Music, w. B. Vinson (mez), J. Bouillat (ten), G. Wieclaw (bass), E. Strosser (pno), C. Desert (pno), J. Sourisse (cnd), Jean Sourisse Ensemble , Vocal Audite Nova Ensemble—Calme des nuits, Op. 68/1; Les fleurs et les arbres, Op. 68/2; Salterelle, Op. 74 FNAC Music ▲ 592224 [DDD]
Strauss, R.:Das Alphorn, w. Hervé Joulain (hn), Denis Pascal (pno) Arion ▲ ARN 68311 [DDD]

Collot, Serge (trb)
Debussy, C.:Son Fl, w. Peter-Lukas Graf (fl), Ursula Holliger (hp) [arr for fl, alt & hp] Claves ▲ CD 50280 [ADD]

Collup, Donald (bar)
Weill, K.:Down in the Valley, w. I. Davidson (sop), M. Acito (ten), J. Mabry (sgr), D. P. Lang (sgr), W. Gundlach (cnd), Westphalia CO, Westphalia Kantorei Capriccio ▲ 60 020-1 [DDD]

Collver, Michael (ct)
Passage, 138 B.C.-A.D. 1611, w. Empire Brass Quintet, Laurie Monahan (sgr), Pete Maunu (acoustic/elec/12string gtr), Doug Lunn (fretless bass), D. Goldblatt (syn), K. Wortman (elec/acoustic perc) *(rec Lenox, MA & Los Angeles, CA May 27-29 & June 28-July)* Telarc ▲ CD 80355 [DDD]

Colmagro, Gianluigi (bar)
Mercadante, S.:Il giuramento, w. P. Wells (sop), B. Wolff (mez), M. Molese (sgr), T. Schippers (cnd), Juilliard Orch, Juilliard Chorus [I] *(rec live, Spoleto, 6/29/70)* Myto 2-▲ 2 MCD 90632 [ADD]
Mercadante, S.:Il giuramento, w. P. Wells (sop), B. Wolff (mez), M. Molese (sgr), T. Schippers (cnd), Juilliard Orch, Juilliard Chorus [I] *(rec live, Spoleto, 6/29/70)* Memories 2-▲ HR 4174/75 (m)

Colombara, Carlo (bass)
Verdi, G.:I masnadieri, w. M. Rowland (sgr), M. Malagnini (sgr), T. Migliorini (sgr), R. Bruson (bar), M. Lanskoy (bar), W. Gönnenwein (cnd), Ludwigsburg Festival Orch, South German Madrigal Choir Bayer 2-▲ BR 500 001/2 [DDD]
Verdi, G.:Requiem Mass, w. C. Vaness (sop), F. Quivar (mez), D. O'Neill (ten), C. Davis (cnd), Bavarian RSO, Bavarian Radio Chorus RCA Red Seal 2-▲ 09026-60902-2

Colombo, Scipio (bar)
Giordano, U.:Fedora, w. Maria Caniglia (sop), Aldo Bertocci (ten), Giacinto Prandelli (ten), Andrea Piccinni (bass), Capozzi (sgr), M. Rossi (cnd), Turin RAI SO, Turin RAI Chorus *(rec 1950)* Cetra Classic 2-▲ Don 35
Rossini, G.:Il turco in Italia, w. Graziella Sciurri (sop), Agostino Lazzari (ten), Sesto Bruscantini (bar), N. Sanzogno (cnd), *(orch & chorus unknown)* *(rec Milan, Feb 25, 1958)* Pantheon 2-▲ PHE 6654 (m)
Verdi, G.:Luisa Miller, w. L. Kelston (sop—Luisa), M.T. Pace (mez—Federica), G. Larui-Volpi (ten—Rodolfo), S. Colombo (bar—Miller), G. Vaghi (bar—Count Walter), D. Baronti (bass—Wurm), M. Rossi (cnd), Rome RAI Orch, Rome RAI Chorus *(rec 1951)* Cetra Classic 2-▲ CDO 17 [AAD]

Colton, Kendra (sop)
Bach, J.S.:Cant 187, w. Wayne Rapier (ob)—Gott versorget alles Leben Boston Records ▲ BR 1013
Vaughan Williams, R.:Blake Songs, w. Wayne Rapier (ob) Boston Records ▲ BR 1013

Colzani, Anselmo (bar)
Donizetti, G.:La favorita, w. F. Cossotto (mez), J. Aragall (ten), E. Gracis (cnd), Turin RAI Orch, Turin RAI Chorus *(rec live)* Melodram 2-▲ MEL 27020
Puccini, G.:La fanciulla del West, w. D. Kirsten (sop), F. Corelli (ten), A. Guadagno (cnd), Philadelphia Lyric Opera Orch, Philadelphia Lyric Opera Chorus [I] *(rec live, 11/10/64)* Melodram 2-▲ MEL 27081 [AAD]
Puccini, G.:Tosca, w. R. Tebaldi (sop—Tosca), F. Corelli (ten—Cavaradossi), A. Colzani (bar—Scarpia), P. L. Latinucci (b-bar—Sacristan), G. Beloni (bass—Angelotti), M. Parenti (cnd), Livorno Teatro La Gran Guardia Orch, Livorno Teatro La Gran Guardia Chorus *(rec live Sept. 21, 1959)* Legato Classics 2-▲ LCD 171-2 [ADD]
Spontini, G.:Agnes von Hohensaufen, w. L. Udovick (sop), D. Dow (sop), F. Corelli (ten), G. Guelfi (bar), V. Gui (cnd), Florence Maggio Musicale Orch, Florence Maggio Musicale Chorus [I] *(rec live 5/9/54)* Melodram 2-▲ MEL 27055 (m) [AAD]
Verdi, G.:Aida, w. A. Stella (sop), F. Barbieri (mez), F. Corelli (ten), M. Petri (bar), V. Gui (cnd), Naples Teatro San Carlo Orch, Naples Teatro San Carlo Chorus [I] *(rec live, Naples 11/2/55)* Golden Age of Opera 2-▲ GAO 116/17 [ADD]
Verdi, G.:La forza del destino, w. E. Farrell (sop), J. Grillo (sop), F. Corelli (ten), E. Flagello (bass), A. Guadagno (cnd), *(orch unknown)* [I] *(rec live, Philadelphia 4/14/65)* Standing Room Only 2-▲ SRO 826-2 [ADD]

Comas (sgr)
Mascagni, P.:Sí, w. Vivian (sop), A. Felle (sop), Maria Gentile (sop), M.G. Liguori (sop), Nicoletti (sgr), S. Sanna (cnd), Montepulciano Arts Center Orch, Montepulciano Arts Center Chorus [I] *(rec live, 7/24/87)* Bongiovanni 2-▲ GB 2050/51 [DDD]

Comboy, Ian (bass)
Davies, P.M.:The Lighthouse, w. Neil Mackie (ten), Christopher Keyte (bass), P. M. Davies (cnd), BBC PO Collins Classics ▲ COL 1415 [DDD]

Comden, Betty (sgr)
Bernstein, L.:Music of, w. Barbara Cook (sop), Adolph Green (sgr), Rosalind Russell (sgr), et al—sels. from Candide, Mass, On the Town, Peter Pan, 1600 Pennsylvania Avenue, Trouble in Tahiti, West Side Story, Wonderful Town *(rec 1950-1973)* CBS ▲ MK 44760 [ADD]
Bernstein, L.:On the Town, w. M. Martin (sgr), N. Walker (sgr), A. Green (sgr), Tutti Camarata Orch, Leonard Joy Orch, Lynn Murray Orch, Lynn Murray Chorus MCA Classics ▲ MCAD 10280 (m) [AAD]

Comencini, Maurizio (ten)
Donizetti, G.:Betly, w. S. Rigacci (sop), R. Scaltriti (bar), B. Rigacci (cnd), Emilia Romagna Arturo Toscanini SO, Lugo Teatro Comunale Rossini Chorus *(rec live, 6/90)* Bongiovanni 2-▲ GB 2091/92 [DDD]
Morlacchi, F.:Nuovo barbiere, w. A. Ruffini (sop), G. Gatti (sop), A. Tomicich (bass), R. Franceschetto (sgr), G. Catalucci (cnd), Orch Giovanile In Canto [I] *(rec live 9/9/89)* Bongiovanni 2-▲ GB 2085/86 [DDD]
Rossini, G.:La cambiale di matrimonio, w. A. Rossi (sop), B. de Simone (bar), B. Praticò (bar), M. Viotti (cnd), English CO [I] Claves 8-▲ CD 9200 [DDD]
Rossini, G.:La cambiale di matrimonio, w. Alessandra Rossi (sop), Bruno Praticò (bar), Bruno De Simone (bar), Valeria Baiano (bass), Francesco Facini (bass), M. Viotti (cnd), English CO Claves ▲ 50-9101
Rossini, G.:The Siege of Corinth, w. L. Serra (sop), D. Raffanti (ten), A. Caforio (bass), M. Lippi (bass), P. Olmi (cnd), Genoa Teatro Carlo Felice Orch, Genoa Teatro Carlo Felice Chorus, Prague Phil Choir *(rec June 2 & 14, 1992)* Nuova Era 3-▲ 7140/42 [DDD]
Wolf-Ferrari, E.:Il campiello, w. D. Mazzucato (Gasparina), G. Devinu (Lucieta), M. Bolgan (Gnese), C. de Mola (Orsola), U. Benelli (Dona Cate Panciana), M. Rene Cosotti (Dona Pasqua Polegana), M. Comencini (Zorozeto), M. Biscotti (Astolfi), I. D'Arcangelo (Anzoleto), C. Striuli (Fabrizio del Ritorti), N. Bareza (cnd), Trieste Teatro Comunale Giuseppe Verdi Orch, Trieste Teatro Comunale G. Verdi Chorus *(rec Feb. 1992)* Ricordi 2-▲ RFCD 2014 [DDD]

Command, Michèle (sop)
Gounod, C.:Sappho, w. S. Coste (sop), C. Popis (ten), E. Faury (bar), P. Fournillier (cnd), St.-Etienne Nouvel Orch Koch Schwann 2-▲ SCH 313112 [DDD]
Massenet, J.:Don Quichotte, w. R. Crespin (sop), G. Bacquier (bar), N. Ghiaurov (bass), R. Bonynge (cnd), Swiss Romande Orch, Swiss Romande Chorus [F] London ("Grand Opera" series) 2-▲ 430636-2 [AAD]
Massenet, J.:Eve, w. Carolyn Sebron (mez), Hervé Lamy (ten), Jean-Philippe Courtis (bass), J.-P. Lore (cnd), French Oratorio Orch, French Oratorio Choir Erol 3-▲ 94002-04
Massenet, J.:Grisélidis, w. Brigitte Desnoues (sop), Jean-Luc Viala (ten), Didier Henry (bar), Maurice Sieyes (bar), Christian Treguier (bar), Jean-Philippe Courtis (bass), Claire Larcher (sgr), P. Fournillier (cnd), Franz Liszt SO, Budapest Lyon Chorus Koch Schwann 2-▲ SCH 312702 [DDD]
Massenet, J.:Marie-Magdeleine, w. Carolyn Sebron (mez), Hervé Lamy (ten), Jean-Philippe Courtis (bass), J.-P. Lore (cnd), French Oratorio Orch, French Oratorio Choir Erol 3-▲ 94002-04
Massenet, J.:La Vierge, w. M. Castets (sop), M. Olmeda (sop), M. Keller (sop), P. Salmon (ten), M. Hacquard (bar), P. Fournillier (cnd), Prague SO, Prague Sym Chorus Koch Schwann 2-▲ CD 313084 [DDD]
Messiaen, O.:Chants de Terre et de Ciel, w. M.-M. Petit (pno) [F] *(rec 1977)* EMI Classics 2-▲ CMS 64092-2 [ADD]
Messiaen, O.:Harawi, w. M.-M. Petit (pno) [F] *(rec 1977)* EMI Classics 2-▲ CMS 64092-2 [ADD]
Messiaen, O.:Mélodies, w. M.-M. Petit (pno) [F] *(rec 1977)* EMI Classics 2-▲ CMS 64092-2 [ADD]
Messiaen, O.:Poèmes pour Mi, w. M.-M. Petit (pno) [F] *(rec 1977)* EMI Classics 2-▲ CMS 64092-2 [ADD]

Como, Perry (sgr)
Rodgers, R.:Music of, w. S. Bass (sgr), J. Andrews (sgr), D. Reese (sgr), J. Jones (sgr), N. Luboff (sgr), M. Gold (sgr), N. Walker (sgr), H. Bowen (sgr), V. Damone (sgr), P. Nero (pno), J. P. Morgan (sgr), E. Fisher (sgr), B. Goodman (cl), Ann-Margaret (sgr), Shorty Rogers (sgr), D. Shore (sgr), T. Martin (sgr), M. King (sgr), A. Newley (sgr) RCA ▲ 8590-2 R ■ 8590-4 R

Comorette, Jean-Louis (ct)
Dupuy, B.A.:Sacred Music, w. Isabelle Poulenard (sop), Erik Gruchet (ten), Dominique Miraille (bar), Jean-Louis Bindi (bass), A. Bourbon (cnd), Baroque Instrumental Ensemble, Toulouse Vocal Group—Noël; Motet; Magnificat Arion ▲ ARN 68330 [DDD]

Comoretto, Jean-Louis (ct)
Handel, G.F.:Cants, w. Isabelle Poulenard (sop), Il Divertimento—Menzognere speranze; Vedendo amor; Figli del mesto cor; Lungi dal mio bel nume Astrée ▲ E 8577
Handel, G.F.:Duets for Various Voices, w. Isabelle Poulenard (sop), Il Divertimento—No, di voi non vo' fidarmi; Troppo curda, troppo fiera; Tanti strali al sen mi scocchi Astrée ▲ E 8577
Josquin Desprez:Missa, "Ave Maris Stella", w. D. Collot (sop), R. Holton (sop), R. Le Chenadec (ct), T. Brehu (ten), H. Lamy (ten), B. Fabre-Garrus (bar), J. Gowings (bar) *(rec Jan. 1993)* Astrée ▲ E 8507 [DDD]
Josquin Desprez:Motets, w. D. Collot (sop), R. Holton (sop), R. Le Chenadec (ct), T. Brehu (ten), H. Lamy (ten), B. Fabre-Garrus (bar), J. Gowings (bar)—Motets à la vierge *(rec Jan. 1993)* Astrée ▲ E 8507 [DDD]
Pergolesi, G.B.:Stabat mater, w. Isabelle Poulenard (sop), J. Malgoire (cnd), La Grande Ecurie et la Chambre du Roy Astrée ▲ E 8556

Compañez, Irene (cta)
Mussorgsky, M.:Khovanshchina, w. Herbert Handt (ten), Mirto Picchi (ten), Boris Christoff (bass), Armedeo Berdini (sgr), Giorgio Canello (sgr), Dmitri Lopatto (sgr), Michele Malaspina (sgr), Jolanda Mancini (sgr), Mario Petri (sgr), A. Rodzinski (cnd), Rome RAI Radio-TV SO, Rome RAI Chorus Stradivarius 2-▲ STV DTM 12320 [ADD]
Mussorgsky, M.:Khovanshchina, w. Jolanda Mancini (sop—Emma), Irene Companez (mez), Amedeo Berdini (ten—Prince Andrei Khovanski), Mirto Picchi (ten—Prince Vasili Golitsin), Herbert Handt (ten—Scribe), Andrea Mineo (bar—Kuzka), Giampiero Malaspina (bar—Shaklovity), Boris Christoff (bass—Dosifei), Mario Petri (bass—Prince Ivan Khovanski), Dimitri Lopatto (Varsonofiev/First Strelyets), Giorgio Conello (Second Strelyets), A. Rodzinski (cnd), *(orch unknown)* [I] *(rec Rome, 1958)* VAI Audio 2-▲ VAIA 1052-2
Ponchielli, A.:La Gioconda, w. M. Callas (sop), F. Cossotto (mez), P. M. Ferraro (ten), P. Cappuccilli (bar), I. Vinco (bass), A. Votto (cnd), La Scala Orch, La Scala Chorus EMI Classics ▲ CDCC 49518
Prokofiev, S.:Alexander Nevsky, w. A. Rodzinski (cnd), Rome RAI Orch, Rome RAI Chorus Stradivarius ▲ STV 10035 [ADD]
Prokofiev, S.:Alexander Nevsky, w. A. Rodzinski (cnd), Rome RAI Orch *(rec May 22, 1958)* Stradivarius ▲ STR 10035 [ADD]

Compton, Judith (alt)
Sowerby, L.:Forsaken of Man, w. Alicia Clark (sop), Thomas Potter (bass), Paul Grizzell (bass), Matthew Greenberg (bass), Bruce Hall (sgr), John Vorassi (sgr), Thomas Weisflog (org), William Ferris (cnd), William Ferris Chorale *(rec St. Thomas the Apostle Church, Chicago, June 1990)* New World ▲ 803942 [AAD]

Conant, Richard (bass)
Mahler, G.:Beethoven's Sym 9, w. Leah Anne Myers (sop), Ilene Sameth (mez), James Clark (ten), P. Tiboris (cnd), Brno State PO, Janáček Opera Chorus Bridge ▲ BCD 9033 [DDD]

Conati, Lorenzo (bar)
Puccini, G.:Manon Lescaut, w. Maria Zamboni (sop), Francesco Merli (ten), L. Molajoli (cnd), La Scala Orch, La Scala Chorus *(rec Milan, 1930)* Phonographe 2-▲ PHG 5006 [ADD]
Puccini, G.:Manon Lescaut, w. Marla Zamboni (sop), Francesco Merli (ten), L. Molajoli (cnd), La Scala Orch, La Scala Chorus *(rec Milan, 1930)* Melodram 2-▲ IMC 202001
Puccini, G.:Manon Lescaut, w. Maria Zamboni (sop—Manon), Anna Masetti-Bassi (mez—Singer), Francesco Merli (ten—Chevalier), Giuseppe Nessi (ten—Edmondo/Dancing Master/ Lamplighter), Lorenzo Conati (bar—Lescaut), Aristide Baracchi (bass—Innkeeper/Sergeant), Attilio Bordonali (bass—Geronte), Natale Villa (bass—Naval Captain), L. Molajoli (cnd), La Scala Orch, Vittore Veneziani (cnd), La Scala Chorus *(rec 1930)* Arkadia ("The 78's" series) 2-▲ 78014 [ADD]

Concari, Sheila (sgr)
Lombardi, D.:Faustimmung, w. Daniele Lombardi (pno—Faust), Sheila Concari (sgr—Fela), Margherita (vc—Margherita) *(rec Emmequattro, Rome, Oct 4, 1987)* Musicaimmagine ▲ MR 10013

Concetti, Andrea (sgr)
Monteverdi, C.:Ballo delle ingrate, w. Carlo Lepore (bass), Daniela Barcellona (sgr), Daniela Ciliberti (sgr), Hans van Dijk (sgr), Remo Guerrini (sgr), Nadia Mantelli (sgr), Elena Marazzi (sgr), Humberto Orellana (sgr), Claudia Pallini (sgr), Luigi Polsini (sgr), Rosa Ricciotti (sgr), Alberto Rota (sgr), Ludovica Scoppola (sgr), *(orch unknown)* Nuova Era ▲ NUO 7224

Condò, Nucci (mez)
Marschner, H.A.:Der Vampyr, w. Carole Farley (sop—Malwina), Nucci Condò (mez—Suse), Oslavio Di Credico (ten—George Dibdin), Josef Protschka (ten—Edgar Aubry), Romano Truffelli (ten—Richard Scrop), Martin Egel (bar—Sir Humphrey Davenaut), Andréa Snarski (bar—Toms Blunt), Siegmund Nimsgern (b-bar—Lord Ruthven), Armando Caforio (bass—Robert Green), Peter Boom (sgr—Il capo dei Vampiri), Carlo Di Giacomo (sgr—James Gadshill), Wolfgang Lenz (sgr—Sir Berkley), Galina Pisarenko (sgr—Janthe), Renzo Scorsoni (sgr—Un servitore di Berkley), Anastasia Tomaszewska Schepis (sgr—Emmy), G. Neuhold (cnd), Rome RAI SO, Rome RAI Chorus *(rec Rome, Jan 26, 1980)* Italia 2-▲ CDC 99 [ADD]
Mozart, W.A.:Nozze di Figaro, w. S. Jurinac (sop), T. Stratas (sop), T. Berganza (mez), A. Lazzari (ten), S. Bruscantini (bar), M. Petri (bass), G. Tadeo (bass), A. Mariotti (bass), Z. Mehta (cnd), *(orch unknown) (rec 1968)* Great Opera Performances 3-▲ GOP 712

Conello, Giorgio (sgr)
Mussorgsky, M.:Khovanshchina, w. Jolanda Mancini (sop—Emma), Irene Companez (mez), Amedeo Berdini (ten—Prince Andrei Khovanski), Mirto Picchi (ten—Prince Vasili Golitsin), Herbert Handt (ten—Scribe), Andrea Mineo (bar—Kuzka), Giampiero Malaspina (bar—Shaklovity), Boris Christoff (bass—Dosifei), Mario Petri (bass—Prince Ivan Khovanski), Dimitri Lopatto (Varsonofiev/First Strelyets), Giorgio Conello (Second Strelyets), A. Rodzinski (cnd), *(orch unknown)* [I] *(rec Rome, 1958)* VAI Audio 2-▲ VAIA 1052-2

Coni, Paolo (bar)
Donizetti, G.:Maria di Rohan (sels), w. M. Nicolesco (sop), G. Morino (ten), M. de Bernart (cnd), Italian International Opera Orch, Slovak Phil Chorus [I] *(rec live)* Nuova Era 2-▲ 6732/33 [DDD]
Leoncavallo, R.:Pagliacci, w. D. Dessì (sop), L. Pavarotti (ten), J. Pons (bar), R. Muti (cnd), Philadelphia Orch [I] Philips ▲ 438132-2
Monteverdi, C.:Orfeo, w. Nuccia Focile (sop), Claudia Clarich (mez), Enrico Facini (ten), James Loomis (bass), H. Handt (cnd), Lucchese CO [orchd Respighi, 1934-35] *(rec live, VII Festival Internazionale di Marlia, 1984)* Claves ▲ CD 9419 [ADD]
Puccini, G.:Manon Lescaut, w. K. Te Kanawa (sop), J. Carreras (ten), I. Tajo (bass), R. Chailly (cnd), Bologna Teatro Comunale Orch [I] London 2-▲ 421426-2 [DDD]
Song Recital, w. Daniela Sbaraglia (pno) Nuova Era ▲ NUO 6827 [DDD]
Tosti, P.F.:Songs, w. D. Sbaraglia (pno) Nuova Era ▲ 6827 [DDD]

Conley, Eugene (ten)
Beethoven, L van:Missa Solemnis, w. M. Marshall (sop), N. Merriman (mez), J. Hines (bass), A. Toscanini (cnd), NBC SO, Robert Shaw Chorale *(rec 1953)* RCA Gold Seal ▲ 60272-2-RG [ADD] ■ 60272-4-RG

Connaughton, Riki (mez)
Stuart, P.:Kill Bear Comes Home, w. Elana Gizzi (sop—Hasty Girl), Mi-Kyung Huh (sop—Cold Feet), Therese Murray (sop—Song Bird), Cherie Pfeil (sop—1st Sister), Renia Shukis (sop—2nd Sister), Riki Connaughton (mez—4th Sister), Lucy Fee (mez—3rd Sister), David Averbach (ten—Song Leader), Mark Schmidt (ten—Kill Bear), Jason Smith (bar—Cheif Wife Hunter), P. Stuart (cnd), Rochester Opera Theater Orch, Rochester Opera Theater Chorus VM ▲ DRK 154 [DDD]

Connell, Elisabeth (sop)
Donizetti, G.:Poliuto, w. N. Martinucci (ten), R. Bruson (bar), J. Latham-König (cnd), Rome Opera Orch, Rome Opera Chorus [I] *(rec live, 1988)* Nuova Era 2-▲ 6776/77 [DDD]
Schreker, F.:Die Gezeichneten, w. Heinz Kruse (ten), Monte Pederson (bar), Alfred Muff (bass), László Polgar (bass), L. Zagrosek (cnd), Berlin German SO London 3-▲ 444442-2
Schubert, Franz:Songs (comp), w. G. Johnson (pno)—13 songs—D.101, 291, 307, 323, 372, 381, 483, 533, 544, 772, 788, 852, 917, 989 [G] Hyperion ▲ CDJ 33005 [DDD]
Verdi, G.:I due Foscari, w. K. Ricciarelli (sop), J. Carreras (ten), V. Bello (ten), M. Antoniak (ten), P. Cappuccilli (bar), S. Ramey (bass), F. Handlos (bass), L. Gardelli (cnd), Austrian RSO, Austrian Radio Chorus Philips 2-▲ 422426-2 [ADD]
Wagner, R.:Lohengrin, w. N. Armstrong (sop), P. Hofmann (ten), L. Roar (bass), B. Weikl (bass), S. Vogel (bass), W. Nelsson (cnd), Bayreuth Festival Orch, Bayreuth Festival Chorus CBS 3-▲ M3K 38594

Connell, John (bass)
Szymanowski, K.:Litany to the Virgin Mary, w. E. Szmytka (sop), F. Quivar (cta), J. Garrison (ten), S. Rattle (cnd), City of Birmingham SO, City of Birmingham Sym Chorus EMI Classics ▲ CDC 55121
Szymanowski, K.:Stabat Mater, w. E. Szmytka (sop), F. Quivar (mez), S. Rattle (cnd), City of Birmingham SO, City of Birmingham Sym Chorus EMI Classics ▲ CDC 55121
Tchaikovsky, P.:Eugene Onegin, w. K. Te Kanawa (sop—Tatiana), P. Bardon (mez—Olga), N. Rosenshein (ten—Lensky), T. Hampson (b-bar—Eugene Onegin), J. Connell (bass—Prince Gremin), C. Mackerras (cnd), Welsh National Opera Orch, Welsh National Opera Chorus [E] EMI Classics ▲ CDCB 55004

Conner, Nadine (sop)
Bach, J.S.:St. Matthew Passion, w. Jean Watson (cta), William Hain (ten), Mack Harrell (bar), Herbert Janssen (bar), Lorenzo Alvary (bass), B. Walter (cnd), New York PO, New York Phil Chorus—Part I Minerva ▲ 20
Bizet, G.:Carmen (sels), w. Risë Stevens (sop), R. Jobin (ten), R. Weede (bar), G. Sébastian (cnd), Metropolitan Opera Orch, New York Metropolitan Opera Chorus [F] Odyssey ■ YT 32102 (m)

Conner, Wayne (ten)
Brahms, J.:Liebeslieder Waltzes SATB, w. B. Valente (sop), M. Kleinman (cta), M. Singher (bar), R. Serkin (pno), L. Fleisher (pno) [G] Sony Classical ("Essential Classics" series) ▲ SBK 48176 ■ SBT 48176

Connery, Sean (nar)
Britten, H.:The Young Person's Guide to the Orchestra, w. A. Dorati (cnd), Royal PO IMP Collectors Series ▲ IMPX 9002 [AAD]
Britten, H.:The Young Person's Guide to the Orchestra, w. A. Dorati (cnd), Royal PO *(rec Kingsway Hall, London, England, Mar 1965)* London ("Phase 4 Stereo" series) ▲ 444104-2 [ADD]
Prokofiev, S.:Peter & the Wolf, w. A. Dorati (cnd), Royal PO *(rec Kingsway Hall, London, England, Mar 1965)* London ("Phase 4 Stereo" series) ▲ 444104-2 [ADD]
Prokofiev, S.:Peter & the Wolf, w. A. Dorati (cnd), Royal PO IMP Collectors Series ▲ IMPX 9002 [AAD]

Connolly, Sarah (cta)
Bach, J.S.:Cant 57, w. Vasiljka Jezovšek (sop), Mark Padmore (ten), Peter Kooy (bass), Phillippe Herreweghe (cnd), Collegium Vocale Harmonia Mundi ▲ HMC 901594
Bach, J.S.:Cant 110, w. Vasiljka Jezovšek (sop), Mark Padmore (ten), Peter Kooy (bass), Phillippe Herreweghe (cnd), Collegium Vocale Harmonia Mundi ▲ HMC 901594
Bach, J.S.:Cant 122, w. Vasiljka Jezovšek (sop), Mark Padmore (ten), Peter Kooy (bass), Phillippe Herreweghe (cnd), Collegium Vocale Harmonia Mundi ▲ HMC 901594

Connors, Carolyn (voc)
Chris Mann & the Impediments, w. C. Mann (voc), Jeannie Marsch (voc), Rik Rue (voc) O.O. Discs ▲ CD 21 [ADD]

Connors, Ursula (sop)
Rameau, J.P.:Les Fêtes d'Hébé, w. R. Leppard (cnd), English CO, Ambrosian Singers EMI Classics ("Baroque" series) ▲ CDK 65732

Conrad, Barbara (mez)
Spirituals, w. Gregory Hopkins (cnd), New England Symphonic Ensemble, Convent Avenue Concert Choir *(rec Convent Avenue Baptist Church, Harlem, NY & Fisher Hall, Santa Rosa)* Naxos ▲ 8.553036 [DDD]

Conrad, Margrit (cta)
Keiser, R.:Passions Oratorium, w. J. Bise (sop), G. Jelden (ten), U. Gilgen (bass), J.E. Dähler (cnd), Bernese Orch, Bernese Chorus [G] *(rec Feb. 1971)* Claves 2-▲ CD 9223/24 [ADD]

Conrad, Richard (bar)
The Age of Bel Canto, w. Joan Sutherland (sop), Marilyn Horne (mez), London SO [cnd:Richard Bonynge], London Sym Chorus London ("The Classic Sound" series) ▲ 448594-2
Sullivan, A.:Songs, w. William Merrill (pno)—Guinevere; O Mistress Mine; A Life That Lives for You; If Dought Deeds; Arabian Love Song; I Would I Were a King; others Pearl ▲ PEA 9636 [DDD]

Consolini, Stefano (ten)
Albanese, G.:Songs, w. Luana Gentile (sop), Antonella Trovarelli (sop), Marina Gentile (mez), Paolo Speca (bar), Andrea De Mele (vn), Sirio Benedetto (sax), Roberto Rupo (pno)—Aria di Natale; Duettino e coro muto (w. Carlo Moreno) [both w. Giorgina Dell'Immagine, Tito Petralia (cnd), EIAR Orch & Chorus]; Passione (M. Gentile); Serenata (Speca); Alzati, o bella... (Trovarelli); Mattinata (Speca); Il sogno d'una suora (Trovarelli); Ninna Nanna (M. Gentile); Barcarola (Rupo); Madrigale (L. Gentile); Ninna nanna...900 (L. Gentile); Variazioni (L. Gentile); Non so qual io mi voglia... (L. Gentile); Io sono un augellin... (L. Gentile); Bravo, bene, bis...(va bene) (Consolini & Di Benedetto); Che caviale (Consolini); Ma non sapete chi sono io? (Consolini & L. & M. Gentile); Grappoli di stelle (Consolini); Notte di Capri (Consolini & Di Mele); Una rosa di ferro battuto (Consolini, Speca & L. & M. Gentile) *(rec Ortona, Teatro Zambra)* Bongiovanni ▲ GB 5054-2 [DDD]

Constantino, Florencio (ten)
Verdi, G.:Il trovatore (sels), w. J. Biel (ten), F. Tamagno (ten), L.-A. Escalaïs (ten), M. Gilion (ten), E. Caruso (ten), A. Paoli (ten), G. Zenatello (ten), J. Sembach (ten), L. Slezak (ten), G. Martinelli (ten), B. De Muro (ten), N. Fusati (ten), N. Piccaluga (ten), G. Lauri-Volpi (ten), A. Pertile (ten), E. Bergamaschi (ten), R. Tauber (ten), J. O'Sullivan (ten), H. Roswaenge (ten), G. Taccani (ten), V. Lois (ten), H. Lazaro (ten), A. Lindi (ten), A. Cortis (ten), F. Merli (ten), F. Völker (ten), J. Kiepura (ten), J. Schmidt (ten), J. Bjoerling (ten), B. Gigli (ten), A. Salvarezza (ten), J. Soler (ten), M. Filippeschi (ten)—34 performances of the Act III tenor aria "Di quella pira!," *(rec from 1903-1956)* Bongiovanni ▲ GB 1051 [AAD]

Conti, Gino (bass)
Giordano, U.:Andrea Chénier, w. Maria Caniglia (sop—Maddalena), Maria Huder (mez—Bersi), Vittoria Palombini (mez—Madelon), Giulietta Simionato (mez—Contessa), Beniamino Gigli (ten—Andrea), Adelio Zagonara (ten—Incroyable/Abbé), Gino Bechi (bar—Carlo), Leone Paci (bar—Mathieu), Giuseppe Taddei (b-bar—Pietro/Fouquier), Italo Tajo (b-bar—Roucher), Gino Conti (bass—Master/Schmidt), O. de Fabritiis (cnd), La Scala Orch, La Scala Chorus *(rec Nov 1941)* Arkadia ("The 78's" series) 2-▲ 78012 [ADD]
Puccini, G.:La fanciulla del West (sels), w. Magda Olivero (sop—Minnie), Corinna Vozza (mez—Wowkle), Paolo Caroli (ten—Harry), Giacomo Lauri-Volpi (ten—Dick Johnson), Marco Rogani (ten—Pony Express Rider), Salvatore di Tommaso (ten—Trin), Adelio Zagonara (ten—Nick), Virgilio Ascorro (bar—Sid), Alfredo Colella (bar—Jake Wallace), Giuseppe Forgione (bar—Bello), Giancarlo Guelfi (bar—Jack Rance), Arturo la Porta (bar—Sonora), Gino Conti (bass—José Castro), Piere Passarotti (bass—Bill), Enzo Titta (bass—Larkens), Giulio Tomei (bass—Ashby), V. Bellezza (cnd), Rome Opera Orch, Rome Opera Chorus—Minnie, dalla mia casa son partito; Laggiù nel Soledad; Chi c'è per farmi i ricci; Oh! Mister Johnson, siete rimasto; Non so ben neppur io; Io non son che una povera fanciulla; No, Minnie, non piangete; Vorrei mettermi queste; Hallo!; Oh, se sapeste; Credo che abbiate torto; Ma ti giuro ch'io non ti lascio più; Vieni fuori!; Una parola sola!...Or son sei mesi; Che c'è di nuovo Jack?; E là; Siete pronto; Ch'ella mi creda; È Minnie!...È Minnie! *(rec Rome, Mar. 30, 1957)* Golden Age of Opera ▲ GAO 180 [ADD]
Puccini, G.:Madama Butterfly, w. Toti dal Monte (sop—Madama Butterfly), Maria Huder (mez—Kate Pinkerton), Beniamino Gigli (ten—B.F. Pinkerton), Adelio Zagonara (ten—Goro), Mario Basiola (bar—Sharpless), Gino Conti (bass—Principe Yamadori), Ernesto Dominici (bass—Il Bonzo), Vittoria Paolombini (sgr—Suzuki), O. de Fabritiis (cnd), Rome Opera Orch, Giuseppe Conca (cnd), Rome Opera Chorus *(rec Aug 1939)* Arkadia 2-▲ CD 78004 (m) [ADD]

Conti, P. (ten)
Verdi, G.:Falstaff, w. E. Norberg-Schulz (sop—Nannetta), L. Serra (sop—Alice), S. Graham (mez—Meg Page), M. Lipovsek (cta—Miss Quickly), K. Begley (ten—Dr. Caius), P. Conti (ten—Ford), M. Luperi (ten—Pistol), J. Van Dam (b-bar—Falstaff), P. LeFebvre (bass—Bardolph), G. Solti (cnd), Berlin PO, Berlin Radio Chorus London ▲ 440650-2 [DDD]

Controbas (sgr)
Mozart, W.A.:Nozze di Figaro (sels), w. Anna Tomowa-Sintow (sop), José van Dam (b-bar), H. von Karajan (cnd), Vienna PO London ▲ 421317-2 [ADD]

Conway, Deborah (sgr)
Nyman, M.:Prospero's Books, w. S. Leonard (sop), U. Lemper (sop), M. Angel (ten), Michael Nyman Band London ▲ 425224-2 [DDD]

Cook, Barbara (sop)
Bernstein, L.:Candide, w. Max Adrian (sgr), Robert Rounseville (ten), et al. Sony Broadway ▲ SK 48017 ■ ST 48017
Bernstein, L.:Music of, w. Betty Comden (sgr), Adolph Green (sgr), Rosalind Russell (sgr), et al—sels. from Candide, Mass, On the Town, Peter Pan, 1600 Pennsylvania Avenue, Trouble in Tahiti, West Side Story, Wonderful Town *(rec 1950-1973)* CBS ▲ MK 44760 [ADD]
Kern, J.:Show Boat, w. W. Warfield (sgr) [1966 revival cast] RCA ▲ 09026-61182-2 [ADD] ■ 09026-61182-4
Kern, J.:Show Boat, w. J. Raitt (sgr), *(other artists unknown)* [1962 studio cast] Columbia ▲ CK 02220 ■ JST 02220
Rodgers, R.:Carousel, w. S. Ramey (bass), S. Brightman (sop), M. Forrester (cta), et al., P. Gemignani (cnd), Royal PO, Ambrosian Singers [1987 studio cast] MCA Classics ▲ MCAD 6209 [DDD] ■ MCAC 6209

Cook, Howard (ten)
Purcell, H.:Odes & Welcome Songs (misc), w. J. Bowman (ct), C. Robson (ct), D. Wilson-Johnson (bar), G. Leonhardt (hpd), G. Leonhardt (cnd), Orch of the Age of Enlightenment Virgin Classics ▲ CDC 59243
Rameau, J.P.:Castor et Pollux, w. V. Gens (sop), A. Mellon (sop), J. Corréas (bass), W. Christie (cnd), Les Arts Florissants Harmonia Mundi France 3-▲ HMC 901435/37

Cook, Terry (bass)
Berlioz, H.:Messe solennelle Bar, w. Gene Tucker (ten), Rosa Lamoreaux (sgr), J. Reilly Lewis (cnd), Washington National Cathedral Choral Society Koch International Classics ▲ KIC 7204 [DDD]
Verdi, G.:Aida (sels), w. A. Millo (sop), D. Zajick (mez), P. Domingo (ten), J. Morris (bar), S. Ramey (bass), J. Levine (cnd), Metropolitan Opera Orch, New York Metropolitan Opera Chorus *(rec New York, May 18-26, 1990)* Sony Classical ("Opera Highlights" series) ▲ SMK 53506 [DDD]

Cooke, Deryck (nar)
Wagner, R.:Der Ring des Nibelungen (sels), w. G. Solti (cnd), Vienna PO—narrated guide to the Ring Cycle w. 193 musical examples London 2-▲ 443581-2

Cookson, Brian (ten)
Walton, W.:Troilus & Cressida, w. Judith Howarth (sop—Cressida), Arthur Davies (ten—Troilus), Nigel Robson (ten—Pandarus), Brian Cookson (ten—3rd Watchman), Peter Bodenham (ten—Priest), Keith Mills (ten—Soldier), Alan Opie (bar—Diomede), James Thornton (bar—Antenor), Clive Bayley (bass—Calkas), David Owen-Lewis (bass—Horaste), R. Hickox (cnd), English Northern Philharmonia, Opera North Chorus Chandos 2-▲ CHAN 9370/71 [DDD]

Cooper (sgr)
Bizet, G.:Carmen, w. Dunn (sgr), P. Domingo (ten), F. Guarrera (bar), A. Guadagno (cnd), Cincinnati Summer Opera Association Orch, Cincinnati Summer Opera Association Chorus [F] *(rec live 7/19/68)* Melodram 2-▲ MEL 27034 (m) [AAD]

Cooper, Sharon (mez)
Klein, G.:Songs, w. Jacqueline Méfano (pno) Arion ▲ ARN 68272 [DDD]
Milhaud, D.:Ani maamin, un chant perdu et retrouvé, w. Sharon Cooper (sop—la Voix), Anna Parus (mez), Bernard Freyd (nar—Isaac), Michel Hermon (nar—le Récitant), Michael Lonsdale (nar—Abraham), Jean Négroni (nar—Jacob), P. Méfano (cnd), Ensemble 2E2M, Madrigal de Bordeaux Arion ▲ ARN 68275 [DDD]
Stravinsky, I.:Les Noces, w. M. Quercia (sop), P. Capelle (ten), P. Marinov (bass), Vieuxtemps (pno), R. Conil (pno), Arzoumanian (pno), Raynaut (pno), R. Hayrabedian (cnd), Strasbourg Percussion Ensemble, Contemporary Choir Pierre Verany ▲ PV 787032 [DDD]

Cooper, Susan (mez)
Somers, H.:Kyrie, w. Roxolana Roslak (sop), Robert Missen (ten), Nelson Lohnes (bass), Timothy Cadan (bass), E. Iseler (cnd), *(orch unknown)*, Elmer Iseler Singers *(rec Flora McRae Eaton Memorial Auditorium & St. Anne's Anglican Church, Toronto)* Centrediscs ▲ CMC 5495 [DDD]

Coppola, Walter (ten)

Bellini, V.:Bianca e Fernando, w. Y. O. Shin (sop), G. Kunde (ten), A. Tomicich (bass), A. Licata (cnd), Catania Teatro Massimo Bellini Orch, Catania Teatro Massimo Bellini Chorus Nuova Era 2-▲ NUO 7076 [DDD]

Dvořák, A.:Mass, w. Dagmar Masková (sop), Marta Benacková (alt), Peter Mikulás (bass), Josef Ksica (org), Josef Pancík (cnd), Prague Chamber Choir *(rec Dvořák Hall, Prague, Nov 1993)* ECM New Series ▲ 78118-21539-2 [DDD]

Janácek, L.:Our Father, w. Josef Ksica (org), Josef Pancík (cnd), Prague Chamber Choir ECM ▲ 21539-2

Corazza, Remy (ten)

Auber, D.-F.:Fra Diavolo, w. M. Mesplé (sop—Zerline), J. Berbié (mez—Lady Pamela), N. Gedda (ten—Fra Diavolo), R. Corazza (ten—Lord Cockburn), T. Dran (ten—Lorenzo), J. Bastin (bass—Matheo), M. Soustrot (cnd), Monte Carlo PO, Jean LaForge Ensemble Choir EMI Classics ▲ CDCB 54810

Charpentier, M.-A.:Magnificat, w. Martha Angelici (sop), Jocelyn Chamonin (sop), André Mallabrera (ct), Georges Abdoun (bar), Jacques Mars (bass), Maurice André (tpt), Marie-Claire Alain (org), L. Martini (cnd), Jean-François Paillard CO, French Jeunesses Musicales Chorale *(rec Paris, Mar 15, 1963)* Vanguard Classics ▲ OVC 8075 [ADD]

Charpentier, M.-A.:Te Deum, H. 146, w. Martha Angelici (sop), Jocelyn Chamonin (sop), André Mallabrera (ct), Georges Abdoun (bar), Jacques Mars (bass), Maurice André (tpt), Marie-Claire Alain (org), L. Martini (cnd), Jean-François Paillard CO, French Jeunesses Musicales Chorale *(rec Paris, Mar 15, 1963)* Vanguard Classics ▲ OVC 8075 [ADD]

Puccini, G.:Turandot, w. Montserrat Caballé (sop—Turandot), Leona Mitchell (sop—Liu), Remy Corazza (ten—Pang), Joseph Franck (ten—Pong), Robert Johnson (ten—Prince of Persia), Raymond Manton (ten—Altoum), Luciano Pavarotti (ten—Calaf), Aldo Bramante (bar—a mandarin), Dale Duesing (bar—Ping), Giorgio Tozzi (bass—Timur), R. Chailly (cnd), *(orch unknown) (rec San Francisco, Nov. 4, 1977)* Legato Classics 2-▲ LCD 188-2

Corbelli, Alessandro (bar)

Cherubini, L.:Lodoïska, w. M. Devia (sop), F. Pedaci (sgr), B. Lombardo (ten), T. Moser (ten), W. Shimell (bar), R. Muti (cnd), La Scala Orch, La Scala Chorus Sony Classical 2-▲ SM2K 47290

Donizetti, G.:Don Pasquale, w. L. Serra (sop), E. Dara (bar), Bartolo (sgr), B. Campanella (cnd), Turin Teatro Regio Orch, Turin Teatro Regio Chorus [I] *(rec live)* Nuova Era 2-▲ 6715/16 [DDD]

Donizetti, G.:Don Pasquale, w. L. Serra (sop), E. Dara (bar), Bartolo (sgr), B. Campanella (cnd), Turin Teatro Regio Orch, Turin Teatro Regio Chorus [I] *(rec live)* Nuova Era ▲ 6766 [DDD]

Donizetti, G.:Rita, or Le mari battu, w. A. Scarabelli (sop), P. Ballo (ten), F. Amendola (cnd), Sicilian CO [I] *(rec live, Palermo 6/19-20/91)* Nuova Era ▲ 7045 [DDD]

Giordano, U.:Fedora, w. Mirella Freni (sop—Principessa Fedora), Adelina Scarabelli (sop—Contessa Olga), Silvia Mazzoni (mez—Dimitri), Monica Minarelli (sgr—Savoiardo), Placido Domingo (ten—Conte Loris), Ernesto Gavazzi (ten—Desiré), Aldo Bottion (ten—Barone Rouvel), Alessandro Corbelli (bar—Siriex), Luigi Roni (bass—Cirillo), Silvestro Sammaritano (bass—Baroff), Alfredo Giacomotti (bass—Gretch), Ernesto Panariello (bass—Lorek), Vincenzo Alaimo (sgr—Nicola), Arnold Bosman (sgr—Boleslao), Bruno Capisani (sgr—Sergio), Renato Zanchetta (sgr—Michele), G. Gavazzeni (cnd), La Scala Orch, La Scala Chorus *(rec La Scala, Apr 5, 1993)* Legato 2-▲ LCD 213-2 [ADD]

Mozart, W.A.:Così fan tutte (sels), w. Felicity Lott (sop), Marie McLaughlin (sop), Nuccia Focile (sop), Jerry Hadley (ten), Gilles Cachemaille (bass) *(rec Usher Hall, Edinburgh, Scotland)* Telarc ▲ CD 80399 [DDD]

Mozart, W.A.:Don Giovanni, w. Christine Brewer (sop—Donna Anna), Nuccia Focile (sop—Zerlina), Felicity Lott (sop—Donna Elvira), Jerry Hadley (ten—Don Ottavio), Bo Skovhus (bar—Don Giovanni), Umberto Chiummo (bass—Masetto/Il Commendatore), Alessandro Corbelli (bass—Leporello), C. Mackerras (cnd), Scottish CO, Scottish Chamber Chorus *(rec Usher Hall, Edinburgh, Scotland, July 31-Aug 11, 1995)* Telarc 3-▲ CD 80420 [DDD]

Mozart, W.A.:Nozze di Figaro, w. Rebecca Evans (sop—Barbarina), Nuccia Focile (sop—Susanna), Suzanne Murphy (sop—Marcellina), Carol Vaness (sop—Countess Almaviva), Susanne Mentzer (mez—Cherubino), Ryland Davies (ten—Don Basilio/Don Curzio), Alessandro Corbelli (bar—Count Almaviva), Alfonso Antoniozzi (bass—Doctor Bartolo/Antonio), Alastair Miles (bass—Figaro), C. Mackerras (cnd), Scottish CO, Scottish Chamber Chorus *(rec Usher Hall, Edingurgh, Scotland, July 31-Aug. 12, 1994)* Telarc 3-▲ CD 80388 [DDD]

Pergolesi, G.B.:Lo frate 'nnamorato, w. N. Focile (sop), A. Felle (sop), B. Manca di Nissa (cta), R. Muti (cnd), La Scala Orch, La Scala Chorus EMI Classics 3-▲ CDCC 54240

Piccinni, N.:La cecchina, ossia la buona figliola, w. Lucia Alberti (sop—Il Cavaliere Armidoro), Emilia Ravaglia (sop—La Marchesa), Margherita Rinaldi (sgr—Cecchina), Elena Zilio (mez—Paoluccia), Ugo Benelli (bar—Il Marchese della Conchiglia), Alessandro Corbelli (bar—Mengotto), Enzo Dara (bar—Tagliaferro), Renata Baldisseri (sgr—Sandrina), G. Gelmetti (cnd), Rome Opera Orch, Rome Opera Chorus *(rec Rome, Feb 4, 1981)* Italia 2-▲ CDC 95 [ADD]

Rossini, G.:Il barbiere di Siviglia, w. J. Larmore (cta), R. Gimeniz (bar), H. Hagegard (bar), S. Ramey (bass), J. López-Cobos (cnd), Lausanne CO, Geneva Grand Théâtre Chorus [I] Teldec 2-▲ 9031-74885-2

Rossini, G.:Il barbiere di Siviglia (sels), w. B. Frittoli (sop), J. Larmore (mez), R. Giménez (ten), Håkan Hagegård (bar), S. Ramey (bass), J. López-Cobos (cnd), Lausanne CO, Geneva Grand Théâtre Chorus Teldec ▲ 93693-2

Rossini, G.:La Cenerentola, w. C. Bartoli (mez—Cenerentola), F. Costa (mez—Clorinda), G. Banditelli (cta—Tisbe), W. Matteuzzi (ten—Don Ramiro), A. Corbelli (bar—Dandini), E. Dara (bar—Don Magnifico), M. Pertusi (bass—Alidoro), R. Chailly (cnd), Bologna Teatro Comunale Orch, Bologna Teatro Comunale Chorus *(rec June 22-July 2, 1992)* London 2-▲ 436902-2 [DDD]

Rossini, G.:La scala di seta, w. Teresa Ringholz (sop), Francesca Provvisionata (mez), Fulvio Massa (ten), Ramon Vargas (ten), Natale de Carolis (b-bar), M. Viotti (cnd), English CO Claves 2-▲ 9219/20

Rossini, G.:Les Soirées musicales, w. J. Anderson (sop), K. Bouleyn (sop), R. Giménez (ten), N. Walker (pno) [I] Nimbus ▲ NI 5132 [DDD]

Corcoran, C. (sgr)

Lloyd Webber, A.:Music of, w. L. Garrett (sgr), Dave Willets (sgr), Gerard Casey (sgr), S. Campbell (sgr), Royal PO, Royal PO Pops Orch, Royal PO Concert Orch—sels from The Phantom of the Opera; Evita; Cats; Joseph & the Amazing Technicolor Dreamcoat; Jesus Christ Superstar; Tell Me on a Sunday; Song & Dance; Starlight Express; Sunset Boulevard Silva America 2-▲ SILCD 1044 [DDD] ■ SILMC 1044

Lloyd Webber, A.:Music of, w. L. Garrett (sgr), Dave Willets (sgr), S. Campbell (sgr), *(other artists unknown)*—The Phantom of the Opera; Aspects of Love; Cats; Evita; Jesus Christ Superstar; Starlight Express Silva America ▲ SILCD 1022 [DDD] ■ SILMC 1022

Cordes, Marcel (bar)

Cherubini, L.:Les Deux journées, w. H. Hillebrecht (sop), F. Wunderlich (ten), R. Hoyem (sgr), H. Müller-Kray (cnd), Stockholm RSO, Stockholm Radio Chorus *(rec live, Stockholm 1960)* Melodram ▲ CDM 19507 [ADD]

Orff, C.:Die Kluge, w. E. Schwarzkopf (sop), R. Christ (ten), P. Kuén (ten), B. Kusche (bar), H. Prey (bar), G. Frick (bass), G. Wieter (bass), W. Sawallisch (cnd), Philharmonia Orch [G] EMI Classics ("Studio" series) 2-▲ CDMB 63712 [ADD]

Strauss, R.:Feuersnot, w. Maud Cunitz (sop—Diemut), Antonia Fahberg (sop—Elsbeth), Irmgard Barth (mez—Wigelis), Liselotte Nölser (sgr—Margret), Karl Ostertag (ten—Schweiker), Marcel Cordes (bar—Kunrad), Kieth Engen (bass—Kofel), Karl Hoppe (bass—Hämerlein), Max Proebstl (bass—Ortolf), Georg Wieter (bass—Jörg), R. Kempe (cnd), Bavarian State Opera Orch, Bavarian State Opera Chorus *(rec Munich Opera Festival, Prince Regent Theater, Aug 14, 1958)* Orfeo d'or 2-▲ 423962

Wagner, R.:Tannhäuser, w. L. Rysanek (sop), J. Lustig (sgr), G. Frick (bass), K. Böhm (cnd), Naples Teatro San Carlo Orch, Naples Teatro San Carlo Chorus [G] *(rec live, Naples, 3/17/56)* Melodram 3-▲ MEL 37073 (m) [AAD]

Cordier, David (ct)

Jones, Robert:Duets for 2 Cts, w. M. Chance (ct), Tragicomedia—eleven duets by Jones, coupled with two duets by John Coprario & Angelo Notari, a solo song by John Dowland, & eight instrumental pieces by Dowland, Giles Farnaby & Tobias Hume Hyperion ▲ CDA 66335 [DDD]

A Musicall Dreame, w. M. Chance (ct), Tragicomedia Hyperion ▲ CDA 66335 [DDD]

Cordier, David (ct) (cont.)

Valls, F.:Scala Arentina Mass, w. S. Paiu (sop), M. van der Sluis (sop), B. Lettinga (alt), J. Elwes (ten), H. van der Kamp (bass), G. Leonhardt (cnd), Netherlands Bach Society Baroque Orch, Netherlands Bach Society Choir Deutsche Harmonia Mundi ▲ 05472-77277-2

Cordoba, L. de (sgr)

Lehár, F.:Eva, w. J. Granados (sop—Prunelles), A. M. Olaria (sop—Eva), A. Kraus (ten—Octavio Flaubert), L. de Cordoba (sgr—Gipsy), S. Ramalle (sgr—Dagoberto), J. Peromingo (sgr—Voisin), E. Estella (cnd), Madrid CO, Spanish National Radio Chorus [Sp] Montilla ▲ CDFM 2036

Cordon, Norman (bass)

Carlo Tagliabue, w. Margherita Carosio (sop), Ettore Bergamaschi (ten), Zinka Milanov (sop), Bruna Castagna (cta), Frederick Jagel (ten), Renata Tebaldi (sop), Alfredo Colella (bass) *(rec in studio and live, 1928-1951)* Bongiovanni ▲ GB 1070-2 [ADD]

Her First Recordings, w. Armand Tokatyan (ten), Lucielle Browning (mez), Pino Bontempi (sgr), Annamary Dickey (sgr), George Cehanovsky (bar), Lorenzo Alvary ((bass), A. Kent (bar), Raoul Jobin (ten) VAI Audio ▲ VAIA 1023 (m) [ADD]

Verdi, G.:Un ballo in maschera, w. Stella Andreva (sop—Oscar), Zinka Milanov (sop—Amelia), Bruna Castagna (cta—Ulrica), Jussi Björling (ten—Riccardo), Lodovico Oliviero (ten—Un Servo D'Amelia), John Cartet (bar—Un Giudice), Alexander Sved (bar—Renato), Normann Cordon (bass—Samuel), Arthur Kent (bass—Silvano), Nicola Moscona (bass—Tom), E. Panizza (cnd), *(orch unknown) (rec live, New York, Dec. 14, 1940)* The Fourties 2-▲ ENT FT 1515

Wagner, R.:Lohengrin (sels), w. Rose Bampton (sop), Arthur Carron (ten), W. Steinberg (cnd), Philadelphia studio musicians, New York studio musicians—Einsam in trüben Tagen; Das süsse Lied verhallt *(rec Academy of Music, Philadelphia & Town Hall, New York, May 27 & 28, 1940)* VAI Audio ▲ VAIA 1084

Corelli, A. (bar)

Spontini, G.:La vestale (sels), w. M. Callas (sop), E. Sordello (bar), A. Votto (cnd), La Scala Orch, La Scala Chorus [I]—3 scenes *(rec live, Milan, 12/7/54)* Verona 2-▲ 28003/04

Corelli, Franco (ten)

At Parma 1961-1971 Myto ▲ MCD 924.64 [ADD]

Bellini, V.:Norma, w. A. Cerquetti (sop), G. Borelli, M. Pirazzini (mez), P. de Palma (ten), G. Neri (bass), G. Santini (cnd), *(orch unknown) (rec Rome, 1958)* Great Opera Performances 2-▲ GOP 722

Bellini, V.:Norma, w. M. Callas (sop), C. Ludwig (mez), N. Zaccaria (bass), T. Serafin (cnd), La Scala Orch, La Scala Chorus [I] EMI Classics ("Studio" series) 3-▲ CDMC 63000 [ADD]

Bellini, V.:Norma, w. M. Callas (sop), E. Nicolai (mez), B. Christoff (bass), A. Votto (cnd), Trieste Teatro Comunale Giuseppe Verdi Orch, Trieste Teatro Comunale G. Verdi Chorus *(rec live 11/19/53)* Melodram 2-▲ CDM 26031 [ADD]

Bellini, V.:Norma (sels), w. M. Callas (sop), M. Pirazzini (mez), P. De Palma (ten), G. Santini (cnd), Rome Opera Orch, Rome Opera Chorus [I] *(rec live 1/2/58)* Melodram ▲ MEL 16000 (m) [AAD]

Bellini, V.:Norma (sels), w. M. Callas (sop), C. Ludwig (mez), N. Zaccaria (bass), T. Serafin (cnd), La Scala Orch, La Scala Chorus EMI Classics ▲ ZDM 63091

Bellini, V.:Norma (sels), w. M. Callas (sop), E. Nicolai (mez), B. Christoff (bass), A. Votto (cnd), Trieste Teatro Comunale Giuseppe Verdi Orch, Trieste Teatro Comunale G. Verdi Chorus—13 arias [I] *(rec live 11/19/53)* Myto 2-▲ 2 MCD 91340 [ADD]

The Best of His Stage Performances Originals ▲ ORI SH 962

Bizet, G.:Carmen, w. Giovanna di Rocco (sop—Frasquita), Grace Bumbry (mez—Carmen), Anita Caminada (mez—Mercedes), Franco Corelli (ten—Don José), Mario Ferrara (ten—Dancario), Franco Bordoni (bar—Escamillo), Carlo Scaravelli (bar—Morales), Giuseppe Morresi (bass—Remendado), Francesco Signor (bass—Zuniga), O. de Fabritiis (cnd), *(orch unknown) (rec Macerata, July 21, 1974)* Golden Age of Opera 2-▲ GAO 181/82 [ADD]

Bizet, G.:Carmen, w. L. Price (sop), M. Freni (sop), R. Merrill (bar), H. von Karajan (cnd), Vienna PO, Vienna State Opera Chorus [F] RCA Gold Seal 3-▲ 6199-2-RG [ADD] 2-■ 6199-4-RG

Bizet, G.:Carmen, w. L. Price (sop), M. Freni (sop), R. Merrill (bar), H. von Karajan (cnd), Vienna PO, Vienna State Opera Chorus [F] RCA Gold Seal ▲ 60190-2-RG [ADD] ■ 60190-4-RG

Bizet, G.:Carmen (sels), w. Mirella Freni (sop), Leontyne Price (sop), H. von Karajan (cnd), Vienna PO, Vienna State Opera Chorus RCA Victor ▲ 09026-68021-2; ■ 09026-68021-4

Bizet, G.:Carmen (sels), w. Margherita Benetti (sop—Micaela), Pia Tassinari (sop—Carmen), Franco Corelli (ten—Don José), Giangiacomo Guelfi (bar—Escamillo), A. Basile (cnd), Turin RAI Orch—[Act. 1] E l'amore uno strano augello; Josèl...Micaela!...Ah! mi parla di lei; Mia madre io vedo ancor, sì, sì; Presso il bastion di Siviglia; Tacer, di, non vuoi tu?; [Act 2] Con voi ber; Alto là! Chi va là ; Il fior che avevi a me tu dato; [Act 3] Andiam, nostra sorte sappiami; [Act 4] Largo! Largo! L'Alcade; Sei tu?...Son io; Più non m'ama il tuo cor? *(rec Torino Dec. 15, 1961)* Myto ▲ MCD 953132

Cilea, F.:Adriana Lecouvreur, w. M. Olivero (sop), G. Simionato (mez), E. Bastianini (bar), M. Rossi (cnd), Naples Teatro San Carlo Orch, Naples Teatro San Carlo Chorus [I] *(rec live 11/28/59)* Melodram 2-▲ MEL 27009 (m) [AAD]

Cilea, F.:Adriana Lecouvreur, w. Magda Olivero (sop), Giulletta Simionato (mez), Ettore Bastianini (bar), M. Rossi (cnd), Naples Teatro San Carlo Orch, Naples Teatro San Carlo Chorus *(rec Naples, Nov 28, 1959)* Agorá Music ("Phoenix" series) 2-▲ 502

Donizetti, G.:Poliuto, w. M. Callas (sop), E. Bastianini (bar), N. Zaccaria (bass), A. Votto (cnd), La Scala Orch, La Scala Chorus [I] *(rec live, 12/7/60)* Arkadia 2-▲ 520 (m) [AAD]

Donizetti, G.:Poliuto, w. M. Callas (sop), E. Bastianini (bar), N. Zaccaria (bass), A. Votto (cnd), La Scala Orch, La Scala Chorus [I] *(rec live, 12/7/60)* Melodram 2-▲ MEL 26006

Donizetti, G.:Poliuto, w. Maria Callas (sop), Ettore Bastianini (bar), A. Votto (cnd), La Scala Orch, La Scala Chorus *(rec live, Milan, 1960)* Enterprise ("Documents" series) 2-▲ ENT LV 977 (m)

Donizetti, G.:Poliuto, w. M. Callas (sop), E. Bastianini (bar), N. Zaccaria (bass), A. Votto (cnd), La Scala Orch, La Scala Chorus [I] *(rec live, Milan 12/7/60)* Verona 2-▲ 28003/04

Franco Corelli, w. Raffaele Mingardo (cnd), Franco Ferraris (cnd) EMI Classics ("Doublefforte" series) 2-▲ CDFB 69530

Franco Corelli, w. *(rec live, 1955-1965)* Memories ("Great Voices" series) 2-▲ MEM 4204 (m)

Franco Corelli Recital, w. *(rec live)* Melodram 2-▲ CDM 26520

Franco Corelli (Vol. 1), w. *(rec live)* Melodram ▲ CDM 16503

Franco Corelli (Vol. 2), w. *(rec live, Munich, 1960)* Melodram ▲ CDM 16521

Gala Operatic Concert, w. M. Caballé (sop), Bonaldi Giaiotti (bass) *(rec live, 1968)* Legato Classics ▲ LCD 101-1 [AAD]

Gala Operatic Concert

Giordano, U.:Andrea Chénier, w. A. Stella (sop—Maddalena), F. Corelli (ten—Andrea Chénier), M. Sereni (bar—Carlo Gerard), G. Santini (cnd), Rome Opera Orch, Rome Opera Chorus EMI Classics ▲ CDMB 65287

Giordano, U.:Andrea Chénier, w. R. Tebaldi (sop), E. Bastianini (bar), L. von Matačić (cnd), *(orch unknown)* —eleven arias [I] *(rec live, Vienna, 6/26/60)* Standing Room Only 2-▲ SRO 821-2 [ADD]

Giordano, U.:Andrea Chénier, w. H. Konetzni (sop—Madelon), M. Sjöstedt (sop—Bersi), R. Tebaldi (sop—Maddalena de Coigny), E. Höngen (cta—La Contessa de Coigny), F. Corelli (ten—Andrea Chénier), E. Bastianini (bar—C. Gérard), K. Paskalis (bar—Pietro Fléville), L. Welter (bar—Fouquier Tinville), A. Pernerstorfer (b-bar—Mathieu), L. von Matačić (cnd), Vienna State Opera Orch, Vienna State Opera Chorus *(rec Vienna, June 26, 1960)* Fortissimo 2-▲ CDE 3003 [ADD]

Giordano, U.:Andrea Chénier, w. Montserrat Caballé (sop), Franco Corelli (ten), R. de Carlo (sgr), D. Dondi (sgr), G. Ellsworth (sgr), J. Fair (sgr), R. Falk (sgr), S. Felter (sgr), E. Green (sgr), H. Hicks (sgr), H. Krauss (sgr), L. Miller (sgr), N. Riggins (sgr), H. Salerno (sgr), A. Guadagno (cnd), Academy of Music Orch, Academy of Music Chorus Great Opera Performances 2-▲ GOP 766

The Golden Years:1962-1966 Standing Room Only ▲ SRO 812-1 [ADD]

Gounod, C.:Faust, w. J. Sutherland (sop), N. Ghiaurov (bass), R. Bonynge (cnd), London SO, Ambrosian Opera Chorus [F] London ("Grand Opera" series) 3-▲ 421240-2 [AAD]

Gounod, C.:Roméo et Juliette, w. G. d'Angelo (sop—Juliette), F. Corelli (ten—Roméo), A. Ferrin (bar—Friar Lawrence), P. Gottlieb (bass—Mercutio), A. Guadagno (cnd), *(orch unknown) (rec live, Philadelphia, 4/14/64)* HRE 2-▲ 1011-2 [ADD]

Gounod, C.:Roméo et Juliette, w. M. Freni (sop—Juliette), F. Corelli (ten—Roméo), H. Gui (bar—Mercutio), C. Câles (bar—Capulet), X. Depraz (bass—Frère Laurent), A. Lombard (cnd), Paris Opera Orch, Paris Opera Chorus EMI Classics ▲ CDMB 65290

Corelli, Franco (ten) (cont.)

Gounod, C.:Roméo et Juliette (sels), w. J. Pilou (sop—Juliette), F. Corelli (ten—Romeo), A. Guadagno (cnd), *(orch unknown)*—8 arias & scenes *(rec live, Philadelphia, 10/24/67)* HRE 2-▲ 1011-2 [ADD]

Homage to Franco Corelli Great Opera Performances 2-▲ GOP 760

Leoncavallo, R.:Pagliacci, w. M. Micheluzzi (sop), M. Carlin (ten), T. Gobbi (bar), L. Puglisi (bar), A. Simonetto (cnd), Milan RAI Orch, Milan RAI Chorus *(rec live 9/26/54 from RAI Milan)* HRE ▲ 1001-1 [ADD]

Leoncavallo, R.:Pagliacci, w. Lucine Amara (sop), Tito Gobbi (bar), L. von Matačić (cnd), La Scala Orch, La Scala Chorus [I] EMI Classics ("Studio" series) 2-▲ CDMB 63967

Mascagni, P.:Cavalleria rusticana, w. V. De los Angeles (sop), G. Santini (cnd), Rome Opera Orch, Rome Opera Chorus [I] EMI Classics ("Studio" series) 2-▲ CDMB 63967

Meyerbeer, G.:Les Huguenots, w. J. Sutherland (sop), F. Cossotto (mez), G. Simionato (mez), V. Ganzarolli (bar), N. Ghiaurov (bass), G. Tozzi (bass), G. Gavezzeni (cnd), La Scala Orch, La Scala Chorus [I] *(rec live 5/28/62)* Melodram 3-▲ MEL 37026 (m) [AAD]

Opera Arias *(rec live, 1955–1970)* Cantabile ("Biographies in Music" series) 2-▲ BIM 702-2 (m/s)

Opera Arias EMI Classics ▲ CDC 47851

Puccini, G.:Arias, w. M. Caballé (sop), M. Chiara (sop), M. Freni (sop), B. Nilsson (sop), J. Sutherland (sop), R. Tebaldi (sop), L. Pavarotti (ten), S. Milnes (bar) London ▲ 421315-2 [ADD]

Puccini, G.:Arias, w. M. Caballé (sop), P. Domingo (ten), *(orch unknown)* EMI Classics ▲ CDE 67782

Puccini, G.:La Bohème, w. R. Tebaldi (sop), Candida (sgr), F. Guarrera (bar), J. Hines (bass), A. Guadagno (cnd), *(orch & chorus unknown)* [I] *(rec live, Philadelphia 12/2/69)* Standing Room Only 2-▲ SRO 821-2 [ADD]

Puccini, G.:La fanciulla del West, w. D. Kirsten (sop), A. Colzani (bar), A. Guadagno (cnd), Philadelphia Lyric Opera Orch, Philadelphia Lyric Opera Chorus [I] *(rec live, 11/10/64)* Melodram 2-▲ MEL 27081 [AAD]

Puccini, G.:Tosca, w. B. Nilsson (sop), D. Fischer-Dieskau (bar), L. Maazel (cnd), St. Cecilia Academy Orch Rome, St. Cecilia Academy Chorus Rome *(rec June 1966)* London ▲ 440051-2

Puccini, G.:Tosca, w. R. Tebaldi (sop—Tosca), F. Corelli (ten—Cavaradossi), A. Colzani (bar—Scarpia), P. L. Latinucci (b-bar—Sacristan), G. Beloni (bass—Angelotti), M. Parenti (cnd), Livorno Teatro La Gran Guardia Orch, Livorno Teatro La Gran Guardia Chorus *(rec live Sept. 21, 1959)* Legato Classics 2-▲ LCD 171-2 [ADD]

Puccini, G.:Turandot, w. B. Nilsson (sop), R. Scotto (sop), B. Giaiotti (bass), F. Molinari-Pradelli (cnd), Rome Opera Orch, Rome Opera Chorus [I] EMI Classics ("Studio" series) 2-▲ CDMB 69327 [ADD]

Puccini, G.:Turandot, w. B. Nilsson (sop—Turnadot), A. Moffo (sop—Liù), F. Corelli (ten—Calaf), C. Anthony (ten—Pong), R. Nagy (ten—Pang), F. Guarrera (bar—Ping), B. Giaiotti (bass—Timur), L. Stokowski (cnd), Metropolitan Opera Orch, New York Metropolitan Opera Chorus *(rec Mar. 4, 1961)* Datum 2-▲ DAT 12301 [ADD]

Puccini, G.:Turandot (sels), w. L. Gencer (sop), L. Udovich (sop), O. de Fabritiis (cnd), Naples Teatro San Carlo Orch, Naples Teatro San Carlo Chorus—Signore ascolta; Il nome che cercate..tu che di gel sei cinta *(rec Jan. 13, 1962)* Golden Age of Opera 2-▲ GAO 143/44 [ADD]

Spontini, G.:Agnes von Hohensaufen, w. L. Udovick (sop), D. Dow (sop), A. Colzani (bar), G. Guelfi (bar), V. Gui (cnd), Florence Maggio Musicale Orch, Florence Maggio Musicale Chorus [I] *(rec live 5/9/54)* Melodram 2-▲ MEL 27055 (m) [AAD]

Spontini, G.:La vestale, w. M. Callas (sop), N. Rossi-Lemeni (bass), E. Sordello (bar), V. Tatozzi (bar), N. Zaccaria (bass), A. Votto (cnd), La Scala Orch, La Scala Chorus Great Opera Performances ▲ GOP 741

Spontini, G.:La vestale, w. M. Callas (sop), E. Sordello (bar), A. Votto (cnd), La Scala Orch, La Scala Chorus [I] *(rec live, Milan, 12/7/54)* Melodram 2-▲ MEL 26008

Verdi, G.:Aida, w. A. Stella (sop), F. Barbieri (mez), A. Colzani (bar), M. Petri (bar), V. Gui (cnd), Naples Teatro San Carlo Orch, Naples Teatro San Carlo Chorus [I] *(rec live, Naples 11/2/55)* Golden Age of Opera 2-▲ GAO 116/17 [ADD]

Verdi, G.:Aida, w. M. C. Verna (sop), M. Pirazzini (cta), G. Guelfi (bar), G. Neri (bass), A. Questa (cnd), Turin RAI SO, Turin RAI Chorus *(rec 1956)* Enterprise ("Palladio") 2-▲ ENT PD 4184 [ADD]

Verdi, G.:Aida (sels), w. B. Nilsson (sop), G. Bumbry (mez), Z. Mehta (cnd), Rome Opera Orch [I] [highlights] EMI Classics (Classics for Pleasure) ▲ CDM 64035

Verdi, G.:La battaglia di Legnano, w. A. Stella (sop), E. Bastianini (bar), G. Gavazzeni (cnd), La Scala Orch, La Scala Chorus [I] *(rec live 12/7/61)* Myto 2-▲ 2 MCD 89010 (m) [ADD]

Verdi, G.:Don Carlos, w. R. Kabaivanska (sop), O. Dominguez (mez), L. Quilico (bar), N. Ghiaurov (bass), N. Ghiuselev (bass), A. Guadagno (cnd), Hartford Opera Orch *(rec live 1966)* Melodram 2-▲ MEL 27511

Verdi, G.:Don Carlos, w. Gundula Janowitz (sop), Shirley Verrett (mez), Eberhard Waechter (bar), Nicolai Ghiaurov (bass), Martti Talvela (bass), H. Stein (cnd), Vienna PO, Vienna State Opera Chorus *(rec Vienna, Oct. 25, 1970)* Pantheon 2-▲ PHE 6614

Verdi, G.:Ernani, w. I. Ligabue (sop), P. Cappuccilli (bar), R. Raimondi (bass), O. de Fabritiis (cnd), Arena di Verona Orch, Arena di Verona Chorus *(rec live, Verona 7/15/72)* Golden Age of Opera 2-▲ GAO 131/32 [ADD]

Verdi, G.:Ernani, w. L. Price (sop), C. Ordassy (sop), C. Anthony (ton), M. Sereni (bar), C. Siepi (bass), C. Russel (bass), T. Schippers (cnd), *(orch unknown)* *(rec 1965)* Great Opera Performances ▲ GOP 702

Verdi, G.:La forza del destino, w. R. Tebaldi (sop), O. Dominguez (mez), R. Capecchi (bar), E. Bastianini (bar), B. Christoff (bass), F. Molinari-Pradelli (cnd), Naples Teatro San Carlo Orch, Naples Teatro San Carlo Chorus *(rec Oct. 1 1958)* Melodram 3-▲ MLO 370102 [ADD]

Verdi, G.:La forza del destino, w. E. Farrell (sop), J. Grillo (sop), A. Colzani (bar), E. Flagello (bass), A. Guadagno (cnd), *(orch unknown)* [I] *(rec live, Philadelphia 4/14/65)* Standing Room Only 2-▲ SRO 826-2 [ADD]

Verdi, G.:La forza del destino (sels), w. R. Tebaldi (sop), F. Molinari-Pradelli (cnd), Naples Teatro San Carlo Orch, Naples Teatro San Carlo Chorus *(rec live Mar. 15, 1958)* Legato Classics 2-▲ LCD 171-2 [ADD]

Verdi, G.:La forza del destino (sels), w. E. Bastianini (bar), F. Molinari-Pradelli (cnd), *(orch unknown)*—Act III, Scene 2 Duet, "Sleale! Il segreto fu dunque violato" [I] *(rec live, Naples 1958)* Standing Room Only 2-▲ SRO 826-2 [ADD]

Verdi, G.:La forza del destino (sels), w. Franco Corelli (ten—Don Alvaro), Giangiacomo Guelfi (bar—Don Carlo), A. Basile (cnd), Turin RAI Orch—[Act 3] La vita è inferno all'infelice...; O tu che in seno agli angeli; Al tradimento...; Amici in vita e in morte; Piano...qui posi...; Solenne in quest'ora; Morir!...tremenda cosa!...; Urna fatale del mio destino; E s'altra prova rinvenir potessi?...; E' salvo! oh gioia immensa; [Act 4] Giunge qualcuno...aprite...; Invano Alvaro ti celasti al mondo; Fratello...; Le minacce, i fieri accenti; Ah, la macchia del tuo stemma *(rec Torino Feb. 6, 1957)* Myto ▲ MCD 953132

Verdi, G.:Il trovatore, w. A. Stella (sop), M. Fiorentini (mez), F. Cossotto (mez), E. Bastianini (bar), I. Vinco (bass), G. Gavazzeni (cnd), La Scala Orch, La Scala Chorus *(rec live, Milan, 12/7/62)* Melodram 2-▲ MEL 27068 (m) [AAD]

Verdi, G.:Il trovatore, w. A. Stella (sop), M. Fiorentini (mez), F. Cossotto (mez), E. Bastianini (bar), I. Vinco (bass), G. Gavazzeni (cnd), La Scala Orch, La Scala Chorus [I] *(rec live, Milan, 12/7/62)* Claque 2-▲ CLQ 2013 (m)

Verdi, G.:Il trovatore, w. Fedora Barbieri (mez), Ettore Bastianini (bar), Agostino Ferrin (bass), Mirella Parutto (sgr), O. de Fabritiis (cnd), Rome Opera Orch, Rome Opera Chorus Stradivarius 2-▲ STV DTM 12313 [ADD]

Vol. 2, w. A. Basile, A. Simonetto, U. Cattini *(various Italian orchs)* Enterprise ("Palladio" series) ▲ ENTPD 4197 [ADD]

Corena, Fernando (bass)

Catalani, A.:La Wally, w. R. Tebaldi (sop), C. Bergonzi (ten), P. Glossop (bar), F. Cleva (cnd), American Opera Society Orch, American Opera Society Chorus *(rec Mar. 13, 1968)* Intaglio 2-▲ ING 764 [ADD]

Donizetti, G.:Don Pasquale, w. G. D'Angelo (sop), A. Kraus (ten), R. Capecchi (bar), U. d'Alessio (sgr), A. Erede (cnd), Naples Teatro San Carlo Orch, Naples Teatro San Carlo Chorus [I] *(rec live in Edinburgh, 9/7/63)* Verona 2-▲ 27023/24 (m) [AAD]

Corena, Fernando (bass) (cont.)

Donizetti, G.:Don Pasquale, w. Gianna D'Angelo (sop), Alfredo Kraus (ten), Renato Capecchi (bar), Ugo D'Alessio (sgr), A. Erede (cnd), Naples Teatro San Carlo Orch, Naples Teatro San Carlo Chorus Great Opera Performances 2-▲ GOP 763

Donizetti, G.:Don Pasquale, w. E. Ravaglia (sop), P. Bottazzo (ten), A. Frati (ten), R. Panerai (bar), R. Muti (cnd), Vienna PO, Vienna State Opera Chorus [I] *(rec live, Salzburg, 8/11/71)* Melodram 2-▲ CDM 27094 [ADD]

Donizetti, G.:Don Pasquale, w. R. Scotto (sop), L. Alva (ten), W. Alberti (bar), B. Rigacci (cnd), Florence Maggio Musicale Orch, Florence Maggio Musicale Chorus [I] *(rec live, Florence 3/1/67)* Claque 2-▲ CLQ 2011 (m)

Mozart, W.A.:Don Giovanni, w. S. Danco (sop), L. della Casa (sop), A. Dermota (ten), C. Siepi (b-bar), J. Krips (cnd), Vienna PO, Vienna State Opera Chorus London 3-▲ 411626-2 [ADD]

Mozart, W.A.:Don Giovanni, w. E. Grümmer (sop), L. Della Casa (sop), R. Streich (sop), L. Simoneau (ten), C. Siepi (b-bar), G. Frick (bass), W. Berry (bass), D. Mitropoulos (cnd), Vienna PO, Vienna State Opera Chorus [I] *(rec live, Salzburg, July 24, 1956)* Arkadia 3-▲ 552 (m) [ADD]

Mozart, W.A.:Don Giovanni, w. E. Grümmer (sop—D. Anna), R. Streich (sop—Zerlina), L. Della Casa (sop—D. Elvira), L. Simoneau (ten—Don Ottavio), C. Siepi (bass-baritone—Don Giovanni), W. Berry (bass—Masetto), G. Frick (bass—Il Commendatore), F. Corena (bass—Leporello), D. Mitropoulos (cnd), Vienna PO, Vienna State Opera Chorus *(rec Salzburg, July 24, 1956)* Sony Classical 3-▲ SM3K 64263 [ADD]

Mozart, W.A.:Don Giovanni, w. Birgit Nilsson (sop—Donna Anna), Leontyne Price (sop—Donna Elvira), Eugenia Ratti (sop—Zerlina), Cesare Valletti (ten—Don Ottavio), Heinz Blankenburg (bar—Masetto), Fernando Corena (b-bar—Leporello), Arnold van Mill (b-bar—Il Commendatore), Cesare Siepi (b-bar—Don Giovanni), E. Leinsdorf (cnd), Vienna PO, Vienna State Opera Chorus [I] London 3-▲ 444594-2 [ADD]

Mozart, W.A.:Entführung, w. Reri Grist (sop—Blondchen), Anneliese Rothenberger (sop—Konstanze), Gerhard Unger (ten—Pedrillo), Fritz Wunderlich (ten—Belmonte), Fernando Corena (bass—Osmin), Michael Heltau (nar—Selim), Z. Mehta (cnd), Vienna PO, Vienna State Opera Chorus *(rec July 28, 1965)* Orfeo d'or ("Festspiel Dokumente" series) 2-▲ 392952 (m)

Mozart, W.A.:Nozze di Figaro, w. G. Gatti (sop), A. Noni (sop), G. Sciurri (sop), J. Gardino (mez), M.T. Pace (mez), A. Mercuriali (ten), S. Bruscantini (bar), I. Tajo (bass), F. Previtali (cnd), Rome RAI Orch [I] *(rec 1951)* Cetra Classic 2-▲ CDO 12

Mozart, W.A.:Nozze di Figaro (sels), w. R. Pütz (sop), T. Stich-Randall (mez), T. Berganza (mez), A.-R. Johnson (ten), G. Bacquier (bar), H. Wallberg (cnd), Swiss Romande Orch, Swiss Romande Chorus—Act IV Melodram 2-▲ CDM 27094 [ADD]

Puccini, G.:La Bohème, w. R. Tebaldi (sop), H. Gueden (sop), G. Prandelli (ten), G. Inghilleri (bar), Raphäel Arié (bass), A. Erede (cnd), St. Cecilia Academy Orch Rome, St. Cecilia Academy Chorus Rome London 2-▲ 440233-2 [ADD]

Puccini, G.:Tosca, w. R. Tebaldi (sop), G. Campora (ten), Enzo Mascherini (bar), A. Erede (cnd), St. Cecilia Academy Orch Rome, St. Cecilia Academy Chorus Rome London 2-▲ 440236-2 [ADD]

Puccini, G.:Tosca, w. Leonie Rysanek (sop), Russell Christopher (ten), Andrea Velis (ten), Clifford Harvuot (bar), Cornell MacNeil (bar), Paul Plishka (bass), F. Molinari-Pradelli (cnd), San Francisco Opera Orch, San Francisco Opera Chorus Melodram 2-▲ CDM 27508

Puccini, G.:Tosca, w. Ranata Tebaldi (sop), Gian Franco Volante (trb), Piero de Palma (ten), Giuseppe Campora (ten), Enzo Mascherini (bar), Dario Caselli (bass), Antonio Sacchetti (bass), A. Erede (cnd), St. Cecilia Academy Orch Rome, St. Cecilia Academy Chorus Rome *(rec 1952)* Andromeda 2-▲ ANR 2539 [ADD]

Puccini, G.:Tosca, w. R. Tebaldi (sop), G. Campora (ten), Enzo Mascherini (bar), A. Erede (cnd), St. Cecilia Academy Orch Rome, St. Cecilia Academy Chorus Rome Enterprise 2-▲ ENTPD 4106 [ADD]

Rossini, G.:Il barbiere di Siviglia, w. R. Peters (sop), C. Valletti (ten), R. Merrill (bar), G. Tozzi (bass), E. Leinsdorf (cnd), Metropolitan Opera Orch, New York Metropolitan Opera Chorus [I] RCA Gold Seal 3-▲ 6505-2-RG [ADD] 2-■ 6505-4-RG (CrO2)

Rossini, G.:Il barbiere di Siviglia, w. Roberta Peters (sop—Rosina), Margaret Roggero (mez—Berta), Cesare Valletti (ten—Count Almaviva), Calvin Marsh (bar—Fiorello/Sergeant), Robert Merrill (bar—Figaro), Fernando Corena (bass—Dr. Bartolo), Carlo Tomanelli (bass—Ambrogio), Giorgio Tozzi (bass—Don Basilio), E. Leinsdorf (cnd), Metropolitan Opera Orch, New York Metropolitan Opera Chorus *(rec Manhattan Center, New York, Sept 1-11, 1958)* RCA Living Stereo 3-▲ 09026-68552-2 [ADD]

Rossini, G.:Il barbiere di Siviglia (sels), w. R. Peters (sop), C. Valletti (ten), R. Merrill (bar), G. Tozzi (bass), E. Leinsdorf (cnd), Metropolitan Opera Orch, New York Metropolitan Opera Chorus RCA Gold Seal ▲ 60188-2-RG [ADD] ■ 60188-4-RG (CrO2)

Verdi, G.:Aida, w. R. Tebaldi (sop), E. Stignani (mez), M. del Monaco (ten), A. Protti (bar), A. Erede (cnd), St. Cecilia Academy Orch Rome, St. Cecilia Academy Chorus Rome London 2-▲ 440239-2 [ADD]

Verdi, G.:Aida, w. Renata Tebaldi (sop—Aida), Ebe Stignani (mez—Amneris), Mario Del Monaco (ten—Radamès), Piero de Palma (ten—Messenger), Aldo Protti (bar—Amonasro), Fernando Corena (bass—King), Dario Caselli (bass—Ramfis), A. Erede (cnd), St. Cecilia Academy Orch Rome, St. Cecilia Academy Chorus Rome *(rec 1952)* Theorema 2-▲ TH 121133/34

Verdi, G.:Falstaff, w. M. Freni (sop), I. Ligabue (sop), L. Alva (ten), R. Capecchi (bar), C. M. Giulini (cnd), Royal Concertgebouw Orch, Netherlands Chamber Choir [I] *(rec live, The Hague 6/20/63)* Verona 2-▲ 27095/96

Verdi, G.:Otello, w. Renata Tebaldi (sop—Desdemona), Luisa Ribacchi (mez—Emilia), Angelo Mercuriali (ten—Roderigo), Mario del Monaco (ten—Otello), Piero de Palma (ten—Cassio), Aldo Protti (bar—Iago), Dario Caselli (bass—A Herald), Fernando Corena (bass—Lodovico), Pierluigi Martinucci (bass—Montano), A. Erede (cnd), St. Cecilia Academy Orch Rome, St. Cecilia Academy Chorus Rome Theorema ▲ TH 121141/142

Verdi, G.:Rigoletto, w. R. Tebaldi (sop), M. del Monaco (ten), A. Protti (bar), P. de Palma (bass), A. Erede (cnd), St. Cecilia Academy Orch Rome, St. Cecilia Academy Chorus Rome London 2-▲ 440245-2 [ADD]

Verdi, G.:Rigoletto, w. Hilde Gueden (sop—Gilda), Piero de Palma (ten—Borsa), Luisa Ribacchi (mez—Giovanna), Giulietta Simionato (mez—Maddalena), Mario del Monaco (ten—Duca de Mantova), Aldo Protti (bar—Rigoletto), Fernando Corena (bass—Conte Monterone), Cesare Siepi (bass—Sparafucile), A. Erede (cnd), St. Cecilia Academy Orch Rome, St. Cecilia Academy Chorus Rome Theorema ▲ TH 121179/180

Cornwell, Joseph (ten)

Blow, J.:Anthems, w. Stephen Varcoe (bar), Robin Blaze (sgr), D. Hill (cnd), Parley of Instruments, Winchester Cathedral Choir Hyperion 2-▲ CDA 67031/32

Blow, J.:The Glorious Day Is Come, w. Suzie le Blanc (sop), Michael Chance (ct), Richard Wistreich (bass), P. Holman (cnd), Parley of Instruments, Playford Consort Hyperion ▲ CDA 66770

Campra, A.:Messe de Requiem, w. Véronique Gens (sop), Anne Gotkovski (sop), Jean-Paul Fouchécourt (alt), Peter Harvey (bar), H. Niquet (cnd), Concert Spirituel Orch, Concert Spirituel Vocal Ensemble Adda ▲ ADD 241952 [DDD]

Campra, A.:Motets, w. Véronique Gens (sop), Anne Gotkovski (sop), Jean-Paul Fouchécourt (alt), Peter Harvey (bar), H. Niquet (cnd), Concert Spirituel Orch, Concert Spirituel Vocal Ensemble—Benedictus Dominus Adda ▲ ADD 241952 [DDD]

Handel, G.F.:Messiah, w. Emma Kirkby (sop), Emily Van Evera (sop), Margaret Cable (mez), James Bowman (ct), David Thomas (bass), A. Parrott (cnd), Taverner Consort, Taverner Choir [E] EMI Classics 2-▲ CDCB 49801 [DDD]

Ryelandt, J.:Agnus Dei, w. Ingrid Kapelle (sop), Lucienne van Deyck (mez), Huub Claessens (bass), Stephan Macleod (bass), G. Llewellyn (cnd), Royal Flanders PO, Altra Voce, Audite Nova *(rec live, Elisabeth Hall, Antwerp, Holland, Dec 9, 1994)* Marco Polo 2-▲ 8.223785/86 [DDD]

Corradi, Giampaolo (bass)

Rossini, G.:Mosè in Egitto, w. Teresa Zylis-Gara (sop), Shirley Verrett (mez), Ottavio Garaventa (ten), Nicolai Ghiaurov (bass), Mario Petri (bass), W. Sawallisch (cnd), Rome RAI Orch, Rome RAI Chorus *(rec live, Rome, 1968)* Italian Opera Rarities 2-▲ IOR 7724 [ADD]

Corréas, Jérôme (bass)

Couperin, F.:Motets, w. Sandrine Piau (sop), C. Pelon (sop), J.–P. Fouchécourt (ten), Les Talens Lyriques—Quatre versets d'un motet composé de l'ordre du Roy (1703); Verset du motet de l'année dernièr; Sept versets d'un motet composé de l'ordre du Roy (1704); Motet à Sainte Suzanne; Sept versets d'un motet composé de l'ordre du Roy (1705); Laudate Pueri Dominum FNAC Music ▲ 592244 [DDD]

Lalande, M.–R. de:Motets, w. V. Gens (sop), S. Piau (sop), A. Steyer (sop), J.–P. Fouchécourt (ten), F. Piolino (ten), W. Christie (cnd), Les Arts Florissants [L] Harmonia Mundi France ▲ HMC 901351

Lalande, M.–R. de:Te Deum, w. V. Gens (sop), S. Piau (sop), A. Steyer (sop), J.–P. Fouchécourt (ten), F. Piolino (ten), W. Christie (cnd), Les Arts Florissants [L] Harmonia Mundi France ▲ HMC 901351

Rameau, J.P.:Castor et Pollux, w. V. Gens (sop), A. Mellon (sop), H. Cook (ten), W. Christie (cnd), Les Arts Florissants Harmonia Mundi France 3–▲ HMC 901435/37

Rameau, J.P.:Les Indes galantes, w. C. McFadden (sop), S. Piau (sop), I. Poulenard (sop), N. Rime (sop), M. Ruggeri (sop), H. Crook (ten), J.–P. Fouchecourt (ten), N. Rivenq (bar), B. Delétré (bass), W. Christie (cnd), Les Arts Florissants [F] Harmonia Mundi France 3–▲ HMC 901367/69

Rameau, J.P.:Nélée et Myrthis, w. A. Mellon (sop—Myrthis), D. Michel–Dansac (sop—Maid), C. Pelon (sop—Maid), F. Semellaz (sop—Corinne), J. Corréas (bass—Nélée), W. Christie (cnd), Les Arts Florissants, Les Arts Florissants Chorus [F] *(rec 5/91)* Harmonia Mundi France ▲ HMC 901381

Corsi, Emilia (sop)

Mozart, W.A.:Don Giovanni (sels), w. Adelina Patti (sop), John McCormack (ten), Mattia Battistini (bar), Ezio Pinza (bass), Landon Ronald (pno), C. Sabajno (cnd)—Alfin Siam liberati...Là ci darem la mano; Finch'han del vino; Batti, batti, o bel Masetto; Il mio tesoro; L'amerò, sarò costante *(rec 1905 - 1944)* Minerva ▲ MN A14 [ADD]

Corsi, Rina (mez)

Donizetti, G.:La fille du régiment, w. Lina Pagliughi (sop), Cesare Valletti (ten), Sesto Bruscantini (bar), Eraldo Coda (bar), M. Rossi (cnd), Milan RAI Lyric Orch, Milan RAI Chorus *(rec 1950)* Cetra Classic 2–▲ CDON 38 [ADD]

Mascagni, P.:L'amico Fritz, w. R. Carteri (sop—Suzel), R. Corsi (mez—Beppe), C. Valletti (ten—Fritz), C. Tagliabue (bar—David), V. Gui (cnd), Milan RAI SO, Milan RAI Chorus *(rec live, Apr. 25, 1953)* Bongiovanni 2–▲ GB 1098/99 [ADD]

Cortés, Hector (nar)

Balada, L.:Maria Sabina, w. América Dunham (nar—Maria Sabina), Burwell Hardy (nar—Town Crier), Guillermo Helguera (nar—Constable), Hector Cortés (nar—Executioner), J. Mester (cnd), Louisville Orch, Richard Spalding (cnd), Univ of Louisville Choir New World ▲ 804982

Balada, L.:Maria Sabina, w. Hector Cortés (nar—Executioner), Amèrica Dunham (nar—Maria Sabina), Burwell Hardy (nar—Town Crier), Guillermo Helguera (nar—Constable), J. Mester (cnd), Louisville Orch, Richard Spalding (cnd), Louisville Univ Chorus *(rec Feb 5, 1973)* New World ▲ 80498–2

Cortez, Miguel (ten)

Donizetti, G.:Requiem Mass, w. L. Pavarotti (ten), R. Bruson (bar), P. Washington (bass), G. Fackler (cnd), Arena di Verona Orch, Arena di Verona Chorus London ("Ovation" series) ▲ 425043–2 [ADD]

Falla, M. de:El retablo de maese Pedro, w. Lourdes Ambriz (sop), Julianne Baird (sop), William Alvarado (bar), Rafael Puyana (hpd), E. Mata (cnd), Mexican Soloists *(rec Sala Nezahualcóyotl, Universidad Nacional Autónoma de Mexico, Mexico City, Oct. 1994)* Dorian ▲ DOR 90214 [DDD]

Verdi, G.:Il trovatore, w. R. Kabaivanska (sop), F. Bonisolli (ten), G. Zancanaro (bar), B. Bartoletti (cnd), Berlin State Opera Orch, Berlin State Opera Chorus [I] Acanta 2–▲ CD 43301 [DDD]

Cortez, Viorica (mez)

Mascagni, P.:Cavalleria rusticana, w. Marina Krilovici (sop—Santuzza), Viorica Cortez (mez—Lola), Milka Nistor (mez—Lucia), Cornel Stavru (ten—Turiddu), David Ohanesian (bar—Alfio), M. Popa (cnd), Bucharest Opera & Ballet Theater Orch, Bucharest Opera & Ballet Theater Chorus *(rec 1966)* Vox Box 2–▲ CDX 5161

Thomas, A.:Hamlet, w. Alexandrina Pendachanska (sop), Boje Skovhus (bar), R. Giovanetti (cnd), ORF SO, Arnold Schoenberg Choir *(rec live, 1994)* Serenissima 3–▲ SER 360147

Verdi, G.:Rigoletto, w. M. Rinaldi (sop), F. Bonisolli (ten), R. Panerai (bar), B. Rundgren (b–bar), F. Molinari–Pradelli (cnd), Dresden State Orch, Dresden State Chorus [I] Acanta 2–▲ CD 41474 [DDD]

Cortis, Antonio (ten)

Antonio Cortis Nimbus ("Prima Voce" series) ▲ NI 7850 [ADD]

Antonio Cortis, 1891–1952, w. La Scala Orch [cnd:Carlo Sabajno] *(rec 1929–30 for HMV)* Preiser ("Lebendige Vergangenheit" series) ▲ PRE 89043 (m) [AAD]

Mozart, W.A.:Così fan tutte, w. M. Adani (sop), T. Stich–Randall (mez), T. Berganza (mez), L. Alva (ten), R. Panerai (bar), H. Rosbaud (cnd), Paris Conservatory Societé des Concerts Orch, Aix–en–Provence Festival Chorus [I] *(rec live, Aix–en–Provence, July 26, 1957)* Melodram 3–▲ MEL 37084 [AAD]

Recordings from 1925–1930 Nimbus ▲ NI 7850

Verdi, G.:Il trovatore (sels), w. J. Biel (ten), F. Tamagno (ten), L.–A. Escalaïs (ten), M. Gilion (ten), E. Caruso (ten), A. Paoli (ten), G. Zenatello (ten), J. Sembach (ten), L. Slezak (ten), F. Constantino (ten), G. Martinelli (ten), B. De Muro (ten), N. Fusati (ten), N. Piccaluga (ten), G. Lauri–Volpi (ten), A. Pertile (ten), E. Bergamaschi (ten), R. Tauber (ten), J. O'Sullivan (ten), H. Roswaenge (ten), G. Taccani (ten), V. Lois (ten), H. Lazaro (ten), A. Lindi (ten), F. Merli (ten), F. Völker (ten), J. Kiepura (ten), J. Schmidt (ten), J. Bjoerling (ten), B. Gigli (ten), A. Salvarezza (ten), J. Soler (ten), M. Filippeschi (ten)—34 performances of the Act III tenor aria "Di quella pira!," *(rec from 1903–1956)* Bongiovanni ▲ GB 1051 [AAD]

Cortis, Marcello (bar)

Massenet, J.:Werther, w. F. Tagliavini (ten), P.L. Latinucci (bass), F. Molinari–Pradelli (cnd), Turin RAI SO *(rec 1953)* Cetra Classic 2–▲ CDO 15 [AAD]

Cosenza, Arthur (bar)

Massenet, J.:Werther, w. J. Guido (sop—Sophie), N. Rankin (sop—Charlotte), C. Valletti (ten—Werther), A. Cosenza (bar—Albert), R. Cellini (cnd), New Orleans Opera Orch *(rec 1956)* Golden Age of Opera 2–▲ GAO 141/42 [ADD]

Puccini, G.:La Bohème, w. Licia Albanese (sop—Mimì), Audrey Schuh (sop—Musetta), Giuseppe di Stefano (ten—Rodolfo), Arthur Cosenza (bar—Schaunard), Giuseppe Valdengo (bar—Marcello), Norman Treigle (bass—Colline), Warren Gadpaille (bass—Benoît/Alcindoro), Thomas Carter (sgr—Parpignol), Harold Crane (sgr—Custom House Official), Steve Harun (sgr—Sergeant), R. Cellini (cnd), New Orleans Opera Orch, New Orleans Opera Chorus *(rec Nov 1959)* VAI Audio 2–▲ VAIA 1119–2 [ADD]

Puccini, G.:Madama Butterfly, w. V. de los Angeles (sop), R. Nadell (mez), B. Faulkner (sgr), W. Fredericks (sgr), J. Thresh (sgr), D. Bernard (sgr), R. Torigi (sgr), W. Herbert (cnd), New Orleans Opera Orch, New Orleans Opera Chorus *(rec live March 18, 1954)* Legato Classics 2–▲ LCD 168–2 [ADD]

Puccini, G.:Madama Butterfly, w. Dorothy Kirsten (sop—Madama Butterfly), Rosalind Nadell (mez—Suzuki), Eileen Ireland (mez—Kate), Daniele Barioni (ten—Pinkerton), Thomas Carter (ten—Goro), Arthur Cosenza (ten—Yamadori), Richard Torigi (bar—Sharpless), Rodney Hall (bass—The Bronze), Harold Crane (bass—Commissioner), R. Cellini (cnd), New Orleans Opera Orch, New Orleans Opera Chorus *(rec live, Mar 1960)* VAI Audio 2–▲ VAIA 1054–2

Saint–Saëns, C.:Samson et Dalila, w. Risë Stevens (mez—Dalila), Ramón Vinay (ten—Samson), Thomas Carter (ten—1st Philistine), Tony Lopez (ten—Philistine Messenger), Joseph Mordino (bar—High Priest), Arthur Cosenza (bass—Abimélech), Joseph Knight (bass—2nd Philistine), Ara Berberian (bass—Old Hebrew), R. Cellini (cnd), New Orleans Opera Orch, New Orleans Opera Chorus *(rec live, Apr 2, 1960)* VAI Audio 2–▲ VAIA 1055–2 [ADD]

Cosenza, Marietta (mez)

Floyd, C.:Susannah, w. Phyllis Curtin (sop—Susannah Polk), Richard Cassilly (ten—Sam Polk), Norman Treigle (bass—Olin Blitch), Marietta Muhs Cosenza (sgr—Mrs. McLean), Marilyn Davidson (sgr—Mrs. Gleaton), Kay Long (sgr—Mrs. Hayes), Jean Young (sgr—Mrs. Ott), Alton Brim (sgr—Elder Hayes), Thomas Carter (sgr—Elder Gleaton), Jack Davis (sgr—Elder McLean), Keith Kaldenberg (sgr—Little Bat McLean), Burton Parker (sgr—Elder Ott), K. Andersson (cnd), New Orleans Opera Orch, New Orleans Opera Chorus *(rec Mar 31, 1962)* VAI Audio 2–▲ VAIA 1115–2 [ADD]

Mascagni, P.:Cavalleria rusticana, w. Zinka Milanov (sop—Santuzza), Jean Craft (mez—Lucia), Marietta Cosenza (mez—Lola), Giuseppe Gismondo (ten—Turiddu), Benjamin Rayson (bar—Alfio), R. Cellini (cnd), New Orleans Opera Orch, New Orleans Opera Chorus *(rec live, 1963)* VAI Audio ▲ VAIA 1053

Cosotti, Max–René (ten)

Wolf–Ferrari, E.:Il campiello, w. D. Mazzucato (Gasparina), G. Devinu (Lucieta), M. Bolgan (Gnese), C. de Mola (Orsola), U. Benelli (Dona Cate Panciana), M. Rene Cosotti (Dona Pasqua Polegana), M. Comencini (Zorozeto), M. Biscotti (Astolfi), I. D'Arcangelo (Anzoleto), C. Striuli (Fabrizio del Ritorti); N. Bareza (cnd), Trieste Teatro Comunale Giuseppe Verdi Orch, Trieste Teatro Comunale G. Verdi Chorus *(rec Feb. 1992)* Ricordi 2–▲ RFCD 2014 [DDD]

Cossa, Dominic (bar)

Donizetti, G.:L'elisir d'amore, w. J. Sutherland (sop), L. Pavarotti (ten), S. Malas (bass), R. Bonynge (cnd), English CO [I] London 2–▲ 414461–2 [ADD]

Meyerbeer, G.:Les Huguenots, w. J. Sutherland (sop), M. Arroyo (sop), H. Tourangeau (mez), A. Vrenios (ten), G. Bacquier (bar), N. Ghiuselev (bass), R. Bonynge (cnd), New Philharmonia Orch, Ambrosian Opera Chorus London ("Grand Opera" series) 4–▲ 430549–2 [AAD]

Sessions, R.:When Lilacs Last in the Dooryard Bloom'd, w. E. Hinds (sop), F. Quivar (mez), S. Ozawa (cnd), Boston SO, Tanglewood Festival Chorus [E] New World ▲ NW 296–2 [AAD]

Cossotto, Fiorenza (mez)

Bellini, V.:I Capuleti e i Montecchi (sels), w. R. Gavarini (ten), V. Tatozzi (bar), L. Maazel (cnd), Rome RAI Orch, Rome RAI Chorus—2 solo tenor arias & 1 mezzo–bass duet [I] *(rec live 10/23/58)* Melodram ("Connaisseur" series) 2–▲ CDM 27509 [ADD]

Bellini, V.:Norma, w. M. Caballé (sop), P. Domingo (ten), R. Raimondi (bass), C.F. Cillario (cnd), London PO, Ambrosian Opera Chorus [I] RCA Gold Seal 3–▲ 6502–2–RG [ADD]

Bellini, V.:Norma, w. Caballé (soprano—Norma), B. Prevedi (ten), J. Carreras (ten), I. Vinco (bass), C. F. Cillario (cnd), Barcelona Teatro Liceo Orch, Barcelona Gran Teatro de Liceo Chorus [I] *(rec live, Barcelona 1/11/70)* Melodram 2–▲ CDM 27089 [ADD]

Bellini, V.:Norma, w. J. Sutherland (sop), C. Craig (ten), I. Vinco (bass), R. Bonynge (cnd), Buenos Aires Teatro Colón Orch, Buenos Aires Teatro Colón Chorus *(rec live 7/2/69)* Ediciones Teatro Colon 3–▲ ETC 101 [AAD]

Bellini, V.:Norma (sels), w. M. Callas (sop), G. Cecchele (ten), I. Vinco (bass), G. Prêtre (cnd), Paris Opera Orch, Paris Opera Chorus—sels. *(rec 1965)* Melodram ▲ MLO 16038 [ADD]

Bellini, V.:La sonnambula, w. M. Callas (sop), N. Monti (ten), N. Zaccaria (bass), A. Votto (cnd), La Scala Orch, La Scala Chorus [I] *(rec live 1957)* Melodram 2–▲ MEL 26003

Bellini, V.:La sonnambula, w. M. Callas (sop), N. Monti (ten), N. Zaccaria (bass), A. Votto (cnd), La Scala Orch, La Scala Chorus [I] *(rec live 1957)* Verona 2–▲ 2704/05 (m) [AAD]

Bellini, V.:La sonnambula, w. M. Callas (sop), N. Monti (ten), N. Zaccaria (bass), A. Votto (cnd), La Scala Orch, La Scala Chorus [I] EMI Classics 2–▲ CDCB 47377 (m)

Bellini, V.:La sonnambula, w. Maria Callas (sop), Nicola Monti (ten), Franco Ricciardi (ten), Dino Mantovani (bar), Nicola Zaccaria (bass), A. Votto (cnd), La Scala Orch, La Scala Chorus Melodram 2–▲ CDM 26037

Bellini, V.:La sonnambula, w. M. Callas (sop), N. Monti (ten), N. Zaccaria (bass), A. Votto (cnd), La Scala Orch, La Scala Chorus [I] *(rec live 1957)* Arkadia 2–▲ 503 (m) [AAD]

Bellini, V.:La sonnambula (sels), w. M. Callas (sop), N. Monti (ten), N. Zaccaria (bass), A. Votto (cnd), La Scala Orch, La Scala Chorus, from Act 2—Oh! se una volta sola rivederio; Ah, non creda mirarti [I] *(rec live, 7/4/57)* Myto 2–▲ 2 MCD 89006 (m) [ADD]

Bizet, G.:Carmen, w. M. Chiara (sop—Micaela), A. Caminada (mez—Mercedes), F. Cossotto (mez—Carmen), F. Andreoli (ten—Il Remendado), P. M. Ferraro (ten—Don José), R. Bruson (bar—Escamillo), G. Zancanaro (bar—Morales), A. Carusi (bass—Il Dancairo), P. Maag (cnd), Venice Teatro La Fenice Orch, Venice Teatro La Fenice Chorus *(rec 1971)* Myto 2–▲ MCD 93487

Cherubini, L.:Médée, w. M. Callas (sop), J. Vickers (ten), N. Zaccaria (bass), N. Rescigno (cnd), Royal Opera House Orch, Royal Opera House Chorus Covent Garden [I] *(rec live, Covent Garden, 6/30/59)* Melodram 2–▲ MEL 26005

Cilea, F.:Adriana Lecouvreur, w. M. Caballé (sop), J. Carreras (ten), A. D'Orazi (bar), G.–F. Masini (cnd), *(orch unknown)* [I] *(rec 1976)* Legato Classics 2–▲ LCD 111–2 [AAD]

Donizetti, G.:La favorita, w. L. Pavarotti (ten), G. Bacquier (bar), N. Ghiaurov (bass), R. Bonynge (cnd), Bologna Teatro Comunale Orch, Bologna Teatro Comunale Chorus London 3–▲ 430038–2 [ADD]

Donizetti, G.:La favorita, w. J. Aragall (ten), A. Colzani (bar), E. Gracis (cnd), Turin RAI Orch, Turin RAI Chorus *(rec live)* Melodram 2–▲ MEL 27020

Donizetti, G.:La favorita (sels), w. M. Zotti (sop), A. Kraus (ten), R. Raimondi (bass), O. de Fabritiis (cnd), NHK SO *(rec Sept. 13, 1971)* Myto 2–▲ MCD 93276

Falla, M. de:La vida breve, w. V. de los Angeles (sop), I. Rivadeneyra (mez), R. Burgos (cnd), Spanish National Orch, Orféon Donostiarra [Sp] EMI Classics ▲ CDM 69590 [ADD]

Gluck, C.W.:Iphigénie en Tauride, w. M. Callas (sop), Albanese (sgr), N. Sanzogno (cnd), La Scala Orch, La Scala Chorus [I] *(rec live 6/1/57)* Melodram 2–▲ MEL 26012 (m)

Mascagni, P.:Cavalleria rusticana, w. C. Bergonzi (ten), G. Guelfi (bar), H. von Karajan (cnd), La Scala Orch, La Scala Chorus [I] Deutsche Grammophon 3–▲ 419257–2 [ADD]

Meyerbeer, G.:Les Huguenots, w. J. Sutherland (sop), G. Simionato (mez), F. Corelli (ten), V. Ganzarolli (bar), N. Ghiaurov (bass), G. Tozzi (bass), G. Gavezzeni (cnd), La Scala Orch, La Scala Chorus [I] *(rec live 5/28/62)* Melodram 3–▲ MEL 37026 (m) [AAD]

Mozart, W.A.:Nozze di Figaro, w. A. Moffo (sop), E. Schwarzkopf (sop), G. Taddei (bar), E. Wächter (bar), C. M. Giulini (cnd), Philharmonia Orch, Philharmonia Chorus [I] EMI Classics ("Studio" series) 2–▲ CDMB 63266 [ADD]

Mozart, W.A.:Nozze di Figaro (sels), w. A. Moffo (sop), E. Schwarzkopf (sop), G. Taddei (bar), E. Wächter (bar), C. M. Giulini (cnd), Philharmonia Orch, Philharmonia Chorus—sels. EMI Classics ("Studio" series) ▲ CDM 63409

Mussorgsky, M.:Khovanshchina, w. Mietta Sighele (sop—Emma), Elena Souliotis (sop—Susanna), Fiorenza Cossotto (mez—Marfa), Herbert Handt (ten—Scribe), Veriano Luchetti (ten—Prince Andrey Khovansky), Ludovic Spiess (ten—Prince Vasily Golitsin), Claudio Strudthoff (ten—Streshnev), Angelo Marchiandi (bar—Kuz'ka), Teodoro Rovetta (bar—1st Strel'tsi), Siegmund Nimsgern (b–bar—Shaklovity), Cesare Siepi (b–bar—Dosifey), Carlo del Bosco (bass—2nd Strel'tsi), Ubaldo Carosi (bass—Varsonofiev), Nicolai Ghiaurov (bass—Prince Ivan Khovnasky), Giovanni Sciarpeletti (bass—Pastor), B. Leskovich (cnd), Rome RAI SO, Rome RAI Chorus—also includes bonus Act V [w Boris Christoff] (Rome, 1958) *(rec Rome, 1973)* Bella Voce 3–▲ BLV 107.402 [AAD]

Opera Arias *(rec live, 1958 & 1961)* Melodram 3–▲ CDM 37038 (m) [AAD]

Ponchielli, A.:La Gioconda, w. M. Callas (sop), I. Companeez (cta), P. M. Ferraro (ten), P. Cappuccilli (bar), I. Vinco (bass), A. Votto (cnd), La Scala Orch, La Scala Chorus EMI Classics ▲ CDCC 49518

Puccini, G.:Madama Butterfly, w. R. Tebaldi (sop), C. Bergonzi (ten), E. Sordello (bar), T. Serafin (cnd), St. Cecilia Academy Orch Rome, St. Cecilia Academy Chorus Rome [I] London 2–▲ 425531–2 [ADD]

Puccini, G.:Madama Butterfly (sels), w. R. Tebaldi (sop), C. Bergonzi (ten), E. Sordello (bar), T. Serafin (cnd), St. Cecilia Academy Orch Rome, St. Cecilia Academy Chorus Rome [I] London ("Opera Gala" series) ▲ 421873–2 [ADD]

Rossini, G.:Il barbiere di Siviglia, w. Luigi Alva (ten), Sesto Bruscantini (bar), Carlo Badioli (bass), Nicolai Ghiaurov (bass), G. Santini (cnd), La Scala Orch, La Scala Chorus *(rec Jan 20, 1964)* Pantheon 2–▲ PHE 6644 (m)

Stella, Cossotto & Monaco, w. Stella, Antonietta (sop), Mario Del Monaco (ten), Ferruccio Scaglia (cnd), Milan RAI SO, Rome RAI SO *(rec Martini & Rossi Concert, 1959 & 1960)* Incontri Memorabili ▲ CDMR 5031

Verdi, G.:Aida, w. M. Caballé (sop), P. Domingo (ten), P. Cappuccilli (bar), N. Ghiaurov (bass), R. Muti (cnd), New Philharmonia Orch, Royal Opera House Chorus Covent Garden [I] EMI Classics 3–▲ CDCC 47271 [ADD]

Verdi, G.:Arias, w. N. Santi (cnd), Royal PO—Ben Io T'Invenni...Anch'io Dischiuso un Giorno...Salga Già del Trono Aurato [from Nabucco]; Egli non Riede Ancora...Non So le Tetre Immagini [from Il Corsaro]; O Don Fatale [from Don Carlo]; Surta È la Notte...Ernani, Ernani Involami [from Ernani]; Ecco L'Orrido Campo...Ma Dall'Arido Stelo & Morró, Ma Prima in Grazia [from Un Ballo in Maschera] Fonit Cetra ("Italia" series) ▲ FCT CDC 89

Verdi, G.:Un ballo in maschera, w. M. Arroyo (sop), R. Grist (sop), P. Domingo (ten), P. Cappuccilli (bar), R. Muti (cnd), New Philharmonia Orch, Royal Opera House Chorus Covent Garden [I] EMI Classics (Studio) 2–▲ CDMB 69576 [ADD]

Cossotto, Fiorenza (mez) (cont.)

Verdi, G.:Don Carlos, w. M. Caballé (sop), P. Domingo (ten), P. Cappuccilli (bar), G. Petkov (bar), E. Inbal (cnd), Arena di Verona Orch, Arena di Verona Chorus [I] *(rec live 7/2/69)* Melodram 3-▲ MEL 37057 (m) [AAD]

Verdi, G.:Don Carlos, w. L. Gencer (sop), B. Prevedi (ten), S. Bruscantini (bar), N. Ghiaurov (bass), F. Previtali (cnd), Rome Opera Orch, Rome Opera Chorus *(rec live)* Melodram 3-▲ MEL 37022

Verdi, G.:Don Carlos, w. Katia Ricciarelli (sop), Fiorenza Cossotto (mez), Guido Fabbris (ten), Veriano Luchetti (ten), Piero Cappuccilli (bar), Gianfranco Casarini (bass), Nicolai Ghiaurov (bass), Alessandro Maddalena (bass), Aracelly Haengel (sgr), Marisa Salimbeni (sgr), Giorgio Zoranca (sgr), G. Prêtre (cnd), *(orch unknown)* Great Opera Performances 3-▲ GOP 777

Verdi, G.:Don Carlos, w. S. Jurinac (sop—Elisabetta), L. Rysanek (sop—Celestial Voice), F. Cossotto (mez—Princess Eboli), L. Dutoit (boy sop—Tebaldo), P. Domingo (ten—Don Carlo), E. Majkut (ten—Count of Lerma), M. Sereni (bar—Rodrigo), C. Siepi (bass—Philip II), I. Vinco (bass—Grand Inquisitor), T. Franc (bass—Friar), S. Varviso (cnd), Vienna State Opera Orch, Vienna State Opera Chorus Standing Room Only 2-▲ SRO 850 [ADD]

Verdi, G.:Un giorno di regno, w. J. Norman (sop), J. Carreras (ten), I. Wixell (bar), V. Sardinero (bar), W. Ganzarolli (bar), P. Elvin (bass), A. Cassinelli (bass), L. Gardelli (cnd), Royal PO, Ambrosian Singers Philips 2-▲ 422429-2 [ADD]

Verdi, G.:Requiem Mass, w. L. Price (sop), L. Pavarotti (ten), N. Ghiaurov (bass), H. von Karajan (cnd), La Scala Orch, La Scala Chorus [L] *(rec live 1/16/67)* Verona 2-▲ 27060/61 (m) [AAD]

Verdi, G.:Requiem Mass, w. L. Price (sop), L. Pavarotti (ten), N. Ghiaurov (bass), H. von Karajan (cnd), La Scala Orch, La Scala Chorus [L] *(rec live 1/16/67)* Melodram 2-▲ MEL 28012

Verdi, G.:Il trovatore, w. A. Stella (sop), M. Fiorentini (mez), F. Corelli (ten), E. Bastianini (bar), I. Vinco (bass), G. Gavazzeni (cnd), La Scala Orch, La Scala Chorus *(rec live, Milan, 12/7/62)* Melodram 2-▲ MEL 27068 (m) [AAD]

Verdi, G.:Il trovatore, w. A. Stella (sop), M. Fiorentini (mez), F. Corelli (ten), E. Bastianini (bar), I. Vinco (bass), G. Gavazzeni (cnd), La Scala Orch, La Scala Chorus [I] *(rec live, Milan, 12/7/62)* Claque 2-▲ CLQ 2013 (m)

Verdi, G.:Il trovatore, w. Carlos Cossutta (ten), Agistino Ferrin (bass), R. Muti (cnd), Florence Teatro Comunale Orch, Florence Teatro Comunale Chorus *(rec live, 1978)* Serenissima 2-▲ SER 306101 [ADD]

Zandonai, R.:I cavalieri di Ekebù, w. Gina Longobardo Fiordaliso (sgr), Lando Bartolini (ten), G. Gavazzeni (cnd), Milan RAI SO, Milan RAI Chorus Fonit Cetra ("Italia" series) 2-▲ FCT CDC 93

Cossutta, Carlo (ten)

Ricci, L.:Crispino e la cornare, w. D. Lojarro (sop), A. Lazzarini (mez), S. Alaimo (bar), R. Coviello (bar), A. Marani (bass), R. Ristori (bass), Benori (sgr), Siclari (sgr), P. Carignani (cnd), San Remo SO, San Remo Sym Chorus [I] *(rec live 11/89)* Bongiovanni 2-▲ GB 2095/96 [DDD]

Verdi, G.:Macbeth, w. C. Ludwig (mez), K. Ridderbusch (bass), S. Milnes (bass), K. Böhm (cnd), Vienna State Opera Orch, Vienna State Opera Chorus *(rec live 1970)* Legato Classics 2-▲ LCD 143-2 [ADD]

Verdi, G.:Il trovatore, w. Fiorenza Cossotto (mez), Agistino Ferrin (bass), R. Muti (cnd), Florence Teatro Comunale Orch, Florence Teatro Comunale Chorus *(rec live, 1978)* Serenissima 2-▲ SER 306101 [ADD]

Cossutta, Enrico (ten)

Verdi, G.:La traviata, w. T. Fabbricini (sop—Violetta), A. Trevisan (mez—Annina), N. Curiel (mez—Flora), R. Alagna (ten—Alfredo), E. Cossutta (ten—Gastone), E. Gavazzi (ten—Giuseppe), O. Mori (bar—Douphol), E. Capuano (bass—d'Obigny), F. Musinu (bass—Grenvil), R. Muti (cnd), La Scala Orch, La Scala Chorus Sony Classical 2-▲ S2K 52486 [DDD]

Costa, Albert da (ten)

Beethoven, L. van:Sym 9, "Choral Sym", w. Emilia Cundari (sop), Nell Rankin (mez), William Wilderman (bass), B. Walter (cnd), Columbia SO, Westminster Sym Choir *(rec American Legion Hall, Los Angeles, CA, Apr. 6, 1954)* Sony Classical ("Bruno Walter Edition, Vol. 2" series) ▲ SMK 64464 [ADD]

Costa, Fernanda (mez)

Puccini, G.:La Bohème, w. A. Moffo (sop), G. Tucker (ten), R. Merrill (bar), G. Tozzi (bass), E. Leinsdorf (cnd), Rome Opera Orch, Rome Opera Chorus [I] RCA Gold Seal 2-▲ 3969-2-RG [ADD] 2-■ 3969-4-RG (CrO2)

Puccini, G.:La Bohème (sels), w. A. Moffo (sop), G. Tucker (ten), R. Merrill (bar), G. Tozzi (bass), E. Leinsdorf (cnd), Rome Opera Orch, Rome Opera Chorus RCA Gold Seal ▲ 60189-2-RG [ADD] ■ 60189-4-RG (CrO2)

Rossini, G.:La Cenerentola, w. C. Bartoli (mez—Cenerentola), F. Costa (mez—Clorinda), G. Banditelli (cta—Tisbe), W. Matteuzzi (ten—Don Ramiro), A. Corbelli (bar—Dandini), E. Dara (bar—Don Magnifico), M. Pertusi (bass—Alidoro), R. Chailly (cnd), Bologna Teatro Comunale Orch, Bologna Teatro Comunale Chorus *(rec June 22–July 2, 1992)* London 2-▲ 436902-2 [DDD]

Costallos, S. (sgr)

Partch, H.:Revelation in the Courthouse Park, w. S. Costallos (sgr—Mom & Agave), C. Durham (ten—Sonny & Pentheus), M. Kimbrough (bar—Vendor & Herdsman), E. Earle (b-bar—Hobo & Tiresias), O. Babatunde (sgr—Dion & Dionysus), C. Roos (sgr—Mayor & Cadmus), O. Williams (sgr—Korypheus), R. Young (sgr—Cop & Guard), D. Mitchell (cnd), Partch Instrumentalists, marching band, *(chorus unknown)* [E] *(rec 10/87)* Tomato 2-▲ R2 70390 [DDD]

Costantino, Florencio (ten)

The World of Singing, Vol 4:The Italian School Part 1:Tenors before World War I, Book 2, w. Edoardo Garbin (ten), Fiorello Giraud (ten), Antonio Paoli (ten), Giuseppe Borgatti (ten), Carlo Albani (ten), Enrico Caruso (ten), Amedeo Bassi (ten), Piero Schivazzi (ten), Elvino Ventura (ten), Giovanni Zenatello (ten) Enterprise ("Vocal Archives" series) 3-▲ ENT VA 2107

Coste, Sharon (sop)

Caplet, A.:Myrrha, w. Marc Duguay (ten), Jean-François Lapointe (bar), J. Grimbert (cnd), Paris Sorbonne Orch, Paris Sorbonne Chorus Marco Polo ▲ 8.223755 [DDD]

Gounod, C.:Sappho, w. M. Command (sop), C. Popis (ten), E. Faury (bar), P. Fournillier (cnd), St.-Etienne Nouvel Orch Koch Schwann 2-▲ SCH 313112 [DDD]

Costello, Elvis (sgr)

Costello, E.:The Juliet Letters, w. Brodsky String Quartet Warner Bros. ▲ 9 45180-2

Coster, Janet (mez)

Holst, G.:A Choral Fant, w. A. Boult (cnd), London PO, John Alldis Choir *(rec Aug. 30, 1967)* Intaglio ▲ ING 740 [ADD]

Verdi, G.:La forza del destino, w. Martina Arroyo (sop—Donna Leonora), Janet Coster (mez—Preziosilla), Kenneth Bowen (ten—Trabuco), Kenneth Collins (ten—Don Alvaro), Peter Glossop (bar—Don Carlo), Roderick Kennedy (bass—Marquis), J. Matheson (cnd), BBC Concert Orch, BBC Concert Chorus *(rec live, early 1980's)* Exclusive 2-▲ EXL 80 [ADD]

Cotrubas, Ileana (sop)

Beethoven, L. van:Missa Solemnis, w. Kathleen Kuhlmann (mez), Robert Tear (ten), Gwynne Howell (bass), J. Pritchard (cnd), BBC SO, BBC Singers IMP ("BBC Radio Classics" series) ▲ IMP 5691552

Bizet, G.:Carmen, w. T. Berganza (mez), P. Domingo (ten), S. Milnes (bar), C. Abbado (cnd), London SO, Ambrosian Opera Chorus [F] Deutsche Grammophon 3-▲ 419636-2 [ADD]

Bizet, G.:Carmen (sels), w. T. Berganza (mez), P. Domingo (ten), S. Milnes (bar), C. Abbado (cnd), London SO, Ambrosian Opera Chorus [F] Deutsche Grammophon ▲ 435401-2 [ADD]

Bizet, G.:Les Pêcheurs de perles, w. A. Vanzo (ten), G. Sarabia (bar), R. Soyer (bass), G. Prêtre (cnd), Paris Opera Orch, Paris Opera Chorus Classics for Pleasure ▲ CDCFP 4721 [ADD]

Brahms, J.:Ein Deutsches Requiem, w. H. Prey (bar), L. Maazel (cnd), New Philharmonia Orch, New Philharmonia Chorus [G] *(rec 1976)* Sony Classical ▲ SK 45853 [ADD]

Charpentier, G.:Louise, w. J. Berbié (mez), P. Domingo (ten), M. Sénéchal (ten), G. Bacqier (bar), G. Prêtre (cnd), New Philharmonia Orch, Ambrosian Opera Chorus [F] Sony Classical 3-▲ S3K 46429 [ADD]

Debussy, C.:La Damoiselle élue, w. G. Maurice (mez), G. Bertini (cnd), Stuttgart RSO, Stuttgart Radio Chorus [F] Orfeo ▲ 012821 [DDD]

Donizetti, G.:Don Pasquale, w. Alfredo Kraus (ten), Wladimiro Ganzarolli (bar), Vincente Sardinero (bar), Sutliff (sgr), B. Bartoletti (cnd), Chicago Lyric Opera Orch, Chicago Lyric Opera Chorus *(rec live, Chicago, Nov. 2, 1974)* Arkadia 2-▲ 490

Cotrubas, Ileana (sop) (cont.)

Donizetti, G.:L'elisir d'amore, w. L. Watson (sop), P. Domingo (ten), G. Evans (bar), I. Wixell (bar), J. Pritchard (cnd), Royal Opera House Orch, Royal Opera House Chorus Covent Garden *(rec 1977)* CBS 2-▲ M2K 34585 [ADD]

Gluck, C.W.:Paride ed Elena, w. S. Greenberg (sop), Fontana (sgr), F. Bonisolli (ten), L. Zagrosek (cnd), Austrian RSO, Austrian Radio Chorus [I] *(rec 1983)* Orfeo 2-▲ 118842 [DDD]

Great Love Scenes, w. P. Domingo, R. Scotto (sop), K. Te Kanawa (sop) CBS ▲ MK 39030 ■ MT 39030

Great Sopranos of Our Time, w. Maria Callas (sop), Joan Sutherland (sop), Renata Scotto (sop), Montserrat Caballé (sop), Elisabeth Schwarzkopf (sop), Victoria de los Angeles (sop), Mirella Freni (sop), Edita Gruberova (sop) Classics for Pleasure ▲ CDEMX 9519 [ADD]

Handel, G.F.:Rinaldo, w. Sophie Boulin (sop—Donna), Ileana Cotrubas (sop—Almirena), Marie-Françoise Jacquelin (sop—Sirene), Nicole Leport (sop—Sirene), Jeanette Scovotti (sop—Armida), Carolyn Watkinson (cta—Rinaldo), Charles Brett (ct—Eustazio), Paul Esswood (ct—Goffredo), Armand Arapian (ten—Mago Christiano/Araldo), Ulrik Cold (bass—Argante), J. Malgoire (cnd), La Grande Écurie et la Chambre du Roy *(rec Paris, 1977)* Sony Classical 3-▲ SM3K 34592

Humperdinck, E.:Hänsel und Gretel, w. E. Söderström (sop), F. von Stade (mez), C. Ludwig (mez), S. Nimsgern (b-bar), J. Pritchard (cnd), Gürzenich Orch [G] CBS 2-▲ M2K 35898 [ADD]

James Levine's 25th Anniversary Metropolitan Opera Gala, w. J. Levine (cnd), Metropolitan Opera Orch, Ileana Cotrubas (sop), Renée Fleming (sop), Hei-Kyung Hong (sop), Karita Mattila (sop), Birgit Nilsson (sop), Ruth Ann Swenson (sop), Kiri Te Kanawa (sop), Deborah Voigt (sop), Grace Bumbry (mez), Heidi Grant Murphy (mez), Anne Sofie von Otter (mez) *(rec live, Metropolitan Opera House, New York, Apr 27, 1996)* Deutsche Grammophon ▲ 449177-2 [DDD]

Mahler, G.:Sym 2, w. Christa Ludwig (cta), Z. Mehta (cnd), Vienna PO, Vienna State Opera Chorus *(rec 1975)* London ("Double Decker" series) 2-▲ 440615-2 [ADD]

Mahler, G.:Sym 8, w. Hanneke van Bork (sop), Heather Harper (sop), Brigit Finnila (mez), Marianne Dieleman (cta), William Cochran (ten), Hermann Prey (bar), Hans Sotin (bass), B. Haitink (cnd), Royal Concertgebouw Orch Philips ("Solo" series) ▲ 446195-2

Mozart, W.A.:Arias, w. Arleen Augér (sop), Kathleen Battle (sop), Irma Beilke (sop), Helena Braun (sop), Lisa Della Casa (sop), Maria Cebotari (sop), Helen Donath (sop), Mirella Freni (sop), Reri Grist (sop), Edita Gruberova (sop), Elisabeth Grümmer (sop), Hilde Güden (sop), Ingeborg Hallstein (sop), Luise Helletsgruber (sop), Gundula Janowitz (sop), Sena Jurinac (sop), Erika Köth (sop), Evelyn Lear (sop), Wilma Lipp (sop), Margaret Marshall (sop), Edith Mathis (sop), Jarmila Novotna (sop), Margherita Perras (sop), Lucia Popp (sop), Elisabeth Rethberg (sop), Anneliese Rothenberger (sop), Elisabeth Schumann (sop), Elisabeth Schwarzkopf (sop), Graziella Sciutti (sop), Irmgard Seefried (sop), Graziella Sciutti (sop), Julia Varady (sop), Agnes Baltsa (mez), Margit Bokor (mez), Brigitte Fassbaender (mez), Christa Ludwig (mez), Ann Murray (mez), Francisco Araiza (ten), Anton Dermota (ten), Helge Rosvaenge (ten), Rudolf Schock (ten), Peter Schreier (ten), Leopold Simoneau (ten), Eric Tappy (ten), Richard Tauber (ten), Gösta Winbergh (ten), Josef Witt (ten), Fritz Wunderlich (ten), Christian Boesch (bar), Willy Domgraf-Fassbaender (bar), Karl Dönch (bar), Dietrich Fischer-Dieskau (bar), Erich Kunz (bar), Eberhard Wächter (bar), Hans Hotter (b-bar), Paul Schöffler (b-bar), Cesare Siepi (b-bar), José Van Dam (b-bar), Walter Berry (bass), Geraint Evans (bass), Nicolai Ghiaurov (bass), Alexander Kipnis (bass), Richard Mayr (bass), Kurt Moll (bass), James Morris (bass), Ezio Pinza (bass), Martti Talvela (bass), Giorgio Tozzi (bass), Hans Duhan (sgr), Res Fischer (sgr), Marie Gerhart (sgr), *(various orchs & cnds)*—sels from Idomeneo, Die Entführung aus der Serail, Le nozze di Figaro, Don Giovanni, Così fan tutte, Die Zauberflöte & various arias Orfeo d'or ("Festspiel Dokumente" series) 5-▲ 408955

Mozart, W.A.:Arias, w. E. Steber (sop), K. Te Kanawa (sop), R. Stevens (mez), P. Domingo (ten), S. Jerusalem (ten), G. London (bar), E. Pinza (bass)—arias & duets from Don Giovanni, Le nozze di Figaro, Die Zauberflöte, etc. *(rec 1941–1978)* CBS Masterworks ▲ MDK 46579 [AAD] ■ MGT 46579

Mozart, W.A.:Arias, w. E. Gruberova (sop), L. Price (sop), J. Varady (sop), L. Popp (mez), F. Araiza (ten), P. Domingo (ten), P. de Palma (ten), P. Schreier (ten), F. Wunderlich (ten), S. Milnes (bar), A. Titus (bar), M. Talvela (bass)—sels. from Entführung aus dem Serail, Così fan tutte, Don Giovanni, Idomeneo, Die Zauberflöte, Le nozze di Figaro Eurodisc ▲ 69256-2-RG [ADD]

Mozart, W.A.:Complete Mozart Edition, w. Jessye Norman (sop), H. Donath (sop), T. Troyanos (mez), W. Hollweg (ten), H. Prey (bar), H. Schmidt-Isserstedt (cnd), North German RSO Philips 3-▲ 422534-2 [ADD]

Mozart, W.A.:Complete Mozart Edition, w. M. Caballé (sop), J. Baker (mez), N. Gedda (ten), C. Davis (cnd), Royal Opera House Orch, Royal Opera House Chorus Covent Garden Philips 3-▲ 422542-2 [ADD]

Mozart, W.A.:Complete Mozart Edition, w. A. Augér (sop), E. Gruberova (sop), A. Baltsa (mez), W. Hollweg (ten), L. Hager (cnd), Salzburg Mozarteum Orch Philips 3-▲ 422529-2 [ADD]

Mozart, W.A.:Missa, K.427, w. K. Te Kanawa (sop), W. Krenn (ten), H. Sotin (bass), R. Leppard (cnd), New Philharmonia Orch, John Alldis Choir [L] EMI Classics ▲ CDC 47385

Mozart, W.A.:Requiem, w. H. Watts (cta), R. Tear (ten), J. Shirley-Quirk (bar), N. Marriner (cnd), Academy of St. Martin in the Fields, Academy of St. Martin in the Fields Chorus [L] London ▲ 417746-2 [ADD]

Puccini, G.:La Bohème, w. Ileana Cotrubas (sop—Mimi), Margherita Guglielmi (sop—Musetta), José Carreras (ten—Rodolfo), Saverio Porzano (ten—Parpignol), Regolo Romani (ten—Vendor), Claudio Giombi (bar—Benoit), Gianni Maffeo (bar—Schaunard), Angelo Romero (bar—Marcello), Alfredo Giacomotti (bass—Alcindoro), Carlo Meliciani (bass—Customs Officer), Giuseppe Morresi (bass—Sergeant), Paolo Washington (bass—Colline), G. Prêtre (cnd), La Scala Orch, La Scala Chorus *(rec Washington D.C., Sept 8, 1976)* Legato Classics 2-▲ LCD 201-2

Puccini, G.:Il trittico, w. R. Scotto (sop), M. Horne (mez), P. Domingo (ten), T. Gobbi (bar), I. Wixell (bar), L. Maazel (cnd), London SO, Philharmonia Orch [I] CBS 3-▲ M3K 35912 [ADD]

Schubert, Franz:Rosamunde, w. W. Boskovsky (cnd), Dresden State Opera Orch, Leipzig Radio Chorus Berlin Classics ▲ BER 9004 [ADD]

Verdi, G.:La traviata, w. G. Aragall (ten), R. Bruson (bar), C. Kleiber (cnd), Bavarian State Orch [I] *(rec 1978)* Artists 2-▲ FED 45 [ADD]

Verdi, G.:La traviata (sels), w. Ileana Cotrubas (sop—Violetta), Elizabeth Bainbridge (mez—Annina), José Carreras (ten—Alfredo), Richard Creeger (ten—Gastone), Victor Braun (bar—Germont), Richard Van Allen (bass—Grenvil), J. Pritchard (cnd), *(orch unknown)*—Libiamo ne' lietialici; Oh, qual pallor!...Un di felice; Ebben? Che diavol fate?...Amor, dunque non piu; E strano!...Ah, fors'e lui; Follie! Follie!...Sempre libera; Lunge da lei...De' miei bollenti spiriti; Che fai?...Amami, Alfredo; Invitato a qui seguirmi...Ogni suo aver tal femmina; Signora...Parigi, o cara; Ah, non piu...Ah, gran Dio, morir si giovine; E strano! Cessarono gli spasimi del dolore *(rec Apr 15, 1974)* Legato Classics 2-▲ LCD 201-2

Cotrubas, M. (sop)

Verdi, G.:Alzira, w. F. Araiza (ten), R. Bruson (bar), L. Gardelli (cnd), Munich RSO, Bavarian Radio Chorus [I] Orfeo 2-▲ 057832 [DDD]

Cottino, Giacomo (ten)

Ponchielli, A.:La Gioconda, w. Zinka Milanov (sop—La Gioconda), Rosalind Elias (mez—Laura), Belan Amparan (cta—La Cieca), Giacomo Cottino (ten—Isepo), Giuseppe Di Stefano (ten—Enzo Grimaldo), Fernando Valentini (bar—Zuane/Un Nocchiero), Leonard Warren (bar—Barnaba), Virgilio Carbonari (bass—Un Cantore), Plinio Clabassi (bass—Alvise Badoero), F. Previtali (cnd), St. Cecilia Academy Orch Rome, St. Cecilia Academy Chorus Rome Theorema 3-▲ TH 121182/184

Counod, Hugues (ten)

Mozart, W.A.:Nozze di Figaro, w. S. Jurinac (sop), G. Sciutti (sop), R. Stevens (mez), M. Sinclair (cta), D. McCoshan (ten), G. Griffith (bar), S. Bruscantini (b-bar), F. Calabrese (bass), V. Gui (cnd), Glyndebourne Festival Orch, Glyndebourne Festival Chorus Classics for Pleasure ▲ CDCFP 4724 [ADD]

Coupe (trb)

Dvořák, A.:Mass, w. S. Taylor (ct), P. Cave (ten), S. Foulkes (bass), A. Pinel (org), M. Archer (cnd), Bristol Cathedral Choir [L] Meridian ▲ CDE 84188

Couperim, Vickie (sgr)

Hildegard Of Bingen:Sacred Songs, w. Jocelyn West (sgr), Vivien Ellis (sgr), Stevie Wishart (sgr/h-g), Hester Briant (sgr), Fiona Cunningham (sgr), Tara Franks (sgr), Emily Levy (sgr), Lucy Steele (sgr), Julie Murphy (sgr), Oxford Girls' Choir—Honey & milk beneath her tongue; Ursula's virgins; The devil's virgins; Place of the ancient heart; Zeal of divinity; O fiery spirit; Red river falling; O orzchis ecclesia, Living-light angels; The clouds are grieving; The firstwoman; From their homeland; But the devil mocked; Song to Ecclesia *(rec Toddington, Gloucestershire, England, May 6–8, 1995)* Celestial Harmonies ▲ 13127-2

Courney, James (bass)
Amram, D.:Songs (3) for America, w. R.A. Clark (cnd), Manhattan CO
Newport Classic ▲ NPD 85546 [DDD]

Courtis, Jean-Philippe (bass)
Berlioz, H.:Les Troyens, w. F. Pollet (sop—Dido), D. Voigt (sop—Cassandre), C. Dubosc (sop—Ascagne), H. Perraguin (cta—Anna), G. Lakes (ten—Aeneas), J.-L. Maurette (ten—Iopas), J. M. Ainsley (ten—Hylas), M. P. (ten—Panthee), G. Cross (ten—Sinon), G. Quilico (bar—Chorebe), J.-P. Courtis (b-bar—Narbal), M. Belleau (bass—Ghost of Hector), R. Schirrer (bass—Priam), C. Dutoit (cnd), Montreal SO, Montreal Sym Chorus London 4-▲ 443693-2 [DDD]
Cherubini, L.:Médée, w. Jano Tamar (sop), Patrizia Ciofi (sgr), Luca Lombardo (sgr), Magali Damonte (sgr), P. Fournillier (cnd), Italian International Opera Orch, Sluk Chamber Chorus Bratislava *(rec Martina Franca Festival, 1995)* Nuova Era 2-▲ NUO 7253
Debussy, C.:Pelléas et Mélisande, w. M. Ewing (sop), C. Ludwig (mez), F. Le Roux (bar), J. Van Dam (bass-bar), C. Abbado (cnd), Vienna PO, Vienna State Opera Chorus
Deutsche Grammophon 2-▲ 435344-2 [DDD]
Haydn, J.:Applausus:Jubilaeum virtutis Palatium, w. Rosemary Musoleno (sop—Temperantia), Kirsten Dolberg (mez—Prudentia), Douglas Johnson (ten—Justitia), Desmond Byrne (bass—Fortitudo), Jean-Philippe Courtis (bass—Theologia), P. Fournillier (cnd), Picardie Orch, Haydn Vocal Ensemble [L] *(rec 9/91)* Opus 111 2-▲ OPS 61-9207/8 [DDD]
Massenet, J.:Eve, w. Michèle Command (sop), Carolyn Sebron (mez), Hervé Lamy (ten), J.-P. Lore (cnd), French Oratorio Orch, French Oratorio Choir Erol 3-▲ 94002-04
Massenet, J.:Grisélidis, w. Michèle Command (sop), Brigitte Desnoues (sop), Jean-Luc Viala (ten), Didier Henry (bar), Maurice Sieyes (bar), Christian Treguier (bar), Claire Larcher (sgr), P. Fournillier (cnd), Franz Liszt SO, Budapest Lyon Chorus Koch Schwann 2-▲ SCH 312702 [DDD]
Massenet, J.:Marie-Magdeleine, w. Michèle Command (sop), Carolyn Sebron (mez), Hervé Lamy (ten), J.-P. Lore (cnd), French Oratorio Orch, French Oratorio Choir Erol 3-▲ 94002-04

Courtneidge, C. (sgr)
Rodgers, R.:Lido Lady (sels), w. P. Dare (sgr), H. French (sgr), *(other artists unknown)*
Pearl ("Flapper" series) ▲ PEA CD 9105 [ADD]

Couture, Michele (sop)
Rorem, N.:A Childhood Miracle, w. Michele Couture (sop—Peony), Darcy Dunn (sgr—Violet), Madeline Tsingopoulos (sgr—Mother), Mary Cidoni (sgr—Emma), Patrick Greene (sgr—Snowman), Peter Castaldi (sgr—Father), R. E. Harrell (cnd), Magic Circle CO Newport Classic ▲ NPT 85594 [DDD]

Covey-Crump, Rogers (ten)
Bach, J.S.:Mass in b, BWV 232, w. E. Kirkby (sop), E. Van Evera (sop), D. Thomas (bass), A. Parrott (cnd), Taverner Consort, Taverner Players, Tölz Boys' Choir [L]
EMI Classics 2-▲ ZDCB 47292-2 [DDD]
Blow, J.:Ode on the Death of Mr. Henry Purcell, w. C. Daniels (ten), P. Holman (cnd), Parley of Instruments Hyperion ▲ CDA 66578 [DDD]
Burgon, G.:The Fall of Lucifer, w. J. Bowman (ct), D. Thomas (bass), G. Burgon (cnd), Endymion Ensemble, M. Greenall (cnd), Elysian Singers London Silva Classics ▲ SIL 6002 [DDD]
Codex Speciálník, w. P. Hillier (cnd), Hillard Ensemble, D. James (ct), J. Potter (ten), G. Jones (bar) *(rec Gönningen City Church, Jan. 1993)* ECM New Series ▲ 78118-21504-2 [DDD]
Kancheli, G.:Evening Prayers, w. David James (ct), John Potter (ten), Gordon Jones (bar), D. R. Davies (cnd), Stuttgart CO *(rec Apr. 1994)* ECM New Series ▲ 78118-21510-2 [DDD]
Mozart, W.A.:Missa, K.317, w. L. Marshall (sop), A. Murray (mez), D. Wilson-Johnson (bar), S. Cleobury (cnd), English CO, King's College Choir Cambridge [L] Argo ▲ 411904-2 [DDD]
Mozart, W.A.:Missa solemnis, K.337, w. L. Marshall (sop), A. Murray (mez), D. Wilson-Johnson (bar), S. Cleobury (cnd), English CO [L] Argo ▲ 411904-2 [DDD]
Mozart, W.A.:Vesperae de Dominica, w. L. Dawson (sop), E. James (mez), P. Hillier (bass), S. Cleobury (cnd), Cambridge Classical Players, Hilliard Ensemble, King's College Choir [L]
EMI Classics ▲ CDC 49672 [DDD]
Mozart, W.A.:Vesperae solennes, w. L. Dawson (sop), E. James (mez), P. Hillier (bass), S. Cleobury (cnd), Cambridge Classical Players, Hilliard Ensemble, King's College Choir [L]
EMI Classics ▲ CDC 49672 [DDD]
Odes on the Death of Henry Purcell, w. Holman, Goodman (cnd), Parley of Instruments, Baroque Orch, Baroque Choir, R. Holton (sop), C. Daniels (ten), S. Birchall (bass) Hyperion ▲ CDA 66578 [DDD]
Officium, w. P. Hillier (cnd), Hillard Ensemble, D. James (ct), J. Potter (ten), G. Jones (bar), J. Gabarek (sop/ten saxs) *(rec Sept. 1993)* ECM New Series ▲ 78118-21525-2
Pärt, A.:Litany, w. David James (ct), John Potter (ten), Gordon Jones (bass), T. Kaljuste (cnd), Tallinn CO, Estonian Phil Chamber Choir *(rec Niguliste Church, Tallinn, Sept 1995)*
ECM New Series ▲ 78118-21592-2 [DDD] ■ 78118-21592-4
Pärt, A.:Passio Domini nostri Jesu Christi secundum Joannem, w. L. Dawson (sop), D. James (alt), J. Potter (ten), G. Jones (bass), M. George (bass), P. Hillier (cnd), Hilliard Ensemble, Western Wind Chamber Chorus [L] ECM New Series ▲ 78118-21370-2 [DDD]; ■ 78118-21370-4 (D)
Purcell, H.:Anthems, w. J. Bowman (ct), C. Daniels (ten), M. George (b-bar), King's Consort, New College Choir Oxford Hyperion ▲ CDA 66656
Purcell, H.:Anthems & Services, w. J. Bowman (ct), C. Daniels (ten), S. Varcoe (bar), M. George (bass), R. King (cnd), King's Consort, New College Choir Oxford—My heart is inditing; The way of God is an undefiled way; Sing unto God; Behold, I bring you glad tidings; Since God so tender a regard; Early, O Lord, my fainting soul; Sleep, Adam, sleep and take thy rest; Awake, ye dead; The earth trembled; Lord not to us but to thy name; O all ye people, clap your hands Hyperion ▲ CDA 66644
Purcell, H.:Anthems & Services, w. James Bowman (ct), Michael George (bass), R. King (cnd), King's Consort, New College Choir Oxford—Behold, now praise the Lord; Blessed are they that fear the Lord; I will give thanks unto Thee, O Lord; My song shall be always Hyperion ▲ CDA 66609
Purcell, H.:Anthems & Services, w. S. Gritton (sop), M. Kennedy (sop), E. O'Dwyer (trb), J. Goodman (trb), J. Bowman (ct), N. Short (ct), C. Daniels (ten), M. Milhofer (ten), M. George (bass), R. Evans (bass), R. King (cnd), King's Consort—I Was Glad When They Said unto Me (coronation & verse anthem); O Consider My Adversity; Beati omnes qui timent Dominum; In the Black Dismal Dungeon of Dispair; Save Me, O God; Te Deum in B♭; Jubilant in B♭; Thy Way, O God, Is Holy
Hyperion ▲ CDA 66677 [DDD]
Purcell, H.:Music for the Funeral of Queen Mary, w. S. Gritton (sop), M. Kennedy (sop), E. O'Dwyer (trb), J. Goodman (trb), J. Bowman (ct), N. Short (ct), C. Daniels (ten), M. Milhofer (ten), M. George (bass), R. Evans (bass), R. King (cnd), King's Consort Hyperion ▲ CDA 66677 [DDD]
Purcell, H.:Music for the Theater, w. E. Kirkby (sop), J. Nelson (sop), J. Bowman (ct), M. Hill (ten), C. Keyte (bass), D. Thomas (bass), C. Hogwood (cnd), Academy of Ancient Music
L'Oiseau-Lyre 6-▲ 425893-2 [ADD]
Purcell, H.:The Prophetess, or The History of Dioclesian, w. L. Dawson (sop), Gillian Fisher (sop), P. Elliot (ten), S. Varcoe (bar), M. George (bass), J.E. Gardiner (cnd), Monteverdi Orch, Monteverdi Choir London Erato ("Gardiner Purcell Collection" series) 2-▲ 96556-2
Purcell, H.:Songs, w. B. Bonney (sop), S. Gritton (sop), J. Bowman (ct), C. Daniels (ten), M. George (bass), D. Miller (archlt/thb/baroque gtr), M. Caudle (b vl), R. King (chamber org)—Draw near, you lovers; While Thyrsis, wrapt in downy sleep; Love, thou canst hear, I lov'd fair Celia; What hope for us remains now he is gone; Pastora's beauties, when unblown; A thousand sev'ral ways I tried; Urge me no more; Farewell all joys; If music be the food of love [1st setting]; Amidst the shades and cool refreshing streams; They say you're angry; Let each gallant heart; This poet sings the Trojan wars; Ah, how pleasant 'tis to love; My heart whenever you appear; On the brow of Richard Hill; Rashly I swore I would disown; Since the pox or the plague; Beneath a dark and melancholy grove; Musing on cares of human fate; Whilst Cynthia sung, all angry winds lay still Hyperion ▲ CDA 66710
Purcell, H.:Songs, w. B. Bonney (sop), S. Gritton (sop), J. Bowman (ct), C. Daniels (ten), M. George (bass), D. Miller (archlt/thb/baroque gtr), M. Caudle (b vl), R. King (org/hpd), King's Consort—Incassum Lesbia; Gentle Shepherds, you that know the charms; I love and I must; Through mournful shades and solitary groves; The Knotting Song Hyperion ▲ CDA 66720 [DDD]

Covey-Crump, Rogers (ten) (cont.)
Purcell, H.:Songs, w. B. Bonney (sop), S. Gritton (sop), J. Bowman (ct), C. Daniels (ten), M. George (bass), R. King (cnd), King's Consort—When Strephon Found; Let Us, Kind Lesbia; Corinna Is Divinely Fair; Olinda in the Shades; If Music Be the Food of Love [3rd setting]; Lovely Albina; I Came, I Saw; No, to What Purpose; Young Thrysis' Fate; She Loves Me and Confesses Too; From Silent Shade (Bess of Bedlam); O Solitude; If Pray'rs and Tears; The Fatal Hour; Sylvia, 'Tis True You're Fair; Amintor, Heedless of His Flocks; Love is Now Become a Trade; Phyllis, I Can Never Forgive It; Who Can Behold?; He Himself Courts His Own Ruin; Let Formal Lovers Still Pursue; Ask Me to Love No More; In Cloris All Soft Charms; Spite of the Godhead Hyperion ▲ CDA 66730
Purcell, H.:Timon of Athens, w. L. Dawson (sop), Gillian Fisher (sop), P. Elliot (ten), S. Varcoe (bar), M. George (bass), J.E. Gardiner (cnd), Monteverdi Orch, Monteverdi Choir London
Erato ("Gardiner Purcell Collection" series) 2-▲ 96556-2
Schütz, H.:Cantiones sacrae, w. Mona Spägele (sop), Ralf Popken (alt), John Potter (ten), Peter Kooj (bass), Thomas Ihlenfeldt (chit), Manfred Cordes (org)—complete 40 motets
CPO 2-▲ 999405-2 [DDD]
Schütz, H.:Symphoniae sacrae 1, w. Barbara Borden (sop), Nele Gramss (sop), John Potter (ten), Douglas Nasrawi (ten), Harry van der Kamp (bass), Concerto Palatino Choir
Accent 2-▲ 9178/79 [DDD]
Stockhausen, K.:Stimmung, w. K. Flowers (sop), P. Walmsley-Clark (sop), Long (sgr), P. Rose (bass), Hillier (sgr) Hyperion ▲ CDA 66115

Coviello, Roberto (bar)
Donizetti, G.:Il furioso all'isola di Santo Domingo, w. P. Antonucci (sop), L. Serra (sop), E. Tandura (mez), L. Canonici (ten), Picconi (sgr), C. Rizzi (cnd), Piacenza SO, Piacenza Chorus [I] *(rec live, 11/10/87)* Bongiovanni 3-▲ GB 2056/58 [DDD]
Donizetti, G.:Torquato Tasso, w. A. D'Auria (sop), L. Serra (sop), N. Ciliento (mez), E. Palacio (ten), S. Alaimo (bass-bar), A. Riva (bass), M.. Bernart (cnd), Genoa Teatro Comunale Orch, Genoa Teatro Comunale Chorus [I] *(rec live 10/16/85)* Bongiovanni 3-▲ GB 2028/30 [DDD]
Ricci, L.:Crispino e la cornare, w. D. Lojarro (sop), A. Lazzarini (mez), Cossutta (ten), S. Alaimo (bar), A. Marani (bass), R. Ristori (bass), Benori (sgr), Siclari (sgr), P. Carignani (cnd), San Remo SO, San Remo Sym Chorus [I] *(rec live 11/89)* Bongiovanni 2-▲ GB 2095/96 [DDD]
Rossini, G.:La scala di seta, w. Luciana Serra (sop), Oslavio di Credico (ten), William Matteuzzi (ten), Natale de Carolis (b-bar), G. Ferro (cnd), Bologna Teatro Comunale Orch
Fonit Cetra ("Ricordi" series) 2-▲ FCT RFCD 2003

Cowan, Richard (bar)
Puccini, G.:Madama Butterfly (sels), w. Ying Huang (sop—Cio-Cio-San), Constance Hauman (mez—Kate Pinkerton), Ning Liang (mez—Suzuki), Richard Troxell (ten—B. F. Pinkerton), Richard Cowan (sgr—Sharpless), Jing Ma Fan (sgr—Goro), Christopheren Nomura (sgr—Prince Yamadori), J. Conlon (cnd), Orch de Paris—Dovunque al Mondo; B. F. Pinkerton Giù; Bimba, Bimba, Non Piangere; Ah! Vieni! Sei Mia!; Un Bel Dì; Ora a Noi; Petali d'Ogni Fior; Coro a Bocca Chiusa; Prelude; Io So Che Alle Sue Pene; Ah! Son Vili; E Sia! A Lui Devo Obbedir; Butterfly! *(rec Olivier Messiaen Auditorium, Paris, 1996)*
Sony Classical ▲ SK 61972 [DDD]

Cowan, Sigmund (bar)
Mascagni, P.:Nerone, w. R. Didonè (sop), D. Di Domenico (ten), M. Dirks (bar), Harry Peeters (bass), Shapero (sgr), Strow-Piccolo (sgr), Tcholakov (sgr), K. Bakels (cnd), Hilversum RSO, Hilversum Chorus [I] Bongiovanni 2-▲ GB 2052/53 [DDD]
Mascagni, P.:Il piccolo Marat, w. S. Neves (sop—Mariella), C. Pfeiler (mez—Principessa di Fleury), D. Galvez-Vallejo (ten—Marat), S. Cowan (bar—Soldier), M. Dirks (bar—Il Ladro), F. Vassar (bass—L'Orco), H. Claessens (bass—Spy), K. Bakels (cnd), Netherlands RSO, Netherlands Radio Chorus *(rec Feb. 9, 1992)* Bongiovanni 2-▲ GB 2168/69 [DDD]
Schreker, F.:Die Gezeichneten, w. M. Schmiege (mez), W. Cochran (ten), W. Oosterkamp (bass), E. de Waart (cnd), Dutch Radio PO, Dutch Radio Phil Chorus Marco Polo 3-▲ 8.223328/30

Cox (sgr)
Janáček, L.:Jenůfa, w. H. Hillebrecht (sop), A. Varnay (sop), W. Cochran (ten), R. Kubelik (cnd), Bavarian State Opera Orch, Bavarian State Opera Chorus [G] *(rec live in Munich, Mar. 17, 1970)*
Myto 2-▲ 2 MCD 90422 [ADD]

Cox, Jean (ten)
Wagner, R.:Die Meistersinger von Nürnberg, w. Hannelore Bode (sop), Klaus Hirte (bar), Karl Ridderbusch (bass), Hans Sotin (bass), S. Varviso (cnd), Bayreuth Festival Orch, Bayreuth Festival Chorus [1974] Philips 32-▲ 434420-2 [ADD/DDD]
Wagner, R.:Die Meistersinger von Nürnberg, w. Hannelore Bode (sop), Klaus Hirte (bar), Karl Ridderbusch (bass), Hans Sotin (bass), S. Varviso (cnd), Bayreuth Festival Orch, Bayreuth Festival Chorus [1974] [G] Philips 4-▲ 434611-2 [ADD]

Cox, Kenneth (bass)
Massenet, J.:Hérodiade, w. Renée Fleming (sop—Salome), Dolora Zajick (mez—Hérodiade), Plácido Domingo (ten—Jean), Juan Pons (bar—Erode), Kenneth Cox (bass—Phanuel), V. Gergiev (cnd), San Francisco Opera Orch, San Francisco Opera Chorus Sony Classical 2-▲ S2K 66847
Massenet, J.:Hérodiade (sels), w. Renée Fleming (sop), Dolora Zajick (mez), Kristin Clayton (sgr), Plácido Domingo (ten), Juan Pons (bar), Hector Vásquez (sgr), V. Gergiev (cnd), San Francisco Opera Orch, San Francisco Opera Chorus—highlights *(rec San Francisco Opera, Nov 1994)*
Sony Classical ▲ SK 61965
Massenet, J.:Hérodiade (sels), w. Renée Fleming (sop—Salomé), Dolora Zajick (mez—Hérodiade), Plácido Domingo (ten—Jean), Juan Pons (bar—Hérode), Hector Vásquez (bar—Vitellius), Kenneth Cox (bass—Phanuel), V. Gergiev (cnd), San Francisco Opera Orch, San Francisco Opera Chorus
Sony Classical ▲ SK 61965

Cozette, Michel (bar)
Gounod, C.:Faust, w. M. Berthon (sop), M. Coiffier (sop), J. Montfort (mez), C. Vezzani (ten), L. Musy (b-bar), M. Journet (bass), H. Busser (cnd), Paris Opera Orch, Paris Opera Chorus [F] *(rec 1930)*
Pearl 2-▲ PEA 9987 [AAD]

Cozzi, Laura (sgr)
Verdi, G.:Un giorno di regno, w. Lina Pagliughi (sop), Mario Carlin (ten), Juan Oncina (ten), Sesto Bruscantini (bar), Renato Capecchi (bar), Cristiano Dalamangas (sgr), A. Simonetto (cnd), Milan RAI Lyric Orch, Milan RAI Chorus *(rec 1951)* Cetra Classic 2-▲ CDON 37 [ADD]

Crabben, Jan van der (bar)
Mozart, W.A.:Music of, w. Philip Defrancq (ten), Reginaldo Pinheiro (ten), Jan Vermeulen (pno), Guy Penson (org), P. Peire (cnd), Collegium Instrumentale Brugense, Capella Brugensis—Zerfliesset heut', geliebte Brüder [song]; Dir Seele des Weltalls [cant]; O heiliges Band der Freundschaft [song]; Die ihr einem Neuen Grade [Maurer-Geselienlied]; Die Maurerfreude [cant]; Maurerische Trauermusik; Die ihr der unermesslichen Weltalls Schöpfer ehrt [Kleine deutsche Kantate]; Laut verkünde unsre Freude [Eine kleine Freimaurerkantate]; Lasst uns mit geschlungen Händen [hymn]; Ihr unsre neuen Leiter [song] *(rec Studio Steurbaut, Gent, Dec 1992)* René Gailly ▲ 92013 [DDD]

Crabtree, Libby (sgr)
Purcell, H.:The Indian Queen, w. Catherine Bott (sop—Orazia/Married Woman), Emma Kirkby (sop—Indian Girl/Zempoalla/Cupid), John Mark Ainsley (ten—Indian Boy/Fame/Follower of Cupid/Aerial Spirits), Julian Podger (ten—Follower of Envy/Aerial Spirit), Gerald Finley (bar—Conjurer/Hymen/Follower of Cupid), Helen Parker (sgr—Aerial Spirits), David Thomas (bass—Envy/High Priest/Married Man/Follower of Cupid), Simon Berridge (sgr—Follower of Envy), Libby Crabtree (sgr—Follower of Hymen/Aerial Spirit), Tommy Williams (sgr—God of Dreams), C. Hogwood (cnd), Academy of Ancient Music *(rec Walthamstow Assembly Hall, London, July 1994)*
L'Oiseau-Lyre ▲ 444339-2 [DDD]

Crabtree, Libby (sop)
Finzi, G.:In terra pax, w. Donald Sweeney (bass), D. Hill (cnd), Bournemouth SO, Winchester Cathedral Choir, Waynflete Singers *(rec Winchester Cathedral, Jan 10-13, 1994)*
London ▲ 444130-2 [DDD]

Crader, Jeannine (sop)
Puccini, G.:Il tabarro, w. P. Domingo (ten), C. Ludgin (bar), J. Rudel (cnd), New York City Opera Orch, New York City Opera Chorus *(rec live 1968; stereo)* Melodram ▲ 17048

Craft, Jean (mez)

Mascagni, P.:Cavalleria rusticana, w. Zinka Milanov (sop—Santuzza), Jean Craft (mez—Lucia), Marietta Cosenza (mez—Lola), Giuseppe Gismondo (ten—Turiddu), Benjamin Rayson (bar—Alfio), R. Cellini (cnd), New Orleans Opera Orch, New Orleans Opera Chorus *(rec live, 1963)* VAI Audio ▲ VAIA 1053

Cragg, Richard (sgr)

Myers, G.:God's Trbn, w. Christine Helfrich (sop), Gordon Myers (bar), Matthew Gillis (sgr), Timothy Pehta (sgr), Paul Norman (sgr), Wendy Catlin (sgr) Katherine Mary Hamilton (sgr), Sharon Hunter (sgr), Gloriae Dei Brass Ensemble Paraclete ▲ CDGD 017 [DDD]; ■ GDC 017

Crahay, Christian (nar)

Pousseur, H.:Traverser la forêt, w. Marianne Pousseur (sop), Peter Harvey (bar), J.-P. Peuvion (cnd), Liège New Music Ensemble, Gerhard Sporken (cnd), Vocal Ensemble Adda ▲ ADD 581295 [DDD]

Craig, Charles (ten)

Bellini, V.:Norma, w. J. Sutherland (sop), F. Cossotto (mez), I. Vinco (bass), R. Bonynge (cnd), Buenos Aires Teatro Colón Orch, Buenos Aires Teatro Colón Chorus *(rec live 7/2/69)* Ediciones Teatro Colon 3-▲ ETC 101 [AAD]

Crain, J. (sgr)

Rodgers, R.:State Fair, w. D. Haymes (sgr), *(other artists unknown)* Classic Int'l Filmusicals ▲ CIFC 3009

Crane, Harold (bass)

Puccini, G.:La Bohème, w. Licia Albanese (sop—Mimì), Audrey Schuh (sop—Musetta), Giuseppe di Stefano (ten—Rodolfo), Arthur Cosenza (bar—Schaunard), Giuseppe Valdengo (bar—Marcello), Norman Treigle (bass—Colline), Warren Gadpaille (bass—Benoît/Alcindoro), Thomas Carter (sgr—Parpignol), Harold Crane (sgr—Custom House Official), Steve Harun (sgr—Sergeant), R. Cellini (cnd), New Orleans Opera Orch, New Orleans Opera Chorus *(rec Nov 1959)* VAI Audio 2-▲ VAIA 1119-2 [ADD]

Puccini, G.:Madama Butterfly, w. Dorothy Kirsten (sop—Madama Butterfly), Rosalind Nadell (mez—Suzuki), Eileen Ireland (mez—Kate), Daniele Barioni (ten—Pinkerton), Thomas Carter (ten—Goro), Arthur Cosenza (ten—Yamadori), Richard Torigi (bar—Sharpless), Rodney Hall (bass—The Bronze), Harold Crane (bass—Commissioner), R. Cellini (cnd), New Orleans Opera Orch, New Orleans Opera Chorus *(rec live, Mar 1960)* VAI Audio 2-▲ VAIA 1054-2

Crasnaru, Gheorghe (bass)

Puccini, G.:Tosca, w. Virginia Zeani (sop—Floria Tosca), Emilia Oprea (mez—Shepherd), Nicolae Andreescu (ten—Spoletta), Corneliu Fanateanu (ten—Mario Cavaradossi), Nicolae Herlea (bar—Baron Scarpia), Gheorghe Crasnaru (bass—Cesare Angelotti), Constantin Gabor (bass—Sacristan), Pompei Harasteanu (bass—Jailer), Adrian Stefanescu (bass—Sciarrone), C. Trailescu (cnd), Romanian Opera Orch, Romanian Opera Chorus *(rec Sept 1977)* Vox Box 2-▲ CDX 5153

Crass, Franz (bass)

Bach, J.S.:Mass in b, BWV 232, w. A. Giebel (sop), J. Baker (mez), N. Gedda (ten), H. Prey (bar), O. Klemperer (cnd), New Philharmonia Orch, BBC Sym Chorus [L] EMI Classics ("Studio" series) 2-▲ ZDMB 63364-2 [ADD]

Beethoven, L. van:Fidelio, w. Ingeborg Hallstein (sop—Marzelline), Christa Ludwig (mez—Leonore/Fidelio), Gerhard Unger (ten—Jaquino), Jon Vickers (ten—Florestan), Walter Berry (bass—Pizarro), Franz Crass (bass—Don Fernando), Gottlob Frick (bass—Rocco), O. Klemperer (cnd), Philharmonia Orch, Philharmonia Chorus EMI Classics 2-▲ CDCB 55170

Beethoven, L. van:Sym 9, "Choral Sym", w. W. Lipp (sop), F. Wunderlich (ten), O. Klemperer (cnd), Philharmonia Orch, Vienna Singverein Arkadia ▲ 759

Brahms, J.:Choral Music, w. Wilma Lipp (sop), Aafje Heynis (cta), W. Sawallisch (cnd), Vienna SO, Vienna Singverein—Ein deutsches Requiem, Op. 45; Academic Festival Ov., Op. 80; Tragic Ov., Op. 81; Schicksalslied, Op. 54; Alto Rhap., Op. 53; Var. on a Theme of Haydn, Op. 56a Philips ▲ 438760-2

Mozart, W.A.:Zauberflöte (sels), w. E. Lear (sop), R. Peters (sop), L. Otto (sop), F. Wunderlich (ten), F. Lenz (ten), D. Fischer-Dieskau (bar), K. Böhm (cnd), Berlin PO, Berlin RIAS Chamber Choir—Scenes & Arias Deutsche Grammophon ▲ 429825-2 [ADD] ■ 429825-4

Orff, C.:Die Kluge, w. L. Popp (sop), J. Van Kesteren (ten), T. Stewart (bar), G. Frick (bass), K. Eichhorn (cnd), Munich RSO Eurodisc 2-▲ 69069-2-RG [ADD]

Orff, C.:Der Mond—Ein kleines Welttheater, w. J. Van Kesteren (ten), T. Stewart (bar), G. Frick (bass), K. Eichhorn (cnd), Munich RSO Eurodisc 2-▲ 69069-2-RG [ADD]

Rossini, G.:Il barbiere di Siviglia, w. Ruth-Margaret Pütz (sop), Annelies Burmeister (mez), Peter Schreier (ten), Hermann Prey (bar), Fritz Ollendorff (bass), O. Suitner (cnd), Berlin State Opera Orch Berlin Classics 2-▲ BER 9021 [ADD]

Smetana, B.:Dalibor, w. Sándor Kónya (ten), Gerd Nienstedt (bass), R. Kubelik (cnd), Bavarian RSO, Bavarian Radio Chorus *(rec live, Munich, 1969)* Serenissima 2-▲ SER 360169

Wagner, R.:Der fliegende Holländer, w. L. Rysanek (sop), A.-M. Bessel (mez), C. Heater (ten), K. Ridderbusch (bass), W. Sawallisch (cnd), La Scala Orch, La Scala Chorus [G] *(rec live, Milan 2/2/66)* Memories 2-▲ HR 4281/82 (m) [ADD]

Wagner, R.:Die Meistersinger von Nürnberg, w. G. Janowitz (sop), B. Fassbaender (mez), S. Kónya (ten), G. Unger (ten), T. Stewart (bar), T. Hemsley (bass), R. Kubelik (cnd), Bavarian RSO, Bavarian Radio Chorus [G] *(rec live, Munich, Oct. 1967)* Myto 4-▲ 4 MCD 92569 [ADD]

Wagner, R.:Die Meistersinger von Nürnberg, w. Gundula Janowitz (sop), Brigitte Fassbaender (mez), Sándor Kónya (ten), Gerhard Unger (ten), Thomas Helmsey (bar), Thomas Stewart (bar), R. Kubelik (cnd), Bavarian RSO, Bavarian Radio Chorus *(rec 1967)* Calig 4-▲ 5097174 [ADD]

Wagner, R.:Parsifal, w. G. Jones (sop), J. King (ten), T. Stewart (bar), D. McIntyre (b-bar), K. Ridderbusch (bass), P. Boulez (cnd), Bayreuth Festival Orch, Bayreuth Festival Chorus [G] *(rec 1970)* Deutsche Grammophon 3-▲ 435718-2 [ADD]

Wagner, R.:Tannhäuser, w. V. de Los Angeles (sop), G. Bumbry (mez), W. Windgassen (ten), G. Stolze (ten), D. Fischer-Dieskau (bar), T. Adam (b-bar), J. Greindl (bass), W. Sawallisch (cnd), Bayreuth Festival Orch, Bayreuth Festival Chorus [G] *(rec 1961)* Myto 3-▲ MCD 93277

Cravcenko, Angelica (mez)

Verdi, G.:Falstaff, w. Augusta Ottrabella (sop—Nannetta), Franca Somigli (sop—Alice), Angelica Cravcenko (mez—Mrs. Quickly), Mita Vasari (mez—Meg), Dino Borgioli (ten—Fenton), Giuseppe Nessi (ten—Bardolfo), Alfredo Tedeschi (ten—Dr. Cajus), Piero Biasini (bar—Ford), Mariano Stabile (bar—Falstaff), Virgilio Lazzari (bass—Pistola), A. Toscanini (cnd), Vienna PO, Vienna State Opera Chorus *(rec Salzburg, Aug 23, 1937)* Minerva 2-▲ MN A36/37 (m) [ADD]

Crawford (sgr)

Verdi, G.:Requiem Mass, w. James (sgr), Shafer (sgr), Farina (sgr), D. Moe (cnd), Oberlin Musical Union Orch [L] Bainbridge 2-▲ BCD 2103 [DDD]

Crawford, M. (sgr)

Lloyd Webber, A.:Music of, w. J. Carreras (ten), S. Brightman (sop), P. Domingo (ten), Royal PO—Cats; Joseph & the Amazing Technicolor Dreamcoat; Requiem; Jesus Christ Superstar; Phantom of the Opera; Aspects of Love; Starlight Express; Evita Polydor ▲ 314 517336-2 ■ 314 517336-4

Lloyd Webber, A.:The Phantom of the Opera, w. S. Brightman (sop) [1986 London cast] Polydor 2-▲ 831273-2 2 ■ 831273-4

Credico, Oslavio di (ten)

Marschner, H.A.:Der Vampyr, w. Carole Farley (sop—Malwina), Nucci Condò (mez—Suse), Oslavio Di Credico (ten—George Dibdin), Josef Protschka (ten—Edgar Aubry), Romano Truffelli (ten—Richard Scrop), Martin Egel (bar—Sir Humphrey Davenaut), Andréa Snarski (bar—Toms Blunt), Siegmund Nimsgern (b-bar—Lord Ruthven), Armando Caforio (bass—Robert Green), Peter Boom (sgr—Il capo dei Vampiri), Carlo Di Giacomo (sgr—James Gadshill), Wolfgang Lenz (sgr—Sir Berkley), Galina Pisarenko (sgr—Janthe), Renzo Scorsoni (sgr—Un servitore di Berkley), Anastasia Tomaszewska Schepis (sgr—Emmy), G. Neuhold (cnd), Rome RAI SO, Rome RAI Chorus *(rec Rome, Jan 26, 1980)* Italia 2-▲ CDC 99 [ADD]

Rossini, G.:La scala di seta, w. Luciana Serra (sop), William Matteuzzi (ten), Roberto Coviello (bar), Natale de Carolis (b-bar), G. Ferro (cnd), Bologna Teatro Comunale Orch Fonit Cetra ("Ricordi" series) 2-▲ FCT RFCD 2003

Salieri, A.:La Locandiera, w. A. Ruffini (sop), G. Sarti (bar), P. Guarnera (bar), F. Luisi (cnd), Emilia Romagna Arturo Toscanini SO [I] *(rec live 1989)* Nuova Era 2-▲ 6888/89 [DDD]

Creech, Philip (ten)

Burleigh, H.T.:Songs, w. Hilda Harris (mez), Steven Cole (ten), Arthur Woodley (bass), Joseph Smith (pno)—Now Sleeps the Crimson Petal; Promis' Lan'; Ethiopia Saluting the Colors; Lovely Dark & Lonely One; Love Watches; Almona; O, Night of Dream & Wonder; His Helmet's Blaze; I Hear His Footsteps, Music Sweet; Thou Art Weary; This is Nirvana; Ahmed's Song of Farewell; Through Moanin' Pines; The Frolic; In de Col' Moonlight; A Jubilee; On Bended Knees; A New Hiding-Place; Worth While; The Jungle Flower; Kashmiri Song; Among the Fuchsias; Till I Wake; By an' By; Ev'ry Time I Feel de Spirit; Deep River; Oh, Didn't it Rain; Swing Low, Sweet Chariot; Wade in de Water; Heav'n, Heav'n Premier ▲ PRCD 1041 [DDD]

Fennimore, J.:Eventide, w. K. Williams (sop), H. Johnsson (mez), T. Rolek (cnd), Chelsea Chamber Ensemble [E] Albany ▲ TROY 023-2 [ADD]

Orff, C.:Carmina burana, w. J. Anderson (sop), B. Weikl (bar), J. Levine (cnd), Chicago SO, Chicago Sym Chorus [G,L] Deutsche Grammophon ▲ 415136-2 [DDD] ■ 415136-4

Creed, Kay (mez)

Puccini, G.:Suor angelica, w. Elisabeth Carron (sop—Angelica), Joan Summers (sop—Genovieffa), Donna Owen (sop—Dolcina), Lou Ann Wyckoff (sop—Alms collector), Hanna Owen (sop—novice), Anthea De Forest (sop—novice), Charlotte Povia (mez—Abbess), Beverly Evans (mez—Monitress), Kay Creed (mez—Mistress), La Vergne Monette (sop/mez—lay sister), Joan August (sop/mez—lay sister), Pearle Goldsmith (sop/mez—other sister), Lila Herbert (sop/mez—other sister), Jodell Kenting (sop/mez—other sister), Ann Pretzat (sop/mez—other sister), Evelyn Sachs (cta—Princess), F. Patanè (cnd), *(orch unknown)* *(rec New York, Feb 23, 1967)* Legato Classics ▲ LCD 212-1 [ADD]

Creeger, Richard (ten)

Verdi, G.:La traviata (sels), w. Ileana Cotrubas (sop—Violetta), Elizabeth Bainbridge (mez—Annina), José Carreras (ten—Alfredo), Richard Creeger (ten—Gastone), Victor Braun (bar—Germont), Richard Van Allen (bass—Grenvil), J. Pritchard (cnd), *(orch unknown)*—Libiamo ne' lietialici; Oh, qual pallor!...Un di felice; Ebben? Che diavol fate?...Amor, dunque non piu; E strano!...Ah, fors'e lui; Follie! Follie!...Sempre libera; Lunge da lei...De' miei bollenti spiriti; Che fai?...Amami, Alfredo; Invitato a qui seguirmi...Ogni suo aver tal femmina; Signora...Parigi, o cara; Ah, non piu...Ah, gran Dio, morir si giovine; E strano! Cessarono gli spasimi del dolore *(rec Apr 15, 1974)* Legato Classics 2-▲ LCD 201-2

Crescini, Laura (sop)

Finzi, A.:Lyrics, w. Simonetta Heger (pno) Nuova Era ▲ NUO 7249

Crespin, Régine (sop)

Beethoven, L. van:Ah, perfido!, w. T. Schippers (cnd), Rome RAI Orch *(rec live 6/6/70)* Melodram 2-▲ CDM 28034 [AAD]

Berlioz, H.:La Damnation de Faust, w. Régine Crespin (sop—Marguerite), Guy Fouché (ten—Faust), Michel Roux (bar—Méphistophélès), Peter van der Bilt (bass—Brander), J. Fournet (cnd), Amsterdam Radio PO, Groot Omroepkoor *(rec Amsterdam, Mar 23, 1963)* Bella Voce 2-▲ BLV 107.202 [AAD]

Berlioz, H.:La Damnation de Faust, w. Andre Turp (ten), Michelle Roux (bar), P. Monteux (cnd), London SO *(rec live, Mar 1962)* Music & Arts 2-▲ CD 928

Debussy, C.:Chansons de Bilitis [F] London ▲ 417813-2 [ADD]

Massenet, J.:Don Quichotte, w. M. Command (sop), G. Bacquier (bar), N. Ghiaurov (bass), R. Bonynge (cnd), Swiss Romande Orch, Swiss Romande Chorus [F] London ("Grand Opera" series) 2-▲ 430636-2 [AAD]

Poulenc, F.:Dialogues des Carmélites, w. D. Duval (sop), L. Berton (sop), D. Scharley (mez), R. Gorr (mez), P. Finel (ten), X. Depraz (bass), P. Dervaux (cnd), Paris Opera Orch [F] EMI Classics 2-▲ CDCB 49331 (m) [ADD]

Poulenc, F.:Songs—7 songs [F] London ▲ 417813-2 [ADD]

Ravel, M.:Shéhérazade Mez, w. E. Ansermet (cnd), Swiss Romande Orch [F] London ▲ 417813-2 [ADD]

Régine Crespin London ("Grandi Voici" series) ▲ 440416-2

Ses Plus Grands Rôles Laserlight ▲ 14263

Strauss, R.:Der Rosenkavalier, w. H. Donath (sop), Y. Minton (mez), M. Jungwirth (bass), G. Solti (cnd), Vienna PO [G] London 3-▲ 417493-2 [ADD]

Wagner, R.:Der Ring des Nibelungen, w. G. Janowitz (sop), C. Ludwig (mez), H. Dernesch (mez), J. Vickers (ten), D. Fischer-Dieskau (bar), D. Thomas (bass), H. von Karajan (cnd), Berlin PO *(rec live at Salzburg Easter Festivals, 1967-1970)* Arkadia 12-▲ 223 (m) [ADD]

Wagner, R.:Der Ring des Nibelungen, w. B. Nilsson (sop), K. Flagstad (sop), C. Watson (sop), C. Ludwig (mez), J. Madeira (mez), S. Svanholm (ten), J. King (ten), G. Stolze (ten), W. Windgassen (ten), G. London (bar), D. Fischer-Dieskau (bar), H. Hotter (b-bar), G. Neidlinger (b-bar), G. Frick (bass), G. Solti (cnd), Vienna PO [G] London 15-▲ 414100-2 [ADD]

Wagner, R.:Der Ring des Nibelungen, w. G. Janowitz (sop), C. Ludwig (mez), H. Dernesch (mez), J. Vickers (ten), D. Fischer-Dieskau (bar), D. Thomas (bass), H. von Karajan (cnd), Berlin PO *(rec late 1960s)* Deutsche Grammophon 15-▲ 435211-2 [ADD]

Wagner, R.:Die Walküre, w. B. Nilsson (sop), C. Ludwig (mez), J. King (ten), H. Hotter (b-bar), G. Frick (bass), G. Solti (cnd), Vienna PO [G] London 4-▲ 414105-2 [ADD]

Crider, Michèle (sop)

Boito, A.:Mefistofele, w. Michèle Crider (sop—Margherita/Elena), Eleonora Jankovic (mez—Marta/Pantalis), Ernesto Gavazzi (ten—Wagner/Nereo), Vincenza La Scola (ten—Faust), Samuel Ramey (bass—Mefistofele), R. Muti (cnd), La Scala Orch, La Scala Chorus *(rec live Mar 3,5 & 8, 1995, Milan)* RCA Victor 2-▲ 09026-68284-2 [DDD]

Verdi, G.:Requiem Mass, w. Markella Hatziano (mez), Gabriel Sadé (ten), Robert Lloyd (bass), R. Hickox (cnd), London SO, London Sym Chorus Chandos ▲ CHAN 9490

Crispi, Massimo (ten)

Scarlatti, A.:Humanità e Lucifero, w. Rossana Bertini (sop), F. Biondi (cnd), Europa Galante Opus 111 ▲ OPS 30-129

Cristoff, Vera de (cta)

Verdi, G.:Rigoletto, w. Lina Pagliughi (sop—Gilda), Linda Brambilla (mez—Countess Ceprano), Vera De Cristoff (cta—Maddalena), Tino Folgar (ten—Duke of Mantua), Giuseppe Nessi (ten—Borsa), Luigi Piazza (bar—Rigoletto), Aristide Baracchi (b-bar—Monterone/Marullo), Salvatore Baccaloni (bass—Sparafucile), Giuseppe Menni (bass—Ceprano), C. Sabajno (cnd), La Scala Orch, La Scala Chorus *(rec La Scala Theatre, Milan, 1927-28)* VAI Audio 2-▲ VAIA 1097-2

Verdi, G.:Rigoletto, w. Lina Pagliughi (sop—Gilda), Linda Brambilla (mez—Contessa di Ceprano), Vera de Cristoff (cta—Maddalena), Tino Folgar (ten—Duca di Mantova), Giuseppe Nessi (ten—Borsa), Aristide Baracchi (bar—Conte di Monterone/Marullo), Luigi Piazza (bar—Rigoletto), Salvatore Baccaloni (bass—Sparafucile), Giuseppe Menni (bass—Conte di Ceprano), C. Sabajno (cnd), La Scala Orch, La Scala Chorus *(rec 1927-28)* Arkadia 2-▲ CD 78003 (m) [ADD]

Criswell, Kim (sop)

The Lorelei, w. London Sinfonietta [cnd:John McGlinn] Angel ▲ CDC 54802

Porter, C.:Anything Goes, w. F. von Stade (mez), J. McGlinn (sgr), C. Groenendaal (sgr), J. Gilford (sgr), London SO, Ambrosian Chorus [original 1934 Broadway version w. original orchestration by Robert Russell Bennett & Hans Spialek] Angel ▲ CDC 49848-2 [DDD]

Porter, C.:Fifty Million Frenchmen, w. H. McGillin (sgr), K. McClelland (sgr), S. Powell (sgr), K. Ziemba (sgr), J. Graae (sgr), J. Harder (sgr), S. Waara (sgr), P. Cass (sgr), J. LeClerc (sgr) [1991 studio cast] New World ▲ 80417-2 [DDD]

Schönberg, C.-M.:Miss Saigon, w. C. Wayne (sgr), M. Freeman (cnd), West End Orch Pickwick ▲ PIC PWKS 4229

Crofoot, Alan (sgr)

Floyd, C.:Markheim, w. Norman Treigle (bass—Markheim), Audrey Schuh (sgr—Tess), Alan Crofoot (sgr—Josiah Creach), William Diard (sgr—Stranger), K. Andersson (cnd), New Orleans Opera Orch, New Orleans Opera Chorus *(rec New Orleans, LA, Mar. 31 & Apr. 2, 1966)* VAI Audio ▲ VAIA 1107

Croft, Dwayne (bar)

Puccini, G.:Manon Lescaut, w. M. Freni (sop—Manon), C. Bartoli (mez—Musici I), L. Pavarotti (ten—Des Grieux), R. Vargas (ten—Edmondo), D. Croft (ten—Lescaut), G. Taddei (bar—Geronte), J. Levine (cnd), Metropolitan Opera Orch, New York Metropolitan Opera Chorus [I] *(rec 1992)* London ▲ 440200-2 [DDD]

Croft, Richard (ten)
Mozart, W.A.:Requiem, w. Ruth Ziesak (sop), Nancy Maultsby (mez), David Arnold (bar), M. Pearlman (cnd), Boston Baroque Orch [completion by Robert Levin; performed on period instruments] *(rec Campion Center, Weston, MA, Nov 2-3, 1994)* Telarc ▲ CD 80410 [DDD]

Crofut, Bill (sgr)
Sing Folk Songs at Tanglewood, w. B. Luxon Omega Classics ▲ OCD 3003 [DDD]
Two Gentlemen Folk, w. B. Luxon Telarc ▲ CD 84401 [DDD] ▮ CS 34401 (D)

Crofut, Bill (sgr/banjo)
Brubeck, C.:Songs, w. Frederica von Stade (sop), Jenny Elkus (sgr), Chris Brubeck (sgr/trbn/pno/db), Mark Vinci (fl), Frank Brown (cl), Edward Arron (vc), Dan Brubeck (dr/perc)—The Distance between Us; La Paloma azul; Strange Meadowlark; Across Your Dreams; Summer Song; Polly; Blue Rondo–A Tribute to Dave; Autumn in Our Town; Thinking of You Thinking of Me; It's a Raggy Waltz; Heart of Winter; In the Grace of Your Room; Lonely on Both Ends of the Road *(rec Sandisfield, MA; Fantasy Studios, Berkeley, CA)* Telarc ▲ CD 80467 [DDD]

Croitoru, Adriana (sop)
Bretan, N.:The Evening Star, w. Adriana Croitoru (sop—King's Daughter), Elena Casian (mez—Lady-in-Waiting), Marius Budoiu (ten—Mariner), Ioan Pojar (ten—Page), Ionel Voineag (ten—Evening Star), Bálint Szabó (bass—Michael the Archangel), B. Hary (cnd), Transylvania PO Cluj *(rec Cluj, Sept 1994)* Nimbus ▲ NI 5463 [DDD]

Crook, Howard (ten)
Bach, J.S.:Cant 73, w. B. Schlick (sop), P. Kooy (bass), P. Herreweghe (cnd), Collegium Vocale Orch, Collegium Vocale Virgin Classics ▲ CDC 59237-2
Bach, J.S.:Cant 80, w. Barbara Schlick (sop), Agnès Mellon (sop), Gérard Lesne (ct), Peter Kooy (bass), P. Herreweghe (cnd), La Chapelle Royale Orch, Collegium Vocale Harmonia Mundi France ∆ HMC 6901326
Bach, J.S.:Cant 105, w. B. Schlick (sop), G. Lesne (mez), P. Kooy (bass), P. Herreweghe (cnd), Collegium Vocale Orch, Collegium Vocale Virgin Classics ▲ CDC 59237-2
Bach, J.S.:Cant 131, w. B. Schlick (sop), G. Lesne (mez), P. Kooy (bass), P. Herreweghe (cnd), Collegium Vocale Orch, Collegium Vocale Virgin Classics ▲ CDC 59237-2
Bach, J.S.:Christmas Oratorio, w. B. Schlick (sop), M. Chance (ct), P. Kooy (bass), P. Herreweghe (cnd), Ghent Collegium Vocale Orch, Ghent Collegium Vocale [G] Virgin Classics (Veritas) 2-▲ ZDCB 59530-2 [DDD]
Bach, J.S.:Magnificat, BWV 243, w. A. Mellon (sop), B. Schlick (sop), G. Lesne (ct), P. Kooy (bass), P. Herreweghe (cnd), La Chapelle Royale Orch, Collegium Vocale [L] Harmonia Mundi France ▲ HMC 901326
Bach, J.S.:Mass in b, BWV 232, w. C. Högman (sop), M. Groop (mez), P. Salomaa (bass), Drottningholm Baroque Ensemble, Mikaeli Chamber Choir Proprius 2-▲ PRCD 9070/71
Bach, J.S.:Mass in b, BWV 232, w. B. Schlick (sop), C. Patriasz (cta), C. Brett (ct), P. Kooy (bass), P. Herreweghe (cnd), Collegium Vocale Orch, Collegium Vocale [L] Virgin Classics ("Veritas" series) 2-▲ CDCB 59517-2 [DDD]
Bach, J.S.:St. John Passion, w. B. Schlick (sop), C. Patriasz (cta), W. Kendall (ten), P. Kooy (bass), P. Lika (bass), P. Herreweghe (cnd), La Chapelle Royale Orch, Ghent Collegium Vocale [G] Harmonia Mundi France 2-▲ HMC 901264/65 [DDD]
Bach, J.S.:St. Matthew Passion, w. B. Bonney (sop), A. Monoyios (sop), A. S. von Otter (mez), M. Chance (ct), A. Rolfe Johnson (ten), O. Bär (bar), A. Schmidt (bar), C. Hauptmann (bass), J. E. Gardiner (cnd), English Baroque Soloists, Monteverdi Choir London [G] Archiv 3-▲ 427648-2 [DDD]
Bach, J.S.:St. Matthew Passion, w. B. Schlick (sop), R. Jacobs (ct), H. P. Blochwitz (ten), U. Cold (bass), P. Kooy (bass), P. Herreweghe (cnd), La Chapelle Royale Orch, Ghent Collegium Vocale [G] Harmonia Mundi France 3-▲ HMC 901155/57
Berlioz, H.:Les Nuits d'été, w. D. Montague (mez), C. Robbin (mez), G. Cachémaille (bar), J.E. Gardiner (cnd), Lyon Opera Orch [F] Erato ("Musifrance" series) ▲ 2292-45517-2 [DDD]
Berlioz, H.:Songs, w. B. Fournier (sop), D. Montague (mez), C. Robbin (mez), G. Cachémaille (bar), J.E. Gardiner (cnd), Lyon Opera Orch—Zaïde [Fournier]; La belle voyageuse [Montague]; La Captive [Robbin]; La mort d'Ophélie [Robbin]; Le jeune pâtre breton [Crook]; Aubade [Crook]; Le Chasseur danois [Cachémaille] [F] Erato ("Musifrance" series) ▲ 2292-45517-2 [DDD]
Charpentier, M.-A.:Leçons de ténèbres, H. 96-110, w. Jan Caals (ten), Harry Ruyl (ten), Luc de Meulenaere (ct), Michel Verschaeve (bar), Kurt Widmer (bass), L. Devos (cnd), Musica Polyphonica Erato 2-▲ ERA 96376 [DDD]
Charpentier, M.-A.:Le Malade imaginaire, w. C. Brua (sop), N. Rime (sop), M. Zanetti (sop), D. Visse (ct), J.-F. Gardeil (bar), W. Christie (cnd), Les Arts Florissants [F] Harmonia Mundi France ▲ HMC 901336
du Mont, H.:Motets pour la chapelle du roy, w. H. Lamy (ten), P. Harvey (bar), O. Schneebeli (cnd), Musica Aeterna, Les Pages de la Chapelle *(rec Sept. 1993)* FNAC Music ▲ 592054 [DDD]
Handel, G.F.:Messiah, w. Arleen Augér (sop), Anne Sofie von Otter (mez), Michael Chance (ct), John Tomlinson (bass), T. Pinnock (cnd), English CO, English Concert Choir [E] Archiv 2-▲ 423630-2 [DDD]
Lalande, M.-R. de:Dies Irae, w. P. Kwella (sop), L. Perillo (sop), H. Lamy (ten), P. Harvey (bar), P. Herreweghe (cnd), La Chapelle Royale Orch, Chapelle Royale Choir [L] Harmonia Mundi France ▲ HMC 901352
Lalande, M.-R. de:Miserere mei, Deus, w. P. Kwella (sop), L. Perillo (sop), H. Lamy (ten), P. Harvey (bar), P. Herreweghe (cnd), La Chapelle Royale Orch, Chapelle Royale Choir [L] Harmonia Mundi France ▲ HMC 901352
Lully, J.-B.:Armide, w. V. Gens (sop), N. Rime (sop), G. Laurens (mez), G. Ragon (ten), P. Herreweghe (cnd), La Chapelle Royale Orch, Collegium Vocale [F] Harmonia Mundi France 2-▲ HMC 901456/57
Lully, J.-B.:Phaëton, w. V. Gens (sop), J. Smith (sop), R. Yakar (sop), J.-P. Fouchécourt (ten), M. Minkowski (cnd), Musiciens du Louvres Erato 2-▲ 91737
Monteverdi, C.:Vespro della Beata Vergine, w. A. Mellon (sop), G. Laurens (mez), D. Thomas (bass), P. Herreweghe (cnd), Toulouse Saqueboutiers, Chapelle Royale Choir, Collegium Vocale [L] Harmonia Mundi France 2-▲ HMC 901247/48 [DDD]
Purcell, H.:Airs & Duets, w. J. Dooley (ct) [E] Elektra/Nonesuch ▮ 71343-4
Purcell, H.:Airs & Duets, w. Jeffrey Dooley (ct) Lyrichord ("Early Music" series) ▲ LYR CD 8024
Purcell, H.:The Fairy Queen, w. Lorraine Hunt (sop), Susan Bickley (mez), Catherine Pierard (mez), Mark Padmore (ten), David Wilson-Johnson (bar), Richard Wistreich (bass), R. Norrington (cnd), London Classical Players, Schütz Choir London EMI Classics ▲ CDCB 55234
Rameau, J.P.:Le Berger fidèle, w. Christine Brandes (sop), Ann Monoyios (sop), Nat Wilson (b-bar), Concert Royal Newport Classic ▲ NPT 85555
Rameau, J.P.:Les Indes galantes, w. C. McFadden (sop), S. Piau (sop), I. Poulenard (sop), N. Rime (sop), M. Ruggeri (sop), H. Crook (ten), J.-P. Fouchecourt (ten), N. Rivenq (bar), J. Corréas (bass), B. Delétré (bass), W. Christie (cnd), Les Arts Florissants [F] Harmonia Mundi France 3-▲ HMC 901367/69
Rameau, J.P.:Pygmalion, w. A. Mellon (sop—Céphise), D. Michel-Dansac (sop—La Statue), S. Piau (sop—L'Amour), H. Crook (ten—Pygmalion), W. Christie (cnd), Les Arts Florissants, Les Arts Florissants Chorus [F] *(rec 5/91)* Harmonia Mundi France ▲ HMC 901381

Crook, Paul (ten)
Handel, G.F.:Messiah (sels), w. Arleen Augér (sop), Anne Sofia von Otter (mez), Michael Chance (ct), John Tomlinson (bass), T. Pinnock (cnd), English CO, English Concert Choir [E] Archiv ▲ 427664-2 [DDD] ▮ 427664-4

Crookes, Anna (sop)
Bach, J.S.:Magnificat, BWV 243, w. Jayne Whitaker (sop), Caroline Trevor (alt), Timothy Robinson (ten), Nicholas Gedge (b-bar), N. Ward (cnd), Northern CO, Oxford Schola Cantorum *(rec St. Peter's Church, Hale, Cheshire, Dec. 2, 1993)* Naxos ▲ 8.550763 [DDD]
Schütz, H.:Weihnachtshistorie, w. Anna Crookes (sop—Angel), Paul Agnew (ct—Evangelist), Michael McCarthy (bass—Herod), Jeremy Summerly (cnd), Oxford Camerata *(rec Oxford, Aug 1995)* Naxos ▲ 8.553514 [DDD]
Vivaldi, A.:Gloria, RV.589, w. Jayne Whitaker (sop), Caroline Trevor (alt), Christine Swain (ob), Robert Glenton (vc), Christopher Stokes (org), N. Ward (cnd), Northern CO, Oxford Schola Cantorum *(rec St. Peter's Church, Hale, Cheshire, Dec. 3, 1993)* Naxos ▲ 8.550767 [DDD]

Crooks, Richard (ten)
The Artistry of Richard Crooks, Vol. 1 *(rec between 1927 & 1941)* Pearl ▲ PEA 9093 [DDD]
Moon of My Delight *(rec 1923-39)* Claremont ▲ GSE 785062
Opera Stars Sing on Radio, Vol. 1:Unpublished Broadcasts from the Fourties, w. Dusolina Giannini (sop), Helen Traubel (sop), Gladys Swarthout (cta), Lauritz Melchoir (ten), Robert Merrill (bar), Lawrence Tibbett (bar), Ezio Pinza (bass) Enterprise ("The Radio Years" series) ▲ ENTRY 11
Richard Crooks in Song:Smilin' Through Happy Days ▲ CDHD 215 [ADD]
Song of Songs Claremont ▲ GSE78 50 53

Croonen, Maria (sgr)
Shostakovich, D.:From Jewish Folk Poetry, w. Annelies Burmeister (mez), Peter Schreier (ten), K. Sanderling (cnd), Berlin SO Berlin Classics ▲ BER 9016 [ADD]

Crosby, Bing (sgr)
Berlin, I.:Blue Skies, w. F. Astaire (sgr), *(other artists unknown)* *(rec Hollywood, CA, 1946)* VJC ▲ VJC 1012-2
Berlin, I.:Blue Skies, w. F. Astaire (sgr), *(other artists unknown)*—sels from the 1946 soundtrack Sandy Hook ▲ CDSH 2095 ▮ CSH 2095
Berlin, I.:Holiday Inn, w. F. Astaire (sgr) *(rec Hollywood, CA, 1942)* VJC ▲ VJC 1012-2
The Decca Masters, Vol. 2 (1944-1946), w. J. Heifetz (vn), Emanuel Bay (pno), Milton Kaye (pno) *(rec 1944-46)* MCA Classics ▲ MCAD 42212 (m) [ADD]
Loesser, F.:Guys and Dolls, w. F. Sinatra (sgr), D. Martin (sgr), J. Stafford (sgr), D. Shore (sgr), D. Reynolds (sgr), C. Dennis (sgr), A. Sherman (sgr), S. Davis Jr. (sgr), *(other artists unknown)* [studio cast] Reprise ▲ 45014-2 [AAD] ▮ 45014-4
Porter, C.:High Society, w. F. Sinatra (sgr), *(other artists unknown)* Capitol ▲ C21S 93787
Rodgers, R.:Music of, w. R. Vallee (sgr), J. Macdonald (sgr), A. Jolson (sgr), et al., Whiteman, Sinatra (cnd), Whiteman Orch, Sinatra Orch, Paramount Studio Orch—On Your Toes; Jumbo; Present Arms; One Damn Thing After Another; The Boys from Syracuse; Heads Up; Lido Lady; Peggy Ann; Love Me Tonight; Higher & Higher; Spring is Here; The Girl Friend; Simple Simon; Hallelujah; I'm a Bum Pearl ("Flapper" series) ▲ PAST CD 9794 [AAD]

Cross, Gregory (ten)
Berlioz, H.:Les Troyens, w. F. Pollet (sop—Dido), D. Voigt (sop—Cassandre), C. Dubosc (sop—Ascagne), H. Perraguin (cta—Anna), G. Lakes (ten—Aeneas), J.-L. Maurette (ten—Iopas), J. M. Ainsley (ten—Hylas), M. P. (ten—Panthee), G. Cross (ten—Sinon), G. Quilico (bar—Chorebe), J.-P. Courtis (b-bar—Narbal), M. Belleau (bass—Ghost of Hector), R. Schirrer (bass—Priam), C. Dutoit (cnd), Montreal SO, Montreal Sym Chorus London 4-▲ 443693-2 [DDD]
Britten, H.:The Turn of the Screw, w. O. Dyer (sop), J. Vyvyan (sop), A. Mandikian (mez), D. Hemmings (trb), P. Pears (ten), B. Britten (cnd), English Opera Group Orch [E] London ▲ 425672-2 (m) [ADD]

Cross, Joan (sop)
Britten, H.:Folksong Arrs, w. P. Pears (ten), B. Britten (pno) EMI Classics ▲ CDMB 64727
Britten, H.:Peter Grimes (sels), w. P. Pears (tenor), R. Goodall (cnd), *(orch unknown)* EMI Classics ▲ CDMB 64727
Britten, H.:The Rape of Lucretia (sels), w. P. Pears (ten), R. Goodall (cnd), *(orch unknown)* EMI Classics ▲ CDMB 64727
Britten, H.:The Rape of Lucretia (sels), w. Joan Cross (sop—Female Chorus), Kathleen Ferrier (cta—Lucretia), Peter Pears (ten—Male Chorus), Otakar Kraus (sgr—Tarquinius), B. Britten (cnd), English Opera Group Orch *(rec Oct 5, 1946)* Music & Arts ▲ CD 901 [ADD]

Cross, Richard (bass)
Bellini, V.:Norma, w. J. Sutherland (sop), M. Horne (mez), J. Alexander (ten), R. Bonynge (cnd), London SO, London Sym Chorus [I] London 3-▲ 425488-2 [ADD]
Bellini, V.:Norma (sels), w. J. Sutherland (sop), M. Horne (mez), J. Alexander (ten), R. Bonynge (cnd), London SO, London Sym Chorus [I] London ("Opera Gala" series) ▲ 421886-2 [ADD]

Crout, Tamara (sop)
Byrd, W.:Songs, w. Lawrence Lipnik (ct), Louis Bagger (hpd), New York Consort of Viols—Rejoice unto the Lord; Delight is dead; Farewell, false love; Who made thee, Hob, forsake the plough?; My mistress had a little dog; Browning (The leaves bee greene); Ye Sacred Muses *(rec Leverett, MA, May 24-26 & June 23, 1993)* Lyrichord ▲ LEMS 8015 [DDD]

Crow, Sheryl (sgr)
Pavarotti & Friends for War Child, w. L. Pavarotti (ten), Eric Clapton (sgr), Elton John (sgr), Liza Minelli (sgr), Joan Osborne (sgr), Jon Secada (sgr), Eric Clapton (gtr), John McLaughlin (gtr), Marco Armiliato, Edoardo Bennato, José Molina, Al DiMeola, Kelly Family, Ligabue, Litfiba, P *(rec Modena, Italy, 1996)* London ▲ 452900-2 ▮ 452900-4

Cruz, Grace de la (sop)
Rossini, G.:Petite messe solennelle, w. M. L. Gilles (cta), H. D. Saretzki (ten), H. G. Grimm (bass), W. A. Albert (cnd), Northwest German PO, Northwest German Phil Choir [orchestral version] [L] *(rec ca. 1970)* Koch Schwann ▲ 3-1345-2 [ADD]

Csapò, Eva (sop)
Bach, J.S.:Cant 18, w. G. Schnaut (mez), A. Kraus (ten), W. Schöne (bass), H. Rilling (cnd), Bach Ensemble [G] *(rec 1975)* Hänssler Classic ▲ 98.877 [AAD]
Bach, J.S.:Cant 106, "Actus tragicus", w. H. Schwarz (cta), A. Kraus (ten), W. Schöne (bass), H. Rilling (cnd), Bach Ensemble *(rec Jan 1975)* Hänssler Classic ▲ 98.830 [AAD]
Bach, J.S.:Cant 143, w. A. Kraus (ten), W. Schöne (bass), H. Rilling (cnd), Stuttgart Bach Collegium [G] Hänssler Classic ▲ 98.870 [AAD]
Holmès, A.:Songs, w. Alicja Masan (pno)—Sérénade d'hiver; Berceuse; Souvenir; Rondel; Chanson du chamelier; Le chemin du ciel; Journée fleurie; L'opprimée; Sérénade de toujours; Sérénade printanière; Sérénade d'été; Sérénade d'automne; Le brick l'espérance; Fleur de neige; Tireli; En chemin; Chanson catalane; Le château de rêve; Le chevalier au lion Accord ▲ ACD 201252 [DDD]
Mozart, W.A.:Davidde penitente, w. G. Koban (sop), A. Baldin (ten), D. Kurz (cnd), Württemberg CO, Württemburg Choir *(rec 1978)* Allegretto ▲ ACD 8164 [ADD] ▮ ACS 8164
Ponchielli, A.:Romances (misc), w. Gérard Wyss (pno)—Un Sogno; Dimenticar Ben Mio; L'Orfana; La Povera Accord ▲ ACD 220682 [DDD]

Csenki, Á. (mez)
Bach, J.S.:St. Matthew Passion, w. R. Kiss (sop), I. Verebics (sop), J. Németh (mez), P. Cser (ten), J. Mukk (ten), I. Gati (bar), F. Korpás (bar), P. Köves (bass), G. Oberfrank (cnd), Hungarian State SO, Hungarian Festival Choir, Hungarian Radio Children's Choir [G] *(rec Feb 1993)* Naxos 3-▲ 8.550832/34 [DDD]

Cser, Péter (bar)
Bach, J.S.:St. Matthew Passion, w. R. Kiss (sop), I. Verebics (sop), Á. Csenki (mez), J. Németh (mez), J. Mukk (ten), I. Gati (bar), F. Korpás (bar), P. Köves (bass), G. Oberfrank (cnd), Hungarian State SO, Hungarian Festival Choir, Hungarian Radio Children's Choir [G] *(rec Feb 1993)* Naxos 3-▲ 8.550832/34 [DDD]
Werner, G.J.:Vesperae de Apostolis, w. Ágnes Dobszay (sop), Péter Patay (cta), Tamás Bubnó (ten), J. Mezei (cnd), Vienna-Szász CO, Budapest Schola Cantorum *(rec St. Columba's Presbyterian Church, Budapest, June 12-15, 1995)* Hungaroton ▲ HCD 31646 [DDD]
Werner, G.J.:Vesperae de Confessoris, w. Éva Bodrogi (sop), Regina Fülöp (cta), Kornél Pechan (ten), János Mezei (org), J. Mezei (cnd), Vienna-Szász CO, Budapest Schola Cantorum *(rec St. Columba's Presbyterian Church, Budapest, June 12-15, 1995)* Hungaroton ▲ HCD 31646 [DDD]

Csonka, Zsuzsa (sop)
Kálmán, I.:Gräfin Mariza (sels), w. Ingrid Kirtesi (sop), János Berkes (ten), L. Kovács (cnd), Hungarian Operetta Orch—Komm mit nach Varasadin *(rec Budapest, Oct 1995)* Naxos ▲ 8.550941 [DDD]
Kálmán, I.:Gräfin Mariza (sels), w. Ingrid Kirtesi (sop), János Berkes (ten), L. Kovács (cnd), Hungarian Operetta Orch—Auftrittsleid Mariza; Komm Zigány; Grüss mir die süssen *(rec Budapest, Jan 1996)* Naxos ▲ 8.550943 [DDD]
Lehár, F.:Operetta Arias, w. Ingrid Kirtesi (sop), János Berkes (ten), L. Kovács (cnd), Hungarian Operetta Orch—Freunde, das Leben ist lebenswert!; Meine Lippen, sie küssen si heiss [both from Giuditta]; O Mädchen, mein Mädchen [from Friedericke]; Dein ist mein ganzes Herz; Wer hat die Liebe uns ins Herz gesenkt?; Immer nur lächeln; Von Apfelblüten einen Kranz [all from Das Land des Lächlens]; Lippen schweigen [from Die lustige Witwe] *(rec Budapest, Oct 1995)* Naxos ▲ 8.550941 [DDD]
Lehár, F.:Paganini (sels), w. Ingrid Kirtesi (sop), János Berkes (ten), L. Kovács (cnd), Hungarian Operetta Orch—Liebe, du Himmel auf Erden *(rec Budapest, Jan 1996)* Naxos ▲ 8.550943 [DDD]

Csonka, Zsuzsa (sop) (cont.)
Stolz, R.:Arias, w. Ingrid Kirtesi (sop), János Berkes (ten), L. Kovács (cnd), Hungarian Operetta Orch—Ich liebe dich! [from Zauber der Bohème]; Zwei gerzen im Dreiviertaltakt; Du sollst der Kaiser meiner Seele sein [both from Der Favorit]; Adieu, mein kleiner Gardeoffizer [from Das Lied ist aus] *(rec Budapest, Jan 1996)* Naxos ▲ 8.550943 [DDD]
Strauss (II), Joh.:Arias, w. Ingrid Kirtesi (sop), János Berkes (ten), L. Kovács (cnd), Hungarian Operetta Orch—Ov; Klänge der Heimat; Trinke Liebchen! Trinke schnell!; Mein Herr Marquis [all from Die Fledermaus]; Laguenwaltzer [from Eine Nacht in Venedig] *(rec Budapest, Jan 1996)* Naxos ▲ 8.550943 [DDD]
Strauss (II), Joh.:Arias, w. Ingrid Kirtesi (sop), János Berkes (ten), L. Kovács (cnd), Hungarian Operetta Orch—Ov; Wer uns getraut; Als flotter Geist [both from Der Zigeunerbaron]; Frühlingstimmen (waltz); Komm in die Gondel [from Eine Nacht in Venedig] *(rec Budapest, Oct 1995)* Naxos ▲ 8.550941 [DDD]
Zeller, C.A.:Vogelhändler (sels), w. Ingrid Kirtesi (sop), János Berkes (ten), L. Kovács (cnd), Hungarian Operetta Orch—Wie mein Ahn'l zwanzig Jahr' *(rec Budapest, Jan 1996)* Naxos ▲ 8.550943 [DDD]

Csordás, Klára (mez)
Bartók, B.:Songs, w. Adrienne Krausz (pno)—8 Hungarian Folksongs, Sz.64; 5 Hungarian Folksongs, Sz.33; 20 Hungarian Folksongs, Sz.92; 5 Songs, Op. 15, Sz.61; Village Scenes, Sz.78 Pyramid ▲ PYR 13509

Cuberli, Lella (sop)
Mozart, W.A.:Così fan tutte (sels), w. J. Rodgers (sop), C. Bartoli (mez), J. Tomlinson (bass), D. Barenboim (cnd), Berlin PO, Berlin RIAS Chamber Choir Erato ▲ 94821
Mozart, W.A.:Don Giovanni (sels), w. J. Rodgers (sop), J. Tomlinson (bass), F. Furlanetto (bass), D. Barenboim (cnd), Berlin PO, Berlin RIAS Chamber Choir Erato ▲ 94823
Mozart, W.A.:Missa, K.427, w. K. Battle (sop), P. Seiffert (ten), K. Moll (bass), J. Levine (cnd), Vienna PO, Vienna State Opera Chorus Deutsche Grammophon ▲ 423664-2 [DDD]
Mozart, W.A.:Nozze di Figaro (sels), w. J. Rodgers (sop), C. Bartoli (mez), A. Schmidt (bar), D. Barenboim (cnd), Berlin PO, Berlin RIAS Chamber Choir Erato ▲ 94822
Vivaldi, A.:La Sena festeggiante, w. H. Müller-Molinari (mez), S. Nimsgern (b-bar), C. Scimone (cnd), Cappella Coloniensis Cetra Classic ▲ CDC 25 [AAD]

Cuccaro, Constanza (sop)
Bach, J.S.:Cant 11, "Ascension Oratorio", w. M. Georg (alt), A. Kraus (ten), A. Schmidt (bass), H. Rilling (cnd), Württemberg CO, Gächinger Kantorei [G] Novalis ▲ 150028 [DDD]
Bach, J.S.:Cant 11, "Ascension Oratorio", w. M. Georg (alt), A. Kraus (ten), A. Schmidt (bass), H. Rilling (cnd), Württemberg CO, Gächinger Kantorei [G] *(rec 1984)* Hänssler Classic 5-▲ 98.976
Bach, J.S.:Cant 145, w. A. Kraus (ten), A. Schmidt (bass), H. Rilling (cnd), Stuttgart Bach Collegium, Gächinger Kantorei [G] Novalis ▲ 150029 [DDD]
Bach, J.S.:Cant 197, w. M. Georg (mez), P. Huttenlocher (bar), H. Rilling (cnd), Bach Ensemble *(rec Feb 1984)* Hänssler Classic ▲ 98.828 [AAD]

Cucciolla, Riccardo (nar)
Petrassi, G.:Laudes creaturarum, w. L. Lanzillotta (cnd), Musica d'Oggi Bongiovanni ▲ GB 5534 [DDD]

Cuénod, Hughes (ten)
Debussy, C.:Songs, w. M. Isepp (pno)—Cinq poèmes de Baudelaire; Trois poèmes de Mallarmé; Nuit d'étoiles; Fleur des blés; Romance; Dans le jardin; Les angélus; L'ombre des arbres; Mandoline; Le son du cor s'afflige; L'échelonnement des haies [F] Nimbus ▲ NI 5231-2 [ADD]
French Songs & Song Cycles, w. G. Parsons (pno) Nimbus ▲ NI 5027
Hugues Cuenod, w. Joel Cohen (lt), Rose Dobos (pno) Memoire Vive ▲ CD 262020 [ADD]
Le Maître de la Melodie, w. Geoffrey Parsons (pno) *(rec ca. 1978)* Nimbus ▲ NI 5337 [ADD]
Martin, F.:Le Mystère de la Nativité, w. Elly Ameling (sop), Aafje Heynis (cta), Louis Devos (ten), Eric Tappy (ten), Pierre Bollet (bar), Derrik Olsen (bar), Charles Clavensy (b-bar), André Vessières (bass), E. Ansermet (cnd), Swiss Romande Orch, Jeunes de l'Eglise Chorus, Ceneva Motet Chorus Cascavelle 2-▲ CVL 2006 [ADD]
Milhaud, D.:Catalogue de fleurs Nimbus ▲ NI 5337 [ADD]
Milhaud, D.:Poèmes de Leo Latil Nimbus ▲ NI 5337 [ADD]
Offenbach, J.:Les Contes d'Hoffmann, w. J. Sutherland (sop), H. Tourangeau (mez), P. Domingo (ten), G. Bacquier (bar), R. Bonynge (cnd), Swiss Romande Orch London 2-▲ 417363-2 [ADD]
Strauss, R.:Ariadne auf Naxos, w. E. Schwarzkopf (sop), I. Seefried (sop), R. Streich (sop), L. Otto (sop), G. Hoffman (mez), R. Schock (ten), G. Unger (ten), H. Prey (bar), F. Ollendorff (bass), H. von Karajan (cnd), Philharmonia Orch [G] *(rec 1954)* EMI Classics ("Studio" series) 2-▲ CDMB 69296 (m) [ADD]
Strauss, R.:Der Rosenkavalier, w. Jarmila Barton (sop—Marianne), Lisa Della Casa (sop—Sophie), Sena Jurinac (sop—Octavian), Ilva Ligabue (sop—Orphan), Elisabeth Schwarzkopf (sop—Marschallin), Else Schürhoff (mez—Annina), Luisa Villa (mez—Milliner), Hugues Cuénod (ten—Marschallin's majordomo), Erich Majkut (ten—Valzacchi), Giuseppe Nessi (ten—Animal seller), Luciano Della Pergola (ten—Lackey/Faninal's majordomo), Antonio Pirino (ten—An Italian Singer), Gino Del Signore (ten—Lackey/Waiter), Erich Kunz (bar—Herr von Faninal), Paolo Pedani (bar—Lackey), Attilo Barbesi (bass—Lackey/Waiter), Enrico Campi (bass—Waiter), Otto Edelmann (bass—Baron Ochs), Bruno Fichtinger (bass—Notary), Franco Taino (bass—Waiter), Maria Amadini (sgr—Orphan), Pina Carrillo (sgr—Orphan), Joszi Trojan Regar (sgr—Innkeeper), H. von Karajan (cnd), La Scala Orch, La Scala Chorus *(rec La Scala Theater, Milan, Jan. 26, 1952)* Legato Classics 3-▲ LCD 197-3

Cullagh, Majella (sop)
Wallace, V.:Maritana, w. Lynda Lee (mez), Paul Charles Clarke (ten), Ian Caddy (bar), Damien Smith (bar), Quentin Hayes (bass), P. O. Duinn (cnd), RTE Concert Orch, RTE Phil Choir *(rec O'Reilly Hall, Dublin, Sept 1995)* Marco Polo 2-▲ 8.223406-7 [DDD]

Cullum, John (bar)
Everybody's Favorite Wedding Music, w. Philharmonic Wedding Ensemble, Bert Lucarelli (cnd), Marni Nixon (sop) Essex Entertainment ▲ ESD 7050 ■ ESC 7050

Cummings, Paul (bar)
Angeli, Music of Angels, w. PAN Ensemble, William Hite (ten), Harlan B. Hokin (ten), Tapestry *(rec Studio A, National Music Center, Lenox, MA, Sept 11-14, 1995)* Telarc ▲ CD 80448 [DDD]

Cundari, Emilia (sop)
Beethoven, L. van:Sym 9, "Choral Sym", w. Nell Rankin (mez), Albert Da Costa (ten), William Wilderman (bass), B. Walter (cnd), Columbia SO, Westminster Sym Choir *(rec American Legion Hall, Los Angeles, CA, Apr. 6, 1954)* Sony Classical ("Bruno Walter Edition, Vol. 2" series) ▲ SMK 64464 [ADD]
Leo, L.:La Morte di Abele, w. Emilia Cundari (sop—Angelo), Giuliana Matteini (sop—Abele), Adriana Lazzarini (mez—Eva), Ferrando Ferrari (ten—Caino), Paolo Montarsolo (bass—Adamo), C. F. Cillario (cnd), Angelicum CO, Turin Polyphonic Chorus Dynamic 2-▲ CDL 144
Mahler, G.:Sym 2, w. M. Forrester (cta), B. Walter (cnd), New York PO, Westminster Choir [G] Odyssey ■ YT 30848

Cunitz, Maud (sop)
Künneke, E.:Die grosse Sünderin (sels), w. R. Schock (ten), Bajew (sgr), Gehly (sgr), Rau (sgr), Schröder (sgr), Weigelt (sgr), Marszalek (cnd), Cologne RSO, Cologne Radio Chorus [G] Acanta ▲ CD 42483 [DDD]
Strauss, R.:Feuersnot, w. Maud Cunitz (sop—Diemut), Antonia Fahberg (sop—Elsbeth), Irmgard Barth (mez—Wigelis), Liselotte Nölser (sgr—Margret), Karl Ostertag (ten—Schweiker), Marcel Cordes (bar—Kunrad), Kieth Engen (bass—Kofel), Karl Hoppe (bass—Hämerlein), Max Proebstl (bass—Ortolf), Georg Wieter (bass—Jörg), R. Kempe (cnd), Bavarian State Opera Orch, Bavarian State Opera Chorus *(rec Munich Opera Festival, Prince Regent Theater, Aug 14, 1958)* Orfeo d'or 2-▲ 423962
Verdi, G.:I vespri siciliani, w. H. Roswaenge (ten), H. Schlusnus (bar), O. von Rohr (bass), K. Schröder (cnd), Hessian RSO, Hesse Radio Chorus *(rec 1951)* Myto 2-▲ MCD 93279
Wagner, R.:Lohengrin, w. Maud Cunitz (sop—Elsa), Margarete Klose (mez—Ortrud), Rudolf Schock (ten—Lohengrin), Josef Metternich (bar—Friedrich von Telramund), Gottlob Frick (bass—King Henry), W. Schüchter (cnd), North German RSO, North German Radio Chorus, West German Radio Men's Chorus *(rec 1953)* EMI Classics 2-▲ CDHC 65517

Cunningham, Fiona (sgr)
Hildegard Of Bingen:Sacred Songs, w. Jocelyn West (sgr), Vivien Ellis (sgr), Stevie Wishart (sgr/h-g), Hester Briant (sgr), Tara Franks (sgr), Emily Levy (sgr), Lucy Steele (sgr), Vickie Couperim (sgr), Julie Murphy (sgr), Oxford Girls' Choir—Honey & milk beneath her tongue; Ursula's virgins; The devil's virgins; Place of the ancient heart; Zeal of divinity; O fiery spirit; Red river falling; O orzchis ecclesia, Living-light angels; The clouds are grieving; The firstwoman; From their homeland; But the devil mocked; Song to Ecclesia *(rec Toddington, Gloucestershire, England, May 6-8, 1995)* Celestial Harmonies ▲ 13127-2

Cunningham, Richard (alt)
Vivaldi, A.:Magnificat, RV.610, w. S. LeBlanc (sop), D. Forget (sop), H. Ingram (ten), J. Lamon (cnd), Tafelmusik, Tafelmusik Chamber Choir [L] Hyperion ▲ CDA 66247 [DDD]

Cunningham, T. (ten)
Handel, G.F.:Messiah, w. Eileen Farrell (sop), Martha Lipton (cta), William Warfield (bar), E. Ormandy (cnd), Philadelphia Orch, Mormon Tabernacle Choir [E] CBS 2-▲ M2K 00607 ■ M2T 00607

Cupido, Alberto (ten)
Boito, A.:Mefistofele, w. Daniela Dessi (sop), Samuel Ramey (bass), B. Bartoletti (cnd), Florence Maggio Musicale Orch, Florence Maggio Musicale Chorus *(rec live, 1989)* Serenissima 2-▲ SER 360114
Cilea, F.:Adriana Lecouvreur (sels), w. M. Olivero (sop—Adriana), M. Moretto (mez—Princess di Bouillon), A. Cupido (ten—Maurizio), O. Mori (bar—Michonnet), C. Gandolfo (pno) *(rec Apr. 1993)* Bongiovanni ▲ GB 2515 [DDD]
Donizetti, G.:Maria di Rudenz, w. Katia Ricciarelli (sop), Leo Nucci (bar), E. Inbal (cnd), Venice Teatro La Fenice Orch, Venice Teatro La Fenice Chorus Serenissima 2-▲ SER 360157 [DDD]
Verdi, G.:Simon Boccanegra, w. Ned Barth (bar), José Van Dam (b-bar), Manfred Schenk (bass), Daniela Longhi (sgr), Dino Musio (sgr), M. Veltri (cnd), Marseille Opera Orch, Marseille Opera Chorus Lyrinx 3-▲ LYX 127 [DDD]

Cura, José (sgr)
Puccini, G.:Le Villi, w. Stefano Antonucci (bar), Nana Gordaze (sgr), B. Aprea (cnd), Italian International Orch Nuova Era ▲ NUO 7218 [DDD]

Curiel, Nicoletta (mez)
Mozart, W.A.:Nozze di Figaro, w. L. Cherici (sop), K. Mattila (sop), M. McLaughlin (sop), M. Bacelli (mez), U. Benelli (ten), L. Gallo (bar), A. Nosotti (bass), M. Pertusi (bass), G. Tadeo (bass), Z. Mehta (cnd), Florence Maggio Musicale Orch, Florence Maggio Musicale Chorus Sony Classical ▲ SK 53286
Verdi, G.:La traviata, w. T. Fabbricini (sop—Violetta), A. Trevisan (mez—Annina), N. Curiel (mez—Flora), R. Alagna (ten—Alfredo), E. Cossutta (ten—Gastone), E. Gavazzi (ten—Giuseppe), O. Mori (bar—Douphol), E. Capuano (bass—d'Obigny), F. Musinu (bass—Grenvil), R. Muti (cnd), La Scala Orch, La Scala Chorus Sony Classical 2-▲ S2K 52486 [DDD]

Curphey, Margaret (sop)
Wagner, R.:Götterdämmerung (sels), w. R. Hunter (sop), A. Remedios (ten), N. Bailey (bar), C. Grant (bass), R. Goodall (cnd), Sadler's Wells Opera Orch, Sadler's Wells Opera Chorus—Act 3, Scenes 2 & 3 [E] Chandos ("Collect" series) ▲ CHAN 6593 [ADD]

Curry, Corrine (mez)
Mahler, G.:Sym 4, w. H. Farberman (cnd), London SO *(rec 1979)* Vox Box 2-▲ CDX 5123

Curry, Diane (cta)
Ahrold, F.:Poems of Sylvia Plath (3), w. H. Farberman (cnd), London SO CRI ■ C 380
Verdi, G.:Requiem Mass, w. V. Dunn (sop), J. Hadley (ten), P. Plishka (bass), R. Shaw (cnd), Atlanta SO, Atlanta Sym Chorus [L] Telarc 2-▲ CD 80152 [DDD] 2-■ CS 30152 (D)

Curtin, Phyllis (sop)
Bach, J.S.:St. John Passion, w. E. Thomann (sop), E. Alberts (cta), W. Kmentt, J. Van Kesteren (ten), R. Springer (bar), O. Wiener (bar), D. Smith (b-bar), F. Guthrie (bass), F. Lukasowsky (bass), H. Scherchen (cnd), Vienna State Opera Orch, Vienna Academy Chorus [G] *(rec ca 1960)* MCA Classics 2-▲ MCAD2-9804
Bach, J.S.:St. John Passion, w. E. Alberts (cta), W. Kmentt (ten), O. Weiner (ten), H. Scherchen (cnd), Vienna State Opera Orch, Vienna Academy Chorus *(rec 1962)* Enterprise ("Documents" series) ▲ ENT LV 925
Beethoven, L. van:Sym 9, "Choral Sym", w. F. Kopleff (cta), J. McCollum (ten), D. Gramm (bass), F. Reiner (cnd), Chicago SO RCA Gold Seal ▲ 09026-61795-2
Floyd, C.:Susannah, w. Phyllis Curtin (sop—Susannah Polk), Richard Cassilly (ten—Sam Polk), Norman Treigle (bass—Olin Blitch), Marietta Muhs Cosenza (sgr—Mrs. McLean), Marilyn Davidson (sgr—Mrs. Gleaton), Kay Long (sgr—Mrs. Hayes), Jean Young (sgr—Mrs. Ott), Alton Brim (sgr—Elder Hayes), Thomas Carter (sgr—Elder Gleaton), Jack Davis (sgr—Elder McLean), Keith Kaldenberg (sgr—Little Bat McLean), Burton Parker (sgr—Elder Ott), K. Andersson (cnd), New Orleans Opera Orch, New Orleans Opera Chorus *(rec Mar 31, 1962)* VAI Audio 2-▲ VAIA 1115-2 [ADD]
Ginastera, A.:Milena, w. B. Priestman (cnd), Denver SO Phoenix ▲ PHCD 107 [AAD]
Rorem, N.:Ariel, w. Joseph Rabbai (cl), Ryan Edwards (pno) Phoenix ▲ PHCD 126
Rorem, N.:Gloria, w. Helen Vanni (mez), Ned Rorem (pno) Phoenix ▲ PHCD 126
Rorem, N.:Some Trees, w. B. Wolff (cta), D. Gramm (bar), N. Rorem (pno) CRI ▲ CD 657 [ADD]
Rorem, N.:Some Trees, w. B. Wolff (mez), D. Gramm (b-bar), N. Rorem (pno) [E] CRI ■ C 238
Rorem, N.:Songs, w. B. Wolff (cta), D. Gramm (bar) [E] CRI ■ C 238
Sibelius, J.:Luonnotar, w. L. Bernstein (cnd), New York PO *(rec Oct. 19, 1965)* Sony Classical 2-▲ SM2K 47619 [ADD]
Ward-Steinman, D.:Fragments from Sappho, w. D. Baron (fl), D. Glazer (cl), D. Ward-Steinman (pno) [E] CRI ■ C 238

Curtis, E. (sop)
Mahin, B.:Shadows, w. A. Wojtera (perc), C. Conger (pno) Capstone ▲ CPS 8061
Mahin, B.:Shadows, w. Al Wojtera (perc), Caryl Conger (pno) Capstone ▲ CPS 8611

Curzi, Cesare (ten)
Strauss (II), Joh.:Eine Nacht in Venedig (sels), w. Christine Gorner (sop), Rita Streich (sop), Nicolai Gedda (ten), Christian Oppleberg (bar), F. Allers (cnd), Graunke SO, Graunke Chorus Emperor Operetta ▲ KO 86345

Cvejic, Biserka (mez)
Strauss (II), Joh.:Der Zigeunerbaron (sels), w. Rita Streich (sop), Grace Bumbry (mez), Gisela Litz (alt), Nicolai Gedda (ten), Hermann Prey (bar), Kurt Bohme (bass), F. Allers (cnd), Munich Bavarian State Opera Orch, Munich Bavarian State Opera Chorus Emperor Operetta ▲ KO 86346

Cyrille, Roseline (cta)
Schubert, Franz:Mass 5, w. S. Chilcott (sop), Vonk (ten), G. Schwarz (bass), R. Delcroix (cnd), Basque Bayonne-Côte Orch, Ametsa D'Irun Choir [L] Forlane ▲ FOR 16649 [DDD]

Czaja, H. (cta)
Rachmaninoff, S.:All-Night Vigil, w. G. Schmitz (ten), Russian Papel College Choir [F. Jockwig (sgr), E. Lohneisen (sgr), P. Blitznetzow (sgr), J. Stojaspal (sgr)]—No. 2 Christophorus ▲ CHR 74609

Czaková, Ilona (sgr)
Mysliveček, J.:Isacco figura, w. Hye Jin Kim (sgr), Tatiana Korovina (sgr), Victoria Luchianez (sgr), Vladimir Dolezal (ten), Ivan Kusnjer (bar), I. Parik (cnd), Prague Sinfonietta, Pavel Kühn (cnd), Kühn Chorus Supraphon 2-▲ SUP 3209

Czaková, Ivana (sop)
Respighi, O.:La bella dormente nel bosco, w. Ivana Czaková (sop—Old Woman/Green Fairy), Adriana Kohútková (sop—Blue Fairy/Nightingale), Henrietta Lednárová (sop—Frog/Spindle), Jana Valásková (sop—Princess), Dagmar Pecková (mez—Cuckoo/Cat), Denisa Šlepkovská (mez—Queen/Duchess), Karol Bernáth (ten—Doctor), Guillermo Dominguez (ten—Prince April), Igor Pasek (ten—Jester), Ján Durčo (bar—Ambassador), Richard Haan (bar—King/Woodcutter), Stanislav Benačka (bass—Doctor), Anton Kúrnava (bass—Doctor), Marián Smolárik (bass—Doctor), M. Adriano (nar—Mr. Dollar Chèques), M. Adriano (cnd), Slovak RSO Bratislava, Ján Rozehnal (cnd), Slovak Phil Chorus *(rec Concert Hall of the Slovak Radio, Bratislava, June 8-20, 1994)* Marco Polo ("Opera Classics" series) ▲ 8.223742 [DDD]

Czerwenka, Oscar (bass)
Albert, E. d':Tiefland, w. G. Brouwenstijn, H. Hopf, W. Kmentt, E. Wächter, P. Schöffler, R. Moralt (cnd), Vienna SO *(rec 1957)* Philips 2-▲ 434781-2

Czerwenka, Oscar (bass) (cont.)
Cornelius, P.:Der Barbier von Bagdad, w. E. Schwarzkopf (sop), G. Hoffman (cta), N. Gedda (ten), G. Unger (ten), E. Leinsdorf (cnd), Philharmonia Orch, Philharmonia Chorus
EMI Classics ▲ CDMB 65284
Einem, G. von:Der Prozess, w. Lisa Della Casa (sop—Frl. Bürstner/Die Frau des Gerichtsdieners/Leni), Peter Klein (ten—Der Direktorstellvertreter/Der Student), Max Lorenz (ten—Josef K.), Erich Majkut (ten—Ein Bursche), László Szemere (ten—Titorelli), Alois Pernerstorfer (b-bar—Willem/Der Gerichtsdiener), Alfred Poell (b-bar—Der Advokat), Walter Berry (bass—Franz/Kanzleidirektor), Oskar Czerwenka (bass—Der Untersuchungsrichter/Der Prügler), Ludwig Hofmann (bass—Der Aufseher/Ein Passant/Der Geistliche/Der Fabrikant), Polly Batic (sgr—Frau Grubach), Endreh Koreh (sgr—Albert K.), Luise Leitner (sgr—Ein buckliges Mädchen), K. Böhm (cnd), Vienna PO, Vienna State Opera Chorus *(rec Aug 17, 1953)* Orfeo d'or ("Festspiel Dokumente" series) 2-▲ 392952 (m)
Mozart, W.A.:Don Giovanni, w. G. Grob-Prandl (sop), H. Konetzni (sop), M. Stabile (bar), A. Pernerstorfer (b-bar), H. Swarowsky (cnd), Vienna SO, Vienna State Opera Chorus *(rec 1950)*
Preiser 2-▲ PRE 90166 [AAD]
Rossini, G.:Il barbiere di Siviglia, w. R. Grist (sop), F. Wunderlich (ten), E. Wächter (bar), Kunz (sgr), K. Böhm (cnd), Vienna State Opera Orch, Vienna State Opera Chorus *(rec live, Vienna 4/28/66)*
Myto 2-▲ 2 MCD 91752 [ADD]

Dachary, Lina (sop)
Gounod, C.:Le Médecin malgré lui, w. Monique Stiot (mez), Michel Hamel (ten), Joseph Peyron (ten), Christophe Benoit (bar), Janine Capderou (sgr), Jean-Louis Soumagnas (sgr), J.-C. Hartemann (cnd), ORTF Lyric Orch Musidisc ▲ MUS 202322 [AAD]
Hahn, R.:O mon del inconnu!, w. Christiane Château (sop), Monique Stiot (mez), Michel Hamel (ten), Joseph Peyron (ten), Aimé Doniat (bar), Dominique Tirmont (bar), Philippe Gaudin (sgr), Jacques Provins (sgr), J. Brebion (cnd), ORTF Lyric Orch Musidisc 2-▲ MUS 202562 [AAD]
Planquette, R.:Rip van Winkle, w. Claudine Collart (sop), Freda Betti (cta), René Lenoty (ten), Joseph Peyron (ten), Charles Daguerressar (bar), Julien Giovannetti (bar), Jacques Pruvost (bar), Lucien Lovano (bass), Patrick Orladey (sgr), Joëlle Pierre (sgr), M. Cariven (cnd), ORTF Lyric Orch, ORTF Lyric Chorale
Musidisc ▲ MUS 201602 [AAD]

Daggett, P. (ten)
Britten, H.:Hymn to St. Cecilia, w. N. Jenkin (sop), R. Dean (sop), C. Trevor (alt), S. Birchall (bass), H. Christophers (cnd), The Sixteen *(rec 1 & 4/91)* Collins Classics ▲ 12862 [DDD]

Dagnino, Giovanni (bass)
Gesualdo, D.C.:Madrigals, w. Elena Cecchi Fedi (sop), Roberta Invernizzi (sop), Daniela Del Monaco (cta), Roberto Balconi (ct), Gian Paolo Fagotto (ten), Giuseppe Zambon (ten), A. Curtis (cnd), I Fegi Armonici—Book 6 [Se la Mia Morte Brami; Beltà Poi Che T'Assenti; Tu Piangi O Fille Mia; Resta di Darmi Noia; Chiaro Risplender Suole; others] Symphonia ▲ SYM 94133
Scarlatti, A.:Abramo, il tuo sembiante, w. S. Piccolo (sop), L. Bacchetta (sop), M. Lazzara (alt), M. Nuvoli (ten), E. Velardi (cnd), Alessandro Stradella Consort [period instrs] [I]
Nuova Era ("Ancient Music" series) ▲ 7117 [DDD]
Stradella, A.:Vocal Music, w. E. Smith (hpd), S. Piccollo (sop), M. Mazzara (alt), R. Balconi (ct), E. Velardi (cnd), Alessandro Stradella Consort—Sinfonia in E from the Cantata "Crudo Mar"; Toccata in a for Harpsichord; Exultate in Deo Fideles, Motet for Bass Solo & Violins; Si Apra al Riso Ogni Labbro, Cantata for 3 Voices & Strings [I,L] Bongiovanni ▲ GB 2123 [DDD]

Dagois, Catherine (cta)
Duparc, H.:Songs, w. E. Teufel (pno)—La vie antérieure; Le manoir de Rosemonde; Extase; Au pays où se fait la guerre; Soupir; Lamento; Phidylé Bayer ▲ 100170
Fauré, G.:Songs, w. E. Teufel (pno)—Fleur jetée; Le secret; Clair de lune; Au bord de l'eau; Automne; Mandoline; Après un rêve; Prison Bayer ▲ 100170

Daguerressar, Charles (bar)
Planquette, R.:Rip van Winkle, w. Claudine Collart (sop), Lina Dachary (sop), Freda Betti (cta), René Lenoty (ten), Joseph Peyron (ten), Julien Giovannetti (bar), Jacques Pruvost (bar), Lucien Lovano (bass), Patrick Orladey (sgr), Joëlle Pierre (sgr), M. Cariven (cnd), ORTF Lyric Orch, ORTF Lyric Chorale
Musidisc ▲ MUS 201602 [AAD]

Dahl, Anne Margrethe (sop)
Gade, N.W.:Frühlings Fant, w. Kirsten Dolberg (cta), Gert Hennig-Jensen (ten), Sten Byriel (bass), Elisabeth Westenholz (pno), M. Schønwandt (cnd), Tivoli SO *(rec Tivoli Concert Hall, Apr 29–30, May 4, 1996)* Marco Polo/Dacapo ▲ 8.224051 [DDD]
Langgaard, R.:Songs, w. Ulrich Staerk (pno)—5 Lieder [text Rittershaus]; Lieder von Goethe; 5 Lieder [text Eichendorff/Heine]; Marienlied [text Eichendorff]; Waldeslieder [text Redwitz]; Aus alten Märchen [text Heine]; Lyriches Intermezzo von Heinrich Heine; Wer zum ersten Male liebt [text Heine] *(rec Frederiksdal Castle, Lolland, Sept. 4–6, 1994)* Marco Polo ("dacapo" series) ▲ 8.224011 [DDD]
Orff, C.:Carmina burana, w. B. Grek (ten), J. Wolanski (bass), I. Stupel (cnd), Artur Rubinstein PO, Artur Rubinstein Phil Chorus *(rec Apr. 1991)* Danacord ▲ DACOCD 400 [DDD]

Dahl, Tracy (sop)
Glitter & Be Gay, w. Calgary PO [cnd:Mario Bernardi] *(rec May 14–16, 1992)*
CBC Records ("SM 5000" series) ▲ SMCD 5125 [DDD]

Dahlberg, Stefan (ten)
Haeffner, J.C.F.:Electra (sels), w. H. Martinpelto (sop), G. Hoffstedt (sop), P.-A. Wahlgren (bar), T. Schuback (cnd), Drottningholm Baroque Ensemble—3 recitatives & arias [Sw] *(rec 1989–90)*
Musica Sveciae ▲ MSCD 426 [DDD]
Naumann, J.G.:Arias, w. G. Hoffstedt (sop), H. Martinpelto (sop), P. A. Wahlgren (bar), T. Schuback (cnd), Drottningholm Baroque Ensemble—sels. from Amphion & Cora och Alonzo [Sw]
Musica Sveciae ▲ MSCD 426 [DDD]
Stenhammar, W.:Sången, w. Iwa Sörenson (sop), Anne Sofie von Otter (mez), Per-Arne Wahlgren (bar), H. Blomstedt (cnd), Swedish RSO, Swedish Radio Chorus, Stockholm State Academy of Music Chamber Choir, Adolf Fredrik Music School Children's Choir Caprice ▲ CAP 21358
Uttini, F.A.B.:Thetis och Pelée (sels), w. H. Martinpelto (sop), G. Hoffstedt (sop), P.-A. Wahlgren (bar), T. Schuback (cnd), Drottningholm Baroque Ensemble [Sw] Musica Sveciae ▲ MSCD 426 [DDD]

Dalamangas, Cristiano (sgr)
Rossini, G.:La Cenerentola, w. Ornella Rovero (sop), Miti Truccato Pace (mez), Giulietta Simionato (mez), Cesare Valletti (ten), Saturno Meletti (bar), Vito Susca (bass), M. Rossi (cnd), Turin RAI Orch, Bruno Erminero (cnd), Turin RAI Chorus Fonit Cetra ("Classic Collection" series) ▲ FCT CDON 34
Verdi, G.:Un giorno di regno, w. Lina Pagliughi (sop), Mario Carlin (ten), Juan Oncina (ten), Sesto Bruscantini (bar), Renato Capecchi (bar), Laura Cozzi (sgr), A. Simonetto (cnd), Milan RAI Lyric Orch, Milan RAI Chorus *(rec 1951)* Cetra Classic 2-▲ CDON 37 [ADD]

Dalayman, Katarina (sgr)
Berwald, F.:Estrella de Soria (sels), w. L. Nordin (sop), S. Smith (sgr), A. Lorentzson (sgr), C. Sköld (sgr), S. Westerberg (cnd), Helsingborg SO, Malmö Chamber Choir Musica Sveciae ▲ MSV 523 [DDD]

Dalberg, Frederick (bass)
Britten, H.:Billy Budd, w. P. Pears (ten), T. Uppman (bar), H. Alan (bar), G. Evans (b-bar), B. Britten (cnd), Royal Opera House Orch, Royal Opera House Chorus Covent Garden *(rec Dec. 1, 1951)*
VAI Audio 3-▲ VAIA 1034-3 [ADD]
Wagner, R.:Götterdämmerung, w. M. Fuchs (sop), H. Scheppan (sop), S. Svanholm (ten), R. Burg (bar), K. Elmendorff (cnd), Bayreuth Festival Orch, Bayreuth Festival Chorus *(rec July 21, 1942)*
Preiser 4-▲ PRE 90164 [AAD]
Wagner, R.:Die Meistersinger von Nürnberg, w. E. Schwarzkopf (sop), I. Malaniuk (cta), H. Hopf (ten), G. Unger (ten), E. Kunz (bar), O. Edelmann (b-bar), H. von Karajan (cnd), Bayreuth Festival Orch, Bayreuth Festival Chorus [G] *(rec 1951)*
EMI Classics ("Great Recordings of the Century" series) 4-▲ CDHD 63500 (m) [ADD]
Wagner, R.:Das Rheingold, w. P. Brivkalne (sop), I. Malaniuk (cta), R. Siewert (cta), Fritz (sgr), Pflanzl (ten), S. Björling (bar), W. Faulhaber (bass), L. Weber (bass), H. von Karajan (cnd), Bayreuth Festival Orch, Bayreuth Festival Chorus [G] *(rec live 8/1/51)* Melodram 2-▲ MEL 26107 (m) [AAD]
Wagner, R.:Siegfried, w. A. Varnay (sop), R. Siewert (cta), B. Aldenhoff (ten), P. Kuen (ten), S. Björling (bar), H. Pflanzl (bass), H. von Karajan (cnd), Bayreuth Festival Orch, Bayreuth Festival Chorus [G] *(rec live 1951)* Melodram 4-▲ MEL 46106 (m) [AAD]

Dale, Clamma (sop)
Back to the Earth, w. I. Tomita (cnd), Plasma SO, Nikolai Demidenko (pno), et al. *(rec live, NYC, 1986)*
RCA Red Seal ▲ 7717-2-RC [DDD]

Dale, Clamma (sop) (cont.)
Bernstein, L.:Songfest, w. R. Elias (mez), N. Williams (mez), N. Rosenshein (ten), J. Reardon (bar), D. Gramm (b-bar), L. Bernstein (cnd), National SO Washington D.C. [E]
Deutsche Grammophon ▲ 415965-2 [ADD]

Dale, Laurence (ten)
Boieldieu, F.-A.:Le Calife de Bagdad, w. L. Mayo (sop), J. Michelini (sop), C. Cheriez (mez), H. Rhys-Evans (ten), A. de Almeida (cnd), Camerata Provence Orch, Provence Camerata Chorus [F]
Sonpact ▲ SPT 93007 [DDD]
Gounod, C.:Messe solennelle de St. Cécile, w. B. Hendricks (sop), J.-P. Lafont (bass), G. Prêtre (cnd), Radio France PO, French Radio Chorus [L] EMI Classics ▲ CDC 47094
Honegger, A.:Le Roi David, w. Alessandra Marc (sop), Sylvie Sullé (mez), D. Mesguich (nar), J.-C. Casadesus (cnd), Lille National Orch EMI Classics ▲ CDC 54793
Monteverdi, C.:Orfeo, w. Efrat Ben Nun (sop—Euridice), Laurence Dale (ten—Orfeo), R. Jacobs (cnd), Concerto Vocale Harmonia Mundi France ▲ HMC 901553.54

Dalena, Maurizio (ten)
Cimarosa, D.:Amor rende sagace, w. G. Bertagnolli (sop), D. Bruera (sop), C. Mantese (sop), E. Dara (bar), M. Nicolini (sgr), F. Neri (cnd), Bolzano Claudio Monteverdi Conservatory Youth Orch [I] *(rec live, Bolzano 7/25–27/91)* Bongiovanni 2-▲ GB 2126/27 [DDD]

Dales, Richard (bar)
Hovhaness, A.:Magnificat, w. Audrey Nossaman (sop), Elizabeth Johnson (cta), Thomas East (ten), R. Whitney (cnd), Louisville Orch, Univ of Louisville Choir Crystal ▲ CD 808

Dalis, Irene (mez)
Wagner, R.:Parsifal, w. J. Thomas (ten), G. London (bar), H. Hotter (b-bar), G. Neidlinger (b-bar), H. Knappertsbusch (cnd), Bayreuth Festival Orch, Bayreuth Festival Chorus [1962] [G]
Philips 4-▲ 416390-2 [ADD]

Dallapozza, Adolf (ten)
Lehár, F.:Friederike (sels), w. Helen Donath (sop), Gabriele Fuchs (sop), H. Wallberg (cnd), Munich RSO, Bavarian Radio Chorus Emperor Operetta ▲ KO 86344
Mozart, W.A.:Idomeneo, w. A. Rothenberger (sop), E. Moser (sop), N. Gedda (ten), P. Schreier (ten), T. Adam (b-bar), H. Schmidt-Isserstedt (cnd), Dresden Staatskapelle, Leipzig Radio Chorus
EMI Classics ("Studio" series) 3-▲ CDMC 63990
Schubert, Franz:Mass 5, w. L. Popp (sop), B. Fassbaender (mez), D. Fischer-Dieskau (bar), W. Sawallisch (cnd), Bavarian RSO, Bavarian Radio Chorus [L] EMI Classics ("Studio" series) ▲ CDM 69222
Schubert, Franz:Tantum ergo, D.962, w. L. Popp (sop), B. Fassbaender (mez), D. Fischer-Dieskau (bar), W. Sawallisch (cnd), Bavarian RSO, Bavarian Radio Chorus [L]
EMI Classics ("Studio" series) ▲ CDM 69223
Strauss (II), Joh.:Wiener Blut, w. H. Papouschek (sop), S. Martikke (sop), E. Kales (sop), K. Ruzicka (ten), E. Kuchar (ten), W. Kandutsch (bar), K. Dönch (bar), O. Kolmann (bass), R. Bibl (cnd), Vienna Volksoper Orch, Vienna Volksoper Chorus Denon 2-▲ CO 8105 [DDD]

dall'Argine, S. (sop)
Boito, A.:Mefistofele, w. R. Noli (sop—Margherita), S. dall'Argine (sop—Elena), G. Poggi (ten—Faust), G. Neri (bass-Mefistofele), F. Capuana (cnd), La Scala Orch, La Scala Chorus [I] *(rec 1952)*
Preiser 2-▲ 90122 (m) [AAD]

Daly, Tyne (sgr)
Bernstein, L.:Music of, w. J. Norman (sop), K. Te Kanawa (sop), J. Anderson (sop), F. von Stade (mez), C. Ludwig (mez), T. Troyanos (mez), J. Carreras (ten), D. Garrison (ten), J. Hadley (ten), T. Hampson (bar), G. Kremer (vn), M. Rostropovich (vc), M.T. Thomas (va), L. Bernstein (cnd), *(orch unknown)* —various popular works Deutsche Grammophon ▲ 439251-2 ■ 439251-4

Dami, Magali (sop)
Fauré, G.:Cantique de Jean Racine, w. P. Harvey (bar), M. Corboz (cnd), Lausanne Instrumental Ensemble, Lausanne Vocal Ensemble [F] *(rec Feb. 14–16, 1992)* FNAC Music ▲ 592097 [DDD]
Fauré, G.:Messe basse (in 3 movts), w. M. Corboz (cnd), Lausanne Instrumental Ensemble, Lausanne Vocal Ensemble [L] *(rec Feb. 14–16, 1992)* FNAC Music ▲ 592097 [DDD]
Fauré, G.:Motets, w. P. Harvey (bar), M. Corboz (cnd), Lausanne Instrumental Ensemble, Lausanne Vocal Ensemble—Maria Mater Gratiae, Op. 47; Ave verum, Op. 65/1; Tantum ergo, Op. 65/2; Tu es Petrus; Tantum ergo [L] *(rec Feb. 14–16, 1992)* FNAC Music ▲ 592097 [DDD]
Fauré, G.:Requiem, w. P. Harvey (bar), M. Corboz (cnd), Lausanne Instrumental Ensemble, Lausanne Vocal Ensemble [L] *(rec Feb. 14–16, 1992)* FNAC Music ▲ 592097 [DDD]

Damisch, Siglinde (sop)
Haydn, M.:Requiem in c, w. Gabriele Schreckenbach (mez), Chris Merritt (ten), Hans Udo Müller (pno), Gerhard Walterskirchen (org), E. Hinreiner (cnd), Salzburg RSO, Mozart Choir *(rec June 1981)*
Koch Treasure ▲ 31608-2 [ADD]

Dam-Jensen, Inger (sop)
Mahler, G.:Sym 4, w. J. Hirokami (cnd), Royal PO *(rec Abbey Road Studio, Apr 25–26, 1995)*
Denon ▲ CO 78832 [DDD]

Damone, V. (sgr)
Rodgers, R.:Music of, w. S. Bass (sgr), J. Andrews (sgr), P. Como (sgr), D. Reese (sgr), J. Jones (sgr), N. Luboff (sgr), M. Gold (sgr), N. Walker (sgr), H. Bowen (sgr), P. Nero (pno), J. P. Morgan (sgr), E. Fisher (sgr), B. Goodman (cl), Ann-Margaret (sgr), Shorty Rogers (sgr), D. Shore (sgr), T. Martin (sgr), M. King (sgr), A. Newley (sgr) RCA ▲ 8590-2 R ■ 8590-4 R
Romberg, S.:Deep in My Heart, w. H. Traubel (sgr), J. Ferrer (sgr), R. Clooney (sgr), Gene Kelly (sgr), F. Kelly (sgr), V. Damone (sgr), J. Powell (sgr), A. Miller (sgr), W. Olvis (sgr), C. Richards (sgr), H. Keel (sgr), T. Martin (sgr), J. Weldon (sgr) Sony Music Special Products ▲ AK 47703

Damonte, Magali (mez)
Cherubini, L.:Médée, w. Jano Tamar (sop), Patrizia Ciofi (sgr), Luca Lombardo (sgr), Jean-Philippe Courtis (bass), P. Fournillier (cnd), Italian International Opera Orch, Sluk Chamber Chorus Bratislava *(rec Martina Franca Festival, 1995)* Nuova Era 2-▲ NUO 7253
Ravel, M.:L'Enfant et les sortilèges, w. M. Lagrange (sop), E. Vidal (sop), M. Mahé (mez), A. Chedel (cta), L. Pezzino (ten), M. Barrard (bar), V. le Texier (b-bar), A. Lombard (cnd), Bordeaux-Aquitaine National Orch, Bordeaux Grand Théâtre Municipal Chorus [F] Valois ▲ V 4670

Danco, Suzanne (sop)
Berlioz, H.:La Damnation de Faust, w. D. Poleri (ten), M. Singher (bar), D. Gramm (bass), C. Munch (cnd), Boston SO, Harvard Glee Club [F] RCA Gold Seal 2-▲ 7940-2-RG [ADD]
Berlioz, H.:La Damnation de Faust, w. David Poleri (ten), Martial Singher (bar), Donald Gramm (bass), McHenry Boatwright (bass), Joseph de Pasquale (va), Louis Speyer (hn), C. Munch (cnd), Boston SO, Harvard Glee Club, Radcliffe Choral Society *(rec Feb 1954)*
RCA Victor Gold Seal 8-▲ 0902-668444-2 [ADD]
Fauré, G.:Requiem, w. G. Souzay (bar), E. Ansermet (cnd), Swiss Romande Orch, Tout le Petiz Union Chorus London ("Weekend Classics" series) ▲ 421026-2 [AAD]
Fauré, G.:Songs, w. Roger Boutry (pno)—Prison Memoire Vive ▲ CD 262024
Mozart, W.A.:Don Giovanni, w. L. della Casa (sop), A. Dermota (ten), C. Siepi (b-bar), F. Corena (bass), J. Krips (cnd), Vienna PO, Vienna State Opera Chorus London 3-▲ 411626-2 [ADD]
Ravel, M.:L'Heure espagnole, w. S. Danco (mez—Concepcion), J. Giraudeau (ten—Gonzalve), M. Hamel (ten—Torquemada), J. Cameron (bar—Ramiro), A. Vessières (bass—Gomez), B. Maderna (cnd), BBC SO *(rec Nov. 1960)* Stradivarius ▲ STR 10062 [ADD]
Suzanne Danco in Concert, w. Roger Boutry (pno) Memoire Vive ▲ 262002 (m) [ADD]

Daneman, Sophie (sop)
Purcell, H.:Dido & Aeneas, w. Véronique Gens (sop—Dido), Sophie Marin-Degor (sop—Belinda), Sophie Daneman (sop—2nd woman/1st witch), Gaëlle Mechaly (sop—2nd witch), Claire Brua (mez—Sorceress), Steve Dugardin (alt—Chorus), Jean-Paul Fouchécourt (ten—Spirit/Sailor), Nathan Berg (b-bar—Aeneas), Jonathan Arnold (bass—Chorus), William Christie (hpd), W. Christie (cnd), Les Arts Florissants *(rec Massy Opera Theatre, Nov. 8–11, 1994)* Erato ▲ 98477-2 [DDD]
Rameau, J.P.:Motets, w. N. Rime (sop), P. Agnew (ct), N. Rivenq (bar), N. Cavallier (bass), W. Christie (cnd), Les Arts Florissants—In convertendo, Quam dilecta, Deus noster refugium *(rec June 8–12, 1994)* Erato ▲ 96967-2 [DDD]

Daner (sgr)
Menotti, G.C.:Goya, w. Josie de Guzman (sgr), Hernandez (sgr), Wentzel (sgr), S. Mercurio (cnd), Spoleto Festival Orch, Westminster Choir [I] *(rec live 1991)* Nuova Era 2-▲ 7060/61 [DDD]

Daniecki, John (ten)

Taneyev, S.:Duet for Romeo & Juliet, w. S. Zambalis (sop), P. Tiboris (cnd), Moscow Radio–TV SO Bridge ▲ BCD 9034 [DDD]

Danieli, Lucia (mez)

Puccini, G.:Madama Butterfly, w. M. Callas (sop), N. Gedda (ten), M. Borriello (bar), H. von Karajan (cnd), La Scala Orch, La Scala Chorus [I] *(rec 1955)* EMI Classics 2-▲ CDCB 47959 (m) [ADD]

Daniels, Barbara (sop)

Rodgers, R.:The Sound of Music, w. E. Farrell (sop), F. von Stade (mez), Håkan Hagegård (ten), L. D. von Schlanbusch (sgr), et al., E. Kunzel (cnd), Cincinnati Pops Orch, May Festival Chorus [1987 studio cast] Telarc ▲ CD 80162 [DDD] ■ CS 30162

Daniels, Charles (ten)

Blow, J.:Ode on the Death of Mr. Henry Purcell, w. R. Covey–Crump (ten), P. Holman (cnd), Parley of Instruments Hyperion ▲ CDA 66578 [DDD]

Clarke, J.:Come, Come Along for a Dance & a Song, w. R. Holton (sop), S. Birchall (bass), R. Goodman (cnd), Parley of Instruments, Parley of Instruments Chorus Hyperion ▲ CDA 66578 [DDD]

Dunstable, J.:Sacred Music, w. Robert Harre Jones (ct), Angus Smith (ten), D. Greig (cnd), Orlando Consort—Missa Rex Seculorum; Ave Maris Stella; Gloria in Canon; O Crux Gloriosa; Descendi in Ortum Meum; Speciosa Facta Es; Sub Tuam Portectionem; Veni Sancte Spiritus; Albanus Roseo Rutilat; Specialis Virgo; Preco Preheminencie; Salve Regina Metronome ▲ 1009

Gay, J.:The Beggar's Opera, w. S. Walker (mez), B. Hoskins (sgr), A. Thompson (ten), I. Caddy (b–bar), J. Barlow (cnd), Broadside Band [E] Hyperion 2-▲ CDA 66591/92

Haydn, J.:Mass 3, "Cäcilienmesse", w. Brigette Fournier (sop), Bernarda Fink (alt), Marcus Fink (bass), M. Corboz (cnd), Lisbon Gulbenkian Foundation Orch, Lisbon Gulbenkian Foundation Chorus *(rec July 1993)* FNAC Music ▲ 592309 [DDD]

Odes on the Death of Henry Purcell, w. Holman, Goodman (cnd), Parley of Instruments, Baroque Orch, Baroque Choir, R. Holton (sop), R. Covey–Crump (ten), S. Birchall (bass) Hyperion ▲ CDA 66578 [DDD]

Purcell, H.:Anthems, w. J. Bowman (ct), R. Covey–Crump (ten), M. George (b–bar), King's Consort, New College Choir Oxford Hyperion ▲ CDA 66656

Purcell, H.:Anthems & Services, w. S. Gritton (sop), M. Kennedy (sop), E. O'Dwyer (trb), J. Goodman (trb), J. Bowman (ct), N. Short (ct), Rogers Covey–Crump (ten), M. Milhofer (ten), M. George (bass), R. Evans (bass), R. King (cnd), King's Consort—I Was Glad When They Said unto Me (coronation & verse anthem); O Consider My Adversity; Beati omnes qui timent Dominum; In the Black Dismal Dungeon of Dispair; Save Me, O God; Te Deum in B♭; Jubilant in B♭; Thy Way, O God, Is Holy Hyperion ▲ CDA 66677 [DDD]

Purcell, H.:Anthems & Services, w. James Bowman (ct), Michael George (bass), Robert Evans (bass), R. King (cnd), King's Consort, New College Choir Oxford—O sing unto the Lord; O praise God in His holiness; Praise the Lord, O Jerusalem; It is a good thing to give thanks; O give thanks unto the Lord; Let mine eyes run down with tears; My beloved spake Hyperion ▲ CDA 66585

Purcell, H.:Anthems & Services, w. J. Bowman (ct), R. Covey–Crump (ten), S. Varcoe (bar), M. George (bass), R. King (cnd), King's Consort, New College Choir Oxford—My heart is inditing; The way of God is an undefiled way; Sing unto God; Behold, I bring you glad tidings; Since God so tender a regard; Early, O Lord, my fainting soul; Sleep, Adam, sleep and take thy rest; Awake, ye dead; The earth trembled; Lord not to us but to thy name; O all ye people, clap your hands Hyperion ▲ CDA 66644

Purcell, H.:Music for the Funeral of Queen Mary, w. S. Gritton (sop), M. Kennedy (sop), E. O'Dwyer (trb), J. Goodman (trb), J. Bowman (ct), N. Short (ct), Rogers Covey–Crump (ten), M. Milhofer (ten), M. George (bass), R. Evans (bass), R. King (cnd), King's Consort Hyperion ▲ CDA 66677 [DDD]

Purcell, H.:Songs, w. B. Bonney (sop), S. Gritton (sop), J. Bowman (ct), R. Covey–Crump (ten), M. George (bass), D. Miller (archlt/thb/baroque gtr), M. Caudle (b vl), R. King (org/hpd), King's Consort—Incassum Lesbia; Gentle Shepherds, you that know the charms; I love and I must; Through mournful shades and solitary groves; The Knotting Song Hyperion ▲ CDA 66720 [DDD]

Purcell, H.:Songs, w. B. Bonney (sop), S. Gritton (sop), J. Bowman (ct), R. Covey–Crump (ten), M. George (bass), D. Miller (archlt/thb/baroque gtr), M. Caudle (b vl), R. King (chamber org)—Draw near, you lovers; While Thyrsis, wrapt in downy sleep; Love, thou canst hear, I lov'd fair Celia; What hope for us remains now he is gone; Pastora's beauties, when unblown; A thousand sev'ral ways I tried; Urge me no more; Farewell all joys; If music be the food of love [1st setting]; Amidst the shades and cool refreshing streams; They say you're angry; Let each gallant heart; This poet sings the Trojan wars; Ah, how pleasant 'tis to love; My heart whenever you appear; On the brow of Richard Hill; Rashly I swore I would disown; Since the pox or the plague; Beneath a dark and melancholy grove; Musing on cares of human fate; Whilst Cynthia sung, all angry winds lay still Hyperion ▲ CDA 66710

Purcell, H.:Songs, w. B. Bonney (sop), S. Gritton (sop), J. Bowman (ct), R. Covey–Crump (ten), M. George (bass), R. King (cnd), King's Consort—When Strephon Found; Let Us, Kind Lesbia; Corinna Is Divinely Fair; Olinda in the Shades; If Music Be the Food of Love [3rd setting]; Lovely Albina; I Came, I Saw; No, to What Purpose; Young Thrysis' Fate; She Loves Me and Confesses Too; From Silent Shade (Bess of Bedlam); O Solitude; If Pray'rs and Tears; The Fatal Hour; Sylvia, 'Tis True You're Fair; Amintor, Heedless of His Flocks; Love is Now Become a Trade; Phyllis, I Can Never Forgive It; Who Can Behold?; He Himself Courts His Own Ruin; Let Formal Lovers Still Pursue; Ask Me to Love No More; In Cloris All Soft Charms, Spite of the Godhead Hyperion ▲ CDA 66730

Daniluk, Pavel (bass)

Dvořák, A.:Armida, w. Joanna Borowska (sop—Armida), Monika Brychtová (sgr—Siren), Wieslaw Ochman (ten—Rinald), Richard Sporka (ten—Dudo), Jan Markvart (bar—Sven), Pavel Daniluk (bass—King), George Fortune (bass—Ismen), Zdenek Harvánek (bass—Ubald), Miloslav Podskalský (bass—Peter), Milan Bürger (sgr—Gernand), Roman Janál (sgr—Muezzin/Hlasatel), Vratislav Kříz (sgr—Gottfried), Vladimír Nacházel (sgr—Roger), G. Albrecht (cnd), Czech PO, Prague Chamber Choir *(rec 1995)* Orfeo 2-▲ 404962 [DDD]

Danson, Ted (nar)

Saint-Saëns, C.:Carnival of the Animals, w. M. Golabek (nar), R. Golabek (nar), F. Savage (nar), C. Heston (nar), J. E. Jones (nar), B. White (nar), L. Redgrave (nar), W. Shatner (nar), J. Rivers (nar), L. Tomlin (nar), D. Raffin (nar), A. Hepburn (nar), D. Moore (nar), W. Matthau (nar), J. Smith (nar), L. Schifrin (cnd), Hollywood CO Dove Audio ▲ DOV 30700

Danz, Ingeborg (mez)

Dvořák, A.:Mass, w. D. Röschmann (sop), C. Elsner (ten), J. Mannov (bass), E. Krapp (org), W. Schäfer (cnd), Frankfurt Kantorei Ars Musici ▲ AM 1083-2 [DDD]

Dvořák, A.:Songs, w. E. Krapp (org)—Vier Geistliche Gesange [Four Spiritual Songs], Op. 19a–d Ars Musici ▲ AM 1083-2 [DDD]

Dvořák, A.:Stabat Mater, w. Marina Shaguch (sop), James Taylor (ten), Thomas Quasthoff (bass), H. Rilling (cnd), Oregon Bach Festival Orch, Oregon Bach Festival Choir *(rec Silva Concert Hall, Hult Center for the Performing Arts, Eugene, Oregon, July 8–11, 1995)* Hänssler Classic ("Exclusive" series) 2-▲ CD 98.935 [DDD]

Haydn, J.:The Seven Last Words of Christ on the Cross, w. Pamela Coburn (sop), Uwe Heilmann (ten), Andreas Schmidt (bar), H. Rilling (cnd), Stuttgart Bach Collegium, Gächinger Kantorei [oratorio version] [G] Hänssler Classic ▲ 98.977 [DDD]

Haydn, M.:Requiem in B♭, w. Pamela Coburn (sop), Andreas Schmidt (bar), H. Rilling (cnd), Stuttgart Bach Collegium, Gächinger Kantorei [L] Hänssler Classic ▲ 98.977 [DDD]

Mozart, W.A.:Requiem, w. C. Oelze (sop), S. Weir (ten), A. Schmidt (bar), H. Rilling (cnd), Stuttgart Bach Collegium, Gächinger Kantorei [L] Hänssler Classic 2-▲ 98.979 [DDD]

Dara, Enzo (bar)

Cimarosa, D.:Amor rende sagace, w. G. Bertagnolli (sop), D. Bruera (sop), C. Mantese (sop), M. Dalena (ten), M. Nicolini (sgr), F. Neri (cnd), Bolzano Claudio Monteverdi Conservatory Youth Orch [I] *(rec live, Bolzano 7/25–27/91)* Bongiovanni 2-▲ GB 2126/27 [DDD]

Cimarosa, D.:Il Matrimonio segreto, w. D. Mazzuccato (sop), B. de Simone (bar), A. Cavallaro (cnd), Marchigiana PO Nuova Era ▲ NUO 7014 [DDD]

Donizetti, G.:Don Pasquale, w. L. Serra (sop), A. Corbelli (bar), Bartolo (sgr), B. Campanella (cnd), Turin Teatro Regio Orch, Turin Teatro Regio Chorus [I] *(rec live)* Nuova Era ▲ 6766 [DDD]

Donizetti, G.:Don Pasquale, w. L. Serra (sop), A. Corbelli (bar), Bartolo (sgr), B. Campanella (cnd), Turin Teatro Regio Orch, Turin Teatro Regio Chorus [I] *(rec live)* Nuova Era 2-▲ 6715/16 [DDD]

Dara, Enzo (bar) (cont.)

Donizetti, G.:L'elisir d'amore, w. K. Battle (sop), D. Upshaw (sop), L. Pavarotti (ten), L. Nucci (bar), J. Levine (cnd), Metropolitan Orch, New York Metropolitan Opera Chorus Deutsche Grammophon 2-▲ 429744-2 [DDD]

Donizetti, G.:La fille du régiment, w. L. Serra (sop), M. Tagliasacchi (sop), W. Matteuzzi (ten), B. Campanella (cnd), Bologna Teatro Comunale Orch, Bologna Teatro Comunale Chorus [I] *(rec live, 2/16–26/89)* Nuova Era 2-▲ 6791/92 [DDD]

Paisiello, G.:Il mondo della luna, w. Gemma Bertagnolli (sop—Clarice), Enzo Dara (bar—Buonafede), Riccardo Ristori (bass—Cecco), Carla Di Censo (sgr—Flaminia), Daniele Gaspari (sgr—Ecclittico), Mattia Nicolini (sgr—Ernesto), F. Neri (cnd), Bolzano Monteverdi Orch *(rec Aug 4–6, 1993)* Bongiovanni 2-▲ GB 2173/74 [DDD]

Piccinni, N.:La cecchina, ossia la buona figliola, w. Lucia Alberti (sop—Il Cavaliere Armidoro), Emilia Ravaglia (sop—La Marchesa), Margherita Rinaldi (sop—Cecchina), Elena Zilio (mez—Paoluccia), Ugo Benelli (bar—Il Marchese della Conchiglia), Alessandro Corbelli (bar—Mengotto), Enzo Dara (bar—Tagliaferro), Renata Baldisseri (sgr—Sandrina), G. Gelmetti (cnd), Rome Opera Orch, Rome Opera Chorus *(rec Rome, Feb 4, 1981)* Italia 2-▲ CDC 95 [ADD]

Puccini, G.:Tosca, w. Raina Kabaivanska (sop—Floria Tosca), Nazzareno Antinori (ten—Mario Cavaradossi), Roumen Doikov (ten—Spoletta), Enzo Dara (bar—Casare Angelotti/Il sagrestano), Nelson Portella (bar—Il Barone Scarpia), Stoyan Balabanov (bass—Sciarrone/Un carceriere), Borislav Peev (sgr—Un Pastore), G. Bellini (cnd), Sofia PO, Bulgarian National Radio Children's Choir, Svetoslav Obrenetov Bulgarian National Chorus *(rec Sophia, Bulgaria, Nov 14–27, 1982)* Arts Music ▲ 47158-2 [DDD]

Rossini, G.:Il barbiere di Siviglia, w. M. Horne (mez), L. Nucci (bar), S. Ramey (bass), R. Chailly (cnd), La Scala Orch, La Scala Chorus [I] CBS 3-▲ M3K 37862 [DDD]

Rossini, G.:Il barbiere di Siviglia (sels), w. M. Horne (mez), R. Pierotti (mez), P. Barbacini (ten), L. Nucci (bar), S. Ramey (bass), S. Sammaritano (bass), R. Chailly (cnd), La Scala Orch, La Scala Chorus *(rec Milan, Jan. 2–18, 1982)* Sony Classical ("Opera Highlights" series) ▲ SMK 53501 [DDD]

Rossini, G.:La cambiale di matrimonio, w. S. Jeun (sop—Fanny), M. Laurenza (sop—Clarina), L. Canonici (ten—Edoardo Milfort), R. Frontali (bar—Slook), E. Dara (bar—Tobia Mill), D. Renzetti (cnd), Turin RAI Orch *(rec Aug. 1991)* Ricordi ▲ RFCD 2011 [DDD]

Rossini, G.:La Cenerentola, w. E. Ravaglia (sop), L. V. Terrani (mez), F. Araiza (ten), G. Ferro (cnd), Cappella Coloniensis, Cologne Radio Chorus [I] Sony Classical 2-▲ S2K 46433 [ADD]

Rossini, G.:La Cenerentola, w. C. Bartoli (mez—Cenerentola), F. Costa (mez—Clorinda), G. Banditelli (cta—Tisbe), W. Matteuzzi (ten—Don Ramiro), A. Corbelli (bar—Dandini), E. Dara (bar—Don Magnifico), M. Pertusi (bass—Alidoro), R. Chailly (cnd), Bologna Teatro Comunale Orch, Bologna Teatro Comunale Chorus *(rec June 22–July 2, 1992)* London 2-▲ 436902-2 [DDD]

Rossini, G.:L'italiana in Algeri, w. L. V. Terrani (mez), L. Rizzi (cta), W. Ganzarolli (bar), G. Ferro (cnd), Capella Coloniensis, Cologne Radio Chorus [period instrs] [I] CBS 2-▲ M2K 39048 [ADD]

Rossini, G.:L'italiana in Algeri, w. T. Berganza (sop), L. Zannini (mez), U. Benelli (ten), A. Romero (bar), P. Montarsolo (bass), C. Abbado (cnd), Florence Teatro Comunale Orch, Florence Teatro Comunale Chorus *(rec 1973)* Great Opera Performances ▲ GOP 740

Rossini, G.:L'italiana in Algeri, w. A. Baltsa (mez), F. Lopardo (ten), R. Raimondi (bass), C. Abbado (cnd), Vienna PO, Vienna State Opera Chorus [I] Deutsche Grammophon 2-▲ 427331-2 [DDD]

Rossini, G.:Il turco in Italia, w. M. Caballé (sop), L. Nucci (bar), S. Ramey (bass), R. Chailly (cnd), National PO London, Ambrosian Opera Chorus [I] CBS 2-▲ M2K 37859 [DDD]

Dare, Phyllis (sgr)

Rodgers, R.:Lido Lady (sels), w. H. French (sgr), C. Courtneidge (sgr), *(other artists unknown)* Pearl ("Flapper" series) ▲ PEA CD 9105 [ADD]

Darian, Anita (sop)

Rorem, N.:Dialogues, w. John Stewart (ten), Richard Cumming (pno), Ned Rorem (pno) Phoenix ▲ PHCD 116 [AAD]

Darling, J. (sgr)

Rodgers, R.:Carousel, w. J. Raitt (sgr), J. Clayton (sgr), C. Johnson (sgr), E. Mattson (sgr), M. Vye (sgr), C. Baxter (sgr), J. Littau (cnd) [1945 cast] MCA Classics ▲ MCAD 10048 [AAD] ■ MCAC 10048

Daróczi, Tamás (ten)

Liszt, F.:An die Künstler, w. A. Molnár (ten), J. Molday (bar), L. Domahidy Jr. (bass), I. Zámbó (cnd), Hungarian State Orch, Hungarian People's Army Male Chorus [G] Hungaroton ▲ HCD 12748 [DDD]

Dash (sgr)

Crumb, G.:Ancient Voices of Children, w. J. DeGaetani (mez), A. Weisberg (cnd), Contemporary Chamber Ensemble—[Sp] Elektra/Nonesuch ▲ 79149-2 [AAD]

Dash, Michael (bar)

de Blasio, C.:All the Way through Evening, w. Chris De Blasio (pno) CRI ▲ CD 729 [DDD]

Daszak, John (ten)

Puccini, G.:Tosca, w. Jane Eaglen (sop—Floria Tosca), Charbel Michael (alt—Shepherd Boy), John Daszak (ten—Spoletta), Dennis O'Neill (ten—Mario Cavaradossi), Christopher Booth-Jones (bar—Sciarrone), Ashley Holland (bar—Jailor), Gregory Yurisich (bar—Baron Scarpia), Peter Rose (bass—Cesare Angelotti), Andrew Shore (bass—Sacristan), D. Parry (cnd), Philharmonia Orch, Geoffrey Mitchell Choir, Peter Kay Children's Chorus Chandos ("Opera in English" series) 2-▲ CHAN 3000

Dávalos, Violeta (sgr)

Morales, M.:Ildegonda, w. Violeta Dávalos (sgr—Ildegonda), Grace Echauri (sgr—Idelbene), Raúl Hernàndez (sgr—Rizzardo), Ricardo Santin (sgr—Rolando), F. Lozano (cnd), Carlos Chávez SO, Escuola Nacional de Música Chorus Forlane 2-▲ FRL 16739 [DDD]

Davené, S. (sop)

Jolivet, A.:Suite liturgique, w. S. Davené (sop) , J. Vandeville (ob), *(not advised of cellist or harpist)* REM ▲ REM 311196 [DDD]

Davenport, Mary (mez)

Handel, G.F.:Judas Maccabaeus, w. Martina Arroyo (sop), Lawrence Avery (ten), Jan Peerce (ten), David Smith (bar), T. Scherman (cnd), Vienna State Opera Orch, Vienna Academy Chorus Vox Box 2-▲ CDX 5125 [ADD]

Davià, Frederico (bass)

Donizetti, G.:Il giovedì grasso, w. J. Gomez (sop), J. Peters (mez), J. Hughes (mez), U. Benelli (bar), B. Donlan (bar), E. Esparza (sgr), D. Atherton (cnd), Eireann Radio–TV SO [I] *(rec live, 1970)* Foyer ▲ FOY 2036 [AAD]

Donizetti, G.:Il giovedì grasso, w. J. Gomez (sop), J. Hughes (mez), J. Peters (mez), U. Benelli (bar), B. Donlan (bar), E. Esparza (sgr), M. Williams (sgr), D. Atherton (cnd), Eireann Radio–TV SO [I] *(rec live, 1970)* Memories ▲ HR 4482 [ADD]

Verdi, G.:Un ballo in maschera (sels), w. Margherita Guglielmi (sop), José Carreras (ten), Giovanni Foiani (bass), F. Molinari–Pradelli (cnd), La Scala Orch, La Scala Chorus—S'avanza il Conte...La rivedrà nell'estasi; Ma se m'è forza perderti...Ah! dessa è là! *(rec Milan, Feb 13, 1975)* Goldies ▲ GLD 63203 [ADD]

David, Jean (sgr/lt)

Cantique des Cantiques Studio SM ▲ D 2310 [DDD]

Davidson, Ilana (sop)

Weill, K.:Down in the Valley, w. M. Acito (ten), D. Collup (bar), J. Mabry (sgr), D. P. Lang (sgr), W. Gundlach (cnd), Westphalia CO, Westphalia Kantorei Capriccio ▲ 60 020-1 [DDD]

Davidson, J. (sgr)

Handel, G.F.:Messiah (reorchd Mozart), w. Andrew Murphy (b–bar), M. Altman (sgr), Peter Elvin (sgr), P. Price (sgr), L. Woodside (cnd), Sinfonia Rubinstein, New York Oratorio Society [Sinfonia Rubinstein is made up from musicians from the Lodz Philharmonic Orchestra and the Lodz Opera of Poland] [E] Koch Schwann 2-▲ SC 100308 [DDD]

Davidson, Marilyn (sgr)

Floyd, C.:Susannah, w. Phyllis Curtin (sop—Susannah Polk), Richard Cassilly (ten—Sam Polk), Norman Treigle (bass—Olin Blitch), Marietta Muhs Cosenza (sgr—Mrs. McLean), Marilyn Davidson (sgr—Mrs. Gleaton), Kay Long (sgr—Mrs. Hayes), Jean Young (sgr—Mrs. Ott), Alton Brim (sgr—Elder Hayes), Thomas Carter (sgr—Elder Gleaton), Jack Davis (sgr—Elder McLean), Keith Kaldenberg (sgr—Little Bat McLean), Burton Parker (sgr—Elder Ott), K. Andersson (cnd), New Orleans Opera Orch, New Orleans Opera Chorus *(rec Mar 31, 1962)* VAI Audio 2-▲ VAIA 1115-2 [ADD]

Davies, Arthur (ten)
Elgar, E.:Caractacus, w. J. Howarth (sop), S. Roberts (bar), D. Wilson-Johnson (bar), A.R. Miles (bass), R. Hickox (cnd), London SO, London Sym Chorus [E] *(rec 1992)* Chandos 2-▲ CHAN 9156/57 [DDD]
Elgar, E.:The Dream of Gerontius, w. F. Palmer (sop), G. Howell (bass), R. Hickox (cnd), London SO, London Sym Chorus [E] Chandos 2-▲ CHAN 8641/42 [DDD]
Elgar, E.:The Kingdom, w. M. Marshall (sop), F. Palmer (sop), D. Wilson-Johnson (bar), R. Hickox (cnd), London SO, London Sym Chorus [E] Chandos 2-▲ CHAN 8788/89 [DDD]
Elgar, E.:The Light of Life, w. J. Howarth (sop), L. Finnie (mez), J. Shirley-Quirk (bar), R. Hickox (cnd), London SO, London Sym Chorus Chandos ▲ CHAN 9208 [DDD]
Handel, G.F.:Messiah, w. Lynn Dawson (sop), Catherine Denley (mez), David James (alt), Michael George (bass), H. Christophers (cnd), The Sixteen Orch, The Sixteen [20-member orchestra, 19-member chorus] [E] *(rec 1986)* Hyperion 2-▲ CDA 66251/52 [DDD]
Mendelssohn, F.:Elijah, w. R. Plowright (sop), L. Finnie (mez), J. Budd (trb), J. White (bass), R. Hickox (cnd), London SO, London Sym Chorus [E] Chandos 2-▲ CHAN 8774/75 [DDD]
Mozart, W.A.:Kyrie, K.341, w. K. Te Kanawa (sop), E. Bainbridge (mez), G. Howell (bass), C. Davis (cnd), London SO, London Sym Chorus [L] Philips ▲ 412873-2
Mozart, W.A.:Requiem, w. H. Donath (sop), Y. Minton (mez), G Nienstedt (bass), C. Davis (cnd), BBC SO, John Alldis Choir [L] Philips ▲ 420353-2 [ADD]
Mozart, W.A.:Requiem, w. Y. Kenny (sop), A. Hodgson (mez), G. Howell (bass), R. Hickox (cnd), Northern Sinfonia of England, London Sym Chorus Virgin Classics ▲ CDZ 59648
Mozart, W.A.:Vesperae solennes, w. K. Te Kanawa (sop), E. Bainbridge (mez), G. Howell (bass), C. Davis (cnd), London SO, London Sym Chorus [L] Philips ▲ 412873-2 [ADD]
Parry, H.:Invocation, w. L. Dawson (sop), B. Rayner Cook (bar), M. Bamert (cnd), London PO, London Phil Chorus [E] Chandos ▲ CHAN 9025 [DDD]
Rossini, G.:Stabat Mater, w. H. Field (sop), D. Jones (mez), R. Earle (bass), R. Hickox (cnd), City of London Sinfonia, London Sym Chorus [L] Chandos ▲ CHAN 8780 [DDD]
Sullivan, A.:The Gondoliers, w. W. Lawson (sop), B. Lewis (cta), D. Oldham (ten), M. Bennett (sop), G. Baker (bar), L. Sheffield (bar), H. Lytton (bar), et al., H. Norris (cnd), D'Oyly Carte Opera Company Orch, D'Oyly Carte Opera Chorus—dialogue omitted *(rec 1927)* Pearl 2-▲ PEAS 9961 (m) [AAD]
Walton, W.:Christopher Columbus (suite), w. L. Finnie (mez), R. Hickox (cnd), City of London Sinfonia, Westminster Singers [E] Chandos ▲ CHAN 8824 [DDD]
Walton, W.:Troilus & Cressida, w. Judith Howarth (sop—Cressida), Arthur Davies (ten—Troilus), Nigel Robson (ten—Pandarus), Brian Cookson (ten—3rd Watchman), Peter Bodenham (ten—Priest), Keith Mills (ten—Soldier), Alan Opie (bar—Diomede), James Thornton (bar—Antenor), Clive Bayley (bass—Calkas), David Owen-Lewis (bass—Horaste), R. Hickox (cnd), English Northern Philharmonia, Opera North Chorus Chandos 2-▲ CHAN 9370/71 [DDD]

Davies, Iestyn (trb)
Purcell, H.:Timon of Athens, w. C. de la Hoyde (trb), J. Bowman (alt), J. M. Ainsley (ten), M. George (bass), R. Hickox (cnd), Collegium Musicum 90—Masque Chandos ("Chaconne" series) ▲ CHAN 0558 [DDD]

Davies, Maldwyn (ten)
Bruckner, A.:Requiem, w. J. Rodgers (sop), C. Denley (mez), M. George (bass), Corydon Singers, M. Best (cnd), English CO Hyperion ▲ CDA 66245 [DDD]
Cherubini, L.:Les Deux journées, w. J. Micheau (sop), P. Gianotti (ten), E. Regnier (ten), C. Paul (bar), T. Beecham (cnd), Royal PO, BBC Theater Chorus *(rec live, London Dec. 19, 1947)* Intaglio 2-▲ INCD 7342 [ADD]
Goss, J.:O Saviour of the World, w. David Wilson-Johnson (bar), Andrew Lucas (org), John Scott (cnd), St. Paul's Cathedral Choir, St. Paul's Cathedral Special Choir Conifer Classics ▲ 75605-51193-2 [DDD]
Handel, G.F.:Semele, w. Norma Burrowes (sop), Patrizia Kwella (sop), Elizabeth Priday (sop), Catherine Denley (mez), Della Jones (mez), Timothy Penrose (alt), Anthony Rolfe-Johnson (ct), Robert Lloyd (b-bar), David Thomas (bass), J. E. Gardiner (cnd), English Baroque Soloists, Monteverdi Choir London Erato 2-▲ 2292-45982-2
Haydn, J.:Mass 11, "Nelsonmesse", "Imperial Mass", "Coronation Mass", w. Felicity Lott (sop), Carolyn Watkinson (cta), David Wilson-Johnson (bar), T. Pinnock (cnd), English CO [L] Archiv ▲ 423097-2 [DDD]
Stainer, J.:The Crucifixion, w. David Wilson-Johnson (bar), Andrew Lucas (org), John Scott (cnd), St. Paul's Cathedral Choir, St. Paul's Cathedral Special Choir Conifer Classics ▲ 75605-51193-2 [DDD]

Davies, Marion (sop)
Milhaud, D.:L'Homme et son désir, w. Yvonne Newman (mez), David Barrett (ten), Anthony Holt (bass), D. Milhaud (cnd), BBC SO IMP ("BBC Radio Classics" series) ▲ IMP 5691512

Davies, Neal (bar)
Dutilleux, H.:Prière pour nous autres charnels, w. Martyn Hill (ten), Y. P. Tortelier (cnd), BBC PO Chandos ▲ CHAN 9504
Dutilleux, H.:Sonnets (2) de Jean Cassou, w. Y. P. Tortelier (cnd), BBC PO [arr bar & orch] Chandos ▲ CHAN 9504

Davies, Rydderch (bass)
Verdi, G.:Macbeth, w. Amy Shuard (sop—Lady Macbeth), Noreen Berry (mez—Lady-in-waiting), John Dobson (ten—Malcolm), André Turp (ten—Macduff), Tito Gobbi (bar—Macbeth), Edgar Boniface (bass—Servant), Rydderch Davies (bass—Doctor), Forbes Robinson (bass—Banco), Jean Holmes (sgr—Apparition), Celia Penny (sgr—Apparition), Glynne Thomas (sgr—Apparition), Brian Wrigt (sgr—Araldo), F. Molinari-Pradelli (cnd), Royal Opera House Orch, Royal Opera House Chorus Covent Garden *(rec London, Apr 8, 1960)* Bella Voce 2-▲ 7203 [AAD]

Davies, Ryland (ten)
Mozart, W.A.:Nozze di Figaro, w. Rebecca Evans (sop—Barbarina), Nuccia Focile (sop—Susanna), Suzanne Murphy (sop—Marcellina), Carol Vaness (sop—Countess Almaviva), Susanne Mentzer (mez—Cherubino), Ryland Davies (ten—Don Basilio/Don Curzio), Alessandro Corbelli (bar—Count Almaviva), Alfonso Antoniozzi (bass—Doctor Bartolo/Antonio), Alastair Miles (bass—Figaro), C. Mackerras (cnd), Scottish CO, Scottish Chamber Chorus *(rec Usher Hall, Edingurgh, Scotland, July 31–Aug. 12, 1994)* Telarc 3-▲ CD 80388 [DDD]

Davies, Sheila (nar)
Davies, S.:What Is the Matter in Amy Glennon?, w. Gregory Whitehead (nar—The Idea), Sheila Davies (nar—Amy Glennon/Chorus), Piers McKenzie (nar—Auctioneer), Fran Smith (sgr), Amy Newburg (sgr), Barney Jones (nar—The Fathers) ▲ WN 0013

Davies, Simon (ten)
Bach, J.S.:Cant 208, "Hunting Cant", w. E. Kirkby (sop), J. Smith (sop), M. George (b-bar), R. Goodman (cnd), Parley of Instruments [G] Hyperion ▲ CDA 66169
Biber, H. von:Requiem à 15, w. E. Bongers (sop), A. Grimm (sop), K. Wessel (alt), P. de Groot (alt), M. Reyans (ten), R. Steur (bass), K.-J. de Koning (bass), T. Koopman (cnd), Amsterdam Baroque Orch, Amsterdam Baroque Choir Erato ▲ 91725
Biber, H. von:Vesperae longiores ac breviores una cum litaniis Laurentanis, w. E. Bongers (sop), A. Grimm (sop), K. Wessel (alt), P. de Groot (alt), M. Reyans (ten), R. Steur (bass), K.-J. de Koning (bass), T. Koopman (cnd), Amsterdam Baroque Orch, Amsterdam Baroque Choir Erato ▲ 91725

Davini, Renata (sgr)
Mascagni, P.:Isabeau, w. Marcella Pobbe (sop—Isabeau), Licia Galvano (mez—Giglietta), Pier Miranda Ferraro (ten—Folco), Orazio Gualtiero (bar—Cornelius), Rinaldo Rola (bass—Re Raimondo), Amelia Bazzini (sgr—Ermyngarde), Piero Benzi (sgr—L'araldo), Renata Davini (sgr—Ermynthrude), Piero Francia (sgr—Il Cavaliere), T. Serafin (cnd), San Remo SO *(rec Sanremo, Jan 13, 1962)* Bongiovanni ("Il Mito dell'Opera" series) 2-▲ GB 1135/36-2 [ADD]

Davis, Agnes (sop)
Beethoven, L. van:Sym 9, "Choral Sym", w. Robert Betts (sgr), Ruth Cathcart (sgr), Eugene Lowenthal (sgr), L. Stokowski (cnd), Philadelphia Orch, Philadelphia Orch Chorus *(rec 1934)* Music & Arts ▲ CD 846 [ADD]
Beethoven, L. van:Sym 9, "Choral Sym", w. Robert Betts (sgr), Ruth Cathcart (sgr), Eugene Lowenthal (sgr), L. Stokowski (cnd), Philadelphia Orch Grammofono 2000 ▲ GRM 78577 (m)

Davis, Agnes (sop) (cont.)
Wagner, R.:Der Ring des Nibelungen, w. F. Jagel (ten), L. Tibbett (bar), L. Stokowski (cnd), Philadelphia Orch *(rec 1933–1939)* Pearl 2-▲ CD 9076 [AAD]

Davis, Jack (sgr)
Floyd, C.:Susannah, w. Phyllis Curtin (sop—Susannah Polk), Richard Cassilly (ten—Sam Polk), Norman Treigle (bass—Olin Blitch), Marietta Muhs Cosenza (sgr—Mrs. McLean), Marilyn Davidson (sgr—Mrs. Gleaton), Kay Long (sgr—Mrs. Hayes), Jean Young (sgr—Mrs. Ott), Alton Brim (sgr—Elder Hayes), Thomas Carter (sgr—Elder Gleaton), Jack Davis (sgr—Elder McLean), Keith Kaldenberg (sgr—Little Bat McLean), Burton Parker (sgr—Elder Ott), K. Andersson (cnd), New Orleans Opera Orch, New Orleans Opera Chorus *(rec Mar 31, 1962)* VAI Audio 2-▲ VAIA 1115-2 [ADD]

Davis, Michael Philip (ten)
Moore, D.:Devil & Daniel Webster, w. Joyce Guyer (sop—Mary Stone), Benjamin Bongers (ten—Walter Butler), Michael Philip Davis (ten—Simon Girty), Matthew Foerschler (ten—Miser Stephens), Darren Keith Woods (ten—Mr. Scratch), Michael Lanman (bass—Blackbeard Teach), David Soxman (bass—Clerk), Brian Steele (bass—Daniel Webster), John Stephens (bass—Jabez Stone), Andrew Stuckey (bass—King Philip), Robert Gibby Brand (actor), Cary Miller (actor), R. Patterson (cnd), Kansas City SO, Kansas City Lyric Opera Chorus *(rec Sept 1995)* Newport Classic ▲ NPD 85585 [DDD]

Davis, Osceola (sgr)
Sing Negro Spirituals, w. Jorma Hynninen (bar) Ondine ▲ ODE 715

Davis Jr., Sammy (sgr)
Loesser, F.:Guys and Dolls, w. F. Sinatra (sgr), B. Crosby (sgr), D. Martin (sgr), J. Stafford (sgr), D. Shore (sgr), D. Reynolds (sgr), C. Dennis (sgr), A. Sherman (sgr), *(other artists unknown)* [studio cast] Reprise ▲ 45014-2 [AAD] ■ 45014-4

Davis, T. (nar)
Speach, B.:Music of, w. J. Schanzer, L. Krech (trbn), J. Williams (gtr), A. de Mare (pno), Michael Pugliese (perc), et al., B. Speach (cnd), Bowery Ensemble—Moto for Trombone, Percussion & Piano (1982); Pensées for Guitar (1983); Trajet for Trombone & Percussion (1983); Sonata for Piano (1986); Shattered Glass for Percussion (1987); Telepathy (Poetry/Music Suite) for Speaker, Contrabas Mode ▲ 16

Davis, Tudor (ten)
Vaughan Williams, R.:Hugh the Dover (sels), w. Mary Lewis (sop), M. Sargent (cnd), *(orch unknown)*—Love Duet *(rec 1924–53)* Beulah ▲ 1PD13

Davislim, Steve (ten)
Bertoni, F.:Orfeo ed Euridice, w. Jeannette Fischer (sop—Euridice), Julia Juon (mez—Orfeo), Steve Davislim (ten—Imeneo), R. Tschupp (cnd), Aargauer SO, Aarau New Canton School Choir *(rec Zurich Radio Studio, Oct 30–Nov 1, 1994)* Jecklin ▲ JEC 700

Davoine, Françoise (nar)
Normandeau, R.:Petit Prince, w. Michel Dumont (nar—Aviator), Martin Pensa (nar—Little Prince), Christine Séguin (nar—Rose), Jean Marchand (nar—King), Luc Durand (nar—Conceited Man), Gilles Dupuis (nar—Drunkard), Guy Nadon (nar—Businessman), Jacques Languirand (nar—Lamplighter), Pierre Bourgault (nar—Geographer), Cynthia Dubois (nar—Snake), Monique Giroux (nar—Flower), Françoise Davoine (nar—Rose Garden), Jean-Louis Millette (nar—Fox), Gérard Poirier (nar—Railway Switchman), Claude Préfontaine (nar—Water Pill Salesman) *(rec Montreal, Aug 1994)* CBC 2-▲ 1091 [DDD]

Davrath, Netania (sop)
Beethoven, L. van:Egmont (incidental music), w. Walther Reyer (nar), M. Abravanel (cnd), Utah SO Vanguard Classics 2-▲ OVC 8084/85 [ADD]
Canteloube, J.:New Songs of the Auvergne, w. G. Kingsley (cnd), *(orch unknown)* [orchd Gershon Kingsley; F dialect] Vanguard Classics 2-▲ SVC 38/39 [AAD]
Canteloube, J.:Songs of Auvergne, w. P. de la Roche (cnd), *(orch unknown)*— complete songs Vanguard Classics 2-▲ OVC 8001/02 [ADD]
Canteloube, J.:Songs of Auvergne, w. P. de la Roche (cnd), *(orch unknown)* [F dialect] Vanguard Classics 2-▲ SVC 38/39 [AAD]
Haydn, J.:Mass 10, "Kriegsmesse", "Paukenmesse", w. Hilde Rössl-Majdan (alt), Anton Dermota (ten), W. Bery (bass), Anton Heiller (org), R. Harand (vc), M. Wöldike (cnd), Vienna State Opera Orch, Vienna State Opera Chorus *(rec May 14–16, 1960)* Vanguard Classics ("The Bach Guild" series) ▲ OVC 2518 [ADD]
Honegger, A.:Judith, w. Blanche Christensen (sop), Madeleine Milhaud (nar), M. Abravanel (cnd), Utah SO, Salt Lake City Symphonic Choir [F] *(rec Dec. 1964)* Vanguard Classics ▲ OVC 8088 [ADD]
Honegger, A.:Le Roi David, w. Jean Preston (mez), Marvin Sorenson (ten), M. Singher (nar), M. Milhaud (nar), M. Abravanel (cnd), Utah SO [F] Vanguard Classics ▲ OVC 4038 [ADD]
Mahler, G.:Sym 4, w. M. Abravanel (cnd), Utah SO [G] *(rec 1974)* Vanguard Classics ▲ OVC 4007 [ADD]
Rachmaninoff, S.:Songs, w. M. Abravanel (cnd), Utah SO—Chanson Georgienne Vanguard Classics ▲ SVC 8 [ADD]
Villa-Lobos, H.:Bachiana brasileira 5, w. L. Bernstein (cnd), New York PO *(rec 1963)* Sony Classical ▲ SMK 47544 [ADD]

Davy, V. (nar)
Stravinsky, I.:L'Histoire du soldat, w. J.-L. Millette (nar—Devil), J. Marchand (nar—soldier), A. Robert (cnd), Chambristes de Montreal CBC ("Musica Viva" series) ▲ MVCD 1049 [DDD]

Davydova, Lioia (sop)
Artyomov, V.:Invocation, w. Mark Pekarsky Percussion Ensemble Olympia ▲ OLY 514 [DDD]

Dawson, Anne (sop)
Boughton, R.:The Immortal Hour, w. D. Wilson-Johnson (bar), R. Kennedy (bass), A. Melville (cnd), English CO, Geoffrey Mitchell Choir [E] Hyperion 2-▲ CDA 66101/02 [DDD]
Ferguson, H.:The Dream of the Rood, w. R. Hickox (cnd), London SO, London Sym Chorus [E] Chandos ▲ CHAN 9082 [DDD]

Dawson, Lynne (sop)
Bach, J.S.:Cant 211, "Coffee Cant", w. N. Robertson (ten), S. Adler (bar), Friends of Apollo [G] Meridian ▲ ECD 84110
Bach, J.S.:Cant 212, "Peasant Cant", w. S. Adler (bar), Friends of Apollo [G] Meridian ▲ ECD 84110
Beethoven, L. van:Syms (comp), w. Jard Van Nes (cta), Anthony Rolfe Johnson (ten), Eike Wilm Schulte (bass), F. Brüggen (cnd), Orch of the 18th Century, Lisbon Gulbenkian Foundation Chorus [on Sym. 9] Philips 5-▲ 442156-2
Gluck, C.W.:Iphigénie en Aulide, w. A. S. von Otter (mez), J. Aler (ten), J. Van Dam (b-bar), Lyon Opera Orch, J. E. Gardiner (cnd), Monteverdi Choir London Erato ("Musifrance" series) 2-▲ 2292-45003-2-ZA [DDD]
Gluck, C.W.:La Recontre imprévue, w. C. Le Coz (sop), L. Dawson (sop), C. Dubosc (sop), S. Marin-Degor (sop), G. Fletcher (sgr), F. Dudziak (ten), G. de Mey (ten), J.-L. Viala (ten), G. Cachémaille (bar), J.-P. Lafont (bass), J. E. Gardiner (cnd), Paris Lyon Opera Orch, Paris Lyon Opera Chorus [F] Erato 2-▲ 2292-45516-2 [DDD]
Graun, K.H.:Cesare e Cleopatra, w. Janet Williams (sop), Iris Vermillion (mez), Robert Gambill (ten), R. Jacobs (cnd), Concerto Cologne Harmonia Mundi France 3-▲ HMC 901561.63
Graun, K.H.:Cesare e Cleopatra, w. Janet Williams (sop), Debora Beronesi (sop), Curtis Rayam (ten), R. Jacobs (cnd), Concerto Cologne, Berlin State Opera Chorus members Serenissima 3-▲ SER 360171 [DDD]
Handel, G.F.:Chandos Anthems (11), w. P. Kwella (sop), J. Bowman (alt), I. Partridge (ten), M. George (bass), H. Christophers (cnd), The Sixteen Orch, The Sixteen Chandos ("Chaconne" series) 4-▲ CHAN 0554 [DDD]
Handel, G.F.:Chandos Anthems (11), w. I. Partridge (ten), M. George (bass), H. Christophers (cnd), The Sixteen Orch, The Sixteen—Nos. 1, 2 & 3 Chandos ("Chaconne" series) ▲ CHAN 0503 [DDD]
Handel, G.F.:Chandos Anthems (11), w. I. Partridge (ten), H. Christophers (cnd), The Sixteen Orch, The Sixteen—Anthem Nos. 10 & 11 [E] Chandos ("Chaconne" series) ▲ CHAN 0509 [DDD]
Handel, G.F.:Chandos Anthems (11), w. I. Partridge (ten), H. Christophers (cnd), The Sixteen Orch, The Sixteen—Anthem Nos. 4-6 [E] Chandos ("Chaconne" series) ▲ CHAN 0504 [DDD]
Handel, G.F.:Dixit Dominus, w. Linda Russell (alt), Charles Brett (ct), Ian Partridge (ten), Michael George (bass), H. Christophers (cnd), The Sixteen Orch, The Sixteen [L] Chandos ("Chaconne" series) ▲ CHAN 0517 [DDD]

1130 ▲ = CD ♦ = Enhanced CD Δ = MD ■ = Cassette Tape □ = DCC

Dawson, Lynne (sop) (cont.)
Handel, G.F.:Dixit Dominus, w. Arleen Augér (sop), Diana Montague (mez), Leigh Nixon (ten), Simon Birchall (bass), S. Preston (cnd), Westminster Abbey Orch, Westminster Abbey Choir [L] Archiv ▲ 423594-2 [DDD]
Handel, G.F.:Giulio Cesare in Egitto, w. Eirian James (mez), Guillemette Laurens (mez), James Bowman (alt), Dominique Visse (alt), Nicolas Rivenq (bar), J. Malgoire (cnd), La Grande Ecurie et la Chambre du Roy Astrée 3-▲ E 8558
Handel, G.F.:Messiah, w. Catherine Denley (mez), David James (alt), Arthur Davies (ten), Michael George (bass), H. Christophers (cnd), The Sixteen Orch, The Sixteen [20-member orchestra, 19-member chorus] [E] *(rec 1986)* Hyperion 2-▲ CDA 66251/52 [DDD]
Handel, G.F.:Messiah, w. Hilary Summers (cta), John Mark Ainsley (ten), Alastair Miles (bass), R. Goodman (cnd), Brandenburg Consort, Stephen Cleobury (cnd), King's College Choir Cambridge [1752 version] Argo 2-▲ 440672-2 [DDD]
Handel, G.F.:Saul, w. D. Brown (sop), D. L. Ragin (ct), J. M. Ainsley (ten), A. Miles (bar), J. E. Gardiner (cnd), English Baroque Soloists, Monteverdi Choir London Philips 3-▲ 426265-2 3PH [DDD]
Handel, G.F.:Silete Venti, w. H. Christophers (cnd), The Sixteen Orch, The Sixteen [L] Chandos ("Chaconne" series) ▲ CHAN 0517 [DDD]
Haydn, J.:Die Schöpfung, w. Neil Rosenshein (ten), John Cheek (bass), J. Revzen (cnd), St. Paul CO, Minnesota Chorale Albany 2-▲ AR 005-6-2
Holst, G.:A Choral Fant, w. H. D. Wetton (cnd), Royal PO, Guildford Choral Society Hyperion ▲ CDA 66660
Holst, G.:First Choral Sym, w. H. D. Wetton (cnd), Royal PO, Guildford Choral Society Hyperion ▲ CDA 66660
Howells, H.:Songs, w. C. Pierard (mez), J.M. Ainsley (ten), B. Luxon (bar), J. Drake (pno)—7 various songs; 2 South African Settings; 3 Folksongs; A Garland for De la Mare; Peacock Pie, Op. 33; 4 French Chansons, Op. 29; In Green Ways, Op. 43; 12 various songs; 3 Children's Songs; 4 Songs, Op. 22 Chandos 2-▲ CHAN 9185/86 [DDD]
Mendelssohn, F.:A Midsummer Night's Dream (comp), w. S. Mentzer (mez), J. Tate (cnd), Rotterdam PO, Toonkunst Chorus, Peter Hall Company EMI Classics 2-▲ CDCB 54348
Mozart, W.A.:Don Giovanni, w. N. Argenta (sop), A. Halgrimson (sop), J. M. Ainsley (ten), G. Finley (ten), A. Miles (bar), A. Schmidt (bar), G. Yurisch (bar), R. Norrington (cnd), London Classical Players, Schütz Choir London EMI Classics ▲ CDCB 54859
Mozart, W.A.:Requiem, w. J. van Nes (cta), K. Lewis (ten), S. Estes (bass), C. M. Giulini (cnd), Philharmonia Orch, Philharmonia Chorus [L] Sony Classical ▲ SK 45577 [DDD]
Mozart, W.A.:Vesperae de Dominica, w. E. James (mez), R. Covey-Crump (ten), P. Hillier (bass), S. Cleobury (cnd), Cambridge Classical Players, Hilliard Ensemble, King's College Choir [L] EMI Classics ▲ CDC 49672 [DDD]
Mozart, W.A.:Vesperae solennes, w. E. James (mez), R. Covey-Crump (ten), P. Hillier (bass), S. Cleobury (cnd), Cambridge Classical Players, Hilliard Ensemble, King's College Choir [L] EMI Classics ▲ CDC 49672 [DDD]
Parry, H.:Invocation, w. A. Davies (ten), B. Rayner Cook (bar), M. Bamert (cnd), London PO, London Phil Chorus [E] Chandos ▲ CHAN 9025 [DDD]
Pärt, A.:Passio Domini nostri Jesu Christi secundum Joannem, w. D. James (alt), R. Covey-Crump (ten), J. Potter (ten), G. Jones (bass), M. George (bass), P. Hillier (cnd), Hilliard Ensemble, Western Wind Chamber Chorus [L] ECM New Series ▲ 78118-21370-2 [DDD]; ■ 78118-21370-4 (D)
Purcell, H.:Dido & Aeneas, w. A. S. von Otter (mez), N. Rogers (ten), S. Varcoe (bar), T. Pinnock (cnd), English Concert, *(chorus unknown)* [E] Archiv ▲ 427624-2 [DDD]
Purcell, H.:The Prophetess, or The History of Dioclesian, w. Gillian Fisher (sop), R. Covey-Crump (ten), P. Elliot (ten), S. Varcoe (bar), M. George (bass), J.E. Gardiner (cnd), Monteverdi Orch, Monteverdi Choir London Erato ("Gardiner Purcell Collection" series) 2-▲ 96556-2
Purcell, H.:Timon of Athens, w. Gillian Fisher (sop), R. Covey-Crump (ten), P. Elliott (ten), S. Varcoe (bar), M. George (bass), J.E. Gardiner (cnd), Monteverdi Orch, Monteverdi Choir London Erato ("Gardiner Purcell Collection" series) 2-▲ 96556-2
Rubbra, E.:Sym 9, w. Della Jones (alt), Stephen Roberts (bar), R. Hickox (cnd), BBC Welsh National SO, BBC Welsh National Chorus Chandos ▲ CHAN 9441
Schumann, R.:Myrthen, w. Ian Partridge (ten), Julius Drake (pno) Chandos ▲ CHAN 9307 [DDD]
Vaughan Williams, R.:Riders to the Sea, w. Ingrid Attrot (sop—Nora), Lynn Dawson (sop—Cathleen), Linda Finnie (mez—Maurya), Karl Daymond (bar—Bartley), R. Hickox (cnd), Northern Sinfonia of England Chandos ▲ CHAN 9392 [DDD]
Vaughan Williams, R.:A Song of Thanksgiving, w. John Gielgud (nar), M. Best (cnd), City of London Sinfonia, London Oratory Junior Choir [E] Hyperion ▲ CDA 66569 [DDD]
Vivaldi, A.:Laudate pueri Dominum, RV.601, w. R. King (cnd), King's Consort [L] *(rec 4/86)* Meridian ▲ CDE 84129

Dawson, Peter (b-bar)
German, E.:Music of, w. W. Booth (ten), Sargent (cnd), *(orchs unknown)*—Nell Gwyn:Overture; Pavane from Romeo & Juliet; Glorious Devon; Henry VIII:Overture; Gipsy Suite; Tom Jones (sels.); The English Rose from Merrie England; Theme & 6 Diversions; Rolling Down to Rio; Valse Gracieuse from Leeds Suite; Berceuse from The Tempter; March Rhapsody on Original Themes *(rec 1920-1939)* Pearl ▲ PEA 9024 [AAD]
A Green & Pleasant Land:Peter Dawson Sings 19 Traditional Favorites *(rec 1912-1937)* Pearl ▲ PEA 9336 (m) [AAD]
Songs & Arias, w. Dawson, Peter (b-bar) Memoir Classics ▲ CDMOIR 434
Songs of the Sea (Stanford) & Other Songs of Sea & Empire *(rec 1925-1937 for HMV)* Pearl ▲ PEA 9384 (m) [AAD]

Day, Doris (sgr)
Broadway, w. Ethel Merman (sgr), Judy Holliday (sgr), Dick van Dyke (sgr), Topol (sgr), Mary Martin (sgr), Jill Haworth (sgr), William Warfield (sgr), et al. Sony Classical ("Greatest Hits" series) ▲ MLK 62365 ■ MLT 62365

Day, Edith (sgr)
Kern, J.:Show Boat (sels), w. P. Robeson (b-bar), J. Bledsoe (sgr), M. Burke (sgr), *(other artists unknown)* [original cast] Pearl ("Flapper" series) ▲ PEA CD 9105 [ADD]

Dayiantis-Straub, Linda (sop)
Caldara, A.:Vaticini di pace, w. Mary Enid Hains (sop), Jennifer Lane (mez), David Arnot (ten), K. Mallon (cnd), Aradia Baroque Ensemble *(rec Toronto, Canada, Jan 1996)* Naxos ▲ 8.553772 [DDD]

Daymond, Karl (bar)
Purcell, H.:Dido & Aeneas, w. Rebecca Evans (sop—Belinda), Maria Ewing (sop—Dido), Mary Plazas (sop—1st witch), Patricia Rozario (sop—2nd woman), Sally Burgess (mez—Sorceress), Pamela Helen Stephens (mez—2nd witch), James Bowman (ct—Spirit), Jamie MacDougal (ten—Sailor), Karl Daymond (bar—Aeneas), R. Hickox (cnd), Collegium Musicum 90 Chandos ("Early Music" series) ▲ CHAN 0586 [DDD]
Vaughan Williams, R.:Riders to the Sea, w. Ingrid Attrot (sop—Nora), Lynn Dawson (sop—Cathleen), Linda Finnie (mez—Maurya), Karl Daymond (bar—Bartley), R. Hickox (cnd), Northern Sinfonia of England Chandos ▲ CHAN 9392 [DDD]

Deam, Donna (sop)
Fauré, G.:Messe basse (in 3 movts), w. J. Scott (org), J. Rutter (cnd), Cambridge Singers [L] Collegium ▲ COLCD 109 [DDD] ■ COLC 109 (D)
Poulenc, F.:Gloria Sop, w. J. Rutter (cnd), City of London Sinfonia, Cambridge Singers [L] Collegium ▲ COLCD 108 [DDD] ■ COLC 108 (D)
Purcell, H.:Dido & Aeneas, w. L. Hunt (sop), L. Saffer (sop), C. Brandes (sop), R. Rainero (sop), E. Rabiner (mez), P. Elliot (ten), M. Dean (bar), N. McGegan (cnd), Philharmonia Baroque Orch, Clare College Choir Cambridge Harmonia Mundi USA ▲ HMU 907110
Purcell, H.:Dido & Aeneas, w. Ruth Holton (sop—Belinda), Elisabeth Priday (sop—2nd Woman), Donna Deam (sop—1st Witch), Shauna Beesley (sop—2nd Witch), Teresa Shaw (mez—Sorceress), Carolyn Watkinson (cta—Dido), Jonathan Peter Kenny (alt—Spirit), Paul Tindall (ten—Sailor), George Mosley (bass—Aeneas), J.E. Gardiner (cnd), English Baroque Soloists, Monteverdi Choir London *(rec Saint George's, Bristol, UK, July 12-14, 1990)* Philips ▲ 432114-2
Rutter, J.:Requiem, w. C. Ashton (sop), J. Rutter (cnd), City of London Sinfonia, Cambridge Singers [E,L] Collegium ▲ COLCD 103 [DDD] ■ COLC 103 (D)

Dean, Benjamin (trb)
Salisbury Cathedral Choir, w. [cnd:Richard Seal], Salisbury Cathedral Choir, Richarl Seal (org) Metronome ▲ MET CD 1016

Dean, Michael (b-bar)
Handel, G.F.:Agrippina, w. S. Bradshaw (sop), W. Hill (sop), L. Saffer (sop), G. Banditelli (cta), D. Minter (alt), R. Popken (alt), B. Szilágyi (bar), N. Isherwood (bass), N. McGegan (cnd), Capella Savaria [period instrs] [I] Harmonia Mundi USA 3-▲ HMU 907063/65 ■ HMU 407063/65
Handel, G.F.:Ottone, Rè di Germania, w. Julianna Gondek (sop), Lisa Saffer (sop), Patricia Spence (mez), Drew Minter (alt), R. Popken (alt), N. McGegan (cnd), Freiburg Baroque Orch *(rec June 9-12, 1992)* Harmonia Mundi USA 3-▲ HMU 907073/75
Handel, G.F.:Radamisto, w. Monika Frimmer (sop), Juliana Gondek (sop), Dana Hanchard (sop), Lisa Saffer (sop), R. Popken (cta), Nicholas Cavallier (bass), N. McGegan (cnd), Freiburg Baroque Orch Harmonia Mundi USA 3-▲ HMU 907111/13
Purcell, H.:Dido & Aeneas, w. L. Hunt (sop), L. Saffer (sop), D. Deam (sop), C. Brandes (sop), R. Rainero (sop), E. Rabiner (mez), P. Elliot (ten), N. McGegan (cnd), Philharmonia Baroque Orch, Clare College Choir Cambridge Harmonia Mundi USA ▲ HMU 907110
Verdi, G.:I lombardi alla prima crociata, w. C. Deutekom (sop), D. Malvisi (sop), M. Aparici (sop), P. Domingo (ten), G. Raimondi (ten), M. Lo Monaco (ten), C. Grant (bass), L. Gardelli (cnd), Royal PO, Ambrosian Singers Philips 2-▲ 422420-2 [ADD]

Dean, Ruth (sop)
Britten, H.:Hymn to St. Cecilia, w. N. Jenkin (sop), C. Trevor (alt), P. Daggett (ten), S. Birchall (bass), H. Christophers (cnd), The Sixteen *(rec 1 & 4/91)* Collins Classics ▲ 12862 [DDD]

Dean, Stafford (bass)
Berlioz, H.:L'Enfance du Christ, w. M. Zimmermann (mez), J. Aler (ten), E. Wilm Schulte (bass), P. Kang (bass), E. Inbal (cnd), Frankfurt RSO, Cologne Radio Chorus [F] Denon 2-▲ CO 76863/4 [DDD]
Donizetti, G.:Lucrezia Borgia, w. J. Sutherland (sop—Lucrezia Borgia), A. Howells (mez—Maffio Orsini), A. Kraus (ten—Gennaro), R. Leggate (ten—Liverotto), J. Summers (bar—Apostolo Gazella), P. Hudson (bass-bar—Gubetta), S. Dean (bass—Don Alfonso), R. Bonynge (cnd), Royal Opera House Orch *(rec London, Apr. 9, 1980)* Ornamenti 2-▲ FE 111 [ADD]
Mozart, W.A.:Requiem, w. Jennifer Smith (sop), Helen Watts (cta), Ian Partridge (ten), M. Atzmon (cnd), BBC Welsh National SO, BBC Choral Society IMP ("BBC Radio" series) ▲ IMP 5691452
Tippett, M.:The Midsummer Marriage, w. Joan Carlyle (sop—Joan), Elizabeth Harwood (sop—Beth), Elizabeth Bainbridge (mez), Helen Watts (cta—Sosostris), Stuart Burrows (ten—Jack), Alberto Remedios (ten—Mark), Raimund Herincx (bass—King Fisher), C. Davis (cnd), Royal Opera House Orch, Royal Opera House Chorus Covent Garden Lyrita 2-▲ SRCD 2217

Deas, Kevin (b-bar)
Bach, J.S.:Magnificat, BWV 243, w. Julianne Baird (sop), Lorie Gratis (mez), David Price (ten), Bronwyn Fix-Keller (hpd), V. Radu (cnd), Ama Deus Ensemble Vox Classics ▲ VOX 7531
Brubeck, D.:To Hope!:A Celebration, w. Shelley Waite (sop), Mark Bleeke (ten), R. Gloyd (cnd), Cathedral Choral Society Orch, Dave Brubeck Quartet, Cathedral Choral Society Chorus *(rec Washington National Cathedral, Washington, D.C., June 12, 1995)* Telarc ▲ CD 80430 [DDD]
Handel, G.F.:Messiah, w. Julianne Baird (sop), Jennifer Lane (mez), David Price (ten), V. Radu (cnd), Ama Deus Ensemble, Ama Deus Ensemble Chorus [period instruments; 1749 Covent Garden version] Vox Classics 2-▲ VOX2 7502 [DDD]
Handel, G.F.:Messiah (sels), w. Julianne Baird (sop), Jennifer Lane (mez), David Price (ten), V. Radu (cnd), Ama Deus Ensemble—[Part 1] Sinf.; Comfort Ye My People; Every Valley Shall Be Exalted; And the Glory of the Lord; O Thou That Tellest Good Tidings to Zion; For Unto Us a Child is Born; Pifa; Rejoice Greatly o Daughter of Zion; He Shall Feed His Flock by Night; [Part 2] He was Despised and Rejected of Men; All We Like Sheep Have Gone Astray; Lift Up Your Heads, O Ye Gates; Why do the Nations So Furiously Rage Together; [Part 3] I Know That My Redeemer Liveth; Behold, I Tell You a Mystery; The Trumpet Shall Sound; Hallelujah Vox Classics ▲ VOX 7508 [DDD]

Debolini, Donatella (sop)
Merchi, J.B.:Ariettes et vaudevilles nouveaux, w. Carlo Mascilli Migliorini (gtr) or Maria Smuraglia (gtr) Entrée ▲ 0073

Decker, Richard (ten)
Mozart, W.A.:Così fan tutte, w. A. C. Antonacci (sop—Fiordiligi), M. Bacelli (sop—Dorabella), L. Cherici (sop—Despina), R. Decker (ten—Ferrando), A. Dohmen (bar—Gugliemo), S. Bruscantini (bar—Don Alfonso), G. Kuhn (cnd), Marchigiana PO, Marchigiana Phil Chorus [I] *(rec live, Teatro Lauro Rossi at the Festival di Macerata, Aug. 3, 1990)* Orfeo 3-▲ 243913 [DDD]

Def-donskaya, Elena (sop)
Prokofiev, S.:Hamlet, w. Sergei Balkov (bar), E. Khachaturian (cnd), USSR Ministry of Culture SO *(rec 1989)* Consonance ▲ 81-5005 [AAD]

Deffai, Emanuela (mez)
Generali, P.:Sacred Music, w. Leila Bersiani (sop), Valentina di Cola (sop), Sella Salvati (cta), Paolo Macedonio (ten), Roberto Bencivenga (ten), Carlo Lepore (bass), E. Brizio (cnd), Czech Radio-TV Orch, Czech Radio-TV Chorus—Magnificat; Domine ad Adjuvandum; Virgam Virtutis; Ecce Virgo; Ave Maria Messe Pastorale; Te Deum *(rec FHS Studios, Prague, 1995)* Studio SM ▲ 2517 [DDD]

Defrancq, Philip (ten)
Mozart, W.A.:Music of, w. Reginaldo Pinhoiro (ten), Jan Van Der Crabben (bar), Jan Vermeulen (pno), Guy Penson (org), P. Peire (cnd), Collegium Instrumentale Brugense, Capella Brugensis—Zerfliesset heut', geliebte Brüder [song]; Dir Seele des Weltalls [cant]; O heiliges Band der Freundschaft [song]; Die ihr einem Neuen Grade [Maurer-Geselienlied]; Die Maurerfreude [cant]; Maurerische Trauermusik; Die ihr der unermesslichen Weltalls Schöpfer ehrt [Kleine deutsche Kantate]; Laut verkünde unsre Freude [Eine kleine Freimaurerkantate]; Lasst uns mit geschlugnen Händen [hymn]; Ihr unsre neuen Leiter [song] *(rec Studio Steurbaut, Gent, Dec 1992)* René Gailly ▲ 92013 [DDD]

DeGaetani, Jan (mez)
Adler, S.:Qt 6 Voc & Strs, w. Fine Arts String Quartet CRI ▲ CD 608 [ADD]
Alfonso El Sabio:Cantigas de Santa Maria, w. C. Cassolas (ten), N. Kepros (troubadour), M. Jaffee (cnd), Waverly Consort [Port] *(rec 1972)* Vanguard Classics ("The Bach Guild" series) ▲ OVC 2013 [ADD]
Benson, W.:5 Lyrics of Louise Bogan, w. Bonita Boyd (fl) [E] Gasparo ▲ GS 261
Berlioz, H.:Les Nuits d'été, w. D. Effron (cnd), Eastman Chamber Ensemble [F] Bridge ▲ BCD 9017 [DDD] ■ BCS 9017 (D)
Brahms, J.:Ernste Gesänge Arabesque ▲ Z 6141
Brahms, J.:Gypsy Songs (8), w. L. Luvisi (pno) *(rec , Aspen Music Festival 7/7/83)* Bridge ▲ BCD 9025 [ADD]
Brahms, J.:Gypsy Songs (8) Arabesque ▲ Z 6141
Brahms, J.:Songs, w. L. Luvisi (pno), L. Dutton (va)—O kühler Wald, Op. 72/3; Verzagen, Op. 72/4; Geistliches Wiegenlied, Op. 91/2 [G] *(rec Aspen Music Festival 7/7/83)* Bridge ▲ BCD 9025 [ADD]
Brahms, J.:Songs, w. G. Kalish (pno)—Eight Gypsy Songs; Ernste Gesänge (4), Op. 121; Fünf Gesänge, Op. 72 [G] Arabesque ▲ Z 6141
Carter, E.:Songs, w. G. Kalish (pno)—2 Songs—Dust of snow; The rose family Elektra/Nonesuch ▲ 79248-2-ZK ■ 79248-4-AW
Carter, E.:Syringa, w. T. Paul (bar), H. Sollberger (cnd), Speculum Musicae, Group for Contemporary Music *(rec 5/81)* CRI ▲ CD 610 [ADD]
Carter, E.:Syringa, w. T. Paul (bar), H. Sollberger (cnd), Speculum Musicae, Group for Contemporary Music [E] *(rec 5/81)* CRI ■ ACS 6003
Chausson, E.:Songs, w. Gilbert Kalish (pno)—Amour d'antan, Op. 8/2; Le Charme, Op. 2/2; Le Temps des lilas, Op. 19; Les Papillons, Op. 2/3; Le Colibri, Op. 2/7; La Caravane, Op. 14 *(rec New York, Apr, 1979)* Arabesque ▲ Z 6673 [ADD]
Copland, A.:Songs (misc), w. L. Smit (pno)—Zion's Walls; At the River; Simple Gifts; 3 Moods; Night Thoughts; 12 Poems of Emily Dickinson; The Little Horses *(rec 1981)* Bridge ▲ BCD 9046 [ADD]
Crumb, G.:Ancient Voices of Children, w. Dash (sgr), A. Weisberg (cnd), Contemporary Chamber Ensemble—[Sp] Elektra/Nonesuch ▲ 79149-2 [AAD]
Crumb, G.:Apparition, w. G. Kalish (pno) [E] *(rec 10/82)* Bridge ▲ BCD 9028 [ADD]
Crumb, G.:Apparition, w. G. Kalish (pno)—[E] Bridge ▲ BCD 9006 [ADD]
Crumb, G.:Madrigals (4 books), w. R. Wernick (cnd), Univ of Pennsylvania Chamber Players—[Sp] New World ▲ NW 357-2

DeGaetani, Jan (mez) (cont.)
Debussy, C.:Songs, w. Gilbert Kalish (pno)—Fêtes galantes I & II; Chansons de Bilitis *(rec New York, Nov 1983)* Arabesque ▲ Z6673 [ADD]
Druckman, J.:Dark Upon the Harp, w. J. Haas (perc), B. Herman (perc), J. Druckman (cnd), American Brass Quintet [E] *(rec Aspen Music Festival 8/6/88)* Bridge ▲ BCD 9023 [ADD]
Falla, M. de:El sombrero de tres picos, w. P. Boulez (cnd), New York PO Sony Classical ("Pierre Boulez Edition" series) ▲ SMK 68333
Falla, M. de:El sombrero de tres picos, w. P. Boulez (cnd), New York PO Odyssey ▲ MBK 44721 [ADD] ■ YT 44721
Fauré, G.:La Chanson d'Eve, w. L. Luvisi (pno) [F] *(rec Aspen Music Festival 7/20/81)* Bridge ▲ BCD 9023 [ADD]
Fine, V.:Missa Brevis, w. Eric Barlett (vc), David Finckel (vc), Michael Finckel (vc), Maxine Neuman (vc) CRI ▲ CD 692 [ADD]
Foster, S.C.:Songs, w. L. Guinn (bar), G. Kalish (pno), Washington Camerata Chorus Elektra/Nonesuch ■ 71333-4
Foster, S.C.:Songs, w. L. Guinn (bar), G. Kalish (pno) Elektra/Nonesuch ▲ 79158-2 [AAD] als
Gideon, M.:Questions on Nature, w. West (ob), S. Lipman (pno), Jekofsky (perc) CRI ■ C 343
Haydn, J.:The Seven Last Words of Christ on the Cross, w. Benita Valente (sop), Jon Humphrey (ten), Thomas Paul (bar), Juilliard String Quartet Sony Classical ▲ SK 44914 [DDD]
Hindemith, P.:When Lilacs Last In The Dooryard Bloom'd, w. William Stone (bar), R. Shaw (cnd), Atlanta SO, Atlanta Sym Chorus [E] Telarc ▲ CD 80132 [DDD]
Ives, C.:Songs, w. G. Kalish (pno)—Down east; Two little flowers; Tom sails away; The see'r; Songs my mother taught me; The side show; The white gulls; West London; Afterglow [E] Bridge ▲ BCD 9006 [ADD]
Ives, C.:Songs, w. G. Kalish (pno)—The Housatonic at Stockbridge; Memories; A—Very Pleasant; B—Rather Sad; From "Paracelsus"; The Things Our Fathers Loved; Ann Street; The Innate; The Circus Band; In the Mornin'; Serenity; Majority; Thoreau; At the River; The Indians; The Cage; Like a Sick Eagle; A Christmas Carol; A Farewell to Land Elektra/Nonesuch ▲ 71325-2 ■ 71325-4
Mahler, G.:Des Knaben Wunderhorn, w. D. Effron (cnd), Eastman Chamber Ensemble [G] Bridge ▲ BCD 9017 [DDD] ■ BCS 9017 (D)
Mahler, G.:Songs from Rückert, w. D. Effron (cnd), Eastman Chamber Ensemble [G] Bridge ▲ BCD 9017 [DDD] ■ BCS 9017 (D)
Mussorgsky, M.:Nursery, w. Gilbert Kalish (pno) *(rec American Academy of Arts & Letters, New York, Jan 23-25, 1984)* Arabesque ▲ Z 6674 [ADD]
Rachmaninoff, S.:Songs, w. Gilbert Kalish (pno)—Oh, Do Not Grieve, Op. 14/8; Lilacs, Op. 21/5; Christ Is Risen, Op. 26/6; The Answer, Op. 21/4; To the Children, Op. 26/7; A Passing Breeze, Op. 34/4; How Long Since Love, Op. 14/3; The Harvest of Sorrow, Op. 4/5 *(rec New York, Apr 1979)* Arabesque ▲ Z 6674 [ADD]
Ravel, M.:Histoires naturelles, w. Gilbert Kalish (pno) *(rec New York, Nov, 1983)* Arabesque ▲ Z 6673 [ADD]
Ronsheim, J.:Bitter-Sweet, w. DesRoches CRI ■ C 301
Schoenberg, A.:Book of the Hanging Gardens, w. G. Kalish (pno) [G] Elektra/Nonesuch ▲ 79237-2-ZK
Schubert, Franz:Songs (misc), w. G. Kalish (pno)—9 Songs [G] *(rec ca. 1975)* Elektra/Nonesuch ▲ 79263-2
Schumann, R.:Frauenliebe und -leben, w. L. Luvisi (pno) [G] *(rec Aspen Music Festival, 7/7/83)* Bridge ▲ BCD 9025 [ADD]
Schumann, R.:Songs, w. G. Kalish (pno)—4 songs from Op. 98a [G] Elektra/Nonesuch ▲ 71364-2
Schumann, R.:Vocal Duets, w. L. Guinn (bar), G. Kalish (pno)—12 duets Elektra/Nonesuch ▲ 71364-2
Shifrin, S.:Satires of Circumstance, w. A. Weisberg (cnd), Contemporary Chamber Ensemble Elektra/Nonesuch ▲ 79222-2-J
Tchaikovsky, P.:Songs, w. Gilbert Kalish (pno)—A Summer Love Tale, Op. 6/2; Blue Eyes of Spring; The Sounds of Day Are Still, Op. 47/4; Was I Not a Blade of Grass?, Op. 47/7; From the Day That I Was Born, Op. 27/5; The Canary, Op. 25/4; It Was in the Early Spring, Op. 38/2; Invocation to Sleep, Op. 27/1; Take away My Heart; None but the Lonely Heart, Op. 6/6 *(rec American Academy of Arts & Letters, New York, Jan 23-25, 1984)* Arabesque ▲ Z 6674 [ADD]
Varèse, E.:Offrandes, w. A. Weisberg (cnd), Contemporary Chamber Ensemble Elektra/Nonesuch ▲ 71269-2
Wernick, R.:Kaddish-Requiem, w. Gilbert, A. Weisberg (cnd), Contemporary Chamber Ensemble Elektra/Nonesuch ▲ 79222-2-J
Wilder, A.:Lullabies & Night Songs, w. R. Wright (cnd), *(orch unknown)* [E] Caedmon ■ CDL5-1777
Wolf, H.:Spanisches Liederbuch (sels), w. G. Kalish (pno)—16 sels. [G] *(rec ca. 1974)* Elektra/Nonesuch ▲ 79263-2

DeGaetani, Jan (spkr)
Schoenberg, A.:Pierrot lunaire, w. A. Weisberg (cnd), Contemporary Chamber Ensemble [G] Elektra/Nonesuch ▲ 79237-2-ZK
Schoenberg, A.:Pierrot lunaire, w. A. Weisberg (cnd), Contemporary Chamber Ensemble [G] Elektra/Nonesuch ■ 71251-4

Degazio, B. (sgr)
Celona, J.:Sum over Histories, w. S. Peet (sgr), R. Sacks (sgr), A. Armin (elecs), R. Armin (elecs), J. Brownell (elecs), D. Hutton (elecs), G. Martynec (elecs), D. Mott (elecs), C. Sokol (elecs) Soundprints ▲ SP 9301

Degelin, Bernadette (sop)
Grétry, A.-E.-M.:Le Jugement de Midas (sels), w. L. Devos (ten), R. Zollman (cnd), Belgium Radio New SO Chamber Ensemble Koch Schwann ▲ SCH 310902 [ADD]

Degeorges, Françoise (sop)
Aperghis, G.:L'origine des espèces, w. Donatienne Michel-Dansac (sop), Emmanuelle Zoll (sop), Valérie Joly (mez), Frédérique Wolf-Michaux (cta), Elena Andreyev (vc) Musique Française d'Aujourd'hui ▲ MFA 216004

Degler, Christa (sop)
Diabelli, A.:Pastoralmesse, w. S. Linden (sop), S. Rauschkolb (cta), D. Clayton (ten), H. Müller (bass), E. Ehret (cnd), Munich St. Michael's Orch, Munich St. Michael Choir [L] Koch Schwann ▲ CD 313015 [ADD]
Mozart, W.A.:Vesperae, w. Margarete Kissel (alt), Desmond Clayton (ten), Hartmut Müller (bass), E. Hinreiner (cnd), Salzburg Mozarteum Camerata Academica Studio SM ▲ 2518

Degos, Damien (trb)
Schubert, Ferdinand:Requiem, w. K. Markus (ten), R. Soyer (bass), J. Galard (org), J.-P. Lore (cnd), French Oratorio Orch, J.-P. Lore Vocal Ensemble, Petits Chanteurs de Notre Dame de la Joie *(rec Nov. 9-11, 1980 & Jan. 25)* Esoldun ▲ MOS 1003 [ADD]
Schubert, Franz:Requiem, w. K. Markus (ten), R. Soyer (bass), J. Galard (org), J.-P. Lore (cnd), French Oratorio Orch, J.-P. Lore Vocal Ensemble, Petits Chanteurs de Notre Dame de la Joie *(rec Nov. 9-11, 1980 & Jan. 25)* Esoldun ▲ MOS 1003 [ADD]

Deis, Lila (sop)
Sargon, S.:Music of, w. Stephen Dubov (ten), Stephen Girko (cl), Christopher Adkins (vc), Vesselin Demirev (vn), Deborah Baron (fl), Simon Sargon (pno)—Shemà [Hear] for Sop, Fl, Cl, Vc & Pno; Before the Ark for Vn & Pno; Wedding Dance for Vn & Pno; Klezmuzik for Cl & Pno; At Gradmother's Knee [5 Yiddish Folk Songs] for Ten & Pno; Meditation for Vc & Pno; At Grandfather's Knee [5 Judeo-Spanish Folk Songs] for Sop & Pno *(rec Caruth Auditorium, SMU, Dallas, TX, Jan 1996)* Gasparo ▲ GAS 318

Delétré, Bernard (bass)
Brossard, S. de:Motets, w. N. Rime (sop), J.-P. Fouchécourt (alt/ten), I. Honeyman (ten), M. Gester (cnd), Parlement de Musique—Salve Rex Christe; Psallite Superi; Qui non diligit te; O Domine quia refugium; Templa nunc fument; Oratorio seu Dialogus Poenitentis animae cum Deo; Festis laeta sonent [L] *(rec 1992)* Opus 111 ▲ OPS 30-69 [DDD]
Charpentier, M.-A.:Médée, w. Isabelle Desrochers (sop—Cleone), Lorraine Hunt (sop—Medee), Noemi Rime (sop—Nerine), Monique Zanetti (sop—Creuse), Mark Padmore (ten—Jason), François Bazola (bar—Arcas), Jean-Marc Salzmann (bar—Oronte), W. Christie (cnd), Les Arts Florissants Erato 3-▲ 96558-2

Delétré, Bernard (bass) (cont.)
Mozart, W.A.:Ave verum corpus, w. Noemi Rime (sop), Christine Batty (mez), Stuart Patterson (ten), G. Vashegyi (cnd), Budapest Orfeo Orch, Patrick Marco (cnd), Maitrise de Paris Pierre Verany ▲ PVY 730058 [DDD]
Mozart, W.A.:Missa, K.317, w. Noemi Rime (sop), Christine Batty (mez), Stuart Patterson (ten), G. Vashegyi (cnd), Budapest Orfeo Orch, Patrick Marco (cnd), Maitrise de Paris Pierre Verany ▲ PVY 730058 [DDD]
Mozart, W.A.:Vesperae solennes, w. Noemi Rime (sop), Christine Batty (mez), Stuart Patterson (ten), G. Vashegyi (cnd), Budapest Orfeo Orch, Patrick Marco (cnd), Maitrise de Paris Pierre Verany ▲ PVY 730058 [DDD]
Rameau, J.P.:Les Indes galantes, w. C. McFadden (sop), S. Piau (sop), I. Poulenard (sop), N. Rime (sop), M. Ruggeri (sop), H. Crook (ten), J.-P. Fouchecourt (ten), N. Riveng (bar), J. Corréas (bass), B. Delétré (bass), W. Christie (cnd), Les Arts Florissants [F] Harmonia Mundi France 3-▲ HMC 901367/69
Rameau, J.P.:Thétis, w. Limoges Baroque Ensemble Soloists *(rec Sept 14-16, 1994)* FNAC Music ▲ CD 592333

Deleuze, Gilles (sgr)
L'Ethique, w. Pinhas, Richard (syns/gtr), J. P. Goude (syn/perc), G. Grunblatt (syn), Patrick Gauthier (syn/bass), Bernard Paganotti (bass), François Auger (drums), Clément Bailly (drums) Cuneiform ▲ Rune 36X

Delille, Jany (sop)
Gluck, C.W.:Orfeo ed Euridice, w. Germaine Féraldy (sop), Alice Raveau (cta), H. Tomasi (cnd), Paris SO [1859 French version, edited by Berlioz & Saint-Saëns] *(rec Paris, 1935)* Pearl 2-▲ PEA 9169 [ADD]

Dellal, Pamela (mez)
Haydn, J.:Mass 11, "Nelsonmesse", "Imperial Mass", "Coronation Mass", w. Janet Baker (sop), Jeffery Thomas (ten), James Maddalena (bar), M. Pearlman (cnd), Banchetto Musicale [L] Arabesque ▲ Z 6560 [DDD]

Deller, Alfred (ct)
Alfred Deller, w. Harold Lester (hpd/org), Robert Spencer (fl), Desmond Dupré (gtr) *(rec between 1965 & 1979)* Memoire Vive ▲ 262004 [ADD]
Britten, H.:A Midsummer Night's Dream, w. E. Harwood (sop), J. Veasey (mez), H. Watts (cta), P. Pears (ten), J. Shirley-Quirk (bar), B. Britten (cnd), London SO, London Sym Chorus [E] London 2-▲ 425663-2 [ADD]
Byrd, W.:Mass in 3 Parts, w. N. Jenkins (ten), M. Bevan (bar), Deller Consort [L] Musique d'Abord ▲ HMA 190211
Byrd, W.:Mass in 4 Parts, w. H. Sheppard (sop), N. Jenkins (ten), M. Bevan (bar), Deller Consort [L] Musique d'Abord ▲ HMA 190211
Byrd, W.:Mass in 5 Parts, w. H. Sheppard (sop), J. Buttrey (ten), N. Jenkins (ten), M. Bevan (bar), Deller Consort [L] Musique d'Abord ▲ HMA 190211
Couperin, F.:Leçons de ténèbres (for Good Friday), w. P. Todd (ten), R. Perulli (va da gamba), M. Chapuis (org) [L] Musique d'Abord ▲ HMA 190210
Couperin, F.:Leçons de ténèbres (for Good Friday), w. Wilfred Brown (ten), Desmond Dupré (vl), Harry Gabb (org) Vanguard Classics ("The Bach Guild" series) ▲ OVC 2525 [ADD]
Dowland, J.:Lt Songs, w. A. Deller [E] Harmonia Mundi France 2-▲ HMC 90244, HMC 90245
Dowland, J.:Songs, w. Robert Spencer (lt) Harmonia Mundi ▲ HMT 790245
Elizabethan & Jacobean Music - Airs & Instrumental Music of England, w. N. Harnoncourt (cnd), Deller Consort, Consort of Viols Vanguard Classics ▲ OVC 8102 [ADD]
Folksongs, w. Mark Deller (ct), Desmond Dupré (lt/gtr) Harmonia Mundi ▲ HMA 190.226
Handel, G.F.:Salve Regina, w. King's Musick [L] Musique d'Abord ▲ HMA 1901054
Handel, G.F.:Sosarme, Rè di Media, w. Margaret Ritchie (sop—Elmira), Alfred Deller (alt—Sosarme), Nancy Evans (mez—Erenice), Helen Watts (cta—Melo), John Kentish (ct—Argone), William Herbert (ten—King Haliate), Ian Wallace (bass—Altomaro), A. Lewis (cnd), St. Cecilia Academy Orch Rome, St. Anthony Singers Theorema 2-▲ TH 121194/195
Monteverdi, C.:Ballo delle ingrate, w. April Cantelo (sop—Una dell' Ingrate), Eileen McLoughlin (sop—Amore), Alfred Deller (alt—Venere), David Ward (bass—Plutone), Julian Bream (lt), Desmond Dupre (vl), A. Deller (cnd), London Chamber Players *(rec Walthamstow Hall, London)* Vanguard Classics ▲ OVC 8100 [ADD]
La Musique de Notre Dame, w. Wilfred Brown (ten), Gerald English (ten), Maurice Bevan (bar) *(rec Jan. 1961 & May 1964)* Vanguard Classics ▲ SVC 36 [AAD]
Purcell, H.:Hail. Bright Cecilia, w. April Cantelo (sop), Wilfred Brown (ten), Maurice Bevan (bar), M. Tippett (cnd), Kalmar CO, Ambrosian Singers Vanguard Classics ▲ OVC 8020 [ADD]
Purcell, H.:King Arthur, w. R. Hardy (sop), H. Sheppard (sop), J. Knibbs (cta), M. Deller (alt), P. Elliott (ten), L. Nixon (ten), M. Bevan (bar), N. Beavan (bass), A. Deller (cnd), Deller Consort, King's Musick [E] Harmonia Mundi France 2-▲ HMC 90252/53
Purcell, H.:Music of, w. April Cantelo (sop), Maurice Bevan (bar), Neville Marriner (vn), Peter Gibbs (vn), Granville Jones (vn), Desmond Dupré (vl), George Malcolm (hpd), Walter Bergmann (hpd)—15 Songs & Airs; Fantasia upon a Ground in d for 3 Violins & Continuo, Z.731; Fantasia upon One Note in F for 5 Viols, Z.745; Hornpipe in e (from The Old Bachelor); Music Lessons 1-12 from Musick's Hand-Maid, Part II; A New Irish Tune, "Lilliburlero," Z.646; Pavan in g for 3 Violins & Bass Viol, Z.752; Sonata in g for Violin & Continuo, Z.780; Sonata No. 9 in F, "Golden Sonata," Z.810 (from Ten Sonatas in Four Parts); Suite in D for Harpsichord, Z.667 Vanguard Classics ("The Bach Guild" series) 2-▲ OVC 2002/03 [ADD]
Purcell, H.:The Prophetess, or The History of Dioclesian, w. H. Sheppard (sop), S. Le Sage (sop), M. Worthley (ten), P. Todd (ten), M. Bevan (bar), A. Deller (cnd), Vienna Concentus Musicus—also includes incidental music from the play *(rec June 1965)* Vanguard Classics ("The Bach Guild" series) ▲ OVC 2517 [ADD]
Purcell, H.:Songs, w. R. Skeaping (vn), W. Kuijken (vl), J. Ryan (vl), W. Christie (hpd), R. Elliott (hpd)—An Evening Hymn; Fairest Isle; From Rosy Bow'rs; I Attempt From Love's Sickness; If Music Be the Food of Love; Not All My Torments; O Lead Me to Some Peaceful Gloom; O Solitude; The Plaint; Retired From My Dear Astrea's Sight; Sweeter Than Roses; Thrice Happy Lovers *(rec April 1979)* Harmonia Mundi ▲ HML 590249
17th & 18th Century Solo English Airs Harmonia Mundi ▲ HMC 90215
Tallis, T.:The Lamentations of Jeremiah, w. Wilfred Brown (ten), Gerald English (ten), Maurice Bevan (bar), John Frost (bass) *(rec Walthamstow Hall, London, 1960)* Vanguard Classics ("The Bach Guild" series) ▲ OVC 2525 [ADD]
The 3 Ravens, w. Desmond Dupré (lt/gtr) *(rec Masonic Temple, Brooklyn, NY, Oct 1955)* Vanguard Classics ("Alfred Deller Edition" series) ▲ OVC 8104 [ADD]
The 3 Ravens:Elizabethan Folk & Minstrel Songs, w. Desmond Dupré (gtr/lt) Vanguard Classics ▲ OVC 8026 (m) [ADD]
The Wraggle Taggle Gypsies, w. Desmond Dupré (lt/gtr), Taylor Recorder Consort *(rec Walthamstow Town Hall, London, Feb 1956)* Vanguard Classics ("Alfred Deller Edition" series) ▲ OVC 8105 [ADD]

Deller, Mark (ct)
Folksongs, w. A. Deller (ct), Desmond Dupré (lt/gtr) Harmonia Mundi ▲ HMA 190.226
Purcell, H.:King Arthur, w. R. Hardy (sop), H. Sheppard (sop), J. Knibbs (cta), A. Deller (ct), P. Elliott (ten), L. Nixon (ten), M. Bevan (bar), N. Beavan (bass), A. Deller (cnd), Deller Consort, King's Musick [E] Harmonia Mundi France 2-▲ HMC 90252/53

Delman, Jacqueline (sop)
Shostakovich, D.:Songs Sop, Op. 127, w. E. Dekov (vn), A. Olofsson (vc), L. Negro (pno) [R] BIS ▲ CD 26 [AAD]

Del Manto, Ivan (sgr)
Verdi, G.:Un ballo in maschera, w. Ghena Dimitrova (sop—Amelia), Isabella Stramaglia (sop—Oscar), Mirna Pecile (cta—Ulrica), Mario Carlin (ten—Un giudice), José Carreras (ten—Riccardo), Piero Cappuccilli (bar—Renato), Massimiliano Malaspina (bass—Samuel), Americo de Santis (bass—Silvano), Francesco Signor (bass—Tom), Ivan Del Manto (sgr—Un servo), G. Patanè (cnd), Parma Teatro Regio Orch *(rec Teatro Regio, Dec. 26, 1972)* Golden Age of Opera 2-▲ GAO 183/84

Delmas, Jean-François (b-bar)
Bizet, G.:Carmen (sels), w. C. Supervia (mez), A. Vavon (sop), A. Bernadet (mez), G. Micheletti (ten), A. Endreze (bar), G. Cloëz (cnd), Paris Opéra-Comique Orch, Paris Opéra-Comique Chorus—14 arias & scenes [F] *(rec Paris, 1930)* The Classical Collector ▲ FDC 2002 (m) [AAD]

Deloire, Annie (mez)
Mozart, W.A.:Thamos, w. T. Stich-Randall (mez), J. Traxel (ten), T. Adam (b-bar), M. Rossi (cnd), Cologne RSO, Cologne Radio Chorus [G] *(rec live, Cologne May 20, 1956)* Melodram 3-▲ CDM 37084 [AAD]

Delorey, John (ct)
French Sacred Music of the 14th Century, Vol. 1, w. Schola Discantus, Bradford Findell (ct), Peter McCabe (ten), Arthur Rawding (ten), Paul Guttry (bar), Kevin Moll (cnd) *(rec Emmanuel Church, Boston, 1994)* Lyrichord ("Early Music" series) ▲ LYR 8012 [DDD]

Delorie, Anny (cta)
Verdi, G.:Un ballo in maschera, w. G. Bouwenstijn (sop), E. Ratti (sop), G. Zampieri (ten), F. Molinari-Pradelli (cnd), Netherlands Opera Orch, Netherlands Opera Chorus *(rec live 1958)* Globe 2-▲ GLO 5109

Del'Orso, Edda (sgr)
Morricone, E.:Giornata, w. E. Morricone (cnd), *(orch unknown)* Point ▲ PRCD 122

de los Angeles, Victoria (sop)—see Angeles, Victoria de los

Delünsch, Mireille (sop)
Berlioz, H.:Herminie, w. P. Herreweghe (cnd), Champs Élysées Theater Orch Harmonia Mundi France ▲ HMC 90152
Chabrier, E.:Fisch-Ton-Kan, w. B. Desnoues (sop), F. Dudziak (ten), C. Mehn (ten), J.-L. Georgel (bar), R. Delage (cnd), Strasbourg Collegium Musicum Orch Arion ▲ ARN 68252 [DDD]
Chabrier, E.:Vaucochard & Son I, w. B. Desnoues (sop), F. Dudziak (ten), C. Mehn (ten), J.-L. Georgel (bar), R. Delage (cnd), Strasbourg Collegium Musicum Orch Arion ▲ ARN 68252 [DDD]
Chabrier, E.:A Wasted Education, w. B. Desnoues (sop), F. Dudziak (ten), C. Mehn (ten), J.-L. Georgel (bar), R. Delage (cnd), Strasbourg Collegium Musicum Orch Arion ▲ ARN 68252 [DDD]
Debussy, C.:La Damoiselle élue, w. S. Sulié (mez), J.-C. Casadesus (cnd), Lille National Orch, Michel Piquemal Vocal Ensemble Harmonia Mundi France ▲ HMC 901490

Demenga, Catrin (sop)
Kancheli, G.:Exil, w. Maacha Deubner (sop), Natalia Pschenitschnikova (a fl/b fl), Ruth Killius (va), Rebecca Firth (vc), Christian Sutter (db) *(rec Propstei St. Gerold, Basel, May 1994)* ECM New Series ▲ 78118-21535-2 [DDD]

Demiris, Leyla (sop)
Sinangil, A.D.:Mevlâna Oratorio (sels), w. Isin Güyer (mez), Mesut Iktu (bar), Mustafa Iktu (bass), Kâmil Sekerkaran (fl), A. D. Sinangil (cnd), Istanbul State Opera Orch, Istanbul State Opera Chorus—Récitatif I; Choral; Récitatif II; V^e partie Gallo ▲ CD 836 [ADD]

Demuth, Leopold (bar)
Wagner, R.:Arias & Scenes, w. Emmy Destinn (sop), Lilly Hafgren (sop), Frida Leider (sop), Emmi Leisner (cta), Ernst Kraus (ten), Lauritz Melchior (ten), Leopold Demuth (bar), Friedrich Schorr (b-bar), Michael Bohynen (bass), Paul Knupfer (bass), Richard Mayr (bass), Heinrich Hensel (sgr), Walter Soomer (sgr) Iron Needle ▲ 1307 (m)

Dench, Judi (nar)
Mendelssohn, F.:A Midsummer Night's Dream (comp), w. Kathleen Battle (sop), Frederica von Stade (mez), S. Ozawa (cnd), Boston SO, Tanglewood Festival Chorus Deutsche Grammophon ▲ 439897-2

Dene, József (bar)
Vivaldi, A.:Juditha triumphans devicta Holofernes barbarie, w. Margit László (sop—Abra), Zsuzsa Barlay (cta—Juditha), József Réti (ten—Servo), Zsolt Bende (bar—Holofernes), József Dene (bar—Ozias), F. Szekeres (cnd), Hungarian State Orch, György Czigány (cnd), Budapest Madrigal Choir, 1968 Classical Diamonds ▲ CLD 4022-23 [ADD]

Dénes, Zsuzsanna (sop)
Mozart, W.A.:Missa, K.427, w. K. Láki (sop), K. Equiluz (ten), R. Holl (bass), N. Harnoncourt (cnd), Vienna Concentus Musicus, Vienna State Opera Chorus [L] Teldec ▲ 2292-43070-2

Deneuve, Catherine (nar)
Debussy, C.:Chansons de Bilitis (recitation), w. Vienna-Berlin Ensemble [F] Deutsche Grammophon ▲ 429738-2 [DDD]

Denize, Nadine (mez)
Berlioz, H.:Roméo et Juliette, w. V. Cole (ten), R. Lloyd (bass), E. Inbal (cnd), Frankfurt RSO, Frankfurt Radio Chorus Denon 2-▲ CO 73210/11 [DDD]
Debussy, C.:Pelléas et Mélisande, w. F. von Stade (mez), G. Raimondi (ten), R. Stilwell (bar), J. Van Dam (bass-bar), H. von Karajan (cnd), Berlin PO, German Opera Chorus [F] EMI Classics 3-▲ CDCC 49350 [ADD]
Gounod, C.:Mors et vita, w. B. Hendricks (sop), J. Aler (ten), J. Van Dam (b-bar), M. Plasson (cnd), Toulouse Capitole Orch, Orféon Donostiarra [F] *(rec 1/92)* EMI Classics 2-▲ CDCB 54459
Massenet, J.:Hérodiade, w. Ernst Blanc (bar), D. Lloyd-Jones (cnd), French Radio Lyric Orch, French Radio Chorus *(rec Paris, Dec 5, 1974)* Agorá ("Phoenix" series) 2-▲ 514
Massenet, J.:Hérodiade, w. Cheryl Studer (sop—Salomé), Nadine Denize (mez—Hérodiade), Ben Heppner (ten—Jean), José Van Dam (b-bar—Phanuel), Thomas Hampson (bass—Hérode), M. Plasson (cnd), Toulouse Capitole Orch, Toulouse Capitole Chorus EMI Classics 3-▲ CDCC 55378
Ravel, M.:Daphnis et Chloé (suite 2), w. J.-C. Casadesus (cnd), Lille National Orch *(rec Oct. 1979)* Harmonia Mundi Plus ▲ HMP 390064
Ravel, M.:Melodies hébraïques, w. J.-C. Casadesus (cnd), Lille National Orch *(rec Oct. 1979)* Harmonia Mundi Plus ▲ HMP 390064
Ravel, M.:Pavane pour une infante défunte, w. J.-C. Casadesus (cnd), Lille National Orch *(rec Oct. 1979)* Harmonia Mundi Plus ▲ HMP 390064
Ravel, M.:Shéhérazade Mez, w. J.-C. Casadesus (cnd), Lille National Orch *(rec Oct. 1979)* Harmonia Mundi Plus ▲ HMP 390064

Denley, Catherine (mez)
Bach, J.S.:Mass in b, BWV 232, w. N. Argenta (sop), M. Tucker (ten), S. Varcoe (b-bar), R. Hickox (cnd), Collegium Musicum 90 Chandos ("Chaconne" series) 2-▲ CHAN 0533/34 [DDD]
Bruckner, A.:Requiem, w. J. Rodgers (sop), M. Davies (ten), M. George (bass), Corydon Singers, M. Best (cnd), English CO Hyperion ▲ CDA 66245 [DDD]
Copland, A.:In the Beginning, w. M. Best (cnd), Corydon Singers [E] Hyperion ▲ CDA 66219 [DDD]
Handel, G.F.:Deborah, w. S. Gritton (sop), Y. Kenny (sop), J. Bowman (alt), M. George (bass), R. King (cnd), King's Consort, Oxford New College Choir Hyperion 2-▲ CDA 66841 [DDD]
Handel, G.F.:Jephtha, w. Julia Gooding (sop), Christiane Oelze (sop), Axel Köhler (ct), John Mark Ainsley (ten), Michael George (bass), M. Creed (cnd), Berlin Academy for Early Music *(rec June 1992)* Berlin Classics 2-▲ BER 1057-2 [DDD]
Handel, G.F.:Joseph & His Brethren, w. Yvonne Kenney (sop), Connor Burrowes (trb), James Bowman (ct), John Mark Ainsley (ten), Michael George (bass), R. King (cnd), King's Consort, New College Choir Oxford, King's Consort Choir Hyperion 3-▲ CDA 67171/3
Handel, G.F.:Messiah, w. Lynn Dawson (sop), David James (alt), Arthur Davies (ten), Michael George (bass), H. Christophers (cnd), The Sixteen Orch, The Sixteen [20-member orchestra, 19-member chorus] [E] *(rec 1986)* Hyperion 2-▲ CDA 66251/52 [DDD]
Handel, G.F.:Messiah (sels), w. Patrizia Kwella (sop), John Mark Ainsley (ten), Bryn Terfel (b-bar), M. Stephenson (cnd), London Musici, London Chamber Choir Conifer Classics ▲ 74321-15354-2
Handel, G.F.:Ottone, Rè di Germania, w. Jennifer Smith (sop—Gismonda), Catherine Denley (mez—Matilda), James Bowman (ct—Ottone), Dominique Visse (ct—Adelberto), Michael George (bass—Emireno), R. King (cnd), King's Consort Hyperion 3-▲ CDA 66751/53
Handel, G.F.:Semele, w. Norma Burrowes (sop), Patrizia Kwella (sop), Elizabeth Priday (sop), Catherine Denley (mez), Della Jones (mez), Timothy Penrose (alt), Anthony Rolfe-Johnson (ct), Maldwyn Davies (ten), Robert Lloyd (b-bar), David Thomas (bass), J. E. Gardiner (cnd), English Baroque Soloists, Monteverdi Choir London Erato 2-▲ 2292-45982-2
Scarlatti, A.:Dixit Dominus, w. N. Argenta (sop), I. Attrot (sop), T. Pinnock (cnd), English Concert, English Chorale Archiv ▲ 423386-2 [DDD]
Telemann, G.P.:Cants, w. P. Kwella (sop), S. Roberts (b-bar), M. George (bass), R. Hickox (cnd), Collegium Musicum 90—Die Donner Ode Chandos ("Chaconne" series) ▲ CHAN 0548 [DDD]

Denley, Catherine (mez) (cont.)
Telemann, G.P.:Motets, w. P. Kwella (sop), S. Roberts (b-bar), M. George (bass), R. Hickox (cnd), Collegium Musicum 90—Deus judicium tuum Chandos ("Chaconne" series) ▲ CHAN 0548 [DDD]
Vivaldi, A.:Gloria, RV.589, w. N. Argenta (sop), I. Attrot (sop), T. Pinnock (cnd), English CO, English Concert Choir Archiv ▲ 423386-2 [DDD]
Vivaldi, A.:Sacred Choral Music, w. Deborah York (sop), James Bowman (ct), R. King (cnd), King's Consort Hyperion ▲ CDA 66779
Vivaldi, A.:Sacred Choral Music, w. Susan Gritton (sop), Lynton Atkinson (trb), David Wilson-Johnson (bar), Lisa Milne (sgr), R. King (cnd), King's Consort—Magnificat; Lauda, Jerusalem; Kyrie eleison; Credo in unum Deum; Dixit Dominus Hyperion ▲ CDA 66769

Denley, Jim (sgr)
Poder à Santa Maria, w. S. Wishart (cnd), Sinfonye, Equidad Barés (sgr), Vivien Ellis (sgr), Paula Chateauneuf (sgr) *(rec Cartuja de Santa María de Cazalla de la Sierra, Seville, Oct. 1993)* Almaviva ▲ 0105 [DDD]

Denning, Angela (sop)
Arriaga, J.C.:Agar, w. J. López-Cobos (cnd), Bilbao SO Discobi 2-▲ DIS 2002/1002
Arriaga, J.C.:Erminia, w. J. López-Cobos (cnd), Bilbao SO Discobi 2-▲ DIS 2002/1002

Dennis, C. (sgr)
Loesser, F.:Guys and Dolls, w. F. Sinatra (sgr), B. Crosby (sgr), D. Martin (sgr), J. Stafford (sgr), D. Shore (sgr), D. Reynolds (sgr), A. Sherman (sgr), S. Davis Jr. (sgr), *(other artists unknown)* [studio cast] Reprise ▲ 45014-2 [AAD] ▮ 45014-4

Denolfo, Ian (ten)
Tchaikovsky, P.:Iolanta, w. Michaela Gurevich (sop—Iolanta), Jaqueline Miura (sop—Brigitta), Tatjana Tabachuk (mez—Martha), Annette Kuhn (mez—Laura), Ian Denolfo (ten—Godefroy), Keith Alexander Bolves (ten—Alméric), Alexander Ben (bar—Robert), Georg Lehner (bar—Ibn-Hakia), Arutiun Kotchinian (bass—René), Kurt Geysen (bass—Bertrand), H. Rotman (cnd), Warsaw PO, ECOV Ensemble Members *(rec Vooruit Center of the Arts, Ghent, Belgium, Aug 28-29, 1993)* CPO 2-▲ CPO 999456-2 [DDD]

Dens, Michel (bar)
Massenet, J.:Manon, w. V. De los Angeles (sop), H. Legay (ten), J. Borthayre (bass), P. Monteux (cnd), Paris Opéra-Comique Orch, Paris Opéra-Comique Chorus [F] EMI Classics 3-▲ CDMC 63549 (m) [ADD]

Dent, Karl (ten)
Janácek, L.:Slavonic Mass, w. C. Brewer (sop), M. Simpson (mez), R. Roloff (bass), R. Shaw (cnd), Atlanta SO, Atlanta Sym Chorus [Sla] Telarc ▲ CD 80287 [DDD]

Denver, John (sgr)
A Love until the End of Time:Domingo's Greatest Love Songs, w. P. Domingo (ten), Lee Holdridge (cnd), Maureen McGovern (sgr) CBS ▲ MK 42520 [ADD/DDD] ▮ FMT 42520
Perhaps Love, w. P. Domingo CBS ▲ MK 37243 ▮ PMT 37243

Denysenko, Wlodzimierz (bass)
Penderecki, K.:Utrenia, w. Delfina Ambroziak (sop), Stefania Woytowicz (sop), Krystyna Szczepanska (mez), Kazimierz Pustelak (ten), Boris Carmeli (bass), A. Markowski (cnd), Warsaw PO, Józef Bok (cnd), Stanislaw Skoraczewski (cnd), Warsaw National Phil Chorus, Pioneer Choir *(rec Warsaw, 1973)* Polskie Nagrania ▲ PNCD 018

Depoltová, Eva (sop)
Fibich, Z.:Šárka, w. Eva Randová (mez), Vilém Přibyl (ten), Vaclav Zítek (bar), J. Štych (cnd), Brno State PO, J. Pancik (cnd), Janáček Opera Chorus *(rec 1978)* Supraphon 2-▲ SUP 0036
Beethoven, L. van:Ah, perfidol, w. F. Vajnar (cnd), Czech PO [I] *(rec 1978)* Supraphonet ▲ 11 1118-2 [AAD]
Dvořák, A.:The Cunning Peasant, w. Václav Zítek (bar), Karel Berman (bass), F. Vajnar (cnd), Prague RSO, Prague Radio Chorus Supraphon 2-▲ SUP 0019 [DDD]
Foerster, J.B.:Eva, w. Anna Barová (mez), Leo Marian Vodicka (ten), Jaroslav Soucek (bar), F. Vajnar (cnd), Prague RSO, Prague Radio Chorus *(rec 1982)* Supraphon 2-▲ SUP 3001
Smetana, B.:The Kiss, w. Libuše Márová (mez), Leo Marian Vodička (ten), F. Vajnar (cnd), Brno Janáček Opera Orch, Brno Janáček Opera Chorus Supraphon 2-▲ SUP 112180 [AAD]

Depraz, Xavier (bass)
Bizet, G.:Les Pêcheurs de perles, w. P. Alerie (sgr), L. Simoneau (ten), J. Fournet (cnd), Lamoureux Orch *(rec 1953)* Philips 2-▲ 434782-2
Debussy, C.:Pelléas et Mélisande, w. J. Micheau (sop), R. Gorr (mez), C. Maurane (bar), M. Roux (bar), J. Fournet (cnd), Lamoureux Orch *(rec 1953* Philips 2-▲ 434783-2
Gounod, C.:Roméo et Juliette, w. M. Freni (sop—Juliette), F. Corelli (ten—Roméo), H. Gui (bar—Mercutio), C. Càles (bar—Capulet), X. Depraz (bass—Frère Laurent), A. Lombard (cnd), Paris Opera Orch, Paris Opera Chorus EMI Classics ▲ CDMB 65290
Landowski, M.:Music of, w. Nadine Sautereau (sop), Jean-Christophe Benoit (bar), Michel Bouquet (spkr), Gilbert Audin (bn), Evelyne Aïello, Didier Bouture, Ludovic Chevalier, Laurent Decker, Françoise Deslogères, Landowski, Tzipine (cnd), Colonne Association des Concerts Orch, Boulogne-Billancourt Orch Conservatory, Paris Conservatory Société des Concerts Orch, L'Itinéraire Ensemble, Harmonia Nova Orch Ensemble—Con Bn; Con pour ondes Martenot; Femme sans passé; Hauts de Hurlevent; Horologe; Mouvement; Notes de Nuit; Souvenir d'un jardin d'enfance; Ventriloque Chamade 3-▲ 5639/40/41 [AAD/DDD]
Poulenc, F.:Dialogues des Carmélites, w. D. Duval (sop), R. Crespin (sop), L. Berton (sop), D. Scharley (mez), R. Gorr (mez), P. Finel (ten), P. Dervaux (cnd), Paris Opera Orch [F] EMI Classics 2-▲ CDCB 49331 (m) [ADD]

Dermota, Anton (ten)
Bach, J.S.:Cant 78, w. T. Stich-Randall (sop), D. Hermann (sop), H. Braun (bar), F. Prohaska (cnd), Bach Guild Orch, Bach Guild Chorus [G] *(rec May 1954)* Vanguard Classics ("The Bach Guild" series) ▲ OVC 2009 [ADD]
Bach, J.S.:Cant 106, "Actus tragicus", w. T. Stich-Randall (sop), D. Hermann (sop), H. Braun (bar), F. Prohaska (cnd), Bach Guild Orch, Bach Guild Chorus [G] *(rec May 1954)* Vanguard Classics ("The Bach Guild" series) ▲ OVC 2009 [ADD]
Bach, J.S.:Magnificat, BWV 243, w. M. Coertse (sop), M. Sjöstedt (sop), H. Rössl-Majdan (mez), F. Guthrie (bass), F. Prohaska (cnd), Vienna State Opera Orch, Vienna State Opera Chorus [L] *(rec June 1957)* Vanguard Classics ("The Bach Guild" series) ▲ OVC 2010 [ADD]
Beethoven, L. van:Leonore (opera), w. H. Zadek (sop), P. Schöffler (b-bar), O. von Rohr (bass), F. Leitner (cnd), Vienna SO, Vienna State Opera Chorus [G] *(rec live, Bregenz 1960)* Melodram 2-▲ CDM 27085 [AAD]
Haydn, J.:Mass 10, "Kriegsmesse", "Paukenmesse", w. Netania Davrath (sop), Hilde Rössl-Majdan (alt), W. Bery (bass), Anton Heiller (org), R. Harand (vc), M. Wöldike (cnd), Vienna State Opera Orch, Vienna State Opera Chorus *(rec May 14-16, 1960)* Vanguard Classics ("The Bach Guild" series) ▲ OVC 2518 [ADD]
Haydn, J.:Die Schöpfung, w. Anny Felbermayer (sop—Eve), Teresa Stich-Randall (sop—Gabriel), Anton Dermota (ten—Uriel), Paul Schöffler (b-bar—Adam), Frederick Guthrie (bass—Raphael), Franz Holletschek (cembalo), M. Wöldike (cnd), Vienna State Opera Orch, Vienna State Opera Chorus *(rec Musikverein, Vienna, Austria, May 1955)* Vanguard Classics 2-▲ SVC 34/35 [ADD]
Mahler, G.:Lied von der Erde, w. Elsa Cavelti (alt), O. Klemperer (cnd), Vienna SO *(rec 1957)* Tuxedo ▲ TUXCD 1036 [ADD]

Dermota, Anton (ten) (cont.)

Mozart, W.A.:Arias, w. Arleen Augér (sop), Kathleen Battle (sop), Irma Beilke (sop), Helena Braun (sop), Lisa Della Casa (sop), Maria Cebotari (sop), Ileana Cotrubas (sop), Helen Donath (sop), Mirella Freni (sop), Reri Grist (sop), Edita Gruberova (sop), Elisabeth Grümmer (sop), Hilde Güden (sop), Ingeborg Hallstein (sop), Luise Helletsgruber (sop), Gundula Janowitz (sop), Sena Jurinac (sop), Erika Köth (sop), Evelyn Lear (sop), Wilma Lipp (sop), Margaret Marshall (sop), Edith Mathis (sop), Jarmila Novotna (sop), Margherita Perras (sop), Lucia Popp (sop), Elisabeth Rethberg (sop), Anneliese Rothenberger (sop), Elisabeth Schumann (sop), Elisabeth Schwarzkopf (sop), Graziella Sciutti (sop), Irmgard Seefried (sop), Graziella Sciutti (sop), Julia Varady (sop), Agnes Baltsa (mez), Margit Bokor (mez), Brigitte Fassbaender (mez), Christa Ludwig (mez), Ann Murray (mez), Francisco Araiza (ten), Helge Rosvaenge (ten), Rudolf Schock (ten), Peter Schreier (ten), Leopold Simoneau (ten), Eric Tappy (ten), Richard Tauber (ten), Gösta Winbergh (ten), Josef Witt (ten), Fritz Wunderlich (ten), Christian Boesch (bar), Willy Domgraf–Fassbaender (bar), Karl Dönch (bar), Dietrich Fischer–Dieskau (bar), Erich Kunz (bar), Eberhard Wächter (bar), Hans Hotter (b–bar), Paul Schöffler (b–bar), Cesare Siepi (b–bar), José Van Dam (b–bar), Walter Berry (bass), Geraint Evans (bass), Nicolai Ghiaurov (bass), Alexander Kipnis (bass), Richard Mayr (bass), Kurt Moll (bass), James Morris (bass), Ezio Pinza (bass), Martti Talvela (bass), Giorgio Tozzi (bass), Hans Duhan (sgr), Res Fischer (sgr), Marie Gerhart (sgr), *(various orchs & cnds)*—sels from Idomeneo, Die Entführung aus der Serail, Le nozze di Figaro, Don Giovanni, Così fan tutte, Die Zauberflöte & various arias Orfeo d'or ("Festspiel Dokumente" series) 5–▲ 408955

Mozart, W.A.:Così fan tutte, w. L. della Casa (sop), E. Loose (sop), C. Ludwig (mez), E. Kunz (bar), P. Schoeffler (bass) London 2–▲ 417185–2 [ADD]

Mozart, W.A.:Così fan tutte (sels), w. Elisabeth Schwarzkopf (sop), Irmgard Seefried (sop), Christa Ludwig (mez), Erich Kunz (bar), Paul Schoeffler (b–bar), K. Böhm (cnd), Vienna PO—Sento, o Dio; Sorella, cosa dici?—Prenderò quel brunettino Orfeo d'or ("Festspiel Dokumente" series) ▲ 394201

Mozart, W.A.:Don Giovanni, w. L. Welitsch (sop), I. Seefried (sop), E. Schwarzkopf (sop), E. Kunz (bar), T. Gobbi (bar), A. Poell (b–bar), J. Greindl (bass), W. Furtwängler (cnd), Vienna PO, Vienna State Opera Chorus *(rec 1950)* Laudis 3–▲ LDS 4001 [AAD]

Mozart, W.A.:Don Giovanni, w. E. Schwarzkopf (sop), E. Grümmer (sop), E. Berger (sop), C. Siepi (b–bar), O. Edelmann (b–bar), W. Berry (bass), W. Furtwängler (cnd), Vienna PO, Vienna State Opera Chorus *(rec Salzburg, Aug. 3, 1953)* EMI Classics ("Great Recordings of the Century" series) 2–▲ CDHB 63860

Mozart, W.A.:Don Giovanni, w. E. Schwarzkopf (sop), E. Grümmer (sop), E. Berger (sop), C. Siepi (b–bar), O. Edelmann (b–bar), W. Berry (bass), W. Furtwängler (cnd), Vienna PO, Vienna State Opera Chorus *(rec 1953)* Arkadia 3–▲ 509 (m) [AAD]

Mozart, W.A.:Don Giovanni, w. S. Danco (sop), L. della Casa (sop), C. Siepi (b–bar), F. Corena (bass), J. Krips (cnd), Vienna PO, Vienna State Opera Chorus London 3–▲ 411626–2 [ADD]

Mozart, W.A.:Don Giovanni (sels), w. Hilde Konetzni (sop), Emmy Loose (sop), Irmgard Seefried (sop), Erich Kunz (bar), Paul Schöffler (b–bar), Herbert Alsen (bass), Böhm, Moralt (cnd), Vienna PO *(rec 1944)* Preiser ▲ PRE 90249 [ADD]

Mozart, W.A.:Entführung, w. S. Barabas (sop), R. Streich (sop), H. Krebs (ten), J. Greindl (bass), F. Fricsay (cnd), Berlin RSO, Berlin Radio Chorus [G] *(rec Jesus–Christuskirche, Berlin–Dahlem, Dec. 19–21, 1949)* Myto 2–▲ 2 MCD 92361 [ADD]

Mozart, W.A.:Entführung (sels), w. Hilde Konetzni (sop), Emmy Loose (sop), Irmgard Seefried (sop), Erich Kunz (bar), Paul Schöffler (b–bar), Herbert Alsen (bass), Böhm, Moralt (cnd), Vienna PO *(rec 1944)* Preiser ▲ PRE 90249 [ADD]

Mozart, W.A.:Requiem, w. Lisa della Casa (sop), Ira Malaniuk (cta), Cesare Siepi (b–bar), B. Walter (cnd), Vienna PO, Vienna State Opera Chorus *(rec Salzburg, July 26, 1956)* Orfeo d'or ("Festspiel Dikumente" series) ▲ C 430961 (m) [ADD]

Mozart, W.A.:Requiem, w. W. Lipp (sop), H. Rössl–Majdan (mez), W. Berry (bass), H. von Karajan (cnd), Berlin PO, Vienna Singverein [L] *(rec 1961)* Deutsche Grammophon ("Resonance" series) ▲ 429160–2 [ADD] ■ 429160–4

Mozart, W.A.:Requiem, w. E. Schumann (sop), K. Thorborg (mez), A. Kipnis (bass), B. Walter (cnd), Vienna PO, Vienna State Opera Chorus EMI Classics ("Great Recordings of the Century" series) 3–▲ CDHC 63912

Mozart, W.A.:Zauberflöte, w. I. Seefried (sop–Pamina), W. Lipp (sop—Queen of the Night), A. Dermota (ten—Tamino), E. Kunz (bar—Papageno), J. Greindl (bass—Sarastro), W. Furtwängler (cnd), Vienna PO, Vienna State Opera Chorus *(rec live 1951)* EMI Classics ▲ CDMC 65356

Mozart, W.A.:Zauberflöte, w. I. Seefried (sop–Pamina), W. Lipp (sop—Queen of the Night), A. Dermota (ten—Tamino), E. Kunz (bar—Papageno), J. Greindl (bass—Sarastro), W. Furtwängler (cnd), Vienna PO, Vienna State Opera Chorus [G] *(rec live, Salzburg, Aug. 6, 1951)* Arkadia 3–▲ 361 [ADD]

Mozart, W.A.:Zauberflöte, w. I. Seefried (sop–Pamina), W. Lipp (sop—Queen of the Night), A. Dermota (ten—Tamino), E. Kunz (bar—Papageno), J. Greindl (bass—Sarastro), W. Furtwängler (cnd), Vienna PO, Vienna State Opera Chorus [G] *(rec live, Salzburg, Aug. 6, 1951)* Foyer 3–▲ FOY 2003 [AAD]

Mozart, W.A.:Zauberflöte, w. I. Seefried (sop–Pamina), W. Lipp (sop—Queen of the Night), A. Dermota (ten—Tamino), E. Kunz (bar—Papageno), J. Greindl (bass—Sarastro), H. von Karajan (cnd), Vienna PO, Musikfreunde Chorus [without dialogue; G] *(rec 1950)* EMI Classics ("Studio" series) 2–▲ CDHB 69631 (m)

Mozart, W.A.:Zauberflöte (sels), w. Hilde Konetzni (sop), Emmy Loose (sop), Irmgard Seefried (sop), Erich Kunz (bar), Paul Schöffler (b–bar), Herbert Alsen (bass), Böhm, Moralt (cnd), Vienna PO *(rec 1944)* Preiser ▲ PRE 90249 [ADD]

Recital, w. Vienna State Opera Orch [cnd:K. Böhm, J. Krips, R. Moralt, et al.] *(rec live, 1942–1970)* Melodram 2–▲ CDM 26522 [AAD]

Schmidt, F.:Das Buch mit sieben Siegeln, w. Hertha Töpper (mez), Thomas Moser (ten), Robert Holl (bass), A.J. Hochstrasser (cnd), Lower Austria Tonkünst Orch, Graezer Concert Choir *(rec 1975)* Preiser 2–▲ PRE 93263 [ADD]

Schmidt, F.:Das Buch mit sieben Siegeln, w. H. Gueden (sop), I. Malaniuk (cta), F. Wunderlich (ten), W. Berry (bass), D. Mitropoulos (cnd), Vienna PO, Vienna Singverein *(rec live, Salzburg Festival 1959)* Melodram 2–▲ MEL 27078

Schmidt, F.:Das Buch mit sieben Siegeln, w. Hilde Gueden (sop), Ira Malaniuk (cta), Fritz Wunderlich (ten), Walter Berry (bass), D. Mitropoulos (cnd), Vienna PO, Vienna Singverein Sony Classical ("Festspiel Dokumente:Salzburger Festspiele" series) 2–▲ SM2K 68442

Still, W.G.:Tristan und Isolde, w. C. Ligendza (sop), R. Baldani (mez), H. Hopf (ten), H. Sotin (bass), G. Neidlinger (bass), C. Kleiber (cnd), Vienna State Opera Orch, Vienna State Opera Chorus *(rec Oct. 7, 1973)* Exclusive 3–▲ EXL 18 [ADD]

Strauss (II), Joh.:Die Fledermaus, w. H. Gueden (sop), J. Patzak (ten), A. Jaresch (ten), A. Poell (b–bar), W. Lipp (sop), S. Wagner (mez), K. Preger (ten), C. Krauss (cnd), Vienna PO *(rec early 1950s)* London ("Historic" series) 2–▲ 425990–2 [AAD]

Strauss (II), Joh.:Die Fledermaus (sels), w. Wilma Lipp (sop), Gerda Scheyer (sop), Christa Ludwig (mez), Walter Berry (bar), Erich Kunz (bar), Eberhard Wachter (bar), O. Ackermann (cnd), Philharmonia Orch, London Phil Chorus Emperor Operetta ▲ KO 86340

Strauss, R.:Arabella, w. L. Della Casa (sop), H. Gueden (sop), I. Malaniuk (cta), W. Kmentt (ten), G. London (bar), O. Edelmann (bass), G. Solti (cnd), Vienna PO [G] London ("Grand Opera" series) 2–▲ 430387–2 [ADD]

Strauss, R.:Daphne (sels), w. M. Reining (sop—Daphne), A. Dermota (ten—Leukippos), R. Moralt (cnd), Vienna State Opera Orch, Vienna State Opera Chorus *(rec May 8, 1942)* Koch Schwann 2–▲ SCH 314552 [ADD]

Strauss, R.:Friedenstag, w. Viorica Ursuleac (sop—Maria), Anton Dermota (ten—Ein Piemonteser), Hans Hotter (b–bar—Kommandant), Herbert Alsen (bass—Wachtmeister), C. Krauss (cnd), Vienna State Opera Orch *(rec Vienna, Oct. 16, 1941)* Koch Schwann 2–▲ SCH 314625 [ADD]

Strauss, R.:Salome (sels), w. E. Schulz (sop—Salome), A. Dermota (ten—Narraboth), J. Witt (ten—Herodes), H. Hotter (bar—Jochanaan), P. Schöffler (b–bar—Jochanaan), R. Strauss (cnd), Vienna State Opera Orch, Vienna State Opera Chorus *(rec Feb. 15 & May 6, 1942)* Koch Schwann 2–▲ SCH 314532 [ADD]

Strauss, R.:Songs, w. H. Konetzni (sop—4 solo songs), A. Dermota (ten—6 solo songs), A. Poell (bar—6 solo songs), Richard Strauss (pno)—Opp. 21/2, 21/3, 69/5, 88/2 *(Konetzni)*; Opp. 15/5, Op. 17/1, 21/1, 32/2, 37/1, 49/2 *(Dermota)*; Opp. 19/1, 21/4, 27/1, 27/3, 36/1, 48/5 *(Poell)* [G] *(rec 1943)* Preiser ▲ 93261 (m) [AAD]

Dermota, Anton (ten) (cont.)

Strauss, R.:Songs, w. M. Reining (sop—6 solo songs), L. Piltti (sop—7 solo songs), A. Dermota (ten—8 solo songs), R. Strauss (pno)—Opp. 10/1, 27/2, 29/1, 37/3, 41/1, 48/1 *(Reining)*; Opp. 15/5, 17/2, 21/1, 29/2, 48/2, 48/3, 49/1 *(Piltti)*; Opp. 10/1, 10/3, 17/1, 19/2, 21/2, 27/3, 32/1, 37/2 *(Dermota)* [G] *(rec Vienna, Apr. 1942)* Preiser ▲ 93262 (m) [AAD]

Verdi, G.:Otello, w. Carla Martinis (sop—Desdemona), Sieglinde Wagner (mez—Emilia), Anton Dermota (ten—Cassio), Paul Schöffler (ten—Iago), Ramon Vinay (ten—Otello), Josef Greindl (bass—Lodovico), W. Furtwängler (cnd), Vienna PO, Vienna State Opera Chorus *(rec live, Salzburg Festival, Aug 7, 1951)* EMI Classics ▲ CDMB 65751

Wagner, R.:Das Liebesverbot, w. H. Zadek (cta), L. Sorell (mez), K. Equiluz (ten), L. Welter (bar), Imdahl (sgr), R. Heger (cnd), Austrian RSO, Austrian Radio Chorus *(rec live, Vienna, 1962)* Melodram 2–▲ MEL 27052 [AAD]

Wagner, R.:Die Meistersinger von Nürnberg, w. M. Reining (sop), H. Noort (ten), H. H. Nissen (bar), H. Alsen (bass), A. Toscanini (cnd), Vienna PO *(rec live, Salzburg, 1937)* Melodram 4–▲ MEL 47041

Dermota, Jovita (sop)

Jovita Dermota Preiser ▲ PRE 90955 [DDD]

Schumann, R.:Frauenliebe und –leben, w. H. Dermota (pno) Preiser ▲ CD 90955 [DDD]

Dernesch, Helga (sop/mez)

Strauss, R.:Arabella, w. K. Te Kanawa (sop), Fontana (sgr), F. Grundheber (bar), J. Tate (cnd), Royal Opera House Orch [G] London 3–▲ 417623–2 [DDD]

Verdi, G.:La forza del destino, w. G. Bumbry (sop—Leonora), H. Dernesch (sop—Preziosilla), N. Gedda (ten—Alvaro), H. Prey (bar—Don Carlos), G. Frick (bass—Pater Guardian), S. Vogel (bass—Marchese), G. Patanè (cnd), Dresden State Orch, Dresden State Opera Chorus *(rec Aug. 1965)* Berlin Classics ("Eterna" series) ▲ BER 2025–2 [ADD]

Wagner, R.:Der Ring des Nibelungen, w. R. Crespin (sop), G. Janowitz (sop), C. Ludwig (mez), J. Vickers (ten), D. Fischer–Dieskau (bar), D. Thomas (bass), H. von Karajan (cnd), Berlin PO *(rec late 1960s)* Deutsche Grammophon 15–▲ 435211–2 [ADD]

Wagner, R.:Der Ring des Nibelungen, w. R. Crespin (sop), G. Janowitz (sop), C. Ludwig (mez), J. Vickers (ten), D. Fischer–Dieskau (bar), D. Thomas (bass), H. von Karajan (cnd), Berlin PO *(rec live at Salzburg Easter Festivals, 1967–1970)* Arkadia 12–▲ 223 (m) [ADD]

Wagner, R.:Tannhäuser, w. C. Ludwig (mez), A. Kollo (ten), H. Braun (bar), H. Sotin (bass), G. Solti (cnd), Vienna PO [Paris version] [G] London 3–▲ 414581–2 [ADD]

Wagner, R.:Tristan und Isolde, w. C. Ludwig (mez), J. Vickers (ten), P. Schreier (ten), B. Weikl (bar), W. Berry (bass), K. Ridderbusch (bass), H. von Karajan (cnd), Berlin PO, German Opera Chorus [G] EMI Classics ("Studio" series) 4–▲ CDMD 69319 [ADD]

Weill, K.:The Threepenny Opera, w. U. Lemper (sop), Milva (sgr), S. Tremper (sgr), R. Kollo (ten), M. Adorf (sgr), W. Reichmann (sgr), J. Mauceri (cnd), Berlin RIAS Sinfonietta, Berlin RIAS Chamber Choir [G] London ▲ 430075–2 [DDD]

Dersen, Elvira (alt)

Draeseke, F.:Mysterium:Christus, w. C. Bischoff (sop), A. Vogel (sop), K. Markus (ten), H.J. Ritzerfeld (ten), P. Langshaw (bar), B. Kämpff (bass), J. Sonnenschmidt (org), U.–R. Follert (cnd), Breslau State PO, Evangelical Boys' Choir Palatine, Heilbronn Vocal Ensemble, Palatine Kurrende Bayer 5–▲ 100175/79

Descrieres, Georges (nar)

Stravinsky, I.:L'Histoire du soldat, w. Jean–Pierre Wallez (vn), D. Debart (cnd), Basse Normandie Instrumental Ensemble Forlane ▲ FRL 16580 [DDD]

Desderi, Claudio (bar)

Bellini, V.:Beatrice di Tenda, w. M. Freni (sop), C. Gonzales (mez), R. Casellato (ten), M. Arena (cnd), *(orch unknown)* *(rec live, Bologna 1976)* Legato Classics 2–▲ LCD 152–2 [ADD]

Mozart, W.A.:Così fan tutte, w. Carol Vaness (sop), Delores Ziegler (mez), C. Watson (cta), J. Aler (ten), D. Duesing (bar), B. Haitink (cnd), London PO, Glyndebourne Festival Chorus EMI Classics 3–▲ CDCC 47727

Rossini, G.:Il Signor Bruschino, w. K. Battle (sop), F. Lopardo (ten), S. Ramey (bass), I. Marin (cnd), English CO Deutsche Grammophon ▲ 435865–2

Desmond, Astra (cta)

Vaughan Williams, R.:Serenade to Music, w. I. Baillie (sop), E. Suddaby (sop), S. Allen (sop), E. Turner (sop), M. Balfour (cta), M. Brunskill (cta), M. Jarred (cta), H. Nash (ten), W. Widdop (ten), P. Jones (ten), F. Titterton (ten), R. Henderson (bass), R. Easton (bass), H. Williams (bass), N. Allin (bass), H. J. Wood (cnd); BBC SO Dutton Laboratories ▲ CDAX 8004 [ADD]

Vaughan Williams, R.:Serenade to Music, w. Isobel Baillie (sop), Lilian Stiles–Allen (sop), Elsie Suddaby (sop), Eva Turner (sop), Margaret Balfour (cta), Muriel Brunskill (cta), Astra Desmond (cta), Mary Jarred (cta), Parry Jones (ten), Heddle Nash (ten), Frank Titterton (ten), Walter Widdop (ten), Roy Henderson (bar), Harold Williams (bar), Norman Allin (bass), Robert Easton (bass), H. Wood (cnd), BBC SO *(rec Abbey Road, Oct 15, 1938)* Claremont ▲ CDGSE 785066

Vaughan Williams, R.:Serenade to Music, w. I. Baillie (sop), E. Suddaby (sop), S. Allen (sop), E. Turner (sop), M. Balfour (cta), A. Desmond (cta), M. Brunskill (cta), M. Jarred (cta), H. Nash (ten), W. Widdop (ten), P. Jones (ten), F. Titterton (ten), R. Henderson (bass), R. Easton (bass), H. Williams (bass), N. Allin (bass), H. Wood (cnd), BBC SO [E] *(rec 10/15/38)* Pearl ▲ GEMMCD 9342 (m) [AAD]

Desnoues, Brigitte (sop)

Chabrier, E.:Fisch–Ton–Kan, w. M. Delunsch (sop), F. Dudziak (ten), C. Mehn (ten), J.–L. Georgel (bar), R. Delage (cnd), Strasbourg Collegium Musicum Orch Arion ▲ ARN 68252 [DDD]

Chabrier, E.:Vaucochard & Son I, w. M. Delunsch (sop), F. Dudziak (ten), C. Mehn (ten), J.–L. Georgel (bar), R. Delage (cnd), Strasbourg Collegium Musicum Orch Arion ▲ ARN 68252 [DDD]

Chabrier, E.:A Wasted Education, w. M. Delunsch (sop), F. Dudziak (ten), C. Mehn (ten), J.–L. Georgel (bar), R. Delage (cnd), Strasbourg Collegium Musicum Orch Arion ▲ ARN 68252 [DDD]

Massenet, J.:Grisélidis, w. Michèle Command (sop), Jean–Luc Viala (ten), Didier Henry (bar), Maurice Sieyes (bar), Christian Treguier (bar), Jean–Philippe Courtis (bass), Claire Larcher (sgr), P. Fournillier (cnd), Franz Liszt SO, Budapest Lyon Chorus Koch Schwann 2–▲ SCH 312702 [DDD]

Mendelssohn, F.:Athalie, w. Danielle Borst (sop), Carolyn Watkinson (cta), Jean–Marc Avocat (sgr), Souad Natech (sgr), B. Tetu (cnd), Lorraine PO, Lyon National Chorus Koch Schwann ▲ SCH 314282 [DDD]

Desrochers, Isabelle (sop)

Charpentier, M.–A.:Médée, w. Isabelle Desrochers (sop—Cleone), Lorraine Hunt (sop—Medee), Noemi Rime (sop—Nerine), Monique Zanetti (sop—Creuse), Mark Padmore (ten—Jason), François Bazola (bar—Arcas), Jean–Marc Salzmann (bar—Oronte), Bernard Deletre (bass–Creon), W. Christie (cnd), Les Arts Florissants Erato 3–▲ 96558–2

Lalande, M.–R. de:Les Leçons de Ténèbres et le Miserere Astrée ▲ E 8592

Lully, J.–B.:Motets, w. D. Favat (sop), R. Duguay (ct), H. Lamy (ten), P. Harvey (bass), H. Niquet (cnd), Concert Spirituel Vocal Ensemble—Te Deum; Miserere; Plaude laetare Gallia *(rec Nov. 22–25, 1993)* FNAC Music ▲ 592308 [DDD]

Rameau, J.P.:Motets, w. V. Gens (sop), J.–P. Fouchecourt (ct), H. Lamy (ten), P. Harvey (bar), M. Loureiro de Sà (bar), S. Imbodem (bass), *(orch unknown)*—Deus noster refugium; Quam dilecta; In convertendo [L] *(rec Apr. 13–18, 1992)* FNAC Music ▲ 592096 [DDD]

Dessay, Nathalie (sop)

Fauré, G.:Songs, w. Béatrice Uria–Monzon (mez), Jean–Paul Fouchécourt (ten), François Le Roux (bar), Jeff Cohen (pno)—complete songs grouped by poets [Leconte de Lisle; Charles Baudelaire; Paul Verlaine; Jean de la Ville de Mirmont; Armand Silvestre; Victor Hugo; Théophile Gautier; 5 Melodies of Venice; Sully Prudhomme; Albert Samain; Louis Pommey; Paul de Chodens; Marc Monnier; Romain Bussine; Victor Wilder; Georgette Deblads; Villiers de l'Isle Adam; Charles Grandmougin; Henri de Régnier; Stéphan Bordèse; Charles Van Lerberghe; Baronne de Brimont; Maurice Maeterlinck; Edmond Haraucourt; Molière REM 4–▲ REM 311179 [DDD]

Mozart, W.A.:Zauberflöte, w. Natalie Dessay (sop—Queen of the Night), Linda Kitchen (sop—Papagena), Rosa Mannion (sop—Pamina), Anna–Maria Panzarella (sop—First Lady), Doris Lamprecht (mez—Second Lady), Delphine Haidan (cta—Third Lady), Hans Peter Blochwitz (ten—Tamino), Steven Cole (ten—Monostatos), Chrisopher Josey (ten—First Priest/First Armed Man), Anton Scharinger (bar—Papageno), Reinhard Hagen (bass—Sarastro), Laurent Naouri (bass—Second Priest/Second Armed Man), Willard White (bass—Speaker), W. Christie (cnd), Les Arts Florissants *(rec Paris Oct 2–9 1995)* Erato 2–▲ 12705–2 [DDD]

Dessay, Nathalie (sop) (cont.)
Orff, C.:Carmina burana, w. Gérard Lesne (ct), Thomas Hampson (bar), M. Plasson (cnd), Toulouse Capitole Orch, Orféon Donostiarra, Midi-Pyrénées Children's Choir *(rec Halle-aux-Grains, Toulouse, Dec. 2, 4 & 6, 1994)* EMI Classics ▲ CDC 55392 [DDD]

Dessi, Daniela (sop)
Boito, A.:Mefistofele, w. Alberto Cupido (ten), Samuel Ramey (bass), B. Bartoletti (cnd), Florence Maggio Musicale Orch, Florence Maggio Musicale Chorus *(rec live, 1989)* Serenissima 2-▲ SER 360114
Leoncavallo, R.:Pagliacci, w. L. Pavarotti (ten), P. Coni (bar), J. Pons (bar), R. Muti (cnd), Philadelphia Orch [I] Philips ▲ 438132-2
Pergolesi, G.B.:Adriano in Siria, w. J. Omilian (sop), L. Mazzaria (sop), S. Anselmi (sop), G. Banditelli (cta), E. di Cesare (ten), M. Panni (cnd), Rome Opera CO [I] *(rec live 12/20/86)* Bongiovanni 3-▲ GB 2078/80 [DDD]
Pergolesi, G.B.:Il flaminio, w. D. Dessì (sop—Flaminio), F. Pediconi (sop—Agata), E. Zilio (mez—Giustina), M. Ferrugia (ten—Fernando), G. Sica (ten—Polidoro), V. Baiano (bass—Checa), S. Pagliuca (bass—Bastiano), M. Panni (cnd), Naples Teatro San Carlo Orch *(rec Nov. 12, 1983)* Fonit Cetra 3-▲ CDC 39 [ADD]
Rossini, G.:Stabat Mater, w. Lucia Mazzaria (sop), Gloria Scalchi (mez), Pietro Ballo (ten), Chris Merritt (ten), Anatoli Kotscherga (bass), Roberto Scandiuzzi (bass), G. Gelmetti (cnd), Stuttgart RSO, North German Radio Chorus, Southwest German Radio Chorus Serenissima 2-▲ SER 360155 [DDD]
Verdi, G.:Falstaff, w. Maureen O'Flynn (sop), Bernadette Manca di Nissa (mez), Delores Ziegler (mez), Ramon Vargas (ten), Ernesto Gavazzi (ten), Paolo Barbacini (ten), Juan Pons (bar), Roberto Frontali (bar), Luigi Roni (bass), R. Muti (cnd), La Scala Orch, La Scala Chorus *(rec Milan La Scala Theater, Italy, Mar. 29 & 31)* Sony Classical ▲ S2K 58961 [DDD]
Verdi, G.:Requiem Mass, w. Lucia Mazzaria (sop), Gloria Scalchi (mez), Pietro Ballo (ten), Chris Merritt (ten), Anatoli Kotscherga (bass), Roberto Scandiuzzi (bass), G. Gelmetti (cnd), Stuttgart RSO, North German Radio Chorus, Southwest German Radio Chorus Serenissima 2-▲ SER 360155 [DDD]

Dessy, D. (mez)
Vivaldi, A.:Il Farnace, w. M. Dupuy (mez), K. Angeloni (mez), P. Malakova (mez), L. Rizzi (cta), R. Garazioti (sgr), M. de Bernart (cnd), San Remo SO [I] *(rec live 12/1/82)* Arkadia-Akademia 2-▲ 110 [ADD]

Dessy-Ceriani (sgr)
Rossini, G.:Ciro in Babilonia, w. C. Calvi (cta), E. Palacio (ten), C. Rizzi (cnd), San Remo SO, San Remo Sym Chorus [I] *(rec live 10/30/88)* Arkadia-Akademia 2-▲ 105 [ADD]

Destain, Robert (sgr)
Lehár, F.:Die lustige Witwe, w. Teresa Stich-Randall (mez—Missia Palmieri), Monique Stiot (mez—Manon), Germaine Duclos (sgr—Praskovia), Linda Felder (sgr—Olga), Christiane Jacquin (sgr—Nadia), Jeannette Levasseur (sgr—Sylviane), Henri Legay (ten—Camille de Coutançon), Joseph Peyron (ten—Kromsky), Robert Destain (sgr—Baron Popoff), Michel Fauche (sgr—Pristich), Gérard Friedmann (sgr—Lerida), Jacques Gilet (sgr—Bogdanowitch), Jean Guy Henneveux (sgr—Prince Danilo), Serge Klin (sgr—Figg), Jacques Villa (sgr—D'Estillac), A. Sibert (cnd), Belgian Radio-TV Orch, Belgian Radio-TV Chorus *(rec Grand Auditorium, Belgium, Apr 30, 1970)* Studio SM 2-▲ 2160 [AAD]

Destal, Fred (bar)
Wagner, R.:Der fliegende Holländer, w. M. Lawrence (sop), A. Kipnis (bass), F. Busch (cnd), Buenos Aires Teatro Colón Orch, Buenos Aires Teatro Colón Chorus [G] *(rec live broadcast 9/19/36)* Pearl 2-▲ PEAS 9910 (m) [ADD]
Wagner, R.:Parsifal (sels), w. Fred Destal (bar—Amfortas), Herbert Alsen (bass—Gurnemanz), Nikolaus Zec (bass—Titurel), H. Knappertsbusch (cnd), Vienna State Opera Orch *(rec Nov. 1, 1937)* Koch Schwann 2-▲ SCH 314632 [ADD]

Destinn, Emmy (sop)
The Complete Destinn, w. E. Caruso (ten), J. McCormack (ten), K. Jörn (ten), G. Martinelli (ten), G. Zenatello (ten), et al. Supraphon 12-▲ SUP 112136 [ADD]
Emmy Destinn Supraphon ("Ultraphon" series) ▲ SUP 111337 [AAD]
Emmy Destinn:The Complete Victor Recordings, 1914-21 Romophone 2-▲ 81002-2
Wagner, R.:Arias & Scenes, w. Lilly Hafgren (sop), Frida Leider (sop), Emmi Leisner (cta), Ernst Kraus (ten), Lauritz Melchior (ten), Leopold Demuth (bar), Friedrich Schorr (b-bar), Michael Bohynen (bass), Paul Knupfer (bass), Richard Mayr (bass), Heinrich Hensel (sgr), Walter Soomer (sgr) Iron Needle ▲ 1307 (m)

Deubner, Maacha (sop)
Kancheli, G.:Exil, w. Catrin Demenga (sop), Natalia Pschenitschnikova (a fl/b fl), Ruth Killius (va), Rebecca Firth (vc), Christian Sutter (db) *(rec Propstei St. Gerold, Basel, May 1994)* ECM New Series ▲ 78118-21535-2 [DDD]

Deutekom, Cristina (sop)
Beethoven, L. van:Christus am Ölberg, w. L. Kozma (ten), F. Lindauer (sgr), R. Muti (cnd), Venice Teatro La Fenice Orch, Venice Teatro La Fenice Chorus [G] *(rec live, Venice 7/4/70)* Arkadia ▲ 743 [ADD]
Bellini, V.:I Puritani, w. F. Raffanelli (sop), N. Gedda (ten), S. Bruscantini (b-bar), A. Ferrin (bass), G. del Vivo (bass), R. Muti (cnd), *(orch unknown)* *(rec 1970)* Great Opera Performances ▲ GOP 735
Donizetti, G.:Lucia di Lammermoor, w. J. Carreras (ten), G. Floravanti (bar), C. Cava (bass), A. Gatto (cnd), *(orch unknown)* [I] *(rec live in Madrid, 1975)* Standing Room Only 2-▲ SRO 809-2 [ADD]
Donizetti, G.:Lucia di Lammermoor (sels), w. Christina Deutekom (sop—Lucia), Luciano Pavarotti (ten—Edgardo), Domenico Trimarchi (bar—Enrico Ashton), Silviano Pagliuca (bass—Raimondo Bidebent), C.M. Guilini (cnd), Naples Teatro San Carlo Orch, Naples Teatro San Carlo Chorus Budget ("The Greatest Voice in Opera" series) ▲ SYP 103
Mozart, W.A.:Zauberflöte, w. P. Lorengar (sop), S. Burrows (ten), H. Prey (bar), D. Fischer-Dieskau (bar), M. Talvela (bass), G. Solti (cnd), Vienna PO [G] London 3-▲ 414568-2
Mozart, W.A.:Zauberflöte (sels), w. Pilar Lorengar (sop), Stuart Burrows (ten), Hermann Prey (bar), Martti Talvela (bass), G. Solti (cnd), Vienna PO London ▲ 421302-2 [ADD]
Rossini, G.:Armida, w. P. Bottazzo (ten), O. Garaventa (ten), E. Gimenez (ten), C. Franci (cnd), Venice Teatro La Fenice Orch, Venice Teatro La Fenice Chorus [I] *(rec live, 4/3/70)* Memories 2-▲ HR 4152/53 (m) [ADD]
Rossini, G.:Armida, w. P. Bottazzo (ten), O. Garaventa (ten), E. Gimenez (ten), B. Trotta (sgr), A. Maddalena (bass), G. Antonini (bass), C. Franci (cnd), Venice Teatro La Fenice Orch, Venice Teatro La Fenice Chorus *(rec live, Venice, 1970)* Foyer 2-▲ FOY 2030 [AAD]
Verdi, G.:Attila, w. G. Raimondi (ten), C. Bergonzi (ten), S. Milnes (bar), L. Gardelli (cnd), Royal PO, Ambrosian Singers Philips 2-▲ 426115-2
Verdi, G.:Un ballo in maschera, w. G. Tucker (ten), R. Bruson (bar), R. Muti (cnd), Florence Teatro Comunale Orch, Florence Teatro Comunale Chorus *(rec live, Florence 1972)* Foyer 2-▲ FOY 2047 [AAD]
Verdi, G.:I lombardi alla prima crociata, w. D. Malvisi (sop), M. Aparici (sop), P. Domingo (ten), G. Raimondi (ten), M. Lo Monaco (ten), M. Dean (b-bar), C. Grant (bass), L. Gardelli (cnd), Royal PO, Ambrosian Singers Philips 2-▲ 422420-2 [ADD]

Deutsch, H. (bar)
Dunstable, J.:Sacred Music, w. A. Teichert-Hailperin (sop), K. Smith (ct), W. Jochens (ten), M. Nitz (ten), Helga Weber Instrumental Circle—Sancta Maria; Beata dei genetrix; Beata mater et innupta virgo; Speciosa facta es; Alma redemptoris mater Entrée ▲ 0041 [ADD]
Hildegard Of Bingen:Sacred Songs, w. A. Teichert-Hailperin (sop), K. Smith (ct), W. Jochens (ten), M. Nitz (ten), Helga Weber Instrumental Circle—Caritas abundat in omnia; O virtus sapientiae; O quam mirabilis; Hodie aperuit nobis clausa porta; Alleluia. O virga, mediatrix; O clarissima mater; O frodens virga Entrée ▲ 0041 [ADD]

Deuveren, Willem-Jan van (ten)
Meijering, Chiel:St. Louis Blues, w. Andrea van Beek (sop), Francine van der Heijden (sop), Jeanette Huizinga (mez), Rein Kolpa (ten), John Vredeveldt (ten), Gérard Bernts (bar), W. Megens (cnd), De Ereprijs Orch [I] *(rec Schouwburg Arnhem, Mar 10, 1995)* Donemus 2-▲ neos 01-02

Devallier, Lucienne (cta)
Beethoven, L. van:Sym 9, "Choral Sym", w. Magda Laszlo (sop), Petre Monteanu (ten), Raffaele Arié (bass), H. Scherchen (cnd), Swiss-Italian RSO, Swiss-Italian Radio-TV Chorus Accord ▲ ACD 201002 [AAD]

DeVerger, Angela (sop)
Constantinides, D.:Vocal Music, w. Cynthia Dewey (nar), Evelyn Petros (sop), Susan Faust Straley (sop), Eugenia Epperson (fl), Richard Jernigan (cl), Kelly Smith Toney (vn), Hye-Yun Chung (hp), Stephen Brown (pno), John Raush (perc), D. Constantinides (cnd), Louisiana State Univ New Music Ensemble—Reflections IV for Sop, Fl, Hp & Pno; Intimations [1 Act Opera]; 4 Songs on Poems by Sappho; Mutability for Sop & Str Qt.; 4 Greek Songs Vestige ▲ 04

Devia, Mariella (sop)
Bellini, V.:I Capuleti e i Montecchi (sels), w. M. Rota (cnd), Swiss-Italian Orch—Oh quante volte *(rec June 4, 1992)* Bongiovanni ▲ GB 2513 [DDD]
Bellini, V.:I Puritani (sels), w. M. Rota (cnd), Swiss-Italian Orch—Qui la voce...Vien diletto *(rec June 4, 1992)* Bongiovanni ▲ GB 2513 [DDD]
Bellini, V.:La sonnambula, w. L. Canonici (ten), A. Verducci (bass), M. Viotti (cnd), Piacenza SO, Piacenza Chorus [I] *(rec live 11/88)* Nuova Era 2-▲ 6764/65 [DDD]
Bellini, V.:La sonnambula (sels), w. M. Rota (cnd), Swiss-Italian Orch—Come per me sereno...Sovra il sen *(rec June 4, 1992)* Bongiovanni ▲ GB 2513 [DDD]
Charpentier, G.:Louise (sels), w. M. Rota (cnd), Swiss-Italian Orch *(rec June 4, 1992)* Bongiovanni ▲ GB 2513 [DDD]
Cherubini, L.:Lodoïska, w. F. Pedaci (sgr), B. Lombardo (ten), T. Moser (ten), A. Corbelli (bar), W. Shimell (bar), R. Muti (cnd), La Scala Orch, La Scala Chorus Sony Classical 2-▲ S2K 47290
Delibes, L.:Lakmé (sels), w. M. Rota (cnd), Swiss-Italian Orch—Aria delle campanelle *(rec June 4, 1992)* Bongiovanni ▲ GB 2513 [DDD]
Donizetti, G.:L'elisir d'amore, w. B. Pratico (bar), P. Spagnoli (bar), M. Viotti (cnd), English CO, Tallis Chamber Choir Erato 2-▲ 4509-91701-2
Donizetti, G.:Linda di Chamounix, w. Mariella Devia (sop—Linda), Sonia Ganassi (mez—Pierotto), Francesca Provvisionato (mez—Maddalena), Luca Canonici (ten—Carlo), Alfonso Antoniozzi (bass—Il Marchese di Boisfleury), Petteri Salomaa (bass—Antonio), Boguslaw Fiksinski (sgr—L'intendente), Donato Di Stefano (sgr—Il Prefetto), G. Bellini (cnd), Eastern Netherlands Orch, Andrew Wise (cnd), National Reisopera Choir *(rec Muziekcentrum Enschede, Holland, June 24-July 2, 1992)* Arts Music 3-▲ 47151-2 [DDD]
Donizetti, G.:Lucia di Lammermoor, w. Vencenzo La Scola (ten), Renato Bruson (bar), S. Ranzani (cnd), La Scala Orch, La Scala Chorus Serenissima 2-▲ SER 360153 [DDD]
Donizetti, G.:Lucia di Lammermoor (sels), w. M. Rota (cnd), Swiss-Italian Orch—Ardon gli incensi *(rec June 4, 1992)* Bongiovanni ▲ GB 2513 [DDD]
Gounod, C.:Roméo et Juliette (sels), w. M. Rota (cnd), Swiss-Italian Orch—Je veux vivre *(rec June 4, 1992)* Bongiovanni ▲ GB 2513 [DDD]
Mozart, W.A.:Entführung, w. Uwe Peper (ten), Kurt Moss (sgr), W. Sawallisch (cnd), La Scala Orch, La Scala Chorus *(rec live, 1994)* Serenissima 2-▲ SER 360161

Devinu, Giusy (sop)
Wolf-Ferrari, E.:Il campiello, w. D. Mazzucato (Gasparina), G. Devinu (Lucieta), M. Bolgan (Gnese), C. de Mola (Orsola), U. Benelli (Dona Cate Panciana), M. Rene Cosotti (Dona Pasqua Polegana), M. Comencini (Zorozeto), M. Biscotti (Astolfi), I. D'Arcangelo (Anzoleto), C. Striuli (Fabrizio del Ritorti), N. Bareza (cnd), Trieste Teatro Comunale Giuseppe Verdi Orch, Trieste Teatro Comunale G. Verdi Chorus *(rec Feb. 1992)* Ricordi 2-▲ RFCD 2014 [DDD]

Devlin, Michael (b-bar)
Haydn, J.:Mass 10, "Kriegsmesse", "Paukenmesse", w. Patricia Wells (sop), Gwendoline Killebrew (mez), Alan Titus (bar), L. Bernstein (cnd), *(orch unknown)*, Norman Scribner Choir [L] *(rec 1973)* Sony Classical ("Bernstein:The Royal Edition" series) 2-▲ SM2K 47563 [ADD]
Offenbach, J.:Les Contes d'Hoffmann, w. Beverly Sills (sop—Olympia/Giulietta/Antonia/Stella), Edith Evans (mez—Nicklausse/Mother's Voice), Michael Devlin (ten—Spalanzani), André Turp (ten—Hoffmann), Luigi Velluci (ten—Andrès/Cochenille/Pitichinaccio/Frantz), Donald Bernard (bar—Luther/Schlemil), Norman Treigle (bass—Lindorf/Coppélius/Dapertutto/Dr. Miracle), John West (bass—Crespel), Alton Brim (sgr—Nathanaël), Rodney Hall (sgr—Hermann), K. Andersson (cnd), New Orleans Opera Orch, New Orleans Opera Chorus *(rec Feb 27, 1964)* VAI Audio 2-▲ VAIA 1121-2 [ADD]
Schoenberg, A.:Moses und Aaron, w. David Pittman-Jennings (nar), Gabriele Fontana (sop—Young Girl), Yvonne Naef (cta—Sick Woman), John Graham-Hall (ten—Young Man/Naked Youth), Pår Lindskog (ten—Youth), Chris Merritt (ten—Aaron), Siegfried Lorenz (bar—Another Man), Michael Devlin (b-bar—Ephraimite), László Polgár (bass—Priest), P. Boulez (cnd), Royal Concertgebouw Orch, Winfried Maczewski (cnd), Netherlands Opera Chorus, Zaans Youth Choir, Waterland Music School *(rec Concertgebouw, Amsterdam, Oct 1995)* Deutsche Grammophon 2-▲ 449 174-2 [DDD]

Devol, Luana (sop)
Schreker, F.:Irrelohe, w. Eva Randová (mez—Old Lola), Michael Pabst (ten—Count Heinrich), Monte Pederson (bar—Peter), Neven Belamaric (sgr—The Parson), Luana Devol (sgr—Eva), Sebastian Holecek (sgr—The Miller), Goran Smimic (sgr—The Forester) Sony Classical 2-▲ S2K 66850

Devos, Louis (ten)
Franck, C.:Messe solennelle, w. P. Bartholomée (cnd), Brussels Radio-TV Instrumentalists, Brussels Radio-TV Chorus [L] *(rec 1976)* Koch Schwann ▲ 3-1044-2 [ADD]
Grétry, A.-E.-M.:Le Jugement de Midas (sels), w. B. Degelin (sop), R. Zollman (cnd), Belgium Radio New SO Chamber Ensemble Koch Schwann ▲ SCH 310902 [ADD]
Lutoslawski, W.:Paroles tissées, w. W. Lutoslawski (cnd), Warsaw PO *(rec Warsaw, 1968)* Polskie Nagrania ▲ PNCD 042 [AAD]
Martin, F.:Le Mystère de la Nativité, w. Elly Ameling (sop), Aafje Heynis (cta), Hugues Cuénod (ten), Eric Tappy (ten), Pierre Bollet (bar), Derrik Olsen (bar), Charles Clavensy (b-bar), André Vessières (bass), E. Ansermet (cnd), Swiss Romande Orch, Jeunes de l'Église Chorus, Geneva Motet Chorus Cascavelle 2-▲ CVL 2006 [ADD]
Orff, C.:Carmina burana, w. N. Burrowes (sop), J. Shirley-Quirk (bar), A. Dorati (cnd), Royal PO, Brighton Festival Chorus [G,L] London ▲ 417714-2 [ADD]
Orff, C.:Carmina burana, w. Norma Burrowes (sop), John Shirley-Quirk (bar), A. Dorati (cnd), Royal PO, Brighton Festival Chorus, Southend Boys' Choir *(rec Kingsway Hall, London, Feb 1976)* London ("Phase 4 Stereo" series) ▲ 444105-2 [ADD]
Rameau, J.P.:Les Indes galantes, w. J. Elwes (ten), P. Huttenlocher (bar), J.-F. Paillard (cnd), Jean-François Paillard CO Erato 3-▲ 95310-2
Schnittke, A.:Faust Cant, w. Mikael Bellini (alt), Inger Blom (cta), Urik Cold (bass), J. DePreist (cnd), Malmö SO, Malmö Sym Chorus BIS ("BIS Twins" series) 2-▲ CD 437/507

Dewey, Cynthia (nar)
Constantinides, D.:Vocal Music, w. Cynthia Dewey (nar), Angela DeVerger (sop), Evelyn Petros (sop), Susan Faust Straley (sop), Eugenia Epperson (fl), Richard Jernigan (cl), Kelly Smith Toney (vn), Hye-Yun Chung (hp), Stephen Brown (pno), John Raush (perc), D. Constantinides (cnd), Louisiana State Univ New Music Ensemble—Reflections IV for Sop, Fl, Hp & Pno; Intimations [1 Act Opera]; 4 Songs on Poems by Sappho; Mutability for Sop & Str Qt.; 4 Greek Songs Vestige ▲ 04

Dewey, Cynthia (sgr)
Constantinides, D.:Intimations, w. Susan Faust Straley (sgr—Ellen), Cynthia Dewey (sgr—Celeste), D. Constantinides (cnd), Louisiana State Univ New Music Ensemble Capstone ▲ CPS 8632

Deyck, Lucienne van (mez)
Brahms, J.:Liebeslieder Waltzes SATB, w. Greta De Reyghere (sop), Guy De Mey (ten), Huub Claessens (bass), Jean-Claude Vanden Eynden (pno), Luc Devos (pno) *(rec Consevatoire Royal, Liège, 1994)* Ricercar ▲ 153138
Brahms, J.:Neue Liebeslieder Waltzes, w. Greta De Reyghere (sop), Guy De Mey (ten), Huub Claessens (bass), Jean-Claude Vanden Eynden (pno), Luc Devos (pno) *(rec Consevatoire Royal, Liège, 1994)* Ricercar ▲ 153138
Hindemith, P.:Die junge Magd, w. Marc Grauwels (fl), Ronald Van Spaendonck (cl), Gaggini String Quartet Syrinx ▲ 95101
Ryelandt, J.:Agnus Dei, w. Ingrid Kapelle (sop), Joseph Cornwell (ten), Huub Claessens (bass), Stephan Macleod (bass), G. Llewellyn (cnd), Royal Flanders PO, Altra Voce, Audite Nova *(rec live, Elisabeth Hall, Antwerp, Holland, Dec 9, 1994)* Marco Polo 2-▲ 8.223785/86 [DDD]

DeYoung, Michelle (mez)

Corigliano, J.:Of Rage & Remembrance, w. Michael Accinno (boy sop), Robert Baker (ten), Michael Forest (ten), Jason Stearns (bar), James Shaffran (bar), L. Slatkin (cnd), National SO Washington D.C., Washington Oratorio Society Men's Chorus *(rec J. F. K. Center for the Performing Arts, Washington, D. C., Nov 9–11, 1995 & Apr 19 &)* RCA Red Seal ▲ 09026-68450-2 [DDD]

Diaconescu, Florin (ten)

Caudella, E.:Dochia, w. P. Sbârcea (cnd), Sibiu PO *(rec 1983)* Electrecord ▲ ELCD 104 [AAD]

Diacovski, Lubomir (ten)

Bach, J.S.:Christmas Oratorio, w. Ludmila Hadjieva (sop), Roumiana Tzatcheva (alt), Plamen Hidjov (bass), Tabakov, Kralev (cnd), Madrigal Chamber Ensemble, Sofia CO Soloists Pentagon 3-▲ 302 [DDD]

Tchaikovsky, P.:Eugene Onegin (sels), w. Alexandrina Pendachanska (sop), Nicolai Ghiaurov (bass), Niko Isakov (sgr), Dresden State Orch, Bulgarian National Chorus—Intro; Peasant's Chorus & Dance; Scene & Aria of Olga; Scene & Quartet; Letter Scene; plus others Laserlight ▲ 14210 [DDD]

Diadkova, Larissa (mez)

Fleischmann, B.:Rothschild's Vn, w. Marina Shaguch (sop), Ilya Levinsky (ten), Konstantin Pluzhnikov (ten), Sergei Leiferkus (bar), G. Rozhdestvensky (cnd), Rotterdam PO *(rec Rotterdam, Netherlands, Aug 24–31, 1995)* RCA Red Seal ▲ 09026-68434-2 [DDD]

Glinka, M.:Russlan & Ludmilla, w. Galina Gorchakova (sop), Irinia Bogachova (sgr), Anna Netrebko (sgr), Yuri Masurin (ten), Konstantin Pluzhnikov (ten), Mikhail Kit (bar), Gennady Bezzubenkov (bass), Vladimir Ognovenko (bass), V. Gergiev (cnd), Kirov Opera Orch, Kirov Opera Chorus Philips ▲ 456 248-2

Shostakovich, D.:From Jewish Folk Poetry, w. Marina Shaguch (sop), Konstantin Pluzhnikov (ten), G. Rozhdestvensky (cnd), Rotterdam PO *(rec Rotterdam, Netherlands, Aug 24–31, 1995)* RCA Red Seal ▲ 09026-68434-2 [DDD]

Tchaikovsky, P.:Iolanta, w. Galina Gorchakova (sop), Nikolai Gassiev (ten), Gegam Grigorian (ten), Dmitri Hvorostovsky (bar), Nikolai Putilin (bar), Sergei Alexashkin (bass), Gennady Bezzubenkov (bass), Olga Korzhenskaya (sgr), Tatyana Kravtsova (sgr), V. Gergiev (cnd), Kirov Opera Orch, Kirov Opera Chorus *(rec Mariinsky Theatre, St. Petersburg)* Philips 2-▲ 442796-2

Diakov, Anton (bass)

Mussorgsky, M.:Boris Godunov, w. N. Dobrianova (sop), S. Jurinac (sop), D. Usunow (ten), N. Ghiaurov (bass), N. Ghiuselev (bass), H. von Karajan (cnd), Vienna PO, Vienna State Opera Chorus [R] *(rec live in Salzburg, 7/26/64)* Arkadia 2-▲ 210 (m) [ADD]

Mussorgsky, M.:Songs & Dances, w. Gérard Wyss (pno) Accord 2-▲ ACD 202152 [DDD]

Diamond, Brad (ten)

Schubert, Franz:Der Graf von Gleichen, w. Gwendolyn Coleman (sop), Karen Driscoll (sop), Tracy Thomas (sop), John M. Koch (bar), G. Samuel (cnd), Cincinnati PO, CCM Chamber Choir *(rec Corbett Auditorium, Univ of Cincinnati, Mar 12–13, 1994)* Centaur 2-▲ 2281/2282 [DDD]

Diana, William (bar)

Berlioz, H.:Lélio, "Le retourà la vie", w. W. Klemperer (nar), G. Siebert (ten), Z. Macal (cnd), Milwaukee Sym Chorus Koss Classics 2-▲ KC 1012 [DDD]

Berlioz, H.:Lélio, "Le retourà la vie", w. G. Siebert (ten), W. Klemperer (nar), Z. Macal (cnd), Milwaukee SO *(rec 1991)* Koss Classics ▲ KC 1017 [DDD]

Diard, William (sgr)

Floyd, C.:Markheim, w. Norman Treigle (bass—Markheim), Audrey Schuh (sgr—Tess), Alan Crofoot (sgr—Josiah Creach), William Diard (sgr—Stranger), K. Andersson (cnd), New Orleans Opera Orch, New Orleans Opera Chorus *(rec New Orleans, LA, Mar. 31 & Apr. 2, 1966)* VAI Audio ▲ VAIA 1107

Diaz, Justino (bass)

Bellini, V.:I Puritani, w. J. Sutherland (sop—Elvira), N. Gedda (ten—Arturo), E. Blanc (bar—Riccardo), J. Diaz (bass—Giorgio), R. Bonynge (cnd), *(orch unknown)* [I] *(rec live, Philadelphia 4/18/63)* Standing Room Only 2-▲ SRO 838-2 [ADD]

Bizet, G.:Carmen, w. G. Bumbry (sop), M. Freni (sop), J. Vickers (ten), H. von Karajan (cnd), Vienna PO, Vienna State Opera Chorus [F] *(rec live, Salzburg 1967)* Arkadia 3-▲ 221 [ADD]

Catalani, A.:La Wally, w. L. Marimpietri (sop), R. Tebaldi (sop), M. del Monaco (ten), P. Cappuccilli (bar), F. Cleva (cnd), Monte Carlo Opera Orch, Turin Lyric Chorus [I] London 2-▲ 425417-2 [ADD]

Cherubini, L.:Mass in d, w. Patricia Wells (sop), Maureen Forrester (cta), George Shirley (ten), N. Jenkins (cnd), Clarion Concerts Orch, Clarion Concerts Chorus *(rec Vanguard's 23rd Street Recording Studio)* Vanguard Classics ▲ SVC-44 [AAD]

Handel, G.F.:Messiah, w. Margaret Price (sop), Yvonne Minton (mez), Alexander Young (ten), J. Somary (cnd), English CO, Amor Artis Chorale [E] *(rec 1970)* Vanguard Classics 2-▲ OVC 4018/19 [ADD]

Handel, G.F.:Messiah, w. Margaret Price (sop), Yvonne Minton (mez), Alexander Young (ten), J. Somary (cnd), English CO, Amor Artis Chorale [E] *(rec 1970)* Vanguard Classics ▲ OVC 4020 [ADD]

Meyerbeer, G.:Les Huguenots, w. Jeanette Scovotti (sop—Urbain), Rita Shane (sop—Marguerite de Valois), Enriqueta Tarrès (sop—Valentine), Nicolai Gedda (ten—Raoul de Nangis), Justino Diaz (bass—Marcel), Dimiter Petkov (bass—Le Comte de Saint-Bris), E. Märzendorfer (cnd), Austrian RSO, Austrian Radio Chorus *(rec Vienna, Feb 17, 1971)* Myto 2-▲ MCD 961141

Offenbach, J.:Les Contes d'Hoffmann, w. E. Gruberova (sop), C. Eder (mez), P. Domingo (ten), M. Sénéchal (ten), Schmidt (sgr), G. Bacquier (bar), J. Morris (bass), S. Ozawa (cnd), French National Orch, French Radio Chorus [F] Deutsche Grammophon 2-▲ 427682-2 [DDD]

Rossini, G.:La pietra del paragone, w. A. Elgar (sop), B. Wolff (mez), E. Bonazzi (mez), J. Carreras (ten), J. Reardon (bar), R. Murcell (bar), A. Foldi (b-bar), N. Jenkins (cnd), Clarion Concerts Orch, Clarion Concerts Chorus [I] *(rec. ca. 1972)* Vanguard Classics 3-▲ OVC 8043/45 [ADD]

Rossini, G.:The Siege of Corinth, w. B. Sills (sop), M. Horne (mez), F. Bonisoli (ten), T. Schippers (cnd), La Scala Orch, La Scala Chorus [I] *(rec live 1969)* Melodram 2-▲ MEL 27043 [AAD]

Rossini, G.:The Siege of Corinth, w. B. Sills (sop), S. Verrett (mez), T. Schippers (cnd), London SO, Ambrosian Opera Chorus [I] *(rec London, 1974)* EMI Classics 3-▲ CDMC 64335

Rossini, G.:Stabat Mater, w. M. Arroyo (sop), B. Wolff (mez), T. del Bianco (ten), T. Schippers (cnd), New York PO, Camerata Singers Sony Classical ▲ SB2K 53252

Verdi, G.:I vespri siciliani, w. M. Caballé (sop), P. Domingo (ten), F. Bordoni (bar), E. Queler (cnd), *(orch unknown)* *(rec live, Barcelona, 1974)* Standing Room Only 2-▲ SRO 837-2 [ADD]

Dibblee, Sally (sop)

Le Souvenir, w. Dibblee, Sally (sop), Russell Braun (bar), Carolyn Maule (pno) Centrediscs ("Lacalée" series) ▲ CMC CD 5696 [DDD]

Dick, van (sgr)

Handel, G.F.:Alcina, w. J. Sutherland (sop), N. Proctor (cta), F. Leitner (cnd), Cappella Coloniensis, Cologne Radio Chorus [I] *(rec live, 1959)* Verona 3-▲ 27011/13 (m) [AAD]

Dicke, Sabine (sop)

Mauersberger, R.:Geh aus, mein Herz, und suche Freude, w. Dorothea Schmidt (sop), Friederike Urban (sop), Annette Bassenge (alt), Christiane Fischer (alt), Sabine Hering (alt), Johannes Unger (org), Wolfgang Unger (dir), Thüringian Academic Sing Circle Thorofon ▲ CTH 2245 [DDD]

Dickerson, Bernard (ten)

Massenet, J.:Sapho, w. Jenny Hill (sop), Laura Sarti (mez), Alexander Oliver (ten), Neilson Taylor (bar), George Macpherson (bass), Milla Andrew (sgr), B. Keefe (cnd), BBC SO, BBC Sym Chorus *(rec live, 1973)* Memories 2-▲ MEM 4601 [AAD]

Dickey, Annamary (sgr)

Her First Recordings, w. E. Steber (sop), Armand Tokatyan (ten), Lucielle Browning (mez), Pino Bontempi (sgr), George Cehanovsky (bar), Lorenzo Alvary ((bass), A. Kent (bar), Raoul Jobin (ten), Norman Cordon (bass) VAI Audio ▲ VAIA 1023 (m) [ADD]

Dickie, John (ten)

Mozart, W.A.:Apollo et Hyacinthus, w. V. Hruba-Frieberger (sop), A. Raunig (alt), R. Popken (alt), M. Pommer (cnd), Leipzig RSO, Leipzig Radio Chorus Berlin Classics 2-▲ BER 1010 [DDD]

Mozart, W.A.:Arias, w. J. Wildner (cnd), Capella Istropolitana—arias from Clemenza di Tito, Così fan tutte, Don Giovanni, Entführung aus dem Serail, Die Zauberflöte *(rec Dec. 1989)* Naxos ▲ 8.550383 [DDD]

Mozart, W.A.:Così fan tutte, w. J. Borowska (sop—Fiordiligi), P. Coles (sop—Despina), R. Yachmi (mez—Dorabella), J. Dickie (ten—Ferrando), A. Martin (bar—Guglielmo), P. Mikulaš (b-bar—Don Alfonso), J. Wildner (cnd), Capella Istropolitana, Slovak Phil Chorus [I] *(rec Feb.–Mar. 1990)* Naxos 3-▲ 8.660008/10 [DDD]

Dickie, John (ten) (cont.)

Mozart, W.A.:Così fan tutte (sels), w. Joanna Borowska (sop—Fiordiligi), Priti Coles (sop—Despina), Rohangiz Yachmi (mez—Dorabella), John Dickie (ten—Ferrando), Andrea Martin (bar—Guglielmo), Peter Mikulaš (bass—Don Alfonso), Milada Synkova (hpd), J. Wildner (cnd), Capella Istropolitana, Slovak Phil Chorus—Ov.; [Act I] La mia Dorabella capace non è; È la fede della femmine; Una bella serenata; Ah guarda, sorella; Vorrei dir, e cor non ho; Sento, o Dio; Bella vita militar!; Soave sia il vento; Smanie implacabili; In uomini, in soldati; Alla bella Despinetta; Come Scoglio; Non siate ritrosi; Un'aura amorosa; [Act II] Una donna a quindici anni; Prenderò quel brunettino; La mano a me date; Ei parte...senti...ah no!; Donne mie la fate a tanti a tanti; Fra gle amplessi; Fortunato l'uom che prende *(rec Slovak Philharmonic Moyzes Hall, Bratislava, Feb.–Apr. 1990)* Naxos ▲ 8.553172 [DDD]

Strauss (II), Joh.:Die Fledermaus (sels), w. Ariane Calix (sop—Ida), Gabriele Fontana (sop—Rosalinde), Brigitte Karwautz (sop—Adele), Rohangiz Yachmi-Caucig (cta—Orlofsky), John Dickie (ten—Eisenstein), Josef Hopferwieser (ten—Alfred), Erich Wessner (ten—Dr. Blind), Andrea Martin (bar—Falke), Alfred Werner (bar—Frank), J. Wildner (cnd), Czech-Slovak RSO Bratislava, Bratislava City Chorus—Ov.; [Act I] Täubchen, das entflattert ist...; Ach, ich darf nicht hin zu dir; Nein, mit solchen Advokaten; Komm mit mir zum Souper; So muss allein ich bleiben; Trinke, Liebchen, trinke schnell; [Act II] Ein Souper heut' uns winkt; Ich lade gern mir Gäste ein; Mein Herr Marquis, ein Mann wie Sie; Dieser Anstand, so manierlich; Klänge der Heimat; Im Feuerstrom der Reben; Marianka komm und tanz me hier; [Act III] Entr'acte; Spiel' ich die Unschuld vom Lande; O Fledermaus, o Fledermaus *(rec Slovak Radio Concert Hall, Bratislava)* Naxos ▲ 8.553171 [DDD]

Dickie, Murray (ten)

Busoni, F.:Arlecchino or Die Fenster, w. E. Malbin (sop), G. Evans (bar), I. Wallace (bar), F. Ollendorf (bass), Glyndeborne Festival Chorus, J. Pritchard (cnd), Glyndebourne Festival Orch EMI Classics ▲ CDMB 65284

Mahler, G.:Des Knaben Wunderhorn, w. L. Popp (sop), J. Baker (mez), D. Fischer-Dieskau (bar), B. Weikl (bar), K. Tennstedt (cnd), London PO EMI Classics ▲ CDZB 62707

Mahler, G.:Das Lied von der Erde, w. L. Popp (sop), J. Baker (mez), D. Fischer-Dieskau (bar), B. Weikl (bar), P. Kletzki (cnd), Philharmonia Orch EMI Classics ▲ CDZB 62707

Monteverdi, C.:Ritorno d'Ulisse, w. P. Esswood (ct), K. Equiluz (ten), N. Rogers (ten), M. Van Egmond (bass), N. Harnoncourt (cnd), Vienna Concentus Musicus Teldec ▲ 42496-2

Mozart, W.A.:Missa, K.317, w. Wilma Lipp (sop), Christa Ludwig (alt), Walter Berry (bass), J. Horenstein (cnd), Vienna SO Vox Legends 2-▲ CDX 5524

Mozart, W.A.:Missa, K.427, w. W. Lipp (sop), C. Ludwig (sop), W. Berry (bass), F. Grossmann (cnd), Pro Musica Orch, Vienna Oratorio Chorus [L] *(rec stereo, 1958)* Preiser ▲ 90053 [AAD]

Mozart, W.A.:Vesperae solennes, w. Wilma Lipp (sop), Christa Ludwig (alt), Walter Berry (bass), J. Horenstein (cnd), Vienna SO Vox Legends 2-▲ CDX 5524

Wagner, R.:Tannhäuser, w. Gré Brouwestijn (sop), Murray Dickie (ten), Karl Liebl (ten), Eberhard Waechter (bar), Alois Pernerstorfer (b-bar), Deszö Ernster (bass), Walter Brunelli (sgr), Peter Harrower (sgr), Rosl Schweiger (sgr), Herta Wilfert (sgr), A. Rodzinski (cnd), Rome RAI Radio-TV SO, Rome RAI Chorus Stradivarius 3-▲ STV 12318

Didonè, Rosanna (sop)

Mascagni, P.:Nerone, w. D. Di Domenico (ten), S. Cowan (bar), M. Dirks (bar), Harry Peeters (bass), Shapero (sgr), Strow-Piccolo (sgr), Tcholakov (sgr), K. Bakels (cnd), Hilversum RSO, Hilversum Chorus [I] Bongiovanni 2-▲ GB 2052/53 [DDD]

Didusch, Reingard (sgr)

Cornelius, P.:Stabat Mater, w. B. Scherler (mez), M. Schmidt (ten), S. Nimsgern (bass-bar), H. Schernus (cnd), Cologne RSO, Cologne Radio Chorus [L] *(rec 1978)* Koch Schwann ▲ 3-1086-2 [ADD]

Diedrich, J. (sgr)

Lloyd Webber, A.:Music of, w. M. Friedman (sgr), C. Carter (sgr), C. Moore (sgr), J. Barrowman (sgr), L. Robertson (sgr), Grania Renihan (sgr), J.O. Edwards (cnd), Munich SO—Cats; Joseph & the Amazing Technicolor Dreamcoat; Phantom of the Opera; Evita; Jesus Christ Superstar; Starlight Express; Song & Dance; Aspects of Love Koch International ▲ CD 340022 [DDD] ▮ MC 340022

Diedrich, Michael (trb)

Mozart, W.A.:Zauberflöte, w. M. Price (sop—Pamina), L. Serra (sop—Queen of the Night), M. Venuti (sop—Papagena), M. McLaughlin (sop—1st Lady), A. Murray (mez—2nd Lady), H. Schwarz (cta—3rd Lady), F. Höher (trb—1st Boy), M. Diedrich (trb—2nd Boy), F. Klos (trb—3rd Boy), P. Schreier (ten—Tamino), R. Tear (ten—Monostatos), R. Goldberg (ten—1st Armoured Man), K. Moll (bass—Sarastro), H. Rech (bass—2nd Armoured Man), C. Davis (cnd), Dresden Staatskapelle, Leipzig Radio Chorus Philips ("Duo" series) 2-▲ 442568-2

Dieleman, Marianne (cta)

Mahler, G.:Sym 8, w. Hanneke van Bork (sop), Ileana Cotrubas (sop), Heather Harper (sop), Brigit Finnila (mez), William Cochran (ten), Hermann Prey (bar), Hans Sotin (bass), B. Haitink (cnd), Royal Concertgebouw Orch Philips ("Solo" series) ▲ 446195-2

Diener, Melanie (sop)

Mendelssohn, F.:St. Paul, w. Annette Markert (mez), James Taylor (ten), Matthias Görne (bass), P. Herreweghe (cnd), Champs Élysées Theater Orch, Chapelle Royale Choir, Collegium Vocale *(rec Stravinsky Auditorium, Montreaux)* Harmonia Mundi France 2-▲ HMC 901584.85

Dieterich, Andreas (trb)

Mozart, W.A.:Zauberflöte, w. Constanze Backes (sop—Papagena), Christiane Oelze (sop—Pamina), Susan Roberts (sop—First Lady), Cyndia Sieden (sop—Queen of the Night), Carola Guber (cta—Second Lady), Maria Jonas (cta—Third Lady), Andreas Dieterich (trb—First Boy), Jan Andreas Mendel (trb—Second Boy), Florian Wöller (trb—Third Boy), Uwe Peper (ten—Monostatos), Nicolas Robertson (ten—First Man in Armor), Michael Schade (ten—Tamino), Gerald Finley (bar—Papageno), Noel Mann (bass—Second Man in Armour), Harry Peeters (bass—Sarastro), Detlef Roth (bass—Speaker/First Priest), Robert Burt (speaker—Third Priest), Robert Johnston (speaker—Second Priest), Wolfgang Knauer (speaker—Fourth Priest), Douglas Welbat (speaker—Second Priest), J. E. Gardiner (cnd), English Baroque Soloists, Monteverdi Choir London *(rec Forum am Schlosspark, Ludwigsburg, July 1995)* Archiv 2-▲ 449166-2

Dietrich, D. (sop)

Feldman, Morton:Rothko Chapel, w. D. Abel (vn), K. Rosenak (pno), W. Winant (perc), Philip Brett (cnd), Univ of California at Berkeley Chamber Chorus *(rec 10/90)* New Albion ▲ NA 039 [DDD]

Dietschy, Véronique (sop)

Bach, J.C.F:Die Auferweckung Lazarus, w. Consuelo Caroli (mez), John Elwes (ten), Philippe Cantor (bar), G. Bezzina (cnd), Nice Baroque Ensemble, Nicole Blanchi Vocal Ensemble Adda ▲ ADD 581182 [DDD]

Boësset, A.:Music of, w. Marcel Bozonnet (nar), Alain Zaepffel (ct), Christophe Le Paludier (ten), Jacques Bone (bass), Claire Antonini (lt), Marianne Muller (vl)—Madame de la fayette; Airs de cour; La princesse de cleves (sels) Adès ▲ ADE 204722

Debussy, C.:Songs, w. Philippe Cassard (pno)—Ariettes oubliées; 5 poèmes de Baudelaire [La balcon; Harmonie du soir; Le jet d'eau; Recueillement; La mort des amants]; Jane; Caprice; Fêtes galantes [En sourdine; Fantoches; Clair de lune] Adès ▲ ADE 202682 [DDD]

Leçons de ténèbres et raga de la nuit avancée, w. Alain Zaepffel (ct), Sulochana Brahaspati (voc), Ensemble Gradiva K617 ▲ 7017 [DDD]

Scarlatti, A.:Cants & Duets, w. Alain Zaepffel (ct), Marianne Muller (vl), Macha Yanuchevskaia (vc), Aline Zylberajch (hpd/org), Yasurnori Imamura (thb)—Il Sonno; Clori e Mirtillo; Marcantonio e Cleopatra; Doralbo e Niso Adès ▲ ADE 202172 [DDD]

Dijck, Jeannette van (sop)

Haydn, J.:Die Schöpfung, w. Peter Schreier (ten), Theo Adam (bass), Hans Plumacher (vc), Heinz Detering (db), Fritz Lehan (hpd), G. Wand (cnd), Cologne Gürzenich Orch, Cologne Gürzenich Chorus Accord 2-▲ ACD 200422 [AAD]

Dijck, Stéphane van (ten)

Sebastiani, J.:St. Matthew Passion, w. Greta de Reyghere (sop), Vincent Gregoire (ct), Hervé Lamy (ten—Evangéliste), Max van Egmond (bass—Christ), P. Pierlot (cnd), Ricercar Consort Ricercar ▲ 160144

Dijk, Hans van (sgr)

Monteverdi, C.:Ballo delle ingrate, w. Carlo Lepore (bass), Daniela Barcellona (sgr), Daniela Ciliberti (sgr), Andrea Concetti (sgr), Remo Guerrini (sgr), Nadia Mantelli (sgr), Elena Marazzi (sgr), Humberto Orellana (sgr), Claudia Pallini (sgr), Luigi Polsini (sgr), Rosa Ricciotti (sgr), Alberto Rota (sgr), Ludovica Scoppola (sgr), *(orch unknown)* Nuova Era ▲ NUO 7224

▲ = CD ♦ = Enhanced CD Δ = MD ▮ = Cassette Tape ▯ = DCC

Dilbèr (sop)
Coloratura Arias, w. Estonia Opera Orch [cnd:Eri Klas] Ondine ▲ ODE 768 [DDD]

Dill Smith, Carolyn (sop)
Mozart, W.A.:Missa brevis, K.194, w. M. Busching (mez), G. Tucker (ten), P. Fay (bar), H. Mardirosian (cnd), St. Thomas Moore Cathedral Orch, St. Thomas Moore Cathedral Chorus [L] Centaur ▲ CRC 2074 [DDD]
Mozart, W.A.:Tantum ergo, w. Marianna Busching (mez), Gene Tucker (ten), Peter Fay (bar), H. Mardirosian (cnd), St. Thomas Moore Cathedral Orch, St. Thomas Moore Cathedral Chorus [L] Centaur ▲ CRC 2074 [DDD]
Mozart, W.A.:Vesperae de Dominica, w. M. Busching (mez), G. Tucker (ten), P. Fay (bar), H. Mardirosian (cnd), St. Thomas Moore Cathedral Orch, St. Thomas Moore Cathedral Chorus [L] Centaur ▲ CRC 2074 [DDD]

Diller, Hermann (ten)
Gassmann, F.L.:La Contessina, w. Susanne Ganglberger (sop—Vespina), Elisabeth Mayer (sop—Contessina), Barbara Eisschiel (mez—Lindoro), Hermann Diller (ten—Gazzetta), Kurt Köller (bar—Pancrazio), Joseph Pichler (Graf Baccellone), H. Dechant (cnd), Collegium Aureum Bayer 2-▲ BR 100 252/3 [DDD]

Dillon, Martil (ten)
Jane's Hand:The Jane Austen Songbooks, w. J. Baird (sop), Elizabeth Henreckson-Farnum (sop), Lorie Gratis (mez), Daniel Pincus (ten), Philip Anderson (ten), Nancy Wilson (bar vn), Peter Segal (bar gtr), Mary Jane Newman (pno/hpd), Anthony Newman (pno) Vox Classics ▲ VOX 7537 [DDD]

Dilova, Penka (mez)
Tchaikovsky, P.:Queen of Spades, w. S. Evstatieva (sop), I. Konsulov (bar), Mazulok (bass), E. Tchakarov (cnd), Sofia Festival Orch, Bulgarian National Chorus [R] Sony Classical 3-▲ S3K 45720

Dilworth, Helen (sop)
Gold, E.:Music of, w. G. Nestor (gtr), F. Benedetti (gtr), R. Gianattosio (pno), Holmby String Quartet—Sonata for Piano (1980); Songs of Love & Parting (1963); Quartet No. 1 for Strings (1948) *(rec 1983 & 1990)* Cambria ▲ CD 1062 [DDD/ADD]

Dima, Elena (sop)
Verdi, G.:Il trovatore, w. Elena Dima (sop—Leonora), Victoria Draganescu (sop—Ines), Zenaida Pally (mez—Azucena), Ion Buzea (ten—Duke of Mantua), Constantin Iliescu (ten—Ruiz), Cornel Stavru (ten—Manrico), Octav Enigarescu (bar—Count di Luna), Constantin Dumitru (bass—Ferrando), E. Massini (cnd), Romanian Opera Orch, Romanian Opera Chorus *(rec 1960–61)* Vox Box 2-▲ CDX 5163

Dimitrova, Ghena (sop)
Mercadante, S.:La Vestale, w. D. Vejzovic (sop), G. Cecchele (ten), Romanò (sgr), Cepreaga (sgr), Kliskic (sgr), Sioli (sgr), Boldrini (sgr), V. Sutej (cnd), Spalato National Theater Orch, Spalato National Theater Chorus [I] *(rec 4/9/87)* Bongiovanni 2-▲ GB 2065/66 [DDD]
Puccini, G.:Turandot, w. C. Gasdia (sop), N. Martinucci (ten), R. Scandiuzzi (bass), D. Oren (cnd), Genoa Teatro Comunale Orch, Genoa Teatro Comunale Chorus [I] *(rec live, 1/20–27/89)* Nuova Era 2-▲ 6786/87 [DDD]
Puccini, G.:Turandot (sels), w. C. Gasdia (sop), N. Martinucci (ten), R. Scandiuzzi (bass), D. Oren (cnd), Genoa Teatro Comunale Orch, Genoa Teatro Comunale Chorus [I] Nuova Era ▲ 6871 [DDD]
Verdi, G.:Aida, w. M. Chiara (sop), L. Pavarotti (ten), L. Nucci (bar), P. Burchuladze (bass), L. Maazel (cnd), La Scala Orch, La Scala Chorus [I] London 3-▲ 417439-2 [DDD] 2-■ 417439-4
Verdi, G.:Aida, w. M. Chiara (sop), L. Pavarotti (ten), L. Nucci (bar), P. Burchuladze (bass), L. Maazel (cnd), La Scala Orch, La Scala Chorus [I] London □ 433162-5
Verdi, G.:Un ballo in maschera, w. Ghena Dimitrova (sop—Amelia), Isabella Stramaglia (sop—Oscar), Mirna Pecile (cta—Ulrica), Mario Carlin (ten—Un giudice), José Carreras (ten—Riccardo), Piero Cappuccilli (bar—Renato), Massimiliano Malaspina (bass—Samuel), Americo de Santis (bass—Silvano), Francesco Signor (bass—Tom), Ivan Del Manto (sgr—Un servo), G. Patanè (cnd), Parma Teatro Regio Orch *(rec Teatro Regio, Dec. 26, 1972)* Golden Age of Opera 2-▲ GAO 183/84
Verdi, G.:Nabucco, w. L. V. Terrani (mez), P. Domingo (ten), P. Cappuccilli (bar), E. Nesterenko (bass), G. Sinopoli (cnd), German Opera Orch, German Opera Chorus [I] Deutsche Grammophon 2-▲ 410512-2 [DDD]
Verdi, G.:Oberto, Conte di San Bonifacio, w. R. Baldani (mez), A. Browner (mez), C. Bergonzi (ten), R. Panerai (bar), L. Gardelli (cnd), Munich RSO, Munich Radio Chorus [I] Orfeo ▲ 175881 [DDD]
Verdi, G.:Oberto, Conte di San Bonifacio, w. R. Baldani (mez), A. Browner (mez), C. Bergonzi (ten), R. Panerai (bar), L. Gardelli (cnd), Munich RSO, Munich Radio Chorus [I] Orfeo 2-▲ 105842 [DDD] 3-■ A 105843 F

Dingman, Robert (ten)
Shewan, S.:Magnificat, w. Erin Stedman (sop), Kimberly Higgins (alt), Alexander Burgess (bar), Paul Shewan (tpt), Barbara Hull (tpt), Nanita Wilson (hn), Scott Emmons (trbn), Kirk Kettinger (tuba), Ann Musser Honeywell (org) Albany ▲ TROY 149 [DDD]
Shewan, S.:The Voice of the Lord in the Storm, w. Erin Stedman (sop), Kimberly Higgins (alt), Alexander Burgess (bar), Paul Shewan (tpt), Barbara Hull (tpt), Nanita Wilson (hn), Scott Emmons (trbn), Kirk Kettinger (tuba), Ann Musser Honeywell (org) Albany ▲ TROY 149 [DDD]

Dinkov, Kosta (bass)
Puccini, G.:Madama Butterfly, w. Raina Kabaivanska (sop—Madama Butterfly), Alexandrina Milcheva (mez—Suzuki), Rossitza Troeva-Mircheva (cta—Kate Pinkerton), Nazzareno Antinori (ten—F.B. Pinkerton), Roumen Doikov (ten—Goro), Werther Vrachovski (ten—Il Principe Yamadori), Nelson Portella (bar—Sharpless), Kosta Dinkov (bass—Lo zio Bonzo), G. Bellini (cnd), Sofia PO, Svetoslav Obrenetov Bulgarian National Chorus *(rec Sophia, Bulgaria, Dec 1–13, 1982)* Arts Music 2-▲ 447161-2 [DDD]

Dirks, Math (bar)
Mascagni, P.:Nerone, w. R. Didonè (sop), D. Di Domenico (ten), S. Cowan (bar), Harry Peeters (bass), Shapero (sgr), Strow-Piccolo (sgr), Tcholakov (sgr), K. Bakels (cnd), Hilversum RSO, Hilversum Chorus [I] Bongiovanni 2-▲ GB 2052/53 [DDD]
Mascagni, P.:Il piccolo Marat, w. S. Neves (sop—Mariella), C. Pfeiler (mez—Principessa di Fleury), D. Galvez-Vallejo (ten—Marat), S. Cowan (bar—Soldier), M. Dirks (bar—Il Ladro), F. Vassar (bass—L'Orco), H. Claessens (bass—Spy), K. Bakels (cnd), Netherlands RSO, Netherlands Radio Chorus *(rec Feb. 9, 1992)* Bongiovanni 2-▲ GB 2168/69 [DDD]

DiSimone, Lorraine (mez)
Mascagni, P.:Silvano, w. Rachel Sparer (sop—Matilde), Lorraine DiSimone (mez—Rosa), Joseph Wolverton (ten—Silvano), Bojan Knezevic (bar—Renzo), P. Tiboris (cnd), Bohuslav Martinů PO *(rec SUNY Performing Arts Center Theatre, Purchase, NY, May 23–25, 1995)* Elysium ▲ GRK 707 [DDD]

Ditlevsen, Jørgen (bass)
Nielsen, C.:Hymnus Amoris, w. I. Nielsen (sop), A. Elkrog (ten), P. Elming (ten), P. Høyer (bar), L. Segerstam (cnd), Danish National RSO, Copenhagen Boys' Choir, Danish National Radio Choir [L] Chandos ▲ CHAN 8853 [DDD]

Dittmannová, Pavla (cta)
Janácek, L.:Music of, w. Zuzana Lapciková (sop), Petr Julícek (ten), L. Svárovský (cnd), Brno State PO, Petr Fiala (cnd), Brno Czech Phil Chorus—Rákos Rákoczy (ballet); folk songs, choruses & dances Supraphon ▲ SUP CD 3129

Diwiak, Dantes (ten)
Steffani, A.:Enrico Leone, w. R. Popken (alt), M. Frimmer (sop), S. Szameit (sop), N. Yoko (cta), C. Guber (cta), G. Faulstich (bar), L. Rovatkay (cnd), Cappela Agostino Steffani [period instrs] [I] Calig ▲ CAL 50855 [DDD]

Dixon, L. (sgr)
Rodgers, R.:Oklahoma!, w. A. Drake (sgr), C. Holm (sgr), J. Roberts (sgr), H. da Silva (sgr), J. Blackton (cnd), *(orch unknown)* MCA Classics ▲ MCAD 10046 [AAD] ■ MCAC 10046

Djokic (sgr)
Mussorgsky, M.:Boris Godunov, w. Cangalovic (sgr), Milosevic (sgr), Petrovic (sgr), D. Miladinovic (cnd), Belgrade National Opera Orch, Belgrade National Opera Chorus *(rec live, La Fenice Theater, Venice, Jan. 3, 1967)* Arkadia 3-▲ 492

Dluha, Kazimierz (sgr)
Moniuszko, S.:Haunted Manor, w. Bozena Betley-Siradzka (sop—Hanna), Anna Witkowska (sop—Marta/Stara Niewiasta), Wiera Baniewicz (mez—Jadwiga), Aleksandra Imalska (mez—Czesnikowa), Kazimierz Dluha (Grzes), Zdzislaw Nikodem (ten—Damazy), Wieslaw Ochman (ten—Stefan), Andrzej Hiolski (bar—Miecznik), Florian Skulski (bar—Maciej), Leonard Mróz (bass—Zbigniew), Andrzej Saciuk (bass—Skoluba), J. Krenz (cnd), Cracow Polish Radio-TV Orch, Cracow Polish Radio-TV Chorus *(rec Cracovia, 1978)* Agorá Music ("Phoenix" series) 3-▲ 509 [ADD]

Doane, David (ten)
Vivier, C.:Kopernikus, "A Ritual Opera of Death", w. Y. Parent (sop), P. Vaillancourt (sop), M.-D. Parent (sop), J. Fleury (cta), M. Ducharme (bar), Y. Saint-Amant (bass), F. Martel (cl), M. Bélanger (vn), L. Bouchard (tpt), L. Vaillancourt (cnd), *(orch unknown)* *(rec Feb. 1991)* CBC ("Musica Viva" series) ▲ MVCD 1047 [DDD]

Dobrev, Ivan (bass)
Schubert, Franz:Mass 2, w. E. Maksimova (sop), H. Kamenov (ten), V. Kazandjiev (cnd), Sofia Soloists CO, Rodina Chorus [L] Musique d'Abord ▲ HMA 190111 [AAD]

Dobrianova, Nadezhda (sop)
Mussorgsky, M.:Boris Godunov, w. S. Jurinac (sop), D. Usunow (ten), N. Ghiaurov (bass), N. Ghiuselev (bass), A. Diakov (bass), H. von Karajan (cnd), Vienna PO, Vienna State Opera Chorus [R] *(rec live in Salzburg, 7/26/64)* Arkadia 2-▲ 210 (m) [ADD]

Dobrowolski, Juri (bass)
Suder, J.:Festival Mass, w. Natalia Kornewa (sop), Maria Neilau (alt), Vladimir Mostomoi (ten), Jessica Hartlieb (vn), Marlene Hinterberger (org), W.A. Albert (cnd), Bavarian State Youth Orch, St. Petersburg Chamber Choir Calig ▲ CAL 50945 [DDD]

Dobson, John (ten)
Janácek, L.:The Cunning Little Vixen, w. L. Watson (sop), E. Bainbridge (mez), G. Knight (mez), D. Montague (mez), R. Tear (ten), T. Allen (bar), G. Howell (bass), S. Rattle (cnd), Royal Opera House Orch [E] EMI Classics 2-▲ CDCB 54212
Verdi, G.:Macbeth, w. Amy Shuard (sop—Lady Macbeth), Noreen Berry (mez—Lady-in-waiting), John Dobson (ten—Malcolm), André Turp (ten—Macduff), Tito Gobbi (bar—Macbeth), Edgar Boniface (bass—Servant), Rydderch Davies (bass—Doctor), Forbes Robinson (bass—Banco), Jean Holmes (sgr—Apparition), Celia Penny (sgr—Apparition), Glynne Thomas (sgr—Apparition), Brian Wrigt (sgr—Araldo), F. Molinari-Pradelli (cnd), Royal Opera House Orch, Royal Opera House Chorus Covent Garden *(rec London, Apr 8, 1960)* Bella Voce 2-▲ 7203 [AAD]

Dobszay, Ágnes (sop)
Werner, G.J.:Vesperae de Apostolis, w. Péter Patay (cta), Tamás Bubnó (ten), Péter Cser (bass), J. Mezei (cnd), Vienna-Szász CO, Budapest Schola Cantorum *(rec St. Columba's Presbyterian Church, Budapest, June 12–15, 1995)* Hungaroton ▲ HCD 31646 [DDD]

Dodge, Charles (sgr)
Dodge, C.:Speech Songs New Albion ▲ NA 043

Doese, Helena (sop)
Beethoven, L. van:Syms (comp), w. Marga Schiml (alt), Peter Schreier (ten), Theo Adam (bass), H. Blomstedt (cnd), Dresden Staatskapelle, Dresden State Opera Chorus, Leipzig Radio Choir *(rec Lukaskirche, Dresden, 1975–80)* Berlin Classics 5-▲ 0021942BC [ADD]
Beethoven, L. van:Syms (comp), w. Marga Schiml (sop), Peter Schreier (ten), Theo Adam (b-bar), H. Blomstedt (cnd), Dresden Staatskapelle, Dresden State Opera Chorus *(rec late 1970's–early 1980's)* Berlin Classics 5-▲ BER 2194 [DDD]

Dohmen, Albert (bar)
Beethoven, L. van:Fidelio (sels), w. Evelyn Herlitzius (sop—Leonore), Ruth Ziesak (sop—Marzelline), Stig Andersen (ten—Florestan), Herbert Lippert (ten—Jaquino), Albert Dohmen (bar—Don Pizarro), Andreas Kohn (bass—Don Fernando), Hans Tschammer (bass—Rocco), G. Solti (cnd), World Orch for Peace, London Voices—Finale Act II *(rec Victoria Hall, Geneva, July 5, 1995)* London ▲ 448901-2 [DDD]
Cornelius, P.:Der Cid, w. Gertrud Ottenthal (sop), Ronnie Johansen (sgr), Robert Schunk (ten), Michael Schopper (bass), Endrik Wottrich (sgr), G. Kuhn (cnd), Berlin RSO, Berlin Radio Chorus Koch Schwann 2-▲ SCH 315222
Mozart, W.A.:Così fan tutte, w. A. C. Antonacci (sop—Fiordiligi), M. Bacelli (sop—Dorabella), L. Cherici (sop—Despina), R. Decker (ten—Ferrando), A. Dohmen (bar—Gugliemo), S. Bruscantini (bar—Don Alfonso), G. Kuhn (cnd), Marchigiana PO, Marchigiana Phil Chorus [I] *(rec live, Teatro Lauro Rossi at the Festival di Macerata, Aug. 3, 1990)* Orfeo 3-▲ 243913 [DDD]

Doikov, Roumen (ten)
Puccini, G.:Madama Butterfly, w. Raina Kabaivanska (sop—Madama Butterfly), Alexandrina Milcheva (mez—Suzuki), Rossitza Troeva-Mircheva (cta—Kate Pinkerton), Nazzareno Antinori (ten—F.B. Pinkerton), Roumen Doikov (ten—Goro), Werther Vrachovski (ten—Il Principe Yamadori), Nelson Portella (bar—Sharpless), Kosta Dinkov (bass—Lo zio Bonzo), G. Bellini (cnd), Sofia PO, Svetoslav Obrenetov Bulgarian National Chorus *(rec Sophia, Bulgaria, Dec 1–13, 1982)* Arts Music 2-▲ 447161-2 [DDD]
Puccini, G.:Tosca, w. Raina Kabaivanska (sop—Floria Tosca), Nazzareno Antinori (ten—Mario Cavaradocci), Roumen Doikov (ten—Spoletta), Enzo Dara (bar—Casare Angelotti/Il sagrestano), Nelson Portella (bar—Il Barone Scarpia), Stoyan Balabanov (bass—Sciarrone/Un carceriere), Borislav Peev (sgr—Un Pastore), G. Bellini (cnd), Sofia PO, Bulgarian National Radio Children's Choir, Svetoslav Obrenetov Bulgarian National Chorus *(rec Sophia, Bulgaria, Nov 14–27, 1982)* Arts Music ▲ 47158-2 [DDD]

Dolberg, Kirsten (mez)
Gade, N.W.:Elverskud, w. Susanne Elmark (sop-Elf-King's Daughter), Guido Paëvatalu (bar-Oluf), M. Schønwandt (cnd), Tivoli SO, Tivoli Concert Choir *(rec Tivoli Concert Hall, Apr 29–30, May 4, 1996)* Marco Polo/Dacapo ▲ 8.224051 [DDD]
Gade, N.W.:Frühlings Fant, w. Anne Margrethe Dahl (sop), Gert Hennig-Jensen (ten), Sten Byriel (bass), Elisabeth Westenholz (pno), M. Schønwandt (cnd), Tivoli SO *(rec Tivoli Concert Hall, Apr 29–30, May 4, 1996)* Marco Polo/Dacapo ▲ 8.224051 [DDD]
Grieg, E.:Songs, w. F. Gürtler (pno)—While I Wait; The First Meeting; With a Water Lily; Two Brown Eyes; I Love You; A Swan Point ▲ PCD 5106
Haydn, J.:Applausus:Jubilaeum virtutis Palatium, w. Rosemary Musoleno (sop—Temperantia), Kirsten Dolberg (mez—Prudentia), Douglas Johnson (ten—Justitia), Desmond Byrne (bass—Fortitudo), Jean-Philippe Courtis (bass—Theologia), P. Fournillier (cnd), Picardie Orch, Haydn Vocal Ensemble [L] *(rec 9/91)* Opus 111 2-▲ OPS 61-9207/8 [DDD]
Koppel, H.D.:Moses, w. Elisabeth Meyer-Topsøe (sop), Kurt Westi (ten), Michael Kristensen (ten), Per Høyer (bar), Christian Christiansen (bass), O.A. Hughes (cnd), Danish National RSO, Jesper Grovw Jørgensen (cnd), Danish National Radio Choir *(rec Danish Radio Concert Hall, Mar 1996)* Marco Polo/Dacapo ▲ 8.224046 [DDD]
Lange-Müller, P.E.:Songs, w. F. Gürtler (pno)—Shulamite's Song in the Wine Garden; Shulamite's Song in the Grove of the Wood-Pigeons; Soloman's song with the Homing Pigeon; Shulamite's Song at the Top of the Mountain; Shulamit'es Song on the Mountains; Shulamite's Song in the Queen's Garden; Shulamite's Song in the Bridal Doorway Point ▲ PCD 5106
Mahler, G.:Sym 2, w. Tina Kiberg (sop), L. Segerstam (cnd), Danish National RSO, Danish National Radio Choir Chandos 2-▲ CHAN 9266/67 [DDD]
Mahler, G.:Sym 8, w. Majken Bjerno (sop), Henriette Bonde-Hansen (sop), Inga Nielsen (sop), Anne Gjevang (alt), Raimo Sirkiä (ten), Jorma Hynninen (bar), Carsten Stabell (bass), L. Segerstam (cnd), Danish National RSO, Copenhagen Boys' Choir, Berlin Phil Choir, Danish National Radio Choir Chandos 2-▲ CHAN 9305/06 [DDD]
Rangström, T.:Songs, w. F. Gürtler (pno)—The Wind and the Tree; The Rain Song; Serenade; The Farewell Point ▲ PCD 5106
Sibelius, J.:Songs, w. F. Gürtler (pno)—The First Kiss; The Girl Came Home from her Lover's Tryst; The Diamond in the March Snow; Little Lasse; Spring Takes Flight Hastily; Reed, Reed, Rustle; Black Roses Point ▲ PCD 5106

Dolezal, Vladimír (ten)
Dvořák, A.:Stabat Mater, w. Eva Jenisova (sop), Hana Stolfova-Bandova (cta), Jiri Sulzenka (bass), L. Svárovský (cnd), Czech PO, Petr Fiala (cnd), Brno Czech Phil Chorus Supraphon 2-▲ SUP CD 3093

Dolezal, Vladimír (ten) (cont.)
Havelka, S.:Music of, w. Brigita Sulcova (sop), Anna Barova (cta), Richard Novak (bass), V. Neumann (cnd), Czech PO, Prague Phil Chorus—Epistola de M. Hieronymi De Praga Supplicio Panton ▲ PAN 810966
Klein, G.:Pvrní hřich *(rec Oct. 20 & 21, 1992)* Koch International Classics ▲ KIC 7230-2 [DDD]
Martinů, B.:Ariadne, w. C. Lindsley (sop), R. Novák (ten), N. Phillips (bar), V. Neumann (cnd), Czech PO, Czech Phil Chorus [Cz] Supraphon ▲ 10 4395-2 [DDD]
Martinů, B.:Mount of 3 Lights, w. R. Novák (bass), P. Haničinec (nar), J. Hora (org), P. Kühn (cnd), Prague Radio Men's Chorus, Kühn Chorus [Cz] *(rec 2-3/88)* Supraphon ▲ 11 0751-2 [DDD]
Mysliveček, J.:Isacco figura, w. Ilona Czaková (sgr), Hye Jin Kim (sgr), Tatiana Korovina (sgr), Victoria Luchianez (sgr), Ivan Kusnjer (bar), I. Parik (cnd), Prague Sinfonietta, Pavel Kühn (cnd), Kühn Chorus Supraphon 2-▲ SUP 3209
Orff, C.:Carmina burana, w. Zdena Kloubová (sop), Ivan Kusnjer (bar), G. Delogu (cnd), Prague SO, Bambini di Praga, Kühn Choir *(rec live, Prague, Dec 12, 1995)* Supraphon ▲ SUP 3160
Orff, C.:Carmina burana, w. E. Jenisová (sop), I. Kusnjer (bar), S. Gunzenhauser (cnd), Czech-Slovak RSO Bratislava, Slovak Phil Chorus Naxos ▲ 8.550196 [DDD] Δ 7.550196 [DDD]
Reicha, A.:Requiem, w. V. Hrubá-Freiberger (sop), A. Barová (mez), L. Vele (bass), L. Mátl (cnd), Dvořák CO, Czech Phil Chorus [L] Supraphon ▲ 11 0332-2 [DDD]
Schnittke, A.:Requiem, w. Zdena Kloubová (sop), Olga Štěpánová (alt), J. Bělohlávek (cnd), Prague SO, Kühn Chorus *(rec live, Smetana Hall, Municipal House, Prague, Dec 19, 1990)* Panton ("60 Years of the Prague SO" series) ▲ PAN 811374 [ADD]
Slavický, K.:Psalmi, w. Salome Losová (sop), Dagmar Pecková (cta), Ludek Vele (bass), Jan Hora (org), P. Kühn (cnd), Kühn Chorus *(rec Dvořák Hall of Rudolfinum, Prague, Mar. 14-16, 1989)* Panton ("Protokol XX" series) ▲ PAN 811142 [DDD]
Zelenka, J.D.:Missa Gratias agimus tibi, w. J. Jonášová (sop), M. Mrázová (cta), P. Mikuláš (bass), J. Bělohlávek (cnd), Czech PO, Czech Phil Chorus [L] Supraphon ▲ 11 0816-2 [DDD]

Dolorian, Marie-Jose (sop)
Ibert, J.:Songs, w. Carlos Cebro (pno)—Berceuse de Galiane; Chanson; Chanson du Rien; 2 Chansons de Melpomène; 4 Chants; Complainte de Florinde; Le Jardin du Ciel; La Verdure dorée; 3 sels from Livre d'Amour; 3 sels from Roi d'Yvetot Media 7 ▲ 007 [DDD]

Dolton, Geoffrey (bar)
Donizetti, G.:Emilia di Liverpool, w. Y. Kenny (sop), A. Mason (sop), B. Mills (sop), C. Merritt (ten), S. Bruscantini (bar), C. Thornton-Holmes (bar), D. Parry (cnd), Philharmonia Orch, Geoffrey Mitchell Choir—complete opera, without dialogue Opera Rara 3-▲ OR 8
Donizetti, G.:L'Eremitaggio di Liverpool, w. Y. Kenny (sop), A. Mason (sop), B. Mills (sop), C. Merritt (ten), S. Bruscantini (bar), C. Thornton-Holmes (bar), D. Parry (cnd), Philharmonia Orch, Geoffrey Mitchell Choir—complete opera, without dialogue Opera Rara 3-▲ OR 8

Dolukhanova, Zara (mez)
Ippolitov-Ivanov, M.:Poems of Tagore, w. N. Svetlanova (pno) *(rec 1952-66)* Russian Disc ▲ RUS 15 015 [ADD]
Kabalevsky, D.:Joyful Songs, w. N. Svetlanova (pno) *(rec 1952-66)* Russian Disc ▲ RUS 15 015 [ADD]
Medtner, N.:Songs—5 songs Russian Disc ▲ RUS 11 342 [AAD]
Prokofiev, S.:Songs Russian Disc ▲ RUS 11 341 [ADD]
Rachmaninoff, S.:Songs—6 songs Russian Disc ▲ RUS 11 342 [AAD]
Scriabin, A.:Songs Russian Disc ▲ RUS 11 342 [AAD]
Shchedrin, R.:Solfeggi, w. N. Svetlanova (pno) *(rec 1971)* Russian Disc ▲ RUS 11 030 [AAD]
Shostakovich, D.:From Jewish Folk Poetry, w. N. Doralik (sop), A. Masennikov (ten), D. Shostakovich (pno) *(rec 1956)* Russian Disc ▲ RUS 15 015 [ADD]
Stravinsky, I.:Songs—2 songs Russian Disc ▲ RUS 11 341 [ADD]
Tchaikovsky, P.:Songs—13 songs Russian Disc ▲ RUS 11 342 [AAD]

Domahidy Jr., L. (bass)
Liszt, F.:An die Künstler, w. A. Molnár (ten), T. Daróczi (ten), J. Molday (bar), I. Zámbó (cnd), Hungarian State Orch, Hungarian People's Army Male Chorus [G] Hungaroton ▲ HCD 12748 [DDD]

Domahidy, László (bass)
Kacsóh, P.:János Vitéz, w. Mária Gyurkovics (sop), Anna Zentai (sop—Iluska), Tivadar Bilicsi (sgr), Hilda Gobbi (sgr), Sándor Pethes (sgr—Bartolo), Róbert Ilosfalvy (ten—Kukorica), György Melis (bar—Bagó), György Radnai (bar—Strázsamester), László Domahidy (bass—Csősz), E. Lukács (cnd), Hungarian State Opera Orch, Hungarian Radio-TV Chorus *(rec Budapest, 1961)* Classical Diamonds 2-▲ CLD 4011-12 [AAD]

Domanínská, Libusé (sop)
Kabeláč, M.:Sym 5, w. K. Ančerl (cnd), Czech PO, Czech Phil Women's Chorus *(rec live)* Panton ▲ 81 1102
Kabeláč, M.:Sym 5, w. K. Ančerl (cnd), Czech PO *(rec 1961)* Praga ▲ PR 255000
Martinů, B.:Bouquet, w. Soňa Červená (alt), Lubomír Havlák (ten), Ladislav Mráz (bass), K. Ančerl (cnd), Czech PO, Czech Phil Chorus *(rec 1967)* Praga ("Karel Ančerl Edition" series) ▲ PR 254061

Domenico, Dino di (ten)
Manfroce, N.A.:Ecuba, w. A. C. Antonacci (sop), F. Piccoli (ten), G. De Bellida (sgr), M. de Bernart (cnd), Italian PO, Italian Phil Chorus [I] *(rec live 1990)* Bongiovanni 2-▲ GB 2119/20 [DDD]
Mascagni, P.:Nerone, w. R. Didoné (sop), S. Cowan (bar), M. Dirks (bar), Harry Peeters (bass), Shapero (sgr), Strow-Piccolo (sgr), Tcholakov (sgr), K. Bakels (cnd), Hilversum RSO, Hilversum Chorus [I] Bongiovanni 2-▲ GB 2052/53 [DDD]
Mercadante, S.:Il bravo, w. J. Perry (sop), A. Tabiadon (mez), S. Bertocchi (ten), S. Antonucci (bar), B. Aprea (cnd), Italian International Orch, Slovak Phil Chorus [I] *(rec live 7/28-31/90)* Nuova Era 3-▲ 6971/73 [DDD]

Domgraf-Fassbaender, Willi (bar)
The Legendary Singers at Lindenoper Berlin (1927-1945)—, w. Gitta Alpar (sop), Erna Berger (sop), Tiana Lemnitz (sop), Maria Müller (sop), Margarete Klose (cta), Peter Anders (ten), Max Lorenz (ten), Walter Ludwig (ten), Lauritz Melchior (ten), Rudolf Schock (ten), Franz Völker (ten), et al. *(rec 1927; 1937; 1941-45)* Minerva ▲ MN A21 [ADD]
Mozart, W.A.:Così fan tutte, w. Irene Eisinger (sop—Despina), Luise Helletsgruber (sop—Dorabella), Ina Souez (sop—Fiordiligi), Heddle Nash (ten—Ferrando), John Brownlee (bass—Don Alfonso), Willi Domgraf-Fassbaender (bass—Guglielmo), F. Busch (cnd), Glyndebourne Festival Orch, Glyndebourne Festival Chorus *(rec June 25-28, 1935)* Arkadia ("The 78's" series) 2-▲ 78011 [ADD]
Mozart, W.A.:Così fan tutte, w. I. Souez (sop), L. Helletsgrüber (sop), I. Eisinger (sop), H. Nash (ten), J. Brownlee (bar), F. Busch (cnd), Glyndebourne Festival Orch, Glyndebourne Festival Chorus [I] *(rec 1935)* Pearl 3-▲ PEAS 9406 (m) [AAD]
Mozart, W.A.:Nozze di Figaro, w. Aulikki Rautawaara (sop), Audrey Mildmay (sop), Constance Willis (mez), John Heddle Nash (ten), Roy Henderson (bar), F. Busch (cnd), Glyndebourne Festival Orch *(rec 1934)* Legend 2-▲ LGD 132 [ADD]
Mozart, W.A.:Nozze di Figaro, w. Luise Helletsgrüber (sop), Audrey Mildmay (sop), Aulikki Rautawaara (sop), Roy Henderson (bar), F. Busch (cnd), Glyndebourne Festival Orch, Glyndebourne Festival Chorus *(rec 1934)* Grammofono 2000 2-▲ GRM 78624
Mozart, W.A.:Nozze di Figaro, w. Aulikki Rautawaara (sop), Audrey Mildmay (sop), Constance Willis (mez), John Heddle Nash (ten), Roy Henderson (bar), F. Busch (cnd), Glyndebourne Festival Orch, Glyndebourne Festival Chorus [I] *(rec 1934-35)* Pearl 2-▲ PEAS 9375 (m) [AAD]
Mozart, W.A.:Nozze di Figaro (sels), w. Luise Helletsgrüber (sop), Audrey Mildmay (sop), Aulikki Rautawaara (sop), Constance Willis (mez), John Heddle Nash (ten), Roy Henderson (bar), Norman Allin (bass), F. Busch (cnd), Glyndebourne Festival Orch Pearl ▲ PEA CD 9230
Mozart, W.A.:Zauberflöte, w. D. Komarek (sop), J. Novotna (sop), J. Osvath (sop), H. Roswaenge (ten), A. Kipnis (bass), A. Toscanini (cnd), Vienna PO, Vienna Phil Chorus [G] *(rec live, Salzburg, July 30, 1937)* Melodram 3-▲ MEL 37040 (m) [AAD]

Domingo, Plácido (ten)
Adoro CBS ▲ MK 37284 ■ FMT 37284
Arias & Duets (1974-1986), w. G. Taddei (bar), L. Pavarotti (ten), et al., Vienna State Opera Orch [var. cnd] Acanta ▲ 49402
The Art of Placido Domingo Replay ▲ BMCD 028 [AAD]
Ave Maria, w. Vienna SO [cnd:Helmuth Froschauer], Vienna Boys Choir RCA Gold Seal ▲ 07863-53835-2

Domingo, Plácido (ten) (cont.)
Ave Maria, w. Mario Lanza (ten), Vienna Boys' Choir, Robert Shaw Chorale RCA Victor ▲ 09026-61838-2 ■ 09026-61838-4
Beethoven, L. van:Missa Solemnis, w. C. Studer (sop), J. Norman (sop), K. Moll (bass), J. Levine (cnd), Vienna PO, Leipzig Radio Chorus, Eric Ericson Chamber Chorus Deutsche Grammophon 2-▲ 435770-2 [DDD]
Beethoven, L. van:Sym 9, "Choral Sym", w. Jessye Norman (sop), Brigitte Fassbaender (mez), Walter Berry (bass), K. Böhm (cnd), Vienna PO, Vienna State Opera Chorus Deutsche Grammophon ("Masters" series) ▲ 445503-2 [DDD]
Bellini, V.:Norma, w. M. Caballé (sop), F. Cossotto (mez), R. Raimondi (bass), C.F. Cillario (cnd), London PO, Ambrosian Opera Chorus [I] RCA Gold Seal 3-▲ 6502-2-RG [ADD]
Best of Deutsche Grammophon ▲ 415366-2 GH [ADD]
The Best of Christmas in Vienna, w. Vienna SO, Charles Aznavour (sgr), José Carreras (ten), Sissel Kyrkjebø (sgr), Dionne Warwick (sgr) *(rec Vienna)* Sony Classical ▲ SK 62696 ■ ST 62696
Bizet, G.:Carmen, w. Cooper (sgr), Dunn (sgr), F. Guarrera (bar), A. Guadagno (cnd), Cincinnati Summer Opera Association Orch, Cincinnati Summer Opera Association Chorus [F] *(rec live 7/19/68)* Melodram 2-▲ MEL 27034 (m) [AAD]
Bizet, G.:Carmen, w. Laura Bustamante (sop—Frasquita), Ximena Riveros (sop—Mercedes), Nancy Stokes (sop—Micaela), Regina Resnik (mez—Carmen), Plácido Domingo (ten—Don José), Ismildo Tedeschi (ten—Remendado), Ramon Vinay (ten—Escamillo), Juan Charles (ten/bar—Dancaire), Agustin Letelier (bar—Morles), Jorge Algorta (bass—Zuniga), A. Guadagno (cnd), Santiago Teatro Municipale Orch, Santiago Teatro Municipale Chorus *(rec Santiago Municipal Theater, Sept. 4, 1967)* Legato Classics 2-▲ LCD 194-2 [ADD]
Bizet, G.:Carmen, w. Kiri Te Kanawa (sop), Shirley Verrett (mez), José Van Dam (b-bar), G. Solti (cnd), Royal Opera House Orch, Royal Opera House Chorus Covent Garden *(rec live, London, 1973)* Arkadia 3-▲ 498
Bizet, G.:Carmen, w. T. Troyanos (mez), K. Te Kanawa (sop), J. Van Dam (b-bar), G. Solti (cnd), London PO [F] London ▲ 421300-2 [ADD]
Bizet, G.:Carmen, w. T. Troyanos (mez), K. Te Kanawa (sop), J. Van Dam (b-bar), G. Solti (cnd), London PO [F] London 3-▲ 414489-2 [ADD]
Bizet, G.:Carmen, w. F. Esham (sop), J. Migenes-Johnson (sop), R. Raimondi (bass), L. Maazel (cnd), French National Orch, French Radio Chorus [F] Erato 3-▲ 2292-45207-2 ZB [DDD]
Bizet, G.:Carmen, w. E. Obraztsova (mez), J. Mazurok (bar), C. Kleiber (cnd), Vienna State Opera Orch, Vienna State Opera Chorus Exclusive 2-▲ EXL 11 [ADD]
Bizet, G.:Carmen, w. I. Cotrubas (sop), T. Berganza (mez), S. Milnes (bar), C. Abbado (cnd), London SO, Ambrosian Opera Chorus [F] Deutsche Grammophon 3-▲ 419636-2 [ADD]
Bizet, G.:Carmen, w. F. Esham (sop), J. Migenes-Johnson (sop), R. Raimondi (bass), L. Maazel (cnd), French National Orch [F] Erato ▲ 2292-45209-2 AW [DDD] ■ 2292-45209-4 AG (D)
Bizet, G.:Carmen (sels), w. Teresa Berganza (mez—Carmen), Plácido Domingo (ten—Don José), C. Abbado (cnd), London SO, John McCarthy (cnd), Patrick Criswell (cnd), Ambrosian Singers, George Watson's College Boys' Chorus—C'est toi? C'est moi Deutsche Grammophon ▲ 447270-2 [ADD] ■ 447 270-4
Bizet, G.:Carmen (sels), w. I. Cotrubas (sop), T. Berganza (mez), S. Milnes (bar), C. Abbado (cnd), London SO, Ambrosian Opera Chorus [F] Deutsche Grammophon ▲ 435401-2 [DDD]
Bizet, G.:Les Pêcheurs de perles (sels), w. Katia Ricciarelli (sop), A. Guadagno (cnd), St. Cecilia Academy Orch Rome—Au fond du temple saint *(rec 1972)* RCA Gold Seal ▲ 09026-62595-2 [ADD]
Boito, A.:Mefistofele, w. M. Caballé (sop), N. Treigle (bass), J. Rudel (cnd), London SO, Ambrosian Opera Chorus [I] EMI Classics 2-▲ CDCB 49522 [ADD]
Boito, A.:Mefistofele, w. E. Marton (sop), S. Ramey (bass), G. Patanè (cnd), Hungarian State SO, Hungarian State Opera Chorus [I] *(rec Budapest, 1988)* Sony Classical 2-▲ S2K 44983 [DDD]
Bravissimo, Domingo!, Vol. 1, w. Leontyne Price (sop), Sherrill Milnes (ten) RCA Red Seal ▲ 07863-57020-2
Bravissimo, Domingo!, Vol. 2 RCA Red Seal ▲ 07863-56211-2
Bretón, T.:La Verbena de la paloma, w. Maria Bayo (sop), Raquel Pierotti (sop), Enrique Baquerizo (sgr), Rafael Castejon (sgr), Milagros Martin (sgr), Silva Tro (sgr), A. Ros-Marbá (cnd), Madrid SO Valois ("Zarauela" series) ▲ V 4725
The Broadway I Love, w. London SO Atlantic ▲ 82350-2 ■ 82350-4
Canta para México Polygram Latino ▲ 419310-2 ■ 419310-4
Canta Para Todos Capitol/EMI Latin ▲ H2Y 42581 ■ H4F 42581
Charpentier, G.:Louise, w. I. Cotrubas (sop), J. Berbié (mez), M. Sénéchal (ten), G. Bacquier (bar), G. Prêtre (cnd), New Philharmonia Orch, Ambrosian Opera Chorus [F] Sony Classical 3-▲ S3K 46429 [ADD]
Christmas' Greatest Voices, w. L. Price (sop), Mario Lanza (sop), et al. RCA ▲ 09026-68265-2; ■ 09026-68265-4
Christmas Sampler, w. James Galway (fl), Vienna Boys' Choir, Boston Pops Orch [cnd:Arthur Fiedler] RCA Victor ▲ 09026-61840-2 ■ 09026-61840-4
Christmas with the Vienna Boys' Choir, w. Vienna Boys' Choir, Hermann Prey (bar) RCA Gold Seal ▲ 7930-2-RG [ADD] ■ 7930-4-RG
Cilea, F.:Adriana Lecouvreur, w. R. Scotto (sop), E. Obraztsova (mez), S. Milnes (bar), J. Levine (cnd), Philharmonia Orch *(rec 1977)* CBS 2-▲ M2K 34588 [ADD]
Cilea, F.:Adriana Lecouvreur, w. M. Olivero (sop), M. L. Nave (mez), E. Sordello (bar), A. Silipigni (cnd), *(orch unknown)* [I] *(rec 1973)* Legato Classics 2-▲ LCD 140-2 [ADD]
Con Amore RCA Victor ▲ 4265-2-RG [ADD] ■ AFK1-4265
Concert for Planet Earth:Rio de Janiero 1992 Sony Classical ▲ SK 52570 ■ ST 52570
Domingo!, w. various orchs CBS ▲ MK 37207 [ADD] ■ MT 37207
Domingo at the Philharmonic, w. New York PO [cnd:Zubin Mehta], Adriana Morell (sop) CBS ▲ MK 44942 [DDD] ■ MT 44942 (D)
Domingo Duets Deutsche Grammophon ▲ 447270-2 ■ 447270-4
The Domingo Edition Deutsche Grammophon ▲ 435401-2 GDE
The Domingo Edition Deutsche Grammophon ▲ 435402-2 GDE
The Domingo Edition Deutsche Grammophon ▲ 435409-2 GDE
The Domingo Edition Deutsche Grammophon ▲ 435410-2 GDE
The Domingo Edition Deutsche Grammophon ▲ 435415-2 GDE
The Domingo Edition Deutsche Grammophon ▲ 435417-2 GDE
The Domingo Edition Deutsche Grammophon ▲ 435418-2 GDE
The Domingo Edition Deutsche Grammophon ▲ 435406-2 GDE
The Domingo Edition Deutsche Grammophon ▲ 435405-2 GDE
Domingo:Greatest Hits RCA Victor ▲ 09026-61406-2 ■ 09026-61406-4
The Domingo Songbook Sony Classical ▲ MDK 48299 ■ MGT 48299
Donizetti, G.:L'elisir d'amore, w. I. Cotrubas (sop), L. Watson (sop), G. Evans (bar), I. Wixell (bar), J. Pritchard (cnd), Royal Opera House Orch, Royal Opera House Chorus Covent Garden *(rec 1977)* CBS 2-▲ M2K 34585 [ADD]
Donizetti, G.:Lucia di Lammermoor, w. C. Studer (sop), J. Pons (bar), S. Ramey (bass), I. Marin (cnd), London SO Deutsche Grammophon 2-▲ 435309-2
Donizetti, G.:Lucia di Lammermoor (sels), w. Cheryl Studer (sop—Lucia), Plácido Domingo (ten—Edgardo), I. Marin (cnd), London SO—Io di te memoria viva... Ah, Verranno a te sull'aure [Act I] Deutsche Grammophon ▲ 447270-2 [DDD] ■ 447 270-4
Donizetti, G.:Roberto Devereux, w. B. Sills (sop), S. Marsee (mez), L. Quilico (bar), J. Rudel (cnd), New York City Opera Orch, New York City Opera Chorus *(rec 1970)* Melodram ▲ MLO 270107 [ADD]
Duets for Voice & Violin, w. Itzhak Perlman (vn) EMI Classics ▲ CDQ 54266 ■ 4DQ 54266
The Essential 3 Tenors, w. José Carreras (ten), Luciano Pavarotti (ten) RCA Gold Seal ▲ 74321-21273-2 [ADD]
Famous Love Duets, Vol. 2, w. Gianna d'Angelo (sop), Montserrat Caballé (sop), Maria Callas (sop), Renata Scotto (sop), Beverly Sills (sop), Renata Tebaldi (sop), José Carreras (ten), Mario Del Monaco (ten), Giuseppe Di Stefano (ten), et al. Enterprise ("Documents" series) ▲ ENTLV 999
From the Official Barcelona Games Ceremony, w. José Carreras (ten), Montserrat Caballé (sop), Giacomo Aragall (ten), Teresa Berganza (mez), Juan Pons (bar) RCA Red Seal ▲ 09026-61204-2 ■ 09026-61204-4 □ 09026-61204-5

1138 ▲ = CD ♦ = Enhanced CD Δ = MD ■ = Cassette Tape □ = DCC

Domingo, Plácido (ten) (cont.)

Giordano, U.:Fedora, w. Mirella Freni (sop—Principessa Fedora), Adelina Scarabelli (sop—Contessa Olga), Silvia Mazzoni (mez—Dimitri), Monica Minarelli (sgr—Savoiardo), Placido Domingo (ten—Conte Loris), Ernesto Gavazzi (ten—Desiré), Aldo Bottion (ten—Barone Rouvel), Alessandro Corbelli (bar—Siriex), Luigi Roni (bass—Cirillo), Silvestro Sammaritano (bass—Baroff), Alfredo Giacomotti (bass—Gretch), Ernesto Panariello (bass—Lorek), Vincenzo Alaimo (sgr—Nicola), Arnold Bosman (sgr—Boleslao), Bruno Capisani (sgr—Sergio), Renato Zanchetta (sgr—Michele), G. Gavazzeni (cnd), La Scala Orch, La Scala Chorus *(rec La Scala, Apr 5, 1993)* Legato 2-▲ LCD 213-2 [ADD]

Gounod, C.:Faust, w. M. Freni (sop), T. Allen (bar), N. Ghiaurov (bass), G. Prêtre (cnd), Paris Opera Orch [F] EMI Classics 3-▲ CDCC 47493 [ADD]

Gounod, C.:Faust (sels), w. M. Freni (sop), T. Allen (bar), N. Ghiaurov (bass), G. Prêtre (cnd), Paris Opera Orch, Orch de Paris, Paris Opera Chorus EMI Classics ▲ ZDM 63090

Gounod, C.:Roméo et Juliette, w. Susan Graham (sop—Stephano), Ruth Ann Swenson (sop—Juliette), Sarah Walker (mez—Gertrude), Paul Charles Clarke (ten—Tybalt), Placido Domingo (ten—Roméo), Kurt Ollmann (bar—Mercutio), Alastair Miles (bass—Frère Laurent), David Pittman-Jennings (bass—Le Duc), Alain Vernhes (bass—Capulet), L. Slatkin (cnd), Munich RSO, Munich Radio Chorus *(rec Studio 1, Bavarian Radio, Munich, Nov 29 - Dec 10, 1995)* RCA Red Seal 2-▲ 09026-68440-2 [DDD]

Granada:The Greatest Hits of Plácido Domingo, w. London SO [cnd:C. Abbado], Los Angeles PO [cnd:C. M. Giulini], Vienna PO [cnd:H. von Karajan], Royal Opera House Orch, Covent Garden [cnd:Z. Mehta], Philharmonia Orch [cnd:Giuseppe Sinopoli] Deutsche Grammophon ▲ 445777-2 ▮ 445777-4

Great Love Scenes, w. R. Scotto (sop), K. Te Kanawa (sop), I. Cotrubas (sop) CBS ▲ MK 39030 ▮ MT 39030

Great Scenes, w. B. Sills (sop) (Rec. live, 1965-1971) Legato Classics ▲ LCD 142-1 [ADD]

Great Voices:Plácido Domingo *(rec 1967-70)* Memories 2-▲ MEM 4558 [ADD]

James Levine's 25th Anniversary Metropolitan Opera Gala, w. J. Levine (cnd), Metropolitan Opera Orch, Ileana Cotrubas (sop), Renée Fleming (sop), Hei-Kyung Hong (sop), Karita Mattila (sop), Birgit Nilsson (sop), Ruth Ann Swenson (sop), Kiri Te Kanawa (sop), Deborah Voigt (sop), Grace Bumbry (mez), Heidi Grant Murphy (mez), Anne Sofie von Otter (mez) *(rec live, Metropolitan Opera House, New York, Apr 27, 1996)* Deutsche Grammophon ▲ 449177-2 [DDD]

Lara, A.:Suite Español—Granada; Clavel Sevillano; Novillero; Murcia; Cuerdas de mi Guitarra; Madrid; Fermin; Sevilla; Españolerias; Valencia; Silverio; Toledo Sony Classical ▲ SK 62625 ▮ ST 62625

Lecuona, E.:Songs, w. L. Holdridge (cnd), Royal PO CBS ▲ MK 38828 ▮ FMT 38828

Leoncavallo, R.:Pagliacci, w. T. Stratas (sop), J. Pons (bar), G. Prêtre (cnd), La Scala Orch, La Scala Chorus [I] Philips 2-▲ 411484-2

Leoncavallo, R.:Pagliacci, w. M. Caballé (sop), S. Milnes (bar), N. Santi (cnd), London SO, John Alldis Choir RCA Gold Seal 2-▲ 09026-60865-2 [ADD]

Leoncavallo, R.:Pagliacci, w. Teresa Stratas (sop—Nedda), Placido Domingo (ten—Canio), Juan Pons (bar—Tonio), G. Prêtre (cnd), La Scala Orch, La Scala Chorus Philips ("Duo" series) 2-▲ 454 265-2

Live in Tokyo 1988, w. Battle, Kathleen (sop), Metropolitan Opera Orch [cnd:James Levine] Deutsche Grammophon ▲ 427686-2 GH [DDD] ▮ 427686-4

Live Recordings, Vol. 1 *(rec 1967-68)* LaserLight ▲ 15230

Live Recordings, Vol. 2 *(rec 1967-68)* LaserLight ▲ 15231

Lloyd Webber, A.:Music of, w. J. Carreras (ten), S. Brightman (sop), M. Crawford (sgr), Royal PO—Cats; Joseph & the Amazing Technicolor Dreamcoat; Requiem; Jesus Christ Superstar; Phantom of the Opera; Aspects of Love; Starlight Express; Evita Polydor ▲ 314 517336-2 ▮ 314 517336-4

Lloyd Webber, A.:Requiem for Soloists, Orch & Chorus, w. Sarah Brightman (sop), Paul Miles-Kingston (trb), L. Maazel (cnd), English CO, Winchester Cathedral Choir *(rec Studio 1, Abbey Road, London, Dec 20-22, 1984)* London ▲ 448616-2 ▮ 48616

Lloyd Webber, A.:Requiem for Soloists, Orch & Chorus, w. Sarah Brightman (sop), Paul Miles-Kingston (trb), L. Maazel (cnd), English CO, Winchester Cathedral Choir [L] EMI Classics ▲ CDC 47146 [DDD] ▮ 4DS 38218 (D)

A Love until the End of Time:Domingo's Greatest Love Songs, w. Lee Holdridge (cnd), Maureen McGovern (sgr), John Denver (sgr) CBS ▲ MK 42520 [ADD/DDD] ▮ FMT 42520

Mascagni, P.:Cavalleria rusticana, w. Ruth Falcon (sop—Lola), Leonie Rysanek (sop—Santuzza), Astrid Varnay (sop—Mamma Lucia), Plácido Domingo (ten—Turiddu), Benito di Bella (bar—Alfio), N. Santi (cnd), Munich National Theater Orch, Munich National Theater Chorus *(rec Munich, Dec 25, 1978)* Legato Classics ▲ LCD 202-1

Mascagni, P.:Cavalleria rusticana, w. Elena Obraztsova (mez—Santuzza), Placido Domingo (ten—Turridu), G. Prêtre (cnd), La Scala Orch, La Scala Chorus Philips ("Duo" series) 2-▲ 454 265-2

Mascagni, P.:Cavalleria rusticana, w. A. Baltsa (mez), S. Mentzer (mez) P. Domingo (ten), J. Pons (bar), G. Sinopoli (cnd), Philharmonia Orch, Royal Opera House Chorus Covent Garden [I] Deutsche Grammophon ▲ 429568-2 [DDD]

Mascagni, P.:Cavalleria rusticana, w. E. Obraztsova (mez), F. Barbieri (mez), R. Bruson (bar), G. Prêtre (cnd), La Scala Orch, La Scala Chorus [I] Philips ▲ 416137-2 [DDD]

Mascagni, P.:Cavalleria rusticana (sels), w. Agnes Baltsa (mez—Santuzza), Plácido Domingo (ten—Turiddu), G. Sinopoli (cnd), Philharmonia Orch—No, no, Turiddu Deutsche Grammophon ▲ 447270-2 [DDD] ▮ 447 270-4

Mascagni, P.:Iris, w. I. Tokody (sop), J. Pons (bar), G. Patanè (cnd), Munich RSO, Bavarian Radio Chorus CBS 2-▲ M2K 45526

Massenet, J.:Le Cid, w. G. Bumbry (mez), P. Plishka (bass), E. Queler (cnd), New York Opera Orch *(rec 1976)* CBS 2-▲ M2K 34211 [ADD]

Massenet, J.:Hérodiade, w. Renée Fleming (sop—Salome), Dolora Zajick (mez—Hérodiade), Plácido Domingo (ten—Jean), Juan Pons (bar—Erode), Kenneth Cox (bass—Phanuel), V. Gergiev (cnd), San Francisco Opera Orch, San Francisco Opera Chorus Sony Classical 2-▲ S2K 66847

Massenet, J.:Hérodiade (sels), w. Renée Fleming (sop—Salomé), Dolora Zajick (mez—Hérodiade), Plácido Domingo (ten—Jean), Juan Pons (bar—Hérode), Hector Vásquez (bar—Vitellius), Kenneth Cox (bass—Phanuel), V. Gergiev (cnd), San Francisco Opera Orch, San Francisco Opera Chorus Sony Classical ▲ SK 61965

Massenet, J.:Hérodiade (sels), w. Renée Fleming (sop), Dolora Zajick (mez), Kristin Clayton (sgr), Kenneth Cox (bass), Juan Pons (bar), Hector Vásquez (sgr), V. Gergiev (cnd), San Francisco Opera Orch, San Francisco Opera Chorus—highlights *(rec San Francisco Opera, Nov 1994)* Sony Classical ▲ SK 61965

Massenet, J.:Manon, w. B. Sills (sop), R. Fredricks (bar), J. Rudel (cnd), New York City Opera Orch, New York City Opera Chorus *(rec live, 1969)* Melodram 2-▲ MEL 27054

Massenet, J.:Manon, w. Beverly Sills (sop—Manon), Plácido Domingo (ten—Des Grieux), Nico Castel (ten—Guillot), Richard Fredricks (bar—Lescaut), Robert Hale (bar—De Brétigny), Malcom Smith (bass—Count de Grieux), J. Rudel (cnd), New York City Opera Orch, New York City Opera Chorus *(rec live, New York, 1969)* Melodram 2-▲ IMC 205008 [ADD]

Meyerbeer, G.:L'Africiane, w. Montserrat Caballe (sop—Selika), Christine Weidinger (sop—Inez), Miriam Ucelay (mez—Anna), Placido Domingo (ten—Vasco de Gama), Guillermo Sarabia (bar—Nelusko), Juan Thomas (b-bar—High Priest of Brahma), Dimiter Petkov (bass—Don Pedro), Juan Pons (bass—Don Diego), Eduardo Soto (bass—Grand Inquisitor), A. de Almeida (cnd), Barcelona Teatro Liceo Orch, Barcelona Gran Teatro de Liceo Chorus *(rec Barcelona, Nov 27, 1977)* Legato Classics 2-▲ LCD 208-2 [ADD]

Moreno Torroba, F.:Luisa Fernanda, w. Verónica Villaroel (sop), Ana Rodrigo (mez), Juan Pons (bar), A. Ros-Marbá (cnd), Madrid SO Valois 2-▲ V 4759

Mozart, W.A.:Arias, w. I. Cotrubas (sop), E. Gruberova (sop), L. Price (sop), J. Varady (sop), L. Popp (mez), F. Araiza (ten), P. de Palma (ten), P. Schreier (ten), F. Wunderlich (ten), S. Milnes (bar), A. Titus (bar), M. Talvela (bass)—sels. from Entführung aus dem Serail, Così fan tutte, Don Giovanni, Idomeneo, Die Zauberflöte, Le nozze di Figaro Eurodisc ▲ 69256-2-RG [ADD]

Mozart, W.A.:Arias, w. E. Steber (sop), I. Cotrubas (sop), K. Te Kanawa (sop), R. Stevens (mez), S. Jerusalem (ten), G. London (bar), E. Pinza (bass)—arias & duets from Don Giovanni, Le nozze di Figaro, Die Zauberflöte, etc. *(rec 1941-1978)* CBS Masterworks ▲ MDK 46579 [AAD] ▮ MGT 46579

Mozart, W.A.:Arias, w. C. Vaness (sop), E. Cohn (cnd), Munich RSO—arias from Clemenza di Tito, Così fan tutte, Don Giovanni, Entführung aus dem Serail, La finta giardineira, Idomeneo, Le nozze di Figaro, Die Zauberflöte EMI Classics ▲ CDC 54329

Domingo, Plácido (ten) (cont.)

Mozart, W.A.:Idomeneo, w. Heidi Grant-Murphy (sop—Ilia), Carol Vaness (sop—Elettra), Cecilia Bartoli (mez—Idamante), Plácido Domingo (ten—Idomeneo), Frank Lopardo (ten—High Priest), Thomas Hampson (bar—Arbace), Bryn Terfel (b-bar—The Voice), J. Levine (cnd), Metropolitan Opera Orch, Raymond Hughes (cnd), New York Metropolitan Opera Chorus *(rec Manhattan Center Studios, New York, Mar & Apr 1994)* Deutsche Grammophon 3-▲ 447 737-2 [DDD]

Mozart, W.A.:Idomeneo, w. Carol Vaness (sop—Elettra), Cecilia Bartoli (mez—Idamante), Heidi Grant Murphy (mez—Ilia), Plácido Domingo (ten— Idomeneo), Thomas Hampson (bar—Arbace), Bryn Terfel (bass-bar—La Voce), J. Levine (cnd), Metropolitan Opera Orch, New York Metropolitan Opera Chorus Deutsche Grammophon ▲ 447737-2

My Life for a Song CBS ▲ MK 37799 ▮ PMT 37799

Offenbach, J.:Les Contes d'Hoffmann, w. E. Gruberova (sop), C. Eder (mez), M. Sénéchal (ten), Schmidt (sgr), G. Bacquier (bar), J. Morris (bass), J. Diaz (bass), S. Ozawa (cnd), French National Orch, French Radio Chorus [F] Deutsche Grammophon 2-▲ 427682-2 [DDD]

Offenbach, J.:Les Contes d'Hoffmann, w. J. Sutherland (sop), H. Tourangeau (mez), H. Cuénod (ten), G. Bacquier (bar), R. Bonynge (cnd), Swiss Romande Orch London 2-▲ 417363-2 [ADD]

Offenbach, J.:Les Contes d'Hoffmann (sels), w. Edita Gruberova (sop—Giulietta), Plácido Domingo (ten—Hoffmann), S. Ozawa (cnd), French National Orch—Malheureux, tu ne comprends done pas Deutsche Grammophon ▲ 447270-2 [DDD] ▮ 447 270-4

Opera Arias EMI Classics ▲ CDM 63103

Opera Classics:His Greatest Recordings EMI Classics ▲ CDC 55017 ▮ 4DS 55017

Opera Favorites Griffin ▲ MACCD 106

Opera Goes to the Movies, w. Roberta Peters (sop), Leontyne Price (sop), et al. RCA Victor ▲ 60841-2-RG ▮ 60841-4-RG

Penella, M.:El gato montés, w. V. Villarroel (sop), T. Berganza (mez), J. Pons (bar), M. Roa (cnd), Madrid SO [Sp] Deutsche Grammophon 2-▲ 435776-2 [DDD]

Perhaps Love, w. John Denver (sgr) CBS ▲ MK 37243 ▮ PMT 37243

Plácido Domingo London ("Grandi Voici" series) ▲ 440410-2

Plácido Domingo, w. Vienna Boys Choir, Vienna SO [cnd:H. Froschauer] RCA Gold Seal ▲ 07863-53835 ▮ ARK1-3835

The Plácido Domingo Album RCA Gold Seal 2-▲ 09026-60866-2 ▮ 09026-60866-4

Plácido Domingo Recital *(rec live)* Melodram 2-▲ CDM 26510

Plácido Domingo Sings Caruso RCA Gold Seal ▲ 09026-61356-2 ▮ 09026-61356-4

Plácido Domingo:The Best of Christmas in Vienna, w. José Carreras (ten), Dionne Warwick (sgr), Charles Aznavour, Sissel Kyrkjebø, Vienna SO [cnd:Vjekoslav Sutej] Sony Classical ▲ SK 62696 ▮ ST 62696

Plácido Domingo:A 25th Anniversary Tribute *(rec 1961-69)* Standing Room Only ("800" series) ▲ SRO 847-1 [ADD]

Ponchielli, A.:La Gioconda (sels), w. Sherrill Milnes (bar), A. Guadagno (cnd), London SO—Enzo Grimaldi, Principe di Santa Fior *(rec 1970)* RCA Gold Seal ▲ 09026-62595-2 [ADD]

Por Fin Juntos Capitol/EMI Latin ▲ H2Y 426241 ▮ H4F 42624

Puccini, G.:Arias, w. M. Caballé (sop), F. Corelli (ten), *(orch unknown)* EMI Classics ▲ CDE 67782

Puccini, G.:La Bohème, w. M. Caballé (sop), J. Blegen (sop), S. Milnes (bar), R. Raimondi (bass), G. Solti (cnd), London PO, John Alldis Choir [I] RCA Red Seal 2-▲ RCD2-0371 2-▮ ARK2-0371

Puccini, G.:La Bohème (sels), w. Sherrill Milnes (bar), A. Guadagno (cnd), London SO—O Mimì, tu più non torni *(rec 1970)* RCA Gold Seal ▲ 09026-62595-2 [ADD]

Puccini, G.:La Bohème (sels), w. M. Cabballé (sop), J. Blegen (sop), S. Milnes (bar), G. Solti (cnd), London PO RCA Victor ▲ 09026-61725-2; ▮ 09026-61725-4 (CrO2)

Puccini, G.:La fanciulla del West, w. M. Zampieri (sop), J. Pons (bar), L. Maazel (cnd), La Scala Orch, La Scala Chorus *(rec live 1991)* Sony Classical 2-▲ S2K 47189

Puccini, G.:La fanciulla del West, w. C. Neblett (sop), S. Milnes (bar), Z. Mehta (cnd), Royal Opera House Orch Covent Garden, Royal Opera House Chorus Covent Garden [I] Deutsche Grammophon 2-▲ 419640-2 [ADD]

Puccini, G.:Madama Butterfly, w. R. Scotto (sop), I. Wixell (bar), L. Maazel (cnd), Philharmonia Orch, Ambrosian Singers [I] CBS 2-▲ M2K 35181 [AAD]

Puccini, G.:Madama Butterfly (sels), w. Katia Ricciarelli (sop), A. Guadagno (cnd), St. Cecilia Academy Orch Rome—Bimba dagli occhi pieni di malia *(rec 1972)* RCA Gold Seal ▲ 09026-62595-2 [ADD]

Puccini, G.:Madama Butterfly (sels), w. L. Price (sop)—Bimba, bimba non piangere RCA Gold Seal ▲ 09026-61634-2

Puccini, G.:Manon Lescaut, w. M. Frèni (sop), R. Bruson (bar), G. Sinopoli (cnd), Philharmonia Orch, Royal Opera House Chorus Covent Garden [I] *(rec 1984)* Deutsche Grammophon 2-▲ 413893-2 [DDD]

Puccini, G.:Manon Lescaut, w. M. Caballé (sop—Manon Lescaut), P. Domingo (ten—Des Grieux), R. Tear (ten—Edmondo), V. Sardinero (bar—Lescaut), N. Mangin (bass—Geronte), B. Bartoletti (cnd), New Philharmonia Orch, Ambrosian Opera Chorus EMI Classics ▲ CDMB 64852

Puccini, G.:Manon Lescaut, w. R. Kabaivanska (sop—Manon), R. Pallini (mez—Singer), P. Domingo (ten—des Grieux), E. Lorenzi (ten—Edmondo), F. Ricciardi (ten—Dancing Master), M. D'Anna (bar—Lescaut), A. Mariotti (bass—Geronte), F. Federici (bass—Innkeeper) Golden Age of Opera 2-▲ GAO 162/63 [ADD]

Puccini, G.:Manon Lescaut (sels), w. Luisa Maragliano (sop), B. Bartoletti (cnd), *(orch unknown)*—Sola, perduta abbandonata *(rec Chicago, 1968)* Golden Age of Opera ▲ GAO 204 [ADD]

Puccini, G.:Manon Lescaut (sels), w. L. Price (sop)—Oh saro la piu bella! RCA Gold Seal ▲ 09026-61634-2

Puccini, G.:Manon Lescaut (sels), w. Montserrat Caballé (sop—Manon), Plácido Domingo (ten—Des Grieux), J. Levine (cnd), Metropolitan Opera Orch—Tu, tu, amore? Tu? [Act II] Deutsche Grammophon ▲ 447270-2 [ADD] ▮ 447270-4

Puccini, G.:La Rondine, w. M. Nicolesco (sop), K. Te Kanawa (sop), D. Rendall (ten), L. Nucci (bar), L. Maazel (cnd), London SO, Ambrosian Opera Chorus [I] CBS 2-▲ M2K 37852 [DDD]

Puccini, G.:Songs, w. Julius Rudel (pno/org)—A te; Vexilla; Salve Regina Ad una morta; Mentia l'avviso; Storiella d'amore; Sole e amore; Avanti Urania; Inno a Diana; E l'uccellino; Terra e mare (performing both autograph & published versions); Canto d'anime; Casa mia, casa mia; Morire?; Inno a Roma [I] CBS ▲ MK 44981 [DDD]

Puccini, G.:Il tabarro, w. J. Crader (sop), C. Ludgin (bar), J. Rudel (cnd), New York City Opera Orch, New York City Opera Chorus *(rec live 1968; stereo)* Melodram ▲ 17048

Puccini, G.:Il tabarro, w. L. Price (sop), S. Milnes (bar), E. Leinsdorf (cnd), New Philharmonia Orch, John Alldis Choir RCA Gold Seal 2-▲ 09026-60865-2 [ADD]

Puccini, G.:Tosca, w. L. Price (sop), S. Milnes (bar), Z. Mehta (cnd), New Philharmonia Orch, John Alldis Choir [I] RCA Victrola 2-▲ RCD2-0105

Puccini, G.:Tosca, w. Raina Kabaivanska (sop), Zanasi (sgr), F.M. Pradelli (cnd), La Scala Orch *(rec live, May 17, 1974)* Arkadia ("Historical Performances" series) 2-▲ 496

Puccini, G.:Tosca, w. M. Freni (sop), S. Ramey (bass), G. Sinopoli (cnd), Philharmonia Orch, Royal Opera House Chorus Covent Garden [I] Deutsche Grammophon 2-▲ 431775-2 [DDD]

Puccini, G.:Tosca, w. R. Scotto (sop), R. Bruson (bar), J. Levine (cnd), Philharmonia Orch, Ambrosian Opera Chorus [I] EMI Classics 2-▲ CDCB 49364 [DDD]

Puccini, G.:Tosca (sels), w. Mirella Freni (sop—Tosca), Plácido Domingo (ten—Cavaradossi), G. Sinopoli (cnd), Philharmonia Orch—Ah, quegli occhi! - Qual occhio al mondo può star [Act I, Part II] Deutsche Grammophon ▲ 447270-2 [DDD] ▮ 447270-4

Puccini, G.:Tosca (sels), w. R. Scotto (sop), R. Bruson (bar), J. Levine (cnd), Philharmonia Orch, Ambrosian Opera Chorus EMI Classics ▲ CDC 54324

Puccini, G.:Tosca (sels), w. L. Price (sop)—Mario, Mario, Mario RCA Gold Seal ▲ 09026-61634-2

Puccini, G.:Il trittico, w. R. Scotto (sop), I. Cotrubas (sop), M. Horne (mez), T. Gobbi (bar), I. Wixell (bar), L. Maazel (cnd), London SO, Philharmonia Orch [I] CBS 3-▲ M3K 35912 [ADD]

Puccini, G.:Turandot, w. K. Ricciarelli (sop), B. Hendricks (sop), R. Raimondi (bass), H. von Karajan (cnd), Vienna PO, Vienna State Opera Chorus [I] Deutsche Grammophon 2-▲ 423855-2 [DDD]

Puccini, G.:Turandot (sels), w. K. Ricciarelli (sop), B. Hendricks (sop), R. Raimondi (bass), H. von Karajan (cnd), Vienna PO, Vienna State Opera Chorus [I] Deutsche Grammophon ▲ 435409-2 [DDD]

Puccini, G.:Le Villi, w. R. Scotto (sop), T. Gobbi (bar), L. Nucci (bar), L. Maazel (cnd), London National PO, Ambrosian Chorus [I] CBS ▲ MK 36669 [ADD]

Domingo, Plácido (ten) (cont.)

Pure Domingo, w. English CO [cnd:Julius Rudel], Madrid SO [cnd:Manuel Moreno–Buendia], Munich RSO [cnd:Eugene Kohn], National PO [cnd:Eugene Kohn], New Philharmonia Orch [cnds:Bruno Bartoletti, Riccardo Muti], Philharmonia Orch [cnd:James Levine] Angel ▲ CDC 55616 [DDD/ADD]

Roman Heroes, w. National PO [cnd:E. Kohn] EMI Classics ▲ CDC 54053

Romanzas de Zarzuelas, w. Manuel Moreno–Buendía, Madrid SO, National Zarzuela Theater Chorus EMI Classics ▲ CDC 49148 [DDD] ■ 4DS 49148 (D)

Rossini, G.:Il barbiere di Siviglia, w. K. Battle (sop), F. Lopardo (ten), L. Gallo (bar), R. Raimondi (bass), C. Abbado (cnd), CO of Europe [I] Deutsche Grammophon 2–▲ 435763–2

Saint–Saëns, C.:Samson et Dalila, w. W. Meier (mez), S. Ramey (bass), A. Fondary (bar), M.–W. Chung (cnd), Bastille Opera Orch, Bastille Opera Chorus EMI Classics 2–▲ CDCB 54470

Saint–Saëns, C.:Samson et Dalila, w. E. Obraztsova (mez), R. Bruson (bar), R. Lloyd (b–bar), D. Barenboim (cnd), Orch de Paris Deutsche Grammophon 2–▲ 413297–2 [ADD]

Save Your Nights for Me CBS ▲ MK 39866 ■ FMT 39866

Schifrin, L.:Cantos Aztecas, w. N. Storojev (bass), C. Julian (sop), M. Felix (sgr), L. Schifrin (cnd), Mexican State SO, Mexico City Chorus [Sp] *(rec live 10/29/88)* Pro Arte ▲ CDD 494 [DDD]

Sings Tangos Deutsche Grammophon ▲ 415120–2 GH [ADD]

Sorozábal, P.:La Tabernera del Puerto, w. María Bayo (sop), Juan Pons (bar), V.P. Pérez (cnd), Galicia SO Auvidis Valois ("Zarzuela Collection" series) ▲ V 4766

Strauss (II), Joh.:Die Fledermaus, w. L. Popp (sop), E. Lind (sop), A. Baltsa (mez), W. Brendel (bar), K. Rydl (bass), P. Domingo (cnd), Munich RSO, Bavarian Radio Chorus [G] EMI Classics 2–▲ CDCB 47480

Strauss, R.:Die Frau ohne Schatten, w. J. Varady (sop), H. Behrens (sop), J. Van Dam (b–bar), G. Solti (cnd), Vienna PO, Vienna State Opera Chorus [G] London 3–▲ 436243–2

Strauss, R.:Der Rosenkavalier, w. G. Jones (sop), L. Popp (sop), C. Ludwig (mez), W. Berry (b–bar), L. Bernstein (cnd), Vienna PO [G] CBS 3–▲ M3K 42564 [ADD]

Tchaikovsky, P.:Eugene Onegin (sels), w. R. Behr (cnd), Philharmonia Orch—Lensky's aria EMI Classics ▲ CDC 55018 ■ 4DS 55018

Tchaikovsky, P.:Songs, w. O. Harnoy (vc)—None but the Lonely Heart EMI Classics ▲ CDC 55018 ■ 4DS 55018

Tenorissimi, Mondiale 90, w. J. Carreras (ten), Luciano Pavarotti (ten) EMI Classics ▲ CDC 54109

Tenors Greatest Hits, w. Luciano Pavarott (ten), José Carerras (ten) RCA Victor ▲ 09026–62709–2 ■ 09026–62709–4

The Three Tenors In Concert, w. J. Carreras (ten), L. Pavarotti (ten), Zubin Mehta (cnd) *(rec Rome, July 7, 1990)* London ▲ 430433–2 ■ 430433–4 □ 430433–5

Verdi, G.:Aida, w. K. Ricciarelli (sop), E. Obraztsova (mez), L. Nucci (bar), N. Ghiaurov (bass), C. Abbado (cnd), La Scala Orch, La Scala Chorus [I] Deutsche Grammophon 3–▲ 410092–2 [DDD]

Verdi, G.:Aida, w. L. Price (sop), G. Bumbry (mez), S. Milnes (bar), R. Raimondi (bass), E. Leinsdorf (cnd), London SO [I] RCA ■ RK 1237

Verdi, G.:Aida, w. L. Price (sop), G. Bumbry (mez), S. Milnes (bar), R. Raimondi (bass), E. Leinsdorf (cnd), London SO [I] RCA Red Seal 3–▲ 6198–2–RC [ADD] 3–■ ARK3–2541

Verdi, G.:Aida, w. A. Millo (sop), D. Zajick (mez), J. Morris (bass), S. Ramey (bass), J. Levine (cnd), Metropolitan Opera Orch, New York Metropolitan Opera Chorus [I] Sony Classical 3–▲ S3K 45973 [DDD] 3–■ S3T 45973 (D)

Verdi, G.:Aida, w. K. Ricciarelli (sop), E. Obraztsova (mez), L. Nucci (bar), N. Ghiaurov (bass), C. Abbado (cnd), La Scala Orch, La Scala Chorus [I] Deutsche Grammophon ▲ 435410–2 [DDD]

Verdi, G.:Aida, w. M. Caballé (sop), F. Cossotto (mez), P. Cappuccilli (bar), N. Ghiaurov (bass), R. Muti (cnd), New Philharmonia Orch, Royal Opera House Chorus Covent Garden [I] EMI Classics 3–▲ CDCC 47271 [ADD]

Verdi, G.:Aida (sels), w. L. Price (sop), G. Bumbry (mez), S. Milnes (bar), E. Leinsdorf (cnd), London SO RCA Victor ▲ 09026–62676–2 ■ 09026–62676–4

Verdi, G.:Aida (sels), w. A. Millo (sop), D. Zajick (mez), J. Morris (bar), S. Ramey (bass), T. Cook (bass), J. Levine (cnd), Metropolitan Opera Orch, New York Metropolitan Opera Chorus *(rec New York, May 18–26, 1990)* Sony Classical ("Opera Highlights" series) ▲ SMK 53506 [DDD]

Verdi, G.:Aida (sels), w. L. Price (sop)—Act IV, Scene 2 RCA Gold Seal ▲ 09026–61634–2

Verdi, G.:Arias, w. K. Ricciarelli (sop), Rome PO—arias & duets from Ballo in maschera, Il Corsaro, Don Carlos, Jerusalem, Giovanna d'Arco, I Masnadieri, Otello, Trovatore, I Vespri siciliani RCA Gold Seal ▲ 6534–2–RG [ADD] ■ 6534–4–RG (CrO2)

Verdi, G.:Arias, w. *(various cnds & orchs)*—nine arias & scenes from Requiem Mass, Traviata, Trovatore *(rec live, 1967–68)* Melodram 3–▲ MEL 37057 (m) [AAD]

Verdi, G.:Arias—arias & scenes from Il Trovatore [w. Leontyne Price (sop), Ryland Davies (ten), Zubin Mehta (cnd), New Philharmonia Orch]; La Traviata [w. Sherrill Milnes (cnd), New Philharmonia Orch]; Rigoletto [w. Sherrill Milnes (cnd), Nello Santo (cnd), London SO, New Philharmonia Orch]; Luisa Miller [w. Edward Downes (cnd), Royal PO]; Simon Boccanegra [w. Edward Downes (cnd), Royal PO]; Un Ballo in maschera [w. Wendy Eathorne (sop), Brian Etheridge (bass), Franklyn Whitely (bass), Nello Santi (cnd), New Philharmonia Orch, John Alldis (cnd), John Alldis Choir]; I Vespri siciliani [w. James Levine (cnd), New Philharmonia Orch]; Aida [w. Erich Leinsdorf (cnd), London SO]; Don Carlo [w. Sherrill Milnes (bar), Anton Guadagno (cnd), London SO]; La Forza del destino [w. Nello Santi (cnd), New Philharmonia Orch]; Otello [w. Katia Ricciarelli (sop), Frank Little (ten), Sherrill Milnes (bar), Malcolm King (bass), Paul Plishka (bass), Anton Guadagno (cnd), Gianandrea Gavazzeni (cnd), James Levine (cnd), London SO, National Academy of Santa Cecilia Orch, National PO] *(rec 1968–78)* RCA Gold Seal ▲ 09026–68446–2 [ADD]

Verdi, G.:Un ballo in maschera, w. Reri Grist (sop), Katia Ricciarelli (sop), Elizabeth Bainbridge (mez), Piero Cappuccilli (bar), C. Abbado (cnd), Royal Opera House Orch, Royal Opera House Chorus Covent Garden *(rec 1975)* Arkadia 2–▲ 488

Verdi, G.:Un ballo in maschera, w. M. Caballé (sop—Amelia), T. Paniagua (sop—Oscar), L. Chookasian (cta—Ulrica), P. Domingo (ten—Riccardo), C. MacNeil (bar—Renato), J. Pons (bar—Tom), C. del Bosco (bass—Samuel), G. Patanè (cnd), *(orch unknown)* Ornamenti 2–▲ FE 103

Verdi, G.:Un ballo in maschera, w. J. Barstow (sop), S. Jo (sop), F. Quivar (mez), L. Nucci (bar), H. von Karajan (cnd), Vienna PO, Vienna State Opera Chorus [I] Deutsche Grammophon 2–▲ 427635–2 [DDD]

Verdi, G.:Un ballo in maschera, w. M. Arroyo (sop), R. Grist (sop), F. Cossotto (mez), P. Cappuccilli (bar), R. Muti (cnd), New Philharmonia Orch, Royal Opera House Chorus Covent Garden [I] EMI Classics (Studio) 2–▲ CDMB 69576 [ADD]

Verdi, G.:Un ballo in maschera (sels), w. L. Price (sop), *(cnd & orch unknown)*—Teco io sto! RCA Gold Seal ▲ 09026–61634–2

Verdi, G.:Don Carlos, w. M. Caballé (sop), F. Cossotto (mez), P. Cappuccilli (bar), G. Petkov (bar), E. Inbal (cnd), Arena di Verona Orch, Arena di Verona Chorus [I] *(rec live 7/2/69)* Melodram 3–▲ MEL 37057 (m) [AAD]

Verdi, G.:Don Carlos, w. S. Jurinac (sop—Elisabetta), L. Rysanek (sop—Celestial Voice), F. Cossotto (mez—Princess Eboli), L. Dutoit (boy sop—Tebaldo), P. Domingo (ten—Don Carlo), E. Majkut (ten—Count of Lerma), M. Sereni (bar—Rodrigo), C. Siepi (bass—Philip II), I. Vinco (bass—Grand Inquisitor), T. Franc (bass—Friar), S. Varviso (cnd), Vienna State Opera Orch, Vienna State Opera Chorus Standing Room Only 2–▲ SRO 850 [ADD]

Verdi, G.:Ernani, w. M. Freni (sop), R. Bruson (bar), N. Ghiaurov (bass), R. Muti (cnd), La Scala Orch, La Scala Chorus [I] EMI Classics 3–▲ CDC 47082 [DDD]

Verdi, G.:Ernani, w. R. Kabaivanska (sop), N. Ghiaurov (bass), Meliciani (sgr), A. Votto (cnd), La Scala Orch, La Scala Chorus *(rec live 12/7/69)* Melodram 2–▲ MEL 27064 (m) [AAD]

Verdi, G.:Ernani (sels), w. Felicia Weathers (sop—Elvira), Delia Wallis (mez—Giovanna), Placido Domingo (ten—Ernani), Wynford Evans (ten—Don Riccardo), Piero Francia (bar—Don Carlo), Agostino Ferrin (bass—Don Ruy Gomex de Silva), Robert Holl (bass—Iago), E. Downes (cnd), Omroep Orch, Omroep Chorus *(rec Amsterdam, Jan 15, 1972)* Bella Voce ▲ BLV 107.004 [AAD]

Verdi, G.:Ernani (sels), w. R. Kabaivanska (sop), La Scala Orch—six solo arias & one chorus *(rec live 12/4/69)* Melodram 2–▲ MEL 27064 (m) [AAD]

Verdi, G.:La forza del destino (sels), w. Sherrill Milnes (bar), A. Guadagno (cnd), London SO—Solenne in quest'ora; Invano, Alvaro, tu calaste al mondo *(rec 1970)* RCA Gold Seal ▲ 09026–62595–2 [ADD]

Domingo, Plácido (ten) (cont.)

Verdi, G.:I lombardi alla prima crociata, w. C. Deutekom (sop), D. Malvisi (sop), M. Aparici (sop), G. Raimondi (ten), M. Lo Monaco (ten), M. Dean (b–bar), C. Grant (bass), L. Gardelli (cnd), Royal PO, Ambrosian Singers Philips 2–▲ 422420–2 [ADD]

Verdi, G.:Luisa Miller, w. A. Millo (sop), F. Quivar (mez), V. Chernov (bar), J. Levine (cnd), Metropolitan Opera Orch, New York Metropolitan Opera Chorus Sony Classical 2–▲ S2K 48073

Verdi, G.:Luisa Miller (sels), w. A. Millo (sop), W. White (mez), F. Quivar (cta), V. Chernov (bar), J.–H. Rootering (bass), P. Plishka (bass), J. Levine (cnd), Metropolitan Opera Orch, New York Metropolitan Opera Chorus *(rec New York, May 2–18, 1991)* Sony Classical ("Opera Highlights" series) ▲ SMK 53508 [DDD]

Verdi, G.:Macbeth, w. Shirley Verrett (mez—Lady Macbeth), Plácido Domingo (ten—Macduff), Piero Cappuccilli (bar—Macbeth), Nicolai Ghiaurov (bass—Banco), C. Abbado (cnd), La Scala Orch, La Scala Chorus Deutsche Grammophon ("The Originals" series) ▲ 449 732–2

Verdi, G.:Nabucco, w. G. Dimitrova (sop), L. V. Terrani (mez), P. Cappuccilli (bar), E. Nesterenko (bass), G. Sinopoli (cnd), German Opera Orch, German Opera Chorus [I] Deutsche Grammophon 2–▲ 410512–2 [DDD]

Verdi, G.:Otello, w. R. Scotto (sop), S. Milnes (bass), J. Levine (cnd), National PO London [I] RCA Red Seal 2–▲ RCD2–2951

Verdi, G.:Otello (sels), w. L. Price (sop)—Gia nella notte RCA Gold Seal ▲ 09026–61634–2

Verdi, G.:Otello (sels), w. Sherrill Milnes (bar), A. Guadagno (cnd), London SO—Sì, pel ciel marmoreo giuro! *(rec 1970)* RCA Gold Seal ▲ 09026–62595–2 [ADD]

Verdi, G.:Requiem Mass, w. A. Marc (sop), W. Meier (mez), F. Furlanetto (bass), D. Barenboim (cnd), Chicago SO, Chicago Sym Chorus Erato 2–▲ 96357–2

Verdi, G.:Il trovatore, w. A. Millo (sop), D. Zajick (mez), S. Kelly (cta), T. Willson (ten), A. Laciura (ten), J. Morris (bass), G. Bater (bass), J. Levine (cnd), Metropolitan Opera Orch, New York Metropolitan Opera Chorus *(rec June 18, 1991)* Sony Classical 2–▲ S2K 48070 [DDD]

Verdi, G.:Il trovatore, w. M. Caballé (sop), E. Sordello (bar), K. Andersson (cnd), New Orleans Opera Orch, New Orleans Opera Chorus [I] *(rec live 3/14/68)* Melodram 2–▲ MEL 27047 [AAD]

Verdi, G.:I vespri siciliani, w. M. Caballé (sop), F. Bordoni (bar), J. Diaz (bass), E. Queler (cnd), *(orch unknown) (rec live, Barcelona, 1974)* Standing Room Only 2–▲ SRO 837–2 [ADD]

Verdi, G.:I vespri siciliani (sels), w. Sherrill Milnes (bar), A. Guadagno (cnd), London SO—Quando al mio sen *(rec 1970)* RCA Gold Seal ▲ 09026–62595–2 [ADD]

Vienna, City of My Dreams, w. Ambrosian Singers, English CO [cnd:J. Rudel] EMI Classics ▲ CDC 47398

Wagner, R.:Lohengrin, w. J. Norman (sop), E. Randová (mez), D. Fischer–Dieskau (bar), S. Nimsgern (b–bar), H. Sotin (bass), G. Solti (cnd), Vienna PO, Vienna State Opera Chorus [G] London ▲ 425530–2 [DDD]

Wagner, R.:Lohengrin, w. J. Norman (sop), E. Randová (mez), D. Fischer–Dieskau (bar), S. Nimsgern (b–bar), H. Sotin (bass), G. Solti (cnd), Vienna PO, Vienna State Opera Chorus [G] London 4–▲ 421053–2 [DDD]

Wagner, R.:Die Meistersinger von Nürnberg, w. C. Ligendza (sop), C. Ludwig (mez), R. Laubenthal (ten), D. Fischer–Dieskau (bar), R. Hermann (bar), P. Lagger (bass), E. Jochum (cnd), German Opera Orch, German Opera Chorus [G] Deutsche Grammophon 4–▲ 415278–2 [ADD]

Wagner, R.:Die Meistersinger von Nürnberg, w. C. Ligendza (sop), C. Ludwig (mez), R. Laubenthal (ten), D. Fischer–Dieskau (bar), R. Hermann (bar), P. Lagger (bass), E. Jochum (cnd), German Opera Orch, German Opera Chorus Deutsche Grammophon ("Domingo Edition" series) ▲ 435406–2

Wagner, R.:Parsifal, w. J. Norman (sop), E. Wlaschiha (bar), K. Moll (bass), J. Morris (bass), J.–H. Rootering (bass), J. Levine (cnd), Metropolitan Opera Orch, New York Metropolitan Opera Chorus Deutsche Grammophon 4–▲ 437501–2

Wagner, R.:Tannhäuser, w. C. Studer (sop), A. Baltsa (mez), A. Schmidt (bar), M. Salminen (bass), G. Sinopoli (cnd), Philharmonia Orch, Royal Opera House Chorus Covent Garden Deutsche Grammophon ▲ 435405–2 [DDD]

Wagner, R.:Tannhäuser, w. C. Studer (sop), A. Baltsa (mez), A. Schmidt (bar), M. Salminen (bass), G. Sinopoli (cnd), Philharmonia Orch, Royal Opera House Chorus Covent Garden [G] Deutsche Grammophon 3–▲ 427625–2 [DDD]

Weber, C.M. von:Oberon, w. B. Nilsson (sop), A. Augér (sop), J. Hamari (mez), H. Prey (bar), R. Kubelik (cnd), Bavarian RSO Deutsche Grammophon 2–▲ 419038–2 [ADD]

Weber, C.M. von:Oberon, w. B. Nilsson (sop), A. Augér (sop), J. Hamari (mez), H. Prey (bar), R. Kubelik (cnd), Bavarian RSO Deutsche Grammophon ("Domingo Edition" series) ▲ 435406–2 [ADD]

The Women in My Life:A Passionate Serenade to Opera's Leading Ladies, w. Deutsche Grammophon ▲ 437743–2 GH ■ 437743–4 GH

Zandonai, R.:Francesca da Rimini, w. R. Kabaivanska (sop), M. Manuguerra (bar), N. Saetta (sgr), E. Queler (cnd), *(orch unknown) (rec live, March 22, 1973)* Standing Room Only 2–▲ SRO 840–2 [ADD]

Zandonai, R.:Francesca da Rimini (sels), w. Katia Ricciarelli (sop), A. Guadagno (cnd), St. Cecilia Academy Orch Rome—Benvenuto, signore mio cognato *(rec 1972)* RCA Gold Seal ▲ 09026–62595–2 [ADD]

Zarzuela Arias, w. Barcelona SO [cnd:Luis A. Garcia–Navarro] Acanta ▲ CD 49390

Zarzuela Arias & Duets, w. Pilar Lorengar (sop) *(rec live, 1981 Salzburg Festival)* CBS ▲ MK 39210 [DDD]

Dominguez, Guilliermo (ten)

Respighi, O.:La bella dormente nel bosco, w. Ivana Czaková (sop—Old Woman/Green Fairy), Adriana Kohútková (sop—Blue Fairy/Nightingale), Henrietta Lednárová (sop—Frog/Spindle), Jana Valásková (sop—Princess), Dagmar Pecková (mez—Cuckoo/Cat), Denisa Slepkovská (mez—Queen/Duchess), Karol Bernáth (ten—Doctor), Guillermo Dominguez (ten—Prince April), Igor Pasek (ten—Jester), Ján Durčo (bar—Ambassador), Richard Haan (bar—King/Woodcutter), Stanislav Benačka (bass—Doctor), Anton Kúrnava (bass—Doctor), Marián Smolárik (bass—Doctor), M. Adriano (nar—Mr. Dollar Chèques), M. Adriano (cnd), Slovak RSO Bratislava, Ján Rozehnal (cnd), Slovak Phil Chorus *(rec Concert Hall of the Slovak Radio, Bratislava, June 8–20, 1994)* Marco Polo ("Opera Classics" series) ▲ 8.223742 [DDD]

Rossini, G.:Petite messe solennelle, w. M. Musacchio (sop), C. Bandera (alt), J. Mannov (bass), U. Koella (pno), N. Clayton (pno), F. Näf (cnd), *(chorus unknown)* Ars Musici ▲ AM 1091 [DDD]

Dominguez, Oralia (mez)

Beethoven, L. van:Sym 9, "Choral Sym", w. Irma Gonzalez (sop), Flavio Becerra (ten), Roberto Banuelas (bar), F. Lozano (cnd), Mexico City PO, Mexico City Chorus Forlane ▲ FRL 18 [AAD]

Borodin, A.:Prince Igor, w. Kalmus (sgr), Infantino (sgr), G. Taddei (ten), B. Christoff (bass), A. La Rosa Parodi (cnd), Rome RAI Orch, Rome RAI Chorus *(rec live 9/19/64)* Melodram 2–▲ MEL 27028 (s)

Boulanger, L.:Du fond de l'abîme, w. Raymond Amade (ten), J. J. Grunenwald (org), I. Markevitch (cnd), Lamoureux Orch, Elisabeth Brasseur Chorale *(rec Salle Pleyel, Paris)* Everest ▲ EVC 9034 [AAD]

Mendelssohn, F.:St. Paul, w. A. Giebel (sop), Theo Altmeyer (ten), S. Nimsgern (b–bar), R. A. El Hage (bass), R. Muti (cnd), Milan RAI Orch, Milan RAI Chorus [G] *(rec live, Milan, 12/15/70)* Memories 2–▲ HR 4267/68 (m) [ADD]

Purcell, H.:Dido & Aeneas, w. Helen Donath (sop—Belinda), Shirley Verrett (sop—Dido), Oralia Dominguez (mez—Sorceress), Carmen Lavani (alt—A Spirit), Margaret Lensky (cta—2nd Witch), Carlo Gaifa (ten—A Sailor), Dan Jordacescu (bar—Aeneas), Rosina Cavicchioli (sgr—A Woman), Lilia Teresita Reyes (sgr—1st Witch), R. Leppard (cnd), Turin RAI SO, Ambrosian Chorus *(rec Torino, May 20, 1971)* Arkadia ▲ 619 [ADD]

Spontini, G.:La vestale, w. R. Scotto (sop), F. Tagliavini (ten), M. Picchi (ten), V. Gui (cnd), Florence Maggio Musicale Orch, Florence Maggio Musicale Chorus [I] *(rec live 5/5/70)* Melodram ("Connaisseur" series) 2–▲ CDM 27512 [ADD]

Verdi, G.:Aida, w. M. Callas (sop), M. Del Monaco (ten), G. Taddei (bar), O. de Fabritiis (cnd), Palacio Bellas Artes Orch, Palacio Bellas Artes Chorus *(rec live, Mexico City 7/3/51)* Melodram 2–▲ CDM 26015

Verdi, G.:Don Carlos, w. R. Kabaivanska (sop), F. Corelli (ten), L. Quilico (bar), N. Ghiaurov (bass), N. Ghiuselev (bass), A. Guadagno (cnd), Hartford Opera Orch *(rec live 1966)* Melodram 2–▲ MEL 27511

Verdi, G.:Falstaff, w. Ilva Ligabue (sop), Luigi Alva (ten), Geraint Evans (bar), Eberhardt Wächter (bar), F. Previtali (cnd), *(orch unknown) (rec Teatro Colon, Buenos Aires, Aug. 30, 1963)* Ornamenti ("Gala Evenings, Teatro Colon") 2–▲ 119

▲ = CD ♦ = Enhanced CD Δ = MD ■ = Cassette Tape □ = DCC

Dominguez, Oralia (mez) (cont.)

Verdi, G.:La forza del destino, w. R. Tebaldi (sop), F. Corelli (ten), R. Capecchi (bar), E. Bastianini (bar), B. Christoff (bass), F. Molinari-Pradelli (cnd), Naples Teatro San Carlo Orch, Naples Teatro San Carlo Chorus *(rec Oct. 1 1958)* Melodram 3-▲ MLO 370102 [AAD]

Verdi, G.:Requiem Mass, w. Gré Brouwenstijn (sop), Giuseppe Zampieri (ten), Nicola Zaccaria (bass), G. Solti (cnd), Cologne RSO, Cologne Radio Chorus *(rec Nov 17, 1958)* Bella Voce 2-▲ 107.201 [AAD]

Verdi, G.:Requiem Mass, w. Elizabeth Schwarzkopf (sop), Giuseppe Di Stefano (ten), Cesare Siepi (b-bar), V. de Sabata (cnd), La Scala Orch, La Scala Chorus Theorema 2-▲ TH 121123/24

Verdi, G.:Requiem Mass, w. Gré Brouwenstijn (sop), Giuseppe Zampieri (ten), Nicola Zaccaria (bass), G. Solti (cnd), West German Radio Orch, West German Radio Chorus Globe 2-▲ GLO 5141 [ADD]

Verdi, G.:Rigoletto (sels), w. C. O'Connor (sop), G. Di Stefano (ten), G. Valdengo (bar), I. Rufino (bass), R. Cellini (cnd), Palacio Bellas Artes Orch, Palacio Bellas Artes Chorus [abridged performance] *(rec live, Mexico City 6/22/48)* Golden Age of Opera 2-▲ GAO 128/29 [ADD]

Verdi, G.:La traviata (sels), w. Elizabeth Schwarzkopf (sop), Giuseppe DiStefano (ten), Cesare Siepi (b-bar), V. de Sabata (cnd), La Scala Orch, La Scala Chorus—Preludes to Acts I & III Theorema 2-▲ TH 121123/24

Dominguez, Rosa (sop)

Caldara, A.:Maddalena ai Piedi di Cristo, w. Maria Cristina Kiehr (sop), Bernarda Fink (cta), Andreas Scholl (ct), Gerd Türk (ten), Ulrich Messthaler (bass), R. Jacobs (cnd), Schola Cantorum Basiliensis Instrumental Ensemble Harmonia Mundi France 2-▲ HMC 905221.22

Dominici, Ernesto (bass)

Puccini, G.:Madama Butterfly, w. Toti dal Monte (sop—Madama Butterfly), Maria Huder (mez—Kate Pinkerton), Beniamino Gigli (ten—B.F. Pinkerton), Adelio Zagonara (ten—Goro), Mario Basiola (bar—Sharpless), Gino Conti (bass—Principe Yamadori), Ernesto Dominici (bass—Il Bonzo), Vittoria Paolombini (sgr—Suzuki), O. de Fabritiis (cnd), Rome Opera Orch, Giuseppe Conca (cnd), Rome Opera Chorus *(rec Aug 1939)* Arkadia 2-▲ CD 78004 (m) [ADD]

Verdi, G.:Rigoletto, w. Mercedes Capsir (sop), Dino Borgioli (ten), Riccardo Stracciari (bar), L. Molajoli (cnd), La Scala Orch, La Scala Chorus Phonographe 2-▲ PHG 5036 [ADD]

Verdi, G.:Rigoletto, w. Mercedes Capsir (sop), Dino Borgioli (ten), Riccardo Stracciari (bar), Duilio Baronti (bass), Anna Masetti Bassi (sgr) *(rec 1930)* Grammofono 2000 2-▲ GRM 78632

Domininská, Libuse (sop)

Janácek, L.:Jenůfa, w. Libuse Domininská (sop—Jenufa), Nadeshda Kniplová (sop—Kostelnicka), Vilém Príbyl (ten—Laca), Ivo Zidek (ten—Steva), B. Gregor (cnd), Prague National Theater Orch, Prague National Theater Chorus EMI Classics 2-▲ CDMB 65476

Donadini, Giovanna (sgr)

Leo, L.:Amor vuol sofferenze, w. Marilena Laurenza (sop), Vitalba Mosca (mez), Piero Guarnera (bar), Domenico Colaianni (sgr), Marilyne Fallot (sgr), Hyun Lee (sgr), D. Moles (cnd), Naples New Scarlatti Orch *(rec Martinafranca Festival, 1994)* Nuova Era 3-▲ NUO 7221

Donaldson, Ann Keri (sop)

Starer, R.:To Think of Time, w. Mariani String Quartet Albany ▲ TROY 151 [DDD]

Donat, Zdzislawa (sop)

Maciejewski, R.:Missa pro defunctis, w. Jadwiga Rappé (alt), Jerzy Knetig (ten), Janusz Niziolek (bass), T. Strugala (cnd), Warsaw PO, Henryk Wojnarowski (cnd), Warsaw National Phil Chorus *(rec National Philharmonic, Warsaw, May 2-15, 1989)* Polskie Nagrania 2-▲ PNCD 039 A/B

Donatella (sop)

Napoli, J.:Arias, w. S. Moltisanti (pno)—Per la tomba; Figlio dormi, dormi Figlio; Filastrocca; Deisperata; Vucca vasata nun perdi vintura; Jesce, Jesce, sole Zuma Records ▲ ZMA 102

Donath, Helen (sop)

Bach, J.S.:Cant 41, w. M. Höffgen (mez), A. Kraus (ten), S. Nimsgern (b-bar), H. Rilling (cnd), Stuttgart Bach Collegium, Gächinger Kantorei [G] Hänssler Classic ▲ 98.870 [AAD]

Bach, J.S.:Cant 51, w. N. Marriner (cnd), Academy of St. Martin in the Fields Classics for Pleasure ("Eminence" series) ▲ CFP 2235

Bach, J.S.:Cant 69, w. J. Hamari (b-bar), A. Kraus (ten), W. Schöne (bass), H. Rilling (cnd), Bach Ensemble *(rec Mar-Apr 1973)* Hänssler Classic ▲ 98.829 [AAD]

Bach, J.S.:Cant 74, w. H. Laurich (cta), A. Kraus (ten), P. Huttenlocher (bar), H. Rilling (cnd), Stuttgart Bach Collegium, Gächinger Kantorei Hänssler Classic ▲ 98.887 [AAD]

Bach, J.S.:Cant 77, w. J. Hamari (mez), A. Kraus (ten), W. Schöne (bar), H. Rilling (cnd), Stuttgart Bach Collegium, Gächinger Kantorei Hänssler Classic ▲ 98.809 [AAD]

Bach, J.S.:Cant 91, w. H. Watts (cta), A. Kraus (ten), W. Schöne (bass), H. Rilling (cnd), Stuttgart Bach Collegium, Württemberg CO, Gächinger Kantorei, Frankfurt Choir [G] *(rec Feb 1972)* Hänssler Classic ▲ 98.822 [AAD]

Bach, J.S.:Cant 94, w. E. Paaske (cta), A. Baldin (ten), H.-F. Kunz (bass), W. Schöne (bass), H. Rilling (cnd), Stuttgart Bach Collegium, Württemberg CO, Gächinger Kantorei Hänssler Classic ▲ 98.808 [AAD]

Bach, J.S.:Cant 96, w. M. Höffgen (mez), A. Kraus (ten), S. Nimsgern (b-bar), H. Rilling (cnd), Stuttgart Bach Collegium, Württemberg CO, Gächinger Kantorei [G] *(rec 1973)* Hänssler Classic ▲ 98.814 [AAD]

Bach, J.S.:Cant 97, w. H. Gardow (sop), A. Kraus (ten), P. Huttenlocher (bar), H. Rilling (cnd), Bach Ensemble *(rec Jan-Feb 1974)* Hänssler Classic ▲ 98.835 [AAD]

Bach, J.S.:Cant 108, w. M. Höffgen (mez), K. Equiluz (ten), H.-F. Kunz (bass), H. Rilling (cnd), Stuttgart Bach Collegium, Gächinger Kantorei [G] *(rec 1980-81)* Hänssler Classic ▲ 98.884 [AAD]

Bach, J.S.:Cant 120, w. H. Laurich (cta), A. Kraus (ten), W. Schöne (bass), H. Rilling (cnd), Bach Ensemble *(rec Mar-Apr 1973)* Hänssler Classic ▲ 98.829 [AAD]

Bach, J.S.:Cant 208, "Hunting Cant", w. Elisabeth Speiser (sop), Wilfrid Jochims (ten), Jakob Stämpfli (bass), H. Rilling (cnd), Stuttgart Bach Collegium, Stuttgart Memorial Church Figuralchor *(rec Southwest Sound Studio, Stuttgart-Bottnang, May 1965)* Musicaphon ▲ 51351 [AAD]

Bach, J.S.:Magnificat, BWV 243, w. Gundula Bernát-Klein (sop), Birgit Finnilä (alt), Peter Schreier (ten), Barry McDaniel (bass), W. Gönnenwein (cnd), German Bach Soloists, South German Madrigal Choir [E♭ version] *(rec Stuttgart Radio, 1966)* Bayer ▲ 100081 [ADD]

Bach, J.S.:Mass in b, BWV 232, w. Brigitte Fassbaender (cta), Claes H. Ahnsjö (ten), Roland Hermann (bar), Robert Holl (bass), E. Jochum (cnd), Bavarian RSO, Bavarian Radio Chorus EMI Classics ("Doublefforte" series) 2-▲ CDFB 68640

Beethoven, L. van:Leonore (opera), w. Edda Moser (sop), Eberhard Büchner (ten), Richard Cassilly (ten), Theo Adam (b-bar), Hermann Christian Polster (bass), Karl Ridderbusch (bass), H. Blomstedt (cnd), Dresden Staatskapelle, Leipzig Radio Chorus Berlin Classics ▲ BER 1140

Beethoven, L. van:Sym 9, "Choral Sym", w. D. Soffel (mez), S. Jerusalem (ten), P. Lika (bass), S. Celibidache (cnd), Munich PO, Munich Phil Chorus *(rec Mar. 19, 1989)* Exclusive ▲ EXL 15 [AAD]

Divas in Song:Marylin Horne, a 60th Birthday Celebration, w. Montserrat Caballé (sop), R. A. Swenson (sop), F. von Stade (mez), R. Fleming (mez), S. Ramey (bass), J. Levine (cnd), M. Katz (pno), W. Jones (pno), K. Donath (pno), Manuel Burgueras (pno) RCA Red Seal ▲ 09026-62547-2

Gluck, C.W.:Orfeo ed Euridice, w. P. Lorengar (sop), M. Horne (mez), G. Solti (cnd), Royal Opera House Orch, Royal Opera House Chorus Covent Garden London 2-▲ 417410-2 [ADD]

Hartmann, K.A.:Simplicius Simplicissimus, w. H. Fricke (cnd), Bavarian RSO Wergo 2-▲ WER 6259-2

Haydn, J.:Die Jahreszeiten, w. A. Kraus (ten), Kurt Widmer (bass), W. Gönnenwein (cnd), Ludwigsburg Festival Orch, South German Madrigal Choir [G] Vox Box 2-▲ CDX 5045 [ADD]

Haydn, J.:Die Schöpfung, w. Scherr (alt), Adalbert Kraus (ten), Kurt Widmer (bass), W. Gönnenwein (cnd), Ludwigsburg Festival Orch, South German Madrigal Choir [G] Vox Box 2-▲ CDX 5025 [ADD]

Kalliwoda, J.W.:Heimatlied, "Treues, stilles Friedensthal", w. D. Klöcker (cl), K. Donath (pno) [G] Acanta ▲ 43508

Lachner, F.P.:Songs Sop, w. D. Klöcker (cl), K. Donath (cl)—Seit ich ihn gesehen, Op. 82; Auf Flügeln Gesanges [G] Acanta ▲ 43508

Lehár, F.:Friederike (sels), w. Gabriele Fuchs (sop), Adolf Dallapozza (ten), H. Wallberg (cnd), Munich RSO, Bavarian Radio Chorus Emperor Operetta ▲ KO 86344

Mahler, G.:Sym 2, w. B. Finnilä (cta), J. Barbirolli (cnd), Stuttgart RSO, Stuttgart Radio Chorus [G] *(rec live 6/19/70)* Arkadia 3-▲ 719 [ADD]

Monteverdi, C.:Incoronazione, w. E. Söderström (sop), C. Berberian (sop), P. Esswood (ct), N. Harnoncourt (cnd), Vienna Concentus Musicus [I] Teldec 4-▲ 2292-42547-2

Donath, Helen (sop) (cont.)

Mozart, W.A.:Arias, w. Arleen Augér (sop), Kathleen Battle (sop), Irma Beilke (sop), Helena Braun (sop), Lisa Della Casa (sop), Maria Cebotari (sop), Ileana Cotrubas (sop), Mirella Freni (sop), Reri Grist (sop), Edita Gruberova (sop), Elisabeth Grümmer (sop), Hilde Güden (sop), Ingeborg Hallstein (sop), Luise Helletsgruber (sop), Gundula Janowitz (sop), Sena Jurinac (sop), Erika Köth (sop), Evelyn Lear (sop), Wilma Lipp (sop), Margaret Marshall (sop), Edith Mathis (sop), Jarmila Novotna (sop), Margherita Perras (sop), Lucia Popp (sop), Elisabeth Rethberg (sop), Anneliese Rothenberger (sop), Elisabeth Schumann (sop), Elisabeth Schwarzkopf (sop), Graziella Sciutti (sop), Irmgard Seefried (sop), Graziella Sciutti (sop), Julia Varady (sop), Agnes Baltsa (mez), Margit Bokor (mez), Brigitte Fassbaender (mez), Christa Ludwig (mez), Ann Murray (mez), Francisco Araiza (ten), Anton Dermota (ten), Helge Rosvaenge (ten), Rudolf Schock (ten), Peter Schreier (ten), Leopold Simoneau (ten), Eric Tappy (ten), Richard Tauber (ten), Gösta Winbergh (ten), Josef Witt (ten), Fritz Wunderlich (ten), Christian Boesch (bar), Willy Domgraf-Fassbaender (bar), Karl Dönch (bar), Dietrich Fischer-Dieskau (bar), Erich Kunz (bar), Eberhard Wächter (bar), Hans Hotter (b-bar), Paul Schöffler (b-bar), Cesare Siepi (b-bar), José Van Dam (b-bar), Walter Berry (bass), Geraint Evans (bass), Nicolai Ghiaurov (bass), Alexander Kipnis (bass), Richard Mayr (bass), Kurt Moll (bass), James Morris (bass), Ezio Pinza (bass), Martti Talvela (bass), Giorgio Tozzi (bass), Hans Duhan (sgr), Res Fischer (sgr), Marie Gerhart (sgr), *(various orchs & cnds)*—sels from Idomeneo, Die Entführung aus der Serail, Le nozze di Figaro, Don Giovanni, Così fan tutte, Die Zauberflöte & various arias Orfeo d'or ("Festspiel Dokumente" series) 5-▲ 408955

Mozart, W.A.:Arias, w. Dieter Klöcker (cl), Josef Suk (vn), Karl-Otto Hartmann (bn), K. Donath (cnd), Suk CO—Cor Sincerum; Jesus Amor Meus; Mens Sancta Deo [2 versions]; Jesu Dulcis Memoria; Salve Regina; Domine Deus Salutis Meae; Plasmator Deus; Die Hoffnung dient zum Stabe *(rec Cultural House, Prague, June 3-10, 1987)* Panton ▲ PAN 810860

Mozart, W.A.:Complete Mozart Edition, w. A. Augér (sop), E. Mathis (sop), J. Varady (sop), P. Schreier (ten), L. Hager (cnd), Salzburg Mozarteum Orch Philips 3-▲ 422532-2 [ADD]

Mozart, W.A.:Complete Mozart Edition, w. Jessye Norman (sop), I. Cotrubas (sop), T. Troyanos (mez), W. Hollweg (ten), H. Prey (bar), H. Schmidt-Isserstedt (cnd), North German RSO Philips 3-▲ 422534-2 [ADD]

Mozart, W.A.:Finta semplice, w. Jutta-Renate Ihloff (sop), Teresa Berganza (mez), A. Rolfe Johnson (ten), Thomas Moser (ten), Robert Lloyd (b-bar), Robert Holl (bass), L. Hager (cnd), Salzburg Mozarteum Orch [I] Orfeo 3-▲ 085843 [DDD]

Mozart, W.A.:Requiem, w. Y. Minton (mez), A. Davies (ten), G Nienstedt (bass), C. Davis (cnd), BBC SO, John Alldis Choir [L] Philips ▲ 420353-2 [ADD]

Mozart, W.A.:Zauberflöte, w. S. Geszty (sop), P. Schreier (ten), G. Leib (bass), T. Adam (bass), O. Suitner (cnd), Dresden Staatskapelle [I] RCA Gold Seal 3-▲ 6511-2 [ADD]

Nicolai, O.:Lustigen Weiber, w. E. Mathis (sop), H. Schwarz (mez), K. Ludwig (ten), K.-E. Mercker (ten), P. Schreier (ten), C. Dormoy (bar), B. Weikl (bar), K. Moll (bass), S. Vogel (bass), B. Klee (cnd), Berlin Staatskapelle, Berlin State Opera Chorus *(rec July 3, 1976)* Berlin Classics ("Eterna" series) ▲ BER 2046-2 [ADD]

Nicolai, O.:Lustigen Weiber, w. E. Mathis (sop), H. Schwarz (cta), P. Schreier (ten), K. Moll (bass), B. Klee (cnd), Berlin Staatskapelle, Berlin State Opera Chorus Berlin Classics 2-▲ BER 2115 [ADD]

Puccini, G.:Gianni Schicchi, w. P. Seiffert (ten), R. Panerai (bar), G. Patanè (cnd), Munich RSO Eurodisc ▲ 7751-2-RC [DDD]

Purcell, H.:Dido & Aeneas, w. Helen Donath (sop—Belinda), Shirley Verrett (sop—Dido), Oralia Dominguez (mez—Sorceress), Carmen Lavani (alt—A Spirit), Margaret Lensky (cta—2nd Witch), Carlo Gaifa (ten—A Sailor), Dan Jordacescu (bar—Aeneas), Rosina Cavicchioli (sgr—A Woman), Lilia Teresita Reyes (sgr—1st Witch), R. Leppard (cnd), Turin RAI SO, Ambrosian Chorus *(rec Torino, May 20, 1971)* Arkadia ▲ 619 [ADD]

Scarlatti, A.:Cants, w. N. Marriner (cnd), Academy of St. Martin in the Fields—Su le sponde del Tebro Classics for Pleasure ("Eminence" series) ▲ CFP 2235

Scarlatti, A.:Su le sponde del Tebro, w. Maurice André (tpt), N. Marriner (cnd), Academy of St. Martin in the Fields EMI Classics ("Baroque" series) ▲ CDK 65735

Schubert, Franz:Der Hirt auf dem Felsen, w. D. Klöcker (cl), K. Donath (pno) [G] Acanta ▲ 43508

Schubert, Franz:Mass 4, w. B. Fassbaender (mez), F. Araiza (ten), D. Fischer-Dieskau (bar), W. Sawallisch (cnd), Bavarian RSO, Bavarian Radio Chorus [L] EMI Classics ("Studio" series) ▲ CDM 69222

Schubert, Franz:Mass 6, w. B. Fassbaender (mez), F. Araiza (ten), D. Fischer-Dieskau (bar), W. Sawallisch (cnd), Bavarian RSO, Bavarian Radio Chorus [L] EMI Classics ("Studio" series) ▲ CDM 69223

Spohr, L.:German Songs , Op. 103, w. D. Klöcker (cl), K. Donath (pno) [G] Acanta ▲ 43508

Strauss, R.:Arabella, w. J. Varady (sop), D. Fischer-Dieskau (bar), A. Schmidt (bar), W. Berry (bass), W. Sawallisch (cnd), Bavarian State Orch Orfeo 2-▲ 169882 [DDD]

Strauss, R.:Der Rosenkavalier, w. R. Crespin (sop), Y. Minton (mez), M. Jungwirth (bass), G. Solti (cnd), Vienna PO [G] London 3-▲ 417493-2 [ADD]

Wagner, R.:Die Meistersinger von Nürnberg, w. R. Hesse (mez), A. Kollo (ten), P. Schreier (ten), T. Adam (b-bar), R. Evans (bass), K. Ridderbusch (bass), H. von Karajan (cnd), Dresden Staatskapelle, Dresden State Chorus, Leipzig Radio Chorus [G] EMI Classics 4-▲ CDCD 49683 [ADD]

Wolf, H.:Der Corregidor, w. D. Soffel (mez), W. Hollweg (ten), P. Maus (ten), K. Moll (bass), D. Fischer-Dieskau (bar), G. Albrecht (cnd), Berlin RSO [G] Koch Schwann 2-▲ CD 314 010

Donath, N. (sop)

Mahler, G.:Sym 4, w. E. Inbal (cnd), Frankfurt RSO [G] Denon ▲ 7952 [DDD]

Donati, Walter (sgr)

Mascagni, P.:Amica, w. Katia Ricciarelli (sop), Monica Minarelli (sgr), Elia Padovan (sgr), Fabio Armiliato (sgr), M. Pace (cnd), Hungarian Radio-TV SO, Hungarian Radio-TV Chorus *(rec Budapest, Nov 1995)* Kicco Classic 2-▲ KC 00296 [DDD]

Donato, Vincenzo di (ten)

Perti, G.A.:Liturgy for Good Friday, w. Patrizia Vaccari (sop), Maura Pederzoli (sop), Cristina Calzolari (sop), Alida Oliva (sop), Claudia Bugli (sop), Lucia Bagnoli (alt), Cinzia Meneghel (alt), Renzo Bez (alt), Alessandro Carmignani (alt), Michel van Goethem (alt), Mauro Collina (ten), Paolo Fanciullacci (ten), Giovanni Caccamo (ten), Paolo Da Col (ten), Sergio Foresti (bass), Marco Scavazza (bass), Luca Ferracin (bass), Paride Montanari (bass), Liuwe Tamminga (org), Sergio Vartolo (org), S. Vartolo (cnd), Bologna San Petronio Capella Musicale Orch—Omnes amici mei; De lamentatione Jeremiae Prophetae:Heth. Cogitavit; Velum templi; Vinea mea; De lamentatione Jeremiae Prophetae:Lamed. Matribus suis; Tamquam ad latronem; Tenebrae factae sunt; Animam meam; Tradiderunt me; Jesum tradidit; De lamentatione Jeremiae Prophetae:Aleph. Ego vir; Caligaverunt *(rec St. Petronio Basilica, Bologna, Mar 28-31, 1995)* Naxos ▲ 8.553321 [DDD]

Dönch, Karl (bar)

Mozart, W.A.:Così fan tutte, w. E. Schwarzkopf (sop—Fiordiligi), C. Ludwig (sop—Dorabella), G. Sciutti (sop—Despina), W. Kmentt (ten—Ferrando), H. Prey (bar—Gugliemo), K. Dönch (bar—D. Alfonso), K. Böhm (cnd), Vienna PO, Vienna State Opera Chorus [I] *(rec live, Salzburg, Aug. 8, 1962)* Arkadia 2-▲ 455 [ADD]

Strauss (II), Joh.:Die Fledermaus, w. E. Schwarzkopf (sop), R. Streich (sop), N. Gedda (ten), H. Krebs (ten), R. Christ (ten), E. Kunz (bar), H. von Karajan (cnd), Philharmonia Orch, Philharmonia Chorus [G] EMI Classics ("Studio" series) 2-▲ CDHB 69531 (m) [ADD]

Strauss (II), Joh.:Wiener Blut, w. H. Papouschek (sop), S. Martikke (sop), E. Kales (sop), A. Dallapozza (ten), K. Ruzicka (ten), E. Kuchar (ten), W. Kandutsch (bar), O. Kolmann (bass), R. Bibl (cnd), Vienna Volksoper Orch, Vienna Volksoper Chorus Denon 2-▲ CO 8105 [DDD]

Strauss (II), Joh.:Der Zigeunerbaron, w. Emmy Loose (sop), Hilde Zadek (sop), Rosette Anday (cta), Julius Patzak (ten), Alfred Poell (bar), Steffi Leverenz (sgr), C. Krauss (cnd), Vienna PO, Vienna State Opera Chorus Phonographe 2-▲ PHG 5020 [AAD]

Dondi, Dino (bar)

Giordano, U.:Andrea Chénier, w. Montserrat Caballé (sop), Franco Corelli (ten), R. de Carlo (sgr), D. Dondi (sgr), G. Ellsworth (sgr), J. Fair (sgr), R. Falk (sgr), S. Felter (sgr), E. Green (sgr), H. Hicks (sgr), H. Krauss (sgr), L. Miller (sgr), N. Riggins (sgr), H. Salerno (sgr), A. Guadagno (cnd), Academy of Music Orch, Academy of Music Chorus Great Opera Performances 2-▲ GOP 766

Donets, S. (sgr)

Prokofiev, S.:Maddalena, w. S. Kulikova (sgr), N. Zagorinskaya (sgr), Y. Melnikova (sgr), S. Yakovlev (sgr), C. Tikhonov (cnd), Moscow Helikon Theater Chamber Ensemble [R] MK ▲ MKA 417056 [DDD]

Donets, S. (sgr) (cont.)

Stravinsky, I.:Mavra, w. S. Kulikova (sgr), N. Zagorinskaya (sgr), Y. Melnikova (sgr), S. Yakovlev (bar), C. Tikhonov (cnd), Moscow Helikon Theater Chamber Ensemble MK ▲ MKA 417056 [DDD]

Doniat, Aimé (bar)

Boieldieu, F.-A.:La Dame blanche, w. Michel Sénéchal (ten—Georges Brown), Aimé Doniat (bar—Dikson), Pierre Héral (bass—Mac-Irton), Adrien Legros (bass—Gaveston), P. Stoll (cnd), Paris SO, Paris Sym Chorus Accord 2-▲ ACD 220862 [AAD]

Hahn, R.:O mon del inconnu!, w. Christiane Château (sop), Lina Dachary (sop), Monique Stiot (mez), Michel Hamel (ten), Joseph Peyron (ten), Dominique Tirmont (bar), Philippe Gaudin (sgr), Jacques Provins (sgr), J. Brebion (cnd), ORTF Lyric Orch Musidisc 2-▲ MUS 202562 [AAD]

Offenbach, J.:Barbe-bleue, w. Henri Legay (ten), René Lenoty (ten), Rene Terrasson (sgr), J. Doussard (cnd), ORTF Lyric Orch, ORTF Lyric Chorale *(rec 1967)* Memories 2-▲ MEM 4591 [ADD]

Donlan, Brian (bar)

Donizetti, G.:Il giovedì grasso, w. J. Gomez (sop), J. Hughes (mez), J. Peters (mez), U. Benelli (bar), F. Davià (bass), E. Esparza (sgr), M. Williams (sgr), D. Atherton (cnd), Eireann Radio-TV SO [I] *(rec live, 1970)* Memories ▲ HR 4482 [ADD]

Donizetti, G.:Il giovedì grasso, w. J. Gomez (sop), J. Peters (mez), J. Hughes (mez), U. Benelli (bar), F. Davià (bass), E. Esparza (sgr), D. Atherton (cnd), Eireann Radio-TV SO [I] *(rec live, 1970)* Foyer ▲ FOY 2036 [AAD]

Donnelly, Patrick (bass)

Mozart, W.A.:Così fan tutte, w. Sophie Marin-Degor (sop—Despina), Laura Polverelli (mez—Dorabella), Sophie Fournier (sgr—Fiordiligi), Nicolas Revenq (bar—Guglielmo), Patrick Donnelly (bass—Don Alfonso), Simon Edwards (sgr—Ferrando), J. Malgoire (cnd), La Grande Écurie et la Chambre du Roy Astrée 8-▲ E 8606

Mozart, W.A.:Don Giovanni, w. Danielle Borst (sop—Donna Anna), Véronique Gens (sop—Donna Elvira), Sophie Marin-Degor (sop—Zerlina), Huub Claessens (bar—Leporello), Nicolas Revenq (bar—Don Giovanni), Patrick Donnelly (bass—Commendatore), Simon Edwards (sgr—Don Ottavio), J. Malgoire (cnd), La Grande Écurie et la Chambre du Roy Astrée 8-▲ E 8606

Mozart, W.A.:Nozze di Figaro, w. Danielle Borst (sop—Countess Almaviva), Claudine Le Coz (sop—Marcellina), Sophie Marin-Degor (sop—Suzanna), Laura Polverelli (mez—Cherubino), Valérie Lecoq (sgr—Barberina), Philippe Cantor (ten—Antonio), Stuart Patterson (ten—Dons Basile & Curzio), Huub Claessens (bar—Figaro), Nicolas Revenq (bar—Count Almaviva), Patrick Donnelly (bass—Bartolo), J. Malgoire (cnd), La Grande Écurie et la Chambre du Roy Astrée 8-▲ E 8606

Donose, Ruxandra (mez)

Mahler, G.:Das Lied von der Erde, w. Thomas Harper (ten), M. Halász (cnd), Irish National SO *(rec National Concert Hall, Dublin, Apr 11-12, 1994)* Naxos ▲ 8.550933 [DDD]

Donovan, J. (sgr)

Lloyd Webber, A.:Joseph and the Amazing Technicolor Dreamcoat [1991 London revival cast] Polydor ▲ 314 511130-2 ■ 314 511130-4

Donzelli, Stefania (sgr)

Grétry, A.-E.-M.:Denys le tyran, w. R. Franceschetto (sgr), C. Di Segni (ten), B. De Simone (bar), F. Vizioli (cnd), Italian International Orch, Ars Pulcherrima Artium Chorus [F] *(rec live, Fermo, Palazzo Sassatelli, 1989)* Memories ▲ DR 3106 [DDD]

Dooley, Jeffery (ct)

Bach, J.S.:Mass in b, BWV 232, w. J. Baird (sop), J. Nelson (sop), F. Hoffmeister (ten), J. Opalach (bass), J. Rifkin (cnd), Bach Ensemble [L] Elektra/Nonesuch 2-▲ 79036-2 [DDD] 2-■ 79036-4 (D)

Furtwängler, W.:Te Deum, w. E. Mathis (sop), S. Wagner (cta), G. Jelden (ten), H. Chemin-Petit (cnd), Berlin PO *(rec live, 1967)* As Disc ▲ ASD 2506

Purcell, H.:Airs & Duets, w. Howard Crook (ten) Lyrichord ("Early Music" series) ▲ LYR CD 8024

Purcell, H.:Airs & Duets, w. H. Crook (ten) [E] Elektra/Nonesuch ■ 71343-4

Dooley, Kathy (sop)

Danova, R.:The Phantom of the Opera on Ice, w. Susannah Glanville (sop), Johnny Logan (ten), Stephen Lee Garden (ten), Mungo Jerry (bar), Nigel Paul (bar), P. Whitfield (cnd), Northern Light SO, Northern Light Choir, Russian Stars on Ice Chorus Plaza ▲ PZA 008

Doralik, Nina (sop)

Shostakovich, D.:From Jewish Folk Poetry, w. Z. Dolukhovna (mez), A. Masennikov (ten), D. Shostakovich (pno) *(rec 1956)* Russian Disc ▲ RUS 15 015 [ADD]

Doré, Doris (sgr)

Wagner, R.:Götterdämmerung (siegfried's funeral), w. Helen Traubel (sop), Herbert Janssen (bar), A. Rodzinski (cnd), New York PO *(rec Carnegie Hall, New York City, Nov 25, 1945)* Enterprise ("The Radio Years" series) ▲ ENT RY 55

Wagner, R.:Das Rheingold (sels), w. Helen Traubel (sop), Herbert Janssen (bar), A. Rodzinski (cnd), New York PO—Entry of the Gods into Valhalla *(rec Carnegie Hall, New York City, Nov 25, 1945)* Enterprise ("The Radio Years" series) ▲ ENT RY 55

Wagner, R.:Siegfried (waldweben), w. Helen Traubel (sop), Herbert Janssen (bar), A. Rodzinski (cnd), New York PO *(rec Carnegie Hall, New York City, Nov 25, 1945)* Enterprise ("The Radio Years" series) ▲ ENT RY 55

Wagner, R.:Die Walküre (act 3), w. Helen Traubel (sop), Herbert Janssen (bar), A. Rodzinski (cnd), New York PO *(rec Carnegie Hall, New York City, Nov 25, 1945)* Enterprise ("The Radio Years" series) ▲ ENT RY 55

Doria, Renée (sop)

Airs d'Opéras français Music Memoria ▲ 30185

Chabrier, E.:Songs, w. Julien Giovannetti (bar), Guy Fouché (sgr), André Rabot (bn), Tasso Janopoulo (pno)—Lied; Tes yeux bleus; Sommation irrespectueuse; Toutes les fleurs; Ruy blas [A quoi bon entendre...]; Credo d'amour; Romance de l'étoile; Villanelle des petits; Les cigales; Ballade des gros dindons; Pastorale des cochons roses; L'île heureuse; Chanson pour jeanne; Duo de l'ouvreuse de l'opéra-comique et de l'employé du bon-marché; L'invitation au voyage Accord ▲ ACD 201392 [AAD]

Fauré, G.:La bonne chanson, w. Berthe Monmart (sop), Pierre Mollet (bar), Simone Gouat (pno) Accord ▲ ACD 204262 [AAD]

Fauré, G.:La Chanson d'Eve, w. Berthe Monmart (sop), Pierre Mollet (bar), Simone Gouat (pno) Accord ▲ ACD 204262 [AAD]

Fauré, G.:L'Horizon chimérique, w. Berthe Monmart (sop), Pierre Mollet (bar), Simone Gouat (pno) Accord ▲ ACD 204262 [AAD]

Fauré, G.:Le Jardin clos, w. Berthe Monmart (sop), Pierre Mollet (bar), Simone Gouat (pno) Accord ▲ ACD 204262 [AAD]

Fauré, G.:Songs, w. Berthe Monmart (sop), Pierre Mollet (bar), Simone Gouat (pno)—Chanson du pêcheur; Lydia; Tristesse; Au bord de l'eau; Puisqu'ici bas; Automne; Poème d'un jour; Les berceaux; Le secret; Aurore; Les roses d'ispahan; Nocturne; Clair de lune; Spleen; La rose; En prière; Mandoline; Green; En sourdine; A Clymène; C'est l'extase; Pleurs d'or; Arpège; Le parfum impérissable; Soir; Dans la forêt de septembre; Le don silencieux; Chanson Accord ▲ ACD 204602 [AAD]

Massé, V.:Les Noces de Jeannette, w. Lucien Huberty (bar), J. Allain (cnd), Pasdeloup Concerts Association Orch Accord ▲ ACD 201192 [AAD]

Dormoy, Claude (bar)

Nicolai, O.:Lustigen Weiber, w. H. Donath (sop), E. Mathis (sop), H. Schwarz (mez), K. Ludwig (ten), K.-E. Mercker (ten), P. Schreier (ten), C. Dormoy (bar), B. Weikl (bar), K. Moll (bass), S. Vogel (bass), B. Klee (cnd), Berlin Staatskapelle, Berlin State Opera Chorus *(rec July 3, 1976)* Berlin Classics ("Eterna" series) ▲ BER 2046-2 [ADD]

Dornbusch, Hans (ten)

Orff, C.:Carmina burana, w. Lena Nordin (sop), Peter Mattei (bar), Love Derwinger (pno), Roland Pöntinen (pno), Kroumata Percussion Ensemble, Cecilia Rydinger Alin (cnd), Allmänna Sången, Uppsala Choir School Children's Chorus [chamber version] *(rec Uppsala Univ Hall, Uppsala, Sweden, June 9-11, 1995)* BIS ▲ CD 734 [DDD]

Dorow, Dorothy (sop)

Dorothy Dorow, w. Gunilla von Bahr (fl), L. Negro (pno) *(rec Aug. 31, 1975 & Jan. 24-2)* BIS ▲ CD 45 [AAD]

Loevendie, T.:Turkish Folk Poems, w. E. Bour (cnd), Residentie Orch The Hague [F] *(rec 1978-82)* Olympia ▲ OCD 506 [AAD]

Messiaen, O.:Harawi, w. C.-A. Dominique (pno) [F] BIS ▲ CD 86

Dorow, Dorothy (sop) (cont.)

Togni, C.:La Guirlande du blois, w. Camillo Togni (pno) Stradivarius ▲ STV DTM 90002 [ADD]

Togni, C.:Helian di Trakl, w. H. Rosbaud (cnd), BBC SO Stradivarius ▲ STV DTM 90002 [ADD]

Togni, C.:Rondeaux per 10, w. S. Gorli (cnd), Divertimento Ensemble Stradivarius ▲ STV DTM 90002 [ADD]

Valen, F.:Orchestral Songs, w. M. Caridis (cnd), Oslo PO—Ave Maria, Op. 4 (1917-21); 2 chinesische Gedichte, Op. 8 (1925-27); Dearest thou now, O soul, Op. 9 (1920-28); The Dark Night of the Soul, Op. 32 (1939) Simax ▲ PSC 3115

Webern, A.:Vocal Chamber Music, w. R. de Leeuw (cnd), Schoenberg Ensemble, Netherlands Chamber Choir—(choral songs) Entflieht auf leichten Kähnen, Op. 2 (1908 & 1914 versions); Two Songs, Op. 19 (1926); (songs for solo voice & instrumental chamber ensemble) Two Songs, Op. 8 (1910); Schmerz, immer blick' nach oben (1913); Three Songs (1913-14); Four Songs, Op. 13 (1914-18); Six Songs, Op. 14 (1917-21); Five Sacred Songs, Op. 15 (1917-22); Five Canons, Op. 16 (1923-24); Three Traditional Rhymes, Op. 17 (1924-25); Three Songs, Op. 18 (1925) [G,L] Koch Schwann ▲ CD 314005 [DDD]

Dorsey, Abner (bass)

Thomson, V.:4 Saints in 3 Acts, w. Inez Matthews (sop—St Settlement), Beatrice Robinson-Wayne (sop—St Teresa I), Altonell Hines (mez—Commère), Ruby Greene (alt—St Teresa II), David Bethea (ten—St Stephen), Charles Holland (ten—St Chavez), Edward Matthews (bar—St Ignatius), Randolph Robinson (bar—St Plan), Abner Dorsey (bass—Compère), V. Thomson (cnd), *(orch unknown)* [abridged by Thompson] *(rec June 25, 1947)* RCA Gold Seal ▲ 09026-68163-2 [ADD]

Dorsey, Leslie (bass)

Schuman, W.:Esses:Short Suite for Singers on Words Beginning with S, w. Rosalind Rees (sop), Gregg Smith (cnd), Gregg Smith Singers Vox Box ("The American Composers" series) 3-▲ CDX 3037

Talma, L.:A Wreath of Blessings, w. Gina Scaggs (sop), April Lindevald (alt), Drew Martin (ten), Gregg Smith (cnd), Gregg Smith Singers Vox Box ("The American Composers" series) 3-▲ CDX 3037

Döse, Helena (sop)

Haydn, J.:Die Schöpfung, w. Helena Döse (sop—Eva), Lucia Popp (sop—Gabriel), Werner Hollweg (ten—Uriel), Benjamin Luxon (bar—Adam), Kurt Moll (bass—Raphael), Jack McCormack (db), David Strange (vc), Antál Dorati (hpd), A. Dorati (cnd), Royal PO, Brighton Festival Chorus *(rec Kingsway Hall, London, Dec 1976)* London 2-▲ 443027-2 [ADD]

Mahler, G.:Das Klagende Lied, w. A. Hodgson (cta), R. Tear (ten), S. Rae, S. Rattle (cnd), City of Birmingham SO, City of Birmingham Sym Chorus EMI ▲ CDC 47089

Wagner, R.:Wesendonck Songs, w. S. Ehrling (cnd), Swedish CO Bluebell ▲ BLU 063 [DDD]

Doublier, Henri (nar)

Honegger, A.:Le Roi David, w. Jacqueline Brumaire (sop), Denise Scharley (alt), Jacques Pottier (ten), S. Baudo (cnd), Paris Opera Orch, Elisabeth Brasseur Chorale Accord ▲ ACD 200822 [AAD]

Dougherty, L. (sop)

Suchy, G.K.:Greek Maxims, w. D. St. Pierre (pno) [E] Capstone ▲ CPS 8613

Douglas, M. (nar)

Stravinsky, I.:L'Histoire du soldat, w. James Mitchell (nar), Alvin Epstein (nar), E. Vardi (cnd), Kapp Sinfonietta [E] MCA Classics 2-▲ MCAD2-9820 [AAD]

Dourian (sgr)

Verdi, G.:Aida, w. G. Jones (sop), J. Vickers (ten), Shaw (sgr), E. Downes (cnd), Royal Opera House Orch, Royal Opera House Chorus Covent Garden [I] *(rec live, Covent Garden, 1/27/68)* Melodram 2-▲ MEL 27019

Douse, Steven (ten)

Delius, F.:Songs, w. A. Ball (pno), Elysian Singers London Continuum ▲ CON 1054

Doussant, Herbert (ten)

Wagner, R.:Der Ring des Nibelungen, w. Liselotte Becker-Egner (sop—Woglinde/Ortlinde/Wellgunde), Angelika Berger (sop—Wellgunde/Waltraute), Siw Ericsdotter (sop—Norn 3), Heidemaria Ferch (sop—Freia/Gerhilde), Bella Jasper (sop—Helmwige/Waldvogel/Woglinde), Ditha Sommer (sop—Sieglinde/Gutrune), Ursula Boese (mez—Erda), Ruth Hesse (mez—Fricka), Nadezda Kniplová (mez—Brünnhilde), Margit Kobeck (mez—Schwertleite/Norn 2), Hilde Rosner (mez—Flosshilde/Siegrunde), Erica Schubert (mez—Grimgerde/Flosshilde), Ingrid Göritz (cta—Rossweisse/Norn 1), Herbert Doussant (ten—Froh), Herold Kraus (ten—Mime), Gerald McKee (ten—Siegmund/Siegfried), Fritz Uhl (ten—Loge), Rudolf Knoll (bar—Gunther/Donner), Rolf Polke (bass-bar—Wotan/Wanderer), Rolf Kühne (bass—Alberich), Takao Okamura (bass—Fafner), Otto von Rohr (bass—Hagen/Fasolt/Hunding), H. Swarowsky (cnd), Czech PO, Prague National Theater Orch *(rec June 3 & 5, July 26-31, A)* Weltbild Classics 14-▲ 703769 [ADD]

Doval, Maria del Mar (sgr)

Nebra, J.:Viento, w. Marta Almajano (sop), Maite Arruabarrena (sop), Raquel Pierotti (sop), Pilar Jurado (sgr), C. Coin (cnd), Limoges Baroque Ensemble Valois ▲ V 4752

Dovenman, Mikhail (ten)

Rachmaninoff, S.:The Bells, w. Yelizaveta Shumskaya (sop), Alexei Bolshakov (bar), K. Kondrashin (cnd), Moscow PO, Alexander Yurlov (cnd), Russian Republican Capelle RCA Gold Seal ▲ 74321-32046-2 [ADD]

Dow, Dorothy (sop)

Spontini, G.:Agnes von Hohensauften, w. L. Udovick (sop), F. Corelli (ten), A. Colzani (bar), G. Guelfi (bar), V. Gui (cnd), Florence Maggio Musicale Orch, Florence Maggio Musicale Chorus [I] *(rec live 5/9/54)* Melodram 2-▲ MEL 27055 (m) [AAD]

Dowd, Ronald (ten)

Berlioz, H.:Requiem, "Grande Messe des Morts", w. C. Davis (cnd), London SO, London Sym Chorus [L] Philips 2-▲ 416283-2 [ADD]

Delius, F.:A Mass of Life, w. K. Te Kanawa (sop), P. Bowden (mez), J. Shirley-Quirk (bar), N. del Mar (cnd), BBC SO, BBC Sym Chorus *(rec live, London 5/3/71)* Intaglio 2-▲ INCD 702-2 [ADD]

Dowling, Denis (bar)

Donizetti, G.:Emilia di Liverpool (sels), w. A. Cantelo (sop), J. Sutherland (sop), W. McAlpine (ten), H. Alan (bass), J. Pritchard (cnd), Royal Liverpool PO, Liverpool Music Group Singers—13 arias from Act 1, & 4 from Act 2 [I] *(rec live, Liverpool Sept. 1957)* Myto ▲ 1 MCD 91545 [ADD]

Sullivan, A.:Iolanthe (sels), w. E. Harwood (sop), S. Bevin (ten), E. Shilling (bar), J. Holmes (bass), A. Faris (cnd), Sadler's Wells Opera Orch, Sadler's Wells Opera Chorus Classics for Pleasure 2-▲ CDCFP 4730 [ADD]

Sullivan, A.:The Mikado, w. M. Studholme (sop), J. Wakefield (ten), C. Revill (bar), J. Holmes (bass), A. Faris (cnd), Sadler's Wells Opera Orch, Sadler's Wells Opera Chorus Classics for Pleasure 2-▲ CDCFP 4730 [ADD]

Downey, S. (sgr)

York, W.:Native Songs, w. N. Armstrong (sop), S. Sylvan (bar), R. Woodhouse (sgr), P. Friedland (fl), J. Fischer (pno), J. Russell Smith (perc) *(rec May 1987)* New World ▲ 80439-2

Downs, Hugh (nar)

Britten, H.:The Young Person's Guide to the Orchestra, w. A. Fiedler (cnd), Boston Pops Orch [commentary Eric Crozier; rec. June 12, 1963] *(rec Symphony Hall, Boston, June 8, 1961)* RCA Living Stereo ▲ 09026-68131-2 [ADD]; ■ 09026-68131-4

Saint-Saëns, C.:Carnival of the Animals, w. Leo Litwin (pno), Samuel Lipman (pno), Martin Hoherman (vc), A. Fiedler (cnd), Boston Pops Orch [verses rec. June 12, 1963] *(rec Symphony Hall, Boston, June 14, 1961)* RCA Living Stereo ▲ 09026-68131-2 [ADD]; ■ 09026-68131-4

Doykov, Roumen (ten)

Verdi, G.:Requiem Mass, w. Maria Belcheva (sop), Stefka Mineva (mez), Dimiter Petkov (bass), P. Tiboris (cnd), Sofia National Opera Orch, Sofia National Opera Chorus *(rec Bulgarian National Radio Studio, Mar 14-17, 1994)* Elysium ▲ GRK 708 [DDD]

Doyle, Allison (sop)

Essentially Christmas, w. East London Chorus, S. Liley (ten), J. Lister (hp), P. Ayres (org), M. Kibbelwhite (cnd), Locke Brass Consort Koch International Classics ▲ KIC 7202 [DDD]

Doyle, Don (nar)

Castelnuovo-Tedesco, M.:Platero y yo, w. Frank Koonce (gtr) *(rec Scottsdale, AZ, 1995)* Summit ▲ SMT 1002 [DDD]

Doyle, Patrick (ten)

Doyle, P.:Henry V, w. S. Rattle (cnd), City of Birmingham SO, Stephen Hill Singers Angel ▲ CDC 49919 ■ 4DS 49919

1142 ▲ = CD ♦ = Enhanced CD Δ = MD ■ = Cassette Tape ▯ = DCC

Draganescu, Victoria (sop)
Verdi, G.:Rigoletto, w. Victoria Draganescu (sop—Countess Ceprano), Magda Ianculescu (sop—Gilda), Dorothea Palade (mez—Maddalena), Valeria Savu (mez—Giovanna), Ion Buzea (ten—Duke of Mantua), Dimitrie Scurtu (ten—Borsa), Nicolae Herlea (bar—Rigoletto), Stefan Petrescu (bar—Marullo), Jean Banescu (bass—Count Ceprano), Nicolae Florei (bass—Monterone), Nicolae Rafael (bass—Sparafucile), J. Bobescu (cnd), Romanian Opera Orch, Romanian Opera Chorus *(rec 1965)* Vox Box 2-▲ CDX 5162
Verdi, G.:Il trovatore, w. Elena Dima (sop—Leonora), Victoria Draganescu (sop—Ines), Zenaida Pally (mez—Azucena), Ion Buzea (ten—Duke of Mantua), Constantin Iliescu (ten—Ruiz), Cornel Stavru (ten—Manrico), Octav Enigarescu (bar—Count di Luna), Constantin Dumitru (bass—Ferrando), E. Massini (cnd), Romanian Opera Orch, Romanian Opera Chorus *(rec 1960–61)* Vox Box 2-▲ CDX 5163

Dragoni, Maria (sop)
Famous Opera Arias, w. Munich Radio Orch [cnd:Gustav Kuhn] Orfeo ▲ C 261921 A [DDD]

Draijer, Jelle (bass)
Monteverdi, C.:Vespro della Beata Vergine, w. Barbara Borden (sop), Maria Cristina Kiehr (sop), Andreas Scholl (alt), John Bowen (ten), Andrew Murgatroyd (ten), Victor Torres (bar), Antonio Abete (bass), René Jacobs (cnd), Concerto Vocale, Netherlands Chamber Choir Harmonia Mundi 2-▲ 901566.67

Drake, Archi (bass)
Monteverdi, C.:Vespro della Beata Vergine, w. Gloria Prosper (sop), Adrienne Albert (mez), Melvin Brown (ten), Richard Levitt (ten), R. Craft (cnd), Columbia Baroque Ensemble, Gregg Smith Singers, Texas Boys' Choir Sony Classical ("Essential Classics" series) 2-▲ SB2K 62656
Porter, C.:Kiss Me, Kate, w. P. Morrison (sgr), *(other artists unknown)* [1958 cast] Broadway Angel ▲ ZDM 64760 ■ EG 64760
Porter, C.:Kiss Me, Kate, w. P. Morrison (sgr), *(other artists unknown)* [1948 Broadway cast] Columbia ▲ CK 04140 ■ JST 04140
Rodgers, R.:Oklahoma!, w. L. Dixon (sgr), C. Holm (sgr), J. Roberts (sgr), H. da Silva (sgr), J. Blackton (cnd), *(orch unknown)* MCA Classics ▲ MCAD 10046 [AAD] ■ MCAC 10046

Drake, Bryan (bar)
Britten, H.:The Rape of Lucretia, w. H. Harper (sop), J. Baker (mez), P. Pears (ten), B. Luxon (bar), J. Shirley-Quirk (bar), B. Britten (cnd), English CO London 2-▲ 425666-2 [ADD]

Dran, Thierry (ten)
Auber, D.-F.:Fra Diavolo, w. M. Mesplé (sop—Zerline), J. Berbié (mez—Lady Pamela), N. Gedda (ten—Fra Diavolo), R. Corazza (ten—Lord Cockburn), T. Dran (ten—Lorenzo), J. Bastin (bass—Matheo), M. Soustrot (cnd), Monte Carlo PO, Jean LaForge Ensemble Choir EMI Classics ▲ CDCB 54810
Messager, A.:Fortunio, w. C. Alliot-Lugaz (sop), G. Cachémaille (bar), R. Schirrer (bar), J. E. Gardiner (cnd), Paris Lyon Opera Orch, Paris Lyon Opera Chorus Erato 2-▲ 45983-2
Ropartz, G.:Sym 3, w. F. Pollet (sop), N. Stutzmann (cta), F. Vassar (b-bar), M. Plasson (cnd), Toulouse Capitole Orch, Orféon Donostiarra EMI Classics ▲ CDM 64689-2

Dressen, Dan (ten)
Smyth, E.:The Boatswain's Mate, w. E. Harrhy (sop), J. Hardy (alt), J. Bohn (bass), P. Brunelle (cnd), Plymouth Music Series Orch, Plymouth Music Series Chorus—Mrs. Water's Aria Virgin Classics ▲ CDC 59022
Smyth, E.:Mass in D, w. E. Harrhy (sop), J. Hardy (alt), J. Bohn (bass), P. Brunelle (cnd), Plymouth Music Series Orch, Plymouth Music Series Chorus Virgin Classics ▲ CDC 59022

Dressen, Elvira (alt)
Schulhoff, E.:The Flames, w. Jane Eaglen (sop—Donna Anna, Nun, Woman, Marguerite), Carola Höhn (sop—Shadow), Celina Lindsley (sop—Shadow), Regina Schudel (sop—Shadow), Iris Vermillion (mez—La Morte), Christiane Berggold (alt—Shadow), Kaja Borris (alt—Shadow), Elvira Dressen (alt—Shadow), Kurt Westi (ten—Don Juan), Johann-Werner Prein (bass—Commendatore), Gerd Wolf (bass—Harlequin), J. Mauceri (cnd), Berlin German SO, Berlin RIAS Chamber Choir *(rec Jesus-Christus Church, Berlin Dahlem, Oct 1993/Apr 1994)* London 2-▲ 444630-2 [DDD]

Dreyfuss, Richard (nar)
Bernstein, L.:Sym 3, "Kaddish", w. G. Levine (cnd), Royal PO *(rec Apr. 7, 1994)* Justice ▲ JR 1801 [DDD]

Driscoll, Karen (sop)
Schubert, Franz:Der Graf von Gleichen, w. Gwendolyn Coleman (sop), Tracy Thomas (sop), Brad Diamond (ten), John M. Koch (bar), G. Samuel (cnd), Cincinnati PO, CCM Chamber Choir *(rec Corbett Auditorium, Univ of Cincinnati, Mar 12–13, 1994)* Centaur 2-▲ 2281/2282 [DDD]

Driscoll, Loren (ten)
Bach, J.S.:Cant 131, w. Robert Oliver (bass), Leonard Arner (ob), R. Craft (cnd), Columbia SO Sony Classical ("Essential Classics" series) 2-▲ SB2K 62656

Drobková, Drahomira (cta)
Báchorek, M.:Hukvald Poem, w. Břetislav Vojkůvka (ten), Pavel Kamas (bar), Otakar Brousek (reciter), O. Trhlík (cnd), Prague SO, Ostrava Female Chamber Chorus, Permoník Children's Chorus *(rec Smetana Hall of Prague's Municipal House, Feb 10 & 11, 1988)* Panton ▲ 811338-2 [DDD]
Báchorek, M.:Music of, w. Osvald Albin (nar), Otakar Brousek (nar), Jan Vlassak (nar), Brigita Šulcová (sop), Karel Průša (bass), Pavel Kamas (sgr), Jan Kyzlink (sgr), Jana Stuperkova-Majtnerova (sgr), Bretislav Vojkuvka (sgr), O. Trhlík (cnd), Ostrava Janáček PO, Praguo SO, Ostrava Janáček Chorus, Ostrava Women's Chamber Chorus, Permoník Children's Chorus—Lidice; Stereofonietta; Hukvald Poem Panton ▲ PAN 811338 [AAD/DDD]
Dvořák, A.:King & Charcoal Burner, w. Viktor Koci (ten), René Tucek (bar), Dalibor Jedlicka (bass), J. Chaloupka (cnd), Prague National Theater Orch, Milan Maly (cnd), Prague National Theater Chorus [final version] *(rec 1989)* Supraphon ("Hidden Treasures from Prague" series) ▲ SUP CD 3078
Janácek, L.:Slavonic Mass, w. Elisabeth Söderström (sop), František Livora (ten), Richard Novák (bass), C. Mackerras (cnd), Czech PO, Czech Phil Chorus Supraphon ▲ SUP 103575 [DDD]
Martinů, B.:Hymn to St. James, w. N. Romanová (sop), R. Novák (ten), P. Haničnec (nar), P. Kühn (cnd), Prague SO members, Prague Radio Chorus [Cz] *(rec 2–3/88)* Supraphon ▲ 11 0751-2 [DDD]
Martinů, B.:The Prophecy of Isaiah, w. N. Romanová (sop), R. Novák (bass), V. Kozderka (tpt), J. Peruška (va), I. Kiezlich (timp), S. Bogunia (pno), P. Kühn (cnd), Prague Radio Men's Chorus, Kühn Chorus [Cz] *(rec 2–3/88)* Supraphon ▲ 11 0751-2 [DDD]

Dry, Marion (cta)
Tcherepnin, I.:Songs Cta, w. Jean-Pierre Dautricourt (fl), Ivan Tcherepnin (elecs) *(rec Harvard University Electronic Music Studio, Oct. & Dec. 1981)* CRI ▲ CD 684 [ADD]

Dua, Octave (ten)
Verdi, G.:La traviata, w. Maria Caniglia (sop—Violetta), Maria Huder (mez—Flora), Gladys Palmer (cta—Annina), Octave Dua (ten—Giuseppe), Beniamino Gigli (ten—Alfredo), Booth Hitchen (ten—D'Obigny), Adelio Zagonara (bar—Gastone), Aristide Baracchi (bar—Douphol), Mario Basiola (bar—Germont), Norman Walker (bass—Dr. Grenville), V. Gui (cnd), London PO, London Phil Chorus *(rec Royal Opera House, Covent Garden, May 22, 1939)* Minerva 2-▲ MN A28/29 (m) [ADD]
Verdi, G.:Il trovatore, w. G. Cigna (sop—Leonora), G. Wettergren (mez—Azucena), M. Huder (mez—Ines), J. Björling (ten—Manrico), O. Dua (ten—Ruiz), C. Zambelli (ten—Ferrando), M. Basiola (bar—Count di Luna), L. Horsman (bar—Old Gypsy), V. Gui (cnd), Royal Opera Orch, Royal Opera House Chorus Covent Garden *(rec May 12, 1939)* Legato Classics 2-▲ LCD 173-2 [ADD]

Dubbini, Agnes (mez)
Puccini, G.:Gianni Schicchi, w. G. Rapisardi (sop), G. Savio (ten), G. Taddei (bar), A. Simonetto (cnd), Turin RAI SO [I] *(rec 10/5/49)* Preiser ▲ 90074 (m) [AAD]

Dubois, Cynthia (nar)
Normandeau, R.:Petit Prince, w. Michel Dumont (nar—Aviator), Martin Pensa (nar—Little Prince), Christine Séguin (nar—Rose), Jean Marchand (nar—King), Luc Durand (nar—Conceited Man), Gilles Dupuis (nar—Drunkard), Guy Nadon (nar—Businessman), Jacques Languirand (nar—Lamplighter), Pierre Bourgault (nar—Geographer), Cynthia Dubois (nar—Snake), Monique Giroux (nar—Flower), Françoise Davoine (nar—Rose Garden), Jean-Louis Millette (nar—Fox), Gérard Poirier (nar—Railway Switchman), Claude Préfontaine (nar—Water Pill Salesman) *(rec Montreal, Aug 1994)* CBC 2-▲ 1091 [DDD]

DuBois, Mark (ten)
Handel, G.F.:Messiah, w. Leslie Fagan (sop), Janis Taylor (mez), Gary Relyea (b-bar), G. Fagan (cnd), Concert Players Orch, Gerald Fagan Singers, London Fanshawe Symphonic Chorus Doremi 2-▲ 9306 [DDD]

DuBois, Mark (ten) (cont.)
Heuberger, R.:Der Opernball (sels), w. J. Kolomyjec (sop), R. Armenian (cnd), Kitchener-Waterloo SO—Im chambre séparée CBC ("SM 5000" series) ▲ SMCD 5126 [DDD]
Kálmán, I.:Die Csárdásfürstin (sels), w. J. Kolomyjec (sop), R. Armenian (cnd), Kitchener-Waterloo SO—Machen wir's den Schwalben nach; Tanzen möcht' ich CBC ("SM 5000" series) ▲ SMCD 5126 [DDD]
Kálmán, I.:Gräfin Mariza, w. L. Boucher (sop), R. Armenian (cnd), Kitchener-Waterloo SO CBC ("SM 5000" series) ▲ SMCD 5045 [DDD]
Kálmán, I.:Gräfin Mariza, w. J. Kolomyjec (sop), R. Armenian (cnd), Kitchener-Waterloo SO—Komm Zigany; Cxárdás CBC ("SM 5000" series) ▲ SMCD 5126 [DDD]
Lavallée, C.:The Widow (sels), w. J. Kolomyjec (sop), R. Armenian (cnd), Kitchener-Waterloo SO—Oh! Trust My Love; Smiling Hope CBC ("SM 5000" series) ▲ SMCD 5126 [DDD]
Lehár, F.:Das Land des Lächelns (sels), w. J. Kolomyjec (sop), R. Armenian (cnd), Kitchener-Waterloo SO—Dei einem Tee ã deux; Dein ist mein ganzes Herz; Ich möcht' wieder einmal die Heimat seh'n CBC ("SM 5000" series) ▲ SMCD 5126 [DDD]
Lehár, F.:Das Land des Lächelns (sels), w. L. Boucher (sop), R. Armenian (cnd), Kitchener-Waterloo SO CBC ("SM 5000" series) ▲ SMCD 5045 [DDD]
Lehár, F.:Die lustige Witwe (sels), w. L. Boucher (sop), R. Armenian (cnd), Kitchener-Waterloo SO CBC ("SM 5000" series) ▲ SMCD 5045 [DDD]
Morawetz, O.:Weaver, w. J. Valdepeñas (cl), P. Parr (pno) Centrediscs ▲ CDCCD 3589 [DDD]
Strauss (II), Joh.:Music of, w. Boucher (sop), R. Armenian (cnd), Kitchener-Waterloo SO—selections from Die Fledermaus & Gypsy Baron CBC ("SM 5000" series) ▲ SMCD 5045 [DDD]
Strauss (II), Joh.:Eine Nacht in Venedig (sels), w. J. Kolomyjec (sop), R. Armenian (cnd), Kitchener-Waterloo SO—Ov.; Sei mir gegrüsst, du holdes Venetia; Polka-Mazurka, Op. 415; Was mir der Zufall gab; Quadrille, Op. 416; Sie sagten meinem Liebesfleh'n; Lagunen-Walzer, Op. 411 CBC ("SM 5000" series) ▲ SMCD 5126 [DDD]
Viens, Gentille Dame:Romantic Arias for Lyric Tenor, w. Kitchener-Waterloo SO [cnd:Raffi Armenian] CBC Records ("SM 5000" series) ▲ SMCD 5077 [DDD] ■ 4-5077 (D)

Dubois, Paul-Alexandre (bar)
Pesson, G.:Music of, w. Donatienne Michel-Dansac (sop), Sandra Roulx (mez), Stuart Patterson (ten), Pascal Sausy (bar), Florence Millet (pno), D. My (cnd), Fa Ensemble, Paris String Quartet—Le gel, par jeu for Fl, Cl, Hn, Bass Mar, Vn & Vc; Qt for Strs; Non Sapremo Mai di Questo Mi for Fl, Vn & Pno; 5 Poèmes de Sandro Penna for Bar, B Cl, Hn, Vn & Vc; La lumière n'a pas de bras pour nous porter for Amplified Pno; La vita è come l'albero di natale for Vn & Pno; Nocturnes en quatuor for Cl, Pno, Vn & Vc; Les chants faëz for Pno & 10 Instrs; Sur-le-champ for 4 Voices & 9 Instrs [from a text by Pierre Alferi] Accord ▲ ACD 204682 [DDD]

Dubosc, Catherine (sop)
Berlioz, H.:Les Troyens, w. F. Pollet (sop—Dido), D. Voigt (sop—Cassandre), C. Dubosc (sop—Ascagne), H. Perraguin (cta—Anna), G. Lakes (ten—Aeneas), J.-L. Maurette (ten—Iopas), J. M. Ainsley (ten—Hylas), M. P. (ten—Panthee), G. Cross (ten—Sinon), G. Quilico (bar—Chorebe), J.-P. Courtis (b-bar—Narbal), M. Belleau (bass—Ghost of Hector), R. Schirrer (bass—Priam), C. Dutoit (cnd), Montreal SO, Montreal Sym Chorus London 4-▲ 443693-2 [DDD]
Gluck, C.W.:La Recontre imprévue, w. C. Le Coz (sop), L. Dawson (sop), C. Dubosc (sop), S. Marin-Degor (sop), G. Fletcher (sgr), F. Dudziak (ten), G. de Mey (ten), J.-L. Viala (ten), G. Cachémaille (bar), J.-P. Lafont (bass), J. E. Gardiner (cnd), Paris Lyon Opera Orch, Paris Lyon Opera Chorus [F] Erato 2-▲ 2292-45516-2 [DDD]
Massenet, J.:Songs, w. Francis Dudziak (bar), Jean-Bernard Dartigolles (pno), Syrille Lacrouts (vc)—Quelques chansons mauves; Dans le sentier, parmi les roses; Tu l'as bien dit; Roses d'Octobre; A Colombine [Sérénade d'Arlequin]; Sérénade de Molière [Musique du temps]; Marquise! [Menuet pour chant]; Les alcyons; Voic que les grands lys; Poème d'amour; L'improvisateur [Souvenir du Transtévère]; Nuit d'Espagne; Elégie; Déclaration; A mignonne; Souhait; Un adieu; Sérénade d'automne; Sonnet; Si tu veux, mignonne; Pensée d'automne; Soir de rêve; On dit; Souvenez-vous, Vierge Marie! Accord ▲ ACD 201632 [DDD]
Poulenc, F.:Dialogues des Carmélites, w. R. Yakar (sop), R. Gorr (mez), M. Dupuy (mez), J. Van Dam (b-bar), K. Nagano (cnd), Lyon Opera Orch Virgin Classics ▲ CDCB 59227
Poulenc, F.:Gloria Sop, w. R. Hickox (cnd), London Sinfonietta, Westminster Singers Virgin Classics ▲ CDC 59286
Poulenc, F.:Stabat mater, w. R. Hickox (cnd), London Sinfonietta, Westminster Singers Virgin Classics ▲ CDC 59286
Prokofiev, S.:The Love for 3 Oranges (suite), w. G. Gautier (ten), J.-L. Viala (ten), G. Bacquier (bar), J. Bastin (bass), K. Nagano (cnd), Paris Lyon Opera Orch, Paris Lyon Opera Chorus [F] Virgin Classics ▲ 59566 [DDD]
Ropartz, G.:Requiem, w. Jacqueline Mayeur (mez), Vincent Le Texier (bar), M. Piquemal (cnd), Jean-Walter Audoli Instrumental Ensemble, French Vittoria Regional Choir Accord ▲ ACD 205132 [DDD]
Rosenthal, M.:Songs, w. J. Kaltenbach (cnd), Nancy SO—Poèmes (3) de Marie Roustan (1933); Poèmes (2) de Jean Cassou (1944); Prières (3) *(rec Salle Poirel, Nancy, France, Sept 6–10, 1994)* Marco Polo ▲ 8.223768 [DDD]

Dubose (sgr)
Campra, A.:Tancrède, w. C. Alliot-Lugaz (sop), D. Evangelatos (cta), G. Reinhart (bar), F. le Roux (bar), P.-Y. le Maigat (bass-bar), J. Malgoire (cnd), La Grande Ecurie et la Chambre du Roy Erato (Musifrance) 2-▲ 2292-45001-2 ZA [DDD]

Dubov, Stephen (ten)
Sargon, S.:Music of, w. Lila Deis (sop), Stephen Girko (cl), Christopher Adkins (vc), Vesselin Demirev (vn), Deborah Baron (fl), Simon Sargon (pno)—Shemà [Hear] for Sop, Fl, Cl, Vc & Pno; Before the Ark for Vn & Pno; Wedding Dance for Vn & Pno; Klezmuzik for Cl & Pno; At Gradmother's Knee [5 Yiddish Folk Songs] for Ten & Pno; Meditation for Vc & Pno; At Grandfather's Knee [5 Judeo-Spanish Folk Songs] for Sop & Pno *(rec Caruth Auditorium, SMU, Dallas, TX, Jan 1996)* Gasparo ▲ GAS 318

Ducharme, Michel (bar)
Vivier, C.:Kopernikus, "A Ritual Opera of Death", w. Y. Parent (sop), P. Vaillancourt (sop), M.-D. Parent (sop), J. Fleury (cta), D. Doane (ten), Y. Saint-Amant (bass), F. Martel (cl), M. Bélanger (vn), L. Bouchard (tpt), L. Vaillancourt (cnd), *(orch unknown)* *(rec Feb. 1991)* CBC ("Musica Viva" series) ▲ MVCD 1047 [DDD]

Duckworth, Laura Lea (sgr)
Caccini, F.:La liberazione di Ruggiero dall'isola d'Alcina, w. Linda De Rungs (sop—Alcian/Vistola), Cecilia Amorocho (sgr—Melissa/Nunzia), Laura Lea Duckworth (sgr—Siren/Harpy), Eric Friedlander (sgr—Monster), L. Ernest Gross (sgr—Enchanted Cypress), Phoebe Jevtovic (sgr—Siren), James Rittenhouse (sgr—Ruggiero/Neptune), Sharon Sim (sgr—Siren), R. Burchard (cnd), Ars Femina Ensemble, TimeChange *(rec Louisville, KY, 1993)* Nannerl ▲ NR-ARS 003; ■ NR-ARS 003

Duclos, Germaine (sgr)
Lehár, F.:Die lustige Witwe, w. Teresa Stich-Randall (mez—Missia Palmieri), Monique Stiot (mez—Manon), Germaine Duclos (sgr—Praskovia), Linda Felder (sgr—Olga), Christiane Jacquin (sgr—Nadia), Jeannette Levasseur (sgr—Sylviane), Henri Legay (ten—Camille de Coutançon), Joseph Peyron (ten—Kromsky), Robert Destain (sgr—Baron Popoff), Michel Fauche (sgr—Pristich), Gérard Friedmann (sgr—Lerida), Jacques Gilet (sgr—Bogdanowitch), Jean Guy Henneveux (sgr—Prince Danilo), Serge Klin (sgr—Figg), Jacques Villa (sgr—D'Estillac), A. Sibert (cnd), Belgian Radio-TV Orch, Belgian Radio-TV Chorus *(rec Grand Auditorium, Belgium, Apr 30, 1970)* Studio SM 2-▲ 2160 [AAD]

Dudarev, Georgy (bass)
Kabalevsky, D.:Colas Breugnon (ov), w. N. Isakova (sop), V. Kayevchenko (sop), L. Boldin (bar), N. Gutorovich (bar), E. Maksimenko (sgr), G. Zhemchuzhin (cnd), Dantchenko Moscow Stanislavsky Music Theater Orch, Dantchenko Moscow Stanislavsky Music Theater Chorus Olympia 2-▲ OLY 291 [ADD]

Dudziak, Francis (bar)
Chabrier, E.:Fisch-Ton-Kan, w. M. Delunsch (sop), B. Desnoues (sop), C. Mehn (ten), J.-L. Georgel (bar), R. Delage (cnd), Strasbourg Collegium Musicum Orch Arion ▲ ARN 68252 [DDD]
Chabrier, E.:Vaucochard & Son I, w. M. Delunsch (sop), B. Desnoues (sop), C. Mehn (ten), J.-L. Georgel (bar), R. Delage (cnd), Strasbourg Collegium Musicum Orch Arion ▲ ARN 68252 [DDD]
Chabrier, E.:A Wasted Education, w. M. Delunsch (sop), B. Desnoues (sop), C. Mehn (ten), J.-L. Georgel (bar), R. Delage (cnd), Strasbourg Collegium Musicum Orch Arion ▲ ARN 68252 [DDD]

Dudziak, Francis (bar) (cont.)
Debussy, C.:Songs, w. Jean-Gernard Dartigolles (pno)—Trois chansons de France [Le temps a laissé son manteau; La grotte; Pour ce que plaisance est morte]; Mandoline; Fêtes galantes II [Les ingénus; Le faune; Colloque sentimental]; Trois mélodies de Paul Verlaine [La mer est plus belle; Le son du cor s'afflige; L'échelonnement des haies]; Huit d'étoiles; Aimons-nous et dormons; Trois ballades de François Villon [Villon à sa mie; Prière à Nostre Dame; Des femmes de Paris]; La belle au bois dormant; Beau soir; Le cloches; Romance; Le promenoir des deux amants [Auprès de cette grotte sombre; Crois mon conseil, Chère Climène; Je tremble en voyant ton visage]; Le Noël des enfants qui n'ont plus de maison Accord ▲ ACD 202302
Gluck, C.W.:La Recontre imprévue, w. C. Le Coz (sop), L. Dawson (sop), C. Dubosc (sop), S. Marin-Degor (sop), G. Fletcher (sgr), G. de Mey (ten), J.-L. Viala (ten), G. Cachémaille (bar), J.-P. Lafont (bass), J. E. Gardiner (cnd), Paris Lyon Opera Orch, Paris Lyon Opera Chorus [F] Erato 2-▲ 2292-45516-2 [DDD]
Massenet, J.:Songs, w. Catherine Dubosc (sop), Jean-Bernard Dartigolles (pno), Syrille Lacrouts (vc)—Quelques chansons mauves; Dans le sentier, parmi les roses; Tu l'as bien dit; Roses d'Octobre; A Colombine [Sérénade d'Arlequin]; Sérénade de Molière [Musique du temps]; Marquise! [Menuet pour chant]; Les alcyons; Voic que les grands lys; Poème d'amour; L'improvisateur [Souvenir du Transtévère]; Nuit d'Espagne; Elégie; Déclaration; A mignonne; Souhait; Un adieu; Sérénade d'automne; Sonnet; Si tu veux, mignonne; Pensée d'automne; Soir de rêve; On dit; Souvenez-vous, Vierge Marie! Accord ▲ ACD 201632 [DDD]

Duesing, Dale (bar)
Barber, S.:The Lovers, w. A. Schenck (cnd), Chicago SO, Chicago Sym Chorus [E] 10/91) Koch International Classics ▲ KIC 7125-2 [DDD]
Bernstein, L.:Arias & Barcarolles, w. Jane Bunnell (mez), G. Schwarz (cnd), Seattle SO [E] Delos ▲ DE 3078 [DDD]
Mozart, W.A.:Così fan tutte, w. Carol Vaness (sop), Delores Ziegler (mez), C. Watson (cta), J. Aler (ten), C. Desderi (bar), B. Haitink (cnd), London PO, Glyndebourne Festival Chorus EMI Classics 3-▲ CDCC 47727
Offenbach, J.:Les Contes d'Hoffmann, w. L. Serra (sop), R. Plowright (sop), J. Norman (sop), A. Murray (mez), J. Taillon (mez), N. Shicoff (ten), A. Oliver (ten), R. Tear (ten), J. Van Dam (b-bar), K. Rydl (bass), S. Cambreling (cnd), Brussels Théâtre de la Monnaie Orch [F] EMI Classics 3-▲ CDCC 49641 [DDD]
Puccini, G.:Turandot, w. Montserrat Caballé (sop—Turandot), Leona Mitchell (sop—Liu), Remy Corazza (ten—Pang), Joseph Franck (ten—Pong), Robert Johnson (ten—Prince of Persia), Raymond Manton (ten—Altoum), Luciano Pavarotti (ten—Calaf), Aldo Bramante (bar—a mandarin), Dale Duesing (bar—Ping), Giorgio Tozzi (bass—Timur), R. Chailly (cnd), *(orch unknown) (rec San Francisco, Nov. 4, 1977)* Legato Classics 2-▲ LCD 188-2
Schnittke, A.:Life with an Idiot, w. T. Ringholz (sop), H. Haskin (ten), M. Rostropovich (cnd), Rotterdam PO, Rotterdam Vocal Ensemble *(rec Amsterdam, world premiere performance, April 13, 1992)* Sony Classical 2-▲ S2K 52495 [DDD]
Zemlinsky, A. von:Lyric Sym, w. E. Söderström (sop), B. Klee (cnd), Berlin RSO [G] Koch Schwann ▲ CD 311 053 [ADD]

Dufour, Oliver (ten)
Mendelssohn, F.:Psalm 42, w. Y. Perrin (sop), M. Schwartz (mez), C. Traube (ten), P. Huttenlocher (bar), C. Ossola (bass), M. Hutin (bass), C. Liang-Sheng (cnd), Geneva SO, Geneva Univ Chorus Gallo ▲ CD 635 [AAD]
Mendelssohn, F.:Psalm 95, w. Y. Perrin (sop), M. Schwartz (mez), C. Traube (ten), P. Huttenlocher (bar), C. Ossola (bass), M. Hutin (bass), C. Liang-Sheng (cnd), Geneva SO, Geneva Univ Chorus Gallo ▲ CD 635 [AAD]
Mendelssohn, F.:Psalm 115, w. Y. Perrin (sop), M. Schwartz (mez), C. Traube (ten), P. Huttenlocher (bar), C. Ossola (bass), M. Hutin (bass), C. Liang-Sheng (cnd), Geneva SO, Geneva Univ Chorus Gallo ▲ CD 635 [AAD]

Dufranne, Hector (bass)
Ravel, M.:L'Heure espagnole, w. Jeanne Krieger (sop—Concepcion), Louis Arnoult (ten—Gonzalve), Raoul Gilles (ten—Torquemada), J. Aubert (bar—Ramiro), Hector Dufranne (bass—Don Inigo Gomez), G. Truc (cnd), *(orch unknown) (rec premiere recording, supervised by Ravel, 1929)* VAI Audio ▲ VAIA 1073

Dugardin, Steve (alt)
Purcell, H.:Dido & Aeneas, w. Véronique Gens (sop—Dido), Sophie Marin-Degor (sop—Belinda), Sophie Daneman (sop—2nd woman/1st witch), Gaëlle Mechaly (sop—2nd witch), Claire Brua (mez—Sorceress), Steve Dugardin (alt—Chorus), Jean-Paul Fouchécourt (ten—Spirit/Sailor), Nathan Berg (b-bar—Aeneas), Jonathan Arnold (bass—Chorus), William Christie (hpd), W. Christie (cnd), Les Arts Florissants *(rec Massy Opera Theatre, Nov. 8-11, 1994)* Erato ▲ 98477-2 [DDD]

Duguay, Marc (ten)
Caplet, A.:Myrrha, w. Sharon Coste (sop), Jean-François Lapointe (bar), J. Grimbert (cnd), Paris Sorbonne Orch, Paris Sorbonne Chorus *(rec Grand Amphithëâtre of the Sorbonne, July 3-5, 1993 & May 8, 1)* Marco Polo ▲ 8.223755 [DDD]

Duguay, Richard (ten)
Un Concert en Nouvelle-France, w. Arion Ensemble *(rec Église St-Paul-de-Joliette, Mar. 7-9, 1994)* CBC Records ("Musica Viva" series) ▲ MVCD 1081 [DDD]
Lully, J.-B.:Motets, w. I. Desrochers (sop), D. Favat (sop), H. Lamy (ten), P. Harvey (bass), H. Niquet (cnd), Concert Spirituel Vocal Ensemble—Te Deum; Miserere; Plaude laetare Gallia *(rec Nov. 22-25, 1993)* FNAC Music ▲ 592308 [DDD]

Dumitru, Constantin (bar)
Verdi, G.:La traviata, w. Elena Simionescu (sop—Annina), Virginia Zeani (sop—Violetta Valery), Elisabeta Neculce-Cartis (mez—Flora Bervoix), Ion Buzea (ten—Alfredo Germont), Vasile Moldoveanu (ten—Gastone/Viconte de Letorieres/Giuseppe), Teodor Panea (ten—Flora's Servant), Constantin Dumitru (bar—Commissioner/Baron Douphol), Nicolae Herlea (bar—Giorgio Germont), Valentin Loghin (bass—Marchese D'Obigny), Nicolae Rafael (bass—Doctor Grenvil), J. Bobescu (cnd), Romanian Opera Orch, Stelian Olariu (cnd), Romanian Opera Chorus *(rec 1968)* Vox Box 2-▲ CDX 5154
Verdi, G.:Il trovatore, w. Elena Dima (sop—Leonora), Victoria Draganescu (sop—Ines), Zenaida Pally (mez—Azucena), Ion Buzea (ten—Duke of Mantua), Constantin Iliescu (ten—Ruiz), Cornel Stavru (ten—Manrico), Octav Enigarescu (bar—Count di Luna), Constantin Dumitru (bass—Ferrando), E. Massini (cnd), Romanian Opera Orch, Romanian Opera Chorus *(rec 1960-61)* Vox Box 2-▲ CDX 5163

Dumont, Michel (nar)
Normandeau, R.:Petit Prince, w. Michel Dumont (nar—Aviator), Martin Pensa (nar—Little Prince), Christine Séguin (nar—Rose), Jean Marchand (nar—King), Luc Durand (nar—Conceited Man), Gilles Dupuis (nar—Drunkard), Guy Nadon (nar—Businessman), Jacques Languirand (nar—Lamplighter), Pierre Bourgault (nar—Geographer), Cynthia Dubois (nar—Snake), Monique Giroux (nar—Flower), Françoise Davoine (nar—Rose Garden), Jean-Louis Millette (nar—Fox), Gérard Poirier (nar—Railway Switchman), Claude Préfontaine (nar—Water Pill Salesman) *(rec Montreal, Aug 1994)* CBC 2-▲ 1091 [DDD]

Dümüller, J. (ten)
Bruckner, A.:Missa solemnis, w. C. Oelze (sop), C. Schubert (alt), R. Hagen (bass), K. A. Rickenbacher (cnd), Bamberg SO, Bamberg Sym Chorus Virgin Classics ▲ CDC 59060
Bruckner, A.:Psalm 112, w. C. Oelze (sop), C. Schubert (alt), R. Hagen (bass), K. A. Rickenbacher (cnd), Bamberg SO, Bamberg Sym Chorus Virgin Classics ▲ CDC 59060
Bruckner, A.:Psalm 114, w. C. Oelze (sop), C. Schubert (alt), R. Hagen (bass), K. A. Richenbacher (cnd), Bamberg SO, Bamberg Sym Chorus Virgin Classics ▲ CDC 59060
Bruckner, A.:Psalm 150, w. C. Oelze (sop), C. Schubert (alt), R. Hagen (bass), K. A. Rickenbacher (cnd), Bamberg SO, Bamberg Sym Chorus Virgin Classics ▲ CDC 59060

Duncan, Todd (sgr)
Gershwin, G.:Porgy & Bess, w. A. Brown (sgr), E. Matthews (sgr), H. Jackson (sgr), H. Dowdy (sgr), A. Long (sgr), Eva Jessye Choir [1940-1942 original cast] MCA Classics ("Broadway Gold" series) ▲ MCAD 10520 ■ MCAC 10520
Gershwin, G.:Porgy & Bess (sels), w. D. Brown (sop), A. Matthews (sop), Jackson (sgr), A. Smallens (cnd), *(orch unknown) (rec 1942 Broadway revival cas)* MCA ■ MCAC 1631 (m)

Dune, Catherine (sop)
Charpentier, M.-A.:In honorem Sancti Xaverii canticum, w. E. Baudry (sop), G. Ragon (ten), P. Colléaux (cnd), Stradivaria Ensemble, Nantes Vocal Ensemble [L] Arion ▲ ARN 68037 [DDD]

Dunham, Amèrica (nar)
Balada, L.:Maria Sabina, w. Hector Cortés (nar—Executioner), Amèrica Dunham (nar—Maria Sabina), Burwell Hardy (nar—Town Crier), Guillermo Helguera (nar—Constable), J. Mester (cnd), Louisville Orch, Richard Spalding (cnd), Louisville Univ Chorus *(rec Feb 5, 1973)* New World ▲ 80498-2

Dunn, D. (sgr)
Bizet, G.:Carmen, w. Cooper (sgr), P. Domingo (ten), F. Guarrera (bar), A. Guadagno (cnd), Cincinnati Summer Opera Association Orch, Cincinnati Summer Opera Association Chorus [F] *(rec live 7/19/68)* Melodram 2-▲ MEL 27034 (m) [AAD]

Dunn, Darcy (sgr)
Rorem, N.:A Childhood Miracle, w. Michele Couture (sop—Peony), Darcy Dunn (sgr—Violet), Madeline Tsingopoulos (sgr—Mother), Mary Cidoni (sgr—Emma), Patrick Greene (sgr—Snowman), Peter Castaldi (sgr—Father), R. E. Harrell (cnd), Magic Circle CO Newport Classic ▲ NPT 85594 [DDD]

Dunn, Darrell (sgr)
Cage, J.:Apartment House 1776, w. Walter Buckingham (sgr—Protestant), Darrell Dunn (sgr—Native American), Semenya McCord (sgr—African American), Chiam Parchi (sgr—Sephardi), New England Conservatory Philharmonia *(rec New England Conservatory of Music, Boston, MA, Mar. 4 & 6, 1991)* Mode ▲ MODE 41

Dunn, Mignon (mez)
Charpentier, G.:Louise, w. B. Sills (sop—Louise), M. Dunn (mez—Louise's Mother), N. Gedda (ten—Julien), J. Van Dam (bass-bar—Louise's Father), J. Rudel (cnd), Paris Opera Orch, Paris Opera Chorus EMI Classics ▲ CDMC 65299
Strauss, R.:Salome, w. G. Jones (sop), D. Fischer-Dieskau (bar), K. Böhm (cnd), Hamburg State Opera Orch *(rec live, 1970)* Deutsche Grammophon 2-▲ 445319-2 [ADD]

Dunn, Susan (sop)
Schoenberg, A.:Gurrelieder, w. B. Fassbaender (mez), S. Jerusalem (ten), P. Haage (ten), H. Becht (bass), H. Hotter (nar), R. Chailly (cnd), Berlin RSO, St. Hedwig's Cathedral Choir, Düsseldorf Municipal Choral Society [G] London 2-▲ 430321-2 [DDD]
Wagner, R.:Die Walküre (act 1), w. K. König (ten), P. Meven (bass), L. Maazel (cnd), Pittsburgh SO [G] Telarc ▲ CD 80258 [DDD]

Dunn, V. (sop)
Verdi, G.:Requiem Mass, w. D. Curry (cta), J. Hadley (ten), P. Plishka (bass), R. Shaw (cnd), Atlanta SO, Atlanta Sym Chorus [L] Telarc 2-▲ CD 80152 [DDD] 2-■ CS 30152 (D)

DuParc, Henri (sgr)
Les Mélodies, w. DuParc, Henri (sgr) Forlane ▲ FOR 16692 [DDD]

Dupard, Marie-Hélène (sop)
Granato, D.:Motets, w. Phillipe Despont (org), Lausanne Ensemble of Female Voices—Crux, moments de la Passion (1990); Homo Quidam (1960); Récitatifs pour la fin du jour (1978); Messe brève (1994); Improvisations rolloises (1958); Rosa vernans (1960); Mariale (1955); Ex Libro Job (1984); Solfeggio sopra'l Jubilate (1968); Petit Magnificat (1980) Gallo ▲ CD 895 [DDD]

Du Plessis, Christian (bar)
Donizetti, G.:Maria Padilla, w. L. McDonall (sop—Maria Padilla), D. Jones (mez—Ines Padilla), G. Clark (ten—Don Ruiz), C. du Plessis (bar—Don Pedro), A. Francis (cnd), London SO, Geoffrey Mitchell Choir [I] *(rec at Henry Wood Hall, London June 1980)* Opera Rara 3-▲ ORC 6
Donizetti, G.:Rosmonda d'Inghilterra, w. Yvonne Kenny (sop), Enid Hartle (mez), Richard Greager (ten), Milla Andreaw (sgr), A. Francis (cnd), Ulster Orch, Opera Rara Chorus *(rec live, 1970's)* Italian Opera Rarities 2-▲ IOR 7730
Donizetti, G.:Ugo, conte di Parigi, w. E. Harrhy (sop), Y. Kenny (sop), J. Price (sop), D. Jones (mez), M. Arthur (ten), A. Francis (cnd), New Philharmonia Orch, Geoffrey Mitchell Choir Opera Rara 3-▲ ORC 1

Dupouy, Jean (ten)
Strauss, R.:Salome, w. K. Huffstodt (sop), H. Jossoud (mez), J.L. Viala (ten), J. van Dam (bar), K. Nagano (cnd), Paris Lyon Opera Orch, Paris Lyon Opera Chorus Virgin Classics 2-▲ CDCB 59054

Dupré, Pierre (bar)
Gounod, C.:Roméo et Juliette, w. Yvonne Gall (sop—Juliette), Champell (sop—Stéphano), Jeanne Goulancourt (mez—Gertrude), Agustarello Affre (ten—Roméo), Edmond Tirmont (ten—Tybalt), Alexis Boyer (bar—Mercutio), Pierre Dupré (bar—Paris), Hypolite Belhomme (bar—Grégorio), Marcel Journet (bass—Frère Laurent), Henri Albers (bass—Capulet), Valermont (bass—The Duke), F. Rühlmann (cnd), Paris Opéra-Comique Orch, Paris Opéra-Comique Chorus *(rec 1912)* VAI Audio ▲ VAIA 1064-3 F

Dupuis, Gilles (nar)
Normandeau, R.:Petit Prince, w. Michel Dumont (nar—Aviator), Martin Pensa (nar—Little Prince), Christine Séguin (nar—Rose), Jean Marchand (nar—King), Luc Durand (nar—Conceited Man), Gilles Dupuis (nar—Drunkard), Guy Nadon (nar—Businessman), Jacques Languirand (nar—Lamplighter), Pierre Bourgault (nar—Geographer), Cynthia Dubois (nar—Snake), Monique Giroux (nar—Flower), Françoise Davoine (nar—Rose Garden), Jean-Louis Millette (nar—Fox), Gérard Poirier (nar—Railway Switchman), Claude Préfontaine (nar—Water Pill Salesman) *(rec Montreal, Aug 1994)* CBC 2-▲ 1091 [DDD]

Dupuy, Martine (mez)
Argento, D.:From the Diary of V. Woolf Gasparo ▲ GS 273 ■ GS 273-C
Benson, W.:Songs for the End of the World Gasparo ▲ GS 273 ■ GS 273-C
Poulenc, F.:Dialogues des Carmélites, w. C. Dubosc (sop), R. Yakar (sop), R. Gorr (mez), J. Van Dam (b-bar), K. Nagano (cnd), Lyon Opera Orch Virgin Classics ▲ CDCB 59227
Vivaldi, A.:Il Farnace, w. K. Angeloni (mez), P. Malakova (mez), D. Dessy (mez), L. Rizzi (cta), R. Garazioti (sgr), M. de Bernart (cnd), San Remo SO [I] *(rec live 12/1/82)* Arkadia-Akademia 2-▲ 110 [ADD]

Durand, Luc (nar)
Normandeau, R.:Petit Prince, w. Michel Dumont (nar—Aviator), Martin Pensa (nar—Little Prince), Christine Séguin (nar—Rose), Jean Marchand (nar—King), Luc Durand (nar—Conceited Man), Gilles Dupuis (nar—Drunkard), Guy Nadon (nar—Businessman), Jacques Languirand (nar—Lamplighter), Pierre Bourgault (nar—Geographer), Cynthia Dubois (nar—Snake), Monique Giroux (nar—Flower), Françoise Davoine (nar—Rose Garden), Jean-Louis Millette (nar—Fox), Gérard Poirier (nar—Railway Switchman), Claude Préfontaine (nar—Water Pill Salesman) *(rec Montreal, Aug 1994)* CBC 2-▲ 1091 [DDD]

Durčo, Ján (bar)
Respighi, O.:La bella dormente nel bosco, w. Ivana Czaková (sop—Old Woman/Green Fairy), Adriana Kohútková (sop—Blue Fairy/Nightingale), Henrietta Lednárová (sop—Frog/Spindle), Jana Valásková (sop—Princess), Dagmar Pecková (mez—Cuckoo/Cat), Denisa Šlepkovská (mez—Queen/Duchess), Karol Bernáth (ten—Doctor), Guillermo Dominguez (ten—Prince April), Igor Pasek (ten—Jester), Ján Durčo (bar—Ambassador), Richard Haan (bar—King/Woodcutter), Stanislav Benačka (bass—Doctor), Anton Kúrnava (bass—Doctor), Marián Smolárik (bass—Doctor), M. Adriano (nar—Mr. Dollar Chèques), M. Adriano (cnd), Slovak RSO Bratislava, Ján Rozehnal (cnd), Slovak Phil Chorus *(rec Concert Hall of the Slovak Radio, Bratislava, June 8-20, 1994)* Marco Polo ("Opera Classics" series) ▲ 8.223742 [DDD]
Respighi, O.:Lucrezia, w. Adriana Kohútková (sop—Venilia), Michela Remor (sop—Lucrezia), Stefania Kaluza (mez—La Voce), Denisa Šlepkovská (mez—Servia), Ludovít Ludha (ten—Collatino), Igor Pasek (ten—Bruto), Ján Durčo (bar—Tito/Valerio), Richard Haan (bar—Tarquinio), Rado Hanák (bass—Arunte/Spurio Lucrezio) *(rec Concert Hall of the Slovak Radio, Bratislava, June 9-16, 1994)* Marco Polo ▲ 8.223717 [DDD]

Durčo, Jan (bass)
Bizet, G.:Carmen (sels), w. D. Palade (sop—Micaëla), A. Liebeck (sop—Frasquita), G. Alperyn (mez—Carmen), D. Schaechter (mez—Mercédès), G. Lamberti (ten—Don José), M. Dvorsky (ten—Remandado), J. Durčo (ten—Cancairo), A. Titus (bar—Escamillo), V. Chmelo (bar—Morales), D. Rigosa (bass—Zuniga), A. Rahbari (cnd), Czech-Slovak RSO Bratislava, Slovak Phil Chorus, Bratislava Children's Choir *(rec July 1990)* Naxos ▲ 8.550727 [DDD]
Puccini, G.:Tosca (sels), w. Nelly Miricioiu (sop—Tosca), Giorgio Lamberti (ten—Cavaradossi), Miroslav Dvorsky (ten—Spoletta), Silvano Carroli (bar—Baron Scarpia), Jozef Spaček (bar—Sacristan), Jan Durco (bass—Sciarrone), Stanislav Benačka (bass—Gaoler), A. Rahbari (cnd), Czech-Slovak RSO Bratislava, Slovak Phil Chorus *(rec Concert Hall of the Slovak Radio, Bratislava, Apr. 7-14, 1990)* Naxos ▲ 8.553153 [DDD]

1144 ▲ = CD ♦ = Enhanced CD Δ = MD ■ = Cassette Tape ▯ = DCC

Durham, C. (ten)

Partch, H.:Revelation in the Courthouse Park, w. S. Costallos (sgr—Mom & Agave), C. Durham (ten—Sonny & Pentheus), M. Kimbrough (bar—Vendor & Herdsman), E. Earle (b-bar—Hobo & Tiresias), O. Babatunde (sgr—Dion & Dionysus), C. Roos (sgr—Mayor & Cadmus), O. Williams (sgr—Korypheus), R. Young (sgr—Cop & Guard), D. Mitchell (cnd), Partch Instrumentalists, marching band, *(chorus unknown)* [E] *(rec 10/87)* Tomato 2-▲ R2 70390 [DDD]

Dürmüller, Jörg (ten)

Haas, P.:The Chosen One, w. Willy Freivogel (fl), Friedhelm Pütz (hn), Monika Hölszky-Wiedemann (vn), Dennis Russell Davies (pno) Orfeo ("Musica Rediviva" series) ▲ 386961 [DDD]

Handel, G.F.:Judas Maccabaeus, w. M. Meier-Schmid (sop), Elisabeth von Magnus (alt), Robert Wörle (ten), Franz-Josef Selig (bass), T. Fey (cnd), Schlierbach CO, Munich Motet Choir [E] Christophorus 2-▲ 77128 [DDD]

Krenek, E.:Der Sprüng über den Schatten, w. D. Amos (sop), L. Kemeny (sop), S. MacLean (mez), U. Neuweiler (ten), J. Pflieger (bar), T. Brüning (sgr), D. de Villiers (cnd), Bielefeld PO, Bielefeld Phil Chorus [G] *(rec live, May 1989)* CPO 2-▲ CPO 999082-2 [DDD]

Vanhal, J.B.:Missa Solemnis, w. Marta Filová (sop), Marta Benačková (mez), Jiří Sulzenko (bass), V. Neumann (cnd), Prague Virtuosi, Prague Chamber Choir—Kyrie eleison, Adagio— Allegro; Christe eleison, Andante; Kyrie eleison, Allegro; Gloria, Allegro moderato; Laudamus te, Andante; Gratias agimus tibi, Allegro moderato; Domine Deus, Rex caelestis, andante; Domine Deus, Agnus Dei, Adagio; Quoniam tu solus sanctus, Allegro moderato, Cum sancto spiritu, Allegro; Credo, Allegro moderato, Et incarnatus est. Adagio; Et resurrexit, Allegro moderato; Sanctus, Adagio—Osanna, Allegro; Benedictus, Andante—Osanna, Allegro; Agnus Dei, Adagio; Dona nobis pacem, Allegro *(rec Evangelische Kirche der böhmischen Brüder, Prag, Sept 25-28, 1994)* Orfeo ▲ C 353 951 A [DDD]

Duske, Joachim (ten)

Zelenka, J.D.:Missa votiva, w. C. Hampe (sop), E. Graf (cta), J. Gebhardt (bass), W. Wehnert (cnd), Hesse Bach Collegium, Marburg Bach Choir [L] Thorofon ▲ CTH 2172 [DDD]

Dussaut, Catherine (sop)

Campra, A.:Tancrède, w. C. Dussaut (sop—Herminie), A. Arapian (ten—Argant), J. Bona (bar—Tancrède), C. Zaffini (cnd), Provence Instrumental Ensemble, Avignon Vocal Ensemble—highlights *(rec 1986)* Pierre Verany ▲ PV.786111 [ADD]

Charpentier, M.-A.:Les Arts florissants, w. J. Feldman (sop), A. Mellon (sop), G. Laurens (mez), D. Visse (ct), P. Cantor (ten), G. Reinhart (bar), W. Christie (cnd), Les Arts Florissants [F] Musique d'Abord ▲ HMA 1901083

Dutoit, Laurence (male sop)

Akademie Chamber Choir & Vienna SO, w. Akademie Chamber Choir [cnd:Ferdinand Grossmann], Vienna SO, Elisabeth Roon (sop), Daagmar Herrmann-Braun (cta), Erich Majkut (ten), W. Berry (bass) Vox 90s ■ V9-9903

Bach, J.S.:Cant 4, w. K. Equiluz (ten), H. Braun (bar), F. Prohaska (cnd), Vienna State Opera Orch, Vienna Chamber Choir [G] *(rec 1959)* Vanguard Classics ("The Bach Guild" series) ▲ OVC 2001 [ADD]

Bach, J.S.:Cant 140, w. K. Equiluz (ten), H. Braun (bar), F. Prohaska (cnd), Vienna State Opera Orch, Vienna State Opera Chorus [G] *(rec 1959)* Vanguard Classics ("The Bach Guild" series) ▲ OVC 2001 [ADD]

Bach, J.S.:Christmas Oratorio, w. E. Roon (sop), D.H. Braun (mez), E. Majkut (ten), W. Berry (bass), B. Seidlhofer (hpd), J. Nebois (org), F. Grossmann (cnd), Vienna SO, Akademie Chamber Choir Vox Box 2-▲ CDX 5096 [ADD]

Schubert, Franz:Mass 1, w. Rose Bahl (alt), Kurt Equiluz (ten), Kunikazu Ohashi (bass), Xaver Mayer (org), G. Barati (cnd), Vienna State Opera Orch, Vienna Academy Chamber Choir *(rec 1960)* Tuxedo ▲ TUXCD 1040 [ADD]

Schubert, Franz:Mass 4, w. Rose Bahl (alt), Kurt Equiluz (ten), Kunikazu Ohashi (bass), Xaver Mayer (org), G. Barati (cnd), Vienna State Opera Orch, Vienna Academy Chamber Choir *(rec 1960)* Tuxedo ▲ TUXCD 1040 [ADD]

Schubert, Franz:Die Verschworenen, w. Ilona Steingruber (sop—Countess), Elizabeth Roon (mez—Helene), Laurence Dutoit (trb—Isella), Walter Anton (ten—Udolin), Walter Berry (bar—Count), Rudolf Kreutzberger (sgr—Astolf), F. Grossmann (cnd), Vienna SO, Vienna Academy Chamber Choir Theorema ▲ TH 121178

Verdi, G.:Don Carlos, w. S. Jurinac (sop—Elisabetta), L. Rysanek (sop—Celestial Voice), F. Cossotto (mez—Princess Eboli), L. Dutoit (boy sop—Tebaldo), P. Domingo (ten—Don Carlo), E. Majkut (ten—Count of Lerma), M. Sereni (bar—Rodrigo), C. Siepi (bass—Philip II), I. Vinco (bass—Grand Inquisitor), T. Franc (bass—Friar), S. Varviso (cnd), Vienna State Opera Orch, Vienna State Opera Chorus Standing Room Only 2-▲ SRO 850 [ADD]

Duval, Denise (sop)

Gluck, C.W.:Orfeo ed Euridice, w. G. Koeman (sop), K. Ferrier (cta), C. Bruck (cnd), Netherlands Opera Orch, Netherlands Opera Chorus *(rec live, 1951)* Verona 2-▲ 27016/17 (m) [AAD]

Poulenc, F.:Dialogues des Carmélites, w. R. Crespin (sop), L. Berton (sop), D. Scharley (mez), R. Gorr (mez), P. Finel (ten), X. Depraz (bass), P. Dervaux (cnd), Paris Opera Orch [F] EMI Classics 2-▲ CDCB 49331 (m) [ADD]

Duval. France (mez)

Massenet, J.:Songs, w. Bruno Laplante (bar), Marc Durand (pno)—Poème d'octobre; Poème d'amour; Poème d'hiver; Poème d'un soir; Lui et Elle [all are song cycles] *(rec Chapelle historique du Bon Pasteur, Montréal, June 1992)* Analekta ▲ AN 2 9406 [DDD]

Words of Love, w. Laplante, Bruno (bar), C. Webster (pno) Analekta ▲ AN29401 [DDD] ■ AN4-9401

Duykers, John (ten)

Giteck, J.:Callin' Home Coyote, w. Deborah Deloria (db), Andy Narell (perc) [E] Mode ▲ 14 ■ 14CS (CrO2)

Harrison, L.:May Rain, w. Julie Steinberg (pno), William Winant (perc) New Albion ▲ NA 055

Dvořáková, Karolina (sop)

Janácek, L.:The Danube Sop & Orch, w. J. Beneš, F. Jílek (cnd), Brno State PO *(rec Jan. 22-25, 1992)* Supraphon ▲ 111522-2 [DDD]

Wagner, R.:Der Ring des Nibelungen, w. B. Nilsson (sop), L. Rysanek (sop), M. Mödl (sop), A. Burmeister (mez), V. Soukupova (mez), E. Wohlfahrt (ten), W. Windgassen (ten), T. Stewart (bar), T. Adam (b-bar), G. Neidlinger (b-bar), K. Böhme (bass), G. Nienstedt (bass), K. Böhm (cnd), Bayreuth Festival Orch, Bayreuth Festival Chorus [G] *(rec live, 1966-67)* Philips 14-▲ 420325-2 [ADD]

Dvorský, Miroslav (ten)

Bizet, G.:Carmen (sels), w. D. Palade (sop—Micaëla), A. Liebeck (sop—Frasquita), G. Alperyn (mez—Carmen), D. Schaechter (mez—Mercédès), G. Lamberti (ten—Don José), M. Dvorsky (ten—Remandado), J. Durco (ten—Cancairo), A. Titus (bar—Escamillo), V. Chmelo (bar—Morales), D. Rigosa (bass—Zuniga), A. Rahbari (cnd), Czech-Slovak RSO Bratislava, Slovak Phil Chorus, Bratislava Children's Choir *(rec July 1990)* Naxos ▲ 8.550727 [DDD]

Janácek, L.:Jenůfa, w. L. Popp (sop), E. Söderström (sop), E. Randová (mez), W. Ochman (ten), C. Mackerras (cnd), Vienna PO [Cz] London 2-▲ 414483-2 [DDD]

Janácek, L.:Our Father, w. G. Landini (pno), C. Gesseney (cnd), Lausanne Euterpe Vocal Ensemble Gallo ▲ CD 784 [DDD]

Puccini, G.:Tosca (sels), w. Nelly Miricioiu (sop—Tosca), Giorgio Lamberti (ten—Cavaradossi), Miroslav Dvorsky (ten—Spoletta), Silvano Carroli (bar—Baron Scarpia), Jozef Spaček (bar—Sacristan), Jan Durco (bass—Sciarrone), Stanislav Benačka (bass—Gaoler), A. Rahbari (cnd), Czech-Slovak RSO Bratislava, Slovak Phil Chorus *(rec Concert Hall of the Slovak Radio, Bratislava, Apr. 7-14, 1990)* Naxos ▲ 8.553153 [DDD]

Respighi, O.:La Primavera, w. Henrietta Lednárová (sop—Prima fanciulla), Jana Valásková (sop—Sirvard), Beata Geriová (mez—Seconda fanciulla), Miroslav Dvorský (ten—Il giovine), Richard Haan (bar—L'orante), Vladimír Kubovčik (bass—Il vecchio), Vera Rasková (fl), M. Adriano (cnd), Slovak RSO Bratislava, Slovak Phil Chorus *(rec Slovak Radio Concert Hall, Bratislava, Jan. 4-9, Feb. 19 & June)* Marco Polo ▲ 8.223595 [DDD]

Verdi, G.:La traviata, w. L. Aliberti (sop), R. Bruson (bar), R. Paternostro (cnd), Tokyo PO, Tokyo Phil Chorus [I] *(rec live, Suntory Hall, Tokyo)* Capriccio 2-▲ 10274/75 [DDD]

Wien, Wien, Schönes Wien, w. M. Cerno (sop), Bratislava RSO [cnd:Jan Pospíchal] Supraphon ▲ SUP CD 3193

Dvorský, Peter (ten)

Dvořák, A.:Songs, w. B. Kulínský (cnd), Prague PO—Oh, My Shepherd Is the Lord; Song of Gladness Will I Sing Thee [from Biblical Songs, Op. 99] Multisonic ▲ 31 0003-2 [ADD]

Dvořák, A.:Stabat Mater, w. G. Benačková (sop), O. Wenkel (cta), J.-H. Rootering (bass), W. Sawallisch (cnd), Czech PO, Czech Phil Chorus [L] Supraphon 2-▲ 10 3561-2 [DDD]

Italian & French Opera Arias, w. Bratislava RSO [cnd:Ondrej Lenárd] Naxos ▲ 8.550343 [DDD]

Janácek, L.:Kát'a Kabanová, w. E. Söderström (sop), N. Kniplová (mez), V. Krejčik (ten), Z. Svehla (ten), D. Jedliča (bass), C. Mackerras (cnd), Vienna PO London 2-▲ 421852-2 [ADD]

Opera Arias, w. Hungarian State Opera Orch [cnd:Andras Mihály] Acanta ▲ 43335

Opera Arias & Duets, w. Fiamma Izzo d'Amico Acanta ▲ CD 43239

Puccini, G.:La Bohème, w. M. Freni (sop), C. Kleiber (cnd), La Scala Orch, La Scala Chorus Artists 2-▲ FED 15 [ADD]

Puccini, G.:La Bohème, w. Veronika Kinsces (sop—Mimi), Sidonia Haljakova (sop—Musette), Peter Dvorsky (ten—Rodolfo), Vijtech Scherenkel (ten—Parpingol), Ian Konsulov (bar—Marcello), Balazs Poka (bar—Schaunard), Stanislav Benacka (bass—Benoit), Dariusz Niemirowicz (bass—Colline), Stefan Janci (bass—Alcindoro), *(cnd & orch unknown)* Griffin ▲ GCD 2942

Puccini, G.:Madama Butterfly, w. V. Kincses (sop), T. Tákacs (mez), L. Miller (bar), G. Patanè (cnd), Hungarian State Opera Orch, Hungarian State Opera Chorus [I] Hungaroton 2-▲ HCD 12256/57

Smetana, B.:The Bartered Bride, w. G. Benačková (sop), R. Novak (bass), Z. Košler (cnd), Czech PO, Czech Phil Chorus [Cz] Supraphon 3-▲ 10 3511-2 [DDD]

Smetana, B.:The Bartered Bride (orch sels), w. Gabriela Benačková (sop), Miroslav Kopp (ten), Z. Košler (cnd), Czech PO, Czech Phil Chorus Supraphon ▲ SUP 112251 [DDD]

Suchon, E.:The Whirlpool, w. G. Benačková (sop), O. Malachovsky (bass), O. Lenárd (cnd), Bratislava RSO Campion 2-▲ 1311/12 [DDD]

Dyadkova, Larissa (mez)

Tchaikovsky, P.:Mazeppa, w. Galina Gorchakoova (sop), Sergei Larin (ten), Sergei Leiferkus (bar), Anatoly Kotscherga (bass), N. Järvi (cnd), Gothenburg SO, Stockholm Royal Opera Chorus Deutsche Grammophon 3-▲ 439906-2

Dyakovski, Lyubomir (ten)

Rimsky-Korsakov, N.:Golden Cockerel, w. Yavora Stoilova (sop—Golden Cockerel), Elena Stoyanova (sop—Queen), Evgenia Babacheva (mez—Amelfa), Lyubomir Bodourov (ten—Prince), Lyubomir Dyakovski (ten—Astrologer), Emil Ugrinov (bar—Afron), Nikolai Stoilov (bass—Tsar), Kosta Videv (bass—Polkan), D. Manolov (cnd), Sofia National Opera Orch, Sofia National Opera Chorus *(rec Sofia, 1985)* Capriccio 2-▲ 10760/61 [DDD]

Rimsky-Korsakov, N.:Snow Maiden, w. Stefka Evstatieva (sop—Kupava), Elena Zemenkova (sop—Snow Maiden), Alexandrina Milcheva (mez—Spring Fairy), Vessela Zorova (mez—wife), Stefka Mineva (alt—Lehl), Avram Andreev (ten—Tsar), Lyubomir Dyakovski (ten—Cottager, Sprite), Lyubomir Videnov (bar—Misgir), Nicola Ghiuselev (bass—King), S. Angelov (cnd), Bulgarian RSO, Bulgarian National Chorus *(rec Sofia, 1985)* Capriccio 3-▲ 10749-51 [DDD]

Dyer, Olive (sop)

Britten, H.:The Turn of the Screw, w. J. Vyvyan (sop), A. Mandikian (mez), D. Hemmings (trb), G. Cross (ten), P. Pears (ten), B. Britten (cnd), English Opera Group Orch [E] London ▲ 425672-2 (m) [ADD]

Dyer-Bennet, Richard (ten)

The Art of Richard Dyer-Bennet Vanguard Classics ▲ OVC 6007 [ADD]

E., Dominique (voc)

East/West, w. Pinhas, Richard (syns/gtr), Norman Spinrad (voc), Patrick Gauthier (syn), G. Grunblatt (syn), François Auger (perc), Steve Shehan (perc), Didier Batard (bass gtr) Cuneiform ▲ Rune 31

Eagan, Seamus (sgr)

Gohl, M.:The West, w. Nana Vasconcelos (sgr), Jay Ungar (vn), Molly Mason (gtr), *(other artists unknown)*, M. Gohl (cnd), Black Elk Voices Sony Classical ▲ SK 62727 ■ ST 62727

Eaglen, Jane (sop)

Beethoven, L. van:Sym 9, "Choral Sym", w. Waltraud Meier (cta), Ben Heppner (ten), Bryn Terfel (bar), C. Abbado (cnd), Berlin PO, Swedish Radio Chorus, Eric Ericson Chamber Choir *(rec Salzburg Easter Festival, 1996)* Sony Classical ▲ SK 62634 △ SM 62634

Bellini, V.:Bianca e Fernando (sels), w. M. Elder (cnd), Orch of the Age of Enlightenment—Sorgi, o padre, e la figlia rimira *(rec Abbey Road Studio, June 16-23, 1996)* Sony Classical ▲ SK 62032 [DDD]

Bellini, V.:Norma, w. Jane Eaglen (sop—Norma), Eva Mei (sop—Adalgisa), Vincenzo La Scola (ten—Pollione), Dmitri Kavrakos (bass—Oroveso), R. Muti (cnd), Florence Maggio Musicale Orch, Florence Maggio Musicale Chorus *(rec live, Alighieri Theater, Florence, July 1994)* EMI Classics 2-▲ CDCC 55471

Bellini, V.:Norma (sels), w. M. Elder (cnd), Orch of the Age of Enlightenment—Casta diva *(rec Abbey Road Studio, Sept 8-10, 1995)* Sony Classical ▲ SK 62032 [DDD]

Bellini, V.:Il pirata (sels), w. M. Elder (cnd), Orch of the Age of Enlightenment—Col sorriso dinnocenza *(rec Abbey Road Studio, Sept 8-10, 1995; June 16-)* Sony Classical ▲ SK 62032 [DDD]

Doyle, P.:Sense & Sensibility, w. Jonathan Snowdon (fl), Richard Morgan (ob), Robert Hill (cl), Tony Hymas (pno), R. Ziegler (cnd), *(orch unknown)* *(rec Air Studios, Lyndhurst Hall)* Sony Classical ▲ SK 62258 [DDD]

Puccini, G.:Tosca, w. Jane Eaglen (sop—Floria Tosca), Charbel Michael (alt—Shepherd Boy), John Daszak (ten—Spoletta), Dennis O'Neill (ten—Mario Cavaradossi), Christopher Booth-Jones (bar—Sciarrone), Ashley Holland (bar—Jailor), Gregory Yurisich (bar—Baron Scarpia), Peter Rose (bass—Cesare Angelotti), Andrew Shore (bass—Sacristan), D. Parry (cnd), Philharmonia Orch, Geoffrey Mitchell Choir, Peter Kay Children's Chorus Chandos ("Opera in English" series) 2-▲ CHAN 3000

Schulhoff, E.:The Flames, w. Jane Eaglen (sop—Donna Anna, Nun, Woman, Marguerite), Carola Höhn (sop—Shadow), Celina Lindsley (sop—Shadow), Regina Schudel (sop—Shadow), Iris Vermillion (mez—La Morte), Christiane Berggold (alt—Shadow), Kaja Borris (alt—Shadow), Elvira Dressen (alt—Shadow), Kurt Westi (ten—Don Juan), Johann-Werner Prein (bass—Commendatore), Gerd Wolf (bass—Harlequin), J. Mauceri (cnd), Berlin German SO, Berlin RIAS Chamber Choir *(rec Jesus-Christus Church, Berlin Dahlem, Oct 1993/Apr 1994)* London 2-▲ 444630-2 [DDD]

Wagner, R.:Götterdämmerung (sels), w. M. Elder (cnd), Royal Opera House Orch—Immolation Scene *(rec Abbey Road Studio, June 16-23, 1996)* Sony Classical ▲ SK 62032 [DDD]

Wagner, R.:Tristan und Isolde (sels), w. M. Elder (cnd), Royal Opera House Orch—Prelude; Liebestod *(rec Abbey Road Studio, June 16-23, 1996)* Sony Classical ▲ SK 62032 [DDD]

Wagner, R.:Tristan und Isolde (prelude & liebestod), w. R. Norrington (cnd), London Classical Players EMI Classics ▲ CDC 55479

Wagner, R.:Die Walküre (sels), w. M. Elder (cnd), Royal Opera House Orch—Brünnhilde's Battle Cry *(rec Abbey Road Studio, June 16-23, 1996)* Sony Classical ▲ SK 62032 [DDD]

Eames, Emma (sop)

Eames & Plançon Nimbus ▲ NI 7860 [ADD]

Eamon, Deltra (sop)

The Art of Laurindo Almeida, w. L. Almeida (gtr) *(rec Hollywood, CA, 1970)* Orion ▲ 7816-2 [AAD]

Earle, E. (bass)

Partch, H.:Revelation in the Courthouse Park, w. S. Costallos (sgr—Mom & Agave), C. Durham (ten—Sonny & Pentheus), M. Kimbrough (bar—Vendor & Herdsman), E. Earle (b-bar—Hobo & Tiresias), O. Babatunde (sgr—Dion & Dionysus), C. Roos (sgr—Mayor & Cadmus), O. Williams (sgr—Korypheus), R. Young (sgr—Cop & Guard), D. Mitchell (cnd), Partch Instrumentalists, marching band, *(chorus unknown)* [E] *(rec 10/87)* Tomato 2-▲ R2 70390 [DDD]

Earle, Roderick (bass)

Rossini, G.:Stabat Mater, w. H. Field (sop), D. Jones (mez), A. Davies (ten), R. Hickox (cnd), City of London Sinfonia, London Sym Chorus [L] Chandos ▲ CHAN 8780 [DDD]

Verdi, G.:La traviata, w. Angela Gheorghiu (sop—Violetta), Leah-Marian Jones (mez—Flora Bervoix), Gillian Knight (mez—Annina), Robin Leggate (ten—Gastone), Frank Lopardo (ten—Alfredo Germont), Rodney Gibson (ten—Servo di Flora), Neil Griffiths (ten—Giuseppe), Mark Beesley (bar—Dottore Grenvile), Leo Nucci (bar—Giorgio Germont), Richard Van Allan (bass—Barone Douphol), Roderick Earle (bass—Marquese d'Obigny), Bryan Secombe (bass—Commissionario), G. Solti (cnd), Royal Opera House Orch, Royal Opera House Chorus Covent Garden *(rec live, Royal Opera House, Covent Garden, Dec. 1994)* London 2-▲ 448119-2

Easley, Lydia Catherine (sop)
Maslanka, D.:Mass, w. Charles Roe (bar), Jane Smith (org), G.I. Hanson (cnd), Univ of Arizona Wind Orch, Univ of Arizona Sym Choir, Arizona Chamber Choir, Tuscon Boys' Chorus *(rec St. Thomas the Apostle Church, Tuscon, Arizona, Apr 29–30, 1996)* Albany 2-▲ TROY 221-22 [DDD]

East, Thomas (ten)
Hovhaness, A.:Magnificat, w. Audrey Nossaman (sop), Elizabeth Johnson (cta), Richard Dales (bar), R. Whitney (cnd), Louisville Orch, Univ of Louisville Choir Crystal ▲ CD 808

Eastman, Julius (bar)
Davies, P.M.:Songs (8) for a Mad King, w. P. M. Davies (cnd), Fires of London *(rec analog rec'g)* Unicorn-Kanchana ▲ DKP CD 9052 [ADD/DDD]

Easton, Robert (bass)
Gounod, C.:Faust, w. M. Licette (sop—Margarita), D. Vane (sop—Siebel), M. Brunskill (cta—Martha), H. Nash (ten—Faust), H. Williams (b-bar—Valentine), R. Easton (bass—Mephistopheles), R. Carr (bass—Wagner), T. Beecham (cnd), BBC SO, BBC Sym Chorus Dutton Laboratories 2-▲ CDAX 2001 [ADD]
Vaughan Williams, R.:Serenade to Music, w. I. Baillie (sop), E. Suddaby (sop), S. Allen (sop), E. Turner (sop), M. Balfour (cta), A. Desmond (cta), M. Brunskill (cta), M. Jarred (cta), H. Nash (ten), W. Widdop (ten), P. Jones (ten), F. Titterton (ten), R. Henderson (bass), H. Williams (bass), N. Allin (bass), H. Wood (cnd), BBC SO [E] *(rec 10/15/38)* Pearl ▲ GEMMCD 9342 (m) [AAD]
Vaughan Williams, R.:Serenade to Music, w. I. Baillie (sop), E. Suddaby (sop), S. Allen (sop), E. Turner (sop), M. Balfour (cta), A. Desmond (cta), M. Brunskill (cta), M. Jarred (cta), H. Nash (ten), W. Widdop (ten), P. Jones (ten), F. Titterton (ten), R. Henderson (bass), H. Williams (bass), N. Allin (bass), H. J. Wood (cnd), BBC SO Dutton Laboratories ▲ CDAX 8004 [ADD]
Vaughan Williams, R.:Serenade to Music, w. Isobel Baillie (sop), Lilian Stiles-Allen (sop), Elsie Suddaby (sop), Eva Turner (sop), Margaret Balfour (cta), Muriel Brunskill (cta), Astra Desmond (cta), Mary Jarred (cta), Parry Jones (ten), Heddle Nash (ten), Frank Titterton (ten), Walter Widdop (ten), Roy Henderson (bar), Harold Williams (bar), Norman Allin (bass), H. Wood (cnd), BBC SO *(rec Abbey Road, Oct 15, 1938)* Claremont ▲ CDGSE 785066

Eberle, K. (mez)
From a Woman's Perspective:Art Songs by Women Composers, w. R. Guy (pno), Kristin Pederson Thelander (hn) Vienna Modern Masters ▲ VMM 2005 [DDD]

Ebert, Elisabeth (sop)
Lortzing, A.:Der Waffenschmied, w. E. Ebert (sop—Marie), G. Prenzlow (mez—Mariens), H. Neukirch (ten—Georg), G. Leib (bar—Ritter), H. Krämer (bass—Hans), H. Fricke (cnd), Berlin State Opera Orch, Berlin State Opera Chorus Berlin Classics ("Eterna" series) ▲ BER 2036-2 [ADD]

Ebrahim, Omar (bar)
Ligeti, G.:The Ligeti Edition, w. Phyllis Bryn-Julson (sop), Rosemary Hardy (sop), Christiane Oelze (sop), Rose Taylor (mez), Sibylle Ehlert (sgr), Pierre-Laurent Aimard (pno), E.-P. Salonen (cnd), Philharmonia Orch, King's Singers—Vocal Works; Madrigals; Mysteries; Adventures; Songs; Nonsense Madrigals Sony Classical ▲ SK 62311

Ebrahim, Omar (nar)
Lieberson, P.:King Gesar, w. Yo-Yo Ma (vc), Emanuel Ax (pno), Peter Serkin (pno), Andras Adorjan (fl), Deborah Marshall (cl), William Purvis (hn), David Taylor (trbn), Stefan Huge (perc) Sony Classical ▲ SK 57971

Echauri, Grace (mez)
Morales, M.:Ildegonda, w. Violeta Dávalos (sgr—Ildegonda), Grace Echauri (sgr—Idelbene), Raúl Hernández (sgr—Rizzardo), Ricardo Santín (sgr—Rolando), F. Lozano (cnd), Carlos Chávez SO, Escuola Nacional de Música Chorus Forlane 2-▲ FRL 16739 [DDD]
Musica para una boda Mexicana:Music for a Mexican Wedding, w. Ambriz, Lourdes (sop), Pro Musica Chorus, Mexico CO Soloists Ensemble [cnd:Luis Sergio Hernandez] Spartacus ▲ 21015

Eckersley, Kate (sop)
Vivaldi, A.:Arias, w. P. Rapson (hpd), P. Rapson (cnd), Fiori Musicali—from La fida Ninfa:Alma oppressa; La Griselda:Agitata da due venti [I] Meridian ▲ CDE 84195
Vivaldi, A.:Motets, w. P. Rapson (hpd), P. Rapson (cnd), Fiori Musicali—In furore [I] Meridian ▲ CDE 84195

Eckert, André (bass)
Bruch, M.:Das Lied von der Glocke, w. Ute Selbig (sop), Elisabeth Graf (alt), Matthias Bleidorn (ten), André Eckert (, Dresden PO *(rec Kreuzkirche Dresden, Jun 24, 1995)* Thorofon 2-▲ DCTH 2291/2 [DDD]

Eckert, R. (sgr)
Dresher, P.:Slow Fire, w. P. Dresher (gtr/kbd/elec), G. Reffkin (perc) [E] Minmax ▲ CD 010

Eckert, Thomasa (sop)
Giteck, J.:Om Shanti, w. New Performance Group New Albion ▲ NA 054
Giteck, J.:Thunder, Like A White Bear Dancing, w. New Performance Group [E] Mode ▲ 14 ■ 14CS (CrO2)

Eda-Pierre, Christiane (sop)
Boieldieu, F.-A.:Le Calife de Bagdad, w. Jane Berbié (mez), Jeannine Collard (mez), Jean Giraudeau (ten), Jean-Paul Vaquelin (sgr), L. Fourestier (cnd), ORTF Lyric Orch, ORTF Lyric Chorale Musidisc ▲ MUS 201852 [AAD]
Britten, H.:Les Illuminations, w. J.-W. Audoli (cnd), Audoli Instrumental Ensemble [F] Arion ▲ ARN 68035 [DDD]
Britten, H.:Phaedra, w. J.-W. Audoli (cnd), Audoli Instrumental Ensemble [E] Arion ▲ ARN 68035 [DDD]
Honegger, A.:Le Roi David, w. Martha Senn (mez), Tibere Raffalli (ten), D. Mesguich (nar), A. Gaillard (nar), S. Baudo (cnd), Czech PO, Czech Chorus [F] Supraphon 2-▲ 11 0132 [DDD]
Inghelbrecht, D.-E.:Requiem, w. Bernard Kruyssen (bar), J. Fournet (cnd), ORTF Lyric Orch, ORTF Choirs Studio SM ("Andre Charlin Collection" series) ▲ 2522
Inghelbrecht, D.-E.:Vézelay, w. Bernard Kruyssen (bar), J. Fournet (cnd), ORTF Lyric Orch, ORTF Choir Studio SM ("Andre Charlin Collection" series) ▲ 2522
Mozart, W.A.:Complete Mozart Edition, w. N. Burrowes (sop), R. Tear (ten), S. Burrows (ten), C. Davis (cnd), Academy of St. Martin in the Fields, John Alldis Choir Philips 2-▲ 422538-2 [DDD]
Rameau, J.P.:Dardanus, w. F. von Stade (mez), G. Gautier (ten), R. Soyer (bar), J. Van Dam (b-bar), R. Leppard (cnd), Paris Lyon Opera Orch, Paris Lyon Opera Chorus Erato 2-▲ 95312-2

Edelman, Gregg (sgr)
Rodgers, R.:Music of, w. V. Clark (sgr), J. Graae (sgr), A. Reed (sgr), L. Wintersteller (sgr)—Oklahoma; Carousel; The Sound of Music; South Pacific; Flower Drum Song; Cinderella & others Varèse Sarabande ▲ VSD 5516 ■ VSC 5516

Edelmann, Otto (bass)
Bach, J.S.:St. Matthew Passion, w. I. Seefried (sop), C. Ludwig (mez), K. Ferrier (cta), P. Schoeffler (bass), H. von Karajan (cnd), Vienna SO, Vienna Singverein *(rec live June 9, 1950)* Verona 3-▲ 27070/72 (m) [AAD]
Bach, J.S.:St. Matthew Passion (sels), w. I. Seefried (sop), C. Ludwig (mez), K. Ferrier (cta), P. Schöffler (bass), H. von Karajan (cnd), Vienna SO, Vienna Singverein Verona ▲ 27076 (m) [AAD]
Beethoven, L. van:Fidelio, w. C. Goltz (sop), S. Jurinac (sop), G. Zampieri (ten), P. Schöffler (b-bar), H. von Karajan (cnd), Vienna PO, Vienna State Opera Chorus [G] *(rec live, Salzburg Festival 7/27/57)* Claque 2-▲ CLQ 2007 (m)
Beethoven, L. van:Fidelio, w. S. Jurinac (sop), M. Mödl (sop), W. Windgassen (ten), A. Poell (bar), G. Frick (bass), W. Furtwängler (cnd), Vienna PO *(rec Oct. 1953)* EMI Classics 2-▲ CDHB 64496
Beethoven, L. van:Syms (comp), w. E. Schwarzkopf (sop), E. Höngen (mez), H. Hopf (ten), W. Furtwängler (cnd), Vienna PO, Bayreuth Festival Orch, Bayreuth Festival Chorus *(rec 1948–54)* EMI Classics 5-▲ CDHE 63606
Beethoven, L. van:Sym 9, "Choral Sym", w. Elisabeth Schwarzkopf (sop), Elsa Cavelti (mez), Ernst Haefliger (ten), W. Furtwängler (cnd), Philharmonia Orch, Lucerne Festival Chorus *(rec Aug 22, 1954)* Music & Arts ▲ CD 790 [ADD]
Gluck, C.W.:Iphigénie en Aulide, w. Inge Borkh (sop—Klytämnestra), Christa Ludwig (mez—Iphigenie), Elisabeth Steiner (mez—Artemis), James King (ten—Achilles), Alois Pernerstorfer (b-bar), Walter Berry (bass), K. Böhm (cnd), Vienna PO, Salzburg Festival Chamber Choir, Vienna State Opera Chorus *(rec Salzburg, Aug 3, 1962)* Orfeo d'or ("Festspiel Dikumente" series) 2-▲ C 428962 (m) [ADD]

Edelmann, Otto (bass) (cont.)
Mozart, W.A.:Don Giovanni, w. E. Schwarzkopf (sop), E. Grümmer (sop), E. Berger (sop), A. Dermota (ten), C. Siepi (b-bar), W. Berry (bass), W. Furtwängler (cnd), Vienna PO, Vienna State Opera Chorus *(rec Salzburg, Aug. 3, 1953)* EMI Classics ("Great Recordings of the Century" series) 2-▲ CDHB 63860
Mozart, W.A.:Don Giovanni, w. E. Schwarzkopf (sop), E. Grümmer (sop), E. Berger (sop), A. Dermota (ten), C. Siepi (b-bar), W. Berry (bass), W. Furtwängler (cnd), Vienna PO, Vienna State Opera Chorus *(rec 1953)* Arkadia 3-▲ 509 (m) [AAD]
Strauss, R.:Arabella, w. L. Della Casa (sop), H. Gueden (sop), I. Malaniuk (cta), A. Dermota (ten), W. Kmentt (ten), G. London (bar), G. Solti (cnd), Vienna PO [G] London ("Grand Opera" series) 2-▲ 430387-2 [ADD]
Strauss, R.:Der Rosenkavalier, w. E. Schwarzkopf (sop—Feldmarschallin), A. Rothenberger (sop—Sophie), S. Jurinac (sop—Octavian), O. Edelmann (bass—Baron Ochs), H. von Karajan (cnd), Vienna PO *(rec live, Salzburg, 8/1/64)* Arkadia 3-▲ 227 [ADD]
Strauss, R.:Der Rosenkavalier, w. Elisabeth Schwarzkopf (sop), Christa Ludwig (mez), Teresa Stich-Randall (mez), H. von Karajan (cnd), Philharmonia Orch, Philharmonia Chorus *(rec 1956)* EMI Classics ▲ CDCC 56113 (m)
Strauss, R.:Der Rosenkavalier, w. Jarmila Barton (sop—Marianne), Lisa Della Casa (sop—Sophie), Sena Jurinac (sop—Octavian), Ilva Ligabue (sop—Orphan), Elisabeth Schwarzkopf (sop—Marschallin), Else Schürhoff (mez—Annina), Luisa Villa (mez—Milliner), Hugues Cuénod (ten—Marschallin's majordomo), Erich Majkut (ten—Valzacchi), Giuseppe Nessi (ten—Animal seller), Luciano Della Pergola (ten—Lackey/Faninal's majordomo), Antonio Pirino (ten—An Italian Singer), Gino Del Signore (ten—Lackey/Waiter), Erich Kunz (bar—Herr von Faninal), Paolo Pedani (bar—Lackey), Attilo Barbesi (bass—Lackey/Waiter), Enrico Campi (bass—Waiter), Otto Edelmann (bass—Baron Ochs), Bruno Fichtinger (bass—Notary), Franco Taino (bass—Waiter), Maria Amadini (sgr—Orphan), Pina Carrillo (sgr—Orphan), Joszi Trojan Regar (sgr—Innkeeper), H. von Karajan (cnd), La Scala Orch, La Scala Chorus *(rec La Scala Theater, Milan, Jan. 26, 1952)* Legato Classics 3-▲ LCD 197-3
Strauss, R.:Der Rosenkavalier, w. E. Schwarzkopf (sop), T. Stich-Randall (sop), C. Ludwig (mez), H. von Karajan (cnd), Philharmonia Orch [G] EMI Classics 3-▲ CDCC 49354 [ADD] 3-■ 3CDX 3970
Strauss, R.:Der Rosenkavalier, w. L. Della Casa (sop), H. Gueden (sop), S. Jurinac (sop), E. Kunz (bar), H. von Karajan (cnd), Vienna PO, Vienna State Opera Chorus [G] *(rec live in Salzburg, 7/26/60)* Arkadia 3-▲ 213 [ADD]
Strauss, R.:Der Rosenkavalier (sels), w. E. Schwarzkopf (sop), T. Stich-Randall (mez), C. Ludwig (mez), H. von Karajan (cnd), Philharmonia Orch, Philharmonia Chorus EMI Classics ▲ ZDM 63452
Wagner, R.:Die Meistersinger von Nürnberg, w. E. Schwarzkopf (sop), E. Kunz (ten), H. von Karajan (cnd), Bayreuth Festival Orch, Bayreuth Festival Chorus *(rec 1951)* Arkadia 4-▲ 224
Wagner, R.:Die Meistersinger von Nürnberg, w. E. Schwarzkopf (sop), I. Malaniuk (cta), H. Hopf (ten), G. Unger (ten), E. Kunz (bar), F. Dalberg (bass), H. von Karajan (cnd), Bayreuth Festival Orch, Bayreuth Festival Chorus [G] *(rec 1951)* EMI Classics ("Great Recordings of the Century" series) 4-▲ CDHD 63500 (m) [ADD]
Wagner, R.:Die Meistersinger von Nürnberg, w. L. Della Casa (sop), I. Malaniuk (cta), H. Hopf (ten), K. Böhme (bass), H. Knappertsbusch (cnd), Bayreuth Festival Orch, Bayreuth Festival Chorus [G] *(rec live, 1952)* Arkadia 4-▲ 440 (m) [AAD]

Eder, Claudia (mez)
Offenbach, J.:Les Contes d'Hoffmann, w. E. Gruberova (sop), P. Domingo (ten), M. Sénéchal (ten), Schmidt (sgr), G. Bacquier (bar), J. Morris (bass), J. Diaz (bass), S. Ozawa (cnd), French National Orch, French Radio Chorus [F] Deutsche Grammophon 2-▲ 427682-2 [DDD]

Eder, Gerhard (bass)
Haydn, J.:Mass 14, "Harmoniemesse", w. Christiane Sorell (sop), Elisabeth Thoman (sop), Rose Bahl (cta), Maura Moreira (cta), Kurt Equiluz (ten), P. Wimburger (bass), G. Barati (cnd), Vienna State Opera Orch, Vienna Academy Chamber Choir *(rec 1964)* Tuxedo ▲ TUXCD 1055 [ADD]

Edgar-Wilson, Richard (ten)
Arne, T.:Artaxerxes, w. Catherine Bott (sop), Patricia Spence (mez), Philippa Hyde (sgr), Christopher Robson (alt), Ian Partridge (ten), R. Goodman (cnd), Parley of Instruments Hyperion ("The English Orpheus" series) 2-▲ CDA 67051/2
Coates, E.:Songs, w. Eugene Asti (pno)—4 Old English Songs; The Mill o' Dreams; Rise up & Reach the Stars; At Vesper Bell; The Young Lover; The Grenadier; Because I Miss You So; Sigh No More, Ladies; Tell Me Where Is Fancy Bred; The Fairy Tales of Ireland; Music of the Night; Betty & Johnny; When I Am Dead; the Little Green Balcony; Ship of Dream; The Outlaw's Song; Your Name; Beautiful Lady Moon; Princess of the Dawn *(rec St. Silas, London, Jan 25–27, 1994)* Marco Polo ▲ 8.223806 [DDD]

Edwards, Jane (nar)
Whiticker, M.:Man, Skin Cancer of the Earth, w. Clive Birch (nar), Matthew Glasgow (nar), Roger Frampton (sax), David Hewitt (perc), R. Peelman (cnd) *(rec Studio 200, ABC Ultimo Centre, Apr 1993)* Tall Poppies ▲ TP 064 [DDD]

Edwards, Joan (cta)
Mozart, W.A.:Songs, w. P. Sharpe (sgr), D. Russell (sgr), D. Hamilton (ten), M. Glasgow (sgr), C. Birch (sgr), P. Hooper (sgr), G. Lancaster (pno) *(rec July 1991)* Tall Poppies ▲ TP009 [DDD]

Edwards, Ronald (ten)
Blitzstein, M.:Songs, w. H. Williams (bar), L. Lehrman (pno)—songs & scenes from Reuben, Reuben [1955], Jane Pickens Show (title theme) [1949], Goloopchik [1946], Idiots First [1962], Juno [1957], New York Opera [1941], No For An Answer [1941], Parade [1935], Sacco & Vanzetti [1959] Premier ▲ PRCD 1005 [DDD]

Edwards, Ryan (sgr)
Donizetti, G.:Caterina Cornaro, w. Montserrat Caballé (sop), Giacomo Aragall (ten), Gwynne Howell (bass), G.-F. Masini (cnd), ORTF Orch *(rec Paris, Nov 25, 1973)* Agorá Music ("Phoenix" series) 2-▲ 505

Edwards, Simon (sgr)
Mozart, W.A.:Così fan tutte, w. Sophie Marin-Degor (sop—Despina), Laura Polverelli (mez—Dorabella), Sophie Fournier (sgr—Fiordiligi), Nicolas Reveng (bar—Guglielmo), Patrick Donnelly (bass—Don Alfonso), Simon Edwards (sgr—Ferrando), J. Malgoire (cnd), La Grande Écurie et la Chambre du Roy Astrée 8-▲ E 8606
Mozart, W.A.:Don Giovanni, w. Danielle Borst (sop—Donna Anna), Véronique Gens (sop—Donna Elvira), Sophie Marin-Degor (sop—Zerlina), Huub Claessens (bar—Leporello), Nicolas Reveng (bar—Don Giovanni), Patrick Donnelly (bass—Commendatore), Simon Edwards (sgr—Don Ottavio), J. Malgoire (cnd), La Grande Écurie et la Chambre du Roy Astrée 8-▲ E 8606

Edwards, Terry (ten)
Machover, T.:Valis, w. A. Azéma (sop), J. Felty (mez), P. Mason (bar), T. Machover (elec), T. Machover (cnd), *(ensemble unknown)* [E] Bridge ▲ BCD 9007 [DDD] ■ BCS 7007 (D)

Een, Robert (sgr)
Monk, M.:Atlas, w. D. Hanchard (sop), S.-Z. Chen (sgr), S. Kalm (bar), M. Monk (cnd), *(orch unknown) (rec June 1992)* ECM New Series ▲ 78118-21491-2 [DDD]
Monk, M.:Boat Song, w. Meredith Monk (org/pno/pitchpipes/voc) ECM New Series ▲ 78118-21482-2 [DDD]
Monk, M.:Facing North, w. Meredith Monk (org/pno/pitchpipes/voc) ECM New Series ▲ 78118-21482-2 [DDD]
Monk, M.:Vessel, w. Meredith Monk (org/pno/pitchpipes/sgr) ECM New Series ▲ 78118-21482-2 [DDD]

Eensalu, Marika (sop)
Tubin, E.:The Parson of Reigi, w. Kempe (ten), Maiste (bar), P. Mägi (cnd), Estonia Opera Co Orch, Estonia Opera Company Chorus Ondine 2-▲ ODE 783-2D [DDD]

Egea, Antonio Belda (nar)
Falla, M. de:El amor brujo, w. S. Aguilar (nar), A. Nafe (nar), J. López-Cobos (cnd), Lausanne CO *(rec Mar. 25–27, 1992)* Denon ▲ CO 75339 [DDD]

Egel, Martin (bass)
Bach, J.S.:Cant 82, w. P.-D. Ponnelle (cnd), Munich Bach Soloists FSM ▲ FCD 97213 [DDD]

▲ = CD ♦ = Enhanced CD Δ = MD ■ = Cassette Tape □ = DCC

Egel, Martin (bass) (cont.)

Marschner, H.A.:Der Vampyr, w. Carole Farley (sop—Malwina), Nucci Condò (mez—Suse), Oslavio Di Credico (ten—George Dibdin), Josef Protschka (ten—Edgar Aubry), Romano Truffelli (ten—Richard Scrop), Martin Egel (bar—Sir Humphrey Davenaut), Andréa Snarski (bar—Toms Blunt), Siegmund Nimsgern (b-bar—Lord Ruthven), Armando Caforio (bass—Robert Green), Peter Boom (sgr—Il capo dei Vampiri), Carlo Di Giacomo (sgr—James Gadshill), Wolfgang Lenz (sgr—Sir Berkley), Galina Pisarenko (sgr—Janthe), Renzo Scorsoni (sgr—Un servitore di Berkley), Anastasia Tomaszewska Schepis (sgr—Emmy), G. Neuhold (cnd), Rome RAI SO, Rome RAI Chorus *(rec Rome, Jan 26, 1980)* Italia 2-▲ CDC 99 [ADD]

Martin, F.:Monologe (6) aus "Jedermann", w. P.-D. Ponnelle (cnd), Nuremberg SO FSM ▲ FCD 97213 [DDD]

Wagner, R.:Arias & Scenes, w. P.-D. Ponnelle (cnd), Monte Carlo PO—arias & scenes from Fliegende Holländer *(Die Frist ist um)*, Das Liebesverbot *(Ja, glühend, wie des Südens Hauch...)*, Parsifal *(Wehvolles Erbe, dem ich verfallen)*, Tannhäuser *(O! du mein holder Abendstern)*, Walküre *(Leb Wohl, du Kühnes)* [G] FSM ▲ FCD 97214 [DDD]

Egerton, Francis (ten)

Bizet, G.:Carmen (sels), w. M. Horne (sop), M. Molese (sgr), M. Pellegrini (sgr), G. Griffiths (bar), D. Bowman (bar), H. Lewis (cnd), Royal PO, Royal Liverpool Phil Choir IMP Collectors Series ▲ IMPX 9016 [AAD]

Tchaikovsky, P.:Eugene Onegin, w. N. Focile (sop), I. Arkhipova (mez), S. Walker (mez), D. Hvorostovsky (bar)., S. Bychkov (cnd), Orch de Paris Philips 2-▲ 438235-2

Eggenhofer, Werner (nar)

Kalitzke, J.:Bericht über den Tod des Musikers Jack Tiergarten, w. Till Krabbe (nar), Brigitte Jäger (sop), Espen Fegran (bar), J. Kalitzke (cnd), North Rhine-Westphalia Musikfabrik *(rec live, Apr 29, 1994)* CPO ▲ 999358-2 [DDD]

Eggers, Anke (cta)

Herzogenberg, H. von:Die Geburt Christi, w. R. Schudel (sop), P. Maus (ten), E. Schramm (bass), C. Grube (cnd), Oriol Ensemble, *(various choruses)* [G] Hänssler Classic 2-▲ 98.574 [AAD]

Egmond, Max van (bass)

Airs de Cour:French Court Music from the 17th Century, w. M.-C. Vallin (sop), Lutz Kirchhof (renaissance lt) Sony Classical ("Vivarte" series) ▲ SK 48250 [DDD]

Bach, J.S.:Cant 1, w. P. Esswood (ct), K. Equiluz (ten), N. Harnoncourt (cnd), Vienna Concentus Musicus, Vienna Boys' Choir [G] Teldec 2-▲ 2292-42497-2 [AAD]

Bach, J.S.:Cant 2, w. P. Esswood (ct), K. Equiluz (ten), N. Harnoncourt (cnd), Vienna Concentus Musicus, Vienna Boys' Choir [G] Teldec 2-▲ 2292-42497-2 [AAD]

Bach, J.S.:Cant 3, w. P. Esswood (ct), K. Equiluz (ten), N. Harnoncourt (cnd), Vienna Concentus Musicus, Vienna Boys' Choir [G] Teldec 2-▲ 2292-42497-2 [AAD]

Bach, J.S.:Cant 4, w. P. Esswood (ct), K. Equiluz (ten), N. Harnoncourt (cnd), Vienna Concentus Musicus, Vienna Boys' Choir [G] Teldec 2-▲ 2292-42497-2 [AAD]

Bach, J.S.:Cant 5, w. P. Esswood (ct), K. Equiluz (ten), N. Harnoncourt (cnd), Vienna Concentus Musicus, Vienna Boys' Choir Teldec 2-▲ 2292-42498-2 [AAD]

Bach, J.S.:Cant 6, w. P. Esswood (ct), K. Equiluz (ten), N. Harnoncourt (cnd), Vienna Concentus Musicus, Vienna Boys' Choir Teldec 2-▲ 2292-42498-2 [AAD]

Bach, J.S.:Cant 7, w. P. Esswood (ct), K. Equiluz (ten), Leonhardt Consort, King's College Choir Cambridge [G] Teldec 2-▲ 2292-42498-2 [AAD]

Bach, J.S.:Cant 8, w. P. Esswood (ct), K. Equiluz (ten), G. Kiefer (bar), Leonhardt Consort, King's College Choir Cambridge [G] Teldec 2-▲ 2292-42498-2 [AAD]

Bach, J.S.:Cant 9, w. P. Esswood (ct), K. Equiluz (ten), Leonhardt Consort, King's College Choir Cambridge [G] Teldec 2-▲ 2292-42499-2 [AAD]

Bach, J.S.:Cant 10, w. P. Esswood (ct), K. Equiluz (ten), Leonhardt Consort, King's College Choir Cambridge [G] Teldec 2-▲ 2292-42499-2 [AAD]

Bach, J.S.:Cant 11, "Ascension Oratorio", w. P. Esswood (ct), K. Equiluz (ten), N. Harnoncourt (cnd), Vienna Concentus Musicus, Vienna Concentus Musicus Chorus [G] Teldec 2-▲ 2292-42499-2 [AAD]

Bach, J.S.:Cant 12, w. P. Esswood (ct), K. Equiluz (ten), Leonhardt Consort, King's College Choir Cambridge [G] Teldec 2-▲ 2292-42500-2 [AAD]

Bach, J.S.:Cant 13, w. P. Esswood (ct), K. Equiluz (ten), Leonhardt Consort, King's College Choir Cambridge [G] Teldec 2-▲ 2292-42500-2 [AAD]

Bach, J.S.:Cant 14, w. M. van Altena (ten), Leonhardt Consort, King's College Choir Cambridge [G] Teldec 2-▲ 2292-42500-2 [AAD]

Bach, J.S.:Cant 16, w. P. Esswood (ct), K. Equiluz (ten), Leonhardt Consort, King's College Choir Cambridge [G] Teldec 2-▲ 2292-42500-2 [AAD]

Bach, J.S.:Cant 17, w. P. Esswood (ct), K. Equiluz (ten), N. Harnoncourt (cnd), Vienna Concentus Musicus, Chorus Viennensis [G] Teldec 2-▲ 2292-42501-2 [AAD]

Bach, J.S.:Cant 18, w. P. Esswood (ct), K. Equiluz (ten), N. Harnoncourt (cnd), Vienna Concentus Musicus, Chorus Viennensis [G] Teldec 2-▲ 2292-42501-2 [AAD]

Bach, J.S.:Cant 19, w. P. Esswood (ct), K. Equiluz (ten), N. Harnoncourt (cnd), Vienna Concentus Musicus, Chorus Viennensis [G] Teldec 2-▲ 2292-42501-2 [AAD]

Bach, J.S.:Cant 20, w. P. Esswood (ct), K. Equiluz (ten), N. Harnoncourt (cnd), Vienna Concentus Musicus, Chorus Viennensis [G] Teldec 2-▲ 2292-42501-2 [AAD]

Bach, J.S.:Cant 22, w. P. Esswood (ct), K. Equiluz (ten), Leonhardt Consort, King's College Choir Cambridge [G] Teldec 2-▲ 2292-42502-2 [AAD]

Bach, J.S.:Cant 23, w. W. Gampert (trb), P. Esswood (ct), M. van Altena (ten), Leonhardt Consort, King's College Choir Cambridge [G] Teldec 2-▲ 2292-42502-2 [AAD]

Bach, J.S.:Cant 24, w. P. Esswood (ct), K. Equiluz (ten), N. Harnoncourt (cnd), Vienna Concentus Musicus, Chorus Viennensis [G] Teldec 2-▲ 2292-42503-2 [AAD]

Bach, J.S.:Cant 25, w. K. Equiluz (ten), N. Harnoncourt (cnd), Vienna Concentus Musicus, Chorus Viennensis [G] Teldec 2-▲ 2292-42503-2 [AAD]

Bach, J.S.:Cant 27, w. R. Hansmann (sop), H. Watts (cta), K. Equiluz (ten), J. Jürgens (cnd), Concerto Amsterdam, Monteverdi Choir London Teldec (Das alte Werke) ▲ 93687

Bach, J.S.:Cant 29, w. P. Esswood (ct), K. Equiluz (ten), N. Harnoncourt (cnd), Vienna Concentus Musicus, Chorus Viennensis [G] Teldec 2-▲ 2292-42504-2 [AAD]

Bach, J.S.:Cant 30, w. P. Esswood (ct), K. Equiluz (ten), N. Harnoncourt (cnd), Vienna Concentus Musicus, Chorus Viennensis [G] Teldec 2-▲ 2292-42504-2 [AAD]

Bach, J.S.:Cant 32, w. W. Gampert (trb), G. Leonhardt (cnd), Leonhardt Consort, Hanover Boys' Choir [G] Teldec 2-▲ 2292-42505-2 [AAD]

Bach, J.S.:Cant 39, w. R. Jacobs (ct), G. Leonhardt (cnd), Leonhardt Consort, Hanover Boys' Choir [G] Teldec 2-▲ 2292-42556-2 [AAD]

Bach, J.S.:Cant 40, w. R. Jacobs (ct), M. van Altena (ten), Leonhardt Consort, Hanover Boys' Choir [G] Teldec 2-▲ 2292-42556-2 [AAD]

Bach, J.S.:Cant 77, w. P. Esswood (ct), A. Kraus (ten), G. Leonhardt (cnd), Leonhardt Consort [G] Teldec 2-▲ 2292-42576-2 [ADD]

Bach, J.S.:Cant 79, w. P. Esswood (ct), G. Leonhardt (cnd), Leonhardt Consort [G] Teldec 2-▲ 2292-42576-2 [ADD]

Bach, J.S.:Cant 83, w. K. Equiluz (ten), N. Harnoncourt (cnd), Vienna Concentus Musicus [G] Teldec 2-▲ 2292-42577-2 [ADD]

Bach, J.S.:Cant 89, w. M. Klein (trb), P. Esswood (ct), G. Leonhardt (cnd), Leonhardt Consort [G] Teldec 2-▲ 2292-42578-2 [ADD]

Bach, J.S.:Cant 90, w. P. Esswood (ct), K. Equiluz (ten), Leonhardt Consort, Ghent Collegium Vocale [G] Teldec 2-▲ 2292-42578-2 [ADD]

Bach, J.S.:Cant 98, w. C. Lengert (trb), P. Esswood (ct), K. Equiluz (ten), Leonhardt Consort [G] Teldec ▲ 2292-42583-2 [ADD]

Bach, J.S.:Cant 100, w. D. Bratschke (trb), P. Esswood (ct), K. Equiluz (ten), G. Leonhardt (cnd), Leonhardt Consort [G] Teldec ▲ 2292-42584-2

Bach, J.S.:Cant 105, w. W. Wiedl (trb), P. Esswood (ct), K. Equiluz (ten), N. Harnoncourt (cnd), Vienna Concentus Musicus, Tölz Boys' Choir [G] Teldec ▲ 2292-42602-2

Bach, J.S.:Cant 106, "Actus tragicus", w. M. Klein (trb), R. Harten (alt), M. van Altena (ten), Leonhardt Consort, Collegium Vocale, Hanover Boys' Chorus [G] Teldec ▲ 2292-42602-2

Egmond, Max van (bass) (cont.)

Bach, J.S.:Cant 107, w. M. Klein (trb), K. Equiluz (ten), Leonhardt Consort, Collegium Vocale [G] Teldec 2-▲ 2292-42603-2

Bach, J.S.:Cant 108, w. P. Esswood (ct), K. Equiluz (ten), N. Harnoncourt (cnd), Vienna Concentus Musicus [G] Teldec 2-▲ 2292-42603-2

Bach, J.S.:Cant 110, w. W. Wiedl (trb), S. Frangoulis (trb), P. Esswood (ct), Stumpf (sgr), K. Equiluz (ten), S. Lorenz (b-bar), N. Harnoncourt (cnd), Vienna Concentus Musicus, Tölz Boys' Choir [G] Teldec 2-▲ 2292-42603-2

Bach, J.S.:Cant 111, w. P. Esswood (ct), K. Equiluz (ten), K. Huber (ten), N. Harnoncourt (cnd), Vienna Concentus Musicus [G] Teldec 2-▲ 2292-42606-2

Bach, J.S.:Cant 112, w. P. Esswood (ct), K. Equiluz (ten), K. Huber (ten), N. Harnoncourt (cnd), Vienna Concentus Musicus [G] Teldec 2-▲ 2292-42606-2

Bach, J.S.:Cant 113, w. S. Hennig (trb), D. Bratschke (trb), R. Jacobs (ct), K. Equiluz (ten), Leonhardt Consort, Collegium Vocale, Hanover Boys' Chorus [G] Teldec 2-▲ 2292-42606-2

Bach, J.S.:Cant 114, w. S. Hennig (trb), R. Jacobs (ct), K. Equiluz (ten), Leonhardt Consort, Collegium Vocale, Hanover Boys' Chorus [G] Teldec 2-▲ 2292-42606-2

Bach, J.S.:Cant 158, w. R. Hansmann (sop), H. Watts (cta), K. Equiluz (ten), J. Jürgens (cnd), Concerto Amsterdam, Monteverdi Choir London Teldec ("Das alte Werke" series) ▲ 93687

Bach, J.S.:Cant 187, w. M. Emmermann (trb), P. Esswood (ct), G. Leonhardt (cnd), Leonhardt Consort, Hanover Men & Boys' Chorus, Collegium Vocale [G] Teldec 2-▲ 2292-44179-2 [DDD]

Bach, J.S.:Cant 198, w. R. Hansmann (sop), H. Watts (cta), K. Equiluz (ten), J. Jürgens (cnd), Concerto Amsterdam, Monteverdi Choir London Teldec (Das alte Werke) ▲ 93687

Bach, J.S.:St. John Passion, w. B. Schlick (sop), K. Ishii (ten), C. de Wolff (cnd), Royal Concertgebouw Orch members, Holland Bach Choir [G] Sound 3-▲ CD 3488/90

Bach, J.S.:St. John Passion, w. K. Equiluz (ten), J. Villisech (bass), N. Harnoncourt (cnd), Vienna Concentus Musicus, Vienna Boys' Choir soloists Teldec ▲ 2292-42492-2

Bach, J.S.:St. Matthew Passion, w. J. Bowman (ct), P. Esswood (ct), T. Sutcliffe (ct), K. Equiluz (ten), N. Harnoncourt (cnd), Vienna Concentus Musicus [G] Teldec 3-▲ 2292-42509-2 [AAD]

Biber, H. von:Requiem à 15, w. G. de Reyghere (sop), J. Feldman (sop), J. Bowman (ct), I. Honeyman (ten), Ricercar Consort, Erik Van Nevel (cnd), Capella Sancti Michaelis [L] *(rec 5/90)* Ricercar ▲ RIC 81063 [DDD]

Bruhns, N.:Cants, w. Jill Feldman (sop), Greta de Reyghere (sop), James Bowman (ct), Ian Honeyman (ten), Guy de Mey (ten), Ricercar Consort—Hemmt eure Tränenflut; Jauchzet dem Herren alle Welt; Wohl dem, der den Herren fürchtet; De profundis; Paratum cor meum; O werter heil'ger Geis; Zeit meines Abschieds; Erstanden ist der heilige Christ; Herr hat seinem Stuhl im Himmel bereitet; Ich liege und schlafe; Mein Herz ist bereit; Muss nicht der Mensch auf dieser Erden in Stetem Streite sein Ricercar In Ecco 2-▲ REC8001/2

Fauré, G.:La bonne chanson, w. Jos Van Immerseel (pno) Channel Classics ▲ CCS 8295

Kerll, J.C.:Missa pro defunctis, w. G. de Reyghere (sop), J. Bowman (alt), I. Honeyman (ten), G. de Mey (ten), E. van Nevel (cnd), Capella Sancti Michaelis, Ricercar Consort [L] *(rec 5/90)* Ricercar ▲ RIC 81063 [DDD]

Love Songs & Dances:Consort Music for Lute & Voices from "Pratum Musicum", w. Kirchhof, Lutz (lt), Marie-Claude Vallin (sop), Claudio Cavina (altus), Sabine Dreier (trns fl), Petra Manz (vl) *(rec Evangelische Kirche, St Osdag, Mandelsloh, Germany, Nov 21-24, 1994)* Sony Classical ("Vivarte" series) ▲ SK 66263 [DDD]

Monteverdi, C.:Orfeo, w. R. Hansmann (sop), C. Berberian (sop), L. Kozma (ten), K. Equiluz (bar), N. Harnoncourt (cnd), Vienna Concentus Musicus, Capella Antiqua München Teldec 2-▲ 42494-2

Monteverdi, C.:Ritorno d'Ulisse, w. P. Esswood (ct), K. Equiluz (ten), M. Dickie (ten), N. Rogers (ten), N. Harnoncourt (cnd), Vienna Concentus Musicus Teldec ▲ 42496-2

Schubert, Franz:Winterreise, w. J. van Immerseel (pno) [G] Channel Classics ▲ CCS 0190 [DDD]

Sebastiani, J.:St. Matthew Passion, w. Greta de Reyghere (sop), Vincent Gregoire (ct), Stéphane van Dijck (ten), Hervé Lamy (ten—Evangéliste), Max van Egmond (bass—Christ), P. Pierlot (cnd), Ricercar Consort Ricercar ▲ 160144

Sweet Was The Song, w. Smithsonian Chamber Players [period instrs] Smithsonian Collection ▲ SMI ND 040

Telemann, G.P.:Der Tag des Gerichts, w. R. Alexander (sop), K. Equiliz (ten), N. Harnoncourt (cnd), Vienna Concentus Musicus, Monteverdi Choir Hamburg Teldec 2-▲ 77621-2

Telemann, G.P.:Ino, w. R. Alexander (sop), K. Equiliz (ten), N. Harnoncourt (cnd), Vienna Concentus Musicus, Monteverdi Choir London Teldec 2-▲ 9031-77621-2

Van Blanckenburg, Q.:Cant, w. T. Koopman (cnd), Residentie Orch The Hague Olympia ▲ OCD 500 [AAD]

Zelenka, J.D.:Lamentationes Jeremiae Prophetae, w. U. Groenewold (cta), H. Meens (ten), R. Shaw (cnd), Academy of the Begynhof Amsterdam [L] Globe ▲ GLO 5050 [DDD]

Ego, Constantino (bar)

Bellini, V.:Il pirata, w. M. Callas (sop—Imogene), P. M. Ferraro (ten—Gualterio), Constantine Ego (bar—Ernesto), N. Rescigno (cnd), American Opera Society Orch, American Opera Society Chorus *(rec 1959)* EMI Classics ▲ CDMB 64938

Bellini, V.:Il pirata, w. M. Callas (sop), P. M. Ferraro (ten), N. Rescigno (cnd), American Opera Society Orch, American Opera Society Chorus [I] *(rec live, New York 1/27/59)* Melodram 2-▲ MEL 26013

Ehlert, Sibylle (sgr)

Ligeti, G.:The Ligeti Edition, w. Phyllis Bryn-Julson (sop), Rosemary Hardy (sop), Christiane Oelze (sop), Rose Taylor (mez), Omar Ebrahim (bar), Pierre-Laurent Aimard (pno), E.-P. Salonen (cnd), Philharmonia Orch, King's Singers—Vocal Works; Madrigals; Mysteries; Adventures; Songs; Nonsense Madrigals Sony Classical ▲ SK 62311

Ehrstedt, Caj (ten)

Braein, E.F.:Anne Pedersdotter, w. K. Ekeberg (sop—Anne Pedersdotter), V. Hanssen (mez—Merete Beyer), R. Eriksen (alt—Herlofs-Marte), I. M. Brekke (alt—Bente), K. M. Sandve (ten—Martin Beyer), C. Ehrstedt (ten—Master Olaus), A. Helleland (ten—David), T. Gilje (ten—Jørund), S. A. Thorsen (bar—Master Johannes), S. Carlsen (bass—Absalon Pedersøn Beyer), T. Stensvold (bass—Master Laurentius), G. Oskarsson (bass—Jens Schelderup), P. Andersson (cnd), Norwegian National Opera Orch, Norwegian National Opera Chorus Simax 2-▲ PSC 3121

Eichhorn, Karoline (nar)

Beethoven, L. van:Leonore Prohaska, w. Sylvia McNair (sop), Marie-Pierre Langlamet (hp), Sascha Reckert (glass hmc), C. Abbado (cnd), Berlin PO, Berlin Radio Chorus *(rec Great Hall, Philharmonie, Berlin)* Deutsche Grammophon ▲ 447748-2 [DDD]

Eipperle, Trude (sop)

Haydn, J.:Die Jahreszeiten, w. Julius Patzak (ten), Georg Hann (bass), C. Krauss (cnd), Vienna PO, Vienna State Opera Chorus [G] *(rec live, June 1942)* Preiser 2-▲ PRE 93053 [AAD]

Haydn, J.:Die Schöpfung, w. Julius Patzak (ten), Georg Hann (bass), C. Krauss (cnd), Vienna PO, Vienna State Opera Chorus *(rec early 1940's)* Preiser 2-▲ PRE 90104 [AAD]

Pfitzner, H.:Von deutscher Seele, w. Luise Willer (mez), Julius Patzak (ten), Ludwig Weber (bass), C. Krauss (cnd), Vienna PO, Vienna State Opera Chorus *(rec Jan 1945)* Preiser 2-▲ PRE 90255 [ADD]

Puccini, G.:La Bohème, w. Hildegarde Ranczak (sop), Alfons Fügel (ten), Carl Kronenberg (bar), Georg Hann (bass), Georg Wieter (bass), Emil Graf (sgr), Otto Hillerbrandt (sgr), Karl Schmidt (sgr), C. Krauss (cnd), Bavarian State Opera Orch, Bavarian State Opera Chorus *(rec 1940)* Preiser 2-▲ PRE 90275

Wagner, R.:Tannhäuser, w. F. Krauss (bar), K. Schmitt-Walter (bar), S. Nilsson (bass), C. Leonhardt (cnd), Stuttgart Radio Orch, Stuttgart Radio Chorus [G] *(rec Oct. 24, 1937, mat. 39695)* Preiser 3-▲ 90133 (m) [AAD]

Eisdell, Hubert (ten)

Handel, G.F.:Messiah, w. Dora Labbette (sop), Muriel Brunskill (cta), Harold Williams (bar), T. Beecham (cnd), BBC SO, BBC Choir *(rec 1927)* Pearl 2-▲ PEA 9456 [DDD]

Eisen, Artur (bass)

Borodin, A.:Prince Igor, w. Elana Obraztsova (mez—Konchakovna), Tatiana Tugarinova (mez—Yaroslavna), Vladimir Atlantov (ten—Vladimir Igoryevich), Artur Eisen (bass—Vladimir Galitsky), Ivan Petrov (bass—Igor Svyatoslavich), Alexander Vedernikov (bass—Konchak), M. Ermler (cnd), Bolshoi Theater Orch, Bolshoi Theater Chorus *(rec Moscow, 1969)* Melodiya ("The Russian Opera" series) 3-▲ 74321-29346-2 [ADD]

Eisenkolb, Susi (sgr)
Waits, T.:The Black Rider:The Casting of Magic Bullets, w. Angelika Thomas (sgr—Anne), Annette Paulmann (sgr—Kätchen), Sona Cervena (sgr—Bird/Messenger/Spoonwoman), Monika Tahal (sgr—Witness/Bird/Shrink/Wilhelm's Double/Skeleton), Susi Eisenkolb (sgr—Bridesmaid/Pegleg's Double), Heinz Vossbrink (sgr—Kuno), Dominique Horwitz (sgr—Pegleg), Gerd Kunath (sgr—Bertram), Stefan Kurt (sgr—Wilhelm), Klaus Schreiber (sgr—Robert/Man on Stag/Georg Schmid), Jörg Holm (Old Uncle/Duke), Jan Moritz Steffen (sgr—Young Kuno/Bird/Shrink/Skeleton), Tom Waits (vocals/coliope/organ/chamberlain/mar/emax/guitar/train whistle), Ralph Carney (saxophone/bass clarinet/baritone horn), Bill Douglas (bass instrument), Kenny Wollesen (perc) Island ▲ 314518559-2

Eisinger, Irene (sop)
Mozart, W.A.:Così fan tutte, w. I. Souez (sop), L. Helletsgrüber (sop), H. Nash (ten), W. Domgraf-Fassbüander (bar), J. Brownlee (bar), F. Busch (cnd), Glyndebourne Festival Orch, Glyndebourne Festival Chorus [I] *(rec 1935)* Pearl 3-▲ PEAS 9406 (m) [AAD]
Mozart, W.A.:Così fan tutte, w. Irene Eisinger (sop—Despina), Luise Helletsgruber (sop—Dorabella), Ina Souez (sop—Fiordiligi), Heddle Nash (ten—Ferrando), John Brownlee (bass—Don Alfonso), Willi Domgraf-Fassbaender (bass—Guglielmo), F. Busch (cnd), Glyndebourne Festival Orch, Glyndebourne Festival Chorus *(rec June 25–28, 1935)* Arkadia ("The 78's" series) 2-▲ 78011 [ADD]

Eisler, David (ten)
Bernstein, L.:Candide, w. E. Mills (sop), Lankston (sgr), J. Mauceri (cnd), New York City Opera Orch, New York Opera Chorus [E] *(rec 1985)* New World 2-▲ NW 340/41-2 2-■ NW 340/41-4

Eisschiel, Barbara (mez)
Gassmann, F.L.:La Contessina, w. Susanne Ganglberger (sop—Vespina), Elisabeth Mayer (sop—Contessina), Barbara Eisschiel (mez—Lindoro), Hermann Diller (ten—Gazzetta), Kurt Köller (bar—Pancrazio), Joseph Pichler (Graf Baccellone), H. Dechant (cnd), Collegium Aureum Bayer 2-▲ BR 100 252/3 [DDD]

Ejsing, Mette (cta)
Nielsen, C.:Aladdin, w. G. Paevatalu (bar), G. Rozhdestvensky (cnd), Danish National RSO, Danish National Radio Chamber Choir Chandos ▲ CHAN 9135 [DDD]
Nielsen, C.:Songs, w. Eva Hess Thaysen (sop), John Laursen (ten), Lars Thodberg Bertelsen (bar), Frode Stengaard (org), Tove Lønskov (pno)—Little Helle; Sir Oluf's Song; Dance-Song; Dawn [all from the play Sir Oluf He Rides]; The Storm Wages over the Dark Waters; My Girl Is as Fair as Amber; The Day the Eagle was Ready to Fly; A Mother was Told at the Feast; The Thistle Crop Looks Promising; Once When Death was Awaited; So Bitter was My Heart; Like a Venturous Fleet at Anchor [all from the play The Mother]; The Sign & the Word of the Cross; Of All the Flowers that Grow on Earth; As the Golden Sun Breaks Through; There is a Path; It Is No Great Struggle; Daffodil, Why Are You Here? [all from Hymns & Sacred Songs]; The Sun Springs Out Like a Rose [from the play Cosmus]; The Great Master Comes; See My Fragile Web; Our Eyes May Rejoice; When Summer's Song is Sung; Earth in Whose Embrace [all from 20 Popular Melodies]; Of What are You Singing? [The Lark]; Teach Me, O Stars of Night [both from 4 Popular Melodies]; Italian Shepherd's Song; We Love You, Our Lofty North!; Vocalise; The Power that Gave Me My Little Song [all from Amor & the Poet]; May Song [Merrily, with Joyful Song!] Rondo Grammofon ▲ RCD 8329

Ekborg, L. (nar)
Larsson, L.-E.:God in Disguise, w. E. Söderström (sop), E. Sandaen (bar), S. Westerberg (cnd), Swedish SO Swedish Society ▲ SCD 1020

Ekdahl, Linnéa (sop)
Nielsen, C.:Choral Music, w. Å. Bäverstam (sop), A. Thors (boy sop), K. M. Sandve (ten), P. Hoyer (bar), E.-P. Salonen (cnd), Swedish RSO, Stockholm Boys' Choir, Swedish Radio Chorus—Springtime in Funen; The Blind Musician; The Old People; Dance Ballad *(rec Sept. 16–18, 1991)* Sony Classical ▲ SK 53276 [DDD]

Ekeberg, Kjersti (sop)
Braein, E.F.:Anne Pedersdotter, w. K. Ekeberg (sop—Anne Pedersdotter), V. Hanssen (mez—Merete Beyer), R. Eriksen (alt—Herlofs-Marte), I. M. Brekke (alt—Bente), K. M. Sandve (ten—Martin Beyer), C. Ehrstedt (ten—Master Olaus), A. Helleland (ten—David), T. Gilje (ten—Jørund), S. A. Thorsen (bar—Master Johannes), S. Carlsen (bass—Absalon Pedersøn Beyer), T. Stensvold (bass—Master Laurentius), G. Oskarsson (bass—Jens Schelderup), P. Andersson (cnd), Norwegian National Opera Orch, Norwegian National Opera Chorus Simax 2-▲ PSC 3121

Eker, Annika Finnilä (cta)
Schnittke, A.:Requiem, w. K. Salomonsson (sop), I. H. Sjöberg (sop), L. Lindholm (sop), N. Högman (ten), S. Parkman (cnd), Stockholm Sinfonietta, Uppsala Academic Chamber Choir [L] BIS ▲ CD 497 [DDD]

Eklöf, Marianne (mez)
Grieg, E.:Peer Gynt, w. B. Bonney (sop), K. M. Sandve (ten), U. Malmberg (bar), N. Järvi (cnd), Gothenburg SO, Gothenburg Sym Chorus [N] Deutsche Grammophon 2-▲ 423079-2 [DDD]
Grieg, E.:Sigurd Jorsalfar, w. B. Bonney (sop), K. M. Sandve (ten), U. Malmberg (bar), N. Järvi (cnd), Gothenburg SO, Gothenburg Sym Chorus [N] Deutsche Grammophon 2-▲ 423079-2 [DDD]
Marianne Eklöf & Stefan Bojsten, w. Stefan Bojsten (pno) MAP ▲ MAPCD 8922
Marschner, H.A.:Hans Heiling, w. M. Hajóssyová (sop), E. Seniglova (sop), K. Markus (ten), T. Mohr (bar), L. Neshyba (bass), E. Körner (cnd), Slovak PO, Slovak Phil Chorus [G] Marco Polo ("Opera Rara" series) 2-▲ 8.223306/07 [DDD]
Sandström, S.-D.:The High Mass, w. Lena Hoel (sop), Sara Olsson (sop), Siri Torjesen (sop), Annika Skoglund (mez), Peter Bengtson (org), L. Segerstam (cnd), Swedish RSO, Eric Ericson Chamber Choir *(rec live, Berwald Hall, Stockholm, Nov. 25 & 26, 1994)* Caprice 2-▲ CAP 22036

Eklund-Tarantino, Anna (sgr)
Kraus, J.M.:Prosperin, w. Hillevi Martinpelto (sop), Susanne Rydén (sop), Peter Mattei (bar), Lars Arvidson (bass), Stephen Smith (sgr), M. Tatlow (cnd), Stockholm CO, Stockholm Chamber Choir Musica Sveciae 2-▲ MSCD 422/23 [DDD]

Elbert, Hartmut (bass)
Keiser, R.:Passions Oratorium, w. T. d'Althann (sop), P. Geitner (sop), M. Paulsen (alt), J. Elbert (ten), C. Brembeck (cnd), Parthenia Baroque, Parthenia Vocal Christophorus ▲ 77143 [DDD]

Elbert, Jochen (ten)
Keiser, R.:Passions Oratorium, w. T. d'Althann (sop), P. Geitner (sop), M. Paulsen (alt), H. Elbert (bass), C. Brembeck (cnd), Parthenia Baroque, Parthenia Vocal Christophorus ▲ 77143 [DDD]

Eles, Sandor (nar)
Bartók, B.:Bluebeard's Castle, w. Anne Sofie von Otter (mez—Judith), John Tomlinson (bass—Duke Bluebeard), B. Haitink (cnd), Berlin PO *(rec Berlin)* EMI Classics ▲ CDC 56162

Elgar, Anne (sop)
Rossini, G.:La pietra del paragone, w. B. Wolff (mez), E. Bonazzi (mez), J. Carreras (ten), J. Reardon (bar), R. Murcell (bar), A. Foldi (b-bar), J. Diaz (bass), N. Jenkins (cnd), Clarion Concerts Orch, Clarion Concerts Chorus [I] *(rec. ca. 1972)* Vanguard Classics 3-▲ OVC 8043/45 [ADD]

El Hage, Robert (bass)
Mendelssohn, F.:St. Paul, w. A. Giebel (sop), O. Dominguez (mez), Theo Altmeyer (ten), S. Nimsgern (b-bar), R. Muti (cnd), Milan RAI Orch, Milan RAI Chorus [G] *(rec live, Milan, 12/15/70)* Memories 2-▲ HR 4267/68 (m) [ADD]
Meyerbeer, G.:Le Prophète, w. M. Rinaldi (sop), M. Horne (mez), N. Gedda (ten), H. Lewis (cnd), Turin RSO, Turin Radio Chorus [F] *(rec live 7/11/70)* Foyer 3-▲ FOY 2035 [AAD]
Righini, V.:Alcide al Bivio, w. L. Serra (sop), S. Browne (cta), W. McKinney (ten), M. Barta (ob), P. Molinari (hpd), T. Gotti (cnd), Swiss-Italian RSO, Swiss-Italian Radio Chorus *(rec 1979)* Bongiovanni 2-▲ GB 2157/58 [ADD]

Elias, Rosalind (mez)
Barber, S.:Vanessa, w. E. Steber (sop), G. Resnik (sop), N. Gedda (ten), G. Tozzi (bass), D. Mitropoulos (cnd), Metropolitan Opera Orch, Metropolitan Opera Chorus [E] RCA Gold Seal ▲ 7899-2-RG [ADD]
Bernstein, L.:Songfest, w. C. Dale (sop), N. Williams (mez), N. Rosenshein (ten), J. Reardon (bar), D. Gramm (b-bar), L. Bernstein (cnd), National SO Washington D.C. [E] Deutsche Grammophon ▲ 415965-2 [ADD]

Elias, Rosalind (mez) (cont.)
Christmas Treasures, w. L. Price (sop), Marian Anderson (cta), Mario Lanza (ten), Giorgio Tozzi (bass), Arthur Fiedler (cnd), Leopold Stokowski (cnd), Robert Shaw Chorale RCA Living Stereo ▲ 09026-61867-2 ■ 09026-61867-4
Haydn, J.:Mass 12, "Theresienmesse", w. Lucia Popp (sop), Robert Tear (ten), Paul Hudson (bass), L. Bernstein (cnd), London SO, London Sym Chorus [L] Sony Classical 2-▲ SM2K 47522 [ADD]
Ponchielli, A.:La Gioconda, w. Zinka Milanov (sop—La Gioconda), Rosalind Elias (mez—Laura), Belan Amparan (cta—La Cieca), Giacomo Cottino (ten—Isepo), Giuseppe Di Stefano (ten—Enzo Grimaldo), Fernando Valentini (bar—Zuane/Un Nocchiero), Leonard Warren (bar—Barnaba), Virgilio Carbonari (bass—Un Cantore), Plinio Clabassi (bass—Alvise Badoero), F. Previtali (cnd), St. Cecilia Academy Orch Rome, St. Cecilia Academy Chorus Rome Theorema 3-▲ TH 121182/184
Prokofiev, S.:Alexander Nevsky, w. F. Reiner (cnd), Chicago SO, Chicago Sym Chorus [E] RCA Gold Seal ▲ 60176-2-RG [ADD] ■ 60176-4-RG (CrO2)
Puccini, G.:Madama Butterfly, w. L. Price (sop), G. Tucker (ten), P. Maero (bar), E. Leinsdorf (cnd), RCA Italian Opera Orch [I] RCA Red Seal 2-▲ 6160-2-RC [ADD]
Puccini, G.:Madama Butterfly, w. A. Moffo (sop), C. Valletti (ten), R. Cesari (bar), E. Leinsdorf (cnd), Rome Opera Orch, Rome Opera Chorus [I] RCA Gold Seal ▲ 60202-2-RG [ADD] ■ 60202-4-RG
Puccini, G.:Madama Butterfly, w. A. Moffo (sop), C. Valletti (ten), R. Cesari (bar), E. Leinsdorf (cnd), Rome Opera Orch, Rome Opera Chorus [I] RCA Gold Seal 2-▲ 4145-2-RG [ADD]
Puccini, G.:Madama Butterfly (sels), w. L. Price (sop), G. Tucker (ten), P. Maero (bar), E. Leinsdorf (cnd), RCA Italian Opera Orch [I] RCA ■ RK 1048
Puccini, G.:Madama Butterfly (sels), w. Leontyne Price (sop), Piero De Palma (ten), Richard Tucker (ten), Phillip Maero (bar), E. Leinsdorf (cnd), RCA Italian Opera Orch, RCA Italiana Opera Chorus RCA Victor ▲ 09026-68089-2; ■ 09026-68089-4
Verdi, G.:Falstaff, w. M. Freni (sop), I. Ligabue (sop), G. Simionato (mez), R. Krause (ten), G. Evans (bar), R. Merrill (bar), G. Solti (cnd), RCA Italian Opera Orch, RCA Italiana Opera Chorus [I] London 2-▲ 417168-2 [ADD]
Verdi, G.:La forza del destino, w. Zinka Milanov (sop), Giuseppe Di Stefano (ten), Leonard Warren (bar), Giorgio Tozzi (bass), Paolo Washington (bass), F. Previtali (cnd), St. Cecilia Academy Orch Rome, St. Cecilia Academy Chorus Rome *(rec 1959)* Theorema 3-▲ TH 121157/59
Verdi, G.:La forza del destino, w. Zinka Milanov (sop—Donna Leonora di Vargas), Rosalind Elias (mez—Preziosilla), Luisa Gioia (sgr—Curra), Angelo Mercuriali (ten—Trabuco), Giuseppe di Stefano (ten—Son Alvaro), Leonard Warren (bar—Don Carlos di Vargas), Giorgio Tozzi (b-bar—Padre guardiano), Dino Mantovani (bar—Fra Melitone), Paolo Washington (b-bar—Il marchese di Calatrava), Virgilio Carbonari (b-bar—un alcalde), Sergio Liviabella (sgr—un chirurgo), F. Previtali (cnd), St. Cecilia Academy Orch Rome, St. Cecilia Academy Chorus Rome [I] London ▲ 443678-2 [ADD]
Verdi, G.:Requiem Mass, w. L. Price (sop), J. Björling (ten), G. Tozzi (bass), F. Reiner (cnd), Vienna PO, Vienna Singverein [L] London 2-▲ 421608-2 [ADD]
Verdi, G.:Requiem Mass, w. Leontyne Price (sop), Jussi Björling (ten), Giorgio Tozzi (bass), F. Reiner (cnd), Vienna PO, French Musical Society Vocal Group *(rec 1959)* London ("Double Decker" series) 2-▲ 444833-2 [ADD]
Verdi, G.:Rigoletto, w. A. Moffo (sop), A. Kraus (ten), R. Merrill (bar), G. Solti (cnd), RCA Italian Opera Orch, RCA Italiana Opera Chorus [I] RCA Gold Seal 2-▲ 6506-2-RG [ADD]
Verdi, G.:Rigoletto, w. A. Moffo (sop), A. Kraus (ten), R. Merrill (bar), G. Solti (cnd), RCA Italian Opera Orch, RCA Italiana Opera Chorus [I] RCA Gold Seal ▲ 60203-2-RG ■ 60203-4-RG
Verdi, G.:Il trovatore, w. L. Price (sop), G. Tucker (ten), L. Warren (bar), G. Tozzi (bass), A. Basile (cnd), Rome Opera Orch RCA Gold Seal 2-▲ 60560-2-RG [ADD] 2-■ 60560-4-RG (CrO2)
The Voices of Living Stereo, Vol. 2, w. E. Farrell (sop), Birgit Nilsson (sop), Roberta Peters (sop), Leontyne Price (sop), Galina Vishnevskaya (sop), Shirley Verrett (mez), Marian Anderson (cta), Maureen Forrester (cta), Sergio Franchi (ten), Mario Lanza (ten), Richard Lewis (ten), Jan Pee, Alexander Dedyukhin (pno), Franz Rupp (pno), Leo Taubman (pno), George Trovillo (pno), Charles Wadsworth (pno), Boston Pops Orch [cnd:Arthur Fiedler], Boston SO [cnd:Charles Munch], Chicago SO [cnd:Fritz Reiner], RCA Victor Orch, RCA Victor Chorus [cnd:Wa *(rec Boston & Chicago & New York & Rome, 1957–1964)* RCA Living Stereo ▲ 09026-68167-2 [ADD]

Eliasson, Göran (ten)
Schnittke, A.:Sym 2, w. Malena Ernman (alt), Mikael Bellini (ct), Torkel Borelius (bass), L. Segerstam (cnd), Royal Stockholm PO, Anders Eby (cnd), Mikaeli Chamber Choir *(rec Stockholm Concert Hall, Sweden, Feb. 24–25, 1994)* BIS ▲ CD 667 [DDD]

Elkins, Margreta (mez)
Donizetti, G.:Lucia di Lammermoor, w. J. McDonald (sop), J. Sutherland (sop), J. Bowman (alt), J. Gibin (ten), J. Rouleau (bass), Shaw (sgr), T. Serafin (cnd), Royal Opera House Orch, Royal Opera House Chorus Covent Garden—3 duets from Act 1, & 3 soprano solo arias from Act 2 [I] Myto ▲ 1 MCD 91545 [ADD]
Handel, G.F.:Rodelinda, Regina de' Longobardi, w. Joan Sutherland (sop—Rodelinda), Margaretha Elkins (mez—Bertarido's sister), Huguette Tourangeau (mez—Bertarido), Cora Canne-Meijer (alt—Unulfo), Eric Tappy (ten—Grimoaldo), Pieter van der Berg (bass—Garibaldo), R. Bonynge (cnd), Netherlands CO *(rec Amsterdam, June 30, 1973)* Bella Voce 2-▲ BLV 107.206 [AAD]

Elkrog, Arne (ten)
Nielsen, C.:Hymnus Amoris, w. I. Nielsen (sop), P. Elming (ten), P. Høyer (bar), J. Ditlevsen (bass), L. Segerstam (cnd), Danish National RSO, Copenhagen Boys' Choir, Danish National Radio Choir [L] Chandos ▲ CHAN 8853 [DDD]

Elkus, Jenny (sgr)
Brubeck, C.:Songs, w. Frederica von Stade (sop), Bill Crofut (sgr/banjo), Chris Brubeck (sgr/trbn/pno/db), Mark Vinci (fl), Frank Brown (cl), Edward Arron (vc), Dan Brubeck (dr/perc)—The Distance between Us; La Paloma azul; Strange Meadowlark; Across Your Dreams; Summer Song; Polly; Blue Rondo-A Tribute to Dave; Autumn in Our Town; Thinking of You Thinking of Me; It's a Raggy Waltz; Heart of Winter; In the Grace of Your Room; Lonely on Both Ends of the Road *(rec Sandisfield, MA; Fantasy Studios, Berkeley, CA)* Telarc ▲ CD 80467 [DDD]

Ellenbeck, Dieter (ten)
Schubert, Franz:Stabat mater, w. G. Zeumer (sop), E. G. Schramm (bass), R. Bader (cnd), Berlin RSO, Berlin Radio Chorus Koch Schwann ▲ CD 313 055 [ADD]
Weill, K.:The Seven Deadly Sins, w. D. Bierett (sop), L. Zagrosek (cnd), Cologne RSO Capriccio ▲ 60028 [DDD]

Elliott, Malia (sgr)
Tanner, J.:Boy with Goldfish, w. L. Siu (sgr), L. Holdridge (cnd), London SO, Nigel Brooks Chorale Albany ▲ TROY 053 [DDD]

Elliott, Paul (ten)
The Age of Cathedrals, w. Theater of Voices [cnd:Paul Hillier], Alan Bennett (ten), Paul Hillier (ten) Harmonia Mundi ▲ HMU 907157 ■ HMU 407157
Bach, J.S.:Magnificat, BWV 243, w. E. Kirkby (sop), J. Nelson (sop), C. Watkinson (cta), D. Thomas (bass), S. Preston (cnd), Academy of Ancient Music, Christ Church Cathedral Choir Oxford [E♭ version; L] L'Oiseau-Lyre ▲ 414678-2 [ADD]
The Early Guitar, w. J. Tyler (lt/baroque gtr/mand), Monica Huggett (baroque vn), Jane Ryan (b vl/baroque vc), Robert Spencer (thb/baroque gtr) Saga Classics ▲ 3356 [ADD]
Gay, J.:The Beggar's Opera (sels), w. P. Kwella (sop), J. Barlow (cnd), Broadside Band—9 songs in 30 versions [E] Harmonia Mundi France ▲ HMC 901071
Handel, G.F.:Israel in Egypt, w. Norma Burrowes (sop), Charles Brett (ct), J.E. Gardiner (cnd), Monteverdi Orch, Monteverdi Choir London Erato 2-▲ 2292-45399-2 ZA
Handel, G.F.:Messiah, w. Emma Kirkby (sop), Judith Nelson (mez), Carolyn Watkinson (cta), David Thomas (bass), C. Hogwood (cnd), Academy of Ancient Music London 2-▲ 430488-2 [DDD]
Handel, G.F.:Messiah, w. Marjanne Kweksilber (sop), James Bowman (ct), G. Reinhart (bar), T. Koopman (cnd), Amsterdam Baroque Orch, The Sixteen Erato 3-▲ 2292-45960-2
Handel, G.F.:The Ways of Zion Do Mourn, w. Norma Burrowes (sop), Charles Brett (ct), J.E. Gardiner (cnd), Monteverdi Orch, Monteverdi Choir London Erato 2-▲ 2292-45399-2 ZA
Lassus, O. de:Paschalis, w. P. Hillier (cnd), Theater of Voices—Exsultet Harmonia Mundi USA ▲ HMU 907076
Lassus, O. de:Passio Domini nostri Jesu Christi secundum Mathheum, w. P. Hillier (cnd), Theater of Voices Harmonia Mundi USA ▲ HMU 907076

▲ = CD ♦ = Enhanced CD Δ = MD ■ = Cassette Tape ▯ = DCC

Elliott, Paul (ten) (cont.)

Lassus, O. de:Sacred Music, w. P. Hillier (cnd), Theater of Voices—Visitatio [from *Easter Dialogue*] Harmonia Mundi USA ▲ HMU 907076

Purcell, H.:Dido & Aeneas, w. L. Hunt (sop), L. Saffer (sop), D. Deam (sop), C. Brandes (sop), R. Rainero (sop), E. Rabiner (mez), M. Dean (bar), N. McGegan (cnd), Philharmonia Baroque Orch, Clare College Choir Cambridge Harmonia Mundi USA ▲ HMU 907110

Purcell, H.:Hail. Bright Cecilia, w. J. Smith (sop), B. Gordon (alt), A. Stafford (alt), S. Varcoe (bar), D. Thomas (bass), J.E. Gardiner (cnd), English Baroque Soloists, Monteverdi Choir London Erato ("Gardiner Purcell Collection" series) ▲ 96554-2

Purcell, H.:King Arthur, w. R. Hardy (sop), H. Sheppard (sop), J. Knibbs (cta), A. Deller (ct), M. Deller (alt), L. Nixon (ten), M. Bevan (bar), N. Beavan (bass), A. Deller (cnd), Deller Consort, King's Musick [E] Harmonia Mundi France 2-▲ HMC 90252/53

Purcell, H.:King Arthur, w. Gillian Fisher (sop), E. Priday (sop), Gill Ross (sop), J. Smith (sop), A. Stafford (alt), S. Varcoe (bar), J.E. Gardiner (cnd), English Baroque Soloists, Monteverdi Choir London Erato ("Gardiner Purcell Collection" series) 2-▲ 96552-2

Purcell, H.:King Arthur, w. J. Smith (sop), G. Fisher (sop), E. Priday (sop), G. Ross (sop), A. Stafford (alt), S. Varcoe (bar), J.E. Gardiner (cnd), English Baroque Soloists, Monteverdi Choir London Erato 2-▲ 2292-45211-2 ZA

Purcell, H.:The Prophetess, or The History of Dioclesian, w. L. Dawson (sop), Gillian Fisher (sop), R. Covey-Crump (ten), S. Varcoe (bar), M. George (bass), J.E. Gardiner (cnd), Monteverdi Orch, Monteverdi Choir London Erato ("Gardiner Purcell Collection" series) 2-▲ 96556-2

Purcell, H.:Timon of Athens, w. L. Dawson (sop), Gillian Fisher (sop), R. Covey-Crump (ten), S. Varcoe (bar), M. George (bass), J.E. Gardiner (cnd), Monteverdi Orch, Monteverdi Choir London Erato ("Gardiner Purcell Collection" series) 2-▲ 96556-2

Songs for a Tudor King, w. P. Hillier (cnd), Hillard Ensemble, Judith Nelson (sop), David James (ct), Leigh Nixon (ten), P. Hillier (bar) Saga Classics ▲ 3378 [ADD]

Vivaldi, A.:Gloria, RV.589, w. J. Nelson (sop), E. Kirkby (sop), C. Watkinson (cta), D. Thomas (bass), S. Preston (cnd), Academy of Ancient Music, Christ Church Cathedral Choir Oxford [L] L'Oiseau-Lyre ▲ 414678-2 [ADD]

Ellis, Vivien (sop)

Hildegard Of Bingen:Sacred Songs, w. Jocelyn West (sgr), Vivien Ellis (sgr), Stevie Wishart (sgr/h-g), Hester Briant (sgr), Fiona Cunningham (sgr), Tara Franks (sgr), Emily Levy (sgr), Lucy Steele (sgr), Vickie Couperin (sgr), Julie Murphy (sgr), Oxford Girls' Choir—Honey & milk beneath her tongue; Ursula's virgins; The devil's virgins; Place of the ancient heart; Zeal of divinity; O fiery spirit; Red river falling; O orzchis ecclesia, Living-light angels; The clouds are grieving; The firstwoman; From their homeland; But the devil mocked; Song to Ecclesia *(rec Toddington, Gloucestershire, England, May 6-8, 1995)* Celestial Harmonies ▲ 13127-2

Old English Nursery Rhymes, w. Tim Laycock (sgr), Broadside Band *(rec Valley Recordings, Littleton-on-Severn, Feb 1996)* Saydisc ▲ CDSDL 419

Poder á Santa Maria, w. S. Wishart (cnd), Sinfonye, Equidad Barés (sgr), Paula Chateauneuf (sgr), Jim Denley (sgr) *(rec Cartuja de Santa María de Cazalla de la Sierra, Seville, Oct. 1993)* Almaviva ▲ 0105 [DDD]

Elloir, Sarah (sgr)

Boieldieu, F.-A.:Le Calife de Bagdad, w. N. Monestier (sop), Ouaki (sgr), Plantak (sgr), Fokenoy (sgr), B. Thomas (cnd), Bernard Thomas CO, Patrick Marco Vocal Ensemble [F] Thésis ▲ THC 82015 [DDD]

Ellsworth, G. (sgr)

Giordano, U.:Andrea Chénier, w. Montserrat Caballé (sop), Franco Corelli (ten), R. de Carlo (sgr), D. Dondi (sgr), G. Ellsworth (sgr), J. Fair (sgr), R. Falk (sgr), S. Felter (sgr), E. Green (sgr), H. Hicks (sgr), H. Krauss (sgr), L. Miller (sgr), N. Riggins (sgr), H. Salerno (sgr), A. Guadagno (cnd), Academy of Music Orch, Academy of Music Chorus Great Opera Performances 2-▲ GOP 766

Ellsworth, Warren (ten)

Wagner, R.:Parsifal, w. Waltraud Meier (mez—Kundry), Warren Ellsworth (ten—Parsifal), Nicholas Folwell (bar—Klingsor), Philip Joll (b-bar—Amfortas), Donald McIntyre (b-bar—Gurnemanz), R. Goodall (cnd), Welsh National Opera Orch, Welsh National Opera Chorus EMI Classics 2-▲ CDMD 65665

Elmark, Susanne (sop)

Gade, N.W.:Elverskud, w. Kirsten Dolberg (cta—Mother), Guido Paevatalu (bar—Oluf), M. Schønwandt (cnd), Tivoli SO, Tivoli Concert Choir *(rec Tivoli Concert Hall, Apr 29-30, May 4, 1996)* Marco Polo/Dacapo ▲ 8.224051 [DDD]

Elming, Paul (ten)

Gade, N.W.:Elverskud, w. E. Johansson (sop), A. Gjevang (cta), D. Kitayenko (cnd), Danish National RSO, Danish National Radio Chamber Choir [Da] Chandos ▲ CHAN 9075 [DDD]

Heise, P.:King & Marshall, w. A. Haugland (bass), C. Christiansen (bass), M. Schønwandt (cnd), Danish National RSO, Danish National Choir Chandos 3-▲ CHAN 9143 [DDD]

Nielsen, C.:Hymnus Amoris, w. I. Nielsen (sop), A. Elkrog (ten), P. Høyer (bar), J. Ditlevsen (bass), L. Segerstam (cnd), Danish National RSO, Copenhagen Boys' Choir, Danish National Radio Choir [L] Chandos ▲ CHAN 8853 [DDD]

Elmo, Cloe (mez)

Verdi, G.:Falstaff, w. Herva Nelli (sop), Teresa Stich-Randall (sop), Frank Guarrera (bar), Giuseppe Valdengo (bar), A. Toscanini (cnd), *(orch unknown) (rec 1950)* Music & Arts 2-▲ CD 248 [ADD]

Verdi, G.:Il trovatore, w. M. Callas (sop), G. Lauri-Volpi (ten), P. Silveri (bar), T. Serafin (cnd), Naples Teatro San Carlo Orch, Naples Teatro San Carlo Chorus [I] *(rec live, Naples, 1/27/51)* Melodram 2-▲ MEL 26001 (m) [AAD]

Verdi, G.:Il trovatore, w. Maria Callas (sop), Giacomo Lauri-Volpi (ten), Paolo Siveri (sgr), T. Serafin (cnd), Naples Teatro San Carlo Orch, Naples Teatro San Carlo Chorus *(rec Theatre of San Carlo, Naples, Jan. 27, 1951)* Pantheon 2-▲ PHE 6636 (m)

Elrod, Pam (mez)

Debussy, C.:Chansons (3) de Charles d'Orléans, w. Julie McCoy (sop), Nanette Soles (mez), Charles Bruffy (ten), Leonard Ratzlaff (bass), Robert Shaw (cnd), Robert Shaw Festival Singers *(rec Church of St. Pierre, Gramat, France, July 26-28, 1994)* Telarc ▲ CD 80408 [DDD]

Elsner, Christian (ten)

Albrechtsberger, J.G.:Missa assumptionis beatae Mariae Virginis, w. F. Schmitt-Bohn (sop), J. Köble (alt), U. Rausch (bass), R. Hug (cnd), Freiburg Baroque Soloists Ars Musici ▲ 0972-2 [DDD]

Bizet, G.:Te Deum, w. Angela Maria Blasi (sop), H.R. Zöbeley (cnd), Munich SO, Munich Motet Choir *(rec live, Herkulessaal, Munich, Mar 13 & 17, 1996)* Calig ▲ CAL 50956 [DDD]

Dvořák, A.:Mass, w. D. Röschmann (sop), I. Danz (alt), J. Mannov (bass), E. Krapp (org), W. Schäfer (cnd), Frankfurt Kantorei Ars Musici ▲ AM 1083-2 [DDD]

Gounod, C.:Messe solennelle de St. Cécile, w. Angela Maria Blasi (sop), Dietrich Henschel (bar), H.R. Zöbeley (cnd), Munich SO, Munich Motet Choir *(rec live, Herkulessaal, Munich, Mar 13 & 17, 1996)* Calig ▲ CAL 50956 [DDD]

Haydn, M.:Missa Sancti Hieronymi, w. Florian Schmitt-Bohn (sop), Joachim Köble (alt), Ulrich Rausch (bass), R. Hug (cnd), Freiburg Baroque Soloists Ars Musici ▲ 0972-2 [DDD]

Elvin, Peter (bass)

Verdi, G.:Un giorno di regno, w. J. Norman (sop), F. Cossotto (mez), J. Carreras (ten), I. Wixell (bar), V. Sardinero (bar), W. Ganzarolli (bar), A. Cassinelli (bass), L. Gardelli (cnd), Royal PO, Ambrosian Singers Philips 2-▲ 422429-2 [ADD]

Elvin, Peter (sgr)

Handel, G.F.:Messiah (reorchd Mozart), w. Andrew Murphy (b-bar), M. Altman (sgr), J. Davidson (sgr), P. Price (sgr), L. Woodside (cnd), Sinfonia Rubinstein, New York Oratorio Society [Sinfonia Rubinstein is made up from musicians from the Lodz Philharmonic Orchestra and the Lodz Opera of Poland] [E] Koch Schwann 2-▲ SC 100308 [DDD]

Elwes, Gervase (ten)

Charpentier, M.-A.:Judicum Salomonis, w. A. Zaepffel (ct), J. Benet (ten), G. Ragon (ten), J. Cabré (bar), G. Reinhart (bar), P. Colléaux (cnd), Stradivaria Ensemble, Nantes Vocal Ensemble [L] Arion ▲ ARN 68037 [DDD]

Song Recital, w. Fredereck B. Kiddle (pno) *(rec 1911-1919 for Columbia)* Opal ▲ CD 9844 (m) [ADD]

Vaughan Williams, R.:On Wenlock Edge, w. F.B. Kiddle (pno), London String Quartet [E] *(rec 1917 for Columbia)* Opal ▲ CD 9844 (m) [AAD]

Elwes, John (ten)

Airs & Dances of Shakespeare's Time, w. C. Mendoze (cnd), Musica Antiqua Ensemble, Stephen Stubbs (lt) Pierre Verany ▲ 787092 [DDD]

Bach, J.C.F:Die Auferweckung Lazarus, w. Véronique Dietschy (sop), Consuelo Caroli (mez), Philippe Cantor (bar), G. Bezzina (cnd), Nice Baroque Ensemble, Nicole Blanchi Vocal Ensemble Adda ▲ ADD 581182 [DDD]

Biber, H. von:Requiem à 15, w. Marta Almajano (sop), Mieke van der Sluis (sop), Mark Padmore (ten), Frans Huijts (bar), Harry van der Kamp (bass), G. Leonhardt (cnd), Netherlands Bach Society Baroque Orch, Netherlands Bach Society Choir *(rec Utrecht, Germany, Oct 22-24, 1994)* Deutsche Harmonia Mundi ▲ 05472-77344-2 [DDD]

Campra, A.:Messe de Requiem, w. E. Baudry (sop), M. Zanetti (sop), J. Benet (ten), S. Varcoe (bar), P. Herreweghe (cnd), La Chapelle Royale Orch [L] Harmonia Mundi France ▲ HMC 901251

Carvalho, J. de S.:Te Deum, w. Brigitte Fournier (sop), Naoko Okada (sop), Elisabeth Graf (cta), Michel Brodard (bar), M. Corboz (cnd), Lisbon Gulbenkian Foundation Orch, Lisbon Gulbenkian Foundation Chorus Cascavelle ▲ CVL 1016 [DDD]

Charpentier, M.-A.:Salve regina à 3 voix pareilles, w. Gérard Lesne (ct), Josep Cabré (bar), J. Savall (cnd), Concert des Nations Astrée ▲ E 8552 [DDD]

Handel, G.F.:Tamerlano, w. Isabelle Poulenard (sop—Irene), Mieke van der Sluis (sop—Asteria), René Jacobs (alt—Andronico), Henri Ledroit (ct—Tamerlano), John Elwes (ten—Bajazet), Gregory Reinhart (bass—Leone), J. Malgoire (cnd), La Grande Écurie et la Chambre du Roy *(rec 1983)* Sony Classical 3-▲ SM3K 37893

Handel, G.F.:Il Trionfo del Tempo e del Disinganno, w. Isabelle Poulenard (sop), Jennifer Smith (sop), Nathalie Stutzmann (cta), M. Minkowski (cnd), Louvre Musicians Erato 2-▲ 2292-45351-2 ZA

L'heritage de Monteverdi, Vol. 2, w. La Fenice, Maria Cristina Kiehr (sop), Ulrich Messthaler (bar) *(rec Eglise de Mormont, Nov 1995)* Ricercar ▲ RIC 166148

Jewels of Early Music, w. Loïnhdana Ensemble, Musica Antiqua, André Isoir (org), Pierre Bardon (org) *(rec 1982-86)* Pierre Verany ▲ 791051 [DDD]

Purcell, H.:Anthems & Services, w. David Cordier (alt), Harry van der Kamp (bass), Peter Kooy (bass), Gustav Leonhardt (org), Tölz Boys' Choir—In thee, O Lord, do I put my trust; My beloved spake; O praise God in His holiness; Praise the Lord, O Jerusalem; Rejoice in the Lord always Sony Classical ("Vivarte" series) ▲ SK 53981

Rameau, J.P.:Les Indes galantes, w. L. Devos (ten), P. Huttenlocher (bar), J.-F. Paillard (cnd), Jean-François Paillard CO Erato 3-▲ 95310-2

Steffani, A.:Stabat Mater, w. Marta Almajano (sop), Mieke van der Sluis (sop), Mark Padmore (ten), Harry van der Kamp (bass), G. Leonhardt (cnd), Netherlands Bach Society Baroque Orch, Netherlands Bach Society Choir *(rec Utrecht, Germany, Oct 22-24, 1994)* Deutsche Harmonia Mundi ▲ 05472-77344-2 [DDD]

Valls, F.:Scala Arentina Mass, w. S. Paiu (sop), M. van der Sluis (sop), B. Lettinga (alt), D. Cordier (ct), H. van der Kamp (bass), G. Leonhardt (cnd), Netherlands Bach Society Baroque Orch, Netherlands Bach Society Choir Deutsche Harmonia Mundi ▲ 05472-77277-2

Ely, Dean (sgr)

Handel, G.F.:Giustino, w. Juliana Gondek (sop), Dawn Kotoski (sop), Dorothea Röschmann (sop), Jennifer Lane (mez), Michael Chance (alt), Drew Minter (alt), Mark Padmore (ten), N. McGegan (cnd), Freiburg Baroque Orch Harmonia Mundi France 3-▲ HMU 907130.32

Emerson, Karen Smith (sop)

Songs of the Nightingale, w. Martin Katz (pno), William Wittig (fl) *(rec Sweeney Concert Hall, Sage Hall, Smith College, Northampton, MA, Jan 3-5, 1994)* Centaur ▲ 2232 [DDD]

Emmermann, Michael (trb)

Bach, J.S.:Cant 187, w. P. Esswood (ct), M. van Egmond (b-bar), G. Leonhardt (cnd), Leonhardt Consort, Hanover Men & Boys' Chorus, Collegium Vocale [G] Teldec 2-▲ 2292-44179-2 [DDD]

Endrèze, Arthur (bar)

Bizet, G.:Carmen (sels), w. C. Supervia (mez), A. Vavon (sop), A. Bernadet (mez), J.-F. Delmas (b-bar), G. Micheletti (ten), G. Cloëz (cnd), Paris Opéra-Comique Orch, Paris Opéra-Comique Chorus—14 arias & scenes [F] *(rec Paris, 1930)* The Classical Collector ▲ FDC 2002 (m) [AAD]

Bizet, G.:Carmen (sels), w. C. Supervia (mez), A. Vavon (sop), A. Bernadet (mez), G. Micheletti (ten), G. Cloëz (cnd), Paris Opéra-Comique Orch, Paris Opéra-Comique Chorus—8 arias & scenes *(rec Paris 1930)* Nimbus ("Prima Voce" series) 2-▲ NI 7836/7 [ADD]

Puccini, G.:Tosca (sels), w. M.-C. Vallin (sop), E. di Mazzei (ten), P. Payen (bar), G. Cloëz (cnd), Paris Opéra-Comique Orch, Paris Opéra-Comique Chorus [abridged version] [F] *(rec 1932)* Music Memoria ▲ 30376

Engeboll, A. (ten)

Gluck, C.W.:Alceste, w. K. Flagstad (sop—Alceste), A. Engeboll (ten—Admetus), N. Moliner (bar—High Priest) [French version] *(rec Apr. 14, 1957)* Eklipse 2-▲ EKR 24

Engel, Jan (bass)

Hummel, J.N.:Alma virgo, w. Amanda Halgrimson (sop), Susan McAdoo (mez), Helmut Wildhaber (ten), Petr Mikuláš (bass), M. Haselböck (cnd), Vienna Academy, Brünn Czech Phil Chorus Koch Schwann ▲ SCH CD 317792

Hummel, J.N.:Mass in E♭, Op. 80, w. Amanda Halgrimson (sop), Susan McAdoo (mez), Helmut Wildhaber (ten), Petr Mikuláš (bass), M. Haselböck (cnd), Vienna Academy, Brünn Czech Phil Chorus Koch Schwann ▲ SCH CD 317792

Hummel, J.N.:Quod quod in orbe, w. Amanda Halgrimson (sop), Susan McAdoo (mez), Helmut Wildhaber (ten), Petr Mikuláš (bass), M. Haselböck (cnd), Vienna Academy, Brünn Czech Phil Chorus Koch Schwann ▲ SCH CD 317792

Engen, Kieth (bass)

Bach, J.S.:Cant 67, w. P. Pears (ten), K. Richter (cnd), Munich Bach Orch, Munich Bach Choir Teldec ▲ 9031-77614-2

Bach, J.S.:Cant 108, w. P. Pears (ten), K. Richter (cnd), Munich Bach Orch, Munich Bach Choir Teldec ▲ 9031-77614-2

Bach, J.S.:Cant 127, w. P. Pears (ten), K. Richter (cnd), Munich Bach Orch, Munich Bach Choir Teldec ▲ 9031-77614-2

Bach, J.S.:St. John Passion, w. Evelyn Lear (sop), Hertha Töpper (mez), Ernst Haefliger (ten), Hermann Prey (bar), K. Richter (cnd), Munich Bach Orch, Munich Bach Choir Deutsche Grammophon ("2CD" series) 2-▲ 453 007-2

Bach, J.S.:St. Matthew Passion, w. I. Seefried (sop), A. Fahberg (sop), H. Töpper (alt), E. Haefliger (ten), D. Fischer-Dieskau (bar), M. Proebstl (bass), K. Richter (cnd), Munich Bach Orch, Munich Bach Choir Archiv ▲ 439338-2 [ADD]

Beethoven, L. van:Fidelio (sels), w. L. Rysanek (sop), I. Seefried (sop), E. Haefliger (ten), F. Lenz (ten), D. Fischer-Dieskau (bar), G. Frick (bass), F. Fricsay (cnd), Bavarian State Orch, Bavarian Opera Chorus—Overture, various arias & scenes, finale [G] IMP Collectors Series ▲ IMPX 9021 [AAD]

Gluck, C.W.:Iphigénie en Tauride, w. S. Jurinac (sop), F. Wunderlich (ten), H. Prey (bar), R. Kubelik (cnd), Bavarian RSO, Bavarian Radio Chorus [1781 J.B. von Alxinger-Gluck German-language version] *(rec live, Munich 1965)* Myto 2-▲ 2 MCD 91544 [ADD]

Haydn, J.:Die Jahreszeiten, w. Agnes Giebel (sop—Hanne), Fritz Wünderlich (ten—Lukas), Kieth Engen (bass—Simon), H. Müller-Kray (cnd), Stuttgart South Radio Orch, Hesse Radio Chorus *(rec Schwetzingen, May 24, 1959)* Bella Voce 2-▲ 7204 [ADD]

Janáček, L.:The Excursions of Mr. Brouček, w. Antonie Fahberg (sop—Piccolo), Wilma Lipp (sop—Málinka), Lilian Benningsen (cta—Fanny Nowak), Paul Kuen (ten—Trambahn-Kondukteur), Karl Ostertag (ten—Vorsitzender des Hausbesitzerverbandes), Fritz Wunderlich (ten—Mazal), Kurt Böhme (b-bar—Sakristan von St. Veit), Kieth Engen (bass—Würfl), J. Keilberth (cnd), Bavarian SO *(rec live, Prinzregententheater, Nov. 19, 1959)* Orfeo 2-▲ 354942 (m)

Mozart, W.A.:Missa brevis, K.220, w. E. Mathis (spo), T. Troyanos (mez), H. Laubenthal (ten) Deutsche Grammophon ▲ 429820-2 [ADD]

Engen, Kieth (bass) (cont.)
Mussorgsky, M.:Boris Godunov, w. Martha Mödl (sop—Marina Mniszek), Lotte Schädle (sop—Xenia), Dorothea Siebert (mez—Fyodor), Hertha Töpper (mez—Xenia's wet-nurs), Karl Hermann Bennert (Boyer Khrushchyov), Lorenz Fehenberger (ten—Prince Shuysky), Hans Hopf (ten—Grigory), Karl Ostertag (ten—Missail), Hans Hotter (b-bar—Boris Godunov), Hermann Uhde (bar—Andrey Shchelkalov), Kurt Böhme (bass—Varlaam), Kim Borg (bass—Pimen), Kieth Engen (bass—Lewicki), Adolf Keil (bass—Nikitich), Benno Kusche (bar—Rangoni), Heinz Maria Linz (bass—Czernikowski), E. Jochum (cnd), Bavarian RSO, Bavarian Radio Chorus *(rec Munich, May 1957)* Myto 3-▲ MCD 953131
Schoenberg, A.:Gurrelieder, w. I. Borkh (sop), H. Schachtschneider (ten), H. Töpper (mez), L. Fehenberger (ten), R. Kubelik (cnd), Bavarian RSO—also includes songs by Berg, Schoenberg & Webern Deutsche Grammophon ("20th Century Classics" series) ▲ 431744-2 [ADD]
Strauss, R.:Feuersnot, w. Maud Cunitz (sop—Diemut), Antonia Fahberg (sop—Elsbeth), Irmgard Barth (mez—Wigelis), Liselotte Nölser (sgr—Margret), Karl Ostertag (ten—Schweiker), Marcel Cordes (bar—Kunrad), Kieth Engen (bass—Kofel), Karl Hoppe (bass—Hämerlein), Max Proebstl (bass—Ortolf), Georg Wieter (bass—Jörg), R. Kempe (cnd), Bavarian State Opera Orch, Bavarian State Opera Chorus *(rec Munich Opera Festival, Prince Regent Theater, Aug 14, 1958)* Orfeo d'or 2-▲ 423962
Wagner, R.:Das Liebesverbot, w. Pamela Coburn (sop—Mariana), Friedrich Lenz (ten—Antonio), Hermann Prey (bar—Friedrich), Keith Engen (bass—Angelo), Raimund Grumbach (bass—Danieli/Wirt), Wolfgang Fassler (sgr—Luzio), Sabine Haas (sgr—Isabella/Claudios Schwester), Alfred Kuhn (sgr—Brighella/Chef der Sbirren), Hermann Sapell (sgr—Pontio Pilato), Robert Schunk (sgr—Claudio), Marianne Seibel (sgr—Dorella), W. Sawallisch (cnd), Bavarian State Orch, Bavarian State Chorus *(rec July 9, 1983)* Orfeo d'or 3-▲ 345953
Wagner, R.:Rienzi, der Letzte der Tribunen, w. Cheryl Studer (sop—Irene), René Kollo (ten—Rienzi), Friedrich Lenz (ten—Gesandte), Norbert Orth (ten—Baroncelli), Bodo Brinkmann (bar—Paolo Orsini), Keith Engen (bass—Cecco del Vecchio), Raimund Grumbach (bass—Gesandte), Jan-Hendrik Rootering (bass—Steffano Colonna), Carmen Anhorn (sgr—Ein Friedensbote), Karl Helm (sgr—Kardinal Orvieto), John Janssen (sgr—Adriano), Alfred Kuhn (sgr—Gesandte), Hans Wilbrink (sgr—Gesandte), W. Sawallisch (cnd), Bavarian State Opera Orch, Bavarian State Opera Chorus *(rec live, July 6, 1983)* Orfeo d'or 3-▲ 346953

Engert-Ely, Ruthlid (mez)
Prokofiev, S.:The Fiery Angel, w. N. Secunde (sop), H. Zednik (ten), S. Lorenz (bar), K. Moll (bass), N. Järvi (cnd), Gothenburg SO, Gothenburg Sym Chorus [R] Deutsche Grammophon 2-▲ 431669-2 [DDD]

Engleman, Robin (nar/perc)
Cahn, W.:The Recital Piece Nexus ▲ 10339 [DDD]

English, Gerald (ten)
Bach, J.S.:Cant 211, "Coffee Cant", w. E. Ameling (sop), S. Nimsgern (b-bar), Collegium Aureum Editio Classica 2-▲ 77151-2-RG [ADD]
Bach, J.S.:Cant 212, "Peasant Cant", w. E. Ameling (sop), S. Nimsgern (b-bar), Collegium Aureum Editio Classica 2-▲ 77151-2-RG [ADD]
Cage, J.:The Wonderful Widow of Eighteen Springs, w. N. Butterly (pno) Tall Poppies ▲ TP 025
Ford, A.:Sacred Places, w. S. Savage (cnd), Griffith Univ Ensemble *(rec live, Basil Jones Theater, Queensland Conservatorium of Music, Brisbane, Sept 1993)* Tall Poppies ▲ TP 053 [DDD]
Ford, A.:Whispers, w. S. Savage (cnd), Griffith Univ Ensemble *(rec live, Basil Jones Theater, Queensland Conservatorium of Music, Brisbane, Sept 1993)* Tall Poppies ▲ TP 053 [DDD]
La Musique de Notre Dame, w. A. Deller (ct), Wilfred Brown (ten), Maurice Bevan (bar) *(rec Jan. 1961 & May 1964)* Vanguard Classics ▲ SVC 36 [AAD]
Orff, C.:Carmina burana, w. S. Armstrong (sop), T. Allen (bar), A. Previn (cnd), London SO, London Sym Chorus, St. Clement Danes Boys' Chorus [G, L] EMI Classics ▲ CDC 47411 ■ 4AM 34770
Tallis, T.:The Lamentations of Jeremiah, w. Alfred Deller (ct), Wilfred Brown (ten), Maurice Bevan (bar), John Frost (bass) *(rec Walthamstow Hall, London, 1960)* Vanguard Classics ("The Bach Guild" series) ▲ OVC 2525 [ADD]

Enhamre, Åse (sop)
Holewa, H.:Concertino 9, w. Magnus Andersson (gtr), C. Merithz (cnd), Strängnäs Sinfonietta Ensemble Phono Suecia ▲ PHN 49 [ADD]

Enigarescu, Octav (bar)
Puccini, G.:Turandot, w. Teodora Lucaciu (sop—Liù), Maria Slatinaru (sop—Princess Turandot), Corneliu Finateanu (ten—Pong), George Mircea (ten—Emperor Altoum), Ludovic Speiss (ten—Prince Calaf), Valentin Teodorian (ten—Pang), Octav Enigarescu (bar—Ping), Dionisie Konya (bar—A Mandarin), Mircea Stefanescu (bar—The Prince of Persia), Nicolae Florei (bass—Timur), C. Litvin (cnd), Romanian Radio-TV Orch, Romanian Radio-TV Chorus *(rec Jan 1970)* Vox Box 2-▲ CDX 5160
Verdi, G.:Il trovatore, w. Elena Dima (sop—Leonora), Victoria Draganescu (sop—Ines), Zenaida Pally (mez—Azucena), Ion Buzea (ten—Duke of Mantua), Constantin Iliescu (ten—Ruiz), Cornel Stavru (ten—Manrico), Octav Enigarescu (bar—Count di Luna), Constantin Dumitru (bass—Ferrando), E. Massini (cnd), Romanian Opera Orch, Romanian Opera Chorus *(rec 1960-61)* Vox Box 2-▲ CDX 5163

Enna, Norma (sop)
Jahn, T.:Music of, w. L'Art Pour L'Art Ensemble—selected vocal arrs. Col Legno ▲ AU 31811

Epperle, T. (sop)
Wagner, R.:Lohengrin, w. H. Braun (sop—Ortrud), T. Epperle (sop—Elsa von Brabant), P. Anders (ten—Lohengrin), C. Kronenberg (bar—Frederich von Telramund), J. Greindl (bass—Heinrich der Vogler), R. Kraus (cnd), Cologne RSO, Cologne Radio Chorus *(rec Nov. 1951)* Myto 3-▲ MCD 93485

Epstein, Alvin (nar)
Stravinsky, I.:L'Histoire du soldat, w. M. Douglas (nar), James Mitchell (nar), E. Vardi (cnd), Kapp Sinfonietta [E] MCA Classics 2-▲ MCAD2-9820 [AAD]

Equiluz, Kurt (ten)
Bach, J.S.:Cant 1, w. P. Esswood (ct), M. van Egmond (b-bar), N. Harnoncourt (cnd), Vienna Concentus Musicus, Vienna Boys' Choir [G] Teldec 2-▲ 2292-42497-2 [AAD]
Bach, J.S.:Cant 2, w. P. Esswood (ct), M. van Egmond (b-bar), N. Harnoncourt (cnd), Vienna Concentus Musicus, Vienna Boys' Choir [G] Teldec 2-▲ 2292-42497-2 [AAD]
Bach, J.S.:Cant 3, w. P. Esswood (ct), M. van Egmond (b-bar), N. Harnoncourt (cnd), Vienna Concentus Musicus, Vienna Boys' Choir [G] Teldec 2-▲ 2292-42497-2 [AAD]
Bach, J.S.:Cant 4, w. L. Dutoit (trb), H. Braun (bar), F. Prohaska (cnd), Vienna State Opera Orch, Vienna Chamber Choir [G] *(rec 1959)* Vanguard Classics ("The Bach Guild" series) ▲ OVC 2001 [ADD]
Bach, J.S.:Cant 4, w. P. Esswood (ct), M. van Egmond (b-bar), N. Harnoncourt (cnd), Vienna Concentus Musicus, Vienna Boys' Choir [G] Teldec 2-▲ 2292-42497-2 [AAD]
Bach, J.S.:Cant 5, w. P. Esswood (ct), M. van Egmond (b-bar), N. Harnoncourt (cnd), Vienna Concentus Musicus, Vienna Boys' Choir Teldec 2-▲ 2292-42498-2 [AAD]
Bach, J.S.:Cant 6, w. P. Esswood (ct), M. van Egmond (b-bar), N. Harnoncourt (cnd), Vienna Concentus Musicus, Vienna Boys' Choir Teldec 2-▲ 2292-42498-2 [AAD]
Bach, J.S.:Cant 7, w. P. Esswood (ct), M. van Egmond (b-bar), Leonhardt Consort, King's College Choir Cambridge [G] Teldec 2-▲ 2292-42498-2 [AAD]
Bach, J.S.:Cant 8, w. P. Esswood (ct), G. Kiefer (bar), M. van Egmond (b-bar), Leonhardt Consort, King's College Choir Cambridge [G] Teldec 2-▲ 2292-42498-2 [AAD]
Bach, J.S.:Cant 9, w. P. Esswood (ct), M. van Egmond (b-bar), Leonhardt Consort, King's College Choir Cambridge [G] Teldec 2-▲ 2292-42499-2 [AAD]
Bach, J.S.:Cant 10, w. P. Esswood (ct), M. van Egmond (b-bar), Leonhardt Consort, King's College Choir Cambridge [G] Teldec 2-▲ 2292-42499-2 [AAD]
Bach, J.S.:Cant 11, "Ascension Oratorio", w. P. Esswood (ct), M. van Egmond (b-bar), N. Harnoncourt (cnd), Vienna Concentus Musicus, Vienna Concentus Musicus Chorus [G] Teldec 2-▲ 2292-42499-2 [AAD]
Bach, J.S.:Cant 12, w. P. Esswood (ct), M. van Egmond (b-bar), Leonhardt Consort, King's College Choir Cambridge [G] Teldec 2-▲ 2292-42500-2 [AAD]
Bach, J.S.:Cant 13, w. P. Esswood (ct), M. van Egmond (b-bar), Leonhardt Consort, King's College Choir Cambridge [G] Teldec 2-▲ 2292-42500-2 [AAD]
Bach, J.S.:Cant 16, w. P. Esswood (ct), M. van Egmond (b-bar), Leonhardt Consort, King's College Choir Cambridge [G] Teldec 2-▲ 2292-42500-2 [AAD]

Equiluz, Kurt (ten) (cont.)
Bach, J.S.:Cant 17, w. P. Esswood (ct), M. van Egmond (b-bar), N. Harnoncourt (cnd), Vienna Concentus Musicus, Chorus Viennensis [G] Teldec 2-▲ 2292-42501-2 [AAD]
Bach, J.S.:Cant 18, w. P. Esswood (ct), M. van Egmond (b-bar), N. Harnoncourt (cnd), Vienna Concentus Musicus, Chorus Viennensis [G] Teldec 2-▲ 2292-42501-2 [AAD]
Bach, J.S.:Cant 19, w. P. Esswood (ct), M. van Egmond (b-bar), N. Harnoncourt (cnd), Vienna Concentus Musicus, Chorus Viennensis [G] Teldec 2-▲ 2292-42501-2 [AAD]
Bach, J.S.:Cant 20, w. P. Esswood (ct), M. van Egmond (b-bar), N. Harnoncourt (cnd), Vienna Concentus Musicus, Chorus Viennensis [G] Teldec 2-▲ 2292-42501-2 [AAD]
Bach, J.S.:Cant 21, w. P. Esswood (ct), W. Wyatt (bass), N. Harnoncourt (cnd), Vienna Concentus Musicus, Chorus Viennensis, Vienna Boys' Choir [G] Teldec 2-▲ 2292-42502-2 [AAD]
Bach, J.S.:Cant 22, w. P. Esswood (ct), M. van Egmond (b-bar), Leonhardt Consort, King's College Choir Cambridge [G] Teldec 2-▲ 2292-42502-2 [AAD]
Bach, J.S.:Cant 24, w. P. Esswood (ct), M. van Egmond (b-bar), N. Harnoncourt (cnd), Vienna Concentus Musicus, Chorus Viennensis [G] Teldec 2-▲ 2292-42503-2 [AAD]
Bach, J.S.:Cant 25, w. M. van Egmond (b-bar), N. Harnoncourt (cnd), Vienna Concentus Musicus, Chorus Viennensis [G] Teldec 2-▲ 2292-42503-2 [AAD]
Bach, J.S.:Cant 26, w. P. Esswood (ct), S. Nimsgern (b-bar), N. Harnoncourt (cnd), Vienna Concentus Musicus, Chorus Viennensis [G] Teldec 2-▲ 2292-42503-2 [AAD]
Bach, J.S.:Cant 27, w. P. Esswood (ct), S. Nimsgern (b-bar), N. Harnoncourt (cnd), Vienna Concentus Musicus, Chorus Viennensis [G] Teldec 2-▲ 2292-42503-2 [AAD]
Bach, J.S.:Cant 27, w. R. Hansmann (sop), H. Watts (cta), M. Van Egmond (b-bar), J. Jürgens (cnd), Concerto Amsterdam, Monteverdi Choir London Teldec (Das alte Werke) ▲ 93687
Bach, J.S.:Cant 28, w. P. Esswood (ct), S. Nimsgern (b-bar), N. Harnoncourt (cnd), Vienna Concentus Musicus, Chorus Viennensis [G] Teldec 2-▲ 2292-42504-2 [AAD]
Bach, J.S.:Cant 29, w. P. Esswood (ct), M. van Egmond (b-bar), N. Harnoncourt (cnd), Vienna Concentus Musicus, Chorus Viennensis [G] Teldec 2-▲ 2292-42504-2 [AAD]
Bach, J.S.:Cant 30, w. P. Esswood (ct), M. van Egmond (b-bar), N. Harnoncourt (cnd), Vienna Concentus Musicus, Chorus Viennensis [G] Teldec 2-▲ 2292-42504-2 [AAD]
Bach, J.S.:Cant 31, w. S. Nimsgern (b-bar), N. Harnoncourt (cnd), Vienna Concentus Musicus, Chorus Viennensis [G] Teldec 2-▲ 2292-42505-2 [AAD]
Bach, J.S.:Cant 34, w. P. Esswood (ct), S. Nimsgern (b-bar), N. Harnoncourt (cnd), Vienna Concentus Musicus [G] Teldec 2-▲ 2292-42505-2 [AAD]
Bach, J.S.:Cant 36, w. P. Esswood (ct), R. van der Meer (bass), N. Harnoncourt (cnd), Vienna Concentus Musicus, Chorus Viennensis Teldec 2-▲ 2292-42506-2 [AAD]
Bach, J.S.:Cant 37, w. P. Esswood (ct), R. van der Meer (bass), N. Harnoncourt (cnd), Vienna Concentus Musicus, Chorus Viennensis [G] Teldec 2-▲ 2292-42506-2 [AAD]
Bach, J.S.:Cant 38, w. P. Esswood (ct), R. van der Meer (bass), N. Harnoncourt (cnd), Vienna Concentus Musicus, Chorus Viennensis [G] Teldec 2-▲ 2292-42506-2 [AAD]
Bach, J.S.:Cant 41, w. P. Esswood (ct), R. van der Meer (bass), N. Harnoncourt (cnd), Vienna Concentus Musicus, Vienna Concentus Musicus Chorus [G] Teldec 2-▲ 2292-42556-2 [AAD]
Bach, J.S.:Cant 42, w. P. Esswood (ct), R. van der Meer (bass), N. Harnoncourt (cnd), Vienna Concentus Musicus, Vienna Concentus Musicus Chorus [G] Teldec 2-▲ 2292-42556-2 [AAD]
Bach, J.S.:Cant 43, w. P. Esswood (ct), R. van der Meer (bass), N. Harnoncourt (cnd), Vienna Concentus Musicus, Vienna Concentus Musicus Chorus [G] Teldec 2-▲ 2292-42559-2 [AAD]
Bach, J.S.:Cant 44, w. P. Esswood (ct), R. van der Meer (bass), N. Harnoncourt (cnd), Vienna Concentus Musicus, Vienna Concentus Musicus Chorus [G] Teldec 2-▲ 2292-42559-2 [AAD]
Bach, J.S.:Cant 45, w. P. Esswood (ct), R. van der Meer (bass), Leonhardt Consort [G] Teldec 2-▲ 2292-42559-2 [AAD]
Bach, J.S.:Cant 46, w. P. Esswood (ct), R. van der Meer (bass), Leonhardt Consort [G] Teldec 2-▲ 2292-42559-2 [AAD]
Bach, J.S.:Cant 48, w. P. Esswood (ct), Vienna Concentus Musicus, Vienna Concentus Musicus Chorus [G] Teldec 2-▲ 2292-42560-2 ZL [AAD]
Bach, J.S.:Cant 55, w. G. Leonhardt (cnd), Leonhardt Consort, Hanover Boys' Choir [G] Teldec 2-▲ 2292-42422-2 [AAD]
Bach, J.S.:Cant 61, w. S. Kronwitter (trb), R. van der Meer (bass), N. Harnoncourt (cnd), Vienna Concentus Musicus, Vienna Boys' Choir [G] Teldec 2-▲ 2292-42565-2 [AAD]
Bach, J.S.:Cant 62, w. P. Esswood (ct), P. Jelosits (ten), R. van der Meer (bass), N. Harnoncourt (cnd), Vienna Concentus Musicus, Vienna Concentus Musicus Chorus [G] Teldec 2-▲ 2292-42565-2 [AAD]
Bach, J.S.:Cant 63, w. P. Esswood (ct), P. Jelosits (ten), R. van der Meer (bass), N. Harnoncourt (cnd), Vienna Concentus Musicus, Vienna Concentus Musicus Chorus [G] Teldec 2-▲ 2292-42565-2 [AAD]
Bach, J.S.:Cant 69, w. W. Wiedl (trb), P. Esswood (ct), R. van der Meer (bass), N. Harnoncourt (cnd), Vienna Concentus Musicus, Concentus Musicus [G] Teldec 2-▲ 2292-42572-2 [ADD]
Bach, J.S.:Cant 70, w. W. Wiedl (trb), P. Esswood (ct), L. Visser (bass), N. Harnoncourt (cnd), Vienna Concentus Musicus, Tölz Boys' Choir [G] Teldec 2-▲ 2292-42572-2 [ADD]
Bach, J.S.:Cant 71, w. W. Wiedl (trb), P. Esswood (ct), R. van der Meer (bass), N. Harnoncourt (cnd), Vienna Concentus Musicus, Vienna Concentus Musicus Chorus [G] Teldec 2-▲ 2292-42572-2 [ADD]
Bach, J.S.:Cant 76, w. P. Esswood (ct), R. van der Meer (bass), N. Harnoncourt (cnd), Vienna Concentus Musicus, Vienna Concentus Musicus Chorus [G] Teldec 2-▲ 2292-42576-2 [ADD]
Bach, J.S.:Cant 78, w. P. Esswood (ct), R. van der Meer (bass), N. Harnoncourt (cnd), Vienna Concentus Musicus, Vienna Concentus Musicus Chorus [G] Teldec 2-▲ 2292-42576-2 [ADD]
Bach, J.S.:Cant 80, w. W. Wiedl (trb), P. Esswood (ct), R. van der Meer (bass), N. Harnoncourt (cnd), Vienna Concentus Musicus [G] Teldec 2-▲ 2292-42577-2 [ADD]
Bach, J.S.:Cant 81, w. P. Esswood (ct), R. van der Meer (bass), N. Harnoncourt (cnd), Vienna Concentus Musicus [G] Teldec 2-▲ 2292-42577-2 [ADD]
Bach, J.S.:Cant 83, w. M. van Egmond (b-bar), N. Harnoncourt (cnd), Vienna Concentus Musicus [G] Teldec 2-▲ 2292-42577-2 [ADD]
Bach, J.S.:Cant 85, w. W. Wiedl (trb), P. Esswood (ct), N. Harnoncourt (cnd), Vienna Concentus Musicus, Vienna Concentus Musicus Chorus [G] Teldec 2-▲ 2292-42578-2 [ADD]
Bach, J.S.:Cant 86, w. W. Wiedl (trb), P. Esswood (ct), N. Harnoncourt (cnd), Vienna Concentus Musicus, Vienna Concentus Musicus Chorus [G] Teldec 2-▲ 2292-42578-2 [ADD]
Bach, J.S.:Cant 87, w. P. Esswood (ct), N. Harnoncourt (cnd), Vienna Concentus Musicus, Vienna Concentus Musicus Chorus [G] Teldec 2-▲ 2292-42578-2 [ADD]
Bach, J.S.:Cant 88, w. M. Klein (trb), P. Esswood (ct), G. Leonhardt (cnd), Leonhardt Consort [G] Teldec 2-▲ 2292-42578-2 [ADD]
Bach, J.S.:Cant 90, w. P. Esswood (ct), M. van Egmond (b-bar), Leonhardt Consort, Ghent Collegium Vocale [G] Teldec 2-▲ 2292-42578-2 [ADD]
Bach, J.S.:Cant 95, w. W. Wiedl (trb), P. Huttenlocher (bar), N. Harnoncourt (cnd), Vienna Concentus Musicus [G] Teldec ▲ 2292-42583-2 [ADD]
Bach, J.S.:Cant 96, w. W. Wiedl (trb), P. Esswood (ct), P. Huttenlocher (bar), N. Harnoncourt (cnd), Vienna Concentus Musicus [G] Teldec ▲ 2292-42583-2 [ADD]
Bach, J.S.:Cant 97, w. W. Wiedl (trb), P. Esswood (ct), P. Huttenlocher (bar), N. Harnoncourt (cnd), Vienna Concentus Musicus [G] Teldec ▲ 2292-42583-2 [ADD]
Bach, J.S.:Cant 98, w. C. Lengert (trb), P. Esswood (ct), M. van Egmond (b-bar), Leonhardt Consort [G] Teldec ▲ 2292-42583-2 [ADD]
Bach, J.S.:Cant 99, w. W. Wiedl (trb), P. Esswood (ct), P. Huttenlocher (bar), N. Harnoncourt (cnd), Vienna Concentus Musicus [G] Teldec ▲ 2292-42584-2
Bach, J.S.:Cant 100, w. D. Bratschke (trb), P. Esswood (ct), M. van Egmond (b-bar), G. Leonhardt (cnd), Leonhardt Consort [G] Teldec ▲ 2292-42584-2
Bach, J.S.:Cant 101, w. W. Wiedl (trb), P. Esswood (ct), P. Huttenlocher (bar), N. Harnoncourt (cnd), Vienna Concentus Musicus [G] Teldec ▲ 2292-42584-2
Bach, J.S.:Cant 102, w. E. Randová (mez), W. Schöne (bass), H. Rilling (cnd), Stuttgart Bach Collegium, Gächinger Kantorei Hänssler Classic ▲ 98.809 [AAD]
Bach, J.S.:Cant 102, w. W. Wiedl (trb), P. Esswood (ct), P. Huttenlocher (bar), N. Harnoncourt (cnd), Vienna Concentus Musicus [G] Teldec ▲ 2292-42584-2

1150 ▲ = CD ♦ = Enhanced CD Δ = MD ■ = Cassette Tape ▯ = DCC

Equiluz, Kurt (ten) (cont.)

Bach, J.S.:Cant 103, w. P. Esswood (ct), P. Huttenlocher (bar), G. Leonhardt (cnd), Leonhardt Consort [G] Teldec ▲ 2292-42602-2

Bach, J.S.:Cant 104, w. P. Huttenlocher (bar), N. Harnoncourt (cnd), Vienna Concentus Musicus, Tölz Boys' Choir [G] Teldec ▲ 2292-42602-2

Bach, J.S.:Cant 105, w. W. Wiedl (trb), P. Esswood (ct), M. van Egmond (b-bar), N. Harnoncourt (cnd), Vienna Concentus Musicus, Tölz Boys' Choir [G] Teldec ▲ 2292-42602-2

Bach, J.S.:Cant 107, w. M. Klein (trb), M. van Egmond (b-bar), Leonhardt Consort, Collegium Vocale [G] Teldec 2-▲ 2292-42603-2

Bach, J.S.:Cant 108, w. H. Donath (sop), M. Höffgen (mez), H.-F. Kunz (bass), H. Rilling (cnd), Stuttgart Bach Collegium, Gächinger Kantorei [G] *(rec 1980-81)* Hänssler Classic ▲ 98.884 [AAD]

Bach, J.S.:Cant 108, w. P. Esswood (ct), M. van Egmond (b-bar), N. Harnoncourt (cnd), Vienna Concentus Musicus [G] Teldec 2-▲ 2292-42603-2

Bach, J.S.:Cant 109, w. G. Schreckenbach (cta), H. Rilling (cnd), Stuttgart Bach Collegium, Gächinger Kantorei [G] *(rec Feb 1981)* Hänssler Classic ▲ 98.818 [AAD]

Bach, J.S.:Cant 109, w. P. Esswood (ct), N. Harnoncourt (cnd), Vienna Concentus Musicus, Tölz Boys' Choir [G] Teldec 2-▲ 2292-42603-2

Bach, J.S.:Cant 110, w. W. Wiedl (trb), S. Frangoulis (trb), P. Esswood (ct), Stumpf (sgr), M. van Egmond (b-bar), S. Lorenz (b-bar), N. Harnoncourt (cnd), Vienna Concentus Musicus, Tölz Boys' Choir [G] Teldec 2-▲ 2292-42603-2

Bach, J.S.:Cant 111, w. P. Esswood (ct), K. Huber (ten), M. van Egmond (b-bar), N. Harnoncourt (cnd), Vienna Concentus Musicus [G] Teldec 2-▲ 2292-42606-2

Bach, J.S.:Cant 112, w. P. Esswood (ct), K. Huber (ten), M. van Egmond (b-bar), N. Harnoncourt (cnd), Vienna Concentus Musicus [G] Teldec 2-▲ 2292-42606-2

Bach, J.S.:Cant 113, w. S. Hennig (trb), D. Bratschke (trb), R. Jacobs (ct), M. van Egmond (b-bar), Leonhardt Consort, Collegium Vocale, Hanover Boys' Chorus [G] Teldec 2-▲ 2292-42606-2

Bach, J.S.:Cant 114, w. S. Hennig (trb), R. Jacobs (ct), M. van Egmond (b-bar), Leonhardt Consort, Collegium Vocale, Hanover Boys' Chorus [G] Teldec 2-▲ 2292-42606-2

Bach, J.S.:Cant 114, w. G. Schnaut (mez), J. Hamari (cta), W. Schöne (bass), H. Rilling (cnd), Stuttgart Bach Collegium, Frankfurt Kantorei, Gächinger Kantorei [G] *(rec 1974)* Hänssler Classic ▲ 98.814 [AAD]

Bach, J.S.:Cant 125, w. M. Höffgen (mez), W. Schöne (bass), H. Rilling (cnd), Bach Ensemble [G] *(rec 1973)* Hänssler Classic ▲ 98.876 [AAD]

Bach, J.S.:Cant 132, w. A. Augér (sop), H. Watts (cta), W. Schöne (bass), H. Rilling (cnd), Stuttgart Bach Collegium, Gächinger Kantorei [G] *(rec Sept 1976 & Jan & Apr 197)* Hänssler Classic ▲ 98.822 [AAD]

Bach, J.S.:Cant 136, w. H. Watts (cta), N. Tüller (bass), H. Rilling (cnd), Stuttgart Bach Collegium, Gächinger Kantorei Hänssler Classic ▲ 98.806 [AAD]

Bach, J.S.:Cant 140, w. L. Dutoit (trb), H. Braun (bar), F. Prohaska (cnd), Vienna State Opera Orch, Vienna State Opera Chorus [G] *(rec 1959)* Vanguard Classics ("The Bach Guild" series) ▲ OVC 2001 [ADD]

Bach, J.S.:Cant 148, w. H. Watts (cta), H. Rilling (cnd), Stuttgart Bach Collegium, Gächinger Kantorei [G] *(rec 1977)* Hänssler Classic ▲ 98.814 [AAD]

Bach, J.S.:Cant 153, w. S. Rampf (ct), T. Hampson (b-bar), N. Harnoncourt (cnd), Vienna Concentus Musicus, Tölz Boys' Choir [G] Teldec 2-▲ 2292-42632-2 [DDD]

Bach, J.S.:Cant 154, w. P. Esswood (ct), T. Hampson (b-bar), N. Harnoncourt (cnd), Vienna Concentus Musicus, Tölz Boys' Choir [G] Teldec 2-▲ 2292-42632-2 [DDD]

Bach, J.S.:Cant 155, w. A. Bergius (trb), P. Esswood (ct), T. Hampson (b-bar), N. Harnoncourt (cnd), Vienna Concentus Musicus, Tölz Boys' Choir [G] Teldec 2-▲ 2292-42632-2 [DDD]

Bach, J.S.:Cant 156, w. P. Esswood (ct), T. Hampson (b-bar), N. Harnoncourt (cnd), Vienna Concentus Musicus, Tölz Boys' Choir [G] Teldec 2-▲ 2292-42632-2 [DDD]

Bach, J.S.:Cant 156, w. H. Laurich (cta), W. Schöne (bass), H. Rilling (cnd), Bach Ensemble [G] *(rec 1973)* Hänssler Classic ▲ 98.875 [AAD]

Bach, J.S.:Cant 158, w. R. Hansmann (sop), H. Watts (cta), M. Van Egmond (b-bar), J. Jürgens (cnd), Concerto Amsterdam, Monteverdi Choir London Teldec ("Das alte Werke" series) ▲ 93687

Bach, J.S.:Cant 162, w. A. Augér (sop), A. Rogers (mez), W. Schöne (bass), H. Rilling (cnd), Stuttgart Bach Collegium, Frankfurt Kantorei [G] *(rec Dec 1975 & Mar 1976)* Hänssler Classic ▲ 98.816 [AAD]

Bach, J.S.:Cant 178, w. G. Schreckenbach (cta), A. Baldin (ten), W. Schöne (bass), H. Rilling (cnd), Stuttgart Bach Collegium, Gächinger Kantorei Hänssler Classic ▲ 98.806 [AAD]

Bach, J.S.:Cant 179, w. A. Augér (sop), W. Schöne (bass), H. Rilling (cnd), Stuttgart Bach Collegium, Gächinger Kantorei Hänssler Classic ▲ 98.808 [AAD]

Bach, J.S.:Cant 181, w. A. Augér (sop), G. Schnaut (mez), G. Schreckenbach (cta), N. Tütler (bass), H. Rilling (cnd), Stuttgart Bach Collegium, Gächinger Kantorei [G] *(rec 1981)* Hänssler Classic ▲ 98.878 [AAD]

Bach, J.S.:Cant 185, w. H. Wittek (trb), P. Esswood (ct), T. Hampson (b-bar), N. Harnoncourt (cnd), Vienna Concentus Musicus, Tölz Boys' Choir [G] Teldec 2-▲ 2292-44179-2 [DDD]

Bach, J.S.:Cant 186, w. A. Augér (sop), H. Watts (cta), H. Rilling (cnd), Stuttgart Bach Collegium, Gächinger Kantorei Hänssler Classic ▲ 98.805 [AAD]

Bach, J.S.:Cant 190, w. H. Watts (cta), N. Tüller (b-bar), H. Rilling (cnd), Stuttgart Bach Collegium, Gächinger Kantorei [G] Hänssler Classic ▲ 98.870 [AAD]

Bach, J.S.:Cant 198, w. R. Hansmann (sop), H. Watts (cta), M. Van Egmond (b-bar), J. Jürgens (cnd), Concerto Amsterdam, Monteverdi Choir London Teldec (Das alte Werke) ▲ 93687

Bach, J.S.:Cant 208, "Hunting Cant", w. A. M. Blasi (sop), J. P. Kenny (alt), R. Holl (bass), N. Harnoncourt (cnd), Vienna Concentus Musicus, Arnold Schoenberg Choir [G] Teldec ▲ 2292-46151-2 [DDD]

Bach, J.S.:Christmas Oratorio, w. P. Esswood (ct), S. Nimsgern (b-bar), N. Harnoncourt (cnd), Vienna Concentus Musicus Teldec 2-▲ 9031-77610-2

Bach, J.S.:Christmas Oratorio, w. P. Esswood (ct), S. Nimsgern (b-bar), N. Harnoncourt (cnd), Vienna Concentus Musicus, Vienna Boys' Choir [G] Teldec ▲ 9031-74893-2

Bach, J.S.:Christmas Oratorio, w. B. Schlick (sop), C. Watkinson (cta), M. Brodard (bar), M. Corboz (cnd), Lausanne CO Erato ▲ 2292-45865-2

Bach, J.S.:Mass in b, BWV 232, w. A. M. Blasi (sop), D. Ziegler (mez), J. Rappé (cta), R. Holl (bass), N. Harnoncourt (cnd), Vienna Concentus Musicus, Arnold Schoenberg Choir [L] Teldec 2-▲ 2292-42676-2 [DDD]

Bach, J.S.:St. John Passion, w. M. Van Egmond (b-bar), J. Villisech (bass), N. Harnoncourt (cnd), Vienna Concentus Musicus, Vienna Boys' Choir soloists Teldec ▲ 2292-42492-2

Bach, J.S.:St. John Passion, w. F. Palmer (sop), B. Finnilä (cta), W. Krenn (ten), P. Huttenlocher (bar), R. van der Meer (bass), M. Corboz (cnd), Lausanne CO, Lausanne Vocal Ensemble Erato 2-▲ 2292-45406-2 FD

Bach, J.S.:St. Luke Passion, w. Christiane Sorell (sop), Maura Moreira (alt), Franz Wimer (bass), Josef Nebois (org), G. Barati (cnd), Vienna State Opera Orch, Akademie Chamber Choir Soloists Sarx 2-▲ SRX 2026 [ADD]

Bach, J.S.:St. Matthew Passion, w. J. Bowman (ct), P. Esswood (ct), T. Sutcliffe (ct), M. van Egmond (b-bar), N. Harnoncourt (cnd), Vienna Concentus Musicus [G] Teldec 3-▲ 2292-42509-2 [AAD]

Bach, J.S.:St. Matthew Passion, w. M. Marshall (sop), C. Watkinson (cta), G. Faulstisch (bar), P. Huttenlocher (bar), R. Johnson (bar), M. Corboz (cnd), Lausanne CO, Lausanne Vocal Ensemble Erato 3-▲ 2292-45375-2 GX

Beethoven, L. van:Fidelio, w. Birgit Nilsson (sop—Leonore), Graziella Sciutti (sop—Marzelline), Kurt Equiluz (ten—Erster Gefangener), Donald Grobe (ten—Jacquino), James McCracken (ten—Florestan), Tom Krause (bar—Don Pizarro), Hermann Prey (bar—Don Fernando), Kurt Böhme (bass—Rocco), Günther Adam (sgr—Zweiter Gefangener), L. Maazel (cnd), Vienna PO, Vienna State Opera Concert Association Chorus *(rec Sofiensaal, Vienna, Mar 1964)* London 2-▲ 448104-2 [ADD]

Benatzky, R.:Im weissen Rössl (sels), w. F. Loor (sop), H. Brauner (cta), K. Terkal (ten), F. Bauer-Theussl (cnd), Vienna Volksoper Orch, Vienna Volksoper Chorus [G] Koch Präsent ▲ CD 399225 [AAD]

Golden Operetta, Vol. 2:Operetta Melodies, w. F. Bauer-Theussl (cnd), Vienna Volksoper Orch, Vienna Volksoper Chorus, Renate Holm (sop), Lotte Rysanek (sop), Dagmar Hermann (mez), Horst Winter (ten), et al. Koch Präsent ▲ 399 224 [AAD]

Haydn, J.:Mass 6, "Nikolai-messe", "6/4-Takt-Messe", w. Elisabeth Thoman (sop), Rose Bahl (cta), G. Barati (cnd), Vienna State Opera Orch, Vienna Academy Chamber Choir *(rec 1964)* Tuxedo ▲ TUXCD 1055 [ADD]

Haydn, J.:Mass 7, "Kleine Orgelmesse", w. Eiko Katonosaka (sop), Elfriede Jahn (alt), Leo Heppe (bass), H. Gillesberger (cnd), Vienna State Opera Orch, Vienna Chamber Choir *(rec 1965)* Tuxedo ▲ TUXCD 1025

Haydn, J.:Mass 14, "Harmoniemesse", w. Christiane Sorell (sop), Elisabeth Thoman (sop), Rose Bahl (cta), Maura Moreira (cta), Gerhard Eder (bass), P. Wimburger (bass), G. Barati (cnd), Vienna State Opera Orch, Vienna Academy Chamber Choir *(rec 1964)* Tuxedo ▲ TUXCD 1055 [ADD]

Krenek, E.:Jonny spielt auf, w. E. Lear (sop—Anita), L. Popp (sop—Yvonne), W. Blankenship (ten—Max), K. Equiluz (ten—Station Announcer), L. Heppe (ten—Manager), T. Stewart (bar—Daniello), G. Feldhof (bass—Jonny), H. Hollreiser (cnd), Vienna State Opera Orch [G] Vanguard Classics ▲ OVC 8048 [ADD]

Lehár, F.:Paganini (sels), w. E. Liebesberg (sop), E. Mechera (sop), Rudolf Christ (ten), F. Bauer-Theussl (cnd), Vienna Volksoper Orch, Vienna Volksoper Chorus [G] Koch Präsent ▲ CD 399226 [AAD]

Monteverdi, C.:Combattimento, w. Joseph Schmidt (ten), Werner Hollweg (ten), N. Harnoncourt (cnd), Vienna Concentus Musicus [I] Teldec ▲ 2292-43036-2

Monteverdi, C.:Lamento della ninfa, w. Schmidt (ten), W. Hollweg (ten), N. Harnoncourt (cnd), Vienna Concentus Musicus [I] Teldec ▲ 2292-43036-2

Monteverdi, C.:Orfeo, w. R. Hansmann (sop), C. Berberian (sop), L. Kozma (ten), M. Van Egmond (bass), N. Harnoncourt (cnd), Vienna Concentus Musicus, Capella Antiqua München Teldec 2-▲ 42494-2

Monteverdi, C.:Ritorno d'Ulisse, w. P. Esswood (ct), M. Dickie (ten), N. Rogers (ten), M. Van Egmond (bass), N. Harnoncourt (cnd), Vienna Concentus Musicus Teldec ▲ 42496-2

Monteverdi, C.:Vespro della Beata Vergine, w. L. Marshall (sop), F. Palmer (sop), P. Langridge (ten), T. Hampson (bar), A. Korn (bass), N. Harnoncourt (cnd), Vienna Concentus Musicus, Hamburg Monteverdi Chorus, Vienna Boys' Chorus [L] Teldec 2-▲ 2292-42671-2

Monteverdi, C.:Vespro della Beata Vergine, w. M. Marshall (sop), F. Palmer (sop), P. Langridge (ten), T. Hampson (bar), A. Korn (bass), N. Harnoncourt (cnd), Vienna Concentus Musicus, Hamburg Monteverdi Chorus, Vienna Boys' Chorus Teldec 2-▲ 92629-2

Mozart, W.A.:Masonic Music, w. K. Rapf (pno/org), P. Maag (cnd), Vienna Volksoper Orch, Vienna Volksoper Chorus—Adagios, K.410 & 411; Adagio & Fugue, K.546; Adagio & Rondo, K.617; Anhang zum Schluss der Freimaurerloge, K.623a; Cants, K.429, 471, 619 & 623; Graduale, K.273; Lieder, K.148, 468, 483 & 484; Maurerische; Motet, K.618; Psalm 129, K.93 *(rec 1966)* Vox Box 2-▲ CDX 5055 [ADD]

Mozart, W.A.:Missa, K.427, w. K. Láki (sop), Z. Dénes (sop), R. Holl (bass), N. Harnoncourt (cnd), Vienna Concentus Musicus, Vienna State Opera Chorus [L] Teldec ▲ 2292-43070-2

Mozart, W.A.:Requiem, w. Rachel Yakar (sop), Ortrun Wenkel (cta), Robert Holl (bass), N. Harnoncourt (cnd), Vienna Concentus Musicus, Vienna State Opera Chorus [L] Teldec ▲ 2292-42911-2

Schubert, Franz:Mass 1, w. Laurence Dutoit (sop), Rose Bahl (alt), Kunikazu Ohashi (bass), Xaver Mayer (org), G. Barati (cnd), Vienna State Opera Orch, Vienna Academy Chamber Choir *(rec 1960)* Tuxedo ▲ TUXCD 1040 [ADD]

Schubert, Franz:Mass 4, w. Laurence Dutoit (sop), Rose Bahl (alt), Kunikazu Ohashi (bass), Xaver Mayer (org), G. Barati (cnd), Vienna State Opera Orch, Vienna Academy Chamber Choir *(rec 1960)* Tuxedo ▲ TUXCD 1040 [ADD]

Telemann, G.P.:Der Tag des Gerichts, w. R. Alexander (sop), M. Van Egmond (bass), N. Harnoncourt (cnd), Vienna Concentus Musicus, Monteverdi Choir Hamburg Teldec 2-▲ 77621-2

Telemann, G.P.:Ino, w. R. Alexander (sop), M. Van Egmond (bar), N. Harnoncourt (cnd), Vienna Concentus Musicus, Monteverdi Choir London Teldec 2-▲ 9031-77621-2

Wagner, R.:Das Liebesverbot, w. H. Zadek (cta), L. Sorell (mez), A. Dermota (ten), L. Welter (bar), Imdahl (sgr), R. Heger (cnd), Austrian RSO, Austrian Radio Chorus *(rec live, Vienna, 1962)* Melodram 2-▲ MEL 27052 [AAD]

Equiluz, Manfred (sgr)

Míca, F.A.:L'origine di Jaromeriz in Moravia, w. Geraldine Cassidy (sgr), Geraldine Geister (sgr), Michael Nowak (sgr), Le Monde Classique [Cz] Supraphon 2-▲ SUP 112192 [DDD]

Erassova, Natalia (sop)

Rachmaninoff, S.:Aleko, w. Galina Borissova (cta), Vitaly Tarastchenko (ten), Vladimir Matorin (bass), Viatcheslav Potchapski (bass), A. Tchistiakov (cnd), Bolshoi Theater Orch, Russian State Choir Russian Season 3-▲ CMX 388053

Rimsky-Korsakov, N.:A May Night, w. Maria Lapina (sop), Elena Okolycheva (cta), Alexander Arkhipov (ten), Vitaly Tarastchenko (ten), Piotr Glouboky (bass), Viatcheslav Potchapski (bass), A. Tchistiakov (cnd), Bolshoi Theater Orch, Russian State Choir Russian Season 4-▲ CMX 388054

Tchaikovsky, P.:The Snow Maiden, w. A. Tchistiakov (cnd), Russian State Choir Russian Season (Russian Season) ▲ LDC 288090

Erato, M. (sop)

Verdi, G.:Un ballo in maschera, w. M. Curtis Verna (sop—Amelia), M. Erato (sop—Oscar), P. Tassinari (cta—Ulrica), F. Tagliavini (ten—Riccardo), G. Valdengo (bar—Renato), A. Albertini (bar—Silvano), M. Stefanoni (bass—Samuel), V. Susca (bass—Tom), A. Questa (cnd), Turin RAI SO, Turin RAI Chorus *(rec 1951)* Cetra Classic 2-▲ CDO 13 [AAD]

Erb, Karl (nar)

Orff, C.:Der Mond—Ein kleines Welttheater, w. Paul Kuen (ten—Lad 3), Josef Knapp (bar—Lad 2), Benno Kusche (bar—Lad 1), Georg Hann (bass—St. Peter), Georg Wieter (bass—Lad 4), Rudolf Wünzer (bass—The Farmer), Karl Hanft (sgr—Innkeeper), Willy Rösner (sgr—The Major), R. Alberth (cnd), Bavarian RSO, Bavarian Radio Chorus *(rec Studio 1, Bavarian Radio, Jan. 19-20, 1950)* Calig ▲ CAL 50948 (m) [ADD]

Erb, Karl (ten)

Bach, J.S.:St. Matthew Passion, w. T. Lemnitz (sop), F. Beckmann (alt), G. Hüsch (bar), S. Schulze (bass), G. Ramin (cnd), Leipzig Gewandhaus Orch, St. Thomas Choir *(abridged performance)* [G] *(rec Mar 1941)* Calig 2-▲ CAL 50 859/60 (m) [AAD]

Karl Erb, w. Erb, Karl (ten) *(rec 1911-14)* Preiser ("Lebendige Vergangenheit" series) ▲ PRE 89095 [AAD]

Lieder Album *(rec between 1934 & 1939)* Preiser 2-▲ PRE 89208 [AAD]

Wolf, H.:Der Corregidor, w. M. Teschemacher (sop), M. Fuchs (sop), J. Herrmann (bar), K. Böhme (b-bar), G. Hann (bass), G. Frick (bass), K. Elmendorff (cnd), Saxon State Orch, Saxon State Chorus *(rec 1944)* Preiser 2-▲ PRE 90182 [AAD]

Erdl, Florian (sgr)

Haydn, J.:Applausus:Jubilaeum virtutis Palatium, w. Gert Füssi (sgr), Christian Graf (sgr), Helmut Wildhaber (ten), Georg Tichy (bass), P. Angerer (cnd), Vienna Concilium Musicum [period instrs] Koch Schwann ▲ SCH 314092

Erdmann, Hildegard (sop)

Haydn, M.:Missa Sancti Aloysii, w. Pieweck (sgr), Wegrzyn (cnd), Hanover Chamber Academy Ars Musici ▲ 1113

Erickson, Kaaren (sop)

Dvořák, A.:Stabat Mater, w. C. Carlson (mez), J. Aler (ten), J. Cheek (bass), Z. Macal (cnd), New Jersey SO, J. Flummerfeldt (cnd), Westminster Sym Choir *(rec Feb. 8-11, 1994)* Delos 2-▲ DE 3161 [DDD]

Getty, G.:The White Election, w. A. Guzelimian (pno) [E] Delos ▲ DCD 3057 [DDD]

Gluck, C.W.:Le Cinesi, w. M. Schiml (sop), A. Milcheva (mez), Moser (sgr), L. Gardelli (cnd), Munich RSO, Munich Radio Chorus [I] Orfeo ▲ 178891 [DDD] ■ MC 178891 (D)

Handel, G.F.:Messiah, w. Sylvia McNair (sop), Alfreda Hodgson (cta), Jon Humphrey (ten), Richard Stilwell (bar), R. Shaw (cnd), Atlanta SO, Atlanta Sym Chorus [E] Telarc ▲ CD 80103 [DDD]; ■ CS 30103 (D)

Handel, G.F.:Messiah, w. Sylvia McNair (sop), Alfreda Hodgson (cta), Jon Humphrey (ten), Richard Stilwell (bar), R. Shaw (cnd), Atlanta SO, Atlanta Sym Chorus [E] Telarc 2-▲ CD 80093-2 [DDD]

Reverie:Romantic Music for Quiet Times, w. N. Rosen (vc), Doris Stevenson (pno), Arturo Delmoni (vn) John Marks Records ▲ JMR 10

Ericsdotter, Siw (sop)

Strauss, R.:Salome, w. Christel Goltz (sop), Helmut Melchert (ten), Ernst Gutstein (bar), O. Suitner (cnd), Dresden Staatskapelle *(rec 1963)* Berlin Classics 2-▲ BER 9101 [ADD]

Ericsdotter, Siw (sop) (cont.)
Wagner, R.:Der Ring des Nibelungen, w. Liselotte Becker-Egner (sop—Woglinde/Ortlinde/Wellgunde), Angelika Berger (sop—Wellgunde/Waltraute), Siw Ericsdotter (sop—Norn 3), Heidemaria Ferch (sop—Freia/Gerhilde), Bella Jasper (sop—Helmwige/Waldvogel/Woglinde), Ditha Sommer (sop—Sieglinde/Gutrune), Ursula Boese (mez—Erda), Ruth Hesse (mez—Fricka), Nadezda Kniplová (mez—Brünnhilde), Margit Kobeck (mez—Schwertleite/Norn 2), Hilde Rosner (mez—Flosshilde/Siegrunde), Erica Schubert (mez—Grimgerde/Flosshilde), Ingrid Göritz (cta—Rossweisse/Norn 1), Herbert Doussant (ten—Froh), Herold Kraus (ten—Mime), Gerald McKee (ten—Siegmund/Siegfried), Fritz Uhl (ten—Loge), Rudolf Knoll (bar—Gunther/Donner), Rolf Polke (bass-bar—Wotan/Wanderer), Rolf Kühne (bass—Alberich), Takao Okamura (bass—Fafner), Otto von Rohr (bass—Hagen/Fasolt/Hunding), H. Swarowsky (cnd), Czech PO, Prague National Theater Orch *(rec June 3 & 5, July 26–31, A)* Weltbild Classics 14–▲ 703769 [ADD]

Ericson, Barbro (mez)
Ligeti, G.:Requiem, w. Lillana Poli (sop), M. Gielen (cnd), Hessian RSO, Hesse Radio Chorus [L] Wergo ▲ WER 60045–50 [ADD]
Verdi, G.:Rigoletto, w. M. Hallin (sop), B. Nordin (sop), K. Meyer (mez), Kjellgren (mez), N. Gedda (ten), O. Sivall (ten), H. Hasslo (bar), I. Wixell (bar), B. Alstergård (bar), A. Tyrén (bass), S. Ehrling (cnd), Stockholm Royal Opera House Orch, Stockholm Royal Opera Chorus *(rec live Jan. 18, 1959)* BIS ▲ CD 296 [AAD]

Eriksen, Randi (alt)
Braein, E.F.:Anne Pedersdotter, w. K. Ekeberg (sop—Anne Pedersdotter), V. Hanssen (mez—Merete Beyer), R. Eriksen (alt—Herlofs-Marte), I. M. Brekke (alt—Bente), K. M. Sandve (ten—Martin Beyer), C. Ehrstedt (ten—Master Olaus), A. Helleland (ten—David), T. Gilje (ten—Jørund), S. A. Thorsen (bar—Master Johannes), S. Carlsen (bass—Absalon Pedersøn Beyer), T. Stensvold (bass—Master Laurentius), G. Oskarsson (bass—Jens Schelderup), P. Andersson (cnd), Norwegian National Opera Orch, Norwegian National Opera Chorus Simax 2–▲ PSC 3121

Ernman, Malena (alt)
Schnittke, A.:Sym 2, w. Mikael Bellini (ct), Göran Eliasson (ten), Torkel Borelius (bass), L. Segerstam (cnd), Royal Stockholm PO, Anders Eby (cnd), Mikaeli Chamber Choir *(rec Stockholm Concert Hall, Sweden, Feb. 24–25, 1994)* BIS ▲ CD 667 [DDD]

Ernster, Deszö (bass)
Wagner, R.:Lohengrin, w. H. Traubel (sop—Elsa), A. Varnay (sop—Ortrud), L. Melchior (ten—Lohengrin), F. Guerrera (bar—Herald), H. Janssen (bar—Telramund), D. Ernster (bass—King Heinrich), F. Stiedry (cnd), Metropolitan Opera Orch, New York Metropolitan Opera Chorus *(rec live Jan. 6, 1950)* Danacord 3–▲ DACOCD 322/24 [AAD]
Wagner, R.:Tannhäuser, w. Gré Brouwestijn (sop), Murray Dickie (ten), Karl Liebl (ten), Eberhard Waechter (bar), Alois Pernerstorfer (b-bar), Walter Brunelli (sgr), Peter Harrower (sgr), Rosl Schweiger (sgr), Herta Wilfert (sgr), A. Rodzinski (cnd), Rome RAI Radio–TV SO, Rome RAI Chorus Stradivarius 3–▲ STV 12318

Ernster, Judd (bass)
Rorem, N.:Miss Julie, w. Theodora Fried (sgr—Miss Julie), Heather Sarris (sgr—Christine, the cook), Laurelyn Watson (sgr—Young Girl), David Blackburn (sgr—Mr. Niels), Mark Mulligan (sgr—Young Boy), Philip Torre (sgr—John, the valet), D. Gilbert (cnd), Manhattan School of Music Opera Orch, Manhattan School of Music Opera Chorus Newport Classic 2–▲ NPT 85605 [DDD]

Erzsébet (sgr)
Kálmán, I.:Die Csárdásfürstin (sels), w. György (sgr), Hanna (sgr), Róbert (sgr), Tamás (cnd), Hungarian Radio–TV SO, Hungarian Radio–TV Chorus Hungaroton ▲ HCD 16780 [AAD]

Escalaïs, Léon (ten)
Verdi, G.:Il trovatore (sels), w. J. Biel (ten), F. Tamagno (ten), M. Gilion (ten), E. Caruso (ten), A. Paoli (ten), G. Zenatello (ten), J. Sembach (ten), L. Slezak (ten), F. Constantino (ten), G. Martinelli (ten), B. De Muro (ten), N. Fusati (ten), N. Piccaluga (ten), G. Lauri–Volpi (ten), A. Pertile (ten), E. Bergamaschi (ten), R. Tauber (ten), J. O'Sullivan (ten), H. Roswaenge (ten), G. Taccani (ten), V. Lois (ten), H. Lazaro (ten), A. Lindi (ten), A. Cortis (ten), F. Merli (ten), F. Völker (ten), J. Kiepura (ten), J. Schmidt (ten), J. Bjoerling (ten), B. Gigli (ten), A. Salvarezza (ten), J. Soler (ten), M. Filippeschi (ten)—34 performances of the Act III tenor aria "Di quella pira!," *(rec from 1903–1956)* Bongiovanni ▲ GB 1051 [AAD]

Eschert, Hasso (ten)
Verdi, G.:Macbeth, w. Astrid Varnay (sop—Lady Macbeth), Trude Roesler (mez—Lady-in-waiting), Hasso Eschert (ten—Malcolm), Walter Geisler (ten—Macduff), Joseph Metternich (bar—Macbeth), Ludwig Weber (bass—Banquo), R. Kraus (cnd), West German Orch, West German Chorus *(rec Cologne, 1954)* Myto 2–▲ 952128

Eschrig, Ralph (ten)
Mozart, W.A.:Bastien und Bastienne, w. D. Schellenberger (sop), R. Pape (bass), M. Pommer (cnd), Leipzig RSO, Leipzig Radio Chorus Berlin Classics 2–▲ BER 1010 [DDD]

Escott, Harry (trb)
Fauré, G.:Requiem, w. David Wilson–Johnson (bar), D. Hill (cnd), City of London Sinfonia, Westminster Cathedral Choir IMP ▲ PCD 2015

Escribano, M. T. (sop)
Debussy, C.:Chansons de Bilitis (recitation), w. F. Cerha (cnd), Die Reihe Ensemble Allegretto ▲ ACD 8159 [ADD] ▮ ACS 8159

Esham, Faith (sop)
Bizet, G.:Carmen, w. J. Migenes–Johnson (sop), P. Domingo (ten), R. Raimondi (bass), L. Maazel (cnd), French National Orch [F] Erato ▲ 2292–45209–2 AW [DDD] ▮ 2292–45209–4 AG (D)
Bizet, G.:Carmen, w. J. Migenes–Johnson (sop), P. Domingo (ten), R. Raimondi (bass), L. Maazel (cnd), French National Orch, French Radio Chorus [F] Erato 3–▲ 2292–45207–2 ZB [DDD]
Danielpour, R.:Sym 3, "Journey Without Distance", w. G. Schwarz (cnd), Seattle SO Delos ▲ DE 3118 [DDD]

Espaillat, Ulises (ten)
Guastavino, C.:Songs, w. P. Zinger (pno)—Desde que te conocí; Viniendo de Chilecito; En los surcos del amor; Mi garganta; Cuando acaba de llover; Préstame tu pañuelito; Ya me voy a retirar; Las puertas de la mañana; Piececitos; Cita; Se equivocó la paloma; Jardin de amores; A volar!; Nana del niño malo; La novia; Geografía Física; Alpuente de la golodrina!; Elegía; La rosa y el sauce; Pueblito, mi pueblo *(rec May 1992)* New Albion ▲ NA 058

Esparza, Elfego (sgr)
Donizetti, G.:Il giovedì grasso, w. J. Gomez (sop), J. Hughes (mez), J. Peters (mez), U. Benelli (bar), B. Donlan (bar), F. Davià (bass), M. Williams (sgr), D. Atherton (cnd), Eireann Radio–TV SO [I] *(rec live, 1970)* Memories ▲ HR 4482 [ADD]
Donizetti, G.:Il giovedì grasso, w. J. Gomez (sop), J. Peters (mez), J. Hughes (mez), U. Benelli (bar), B. Donlan (bar), F. Davià (bass), D. Atherton (cnd), Eireann Radio–TV SO [I] *(rec live, 1970)* Foyer ▲ FOY 2036 [AAD]

Esposito, Andrée (sop)
Chausson, E.:Chanson perpétuelle, w. J.–P. Jacquillat (cnd), Lamoureux Concerts Orch EMI Classics ▲ CDM 64365
Satie, E.:Geneviève de Brabant, w. A. Guiot (sop), M. Mesplé (sop), D. Millet (sop), J.C. Benoit (bar), A. Ciccolini (pno), P. Dervaux (cnd), Orch de Paris, Paris Opera Chorus Virgin Classics 2–▲ CDZB 62877
Satie, E.:Socrate, w. A. Guiot (sop), M. Mesplé (sop), D. Millet (sop), J. C. Benoit (bar), P. Dervaux (cnd), Orch de Paris, Paris Opera Chorus Virgin Classics 2–▲ CDZB 62877
Vivaldi, A.:Gloria, RV.589, w. Solange Michel (sop), Janine Collard (cta), R. Wagner (cnd), Paris Conservatory Societé des Concerts Orch, Roger Wagner Chorale EMI Classics ("Baroque" series) ▲ CDK 65737

Esposito, F. (sgr)
Menichetti, D.:L'Epifania del Signore, w. K. Gamberucci (sop), F. Facini (bass), A. Palombi (sgr), A. Della Santa (sgr), H. Handt (cnd), Toscana Accademia Strumentale, Polifonica Lucchese Bongiovanni ▲ GB 5033 [DDD]

Essex, Violet (sop)
Sullivan, A.:The Gondoliers—Kind Sir you cannot; J. Coates—Take a pair of sparkling eyes; C. Herwin—The Duchess' song Symposium ▲ 1123

Esswood, Paul (ct)
Bach, J.S.:Cant 1, w. K. Equiluz (ten), M. van Egmond (b–bar), N. Harnoncourt (cnd), Vienna Concentus Musicus, Vienna Boys' Choir [G] Teldec 2–▲ 2292–42497–2 [AAD]
Bach, J.S.:Cant 2, w. K. Equiluz (ten), M. van Egmond (b–bar), N. Harnoncourt (cnd), Vienna Concentus Musicus, Vienna Boys' Choir [G] Teldec 2–▲ 2292–42497–2 [AAD]
Bach, J.S.:Cant 3, w. K. Equiluz (ten), M. van Egmond (b–bar), N. Harnoncourt (cnd), Vienna Concentus Musicus, Vienna Boys' Choir [G] Teldec 2–▲ 2292–42497–2 [AAD]
Bach, J.S.:Cant 4, w. K. Equiluz (ten), M. van Egmond (b–bar), N. Harnoncourt (cnd), Vienna Concentus Musicus, Vienna Boys' Choir [G] Teldec 2–▲ 2292–42497–2 [AAD]
Bach, J.S.:Cant 5, w. K. Equiluz (ten), M. van Egmond (b–bar), N. Harnoncourt (cnd), Vienna Concentus Musicus, Vienna Boys' Choir Teldec 2–▲ 2292–42498–2 [AAD]
Bach, J.S.:Cant 6, w. K. Equiluz (ten), M. van Egmond (b–bar), N. Harnoncourt (cnd), Vienna Concentus Musicus, Vienna Boys' Choir Teldec 2–▲ 2292–42498–2 [AAD]
Bach, J.S.:Cant 7, w. K. Equiluz (ten), M. van Egmond (b–bar), Leonhardt Consort, King's College Choir Cambridge [G] Teldec 2–▲ 2292–42498–2 [AAD]
Bach, J.S.:Cant 8, w. K. Equiluz (ten), G. Kiefer (bar), M. van Egmond (b–bar), Leonhardt Consort, King's College Choir Cambridge [G] Teldec 2–▲ 2292–42498–2 [AAD]
Bach, J.S.:Cant 9, w. K. Equiluz (ten), M. van Egmond (b–bar), Leonhardt Consort, King's College Choir Cambridge [G] Teldec 2–▲ 2292–42499–2 [AAD]
Bach, J.S.:Cant 10, w. K. Equiluz (ten), M. van Egmond (b–bar), Leonhardt Consort, King's College Choir Cambridge [G] Teldec 2–▲ 2292–42499–2 [AAD]
Bach, J.S.:Cant 11, "Ascension Oratorio", w. K. Equiluz (ten), M. van Egmond (b–bar), N. Harnoncourt (cnd), Vienna Concentus Musicus, Vienna Concentus Musicus Chorus [G] Teldec 2–▲ 2292–42499–2 [AAD]
Bach, J.S.:Cant 12, w. K. Equiluz (ten), M. van Egmond (b–bar), Leonhardt Consort, King's College Choir Cambridge [G] Teldec 2–▲ 2292–42500–2 [AAD]
Bach, J.S.:Cant 13, w. K. Equiluz (ten), M. van Egmond (b–bar), Leonhardt Consort, King's College Choir Cambridge [G] Teldec 2–▲ 2292–42500–2 [AAD]
Bach, J.S.:Cant 16, w. K. Equiluz (ten), M. van Egmond (b–bar), Leonhardt Consort, King's College Choir Cambridge [G] Teldec 2–▲ 2292–42500–2 [AAD]
Bach, J.S.:Cant 17, w. K. Equiluz (ten), M. van Egmond (b–bar), N. Harnoncourt (cnd), Vienna Concentus Musicus, Chorus Viennensis [G] Teldec 2–▲ 2292–42501–2 [AAD]
Bach, J.S.:Cant 18, w. K. Equiluz (ten), M. van Egmond (b–bar), N. Harnoncourt (cnd), Vienna Concentus Musicus, Chorus Viennensis [G] Teldec 2–▲ 2292–42501–2 [AAD]
Bach, J.S.:Cant 19, w. K. Equiluz (ten), M. van Egmond (b–bar), N. Harnoncourt (cnd), Vienna Concentus Musicus, Chorus Viennensis [G] Teldec 2–▲ 2292–42501–2 [AAD]
Bach, J.S.:Cant 20, w. K. Equiluz (ten), M. van Egmond (b–bar), N. Harnoncourt (cnd), Vienna Concentus Musicus, Chorus Viennensis [G] Teldec 2–▲ 2292–42501–2 [AAD]
Bach, J.S.:Cant 21, w. K. Equiluz (ten), W. Wyatt (bass), N. Harnoncourt (cnd), Vienna Concentus Musicus, Chorus Viennensis, Vienna Boys' Choir [G] Teldec 2–▲ 2292–42502–2 [AAD]
Bach, J.S.:Cant 22, w. K. Equiluz (ten), M. van Egmond (b–bar), Leonhardt Consort, King's College Choir Cambridge [G] Teldec 2–▲ 2292–42502–2 [AAD]
Bach, J.S.:Cant 23, w. W. Gampert (trb), M. van Altena (ten), M. van Egmond (b–bar), Leonhardt Consort, King's College Choir Cambridge [G] Teldec 2–▲ 2292–42502–2 [AAD]
Bach, J.S.:Cant 24, w. K. Equiluz (ten), M. van Egmond (b–bar), N. Harnoncourt (cnd), Vienna Concentus Musicus, Chorus Viennensis [G] Teldec 2–▲ 2292–42503–2 [AAD]
Bach, J.S.:Cant 26, w. K. Equiluz (ten), S. Nimsgern (b–bar), N. Harnoncourt (cnd), Vienna Concentus Musicus, Chorus Viennensis [G] Teldec 2–▲ 2292–42503–2 [AAD]
Bach, J.S.:Cant 27, w. K. Equiluz (ten), S. Nimsgern (b–bar), N. Harnoncourt (cnd), Vienna Concentus Musicus, Chorus Viennensis [G] Teldec 2–▲ 2292–42503–2 [AAD]
Bach, J.S.:Cant 28, w. K. Equiluz (ten), S. Nimsgern (b–bar), N. Harnoncourt (cnd), Vienna Concentus Musicus, Chorus Viennensis [G] Teldec 2–▲ 2292–42504–2 [AAD]
Bach, J.S.:Cant 29, w. K. Equiluz (ten), M. van Egmond (b–bar), N. Harnoncourt (cnd), Vienna Concentus Musicus, Chorus Viennensis [G] Teldec 2–▲ 2292–42504–2 [AAD]
Bach, J.S.:Cant 30, w. K. Equiluz (ten), M. van Egmond (b–bar), N. Harnoncourt (cnd), Vienna Concentus Musicus, Chorus Viennensis [G] Teldec 2–▲ 2292–42504–2 [AAD]
Bach, J.S.:Cant 34, w. K. Equiluz (ten), S. Nimsgern (b–bar), N. Harnoncourt (cnd), Vienna Concentus Musicus [G] Teldec 2–▲ 2292–42505–2 [AAD]
Bach, J.S.:Cant 35, w. N. Harnoncourt (cnd), Vienna Concentus Musicus, Chorus Viennensis [G] Teldec 2–▲ 2292–42506–2 [AAD]
Bach, J.S.:Cant 36, w. K. Equiluz (ten), R. van der Meer (bass), N. Harnoncourt (cnd), Vienna Concentus Musicus, Chorus Viennensis Teldec 2–▲ 2292–42506–2 [AAD]
Bach, J.S.:Cant 37, w. K. Equiluz (ten), R. van der Meer (bass), N. Harnoncourt (cnd), Vienna Concentus Musicus, Chorus Viennensis [G] Teldec 2–▲ 2292–42506–2 [AAD]
Bach, J.S.:Cant 38, w. K. Equiluz (ten), R. van der Meer (bass), N. Harnoncourt (cnd), Vienna Concentus Musicus, Chorus Viennensis [G] Teldec 2–▲ 2292–42506–2 [AAD]
Bach, J.S.:Cant 41, w. K. Equiluz (ten), R. van der Meer (bass), N. Harnoncourt (cnd), Vienna Concentus Musicus, Vienna Concentus Musicus Chorus [G] Teldec 2–▲ 2292–42556–2 [AAD]
Bach, J.S.:Cant 42, w. K. Equiluz (ten), R. van der Meer (bass), N. Harnoncourt (cnd), Vienna Concentus Musicus, Vienna Concentus Musicus Chorus [G] Teldec 2–▲ 2292–42556–2 [AAD]
Bach, J.S.:Cant 43, w. K. Equiluz (ten), R. van der Meer (bass), N. Harnoncourt (cnd), Vienna Concentus Musicus, Vienna Concentus Musicus Chorus [G] Teldec 2–▲ 2292–42559–2 [AAD]
Bach, J.S.:Cant 44, w. K. Equiluz (ten), R. van der Meer (bass), N. Harnoncourt (cnd), Vienna Concentus Musicus, Vienna Concentus Musicus Chorus [G] Teldec 2–▲ 2292–42559–2 [AAD]
Bach, J.S.:Cant 45, w. K. Equiluz (ten), R. van der Meer (bass), Leonhardt Consort [G] Teldec 2–▲ 2292–42559–2 [AAD]
Bach, J.S.:Cant 46, w. K. Equiluz (ten), R. van der Meer (bass), Leonhardt Consort [G] Teldec 2–▲ 2292–42559–2 [AAD]
Bach, J.S.:Cant 48, w. K. Equiluz (ten), Vienna Concentus Musicus, Vienna Concentus Musicus Chorus [G] Teldec 2–▲ 2292–42560–2 ZL [AAD]
Bach, J.S.:Cant 54, w. G. Leonhardt (cnd), Leonhardt Consort [G] Teldec 2–▲ 2292–42422–2 [AAD]
Bach, J.S.:Cant 62, w. P. Jelosits (ten), K. Equiluz (ten), R. van der Meer (bass), N. Harnoncourt (cnd), Vienna Concentus Musicus, Vienna Concentus Musicus Chorus [G] Teldec 2–▲ 2292–42565–2 [AAD]
Bach, J.S.:Cant 63, w. P. Jelosits (ten), K. Equiluz (ten), R. van der Meer (bass), N. Harnoncourt (cnd), Vienna Concentus Musicus, Vienna Concentus Musicus Chorus [G] Teldec 2–▲ 2292–42565–2 [AAD]
Bach, J.S.:Cant 64, w. P. Jelosits (ten), R. van der Meer (bass), N. Harnoncourt (cnd), Vienna Concentus Musicus, Vienna Boys' Choir [G] Teldec 2–▲ 2292–42565–2 [AAD]
Bach, J.S.:Cant 69, w. W. Wiedl (trb), K. Equiluz (ten), R. van der Meer (bass), N. Harnoncourt (cnd), Vienna Concentus Musicus, Concentus Musicus [G] Teldec 2–▲ 2292–42572–2 [ADD]
Bach, J.S.:Cant 70, w. W. Wiedl (trb), K. Equiluz (ten), L. Visser (bass), N. Harnoncourt (cnd), Vienna Concentus Musicus, Tölz Boys' Choir [G] Teldec 2–▲ 2292–42572–2 [ADD]
Bach, J.S.:Cant 71, w. W. Wiedl (trb), K. Equiluz (ten), R. van der Meer (bass), N. Harnoncourt (cnd), Vienna Concentus Musicus, Vienna Concentus Musicus Chorus [G] Teldec 2–▲ 2292–42572–2 [ADD]
Bach, J.S.:Cant 72, w. W. Wiedl (trb), R. van der Meer (bass), N. Harnoncourt (cnd), Vienna Concentus Musicus, Tölz Boys' Choir [G] Teldec 2–▲ 2292–42572–2 [ADD]
Bach, J.S.:Cant 76, w. K. Equiluz (ten), R. van der Meer (bass), N. Harnoncourt (cnd), Vienna Concentus Musicus, Vienna Concentus Musicus Chorus [G] Teldec 2–▲ 2292–42576–2 [ADD]
Bach, J.S.:Cant 77, w. A. Kraus (ten), M. van Egmond (b–bar), G. Leonhardt (cnd), Leonhardt Consort [G] Teldec 2–▲ 2292–42576–2 [ADD]
Bach, J.S.:Cant 78, w. K. Equiluz (ten), R. van der Meer (bass), N. Harnoncourt (cnd), Vienna Concentus Musicus, Vienna Concentus Musicus Chorus [G] Teldec 2–▲ 2292–42576–2 [ADD]
Bach, J.S.:Cant 79, w. M. van Egmond (b–bar), G. Leonhardt (cnd), Leonhardt Consort [G] Teldec 2–▲ 2292–42576–2 [ADD]
Bach, J.S.:Cant 80, w. W. Wiedl (trb), K. Equiluz (ten), R. van der Meer (bass), N. Harnoncourt (cnd), Vienna Concentus Musicus [G] Teldec 2–▲ 2292–42577–2 [ADD]

1152 ▲ = CD ⧫ = Enhanced CD Δ = MD ▮ = Cassette Tape ▯ = DCC

Esswood, Paul (ct) (cont.)

Bach, J.S.:Cant 81, w. K. Equiluz (ten), R. van der Meer (bass), N. Harnoncourt (cnd), Vienna Concentus Musicus [G] Teldec 2-▲ 2292-42577-2 [ADD]

Bach, J.S.:Cant 85, w. W. Wiedl (trb), K. Equiluz (ten), N. Harnoncourt (cnd), Vienna Concentus Musicus, Vienna Concentus Musicus Chorus [G] Teldec 2-▲ 2292-42578-2 [ADD]

Bach, J.S.:Cant 86, w. W. Wiedl (trb), K. Equiluz (ten), N. Harnoncourt (cnd), Vienna Concentus Musicus, Vienna Concentus Musicus Chorus [G] Teldec 2-▲ 2292-42578-2 [ADD]

Bach, J.S.:Cant 87, w. K. Equiluz (ten), N. Harnoncourt (cnd), Vienna Concentus Musicus, Vienna Concentus Musicus Chorus [G] Teldec 2-▲ 2292-42578-2 [ADD]

Bach, J.S.:Cant 88, w. M. Klein (trb), K. Equiluz (ten), G. Leonhardt (cnd), Leonhardt Consort [G] Teldec 2-▲ 2292-42578-2 [ADD]

Bach, J.S.:Cant 89, w. M. Klein (trb), M. van Egmond (b–bar), G. Leonhardt (cnd), Leonhardt Consort [G] Teldec 2-▲ 2292-42578-2 [ADD]

Bach, J.S.:Cant 90, w. K. Equiluz (ten), M. van Egmond (b–bar), Leonhardt Consort, Ghent Collegium Vocale [G] Teldec 2-▲ 2292-42578-2 [ADD]

Bach, J.S.:Cant 96, w. W. Wiedl (trb), K. Equiluz (ten), P. Huttenlocher (bar), N. Harnoncourt (cnd), Vienna Concentus Musicus [G] Teldec ▲ 2292-42583-2 [ADD]

Bach, J.S.:Cant 97, w. W. Wiedl (trb), K. Equiluz (ten), P. Huttenlocher (bar), N. Harnoncourt (cnd), Vienna Concentus Musicus [G] Teldec ▲ 2292-42583-2 [ADD]

Bach, J.S.:Cant 98, w. C. Lengert (trb), K. Equiluz (ten), M. van Egmond (b–bar), Leonhardt Consort [G] Teldec ▲ 2292-42583-2 [ADD]

Bach, J.S.:Cant 99, w. W. Wiedl (trb), K. Equiluz (ten), P. Huttenlocher (bar), N. Harnoncourt (cnd), Vienna Concentus Musicus [G] Teldec ▲ 2292-42584-2

Bach, J.S.:Cant 100, w. D. Bratschke (trb), K. Equiluz (ten), M. van Egmond (b–bar), G. Leonhardt (cnd), Leonhardt Consort [G] Teldec ▲ 2292-42584-2

Bach, J.S.:Cant 101, w. W. Wiedl (trb), K. Equiluz (ten), P. Huttenlocher (bar), N. Harnoncourt (cnd), Vienna Concentus Musicus [G] Teldec ▲ 2292-42584-2

Bach, J.S.:Cant 102, w. W. Wiedl (trb), K. Equiluz (ten), P. Huttenlocher (bar), N. Harnoncourt (cnd), Vienna Concentus Musicus [G] Teldec ▲ 2292-42584-2

Bach, J.S.:Cant 103, w. K. Equiluz (ten), P. Huttenlocher (bar), G. Leonhardt (cnd), Leonhardt Consort [G] Teldec ▲ 2292-42602-2

Bach, J.S.:Cant 105, w. W. Wiedl (trb), K. Equiluz (ten), M. van Egmond (b–bar), N. Harnoncourt (cnd), Vienna Concentus Musicus, Tölz Boys' Choir [G] Teldec ▲ 2292-42602-2

Bach, J.S.:Cant 108, w. K. Equiluz (ten), M. van Egmond (b–bar), N. Harnoncourt (cnd), Vienna Concentus Musicus [G] Teldec 2-▲ 2292-42603-2

Bach, J.S.:Cant 109, w. K. Equiluz (ten), N. Harnoncourt (cnd), Vienna Concentus Musicus, Tölz Boys' Choir [G] Teldec 2-▲ 2292-42603-2

Bach, J.S.:Cant 110, w. W. Wiedl (trb), S. Frangoulis (trb), Stumpf (sgr), K. Equiluz (ten), M. van Egmond (b–bar), S. Lorenz (b–bar), N. Harnoncourt (cnd), Vienna Concentus Musicus, Tölz Boys' Choir [G] Teldec 2-▲ 2292-42603-2

Bach, J.S.:Cant 111, w. K. Equiluz (ten), K. Huber (ten), M. van Egmond (b–bar), N. Harnoncourt (cnd), Vienna Concentus Musicus [G] Teldec 2-▲ 2292-42606-2

Bach, J.S.:Cant 112, w. K. Equiluz (ten), K. Huber (ten), M. van Egmond (b–bar), N. Harnoncourt (cnd), Vienna Concentus Musicus [G] Teldec 2-▲ 2292-42606-2

Bach, J.S.:Cant 154, w. K. Equiluz (ten), T. Hampson (b–bar), N. Harnoncourt (cnd), Vienna Concentus Musicus, Tölz Boys' Choir [G] Teldec 2-▲ 2292-42632-2 [DDD]

Bach, J.S.:Cant 155, w. A. Bergius (trb), K. Equiluz (ten), T. Hampson (b–bar), N. Harnoncourt (cnd), Vienna Concentus Musicus, Tölz Boys' Choir [G] Teldec 2-▲ 2292-42632-2 [DDD]

Bach, J.S.:Cant 156, w. K. Equiluz (ten), T. Hampson (b–bar), N. Harnoncourt (cnd), Vienna Concentus Musicus, Tölz Boys' Choir [G] Teldec 2-▲ 2292-42632-2 [DDD]

Bach, J.S.:Cant 185, w. H. Wittek (trb), K. Equiluz (ten), T. Hampson (b–bar), N. Harnoncourt (cnd), Vienna Concentus Musicus, Tölz Boys' Choir [G] Teldec 2-▲ 2292-44179-2 [DDD]

Bach, J.S.:Cant 187, w. M. Emmermann (trb), M. van Egmond (b–bar), G. Leonhardt (cnd), Leonhardt Consort, Hanover Men & Boys' Chorus, Collegium Vocale [G] Teldec 2-▲ 2292-44179-2 [DDD]

Bach, J.S.:Christmas Oratorio, w. K. Equiluz (ten), S. Nimsgern (b–bar), N. Harnoncourt (cnd), Vienna Concentus Musicus Teldec-2-▲ 9031-77610-2

Bach, J.S.:Christmas Oratorio, w. K. Equiluz (ten), S. Nimsgern (b–bar), N. Harnoncourt (cnd), Vienna Concentus Musicus, Vienna Boys' Choir [G] Teldec ▲ 9031-74893-2

Bach, J.S.:St. Matthew Passion, w. J. Bowman (ct), T. Sutcliffe (ct), K. Equiluz (ten), M. van Egmond (b–bar), N. Harnoncourt (cnd), Vienna Concentus Musicus [G] Teldec 3-▲ 2292-42509-2 [AAD]

Bononcini, A.:Stabat Mater, w. Felicity Palmer (sop), Philip Langridge (ten), Christopher Keyte (bass), John Scott (org), John Willison (vn), Chris Wellington (va), Don McVeigh (va), G. Guest (cnd), Philomusica Antiqua of London, St. John's College Choir Cambridge *(rec 1977)* London 2-▲ 443868-2 [ADD]

Britten, H.:Canticles I–V, w. J. Griffett (ten), J. Ridgway (pno), T. Walker (gtr)—Canticle II IMP Masters ▲ IMPMCD 57 [DDD]

Britten, H.:Folksong Arrs, w. J. Griffett (ten), J. Ridgway (pno), T. Walker (gtr) IMP Masters ▲ IMPMCD 57 [DDD]

Britten, H.:Songs from the Chinese, w. J. Griffet (ten), T. Walker (gtr) IMP Masters ▲ IMPMCD 57 [DDD]

Caldara, A.:Crucifixus, w. Felicity Palmer (sop), Philip Langridge (ten), Christopher Keyte (bass), John Scott (org), John Willison (vn), Chris Wellington (va), Don McVeigh (va), G. Guest (cnd), Philomusica Antiqua of London, St. John's College Choir Cambridge *(rec 1977)* London 2-▲ 443868-2 [ADD]

Glass, Philip:Songs from the Trilogy, w. M. Vargas (sop), L. Childs (spkr), P. Esswood, D. Perry (ten), Philip Glass Ensemble CBS ▲ MK 45580 ■ FMT 45580

Handel, G.F.:Messiah, w. Elisabeth Harwood (sop), Janet Baker (mez), Robert Tear (ten), Raimund Herincx (bass), C. Mackerras (cnd), English CO, Ambrosian Singers [E] Angel ("Studio" series) 2-▲ CDMB 62748 [ADD]

Handel, G.F.:Messiah, w. Oliver Johnston (trb), Rae Woodland (sop), Norma Proctor (cta), Stephen Roberts (bar), J. Tobin (cnd), English SO, London Choral Society [Handel's original orchestration] [E] *(rec 1976)* Protone ■ CSPR 166/67

Handel, G.F.:Messiah, w. Elisabeth Harwood (sop), Janet Baker (mez), Robert Tear (ten), Raimund Herincx (bass), C. Mackerras (cnd), English CO, Ambrosian Singers [E] Angel ("Studio" series) ▲ CDM 69040

Handel, G.F.:Rinaldo, w. Sophie Boulin (sop—Donna), Ileana Cotrubas (sop—Almirena), Marie–Françoise Jacquelin (sop—Sirene), Nicole Leport (sop—Sirene), Jeanette Scovotti (sop—Armida), Carolyn Watkinson (cta—Rinaldo), Charles Brett (ct—Eustazio), Paul Esswood (ct—Goffredo), Armand Arapian (ten—Mago Christiano/Araldo), Ulrik Cold (bass—Argante), J. Malgoire (cnd), La Grande Écurie et la Chambre du Roy *(rec Paris, 1977)* Sony Classical 3-▲ SM3K 34592

Handel, G.F.:Serse, w. Barbara Hendricks (sop—Romilda), Anne–Marie Rodde (sop—Atalanta), Carolyn Watkinson (cta—Xerxes), Otrun Wenkel (cta—Amastre), Paul Esswood (ct—Arsamene), Ulrich Studer (bar—Elviro), Ulrik Cold (bass—Ariodate), J. Malgoire (cnd), La Grande Écurie et la Chambre du Roy *(rec Paris, 1979)* Sony Classical 3-▲ SM3K 36941

Lotti, A.:Crucifixus, w. Felicity Palmer (sop), Philip Langridge (ten), Christopher Keyte (bass), John Scott (org), John Willison (vn), Chris Wellington (va), Don McVeigh (va), G. Guest (cnd), Philomusica Antiqua of London, St. John's College Choir Cambridge *(rec 1977)* London 2-▲ 443868-2 [ADD]

Monteverdi, C.:Incoronazione, w. H. Donath (sop), E. Söderström (sop), C. Berberian (sop), N. Harnoncourt (cnd), Vienna Concentus Musicus [I] Teldec 4-▲ 2292-42547-2

Monteverdi, C.:Ritorno d'Ulisse, w. K. Equiluz (ten), M. Dickie (ten), N. Rogers (ten), M. Van Egmond (bass), N. Harnoncourt (cnd), Vienna Concentus Musicus Teldec ▲ 42496-2

Estep, Craig (ten)

Rossini, G.:Music of, w. M. Fortuna (sop), M. Lerner (sop), D. Voigt (sop), M. Horne (mez), K. Kuhlmann (mez), F. von Stade (mez), R. Blake (ten), C. Merritt (ten), T. Hampson (b–bar), H. Runey (b–bar), J. Opalach (bass), S. Ramey (bass), R. Norrington (cnd), Orch of St. Luke's, New York Concert Chorale EMI Classics ▲ CDC 54643

Estes, Simon (bass)

Bizet, G.:Carmen, w. J. Norman (sop), M. Freni (sop), N. Shicoff (ten), S. Ozawa (cnd), French National Orch, French Radio Chorus [F] Philips ▲ 426040-2 [DDD] ■ 426040-4 □ 426040-5

Estes, Simon (bass) (cont.)

Bizet, G.:Carmen, w. J. Norman (sop), M. Freni (sop), N. Shicoff (ten), S. Ozawa (cnd), French National Orch, French Radio Chorus [F] Philips 3-▲ 422366-2 [DDD]

Falla, M. de:Atlántida, w. M. Bayo (sop), T. Berganza (mez), E. Colomer (cnd), Spanish National Youth Orch Valois 2-▲ V 4685

Gershwin, G.:Porgy & Bess (sels), w. R. Alexander (sop), L. Slatkin (cnd), Berlin RSO, Berlin Radio Chorus [E] Philips ▲ 412720-2 [DDD]

Haydn, J.:Mass 11, "Nelsonmesse", "Imperial Mass", "Coronation Mass", w. Judith Blegen (sop), Gwendolen Killebrew (mez), Kenneth Riegel (ten), L. Bernstein (cnd), New York PO, Westminster Choir [L] *(rec 1976)* Sony Classical ("Bernstein:The Royal Edition" series) 2-▲ SM2K 47563 [ADD]

Haydn, J.:Mass 14, "Harmoniemesse", w. Judith Blegen (sop), Fredrica von Stade (mez), Kenneth Riegel (ten), L. Bernstein (cnd), New York PO, Westminster Choir [L] *(rec 1966)* Sony Classical 2-▲ SM2K 47560 [ADD]

Mozart, W.A.:Requiem, w. L. Dawson (sop), J. van Nes (cta), K. Lewis (ten), C. M. Guilini (cnd), Philharmonia Orch, Philharmonia Chorus [L] Sony Classical ▲ SK 45577 [DDD]

Saint–Saëns, C.:Samson et Dalila, w. J. Carreras (ten), A. Baltsa (mez), Summers (bar), Burchuladze (bass), C. Davis (cnd), Bavarian RSO, Bavarian Radio Chorus Philips 2-▲ 426243-2 [DDD]

Saint–Saëns, C.:Samson et Dalila (sels), w. A. Baltsa (mez), J. Carreras (ten), D. George (ten), J. Summers (bar), P. Burchuladze (bass), C. Davis (cnd), Bavarian RSO Philips ▲ 438504-2

Stravinsky, I.:Oedipus Rex, w. A. S. von Otter (mez/sop), V. Cole (ten), N. Gedda (ten), H. Sotin (bass), P. Chéreau (nar), E.–P. Salonen (cnd), Swedish RSO, *(chorus unknown)* Sony Classical ▲ SK 48057

Verdi, G.:Don Carlos, w. M. Caballé (sop—Elisabeth de Valois), G. Bumbry (mez—Princess Eboli), J. Aragall (ten—Don Carlos), R. Bruson (bar—Rodrigue), S. Estes (bass—Philip II), T. Fulton (cnd), *(orch unknown)* *(rec Orange, France, 1979)* Ornamenti 2-▲ FE 110 [ADD]

Wagner, R.:Der fliegende Holländer, w. L. Balsev (sop), R. Schunk (ten), M. Salminen (bass), W. Nelsson (cnd), Bayreuth Festival Orch, Bayreuth Festival Chorus [G] Philips 2-▲ 434599-2 [DDD]

Wagner, R.:Parsifal, w. W. Meier (mez), P. Hofmann (ten), F. Mazura (bar), H. Sotin (bass), M. Salminen (bass), J. Levine (cnd), Bayreuth Festival Orch, Bayreuth Festival Chorus [1985] [G] Philips 4-▲ 434616-2 [DDD]

Esteve, V. (bar)

Massenet, J.:Hérodiade, w. M. Caballé (sop—Salomé), D. Vejzovic (mez—Hérodiade), J. Carreras (ten—Jean), J. Pons (bar—Hérode), E. Serra (bar—Vitellius), V. Esteve (bar—High Priest), R. Kennedy (bass—Phanuel), J. Delacôte (cnd), Barcelona Teatro Liceo Orch, Barcelona Gran Teatro de Liceo Chorus *(rec Jan. 6, 1984)* Legato Classics 2-▲ LCD 182 [ADD]

Esteves, José Alberto (ten)

Gottschalk, L.M.:Music of, w. Trinidad Paniagua (sop), Pablo Garcia (bar), Eugene List (pno), Cary Lewis (pno), Brady Millican (pno), Adler, Buketoff (cnd), Berlin SO, Vienna State Opera Orch—Grande Tarantelle for Piano & Orchestra, Op. 67; Symphony No. 1, "La nuit des tropiques"; Symphony No. 2, "A Montevideo"; The Union (concert paraphrase on American national airs) for Piano & Orchestra, Op. 48; Variations on the Portuguese National Hymn for Piano & Orchestra, Op. 91; Grande fantaisie triomphale sur l'hymne national brésilien for Piano & Orchestra, Op. 69; Marche solennelle for Orchestra; Marcha triunfal y final de opera for Orchestra; Escenas campestres (opera in one act); Five Pieces for Piano Duet [Radieuse, Op. 72; Ses yeux, Op. 66; La Gallina, Op. 53; Ojos criollos, Op. 37; Pasquinade, Op. 59] Vox Box 2-▲ CDX 5009 [ADD]

Ettl, Karl (bass)

Mozart, W.A.:Don Giovanni, w. L. Helletsgruber (sop), E. Rethberg (sop), M. Bokor (mez), D. Borgioli (ten), E. Pinza (bass), B. Walter (cnd), Vienna PO, Vienna State Opera Chorus *(rec Salzburg, Aug. 2, 1937)* Melodram 3-▲ MLO 37506 [ADD]

Wagner, R.:Rienzi, der Letzte der Tribunen (sels), w. Rosette Andsy (cta—Adriano), Hermann Gallos (ten—Baroncelli), Franz Völker (tenor-Rienzi), Karl Ettl (bass—Cecco), J. Krips (cnd), Vienna State Opera Orch *(rec Vienna, May 15, 1933)* Koch Schwann 2-▲ SCH 314662 [ADD]

Eustrati, Diana (cta)

Beethoven, L. van:Sym 9, "Choral Sym", w. Anny Schlemm (sop), Gert Lutze (ten), Thomas Paul (bass), H. Abendroth (cnd), Leipzig RSO *(rec 1953)* Arlecchino ARL

Evangelatos, Daphné (cta)

Campra, A.:Tancrède, w. C. Alliot–Lugaz (sop), G. Reinhart (bar), F. le Roux (bar), P.–Y. le Maigat (bass–bar), Dubose (sgr), J. Malgoire (cnd), La Grande Écurie et la Chambre du Roy Erato (Musifrance) 2-▲ 2292-45001-2 ZA [DDD]

Straus, O.:The Merry Nibelungs, w. Lisa Griffith (sop—Kriemhild), Gudrun Volkert (sop—Brunhilde), Daphne Evangelatos (cta—Ute), Gabriele Henkel (sgr—Giselher), Christine Mann (sgr—Vogel), Hein Heidbüchel (ten—Volker), Martin Gantner (sgr—Gunther), Gerd Grochowski (sgr—Dankwart), Michael Nowak (sgr—Siegfried), Josef Otten (sgr—Hagen), S. Köhler (cnd), Cologne RSO, Cologne Radio Chorus *(rec Cologne, Jan 31–Feb 17, 1995)* Capriccio ▲ 10752 [DDD]

Evans, Anne (sop)

Wagner, R.:Götterdämmerung, w. A. Evans (sop—Brünnhilde), E.–M. Bundschuh (sop—Gutrune), H. Leidland (sop—Woglinde), A. Küttenbaum (sop—Wellgunde), W. Meier (mez—Waltraute), B. Svendén (mez—1st Norn), J. Turner (mez), *(cnd & orch unknown)* Teldec 4-▲ 4509-94194-2 [DDD]

Wagner, R.:Siegfried, w. A. Evans (sop—Brünnhilde), H. Leidland (sop—Waldvogel), B. Svendén (mez—Erda), S. Jerusalem (ten—Siegfried), G. Clark (ten—Mime), J. Tomlinson (bass—Der Wanderer), G. von Kannen (bass—Alberich), P. Kang (bass), *(cnd & orch unknown)* Teldec 4-▲ 4509-94193-2 [DDD]

Evans, Beverly (sop)

Puccini, G.:Suor angelica, w. Elisabeth Carron (sop—Angelica), Joan Summers (sop—Genovieffa), Donna Owen (sop—Dolcina), Lou Ann Wyckoff (sop—Alms collector), Hanna Owen (sop—novice), Anthea De Forest (sop—novice), Charlotte Povia (mez—Abbess), Beverly Evans (mez—Monitress), Kay Creed (mez—Mistress), La Vergne Monette (sop/mez—lay sister), Joan August (sop/mez—lay sister), Pearle Goldsmith (sop/mez—other sister), Lila Herbert (sop/mez—other sister), Jodell Kenting (sop/mez—other sister), Ann Pretzat (sop/mez—other sister), Evelyn Sachs (cta—Princess), F. Patanè (cnd), *(orch unknown)* *(rec New York, Feb 23, 1967)* Legato Classics ▲ LCD 212-1 [ADD]

Verdi, G.:Rigoletto, w. P. Wise (sop—Gilda), B. Evans (sop—Giovanna), M. Yauger (mez—Maddalena), J. Carreras (ten—Duke), L. Quilico (bar—Rigoletto), J. Rudel (cnd), *(orch unknown)* *(rec Apr. 22, 1973)* Standing Room Only 2-▲ SRO 843 [ADD]

Evans, Damon (ten)

Gershwin, G.:Porgy & Bess, w. C. Haymon (sop—Bess), C. Clarey (sop—Serena), M. Simpson (sop—Maria), D. Evans (ten—Sporting Life), G. Baker (bar—Crown), W. White (bar—Porgy), S. Rattle (cnd), London PO, Glyndebourne Festival Chorus EMI Classics 3-▲ CDCC 49568

Gershwin, G.:Porgy & Bess (sels), w. Cynthia Clarey (sop—Serena), Cynthia Haymon (sop—Bess), Damon Evans (ten—Sportin' Life), Gordon Hawkins (bar—Porgy), Andrew Litton (pno), A. Litton (cnd), Dallas SO, Dallas Sym Chorus—Intro/Jasbo Brown; Summertime; A Woman Is a Sometime Thing; Gone, Gone, Gone; My Man's Gone Now; Leavin' for the Promise' Lan'; Oh I Got Plenty O' Nuttin'; Bess, You Is My Woman Now; Oh, I Can't Sit Down; I Ain't Got No Shame; It Ain't Necessarily So; Shame on All You Sinners; I Loves You, Porgy; Hurricane; There's a Boat Dat's Leavin' Soon for New York; Act 3, Scene 3 Orchestral Intro; Good Mornin', Sistuh; Oh Lawd, I'm on My Way! [concert suite arr A. Litton] *(rec Eugene McDermott Hall, Dallas, May 1995)* Dorian ▲ DOR 90223 [DDD]

Evans, Edith (mez)

Offenbach, J.:Les Contes d'Hoffmann, w. Beverly Sills (sop—Olympia/Giulietta/Antonia/Stella), Edith Evans (mez—Nicklausse/Mother's Voice), Michael Devlin (ten—Spalanzani), André Turp (ten—Hoffmann), Luigi Vellucci (ten—Andrès/Cochenille/Pitichinaccio/Frantz), Donald Bernard (bar—Luther/Schlemil), Norman Treigle (bass—Lindorf/Coppélius/Dapertutto/Dr. Miracle), John West (bass—Crespel), Alton Brim (sgr—Nathanaël), Rodney Hall (sgr—Hermann), K. Andersson (cnd), New Orleans Opera Orch, New Orleans Opera Chorus *(rec Feb 27, 1964)* VAI Audio 2-▲ VAIA 1121-2 [ADD]

Evans, Geraint (bar)

Britten, H.:Billy Budd, w. P. Pears (ten), T. Uppman (bar), H. Alan (bar), F. Dalberg (bass), B. Britten (cnd), Royal Opera House Orch, Royal Opera House Chorus Covent Garden *(rec Dec. 1, 1951)* VAI Audio 3-▲ VAIA 1034-3 [ADD]

Britten, H.:Peter Grimes, w. C. Watson (sop), P. Pears (ten), B. Britten (cnd), Royal Opera House Orch, Royal Opera House Chorus Covent Garden [E] London 3-▲ 414577-2 [ADD]

Evans, Geraint (bar) (cont.)

Busoni, F.:Arlecchino or Die Fenster, w. E. Malbin (sop), M. Dickie (ten), I. Wallace (bar), F. Ollendorf (bass), Glyndeborne Festival Chorus, J. Pritchard (cnd), Glyndebourne Festival Orch — EMI Classics ▲ CDMB 65284

Donizetti, G.:Don Pasquale, w. Edoardo Gimenez (ten), Mario D'Anna (sgr), Carol Webber (sgr), H. Holt (cnd), *(orch unknown)* *(rec Seattle, 1981)* — Ornamenti ("Gala Evenings, Teatro Colon" series) 2–▲ 121

Donizetti, G.:L'elisir d'amore, w. I. Cotrubas (sop), L. Watson (sop), P. Domingo (ten), I. Wixell (bar), J. Pritchard (cnd), Royal Opera House Orch, Royal Opera House Chorus Covent Garden *(rec 1977)* — CBS 2–▲ M2K 34585 [ADD]

Mahler, G.:Des Knaben Wunderhorn, w. Janet Baker (mez), Roland Hermann (bar), W. Morris (cnd), London PO, London Symphonica — IMP ▲ PCD 2020

Mahler, G.:Lieder eines fahrenden Gesellen, w. Janet Baker (mez), Roland Hermann (bar), W. Morris (cnd), London PO, London Symphonica — IMP ▲ PCD 2020

Mathias, W.:Ave Rex, w. Janet Price (sop), Kenneth Bowen (ten), Michael Rippon (bar), Atherton, Willcocks (cnd), London SO, New Philharmonia Orch, Welsh National Opera Chorus, Windsor Bach Choir, St. George's Chapel Choristers — Lyrita ▲ SRCD .324

Mozart, W.A.:Così fan tutte, w. M. Price (sop), L. Popp (sop), Y. Minton (mez), L. Alva (ten), H. Sotin (bass), O. Klemperer (cnd), New Philharmonia Orch, John Alldis Choir — EMI Classics 3–▲ CDMC 63845

Mozart, W.A.:Nozze di Figaro, w. E. Söderström (sop), R. Grist (sop), T. Berganza (mez), O. Klemperer (cnd), New Philharmonia Orch, John Alldis Choir — EMI Classics 3–▲ CDMC 63849

Mozart, W.A.:Nozze di Figaro, w. H. Harper (sop), J. Blegen (sop), T. Berganza (mez), D. Fischer-Dieskau (bar), D. Barenboim (cnd), English CO, John Alldis Choir [I] — EMI Classics ("Studio" series) 3–▲ CDMC 63646 [ADD]

Puccini, G.:Madama Butterfly, w. V. de los Angeles (sop—Madama Butterfly), B. Howitt (mez—Suzuki), J. Livingston (mez—Kate), J. Lanigan (ten—Pinkerton), D. Tree (ten—Goro), D. A. (ten—Yamadori), G. Evans (bar—Sharpless), M. Langdon (bass—Bonzo), R. Kempe (cnd), Royal Opera House Orch, Royal Opera House Chorus Covent Garden *(rec London, May 1957)* — Ornamenti 2–▲ FE 112 [ADD]

Sullivan, A.:The Gondoliers, w. A. Young (ten), O. Brannigan (bass), R. Lewis (ten), M. Sargent (cnd), Pro Arte Orch, Glyndebourne Festival Chorus — EMI Classics 2–▲ CDMB 64394

Sullivan, A.:The Mikado, w. O. Brannigan (bass), R. Lewis (ten), I. Wallace (bass), M. Sargent (cnd), Pro Arte Orch, Glyndebourne Festival Chorus — EMI Classics 2–▲ CDMB 64403

Verdi, G.:Falstaff, w. M. Freni (sop), I. Ligabue (sop), G. Simionato (mez), R. Elias (mez), R. Krause (ten), R. Merrill (bar), G. Solti (cnd), RCA Italian Opera Orch, RCA Italiana Opera Chorus [I] — London 2–▲ 417168–2 [ADD]

Verdi, G.:Falstaff, w. Ilva Ligabue (sop), Oralia Dominguez (mez), Luigi Alva (ten), Eberhardt Wächter (bar), F. Previtali (cnd), *(orch unknown)* *(rec Teatro Colon, Buenos Aires, Aug. 30, 1963)* — Ornamenti ("Gala Evenings, Teatro Colon") 2–▲ 119

Evans, Glyn (ten)

Mahler, G.:Des Knaben Wunderhorn, w. J. Baker (mez), W. Morris (cnd), London PO [G] *(rec 1966)* — Nimbus ▲ NI 5084 [AAD]

To God Sing Praise, w. Douglas Bodle (org) — Pro Arte ▲ CDD 3403 [DDD]

Evans, Mark (bar)

Britten, H.:Curlew River, w. Hugo Ticciati (trb), Mark Milhofer (ten), Gwynn Hughes Jones (bar), Matthew Hargreaves (bass), D. Angus (cnd), Guildhall Chamber Ensemble — Koch Schwann ▲ SCH 313972

Evans, Nancy (mez)

Handel, G.F.:Sosarme, Rè di Media, w. Margaret Ritchie (sop—Elmira), Alfred Deller (mez—Sosarme), Nancy Evans (mez—Erenice), Helen Watts (cta—Melo), John Kentish (ct—Argone), William Herbert (ten—King Haliate), Ian Wallace (bass—Altomaro), A. Lewis (cnd), St. Cecilia Academy Orch Rome, St. Anthony Singers — Theorema 2–▲ TH 121194/195

Evans, Peter Lloyd (ten)

Sullivan, A.:The Yeomen of the Guard, w. Felicity Palmer (sop—Dame Carruthers), Pamela Helen Stephens (mez—Phoebe Meryll), Neill Archer (ten—Col Fairfax), Peter Hoare (ten—Leonard Meryll), Ralph Mason (ten—1st Yeoman), Donald Maxwell (bar—Wilfred Shadbolt), Peter Savidge (bar—Lieutenant Sir Richard Cholmondely), Donald Adams (bass—Sergeant Meryll), Richard Suart (bass—Jack Point), Peter Lloyd Evans (sgr—2nd Yeoman), Alwyn Mellor (sgr—Elsie Maynard), Clare O'Neill (sgr—Kate), C. Mackerras (cnd), Welsh National Opera Orch, Welsh National Opera Chorus *(rec Brangwyn Hall, Swasea, Wales, Apr 18–30 & May 1, 1995)* — Telarc 2–▲ CD 80404 [DDD]

Evans, Rebecca (sop)

Mozart, W.A.:Nozze di Figaro, w. Rebecca Evans (sop—Barbarina), Nuccia Focile (sop—Susanna), Suzanne Murphy (sop—Marcellina), Carol Vaness (sop—Countess Almaviva), Susanne Mentzer (mez—Cherubino), Ryland Davies (ten—Don Basilio/Don Curzio), Alessandro Corbelli (bar—Count Almaviva), Alfonso Antoniozzi (bass—Doctor Bartolo/Antonio), Alastair Miles (bass—Figaro), C. Mackerras (cnd), Scottish CO, Scottish Chamber Chorus *(rec Usher Hall, Edingurgh, Scotland, July 31–Aug. 12, 1994)* — Telarc 3–▲ CD 80388 [DDD]

Purcell, H.:Dido & Aeneas, w. Rebecca Evans (sop—Belinda), Maria Ewing (sop—Dido), Mary Plazas (sop—1st witch), Patricia Rozario (sop—2nd woman), Sally Burgess (mez—Sorceress), Pamela Helen Stephens (mez—2nd witch), James Bowman (ct—Spirit), Jamie MacDougal (ten—Sailor), Karl Daymond (bar—Aeneas), R. Hickox (cnd), Collegium Musicum 90 — Chandos ("Early Music" series) ▲ CHAN 0586 [DDD]

Sullivan, A.:HMS Pinafore, w. F. Palmer (sop—Little Buttercup), R. Evans (mez—Josephine), M. Schade (ten—Ralph Rackstraw), T. Allen (bar—Capt. Corcoran), R. Suart (bass—Rt. Hon. Sir Joseph Porter, K.C.B.), D. Adams (bass—Dick Deadeye), R. Van A. (bass—Bill Bobstay), C. Mackerras (cnd), Welsh National Opera Orch, Welsh National Opera Chorus *(rec Swansea, Wales, June 5–8, 1994)* — Telarc ▲ CD 80374 [DDD]

Sullivan, A.:The Pirates of Penzance, w. R. Evans (sop—Mabel), G. Knight (mez—Ruth), J. Gossage (mez—Edith), J. M. Ainsley (ten—Frederic), R. Suart (bar—Maj.-Gen. Stanley), N. Folwell (bar—Samuel), D. Adams (b-bar—Pirate King), R. Van Allan (bass—Sergeant of Police), C. Mackerras (cnd), Welsh National Opera Orch, Welsh National Opera Chorus *(rec May 4–6, 1993)* — Telarc ▲ CD 80353 [DDD]; ■ CS 30353

Sullivan, A.:Trial by Jury, w. Rebecca Evans (sop—Plaintiff), Barry Banks (ten—Defendant), Gareth Rhys-Davies (bar—Foreman of the Jury), Peter Savidge (bar—Counsel for the Plaintiff), Donald Adams (bass—Usher), Richard Suart (bass—The Learned Judge), C. Mackerras (cnd), Welsh National Opera Orch, Welsh National Opera Chorus *(rec Brangwyn Hall, Swasea, Wales, Apr 18–30 & May 1, 1995)* — Telarc 2–▲ CD 80404 [DDD]

Vaughan Williams, R.:Hugh the Dover, w. S. Walker (mez), B. Bottone (ter), N. Jenkins (ten), A. Opie (bar), R. Van Allan (bass), M. Best (cnd), Corydon Orch, Corydon Singers, New London Children's Choir — Hyperion 2–▲ CDA 66901/02

Evans, Robert (bass)

Purcell, H.:Anthems & Services, w. S. Gritton (sop), M. Kennedy (sop), E. O'Dwyer (trb), J. Goodman (trb), J. Bowman (ct), N. Short (ct), Rogers Covey-Crump (ten), C. Daniels (ten), M. Milhofer (ten), M. George (bass), R. King (cnd), King's Consort—I Was Glad When They Said unto Me (coronation & verse anthem); O Consider My Adversity; Beati omnes qui timent Dominum; In the Black Dismal Dungeon of Dispair; Save Me, O God; Te Deum in B♭; Jubilant in B♭; Thy Way, O God, Is Holy — Hyperion ▲ CDA 66677 [DDD]

Purcell, H.:Anthems & Services, w. James Bowman (ct), Charles Daniels (ten), Michael George (bass), R. King (cnd), King's Consort, New College Choir Oxford—O sing unto the Lord; O praise God in His holiness; Praise the Lord, O Jerusalem; It is a good thing to give thanks; O give thanks unto the Lord; Let mine eyes run down with tears; My beloved spake — Hyperion ▲ CDA 66585

Purcell, H.:Music for the Funeral of Queen Mary, w. S. Gritton (sop), M. Kennedy (sop), E. O'Dwyer (trb), J. Goodman (trb), J. Bowman (ct), N. Short (ct), Rogers Covey-Crump (ten), C. Daniels (ten), M. Milhofer (ten), M. George (bass), R. King (cnd), King's Consort — Hyperion ▲ CDA 66677 [DDD]

Wagner, R.:Die Meistersinger von Nürnberg, w. H. Donath (sop), R. Hesse (mez), A. Kollo (ten), P. Schreier (ten), T. Adam (b-bar), K. Ridderbusch (bass), H. von Karajan (cnd), Dresden Staatskapelle, Dresden State Chorus, Leipzig Radio Chorus [G] — EMI Classics 4–▲ CDCD 49683 [ADD]

Evans, Timothy Leigh (sgr)

Monteverdi, C.:Orfeo, w. Jennifer Lane (mez), Jeffrey Thomas (ten), Michael Brown (sgr), Dana Hanchard (sgr), Paul Shipper (sgr), G. Toth (cnd), ARTEK — Lyrichord 2–▲ LYR 9002 [DDD]

Evans, Wynford (ten)

Verdi, G.:Ernani (sels), w. Felicia Weathers (sop—Elvira), Delia Wallis (mez—Giovanna), Placido Domingo (ten—Ernani), Wynford Evans (ten—Don Riccardo), Piero Francia (bar—Don Carlo), Agostino Ferrin (bass—Don Ruy Gomex de Silva), Robert Holl (bass—Iago), E. Downes (cnd), Omroep Orch, Omroep Chorus *(rec Amsterdam, Jan 15, 1972)* — Bella Voce ▲ BLV 107.004 [AAD]

Evitts, David (bar)

Paine, J.K.:St. Peter, w. J. Ommerlé (sop), A. Fortunato (mez), P. Kelly (ten), G. Schuller (cnd), Boston Pro Arte CO, Back Bay Chorale [E] *(rec live in concert at Sanders Theater, Cambridge, Mass., 5/21/89)* — GM 2–▲ 2027CD 2

Stravinsky, I.:L'Histoire du soldat, w. Catherine Ciesinski (mez), Jon Humphries (ten), Mark Wajt (pno), R. Craft (cnd), Orch of St. Luke, Gregg Smith Singers — MusicMasters ▲ 01612–67152–2

Evseeva, Elena (sop)

Haydn, J.:The Seven Last Words of Christ on the Cross, w. Margarita Maruna (mez), Arkady Mishenkin (ten), Boris Bezhko (bass), A. de Almeida (cnd), Moscow SO, Stanislav Gussev (cnd), Russian State Academy Chorus *(rec Mosfilm Studio, Moscow, Jan 27–28, 1995)* — SOMM ▲ SOMMCD 203 [DDD]

Evstatieva, Stefka (sop)

Borodin, A.:Prince Igor, w. A. Milcheva (mez), B. Martinovich (b-bar), N. Ghiaurov (bass), N. Ghiuselev (bass), E. Tchakarov (cnd), Sofia Festival Orch, Sofia National Opera Chorus [R] — Sony Classical 3–▲ S3K 44878 [DDD]

Rimsky-Korsakov, N.:Snow Maiden, w. Stefka Evstatieva (sop—Kupava), Elena Zemenkova (sop—Snow Maiden), Alexandrina Milcheva (mez—Spring Fairy), Vessela Zorova (mez—wife), Stefka Mineva (alt—Lehl), Avram Andreev (ten—Tsar), Lyubomir Dyakovski (ten—Cottager, Sprite), Lyubomir Videnov (bar—Misgir), Nicola Ghiuselev (bass—King), S. Angelov (cnd), Bulgarian RSO, Bulgarian National Chorus *(rec Sofia, 1985)* — Capriccio 3–▲ 10749–51 [DDD]

Tchaikovsky, P.:Queen of Spades, w. P. Dilova (mez), I. Konsulov (bar), Mazulok (bass), E. Tchakarov (cnd), Sofia Festival Orch, Bulgarian National Chorus [R] — Sony Classical 3–▲ S3K 45720

Ewing, Alan (bass)

Monteverdi, C.:Volgendo il ciel, w. E. Kirkby (sop), S. LeBlanc (sop), M. Nichols (mez), P. Agnew (ct), A. Rooley (cnd), Consort of Musicke [I] — Virgin Classics ▲ 59606 [DDD]

Ewing, Maria (sop)

Debussy, C.:Pelléas et Mélisande, w. C. Ludwig (mez), F. Le Roux (bar), J. Van Dam (bass-bar), J.-P. Courtis (bass), C. Abbado (cnd), Vienna PO, Vienna State Opera Chorus — Deutsche Grammophon 2–▲ 435344–2 [DDD]

Monteverdi, C.:Ballo delle ingrate, w. Evelyn Tubb (sop), Emma Kirkby (sop), Barbara Nichols (sop), A. Rooley (cnd), Consort of Musicke [I] — Virgin Classics ▲ 59606 [DDD]

Mozart, W.A.:Don Giovanni, w. C. Vaness (sop), E. Gale (sop), K. Lewis (ten), T. Allen (bar), R. Van Allan (bass), B. Haitink (cnd), London PO, Glyndebourne Festival Chorus [I] — EMI Classics 3–▲ CDCC 47036 [DDD]

Mozart, W.A.:Requiem, w. M. McLaughlin (sop), J. Hadley (ten), C. Hauptmann (bass), L. Bernstein (cnd), Bavarian RSO, Bavarian Radio Chorus [L] — Deutsche Grammophon ▲ 427353–2 [DDD]

Purcell, H.:Dido & Aeneas, w. Rebecca Evans (sop—Belinda), Maria Ewing (sop—Dido), Mary Plazas (sop—1st witch), Patricia Rozario (sop—2nd woman), Sally Burgess (mez—Sorceress), Pamela Helen Stephens (mez—2nd witch), James Bowman (ct—Spirit), Jamie MacDougal (ten—Sailor), Karl Daymond (bar—Aeneas), R. Hickox (cnd), Collegium Musicum 90 — Chandos ("Early Music" series) ▲ CHAN 0586 [DDD]

Ravel, M.:Shéhérazade Mez, w. S. Rattle (cnd), City of Birmingham SO — EMI Classics ▲ CDC 54204

Shostakovich, D.:Lady Macbeth of Mtsensk, w. E. Zaremba (mez), P. Langridge (ten), H. Zednik (ten), A. Haugland (bass), A. Kotcherga (bass), K. Moll (bass), S. Larin (bass), M.-W. Chung (cnd), Bastille Opera Orch, Bastille Opera Chorus — Deutsche Grammophon 2–▲ 437511–2

Eythe, W. (sgr)

Porter, C.:Out of This World, w. C. Greenwood (sgr), P. Gillette (sgr) — Sony Broadway ▲ SK 48223 ■ ST 48223

Fabbri, Franca (sgr)

Verdi, G.:Un giorno di regno, w. Maria Casula (sop), Angelo Romero (bar), Enrico Fissore (bass), Michele Guento (sgr), Islen Moubayed (sgr), Ruggero Rado (sgr), Bernardino Trotta (sgr), A. Zedda (cnd), *(orch unknown)* — Great Opera Performances 2–▲ GOP 782

Fabbricini, Tiziana (sop)

Verdi, G.:La traviata, w. T. Fabbricini (sop—Violetta), A. Trevisan (mez—Annina), N. Curiel (mez—Flora), R. Alagna (ten—Alfredo), E. Cossutta (ten—Gastone), E. Gavazzi (ten—Giuseppe), O. Mori (bar—Douphol), E. Capuano (bass—d'Obigny), F. Musinu (bass—Grenvil), R. Muti (cnd), La Scala Orch, La Scala Chorus — Sony Classical 2–▲ S2K 52486 [DDD]

Fabbris, Guido (ten)

Donizetti, G.:Roberto Devereux, w. Montserrat Caballé (sop), Beverly Wolff (mez), Gianni Raimondi (ten), Walter Alberti (bar), Paolo Badoer (sgr), Carlo Micalucci (sgr), Carlo Padoan (sgr), B. Bartoletti (cnd), Venice Teatro La Fenice Orch, Venice Teatro La Fenice Chorus — Great Opera Performances 2–▲ GOP 764

Verdi, G.:Don Carlos, w. Katia Ricciarelli (sop), Fiorenza Cossotto (mez), Guido Fabbris (ten), Veriano Luchetti (ten), Piero Cappuccilli (bar), Gianfranco Casarini (bass), Nicolai Ghiaurov (bass), Alessandro Maddalena (bass), Aracelly Haengel (sgr), Marisa Salimbeni (sgr), Giorgio Zoranca (sgr), G. Prêtre (cnd), *(orch unknown)* — Great Opera Performances 3–▲ GOP 777

Fabre-Garrus, Bernard (bar)

Josquin Desprez:Missa, "Ave Maris Stella", w. D. Collot (sop), R. Holton (sop), J.-L. Comoretto (ct), R. Le Chenadec (ct), T. Brehu (ten), H. Lamy (ten), J. Gowings (bar) *(rec Jan. 1993)* — Astrée ▲ E 8507 [DDD]

Josquin Desprez:Motets, w. D. Collot (sop), R. Holton (sop), J.-L. Comoretto (ct), R. Le Chenadec (ct), T. Brehu (ten), H. Lamy (ten), J. Gowings (bar)—Motets à la vierge *(rec Jan. 1993)* — Astrée ▲ E 8507 [DDD]

Fabuel, Gloria (sop)

Martin Y Soler, V.:Una Cosa rara, w. M. A. Peters (sop), M. Figueras (sop), E. Palacio (ten), F. Belaza-Leoz (bar), S. Palatchi (bass), F. Garrigosa (bass), I. Fresán (sgr), J. Savall (cnd), Concert des Nations, La Capella Reial de Catalunya [I] *(rec 1991)* — Astrée 3–▲ E 8760 [DDD]

Facini, Enrico (ten)

Monteverdi, C.:Orfeo, w. Nuccia Focile (sop), Claudia Clarich (mez), Paolo Coni (bar), James Loomis (bass), H. Handt (cnd), Lucchese CO [orchd Respighi, 1934–35] *(rec live, VII Festival Internazionale di Marlia, 1984)* — Claves ▲ CD 9419 [ADD]

Verdi, G.:Il trovatore, w. Antonella Banaudi (sop—Leonora), Barbara Frittoli (sop—Ines), Shirley Verrett (mez—Azucena), Enrico Facini (ten—Un messo), Piero de Palma (ten—Ruiz), Luciano Pavarotti (ten—Marico), Leo Nucci (bar—Il Conte di Luna), Roberto Scaltriti (bar—Un vecchio zingaro), Francesco Ellero d'Artegna (bass—Ferrando), Z. Mehta (cnd), Florence Maggio Musicale Orch, Florence Maggio Musicale Chorus *(rec Maggio Musicale Fiorentino Community Theater, June 18–July 2, 1990)* — London 2–▲ 430694–2

Facini, Francesco (bass)

Mayr, S.:La rosa bianca e la rosa rossa, w. Susanna Anselmi (sop), Anna Caterina Antonacci (sop), Silvia Mazzoni (mez), Luca Canonici (ten), Danilo Serraiocco (bass), T. Briccetti (cnd), Bergamo Stabile Orch — Fonit Cetra ("Ricordi" series) 2–▲ FCT RFCD 2007

Menichetti, D.:L'Epifania del Signore, w. K. Gamberucci (sop), A. Palombi (sgr), A. Della Santa (sgr), F. Esposito (sgr), H. Handt (cnd), Toscana Accademia Strumentale, Polifonica Lucchese — Bongiovanni ▲ GB 5033 [DDD]

Rossini, G.:La cambiale di matrimonio, w. Alessandra Rossi (sop), Maurizio Comencini (ten), Bruno Praticò (bar), Bruno De Simone (bar), Valeria Baiano (bass), M. Viotti (cnd), English CO — Claves ▲ 50-9101

Fagan, Leslie (sop)

Handel, G.F.:Messiah, w. Janis Taylor (mez), Mark Dubois (ten), Gary Relyea (b-bar), G. Fagan (cnd), Concert Players Orch, Gerald Fagan Singers, London Fanshawe Symphonic Chorus — Doremi 2–▲ 9306 [DDD]

▲ = CD ♦ = Enhanced CD Δ = MD ■ = Cassette Tape ▯ = DCC

Fagotto, Gianpaolo (ten)

Gesualdo, D.C.:Madrigals, w. Elena Cecchi Fedi (sop), Roberta Invernizzi (sop), Daniela Del Monaco (cta), Roberto Balconi (ct), Giuseppe Zambon (ten), Giovanni Dagnino (bass), A. Curtis (cnd), I Fegi Armonici—Book 6 [Se la Mia Morte Brami; Beltà Poi Che T'Assenti; Tu Piangi Ô Fille Mia; Resta di Darmi Noia; Chiaro Risplender Suole; others] Symphonia ▲ SYM 94133

Peri, J.:Euridice, w. Monica Benvenuti (sop—Ninfa I/Venere), Rossana Bertini (sop—Dafne/Ninfa II), Gloria Banditelli (cta—Euridice/Ninfa III/Tragedia/Proserpina), Mario Cecchetti (ten—Aminta/Radamanto), Paolo Da Col (ten—Tirsi), Gianpaolo Fagotto (ten—Orfeo), Giuseppe Zambon (ct—Arcetro), Sergio Foresti (bass—Caronte/Pastore), Furio Zanasi (bass—Plutone), R. de Caro (cnd), Arpeggione Ensemble *(rec Bologna, Italy, Nov 1992)* Arts Music 2-▲ 47276-2 [DDD]

Scarlatti, A.:Cants & Duets, w. C. Miatello (sop), C. Cavina (alt), L. Scoppola (sgr), P. Pandolfo (ctb), R. Sensi (sgr), R. Alessandrini (cnd)—Clori mia, Clori bella (cantata for soprano, flute & bass continuo); Dimmi crudele, e quando (duet for soprano, alto & bass continuo); Son pur care le catene (duet for soprano, alto & bass continuo); Sovente Amor mi chiama (cantata for alto & bass continuo); Ammore, brutto figlio de pottana (cantata for tenor & bass continuo) [I] Tactus ▲ TC 661901

Scarlatti, A.:Lamentazioni par la Settimana Santa, w. C. Miatello (sop), Aurora Ensemble Symphonia ▲ SYM 92D17 [DDD]

Stradella, A.:Cants, w. Cristina Miatello (sop), Antonio Abete (sgr), Roberto Balconi (sgr), Lavinia Bertotti (sgr), Roberta Giua (sgr), S. Balestracci (cnd), Santo Spirito Academy Orch, Santo Spirito Academy Chorus—for 5 w. vns [For Holy Christmas]; for 5 w. instruments [For the Souls in Purgatory] Stradivarius ▲ STV 33392 [DDD]

Fahberg, Antonia (sop)

Bach, J.S.:Cant 80, w. Bargarete Bence (cta), Theophil Maier (ten), Ulrich Schaible (bass), H. Rilling (cnd), Württemberg CO, Stuttgart Memorial Church Figuralchor *(rec 1964)* Vox Box 3-▲ CD3X 3039

Bach, J.S.:St. Matthew Passion, w. I. Seefried (sop), H. Töpper (alt), E. Haefliger (ten), D. Fischer-Dieskau (bar), K. Engen (bass), M. Proebstl (bass), K. Richter (cnd), Munich Bach Orch, Munich Bach Choir Archiv ▲ 439338-2 [ADD]

Janácek, L.:The Excursions of Mr. Brouček, w. Antonie Fahberg (sop—Piccolo), Wilma Lipp (sop—Málinka), Lilian Benningsen (cta—Fanny Nowak), Paul Kuen (ten—Trambahn-Kondukteur), Karl Ostertag (ten—Vorsitzender des Hausbesitzerverbandes), Fritz Wunderlich (ten—Mazal), Kurt Böhme (b-bar—Sakristan von St. Veit), Kieth Engen (bass—Würfl), J. Keilberth (cnd), Bavarian SO *(rec live, Prinzregententheater, Nov. 19, 1959)* Orfeo 2-▲ 354942 (m)

Schubert, Franz:Lazarus, or Die Feier der Auferstehung, w. H. Banzhaf (cnd), Pro Musica Sacra Orch, Pro Musica Sacra Chorus Studio SM ▲ 2498

Strauss, R.:Feuersnot, w. Maud Cunitz (sop—Diemut), Antonia Fahberg (sop—Elsbeth), Irmgard Barth (mez—Wigelis), Liselotte Nölser (sgr—Margret), Karl Ostertag (ten—Schweiker), Marcel Cordes (bar—Kunrad), Kieth Engen (bass—Kofel), Karl Hoppe (bass—Hämerlein), Max Proebstl (bass—Ortolf), Georg Wieter (bass—Jörg), R. Kempe (cnd), Bavarian State Opera Orch, Bavarian State Opera Chorus *(rec Munich Opera Festival, Prince Regent Theater, Aug 14, 1958)* Orfeo d'or 2-▲ 423962

Fair, J. (sgr)

Giordano, U.:Andrea Chénier, w. Montserrat Caballé (sop), Franco Corelli (ten), R. de Carlo (sgr), D. Dondi (sgr), G. Ellsworth (sgr), R. Falk (sgr), S. Felter (sgr), E. Green (sgr), H. Hicks (sgr), H. Krauss (sgr), L. Miller (sgr), N. Riggins (sgr), H. Salerno (sgr), A. Guadagno (cnd), Academy of Music Orch, Academy of Music Chorus Great Opera Performances 2-▲ GOP 766

Fairbanks, Nola (sgr)

Strauss (II), Joh.:Eine Nacht in Venedig, w. Nola Fairbanks (sgr—Ciboletta), Thomas Tibbett Hayward (sgr—Mario), Laurel Hurley (sgr—Nina), David Kurlan (sgr—Senator Bartoldi), Guen Omeron (sgr—Barbara), Jack Russell (sgr—Duke of Palobino), Kenneth Schon (sgr—Filippo Del Aqua), Norwood Smith (sgr—Caramello), Enzo Stuarti (sgr—Pappacoda) *(rec Belock Recording Studio, Bayside, NY)* Everest ▲ EVC 9036 [AAD]

Faithfull, Marianne (sgr)

Badalamenti, A.:The City of Lost Children [original film score] Point Music ▲ 314-532047-2

Falchi, R. de (bar)

Verdi, G.:Aida (sels), w. M. Callas (sop), E. Stignani (mez), M. Picchi (ten), G. Neri (bass), V. Bellezza (cnd), Rome Opera Orch—five arias with Callas (solo, three duets & quintet) *(rec live 10/2/50)* Melodram 2-▲ CDM 26019 [AAD]

Falcon, Ruth (sop)

Mascagni, P.:Cavalleria rusticana, w. Ruth Falcon (sop—Lola), Leonie Rysanek (sop—Santuzza), Astrid Varnay (sop—Mamma Lucia), Plácido Domingo (ten—Turiddu), Benito di Bella (bar—Alfio), N. Santi (cnd), Munich National Theater Orch, Munich National Theater Chorus *(rec Munich, Dec 25, 1978)* Legato Classics ▲ LCD 202-1

Falewicz, Magdalena (sop)

Gluck, C.W.:Orfeo ed Euridice, w. M. Kweksilber (sop), R. Jacobs (alt), S. Kuijken (cnd), La Petite Bande, Collegium Vocale Accent 2-▲ 48223/24 [DDD]

Schubert, Franz:Alfonso und Estrella, w. E. Mathis (sop), P. Schreier (ten), H. Prey (bar), D. Fischer-Dieskau (bar), T. Adam (b-bar), O. Suitner (cnd), Berlin Staatskapelle, Berlin Radio Chorus Berlin Classics 3-▲ BER 2156 [ADD]

Falk, Julianna (cta)

Handel, G.F.:Judas Maccabaeus, w. Agnes Giebel (sop), Fritz Wunderlich (ten), L. Welter (bar), Pöld (sgr), R. Kubelik (cnd), Bavarian RSO, Bavarian Chorus [G] *(rec live 10/25/63)* Melodram 2-▲ MEL 28026 [AAD]

Falk, R. (sgr)

Giordano, U.:Andrea Chénier, w. Montserrat Caballé (sop), Franco Corelli (ten), R. de Carlo (sgr), D. Dondi (sgr), G. Ellsworth (sgr), J. Fair (sgr), S. Felter (sgr), E. Green (sgr), H. Hicks (sgr), H. Krauss (sgr), L. Miller (sgr), N. Riggins (sgr), H. Salerno (sgr), A. Guadagno (cnd), Academy of Music Orch, Academy of Music Chorus Great Opera Performances 2-▲ GOP 766

Fallot, Marilyne (sgr)

Leo, L.:Amor vuol sofferenze, w. Marilena Laurenza (sop), Vitalba Mosca (mez), Piero Guarnera (bar), Domenico Colaianni (sgr), Giovanna Donadini (sgr), Hyun Lee (sgr), D. Moles (cnd), Naples New Scarlatti Orch *(rec Martinafranca Festival, 1994)* Nuova Era 3-▲ NUO 7221

Fan, Jing Ma (sgr)

Puccini, G.:Madama Butterfly (sels), w. Ying Huang (sop—Cio-Cio-San), Constance Hauman (mez—Kate Pinkerton), Ning Liang (mez—Suzuki), Richard Troxell (ten—B. F. Pinkerton), Richard Cowan (sgr—Sharpless), Jing Ma Fan (sgr—Goro), Christopheren Nomura (sgr—Prince Yamadori), J. Conlon (cnd), Orch de Paris—Dovunque al Mondo; B. F. Pinkerton Giù; Bimba, Bimba, Non Piangere; Ah! Vien! Sei Mia!; Un Bel Dí; Ora a Noi; Petali d'Ogni Fior; Coro a Bocca Chiusa; Prelude; Io So Che Alle Sue Pene; Ah! Son Vil!; E Sia! A Lui Devo Obbedir; Butterfly! *(rec Olivier Messiaen Auditorium, Paris, 1996)* Sony Classical ▲ SK 61972 [DDD]

Fanateanu, Corneliu (ten)

Puccini, G.:Tosca, w. Virginia Zeani (sop—Floria Tosca), Emilia Oprea (mez—Shepherd), Nicolae Andreescu (ten—Spoletta), Corneliu Fanateanu (ten—Mario Cavaradossi), Nicolae Herlea (bar—Baron Scarpia), Gheorghe Crasnaru (bass—Cesare Angelotti), Constantin Gabor (bass—Sacristan), Pompei Harasteanu (bass—Jailer), Adrian Stefanescu (bass—Sciarrone), C. Trailescu (cnd), Romanian Opera Orch, Romanian Opera Chorus *(rec Sept 1977)* Vox Box 2-▲ CDX 5153

Fanciullacci, Paolo (ten)

Perti, G.A.:Liturgy for Good Friday, w. Patrizia Vaccari (sop), Maura Pederzoli (sop), Cristina Calzolari (sop), Alida Oliva (sop), Claudia Bugli (sop), Lucia Bagnoli (alt), Cinzia Meneghel (alt), Renzo Bez (alt), Alessandro Carmignani (alt), Michel van Goethem (alt), Mauro Collina (ten), Vincenzo Di Donato (ten), Paolo Fanciullacci (ten), Giovanni Caccamo (ten), Paolo Da Col (ten), Sergio Foresti (bass), Marco Scavazza (bass), Luca Ferracin (bass), Paride Montanari (bass), Liuwe Tamminga (org), Sergio Vartolo (org), S. Vartolo (cnd), Bologna San Petronio Capella Musicale Orch—Omnes amici mei; De lamentatione Jeremiae Prophetae:Heth. Cogitavit; Velum templi; Vinea mea; De lamentatione Jeremiae Prophetae:Lamed. Matribus suis; Tamquam ad latronem; Tenebrae factae sunt; Animam meam; Tradiderunt me; Jesum tradidit; De lamentatione Jeremiae Prophetae:Aleph. Ego vir; Caligaverunt *(rec St. Petronio Basilica, Bologna, Mar 28-31, 1995)* Naxos ▲ 8.553321 [DDD]

Fandrey, Birgit (sgr)

Künneke, E.:The Alluring Flame, w. Birgit Fandrey (sgr—Dolores), Christianne Hossfeld (sgr—Lisbeth), Maria Mallé (sgr), Jürgen Sacher (ten—Master), Ralf Lukas (bar—Hoffman), Gerd Grochowski (sgr—1st Neighbor), Gerhard Peters (sgr—Friedrich), Zoran Todorovic (sgr—Jacinto), Theodor Weimer (sgr—2nd Neighbor), P. Falk (cnd), Cologne RSO, Cologne Radio Chorus *(rec Cologne, Nov 7-26, 1994)* Capriccio ▲ 10753 [DDD]

Fanelli, Maria Luisa (sop)

Verdi, G.:Requiem Mass, w. Irene Minghini-Cattaneo (mez), Fracno Lo Giudice (ten), E. Pinza (bass), C. Sabajno (cnd), La Scala Orch, La Scala Chorus *(rec 1927 for HMV)* Pearl ▲ GEMMCD 9374 (m) [AAD]

Fanjat (sop)

Nivers, G.G.:Motets, w. J. Nicolas (sop), Boraly (sgr), Malardenti (sgr), Maréchal (sgr), Houbart (org)—Motet a la Sainte Vierge pour le temps de Paques; Motet pour L'Elévation; Motet pour le Saint Sacrament; Motet du temps de carême pour le Saint Sacrement; Motet du temps de Noël pour le Saint Sacrement; Motet final du tout office pour le Roy [L] Pierre Verany ▲ PV.791101 [DDD]

Faragó (sop)

Bartók, B.:Village Scenes, w. Adám (sop), A. Dorati (cnd), Budapest Chamber Ensemble, Györ Girls' Choir [Slovak] Hungaroton ▲ HCD 31047 [ADD]

Szokolay, S.:Blood Wedding, w. E. Házy (sop), O. Szönyi (sop), E. Komlóssy (cta), A. Kórodi (cnd), Hungarian State Opera Orch, Hungarian State Opera Chorus [Hun] Hungaroton 2-▲ HCD 11262/63 [ADD]

Fardilha, Josè (bass)

Rossini, G.:La pietra del paragone, w. Tiziana Carraro (sop—Fulvia), Elisabetta Gutierrez (mez—Baronessa Aspasia), Sara Mingardo (cta—Clarice), William Matteuzzi (ten—Giocondo), Marco Camastra (bar—Pacuvio), Pietro Spagnoli (bar—Conte Asdrubale), Gioacchino Zarrelli (bar—Fabrizio), Josè Fardilha (bass—Macrobio), B. Aprea (cnd), Graz SO, Sluk Chamber Chorus Bratislava *(rec 1993)* Bongiovanni 2-▲ GB 2179/80 [DDD]

Farina, Ida (sgr)

Massenet, J.:Manon (sels), w. Mirella Freni (sop), Luciano Pavarotti (ten), Franco Ricciardi (ten), Wladimiro Ganzarolli (bar), Giuseppe Morresi (bass), Antonio Zerbini (bass), P. Maag (cnd), La Scala Orch, La Scala Chorus *(rec live, Milan, 1969)* Budget ("The Greatest Voice in Opera" series) ▲ SYP 110

Verdi, G.:Requiem Mass, w. James (sgr), Shafer (sgr), Crawford (sgr), D. Moe (cnd), Oberlin Musical Union Orch [L] Bainbridge 2-▲ BCD 2103 [DDD]

Farinelli, Hanna (sop)

Dittersdorf, K.D. von:Sacred Music, w. Birgit Calm (alt), Heiner Hopfner (ten), Nikolaus Hillebrand (bass), G. Ratzinger (cnd), Munich Consortium Musicum, Regensburg Cathedral Choir—Requiem in c; Offertorium zu Ehren des Heiligen Johann von Nepomuk; Laurentanische Litanei Ars Musici ▲ AM 1158-2 [DDD]

Faringer, Solveig (sop)

Burkhart, F.:Adventslieder (3), w. Clas Pehrsson (rcr), Jörgen Rörby (gtr) *(rec Castle Wik, Sweden, Jan 19, 20 & 26, 1974)* BIS ▲ CD 202 [AAD]

Kukuck, F.:Die Brücke, w. Clas Pehrsson (rcr), Jörgen Rörby (gtr) *(rec Castle Wik, Sweden, Jan 19, 20 & 26, 1974)* BIS ▲ CD 202 [AAD]

Lundén, L.:Little Toe & Nine More, w. Clas Pehrsson (rcr), Jörgen Rörby (gtr) *(rec Castle Wik, Sweden, Jan 19, 20 & 26, 1974)* BIS ▲ CD 202 [AAD]

Sonninen, A.:El amor pasa, w. Gunilla von Bahr (fl), S. Westerberg (cnd), Swedish RSO members *(rec Stockholm Concert Hall, Sweden, Sept. 17, 1974)* BIS ▲ CD 11 [AAD]

Farkas, Katalin (sop)

Handel, G.F.:Brockes-Passion, w. M. Zádori (sop), D. Minter (alt), J. Bándi (ten), M. Klietmann (ten), G. de Mey (ten), I. Gáti (bar), N. McGegan (cnd), Capella Savaria, Hallé State Chorus [period instrs] [G] Hungaroton 3-▲ HCD 12734/36 [DDD]

Pergolesi, G.B.:La serva padrona, w. J. Gregor (bass), P. Németh (cnd), Capella Savaria [period instrs] [F,I] Hungaroton ▲ HCD 12846 [DDD]

Farley, Carole (sop)

Britten, H.:Les Illuminations, w. J. Serebrier (cnd), Scottish CO Phoenix ▲ PHCD 111 [DDD]

Lemeland, A.:Omaha:Chant pour les soldats morts, w. M. Tardue (cnd), Grenoble Instrumental String Ensemble Skarbo ▲ SKR 2338 [DDD]

Marschner, H.A.:Der Vampyr, w. Carole Farley (sop—Malwina), Nucci Condò (mez—Suse), Oslavio Di Credico (ten—George Dibdin), Josef Protschka (ten—Edgar Aubry), Romano Truffelli (ten—Richard Scrop), Martin Egel (bar—Sir Humphrey Davenaut), Andréa Snarski (bar—Toms Blunt), Siegmund Nimsgern (b-bar—Lord Ruthven), Armando Caforio (bass—Robert Green), Peter Boom (sgr—Il capo dei Vampiri), Carlo Di Giacomo (sgr—James Gadshill), Wolfgang Lenz (sgr—Sir Berkley), Galina Pisarenko (sgr—Janthe), Renzo Scorsoni (sgr—Un servitore di Berkley), Anastasia Tomaszewska Schepis (sgr—Emmy), G. Neuhold (cnd), Rome RAI SO, Rome RAI Chorus *(rec Rome, Jan 26, 1980)* Italia 2-▲ CDC 99 [ADD]

Poulenc, F.:La Voix humaine, w. J. Serebrier (cnd), Adelaide SO [F] Chandos ▲ CHAN 8331 [DDD]

Prokofiev, S.:Songs, w. R. Vignoles (pno)—Five Poems, Op. 23; Five Melodies, Op. 35; Three Children's Songs, Op. 68; Two Russian Songs, Op. 104 [R] ASV ▲ ASV 669 [DDD]

Prokofiev, S.:The Ugly Duckling, w. R. Vignoles (pno) [R] ASV ▲ ASV 669 [DDD]

Tchaikovsky, P.:Arias, w. J. Serebrier (cnd), Melbourne SO, Sicilian SO—15 arias from composer's 8 major operas IMP Masters ▲ IMPMCD 64 [DDD]

Tchaikovsky, P.:Eugene Onegin (sels), w. J. Serebrier (cnd), Melbourne SO—Tatiana's Letter Scene IMP ("Concert Classics" series) ▲ IMP PCD 1102

Weill, K.:Songs, w. R. Vignoles (pno)—(songs from 1914-1950) including Reiterlied; Speak low; Is it him or is it me; The saga of Jenny; That's him; One life to live; Foolish heart; Matrosen-Tango; Alabama Song; Havanna-Lied; Das schöne Kind; Polly's Lied (Hübsch als es währte); Denn wie man sich bettet, so liegt man; etc. ASV ▲ ASV 790

Farrar, Geraldine (sop)

Bizet, G.:Carmen (sels), w. Geraldine Farrar (sop—Carmen), Giovanni Martinelli (ten—Don José), Pasquale Amato (bar—Escamillo), W. Rogers (cnd), *(orch unknown)*—L'amour est un oiseau rebelle; Près des remparts; Les tringles des sistres; Couplets du Toréador; Halte là! Qui va là?; Au quartier! pour l'appel!; La fleur que tu m'avais jetée; Non, tu ne m'aimes pas...Là-bas, dans la montagne; Voyons que j'essaie; Je dis que rien ne m'épouvante; Aragonaise [Prelude to Act 4; w. Arturo Toscanini (cnd), La Scala Orch]; Si tu m'aimes, Carmen; C'est toi! C'est moi!; Mais moi, Carmen, je t'aime encore Nimbus ▲ NI 7872 [ADD]

Caruso, Ferrar & Journet:Highlights from Faust & French Opera, w. E. Caruso (ten), Marcel Journet (bass) Nimbus ▲ NI 7859 [ADD]

The Complete Odéon & Victor Recordings, w. E. Clément (ten), Marcel Journet (bass), Frank La Forge (pno), Rosario Bourdon (cnd) *(rec Odeon 1905; Victor 1911-1)* Romophone ▲ 82002-2

18 Arias, w. G. Farrar (sop) Pearl ▲ PEA 9420 (m) [AAD]

Ferrar in Italian Opera, w. G. Farrar (sop) *(rec 1908-13)* Nimbus ▲ NI 7857 [ADD]

Gounod, C.:Roméo et Juliette (sels), w. *(orch unknown)*—Je veux vivre dans ce rêve; Ange adorable [w. Edmond Clément (ten)] Nimbus ▲ NI 7872 [ADD]

Massenet, J.:Manon (sels), w. *(cnd & orch unknown)*—Allons! Il le faut...Adieu, notre petite table *(rec Dec. 8, 1908)* Nimbus ▲ NI 7872 [ADD]

Massenet, J.:Thaïs (sels)—Te souvient-il du lumineux voyage *(rec Apr. 2, 1918)* Nimbus ▲ NI 7872 [ADD]

Offenbach, J.:Les Contes d'Hoffmann (sels), w. Antonio Scotti (bar), *(orch unknown)*—Belle nuit, ô nuit d'amour *(rec Oct. 6, 1909)* Nimbus ▲ NI 7872 [ADD]

Thomas, A.:Mignon (sels), w. Fritz Kreisler (vn), W. Rogers (cnd), *(orch unknown)*—Connais-tu le pays? *(rec May 24, 1915)* Nimbus ▲ NI 7872 [ADD]

Farrell, Eileen (sop)

Beethoven, L. van:Missa Solemnis, w. C. Smith (mez), R. Lewis (ten), K. Borg (bass), L. Bernstein (cnd), New York PO, Westminster Choir [L] Sony Classical 2-▲ SM2K 47522 [ADD]

Beethoven, L. van:Music of, w. Anthony Newman (kbd), *(other artists unknown)*, Giulini (cnd), *(orchs unknown)*—sels from Syms 5, 7 & 9; Son No. 8 for Pno; sels from Fidelio; plus others Sony Classical ("Greatest Hits" series) ▲ MLK 62681 ■ MLT 62681

Farrell, Eileen (sop) (cont.)

Berg, A.:Wozzeck, w. F. Jagel (ten), M. Harrell (bar), R. Lloyd (bass), D. Mitropoulos (cnd), New York PO *(rec live 1950)* Andromeda ▲ ANR 2514 [ADD]

Handel, G.F.:Messiah, w. Martha Lipton (cta), T. Cunningham (ten), William Warfield (bar), E. Ormandy (cnd), Philadelphia Orch, Mormon Tabernacle Choir [E] CBS 2-▲ M2K 00607 ■ M2T 00607

Love Is Letting Go DRG ▲ DRG 91436 [ADD]

Opera Arias & Songs, w. George Trovillo (pno), Philharmonia Orch [cnd:Thomas Schippers] Testament ▲ SBT 1073

Rodgers, R.:The Sound of Music, w. F. von Stade (mez), Håkan Hagegård (ten), B. Daniels (sgr), L. D. von Schlanbusch (sgr), et al., E. Kunzel (cnd), Cincinnati Pops Orch, May Festival Chorus [1987 studio cast] Telarc ▲ CD 80162 [DDD] ■ CS 30162

Verdi, G.:Arias, w. G. Tucker (ten) [duets] Odyssey ■ YT 35935

Verdi, G.:La forza del destino, w. J. Grillo (sop), F. Corelli (ten), A. Colzani (bar), E. Flagello (bass), A. Guadagno (cnd), *(orch unknown)* [I] *(rec live, Philadelphia 4/14/65)* Standing Room Only 2-▲ SRO 826-2 [ADD]

Verdi, G.:Music of, w. Richard Tucker (ten) [w. Vienna State Opera Orch [cnd:Nello Santi], Columbia SO [cnd:Fausto Cleva], New Philharmonia Orch [cnd:Franz Allers]]—arias & duets from Aida; Un ballo in maschera; I Lombardi; I due Foscari; Simon Boccanegra; Il trovatore; Luisa Miller; Rigoletto; I vespri siciliani; La forza del destino; Otello Sony Classical ("Masterworks Heritage" series) ▲ MHK 62357

Verdi, G.:Music of [w. Richard Tucker (ten), Columbia SO [cnds:Max Rudolf & Fausto Cleva]]—arias & 1 duet from Aida; Il trovatore; Don Carlo; Otello; La forza del destino; Simon Boccanegra; Un ballo in maschera Sony Classical ("Masterworks Heritage" series) ▲ MHK 62358

The Voices of Living Stereo, Vol. 2, w. Birgit Nilsson (sop), Roberta Peters (sop), Leontyne Price (sop), Galina Vishnevskaya (sop), Rosalind Elias (mez), Shirley Verrett (mez), Marian Anderson (cta), Maureen Forrester (cta), Sergio Franchi (ten), Mario Lanza (ten), Richard Lewis (ten), Jan Pee, Alexander Dedyukhin (pno), Franz Rupp (pno), Leo Taubman (pno), George Trovillo (pno), Charles Wadsworth (pno), Boston Pops Orch [cnd:Arthur Fiedler], Boston SO [cnd:Charles Munch], Chicago SO [cnd:Fritz Reiner], RCA Victor Orch, RCA Victor Chorus [cnd:Wa *(rec Boston & Chicago & New York & Rome, 1957–1964)* RCA Living Stereo ▲ 09026-68167-2 [ADD]

Wagner, R.:Götterdämmerung (immolation scene), w. C. Munch (cnd), Boston SO RCA Gold Seal ▲ 09026-60686-2

Wagner, R.:Götterdämmerung (immolation scene), w. V. de Sabata (cnd), New York PO *(rec 1951)* Arkadia ▲ 512 (m) [AAD]

Wagner, R.:Ovs, Preludes & Orch Sels, w. L. Bernstein (cnd), New York PO—Tannhäuser:Ov.; Götterdämmerung:Finale Act 3; Tristan und Isolde:Prelude Act 1 *(rec 1961 & 1967)* Sony Classical ▲ SMK 47644 [ADD]

Farrow, Norman (b-bar)

Bach, J.S.:Arias, w. Lois Marshall (sop), Maureen Forrester (alt), Richard Lewis (ten), Oscar Shumsky (vn), Brian Priestman (cnd), *(chorus unknown)*—Arias Nos. 32, 42, 120a, 132, & 182; Duet from Cant. 205 Vox Box 2-▲ CDX 5127 [ADD]

Bach, J.S.:Cant 3, w. Lois Marshall (sop), Maureen Forrester (alt), Richard Lewis (ten), B. Priestman (cnd), *(orch unknown)*, *(chorus unknown)* Vox Box 2-▲ CDX 5127 [ADD]

Bach, J.S.:Cant 102, w. Maureen Forrester (alt), Richard Lewis (ten), G. Leonhardt (cnd), Leonhardt Consort, Brian Priestman (cnd), *(chorus unknown)* Vox Box 2-▲ CDX 5127 [ADD]

Fassbaender, Brigitte (mez)

Bach, J.S.:Christmas Oratorio, w. E. Ameling (sop), H. Laubenthal (ten), H. Prey (bar), E. Jochum (cnd), Tölz SO, Bavarian Radio Boys' Chorus—highlights Philips ("Silver Line" series) ▲ 422252-2 [ADD]

Bach, J.S.:Mass in b, BWV 232, w. Helen Donath (sop), Claes H. Ahnsjö (ten), Roland Hermann (bar), Robert Holl (bass), E. Jochum (cnd), Bavarian RSO, Bavarian Radio Chorus EMI Classics ("Doublefforte" series) 2-▲ CDFB 68640

Bach, J.S.:St. John Passion (sels), w. W. Gönnenwein (cnd), Consortium Musicum, South German Madrigal Choir—Es ist vollbracht; Ruht wohl, ihr heiligen Gebeine *(rec Église de Schwaigern, Oct. 1969)* EMI Classics ▲ CDK 65334 [ADD]

Beethoven, L. van:Sym 9, "Choral Sym", w. Jessye Norman (sop), Plácido Domingo (ten), Walter Berry (bass), K. Böhm (cnd), Vienna PO, Vienna State Opera Chorus Deutsche Grammophon ("Masters" series) ▲ 445503-2 [DDD]

Berg, A.:Lulu, w. P. Wise (sop—Lulu), B. Fassbaender (mez—Countess Geschwitz), H. Hotter (b-bar—Schigolch), J. Tate (cnd), French National Orch—Act 3 [G] *(rec live 9 & 10/91)* EMI Classics 3-▲ CDCC 54622 [DDD]

Berg, A.:Lulu, w. A. Silja (sop), W. Berry (b-bar), K. Moll (bass), H. Hotter (b-bar), A. Szramek (sgr), C. von Dohnányi (cnd), Vienna PO London 2-▲ 430415-2 [ADD]

Berg, A.:Songs, Op. 2, w. John Wustman (pno) [G] Acanta ▲ 43579

Berlioz, H.:Roméo et Juliette, w. N. Gedda (ten), J. Shirley-Quirk (bar), L. Gardelli (cnd), ORF SO, Vienna State Opera Chorus [F] Orfeo 2-▲ 087842 [DDD]

Brahms, J.:Ernste Gesänge, w. E. Leonskaja (pno) Teldec ▲ 74872-2

Brahms, J.:Liebeslieder Waltzes SATB, w. E. Mathis (sop), P. Schreier (ten), D. Fischer-Dieskau (bar), K. Engel (pno), W. Sawallisch (pno) [G] Deutsche Grammophon ▲ 423133-2 [DDD]

Brahms, J.:Neue Liebeslieder Waltzes, w. E. Mathis (sop), P. Schreier (ten), D. Fischer-Dieskau (bar), K. Engel (pno), W. Sawallisch (pno) [G] Deutsche Grammophon ▲ 423133-2 [DDD]

Brahms, J.:Romanzen aus Tieck's *Magelone*, w. E. Leonskaja (pno) *(rec Berlin, March 1993)* Teldec ▲ 90854-2 [DDD]

Brahms, J.:Songs, w. I. Gage (pno)—18 songs [G] Acanta ▲ 43507

Brahms, J.:Songs, w. E. Leonskaja (pno) Teldec ▲ 74872-2

Dvořák, A.:Requiem Mass, w. G. Benačková (sop), T. Moser (ten), J.-H. Rootering (bass), W. Sawallisch (cnd), Czech PO, Czech Chorus [L] Supraphon 2-▲ 10 4241 [DDD]

Enescu, G.:Oedipe, w. B. Hendricks (sop), M. Lipovšek (mez), J. Taillon (mez), N. Gedda (ten), J. Aler (ten), G. Bacquier (bar), Quilico (bar), J. Van Dam (bass-bar), L. Foster (cnd), Monte Carlo PO, Orféon Donostiarra, Petits Chanteurs de Monaco [F] EMI Classics 2-▲ CDCB 54011 [DDD]

Fall, L.:Der fidele Bauer (sels), w. Sonja Knittel (sop), Heinz Hoppe (ten), Fritz Wunderlich (ten), Benno Kusche (bass), C. Michalski (cnd), Graunke SO, Rudolf Lamy Singers Emperor Operetta ▲ KO 86353

Famous Arias Orfeo ▲ 096841 [DDD]

Gounod, C.:Faust, w. C. Gasdia (sop), S. Mentzer (mez), J. Hadley (ten), A. Agache (bar), P. Fourcade (bass), C. Rizzi (cnd), Welsh National Opera Orch, Welsh National Opera Chorus Teldec 3-▲ 90872

Haydn, J.:Mass 10, "Kriegsmesse", "Paukenmesse", w. Judith Blegen (sop), Claes Hakan Ahnsjö (ten), Hans Sotin (bass), L. Bernstein (cnd), Bavarian RSO, Bavarian Radio Chorus [L] Philips ▲ 412734-2 [DDD]

Hindemith, P.:When Lilacs Last In The Dooryard Bloom'd, w. D.Fischer-Dieskau (bar), W. Sawallisch (cnd), Vienna SO, Vienna State Opera Chorus [E] *(rec live, 11/1/83)* Orfeo ▲ 112851 [DDD]

Humperdinck, E.:Hänsel und Gretel, w. L. Popp (sop), J. Hamari (mez), A. Schlemm (mez), W. Berry (bass), G. Solti (cnd), Vienna PO London 2-▲ 421111-2 [ADD]

Mahler, G.:Des Knaben Wunderhorn, w. John Wustman (pno)—6 sels. [G] Acanta ▲ 43579

Mahler, G.:Das Lied von der Erde, w. T. Moser (ten), C. Katsaris (pno)—the first recording of Mahler's original piano/vocal score version [G] Teldec ▲ 2292-46276-2 ZK [DDD]

Mahler, G.:Das Lied von der Erde, w. F. Araiza (ten), C. M. Giulini (cnd), Berlin PO [G] Deutsche Grammophon ▲ 413459-2 [DDD]

Mahler, G.:Lieder eines fahrenden Gesellen, w. G. Sinopoli (cnd), Philharmonia Orch [G] Deutsche Grammophon 2-▲ 415959-2 [DDD]

Mahler, G.:Sym 2, w. R. Plowright (sop), G. Sinopoli (cnd), Philharmonia Orch, Philharmonia Chorus [G] Deutsche Grammophon 2-▲ 415959-2 [DDD]

Mendelssohn, F.:A Midsummer Night's Dream (comp), w. Edith Mathis (sop), O. Klemperer (cnd), Bavarian RSO, Bavarian Radio Chorus *(rec live, May 23, 1969)* Originals ▲ ORI SH 917

Fassbaender, Brigitte (mez) (cont.)

Mozart, W.A.:Arias, w. Arleen Augér (sop), Kathleen Battle (sop), Irma Beilke (sop), Helena Braun (sop), Lisa Della Casa (sop), Maria Cebotari (sop), Ileana Cotrubas (sop), Helen Donath (sop), Mirella Freni (sop), Reri Grist (sop), Edita Gruberova (sop), Elisabeth Grümmer (sop), Hilde Güden (sop), Ingeborg Hallstein (sop), Luise Helletsgruber (sop), Gundula Janowitz (sop), Sena Jurinac (sop), Erika Köth (sop), Evelyn Lear (sop), Wilma Lipp (sop), Margaret Marshall (sop), Edith Mathis (sop), Jarmila Novotna (sop), Margherita Perras (sop), Lucia Popp (sop), Elisabeth Rethberg (sop), Anneliese Rothenberger (sop), Elisabeth Schumann (sop), Elisabeth Schwarzkopf (sop), Graziella Sciutti (sop), Irmgard Seefried (sop), Graziella Sciutti (sop), Julia Varady (sop), Agnes Baltsa (mez), Brigitte Fassbaender (mez), Christa Ludwig (mez), Ann Murray (mez), Francisco Araiza (ten), Anton Dermota (ten), Helge Rosvaenge (ten), Rudolf Schock (ten), Peter Schreier (ten), Leopold Simoneau (ten), Eric Tappy (ten), Richard Tauber (ten), Gösta Winbergh (ten), Josef Witt (ten), Fritz Wunderlich (ten), Christian Boesch (bar), Willy Domgraf-Fassbaender (bar), Karl Dönch (bar), Dietrich Fischer-Dieskau (bar), Erich Kunz (bar), Eberhard Wächter (bar), Hans Hotter (b-bar), Paul Schöffler (b-bar), Cesare Siepi (b-bar), José Van Dam (b-bar), Walter Berry (bass), Geraint Evans (bass), Nicolai Ghiaurov (bass), Alexander Kipnis (bass), Richard Mayr (bass), Kurt Moll (bass), James Morris (bass), Ezio Pinza (bass), Martti Talvela (bass), Giorgio Tozzi (bass), Hans Duhan (sgr), Res Fischer (sgr), Marie Gerhart (sgr), *(various orchs & cnds)*—sels from Idomeneo, Die Entführung aus der Serail, Le nozze di Figaro, Don Giovanni, Così fan tutte, Die Zauberflöte & various arias Orfeo d'or ("Festspiel Dokumente" series) 5-▲ 408955

Mozart, W.A.:Clemenza, w. M. Casula (sop), L. Popp (sop), T. Berganza (mez), T. Franc (bass), F. Krenn (bass), I. Kertész (cnd), Vienna State Opera Orch, Vienna State Opera Chorus London ("Grand Opera" series) 2-▲ 430105-2 [ADD]

Mozart, W.A.:Complete Mozart Edition, w. T. Moser (ten), B. McDaniel (bar), L. Hager (cnd), Salzburg Mozarteum Orch Philips 3-▲ 422533-2 [ADD]

Mozart, W.A.:Così fan tutte, w. G. Janowitz (sop), R. Grist (sop), P. Schreier (ten), H. Prey (bar), D. Fischer-Dieskau (bar), K. Böhm (cnd), Vienna PO *(rec live, 1972)* Foyer 2-▲ FOY 2066 [ADD]

Mozart, W.A.:Così fan tutte (sels), w. G. Janowitz (sop), R. Grist (sop), P. Schreier (ten), H. Prey (bar), R. Panerai (bar), K. Böhm (cnd), Vienna PO, Vienna State Opera Chorus—scenes & arias Deutsche Grammophon ▲ 429824-2 [ADD]

Mussorgsky, M.:Songs & Dances, w. N. Järvi (cnd), Gothenburg SO Deutsche Grammophon ▲ 437785-2 [DDD]

Ogermann, C.:Tagore-Lieder, w. John Wustman (pno)—set of 7 songs [G] Acanta ▲ 43579

Schoeck, O.:Das Schloss Dürande (sels), w. Maria Cebotari (sop—Gabriele), Marta Fuchs (sop—Gräfin Morvaille), Brigitte Fassbaender (mez—Renald Willi Domgraf), Rut Berglund (cta—Priorin), Peter Anders (ten—Armand), Benno Arnold (ten—Jäger), Josef Greindl (bass—Nicole), Hans Wrana (bass—Jäger), Vasso Argyris (sgr—Volksredner), Otto Hüsch (sgr—Wildhüter), Leo Laschet (sgr—Jäger), Fritz Marcks (sgr—Jäger), Felix Schneider (sgr—Jäger), R. Heger (cnd)—Text; Ich kann es nicht glauben [from Act 1]; Text; Heil dir, du Feuerquelle [from Act 2]; Text; Gesucht und nicht gefunden [from Act 3]; Text; Der Jäger ist frei! [Act 3 Finale]; Text; Sie kommen mit Flinten und Stangen [Act 4]; Text; Du Narr des vermeintlichen Rechts [Act 4 finale]; Text *(rec live, Apr 1943)* Jecklin ▲ JD 692

Schoenberg, A.:Gurrelieder, w. S. Dunn (sop), S. Jerusalem (ten), P. Haage (ten), H. Becht (bass), H. Hotter (nar), R. Chailly (cnd), Berlin RSO, St. Hedwig's Cathedral Choir, Düsseldorf Municipal Choral Society [G] London 2-▲ 430321-2 [DDD]

Schubert, Franz:Mass 4, w. H. Donath (sop), F. Araiza (ten), D. Fischer-Dieskau (bar), W. Sawallisch (cnd), Bavarian RSO, Bavarian Radio Chorus [L] EMI Classics ("Studio" series) ▲ CDM 69222

Schubert, Franz:Mass 5, w. L. Popp (sop), A. Dallapozza (ten), D. Fischer-Dieskau (bar), W. Sawallisch (cnd), Bavarian RSO, Bavarian Radio Chorus [L] EMI Classics ("Studio" series) ▲ CDM 69222

Schubert, Franz:Mass 6, w. H. Donath (sop), F. Araiza (ten), D. Fischer-Dieskau (bar), W. Sawallisch (cnd), Bavarian RSO, Bavarian Radio Chorus [L] EMI Classics ("Studio" series) ▲ CDM 69223

Schubert, Franz:Schwanengesang, w. A. Reimann (pno) [G] Deutsche Grammophon ▲ 429766-2 [DDD]

Schubert, Franz:Songs (comp), w. G. Johnson (pno)—12 songs—D.59, 116, 433, 474, 584, 672, 744, 753, 754, 801, 871, 989 [G] Hyperion ▲ CDJ 33011

Schubert, Franz:Songs (misc), w. C. Garben (pno)—19 songs—D.138, 149, 216, 224, 225, 226, 257, 259, 295, 321, 328, 478, 544, 558, 719, 764, 766, 768, 877 [G] Sony Classical ▲ SK 53104 [DDD]

Schubert, Franz:Songs (misc), w. A. Reimann (pno)—5 Lieder [G] Deutsche Grammophon ▲ 429766-2 [DDD]

Schubert, Franz:Tantum ergo, D.962, w. L. Popp (sop), A. Dallapozza (ten), D. Fischer-Dieskau (bar), W. Sawallisch (cnd), Bavarian RSO, Bavarian Radio Chorus [L] EMI Classics ("Studio" series) ▲ CDM 69223

Schumann, R.:Liederkreis, Op. 39, w. E. Leonskaja (pno) Teldec ▲ 74872-2

Strauss (II), Joh.:Die Fledermaus, w. K. Te Kanawa (sop), E. Gruberová (sop), W. Brendel (bar), R. Leech (ten), O. Bär (bar), T. Krause (bar), A. Previn (cnd), Vienna PO, Vienna State Opera Chorus [G] Philips 2-▲ 432157-2 [DDD]

Strauss (II), Joh.:Die Fledermaus (sels), w. K. Te Kanawa (sop), E. Gruberova (sop), R. Leech (ten), W. Brendel (bar), O. Bär (bar), A. Previn (cnd), Vienna PO Philips ▲ 438503-2

Strauss, R.:Capriccio, w. Kiri Te Kanawa (sop—Gräfin), Brigitte Fassbaender (mez—Clairon), Uwe Heilmann (ten—Flamand), Werner Hollweg (ten—Taupe), Olaf Bär (bar—Olivier), Håkan Hagegård (bar—Graf), Victor von Halem (b-bar—La Roche), U. Schirmer (cnd), Vienna PO [G] *(rec Vienna, Dec 1993)* London 2-▲ 444405-2 [DDD]

Strauss, R.:Der Rosenkavalier, w. Erika Köth (sop—Sophie), Annelie Waas (sop—Marianne), Claire Watson (sop—Marschallin), Hertha Töpper (mez—Octavian), Brigitte Fassbaender (cta—Annina), Gerhard Stolze (ten—Valzacchi), Fritz Wunderlich (ten—Singer), Otto Wiener (bar—Faninal), Kurt Böhme (bass—Baron), J. Keilberth (cnd), Bavarian State Opera Orch, Bavarian State Opera Chorus *(rec Munich Opera Festival, National Theater, May 21, 1965)* Orfeo d'or 3-▲ 425963

Strauss, R.:Der Rosenkavalier, w. Claire Watson (sop—Feldmarschallin), Lucia Popp (sop—Sophie), Annelie Waas (sop—Marianne), Brigitte Fassbaender (mez—Octavian), Margaretthe Bence (ct—Annina), David Thaw (ten—Valzacchi), Karl Ridderbusch (bass—Baron Ochs), Benno Kusche (bass—Herr von Faninal), Albrecht Peter (bass—Police Inspector), C. Kleiber (cnd), Bavarian State Orch, Bavarian State Chorus *(rec live, Münchner Festspiele, July 20, 1974)* Arkadia 3-▲ 486 [ADD]

Strauss, R.:Der Rosenkavalier, w. C. Watson (sop), K. Ridderbusch (bass), C. Kleiber (cnd), Bavarian State Opera Orch *(rec 1977)* Exclusive 3-▲ EXL 49 [ADD]

Strauss, R.:Salome, w. E. Martón (sop), H. Zednik (ten), R. Lewis (ten), B. Weikl (bar), Z. Mehta (cnd), Berlin PO *(rec live)* Sony Classical 2-▲ S2K 46717

Verdi, G.:Rigoletto, w. E. Gruberova (sop), Schicoff (ten), R. Bruson (bar), R. Lloyd (b-bar), G. Sinopoli (cnd), St. Cecilia Academy Orch Rome, St. Cecilia Academy Chorus Rome [I] Philips 2-▲ 412592-2 [DDD]

Wagner, R.:Die Meistersinger von Nürnberg, w. Gundula Janowitz (sop), Sándor Kónya (ten), Gerhard Unger (ten), Thomas Helmsey (bar), Thomas Stewart (bar), Franz Crass (bass), R. Kubelik (cnd), Bavarian RSO, Bavarian Radio Chorus *(rec 1967)* Calig 4-▲ 5097174 [ADD]

Wagner, R.:Die Meistersinger von Nürnberg, w. G. Janowitz (sop), S. Kónya (ten), G. Unger (ten), T. Stewart (bar), F. Crass (bass), T. Hemsley (bass), R. Kubelik (cnd), Bavarian RSO, Bavarian Radio Chorus [G] *(rec live, Munich, Oct. 1967)* Myto 4-▲ 4 MCD 92569 [ADD]

Wagner, R.:Tristan und Isolde, w. M. Price (sop), A. Kollo (ten), D. Fischer-Dieskau (bar), K. Moll (bass), C. Kleiber (cnd), Dresden State Opera Orch [G] Deutsche Grammophon 4-▲ 413315-2 [DDD]

Weill, K.:The Seven Deadly Sins, w. K.-H. Brandt (ten), H. Sojer (ten), H. Komatsu (bass), I. Urbas (bass), C. Garben (cnd), North German Radio PO Harmonia Mundi France ▲ HMC 901420

Weill, K.:Songs, w. C. Garben (pno)—Complainte de la Seine; Youkali; Es regnet; Wie lange noch?; Nanna's Lied; Berlin im Licht Harmonia Mundi France ▲ HMC 901420

Wolf, H.:Mörike-Lieder (sels), w. J.-Y. Thibaudet (pno)—Zum neuen Jahr; Gebet; Fubreise; Auf einer wanderung;Peregrina 1 & 2; Lebe wohl; Verborgenheit; Auf ein altes Bild; Schlafendes Jesuskind; An den Schlaf; Das verlassene Mägdlein; In der Frühe; Gesang Weylas; Im Frühling; Denk es, o Seele!; Dr Gärtner; Begegnung; Nimmersatte Liebe; Der Knabe und das Immlein; Bel einer Trauung; Storchenbotschaft; SelbstgestUandnis; Jägerlied; Der Feulerreiter London ▲ 440208-2 [DDD]

Fassbender, Hedwig (mez)

Berio, L.:Chamber Music, w. J. Henneberger (cnd), Zurich New Music Ensemble—Strings in the Earth; All day; Winds of May *(rec 1993)* Jecklin-Disco ▲ JD 684-2 [DDD]

▲ = CD ♦ = Enhanced CD Δ = MD ■ = Cassette Tape ▯ = DCC

Fassbender, Hedwig (mez) (cont.)
Berio, L.:Folk Songs Mez, w. J. Henneberger (cnd), Zurich New Music Ensemble—[arr. by Berio] Black is the color (USA); I wonder as I wander (USA); The moon has risen (Armenian); Little nightingale (France); May the Lord send fine weather... (Italy); The ideal woman (Italy); Dance (Italy); Songs of sadness (Sardinia); Wretched is he (France); The Spinner (France); Azerbaijan love song (Azerbaijan) *(rec 1993)* Jecklin-Disco ▲ JD 684-2 [DDD]
Denisov, E.:La Vie en Rouge, w. J. Henneberger (cnd), Zurich New Music Ensemble—I'd like; A real joke; The atom-bomb waltz; The yellow waltz; The Prisoner; What I live for; The last waltz *(rec 1993)* Jecklin-Disco ▲ JD 684-2 [DDD]
Holliger, H.:Glühende Rätsel, w. H. Holliger (cnd), Contrechamps Ensemble Accord ▲ ACD 201922 [DDD]
Schoeck, O.:Songs (comp), w. Aziz Kortel (pno)—Das stille Leuchten, Op. 60; Geheimnis und Gleichnis; Berg und See *(rec 1994)* Jecklin ▲ JD 680
Zemlinsky, A. von:Songs (misc), w. V. Neumann (cnd), Czech PO—6 Gesänge, Op. 13 [G] Supraphon ▲ SUP 11 1811 [DDD]

Fassler, Hedy (sop)
Weill, K.:The Threepenny Opera, w. Liane (sop—Polly Peachum), A. Felbermayer (sop—Lucy), H. Fassler (sop—Jenny), R. Anday (cta—Mrs. Peachum), K. Preger (ten—Macheath), H. Roswaenge (ten—Street Crier), A. Jerger (bar—Peachum), F. Gutherie (bar), *(cnd & orch unknown)* Vanguard Classics ▲ OVC 8057 [ADD]

Fassler, Wolfgang (sgr)
Wagner, R.:Das Liebesverbot, w. Pamela Coburn (sop—Mariana), Friedrich Lenz (ten—Antonio), Hermann Prey (bar—Friedrich), Keith Engen (bass—Angelo), Raimund Grumbach (bass—Danieli/Wirt), Wolfgang Fassler (sgr—Luzio), Sabine Haas (sgr—Isabella/Claudios Schwester), Alfred Kuhn (sgr—Brighella/Chef der Sbirren), Hermann Sapell (sgr—Pontio Pilato), Robert Schunk (sgr—Claudio), Marianne Seibel (sgr—Dorella), W. Sawallisch (cnd), Bavarian State Orch, Bavarian State Chorus *(rec July 9, 1983)* Orfeo d'or 3-▲ 345953

Fath, Bruno (sgr)
Henze, H.-W.:Elegy for Young Lovers, w. Regina Schudel (sop), Richard Lloyd Morgan (bass), Lawrence Richard (bass), Helmut Bernhofen (sgr), Aurelia Hajek (sgr), Silvia Weiss (sgr), B. Jones (cnd), Berlin Chamber Opera Orch *(rec Berlin)* Deutsche Schallplatten 2-▲ DS 1050

Fauché, Françoise (bass)
Lassus, O. de:Motets, w. La Fenice Ensemble—Haec quae ter triplici; Suzanne un jour; Susana un jour; Suzanne un giur; Bonjour mon coeu; Bonn jour mon cueur; Mr Buctons galiard; Et d'où venez vous, Madame Lucette Ricercar ▲ 152137
Palestrina, G.:Motets, w. La Fenice Ensemble—Io son ferito, ahi lasso; Vestiva i colli; Io son ferito; Ricercar noni toni; Pulchra es amica mea; Vestiva i colli; Pulchra es amica mea Ricercar ▲ 152137

Fauchecourt, Jean-Paul (ct)
Campra, A.:Motets, w. Véronique Gens (sop), Anne Gotkovsky (sop), Hervé Lamy (ten), Peter Harvey (bass), H. Niquet (cnd), Concert Spirituel Orch, Concert Spirituel Vocal Ensemble—2 Noster Refugium; Cantate Domino; De Profundis Adda ▲ ADD 243912

Fauchey, Michel (sgr)
Lehár, F.:Die lustige Witwe, w. Teresa Stich-Randall (mez—Missia Palmieri), Monique Stiot (mez—Manon), Germaine Duclos (sgr—Praskovia), Linda Felder (sgr—Olga), Christiane Jacquin (sgr—Nadia), Jeannette Levasseur (sgr—Sylviane), Henri Legay (ten—Camille de Coutançon), Joseph Peyron (ten—Kromsky), Robert Destain (sgr—Baron Popoff), Michel Fauche (sgr—Pristich), Gérard Friedmann (sgr—Lerida), Jacques Gilet (sgr—Bogdanowitch), Jean Guy Henneveux (sgr—Prince Danilo), Serge Klin (sgr—Figg), Jacques Villa (sgr—D'Estillac), A. Sibert (cnd), Belgian Radio-TV Orch, Belgian Radio-TV Chorus *(rec Grand Auditorium, Belgium, Apr 30, 1970)* Studio SM 2-▲ 2160 [AAD]

Faulhaber, Werner (bass)
Wagner, R.:Das Rheingold, w. P. Brivkalne (sop), I. Malaniuk (cta), R. Siewert (cta), Fritz (sgr), Pflanzl (ten), S. Björling (bar), L. Weber (bass), F. Dalberg (bass), H. von Karajan (cnd), Bayreuth Festival Orch, Bayreuth Festival Chorus [G] *(rec live 8/1/51)* Melodram 2-▲ MEL 26107 (m) [AAD]

Faulkner, B. (sgr)
Puccini, G.:Madama Butterfly, w. V. de los Angeles (sop), R. Nadell (mez), W. Fredericks (sgr), J. Thresh (sgr), D. Bernard (sgr), R. Torigi (sgr), A. Cosenza (bar), W. Herbert (cnd), New Orleans Opera Orch, New Orleans Opera Chorus *(rec live March 18, 1954)* Legato Classics 2-▲ LCD 168-2 [ADD]

Faulkner, Julie (sop)
Pergolesi, G.B.:Orfeo, w. M. Halász (cnd), Budapest Camerata *(rec Festetich Castle, Budapest, Sept. 1994)* Naxos ▲ 8.550766 [DDD]
Pergolesi, G.B.:Stabat mater, w. Anna Gonda (alt), M. Halász (cnd), Camerata Budapest *(rec Festetich Castle, Budapest, Sept. 1994)* Naxos ▲ 8.550766 [DDD]
Schumann, R.:Genoveva, w. J. Faulkner (sop—Genoveva), R. Behle (sop—Margaretha), K. Lewis (ten—Golo), A. Titus (bar—Siegfried), H. Stamm (bass—Hidulfus, Caspar), J. Tilli (bass—Balthasar), G. Albrecht (cnd), Hamburg State PO, Hamburg State Opera Chorus [G] *(rec 1992)* Orfeo 2-▲ 289932 [DDD]

Faull, Ellen (sop)
Schoenberg, A.:Songs, w. Helen Vanni (mez), Donald Gramm (b-bar), Glenn Gould (pno)—Zwei Gesange, Op. 1; Vier Lieder, Op. 2; Das Buch der hängenden Gärten; Sechs Lieder, Op. 3; Zwei Balladen, Op. 12; Drei Lieder, Op. 48; Zwei Lieder, Op. 14; Zwei Lieder, Op. Posth.; Acht Lieder, Op. 6 Sony Classical ("Glen Gould Edition" series) 2-▲ SM2K 52667

Faulstich, Gerhard (bar)
Bach, J.S.:St. Matthew Passion, w. M. Marshall (sop), C. Watkinson (cta), K. Equiluz (ten), P. Huttenlocher (bar), R. Johnson (bar), M. Corboz (cnd), Lausanne CO, Lausanne Vocal Ensemble Erato 3-▲ 2292-45375-2 GX
Mozart, W.A.:Requiem, w. Edith Wiens (sop), Gabriele Schreckenbach (mez), Aldo Baldin (ten), U. Gronostay (cnd), Berlin RSO, Berlin RIAS Chamber Choir [L] LaserLight ▲ 15 882 [DDD]
Steffani, A.:Enrico Leone, w. R. Popken (alt), M. Frimmer (sop), S. Szameit (sop), N. Yoko (cta), C. Guber (cta), D. Diwiak (ten), L. Rovatkay (cnd), Cappela Agostino Steffani [period instrs] [I] Calig ▲ CAL 50855 [DDD]

Fauqueur, Alain (boy sop)
Boulanger, L.:Pie Jesu, w. J. J. Grunenwald (org), I. Markevitch (cnd), Lamoureux Orch members *(rec Salle Pleyel, Paris)* Everest ▲ EVC 9034 [AAD]

Fauré, André (nar)
Schibler, A.:La Folie de Tristan, w. Audrey Michael (sop—Iseut), Arlette Chédel (mez—Brangien), Pierre-André Blaser (ten—Tristan), Philippe Huttenlocher (bar—Le roi Marc/Le pêcheur/Le portier), William Jacques (nar), Snezana Zivojinovic (nar), J. Auberson (cnd), Lausanne CO, Romande Instrumental Group Rockband, Swiss Romande Radio Choir *(rec live, Festival de Montreux, Sept 15, 1980)* Jecklin ▲ JD 695

Faury, E. (bar)
Gounod, C.:Sappho, w. M. Command (sop), S. Coste (sop), C. Popis (ten), P. Fournillier (cnd), St.-Etienne Nouvel Orch Koch Schwann 2-▲ SCH 313112 [DDD]

Favat, Dominique (sop)
Lully, J.-B.:Motets, w. I. Desrochers (sop), R. Duguay (ct), H. Lamy (ten), P. Harvey (bass), H. Niquet (cnd), Concert Spirituel Vocal Ensemble—Te Deum; Miserere; Plaude laetare Gallia *(rec Nov. 22-25, 1993)* FNAC Music ▲ 592308 [DDD]

Favero, Mafalda (sop)
Arias & Duets *(rec 1928-1946)* VAI Audio ▲ VAIA 1071
Boito, A.:Mefistofele, w. Giannina Arangi-Lombardi (sop), Antonio Melandri (ten), Giuseppe Nessi (ten), Nazzareno de Angelis (bass), L. Molajoli (cnd), La Scala Orch, La Scala Chorus Grammofono 2000 2-▲ GRM 78606 (m)
Massenet, J.:Manon (sels), w. G. Di Stefano (ten), M. Borriello (bar), M. Mainardi (bar), A. Guarnieri (cnd), La Scala Orch, La Scala Chorus *(rec live, Milan, 3/15/47)* Myto ▲ 1 MCD 90526 [ADD]
Il mito dell'opera Bongiovanni ▲ 1078
Puccini, G.:Manon Lescaut (sels), w. R. Tebaldi (sop), J. Gardino (mez), G. Malipiero (ten), G. Nessi (ten), M. Stabile (bar), T. Pasero (b-bar), C. Forti (bass), A. Toscanini (cnd), La Scala Orch, La Scala Chorus—Intermezzo; Act 3 *(rec live, Milan, May 18, 1946)* Arkadia ("Historical Performances" series) 2-▲ 604 (m)

Fay, Peter (bar)
Mozart, W.A.:Missa brevis, K.194, w. M. Busching (mez), G. Tucker (ten), C. Dill Smith (sgr), H. Mardirosian (cnd), St. Thomas Moore Cathedral Orch, St. Thomas Moore Cathedral Chorus [L] Centaur ▲ CRC 2074 [DDD]
Mozart, W.A.:Tantum ergo, w. Carolyn Dill Smith (sop), Marianna Busching (mez), Gene Tucker (ten), H. Mardirosian (cnd), St. Thomas Moore Cathedral Orch, St. Thomas Moore Cathedral Chorus [L] Centaur ▲ CRC 2074 [DDD]
Mozart, W.A.:Vesperae de Dominica, w. C. Dill Smith (sop), M. Busching (mez), G. Tucker (ten), H. Mardirosian (cnd), St. Thomas Moore Cathedral Orch, St. Thomas Moore Cathedral Chorus [L] Centaur ▲ CRC 2074 [DDD]

Fazah, Adib (sgr)
Donizetti, G.:Lucrezia Borgia, w. Montserrat Caballé (sop), Jane Berbié (mez), Alain Vanzo (ten), Kostas Paskalis (bar), Arnold Voketaitis (bass-bar), L. D. Clements (sgr), Mauro Lampi (sgr), Vern Shinall (sgr), Jerold Siena (sgr), William Wiederanders (sgr), J. Perlea (cnd), New York City Opera Orch, New York City Chorus Great Opera Performances 2-▲ GOP 769

Federici, Franco (bass)
Puccini, G.:Manon Lescaut, w. R. Kabaivanska (sop—Manon), R. Pallini (mez—Singer), P. Domingo (ten—des Grieux), E. Lorenzi (ten—Edmondo), F. Ricciardi (ten—Dancing Master), M. D'Anna (bar—Lescaut), A. Mariotti (bass—Geronte), F. Federici (bass—Innkeeper) Golden Age of Opera 2-▲ GAO 162/63 [ADD]
Puccini, G.:Tosca, w. R. Kaibaivanska (sop—Floria), L. Pavarotti (ten—Mario), I. Wixell (bar—Scarpia), F. Federici (bass—Angelotti), D. Oren (cnd), Rome Opera Orch, Rome Opera Chorus RCA Red Seal ▲ 09026-61807-2; ■ 09026-61807-4
Puccini, G.:Tosca, w. R. Kaibaivanska (sop—Floria), L. Pavarotti (ten—Mario), I. Wixell (bar—Scarpia), F. Federici (bass—Angelotti), D. Oren (cnd), Rome Opera Orch, Rome Opera Chorus RCA Red Seal 2-▲ 09026-61806-2
Verdi, G.:Nabucco, w. Monica Pick-Hieronimi (sop), Anna Schiatti (sop), Mina Blum (sop), Angelo Casertano (ten), Gilberto Maffezzoni (ten), Paolo Gavanelli (bass), Paata Burchuladze (bass), A. Guadagno (cnd), Arena di Verona Orch, Arena di Verona Chorus *(rec Berlin, Spring 1996)* Koch Schwann 2-▲ SCH CD 364272

Fedi, Elena Cecchi (sop)
Gesualdo, D.C.:Madrigals, w. Roberta Invernizzi (sop), Daniela Del Monaco (cta), Roberto Balconi (ct), Gian Paolo Fagotto (ten), Giuseppe Zambon (ten), Giovanni Dagnino (bass), A. Curtis (cnd), I Fegi Armonici—Book 6 [Se la Mia Morte Brami; Beltà Poi Che T'Assenti; Tu Piangi O Fille Mia; Resta di Darmi Noia; Chiaro Risplender Suole; others] Symphonia ▲ SYM 94133

Fedin, Alexander (ten)
Mussorgsky, M.:Boris Godunov, w. V. Valente (sop—Xenia), E. Gorochovskaya (mez—Nurse), L. Nichiteanu (mez—Fyodor), E. Zarmeba (mez—Hostess), M. Lipovšek (cta—Marina), P. Langridge (ten—Prince Shuisky), H. Wildhaber (ten—Misail), A. Fedin (ten—Simpleton), S. Leiferkus (bar—Rangoni), A. Kotcherga (bass—B. Godounov), A. Shagidullin (bass—Shchelkalov), S. Ramey (bass—Pimen), S. Larin (bass—Girgory), G. Nikolsky (bass—Varlaam), C. Abbado (cnd), Berlin PO, Tölz Boys' Choir, Berlin Radio Chorus, Slovak Phil Chorus *(rec Nov. 7-30, 1993)* Sony Classical 3-▲ S3K 58977 [DDD]
Tchaikovsky, P.:Eugene Onegin, w. Lidiya Chernikh (sop), Tamara Sinyavskaya (mez), Alexander Vedernikov (bass), Yuri Mazurok (sgr), V. Fedoseyev (cnd), USSR SO, Moscow SO, Fernseh SO Audiophile Classics ("Legacy Collection" series) 2-▲ 101.751

Fee, Lucy (mez)
Stuart, P.:Kill Bear Comes Home, w. Elana Gizzi (sop—Hasty Girl), Mi-Kyung Huh (sop—Cold Feet), Therese Murray (sop—Song Bird), Cherie Pfeil (sop—1st Sister), Renia Shukis (sop—2nd Sister), Riki Connaughton (mez—4th Sister), Lucy Fee (mez—3rd Sister), David Averbach (ten—Song Leader), Mark Schmidt (ten—Kill Bear), Jason Smith (bar—Cheif Wife Hunter), P. Stuart (cnd), Rochester Opera Theater Orch, Rochester Opera Theater Chorus VM ▲ DRK 154 [DDD]

Fegran, Espen (bar)
Kalitzke, J.:Bericht über den Tod des Musikers Jack Tiergarten, w. Werner Eggenhofer (nar), Till Krabbe (nar), Brigitte Jäger (sop), J. Kalitzke (cnd), North Rhine-Westphalia Musikfabrik *(rec live, Apr 29, 1994)* CPO ▲ 999358-2 [DDD]

Fehenberger, Lorenz (ten)
Mussorgsky, M.:Boris Godunov, w. Martha Mödl (sop—Marina Mniszek), Lotte Schädle (sop—Xenia), Dorothea Siebert (mez—Fyodor), Hertha Töpper (mez—Xenia's wet-nurs), Karl Hermann Bennert (Boyer Khrushchyov), Lorenz Fehenberger (ten—Prince Shuysky), Hans Hopf (ten—Grigory), Karl Ostertag (ten—Missail), Hans Hotter (b-bar—Boris Godunov), Hermann Uhde (bar—Andrey Shchelkalov), Kurt Böhme (bass—Varlaam), Kim Borg (bass—Pimen), Kieth Engen (bass—Lewicki), Adolf Keil (bass—Nikitich), Benno Kusche (bar—Rangoni), Heinz Maria Linz (bass—Czernikowski), E. Jochum (cnd), Bavarian RSO, Bavarian Radio Chorus *(rec Munich, May 1957)* Myto 3-▲ MCD 953131
Schoenberg, A.:Gurrelieder, w. I. Borkh (sop), H. Schachtschneider (ten), H. Töpper (mez), K. Engen (bass), R. Kubelik (cnd), Bavarian RSO—also includes songs by Berg, Schoenberg & Webern Deutsche Grammophon ("20th Century Classics" series) ▲ 431744-2 [ADD]
Verdi, G.:Un ballo in maschera, w. Martha Mödl (sop—Ulrica), Walburga Wegner (sop—Amelia), Anny Schlemm (mez—Oscar), Lorenz Fehenberger (ten—Ricardo), Dietrich Fischer-Dieskau (bar—Renato), Wilhelm Schirp (bass—Samuel), Willy Schoneweib (bass—Tom), Gunther Wilhelms (bass—Silvan), Fritz Augustin (sgr—Ein Richter), Friedrich Himmelmann (sgr—Ein Diener Amelia), F. Busch (cnd), Cologne RSO, Bernhard Alois Zimmermann (cnd), Cologne Radio Chorus Calig 2-▲ 50946/47 (m) [ADD]

Fehn, Helmut (bass)
Rossini, G.:Stabat Mater, w. E. Grümmer (sop), M. von Ilosvay (mez), C. Ludwig (mez), F. Fricsay (cnd), Cologne RSO, Cologne Radio Chorus [L] *(rec 1953)* Melodram ▲ CDM 16523 [AAD]

Fehringer, Franz (ten)
Jessel, L.:Schwarzwaldmädel (sels), w. E. Lind (sop), B. Kusche (bar), Hofmann (sgr), Schörg (sgr), Schubert (sgr), Marszalek (cnd), Cologne RSO, Cologne Radio Chorus [G] Acanta ▲ CD 42552 [DDD]
Kálmán, I.:Die Csárdásfürstin (sels), w. E. Köth (sop), B. Kusche (bar), Heusser (sgr), Hofmann (sgr), Marszalek (cnd), Cologne Radio Orch, Cologne Radio Chorus [G] Acanta ▲ CD 42435 [DDD]
Strauss, R.:Salome, w. I. Borkh (sop—Salome), M. Klose (mez—Herodias), C. Ludwig (mez—Page), M. Lorenz (ten—Herodes), F. Fehringer (ten—Narraboth), F. Frantz (bar—Jokanaan), K. Schröder (cnd), Hessian RSO *(rec 1952)* Myto 2-▲ 93592

Feilhaber, Alfred (ten)
Wagner, S.:Der Bärenhäuter, w. B. Johanning (sop—Luise), K. Likic (sop—Lene), T. Koon (sop—Gunda), V. Horn (ten—Hans Kraft), A. Feilhaber (ten—Nikolaus Spitz), R. Hartmann (bar—Kaspar Wild), A. Wenhold (bar—Stranger), A. Waller (bass—Devil), H. Kiichli (bass—Melchior Fröhlich), K. Bach (cnd), Thüringian SO, Thüringian State Theater Chorus *(rec Rudolstadt, July 25-31, 1993)* Marco Polo ("Opera Classics" series) 2-▲ 8.223713/4 [DDD]

Feinsinger, Mary (mez)
Asia, D.:Sand II, w. Reconnaissance Chamber Ensemble Albany ▲ TROY 106 [DDD]

Feis, Doreen de (sop)
Górecki, H.-M.:Sym 3, "Sym of Sorrowful Songs", w. A. Leaper (cnd), Gran Canaria PO *(rec Iglesia de San Francisco, Telde, Gran Canaria, Apr 11, 1995)* RCA Gold Seal ▲ 09026-68387-2 [DDD]

Felbermayer, Anny (sop)
Bach, J.S.:Cant 70, w. E. Wiens (sop), H. M. Welfing (ten), N. Foster (bass), F. Prohaska (cnd), Vienna State Opera Orch, Vienna State Opera Chorus [G] *(rec June 1957)* Vanguard Classics ("The Bach Guild" series) ▲ OVC 2010 [ADD]
Haydn, J.:Die Schöpfung, w. Anny Felbermayer (sop—Eve), Teresa Stich-Randall (sop—Gabriel), Anton Dermota (ten—Uriel), Paul Schöffler (b-bar—Adam), Frederick Guthrie (bass—Raphael), Franz Holletschek (cembalo), M. Wöldike (cnd), Vienna State Opera Orch, Vienna State Opera Chorus *(rec Musikverein, Vienna, Austria, May 1955)* Vanguard Classics 2-▲ SVC 34/35 [AAD]
Humperdinck, E.:Hänsel und Gretel, w. E. Schwarzkopf (sop), E. Grümmer (sop), M. von Ilosvay (mez), E. Schürhoff (mez), J. Metternich (bar), H. von Karajan (cnd), Philharmonia Orch, Loughton High School Chorus, Bancroft's School Chorus [G] *(rec 1953)* EMI Classics ("Studio" series) 2-▲ CDMB 69293 (m) [ADD]

Felbermayer, Anny (sop) (cont.)

Weill, K.:The Threepenny Opera, w. Liane (sop—Polly Peachum), A. Felbermayer (sop—Lucy), H. Fassler (sop—Jenny), R. Anday (cta—Mrs. Peachum), K. Preger (ten—Macheath), H. Roswaenge (ten—Street Crier), A. Jerger (bar—Peachum), F. Gutherie (bar), *(cnd & orch unknown)* Vanguard Classics ▲ OVC 8057 [ADD]

Felder, Linda (sop)

Lehár, F.:Die lustige Witwe, w. Teresa Stich-Randall (mez—Missia Palmieri), Monique Stiot (mez—Manon), Germaine Duclos (sgr—Praskovia), Linda Felder (sgr—Olga), Christiane Jacquin (sgr—Nadia), Jeannette Levasseur (sgr—Sylviane), Henri Legay (ten—Camille de Coutançon), Joseph Peyron (ten—Kromsky), Robert Destain (sgr—Baron Popoff), Michel Fauche (sgr—Pristich), Gérard Friedmann (sgr—Lerida), Jacques Gilet (sgr—Bogdanowitch), Jean Guy Henneveux (sgr—Prince Danilo), Serge Klin (sgr—Figg), Jacques Villa (sgr—D'Estillac), A. Sibert (cnd), Belgian Radio-TV Orch, Belgian Radio-TV Chorus *(rec Grand Auditorium, Belgium, Apr 30, 1970)* Studio SM 2-▲ 2160 [AAD]

Feldhoff, Gerd (bass)

Hindemith, P.:Mathis der Maler, w. Urszula Koszut (sop), Trudeliese Schmidt (mez), Rose Wagemann (mez), William Cochran (ten), Donald Grobe (ten), James King (ten), Manfred Schmidt (ten), Dietrich Fischer-Dieskau (bar), Alexander Malta (bass), Peter Meven (bass), Karl Kreile (sgr), R. Kubelik (cnd), Bavarian RSO, Bavarian Radio Chorus EMI Classics 2-▲ CDCC 55237

Krenek, E.:Jonny spielt auf, w. E. Lear (sop—Anita), L. Popp (sop—Yvonne), W. Blankenship (ten—Max), K. Equiluz (ten—Station Announcer), L. Heppe (ten—Manager), T. Stewart (bar—Daniello), G. Feldhof (bass—Jonny), H. Hollreiser (cnd), Vienna State Opera Orch [G] Vanguard Classics ▲ OVC 8048 [ADD]

Feldman, Jill (sop)

Bernstein, C.H.:Leda & the 6 Songs without Words, w. Adam Korniszewski (vn) Arcobaleno 2-▲ AAOC 93922

Biber, H. von:Requiem à 15, w. G. de Reyghere (sop), J. Bowman (ct), I. Honeyman (ten), M. van Egmond (bass), Ricercar Consort, Erik Van Nevel (cnd), Capella Sancti Michaelis [L] *(rec 5/90)* Ricercar ▲ RIC 81063 [DDD]

Bruhns, N.:Cants, w. Greta de Reyghere (sop), James Bowman (ct), Ian Honeyman (ten), Guy de Mey (ten), Max Van Egmond (bass), Ricercar Consort—Hemmt eure Tränenflut; Jauchzet dem Herren alle Welt; Wohl dem, der den Herren fürchtet; De profundis; Paratum cor meum; O werter heil'ger Geis; Zeit meines Abschieds; Erstanden ist der heilige Christ; Herr hat seinem Stuhl im Himmel bereitet; Ich liege und schlafe; Mein Herz ist bereit; Muss nicht der Mensch auf dieser Erden in Stetem Streite sein Ricercar In Ecco 2-▲ REC8001/2

Charpentier, M.-A.:Les Arts florissants, w. C. Dussaut (sop), A. Mellon (sop), G. Laurens (mez), D. Visse (ct), P. Cantor (ten), G. Reinhart (bar), W. Christie (cnd), Les Arts Florissants [F] Musique d'Abord ▲ HMA 1901083

Charpentier, M.-A.:Le Malade imaginaire, w. I. Poulenard (sop), M. Minkowski (cnd), Louvre Musicians Erato (Musifrance) ▲ 2292-45002-2 ZK

Colonna, G.P.:Magnificat, w. S. Vartolo (cnd), St. Petronio Cappella Musicale, San Petronio Cappella Musicale [L] Tactus 2-▲ TC 630390 [DDD]

Couperin, F.:Motets, w. I. Poulenard (sop), G. Reinhart (bass), J. ter Linden (bass vl), D. Moroney (hpd)—[L] Musique d'Abord ▲ HMA 1901150

Handel, G.F.:Clori, Tirsi e Fileno, w. L. Hunt (sop), D. Minter (alt), N. McGegan (cnd), Philharmonia Baroque Orch [I] Harmonia Mundi USA ▲ HMU 907045

Handel, G.F.:Susanna, w. Lorraine Hunt (sop), Drew Minter (alt), Jeffery Thomas (ten), William Parker (bar), David Thomas (bass), N. McGegan (cnd), Philharmonia Baroque Orch, Univ of California at Berkeley Chamber Chorus [E] Harmonia Mundi USA 3-▲ HMU 907030/32

Handel, G.F.:Susanna (sels), w. Lorraine Hunt (sop), Drew Minter (alt), Jeffery Thomas (ten), William Parker (bar), David Thomas (bass), N. McGegan (cnd), Philharmonia Baroque Orch, Univ of California at Berkeley Chamber Chorus [E] Harmonia Mundi USA ("Nightingale" series) ▲ HMN 907601

Handel, G.F.:Susanna (sels), w. Lorraine Hunt (sop), Drew Minter (alt), Jeffrey Thomas (ten), William Parker (bar), David Thomas (bass), N. McGegan (cnd), Philharmonia Baroque Orch Harmonia Mundi France ▲ HMU 907168

Purcell, H.:Ayres & Songs, w. Nigel North (lt), Sarah Cunningham (b vl) Arcana ▲ ACA 2 [DDD]

Purcell, H.:Dido & Aeneas, w. G. Laurens (mez), P. Cantor (ten), W. Christie (cnd), Les Arts Florissants [E] Harmonia Mundi France ▲ HMC 905173

Feldshuh, Tovah (nar)

A Portrait in Song of the Spanish Jews, w. Western Wind Western Wind ▲ 1836 CD [DDD] ▮ 1836 CT (D)

Felix, M. (sgr)

Schifrin, L.:Cantos Aztecas, w. P. Domingo (ten), N. Storojev (bass), C. Julian (sop), L. Schifrin (cnd), Mexican State SO, Mexico City Chorus [Sp] *(rec live 10/29/88)* Pro Arte ▲ CDD 494 [DDD]

Félix, Thierry (bar)

Debussy, C.:Songs, w. Stany David Lasry (pno) Arcana ▲ ACA 44

Fauré, G.:songs, w. Erika Guiomar (pno)—Arpège, Op. 76/2; L'horizon chimérique, Op. 118; La bonne chanson, Op. 61; Le parfum impérissable, Op. 76/1; Mélodies de Venise, Op. 58; Mirages, Op. 113; Prison, Op. 83/1; Soir, Op. 83/2 Arcana ▲ ACA 28 [DDD]

Felle, Amelia (sop)

Ferrero, L.:Mare nostro, w. A. Felle (sop—Candeggina), E. Jankovic (mez—Astradiva), C. Di Segni (ten—Rimestino), D. Serraiocco (bass-bar—Marchingello), A. Antoniozzi (bass-bar—Pigliatutto), G. Maisni (cnd), Venezze di Rovigo Conservatory of Music Orch, Venezze di Rovigo Conservatory of Music Chorus *(rec Oct. 21–24, 1991)* Ricordi 2-▲ RFCD 2016 [DDD]

Mascagni, P.:Sì, w. Vivian (sop), Maria Gentile (sop), M.G. Liguori (sop), Nicoletti (sgr), Comas (sgr), S. Sanna (cnd), Montepulciano Arts Center Orch, Montepulciano Arts Center Chorus [I] *(rec live, 7/24/87)* Bongiovanni 2-▲ GB 2050/51 [DDD]

Pergolesi, G.B.:Lo frate 'nnamorato, w. N. Focile (sop), B. Manca di Nissa (cta), A. Corbelli (bar), R. Muti (cnd), La Scala Orch, La Scala Chorus EMI Classics 3-▲ CDCC 54240

Rossini, G.:Il barbiere di Siviglia, w. S. Mentzer (mez), J. Hadley (ten), T. Hampson (bass), S. Ramey (bass), G. Gelmetti (cnd), Tuscan Orch EMI ▲ 54863-2

Rossini, G.:L'inganno felice, w. Iorio Zennaro (ten), Fabio Previati (bar), Natale de Carolis (b-bar), Danilo Serraiocco (bass), M. Viotti (cnd), English CO Claves ▲ 50-9211

Rossini, G.:L'inganno felice, w. I. Zennaro (ten), F. Previati (bar), N. de Carolis (b-bar), D. Serraiocco (b-bar), M. Viotti (cnd), English CO [I] Claves 8-▲ CD 9200 [DDD]

Feller, Carlos (bass)

Mozart, W.A.:Così fan tutte, w. A. Roocroft (sop), E. James (mez), R. Gilfrey (bar), J. E. Gardiner (cnd), English Baroque Soloists Archiv 3-▲ 437829-2 [DDD]

Felter, S. (sgr)

Giordano, U.:Andrea Chénier, w. Montserrat Caballé (sop), Franco Corelli (ten), R. de Carlo (sgr), D. Dondi (sgr), G. Ellsworth (sgr), J. Fair (sgr), R. Falk (sgr), E. Green (sgr), H. Hicks (sgr), H. Krauss (sgr), L. Miller (sgr), N. Riggins (sgr), H. Salerno (sgr), A. Guadagno (cnd), Academy of Music Orch, Academy of Music Chorus Great Opera Performances 2-▲ GOP 766

Felty, Janice (mez)

Harbison, J.:The Natural World, w. J. Harbison (cnd), Los Angeles Phil New Music Group [E] New World ▲ 80395-2 [DDD]

Machover, T.:Valis, w. A. Azéma (sop), T. Edwards (ten), P. Mason (bar), T. Machover (elec), T. Machover (cnd), *(ensemble unknown)* [E] Bridge ▲ BCD 9007 [DDD] ▮ BCS 7007 (D)

Sims, E.:Come Away, w. D. Hoose (cnd), Dinosaur Annex Music Ensemble [E] CRI ▲ CD 578 [DDD]

Féraldy, Germaine (sop)

Charpentier, G.:Songs, w. J. Planel (ten), J. Lanzone (bar), G. Charpentier (cnd), *(orch & chorus unknown)* —Chanson du chemin; Ronde des campagnons; A mules; Les chevaux de bois; Sérénade à Watteau; Les yeux de Berthe [F] *(rec 1934)* Music Memoria 3-▲ 30223

Gluck, C.W.:Orfeo ed Euridice, w. Jany Delille (sop), Alice Raveau (cta), H. Tomasi (cnd), Paris SO [1859 French version, edited by Berlioz & Saint-Saëns] *(rec Paris, 1935)* Pearl 2-▲ PEA 9169 [ADD]

Massenet, J.:Manon, w. J. Rogatchewsky (ten), L. Guénot (bass), E. Cohen (cnd), Paris Opéra-Comique Orch, Paris Opéra-Comique Chorus [F] *(rec 1928–29 for Columbia)* Classical Collector 2-▲ FDC 2 2001 (m) [AAD]

Ferch, Heidemaria (sop)

Wagner, R.:Der Ring des Nibelungen, w. Liselotte Becker-Egner (sop—Woglinde/Ortlinde/Wellgunde), Angelika Berger (sop—Wellgunde/Waltraute), Siw Ericsdotter (sop—Norn 3), Heidemaria Ferch (sop—Freia/Gerhilde), Bella Jasper (sop—Helmwige/Waldvogel/Woglinde), Ditha Sommer (sop—Sieglinde/Gutrune), Ursula Boese (mez—Erda), Ruth Hesse (mez—Fricka), Nadezda Kniplová (mez—Brünnhilde), Margit Kobeck (mez—Schwertleite/Norn 2), Hilde Rosner (mez—Flosshilde/Siegrunde), Erica Schubert (mez—Grimgerde/Flosshilde), Ingrid Göritz (cta—Rossweisse/Norn 1), Herbert Doussant (ten—Froh), Herold Kraus (ten—Mime), Gerald McKee (ten—Siegmund/Siegfried), Fritz Uhl (ten—Loge), Rudolf Knoll (bar—Gunther/Donner), Rolf Polke (bass-bar—Wotan/Wanderer), Rolf Kühne (bass—Alberich), Takao Okamura (bass—Fafner), Otto von Rohr (bass—Hagen/Fasolt/Hunding), H. Swarowsky (cnd), Czech PO, Prague National Theater Orch *(rec June 3 & 5, July 26–31, A)* Weltbild Classics 14-▲ 703769 [ADD]

Fernandez, Wilhelmina (sop)

Sings Favorite Spirituals, w. George Darden (pno) Kem-Disc ▲ 1010 [DDD]

Fernandi, Eugenio (ten)

Donizetti, G.:Lucia di Lammermoor, w. Maria Callas (sop), Rolando Panerai (bar), Giuseppe Modesti (bass), T. Serafin (cnd), Rome RAI SO, Rome RAI Chorus *(rec live, Rome, 1957)* Enterprise ("Documents" series) 2-▲ ENTLV 973 [ADD]

Il Mito Dell'Opera:Eugenio Fernandi, w. (rec. 1957–66) Bongiovanni ▲ GB 1086 [ADD]

Puccini, G.:Turandot, w. M. Callas (sop), E. Schwarzkopf (sop), N. Zaccaria (bass), T. Serafin (cnd), La Scala Orch, La Scala Chorus [I] *(rec 1957)* EMI Classics 2-▲ CDCB 47971 (m) [ADD]

Verdi, G.:Don Carlos, w. S. Jurinac (sop), G. Simionato (mez), E. Bastianini (bar), C. Siepi (b-bar), H. von Karajan (cnd), Vienna PO, Vienna State Opera Chorus [I] *(rec live, Salzburg 7/26/58)* Arkadia 2-▲ 220 [ADD]

Ferracin, Luca (bass)

Perti, G.A.:Liturgy for Good Friday, w. Patrizia Vaccari (sop), Maura Pederzoli (sop), Cristina Calzolari (sop), Alida Oliva (sop), Claudia Bugli (sop), Lucia Bagnoli (alt), Cinzia Meneghel (alt), Renzo Bez (alt), Alessandro Carmignani (alt), Michel van Goethem (alt), Mauro Collina (ten), Vincenzo Di Donato (ten), Paolo Fanciullacci (ten), Giovanni Caccamo (ten), Paolo Da Col (ten), Sergio Foresti (bass), Marco Scavazza (bass), Paride Montanari (bass), Liuwe Tamminga (org), Sergio Vartolo (org), S. Vartolo (cnd), Bologna San Petronio Capella Musicale Orch—Omnes amici mei; De lamentatione Jeremiae Prophetae:Heth. Cogitavit; Velum templi; Vinea mea; De lamentatione Jeremiae Prophetae:Lamed. Matribus suis; Tamquam ad latronem; Tenebrae factae sunt; Animam meam; Tradiderunt me; Jesum tradidit; De lamentatione Jeremiae Prophetae:Aleph. Ego vir; Caligaverunt *(rec St. Petronio Basilica, Bologna, Mar 28–31, 1995)* Naxos ▲ 8.553321 [DDD]

Ferracini, Maria-Grazia (sop)

Caldara, A.:Il gioco del quadriglio, w. Basia Retchitzka (sop), Elana Rizzieri (sop), Maria Minetto (cta), E. Loehrer (cnd), Lugano Chamber Society Orch, Minetto Chorus Dynamic ▲ CDL 140

Cimarosa, D.:I Finti nobili (sels), w. C. Cadelo (sop), R. Cassinelli (ten), R. Malacarne (ten), G. Sarti (bar), B. Marinotti (cnd), RTSI Orch—Li sposi per accidente (Act 3) *(rec 1970)* Foyer ▲ FOY 2057 [AAD]

Pergolesi, G.B.:Mass in F, w. B. Retchitzka (sop), M. Minetto (cta), V. Gohl (cta), C. Jauquier (ten), J. Loomis (bass), Milan Solisti, Plifonia Choir *(rec 1967)* Rivoalto ▲ RIV 8922 [ADD]

Ferradini, M. (ten)

Milesi, P.:Modi 2, w. L. M. Pickova (sop), Françoise Goddard (alt), B. Andersen (bass), D. Cassamagnaghi (fl), S. Scanziani (ob), A. Bianchi (cl/b cl), E. Crisafulli (bn), C. Gazzola (hn), F. Gualandris (tuba), A. Girardi (celtic hp), R. Anedda (vn), E. Groppo (vn), M. Pagani (vn), M. Ravasio (va), S. Righini (vc), P. Rizzi (db), J. Scully (perc), P. Milesi (cnd) Cuneiform ▲ RUNE 63

Ferrante, A. M. (sop)

Carissimi, G.:Oratorio della Santissima Vergine, w. P. Borri (sop), P. Pace (sop), A. Christofellis (alt), L. Petroni (ten), F. Sclaverano (ten), R. Abbondanza (bass), M. Mondelli (bass), P. Spagnoli (bass), F. Colusso (cnd), Seicentonovecento Ensemble [I] Bongiovanni ▲ GB 10011 [DDD]

Carissimi, G.:Oratorio di Daniele Profeta, w. P. Borri (sop), P. Pace (sop), A. Christofellis (alt), L. Petroni (ten), F. Sclaverano (ten), R. Abbondanza (bass), M. Mondelli (bass), P. Spagnoli (bass), F. Colusso (cnd), Seicentonovecento Ensemble [I] Bongiovanni ▲ GB 10011 [DDD]

Ferrante, Nel de (sgr)

Bruynèl, T.:Elegy Donemus ▲ NEAR 01 [DDD]

Ferrara, Mario (ten)

Bizet, G.:Carmen, w. Giovanna di Rocco (sop—Frasquita), Grace Bumbry (mez—Carmen), Anita Caminada (mez—Mercedes), Franco Corelli (ten—Don José), Mario Ferrara (ten—Dancario), Franco Bordoni (bar—Escamillo), Carlo Scaravelli (bar—Morales), Giuseppe Morresi (bass—Remendado), Francesco Signor (bass—Zuniga), O. de Fabritiis (cnd), *(orch unknown)* *(rec Macerata, July 21, 1974)* Golden Age of Opera 2-▲ GAO 181/82 [ADD]

Zandonai, R.:Francesca da Rimini, w. L. Gencer (sop—Francesca), R. Cioni (ten—Paolo), M. Ferrara (ten—Malatesino), F. Capuana (cnd), Trieste Teatro Comunale Giuseppe Verdi Orch, Trieste Teatro Comunale G. Verdi Chorus *(rec Mar. 19. 1961)* Arkadia 2-▲ 597 [ADD]

Ferrari, Cesira (mez)

Puccini, G.:Madama Butterfly, w. Rosetta Pampanini (sop—Madama Butterfly), Conchita Velasquez (mez—Suzuki), Cesira Ferrari (mez—Kate Pinkerton), Alessandro Granda (ten—F. B. Pinkerton), Giuseppe Nessi (ten—Goro), Aristide Baracchi (bar—Il Principe Yamadori), Gino Vanelli (bar—Sharpless), Lino Bonardi (bass—Il Commissario Imperiale), Salvatore Baccaloni (bass—Lo zio Bonzo), L. Molajoli (cnd), La Scala Orch, La Scala Chorus Bongiovanni 2-▲ 1123/24 [ADD]

Rossini, G.:Il barbiere di Siviglia, w. Cesira Ferrari (mez—Berta), Mercedes Capsir (cta—Rosina), Dino Borgioli (ten—Count), Salvatore Baccaloni (bar—Bortolo), Aristide Baracchi (bar—Officer), Riccardo Stracciari (bar—Figaro), Vincenzo Bettoni (bass—Don Basilio), Attilo Bordonali (bass—Fiorello), L. Molajoli (cnd), La Scala Orch, La Scala Chorus *(rec 1930)* Arkadia ("The 78's" series) 2-▲ 78008 [ADD]

Ferrari, Fernando (ten)

Cilea, F.:Adriana Lecouvreur, w. M. Olivero (sop—Adriana), F. Ferrari (ten—Maurizio), R. Capecchi (bar—Michonnet), F. Vernizzi (cnd), *(orch unknown)* [I] *(rec live, Amsterdam 11/6/65)* Verona 2-▲ 27077/78

Leo, L.:La Morte di Abele, w. Emilia Cundari (sop—Angelo), Giuliana Matteini (sop—Abele), Adriana Lazzarini (mez—Eva), Ferrando Ferrari (ten—Caino), Paolo Montarsolo (bass—Adamo), C. F. Cillario (cnd), Angelicum CO, Turin Polyphonic Chorus Dynamic 2-▲ CDL 144

Ricci, F.P.:Lezione terza per il Mercoldi Santo, w. Caterina Calvi (cta) Nuova Era ▲ NUO 7244

Ferrarini, Alido (sop)

Verdi, G.:Rigoletto, w. Y. Ramiro (ten), E. Tumagian (bar), J. Spaček (bar), A. Rahbari (cnd), Czech-Slovak RSO Bratislava, Slovak Phil Chorus [I] Naxos 2-▲ 8.660013/14 [DDD]

Ferraro, Pier Miranda (ten)

Bellini, V.:Il pirata, w. M. Callas (sop), C. Ego (bar), N. Rescigno (cnd), American Opera Society Orch, American Opera Society Chorus [I] *(rec live, New York 1/27/59)* Melodram 2-▲ MEL 26013

Bellini, V.:Il pirata, w. M. Callas (sop—Imogene), P. M. Ferraro (ten—Gualterio), Constantine Ego (bar—Ernesto), N. Rescigno (cnd), American Opera Society Orch, American Opera Society Chorus *(rec 1959)* EMI Classics ▲ CDMB 64938

Bizet, G.:Carmen, w. M. Chiara (sop—Micaela), A. Caminada (mez—Mercedes), F. Cossotto (mez—Carmen), F. Andreoli (ten—Il Remendado), P. M. Ferraro (ten—Don José), R. Bruson (bar—Escamillo), G. Zancanaro (bar—Morales), A. Carusi (bass—Il Dancairo), P. Maag (cnd), Venice Teatro La Fenice Orch, Venice Teatro La Fenice Chorus *(rec 1971)* Myto 2-▲ MCD 93487

Mascagni, P.:Guglielmo Ratcliff, w. R. Mattioli (sop), F. Mazzoli (bass), A. La Rosa Parodi (cnd), RAI SO *(rec 1963)* Memories ▲ MEM 4515 [ADD]

Mascagni, P.:Isabeau, w. Marcella Pobbe (sop—Isabeau), Licia Galvano (mez—Giglietta), Pier Miranda Ferraro (ten—Folco), Orazio Gualtiero (bar—Cornelius), Rinaldo Rola (bass—Re Raimondo), Amelia Bazzini (sgr—Ermyngarde), Piero Benzi (sgr—L'araldo), Renata Davini (sgr—Ermynthrude), Piero Francia (sgr—Il Cavaliere), T. Serafin (cnd), San Remo SO *(rec Sanremo, Jan 13, 1962)* Bongiovanni ("Il Mito dell'Opera" series) 2-▲ GB 1135/36-2 [ADD]

Mascagni, P.:Isabeau (sels), w. Marcella Pobbe (sop), Rinaldo Rosa (sgr), San Remo SO Cetra Classic ▲ CDON 44

Ponchielli, A.:La Gioconda, w. M. Callas (sop), F. Cossotto (mez), I. Companeez (cta), P. Cappuccilli (bar), I. Vinco (bass), A. Votto (cnd), La Scala Orch, La Scala Chorus EMI Classics ▲ CDCC 49518

Ferrer, J. (nar)
Prokofiev, S.:Peter & the Wolf, w. E. Goossens (cnd), Vienna State Opera Orch—two separate performances, in English & Spanish *(rec ca. 1960)* MCA Classics 2-▲ MCAD2-9820 [AAD]

Ferrer, J. (sgr)
Romberg, S.:Deep in My Heart, w. H. Traubel (sgr), R. Clooney (sgr), Gene Kelly (sgr), F. Kelly (sgr), V. Damone (sgr), J. Powell (sgr), A. Miller (sgr), W. Olvis (sgr), C. Richards (sgr), H. Keel (sgr), T. Martin (sgr), J. Weldon (sgr) Sony Music Special Products ▲ AK 47703

Ferrier, Kathleen (cta)
The Art of Kathleen Ferrier, w. Isobel Baillie (sop), Gerald Moore (pno), Netherlands Opera Orch [cnd:Charles Bruck] EMI Classics ("Great Recordings of the Century" series) ▲ CDH 61003 (m)
Bach, J.S.:Mass in b, BWV 232, w. E. Schwarzkopf (sop), A. Galliera (cnd), Philharmonia Orch EMI Classics ▲ CDM 63655
Bach, J.S.:Mass in b, BWV 232, w. E. Schwarzkopf (sop), C. Ludwig (mez), A. Poell (b–bar), Schöffler (bass), H. von Karajan (cnd), Vienna SO [L] *(rec live at Vienna's International Bach Festival, June 15, 1950)* Verona 2-▲ 27073/74 (m) [AAD]
Bach, J.S.:Mass in b, BWV 232, w. E. Schwarzkopf (sop), C. Ludwig (mez), A. Poell (b–bar), Schöffler (bass), H. von Karajan (cnd), Vienna SO, Vienna Singverein—6 arias excerpted from the above rec'g Verona ▲ 27076 (m) [AAD]
Bach, J.S.:St. Matthew Passion, w. I. Seefried (sop), C. Ludwig (mez), O. Edelmann (b–bar), P. Schoeffler (bass), H. von Karajan (cnd), Vienna SO, Vienna Singverein [G] *(rec live June 9, 1950)* Verona 3-▲ 27070/72 (m) [AAD]
Bach, J.S.:St. Matthew Passion (sels), w. I. Seefried (sop), C. Ludwig (mez), O. Edelmann (b–bar), P. Schöffler (bass), H. von Karajan (cnd), Vienna SO, Vienna Singverein Verona ▲ 27076 (m) [AAD]
Brahms, J.:Alto Rhap, w. F. Busch (cnd), Danish National RSO, Danish National Radio Choir [G] *(rec 10/6/49)* Danacord ▲ DACOCD 301 (m)
Brahms, J.:Songs, w. P. Spurr (pno) [G] Danacord ▲ DACOCD 301 (m)
Britten, H.:The Rape of Lucretia (sels), w. Joan Cross (sop—Female Chorus), Kathleen Ferrier (cta—Lucretia), Peter Pears (ten—Male Chorus), Otakar Kraus (sgr—Tarquinius), B. Britten (cnd), English Opera Group Orch *(rec Oct 5, 1946)* Music & Arts ▲ CD 901 [ADD]
Gluck, C.W.:Orfeo ed Euridice, w. G. Koeman (sop), D. Duval (sop), C. Bruck (cnd), Netherlands Opera Orch, Netherlands Opera Chorus *(rec live, 1951)* Verona 2-▲ 27016/17 (m) [AAD]
Gluck, C.W.:Orfeo ed Euridice (sels), w. A. Ayars (sop), Z. Vlachopoulos (sop), F. Stiedry (cnd), Southern PO, Glyndebourne Festival Chorus *(rec 1947)* Enterprise ("Palladio" series) ▲ ENTPD 4171 [ADD]
Kathleen Ferrier Edition, Vols. 1–10 London 10-▲ 433802-2 LM [ADD]
Kathleen Ferrier Edition, Vol. 3, w. Malcolm Sargent (cnd), London SO, Boyd Neel String Orch, Jacques Orch *(rec 1946 & 1949)* London ▲ 433470-2 LM [ADD]
Kathleen Ferrier Edition, Vol. 4, w. Benjamin Britten (pno) *(rec 1948)* London ▲ 433471-2 LM [ADD]
Kathleen Ferrier Edition, Vol. 7, w. London PO [cnd:G. Boult] *(rec 1952)* London ▲ 433474-2 LM [ADD]
Kathleen Ferrier Edition, Vol. 8:Blow The Wind Southerly London ▲ 433475-2 LM [ADD]
Kathleen Ferrier Edition, Vol. 9, w. Bruno Walter (pno) London ▲ 433476-2 LM [ADD]
Kathleen Ferrier Edition, Vol. 10 London ▲ 433477-2 LM [ADD]
Mahler, G.:Kindertotenlieder, w. B. Walter (cnd), Vienna PO [G] EMI Classics ("Great Recordings of the Century" series) ▲ CDH 61003 (m)
Mahler, G.:Sym 2, w. J. Vincent (sop), O. Klemperer (cnd), Royal Concertgebouw Orch—abridged version of the 4th movt., "Urlicht," from the above rec'g Verona ▲ 27076 (m) [AAD]
Mahler, G.:Sym 2, w. J. Vincent (sop), O. Klemperer (cnd), Royal Concertgebouw Orch [G] *(rec 7/12/51)* Verona 2-▲ 27062/63 (m) [AAD]
Recital Laserlight ▲ 14262

Ferrin, Agostino (bass)
Bellini, V.:I Capuleti e i Montecchi, w. R. Scotto (sop), G. Aragall (ten), L. Pavarotti (ten), A. Giacomotti (bass), C. Abbado (cnd), La Scala Orch, La Scala Chorus *(rec live 1967)* Butterfly Music 2-▲ BMC 12 [AAD]
Bellini, V.:Norma, w. Margherita Rinaldi (sop—Adalgisa), Renata Scotto (sop—Norma), Giuseppina Arista (mez—Clotilde), Ermanno Mauro (ten—Pollione), Giancarlo Turati (ten—Flavio), Agostino Ferrin (bass—Oroveso), R. Muti (cnd), Florence Teatro Comunale Orch, Florence Teatro Comunale Chorus *(rec Florence, Dec 19, 1978)* Legato Classics 2-▲ LCD 203-2
Bellini, V.:I Puritani, w. C. Deutekom (sop), F. Raffanelli (sop), N. Gedda (ten), S. Bruscantini (b–bar), G. del Vivo (bass), R. Muti (cnd), *(orch unknown)* *(rec 1970)* Great Opera Performances ▲ GOP 735
Boito, A.:Nerone, w. I. Ligabue (sop), R. Baldani (mez), B. Prevedi (bar), G. Gavazzeni (cnd), Turin RAI SO, Turin RAI Chorus *(rec live 1975)* Italian Opera Rarities 2-▲ IOR 7704 [ADD]
Donizetti, G.:Marino Faliero, w. M. Roberti (sop), O. Mori (bar), Meliciani (sgr), A. Camozzo (cnd), *(orch & chorus unknown)* [I] *(rec live, Bergamo 1966)* Melodram 2-▲ MEL 27030
Gounod, C.:Roméo et Juliette, w. G. d'Angelo (sop—Juliette), F. Corelli (ten—Romeo), A. Ferrin (bar—Friar Lawrence), P. Gottlieb (bass—Mercutio), A. Guadagno (cnd), *(orch unknown)* *(rec live, Philadelphia, 4/14/64)* HRE 2-▲ 1011-2 [ADD]
Verdi, G.:Ernani (sels), w. Felicia Weathers (sop—Elvira), Delia Wallis (mez—Giovanna), Placido Domingo (ten—Ernani), Wynford Evans (ten—Don Riccardo), Piero Francia (bar—Don Carlo), Agostino Ferrin (bass—Don Ruy Gomex de Silva), Robert Holl (bass—Iago), E. Downes (cnd), Omroep Orch, Omroep Chorus *(rec Amsterdam, Jan 15, 1972)* Bella Voce ▲ BLV 107.004 [ADD]
Verdi, G.:Macbeth, w. Grace Bumbry (mez—Lady Macbeth), Luciano Saldari (ten—Macduff), Paride Venturi (ten—Malcolm), Renato Bruson (bar—Macbeth), Agostino Ferrin (bass—Banquo), A. Gatto (cnd), Bologna Teatro Comunale Orch, Bologna Teatro Comunale Chorus *(rec Bologna, Mar. 18, 1975)* Golden Age of Opera 2-▲ GAO 185/86 [ADD]
Verdi, G.:Il trovatore, w. Fedora Barbieri (mez), Franco Corelli (ten), Ettore Bastianini (bar), Mirella Parutto (sgr), O. de Fabritiis (cnd), Rome Opera Orch, Rome Opera Chorus Stradivarius 2-▲ STV DTM 12313 [ADD]
Verdi, G.:Il trovatore, w. Fiorenza Cossotto (mez), Carlos Cossutta (ten), R. Muti (cnd), Florence Teatro Comunale Orch, Florence Teatro Comunale Chorus *(rec live, 1978)* Serenissima 2-▲ SER 306101 [ADD]

Ferrin, Gaetano (bass)
Bellini, V.:I Capuleti e i Montecchi (sels), w. Luciano Pavarotti (ten), Alfredo Giacomotti (bass), C. Abbado (cnd), La Scala Orch, La Scala Chorus—O di Cappelio generoso amici...E serbato a questo acciaro *(rec live, Nov. 20, 1969)* RCA Gold Seal ▲ 09026-68014-2 [ADD]
Gounod, C.:Roméo et Juliette (sels), w. Renata Scotto (sop—Juliet), Giacomo Aragall (ten—Romeo), Luciano Pavarotti (ten—Tebaldo), Gaetano Ferrin (bass—Capellio), Alfredo Giacomotti (bass—Lorenzo), C. Abbado (cnd), La Scala Orch, La Scala Chorus Budget ("The Greatest Voice in Opera" series) ▲ SYP 111

Ferrugia, M. (ten)
Pergolesi, G.B.:Il flaminio, w. D. Dessi (sop—Flaminio), F. Pediconi (sop—Agata), E. Zilio (mez—Giustina), M. Ferrugia (ten—Fernando), G. Sica (ten—Polidoro), V. Baiano (bass—Checa), S. Pagliuca (bass—Bastiano), M. Panni (cnd), Naples Teatro San Carlo Orch *(rec Nov. 12, 1983)* Fonit Cetra 3-▲ CDC 39 [ADD]

Fers, Márta (sop)
Esterházy, P.:Harmonia caelestis, w. M. Zádori (sop), K. Gémes (mez), K. Károlyi (cta), G. Kállay (ten), J. Moldvay (bass), P. Németh (cnd), Capella Savaria, Savaria Vocal Ensemble [period instrs] [L] Hungaroton 2-▲ HCD 31148/49 [DDD]
Graun, K.H.:Der Tod Jesu, w. M. Zádori (sop), M. Klietmann (ten), K. Mertens (b–bar), P. Németh (cnd), Capella Savaria Musique d'Abord ▲ HMA 1903061

Fersch, Jürgen (sgr)
Schnittke, A.:Historia von D. Johann Fausten, w. Hanna Schwarz (mez—Fair Helen), Arno Raunig (alt—Mephostophiles), Eberhard Büchner (ten—Old Man), Jürgen Freier (bar—Dr. Johann Faustus), Jonathan Barreto-Ramos (sgr—Student), Jürgen Fersch (sgr—Student), Eberhard Lorenz (sgr—Erzähler), Christoph Johannes Wendel (sgr—Student), G. Albrecht (cnd), Hamburg State PO, Hamburg State Opera Chorus *(rec live, Hamburg, Germany)* RCA Red Seal 2-▲ 09026-68413-2

Feubel, Manon (sop)
Chi Il Bel Sogno, w. Laval SO [cnd:Jacques Lacombe] *(rec Laval, Quebec, Mar 29–31, 1995)* CBC ▲ SMCD 5156 [DDD]
Chi il Bel Sogno..., w. Laval SO [cnd:Jacques Lacombe] CBC Records ▲ SM5 5156 [DDD]

Feuss (sgr)
Verdi, G.:Il trovatore (sels), w. M. Callas (sop), C. Sagarminaga (ten), K. Baum (ten), L. Warren (bar), G. Picco (cnd), Palacio Bellas Artes Orch, Palacio Bellas Artes Chorus—ten selections from Acts 1 & 4 [I] *(rec live, Mexico City 6/20/50)* Myto 2-▲ 2 MCD 90213 (m) [ADD]

Feux (sgr)
Verdi, G.:Un ballo in maschera (sels), w. A. Schuh (sgr), Larrimore (sgr), J. Björling (ten), M. Rothmüller (bar), N. Treigle (bass), J. Morris (bass), W. Herbert (cnd), *(orch unknown)* [I] *(rec live, New Orleans, 4/22/50)* Legato Classics ▲ LCD 154-1 (m) [ADD]

Fez, Elisabeth (cta)
Strauss (II), Joh.:Der Zigeunerbaron, w. Emmy Loose (sop—Arsena), Gerda Scheyrer (sop—Saffi), Elisabeth Fez (cta—Mirabella), Hilde Rössl-Majdan (cta—Czipra), Waldemar Kmentt (ten—Barinkay), Paul Spani (ten—Ottokar), Erich Kunz (bar—Homonay), Kurt Preger (bar—Zsupan), Eberhard Wächter (bass—Carnero), A. Paulik (cnd), Vienna State Opera Orch, Vienna State Opera Chorus *(rec Brahmssaal, Vienna, Austria, June 1956)* Vanguard Classics 2-▲ OVC 8082/83 [ADD]

Fichtinger, Bruno (bass)
Strauss, R.:Der Rosenkavalier, w. Jarmila Barton (sop—Marianne), Lisa Della Casa (sop—Sophie), Sena Jurinac (sop—Octavian), Ilva Ligabue (sop—Orphan), Elisabeth Schwarzkopf (sop—Marschallin), Else Schürhoff (mez—Annina), Luisa Villa (mez—Milliner), Hugues Cuénod (ten—Marschallin's majordomo), Erich Majkut (ten—Valzacchi), Giuseppe Nessi (ten—Animal seller), Luciano Della Pergola (ten—Lackey/Faninal's majordomo), Antonio Pirino (ten—An Italian Singer), Gino Del Signore (ten—Lackey/Waiter), Erich Kunz (bar—Herr von Faninal), Paolo Pedani (bar—Lackey), Attilo Barbesi (bass—Lackey/Waiter), Enrico Campi (bass—Waiter), Otto Edelmann (bass—Baron Ochs), Bruno Fichtinger (bass—Notary), Franco Taino (bass—Waiter), Maria Amadini (sgr—Orphan), Pina Carrillo (sgr—Orphan), Joszi Trojan Regar (sgr—Innkeeper), H. von Karajan (cnd), La Scala Orch, La Scala Chorus *(rec La Scala Theater, Milan, Jan. 26, 1952)* Legato Classics 3-▲ LCD 197-3

Fiddle, H. (sgr)
Grieg, E.:Norwegian Folk Songs, Op. 66, w. K. Hamre (sgr), R. Horvei (sgr), G. Botnen (pno) Simax ▲ PSC 1102
Grieg, E.:Norwegian Peasant Dances, Op. 72, w. K. Hamre (sgr), R. Horvei (sgr), G. Botnen (pno) Simax ▲ PSC 1102

Fiedler, Ursula (sop)
Mozart, W.A.:Arias, w. C. Eisenberger (vn), C. Traunfellner (cnd), Vienna CO—Exsultate, Jubilate; Voi avete un cor fedele; Misera, dove son!; Non temer, amato bene; Vedrai carino, se sei buonino; Bella mia fiamma, addio; Alma grande e nobil core; Chi sa, chi sa, qual sia Camerata ▲ 30CM-343

Field, Helen (sop)
Arias for Soprano & Trumpet, w. John Wallace (tpt), Philharmonia Orch [cnd:Simon Wright] Nimbus ▲ NI 5123 [DDD]
Martinů, B.:The Greek Passion, w. John Mitchinson (ten), Phillip Joll (b–bar), John Tomlinson (bass), C. Mackerras (cnd), Brno State PO, Czech Phil Chorus [E] *(rec 1981)* Supraphon 2-▲ 10 3611-2 [DDD]
Rossini, G.:Stabat Mater, w. D. Jones (mez), A. Davies (ten), R. Earle (bass), R. Hickox (cnd), City of London Sinfonia, London Sym Chorus [L] Chandos ▲ CHAN 8780 [DDD]

Field, Julia (alt)
Howells, H.:Requiem, w. Sally Barber (sop), Mark Johnstone (ten), Andrew Angus (bar), Jeremy Backhouse (cnd), Vasari Singers *(rec All Hallows, Gospel Oak, Feb 18–20, 1994)* United ▲ CAL 88033 [DDD]

Field, L. (sop)
Crawford, R.:Songs (5), w. H. Wingreen (pno) [E] *(rec 1987)* Cambria ▲ CD 1037 [DDD]
Gideon, M.:Morning Songs (4) of Childhood on Hebrew Texts, w. H. Wingreen (pno) [He] *(rec 1987)* Cambria ▲ CD 1037 [DDD]
Price, F.B.:Songs, w. H. Wingreen (pno)—Travel's End; To My Little Son; Night; To the Dark Virgin [E] *(rec 1987)* Cambria ▲ CD 1037 [DDD]
Rogers, P.:Sonja, w. H. Wingreen (pno)—5 songs [E] *(rec 1987)* Cambria ▲ CD 1037 [DDD]
Van De Vate, N.:Songs for the 4 Parts of the Night, w. H. Wingreen (pno) [E] *(rec 1987)* Cambria ▲ CD 1037 [DDD]

Field, Margaret (sop)
Borodin, A.:Prince Igor (sels), w. G. Simon (cnd), Philharmonia Orch Off-stage Brass, BBC Sym Chorus—Suite [orchd Glazunov & Rimsky-Korsakov] *(rec All Hallows Church, Gospel Oak, London)* Cala ▲ CAL 1011 [DDD]

Figacci, S. (sgr)
Donizetti, G.:Rita, or Le mari battu, w. U. Benelli (bar), R. Franceschetto (sgr), G. Manini (sgr), F. Maestri (cnd), In Canto CO *(rec Sept. 1990)* Bongiovanni 2-▲ GB 2109/10 [DDD]

Figner, Nicolai (ten)
The World of Singing, Vol. 2:Singers of Imperial Russia, w. Nina Koshetz (sop), Evgenia Zbruova (cta), Feodor Chaliapin (bass), Nina Friede (sgr), Maria Kouznetsova (sgr), Anastacia Vialtzeva (sgr) Enterprise ("Vocal Archives" series) 2-▲ ENT VA 2102

Figueras, Montserrat (sop)
Caccini, G.:Le nuove musiche, w. J. Savall (vl), R. Clancy (baroque gtr), H. Smith (baroque gtr), X. Schindler (hp), Schola Cantorum Basiliensis Editio Classica ▲ 77164-2-RG [ADD]
El Cant de la Sibil-la, Vol. 1, w. Capella Reial de Catalunya [cnd:Jordi Savall] Fontalis ▲ ES 8705
El Canto de la Sibila II, w. La Capella Reial de Catalunya [cnd:Jordi Savall] Fontalis ▲ 9900
Lope de Vega:Intermedios del Barroco Hispánico, w. J. Savall (cnd), Hespèrion XX Astrée ▲ E 8729
Martin Y Soler, V.:Una Cosa rara, w. M. A. Peters (sop), G. Fabuel (sop), E. Palacio (ten), F. Belaza-Leoz (bar), S. Palatchi (bass), F. Garrigosa (bass), I. Fresán (sgr), J. Savall (cnd), Concert des Nations, La Capella Reial de Catalunya [I] *(rec 1991)* Astrée 3-▲ E 8760 [DDD]
Merula, T.:Arias & Capriccios, w. J.-P. Canihac (cnt), T. Koopman (hpd), J. Savall (vl), R. Lislevand (thb), A. Lawrence-King (hp), L. Duftschmid (vn) Astrée ▲ E 8503
Milán, L. de:Maestro (sels), w. H. Smith (vihuela)—sel. of 16 sonetos, villancicos & romances, sung in Castilian, Portuguese & Italian Astrée ▲ E 7777 [ADD]
Monteverdi, C.:Arie e Lamenti, w. T. Koopman (hpd/org), A. Lawrence-King (hp), R. Lislevand (thb) Astrée ▲ E 8710
Mozart, W.A.:Requiem, w. C. Schubert (alt), G. Türk (ten), J. Schreckenberger (bass), J. Savall (cnd), La Capella Reial de Catalunya, Le Concert des Nations Astrée ▲ E 8759
Mudarra, A.:Libros de musica (sels), w. Hopkins Smith (vih)—Book 3:Si me llaman a mi; Si viesse e melevasse; La vita fugge; O gelosia d'amanti; Triste estava el rey David; Israel, mira tus montes; Beatus ille; Dulces exuviae; Regia qui mesto Por asperos caminos; Que llanto son aquestos; Claros y frescos rios; Isabel, perdiste la tu faxa; Gentil cavallero; Recuerde el alma dormida Astrée 2-▲ E 8533
Music at the Time of Beaumarchais, w. Lawrence Monteyro (sop), Raphel Oleg (vn), Miguel da Silva (va), Christophe Coin (vc), Marc Coppey (vc), José Miguel Moreno (gtr), Paul Badura-Skoda (pno), Philippe Cassard (pno), Eric Le Sage (pno), Bob Van Asperen (h Valois ▲ V 4767
Savall, J.:Joan of Arc, w. J. Savall (vl), Hespèrion XX, La Capella Reial de Catalunya Harmonia Mundi ▲ K 1006-2 ■ K 51006-4
The Voice of Emotion Fontalis ▲ ES 9901

Fiil, Laila (sop)
Johansson, O.:This Music is Called 4 Screaming Songs for Me *(rec Oct 1979)* Point ▲ PCD 5118

Fiksinski, Boguslaw (sgr)
Donizetti, G.:Linda di Chamounix, w. Mariella Devia (sop—Linda), Sonia Ganassi (mez—Pierotto), Francesca Provvisionato (mez—Maddalena), Luca Canonici (ten—Carlo), Alfonso Antoniozzi (bass—Il Marchese di Boisfleury), Petteri Salomaa (bass—Antonio), Boguslaw Fiksinski (sgr—L'intendente), Donato Di Stefano (sgr—Il Prefetto), G. Bellini (cnd), Eastern Netherlands Orch, Andrew Wise (cnd), National Reisopera Choir *(rec Muziekcentrum Enschede, Holland, June 24–July 2, 1992)* Arts Music 3-▲ 47151-2 [DDD]

VOCALISTS

Filacuridi, Nicola (ten)

Bellini, V.:I Puritani (sels), w. J. Sutherland (sop), E. Blanc (bar), G. Modesti (bass), *(orch unknown)* *(rec live, Edinburgh, Sept. 8, 1960)* Standing Room Only 2-▲ SRO 841-2 [ADD]

Maria Callas & Nicola Filacuridi, w. M. Callas (sop), Turin RAI SO [cnd:Oliviero De Fabritiis] *(rec Milan, Feb. 18, 1952)* Incontri memorabili ("Martini & Rossi Concert" series) ▲ CDMR 5001 [ADD]

Verdi, G.:La traviata (sels), w. R. Tebaldi (sop), U. Savarese (bar), T. Serafin (cnd), Florence Maggio Musicale Orch, Florence Maggio Musicale Chorus *(rec live, Florence 1956)* Melodram ▲ MEL 15006

Filippeschi, Mario (ten)

Bellini, V.:Norma, w. M. Callas (sop), E. Stignani (mez), N. Rossi-Lemeni (bass), T. Serafin (cnd), La Scala Orch, La Scala Chorus [I] EMI Classics 3-▲ CDC 47303 (m)

Bellini, V.:I Puritani, w. Lina Pagliughi (sop), Rolando Panerai (bar), Sesto Bruscantini (bass), F. Previtali (cnd), Rome RAI SO, Rome RAI Chorus *(rec Rome, Jan. 4 & 5, 1952)* Pantheon 2-▲ PHE 6640 (m)

Gounod, C.:Faust (sels), w. R. Tebaldi (sop), F. Cadoni (mez), R. Panerai (bar), I. Tajo (bass), F. Patanè (cnd), Naples Teatro San Carlo Orch, Naples Teatro San Carlo Chorus—Act IV, Scenes 1 & 2 & Act V, Scene 2 *(rec live, 4/26/51)* Standing Room Only 2-▲ SRO 810-2 [ADD]

Mario Filippeschi, w. various Italian orchs *(rec live, 1955-1957)* Bongiovanni ▲ GB 1059-2 [ADD]

Mario Filippeschi, Vol. 2 *(rec between 1950 & 1957)* Bongiovanni ▲ GB 1084 [ADD]

Puccini, G.:Tosca, w. M. Callas (sop), R. Weede (bar), U. Mugnai (cnd), Palacio Bellas Artes Orch, Palacio Bellas Artes Chorus [I] *(rec live, Mexico City, 6/8/50)* Standing Room Only 2-▲ SRO 820-2 [ADD]

Puccini, G.:Tosca, w. Maria Callas (sop), Carlos Sagarminaga (ten), Robert Weede (bar), Ramon Alonso (bass), U. Mugnai (cnd), Palacio Bellas Artes Orch, Palacio Bellas Artes Chorus Melodram 3-▲ CDM 36032

Rossini, G.:Armida, w. L. Albanese (sop), M. Callas (sop), G. Raimondi (ten), T. Serafin (cnd), Florence Teatro Comunale Orch, Florence Teatro Comunale Chorus [I] *(rec live, Florence, 4/26/52)* Melodram 2-▲ MEL 26024

Verdi, G.:Aida (sels), w. O. Rovere (sop), E. Stignani (mez), C. Cava (bass), B. McFerrin (sgr), V. Bellezza (cnd), Naples Teatro San Carlo Orch, Naples Teatro San Carlo Chorus [I] [highlights] *(rec live, Arena Flegrea, Naples, 7/15/56)* Golden Age of Opera ▲ GAO 130 [ADD]

Verdi, G.:Simon Boccanegra (sels), w. Celia Garcia (sop—Maria Boccanegra), Mario Filippeschi (ten—Gabriele Adorno), Ignacio Ruffino (ten—Pietro), Leonard Warren (bar—Simon Boccanegra), Roberto Silva (bass—Jacopo Fiesco), Carlo Morelli (bass—Paolo), R. Cellini (cnd), Mexican National Opera Orch, Mexican National Opera Chorus *(rec Palacio de las Bellas Artes, Mexico City, July 4, 1950)* Legato Classics ▲ LCD 185-1 [ADD]

Verdi, G.:Il trovatore (sels), w. J. Biel (ten), F. Tamagno (ten), L.-A. Escalaïs (ten), M. Gilion (ten), E. Caruso (ten), A. Paoli (ten), G. Zenatello (ten), J. Sembach (ten), L. Slezak (ten), F. Constantino (ten), G. Martinelli (ten), B. De Muro (ten), N. Fusati (ten), N. Piccaluga (ten), G. Lauri-Volpi (ten), A. Pertile (ten), E. Bergamaschi (ten), R. Tauber (ten), J. O'Sullivan (ten), H. Roswaenge (ten), G. Taccani (ten), V. Lois (ten), H. Lazaro (ten), A. Lindi (ten), A. Cortis (ten), F. Merli (ten), F. Völker (ten), J. Kiepura (ten), J. Schmidt (ten), J. Bjoerling (ten), B. Gigli (ten), A. Salvarezza (ten), J. Soler (ten)—34 performances of the Act III tenor aria "Di quella pira!," *(rec from 1903-1956)* Bongiovanni ▲ GB 1051 [AAD]

Verdi, G.:I vespri siciliani, w. A. Stella (sop—Elena), M. Filippeschi (ten—Arrigo), G. Taddei (bar—Monforte), B. Ladysz (bass—Procida), T. Serafin (cnd), Palermo Teatro Massimo Orch, Palermo Teatro Massimo Chorus *(rec Jan. 18, 1957)* Golden Age of Opera 2-▲ GAO 145/46 [ADD]

Filová, Marta (sop)

Vanhal, J.B.:Missa Solemnis, w. Marta Benačková (mez), Jörg Dürmüller (ten), Jiři Sulzenko (bass), V. Neumann (cnd), Prague Virtuosi, Prague Chamber Choir—Kyrie eleison, Adagio— Allegro; Christe eleison, Andante; Kyrie eleison, Allegro; Gloria, Allegro moderato; Laudamus te, Andante; Gratias agimus tibi, Allegro moderato; Domine Deus, Rex caelestis, andante; Domine Deus, Agnus Dei, Adagio; Quoniam tu solus sanctus, Allegro moderato, Cum sancto spiritu, Allegro; Credo, Allegro moderato, Et incarnatus est. Adagio; Et resurrexit, Allegro moderato; Sanctus, Adagio—Osanna, Allegro; Benedictus, Andante—Osanna, Allegro; Agnus Dei, Adagio; Dona nobis pacem, Allegro *(rec Evangelische Kirche der böhmischen Brüder, Prag, Sept 25-28, 1994)* Orfeo ▲ C 353 951 A [DDD]

Finateanu, Corneliu (ten)

Puccini, G.:Turandot, w. Teodora Lucaciu (sop—Liù), Maria Slatinaru (sop—Princess Turandot), Corneliu Finateanu (ten—Pong), George Mircea (ten—Emperor Altoum), Ludovic Speiss (ten—Prince Calaf), Valentin Teodorian (ten—Pang), Octav Enigarescu (bar—Ping), Dionisie Konya (bar—A Mandarin), Mircea Stefanescu (bar—The Prince of Persia), Nicolae Florei (bass—Timur), C. Litvin (cnd), Romanian Radio-TV Orch, Romanian Radio-TV Chorus *(rec Jan 1970)* Vox Box 2-▲ CDX 5160

Findell, Bradford (ct)

French Sacred Music of the 14th Century, Vol. 1, w. Schola Discantus, John Delorey (ct), Peter McCabe (ten), Arthur Rawding (ten), Paul Guttry (bar), Kevin Moll (cnd) *(rec Emmanuel Church, Boston, 1994)* Lyrichord ("Early Music" series) ▲ LYR 8012 [DDD]

Finel, Paul (ten)

Poulenc, F.:Dialogues des Carmélites, w. D. Duval (sop), R. Crespin (sop), L. Berton (sop), D. Scharley (mez), R. Gorr (mez), X. Depraz (bass), P. Dervaux (cnd), Paris Opera Orch [F] EMI Classics 2-▲ CDCB 49331 (m) [ADD]

Fineschi, Ornella (sop)

De Cavalieri, Fineschi, Olivero, Stignani, Tassinari, w. A. de Cavalieri (sop), Magda Olivero (sop), Ebe Stignani (mez), Pia Tassinari (mez), Rome RAI SO, Milan RAI SO *(rec 1953-58)* Incontri Memorabili ("Martini & Rossi Concerts" series) ▲ 5020

Fink, Bernarda (cta)

Caldara, A.:Maddalena ai Piedi di Cristo, w. Maria Cristina Kiehr (sop), Rosa Dominguez (sop), Andreas Scholl (ct), Gerd Türk (ten), Ulrich Messthaler (bass), R. Jacobs (cnd), Schola Cantorum Basiliensis Instrumental Ensemble Harmonia Mundi France 2-▲ HMC 905221.22

Handel, G.F.:Amadigi di Gaula, w. E. Harrhy (sop—Melissa), J. Smith (sop—Oriana), P. Bertin (mez—Orgando), B. Fink (cta—Dardano), N. Stutzmann (cta—Amadigi), M. Minkowski (cnd), Louvre Musicians, Louvre Choir [I] Erato 2-▲ 2292-45490-2 [DDD]

Handel, G.F.:Giulio Cesare in Egitto, w. Barbara Schlick (sop), Jennifer Larmore (mez), Marianne Rørholm (mez), Derek Lee Ragin (ct), Dominique Visse (ct), Oliver Lallouette (bass), Furio Zanasi (bass), R. Jacobs (cnd), Concerto Cologne [period instrs] Harmonia Mundi France 3-▲ HMC 901385/87

Handel, G.F.:Giulio Cesare in Egitto (sels), w. Barbara Schlick (sop), Jennifer Larmore (mez), Marianne Rørholm (mez), Derek Lee Ragin (ct), R. Jacobs (cnd), Concerto Cologne Harmonia Mundi France ▲ HMC 901458

Handel, G.F.:Poro, Rè dell'Indie, w. Rossana Bertini (sop), Gloria Banditelli (cta), Gérard Lesne (ct), F. Biondi (cnd), Europa Galante Opus 111 3-▲ OPS 30-113/15

Haydn, J.:Mass 3, "Căcilienmesse", w. Brigette Fournier (sop), Charles Daniels (ten), Marcus Fink (bass), M. Corboz (cnd), Lisbon Gulbenkian Foundation Orch, Lisbon Gulbenkian Foundation Chorus *(rec July 1993)* FNAC Music ▲ 592309 [DDD]

Haydn, J.:Mass 5, "Missa Sancti Josephi", "Grosse Orgelmesse", w. Dorthea Röschmann (sop), Helmut Wildhaber (ten), Klaus Mertens (bar), M. Haselböck (cnd), Vienna Academy, Hugo Distler Choir Novalis ▲ 150095 [DDD]

Haydn, J.:Mass 7, "Kleine Orgelmesse", w. Dorthea Röschmann (sop), Helmut Wildhaber (ten), Klaus Mertens (bar), M. Haselböck (cnd), Vienna Academy, Hugo Distler Choir Novalis ▲ 150095 [DDD]

Haydn, J.:Salve regina, H.XXIIIb/2, w. Dorthea Röschmann (sop), Helmut Wildhaber (ten), Klaus Mertens (bar), M. Haselböck (cnd), Vienna Academy, Hugo Distler Choir Novalis ▲ 150095 [DDD]

Monteverdi, C.:Incoronazione, w. Constanze Backes (sop—Valletto), Catherine Bott (sop—Drusilla/Pallade/La Virtù), Dana Hanchard (sop—Nerone), Sylvia McNair (sop—Poppea), Marinella Pennicchi (sop—Amore/Damigella), Annie Sofie von Otter (mez—Ottavia/Venere/La Fortuna), Julian Clarkson (alt—Littore/Mercurio), Bernarda Fink (cta—Arnalta), Roberto Balconi (ct—Nutrice), Michael Chance (ct—Ottone), Nigel Robson (ten—Liberto/Soldato Secondo), Mark Tucker (ten—Lucano/Soldato Primo), Francesco Ellero d'Artegna (bass—Seneca), J. E. Gardiner (cnd), English Baroque Soloists *(rec Queen Elizabeth Hall, South Bank Ctr, London, Dec 1993)* Archiv 3-▲ 447088-2

Fink, Bernarda (cta) (cont.)

Monteverdi, C.:Ritorno d'Ulisse, w. L. Hunt (sop), C. Högman (sop), D. Vissé (ct), C. Prégardien (ten), G. Tucker (ten), D. Thomas (bass), R. Jacobs (cnd), Concerto Vocale [I] Harmonia Mundi France 3-▲ HMC 901427/29

Rameau, J.P.:Hippolyte et Aricie, w. Véronique Gens (sop), Jean-Paul Fouchécourt (ten), Laurent Naouri (bar), Russell Smythe (bar), M. Minkowski (cnd), Louvre Musicians, Sagittarius Vocal Ensemble Archiv 3-▲ 445853-2

Fink, Marcus (bass)

Handel, G.F.:Messiah (reorchd Mozart), w. Audrey Michael (sop), Jard van Nes (cta), Hans-Peter Blochwitz (tenor), M. Corboz (cnd), Lausanne Instrumental Ensemble, Lausanne Vocal Ensemble [G] Erato 2-▲ 2292-45497-2 [DDD]

Haydn, J.:Mass 3, "Căcilienmesse", w. Brigette Fournier (sop), Bernarda Fink (alt), Charles Daniels (ten), M. Corboz (cnd), Lisbon Gulbenkian Foundation Orch, Lisbon Gulbenkian Foundation Chorus *(rec July 1993)* FNAC Music ▲ 592309 [DDD]

Fink, Walter (bass)

Wagner, R.:Das Rheingold, w. Gabriele Fontana (sop—Woglinde), Nancy Gustafson (sop—Freia), Ildiko Komlosi (mez—Wellgunde), Hanna Schwarz (mez—Fricka), Elena Zaremba (mez—Erda), Margareta Hintermeier (cta—Flosshilde), Kim Begley (ten—Loge), Peter Schreier (ten—Mime), Thomas Sunnegardh (ten—Froh), Robert Hale (bass-bar—Wotan), Walter Fink (bass—Fafner), Franz-Josef Kapellmann (bass—Alberich), Jan-Hendrik Rootering (bass—Fasolt), Eike Wilm Schulte (bass—Donner), C. von Dohnányi (cnd), Cleveland Orch *(rec Severance Hall, Cleveland, Ohio, Dec 1993)* London 2-▲ 443690-2

Finke, Martin (ten)

Dittersdorf, K.D. von:Doctor und Apotheker, w. Hildegard Uhrmacher (sop—Leonore), Donna Woodward (sop—Rosalia), Waltraud Meier (mez—Claudia), Martin Finke (ten—Sichel), Frieder Lang (ten—Gotthold), Alois Perl (ten—Gallus), Gerhard Unger (ten—Sturmwald), Thomas Pfeiffer (bar—Police Commisioner), Wolfgang Schöne (bar—Krautmann), Harald Stamm (bass—Stössel), J. Lockhart (cnd), Rhine State PO Bayer 2-▲ BR 100 238/39 [DDD]

Finley, Gerald (bar)

Brahms, J.:Ein Deutsches Requiem, w. Christiane Oelze (sop), P. Herreweghe (cnd), Champs Élysées Theater Orch, Chapelle Royale Choir, Collegium Vocale Harmonia Mundi ▲ HMC 901608 ■ HMC 401608

Haydn, J.:Die Schöpfung, w. Donna Brown (sop), Sylvia McNair (sop), Michael Schade (ten), Rodney Gilfry (bar), J. E. Gardiner (cnd), English Baroque Soloists, Monteverdi Choir London Archiv ▲ 449 217-2

Mozart, W.A.:Zauberflöte, w. Constanze Backes (sop—Papagena), Christiane Oelze (sop—Pamina), Susan Roberts (sop—First Lady), Cyndia Sieden (sop—Queen of the Night), Carola Guber (cta—Second Lady), Maria Jonas (cta—Third Lady), Andreas Dieterich (trb—First Boy), Jan Andreas Mendel (trb—Second Boy), Florian Wöller (trb—Third Boy), Uwe Peper (ten—Monostatos), Nicolas Robertson (ten—First Man in Armor), Michael Schade (ten—Tamino), Gerald Finley (bar—Papageno), Noel Mann (bass—Second Man in Armour), Harry Peeters (bass—Sarastro), Detlef Roth (bass—Speaker/First Priest), Robert Burt (speaker—Third Priest), Robert Johnston (speaker—Second Priest), Wolfgang Knauer (speaker—Fourth Priest), Douglas Welbat (speaker—Second Priest), J. E. Gardiner (cnd), English Baroque Soloists, Monteverdi Choir London *(rec Forum am Schlosspark, Ludwigsburg, July 1995)* Archiv 2-▲ 449166-2

Purcell, H.:The Indian Queen, w. Catherine Bott (sop—Orazia/Married Woman), Emma Kirkby (sop—Indian Girl/Zempoalla/Cupid), John Mark Ainsley (ten—Indian Boy/Fame/Follower of Cupid/Aerial Spirits), Julian Podger (ten—Follower of Envy/Aerial Spirit), Gerald Finley (bar—Conjurer/Hymen/Follower of Cupid), Helen Parker (sgr—Aerial Spirits), David Thomas (bass—Envy/High Priest/Married Man/Follower of Cupid), Simon Berridge (sgr—Follower of Envy), Libby Crabtree (sgr—Follower of Hymen/Aerial Spirit), Tommy Williams (sgr—God of Dreams), C. Hogwood (cnd), Academy of Ancient Music *(rec Walthamstow Assembly Hall, London, July 1994)* L'Oiseau-Lyre ▲ 444339-2 [DDD]

Purcell, H.:King Arthur, w. N. Argenta (sop), J. Gooding (sop), L. Perillo (sop), J. MacDougall (ten), M. Tucker (ten), B. Bannatyne-Scott (bass), T. Pinnock (cnd), English Concert, *(chorus unknown)* Archiv 2-▲ 435490-2 [DDD]

Webern, A.:music of, w. Christiane Oelze (sop), P. Boulez (cnd), Berlin PO, BBC Singers—Sym, Op. 21; Cants, Opp. 29 & 31; 3 Songs; Das Augenlicht; Vars, Op. 30; 5 Pieces Deutsche Grammophon ▲ 447 765-2

Finley, Gerald (ten)

Berlioz, H.:L'Enfance du Christ, w. Jean Rigby (mez), John Aler (ten), Alastair Miles (bar), Gwynne Howell (bass), M. Best (cnd), Cordon Orch, Corydon Singers, St. Paul's Cathedral Choir Hyperion 2-▲ CDA 66991/2

Mozart, W.A.:Don Giovanni, w. N. Argenta (sop), A. Halgrimson (sop), L. Dawson (sop), J. M. Ainsley (ten), A. Miles (bar), A. Schmidt (bar), G. Yurisch (bar), R. Norrington (cnd), London Classical Players, Schütz Choir London EMI Classics ▲ CDCB 54859

Finnie, Linda (mez)

Bliss, A.:The Enchantress, w. V. Handley (cnd), Ulster Orch [E] Chandos ▲ CHAN 8818 [DDD]

Brahms, J.:Ernste Gesänge, w. A. Legge (pno)—Nos. 1-4 [G] Chandos ▲ CHAN 8786 [DDD]

Brahms, J.:Songs, Op. 91, w. J. Harrington (va), A. Legge (pno) [G] Chandos ▲ CHAN 8786 [DDD]

Britten, H.:Spring Sym, w. Eiddwen Harrhy (sop), Robert Tear (ten), G. Rozhdestvensky (cnd), BBC SO, BBC Sym Chorus, London Voices, Southend Boys' Choir IMP ("BBC Radio Classics" series) ▲ IMP 5691752

Chausson, E.:Poème de l'amour et de la mer, w. Y.P. Tortelier (cnd), Ulster Orch [F] Chandos ▲ CHAN 8952 [DDD]

Elgar, E.:The Light of Life, w. J. Howarth (sop), A. Davies (ten), J. Shirley-Quirk (bar), R. Hickox (cnd), London SO, London Sym Chorus Chandos ▲ CHAN 9208 [DDD]

Elgar, E.:The Music Makers, w. B. Thomson (cnd), London PO, London Phil Chorus [E] Chandos ▲ CHAN 9022 [DDD]

Elgar, E.:Sea Pictures, w. B. Thomson (cnd), London PO, London Phil Chorus [E] Chandos ▲ CHAN 9022 [DDD]

Handel, G.F.:Messiah, w. Helen Kucharek (sop), Jennifer Smith (sop), Niel Mackie (ten), Rodney Macann (b-bar), T. Dean (cnd), Pro Christe Orch, Pro Christe Choir *(rec St. Augustine's Church, Kilburn, London, 1986)* Guild 2-▲ GMDD 7112/3 [ADD]

Handel, G.F.:Messiah (sels), w. Felicity Lott (sop), Glenn Winslade (ten), Henry Herford (bar), G. Malcolm (cnd), Scottish CO, Scottish Phil Singers IMP ("Classic" series) ▲ IMP 2031

Korngold, E.W.:Abschiedslieder, w. E. Downes (cnd), BBC PO Chandos ▲ CHAN 9171 [DDD]

Mahler, G.:Kindertotenlieder, w. N. Järvi (cnd), Royal Scottish Orch [G] Chandos 2-▲ CHAN 9117/18 [DDD]

Mahler, G.:Das Klagende Lied, w. J. Rodgers (sop), H. P. Blochwitz (ten), R. Hickox (cnd), Bournemouth SO, Bath Festival Chorus, Waynflete Singers Chandos ▲ CHAN 9247 [DDD]

Mahler, G.:Lieder eines fahrenden Gesellen, w. N. Järvi (cnd), Royal Scottish Orch [G] Chandos ▲ CHAN 8951 [DDD]

Mahler, G.:Sym 3, w. N. Järvi (cnd), Royal Scottish Orch, Royal Scottish Chorus [G] Chandos 2-▲ CHAN 9117/18 [DDD]

Mahler, G.:Sym 4, w. N. Järvi (cnd), Royal Scottish Orch [G] Chandos ▲ CHAN 8951 [DDD]

Mendelssohn, F.:Elijah, w. R. Plowright (sop), J. Budd (trb), A. Davies (ten), J. White (bass), R. Hickox (cnd), London SO, London Sym Chorus [E] Chandos 2-▲ CHAN 8774/75 [DDD]

Prokofiev, S.:Alexander Nevsky, w. N. Järvi (cnd), Scottish National Orch, Scottish National Chorus Chandos ▲ CHAN 8584 [DDD]

Prokofiev, S.:Ivan the Terrible Cta, w. N. Storojev (bass), N. Järvi (cnd), Philharmonia Orch, Philharmonia Chorus Chandos ▲ CHAN 8977 [DDD]

Ravel, M.:L'Enfant et les sortilèges, w. Arleen Augér (sop), Marilyn Richardson (sop), Jane Berbié (mez), Jocelyne Taillon (mez), Davenny Wyner (mez), Philip Langridge (ten), Philippe Huttenlocher (bar), Jules Bastin (bass), A. Previn (cnd), London SO, Ambrosian Opera Chorus Classics for Pleasure ("Eminence" series) ▲ CFP 2241

Ravel, M.:Shéhérazade Mez, w. Y.P. Tortelier (cnd), Ulster Orch Chandos ▲ CHAN 8914 [DDD]

Respighi, O.:Aretusa, w. R. Hickox (cnd), BBC PO Chandos ▲ CHAN 9453

Respighi, O.:La Sensitiva, w. R. Hickox (cnd), BBC PO Chandos ▲ CHAN 9453

▲ = CD ♦ = Enhanced CD Δ = MD ■ = Cassette Tape ◻ = DCC

Finnie, Linda (mez) (cont.)
Respighi, O.:Il Tramonto, w. T. Vásáry (cnd), Bournemouth Sinfonietta [I] Chandos ▲ CHAN 8913 [DDD]
Schumann, R.:Frauenliebe und -leben, w. A. Legge (pno) [G] Chandos ▲ CHAN 8786 [DDD]
Songs of the British Isles, w. Anthony Legge (pno) Chandos ▲ CHAN 8749 [DDD]
Strauss, R.:Songs, w. N. Järvi (cnd), Scottish National Orch—Notturno, Op. 44, No. 1 [G] Chandos ▲ CHAN 8834 [DDD]
Vaughan Williams, R.:Riders to the Sea, w. Ingrid Attrot (sop—Nora), Lynn Dawson (sop—Cathleen), Linda Finnie (mez—Maurya), Karl Daymond (bar—Bartley), R. Hickox (cnd), Northern Sinfonia of England Chandos ▲ CHAN 9392 [DDD]
Wagner, R.:Das Rheingold, w. L. Finnie (mez—Fricka), G. Clark (ten—Loge), J. Tomlinson (bar—Wotan), B. Brinkmann (bar—Donner), D. Barenboim (cnd), Bayreuth Festival Orch, Bayreuth Festival Chorus [G] Teldec 2-▲ 4509-91185-2
Walton, W.:Christopher Columbus (suite), w. A. Davies (ten), R. Hickox (cnd), City of London Sinfonia, Westminster Singers [E] Chandos ▲ CHAN 8824 [DDD]

Finnilä, Birgit (mez)
Bach, J.S.:Magnificat, BWV 243, w. Helen Donath (sop), Gundula Bernát-Klein (sop), Peter Schreier (ten), Barry McDaniel (bass), W. Gönnenwein (cnd), German Bach Soloists, South German Madrigal Choir [E♭ version] *(rec Stuttgart Radio, 1966)* Bayer ▲ 100081 [ADD]
Bach, J.S.:St. John Passion, w. F. Palmer (sop), K. Equiluz (ten), W. Krenn (ten), P. Huttenlocher (bar), R. van der Meer (bass), M. Corboz (cnd), Lausanne CO, Lausanne Vocal Ensemble Erato 2-▲ 2292-45406-2 FD
Bach, J.S.:St. Matthew Passion, w. E. Ameling (sop), E. Haefliger (ten), S. McCoy (ten), B. Luxon (bar), B. McDaniel (bar), J. Somary (cnd), English CO, Ambrosian Singers *(rec 1977)* Vanguard Classics 3-▲ OVC 4060/62 [ADD]
Bach, J.S.:St. Matthew Passion (sels), w. E. Ameling (sop), E. Haefliger (ten), S. McCoy (ten), B. Luxon (bar), B. McDaniel (bar), J. Somary (cnd), English CO, Ambrosian Singers Vanguard Classics ▲ OVC 4063 [ADD]
Elgar, E.:Sea Pictures, w. Geoffrey Parsons (pno) *(rec Nacka Aula, Nacka, Sweden, Sept 21, 1975)* BIS ▲ CD 127 [AAD]
Hallnäs, H.:Songs, w. Marta Schele (sop), Rolf Leanderson (bar), Elisef Lunden (pno)—3 sels BIS ▲ CD 38
Mahler, G.:Sym 2, w. H. Donath (sop), J. Barbirolli (cnd), Stuttgart RSO, Stuttgart Radio Chorus [G] *(rec live 6/19/70)* Arkadia 3-▲ 719 [ADD]
Mahler, G.:Sym 8, w. Hanneke van Bork (sop), Ileana Cotrubas (sop), Heather Harper (sop), Marianne Dieleman (cta), William Cochran (ten), Hermann Prey (bar), Hans Sotin (bass), B. Haitink (cnd), Royal Concertgebouw Orch Philips ("Solo" series) ▲ 446195-2
Nystroem, G.:Songs, w. Marta Schele (sop), Rolf Leanderson (bar), Elisef Lunden (pno)—3 sels BIS ▲ CD 38
Nystroem, G.:Songs at the Sea, w. Marta Schele (sop), Rolf Leanderson (bar), Elisef Lunden (pno) BIS ▲ CD 38
Rosenberg, H.:Chinese Songs, w. Marta Schele (sop), Rolf Leanderson (bar), Elisef Lunden (pno) BIS ▲ CD 38
Shostakovich, D.:Lady Macbeth of Mtsensk, w. G. Vishnevskaya (sop), N. Gedda (ten), A. Haugland (bass), M. Rostropovich (cnd), London PO, Ambrosian Opera Chorus [R] EMI Classics 2-▲ CDCB 49955 [ADD]
Strauss, R.:Die ägyptische Helena, w. G. Jones (sop), M. Kastu (ten), B. Hendricks (sop), W. White (bass), C. Rayam (ten), A. Dorati (cnd), Detroit SO London ("Grand Opera" series) 2-▲ 430381-2 [AAD]
Werle, L.J.:Night Hunt, w. Marta Schele (sop), Rolf Leanderson (bar), Elisef Lunden (pno) BIS ▲ CD 38

Fioravanti, Giulio (bar)
Donizetti, G.:La fille du régiment, w. A. Moffo (sop), J. Gardino (mez), G. Campora (ten), F. Mannino (cnd), Milan RAI Orch, Milan RAI Chorus *(rec live Dec 2, 1960)* Melodram 2-▲ MEL 27018 [ADD]
Donizetti, G.:Lucia di Lammermoor, w. C. Deutekom (sop), J. Carreras (ten), C. Cava (bass), A. Gatto (cnd), *(orch unknown)* [I] *(rec live in Madrid, 1975)* Standing Room Only 2-▲ SRO 809-2 [ADD]
Leoncavallo, R.:Edipo re, w. L. Infantino (ten), G. Malaspina (bar), R. Parodi (cnd), Naples Teatro San Carlo Orch, Naples Teatro San Carlo Chorus *(rec live, Naples, 1970)* Italian Opera Rarities ▲ IOR 7723 [ADD]
Puccini, G.:Manon Lescaut, w. M. Callas (sop), G. di Stefano (ten), T. Serafin (cnd), La Scala Orch, La Scala Chorus [I] EMI Classics 2-▲ CDCB 47392 (m)
Puccini, G.:Tosca, w. M. Olivero (sop), A. Misciano (ten), F. Vernizzi (cnd), Turin RAI Orch, Turin RAI Chorus *(rec live 1960)* Melodram 2-▲ MEL 27026
Verdi, G.:Stiffelio, w. A. Gulin (sop—Lina), M. del Monaco (ten—Stiffelio), A. Marchiandi (ten—Raffaele), G. Fioravanti (bar—Stankar), J. Hecht (bass—Jorg), O. de Fabritiis (cnd), Naples Teatro San Carlo Orch, Naples Teatro San Carlo Chorus *(rec Dec. 26, 1972)* Standing Room Only 2-▲ SRO 169-2

Fiordaliso, Gina Longobardo (sgr)
Zandonai, R.:I cavalieri di Ekebù, w. Fiorenza Cossotto (sop), Lando Bartolini (ten), G. Gavazzeni (cnd), Milan RAI SO, Milan RAI Chorus Fonit Cetra ("Italia" series) 2-▲ FCT CDC 93

Flore, Janice (sop)
Cacioppo, C.:Wolf, w. David Geber (vc), Curt Cacioppo (pno) Capstone ▲ CPS 8632

Fiorentini, Mirella (mez)
Bellini, V.:I Puritani, w. Mirella Freni (sop), Luciano Pavarotti (ten), Emilio Venturini (ten), Sesto Bruscantini (bar), Giovanni Antonini (bass), Bonaldo Giaiotti (bass), R. Muti (cnd), Rome RAI SO, Rome RAI Chorus Melodram 2-▲ CDM 27062
Verdi, G.:Il trovatore, w. A. Stella (sop), F. Cossotto (mez), F. Corelli (ten), E. Bastianini (bar), I. Vinco (bass), G. Gavazzeni (cnd), La Scala Orch, La Scala Chorus *(rec live, Milan, 12/7/62)* Melodram 2-▲ MEL 27068 (m) [AAD]
Verdi, G.:Il trovatore, w. A. Stella (sop), F. Cossotto (mez), F. Corelli (ten), E. Bastianini (bar), I. Vinco (bass), G. Gavazzeni (cnd), La Scala Orch, La Scala Chorus [I] *(rec live, Milan, 12/7/62)* Claque 2-▲ CLQ 2013 (m)

Fiorini (sgr)
Mercadante, S.:Elisa e Claudio, w. Virginia Zeani (sop), Agostino Lazzari (ten), Domenico Trimarchi (bar), Ugo Trama (bass), U. Rapalo (cnd), Naples Teatro San Carlo Orch, Naples Teatro San Carlo Chorus *(rec live, Naples, 1/31/71)* Melodram 2-▲ MEL 27099 [ADD]

Firestone, Adria (cta)
Cage, J.:Songs—5 Songs for Cta Wergo ▲ WER 61592

Fischer, Belá (alt)
Schubert, Franz:Mass 3, w. Alexander Nader (sop), Thomas Puchegger (sop), Georg Leskovich (alt), Jörg Hering (ten), Harry Van der Kamp (bass), Arno Hartmann (org), B. Weil (cnd), Orch of the Age of Enlightenment, Chorus Viennensis, Vienna Boys' Choir Sony Classical ("Vivarte" series) ▲ SK 68248
Schubert, Franz:Mass 4, w. Alexander Nader (sop), Thomas Puchegger (sop), Georg Leskovich (alt), Jörg Hering (ten), Harry Van der Kamp (bass), Arno Hartmann (org), B. Weil (cnd), Orch of the Age of Enlightenment, Chorus Viennensis, Vienna Boys' Choir Sony Classical ("Vivarte" series) ▲ SK 68248

Fischer, Carola (cta)
Matthus, S.:Mirabeau, w. Carola Höhn (sop—Marie Antoinette), Carola Fischer (cta—Eveline Le Jay), Peter-Jürgend Schmidt (ten—Ludwig XVI), Jürgen Freier (bar—Honoré-Gabriel de Riqueti), Gerd Wolf (bass—Victor Riqueti), H. Fricke (cnd), Berlin State Opera Orch, Berlin State Opera Chorus *(rec Berlin, 1989)* Berlin Classics 2-▲ BER 1075 [DDD]

Fischer, Christiane (alt)
Mauersberger, R.:Geh aus, mein Herz, und suche Freude, w. Sabine Dicke (sop), Dorothea Schmidt (sop), Friederike Urban (sop), Annette Bassenge (alt), Sabine Hering (alt), Johannes Unger (org), Wolfgang Unger (dir), Thüringian Academic Sing Circle Thorofon ▲ CTH 2245 [DDD]

Fischer, Jeannette (sop)
Bertoni, F.:Orfeo ed Euridice, w. Jeannette Fischer (sop—Euridice), Julia Juon (mez—Orfeo), Steve Davislim (ten—Imeneo), R. Tschupp (cnd), Aargauer SO, Aarau New Canton School Choir *(rec Zurich Radio Studio, Oct 30-Nov 1, 1994)* Jecklin ▲ JEC 700
Maggini, E.:Zwischen Himmel und Erde, w. Werner Zumsteg (fl)—Als ob die Nacht; Im Wärmezirkel; Komm ich weiss; Greift ein Engel; So wie du daliegst; Er sagte; Als ob ein Jubel; Wenn die Tische; Gib mir die Hand *(rec RTSI, Rete 2, Dec 1993)* Jecklin ▲ JS 311-2 [DDD]

Fischer, Jeannette (sop) (cont.)
Marek, C.:Rural Scenes, w. R. Tschupp (cnd), Zurich Camerata *(rec Dec 1993-Dec 1994)* Jecklin ▲ JEC 306

Fischer, L. (cta)
Verdi, G.:Requiem Mass, w. I. Auez (sop), L. van Tulder (ten), H. Schey (bar), C. Schuricht (cnd), Royal Concertgebouw Orch, Amsterdam Toonkunst Choir *(rec live, Amsterdam, Nov. 2, 1939)* Archipon 2-▲ ARC 3.2/3 (m) [ADD]

Fischer, Thomas (ten)
Weill, K.:Der Jasager, w. H. Helling (cta), T. Schmeisser (treb), T. Bräutigam (ten), U. Schütte (bar), M. Knöppel (bass), W. Gundlach (cnd), Westphalia CO, Westphalia Kantorei Capriccio ▲ 60 020-1 [DDD]

Fischer-Dieskau, Dietrich (bar)
Bach, J.S.:Cant 26, w. E. Mathis (sop), P. Schreier (ten), A. Schmidt (bar), K. Richter (cnd), Munich Bach Orch, Munich Bach Choir Archiv ▲ 427130-2 [ADD]
Bach, J.S.:Cant 56, w. H. Rilling (cnd), Stuttgart Bach Collegium, Gächinger Kantorei [G] Novalis ▲ 150029 [DDD]
Bach, J.S.:Cant 56, w. H. Rilling (cnd), Stuttgart Bach Collegium, Gächinger Kantorei [G] *(rec ca 1986)* Hänssler Classic ▲ 98.903 [AAD]
Bach, J.S.:Cant 56, w. K. Richter (cnd), Munich Bach Orch [G] Archiv ▲ 427128-2 [ADD]
Bach, J.S.:Cant 80, w. E. Mathis (sop), T. Schmidt (mez), P. Schreier (ten), K. Richter (cnd), Munich Bach Orch, Munich Bach Choir Archiv ▲ 427130-2 [ADD]
Bach, J.S.:Cant 82, w. H. Rilling (cnd), Stuttgart Bach Collegium, Gächinger Kantorei [G] Novalis ▲ 150028 [DDD]
Bach, J.S.:Cant 82, w. K. Richter (cnd), Munich Bach Orch [G] Archiv ▲ 427128-2 [ADD]
Bach, J.S.:Cant 82, w. H. Rilling (cnd), Stuttgart Bach Collegium, Gächinger Kantorei [G] *(rec ca 1986)* Hänssler Classic ▲ 98.903 [AAD]
Bach, J.S.:Cant 116, w. E. Mathis (sop), T. Schmidt (mez), P. Schreier (ten), K. Richter (cnd), Munich Bach Orch, Munich Bach Choir Archiv ▲ 427130-2 [ADD]
Bach, J.S.:Cant 140, w. E. Mathis (sop), P. Schreier (ten), K. Richter (cnd), Munich Bach Orch, Munich Bach Choir [G] Deutsche Grammophon ("Galleria" series) ▲ 419466-2 [ADD]
Bach, J.S.:Cant 203, w. Aurèle Nicolet (fl), Helmut Keller (vn), Irmgard Poppen (vc), Edith Picht-Axenfeld (hpd) EMI Classics ("Baroque" series) ▲ CDK 65729
Bach, J.S.:Cant 208, "Hunting Cant", w. Erika Köth (sop), K. Forster (cnd), Berlin SO, St. Hedwig's Cathedral Choir EMI Classics ("Baroque" series) ▲ CDK 65729
Bach, J.S.:Christmas Oratorio, w. Elly Ameling (sop), Janet Baker (mez), Robert Tear (ten), P. Ledger (cnd), Academy of St. Martin in the Fields, King's College Choir Cambridge *(rec 1976)* EMI Classics ("Doublefforte" series) 2-▲ CDFB 69503
Bach, J.S.:Magnificat, BWV 243, w. M. Stader (sop), H. Töpper (cta), E. Haefliger (ten), K. Richter (cnd), Munich Bach Orch, Munich Bach Choir [L] Deutsche Grammophon ("Galleria" series) ▲ 419466-2 [ADD]
Bach, J.S.:St. Matthew Passion, w. G. Janowitz (sop), C. Ludwig (mez), H. Laubenthal (ten), P. Schreier (ten), W. Berry (bar), H. von Karajan (cnd), Berlin PO, Vienna Singverein, German Opera Chorus [G] Deutsche Grammophon 3-▲ 419789-2 [ADD]
Bach, J.S.:St. Matthew Passion, w. E. Schwarzkopf (sop), C. Ludwig (mez), N. Gedda (ten), W. Berry (bass), O. Klemperer (cnd), Philharmonia Orch EMI Classics 3-▲ ZDMC 63058
Bach, J.S.:St. Matthew Passion, w. I. Seefried (sop), A. Fahberg (sop), H. Töpper (alt), E. Haefliger (ten), K. Engen (bass), M. Proebstl (bass), K. Richter (cnd), Munich Bach Orch, Munich Bach Choir Archiv ▲ 439338-2 [ADD]
Barber, S.:Dover Beach, w. Juilliard String Quartet [E] *(rec 1967)* Sony Masterworks ("Portrait" series) ▲ MPK 46727 [ADD]
Beethoven, L. van:Fidelio, w. G. Janowitz (sop), L. Popp (sop), R. Kollo (ten), H. Sotin (bass), L. Bernstein (cnd), Vienna PO, Vienna State Opera Chorus [G] Deutsche Grammophon 2-▲ 419436-2 [ADD]
Beethoven, L. van:Fidelio (sels), w. L. Rysanek (sop), I. Seefried (sop), E. Haefliger (ten), F. Lenz (ten), K. Engen (bass), G. Frick (bass), F. Fricsay (cnd), Bavarian State Orch, Bavarian Opera Chorus—Overture, various arias & scenes, finale [G] IMP Collectors Series ▲ IMPX 9021 [AAD]
Beethoven, L. van:Songs, w. Hertha Klust (pno)—7 Goethe-Lieder; 6 Lieder von Gellert, Op. 48; 14 Lieder Nach Verschiedenen Dichtern Testament ▲ TES 1057 [ADD]
Berg, A.:Lulu, w. E. Lear (sop—Lulu), P. Johnson (mez—Countess Geschwitz), D. Grobe (ten—Alwa), Fischer-Dieskau (bar—Dr. Schön), K. Böhm (cnd), German Opera Orch, German Opera Chorus [G] *(rec 1968)* Deutsche Grammophon 3-▲ 435705-2 [ADD]
Berg, A.:Wozzeck, w. E. Lear (sop—Marie), F. Wunderlich (ten—Andres), G. Stoltze (ten—The Captain), D. Fischer-Dieskau (bar—Wozzeck), K. Böhm (cnd), German Opera Orch, German Opera Chorus [G] *(rec 1965)* Deutsche Grammophon 3-▲ 435705-2 [ADD]
Brahms, J.:Ein Deutsches Requiem, w. E. Grümmer (sop), R. Kempe (cnd), Berlin PO, St. Hedwig's Cathedral Choir [G] EMI Classics ▲ CDH 64705
Brahms, J.:Ein Deutsches Requiem, w. E. Schwarzkopf (sop), O. Klemperer (cnd), Philharmonia Orch, Philharmonia Chorus [G] EMI Classics 2-▲ CDC 47238
Brahms, J.:Duets, Op. 28, w. Janet Baker (mez), Daniel Barenboim (pno) EMI Classics ("Doubleforte" series) 2-▲ CDFB 68667
Brahms, J.:Liebeslieder Waltzes SATB, w. E. Mathis (sop), B. Fassbaender (mez), P. Schreier (ten), K. Engel (pno), W. Sawallisch (pno) [G] Deutsche Grammophon ▲ 423133-2 [DDD]
Brahms, J.:Neue Liebeslieder Waltzes, w. E. Mathis (sop), B. Fassbaender (mez), P. Schreier (ten), K. Engel (pno), W. Sawallisch (pno) [G] Deutsche Grammophon ▲ 423133-2 [DDD]
Brahms, J.:Romanzen aus Tieck's *Magelone*, w. Sviatoslav Richter (pno) *(rec live, 1965)* As Disc ▲ ASD 2602
Brahms, J.:Romanzen aus Tieck's *Magelone*, w. S. Richter (pno) *(rec 1965)* Historical Performers ▲ HPS 1 [ADD]
Brahms, J.:Songs, w. S. Richter (pno)—Op. 33 *(rec 1965)* Historical Performers ▲ HPS 1 [ADD]
Brahms, J.:Songs, w. H. Höll (pno)—Opp. 19/5; 32/1,2,4,5 & 9; 48/1; 49/5; 59/2; 69/5; 70/3 & 4; 71/1 & 3; 72/5; 86/1 & 2; 95/2; 96/3 & 4; 105/4; 107/4 [G] Bayer ▲ 100006 [DDD]
Britten, H.:Songs & Proverbs of William Blake, w. P. Pears (ten) [E] London 3-▲ 417428-2 [ADD]
Britten, H.:War Requiem, w. G. Vishnevskaya (sop), P. Pears (ten), B. Britten (cnd), London SO, London Sym Chorus [E,L] London 2-▲ 414383-2 [ADD]
Busoni, F.:Doktor Faust, w. H. Hillebrecht (sop), W. Cochran (ten), K. C. Kohn (bass), F. Leitner (cnd), Bavarian RSO, Bavarian Radio Sym Chorus [G] Deutsche Grammophon ("20th Century Classics" series) 3-▲ 427413-2 [ADD]
Debussy, C.:L'Enfant prodigue, w. J. Norman (sop), J. Carreras (ten), G. Bertini (cnd), Stuttgart RSO, Stuttgart Radio Chorus [F] Orfeo ▲ 012821
Debussy, C.:Songs, w. Hartmut Höll (pno) Claves ▲ 50-8809
Debussy, C.:Songs, w. Hartmut Höll (pno)—Beau soir; Mandoline; Le jet d'eau; Chevaux de bois; Green; Les cloches; Dans le jardin; La mer est plus belle; Le son du cor; L'échelonnement des haies; En sourdine; Clair de lune; Fantoches; Fleur des blés; Recueillement; De soir; Les ingénus; Le faune; Colloque sentimental [F] *(rec 1988)* Claves ▲ CD 8809 [DDD]
Dehmel Lieder, w. Kolja Blacher (vn), Aribert Reimann (pno) Orfeo d'or ▲ 390951
Duets, w. C. Bergonzi (ten) Orfeo ▲ C 028821 [DDD]
Dvořák, A.:Biblical Songs, Op. 99, w. Jörg Demus (pno) Deutsche Grammophon ("Double" series) 2-▲ 437377-2
Fauré, G.:Pavane Orch, w. S. Armstrong (sop), Orch de Paris, Edinburgh Festival Chorus EMI Classics ▲ CDM 64634
Fauré, G.:Requiem, w. V. de los Angeles (sop), A. Cluytens (cnd), Paris Conservatory Société des Concerts Orch, Brasseur Choir [L] EMI Classics ▲ CDC 47836
Fauré, G.:Requiem, w. S. Armstrong (sop), Orch de Paris, Edinburgh Festival Chorus EMI Classics ▲ CDM 64634
Gluck, C.W.:Iphigénie en Tauride, w. P. Lorengar (sop), F. Bonisolli (ten), W. Grönroos (bar), L. Gardelli (cnd), Bavarian RSO, Bavarian Radio Chorus [F] Orfeo 2-▲ 052832 [DDD]
Gluck, C.W.:Orfeo ed Euridice, w. Ruth-Margret Pütz (sop), Elisabeth Söderström (sop), F. Leitner (cnd), Cappella Coloniensis, Cologne Radio Chorus *(rec live, Cologne, Nov. 8, 1964)* Orfeo d'or 2-▲ 391952

VOCALISTS

Fischer–Dieskau, Dietrich (bar) (cont.)

Goethe Lieder:Songs on Texts by Johann Wolfgang von Goethe, w. Karl Engel (pno) *(rec live, Stockholm, 1970)* Orfeo d'or ▲ 389951 (m) [ADD]
Haydn, J.:Die Jahreszeiten, w. Edith Mathis (sop), Sigfried Jerusalem (ten), N. Marriner (cnd), Academy of St. Martin in the Fields Philips ("Duo" series) 2–▲ 438715–2
Haydn, J.:Die Schöpfung, w. Gunalda Janowitz (sop), Fritz Wunderlich (ten), H. von Karajan (cnd), Berlin PO, Vienna Singverein *(rec 1966 & 1968)* Deutsche Grammophon ("Galleria" series) 2–▲ 435077–2 [ADD]
Hindemith, P.:Cardillac, w. Leonore Kirschstein (sop), Donald Grobe (ten), J. Keilberth (cnd), Cologne RSO [G] Deutsche Grammophon ("20th Century Classics" series) 2–▲ 431741–2 [ADD]
Hindemith, P.:Mathis der Maler, w. Urszula Koszut (sop), Trudeliese Schmidt (mez), Rose Wagemann (mez), William Cochran (ten), Donald Grobe (ten), James King (ten), Manfred Schmidt (ten), Gerd Feldhoff (bass), Alexander Malta (bass), Peter Meven (bass), Karl Kreile (sgr), R. Kubelik (cnd), Bavarian RSO, Bavarian Radio Chorus EMI Classics 2–▲ CDCC 55237
Hindemith, P.:Mathis der Maler, w. P. Lorengar (sop), D. Grobe (ten), L. Ludwig (cnd), Berlin RSO [G]—sels Deutsche Grammophon ("20th Century Classics" series) 2–▲ 431741–2 [ADD]
Hindemith, P.:Songs, w. Aribert Reimann (pno)—19 songs:Sonnenuntergang; The wild flower's song; The moon; Sing on there in the swamp; On hearing "The Last rose of Summer"; Ehemals und jetzt; Brautgesang; Singet leise; Das ganze, nicht das Einzelne; Des Morgens; Fragment; Der Tod; Ich will nicht klagen mehr; Hymne; Abendphantasie; O, nun heb du an, dort in deinem Moor (1919); Vor dir schein' ich aufgewacht (1920); Die Sonne sinkt; An die Parzen [E,G] Orfeo ▲ 156861 [DDD]
Hindemith, P.:When Lilacs Last In The Dooryard Bloom'd, w. B. Fassbaender (mez), W. Sawallisch (cnd), Vienna SO, Vienna State Opera Chorus [E] *(rec live, 11/1/83)* Orfeo ▲ 112851 [DDD]
Les introuvables de Dietrich Fischer–Dieskau, w. Kark Engel (pno), Hertha Klust (pno), Gerald Moore (pno), Aribert Reimann (pno), Robert Veyron–Lacroix (hpd) EMI Classics 6–▲ CDZF 68509
Lieder der Romantik, w. Dieter Klöcker (cl), Klaus Wallendorf (hn), Hartmut Höll (pno) Orfeo ▲ 153861
Liszt, F.:Choral Music, w. U. Gronostay (cnd), Netherlands Chamber Choir—Es war einmal ein König; Arbeiter Chor; Sankt Christoph; Qui Mariam absolvisti; Rosario; Die Seligkeiten *(rec 10/89)* Globe ▲ GLO 5070 [DDD]
Mahler, G.:Kindertotenlieder, w. R. Kempe (cnd), Berlin PO [G] EMI Classics ▲ CDC 47657 (m) [ADD]
Mahler, G.:Des Knaben Wunderhorn, w. D. Barenboim (cnd), Berlin PO [G] Sony Classical ▲ SK 44935 [DDD]
Mahler, G.:Des Knaben Wunderhorn, w. E. Schwarzkopf (sop), G. Szell (cnd), London SO EMI Classics ▲ CDC 47277
Mahler, G.:Des Knaben Wunderhorn, w. L. Popp (sop), J. Baker (mez), M. Dickie (ten), B. Weikl (bar), K. Tennstedt (cnd), London PO EMI Classics ▲ CDZB 62707
Mahler, G.:Das Lied von der Erde, w. M. King (mez), L. Bernstein (cnd), Vienna PO [G] London ▲ 417783–2 [ADD]
Mahler, G.:Das Lied von der Erde, w. L. Popp (sop), J. Baker (mez), M. Dickie (ten), B. Weikl (bar), P. Kletzki (cnd), Philharmonia Orch EMI Classics ▲ CDZB 62707
Mahler, G.:Lieder eines fahrenden Gesellen, w. L. Bernstein (pno) [G] *(rec live at Lincoln Center, New York, 11/8/68)* Myto ▲ 1 MCD 89008 (m) [ADD]
Mahler, G.:Lieder eines fahrenden Gesellen, w. D. Barenboim (cnd), Berlin PO [G] Sony Classical ▲ SK 44935 [DDD]
Mahler, G.:Lieder eines fahrenden Gesellen, w. W. Furtwängler (cnd), Vienna PO [G] *(rec Salzburg, 8/19/51)* Verona 2–▲ 27062/63 (m) [AAD]
Mahler, G.:Lieder eines fahrenden Gesellen, w. W. Furtwängler (cnd), Philharmonia Orch [G] EMI Classics ▲ CDC 47657 (m) [ADD]
Mahler, G.:Songs from Rückert, w. D. Barenboim (pno) [G] EMI Classics ▲ CDC 47657 [ADD]
Mahler, G.:Songs from Rückert, w. L. Bernstein (pno)—4 songs:Blicke mir nicht in die Lieder; Ich atmet' einen Linden Duft; Ich bin der Welt abhanden; Um Mitternacht [G] *(rec live at Lincoln Center, New York, 11/8/68)* Myto ▲ 1 MCD 89008 (m) [ADD]
Matthus, S.:Holofernes, w. K. Masur (cnd), Leipzig Gewandhaus Orch *(rec 1981)* Berlin Classics ▲ BER 2072 [ADD]
Mendelssohn, F.:Elijah, w. Gwyneth Jones (sop), Janet Baker (mez), Simon Woolf (trb), Nicolai Gedda (ten), R. Frühbeck de Burgos (cnd), New Philharmonia Orch, New Philharmonia Chorus, Wandsworth School Boys' Choir *(rec 1968)* EMI Classics ("Doublefforte" series) 2–▲ CDFB 68601
Mendelssohn, F.:Songs, w. H. Holl (pno)—Der Verlassene; Ich weiss mir 'n Mädchen; Mary's dream; We've a bonnie wee flower; Minnelied im Mai; Pilgerspruch; Maienlied; Im Grünen; Abendlied; Wartend; Im Frühling; Im Herbst; Frühlingslaue; Das Schifflein; Lieblingsplätzchen; Altdeutsches Frühlingslied; Minnelied; Meerfahrt; Weiter, rastlos; Der Blumenstrauss; Frühlingslied; Herbstlied; Erntelied *(rec 1989 & 1991)* Claves ▲ CD 9009 [DDD]
Mozart, W.A.:Così fan tutte, w. G. Janowitz (sop), R. Grist (sop), B. Fassbaender (mez), P. Schreier (ten), H. Prey (bar), K. Böhm (cnd), Vienna PO *(rec live, 1972)* Foyer 2–▲ FOY 2066 [ADD]
Mozart, W.A.:Don Giovanni, w. I. Seefried (sop), S. Jurinac (sop), M. Stader (sop), E. Haefliger (ten), K. C. Kohn (bass), F. Fricsay (cnd), Berlin RSO Deutsche Grammophon 3–▲ 437341–2
Mozart, W.A.:Don Giovanni (sels), w. R. Grist (sop), B. Nilsson (sop), M. Arroyo (sop), P. Schreier (ten), M. Talvela (bass), K. Böhm (cnd), Prague National Theater Orch IMP Collectors Series ▲ IMPX 9023 [AAD]
Mozart, W.A.:Notturnos Sops, w. C. Schäfer (sop), G. Hintz (sop), Berlin PO Winds Orfeo ▲ 218911 (m) [DDD]
Mozart, W.A.:Nozze di Figaro, w. H. Harper (sop), J. Blegen (sop), T. Berganza (mez), G. Evans (bar), D. Barenboim (cnd), English CO, John Alldis Choir [I] EMI Classics ("Studio" series) 3–▲ CDMC 63646 [ADD]
Mozart, W.A.:Nozze di Figaro, w. M. Stader (sop), I. Seefried (sop), H. Töpper (mez), R. Capecchi (bar), I. Sardi (bass), F. Fricsay (cnd), Berlin RSO [G] *(rec 1960)* Deutsche Grammophon 3–▲ 437671–2
Mozart, W.A.:Nozze di Figaro (sels), w. G. Janowitz (sop), E. Mathis (sop), T. Troyanos (mez), H. Prey (bar), K. Böhm (cnd), Berlin German Opera Orch—Scenes & Arias Deutsche Grammophon ▲ 429822–2 [ADD]
Mozart, W.A.:Più non si trovano, w. C. Schäfer (sop), G. Hintz (sop), Berlin PO Winds Orfeo ▲ 218911 [DDD]
Mozart, W.A.:Zauberflöte, w. P. Lorengar (sop), C. Deutekom (sop), S. Burrows (ten), H. Prey (bar), M. Talvela (bass), G. Solti (cnd), Vienna PO [G] London 3–▲ 414568–2
Mozart, W.A.:Zauberflöte (sels), w. E. Lear (sop), R. Peters (sop), L. Otto (sop), F. Wunderlich (ten), F. Lenz (ten), F. Crass (bass), K. Böhm (cnd), Berlin PO, Berlin RIAS Chamber Choir—Scenes & Arias Deutsche Grammophon ▲ 429825–2 [ADD] ■ 429825–4
Orff, C.:Carmina burana, w. G. Janowitz (sop), G. Stolze (ten), G.L. Jochum (cnd), German Opera Orch, German Opera Chorus [G, L] Deutsche Grammophon ("Galleria" series) ▲ 423886–2 [ADD]
Orff, C.:Carmina burana, w. Gundula Janowitz (sop), Gerhard Stolze (ten), E. Jochum (cnd), Berlin German Opera Orch, Berlin German Opera Chorus *(rec Ufa–Studio, Berlin, Oct 1967)* Deutsche Grammophon ▲ 447437–2 [ADD]
Pfitzner, H.:Songs, w. H. Höll (pno) [G] Orfeo ▲ 036821 [DDD]
Puccini, G.:Tosca, w. B. Nilsson (sop), F. Corelli (ten), L. Maazel (cnd), St. Cecilia Academy Orch Rome, St. Cecilia Academy Chorus Rome *(rec June 1966)* London ▲ 440051–2
Ravel, M.:Chants populaires, w. H. Höll (pno) Orfeo ▲ 061831 [DDD]
Ravel, M.:Epigrammes de Clément Marot, w. H. Höll (pno) Orfeo ▲ 061831 [DDD]
Ravel, M.:Histoires naturelles, w. H. Höll (pno) Orfeo ▲ 061831 [DDD]
Ravel, M.:Mélodies populaires grecques, w. H. Höll (pno) Orfeo ▲ 061831 [DDD]
Ravel, M.:Songs, w. H. Höll (pno) [F] Orfeo ▲ 061831 [DDD]
Reger, M.:Orchestral Songs, w. G. Albrecht (cnd), Hamburg PO, Monteverdi Choir London, St. Michael's Choir—Der Einsiedler, Op. 144a; Hymnus der Liebe, Op. 136; Requiem, Op. 144b; An die Hoffnung, Op. 124 [G] Orfeo ▲ 209901 [DDD]
Reichardt, J.F.:Lieder, w. M. Graf (hp)—20 lieder, most set to texts by Goethe or Schiller [G] *(rec 1990)* Orfeo ▲ 245921 [DDD]
Reimann, A.:Shine & Dark, w. A. Reimann (pno) Orfeo ▲ 212901
Reimann, A.:Unrevealed, w. Cherubini String Quartet Orfeo ▲ 212901
Rihm, W.:umsungen, w. E. Bour (cnd), Ensemble Modern Ars Musici ▲ 0825 [DDD]
Ruzicka, P.:Der die Gesänge zerschlug, w. E. Bour (cnd), Ensemble Modern Ars Musici ▲ 0825 [DDD]
Schoeck, O.:Das holde Bescheiden, w. M. Shirai (mez), H. Höll (pno) Claves 2–▲ CD 9308/9 [DDD]

Fischer–Dieskau, Dietrich (bar) (cont.)

Schoeck, O.:Das stille Leuchten, w. Hartmut Höll (pno) Claves ▲ 50–8910
Schoeck, O.:Unter Sternen, w. Hartmut Höll (pno) Claves ▲ 50–8606
Schubert, Franz:Alfonso und Estrella, w. E. Mathis (sop), M. Falewicz (sop), P. Schreier (ten), H. Prey (bar), T. Adam (b–bar), O. Suitner (cnd), Berlin Staatskapelle, Berlin Radio Chorus Berlin Classics 3–▲ BER 2156 [ADD]
Schubert, Franz:Mass 4, w. H. Donath (sop), B. Fassbaender (mez), F. Araiza (ten), W. Sawallisch (cnd), Bavarian RSO, Bavarian Radio Chorus [L] EMI Classics ("Studio" series) ▲ CDM 69222
Schubert, Franz:Mass 5, w. L. Popp (sop), B. Fassbaender (mez), A. Dallapozza (ten), W. Sawallisch (cnd), Bavarian RSO, Bavarian Radio Chorus [L] EMI Classics ("Studio" series) ▲ CDM 69222
Schubert, Franz:Mass 6, w. H. Donath (sop), B. Fassbaender (mez), F. Araiza (ten), W. Sawallisch (cnd), Bavarian RSO, Bavarian Radio Chorus [L] EMI Classics ("Studio" series) ▲ CDM 69223
Schubert, Franz:Die Schöne Müllerin, w. Gerald Moore (pno) [G] *(rec 1951)* EMI Classics ("Studio" series) 3–▲ CDMC 63559 (m) [ADD]
Schubert, Franz:Die Schöne Müllerin, w. Gerald Moore (pno) [G] Deutsche Grammophon ▲ 415186–2 [ADD]
Schubert, Franz:Schwanengesang, w. G. Moore (pno) [G] *(rec 1951–58)* EMI Classics ("Studio" series) 3–▲ CDMC 63559 (m) [ADD]
Schubert, Franz:Schwanengesang, w. G. Moore (pno) [G] Deutsche Grammophon ▲ 415188–2 [ADD]
Schubert, Franz:Schwanengesang, w. K. Billing (pno) [G] *(rec live, Berlin, 1/19–25/48)* Melodram ▲ MEL 18017
Schubert, Franz:Schwanengesang, w. A. Brendel (pno) [G] Philips ▲ 411051–2 [DDD]
Schubert, Franz:Songs (comp), w. G. Moore (pno)—171 songs [G] Deutsche Grammophon 9–▲ 437225–2
Schubert, Franz:Songs (misc), w. K. Billing (pno)—7 songs—D.138; D.771; D.911 [Winterreise], Nos. 1,11,13 & 24; D.932 [G] *(rec live, Berlin, 1/19–25/48)* Melodram ▲ MEL 18017
Schubert, Franz:Songs (misc), w. G. Moore (pno)—234 songs [G] Deutsche Grammophon 9–▲ 437215–2 [ADD]
Schubert, Franz:Songs (misc), w. G. Moore (pno)—D.257, 300, 314, 328, 343, 456, 531, 536, 545, 550, 565, 649, 741, 765, 774, 785, 871, 889, 917, 938 [G] EMI Classics ("Studio" series) ▲ CDM 69503 [ADD]
Schubert, Franz:Songs (misc), w. G. Moore (pno), K. Engel (pno)—37 songs *(rec 1958–65)* EMI Classics ("Studio" series) 2–▲ CDMB 63566 [ADD]
Schubert, Franz:Tantum ergo, D.962, w. L. Popp (sop), B. Fassbaender (mez), A. Dallapozza (ten), W. Sawallisch (cnd), Bavarian RSO, Bavarian Radio Chorus [L] EMI Classics ("Studio" series) ▲ CDM 69223
Schubert, Franz:Winterreise, w. G. Moore (pno) [G] *(rec 1955)* EMI Classics ("Studio" series) 3–▲ CDMC 63559 (m) [ADD]
Schubert, Franz:Winterreise, w. M. Perahia (pno) Sony Classical ▲ SK 48237 [DDD]
Schubert, Franz:Winterreise, w. H. Reutter (pno) [G] *(rec broadcast, 1952)* Verona ▲ 2702 (m) [AAD]
Schubert, Franz:Winterreise, w. Jörg Demus (pno) *(rec 1965)* Deutsche Grammophon ("The Originals" series) ▲ 447421–2
Schubert, Franz:Winterreise, w. G. Moore (pno) [G] Deutsche Grammophon ▲ 415187–2 [ADD]
Schubert, Franz:Winterreise, w. H. Klust (pno) *(rec live 1953)* Melodram ▲ MEL 18016
Schubert, Franz:Winterreise, w. A. Brendel (pno) Philips ▲ 411463–2 [DDD]
Schumann, R.:Dichterliebe, w. A. Brendel (pno) [G] Philips ▲ 416352–2 [DDD]
Schumann, R.:Genoveva, w. E. Moser (sop), P. Schreier (ten), S. Lorenz (b–bar), K. Masur (cnd), Leipzig Gewandhaus Orch, Berlin Radio Chorus Berlin Classics ("Eterna" series) 2–▲ BER 2056 [ADD]
Schumann, R.:Liederkreis, Op. 39, w. A. Brendel (pno) [G] Philips ▲ 416352–2 [DDD]
Schumann, R.:Scenes from Goethe's "Faust", w. E. Mathis (sop), B. Rayner Cook (bar), G. Howell (bass), P. Boulez (cnd), BBC SO, BBC Sym Chorus *(rec live, London, March 7, 1973)* Memories 2–▲ HR 4489/90 [ADD]
Shostakovich, D.:Sym 14, w. J. Varady (sop), O. Wenkel (cta), B. Haitink (cnd), Royal Concertgebouw Orch London ▲ 417514–2 [DDD]
Spohr, L.:Jessonda, w. J. Varady (sop), R. Behle (sop), T. Moser (ten), K. Moll (bass), G. Albrecht (cnd), Hamburg State PO, Hamburg State Opera Chorus [G] Orfeo 2–▲ 240912 [DDD]
Spohr, L.:Songs, w. H. Höll (pno) [G] Orfeo ▲ 103841 [DDD] ■ M 103841A
Spohr, L.:Songs Bar, Op. 154, w. D. Sitkovetzky (vn), H. Höll (pno) [G] Orfeo ▲ 103841 [DDD] ■ M 103841A
Spontini, G.:Olympia, w. J. Varady (sop), S. Toczyska (mez), F. Tagliavini (ten), G. Fortune (bass), J. Becker (bass), G. Albrecht (cnd), Berlin RSO, Berlin Radio Chorus [Paris version] Orfeo 2–▲ 137862 [DDD]
Strauss, R.:Arabella, w. H. Donath (sop), J. Varady (sop), A. Schmidt (bar), W. Berry (bass), W. Sawallisch (cnd), Bavarian State Orch Orfeo 2–▲ 169882 [DDD]
Strauss, R.:Ariadne auf Naxos, w. J. Norman (sop), J. Varady (sop), E. Gruberova (sop), P. Frey (ten), O. Bär (bar), K. Masur (cnd), Leipzig Gewandhaus Orch [G] Philips 2–▲ 422084–2 [DDD]
Strauss, R.:Capriccio, w. E. Schwarzkopf (sop), A. Moffo (sop), C. Ludwig (mez), N. Gedda (ten), E. Wächter (bar), H. Hotter (b–bar), W. Sawallisch (cnd), Philharmonia Orch [G] EMI Classics 2–▲ CDCB 49014 (m) [ADD]
Strauss, R.:Elektra, w. I. Borkh (sop), M. Schech (sop), J. Madeira (mez), K. Böhm (cnd), Dresden Staatskapelle [G] *(rec 1961)* Deutsche Grammophon 2–▲ 445329–2
Strauss, R.:Salome, w. G. Jones (sop), M. Dunn (mez), K. Böhm (cnd), Hamburg State Opera Orch *(rec live, 1970)* Deutsche Grammophon 2–▲ 445319–2 [ADD]
Strauss, R.:Salome, w. L. Rysanek (sop), A. Varnay (sop/mez), G. Stolze (ten), F. Leitner (cnd), Bavarian State Opera Orch *(rec live, Monaco, 1971)* Melodram 2–▲ MEL 27098
Strauss, R.:Songs, w. G. Moore (pno)—contains "all Strauss lieder suited to the baritone voice" [G] EMI Classics 6–▲ CDMF 63995
Stravinsky, I.:Abraham & Isaac, w. G. Bertini (cnd), Stuttgart RSO [E] Orfeo ▲ 015821 [DDD]
Stravinsky, I.:Babel, w. Bertini, Stuttgart RSO [E] Orfeo ▲ 015821 [DDD]
Stravinsky, I.:Elegy for J.F.K., w. H. Gruber (cl), K. T. Adler (cl), K. Berger (cl) [E] Orfeo ▲ 015821 [DDD]
Stravinsky, I.:Songs, w. G. Bertini (cnd), Stuttgart RSO—2 Verlaine Songs, Op. 9 [F] Orfeo ▲ 015821 [DDD]
Telemann, G.P.:Cants, w. Aurèle Nicolet (fl), Helmut Keller (vn), Irmgard Poppen (vc), Edith Picht–Axenfeld (hpd)—Die Hoffnung ist mein Leben EMI Classics ("Baroque" series) ▲ CDK 65729
Verdi, G.:Un ballo in maschera, w. Martha Mödl (sop—Ulrica), Walburga Wegner (sop—Amelia), Anny Schlemm (mez—Oscar), Lorenz Fehenberger (ten—Ricardo), Dietrich Fischer–Dieskau (bar—Renato), Wilhelm Schirp (bass—Samuel), Willy Schoneweib (bass—Tom), Gunther Wilhelms (bass—Silvan), Fritz Augustin (sgr—Ein Richter), Friedrich Himmelmann (sgr—Ein Diener Amelia), F. Busch (cnd), Cologne RSO, Bernhard Alois Zimmermann (cnd), Cologne Radio Chorus Calig 2–▲ 50946/47 (m) [ADD]
Verdi, G.:Don Carlos, w. R. Tebaldi (sop), G. Bumbry (mez), C. Bergonzi (ten), N. Ghiaurov (bass), G. Solti (cnd), Royal Opera House Orch Covent Garden, Royal Opera House Chorus Covent Garden [1886 5–act Italian version] [I] London 3–▲ 421114–2 [ADD]
Verdi, G.:Otello, w. G. Jones (sop—Desdemona), A. di Stasio (mez—Emilia), J. McCracken (ten—Otello), P. de Palma (ten—Cassio), D. Fischer–Dieskau (bar—Iago), J. Barbirolli (cnd), New Philharmonia Orch, Ambrosian Opera Chorus EMI Classics ▲ CDMB 65296
Verdi, G.:La traviata, w. P. Lorengar (sop), S. Malagu (mez), G. Aragall (ten), L. Maazel (cnd), Berlin German Opera Orch, Berlin German Opera Chorus London ("Double Decker" series) 2–▲ 443000–2
Wagner, R.:Der fliegende Holländer, w. M. Schech (sop), S. Wagner (mez), G. Frick (ten), F. Wunderlich (ten), R. Schock (ten), F. Konwitschny (cnd), Berlin Staatskapelle Berlin Classics ("Eterna" series) 2–▲ BER 2097 [ADD]
Wagner, R.:Der fliegende Holländer (sels), w. Marianne Schech (sop), Fritz Wunderlich (ten), Gottlob Frick (bass), F. Konwitschny (cnd), Berlin Staatskapelle Berlin Classics ▲ BER 9080 [ADD]
Wagner, R.:Götterdämmerung, w. B. Nilsson (sop), J. Watson (sop), C. Ludwig (mez), W. Windgassen (ten), G. Frick (bass), G. Solti (cnd), Vienna PO [G] London 4–▲ 414115–2 [ADD]
Wagner, R.:Lohengrin, w. E. Grümmer (sop), C. Ludwig (mez), J. Thomas (ten), G. Frick (bass), R. Kempe (cnd), Vienna PO, Vienna State Opera Chorus [G] EMI Classics 3–▲ CDCC 49017 [ADD]
Wagner, R.:Lohengrin, w. J. Norman (sop), E. Randová (mez), P. Domingo (ten), S. Nimsgern (b–bar), H. Sotin (bass), G. Solti (cnd), Vienna PO, Vienna State Opera Chorus [G] London ▲ 425530–2 [DDD]

▲ = CD ♦ = Enhanced CD Δ = MD ■ = Cassette Tape □ = DCC

Fischer-Dieskau, Dietrich (bar) (cont.)

Wagner, R.:Lohengrin, w. J. Norman (sop), E. Randová (mez), P. Domingo (ten), S. Nimsgern (b–bar), H. Sotin (bass), G. Solti (cnd), Vienna PO, Vienna State Opera Chorus [G] London 4–▲ 421053–2 [DDD]

Wagner, R.:Die Meistersinger von Nürnberg, w. C. Ligendza (sop), C. Ludwig (mez), P. Domingo (ten), R. Laubenthal (ten), R. Hermann (bar), P. Lagger (bass), E. Jochum (cnd), German Opera Orch, German Opera Chorus [G] Deutsche Grammophon 4–▲ 415278–2 [ADD]

Wagner, R.:Die Meistersinger von Nürnberg, w. C. Ligendza (sop), C. Ludwig (mez), P. Domingo (ten), R. Laubenthal (ten), R. Hermann (bar), P. Lagger (bass), E. Jochum (cnd), German Opera Orch, German Opera Chorus Deutsche Grammophon ("Domingo Edition" series) ▲ 435406–2

Wagner, R.:Parsifal, w. C. Ludwig (mez), A. Kollo (ten), Z. Kelemen (bar), G. Frick (bass), G. Solti (cnd), Vienna PO, Vienna State Opera Chorus, Vienna Boys' Choir [G] London 4–▲ 417143–2 [ADD]

Wagner, R.:Der Ring des Nibelungen, w. R. Crespin (sop), G. Janowitz (sop), C. Ludwig (mez), H. Dernesch (mez), J. Vickers (ten), D. Thomas (bass), H. von Karajan (cnd), Berlin PO *(rec late 1960s)* Deutsche Grammophon 15–▲ 435211–2 [ADD]

Wagner, R.:Der Ring des Nibelungen, w. R. Crespin (sop), G. Janowitz (sop), C. Ludwig (mez), H. Dernesch (mez), J. Vickers (ten), D. Thomas (bass), H. von Karajan (cnd), Berlin PO *(rec live at Salzburg Easter Festivals, 1967–1970)* Arkadia 12–▲ 223 (m) [ADD]

Wagner, R.:Der Ring des Nibelungen, w. B. Nilsson (sop), K. Flagstad (sop), R. Crespin (sop), C. Watson (sop), C. Ludwig (mez), J. Madeira (mez), S. Svanholm (ten), J. King (ten), G. Stolze (ten), W. Windgassen (ten), G. London (bar), H. Hotter (b–bar), G. Neidlinger (b–bar), G. Frick (bass), G. Solti (cnd), Vienna PO [G] London 15–▲ 414100–2 [ADD]

Wagner, R.:Tannhäuser, w. G. Brouwenstijn (sop), R. Vinay (ten), J. Greindl (bass), J. Keilberth (cnd), Bayreuth Festival Orch, Bayreuth Festival Chorus *(rec live, Bayreuth, 1954)* Melodram 3–▲ MEL 36105

Wagner, R.:Tannhäuser, w. E. Grümmer (sop), M. Schech (sop), H. Hopf (ten), F. Wunderlich (ten), G. Frick (bass), F. Konwitschny (cnd), Berlin State Opera Orch, Berlin State Opera Chorus [G] EMI Classics ("Studio" series) 3–▲ CDMC 63214 [ADD]

Wagner, R.:Tannhäuser, w. V. de Los Angeles (sop), G. Bumbry (mez), W. Windgassen (ten), G. Stolze (ten), T. Adam (b–bar), J. Greindl (bass), F. Crass (bass), W. Sawallisch (cnd), Bayreuth Festival Orch, Bayreuth Festival Chorus [G] *(rec 1961)* Myto 3–▲ MCD 93277

Wagner, R.:Tristan und Isolde, w. M. Price (sop), B. Fassbaender (mez), A. Kollo (ten), K. Moll (bass), C. Kleiber (cnd), Dresden State Opera Orch [G] Deutsche Grammophon 4–▲ 413315–2 [DDD]

Weber, C.M. von:Songs, w. H. Höll (pno)—Meine Lieder, meine Sänge; Klage; Der kleine Fritz; Was zieht zu deinem Zauberkreise; Ich sah ein Röschen am Wege steh'n; Er an Sie; Meine Farben; Liebe-Glühen; Über die Berge mit Ungestüm; Es stürmt auf der Flur; Minnelied; Reigen; Sind es Schmerzen; Mein Verlangen; Wenn ich ein Vöglein wär'; Mein Schatzerl ist hübsch; Liebesgruss aus der Ferne; Herzchen, mein Schätzchen; Das Veilchen im Thale; Ich denke dein; Serenade:Horch'! Leise horch', Geliebte!; Romanze:Sie war so hold Claves ▲ CD 9118 [DDD]

Weber, C.M. von:Songs, w. Hartmut Höll (pno)—22 sels Claves ▲ 50–9118

Wolf, H.:Der Corregidor, w. H. Donath (sop), D. Soffel (mez), W. Hollweg (ten), P. Maus (ten), K. Moll (bass), G. Albrecht (cnd), Berlin RSO [G] Koch Schwann 2–▲ CD 314 010

Wolf, H.:Italienische Liederbücher (sels), w. E. Schwarzkopf (sop), G. Moore (pno) EMI Classics ▲ CDM 63732

Wolf, H.:Mörike-Lieder (sels), w. Sviatoslav Richter (pno)—26 sels Music & Arts ▲ CD 870

Wolf, H.:Songs (misc), w. Hartmut Höll (pno)—21 songs [texts Heinrich Heine & Joseph von Eichendorff] Claves ▲ 50–8706

Wolf, H.:Songs (misc), w. S. Soltesz (cnd), Munich RSO—5 Goethe-Lieder, 5 Mörike-Lieder, Drei Michelangelo-Lieder, & 4 more [G] *(rec in studio, 1990)* Orfeo ▲ 219911 [DDD]

Zelter, C.F.:Songs, w. A. Reimann (pno) [G] Orfeo ▲ 097841 [DDD]

Fischer-Dieskau, Dietrich (nar)

Schubert, Franz:Die Schöne Müllerin, w. Ian Bostridge (ten), Graham Johnson (pno)—5 additional poems read by Fischer-Dieskau Hyperion ▲ CDJ 33025

Fischer-Kunz, Annemarie (cta)

Mendelssohn, Fanny:Oratorio, w. I. Lippitz (sop), H. Hatano (ten), T. Thomaschke (bass), E.M. Blankenburg (cnd), Cologne Youth Orch, Cologne Youth Chorus CPO ▲ CPO 999009–2 [DDD]

Fisher, E. (sgr)

Rodgers, R.:Music of, w. S. Bass (sgr), J. Andrews (sgr), P. Como (sgr), D. Reese (sgr), J. Jones (sgr), N. Luboff (sgr), M. Gold (sgr), N. Walker (sgr), H. Bowen (sgr), V. Damone (sgr), P. Nero (pno), J. P. Morgan (sgr), E. Fisher (sgr), B. Goodman (cl), Ann-Margaret (sgr), Shorty Rogers (sgr), D. Shore (sgr), T. Martin (sgr), M. King (sgr), A. Newley (sgr) RCA ▲ 8590–2 R ■ 8590–4 R

Fisher, Gillian (sop)

Handel, G.F.:Aminta e Fillide, w. P. Kwella (sop), D. Darlow (cnd), London Handel Orch [I] Hyperion ▲ CDA 66118

Handel, G.F.:The Triumph of Time & Truth, w. James Goodman (trb), Emma Kirkby (sop), Charles Brett (ct), Ian Partridge (ten), Stephen Varcoe (bar), D. Darlow (cnd), London Handel Orch, London Handel Chorus [E] Hyperion 2–▲ CDA 66071/72

Lalande, M.-R. de:Confitebor tibi, Domine, w. O. Johnston (trb), C. Daniels (ct), A. Smith (ten), S. Varcoe (bass), E. Higginbottom (cnd), King's Consort, Oxford New College Choir [L] Erato (Musifrance) ▲ 2292–45014–2 [DDD]

Lalande, M.-R. de:De profundis solo Voices, Orch & Chorus, w. O. Johnston (trb), C. Daniels (ct), A. Smith (ten), S. Varcoe (bass), E. Higginbottom (cnd), King's Consort, New College Choir Oxford [L] Erato (Musifrance) ▲ 2292–45014–2 [DDD]

Lalande, M.-R. de:Miserere, w. O. Johnston (trb), C. Daniels (ct), A. Smith (ten), S. Varcoe (bass), E. Higginbottom (cnd), King's Consort, Oxford New College Choir [L] Erato (Musifrance) ▲ 2292–45014–2 [DDD]

Purcell, H.:King Arthur, w. J. Smith (sop), E. Priday (sop), G. Ross (sop), A. Stafford (alt), P. Elliott (ten), S. Varcoe (bar), J.E. Gardiner (cnd), English Baroque Soloists, Monteverdi Choir London Erato 2–▲ 2292–45211–2 ZA

Purcell, H.:King Arthur, w. E. Priday (sop), Gill Ross (sop), J. Smith (sop), A. Stafford (alt), P. Elliot (ten), S. Varcoe (bar), J.E. Gardiner (cnd), English Baroque Soloists, Monteverdi Choir London Erato ("Gardiner Purcell Collection" series) 2–▲ 96552–2

Purcell, H.:King Arthur (sels), w. J. Smith (sop), E. Priday (sop), G. Ross (sop), J. E. Gardiner (cnd), English Baroque Soloists, Monteverdi Choir Erato ▲ 45919–2

Purcell, H.:The Prophetess, or The History of Dioclesian, w. L. Dawson (sop), R. Covey-Crump (ten), P. Elliot (ten), S. Varcoe (bar), M. George (bass), J.E. Gardiner (cnd), Monteverdi Orch, Monteverdi Choir London Erato ("Gardiner Purcell Collection" series) 2–▲ 96556–2

Purcell, H.:Timon of Athens, w. L. Dawson (sop), R. Covey-Crump (ten), P. Elliot (ten), S. Varcoe (bar), M. George (bass), J.E. Gardiner (cnd), Monteverdi Orch, Monteverdi Choir London Erato ("Gardiner Purcell Collection" series) 2–▲ 96556–2

Fisher, Sylvia (sop)

Britten, H.:Albert Herring, w. A. Cantelo (sop), S. Rex (mez), P. Pears (ten), J. Noble (bar), O. Brannigan (bass), B. Britten (cnd), English CO [E] London 2–▲ 421849–2 [ADD]

Britten, H.:Owen Wingrave, w. J. Vyvyan (Mrs. Julian), H. Harper (Mrs. Coyle), J. Baker (Kate), P. Pears (Sir P. Wingrave; Narrator), B. Luxon (Owen Wingrave), J. Shirley-Quirk (Coyle), B. Britten, Wandworth School Boys' Choir, English CO London 2–▲ 433200–2

Fisichella, Salvatore (ten)

Leoncavallo, R.:Nuit de mai, w. N. Santi (cnd), Swiss-Italian Orch Accord ▲ ACD 201582 [DDD]

Rossini, G.:Otello, w. F. von Stade (mez), J. Carreras (ten), S. Ramey (bass), J. López-Cobos (cnd), Philharmonia Orch, Ambrosian Opera Chorus [I] Philips 2–▲ 432456–2 [ADD]

Verdi, G.:Giovanna d'Arco, w. Edita Gruberova (sop), Giorgio Zancanaro (bar), G.-F. Masini (cnd), Vienna SO *(rec live, 1985)* Serenissima 2–▲ SER 360133

Fissore, Enrico (b-bar)

Donizetti, G.:Gianni di Parigi, w. L. Serra (sop), E. Zilio (mez), G. Morino (ten), A. Romero (bar), S. Manga (sgr), C. F. Cillario (cnd), Milan RAI Orch, Milan RAI Chorus [I] *(rec live)* Nuova Era 2–▲ 6752/53 [DDD]

Donizetti, G.:I pazzi per progetto, w. S. Rigacci (sop), A. Cicogna (mez), G. Polidori (bar), G. Sarti (bar), V. M. Brunetti (bass), L. Monreale (bass), G. Micheli (cnd), Emilia Romagna Arturo Toscanini SO [I] *(rec live, 12/88)* Bongiovanni ▲ GB 2070 [DDD]

Fissore, Enrico (b-bar) (cont.)

Lattuada, F.:Le Preziose ridicole, w. S. Valayre (sop—Madelon), A. Catarci (sop—Marotte), A. Cicogna (mez—Cathos), S. Tedesco (ten—La Grange), E. Di Cesare (ten—Mascarille), A. Veccia (bar—Croissy), R. Servile (bar—Jodelet), E. Fissore (bass—Gorgibus), E. Romagna (cnd), Toscanini SO, G. Masini (cnd), Rossini Teatro Comunale Chorus [I] *(rec live, 1991)* Ermitage ▲ ERM 404 [DDD]

Puccini, G.:La Bohème, w. Leontina Vaduva (sop—Mimi), Ruth Ann Swenson (sop—Musetta), Roberto Alagna (ten—Rodolfo), Simon Keenlyside (bar—Schaunard), Thomas Hampson (bar—Marcello), Samuel Ramey (bass—Colline), Enrico Fissore (bass—Benoit), A. Pappano (cnd), Philharmonia Orch EMI Classics 2–♦ CDCB 56120

Rossini, G.:La cambiale di matrimonio, w. V. Gui (cnd), Milan RAI SO *(rec 1971)* Memories ▲ MEM 4506 [AAD]

Verdi, G.:Un giorno di regno, w. Maria Casula (sop), Angelo Romero (bar), Franca Fabbri (sgr), Michele Guento (sgr), Islen Moubayed (sgr), Ruggero Rado (sgr), Bernardino Trotta (sgr), A. Zedda (cnd), *(orch unknown)* Great Opera Performances 2–▲ GOP 782

Fithian, Bruce (ten)

Viens, M.:Color Scope, w. Michael C. Viens (pno) MMC ▲ MMC 2040 [DDD]

Viens, M.:Star Blaze, w. Michael C. Viens (pno) MMC ▲ MMC 2040 [DDD]

Viens, M.:Sundown Voyager, w. Michael C. Viens (pno) MMC ▲ MMC 2040 [DDD]

Fitz, Heinz (spkr)

Corghi, A.:Divara—Wasser und Blut, w. Susanna von der Burg (sop—Divara), Suzanne McLeod (mez—Else Windscherer), Eva Lillian Thingboe (mez—Hille Feiken), Robert Schwarts (ten—Lame Man), Heinz Fitz (spkr—Bernd Knipperdollinck), Hanslutz Hildmann (spkr—Jan Matthys), Michael Holm (spkr—Bernhard Rothmann), Christopher Krieg (spkr—Jan van Leiden), W. Humburg (cnd), Münster SO, Münster City Theater Chorus [G] *(rec Grosses Haus, Münster State Theater, Nov. 27–29, 1993)* Marco Polo 2–▲ 8.223706/07 [DDD]

Flagello, Ezio (bass)

Bellini, V.:I Capuleti e i Montecchi, w. L. Hurley (sop), G. Simionato (mez), R. Cassily (ten), A. Gamson (cnd), American Opera Society Orch, American Opera Society Chorus [I] *(rec live, New York 10/14/58)* Melodram ("Connaisseur" series) 2–▲ CDM 27509 [ADD]

Bellini, V.:La sonnambula, w. J. Sutherland (sop), R. Cioni (ten), *(cnd & orch unknown)* *(rec live Dec. 5, 1961")* Standing Room Only 2–▲ SRO 841–2 [ADD]

Donizetti, G.:Lucia di Lammermoor, w. A. Moffo (sop), C. Bergonzi (ten), M. Sereni (bar), G. Prêtre (cnd), RCA Italian Opera Orch [I] RCA Gold Seal 2–▲ 6504–2–RG [ADD]

Donizetti, G.:Lucrezia Borgia, w. M. Caballé (sop), A. M. Rota (cta), G. Raimondi (ten), E. Gracis (cnd), La Scala Orch, La Scala Chorus [I] *(rec live, 3/2/70)* Myto 2–▲ 2 MCD 90423 [ADD]

Flagello, N.:The Land, w. N. Flagello (cnd), Rome CO Citadel ▲ CTD 88115 [ADD/DDD]

Puccini, G.:La Bohème, w. L. Albanese (sop), L. Hurley (sop), C. Bergonzi (ten), C. Harvuot (bar), M. Sereni (bar), N. Scott (bass), T. Schippers (cnd), New York Metropolitan Opera Orch, New York Metropolitan Opera Chorus *(rec Feb. 15, 1958)* Golden Age of Opera 2–▲ GAO 139/40 [ADD]

Verdi, G.:Ernani, w. L. Price (sop), C. Bergonzi (ten), M. Sereni (bar), T. Schippers (cnd), RCA Italian Opera Orch [I] RCA Gold Seal 2–▲ 6503–2–RG [ADD]

Verdi, G.:La forza del destino, w. E. Farrell (sop), J. Grillo (sop), F. Corelli (ten), A. Colzani (bar), A. Guadagno (cnd), *(orch unknown)* [I] *(rec live, Philadelphia 4/14/65)* Standing Room Only 2–▲ SRO 826–2 [ADD]

Verdi, G.:Simon Boccanegra, w. Renata Tebaldi (sop—Maria Boccanegra), Penelope Jensen (mez—Maria's Maidservant), Richard Tucker (ten—Gabriele Adorno), Rod MacWerter (ten—Paolo), Cornell MacNeil (bar—Simon Boccanegra), Ara Berberian (bar—Pietro), Ezio Flagello (bass—Jacopo Fiesco), Franco Iglesias (bass—Paolo), J. Levine (cnd), *(orch unknown)* *(rec live, Miami, 1970)* Legato Classics 2–▲ LCD 189–2 [ADD]

Flagstad, Kirsten (sop)

Beethoven, L. van:Fidelio, w. J. Patzak (ten), P. Schöffler (b–bar), J. Greindl (bass), W. Furtwängler (cnd), Vienna PO, Vienna State Opera Chorus [G] *(rec live 1950)* Arkadia 2–▲ 354

Beethoven, L. van:Fidelio, w. J. Patzak (ten), J. Griendl (bass), W. Furtwängler (cnd), Vienna PO, Vienna State Opera Chorus EMI Classics 2–▲ CDC 64901

Beethoven, L. van:Fidelio, w. J. Patzak (ten), P. Schöffler (b–bar), J. Greindl (bass), W. Furtwängler (cnd), Vienna PO, Vienna State Opera Chorus [G] *(rec live, Salzburg 8/5/50)* Verona 2–▲ 27044/45 (m) [AAD]

Beethoven, L. van:Fidelio (sels), w. B. Walter (cnd), New York Metropolitan Opera Orch—Act 1 aria, "Abscheulicher! Wo eilst du hin?" *(rec 1940)* Memories 2–▲ HR 4456/57 [ADD]

Beethoven, L. van:Fidelio (sels), w. Lauritz Melchior (ten) *(other artists unknown)*—Abscheulicher! Wo eilst du hin? Enterprise ("Vocal Archives" series) ▲ ENT VA 1128

Beethoven, L. van:Songs, w. Waldemar Alme (pno), An die Hoffnung, Op. 94 [G] Acanta ▲ 43189

The Complete 1937 Victor Recordings, w. Philadelphia Orch [cnd:Eugene Ormandy] Romophone ▲ 81023–2

Flagstad & Melchior Sing Wagner, w. Lauritz Melchior (ten) *(rec 1935–40)* Pearl ▲ PEA 9049 [AAD]

Flagstad in Song Nimbus ▲ NI 7871 [ADD]

Gluck, C.W.:Alceste, w. K. Flagstad (sop—Alceste), A. Engeboll (ten—Admetus), N. Moliner (bar—High Priest) [French version] *(rec Apr. 14, 1957)* Eklipse 2–▲ EKR 24

Gluck, C.W.:Alceste (sels), w. J. Hye-Knudsen (cnd), Danish Radio Concert Orch, Danish National Radio Choir—five arias & scenes *(rec live 4/14/57)* Melodram 2–▲ MEL 26514 (m) [AAD]

Grieg, E.:Songs—19 songs, most with orch.:A mother's grief; Solvelg's song *[1929]*; With a primrose; And I would have a sweetheart *[1937]*; Spring; Youth; The goal; From Monte Pincio; The first meeting; Hope; A swan; Eros; I love thee; Return to Rundarme *[1953]* *(rec 1929, 1937 & 1953)* Memories 2–▲ HR 4456/57 [ADD]

Grieg, E.:Songs, w. M. Sargent (cnd), BBC SO—Spring, Op. 33/10; The Youth, Op. 33/9; On the way home, Op. 33/8; My goal, Op. 33/1; From Monte Pincio, Op. 39; The first meeting, Op. 21/1; Hope, Op. 26/1; A swan, Op. 25/2; Eros, Op. 70/1; I love thee, Op. 5/3 *(rec live, Royal Albert Hall, 9/7/57)* Arkadia 2–▲ 576 [ADD]

In Copenhagen, w. Flagstad, Kirsten (sop), Edwin McArthur (pno) Danacord ▲ DACOCD 325 (m)

Kirsten Flagstad Recordings from 1935–39, w. Flagstad, Kirsten (sop), San Francisco Opera Orch [cnd:Edwin McArthur], Philadelphia Orch [cnd:Eugene Ormandy], Hans Lange (cnd) Nimbus ▲ NI 7847

Sinding, C.:Songs, w. W. Alme (pno)—Eg vil deg'kje elske; Eg tykkjer det er reint langsmt; Eg tarv ikkje ljose aa kveikje Acanta ▲ 43189

Still, W.G.:Tristan und Isolde, w. Kerstin Thorborg (mez), Lauritz Melchoir (ten), Ludwig Hofmann (bass), Julius Huehn (sgr), A. Bodanzky (cnd), *(orch unknown)* *(rec Jan 2, 1937)* Enterprise ("The Fourties" series) 3–▲ ENT 304

Strauss, R.:Arias, w. G. Sébastian (cnd), Berlin City Opera Orch—from Elektra—Orest!...Orest! [from Recognition Scene] [G] *(rec live, 5/9/52)* Melodram 2–▲ MEL 26514 (m) [AAD]

Strauss, R.:Arias, w. G. Sébastian (cnd), Berlin City Opera Orch—from Elektra—Orest!...Orest! [from Recognition Scene] [G] *(rec live, 5/9/52)* Arkadia 2–▲ 576 (m) [ADD]

Strauss, R.:4 Last Songs, w. G. Sébastian (cnd), Berlin City Opera Orch—3 songs only, omitting Frühling *(rec live, 5/9 or 5/11/52)* Arkadia 2–▲ 576 [ADD]

Strauss, R.:4 Last Songs, w. G. Sébastian (cnd), Berlin City Opera Orch—3 songs only, omitting Frühling *(rec live, 5/9 or 5/11/52)* Melodram 2–▲ MEL 26514 (m) [AAD]

Strauss, R.:4 Last Songs, w. W. Furtwängler (cnd), London PO *(rec live, London, 1949)* Melodram 2–▲ CDM 25009 [ADD]

Strauss, R.:Songs, w. W. Alme (pno)—Im Abendrot, Op. 4 [G] Acanta ▲ 43189

Studio & Live Performances 1923–1953, w. Flagstad, Kirsten (sop), Lauritz Melchior (ten) Memories 2–▲ MEM 4456 [ADD]

Wagner, R.:Arias & Scenes, w. G. Sébastian (cnd), Berlin City Opera Orch—12 arias & scenes from Götterdämmerung, Parsifal, Tristan *(rec live 5/9 & 11/52)* Melodram 2–▲ MEL 26514 (m) [AAD]

Wagner, R.:Arias & Scenes, w. L. Melchior (ten), Walter, MacArthur, Sargent (cnd), New York PO, RCA Victor SO, San Francisco Opera Orch, BBC SO—selections from Götterdämering; Tristan & Isolde; Lohengrin Memories 2–▲ HR 4456/57 [ADD]

Wagner, R.:Arias & Scenes, w. Lauritz Melchior (bar), Ormandy, McArthur, Walter (cnd), Philadelphia Orch, San Francisco Opera Orch, RCA Victor SO, New York PO—arias & duets from Lohengrin, Tristan & Isolde, Götterdämmerung, Parsifal & Fidelio *(rec New York City, 1939–41)* Grammofono 2000 ▲ GRM 78526 (m)

Flagstad, Kirsten (sop) (cont.)

Wagner, R.:Arias & Scenes, w. Ormandy, Lange (cnd), Philadelphia Orch—arias from Die Walküre; Tristan und Isolde; Tannhäuser; Lohengrin IMP ("Golden Legacy" series) ▲ IMPGLRS 105 [ADD]

Wagner, R.:Arias & Scenes, w. Lauritz Melchior (ten), E. McArthur (cnd), San Francisco Opera Orch, RCA Victor SO—duets from Lohengrin; Tristan und Isolde; Götterdämmerung; Parsifal Pearl ▲ PEA 9190

Wagner, R.:Arias & Scenes, w. K. Flagstad (sop), E. Rethberg (sop), B. Nilsson (sop), E. Schumann (sop), F. Leider (sop), L. Melchior (ten), G. Thill (ten), A. Pertile (ten), G. Hüsch (bar), F. Schorr (b–bar), H. Hotter (b–bar), A. Kipnis (bass), *(orch unknown)* EMI Classics ("Studio" series) 4–▲ CDMC 64008

Wagner, R.:Arias & Scenes, w. Lauritz Melchior (ten) *(other artists unknown)*—Das süsse Lied verhallt [from Lohengrin]; O sink' hernieder [from Tristan und Isolde]; Zu neuen Taten [from Götterdämmerung]; Nur eine Waffe taugt [from Parsifal] Enterprise ("Vocal Archives" series) ▲ ENT VA 1128

Wagner, R.:Arias & Scenes, Philharmonia Orch—Tannhäuser:Allmächt'ge Jungfrau! *[cond. Issay Dobrowen; rec. 4/1/48]*; Siegfried:Ewig war ich *[w. Set Svanholm, tenor, cond. Georges Sebastian; rec. 6/12–13/51]*; Götterdämmerung:Starke Scheite schichtet mir dort (Brünnhilde's Immolation) *[cond. Furtwängler; rec. 3/26/48]*; Tristan und Isolde:Doch nun von Tristan genau will ich's vernehmen! (Isolde's Narrative and Curse) *[w. Elisabeth Höngen, mezzo, cond. Dobrowen; rec. 3/31/48]*; Mild und leise (Liebestod) *[cond. Dobrowen, rec. 4/1/48]* [G] EMI Classics ("Great Recordings of the Century" series) ▲ CDH 63030 (m) [ADD]

Wagner, R.:Arias & Scenes—selections from Götterdämmerung *(Zu neuen Thaten, w. Melchior; Immolation Scene)*, Lohengrin *(Euch Lüften, die mein Klagen)*, Parsifal *(Ich sah' das Kind)*, Tristan *(Liebestod)*, Walküre *(Du bist der Lenz; Ho–jo–to–ho)* RCA Gold Seal ▲ 7915–2–RG (m) [ADD] ■ 7915–4–RG (CrO2)

Wagner, R.:Der fliegende Holländer (sels), w. M. Lorenz (ten), H. Janssen (bar), L. Weber (bass), F. Reiner (cnd), Royal Opera House Orch, Royal Opera House Chorus Covent Garden [G] *(rec live, Covent Garden, 6/11/37)* Standing Room Only ▲ SRO 808–1 (m) [ADD]

Wagner, R.:Der fliegende Holländer (sels), w. Tiana Lemnitz (sop), Torsten Ralf (ten), Rudolf Bockelmann (b–bar), Ludwig Weber (bass), T. Beecham (cnd), Royal Opera House Orch, Royal Opera House Chorus Covent Garden Memories ("Golden" series) ▲ MEM 3003

Wagner, R.:Götterdämmerung (sels), w. B. Walter (cnd), *(orch unknown)*—Brünnhilde's Immolation Scene *(rec 1944–52)* Music & Arts ▲ CD 838 [AAD]

Wagner, R.:Götterdämmerung (sels), w. Tiana Lemnitz (sop), Torsten Ralf (ten), Rudolf Bockelmann (b–bar), Ludwig Weber (bass), T. Beecham (cnd), Royal Opera House Orch, Royal Opera House Chorus Covent Garden Memories ("Golden" series) ▲ MEM 3003

Wagner, R.:Götterdämmerung (immolation scene), w. G. Sébastian (cnd), Berlin City Opera Orch [G] *(rec live, 5/9/52)* Arkadia 2–▲ 576 [ADD]

Wagner, R.:Götterdämmerung (immolation scene), w. E. Kleiber (cnd), Buenos Aires Teatro Colón Orch [G] *(rec live broadcast, Sept. 1948)* Pearl 2–▲ PEAS 9910 (m) [ADD]

Wagner, R.:Lohengrin (sels), w. Tiana Lemnitz (sop), Torsten Ralf (ten), Rudolf Bockelmann (b–bar), Ludwig Weber (bass), T. Beecham (cnd), Royal Opera House Orch, Royal Opera House Chorus Covent Garden Memories ("Golden" series) ▲ MEM 3003

Wagner, R.:Die Meistersinger von Nürnberg (sels), w. Tiana Lemnitz (sop), Torsten Ralf (ten), Rudolf Bockelmann (b–bar), Ludwig Weber (bass), T. Beecham (cnd), Royal Opera House Orch, Royal Opera House Chorus Covent Garden Memories ("Golden" series) ▲ MEM 3003

Wagner, R.:Parsifal (sels), w. L. Melchior (ten), E. McArthur (cnd), RCA Victor SO—Act 2 *(Dies alles hab' ich nun geträumt [Herzenleide Scene])* RCA Gold Seal ▲ 7915–2–RG (m) [ADD] ■ 7915–4–RG (CrO2)

Wagner, R.:Das Rheingold, w. J. Madeira (mez), S. Svanholm (ten), G. London (bar), G. Neidlinger (b–bar), K. Böhme (bass), G. Solti (cnd), Vienna PO [G] London 3–▲ 414101–2 [ADD]

Wagner, R.:Der Ring des Nibelungen, w. B. Nilsson (sop), R. Crespin (sop), C. Watson (sop), C. Ludwig (mez), J. Madeira (mez), S. Svanholm (ten), J. King (ten), G. Stolze (ten), W. Windgassen (ten), G. London (bar), D. Fischer–Dieskau (bar), H. Hotter (b–bar), G. Neidlinger (b–bar), G. Frick (bass), G. Solti (cnd), Vienna PO [G] London 15–▲ 414100–2 [ADD]

Wagner, R.:Der Ring des Nibelungen, w. H. Konetzni (sop), E. Höngen (cta), G. Treptow (ten), S. Svanholm (ten), M. Lorenz (ten), F. Frantz (b–bar), L. Weber (bass), B. Herrmann (bass), W. Furtwängler (cnd), La Scala Orch, La Scala Chorus *(rec live 1950)* Arkadia 12–▲ 351 [ADD]

Wagner, R.:Der Ring des Nibelungen, w. Hilde Konetzni (sop), Elisabeth Höngen (cta), Max Lorenz (ten), Set Svanholm (ten), Günther Treptow (ten), Josef Hermann (bar), Ludwig Weber (bass), Ferdinand Franz (sgr), W. Furtwängler (cnd), La Scala Orch, La Scala Chorus *(rec Milan, 1950)* Music & Arts 12–▲ CD 914

Wagner, R.:Tristan und Isolde, w. L. Melchior (ten), H. Janssen (bar), P. Schoeffler (b–bar), T. Beecham (cnd), Royal Opera House Orch, Royal Opera House Chorus Covent Garden *(rec live, Covent Garden, 6/18 & 22/37)* Melodram 3–▲ MEL 37029 (m) [AAD]

Wagner, R.:Tristan und Isolde, w. Sabine Kalter (cta), Lauritz Melchoir (ten), Emmanuel List (bass), F. Reiner (cnd), London PO Enterprise ("The Radio Years" series) 3–▲ ENT 39 (m)

Wagner, R.:Tristan und Isolde, w. S. Kalter (cta), L. Melchior (ten), H. Janssen (bar), E. List (bass), F. Reiner (cnd), Royal Opera House Orch, Royal Opera House Chorus Covent Garden [G] *(rec live, Covent Garden May/June 1936)* VAI Audio 3–▲ VAIA 1004–3 (m) [ADD]

Wagner, R.:Tristan und Isolde, w. M. Klose (cta), L. Melchior (ten), H. Janssen (bar), S. Nilsson (bass), Beecham, Reiner (cnd), *(orch unknown)*—a compilation of two 1937 live performance recordings, with some passages conducted by Beecham, others by Reiner [G] EMI Classics ("Great Recordings of the Century" series) 3–▲ CDHC 64037

Wagner, R.:Tristan und Isolde, w. Margarete Klose (mez), Lauritz Melchior (ten/bar), Herbert Janssen (bar), Sven Nilsson (bass), T. Beecham (cnd), Philharmonia Orch, Royal Opera House Chorus Covent Garden *(rec 1937)* Grammofono 2000 3–▲ GRM 78570 (m)

Wagner, R.:Tristan und Isolde (sels), w. G. Sébastian (cnd), Berlin City Opera Orch—Act 1 *(Wie lachend sie mir Lieder singen)*, Act 3 *(Tristan!...Ich bins, ich bins; Mild und leise [Liebestod]) [G] (rec live May 9, 1952)* Arkadia 2–▲ 576 (m) [ADD]

Wagner, R.:Tristan und Isolde (sels), w. V. Ursuleac (sop), S. Svanholm (ten), H. Hotter (b–bar), E. Kleiber (cnd), Buenos Aires Teatro Colón Orch, Buenos Aires Teatro Colón Chorus—highlights from Acts 1–3 [G] *(rec live, 1948)* Melodram 2–▲ MEL 25007 (m) [AAD]

Wagner, R.:Tristan und Isolde (sels), w. Tiana Lemnitz (sop), Torsten Ralf (ten), Rudolf Bockelmann (b–bar), Ludwig Weber (bass), T. Beecham (cnd), Royal Opera House Orch, Royal Opera House Chorus Covent Garden Memories ("Golden" series) ▲ MEM 3003

Wagner, R.:Die Walküre (act 2), w. L. Lehmann (sop), L. Melchior (ten), F. Schorr (b–bar), F. Reiner (cnd), *(orch unknown)* [G] *(rec 1936)* Legato Classics ▲ LCD 133–1 (m) [AAD]

Wagner, R.:Die Walküre (act 3), w. K. Flagstad (sop—Brünnhilde), M. Müller (sop—Sieglinde), R. Bockelmann (b–bar—Wotan), W. Furtwängler (cnd), Royal Opera House Orch [G] *(rec Covent Garden, 5/26/37)* Myto ▲ 1 MCD 91443 [ADD]

Wagner, R.:Wesendonck Songs, w. G. Sébastian (cnd), Berlin City Opera Orch [G] *(rec live, 5/9 or 5/11/52)* Melodram 2–▲ MEL 26514 (m) [AAD]

Wagner, R.:Wesendonck Songs, w. G. Sébastian (cnd), Berlin City Opera Orch [G] *(rec live, 5/9 or 5/11/52)* Arkadia 2–▲ 576 [ADD]

Wagner, R.:Wesendonck Songs, w. Bruno Walter (pno) *(rec 1944–52)* Music & Arts ▲ CD 838 [AAD]

Wagner, R.:Wesendonck Songs, w. Gerald Moore (pno) [G] *(rec 5/25–26/48)* EMI Classics ("Great Recordings of the Century" series) ▲ CDH 63030 (m) [ADD]

Wagner, R.:Wesendonck Songs, w. Bruno Walter (pno) *(rec live, 1952)* Legend ▲ LGD 119

Wagner, R.:Wesendonck Songs, w. M. Sargent (cnd), BBC SO *(rec 1953)* Memories 2–▲ HR 4456/57 [ADD]

Wagner, R.:Wesendonck Songs, w. Ø. Fjeldstad (cnd), Oslo PO [G] Acanta ▲ 43189

Wagner, R.:Wesendonck Songs, w. Bruno Walter (pno) *(rec live, 1952)* Historical Performers ▲ HPS 27

Flamm, Carol (sgr)

Rorem, N.:3 Sisters Who Are Not Sisters, w. Andrea Matthews (sop—Jenny), Carol Flamm (sgr—Helen), Madeline Tsingopoulos (sgr—Ellen), Frederick Urrey (ten—Samuel), Mark Singer (sgr—Sylvester), John Van Buskirk (pno) Newport Classic ▲ NPT 85594 [DDD]

Flanders, Michael (nar)

Britten, H.:The Young Person's Guide to the Orchestra, w. Royal Liverpool PO, Groves, Kurtz (cnd), Philharmonia Orch EMI Classics ▲ CDM 63177

Prokofiev, S.:Peter & the Wolf, w. E. Kurtz (cnd), Philharmonia Orch EMI Classics ▲ CDM 63177

Saint–Saëns, C.:Carnival of the Animals, w. E. Kurtz (cnd), Philharmonia Orch EMI Classics ▲ CDM 63177

Flanders, T. (sop)

Kassel, R.:Celebrating, w. C. Schadeberg (sop) Mode ▲ 23

Kassel, R.:Gathering, w. C. Schadeberg (sop) Mode ▲ 23

Flebbe, Herta (sop)

Schütz, H.:St. John Passion, w. Johannes Hoeflin (ten—Evangelist), Rolf Bössow (ten—Pilate), Gert Spierting (ten), Jakob Stämpfli (bass—Jesus), Teinhard Tuge (bass—soliloquies), W. Ehmann (cnd), Westphalia Kantorei *(rec Münster zu Herfor, Sept. 1961)* Cantate ▲ 57602 [ADD]

Flechter, Guy (ten)

Handel, G.F.:Scipione, w. Doris Lamprecht (sop), Sandrine Piau (sop), Vandaa Tabery (mez), Oliver Lalouette (bass), C. Rousset (cnd), Les Talens Lyriques [I] FNAC Music 3–▲ 592245 [DDD]

Fleckenstein, Barbara (sgr)

Wagner, R.:Lohengrin, w. Sharon Sweet (sop—Elsa), Eva Marton (sop—Ortrud), Ben Heppner (ten—Lohengrin), Anton Rosner (ten—Nobleman), Heinrich Weber (ten—Nobleman), Jan–Hendrik Rootering (bar—Heinrich der Vögler), Sergei Leiferkus (bar—Friedrich von Telramund), Bryn Terfel (b–bar—King's Herald), Barbara Fleckenstein (sgr—Page), Atsuko Suzuki (sgr—Page), Gisela Ulmann (sgr—Page), Marion Rambausek (sgr—Page), Dankwart Siegele (sgr—Nobleman), Jürgen Weiss (sgr—Nobleman), C. Davis (cnd), Bavarian SO, Bavarian State Opera Chorus, Bavarian Radio Chorus *(rec Residenz Herkulesaal, Munich, May 14–28, 1994)* RCA Red Seal 3–▲ 09026–62646–2 [DDD]

Wagner, R.:Lohengrin (sels), w. Eva Marton (sop—Ortrud), Sharon Sweet (sop—Elsa von Brabant), Barbara Fleckenstein (sgr—Page), Marion Rambausek (sgr—Page), Atsuko Suzuki (sgr—Page), Gisela Ulmann (sgr—Page), Ben Heppner (ten—Lohengrin), Anton Rosner (ten—Nobleman), Heinrich Weber (ten—Nobleman), Sergei Leiferkus (bar—Friedrich von Telramund), Bryn Terfel (b–bar—King's Herald), Jan–Hendrik Rootering (bass—Henry the Fowler), Dankwart Siegele (sgr—Nobleman), Jürgen Weiss (sgr—Nobleman), C. Davis (cnd), Bavarian RSO, Michael Gläser (cnd), Udo Mehrpohl (cnd), Bavarian Radio Chorus, Bavarian State Opera Chorus—Seht! Seht! [from Act 1, Scene 2]; Nun sei bedankt, mein lieber Schwan!; Wenn ich im Kampfe für dich siege; Welch holde Wunder muss ich sehen?; Nun höret mich und achtet wohl; Durch Gottes Sieg ist jetzt dein Leben mein [all from Act 1, Scene 3]; Treulich geführt ziehet dahin [from Act 3, Scene 1]; Wie hehr erkenn' ich unsrer Liebe Wesen!; Höchstes Vertrau'n hast du mir schon zu danken; Weh' nun ist all' unser Glück dahin! [all from Act 3, Scene 2]; In fernem Land, unnahbar euren Schritten [from Act 3, Scene 3] *(rec Munich, Mar 14–28, 1994)* RCA Red Seal ▲ 09026–68239–2 [DDD]

Fleet, E. (sgr)

Gay, J.:The Beggar's Opera (sels), w. P. Clark (sop), A. Jenkins (sop), M. Cable (mez), E. Lane (mez), S. Minty (mez), P. Hall (ten), V. Midgley (ten), N. Rogers (ten), J. Noble (bar), D. Stevens (cnd), Accademia Monteverdiana Orch, Accademia Monteverdiana Chorus—59 songs *(rec Aug. 1978)* Koch Treasure ▲ 31621–2 [ADD]

Fleischer, E. (cta)

Weber, C.M. von:Kampf und Sieg, w. L. Schmidt–Glänzel (sop), G. Lutze (ten), H. Krämer (bar), H. Kegel (cnd), Leipzig RSO, Leipzig Radio Chorus [G] Forlane ▲ FOR 16572 (m) [AAD]

Fleming, Renée (sop)

Divas in Song:Marylin Horne, a 60th Birthday Celebration, w. Montserrat Caballé (sop), H. Donath (sop), R. A. Swenson (sop), F. von Stade (mez), S. Ramey (bass), J. Levine (cnd), M. Katz (pno), W. Jones (pno), K. Donath (pno), Manuel Burgueras (pno) RCA Red Seal ▲ 09026–62547–2

Hodkinson, S.:Chansons de Jadis, w. P. Phillips (cnd), Eastern Connecticut SO [E] Centaur ▲ CRC 2073 [DDD]

James Levine's 25th Anniversary Metropolitan Opera Gala, w. J. Levine (cnd), Metropolitan Opera Orch, Ileana Cotrubas (sop), Hei–Kyung Hong (sop), Karita Mattila (sop), Birgit Nilsson (sop), Ruth Ann Swenson (sop), Kiri Te Kanawa (sop), Deborah Voigt (sop), Grace Bumbry (mez), Heidi Grant Murphy (mez), Anne Sofie von Otter (mez) *(rec live, Metropolitan Opera House, New York, Apr 27, 1996)* Deutsche Grammophon ▲ 449177–2 [DDD]

Massenet, J.:Hérodiade, w. Renée Fleming (sop—Salome), Dolora Zajick (mez—Hérodiade), Plácido Domingo (ten—Jean), Juan Pons (bar—Erode), Kenneth Cox (bass—Phanuel), V. Gergiev (cnd), San Francisco Opera Orch, San Francisco Opera Chorus Sony Classical 2–▲ S2K 66847

Massenet, J.:Hérodiade (sels), w. Renée Fleming (sop—Salomé), Dolora Zajick (mez—Hérodiade), Plácido Domingo (ten—Jean), Juan Pons (bar—Hérode), Hector Vásquez (bar—Vitellius), Kenneth Cox (bass—Phanuel), V. Gergiev (cnd), San Francisco Opera Orch, San Francisco Opera Chorus Sony Classical ▲ SK 61965

Massenet, J.:Hérodiade (sels), w. Dolora Zajick (mez), Kristin Clayton (sgr), Plácido Domingo (ten), Kenneth Cox (bass), Juan Pons (bar), Hector Vásquez (sgr), V. Gergiev (cnd), San Francisco Opera Orch, San Francisco Opera Chorus—highlights *(rec San Francisco Opera, Nov 1994)* Sony Classical ▲ SK 61965

Mozart, W.A.:Così fan tutte, w. Renée Fleming (sop—Fiordiligi), Adelina Scarabelli (sop—Despina), Anne Sofie Von Otter (mez—Dorabella), Frank Lopardo (ten—Ferrando), Olaf Bar (bar—Guglielmo), Michele Pertusi (bass—Don Alfonso), G. Solti (cnd), CO of Europe London 3–▲ 444174–2

Rossini, G.:Armida, w. C. Bosi (ten), B. Fowler (ten), J. Francis (ten), D. Kaasch (ten), G. Kunde (ten), I. Zennaro (ten), I. D'Arcangelo (bass), S. Zadvorny (bass), D. Gatti (cnd), Bologna Teatro Comunale Orch, Bologna Teatro Comunale Chorus *(rec Pesaro, Italy, Aug. 6–17, 1993)* Sony Classical 3–▲ S3K 58968 [DDD]

Strauss, R.:4 Last Songs, w. C. Eschenbach (cnd), Houston SO *(rec Jones Hall, Houston, TX, Mar 14 & 20, 1995)* RCA Red Seal ▲ 09026–68539–2 [DDD]

Strauss, R.:Der Rosenkavalier (sels), w. K. Battle (sop), F. von Stade (mez), A. Schmidt (bar), C. Abbado (cnd), Berlin PO *(rec Dec. 31, 1992)* Sony Classical ▲ SK 52565

Strauss, R.:Der Rosenkavalier (suite), w. C. Eschenbach (cnd), Houston SO *(rec Jones Hall, Houston, TX, May 8, 1995)* RCA Red Seal ▲ 09026–68539–2 [DDD]

Strauss, R.:Songs, w. C. Eschenbach (cnd), Houston SO—Befreit, Op. 39/4; Muttertändelei, Op. 43/2; Wiegenlied, Op. 41/1; Waldseligkeit, Op. 49/1; Cäcilie, Op. 27/2 *(rec Jones Hall, Houston, TX, May 8, 1995)* RCA Red Seal ▲ 09026–68539–2 [DDD]

Villa–Lobos, H.:The Forest of the Amazon, w. A. Heller (cnd), Moscow RSO Consonance ▲ 81 0012 [DDD]

Flesch, Ella (sop)

Wagner, R.:Die Walküre (act 2), w. M. Fuchs (sop), L. Lehmann (sop), M. Klose (cta), L. Melchior (ten), H. Hotter (b–bar), A. Jerger (b–bar), E. List (bass), B. Walter (cnd), Berlin State Opera Orch [G] *(rec 9/38 & 6/22/35)* Danacord 2–▲ DACOCD 317/18 (m)

Wagner, R.:Die Walküre (act 2), w. M. Fuchs (sop), L. Lehmann (sop), M. Klose (cta), L. Melchior (ten), H. Hotter (b–bar), A. Jerger (b–bar), E. List (bass), B. Walter (cnd), Berlin State Opera Orch [G] *(rec 9/38 & 6/22/35)* EMI Classics ("References" series) ▲ CDH 64255

Fleta, Miguel (ten)

Leoncavallo, R.:Pagliacci (sels), w. Enrico Caruso (ten), Antonio Paoli (ten), Giovanni Zenatello (ten), Amedeo Bassi (ten), Hermann Jadlowker (ten), Fernand Ansseau (ten), Hipolito Lazaro (ten), Nino (Filippo) Piccaluga (ten), Mario Chamlee (ten), Giacomo Lauri–Volpi (ten), Giovanni Martinelli (ten), Aureliano Pertile (ten), Georges Thill (ten), Alessandro Valente (ten), Francesco Merli (ten), Lauritz Melchior (ten), Marcel Wittrisch (ten), Joseph Schmidt (ten), Beniamino Gigli (ten), Giuseppe Lugo (ten), Helge Roswaenge (ten), Jussi Bjoerling (ten)—23 versions of the tenor aria "Vesti la giubba" *(rec 1907–1944)* Bongiovanni ▲ GB 1071 [ADD]

Miguel Fleta *(rec 1922–1927 for HMV)* Preiser ("Lebendige Vergangenheit" series) ▲ PRE 89002 (m) [AAD]

Miguel Fleta, Vol. 2 *(rec 1927–31)* Preiser ("Lebendige Vergangenheit" series) ▲ PRE 89093 [AAD]

Fletcher (ten)

Schubert, Franz:Mass 2, w. M. Pares–Reyna (sop), P. Fourcade (bass), M. Piquemal (cnd), Harmonia Nova Orch Ensemble, Michel Piquemal Vocal Ensemble [L] Gallo ▲ CD 584 [DDD]

Schubert, Franz:Mass 4, w. M. Pares–Reyna (sop), N. Stutzmann (alt), P. Fourcade (bass), M. Piquemal (cnd), Harmonia Nova Orch Ensemble, Michel Piquemal Vocal Ensemble [L] Gallo ▲ CD 584 [DDD]

Fletcher, Graham (sgr)

Gluck, C.W.:La Recontre imprévue, w. C. Le Coz (sop), L. Dawson (sop), C. Dubosc (sop), S. Marin-Degor (sop), F. Dudziak (ten), G. de Mey (ten), J.-L. Viala (ten), G. Cachémaille (bar), J.-P. Lafont (bass), J. E. Gardiner (cnd), Paris Lyon Opera Orch, Paris Lyon Opera Chorus [F] Erato 2-▲ 2292-45516-2 [DDD]

Fleury, Jocelyne (cta)

Vivier, C.:Kopernikus, "A Ritual Opera of Death", w. Y. Parent (sop), P. Vaillancourt (sop), M.-D. Parent (sop), D. Doane (ten), M. Ducharme (bar), Y. Saint-Amant (bass), F. Martel (cl), M. Bélanger (vn), L. Bouchard (tpt), L. Vaillancourt (cnd), *(orch unknown)* *(rec Feb. 1991)* CBC ("Musica Viva" series) ▲ MVCD 1047 [DDD]

Flight, P. (ct)

Howells, H.:Requiem, w. J. Barton (trb), D. Honoré (ten), T. Woody (bar), F. Burgomeister (cnd), Indianapolis Festival Orch, Christ Church Cathedral Men & Boys Choir Oxford Gothic ▲ G 49062 [DDD]

Flimm, Jurgen (sgr)

Strauss (II), Joh.:Der Zigeunerbaron, w. Pamela Coburn (sop), Christiane Oelze (sop), Julia Hamari (mez), Elisabeth von Magnus (alt), Herbert Lippert (ten), Rudolf Schasching (ten), Wolfgang Holzmair (bar), Robert Florianschutz (sgr), Hans-Jurgen Lazar (sgr), N. Harnoncourt (cnd), Vienna SO, Arnold Schoenberg Choir *(rec Vienna, 1994)* Teldec 2-▲ 94555-2

Flint, A. (sgr)

Pugnani, G.:Werther, w. M. Cei (sgr), A. Andreani (sgr), T. Yamashita (sgr), M. Andreae (cnd), Swiss-Italian Radio-TV Orch *(rec Dec. 14, 1989)* Bongiovanni 2-▲ GB 5028/29 [DDD]

Flore, A. (voc)

Amendola, F.:Ricercari, w. D. Patumi (db), A. Frederico (elecs/pno), G. Lanzini (cl), L. Ciolfi (vn), C. Cavalieri (vn), C. Sanzo (vc), O. Mangiavacchi (perc), Donizetti Ensemble Bongiovanni ▲ GB 5519 [DDD]

Florei, Nicolae (bass)

Puccini, G.:Turandot, w. Teodora Lucaciu (sop—Liù), Maria Slatinaru (sop—Princess Turandot), Corneliu Finateanu (ten—Pong), George Mircea (ten—Emperor Altoum), Ludovic Speiss (ten—Prince Calaf), Valentin Teodorian (ten—Pang), Octav Enigarescu (bar—Ping), Dionisie Konya (bar—A Mandarin), Mircea Stefanescu (bar—The Prince of Persia), Nicolae Florei (bass—Timur), C. Litvin (cnd), Romanian Radio-TV Orch, Romanian Radio-TV Chorus *(rec Jan 1970)* Vox Box 2-▲ CDX 5160

Verdi, G.:La forza del destino, w. Maria Nistor-Slatinaru (sop—Donna Leonora), Mihaela Mariacineanu (mez—Curra), Zenaida Pally (mez—Preziosilla), Ludovic Speiss (ten—Don Alvaro), Ion Stoian (ten—Trabucco), Nicolae Herlea (bar—Don Carlo), Nicolae Florei (bass—Padre Guardiano) Constantin Gabor (bass—Fra Melitone), Dan Musetescu (bass—An Alcalde), Mihai Panghe (bass—Marquis of Calatrava), C. Litvin (cnd), Romanian Radio-TV Orch, Romanian Radio-TV Chorus *(rec Jan 1970)* Vox Box 3-▲ CD3X 3038

Verdi, G.:Rigoletto, w. Victoria Draganescu (sop—Countess Ceprano), Magda Ianculescu (sop—Gilda), Dorothea Palade (mez—Maddalena), Valeria Savu (mez—Giovanna), Ion Buzea (ten—Duke of Mantua), Dimitrie Scurtu (ten—Borsa), Nicolae Herlea (bar—Rigoletto), Stefan Petrescu (bar—Marullo), Jean Banescu (bass—Count Ceprano), Nicolae Florei (bass—Monterone), Nicolae Rafael (bass—Sparafucile), J. Bobescu (cnd), Romanian Opera Orch, Romanian Opera Chorus *(rec 1965)* Vox Box 2-▲ CDX 5162

Florescu, Arta (sop)

Leoncavallo, R.:Pagliacci, w. Arta Florescu (sop—Nedda), Cornel Stavru (ten—Canio), Valentin Teodorian (ten—Beppe), Nicolae Herlea (bar—Tonio), Ladislau Konya (bar—Silvio), M. Popa (cnd), Bucharest Opera & Ballet Theater Orch, Bucharest Opera & Ballet Theater Chorus *(rec 1966)* Vox Box 2-▲ CDX 5161

Florez, Juan Diego (ten)

Martin Y Soler, V.:Il Tutore Burlato, w. Liliana Marzano (sop—Menica), Maria Angeles Peters (sop—Violante), Juan Diego Florez (ten—Anselmo), Ernesto Palacio (ten—Il Cavaliere), Marcello Lippi (bar—Pippo), Giancarlo Tosi (bass—Don Fabrizio), Michela Forgione (hpd), M. Harth-Bedoya (cnd), Dianopolis Bulgarian CO *(rec VI Festival Internazionale di Gerace nella Chiesa di San Francesco, Aug 16, 1994)* Bongiovanni 2-▲ GB 2175/76-2 [DDD]

Zingarelli, N.A.:La passione di Gesù Cristo, w. Ernesto Palacio (ten), Simone Alaimo (b-bar), P. Pelucchi (cnd), Bergamo Collegium Musicum *(rec S. Martino Church, Tirano, June 30, 1995)* Agorá ▲ 018 [DDD]

Florianschütz, Robert (bass)

Strauss (II), Joh.:Der Zigeunerbaron, w. Pamela Coburn (sop), Christiane Oelze (sop), Julia Hamari (mez), Elisabeth von Magnus (alt), Herbert Lippert (ten), Rudolf Schasching (ten), Wolfgang Holzmair (bar), Jurgen Flimm (sgr), Hans-Jurgen Lazar (sgr), N. Harnoncourt (cnd), Vienna SO, Arnold Schoenberg Choir *(rec Vienna, 1994)* Teldec 2-▲ 94555-2

Flöth, Michael (bass)

Haydn, M.:German Masses, w. R. van Husen (ten), H.-G. Freimuth (cnd), Münster Wind Ensemble, Münster Cathedral Choir—No. 1 Calig ▲ CAL 50824 [ADD]

Schubert, Franz:Deutsche Messe, w. R. van Husen (ten), H.-G. Freimuth (cnd), Münster Wind Ensemble, Münster Cathedral Choir Calig ▲ CAL 50824 [ADD]

Flowers, Kate (sop)

Stockhausen, K.:Stimmung, w. P. Walmsley-Clark (sop), Long (sgr), R. Covey-Crump (ten), P. Rose (bass), Hillier (sgr) Hyperion ▲ CDA 66115

Floyd, Victor (ten)

Britten, H.:Rejoice in the Lamb, w. Susan Ashe (sop), Cynthia Calabrese (alt), Charles Sprawls (bass), Alfred Calabrese (cnd), Britten Singers ACA Digital Recording ▲ CM 20039

Flynn, Renée (sop)

Vaughan Williams, R.:Dona nobis pacem, w. R. Henderson (bar), R. Vaughan Williams (cnd), BBC SO, BBC Sym Chorus [E,L] *(rec 11/36)* Pearl ▲ GEMMCD 9342 (m) [AAD]

Focile, Nuccia (sop)

Donizetti, G.:Arias, w. Michael Pollock (pno)—6 arias Unicorn-Kanchana ▲ DKPCD 9161

Donizetti, G.:Songs, w. Michael Pollock (pno)—Canzone Napoletane Unicorn-Kanchana ▲ DKPCD 9161

Monteverdi, C.:Orfeo, w. Claudia Clarich (mez), Enrico Facini (ten), Paolo Coni (bar), James Loomis (bass), H. Handt (cnd), Lucchese CO [orchd Respighi, 1934-35] *(rec live, VII Festival Internazionale di Marlia, 1984)* Claves ▲ CD 9419 [ADD]

Mozart, W.A.:Così fan tutte (sels), w. Felicity Lott (sop), Marie McLaughlin (sop), Jerry Hadley (ten), Alessandro Corbelli (bass), Gilles Cachemaille (bass) *(rec Usher Hall, Edinburgh, Scotland)* Telarc ▲ CD 80399 [DDD]

Mozart, W.A.:Don Giovanni, w. Christine Brewer (sop—Donna Anna), Nuccia Focile (sop—Zerlina), Felicity Lott (sop—Donna Elvira), Jerry Hadley (ten—Don Ottavio), Bo Skovhus (bar—Don Giovanni), Umberto Chiummo (bass—Masetto/Il Commendatore), Alessandro Corbelli (bass—Leporello), C. Mackerras (cnd), Scottish CO, Scottish Chamber Chorus *(rec Usher Hall, Edinburgh, Scotland, July 31-Aug 11, 1995)* Telarc 3-▲ CD 80420 [DDD]

Mozart, W.A.:Nozze di Figaro, w. Rebecca Evans (sop—Barbarina), Nuccia Focile (sop—Susanna), Suzanne Murphy (sop—Marcellina), Carol Vaness (sop—Countess Almaviva), Susanne Mentzer (mez—Cherubino), Ryland Davies (ten—Don Basilio/Don Curzio), Alessandro Corbelli (bar—Count Almaviva), Alfonso Antoniozzi (bass—Doctor Bartolo/Antonio), Alastair Miles (bass—Figaro), C. Mackerras (cnd), Scottish CO, Scottish Chamber Chorus *(rec Usher Hall, Edingurgh, Scotland, July 31-Aug. 12, 1994)* Telarc 3-▲ CD 80388 [DDD]

My Heart's Delight, w. L. Pavarotti (ten), Royal PO [cnd:M. Benini] *(rec 1993)* London ▲ 433260-2 △ 433260-4 ■ 433260-4

Pergolesi, G.B.:Lo frate 'nnamorato, w. A. Felle (sop), B. Manca di Nissa (cta), A. Corbelli (bar), R. Muti (cnd), La Scala Orch, La Scala Chorus EMI Classics 3-▲ CDCC 54240

Puccini, G.:Songs, w. Michael Pollock (pno)—Storiella d'amore; Sole e amore; A l'uccellino; Casa mio; Morire; Canto d'anime Unicorn-Kanchana ▲ DKPCD 9161

Tchaikovsky, P.:Eugene Onegin, w. I. Arkhipova (mez), S. Walker (mez), F. Egerton (ten), D. Hvorostovsky (bar)., S. Bychkov (cnd), Orch de Paris Philips 2-▲ 438235-2

Focile, Nuccia (sop) (cont.)

Verdi, G.:Songs, w. Michael Pollock (pno)—Brindisi I & II; Perduta ho la pace; Deh pietoso, ho Addolorata; Stornello; L'Abandonée; E la vita; La Zingara; Il Tramonto Unicorn-Kanchana ▲ DKPCD 9161

Fodor, János (bar)

Verdi, G.:Rigoletto (sels), w. Mária Gyurkovics (sop), Olga Szönyi (mez), Ernö Kenéz (ten), Alexander Svéd (bar), József Bódy (bass), Kórodi, Molinari-Pradelli (cnd), Hungarian State Opera Orch—Pari siamo!; Figlia! Mio padre! A te dappresso; Cortigiani! Vil' razza dannata; Tutte le feste al tempio...Ah! solo per me!; Chi è mai... *(rec 1955-56)* Hungaroton ("Great Hungarian Voices" series) ▲ HCD 31614 [ADD]

Foerschler, Matthew (ten)

Moore, D.:Devil & Daniel Webster, w. Joyce Guyer (sop—Mary Stone), Benjamin Bongers (ten—Walter Butler), Michael Philip Davis (ten—Simon Girty), Matthew Foerschler (ten—Miser Stephens), Darren Keith Woods (ten—Mr. Scratch), Michael Lanman (bass—Blackbeard Teach), David Soxman (bass—Clerk), Brian Steele (bass—Daniel Webster), John Stephens (bass—Jabez Stone), Andrew Stuckey (bass—King Philip), Robert Gibby Brand (actor), Cary Miller (actor), R. Patterson (cnd), Kansas City SO, Kansas City Lyric Opera Chorus *(rec Sept 1995)* Newport Classic ▲ NPD 85585 [DDD]

Foiani, Giovanni (bass)

Puccini, G.:Manon Lescaut, w. Magda Olivero (sop—Manon), Tine Appelman (mez—Singer), Umberto Borso (ten—Chevalier), Mario Carlin (ten—Edmondo/Dancing Master/Lamplighter), Ferdinando Lidonni (bar—Lescaut), Giovanni Foiani (bass—Geronte/Sergeant/Captain), Joop Ruivenkamp (bass—Innkeeper), F. Vernizzi (cnd), Groot Omroep Orch, Groot Omroep Choir *(rec Amsterdam, Oct 31, 1964)* Bella Voce 2-▲ BLV 107.221 [AAD]

Verdi, G.:Un ballo in maschera (sels), w. Margherita Guglielmi (sop), José Carreras (ten), Frederico Davià (bass), F. Molinari-Pradelli (cnd), La Scala Orch, La Scala Chorus—S'avanza il Conte...La rivedrà nell'estasi; Ma se m'è forza perderti...Ah! dessa è là! *(rec Milan, Feb 13, 1975)* Goldies ▲ GLD 63203 [ADD]

Fokenoy (sgr)

Boieldieu, F.-A.:Le Calife de Bagdad, w. N. Monestier (sop), Ouaki (sgr), S. Elloir (sgr), Plantak (sgr), B. Thomas (cnd), Bernard Thomas CO, Patrick Marco Vocal Ensemble [F] Thésis ▲ THC 82015 [DDD]

Folan, Andrea (sop)

Haydn, J.:Arianna a Naxos, w. Tom Beghin (pno) *(rec Sage Chapel, Cornell Univ., Itahca, NY, Mar 21-23, 1995)* Bridge ▲ BCD 9059 [DDD]

Haydn, J.:Songs (52) solo Voice & Kbd, w. Tom Beghin (pno)—Das strickende Mädchen; Cupido; Der erste Kuss; Eine sehr gewöhnliche Geschichte; Die Verlassene; Der Gleichsinn; An Iris; An Thyrsis; Trost unglücklicher Liebe; Die Landlust; Liebeslied; Die zu späte Ankunft der Mutter [H.XXVIa/1-12] *(rec Sage Chapel, Cornell Univ., Itahca, NY, Mar 21-23, 1995)* Bridge ▲ BCD 9059 [DDD]

Foldi, Andrew (b-bar)

Rossini, G.:La pietra del paragone, w. A. Elgar (sop), B. Wolff (mez), E. Bonazzi (mez), J. Carreras (ten), J. Reardon (bar), R. Murcell (bar), J. Diaz (bass), N. Jenkins (cnd), Clarion Concerts Orch, Clarion Concerts Chorus [I] *(rec. ca. 1972)* Vanguard Classics 3-▲ OVC 8043/45 [ADD]

Folgar, Tino (ten)

Verdi, G.:Rigoletto, w. Lina Pagliughi (sop—Gilda), Linda Brambilla (mez—Countess Ceprano), Vera De Cristoff (cta—Maddalena), Tino Folgar (ten—Duke of Mantua), Giuseppe Nessi (ten—Borsa), Luigi Piazza (bar—Rigoletto), Aristide Baracchi (b-bar—Monterone/Marullo); Salvatore Baccaloni (bass—Sparafucile), Giuseppe Menni (bass—Ceprano), C. Sabajno (cnd), La Scala Orch, La Scala Chorus *(rec La Scala Theatre, Milan, 1927-28)* VAI Audio 2-▲ VAIA 1097-2

Verdi, G.:Rigoletto, w. Lina Pagliughi (sop), Salvatore Baccaloni (bass), Luigi Piazza (sgr), C. Sabajno (cnd), La Scala Orch, La Scala Chorus Pearl 2-▲ PEA 9180 [ADD]

Verdi, G.:Rigoletto, w. Lina Pagliughi (sop—Gilda), Linda Brambilla (mez—Contessa di Ceprano), Vera de Cristoff (cta—Maddalena), Tino Folgar (ten—Duca di Mantova), Giuseppe Nessi (ten—Borsa), Aristide Baracchi (bar—Conte di Monterone/Marullo), Luigi Piazza (bar—Rigoletto), Salvatore Baccaloni (bass—Sparafucile), Giuseppe Menni (bass—Conte di Ceprano), C. Sabajno (cnd), La Scala Orch, La Scala Chorus *(rec 1927-28)* Arkadia 2-▲ CD 78003 (m) [ADD]

Foltyn, Maria (sop)

Moniuszko, S.:Halka (sels), w. Franciszek Arno (ten), Rezler, Latoszewski (cnd), Polish National RSO Katowice, Warsaw Opera Orch—Gdyby rannym slonkiem; O mój malenki Polskie Nagrania ▲ PNCD 275

Puccini, G.:Arias, w. Franciszek Arno (ten), Latoszewski, Rezler (cnd), Polish National RSO Katowice, Warsaw Opera Orch—Mi chiamano Mimi [from Cyganeria]; Ah! que gli ochi; Vissi d'arte [both from Tosca] Polskie Nagrania ▲ PNCD 275

Verdi, G.:Arias, w. Franciszek Arno (ten), Rezler, Latoszewski (cnd), Polish National RSO Katowice, Warsaw Opera Orch—O Patria mia [from Aida]; Ma dall'arido stelo [from Bal Maskowy]; Pace, pace, mio Dio [from Moc Przeznaczenia] Polskie Nagrania ▲ PNCD 275

Wagner, R.:Lohengrin (sels), w. Franciszek Arno (ten), Rezler, Latoszewski (cnd), Polish National RSO Katowice, Warsaw Opera Orch—Einsam in truben Tagen Polskie Nagrania ▲ PNCD 275

Folwell, Nicholas (bar)

Sullivan, A.:The Mikado, w. M. McLaughlin (sop), A. Howells (mez), J. Watson (sop), F. Palmer (sop/mez), D. Adams (bass), A. Rolfe Johnson (ten), R. Stuart (bar), R. Van Allan (bass), C. Mackerras (cnd), Welsh National Opera Orch, Welsh National Opera Chorus—Ov & dialogue omitted [E] Telarc ▲ CD 80284 [DDD]; ■ CS 30284 (D)

Sullivan, A.:The Pirates of Penzance, w. R. Evans (sop—Mabel), G. Knight (mez—Ruth), J. Gossage (mez—Edith), J. M. Ainsley (ten—Frederic), R. Suart (bar—Maj.-Gen. Stanley), N. Folwell (bar—Samuel), D. Adams (b-bar—Pirate King), R. Van Allan (bass—Sergeant of Police), C. Mackerras (cnd), Welsh National Opera Orch, Welsh National Opera Chorus *(rec May 4-6, 1993)* Telarc ▲ CD 80353 [DDD]; ■ CS 30353

Wagner, R.:Parsifal, w. Waltraud Meier (mez—Kundry), Warren Ellsworth (ten—Parsifal), Nicholas Folwell (bar—Klingsor), Philip Joll (b-bar—Amfortas), Donald McIntyre (b-bar—Gurnemanz), R. Goodall (cnd), Welsh National Opera Orch, Welsh National Opera Chorus EMI Classics 2-▲ CDMD 65665

Weir, J.:Blond Eckbert, w. Anne-Marie Owens (mez), Nerys Jones (sgr), Christopher Ventris (sgr), S. Edwards (cnd), English National Opera Orch Collins Classics ▲ COL 1461

Fomina, Nina (sop)

Glinka, M.:Russlan & Ludmilla, w. Nina Fomina (sop—Gorislava), Bela Rudenko (sop—Ludmilla), Tamara Sinyavskaya (mez—Ratmir), Boris Morozov (bass—Farlaf), Evgeny Nesterenko (bass—Russlan), Valeri Yaroslavtsev (bass—Svetozar), Y. Simonov (cnd), Bolshoi Theater Orch, Bolshoi Theater Chorus *(rec Moscow, 1978-1979)* Melodiya ("The Russian Opera" series) 3-▲ 74321-29348-2 [ADD]

Fonda, Henry (nar)

Copland, A.:Lincoln Portrait, w. A. Copland (cnd), London SO CBS ▲ MK 42431 [ADD]

Copland, A.:Lincoln Portrait, w. A. Copland (cnd), London SO [E] CBS ■ MT 30649

Fondary, Alain (bar)

Massenet, J.:Don Quichotte, w. T. Berganza (mez—La Belle Dulcinée), A. Fondary (bar—Sancho Pana), J. Van Dam (b-bar—Don Quichotte), M. Plasson (cnd), Toulouse Capitole Orch, Toulouse Capitole Chorus EMI Classics ▲ CDCB 54767

Puccini, G.:La fanciulla del West, w. Eva Martón (sop), Dennis O'Neill (ten), Walter Planté (ten), L. Slatkin (cnd), Munich RSO RCA Red Seal ▲ 09026-60597-2

Saint-Saëns, C.:Samson et Dalila, w. W. Meier (mez), P. Domingo (ten), S. Ramey (bass), M.-W. Chung (cnd), Bastille Opera Orch, Bastille Opera Chorus EMI Classics 2-▲ CDCB 54470

Fontana, Gabriele (sop)

Schmidt, F.:Das Buch mit sieben Siegeln, w. Margareta Hintermeier (alt), Kurt Azesberger (ten), Eberhard Büchner (ten—Johannes), Robert Holl (bass—Voice of the Lord), Robert Holzer (bass), Martin Haselböck (org), H. Stein (cnd), Vienna SO, Vienna Sym Chorus *(rec live, Vienna Music Hall, May 1996)* Calig 2-▲ CAL 50978/9 [DDD]

Schoenberg, A.:Moses und Aaron, w. David Pittman-Jennings (nar), Gabriele Fontana (sop—Young Girl), Yvonne Naef (cta—Sick Woman), John Graham-Hall (ten—Young Man/Naked Youth), Pår Lindskog (ten—Youth), Chris Merritt (ten—Aaron), Siegfried Lorenz (bar—Another Man), Michael Devlin (b-bar—Ephraimite), László Polgár (bass—Priest), P. Boulez (cnd), Royal Concertgebouw Orch, Winfried Maczewski (cnd), Netherlands Opera Chorus, Zaans Youth Choir, Waterland Music School *(rec Concertgebouw, Amsterdam, Oct 1995)* Deutsche Grammophon 2-▲ 449 174-2 [DDD]

Schumann, C.:Songs, w. Konstanze Eickhorst (pno) CPO ▲ CPO 999127 [DDD]

Fontana, Gabriele (sop) (cont.)

Strauss (II), Joh.:Die Fledermaus (sels), w. Ariane Calix (sop—Ida), Gabriele Fontana (sop—Rosalinde), Brigitte Karwautz (sop—Adele), Rohangiz Yachmi-Caucig (cta—Orlofsky), John Dickie (ten—Eisenstein), Josef Hopferwieser (ten—Alfred), Erich Wessner (ten—Dr. Blind), Andrea Martin (bar—Falke), Alfred Werner (bar—Frank), J. Wildner (cnd), Czech-Slovak RSO Bratislava, Bratislava City Chorus—Ov.; [Act I] Täubchen, das entflattert ist...; Ach, ich darf nicht hin zu dir; Nein, mit solchen Advokaten; Komm mit mir zum Souper; So muss allein ich bleiben; Trinke, Liebchen, trinke schnell; [Act II] Ein Souper heut' uns winkt; Ich lade gern mir Gäste ein; Mein Herr Marquis, ein Mann wie Sie; Dieser Anstand, so manierlich; Klänge der Heimat; Im Feuerstrom der Reben; Marianka komm und tanz me hier; [Act III] Entr'acte; Spiel' ich die Unschuld vom Lande; O Fledermaus, o Fledermaus *(rec Slovak Radio Concert Hall, Bratislava)* Naxos ▲ 8.553171 [DDD]

Wagner, R.:Das Rheingold, w. Gabriele Fontana (sop—Woglinde), Nancy Gustafson (sop—Freia), Ildiko Komlosi (mez—Wellgunde), Hanna Schwarz (mez—Fricka), Elena Zaremba (mez—Erda), Margareta Hintermeier (cta—Flosshilde), Kim Begley (ten—Loge), Peter Schreier (ten—Mime), Thomas Sunnegardh (ten—Froh), Robert Hale (bass-bar—Wotan), Walter Fink (bass—Fafner), Franz-Josef Kapellmann (bass—Alberich), Jan-Hendrik Rootering (bass—Fasolt), Eike Wilm Schulte (bass—Donner), C. von Dohnányi (cnd), Cleveland Orch *(rec Severance Hall, Cleveland, Ohio, Dec 1993)* London 2-▲ 443690-2

Zimmermann, U.:Die weisse Rose (sels), w. L.-M. Harder (ten), U. Zimmermann (cnd), *(ensemble unknown)* [scenes for 2 solo voices & instrumental ensemble] [G] Orfeo ▲ 162871 [DDD]

Fontana, Nancy (sgr)

Gluck, C.W.:Paride ed Elena, w. I. Cotrubas (sop), S. Greenberg (sop), F. Bonisolli (ten), L. Zagrosek (cnd), Austrian RSO, Austrian Radio Chorus [I] *(rec 1983)* Orfeo 2-▲ 118842 [DDD]

Strauss, R.:Arabella, w. K. Te Kanawa (sop), H. Dernesch (sop/mez), F. Grundheber (bar), J. Tate (cnd), Royal Opera House Orch [G] London 3-▲ 417623-2 [DDD]

Fontana, Teresita (sgr)

Distel, H.:La Stazione, w. Valeria Manzoni (sgr), Malwida Meysenbug (sgr), Federico Paternina (sgr), Arturo Schwarz (sgr) *(rec Milan, Italy & Bern, Switzerland, 1987 & May 1990)* Hat Hut ("NOW." series) ▲ hat ART CD 6060 [AAD]

Forbes, Patricia (sop)

Walton, W.:The Twelve, w. R. Gleave (mez), S. Gay (alt), J. Oxley (ten), P. Harvey (bar), R. Hickox (cnd), City of London Sinfonia [E] Chandos ▲ CHAN 8824 [DDD]

Ford, B. (sop)

Harrison, C.:Songs from a Child's Garden, w. B. K. Vaughn (pno) [E] CRS ▲ 9255

Ford, Bruce (ten)

Auber, D.-F.:Le Domino noir, w. Sumi Jo (sop), Doris Lamprecht (sop), Martine Olmeda (sop), Isabelle Vernet (sop), Jocelyne Taillon (mez), Patrick Power (ten), Gilles Cachemaille (bar), Jules Bastin (bass), R. Bonynge (cnd), English CO, London Voices London 2-▲ 440646-2

Bertoni, F.:Orfeo ed Euridice, w. Cecilia Gasdia (sop—Euridice), Delores Ziegler (mez—Orfeo), Bruce Ford (ten—Imeneo), C. Scimone (cnd), Venice Solisti, John McCarthy (cnd), Ambrosian Opera Chorus *(rec Vicenza, Italy, Aug 3-7, 1990)* Arts Music ▲ 47118-2 [DDD]

Handel, G.F.:Messiah, w. Patricia Schuman (sop), Lucia Valentini Terrani (alt), Gwynne Howell (bass), Bernard Soustrot (tpt), C. Scimone (cnd), Venice Solisti, John McCarthy (cnd), Ambrosian Singers *(rec S. Francisco Church, Schio, Italy, June 23-30, 1989)* Arts 2-▲ 471052 [DDD]

Handel, G.F.:Messiah, w. Patricia Schuman (sop), Lucia Valentini Terrani (alt), Gwynne Howell (bass), C. Scimone (cnd), Venice Solisti, John McCarthy (cnd), Ambrosian Singers *(rec Schio, Italy, June 23-30, 1989)* Arts 2-▲ 47105-2 [DDD]

Meyerbeer, G.:Il crociato, w. Linda Kitchen (sop), Y. Kenny (sop), R. Platt (sop), D. Montague (mez), D. Jones (mez), U. Benelli (bar), D. Parry (cnd), Royal PO, Geoffrey Mitchell Choir [I] *(rec CTS Studios, Wembley, London, Dec. 1990-June 1991)* Opera Rara 4-▲ OR 10

Ford-Livene, Nmon (ten)

Axelrod, L.:Songs, w. Louisa Ann Parks (sop), Michael Horton (ten), Malcolm Mackenzie (bar), Richard Bernstein (bass), M. Beltrami (cnd)—sels w. lyrics by Burns, Browning, Byron, Keats, Morris, Poe, Rossetti, Shelley, Wordsworth & Yeats Marquis ▲ MAR 171

Foreman, M. (sgr)

Argento, D.:Postcard from Morocco, w. S. Roche, B. Brandt, J. Hardy, Y. Marshall, V. Sutton, B. Busse, M. Foreman, P. Brunelle (cnd), Minnesota Opera Orch CRI 2-▲ CD 614 [ADD]

Forese, Angelo Lo (ten)

Cherubini, L.:Médée, w. M. Olivero (sop), E. Baggiore (sgr), L. Ganbelli (bass), N. Rescigno (cnd), Mantova Teatro Sociale Orch, Mantova Teatro Sociale Chorus [I] *(rec live, Mantova 1/23/71)* Myto 2-▲ 2 MCD 91136 [ADD]

Giordano, U.:Andrea Chénier (sels), w. Luisa Maragliano (sop), U. Rapalo (cnd), *(orch unknown)*—Vicino a te s'acqueta' *(rec Naples, 1969)* Golden Age of Opera ▲ GAO 204 [ADD]

Forest, Anthea de (sop)

Puccini, G.:Suor angelica, w. Elisabeth Carron (sop—Angelica), Joan Summers (sop—Genovieffa), Donna Owen (sop—Dolcina), Lou Ann Wyckoff (sop—Alms collector), Hanna Owen (sop—novice), Anthea De Forest (sop—novice), Charlotte Povia (mez—Abbess), Beverly Evans (mez—Monitress), Kay Creed (mez—Mistress), La Vergne Monette (sop/mez—lay sister), Joan August (sop/mez—lay sister), Pearle Goldsmith (sop/mez—other sister), Lila Herbert (sop/mez—other sister), Jodell Kenting (sop/mez—other sister), Ann Pretzat (sop/mez—other sister), Evelyn Sachs (cta—Princess), F. Patanè (cnd), *(orch unknown)* *(rec New York, Feb 23, 1967)* Legato Classics ▲ LCD 212-1 [ADD]

Forest, Jean-Michel (spkr)

Dussek, J.L.:The Sufferings of the Queen of France, w. Andreas Staier (pno), Jean-Michel Forest (speaker—Marie-Antoinette) *(rec German Radio, Cologne, Nov 24-28, 1992)* Capriccio ▲ 10 444 [DDD]

Forest, Michael (ten)

Corigliano, J.:Of Rage & Remembrance, w. Michelle DeYoung (mez), Michael Accinno (boy sop), Robert Baker (ten), Jason Stearns (bar), James Shaffran (bar), L. Slatkin (cnd), National SO Washington D.C., Washington Oratorio Society Men's Chorus *(rec J. F. K. Center for the Performing Arts, Washington, D. C., Nov 9-11, 1995 & Apr 19 &)* RCA Red Seal ▲ 09026-68450-2 [DDD]

Foresti, Sergio (bass)

Frescobaldi, G.:Arie musicali per cantarsi, w. G. Banditelli (mez), R. Bertini (sop), C. Cavina (alt), G. Maletto (ten), S. Naglia (ten), R. Alessandrini (cnd), Concerto Italiano Opus 111 2-▲ OPS 30-105/106

Peri, J.:Euridice, w. Monica Benvenuti (sop—Ninfa I/Venere), Rossana Bertini (sop—Dafne/Ninfa II), Gloria Banditelli (cta—Euridice/Ninfa III/Tragedia/Proserpina), Mario Cecchetti (ten—Aminta/Radamanto), Paolo Da Col (ten—Tirsi), Gianpaolo Fagotto (ten—Orfeo), Giuseppe Zambon (ct—Arcetro), Sergio Foresti (bass—Caronte/Pastore), Furio Zanasi (bass—Plutone), R. de Caro (cnd), Arpeggione Ensemble *(rec Bologna, Italy, Nov 1992)* Arts Music 2-▲ 47276-2 [DDD]

Perti, G.A.:Liturgy for Good Friday, w. Patrizia Vaccari (sop), Maura Pederzoli (sop), Cristina Calzolari (sop), Alida Oliva (sop), Claudia Bugli (sop), Lucia Bagnoli (alt), Cinzia Meneghel (alt), Renzo Bez (alt), Alessandro Carmignani (alt), Michel van Goethem (alt), Mauro Collina (ten), Vincenzo Di Donato (ten), Paolo Fanciullacci (ten), Giovanni Caccamo (ten), Paolo Da Col (ten), Marco Scavazza (bass), Luca Ferracin (bass), Paride Montanari (bass), Liuwe Tamminga (org), Sergio Vartolo (org), S. Vartolo (cnd), Bologna San Petronio Capella Musicale Orch—Omnes amici mei; De lamentatione Jeremiae Prophetae:Heth. Cogitavit; Velum templi; Vinea mea; De lamentatione Jeremiae Prophetae:Lamed. Matribus suis; Tamquam ad latronem; Tenebrae factae sunt; Animam meam; Tradiderunt me; Jesum tradidit; De lamentatione Jeremiae Prophetae:Aleph. Ego vir; Caligaverunt *(rec St. Petronio Basilica, Bologna, Mar 28-31, 1995)* Naxos ▲ 8.553321 [DDD]

Viadana, L. da:Vespri per l'Assunzione, w. S. Pozzer (sop), C. Calvino (alt), U. Müller Adam (ten), J. Clement (ten), L'Amaltea Ensemble, Vox Hesperia, St. Marco Capella Musicale Fonè ▲ FON 92F 08 [DDD]

Forget, Danièle (sop)

Campra, A.:Cants françaises, w. Arion Ensemble—Arion Analekta Fleur de Lys ▲ FL 2 3018

Clérambault, L.N.:Cants, w. Arion Ensemble—Léandre et Héro; Orphée Analekta Fleur de Lys ▲ FL 2 3018

Montéclair, M.P. de:Cants, w. Arion Ensemble—Pan et Syrinx Analekta Fleur de Lys ▲ FL 2 3018

Vivaldi, A.:Magnificat, RV.610, w. S. LeBlanc (sop), R. Cunningham (alt), H. Ingram (ten), J. Lamon (cnd), Tafelmusik, Tafelmusik Chamber Choir [L] Hyperion ▲ CDA 66247 [DDD]

Forgione, Giuseppe (bar)

Puccini, G.:La fanciulla del West (sels), w. Magda Olivero (sop—Minnie), Corinna Vozza (mez—Wowkle), Paolo Caroli (ten—Harry), Giacomo Lauri-Volpi (ten—Dick Johnson), Marco Rogani (ten—Pony Express Rider), Salvatore di Tommaso (ten—Trin), Adelio Zagonara (ten—Nick), Virgilio Ascorro (bar—Sid), Alfredo Colella (bar—Jake Wallace), Giuseppe Forgione (bar—Bello), Giancarlo Guelfi (bar—Jack Rance), Arturo la Porta (bar—Sonora), Gino Conti (bass—José Castro), Piere Passarotti (bass—Bill), Enzo Titta (bass—Larkens), Giulio Tomei (bass—Ashby), V. Bellezza (cnd), Rome Opera Orch, Rome Opera Chorus—Minnie, dalla mia casa son partito; Laggiù nel Soledad; Chi c'è per farmi i ricci; Oh! Mister Johnson, siete rimasto; Non so ben neppur io; Io non son che una povera fanciulla; No, Minnie, non piangete; Vorrei mettermi queste; Hallo!; Oh, se sapeste; Credo che abbiate torto; Ma ti giuro ch'io non ti lascio più; Vieni fuori!; Una parola sola!...Or son sei mesi; Che c'è di nuovo Jack?; È là; Siete pronto; Ch'ella mi creda; È Minnie!...È Minnie! *(rec Rome, Mar. 30, 1957)* Golden Age of Opera ▲ GAO 180 [ADD]

Forgues, Michel (nar)

Provost, S.:L'Adorable verrotière, w. Pauline Vaillancourt (sop), L. Vaillancourt (cnd), Nouvel Ensemble Moderne *(rec Studio 12, Maison de Radio-Canada, Montreal, May 12, 1993)* Ummus ▲ UMM 109

Forkush, Tony (nar)

Vees, J.:Rocket Baby, w. Jeff Krieger (elec vc/elec) CRI ("Emergency Music" series) ▲ CD 730 [DDD]

Formichi, Cesare (bar)

Cesare Formichi, w. A. Ketelby (cnd), H. Harty (cnd) *(rec 1916-32)* Preiser ("Lebendige Vergangenheit" series) ▲ PRE 89055 [ADD]

Forrester, Maureen (cta)

The Art of Maureen Forrester, w. Andrew Davis (pno) Mastersound ▲ DFCDI 212 [DDD]

Bach, J.S.:Arias, w. Lois Marshall (sop), Richard Lewis (ten), Norman Farrow (b-bar), Oscar Shumsky (vn), Brian Priestman (cnd), *(chorus unknown)*—Arias Nos. 32, 42, 120a, 132, & 182; Duet from Cant. 205 Vox Box 2-▲ CDX 5127 [ADD]

Bach, J.S.:Cant 3, w. Lois Marshall (sop), Richard Lewis (ten), Norman Farrow (b-bar), B. Priestman (cnd), *(orch unknown)*, *(chorus unknown)* Vox Box 2-▲ CDX 5127 [ADD]

Bach, J.S.:Cant 102, w. Richard Lewis (ten), Norman Farrow (b-bar), G. Leonhardt (cnd), Leonhardt Consort, Brian Priestman (cnd), *(chorus unknown)* Vox Box 2-▲ CDX 5127 [ADD]

Beethoven, L. van:Missa Solemnis, w. M. Arroyo (sop), R. Lewis (ten), C. Siepi (b-bar), E. Ormandy (cnd), Philadelphia Orch, Singing City Choir *(rec Mar. 29-30, 1967)* Sony Classical ("Essential Classics" series) ▲ SBK 53517 [ADD] ■ SBT 53517

Cherubini, L.:Mass in d, w. Patricia Wells (sop), George Shirley (ten), Justino Diaz (bass), N. Jenkins (cnd), Clarion Concerts Orch, Clarion Concerts Chorus *(rec Vanguard's 23rd Street Recording Studio* Vanguard Classics ▲ SVC-44 [AAD]

Duets:Ofra Harnoy & Friends, w. O. Harnoy (vc), Michael Dussek (pno), Orford String Quartet, Andrew Davis (pno), Jeanne Baxtresser (fl), Catherine Wilson (pno), Paul Brodie (sax), Shauna Rolston (vc), Armin Strings, Canadian Piano Trio, Adele Armin (vn) Mastersound ▲ MST 30 [DDD]

Gluck, C.W.:Orfeo ed Euridice, w. H. Steffek (sop—Amore), T. Stich-Randall (mez—Euridice), M. Forrester (cta—Orfeo), C. Mackerras (cnd), Vienna State Opera Orch, Vienna State Opera Chorus [Italian version w. additions composed for the French production] *(rec 6/66)* Vanguard Classics 2-▲ OVC 4039/40 [ADD]

Handel, G.F.:Arias, *(various orchs)*—arias from Giulio Cesare; Ottone; Hercules; Jephtha; Rodelinda; Samson; Serse; Theodora [E,I] *(rec 1960s)* CBC ("SM 5000" series) ▲ SMCD 5094 [ADD]

Handel, G.F.:Giulio Cesare in Egitto, w. Beverly Sills (sop), Fritz Wolff (ten), Spiro Malas (bass), Norman Treigle (bass), J. Redel (cnd), New York City Opera Orch, New York City Opera Chorus RCA Gold Seal 2-▲ 6182-2-RG [ADD]

Handel, G.F.:Theodora, w. H. Harper (sop), M. Lehane (mez), A. Young (ten), J. Lawrenson (bar), J. Somary (cnd), English CO, Amor Artis Chorale [E] *(rec 1968)* Vanguard Classics 2-▲ OVC 4074/5 [ADD]

Lullabies, w. John Arpin (pno) *(rec 5/88)* Pro Arte ▲ CDD 411 [DDD]

Mahler, G.:Des Knaben Wunderhorn, w. H. Rehfuss (b-bar), F. Prohaska (cnd), Vienna Festival Orch *(rec 5 & 6/63)* Vanguard Classics ▲ OVC 4045 [ADD]

Mahler, G.:Das Lied von der Erde, w. R. Lewis (ten), F. Reiner (cnd), Chicago SO [G] RCA Gold Seal ▲ 60178-2-RG [ADD]

Mahler, G.:Syms, w. E. Ameling (sop), H. Harper (mez), H. Prey (bar), B. Haitink (cnd), Royal Concertgebouw Orch Philips 10-▲ 442050-2

Mahler, G.:Sym 2, w. B. Valente (sop), G. Kaplan (cnd), London SO, London Sym Chorus MCA Classics 2-▲ MCAD 11011 [DDD]; 2-■ MCAC 11011 (D)

Mahler, G.:Sym 2, w. Benita Valente (sop), G. Kaplan (cnd), London SO, Ardwyn Singers, BBC Welsh Chorus, Cardiff Polyphonic Choir, Dyfed Choir Conifer Classics 2-▲ 75605-51277-2 [DDD]

Mahler, G.:Sym 2, w. K. Battle (sop), L. Slatkin (cnd), St. Louis SO, St. Louis Sym Chorus Telarc 2-▲ CD 80081/82 [DDD]

Mahler, G.:Sym 2, w. E. Cundari (sop), B. Walter (cnd), New York PO, Westminster Choir [G] Odyssey ■ YT 30848

Mahler, G.:Sym 3, w. Z. Mehta (cnd), Los Angeles PO London ("Double Decker" series) 2-▲ 443030-2

Ofra Harnoy & Friends, w. O. Harnoy (vc), Orford String Quartet, J. Baxtresser (fl), P. Brodie (sax), M. Dussek (pno), et al. Pro Arte ▲ CDD 552 [DDD]

Prokofiev, S.:Summer Day, Metropolitan Orch [E] CBC ("SM 5000" series) 2-▲ SMCD 5118-2 [DDD]

Respighi, O.:Lauda per la Natività del Signore, w. Valente (sop), Gordon (ten), M. Korn (cnd), Concerto Soloists Instrumental Ensemble, Philadelphia Singers RCA Red Seal ▲ 7787-2-RC [DDD] ■ 7787-4-RC (CrO2)

Rodgers, R.:Carousel, w. B. Cook (sop), S. Ramey (bass), S. Brightman (sop), et al., P. Geminiani (cnd), Royal PO, Ambrosian Singers [1987 studio cast] MCA Classics ▲ MCAD 6209 [DDD] ■ MCAC 6209

Tchaikovsky, P.:Queen of Spades, w. M. Freni (sop), V. Atlantov (ten), D. Hvorostovsky (bar), S. Ozawa (cnd), Boston SO, Tanglewood Festival Chorus RCA Red Seal ▲ 09026-61227-2 [DDD] □ 09026-61227-5

Tchaikovsky, P.:Queen of Spades, w. M. Freni (sop), V. Atlantov (ten), D. Hvorostovsky (bar), S. Ozawa (cnd), Boston SO, Tanglewood Festival Chorus RCA Red Seal 3-▲ 09026-60992-2 [DDD]

Verdi, G.:Requiem Mass, w. L. Amara (sop), R. Tucker (ten), G. London (bar), E. Ormandy (cnd), Philadelphia Orch, Westminster Choir Sony Classical ▲ SB2K 53252

Verdi, G.:Requiem Mass, w. L. Amara (sop), R. Tucker (ten), G. London (bar), E. Ormandy (cnd), Philadelphia Orch, Westminster Choir [L] Odyssey ■ YT 35230

The Voices of Living Stereo, Vol. 2, w. E. Farrell (sop), Birgit Nilsson (sop), Roberta Peters (sop), Leontyne Price (sop), Galina Vishnevskaya (sop), Rosalind Elias (mez), Shirley Verrett (mez), Marian Anderson (cta), Sergio Franchi (ten), Mario Lanza (ten), Richard Lewis (ten), Jan Pee, Alexander Dedyukhin (pno), Franz Rupp (pno), Leo Taubman (pno), George Trovillo (pno), Charles Wadsworth (pno), Boston Pops Orch [cnd:Arthur Fiedler], Boston SO [cnd:Charles Munch], Chicago SO [cnd:Fritz Reiner], RCA Victor Orch, RCA Victor Chorus [cnd:Wa *(rec Boston & Chicago & New York & Rome, 1957-1964)* RCA Living Stereo ▲ 09026-68167-2 [ADD]

Forrester, Maureen (nar)

Prokofiev, S.:Peter & the Wolf, w. A. Grossmann (cnd), Metropolitan Orch [E] CBC ("SM 5000" series) 2-▲ SMCD 5118-2 [DDD]

Prokofiev, S.:Winter Bonfire, w. A. Grossmann (cnd), Metropolitan Orch, Les Petits Chanteurs du Mont-Royal [E] CBC ("SM 5000" series) 2-▲ SMCD 5118-2 [DDD]

Forsini, Mario (bass)

Verdi, G.:I vespri siciliani, w. Maria Callas (sop—Duchess), Giorgio Kokolios Bardi (ten—Arrigo), Gino Sarri (ten—Danieli), Enzo Mascherini (bar—Guido di Monforte), Boris Christoff (bass—Giovanni da Procida), Mario Forsini (bass—Count Vaudemont), Bruneo Carmassi (bass—Bethune), E. Kleiber (cnd), Florence Teatro Comunale Orch, Florence Teatro Comunale Chorus *(rec live, Florence, 1951)* Melodram 3-▲ IMC 303016 [ADD]

Forst, Judith (mez)

French & Italian Opera Arias, w. Vancouver SO [cnd:Mario Bernardi] CBC Records ("SM 5000" series) ▲ SMCD 5063 [DDD]

1166

▲ = CD ♦ = Enhanced CD Δ = MD ■ = Cassette Tape □ = DCC

Förster, Jürgen (ten)

Mozart, W.A.:Entführung, w. Rosemarie Ronisch (sop), Jutta Vulpius (sop), Rolf Apreck (ten), Arnold van Mill (bass), O. Suitner (cnd), Dresden State Opera Orch, Dresden State Opera Chorus
Berlin Classics 2-▲ BER 9116

Forte, Cinzia (sgr)

Haydn, J.:Lo Speziale, w. Gil Manuel Beltran (ten—Sempronio), Daniela Broganelli (sgr—Volpino), Cinzia Forte (sgr—Grilletta), Paolo Pellegrini (sgr—Mengone), Maurizio Gambini (vc), Marco Tinarelli (db), Gabriele Catalucci (hpd), F. Maestri (cnd), In Canto CO *(rec 1993)*
Bongiovanni 2-▲ GB 2171/72 [DDD]

Fortes, Paulo (bar)

Gomes, A.C.:Il Guarany, w. Niza De Castro Tank (sop—Cecilia), Roque Lotti (ten—Ruy Bento), Manrico Patassini (ten—Pery), Paschoal Raymundo (ten—Don Alvaro), Paulo Fortes (bar—Gonzales), Juan Carlos Ortiz (b-bar—Il Cacico), Waldomiro Furlan (bass—Alonso), Josè Perrotta (bass—Don Antonio De Mariz), A. Belardi (cnd), Saõ Paulo Teatro Municipale Orch, Saõ Paulo Teatro Municipale Chorus *(rec Studios of the Teatro Municipal, Saõ Paulo, Brazil, 1959)*
Arkadia 2-▲ HP 617.2 [ADD]

Forti, Carlo (bass)

Puccini, G.:Manon Lescaut (sels), w. M. Favero (sop), R. Tebaldi (sop), J. Gardino (mez), G. Malipiero (ten), G. Nessi (ten), M. Stabile (bar), T. Pasero (b-bar), A. Toscanini (cnd), La Scala Orch, La Scala Chorus—Intermezzo; Act 3 *(rec live, Milan, May 18, 1946)*
Arkadia ("Historical Performances" series) 2-▲ 604 (m)

Fortuna, Maria (sop)

Rossini, G.:Music of, w. M. Lerner (sop), D. Voigt (sop), M. Horne (mez), K. Kuhlmann (mez), F. von Stade (mez), R. Blake (ten), C. Estep (ten), C. Merritt (ten), T. Hampson (b-bar), H. Runey (b-bar), J. Opalach (bass), S. Ramey (bass), R. Norrington (cnd), Orch of St. Luke's, New York Concert Chorale
EMI Classics ▲ CDC 54643

Fortunato, D'Anna (mez)

An American Collage:Music for Solo Voice & Chorus, w. Rooke Chapel Choir [cnd:W. Payn]
Albany ▲ TROY 098 [ADD]

American Works for Solo Voice and Chorus
Albany ▲ TROY 098 [DDD]

Battistin, J.B.:Héraclitie et Démocrite, w. J. Ostendorf (b-bar), E. Brewer (hpd), R. Palmer (cnd), Brewer CO [period instrs] *(rec 1985)*
Erasmus ▲ WVH 071 [DDD]

Beach, A.M.C.:Songs, w. Virginia Eskin (pno)—Ariette, Op. 1/4; Ah, Love But a Day, Op. 44/2; Just For This!, Op. 26/2; Dearie, Op. 43/1; Ye Banks and Braes o' Bonny Doone, Op. 12/2; Hymn of Trust, Op. 13; Chanson d'amour, Op. 21/1; Juni, Op. 51/3; Dark Garden, Op. 131; Elle et moi, Op. 21/3; Ecstasy, Op. 19/2; Dark is the Night, Op. 11/11; Rendezvous, Op. 120
Northeastern ▲ NR 9004-CD

Clérambault, L.N.:Cants, w. J. Ostendorf (bass-bar), E. Brewer (org), R. Palmer (cnd), Brewer CO—Le Soleil vainqueur (1721); Léandre et Héro [from Livre II (1713)] *(rec 1985)*
Erasmus ▲ WVH 071 [DDD]

Flowering of Vocal Music in America, 1767-1823, w. Susan Belling (sop), Cynthia Clarey (sop), Barbara Wallace (sop), Debra Vanderlinde (sop), Evelyn Petros (mez), Charles Bressler (ten), Richard Anderson (bar), James Tyeska (bar), Joseph McKee (bass), Cynthia Otis (hp), Leonard Rav
New World ▲ 80467-2

Handel, G.F.:Berenice, w. Julianne Baird (sop—Berenice), Andrea Matthews (sop—Alessandro), D'Anna Fortunato (mez—Selene), Jennifer Lane (mez—Demetrio), Drew Minter (alt—Arsace), John McMaster (ten—Fabio), Jan Opalach (bass—Aristobolo), R. Palmer (cnd), Brewer CO
Newport Classic 3-▲ NPD 85620/3 [DDD]

Handel, G.F.:Ezio, w. Julianne Baird (sop—Fulvia), Jennifer Lane (mez—Onoria), D'Anna Fortunato (cta—Ezio), Raymond Pellerin (alt—Emperor), Frederick Urrey (ten—Massimo), Nathaniel Watson (bar—Varo), Johannes Somary (org), R.A. Clark (cnd), Manhattan CO *(rec St. Jean Baptiste Church, New York, Mar. 1994)*
Vox Classics 2-▲ VOX 27503 [DDD]

Handel, G.F.:Faramondo, w. Julianne Baird (sop—Clotilde), Mary Ellen Callahan (sop—Adolfo), D'Anna Fortunado (mez—Faramondo), Jennifer Lane (mez—Rosimonda), Drew Minter (alt—Gernando), Peter Castaldi (bar—Gustavo), Mark Singer (bar—Tebaldo), Edward Brewer (hpd), R. Palmer (cnd), Brewer CO [period instrs]
Vox Classics 3-▲ VOX3 7536 [DDD]

Handel, G.F.:Imeneo, w. Julianne Baird (sop—Rosmene), Beverly Hoch (sop—Clomiri), D'Anna Fortunato (cta—Tirinto), Jan Opalach (bass—Argenio), John Ostendorf (bass—Imeneo), Edward Brewer (hpd), R. Palmer (cnd), Brewer CO
Vox Box 2-▲ CDX 5135 [DDD]

Handel, G.F.:Joshua, w. Julianne Baird (sop), John Aler (ten), John Ostendorf (b-bar), R. Palmer (cnd), Brewer CO, Brewer Chorus [period instrs]
Newport Classic 2-▲ NPD 85515/1-2 [DDD]

Handel, G.F.:Muzio Scevola, w. Julianne Baird (sop—Clelia), Andrea Matthews (sop—Fidalma), Erie Mills (sop—Orazio), D'Anna Fortunato (mez—Muzio), Jennifer Lane (mez—Irene), Frederick Urrey (ten—Tarquino), John Ostendorf (b-bar—Porsenna), R. Palmer (cnd), Brewer Baroque CO [period instrs] [l] *(rec 10/91)*
Newport Classic 2-▲ NPD 85540/2 [DDD]

Handel, G.F.:Siroe, Rè di Persia, w. Andrea Matthews (sop), Julianne Baird (mez), Steven Rickards (ct), Frederick Urrey (ten), John Ostendorf (b-bar), R. Palmer (cnd), Brewer Baroque CO [period instrs] [l]
Newport Classic 3-▲ NCD 60125 [DDD]

Handel, G.F.:Sosarme, Rè di Media, w. Julinne Baird (sop—Elmira), D'Anna Fortunato (mez—Sosarmo), Jennifer Lane (mez—Erenice), Drew Minter (ct—Melo), Rarmond Pellerin (ct—Argone), John Aler (ten—King Haliate), Nathaniel Watson (bass—Varo), Edward Brewer (hpd)
Newport Classic 2-▲ NPT 85575 [DDD]

Haydn, J.:La Cantarina, w. Brenda Harris (sop—Gasparina), Joyce Guyer (sop—Don Ettore), D'Anna Fortunato (mez—Apollonia), Jon Garrison (ten—Don Pelagio), R. Palmer (cnd), Palmer CO *(rec St. Michael's Church, New York City, Apr. 1994)*
Newport Classic ▲ NPD 85595 [DDD]

Jaffe, S.:Songs with Ensemble, w. W. Purvis (cnd), Speculum Musicae *(rec Oct. 22 & 23, 1993)*
Bridge ▲ BCD 9047 [DDD]

Mozart, W.A.:Requiem, w. Lorna Haywood (sop), Partick Romero (ten), John Cheek (bass), J. Sommary (cnd), Amor Artis Orch, Amor Artis Chorale [period instrs] *(rec St. Jean Baptiste Church, New York City, Mar 1996)*
Vox Classics ▲ VOX 7534 [DDD]

On This Day Earth Shall Ring!, w. Rooke Chapel Choir, Rooke Chapel Ringers, Elizabeth Etters-Asmus (hp), David Cover (org), William Payn (cnd) *(rec Rooke Chapel, Bucknell Univ, Feb & May 1995)*
Albany ▲ TROY 177 [DDD]

Paine, J.K.:St. Peter, w. J. Ommerlé (sop), P. Kelly (ten), D. Evitts (bar), G. Schuller (cnd), Boston Pro Arte CO, Back Bay Chorale [E] *(rec live in concert at Sanders Theater, Cambridge, Mass., 5/21/89)*
GM 2-▲ 2027CD 2

Regondi, G.:Songs, w. Julie Lustman (pno)—As Slowly Part the Shades of Night; L'Avviso; Tell Me Heart! Why So Desponding?; Absence *(rec Feb. & May, 1994)*
Bridge ▲ BCD 9055 [DDD]

Sowerby, L.:Songs, w. Veronica Macchia-Kadlubkiewicz (vn), Tessa van Buskirk (vn), Virginia Christensen (va), Michael Curry (vc)—Premonition; Kisses; Midnight; Reassurance; Adventure [all text L. E. Thomas]
Gasparo ▲ GSCD 315 [DDD]

Sowerby, L.:Songs of Resignation, w. Veronica Macchia-Kadlubkiewicz (vn), Steven Jackson (cl), Anthony de Mare (pno)
Gasparo ▲ GSCD 315 [DDD]

Thomson, V.:Lord Byron, w. J. Ommerlé (sop), M. Lord (ten), R. Zeller (bar), R. Johnson (bar), J. Bolle (cnd), Monadnock Music Festival Orch [E] *(rec live, Aug. 31 & Sept. 2, 1991)*
Koch International Classics 2-▲ KIC 7124-2 [DDD]

Fortune, George (bass)

Dvořák, A.:Armida, w. Joanna Borowska (sop—Armida), Monika Brychtová (sgr—Siren), Wieslaw Ochman (ten—Rinald), Richard Sporka (ten—Dudo), Jan Markvart (bar—Sven), Pavel Daniluk (bass—King), George Fortune (bass—Ismen), Zdenek Harvánek (bass—Ubald), Miloslav Podskalský (bass—Peter), Milan Bürger (sgr—Gernand), Roman Janál (sgr—Muezzin/Hlasatel), Vratislav Kříz (sgr—Gottfried), Vladimír Nacházel (sgr—Roger), G. Albrecht (cnd), Czech PO, Prague Chamber Choir *(rec 1995)*
Orfeo 2-▲ 404962 [DDD]

Massenet, J.:Thérèse, w. Agnes Baltsa (mez—Thèrése), Francisco Araiza (ten—Armand), Gino Sinimberghi (ten—Officer), George Fortune (bass—André), Giancarlo Luccardi (bass—Morel), Eftimios Michalopoulos (sgr—Officer/Municipal Officer), G. Albrecht (cnd), Rome RAI SO, Giuseppe Piccillo (cnd), Rome RAI Chorus
Orfeo ▲ 387961 [DDD]

Fortune, George (bass) (cont.)

Spontini, G.:Olympia, w. J. Varady (sop), S. Toczyska (mez), F. Tagliavini (ten), D. Fischer-Dieskau (bar), J. Becker (bass), G. Albrecht (cnd), Berlin RSO, Berlin Radio Chorus [Paris version]
Orfeo 2-▲ 137862 [DDD]

Wolf-Ferrari, E.:La vita nuova, w. Celina Lindsley (sop), R. Bader (cnd), Berlin RSO, St. Hedwig's Cathedral Children's Choir
Koch Schwann ▲ SCH 312672 [DDD]

Foscale, M. C. (sgr)

Puccini, G.:Madama Butterfly, w. C. Petrella (sop—Madama Butterfly), M. Masini (mez—Suzuki), M. C. Foscale (sgr—Kate Pinkerton), F. Tagliavini (ten—Pinkerton), M. Caruso (ten—Goro), G. Taddei (bar—Sharpless), A. Albertini (bar—Yamadori), A. Biancardo (bass—Bonze), A. Questa (cnd), Turin RAI Orch, Cetra Chorus *(rec 1953)*
Cetra Classic 2-▲ CDO 10 [AAD]

Foster, Norman (bass)

Bach, J.S.:Cant 70, w. A. Felbermayer (sop), E. Wiens (sop), H. M. Welfing (ten), F. Prohaska (cnd), Vienna State Opera Orch, Vienna State Opera Chorus [G] *(rec June 1957)*
Vanguard Classics ("The Bach Guild" series) ▲ OVC 2010 [ADD]

Mahler, G.:Kindertotenlieder, w. J. Horenstein (cnd), Bamberg SO *(rec 1955)*
Vox Box ("Legends" series) 2-▲ CDX2 5509 [ADD]

Mahler, G.:Lieder eines fahrenden Gesellen, w. J. Horenstein (cnd), Bamberg SO *(rec Bamberg, 1954)*
Vox Legends 2-▲ CDX2 5529

Foster, Susan (sop)

Weisgall, H.:Six Characters in Search of an Author, w. E. Byrne (sop—Stepdaughter), S. Foster (sop—Prompter), E. Furtal (sop—Coloratura), J. King (mez—Mezzo), N. Maultsby (mez—Mother), P. LoVerne (cta—Madame Pace), D. Pritchett (alt—Wardrobe Mistress), B. Fowler (ten—Tenore Boffo), K. Anderson (ten—Director), A. Schroeder (bar—Accompanist), P. Zawisza (bar—Stage Manager), R. Orth (bar—Father), G. Lehman (bar—Son), M. Wadsworth (b-bar—Basso Cantante), L. Schaenen (cnd), Chicago Lyric Opera Orch, Lyric Opera Center Chorus *(rec Chicago, June 14 & 16, 1990)*
New World 2-▲ 80454-2

Fouché, Guy (ten)

Berlioz, H.:La Damnation de Faust, w. Régine Crespin (sop—Marguerite), Guy Fouché (ten—Faust), Michel Roux (bar—Méphistophélès), Peter van der Bilt (bass—Brander), J. Fournet (cnd), Amsterdam Radio PO, Groot Omroepkoor *(rec Amsterdam, Mar 23, 1963)*
Bella Voce 2-▲ BLV 107.202 [AAD]

Chabrier, E.:Songs, w. Renée Doria (sop), Julien Giovannetti (bar), André Rabot (bn), Tasso Janopoulo (pno)—Lied; Tes yeux bleus; Sommation irrespectueuse; Toutes les fleurs; Ruy blas [A quoi bon entendre...]; Credo d'amour; Romance de l'étoile; Villanelle des petits; Les cigales; Ballade des gros dindons; Pastorale des cochons roses; L'île heureuse; Chanson pour jeanne; Duo de l'ouvreuse de l'opéra-comique et de l'employé du bon-marché; L'invitation au voyage
Accord ▲ ACD 201392 [AAD]

Fouchécourt, Jean-Paul (ten)

Brossard, S. de:Motets, w. N. Rime (sop), I. Honeyman (ten), B. Deletré (bass), M. Gester (cnd), Parlement de Musique—Salve Rex Christe; Psallite Superi; Qui non diligit te; O Domine quia refugium; Templa nunc fument; Oratorio seu Dialogus Poenitentis animae cum Deo; Festis laeta sonent [L] *(rec 1992)*
Opus 111 ▲ OPS 30-69 [DDD]

Campra, A.:Messe de Requiem, w. Véronique Gens (sop), Anne Gotkovski (sop), Joseph Cornwell (ten), Peter Harvey (bar), H. Niquet (cnd), Concert Spirituel Orch, Concert Spirituel Vocal Ensemble
Adda ▲ ADD 241952 [DDD]

Campra, A.:Motets, w. Véronique Gens (sop), Anne Gotkovski (sop), Joseph Cornwell (ten), Peter Harvey (bar), H. Niquet (cnd), Concert Spirituel Orch, Concert Spirituel Vocal Ensemble—Benedictus Dominus
Adda ▲ ADD 241952 [DDD]

Campra, A.:Motets, w. Véronique Gens (sop), Anne Gotkovski (sop), Douglas Nasrawi (ten), Peter Harvey (bar), Marcos Loureiro de Sà (bar), Kevin Mallon (vn), H. Niquet (cnd), Concert Spirituel Orch, Concert Spirituel Vocal Ensemble—Te Deum; Notus in Judea Deus; Deus in Nomine Tuo
Adda ▲ ADD 241942 [DDD]

Clérambault, L.N.:Cants, w. Noémi Rime (sop), Nicolas Rivenq (bass), Hiro Kurosaki (vn), Ryo Terakado (vn), Marc Hantaï (fl), Eric Bellocq (thb), Elisabeth Matiffa (b vl), Bruno Croscet (basse de vn), W. Christie (cnd), Les Arts Florissants—Pyrame et Tisbé, La Muse de l'opéra ou les Caractères Lyriques, La Mort d'Hercule, Orphée
Musique d'Abord ▲ HMA 1901329

Couperin, F.:Motets, w. Sandrine Piau (sop), C. Pelon (sop), J. Corréas (bass), Les Talens Lyriques—Quatre versets d'un motet composé de l'ordre du Roy (1703); Verset du motet de l'année dernièr; Sept versets d'un motet composé de l'ordre du Roy (1704); Motet à Sainte Suzanne; Sept versets d'un motet composé de l'ordre du Roy (1705); Laudate Pueri Dominum rec. May 25-28, 1993
FNAC Music ▲ 592244 [DDD]

Desmarets, H.:Motets, w. Sarah Leonard (sop), Norman Richard (b-bar), C. Jackson (cnd), Montreal Ancient Music Ensemble, Les Violons du Roy—Domine ne in furore; Usquequo Domine Confitebor Tibi Domine; Lauda Jerusalem; Marche Lorraine
K617 2-▲ 7053

Fauré, G.:Songs, w. Natalie Dessay (sop), Béatrice Uria-Monzon (mez), François Le Roux (bar), Jeff Cohen (pno)—complete songs grouped by poets [Leconte de Lisle; Charles Baudelaire; Paul Verlaine; Jean de la Ville de Mirmont; Armand Silvestre; Victor Hugo; Théophile Gautier; 5 Melodies of Venice; Sully Prudhomme; Albert Samain; Louis Pommey; Paul de Chodens; Marc Monnier; Romain Bussine; Victor Wilder; Georgette Deblads; Villiers de l'Isle Adam; Charles Grandmougin; Henri de Régnier; Stéphan Bordèse; Charles Van Lerberghe; Baronne de Brimont; Maurice Maeterlinck; Edmond Haraucourt; Molière
REM 4-▲ REM 311179 [DDD]

Lalande, M.-R. de:Motets, w. V. Gens (sop), S. Piau (sop), A. Steyer (sop), F. Piolino (ten), J. Corréas (bass), W. Christie (cnd), Les Arts Florissants [L]
Harmonia Mundi France ▲ HMC 901351

Lalande, M.-R. de:Te Deum, w. V. Gens (sop), S. Piau (sop), A. Steyer (sop), F. Piolino (ten), J. Corréas (bass), W. Christie (cnd), Les Arts Florissants [L]
Harmonia Mundi France ▲ HMC 901351

Lully, J.-B.:Phaëton, w. V. Gens (sop), J. Smith (sop), R. Yakar (sop), H. Crook (ten), M. Minkowski (cnd), Musiciens du Louvres
Erato 2-▲ 91737

Purcell, H.:Dido & Aeneas, w. Véronique Gens (sop—Dido), Sophie Marin-Degor (sop—Belinda), Sophie Daneman (sop—2nd woman/1st witch), Gaëlle Mechaly (sop—2nd witch), Claire Brua (mez—Sorceress), Steve Dugardin (alt—Chorus), Jean-Paul Fouchécourt (ten—Spirit/Sailor), Nathan Berg (b-bar—Aeneas), Jonathan Arnold (bass—Chorus), William Christie (hpd), W. Christie (cnd), Les Arts Florissants *(rec Massy Opera Theatre, Nov. 8-11, 1994)*
Erato ▲ 98477-2 [DDD]

Rameau, J.P.:Hippolyte et Aricie, w. Véronique Gens (sop), Bernarda Fink (cta), Laurent Naouri (bar), Russell Smythe (bar), M. Minkowski (cnd), Louvre Musicians, Sagittarius Vocal Ensemble
Archiv 3-▲ 445853-2

Rameau, J.P.:Les Indes galantes, w. C. McFadden (sop), S. Piau (sop), I. Poulenard (sop), N. Rime (sop), M. Ruggeri (sop), H. Crook (ten), J.-P. Fouchecourt (ten), N. Rivenq (bar), J. Corréas (bass), B. Delétré (bass), W. Christie (cnd), Les Arts Florissants [F]
Harmonia Mundi France 3-▲ HMC 901367/69

Rameau, J.P.:Motets, w. I. Desrochers (sop), V. Gens (sop), H. Lamy (ten), P. Harvey (bar), M. Loureiro de Sà (bar), S. Imbodem (bass), *(orch unknown)*—Deus noster refugium; Quam dilecta; In convertendo [L] *(rec Apr. 13-18, 1992)*
FNAC Music ▲ 592096 [DDD]

Strauss, R.:Krämerspiegel, w. Christian Ivaldi (pno)
Adès ▲ ADE 141772

Varèse, E.:Un Grand sommeil noir, w. Haridas Greif (pno)
Memoire Vive ▲ CD 262024

Foulkes, Stephen (bar)

Dvořák, A.:Mass, w. Coupe (trb), S. Taylor (ct), P. Cave (ten), A. Pinel (org), M. Archer (cnd), Bristol Cathedral Choir [L]
Meridian ▲ CDE 84188

Tučapsky, A.:The Sacrifice, w. Colin Hunt (org), Nigel Perrin (cnd), Bath Camerata *(rec Wells Cathedral, Jan 27, 1996)*
SOMM ▲ SOMMCD 205 [DDD]

Fourcade, Philippe (bass)

Donizetti, G.:La fille du régiment, w. Edita Gruberová (sop), Rosa Laghezza (mez), Deon van der Walt (sgr), François Castel (sgr), M. Panni (cnd), Munich RSO, Bavarian Radio Chorus
Nightingale Classics 2-▲ NIG 70566

Gounod, C.:Faust, w. C. Gasdia (sop), B. Fassbaender (mez), S. Mentzer (mez), J. Hadley (ten), A. Agache (bar), C. Rizzi (cnd), Welsh National Opera Orch, Welsh National Opera Chorus
Teldec 3-▲ 90872

Schubert, Franz:Mass 2, w. M. Pares-Reyna (sop), Fletcher (sgr), M. Piquemal (cnd), Harmonia Nova Orch Ensemble, Michel Piquemal Vocal Ensemble [L]
Gallo ▲ CD 584 [DDD]

Fourcade, Philippe (bass) (cont.)
Schubert, Franz:Mass 4, w. M. Pares-Reyna (sop), N. Stutzmann (alt), Fletcher (ten), M. Piquemal (cnd), Harmonia Nova Orch Ensemble, Michel Piquemal Vocal Ensemble [L] Gallo ▲ CD 584 [DDD]

Fourié, George (sgr)
Refice, L.:Cecilia, w. R. Scotto (sop), H. Theyard (ten), A. Campori (cnd), *(orch unknown)*—abriged version *(rec live 1976)* Vai Audio ▲ VAIA 1042 [ADD]

Fournet, Anne (nar)
Stravinsky, I.:Perséphone, w. Anthony Rolf-Johnson (ten), K. Nagano (cnd), London PO Virgin Classics ▲ ZDMB 61249
Stravinsky, I.:Perséphone, w. A. Rolfe-Johnson (ten), K. Nagano (cnd), London PO, Tiffin Boys' School Choir, London Phil Chorus [F] Virgin Classics 2-▲ 59077 [DDD]

Fournier, Brigitte (sop)
Berlioz, H.:Songs, w. D. Montague (mez), C. Robbin (mez), H. Crook (ten), G. Cachémaille (bar), J.E. Gardiner (cnd), Lyon Opera Orch—Zaïde [Fournier]; La belle voyageuse [Montague]; La Captive [Robbin]; La mort d'Ophélie [Robbin]; Le jeune pâtre breton [Crook]; Aubade [Crook]; Le Chasseur danois [Cachémaille] [F] Erato ("Musifrance" series) ▲ 2292-45517-2 [DDD]
Carvalho, J. de S.:Te Deum, w. Naoko Okada (sop), Elisabeth Graf (cta), John Elwes (ten), Michel Brodard (bar), M. Corboz (cnd), Lisbon Gulbenkian Foundation Orch, Lisbon Gulbenkian Foundation Chorus Cascavelle ▲ CVL 1016 [DDD]
Haydn, J.:Mass 3, "Cäcilienmesse", w. Bernarda Fink (alt), Charles Daniels (ten), Marcus Fink (bass), M. Corboz (cnd), Lisbon Gulbenkian Foundation Orch, Lisbon Gulbenkian Foundation Chorus *(rec July 1993)* FNAC Music ▲ 592309 [DDD]
Orff, C.:Carmina burana, w. Peter Sigrist (ten), Michel Brodard (bar), Jean-Jacques Balet (pno), Mayumi Kameda (pno), Geneva Percussion Ensemble [version for 2 pnos & perc] Cascavelle ▲ CVL 1009 [DDD]
Pergolesi, G.B.:Stabat mater, w. Artur Stefanowicz (ct), A. Mysinski (cnd), Warsaw Soloists *(rec Warsaw Philharmonic Concert Hall, Warsaw, 1992)* Elysium ▲ GRK 705 [DDD]
Poulenc, F.:Gloria Sop, w. P. Crispini (cnd), European Concerts Orch, Evoe Choir Doron ▲ DRC 3022 [DDD]
Vivaldi, A.:Stabat Mater, w. Artur Stefanowicz (ct), A. Mysinski (cnd), Warsaw Soloists *(rec Warsaw Philharmonic Concert Hall, Warsaw, 1992)* Elysium ▲ GRK 705 [DDD]

Fournier, Sophie (sop)
Lefébure-Wély, L.J.A.:Music of, w. Sylvie de May (sop), Catherine Ravenne (alt), Antoine Espagno (db), Vincent Genvrin (org), La Lyre Seraphique, Pythagore Vocal Ensemble—Sainte cité, demeure permanente; Récit de Hautbois ou de Trompette harmonique; L'Encens divin; Offertoire [grand choeur]; Seigneur dès ma première enfance; Verset; Pleins de ferveur; Marche; Jour heureux, sainte allégresse; Esprit divin, Dieu de lumière; Andante, choeur de voix humaines; Afin d'être docile et sage; Mon fils, pour apprendre; Andante; Motet à la Sainte-Vierge; Andante; Du Roi des cieux tout célèbre la gloire; Scène pastorale; Andantino Media 7 ▲ 004 [DDD]
Mozart, W.A.:Così fan tutte, w. Sophie Marin-Degor (sop—Despina), Laura Polverelli (mez—Dorabella), Sophie Fournier (sgr—Fiordiligi), Nicolas Reveng (bar—Guglielmo), Patrick Donnelly (bass—Don Alfonso), Simon Edwards (sgr—Ferrando), J. Malgoire (cnd), La Grande Écurie et la Chambre du Roy Astrée 8-▲ E 8606

Fowler, Bruce (ten)
Handel, G.F.:Messiah, w. Karen Clift (sop), Catherine Robbin (mez), Victor Ledbetter (bar), M. Pearlman (cnd), Boston Baroque Orch, Boston Baroque Chorus [E] Telarc 2-▲ CD 80322 [DDD]
Handel, G.F.:Messiah (sels), w. Karen Clift (sop), Catherine Robbin (mez), Victor Ledbetter (bar), M. Pearlman (cnd), Boston Baroque Orch, Boston Baroque Chorus—Sinfonia; Comfort ye, my people; Every valley shall be exalted; And the glory of the Lord; And He shall purify; Behold, a virgin shall conceive; O thou that tellest good tidings to Zion; For unto us a Child is born; Rejoice greatly, O daughter of Zion; His yoke is easy; All we like sheep; Lift up your heads; The Lord gave the word; Their sound is gone out; Why do the nations?; Let us break their bonds asunder; He that dwelleth in heaven; Thou shalt break them; Hallelujah; I know that my Redeemer liveth; Since by man came death; Behold, I tell you a mystery; The trumpet shall sound; Then shall be brought to pass; O death, where is thy sting?; But thanks be to God; Worthy is the Lamb...Amen *(rec May 18–22, 1992)* Telarc ▲ CD 80348 [DDD]
Rossini, G.:Armida, w. R. Fleming (sop), C. Bosi (ten), J. Francis (ten), D. Kaasch (ten), G. Kunde (ten), I. Zennaro (ten), I. D'Arcangelo (bass), S. Zadvorny (bass), D. Gatti (cnd), Bologna Teatro Comunale Orch, Bologna Teatro Comunale Chorus *(rec Pesaro, Italy, Aug. 6–17, 1993)* Sony Classical 3-▲ S3K 58968 [DDD]
Telemann, G.P.:Der Tag des Gerichts, w. Patrice Michaels Bell (sop), Sandra Walker (mez), Karen Brunssen (mez), Kurt R. Hansen (ten), William Stone (bar), Douglas Anderson (bar), T. Wikman (cnd), Music of the Baroque Orch, Baroque Music Chorus *(rec live, St. Paul's United Church of Christ, Feb 23, 1992)* Music of the Baroque 2-▲ MB 107
Weisgall, H.:Six Characters in Search of an Author, w. E. Byrne (sop—Stepdaughter), S. Foster (sop—Prompter), E. Furtal (sop—Coloratura), J. King (mez—Mezzo), N. Maultsby (mez—Mother), P. LoVerne (cta—Madame Pace), D. Pritchett (alt—Wardrobe Mistress), B. Fowler (ten—Tenore Boffo), K. Anderson (ten—Director), A. Schroeder (bar—Accompanist), P. Zawisza (bar—Stage Manager), R. Orth (bar—Father), G. Lehman (bar—Son), M. Wadsworth (b-bar—Basso Cantante), L. Schaenen (cnd), Chicago Lyric Opera Orch, Lyric Opera Center Chorus *(rec Chicago, June 14 & 16, 1990)* New World 2-▲ 80454-2

Franc, Tugomir (bass)
Mozart, W.A.:Clemenza, w. M. Casula (sop), L. Popp (sop), T. Berganza (mez), B. Fassbaender (mez), F. Krenn (bass), I. Kertész (cnd), Vienna State Opera Orch, Vienna State Opera Chorus London ("Grand Opera" series) 2-▲ 430105-2 [ADD]
Mozart, W.A.:Requiem, w. E. Ameling (sop), M. Horne (mez), U. Benelli (bar), I. Kertész (cnd), Vienna PO, Vienna State Opera Chorus London ("Weekend Classics" series) ▲ 417681-2 [ADD] ▮ 417681-4
Verdi, G.:Don Carlos, w. S. Jurinac (sop—Elisabetta), L. Rysanek (sop—Celestial Voice), F. Cossotto (mez—Princess Eboli), L. Dutoit (boy sop—Tebaldo), P. Domingo (ten—Don Carlo), E. Majkut (ten—Count of Lerma), M. Sereni (bar—Rodrigo), C. Siepi (bass—Philip II), I. Vinco (bass—Grand Inquisitor), T. Franc (bass—Friar), S. Varviso (cnd), Vienna State Opera Orch, Vienna State Opera Chorus Standing Room Only 2-▲ SRO 850 [ADD]
Wagner, R.:Parsifal, w. C. Ludwig (mez), E. Höngen (cta), H.-M. Uhle (ten), H. Hotter (b-bar), W. Berry (bass), H. von Karajan (cnd), Vienna State Opera Orch, Vienna State Opera Chorus [G] *(rec live 4/1/61)* Arkadia 3-▲ 219 (m) [ADD]

Francardi, L. (ten)
Verdi, G.:Nabucco, w. C. Mancini (sop—Abigaille), G. Gatti (sop—Fenena), B. Preziosa (sop—Anna), M. Binci (ten—Ismaele), L. Francardi (ten—Abdallo), P. Silveri (bar—Nabucodonosor), A. Cassinelli (bass—Zaccaria), A. Gaggi (bass—High Priest of Baal), F. Previtali (cnd), Rome RAI Orch, Rome RAI Chorus *(rec Rome, 1951)* Cetra Classic 2-▲ CDO 26 [ADD]

Franceschetto, Romano (bass)
Donizetti, G.:La bella prigioniera, w. S. Rigacci (sop), P. Pellegrini (sgr), F. Maestri (cnd), In Canto CO *(rec Apr. 1992)* Bongiovanni 2-▲ GB 2109/10 [DDD]
Donizetti, G.:Rita, or Le mari battu, w. U. Benelli (bar), S. Figacci (sgr), G. Manini (sgr), F. Maestri (cnd), In Canto CO *(rec Sept. 1990)* Bongiovanni 2-▲ GB 2109/10 [DDD]
Grétry, A.-E.-M.:Denys le tyran, w. S. Donzelli (sgr), C. Di Segni (ten), B. De Simone (bar), F. Vizioli (cnd), Italian International Orch, Ars Pulcherrima Artium Chorus [F] *(rec live, Fermo, Palazzo Sassatelli, 1989)* Memories ▲ DR 3106 [DDD]
Hasse, J.A.:La Contadina, w. Susanna Rigacci (sop), F. Maestri (cnd), In Canto CO [I] *(rec Oct. 5, 1991)* Bongiovanni ▲ GB 2128 [DDD]
Marcello, B.:Il pianto e il riso delle quattro stagioni, w. S. Piccollo (sop—Primavera), A. Carmignani (ct—Estate), M. Beasley (ten—Autunno), F. Ghiglione (cnd), Don Milani Cultural Association Orch, G. B. Trofello Schola Cantorum *(rec Mar. 29, 1992)* Bongiovanni 2-▲ GB 2159/60 [DDD]
Morlacchi, F.:Nuovo barbiere, w. A. Ruffini (sop), G. Gatti (sop), M. Comencini (ten), A. Tomicich (bass), G. Catalucci (cnd), Orch Giovanile In Canto [I] *(rec live 9/9/89)* Bongiovanni 2-▲ GB 2085/86 [DDD]

Franchi, Bruno (sgr)
Verdi, G.:I lombardi alla prima crociata, w. Renata Broilo (sop), Maria Vitale (sop), Miriam Pirazzini (mez), Aldo Bertocci (ten), Mario Frosini (sgr), Mario Petri (bass), Gustavo Gallo (sgr), Renato Pasquali (sgr), M. Wolf-Ferrari (cnd), Milan RAI Lyric Orch, Milan RAI Chorus *(rec 1954)* Cetra Classic 2-▲ CDON 41 [ADD]

Franchi, Sergio (ten)
The Voices of Living Stereo, Vol. 2, w. E. Farrell (sop), Birgit Nilsson (sop), Roberta Peters (sop), Leontyne Price (sop), Galina Vishnevskaya (sop), Rosalind Elias (mez), Shirley Verrett (mez), Marian Anderson (cta), Maureen Forrester (cta), Mario Lanza (ten), Richard Lewis (ten), Jan Peerce, Alexander Dedyukhin (pno), Franz Rupp (pno), Leo Taubman (pno), George Trovillo (pno), Charles Wadsworth (pno), Boston Pops Orch [cnd:Arthur Fiedler], Boston SO [cnd:Charles Munch], Chicago SO [cnd:Fritz Reiner], RCA Victor Orch, RCA Victor Chorus [cnd:Wa *(rec Boston & Chicago & New York & Rome, 1957–1964)* RCA Living Stereo ▲ 09026-68167-2 [ADD]

Franci, Benvenuto (bar)
Bizet, G.:Carmen, w. Ines Alfani Tellini (sop), Aurora d'Alessio Buades (cta), Aureliano Pertile (ten), L. Molajoli (cnd), La Scala Orch, La Scala Chorus *(rec Milan, 1933)* Phonographe 2-▲ PHG 5013 [ADD]
Iva Pacetti, w. Pacetti, Iva (sop), Beniamino Gigli (ten), Mario Basiola (bar) *(rec 1928–40)* Preiser ("Lebendige Vergangenheit" series) ▲ PRE 89124
Verdi, G.:Otello (sels), w. C. Muzio (sop), R. Ponselle (sop), H. Spani (sop), E. Caruso (ten), N. Fusati (ten), L. Melchior (ten), F. Merli (ten), F. Tamagno (ten), V. Maurel (bar), R. Stracciari (bar), T. Ruffo (bar) *(rec 1906–1933)* Music Memoria ▲ 30219

Francia, Piero (bar)
Verdi, G.:Ernani (sels), w. Felicia Weathers (sop—Elvira), Delia Wallis (mez—Giovanna), Placido Domingo (ten—Ernani), Wynford Evans (ten—Don Riccardo), Piero Francia (bar—Don Carlo), Agostino Ferrin (bass—Don Ruy Gomex de Silva), Robert Holl (bass—Iago), E. Downes (cnd), Omroep Orch, Omroep Chorus *(rec Amsterdam, Jan 15, 1972)* Bella Voce ▲ BLV 107.004 [AAD]

Francia, Piero (sgr)
Mascagni, P.:Isabeau, w. Marcella Pobbe (sop—Isabeau), Licia Galvano (mez—Giglietta), Pier Miranda Ferraro (ten—Folco), Orazio Gualtiero (bar—Cornelius), Rinaldo Rola (bass—Re Raimondo), Amelia Bazzini (sgr—Ermyngarde), Piero Benzi (sgr—L'araldo), Renata Davini (sgr—Ermynthrude), Piero Francia (sgr—Il Cavaliere), T. Serafin (cnd), San Remo SO *(rec Sanremo, Jan 13, 1962)* Bongiovanni ("Il Mito dell'Opera" series) 2-▲ GB 1135/36-2 [ADD]

Francis, Jeffery (ten)
Jommelli, N.:La Passione di Gesù Cristo, w. Debora Beronesi (sop), Anke Herrmann (sgr), Maurizio Picconi (sgr), A. de Marchi (cnd), Berlin Baroque Academy, Eufonia, Sigismondo D'India *(rec Mar 31–Apr 4, 1996)* K617 2-▲ 7063 [DDD]
Rossini, G.:Armida, w. R. Fleming (sop), C. Bosi (ten), B. Fowler (ten), D. Kaasch (ten), G. Kunde (ten), I. Zennaro (ten), I. D'Arcangelo (bass), S. Zadvorny (bass), D. Gatti (cnd), Bologna Teatro Comunale Orch, Bologna Teatro Comunale Chorus *(rec Pesaro, Italy, Aug. 6–17, 1993)* Sony Classical 3-▲ S3K 58968 [DDD]
Thome, D.:3 Psalms, w. Joan Catoni Conlon (cnd), Univ of Washington Chorale [E] Capstone ▲ CPS 8613

Franck, Joseph (ten)
Puccini, G.:Turandot, w. Montserrat Caballé (sop—Turandot), Leona Mitchell (sop—Liu), Remy Corazza (ten—Pang), Joseph Franck (ten—Pong), Robert Johnson (ten—Prince of Persia), Raymond Manton (ten—Altoum), Luciano Pavarotti (ten—Calaf), Aldo Bramante (bar—a mandarin), Dale Duesing (bar—Ping), Giorgio Tozzi (bass—Timur), R. Chailly (cnd), *(orch unknown) (rec San Francisco, Nov. 4, 1977)* Legato Classics 2-▲ LCD 188-2

Franco, Loretta di (sop)
Verdi, G.:La traviata (sels), w. Joan Sutherland (sop), Frederica von Stade (mez), Leo Goeke (ten), Lou Marcella (ten), Luciano Pavarotti (ten), Gene Boucher (bar), Raymond Gibbs (bar), Sherrill Milnes (bar), Louis Sgarro (bar), John Trehy (bar) Budget ("The Greatest Voice in Opera" series) ▲ SYP 112

Franco, Olga de (sop)
Mascagni, P.:Cavalleria rusticana, w. Delia Sanzio (sop—Santuzza), Mimma Pennaloni (mez—Lola), Olga de Franco (cta—Lucia), Giovanni Breviario (ten—Turiddu), Piero Biasini (bar—Alfio), C. Sabajno (cnd), La Scala Orch, La Scala Chorus VAI Audio ▲ VAIA 1082-2
Verdi, G.:La traviata, w. Olga de Franco (sop—Flora Bervoix/Annina), Anna Rosza (sop—Violetta Valery), Giordano Callegari (ten—Gastone), Alessandro Ziliani (ten—Alfredo Germont), Luigi Borgonovo (bar—Giorgio Germont), Arnoldo Lenzi (bar—Barone Douphol), Antonio Gelli (bass—Marchese d'Obigny/Dottor Grenvil), C. Sabajno (cnd), La Scala Orch, Vittore Veneziani (cnd), La Scala Chorus *(rec Oct–Nov 1930)* Arkadia 2-▲ CD 78001 (m) [ADD]
Verdi, G.:La traviata, w. Olga de Franco (sop—Flora Bervoix/Annina), Anna Rosza (sop—Violetta Valéry), Giordano Callegari (ten—Gastone), Alessandro Ziliani (ten—Alfredo Germont), Luigi Borgonovo (bar—Giorgio Germont), Arnoldo Lenzi (bar—Baron Douphol), Antonio Gelli (bass—Marquis d'Obigny/Dr. Grenvil), C. Sabajno (cnd), La Scala Orch, La Scala Chorus *(rec La Scala Theatre, Milan, Oct.–Nov. 1930)* VAI Audio 2-▲ VAIA 1108-2
Verdi, G.:Il trovatore, w. Maria Carena (sop—Leonora), Olga De Franco (sop—Ines), Irene Minghini Cattaneo (mez—Azucena), Aureliano Pertile (ten—Manrico), Giordano Callegari (ten—Ruiz/Messenger), Apollo Granforte (bar—Count), Bruno Carmassi (bass—Ferrando), Antonio Gelli (bass—Old Gypsy), C. Sabajno (cnd), La Scala Orch, Vittore Veneziani (cnd), La Scala Chorus *(rec 1930)* Arkadia ("The 78's" series) 2-▲ 78007 [ADD]

Frangoulis, Stefan (trb)
Bach, J.S.:Cant 110, w. W. Wiedl (trb), P. Esswood (ct), Stumpf (sgr), K. Equiluz (ten), M. van Egmond (b-bar), S. Lorenz (b-bar), N. Harnoncourt (cnd), Vienna Concentus Musicus, Tölz Boys' Choir [G] Teldec 2-▲ 2292-42603-2

Frank, Peter (bass)
Caldara, A.:Stabat Mater, w. Monika Frimmer (sop), Gloria Banditelli (mez), Gerd Türk (ten), L. Rovatkay (cnd), Capella Agostino Steffani, Westphalia Kantorei EMI Classics ▲ CDC 54845
Pergolesi, G.B.:Stabat mater, w. Monika Frimmer (sop), Gloria Banditelli (mez), Gerd Türk (ten), L. Rovatkay (cnd), Capella Agostino Steffani, Westphalia Kantorei EMI Classics ▲ CDC 54845
Vivaldi, A.:Son al St. Sepolcro, w. Monika Frimmer (sop), Gloria Banditelli (mez), Gerd Türk (ten), L. Rovatkay (cnd), Capella Agostino Steffani, Westphalia Kantorei EMI Classics ▲ CDC 54845

Frank, Susan Storey (sop)
Music from Cranberry Isles, w. Julius Baker (fl), Sara Lambert Bloom (ob), et al. Centaur ▲ CRC 2084

Franklin, T. (bar)
Mozart, W.A.:Don Giovanni, w. I. Souez (sop), L. Helletsgrüber (sop), A. Mildmay (sop), K. von Pataky (ten), J. Brownlee (bar), R. Henderson (bar), S. Baccaloni (bass), F. Busch (cnd), Glyndebourne Festival Orch, Glyndebourne Festival Chorus [I] *(rec 1936, orig. issued by HMV)* Pearl 3-▲ PEAS 9369 (m) [AAD]

Franks, Tara (sgr)
Hildegard Of Bingen:Sacred Songs, w. Jocelyn West (sgr), Vivien Ellis (sgr), Stevie Wishart (sgr/h-g), Hester Briant (sgr), Fiona Cunningham (sgr), Tara Franks (sgr), Emily Levy (sgr), Lucy Steele (sgr), Vickie Couperim (sgr), Julie Murphy (sgr), Oxford Girls' Choir—Honey & milk beneath her tongue; Ursula's virgins; The devil's virgins; Place of the ancient heart; Zeal of divinity; O fiery spirit; Red river falling; O orzchis ecclesia, Living-light angels; The clouds are grieving; The firstwoman; From their homeland; But the devil mocked; Song to Ecclesia *(rec Toddington, Gloucestershire, England, May 6–8, 1995)* Celestial Harmonies ▲ 13127-2

Frantz, Ferdinand (b-bar)
Beethoven, L. van:Fidelio (sels), w. E. Schlüte (sop), L. della Casa (sop), J. Patzak (ten), R. Schock (ten), H. Alsen (bass), W. Furtwängler (cnd), Vienna State Opera Orch, Vienna State Opera Chorus—Overture, 16 arias & choruses *(rec live, Salzburg Festspielhaus Aug. 3, 1948)* Melodram 2-▲ CDM 25009 [ADD]
Strauss, R.:Die Liebe der Danae (sels), w. L. Rysanek (sop), R. Kempe (cnd), Bavarian State Opera Orch—eleven arias from Acts 1,2 & 3 [G] *(rec 1953)* Melodram 3-▲ MEL 37061 (m) [AAD]
Strauss, R.:Salome, w. I. Borkh (sop—Salome), M. Klose (mez—Herodias), C. Ludwig (mez—Page), M. Lorenz (ten—Herodes), F. Fehringer (ten—Narraboth), F. Frantz (bar—Jokanaan), K. Schröder (cnd), Hessian RSO *(rec 1952)* Myto 2-▲ 93592

▲ = CD ♦ = Enhanced CD Δ = MD ▮ = Cassette Tape ▯ = DCC

Frantz, Ferdinand (b–bar) (cont.)

Wagner, R.:Die Meistersinger von Nürnberg, w. E. Grümmer (sop), M. Höffgen (cta), R. Schock (ten), G. Unger (ten), H. Prey (bar), B. Kusche (bar), G. Frick (bass), R. Kempe (cnd), Berlin PO *(rec 1956)* EMI Classics 4–▲ CDMD 64154

Wagner, R.:Die Meistersinger von Nürnberg, w. Tiana Lemnitz (sop—Eva), Bernd Aldenhoff (ten—Walther von Stolzing), Gerhard Unger (ten—David), Ferdinand Frantz (b–bar—Hans Sachs), Kurt Boehme (bass—Veit Pogner), Heinrich Pflanzl (bass—Sixtus Beckmesser), R. Kempe (cnd), Saxon State Orch *(rec Dresden, 1951)* Myto 4–▲ MCD 961138

Wagner, R.:Das Rheingold, w. L. Otto (sop), M. Muszely (sop), J. Blatter (mez), R. Stewart (mez), S. Wagner (mez), R. Schock (ten), H. Melchert (ten), B. Kusche (bass), J. Metternich (bass), R. Kempe (cnd), Berlin Staatskapelle *(rec Mar. 1959)* Berlin Classics ("Eterna" series) ▲ BER 2035 [ADD]

Wagner, R.:Der Ring des Nibelungen, w. K. Flagstad (sop), H. Konetzni (sop), E. Höngen (cta), G. Treptow (ten), S. Svanholm (ten), M. Lorenz (ten), L. Weber (bass), B. Herrmann (bass), W. Furtwängler (cnd), La Scala Orch, La Scala Chorus *(rec live 1950)* Arkadia 12–▲ 351 [ADD]

Wagner, R.:Der Ring des Nibelungen, w. Kirsten Flagstad (sop), Hilde Konetzni (sop), Elisabeth Höngen (cta), Max Lorenz (ten), Set Svanholm (ten), Günther Treptow (ten), Josef Hermann (bar), Ludwig Weber (bass), W. Furtwängler (cnd), La Scala Orch, La Scala Chorus *(rec Milan, 1950)* Music & Arts 12–▲ CD 914

Wagner, R.:Tristan und Isolde, w. Helena Braun (sop—Isolde), Margarete Klose (mez—Brangäne), Günther Treptow (ten—Tristan), Paul Kuen (ten—Ein Hirte), Albrecht Peter (bar—Melot), Fritz Richard Bender (bar—Ein Steuermann), Ferdinand Frantz (b–bar—König Marke), Paul Schöffler (b–bar—Kurwenal), H. Knappertsbusch (cnd), Bavarian State Opera Orch, Bavarian State Opera Chorus *(rec live, Prinzregententheater, July 23, 1950)* Orfeo 3–▲ 355

Franz, Paul (ten)

Paul Franz:Great Recordings *(rec 1911–29)* Preiser ("Lebendige Vergangenheit" series) ▲ PRE 89099 [ADD]

Franzen, Hans (bass)

Zemlinsky, A. von:Kleider machen Leute, w. E. Mathis (sop), H. Winkler (ten), V. Vogel (ten), C. Otelli (bar), R. Scholze (bass), W. Slabbert (sgr), R. Weikert (cnd), Zurich Opera Orch, Zurich Opera House Chorus [G] *(rec live, Zurich Opera House, 6/29/90)* Koch Schwann 2–▲ CD 314 069 [DDD]

Franzini, Carlo (sgr)

Wagner, R.:Die Meistersinger von Nürnberg, w. Bruna Rizzoli (sop), Fernanda Cadoni (mez), Luigi Infantino (ten), Vito Tatone (ten), Renato Capecchi (bar), Giuseppe Taddei (bar), Boris Christoff (bass), Giovanni Ciavola (bass), James Loomis (bass), Silvo Maionica (bass), Vito Susca (bass), Raimondo Botteghelli (sgr), Walter Brunelli (sgr), Ezio de Giorgi (sgr), Renzo Gonzales (sgr), L. von Matačić (cnd), Turin RAI Radio–TV SO, Turin RAI Chorus Stradivarius 4–▲ STV 12310

Frascati, Tommaso (ten)

Massenet, J.:Don Quichotte, w. Teresa Berganza (mez), Pina Malgarini (mez), Carlo Badioli (bass), Boris Christoff (bass), A. Simonetto (cnd), Milan RAI SO, Milan RAI Chorus Melodram 2–▲ CDM 27027

Puccini, G.:Turandot, w. Birgit Nilsson (sop—Turandot), Renata Tebaldi (sop—Liù), Jussi Björling (ten—Calaf), Alessio De Paolis (ten—Emperor Altoum), Piero de Palma (ten—Pang), Mario Sereni (bar—Ping), Adelio Zagonara (bar—Prince of Persia), Giorgio Tozzi (bass—Timur), Tommaso Frascati (bass—Pong), Leonardo Monreale (bass—Mandarin), E. Leinsdorf (cnd), Rome Opera Orch, Rome Opera Chorus *(rec Rome Opera House, July 3–11, 1959)* RCA Living Stereo 2–▲ 09026–62687–2 [ADD]

Fratarcangeli, M. (sgr)

Wolf–Ferrari, E.:I quatro rusteghi, w. A. P (Margarita), D. Lombardi (Lucieta), G. Merrino (Marina), M. Fratarcangeli (Felice) L. Belluso (Servant), A. Abete (Lunardo), M. Nicolini (Maurizio), G. Sorrentino (Filipeto), M. Peirone (Simon), D. Baronchelli (Cancian), A. Lemmo (Count Riccard) Arkadia–Akademia 2–▲ 139 [DDD]

Frati, Augusto (ten)

Donizetti, G.:Don Pasquale, w. E. Ravaglia (sop), P. Bottazzo (ten), R. Panerai (bar), F. Corena (bass), R. Muti (cnd), Vienna PO, Vienna State Opera Chorus [I] *(rec live, Salzburg, 8/11/71)* Melodram 2–▲ CDM 27094 [ADD]

Frauchiger, Ingrid (sop)

Daetwyler, J.:Rilke Songs (3), w. Reist String Quartet—[G] Grammont ▲ CTSP 15–2

Fredericks, W. (sgr)

Puccini, G.:Madama Butterfly, w. V. de los Angeles (sop), R. Nadell (mez), B. Faulkner (sgr), J. Thresh (sgr), D. Bernard (sgr), R. Torigi (sgr), A. Cosenza (bar), W. Herbert (cnd), New Orleans Opera Orch, New Orleans Opera Chorus *(rec live March 18, 1954)* Legato Classics 2–▲ LCD 168–2 [ADD]

Fredricks, Richard (bar)

Massenet, J.:Manon, w. B. Sills (sop), P. Domingo (ten), J. Rudel (cnd), New York City Opera Orch, New York City Opera Chorus *(rec live, 1969)* Melodram 2–▲ MEL 27054

Massenet, J.:Manon, w. Beverly Sills (sop—Manon), Plácido Domingo (ten—Des Grieux), Nico Castel (ten—Guillot), Richard Fredricks (bar—Lescaut), Robert Hale (bar—De Brétigny), Malcom Smith (bass—Count de Grieux), J. Rudel (cnd), New York City Opera Orch, New York City Opera Chorus *(rec live, New York, 1969)* Melodram 2–▲ IMC 205008 [ADD]

Puccini, G.:Tosca, w. Birgit Nilsson (sop—Floria Tosca), Puli Toro (mez—Shepherd), Jose Carreras (ten—Mario Cavaradossi), Joaquin Romaguera (ten—Spoleta), James Billings (bar—Sacristan), Richard Fredricks (bar—Baron Scarpa), Samuel Ramey (bass—Cesare Angelotti), William Ledbetter (sgr—Sciarrone), Richard Park (sgr—Cardinal), Don Yule (sgr—Jailer), J. Rudel (cnd), *(orch & chorus unknown)* *(rec Nov 13, 1974)* Legato Classics 2–▲ LCD–200–2

Freeman, Carroll (ten)

Sullivan, A.:HMS Pinafore, w. D. Hays (sop), M. Rawlins (sgr), E. Schilling (sgr), E. Johnson (cta), M. Elder (cnd), Rochester PO, Eastman Chorale members—highlights *(rec 11/89)* Pro Arte ▲ CDd 480 [DDD]

Sullivan, A.:The Mikado, w. D. Hays (sop), M. Rawlins (sgr), E. Schilling (sgr), E. Johnson (cta), M. Elder (cnd), Rochester PO, Eastman Chorale members—highlights *(rec 11/89)* Pro Arte ▲ CDd 480 [DDD]

Sullivan, A.:The Pirates of Penzance, w. D. Hays (sgr), M. Rawlins (sgr), E. Schilling (sgr), E. Johnson (cta), M. Elder (cnd), Rochester PO, Eastman Chorale members—highlights *(rec 11/89)* Pro Arte ▲ CDd 480 [DDD]

Freeney, Dionne (alt)

Soldier, D.:War Prayer, w. Jason White (ten), Wilbur Pauley (bass), R.A. Clark (cnd), Manhattan CO, Gospel Singers Newport Classic ▲ NPD 85589 [DDD]

Freier, Jürgen (bar)

Matthus, S.:Mirabeau, w. Carola Höhn (sop—Marie Antoinette), Carola Fischer (cta—Eveline Le Jay), Peter–Jürgend Schmidt (ten—Ludwig XVI), Jürgen Freier (bar—Honoré–Gabriel de Riqueti), Gerd Wolf (bass—Victor Riqueti), H. Fricke (cnd), Berlin State Opera Orch, Berlin State Opera Chorus *(rec Berlin, 1989)* Berlin Classics 2–▲ BER 1075 [DDD]

Schnittke, A.:Historia von D. Johann Fausten, w. Hanna Schwarz (mez—Fair Helen), Arno Raunig (alt—Mephostophiles), Eberhard Büchner (ten—Old Man), Jürgen Freier (bar—Dr. Johann Faustus), Jonathan Barreto–Ramos (sgr—Student), Jürgen Fersch (sgr—Student), Eberhard Lorenz (sgr—Erzähler), Christoph Johannes Wendel (sgr—Student), G. Albrecht (cnd), Hamburg State PO, Hamburg State Opera Chorus *(rec live, Hamburg, Germany)* RCA Red Seal 2–▲ 09026–68413–2

Freiman, Mark (bass)

Moore, D.:Ballad of Baby Doe, w. Jan Grissom (sop—Baby Doe), Dana Kreuger (mez—Augusta), Myrna Paris (cta—Mama), Brian Steele (bar—Horace), Mark Freiman (b–bar—W. J. Bryan), J. Moriarty (cnd), Central City Opera Orch, Central City Opera Chorus *(rec Central City, CO)* Newport Classic 2–▲ NPD 85593/2 [DDD]

Frellesvig, Anne (sgr)

Kuhlau, F.:Lulu, w. T. Kiberg (sop), K. von Binzer (ten), R. Saarman (ten), U. Cold (bass), E. Harbo (sgr), M. Schønwandt (cnd), Danish National RSO, Danish National Radio Choir [Da] Kontrapunkt 3–▲ 32009/11 [DDD]

Frémeau, Jean–Marie (bar)

Chaynes, C.:Jocaste, w. René Boutet (ten), André Cognet (b–bar), F. Chaslin (cnd), Rouen SO, Théâtre des Arts Chorus *(rec Rouen Theater, Rouen, France, 1993)* Chamade 2–▲ 5633/34

Fauré, G.:Requiem, w. Antoine Brouquet (sop), J.–P. Salanne (cnd), Domaine Musical Orch, Tarbes Midi–Pyrénées Régional Choir Adès ▲ ADE 204782 [DDD]

French, H. (sgr)

Rodgers, R.:Lido Lady (sels), w. P. Dare (sgr), C. Courtneidge (sgr), *(other artists unknown)* Pearl ("Flapper" series) ▲ PEA CD 9105 [ADD]

Freni, Mirella (sop)

Arias & Duets, w. L. Pavarotti (ten) London ▲ 421878–2 LA [ADD/DDD]

Bellini, V.:Beatrice di Tenda, w. C. Gonzales (mez), C. Desderi (bar), R. Casellato (ten), M. Arena (cnd), *(orch unknown)* *(rec live, Bologna 1976)* Legato Classics 2–▲ LCD 152–2 [ADD]

Bellini, V.:I Puritani, w. L. Pavarotti (ten), S. Bruscantini (bar), B. Giaotti (bass), R. Muti (cnd), Rome RAI SO, Rome RAI Chorus [I] *(rec live, Rome 7/8/69)* Verona 3–▲ 27029/31

Bellini, V.:I Puritani, w. Luciano Pavarotti (ten), Sesto Bruscantini (b–bar), R. Muti (cnd), Rome RAI SO, Rome RAI Chorus *(rec Rome, 1969)* Enterprise ("Palladio" series) 3–▲ ENTPD 4205 [ADD]

Bellini, V.:I Puritani, w. Mirelle Fiorentini (mez), Luciano Pavarotti (ten), Emilio Venturini (ten), Sesto Bruscantini (bar), Giovanni Antonini (bass), Bonaldo Giaiotti (bass), R. Muti (cnd), Rome RAI SO, Rome RAI Chorus Melodram 2–▲ CDM 27062

Bellini, V.:I Puritani, w. Mirella Freni (sop—Elvira), Rita Bezzi (mez—Enrichetta), Alfredo Kraus (ten—Arturo Talbot), Augusto Pedroni (ten—Sir Bruno Robertson), Attilio d'Orazi (bar—Sir Riccardo Forth), Raffaele Arié (bass—Sir Giorgio), Bruno Cioni (bass—Lord Gualtiero Walton), N. Verchi (cnd), Modena Teatro Comunale Orch, Modeno Teatro Comunale Chorus *(rec Modena Teatro Comunale, Dec. 26, 1962)* Legato Classics 2–▲ LCD 195–2 [ADD]

Bellini, V.:I Puritani (sels), w. Luciano Pavarotti (ten), Giovanni Antonini (bass), Bonaldo Giaiotti (bass), R. Muti (cnd), Rome RAI SO, Rome RAI Chorus—A te, o cara *(rec Rome, July 8, 1969)* Goldies ▲ GLD 63202 [ADD]

Bellini, V.:I Puritani (sels), w. Luciano Pavarotti (ten), Bonaldo Giaiotti (bass), R. Muti (cnd), Rome SO, Rome Sym Chorus—A te, o cara, amor talora *(rec live, Oct. 7, 1969)* RCA Gold Seal ▲ 09026–68014–2 [ADD]

Bizet, G.:Carmen, w. L. Price (sop), F. Corelli (ten), R. Merrill (bar), H. von Karajan (cnd), Vienna PO, Vienna State Opera Chorus [F] RCA Gold Seal 3–▲ 6199–2–RG [ADD] 2–■ 6199–4–RG

Bizet, G.:Carmen, w. L. Price (sop), F. Corelli (ten), R. Merrill (bar), H. von Karajan (cnd), Vienna PO, Vienna State Opera Chorus [F] RCA Gold Seal ▲ 60190–2–RG [ADD] ■ 60190–4–RG

Bizet, G.:Carmen, w. J. Norman (sop), N. Shicoff (ten), S. Estes (bass), S. Ozawa (cnd), French National Orch, French Radio Chorus [F] Philips 3–▲ 422366–2 [DDD]

Bizet, G.:Carmen, w. J. Norman (sop), N. Shicoff (ten), S. Estes (bass), S. Ozawa (cnd), French National Orch, French Radio Chorus [F] Philips ▲ 426040–2 [DDD] ■ 426040–4 □ 426040–5

Bizet, G.:Carmen, w. G. Bumbry (sop), J. Vickers (ten), J. Diaz (bass), H. von Karajan (cnd), Vienna PO, Vienna State Opera Chorus [F] *(rec live, Salzburg 1967)* Arkadia 3–▲ 221 [ADD]

Bizet, G.:Carmen, w. G. Bumbry (mez), J. Vickers (ten), K. Paskalis (bar), R. Frühbeck de Burgos (cnd), Paris Opera Orch, Paris Opera Chorus [opéra comique version] [F] EMI Classics ("Studio" series) 2–▲ CDMB 63643 [ADD]

Bizet, G.:Carmen (sels), w. Grace Bumbry (mez), Jon Vickers (ten), H. von Karajan (cnd), Vienna PO *(rec Salzburg, 1967)* Arkadia 3–▲ 498

Bizet, G.:Carmen (sels), w. Leontyne Price (sop), Franco Corelli (ten), H. von Karajan (cnd), Vienna PO, Vienna State Opera Chorus RCA Victor ▲ 09026–68021–2; ■ 09026–68021–4

Boito, A.:Mefistofele, w. M. Caballé (sop), L. Pavarotti (ten), N. Ghiaurov (bass), O. de Fabritiis (cnd), National PO London [I] London 3–▲ 410175–2 [DDD]

A Celebration Cantabile ("Biographies in Music" series) 2–▲ BIM 703–2

Donizetti, G.:Don Pasquale, w. G. Winbergh (ten), S. Bruscantini (bar), L. Nucci (bar), R. Muti (cnd), Philharmonia Orch, Ambrosian Opera Chorus EMI Classics 2–▲ CDCB 47068

Donizetti, G.:Don Pasquale (sels), w. G. Winbergh (ten), S. Bruscantini (bar), L. Nucci (bar), R. Muti (cnd), Philharmonia Orch, Ambrosian Opera Chorus EMI Classics ▲ CDC 54490

Donizetti, G.:L'elisir d'amore, w. N. Gedda (ten), R. Capecchi (bar), M. Sereni (bar), F. Molinari–Pradelli (cnd), Rome Opera Orch [I] EMI Classics (Studio) 2–▲ CDMB 69897 [ADD]

Donizetti, G.:La fille du régiment, w. L. Pavarotti (ten), W. Ganzarolli (bar), N. Sanzogno (cnd), La Scala Orch, La Scala Chorus *(rec 1969)* Memories 2–▲ MEM 4507 [AAD]

Donizetti, G.:La fille du régiment, w. A. di Stasio (mez), L. Pavarotti (ten), W. Ganzarolli (bar), W. Monachesi (bar), N. Sanzogno (cnd), La Scala Orch, La Scala Chorus [I] *(rec live, 2/11/69)* Melodram 2–▲ MEL 27045

Donizetti, G.:La fille du régiment, w. A. di Stasio (mez), L. Pavarotti (ten), W. Ganzarolli (bar), W. Monachesi (bar), N. Sanzogno (cnd), La Scala Orch, La Scala Chorus [I] *(rec live, 2/11/69)* Verona 2–▲ 27046/47 (m) [AAD]

Donizetti, G.:La fille du régiment (sels), w. Anna di Stasio (mez), Angelo Mercuriali (ten), Luciano Pavarotti (ten), Wladimiro Ganzarolli (bar), Walter Monachesi (bar), Giuseppe Morresi (bass), V. Gullino (sgr), Luisa Rezzadore (sgr), N. Sanzogno (cnd), La Scala Orch, La Scala Chorus Budget ("The Greatest Voice in Opera" series) ▲ SYP 108

Giordano, U.:Fedora, w. Mirella Freni (sop—Principessa Fedora), Adelina Scarabelli (sop—Contessa Olga), Silvia Mazzoni (mez—Dimitri), Monica Minarelli (sgr—Savoiardo), Placido Domingo (ten—Conto Loris), Ernesto Gavazzi (ten—Desiré), Aldo Bottion (ten—Barone Rouvel), Alessandro Corbelli (bar—Siriex), Luigi Roni (bass—Cirillo), Silvestro Sammaritano (bass—Baroff), Alfredo Giacomotti (bass—Gretch), Ernesto Panariello (bass—Lorek), Vincenzo Alaimo (sgr—Nicola), Arnold Bosman (sgr—Boleslao), Bruno Capisani (sgr—Sergio), Renato Zanchetta (sgr—Michele), G. Gavazzeni (cnd), La Scala Orch, La Scala Chorus *(rec La Scala, Apr 5, 1993)* Legato 2–▲ LCD 213–2 [ADD]

Gounod, C.:Faust, w. P. Domingo (ten), T. Allen (bar), N. Ghiaurov (bass), G. Prêtre (cnd), Paris Opera Orch [F] EMI Classics 3–▲ CDCC 47493 [ADD]

Gounod, C.:Faust, w. G. Raimondi (ten), N. Ghiaurov (bass), G. Prêtre (cnd), La Scala Orch, La Scala Chorus *(rec live 1967)* Melodram 3–▲ MEL 37005

Gounod, C.:Faust (sels), w. P. Domingo (ten), T. Allen (bar), N. Ghiaurov (bass), G. Prêtre (cnd), Paris Opera Orch, Orch de Paris, Paris Opera Chorus EMI Classics ▲ ZDM 63090

Gounod, C.:Roméo et Juliette, w. M. Freni (sop—Juliette), F. Corelli (ten—Roméo), H. Gui (bar—Mercutio), C. Càles (bar—Capulet), X. Depraz (bass—Frère Laurent), A. Lombard (cnd), Paris Opera Orch, Paris Opera Chorus EMI Classics ▲ CDMB 65290

Great Sopranos of Our Time, w. Maria Callas (sop), Joan Sutherland (sop), Renata Scotto (sop), Montserrat Caballé (sop), Elisabeth Schwarzkopf (sop), Victoria de los Angeles (sop), Ileana Cotrubas (sop), Edita Gruberova (sop) Classics for Pleasure ▲ CDEMX 9519 [ADD]

Handel, G.F.:Alcina, w. J. Sutherland (sop), T. Berganza (mez), R. Bonynge (cnd), London SO London ("Grand Opera" series) 3–▲ 433723–2 [ADD]

Leoncavallo, R.:Pagliacci, w. L. Pavarotti (ten), I. Wixell (bar), G. Patanè (cnd), National PO London, National Phil London Chorus [I] London 2–▲ 414590–2 [ADD]

Leoncavallo, R.:Pagliacci (sels), w. J. Varady (sop), L. Pavoratti (ten), P. Cappuccilli (bar), I. Wixell (bar), G. Gavazzeni (cnd), National PO London London ▲ 421870–2 [ADD]

Martucci, G.:La canzone dei ricordi, w. R. Muti (cnd), La Scala Orch *(rec Teatro Abanella, Milan, Italy, Jan 17–22, 1995)* Sony Classical ▲ SK 64582 [DDD]

Mascagni, P.:L'amico Fritz, w. L. Pavarotti (ten), V. Sardinero (bar), G. Gavazzeni (cnd), Royal Opera House Orch Covent Garden, Royal Opera House Chorus Covent Garden [I] EMI Classics 2–▲ CDCB 47905 [ADD]

Mascagni, P.:Cavalleria rusticana (sels), w. Julia Varady (sop), Luciano Pavoratti (ten), Piero Cappuccilli (bar), Ingvar Wixel (bar), G. Gavazzeni (cnd), National PO London London ▲ 421870–2 [ADD]

Massenet, J.:Manon, w. L. Pavarotti (ten), R. Panerai (bar), P. Maag (cnd), La Scala Orch, La Scala Chorus [I] *(rec live, 6/3/69)* Verona 2–▲ 27052/53 (m) [AAD]

Massenet, J.:Manon, w. L. Pavarotti (ten), R. Panerai (bar), P. Maag (cnd), La Scala Orch, La Scala Chorus [I] *(rec live, 6/3/69)* Melodram 2–▲ MEL 27046 [AAD]

Massenet, J.:Manon (sels), w. Luciano Pavarotti (ten), Franco Ricciardi (ten), Wladimiro Ganzarolli (bar), Giuseppe Morresi (bass), Antonio Zerbini (bass), Ida Farina (sgr), P. Maag (cnd), La Scala Orch, La Scala Chorus *(rec live, Milan, 1969)* Budget ("The Greatest Voice in Opera" series) ▲ SYP 110

Mirella Freni:40th Anniversary London ("Grandi Voici" series) ▲ 440412–2

Freni, Mirella (sop) (cont.)

Mozart, W.A.:Arias, w. Arleen Augér (sop), Kathleen Battle (sop), Irma Beilke (sop), Helena Braun (sop), Lisa Della Casa (sop), Maria Cebotari (sop), Ileana Cotrubas (sop), Helen Donath (sop), Reri Grist (sop), Edita Gruberova (sop), Elisabeth Grümmer (sop), Hilde Güden (sop), Ingeborg Hallstein (sop), Luise Helletsgruber (sop), Gundula Janowitz (sop), Sena Jurinac (sop), Erika Köth (sop), Evelyn Lear (sop), Wilma Lipp (sop), Margaret Marshall (sop), Edith Mathis (sop), Jarmila Novotna (sop), Margherita Perras (sop), Lucia Popp (sop), Elisabeth Rethberg (sop), Anneliese Rothenberger (sop), Elisabeth Schumann (sop), Elisabeth Schwarzkopf (sop), Graziella Sciutti (sop), Irmgard Seefried (sop), Graziella Sciutti (sop), Julia Varady (sop), Agnes Baltsa (mez), Margit Bokor (mez), Brigitte Fassbaender (mez), Christa Ludwig (mez), Ann Murray (mez), Francisco Araiza (ten), Anton Dermota (ten), Helge Rosvaenge (ten), Rudolf Schock (ten), Peter Schreier (ten), Leopold Simoneau (ten), Eric Tappy (ten), Richard Tauber (ten), Gösta Winbergh (ten), Josef Witt (ten), Fritz Wunderlich (ten), Christian Boesch (bar), Willy Domgraf-Fassbaender (bar), Karl Dönch (bar), Dietrich Fischer-Dieskau (bar), Erich Kunz (bar), Eberhard Wächter (bar), Hans Hotter (b-bar), Paul Schöffler (b-bar), Cesare Siepi (b-bar), José Van Dam (b-bar), Walter Berry (bass), Geraint Evans (bass), Nicolai Ghiaurov (bass), Alexander Kipnis (bass), Richard Mayr (bass), Kurt Moll (bass), James Morris (bass), Ezio Pinza (bass), Martti Talvela (bass), Giorgio Tozzi (bass), Hans Duhan (sgr), Res Fischer (sgr), Marie Gerhart (sgr), *(various orchs & cnds)*—sels from Idomeneo, Die Entführung aus der Serail, Le nozze di Figaro, Don Giovanni, Così fan tutte, Die Zauberflöte & various arias — Orfeo d'or ("Festspiel Dokumente" series) 5-▲ 408955

Mozart, W.A.:Complete Mozart Edition, w. K. Te Kanawa (sop), M. Arroyo (sop), S. Burrows (ten), I. Wixell (bar), C. Davis (cnd), Royal Opera House Orch, Royal Opera House Chorus Covent Garden — Philips 3-▲ 422541-2 [ADD]

Mozart, W.A.:Complete Mozart Edition, w. J. Norman (sop), Y. Minton (mez), I. Wixell (bar), C. Davis (cnd), BBC SO, BBC Sym Chorus — Philips 3-▲ 422540-2 [ADD]

Mozart, W.A.:Don Giovanni, w. G. Janowitz (sop), T. Zylis-Gara (sop), A. Kraus (ten), R. Panerai (bar), V. von Halem (bass), N. Ghiaurov (bass), H. von Karajan (cnd), Vienna PO, Vienna State Opera Chorus [I] *(rec live, Salzburg, Aug. 1, 1969)* — Memories 3-▲ HR 4362/64 (m) [ADD]

Mozart, W.A.:Nozze di Figaro, w. Gundula Janowitz (sop), Jane Berbié (mez), Frederica von Stade (mez), Michel Sénéchal (ten), José Van Dam (b-bar), Kurt Moll (bass), G. Solti (cnd), Paris Opera Orch, Paris Opera Chorus *(rec live, Paris, Apr 7, 1973)* — Agorá ("Phoenix" series) 3-▲ 515

Mozart, W.A.:Nozze di Figaro, w. Daniela Mazzucato (sop), Teresa Berganza (mez), Mirto Picchi (ten), Hermann Prey (bar), José Van Dam (b-bar), Paolo Montarsolo (bass), C. Abbado (cnd), La Scala Orch, La Scala Chorus *(rec live, Apr 22, 1974)* — Arkadia 3-▲ 614

Opera Arias, w. Freni, Mirella (sop) — EMI Classics ▲ CDM 63110

Piccinni, N.:La cecchina (sels), w. I. Hollweg (sop), S. Bruscantini (bar), R. Panerai (bar), F. Caracciolo (cnd), Naples RAI Orch—13 arias *(rec live 11/25/69)* — Arkadia 2-▲ 596 [ADD]

Puccini, G.:Arias, w. M. Caballé (sop), M. Chiara (sop), B. Nilsson (sop), J. Sutherland (sop), R. Tebaldi (sop), F. Corelli (ten), L. Pavarotti (ten), S. Milnes (bar) — London ▲ 421315-2 [ADD]

Puccini, G.:La Bohème, w. M. Adani (sop), L. Pavarotti (ten), L. Saccomani (bar), M. Wolf-Ferrari (cnd), Genoa Teatro Comunale Orch, Genoa Teatro Comunale Chorus [I] *(rec live 4/12/69)* — Verona 2-▲ 27079/80

Puccini, G.:La Bohème, w. M. Adani (sop), L. Pavarotti (ten), L. Saccomani (bar), M. Wolf-Ferrari (cnd), Genoa Teatro Comunale Orch, Genoa Teatro Comunale Chorus *(rec live, Apr 12, 1969)* — Melodram 2-▲ MEL 27031 [AAD]

Puccini, G.:La Bohème, w. E. Harwood (sop), L. Pavarotti (ten), R. Panerai (bar), H. von Karajan (cnd), Berlin PO, German Opera Chorus [I] — London 2-▲ 421049-2 [ADD] 2-▮ 421049-4

Puccini, G.:La Bohème, w. H. Gueden (sop), G. Raimondi (ten), G. Taddei (bar), H. von Karajan (cnd), Vienna State Opera Orch, Vienna State Opera Chorus [I] *(rec live 11/30/63)* — Melodram 2-▲ MELCD 27007

Puccini, G.:La Bohème, w. N. Gedda (ten), M. Sereni (bar), T. Schippers (cnd), Rome Opera Orch, Rome Opera Chorus [I] — EMI Classics ("Studio" series) 2-▲ CDMB 69657

Puccini, G.:La Bohème, w. P. Dvorsky (ten), C. Kleiber (cnd), La Scala Orch, La Scala Chorus — Artists 2-▲ FED 15 [ADD]

Puccini, G.:La Bohème (sels), w. N. Gedda (ten), M. Sereni (bar), T. Schippers (cnd), Rome Opera Orch, Rome Opera Chorus — EMI Classics ("Studio" series) ▲ CDM 63932 ▮ EG 63932

Puccini, G.:La Bohème (sels), w. H. Gueden (sop), G. Raimondi (ten), R. Panerai (bar), H. von Karajan (cnd), Vienna State Opera Orch—7 arias & scenes [I] *(rec live 11/9/63)* — Verona 2-▲ 27079/80

Puccini, G.:La Bohème (sels), w. E. Harwood (sop), L. Pavarotti (ten), R. Panerai (bar), H. von Karajan (cnd), Berlin PO, German Opera Chorus — London ▲ 421245-2 [DDD] ▮ 421245-4

Puccini, G.:Madama Butterfly, w. T. Berganza (mez), J. Carreras (ten), J. Pons (bar), G. Sinopoli (cnd), Philharmonia Orch, Ambrosian Opera Chorus [I] — Deutsche Grammophon 3-▲ 423567-2 [DDD]

Puccini, G.:Madama Butterfly, w. C. Ludwig (mez), L. Pavarotti (ten), R. Kerns (bar), H. von Karajan (cnd), Vienna PO [I] — London 3-▲ 417577-2 [ADD]

Puccini, G.:Madama Butterfly (sels), w. C. Ludwig (mez), L. Pavarotti (ten), R. Kerns (bar), H. von Karajan (cnd), Vienna PO [I] — London ▲ 421247-2 [ADD] ▮ 421247-4

Puccini, G.:Manon Lescaut, w. P. Domingo (ten), R. Bruson (bar), G. Sinopoli (cnd), Philharmonia Orch, Royal Opera House Chorus Covent Garden [I] *(rec 1984)* — Deutsche Grammophon 2-▲ 413893-2 [DDD]

Puccini, G.:Manon Lescaut, w. M. Freni (sop—Manon), C. Bartoli (mez—Musici I), L. Pavarotti (ten—Des Grieux), R. Vargas (ten—Edmondo), D. Croft (ten—Lescaut), G. Taddei (bar—Geronte), J. Levine (cnd), Metropolitan Opera Orch, New York Metropolitan Opera Chorus [I] *(rec 1992)* — London ▲ 440200-2 [DDD]

Puccini, G.:Tosca, w. L. Pavarotti (ten), S. Milnes (bar), N. Rescigno (cnd), National PO London [I] — London 2-▲ 414036-2 [ADD]

Puccini, G.:Tosca, w. P. Domingo (ten), S. Ramey (bass), G. Sinopoli (cnd), Philharmonia Orch, Royal Opera House Chorus Covent Garden [I] — Deutsche Grammophon 2-▲ 431775-2 [DDD]

Puccini, G.:Tosca (sels), w. Mirella Freni (sop—Tosca), Plácido Domingo (ten—Cavaradossi), G. Sinopoli (cnd), Philharmonia Orch—Ah, quegli occhi! - Qual occhio al mondo può star [Act I, Part II] — Deutsche Grammophon ▲ 447270-2 [DDD] ▮ 447270-4

Puccini, G.:Il trittico, w. E. Souljois (sop), G. Giacomini (ten), R. Alagna (ten), J. Pons (bar), L. Nucci (bar), B. Bartoletti (cnd), Florence Maggio Musicale Orch, Florence Maggio Musicale Chorus — London 3-▲ 436261-2 [DDD]

Puccini, G.:Turandot, w. M. Caballé (sop—Turnadot), M. Freni (sop—Liu), J. Carreras (ten—Calaf), M. Sénéchal (ten—Emperor Altoum), V. Sardinero (bar—Ping), P. Plishka (bass—Timur), A. Lombard (cnd), Strasbourg PO, Maîtrise de la Cathédrale, Rhine Opera Chorus — EMI Classics ▲ CDMB 65293

Puccini, G.:Turandot (sels), w. M. Caballé (sop), J. Carreras (ten), M. Sénéchal (ten), A. Lombard (cnd), Strasbourg PO, Rhine Opera Chorus — EMI Classics ("Studio" series) ▲ CDM 63410

Scarlatti, A.:La Griselda, w. L. Alva (ten), V. Luchetti (ten), R. Panerai (bar), S. Bruscantini (bar), N. Sanzogno (cnd), Naples Alessandro Scarlatti RAI Orch, Naples Scarlatti Chorus [I] *(rec live 10/29/70)* — Memories 2-▲ HR 4154/55 (m) [ADD]

Strauss, R.:4 Last Songs, w. V. Smetáček (cnd), Bologna SO [G] *(rec live, 11/73)* — Cantabile 2-▲ BIM 703-2

Tchaikovsky, P.:Queen of Spades, w. M. Forrester (cta), V. Atlantov (ten), D. Hvorostovsky (bar), S. Ozawa (cnd), Boston SO, Tanglewood Festival Chorus — RCA Red Seal 3-▲ 09026-60992-2 [DDD]

Tchaikovsky, P.:Queen of Spades, w. M. Forrester (cta), V. Atlantov (ten), D. Hvorostovsky (bar), S. Ozawa (cnd), Boston SO, Tanglewood Festival Chorus — RCA Red Seal ▲ 09026-61227-2 [DDD] ☐ 09026-61227-5

Verdi, G.:Aida, w. K. Ricciarelli (sop), A. Baltsa (mez), J. Carreras (ten), P. Cappuccilli (bar), G. Raimondi (ten), J. Van Dam (b-bar), H. von Karajan (cnd), Vienna PO, Vienna State Opera Chorus [I] — EMI Classics (Studio) 3-▲ CDMC 69300 [ADD]

Verdi, G.:Ernani, w. P. Domingo (ten), R. Bruson (bar), N. Ghiaurov (bass), R. Muti (cnd), La Scala Orch, La Scala Chorus [I] — EMI Classics 3-▲ CDC 47082 [DDD]

Verdi, G.:Falstaff, w. I. Ligabue (sop), L. Alva (ten), R. Capecchi (bar), F. Corena (bass), C. M. Giulini (cnd), Royal Concertgebouw Orch, Netherlands Chamber Choir [I] *(rec live, The Hague 6/20/63)* — Verona 2-▲ 27095/96

Verdi, G.:Falstaff, w. I. Ligabue (sop), G. Simionato (mez), R. Elias (mez), R. Krause (ten), G. Evans (bar), R. Merrill (bar), G. Solti (cnd), RCA Italian Opera Orch, RCA Italiana Opera Chorus [I] — London 2-▲ 417168-2 [ADD]

Freni, Mirella (sop) (cont.)

Verdi, G.:Otello, w. J. Vickers (ten), P. Glossop (bar), H. von Karajan (cnd), Vienna PO *(rec 1971)* — Memories 2-▲ MEM 4533 [ADD]

Verdi, G.:La traviata, w. F. Bonisolli (ten), S. Bruscantini (bar), L. Gardelli (cnd), Berlin State Opera Orch, Berlin State Opera Chorus [I] — Acanta 2-▲ CD 41644 [DDD]

Verdi, G.:La traviata, w. R. Righetti (mez), R. Cioni (ten), M. Sereni (bar), H. von Karajan (cnd), La Scala Orch, La Scala Chorus *(rec Milan, 1964)* — Legend 2-▲ LGD 125 [ADD]

Verismo Arias, w. La Fenice Theater Orch [cnd:Roberto Abbado] — London ▲ 433316-2 LH [DDD]

Frenk, Ruth (mez)

Der letzte Schmetterling:Kabarett und Lieder aus Theresienstadt — Erasmus ▲ WVH 037 [DDD]

Fresán, Iñaki (sgr)

Martín Y Soler, V.:Una Cosa rara, w. M. A. Peters (sop), M. Figueras (sop), G. Fabuel (sop), E. Palacio (ten), F. Belaza-Leoz (bar), S. Palatchi (bass), F. Garrigosa (bass), J. Savall (cnd), Concert des Nations, La Capella Reial de Catalunya [I] *(rec 1991)* — Astrée 3-▲ E 8760 [DDD]

Freund, Pia (sop)

Villa-Lobos, H.:Bachiana brasileira 5, w. Timo Korhonen (gtr), chamber ensemble — Ondine ▲ ODE 838

Villa-Lobos, H.:Distribution de fleurs, w. Timo Korhonen (gtr) — Ondine ▲ ODE 838

Villa-Lobos, H.:Modinha, w. Timo Korhonen (gtr) — Ondine ▲ ODE 838

Frey, Paul (ten)

Strauss, R.:Ariadne auf Naxos, w. J. Norman (sop), J. Varady (sop), E. Gruberova (sop), O. Bär (bar), D. Fischer-Dieskau (bar), K. Masur (cnd), Leipzig Gewandhaus Orch [G] — Philips 2-▲ 422084-2 [DDD]

Wagner, R.:Lohengrin, w. C. Studer (sop), M. Schenk (bass), P. Schneider (cnd), Bayreuth Festival Orch, Bayreuth Festival Chorus [G] — Philips 4-▲ 434602-2 [DDD]

Wagner, R.:Lohengrin, w. C. Studer (sop), M. Schenk (bass), P. Schneider (cnd), Bayreuth Festival Orch, Bayreuth Festival Chorus — Philips 32-▲ 434420-2 [ADD/DDD]

Wagner, R.:Lohengrin (sels), w. C. Studer (sop), G. Schnaut (sop), M. Schenk (bass), P. Schneider (cnd), Bayreuth Festival Orch, Bayreuth Festival Chorus — Philips ▲ 438500-2

Freyd, Bernard (nar)

Milhaud, D.:Ani maamin, un chant perdu et retrouvé, w. Sharon Cooper (sop—la Voix), Anna Parus (mez), Bernard Freyd (nar—Isaac), Michel Hermon (nar—le Récitant), Michael Lonsdale (nar—Abraham), Jean Négroni (nar—Jacob), P. Méfano (cnd), Ensemble 2E2M, Madrigal de Bordeaux — Arion ▲ ARN 68275 [DDD]

Frick, Gottlob (bass)

Beethoven, L. van:Fidelio, w. Ingeborg Hallstein (sop—Marzelline), Christa Ludwig (mez—Leonore/Fidelio), Gerhard Unger (ten—Jaquino), Jon Vickers (ten—Florestan), Walter Berry (bass—Pizarro), Franz Crass (bass—Don Fernando), Gottlob Frick (bass—Rocco), O. Klemperer (cnd), Philharmonia Orch, Philharmonia Chorus — EMI Classics 2-▲ CDCB 55170

Beethoven, L. van:Fidelio, w. I. Hallstein (sop), C. Ludwig (mez), J. Vickers (ten), G. Unger (ten), W. Berry (bass), O. Klemperer (cnd), Philharmonia Orch, Philharmonia Chorus [G]; w. minimal dialog — EMI Classics ("Studio" series) 2-▲ CDMB 69324 [ADD]

Beethoven, L. van:Fidelio, w. S. Jurinac (sop), M. Mödl (sop), W. Windgassen (ten), A. Poell (bar), O. Edelmann (bass), W. Furtwängler (cnd), Vienna PO *(rec Oct. 1953)* — EMI Classics 2-▲ CDHB 64496

Beethoven, L. van:Fidelio, w. S. Jurinac (sop), J. Vickers (ten), H. Hotter (b-bar), O. Klemperer (cnd), Royal Opera House Orch, Royal Opera House Chorus Covent Garden [G] *(rec live, Covent Garden, 3/7/61)* — Melodram 2-▲ MEL 27076 (m) [AAD]

Beethoven, L. van:Fidelio (sels), w. L. Rysanek (sop), I. Seefried (sop), E. Haefliger (ten), F. Lenz (ten), D. Fischer-Dieskau (bar), K. Engen (bass), F. Fricsay (cnd), Bavarian State Orch, Bavarian Opera Chorus—Overture, various arias & scenes, finale [G] — IMP Collectors Series ▲ IMPX 9021 [AAD]

Bruckner, A.:Te Deum, w. Hilde Gueden (sop), Hilde Zadeck (cta), Erich Majkut (ten), B. Walter (cnd), Vienna PO, Vienna State Opera Chorus *(rec live, 1955)* — Enterprise ("Palladio" series) ▲ ENTPD 4209 [ADD]

Cornelius, P.:Der Barbier von Bagdad, w. S. Jurinac (sop), H. Rössl-Majdan (mez), E. Majkut (ten), R. Schock (ten), A. Poell (bass-bar), H. Hollreiser (cnd), Austrian RSO, Austrian Radio Chorus *(rec live Vienna 1952)* — Melodram 2-▲ MEL 27050 (m) [AAD]

Cornelius, P.:Der Barbier von Bagdad, w. S. Jurinac (sop), H. Rössl-Majdan (mez), E. Majkut (ten), R. Schock (ten), A. Poell (bass-bar), H. Hollreiser (cnd), Austrian RSO, Austrian Radio Chorus [G] *(rec live Vienna, 1952)* — Verona 2-▲ 27050/51 (m) [AA

Haydn, J.:Mass 6, "Nikolai-messe", "6/4-Takt-Messe", w. Agnes Giebel (sop), Waldemar Kmentt (ten), E. Jochum (cnd), Bavarian RSO, Vienna Cathedral Choir, Vienna Boys' Choir — Philips ("Two-Fers" series) 2-▲ 446175-2

Haydn, J.:Mass 7, "Kleine Orgelmesse", w. Agnes Giebel (sop), Waldemar Kmentt (ten), E. Jochum (cnd), Bavarian RSO, Vienna Cathedral Choir, Vienna Boys' Choir — Philips ("Two-Fers" series) 2-▲ 446175-2

Haydn, J.:Die Schöpfung, w. Agnes Giebel (sop), Waldemar Kmentt (ten), E. Jochum (cnd), Bavarian RSO, Vienna Cathedral Choir, Vienna Boys' Choir — Philips ("Two-Fers" series) 2-▲ 446175-2

Mozart, W.A.:Arias, w. I. Hollweg (sop), L. Marshall (sop), L. Simoneau (ten), G. Unger (ten), T. Beecham (cnd), Royal PO, Beecham Choral Society — EMI Classics 2-▲ CDHB 63715

Mozart, W.A.:Don Giovanni, w. E. Grümmer (sop), L. Della Casa (sop), R. Streich (sop), L. Simoneau (ten), C. Siepi (b-bar), W. Berry (bass), F. Corena (bass), D. Mitropoulos (cnd), Vienna PO, Vienna State Opera Chorus [I] *(rec live, Salzburg, July 24, 1956)* — Arkadia 3-▲ 552 (m) [ADD]

Mozart, W.A.:Don Giovanni, w. M. Schech (sop), M. Teschemacher (sop), H. Hopf (ten), M. Ahlersmeyer (bar), K. Böhme (bass), K. Elmendorff (cnd), Saxon State Orch, Dresden State Opera Chorus [G] *(rec 1943)* — Berlin Classics ("Dokumente" series) 3-▲ BER 2048 [ADD]

Mozart, W.A.:Don Giovanni, w. E. Grümmer (sop—D. Anna), R. Streich (sop—Zerlina), L. Della Casa (sop—D. Elvira), L. Simoneau (ten—Don Ottavio), C. Siepi (bass-baritone—Don Giovanni), W. Berry (bass—Masetto), G. Frick (bass—Il Commendatore), F. Corena (bass—Leporello), D. Mitropoulos (cnd), Vienna PO, Vienna State Opera Chorus *(rec Salzburg, July 24, 1956)* — Sony Classical 3-▲ SM3K 64263 [ADD]

Mozart, W.A.:Entführung, w. I. Hollweg (sop), L. Marshall (sop), L. Simoneau (ten), G. Unger (ten), T. Beecham (cnd), Royal PO, Beecham Choral Society — EMI Classics 2-▲ CDHB 63715

Mozart, W.A.:Songs, w. M. Callas (sop), E. Grümmer (sop), E. Schwarzkopf (sop), R. Scotto (sop), T. Lemnitz (sop), E. Berger (sop), S. Jurinac (sop), E. Schumann (sop), I. Souez (sop), E. Rethberg (sop), L. Lehmann (sop), N. Gedda (ten), J. McCormack (ten), H. Roswenge (ten), H. Nash (ten), T. Gobbi (bar), G. Hüsch (bar), E. Kunz (bar), E. Pinza (bass), A. Kipnis (bass) — EMI Classics 4-▲ CDMD 63750

Mozart, W.A.:Zauberflöte, w. G. Janowitz (sop), L. Popp (sop), R. Pütz (sop), N. Gedda (ten), W. Berry (bass), O. Klemperer (cnd), Philharmonia Orch, Philharmonia Chorus [without dialog; G] — EMI Classics ("Studio" series) 2-▲ CDMB 69971 [ADD]

Mozart, W.A.:Zauberflöte, w. Gundula Janowitz (sop—Pamina), Lucia Popp (sop—Queen of the Night), Nicolai Gedda (ten-Tamina), Walter Berry (bass—Papageno), Gottlob Frick (bass—Sarastro), O. Klemperer (cnd), Philharmonia Orch, Philharmonia Chorus — EMI Classics 2-▲ CDCB 55173

Orff, C.:Die Kluge, w. E. Schwarzkopf (sop), R. Christ (ten), P. Kuén (ten), M. Cordes (bar), B. Kusche (bar), H. Prey (bar), G. Wieter (bass), W. Sawallisch (cnd), Philharmonia Orch [G] — EMI Classics ("Studio" series) 2-▲ CDMB 63712 [ADD]

Orff, C.:Die Kluge, w. L. Popp (sop), J. Van Kesteren (ten), T. Stewart (bar), F. Crass (bass), K. Eichhorn (cnd), Munich RSO — Eurodisc 2-▲ 69069-2-RG [ADD]

Orff, C.:Der Mond—Ein kleines Welttheater, w. J. Van Kesteren (ten), T. Stewart (bar), F. Crass (bass), K. Eichhorn (cnd), Munich RSO — Eurodisc 2-▲ 69069-2-RG [ADD]

Pfitzner, H.:Palestrina, w. S. Jurinac (sop), C. Ludwig (mez), F. Wunderlich (ten), G. Stolze (ten), O. Wiener (bar), W. Berry (bass), R. Heger (cnd), Vienna State Opera Orch, Vienna State Opera Chorus *(rec live, Vienna 12/16/64)* — Myto 3-▲ 3 MCD 92259 [ADD]

Smetana, B.:The Bartered Bride, w. P. Lorengar (sop), F. Wunderlich (ten), R. Kempe (cnd), Bamberg SO, Bamberg RIAS Chorus [G] *(rec ca. 1963)* — EMI Classics ("Studio" series) 2-▲ CDMB 64002

Verdi, G.:La forza del destino, w. G. Bumbry (sop—Leonora), H. Dernesch (sop—Preziosilla), N. Gedda (ten—Alvaro), H. Prey (bar—Don Carlos), G. Frick (bass—Pater Guardian), S. Vogel (bass—Marchese), G. Patanè (cnd), Dresden State Orch, Dresden State Opera Chorus *(rec Aug. 1965)* — Berlin Classics ("Eterna" series) ▲ BER 2025-2 [ADD]

Verdi, G.:Requiem Mass, w. M. Stader (sop), M. Höffgen (cta), F. Wunderlich (ten), H. Müller-Kray (cnd), South German RSO, South German Radio Sym Chorus *(rec live, Stuttgart, 11/2/60)* — Myto 2-▲ 2 MCD 91648 [ADD]

▲ = CD ♦ = Enhanced CD Δ = MD ▮ = Cassette Tape ☐ = DCC

Frick, Gottlob (bass) (cont.)

Wagner, R.:Der fliegende Holländer, w. M. Schech (sop), S. Wagner (mez), F. Wunderlich (ten), R. Schock (ten), D. Fischer-Dieskau (bar), F. Konwitschny (cnd), Berlin Staatskapelle — Berlin Classics ("Eterna" series) 2-▲ BER 2097 [ADD]

Wagner, R.:Der fliegende Holländer (sels), w. Marianne Schech (sop), Fritz Wunderlich (ten), Dietrich Fischer-Dieskau (bar), F. Konwitschny (cnd), Berlin Staatskapelle — Berlin Classics ▲ BER 9080 [ADD]

Wagner, R.:Götterdämmerung, w. B. Nilsson (sop), J. Watson (sop), C. Ludwig (mez), W. Windgassen (ten), D. Fischer-Dieskau (bar), G. Solti (cnd), Vienna PO [G] — London 4-▲ 414115-2 [ADD]

Wagner, R.:Götterdämmerung, w. Birgit Nilsson (sop—Brünnhilde), Leonie Rysanek (sop—Gutrune), Gerda Sommerschuh (sop—Woglinde), Elisabeth Lindermeier (sop—Wellgunde), Ruth Michaelis (sop—Flohilde), Marianne Schech (sop—Dritte Norne), Ira Malaniuk (mez—Waltraute), Irmgarth Barth (mez—Erste Norne), Hertha Töpper (mez—Zweite Norne), Bernd Aldenhoff (ten—Siegfried), Hermann Uhde (bar—Gunther), Gottlob Frick (bass—Hagen), H. Knappertsbusch (cnd), Bavarian State Opera Orch, Bavarian State Opera Chorus *(rec live, Prinzregententheater, Sept. 1, 1955)* — Orfeo 4-▲ 356944 (m)

Wagner, R.:Götterdämmerung (sels), w. A. Varnay (sop), E. Grümmer (sop), B. Aldenhoff (ten), H. Uhde (bar), J. Greindl (bass), H. Knappertsbusch (cnd), Bavarian State Opera Orch, Bayreuth Festival Orch, Bavarian State Opera Chorus, Bayreuth Festival Chorus [G] *(rec live 1955 & 1957)* — Melodram 4-▲ MEL 46106 (m) [AAD]

Wagner, R.:Lohengrin, w. E. Grümmer (sop), C. Ludwig (mez), J. Thomas (ten), D. Fischer-Dieskau (bar), R. Kempe (cnd), Vienna PO, Vienna State Opera Chorus [G] — EMI Classics 3-▲ CDCC 49017 [ADD]

Wagner, R.:Lohengrin, w. Maud Cunitz (sop—Elsa), Margarete Klose (mez—Ortrud), Rudolf Schock (ten—Lohengrin), Josef Metternich (bar—Friedrich von Telramund), Gottlob Frick (bass—King Henry), W. Schüchter (cnd), North German RSO, North German Radio Chorus, West German Radio Men's Chorus *(rec 1953)* — EMI Classics 2-▲ CDHC 65517

Wagner, R.:Die Meistersinger von Nürnberg, w. E. Grümmer (sop), M. Höffgen (cta), R. Schock (ten), G. Unger (ten), H. Prey (bar), B. Kusche (bar), F. Frantz (b-bar), R. Kempe (cnd), Berlin PO *(rec 1956)* — EMI Classics 4-▲ CDMD 64154

Wagner, R.:Parsifal, w. C. Ludwig (mez), A. Kollo (ten), D. Fischer-Dieskau (bar), Z. Kelemen (bar), G. Solti (cnd), Vienna PO, Vienna State Opera Chorus, Vienna Boys' Choir [G] — London 4-▲ 417143-2 [ADD]

Wagner, R.:Der Ring des Nibelungen, w. B. Nilsson (sop), K. Flagstad (sop), R. Crespin (sop), C. Watson (sop), C. Ludwig (mez), J. Madeira (mez), S. Svanholm (ten), J. King (ten), G. Stolze (ten), W. Windgassen (ten), G. London (bar), D. Fischer-Dieskau (bar), H. Hotter (b-bar), G. Neidlinger (b-bar), G. Frick (bass), G. Solti (cnd), Vienna PO [G] — London 15-▲ 414100-2 [ADD]

Wagner, R.:Tannhäuser, w. E. Grümmer (sop), M. Schech (sop), H. Hopf (ten), F. Wunderlich (ten), D. Fischer-Dieskau (bar), F. Konwitschny (cnd), Berlin State Opera Orch, Berlin State Opera Chorus [G] — EMI Classics ("Studio" series) 3-▲ CDMC 63214 [ADD]

Wagner, R.:Tannhäuser, w. L. Rysanek (sop), J. Lustig (sgr), M. Cordes (bar), K. Böhm (cnd), Naples Teatro San Carlo Orch, Naples Teatro San Carlo Chorus [G] *(rec live, Naples, 3/17/56)* — Melodram 3-▲ MEL 37073 (m) [AAD]

Wagner, R.:Tristan und Isolde (acts 2 & 3), w. E. Schlüter (sop), M. Klose (cta), L. Suthaus (ten), J. Prohaska (ten), W. Furtwängler (cnd), Berlin State Opera Orch, Berlin State Opera Chorus [G] *(rec live, Berlin, 10/3/47)* — Arkadia 2-▲ 358 [ADD]

Wagner, R.:Die Walküre, w. B. Nilsson (sop), R. Crespin (sop), C. Ludwig (mez), J. King (ten), H. Hotter (b-bar), G. Solti (cnd), Vienna PO [G] — London 4-▲ 414105-2 [ADD]

Wolf, H.:Der Corregidor, w. M. Teschemacher (sop), M. Fuchs (sop), K. Erb (ten), J. Herrmann (bar), K. Böhme (b-bar), G. Hann (bass), K. Elmendorff (cnd), Saxon State Orch, Saxon State Chorus *(rec 1944)* — Preiser 2-▲ PRE 90182 [AAD]

Fricke, Peter (nar)

Stravinsky, I.:L'Histoire du soldat, w. E. Sebestyen (cnd), Bavarian RSO *(rec Jan. 31, 1987)* — Calig ▲ CAL 50894 [DDD]

Friday, Elisabeth (sgr)

Handel, G.F.:Israel in Egypt, w. Ruth Holton (sop), Michael Chance (alt), Philip Salmon (ten), Paul Tindall (sgr), J. E. Gardiner (cnd), English Baroque Soloists, Monteverdi Choir London — Philips ▲ 432110-2

Fried, Theodora (sop)

Rorem, N.:Miss Julie, w. Theodora Fried (sgr—Miss Julie), Heather Sarris (sgr—Christine, the cook), Laurelyn Watson (sgr—Young Girl), David Blackburn (sgr—Mr. Niels), Mark Mulligan (sgr—Young Boy), Philip Torre (sgr—John, the valet), Judd Ernster (bass), D. Gilbert (cnd), Manhattan School of Music Opera Orch, Manhattan School of Music Opera Chorus — Newport Classic 2-▲ NPT 85605 [DDD]

Friedauer, Harry (ten)

Fall, L.:Die Dollarprinzessin (sels), w. Sari Barabas (sop), Christine Gorner (sop), Heinz Hoppe (ten), C. Michalski (cnd), Graunke SO, Botho Lucas Chorus — Emperor Operetta ▲ KO 86353

Lehár, F.:Zigeunerliebe (sels), w. Sari Barabas (sop), Christine Gorner (sop), Heinz Hoppe (ten), C. Michalski (cnd), Graunke SO, Rudolf Lamy Singers — Emperor Operetta ▲ KO 86342

Friede, Nina (sgr)

The World of Singing, Vol. 2:Singers of Imperial Russia, w. Nina Koshetz (sop), Evgenia Zbrueva (cta), Nicolai Figner (ten), Feodor Chaliapin (bass), Maria Kouznetsova (sgr), Anastasia Vialtzeva (sgr) — Enterprise ("Vocal Archives" series) 2-▲ ENT VA 2102

Friedlander, Eric (sgr)

Caccini, F.:La liberazione di Ruggiero dall'isola d'Alcina, w. Linda De Rungs (sop—Alcian/Vistola), Cecilia Amorocho (sgr—Melissa/Nunzia), Laura Lea Duckworth (sgr—Siren/Harpy), Eric Friedlander (sgr—Monster), L. Ernest Gross (sgr—Enchanted Cypress), Phoebe Jevtovic (sgr—Siren), James Rittenhouse (sgr—Ruggiero/Neptune), Sharon Sim (sgr—Siren), R. Burchard (cnd), Ars Femina Ensemble, TimeChange *(rec Louisville, KY, 1993)* — Nannerl ▲ NR-ARS 003; ■ NR-ARS 003

Friedli, Irène (mez)

Kelterborn, R.:Ensemble-Buch II, w. D. Cichewiecz (cnd), Hamburg das neue werk Ensemble *(rec North German Radio Studio 10, Hamburg, Aug 14-25, 1995)* — Musicaphon ▲ M 55706 [DDD]

Stravinsky, I.:Canticum sacrum, w. Frieder Lang (ten), N. Järvi (cnd), Swiss Romande Orch, Lausanne Pro Arte Choir — Chandos ▲ CHAN 9408 [DDD]

Stravinsky, I.:Chorale Variations on the German Christmas Carol "Vom Himmel hoch da komm' ich her", w. Frieder Lang (ten), N. Järvi (cnd), Swiss Romande Orch, Lausanne Pro Arte Choir — Chandos ▲ CHAN 9408 [DDD]

Stravinsky, I.:Requiem Canticles, w. Michel Brodard (bass), N. Järvi (cnd), Swiss Romande Orch, Lausanne Pro Arte Choir, Romande Chamber Choir — Chandos ▲ CHAN 9408 [DDD]

Friedman, Maria (sgr)

Lloyd Webber, A.:Music of, w. C. Carter (sgr), C. Moore (sgr), J. Barrowman (sgr), L. Robertson (sgr), J. Diedrich (sgr), Grania Renihan (sgr), J.O. Edwards (cnd), Munich SO—Cats; Joseph & the Amazing Technicolor Dreamcoat; Phantom of the Opera; Evita; Jesus Christ Superstar; Starlight Express; Song & Dance; Aspects of Love — Koch International ▲ CD 340022 [DDD] ■ MC 340022

Friedman, Stephanie (mez)

Adams, J.:The Death of Klinghoffer, w. S. Sylvan (bar), J. Maddalena (bar), T. Hammons (bar), K. Nagano (cnd), Lyon Opera Orch, English Opera Group Chorus — Elektra/Nonesuch 2-▲ 79281-2 2-■ 79281-4

Lewis, P.S.:Where the Heart Is Pure, w. L. Pillot (cnd), Berkeley SO *(rec St. Stephen's Church, Belvedere, CA, Oct 1994 & June 1995)* — New Albion ▲ NA 079

More Than Sax:Baroque, Blues & Beyond, w. Wolford, Dale (a sax/s sax), Ivan Rosenblum (pno) *(rec Belmont, CA & Richmond, CA, Aug. 17-20, 1993 & Jan. 2)* — Gliddon ▲ GP 001 [DDD]

Thow, J.:Songs, w. San Francisco Contemporary Music Players — Music & Arts ▲ CD 915

Friedmann, Gérard (sgr)

Lehár, F.:Die lustige Witwe, w. Teresa Stich-Randall (mez—Missia Palmieri), Monique Stiot (mez—Manon), Germaine Duclos (sgr—Praskovia), Linda Felder (sgr—Olga), Christiane Jacquin (sgr—Nadia), Jeannette Levasseur (sgr—Sylviane), Henri Legay (ten—Camille de Coutançon), Joseph Peyron (ten—Kromsky), Robert Destain (sgr—Baron Popoff), Michel Fauche (sgr—Pristich), Gérard Friedmann (sgr—Lerida), Jacques Gilet (sgr—Bogdanowitch), Jean Guy Henneveux (sgr—Prince Danilo), Serge Klin (sgr—Figg), Jacques Villa (sgr—D'Estillac), A. Sibert (cnd), Belgian Radio-TV Orch, Belgian Radio-TV Chorus *(rec Grand Auditorium, Belgium, Apr 30, 1970)* — Studio SM 2-▲ 2160 [AAD]

Friedrich, Elisabeth (sop)

Wagner, R.:Die Walküre (sels), w. G. Rünger (sop), K. Buschmann (ten), W. Rode (bar), W. Brückner-Rüggeberg (cnd), Reich Radio Königsberg Large Orch—Act II, Scenes 2,3 & 4 & Act III, Scenes 1,2 & 3 [G] *(rec live 2/17 & 5/1 1938)* — Preiser 2-▲ 90075 (m) [AAD]

Friedrich, Karl (ten)

Strauss (II), Joh.:Eine Nacht in Venedig, w. E. Réthy (sop), M. Schober (sop), R. Boesch (bar), A. Jerger (b-bar), K. Preger (ten), A. Paulik (cnd), Vienna SO, Bregenz Festival Choir [G] *(rec 1951)* — Koch Schwann ▲ 3-1272-2 [ADD]

Strauss, R.:Salome, w. Maria Cebotari (sop—Salome), Elisabeth Höngen (mez—Herodias), Karl Friedrich (ten—Narraboth), Julius Patzak (ten—Herod), Marko Rothmüller (bar—Jokanaan), C. Krauss (cnd), Vienna State Opera Orch, Vienna State Opera Chorus *(rec Covent Garden, London, Sept 30, 1947)* — Legato 2-▲ LCD 211-2 [ADD]

Friedrich, Wolf Matthias (bass)

Cherubini, L.:Masses, w. Monika Wiebe (sop), Helena Jungwirth (alt), Rodrigo Orrego (ten), H.R. Zöbeley (cnd), Munich SO, Munich Motet Choir—Missa Solemnis — Calig ▲ CAL 50914

Friesenhausen, Maria (sop)

Bach, J.S.:Cant 187, w. H. Laurich (mez), W. Schöne (bass), H. Rilling (cnd), Stuttgart Bach Collegium, Gächinger Kantorei — Hänssler Classic ▲ 98.806 [AAD]

Romberg, A.:Der Lied von der Glocke, w. R. Naber (alt), H. Hopfner (ten), K. Ridderbusch (bass), G. Knüsel (cnd), Essen CO, Duisburg State Concert Chorus — Calig ▲ CAL 50942

Frijsh, Povla (sop)

Great Voices of the Century, w. Elena Gerhardt (sop), Lotte Lehmann (sop), Gerald Moore (pno) *(rec 1929-1939)* — Sanctus ▲ 001 [ADD]

Frimmer, Monika (sop)

Bach, J.S.:Cant 14, w. E. Büchner (ten), A. Scheibner (bar), M. Pommer (cnd), Leipzig New Bach Collegium Musicum, Leipzig St. Thomas Church Choir [G] — Capriccio ▲ CDC 10027

Bach, J.S.:Cant 51, w. M. Pommer (cnd), Leipzig New Bach Collegium Musicum, Leipzig St. Thomas Church Choir [G] — Capriccio ▲ CDC 10027 [DDD]

Bach, J.S.:Cant 143, w. E. Büchner (ten), A. Scheibner (bar), M. Pommer (cnd), Leipzig New Bach Collegium Musicum, Leipzig St. Thomas Church Choir [G] — Capriccio ▲ CDC 10027 [DDD]

Bach, J.S.:St. Matthew Passion, w. Veronika Winter (sop), Lena Susanne Norin (alt), Wilfried Jochens (ten), Christoph Prégardien (ten), Klaus Mertens (bass), Hans-Georg Wimmer (bass), H. Max (cnd), Das Kliene Konzert, Rhineland Kantorei — Capriccio 2-▲ 60 046 [DDD]

Caldara, A.:Stabat Mater, w. Gloria Banditelli (mez), Gerd Türk (ten), Peter Frank (bass), L. Rovatkay (cnd), Capella Agostino Steffani, Westphalia Kantorei — EMI Classics ▲ CDC 54845

Durante, F.:Lamentationes Jeremiae Prophetae, w. Mechthild Bach (sop), Margarete Joswig (sgr), P. Neumann (cnd), Collegium Cartusianum, Cologne Chamber Choir — CPO ▲ CPO 999325

Handel, G.F.:Radamisto, w. Juliana Gondek (sop), Dana Hanchard (sop), Lisa Saffer (sop), R. Popken (cta), Michael Dean (b-bar), Nicholas Cavallier (bass), N. McGegan (cnd), Freiburg Baroque Orch — Harmonia Mundi USA 3-▲ HMU 907111/13

Mangold, C.A.:Abraham, w. Georg Mechthild (mez), B Gärtner (ten), Gerd Türk (ten), Giles Cachemaille (bar), Philadelphia Orch, Darmstadt Concert Choir — Christophorus 2-▲ 77172

Mozart, W.A.:Missa, K.427, w. Barbara Schlick (sop), Christoph Prégardien (ten), Klaus Mertens (bass), P. Neumann (cnd), Collegium Cartusianum, Cologne Chamber Choir — Virgin Classics ▲ CDM 61167

Pergolesi, G.B.:Stabat mater, w. Gloria Banditelli (mez), Gerd Türk (ten), Peter Frank (bass), L. Rovatkay (cnd), Capella Agostino Steffani, Westphalia Kantorei — EMI Classics ▲ CDC 54845

Steffani, A.:Enrico Leone, w. R. Popken (alt), S. Szameit (sop), N. Yoko (cta), C. Guber (cta), D. Diwiak (ten), G. Faulstich (bar), L. Rovatkay (cnd), Cappela Agostino Steffani [period instrs] [I] — Calig ▲ CAL 50855 [DDD]

Telemann, G.P.:Auferstehung und Himmelfahrt Jesu, w. Veronika Winter (sop), Matthias Koch (alt), Nico Van der Meel (ten), Klaus Mertens (bass), H. Max (cnd), Das Kliene Konzert, Rhineland Kantorei — Capriccio ▲ CD 10596 [DDD]

Vivaldi, A.:Son al St. Sepolcro, w. Gloria Banditelli (mez), Gerd Türk (ten), Peter Frank (bass), L. Rovatkay (cnd), Capella Agostino Steffani, Westphalia Kantorei — EMI Classics ▲ CDC 54845

Zelenka, J.D.:Missa sanctissimae trinitatis, w. Elisabeth Graf (cta), Markus Brutscher (ten), W. Wehnert (cnd), Marburg Bach Choir — Thorofon ▲ CTH 2265

Frind, Anni (sop)

From Opera & Operetta — Centaur ("Historic Recordings" series) ▲ CRC 2116

Frisani, Rosita (sop)

Porpora, N.A.:Cant per la notte di Natale, w. Rosita Frisani (sop—Dorindo), Roberta Invernizzi (sop—Angelo), Marco Lazzara (cta—Montano), E. Velardi (cnd), Alessandro Stradella Consort *(rec Genoa, Jan 29-30, 1995)* — Bongiovanni 2-▲ GB 2181/2

Frittoli, Barbara (sop)

Rossini, G.:Il barbiere di Siviglia (sels), w. J. Larmore (mez), R. Giménez (ten), Håkan Hagegård (bar), A. Corbelli (bar), S. Ramey (bass), J. López-Cobos (cnd), Lausanne CO, Geneva Grand Théâtre Chorus — Teldec ▲ 93693-2

Verdi, G.:Il trovatore, w. Antonella Banaudi (sop—Leonora), Barbara Frittoli (sop—Ines), Shirley Verrett (mez—Azucena), Enrico Facini (ten—Un messo), Piero de Palma (ten—Ruiz), Luciano Pavarotti (ten—Manrico), Leo Nucci (bar—Il Conte di Luna), Roberto Scaltriti (bar—Un vecchio zingaro), Francesco Ellero d'Artegna (bass—Ferrando), Z. Mehta (cnd), Florence Maggio Musicale Orch, Florence Maggio Musicale Chorus *(rec Maggio Musicale Fiorentino Community Theater, June 18-July 2, 1990)* — London 2-▲ 430694-2

Fritz (sgr)

Wagner, R.:Das Rheingold, w. P. Brivkalne (sop), I. Malaniuk (cta), R. Siewert (cta), Pflanzl (ten), S. Björling (bar), W. Faulhaber (bass), L. Weber (bass), F. Dalberg (bass), H. von Karajan (cnd), Bayreuth Festival Orch, Bayreuth Festival Chorus [G] *(rec live 8/1/51)* — Melodram 2-▲ MEL 26107 (m) [AAD]

Fritz, Bruno (bar)

Straus, O.:Ein Walzertraum (sels), w. Melita Muszely (sop), Lisa Otto (sop), Rudolf Schock (ten), W. Schüchter (cnd), Berlin Orch, Berlin Chorus — Emperor Operetta ▲ KO 86346

Froboess, Cornelia (nar)

Brahms, J.:Romanzen aus Tieck's *Magelone*, w. Hans Peter Blochwitz (ten), Eric Schneider (pno) — Berlin Classics ▲ BER 1125 [DDD]

Froerer, Laverne G. (mez)

Bernhard, C.:Missa "Durch Adams Fall", w. Henriette Schellenberg (sop), Keith Boldt (ten), George Roberts (bar), J. Washburn (cnd), CBC Vancouver SO, Vancouver Chamber Choir *(rec Ryerson United Church & The Orpheum, Vancouver, May 4-7, 1992)* — CBC ▲ 5160 [DDD]

Fauré, G.:Messe basse, w. Henriette Schellenberg (sop), Keith Boldt (ten), George Roberts (bar), J. Washburn (cnd), CBC Vancouver SO, Vancouver Chamber Choir [orchd J. Washburn] *(rec Ryerson United Church & The Orpheum, Vancouver, May 4-7, 1992)* — CBC ▲ 5160 [DDD]

Haydn, J.:Mass 7, "Kleine Orgelmesse", w. Henriette Schellenberg (sop), Keith Boldt (ten), George Roberts (bar), J. Washburn (cnd), CBC Vancouver SO, Vancouver Chamber Choir *(rec Ryerson United Church & The Orpheum, Vancouver, May 4-7, 1992)* — CBC ▲ 5160 [DDD]

Weber, C.M. von:Missa sancta 2, w. Henriette Schellenberg (sop), Keith Boldt (ten), George Roberts (bar), J. Washburn (cnd), CBC Vancouver SO, Vancouver Chamber Choir *(rec Ryerson United Church & The Orpheum, Vancouver, May 4-7, 1992)* — CBC ▲ 5160 [DDD]

Frohnmayer, Eilen (sop)

Dankner, S.:Songs of Bygone Days, w. P. Frohnmayer (bar), H.J. McCracken (pno) — Albany ▲ TROY 067 [DDD]

Frohnmayer, Philip (bar)

Dankner, S.:Songs of Bygone Days, w. E. Frohnmayer (sop), H.J. McCracken (pno) — Albany ▲ TROY 067 [DDD]

Frontali, Roberto (bar)

Bellini, V.:La straniera, w. L. Alberti (sop—Alaide), S. Mingardo (mez—Isoletta), V. Bello (ten—Arturo), R. Frontale (bar—Il Barone di Valdeburgo), V. Sagona (bass—Il signore di Montalino), P. Zizich (bass—Osburgo), G. Masini (cnd), Trieste Teatro Comunale Giuseppe Verdi Orch, Trieste Teatro Comunale G. Verdi Chorus *(rec Dec. 1990)* — Ricordi ▲ RFCD 2015 [DDD]

Frontali, Roberto (bar) (cont.)
Donizetti, G.:L'elisir d'amore, w. Alessandra Ruffini (sop—Adina), Mariangela Spotorno (sop—Gianetta), Vincenzo La Scola (ten—Nemorino), Simone Alaimo (bar—Dulcamara), Roberto Frontali (bar—Belcore), P.G. Morandi (cnd), Hungarian State Opera Orch, Anikó Katona (cnd), Hungarian State Opera Chorus *(rec Budapest, July 1995)* Naxos 2-▲ 8.60045-6 [DDD]
Rossini, G.:La cambiale di matrimonio, w. S. Jeun (sop—Fanny), M. Laurenza (sop—Clarina), L. Canonici (ten—Edoardo Milfort), R. Frontali (bar—Slook), E. Dara (bar—Tobia Mill), D. Renzetti (cnd), Turin RAI Orch *(rec Aug. 1991)* Ricordi ▲ RFCD 2011 [DDD]
Verdi, G.:Falstaff, w. Maureen O'Flynn (sop), Daniela Dessi (sop), Bernadette Manca di Nissa (mez), Delores Ziegler (mez), Ramon Vargas (ten), Ernesto Gavazzi (ten), Paolo Barbacini (ten), Juan Pons (bar), Roberto Frontali (bar), Luigi Roni (bass), R. Muti (cnd), La Scala Orch, La Scala Chorus *(rec Milan La Scala Theater, Italy, Mar. 29 & 31)* Sony Classical ▲ S2K 58961 [DDD]

Frontali, Roberto (sgr)
Bellini, V.:Il pirata, w. Lucia Aliberti (sop), Stuart Neill (sgr), José Guadalupe Reyes (sgr), M. Viotti (cnd), Berlin German Opera Orch, Berlin German Opera Chorus Berlin Classics 2-▲ BER 1115 [DDD]

Frosini, Mario (bass)
Verdi, G.:I lombardi alla prima crociata, w. Renata Broilo (sop), Maria Vitale (sop), Miriam Pirazzini (mez), Aldo Bertocci (ten), Mario Petri (bass), Bruno Franchi (sgr), Gustavo Gallo (sgr), Renato Pasquali (sgr), M. Wolf-Ferrari (cnd), Milan RAI Lyric Orch, Milan RAI Chorus *(rec 1954)* Cetra Classic 2-▲ CDON 41 [ADD]

Frost, Jenni (sop)
Songs from the Heart, w. Julie Frost (pno) *(rec Studio P, Bala Cynwyd, Pennsylvania, Oct. 31, Dec. 12, 1994, J)* Albany ▲ TROY 165 [DDD]

Frost, John (bass)
Tallis, T.:The Lamentations of Jeremiah, w. Alfred Deller (ct), Wilfred Brown (ten), Gerald English (ten), Maurice Bevan (bar) *(rec Walthamstow Hall, London, 1960)* Vanguard Classics ("The Bach Guild" series) ▲ OVC 2525 [ADD]

Frush, Povla (sgr)
The Complete Recordings *(rec 1926–55)* Pearl 2-▲ PEA 9095 [ADD]

Frusoni, Maurizio (ten)
Boito, A.:Mefistofele (sels), w. M. Olivero (sop—Margherita), M. Frusoni (ten—Faust), H. Smit (b-bar—Mefistofele), A. Kerjens (cnd), *(orch unknown)*—Act III *(rec live May 5, 1973)* VAI Audio 2-▲ VAIA 1062 [ADD]
Catalani, A.:Edmea, w. M. Sokolinska Noto (sop), M. Chingari (bar), P. Lefebvre (bass), A. Nosotti (bass), G. Pasella (bass), G. del Vivo (bass), M. de Bernart (cnd), Lucca Teatro Comunale Giglio Orch, Lucca Teatro Comunale del Giglio Chorus [l] *(rec live 9/89)* Bongiovanni 2-▲ GB 2093/94 [DDD]
Catalani, A.:Mass, w. C. Basto (sop), A. Cipriani (cta), P. Janowski (bass), G. Cosmi (cnd), Lucca Teatro Comunale Giglio Orch [L] *(rec 1985)* Bongiovanni ▲ GB 2027 [DDD]
Catalani, A.:La Wally (sels), w. M. Olivero (sop—Wally), M. Frusoni (ten—Hagenbach), A. Kerjens (cnd), *(orch unknown)*—Act IV *(rec live May 5, 1973)* VAI Audio 2-▲ VAIA 1062 [ADD]
Cilea, F.:Adriana Lecouvreur (sels), w. M. Olivero (sop—Adriana), M. Frusoni (ten—Maurizio), H. Smit (bass-bar—Michonnet), A. Kerjens (cnd), *(orch unknown)*—Act IV *(rec live May 5, 1973)* VAI Audio 2-▲ VAIA 1062 [ADD]
Puccini, M.:Kyrie, w. G. Cosmi (cnd), Lucca Teatro Comunale del Giglio Orch, St. Cecilia Cappella Musicale [L] Bongiovanni ▲ GB 2047 [DDD]
Puccini, M.:Magnificat, w. Nenci (ten), Di Benedetto (bass), G. Cosmi (cnd), Lucca Teatro Comunale del Giglio Orch, St. Cecilia Cappella Musicale [L] Bongiovanni ▲ GB 2047 [DDD]

Fry, Leslie (bar)
Delius, F.:Hassan, w. T. Beecham (cnd), Royal PO, BBC Sym Chorus *(rec 1955–56)* Sony Masterworks (Portrait) ▲ MPK 47680 [ADD]

Fryatt, John (ten)
Stravinsky, I.:Pulcinella, w. J. Smith (sop), M. King (bass), S. Rattle (cnd), Northern Sinfonia of England EMI Classics ▲ CDM 64739

Fuchs, Barbara (sgr)
Schoenberg, A.:Die Jakobsleiter, w. Barbara Kilduff (sop—Seele 1), Jadwiga Rappé (cta—Sterbende), Wilfried Gahmlich (ten—Aufrührerischer), Cornelius Hauptmann (ten—Gabriel), Keith Lewis (ten—Berfener), Kurt Azesberger (bar—Mönch), Barbara Fuchs (sgr—Seele 2), Matteo de Monti (sgr—Ringender), Bjorn Waag (sgr—Auserwählter), E. Inbal (cnd), Frankfurt RSO, Robin Gritton (cnd), Berlin Radio Chorus *(rec Alte Oper, Frankfurt, Sept 6–9, 1994)* Denon ▲ CO 78977 [DDD]

Fuchs, Eugen (bar)
Flotow, F. von:Martha, w. Erna Berger (sop), Peter Anders (ten), Josef Greindl (bass), J. Schüler (cnd), Berlin German Opera Orch, Berlin German Opera Chorus Phonographe 2-▲ PHG 5050
Flotow, F. von:Martha, w. E. Berger (sop), P. Anders (ten), J. Greindl (bass), J. Schüler (cnd), Berlin State Opera Orch *(rec 1944)* Berlin Classics 2-▲ BER 2163 [ADD]
Wagner, R.:Die Meistersinger von Nürnberg (sels), w. T. Lemnitz (sop), E. Laholm (ten), R. Bockelmann (bar), W. Furtwängler (cnd), Vienna State Opera Orch, Vienna State Opera Chorus *(rec Sept. 5, 1938)* Koch Schwann 2-▲ SCH 314522 [ADD]
Wagner, R.:Die Meistersinger von Nürnberg (sels), w. M. Teschemacher (sop), H. Jung (mez), M. Kremer (ten), T. RA. (ten), H.-H. Nissen (bar), S. Nilsson (bass), K. Böhm (cnd), Saxon State Orch—Act. 3 *(rec 1939)* Pearl 2-▲ PEA 9121 [ADD]

Fuchs, Gabriele (sop)
Lehár, F.:Friederike (sels), w. Helen Donath (sop), Adolf Dallapozza (ten), H. Wallberg (cnd), Munich RSO, Bavarian Radio Chorus Emperor Operetta ▲ KO 86344
Mozart, W.A.:Exsultate, w. E. Hinreiner (cnd), Salzburg Mozarteum Orch [L] Pro Arte ▲ CDD 471 [DDD]
Mozart, W.A.:Missa, K.317, w. Novak (alt), Sailer (ten), H. Müller (bass), E. Hinreiner (cnd), Salzburg Mozarteum Orch, Salzburg Mozarteum Chorus [L] Pro Arte ▲ CDD 471 [DDD]
Mozart, W.A.:Sacred Music, w. S. Sass (sop), *(cnd & orch unknown)*—Ah, lo previdi...Ah, t'invola agl'occhi miei, K.272; Ave Verum Corpus, K.618; Exsultate, jubilate, K.165; Laudate Dominum, K.321 [L] LaserLight ▲ 15 884 [DDD]

Fuchs, Marta (sop)
Schoeck, O.:Das Schloss Dürande (sels), w. Maria Cebotari (sop—Gabriele), Marta Fuchs (sgr—Gräfin Morvaille), Brigitte Fassbaender (mez—Renald Willi Domgraf), Rut Berglund (cta—Priorin), Peter Anders (ten—Armand), Benno Arnold (ten—Jäger), Josef Greindl (bass—Nicole), Hans Wrana (bass—Jäger), Vasso Argyris (sgr—Volksredner), Otto Hüsch (sgr—Wildhüter), Leo Laschet (sgr—Jäger), Fritz Marcks (sgr—Jäger), Felix Schneider (sgr—Jäger), R. Heger (cnd)—Text; Ich kann es nicht glauben [from Act 1]; Text; Heil dir, du Feuerquelle [from Act 2]; Text; Gesucht und nicht gefunden [from Act 3]; Text; Der Jäger ist frei [Act 3 Finale]; Text; Sie kommen mit Flinten und Stangen [Act 4]; Text; Du Narr des vermeintlichen Rechts [Act 4 finale]; Text *(rec live, Apr 1943)* Jecklin ▲ JD 692
Wagner, R.:Götterdämmerung, w. H. Scheppan (sop), S. Svanholm (ten), R. Burg (bar), F. Dalberg (bass), K. Elmendorff (cnd), Bayreuth Festival Orch, Bayreuth Festival Chorus *(rec July 21, 1942)* Preiser 4-▲ PRE 90164 [AAD]
Wagner, R.:Die Walküre (act 2), w. E. Flesch (sop), L. Lehmann (sop), M. Klose (cta), L. Melchior (ten), H. Hotter (b-bar), A. Jerger (b-bar), E. List (bass), B. Walter (cnd), Berlin State Opera Orch [G] *(rec 9/38 & 6/22/35)* Danacord 2-▲ DACOCD 317/18 (m)
Wagner, R.:Die Walküre (act 2), w. E. Flesch (sop), L. Lehmann (sop), M. Klose (cta), L. Melchior (ten), H. Hotter (b-bar), A. Jerger (b-bar), E. List (bass), B. Walter (cnd), Berlin State Opera Orch [G] *(rec 9/38 & 6/22/35)* EMI Classics ("References" series) ▲ CDH 64255
Wolf, H.:Der Corregidor, w. M. Teschemacher (sop), K. Erb (ten), J. Herrmann (bar), K. Böhme (b-bar), G. Hann (bass), G. Frick (bass), K. Elmendorff (cnd), Saxon State Orch, Saxon State Chorus *(rec 1944)* Preiser 2-▲ PRE 90182 [AAD]

Fuchsberger, V. (sgr)
Caprioli, A.:Serenata per Francesca, w. G. Schneider (vn), S. Winiarczyk (ob), A. Aigmüller (dr), R. Crow (instr), R. Huber (instr), K. Ager (cnd), Austrian Ensemble for New Music *(rec 1987)* Pro Viva ▲ ISPV 148 CD [ADD]

Fueter, D. (sop)
Keller, A.:Der enthüllte Stern, w. D. Fueter (sop), K. Graf (sop), A. K. Graf (fl), L. Pellerin (ob), E. Schmid (cl), U. Walker (vn), C. Schiller (va), P. Demenga (vc), P. Hug-Rutti (hp), F. Eberle (dr) [G] Grammont ▲ CTSP 19–2 [ADD]

Fueter, D. (sop) (cont.)
Keller, A.:Ewiger Augenblick, w. K. Graf (sop), A. K. Graf (fl), E. Schmid (cl), D. Isler (cel), P. Hug-Rutti (hp), U. Walker (vn), P. Demenga (vc) [G] Grammont ▲ CTSP 19–2 [ADD]

Fuge, K. (sop)
Prokofiev, S.:Eugene Onegin, w. T. West (nar), P. im Thurn (bar), J. Walker (bass), E. Downes (cnd), Sinfonia 21, New Company Chandos 2-▲ CHAN 9318/19 [DDD]

Fügel, Alfons (ten)
Puccini, G.:La Bohème, w. Trude Eipperle (sop), Hildegarde Ranczak (sop), Carl Kronenberg (bar), Georg Hann (bass), Georg Wieter (bass), Emil Graf (sgr), Otto Hillerbrandt (sgr), Karl Schmidt (sgr), C. Krauss (cnd), Bavarian State Opera Orch, Bavarian State Opera Chorus *(rec 1940)* Preiser 2-▲ PRE 90275

Fujihara, Hinako (sop)
Hovhaness, A.:Celestial Canticle, w. Scott Goff (fl), A. Hovhaness (cnd), Northwest Sinfonia *(rec St Thomas Center Chapel, Bothell, WA, Jan 1995)* Crystal ▲ CD 811 [DDD]
Hovhaness, A.:Tale of the Sun Goddess Going into the Stone House (sels), w. Scott Goff (fl), A. Hovhaness (cnd), Northwest Sinfonia—O, Joy at the Dawn of Spring *(rec St Thomas Center Chapel, Bothell, WA, Jan 1995)* Crystal ▲ CD 811 [DDD]

Fullone, Martino (sgr)
Rossini, G.:Demetrio e Polibio, w. Christine Weidinger (sop—Lisinga), Sara Mingardo (cta—Siveno), Anna Laura Longo (sgr—Olmira), Dalmacio Gonzales (ten—Demetrio/Eumene), Giorgio Surjan (bass—Polibio), Martino Fullone (sgr—Onao), M. Carraro (cnd), Graz SO, Bratislava Chamber Chorus *(rec live, Martina Franca Opera Festival, Italy, July 27, 1992)* Dynamic 2-▲ CDS 171/1-2 [DDD]

Fülöp, Attila (ten)
Durkó, Z.:Burial Prayer, w. Endre Ütő (bass), G. Lehel (cnd), Budapest SO, Ferenc Sapszon (cnd), Hungarian Radio-TV Chorus *(rec 1975)* Hungaroton ▲ HCD 31654 [AAD]

Fülöp, Regina (cta)
Werner, G.J.:Vesperae de Confessoris, w. Éva Bodrogi (sop), Kornél Pechan (ten), Péter Cser (bass), János Mezei (org), J. Mezei (cnd), Vienna-Szász CO, Budapest Schola Cantorum *(rec St. Columba's Presbyterian Church, Budapest, June 12–15, 1995)* Hungaroton ▲ HCD 31646 [DDD]

Fünger, Gertrude (cta)
Wagner, R.:Parsifal (sels), w. Gertrude Fünger (cta—Kundry), Gunnar Graarud (ten—Parsifal), Emil Schipper (bar—Amfortas), Josef von Manowarda (bass—Gurnemanz), C. Krauss (cnd), Vienna State Opera Orch *(rec Apr. 13, 1933)* Koch Schwann 2-▲ SCH 314642 [ADD]

Furdui, Svetlana (mez)
Tchaikovsky, P.:Moscow, w. Vassily Gerello (bar), A. Litton (cnd), Dallas SO, Dallas Sym Chorus *(rec McDermott Hall, Meyerson Center, Dallas, TX, Nov 16–18, 1995)* Delos ("Virtual Reality Recording" series) ▲ DE 3196 [DDD]

Furlan, Waldomiro (bass)
Gomes, A.C.:Il Guarany, w. Niza De Castro Tank (sop—Cecilia), Roque Lotti (ten—Ruy Bento), Manrico Patassini (ten—Pery), Paschoal Raymundo (ten—Don Alvaro), Paulo Fortes (bar—Gonzales), Juan Carlos Ortiz (b-bar—Il Cacico), Waldomiro Furlan (bass—Alonso), José Perrotta (bass—Don Antonio De Mariz), A. Belardi (cnd), São Paulo Teatro Municipale Orch, São Paulo Teatro Municipale Chorus *(rec Studios of the Teatro Municipal, São Paulo, Brazil, 1959)* Arkadia 2-▲ HP 617.2 [ADD]

Furlanetto, Ferruccio (bass)
Donizetti, G.:Les Martyrs, w. L. Gencer (sop), R. Bruson (bar), O. Garaventa (bar), G. Gelmetti (cnd), Venice Teatro La Fenice Orch, Venice Teatro La Fenice Chorus *(rec 1978)* Italian Opera Rarities ▲ IOR 7716 [ADD]
Gazzaniga, G.:Don Giovanni, w. L. Serra (sop), E. Szmytka (sop), E. Schmid-Lienbacher (sop), D. Johnson (sgr), B. Weil (cnd), Tafelmusik Sony Classical ("Vivarte" series) ▲ SK 46693
Mozart, W.A.:Arias, w. I. Marin (cnd), Vienna SO—(15 arias) from Così fan tutte *(Donne mie; Rivolgete a lui lo sguardo)*, Don Giovanni *(Deh, vienni alla finestra; Finch'han dal vino; Ho, capito, Signor, si; Madamina! il catologo è questo; Metà di voi qua vadano)*, Le nozze di Figaro *(Hai già vinta la causa; Non più andrai; La vendetta; Se vuol ballare; Tutte è disposto)*, Die Zauberflöte *(In diesen heiligen Hallen; Ein Mädchen oder Weibchen; Der Vogelfänger bin ich ja)* [G,l] Sony Classical ▲ SK 47192
Mozart, W.A.:Don Giovanni, w. A. Tomowa-Sintow (sop), K. Battle (sop), A. Baltsa (mez), G. Winbergh (ten), S. Ramey (bass), P. Burchuladze (bass), H. von Karajan (cnd), Berlin PO, German Opera Chorus [l] Deutsche Grammophon 3-▲ 419179-2 [DDD]
Mozart, W.A.:Don Giovanni (sels), w. A. Tomowa-Sintow (sop), K. Battle (sop), A. Baltsa (mez), G. Winbergh (ten), S. Ramey (bass), P. Burchuladze (bass), H. von Karajan (cnd), Berlin PO, German Opera Chorus [l] Deutsche Grammophon ▲ 419635-2 [DDD]
Mozart, W.A.:Don Giovanni (sels), w. L. Cuberli (sop), J. Rodgers (sop), J. Tomlinson (bass), D. Barenboim (cnd), Berlin PO, Berlin RIAS Chamber Choir Erato ▲ 94823
Mozart, W.A.:Music of, w. Isaac Stern (vn), N. Marriner (cnd), Academy of St. Martin in the Fields, Canadian Brass—Eine kleine Nachtmusik; Syms 38 & 41; sels from Die Zauberflöte; plus others Sony Classical ("Greatest Hits" series) ▲ MLK 62682 ■ MLT 62682
Verdi, G.:Don Carlos (sels), w. J. Bunnell (sop), A. Millo (sop), D. Zajick (mez), M. Sylvester (ten), V. Chernov (bar), P. Plishka (bass), J. Levine (cnd), Metropolitan Opera Orch, New York Metropolitan Opera Chorus *(rec New York, Apr. 20–May 14, 1992)* Sony Classical ("Opera Highlights" series) ▲ SMK 53507 [DDD]
Verdi, G.:Requiem Mass, w. A. Marc (sop), W. Meier (mez), P. Domingo (ten), D. Barenboim (cnd), Chicago SO, Chicago Sym Chorus Erato 2-▲ 96357-2

Furlanetto, Giovanni (bar)
Bellini, V.:La sonnambula, w. Maria Costanza Nocentini (sop), Vitalba Mosca (mez), Giuseppe Morino (ten), Patrizia Ciofi (sgr), Etienne Ligot (sgr), Walter Mikus (sgr), G. Carella (cnd), Italian International Orch Nuova Era 2-▲ NUO 7215 [DDD]
Mozart, W.A.:Così fan tutte, w. Kiri Te Kanawa (sop), Marie McLaughlin (sop), Ann Murray (mez), Hans-Peter Blochwitz (ten), Thomas Hampson (bar), J. Levine (cnd), Vienna PO, Vienna State Opera Chorus [l] Deutsche Grammophon 3-▲ 423897-2 [DDD]

Furmančoková, Zdena (sgr)
Liebermann, R.:Medea, w. Françoise Pollet (sop—Medea), Yvi Jänicke (cta—Chalkiope), Zdena Furmančoková (sgr—Syrinx), Dagmar Hesse (sgr—Aiglaia), Hanne Krogen (sgr—Kore), Michaela Lucas (sgr—Oinone), Renate Spingler (sgr—Silene), Jochen Kowalski (ct—Kreon), Aage Haugland (bass—Jason), G. Albrecht (cnd), Hamburg State PO, Hamburg State Opera Chorus *(rec live, Hamburg, Germany, Sept 24, 1995)* Musiques Suisses ▲ 6126 [DDD]

Furnival, Anthony (spkr)
Honegger, A.:Christophe Colomb, w. E. Knecht (speaker—Queen Isabella), S. Rawson (speaker—The Magician), N. Garvey (speaker—Christopher Columbus), A. Furnival (speaker—King Ferdinand), D. McCabe (bar), C. Peltz (cnd), Buffalo Opera Sacra Orch, Buffalo Opera Sacra Chorus [E] *(rec Buffalo, New York, Oct. 30–31, 1992)* Mode ▲ MOD 35 [DDD]

Furtal, E. (sop)
Weisgall, H.:Six Characters in Search of an Author, w. E. Byrne (sop—Stepdaughter), S. Foster (sop—Prompter), E. Furtal (sop—Coloratura), J. King (mez—Mezzo), N. Maultsby (mez—Mother), P. LoVerne (cta—Madame Pace), D. Pritchett (alt—Wardrobe Mistress), B. Fowler (ten—Tenore Boffo), K. Anderson (ten—Director), A. Schroeder (bar—Accompanist), P. Zawisza (bar—Stage Manager), R. Orth (bar—Father), G. Lehman (bar—Son), M. Wadsworth (b-bar—Basso Cantante), L. Schaenen (cnd), Chicago Lyric Opera Orch, Lyric Opera Center Chorus *(rec Chicago, June 14 & 16, 1990)* New World 2-▲ 80454-2

Furusawa, Yoskiko (sop)
Stravinsky, I.:Japanese Lyrics, w. E. Ansermet (cnd), Swiss Romande Orch members *(rec 11/3/50)* Claves ▲ CD 8918 (m) [ADD]

Fusati, Nicola (ten)
Verdi, G.:Otello, w. Maria Carbone (sgr), Piero Girardi (ten), Corrado Zambelli (ten), Apollo Granforte (bar), Enrico Spada (sgr), C. Sabajno (cnd), La Scala Orch, La Scala Chorus Grammofono 2000 2-▲ GRM 78651
Verdi, G.:Otello (sels), w. C. Muzio (sop), R. Ponselle (sop), H. Spani (sop), E. Caruso (tenL Melchior (ten), F. Merli (ten), F. Tamagno (ten), B. Franci (bar), V. Maurel (bar), R. Stracciari (bar), T. Ruffo (bar) *(rec 1906–1933)* Music Memoria ▲ 30219

1172 ▲ = CD ♦ = Enhanced CD Δ = MD ■ = Cassette Tape □ = DCC

Fusati, Nicola (ten) (cont.)
Verdi, G.:Il trovatore (sels), w. J. Biel (ten), F. Tamagno (ten), L.-A. Escalaïs (ten), M. Gilion (ten), E. Caruso (ten), A. Paoli (ten), G. Zenatello (ten), J. Sembach (ten), L. Slezak (ten), F. Constantino (ten), G. Martinelli (ten), B. De Muro (ten), N. Piccaluga (ten), G. Lauri-Volpi (ten), A. Pertile (ten), E. Bergamaschi (ten), R. Tauber (ten), J. O'Sullivan (ten), H. Roswaenge (ten), G. Taccani (ten), V. Lois (ten), H. Lazaro (ten), A. Lindi (ten), A. Cortis (ten), F. Merli (ten), F. Völker (ten), J. Kiepura (ten), J. Schmidt (ten), J. Bjoerling (ten), B. Gigli (ten), A. Salvarezza (ten), J. Soler (ten), M. Filippeschi (ten)—34 performances of the Act III tenor aria "Di quella pira!," *(rec from 1903–1956)* Bongiovanni ▲ GB 1051 [AAD]

Fusco, Cecilia (sop)
Rossini, G.:L'occassione fa il ladro, w. M. T. Pace (mez), G. Sinimberghi (ten), I. Tajo (bass), R. Gonzales (sgr), L. Colonna (cnd), Naples Alessandro Scarlatti RAI Orch [I] *(rec live, Naples, Sept. 29, 1963)* Arkadia ▲ 602 [ADD]

Füssi, Gert (sgr)
Haydn, J.:Applausus:Jubilaeum virtutis Palatium, w. Florian Erdl (sgr), Christian Graf (sgr), Helmut Wildhaber (ten), Georg Tichy (bass), P. Angerer (cnd), Vienna Concilium Musicum [period instrs] Koch Schwann ▲ SCH 314092

Fyson, Leslie (bar)
Hovhaness, A.:Lady of Light, w. Patricia Clark (sop), A. Hovhaness (cnd), Royal PO, Ambrosian Chorus Crystal ▲ CD 806

Gabarain, Marina de (mez)
Rossini, G.:La Cenerentola, w. A. Noni (sop), F. Cadoni (mez), H. Alan (bass), V. Gui (cnd), Glyndebourne Festival Orch, Glyndebourne Festival Chorus *(rec 1955)* EMI Classics 2-▲ CDMB 64183

Gabor, Constantin (bass)
Puccini, G.:La Bohème, w. Elvira Cirje-Druica (sop—Musetta), Eugenia Moldoveanu (sop—Mimi), Andrei Borsos (ten—Parpignol), Constantin Gabor (ten—Alcindoro), Ludovic Spiess (ten—Rodolfo), Lucian Marinescu (bar—Schaunard), David Ohanesian (bar—Marcello), Pompei Harasteanu (bass—Benoit), Dan Zancu (bass—Colline), C. Petrovici (cnd), Romanian Opera Orch, Romanian Opera Chorus *(rec 1982)* Vox Box 2-▲ CDX 5156

Puccini, G.:Tosca, w. Virginia Zeani (sop—Floria Tosca), Emilia Oprea (mez—Shepherd), Nicolae Andreescu (ten—Spoletta), Corneliu Fanateanu (ten—Mario Cavaradossi), Nicolae Herlea (bar—Baron Scarpia), Gheorghe Crasnaru (bass—Cesare Angelotti), Constantin Gabor (bass—Sacristan), Pompei Harasteanu (bass—Jailer), Adrian Stefanescu (bass—Sciarrone), C. Trailescu (cnd), Romanian Opera Orch, Romanian Opera Chorus *(rec Sept 1977)* Vox Box 2-▲ CDX 5153

Rossini, G.:Il barbiere di Siviglia, w. Magda Ianculescu (sop—Rosina), Maria Sandulescu (mez—Berta), Valentin Teodorian (ten—Count Almaviva), Nicolae Herlea (bar—Figaro), Stefan Petrescu (bar—Fiorello), Constantin Gabor (bass—Don Bartolo), Valentin Loghin (bass—Don Basilio), M. Brediceanu (cnd), Romanian Opera Orch, Romanian Opera Chorus *(rec 1960–61)* Vox Box 2-▲ CDX 5159

Verdi, G.:La forza del destino, w. Maria Nistor-Slatinaru (sop—Donna Leonora), Mihaela Mariacineanu (mez—Curra), Zenaida Pally (mez—Preziosilla), Ludovic Speiss (ten—Don Alvaro), Ion Stoian (ten—Trabucco), Nicolae Herlea (bar—Don Carlo), Nicolae Florei (bass—Padre Guardiano) Constantin Gabor (bass—Fra Melitone), Dan Musetescu (bass—An Alcalde), Mihai Panghe (bass—Marquis of Calatrava), C. Litvin (cnd), Romanian Radio-TV Orch, Romanian Radio-TV Chorus *(rec Jan 1970)* Vox Box 3-▲ CD3X 3038

Gabrovska, Theodora (sop)
Pergolesi, G.B.:Stabat mater, w. H. Angelakova (alt), A. Blagoeva (cnd), New CO, Sofia Boys' Choir Gega ▲ GD 153 [DDD]

Gabry, Edith (sgr)
Mozart, W.A.:Mitridate, w. M. Zara (sop), G. Stanley (sgr), L. Hager (cnd), Salzburg Mozarteum Orch [I] *(rec live in Salzburg, Jan. 31, 1970)* Memories 2-▲ HR 4156/57 (m) [ADD]

Gadd, Stephen (bass)
Maccunn, H.:The Dowie Dens o'Yarrow, w. Lisa Milne (sop), Janice Watson (sop), Jamie MacDougall (ten), Peter Sidhom (bar), M. Brabbins (cnd), BBC Scottish SO, Scottish Opera Chorus Hyperion ▲ CDA 66815

Maccunn, H.:Jeanie Deans (sels), w. Lisa Milne (sop), Janice Watson (sop), Jamie MacDougall (ten), Peter Sidhom (bar), M. Brabbins (cnd), BBC Scottish SO, Scottish Opera Chorus Hyperion ▲ CDA 66815

Maccunn, H.:Lay of Last Minstrel, w. Lisa Milne (sop), Janice Watson (sop), Jamie MacDougall (ten), Peter Sidhom (bar), M. Brabbins (cnd), BBC Scottish SO, Scottish Opera Chorus Hyperion ▲ CDA 66815

Maccunn, H.:Ship o' the Fiend, w. Lisa Milne (sop), Janice Watson (sop), Jamie MacDougall (ten), Peter Sidhom (bar), M. Brabbins (cnd), BBC Scottish SO, Scottish Opera Chorus Hyperion ▲ CDA 66815

Mozart, W.A.:Missa, K.317, w. Barbara Bonney (sop), Catherine Wyn-Rogers (cta), Jamie MacDougall (ten), T. Pinnock (cnd), English CO, English Concert Choir Archive ▲ 445353-2

Mozart, W.A.:Vesperae solennes, w. Barbara Bonney (sop), Catherine Wyn-Rogers (cta), Jamie MacDougall (ten), T. Pinnock (cnd), English CO, English Concert Choir Archive ▲ 445353-2

Gadjev, Zdravko (ten)
Mussorgsky, M.:Khovanshchina, w. A. Miltcheva (mez), M. Popov (ten), K. Kaludov (ten), N. Ghiaurov (bass), N. Ghiuselev (bass), E. Tchakarov (cnd), Sofia National Opera Orch, Sofia National Opera Chorus Sony Classical 3-▲ S3K 45831

Gadpaille, Warren (bass)
Puccini, G.:La Bohème, w. Licia Albanese (sop—Mimi), Audrey Schuh (sop—Musetta), Giuseppe di Stefano (ten—Rodolfo), Arthur Cosenza (bar—Schaunard), Giuseppe Valdengo (bar—Marcello), Norman Treigle (bass—Colline), Warren Gadpaille (bass—Benoît/Alcindoro), Thomas Carter (sgr—Parpignol), Harold Crane (sgr—Custom House Official), Steve Harun (sgr—Sergeant), R. Cellini (cnd), New Orleans Opera Orch, New Orleans Opera Chorus *(rec Nov 1959)* VAI Audio 2-▲ VAIA 1119-2 [ADD]

Gadulanka, Jadwiga (sop)
Penderecki, K.:Als Jakob erwachte, w. Zahos Terzakis (ten), Piotr Nowacki (bass), K. Penderecki (cnd), Royal Stockholm PO, Stockholm Royal Theater Opera Chorus Chandos 2-▲ CHAN 9459

Penderecki, K.:Polish Requiem, w. Zahos Terzakis (ten), Piotr Nowacki (bass), K. Penderecki (cnd), Royal Stockholm PO, Stockholm Royal Theater Opera Chorus Chandos 2-▲ CHAN 9459

Szymanowski, K.:Stabat Mater, w. K. Szostek-Radkowa (mez), A. Hlolski (bar), K. Stryja (cnd), Polish State PO, Polish State Phil Chorus Marco Polo ▲ 8.223293 [DDD]

Gaetani, Jan de (mez)
Crumb, G.:Night Music I, w. J. Thome (cnd), Orch of Our Time Vox Box 2-▲ CDX 5144

Kupferman, M.:Mask of Electra, w. Ronald Roseman (ob), Joel Spiegelman (elec hpd) Soundspells ▲ SP 112 [ADD]

Kurtág, G.:Scenes from a Novel, w. Speculum Musicae *(rec live, New York City, 1987)* Bridge ▲ BCD 9048 [ADD]

Moore, T.:Irish Melodies, w. L. Shelton (sop), F. Kelley (ten), W. Sharp (bar), I. Kipnis (pno) [E] Elektra/Nonesuch ▮ 79059-4 (D)

Mozart, W.A.:Missa, K.317, w. C. Bogard (sop), R. White (ten), T. Paul (bass), D. Zinman (cnd), Rochester PO, Roberts Wesleyan College Chorale *(rec 1978)* Allegretto ▲ ACD 8164 [ADD] ▮ ACS 8164

Ronsheim, J.:Easter-Wings, w. R. DesRoches (perc) CRI ▮ C 301

Shostakovich, D.:From Jewish Folk Poetry, w. Benita Valente (sop), Jon Humphrey (ten), Samuel Lipman (pno) *(rec live, Aspen Music Festival, 1980)* Bridge ▲ BCD 9048 [ADD]

Welcher, D.:Abeja Blanca, w. Philip West (E hn), Robert Spillman (pno) Bridge ▲ BCD 9048 [ADD]

Gaetze, Christa (sop)
Pantillon, F.:Le Noël des Bergers, w. Philippe Laubscher (org), François Pantillon (cnd), Bern Vocal Ensemble *(rec La Salle Musica de La Chaux-de-Fonds)* Gallo ▲ CD 884 [DDD]

Gafni, Miklos (ten)
Miklos Gafni Sings, w. Vienna Operetta Orch, Philharmonica Hungarica Orch Aurora ▲ AUR 5051 [ADD]

Gaggi, Albino (bass)
Verdi, G.:La battaglia di Legnano, w. Caterina Mancini (sop), Amedeo Berdini (bar), Rolando Panerai (bar), Edmea Limberti (sgr), Manfredi Ponz de Leon (sgr), F. Previtali (cnd), Rome RAI SO, Rome RAI Chorus *(rec 1951)* Cetra Classic 2-▲ CDON 40 [ADD]

Gaggi, Albino (bass) (cont.)
Verdi, G.:Don Carlos, w. M. Caniglia (sop—Elisabeth de Valois), G. Sciutti (sop—Page), E. Stignani (mez—Princess Eboli), M. Picchi (ten—Don Carlos), M. Ponz de L. (ten—Count of Lerma), P. Silveri (bar—Rodrigue), N. Rossi Lemeni (bass—Philip II), G. Neri (bass—Grand Inquisitor), A. Gaggi (bass—Old Monk), F. Previtali (cnd), Rome RAI SO, Rome RAI Chorus *(rec Rome, 1951)* Cetra Classic 3-▲ CDO 25 [ADD]

Verdi, G.:Nabucco, w. C. Mancini (sop—Abigaille), G. Gatti (sop—Fenena), B. Preziosa (sop—Anna), M. Binci (ten—Ismaele), L. Francardi (ten—Abdallo), P. Silveri (bar—Nabucodonosor), A. Cassinelli (bass—Zaccaria), A. Gaggi (bass—High Priest of Baal), F. Previtali (cnd), Rome RAI Orch, Rome RAI Chorus *(rec Rome, 1951)* Cetra Classic 2-▲ CDO 26 [ADD]

Gagliardo, Tulio (bass)
Verdi, G.:Rigoletto, w. Renata Scotto (sop—Gilda), Stella Maris Silva (sop—Giovanna), Martha Carrizo (mez—Page), Carmen de la Mata (mez—Countess Ceprano), Noemi Souza (cta—Maddalena), Horacio Mastrango (ten—Borso), Richard Tucker (ten—Duke of Mantua), Cornell MacNeil (bar—Rigoletto), Riccardo Yost (bar—Marullo), Guerrino Boschetti (bass—Usher), Tulio Gagliardo (bass—Count Ceprano), Victor de Narké (bass—Monterone), William Wilderman (bass—Sparafucile), F. Previtali (cnd), Buenos Aires Teatro Colón Orch, Buenos Aires Teatro Colón Chorus *(rec Colon Theater, Buenos Aires, Aug. 22, 1967)* Legato Classics 2-▲ LCD 198-2

Gahmlich, Wilfried (ten)
Mozart, W.A.:Entführung, w. S. Greenburg (sop), J. Thames (sop), J. van der Schaaf (ten), K. Rydl (bass), Trissenaar (sgr), M. Viotti (cnd), Frankfurt RSO, Bamberg Sym Chorus Capriccio 2-▲ 10 403/04

Mozart, W.A.:Entführung, w. S. Greenberg (sop), J. Thames (sop), J. Van Der Schaaf (ten), K. Rydl (bass), M. Viotti (cnd), Frankfurt RSO, Bamberg Sym Chorus LaserLight ▲ 14117 [DDD]

Schoenberg, A.:Die Jakobsleiter, w. Barbara Kilduff (sop—Seele 1), Jadwiga Rappé (cta—Sterbende), Wilfried Gahmlich (ten—Aufrührerischer), Cornelius Hauptmann (ten—Gabriel), Keith Lewis (ten—Berfener), Kurt Azesberger (bar—Mönch), Barbara Fuchs (sgr—Seele 2), Matteo de Monti (sgr—Ringender), Bjorn Waag (sgr—Auserwählter), E. Inbal (cnd), Frankfurt RSO, Robin Gritton (cnd), Berlin Radio Chorus *(rec Alte Oper, Frankfurt, Sept 6–9, 1994)* Denon ▲ CO 78977 [DDD]

Gaifa, Carlo (ten)
Bellini, V.:I Puritani, w. K. Ricciarelli (sop), E. Jankovic (mez), C. Merritt (ten), A. Riva (bass), R. Scandiuzzi (bass), G. Ferro (cnd), Sicilian SO, Bari Teatro Petruzzelli Chorus *(rec Apr. 10, 1986)* Cetra Classic ▲ CDC 20 [ADD]

Bellini, V.:I Puritani, w. Katia Ricciarelli (sop), Eleonora Jankovic (mez), Juan Luque Carmona (ten), Chris Merritt (ten), Roberto Scandiuzzi (bass), G. Ferro (cnd), Sicilian SO, Bari Teatro Petruzzelli Chorus Fonit Cetra ("Digital Operas" series) 3-▲ FCT CDC 20

Canzoni da Battello, w. Cristina Miatellp (sop), instr accompaniment Tactus ▲ TC 700001 [DDD]

Puccini, G.:Manon Lescaut (sels), w. Giuseppe Giacomini (ten), Guido Mazzini (bass), Giorgio Tadeo (bass), Angeles Gulin (sgr), M. Arena (cnd), *(orch unknown)*—Tra voi belle; Cortese damigella; Donna non vidi mai; Vedete, io son fedele; Tu, tu, amore; Ah! Manon, mi tradisce; Lescaut!; Ansia eterna crudel; No, pazzo son; Tutta su me ti posa; Manon...senti amor mio *(rec Treviso, Oct. 16, 1974)* Golden Age of Opera 2-▲ GAO 189/90 [ADD]

Purcell, H.:Dido & Aeneas, w. Helen Donath (sop—Belinda), Shirley Verrett (sop—Dido), Oralia Dominguez (mez—Sorceress), Carmen Lavani (alt—A Spirit), Margaret Lensky (cta—2nd Witch), Carlo Gaifa (ten—A Sailor), Dan Jordacescu (bar—Aeneas), Rosina Cavicchioli (sgr—A Woman), Lilia Teresita Reyes (sgr—1st Witch), R. Leppard (cnd), Turin RAI SO, Ambrosian Chorus *(rec Torino, May 20, 1971)* Arkadia ▲ 619 [ADD]

Respighi, O.:Christus, w. R. Hermann (bar), G. Sarti (bar), M. Balderi (cnd), Swiss-Italian Orch, Swiss-Italian Chorus [L] Claves ▲ CD 9203 [DDD]

Gaillard, Annie (nar)
Honegger, A.:Le Roi David, w. Christiane Eda-Pierre (sop), Martha Senn (mez), Tibere Raffalli (ten), D. Mesguich (nar), S. Baudo (cnd), Czech PO, Czech Chorus [F] Supraphon 2-▲ 11 0132 [DDD]

Galante, Inessa (sop)
Goldins, M.:Jewish Folksongs (18) Campion ▲ 1340

Heroines, w. Latvian Opera Orch [cnd:Alexander Vilumanis] Campion ▲ 1338 [DDD]

Lyric, Coloratura, Dramatic, w. Latvian National SO [cnd:Vilumanis] Campion ▲ 1335

Rachmaninoff, S.:Songs, w. Vladimir Chochlov (pno)—Sing Not to Me Beautiful Maiden [from Songs (6), Op. 4/4 (1890–93)]; They Answered; How Fair This Place [both from Songs (12), Op. 21/4 & 7 (1902)]; Before My Window [from Songs (15), Op.26/10 (1906)] Campion ▲ 1340 [AAD]

Gale, Elizabeth (sop)
Britten, H.:Spring Sym, w. A. Hodgson (cta), M. Hill (ten), R. Hickox (cnd), London SO, London Sym Chorus, Southend Boys' Choir [E] Chandos ▲ CHAN 8855 [DDD]

Gluck, C.W.:Orfeo ed Euridice, w. E. Speiser (sop), J. Baker (mez), R. Leppard (cnd), London PO Erato 2-▲ 2292-45864-2

Handel, G.F.:Israel in Egypt, w. James Bowman (alt), Ian Partridge (ten), Tom McDonnell (bar), Alan Watt (bass), Watson (sgr), S. Preston (cnd), English CO, Christ Church Cathedral Choir Oxford London ("Jubilee" series) 2-▲ 421602-2 [ADD]

Handel, G.F.:Israel in Egypt, w. Lillian Watson (sop), James Bowman (alt), Ian Partridge (ten), Tom McDonnell (bass), Alan Watt (bass), S. Preston (cnd), English CO, Christ Church Cathedral Choir Oxford *(rec Chapel of Merton College, Oxford, 1975)* London 2-▲ 443470-2 [ADD]

Handel, G.F.:Messiah, w. Marjana Lipovšek (mez), Werner Hollweg (ten), Roderick Kennedy (bass), N. Harnoncourt (cnd), Vienna Concentus Musicus Teldec 2-▲ 9031-77615-2

Handel, G.F.:Messiah (sels), w. Marjana Lipovsek (mez), Werner Hollweg (ten), Roderick Kennedy (bass), N. Harnoncourt (cnd), Vienna Concentus Musicus, Stockholm Chamber Choir [E] Teldec ▲ 2292-42409-2

Mozart, W.A.:Don Giovanni, w. C. Vaness (sop), M. Ewing (sop), K. Lewis (ten), T. Allen (bar), R. Van Allan (bass), B. Haitink (cnd), London PO, Glyndebourne Festival Chorus [I] EMI Classics 3-▲ CDCC 47036 [DDD]

Galeffi, Carlo (bar)
The Italian Vocal Tradition, Vol. 1:The Voices of Toscanini, w. Toti dal Monte (sop), Claudio Muzio (sop), Rosetta Pampanini (sop), Biata Scacciati (sop), Giacomo Lauri-Volpi (ten), Francesco Merli (ten), Aureliano Pertile (ten), Mariano Stabile (bar), Riccardo Stracciari (bar), Nazzareno de Angel *(rec 1921–35)* Iron Needle ▲ 1304

Leoncavallo, R.:Pagliacci, w. Rosetta Pampanini (sop), Francesco Merli (ten), Giuseppe Nessi (ten), L. Molajoli (cnd), La Scala Orch, La Scala Chorus *(rec Milan, 1930)* Phonographe 2-▲ PHG CD 5066

Leoncavallo, R.:Pagliacci, w. Rosetta Pampanini (sop), Francesco Merli (ten), Giuseppe Nessi (ten), Gino Vanelli (bar), *(orch unknown)* *(rec Milan, 1930)* Melodram ▲ IMC 102003

Mascagni, P.:Cavalliera rusticana, w. Lina Bruna-Rasa (sop), Giulietta Simionato (mez), Benia Gigli (ten), Giuseppe Nessi (ten), Gino Bechi (bar), P. Mascagni (cnd), La Scala Orch, La Scala Chorus *(rec Milan, 1940)* Phonographe 2-▲ PHG CD 5066

Opera Arias *(rec from EMI Columbia 78 rpm discs 1926–30)* Preiser ("Lebendige Vergangenheit" series) ▲ PRE 89040 (m) [AAD]

Verdi, G.:Un ballo in maschera (sels), w. Maria Caniglia (sop), Gina Cigna (sop), Fedora Barbieri (mez), Enrico Carusa (ten), Beniamino Gigli (ten), Giovanni Zenatello (ten), Lawrence Tibbett (bar), *(various orchs & cnds)* *(rec 1911–43)* Grammofono 2000 ▲ GRM 78527 (m)

Galgani, Ilaria (sop)
Marinuzzi, G.:Jacquerie, w. Antonio Salvadori (bar), Miro Solman (sgr), Martine Surais (sgr), A. Licata (cnd), Catania Teatro Massimo Bellini Orch, Catania Teatro Massimo Bellini Chorus *(rec Catania, 1994)* Nuova Era 2-▲ NUO 7200 [DDD]

Scarlatti, A.:Concerti sacri, motetti, w. Susanna Anselmi (cta), Luca Casalin (ten), Daniele Tonini (bass), Il Ruggiero—Nos. 1–5 Tactus ▲ TC 661903 [DDD]

Scarlatti, A.:Concerti sacri, motetti, w. Susanna Anselmi (cta), Luca Casalin (ten), Daniele Tonini (bass), Il Ruggiero—Nos. 6–10 Tactus ▲ TC 661904 [DDD]

Galka, Czeslaw (bar)
Elsner, J.:Passio Domini Nostri Jesu Christi, w. B. Harasimowicz (sop), K. Szmyt (ten), P. Nowacki (bass), K. Kord (cnd), Warsaw National Philharmonic SO, Warsaw National Philharmonic Sym Chorus *(rec 1990)* Muza ▲ PNCD 078 [DDD]

Galka, Czeslaw (bar) (cont.)
Elsner, J.:Passio Domini Nostri Jesu Christi, w. Bozena Harasimowicz (sop), Krzysztof Szmyt (ten), Bogdan Sliwa (bar), Piotr Nowacki (bass), K. Kord (cnd), Warsaw PO, Henryk Wojnarowski (cnd), Ewa Marchwicka (cnd), Warsaw National Phil Chorus, E. Mlynarski State School of Music Children's Choir *(rec National Philharmonic, Warsaw, 1990)* Polskie Nagrania ▲ PNCD 078 [DDD]
Nicolai, O.:Te Deum, w. Bozena Betley (sop), Zofie Kilanowicz (sop), Katarztna Suska (cta), Henryk Grychnik (ten), Jerzy Gruszcynski (bass), R. Bader (cnd), Cracow PO, Cracow Phil Chorus Koch Schwann ▲ SCH CD 310872

Galka, Czeslaw (bass)
Gloria Tibi Trinitas:Sacred Music of Slav Composers 18th–20th Centuries, w. Warsaw Cathedral Choir [cnd:Andrzej Filaber], Jolanta Kaufman (sop), Anna Lubanska (alt), Ryszard Wróblewski (ten), Maciej Piwowarski (org) Polskie Nagrania Edition ▲ ECD 057 [DDD]

Gall, Jeffrey (ct)
Bach, J.S.:Magnificat, BWV 243, w. J. Bryden (sop), J. Baird (sop), F. Hoffmeister (ten), J. Opalach (bass), J. Rifkin (cnd), Bach Ensemble [L] Pro Arte ▲ CDD 185 [DDD]

Gall, Yvonne (sop)
Gounod, C.:Roméo et Juliette, w. Yvonne Gall (sop—Juliette), Champell (sop—Stéphano), Jeanne Goulancourt (mez—Gertrude), Agustarello Affre (ten—Roméo), Edmond Tirmont (ten—Tybalt), Alexis Boyer (bar—Mercutio), Pierre Dupré (bar—Paris), Hypolite Belhomme (bar—Grégorio), Marcel Journet (bass—Frère Laurent), Henri Albers (bass—Capulet), Valermont (bass—The Duke), F. Rühlmann (cnd), Paris Opéra-Comique Orch, Paris Opéra-Comique Chorus *(rec 1912)* VAI Audio ▲ VAIA 1064–3 F

Galla, Ján (bass)
Suk, J.:Epilogue, w. Zora Jehličková (sop), Iván Kusnjer (bar), V. Neumann (cnd), Czech PO Supraphon 2–▲ SUP 111962 [DDD]
Suk, J.:Epilogue, w. Z. Jehličková (sop), I. Kusnjer (bar), V. Neumann (cnd), Czech PO, Czech Phil Chorus [Cz] Supraphon ▲ 11 0116–2 [DDD]

Gallagher, H. (sgr)
Rodgers, R.:Pal Joey, w. P. Northrop (sgr), E. Stritch (sgr) [1952 revival cast] Broadway Angel ▲ ZDM 64696 ■ EG 64696

Galli, Emanuela (sop)
Marini, B.:Music of, w. P. Beier (cnd), Galilei Ensemble Stradivarius ▲ STV 33446 [DDD]

Galli, Gianni (bar)
Cilea, F.:L'Arlesiana, w. L. di Lelio (sop), P. Tassinari (sop), F. Tagliavini (ten), P. Silveri (bar), B. Carmassi (bass), A. Zerbini (bass), A. Basile (cnd), Turin RAI Orch, Turin RAI Chorus *(rec 1951)* Cetra Classics ▲ CDO 21 [AAD]

Galliard, Peter (ten)
Dessau, P.:Haggada, w. Sabine Ritterbusch (sop), Renate Spingler (sop), Yvi Jänicke (alt), Peter Galliard (ten—Rabbi Tarfon/Jude/ten solo), Gabriel Sadé (ten—Pharaoh), Jochen Schmeckenbecher (bar—Rabbi Jehoschua), Bernd Weikl (bar—Moses), Matthias Hölle (bass—Speaker/Rabbi Akiwa), Alfred Muff (bass—Father/Rabbi Eleasar), Johann Tilli (bass—Rabbi Elieser/bass solo), G. Albrecht (cnd), Hamburg State PO, Berlin Carl Maria Von Weber Men's Choir, Hamburg Alsterspatzen, North German Radio Chorus [G] *(rec Musikhalle, Hamburg, Sept 4 & 5, 1994)* Capriccio 2–▲ 10590/91 [DDD]

Galli-Curci, Amelita (sop)
Amelita Galli-Curci:The Victor Recordings (1930) *(rec 1930)* Romophone ▲ 81021–2
Amelita Galli-Curci:The Complete Acoustic Recordings, Vol. 1 *(rec. 1916–20)* Romophone 2–▲ 81003–2
Amelita Galli-Curci in Opera & Song w. Rosario Bourdon (cnd), Metropolitan Opera Orch [cnd:Giulio Setti] Happy Days ▲ CDHD 201 [ADD]
Amelita Galli-Curci *(rec 1917–1930)* Nimbus ("Prima Voce" series) ▲ NI 7806 (m) [ADD]
Amelita Galli-Curci, Vol. 2 *(rec. 1917–1930)* Pearl ▲ PEA 9450 (m) [AAD]
Galli-Curci Favorites RCA Gold Seal ▲ 09026–61413–2
Lo! Here the Gentle Lark *(rec 1917–28)* ASV Living Era ▲ ASL 5201
The Recordings, 1916–20 Minerva ▲ MN A26 (m) [ADD]
Verdi, G.:Rigoletto (sels), w. Giuseppe De Luca (bar)—Ah, veglia o donna; Piangi, piangi, fanciulla; Oh mia Gilda, fanciulla *(rec 1927 & 1918)* Minerva ▲ MN–A23 [ADD]
Verdi, G.:La traviata (sels), w. Tito Schipa (ten), *(orch unknown)* Forlane ▲ FRL 16718 [ADD]
Verdi, G.:La traviata (sels), w. Giuseppe De Luca (bar)—Dite alla giovine *(rec 1927)* Minerva ▲ MN–A23 [ADD]
The Victor Recordings 1925–28 *(rec 1925–28)* Romophone 2–▲ 810202

Gallo, Gustavo (sgr)
Verdi, G.:I lombardi alla prima crociata, w. Renata Broilo (sop), Maria Vitale (sop), Miriam Pirazzini (mez), Aldo Bertocci (ten), Mario Frosini (sgr), Mario Petri (bass), Bruno Franchi (sgr), Renato Pasquali (sgr), M. Wolf-Ferrari (cnd), Milan RAI Lyric Orch, Milan RAI Chorus *(rec 1954)* Cetra Classic 2–▲ CDON 41 [AAD]

Gallo, Lucio (bar)
Mozart, W.A.:Nozze di Figaro, w. L. Cherici (sop), K. Mattila (sop), M. McLaughlin (sop), M. Bacelli (mez), N. Curiel (mez), U. Benelli (ten), A. Nosotti (bass), M. Pertusi (bass), G. Tadeo (bass), Z. Mehta (cnd), Florence Maggio Musicale Orch, Florence Maggio Musicale Chorus Sony Classical ▲ SK 53286
Mozart, W.A.:Nozze di Figaro, w. Cecilia Bartoli (sop—Cherubino), Sylvia McNair (sop—Susanna), Cheryl Studer (sop—Countess Almaviva), Lucio Gallo (bar—Figaro), Boje Skovhus (bar—Count Almaviva), C. Abbado (cnd), Vienna PO, Vienna State Opera Chorus Deutsche Grammophon 3–▲ 445903–2
Rossini, G.:Il barbiere di Siviglia, w. K. Battle (sop), P. Domingo (ten), F. Lopardo (ten), R. Raimondi (bass), C. Abbado (cnd), CO of Europe [I] Deutsche Grammophon 2–▲ 435763–2

Gallos, Hermann (ten)
Mozart, W.A.:Requiem, w. Hanna Seebach-Ziegler (sop), Jella von Braun (alt), Richard Mayr (bass), J. Messner (cnd), Cathedral Choral Society Orch, Salzburg Cathedral Choir *(rec Aug 9, 1931)* Orfeo d'or ("Festspiel Dokumente" series) ▲ 396951
Wagner, R.:Rienzi, der Letzte der Tribunen (sels), w. Rosette Andsy (cta—Adriano), Hermann Gallos (ten—Baroncelli), Franz Völker (tenor-Rienzi), Karl Ettl (bass—Cecco), J. Krips (cnd), Vienna State Opera Orch *(rec Vienna, May 15, 1933)* Koch Schwann 2–▲ SCH 314662 [ADD]

Galloway, M. (ten)
Rorem, N.:Hearing, w. R. Rees (sop), K. Wheeler (mez), M. Galloway (ten), R. Hilley (bar), R. Wagner (cl), J. Hamlin (tpt), D. Starobin (mand), D. Davidson (vn), K. Askew (va), J. Babich (db), P. Suits (pno), D. Druckman (perc), G. Smith (cnd) Premier ▲ PRCD 1035 [ADD]

Galusin, Vladimir (ten)
Mussorgsky, M.:Khovanshchina, w. O. Borodina (mez), B. Minjelkiev (bass), Ohotnikav (sgr), V. Gergiev (cnd), Kirov Opera Orch, Kirov Opera Chorus [R] Philips 3–▲ 432147–2 [DDD]

Galvano, Licia (sop)
Mascagni, P.:Isabeau, w. Marcella Pobbe (sop—Isabeau), Licia Galvano (mez—Giglietta), Pier Miranda Ferraro (ten—Folco), Orazio Gualtiero (bar—Cornelius), Rinaldo Rola (bass—Re Raimondo), Amelia Bazzini (sgr—Ermyngarde), Piero Benzi (sgr—L'araldo), Renata Davini (sgr—Ermynthrude), Piero Francia (sgr—Il Cavaliere), T. Serafin (cnd), San Remo SO *(rec Sanremo, Jan 13, 1962)* Bongiovanni ("Il Mito dell'Opera" series) 2–▲ GB 1135/36–2 [ADD]
Verdi, G.:Ernani, w. Licia Galvano (sop—Giovanna), Leyla Gencer (sop—Elvira), Carlo Bergonzi (ten—Ernani), Nino Valori (ten—Don Riccardo), Piero Cappuccilli (bar—Don Carlo), Alessandro Cassis (bar—Jago), Ruggero Raimondi (bass—Don Ruy Gomez de Silva), G. Gavazzeni (cnd), Catania Teatro Massimo Bellini Orch, Catania Teatro Massimo Bellini Chorus *(rec live, Catania, Jan 15, 1972)* Arkadia 2–▲ 621 [ADD]

Galvany, Maria (sop)
Fernando de Lucia, w. Fernando de Lucia (ten), Antonio Pini-Corsi (bar), Josefina Huguet (sop), Ernesto Badini (bar), Celestina Boninsegna (sop) Symposium ▲ SYM 1149
Mozart, W.A.:Zauberflöte (sels), w. Marcel Wittrisch (ten), Alexander Kipnis (b), Eide Norena (sop), C. Schmalstich (cnd), Berlin State Opera Orch—Dies Bildnis (Act 1); O Isis und Osiris; Der Hölle Rache; Ach, ich fühl's *(rec 1905 - 1944)* Minerva ▲ MN A14 [ADD]

Galvez-Vallejo, Daniel (ten)
Liszt, F.:Requiem, w. Jacques Maresch (ten), Lionel Peintre (bar), Bertrand Bontoux (bass), Francois-Henri Houbart (org), Y. Parmentier (cnd), Republican Guard Brass & Percussion, French Army Chorus Adès ▲ ADE 203032

Galvez-Vallejo, Daniel (ten) (cont.)
Mascagni, P.:Il piccolo Marat, w. S. Neves (sop—Mariella), C. Pfeiler (mez—Principessa di Fleury), D. Galvez-Vallejo (ten—Marat), S. Cowan (bar—Soldier), M. Dirks (bar—Il Ladro), F. Vassar (bass—L'Orco), H. Claessens (bass—Spy), K. Bakels (cnd), Netherlands RSO, Netherlands Radio Chorus *(rec Feb. 9, 1992)* Bongiovanni 2–▲ GB 2168/69 [DDD]
Tournemire, C.:Sym 6, w. P. Bartholomée (cnd), Liège PO, Brussels Polyphonia Choir Valois ▲ V 4757

Gambarini, Erina (sop)
Melani, A.:Cants, w. G. Cassone (nat tpt), Pian e Forte Ensemble—"All'armi, pensieri" & "Qual bellici, accenti" [I] Nuova Era ("Ancient Music" series) ▲ 7009 [DDD]
Scarlatti, A.:Su le sponde del Tebro, w. G. Cassone (tpt), Pian e Forte Ensemble [I] Nuova Era ("Ancient Music" series) ▲ 7009 [DDD]

Gambelli, Loris (bass)
Mercadante, S.:Il bravo, w. Miwako Matsumoto (sop—Violetta), Giovanna di Rocco (sop—Michelina), William Johns (ten—Il Bravo), Antonio Savastano (ten—Pisani), Gino Sinimberghi (ten—Cappello), Loris Gambelli (bass—Marco), Mario Machì (bass—Luigi), Paolo Washington (bass—Foscari), Maria Parazzini (sgr—Teodora), G. Ferro (cnd), Rome Opera Orch, Rome Opera Chorus *(rec Rome, Dec 30, 1976)* Italia 3–▲ CDC 94 [ADD]
Verdi, G.:Rigoletto, w. Cecilia Nunez Albanese (sop—Gilda), Wilma Borrelli (cta—Maddalena), Jaime Aragall (ten—Duke of Mantua), Renato Bruson (bar—Rigoletto), Loris Gambelli (bass—Sparafucile), G. Campanino (cnd), Naples Teatro San Carlo Orch, Naples Teatro San Carlo Chorus *(rec San Carlo Theatre, Naples, Feb. 1973)* Golden Age of Opera 2–▲ GAO 177–78 [ADD]

Gamberucci, Kate (sop)
Menichetti, D.:L'Epifania del Signore, w. F. Facini (bass), A. Palombi (sgr), A. Della Santa (sgr), F. Esposito (sgr), H. Handt (cnd), Toscana Accademia Strumentale, Polifonica Lucchese Bongiovanni ▲ GB 5033 [DDD]
Pergolesi, G.B.:San Guglielmo Duca d'Aquitania, w. Caldini (sgr), B. Lucarini (sop), R. Girolami (bass), G. Gatti (bar), Herron (sgr), F. Maestri (cnd), Terni CO [I] *(rec live, 12/18/86)* Bongiovanni 2–▲ GB 2060/61 [DDD]
Scarlatti, D.:La Dirindina, w. G. Gatti (ten), Mari (bar), F. Maestri (cnd), *(ensemble unknown)* [I] *(rec live, 1985)* Bongiovanni ▲ GB 2026 [DDD]

Gambill, Robert (ten)
Gluck, C.W.:La Recontre imprévue, w. J. Kaufmann (sop—Rezia), A. Stumphius (sop—Dardané), A.-M. Rodde (sop—Amine), I. Vermillion (mez—Balkis), R. Gambill (ten—Ali), C. H. Ahnsjö (ten—Osmin), J.-H. Rootering (bass—Un Calender), L. Hager (cnd), Munich RSO Orfeo 2–▲ 242912 [DDD]
Graun, K.H.:Cesare e Cleopatra, w. Janet Williams (sop), Lynne Dawson (sop), Iris Vermillion (mez), R. Jacobs (cnd), Concerto Cologne Harmonia Mundi France 3–▲ HMC 901561.63
Handel, G.F.:Acis & Galatea [arr Mozart], w. E. Mathis (sop), A R. Johnson (ten), R. Lloyd (b-bar), P. Schreier (cnd), Austrian RSO, Austrian Radio Chorus [E] Orfeo 2–▲ 133852 [DDD]
Mozart, W.A.:Entführung, w. C. Studer (sop), E. Szmytka (sop), K. Streit (ten), G. Missenhardt (bar), M. Heltau (nar), B. Weil (cnd), Vienna SO, Vienna State Opera Chorus Sony Classical 2–▲ S2K 48053
Mozart, W.A.:Entführung (sels), w. C. Studer (sop), E. Szmytka (sop), K. Streit (ten), Gunter Missenhardt (bar), B. Weil (cnd), Vienna SO, Vienna State Opera Chorus *(rec Vienna, Apr. 2–10, 1991)* Sony Classical ("Opera Highlights" series) ▲ SMK 53500 [DDD]
Rossini, G.:Messa di gloria, w. A. C. Antonacci (sop), B. Manca Di Nissa (cta), F. Araiza (ten), P. Spagnoli (bar), S. Accardo (cnd), St. Cecilia Academy Orch Rome, St. Cecilia Academy Chorus Rome *(rec Mar. 1–2, 1992)* Ricordi ▲ RFCD 2012 [DDD]
Rossini, G.:Stabat Mater, w. R. Muti (cnd), Florence Maggio Musicale Orch—Cujus animam gementem EMI Classics ("Encore" series) ▲ CDE 68308 [ADD/DDD]
Schubert, Franz:Fierrabras, w. K. Mattila (sop), C. Studer (sop), T. Hampson (bar), R. Holl (bass), L. Polgar (bass), C. Abbado (cnd), CO of Europe, Arnold Schoenberg Choir [G] *(rec live)* Deutsche Grammophon 2–▲ 427341–2 [DDD]

Gamlich, Wilfried (ten)
Mozart, W.A.:Entführung, w. Yvonne Kenny (sop), Carolyn Watson (cta), Peter Schreier (ten), Matti Salminen (bass), Wolfgang Reichmann (nar), N. Harnoncourt (cnd), Zurich Mozart Opera Orch, Zurich Mozart Opera Chorus [G] Teldec 2–▲ 2292–42643–2

Gamo-Yamamoto, Nobuko (sop)
Bach, J.S.:Cant 151, w. H. Laurich (cta), A. Kraus (ten), H.-F. Kunz (bass), H. Rilling (cnd), Stuttgart Bach Collegium, Frankfurt Kantorei [G] *(rec Feb 1971)* Hänssler Classic ▲ 98.825 [AAD]

Gampert, Walter (trb)
Bach, J.S.:Cant 23, w. P. Esswood (ct), M. van Altena (ten), M. van Egmond (b-bar), Leonhardt Consort, King's College Choir Cambridge [G] Teldec 2–▲ 2292–42502–2 [AAD]
Bach, J.S.:Cant 32, w. M. van Egmond (b-bar), G. Leonhardt (cnd), Leonhardt Consort, Hanover Boys' Choir [G] Teldec 2–▲ 2292–42505–2 [AAD]

Ganassi, Sonia (mez)
Donizetti, G.:Linda di Chamounix, w. Mariella Devia (sop—Linda), Sonia Ganassi (mez—Pierotto), Francesca Provvisionato (mez—Maddalena), Luca Canonici (ten—Carlo), Alfonso Antoniozzi (bass—Il Marchese di Boisfleury), Petteri Salomaa (bass—Antonio), Boguslaw Fiksinski (sgr—L'intendente), Donato Di Stefano (sgr—Il Prefetto), G. Bellini (cnd), Eastern Netherlands Orch, Andrew Wise (cnd), National Reisopera Choir *(rec Muziekcentrum Enschede, Holland, June 24–July 2, 1992)* Arts Music 3–▲ 47151–2 [DDD]
Rossini, G.:Il barbiere di Siviglia, w. I. Kertesi (sop—Berta), S. Ganassi (mez—Rosina), R. Vargas (ten—Almaviva), A. Romero (bar—Dr. Bartolo), R. Servile (bar—Figaro), F. de Grandis (bass—Basilio), K. Sárkány (bass—Fiorello), A. Déri (pno), B. Sztankovits (gtr), W. Humburg (cnd), Failoni CO, Hungarian Radio Chorus *(rec Nov. 16–28, 1992)* Naxos 3–▲ 8.660027/29 [DDD]

Ganbelli, Loris (bass)
Cherubini, L.:Médée, w. M. Olivero (sop), E. Baggiore (sgr), A. Lo Forese (sgr), N. Rescigno (cnd), Mantova Teatro Sociale Orch, Mantova Teatro Sociale Chorus [I] *(rec live, Mantova 1/23/71)* Myto 2–▲ 2 MCD 91136 [ADD]

Gandolfi, Alfredo (bar)
Verdi, G.:La traviata, w. Rosa Ponselle (sop—Violetta), Henriette Wakefield (sop—Annina), Frederick Jagel (ten—Alfredo), Alfredo Gandolfi (bar—Baron), Lawrence Tibbett (bar—Giorgio), E. Panizza (cnd), *(orch unknown) (rec live, New York, Jan. 5, 1935)* The Fourties 2–▲ ENT FT 1513

Ganglberger, Susanne (sop)
Gassmann, F.L.:La Contessina, w. Susanne Ganglberger (sop—Vespina), Elisabeth Mayer (sop—Contessina), Barbara Eisschiel (mez—Lindoro), Hermann Diller (ten—Gazzetta), Kurt Köller (bar—Pancrazio), Joseph Pichler (Graf Baccellone), H. Dechant (cnd), Collegium Aureum Bayer 2–▲ BR 100 252/3 [DDD]

Gant, Andrew (ten)
Purcell, H.:Anthems & Services, w. Tom Seligman (trb), James Bowman (ct), Ashley Stafford (ct), John Mark Ainsley (ten), Michael George (bass), Charles Pott (bass), R. King (cnd), King's Consort, King's Consort—O Sing unto the Lord; My beloved spake *(rec St Jude-on-the-Hill, London, Dec 20–21, 1968)* United ▲ CAL 88002 [DDD]

Gantner, Martin (ten)
Straus, O.:The Merry Nibelungs, w. Lisa Griffith (sop—Kriemhild), Gudrun Volkert (sop—Brunhilde), Daphne Evangelatos (cta—Ute), Gabriele Henkel (sgr—Giselher), Christine Mann (sgr—Vogel), Hein Heidbüchel (ten—Volker), Martin Gantner (sgr—Gunther), Gerd Grochowski (sgr—Dankwart), Michael Nowak (sgr—Siegfried), Josef Otten (sgr—Hagen), S. Köhler (cnd), Cologne RSO, Cologne Radio Chorus *(rec Cologne, Jan 31–Feb 17, 1995)* Capriccio ▲ 10752 [DDD]

Ganz, Bruno (nar)
Beethoven, L. van:Die Weihe des Hauses (incidental music), w. Sylvia McNari (sop), Byrn Terfel (bar), C. Abbado (cnd), Berlin PO, Berlin Radio Chorus *(rec Great Hall, Philharmonie, Berlin)* Deutsche Grammophon ▲ 447748–2 [DDD]
Maderna, B.:Hyperion, w. P Walmsley-Clark (sop), J. Zoon (fl), P. Eötvös (cnd), Asko Ensemble, Les Jeunes Solistes Vocal Ensemble Montaigne 2–▲ MO 782014 [DDD]
Nono, L.:Canto sospeso, w. B. Bonney (sop), S. Otto (alt), M. Torzewski (ten), S. Lothar (nar), Berlin Radio Chorus *(rec Dec. 9–11, 1992)* Sony Classical ▲ SK 53360 [DDD]

Ganz, Isabelle (mez)
Viens, M.:Voices in the Still, w. Michael C. Viens (pno) MMC ▲ MMC 2040 [DDD]

Ganz, Sara (sop)
Martin, F.:Maria–Triptychon, w. Stuart Canin (vn), K. Nagano (cnd), Berkeley SO *(rec Los Medanos College, Pittsburgh, CA, Feb 25–26, 1995)* New Albion ▲ NA 086

Ganzarolli, Wladimiro (bar)
Cherubini, L.:Ali Baba, ou Les Quarante voleurs, w. T. Stich–Randall (sop), A. Kraus (ten), N. Sanzogno (cnd), La Scala Orch, La Scala Chorus *(rec 1963)* Memories 2–▲ MEM 4513 [ADD]
Donizetti, G.:Don Pasquale, w. Ileana Cotrubas (sop), Alfredo Kraus (ten), Vincente Sardinero (bar), Sutliff (sgr), B. Bartoletti (cnd), Chicago Lyric Opera Orch, Chicago Lyric Opera Chorus *(rec live, Chicago, Nov. 2, 1974)* Arkadia 2–▲ 490
Donizetti, G.:Il Duca d'Alba, w. Renato Cioni (ten), Franco Ventriglia (bass), T. Schippers (cnd), Trieste PO Melodram ▲ CDM 27036
Donizetti, G.:Il Duca d'Alba, w. Louis Quilico (bar), Enzo Tei (sgr), Ivana Tosini (sgr), T. Schippers (cnd), Trieste PO *(rec live at the Spoleto Festival, June 11, 1959)* Memories 2–▲ MEM 4579 [ADD]
Donizetti, G.:La fille du régiment, w. M. Freni (sop), A. di Stasio (mez), L. Pavarotti (ten), W. Monachesi (bar), N. Sanzogno (cnd), La Scala Orch, La Scala Chorus [I] *(rec live, 2/11/69)* Melodram 2–▲ MEL 27045
Donizetti, G.:La fille du régiment, w. M. Freni (sop), L. Pavarotti (ten), N. Sanzogno (cnd), La Scala Orch, La Scala Chorus *(rec 1969)* Memories 2–▲ MEM 4507 [AAD]
Donizetti, G.:La fille du régiment, w. M. Freni (sop), A. di Stasio (mez), L. Pavarotti (ten), W. Monachesi (bar), N. Sanzogno (cnd), La Scala Orch, La Scala Chorus [I] *(rec live, 2/11/69)* Verona 2–▲ 27046/47 (m) [AAD]
Donizetti, G.:La fille du régiment (sels), w. Mirella Freni (sop), Anna di Stasio (mez), Angelo Mercuriali (ten), Luciano Pavarotti (ten), Walter Monachesi (bar), Giuseppe Morresi (bass), V. Gullino (sgr), Luisa Rezzadore (sgr), N. Sanzogno (cnd), La Scala Orch, La Scala Chorus Budget ("The Greatest Voice in Opera" series) ▲ SYP 108
Massenet, J.:Manon (sels), w. Mirella Freni (sop), Luciano Pavarotti (ten), Franco Ricciardi (ten), Giuseppe Morresi (bass), Antonio Zerbini (bass), Ida Farina (sgr), P. Maag (cnd), La Scala Orch, La Scala Chorus *(rec live, Milan, 1969)* Budget ("The Greatest Voice in Opera" series) ▲ SYP 110
Meyerbeer, G.:Les Huguenots, w. J. Sutherland (sop), F. Cossotto (mez), G. Simionato (mez), F. Corelli (ten), N. Ghiaurov (bass), G. Tozzi (bass), G. Gavezzeni (cnd), La Scala Orch, La Scala Chorus [I] *(rec live 5/28/62)* Melodram 3–▲ MEL 37026 (m) [AAD]
Rossini, G.:L'italiana in Algeri, w. L. V. Terrani (mez), L. Rizzi (cta), E. Dara (bar), G. Ferro (cnd), Capella Coloniensis, Cologne Radio Chorus [period instrs] [I] CBS 2–▲ M2K 39048 [ADD]
Verdi, G.:Un giorno di regno, w. J. Norman (sop), F. Cossotto (mez), J. Carreras (ten), I. Wixell (bar), V. Sardinero (bar), P. Elvin (bass), A. Cassinelli (bass), L. Gardelli (cnd), Royal PO, Ambrosian Singers Philips 2–▲ 422429–2 [ADD]

Gaponova, Nina (sop)
Scriabin, A.:Sym 1, w. Andrei Salynikov (ten), E. Svetlanov (cnd), USSR SO, USSR Radio Chorus *(rec live, Moscow, April 14, 1990)* Russian Disc ▲ RC CD 11 056 [ADD]

Garaventa, Ottavio (ten)
Catalani, A.:Dejanice, w. C. Basto (sop), M. L. Garbato (sop), R. Massis (bar), C. Zardo (bass), J. Latham–König (cnd), Lucca Teatro Comunale del Giglio Orch, Lucca Teatro Comunale del Giglio Chorus [I] *(rec 9/6/85)* Bongiovanni 2–▲ GB 2031/32 [DDD]
Donizetti, G.:Maria Stuarda, w. M. Caballé (sop), S. Verrett (mez), C.F. Cillario (cnd), La Scala Orch, La Scala Chorus [I] *(rec live, Milan 4/20/71)* Myto 2–▲ 2 MCD 91137 [ADD]
Donizetti, G.:Les Martyrs, w. L. Gencer (sop), R. Bruson (bar), F. Furlanetto (bass), G. Gelmetti (cnd), Venice Teatro La Fenice Orch, Venice Teatro La Fenice Chorus *(rec 1978)* Italian Opera Rarities ▲ IOR 7716 [ADD]
Rossini, G.:Armida, w. C. Deutekom (sop), P. Bottazzo (ten), E. Gimenez (ten), B. Trotta (sgr), A. Maddalena (bass), G. Antonini (bass), C. Franci (cnd), Venice Teatro La Fenice Orch, Venice Teatro La Fenice Chorus *(rec live, Venice, 1970)* Foyer 2–▲ FOY 2030 [AAD]
Rossini, G.:Armida, w. C. Deutekom (sop), P. Bottazzo (ten), E. Gimenez (ten), C. Franci (cnd), Venice Teatro La Fenice Orch, Venice Teatro La Fenice Chorus [I] *(rec live, 4/3/70)* Memories 2–▲ HR 4152/53 (m) [ADD]
Rossini, G.:Mosè in Egitto, w. Teresa Zylis–Gara (sop), Shirley Verrett (mez), Giampaolo Corradi (bass), Nicolai Ghiaurov (bass), Mario Petri (bass), W. Sawallisch (cnd), Rome RAI Orch, Rome RAI Chorus *(rec live, Rome, 1968)* Italian Opera Rarities 2–▲ IOR 7724 [ADD]

Garazioti, Rena (sgr)
Vivaldi, A.:Il Farnace, w. M. Dupuy (mez), K. Angeloni (mez), P. Malakova (mez), D. Dessy (mez), L. Rizzi (cta), M. de Bernart (cnd), San Remo SO [I] *(rec live 12/1/82)* Arkadia–Akademia 2–▲ 110 [ADD]

Garbato, Maria Luisa (sop)
Catalani, A.:Dejanice, w. C. Basto (sop), O. Garaventa (ten), R. Massis (bar), C. Zardo (bass), J. Latham–König (cnd), Lucca Teatro Comunale del Giglio Orch, Lucca Teatro Comunale del Giglio Chorus [I] *(rec 9/6/85)* Bongiovanni 2–▲ GB 2031/32 [DDD]
Catalani, A.:Loreley, w. M. Colalillo (sop), P. Visconti (ten), A. Cassis (bar), N. Annovazzi (cnd), Lucca Teatro Comunale del Giglio Orch, Lucca Teatro Comunale del Giglio Chorus *(rec live 9/19/82)* Bongiovanni 2–▲ GB 2015/16 [ADD]

Garber, Lin (bar)
Rorem, N.:Missa Brevis, w. Rosalind Rees (sop), Priscilla Magdamo (alt), Gregg Smith (cnd), Gregg Smith Singers Vox Box ("The American Composers" series) 3–▲ CDX 3037

Garbin, Edoardo (ten)
The World of Singing, Vol. 3:The Italian School, Part 1:The Italian Tenors Before World War I (1902–13), w. Antonio Aramburo (ten), Alessandro Bonci (ten), Giuseppe Borgatti (ten), Enrico Caruso (ten), Fiorello Giraud (ten), Fernando de Lucia (ten), Francesco Marconi (ten), Giovanni Battista de Negri (ten), Antonio Paoli (ten), et al. Enterprise ("Vocal Archives" series) 3–▲ ENT VA 2104
The World of Singing, Vol 4:The Italian School Part 1:Tenors before World War I, Book 2, w. Fiorello Giraud (ten), Florencio Costantino (ten), Antonio Paoli (ten), Giuseppe Borgatti (ten), Carlo Albani (ten), Enrico Caruso (ten), Amedeo Bassi (ten), Piero Schivazzi (ten), Elvino Ventura (ten), Giovanni Zenatello (ten) Enterprise ("Vocal Archives" series) 3–▲ ENT VA 2107

Garcia, Celia (sop)
Verdi, G.:Simon Boccanegra (sels), w. Celia Garcia (sop—Maria Boccanegra), Mario Filippeschi (ten—Gabriele Adorno), Ignacio Ruffino (ten—Pietro), Leonard Warren (bar—Simon Boccanegra), Roberto Silva (bass—Jacopo Fiesco), Carlo Morelli (bass—Paolo), R. Cellini (cnd), Mexican National Opera Orch, Mexican National Opera Chorus *(rec Palacio de las Bellas Artes, Mexico City, July 4, 1950)* Legato Classics ▲ LCD 185–1 [ADD]

Garcia, Pablo (bar)
Gottschalk, L.M.:Music of, w. Trinidad Paniagua (sop), José Alberto Esteves (ten), Eugene List (pno), Cary Lewis (pno), Brady Millican (pno), Adler, Buketoff (cnd), Berlin SO, Vienna State Opera Orch—Grande Tarantelle for Piano & Orchestra, Op. 67; Symphony No. 1, "La nuit des tropiques"; Symphony No. 2, "A Montevideo"; The Union (concert paraphrase on American national airs) for Piano & Orchestra, Op. 48; Variations on the Portuguese National Hymn for Piano & Orchestra, Op. 91; Grande fantaisie triomphale sur l'hymne national brésilien for Piano & Orchestra, Op. 69; Marche solennelle for Orchestra; Marcha triunfal y final de opera for Orchestra; Escenas campestres (opera in one act); Five Pieces for Piano Duet [Radieuse, Op. 72; Ses yeux, Op. 66; La Gallina, Op. 53; Ojos criollos, Op. 37; Pasquinade, Op. 59] Vox Box 2–▲ CDX 5009 [ADD]

Garde, Annie Birgit (sop)
Sings Danish Romances, w. Henning Wellejus (pno) Danacord ▲ DACOCD 348 [DDD]

Gardeil, Jean–François (bar)
Charpentier, M.–A.:Le Malade imaginaire, w. C. Brua (sop), N. Rime (sop), M. Zanetti (sop), D. Visse (ct), H. Crook (ten), W. Christie (cnd), Les Arts Florissants [F] Harmonia Mundi France ▲ HMC 901336
Chausson, E.:Mélodies (comp), w. Sandrine Piau (sop), Brigitte Balleys (mez), Billy Eidi (pno), Ludwig String Quartet Timpani 2–▲ 2C 2028
Debussy, C.:Songs, w. Billy Eidi (pno)—Fêtes galantes 1er cahier; Fêtes galantes 2e cahier; 3 ballades de François Villon; Le promenoir des 2 amants; 3 poèmes de Stéphanie Mallarmé Adda ▲ ADD 581307

Gardeil, Jean–François (bar) (cont.)
Honegger, A.:Songs, w. Brigitte Balleys (mez), Billy Eidi (pno)—Mimaamaquim; Nature morte; O Salutaris; O Temps suspends ton Vol; Panis Angelicus; Petit Cours de Morale; Quatre Chansons pour voix grave; Quatre Poèms; Saluste du Bartas; Six Poésie de Jean Cocteau; Trois Poèmes de Claudel; Trois Poèmes de Paul Fort; Trois Psaumes; Vocalise–Etude [F,L,Heb] *(rec Aug. 1992)* Timpani ▲ 1C1015 [DDD]
Lully, J.–B.:Atys, w. Agnés Mellon (sop), Guillemette Laurens (mez), Guy de Mey (ten), W. Christie (cnd), Les Arts Florissants, Les Arts Florissants Chorus [F] Harmonia Mundi France 3–▲ HMC 901257/59 [DDD];
Poulenc, F.:Banalités, w. Billy Eidi (pno) Adda ▲ ADD 581210 [DDD]
Poulenc, F.:Le Bestiarire, w. Billy Eidi (pno) Adda ▲ ADD 581210 [DDD]
Poulenc, F.:Poèmes, w. Billy Eidi (pno) Adda ▲ ADD 581210 [DDD]
Ravel, M.:Don Quichotte à Dulcinée, w. Billy Eidi (pno) Adda ▲ ADD 581210 [DDD]
Ravel, M.:Histoires naturelles, w. Billy Eidi (pno) Adda ▲ ADD 581210 [DDD]
Ravel, M.:Mélodies populaires grecques, w. Billy Eidi (pno) Adda ▲ ADD 581210 [DDD]
Roussel, A.:Songs, w. Billy Eidi (pno)—2 mélodies, Op. 20; 2 mélodies, Op. 50; 2 mélodies, Op. 55; Odes anacréontiques, Opp. 31 & 32 Adda ▲ ADD 581307

Garden, Mary (sop)
Selection of Her Finest Recordings *(rec. between 1903 & 1929)* Pearl ▲ PEA 9067 [AAD]

Garden, Stephen Lee (ten)
Danova, R.:The Phantom of the Opera on Ice, w. Susannah Glanville (sop), Kathy Dooley (sop), Johnny Logan (ten), Mungo Jerry (bar), Nigel Paul (bar), P. Whitfield (cnd), Northern Light SO, Northern Light Choir, Russian Stars on Ice Chorus Plaza ▲ PZA 008

Gardino, Jolanda (mez)
Catalani, A.:La Wally, w. R. Scotto (sop—Walter), R. Tebaldi (sop—Wally), J. Gardino (mez—Afra), M. Del Monaco (ten—Giuseppe Hagenbach), G.G. Guelfi (bar—Vincenzo Gellner), G. Tozzi (bass—Stromminger), C. M. Giulini (cnd), La Scala Orch, La Scala Chorus *(rec Dec. 7, 1953)* Legato Classics 2–▲ LCD 177–2 [ADD]
Donizetti, G.:La fille du régiment, w. A. Moffo (sop), G. Campora (ten), G. Fioravanti (bar), F. Mannino (cnd), Milan RAI Orch, Milan RAI Chorus *(rec live Dec 2, 1960)* Melodram 2–▲ MEL 27018 [ADD]
Mozart, W.A.:Nozze di Figaro, w. G. Gatti (sop), A. Noni (sop), G. Sciurri (sop), M.T. Pace (mez), A. Mercuriali (ten), S. Bruscantini (bar), I. Tajo (bass), F. Corena (bass), F. Previtali (cnd), Rome RAI Orch [I] *(rec 1951)* Cetra Classic 2–▲ CDO 12
Puccini, G.:Manon Lescaut (sels), w. M. Favero (sop), R. Tebaldi (sop), G. Malipiero (ten), G. Nessi (ten), M. Stabile (bar), T. Pasero (b–bar), C. Forti (bass), A. Toscanini (cnd), La Scala Orch, La Scala Chorus—Intermezzo; Act 3 *(rec live, Milan, May 18, 1946)* Arkadia ("Historical Performances" series) 2–▲ 604 (m)

Gardner, A. (sgr)
Kern, J.:Show Boat, w. K. Grayson (sgr), H. Keel (sgr), *(other artists unknown) .(rec 1951)* Sony Music Special Products ▲ AK 45436 ■ AT 45436
Kern, J.:Show Boat, w. K. Grayson (sgr), H. Keel (sgr) *(rec 1951)* TCM ▲ R2 71998

Gardow, Helrun (sop)
Bach, J.S.:Cant 97, w. H. Donath (sop), A. Kraus (ten), P. Huttenlocher (bar), H. Rilling (cnd), Bach Ensemble *(rec Jan–Feb 1974)* Hänssler Classic ▲ 98.835 [AAD]
Bach, J.S.:Cant 110, w. K. Graf (sop), A. Baldin (ten), W. Schöne (bass), H. Rilling (cnd), Stuttgart Bach Collegium, Gächinger Kantorei [G] *(rec Jan–Feb 1974)* Hänssler Classic ▲ 98.824 [AAD]
Bach, J.S.:Cant 167, w. K. Graf (sop), A. Kraus (ten), N. Tüller (bass), H. Rilling (cnd), Stuttgart Bach Collegium, Remembrance Florid Church Chorus Hänssler Classic ▲ 98.803 [AAD]

Gari, Suzanne (sop)
Hasse, J.A.:Piramo e Tisbe, w. Barbara Schlick (sop), Michel LeCocq (ten), H. Müller–Brühl (cnd), Capella Clementina Koch Schwann 2–▲ SCH 310882 [DDD]

Gariboldi, Luigi (ten)
Vivaldi, A.:Gloria, RV.589, w. R. Invernizzi (sop), P. Vaccari (sop), R. Balconi (ct), C. Gubert (cnd), Padua Bach Academy CO, Padua Bach Academy Chamber Chorus Rivoalto ▲ RIV 9301 [DDD]
Vivaldi, A.:Magnificat, RV.610, w. R. Invernizzi (sop), P. Vaccari (sop), R. Balconi (ct), C. Gubert (cnd), Padua Bach Academy CO, Padua Bach Academy Chamber Chorus Rivoalto ▲ RIV 9301 [DDD]

Garin, Remi (ten)
Rossini, G.:Petite messe solennelle, w. E. Schmitt (sop), S. Gregoire (cta), A. Golven (bass), F. Maciocchi (pno) J.–F. Hatton (harm), Paris Opéra–Comique Chorus IMP Masters ▲ IMP MCD61

Garino, Gérard (ten)
Berlioz, H.:Choral Music, w. R. van der Meer (bass), L. Visser (bass), J. Fournet (cnd), Dutch RSO, Dutch Radio Chorus—Le cinq mai, Op. 6; L'impériale, Op. 26; La mort d'Orphée; La révolution grecque, scène héroïque Denon ▲ CO 72886 [DDD]
Chabrier, E.:Gwendoline, w. Adriana Kohútková (sop—Gwendoline), Gérard Garino (ten—Armel), Didier Henry (bar—Harald), J.–P. Pepin (cnd), Slovak PO, Czech Phil Chorus, Slovak Phil Chorus L'Empreinte Digitale 2–▲ ED 13059

Garland, Judy (sgr)
Berlin, I.:Annie Get Your Gun, w. K. Wynn (sgr), H. Keel (sgr), F. Morgan (sgr), *(other artists unknown) (rec 1949 soundtrack)* Sandy Hook ▲ CSH 2053
Porter, C.:The Pirate, w. Gene Kelly (sgr) Sony Music Special Products ▲ AK 48608

Garrard, Don (bass)
Berlioz, H.:Benvenuto Cellini, w. J. Carlyle (sop), J. Veasey (mez), K. Lewis (ten), Kentish, Cameron, Bushby, Ward, A. Dorati (cnd), BBC SO, BBC Sym Chorus [E] *(rec live, Royal Festival Hall, 1964)* Music & Arts 2–▲ CD 618 (m) [AAD]

Garrett, Eric (bar)
Puccini, G.:Tosca, w. Maria Callas (sop—Floria Tosca), Robert Bowman (ten—Spoletta), Renato Cioni (ten—Mario Cavaradossi), Eric Garrett (bar—Il Sagrestano), Tito Gobbi (bar—Scarpia), Victor Godfrey (bass—Casare Angelotti), Dennis Wicks (bass—Sciarrone), C. F. Cillario (cnd), Royal Opera House Orch, Royal Opera House Chorus Covent Garden *(rec London, 1964)* Melodram 2–▲ CDI 203003 [ADD]

Garrett, Lesley (sop)
Burgon, G.:Film Music, Philharmonia Orch—Brideshead Revisited; The Chronicles of Narnia; Bleak House; The Testament of Youth; Tinker, Tailor, Soldier, Spy Silva America ▲ SSD 1005 [DDD] ■ SSC 1005
Diva!:A Soprano at the Movies, w. Philharmonia Orch [cnd:Andrew Greenwood] Silva America ▲ SIL 1007 [DDD] ■ SSC 1007 (D)
Lesley Garrett:Prima Donna, w. Philharmonia Orch [cnd:Ivor Bolton], *(rec. July–Aug., 1992)* Silva America ▲ SIL 1023 [DDD] ■ SIL MC1023
Lloyd Webber, A.:Music of, w. Dave Willets (sgr), C. Corcoran (sgr), Gerard Casey (sgr), S. Campbell (sgr), Royal PO, Royal PO Pops Orch, Royal PO Concert Orch—sels from The Phantom of the Opera; Evita; Cats; Joseph & the Amazing Technicolor Dreamcoat; Jesus Christ Superstar; Tell Me on a Sunday; Song & Dance; Starlight Express; Sunset Boulevard Silva America 2–▲ SILCD 1044 [DDD] ■ SILMC 1044
Lloyd Webber, A.:Music of, w. P. Bateman (cnd), Royal Concert PO Silva America ▲ SSD 1029 ■ SSC 1029
Lloyd Webber, A.:Music of, w. Dave Willets (sgr), C. Corcoran (sgr), S. Campbell (sgr), *(other artists unknown)*—The Phantom of the Opera; Aspects of Love; Cats; Evita; Jesus Christ Superstar; Starlight Express Silva America ▲ SILCD 1022 [DDD] ■ SILMC 1022
Roylance, D.:Battle of the Atlantic Suite, w. B. Connor (cnd), Hallé Orch, Hallé State Chorus Conifer Classics ▲ 74321–15008–2
Simple Gifts, w. Royal PO [cnd:P. Robinson] Silva Classics ▲ SIL 6004 [DDD] ■ SIL MC 6004
Soprano in Hollywood, w. BBC Concert Orch [cnd:Paul Bateman] Silva Classics ▲ SIL CD 6013
A Soprano in Red, w. Royal Philharmonic Concert Orch [cnd:James Holmes] Silva Classics ▲ SIL 6008 ■ SIL 6008
Sullivan, A.:The Mikado, w. J. Rigby (mez), S. Bullock (sop), F. Palmer (sop/mez), B. Bottone (ten), R. Angas (bass), E. Idle (bar), R. Van Allan (bass), M. Richardson (bar), P. Robinson (cnd), English National Opera Orch, English Opera Group Chorus—sels [E] MCA Classics ▲ MCAD 6215 [DDD]; ■ MCAC 6215 (D)
Taylor, B.J.:Wuthering Heights, w. Dave Willets (sgr), C. Carter (sgr), J. Sladdon (sgr), S. Campbell (sgr), Philharmonia Orch, Contorum Choir Silva America ▲ SSD 1008 ■ SSC 1008

Garrigosa, Francesc (ten)

Albéniz, I.:Pepita Jiminez (suite), w. Susan Chilcott (sop), Barcelona Children's Choir, J. Pons (cnd), Barcelona's Free Theater CO Harmonia Mundi France ▲ HMC 901537

Martin Y Soler, V.:Una Cosa rara, w. M. A. Peters (sop), M. Figueras (sop), G. Fabuel (sop), E. Palacio (ten), F. Belaza-Leoz (bar), S. Palatchi (bass), I. Fresán (sgr), J. Savall (cnd), Concert des Nations, La Capella Reial de Catalunya [I] *(rec 1991)* Astrée 3-▲ E 8760 [DDD]

Garrison, David (ten)

Bernstein, L.:Music of, w. J. Norman (sop), K. Te Kanawa (sop), J. Anderson (sop), F. von Stade (mez), C. Ludwig (mez), T. Troyanos (mez), J. Carreras (ten), J. Hadley (ten), T. Hampson (bar), T. Daly (sgr), G. Kremer (vn), M. Rostropovich (vc), M.T. Thomas (va), L. Bernstein (cnd), *(orch unknown)*—various popular works Deutsche Grammophon ▲ 439251-2 ▮ 439251-4

Kern, J.:Show Boat, w. P. O'Hara (sop), T. Stratas (sop), K. Burns (mez), F. von Stade (mez), J. Hadley (ten), B. Hubbard (bar), J. McGlinn (cnd), London Sinfonietta, Ambrosian Opera Chorus EMI Classics ▲ ZDC 49847

Kern, J.:Show Boat, w. P. O'Hara (sop), T. Stratas (sop), K. Burns (mez), F. von Stade (mez), J. Hadley (ten), B. Hubbard (bar), J. McGlinn (cnd), London Sinfonietta, Ambrosian Opera Chorus, Ambrosian Singers EMI Classics 3-▲ A23 49108

Garrison, Jon (ten)

Carter, E.:In Sleep, In Thunder, w. R. Black (cnd), Speculum Musicae [E] Bridge ▲ BCD 9014 [DDD]

Haydn, J.:La Cantarina, w. Brenda Harris (sop—Gasparina), Joyce Guyer (sop—Don Ettore), D'Anna Fortunato (mez—Apollonia), Jon Garrison (ten—Don Pelagio), R. Palmer (cnd), Palmer CO *(rec St. Michael's Church, New York City, Apr. 1994)* Newport Classic ▲ NPD 85595 [DDD]

Stravinsky, I.:The Rake's Progress, w. J. West (sop—Anne Trulove), S. Love (mez—Mother Goose), W. White (mez—Baba the Turk), J. Garrison (ten—Tome Rakewell), M. Lowrey (ten—Sellem), A. Woodley (bar—Father Truelove), J. Cheek (b-bar), *(orch unknown)* MusicMasters 2-▲ 01612-67131-2 [DDD]

Szymanowski, K.:Litany to the Virgin Mary, w. E. Szmytka (sop), F. Quivar (cta), J. Connell (bass), S. Rattle (cnd), City of Birmingham SO, City of Birmingham Sym Chorus EMI Classics ▲ CDC 55121

Szymanowski, K.:Sym 3, w. S. Rattle (cnd), City of Birmingham SO, City of Birmingham Sym Chorus EMI Classics ▲ CDC 55121

Garth, J. (sgr)

Berlin, I.:Annie Get Your Gun, w. E. Merman (sgr), R. Middleton (sgr), L. Bibb (sgr), K. Carnes (sgr), R. Lenn (sgr), C. Turner (sgr), J. Blackton (cnd) [1946 cast] MCA Classics ▲ MCAD 10047 [AAD] ▮ MCAC 10047

Gärtner, Barnhard (ten)

Mangold, C.A.:Abraham, w. Monika Frimmer (sop), Georg Mechthild (mez), Gerd Türk (ten), Giles Cachemaille (bar), Philadelphia Orch, Darmstadt Concert Choir Christophorus 2-▲ 77172

Mozart, W.A.:Missa Solemnis, w. Christa Goetze (sop), Anna Schaffner (alt), Rudolf Rosen (bass), Philippe Laubscher (org), F. Pantillon (cnd), Bieler SO, Pro Arte Chorale, Bern Vocal Ensemble Gallo ▲ CD 893 [DDD]

Garvey, Neil (spkr)

Honegger, A.:Christophe Colomb, w. E. Knecht (speaker—Queen Isabella), S. Rawson (speaker—The Magician), N. Garvey (speaker—Christopher Columbus), A. Furnival (speaker—King Ferdinand), D. McCabe (bar), C. Peltz (cnd), Buffalo Opera Sacra Orch, Buffalo Opera Sacra Chorus [E] *(rec Buffalo, New York, Oct. 30-31, 1992)* Mode ▲ MOD 35 [DDD]

Garvin, G. Bradley (b-bar)

Eaton, J.:Ajax, w. C. Baker (cnd), Indiana Univ New Music Ensemble *(rec Musical Arts Ctr, Bloomington, IN, Oct 19, 1989)* Indiana Univ School of Music ▲ 0-253-31842-4

Gasa, Francesco (alt)

Britten, H.:A Ceremony of Carols, w. S. Bardolet (trb), X. Canadell (trb), J. Pieres (alt), M. L. Ibañez (hp), G. Estrada (org), Escolania de Montserrat, I. Segarra (cnd) *(rec 1978?)* Koch Treasure ▲ 31624-2 [ADD]

Mendelssohn, F.:Motets, Op. 39, w. S. Bardolet (trb), X. Canadell (trb), J. Pieres (alt), M. L. Ibañez (hp), G. Estrada (org), I. Segarra (cnd), Montserrat Escolania *(rec 1978?)* Koch Treasure ▲ 31624-2 [ADD]

Gasdia, Cecilia (sop)

Bertoni, F.:Orfeo ed Euridice, w. Cecilia Gasdia (sop—Euridice), Delores Ziegler (mez—Orfeo), Bruce Ford (ten—Imeneo), C. Scimone (cnd), Venice Solisti, John McCarthy (cnd), Ambrosian Opera Chorus *(rec Vicenza, Italy, Aug 3-7, 1990)* Arts Music ▲ 47118-2 [DDD]

Cecilia Gasdia, Leo Nucci & Ruggero Raimondi:In Concerto, w. Leo Nucci (bar), Ruggero Raimondi (bass) Bongiovanni ▲ GB 2516-2

Donizetti, G.:L'Esule di Roma, w. E. Palacio (ten), A. Ariostini (bar), S. Alaimo (bass-bar), M. de Bernart (cnd), Piacenza SO, Paris Opéra-Comique Chorus *(rec live, 10/14/86)* Bongiovanni 2-▲ GB 2045/46 [DDD]

Gounod, C.:Faust, w. B. Fassbaender (mez), S. Mentzer (mez), J. Hadley (ten), A. Agache (bar), P. Fourcade (bass), C. Rizzi (cnd), Welsh National Opera Orch, Welsh National Opera Chorus Teldec 3-▲ 90872

Handel, G.F.:Rinaldo, w. Christine Weidinger (sop), Marylin Horne (mez), Ernesto Palacio (ten), J. Fisher (cnd), Venice Teatro La Fenice Orch *(rec live 1989)* Nuova Era 2-▲ 6813/14 [DDD]

Puccini, G.:Turandot, w. G. Dimitrova (sop), N. Martinucci (ten), R. Scandiuzzi (bass), D. Oren (cnd), Genoa Teatro Comunale Orch, Genoa Teatro Comunale Chorus [I] *(rec live, 1/20-27/89)* Nuova Era 2-▲ 6786/87 [DDD]

Puccini, G.:Turandot (sels), w. G. Dimitrova (sop), N. Martinucci (ten), R. Scandiuzzi (bass), D. Oren (cnd), Genoa Teatro Comunale Orch, Genoa Teatro Comunale Chorus [I] Nuova Era ▲ 6871 [DDD]

Verdi, G.:Luisa Miller, w. Mazzareno Antinori (ten), Simone Alaimo (b-bar), G. Gavazzeni (cnd), Parma Teatro Regio Orch, Parma Teatro Regio Chorus *(rec live, 1981)* Serenissima 2-▲ SER 360143

Vivaldi, A.:Catone in Utica, w. Susanna Rigacci (sop), Marilyn Schmiege (sop), Lucretia Lendi (mez), Margarita Zimmerman (mez), C. Scimone (cnd), Venice Solisti Erato 2-▲ ERA SEL 11232 [DDD]

Gaspari, Daniele (sgr)

Paisiello, G.:Il mondo della luna, w. Gemma Bertagnolli (sop—Clarice), Enzo Dara (bar—Buonafede), Riccardo Ristori (bass—Cecco), Carla Di Censo (sgr—Flaminia), Daniele Gaspari (sgr—Ecclittico), Mattia Nicolini (sgr—Ernesto), F. Neri (cnd), Bolzano Monteverdi Orch *(rec Aug 4-6, 1993)* Bongiovanni 2-▲ GB 2173/74 [DDD]

Gasparini, Annamaria (mez)

Zandonai, R.:Francesca da Rimini (sels), w. M. Olivero (sop), A. Cesarini (ten), M. del Monaco (ten), V. Carbonari (bass), N. Rescigno (cnd), Monte Carlo Opera Orch London ("Grand Opera" series) 2-▲ 433033-2 [ADD]

Gassiev, Nikolai (ten)

Tchaikovsky, P.:Iolanta, w. Galina Gorchakova (sop), Gegam Grigorian (ten), Dmitri Hvorostovsky (bar), Nikolai Putilin (bar), Sergei Alexashkin (bass), Gennady Bezzubenkov (bass), Larissa Diadkova (sgr), Olga Korzhenskaya (sgr), Tatyana Kravtsova (sgr), V. Gergiev (cnd), Kirov Opera Orch, Kirov Opera Chorus *(rec Mariinsky Theatre, St. Petersburg)* Philips 2-▲ 442796-2

Gáti, Istvan (bar)

Bach, J.S.:Cant 51, w. I. Kertesi (sop), J. Pászthy (sop), J. Nemeth (mez), J. Mukk (ten), M. Antal (cnd), Failoni CO, Hungarian Radio Chorus Naxos ▲ 8.550643 [DDD]

Bach, J.S.:Cant 80, w. I. Kertesi (sop), J. Nemeth (alt), J. Mukk (ten), M. Antal (cnd), Failoni CO, Hungarian Radio Chorus *(rec Jan 1992)* Naxos ▲ 8.550642 [DDD]

Bach, J.S.:Cant 147, w. I. Kertesi (sop), J. Nemeth (alt), J. Mukk (ten), M. Antal (cnd), Failoni CO, Hungarian Radio Chorus *(rec Jan 1992)* Naxos ▲ 8.550642 [DDD]

Bach, J.S.:Cant 208, "Hunting Cant", w. I. Kertesi (sop), J. Pászthy (sop), J. Nemeth (mez), J. Mukk (ten), M. Antal (cnd), Failoni CO, Hungarian Radio Chorus Naxos ▲ 8.550643 [DDD]

Bach, J.S.:Cant 211, "Coffee Cant", w. I. Kertesi (sop), J. Mukk (ten), M. Antal (cnd), Failoni CO *(rec 1992)* Naxos ▲ 8.550641 [DDD]

Bach, J.S.:Cant 212, "Peasant Cant", w. I. Kertesi (sop), J. Mukk (ten), M. Antal (cnd), Failoni CO *(rec 1992)* Naxos ▲ 8.550641 [DDD]

Gáti, Istvan (bar) (cont.)

Bach, J.S.:St. Matthew Passion, w. R. Kiss (sop), I. Verebics (sop), Á. Csenki (mez), J. Németh (mez), P. Cser (ten), J. Mukk (ten), F. Korpás (bar), P. Kóves (bass), G. Oberfrank (cnd), Hungarian State SO, Hungarian Festival Choir, Hungarian Radio Children's Choir [G] *(rec Feb 1993)* Naxos 3-▲ 8.550832/34 [DDD]

Erkel, F.:Hunyadi László, w. M. Kalmár (sop), S. Sass (sop), D. Gulyás (ten), A. Molnar (ten), S. Sólyom-Nagy (bar), J. Kovács (cnd), Hungarian State Opera Orch, Hungarian State Opera Chorus [Hun] Hungaroton 3-▲ HCD 12581/83 [DDD]

Handel, G.F.:Brockes-Passion, w. K. Farkas (sop), M. Zádori (sop), D. Minter (alt), J. Bándi (ten), M. Klietmann (ten), G. de Mey (ten), N. McGegan (cnd), Capella Savaria, Hallé State Chorus [period instrs] [G] Hungaroton 3-▲ HCD 12734/36 [DDD]

Strauss, R.:Guntram, w. I. Tokody (sop), R. Goldberg (ten), S. Sólyom-Nágy (bar), E. Queler (cnd), Hungarian State Orch, Hungarian People's Army Male Chorus [G] CBS 2-▲ M2K 39737 [DDD]

Telemann, G.P.:Brockes Passion, w. M. Zádori (sop), A. Markert (cta), M. Klietmann (ten), G. De Mey (ten), N. McGegan (cnd), Capella Savaria, Hallé State Chorus [period instrs] Hungaroton 3-▲ HCD 31130/32 [DDD]

Vivaldi, A.:L'Olimpiade (sels), w. M. Zempléni (sop), T. Takács (mez), Horváth (sgr), Káplán (sgr), L. Miller (bar), K. Kováts (bass), F. Szekeres (cnd), Hungarian State Orch, Budapest Madrigal Choir [I] White Label ▲ HRC 073 [ADD]

Gatta, Dora (sop)

Gatta, Moffo, Rizzieri, Christoff & Mazzolli, w. Anna Moffo (sop), Elena Rizzieri (sop), Boris Christoff (bass), Ferruccio Mazzoli (bass), Rome RAI SO, Turin RAI SO *(rec Martini & Rossi Concert)* Incontri Memorabili ▲ CDMR 5033

Massenet, J.:Werther, w. D. Gatta (sop—Sofia), I. Ligabue (sop—Kaethlen), G. Simionato (mez—Charlotte), F. Tagliavini (ten—Werther), V. Pandano (ten—Schmidt), E. Campi (bass—Johann), S. Bruscantini (bass—Le Bailli), F. Capuana (cnd), La Scala Orch, La Scala Chorus *(rec Apr. 21, 1951)* Bongiovanni 2-▲ GB 1101/02 [ADD]

Rossini, G.:Il barbiere di Siviglia, w. C. Valletti (ten), G. Bechi (bar), N. Rossi-Lemeni (bass), V. de Sabata (cnd), La Scala Orch, La Scala Chorus *(rec 1952)* Memories 2-▲ MEM 4525 [AAD]

Gatti, Gabriella (sop)

Morlacchi, F.:Nuovo barbiere, w. A. Ruffini (sop), M. Comencini (ten), A. Tomicich (bass), R. Franceschetto (sgr), G. Catalucci (cnd), Orch Giovanile In Canto [I] *(rec live 9/9/89)* Bongiovanni 2-▲ GB 2085/86 [DDD]

Mozart, W.A.:Nozze di Figaro, w. A. Noni (sop), G. Sciurri (sop), J. Gardino (mez), M.T. Pace (mez), A. Mercuriali (ten), S. Bruscantini (bar), I. Tajo (bass), F. Corena (bass), F. Previtali (cnd), Rome RAI Orch [I] *(rec 1951)* Cetra Classic 2-▲ CDO 12

Verdi, G.:Nabucco, w. C. Mancini (sop—Abigaille), G. Gatti (sop—Fenena), B. Preziosa (sop—Anna), M. Binci (ten—Ismaele), L. Francardi (ten—Abdallo), P. Silveri (bar—Nabucodonosor), A. Cassinelli (bass—Zaccaria), A. Gaggi (bass—High Priest of Baal), F. Previtali (cnd), Rome RAI Orch, Rome RAI Chorus *(rec Rome, 1951)* Cetra Classic 2-▲ CDO 26 [ADD]

Gatti, Giorgio (bar)

Cavalli, P.F.:Ormindo, w. E. Zilio (mez), V. Manno (ten), A. Rinaldi (bar), R. Fasano (cnd), Rome Virtuosi Stradivarius 2-▲ DAT 12307

Cherubini, L.:Il Giuocatore, w. Monica Bacelli (sop), G. Bernasconi (cnd), Italian Instrumental Academy *(rec Parma, Mar 20-22, 1989)* Agorá Music ("Phoenix" series) ▲ 504

Cimarosa, D.:Il Maestro di cappella, w. R. Cirri (cnd), Ars Cantus *(rec Sept 7-10, 1995)* Bongiovanni ▲ GB 2184 [DDD]

Fioravanti, V.:Le cantatrici villane, w. G. Manci (sop—Agata), M. Mauro (sop—Nunziella), M. A. Peters (sop—Rosa), F. Sovilla (mez—Giannetta), E. Palacio (ten—Carlino), G. Gatti (bar—Don Bucefalo), D. Serraiocco (bass—Don Marco), R. Tigani (cnd), Frosinone Licinio Refice Conservatory SO *(rec Oct. 22, 23 & 25, 1992; [])* Bongiovanni 2-▲ GB 2135/36 [DDD]

Hasse, J.A.:Larinda e Vanesio, w. Silvia Piccollo (sop—Larinda), Giorgio Gatti (bar—Vanesio), S. Carchiolo (cnd), Catania Baroque Orch *(rec Sept. 29, 1992)* Bongiovanni ▲ GB 2137

Hasse, J.A.:La Serva scaltra, w. Bernadette Lucarini (sop), G. Catalucci (cnd), Sassari SO Ensemble [I] Bongiovanni ▲ GB 2101 [DDD]

Pergolesi, G.B.:San Guglielmo Duca d'Aquitania, w. K. Gamberucci (sop), Caldini (sgr), B. Lucarini (sop), R. Girolami (bass), Herron (sgr), F. Maestri (cnd), Terni CO [I] *(rec live, 12/18/86)* Bongiovanni 2-▲ GB 2060/61 [DDD]

Rossini, G.:L'inganno felice, w. S. Rigacci (sop—Isabella), E. Palacio (ten—Duke Bertrando), G. Gatti (bar—Batone), R. Ripesi (bass—Tarabotto), G. Casali (bass—Ormondo), F. Maestri (cnd), In Canto CO *(rec Dec. 1992)* Bongiovanni 2-▲ GB 2133/34 [DDD]

Sacchini, A.:La contandina in corte, w. S. Rigacci (sop—Tancia), E. Palacio (ten—Ruggiero), G. Gatti (bar—Berto), C. Boersma (vc), M. Clavenna (db), M. T. Conti (hpd), G. Catalucci (cnd), Sassari SO *(rec Dec. 17-18, 1991)* Bongiovanni 2-▲ GB 2145/46 [DDD]

Salieri, A.:Arlecchinata, w. U. Benelli (bar), P. Pellegrini (sgr), G. Catalucci (cnd), In Canto di Terni Youth Orch [I] *(rec live 9/90)* Bongiovanni 2-▲ GB 2111/12 [DDD]

Sarro, D.N.:Dorina e Nibbio, w. S. Mingardo (cta—Dorina), G. Gatti (bar—Nibbio), G. Catalucci (cnd), In Canto CO *(rec Dec. 8, 1992)* Bongiovanni ▲ GB 2147 [DDD]

Scarlatti, D.:La Dirindina, w. K. Gamberucci (sop), Mari (bar), F. Maestri (cnd), *(ensemble unknown)* [I] *(rec live, 1985)* Bongiovanni ▲ GB 2026 [DDD]

Gauci, Miriam (sop)

Beethoven, L. van:Egmont (ov), w. A. Rahbari (cnd), Brussels Belgian Radio-TV PO Discover International ▲ DICD 920114 [DDD]

Beethoven, L. van:Sym 9, "Choral Sym", w. A. Rahbari (cnd), Brussels Belgian Radio-TV PO, Bruges Cantores Oratorio Choir Discover International ▲ DICD 920151 [DDD]

Brahms, J.:Ein Deutsches Requiem, w. E. Tumagian (bar), A. Rahbari (cnd), Czech-Slovak RSO Bratislava, Slovak Phil Chorus *(rec June 1992)* Naxos ▲ 8.550213 [DDD]

Puccini, G.:Madama Butterfly, w. N. Boschkowá (mez), A. Michalková (mez), Y. Ramiro (ten), A. Rahbari (cnd), Czech-Slovak RSO Bratislava, Slovak Phil Chorus [I] Naxos 2-▲ 8.660015/16 [DDD]

Puccini, G.:Madama Butterfly (sels), w. Miriam Gauci (sop—Madama Butterfly), Nelly Boschkowa (mez—Suzuki), Yordi Ramiro (ten—F.B. Pinkerton), Jozef Abel (ten—Goro), Georg Tichy (bass—Sharpless), Anna Tomkovicová (sgr), Mária Stahelová (sgr), Elena Hanzelová (sgr) *(rec Concert Hall of the Czecho-Slovak Radio, Bratislava, May 2-10, 1991)* Naxos ▲ 8.553152 [DDD]

Soprano Arias from Italian Operas, w. Brussels BRT PO [cnd:Alexander Rahbari] *(rec. Jan. 14-17, 1992)* Naxos ▲ 8.550606 [DDD] Δ 7.550606 [DDD]

Gaudel, Christiane (mez)

Charpentier, G.:Louise, w. N. Vallin (sop—Louise), C. Gaudel (sop—Irma), A. Lecouvreur (mez—Mother), G. Thill (ten—Julien), A. Pernet (bass—Father), E. Bigot (cnd), Raugel Orch, Raugel Chorus *(rec 1936)* Nimbus (Prima Voce) ▲ NI 7829 (m) [ADD]

Charpentier, G.:Louise (abridged ed), w. N. Vallin (sop—Louise), C. Gaudel (mez—Irma), A. Lecouvreur (cta—La Mère), G. Thill (ten—Julien), A. Pernet (bass—La Père), E. Bigot (cnd), *(orch & chorus unknown)* [F] *(rec 1935 for Columbia Records)* Music Memoria 3-▲ 30223

Gaudin, Philippe (sgr)

Hahn, R.:O mon bel inconnul, w. Christiane Château (sop), Lina Dachary (sop), Monique Stiot (mez), Michel Hamel (ten), Joseph Peyron (ten), Aimé Doniat (bar), Dominique Tirmont (bar), Jacques Provins (sgr), J. Brebion (cnd), ORTF Lyric Orch Musidisc 2-▲ MUS 202562 [AAD]

Gaudioso, Gerardo (bar)

Verdi, G.:La traviata (sels), w. Anna de Santis (sop—Annina), Renata Tebaldi (sop—Violetta), Giuseppe Campora (ten—Alfredo), Gerardo Gaudioso (bar—Douphol), Giuseppe Taddei (bar—Germont), Antonio Picillo (bass—Grenvil), G. Santini (cnd), Naples Teatro San Carlo Orch, Naples Teatro San Carlo Chorus—E strano...Ah, fors'e lui; Follie!...Sempre libera; Pero l'attendo...Amami, Alfredo; Invitato a qui seguirmi; Alfredo, Alfredo, di questo core; Teneste la promessa...Addio del passato; Ma se tornando...Ah! Gran Dio! Morir si giovine; Se una pudica vergine *(rec San Carlo Theater, Naples, Jan. 17, 1952)* Legato Classics 2-▲ LCD 193-2 [DDD]

Gautier, Caroline (nar)

Poulenc, F.:L'Histoire de Babar, w. William Nabore (pno) Accord ▲ ACD 200592 [DDD]

Gautier, Caroline (sgr)

Benda, G.A.:Medea, w. O. Cuendet (cnd), Lausanne CO Accord ▲ ACD 202622

1176 ▲ = CD ♦ = Enhanced CD Δ = MD ▮ = Cassette Tape ◻ = DCC

Gautier, Georges (ten)

Prokofiev, S.:The Love for 3 Oranges (suite), w. C. Dubosc (sop), J.-L. Viala (ten), G. Bacquier (bar), J. Bastin (bass), K. Nagano (cnd), Paris Lyon Opera Orch, Paris Lyon Opera Chorus [F] Virgin Classics ▲ 59566 [DDD]

Rameau, J.P.:Dardanus, w. C. Eda-Pierre (sop), F. von Stade (mez), R. Soyer (bar), J. Van Dam (b-bar), R. Leppard (cnd), Paris Lyon Opera Orch, Paris Lyon Opera Chorus Erato 2-▲ 95312-2

Gauvin, Katrina (sop)

Little Notebook for Anna Magdalena Bach, w. Gauvin, Katrina (sop), Luc Beauséjour (hpd), Sergeï Istomin (vc) Analekta Fleur de Lys ▲ FL 23064 [DDD]

Gavanelli, Paolo (bass)

Bellini, V.:Beatrice di Tenda, w. L. Aliberti (sop), C. Capasso (treble), M. Thompson (ten), F. Luisi (cnd), Berlin German Opera Orch, Berlin German Opera Chorus Berlin Classics 2-▲ BER 1042 [DDD]

Verdi, G.:Nabucco, w. Monica Pick-Hieronimi (sop), Anna Schiatti (sop), Mina Blum (sop), Angelo Casertano (ten), Gilberto Maffezzoni (ten), Paata Burchuladze (bass), Franco Federici (bass), A. Guadagno (cnd), Arena di Verona Orch, Arena di Verona Chorus *(rec Berlin, Spring 1996)* Koch Schwann 2-▲ SCH CD 364272

Gavarini, Renato (ten)

Bellini, V.:I Capuleti e i Montecchi (sels), w. F. Cossotto (mez), V. Tatozzi (bar), L. Maazel (cnd), Rome RAI Orch, Rome RAI Chorus—2 solo tenor arias & 1 mezzo-bass duet [I] *(rec live 10/23/58)* Melodram ("Connaisseur" series) 2-▲ CDM 27509 [ADD]

Gluck, C.W.:Alceste, w. M. Callas (sop), R. Panerai (bar), S. Maionica (bass), C. M. Giulini (cnd), La Scala Orch, La Scala Chorus—plus "Callas Sings Gluck & Rossini" [French version] *(rec live, La Scala, 4/4/54)* Melodram 2-▲ MEL 26026

Gavazzeni, Mazzola (ten)

Verdi, G.:Arias, w. M. Callas (sop), G. Di Stefano (ten), C.M. Giulini (cnd), La Scala Orch—E strano...Sempre libera;—Ecco l'orrido campo...Ma dall' arido stelo Myto 2-▲ MCD 89003 (m) [ADD]

Gavazzi, Carla (sop)

Cilea, F.:Adriana Lecouvreur, w. Miti Truccato Pace (mez), Giacinto Prandelli (ten), Saturno Meletti (bar), A. Simonetto (cnd), Milan RAI Lyric Orch, Milan RAI Chorus Fonit Cetra ("Classic Collection" series) 2-▲ FCT CDO 20

Leoncavallo, R.:Pagliacci, w. C. Gavazzi (sop—Nedda), C. Bergonzi (ten—Canio), S. Di Tommaso (ten—Beppe), C. Tagliabue (bar—Tonio), M. Rossi (bar—Silvio), A. Simonetto (cnd), Turin RAI SO, Turin RAI Chorus *(rec Turin, 1951)* Cetra Classic 2-▲ CDO 27 [ADD]

Gavazzi, Ernesto (ten)

Boito, A.:Mefistofele, w. Michèle Crider (sop—Margherita/Elena), Eleonora Jankovic (mez—Marta/Pantalis), Ernesto Gavazzi (ten—Wagner/Nereo), Vincenza La Scola (ten—Faust), Samuel Ramey (bass—Mefistofele), R. Muti (cnd), La Scala Orch, La Scala Chorus *(rec live Mar 3,5 & 8, 1995, Milan)* RCA Victor 2-▲ 09026-68284-2 [DDD]

Giordano, U.:Fedora, w. Mirella Freni (sop—Principessa Fedora), Adelina Scarabelli (sop—Contessa Olga), Silvia Mazzoni (mez—Dimitri), Monica Minarelli (sgr—Savoiardo), Placido Domingo (ten—Conte Loris), Ernesto Gavazzi (ten—Desiré), Aldo Bottion (ten—Barone Rouvel), Alessandro Corbelli (bar—Siriex), Luigi Roni (bass—Cirillo), Silvestro Sammaritano (bass—Baroff), Alfredo Giacomotti (bass—Gretch), Ernesto Panariello (bass—Lorek), Vincenzo Alaimo (sgr—Nicola), Arnold Bosman (sgr—Boleslao), Bruno Capisani (sgr—Sergio), Renato Zanchetta (sgr—Michele), G. Gavazzeni (cnd), La Scala Orch, La Scala Chorus *(rec La Scala, Apr 5, 1993)* Legato 2-▲ LCD 213-2 [ADD]

Verdi, G.:Falstaff, w. Maureen O'Flynn (sop), Daniela Dessi (sop), Bernadette Manca di Nissa (mez), Delores Ziegler (mez), Ramon Vargas (ten), Ernesto Gavazzi (ten), Paolo Barbacini (ten), Juan Pons (bar), Roberto Frontali (bar), Luigi Roni (bass), R. Muti (cnd), La Scala Orch, La Scala Chorus *(rec Milan La Scala Theater, Italy, Mar. 29 & 31)* Sony Classical ▲ S2K 58961 [DDD]

Verdi, G.:La traviata, w. T. Fabbricini (sop—Violetta), A. Trevisan (mez—Annina), N. Curiel (mez—Flora), R. Alagna (ten—Alfredo), E, Cossutta (ten—Gastone), E. Gavazzi (ten—Giuseppe), O. Mori (bar—Douphol), E. Capuano (bass—d'Obigny), F. Musinu (bass—Grenvil), R. Muti (cnd), La Scala Orch, La Scala Chorus Sony Classical 2-▲ S2K 52486 [DDD]

Gay, Paul (bass)

Bach, J.S.:Mass in b, BWV 232, w. Hélène Obadia (sop), Madeleine Jalbert (alt), Adrian Brand (ten), Eric Aubier (tpt), P. Kuentz (cnd), Paul Kuentz Orch, Paul Kuentz Choir Pierre Verany ▲ PVY 730060 [DDD]

Gay, Simon (alt)

Walton, W.:The Twelve, w. P. Forbes (sop), R. Gleave (mez), J. Oxley (ten), P. Harvey (bar), R. Hickox (cnd), City of London Sinfonia [E] Chandos ▲ CHAN 8824 [DDD]

Gayer, Catherine (sop)

Dallapiccola, L.:Ulisse, w. E. Saedén (bar), V. von Halem (bass), A. Bernard (sgr), L. Maazel (cnd), Berlin German Opera Orch, Berlin German Opera Chorus *(rec live, Berlin 9/28/68)* Stradivarius 2-▲ STR 10063 [ADD]

Kahn, E.I.:Chansons Populaires, w. F. Maus (pno) CRI ▲ CD 563 [DDD]

Kahn, E.I.:Pieces on Medieval German Poems, w. F. Maus (pno) [G,F] CRI ▲ CD 563 [DDD]

Tal, J.:Else-Hommage, w. J. Bliese (nar), H. Ganz (va), G. Teutsch (vc), N. Hauptmann (hn), K. Helwig (pno), J. Tal (cnd) Academy ▲ ACA 8506 [ADD]

Gaynes, George (sgr)

Janácek, L.:Slavonic Mass, w. H. Pilarczyk (sop), J. Martin (mez), N. Gedda (ten), L. Bernstein (cnd), New York PO, Westminster Choir *(rec 1963)* Sony Classical ("Bernstein:The Royal Edition" series) ▲ SMK 47569 [ADD]

Gaze, Christopher (nar)

Songs of War & Peace, w. Leoni Men's Chorus [cnd:Diane Loomer], Stephen Smith (pno), Philip Crewe (perc), Salvador Ferreras (perc) Skylark ▲ 9501 [DDD]

Gebhardt, Joachim (bass)

Haydn, M.:Missa in honorem Sanctae Ursulae, w. Mechthild Bach (sop), Gabriele Binder (cta), Karl-Heinz Lampe (ten), H.R. Zöbeley (cnd), Munich Residenz Orch, Munich Motet Choir Calig ▲ CAL 50901 [DDD]

Zelenka, J.D.:Missa votiva, w. C. Hampe (sop), E. Graf (cta), J. Duske (ten), W. Wehnert (cnd), Hesse Bach Collegium, Marburg Bach Choir [L] Thorofon ▲ CTH 2172 [DDD]

Gedda, Nicolai (ten)

Auber, D.-F.:Fra Diavolo, w. M. Mesplé (sop—Zerline), J. Berbié (mez—Lady Pamela), N. Gedda (ten—Fra Diavolo), R. Corazza (ten—Lord Cockburn), T. Dran (ten—Lorenzo), J. Bastin (bass—Matheo), M. Soustrot (cnd), Monte Carlo PO, Jean LaForge Ensemble Choir EMI Classics ▲ CDCB 54810

Bach, J.S.:Mass in b, BWV 232, w. A. Giebel (sop), J. Baker (mez), H. Prey (bar), F. Crass (bass), O. Klemperer (cnd), New Philharmonia Orch, BBC Sym Chorus [L] EMI Classics ("Studio" series) 2-▲ ZDMB 63364-2 [ADD]

Bach, J.S.:St. Matthew Passion, w. E. Schwarzkopf (sop), C. Ludwig (mez), S. Fischer-Dieskau (bar), W. Berry (bass), O. Klemperer (cnd), Philharmonia Orch EMI Classics 3-▲ ZDMC 63058

Barber, S.:Vanessa, w. E. Steber (sop), G. Resnik (sop), R. Elias (mez), G. Tozzi (bass), D. Mitropoulos (cnd), Metropolitan Opera Orch, Metropolitan Opera Chorus [E] RCA Gold Seal ▲ 7899-2-RG [ADD]

Bellini, V.:I Puritani, w. C. Deutekom (sop), F. Raffanelli (sop), S. Bruscantini (b-bar), A. Ferrin (bass), G. del Vivo (bass), R. Muti (cnd), *(orch unknown)* *(rec 1970)* Great Opera Performances ▲ GOP 735

Bellini, V.:I Puritani, w. J. Sutherland (sop—Elvira), N. Gedda (ten—Arturo), E. Blanc (bar—Riccardo), J. Diaz (bass—Giorgio), R. Bonynge (cnd), *(orch unknown)* [I] *(rec live, Philadelphia 4/18/63)* Standing Room Only 2-▲ SRO 838-2 [ADD]

Berlioz, H.:La Damnation de Faust, w. M. Horne (mez—Marguerite), N. Gedda (ten—Faust), R. Soyer (bass—Mephistofeles), D. Petkov (bass—Brander), G. Prêtre (cnd), Rome RAI SO, Rome RAI Chorus *(rec live 1/11/69)* Arkadia 4-▲ 461 [ADD]

Berlioz, H.:La Damnation de Faust, w. J. Veasey (mez), G. Bastin (bar), C. Davis (cnd), London SO, London Sym Chorus, Ambrosian Singers [F] Philips 2-▲ 416395-2 [ADD]

Berlioz, H.:La Damnation de Faust, w. Janet Baker (mez), Gabriel Bacquier (bar), G. Prêtre (cnd), Orch de Paris, Paris Opera Chorus EMI Classics 2-▲ CDFB 68583

Berlioz, H.:L'Enfance du Christ, w. Victoria de los Angeles (sop), Roger Soyer (bar), Ernest Blanc (bar), A. Cluytens (cnd), Paris Conservatory Societé des Concerts Orch, René DuClos Chorus EMI Classics ("Doublefforte" series) 2-▲ CDFB 68586

Gedda, Nicolai (ten) (cont.)

Berlioz, H.:Roméo et Juliette, w. B. Fassbaender (mez), J. Shirley-Quirk (bar), L. Gardelli (cnd), ORF SO, Vienna State Opera Chorus [F] Orfeo 2-▲ 087842 [DDD]

Berlioz, H.:Les Troyens, w. M. Horne (mez), S. Verrett (mez), V. Luchetti (ten), R. Massard (bar), G. Prêtre (cnd), Rome RAI SO, Rome RAI Chorus [F] *(rec live 5/30/69)* Melodram 3-▲ MEL 37060 [AAD]

Berlioz, H.:Les Troyens, w. M. Horne (mez), S. Verrett (mez), V. Luchetti (ten), R. Massard (bar), G. Prêtre (cnd), Rome RAI SO, Rome RAI Chorus *(rec live 5/30/69)* Arkadia 4-▲ 461 [ADD]

Bernstein, L.:Candide (restored), w. J. Anderson (sop), C. Ludwig (mez), D. Jones (mez), J. Hadley (ten), A. Green (sgr), K. Ollmann (bar), L. Bernstein (cnd), London SO, London Sym Chorus *(rec 1989)* Deutsche Grammophon ▲ 429734-2 [DDD] ■ 429734-4

Bernstein, L.:Candide (restored), w. J. Anderson (sop), C. Ludwig (mez), D. Jones (mez), J. Hadley (ten), A. Green (sgr), K. Ollmann (bar), L. Bernstein (cnd), London SO, London Sym Chorus Deutsche Grammophon ■ 437328-4

Bizet, G.:Carmen, w. J. Micheau (sop), V. de los Angeles (sop), E. Blanc (bar), T. Beecham (cnd), *(orch unknown)* [F] EMI Classics 3-▲ CDCC 49240 [ADD]

Bizet, G.:Carmen, w. H. Gueden (sop), G. Simionato (mez), H. von Karajan (cnd), Vienna SO, Vienna Singverein *(rec live, Vienna Oct. 1954)* Melodram 2-▲ MEL 27012

Bizet, G.:Carmen, w. M. Callas (sop), A. Guiot (sop), R. Massard (bar), G. Prêtre (cnd), Paris Opera Orch, Paris Opera Chorus [F] EMI Classics 2-▲ CDCB 54368

Bizet, G.:Carmen (sels), w. M. Callas (sop), A. Guiot (sop), R. Massard (bar), G. Prêtre (cnd), Paris Opera Orch [F] EMI Classics ▲ CDM 63075 ■ EG 63075

Bizet, G.:Les Pêcheurs de perles, w. J. Micheau (sop), E. Blanc (bar), J. Mars (bar), P. Dervaux (cnd), Paris Opéra-Comique Orch, Paris Opéra-Comique Chorus [F] EMI Classics ("Studio" series) 2-▲ CDMB 69704 [ADD]

Charpentier, G.:Louise, w. B. Sills (sop—Louise), M. Dunn (mez—Louise's Mother), N. Gedda (ten—Julien), J. Van Dam (bass-bar—Louise's Father), J. Rudel (cnd), Paris Opera Orch, Paris Opera Chorus EMI Classics ▲ CDMC 65299

Cornelius, P.:Der Barbier von Bagdad, w. E. Schwarzkopf (sop), G. Hoffman (cta), G. Unger (ten), O. Czerwenka (bass), E. Leinsdorf (cnd), Philharmonia Orch, Philharmonia Chorus EMI Classics ▲ CDMB 65284

Donizetti, G.:L'elisir d'amore, w. M. Freni (sop), R. Capecchi (bar), M. Sereni (bar), F. Molinari-Pradelli (cnd), Rome Opera Orch [I] EMI Classics (Studio) 2-▲ CDMB 69897 [ADD]

Enescu, G.:Oedipe, w. B. Hendricks (sop), B. Fassbaender (mez), M. Lipovšek (mez), J. Taillon (mez), J. Aler (ten), G. Bacquier (bar), Quilico (bar), J. Van Dam (bass-bar), L. Foster (cnd), Monte Carlo PO, Orféon Donostiarra, Petits Chanteurs de Monaco [F] EMI Classics 2-▲ CDCB 54011 [DDD]

Gade, N.W.:Kalanus, w. M. Rørholm (méz), L. Mróz (bar), F. Rasmussen (cnd), Collegium Musicum, Canzone Choir Kontrapunkt ▲ 32072 [DDD]

Gluck, C.W.:Alceste, w. J. Norman (sop), B. Weikl (bar), T. Krause (bar), S. Nimsgern (b-bar), S. Baudo (cnd), Bavarian RSO, Bavarian Radio Chorus [French version] Orfeo 3-▲ 027823 [DDD]

Gluck, C.W.:Alceste, w. J. Norman (sop), B. Weikl (bar), T. Krause (bar), S. Nimsgern (b-bar), S. Baudo (cnd), Bavarian RSO, Bavarian Radio Chorus, *(highlights of above)* Orfeo ▲ 027901 [DDD]

Gounod, C.:Faust, w. V. de los Angeles (sop), L. Berton (sop), R. Gorr (mez), E. Blanc (bar), B. Christoff (bass), A. Cluytens (cnd), Paris Opera Orch [F] Angel ("Studio" series) 3-▲ CDMC 69983 [ADD]

Gounod, C.:Faust (sels), w. Liliane Berton (sop), Victoria de los Angeles (sop), Rita Gorr (mez), Victor Autran (bar), Ernest Blanc (bar), Boris Christoff (bass), A. Cluytens (cnd), Paris Opera Orch, Paris Opera Chorus Classics for Pleasure ("Eminence" series) ▲ CDEMX 2215 [DDD]

Handel, G.F.:Messiah, w. Elisabeth Schwarzkopf (sop), Grace Hoffman (cta), Jerome Hines (bass), O. Klemperer (cnd), Philharmonia Orch, Philharmonia Chorus EMI Classics 3-▲ ZDMC 63621

Haydn, J.:L'Anima del filosofo, or Orfeo ed Euridice, w. Joan Sutherland (sop), R. Bonynge (cnd), Scottish National Orch [I] *(rec live Edinburgh International Festival, 1967)* Myto 2-▲ 2 MCD 90529 [ADD]

Haydn, J.:L'Anima del filosofo, or Orfeo ed Euridice, w. Joan Sutherland (sop), R. Bonynge (cnd), Scottish National Orch, Scottish National Chorus *(rec live)* Verona 2-▲ VER 28018

In Recital, w. Pieralba Soroga (pno) Fonè ▲ 85F 02-6 [ADD]

Janácek, L.:The Diary of One Who Disappeared, w. Véra Soukupová (mez), Stepanka Stepanova (mez), Beno Blachut (ten), Josef Paleníček (pno), Prague Radio Women's Chorus, Czech Chamber Singers Female Chorus—contains 2 complete performances *(rec 1984 & 1956)* Supraphon ▲ SUP 0022 [DDD/ADD]

Janácek, L.:Slavonic Mass, w. H. Pilarczyk (sop), J. Martin (mez), G. Gaynes (sgr), L. Bernstein (cnd), New York PO, Westminster Choir *(rec 1963)* Sony Classical ("Bernstein:The Royal Edition" series) ▲ SMK 47569 [ADD]

Korngold, E.W.:Das Wunder der Heliane, w. A. Tomowa-Sintow (sop), R. Runkel (cta), J. D. de Haan (ten), H. Welker (bar), R. Pape (bass), J. Mauceri (cnd), Berlin RSO [G] London 3-▲ 436636-2 [DDD]

Lehár, F.:Giuditta (sels), w. Anneliese Rothenberger (sop), W. Mattes (cnd), Graunke SO, Munich Theater Gartnerplatz Chorus Emperor Operetta ▲ KO 86342

Lehár, F.:Das Land des Lächelns (sels), w. Renato Holm (sop), Anneliese Rothenberger (sop), W. Mattes (cnd), Graunke SO, Bavarian Radio Chorus Emperor Operetta ▲ KO 86341

Lehár, F.:Die lustige Witwe, w. E. Schwarzkopf (sop), E. Loose (sop), E. Kunz (bar), A. Kraus (ten), O. Ackermann (cnd), Philharmonia Orch, Philharmonia Chorus [G] EMI Classics ("Studio" series) ▲ CDH 69520 (m) [ADD]

Lehár, F.:Die lustige Witwe, w. E. Schwarzkopf (sop), H. Steffek (sop), E. Wächter (bar), L. von Matačić (cnd), Philharmonia Orch, Philharmonia Chorus [G] EMI Classics 2-▲ CDCB 47177

Lehár, F.:Die lustige Witwe (sels), w. Erika Koth (sop), Anneliese Rothenberger (sop), Robert Ilosfalvy (ten), W. Mattes (cnd), Graunke SO, Bavarian Radio Chorus Emperor Operetta ▲ KO 86343

Lehár, F.:Operetta Arias, w. W. Mattes (cnd), Graunke SO—sels from Das Land des Lächelns; Frasquita; Friederike; Giuditta; Der Zarewitsch; Schön ist der Welt; Die lustige Witwe; Der Graf von Luxembourg Emperor Operetta ▲ KO 86354

Liebermann, R.:Die Schule der Frauen, w. Anneliese Rothenberger (sop—Agnes), Christa Ludwig (mez—Georgette), Nicolai Gedda (ten—Horace), Alois Pernerstorfer (b-bar—Gronte), Walter Berry (bass—Poquelin), Kurt Böhme (bass—Arnolphe), G. Szell (cnd), Vienna PO *(rec Salzburg, Aug 17, 1957)* Orfeo d'or ("Festspiel Dikumente" series) 2-▲ C 429962 (m) [ADD]

Massenet, J.:Cendrillon, w. R. Welting (sop), F. von Stade (mez), J. Bastin (bass), J. Rudel (cnd), Philharmonia Orch, Ambrosian Opera Chorus [F] CBS 2-▲ M2K 35194 [ADD]

Massenet, J.:Manon, w. B. Sills (sop), G. Souzay (bar), G. Bacquier (bar), J. Rudel (cnd), New Philharmonia Orch, Ambrosian Opera Chorus [F] EMI Classics ("Studio" series) 3-▲ CDMC 69831 [ADD]

Massenet, J.:Thaïs, w. Beverly Sills (sop—Thaïs), Nicolai Gedda (ten—Nicias), Sherrill Milnes (bar—Athanaël), L. Maazel (cnd), New Philharmonia Orch, John Alldis Choir EMI Classics 2-▲ CDMB 65479

Massenet, J.:Werther, w. V. De los Angeles (sop), M. Mesplé (sop), G. Prêtre (cnd), Orch de Paris, Paris Chorus [F] EMI Classics ("Studio" series) 2-▲ CDMB 63973

Mendelssohn, F.:Elijah, w. Gwyneth Jones (sop), Janet Baker (mez), Simon Woolf (trb), Dietrich Fischer-Dieskau (bar), R. Frühbeck de Burgos (cnd), New Philharmonia Orch, New Philharmonia Chorus, Wandsworth School Boys' Choir *(rec 1968)* EMI Classics ("Doublefforte" series) 2-▲ CDFB 68601

Meyerbeer, G.:Les Huguenots, w. Jeanette Scovotti (sop—Urbain), Rita Shane (sop—Marguerite de Valois), Enriqueta Tarrès (sop—Valentine), Nicolai Gedda (ten—Raoul de Nangis), Justino Diaz (bass—Marcel), Dimiter Petkov (bass—Le Comte de Saint-Bris), E. Märzendorfer (cnd), Austrian RSO, Austrian Radio Chorus *(rec Vienna, Feb 17, 1971)* Myto 2-▲ MCD 961141

Meyerbeer, G.:Le Prophète, w. M. Rinaldi (sop), M. Horne (mez), R. El Hage (bass), H. Lewis (cnd), Turin RSO, Turin Radio Chorus [F] *(rec live 7/11/70)* Foyer 3-▲ FOY 2035 [AAD]

Mozart, W.A.:Complete Mozart Edition, w. M. Caballé (sop), I. Cotrubas (sop), J. Baker (mez), C. Davis (cnd), Royal Opera House Orch, Royal Opera House Chorus Covent Garden Philips 3-▲ 422542-2 [ADD]

Mozart, W.A.:Don Giovanni, w. C. Watson (sop), C. Ludwig (mez), N. Ghiaurov (bass), O. Klemperer (cnd), New Philharmonia Orch, New Philharmonia Chorus EMI Classics 3-▲ CDMC 63841

Gedda, Nicolai (ten) (cont.)
Mozart, W.A.:Entführung, w. Teresa Stich-Randall (mez), Michel Sénéchal (ten), Carmen Prieto (sgr), H. Rosbaud (cnd), Paris Conservatory Societé des Concerts Orch, Elisabeth Brasseur Chorale *(rec Aix-en-Provence Festival, France, 1954)* Agorá ("Phoenix" series) 2-▲ 512
Mozart, W.A.:Idomeneo, w. A. Rothenberger (sop), E. Moser (sop), A. Dallapozza (ten), P. Schreier (ten), T. Adam (b-bar), H. Schmidt-Isserstedt (cnd), Dresden Staatskapelle, Leipzig Radio Chorus EMI Classics ("Studio" series) 3-▲ CDMC 63990
Mozart, W.A.:Songs, w. M. Callas (sop), E. Grümmer (sop), E. Schwarzkopf (sop), R. Scotto (sop), T. Lemnitz (sop), E. Berger (sop), S. Jurinac (sop), E. Schumann (sop), I. Souez (sop), E. Rethberg (sop), L. Lehmann (sop), J. McCormack (ten), H. Roswenge (ten), H. Nash (ten), T. Gobbi (bar), G. Hüsch (bar), E. Kunz (bar), G. Frick (bass), E. Pinza (bass), A. Kipnis (bass) EMI Classics 4-▲ CDMD 63750
Mozart, W.A.:Zauberflöte, w. E. Schwarzkopf (sop), R. Streich (sop), A. Noni (sop), G. Taddei (bar), M. Petri (bass), H. von Karajan (cnd), Rome Radio Orch, Rome RAI Chorus [I] *(rec live, Dec. 19, 1953)* Myto 2-▲ 2 MCD 89007 (m) [ADD]
Mozart, W.A.:Zauberflöte, w. G. Janowitz (sop), L. Popp (sop), R. Pütz (sop), W. Berry (bass), G. Frick (bass), O. Klemperer (cnd), Philharmonia Orch, Philharmonia Chorus [without dialog; G] EMI Classics ("Studio" series) 2-▲ CDMB 69971 [ADD]
Mozart, W.A.:Zauberflöte, w. Gundula Janowitz (sop—Pamina), Lucia Popp (sop—Queen of the Night), Walter Berry (bass—Papageno), Gottlob Frick (bass—Sarastro), O. Klemperer (cnd), Philharmonia Orch, Philharmonia Chorus EMI Classics 2-▲ CDCB 55173
Mussorgsky, M.:Boris Godunov, w. G. Vishnevskaya (sop), G. Raimondi (ten), M. Rostropovich (cnd), National SO Washington D.C., Washington Oratorio Society, Choral Arts Society [R] Erato 3-▲ 2292-45418-2 ZB [DDD]
Mussorgsky, M.:Boris Godunov, w. N. Gedda (ten—Dmitri), M. Talvela (bass—Boris), J. Semkow (cnd), Cracow RSO, Cracow Radio Chorus EMI Classics ▲ CDCC 54377
Naumann, J.G.:Gustaf Wasa, w. Anders Andersson (ten—Gustav Wasa), Nicolai Gedda (ten—Christjern), P. Brunelle (cnd), Royal Swedish Opera Orch, Stockholm Royal Theater Opera Chorus Virgin Classics ▲ CDCB 45148
Nicolai Gedda:The First 10 Years, 1952-1962 Bluebell ▲ BLU 056 [ADD]
Nicolai Gedda in Recital, w. E. Werba (pno), *(rec. live at the Salzburg Festival, Aug. 1961)* EMI Classics ▲ CDM 65352
Northern & Russian Songs *(rec live, Queen Elisabeth Hall, London, Nov. 21, 1971)* Arkadia ▲ 806
Offenbach, J.:Les Contes d'Hoffmann, w. E. Schwarzkopf (sop), G. d'Angelo (sop), V. de los Angeles (sop), G. London (bar), E. Blanc (bar), A. Cluytens (cnd), Paris Conservatory Société des Concerts Orch, René DuClos Chorus [F] EMI Classics ("Studio" series) 2-▲ CDMB 63222 [ADD]
Puccini, G.:La Bohème, w. M. Freni (sop), M. Sereni (bar), T. Schippers (cnd), Rome Opera Orch, Rome Opera Chorus [I] EMI Classics ("Studio" series) 2-▲ CDMB 69657
Puccini, G.:La Bohème (sels), w. M. Freni (sop), M. Sereni (bar), T. Schippers (cnd), Rome Opera Orch, Rome Opera Chorus EMI Classics ("Studio" series) ▲ CDM 63932 ■ EG 63932
Puccini, G.:Madama Butterfly, w. M. Callas (sop), L. Danieli (mez), M. Borriello (bar), H. von Karajan (cnd), La Scala Orch, La Scala Chorus [I] *(rec 1955)* EMI Classics 2-▲ CDCB 47959 (m) [ADD]
Recital Myto ▲ MCD 916.46 [ADD]
Rossini, G.:Arias, w. June Anderson (sop), Montserrat Caballé (sop), Maria Callas (sop), Edita Gruberova (sop), Pilar Lorengar (sop), Mady Mesplé (sop), Tito Gobbi (bar), Samuel Ramey (bass), *(orchs unknown)* —from Barbiere di Siviglia; La Cenerentola; La Gazza ladra; Petite messe solennelle; Semiramide; Stabat Mater *(rec 1958–89)* EMI Classics 2-▲ CZS 67440-2 [ADD/DDD]
Rossini, G.:Il barbiere di Siviglia, w. Beverly Sills (sop), Fedora Barbieri (mez), Renato Capecchi (bar), Sherill Milnes (bar), Ruggero Raimondi (bass), J. Levine (cnd), London SO, John Alldis Choir EMI Classics 2-▲ CDMB 66040
Rossini, G.:Guillaume Tell, w. M. Caballé (sop), M. Mesplé (sop), C. Burles (ten), G. Bacquier (bar), G. Howell (bass), L. Gardelli (cnd), Royal PO, Ambrosian Opera Chorus EMI Classics 4-▲ CDMD 69951
Russian Liturgical Chant, w. Paris Russian Orthodox Cathedral Choir Philips ("Collector" series) ▲ 434174-2 PM [ADD]
Shostakovich, D.:Lady Macbeth of Mtsensk, w. G. Vishnevskaya (sop), B. Finnilä (mez), A. Haugland (bass), M. Rostropovich (cnd), London PO, Ambrosian Opera Chorus [R] EMI Classics 2-▲ CDCB 49955 [ADD]
Stenhammar, W.:Serenade, w. E. Söderström (sop), R. Kubelik (cnd), Stockholm PO Swedish Society ▲ SCD 1016
Strauss (II), Joh.:Die Fledermaus, w. E. Schwarzkopf (sop), R. Streich (sop), H. Krebs (ten), R. Christ (ten), E. Kunz (bar), K. Dönch (bar), H. von Karajan (cnd), Philharmonia Orch, Philharmonia Chorus [G] EMI Classics ("Studio" series) 2-▲ CDHB 69531 (m) [ADD]
Strauss (II), Joh.:Eine Nacht in Venedig (sels), w. Christine Gorner (sop), Rita Streich (sop), Cesare Curzi (ten), Christian Oppleberg (bar), F. Allers (cnd), Graunke SO, Graunke Chorus Emperor Operetta ▲ KO 86345
Strauss (II), Joh.:Wiener Blut (sels), w. Christine Gorner (sop), Anneliese Rothenberger (sop), W. Mattes (cnd), Graunke SO, Munich Theater Gartnerplatz Chorus Emperor Operetta ▲ KO 86345
Strauss (II), Joh.:Der Zigeunerbaron (sels), w. Rita Streich (sop), Grace Bumbry (mez), Biserka Cvejic (mez), Gisela Litz (alt), Hermann Prey (bar), Kurt Bohme (bass), F. Allers (cnd), Munich Bavarian State Opera Orch, Munich Bavarian State Opera Chorus Emperor Operetta ▲ KO 86346
Strauss, R.:Capriccio, w. E. Schwarzkopf (sop), A. Moffo (sop), C. Ludwig (mez), D. Fischer-Dieskau (bar), E. Wächter (bar), H. Hotter (b-bar), W. Sawallisch (cnd), Philharmonia Orch [G] EMI Classics 2-▲ CDCB 49014 (m) [ADD]
Stravinsky, I.:Oedipus Rex, w. M. Laszlò (mez—Jocasta), N. Gedda (ten—Oedipus), A. Bertocci (ten—Shepherd), M. Petri (bar—Creon & Tireseus), N. Catalani (bar—Messenger), A. Foà (speaker), H. von Karajan (cnd), Rome RAI SO, Rome RAI Chorus *(rec Dec. 20, 1952)* Stradivarius ▲ DAT 12311 [ADD]
Stravinsky, I.:Oedipus Rex, w. A. S. von Otter (mez/sop), V. Cole (ten), S. Estes (bass), H. Sotin (bass), P. Chéreau (nar), E.-P. Salonen (cnd), Swedish RSO, *(chorus unknown)* Sony Classical ▲ SK 48057
Tchaikovsky, P.:Eugene Onegin, w. A. Tomowa-Sintow (sop), R. Troava-Mircheva (cta), Y. Mazurok (bar), N. Ghiuselev (bass), E. Tchakarov (cnd), Sofia Festival Orch, Sofia National Opera Chorus [R] Sony Classical 2-▲ S2K 45539 [DDD]
Tchaikovsky, P.:Iolanta, w. G. Vishnevskaya (sop), W. Groenroos (bar), M. Rostropovich (cnd), Orch de Paris Erato 2-▲ 45793-2
Verdi, G.:La forza del destino, w. G. Bumbry (sop—Leonora), H. Dernesch (sop—Preziosilla), N. Gedda (ten—Alvaro), H. Prey (bar—Don Carlos), G. Frick (bass—Pater Guardian), S. Vogel (bass—Marchese), G. Patanè (cnd), Dresden State Orch, Dresden State Opera Chorus *(rec Aug. 1965)* Berlin Classics ("Eterna" series) ▲ BER 2025-2 [ADD]
Verdi, G.:Requiem Mass, w. E. Schwarzkopf (sop), C. Ludwig (mez), N. Ghiaurov (bass), C. M. Giulini (cnd), Philharmonia Orch, London Phil Choir [L] EMI Classics 2-▲ CDCB 47257 [ADD]
Verdi, G.:Rigoletto, w. M. Hallin (sop), B. Nordin (sop), K. Meyer (mez), B. Ericson (mez), Kjellgren (mez), O. Sivall (ten), H. Hasslo (bar), I. Wixell (bar), B. Alstergård (bar), A. Tyrén (bass), S. Ehrling (cnd), Stockholm Royal Opera House Orch, Stockholm Royal Opera Chorus *(rec live Jan. 18, 1959)* BIS ▲ CD 296 [AAD]
Weber, C.M. von:Euryanthe, w. Jessye Norman (sop), Rita Hunter (sop), Tom Krause (bar), M. Janowski (cnd), Dresden Staatskapelle, Leipzig Radio Chorus Berlin Classics 3-▲ BER 1108 [ADD]

Gedge, Nicholas (b-bar)
Bach, J.S.:Magnificat, BWV 243, w. Anna Crookes (sop), Jayne Whitaker (sop), Caroline Trevor (alt), Timothy Robinson (ten), N. Ward (cnd), Northern CO, Oxford Schola Cantorum *(rec St. Peter's Church, Hale, Cheshire, Dec. 2, 1993)* Naxos ▲ 8.550763 [DDD]
Fauré, G.:Requiem, w. Lisa Beckley (sop), Colm Carey (org), J. Summerly (cnd), Oxford Camerata, Oxford Schola Cantorum *(rec Hertford College Chapel, Oxford, May 17 & 18, 1993)* Naxos ▲ 8.550765 [DDD]

Geer, E. (nar)
Kraft, William:Der Imagistes, w. M. Kermoyan (nar), Los Angeles Percussion Ensemble [E] *(rec 1977)* CRI ▲ CD 639 [ADD/DDD]

Gehly (sgr)
Künneke, E.:Die grosse Sünderin (sels), w. M. Cunitz (sop), R. Schock (ten), Bajew (sgr), Rau (sgr), Schröder (sgr), Weigelt (sgr), Marszalek (cnd), Cologne RSO, Cologne Radio Chorus [G] Acanta ▲ CD 42483 [DDD]

Gehly (sgr) (cont.)
Lehár, F.:Paganini (sels), w. A. Schlemm (mez), Lisolette Losch (sop), P. Anders (ten), Hofmann (sgr), Schneider (sgr), Marszalek (cnd), Cologne RSO, Cologne Radio Chorus [G] Acanta ▲ CD 43810 [DDD]

Gehrman, S. (alt)
Duparc, H.:Songs, w. A. Farmer (pno)—Chanson triste; L'invitation du voyage; Extase; Lamento Nimbus ▲ NI 5396 [DDD]
Fauré, G.:Songs, w. A. Farmer (pno)—L'horizon chimerique, Op. 118; Le secret; Tristesse; Au bord de l'eau; La chanson du pecheur; Automne; Les berceaux; Apres un rève, Mirages, Op. 113 Nimbus ▲ NI 5396 [DDD]

Gehrman, Shura (bass)
Brahms, J.:Ernste Gesänge, w. N. Walker (pno) [G] Nimbus ▲ NI 5024 [AAD]
Brahms, J.:Songs, w. N. Walker (pno) [G] Nimbus ▲ NI 5024 [AAD]
Butterworth, G.:Songs (6) from *A Shropshire Lad*, w. A. Farmer (pno) [E] Nimbus ▲ NI 5033 [ADD]
Folk Songs Of The British Isles, w. Adrian Farmer (pno) Nimbus ▲ NI 5082 [DDD]
Ibert, J.:Chansons de Don Quichotte, w. W. Farmer (pno) [F] Nimbus ▲ NI 5029
The Male Alto Voice, w. A. Farmer (pno) Nimbus ▲ NI 5395
Milhaud, D.:Soirées de Pétrograd, w. A. Farmer (pno) [F] Nimbus ▲ NI 5029
Mussorgsky, M.:Songs & Dances, w. Nina Walker (pno) Nimbus ▲ NI 1414 [ADD]
Poulenc, F.:Le Bestiarie, w. W. Farmer (pno) [F] [arr bar & pno] Nimbus ▲ NI 5029
Ravel, M.:Chants populaires, w. W. Farmer (pno) Nimbus ▲ NI 5029
Ravel, M.:Mélodies populaires grecques, w. W. Farmer (pno) Nimbus ▲ NI 5029
Schubert, Franz:Die Schöne Müllerin, w. Nina Walker (pno) [E] Nimbus ▲ NI 5023 [AAD]
Schubert, Franz:Die Schöne Müllerin, w. Nina Walker (pno) [G] Nimbus ▲ NI 5253 [ADD]
Schubert, Franz:Schwanengesang, w. N. Walker (pno) [G] Nimbus ▲ NI 5022
Schubert, Franz:Songs (misc), w. N. Walker (pno)—5 songs [G] Nimbus ▲ NI 5024 [AAD]
Schubert, Franz:Songs (misc), w. N. Walker (pno)—7 songs [G] Nimbus ▲ NI 5022
Schubert, Franz:Winterreise, w. N. Walker (pno) [E] Nimbus ▲ NI 5282 [ADD]
Schumann, R.:Dichterliebe, w. N. Walker (pno) [G] Nimbus ▲ NI 5024 [AAD]
Vaughan Williams, R.:Songs of Travel, w. W. Farmer (pno) [E] Nimbus ▲ NI 5033 [ADD]

Geijsen, Gaudia (mez)
Brahms, J.:Ernste Gesänge, w. J. Gruithuyzen (pno) Erasmus ▲ WVH 041 [DDD]
Duparc, H.:Songs, w. J. Gruithuyzen (pno)—La Vie antérieure; La Manoir de Rosemonde; Au pays où se fait la Guerre Erasmus ▲ WVH 041 [DDD]
Granados, E.:Songs, w. J. Gruithuyzen (pno)—La maja Dolorosa, Nos. 1-3 Erasmus ▲ WVH 041 [DDD]
Sibelius, J.:Songs, w. J. Gruithuyzen (pno)—Till Kvällen; Den första Kyssen; Flickan kom ifrån sin Älsklings möte; se'n har jag ej frågat mera; Svarta Rosor; Kom nu hit, död Erasmus ▲ WVH 041 [DDD]
Turina, J.:Songs, w. J. Gruithuyzen (pno)—cantares Erasmus ▲ WVH 041 [DDD]

Geisen, Erik (ten)
Romberg, S.:The Student Prince (operetta), w. C. Jeffreys (sop), D. Honig (b-bar), S. Gyártó (cnd), Hamburg State Opera Orch, Hamburg State Opera Chorus [G] Bayer ▲ 150004

Geiser-Payer, B. (alt)
Suter, R.:Musikalisches Tagesbuch 1, w. H. Haldemann (pic/fl), H. Holliger (ob), H. Bochet (bn), J. Joubert (vn), J. Semper (va), W. Eugster (vc), M. Dellanoy (db) *(rec 1962)* Grammont ▲ CSTP 6-2 [AAD]

Geisler, Walter (ten)
Verdi, G.:Macbeth, w. Astrid Varnay (sop—Lady Macbeth), Trude Roesler (mez—Lady-in-waiting), Hasso Eschert (ten—Malcolm), Walter Geisler (ten—Macduff), Joseph Metternich (bar—Macbeth), Ludwig Weber (bass—Banquo), R. Kraus (cnd), West German Orch, West German Chorus *(rec Cologne, 1954)* Myto 2-▲ 952128

Geister, Geraldine (sgr)
Mica, F.A.:L'origine di Jaromeriz in Moravia, w. Geraldine Cassidy (sgr), Manfred Equiluz (sgr), Michael Nowak (sgr), Le Monde Classique [Cz] Supraphon 2-▲ SUP 112192 [DDD]

Geitner, Petra (sop)
Keiser, R.:Passions Oratorium, w. T. d'Althann (sop), M. Paulsen (alt), J. Elbert (ten), H. Elbert (bass), C. Brembeck (cnd), Parthenia Baroque, Parthenia Vocal Christophorus ▲ 77143 [DDD]
Scarlatti, A.:Passion Oratorio, w. M. Bach (sop), K. Wessel (alt), M. Schneider (cnd), La Stagione, Frankfurt Vocal Ensemble Capriccio 2-▲ CD 10 411/12

Geldern, Harold von (bar)
Rich, F.C.:The Hudson Oratorio, w. Kathryn Radcliffe (sop), Rick Hamelin (ten), F.C. Rich (cnd), Juilliard Orch members *(rec Church of the Epiphany, New York City, July 1996)* Albany ▲ TROY 217 [DDD]

Geleva, Alexey (bass)
Mussorgsky, M.:Boris Godunov, w. Irina Arkhipova (mez—Marina Mnishek), Evgenya Verbitskaya (mez—Nurse to Xenia), Valentina Klepatskaya (sgr—Fyodor), Tamara Sorokina (sgr—Xenia), Anton Grigoryev (ten—Simpleton), Vladimir Ivanovsky (ten—Grigory, the Pretender), Gyorgy Shulpin (bar—Prince Shuisky), Alexey Geleva (bass—Varlaam), Ivan Petrov (bass—Boris Godounov), Mark Reshetin (bass—Pimen), Alexi Ivanov (sgr—Andrei Shchelkalov), Evgeny Kibkalo (sgr—Rangoni), A. Melik-Pashayev (cnd), Bolshoi Theater Orch, Bolshoi Theater Chorus *(rec Moscow, 1962)* Melodiya ("The Russian Opera" series) 3-▲ 74321-29349-2 [ADD]

Gelli, Antonio (bass)
Puccini, G.:Tosca, w. C. Melis (sop—Tosca), P. Pauloi (ten—Cavarodossi), N. Palai (ten—Spoletta), A. Granforte (bar—Scarpia), G. Azzimonti (bass—Sciarrone/Angelotti), A. Gelli (bass—Sacristan), C. Sabajno (cnd), La Scala Orch, La Scala Chorus [I] *(rec Milan, Nov. 1929)* VAI Audio 2-▲ VAIA 1076-2 (m) [ADD]
Puccini, G.:Tosca, w. Carmen Melis (sop—Tosca), Nello Palai (ten—Spoletta), Piero Pauli (ten—Cavaradossi), Apollo Granforte (bar—Scarpia), Giovanni Azzimonti (bass—Angelotti/Sciarrone), Antonio Gelli (bass—Sagrestano), C. Sabajno (cnd), La Scala Orch, La Scala Chorus *(rec Nov 1929)* Arkadia 2-▲ CD 78002 (m) [ADD]
Verdi, G.:La traviata, w. Olga de Franco (sop—Flora Bervoix/Annina), Anna Rosza (sop—Violetta Valéry), Giordano Callegari (ten—Gastone), Alessandro Ziliani (ten—Alfredo Germont), Luigi Borgonovo (bar—Giorgio Germont), Arnoldo Lenzi (bar—Baron Douphol), Antonio Gelli (bass—Marquis d'Obigny/Dr. Grenvil), C. Sabajno (cnd), La Scala Orch, La Scala Chorus *(rec La Scala Theatre, Milan, Oct.-Nov. 1930)* VAI Audio 2-▲ VAIA 1108-2
Verdi, G.:La traviata, w. Olga de Franco (sop—Flora Bervoix/Annina), Anna Rosza (sop—Violetta Valery), Giordano Callegari (ten—Gastone), Alessandro Ziliani (ten—Alfredo Germont), Luigi Borgonovo (bar—Giorgio Germont), Arnoldo Lenzi (bar—Barone Douphol), Antonio Gelli (bass—Marchese d'Obigny/Dottor Grenvil), C. Sabajno (cnd), La Scala Orch, Vittore Veneziani (cnd), La Scala Chorus *(rec Oct-Nov 1930)* Arkadia 2-▲ CD 78001 (m) [ADD]
Verdi, G.:Il trovatore, w. Maria Carena (sop—Leonora), Olga De Franco (sop—Ines), Irene Minghini Cattaneo (mez—Azucena), Aureliano Pertile (ten—Manrico), Giordano Callegari (ten—Ruiz/Messenger), Apollo Granforte (bar—Count), Bruno Carmassi (bass—Ferrando), Antonio Gelli (bass—Old Gypsy), C. Sabajno (cnd), La Scala Orch, Vittore Veneziani (cnd), La Scala Chorus *(rec 1930)* Arkadia ("The 78's" series) 2-▲ 78007 [ADD]

Gémes, Katalin (mez)
Bengraf, J.:Sacred Music, w. Ingrid Kertesi (sop), Gábor Kállay (ten), Ákos Ambrus (bar), István Ella (org), Zsolt Kovács (vc), Balázs Arnóth (bn), Vilmos Buza (db), J. Dobra (cnd), Vienna-Szász CO, Tomkins Vocal Ensemble—Te Deum; O sacrum convivium; Libera me; Gloria [from Missa solemnis in D] Hungaroton ▲ HCD 31609 [DDD]
Druschetzky, G.:Missa solemnis, w. Ingrid Kertesi (sop), Gábor Kállay (ten), Ákos Ambrus (bar), István Ella (org), Zsolt Kovács (vc), Balázs Arnóth (bn), Vilmos Buza (db), J. Dobra (cnd), Vienna-Szász CO, Tomkins Vocal Ensemble Hungaroton ▲ HCD 31609 [DDD]
Esterházy, P.:Harmonia caelestis, w. M. Fers (sop), M. Zádori (sop), K. Károlyi (cta), G. Kállay (ten), J. Moldvay (bass), P. Németh (cnd), Capella Savaria, Savaria Vocal Ensemble [period instrs] [L] Hungaroton 2-▲ HCD 31148/49 [DDD]
Vivaldi, A.:Juditha triumphans devicta Holofernes barbarie, w. M. Zádori (sop), J. Németh (mez), G. Banditelli (cta), A. Markert (cta), N. McGegan (cnd), Capella Savaria, Savaria Vocal Ensemble [L] Hungaroton 2-▲ HCD 31063/64 [DDD]

▲ = CD ♦ = Enhanced CD ∆ = MD ■ = Cassette Tape ◻ = DCC

Genaux, Vivica (mez)

Puccini, G.:Madama Butterfly, w. Maria Spacagna (sop), Sharon Grahm (mez), Richard di Renzi (ten), Richard Markley (ten), Erich Parce (bar), James Butler (bass), C. Rosenkrans (cnd), Hungarian State Opera Orch, Anikó Katona (cnd), Hungarian State Opera Chorus—3 versions *(rec Italian Institute, Budapest, Sept 5-21, 1995)* Vox Classics 4-▲ VOX4 7525 [DDD]

Gencer, Leyla (sop)

Bellini, V.:Beatrice di Tenda, w. J. Oncina (ten), M. Zanasi (bar), V. Gui (cnd), Venice Teatro La Fenice Orch, Venice Teatro La Fenice Chorus *(rec 1964)* Memories 2-▲ MEM 4543 [ADD]

Catalani, A.:La Wally (sels), Turin RAI SO—Aria Cetra Classic ("Classics Collection" series) ▲ 112 [ADD]

Chopin, F.:Songs Sop (comp), w. N. Magaloff (pno) [Pol] Arkadia-Akademia ▲ 101 [ADD]

Cilea, F.:Adriana Lecouvreur, w. L. Gencer (sop—Adriana), A. Lazzarini (mez—Princess), F. Ricciardi (ten—Abbot), A. Zambon (ten—Maurizio), E. Sordello (bar—Michonnet), A. Zerbini (bass—Prince), O. de Fabritiis (cnd), Naples Teatro San Carlo Orch, Naples Teatro San Carlo Chorus *(rec Dec. 17, 1966)* Golden Age of Opera 2-▲ GAO 143/44 [ADD]

Donizetti, G.:Anna Bolena, w. G. Simionato (mez), A. Bertocci (ten), P. Clabassi (bass), G. Gavazzeni (cnd), Milan RAI SO, Milan RAI Chorus *(rec 1958)* Memories 2-▲ MEM 4517 [AAD]

Donizetti, G.:Anna Bolena, w. Giulieta Simionato (mez), Aldo Bertocci (ten), Plinio Clabassi (bass), G. Gavazzeni (cnd), Milan RAI SO, Milan RAI Chorus *(rec July 11, 1958)* Agorá Music ("Phoenix" series) 2-▲ 503

Donizetti, G.:Arias, Turin RAI SO—arias from Catarina Cornaro; Roberto Devereux; Maria Stuarda & Lucrezia Borgia Cetra Classic ("Classics Collection" series) ▲ 112 [ADD]

Donizetti, G.:Belisario, w. M. Pecile (cta), U. Grilli (ten), G. Taddei (bar), N. Zaccaria (bass), G. Gavazzeni (cnd), Venice Teatro La Fenice Orch, Venice Teatro La Fenice Chorus [l] *(rec live, Venice 5/14/69)* Melodram 2-▲ MEL 27051 [AAD]

Donizetti, G.:Belisario, w. M. Pecile (cta), U. Grilli (ten), G. Taddei (bar), N. Zaccaria (bass), G. Gavazzeni (cnd), Venice Teatro La Fenice Orch, Venice Teatro La Fenice Chorus [l] *(rec live in Venice, 5/14/69)* Verona 2-▲ 27048/49 (m) [AAD]

Donizetti, G.:Caterina Cornaro, w. G. Aragall (ten), R. Bruson (bar), C.F. Cillario (cnd), Naples Teatro San Carlo Orch, Naples Teatro San Carlo Chorus [l] *(rec live, Naples 5/28/72)* Memories 2-▲ HR 4448/49 (m) [ADD]

Donizetti, G.:Caterina Cornaro, w. G. Aragall (ten), R. Bruson (bar), L. Risani (sgr), C.F. Cillario (cnd), Naples Teatro San Carlo Orch, Naples Teatro San Carlo Chorus *(rec live, 5/28/72)* Myto 2-▲ 2 MCD 92153 [ADD]

Donizetti, G.:Lucia di Lammermoor (sels), w. G. Prandelli (ten), N. Carta (bar), R. Botteghelli (bass), Hussu (sgr), Sabatucci (sgr), O. de Fabritiis (cnd), Trieste Teatro Comunale Giuseppe Verdi Orch, Trieste Teatro Comunale G. Verdi Chorus *(rec live 12/13/57 & 2/10/58)* Melodram ▲ MEL 15003 (m) [AAD]

Donizetti, G.:Lucrezia Borgia, w. T. Troyanos (mez), J. Carrerras (ten), N. Rescigno (cnd), Dallas Civic Opera Orch, Dallas Civic Opera Chorus *(rec 1973)* Melodram 2-▲ MLO 270109 [ADD]

Donizetti, G.:Lucrezia Borgia (sels), w. G. Raimondi (ten), L. Roni (bass-bar), E. Gracis (cnd), La Scala Orch, La Scala Chorus—8 scenes & arias [l] *(rec live, 3/12/70)* Myto 2-▲ 2 MCD 90423 [ADD]

Donizetti, G.:Lucrezia Borgia (sels), w. L. Gencer (sop—Lucrezia), U. Grilli (ten—Gennaro), A. Camozzo (cnd), Bergamo Teatro Donizetti Orch—sels. *(rec live, 10/4/71)* Myto 2-▲ 2 MCD 92153 [ADD]

Donizetti, G.:Maria Stuarda, w. S. Verrett (mez), F. Tagliavini (ten), F. Molinari-Pradelli (cnd), Florence Maggio Musicale Orch, Florence Maggio Musicale Chorus *(rec 1967)* Memories 2-▲ MEM 4504 [AAD]

Donizetti, G.:Maria Stuarda (sels), w. S. Verrett (mez), F. Tagliavini (ten), F. Molinari-Pradelli (cnd), Florence Maggio Musicale Orch, Florence Maggio Musicale Chorus, 11 arias from Acts 2 & 3 [l] *(rec 5/2/67)* Myto 2-▲ 2 MCD 91137 [ADD]

Donizetti, G.:Les Martyrs, w. R. Bruson (bar), O. Garaventa (bar), F. Furlanetto (bass), G. Gelmetti (cnd), Venice Teatro La Fenice Orch, Venice Teatro La Fenice Chorus *(rec 1978)* Italian Opera Rarities ▲ IOR 7716 [ADD]

Gencer & Infantino, w. Luigi Infantino (ten), Milan RAI SO [cnd:Alfredo Simonetto] *(rec Martini & Rossi Concert, 1958)* Incontri Memorabili ▲ CDMR 5017

Leyla Gencer Memories ("Great Voices" series) 2-▲ MEM 4239 (m)

Leyla Gencer:The Queen of Live Recordings *(rec live, 1958-69)* Enterprise ("Documents" series) ▲ ENTLV 971 [ADD]

Massenet, J.:Werther, w. F. Tagliavini (ten)., C.F. Cillario (cnd), Trieste Teatro Comunale Giuseppe Verdi Orch *(rec 1959)* Memories 2-▲ MEM 4554 [ADD]

Massenet, J.:Werther, w. L. Gencer (sop—Carlotta), G. Tavolaccini (sop—Sofia), F. Tagliavini (ten—Werther), M. Borriello (bar—Alberto), E. Mocchiutti (bar—Johann), V. Susca (bass—Il Podestà), R. Botteghelli (bass—Schmidt), C.F. Cillario (cnd), *(orch unknown)* Arkadia 2-▲ 599 [ADD]

Mozart, W.A.:Don Giovanni, w. Leyla Gencer (sop—Donn'Elvra), Teresa Stich-Randall (mez—Donn'Anna), Sesto Bruscantini (bar—Leporello), Mario Petri (bar—Don Giovanni), F. Molinari-Pradelli (cnd), Milan RAI SO, Milan RAI Chorus Stradivarius 3-▲ STV DTM 12321 [ADD]

Pacini, G.:Saffo, w. F. Mattiucci (mez), T. del Bianco (ten), L. Quilico (bar), F. Capuana (cnd), Naples Teatro San Carlo Orch, Naples Teatro San Carlo Chorus [l] *(rec live, 4/7/67)* Arkadia 2-▲ 541 (m) [AAD]

Ponchielli, A.:La Gioconda, w. Anna di Stasio (mez), Gianni Raimondi (ten), Ruggero Raimondi (bass), B. Bartoletti (cnd), Rome Opera Orch, Rome Opera Chorus Melodram 3-▲ CDM 37092

Puccini, G.:Tosca, w. Giuseppe Taddei (bar), Melchiorre Luise (bass), Vittorio de Santis (sgr), V. Bellezza (cnd), *(orch & chorus unknown)* *(rec live, Naples, Mar. 21, 1955)* Great Opera Performances 2-▲ GOP 751

Puccini, G.:Turandot (sels), w. L. Udovich (sop), F. Corelli (ten), O. de Fabritiis (cnd), Naples Teatro San Carlo Orch, Naples Teatro San Carlo Chorus—Signore ascolta; Il nome che cercate..tu che di gel sei cinta *(rec Jan. 13, 1962)* Golden Age of Opera 2-▲ GAO 143/44 [ADD]

Rossini, G.:Elisabetta, regina d'Inghilterra, w. S. Geszty (sop), U. Grilli (ten), P. Bottazzo (ten), N. Sanzogno (cnd), Palermo Teatro Massimo Orch, Palermo Teatro Massimo Chorus [l] *(rec live, 11/24/70)* Myto 2-▲ 2 MCD 90530 [ADD]

Smareglia, A.:La falena, w. Leyla Gencer (sop—La Falena), Rita Lantieri (sop—Albina, sua figlia), Ruggero Bondino (ten—Re Stellio), Dario Zerial (ten—Il ladro), Mario D'Anna (bar—Il vecchio Uberto), Aurio Tomicich (bass—Morio), Giuseppe Botta (sgr—Un marinaio), G. Gavazzeni (cnd), Trieste Teatro Comunale Giuseppe Verdi Orch, Trieste Teatro Comunale G. Verdi Chorus *(rec Trieste, Mar 18, 1876)* Bongiovanni 2-▲ GB 1131/32

Tchaikovsky, P.:Queen of Spades (sels), w. L. Gencer (sop—Liza), A. Annaloro (ten—Hermann), N. Sanzogno (cnd), La Scala Orch [l] *(rec Feb. 2, 1960)* Arkadia 2-▲ 599 [ADD]

Verdi, G.:Arias, Turin RAI SO—arias from Il Trovatore; La Forza del Destino; Aida; La Traviata Cetra Classic ("Classics Collection" series) ▲ 112 [ADD]

Verdi, G.:Un ballo in maschera, w. Adriana Lazzarini (mez), Carlo Bergonzi (ten), Mario Zanasi (bar), O. de Fabritiis (cnd), Bologna Teatro Comunale Orch, Bologna Teatro Comunale Chorus *(rec live, Nov 28, 1961)* Arkadia 2-▲ 622

Verdi, G.:La battaglia di Legnano (sels), w. J. Gibin (ten), U. Savarese (bar), F. Molinari-Pradelli (cnd), Trieste Teatro Comunale Giuseppe Verdi Orch, Trieste Teatro Comunale G. Verdi Chorus—extensive selections from Acts 1,3 & 4 [l] *(rec live 3/8/63)* Myto 2-▲ 2 MCD 89010 (m) [ADD]

Verdi, G.:Don Carlos, w. F. Cossotto (mez), B. Prevedi (ten), S. Bruscantini (bar), N. Ghiaurov (bass), F. Previtali (cnd), Rome Opera Orch, Rome Opera Chorus *(rec live)* Melodram 3-▲ MEL 37022

Verdi, G.:Ernani, w. Licia Galvano (sop—Giovanna), Leyla Gencer (sop—Elvira), Carlo Bergonzi (ten—Ernani), Nino Valori (ten—Don Riccardo), Piero Cappuccilli (bar—Don Carlo), Alessandro Cassis (bar—Jago), Ruggero Raimondi (bass—Don Ruy Gomez de Silva), G. Gavazzeni (cnd), Catania Teatro Massimo Bellini Orch, Catania Teatro Massimo Bellini Chorus *(rec live, Catania, Jan 15, 1972)* Arkadia 2-▲ 621 [ADD]

Verdi, G.:La forza del destino, w. G. Carturan (mez), G. Di Stefano (ten), A. Priotti (bar), C. Siepi (b-bar), A. Votto (cnd), *(orch unknown)* *(rec live, Cologne 1957)* Melodram 3-▲ MEL 37010

Verdi, G.:La forza del destino, w. Giuseppe di Stefano (ten), Aldo Protti (bar), Cesare Siepi (bass), A. Votto (cnd), La Scala Orch, La Scala Chorus *(rec La Scala Theatre, Milan, July 5, 1957)* Pantheon 3-▲ PHE 6627 (m)

Gencer, Leyla (sop) (cont.)

Verdi, G.:La forza del destino, w. Leyla Gencer (sop—Leonora), Gabriella Carturan (mez—Preziosilla), Giuseppe di Stefano (ten—Don Alvaro), Aldo Protti (bar—Don Carlo), Cesare Siepi (b-bar), Franco Calabrese (bass—Marchese di Calatrava), Enrico Campi (bass—Fra Melitone), A. Votto (cnd), La Scala Orch, La Scala Chorus *(rec Bühnen der Stadt, Köln, July 5, 1957)* Agorá Music ("Phoenix" series) 3-▲ 510 [ADD]

Verdi, G.:Jérusalem, w. Giacomo Aragall (ten), Giancarlo Guelfi (bar), G. Gavazzeni (cnd), Venice Teatro La Fenice Orch, Venice Teatro La Fenice Chorus [l] *(rec live 9/24/63)* Melodram 2-▲ MEL 27004

Verdi, G.:Jérusalem, w. Giacomo Aragall (ten), Giancarlo Guelfi (bar), G. Gavazzeni (cnd), Venice Teatro La Fenice Orch [l] *(rec live 9/24/63)* Verona 2-▲ 27040/41 (m) [AAD]

Verdi, G.:Jérusalem, w. Giacomo Aragall (ten), Giancarlo Guelfi (bar), G. Gavazzeni (cnd), Venice Teatro La Fenice Orch, Venice Teatro La Fenice Chorus *(rec Venice, Sept 24, 1963)* Agorá Music ("Phoenix" series) 2-▲ 506

Verdi, G.:Macbeth, w. Mirto Picchi (ten), Giuseppe Taddei (bar), Ferruccio Mazzoli (bass), V. Gui (cnd), Palermo Teatro Massimo Orch, Palermo Teatro Massimo Chorus *(rec Palermo, Jan. 14, 1960)* Pantheon 2-▲ PHE 6604 (m)

Verdi, G.:Macbeth (sels), w. G. Lamberti (ten), G. Guelfi (bar), G. Gavazzeni (cnd), Venice Teatro La Fenice Orch, Venice Teatro La Fenice Chorus [l] [highlights] *(rec live 4/9/68)* Melodram ▲ MEL 15002

Verdi, G.:Simon Boccanegra, w. Glade Peterson (ten), Giuseppe Zampieri (ten), Tito Gobbi (bar), Rolando Panerai (bar), Vito Susca (bass), Giorgio Tozzi (bass), G. Gavazzeni (cnd), *(orch unknown)* Great Opera Performances 2-▲ GOP 767

Verdi, G.:La traviata (sels), w. F. Labò (ten), P. Cappuccilli (bar), N. Rescigno (cnd), Rio de Janeiro Teatro Municipale Orch, Rio de Janeiro Teatro Municipale Chorus *(rec live 8/8/64)* Golden Age of Opera ▲ GAO 120 [ADD]

Verdi, G.:Il trovatore, w. Leyla Gencer (sop—Leonora), Laura Londi (sop—Ines), Fedora Barbieri (mez—Azucena), Mario del Monaco (ten—Manrico), Athos cesarini (ten—Ruiz), Walter Artioli (ten—Messanger) Ettore Bastianini (bar—Count Luna), Plinio Clabassi (bass—Ferrando), Sergio Liliani (bass—Gypsy), F. Previtali (cnd), Milan RAI SO, Milan RAI Chorus *(rec live, Milan, May 29, 1957)* Arkadia 2-▲ 483 [ADD]

Verdi, G.:Il trovatore (sels), w. Leyla Gencer (sop—Leonora), Laura Londi (sop—Ines), Athos Cesarini (ten—Ruiz), Mario del Monaco (ten—Manrico), Ettore Bastianini (bar), F. Previtali (cnd), Milan RAI SO, Milan RAI Chorus *(rec Milan, May 18, 1957)* Agorá Music ("Phoenix" series) 3-▲ 510 [ADD]

Verdi, G.:I vespri siciliani, w. Giangiacomo Guelfi (bar), Nicola Rossi-Lemeni (bass), Gastone Limarilli (sgr), G. Gavazzeni (cnd), Rome Opera Orch, Rome Opera Chorus *(rec Dec 5, 1964)* Pantheon 2-▲ PHE 6770

Verdi, G.:I vespri siciliani, w. G. Limarilli (ten), G. Guelfi (bar), N. Rossi-Lemeni (bass), G. Gavazzeni (cnd), Rome Opera Orch, Rome Opera Chorus [l] *(rec live, Rome 1964)* Melodram 2-▲ MEL 27037 [ADD]

Verdi, G.:I vespri siciliani (sels), w. G. Casellato-Lamberti (ten), La Scala Orch, La Scala Chorus—one solo soprano aria & three duets from Act 4 [l] Myto 2-▲ 2 MCD 90524 [ADD]

Zandonai, R.:Francesca da Rimini, w. L. Gencer (sop—Francesca), R. Cioni (ten—Paolo), M. Ferrara (ten—Malatesino), F. Capuana (cnd), Trieste Teatro Comunale Giuseppe Verdi Orch, Trieste Teatro Comunale G. Verdi Chorus *(rec Mar. 19. 1961)* Arkadia 2-▲ 597 [ADD]

Genhardt (bass)

Brixi, F.X.:Missa Interga, w. I. Verebics (sop), C. Borchers (cta), S. Weir (ten), H. Rilling (cnd), Prague CO, Kühn Chorus Supraphon ▲ 11 0092-2 [DDD]

Brixi, F.X.:Opus Patheticum de Septem Doloribus Beatae Mariae Virginis, w. I. Verebics (sop), C. Borchers (cta), S. Weir (ten), H. Rilling (cnd), Prague CO, Kühn Chorus Supraphon ▲ 11 0092-2 [DDD]

Genova, Tiha (sop)

Mahler, G.:Sym 2, w. Vessela Zorova (alt), E. Tabakov (cnd), Sofia PO, Bulgarian National Chorus *(rec Bulgarian Concert Hall, Sofia, Jan 1987)* Capriccio 15-▲ 49043 [DDD]

Pergolesi, G.B.:Stabat mater, w. Bozhkova (sgr), V. Kazandjiev (cnd), Bulgarian PO, Bulgarian Phil Chorus [L] Vivace 2-▲ 140141 [ADD/DDD]

Gens, Véronique (sop)

Campra, A.:Messe de Requiem, w. Anne Gotkovski (sop), Jean-Paul Fouchécourt (alt), Joseph Cornwell (ten), Peter Harvey (bar), H. Niquet (cnd), Concert Spirituel Orch, Concert Spirituel Vocal Ensemble Adda ▲ ADD 241952 [DDD]

Campra, A.:Motets, w. Anne Gotkovski (sop), Jean-Paul Fouchécourt (alt), Douglas Nasrawi (ten), Peter Harvey (bar), Marcos Loureiro de Sà (bar), Kevin Mallon (vn), H. Niquet (cnd), Concert Spirituel Orch, Concert Spirituel Vocal Ensemble—Te Deum; Notus in Judea Deus; Deus in Nomine Tuo Adda ▲ ADD 241942 [DDD]

Campra, A.:Motets, w. Anne Gotkovski (sop), Jean-Paul Fouchécourt (alt), Joseph Cornwell (ten), Peter Harvey (bar), H. Niquet (cnd), Concert Spirituel Orch, Concert Spirituel Vocal Ensemble—Benedictus Dominus Adda ▲ ADD 241952 [DDD]

Campra, A.:Motets, w. Anne Gotkovsky (sop), Jean-Paul Fauchecourt (ct), Hervé Lamy (ten), Peter Harvey (bass), H. Niquet (cnd), Concert Spirituel Orch, Concert Spirituel Vocal Ensemble—2 Noster Refugium; Cantate Domino; De Profundis Adda ▲ ADD 243912

Lalande, M.-R. de:Motets, w. S. Piau (sop), A. Steyer (sop), J.-P. Fouchécourt (ten), F. Piolino (ten), J. Corréas (bass), W. Christie (cnd), Les Arts Florissants [L] Harmonia Mundi France ▲ HMC 901351

Lalande, M.-R. de:Te Deum, w. S. Piau (sop), A. Steyer (sop), J.-P. Fouchécourt (ten), F. Piolino (ten), J. Corréas (bass), W. Christie (cnd), Les Arts Florissants [L] Harmonia Mundi France ▲ HMC 901351

Lully, J.-B.:Armide, w. N. Rime (sop), G. Laurens (mez), H. Crook (ten), G. Ragon (ten), P. Herreweghe (cnd), La Chapelle Royale Orch, Collegium Vocale [F] Harmonia Mundi France 2-▲ HMC 901456/57

Lully, J.-B.:Phaëton, w. J. Smith (sop), R. Yakar (sop), H. Crook (ten), J.-P. Fouchécourt (ten), M. Minkowski (cnd), Musiciens du Louvres Erato 2-▲ 91737

Mozart, W.A.:Don Giovanni, w. Danielle Borst (sop—Donna Anna), Véronique Gens (sop—Donna Elvira), Sophie Marin-Degor (sop—Zerlina), Huub Claessens (bar—Leporello), Nicolas Revenq (bar—Don Giovanni), Patrick Donnelly (bass—Commendatore), Simon Edwards (sgr—Don Ottavio), J. Malgoire (cnd), La Grande Écurie et la Chambre du Roy Astrée 8-▲ E 8606

Purcell, H.:Dido & Aeneas, w. Véronique Gens (sop—Dido), Sophie Marin-Degor (sop—Belinda), Sophie Daneman (sop—2nd woman/1st witch), Gaëlle Mechaly (sop—2nd witch), Claire Brua (mez—Sorceress), Steve Dugardin (alt—Chorus), Jean-Paul Fouchécourt (ten—Spirit/Sailor), Nathan Berg (b-bar—Aeneas), Jonathan Arnold (bass—Chorus), William Christie (hpd), W. Christie (cnd), Les Arts Florissants *(rec Massy Opera Theatre, Nov. 8-11, 1994)* Erato ▲ 98477-2 [DDD]

Rameau, J.P.:Castor et Pollux, w. A. Mellon (sop), H. Cook (ten), J. Corréas (bass), W. Christie (cnd), Les Arts Florissants Harmonia Mundi France 3-▲ HMC 901435/37

Rameau, J.P.:Hippolyte et Aricie, w. Bernarda Fink (cta), Jean-Paul Fouchécourt (ten), Laurent Naouri (bar), Russell Smythe (bar), M. Minkowski (cnd), Louvre Musicians, Sagittarius Vocal Ensemble Archiv 3-▲ 445853-2

Rameau, J.P.:Motets, w. I. Desrochers (sop), J.-P. Fouchecourt (ct), H. Lamy (ten), P. Harvey (bar), M. Loureiro de Sà (bar), S. Imbodem (bass), *(orch unknown)*—Deus noster refugium; Quam dilecta; In convertendo [L] *(rec Apr. 13-18, 1992)* FNAC Music ▲ 592096 [DDD]

Gentile, Luana (sop)

Albanese, G.:Songs, w. Antonella Trovarelli (sop), Marina Gentile (mez), Stefano Consolini (ten), Paolo Speca (bar), Andrea De Mele (vn), Sirio Benedetto (sax), Roberto Rupo (pno)—Madrigale, Ninna nanna...900, Variazioni, Non so qual io mi voglia..., Io sono un augellin..., Ma non sapete chi sono io?, Una rosa di ferro battuto *(rec Ortona, Teatro Zambra, Feb 21, 22, 23 & Mar 1 &)* Bongiovanni ▲ GB 5054-2 [DDD]

Gentile, Maria (sop)

Bizet, G.:Don Procopio, w. Muscente (sgr), Carmona (sgr), Barry (sgr), A. Antoniozzi (bar), S. Sanna (cnd), Berlin Radio Youth Orch, Symbolon Ensemble Chorus [l] *(rec live 5/25/86)* Bongiovanni 2-▲ GB 2043/44 [DDD]

Mascagni, P.:Sí, w. Vivian (sop), A. Felle (sop), M.G. Liguori (sop), Nicoletti (sgr), Comas (sgr), S. Sanna (cnd), Montepulciano Arts Center Orch, Montepulciano Arts Center Chorus [l] *(rec live, 7/24/87)* Bongiovanni 2-▲ GB 2050/51 [DDD]

Gentile, Marina (mez)

Albanese, G.:Songs, w. Luana Gentile (sop), Antonella Trovarelli (sop), Stefano Consolini (ten), Paolo Speca (bar), Andrea De Mele (vn), Sirio Benedetto (sax), Roberto Rupo (pno)—Ninna Nanna , Ma non sapete chi sono io?, Una rosa di ferro battuto *(rec Ortona, Teatro Zambra, Feb 21, 22, 23 & Mar 1 &)* Bongiovanni ▲ GB 5054–2 [DDD]

Tosti, P.F.:Canti populari e romanze abruzzesi, w. C. Di Censo (sop), W. Omaggio (ten), P. Speca (sgr), I. Crissante (pno) Nuova Era ▲ NUO 7166 [DDD]

Genz, Stephan (bar)

Wolf, H.:Goethe–Lieder (sels), w. Locky Chung (bar), Markus Hadulla (pno), Claar Ter Horst (pno)—24 sels Claves ▲ 50–9517

Georg, Mechthild (mez)

Bach, J.S.:Cant 11, "Ascension Oratorio", w. C. Cuccaro (sop), A. Kraus (ten), A. Schmidt (bass), H. Rilling (cnd), Württemberg CO, Găchinger Kantorei [G] *(rec 1984)* Hänssler Classic 5–▲ 98.976

Bach, J.S.:Cant 11, "Ascension Oratorio", w. C. Cuccaro (sop), A. Kraus (ten), A. Schmidt (bass), H. Rilling (cnd), Württemberg CO, Găchinger Kantorei [G] Novalis ▲ 150028 [DDD]

Bach, J.S.:Cant 117, w. A. Kraus (ten), A. Schmidt (bar), H. Rilling (cnd), Stuttgart Bach Collegium, Găchinger Kantorei [G] Novalis ▲ 150028 [DDD]

Bach, J.S.:Cant 149, w. A. Augér (sop), A. Baldin (ten), P. Huttenlocher (bar), H. Rilling (cnd), Stuttgart Bach Collegium, Găchinger Kantorei [G] *(rec 1984)* Hänssler Classic ▲ 98.815 [AAD]

Bach, J.S.:Cant 197, w. C. Cuccaro (sop), P. Huttenlocher (bar), H. Rilling (cnd), Bach Ensemble *(rec Feb 1984)* Hänssler Classic ▲ 98.828 [AAD]

Bach, J.S.:Cant 200, w. H. Rilling (cnd), Bach Ensemble [G] *(rec 1984)* Hänssler Classic 5–▲ 98.976

Mozart, W.A.:Missa, K.317, w. Barbara Schlick (sop), Alexander Stevenson (ten), Philip Langshaw (bass), P. Kuentz (cnd), Paul Kuentz Orch, Paul Kuentz Choir Pierre Verany ▲ PVY 730041

Rossini, G.:Péchés de vieillesse (sels), w. M. Castets (sop), J.–L. Maurette (ten), M. Brodard (bar), R. Nolte (bass), E. Kalvelage (pno), C. Spering (org), M. Jorand (perc), Cologne Chorus Musicus—Toast pour le nouvel an, Roméo, La Grande Coquette, Un sou, Chanson de Zora, La Nuit de Noël, Le Dodo des enfants, Le Lazzarone, Adieux à la vie!, Soupirs et sourire, L'Orpheline du Tyrol, Choeur de chasseurs démocrates; *Morceaux réservés*—Ave Maria, Les Amants de Séville, Le Chant des Titans, Chant funèbre [F] *(rec Aug. 1992)* Opus 111 ▲ OPS 30–70 [DDD]

Telemann, G.P.:Cants, w. Constanze Backes (sop), Klaus Mertens (bar), Andreas Post (sgr), L. Rémy (cnd), Telemann CO, Helko Siede (cnd), Michaelstein Chamber Choir—Christmas cantatas, "Siehe, ich verkündige Euch" (1761) & "Der Herr hat offenbaret" (1762) *(rec Apr 28–May 2, 1996)* CPO ▲ CPO 999419–2 [DDD]

Telemann, G.P.:Hirten an der Krippe zu Bethlehem, w. Constanze Backes (sop), Klaus Mertens (bar), Andreas Post (sgr), L. Rémy (cnd), Telemann CO, Helko Siede (cnd), Michaelstein Chamber Choir *(rec Apr 28–May 2, 1996)* CPO ▲ CPO 999419–2 [DDD]

George, Donald (ten)

Saint–Saëns, C.:Samson et Dalila (sels), w. A. Baltsa (mez), J. Carreras (ten), J. Summers (bar), S. Estes (bass), P. Burchuladze (bass), C. Davis (cnd), Bavarian RSO Philips ▲ 438504–2

George, Michael (bass)

Bach, J.S.:Cant 208, "Hunting Cant", w. E. Kirkby (sop), J. Smith (sop), S. Davies (ten), R. Goodman (cnd), Parley of Instruments [G] Hyperion ▲ CDA 66169

Bach, J.S.:St. John Passion, w. P. Kwella (sop), D. James (ct), W. Kendall (ten), I. Partridge (ten), D. Wilson–Johnson (b–bar), H. Christophers (cnd), The Sixteen Orch, The Sixteen [G] Chandos ("Chaconne" series) 2–▲ CHAN 0507/08 [DDD]

Beethoven, L. van:Missa Solemnis, w. M. Hirsti (sop), C. Watkinson (cta), A. Murgatroyd (ten), T. Kvam (cnd), Hanover Band, Oslo Cathedral Choir [period instrs] [L] Nimbus ▲ NI 5109 [DDD]

Blow, J.:Songs, w. James Bowman (ct), John Mark Ainsley (ten), Charles Pott (bass), R. King (cnd), King's Consort—Sing unto the Lord, Oh ye Saints *(rec St Jude–on–the–Hill, London, Dec 20–21, 1968)* United ▲ CAL 88002 [DDD]

Bruckner, A.:Requiem, w. J. Rodgers (sop), C. Denley (mez), M. Davies (ten), Corydon Singers, M. Best (cnd), English CO Hyperion ▲ CDA 66245 [DDD]

Chabrier, E.:Briséïs, ou Les Amants de Corinthe, w. Kathryn Harries (sop), Simon Keenlyside (trb), Mark Padmore (ten), Joan Rodgers (sgr), J. Y. Ossonce (cnd), BBC Scottish SO Hyperion ▲ CDA 66803

Dodgson, S.:Last of the Leaves, w. John Bradbury (cl), R. Zollman (cnd), Northern Sinfonia of England *(rec St Nicholas Hospital, Newcastle–upon–Tyne, Oct 23–24, 1992)* Biddulph ▲ LAW 013 [DDD]

The Essential Gregorian Chant, w. Pro Cantione Antiqua [cnd:James O'Donnell], James Griffett (ten), Ian Partridge (ten), Stephen Roberts (bar), Gordon Jones (bass) Cala ▲ CAL CACD 88035 [DDD]

The Essential Gregorian Chant, w. James Griffett (ten), Ian Partridge (ten), Stephen Roberts (b–bar), Gordon Jones (bass), Pro Cantione Antique [cnd:James O'Donnell] United ▲ UNI 88035 [DDD]

Fauré, G.:Requiem, w. I. Poulenard (sop), M. Best (cnd), English CO, Corydon Singers [1893 version] Hyperion ▲ CDA 66292

Gregorian Lent & Easter, w. [cnd:James O'Donnell], Pro Cantione Antiqua, J. Griffett (ten), I. Partridge (ten), S. Roberts (bar), G. Jones (bass) *(rec All Saints, East Finchley, Dec 7–9, 1993)* United ▲ UNI 88016 [DDD]

Handel, G.F.:Alexander's Feast (ode), w. N. Argenta (sop), I. Partridge (ten), H. Christophers (cnd), The Sixteen Orch, The Sixteen Chorus Collins Classics 2–▲ COL 7016 [DDD]

Handel, G.F.:Apollo e Dafne, w. N. Argenta (sop), S. Standage (cnd), Collegium Musicum 90 Chandos ("Early Music" series) ▲ CHAN 0583 [DDD]

Handel, G.F.:Chandos Anthems (11), w. L. Dawson (sop), I. Partridge (ten), H. Christophers (cnd), The Sixteen Orch, The Sixteen—Nos. 1, 2 & 3 Chandos ("Chaconne" series) ▲ CHAN 0503 [DDD]

Handel, G.F.:Chandos Anthems (11), w. P. Kwella (sop), J. Bowman (ct), I. Partridge (ten), H. Christophers (cnd), The Sixteen Orch, The Sixteen—Anthem Nos. 7–9 [E] Chandos ("Chaconne" series) ▲ CHAN 0505 [DDD]

Handel, G.F.:Chandos Anthems (11), w. L. Dawson (sop), P. Kwella (sop), J. Bowman (alt), I. Partridge (ten), H. Christophers (cnd), The Sixteen Orch, The Sixteen Chandos ("Chaconne" series) 4–▲ CHAN 0554 [DDD]

Handel, G.F.:Deborah, w. S. Gritton (sop), Y. Kenny (sop), C. Denley (mez), J. Bowman (alt), R. King (cnd), King's Consort, Oxford New College Choir Hyperion 2–▲ CDA 66841 [DDD]

Handel, G.F.:Dixit Dominus, w. Lynn Dawson (sop), Linda Russell (alt), Charles Brett (ct), Ian Partridge (ten), H. Christophers (cnd), The Sixteen Orch, The Sixteen [L] Chandos ("Chaconne" series) ▲ CHAN 0517 [DDD]

Handel, G.F.:Jephtha, w. Julia Gooding (sop), Christiane Oelze (sop), Catherine Denley (mez), Axel Köhler (ct), John Mark Ainsley (ten), M. Creed (cnd), Berlin Academy for Early Music *(rec June 1992)* Berlin Classics 2–▲ BER 1057–2 [DDD]

Handel, G.F.:Joseph & His Brethren, w. Yvonne Kenney (sop), Catherine Denley (mez), Connor Burrowes (trb), James Bowman (ct), John Mark Ainsley (ten), R. King (cnd), King's Consort, New College Choir Oxford, King's Consort Choir Hyperion 3–▲ CDA 67171/3

Handel, G.F.:Messiah, w. Lynn Dawson (sop), Catherine Denley (mez), David James (alt), Arthur Davies (ten), H. Christophers (cnd), The Sixteen Orch, The Sixteen [20–member orchestra, 19–member chorus] [E] *(rec 1986)* Hyperion 2–▲ CDA 66251/52 [DDD]

Handel, G.F.:Nisi Dominus, w. Charles Brett (ct), Ian Partridge (ten), H. Christophers (cnd), The Sixteen Orch, The Sixteen [L] Chandos ("Chaconne" series) ▲ CHAN 0517 [DDD]

Handel, G.F.:Occasional Oratorio, w. Susan Gritton (sop), Lisa Milne (sop), James Brown (ct), John Mark Ainsley (ten), R. King (cnd), King's Consort, New College Choir Oxford Hyperion 2–▲ CDA 66961/62

Handel, G.F.:Ottone, Rè di Germania, w. Jennifer Smith (sop—Gismonda), Catherine Denley (mez—Matilda), James Bowman (ct—Ottone), Dominique Visse (ct—Adelberto), Michael George (bass—Emireno), R. King (cnd), King's Consort Hyperion 3–▲ CDA 66751/53

Handel, G.F.:La Rezurrezione, w. Linda Saffer (sop), Judith Nelson (mez), Patricia Spence (mez), Jeffery Thomas (ten), N. McGegan (cnd), Philharmonia Baroque Orch [I] Harmonia Mundi USA 2–▲ HMU 907027/28

Haydn, J.:Mass 7, "Kleine Orgelmesse", w. Linda Russell (alto), Catherine Wyn–Rogers (alt), William Kendall (ten), D. Hill (cnd), Brandenburg Orch, Winchester Cathedral Choir Hyperion ▲ CDA 66508 [DDD]

George, Michael (bass) (cont.)

Haydn, J.:Mass 14, "Harmoniemesse", w. Linda Russell (alto), Catherine Wyn–Rogers (alt), William Kendall (ten), D. Hill (cnd), Brandenburg Orch, Winchester Cathedral Choir Hyperion ▲ CDA 66508 [DDD]

Haydn, J.:Die Schöpfung, w. Emma Kirkby (sop), Anthony Rolfe Johnson (ten), C. Hogwood (cnd), Academy of Ancient Music, New College Choir Oxford [E] L'Oiseau–Lyre 2–▲ 430397–2 [DDD]

Lloyd, G.:John Socman (sels), w. J. Watson (sop), D. Montague (mez), T. Booth (ten), D. Wilson–Johnson (bar), M. Rivers (bar), G. Lloyd (cnd), Philharmonia Orch, London Voices Albany ▲ TROY 131 [DDD]

Mozart, W.A.:Missa, K.317, w. E. Kirkby (sop), C. Robbin (mez), J.M. Ainsley (ten), C. Hogwood (cnd), Academy of Ancient Music, Winchester Cathedral Choir Argo ▲ 436585–2 [DDD]

Pärt, A.:Passio Domini nostri Jesu Christi secundum Joannem, w. L. Dawson (sop), D. James (alt), R. Covey–Crump (ten), J. Potter (ten), G. Jones (bass), P. Hillier (cnd), Hilliard Ensemble, Western Wind Chamber Chorus [L] ECM New Series ▲ 78118–21370–2 [DDD]; ■ 78118–21370–4 (D)

Purcell, H.:Anthems, w. J. Bowman (ct), R. Covey–Crump (ten), C. Daniels (ten), King's Consort, New College Choir Oxford Hyperion ▲ CDA 66656

Purcell, H.:Anthems & Services, w. James Bowman (ct), Roger Covey–Crump (ten), R. King (cnd), King's Consort, New College Choir Oxford—Behold, now praise the Lord; Blessed are they that fear the Lord; I will give thanks unto Thee, O Lord; My song shall be always Hyperion ▲ CDA 66609

Purcell, H.:Anthems & Services, w. S. Gritton (sop), M. Kennedy (sop), E. O'Dwyer (trb), J. Goodman (trb), J. Bowman (ct), N. Short (ct), Rogers Covey–Crump (ten), C. Daniels (ten), M. Milhofer (ten), M. George (bass), R. Evans (bass), R. King (cnd), King's Consort—I Was Glad When They Said unto Me (coronation & verse anthem); O Consider My Adversity; Beati omnes qui timent Dominum; In the Black Dismal Dungeon of Dispair; Save Me, O God; Te Deum in B♭; Jubilant in B♭; Thy Way, O God, Is Holy Hyperion ▲ CDA 66677 [DDD]

Purcell, H.:Anthems & Services, w. James Bowman (ct), Charles Daniels (ten), Robert Evans (bass), R. King (cnd), King's Consort, New College Choir Oxford—O sing unto the Lord; O praise God in His holiness; Praise the Lord, O Jerusalem; It is a good thing to give thanks; O give thanks unto the Lord; Let mine eyes run down with tears; My beloved spake Hyperion ▲ CDA 66585

Purcell, H.:Anthems & Services, w. J. Bowman (ct), R. Covey–Crump (ten), C. Daniels (ten), S. Varcoe (bar), R. King (cnd), King's Consort, New College Choir Oxford—My heart is inditing; The way of God is an undefiled way; Sing unto God; Behold, I bring you glad tidings; Since God so tender a regard; Early, O Lord, my fainting soul; Sleep, Adam, sleep and take thy rest; Awake, ye dead; The earth trembled; Lord not to us but to thy name; O all ye people, clap your hands Hyperion ▲ CDA 66644

Purcell, H.:Anthems & Services, w. Tom Seligman (trb), James Bowman (ct), Ashley Stafford (ct), John Mark Ainsley (ten), Andrew Gant (ten), Charles Pott (bass), R. King (cnd), King's Consort, King's Consort—O Sing unto the Lord; My beloved spake *(rec St Jude–on–the–Hill, London, Dec 20–21, 1968)* United ▲ CAL 88002 [DDD]

Purcell, H.:Music for the Funeral of Queen Mary, w. S. Gritton (sop), M. Kennedy (sop), E. O'Dwyer (trb), J. Goodman (trb), J. Bowman (ct), N. Short (ct), Rogers Covey–Crump (ten), C. Daniels (ten), M. Milhofer (ten), R. Evans (bass), R. King (cnd), King's Consort Hyperion ▲ CDA 66677 [DDD]

Purcell, H.:The Prophetess, or The History of Dioclesian, w. L. Dawson (sop), Gillian Fisher (sop), R. Covey–Crump (ten), P. Elliot (ten), S. Varcoe (bar), J.E. Gardiner (cnd), Monteverdi Orch, Monteverdi Choir London Erato ("Gardiner Purcell Collection" series) 2–▲ 96556–2

Purcell, H.:The Prophetess, or The History of Dioclesian, w. C. Pierard (sop), J. Bowman (alt), J. M. Ainsley (ten), I. Bostridge (ten), R. Hickox (cnd), Collegium Musicum 90—Masque Chandos ("Chaconne" series) ▲ CHAN 0558 [DDD]

Purcell, H.:The Prophetess, or The History of Dioclesian, w. Catherine Pierard (sop), James Bowman (alt), John Mark Ainsley (ten), R. Hickox (cnd), Collegium Musicum 90 Chandos ▲ CHAN 0569/70 [DDD]

Purcell, H.:Songs, w. B. Bonney (sop), S. Gritton (sop), J. Bowman (ct), R. Covey–Crump (ten), C. Daniels (ten), R. King (cnd), King's Consort—When Strephon Found; Let Us, Kind Lesbia; Corinna Is Divinely Fair; Olinda in the Shades; If Music Be the Food of Love [3rd setting]; Lovely Albina; I Came, I Saw; No, to What Purpose; Young Thrysis' Fate; She Loves Me and Confesses Too; From Silent Shade (Bess of Bedlam); O Solitude; If Pray'rs and Tears; The Fatal Hour; Sylvia, 'Tis True You're Fair; Amintor, Heedless of His Flocks; Love is Now Become a Trade; Phyllis, I Can Never Forgive It; Who Can Behold?; He Himself Courts His Own Ruin; Let Formal Lovers Still Pursue; Ask Me to Love No More; In Cloris All Soft Charms; Spite of the Godhead Hyperion ▲ CDA 66730

Purcell, H.:Songs, w. B. Bonney (sop), S. Gritton (sop), J. Bowman (ct), R. Covey–Crump (ten), C. Daniels (ten), D. Miller (archlt/thb/baroque gtr), M. Caudle (b vl), R. King (chamber org)—Draw near, you lovers; While Thyrsis, wrapt in downy sleep; Love, thou canst hear, I lov'd fair Celia; What hope for us remains now he is gone; Pastora's beauties, when unblown; A thousand sev'ral ways I tried; Urge me no more; Farewell all joys; If music be the food of love [1st setting]; Amidst the shades and cool refreshing streams; They say you're angry; Let each gallant heart; This poet sings the Trojan wars; Ah, how pleasant 'tis to love; My heart whenever you appear; On the brow of Richard Hill; Rashly I swore I would disown; Since the pox or the plague; Beneath a dark and melancholy grove; Musing on cares of human fate; Whilst Cynthia sung, all angry winds lay still Hyperion ▲ CDA 66710

Purcell, H.:Songs, w. B. Bonney (sop), S. Gritton (sop), J. Bowman (ct), R. Covey–Crump (ten), C. Daniels (ten), D. Miller (archlt/thb/baroque gtr), M. Caudle (b vl), R. King (org/hpd), King's Consort—Incassum Lesbia; Gentle Shepherds, you that know the charms; I love and I must; Through mournful shades and solitary groves; The Knotting Song Hyperion ▲ CDA 66720 [DDD]

Purcell, H.:Timon of Athens, w. I. Davies (trb), C. de la Hoyde (trb), J. Bowman (alt), J. M. Ainsley (ten), R. Hickox (cnd), Collegium Musicum 90—Masque Chandos ("Chaconne" series) ▲ CHAN 0558 [DDD]

Purcell, H.:Timon of Athens, w. L. Dawson (sop), Gillian Fisher (sop), R. Covey–Crump (ten), P. Elliot (ten), S. Varcoe (bar), J.E. Gardiner (cnd), Monteverdi Orch, Monteverdi Choir London Erato ("Gardiner Purcell Collection" series) 2–▲ 96556–2

Schubert, Franz:Songs (comp), w. John Mark Ainsley (ten), Simon Keenlyside (bass), Graham Schäfer (sgr), Graham Johnson (cnd), London Schubert Chorale—settings of Goethe's poetry Hyperion ▲ CDJ 33024

Schubert, Franz:Songs (comp), w. P. Rozario (sop), J.M. Ainsley (ten), I. Bostridge (ten), G. Johnson (pno), S. Layton (cnd), London Schubert Chorale—Winterlied; Ossians Lied nach dem Falle Nathos; Das Mädchen von Inistore; Als ich sie erröten; Schwangesang; Totenkranz für ein Kind; Die Fröhlichkeit; Der Zufriedene; Alles um Liebe; Geist der Liebe; Dei erste Liebe; Die Täuschung; Liebesrausch; Huldigung; Heidenröslein; Nachtgesang; Der Morgenstern; Der Knappenlied; Trinklied vor der Schlacht; Schwertlied; Begräbnislied; Grablied; Osterlied; Hoffnung; Punschlied; Klage um Ali Bey; Abendständchen; Tische'rlied; Wiegenlied; Die Macht der Liebe; Trinklied, D.183; Trinklied, D.267 Hyperion ▲ CDJ 33020

Stainer, J.:The Crucifixion, w. J. Griffett (ten), A. Newberry (vc), S. Vann (cnd), Peterborough Cathedral Choir ASV Quicksilva ▲ ASQ 6100 [ADD]

Telemann, G.P.:Cants, w. P. Kwella (sop), C. Denley (mez), S. Roberts (b–bar), R. Hickox (cnd), Collegium Musicum 90—Die Donner Ode Chandos ("Chaconne" series) ▲ CHAN 0548 [DDD]

Telemann, G.P.:Motets, w. P. Kwella (sop), C. Denley (mez), S. Roberts (b–bar), R. Hickox (cnd), Collegium Musicum 90—Deus judicium tuum Chandos ("Chaconne" series) ▲ CHAN 0548 [DDD]

Vaughan Williams, R.:Songs, w. Ian Bostridge (ten), Stephen Layton (cnd), Holst Singers—Loch Lomand; 3 Shakespeare Songs; Alister McAlpine's Lament; An Acre of Land; The Seeds of Love; Ca' the yowes; 5 English Folksongs; The Winter Is Gone; Mannin Veen; Bushes & Briars; Down among the Dead Men; 3 Elizabethan Songs; Greensleeves; Rest; Heart's Music; Come away, Death; The Turtle Dove Hyperion ▲ CDA 66777

Georgel, Jean–Louis (bar)

Chabrier, E.:Fisch–Ton–Kan, w. M. Delunsch (sop), B. Desnoues (sop), F. Dudziak (ten), C. Mehn (ten), R. Delage (cnd), Strasbourg Collegium Musicum Orch Arion ▲ ARN 68252 [DDD]

Chabrier, E.:Vaucochard & Son I, w. M. Delunsch (sop), B. Desnoues (sop), F. Dudziak (ten), C. Mehn (ten), R. Delage (cnd), Strasbourg Collegium Musicum Orch Arion ▲ ARN 68252 [DDD]

Chabrier, E.:A Wasted Education, w. M. Delunsch (sop), B. Desnoues (sop), F. Dudziak (ten), C. Mehn (ten), R. Delage (cnd), Strasbourg Collegium Musicum Orch Arion ▲ ARN 68252 [DDD]

Georgescu, Florin (ten)
Donizetti, G.:Lucia di Lammermoor, w. Silvia Voinea (sop—Lucia), Lucia Cicoara (mez—Alisa), Florin Georgescu (ten—Edgardo), Gabriel Nastase (ten—Arturo), Nicolae Herlea (bar—Lord Enrico), Pompei Harasteanu (bass—Raimondo), C. Petrovici (cnd), Romanian Opera Orch, Romanian Opera Chorus *(rec 1984)* Vox Box 2-▲ CDX 5164

Geraerts, Harry (ct)
Desmarets, H.:Sacred Music, w. Barbara Schlick (sop), Mieke Van der Sluis (sop), Fiori Musicali, New College Choir Oxford—Deux grands motets lorrains; Mystères de notre seigneur Jésus-Christ Erato ▲ ERA SEL 98529 [ADD]

Gerasimova, Natalia (sop)
A Collection Of 19th Century Songs, w. Vladimir Skanavi (pno) Art & Electronics ▲ AED 68020 [DDD]
Mussorgsky, M.:Sunless, w. E. Svetlanov (cnd), Russia State SO *(rec L'Arsenal, Metz, France, July 5-9, 1994)* RCA Red Seal ▲ 09026-68406-2 [DDD]

Gerbert, M. (sgr)
Zinsstag, G.:Trauma, w. M. Bair-Ivenz, G. Schatz, K. M. Ziegler, South German Radio Chorus *(rec April 14, 1981)* Grammont ▲ CTSP 36-2 [ADD]

Gerdesits, Ferenc (ten)
Puccini, G.:Tosca (sels), w. E. Marton (sop), B. Heja (trb), J. Carreras (ten), J. Pons (bar), J. Nemeth (bar), J. Gregor (bass), M. Tilson Thomas (cnd), Hungarian State Orch, Hungarian Radio-TV Chorus *(rec Budapest, Dec. 14-22, 1988)* Sony Classical ("Opera Highlights" series) ▲ SMK 53500 [DDD]

Gerello, Vassily (bar)
Tchaikovsky, P.:Moscow, w. Svetlana Furdui (mez), A. Litton (cnd), Dallas SO, Dallas Sym Chorus *(rec McDermott Hall, Meyerson Center, Dallas, TX, Nov 16-18, 1995)* Delos ("Virtual Reality Recording" series) ▲ DE 3196 [DDD]

Gergalov, Alexander (bar)
Prokofiev, S.:War & Peace, w. Y. Prokina (sop), O. Borodina (mez), G. Gregoriam (ten), V. Gergiev (cnd), Kirov Orch, Kirov Opera Chorus [R] Philips 3-▲ 434097-2

Gerhardt, Elena (sop)
Great Voices of the Century, w. Povla Frijsh (sop), Lotte Lehmann (sop), Gerald Moore (pno) *(rec 1929-1939)* Sanctus ▲ 001 [ADD]

Gerhart, Maria (sop)
Mozart, W.A.:Rè pastore (sels), w. Gustav Liebich (vn), Victor Boschetti (pno) *(rec 1905 - 1944)* Minerva ▲ MN A14 [ADD]

Geriová, Beata (mez)
Respighi, O.:La Primavera, w. Henrietta Lednárová (sop—Prima fanciulla), Jana Valásková (sop—Sirvard), Beata Geriová (mez—Seconda fanciulla), Miroslav Dvorský (ten—Il giovine), Richard Haan (bar—L'orante), Vladimír Kubovčik (bass—Il vecchio), Vera Rasková (fl), M. Adriano (cnd), Slovak RSO Bratislava, Slovak Phil Chorus *(rec Slovak Radio Concert Hall, Bratislava, Jan. 4-9, Feb. 19 & June)* Marco Polo ▲ 8.223595 [DDD]

Gerishen, Franz (bar)
Bach, J.S.:Cant 39, w. A. Augér (sop), G. Schreckenbach (cta), H. Rilling (cnd), Stuttgart Bach Collegium, Gächinger Kantorei Hänssler Classic ▲ 98.802 [AAD]

Gérome, Raymond (nar)
Milhaud, D.:Les Mariés de la tour eiffel, w. Jean-Pierre Aumont (nar), B. Desgraupes (cnd), Erwartung Ensemble *(rec L'Opéra Comique, Paris, Dec 1989 & May 1990)* Marco Polo ▲ 8.223788 [DDD]

Gerron, Kurt (sgr)
Weill, K.:The Threepenny Opera, w. L. Lenya (sop), E. Helmke (sop), T. Mackeben (cnd), *(orch unknown)* [G] *(rec original German cast, 1930)* Mastersound ▲ DFCD1-110 (m) [ADD]
Weill, K.:The Threepenny Opera, w. L. Lenya (sop), E. Helmke (sop), T. Mackeben (cnd), *(orch unknown)* [G] *(rec original German cast, 1930)* Teldec ▲ 9031-72025-2 [ADD]

Gerstenhaber, Cyrille (sop)
Gouvy, T.:Songs, w. Hélène Lucas (pno)—sels from 40 poèmes of Ronsard & 18 sonnets & chansons of Desportes *(rec l'Auditorium Tibor Varga à Sion, July 27 - Aug 1, 1995)* K617 ▲ 7054 [DDD]

Gerville-Réache, Jeanne (mez)
The Complete Recordings, 1909-1913 Pearl ▲ PEA 9853 [ADD]

Geszty, Sylvia (sop)
Beethoven, L. van:Music of, w. Jozsef Reti (ten), Hermann Christian Polster (bass), Koch (cnd), Berlin RSO, Berlin State Orch, Berlin Soloists—Christ on the Mount of Olives (oratorio); Con in E♭ Pno; Irish Songs; Minuets; Canons; Epigrams; Joke Pieces; Incidental & Ballet Music Berlin Classics 3-▲ BER 9132
Handel, G.F.:Imeneo, w. Renate Krahmer (sop), Hans-Joachim Rotzsch (ten), Günther Leib (bass), Siegfried Vogel (bass), H.-T. Margraf (cnd), Halle Handel Festival Orch, Leipzig Radio Chorus *(rec 1966)* Berlin Classics ▲ BER 9110
Mozart, W.A.:Schauspieldirektor, w. Peter Schreier (ten), Hermann Christian Polster (bass), H. Koch (cnd), Berlin CO—features complete dialog *(rec 1968)* Berlin Classics ▲ BER 9136 [DDD]
Mozart, W.A.:Schuldigkeit, w. A. Augér (sop), K. Láki (sop), W. Hollweg (ten), C. H. Ahnsjö (ten), R. Bader (cnd), Berlin Cathedral Choir [G] *(rec 1980)* Koch Schwann 2-▲ CD 313065 [ADD]
Mozart, W.A.:Zauberflöte, w. H. Donath (sop), P. Schreier (ten), G. Leib (bass), T. Adam (bass), O. Suitner (cnd), Dresden Staatskapelle [I] RCA Gold Seal 3-▲ 6511-2 [ADD]
Rossini, G.:Elisabetta, regina d'Inghilterra, w. L. Gencer (sop), U. Grilli (ten), P. Bottazzo (ten), N. Sanzogno (cnd), Palermo Teatro Massimo Orch, Palermo Teatro Massimo Chorus [I] *(rec live, 11/24/70)* Myto 2-▲ 2 MCD 90530 [ADD]

Geyer, Stefan (bar)
Telemann, G.P.:Cants, w. Greetje Anthoni (sop), Yves Saelens (ten), F. Heyerick (cnd), Le Mercure Galant Baroque Orch, Ex Tempore Vocal Ensemble—Der Tod Jesu *(rec Studio Steurbaut, Gent, June 1995)* René Gailly ▲ 92025 [DDD]

Geysen, Kurt (bass)
Tchaikovsky, P.:Iolanta, w. Michaela Gurevich (sop—Iolanta), Jaqueline Miura (sop—Brigitta), Tatjana Tabachuk (mez—Martha), Annette Kuhn (mez—Laura), Ian Denolfo (ten—Godefroy), Keith Alexander Bolves (ten—Alméric), Alexander Ben (bar—Robert), Georg Lehner (bar—Ibn-Hakia), Arutiun Kotchinian (bass—René), Kurt Geysen (bass—Bertrand), H. Rotman (cnd), Warsaw PO, ECOV Ensemble Members *(rec Vooruit Center of the Arts, Ghent, Belgium, Aug 28-29, 1993)* CPO 2-▲ CPO 999456-2 [DDD]

Ghaffarpour, Pouran (voc)
Battiato, F.:Haiku, w. Franco Battiato (voc), Pouran Ghaffarpour (voc), Antonio Ballista (pno), Marco Boni (vc), Guido Corti (cnt), Filippo Destrieri (kbd/computer), John Giblin (bass), Gavin Harrison (dr/perc), Jakko Jakszyk (gtr), Roberto Mazza (ob), Fabrizio Merlini (va), Angelo Privitera (kbd/computer), Mino Bordignon (cnd), Milan Chamber Music Choir Hemisphere ▲ 837234-2

Ghazarian, Sona (sop)
Beethoven, L. van:Fidelio, w. H. Behrens (sop), P. Hofmann (ten), T. Adam (b-bar), H. Sotin (bass), G. Solti (cnd), Chicago SO, Chicago Sym Chorus [G] London 2-▲ 410227-2 [DDD]
Mozart, W.A.:Don Giovanni, w. G. Ottenthal (sop), P. Pace (sop), G. Sabbatini (ten), R. Bruson (bar), A> Rinaldi-Miliani (bar), F. De Grandis (bass), N. Ghiuselev (bass), N. Järvi (cnd), Cologne RSO, Cologne Radio Chorus [I] Chandos 3-▲ CHAN 8920/22 [DDD]

Gheorghiu, Angela (sop)
Puccini, G.:Arias, w. Nina Rautio (sop), Johan Botha (ten), Anthony Michaels-Moore (bar), E. Downes (cnd), Royal Opera House Orch, Royal Opera House Chorus Covent Garden—Se come voi piccina io fossi [from Le villi]; Addio mio dolce amor [from Edgar]; Donna non vidi mai; Sola, perduta, abbandonata [both from Manon Lescaut]; Donde lieta usci [from La Bohème]; Act 1 Finale; E lucevan le stelle [both from Tosca]; Un tal baccano in chiesa; Or tutto è chiaro; Tre sbirri, una carrozza; Un bel dì [from Madama Butterfly]; Ch'ella mi creda [from La fanciulla del West]; Chi il bel sogno di Doretta [from La rondine]; Nulla, silenzio [from Il tabarro]; Senza mamma [from Suor Angelica]; O mio babbino caro [from Gianni Schicchi]; Act I Finale; Nessun dorma [both from Turandot]; Signore, acolta; Non piangere, Liù *(rec Henry Wood Hall, London, Feb 12-27 & Mar 5, 1995)* Conifer Classics ("Royal Opera House" series) ▲ 75605-55013-2 [DDD]

Gheorghiu, Angela (sop) (cont.)
Verdi, G.:La traviata, w. Angela Gheorghiu (sop—Violetta), Leah-Marian Jones (mez—Flora Bervoix), Gillian Knight (mez—Annina), Robin Leggate (ten—Gastone), Frank Lopardo (ten—Alfredo Germont), Rodney Gibson (ten—Servo di Flora), Neil Griffiths (ten—Giuseppe), Mark Beesley (bar—Dottore Grenvile), Leo Nucci (bar—Giorgio Germont), Richard Van Allan (bass—Barone Douphol), Roderick Earle (bass—Marquese d'Obigny), Bryan Secombe (bass—Commissionario), G. Solti (cnd), Royal Opera House Orch, Royal Opera House Chorus Covent Garden *(rec live, Royal Opera House, Covent Garden, Dec. 1994)* London 2-▲ 448119-2

Gherman, Emil (ten)
Puccini, G.:Madama Butterfly, w. Eugenia Moldoveanu (sop—Madama Butterfly), Mihaela Agachi (mez—Suzuki), Corina Circa (mez—Kate Pinkerton), Emil Gherman (ten—B.F. Pinkerton), Stefan Popescu (ten—Goro), Ioan Soanea (bar—The Bonze/Yakuside), Eduard Tumageanian (bar—Sharpless), Alexandru Kopeczi (bass—Prince Yamadori), Mircea Moisa (bass—Commissioner), P. Popescu (cnd), Satu Mare PO, Cluj-Napoca Phil Chorus *(rec 1979)* Vox Box 2-▲ CDX 5155

Ghiaurov, Nicolai (bass)
The Art of Nikolai Ghiaurov, w. various Bulgarian orchs Forlane ▲ FOR 16559 [AAD]
Bellini, V.:I Puritani, w. J. Sutherland (sop), L. Pavarotti (ten), P. Cappuccilli (bar), R. Bonynge (cnd), London SO [I] London 3-▲ 417588-2 [ADD]
Bellini, V.:La sonnambula, w. J. Sutherland (sop), L. Pavarotti (ten), R. Bonynge (cnd), National PO London [I] London 2-▲ 417424-2 [DDD]
Boito, A.:Mefistofele, w. R. Tebaldi (sop—Margheritta), E. Souliotis (sop—Elena), M. Mackenzie (mez—Marta), M. Ruggiero (mez—Pantalis), A. Kraus (ten—Faust), H. Kraus (ten—Wagner), N. Ghiaurov (bass—Mefistofele), N. Sanzogno (cnd), *(orch unknown)* Ornamenti 2-▲ FE 101
Boito, A.:Mefistofele, w. M. Freni (sop), M. Caballé (sop), L. Pavarotti (ten), O. de Fabritiis (cnd), National PO London [I] London 3-▲ 410175-2 [DDD]
Boito, A.:Mefistofele, w. R. Tebaldi (sop), C. Bergonzi (ten), L. Gardelli (cnd), *(orch unknown)* *(rec live, New York 1/25/66)* Standing Room Only 2-▲ SRO 824-2 [ADD]
Borodin, A.:Prince Igor, w. S. Evstatieva (sop), A. Milcheva (mez), B. Martinovich (b-bar), N. Ghiuselev (bass), E. Tchakarov (cnd), Sofia Festival Orch, Sofia National Opera Chorus [R] Sony Classical 3-▲ S3K 44878 [DDD]
Donizetti, G.:La favorita, w. F. Cossotto (mez), L. Pavarotti (ten), G. Bacquier (bar), R. Bonynge (cnd), Bologna Teatro Comunale Orch, Bologna Teatro Comunale Chorus London 3-▲ 430038-2 [ADD]
Donizetti, G.:Lucia di Lammermoor, w. J. Sutherland (sop), L. Pavarotti (ten), S. Milnes (bar), R. Bonynge (cnd), Royal Opera House Orch [I] London 3-▲ 410193-2 [ADD]
Donizetti, G.:Lucia di Lammermoor (sels), w. J. Sutherland (sop), L. Pavarotti (ten), S. Milnes (bar), R. Bonynge (cnd), Royal Opera House Orch, Royal Opera House Chorus Covent Garden [I] London ("Opera Gala" series) ▲ 421885-2 [ADD]
Gounod, C.:Faust, w. J. Sutherland (sop), F. Corelli (ten), R. Bonynge (cnd), London SO, Ambrosian Opera Chorus [F] London ("Grand Opera" series) 3-▲ 421240-2 [AAD]
Gounod, C.:Faust, w. R. Scotto (sop), A. Kraus (ten), P. Ethuin, *(orch unknown)* [F] *(rec live, Tokyo, 1973)* Standing Room Only 3-▲ SRO 811-3 [ADD]
Gounod, C.:Faust, w. M. Freni (sop), G. Raimondi (ten), G. Prêtre (cnd), La Scala Orch, La Scala Chorus *(rec live 1967)* Melodram 3-▲ MEL 37005
Gounod, C.:Faust, w. M. Freni (sop), P. Domingo (ten), T. Allen (bar), G. Prêtre (cnd), Paris Opera Orch [F] EMI Classics 3-▲ CDCC 47493 [ADD]
Gounod, C.:Faust (sels), w. M. Freni (sop), P. Domingo (ten), T. Allen (bar), G. Prêtre (cnd), Paris Opera Orch, Orch de Paris, Paris Opera Chorus EMI Classics ▲ ZDM 63090
Gounod, C.:Faust (sels), w. Alexandrina Pendachanska (sop—Margarethe), Giuseppe Sabbatini (ten—Faust), György Melis (bar—Valentin), Nicolai Ghiaurov (bass—Méphistophélès), Nikola Ghiuselev (bass—Méphistophélès), Berlin RSO, Vienna SO, Hungarian State Opera Orch, Bulgarian RSO, Sofia SO, Bulgarian National Chorus, Bulgarian National Chorus Radio Choir—Intro; Vien ou bière; O sainte médaille...Avant de quitter ces lieux; Le veau d'or [all from Act 2]; Quel trouble inconnu me pénètre!...Salut! demeure chaste et pure; Je voudrais bien savoir...Il était un roi de Thule; Un bouquet!...O Dieu! que de bijoux [both from Act 3]; Gloire immortelle de nos aieux; Vous qui faites l'endormie [both from Act 4]; Intermezzo; Walpurgis Night [both from Act 5] Laserlight ▲ 14209 [DDD]
Massenet, J.:Don Quichotte, w. R. Crespin (sop), M. Command (sop), G. Bacquier (bar), R. Bonynge (cnd), Swiss Romande Orch, Swiss Romande Chorus [F] London ("Grand Opera" series) 2-▲ 430636-2 [AAD]
Massenet, J.:Le Roi de Lahore, w. J. Sutherland (sop), L. Lima (ten), S. Milnes (bar), R. Bonynge (cnd), National PO London, London Voices London ("Grand Opera" series) 2-▲ 433851-2 [DDD]
Meyerbeer, G.:Les Huguenots, w. J. Sutherland (sop), F. Cossotto (mez), G. Simionato (mez), F. Corelli (ten), V. Ganzarolli (bar), G. Tozzi (bass), G. Gavezzeni (cnd), La Scala Orch, La Scala Chorus [I] *(rec live 5/28/62)* Melodram 3-▲ MEL 37026 (m) [AAD]
Mozart, W.A.:Don Giovanni, w. C. Watson (sop), C. Ludwig (mez), N. Gedda (ten), O. Klemperer (cnd), New Philharmonia Orch, New Philharmonia Chorus EMI Classics 3-▲ CDMC 63841
Mozart, W.A.:Don Giovanni, w. G. Janowitz (sop), T. Zylis-Gara (sop), M. Freni (sop), A. Kraus (ten), R. Panerai (bar), V. von Halem (bass), H. von Karajan (cnd), Vienna PO, Vienna State Opera Chorus [I] *(rec live, Salzburg, Aug. 1, 1969)* Memories 3-▲ HR 4362/64 (m) [ADD]
Mozart, W.A.:Don Giovanni, w. G. Janowitz (sop), S. Jurinac (sop), G. von Milivkovic (mez), A. Kraus (ten), C. M. Giulini (cnd), Rome RAI Orch, Rome RAI Chorus *(rec live, May 12, 1970)* Melodram 3-▲ MEL 37080
Mussorgsky, M.:Boris Godunov, w. S. Mineva (mez—Marina), M. Svetlev (ten—Gregory), N. Ghiaurov (bass—Boris), N. Ghiuselev (bass—Pimen), E. Tchakarov (cnd), Sofia Festival Orch, Sofia National Opera Chorus [R] Sony Classical ("Russian Opera" series) 3-▲ S3K 45763
Mussorgsky, M.:Boris Godunov, w. N. Dobrianova (sop), S. Jurinac (sop), D. Usunow (ten), N. Ghiuselev (bass), A. Diakov (bass), H. von Karajan (cnd), Vienna PO, Vienna State Opera Chorus [R] *(rec live in Salzburg, 7/26/64)* Arkadia 2-▲ 210 (m) [ADD]
Mussorgsky, M.:Khovanshchina, w. A. Miltcheva (mez), M. Popov (ten), K. Kaludov (ten), Z. Gadjev (bass), N. Ghiuselev (bass), E. Tchakarov (cnd), Sofia National Opera Orch, Sofia National Opera Chorus Sony Classical 3-▲ S3K 45831
Mussorgsky, M.:Khovanshchina, w. Mietta Sighele (sop—Emma), Elena Souliotis (sop—Susanna), Fiorenza Cossotto (mez—Marfa), Herbert Handt (ten—Scribe), Veriano Luchetti (ten—Prince Andrey Khovansky), Ludovic Spiess (ten—Prince Vasily Golitsin), Claudio Strudthoff (ten—Streshnev), Angelo Marchiandi (bar—Kuz'ka), Teodoro Rovetta (bar—1st Strel'tsi), Siegmund Nimsgern (b-bar—Shaklovity), Cesare Siepi (b-bar—Dosifey), Carlo del Bosco (bass—2nd Strel'tsi), Ubaldo Carosi (bass—Varsonofiev), Nicolai Ghiaurov (bass—Prince Ivan Khovnasky), Giovanni Sciarpeletti (bass—Pastor), B. Leskovich (cnd), Rome RAI SO, Rome RAI Chorus—also includes bonus Act V [w Boris Christoff] (Rome, 1958) *(rec Rome, 1973)* Bella Voce 3-▲ BLV 107.402 [AAD]
Opera Arias & Songs *(rec 1961-70)* Arkadia ▲ 807
Ponchielli, A.:La Gioconda, w. M. Caballé (sop), A. Baltsa (mez), L. Pavarotti (ten), S. Milnes (bar), B. Bartoletti (cnd), National PO [I] London 3-▲ 414349-2 [DDD]
Public Performances 1966-1970 Memories ("Great Voices" series) 2-▲ HR 4223 [ADD]
Puccini, G.:Turandot, w. J. Sutherland (sop), M. Caballé (sop), L. Pavarotti (ten), Z. Mehta (cnd), London PO, John Alldis Choir [I] London 2-▲ 414274-2 [ADD]
Puccini, G.:Turandot (sels), w. J. Sutherland (sop), M. Caballé (sop), L. Pavarotti (ten), Z. Mehta (cnd), London PO London ▲ 421320-2 [ADD] ■ 421320-4
Rossini, G.:Il barbiere di Siviglia, w. Fiorenza Cossotto (mez), Luigi Alva (ten), Sesto Bruscantini (bar), Carlo Badioli (bass), G. Santini (cnd), La Scala Orch, La Scala Chorus *(rec Jan 20, 1964)* Pantheon 2-▲ PHE 6644 (m)
Rossini, G.:Mosè in Egitto, w. Teresa Zylis-Gara (sop), Shirley Verrett (mez), Ottavio Garàventa (ten), Giampaolo Corradi (bass), Mario Petri (bass), W. Sawallisch (cnd), Rome RAI Orch, Rome RAI Chorus *(rec live, Rome, 1968)* Italian Opera Rarities 2-▲ IOR 7724 [ADD]
Russian Romances, w. Pavlina Dokovska (pno) RCA Red Seal ▲ 09026-62501-2
Tchaikovsky, P.:Eugene Onegin (sels), w. Alexandrina Pendachanska (sop), Lyubomir Diakovski (sgr), Niko Isakov (sgr), Dresden State Orch, Bulgarian National Chorus—Intro; Peasant's Chorus & Dance; Scene & Aria of Olga; Scene & Quartet; Letter Scene; plus others Laserlight ▲ 14210 [DDD]
Verdi, G.:Aida, w. K. Ricciarelli (sop), E. Obraztsova (mez), P. Domingo (ten), L. Nucci (bar), C. Abbado (cnd), La Scala Orch, La Scala Chorus [I] Deutsche Grammophon 3-▲ 410092-2 [DDD]

Ghiaurov, Nicolai (bass) (cont.)

Verdi, G.:Aida, w. K. Ricciarelli (sop), E. Obraztsova (mez), P. Domingo (ten), L. Nucci (bar), C. Abbado (cnd), La Scala Orch, La Scala Chorus [I] Deutsche Grammophon ▲ 435410-2 [DDD]

Verdi, G.:Aida, w. M. Caballé (sop), F. Cossotto (mez), P. Domingo (ten), P. Cappuccilli (bar), R. Muti (cnd), New Philharmonia Orch, Royal Opera House Chorus Covent Garden [I] EMI Classics 3-▲ CDCC 47271 [ADD]

Verdi, G.:Attila, w. Rita Orlandi Malaspina (sop—Odabella), Veriano Luchetti (ten—Foresto), Piero de Palma (ten—Uldino), Piero Cappuccilli (bar—Ezio), Nicolai Ghiaurov (bass—Attila), Luigi Roni (bass—Leone), G. Patanè (cnd), La Scala Orch, La Scala Chorus *(rec Milan, May 15, 1972)* Golden Age of Opera 2-▲ GAO 187/88 [ADD]

Verdi, G.:Attila, w. Rita Orlandi Malaspina (sop—Odabella), Veriano Luchetti (ten—Foresto), Piero De Palma (ten—Uldino), Piero Cappuccilli (bar—Ezio), Nicolai Ghiaurov (bass—Attila), Luigi Roni (bass—Leone), G. Patanè (cnd), La Scala Orch, La Scala Chorus *(rec Milan, May 12, 1975)* Myto 2-▲ MCD 961140

Verdi, G.:Don Carlos, w. L. Gencer (sop), F. Cossotto (mez), B. Prevedi (ten), S. Bruscantini (bar), F. Previtali (cnd), Rome Opera Orch, Rome Opera Chorus *(rec live)* Melodram 3-▲ MEL 37022

Verdi, G.:Don Carlos, w. R. Kabaivanska (sop), O. Dominguez (mez), F. Corelli (ten), L. Quilico (bar), N. Ghiuselev (bass), A. Guadagno (cnd), Hartford Opera Orch *(rec live 1966)* Melodram 2-▲ MEL 27511

Verdi, G.:Don Carlos, w. Gundula Janowitz (sop), Shirley Verrett (mez), Franco Corelli (ten), Eberhard Waechter (bar), Martti Talvela (bass), H. Stein (cnd), Vienna PO, Vienna State Opera Chorus *(rec Vienna, Oct. 25, 1970)* Pantheon 2-▲ PHE 6614

Verdi, G.:Don Carlos, w. Katia Ricciarelli (sop), Fiorenza Cossotto (mez), Guido Fabbris (ten), Veriano Luchetti (ten), Piero Cappuccilli (bar), Gianfranco Casarini (bass), Alessandro Maddalena (bass), Aracelly Haengel (sgr), Marisa Salimbeni (sgr), Giorgio Zoranca (sgr), G. Prêtre (cnd), *(orch unknown)* Great Opera Performances 3-▲ GOP 777

Verdi, G.:Don Carlos, w. R. Tebaldi (sop), G. Bumbry (mez), C. Bergonzi (ten), D. Fischer-Dieskau (bar), G. Solti (cnd), Royal Opera House Orch Covent Garden, Royal Opera House Chorus Covent Garden [1886 5-act Italian version] [I] London 3-▲ 421114-2 [ADD]

Verdi, G.:Ernani, w. M. Freni (sop), P. Domingo (ten), R. Bruson (bar), R. Muti (cnd), La Scala Orch, La Scala Chorus [I] EMI Classics 3-▲ CDC 47082 [DDD]

Verdi, G.:Ernani, w. R. Kabaivanska (sop), P. Domingo (ten), Meliciani (sgr), A. Votto (cnd), La Scala Orch, La Scala Chorus *(rec live 12/7/69)* Melodram 2-▲ MEL 27064 (m) [AAD]

Verdi, G.:Macbeth, w. Shirley Verrett (mez—Lady Macbeth), Plácido Domingo (ten—Macduff), Piero Cappuccilli (bar—Macbeth), Nicolai Ghiaurov (bass—Banco), C. Abbado (cnd), La Scala Orch, La Scala Chorus Deutsche Grammophon ("The Originals" series) ▲ 449 732-2

Verdi, G.:Nabucco, w. Gloria Lane (mez), Gianni Raimondi (ten), Giangiacomo Guelfi (bar), Elena Saliotis (sgr), G. Gavazzeni (cnd), La Scala Orch, La Scala Chorus *(rec La Scala Theater, Milan, Dec. 7, 1966)* Pantheon 2-▲ PHE 6757 (m)

Verdi, G.:Requiem Mass, w. L. Price (sop), F. Cossotto (mez), L. Pavarotti (ten), H. von Karajan (cnd), La Scala Orch, La Scala Chorus [L] *(rec live 1/16/67)* Verona 2-▲ 27060/61 (m) [AAD]

Verdi, G.:Requiem Mass, w. E. Schwarzkopf (sop), C. Ludwig (mez), N. Gedda (ten), C. M. Giulini (cnd), Philharmonia Orch, London Phil Choir [L] EMI Classics 2-▲ CDCB 47257 [ADD]

Verdi, G.:Requiem Mass, w. L. Price (sop), F. Cossotto (mez), L. Pavarotti (ten), H. von Karajan (cnd), La Scala Orch, La Scala Chorus [L] *(rec live 1/16/67)* Melodram 2-▲ MEL 28012

Verdi, G.:Rigoletto (sels), w. J. Anderson (sop), S. Verrett (mez), L. Pavarotti (ten), L. Nucci (bar), R. Chailly (cnd), Bologna Teatro Comunale Orch, Bologna Teatro Comunale Chorus London ▲ 436097-2 [DDD]

Verdi, G.:Il trovatore, w. J. Sutherland (sop), M. Horne (mez), L. Pavarotti (ten), I. Wixell (bar), R. Bonynge (cnd), National PO London [I] London 2-▲ 417137-2 [ADD]

Ghirardini, Emilio (bar)

Verdi, G.:Falstaff, w. Pia Tassinari (sop—Alice Ford), Ines Alfani Tellini (sop—Nannetta), Aurora Buades (mez—Quickly), Rita Monticone (mez—Meg Page), Roberto D'Alessio (ten—Fenton), Giuseppe Nessi (ten—Bardolfo), Emilio Venturini (ten—Dr. Caius), Emilio Ghirardini (bar—Ford), Giacomo Rimini (bar—Sir John Falstaff), Salvatore Baccaloni (bass—Pistola), L. Molajoli (cnd), Milan SO, La Scala Chorus *(rec La Scala Theatre, Milan, Apr. 1932)* VAI Audio 2-▲ VAIA 1098-2

Verdi, G.:La forza del destino (sels), w. G. Cigna (sop—Leonora), E. Ghirardini (bar—Melitone), G. Vaghi (bar—Guardiano), O. de Fabritiis (cnd), Rome RAI Orch, Rome RAI Chorus *(rec Oct. 10, 1938)* Legato Classics 2-▲ LCD 173-2 [ADD]

Ghiuselev, Nikola (bass)

Nicola Ghiuselev, w. Sofia SO [cnd:Metodii Matakiev], Bulgarian National Phil Choir Gega ▲ GD 200 [DDD]

Orthodox Chants Jade ▲ JAD C 064

Bellini, V.:I Puritani (sels), w. J. Sutherland (sop), D. Cole (sop), A. Kraus (ten), R. Wolansky (bar), R. Bonynge (cnd), San Francisco Opera Orch, San Francisco Opera Chorus *(rec live, San Francisco, 9/2/66)* Golden Age of Opera ▲ GAO 133 [ADD]

Borodin, A.:Prince Igor, w. S. Evstatieva (sop), A. Milcheva (mez), B. Martinovich (b-bar), N. Ghiaurov (bass), E. Tchakarov (cnd), Sofia Festival Orch, Sofia National Opera Chorus [R] Sony Classical 3-▲ S3K 44878 [DDD]

Cherubini, L.:Médée, w. L. Popp (sop), L. Rysanek (sop), M. Lilowa (mez), B. Prevedi (ten), H. Stein (cnd), Vienna State Opera Orch, Vienna State Opera Chorus *(rec live, Vienna 1/31/72)* Melodram 2-▲ CDM 27087 [ADD]

Donizetti, G.:Anna Bolena, w. Katia Ricciarelli (sop), Doris Soffel (cta), Pietro Ballo (ten), E. Pidò (cnd), Palermo Teatro Massimo Orch, Palermo Teatro Massimo Chorus *(rec live, 1991)* Serenissima 3-▲ SER 360111

Gounod, C.:Faust (sels), w. Alexandrina Pendachanska (sop—Margarethe), Giuseppe Sabbatini (ten—Faust), György Melis (bar—Valentin), Nicolai Ghiaurov (bass—Méphistophélès), Nikola Ghiuselev (bass—Méphistophélès), Berlin RSO, Vienna SO, Hungarian State Opera Orch, Bulgarian RSO, Sofia SO, Bulgarian National Chorus, Bulgarian National Chorus Radio Choir—Intro; Vien ou bière; O sainte médaille...Avant de quitter ces lieux; Le veau d'or [all from Act 2]; Quel trouble inconnu me pénètre!...Salut! demeure chaste et pure; Je voudrais bien savoir...Il était un roi de Thule; Un bouquet!...O Dieu! que de bijoux [both from Act 3]; Gloire immortelle de nos aieux; Vous qui faites l'endormie [both from Act 4]; Intermezzo; Walpurgis Night [both from Act 5] Laserlight ▲ 14209 [DDD]

Meyerbeer, G.:Les Huguenots, w. J. Sutherland (sop), M. Arroyo (sop), H. Tourangeau (mez), A. Vrenios (ten), D. Cossa (bar), G. Bacquier (bar), R. Bonynge (cnd), New Philharmonia Orch, Ambrosian Opera Chorus London ("Grand Opera" series) 4-▲ 430549-2 [AAD]

Mozart, W.A.:Don Giovanni, w. S. Ghazarian (sop), G. Ottenthal (sop), P. Pace (sop), G. Sabbatini (ten), R. Bruson (bar), S. Rinaldi-Miliani (bar), F. De Grandis (bass), N. Järvi (cnd), Cologne RSO, Cologne Radio Chorus [I] Chandos 3-▲ CHAN 8920/22 [DDD]

Mussorgsky, M.:Boris Godunov, w. S. Mineva (mez—Marina), M. Svetlev (ten—Gregory), N. Ghiaurov (bass—Boris), N. Ghiuselev (bass—Pimen), E. Tchakarov (cnd), Sofia Festival Orch, Sofia National Opera Chorus [R] Sony Classical ("Russian Opera" series) 3-▲ S3K 45763

Mussorgsky, M.:Boris Godunov, w. N. Dobrianova (sop), S. Jurinac (sop), D. Usunow (ten), N. Ghiaurov (bass), A. Diakov (bass), H. von Karajan (cnd), Vienna PO, Vienna State Opera Chorus [R] *(rec live in Salzburg, 7/26/64)* Arkadia 2-▲ 210 (m) [ADD]

Mussorgsky, M.:Khovanshchina, w. A. Miltcheva (mez), M. Popov (ten), K. Kaludov (ten), Z. Gadjev (bass), N. Ghiaurov (bass), E. Tchakarov (cnd), Sofia National Opera Orch, Sofia National Opera Chorus Sony Classical 3-▲ S3K 45831

Rimsky-Korsakov, N.:Snow Maiden, w. Stefka Evstatieva (sop—Kupava), Elena Zemenkova (sop—Snow Maiden), Alexandrina Milcheva (mez—Spring Fairy), Vessela Zorova (mez—wife), Stefka Mineva (alt—Lehl), Avram Andreev (ten—Tsar), Lyubomir Dyakovski (ten—Cottager, Sprite), Lyubomir Videnov (bar—Misgir), Nicola Ghiuselev (bass—King), S. Angelov (cnd), Bulgarian RSO, Bulgarian National Chorus *(rec Sofia, 1985)* Capriccio 3-▲ 10749-51 [DDD]

Tchaikovsky, P.:Eugene Onegin, w. A. Tomowa-Sintow (sop), R. Troava-Mircheva (cta), N. Gedda (ten), Y. Mazurok (bar), E. Tchakarov (cnd), Sofia Festival Orch, Sofia National Opera Chorus [R] Sony Classical 2-▲ S2K 45539 [DDD]

Verdi, G.:Attila, w. Maria Chiara (sop), Silvano Carroli (bar), N. Santi (cnd), Turin Teatro Regio Orch, Turin Teatro Regio Chorus *(rec live, 1980)* Serenissima 2-▲ SER 360138

Ghiuselev, Nikola (bass) (cont.)

Verdi, G.:La battaglia di Legnano, w. K. Ricciarelli (sop), J. Carreras (ten), M. Manuguerra (bar), L. Gardelli (cnd), ORF SO, ORTF Choir Philips 2-▲ 422435-2 [ADD]

Verdi, G.:Don Carlos, w. R. Kabaivanska (sop), O. Dominguez (mez), F. Corelli (ten), L. Quilico (bar), N. Ghiaurov (bass), A. Guadagno (cnd), Hartford Opera Orch *(rec live 1966)* Melodram 2-▲ MEL 27511

Verdi, G.:I lombardi alla prima crociata, w. S. Sass (sop), J. Carreras (ten), L. Gardelli (cnd), *(orch unknown)* [I] *(rec live, London, 1976)* Standing Room Only 2-▲ SRO 829-2 [ADD]

Verdi, G.:Requiem Mass, w. Wiener-Chenisheva (sop), A. Milcheva-Nonova (mez), L. Bodourov (ten), I. Marinov (cnd), Sofia State PO, Sofia State Chorus [L] Vivace 3-▲ E 326 [ADD]

Giacomini, Giuseppe (ten)

Donizetti, G.:Fausta, w. R. Kabaiwanska (sop), R. Bruson (bar), D. Oren (cnd), Rome Opera Orch, Rome Opera Chorus *(rec live, 1981)* Italian Opera Rarities 3-▲ IOR 7701 [ADD]

Giordano, U.:Fedora (sels), w. Magda Olivero (sop), Franco Piva (ten), Elena Baggiore (sgr), M. Braggio (cnd), *(orch unknown)*—Amor ti vieta; Loris Ipanoff, oggi lo Zar; Muta è mia madre, muto il fratello *(rec Piacenza, Jan. 9, 1972)* Golden Age of Opera 2-▲ GAO 189/90 [ADD]

Mascagni, P.:Cavalleria rusticana, w. J. Norman (sop), M. Senn (mez), R. Laghezza (mez), D. Hvorostovsky (bar), S. Bychkov (cnd), Orch de Paris Philips ▲ 432105-2 [DDD]

Mascagni, P.:Cavalleria rusticana (sels), w. Aldo Protti (bar), Maria Luisa Nave (sgr), M. Gusella (cnd), *(orch unknown)*—O Lola ch'hai di latti la cammisa; Tu qui Santuzza; Intanto amici qua; Mamma, quel vino è generoso *(rec Parma, Feb. 6, 1969)* Golden Age of Opera 2-▲ GAO 189/90 [ADD]

Puccini, G.:Manon Lescaut (sels), w. Carlo Gaifa (ten), Guido Mazzini (bass), Giorgio Tadeo (bass), Angeles Gulin (sgr), M. Arena (cnd), *(orch unknown)*—Tra voi belle; Cortese damigella; Donna non vidi mai; Vedete, io son fedele; Tu, tu, amore; Ah! Manon, mi tradisce; Lescaut!; Ansia eterna crudel; No, pazzo son; Tutta su me ti posa; Manon...senti amor mio *(rec Treviso, Oct. 16, 1974)* Golden Age of Opera 2-▲ GAO 189/90 [ADD]

Puccini, G.:Il trittico, w. M. Freni (sop), E. Souljois (sop), R. Alagna (ten), J. Pons (bar), L. Nucci (bar), B. Bartoletti (cnd), Florence Maggio Musicale Orch, Florence Maggio Musicale Chorus London 3-▲ 436261-2 [DDD]

Verdi, G.:La forza del destino (sels), w. Raina Kabaivanska (sop), Kurt Moll (bass), Norman Mittelmann (sgr), J. Rudel (cnd), *(orch unknown)*—Ah per sempre o mio bell'angiol; La vita è inferno all'infelice; Fuggir...ferito siete; Solenne in quest'ora; Fratello...Riconoscimi; Io muoio...confession *(rec Parigi, May 27, 1975)* Golden Age of Opera 2-▲ GAO 189/90 [ADD]

Giacomo, Carlo di (sgr)

Marschner, H.A.:Der Vampyr, w. Carole Farley (sop—Malwina), Nucci Condò (mez—Suse), Oslavio Di Credico (ten—George Dibdin), Josef Protschka (ten—Edgar Aubry), Romano Truffelli (ten—Richard Scrop), Martin Egel (bar—Sir Humphrey Davenaut), Andréa Snarski (bar—Toms Blunt), Siegmund Nimsgern (b-bar—Lord Ruthven), Armando Caforio (bass—Robert Green), Peter Boom (sgr—Il capo dei Vampiri), Carlo Di Giacomo (sgr—James Gadshill), Wolfgang Lenz (sgr—Sir Berkley), Galina Pisarenko (sgr—Janthe), Renzo Scorsoni (sgr—Un servitore di Berkley), Anastasia Tomaszewska Schepis (sgr—Emmy), G. Neuhold (cnd), Rome RAI SO, Rome RAI Chorus *(rec Rome, Jan 26, 1980)* Italia 2-▲ CDC 99 [ADD]

Giacomotti, Alfredo (bass)

Bellini, V.:I Capuleti e i Montecchi, w. R. Scotto (sop), G. Aragall (ten), L. Pavarotti (ten), A. Ferrin (bass), C. Abbado (cnd), La Scala Orch, La Scala Chorus *(rec live 1967)* Butterfly Music 2-▲ BMC 12 [AAD]

Bellini, V.:I Capuleti e i Montecchi (sels), w. Luciano Pavarotti (ten), Gaetano Ferrin (bass), C. Abbado (cnd), La Scala Orch, La Scala Chorus—O di Cappelio generoso amici...È serbato a questo acciaro *(rec live, Nov. 20, 1969)* RCA Gold Seal ▲ 09026-68014-2 [ADD]

Giordano, U.:Fedora, w. Mirella Freni (sop—Principessa Fedora), Adelina Scarabelli (sop—Contessa Olga), Silvia Mazzoni (mez—Dimitri), Monica Minarelli (sgr—Savoiardo), Placido Domingo (ten—Conte Loris), Ernesto Gavazzi (ten—Desiré), Aldo Bottion (ten—Barone Rouvel), Alessandro Corbelli (bar—Siriex), Luigi Roni (bass—Cirillo), Silvestro Sammaritano (bass—Baroff), Alfredo Giacomotti (bass—Gretch), Ernesto Panariello (bass—Lorek), Vincenzo Alaimo (sgr—Nicola), Arnold Bosman (sgr—Boleslao), Bruno Capisani (sgr—Sergio), Renato Zanchetta (sgr—Michele), G. Gavazzeni (cnd), La Scala Orch, La Scala Chorus *(rec La Scala, Apr 5, 1993)* Legato 2-▲ LCD 213-2 [ADD]

Gounod, C.:Roméo et Juliette (sels), w. Renata Scotto (sop—Juliet), Giacomo Aragall (ten—Romeo), Luciano Pavarotti (ten—Tebaldo), Gaetano Ferrin (bass—Capellio), Alfredo Giacomotti (bass—Lorenzo), C. Abbado (cnd), La Scala Orch, La Scala Chorus Budget ("The Greatest Voice in Opera" series) ▲ SYP 111

Puccini, G.:La Bohème, w. Ileana Cotrubas (sop—Mimi), Margherita Guglielmi (sop—Musetta), José Carreras (ten—Rodolfo), Saverio Porzano (ten—Parpignol), Regolo Romani (ten—Vendor), Claudio Giombi (bar—Benoit), Gianni Maffeo (bar—Schaunard), Angelo Romero (bar—Marcello), Alfredo Giacomotti (bass—Alcindoro), Carlo Meliciani (bass—Customs Officer), Giuseppe Morresi (bass—Sergeant), Paolo Washington (bass—Colline), G. Prêtre (cnd), La Scala Orch, La Scala Chorus *(rec Washington D.C., Sept 8, 1976)* Legato Classics 2-▲ LCD 201-2

Giaiotti, Bonaldo (bass)

Bellini, V.:I Puritani, w. Mirella Freni (sop), Mirelle Fiorentini (mez), Luciano Pavarotti (ten), Emilio Venturini (ten), Sesto Bruscantini (bar), Giovanni Antonini (bass), R. Muti (cnd), Rome RAI SO, Rome RAI Chorus Melodram 2-▲ CDM 27062

Bellini, V.:I Puritani (sels), w. Mirella Freni (sop), Luciano Pavarotti (ten), R. Muti (cnd), Rome SO, Rome Sym Chorus—A te, o cara, amor talora *(rec live, Oct. 7, 1969)* RCA Gold Seal ▲ 09026-68014-2 [ADD]

Bellini, V.:I Puritani (sels), w. Mirella Freni (sop), Luciano Pavarotti (ten), Giovanni Antonini (bass), R. Muti (cnd), Rome RAI SO, Rome RAI Chorus—A te, o cara *(rec Rome, July 8, 1969)* Goldies ▲ GLD 63202 [ADD]

Gala Operatic Concert, w. Montserrat Caballé (sop), Franco Corelli (ten) *(rec live, 1968)* Legato Classics ▲ LCD 101-1 [AAD]

Ponchielli, A.:La Gioconda, w. M. Caballé (sop—Gioconda), M. L. Nave (mez—Laura), P. Payne (mez—La Cieca), J. Carreras (ten—Enzo), M. Manuguerra (bar—Barnaba), B. Giaiotti (bass—Alvise), J. López-Cobos (cnd), *(orch unknown)* *(rec Dec. 6, 1979)* Legato Classics ▲ LCD 170-2 [ADD]

Puccini, G.:Turandot, w. B. Nilsson (sop—Turnadot), A. Moffo (sop—Liù), F. Corelli (ten—Calaf), C. Anthony (ten—Pong), R. Nagy (ten—Pang), F. Guarrera (bar—Ping), B. Giaiotti (bass—Timur), L. Stokowski (cnd), Metropolitan Opera Orch, New York Metropolitan Opera Chorus *(rec Mar. 4, 1961)* Datum 2-▲ DAT 12301 [ADD]

Puccini, G.:Turandot, w. B. Nilsson (sop), R. Scotto (sop), F. Corelli (ten), F. Molinari-Pradelli (cnd), Rome Opera Orch, Rome Opera Chorus [I] EMI Classics ("Studio" series) 2-▲ CDMB 69327 [ADD]

Giannini, Dusolina (sop)

Dusolina Giannini Preiser ("Lebendige Vergangenheit" series) ▲ PRE 89044 (m) [AAD]

Gigli:Arias, Duets & Songs, w. Beniamino Gigli (ten), Maria Caniglia (sop), Titta Ruffo (bar), John Barbirolli (cnd), Eugene Goossens (cnd), Carlo Sabajno (cnd), et al. *(rec 1926-37)* Pearl 2-▲ PEA 9176 [ADD]

Opera Stars Sing on Radio, Vol. 1:Unpublished Broadcasts from the Fourties, w. Helen Traubel (sop), Gladys Swarthout (cta), Richard Crooks (ten), Lauritz Melchoir (ten), Robert Merrill (bar), Lawrence Tibbett (bar), Ezio Pinza (bass) Enterprise ("The Radio Years" series) ▲ ENTRY 11

Verdi, G.:Aida, w. Dusolina Giannini (sop—Aida), Irene Minghini-Cattaneo (mez—Amneris), Giuseppe Nessi (ten—Messenger), Aureliano Pertile (ten—Radames), Giovanni Inghilleri (bar—Amonasro), Luigi Manfrini (bass—Ramfis), Guglielmo Masini (bass—King), C. Sabajno (cnd), La Scala Orch, Vittore Veneziani (cnd), La Scala Chorus *(rec 1928)* Arkadia ("The 78's" series) 2-▲ 78013 [ADD]

Verdi, G.:Aida, w. I. Minghini-Cattaneo (cta), A. Pertile (ten), G. Inghilleri (bar), L. Manfrini (bass), C. Sabajno (cnd), La Scala Orch, La Scala Chorus [I] *(rec 1928 for HMV)* Pearl 2-▲ CDS 9402 (m) [AAD]

Verdi, G.:Aida, w. Irene Minghini-Cattaneo (cta), Aureliano Pertile (ten), C. Sabajno (cnd), La Scala Orch, La Scala Chorus *(rec Milan, 1928)* Phonographie 2-▲ PHG 5004 [ADD]

Giannotti, Armando (ten)

Donizetti, G.:Lucia di Lammermoor, w. Lina Pagliughi (sop—Lucia), Maria Vinciguerra (mez—Alisa), Armando Giannotti (ten—Normanno), Muzio Giovagnoli (ten—Arturo), Giovanni Malipiero (ten—Edgardo), Giuseppe Manacchini (bar—Enrico), Luciano Neroni (bass—Raimondo), U. Tansini (cnd), EIAR Orch, EIAR Chorus *(rec 1938)* Bongiovanni ("Il mito dell'opera" series) 2-▲ GB 1122-2 [ADD]

Donizetti, G.:Lucia di Lammermoor, w. Lina Pagliughi (sop—Lucia), Maria Vinciguerra (mez—Alisa), Armando Giannotti (ten—Normanno), Muzio Giovannoli (ten—Lord Arturo), Giovanni Malipiero (ten—Edgardo), Giuseppe Manacchini (bar—Lord Enrico), Luciano Neroni (bass—Raimondo), U. Tansini (cnd), EIAR Orch, EIAR Chorus *(rec Turin, 1942)* Melodram 2-▲ IMC 202004 [ADD]

Mascagni, P.:L'amico Fritz, w. P. Tassinari (sop—Suzel), A. Pini (mez—Beppe), F. Tagliavini (ten—Fritz), A. Giannotti (ten—Frederico), S. Meletti (bar—David), P. L. Latinucci (bass—Hanezò), P. Mascagni (cnd), Turin RSO, Turin Radio Chorus *(rec 1941)* Cetra Classic 2-▲ CDO 18

Gianotti, Pierre (ten)

Cherubini, L.:Les Deux journées, w. J. Micheau (sop), M. Davies (ten), E. Regnier (ten), C. Paul (bar), T. Beecham (cnd), Royal PO, BBC Theater Chorus *(rec live, London Dec. 19, 1947)* Intaglio 2-▲ INCD 7342 [ADD]

Giaotti, B. (bass)

Bellini, V.:I Puritani, w. M. Freni (sop), L. Pavarotti (ten), S. Bruscantini (bar), R. Muti (cnd), Rome RAI SO, Rome RAI Chorus [I] *(rec live, Rome 7/8/69)* Verona 3-▲ 27029/31

Giband, Félix (bass)

Gounod, C.:Philémon et Baucis, w. Anne-Marie Rodde (sop), Jean-Claude Orliac (ten), Pierre Néquecaur (bar), H. Gallois (cnd), French Radio Lyric Orch Musidisc ▲ MUS 202342 [AAD]

Gibbons, Mark (voc)

Spasm, w. Lowenstern, Michael (b cl), Heather Barringer (voc), Jay Johnson (voc), Jerome Kitzke (voc), Matt Lambiase (voc), Tom Linker (voc), Ed Lowenstern (voc), Michael Lowenstern (voc) *(rec Creation Audio, Minneapolis, NYU Studios, New York City & Studio A, Stony Brook, Aug 1994–July 1996)* New World ▲ 80468-2

Gibbs, Raymond (bar)

Verdi, G.:La traviata (sels), w. Loretta di Franco (sop), Joan Sutherland (sop), Frederica von Stade (mez), Leo Goeke (ten), Lou Marcella (ten), Luciano Pavarotti (ten), Gene Boucher (bar), Sherrill Milnes (bar), Louis Sgarro (bar), John Trehy (bar) Budget ("The Greatest Voice in Opera" series) ▲ SYP 112

Gibin, João (ten)

Donizetti, G.:Lucia di Lammermoor, w. J. McDonald (sop), J. Sutherland (sop), M. Elkins (mez), J. Bowman (alt), J. Rouleau (bass), Shaw (sgr), T. Serafin (cnd), Royal Opera House Orch, Royal Opera House Chorus Covent Garden—3 duets from Act 1, & 3 soprano solo arias from Act 2 [I] Myto ▲ 1 MCD 91545 [ADD]

Puccini, G.:La fanciulla del West, w. B. Nilsson (sop), A. Mongelli (bar), L. von Matačič (cnd), La Scala Orch, La Scala Chorus [I] EMI Classics ("Studio" series) 2-▲ CDMB 63970

Verdi, G.:La battaglia di Legnano (sels), w. L. Gencer (sop), U. Savarese (bar), F. Molinari-Pradelli (cnd), Trieste Teatro Comunale Giuseppe Verdi Orch, Trieste Teatro Comunale G. Verdi Chorus—extensive selections from Acts 1,3 & 4 [I] *(rec live 3/8/63)* Myto 2-▲ 2 MCD 89010 (m) [ADD]

Gibson, Barbara (sop)

Gluck, C.W.:Orfeo ed Euridice (sels), w. N. Merriman (mez), A. Toscanini (cnd), NBC SO, Robert Shaw Chorale—Act 2 RCA Gold Seal ▲ 60280-2-RG; ▮ 60280-4-RG

Gibson, Nancy (sop)

Berlinski, H.:Das Gebet Bonhoeffers, w. Matthias Weichert (bass), Olaf Georgi (fl), Bernhard Hentrich (vc), Herman Berlinski (org), Holger Miersch (cel), Martin Homann (perc), Hans-Christoph Rademann (cnd), Dresden Chamber Choir Vienna Modern Masters ▲ VMM 3027 [DDD]

Helmschrott, R.:Cross & Freedom, w. Helmut Schatz, Frieder Aurich (ten), Matthias Weichert (bass), Manfred Ball (nar), Anett Baumann (vn), Frank Philliptsch, Linda Robbins, Gerhard Wolf, Martin Homann (perc), Robert M. Helmschrott (org), H.-C. Rademann (cnd), Munich Trombone Quartet, Dresden Chamber Choir Vienna Modern Masters ▲ VMM 3027 [DDD]

Warren, E.R.:Singing Earth, w. E. R. Warren (pno), F. Smith (fl)—The wind sings welcome; Summer stars; Tawny days; Great memories [E] Cambria ▲ CD 1028 [DDD]

Warren, E.R.:Songs Sop, w. E. R. Warren (pno), F. Smith (fl)—22 songs [E] Cambria ▲ CD 1028 [DDD]

Gibson, Rodney (ten)

Verdi, G.:La traviata, w. Angela Gheorghiu (sop—Violetta), Leah-Marian Jones (mez—Flora Bervoix), Gillian Knight (mez—Annina), Robin Leggate (ten—Gastone), Frank Lopardo (ten—Alfredo Germont), Rodney Gibson (ten—Servo di Flora), Neil Griffiths (ten—Giuseppe), Mark Beesley (bar—Dottore Grenvile), Leo Nucci (bar—Giorgio Germont), Richard Van Allan (bass—Barone Douphol), Roderick Earle (bass—Marquese d'Obigny), Bryan Secombe (bass—Commissionario), G. Solti (cnd), Royal Opera House Orch, Royal Opera House Chorus Covent Garden *(rec live, Royal Opera House, Covent Garden, Dec. 1994)* London 2-▲ 448119-2

Giebel, Agnes (sop)

Bach, J.S.:Mass in b, BWV 232, w. J. Baker (mez), N. Gedda (ten), H. Prey (bar), F. Crass (bass), O. Klemperer (cnd), New Philharmonia Orch, BBC Sym Chorus [L] EMI Classics ("Studio" series) 2-▲ ZDMB 63364-2 [ADD]

Bach, J.S.:Masses, BWV 233-30, "Lutheran Masses", w. G. Litz (mez), H. Prey (bar), K. Redel (cnd), Pro Arte Orch, Pro Arte Chorale—BWV 233 in F Philips 2-▲ 438739-2

Handel, G.F.:Judas Maccabaeus, w. Julianna Falk (cta), Fritz Wunderlich (ten), L. Welter (bar), Pöld (sgr), R. Kubelik (cnd), Bavarian RSO, Bavarian Chorus [G] *(rec live 10/25/63)* Melodram 2-▲ MEL 28026 [AAD]

Haydn, J.:Die Jahreszeiten, w. Agnes Giebel (sop—Hanne), Fritz Wünderlich (ten—Lukas), Kieth Engen (bass—Simon), H. Müller-Kray (cnd), Stuttgart South Radio Orch, Hesse Radio Chorus *(rec Schwetzingen, May 24, 1959)* Bella Voce 2-▲ 7204 [AAD]

Haydn, J.:Mass 6, "Nikolai-messe", "6/4-Takt-Messe", w. Waldemar Kmentt (ten), Gottlob Frick (bass), E. Jochum (cnd), Bavarian RSO, Vienna Cathedral Choir, Vienna Boys' Choir Philips ("Two-Fers" series) 2-▲ 446175-2

Haydn, J.:Mass 7, "Kleine Orgelmesse", w. Waldemar Kmentt (ten), Gottlob Frick (bass), E. Jochum (cnd), Bavarian RSO, Vienna Cathedral Choir, Vienna Boys' Choir Philips ("Two-Fers" series) 2-▲ 446175-2

Haydn, J.:Die Schöpfung, w. Waldemar Kmentt (ten), Gottlob Frick (bass), E. Jochum (cnd), Bavarian RSO, Vienna Cathedral Choir, Vienna Boys' Choir Philips ("Two-Fers" series) 2-▲ 446175-2

Mendelssohn, F.:St. Paul, w. O. Dominguez (mez), Theo Altmeyer (ten), S. Nimsgern (b-bar), R. A. El Hage (bass), R. Muti (cnd), Milan RAI Orch, Milan RAI Chorus [G] *(rec live, Milan, 12/15/70)* Memories 2-▲ HR 4267/68 (m) [ADD]

Mozart, W.A.:Missa, K.427, w. E. Lear (sop), P. Munteanu (ten), F. Gutherie (bass), S. Celibidache (cnd), Rome RAI SO, Rome RAI Chorus *(rec Mar. 26, 1960)* Emozioni ▲ CDAR 2007 [ADD]

Gielgud, John (nar)

Picker, T.:The Encantadas, w. C. Eschenbach (cnd), Houston SO [E] Virgin Classics ▲ 59007 [DDD]

Prokofiev, S.:Peter & the Wolf, w. R. Stamp (cnd), Academy of London Orch Virgin Classics ▲ 59533 [DDD]

Prokofiev, S.:Peter & the Wolf, w. R. Stamp (cnd), Academy of London Orch Virgin Classics ("Ultraviolet" series) ▲ CUV 61137

Ravel, M.:Gaspard de la nuit, w. Gina Bachauer (pno)—includes readings of poems by Bertrand [Ondine, Le Gibet & Scarbo] Mercury Living Presence ▲ 434359-2

Saint-Saëns, C.:Carnival of the Animals, w. R. Stamp (cnd), Academy of London Orch Virgin Classics ("Ultraviolet" series) ▲ CUV 61137

Vaughan Williams, R.:A Song of Thanksgiving, w. L. Dawson (sop), M. Best (cnd), City of London Sinfonia, London Oratory Junior Choir [E] Hyperion ▲ CDA 66569 [DDD]

Walton, W.:As You Like It (sels), w. N. Marriner (cnd), Academy of St. Martin in the Fields—Prelude; Moonlight Chandos ("7000" series) ▲ CHAN 7041

Walton, W.:Hamlet, w. N. Marriner (cnd), Academy of St. Martin in the Fields Chandos ▲ CHAN 8842 [DDD]

Walton, W.:Hamlet (sels), w. N. Marriner (cnd), Academy of St. Martin in the Fields—Fanfare; Soliloquy; The Ghost; The Question; To Be or Not to Be; Threnody; Finale Chandos ("7000" series) ▲ CHAN 7041

Gielgud, John (nar) (cont.)

Walton, W.:Richard III (shakespeare scenario), w. N. Marriner (cnd), Academy of St. Martin in the Fields Chandos ▲ CHAN 8841 [DDD]

Walton, W.:Richard III (sels), w. N. Marriner (cnd), Academy of St. Martin in the Fields—Prelude; Now Is the Winter of Our Discontent; The Princes in the Tower; Death of Richard & Finale Chandos ("7000" series) ▲ CHAN 7041

Gierlach, Robert (bar)

Traetta, T.:Litanies, w. S. Krasteva (sop), I. Aramayo Sandivari (sgr), A. De Lucia (sgr), I. Lo Vetere (cnd), Giovanile Ambrosiano Ensemble Bongiovanni ▲ GB 2127 [DDD]

Traetta, T.:Stabat Mater, w. S. Krasteva (sop), I. Aramayo Sandivari (sgr), A. De Lucia (sgr), I. Lo Vetere (cnd), Giovanile Ambrosiano Ensemble, Piacenza Polifonico Farnesiano Chorus Bongiovanni ▲ GB 2127 [DDD]

Gigli, Beniamino (ten)

The Acoustic Records, Part 2:1918-23 Enterprise ("Vocal Archives" series) ▲ ENT VA 1127

American & European Recordings *(rec. 1925-35)* Pearl ▲ PEA 9033 [AAD]

Arias & Duets w. Iva Pacetti (sop), Giulio Tomei (bar) EMI Classics ▲ CDH 61052

Beniamino Gigli Phonographe ("Great Voices" series) 2-▲ PHG 5058

Beniamino Gigli RCA Gold Seal ▲ 7811-2-RG (m) [ADD] ▮ 7811-4-RG

Beniamino Gigli Memoir Classics ("Great Voices of the Century" series) ▲ CDMOIR 417 [AAD]

Beniamino Gigli *(rec Vienna, 1955)* Bongiovanni 2-▲ GB 1055/56-2 [ADD]

Beniamino Gigli in Opera & Song *(rec London; Liederkranz Hall, New York; Milan; Berlin)* Happy Days ▲ CDHD 227 [AAD]

The Best of Gigli Pearl ▲ PEA 7083

Bizet, G.:Carmen (sels), w. R. Gigli (sop), E. Stignani (mez), *(orch unknown)* Melodram ▲ CD 15005 (m)

Bizet, G.:Les Pêcheurs de perles (sels), w. Giuseppe De Luca (bar)—Del tempio al limitar *(rec 1927)* Minerva ▲ MN-A23 [ADD]

Callas, Gigli, w. Maria Callas (sop), Milan RAI SO [cnd:Alfredo Simonetto] *(rec Casino Municipale Opera Theatre, Sanremo, Dec. 27, 1954)* Incontri Memorabili ▲ CDMR 5002

Canti Sacri EMI Classics ▲ CDM 69235

The Complete Operatic Acoustical Recordings, w. Carlo Sabajno (cnd), Joseph Pasternack (cnd), Rosario Bourdon (cnd), et al. *(rec Milan & New York/Camden)* Pearl 2-▲ PEA 9423 (m) [AAD]

The Complete Victor Recordings, Vol. 1 (1921-25) Romophone 2-▲ 82003-2

The Complete Victor Recordings, Vol. 2 Romophone 2-▲ 82004-2

The Complete Victor Recordings, Volume 3:(1929-32) Romophone ▲ 82005-2

Donizetti, G.:Lucia di Lammermoor (sels), w. Ezio Pinza (bar), *(orch unknown)* Forlane ▲ FRL 16718 [ADD]

The Essential Gigli Mastersound ▲ MST 115 [ADD]

Una Furtiva Lacrima *(rec. live 1927-46)* Foyer ▲ FOY 2081 [AAD]

Gigli in Song Nimbus ▲ NI 7874 [ADD]

Gigli in Song Pearl ▲ PEA 9915 (m) [AAD]

Gigli, Vol. 1 *(rec 1918-24)* Nimbus ("Prima Voce" series) ▲ NI 7807 (m) [ADD]

Gigli, Vol. 2 *(rec 1925-40)* Nimbus ("Prima Voce" series) ▲ NI 7817 [ADD]

Gigli:Arias, Duets & Songs, w. Maria Caniglia (sop), Dusolina Giannini (sop), Titta Ruffo (bar), John Barbirolli (cnd), Eugene Goossens (cnd), Carlo Sabajno (cnd), et al. *(rec 1926-37)* Pearl 2-▲ PEA 9176 [ADD]

Giordano, U.:Andrea Chénier, w. M. Caniglia (sop), G. Simionato (mez), G. Bechi (bar), G. Taddei (bar), I. Tajo (bass), O. de Fabritiis (cnd), La Scala Orch, La Scala Chorus [I] *(rec 1941, HMV DB 5423/35)* Angel ("Studio" series) 2-▲ CDHB 69996 (m) [ADD]

Giordano, U.:Andrea Chénier, w. Maria Caniglia (sop—Maddalena), Maria Huder (mez—Bersi), Vittoria Palombini (mez—Madelon), Giulietta Simionato (mez—Contessa), Beniamino Gigli (ten—Andrea), Adelio Zagonara (ten—Incroyable/Abbé), Gino Bechi (bar—Carlo), Leone Paci (bar—Mathieu), Giuseppe Taddei (b-bar—Pietro/Fouquier), Italo Tajo (b-bar—Roucher), Gino Conti (bass—Master/Schmidt), O. de Fabritiis (cnd), La Scala Orch, La Scala Chorus *(rec Nov 1941)* Arkadia ("The 78's" series) 2-▲ 78012 [ADD]

His Greatest Hits during the Italian 30's Enterprise ("The Radio Years" series) ▲ ENT RY 59

Iva Pacetti, w. Iva Pacetti (sop), Mario Basiola (bar), Benvenuto Franci (bar) *(rec 1928-40)* Preiser ("Lebendige Vergangenheit" series) ▲ PRE 89124

Legendary Three Tenors, w. Enrico Caruso (ten), John McCormack (ten), Ruggiero Leoncavallo (pno), Edwin Schneider (pno), Metropolitan Opera Orch, Metropolitan Opera Chorus [cnd:Giulio Setti], Philharmonia Orch, Philharmonia Chorus [cnd:Stanford Robinson] *(rec 1904-1950)* RCA Gold Seal ▲ 09026-68534-2 [ADD] ▮ 09026-68534-4

Leoncavallo, R.:Pagliacci, w. I. Pacetti (sop—Nedda), B. Gigli (ten—Canio), G. Nessi (ten—Peppe), M. Basiola (bar—Tonio), F. Ghione (cnd), La Scala Orch, La Scala Chorus [I] *(rec 1934)* EMI Classics ("Studio" series) ▲ CDH 63309 (m) [ADD]

Leoncavallo, R.:Pagliacci, w. I. Pacetti (sop—Nedda), B. Gigli (ten—Canio), G. Nessi (ten—Peppe), M. Basiola (bar—Tonio), F. Ghione (cnd), La Scala Orch, La Scala Chorus [I] *(rec July 1934)* Nimbus 2-▲ NI 7843/44 [ADD]

Leoncavallo, R.:Pagliacci, w. I. Pacetti (sop—Nedda), B. Gigli (ten—Canio), G. Nessi (ten—Peppe), M. Basiola (bar—Tonio), F. Ghione (cnd), La Scala Orch, La Scala Chorus [I] *(rec 1934 for HMV)* Music Memoria ▲ 30275

Leoncavallo, R.:Pagliacci (sels), w. Enrico Caruso (ten), Antonio Paoli (ten), Giovanni Zenatello (ten), Amedeo Bassi (ten), Hermann Jadlowker (ten), Fernand Ansseau (ten), Hipolito Lazaro (ten), Nino (Filippo) Piccaluga (ten), Mario Chamlee (ten), Giacomo Lauri-Volpi (ten), Miguel Fleta (ten), Giovanni Martinelli (ten), Aureliano Pertile (ten), Georges Thill (ten), Alessandro Valente (ten), Francesco Merli (ten), Lauritz Melchior (ten), Marcel Wittrisch (ten), Joseph Schmidt (ten), Beniamino Gigli (ten), Giuseppe Lugo (ten), Helge Roswaenge (ten), Jussi Bjoerling (ten)—23 versions of the tenor aria "Vesti la giubba" *(rec 1907-1944)* Bongiovanni ▲ GB 1071 [ADD]

Live Recordings *(rec 1935-55)* Legato Classics ▲ LCD 106-1 (m) [AAD]

The Magnificent Gigli IMP Classics ▲ GLRS 102 [ADD]

Mascagni, P.:Arias [I] EMI Classics ("Studio" series) 2-▲ CDHB 69987 (m) [ADD]

Mascagni, P.:Cavalleria rusticana, w. L.B. Rasa (sop), M. Marucucci (mez), G. Simionato (mez), G. Bechi (bar), P. Mascagni (cnd), La Scala Orch, La Scala Chorus *(rec 1940)* Nimbus 2-▲ NI 7843/44 [ADD]

Mascagni, P.:Cavalliera rusticana, w. Lina Bruna-Rasa (sop), Giulietta Simionato (mez), Giuseppe Nessi (ten), Gino Bechi (bar), Carlo Galeffi (bar), P. Mascagni (cnd), La Scala Orch, La Scala Chorus *(rec Milan, 1940)* Phonographe 2-▲ PHG CD 5066

Mascagni, P.:Cavalleria rusticana, w. L. Bruna Rasa (sop), G. Simionato (mez), G. Bechi (bar), P. Mascagni (cnd), La Scala Orch, La Scala Chorus [I] *(rec 1940)* EMI Classics ("Studio" series) 2-▲ CDHB 69987 (m) [ADD]

'O Sole Mio *(rec. 1918-49)* EMI Classics 2-▲ ZDHB 63390

Opera Arias EMI Classics ("Great Recordings of the Century" series) ▲ CDH 61051 (m) [ADD]

Ponchielli, A.:La Gioconda (sels), w. Giuseppe De Luca (bar)—Enzo Grimaldo *(rec 1927)* Minerva ▲ MN-A23 [ADD]

Puccini, G.:La Bohème, w. L. Albanese (sop), T. Menotti (sop), A. Poli (bar), U. Berrettoni (cnd), La Scala Orch, La Scala Chorus [I] *(rec 1937)* EMI Classics ("Studio" series) 2-▲ CDHB 63335 (m) [ADD]

Puccini, G.:La Bohème, w. Licia Albanese (sop), Tatiana Menotti (sop), Afro Poli (bar), U. Berrettoni (cnd), La Scala Orch, La Scala Chorus *(rec Milan, 1938)* Phonographe 2-▲ PHG CD 5071

Puccini, G.:La Bohème, w. Licia Albanese (sop—Mimì), Tatiana Menotti (sop—Musetta), Beniamino Gigli (ten—Rodolfo), Nello Palai (ten—Parpignol), Aristide Baracchi (bar—Schaunard), Afro Poli (bar—Marcello), Duilio Baronti (bass—Colline), Carlo Scattola (bass—Benoit/Alcindoro), U. Berrettoni (cnd), La Scala Orch, Vittore Veneziani (cnd), La Scala Chorus *(rec Feb-Mar 1938)* Arkadia ("The 78's" series) 2-▲ 78009 [ADD]

Puccini, G.:La Bohème, w. L. Albanese (sop—Mimì), T. Menotti (sop—Musetta), B. Gigli (ten—Rodolfo), N. Palai (ten—Parpignol), A. Poli (bar—Marcello), A. Baracchi (bar—Schaunard), D. Baronti (bass—Colline), C. Scattola (bass—Benoit/Alcindoro), U. Berrettoni (cnd), La Scala Orch, La Scala Chorus [I] *(rec Milan, May 1938)* Nimbus 2-▲ NI 7862/63 [ADD]

Puccini, G.:La Bohème (sels), w. Maria Caniglia (sop), *(orch unknown)* Forlane ▲ FRL 16718 [ADD]

Gigli, Beniamino (ten) (cont.)
Puccini, G.:La Bohème (sels), w. Giuseppe De Luca (bar)—Ah Mimì, tu più non torni *(rec 1927)* Minerva ▲ MN–A23 [ADD]
Puccini, G.:Madama Butterfly, w. Toti dal Monte (sop—Madama Butterfly), Maria Huder (mez—Kate Pinkerton), Beniamino Gigli (ten—B.F. Pinkerton), Adelio Zagonara (ten—Goro), Mario Basiola (bar—Sharpless), Gino Conti (bass—Principe Yamadori), Ernesto Dominici (bass—Il Bonzo), Vittoria Paolombini (sgr—Suzuki), O. de Fabritiis (cnd), Rome Opera Orch, Giuseppe Conca (cnd), Rome Opera Chorus *(rec Aug 1939)* Arkadia 2–▲ CD 78004 (m) [ADD]
Puccini, G.:Manon Lescaut (sels), w. B. Guerrini (mez), M. Borriello (bar), *(orch unknown)* *(rec Milan, 1950)* Melodram ▲ CD 15005 (m)
Puccini, G.:Tosca, w. Maria Caniglia (sop), Armando Borgioli (bar), O. de Fabritiis (cnd), Rome Teatro Reale Opera Orch, Reale Theater Chorus *(rec 1938)* Grammofono 2000 2–▲ GRM 78591 (m)
Rosanna Carteri, Antonietta Stella & Beniamino Gigli, w. Rosanna Carteri (sop), Antonietta Stella (sop), Rome RAI SO, Rome RAI Chorus [cnd:Nino Antonellini], Milan RAI SO [cnd:Nino Sanzogno] *(rec Milan & Sanremo, Feb. 9, 1953 & Dec. 21, 1)*
Incontri memorabili ("Martini & Rossi Concert" series) ▲ CDMR 5005 [ADD]
Three Legendary Tenors:In Opera & Song, w. Jussi Björling (ten), Enrico Caruso (ten), Giuseppe de Luca (bar) Nimbus ▲ NI 1434 [ADD]
Verdi, G.:Aida, w. Maria Caniglia (sop—Aida), Ebe Stignani (mez—Amneris), Beniamino Gigli (ten—Radamés), Armando Borgioli (bar—Amonasro), T. Beecham (cnd), London SO, London Sym Chorus *(rec Royal Opera House, Covent Garden, May 24, 1939)*
Enterprise ("The Radio Years" series) 2–▲ ENT RY 62
Verdi, G.:Aida (sels), *(orch unknown)* Forlane ▲ FRL 16718 [ADD]
Verdi, G.:Aida (sels), w. Maria Nemeth (sop—Aida), Rosette Anday (cta—Amneris), Benjamino Gigli (ten—Radames), Alexander Kipnis (bass—Ramfis), K. Alwin (cnd), Vienna State Opera Orch *(rec May 23, 1937)* Koch Schwann 2–▲ SCH 314632 [ADD]
Verdi, G.:Un ballo in maschera, w. Maria Caniglia (sop—Amelia), Fedora Barbieri (mez—Ulrica), Beniamino Gigli (ten—Riccardo), Gino Bechi (bar—Renato), Tancredi Pasero (bass—Samuel), Blando Giusti (sgr—Un Giudice), Nicola Niccolini (sgr—Silvano), Ugo Novelli (sgr—Tom), Elda Ribetti (sgr—Oscar), T. Serafin (cnd), Rome Opera Orch, Giuseppe Conca (cnd), Rome Opera Chorus *(rec 1943)* Arkadia 2–▲ CD 78005 (m) [ADD]
Verdi, G.:Un ballo in maschera, w. Maria Caniglia (sop), Fedora Barbieri (cta), Gino Bechi (bar), T. Serafin (cnd), Rome Opera Orch, Rome Opera Chorus *(rec Rome, July, 1943)*
Grammofono 2000 2–▲ GRM 78556
Verdi, G.:Un ballo in maschera (sels), w. Maria Caniglia (sop), Gina Cigna (sop), Fedora Barbieri (mez), Enrico Carusa (ten), Giovanni Zenatello (ten), Carlo Galeffi (bar), Lawrence Tibbett (bar), *(various orchs & cnds)* *(rec 1911–43)* Grammofono 2000 ▲ GRM 78527 (m)
Verdi, G.:La forza del destino (sels), w. Barbato (sop), E. Mascherini (bar), G. Neri (bass), A. Votto (cnd), Rio de Janeiro Teatro Municipale Orch, Rio de Janeiro Teatro Municipale Chorus [I] *(rec live 8/16/51)* Standing Room Only ▲ SRO 807–1 (m) [ADD]
Verdi, G.:La forza del destino (sels), w. Giuseppe De Luca (bar)—Solenne in quest'ora *(rec 1927)*
Minerva ▲ MN–A23 [ADD]
Verdi, G.:Requiem Mass, w. Maria Caniglia (sop), Ebe Stignani (cta), Ezio Pinza (bass), T. Serafin (cnd), La Scala Orch, La Scala Chorus *(rec 1939)* Phonographie ▲ PHG 5012 [ADD]
Verdi, G.:Requiem Mass, w. Maria Caniglia (sop), Ebe Stignani (cta), Ezio Pinza (bass), T. Serafin (cnd), Rome Opera Orch, Rome Opera Chorus *(rec 1939)* Pearl ▲ PEA 9162 [ADD]
Verdi, G.:Requiem Mass (sels), w. M. Caniglia (sop), E. Stignani (mez), T. Pasero (bass), V. de Sabata (cnd), Rome CO, Rome RAI Chorus, Turin RAI Chorus—Dies irae; Sanctus; Libera me *(rec Dec. 14, 1940)* Legato Classics 2–▲ LCD 178–2
Verdi, G.:La traviata, w. Maria Caniglia (sop), Mario Basiola (bar), V. Gui (cnd), London PO, London Phil Chorus *(rec Royal Opera House, Covent Garden, May 22, 1939)*
Enterprise ("The Fourties" series) 2–▲ ENT 313
Verdi, G.:La traviata, w. Maria Caniglia (sop—Violetta), Maria Huder (mez—Flora), Gladys Palmer (cta—Annina), Octave Dua (ten—Giuseppe), Beniamino Gigli (ten—Alfredo), Booth Hitchen (ten—D'Obigny), Adelio Zagonara (bar—Gastone), Aristide Baracchi (bar—Douphol), Mario Basiola (bar—Germont), Norman Walker (bass—Dr. Grenville), V. Gui (cnd), London PO, London Phil Chorus *(rec Royal Opera House, Covent Garden, May 22, 1939)* Minerva 2–▲ MN A28/29 (m) [ADD]
Verdi, G.:La traviata, w. Maria Caniglia (sop—Violetta), Baniamino Gigli (ten—Alfredo), Mario Basiola (bar—Germont), V. Gui (cnd), London SO, London Sym Chorus
Enterprise ("The Radio Years" series) 2–▲ ENT RY 64
Verdi, G.:Il trovatore (sels), w. J. Biel (ten), F. Tamagno (ten), L.-A. Escalaïs (ten), M. Gilion (ten), E. Caruso (ten), A. Paoli (ten), G. Zenatello (ten), J. Sembach (ten), L. Slezak (ten), F. Constantino (ten), G. Martinelli (ten), B. De Muro (ten), N. Fusati (ten), N. Piccaluga (ten), G. Lauri-Volpi (ten), A. Pertile (ten), E. Bergamaschi (ten), R. Tauber (ten), J. O'Sullivan (ten), H. Roswaenge (ten), G. Taccani (ten), V. Lois (ten), H. Lazaro (ten), A. Lindi (ten), A. Cortis (ten), F. Merli (ten), F. Völker (ten), J. Kiepura (ten), J. Schmidt (ten), J. Bjoerling (ten), A. Salvarezza (ten), J. Soler (ten), M. Filippeschi (ten)—34 performances of the Act III tenor aria "Di quella pira!," *(rec from 1903–1956)*
Bongiovanni ▲ GB 1051 [AAD]
The Victor Recordings, Vol. 2 *(rec 1927–30)* Pearl ▲ PEA 9367 (m) [AAD]

Gigli, Rina (sop)
Bizet, G.:Carmen (sels), w. E. Stignani (mez), B. Gigli (ten), *(orch unknown)* Melodram ▲ CD 15005 (m)

Gijsegem, Ludwig van (ten)
Messiaen, O.:La Transfiguration de Notre Seigneur Jésus-Christ, w. Yvonne Loriod (pno), R. de Leeuw (cnd), Hilversum RSO, BRT Choir Montaigne 2–▲ MO 782040

Gilbert (voc)
Wernick, R.:Kaddish-Requiem, w. J. DeGaetani (mez), A. Weisberg (cnd), Contemporary Chamber Ensemble Elektra/Nonesuch ▲ 79222-2-J

Gilet, Jacques (sgr)
Lehár, F.:Die lustige Witwe, w. Teresa Stich-Randall (mez—Missia Palmieri), Monique Stiot (mez—Manon), Germaine Duclos (sgr—Praskovia), Linda Felder (sgr—Olga), Christiane Jacquin (sgr—Nadia), Jeannette Levasseur (sgr—Sylviane), Henri Legay (ten—Camille de Coutançon), Joseph Peyron (ten—Kromsky), Robert Destain (sgr—Baron Popoff), Michel Fauche (sgr—Pristich), Gérard Friedmann (sgr—Lerida), Jacques Gilet (sgr—Bogdanowitch), Jean Guy Henneveux (sgr—Prince Danilo), Serge Klin (sgr—Figg), Jacques Villa (sgr—D'Estillac), A. Sibert (cnd), Belgian Radio-TV Orch, Belgian Radio-TV Chorus *(rec Grand Auditorium, Belgium, Apr 30, 1970)* Studio SM 2–▲ 2160 [AAD]

Gilford, Jack (ten)
Gershwin, G.:Let 'Em Eat Cake, w. L. Kert McGovern (sgr), M. Thomas (cnd), Orch of St. Luke, New York Choral Artists [E] CBS 2–▲ M2K 42522 [DDD]
Gershwin, G.:Of Thee I Sing, w. L. Kert McGovern (sgr), M. Thomas (cnd), Orch of St. Luke, New York Choral Artists [E] CBS 2–▲ M2K 42522 [DDD]
Porter, C.:Anything Goes, w. F. von Stade (mez), J. McGlinn (sgr), K. Criswell (sop), C. Groenendaal (sgr), London SO, Ambrosian Chorus [original 1934 Broadway version w. original orchestration by Robert Russell Bennett & Hans Spialek] Angel ▲ CDC 49848-2 [DDD]

Gilfry, Rodney (bar)
Brahms, J.:Ein Deutsches Requiem, w. C. Margiono (sop), J. E. Gardiner (cnd), Orch Révolutionnaire et Romantique, Monteverdi Choir London [period instrs] Philips ▲ 432140-2 [DDD] □ 432140-5
Haydn, J.:Die Schöpfung, w. Donna Brown (sop), Sylvia McNair (sop), Michael Schade (ten), Gerald Finley (bar), J. E. Gardiner (cnd), English Baroque Soloists, Monteverdi Choir London
Archiv ▲ 449 217-2
Mozart, W.A.:Così fan tutte, w. A. Roocroft (sop), E. James (mez), C. Feller (bass), J. E. Gardiner (cnd), English Baroque Soloists Archiv 3–▲ 437829-2 [DDD]
Mozart, W.A.:Don Giovanni, w. Charlotte Margiono (sop—Donna Elvira), Luba Orgonasova (sop—Donna Anna), Eirian James (mez—Zerlina), Julian Clarkson (alt—Masetto), Christoph Prégardien (ten—Don Ottavio), Rodney Gilfry (bar—Don Giovanni), Ildebrando d'Arcangelo (bass—Leporello), Andrea Silvestrelli (bass—Il Commendatore), J. E. Gardiner (cnd), English Baroque Soloists, Monteverdi Choir London Deutsche Grammophon ("4D Audio" series) 3–▲ 445870-2
Mozart, W.A.:Nozze di Figaro, w. A. Hagley (sop), H. Martinpelto (sop), B. Terfel (b-bar), J. E. Gardiner (cnd), English Baroque Soloists, Monteverdi Choir London [G] Archiv 3–▲ 439871-2 [DDD]

Gilgen, Ulrich (bass)
Keiser, R.:Passions Oratorium, w. J. Bise (sop), M. Conrad (cta), G. Jelden (ten), J.E. Dähler (cnd), Bernese Orch, Bernese Chorus [G] *(rec Feb. 1971)* Claves 2–▲ CD 9223/24 [ADD]

Gilhuus, Ivar (ten)
Jensen, L.I.:The Return, w. A. Bolstad (sop), R. Sterne (alt), H. Bjørkey (ten), P. Vollestad (bar), C. Stabell (bass), O.K. Ruud (cnd), Trondheim SO, Trondheim Sym Chorus, Nidarso Cathedral Choir
Simax 2–▲ PSC 3109

Gilion, Mario (ten)
Il mito dell'opera Bongiovanni ▲ GB 1076 [ADD]
Verdi, G.:Il trovatore (sels), w. J. Biel (ten), F. Tamagno (ten), L.-A. Escalaïs (ten), E. Caruso (ten), A. Paoli (ten), G. Zenatello (ten), J. Sembach (ten), L. Slezak (ten), F. Constantino (ten), G. Martinelli (ten), B. De Muro (ten), N. Fusati (ten), N. Piccaluga (ten), G. Lauri-Volpi (ten), A. Pertile (ten), E. Bergamaschi (ten), R. Tauber (ten), J. O'Sullivan (ten), H. Roswaenge (ten), G. Taccani (ten), V. Lois (ten), H. Lazaro (ten), A. Lindi (ten), A. Cortis (ten), F. Merli (ten), F. Völker (ten), J. Kiepura (ten), J. Schmidt (ten), J. Bjoerling (ten), B. Gigli (ten), A. Salvarezza (ten), J. Soler (ten), M. Filippeschi (ten)—34 performances of the Act III tenor aria "Di quella pira!," *(rec from 1903–1956)*
Bongiovanni ▲ GB 1051 [AAD]

Gilje, Tor (ten)
Braein, E.F.:Anne Pedersdotter, w. K. Ekeberg (sop—Anne Pedersdotter), V. Hanssen (mez—Merete Beyer), R. Eriksen (alt—Herlofs-Marte), I. M. Brekke (alt—Bente), K. M. Sandve (ten—Martin Beyer), C. Ehrstedt (ten—Master Olaus), A. Helleland (ten—David), T. Gilje (ten—Jørund), S. A. Thorsen (bar—Master Johannes), S. Carlsen (bass—Absalon Pedersøn Beyer), T. Stensvold (bass—Master Laurentius), G. Oskarsson (bass—Jens Schelderup), P. Andersson (cnd), Norwegian National Opera Orch, Norwegian National Opera Chorus Simax 2–▲ PSC 3121

Gillert, Christopher (ten)
Elgar, E.:The Kingdom, w. Y. Kenny (sop), A. Hodgson (alt), B. Luxon (bass), L. Slatkin (cnd), London PO, London Phil Chorus RCA Red Seal 2–▲ 07863-57862-2

Gilles, Jean Villard (nar)
Stravinsky, I.:L'Histoire du soldat, w. F. Simon (the Soldier), W. Jacques (the Devil), E. Ansermet (cnd), Swiss Romande Orch members [F] *(rec 4/17/52)* Claves ▲ CD 8918 (m) [ADD]

Gilles, Marie Louise (cta)
Rossini, G.:Petite messe solennelle, w. G. de la Cruz (sop), H. D. Saretzki (ten), H. G. Grimm (bass), W. A. Albert (cnd), Northwest German PO, Northwest German Phil Choir [orchestral version] [L] *(rec ca. 1970)* Koch Schwann ▲ 3-1345-2 [ADD]

Gilles, Raoul (ten)
Ravel, M.:L'Heure espagnole, w. Jeanne Krieger (sop—Concepcion), Louis Arnoult (ten—Gonzalve), Raoul Gilles (ten—Torquemada), J. Aubert (bar—Ramiro), Hector Dufranne (bass—Don Inigo Gomez), G. Truc (cnd), *(orch unknown)* *(rec premiere recording, supervised by Ravel, 1929)*
VAI Audio ▲ VAIA 1073

Gillett, Christopher (ten)
Loevendie, T.:Gassir, the Hero, w. Claron McFadden (sop—Partridge/Priestess), Timothy Wilson (alt—Shamsi), Christopher Gillett (ten—Safi), Robert Poulton (bar—Gassir), Lieuwe Visser (bass—Yemni), Roger Smeets (sgr—Rafi), D. Porcelijn (cnd), Asko Ensemble *(rec live, Amsterdam Studios, June 14–15, 1993)* Donemus ▲ CV 35

Gillette, P. (sgr)
Porter, C.:Out of This World, w. C. Greenwood (sgr), W. Eythe (sgr)
Sony Broadway ▲ SK 48223 ▮ ST 48223

Gillis, Matthew (sgr)
Myers, G.:God's Trbn, w. Christine Helfrich (sop), Gordon Myers (bar), Richard Cragg (sgr), Timothy Pehta (sgr), Paul Norman (sgr), Wendy Catlin (sgr) Katherine Mary Hamilton (sgr), Sharon Hunter (sgr), Gloriae Dei Brass Ensemble Paraclete ▲ CDGD 017 [DDD]; ▮ GDC 017

Gilvan, R. (ten)
McLeod, J.:Lieder der Jugend, w. J. McLeod (cnd), Polish Radio-TV SO
Vienna Modern Masters ▲ VMM 3026 [DDD]

Gimenez, Edoardo (ten)
Donizetti, G.:Don Pasquale, w. Geraint Evans (bar), Mario D'Anna (sgr), Carol Webber (sgr), H. Holt (cnd), *(orch unknown)* *(rec Seattle, 1981)*
Ornamenti ("Gala Evenings, Teatro Colon" series) 2–▲ 121
Gounod, C.:Faust, w. Renata Scotto (sop—Margherita), Anna di Stasio (mez—Marta), Flaviano Labò (ten—Faust), Edoardo Gimenez (ten—Siebel), Piero Cappuccilli (bar—Valentino), Bruno Grella (bar—Wagner), Ruggero Raimondi (bass—Mefistofele), M. Gusella (cnd), Margherita Theater Orch, Margherita Theater Chorus *(rec Genova, 1970)* Golden Age of Opera 2–▲ GAO 170/71 [ADD]
Rossini, G.:Armida, w. C. Deutekom (sop), P. Bottazzo (ten), O. Garaventa (ten), C. Franci (cnd), Venice Teatro La Fenice Orch, Venice Teatro La Fenice Chorus [I] *(rec live, 4/3/70)*
Memories 2–▲ HR 4152/53 (m) [ADD]
Rossini, G.:Armida, w. C. Deutekom (sop), P. Bottazzo (ten), O. Garaventa (ten), B. Trotta (sgr), A. Maddalena (bass), G. Antonini (bass), C. Franci (cnd), Venice Teatro La Fenice Orch, Venice Teatro La Fenice Chorus *(rec live, Venice, 1970)* Foyer 2–▲ FOY 2030 [AAD]

Giménez, Raúl (ten)
Argentinian Songs, w. Giménez, Raúl (ten), Nina Walker (pno) Nimbus ▲ NI 5107 [DDD]
Bellini, V.:Arias, w. M. Veltri (cnd), Scottish CO—arias from I Puritani, La Sonnambula
Nimbus ▲ NI 5224 [DDD]
Donizetti, G.:Arias, w. M. Veltri (cnd), Scottish CO—arias from Don Pasquale, Elisir d'amore, La Favorita, Fille du régiment, Lucia di Lammermoor Nimbus ▲ NI 5224 [DDD]
Mozart, W.A.:Arias, w. B. Wordsworth (cnd), Royal Opera House Orch—9 arias from Clemenza di Tito, Così fan tutte, Don Giovanni, La finta giardiniera, Il re pastore, Die Zauberflöte; Misero! o sogno, o son desto? (concert aria), K.431 Nimbus ▲ NI 5300 [DDD]
Mysliveček, J.:Belerofonte, w. C. Lindsleyová (sop), G. Mayová (sop), K. Lakiová (sop), D. Ahlstedt (ten), S. Margita (ten), Z. Peskó (cnd), Prague CO, Czech Phil Chorus [I] *(rec 1987)*
Supraphon 3–▲ 11 0006-2 [DDD]
Rossini, G.:Arias, w. M. Veltri (cnd), Scottish CO, Scottish Chamber Chorus Nimbus ▲ NI 5106 [DDD]
Rossini, G.:Il barbiere di Siviglia, w. J. Larmore (cta), A. Corbelli (bar), H. Hagegard (bar), S. Ramey (bass), J. López-Cobos (cnd), Lausanne CO, Geneva Grand Théâtre Chorus [I]
Teldec 2–▲ 9031-74885-2
Rossini, G.:Il barbiere di Siviglia (sels), w. B. Frittoli (sop), J. Larmore (mez), Håkan Hagegård (bar), A. Corbelli (bar), S. Ramey (bass), J. López-Cobos (cnd), Lausanne CO, Geneva Grand Théâtre Chorus
Teldec ▲ 93693-2
Rossini, G.:Les Soirées musicales, w. J. Anderson (sop), K. Bouleyn (sop), A. Corbelli (bar), N. Walker (pno) [I] Nimbus ▲ NI 5132 [DDD]
Rossini, G.:Stabat Mater, w. Luba Orgonasova (sop), Cecilia Bartoli (mez), Roberto Scandiuzzi (bass), M.-W. Chung (cnd), Vienna PO, Vienna State Opera Chorus Deutsche Grammophon ▲ 449 178-2

Ginn, Michael (trb)
Handel, G.F.:L'Allegro, Il Penseroso ed il Moderato, w. Patrizia Kwella (sop), Marie McLaughlin (sop), J. E. Gardiner (cnd), English Baroque Soloists, Monteverdi Choir London
Erato 2–▲ 2292-45377-2 ZA

Gioia, Luisa (sgr)
Verdi, G.:La forza del destino, w. Zinka Milanov (sop—Donna Leonora di Vargas), Rosalind Elias (mez—Preziosilla), Luisa Gioia (sgr—Curra), Angelo Mercuriali (ten—Trabuco), Giuseppe di Stefano (ten—Son Alvaro), Leonard Warren (bar—Don Carlos di Vargas), Giorgio Tozzi (b-bar—Padre guardiano), Dino Mantovani (bar—Fra Melitone), Paolo Washington (b-bar—Il marchese di Calatrava), Virgilio Carbonari (b-bar—un alcalde), Sergio Liviabella (sgr—un chirurgo), F. Previtali (cnd), St. Cecilia Academy Orch Rome, St. Cecilia Academy Chorus Rome [I] London ▲ 443678-2 [ADD]

 ▲ = CD ♦ = Enhanced CD Δ = MD ▮ = Cassette Tape □ = DCC

Giombi, Claudio (bar)
Puccini, G.:La Bohème, w. Ileana Cotrubas (sop—Mimi), Margherita Guglielmi (sop—Musetta), José Carreras (ten—Rodolfo), Saverio Porzano (ten—Parpignol), Regolo Romani (ten—Vendor), Claudio Giombi (bar—Benoit), Gianni Maffeo (bar—Schaunard), Angelo Romero (bar—Marcello), Alfredo Giacomotti (bass—Alcindoro), Carlo Meliciani (bass—Customs Officer), Giuseppe Morresi (bass—Sergeant), Paolo Washington (bass—Colline), G. Prêtre (cnd), La Scala Orch, La Scala Chorus *(rec Washington D.C., Sept 8, 1976)* Legato Classics 2-▲ LCD 201-2
Puccini, G.:La Bohème, w. Katia Ricciarelli (sop), Francisco Araiza (ten), Angelo Casertano (ten), Stefano Antonucci (bar), Paata Burchuladze (bass), Alfredo Mariotti (bass), Alberto Noli (bass), Andrea Piccinni (bass), Lauren Broglia (sgr), A. Guadagno (cnd), Arena di Verona Orch, Limburg Cathedral Boys' Chorus Koch Schwann 2-▲ SCH 315922

Giorgetti, Giorgio (bar)
Rossini, G.:Il barbiere di Siviglia (sels), w. G. d' Angelo (sop), G. Carturan (mez), N. Monti (ten), R. Capecchi (bar), C. Cava (bass), G. Tadeo (bass), B. Bartoletti (cnd), Bavarian RSO IMP Collectors Series ▲ IMPX 9022 [AAD]
Verdi, G.:Simon Boccanegra, w. A. Stella (sop—Maria), C. Bergonzi (ten—Gabriele), G. Giorgetti (bar—Pietro), W. Monachesi (bar—Paolo), M. Petri (bar—Jacopo), P. Silveri (bar—Simon), F. Molinari-Pradelli (cnd), Rome Radio Orch, Rome RAI Chorus *(rec 1951)* Cetra Classic ▲ CDO 23 [ADD]

Giorgi, Ezio de (sgr)
Wagner, R.:Die Meistersinger von Nürnberg, w. Bruna Rizzoli (sop), Fernanda Cadoni (mez), Luigi Infantino (ten), Vito Tatone (ten), Renato Capecchi (bar), Giuseppe Taddei (bar), Boris Christoff (bass), Giovanni Ciavola (bass), James Loomis (bass), Silvo Maionica (bass), Vito Susca (bass), Raimondo Botteghelli (sgr), Walter Brunelli (sgr), Carlo Franzini (sgr), Renzo Gonzales (sgr), L. von Matačić (cnd), Turin RAI Radio-TV SO, Turin RAI Chorus Stradivarius 4-▲ STV 12310

Giorgini, Aristodemo (ten)
Puccini, G.:La Bohème, w. Rosina Torri (sop—Mimi), Thea Vitulli (sop—Musetta), Aristodemo Giorgini (ten—Rodolfo), Giuseppe Nessi (ten—Parpignol), Ernesto Badini (bar—Marcello), Aristide Baracchi (bar—Schaunard), Luigi Manfrini (bass—Colline), Salvatore Baccaloni (bass—Benoit/Alcindoro), C. Sabajno (cnd), La Scala Orch, La Scala Chorus *(rec 1928)* VAI Audio 2-▲ VAIA 1078-2
Puccini, G.:La Bohème, w. R. Torri (sop), T. Vitulli (sop), E. Badini (bar), L. Manfrini (bass), C. Sabajno (cnd), La Scala Orch [I] *(rec 1927)* InSync 2-■ C 4131/2 (m)

Giovagnoli, Muzio (ten)
Donizetti, G.:Lucia di Lammermoor, w. Lina Pagliughi (sop—Lucia), Maria Vinciguerra (mez—Alisa), Armando Giannotti (ten—Normanno), Muzio Giovagnoli (ten—Arturo), Giovanni Malipiero (ten—Edgardo), Giuseppe Manacchini (bar—Enrico), Luciano Neroni (bass—Raimondo), U. Tansini (cnd), EIAR Orch, EIAR Chorus *(rec 1938)* Bongiovanni ("Il mito dell'opera" series) 2-▲ GB 1122-2 [ADD]

Giovannetti, Julien (bar)
Chabrier, E.:Songs, w. Renée Doria (sop), Guy Fouché (sgr), André Rabot (bn), Tasso Janopoulo (pno)—Lied; Tes yeux bleus; Sommation irrespectueuse; Toutes les fleurs; Ruy blas [A quoi bon entendre...]; Credo d'amour; Romance de l'étoile; Villanelle des petits; Les cigales; Ballade des gros dindons; Pastorale des cochons roses; L'île heureuse; Chanson pour jeanne; Duo de l'ouvreuse de l'opéra-comique et de l'employé du bon-marché; L'invitation au voyage Accord ▲ ACD 201392 [AAD]
Massenet, J.:Werther, w. Mady Mesplé (sop—Sophie), Rita Gorr (mez—Charlotte), Robert Andreozzi (ten—Schmidt), Albert Lance (ten—Werther), Gabriel Bacquier (bar—Albert), Julien Giovannetti (bar—Le Bailli), Jacques Mars (bar—Johann), J. Etcheverry (cnd), *(orch unknown)* Adès 2-▲ ADE 140832 [AAD]
Planquette, R.:Rip van Winkle, w. Claudine Collart (sop), Lina Dachary (sop), Freda Betti (cta), René Lenoty (ten), Joseph Peyron (ten), Charles Daguerressar (bar), Jacques Pruvost (bar), Lucien Lovano (bass), Patrick Orladey (sgr), Joëlle Pierre (sgr), M. Cariven (cnd), ORTF Lyric Orch, ORTF Lyric Chorale Musidisc ▲ MUS 201602 [AAD]

Giovannoli, Muzio (ten)
Donizetti, G.:Lucia di Lammermoor, w. Lina Pagliughi (sop—Lucia), Maria Vinciguerra (mez—Alisa), Armando Giannotti (ten—Normanno), Muzio Giovannoli (ten—Lord Arturo), Giovanni Malipiero (ten—Edgardo), Giuseppe Manacchini (bar—Lord Enrico), Luciano Neroni (bass—Raimondo), U. Tansini (cnd), EIAR Orch, EIAR Chorus *(rec Turin, 1942)* Melodram 2-▲ IMC 202004 [ADD]

Girardi, Piero (ten)
Verdi, G.:Otello, w. Maria Carbone (sgr), Nicola Fusati (ten), Corrado Zambelli (ten), Apollo Granforte (bar), Enrico Spada (sgr), C. Sabajno (cnd), La Scala Orch, La Scala Chorus Grammofono 2000 2-▲ GRM 78651

Girardi, Sulie (mez)
Dembski, S.:Of Mere Being, w. S. Kawalla (cnd), Polish Radio-TV SO Vienna Modern Masters ▲ VMM 3002 [DDD]
Scott, D.:Arras:A Garden of Cinema, w. S. Kawalla (cnd), Koszalin State PO, Silesian Univ Choir Vienna Modern Masters ▲ VMM 3022 [DDD]
Van De Vate, N.:Letter to a Friend's Lonliness, w. Bohuslav Martinů Philharmonic String Quartet Vienna Modern Masters ▲ VMM 2006 [DDD]
Van De Vate, N.:Voices for Women, w. S. Kawalla (cnd), Koszalin State PO, Silesian Univ Choir Vienna Modern Masters ▲ VMM 3022 [DDD]

Giraud, Fiorello (ten)
The World of Singing, Vol. 3:The Italian School, Part 1:The Italian Tenors Before World War I (1902-13), w. Antonio Aramburo (ten), Alessandro Bonci (ten), Giuseppe Borgatti (ten), Enrico Caruso (ten), Edoardo Garbin (ten), Fernando de Lucia (ten), Francesco Marconi (ten), Giovanni Battista de Negri (ten), Antonio Paoli (ten), Francesco T Enterprise ("Vocal Archives" series) 3-▲ ENT VA 2104
The World of Singing, Vol 4:The Italian School Part 1:Tenors before World War I, Book 2, w. Edoardo Garbin (ten), Florencio Costantino (ten), Antonio Paoli (ten), Giuseppe Borgatti (ten), Carlo Albani (ten), Enrico Caruso (ten), Amedeo Bassi (ten), Piero Schivazzi (ten), Elvino Ventura (ten), Giovanni Zenatello (ten) Enterprise ("Vocal Archives" series) 3-▲ ENT VA 2107

Giraudeau, Jean (ten)
Boieldieu, F.-A.:Le Calife de Bagdad, w. Christiane Eda-Pierre (sop), Jane Berbié (mez), Jeannine Collard (mez), Jean-Paul Vaquelin (sgr), L. Fourestier (cnd), ORTF Lyric Orch, ORTF Lyric Chorale Musidisc ▲ MUS 201852 [AAD]
Escher, R.:Univers de Rimbaud, w. F. Leitner (cnd), Residentie Orch The Hague [F] *(rec 1978-82)* Olympia ▲ OCD 506 [AAD]
Milhaud, D.:Les Malheurs d'Orphée (sels), w. Jacqueline Brumaire (sop), D. Milhaud (cnd), Paris Opera Orch Adès ▲ ADE 203452 [AAD]
Milhaud, D.:Pauvre matelot (sels), w. Jacqueline Brumaire (sop), D. Milhaud (cnd), Paris Opera Orch Adès ▲ ADE 203452 [AAD]
Ravel, M.:L'Heure espagnole, w. S. Danco (mez—Concepcion), J. Giraudeau (ten—Gonzalve), M. Hamel (ten—Torquemada), J. Cameron (bar—Ramiro), A. Vessières (bass—Gomez), B. Maderna (cnd), BBC SO *(rec Nov. 1960)* Stradivarius ▲ STR 10062 [ADD]

Girolami, R. (bass)
Pergolesi, G.B.:San Guglielmo Duca d'Aquitania, w. K. Gamberucci (sop), Caldini (sgr), B. Lucarini (sop), G. Gatti (bar), Herron (sgr), F. Maestri (cnd), Terni CO [I] *(rec live, 12/18/86)* Bongiovanni 2-▲ GB 2060/61 [DDD]
Scarlatti, D.:Cants, w. A. Rossi (sop), F. Maestri (cnd), *(ensemble unknown)*—"Amenissimi prati," for Bass & Instrumental Ensemble; "Se fedele tu m'adori," for Soprano & Ensemble [I] *(rec live, 1988)* Bongiovanni ▲ GB 2026 [DDD]

Giron (sgr)
Verdi, G.:La traviata, w. M. Callas (sop), C. Valletti (ten), G. Taddei (bar), O. de Fabritiis (cnd), Palacio Bellas Artes Orch, Palacio Bellas Artes Chorus [I] *(rec live, Mexico City, 7/17/51)* Melodram 2-▲ CDM 26019 [AAD]

Giroux, Monique (nar)
Normandeau, R.:Petit Prince, w. Michel Dumont (nar—Aviator), Martin Pensa (nar—Little Prince), Christine Séguin (nar—Rose), Jean Marchand (nar—King), Luc Durand (nar—Conceited Man), Gilles Dupuis (nar—Drunkard), Guy Nadon (nar—Businessman), Jacques Languirand (nar—Lamplighter), Pierre Bourgault (nar—Geographer), Cynthia Dubois (nar—Snake), Monique Giroux (nar—Flower), Françoise Davoine (nar—Rose Garden), Jean-Louis Millette (nar—Fox), Gérard Poirier (nar—Railway Switchman), Claude Préfontaine (nar—Water Pill Salesman) *(rec Montreal, Aug 1994)* CBC 2-▲ 1091 [DDD]

Gismondo, Giuseppe (ten)
Alfano, F.:Risurrezione, w. M. Olivero (Katiusha), A. Di Stasio (Matrena), A. Boyer (Simonson), E. Boncompagni (cnd), Turin RAI Orch [I] *(rec live, Oct 22, 1971)* Standing Room Only 2-▲ SRO 839-2 [ADD]
Mascagni, P.:Cavalleria rusticana, w. Zinka Milanov (sop—Santuzza), Jean Craft (mez—Lucia), Marietta Cosenza (mez—Lola), Giuseppe Gismondo (ten—Turiddu), Benjamin Rayson (bar—Alfio), R. Cellini (cnd), New Orleans Opera Orch, New Orleans Opera Chorus *(rec live, 1963)* VAI Audio ▲ VAIA 1053
Mascagni, P.:Iris (sels), w. M. Olivero (sop—Iris), G. Gismondo (ten—Osaka), M. Basiola II (bar—Kyoto), O. de Fabritiis (cnd), *(orch unknown)*—scenes from Acts II & III *(rec live, June 3, 1966)* VAI Audio 2-▲ VAIA 1062 (m) [ADD]

Giua, Roberta (sgr)
Stradella, A.:Cants, w. Cristina Miatello (sop), Gianpaolo Fagotto (ten), Antonio Abete (sgr), Roberto Balconi (sgr), Lavinia Bertotti (sgr), S. Balestracci (cnd), Santo Spirito Academy Orch, Santo Spirito Academy Chorus—for 5 w. vns [For Holy Christmas]; for 5 w. instruments [For the Souls in Purgatory] Stradivarius ▲ STV 33392 [DDD]

Giudice, Franco Lo (ten)
Verdi, G.:Requiem Mass, w. Maria Luisa Fanelli (sop), Irene Minghini-Cattaneo (mez), E. Pinza (bass), C. Sabajno (cnd), La Scala Orch, La Scala Chorus *(rec 1927 for HMV)* Pearl ▲ GEMMCD 9374 (m) [AAD]

Giusti, Blando (sgr)
Verdi, G.:Un ballo in maschera, w. Maria Caniglia (sop—Amelia), Fedora Barbieri (mez—Ulrica), Beniamino Gigli (ten—Riccardo), Gino Bechi (bar—Renato), Tancredi Pasero (bass—Samuel), Blando Giusti (sgr—Un Giudice), Nicola Niccolini (sgr—Silvano), Ugo Novelli (sgr—Tom), Elda Ribetti (sgr—Oscar), T. Serafin (cnd), Rome Opera Orch, Giuseppe Conca (cnd), Rome Opera Chorus *(rec 1943)* Arkadia 2-▲ CD 78005 (m) [ADD]

Gizzi, Elana (sop)
Stuart, P.:Kill Bear Comes Home, w. Elana Gizzi (sop—Hasty Girl), Mi-Kyung Huh (sop—Cold Feet), Therese Murray (sop—Song Bird), Cherie Pfeil (sop—1st Sister), Renia Shukis (sop—2nd Sister), Riki Connaughton (mez—4th Sister), Lucy Fee (mez—3rd Sister), David Averbach (ten—Song Leader), Mark Schmidt (ten—Kill Bear), Jason Smith (bar—Cheif Wife Hunter), P. Stuart (cnd), Rochester Opera Theater Orch, Rochester Opera Theater Chorus VM ▲ DRK 154 [DDD]

Gjerris, Helene (sop)
Borup-Jørgensen, A.:Songs, w. Erik Skjoldan (pno)—O Barn; Verirrt; Sehnsucht; Über die Heide; Ende des Herbstes; Schluszstück Point ▲ PCD 5117

Gjevang, Anne (mez)
Gade, N.W.:Elverskud, w. E. Johansson (sop), P. Elming (ten), D. Kitayenko (cnd), Danish National RSO, Danish National Radio Chamber Choir [Da] Chandos ▲ CHAN 9075 [DDD]
Handel, G.F.:Messiah, w. Kiri Te Kanawa (sop), Richard Lewis (ten), Gwynne Howell (bass), G. Solti (cnd), Chicago SO, Chicago Sym Chorus [E] London 2-▲ 414396-2 [DDD]
Handel, G.F.:Messiah (sels), w. Kiri Te Kanawa (sop), Richard Lewis (ten), Gwynne Howell (bass), G. Solti (cnd), Chicago SO, Chicago Sym Chorus—arias & choruses London ▲ 430098-2 [DDD] ■ 430098-4
Mahler, G.:Des Knaben Wunderhorn, w. Einar Steen-Nøkleberg (pno)—Um schlimme Kinder artig zu machen; Ablösung im Sommer; Zu Strassburg auf der Schanz'; Starke Einbildungskraft; Scheiden und Meiden; Verlorne Müh'; Irdische Leben; Rheinlegendchen; Lob des hohen Verstands *(rec Jar Church, Sept 1995)* Victoria ▲ VCD 19069
Mahler, G.:Sym 3, w. L. Segerstam (cnd), Danish National RSO, Danish National Radio Choir [G] Chandos 2-▲ CHAN 8970/71 [DDD]
Mahler, G.:Sym 8, w. Majken Bjerno (sop), Henriette Bonde-Hansen (sop), Inga Nielsen (sop), Kirsten Dolberg (alt), Raimo Sirkiä (ten), Jorma Hynninen (bar), Carsten Stabell (bass), L. Segerstam (cnd), Danish National RSO, Copenhagen Boys' Choir, Berlin Phil Choir, Danish National Radio Choir Chandos 2-▲ CHAN 9305/06 [DDD]
Nielsen, C.:Saul & David, w. T. Kiberg (sop), P. Lindroos (ten), K. Westi (ten), C. Christiansen (bass), A. Haugland (bass), J. Klint (bass), N. Järvi (cnd), Danish National RSO, Danish National Radio Choir [Da] Chandos 2-▲ CHAN 8911/12 [DDD]
Pfitzner, H.:Songs, w. Einar Steen-Nøkleberg (pno)—Hast du von den Fischerkinden das alte Märchen vernommen?; Velassene Mägdlein; Denk es, o Seele; Ist der Himmel im Lenz so blau? *(rec Jar Church, Sept 1995)* Victoria ▲ VCD 19069
Werfel, A.M.:Songs, w. Einar Steen-Nøkleberg (pno)—Stille Stadt; In meines Vaters Garten; Laue Sommernacht; Bei dir ist es Traut; Ich wandle unter Baumen *(rec Jar Curch, Sept 1995)* Victoria ▲ VCD 19069
Zemlinsky, A. von:Songs, w. Einar Steen-Nøkleberg (pno)—3 Schwestern; Mädchen mit den verbundenen Augen; Lied der Jungfrau; Als ihr Geliebter schied; Und kehrt er einst Heim; Sie kam zum Schloss gegangen *(rec Jar Curch, Sept 1995)* Victoria ▲ VCD 19069

Glanville, Susannah (sop)
Danova, R.:The Phantom of the Opera on Ice, w. Kathy Dooley (sop), Johnny Logan (ten), Stephen Lee Garden (ten), Mungo Jerry (bar), Nigel Paul (bar), P. Whitfield (cnd), Northern Light SO, Northern Light Choir, Russian Stars on Ice Chorus Plaza ▲ PZA 008

Glasgow, Matthew (nar)
Whiticker, M.:Man, Skin Cancer of the Earth, w. Clive Birch (nar), Jane Edwards (nar), Roger Frampton (sax), David Hewitt (perc), R. Peelman (cnd) *(rec Studio 200, ABC Ultimo Centre, Apr 1993)* Tall Poppies ▲ TP 064 [DDD]

Glasgow, Matthew (sgr)
Mozart, W.A.:Songs, w. J. Edwards (cta), P. Sharpe (sgr), D. Russell (sgr), D. Hamilton (ten), C. Birch (sgr), P. Hooper (sgr), G. Lancaster (pno) *(rec July 1991)* Tall Poppies ▲ TP009 [DDD]

Glashof, Wolfgang (bar)
Bizet, G.:Les Pêcheurs de perles (sels), w. B. Lazzaretti (ten), H.-M. Schneidt (cnd), Berlin RSO—Act 1 duet, "Au fond du temple saint" Capriccio ▲ 10 380 [DDD]

Gleason, Helen (sop)
Joseph Schmidt, w. Schmidt, Joseph (ten), Berlin RSO [cnd:Rudolf Hindemith, Bruno Seidler-Winkler, Hermann Scherchen, Fritz Stiedry, Max von Schillings], unknown orchestra [cnd:Idris Lewis], General Motors SO, General Motors Sym Chorus [cnd:Erno Rapee, José Iturbi, Oscar Straus], Helen Gleas Koch Schwann ▲ SCH 312572 [ADD]

Gleave, Ruth (mez)
Walton, W.:The Twelve, w. P. Forbes (sop), S. Gay (alt), J. Oxley (ten), P. Harvey (bar), R. Hickox (cnd), City of London Sinfonia [E] Chandos ▲ CHAN 8824 [DDD]

Glen, Judy (nar)
Bremner, A.:In the Shrubbery, w. David Miller (pno), Gerard Willems (pno), Philip South (perc), Roland Peelman (cnd), Song Company *(rec Studio 200, ABC Ultimo Centre, Apr 1993)* Tall Poppies ▲ TP 064 [DDD]

Glennon, Jean (sop)
Beethoven, L. van:Syms (comp), w. Dalia Schaechter (cta), Algridas Janutas (ten), Benno Schollum (bass), Y. Menuhin (cnd), Sinfonia Varsovia, Kuanas State Choir Lithuania IMP ("IMG" series) 5-▲ IMP 6800025

Glossop, Peter (bar)
Berlioz, H.:Les Troyens, w. B. Lindholm (sop), J. Veasey (mez), J. Vickers (ten), R. Soyer (bass), C. Davis (cnd), Royal Opera House Orch [F] Philips 4-▲ 416432-2 [ADD]
Britten, H.:Billy Budd, w. P. Pears (ten), J. Shirley-Quirk (bar), B. Luxon (bar), M. Langdon (bass), O. Brannigan (bass), B. Britten (cnd), London SO, Ambrosian Singers [E] London 3-▲ 417428-2 [ADD]

Glossop, Peter (bar) (cont.)

Catalani, A.:La Wally, w. R. Tebaldi (sop), C. Bergonzi (ten), F. Corena (bass), F. Cleva (cnd), American Opera Society Orch, American Opera Society Chorus *(rec Mar. 13, 1968)* Intaglio 2-▲ ING 764 [ADD]

Verdi, G.:Ernani, w. Montserrat Caballè (sop), Bruno Prevedi (ten), Boris Christoff (bass), G. Gavazzeni (cnd), Milan RAI SO, Milan RAI Chorus *(rec Milan, Mar. 25, 1969)* Pantheon 2-▲ PHE 6634 (m)

Verdi, G.:La forza del destino, w. Martina Arroyo (sop—Donna Leonora), Janet Coster (mez—Preziosilla), Kenneth Bowen (ten—Trabuco), Kenneth Collins (ten—Don Alvaro), Peter Glossop (bar—Don Carlo), Roderick Kennedy (bass—Marquis), J. Matheson (cnd), BBC Concert Orch, BBC Concert Chorus *(rec live, early 1980's)* Exclusive 2-▲ EXL 80 [ADD]

Verdi, G.:Otello, w. M. Freni (sop), J. Vickers (ten), H. von Karajan (cnd), Vienna PO *(rec 1971)* Memories 2-▲ MEM 4533 [ADD]

Verdi, G.:La traviata, w. R. Scotto (sop), L. Pavarotti (ten), C. F. Cillario (cnd), Royal Opera House Orch, Royal Opera House Chorus Covent Garden *(rec live 1965)* Memories 2-▲ HR 4404/05 (m)

Glossup, Peter (bar)

Purcell, H.:Dido & Aeneas, w. Victoria de los Angeles (sop—Dido), Heather Harper (sop—Belinda), Patricia Johnson (mez—Sorceress), Peter Glossup (bar—Aeneas), J. Barbirolli (cnd), English CO, Ambrosian Singers EMI Classics 2-▲ ZDM 65664

Glouboky, Piotr (bass)

Karetnikov, N.:Till Eulenspiegel, w. E. Mazo (sop), L. Mkrtchian (cta), A. Proujanski (ten), B. Koudriavtsev (bar), A. Motchalov (bass), A. Martinov (sgr), Polianski (cnd), Soviet Cinema Orch, Soviet Cinema Chorus *(rec Moscow, 1988)* Russian Season ("Russian Season" Series) 2-▲ LDC 288029/30 [DDD]

Rachmaninoff, S.:The Miserly Knight, w. Mikhail Krutikov (sgr), Vladimir Kudriashov (sgr), Alexander Arkhipov (sgr), Vladislav Verestnikov (sgr), A. Tchistiakov (cnd), Bolshoi Theater Orch, Russian State Choir Russian Season 3-▲ CMX 388053

Rimsky-Korsakov, N.:A May Night, w. Maria Lapina (sop), Natalia Erassova (mez), Elena Okolycheva (cta), Alexander Arkhipov (ten), Vitaly Tarastchenko (ten), Viatcheslav Potchapski (bass), A. Tchistiakov (cnd), Bolshoi Theater Orch, Russian State Choir Russian Season 4-▲ CMX 388054

Shostakovich, D.:4 Verses by Captain Lebyadkin, w. Natalia Rassoudova (pno) Russian Season ▲ RUS 288089

Shostakovich, D.:Songs, Op. 46, w. Natalia Rassoudova (pno) Russian Season ▲ RUS 288089

Shostakovich, D.:Songs, Op. 62, w. Natalia Rassoudova (pno) Russian Season ▲ RUS 288089

Shostakovich, D.:Songs, Op. 121, w. Natalia Rassoudova (pno) Russian Season ▲ RUS 288089

Glover, Cynthia (sop)

Elgar, E.:The Starlight Express (suite), w. J. Lawrenson (bar), G. Hurst (cnd), Bournemouth Sinfonietta Chandos ("Collect" series) ▲ CHAN 6582 [ADD]

Gmyrja, Boris (bass)

Lebendige Vergangenheit, w. Gmyrja, Boris (bass) Preiser ▲ PRE CD 89119

Gobbi, Hilda (sgr)

Kacsóh, P.:János Vitéz, w. Mária Gyurkovics (sop), Anna Zentai (sop—Iluska), Tivadar Bilicsi (sgr), Sándor Pethes (sgr—Bartolo), Róbert Ilosfalvy (ten—Kukorica), György Melis (bar—Bagó), György Radnai (bar—Strázsamester), László Domahidy (bass—Csősz), E. Lukács (cnd), Hungarian State Opera Orch, Hungarian Radio-TV Chorus *(rec Budapest, 1961)* Classical Diamonds 2-▲ CLD 4011-12 [AAD]

Gobbi, Tito (bar)

Cilea, F.:L'Arlesiana (sels)—Come Due Tizzi Accesi Legato Classics 2-▲ LCD 206-2 [ADD]

Donizetti, G.:Lucia di Lammermoor, w. M. Callas (sop), G. di Stefano (ten), R. Arie (bass), T. Serafin (cnd), Florence Maggio Musicale Orch [I] EMI Classics (Studio) 2-▲ CDMB 69980 (m) [ADD]

Giordano, U.:Fedora, w. M. Olivero (sop), M. del Monaco (ten), L. Gardelli (cnd), Monte Carlo Opera Orch London ("Grand Opera" series) 2-▲ 433033-2 [ADD]

Leoncavallo, R.:Pagliacci, w. M. Micheluzzi (sop), F. Corelli (ten), M. Carlin (ten), L. Puglisi (bar), A. Simonetto (cnd), Milan RAI Orch, Milan RAI Chorus *(rec live 9/26/54 from RAI Milan)* HRE ▲ 1001-1 [ADD]

Leoncavallo, R.:Pagliacci, w. M. Callas (sop), G. di Stefano (ten), R. Panerai (bar), T. Serafin (cnd), La Scala Orch [I] EMI Classics 3-▲ CDCC 47981 [ADD]

Leoncavallo, R.:Pagliacci, w. Lucine Amara (sop), France Corelli (ten), L. von Matačić (cnd), La Scala Orch, La Scala Chorus [I] EMI Classics ("Studio" series) 2-▲ CDMB 63967

Leoncavallo, R.:Zazà (sels)—Zaza, Piccola Zingara Legato Classics 2-▲ LCD 206-2 [ADD]

Mascagni, P.:Cavalleria rusticana, w. E. Suliotis (sop), S. Malagu (mez), A. Di Stasio (mez), M. Del Monaco (ten), S. Varviso (cnd), Rome Opera Orch, Rome Opera Chorus [I] IMP Collectors Series ▲ IMPX 9018 [AAD]

Mozart, W.A.:Don Giovanni, w. L. Welitsch (sop), I. Seefried (sop), E. Schwarzkopf (sop), A. Dermota (ten), E. Kunz (bar), A. Poell (b-bar), J. Greindl (bass), W. Furtwängler (cnd), Vienna PO, Vienna State Opera Chorus *(rec 1950)* Laudis 3-▲ LDS 4001 [AAD]

Mozart, W.A.:Don Giovanni (sels)—De Viene alla Finestra Legato Classics 2-▲ LCD 206-2 [ADD]

Mozart, W.A.:Nozze di Figaro (sels), w. A. Simonetto (cnd), Milan Italian Radio-TV Orch—Aprite un Po' Quegli Occhi Fonit Cetra ("Martini & Rossi" series) ▲ FCT CDMR 5008

Mozart, W.A.:Nozze di Figaro (sels)—Aprite un Po' Quegli Occhi Legato Classics 2-▲ LCD 206-2 [ADD]

Mozart, W.A.:Songs, w. M. Callas (sop), E. Grümmer (sop), E. Schwarzkopf (sop), R. Scotto (sop), T. Lemnitz (sop), E. Berger (sop), S. Jurinac (sop), E. Schumann (sop), I. Souez (sop), E. Rethberg (sop), L. Lehmann (sop), N. Gedda (ten), J. McCormack (ten), H. Roswenge (ten), H. Nash (ten), T. Gobbi (bar), G. Hüsch (bar), E. Kunz (bar), G. Frick (bass), E. Pinza (bass), A. Kipnis (bass) EMI Classics 4-▲ CDMD 63750

Public Performances, w. Gobbi, Tito (bar) *(rec 1950-64)* Memories ("Great Voices" series) 2-▲ MEM 4376 (m) [ADD]

Puccini, G.:La Bohème, w. R. Tebaldi (sop), E. Ribetti (mez), E. Avolanti (ten), G. Lauri Volpi (ten), S. Meletti (bar), C. Badioli (bass), G. Neri (bass), G. Santini (cnd), *(orch unknown)* *(rec 1951)* Great Opera Performances ▲ GOP 743

Puccini, G.:La Bohème (sels), w. R. Scotto (sop), G. Poggi (ten), Maneguzzer (sgr), A. Votto (cnd), Florence Maggio Musicale IMP Collectors Series ▲ IMPX 9024 [AAD]

Puccini, G.:La fanciulla del West (sels)—Minnie dalla Mia Casa Son Partito Legato Classics 2-▲ LCD 206-2 [ADD]

Puccini, G.:Tosca, w. M. Callas (sop), R. Cioni (ten), C. F. Cillario (cnd), Royal Opera House Orch, Royal Opera House Chorus Covent Garden [I] *(rec live 1/21/64)* Melodram 2-▲ MEL 26011

Puccini, G.:Tosca, w. M. Callas (sop), R. Cioni (ten), C. F. Cillario (cnd), Royal Opera House Orch, Royal Opera House Chorus Covent Garden [I] *(rec live, 1/21/64)* Verona 2-▲ 27027/28 (m) [AAD]

Puccini, G.:Tosca, w. Maria Callas (sop—Floria Tosca), Robert Bowman (ten—Spoletta), Renato Cioni (ten—Mario Cavaradossi), Eric Garrett (bar—Il Sagrestano), Tito Gobbi (bar—Scarpia), Victor Godfrey (bass—Casare Angelotti), Dennis Wicks (bass—Sciarrone), C. F. Cillario (cnd), Royal Opera House Orch, Royal Opera House Chorus Covent Garden *(rec London, 1964)* Melodram 2-▲ CDI 203003 [ADD]

Puccini, G.:Tosca, w. R. Tebaldi (sop), F. Tagliavini (ten), F. Molinari-Pradelli (cnd), Royal Opera House Orch, Royal Opera House Chorus Covent Garden [I] *(rec live at Covent Garden, 6/30/55)* Legato Classics 2-▲ LCD 157-2 (m) [ADD]

Puccini, G.:Tosca, w. M. Callas (sop), C. Bergonzi (ten), G. Prêtre (cnd), Paris Conservatory Société des Concerts Orch, Paris Opera Chorus [I] EMI Classics ("Studio" series) 2-▲ CDMB 69974 [ADD]

Puccini, G.:Tosca, w. M. Callas (sop), R. Cioni (ten), N. Rescigno (cnd), Paris Opera Orch, Paris Opera Chorus *(rec live, Paris March 3, 1965)* Melodram 2-▲ CDM 26033 [ADD]

Puccini, G.:Tosca, w. M. Callas (sop), G. di Stefano (ten), V. de Sabata (cnd), La Scala Orch, La Scala Chorus [I] *(rec 1953)* EMI Classics 2-▲ CDCB 47174 (m) 2-■ 4AV 34047 (m)

Puccini, G.:Tosca (sels), w. M. Callas (sop), R. Scotto (sop), C. Bergonzi (ten), A. Kraus (ten), G. Prêtre (cnd), Orch de Paris EMI Classics ▲ ZDM 63087

Puccini, G.:Il trittico, w. R. Scotto (sop), I. Cotrubas (sop), M. Horne (mez), P. Domingo (ten), I. Wixell (bar), L. Maazel (cnd), London SO, Philharmonia Orch [I] CBS 3-▲ M3K 35912 [ADD]

Puccini, G.:Il trittico, w. V. de los Angeles (sop), F. Barbieri (mez), G. Prandelli (ten), *(other soloists unknown)*, Rome Opera Orch, Rome Opera Chorus *(rec Rome, 1950s)* EMI Classics 3-▲ CDMC 64165 (m)

Gobbi, Tito (bar) (cont.)

Puccini, G.:Turandot, w. B. Nilsson (sop), L. Price (sop), G. di Stefano (ten), F. Molinari-Pradelli (cnd), Vienna State Opera Orch, Vienna State Opera Chorus [I] *(rec live, 6/22/61)* Legato Classics 2-▲ LCD 153-2 (m) [ADD]

Puccini, G.:Le Villi, w. R. Scotto (sop), P. Domingo (ten), L. Nucci (bar), L. Maazel (cnd), London National PO, Ambrosian Chorus [I] CBS ▲ MK 36669 [ADD]

Rosanna Carteri, Tito Gobbi, w. Carteri, Rosanna (sop), Milan RAI SO [cnd:Alfredo Simonetto] *(rec Dec. 24, 1956)* Incontri Memorabili ("Martini & Rossi Concerts" series) ▲ 5008

Rossini, G.:Arias, w. June Anderson (sop), Montserrat Caballé (sop), Maria Callas (sop), Edita Gruberova (sop), Pilar Lorengar (sop), Mady Mesplé (sop), Nicolai Gedda (ten), Samuel Ramey (bass), *(orchs unknown)*—from Barbiere di Siviglia; La Cenerentola; La Gazza ladra; Petite messe solennelle; Semiramide; Stabat Mater *(rec 1958-89)* EMI Classics 2-▲ CZS 67440-2 [ADD/DDD]

Rossini, G.:Il barbiere di Siviglia, w. M. Callas (sop), L. Alva (ten), N. Zaccaria (bass), F. Ollendorf (bass), A. Galliera (cnd), Philharmonia Orch EMI Classics ▲ ZDM 63076

Rossini, G.:Il barbiere di Siviglia, w. M. Callas (sop), L. Alva (ten), A. Galliera (cnd), Philharmonia Orch [I] *(rec 1957)* EMI Classics 2-▲ CDCB 47634 [ADD]

Rossini, G.:Il barbiere di Siviglia, w. M. Callas (sop), L. Alva (ten), C. M. Giulini (cnd), La Scala Orch, La Scala Chorus [I] *(rec live 1956)* Melodram 2-▲ MEL 26020

Rossini, G.:Il barbiere di Siviglia (sels)—Largo al Factotum Legato Classics 2-▲ LCD 206-2 [ADD]

Rossini, G.:Guillaume Tell (sels), w. A. Simonetto (cnd), Milan Italian Radio-TV Orch—Resta Immobile Fonit Cetra ("Martini & Rossi" series) ▲ FCT CDMR 5008

Verdi, G.:Aida, w. M. Callas (sop), F. Barbieri (mez), G. Tucker (ten), N. Zaccaria (bass), T. Serafin (cnd), La Scala Orch, La Scala Chorus [I] EMI Classics 3-▲ CDCC 49030 [ADD]

Verdi, G.:Un ballo in maschera, w. M. Callas (sop), E. Ratti (sop), F. Barbieri (mez), G. Di Stefano (ten), A. Votto (cnd), La Scala Orch, La Scala Chorus [I] *(rec 1956)* EMI Classics 2-▲ CDCB 47498 (m)

Verdi, G.:Don Carlos, w. G. Brouwenstein (sop—Elisabeta di Valois), F. Barbieri (mez—Princess Eboli), J. Vickers (ten—Don Carlo), T. Gobbi (bar—Rodrigo), B. Christoff (bass—Fillipo), C. M. Giulini (cnd), Royal Opera House Orch, Royal Opera House Chorus Covent Garden *(rec 1958)* Myto 3-▲ MCD 94197

Verdi, G.:Don Carlos (sels), *(cnd & orch unknown)*—Convien qui dirci addio...Per me giunto; O Carlo, ascolta la madre t'aspetta Legato Classics 2-▲ LCD 206-2 [ADD]

Verdi, G.:Don Carlos (sels), w. A. Simonetto (cnd), Milan Italian Radio-TV Orch—O Carlo Ascolta Fonit Cetra ("Martini & Rossi" series) ▲ FCT CDMR 5008

Verdi, G.:Falstaff, w. Anna Moffo (sop—Nannetta), Renata Tebaldi (sop—Alice Ford), Anna Maria Canali (mez—Meg Page), Giulietta Simionato (mez—Dame Quickly), Mariano Caruso (ten—Doctor Caius), Alvinio Misciano (ten—Fenton), Luigi Vellucci (ten—Bardolfo), Tito Gobi (bar—Falstaff), Carnell MacNeil (bar—Ford), Kenneth Smith (bass-Pistola), T. Serafin (cnd), *(orch unknown)* *(rec Chicago, 1958)* Legato Classics 2-▲ LCD 206-2 [ADD]

Verdi, G.:Macbeth, w. Amy Shuard (sop—Lady Macbeth), Noreen Berry (mez—Lady-in-waiting), John Dobson (ten—Malcolm), André Turp (ten—Macduff), Tito Gobbi (bar—Macbeth), Edgar Boniface (bass—Servant), Rydderch Davies (bass—Doctor), Forbes Robinson (bass—Banco), Jean Holmes (sgr—Apparition), Celia Penny (sgr—Apparition), Glynne Thomas (sgr—Apparition), Brian Wrigt (sgr—Araldo), F. Molinari-Pradelli (cnd), Royal Opera House Orch, Royal Opera House Chorus Covent Garden *(rec London, Apr 8, 1960)* Bella Voce 2-▲ 7203 [AAD]

Verdi, G.:Nabucco, w. E. Suliotis (sop), B. Prevedi (ten), C. Cava (bass), L. Gardelli (cnd), Vienna State Opera Orch, Vienna State Opera Chorus [I] London 2-▲ 417407-2 [ADD]

Verdi, G.:Otello, w. Raina Kabaivanska (sop), Josephine Veasey (mez), John Lanigan (ten), Mario del Monaco (ten), G. Solti (cnd), Royal Opera House Orch, Royal Opera House Covent Garden Chorus *(rec June 30, 1962)* Memories ▲ MEM 4583 [AAD]

Verdi, G.:Otello, w. Raina Kabaivanska (sop), Mario del Monaco (ten), G. Solti (cnd), Royal Opera House Orch, Royal Opera House Chorus Covent Garden Pantheon 2-▲ PHE 6608

Verdi, G.:Otello (sels), *(cnd & orch unknown)*—Era la Notte; Credo in un Dio Crudel Legato Classics 2-▲ LCD 206-2 [ADD]

Verdi, G.:Otello (sels), w. Mario del Monaco (ten), Tito Gobbi (bar—Iago), A. Erede (cnd), Japanese RSO—Esultate! L'orgoglio musulmano; Tu?! Indietro!...Ora e per sempre addio; Ah! Mille vite...Si, pel ciel; Dio! mi potevi scagliar; Niun mi tema *(rec Tokyo, Feb. 4, 1952)* Melodram ▲ CDI 104006 [ADD]

Verdi, G.:Otello (sels), w. Mario Del Monaco (ten—Otello), Tito Gobbi (bar—Iago), N. Sanzogno (cnd), Palermo Teatro Massimo Orch *(rec Palermo, Jan 1, 1962)* Bella Voce 2-▲ 7203 [AAD]

Verdi, G.:Rigoletto (sels), w. L. Pagliughi (sop), G. Lauri-Volpi (ten), F. Previtali (cnd), Rome RAI Orch, Rome RAI Chorus [highlights] *(rec 1947)* Melodram ▲ MEL 15008

Verdi, G.:Simon Boccanegra, w. Leyla Gencer (sop), Glade Peterson (ten), Giuseppe Zampieri (ten), Rolando Panerai (bar), Vito Susca (bass), Giorgio Tozzi (bass), G. Gavazzeni (cnd), *(orch unknown)* Great Opera Performances 2-▲ GOP 767

Gøbel, Bodil (sop)

Kuhlau, F.:Elverhøj, w. Gurli Plesner (cta), Mogens Schmidt Johansen (bar), J. Frandsen (cnd), Danish National RSO, Danish National Radio Choir *(rec Danish Radio Concert Hall, Aug 1974)* Marco Polo/Dacapo ▲ 8.224053 [AAD]

Goddard, Françoise (alt)

Milesi, P.:Modi 2, w. L. M. Pickova (sop), M. Ferradini (ten), B. Andersen (bass), D. Cassamagnaghi (fl), S. Scanziani (ob), A. Bianchi (cl/b cl), E. Crisafulli (bn), C. Gazzola (hn), F. Gualandris (tuba), A. Girardi (celtic hp), R. Anedda (vn), E. Groppo (vn), M. Pagani (vn), M. Ravasio (va), S. Righini (vc), P. Rizzi (db), J. Scully (perc), P. Milesi (cnd) Cuneiform ▲ RUNE 63

Godfrey, Victor (bass)

Puccini, G.:Tosca, w. Maria Callas (sop—Floria Tosca), Robert Bowman (ten—Spoletta), Renato Cioni (ten—Mario Cavaradossi), Eric Garrett (bar—Il Sagrestano), Tito Gobbi (bar—Scarpia), Victor Godfrey (bass—Casare Angelotti), Dennis Wicks (bass—Sciarrone), C. F. Cillario (cnd), Royal Opera House Orch, Royal Opera House Chorus Covent Garden *(rec London, 1964)* Melodram 2-▲ CDI 203003 [ADD]

Goedhart, Peter (bar)

Theodorakis, M.:Songs, w. Wim Spruijt (gtr)—Ballad of Mauthausen; Songs (4) from "Epitaph"; Romancero Gitano [after Garcia Lorca] [arr Stephen Dodgson for voc & gtr] Erasmus ▲ WVH 167

Goeke, Leo (ten)

Verdi, G.:La traviata (sels), w. Loretta di Franco (sop), Joan Sutherland (sop), Frederica von Stade (mez), Lou Marcella (ten), Luciano Pavarotti (ten), Gene Boucher (bar), Raymond Gibbs (bar), Sherrill Milnes (bar), Louis Sgarro (bar), John Trehy (bar) Budget ("The Greatest Voice in Opera" series) ▲ SYP 112

Goerke, Christine (sop)

Britten, H.:Hymn to St. Cecilia, w. Nanette Soles (mez), Matthew Pittman (ten), Leonard Ratzlaff (bass), Robert Shaw (cnd), Robert Shaw Festival Singers *(rec Church of St. Pierre, Gramat, France, July 26-28, 1994)* Telarc ▲ CD 80408 [DDD]

Poulenc, F.:Stabat mater, w. R. Shaw (cnd), Atlanta SO, Atlanta Sym Chorus *(rec Atlanta, Nov. 7-8, 1993)* Telarc ▲ CD 80362 [DDD]

Szymanowski, K.:Stabat Mater, w. M. Simpson (mez), V. Ledbetter (bar), R. Shaw (cnd), Atlanta SO, Atlanta Sym Chorus *(rec Atlanta, Nov. 7-8, 1993)* Telarc ▲ CD 80362 [DDD]

Goethem, Michel van (alt)

Perti, G.A.:Liturgy for Good Friday, w. Patrizia Vaccari (sop), Maura Pederzoli (sop), Cristina Calzolari (sop), Alida Oliva (sop), Claudia Bugli (sop), Lucia Bagnoli (alt), Cinzia Meneghel (alt), Renzo Bez (alt), Alessandro Carmignani (alt), Mauro Collina (ten), Vincenzo Di Donato (ten), Paolo Fanciullacci (ten), Giovanni Caccamo (ten), Paolo Da Col (ten), Sergio Foresti (bass), Marco Scavazza (bass), Luca Ferracin (bass), Paride Montanari (bass), Liuwe Tamminga (org), Sergio Vartolo (org), S. Vartolo (cnd), Bologna San Petronio Capella Musicale Orch—Omnes amici mei; De lamentatione Jeremiae Prophetae:Heth. Cogitavit; Velum templi; Vinea mea; De lamentatione Jeremiae Prophetae:Lamed. Matribus suis; Tamquam ad latronem; Tenebrae factae sunt; Animam meam; Tradiderunt me; Jesum tradidit; De lamentatione Jeremiae Prophetae:Aleph. Ego vir; Caligaverunt *(rec St. Petronio Basilica, Bologna, Mar 28-31, 1995)* Naxos ▲ 8.553321 [DDD]

Goetz, L. (sop)

Pfitzner, H.:Songs, w. R. Schwarz (pno)—16 songs (Opp. 5, 11 & 33) [G] Ars Produktion ▲ ARS 368301 [AAD]

Schumann, R.:Liederkreis, Op. 39, w. U. Gefe (pno) [G] Ars Produktion ▲ FCD 368302

Wolf, H.:Italienische Liederbücher (sels), w. U. Gefe (pno)—19 songs [G] Ars Produktion ▲ FCD 368302

Goetze, Christa (sop)
Mozart, W.A.:Missa Solemnis, w. Anna Schaffner (alt), Barnhard Gärtner (ten), Rudolf Rosen (bass), Philippe Laubscher (org), F. Pantillon (cnd), Bieler SO, Pro Arte Chorale, Bern Vocal Ensemble Gallo ▲ CD 893 [DDD]
Pantillon, F.:Bethlehem, w. Rudolf Rosen (nar), Philippe Laubscher (org), F. Pantillon (cnd), Bieler SO, Pro Arte Chorale, Bern Vocal Ensemble Gallo ▲ CD 893 [DDD]

Gohl, Verena (cta)
Bach, J.S.:Cant 20, w. M. Kessler (mez), T. Altmeyer (ten), A. Kraus (ten), W. Schöne (bass), H. Rilling (cnd), Stuttgart Bach Collegium, Frankfurt Kantorei Hänssler Classic ▲ 98.801 [AAD]
Bach, J.S.:Cant 40, w. A. Kraus (ten), S. Nimsgern (b–bar), H. Rilling (cnd), Stuttgart Bach Collegium, Stuttgart Gedächtnis Figural Choir [G] *(rec June–July 1970)* Hänssler Classic ▲ 98.824 [AAD]
Bach, J.S.:Cant 75, w. I. Reichelt, J. Hamari (cta), A. Baldin (ten), A. Kraus (ten), H.–F. Kunz (bass), H. Rilling (cnd), Stuttgart Bach Collegium, Frankfurt Kantorei [G] *(rec 1970)* Hänssler Classic ▲ 98.891 [AAD]
Bach, J.S.:Cant 88, w. I. Reichelt (sop), A. Kraus (ten), W. Schöne (bass), H. Rilling (cnd), Stuttgart Bach Collegium, Remembrance Florid Church Chorus Hänssler Classic ▲ 98.804 [AAD]
Mäder, U.:Mit Nacht beladen, w. Michael Gohl (cl), P. Siegwart (cnd), Zurich Collegium Musicum *(rec 1996)* Jecklin ▲ JS 3072 [DDD]
Mozart, W.A.:Notturnos Sops, w. E. Speiser (sop), K. Widmer (bass), H.R. Stalder (cl), R. Kubli (bas hn), H. Leuthold (bas hn) [I] *(rec 1968)* Jecklin–Disco ▲ JD 549–2 [ADD]
Mozart, W.A.:Più non si trovano, w. E. Speiser (sop), K. Widmer (bass), H.R. Stalder (cl), R. Kubli (bas hn), H. Leuthold (bas hn) [I] *(rec 1968)* Jecklin–Disco ▲ JD 549–2 [ADD]
Pergolesi, G.B.:Mass in F, w. B. Retchitzka (sop), G. Ferracini (sop), M. Minetto (cta), C. Jauquier (ten), J. Loomis (bass), Milan Solisti, Plifonia Choir *(rec 1967)* Rivoalto ▲ RIV 8922 [ADD]
Perrin, J.:German Songs, w. V. Desarzens (cnd), Lausanne CO *(rec Radio Lausanne, May 22, 1970)* Grammont ▲ CTSP 45 [AAD]

Golabek, M. (nar)
Saint-Saëns, C.:Carnival of the Animals, w. R. Golabek (nar), F. Savage (nar), C. Heston (nar), J. E. Jones (nar), B. White (nar), L. Redgrave (nar), W. Shatner (nar), J. Rivers (nar), T. Danson (nar), L. Tomlin (nar), D. Raffin (nar), A. Hepburn (nar), D. Moore (nar), W. Matthau (nar), J. Smith (nar), L. Schifrin (cnd), Hollywood CO Dove Audio ▲ DOV 30700

Golabek, R. (nar)
Saint-Saëns, C.:Carnival of the Animals, w. M. Golabek (nar), F. Savage (nar), C. Heston (nar), J. E. Jones (nar), B. White (nar), L. Redgrave (nar), W. Shatner (nar), J. Rivers (nar), T. Danson (nar), L. Tomlin (nar), D. Raffin (nar), A. Hepburn (nar), D. Moore (nar), W. Matthau (nar), J. Smith (nar), L. Schifrin (cnd), Hollywood CO Dove Audio ▲ DOV 30700

Gold, M. (sgr)
Rodgers, R.:Music of, w. S. Bass (sgr), J. Andrews (sgr), P. Como (sgr), D. Reese (sgr), J. Jones (sgr), N. Luboff (sgr), N. Walker (sgr), H. Bowen (sgr), V. Damone (sgr), P. Nero (pno), J. P. Morgan (sgr), E. Fisher (sgr), B. Goodman (cl), Ann–Margaret (sgr), Shorty Rogers (sgr), D. Shore (sgr), T. Martin (sgr), M. King (sgr), A. Newley (sgr) RCA ▲ 8590–2 R ■ 8590–4 R

Goldberg, Reiner (ten)
Beethoven, L. van:Fidelio, w. J. Norman (sop), P. Coburn (sop), H.–P. Blochwitz (ten), K. Möll (bass), B. Haitink (cnd), Dresden Staatskapelle, Dresden State Chorus Philips ▲ 438496–2
Beethoven, L. van:Fidelio, w. J. Norman (sop), P. Coburn (sop), H.–P. Blochwitz (ten), A. Schmidt (bar), E. Wlaschiha (bass), K. Moll (bass), B. Haitink (cnd), Dresden Staatskapelle, Dresden State Chorus [G] Philips 2–▲ 426308–2 [DDD]
Beethoven, L. van:Sym 9, "Choral Sym", w. E. Wiens (sop), U. Walther (cta), K.–H. Stryczek (bass), H. Blomstedt (cnd), Dresden Staatskapelle, Dresden State Opera Chorus, Dresden Sym Chorus—final chorus Capriccio ▲ 10 914 [DDD]
Berg, A.:Wozzeck, w. G. Schröter (mez), H. Hiestermann (ten), T. Adam (b–bar), H. Kegel (cnd), Leipzig RSO *(rec Apr. 9, 1973)* Berlin Classics ("Eterna" series) 2–▲ BER 2068 [ADD]
Mahler, G.:Das Klagende Lied, w. C. Studer (sop), W. Meier (mez), T. Allen (bar), G. Sinopoli (cnd), Philharmonia Orch, Shin–Yuh Kai Chorus *(rec live, Japan 1990)* Deutsche Grammophon ▲ 435382–2 [DDD]
Mozart, W.A.:Zauberflöte, w. M. Price (sop—Pamina), L. Serra (sop—Queen of the Night), M. Venuti (sop—Papagena), M. McLaughlin (sop—1st Lady), A. Murray (mez—2nd Lady), H. Schwarz (cta—3rd Lady), F. Höher (trb—1st Boy), M. Diedrich (trb—2nd Boy), F. Klos (trb—3rd Boy), P. Schreier (ten—Tamino), R. Tear (ten—Monostatos), R. Goldberg (ten—1st Armoured Man), K. Moll (bass—Sarastro), H. Rech (bass—2nd Armoured Man), C. Davis (cnd), Dresden Staatskapelle, Leipzig Radio Chorus Philips ("Duo" series) 2–▲ 442568–2
Operatic Arias, w. Berlin State Orch [cnd:Siegfried Kurz] Capriccio ▲ 10056 [DDD]
Schoenberg, A.:Moses und Aaron, w. Renate Krahmer (sop), Gisela Pohl (cta), Werner Haseleu (nar), H. Kegel (cnd), Leipzig RSO, Leipzig Radio Chorus Berlin Classics 2–▲ BER 1116 [ADD]
Strauss, R.:Guntram, w. I. Tokody (sop), S. Sólyom–Nágy (bar), I. Gáti (bar), E. Queler (cnd), Hungarian State Orch, Hungarian People's Army Male Chorus [G] CBS 2–▲ M2K 39737 [DDD]
Wagner, R.:Götterdämmerung, w. H. Behrens (sop), C. Studer (sop), H. Schwarz (mez), B. Weikl (bar), E. Wlaschiha (bar), M. Salminen (bass), J. Levine (cnd), Metropolitan Opera Orch, New York Metropolitan Opera Chorus Deutsche Grammophon 4–▲ 429385–2 [DDD]
Wagner, R.:Der Ring des Nibelungen (sels), w. E. Marton (sop), C. Studer (sop), K. Te Kanawa (sop), M. Lipovšek (mez), S. Jerusalem (ten), P. Haage (ten), J. Morris (bass), B. Haitink (cnd), Bayer RSO EMI Classics ▲ ZDC 54633
Wagner, R.:Der Ring des Nibelungen (sels), w. J. Norman (sop), H. Behrens (sop), K. Battle (sop), J. Morris (mez), C. Ludwig (mez), S. Jerusalem (ten), E. Wlaschiha (bar), M. Salminen (bass), J. Levine (cnd), Metropolitan Opera Orch—The Compact Ring—Ride of the Valkyries Wotan's Farewell & Magic Fire Music, Forest Murmurs, Brünnhilde's Awakening, Siegfried's Funeral Music, Brünnhilde's Immolation, & others Deutsche Grammophon ▲ 437825–2
Wagner, R.:Siegfried, w. H. Behrens (sop), B. Svenden (sop), J. Morris (bass), J. Levine (cnd), Metropolitan Opera Orch, New York Metropolitan Opera Chorus [G] Deutsche Grammophon 4–▲ 429407–2 [DDD]
Wagner, R.:Tannhäuser (sels), w. Sylvia Sass (sop), Hermann Prey (bar), Bavarian State Opera Orch, Bavarian State Opera Chorus—Ov; Venusberg Bacchanal; Dich, teure halle, grüb' ich wieder; Freudig Begrüben wir die edle Halle; Intro; die Pilger sind's - Beglückt darf nun dich, o Heimat, ich schauen; plus others Laserlight ▲ 14211 [DDD]

Golden, Ruth (sop)
Barber, S.:Knoxville:Summer of 1915, w. D. Barra (cnd), San Diego CO Koch International Classics ▲ KIC 7206 [DDD]
Delius, F.:Songs, w. S. Sulich (pno)—18 songs, composed 1888–1895 [E,F,G]—The bird's story; Twilight fancies; Young Venevil; Three Songs by Percy Shelley (1891); Four Poems of Paul Verlaine (1895); The homeward way; Cradle song; Hidden love; Dreamy nights; Nachtigall; Am schönsten Sonnerabend war's; Sehnsucht; Beim Sonnenuntergang Koch International Classics ▲ KIC 7043–2 [DDD]
Rodrigo, J.:Madrigales amatorias, w. D. Barra (cnd), San Diego CO Koch International Classics ▲ KIC 7160–2 [DDD]
Vaughan Williams, R.:Songs, w. T. Woodman (bar), N. Bean (vn), L. Rothfuss (pno)—From the House of Life; 4 Last Songs; Linden Lea; The Sky Above the Roof; Dreamland; Claribel; If I Were a Queen; 4 Poems by Fredegond Shove; Adieu; Think of Me; Along the Field *(rec Apr. 1992)* Koch International Classics ▲ KIC 7168 [DDD]
Warlock, P.:Songs Sop, w. L. Rothfuss (pno)—(21) Late summer; I have a garden; My own country; Lullaby; Sweet content; Ha'nacker Mill; The night; To the memory of a great singer; The bords; Frostbound wood; The first mercy; Pretty ring time; Have you seen but a white lily grow; Cradle song; The cloths of heaven; Sleep; Lilygay [song cycle] Koch International Classics ▲ KIC 7118–2 [DDD]

Goldsmith, Pearle (sop/mez)
Puccini, G.:Suor angelica, w. Elisabeth Carron (sop—Angelica), Joan Summers (sop—Genovieffa), Donna Owen (sop—Dolcina), Lou Ann Wyckoff (sop—Alms collector), Hanna Owen (sop—novice), Anthea De Forest (sop—novice), Charlotte Povia (mez—Abbess), Beverly Evans (mez—Monitress), Kay Creed (mez—Mistress), La Vergne Monette (sop/mez—lay sister), Joan August (sop/mez—lay sister), Pearle Goldsmith (sop/mez—other sister), Lila Herbert (sop/mez—other sister), Jodell Kenting (sop/mez—other sister), Ann Pretzat (sop/mez—other sister), Evelyn Sachs (cta—Princess), F. Patanè (cnd), *(orch unknown) (rec New York, Feb 23, 1967)* Legato Classics ▲ LCD 212–1 [ADD]

Golfier, Françoise (sop)
Debussy, C.:Pelléas et Mélisande, w. C. Alliot–Lugaz (sop), C. Carlson (mez), D. Henry (ten), G. Cachemaille (bar), P. Thau (bass), C. Dutoit (cnd), Montreal SO, Montreal Sym Chorus [F] London 2–▲ 430502–2 [DDD]

Goltz, Christel (sop)
Beethoven, L. van:Fidelio, w. S. Jurinac (sop), G. Zampieri (ten), P. Schöffler (b–bar), O. Edelmann (bass), H. von Karajan (cnd), Vienna PO, Vienna State Opera Chorus [G] *(rec live, Salzburg Festival 7/27/57)* Claque 2–▲ CLQ 2007 (m)
Orff, C.:Antigonae, w. Paul Kuen (ten), Karl Ostertag (ten), Benno Kusche (bar), Hermann Uhde (bar), N. Barth (bar), G. Solti (cnd), Bavarian State Opera Orch, Bavarian State Opera Chorus *(rec Prinzregententheater, Jan. 12, 1951)* Orfeo d'or 2–▲ 407952
Strauss, R.:Die Frau ohne Schatten (sels), w. E. Steber (sop), I. Steingruber (sop), S. Svanholm (ten), O. Wiener (bass), K. Böhm (cnd), *(orch unknown)*—selections from Act Two (Sieh, Amme, sieh...Würde ich lieber selber zu Stein!) & Act Three (Vater, bist du's?...) *(rec live, Munich, 6/4/53)* VAI Audio ▲ VAIA 1012 (m/s) [ADD]
Strauss, R.:Salome, w. Helmut Melchert (ten), Ernst Gutstein (bar), Siw Ericsdotter (sgr), O. Suitner (cnd), Dresden Staatskapelle *(rec 1963)* Berlin Classics 2–▲ BER 9101 [ADD]

Golven, Alain (bass)
Rossini, G.:Petite messe solennelle, w. E. Schmitt (sop), S. Gregoire (cta), R. Garin (ten), F. Maciocchi (pno) J.–F. Hatton (harm), Paris Opéra–Comique Chorus IMP Masters ▲ IMP MCD61

Gomez, Jill (sop)
Alwyn, W.:Invocations, w. A. R. Johnson (pno) *(rec Sept 1983)* Chandos ▲ CHAN 9220 [DDD]
Alwyn, W.:A Leave–Taking, w. A. R. Johnson (pno) *(rec Apr 1984)* Chandos ▲ CHAN 9220 [DDD]
American Music Sampler, w. Gomez, Jill (sop), Crispian Steele (tpt), Helen McQueen (E hn), Wayne Marshall (pno), City of London Sinfonia [cnd:R. Hickox] Virgin Classics 2–▲ CDC 59089
Barber, S.:Knoxville:Summer of 1915, w. R. Hickox (cnd), City of London Sinfonia [E] Virgin Classics ▲ 59520 [DDD]
Berlioz, H.:Songs, w. John Constable (pno)—Le Coucher de soleil; L'Origine de la harpe; La Belle voyageuse Saga Classics ▲ EC 3333
Bizet, G.:Songs, w. John Constable (pno)—Chanson d'avril; Adieux de l'hôtesse arabe; Vous ne priez pas; La Chanson de la rose Saga Classics ▲ EC 3333
Britten, H.:Chanson françaises (4), w. S. Rattle (cnd), City of Birmingham SO [F] *(rec 4/82)* EMI Classics 2–▲ ZDCB 54270 [DDD]
Britten, H.:A Midsummer Night's Dream, w. D. Jones (sop), J. Bowman (ct), N. Bailey (bar), H. Herford (bar), R. Hickox (cnd), City of London Sinfonia Virgin Classics ▲ CDCB 59305
Britten, H.:Songs, w. M. Jones (pno), *(ensemble unknown)*—O tell me the truth about love; Funeral Blues; Johnny; Calypso; When you're feeling like expressing your affection; As it is, plenty; The Spider and the Fly; Blues from *Paul Bunyan*; The clock on the wall; Boogie–woogie Unicorn–Kanchana ▲ DKP CD 9138
Cabaret Classics, w. Gomez, Jill (sop), John Constable (pno) Unicorn–Kanchana ▲ DKPCD 9055
Debussy, C.:Proses lyriques, w. John Constable (pno) Saga Classics ▲ EC 3333
Debussy, C.:Songs, w. John Constable (pno)—Noël des enfants qui n'ont plus de maisons Saga Classics ▲ EC 3333
Donizetti, G.:Il giovedì grasso, w. J. Peters (mez), J. Hughes (mez), U. Benelli (bar), B. Donlan (bar), F. Davià (bass), E. Esparza (sgr), D. Atherton (cnd), Eireann Radio–TV SO [I] *(rec live, 1970)* Foyer ▲ FOY 2036 [AAD]
Donizetti, G.:Il giovedì grasso, w. J. Hughes (mez), J. Peters (mez), U. Benelli (bar), B. Donlan (bar), F. Davià (bass), E. Esparza (sgr), M. Williams (sgr), D. Atherton (cnd), Eireann Radio–TV SO [I] *(rec live, 1970)* Memories ▲ HR 4482 [ADD]
Falla, M. de:El corregidor y la molinera, w. Aquarius, N. Cleobury (cnd) Virgin Classics ("Ultraviolet" series) ▲ CUV 61138
Falla, M. de:El sombrero de tres picos, w. Y. P. Tortelier (cnd), Philharmonia [Sp] Chandos ▲ CHAN 8904 [DDD]
Handel, G.F.:Ode for St. Cecilia's Day, w. Robert Tear (ten), P. Ledger (cnd), English CO, King's College Choir Cambridge ASV ▲ ASV CD 512
Handel, G.F.:Ode for St. Cecilia's Day, w. Robert Tear (ten), P. Ledger (cnd), English CO, King's College Choir Cambridge [E] ASV ▲ ASV 512 [DDD]
Porter, C.:Songs, w. M. Jones (pno)—Let's Do It; Night and Day; My Heart Belongs to Daddy; Miss Otis Regrets; The Physician Unicorn–Kanchana ▲ DKP CD 9138
Rameau, J.P.:La Danse, w. A.–M. Rodde (sop), J.–C. Orliac (ten), J.E. Gardiner (cnd), Monteverdi Orch, Monteverdi Choir London Erato ▲ 45985–2
Ravel, M.:Poèmes de Mallarmé, w. P. Boulez (cnd), BBC SO [F] CBS ▲ MK 39023
A Spanish Songbook, w. Gomez, Jill (sop), John Constable (pno) Conifer Classics ▲ 75605–51243–2 [DDD]
Tippett, M.:A Child Of Our Time, w. Helen Watts (cta), Kenneth Wooliam (ten), John Shirley–Quirk (bar), G. Rozhdestvensky (cnd), BBC SO, BBC Sym Chorus IMP ("BBC Radio Classics" series) ▲ IMP 9130
Villa–Lobos, H.:Bachiana brasileira 5, w. Pleeth Cello Octet Hyperion ▲ CDA 66257 [DDD]
Walton, W.:A Song for the Lord Mayor's Table, w. R. Hickox (cnd), City of London Sinfonia [E] Chandos ▲ CHAN 8824 [DDD]
Walton, W.:Songs after Edith Sitwell, w. R. Hickox (cnd), City of London Sinfonia [E] Chandos ▲ CHAN 8824 [DDD]

Gonda, Anna (alt)
Pergolesi, G.B.:Stabat mater, w. Julia Faulkner (sop), M. Halász (cnd), Camerata Budapest *(rec Festetich Castle, Budapest, Sept. 1994)* Naxos ▲ 8.550766 [DDD]

Gondek, Juliana (sop)
Handel, G.F.:Ariodante, w. L. Saffer (sop), L. Hunt (mez), Jennifer Lane (mez), J. Lindemann (ten), R. Müller (ten), N. Cavallier (bass), N. McGegan (cnd), Freiburg Baroque Orch, Ralf Popken (cnd), Wilhelmshaven Vocal Ensemble [172–page libretto w. production photos] Harmonia Mundi France 3–▲ HMC 907146.48
Handel, G.F.:Giustino, w. Dawn Kotoski (sop), Dorothea Röschmann (sop), Jennifer Lane (mez), Michael Chance (alt), Drew Minter (alt), Mark Padmore (ten), Dean Ely (sgr), N. McGegan (cnd), Freiburg Baroque Orch Harmonia Mundi France 3–▲ HMU 907130.32
Handel, G.F.:Ottone, Rè di Germania, w. Lisa Saffer (sop), Patricia Spence (mez), Drew Minter (alt), R. Popken (alt), Michael Dean (b–bar), N. McGegan (cnd), Freiburg Baroque Orch *(rec June 9–12, 1992)* Harmonia Mundi USA 3–▲ HMU 907073/75
Handel, G.F.:Radamisto, w. Monika Frimmer (sop), Dana Hanchard (sop), Lisa Saffer (sop), R. Popken (cta), Michael Dean (b–bar), Nicholas Cavallier (bass), N. McGegan (cnd), Freiburg Baroque Orch Harmonia Mundi USA 3–▲ HMU 907111/13

Gonzales, Carmen (mez)
Bellini, V.:Beatrice di Tenda, w. M. Freni (sop), C. Desderi (bar), R. Casellato (ten), M. Arena (cnd), *(orch unknown) (rec live, Bologna 1976)* Legato Classics 2–▲ LCD 152–2 [ADD]
Puccini, G.:La Bohème, w. L. Orgonasova (sop), J. Welch (ten), F. Previati (bar), W. Humburg (cnd), *(orch unknown)*, Bratislava Children's Choir [I] Naxos 2–▲ 8.660003/04 [DDD]
Puccini, G.:La Bohème (sels), w. Luba Orgonasova (sop—Mimi), Carmen Gonzales (sop—Musetta), Jonathan Welch (ten—Rudolfo), Fabio Previati (bar—Marcello), Boaz Senator (bar—Schaunard), Ivan Urbas (bass—Colline), Jiri Sulzenko (bass—Alcindoro), W. Humburg (cnd), Czech–Slovak RSO Bratislava, Bratislava Children's Choir, Slovak Phil Chorus *(rec Concert Hall, Czecho–Slovak Radio, Bratislava, Apr. 23–May 4, 1990)* Naxos ▲ 8.553151 [DDD]

VOCALISTS

Gonzales, Carmen (mez) (cont.)
Vivaldi, A.:Orlando Furioso, w. V. de los Angeles (sop), M. Horne (mez), L. Valentini-Terrani (mez), Kosma (sgr), S. Bruscantini (bar), N. Zaccaria (bass), C. Scimone (cnd), Venice Solisti
Erato 3-▲ 2292-45147-2 ZB

Gonzales, Dalmacio (ten)
Rossini, G.:Demetrio e Polibio, w. Christine Weidinger (sop—Lisinga), Sara Mingardo (cta—Siveno), Anna Laura Longo (sgr—Olmira), Dalmacio Gonzales (ten—Demetrio/Eumene), Giorgio Surjan (bass—Polibio), Martino Fullone (sgr—Onao), M. Carraro (cnd), Graz SO, Bratislava Chamber Chorus *(rec live, Martina Franca Opera Festival, Italy, July 27, 1992)* Dynamic 2-▲ CDS 171/1-2 [DDD]

Gonzales, Renzo (sgr)
Rossini, G.:L'occassione fa il ladro, w. C. Fusco (sop), M. T. Pace (mez), G. Sinimberghi (ten), I. Tajo (bass), L. Colonna (cnd), Naples Alessandro Scarlatti RAI Orch [I] *(rec live, Naples, Sept. 29, 1963)*
Arkadia ▲ 602 [ADD]
Wagner, R.:Die Meistersinger von Nürnberg, w. Bruna Rizzoli (sop), Fernanda Cadoni (mez), Luigi Infantino (ten), Vito Tatone (ten), Renato Capecchi (bar), Giuseppe Taddei (bar), Boris Christoff (bass), Giovanni Ciavola (bass), James Loomis (bass), Silvo Maionica (bass), Vito Susca (bass), Raimondo Botteghelli (sgr), Walter Brunelli (sgr), Carlo Franzini (sgr), Ezio de Giorgi (sgr), Renzo Gonzales (sgr), L. von Matačić (cnd), Turin RAI Radio-TV SO, Turin RAI Chorus Stradivarius 4-▲ STV 12310

Gonzalez, Fabienne (sop)
Essyad, A.:Le Collier des ruses, w. C. Bonnet (sop), V. Reinbold (mez), P. Nahon (cnd), Ensemble Instrumental K617 2-▲ 7051

Gonzalez, Irma (sop)
Beethoven, L. van:Sym 9, "Choral Sym", w. Oralia Dominguez (cta), Flavio Becerra (ten), Roberto Banuelas (bar), F. Lozano (cnd), Mexico City PO, Mexico City Chorus Forlane ▲ FRL 18 [AAD]
Revueltas, S.:Canciones para niños, w. F. Lozano (cnd), Mexico City PO Spartacus ▲ 21020

Gonzalo (sgr)
Falla, M. de:El retablo de maese Pedro, w. Seoane (sop), Navarro (sgr), E. Halffter (cnd), Champs Élysées Theater Orch *(rec ca. 1959)* MCA Classics ▲ MCAD 10481 (m/s) [ADD]

Goodall, Valorie (sop)
Lehár, F.:Das Land des Lächelns, w. Dagmar Koller (sop), Guiseppe di Stefano (ten), Heinz Holecek (bass), H. Lambrecht (cnd), Vienna Volksoper Orch [G] *(rec 1967)* Preiser ▲ 93144 [ADD]

Gooding, Julia (sop)
Handel, G.F.:Jephtha, w. Christiane Oelze (sop), Catherine Denley (mez), Axel Köhler (ct), John Mark Ainsley (ten), Michael George (bass), M. Creed (cnd), Berlin Academy for Early Music *(rec June 1992)*
Berlin Classics 2-▲ BER 1057-2 [DDD]
Linley, T.:Cants, w. P. Nicholson (cnd), Parley of Instruments—In yonder grove; Ye nymphs of Albion's beauty-blooming isle; Daughter of Heav'n, fair art thou! Hyperion ▲ CDA 66767
Linley, T.:Theatre Music, w. P. Nicholson (cnd), Parley of Instruments—Music for The Tempest; Ov. to The Duenna Hyperion ▲ CDA 66767
Purcell, H.:King Arthur, w. N. Argenta (sop), L. Perillo (sop), J. MacDougall (ten), M. Tucker (ten), G. Finley (bar), B. Bannatyne-Scott (bass), T. Pinnock (cnd), English Concert, *(chorus unknown)*
Archiv 2-▲ 435490-2 [DDD]

Goodman, James (trb)
Handel, G.F.:The Triumph of Time & Truth, w. Fisher (sop), Emma Kirkby (sop), Charles Brett (ct), Ian Partridge (ten), Stephen Varcoe (bar), D. Darlow (cnd), London Handel Orch, London Handel Chorus [E]
Hyperion 2-▲ CDA 66071/72
Purcell, H.:Anthems & Services, w. S. Gritton (sop), M. Kennedy (sop), E. O'Dwyer (trb), J. Goodman (trb), J. Bowman (ct), N. Short (ct), Rogers Covey-Crump (ten), C. Daniels (ten), M. Milhofer (ten), M. George (bass), R. Evans (bass), R. King (cnd), King's Consort—I Was Glad When They Said unto Me (coronation & verse anthem); O Consider My Adversity; Beati omnes qui timent Dominum; In the Black Dismal Dungeon of Dispair; Save Me, O God; Te Deum in B♭; Jubilant in B♭; Thy Way, O God, Is Holy
Hyperion ▲ CDA 66677 [DDD]
Purcell, H.:Music for the Funeral of Queen Mary, w. S. Gritton (sop), M. Kennedy (sop), E. O'Dwyer (trb), J. Goodman (trb), J. Bowman (ct), N. Short (ct), Rogers Covey-Crump (ten), C. Daniels (ten), M. Milhofer (ten), M. George (bass), R. Evans (bass), R. King (cnd), King's Consort Hyperion ▲ CDA 66677 [DDD]

Góralski, Jan (ten)
Moniuszko, S.:Halka, w. Barbara Nieman (sop), Halina Sloniowska (sop), Bogdan Paprocki (ten), Leslaw Pawluk (ten), Kazimierz Pustelak (ten), Andrzej Hiolski (bar), Edmund Kossowski (bass), Edward Pawlak (bass), Z. Gorzynski (cnd), Warsaw State Opera House Orch, Warsaw National Opera Chorus *(rec Warsaw, 1965)* Polskie Nagrania ▲ PNCD 092 [AAD]

Gorchakoova, Galina (sop)
Tchaikovsky, P.:Mazeppa, w. Larissa Dyadkova (mez), Sergei Larin (ten), Sergei Leiferkus (bar), Anatoly Kotscherga (bass), N. Järvi (cnd), Gothenburg SO, Stockholm Royal Opera Chorus
Deutsche Grammophon 3-▲ 439906-2

Gorchakova, Galina (sop)
Glinka, M.:Russlan & Ludmilla, w. Larissa Diadkova (cta), Irinia Bogachova (sgr), Anna Netrebko (sgr), Yuri Masurin (ten), Konstantin Pluzhnikov (ten), Mikhail Kit (bar), Gennady Bezzubenkov (bass), Vladimir Ognovenko (bass), V. Gergiev (cnd), Kirov Opera Orch, Kirov Opera Chorus Philips ▲ 456 248-2
Tchaikovsky, P.:Arias, w. V. Gergiev (cnd), Kirov Orch, Kirov Opera Chorus—Letter Scene [from Eugene Onegin]; Zachem eti sl'ozy [Pique Dame]; Gde zhe ty, moj zjelannyj? [from Sorceress]; Pachudilis' mne butta galasa [from Oprichnik] Philips ▲ 446405-2
Tchaikovsky, P.:Iolanta, w. Galina Gorchakova (sop), Nikolai Gassiev (ten), Gegam Grigorian (ten), Dmitri Hvorostovsky (bar), Nikolai Putilin (bar), Sergei Alexashkin (bass), Gennady Bezzubenkov (bass), Larissa Diadkova (sgr), Olga Korzhenskaya (sgr), Tatyana Kravtsova (sgr), V. Gergiev (cnd), Kirov Opera Orch, Kirov Opera Chorus *(rec Mariinsky Theatre, St. Petersburg)* Philips 2-▲ 442796-2
Verdi, G.:Arias, w. V. Gergiev (cnd), Kirov Orch, Kirov Opera Chorus—Madre, pietosa Vergine; Pace, pace mio dio [both from La Forze del destino]; Qui Radamès verrà—Oh patria mia [from Aida]; Tacea la notte placida—Di tale amor [from Il Trovatore]; Mia madre aveva; Piangea cantando; Ave Maria (Willow Song) [all from Otello] Philips ▲ 446405-2

Gordaze, Nana (sgr)
Mercadante, S.:Caritea, regina di Spagna, w. Sonia Lee (sgr), Jacek Laszczkowski (sgr), Nicolas Rivenq (bar), Gregory Bonfatti (sgr), Ayhan Ustuk (sgr), G. Carella (cnd), Italian International Opera Orch, Bratislava Camera Chorus *(rec Italy, 1995)* Nuova Era 3-▲ NUO 7258
Puccini, G.:Le Villi, w. Stefano Antonucci (bar), José Cura (sgr), B. Aprea (cnd), Italian International Orch
Nuova Era ▲ NUO 7218 [DDD]

Gordon, Brian (alt)
Purcell, H.:Hail. Bright Cecilia, w. J. Smith (sop), A. Stafford (alt), P. Elliot (ten), S. Varcoe (bar), D. Thomas (bass), J.E. Gardiner (cnd), English Baroque Soloists, Monteverdi Choir London
Erato ("Gardiner Purcell Collection" series) ▲ 96554-2

Gordon, David (ten)
Bach, J.S.:Arias, w. Emily Newbold (fl), Loretta O'Sullivan (vc), Charlotte Mattax (hpd), G. Funfgeld (cnd), Bethlehem Bach Festival Orch—Ermunter dich [from Cant.180]; Der Ewigkeit [from Cant. 198]; Ach, schlage doch [from Cant. 95]; Benedictus [from Mass in b, BWV 232]; Woferne du [from Cant. 41]; O Seelenparadies [from Cant. 172]; Frohe Hirten [from Christmas Oratorio, BWV 248] *(rec St. Michael's Church, New York City, June 1994)* Newport Classic ▲ NPD 85582 [DDD]
Bach, J.S.:Cant 63, w. S. McNair (sop), J. Taylor (mez), D. Lichti (b-bar), G. Funfgeld (cnd), Bach Festival Orch, Bethlehem Bach Choir—plus Sanctus from Mass in b, BWV 232 [G]
Dorian ▲ DOR 90113 [DDD]
Bach, J.S.:Cant 65, w. D. Lichti (b-bar), G. Funfgeld (cnd), Bach Festival Orch, Bethlehem Bach Choir [G] Dorian ▲ DOR 90113 [DDD]
Bach, J.S.:Cant 140, w. H. Schellenberg (sop), D. Lichti (b-bar), G. Funfgeld (cnd), Bach Festival Orch, Bethlehem Bach Choir [G] Dorian ▲ DOR 90127 [DDD]
Bach, J.S.:Magnificat, BWV 243, w. P. Jensen (sop), D. Upshaw (sop), M. Simpson (mez), W. Stone (bar), R. Shaw (cnd), Atlanta SO, Atlanta Chamber Chorus Telarc ▲ CD 80194 [DDD]
Handel, G.F.:Acis & Galatea, w. D. Kotoski (sop—Galatea), D. Gordon (ten—Acis), G. Siebert (ten—Damon), J. Opalach (bass—Polyphemus), G. Schwarz (cnd), Seattle SO, Seattle Chorale [E]
Delos 2-▲ DE 3107 [DDD]

Gordon, David (ten) (cont.)
Respighi, O.:Lauda per la Natività del Signore, w. Valente (sop), M. Forrester (cta), M. Korn (cnd), Concerto Soloists Instrumental Ensemble, Philadelphia Singers
RCA Red Seal ▲ 7787-2-RC [DDD] ■ 7787-4-RC (CrO2)
Schubert, Franz:Mass 2, w. D. Upshaw (sop), W. Stone (bass), R. Shaw (cnd), Atlanta SO, Atlanta Sym Chorus [L] Telarc ▲ CD 80212 [DDD]
Vivaldi, A.:Gloria, RV.589, w. D. Upshaw (sop), P. Jensen (sop), M. Simpson (mez), W. Stone (bar), R. Shaw (cnd), Atlanta SO, Atlanta Chamber Chorus Telarc ▲ CD 80194 [DDD]

Gorgoza, Emilio de (bar)
Emilio de Gorgoza, w. Gorgoza, Emilio de (bar) *(rec between 1906 & 1925)*
Pearl ▲ PEA 9089 [ADD]

Göritz, Ingrid (cta)
Wagner, R.:Der Ring des Nibelungen, w. Liselotte Becker-Egner (sop—Woglinde/Ortlinde/Wellgunde), Angelika Berger (sop—Wellgunde/Waltraute), Siw Ericsdotter (sop—Norn 3), Heidemaria Ferch (sop—Freia/Gerhilde), Bella Jasper (sop—Helmwige/Waldvogel/Woglinde), Ditha Sommer (sop—Sieglinde/Gutrune), Ursula Boese (mez—Erda), Ruth Hesse (mez—Fricka), Nadezda Kniplová (mez—Brünnhilde), Margit Kobeck (mez—Schwertleite/Norn 2), Hilde Rosner (mez—Flosshilde/Siegrunde), Erica Schubert (mez—Grimgerde/Flosshilde), Ingrid Göritz (cta—Rossweisse/Norn 1), Herbert Doussant (ten—Froh), Herold Kraus (ten—Mime), Gerald McKee (ten—Siegmund/Siegfried), Fritz Uhl (ten—Loge), Rudolf Knoll (bar—Gunther/Donner), Rolf Polke (bass-bar—Wotan/Wanderer), Rolf Kühne (bass—Alberich), Takao Okamura (bass—Fafner), Otto von Rohr (bass—Hagen/Fasolt/Hunding), H. Swarowsky (cnd), Czech PO, Prague National Theater Orch *(rec June 3 & 5, July 26-31, A)* Weltbild Classics 14-▲ 703769 [ADD]

Görne, Matthias (bar)
Eisler, H.:Deutsche Sinfonie, w. Hendrikje Wangemann (sop), Annette Markert (alt), Peter Lika (bass), Gert Gütschow (speaker), Volker Schwarz (speaker), L. Zagrosek (cnd), Leipzig Gewandhaus Orch, Ernst Senff Chorus *(rec Gewandhaus, Leipzig, May 1995)*
London ("Entartet Musik" series) ▲ 448389-2 [DDD]
Schubert, Franz:Songs (comp), w. Christine Schäfer (sop), Graham Johnson (pno)—22 songs including D.395, 410, 628-631, 633, 634, 646, 649, 652, 684, 690-694, 708, 711, 745, 854, 855
Hyperion ▲ 33027

Görne, Matthias (bass)
Braunfels, W.:Die Vögel, w. Helen Kwon (sop—Nightingale), Wolfgang Holzmair (bar—Hoopoe), Matthias Gorne (b-bar—Prometheus), Michael Krause (sgr—Loyal Friend), Endrik Wottrich (sgr—Good Hope), L. Zagrosek (cnd), Berlin German SO, Berlin Radio Chorus
London ("Entartete Musik" series) ▲ 448 679-2
Mendelssohn, F.:St. Paul, w. Melanie Diener (sop), Annette Markert (mez), James Taylor (ten), P. Herreweghe (cnd), Champs Élysées Theater Orch, Chapelle Royale Choir, Collegium Vocale *(rec Stravinsky Auditorium, Montreaux)* Harmonia Mundi France 2-▲ HMC 901584.85

Görner, A. (sop)
Kálmán, I.:Gräfin Mariza, w. F. Wunderlich (ten), B. Kusche (bar), Hartung (sgr), Hofmann (sgr), Marszalek (cnd), Cologne Radio Orch, Cologne Radio Chorus [G] Acanta ▲ CD 42479 [DDD]

Gorner, Christine (sop)
Fall, L.:Die Dollarprinzessin (sels), w. Sari Barabas (sop), Harry Friedauer (ten), Heinz Hoppe (ten), C. Michalski (cnd), Graunke SO, Botho Lucas Chorus Emperor Operetta ▲ KO 86353
Fall, L.:Der liebe Augustin (sels), w. Sari Barabas (sop), Heinz Hoppe (ten), Benno Kusche (b-bar), C. Michalski (cnd), Graunke SO, Rudolf Lamy Singers Emperor Operetta ▲ KO 86352
Fall, L.:Die Rose von Stambul (sels), w. Melita Muszely (sop), Fritz Wunderlich (ten), C. Michalski (cnd), Graunke SO Emperor Operetta ▲ KO 86353
Lehár, F.:Der Zarewitsch (sels), w. Melita Muszely (sop), Fritz Wunderlich (ten), Willy Hagara (bar), C. Michalski (cnd), Bavarian SO Emperor Operetta ▲ KO 86341
Lehár, F.:Zigeunerliebe (sels), w. Sari Barabas (sop), Harry Friedauer (ten), Heinz Hoppe (ten), C. Michalski (cnd), Graunke SO, Rudolf Lamy Singers Emperor Operetta ▲ KO 86342
Strauss (II), Joh.:Eine Nacht in Venedig (sels), w. Rita Streich (sop), Cesare Curzi (ten), Nicolai Gedda (ten), Christian Oppleberg (bar), F. Allers (cnd), Graunke SO, Graunke Chorus
Emperor Operetta ▲ KO 86345
Strauss (II), Joh.:Wiener Blut (sels), w. Anneliese Rothenberger (sop), Nicolai Gedda (ten), W. Mattes (cnd), Graunke SO, Munich Theater Gartnerplatz Chorus Emperor Operetta ▲ KO 86345

Gorochovskaya, Evgenia (mez)
Mussorgsky, M.:Boris Godunov, w. V. Valente (sop—Xenia), E. Gorochovskaya (mez—Nurse), L. Nichiteanu (mez—Fyodor), E. Zarmeba (mez—Hostess), M. Lipovšek (cta—Marina), P. Langridge (ten—Prince Shuisky), H. Wildhaber (ten—Misail), A. Fedin (ten—Simpleton), S. Leiferkus (bar—Rangoni), A. Kotcherga (bass—B. Godounov), A. Shagidullin (bass—Shchelkalov), S. Ramey (bass—Pimen), S. Larin (bass—Girgory), G. Nikolsky (bass—Varlaam), C. Abbado (cnd), Berlin PO, Tölz Boys' Choir, Berlin Radio Chorus, Slovak Phil Chorus *(rec Nov. 7-30, 1993)*
Sony Classical 3-▲ S3K 58977 [DDD]
Prokofiev, S.:Alexander Nevsky, w. Y. Temirkanov (cnd), St. Petersburg PO *(rec Philharmonia Hall, St. Petersburg, Mar 16 & 17, 1993)* RCA Red Seal ▲ 0902-668642-2 [DDD]

Gorr, Rita (mez)
Debussy, C.:Pelléas et Mélisande, w. J. Micheau (sop), C. Maurane (bar), M. Roux (bar), X. Depraz (bass), J. Fournet (cnd), Lamoureux Orch *(rec 1953* Philips 2-▲ 434783-2
Gounod, C.:Faust, w. V. de los Angeles (sop), L. Berton (sop), N. Gedda (ten), E. Blanc (bar), B. Christoff (bass), A. Cluytens (cnd), Paris Opera Orch [F] Angel ("Studio" series) 3-▲ CDMC 69983 [ADD]
Gounod, C.:Faust (sels), w. Liliane Berton (sop), Victoria de los Angeles (sop), Nicolai Gedda (ten), Victor Autran (bar), Ernest Blanc (bar), Boris Christoff (bass), A. Cluytens (cnd), Paris Opera Orch, Paris Opera Chorus Classics for Pleasure ("Eminence" series) ▲ CDEMX 2215 [DDD]
Massenet, J.:Werther, w. Mady Mesplé (sop—Sophie), Rita Gorr (mez—Charlotte), Robert Andreozzi (ten—Schmidt), Albert Lance (ten—Werther), Gabriel Bacquier (bar—Albert), Julien Giovannetti (bar—Le Bailli), Jacques Mars (bar—Johann), J. Etcheverry (cnd), *(orch unknown)*
Adès 2-▲ ADE 140832 [AAD]
Poulenc, F.:Dialogues des Carmélites, w. C. Dubosc (sop), R. Yakar (sop), M. Dupuy (mez), J. Van Dam (b-bar), K. Nagano (cnd), Lyon Opera Orch Virgin Classics ▲ CDCB 59227
Poulenc, F.:Dialogues des Carmélites, w. D. Duval (sop), R. Crespin (sop), L. Berton (sop), D. Scharley (mez), P. Finel (ten), X. Depraz (bass), P. Dervaux (cnd), Paris Opera Orch [F]
EMI Classics 2-▲ CDCB 49331 (m) [ADD]
Saint-Saëns, C.:Samson et Dalila, w. J. Vickers (ten), E. Blanc (bar), G. Prêtre (cnd), Paris Opera Orch, René DuClos Chorus [F] EMI Classics 2-▲ CDCB 47895
Saint-Saëns, C.:Samson et Dalila (sels), w. J. Vickers (ten), E. Blanc (bar), G. Prêtre (cnd), Paris Opera Orch EMI Classics ▲ ZDM 63935
Verdi, G.:Aida, w. L. Price (sop), J. Vickers (ten), R. Merrill (bar), G. Tozzi (bass), G. Solti (cnd), Rome Opera Orch, Rome Opera Chorus [I] London ▲ 421860-2 [ADD]
Verdi, G.:Aida, w. L. Price (sop), J. Vickers (ten), R. Merrill (bar), G. Tozzi (bass), G. Solti (cnd), Rome Opera Orch, Rome Opera Chorus [I] London 3-▲ 417416-2 [ADD]
Wagner, R.:Das Rheingold, w. E. Grümmer (sop), A. Andersson (ten), S. Konya (ten), T. Adam (b-bar), H. Hotter (b-bar), J. Greindl (bass), H. Knappertsbusch (cnd), Bayreuth Festival Orch, Bayreuth Festival Chorus [G] *(rec live 1958)* Arkadia 2-▲ 441 [AAD]

Górzynska, Halina (sop)
Gluck, C.W.:La Corona, w. A. Slowakiewicz (sop), L. Juranek (sop), B. Nowicka (mez), T. Bugaj (cnd), Warsaw Sinfonia [I] Orfeo 2-▲ 135872 [DDD]

Gossage, Julia (mez)
Sullivan, A.:The Pirates of Penzance, w. R. Evans (sop—Mabel), G. Knight (mez—Ruth), J. Gossage (mez—Edith), J. M. Ainsley (ten—Frederic), R. Suart (bar—Maj.-Gen. Stanley), N. Folwell (bar—Samuel), D. Adams (b-bar—Pirate King), R. Van Allan (bass—Sergeant of Police), C. Mackerras (cnd), Welsh National Opera Orch, Welsh National Opera Chorus *(rec May 4-6, 1993)*
Telarc ▲ CD 80353 [DDD]; ■ CS 30353

Gotkovsky, Anne (sop)
Campra, A.:Messe de Requiem, w. Véronique Gens (sop), Jean-Paul Fouchécourt (alt), Joseph Cornwell (ten), Peter Harvey (bar), H. Niquet (cnd), Concert Spirituel Orch, Concert Spirituel Vocal Ensemble
Adda ▲ ADD 241952 [DDD]

Gotkovsky, Anne (sop) (cont.)
Campra, A.:Motets, w. Véronique Gens (sop), Jean-Paul Fouchécourt (alt), Joseph Cornwell (ten), Peter Harvey (bar), H. Niquet (cnd), Concert Spirituel Orch, Concert Spirituel Vocal Ensemble—Benedictus Dominus Adda ▲ ADD 241952 [DDD]
Campra, A.:Motets, w. Véronique Gens (sop), Jean-Paul Fauchecourt (ct), Hervé Lamy (ten), Peter Harvey (bass), H. Niquet (cnd), Concert Spirituel Orch, Concert Spirituel Vocal Ensemble—2 Noster Refugium; Cantate Domino; De Profundis Adda ▲ ADD 243912
Campra, A.:Motets, w. Véronique Gens (sop), Jean-Paul Fouchécourt (alt), Douglas Nasrawi (ten), Peter Harvey (bar), Marcos Loureiro de Sá (bar), Kevin Mallon (vn), H. Niquet (cnd), Concert Spirituel Orch, Concert Spirituel Vocal Ensemble—Te Deum; Notus in Judea Deus; Deus in Nomine Tuo Adda ▲ ADD 241942 [DDD]

Goud, Ananda (mez)
Straesser, J.:Gedanken der Nacht, w. J. Sligter (cnd), Basho Ensemble *(rec live, Vredenburg, Utrecht, Jan. 17, 1993)* Donemus ▲ CV 44

Goulancourt, Jeanne (mez)
Gounod, C.:Roméo et Juliette, w. Yvonne Gall (sop—Juliette), Champell (sop—Stéphano), Jeanne Goulancourt (mez—Gertrude), Agustarello Affre (ten—Roméo), Edmond Tirmont (ten—Tybalt), Alexis Boyer (bar—Mercutio), Pierre Dupré (bar—Paris), Hypolite Belhomme (bar—Grégorio), Marcel Journet (bass—Frère Laurent), Henri Albers (bass—Capulet), Valermont (bass—The Duke), F. Rühlmann (cnd), Paris Opéra-Comique Orch, Paris Opéra-Comique Chorus *(rec 1912)* VAI Audio ▲ VAIA 1064-3 F

Gowings, J. (bar)
Josquin Desprez:Missa, "Ave Maris Stella", w. D. Collot (sop), R. Holton (sop), J.-L. Comoretto (ct), R. Le Chenadec (ct), T. Brehu (ten), H. Lamy (ten), B. Fabre-Garrus (bar) *(rec Jan. 1993)* Astrée ▲ E 8507 [DDD]
Josquin Desprez:Motets, w. D. Collot (sop), R. Holton (sop), J.-L. Comoretto (ct), R. Le Chenadec (ct), T. Brehu (ten), H. Lamy (ten), B. Fabre-Garrus (bar)—Motets à la vierge *(rec Jan. 1993)* Astrée ▲ E 8507 [DDD]

Graae, Jason (sgr)
Porter, C.:Fifty Million Frenchmen, w. H. McGillin (sgr), K. Criswell (sop), K. McClelland (sgr), S. Powell (sgr), K. Ziemba (sgr), J. Harder (sgr), S. Waara (sgr), P. Cass (sgr), J. LeClerc (sgr) [1991 studio cast] New World ▲ 80417-2 [DDD]
Rodgers, R.:Music of, w. V. Clark (sgr), Gregg Edelman (sgr), A. Reed (sgr), L. Wintersteller (sgr)—Oklahoma; Carousel; The Sound of Music; South Pacific; Flower Drum Song; Cinderella & others Varèse Sarabande ▲ VSD 5516 ■ VSC 5516

Graaner, Irene (sop)
Liszt, F.:Missa choralis, w. Else Paaske (alt), Kai Hansen (ten), Michael Hansen (bar), Hans Christian Andersen (bass), Niels Henrik Nielsen (org), Tamás Vetö (cnd), Copenhagen Univ Choir Point ▲ PCD 5075 [ADD]

Graarud, Gunnar (ten)
Wagner, R.:Parsifal (sels), w. Gertrude Fünger (cta—Kundry), Gunnar Graarud (ten—Parsifal), Emil Schipper (bar—Amfortas), Josef von Manowarda (bass—Gurnemanz), C. Krauss (cnd), Vienna State Opera Orch *(rec Apr. 13, 1933)* Koch Schwann 2-▲ SCH 314642 [ADD]

Grabowski, B. (bar)
Berlioz, H.:Lélio, "Le retour à la vie", w. M. Rabsilber (ten), H.-P. Minetti (nar), R. Reuter (cnd), Berlin Comic Opera Orch, Berlin Radio Chorus [F; narration G] Berlin Classics ▲ BER 2149 [DDD]

Grace, Nickolas (bar)
Porter, C.:A Swell Party, w. A. Richards (sgr), A. Woods (sgr), D. Keman (sgr), M. Smith (sgr), *(other artists unknown)* [1992 London cast] Silva America ▲ SSD 1006 [DDD] ■ SSC 1006

Graf, Christian (sgr)
Haydn, J.:Applausus:Jubilaeum virtutis Palatium, w. Florian Erdl (sgr), Gert Füssi (sgr), Helmut Wildhaber (ten), Georg Tichy (bass), P. Angerer (cnd), Vienna Concilium Musicum [period instrs] Koch Schwann ▲ SCH 314092

Graf, Elisabeth (cta)
Bruch, M.:Das Lied von der Glocke, w. Ute Selbig (sop), Matthias Bleidorn (ten), André Eckert (bass), Dresden PO *(rec Kreuzkirche Dresden, Jun 24, 1995)* Thorofon 2-▲ DCTH 2291/2 [DDD]
Carvalho, J. de S.:Te Deum, w. Brigitte Fournier (sop), Naoko Okada (sop), John Elwes (ten), Michel Brodard (bar), M. Corboz (cnd), Lisbon Gulbenkian Foundation Orch, Lisbon Gulbenkian Foundation Chorus Cascavelle ▲ CVL 1016 [DDD]
Zelenka, J.D.:Missa sanctissimae trinitatis, w. Monika Frimmer (sop), Markus Brutscher (ten), W. Wehnert (cnd), Marburg Bach Choir Thorofon ▲ CTH 2265
Zelenka, J.D.:Missa votiva, w. C. Hampe (sop), J. Duske (ten), J. Gebhardt (bass), W. Wehnert (cnd), Hesse Bach Collegium, Marburg Bach Choir [L] Thorofon ▲ CTH 2172 [DDD]

Graf, Emil (bass)
Puccini, G.:La Bohème, w. Trude Eipperle (sop), Hildegarde Ranczak (sop), Alfons Fügel (ten), Carl Kronenberg (bar), Georg Hann (bass), Georg Wieter (bass), Otto Hillerbrandt (sgr), Karl Schmidt (sgr), C. Krauss (cnd), Bavarian State Opera Orch, Bavarian State Opera Chorus *(rec 1940)* Preiser 2-▲ PRE 90275
Strauss, R.:Salome, w. Astrid Varnay (sop—Salome), Hertha Töpper (mez—Der Page der Herodias), Margarete Klose (cta—Herodias), Hans Hopf (ten—Narraboth), Karl Hoppe (ten—1st Nazarene), Karl Ostertag (ten—1st Jew), Julius Patzak (ten—Herodes), Hans Braun (bar—Jochanaan), Benno Kusche (bar—2nd Soldier), Adolf Keil (bass—1st Soldier), Hans Hermann Nissen (bass—Ein Kappadozier), Max Proebstl (bass—2nd Nazarene), Walter Carnotch (sgr—4th Jew), Emil Graf (sgr—3rd Jew), Paul Kaussen (sgr—2nd Jew), Hildegard Limmer (sgr—A slave), Georg Witter (sgr—5th Jew), H. Weigert (cnd), Bavarian RSO *(rec June 21-25, 1953)* Bella Voce 2-▲ BLV 7210 [AAD]

Graf, Kathrin (sop)
Bach, J.S.:Arias, w. Peter-Lukas Graf (fl), Raffaele Altwegg (vc), Michio Kobayashi (hpd/pno)—Meine Seele sie vergnügt [from Cantata No. 204, Von der Vergnügsamkeit] *(rec Protestant Chuch Seon, 1976)* Claves ("Favor Collection" series) ▲ CD 604 [ADD]
Bach, J.S.:Cant 110, w. H. Gardow (sop), A. Baldin (ten), W. Schöne (bass), H. Rilling (cnd), Stuttgart Bach Collegium, Gächinger Kantorei [G] *(rec Jan-Feb 1974)* Hänssler Classic ▲ 98.824 [AAD]
Bach, J.S.:Cant 167, w. H. Gardow (sop), A. Kraus (ten), N. Tüller (bass), H. Rilling (cnd), Stuttgart Bach Collegium, Remembrance Florid Church Chorus Hänssler Classic ▲ 98.803 [AAD]
Handel, G.F.:Arias, w. P. Graf (fl), R.Altwegg (vc), M. Kobayashi (hpd/pno)—Meine Seele hört im Sehen [from 9 German Arias] *(rec Protestant Chuch Seon, 1976)* Claves ("Favor Collection" series) ▲ CD 604 [ADD]
Keller, A.:Der enthüllte Stern, w. D. Fueter (sop), A. K. Graf (fl), L. Pellerin (ob), E. Schmid (cl), U. Walker (vn), C. Schiller (va), P. Demenga (vc), P. Hug-Rutti (hp), F. Eberle (dr) [G] Grammont ▲ CTSP 19-2 [ADD]
Keller, A.:Ewiger Augenblick, w. D. Fueter (sop), A. K. Graf (fl), E. Schmid (cl), D. Isler (cel), P. Hug-Rutti (hp), U. Walker (vn), P. Demenga (vc) [G] Grammont ▲ CTSP 19-2 [ADD]
Koechlin, C.:Premier album de Lilian, w. Philippe Racine (fl), Daniel Cholette (pno), Christine Simonin (ondes martinot) Accord ▲ ACD 201232 [DDD]
Lehmann, H.U.:Kammermusik, w. A.-K. Graf (fl), E. Schmid (cl), W. Grimmer (vc), I. Nakamura (perc) Jecklin ▲ JD 689
Martin, F.:Chants de Noël, w. Peter-Lukas Graf (fl), Michio Kobayashi (pno) *(rec Protestant Chuch Seon, 1976)* Claves ("Favor Collection" series) ▲ CD 604 [ADD]
Missa in festo Pentecostes, w. Einsiedein & Lucerne Choralschola [cnd:Roman Bannwart], E. Schmid, C. Schiller, T. Käser *(rec 1987)* Jecklin ▲ JEC 617-2 [DDD]
Moser, R.:Wortabend, w. N. Tüller (bass), M. Venzago (cnd), Basel RSO Soloists [G] Grammont ▲ CTSP 12-2 [ADD]
Rameau, J.P.:Music of, w. Peter-Lukas Graf (fl), Alexander van Wijnkoop (vn), Michio Kobayashi (hpd/pno)—Rossignols amoureux *(rec Protestant Chuch Seon, 1976)* Claves ("Favor Collection" series) ▲ CD 604 [ADD]
Ravel, M.:Chansons madécasses, w. Peter-Lukas Graf (fl), Raffaele Altwegg (vc), Michio Kobayashi (hpd/pno) *(rec Protestant Chuch Seon, 1976)* Claves ("Favor Collection" series) ▲ CD 604 [ADD]
Roussel, A.:Poèmes de Ronsard, w. Peter-Lukas Graf (fl) *(rec Protestant Chuch Seon, 1976)* Claves ("Favor Collection" series) ▲ CD 604 [ADD]
Satie, E.:Socrate, w. Werner Bärtschi (pno) Accord ▲ ACD 220522 [DDD]

Graf, Kathrin (sop) (cont.)
Scarlatti, A.:Solitudini amene, apriche collinette, w. Peter-Lukas Graf (fl), Raffaele Altwegg (vc), Michio Kobayashi (hpd/pno) *(rec Protestant Chuch Seon, 1976)* Claves ("Favor Collection" series) ▲ CD 604 [ADD]
Wildberger, J.:Die Stimme, die alte, schwächer werdende Stimme, w. S. Palm (vc), L. Zagrosek (cnd), Southwest German RSO Baden-Baden [G] *(rec May 30, 1980)* Grammont ▲ CTSP 25-2 [ADD]

Graham, Sandra (mez)
Verdi, G.:Falstaff, w. E. Norberg-Schulz (sop—Nannetta), L. Serra (sop—Alice), S. Graham (mez—Meg Page), M. Lipovsek (cta—Miss Quickly), K. Begley (ten—Dr. Caius), P. Conti (ten—Ford), M. Luperi (ten—Pistol), J. Van Dam (b-bar—Falstaff), P. LeFebvre (bass—Bardolph), G. Solti (cnd), Berlin PO, Berlin Radio Chorus London ▲ 440650-2 [DDD]

Graham, Susan (sop)
Gounod, C.:Roméo et Juliette, w. Susan Graham (sop—Stephano), Ruth Ann Swenson (sop—Juliette), Sarah Walker (mez—Gertrude), Paul Charles Clarke (ten—Tybalt), Placido Domingo (ten—Roméo), Kurt Ollmann (bar—Mercutio), Alastair Miles (bass—Frère Laurent), David Pittman-Jennings (bass—Le Duc), Alain Vernhes (bass—Capulet), L. Slatkin (cnd), Munich RSO, Munich Radio Chorus *(rec Studio 1, Bavarian Radio, Munich, Nov 29 - Dec 10, 1995)* RCA Red Seal 2-▲ 09026-68440-2 [DDD]

Grahame, Gloria (sgr)
Rodgers, R.:Oklahoma!, w. Gordon MacRae (sgr), S. Jones (sgr), R. Steiger (sgr), Gene Nelson (sgr), C. Greenwood (sgr), J. Whitmore (sgr) *(rec 1955)* Broadway Angel ▲ ZDM 64691 ■ EG 64691

Graham-Hall, John (ten)
The Best of Richard Hickox, w. R. Hickox (cnd), London SO, London Sym Chorus, Penelope Walmsley-Clark (sop), D. Maxwell (bar), Southend Boys' Choir, London Voices IMP Classics 3-▲ TCD 1073 [DDD]
Lloyd Webber, W.S.:Arias, w. P. Ledger (org)—Arias:The King of Love & Thou Art the King, from cantatas *The Saviour* & *The Divine Compassion*; Songs—A rent for love; Utopia; Over the bridge; The pretty washer-maiden; So lovely the rose [E] ASV ▲ ASV 584 [DDD]
Lloyd Webber, W.S.:Songs Ten & Pno, w. P. Ledger (pno)—Arias:The King of Love & Thou Art the King, from cantatas *The Saviour* & *The Divine Compassion*; Songs—A rent for love; Utopia; Over the bridge; The pretty washer-maiden; So lovely the rose [E] ASV ▲ ASV 584 [DDD]
Lloyd Webber, W.S.:Songs, w. *(pianist unknown)*—5 Songs ASV ▲ ASV 961
Orff, C.:Carmina burana, w. P. Walmsley-Clark (sop), D. Maxwell (bar), R. Hickox (cnd), London SO, London Sym Chorus [G, L] IMP Classics ▲ PCD 855
Schoenberg, A.:Moses und Aaron, w. David Pittman-Jennings (nar), Gabriele Fontana (sop—Young Girl), Yvonne Naef (cta—Sick Woman), John Graham-Hall (ten—Young Man/Naked Youth), Pår Lindskog (ten—Youth), Chris Merritt (ten—Aaron), Siegfried Lorenz (bar—Another Man), Michael Devlin (b-bar—Ephraimite), László Polgár (bass—Priest), P. Boulez (cnd), Royal Concertgebouw Orch, Winfried Maczewski (cnd), Netherlands Opera Chorus, Zaans Youth Choir, Waterland Music School *(rec Concertgebouw, Amsterdam, Oct 1995)* Deutsche Grammophon 2-▲ 449 174-2 [DDD]
Stravinsky, I.:Pulcinella, w. G. Wilson (ten), J. Opalach (bass), G. Schwarz (cnd), Seattle SO Delos ▲ DE 3100 [DDD]

Grahl, Hans (ten)
Wagner, R.:Parsifal (sels), w. A. Konetzni (sop), H. Weidemann (bar), H. Alsen (bass), H. Knappertsbusch (cnd), Vienna State Opera Orch, Vienna State Opera Chorus *(rec Apr. 6, 1939)* Koch Schwann 2-▲ SCH 314522 [ADD]

Grahm, Sharon (mez)
Puccini, G.:Madama Butterfly, w. Maria Spacagna (sop), Vivica Genaux (mez), Richard di Renzi (ten), Richard Markley (ten), Erich Parce (bar), James Butler (bass), C. Rosenkrans (cnd), Hungarian State Opera Orch, Anikó Katona (cnd), Hungarian State Opera Chorus—3 versions *(rec Italian Institute, Budapest, Sept 5-21, 1995)* Vox Classics 4-▲ VOX4 7525 [DDD]

Graml, Helmut (bar)
Orff, C.:Der Mond—Ein kleines Welttheater, w. R. Christ (ten), P. Kuén (ten), K. Schmitt-Walter (bar), H. Hotter (b-bar), P. Lagger (bass), W. Sawallisch (cnd), Philharmonia Orch, Philharmonia Chorus [G] EMI Classics ("Studio" series) 2-▲ CDMB 63712 [ADD]

Gramm, Donald (bass)
Beethoven, L. van:Sym 9, "Choral Sym", w. P. Curtin (sop), F. Kopleff (cta), J. McCollum (ten), F. Reiner (cnd), Chicago SO RCA Gold Seal ▲ 09026-61795-2
Berlioz, H.:La Damnation de Faust, w. S. Danco (sop), D. Poleri (ten), M. Singher (bar), C. Munch (cnd), Boston SO, Harvard Glee Club [F] RCA Gold Seal 2-▲ 7940-2-RG [ADD]
Berlioz, H.:La Damnation de Faust, w. Suzanne Danco (sop), David Poleri (ten), Martial Singher (bar), McHenry Boatwright (bass), Joseph de Pasquale (va), Louis Speyer (hn), C. Munch (cnd), Boston SO, Harvard Glee Club, Radcliffe Choral Society *(rec Feb 1954)* RCA Victor Gold Seal 8-▲ 0902-668444-2 [ADD]
Bernstein, L.:Songfest, w. C. Dale (sop), R. Elias (mez), N. Williams (mez), N. Rosenshein (ten), J. Reardon (bar), L. Bernstein (cnd), National SO Washington D.C. [E] Deutsche Grammophon ▲ 415965-2 [ADD]
Donizetti, G.:Don Pasquale, w. Beverly Sills (sop), Alfredo Kraus (ten), Alan Titus (bar), S. Caldwell (cnd), London SO, Ambrosian Opera Chorus EMI Classics 2-▲ CDMB 66030
La Montaine, J.:Wilderness Journal, w. Paul Callaway (org), A. Dorati (cnd), National SO Washington D.C. *(rec live, Kennedy Center, Oct 10, 1972)* Fredonia Discs ▲ FDCD 12
La Montaine, J.:Wilderness Journal, w. Paul Callaway (org), A. Dorati (cnd), National SO Washington D.C. *(rec live, Kennedy Center, Oct 10, 1972)* Fredonia Discs ■ FDC 11
Love's Secrets & Other Songs By American Composers, w. Eleanor Steber (sop), Mildred Miller (mez), John McCollum (ten), Edwin Biltcliffe (pno), Richard Cumming (pno) Vox Box ("The American Composers" series) 2-▲ CDX 5129
Rorem, N.:Some Trees, w. P. Curtin (sop), B. Wolff (mez), N. Rorem (pno) [E] CRI ■ C 238
Rorem, N.:Some Trees, w. P. Curtin (sop), B. Wolff (cta), N. Rorem (pno) CRI ▲ CD 657 [ADD]
Rorem, N.:Songs, w. P. Curtin (sop), B. Wolff (cta) [E] CRI ■ C 238
Rorem, N.:War Scenes, w. Eugene Istomin (pno) Phoenix ▲ PHCD 116 [AAD]
Schoenberg, A.:Songs, w. Ellen Faull (sop), Helen Vanni (mez), Glenn Gould (pno)—Zwei Gesange, Op. 1; Vier Lieder, Op. 2; Das Buch der hängenden Gärten; Sechs Lieder, Op. 3; Zwei Balladen, Op. 12; Drei Lieder, Op. 48; Zwei Lieder, Op. 14; Zwei Lieder, Op. Posth.; Acht Lieder, Op. 6 Sony Classical ("Glen Gould Edition" series) 2-▲ SM2K 52667

Gramss, Nele (sop)
Schütz, H.:Symphoniae sacrae 1, w. Barbara Borden (sop), Rogers Covey-Crump (ten), John Potter (ten), Douglas Nasrawi (ten), Harry van der Kamp (bass), Concerto Palatino Choir Accent 2-▲ 9178/79 [DDD]

Granados, J. (bass)
Lehár, F.:Eva, w. J. Granados (sop—Prunelles), A. M. Olaria (sop—Eva), A. Kraus (ten—Octavio Flaubert), L. de Cordoba (sgr—Gipsy), S. Ramalle (sgr—Dagoberto), J. Perominge (sgr—Voisin), E. Estella (cnd), Madrid CO, Spanish National Radio Chorus [Sp] Montilla ▲ CDFM 2036

Granda, Alessandro (ten)
Puccini, G.:Madama Butterfly, w. R. Pampanini (sop), G. Nessi (ten), G. Vanelli (bar), S. Baccaloni (bass), L. Malajoli (cnd), La Scala Orch, La Scala Chorus *(rec 1928)* Centaur 2-▲ CRC 2196/97
Puccini, G.:Madama Butterfly, w. Rosetta Pampanini (sop—Madam Butterfly), Conchita Velasquez (mez—Suzuki), Cesira Ferrari (mez—Kate Pinkerton), Alessandro Granda (ten—F. B. Pinkerton), Giuseppe Nessi (ten—Goro), Aristide Baracchi (bar—Il Principe Yamadori), Gino Vanelli (bar—Sharpless), Lino Bonardi (bass—Il Commissario Imperiale), Salvatore Baccaloni (bass—Lo zio Bonzo), L. Molajoli (cnd), La Scala Orch, La Scala Chorus Bongiovanni 2-▲ 1123/24 [ADD]

Grandis, Franco de (bass)
Mozart, W.A.:Don Giovanni, w. S. Ghazarian (sop), G. Ottenthal (sop), P. Pace (sop), G. Sabbatini (ten), R. Bruson (bar), S. Rinaldi-Miliani (bar), N. Ghiuselev (bass), N. Järvi (cnd), Cologne RSO, Cologne Radio Chorus [I] Chandos 3-▲ CHAN 8920/22 [DDD]
Rossini, G.:Il barbiere di Siviglia, w. I. Kertesi (sop—Berta), S. Ganassi (mez—Rosina), R. Vargas (ten—Almaviva), A. Romero (bar—Dr. Bartolo), R. Servile (bar—Figaro), F. de Grandis (bass—Basilio), K. Sárkány (bass—Fiorello), A. Déri (pno), B. Sztankovits (gtr), W. Humburg (cnd), Failoni CO, Hungarian Radio Chorus *(rec Nov. 16-28, 1992)* Naxos 3-▲ 8.660027/29 [DDD]
Spontini, G.:La vestale, w. R. Plowright (sop), G. Pasino (mez), F. Araiza (ten), P. Lefèbvre (ten), A. Cauli (bar), G. Kuhn (cnd), Munich RSO, Munich Radio Chorus [F] Orfeo 2-▲ 256922 [DDD]

Granforte, Apollo (bar)
Apollo Granforte, 1886–1975, w. Apollo Granforte (bar), La Scala Orch, La Scala Chorus [cnd:Carlo Sabajno] *(rec HMV 1928–31)* Preiser ("Lebendige Vergangenheit" series) ▲ PRE 89048 (m) [AAD]
Leoncavallo, R.:Pagliacci, w. Adelaide Saraceni (sop—Nedda), Alessandro Valente (ten—Canio), Nello Palai (ten—Beppe), Apollo Granforte (bar—Tonio), Leonildo Basi (bass—Silvio), C. Sabajno (cnd), La Scala Orch, La Scala Chorus *(rec Apr, Sept 1929 & Jan 1930)* VAI Audio 2–▲ VAIA 1082–2
Puccini, G.:Tosca, w. C. Melis (sop—Tosca), P. Pauloi (ten—Cavarodossi), N. Palai (ten—Spoletta), A. Granforte (bar—Scarpia), G. Azzimonti (bass—Sciarrone/Angelotti), A. Gelli (bass—Sacristan), C. Sabajno (cnd), La Scala Orch, La Scala Chorus [I] *(rec Milan, Nov. 1929)* VAI Audio 2–▲ VAIA 1076–2 (m) [ADD]
Puccini, G.:Tosca, w. Carmen Melis (sop—Tosca), Nello Palai (ten—Spoletta), Piero Pauli (ten—Cavaradossi), Apollo Granforte (bar—Scarpia), Giovanni Azzimonti (bass—Angelotti/Sciarrone), Antonio Gelli (bass—Sagrestano), C. Sabajno (cnd), La Scala Orch, La Scala Chorus *(rec Nov 1929)* Arkadia 2–▲ CD 78002 (m) [ADD]
Verdi, G.:Arias—12 arias from Otello, Rigoletto, Traviata & Trovatore *(rec 1928–31)* Preiser ("Lebendige Vergangenheit" series) ▲ 89048 (m) [AAD]
Verdi, G.:Otello, w. Maria Carbone (sgr), Nicola Fusati (ten), Piero Girardi (ten), Corrado Zambelli (ten), Enrico Spada (sgr), C. Sabajno (cnd), La Scala Orch, La Scala Chorus Grammofono 2000 2–▲ GRM 78651
Verdi, G.:Il trovatore, w. Maria Caniglia (sop), Aureliano Pertile (ten), C. Sabajno (cnd), La Scala Orch, La Scala Chorus *(rec Milan, Sept.–Oct. 1930)* Phonographie 2–▲ PHG 5002 [ADD]
Verdi, G.:Il trovatore, w. Maria Carena (sop—Leonora), Olga De Franco (sop—Ines), Irene Minghini Cattaneo (mez—Azucena), Aureliano Pertile (ten—Manrico), Giordano Callegari (ten—Ruiz/Messenger), Apollo Granforte (bar—Count), Bruno Carmassi (bass—Ferrando), Antonio Gelli (bass—Old Gypsy), C. Sabajno (cnd), La Scala Orch, Vittore Veneziani (cnd), La Scala Chorus *(rec 1930)* Arkadia ("The 78's" series) 2–▲ 78007 [ADD]

Grant (sgr)
Rossini, G.:Semiramide, w. J. Sutherland (sop), M. Horne (mez), Myers (sgr), R. Bonynge (cnd), New Philharmonia Orch, Ambrosian Opera Chorus [I] *(rec live at the Theatre Royal, Drury Lane, 2/9/69)* Arkadia 2–▲ 579 (m) [ADD]

Grant, Clifford (bass)
Elgar, E.:The Apostles, w. S. Armstrong (sop), H. Watts (cta), R. Tear (ten), J. C. Case (bar), B. Luxon (bar), A. Boult (cnd), London PO, London Phil Chorus, Downe House School Choir [E] EMI Classics ▲ CDMB 64206
Verdi, G.:I lombardi alla prima crociata, w. C. Deutekom (sop), D. Malvisi (sop), M. Aparici (sop), P. Domingo (ten), G. Raimondi (ten), M. Lo Monaco (ten), M. Dean (b–bar), L. Gardelli (cnd), Royal PO, Ambrosian Singers Philips 2–▲ 422420–2 [ADD]
Wagner, R.:Götterdämmerung (sels), w. M. Curphey (sop), R. Hunter (sop), A. Remedios (ten), N. Bailey (bar), R. Goodall (cnd), Sadler's Wells Opera Orch, Sadler's Wells Opera Chorus—Act 3, Scenes 2 & 3 [E] Chandos ("Collect" series) ▲ CHAN 6593 [ADD]

Grant–Murphy, Heidi (sop)
Mozart, W.A.:Idomeneo, w. Heidi Grant–Murphy (sop—Ilia), Carol Vaness (sop—Elettra), Cecilia Bartoli (mez—Idamante), Plácido Domingo (ten—Idomeneo), Frank Lopardo (ten—High Priest), Thomas Hampson (bar—Arbace), Bryn Terfel (b–bar—The Voice), J. Levine (cnd), Metropolitan Opera Orch, Raymond Hughes (cnd), New York Metropolitan Opera Chorus *(rec Manhattan Center Studios, New York, Mar & Apr 1994)* Deutsche Grammophon 3–▲ 447 737–2 [DDD]

Granzer, Robert (bar)
Strauss (II), Joh.:Die Fledermaus, w. M. Irosch (sop), D. Koller (sop), M. Holliday (sop), W. Kmentt (ten), R. Karczykowski (ten), H. Kraemmer (bar), E. Binder (cnd), Vienna Volksoper Orch, Vienna Volksoper Chorus [G] Denon 2–▲ CO 8101 [DDD]

Gratis, Lorie (mez)
Bach, J.S.:Magnificat, BWV 243, w. Julianne Baird (sop), David Price (ten), Kevin Deas (bass–bar), Bronwyn Fix–Keller (hpd), V. Radu (cnd), Ama Deus Ensemble Vox Classics ▲ VOX 7531
Jane's Hand:The Jane Austen Songbooks, w. Baird, Julianne (sop), Elizabeth Henreckson–Farnum (sop), Daniel Pincus (ten), Philip Anderson (ten), Martil Dillon (ten), Nancy Wilson (bar vn), Peter Segal (bar gtr), Mary Jane Newman (pno/hpd), Anthony Newman (pno) Vox Classics ▲ VOX 7537 [DDD]

Graves, Denyce (mez)
Heroines of Romantic French Opera, w. Monte Carlo PO [cnd:M. Soustrot] Fnac Music ▲ 592056
Spontini, G.:La vestale, w. Karen Huffstodt (sop—Julie), Denyce Graves (mez—La Grande Vestale), Patrick Raftery (ten—Cinna), Anthony Michaels–Moore (bar—Licinius), R. Muti (cnd), La Scala Orch, La Scala Chorus Sony Classical 3–▲ S3K 66357
Thomas, A.:Hamlet, w. J. Anderson (sop—Ophelie), D. Graves (mez—Gertrude); G. Kunde (ten—Laerte), T. Hampson (bar—Hamlet), S. Ramey (bass—Claudius), A. de Almeida (cnd), London PO, Ambrosian Singers EMI Classics 3–▲ CDCC 54820

Gray, Linda Esther (sop)
Wagner, R.:Die Feen, w. K. Lövaas (sop), K. Láki (sop), Anderson (sop), R. Alexander (sop), R. Hermann (bar), K. Moll (bass), W. Sawallisch (cnd), Bavarian RSO, Bavarian Radio Chorus [G] *(rec live, Munich Opera Fest. 1983)* Orfeo 3–▲ 062833 [DDD]

Grayson, K. (sgr)
Kern, J.:Show Boat, w. H. Keel (sgr), A. Gardner (sgr) *(rec 1951)* TCM ▲ R2 71998
Kern, J.:Show Boat, w. H. Keel (sgr), A. Gardner (sgr), *(other artists unknown) (rec 1951)* Sony Music Special Products ▲ AK 45436 ▮ AT 45436

Grayston, Jean (cta)
Music for a Grand Hotel, w. Max Jaffa Trio, Max Jaffa (vn), Grand Hotel Orch Valentine ▲ VALD 8057 [DDD]
Music for a Palm Court, w. Max Jaffa Trio Valentine ▲ VALD 8061 [DDD]

Greager, Richard (ten)
Donizetti, G.:Rosmonda d'Inghilterra, w. Yvonne Kenny (sop), Enid Hartle (mez), Christian du Plessis (bar), Milla Andreaw (sgr), A. Francis (cnd), Ulster Orch, Opera Rara Chorus *(rec live, 1970's)* Italian Opera Rarities 2–▲ IOR 7730

Grebner, A. (spkr)
Stern, A.:The Fairy's Gift, w. A. Stern (cnd), XTET Delos ▲ DE 6001 [DDD] ▮ CS 6001 (D)

Greco, B. (sgr)
Mancini, H.:Film Music, w. A. Williams (sgr), J. Mathis (sgr), L. Albright (sgr), B. Hackett (sgr), C. Byrd (sgr), P. Page (sgr), Mancini (cnd), Costa Orch, Conniff Orch, Mancini Orch—sels from Breakfast at Tiffany's; Peter Gunn; Mr. Lucky & others Columbia/Legacy ▲ CK 66505

Greco, Norina (sop)
Verdi, G.:Il trovatore, w. Norina Greco (sop—Leonora), Bruna Castagna (cta—Azucena), Jussi Björling (ten—Manrico), Francesco Valentino (bar—Count di Luna), Nicola Moscona (bass—Ferrando), F. Calusio (cnd), *(orch unknown) (rec live, New York, Jan. 11, 1941)* The Fourties 2–▲ ENT FT 1507
Verdi, G.:Il trovatore, w. Bruna Castagna (mez), Jussi Björling (ten), Nicola Moscona (bass), Francesco Valentino (sgr), F. Calusio (cnd), *(orch & chorus unknown)* Enterprise ("The Radio Years" series) 2–▲ ENT 44 (m)

Green, Adolph (sgr)
Bernstein, L.:Candide (restored), w. J. Anderson (sop), C. Ludwig (mez), D. Jones (mez), J. Hadley (ten), N. Gedda (ten), K. Ollmann (bar), L. Bernstein (cnd), London SO, London Sym Chorus Deutsche Grammophon ▮ 437328–4
Bernstein, L.:Candide (restored), w. J. Anderson (sop), C. Ludwig (mez), D. Jones (mez), J. Hadley (ten), N. Gedda (ten), K. Ollmann (bar), L. Bernstein (cnd), London SO, London Sym Chorus *(rec 1989)* Deutsche Grammophon ▲ 429734–2 [DDD] ▮ 429734–4
Bernstein, L.:Music of, w. Barbara Cook (sop), Betty Comden (sgr), Rosalind Russell (sgr), et al—sels. from Candide, Mass, On the Town, Peter Pan, 1600 Pennsylvania Avenue, Trouble in Tahiti, West Side Story, Wonderful Town *(rec 1950–1973)* CBS ▲ MK 44760 [ADD]
Bernstein, L.:On the Town, w. M. Martin (sgr), N. Walker (sgr), B. Comden (sgr), Tutti Camarata Orch, Leonard Joy Orch, Lynn Murray Orch, Lynn Murray Chorus MCA Classics ▲ MCAD 10280 (m) [AAD]

Green, Barton (ten)
Lovenstein, J.:Music of, w. Mary Brockenbrough (sop), Laura Sanders (sop), Rockland Osgood (ten), David Murray (bar), Benjamin Sears (bar), Jonathan Lovenstein (pno), Heather O'Donnell (pno), James Silvers (pno), Rocy Reider (fl), Jason Horowitz (vn), Adrianna Hulscher (vn), James Johnston (vn), Mimi Ragson (vn), Peter Landeen (vc), Reinmar Seidler (vc)—Blake Songs; other works Titanic ▲ Ti 221 [DDD]

Green, Eugene (bass)
Giordano, U.:Andrea Chénier, w. Montserrat Caballé (sop), Franco Corelli (ten), R. de Carlo (sgr), D.. Dondi (sgr), G. Ellsworth (sgr), J. Fair (sgr), R. Falk (sgr), S. Felter (sgr), H. Hicks (sgr), H. Krauss (sgr), L. Miller (sgr), N. Riggins (sgr), H. Salerno (sgr), A. Guadagno (cnd), Academy of Music Orch, Academy of Music Chorus Great Opera Performances 2–▲ GOP 766
Mahler, G.:Sym 8, w. Oksana Krovytska (sop—Magna Peccatrix), Sheila Smith (sop—Una poenitentium), Shauna Southwick (sop—Mater gloriosa), Kristine Jepson (mez—Maria Aegyptiaca), Julie Simson (mez—Mulier Samaritana), Kurt Hansen (ten—Doctor Marianus), Brian Steele (bar—Pater ecstaticus), Eugene Green (b–bar—Pater profundus), R. Olson (cnd), Colorado MahlerFest Orch, Colorado MahlerFest Chorale, Colorado Mormon Chorale, Colorado Children's Chorale *(rec MahlerFest VIII, Boulder, CO, Jan 14–15, 1995)* MahlerFest 2–▲ MF8–1

Greenawald, Sheir (sop)
Blitzstein, M.:Regina, w. A. Réaux (sop), K. Ciesinski (mez), S. Ramey (bass), J. Mauceri (cnd), Scottish Opera Orch, Scottish Opera Chorus [E] London 2–▲ 433812–2 [DDD]
Summerdays:From the Musical Masterworks Festival at Old Lyme, w. Sheir Greenawald (sop), Beverly Hoch (sop), John Koch (ten), Aloysia Friedman (vn), Michele Sidener (va), Norman Krieger (cnd), Norman Krieger (pno) Well–Tempered Productions ▲ WTP 5173 [DDD]

Greenberg, Matthew (bass)
Sowerby, L.:Forsaken of Man, w. Alicia Clark (sop), Judith Compton (alt), Thomas Potter (bass), Paul Grizzell (bass), Bruce Hall (sgr), John Vorassi (sgr), Thomas Weisflog (org), William Ferris (cnd), William Ferris Chorale *(rec St. Thomas the Apostle Church, Chicago, June 1990)* New World ▲ 803942 [AAD]

Greenberg, Sylvia (sop)
Gluck, C.W.:Paride ed Elena, w. I. Cotrubas (sop), Fontana (sgr), F. Bonisolli (ten), L. Zagrosek (cnd), Austrian RSO, Austrian Radio Chorus [I] *(rec 1983)* Orfeo 2–▲ 118842 [DDD]
Mozart, W.A.:Entführung, w. J. Thames (sop), J. van der Schaaf (ten), W. Gahmlich (ten), K. Rydl (bass), Trissenaar (sgr), M. Viotti (cnd), Frankfurt RSO, Bamberg Sym Chorus Capriccio 2–▲ 10 403/04
Mozart, W.A.:Entführung, w. J. Thames (sop), J. Van Der Schaaf (ten), W. Gahmlich (ten), K. Rydl (bass), M. Viotti (cnd), Frankfurt RSO, Bamberg Sym Chorus LaserLight ▲ 14117 [DDD]
Schmidt, F.:Das Buch mit sieben Siegeln, w. Carolyn Watkinson (cta), Peter Schreier (ten), Thomas Moser (ten), Robert Holl (bass), Kurt Rydl (bass), L. Zagrosek (cnd), Austrian RSO, Vienna State Opera Chorus [G] Orfeo 2–▲ 143862 [DDD]

Greene, Patrick (sgr)
Rorem, N.:A Childhood Miracle, w. Michele Couture (sop—Peony), Darcy Dunn (sgr—Violet), Madeline Tsingopoulos (sgr—Mother), Mary Cidoni (sgr—Emma), Patrick Greene (sgr—Snowman), Peter Castaldi (sgr—Father), R. E. Harrell (cnd), Magic Circle CO Newport Classic ▲ NPT 85594 [DDD]

Greene, Ruby (alt)
Thomson, V.:4 Saints in 3 Acts, w. Inez Matthews (sop—St Settlement), Beatrice Robinson–Wayne (sop—St Teresa I), Altonell Hines (mez—Commère), Ruby Greene (alt—St Teresa II), David Bethea (ten—St Stephen), Charles Holland (ten—St Chavez), Edward Matthews (bar—St Ignatius), Randolph Robinson (bar—St Plan), Abner Dorsey (bass—Compère), V. Thomson (cnd), *(orch unknown)* [abridged by Thompson] *(rec June 25, 1947)* RCA Gold Seal ▲ 09026–68163–2 [ADD]

Greenwood, Charlotte (sgr)
Porter, C.:Out of This World, w. W. Eythe (sgr), P. Gillette (sgr) Sony Broadway ▲ SK 48223 ▮ ST 48223
Rodgers, R.:Oklahoma!, w. Gordon MacRae (sgr), S. Jones (sgr), R. Steiger (sgr), Gloria Grahame (sgr), Gene Nelson (sgr), J. Whitmore (sgr) *(rec 1955)* Broadway Angel ▲ ZDM 64691 ▮ EG 64691

Greevy, Bernadette (mez)
Berlioz, H.:Les Nuits d'été, w. Y.P. Tortelier (cnd), Ulster Orch [F] Chandos ▲ CHAN 8735 [DDD]
Boulanger, L.:Du fond de l'abîme, w. I. Partridge (ten), N. Boulanger (cnd), BBC SO, BBC Sym Chorus *(rec live, London Nov. 1968)* Intaglio ▲ INCD 703–1 [ADD]
Duparc, H.:Songs, w. Y.P. Tortelier (cnd), Ulster Orch—Chanson triste; Le Manoir de Rosemonde; L'invitation au voyage; Soupir; Phidylé; La vie antérieure; Sérénade florentine [F] Chandos ▲ CHAN 8735 [DDD]
Elgar, E.:Sea Pictures, w. V. Handley (cnd), London PO Classics for Pleasure ▲ CDCFP 9004 [AAD]
Green, P.:Mass of St. Francis of Assisi, "Let Me Bring Love", w. Sydney MacEwan (bar), David Budway (pno), Cork Children's Choir Alanna ▲ ALA 5553

Gregoire, Soazig (cta)
Rossini, G.:Petite messe solennelle, w. E. Schmitt (sop), R. Garin (ten), A. Golven (bass), F. Maciocchi (pno) J.–F. Hatton (harm), Paris Opéra–Comique Chorus IMP Masters ▲ IMP MCD61

Gregoire, Thierry (alt)
Palestrina, G.:Sacred Music, w. Catherine Greuillet (sop), Pierre Sciema (alt), Bruno Boterf (ten), Joel Suhubiette (ten), Jean–Luc Baudoin (ten), Jean–Claude Sarragosse (bass), Laurent Stewart (org), Françoise Lasserre (cnd), Champagne–Ardenne Akademia Regional Vocal Ensemble—Ave maria; Salve regina; Vergine bella; Vergine saggia; Virgine pura; Virgine santa; Vergine sola; Vergine chiara; Vergine, quante lagrime; Vergine, tale è terra; Ave mundi spes; Ave regina coelorum; Alma redemptoris mater; Regina coieli laetare; Salve regina; Magnificat; others *(rec Convent of the Annunciation Dominican Church, Paris, Jan., 1994)* Pierre Verany ▲ PVY 794041 [DDD]

Gregoire, Vincent (ct)
Sebastiani, J.:St. Matthew Passion, w. Greta de Reyghere (sop), Stéphane van Dijck (ten), Hervé Lamy (ten—Evangéliste), Max van Egmond (bass—Christ), P. Pierlot (cnd), Ricercar Consort Ricercar ▲ 160144

Gregor, József (bass)
Bartók, B.:Cant Profana, "The Giant Stags", w. József Réti (ten), A. Dorati (cnd), Budapest SO, Hungarian Radio–TV Chorus Hungaroton ▲ HCD 31503 [ADD]
Cimarosa, D.:Il Maestro di cappella, w. T. Pál (cnd), Corelli CO [I] Hungaroton ▲ HCD 12573 [DDD]
Giordano, U.:Fedora, w. V. Kincses (sop), E. Martón (sop), J. Carreras (ten), G. Patanè (cnd), Hungarian Radio–TV SO, Hungarian Radio–TV Chorus [I] CBS 2–▲ M2K 42181 [DDD]
Kodály, Z.:Háry János, w. T. Takács (mez), S. Sólyom–Nagy (bar), J. Ferencsik (cnd), Hungarian State Opera Orch [Hun] Hungaroton 2–▲ HCD 12837/38
Liszt, F.:Missa solemnis, w. V. Kincses (mez), T. Takács (mez), G. Korondy (ten), A. Ferencsik (cnd), Budapest SO, Budapest Sym Chorus [L] Hungaroton ▲ HCD 11861
Pergolesi, G.B.:La serva padrona, w. K. Farkas (sop), P. Németh (cnd), Capella Savaria [period instrs] [F,I] Hungaroton ▲ HCD 12846 [DDD]
Puccini, G.:Tosca (sels), w. E. Marton (sop), B. Heja (trb), J. Carreras (ten), F. Gerdesits (ten), J. Pons (bar), J. Nemeth (bar), M. Tilson Thomas (cnd), Hungarian State Orch, Hungarian Radio–TV Chorus *(rec Budapest, Dec. 14–22, 1988)* Sony Classical ("Opera Highlights" series) ▲ SMK 53500 [DDD]
Schumann, R.:Requiem, Op. 148, w. E. Andor (sop), Barlay (sgr), Korondy (sgr), M. Forrai (cnd), Hungarian State Orch, Budapest Chorus [L] Hungaroton ▲ HCD 11809
Schumann, R.:Requiem Mignon, w. E. Andor (sop), Barlay (sgr), Korondy (sgr), M. Forrai (cnd), Hungarian State Orch, Budapest Chorus [L] Hungaroton ▲ HCD 11809
Telemann, G.P.:Der Schulmeister, w. T. Pál (cnd), Corelli CO, Schola Hungarica Boys' Chorus [G] Hungaroton ▲ HCD 12573 [DDD]

Gregoriam, G. (ten)
Prokofiev, S.:War & Peace, w. Y. Prokina (sop), O. Borodina (mez), A. Gergalov (bar), V. Gergiev (cnd), Kirov Orch, Kirov Opera Chorus [R] Philips 3–▲ 434097–2

Greindl, Josef (bass)
Beethoven, L. van:Fidelio, w. K. Flagstad (sop), J. Patzak (ten), P. Schöffler (b–bar), W. Furtwängler (cnd), Vienna PO, Vienna State Opera Chorus [G] *(rec live 1950)* Arkadia 2–▲ 354
Beethoven, L. van:Fidelio, w. K. Flagstad (sop), J. Patzak (ten), W. Furtwängler (cnd), Vienna PO, Vienna State Opera Chorus EMI Classics 2–▲ CDC 64901

▲ = CD ♦ = Enhanced CD Δ = MD ▮ = Cassette Tape ▯ = DCC

Greindl, Josef (bass) (cont.)

Beethoven, L. van:Fidelio, w. K. Flagstad (sop), J. Patzak (ten), P. Schöffler (b–bar), W. Furtwängler (cnd), Vienna PO, Vienna State Opera Chorus [G] *(rec live, Salzburg 8/5/50)* Verona 2–▲ 27044/45 (m) [AAD]

Flotow, F. von:Martha, w. Erna Berger (sop), Peter Anders (ten), Eugene Fuchs (bar), J. Schüler (cnd), Berlin German Opera Orch, Berlin German Opera Chorus Phonographe 2–▲ PHG 5050

Flotow, F. von:Martha, w. E. Berger (sop), P. Anders (ten), E. Fuchs (bar), J. Schüler (cnd), Berlin State Opera Orch *(rec 1944)* Berlin Classics 2–▲ BER 2163 [ADD]

Haydn, J.:Mass 3, "Cäcilienmesse", w. Maria Stader (sop), Marga Höffgen (cta), Richard Holm (ten), E. Jochum (cnd), Bavarian RSO, Bavarian Radio Chorus Deutsche Grammophon 2–▲ 437383–2 [ADD]

The Legendary Singers at Lindenoper Berlin (1927–1945)—, w. Gitta Alpar (sop), Erna Berger (sop), Tiana Lemnitz (sop), Maria Müller (sop), Margarete Klose (cta), Peter Anders (ten), Max Lorenz (ten), Walter Ludwig (ten), Lauritz Melchior (ten), Rudolf Schock (ten), Franz Völker (ten), Willi Domgraf–Fassb *(rec 1927; 1937; 1941–45)* Minerva ▲ MN A21 [ADD]

Mozart, W.A.:Don Giovanni, w. L. Welitsch (sop), I. Seefried (sop), E. Schwarzkopf (sop), A. Dermota (ten), E. Kunz (bar), T. Gobbi (bar), A. Poell (b–bar), W. Furtwängler (cnd), Vienna PO, Vienna State Opera Chorus *(rec 1950)* Laudis 3–▲ LDS 4001 [AAD]

Mozart, W.A.:Entführung, w. S. Barabas (sop), R. Streich (sop), A. Dermota (ten), H. Krebs (ten), F. Fricsay (cnd), Berlin RSO, Berlin Radio Chorus [G] *(rec Jesus–Christuskirche, Berlin–Dahlem, Dec. 19–21, 1949)* Myto 2–▲ 2 MCD 92361 [ADD]

Mozart, W.A.:Missa, K.317, w. Maria Stader (sop), Sieglinde Wagner (mez), Helmut Krebs (ten), I. Markevitch (cnd), Berlin PO, St. Hedwig's Cathedral Choir Deutsche Grammophon 2–▲ 437383–2

Mozart, W.A.:Zauberflöte, w. I. Seefried (sop–Pamina), W. Lipp (sop—Queen of the Night), A. Dermota (ten—Tamino), E. Kunz (bar—Papageno), J. Greindl (bass—Sarastro), W. Furtwängler (cnd), Vienna PO, Vienna State Opera Chorus [G] *(rec live, Salzburg, Aug. 6, 1951)* Foyer 3–▲ FOY 2003 [AAD]

Mozart, W.A.:Zauberflöte, w. I. Seefried (sop–Pamina), W. Lipp (sop—Queen of the Night), A. Dermota (ten—Tamino), E. Kunz (bar—Papageno), J. Greindl (bass—Sarastro), W. Furtwängler (cnd), Vienna PO, Vienna State Opera Chorus *(rec live 1951)* EMI Classics ▲ CDMC 65356

Mozart, W.A.:Zauberflöte, w. Wilma Lipp (sop), Irmgard Seefried (sop), Peter Klein (ten), Walther Ludwig (ten), Karl Schmitt–Walter (bar), Paul Schöffler (sgr), W. Furtwängler (cnd), Vienna PO, Vienna State Opera Chorus *(rec 1949)* Music & Arts 3–▲ CD 882 [AAD]

Mozart, W.A.:Zauberflöte, w. I. Seefried (sop–Pamina), W. Lipp (sop—Queen of the Night), A. Dermota (ten—Tamino), E. Kunz (bar—Papageno), J. Greindl (bass—Sarastro), W. Furtwängler (cnd), Vienna PO, Vienna State Opera Chorus [G] *(rec live, Salzburg, Aug. 6, 1951)* Arkadia 3–▲ 361 [ADD]

Mozart, W.A.:Zauberflöte, w. I. Seefried (sop–Pamina), W. Lipp (sop—Queen of the Night), A. Dermota (ten—Tamino), E. Kunz (bar—Papageno), J. Greindl (bass—Sarastro), H. von Karajan (cnd), Vienna PO, Musikfreunde Chorus [without dialogue; G] *(rec 1950)* EMI Classics ("Studio" series) 2–▲ CDHB 69631 (m)

Mozart, W.A.:Zauberflöte (sels), w. I. Seefried (sop), W. Lipp (sop), W. Ludwig (ten), K. Schmitt–Walter (bar), W. Furtwängler (cnd), Vienna PO, Vienna State Opera Chorus—Ov. & 11 arias *(rec live, Salzburg, July, 27, 1949)* Arkadia 3–▲ 361 [ADD]

Orff, C.:De temporum fine comoedia, w. C. Ludwig (mez), P. Schreier (ten), H. von Karajan (cnd), Cologne RSO, Cologne Radio Chorus [L] Deutsche Grammophon ("20th Century Classics" series) ▲ 429859–2 [ADD]

Schoeck, O.:Das Schloss Dürande (sels), w. Maria Cebotari (sop—Gabriele), Marta Fuchs (sop—Gräfin Morvaille), Brigitte Fassbaender (mez—Renald Willi Domgraf), Rut Berglund (cta—Priorin), Peter Anders (ten—Armand), Benno Arnold (ten—Jäger), Josef Greindl (bass—Nicole), Hans Wrana (bass—Jäger), Vasso Argyris (sgr—Volksredner), Otto Hüsch (sgr—Wildhüter), Leo Laschet (sgr—Jäger), Fritz Marcks (sgr—Jäger), Felix Schneider (sgr—Jäger), R. Heger (cnd)—Text; Ich kann es nicht glauben [from Act 1]; Text; Heil dir, du Feuerquelle [from Act 2]; Text; Gesucht und nicht gefunden [from Act 3]; Text; Der Jäger ist frei! [Act 3 Finale]; Text; Sie kommen mit Flinten und Stangen [Act 4]; Text; Du Narr des vermeintlichen Rechts [Act 4 finale]; Text *(rec live, Apr 1943)* Jecklin ▲ JD 692

Verdi, G.:Otello, w. Carla Martinis (sop—Desdemona), Sieglinde Wagner (mez—Emilia), Anton Dermota (ten—Cassio), Paul Schöffler (ten—Iago), Ramon Vinay (ten—Otello), Josef Greindl (bass—Lodovico), W. Furtwängler (cnd), Vienna PO, Vienna State Opera Chorus *(rec live, Salzburg Festival, Aug 7, 1951)* EMI Classics ▲ CDMB 65751

Verdi, G.:Rigoletto, w. E. Berger (sop), R. Jacobs (alt), H. Roswaenge (ten), H. Schlusnus (bass), R. Heger (cnd), Berlin State Opera Orch, Berlin State Opera Chorus [G] *(rec 11/20–22/44)* Preiser 2–▲ 90036 (m) [AAD]

Wagner, R.:Choruses, w. E. Schärtel (mez), W. Pitz (cnd), Bayreuth Festival Orch, Bayreuth Festival Chorus—choruses from Lohengrin, Götterdämmerung, Parsifal, Fliegende Holländer, Tannhäuser, Meistersinger Deutsche Grammophon ("Resonance" series) ▲ 429169–2 [ADD]

Wagner, R.:Der fliegende Holländer, w. L. Rysanek (sop), G. London (bar), W. Sawallisch (cnd), Bayreuth Festival Orch, Bayreuth Festival Chorus [G] *(rec live, Bayreuth 1959)* Melodram 2–▲ MEL 26101

Wagner, R.:Der fliegende Holländer, w. Annelies Kupper (sop—Senta), Sieglinde Wagner (mez—Mary), Ernst Haefliger (ten—Steersman), Wolfgang Windgassen (ten—Erik), Josef Metternich (ten—Dutchman), Josef Greindi (bass—Daland), F. Fricsay (cnd), Berlin RIAS SO, Berlin RIAS Chamber Choir *(rec 1953)* Deutsche Grammophon 2–▲ 439714–2 (m) [ADD]

Wagner, R.:Götterdämmerung (sels), w. A. Varnay (sop), E. Grümmer (sop), B. Aldenhoff (ten), H. Uhde (bar), G. Frick (bass), H. Knappertsbusch (cnd), Bavarian State Opera Orch, Bayreuth Festival Orch, Bavarian State Opera Chorus, Bayreuth Festival Chorus [G] *(rec live 1955 & 1957)* Melodram 4–▲ MEL 46106 (m) [AAD]

Wagner, R.:Lohengrin, w. E. Steber (sop), A. Varnay (sop), W. Windgassen (ten), H. Uhde (bar), J. Keilberth (cnd), Bayreuth Festival Orch, Bayreuth Festival Chorus *(rec live, Bayreuth Festival, 1953)* Teldec ("Historic" series) 4–▲ 93674

Wagner, R.:Lohengrin, w. H. Braun (sop—Ortrud), T. Epperle (sop—Elsa von Brabant), P. Anders (ten—Lohengrin), C. Kronenberg (bar—Frederich von Telramund), J. Greindl (bass—Heinrich der Vogler), R. Kraus (cnd), Cologne RSO, Cologne Radio Chorus *(rec Nov. 1951)* Myto 3–▲ MCD 93485

Wagner, R.:Die Meistersinger von Nürnberg, w. E. Grümmer (sop), W. Windgassen (ten), T. Adam (b–bar), H. Knappertsbusch (cnd), Bayreuth Festival Orch, Bayreuth Festival Chorus [G] *(rec live, Bayreuth, 1960)* Melodram 4–▲ MEL 46103

Wagner, R.:Die Meistersinger von Nürnberg, w. Maria Müller (sop), Max Lorenz (ten), Jaro Prohaska (bar), Bayreuth Festival Orch, Bayreuth Festival Chorus *(rec live, July–Aug 1943)* Grammofono 2000 4–▲ GRM 78602

Wagner, R.:Das Rheingold, w. E. Grümmer (sop), R. Gorr (mez), A. Andersson (ten), S. Konya (ten), T. Adam (b–bar), H. Hotter (b–bar), H. Knappertsbusch (cnd), Bayreuth Festival Orch, Bayreuth Festival Chorus [G] *(rec live 1958)* Arkadia 2–▲ 441 [AAD]

Wagner, R.:Der Ring des Nibelungen, w. Gré Brouwenstein (sop—Freia/Sieglinde), Ilse Hollweg (sop—Waldvogel), Gerda Lammers (sop—Ortlinde), Paula Lenchner (sop—Wellgunde/Gerhilde), Hilde Scheppan (sop—Helmwige), Astrid Varnay (sop—Brünnilde/3rd Norn), Lore Wissmann (sop—Woglinde), Maria von Ilosvay (mez—Flosshilde/Schwertleite/2nd Norn), Louise Charlotte Kamps (mez—Siegrune), Jean Madeira (mez—Erda/Rossweisse/1st Norn), Georgine van Milinkovic (mez—Fricka/Grimgerde), Elisabeth Schärtel (mez—Waltraute), Paul Kuën (ten—Mime), Ludwig Suthaus (ten—Loge), Josef Traxel (ten—Froh), Wolfgang Windgassen (ten—Siegmund/Siegfried), Alfons Herwig (bar—Donner), Hermann Uhde (bar—Gunther), Hans Hotter (b–bar—Wotan), Gustav Neidlinger (b–bar—Alberich), Josef Griendl (bass—Fasolt/Hunding/Hagen), Arnold van Mill (bass—Fafner), H. Knappertsbusch (cnd), Bayreuth Festival Orch, Bayreuth Festival Chorus *(rec live, Bayreuth, Aug 13–17, 1956)* Golden Melodram 14–▲ GM 1.001 [ADD]

Wagner, R.:Der Ring des Nibelungen (sels), w. Birgit Nilsson (sop—Brünnhilde), Leonie Rysanek (sop—Sieglinde), James King (ten—Siegmund), Wolfgang Windgassen (ten), Theo Adam (b–bar—Wotan), Gustav Neidlinger (b–bar), K. Böhm (cnd), Bayreuth Festival Orch *(rec Bayreuth, 1967)* Philips 2–▲ 454020–2

Wagner, R.:Siegfried, w. A. Varnay (sop), W. Windgassen (ten), A. Andersson (ten), G. Stoltze (ten), H. Hotter (b–bar), H. Knappertsbusch (cnd), Bayreuth Festival Orch, Bayreuth Festival Chorus [G] *(rec live 1958)* Arkadia 4–▲ 443 [AAD]

Wagner, R.:Tannhäuser, w. V. de Los Angeles (sop), G. Bumbry (mez), W. Windgassen (ten), G. Stolze (ten), D. Fischer–Dieskau (bar), T. Adam (b–bar), F. Crass (bass), W. Sawallisch (cnd), Bayreuth Festival Orch, Bayreuth Festival Chorus [G] *(rec 1961)* Myto 3–▲ MCD 93277

Greindl, Josef (bass) (cont.)

Wagner, R.:Tannhäuser, w. A. Silja (sop), G. Bumbry (mez), W. Windgassen (ten), E. Wächter (bar), W. Sawallisch (cnd), Bayreuth Festival Orch, Bayreuth Festival Chorus [Dresden version with Paris Venusberg music] [G] Philips 3–▲ 434607–2 [ADD]

Wagner, R.:Tannhäuser, w. G. Brouwenstijn (sop), R. Vinay (ten), D. Fischer–Dieskau (bar), J. Keilberth (cnd), Bayreuth Festival Orch, Bayreuth Festival Chorus *(rec live, Bayreuth, 1954)* Melodram 3–▲ MEL 36105

Grek, Blazej (ten)

Orff, C.:Carmina burana, w. A. M. Dahl (sop), J. Wolanski (bass), I. Stupel (cnd), Artur Rubinstein PO, Artur Rubinstein Phil Chorus *(rec Apr. 1991)* Danacord ▲ DACOCD 400 [DDD]

Grella, Bruno (bar)

Gounod, C.:Faust, w. Renata Scotto (sop—Margherita), Anna di Stasio (mez—Marta), Flaviano Labò (ten—Faust), Edoardo Gimenez (ten—Siebel), Piero Cappuccilli (bar—Valentino), Bruno Grella (bar—Wagner), Ruggero Raimondi (bass—Mefistofele), M. Gusella (cnd), Margherita Theater Orch, Margherita Theater Chorus *(rec Genova, 1970)* Golden Age of Opera 2–▲ GAO 170/71 [ADD]

Gremillion, Randall (bass)

Blumenfeld, H.:Ange de flamme et de glaçe, w. Christine Schadeberg (sop), G. Samuel (cnd), Cincinnati PO Centaur ▲ CRC 2277

Blumenfeld, H.:La Face cendrée, w. Christine Schadeberg (sop), G. Samuel (cnd), Cincinnati PO Centaur ▲ CRC 2277

Blumenfeld, H.:Illuminations, w. Christine Schadeberg (sop), G. Samuel (cnd), Cincinnati PO Centaur ▲ CRC 2277

Grenier, G. (voc)

Ashley, R.:Yellow Man with Heart with Wings, w. R. Ashley (English voc/all instrs except clavinet), "Blue" Gene Tyranny (clavinet) Lovely Music ▲ LCD 1003 [ADD]

Grenzberg, Willy (bar)

Armanini, M.:Poems, w. J. Zoltek (cnd), Bohuslav Martinů PO Chroma ▲ CHR CD 10001 [DDD]

Greuillet, Catherine (sop)

Palestrina, G.:Sacred Music, w. Thierry Gregoire (alt), Pierre Sciema (alt), Bruno Boterf (ten), Joel Suhubiette (ten), Jean–Luc Baudoin (ten), Jean–Claude Sarragosse (bass), Laurent Stewart (org), Françoise Lasserre (cnd), Champagne–Ardenne Akademia Regional Vocal Ensemble—Ave maria; Salve regina; Vergine bella; Vergine saggia; Virgine pura; Virgine santa; Vergine sola; Vergine chiara; Vergine, quante lagrime; Vergine, tale è terra; Ave mundi spes; Ave regina coelorum; Alma redemptoris mater; Regina coieli laetare; Salve regina; Magnificat; others *(rec Convent of the Annunciation Dominican Church, Paris, Jan., 1994)* Pierre Verany ▲ PVY 794041 [DDD]

Grey, Madeleine (sop)

The Art Of, w. Elie Cohen (cnd), Maurice Ravel (cnd) InSync ■ C 4143

Canteloube, J.:Songs of Auvergne, w. Cohen (cnd), *(orch unknown)* *(rec 1930)* InSync ■ C 4143

Ravel, M.:Chansons madécasses, w. Ravel Ensemble [F] *(rec 1932)* InSync ■ C 4143

Ravel, M.:Chants populaires, w. M. Ravel (pno)—No. 4, Chanson hébraîque [He] *(rec 1932)* InSync ■ C 4143

Ravel, M.:Melodies hébraïques, w. M. Ravel (pno) *(rec 1932)* InSync ■ C 4143

Griffelt, James (ten)

Warlock, P.:The Curlew, w. Haffner String Quartet ASV ("Quicksilva" series) ▲ ASQ 6143 [DDD]

Warlock, P.:Songs Ten, w. Haffner String Quartet ASV ("Quicksilva" series) ▲ ASQ 6143 [DDD]

Griffett, James (ten)

Beethoven, L. van:Songs, w. Franzjosef Maier (vn), Rudolf Mandalka (vc), Bradford Tracey (pno)—To the Aeolian Harp; Sally in Our Alley; The Soldier; Sympathy; The Farewell Song; Come, Darby Dear, Easy; The Shepherd's Song; The British Light Dragoons Ars Musici ▲ 1142 [ADD]

Blow, J.:Songs, w. T. Penrose (ct), M. Venhoda (cnd), Chamber Ensemble of Early Instruments—Welcome Ev'ry Guest; Ah, Heav'n! What Is't I Hear; Loving Above Himself; If I My Celia Could Persuade; The Fair Lover And His Black Mistress; Why Weeps Asteria?; The Spheres, Those Instruments Divine; Hark! How the Wakened Strings Resound Campion ▲ 1323 [DDD]

Britten, H.:Canticles I–V, w. P. Esswood (ct), J. Ridgway (pno), T. Walker (gtr)—Canticle II IMP Masters ▲ IMPMCD 57 [DDD]

Britten, H.:Folksong Arrs, w. P. Esswood (ct), J. Ridgway (pno), T. Walker (gtr) IMP Masters ▲ IMPMCD 57 [DDD]

Britten, H.:Songs from the Chinese, w. P. Esswood (ct), T. Walker (gtr) IMP Masters ▲ IMPMCD 57 [DDD]

The Essential Gregorian Chant, w. James Griffett (ten), Ian Partridge (ten), Michael George (b–bar), Stephen Roberts (b–bar), Gordon Jones (bass), Pro Cantione Antique [cnd:James O'Donnell] United ▲ UNI 88035 [DDD]

The Essential Gregorian Chant, w. Pro Cantione Antiqua [cnd:James O'Donnell], Ian Partridge (ten), Stephen Roberts (bar), Michael George (bass), Gordon Jones (bass) Cala ▲ CAL CACD 88035 [DDD]

Gregorian Lent & Easter, w. Pro Cantione Antiqua [cnd:James O'Donnell], I. Partridge (ten), S. Roberts (bar), M. George (bass), G. Jones (bass) *(rec All Saints, East Finchley, Dec 7–9, 1993)* United ▲ UNI 88016 [DDD]

Handel, G.F.:Messiah, w. Ruth Holton (sop), Vanessa Williamson (mez), Lawrence Albert (bass), U. Walser (tpt), M. Brown (cnd), Gioia della Musica, Bmensky Akademicky Sbor Allegro 2–▲ ALGDPCD 1068 [DDD]

Handel, G.F.:Messiah (sels), w. Ruth Holton (sop), Vanessa Williamson (mez), L. Albert (bass), M. Brown (cnd), Gioia della Musica, Bmensky Akademicky Sbor Allegro ▲ ALG PCD 1078 [DDD]

Haydn, J.:Canzonettas, w. Bradford Tracey (pno)—Nos. 25–36 Teldec ▲ TEL SEL 97503 [ADD]

Haydn, J.:Songs, w. Franzjosef Maier (vn), Rudolf Mandalka (vc), Bradford Tracey (pno)—Will Ye Got to Flanders; The Glancing of Her Apron; Jockie & Sandy; O Can Ye Sew Cushions; Margret's Ghost; Up in the Morning Early; Barbara Allen; Green Grow the Rashes; Lizae Baillie; Blue Bonnets Ars Musici ▲ 1142 [ADD]

Kozeluch, L.:Original Scottish Airs, w. J. Krejci (vn), P. Hejny (vc), R. Zelenka (pno) [arr. J. Griffett; lyrics by Robert Burns]—Nae gentle dames; Here's a health to ane I lo'e dear; Ye banks and braes of bonie Doon; Blythe, blythe and merry was she; Lord Gregory; My Nannie's awa'; And ye shall walk in silk attire; Turn again, thou fair Eliza; Contented wi' little; The day returns; On a bank of flowers; Adieu ye streams; All Water; My love she's but a lassie yet; True hearted was he, the sad swain o' the Yarrow; She's fair and fause; O this is no my aine lassie; The Tears of Scotland Campion ▲ 1322 [DDD]

Mozart, W.A.:Ave verum corpus, w. E. Mirgova (sop), M. Kozená (cta), J. Klecker (bass), A. Kroper (cnd), Prague Concertino Nutturno Allegro ▲ ALG PCD 1022 [DDD]

Mozart, W.A.:Requiem, w. E. Mirgova (sop), M. Kozená (cta), J. Klecker (bass), A. Kroper (cnd), Prague Concertino Nutturno, Brnensky Academy Choir Allegro ▲ ALG PCD 1022 [DDD]

Purcell, H.:Songs, w. T. Penrose (ct)—Ah, How Happy We Are; So! When the Glittering Queen of the Night; In Vain the Amorous Flute; Yes, Daphne; Crown the Altar; After War's Alarms Repeated Campion ▲ 1323 [DDD]

Shakespearian Songbook, w. James Griffett (ten), Brian Wright (lt) Carlton ("Musick's Monument" series) ▲ MSK 6500022

Stainer, J.:The Crucifixion, w. M. George (bass), A. Newberry (vc), S. Vann (cnd), Peterborough Cathedral Choir ASV Quicksilva ▲ ASQ 6100 [ADD]

Griffey, Anthony (ten)

Starer, R.:Night Thoughts, w. Theresa Santiago (sop), Jennifer Hines (mez), Neil Michaels (bar), Adelaide Roberts (pno), Edgar Roberts (pno) Albany ▲ TROY 151 [DDD]

Griffies, E. (sgr)

Berlin, I.:Miss Liberty, w. E. Albert (sgr), A. McLerie (sgr), M. McCarty (sgr) [1949 Broadway cast] Sony Broadway ▲ SK 48015 ■ ST 48015

Griffith, Beth (sop)

Cage, J.:Four Walls, w. John McAlpine (pno) *(rec DeutschlandRadio Cologne Recording House, Apr 29–30, 1994)* Largo ▲ 5132 [DDD]

Griffith, David (ten)

La Montaine, J.:Lessons of Christmas, w. Polly Jo Baker (sop), Carol Baum (hp), Scott Shepherd (perc), J. Montaine (cnd), Fredonia Singers Fredonia Discs ▲ FDCD 14

Griffith, Lisa (sop)
Orff, C.:Carmina burana, w. Ulrich Ress (ten), Thomas Mohr (bar), M. Tang (cnd), Royal Flemish PO, Frankfurt Figuralchor, Frankfurt Children's Choir, Frankfurt Choral Society, Goethe Academy Children's Choir *(rec Oct. 1993)* Wergo ▲ WER 6602-2 [DDD]
Orff, C.:Carmina burana, w. Susan Roberts (sop), Frankfurt Kantorei, Frankfurt Singakademie Wergo 2-▲ WER 6275-2
Orff, C.:Catulli Carmina, w. Susan Roberts (sop), Frankfurt Kantorei, Frankfurt Singakademie Wergo ▲ WER 6275-2
Orff, C.:Trionfo di Afrodite, w. Susan Roberts (sop), Frankfurt Kantorei, Frankfurt Singakademie Wergo ▲ WER 6275-2
Straus, O.:The Merry Nibelungs, w. Lisa Griffith (sop—Kriemhild), Gudrun Volkert (sop—Brunhilde), Daphne Evangelatos (cta—Ute), Gabriele Henkel (sgr—Giselher), Christine Mann (sgr—Vogel), Hein Heidbüchel (ten—Volker), Martin Gantner (sgr—Gunther), Gerd Grochowski (sgr—Dankwart), Michael Nowak (sgr—Siegfried), Josef Otten (sgr—Hagen), S. Köhler (cnd), Cologne RSO, Cologne Radio Chorus *(rec Cologne, Jan 31–Feb 17, 1995)* Capriccio ▲ 10752 [DDD]

Griffiths, Gwyn (bar)
Bizet, G.:Carmen (sels), w. M. Horne (sop), M. Molese (sgr), M. Pellegrini (sgr), D. Bowman (bar), F. Egerton (ten), H. Lewis (cnd), Royal PO, Royal Liverpool Phil Choir IMP Collectors Series ▲ IMPX 9016 [AAD]
Mozart, W.A.:Nozze di Figaro, w. S. Jurinac (sop), G. Sciutti (sop), R. Stevens (mez), M. Sinclair (cta), D. McCoshan (ten), H. Counod (ten), S. Bruscantini (b-bar), F. Calabrese (bass), V. Gui (cnd), Glyndebourne Festival Orch, Glyndebourne Festival Chorus Classics for Pleasure ▲ CDCFP 4724 [ADD]

Griffiths, Neil (ten)
Verdi, G.:La traviata, w. Angela Gheorghiu (sop—Violetta), Leah-Marian Jones (mez—Flora Bervoix), Gillian Knight (mez—Annina), Robin Leggate (ten—Gastone), Frank Lopardo (ten—Alfredo Germont), Rodney Gibson (ten—Servo di Flora), Neil Griffiths (ten—Giuseppe), Mark Beesley (bar—Dottore Grenvile), Leo Nucci (bar—Giorgio Germont), Richard Van Allan (bass—Barone Douphol), Roderick Earle (bass—Marquese d'Obigny), Bryan Secombe (bass—Commissionario), G. Solti (cnd), Royal Opera House Orch, Royal Opera House Chorus Covent Garden *(rec live, Royal Opera House, Covent Garden, Dec. 1994)* London 2-▲ 448119-2

Grigorescu, Elena (sop)
Schreker, F.:Der ferne Klang, w. T. Harper (ten), M. Halász (cnd), Hagen PO, Hagen Phil Chorus [G] Marco Polo 2-▲ 8.223270/271 [DDD]

Grigorian, Gegam (ten)
Tchaikovsky, P.:Iolanta, w. Galina Gorchakova (sop), Nikolai Gassiev (ten), Dmitri Hvorostovsky (bar), Nikolai Putilin (bar), Sergei Alexashkin (bass), Gennady Bezzubenkov (bass), Larissa Diadkova (sgr), Olga Korzhenskaya (sgr), Tatyana Kravtsova (sgr), V. Gergiev (cnd), Kirov Opera Orch, Kirov Opera Chorus *(rec Mariinsky Theatre, St. Petersburg)* Philips 2-▲ 442796-2
Tchaikovsky, P.:Queen of Spades, w. M. Gulegina (sop), O. Borodina (mez), V. Gergiev (cnd), Kirov Opera Orch, Kirov Opera Chorus Philips ▲ 438141-2

Grigorova, Petya (sop)
Keiser, R.:Croesus, w. M. Klietmann (ten), S. Mizugushi (bass), R. Clemencic (cnd), Clemencic Consort, La Cappella Vocal Ensemble [G] Nuova Era ("Ancient Music" series) 2-▲ 6934/35 [DDD]

Grigoryev, Anton (ten)
Mussorgsky, M.:Boris Godunov, w. Irina Arkhipova (mez—Marina Mnishek), Evgenya Verbitskhaya (mez—Nurse to Xenia), Valentina Klepatskaya (sgr—Fyodor), Tamara Sorokina (sgr—Xenia), Anton Grigoryev (ten—Simpleton), Vladimir Ivanovsky (ten—Grigory, the Pretender), Gyorgy Shulpin (bar—Prince Shuisky), Alexey Geleva (bass—Varlaam), Ivan Petrov (bass—Boris Godounov), Mark Reshetin (bass—Pimen), Alexi Ivanov (sgr—Andrei Shchelkalov), Evgeny Kibkalo (sgr—Rangoni), A. Melik-Pashayev (cnd), Bolshoi Theater Orch, Bolshoi Theater Chorus *(rec Moscow, 1962)* Melodiya ("The Russian Opera" series) 3-▲ 74321-29349-2 [ADD]

Grilli, Umberto (ten)
Donizetti, G.:Belisario, w. L. Gencer (sop), M. Pecile (cta), G. Taddei (bar), N. Zaccaria (bass), G. Gavazzeni (cnd), Venice Teatro La Fenice Orch, Venice Teatro La Fenice Chorus [I] *(rec live, Venice 5/14/69)* Melodram 2-▲ MEL 27051 [AAD]
Donizetti, G.:Belisario, w. L. Gencer (sop), M. Pecile (cta), G. Taddei (bar), N. Zaccaria (bass), G. Gavazzeni (cnd), Venice Teatro La Fenice Orch, Venice Teatro La Fenice Chorus [I] *(rec live in Venice, 5/14/69)* Verona 2-▲ 27048/49 (m) [ADD]
Donizetti, G.:Lucrezia Borgia (sels), w. L. Gencer (sop—Lucrezia), U. Grilli (ten—Gennaro), A. Camozzo (cnd), Bergamo Teatro Donizetti Orch—sels. *(rec live, 10/4/71)* Myto 2-▲ 2 MCD 92153 [ADD]
Donizetti, G.:Maria di Rohan, w. R. Scotto (sop—Maria), E. Zilio (mez—Armando di Gondi), U. Grilli (ten—Riccardo), R. Bruson (bar—Enrico), G. Gavazzeni (cnd), Venice Teatro La Fenice Orch, Venice Teatro La Fenice Chorus *(rec live Mar. 26, 1974)* Golden Age of Opera 2-▲ GAO 156/57 [ADD]
Rossini, G.:Elisabetta, regina d'Inghilterra, w. L. Gencer (sop), S. Geszty (sop), P. Bottazzo (ten), N. Sanzogno (cnd), Palermo Teatro Massimo Orch, Palermo Teatro Massimo Chorus [I] *(rec live, 11/24/70)* Myto 2-▲ 2 MCD 90530 [ADD]

Grillo, Joann (sop)
Flagello, N.:She Walks In Beauty, w. N. Flagello (cnd), Rome SO Phoenix ▲ PHCD 125 [ADD]
Verdi, G.:La forza del destino, w. E. Farrell (sop), F. Corelli (ten), A. Colzani (bar), E. Flagello (bass), A. Guadagno (cnd), *(orch unknown)* [I] *(rec live, Philadelphia 4/14/65)* Standing Room Only 2-▲ SRO 826-2 [ADD]

Grimm, Anne (sop)
Biber, H. von:Requiem à 15, w. E. Bongers (sop), K. Wessel (alt), P. de Groot (alt), M. Reyans (ten), S. Davies (ten), R. Steur (bass), K.-J. de Koning (bass), T. Koopman (cnd), Amsterdam Baroque Orch, Amsterdam Baroque Choir Erato ▲ 91725
Biber, H. von:Vesperae longiores ac breviores una cum litaniis Laurentanis, w. E. Bongers (sop), K. Wessel (alt), P. de Groot (alt), M. Reyans (ten), S. Davies (ten), R. Steur (bass), K.-J. de Koning (bass), T. Koopman (cnd), Amsterdam Baroque Orch, Amsterdam Baroque Choir Erato ▲ 91725

Grimm, Hans Günter (bass)
Rossini, G.:Petite messe solennelle, w. G. de la Cruz (sop), M. L. Gilles (cta), H. D. Saretzki (ten), W. A. Albert (cnd), Northwest German PO, Northwest German Phil Choir [orchestral version] [L] *(rec ca. 1970)* Koch Schwann ▲ 3-1345-2 [ADD]

Gripekoven, Margot (sop)
Lortzing, A.:Zar und Zimmermann, w. M. Gripekoven (sop—Marie), E. Mayer (cta—Widow Browe), H. Buchta (ten—Peter Ivanov), H. Schmid-Berikoven (ten—Marquis de Chateauneuf), G. Hann (b-bar—Tsar Peter I), W. Strienz (b-bar—Van Bett), B. Müller (bass) Myto 2-▲ MCD 943103

Grishko, Vladimir (ten)
Tchaikovsky, P.:The Snow Maiden, w. Irina Mishura-Lekhtman (mez), N. Järvi (cnd), Detroit SO, Univ Musical Society Choral Union Chandos ▲ CHAN 9324 [DDD]

Grissom, Jan (sop)
Moore, D.:Ballad of Baby Doe, w. Jan Grissom (sop—Baby Doe), Dana Kreuger (mez—Augusta), Myrna Paris (cta—Mama), Brian Steele (bar—Horace), Mark Freiman (b-bar—W. J. Bryan), J. Moriarty (cnd), Central City Opera Orch, Central City Opera Chorus *(rec Central City, CO)* Newport Classic 2-▲ NPD 85593/2 [ADD]

Grist, Reri (sop)
Donizetti, G.:L'elisir d'amore (sels), w. Luciano Pavarotti (ten), Sesto Bruscantini (bar), Ingvar Wixell (bar), Maria Ambrosio (sgr), G. Patanè (cnd), San Francisco War Memorial Opera House Orch, San Francisco War Memorial Opera House Chorus *(rec live, San Francisco, 1969)* Budget ("The Greatest Voice in Opera" series) ▲ SYP 109
Mahler, G.:Sym 4, w. L. Bernstein (cnd), New York PO *(rec 1960)* Sony Classical ("Bernstein:The Royal Edition" series) ▲ SMK 47579 [ADD]

Grist, Reri (sop) (cont.)
Mozart, W.A.:Arias, w. Arleen Augér (sop), Kathleen Battle (sop), Irma Beilke (sop), Helena Braun (sop), Lisa Della Casa (sop), Maria Cebotari (sop), Ileana Cotrubas (sop), Helen Donath (sop), Mirella Freni (sop), Edita Gruberova (sop), Elisabeth Grümmer (sop), Hilde Güden (sop), Ingeborg Hallstein (sop), Luise Helletsgruber (sop), Gundula Janowitz (sop), Sena Jurinac (sop), Erika Köth (sop), Evelyn Lear (sop), Wilma Lipp (sop), Margaret Marshall (sop), Edith Mathis (sop), Jarmila Novotna (sop), Margherita Perras (sop), Lucia Popp (sop), Elisabeth Rethberg (sop), Anneliese Rothenberger (sop), Elisabeth Schumann (sop), Elisabeth Schwarzkopf (sop), Graziella Sciutti (sop), Irmgard Seefried (sop), Graziella Sciutti (sop), Julia Varady (sop), Agnes Baltsa (mez), Margit Bokor (mez), Brigitte Fassbaender (mez), Christa Ludwig (mez), Ann Murray (mez), Francisco Araiza (ten), Anton Dermota (ten), Helge Rosvaenge (ten), Rudolf Schock (ten), Peter Schreier (ten), Leopold Simoneau (ten), Eric Tappy (ten), Richard Tauber (ten), Gösta Winbergh (ten), Josef Witt (ten), Fritz Wunderlich (ten), Christian Boesch (bar), Willy Domgraf-Fassbaender (bar), Karl Dönch (bar), Dietrich Fischer-Dieskau (bar), Erich Kunz (bar), Eberhard Wächter (bar), Hans Hotter (b-bar), Paul Schöffler (b-bar), Cesare Siepi (b-bar), José Van Dam (b-bar), Walter Berry (bass), Geraint Evans (bass), Nicolai Ghiaurov (bass), Alexander Kipnis (bass), Richard Mayr (bass), Kurt Moll (bass), James Morris (bass), Ezio Pinza (bass), Martti Talvela (bass), Giorgio Tozzi (bass), Hans Duhan (sgr), Res Fischer (sgr), Marie Gerhart (sgr), *(various orchs & cnds)* —sels from Idomeneo, Die Entführung aus der Serail, Le nozze di Figaro, Don Giovanni, Così fan tutte, Die Zauberflöte & various arias Orfeo d'or ("Festspiel Dokumente" series) 5-▲ 408955
Mozart, W.A.:Così fan tutte, w. G. Janowitz (sop), B. Fassbaender (mez), P. Schreier (ten), H. Prey (bar), D. Fischer-Dieskau (bar), K. Böhm (cnd), Vienna PO *(rec live, 1972)* Foyer 2-▲ FOY 2066 [ADD]
Mozart, W.A.:Così fan tutte (sels), w. G. Janowitz (sop), B. Fassbaender (mez), P. Schreier (ten), H. Prey (bar), R. Panerai (bar), K. Böhm (cnd), Vienna PO, Vienna State Opera Chorus—scenes & arias Deutsche Grammophon ▲ 429824-2 [ADD]
Mozart, W.A.:Don Giovanni (sels), w. B. Nilsson (sop), M. Arroyo (sop), P. Schreier (ten), D. Fischer-Dieskau (bar), M. Talvela (bass), K. Böhm (cnd), Prague National Theater Orch IMP Collectors Series ▲ IMPX 9023 [AAD]
Mozart, W.A.:Entführung, w. Reri Grist (sop—Blondchen), Anneliese Rothenberger (sop—Konstanze), Gerhard Unger (ten—Pedrillo), Fritz Wunderlich (ten—Belmonte), Fernando Corena (bass—Osmin), Michael Heltau (nar—Selim), Z. Mehta (cnd), Vienna PO, Vienna State Opera Chorus *(rec July 28, 1965)* Orfeo d'or ("Festspiel Dokumente" series) 2-▲ 392952 (m)
Mozart, W.A.:Nozze di Figaro, w. E. Söderström (sop), T. Berganza (mez), G. Evans (bar), O. Klemperer (cnd), New Philharmonia Orch, John Alldis Choir EMI Classics 3-▲ CDMC 63849
Mozart, W.A.:Zauberflöte, w. Edita Gruberová (sop), Edith Mathis (sop), Rene Kollo (ten), Gerhard Unger (ten), Hermann Prey (bar), José Van Dam (b-bar), Peter Meven (bass), H. von Karajan (cnd), Vienna PO, Vienna State Opera Chorus *(rec live, Salzburg, July 26, 1974)* Arkadia 2-▲ 233
Rossini, G.:Il barbiere di Siviglia, w. F. Wunderlich (ten), E. Wächter (bar), O. Czerwenka (bass), Kunz (sgr), K. Böhm (cnd), Vienna State Opera Orch, Vienna State Opera Chorus *(rec live, Vienna 4/28/66)* Myto 2-▲ 2 MCD 91752 [ADD]
Verdi, G.:Un ballo in maschera, w. M. Arroyo (sop), F. Cossotto (mez), P. Domingo (ten), P. Cappuccilli (bar), R. Muti (cnd), New Philharmonia Orch, Royal Opera House Chorus Covent Garden [I] EMI Classics (Studio) 2-▲ CDMB 69576 [ADD]
Verdi, G.:Un ballo in maschera, w. Katia Ricciarelli (sop), Elizabeth Bainbridge (mez), Plácido Domingo (ten), Piero Cappuccilli (bar), C. Abbado (cnd), Royal Opera House Orch, Royal Opera House Chorus Covent Garden *(rec 1975)* Arkadia 2-▲ 488

Gritton, Susan (sop)
Britten, H.:A Boy Was Born, w. Catherine Wyn-Rogers (sgr), David Goode (org), Stephen Layton (cnd), Holst Singers Hyperion ▲ CDA 66825
Britten, H.:Choral Music, w. Catherine Wyn-Rogers (sgr), David Goode (org), Stephen Layton (cnd), Holst Singers—Christ's Nativity; A Shepherd's Carol; Jubilate in C Hyperion ▲ CDA 66825
Britten, H.:A Hymn to the Virgin, w. Catherine Wyn-Rogers (sgr), David Goode (org), Stephen Layton (cnd), Holst Singers Hyperion ▲ CDA 66825
Britten, H.:Purcell Realizations, w. Felicity Lott (sop), Sarah Walker (mez), James Bowman (alto), John Mark Ainsley (ten), Anthony Rolfe Johnson (ten), Richard Jackson (bass), Simon Keenlyside (bass), Ian Bostridge (sgr), Graham Johnson (pno) Hyperion 2-▲ CDA 67061/62
Britten, H.:Te Deum, w. Catherine Wyn-Rogers (sgr), David Goode (org), Stephen Layton (cnd), Holst Singers Hyperion ▲ CDA 66825
British Music on Hyperion, w. Parley of Instruments, Roy Goodman (cnd), John Mark Ainsley (ten), Graham Johnson (pno), Salomon Quartet, BBC Scottish SO, Anthony Rolfe Johnson (ten), Royal PO, St. Paul's Cathedral Choir, Nash Ensemble, Martyn Hill (ten), Susan Gritton (sop), et al. Hyperion ▲ HYP 15
Handel, G.F.:Arias, w. J. Bowman (ct), R. King (cnd), King's Consort—Yet can I hear that dulcet lay; How can I stay, when love invites; O fairest of 10 thousand fair; Great God! Who yet but darkly known; The raptur'd soul; Father of Heaven; Ov to Esther; O Lord, whose mercies numberless; What though I trace each herb; Martial Sym & Destructive War; Welcome as the dawn of day; Kind Heaven if virtue be thy care; Almighty pow'r; Tune your harps Hyperion ▲ CDA 66797
Handel, G.F.:Deborah, w. Y. Kenny (sop), C. Denley (mez), J. Bowman (alt), M. George (bass), R. King (cnd), King's Consort, Oxford New College Choir Hyperion 2-▲ CDA 66841 [DDD]
Handel, G.F.:Occasional Oratorio, w. Lisa Milne (sop), James Brown (ct), John Mark Ainsley (ten), Michael George (bass), R. King (cnd), King's Consort, New College Choir Oxford Hyperion 2-▲ CDA 66961/62
Purcell, H.:Anthems & Services, w. M. Kennedy (sop), E. O'Dwyer (trb), J. Goodman (trb), J. Bowman (ct), N. Short (ct), Rogers Covey-Crump (ten), C. Daniels (ten), M. Milhofer (ten), M. George (bass), R. Evans (bass), R. King (cnd), King's Consort—I Was Glad When They Said unto Me (coronation & verse anthem); O Consider My Adversity; Beati omnes qui timent Dominum; In the Black Dismal Dungeon of Dispair; Save Me, O God; Te Deum in B♭; Jubilant in B♭; Thy Way, O God, Is Holy Hyperion ▲ CDA 66677 [DDD]
Purcell, H.:Music for the Funeral of Queen Mary, w. M. Kennedy (sop), E. O'Dwyer (trb), J. Goodman (trb), J. Bowman (ct), N. Short (ct), Rogers Covey-Crump (ten), C. Daniels (ten), M. Milhofer (ten), M. George (bass), R. Evans (bass), R. King (cnd), King's Consort Hyperion ▲ CDA 66677 [DDD]
Purcell, H.:Songs, w. B. Bonney (sop), J. Bowman (ct), R. Covey-Crump (ten), C. Daniels (ten), M. George (bass), D. Miller (archlt/thb/baroque gtr), M. Caudle (b vl), R. King (org/hpd), King's Consort—Incassum Lesbia; Gentle Shepherds, you that know the charms; I love and I must; Through mournful shades and solitary groves; The Knotting Song Hyperion ▲ CDA 66720 [DDD]
Purcell, H.:Songs, w. B. Bonney (sop), J. Bowman (ct), R. Covey-Crump (ten), C. Daniels (ten), M. George (bass), D. Miller (archlt/thb/baroque gtr), M. Caudle (b vl), R. King (chamber org)—Draw near, you lovers; While Thyrsis, wrapt in downy sleep; Love, thou canst hear, I lov'd fair Celia; What hope for us remains now he is gone; Pastora's beauties, when unblown; A thousand sev'ral ways I tried; Urge me no more; Farewell all joys; If music be the food of love [1st setting]; Amidst the shades and cool refreshing streams; They say you're angry; Let each gallant heart; This poet sings the Trojan wars; Ah, how pleasant 'tis to love; My heart whenever you appear; On the brow of Richard Hill; Rashly I swore I would disown; Since the pox or the plague; Beneath a dark and melancholy grove; Musing on cares of human fate; Whilst Cynthia sung, all angry winds lay still Hyperion ▲ CDA 66710
Purcell, H.:Songs, w. B. Bonney (sop), J. Bowman (ct), R. Covey-Crump (ten), C. Daniels (ten), M. George (bass), R. King (cnd), King's Consort—When Strephon Found; Let Us, Kind Lesbia; Corinna Is Divinely Fair; Olinda in the Shades; If Music Be the Food of Love [3rd setting]; Lovely Albina; I Came, I Saw; No, to What Purpose; Young Thrysis' Fate; She Loves Me and Confesses Too; From Silent Shade (Bess of Bedlam); O Solitude; If Pray'rs and Tears; The Fatal Hour; Sylvia, 'Tis True You're Fair; Amintor, Heedless of His Flocks; Love is Now Become a Trade; Phyllis, I Can Never Forgive It; Who Can Behold?; He Himself Courts His Own Ruin; Let Formal Lovers Still Pursue; Ask Me to Love No More; In Cloris All Soft Charms; Spite of the Godhead Hyperion ▲ CDA 66730
Vivaldi, A.:Sacred Choral Music, w. Catherine Denley (mez), Lynton Atkinson (trb), David Wilson-Johnson (bar), Lisa Milne (sgr), R. King (cnd), King's Consort—Magnificat; Lauda, Jerusalem; Kyrie eleison; Credo in unum Deum; Dixit Dominus Hyperion ▲ CDA 66769

Grizzell, Paul (bass)
Sowerby, L.:Forsaken of Man, w. Alicia Clark (sop), Judith Compton (alt), Thomas Potter (bass), Matthew Greenberg (bass), Bruce Hall (sgr), John Vorassi (sgr), Thomas Weisflog (org), William Ferris (cnd), William Ferris Chorale *(rec St. Thomas the Apostle Church, Chicago, June 1990)* New World ▲ 803942 [AAD]

▲ = CD ♦ = Enhanced CD Δ = MD ■ = Cassette Tape □ = DCC

Grobe, Daniel (ten)

Beethoven, L. van:Fidelio, w. Birgit Nilsson (sop—Leonore), Graziella Sciutti (sop—Marzelline), Kurt Equiluz (ten—Erster Gefangener), Donald Grobe (ten—Jacquino), James McCracken (ten—Florestan), Tom Krause (bar—Don Pizarro), Hermann Prey (bar—Don Fernando), Kurt Böhme (bass—Rocco), Günther Adam (sgr—Zweiter Gefangener), L. Maazel (cnd), Vienna PO, Vienna State Opera Concert Association Chorus *(rec Sofiensaal, Vienna, Mar 1964)* London 2-▲ 448104-2 [ADD]

Berg, A.:Lulu, w. E. Lear (sop—Lulu), P. Johnson (mez—Countess Geschwitz), D. Grobe (ten—Alwa), Fischer-Dieskau (bar—Dr. Schön), K. Böhm (cnd), German Opera Orch, German Opera Chorus [G] *(rec 1968)* Deutsche Grammophon 3-▲ 435705-2 [ADD]

Hindemith, P.:Cardillac, w. Leonore Kirschstein (sop), Dietrich Fischer-Dieskau (bar), J. Keilberth (cnd), Cologne RSO [G] Deutsche Grammophon ("20th Century Classics" series) 2-▲ 431741-2 [ADD]

Hindemith, P.:Mathis der Maler, w. Urszula Koszut (sop), Trudeliese Schmidt (mez), Rose Wagemann (mez), William Cochran (ten), James King (ten), Manfred Schmidt (ten), Dietrich Fischer-Dieskau (bar), Gerd Feldhoff (bass), Alexander Malta (bass), Peter Meven (bass), Karl Kreile (sgr), R. Kubelik (cnd), Bavarian RSO, Bavarian Radio Chorus EMI Classics 2-▲ CDCC 55237

Hindemith, P.:Mathis der Maler, w. P. Lorengar (sop), D. Fischer-Dieskau (bar), L. Ludwig (cnd), Berlin RSO [G]—sels Deutsche Grammophon ("20th Century Classics" series) 2-▲ 431741-2 [ADD]

Marschner, H.A.:Der Vampyr, w. Arleen Augér (sop), Roland Hermann (bar), Nikolas Hillebrand (bass), F. Rieger (cnd), Bavarian RSO, Bavarian Radio Chorus *(rec live, Munich, 1974)* Enterprise ("Documents" series) 2-▲ ENT 1009

Grob-Prandl, Gertrud (sop)

Gertrud Grob-Prandl, Ferruccio Tagliavini, w. Ferruccio Tagliavini (ten), Milan RAI SO [cnd:Oliviero de Fabritiis] *(rec Dec. 24, 1953)* Incontri Memorabili ("Martini & Rossi Concerts" series) ▲ 5004

Mozart, W.A.:Don Giovanni, w. H. Konetzni (sop), M. Stabile (bar), A. Pernerstorfer (b-bar), O. Czerwenka (bass), H. Swarowsky (cnd), Vienna SO, Vienna State Opera Chorus *(rec 1950)* Preiser 2-▲ PRE 90166 [AAD]

Grochowski, Gerd (sgr)

Künneke, E.:The Alluring Flame, w. Birgit Fandrey (sgr—Dolores), Christianne Hossfeld (sgr—Lisbeth), Maria Mallé (sgr), Jürgen Sacher (ten—Master), Ralf Lukas (bar—Hoffman), Gerd Grochowski (sgr—1st Neighbor), Gerhard Peters (sgr—Friedrich), Zoran Todorovic (sgr—Jacinto), Theodor Weimer (sgr—2nd Neighbor), P. Falk (cnd), Cologne RSO, Cologne Radio Chorus *(rec Cologne, Nov 7-26, 1994)* Capriccio ▲ 10753 [DDD]

Straus, O.:The Merry Nibelungs, w. Lisa Griffith (sop—Kriemhild), Gudrun Volkert (sop—Brunhilde), Daphne Evangelatos (cta—Ute), Gabriele Henkel (sgr—Giselher), Christine Mann (sgr—Vogel), Hein Heidbüchel (ten—Volker), Martin Gantner (sgr—Gunther), Gerd Grochowski (sgr—Dankwart), Michael Nowak (sgr—Siegfried), Josef Otten (sgr—Hagen), S. Köhler (cnd), Cologne RSO, Cologne Radio Chorus *(rec Cologne, Jan 31-Feb 17, 1995)* Capriccio ▲ 10752 [DDD]

Groenendaal, Cris (ten)

Porter, C.:Anything Goes, w. F. von Stade (mez), J. McGlinn (sgr), K. Criswell (sop), J. Gilford (sgr), London SO, Ambrosian Chorus [original 1934 Broadway version w. original orchestration by Robert Russell Bennett & Hans Spialek] Angel ▲ CDC 49848-2 [DDD]

Groener, Harry (sgr)

Gershwin, G.:Crazy for You, w. J. Benson (sgr) [1992 Broadway cast] Broadway Angel ▲ CDQ 54618 ■ 4DQ 54618

Groenewold, Ulla (cta)

Homilius, G.A.:St. Matthew Passion, w. A. Monoyios (sop), G. Türk, C. Prégardien (ten), K. Mertens (b-bar), H.-G. Wimmer (bass), Berlin Academy for Early Music, Leverkusen Cappella Vocale Berlin Classics 2-▲ BER 1046 [DDD]

Mozart, W.A.:Missa [longa], K.262, w. Regina Schudel (sop), Peter Maus (ten), Berthold Possemeyer (bar), U. Gronostay (cnd), Berlin Radio Sinfonietta, Berlin Radio Chamber Choir [L] Koch Schwann ▲ CD 313 021 [ADD/DDD]

Mozart, W.A.:Missa brevis, K.258, w. Regina Schudel (sop), Peter Maus (ten), Berthold Possemeyer (bar), U. Gronostay (cnd), Berlin Radio Sinfonietta, Berlin Chamber Chorus [L] Koch Schwann ▲ CD 313 021 [ADD/DDD]

Zelenka, J.D.:Lamentationes Jeremiae Prophetae, w. H. Meens (ten), M. van Egmond (bass), R. Shaw (cnd), Academy of the Begynhof Amsterdam [L] Globe ▲ GLO 5050 [DDD]

Groh, Herbert Ernst (ten)

Herbert Ernst Groh Pearl ▲ PEA 9419 (m) [AAD]

Gronlund, Peter (ten)

Nielsen, C.:Springtime, w. I. Nielsen (sop), S. Byriel (b-bar), L. Segerstam (cnd), Danish National RSO, Danish National Radio Choir, Danish National Radio Children's Choir [Da] Chandos ▲ CHAN 8853 [DDD]

Grönroos, Walton (bar)

Brahms, J.:Romanzen aus Tieck's *Magelone*, w. R. Gothóni (pno) *(rec Nacka Aula, Nacka Sweden, July 26-27, 1976)* BIS ▲ CD 70 [AAD]

Gluck, C.W.:Iphigénie en Tauride, w. P. Lorengar (sop), F. Bonisolli (ten), D. Fischer-Dieskau (bar), L. Gardelli (cnd), Bavarian RSO, Bavarian Radio Chorus [F] Orfeo 2-▲ 052832 [DDD]

Kokkonen, J.:Erekhtheion, w. S. Vihavainen (sop), O. Vänskä (cnd), Lahti SO, Academic Choral Society [Fin] BIS ▲ CD 498 [DDD]

Kokkonen, J.:Requiem (in memoriam Maija Kokkonen), w. S. Isokoski (sop), U. Söderblom (cnd), Lahti SO, Savonlinna Opera Festival Chorus [L] BIS ▲ CD 508 [DDD]

Liszt, F.:Cantico del sol di Dan Francesco d'Assisi, w. G. Albrecht (cnd), Berlin RSO, Berlin RIAS Men's Chamber Choir Koch Schwann ▲ CD 311 055

Mozart, W.A.:Missa solemnis, K.139, w. M. Lindsay (sop), G. Schreckenbach (mez), W. Hollweg (ten), M. Creed (cnd), Berlin RSO, Berlin RIAS Chamber Choir [L] Capriccio ▲ 10169 [DDD]

Mozart, W.A.:Missa solemnis, K.139, w. M. Lindsay (sop), G. Schreckenbach (mez), W. Hollweg (ten), M. Creed (cnd), Berlin RSO, Berlin RIAS Chamber Choir [L] LaserLight ▲ 15 883 [DDD]

Mozart, W.A.:Missa brevis, K.65, w. C. Malone (sop), G. Schreckenbach (mez), K. Markus (ten), R. Bader (cnd), Berlin RSO, St. Hedwig's Cathedral Choir [L] Koch Schwann ▲ SCH 313021 [ADD/DDD]

Rangström, T.:Ur kung Eriks visor, w. Ralf Gothóni (pno) *(rec Nacka Aula, Nacka, Sweden, July 26-27, 1976)* BIS ▲ CD 43 [AAD]

Schumann, R.:Dichterliebe, w. R. Gothóni (pno) *(rec 1977)* BIS ▲ CD 92 [AAD]

Schumann, R.:Liederkreis, Op. 24, w. R. Gothóni (pno) *(rec 1977)* BIS ▲ CD 92 [AAD]

Sibelius, J.:Songs, w. Ralf Gothóni (pno)—Diamond on the March Snow, Op. 36/6; The Young Huntsman, Op. 13/7; Astray, Op. 17/4; Sunrise, Op. 38/3; Romeo, Op. 61/4 *(rec Nacka Aula, Nacka, Sweden, July 26-27, 1976)* BIS ▲ CD 43 [AAD]

Gronroos, Walton (bar)

Tchaikovsky, P.:Iolanta, w. G. Vishnevskaya (sop), N. Gedda (ten), M. Rostropovich (cnd), Orch de Paris Erato 2-▲ 45793-2

Groop, Monica (mez)

Bach, J.S.:Christmas Oratorio, w. Ruth Ziesak (sop), Christoph Pregardien (ten), Klaus Mertens (bass), R. Otto (cnd), Concerto Cologne, Frankfurt Vocal Ensemble *(rec Festeburgkirche Frankfurt, Jan 9-16, 1991 & May 12-1)* Capriccio 2-▲ 60025-2 [DDD]

Bach, J.S.:Mass in b, BWV 232, w. C. Högman (sop), H. Crook (ten), P. Salomaa (bass), Drottningholm Baroque Ensemble, Mikaeli Chamber Choir Proprius 2-▲ PRCD 9070/71

Donizetti, G.:Linda di Chamounix, w. Edita Gruberová (sop), Don Bernardini (sgr), Ettore Kim (sgr), F. Haider (cnd), Swedish RSO, Mikaeli Chamber Choir Nightingale Classics 3-▲ NIG 70561

Grieg, E.:Songs, w. Ilmo Ranta (pno)—Romancer, Op. 15; Romancer, Op. 39; Romancer og Ballader af Andreas Munch, Op. 9; Digte af Vilhelm Krag, Op. 60; 4 Songs without Opus numbers *(rec Danderyd Grammar School, Sweden, Jan 11-14, 1996)* BIS ▲ CD 787 [DDD]

Grieg, E.:Songs, w. L. Derwinger (pno)—Sex digte [6 Poems], Op. 4/1-6; Hjertets melodier [The Heart's Melody], Op. 5/1-4; Sex digte of Ibsen, Op. 25/1-6; Songs from Rolfsen's Laesebog, Op. 61/1-7; Haugtussa (song cycle), Op. 67/1-8 BIS ▲ CD 637 [DDD]

Haydn, J.:Mass 10, "Kriegsmesse", "Paukenmesse", w. Ann Monoyios (sop), Jörg Hering (ten), Harry van der Kamp (bass), B. Weil (cnd), Tafelmusik, Tölz Boys' Choir Sony Classical ("Vivarte" series) ▲ SK 68255

Kokkonen, J.:The Hades of the Birds, w. U. Söderblom (cnd), Lahti SO [Fin] BIS ▲ CD 485 [DDD]

Groop, Monica (mez) (cont.)

Mozart, W.A.:Così fan tutte, w. S. Isokoski (sop—Fiordiligi), N. Argenta (sop—Despina), M. Groop (mez—Dorabella), M. Schäfer (ten—Ferrando), P. Vollestad (bar—Guglielmo), H. Claessens (b-bar—Don Alfonso)., S. Kuijken (cnd), La Petite Bande, La Petite Bande Chorus Accent 3-▲ ACC 9296/98

Schubert, Franz:Songs (misc), w. Rudolf Jansen (pno)—Fischerweise; Seligkeit; Lied der Mignon; Die Forelle; Romanz aus Rosamunde; Lachen und wienen; Auf dem Wasser zu singen; Schäfers Klaglied; Pax Vobiscum; Die männer sind mechant!; An die Musik; An Silvia; Du bist die Ruh; Ganymed; Wiegenlied; Der Musenshon; Meeres Stille; Ave Maria; Ständchen Ondine ▲ ODE CD 886

Sibelius, J.:Songs, w. L. Derwinger (pno)—The Fool's Song of the Spider, Op. 27/4 [from *King Christian I*]; 5 Christmas Songs, Op. 1; 8 Songs, Op. 57; Hymn to Thaïs; 6 Songs, Op. 72; 6 Songs, Op. 86; The Little Girls BIS ▲ CD 657 [DDD]

Sibelius, J.:The Tempest, w. R. Viljakainen (sop), J. Silvasti (ten), J. Hynninen (bar), S. Tiilikainen (bar), J.-P. Saraste (cnd), Finnish RSO, Finnish Opera Festival Chorus Ondine ▲ ODE 813 [DDD]

Trombone & Voice in the Hapsburg Empire, w. Christian Lindberg (trbn) *(rec 1992)* BIS ▲ CD 548 [DDD]

Groot, Peter de (alt)

Biber, H. von:Requiem à 15, w. E. Bongers (sop), A. Grimm (sop), K. Wessel (alt), M. Reyans (ten), S. Davies (ten), R. Steur (bass), K.-J. de Koning (bass), T. Koopman (cnd), Amsterdam Baroque Orch, Amsterdam Baroque Choir Erato ▲ 91725

Biber, H. von:Vesperae longiores ac breviores una cum litaniis Laurentanis, w. E. Bongers (sop), A. Grimm (sop), K. Wessel (alt), M. Reyans (ten), S. Davies (ten), R. Steur (bass), K.-J. de Koning (bass), T. Koopman (cnd), Amsterdam Baroque Orch, Amsterdam Baroque Choir Erato ▲ 91725

Grootel, Suze van (sop)

Hollander, H.:Sacred Music, w. K. van der Poel (mez), J. Boswinkel (bass), P. Rikkers (vn), J. van der Meer (db), T. van Eijk (org), Cappella Breda—Cantabant sancti; Domine Jesu Christe; Domine Deus; Ecce vicit leo; O nomen Jesu; Recipe me; Quem vidistis pastores; Sanctus Jacobus; Quid est hoc; O vos omnes; Ecce clamo; Ave Maria; O Beatum Virum; O bone Jesu; Te gloriosus Erasmus ▲ WVH 047 [DDD]

Gross, L. Ernest (sgr)

Caccini, F.:La liberazione di Ruggiero dall'isola d'Alcina, w. Linda De Rungs (sop—Alcian/Vistola), Cecilia Amorocho (sgr—Melissa/Nunzia), Laura Lea Duckworth (sgr—Siren/Harpy), Eric Friedlander (sgr—Monster), L. Ernest Gross (sgr—Enchanted Cypress), Phoebe Jevtovic (sgr—Siren), James Rittenhouse (sgr—Ruggiero/Neptune), Sharon Sim (sgr—Siren), R. Burchard (cnd), Ars Femina Ensemble, TimeChange *(rec Louisville, KY, 1993)* Nannerl ▲ NR-ARS 003; ■ NR-ARS 003

Grossberger, Dina (mez)

Hasse, J.A.:Miserere in e, w. Greta de Reyghere (sop), Ian Honeyman (ten), D Snellincks (bass), Il Fondamento Opus 111 ▲ OPS 3080

Hasse, J.A.:Requiem, w. Greta de Reyghere (sop), Ian Honeyman (ten), D. Snellincks (bass), Il Fondamento Ensemble Opus 111 ▲ OPS 3080

Grossmann, Walter (bass)

Wagner, R.:Die Walküre (sels), w. Anny Konetzni (sop—Brunnhilde), Maria Müller (sop—Sieglinde), Franz Völker (ten—Siegmund), Walter Grossmann (bass—Wotan), W. Furtwängler (cnd), Vienna State Opera Orch *(rec Vienna, Feb. 13-17, 1936)* Koch Schwann 2-▲ SCH 314702 [ADD]

Grossmeyer, Cilla (sop)

Fleischer, T.:Lamentation, w. A. Haroz (hp), E. Lavry (hp), D. Kovalsky (perc), Zimrat Women's Chorus Opus One ▲ Cd 158 [DDD]

Groves, Charles (ten)

Vaughan Williams, R.:The Pilgrim's Progress, w. Delyth Jones (sop), Elsa Kendal (cta), Robin Leggate (ten), V. Handley (cnd), BBC Northern SO, BBC Northern Singers IMP ("BBC Radio Classics" series) ▲ IMP 5691662

Groves, Olives (sgr)

Dibdin, C.:Lionel & Clarissa (sels), w. W. Temple (sgr), A. Reynolds (cnd), Hammersmith Lyric Theater Orch *(rec 1925 for HMV)* Pearl ▲ PEA 9917 (m) [AAD]

Gruber, Heinz Karl (bar)

Weill, K.:Songs, w. R. Hardy (sop), H. K. Gruber (cnd), Ensemble Modern—Berlin im Licht; Slow Fox and Algi-Song; Klopslied; Ach, wär mein Lieb ein brünnlein Kalt; Frauentanz, Op. 10; Bastille Musik; Ol-Musik; Suite panaméenne; Cowboy Song; Captain Valentine's Song; Die stille Stadt Largo ▲ 5114 [DDD]

Gruber, Heinz Karl (reader)

Cerha, F.:Eine Art Chanson, w. H.C. Artmann (reader), J. Holland (reader), M. Jones (reader), R. McGee (reader), G. Rühm (reader) *(rec live Apr. 30, 1993)* Largo ▲ 5126 [DDD]

Gruberová, Edita (sop)

The Anniversary Concert, w. Tokyo PO [cnd:Friedrich Haider] Nightingale Classics ▲ NIG CD 90560

The Art of the Coloratura Orfeo ▲ C 072831 [DDD]

Bellini, V.:Beatrice di Tenda, w. E. Gruberová (sop—Beatrice), V. Kasarova (mez—Agnese), D. Bernardini (ten—Orombello), B. Robinšak (ten—Anichino), I. Morosov (ten—Filippo Maria Visconti), D. Sumegi (bass—Rizzardo), P. Steinberg (cnd), Austrian RSO, Austrian Radio Chorus [I] *(rec live, Vienna Concert House 1/30 & 2/1/92)* Nightingale Classics 2-▲ NC 070560-2 [DDD]

Bellini, V.:I Capuleti e i Montecchi, w. E. Guberova (sop—Giulietta), A. Baltsa (mez—Romeo), D. Raffanti (ten—Tebaldo), R. Muti (cnd), Royal Opera House Orch, Royal Opera House Chorus Covent Garden EMI Classics ▲ CDMB 64846

Bellini, V.:I Puritani, w. Katia Lytting (mez), Justin Lavender (ten), Carlo Tuand (ten), Ettore Kim (bar), Francesco Ellero d'Artegna (bass), Dankwart Siegele (bass), F. Luisi (cnd), Munich RSO, Bavarian Radio Chorus Nightingale Classics 3-▲ NIG 70562

Brahms, J.:Songs, w. E. Werba (pno)—Opp. 70/1, 85/6, 95/1, 106/2 Orfeo ▲ 066831 [DDD]

Children's Songs of the World, w. International Children's Choir, Rudolfsheimer Children's Choir Nightingale Classics ▲ NIG CD 70660

Delibes, L.:Lakmé (sels), w. G. Kuhn (cnd), Munich RSO—Ou va la jeune Indoue? Classics for Pleasure ("Eminence" series) ▲ CFP 2234

Donizetti, G.:Anna Bolena, w. Delores Ziegler (mez), Stefano Palatchi (bass), E. Boncompagni (cnd), Hungarian RSO, Hungarian Radio Chorus Nightingale Classics 3-▲ NIG 70565

Donizetti, G.:La fille du régiment, w. Rosa Laghezza (mez), Deon van der Walt (sgr), Philippe Fourcade (bass), François Castel (sgr), M. Panni (cnd), Munich RSO, Bavarian Radio Chorus Nightingale Classics 2-▲ NIG 70566

Donizetti, G.:Linda di Chamounix, w. Monica Groop (mez), Don Bernardini (sgr), Ettore Kim (sgr), F. Haider (cnd), Swedish RSO, Mikaeli Chamber Choir Nightingale Classics 3-▲ NIG 70561

Donizetti, G.:Lucia di Lammermoor, w. A. Kraus (ten), D. Lloyd (ten), R. Bruson (bar), Royal PO, Ambrosian Opera Chorus *(rec 1983)* EMI Classics ▲ CDMB 64622

Donizetti, G.:Lucia di Lammermoor (sels), w. G. Kuhn (cnd), Munich RSO—Il dolce suono-Ardon gl'incensi Classics for Pleasure ("Eminence" series) ▲ CFP 2234

Donizetti, G.:Lucia di Lammermoor (sels), w. A. Agache (ten), A. Miles (bass), R. Bonynge (cnd), London SO, Ambrosian Singers—Oh giusto cielo...Il dolce suono; Ohimè! sorge il tremendo fantasma; S'avanza Enrico; Spargi d'amore pianto Teldec ▲ 4509-93691-2 [DDD]

Donizetti, G.:Roberto Devereux, w. Delores Ziegler (mez), Don Bernardini (sgr), Ettore Kim (sgr), F. Haider (cnd), Strasbourg PO, Rhine Opera Chorus Nightingale Classics 2-▲ NIG 70563

Dvořák, A.:Songs, w. E. Werba (pno)—Liebeslieder, Op. 83 Orfeo ▲ 066831 [DDD]

Famous Opera Arias, w. Munich Radio Orch [cnd:L. Gardelli] Orfeo ▲ C 101841

Gluck, C.W.:Orfeo ed Euridice, w. Marshall (sop), A. Baltsa (mez), R. Muti (cnd), Philharmonia Orch, Ambrosian Opera Chorus Angel ("Studio" series) 2-▲ CDMB 63637 [DDD]

Gounod, C.:Roméo et Juliette (sels), w. G. Kuhn (cnd), Munich RSO—Ah! je veux vivre Classics for Pleasure ("Eminence" series) ▲ CFP 2234

Great Sopranos of Our Time, w. Maria Callas (sop), Joan Sutherland (sop), Renata Scotto (sop), Montserrat Caballé (sop), Elisabeth Schwarzkopf (sop), Victoria de los Angeles (sop), Mirella Freni (sop), Ileana Cotrubas (sop) Classics for Pleasure ▲ CDEMX 9519 [ADD]

Handel, G.F.:Arias, w. W. Marsalis (tpt), R. Leppard (cnd), English CO, "Eternal Source of Light Divine," from *Birthday Ode for Queen Anne* & "Let the Bright Seraphim," from *Samson* [E] CBS ▲ MK 39061 [DDD]; ■ IMT 39061 (D)

Haydn, J.:Die Schöpfung, w. Josef Protschka (ten), Robert Holl (bass), N. Harnoncourt (cnd), Vienna SO, Arnold Schoenberg Choir [G] Teldec 2-▲ 2292-42682-2

Gruberová, Edita (sop) (cont.)

Humperdinck, E.:Hänsel und Gretel, w. G. Jones (sop), B. Bonney (sop), C. Oelze (sop), A. Murray (mez), C. Ludwig (mez), F. Grundheber (bar), C. Davis (cnd), Dresden Staatskapelle Philips 2–▲ 438013–2

Mad Scenes, w. Munich RSO [cnd:Fabio Luisi], Bavarian Radio Chorus Nightingale Classics ▲ NIG CD 110560

Mahler, G.:Sym 4, w. G. Sinopoli (cnd), Philharmonia Orch Deutsche Grammophon ▲ 437527–2

Meyerbeer, G.:Les Huguenots (sels), w. G. Kuhn (cnd), Munich RSO—Nobles seigneurs, salut! Classics for Pleasure ("Eminence" series) ▲ CFP 2234

Mozart, W.A.:Arias, w. N. Harnoncourt (cnd), CO of Europe—concert arias K.217, 368, 369, 374, 416, 418, 419, 538 Teldec ▲ 9031–72302–2 ZK

Mozart, W.A.:Arias, w. N. Harnoncourt (cnd)—Vorrei spiegarvi, oh Dio!, K.418; Ah, se in ciel, benigne stelle, K.538 [both w. CO of Europe]; Der Hölle Rache kocht in meinem Herzen [from Die Zauberflöte; w. Zurich Opera Orch.]; Or sai ch Teldec ▲ 450993691–2 [DDD]

Mozart, W.A.:Arias, w. I. Cotrubas (sop), L. Price (sop), J. Varady (sop), L. Popp (mez), F. Araiza (ten), P. Domingo (ten), P. de Palma (ten), P. Schreier (ten), F. Wunderlich (ten), S. Milnes (bar), A. Titus (bar), M. Talvela (bass)—sels. from Entführung aus dem Serail, Così fan tutte, Don Giovanni, Idomeneo, Die Zauberflöte, Le nozze di Figaro Eurodisc ▲ 69256–2–RG [ADD]

Mozart, W.A.:Arias, w. Arleen Augér (sop), Kathleen Battle (sop), Irma Beilke (sop), Helena Braun (sop), Lisa Della Casa (sop), Maria Cebotari (sop), Ileana Cotrubas (sop), Helen Donath (sop), Mirella Freni (sop), Reri Grist (sop), Elisabeth Grümmer (sop), Hilde Güden (sop), Ingeborg Hallstein (sop), Luise Helletsgruber (sop), Gundula Janowitz (sop), Sena Jurinac (sop), Erika Köth (sop), Evelyn Lear (sop), Wilma Lipp (sop), Margaret Marshall (sop), Edith Mathis (sop), Jarmila Novotna (sop), Margherita Perras (sop), Lucia Popp (sop), Elisabeth Rethberg (sop), Anneliese Rothenberger (sop), Elisabeth Schumann (sop), Elisabeth Schwarzkopf (sop), Graziella Sciutti (sop), Irmgard Seefried (sop), Graziella Sciutti (sop), Julia Varady (sop), Agnes Baltsa (mez), Margit Bokor (mez), Brigitte Fassbaender (mez), Christa Ludwig (mez), Ann Murray (mez), Francisco Araiza (ten), Anton Dermota (ten), Helge Rosvaenge (ten), Rudolf Schock (ten), Peter Schreier (ten), Leopold Simoneau (ten), Eric Tappy (ten), Richard Tauber (ten), Gösta Winbergh (ten), Josef Witt (ten), Fritz Wunderlich (ten), Christian Boesch (bar), Willy Domgraf–Fassbaender (bar), Karl Dönch (bar), Dietrich Fischer–Dieskau (bar), Erich Kunz (bar), Eberhard Wächter (bar), Hans Hotter (b–bar), Paul Schöffler (b–bar), Cesare Siepi (b–bar), José Van Dam (b–bar), Walter Berry (bass), Geraint Evans (bass), Nicolai Ghiaurov (bass), Alexander Kipnis (bass), Richard Mayr (bass), Kurt Moll (bass), James Morris (bass), Ezio Pinza (bass), Martti Talvela (bass), Giorgio Tozzi (bass), Hans Duhan (sgr), Res Fischer (sgr), Marie Gerhart (sgr), *(various orchs & cnds)*—sels from Idomeneo, Die Entführung aus der Serail, Le nozze di Figaro, Don Giovanni, Così fan tutte, Die Zauberflöte & various arias Orfeo d'or ("Festspiel Dokumente" series) 5–▲ 408955

Mozart, W.A.:Bastien und Bastienne, w. V. Cole (ten), L. Polgár (bass), R. Leppard (cnd), Franz Liszt CO Sony Classical ▲ SK 45855

Mozart, W.A.:Complete Mozart Edition, w. E. Mathis (sop), L. Popp (mez), F. Araiza (ten), P. Schreier (ten), W. Berry (bass), Salzburg Mozarteum Orch Philips 8–▲ 422523–2 [ADD]

Mozart, W.A.:Complete Mozart Edition, w. E. Mathis (sop), E. Moser (sop), L. Popp (mez), P. Schreier (ten), L. Hager (cnd), Salzburg Mozarteum Orch Philips 2–▲ 422531–2 [ADD]

Mozart, W.A.:Complete Mozart Edition, w. A. Augér (sop), I. Cotrubas (sop), A. Baltsa (mez), W. Hollweg (ten), L. Hager (cnd), Salzburg Mozarteum Orch Philips 3–▲ 422529–2 [ADD]

Mozart, W.A.:Don Giovanni, w. B. Bonney (sop), R. Alexander (sop), T. Hampson (bar), N. Harnoncourt (cnd), Royal Concertgebouw Orch [I] Teldec 3–▲ 2292–44184–2 [DDD]

Mozart, W.A.:Entführung, w. F. Araiza (ten), R. Orth (bar), R. Bracht (bass), H. Wallberg (cnd), Munich RSO Eurodisc 2–▲ 7792–2 [ADD]

Mozart, W.A.:Entführung, w. K. Battle (sop), G. Winbergh (ten), H. Zednik (ten), M. Talvela (bass), Will Quadflieg (nar), G. Solti (cnd), Vienna PO [G] London 2–▲ 417402–2 [DDD]

Mozart, W.A.:Finta giardiniera, w. C. Margiono (sop), M. Bacelli (sop), D. Upshaw (sop), U. Heilmann (ten), A. Scharinger (bass), N. Harnoncourt (cnd), Vienna Concentus Musicus Teldec 3–▲ 72309–2

Mozart, W.A.:Idomeneo, w. L. Popp (sop), A. Baltsa (mez), L. Pavarotti (ten), L. Nucci (bar), J. Pritchard (cnd), Vienna PO, Vienna State Opera Chorus [I] London 3–▲ 411805–2 [DDD]

Mozart, W.A.:Zauberflöte, w. Reri Grist (sop), Edith Mathis (sop), Rene Kollo (ten), Gerhard Unger (ten), Hermann Prey (bar), José Van Dam (b–bar), Peter Meven (bass), H. von Karajan (cnd), Vienna PO, Vienna State Opera Chorus *(rec live, Salzburg, July 26, 1974)* Arkadia 2–▲ 233

Mozart, W.A.:Zauberflöte, w. L. Popp (sop), S. Jerusalem (ten), W. Brendel (bar), R. Bracht (bass), B. Haitink (cnd), Bavarian RSO, Bavarian Radio Chorus [G] EMI Classics 3–▲ CDCC 47951 [DDD]

Mozart, W.A.:Zauberflöte, w. B. Bonney (sop), G. Schmid (sop), H.–P. Blochwitz (ten), T. Hampson (bar), M. Salminen (bass), A. Scharinger (bass), N. Harnoncourt (cnd), Zurich Opera Orch, Zurich Opera House Chorus [G] Teldec 2–▲ 2292–42716–2

Mozart, W.A.:Zauberflöte (sels), w. L. Popp (sop), S. Jerusalem (ten), W. Brendel (bar), R. Bracht (bass), B. Haitink (cnd), Bavarian RSO, Bavarian Radio Chorus [G] EMI Classics ▲ CDC 47008 [DDD]

Offenbach, J.:Les Contes d'Hoffmann, w. C. Eder (mez), P. Domingo (ten), M. Sénéchal (ten), Schmidt (sgr), G. Bacquier (bar), J. Morris (bass), J. Diaz (bass), S. Ozawa (cnd), French National Orch, French Radio Chorus [F] Deutsche Grammophon 2–▲ 427682–2 [DDD]

Offenbach, J.:Les Contes d'Hoffmann (sels), w. Edita Gruberova (sop—Giulietta), Plácido Domingo (ten—Hoffmann), S. Ozawa (cnd), French National Orch—Malheureux, tu ne comprends done pas Deutsche Grammophon ▲ 447270–2 [DDD] ■ 447 270–4

Operetta Gala, w. Munich RSO [cnd:Rudolf Bibl] Nightingale Classics ▲ NIG CD 100560

Orff, C.:Carmina burana, w. J. Aler (ten), T. Hampson (bar), S. Ozawa (cnd), Berlin PO, Berlin Cathedral Boys' Choir, Shin–Yuh Kai Chorus [G, L] Philips ▲ 422363–2 [DDD] □ 422363–5

Purcell, H.:Music of, w. W. Marsalis (tpt), R. Leppard (cnd), English CO—sels. from *The Indian Queen, King Arthur* & *Come Ye Sons of Art* CBS ▲ MK 39061 [DDD] ■ IMT 39061 (D)

Rossini, G.:Arias, w. June Anderson (sop), Montserrat Caballé (sop), Maria Callas (sop), Pilar Lorengar (sop), Mady Mesplé (sop), Nicolai Gedda (ten), Tito Gobbi (bar), Samuel Ramey (bass), *(orchs unknown)* —from Barbiere di Siviglia; La Cenerentola; La Gazza ladra; Petite messe solennelle; Semiramide; Stabat Mater *(rec 1958–89)* EMI Classics 2–▲ CZS 67440–2 [ADD/DDD]

Rossini, G.:Il barbiere di Siviglia (sels), w. G. Kuhn (cnd), Munich RSO—Una voce poco fa Classics for Pleasure ("Eminence" series) ▲ CFP 2234

Rossini, G.:Semiramide (sels), w. G. Kuhn (cnd), Munich RSO—Bel raggio lusinghier [Act. I] EMI Classics ("Encore" series) ▲ CDE 68308 [ADD/DDD]

Rossini, G.:Semiramide (sels), w. G. Kuhn (cnd), Munich RSO—Bel raggio lushinghier Classics for Pleasure ("Eminence" series) ▲ CFP 2234

Songs of Mendelssohn, Schubert & Brahms, w. Peter Schmidl (cl), Friedrich Haider (pno) Nightingale Classics ▲ NIG CD 70860

Strauss (II), Joh.:Die Fledermaus, w. K. Te Kanawa (sop), B. Fassbaender (mez), W. Brendel (bar), R. Leech (ten), O. Bär (bar), T. Krause (bar), A. Previn (cnd), Vienna PO, Vienna State Opera Chorus [G] Philips 2–▲ 432157–2 [DDD]

Strauss (II), Joh.:Die Fledermaus (sels), w. K. Te Kanawa (sop), B. Fassbaender (mez), R. Leech (ten), W. Brendel (bar), O. Bär (bar), A. Previn (cnd), Vienna PO Philips ▲ 438503–2

Strauss (II), Joh.:Die Fledermaus (sels), w. B. Bonney (sop), M. Lipovšek (mez), W. Kmentt (ten), W. Hollweg (ten), J. Protschka (ten), C. Boesch (bar), A. Scharinger (bass), N. Harnoncourt (cnd), Royal Concertgebouw Orch, Netherlands Opera Chorus Teldec ▲ 42427–2

Strauss (II), Joh.:Die Fledermaus (sels), w. N. Harnoncourt (cnd), Royal Concertgebouw Orch—Klänge der Heimat Teldec ▲ 450993691–2 [DDD]

Strauss, R.:Ariadne auf Naxos, w. J. Norman (sop), J. Varady (sop), P. Frey (ten), O. Bär (bar), D. Fischer–Dieskau (bar), K. Masur (cnd), Leipzig Gewandhaus Orch [G] Philips 2–▲ 422084–2 [DDD]

Strauss, R.:Ariadne auf Naxos, w. L. Price (sop), R. Kollo (ten), G. Solti (cnd), London PO [G] London ("Grand Opera" series) 2–▲ 430384–2 [ADD]

Strauss, R.:Songs, w. E. Werba (pno)—10 songs—Opp. 22/1–4; 48/1–2; 68/1,2 & 5; 69/5 Orfeo ▲ 066831 [DDD]

Strauss, R.:Songs, Op. 68, w. M. Tilson Thomas (cnd), London SO *(rec Feb. 6–7, 1991)* Sony Classical ▲ SK 48242 [DDD]

Thomas, A.:Hamlet (sels), w. G. Kuhn (cnd), Munich RSO—A vos jeux, mes amis–Partagez–vous mes fleurs Classics for Pleasure ("Eminence" series) ▲ CFP 2234

Verdi, G.:Giovanna d'Arco, w. Salvatore Fisichella (ten), Giorgio Zancanaro (bar), G.–F. Masini (cnd), Vienna SO *(rec live, 1985)* Serenissima 2–▲ SER 360133

Gruberová, Edita (sop) (cont.)

Verdi, G.:Rigoletto, w. B. Fassbaender (mez), Schicoff (ten), R. Bruson (bar), R. Lloyd (b–bar), G. Sinopoli (cnd), St. Cecilia Academy Orch Rome, St. Cecilia Academy Chorus Rome [I] Philips 2–▲ 412592–2 [DDD]

Verdi, G.:La traviata, w. N. Shicoff (ten), G. Zancanaro (bar), C. Rizzi (cnd), London SO, Ambrosian Singers Teldec 2–▲ 9031–76348–2 PL

Verdi, G.:La traviata (sels), w. C. Rizzi (cnd), London SO—È stranolè strano...Ah, fors'è lui Teldec ▲ 450993691–2 [DDD]

Verdi, G.:La traviata (sels), w. N. Shicoff (ten), G. Zancanaro (bar), C. Rizzi (cnd), London SO [I] Teldec ▲ 4509–91975–2

Gruchet, Erik (ten)

Dupuy, B.A.:Sacred Music, w. Isabelle Poulenard (sop), Jean–Louis Comorette (ct), Dominique Miraille (bar), Jean–Louis Bindi (bass), A. Bourbon (cnd), Baroque Instrumental Ensemble, Toulouse Vocal Group—Noël; Motet; Magnificat Arion ▲ ARN 68330 [DDD]

Grumbach, Raimund (bass)

Wagner, R.:Das Liebesverbot, w. Pamela Coburn (sop—Mariana), Friedrich Lenz (ten—Antonio), Hermann Prey (bar—Friedrich), Keith Engen (bass—Angelo), Raimund Grumbach (bass—Danieli/Wirt), Wolfgang Fassler (sgr—Luzio), Sabine Haas (sgr—Isabella/Claudios Schwester), Alfred Kuhn (sgr—Brighella/Chef der Sbirren), Hermann Sapell (sgr—Pontio Pilato), Robert Schunk (sgr—Claudio), Marianne Seibel (sgr—Dorella), W. Sawallisch (cnd), Bavarian State Orch, Bavarian State Chorus *(rec July 9, 1983)* Orfeo d'or 3–▲ 345953

Wagner, R.:Rienzi, der Letzte der Tribunen, w. Cheryl Studer (sop—Irene), René Kollo (ten—Rienzi), Friedrich Lenz (ten—Gesandte), Norbert Orth (ten—Baroncelli), Bodo Brinkmann (bar—Paolo Orsini), Keith Engen (bass—Cecco del Vecchio), Raimund Grumbach (bass—Gesandte), Jan–Hendrik Rootering (bass—Steffano Colonna), Carmen Anhorn (sgr—Ein Friedensbote), Karl Helm (sgr—Kardinal Orvieto), John Janssen (sgr—Adriano), Alfred Kuhn (sgr—Gesandte), Hans Wilbrink (sgr—Gesandte), W. Sawallisch (cnd), Bavarian State Opera Orch, Bavarian State Opera Chorus *(rec live, July 6, 1983)* Orfeo d'or 3–▲ 346953

Grümmer, Elisabeth (sop)

Brahms, J.:Ein Deutsches Requiem, w. D. Fischer–Dieskau (bar), R. Kempe (cnd), Berlin PO, St. Hedwig's Cathedral Choir [G] EMI Classics ▲ CDH 64705

Brahms, J.:Songs, w. Gerald Moore (pno)—Regenlied; Das Mädchen; Geheimnis; Mädchenlied; Wiegenlied Testament ▲ 1086

Grieg, E.:Peer Gynt (sels), w. Gerald Moore (pno)—Der Winter mag scheiden Testament ▲ 1086

Grieg, E.:Songs, w. Gerald Moore (pno)—Schlaf, du teuerster Knabe mein! Testament ▲ 1086

Humperdinck, E.:Hänsel und Gretel, w. E. Schwarzkopf (sop), A. Felbermayer (sop), M. von Ilosvay (mez), E. Schürhoff (mez), J. Metternich (bar), H. von Karajan (cnd), Philharmonia Orch, Loughton High School Chorus, Bancroft's School Chorus [G] *(rec 1953)* EMI Classics ("Studio" series) 2–▲ CDMB 69293 (m) [ADD]

Mozart, W.A.:Arias, w. Arleen Augér (sop), Kathleen Battle (sop), Irma Beilke (sop), Helena Braun (sop), Lisa Della Casa (sop), Maria Cebotari (sop), Ileana Cotrubas (sop), Helen Donath (sop), Mirella Freni (sop), Reri Grist (sop), Edita Gruberova (sop), Hilde Güden (sop), Ingeborg Hallstein (sop), Luise Helletsgruber (sop), Gundula Janowitz (sop), Sena Jurinac (sop), Erika Köth (sop), Evelyn Lear (sop), Wilma Lipp (sop), Margaret Marshall (sop), Edith Mathis (sop), Jarmila Novotna (sop), Margherita Perras (sop), Lucia Popp (sop), Elisabeth Rethberg (sop), Anneliese Rothenberger (sop), Elisabeth Schumann (sop), Elisabeth Schwarzkopf (sop), Graziella Sciutti (sop), Irmgard Seefried (sop), Graziella Sciutti (sop), Julia Varady (sop), Agnes Baltsa (mez), Margit Bokor (mez), Brigitte Fassbaender (mez), Christa Ludwig (mez), Ann Murray (mez), Francisco Araiza (ten), Anton Dermota (ten), Helge Rosvaenge (ten), Rudolf Schock (ten), Peter Schreier (ten), Leopold Simoneau (ten), Eric Tappy (ten), Richard Tauber (ten), Gösta Winbergh (ten), Josef Witt (ten), Fritz Wunderlich (ten), Christian Boesch (bar), Willy Domgraf–Fassbaender (bar), Karl Dönch (bar), Dietrich Fischer–Dieskau (bar), Erich Kunz (bar), Eberhard Wächter (bar), Hans Hotter (b–bar), Paul Schöffler (b–bar), Cesare Siepi (b–bar), José Van Dam (b–bar), Walter Berry (bass), Geraint Evans (bass), Nicolai Ghiaurov (bass), Alexander Kipnis (bass), Richard Mayr (bass), Kurt Moll (bass), James Morris (bass), Ezio Pinza (bass), Martti Talvela (bass), Giorgio Tozzi (bass), Hans Duhan (sgr), Res Fischer (sgr), Marie Gerhart (sgr), *(various orchs & cnds)*—sels from Idomeneo, Die Entführung aus der Serail, Le nozze di Figaro, Don Giovanni, Così fan tutte, Die Zauberflöte & various arias Orfeo d'or ("Festspiel Dokumente" series) 5–▲ 408955

Mozart, W.A.:Don Giovanni, w. E. Schwarzkopf (sop), E. Berger (sop), A. Dermota (ten), C. Siepi (b–bar), O. Edelmann (b–bar), W. Berry (bass), W. Furtwängler (cnd), Vienna PO, Vienna State Opera Chorus *(rec 1953)* Arkadia 3–▲ 509 (m) [AAD]

Mozart, W.A.:Don Giovanni, w. E. Grümmer (sop—D. Anna), R. Streich (sop—Zerlina), L. Della Casa (sop—D. Elvira), L. Simoneau (ten—Don Ottavio), C. Siepi (bass–baritone—Don Giovanni), W. Berry (bass—Masetto), G. Frick (bass—Il Commendatore), F. Corena (bass—Leporello), D. Mitropoulos (cnd), Vienna PO, Vienna State Opera Chorus *(rec Salzburg, July 24, 1956)* Sony Classical 3–▲ SM3K 64263 [ADD]

Mozart, W.A.:Don Giovanni, w. E. Schwarzkopf (sop), E. Berger (sop), A. Dermota (ten), C. Siepi (b–bar), O. Edelmann (b–bar), W. Berry (bass), W. Furtwängler (cnd), Vienna PO, Vienna State Opera Chorus *(rec Salzburg, Aug. 3, 1953)* EMI Classics ("Great Recordings of the Century" series) 2–▲ CDHB 63860

Mozart, W.A.:Don Giovanni, w. L. Della Casa (sop), R. Streich (sop), L. Simoneau (ten), C. Siepi (b–bar), G. Frick (bass), W. Berry (bass), F. Corena (bass), D. Mitropoulos (cnd), Vienna PO, Vienna State Opera Chorus [I] *(rec live, Salzburg, July 24, 1956)* Arkadia 3–▲ 552 (m) [ADD]

Mozart, W.A.:Songs, w. M. Callas (sop), E. Schwarzkopf (sop), R. Scotto (sop), T. Lemnitz (sop), E. Berger (sop), S. Jurinac (sop), E. Schumann (sop), I. Souez (sop), E. Rethberg (sop), L. Lehmann (sop), N. Gedda (ten), J. McCormack (ten), H. Roswenge (ten), H. Nash (ten), T. Gobbi (bar), G. Hüsch (bar), E. Kunz (bar), G. Frick (bass), E. Pinza (bass), A. Kipnis (bass) EMI Classics 4–▲ CDMD 63750

Rossini, G.:Stabat Mater, w. M. von Ilosvay (mez), C. Ludwig (mez), H. Fehn (bass), F. Fricsay (cnd), Cologne RSO, Cologne Radio Chorus [L] *(rec 1953)* Melodram ▲ CDM 16523 [AAD]

Schubert, Franz:Songs (misc), w. Gerald Moore (pno)—Suleikas Gesang II; Auf dem Wasser zu singen; Wiegenlied; Rastlose Liebe; Vor meiner Wiege; Die Forelle; Fischerweise Testament ▲ 1086

Strauss, R.:4 Last Songs, w. R. Kraus (cnd), Berlin RSO [G] *(rec 1970)* Melodram ▲ CDM 16523 [AAD]

Verdi, G.:Otello (sels), w. Gerald Moore (pno)—Nun in der Nächt'gen Stille [Love Duet, Act I] Testament ▲ 1086

Verdi, G.:Songs, w. Gerald Moore (pno)—Ave Maria; Lied von der Weide (Willow Song) Testament ▲ 1086

Wagner, R.:Götterdämmerung (sels), w. A. Varnay (sop), B. Aldenhoff (ten), H. Uhde (bar), G. Frick (bass), J. Greindl (bass), H. Knappertsbusch (cnd), Bavarian State Opera Orch, Bayreuth Festival Orch, Bavarian State Opera Chorus, Bayreuth Festival Chorus [G] *(rec live 1955 & 1957)* Melodram 4–▲ MEL 46106 (m) [AAD]

Wagner, R.:Lohengrin, w. C. Ludwig (mez), J. Thomas (ten), D. Fischer–Dieskau (bar), G. Frick (bass), R. Kempe (cnd), Vienna PO, Vienna State Opera Chorus [G] EMI Classics 3–▲ CDCC 49017 [ADD]

Wagner, R.:Die Meistersinger von Nürnberg, w. M. Höffgen (cta), R. Schock (ten), G. Unger (ten), H. Prey (bar), B. Kusche (bar), F. Frantz (b–bar), G. Frick (bass), R. Kempe (cnd), Berlin PO *(rec 1956)* EMI Classics 4–▲ CDMD 64154

Wagner, R.:Die Meistersinger von Nürnberg, w. W. Windgassen (ten), T. Adam (b–bar), J. Greindl (bass), H. Knappertsbusch (cnd), Bayreuth Festival Orch, Bayreuth Festival Chorus [G] *(rec live, Bayreuth, 1960)* Melodram 4–▲ MEL 46103

Wagner, R.:Das Rheingold, w. R. Gorr (mez), A. Andersson (ten), S. Konya (ten), T. Adam (b–bar), H. Hotter (b–bar), J. Greindl (bass), H. Knappertsbusch (cnd), Bayreuth Festival Orch, Bayreuth Festival Chorus [G] *(rec live 1958)* Arkadia 2–▲ 441 [AAD]

Wagner, R.:Tannhäuser, w. M. Schech (sop), H. Hopf (ten), F. Wunderlich (ten), D. Fischer–Dieskau (bar), G. Frick (bass), F. Konwitschny (cnd), Berlin State Opera Orch, Berlin State Opera Chorus [G] EMI Classics ("Studio" series) 3–▲ CDMC 63214 [ADD]

Grundheber, Franz (bar)

Berg, A.:Wozzeck, w. H. Behrens (sop), P. Langridge (ten), H. Zednik (ten), A. Haugland (bass), C. Abbado (cnd), Vienna PO, Vienna State Opera Chorus, Vienna Boys' Choir [G] *(rec live, 6/88)* Deutsche Grammophon 2–▲ 423587–2 [DDD]

Grundheber, Franz (bar) (cont.)
Hindemith, P.:Mörder, Hoffnug der Frauen, w. Gabriele Schnaut (sop), G. Albrecht (cnd), Berlin RSO Wergo ▲ WER 60132-50 [DDD]
Humperdinck, E.:Hänsel und Gretel, w. E. Gruberova (sop), G. Jones (sop), B. Bonney (sop), C. Oelze (sop), A. Murray (mez), C. Ludwig (mez), C. Davis (cnd), Dresden Staatskapelle Philips 2-▲ 438013-2
Strauss, R.:Arabella, w. K. Te Kanawa (sop), Fontana (sgr), H. Dernesch (sop/mez), J. Tate (cnd), Royal Opera House Orch [G] London 3-▲ 417623-2 [DDD]
Zemlinsky, A. von:Der König Kandaules (sels), w. G. Albrecht (cnd), Hamburg PO—Prelude & Gyge's Monologue Capriccio ▲ 10448 [DDD]
Zemlinsky, A. von:Symphonische Gesänge, w. G. Albrecht (cnd), Hamburg PO Capriccio ▲ 10448 [DDD]

Grünenpült, Kirsten (sgr)
Austin, E.:An Die Nachgeborenen, w. Alex Bassermann (sgr), Veronika Winter (sgr), Sibylle Dotzauer (pno), Gerald Kegelmann (cnd), Heidelberg-Mannheim State Univ Chamber Choir Capstone ▲ CPS 8625

Gruszcynski, Jerzy (bass)
Nicolai, O.:Te Deum, w. Bozena Betley (sop), Zofie Kilanowicz (sop), Katarztna Suska (cta), Henryk Grychnik (ten), Czeslaw Galka (bar), R. Bader (cnd), Cracow PO, Cracow Phil Chorus Koch Schwann ▲ SCH CD 310872

Grychnik, Henryk (ten)
Nicolai, O.:Te Deum, w. Bozena Betley (sop), Zofie Kilanowicz (sop), Katarztna Suska (cta), Czeslaw Galka (bar), Jerzy Gruszcynski (bass), R. Bader (cnd), Cracow PO, Cracow Phil Chorus Koch Schwann ▲ SCH CD 310872
Szymanowski, K.:King Roger, w. B. Zagòrzanka (sop), A. Malewicz-Madey (cta), W. Ochman (ten), A. Hiolski (bar), L. A. Mròz (bass), K. Stryja (cnd), Polish State PO Katowice, Cracow Phil Boys' Chorus, Polish State Phil Chorus *(rec Apr. 7-9, 1990)* Marco Polo ("Opera Classics" series) 2-▲ 8.223339/40 [DDD]

Gualtiero, Orazio (bar)
Mascagni, P.:Isabeau, w. Marcella Pobbe (sop—Isabeau), Licia Galvano (mez—Giglietta), Pier Miranda Ferraro (ten—Folco), Orazio Gualtiero (bar—Cornelius), Rinaldo Rola (bass—Re Raimondo), Amelia Bazzini (sgr—Ermyngarde), Piero Benzi (sgr—L'araldo), Renata Davini (sgr—Ermynthrude), Piero Francia (sgr—Il Cavaliere), T. Serafin (cnd), San Remo SO *(rec Sanremo, Jan 13, 1962)* Bongiovanni ("Il Mito dell'Opera" series) 2-▲ GB 1135/36-2 [ADD]

Guarino, Robert (ten)
Donaudy, S.:Airs de style ancien, w. Dennis Helmrich (pno) *(rec Trenton State College, Spring 1996)* Newport Classic ▲ NPD 85607 [DDD]

Guarnera, Piero (bar)
Leo, L.:Amor vuol sofferenze, w. Marilena Laurenza (sop), Vitalba Mosca (mez), Domenico Colaianni (sgr), Giovanna Donadini (sgr), Marilyne Fallot (sgr), Hyun Lee (sgr), D. Moles (cnd), Naples New Scarlatti Orch *(rec Martinafranca Festival, 1994)* Nuova Era 3-▲ NUO 7221
Salieri, A.:La Locandiera, w. A. Ruffini (sop), G. Sarti (bar), O. Di Credico (ten), F. Luisi (cnd), Emilia Romagna Arturo Toscanini SO [I] *(rec live 1989)* Nuova Era 2-▲ 6888/89 [DDD]

Guarneri, Guido (sgr)
Leoncavallo, R.:Zingari, w. Aldo Bottion (ten), Gianna Galli (sgr), Renzo Scarsoni (sgr), E. Boncompagni (cnd), Turin RAI Orch, Turin RAI Chorus *(rec live, 1975)* Italian Opera Rarities ▲ IOR 7729 [ADD]

Guarrera, Frank (bar)
Bizet, G.:Carmen, w. Cooper (sgr), Dunn (sgr), P. Domingo (ten), A. Guadagno (cnd), Cincinnati Summer Opera Association Orch, Cincinnati Summer Opera Association Chorus [F] *(rec live 7/19/68)* Melodram 2-▲ MEL 27034 (m) [AAD]
Puccini, G.:La Bohème, w. R. Tebaldi (sop), Candida (sgr), F. Corelli (ten), J. Hines (bass), A. Guadagno (cnd), *(orch & chorus unknown)* [I] *(rec live, Philadelphia 12/2/69)* Standing Room Only 2-▲ SRO 821-2 [ADD]
Puccini, G.:Turandot, w. B. Nilsson (sop—Turnadot), A. Moffo (sop—Liù), F. Corelli (ten—Calaf), C. Anthony (ten—Pong), R. Nagy (ten—Pang), F. Guarrera (bar—Ping), B. Giaiotti (bass—Timur), L. Stokowski (cnd), Metropolitan Opera Orch, New York Metropolitan Opera Chorus *(rec Mar. 4, 1961)* Datum 2-▲ DAT 12301 [ADD]
Verdi, G.:Falstaff, w. Herva Nelli (sop), Teresa Stich-Randall (sop), Cloë Elmo (cta), Giuseppe Valdengo (bar), A. Toscanini (cnd), *(orch unknown)* *(rec 1950)* Music & Arts 2-▲ CD 248 [ADD]

Guber, Carola (cta)
Duruflé, M.:Requiem, w. P. Sefcik (baritone), C. O. Beyer (cello), T. Götting (organ), Kammerorchester, H. Hennig (cnd), H. Hennig (cnd), Hanover Youth Choir Ars Musici ▲ AM 1098-2 [DDD]
Mozart, W.A.:Zauberflöte, w. Constanze Backes (sop—Papagena), Christiane Oelze (sop—Pamina), Susan Roberts (sop—First Lady), Cyndia Sieden (sop—Queen of the Night), Carola Guber (cta—Second Lady), Maria Jonas (cta—Third Lady), Andreas Dieterich (trb—First Boy), Jan Andreas Mendel (trb—Second Boy), Florian Wöller (trb—Third Boy), Uwe Peper (ten—Monostatos), Nicolas Robertson (ten—First Man in Armor), Michael Schade (ten—Tamino), Gerald Finley (bar—Papageno), Noel Mann (bass—Second Man in Armour), Harry Peeters (bass—Sarastro), Detlef Roth (bass—Speaker/First Priest), Robert Burt (speaker—Third Priest), Robert Johnston (speaker—Second Priest), Wolfgang Knauer (speaker—Fourth Priest), Douglas Welbat (speaker—Second Priest), J. E. Gardiner (cnd), English Baroque Soloists, Monteverdi Choir London *(rec Forum am Schlosspark, Ludwigsburg, July 1995)* Archiv 2-▲ 449166-2
Steffani, A.:Enrico Leone, w. R. Popken (alt), M. Frimmer (sop), S. Szameit (sop), N. Yoko (cta), D. Diwiak (ten), G. Faulstich (bar), L. Rovatkay (cnd), Cappela Agostino Steffani [period instrs] [I] Calig ▲ CAL 50855 [DDD]
Vierne, L.:Messe solennelle, w. P. Sefcik (bar), T. Götting (org), H. Hennig (cnd), Hanover CO, Hanover Youth Choir Ars Musici ▲ AM 1098-2 [DDD]

Gubrud, I. (sop)
Aitken, H.:Soledades, Cantata VII, w. M. Garrett (pno) CRI ▲ CD 595 [DDD]

Gubsky, Vladimir (sgr)
Shvedov, K.:Liturgy of St. John Chrysostom, w. Elena Rastvorova (cnd), Moscow New Choir Olympia ▲ OLY 481 [DDD]

Gudbjörnsson, Gunnar (ten)
Classical Spectacular 2, w. Royal PO, Michael Reed (cnd), J. Howard (bar), Scots Guards Band, Welsh Guards Band, London Choral Society RPO Records ▲ CDRPO 5010 [DDD]

Gueden, Hilde (sop)
Bizet, G.:Carmen, w. G. Simionato (mez), N. Gedda (ten), H. von Karajan (cnd), Vienna SO, Vienna Singverein *(rec live, Vienna Oct. 1954)* Melodram 2-▲ MEL 27012
Bruckner, A.:Te Deum, w. Hilde Zadeck (cta), Erich Majkut (ten), Gottlob Frick (bass), B. Walter (cnd), Vienna PO, Vienna State Opera Chorus *(rec live, 1955)* Enterprise ("Palladio" series) ▲ ENTPD 4209 [ADD]
Cimarosa, D.:Il Matrimonio segreto (sels), w. A. Noni (sop), F. Barbieri (mez), T. Schipa (ten), S. Bruscantini (bar), B. Christoff (bass), M. Rossi (cnd), La Scala Orch—Act I highlights [I] *(rec live, Milan March 22, 1949)* Melodram 2-▲ CDM 29505 [ADD]
The Early Recordings *(rec between 1942 & 1951)* Preiser ▲ PRE 90176 [AAD]

Gueden, Hilde (sop) (cont.)
Mozart, W.A.:Arias, w. Arleen Augér (sop), Kathleen Battle (sop), Irma Beilke (sop), Helena Braun (sop), Lisa Della Casa (sop), Maria Cebotari (sop), Ileana Cotrubas (sop), Helen Donath (sop), Mirella Freni (sop), Reri Grist (sop), Edita Gruberova (sop), Elisabeth Grümmer (sop), Ingeborg Hallstein (sop), Luise Helletsgruber (sop), Gundula Janowitz (sop), Sena Jurinac (sop), Erika Köth (sop), Evelyn Lear (sop), Wilma Lipp (sop), Margaret Marshall (sop), Edith Mathis (sop), Jarmila Novotna (sop), Margherita Perras (sop), Lucia Popp (sop), Elisabeth Rethberg (sop), Anneliese Rothenberger (sop), Elisabeth Schumann (sop), Elisabeth Schwarzkopf (sop), Graziella Sciutti (sop), Irmgard Seefried (sop), Graziella Sciutti (sop), Julia Varady (sop), Agnes Baltsa (mez), Margit Bokor (mez), Brigitte Fassbaender (mez), Christa Ludwig (mez), Ann Murray (mez), Francisco Araiza (ten), Anton Dermota (ten), Helge Rosvaenge (ten), Rudolf Schock (ten), Peter Schreier (ten), Leopold Simoneau (ten), Eric Tappy (ten), Richard Tauber (ten), Gösta Winbergh (ten), Josef Witt (ten), Fritz Wunderlich (ten), Christian Boesch (bar), Willy Domgraf-Fassbaender (bar), Karl Dönch (bar), Dietrich Fischer-Dieskau (bar), Erich Kunz (bar), Eberhard Wächter (bar), Hans Hotter (b-bar), Paul Schöffler (b-bar), Cesare Siepi (b-bar), José Van Dam (b-bar), Walter Berry (bass), Geraint Evans (bass), Nicolai Ghiaurov (bass), Alexander Kipnis (bass), Richard Mayr (bass), Kurt Moll (bass), James Morris (bass), Ezio Pinza (bass), Martti Talvela (bass), Giorgio Tozzi (bass), Hans Duhan (sgr), Res Fischer (sgr), Marie Gerhart (sgr), *(various orchs & cnds)*—sels from Idomeneo, Die Entführung aus der Serail, Le nozze di Figaro, Don Giovanni, Così fan tutte, Die Zauberflöte & various arias Orfeo d'or ("Festspiel Dokumente" series) 5-▲ 408955
Mozart, W.A.:Don Giovanni, w. L. Price (sop), G. Sciurri (sop), F. Wunderlich (ten), E. Wächter (bar), W. Berry (bass), H. von Karajan (cnd), Vienna PO, Vienna State Opera Chorus [I] *(rec live, 1963)* Verona 3-▲ 27065/67 (m) [AAD]
Mozart, W.A.:Nozze di Figaro, w. Anneliese Rothenberger (sop), Edith Mathis (sop), Peter Schreier (ten), Walter Berry (bar), Hermann Prey (bar), O. Suitner (cnd), Dresden Staatskapelle Berlin Classics 3-▲ BER 2096 [ADD]
Mozart, W.A.:Nozze di Figaro, w. Elisabeth Schwarzkopf (sop—Countess), Irmgard Seefried (sop—Susanna), Hilde Güden (mez—Cherubino), Paul Schöffler (bar—Almaviva), Erich Kunz (bass—Figaro), W. Furtwängler (cnd), Vienna PO, Vienna State Opera Chorus *(rec Salzburg Festival, Aug 8, 1953)* EMI Classics 3-▲ CDHC 66080
Mozart, W.A.:Nozze di Figaro (sels), w. Anneliese Rothenberger (sop), Hermann Prey (bar), Walter Berry (bass), O. Suitner (cnd), Dresden Staatskapelle Berlin Classics ▲ BER 9079 [ADD]
Mozart, W.A.:Zauberflöte, w. W. Lipp (sop), L. Simoneau (ten), W. Berry (bass), K. Bohme (bass), K. Böhm (cnd), Vienna PO, Vienna State Opera Chorus London ("Grand Opera" series) 2-▲ 414362-2 [ADD]
Puccini, G.:La Bohème, w. M. Freni (sop), G. Raimondi (ten), G. Taddei (bar), H. von Karajan (cnd), Vienna State Opera Orch, Vienna State Opera Chorus [I] *(rec live 11/30/63)* Melodram 2-▲ MELCD 27007
Puccini, G.:La Bohème, w. R. Tebaldi (sop), G. Prandelli (ten), G. Inghilleri (bar), F. Corena (bass), Raphäel Arié (bass), A. Erede (cnd), St. Cecilia Academy Orch Rome, St. Cecilia Academy Chorus Rome London 2-▲ 440233-2 [ADD]
Puccini, G.:La Bohème (sels), w. M. Freni (sop), G. Raimondi (ten), R. Panerai (bar), H. von Karajan (cnd), Vienna State Opera Orch—7 arias & scenes [I] *(rec live 11/9/63)* Verona 2-▲ 27079/80
Schmidt, F.:Das Buch mit sieben Siegeln, w. I. Malaniuk (cta), A. Dermota (ten), F. Wunderlich (ten), W. Berry (bass), D. Mitropoulos (cnd), Vienna PO, Vienna Singverein *(rec live, Salzburg Festival 1959)* Melodram 2-▲ MEL 27078
Schmidt, F.:Das Buch mit sieben Siegeln, w. Ira Malaniuk (cta), Anton Dermota (ten), Fritz Wunderlich (ten), Walter Berry (bass), D. Mitropoulos (cnd), Vienna PO, Vienna Singverein Sony Classical ("Festspiel Dokumente:Salzburger Festspiele" series) 2-▲ SM2K 68442
Strauss (II), Joh.:Die Fledermaus, w. R. Streich (sop), G. Di Stefano (ten), G. Stolze (ten), G. Zampieri (ten), E. Wächter (bar), W. Berry (bass), E. Kunz (bar), H. von Karajan (cnd), Vienna State Opera Orch, Vienna State Opera Chorus [G] Arkadia 3-▲ 215 (m) [ADD]
Strauss (II), Joh.:Die Fledermaus, w. E. Köth (sop), R. Resnik (mez), W. Kmentt (ten), G. Zampieri (ten), E. Wächter (bar), W. Berry (bass), E. Kunz (bar), H. von Karajan (cnd), Vienna PO, Vienna State Opera Chorus, with Gala Sequence [G] London 2-▲ 421046-2 [ADD]
Strauss (II), Joh.:Die Fledermaus, w. J. Patzak (ten), A. Dermota (ten), A. Jaresch (ten), A. Poell (b-bar), W. Lipp (sop), S. Wagner (mez), K. Preger (ten), C. Krauss (cnd), Vienna PO *(rec early 1950s)* London ("Historic" series) 2-▲ 425990-2 [ADD]
Strauss (II), Joh.:Music of, w. H. von Karajan (cnd), Vienna PO, Vienna Men's Choral Association—5 waltzes & polkas—Blue Danube; Annen-Polka; Pizzicato Polka; Voices of Spring; Imperial Waltz [G] Arkadia 3-▲ 215 (m) [ADD]
Strauss (II), Joh.:Wiener Blut (sels), w. M. Schramm (sop), R. Schock (ten), B. Kusche (bar), R. Stolz (cnd), Vienna SO [G] Eurodisc ▲ 25-8370 [ADD]
Strauss, R.:Arabella, w. L. Della Casa (sop), I. Malaniuk (cta), A. Dermota (ten), W. Kmentt (ten), G. London (bar), O. Edelmann (bass), G. Solti (cnd), Vienna PO [G] London ("Grand Opera" series) 2-▲ 430387-2 [ADD]
Strauss, R.:Ariadne auf Naxos, w. L. Della Casa (sop), I. Seefried (sop), R. Schock (ten), P. Schöffler (bass), K. Böhm (cnd), Vienna PO *(rec Salzburg Festival, 1954)* Deutsche Grammophon 2-▲ 445332-2 (m) [ADD]
Strauss, R.:Daphne, w. F. Wunderlich (ten), J. King (ten), P. Schöffler (bass), K. Böhm (cnd), Vienna SO, Vienna State Opera Chorus *(rec live 1963)* Deutsche Grammophon 2-▲ 445322-2
Strauss, R.:Der Rosenkavalier, w. L. Della Casa (sop), S. Jurinac (sop), E. Kunz (bar), O. Edelmann (b-bar), H. von Karajan (cnd), Vienna PO, Vienna State Opera Chorus [G] *(rec live in Salzburg, 7/26/60)* Arkadia 3-▲ 213 [ADD]
Strauss, R.:Der Rosenkavalier, w. M. Reining (sop), S. Jurinac (sop), L. Weber (bass), E. Kleiber (cnd), Vienna PO, Vienna State Opera Chorus [G] London ("Historic" series) ▲ 425950-2 (m) [ADD]
Strauss, R.:Die Schweigsame Frau, w. F. Wunderlich (ten), H. Prey (bar), H. Hotter (b-bar), K. Böhm (cnd), Vienna PO *(rec Salzburg Festival, 1959)* Deutsche Grammophon 2-▲ 445335-2 (m) [ADD]
Verdi, G.:Otello, w. G. Simionato (mez), M. del Monaco (ten), A. Protti (bar), C. Siepi (b-bar), A. Erede (cnd), St. Cecilia Academy Orch Rome, St. Cecilia Academy Chorus Rome London 2-▲ 440242-2 [ADD]
Verdi, G.:Rigoletto, w. Hilde Gueden (sop—Gilda), Piero de Palma (ten—Borsa), Luisa Ribacchi (mez—Giovanna), Giulietta Simionato (mez—Maddalena), Mario del Monaco (ten—Duca de Mantova), Aldo Protti (bar—Rigoletto), Fernando Corena (bass—Conte Monterone), Cesare Siepi (bass—Sparafucile), A. Erede (cnd), St. Cecilia Academy Orch Rome, St. Cecilia Academy Chorus Rome Theorema ▲ TH 121179/180
Wie die Welt sie kannte Preiser ▲ PRE 90227 [ADD]

Guelfi, Giangiacomo (bar)
Bizet, G.:Carmen (sels), w. Margherita Benetti (sop—Micaela), Pia Tassinari (sop—Carmen), Franco Corelli (ten—Don José), Giangiacomo Guelfi (bar—Escamillo), A. Basile (cnd), Turin RAI Orch—[Act. 1] È l'amore uno strano augello; Josè!...Micaela!...Ah! mi parla di lei; Mia madre io vedo ancor, si, si; Presso il bastion di Siviglia; Tacer, dì, non vuoi tu?; [Act 2] Con voi ber; Alto là! Chi va là ; Il fior che avevi a me tu dato; [Act 3] Andiam, nostra sorte sappiam!; [Act 4] Largo! Largo! L'Alcade; Sei tu?...Son io; Più non m'ama il tuo cor? *(rec Torino Dec. 15, 1961)* Myto ▲ MCD 953132
Catalani, A.:La Wally, w. R. Scotto (sop), R. Tebaldi (sop), M. del Monaco (ten), C.M. Giulini (cnd), *(orch unknown)* *(rec Milan, 1953)* Great Opera Performances 2-▲ GOP 734
Catalani, A.:La Wally, w. R. Scotto (sop—Walter), R. Tebaldi (sop—Wally), J. Gardino (mez—Afra), M. Del Monaco (ten—Giuseppe Hagenbach), G.G. Guelfi (bar—Vincenzo Gellner), G. Tozzi (bass—Stromminger), C. M. Giulini (cnd), La Scala Orch, La Scala Chorus *(rec Dec. 7, 1953)* Legato Classics 2-▲ LCD 177-2 [ADD]
Mascagni, P.:Cavalleria rusticana, w. F. Cossotto (mez), C. Bergonzi (ten), H. von Karajan (cnd), La Scala Orch, La Scala Chorus [I] Deutsche Grammophon 3-▲ 419257-2 [ADD]
Puccini, G.:La fanciulla del West, w. E. Steber (sop), M. del Monaco (ten), D. Mitropoulos (cnd), Venice Teatro La Fenice Orch, Venice Teatro La Fenice Chorus *(rec live, 6/15/54)* Arkadia 2-▲ 565 (m)

Guelfi, Giangiacomo (bar) (cont.)
Puccini, G.:La fanciulla del West (sels), w. Magda Olivero (sop—Minnie), Corinna Vozza (mez—Wowkle), Paolo Caroli (ten—Harry), Giacomo Lauri-Volpi (ten—Dick Johnson), Marco Rogani (ten—Pony Express Rider), Salvatore di Tommaso (ten—Trin), Adelio Zagonara (ten—Nick), Virgilio Ascorro (bar—Sid), Alfredo Colella (bar—Jake Wallace), Giuseppe Forgione (bar—Bello), Giancarlo Guelfi (bar—Jack Rance), Arturo la Porta (bar—Sonora), Gino Conti (bass—José Castro), Piere Passarotti (bass—Bill), Enzo Titta (bass—Larkens), Giulio Tomei (bass—Ashby), V. Bellezza (cnd), Rome Opera Orch, Rome Opera Chorus—Minnie, dalla mia casa son partito; Laggiù nel Soledad; Chi c'è per farmi i ricci; Oh! Mister Johnson, siete rimasto; Non so ben neppur io; Io non son che una povera fanciulla; No, Minnie, non piangete; Vorrei mettermi queste; Hallo!; Oh, se sapeste; Credo che abbiate torto; Ma ti giuro ch'io non ti lascio più; Vieni fuori!; Una parola sola!...Or son sei mesi; Che c'è di nuovo Jack?; È là; Siete pronto; Ch'ella mi creda; È Minnie!...È Minnie! *(rec Rome, Mar. 30, 1957)* Golden Age of Opera ▲ GAO 180 [ADD]
Spontini, G.:Agnes von Hohensauften, w. L. Udovick (sop), D. Dow (sop), F. Corelli (ten), A. Colzani (bar), V. Gui (cnd), Florence Maggio Musicale Orch, Florence Maggio Musicale Chorus [I] *(rec live 5/9/54)* Melodram 2-▲ MEL 27055 (m) [AAD]
Spontini, G.:Agnes von Hohensauften, w. M. Caballé (sop), A. Stella (sop), B. Prevedi (ten), R. Muti (cnd), Rome Radio Orch, Rome RAI Chorus [I] *(rec live, 4/30/70)* Myto 2-▲ 2 MCD 90215 (m) [ADD]
Verdi, G.:Aida, w. Antonietta Stella (sop—Aida), Mirella Parutto (sop—Priestess), Giulietta Simionato (mez—Amneris), Giuseppe DiStefano (ten—Radames), Giuseppe Zampiere (ten—Messenger), Giangiacomo Guelfi (bar—Amonasro), Silvio Maionica (bass—King of Egypt), Nicola Zaccaria (bass–Ramfis), A. Votto (cnd), La Scala Orch, La Scala Chorus *(rec Milan, Dec 7, 1956)* Legato Classics 2-▲ LCD 204-2 [ADD]
Verdi, G.:Aida, w. M. C. Verna (sop), M. Pirazzini (cta), F. Corelli (ten), G. Neri (bass), A. Questa (cnd), Turin RAI SO, Turin RAI Chorus *(rec 1956)* Enterprise ("Palladio") 2-▲ ENT PD 4184 [ADD]
Verdi, G.:Aida (sels), w. Luisa Maragliano (sop), G. Gavazzeni (cnd)—Ciel! Mio padre; Pur ti riveggo, mia dolce Aida; La fatal pietra *(rec 1960 & 72)* Golden Age of Opera ▲ GAO 204 [ADD]
Verdi, G.:Aida (sels), w. A. Cerquetti (sop), E. Nicolai (mez), G. Penno (ten), B. Christoff (bass), G. Santini (cnd), Naples Teatro San Carlo Orch, Naples Teatro San Carlo Chorus [I] [highlights] *(rec live, Naples, July 24, 1954)* Golden Age of Opera ▲ GAO 134 [ADD]
Verdi, G.:Attila, w. Antonietta Stella (sop), Gianfranco Cecchele (ten), Ruggiero Raimondi (bass), R. Muti (cnd), Rome RAI Orch, Rome RAI Chorus *(rec live 1970)* Memories 2-▲ HR 4178/79 (m)
Verdi, G.:Attila, w. Antonietta Stella (sop), Gianfranco Cecchele (ten), Ruggiero Raimondi (bass), R. Muti (cnd), Rome RAI SO, Rome RAI Chorus *(rec Rome, Nov. 21, 1970)* Pantheon 2-▲ PHE 6642 (m)
Verdi, G.:Attila, w. M. Roberti (sop—Odabella), G. Limarilli (tenor—Foresto), G. Guelfi (baritone—Ezio), B. Christoff (bass—Attila), B. Bartoletti (cnd), Florence Teatro Comunale Orch, Florence Teatro Comunale Chorus *(rec Jan. 12, 1962)* Myto 2-▲ MCD 93589 [DDD]
Verdi, G.:La forza del destino (sels), w. Franco Corelli (ten—Don Alvaro), Giangiacomo Guelfi (bar—Don Carlo), A. Basile (cnd), Turin RAI Orch—[Act 3] La vita è inferno all'infelice...; O tu che in seno agli angeli; Al tradimento...; Amici in vita e in morte; Piano...qui posi...; Solenne in quest'ora; Morir!...tremenda cosa!...; Urna fatale del mio destino; E s'altra prova rinvenir potessi?...; E' salvo! oh gioia immensa; [Act 4] Giunge qualcuno...aprite...; Invano Alvaro ti celasti al mondo; Fratello...; Le minacce, i fieri accenti; Ah, la macchia del tuo stemma *(rec Torino Feb. 6, 1957)* Myto ▲ MCD 953132
Verdi, G.:Jérusalem, w. Leyla Gencer (sop), Giacomo Aragall (ten), G. Gavazzeni (cnd), Venice Teatro La Fenice Orch, Venice Teatro La Fenice Chorus *(rec Venice, Sept 24, 1963)* Agorá Music ("Phoenix" series) 2-▲ 506
Verdi, G.:Jérusalem, w. Leyla Gencer (sop), Giacomo Aragall (ten), G. Gavazzeni (cnd), Venice Teatro La Fenice Orch, Venice Teatro La Fenice Chorus [I] *(rec live 9/24/63)* Melodram 2-▲ MEL 27004
Verdi, G.:Jérusalem, w. Leyla Gencer (sop), Giacomo Aragall (ten), G. Gavazzeni (cnd), Venice Teatro La Fenice Orch [I] *(rec live 9/24/63)* Verona 2-▲ 27040/41 (m) [AAD]
Verdi, G.:Macbeth (sels), w. L. Gencer (sop), G. Lamberti (ten), G. Gavazzeni (cnd), Venice Teatro La Fenice Orch, Venice Teatro La Fenice Chorus [I] [highlights] *(rec live 4/9/68)* Melodram ▲ MEL 15002
Verdi, G.:Nabucco, w. Gloria Lane (mez), Gianni Raimondi (ten), Nicolai Ghiaurov (bass), Elena Saliotis (sgr), G. Gavazzeni (cnd), La Scala Orch, La Scala Chorus *(rec La Scala Theater, Milan, Dec. 7, 1966)* Pantheon 2-▲ PHE 6757 (m)
Verdi, G.:Stiffelio, w. Gulin–Dominguez (sop), G. Limarilli (ten), G. Gavazzeni (cnd), Rome Opera Orch, Rome Opera Chorus *(rec live, Rome 1964)* Melodram 2-▲ MEL 27033
Verdi, G.:I vespri siciliani, w. L. Gencer (sop), G. Limarilli (ten), N. Rossi–Lemeni (bass), G. Gavazzeni (cnd), Rome Opera Orch, Rome Opera Chorus [I] *(rec live, Rome 1964)* Melodram 2-▲ MEL 27037 [ADD]
Verdi, G.:I vespri siciliani, w. Leyla Gencer (sop), Nicola Rossi–Lemeni (bass), Gastone Limarilli (sgr), G. Gavazzeni (cnd), Rome Opera Orch, Rome Opera Chorus *(rec Dec 5, 1964)* Pantheon 2-▲ PHE 6770
Wagner, R.:Lohengrin (sels), w. R. Tebaldi (sop—Elsa), E. Nicolai (mez—Ortrud), G. Penno (ten—Lohengrin), G. Guelfi (bar—Telramund), G. Neri (bass—Heinrich), G. Santini (cnd), Naples Teatro San Carlo Orch, Naples Teatro San Carlo Chorus—8 soprano duets/trio from Acts 1–3 [I] *(rec live, Naples, 12/26/54)* Standing Room Only ▲ SRO 834-1 [ADD]

Guénot, L. (bass)
Massenet, J.:Manon, w. G. Féraldy (sop), J. Rogatchewsky (ten), E. Cohen (cnd), Paris Opéra–Comique Orch, Paris Opéra–Comique Chorus [F] *(rec 1928–29 for Columbia)* Classical Collector 2-▲ FDC 2 2001 (m) [AAD]

Guento, Michele (sgr)
Verdi, G.:Un giorno di regno, w. Maria Casula (sop), Angelo Romero (bar), Enrico Fissore (bass), Franca Fabbri (sgr), Islen Moubayed (sgr), Ruggero Rado (sgr), Bernardino Trotta (sgr), A. Zedda (cnd), *(orch unknown)* Great Opera Performances 2-▲ GOP 782

Guerassimova, Natalia (sop)
Mahler, G.:Sym 2, w. Olga Alexandrova (alt), E. Svetlanov (cnd), Russian State SO, Russian Radio–TV Large Academic Choir Russian Season 2-▲ 288136.37
Mahler, G.:Sym 4, w. E. Svetlanov (cnd), Russian State SO Russian Season ▲ RUS 288133
Shostakovich, D.:Suite 1 Jazz Orch, w. Moscow Trio Russian Season ("Russian Season" series) ▲ RUS 288088

Guerrera, Frank (bar)
Wagner, R.:Lohengrin, w. H. Traubel (sop—Elsa), A. Varnay (sop—Ortrud), L. Melchior (ten—Lohengrin), F. Guerrera (bar—Herald), H. Janssen (bar—Telramund), D. Ernster (bass—King Heinrich), F. Stiedry (cnd), Metropolitan Opera Orch, New York Metropolitan Opera Chorus *(rec live Jan. 6, 1950)* Danacord 3-▲ DACOCD 322/24 [AAD]

Guerrini, Barbara (mez)
Puccini, G.:Manon Lescaut (sels), w. B. Gigli (ten), M. Borriello (bar), *(orch unknown)* *(rec Milan, 1950)* Melodram ▲ CD 15005 (m)

Guerrini, Remo (sgr)
Monteverdi, C.:Ballo delle ingrate, w. Carlo Lepore (bass), Daniela Barcellona (sgr), Daniela Ciliberti (sgr), Andrea Concetti (sgr), Hans van Dijk (sgr), Nadia Mantelli (sgr), Elena Marazzi (sgr), Humberto Orellana (sgr), Claudia Pallini (sgr), Luigi Polsini (sgr), Rosa Ricciotti (sgr), Alberto Rota (sgr), Ludovica Scoppola (sgr), *(orch unknown)* Nuova Era ▲ NUO 7224

Guglielmi, Margherita (sop)
Donizetti, G.:Don Pasquale, w. Margherita Guglielmi (sop—Norina), Alfredo Kraus (ten—Ernesto), Rolando Panerai (bar—Malatesta), Paolo Montarsolo (bass—Don Pasquale), P. Bellugi (cnd), La Scala Orch, La Scala Chorus *(rec Jan 13, 1974)* Golden Age of Opera 2-▲ GAO 202/203 [ADD]
Puccini, G.:La Bohème, w. Ileana Cotrubas (sop—Mimi), Margherita Guglielmi (sop—Musetta), José Carreras (ten—Rodolfo), Saverio Porzano (ten—Parpignol), Regolo Romani (ten—Vendor), Claudio Giombi (bar—Benoit), Gianni Maffeo (bar—Schaunard), Angelo Romero (bar—Marcello), Alfredo Giacomotti (bass—Alcindoro), Carlo Meliciani (bass—Customs Officer), Giuseppe Morresi (bass—Sergeant), Paolo Washington (bass—Colline), G. Prêtre (cnd), La Scala Orch, La Scala Chorus *(rec Washington D.C., Sept 8, 1976)* Legato Classics 2-▲ LCD 201-2
Rossini, G.:L'equivoco Stravagante, w. G. Baratti (ten), R. Panerai (bar), S. Bruscantini (b-bar), B. Rigacci (cnd), *(orch unknown)* [I] *(rec Naples, 1974)* Golden Age of Opera 2-▲ GAO 154/55

Guglielmi, Margherita (sop) (cont.)
Verdi, G.:Un ballo in maschera (sels), w. José Carreras (ten), Frederico Davià (bass), Giovanni Foiani (bass), F. Molinari–Pradelli (cnd), La Scala Orch, La Scala Chorus—S'avanza il Conte...La rivedrà nell'estasi; Ma se m'è forza perderti...Ah! dessa è là! *(rec Milan, Feb 13, 1975)* Goldies ▲ GLD 63203 [ADD]

Gui, Henri (bar)
Gounod, C.:Roméo et Juliette, w. M. Freni (sop—Juliette), F. Corelli (ten—Roméo), H. Gui (bar—Mercutio), C. Càles (bar—Capulet), X. Depraz (bass—Frère Laurent), A. Lombard (cnd), Paris Opera Orch, Paris Opera Chorus EMI Classics ▲ CDMB 65290

Guido, J. (sop)
Massenet, J.:Werther, w. J. Guido (sop—Sophie), N. Rankin (sop—Charlotte), C. Valletti (ten—Werther), A. Cosenza (bar—Albert), R. Cellini (cnd), New Orleans Opera Orch *(rec 1956)* Golden Age of Opera 2-▲ GAO 141/42 [ADD]

Guillaume, Edith (mez)
Gade, N.W.:Elverskud, w. L. Balslev (sop), M. Melbye (bar), F. Rasmussen (cnd), Collegium Musicum, Canzone Choir [Da] Kontrapunkt ▲ 32070 [DDD]
Klit, L.:The Last Virtuoso, w. Hanne Andersen (sop), Jan Lund (ten), Jesper Buhl (bar), Jørgen Ole Børch (bass), S. A. Johansen (cnd), *(ensemble unknown)* Kontrapunkt ▲ KPT 32221

Guimaraes, Leila (sop)
Villa–Lobos, H.:Bachianas brasileiras (comp), w. Nelson Freire (pno), I. Karabtchevsky (cnd), Brazil SO *(rec June–Sept 1987)* Iris 3-▲ 143/3 [ADD]

Guinn, Leslie (bar)
Foster, S.C.:Songs, w. Jan DeGaetani (mez), G. Kalish (pno) Elektra/Nonesuch ▲ 79158-2 [AAD] als
Foster, S.C.:Songs, w. Jan DeGaetani (mez), G. Kalish (pno), Washington Camerata Chorus Elektra/Nonesuch ■ 71333-4
Rouse, C.:Mitternachtlieder, w. S. Hodkinson (cnd), Eastman Musica Nova Ensemble *(rec Eastman Theater, Nov 29, 1983)* Albany ▲ TROY 192 [ADD]
Schumann, R.:Vocal Duets, w. J. DeGaetani (mez), G. Kalish (pno)—12 duets Elektra/Nonesuch ▲ 71364-2

Guiot, Andrée (sop)
Bizet, G.:Carmen, w. M. Callas (sop), N. Gedda (ten), R. Massard (bar), G. Prêtre (cnd), Paris Opera Orch, Paris Opera Chorus [F] EMI Classics 2-▲ CDCB 54368
Bizet, G.:Carmen (sels), w. M. Callas (sop), N. Gedda (ten), R. Massard (bar), G. Prêtre (cnd), Paris Opera Orch [F] EMI Classics ▲ CDM 63075 ■ EG 63075
Offenbach, J.:Les Contes d'Hoffmann (sels), w. Andréa Guiot (sop—Antonia), Mady Mesplé (sop—Olympia), Suzanne Sarroca (sop—Giulietta), Albert Lance (ten—Hoffmann), Gabriel Bacquier (bar—Docteur Miracle), Robert Massard (bar—Dapertutto), J. Etcheverry (cnd), *(orch unknown)* —Prologue; Dans les rôles d'amoureux...; Il était une fois...; Allons! Courage et confiance...; C'est moi, coppélius!...; Les oiseaux dans la charmille; Barcarolle; Scintille, diamant...; Malheureux, tu ne comprends donc pas...; Hélas! Mon coeur s'égare encore...; Elle a fui, la touterelle...; Eh bien! Quoi! Toujours en colère!...; Tu ne chanteras plus?... Adès ▲ ADE 202702 [AAD]
Satie, E.:Geneviéve de Brabant, w. M. Mesplé (sop), D. Millet (sop), A. Esposito (sop), J.C. Benoit (bar), A. Ciccolini (pno), P. Dervaux (cnd), Orch de Paris, Paris Opera Chorus Virgin Classics 2-▲ CDZB 62877
Satie, E.:Socrate, w. M. Mesplé (sop), D. Millet (sop), A. Esposito (sop), J. C. Benoit (bar), P. Dervaux (cnd), Orch de Paris, Paris Opera Chorus Virgin Classics 2-▲ CDZB 62877

Guittard (sgr)
Rodgers, R.:Oklahoma!, w. Andreas (sgr), *(other artists unknown)* [1979 Broadway revival cast] RCA ▲ RCD 13572 ■ CBK 13572

Gulegina, Maria (sop)
Tchaikovsky, P.:Queen of Spades, w. O. Borodina (mez), G. Grigorian (ten), V. Gergiev (cnd), Kirov Opera Orch, Kirov Opera Chorus Philips ▲ 438141-2

Gulin, Angeles (sop)
Bellini, V.:Beatrice di Tenda, w. E. Zilio (mez), J. Carreras (ten), R. Bruson (bar), F. Mannino (cnd), Turin RAI Orch, Turin RAI Chorus [I] *(rec live Oct. 9, 1973)* Golden Age of Opera 2-▲ GAO 158/59 [ADD]
Giordano, U.:Andrea Chénier, w. A. Gulin (sop—Maddalena), C. Bergonzi (ten—Andrea Chenier), S. Milnes (bar—Gérard), A. Guadagno (cnd), New Philharmonia Orch, Ambrosian Chorus *(rec live, London, 2/8/70)* Myto 2-▲ 2 MCD 91750 [ADD]
Puccini, G.:Manon Lescaut (sels), w. Carlo Gaifa (ten), Giuseppe Giacomini (ten), Guido Mazzini (bass), Giorgio Tadeo (bass), M. Arena (cnd), *(orch unknown)*—Tra voi belle; Cortese damigella; Donna non vidi mai; Vedete, io son fedele; Tu, tu, amore; Ah! Manon, mi tradisce; Lescaut!; Ansia eterna crudel; No, pazzo son; Tutta su me ti posa; Manon...senti amor mio *(rec Treviso, Oct. 16, 1974)* Golden Age of Opera 2-▲ GAO 189/90 [ADD]
Verdi, G.:Stiffelio, w. A. Gulin (sop—Lina), M. del Monaco (ten—Stiffelio), A. Marchiandi (ten—Raffaele), G. Fioravanti (bar—Stankar), J. Hecht (bass—Jorg), O. de Fabritiis (cnd), Naples Teatro San Carlo Orch, Naples Teatro San Carlo Chorus *(rec Dec. 26, 1972)* Standing Room Only 2-▲ SRO 169-2

Gulin–Dominguez (sop)
Verdi, G.:Stiffelio, w. G. Limarilli (ten), G. Guelfi (bar), G. Gavazzeni (cnd), Rome Opera Orch, Rome Opera Chorus *(rec live, Rome 1964)* Melodram 2-▲ MEL 27033

Gullino, V. (sgr)
Donizetti, G.:La fille du régiment (sels), w. Mirella Freni (sop), Anna di Stasio (mez), Angelo Mercuriali (ten), Luciano Pavarotti (ten), Wladimiro Ganzarolli (bar), Walter Monachesi (bar), Giuseppe Morresi (bass), Luisa Rezzadore (sgr), N. Sanzogno (cnd), La Scala Orch, La Scala Chorus Budget ("The Greatest Voice in Opera" series) ▲ SYP 108

Gulyás, Dénes (ten)
Caldara, A.:Magnificat, w. M. Szücs (sop), K. Takács (cta), T. Bátor (bass), F. Szekeres (cnd), Budapest Strings, Budapest Madrigal Choir [L] Hungaroton ▲ HCD 31259 [DDD]
Erkel, F.:Hunyadi László, w. M. Kalmár (sop), S. Sass (sop), A. Molnar (ten), I. Gáti (bar), S. Sólyom–Nagy (bar), J. Kovács (cnd), Hungarian State Opera Orch, Hungarian State Opera Chorus [Hun] Hungaroton 3-▲ HCD 12581/83 [DDD]
Liszt, F.:Hungarian Coronation Mass, w. V. Kincses (sop), T. Tákacs (mez), L. Polgar (bass), G. Lehel (cnd), Budapest SO, Hungarian Radio Chorus [L] Hungaroton ▲ HCD 12148
Mahler, G.:Das Klagende Lied, w. Katalin Szendrényi (sop), Klára Takács (cta), A. Ligeti (cnd), Budapest SO, Péter Erdei (cnd), Hungarian Radio–TV Chorus Classical Diamonds ▲ CLD 4010 [DDD]
Sammartini, G.B.:Magnificat in B♭, w. Szücs (sop), Takács (alt), Bátor (bass), F. Szekeres (cnd), Budapest Strings, Budapest Madrigal Choir [L] Hungaroton ▲ HCD 31259 [DDD]
Vivaldi, A.:Magnificat, RV.610, w. T. Takács (mez), T. Bátor (bass), R. Szücs (bass), F. Szekeres (cnd), Budapest Strings, Budapest Madrigal Choir [L] Hungaroton ▲ HCD 31259 [DDD]

Gunson, Ameral (mez)
Britten, H.:The Rape of Lucretia (sels), w. C. Pierard (sop), P. Rozario (sop), J. Rigby (cta), N. Robson (ten), D. Maxwell (bar), A. Opie (bar), A. Miles (bass), R. Hickox (cnd), City of London Sinfonia Chandos 2-▲ CHAN 9254/55 [DDD]
Janácek, L.:Slavonic Mass, w. F. Palmer (sop), M. King (mez), J. Mitchinson (ten), J. Parker–Smith (org), S. Rattle (cnd), City of Birmingham SO, City of Birmingham Sym Chorus EMI ▲ CDC 47504
Walton, W.:Gloria, w. N. Mackie (ten), S. Roberts (bar), D. Willcocks (cnd), Philharmonia Orch, Bach Choir [L] Chandos ▲ CHAN 8760 [DDD]

Gurevich, Michaela (sop)
Tchaikovsky, P.:Iolanta, w. Michaela Gurevich (sop—Iolanta), Jaqueline Miura (sop—Brigitta), Tatjana Tabachuk (mez—Martha), Annette Kuhn (mez—Laura), Ian Denolfo (ten—Godefroy), Keith Alexander Bolves (ten—Alméric), Alexander Ben (bar—Robert), Georg Lehner (bar—Ibn–Hakia), Arutiun Kotchinian (bass—René), Kurt Geysen (bass—Bertrand), H. Rotman (cnd), Warsaw PO, ECOV Ensemble Members *(rec Vooruit Center of the Arts, Ghent, Belgium, Aug 28–29, 1993)* CPO 2-▲ CPO 999456-2 [DDD]

Gustafson, Nancy (sop)
Lehár, F.:Das Land des Lächelns, w. Nancy Gustafson (sop—Lisa), Naomi Itami (sop—Mi), Lynton Atkinson (ten—Gustl), Jerry Hadley (ten—Prince Sou Chong), R. Bonynge (cnd), English CO *(rec EMI Abbey Road, Studio One, London, England; Aug 2–25, 1995)* Telarc ▲ CD-80419 [DDD]

▲ = CD ♦ = Enhanced CD Δ = MD ■ = Cassette Tape □ = DCC

Gustafson, Nancy (sop) (cont.)

Lehár, F.:Der Zarewitsch, w. Nancy Gustafson (sop—Sonia), Naomi Itami (sop—Mascha), Lynton Atkinson (ten—Ivan), Jerry Hadley (ten—the Czarevitch), Jeffrey Carl (bar—Grand Duke/Soldier), R. Bonynge (cnd), English CO *(rec EMI Abbey Road, Studio One, London, England; Aug 25–27, 1995)* Telarc ▲ CD-80395 [DDD]

Mahler, G.:Sym 2, w. Florence Quivar (mez), Z. Mehta (cnd), Israel PO, Prague Phil Chorus *(rec Fredric R. Mann Auditorium, Tel Aviv, Jan–Feb. 1994)* Teldec ▲ 94545-2 [DDD]

Pavarotti & Friends 2, w. Luciano Pavarotti (ten), Bryan Adams (sgr), Andreas Vollenweider (kbd), Michael Kamen (cnd), Leone Mageira (cnd), Bologna Community Theater Orch London ▲ 444460–2 ■ 444460–4

Wagner, R.:Das Rheingold, w. Gabriele Fontana (sop—Woglinde), Nancy Gustafson (sop—Freia), Ildiko Komlosi (mez—Wellgunde), Hanna Schwarz (mez—Fricka), Elena Zaremba (mez—Erda), Margareta Hintermeier (cta—Flosshilde), Kim Begley (ten—Loge), Peter Schreier (ten—Mime), Thomas Sunnegardh (ten—Froh), Robert Hale (bass-bar—Wotan), Walter Fink (bass—Fafner), Franz-Josef Kapellmann (bass—Alberich), Jan-Hendrik Rootering (bass—Fasolt), Eike Wilm Schulte (bass—Donner), C. von Dohnányi (cnd), Cleveland Orch *(rec Severance Hall, Cleveland, Ohio, Dec 1993)* London 2–▲ 443690–2

Gustavson, Eva (mez)

Verdi, G.:Aida, w. H. Nelli (sop), G. Tucker (ten), G. Valdengo (bar), A. Toscanini (cnd), NBC SO, Robert Shaw Chorale [I] RCA Gold Seal 7–▲ 60326–2–RG (m) [ADD] 6–■ 60326–4–RG (CrO2)

Verdi, G.:Aida, w. H. Nelli (sop), G. Tucker (ten), G. Valdengo (bar), A. Toscanini (cnd), NBC SO, Robert Shaw Chorale [I] RCA Gold Seal 3–▲ 60251–2–RG (m) [ADD] 2–■ 60251–4–RG (CrO2)

Guthrie, Frederick (bass)

Bach, J.S.:Magnificat, BWV 243, w. M. Coertse (sop), M. Sjöstedt (sop), H. Rössl–Majdan (mez), A. Dermota (ten), F. Prohaska (cnd), Vienna State Opera Orch, Vienna State Opera Chorus [L] *(rec June 1957)* Vanguard Classics ("The Bach Guild" series) ▲ OVC 2010 [ADD]

Bach, J.S.:St. John Passion, w. P. Curtin (sop), E. Thomann (sop), E. Alberts (cta), W. Kmentt, J. Van Kesteren (ten), R. Springer (bar), O. Wiener (bar), D. Smith (b–bar), F. Guthrie (bass), F. Lukasowsky (bass), H. Scherchen (cnd), Vienna State Opera Orch, Vienna Academy Chorus [G] *(rec ca 1960)* MCA Classics 2–▲ MCAD2–9804

Haydn, J.:Die Schöpfung, w. Anny Felbermayer (sop—Eve), Teresa Stich–Randall (sop—Gabriel), Anton Dermota (ten—Uriel), Paul Schöffler (b–bar—Adam), Frederick Guthrie (bass—Raphael), Franz Holletschek (cembalo), M. Wöldike (cnd), Vienna State Opera Orch, Vienna State Opera Chorus *(rec Musikverein, Vienna, Austria, May 1955)* Vanguard Classics 2–▲ SVC 34/35 [AAD]

Mozart, W.A.:Missa, K.427, w. A. Giebel (sop), E. Lear (sop), P. Munteanu (ten), S. Celibidache (cnd), Rome RAI SO, Rome RAI Chorus *(rec Mar. 26, 1960)* Emozioni ▲ CDAR 2007 [ADD]

Mozart, W.A.:Requiem, w. S. Jurinac (sop), L. West (alt), H. Loeffler (ten), H. Scherchen (cnd), Vienna State Opera Orch, Vienna State Opera Chorus *(rec 1958)* Andromeda ▲ ANR 2525 [ADD]

Mozart, W.A.:Requiem, w. S. Jurinac (sop), L. West (alt), H. Loeffler (ten), R. Leibowitz (cnd), Vienna State Opera Orch, Vienna State Opera Chorus [L] *(rec 1958)* MCA Classics 2–▲ MCAD2 9816 [AAD]

Weill, K.:The Threepenny Opera, w. Liane (sop—Polly Peachum), A. Felbermayer (sop—Lucy), H. Fassler (sop—Jenny), R. Anday (cta—Mrs. Peachum), K. Preger (ten—Macheath), H. Roswaenge (ten—Street Crier), A. Jerger (bar—Peachum), *(cnd & orch unknown)* Vanguard Classics ▲ OVC 8057 [ADD]

Guthrie, Thomas (bass)

Purcell, H.:Odes & Welcome Songs (misc), w. Jeni Bern (sop), Susan Bisatt (sop), William Purefoy (ct), Christopher Robson (ct), Ian Honeyman (ten), R. Glenton (cnd), Orch of the Golden Age, Golden Age Choir—The noise of foreign wars (fragment) [ed. by Bruce Wood] *(rec Manchester Grammar School, England, May 13 & 14, 1995)* Naxos ▲ 8.553444 [DDD]

Purcell, H.:Raise, Raise the Voice, w. Jeni Bern (sop), Susan Bisatt (sop), William Purefoy (ct), Christopher Robson (ct), Ian Honeyman (ten), R. Glenton (cnd), Orch of the Golden Age, Golden Age Choir *(rec Manchester Grammar School, England, May 13 & 14, 1995)* Naxos ▲ 8.553444 [DDD]

Purcell, H.:Te Deum & Jubilate, w. Jeni Bern (sop), Susan Bisatt (sop), William Purefoy (ct), Christopher Robson (ct), Ian Honeyman (ten), David Staff (tpt), R. Glenton (cnd), Orch of the Golden Age, Golden Age Choir *(rec Manchester Grammar School, England, May 13 & 14, 1995)* Naxos ▲ 8.553444 [DDD]

Purcell, H.:Welcome to All the Pleasures, w. Jeni Bern (sop), Susan Bisatt (sop), William Purefoy (ct), Christopher Robson (ct), Ian Honeyman (ten), R. Glenton (cnd), Orch of the Golden Age, Golden Age Choir *(rec Manchester Grammar School, England, May 13 & 14, 1995)* Naxos ▲ 8.553444 [DDD]

Gutierrez, Elisabetta (mez)

Rossini, G.:La pietra del paragone, w. Tiziana Carraro (sop—Fulvia), Elisabetta Gutierrez (mez—Baronessa Aspasia), Sara Mingardo (cta—Clarice), William Matteuzzi (ten—Giocondo), Marco Camastra (bar—Pacuvio), Pietro Spagnoli (bar—Conte Asdrubale), Gioacchino Zarrelli (bar—Fabrizio), Josè Fardilha (bass—Macrobio), B. Aprea (cnd), Graz SO, Sluk Chamber Chorus Bratislava *(rec 1993)* Bongiovanni 2–▲ GB 2179/80 [DDD]

Gutorovich, Nikolai (ten)

Kabalevsky, D.:Colas Breugnon (ov), w. N. Isakova (sop), V. Kayevchenko (sop), L. Boldin (bar), G. Dudarev (bass), E. Maksimenko (sgr), G. Zhemchuzhin (cnd), Dantchenko Moscow Stanislavsky Music Theater Orch, Dantchenko Moscow Stanislavsky Music Theater Chorus Olympia 2–▲ OLY 291 [ADD]

Gütschow, Gert (spkr)

Eisler, H.:Deutsche Sinfonie, w. Hendrikje Wangemann (sop), Annette Markert (alt), Matthias Görne (bar), Peter Lika (bass), Volker Schwarz (speaker), L. Zagrosek (cnd), Leipzig Gewandhaus Orch, Ernst Senff Chorus *(rec Gewandhaus, Leipzig, May 1995)* London ("Entartet Musik" series) ▲ 448389–2 [DDD]

Gutstein, Ernst (bar)

Strauss, R.:Salome, w. Christel Goltz (sop), Helmut Melchert (ten), Siw Ericsdotter (sgr), O. Suitner (cnd), Dresden Staatskapelle *(rec 1963)* Berlin Classics 2–▲ BER 9101 [ADD]

Guttry, Paul (bar)

French Sacred Music of the 14th Century, Vol. 1, w. Schola Discantus, Bradford Findell (ct), John Delorey (ct), Peter McCabe (ten), Arthur Rawding (ten), Kevin Moll (cnd) *(rec Emmanuel Church, Boston, 1994)* Lyrichord ("Early Music" series) ▲ LYR 8012 [DDD]

Guy, Christine (alt)

Kraft, Walter:Christus, w. Anna Senn–Dähler (sop), Barbara Künzler (sop), Barbara Sutter (sop), Heidi Uhlmann (alt), Daniel Zellweger (alt), Matthias Senn (ten), Mikoto Usami (ten), Wolfgang Pailer (bass), Heinz Suter (bass), Klaus Knall (cnd), Evangelische Singgemeinde Choirs *(rec Ostdorf bei Balingen, Oct. 8–11, 1986)* Cantate 2–▲ 58004 [DDD]

Güyer, I. (mez)

Sinangil, A.D.:Mevlâna Oratorio (sels), w. Leyla Demiris (sop), Mesut Iktu (bar), Mustafa Iktu (bass), Kâmil Sekerkaran (fl), A. D. Sinangil (cnd), Istanbul State Opera Orch, Istanbul State Opera Chorus—Récitatif I; Choral; Récitatif II; V^5 partie Gallo ▲ CD 836 [ADD]

Guyer, Joyce (sop)

Haydn, J.:La Cantarina, w. Brenda Harris (sop—Gasparina), Joyce Guyer (sop—Don Ettore), D'Anna Fortunato (mez—Apollonia), Jon Garrison (ten—Don Pelagio), R. Palmer (cnd), Palmer CO *(rec St. Michael's Church, New York City, Apr. 1994)* Newport Classic ▲ NPD 85595 [DDD]

Moore, D.:Devil & Daniel Webster, w. Joyce Guyer (sop—Mary Stone), Benjamin Bongers (ten—Walter Butler), Michael Philip Davis (ten—Simon Girty), Matthew Foerschler (ten—Miser Stephens), Darren Keith Woods (ten—Mr. Scratch), Michael Lanman (bass—Blackbeard Teach), David Soxman (bass—Clerk), Brian Steele (bass—Daniel Webster), John Stephens (bass—Jabez Stone), Andrew Stuckey (bass—King Philip), Robert Gibby Brand (actor), Cary Miller (actor), R. Patterson (cnd), Kansas City SO, Kansas City Lyric Opera Chorus *(rec Sept 1995)* Newport Classic ▲ NPD 85585 [DDD]

Guyer, Joyce (sop) (cont.)

Sousa, J.P.:Songs, w. M. Wilson (sgr), D. Buck (sgr)—(6 soprano solos, 7 baritone solos, & 5 duets) I've made my plans for the summer (1907); The love that lives forever (1917); Valse song [The Crystal lute – from *The American Maid*, 1909]; Oh, ye lilies white (1887); Girls who have loved [or The Mystery of History – from *The Free Lance*, 1905]; There's a mery brown thrush (1926); The fighting race (1919); A Serenade in Seville (1924); My own, my Geraldine (1887); Sweet Miss Industry (1887); I wonder (1888); You cannot tell how old they are by looking at their skirts (1923); Forever and a day (1927); Sweetheart, I'm waiting (1895); Blue Ridge, I'm coming back to you (1917); Love's radiant hour (1928); A rare old fellow (1881); The Stars and Stripes forever (1898) [E] Premier ▲ PRCD 1011 [DDD]

Villanelle:French Masterworks for Horn, w. David Jolley (hn), Nancy Allen (hp), Samuel Sanders (pno) *(rec SUNY, Purchase Recital Hall, May 24–26, 1995)* Arabesque ▲ Z 6678 [DDD]

Guzman, Josie de (sgr)

Menotti, G.C.:Goya, w. Daner (sgr), Hernandez (sgr), Wentzel (sgr), S. Mercurio (cnd), Spoleto Festival Orch, Westminster Choir [I] *(rec live 1991)* Nuova Era 2–▲ 7060/61 [DDD]

Guzman, Salvador (ten)

Mozart, W.A.:Zauberflöte, w. Birgit Been (sop), Nathalie Boissy (sop), Marianne Seibel (sop), Renate Springer (sop), Elizabeth Vidal (sop), Eleanor James (mez), Salvador Guzman (ten), Herbert Hechenberger (ten), Wolfgang Newmann (ten), Klaus Häger (bass), Philip Langshaw (bass), Hans–Georg Moser (bass), P. Kuentz (cnd), Paul Kuentz Orch, Francis Bardot (cnd), Maitrise des Hauts–de–Seine members, Paul Kuentz Choirs Pierre Verany 2–▲ PVY 730055 [DDD]

Gwynne, Peter (nar)

Lumsdaine, D.:Aria for Edward John Eyre, w. M. Qualfe (sop), J. Tong (nar), D. Stanhope (cnd), Seymour Group Vox Australis ▲ VAST 011

Gwynne, Robert (sgr)

Mussorgsky, M.:Boris Godunov (sels), w. Walter Widdop (ten), Edward Halland (bass), Franklin Kelsey (sgr), A. Coates (cnd), *(orch unknown)*—Revolutionary Scene, Act. IV *(rec Hayes, Studio B, Nov. 3, 1925)* Claremont ▲ GSE 785061

György (sgr)

Kálmán, I.:Die Csárdásfürstin (sels), w. Erzsébet (sgr), Hanna (sgr), Róbert (sgr), Tamás (cnd), Hungarian Radio–TV SO, Hungarian Radio–TV Chorus Hungaroton ▲ HCD 16780 [AAD]

Gyurkovics, Mária (sop)

Kacsóh, P.:János Vitéz, w. Anna Zentai (sop—Iluska), Tivadar Bilicsi (sgr), Hilda Gobbi (sgr), Sándor Pethes (sgr—Bartolo), Róbert Ilosfalvy (ten—Kukorica), György Melis (bar—Bagó), György Radnai (bar—Strázsamester), László Domahidy (bass—Csősz), E. Lukács (cnd), Hungarian State Opera Orch, Hungarian Radio–TV Chorus *(rec Budapest, 1961)* Classical Diamonds 2–▲ CLD 4011–12 [AAD]

Verdi, G.:Rigoletto (sels), w. Olga Szönyi (mez), Ernö Kenéz (ten), János Fodor (bar), Alexander Svéd (bar), József Bódy (bass), Kórodi, Molinari–Pradelli (cnd), Hungarian State Opera Orch—Pari siamo!; Figlia! Mio padre! A te dappresso; Cortigiani! Vil' razza dannata; Tutte le feste al tempio...Ah! solo per me!; Chi è mai... *(rec 1955–56)* Hungaroton ("Great Hungarian Voices" series) ▲ HCD 31614 [ADD]

Gyuselev (sgr)

Rachmaninoff, S.:Aleko, w. Karnobatlova (sgr), Kaychev (sgr), *(orch & chorus unknown)* [R] Monitor 2–■ 55004

Haage, Peter (ten)

Schoenberg, A.:Gurrelieder, w. S. Dunn (sop), B. Fassbaender (mez), S. Jerusalem (ten), H. Becht (bass), H. Hotter (nar), R. Chailly (cnd), Berlin RSO, St. Hedwig's Cathedral Choir, Düsseldorf Municipal Choral Society [G] London 2–▲ 430321–2 [DDD]

Wagner, R.:Das Rheingold, w. M. Lipovšek (mez), J. Rappé (ten), H. Zednik (ten), A. Schmidt (bar), T. Adam (b–bar), H. Tschammer (bass), K. Rydl (bass), J. Morris (bass), B. Haitink (cnd), Bavarian RSO [G] EMI Classics 2–▲ CDCB 49853 [DDD]

Wagner, R.:Der Ring des Nibelungen (sels), w. E. Marton (sop), C. Studer (sop), K. Te Kanawa (sop), M. Lipovšek (mez), S. Jerusalem (ten), R. Goldberg (ten), J. Morris (bass), B. Haitink (cnd), Bayer RSO EMI Classics ▲ ZDC 54633

Wagner, R.:Siegfried, w. K. Te Kanawa (sop), E. Marton (sop), S. Jerusalem (ten), J. Morris (bass), B. Haitink (cnd), Bavarian RSO [G] EMI Classics 4–▲ CDCD 54290

Weill, K.:Mahagonny, w. U. Lemper (sop), H. Jungwirth (sop), H. Wildhaber (ten), T. Mohr (bar), S. Tremper (sgr), Jeffrey Cohen (pno), J. Mauceri (cnd), Berlin RIAS Chamber Ensemble [G] London ▲ 430168–2 [DDD]

Weill, K.:The Seven Deadly Sins, w. U. Lemper (sop), H. Jungwirth (sop), H. Wildhaber (ten), T. Mohr (bar), S. Tremper (sgr), J. Mauceri (cnd), Berlin RIAS Chamber Ensemble [G] London ▲ 430168–2 [DDD]

Zemlinsky, A. von:Der Traumgörge, w. P. Coburn (sop), J. Martin (sop), G. M. Ronge (sop), B. Calm (mez), H. Kruse (ten), J. Protschka (ten), H. Welker (bar), M. Blasius (bass), V. von Halem (bass), G. Albrecht (cnd), Frankfurt RSO [G] Capriccio 2–▲ CD 10241/2 [DDD]

Haan, John David de (ten)

Korngold, E.W.:Das Wunder der Heliane, w. A. Tomowa–Sintow (sop), R. Runkel (cta), N. Gedda (ten), H. Welker (bar), R. Pape (bass), J. Mauceri (cnd), Berlin RSO [G] London 3–▲ 436636–2 [DDD]

Haan, Richard (bar)

Respighi, O.:La bella dormente nel bosco, w. Ivana Czaková (sop—Old Woman/Green Fairy), Adriana Kohútková (sop—Blue Fairy/Nightingale), Henrietta Lednárová (sop—Frog/Spindle), Jana Valásková (sop—Princess), Dagmar Pecková (mez—Cuckoo/Cat), Denisa Šlepkovská (mez—Queen/Duchess), Karol Bernáth (ten—Doctor), Guillermo Dominguez (ten—Prince April), Igor Pasek (ten—Jester), Ján Durčo (bar—Ambassador), Richard Haan (bar—King/Woodcutter), Stanislav Benačka (bass—Doctor), Anton Kúrnava (bass—Doctor), Marián Smolárik (bass—Doctor), M. Adriano (nar—Mr. Dollar Chèques), M. Adriano (cnd), Slovak RSO Bratislava, Ján Rozehnal (cnd), Slovak Phil Chorus *(rec Concert Hall of the Slovak Radio, Bratislava, June 8–20, 1994)* Marco Polo ("Opera Classics" series) ▲ 8.223742 [DDD]

Respighi, O.:Lucrezia, w. Adriana Kohútková (sop—Venilia), Michela Remor (sop—Lucrezia), Stefania Kaluza (mez—La Voce), Denisa Šlepkovská (mez—Servia), Ludovít Ludha (ten—Collatino), Igor Pasek (ten—Bruto), Ján Durčo (bar—Tito/Valerio), Richard Haan (bar—Tarquinio), Rado Hanák (bass—Arunte/Spurio Lucrezio) *(rec Concert Hall of the Slovak Radio, Bratislava, June 9–16, 1994)* Marco Polo ▲ 8.223717 [DDD]

Respighi, O.:La Primavera, w. Henrietta Lednárová (sop—Prima fanciulla), Jana Valásková (sop—Sirvard), Beata Geriová (mez—Seconda fanciulla), Miroslav Dvorský (ten—Il giovine), Richard Haan (bar—L'orante), Vladimír Kubovčik (bass—Il vecchio), Vera Rasková (fl), M. Adriano (cnd), Slovak RSO Bratislava, Slovak Phil Chorus *(rec Slovak Radio Concert Hall, Bratislava, Jan. 4–9, Feb. 19 & June)* Marco Polo ▲ 8.223595 [DDD]

Haan, S. de (sgr)

Vine, C.:Love Song *(rec March 1992)* Tall Poppies ▲ TP013 [DDD]

Haas, Sabine (sgr)

Wagner, R.:Das Liebesverbot, w. Pamela Coburn (sop—Mariana), Friedrich Lenz (ten—Antonio), Hermann Prey (bar—Friedrich), Keith Engen (bass—Angelo), Raimund Grumbach (bass—Danieli/Wirt), Wolfgang Fassler (sgr—Luzio), Sabine Haas (sgr—Isabella/Claudios Schwester), Alfred Kuhn (sgr—Brighella/Chef der Sbirren), Hermann Sapell (sgr—Pontio Pilato), Robert Schunk (sgr—Claudio), Marianne Seibel (sgr—Dorella), W. Sawallisch (cnd), Bavarian State Orch, Bavarian State Chorus *(rec July 9, 1983)* Orfeo d'or 3–▲ 345953

Hackett, B. (sgr)

Mancini, H.:Film Music, w. A. Williams (sgr), J. Mathis (sgr), L. Albright (sgr), B. Greco (sgr), C. Byrd (sgr), P. Page (sgr), Mancini (cnd), Costa Orch, Conniff Orch, Mancini Orch—sels from Breakfast at Tiffany's; Peter Gunn; Mr. Lucky & others Columbia/Legacy ▲ CK 66505

Hacquard, Mario (bar)

Massenet, J.:Cléopâtre, w. B. Harries (sop), Daniéle Streiff (sop), M. Olmeda (sop), J. Maurette (ten), D. Henry (bar), P. Fournillier (cnd), St.–Etienne Nouvel Orch, Saint–Etienne Nouvel Chorus [F] *(rec live, Massenet Festival in Saint–Etienne 1990)* Koch Schwann 2–▲ 3–1032–2 [DDD]

Massenet, J.:La Vierge, w. M. Command (sop), M. Castets (sop), M. Olmeda (sop), M. Keller (sop), P. Salmon (ten), P. Fournillier (cnd), Prague SO, Prague Sym Chorus Koch Schwann 2–▲ CD 313084 [DDD]

Hadjieva, Ludmila (sop)
Bach, J.S.:Christmas Oratorio, w. Roumiana Tzatcheva (alt), Lubomir Diacovski (ten), Plamen Hidjov (bass), Tabakov, Kralev (cnd), Madrigal Chamber Ensemble, Sofia CO Soloists
Pentagon 3-▲ 302 [DDD]

Hadley, Jerry (ten)
Beethoven, L. van:Sym 9, "Choral Sym", w. B. Valente (sop), F. Kopleff (cta), J. Cheek (bass), R. Shaw (cnd), Atlanta SO, Atlanta Sym Chorus Pro Arte ▲ CDD 245 [DDD]
Bernstein, L.:Candide (restored), w. J. Anderson (sop), C. Ludwig (mez), D. Jones (mez), N. Gedda (ten), A. Green (sgr), K. Ollmann (bar), L. Bernstein (cnd), London SO, London Sym Chorus
Deutsche Grammophon ■ 437328-4
Bernstein, L.:Candide (restored), w. J. Anderson (sop), C. Ludwig (mez), D. Jones (mez), N. Gedda (ten), A. Green (sgr), K. Ollmann (bar), L. Bernstein (cnd), London SO, London Sym Chorus *(rec 1989)*
Deutsche Grammophon ▲ 429734-2 [DDD] ■ 429734-4
Bernstein, L.:Music of, w. J. Norman (sop), K. Te Kanawa (sop), J. Anderson (sop), F. von Stade (mez), C. Ludwig (mez), T. Troyanos (mez), J. Carreras (ten), D. Garrison (ten), J. Hadley (ten), T. Hampson (bar), T. Daly (sgr), G. Kremer (vn), M. Rostropovich (vc), M.T. Thomas (va), L. Bernstein (cnd), *(orch unknown)*—various popular works Deutsche Grammophon ▲ 439251-2 ■ 439251-4
Britten, H.:Les Illuminations, w. W. Boughton (cnd), English String Orch Nimbus ▲ 5234-2 [DDD]
Britten, H.:Nocturne, w. W. Boughton (cnd), English String Orch Nimbus ▲ 5234-2 [DDD]
Britten, H.:Serenade, Op. 31, w. A. Halstead (hn), W. Boughton (cnd), English String Orch
Nimbus ▲ 5234-2 [DDD]
Donizetti, G.:Anna Bolena, w. J. Sutherland (sop), S. Mentzer (mez), B. Manca di Nissa (cta), S. Ramey (bass), R. Bonynge (cnd), Welsh National Opera Orch [I] London 3-▲ 421096-2 [DDD]
Floyd, C.:Susannah, w. C. Studer (sop—Sussanah Polk), J. Hadley (ten—Sam Polk), S. Ramey (bass—Rev. Olin Blitch), K. Nagano (cnd), Paris Lyon Opera Orch, Paris Lyon Opera Chorus
Virgin Classics ▲ CDCB 45039
Golden Days, w. Tony Randall (sgr), Mario Lanza (ten), American Theater Orch [cnd:Paul Gemignani], Harvard Glee Club RCA Victor ▲ 09026-62681-2 ■ 09026-62681-2
Gounod, C.:Faust, w. C. Gasdia (sop), B. Fassbaender (mez), S. Mentzer (mez), A. Agache (bar), P. Fourcade (bass), C. Rizzi (cnd), Welsh National Opera Orch, Welsh National Opera Chorus
Teldec 3-▲ 90872
Hadley & Hampson, w. Thomas Hampson (bass), Welsh National Opera Orch [cnd:Carlo Rizzi]
Teldec ▲ 73283-2
Handel, G.F.:Messiah, w. Sylvia McNair (sop), Anne Sofie von Otter (mez), Michael Chance (alt), Robert Lloyd (b-bar), N. Marriner (cnd), Academy of St. Martin in the Fields [E] *(rec live, Dublin 4/13/92)*
Philips 2-▲ 434695-2 [DDD]
In the Real World, w. American Theater Orch [cnd:Paul Gemignani] RCA Victor ▲ 09026-61937-2
James Levine's 25th Anniversary Metropolitan Opera Gala, w. J. Levine (cnd), Metropolitan Opera Orch, Ileana Cotrubas (sop), Renée Fleming (sop), Hei-Kyung Hong (sop), Karita Mattila (sop), Birgit Nilsson (sop), Ruth Ann Swenson (sop), Kiri Te Kanawa (sop), Deborah Voigt (sop), Grace Bumbry (mez), Heidi Grant Murphy (mez), Anne Sofie von Otter (mez) *(rec live, Metropolitan Opera House, New York, Apr 27, 1996)* Deutsche Grammophon ▲ 449177-2 [DDD]
Kern, J.:Show Boat, w. F. von Stade (mez), T. Stratas (sop), B. Hubbard (bar), P. O'Hara (sgr), K. Burns (mez), N. Kulp (sgr), J. McGlinn (cnd), London Sinfonietta, Ambrosian Chorus [original orchd Robert Russell Bennett]—also includes 45 minutes of music intended for the original performance but never included, plus music from revivals and films [1988 studio cast] Angel 3-▲ A23 49108 [DDD]
Kern, J.:Show Boat, w. P. O'Hara (sop), T. Stratas (sop), K. Burns (mez), F. von Stade (mez), D. Garrison (ten), B. Hubbard (bar), J. McGlinn (cnd), London Sinfonietta, Ambrosian Opera Chorus, Ambrosian Singers EMI Classics 3-▲ A23 49108
Kern, J.:Show Boat, w. P. O'Hara (sop), T. Stratas (sop), K. Burns (mez), F. von Stade (mez), D. Garrison (ten), B. Hubbard (bar), J. McGlinn (cnd), London Sinfonietta, Ambrosian Opera Chorus
EMI Classics ▲ ZDC 49847
Lehár, F.:Das Land des Lächelns, w. Nancy Gustafson (sop—Lisa), Naomi Itami (sop—Mi), Lynton Atkinson (ten—Gustl), Jerry Hadley (ten—Prince Sou Chong), R. Bonynge (cnd), English CO *(rec EMI Abbey Road, Studio One, London, England; Aug 2-25, 1995)* Telarc ▲ CD-80419 [DDD]
Lehár, F.:Der Zarewitsch, w. Nancy Gustafson (sop—Sonia), Naomi Itami (sop—Mascha), Lynton Atkinson (ten—Ivan), Jerry Hadley (ten—the Czarevitch), Jeffrey Carl (bar—Grand Duke/Soldier), R. Bonynge (cnd), English CO *(rec EMI Abbey Road, Studio One, London, England; Aug 25-27, 1995)*
Telarc ▲ CD-80395 [DDD]
McCartney, P.:Liverpool Oratorio, w. K. Te Kanawa (sop), S. Burgess (mez), W. White (bass), C. Davis (cnd), Royal Liverpool PO, Royal Liverpool Phil Choir
EMI Classics 2-▲ CDQB 54371 2-■ 4D2Q 54371
Mad About Love, w. Cheryl Studer (sop), Kiri Te Kanawa (sop), José Carreras (ten), Philharmonia Orch [cnd:Giuseppe Sinopoli], Bastille Opera Orch [cnd:Myung-Whun Chung], Boston SO [cnd:Seiji Ozawa], Vienna PO [cnd:John Eliot Gardiner, James Levine]
Deutsche Grammophon ▲ 449112-2 ■ 449112-4
Mendelssohn, F.:Elijah, w. Barbara Bonney (sop), Henriette Schellenberg (sop), Florence Quivar (mez), Marietta Simpson (mez), Reid Bartelme (trb), Richard Clement (ten), Thomas Hampson (bar), Thomas Paul (bar), R. Shaw (cnd), Atlanta SO, Atlanta Sym Chorus [E] *(rec Symphony Hall, Woodruff Arts Center, Atlanta, GA, Nov. 5-7, 1994)* Telarc 2-▲ CD 80389 [DDD]
Mozart, W.A.:Complete Mozart Edition, w. A. M. Blasi (sop), S. McNair (sop), I. Vermillion (mez), C. H. Ahnsjö (ten), N. Marriner (cnd), Academy of St. Martin in the Fields Philips 2-▲ 422535-2 [ADD]
Mozart, W.A.:Così fan tutte (sels), w. Felicity Lott (sop), Marie McLaughlin (sop), Nuccia Focile (sop), Alessandro Corbelli (bass), Gilles Cachemaille (bass) *(rec Usher Hall, Edinburgh, Scotland)*
Telarc ▲ CD 80399 [DDD]
Mozart, W.A.:Don Giovanni, w. Christine Brewer (sop—Donna Anna), Nuccia Focile (sop—Zerlina), Felicity Lott (sop—Donna Elvira), Jerry Hadley (ten—Don Ottavio), Bo Skovhus (bar—Don Giovanni), Umberto Chiummo (bass—Masetto/Il Commendatore), Alessandro Corbelli (bass—Leporello), C. Mackerras (cnd), Scottish CO, Scottish Chamber Chorus *(rec Usher Hall, Edinburgh, Scotland, July 31-Aug 11, 1995)* Telarc 3-▲ CD 80420 [DDD]
Mozart, W.A.:Requiem, w. M. McLaughlin (sop), M. Ewing (sop), C. Hauptmann (bass), L. Bernstein (cnd), Bavarian RSO, Bavarian Radio Chorus [L] Deutsche Grammophon ▲ 427353-2 [DDD]
Mozart, W.A.:Requiem, w. A. Augér (sop), D. Ziegler (mez), T. Krause (bar), R. Shaw (cnd), Atlanta SO, Atlanta Sym Chorus [L] Telarc ▲ CD 80128 [DDD]
Mozart, W.A.:Zauberflöte, w. B. Hendricks (sop—Pamina), J. Anderson (sop—Queen of the Night), U. Steinsky (sop—Papagena), J. Hadley (ten—Tamino), T. Allen (bar—Papageno), R. Lloyd (bass—Sarastro), C. Mackerras (cnd), Scottish CO, Scottish Chamber Chorus [G] Telarc 2-▲ CD 80302 [DDD]
Noël, w. Canadian Brass, Canadian Brass Jazz All-Stars, Angel Romero (gtr), *(children's choir unknown)*, Richard Stoltzman (cl), Harolyn Blackwell (sop), King's Singers, James Galway (fl) *(rec Apr. 17-20, 1994)* RCA Victor ▲ 09026-62683-2 ■ 09026-62683-4
Rossini, G.:Il barbiere di Siviglia, w. A. Felle (sop), S. Mentzer (mez), T. Hampson (bass), S. Ramey (bass), G. Gelmetti (cnd), Tuscan Orch EMI ▲ 54863-2
Standing Room Only:Broadway Favorites, w. American Theater Orch [cnd:Paul Gemignani]
RCA Victor ▲ 09026-61370-2 [ADD] ■ 09026-61370-4 (CrO2) □ 09026-61370-5
Verdi, G.:Requiem Mass, w. V. Dunn (sop), D. Curry (cta), P. Plishka (bass), R. Shaw (cnd), Atlanta SO, Atlanta Sym Chorus [L] Telarc 2-▲ CD 80152 [DDD] 2-■ CS 30152 (D)
Weill, K.:Street Scene, w. J. Barstow (sop), A. Réaux (sop), S. Ramey (bass), J. Mauceri (cnd), Scottish Opera Orch, Scottish Opera Chorus [E] London 2-▲ 433371-2 [DDD]

Hadrabavá, Eva (sop)
Strauss, R.:Der Rosenkavalier (sels), w. Lotte Lehmann (sop—Feldmarschallin), Elisabeth Schumann (sop—Sophie), Eva Hadrabavá (sop—Octavian), H. Knappertsbusch (cnd), Vienna State Opera Orch *(rec Vienna, Apr. 22, 1936)* Koch Schwann 2-▲ SCH 314622 [ADD]

Hadzhieva, Lyudmila (sop)
Mahler, G.:Sym 4, w. E. Tabakov (cnd), Sofia PO *(rec Bulgarian Concert Hall, Sofia, Jan 1990)*
Capriccio 15-▲ 49043 [DDD]

Hadzhieva, Lyudmila (sop) (cont.)
Mahler, G.:Sym 8, w. Maria Temeshi (sop), Darina Takova (sop), Tamara Takac (alt), Boryana Tabakova (alt), Janos Bandi (ten), Pal Kovacs (bar), Tamash Syule (bass), E. Tabakov (cnd), Sofia PO, Bulgarian National Chorus, Bulgarian National Radio Chorus, Bulgarian National Radio Children's Choir *(rec National Palace of Culture, Sofia, June 1991)* Capriccio 15-▲ 49043 [DDD]

Haefliger, Ernst (ten)
Bach, J.S.:Magnificat, BWV 243, w. M. Stader (sop), H. Töpper (cta), D. Fischer-Dieskau (bar), K. Richter (cnd), Munich Bach Orch, Munich Bach Choir [L]
Deutsche Grammophon ("Galleria" series) ▲ 419466-2 [ADD]
Bach, J.S.:Mass in b, BWV 232, w. Maria Stader (sop), Sieglinde Wagner (mez), Theo Adam (b-bar), R. Mauersberger (cnd), Dresden State Orch, Dresden Kreuz Choir *(rec 1958)*
Berlin Classics ▲ BER 9171
Bach, J.S.:St. John Passion, w. Evelyn Lear (sop), Hertha Töpper (mez), Hermann Prey (bar), Kieth Engen (bass), K. Richter (cnd), Munich Bach Orch, Munich Bach Choir
Deutsche Grammophon ("2CD" series) 2-▲ 453 007-2
Bach, J.S.:St. Matthew Passion, w. E. Ameling (sop), B. Finnilä (cta), S. McCoy (ten), B. Luxon (bar), B. McDaniel (bar), J. Somary (cnd), English CO, Ambrosian Singers *(rec 1977)*
Vanguard Classics 3-▲ OVC 4060/62 [ADD]
Bach, J.S.:St. Matthew Passion, w. I. Seefried (sop), A. Fahberg (sop), H. Töpper (alt), D. Fischer-Dieskau (bar), K. Engen (bass), M. Proebstl (bass), K. Richter (cnd), Munich Bach Orch, Munich Bach Choir Archiv ▲ 439338-2 [ADD]
Bach, J.S.:St. Matthew Passion (sels), w. E. Ameling (sop), B. Finnilä (cta), S. McCoy (ten), B. Luxon (bar), B. McDaniel (bar), J. Somary (cnd), English CO, Ambrosian Singers
Vanguard Classics ▲ OVC 4063 [ADD]
Beethoven, L. van:Fidelio (sels), w. L. Rysanek (sop), I. Seefried (sop), F. Lenz (ten), D. Fischer-Dieskau (bar), K. Engen (bass), G. Frick (bass), F. Fricsay (cnd), Bavarian State Orch, Bavarian Opera Chorus—Overture, various arias & scenes, finale [G] IMP Collectors Series ▲ IMPX 9021 [AAD]
Beethoven, L. van:Missa Solemnis, w. M. Stader (sop), E. Cavalti (mez), H. Rehfuss (bass), C. Schuricht (cnd), Hamburg SO, St. Hedwig's Cathedral Choir *(rec Sept. 15, 1957)*
Archipon 2-▲ ARCH 2.1CD (m) [ADD]
Beethoven, L. van:Sym 9, "Choral Sym", w. Elisabeth Schwarzkopf (sop), Elsa Cavelti (mez), Otto Edelmann (bass), W. Furtwängler (cnd), Philharmonia Orch, Lucerne Festival Chorus *(rec Aug 22, 1954)* Music & Arts ▲ CD 790 [ADD]
Bruckner, A.:Mass 3, w. M. Stader (sop), C. Hellmann (mez), K. Borg (bass), E. Jochum (cnd), Bavarian RSO, Bavarian Radio Chorus Deutsche Grammophon ("The Originals" series) 2-▲ 447409-2
Bruckner, A.:Mass 3, w. M. Stader (sop), A. Hellmann (alt), K. Borg (bass), E. Jochum (cnd), Bavarian RSO, Bavarian Radio Chorus [L] Deutsche Grammophon 4-▲ 423127-2 [ADD]
Bruckner, A.:Te Deum, w. M. Stader (sop), S. Wagner (mez), P. Lagger (bass), E. Jochum (cnd), Berlin PO, German Opera Chorus [L] Deutsche Grammophon 4-▲ 423127-2 [ADD]
Debussy, C.:Pelléas et Mélisande, w. E. Schwarzkopf (sop), M. Roux (bar), M. Petri (bass), H. von Karajan (cnd), Rome Radio Orch, Rome RAI Chorus [F] *(rec live, 12/19/54)*
Arkadia 2-▲ 218 (m) [ADD]
Dvořák, A.:Requiem Mass, w. Maria Stader (sop), Sieglinde Wagner (cta), Kim Borg (b-bar), K. Ancerl (cnd), Czech PO, Czech Chorus Deutsche Grammophon ("Double" series) 2-▲ 437377-2
Handel, G.F.:Judas Maccabaeus, w. Gundula Janowitz (sop), Hertha Töpper (alt), Peter Schreier (ten), Theo Adam (bass), Siegfried Vogel (bass), H. Koch (cnd), Berlin RSO, Berlin Radio Chorus
Berlin Classics 2-▲ BER 9112
Mahler, G.:Das Klagende Lied, w. E. Lear (sop), E. Söderström (sop), G. Hoffman (mez), S. Burrows (ten), G. Nienstedt (bass), P. Boulez (cnd), London SO, London Sym Chorus
Sony Classical ("Pierre Boulez Edition" series) ▲ SK 45841
Mahler, G.:Das Lied von der Erde, w. Grace Hoffman (mez), H. Rosbaud (cnd), Cologne RSO *(rec live, Cologne, Germany, Apr 18, 1955)* Agorá Music ("Phoenix" series) ▲ 701 [ADD]
Mahler, G.:Das Lied von der Erde, w. M. Miller (mez), B. Walter (cnd), New York PO [G]
CBS ▲ MK 42034
Mieg, P.:Mit Nacht, w. E. Schmid (cnd), Beromünster RSO *(rec 1966)* Jecklin ▲ JS 314-2 [DDD]
Mozart, W.A.:Arias, w. J.E. Dähler (cnd), English CO—Un'aura amorosa; Il mio tesoro; Dalla sua pace; Misero! O sogno, o son desto?; Ich baue ganz auf deine Stärke; Dies Bildnis ist bezaubernd schön; Se all'Impero; Torna la pace; Per pietà, non ricercate *(rec St. Jude's Church, London, Apr 1983)*
Claves ▲ CD 508305 [DDD]
Mozart, W.A.:Arias, w. J.E. Dähler (cnd), English CO—includes O sogno, o son desto?; Per pieta, non ricertate; arias from Don Giovanni; Così fan tutte; Titus; Idomeneo; Die Zauberflöte; Die Entführung aus dem Serail Claves ▲ 50-8305
Mozart, W.A.:Don Giovanni, w. I. Seefried (sop), S. Jurinac (sop), M. Stader (sop), D. Fischer-Dieskau (bar), K. C. Kohn (bass), F. Fricsay (cnd), Berlin RSO Deutsche Grammophon 3-▲ 437341-2
Old German Christmas Songs, w. Consilium Musicum [cnd:Paul Angerer] Claves ▲ CD 8408 [DDD]
Schoeck, O.:Der Postillon, w. K. Grenacher (pno), Wettinger CO, Wettinger Chamber Chorus, Seminarchor Wettingen [G] *(rec 1967)* Jecklin-Disco ▲ JD 504-2 [ADD]
Schoeck, O.:Songs (misc), w. K. Grenacher (pno), Wettinger CO, Wettinger Chamber Chorus, Seminarchor Wettingen [G] *(rec 1967)* Jecklin-Disco ▲ JD 504-2 [ADD]
Schoeck, O.:Spielmannsweisen, w. C. Eisenhoffer (hp) [G] Gallo ▲ CD 622 [AAD]
Schubert, Franz:Die Schöne Müllerin, w. Erik Werba (pno) *(rec 1967)*
Sony Classical ("Essential Classics" series) ▲ SBK 48287 [AAD] ■ SBT 48287
Schubert, Franz:Die Schöne Müllerin, w. Jörg Ewald Dähler (pno) *(rec Kirche Seon, June 1982)*
Claves ▲ CD 508301 [DDD]
Schubert, Franz:Die Schöne Müllerin, w. Jörg Ewald Dähler (pno) Claves ▲ 50-8301
Schubert, Franz:Schwanengesang, w. Jörg Ewald Dähler (pno) Claves ▲ 50-8506
Schubert, Franz:Songs (misc), w. Jörg Ewald Dähler (pno)—23 songs Claves ▲ 50-8611
Schubert, Franz:Winterreise, w. Jörg Ewald Dähler (pno) Claves ▲ 50-8008
Schubert, Franz:Winterreise, w. Jörg Ewald Dähler (pno) *(rec Kirche Saanen, Sept 1980)*
Claves ▲ CD 508008 [DDD]
Wagner, R.:Der fliegende Holländer, w. Annelies Kupper (sop—Senta), Sieglinde Wagner (mez—Mary), Ernst Haefliger (ten—Steersman), Wolfgang Windgassen (ten—Erik), Josef Metternich (ten—Dutchman), Josef Greindl (bass—Daland), F. Fricsay (cnd), Berlin RIAS SO, Berlin RIAS Chamber Choir *(rec 1953)*
Deutsche Grammophon 2-▲ 439714-2 (m) [ADD]

Haengel, Aracelly (sgr)
Verdi, G.:Don Carlos, w. Katia Ricciarelli (sop), Fiorenza Cossotto (mez), Guido Fabbris (ten), Veriano Luchetti (ten), Piero Cappuccilli (bar), Gianfranco Casarini (bass), Nicolai Ghiaurov (bass), Alessandro Maddalena (bass), Marisa Salimbeni (sgr), Giorgio Zoranca (sgr), G. Prêtre (cnd), *(orch unknown)*
Great Opera Performances 3-▲ GOP 777

Hafgren, Lily (sop)
Wagner, R.:Arias & Scenes, w. Emmy Destinn (sop), Frida Leider (sop), Emmi Leisner (cta), Ernst Kraus (ten), Lauritz Melchior (ten), Leopold Demuth (bar), Friedrich Schorr (b-bar), Michael Bohynen (bass), Paul Knupfer (bass), Richard Mayr (bass), Heinrich Hensel (sgr), Walter Soomer (sgr)
Iron Needle ▲ 1307 (m)

Hagara, Willy (bar)
Lehár, F.:Der Zarewitsch (sels), w. Christine Gorner (sop), Melita Muszely (sop), Fritz Wunderlich (ten), C. Michalski (cnd), Bavarian SO Emperor Operetta ▲ KO 86341

Hagegård, Erland (ten)
Brahms, J.:Duets, Op. 28, w. E. Thallaug (alt), L. Negro (pno) *(rec Nacka Aula, Nacka Sweden, Dec. 20-22, 1976)* BIS ▲ CD 70 [AAD]
Brahms, J.:Duets, Op. 28, w. Edith Thallaug (alt), Lucia Negro (pno) *(rec Nacka Aula, Nacka, Sweden, 1976)* BIS ▲ CD 77 [AAD]
Pettersson, G.A.:Vox Humana, w. Marianne Mellnäs (sop), Margot Rödin (alt), Sven-Erik Alexandersson (ten), S. Westerberg (cnd), Swedish RSO, Swedish Radio Chorus *(rec Royal Swedish Academy of Music, Stockholm, Sweden, Mar. 22 & May 24, 1976)* BIS ▲ CD 55 [AAD]
Schumann, R.:Songs, w. Lucia Negro (pno)—Der Contrabandiste *(rec Nacka Aula, Nacka, Sweden, 1976)*
BIS ▲ CD 77 [AAD]
Schumann, R.:Spanisches Liederspiel, w. Märta Schéle (sop), Edith Thallaug (alt), Gösta Winbergh (ten), Lucia Negro (pno) *(rec Nacka Aula, Nacka, Sweden, 1976)* BIS ▲ CD 77 [AAD]

1198 ▲ = CD ♦ = Enhanced CD Δ = MD ■ = Cassette Tape □ = DCC

Hagegård, Erland (ten) (cont.)
Sibelius, J.:The Maiden in the Tower, w. M. A. Häggander (sop), J. Hynninen (bar), T. Kruse (cta), N. Järvi (cnd), Gothenburg SO, Gothenburg Chorus [Fin] BIS ▲ CD 250 [DDD]

Hagegård, Håkan (bar)
Basic 100, Vol. 60, w. Barbara Hendricks (sop), John Aler (ten), London SO [cnd:Eduardo Mata] RCA Victor ▲ 09026-68085-2 ■ 09026-68085-4
Brahms, J.:Ein Deutsches Requiem, w. K. Battle (sop), J. Levine (cnd), Chicago SO, Chicago Sym Chorus [G] *(rec ca. 1984)* RCA Gold Seal ▲ 09026-61349-2 ■ 09026-61349-4
Diepenbrock, A.:Im grossen Schweigen, w. R. Chailly (cnd), Royal Concertgebouw Orch London 2-▲ 444446-2
Grieg, E.:Salmer, w. T. Kvam (cnd), Oslo Cathedral Choir Nimbus ▲ NI 5171 [DDD]
Grieg, E.:Songs, w. W. Jones (pno) [Disc 1]—Melodies of the Heart by Hans Christian Andersen, Op. 5; 9 Songs, Op. 18; 6 Songs by Henrik Ibsen, Op. 25; Last Spring, Op. 33/2; The Mountain Thrall, Op. 32; Rocking, Rocking, Op. 49/2; Henrik Wergeland, Op. 58/3; [Disc 2]—Songs & Ballads by Andreas Munch, Op. 9; 4 Songs by Bjornstjerne Bjornson, Op. 21; 5 Songs by John Paulsen, Op. 26; Songs, Op. 39, Reminiscences from Mountain & Fjord by Holger Drachmann, Op. 44 RCA Red Seal 2-▲ 09026-61630-2
Haydn, J.:Die Jahreszeiten, w. Arleen Auger (sop), John Aler (ten), J. Revzen (cnd), St. Paul CO, Minnesota Chorale [G] Koch International Classics 2-▲ KIC 7065-2 [DDD]
James Levine's 25th Anniversary Metropolitan Opera Gala, w. J. Levine (cnd), Metropolitan Opera Orch, Ileana Cotrubas (sop), Renée Fleming (sop), Hei-Kyung Hong (sop), Karita Mattila (sop), Birgit Nilsson (sop), Ruth Ann Swenson (sop), Kiri Te Kanawa (sop), Deborah Voigt (sop), Grace Bumbry (mez), Heidi Grant Murphy (mez), Anne Sofie von Otter (mez) *(rec live, Metropolitan Opera House, New York, Apr 27, 1996)* Deutsche Grammophon ▲ 449177-2 [DDD]
Larsson, L.-E.:God in Disguise, w. B. Nordin (sop), Jonsson (nar), S. Frykberg (cnd), Helsingborg SO, Helsingborg Sym Chorus [Sw] BIS ▲ CD 96 [AAD]
Lidholm, I.:A Dream Play, w. Hillevi Martinpelto (sop), K. Ingebretsen (cnd), Royal Stockholm Orch Caprice 2-▲ CAP 22029
Mendelssohn, F.:Psalms, Op. 78, w. T. Kvam (cnd), Oslo Cathedral Choir Nimbus ▲ NI 5171 [DDD]
Mozart, W.A.:Missa solemnis, K.139, w. B. Bonney (sop), J. Rappé (ten), J. Protschka (ten), N. Harnoncourt (cnd), Vienna Concentus Musicus, Arnold Schoenberg Choir [L] Teldec ▲ 2292-44180-2 [DDD]
Mozart, W.A.:Nozze di Figaro, w. A. Augér (sop), B. Bonney (sop), A. Nafé (mez), P. Salomaa (bass), A. Östman (cnd), Drottningholm Court Theater Orch, Drottningholm Court Thea Chorus [I] L'Oiseau-Lyre 3-▲ 421333-2 [DDD]
Mozart, W.A.:Zauberflöte, w. S. Jo (sop), L. Orgonasova (sop), Martina Bovet (sop), G. Winbergh (ten), A. Jordan (cnd), Paris Orchestral Ensemble, Romande Chamber Choir, Pro Arte Lausanne Erato 2-▲ 2292-45469-2 [DDD]
Orff, C.:Carmina burana, w. S. McNair (sop), J. Aler (ten), L. Slatkin (cnd), St. Louis SO RCA Red Seal ▲ 09026-61673-2; ■ 09026-61673-4
Orff, C.:Carmina burana, w. Barbara Hendricks (sop), John Aler (ten), E. Mata (cnd), London SO, London Sym Chorus RCA Victor ▲ 09026-68085-2; ■ 09026-68085-4
Orff, C.:Carmina burana, w. J. Blegen (sop), W. Brown (ten), R. Shaw (cnd), Atlanta SO, Atlanta Sym Chorus [G, L] Telarc ▲ CD 80056 [DDD]
Paulus, S.:Bittersuite, w. W. Jones (pno) [E] Albany ▲ TROY 036-2 [DDD]
Rangström, T.:Songs, w. B. Svendén (sop), T. Schuback (pno) Musica Sveciae ▲ MSV 629 [DDD]
Rodgers, R.:The Sound of Music, w. E. Farrell (sop), F. von Stade (mez), B. Daniels (sgr), L. D. von Schlanbusch (sgr), et al., E. Kunzel (cnd), Cincinnati Pops Orch, May Festival Chorus [1987 studio cast] Telarc ▲ CD 80162 [DDD] ■ CS 30162
Rosenberg, H.:Sym 4, w. S. Ehrling (cnd), Gothenburg SO, Rilke Ensemble members, Pro Musica Chamber Choir, Swedish Radio Chorus Caprice ▲ CAP 21429 [DDD]
Rossini, G.:Il barbiere di Siviglia, w. J. Larmore (cta), A. Corbelli (bar), R. Gimeniz (bar), S. Ramey (bass), J. López-Cobos (cnd), Lausanne CO, Geneva Grand Théâtre Chorus [I] Teldec 2-▲ 9031-74885-2
Rossini, G.:Il barbiere di Siviglia (sels), w. B. Frittoli (sop), J. Larmore (mez), R. Giménez (ten), A. Corbelli (bar), S. Ramey (bass), J. López-Cobos (cnd), Lausanne CO, Geneva Grand Théâtre Chorus Teldec ▲ 93693-2
Schubert, Franz:Die Schöne Müllerin, w. E. Ax (pno) RCA Red Seal ▲ 09026-61705-2
Stenhammar, W.:Ithaka, w. K. Ingebretsen (cnd), Swedish RSO Caprice ▲ CAP 21358
Stenhammar, W.:Songs, w. A. S. von Otter (mez), B. Forsberg (pno), T. Schuback (pno) Musica Sveciae ▲ MSCD 623
Strauss, R.:Capriccio, w. Kiri Te Kanawa (sop—Gräfin), Brigitte Fassbaender (mez—Clairon), Uwe Heilmann (ten—Flamand), Werner Hollweg (ten—Taupe), Olaf Bär (bar—Olivier), Håkan Hagegård (bar—Graf), Victor von Halem (b-bar—La Roche), U. Schirmer (cnd), Vienna PO [G] *(rec Vienna, Dec 1993)* London 2-▲ 444405-2 [DDD]
Wagner, R.:Tannhäuser (sels), w. K. Te Kanawa (sop), W. Meier (mez), R. Kollo (ten), M. Janowski (cnd), Philharmonia Orch, Ambrosian Singers Teldec ▲ 46336-2 ■ 46336-4
Wagner, R.:Tannhäuser (sels), w. K. Te Kanawa (sop), R. Kollo (ten), W. Meier (mez), M. Holle (bass), M. Janowski (cnd), Philharmonia Orch, Ambrosian Singers; music from film soundtrack for Meeting Venus Teldec ▲ 2292 46336-2 [DDD] ■ 2292 46336-4 □ 2292 46336-5
Wolf, H.:Italienische Liederbücher (comp), w. B. Bonney (sop), G. Parsons (pno) Teldec ▲ 72301
Zemlinsky, A. von:Lyric Sym, w. Alessandra Marc (sop), R. Chailly (cnd), Royal Concertgebouw Orch London ("Entartete Musik" series) ▲ 443569-2 [DDD]
Zueignung [Dedication], w. Thomas Schuback (pno) BIS ▲ CD 54 [AAD]

Hagemeier, B. (sop)
Van Appledorn, M.J.:Missa Brevis, w. J. D. Maynard (org) CRS ▲ CD 9052

Hagen, Reinhard (bass)
Bach, J.S.:St. John Passion, w. C. Schäfer (sop), Y. Jänicke (mez), A. Kraus (ten), B. Possemeyer (bass), E. Weyand (cnd), Stuttgart Hymnus Chor, Stuttgart Hymnus Boys' Choir [G] *(rec 1990)* Hänssler Classic 2-▲ 98.968
Bruckner, A.:Missa solemnis, w. C. Oelze (sop), C. Schubert (alt), J. Dümüller (ten), K. A. Rickenbacher (cnd), Bamberg SO, Bamberg Sym Chorus Virgin Classics ▲ CDC 59060
Bruckner, A.:Psalm 112, w. C. Oelze (sop), C. Schubert (alt), J. Dümüller (ten), K. A. Rickenbacher (cnd), Bamberg SO, Bamberg Sym Chorus Virgin Classics ▲ CDC 59060
Bruckner, A.:Psalm 114, w. C. Oelze (sop), C. Schubert (alt), J. Dümüller (ten), K. A. Richenbacher (cnd), Bamberg SO, Bamberg Sym Chorus Virgin Classics ▲ CDC 59060
Bruckner, A.:Psalm 150, w. C. Oelze (sop), C. Schubert (alt), J. Dümüller (ten), K. A. Rickenbacher (cnd), Bamberg SO, Bamberg Sym Chorus Virgin Classics ▲ CDC 59060
Mozart, W.A.:Zauberflöte, w. Natalie Dessay (sop—Queen of the Night), Linda Kitchen (sop—Papagena), Rosa Mannion (sop—Pamina), Anna-Maria Panzarella (sop—First Lady), Doris Lamprecht (mez—Second Lady), Delphine Haidan (cta—Third Lady), Hans Peter Blochwitz (ten—Tamino), Steven Cole (ten—Monostatos), Chrisopher Josey (ten—First Priest/First Armed Man), Anton Scharinger (bar—Papageno), Reinhard Hagen (bass—Sarastro), Laurent Naouri (bass—Second Priest/Second Armed Man), Willard White (bass—Speaker), W. Christie (cnd), Les Arts Florissants *(rec Paris Oct 2-9 1995)* Erato 2-▲ 12705-2 [DDD]

Hagen-William, Louis (b-bar)
Mozart, W.A.:Arias, w. W. Proost (cnd), Sinfonia D'Anvers—10 opera arias from Betulia liberata, Così fan tutte, Don Giovanni, Finta semplice, Le nozze di Figaro, Zaide; 5 concert arias, K.513, 539, 549, 612, 621a Quantum ▲ QM 6896 [DDD] ■ QM 1991 (D)

Häger, Klaus (bass)
Bach, J.S.:Cant 205, w. Efrat Ben-Nunn (sop), Katharina Kammerloher (alt), Christoph Prégardien (ten), R. Jacobs (cnd), Berlin Academy for Early Music, Berlin Chamber Chorus Harmonia Mundi France 2-▲ HMC 901544.45
Bach, J.S.:Cant 213, w. Efrat Ben-Nun (sop), Andreas Scholl (ct), James Taylor (ten), R. Jacobs (cnd), Berlin Academy for Early Music, Berlin Chamber Chorus Harmonia Mundi France 2-▲ HMC 901544.45

Häger, Klaus (bass) (cont.)
Mozart, W.A.:Zauberflöte, w. Birgit Been (sop), Nathalie Boissy (sop), Marianne Seibel (sop), Renate Springer (sop), Elizabeth Vidal (sop), Eleanor James (mez), Salvador Guzman (ten), Herbert Hechenberger (ten), Wolfgang Newmann (ten), Philip Langshaw (bass), Hans-Georg Moser (bass), P. Kuentz (cnd), Paul Kuentz Orch, Francis Bardot (cnd), Maitrise des Hauts-de-Seine members, Paul Kuentz Choirs Pierre Verany 2-▲ PVY 730055 [DDD]

Häggander, Mari Anne (sop)
Brahms, J.:Ein Deutsches Requiem, w. M. Lorenz (ten), H. Kegel (cnd), Leipzig RSO, Leipzig Radio Chorus [G] Capriccio ▲ 10095 [DDD]
Grieg, E.:Peer Gynt, w. U. Malmberg (bar), H. Blomstedt (cnd), San Francisco SO, *(chorus unknown)* [N] London ▲ 425448-2 [DDD]
Lindblad, A.F.:Songs, w. Mikael Samuelson (bar), Thomas Schuback (pno), sels. unknown Caprice ▲ CAP 21425 [DDD]
Olsson, O.:Requiem, w. E. Paaske (cta), A. Andersson (ten), L. Wedin (bar), A. Öhrwall (cnd), Stockholm PO, Stockholm Phil Chorus Caprice ▲ CAP 21368 [DDD]
Sibelius, J.:Luonnotar, w. J. Panula (cnd), Gothenburg SO [Fin] BIS ▲ CD 270 [DDD]
Sibelius, J.:The Maiden in the Tower, w. E. Hagegard (ten), J. Hynninen (bar), T. Kruse (cta), N. Järvi (cnd), Gothenburg SO, Gothenburg Chorus [Fin] BIS ▲ CD 250 [DDD]
Sibelius, J.:Songs, w. J. Hynninen (bar), J. Panula (cnd), Gothenburg SO (for solo voice & orchestra) [Fin, Sw] BIS ▲ CD 270 [DDD]

Häggstam, Alf (bass)
Wikström, I.:Den Brottsliga Modern, w. E. Saeden (bar), M. Tretom (sop), Nordisk CO Proprius ▲ 9069

Hagley, Alison (sop)
Mendelssohn, F.:Sym 2, w. C. Haymon (sop), P. Straka (ten), W. Weller (cnd), Philharmonia Orch, Philharmonia Chorus [G] Chandos ▲ CHAN 8995 [DDD]
Mozart, W.A.:Nozze di Figaro, w. H. Martinpelto (sop), R. Gilfrey (bar), B. Terfel (b-bar), J. E. Gardiner (cnd), English Baroque Soloists, Monteverdi Choir London [G] Archiv 3-▲ 439871-2 [DDD]

Haidan, Delphine (cta)
Mozart, W.A.:Zauberflöte, w. Natalie Dessay (sop—Queen of the Night), Linda Kitchen (sop—Papagena), Rosa Mannion (sop—Pamina), Anna-Maria Panzarella (sop—First Lady), Doris Lamprecht (mez—Second Lady), Delphine Haidan (cta—Third Lady), Hans Peter Blochwitz (ten—Tamino), Steven Cole (ten—Monostatos), Chrisopher Josey (ten—First Priest/First Armed Man), Anton Scharinger (bar—Papageno), Reinhard Hagen (bass—Sarastro), Laurent Naouri (bass—Second Priest/Second Armed Man), Willard White (bass—Speaker), W. Christie (cnd), Les Arts Florissants *(rec Paris Oct 2-9 1995)* Erato 2-▲ 12705-2 [DDD]

Haik-Vantoura, Suzanne (mez)
Haik-Vantoura, S.:The Song of Songs, w. M.-L. Banzet (bar), R. Boschiero (hp), S. Chefson (fl), E. Dutrieux (cnd), *(chorus unknown)* [He] *(rec 1986)* Alienor ▲ AL 1045 [DDD]

Hain, Walter (ten)
Bach, J.S.:St. Matthew Passion, w. Nadine Conner (sop), Jean Watson (cta), Mack Harrell (bar), Herbert Janssen (bar), Lorenzo Alvary (bass), B. Walter (cnd), New York PO, New York Phil Chorus—Part I Minerva ▲ 20

Hains, Mary Enid (sop)
Caldara, A.:Vaticini di pace, w. Linda Dayiantis-Straub (sop), Jennifer Lane (mez), David Arnot (ten), K. Mallon (cnd), Aradia Baroque Ensemble *(rec Toronto, Canada, Jan 1996)* Naxos ▲ 8.553772 [DDD]

Hajek, Aurelia (sgr)
Henze, H.-W.:Elegy for Young Lovers, w. Regina Schudel (sop), Richard Lloyd Morgan (bass), Lawrence Richard (bass), Helmut Bernhofen (sgr), Bruno Fath (sgr), Silvia Weiss (sgr), B. Jones (cnd), Berlin Chamber Opera Orch *(rec Berlin)* Deutsche Schallplatten 2-▲ DS 1050

Hajóssyová, Magdaléna (sop)
Janáček, L.:The Cunning Little Vixen, w. G. Benačková (sop—Goldskin), M. Hajóssyová (sop—Cunning Little Vixen), R. Novák (bass—Forester), V. Neumann (cnd), Czech PO, Czech Phil Chorus, Kühn Children's Chorus [Cz] *(rec 1979-80)* Supraphon 2-▲ 10 3471-2 [AAD]
Janáček, L.:Fate, w. Vladimír Krejčík (ten), Vilém Přibyl (ten), F. Jílek (cnd), Brno Janáček Opera Orch, Brno Janáček Opera Chorus Supraphon ▲ SUP 0045 [AAD]
Magdalena Hajóssyova:Soprano, w. M. Lapsansky (pno) Multisonic ▲ MUL 310195 [DDD]
Mahler, G.:Sym 4, w. V. Neumann (cnd), Czech PO [G] *(rec 1980)* Supraphon ▲ 11 1975-2 [AAD]
Marschner, H.A.:Hans Heiling, w. E. Seniglova (sop), M. Eklöf (mez), K. Markus (ten), T. Mohr (bar), L. Neshyba (bass), E. Körner (cnd), Slovak PO, Slovak Phil Chorus [G] Marco Polo ("Opera Rara" series) 2-▲ 8.223306/07 [DDD]
Mozart, W.A.:Requiem, w. J. Horská (cta), J. Kundlák (ten), P. Mikuláš (bass), Z. Košler (cnd), Slovak PO, Slovak Phil Chorus Naxos ▲ 8.550235 [DDD] △ 7.550235 [DDD]
Reicha, A.:Der neue Psalm, w. Anna Barová (mez), Andreas Schmidt (bar), Karel Průša (bass), L. Mátl (cnd), Dvořák CO, Czech Phil Chorus Panton ▲ PAN 810758 [DDD]
Schubert, Franz:Sacred Music, w. P. Schreier (ten), D. Knothe (cnd), Berlin RSO, Berlin Radio Chorus—Offertorium, D.963; Offertorium, D.223; Tantum ergo, D.962; Psalm 23, D.706; An die Sonne, D.439; Offertorium, D.136; Salve Regina, D.106; Salve Regina, D.386; Psalm 92, D.953; Chor der Engel, D.440 [G,L] Capriccio ▲ 10096 [DDD]
Shostakovich, D.:Sym 14, w. P. Mikuláš (bass), L. Slovák (cnd), Czech-Slovak RSO Bratislava *(rec Feb. 22-Mar. 4, 1991)* Naxos ▲ 8.550631 [ADD]
Tomášek, V.J.K.:Songs, w. Marián Lapsansky (pno)—Dauernder Frühling, Op. 77; Der Nachtigall letzter Gesang, Op. 77; Des Dichters Lied, Op. 77; Heideröslein, Op. 53/1; Nähe des Geliebten, Op. 53/2; Mailied, Op. 53/3; Mignons Sehnsucht, Op. 54/1; Die Spröde, Op. 54/2; Die Bekehrte, Op. 54/3; Mit einem gemahlten Bande, Op. 55/4; Die Nacht, Op. 55/5; An den Mond, Op. 56/4; Das Veilchen, Op. 57/1; Rastlose Liebe, Op. 58/1; Wanderers Nachtlied, Op. 58/4; Vorschlag zur Güte, Op. 60/2; Die Erwartung; Das Lied; Das Mädchen, Op. 33; Des Pilgers Nachtlied, Op. 33; Der Knabe, Op. 33; In die Ferne, Op. 92; Mein Lieb, Op. 92; Mein Hochland, Op. 92 Multisonic ▲ MUL 310248 [DDD]

Haken, Eduard (bass)
Dvořák, A.:Rusalka, w. Milada Šubrtová (sop), Ivo Žídek (ten), Z. Chalabala (cnd), Prague National Theater Orch, Prague National Theater Chorus Supraphon 2-▲ SUP 0013 [AAD]
Eduard Haken, w. Prague National Theater Orch, Prague National Theater Chorus, Prague Smetana Theater Orch, Prague CO, Prague RSO Supraphon ▲ SUP 3186
Smetana, B.:The Bartered Bride, w. Drahomíra Tikalová (sop), Ivo Žídek (ten), Z. Chalabala (cnd), Prague National Theater Orch, Prague National Theater Chorus Supraphon 2-▲ SUP 0040 [AAD]

Halac, Desirée (mez)
Purcell, H.:Dido & Aeneas, w. Cassandra Hoffman (sop—Belinda), Arlene Travis (sop—2nd Witch), Desirée Halac (mez—Sorceress/Spirit), Jennifer Lane (mez—Dido), Elizabeth Norman (alt), Thomas Bogdan (ten—A Sailor), Michael Brown (bar—Aeneas), Curtis Streetman (bar), Caitriona O'Leary (sgr—2nd Woman), Sarah Pillow (sgr—1st Witch), B. Brookshire (cnd), San Cassiano Musici *(rec St. Ignatius of Antioch Episcopal Church, New York City, Spring 1995)* Vox Classics ▲ VOX 7518

Haldas, Béatrice (sop)
Rossini, G.:Stabat Mater, w. Lucia V. Terrani (mez), Antonio Savastano (ten), Raffaele Arié (bass), E. Loehrer (cnd), Swiss-Italian Radio-TV Orch, Swiss-Italian Radio-TV Chorus Accord ▲ ACD 201752 [AAD]
Zemlinsky, A. von:Der Geburtstag der Infantin, w. I. Nielsen (sop), K. Riegel (ten), D. Weller (bass), G. Albrecht (cnd), Berlin RSO, Berlin RIAS Women's Chamber Choir [G] Koch Schwann ▲ CD 314 013 [DDD]

Hale, B. (sgr)
Kern, J.:Sunny (sels), w. J. Buchanan (sgr), C. Hulbert (sgr), *(other artists unknown)* Pearl ("Flapper" series) ▲ PEA CD 9105 [ADD]

Hale, R. (nar)
Prokofiev, S.:Peter & the Wolf, w. S. Koussevitzky (cnd), Boston SO *(rec 1939 for Victor/HMV)* Pearl ▲ PEA 9487 (m) [AAD]

Hale, Robert (b–bar)
Donizetti, G.:Lucia di Lammermoor (sels), w. Renata Scotto (sop—Lucia), Ruth Carron (mez—Alisa), Richard Tucker (ten—Edgardo), Matteo Manuguerra (bar—Enrico), Robert Hale (bass–bar—Raimondo), A. Guadagno (cnd), *(orch & chorus unknown)*—Lucia, perdona...Verranno a te; Sconsigliato! In queste porte; Il dolce suono; Non mi guardar si fiero...Spargi d'amaro pianto; Tombe degli avi miei...Fra poco a me ricovero; Tu che a Dio spiegasti l'ali *(rec Philadelphia, 1973)* Legato Classics 2-▲ LCD 198-2
Handel, G.F.:Messiah, w. Saul Quirke (trb), Margaret Marshall (sop), Catherine Robbin (mez), Charles Brett (ct), Anthony Rolfe Johnson (ten), J. E. Gardiner (cnd), English Baroque Soloists, Monteverdi Choir London [E] Philips 3-▲ 411041-2 [DDD]
Handel, G.F.:Messiah, w. Saul Quirke (trb), Margaret Marshall (sop), Catherine Robbin (mez), Charles Brett (ct), Anthony Rolfe Johnson (ten), J. E. Gardiner (cnd), English Baroque Soloists, Monteverdi Choir London [E] Philips ▲ 412267-2 [DDD]
Massenet, J.:Manon, w. Beverly Sills (sop—Manon), Plácido Domingo (ten—Des Grieux), Nico Castel (ten—Guillot), Richard Fredricks (bar—Lescaut), Robert Hale (bar—De Brétigny), Malcom Smith (bass—Count de Grieux), J. Rudel (cnd), New York City Opera Orch, New York City Opera Chorus *(rec live, New York, 1969)* Melodram 2-▲ IMC 205008 [ADD]
Wagner, R.:Der fliegende Holländer, w. H. Beherns (sop—Senta), I. Vermillion (mez—Mary), U. Heilmann (ten—Helmsman), J. Protschka (ten—Erik), R. Hale (bar—The Dutchman), K. Rydl (bass—Daland), C. von Dohnányi (cnd), Vienna PO, Vienna State Opera Chorus London 2-▲ 436418-2 [DDD]
Wagner, R.:Das Rheingold, w. Gabriele Fontana (sop—Woglinde), Nancy Gustafson (sop—Freia), Ildiko Komlosi (mez—Wellgunde), Hanna Schwarz (mez—Fricka), Elena Zaremba (mez—Erda), Margareta Hintermeier (cta—Flosshilde), Kim Begley (ten—Loge), Peter Schreier (ten—Mime), Thomas Sunnegardh (ten—Froh), Robert Hale (bass–bar—Wotan), Walter Fink (bass—Fafner), Franz-Josef Kapellmann (bass—Alberich), Jan-Hendrik Rootering (bass—Fasolt), Eike Wilm Schulte (bass—Donner), C. von Dohnányi (cnd), Cleveland Orch *(rec Severance Hall, Cleveland, Ohio, Dec 1993)* London 2-▲ 443690-2

Halem, Victor von (bass)
Beethoven, L. van:Christus am Ölberg, w. M. Pick-Hieronimi (sop), J. Anderson (sop), S. Baudo (cnd), Lyon National Orch, Lyon National Chorus [G] Harmonia Mundi France ▲ HMC 905181
Dallapiccola, L.:Ulisse, w. C. Gayer (sop), E. Saedén (bar), A. Bernard (sgr), L. Maazel (cnd), Berlin German Opera Orch, Berlin German Opera Chorus *(rec live, Berlin 9/28/68)* Stradivarius 2-▲ STR 10063 [ADD]
Hindemith, P.:Mathis der Maler, w. Josef Protschka (ten), Hermann Winkler (ten), Roland Hermann (bar), Harold Stamm (bass), G. Albrecht (cnd), Cologne RSO Wergo 3-▲ WER 6255-2
Mozart, W.A.:Don Giovanni, w. G. Janowitz (sop), T. Zylis-Gara (sop), M. Freni (sop), A. Kraus (ten), R. Panerai (bar), N. Ghiaurov (bass), H. von Karajan (cnd), Vienna PO, Vienna State Opera Chorus [I] *(rec live, Salzburg, Aug. 1, 1969)* Memories 3-▲ HR 4362/64 (m) [ADD]
Righini, V.:Te Deum, w. G. Resick (sop), M. Schiml (sop), R. Wohlers (ten), G. Albrecht (cnd), Berlin RSO, Berlin Radio Chorus [L] Koch Schwann ▲ CD 313052 [ADD]
Strauss, R.:Capriccio, w. Kiri Te Kanawa (sop—Gräfin), Brigitte Fassbaender (mez—Clairon), Uwe Heilmann (ten—Flamand), Werner Hollweg (ten—Taupe), Olaf Bär (bar—Olivier), Håkan Hagegård (bar—Graf), Victor von Halem (b–bar—La Roche), U. Schirmer (cnd), Vienna PO [G] *(rec Vienna, Dec 1993)* London 2-▲ 444405-2 [DDD]
Zemlinsky, A. von:Der Traumgörge, w. P. Coburn (sop), J. Martin (sop), G. M. Ronge (sop), B. Calm (mez), P. Haage (ten), H. Kruse (ten), J. Protschka (ten), H. Welker (bar), M. Blasius (bass), G. Albrecht (cnd), Frankfurt RSO [G] Capriccio 2-▲ CD 10241/2 [DDD]

Halgrimson, Amanda (sop)
Hummel, J.N.:Alma virgo, w. Susan McAdoo (mez), Helmut Wildhaber (ten), Petr Mikuláš (bass), Jan Engel (bass), M. Haselböck (cnd), Vienna Academy, Brünn Czech Phil Chorus Koch Schwann ▲ SCH CD 317792
Hummel, J.N.:Mass in E♭, Op. 80, w. Susan McAdoo (mez), Helmut Wildhaber (ten), Petr Mikuláš (bass), Jan Engel (bass), M. Haselböck (cnd), Vienna Academy, Brünn Czech Phil Chorus Koch Schwann ▲ SCH CD 317792
Hummel, J.N.:Quod quod in orbe, w. Susan McAdoo (mez), Helmut Wildhaber (ten), Petr Mikuláš (bass), Jan Engel (bass), M. Haselböck (cnd), Vienna Academy, Brünn Czech Phil Chorus Koch Schwann ▲ SCH CD 317792
Mozart, W.A.:Don Giovanni, w. N. Argenta (sop), L. Dawson (sop), J. M. Ainsley (ten), G. Finley (ten), A. Miles (bar), A. Schmidt (bar), G. Yurisch (bar), R. Norrington (cnd), London Classical Players, Schütz Choir London EMI Classics ▲ CDCB 54859

Haljakova, Sidonia (sop)
Puccini, G.:La Bohème, w. Veronika Kinsces (sop—Mimi), Sidonia Haljakova (sop—Musette), Peter Dvorsky (ten—Rodolfo), Vijtech Scherenkel (ten—Parpingol), Ian Konsulov (bar—Marcello), Balazs Poka (bar—Schaunard), Stanislav Benacka (bass—Benoit), Dariusz Niemirowicz (bass—Colline), Stefan Janci (bass—Alcindoro), *(cnd & orch unknown)* Griffin ▲ GCD 2942

Hall, Aled (ten)
Pacini, G.:Saffo, w. Francesca Pedaci (sop—Saffo), Gemma Bertagnolli (sop—Dirce), Mariana Pentcheva (mez—Climene), Carlo Ventre (ten—Faone), Aled Hall (ten—Ippia), Roberto de Candia (bar—Alcandro), Davide Baronchelli (bass—Lisimaco), M. Benini (cnd), Irish National SO, Lubomír Mátl (cnd), Wexford Festival Opera Chorus *(rec Wexford, Oct & Nov 1995)* Marco Polo 2-▲ 8.223883-4 [DDD]

Hall, Bruce (sgr)
Sowerby, L.:Forsaken of Man, w. Alicia Clark (sop), Judith Compton (alt), Thomas Potter (bass), Paul Grizzell (bass), Matthew Greenberg (bass), John Vorassi (sgr), Thomas Weisflog (org), William Ferris (cnd), William Ferris Chorale *(rec St. Thomas the Apostle Church, Chicago, June 1990)* New World ▲ 803942 [AAD]

Hall, J. (sgr)
Rodgers, R.:Flower Drum Song, w. P. Suzuki (sgr), M. Umeki (sgr) [1958 cast] Columbia ▲ CK 02009 ▮ JST 02009

Hall, John (bar)
Casken, J.:Golem, w. P. Rozario (sop), C. Robson (ct), A. Clarke (bar), R. Bernas (cnd), Music Projects London Virgin Classics 2-▲ CDC 59028

Hall, Kent (b–bar)
Parker, H.:Hora novissima, w. A. Soranno (sop), J. Simson (mez), D. Andersen (b–bar), J. Levick (cnd), Nebraska CO, Abendmusik Chorus, Nebraska Wesleyan Univ Choir Albany 2-▲ TROY 124/25

Hall, Meredith (sop)
Purcell, H.:Dido & Aeneas, w. Meredith Hall (sop—2nd Witch/Spirit), Ann Monoyios (sop—Belinda), Shari Saunders (sop—2nd Woman/1st Woman), Jennifer Lane (mez—Dido/Sorceress), Benjamin Butterfield (ten—Sailor), Russell Braun (bar—Aeneas), J. Lamon (cnd), Tafelmusik, Tafelmusik Chamber Choir *(rec Glenn Gould Studio, CBC Toronto, Apr 26-29, 1995)* CBC ▲ SM5 5147 [DDD]

Hall, Peter (ten)
Britten, H.:A Boy Was Born, w. S. Leonard (sop), N. Tibbels (sop), S. Bickley (mez), G. Jess (bass), T. Edwards (cnd), London Sinfonietta Chorus, St. Paul's Cathedral Choristers Virgin Classics ▲ CDC 59136
Britten, H.:Hymn to St. Cecilia, w. S. Leonard (sop), N. Tibbels (sop), S. Bickley (mez), G. Jess (bass), T. Edwards (cnd), London Sinfonietta Chorus, St. Paul's Cathedral Choir Virgin Classics ▲ CDC 59136
Britten, H.:Sonnets of Michelangelo, w. S. Leonard (sop), N. Tibbels (sop), S. Bickley (mez), G. Jess (bass), T. Edwards (cnd), London Sinfonietta Chorus, Choristers of St. Paul's Cathedral Virgin Classics ▲ CDC 59136
Gay, J.:The Beggar's Opera (sels), w. P. Clark (sop), A. Jenkins (sop), M. Cable (mez), E. Lane (mez), S. Minty (mez), E. Fleet (sgr), P. Hall (ten), V. Midgley (ten), N. Rogers (ten), J. Noble (bar), D. Stevens (cnd), Accademia Monteverdiana Orch, Accademia Monteverdiana Chorus—59 songs *(rec Aug. 1978)* Koch Treasure ▲ 3162I-2 [ADD]
Nono, L.:Prometeo, w. I. Ade-Jesemann (sop), M. Bair-Ivenz (sop), S. Otto (alt), U. Krumbiegel (nar), M. Schadock (nar), C. Abbado (cnd), Berlin PO, Freiburg Soloists Choir *(rec May 23-25, 1993)* Sony Classical ▲ SK 53978 [DDD]
Orff, C.:Carmina burana, w. S. Armstrong (sop), B. Rayner Cook (bar), M. Handford (cnd), Hallé Orch, Hallé State Chorus Classics for Pleasure ▲ CDCFP 9005 [ADD]

Hall, Peter (ten) (cont.)
Purcell, H.:Songs, w. Jean Nibbs (sop), Geoffrey Mitchell (ct), David Thomas (bass), Margaret Phillips (org), Michael Howard (cnd), Cantores in Ecclesia—Hear My Prayer, O Lord; Song of the 3 Children; Remember Not, Lord, Our Offences; Voluntary for Single Organ; Magnificat & Nunc Dimittis in g; Thy Work is a Lantern; Burial Sentences for Queen Mary [Man That is Born of a Woman; In the Midst of Life We Are in Death; Thou Knowest, Lord, the Secrets of Our Hearts]; O God, Thou Art My God; Magnificat & Nunc Dimittis in B♭; Voluntary on the 100th Psalm Tune; Turn Thou Us, O Good Lord; O Give Thanks Unto the Lord [Psalm 106] IMP ("BBC Radio Classics" series) ▲ IMP 9126
Tippett, M.:King Priam, w. Heather Harper (sop—Hecuba), Linda Hirst (sop—Serving Woman), Felicity Palmer (sop—Andromache), Julian Saipe (sop—Paris), Yvonne Minton (mez—Helen), Ann Murray (mez—Nurse), Kenneth Bowen (ten—Hermes), Peter Hall (ten—Young Guard), Philip Langridge (ten—Paris), Robert Tear (ten—Achilles), Thomas Allen (bar—Hector), Norman Bailey (bar—Priam), Stephen Roberts (bar—Patroclus), David Wilson-Johnson (bar—Old Man), D. Atherton (cnd), London Sinfonietta, London Sinfonietta Chorus Chandos ▲ CHAN 9406/7 [DDD]

Hall, Robert (bass)
Schubert, Franz:Schwanengesang, w. David Lutz (pno) Preiser ▲ PRE 93402 [DDD]
Schubert, Franz:Songs (misc), w. David Lutz (pno)—selected Mayrhofer Lieder [Am Strome; Auf der Donau; Heliopolis I & II; Nach einem Gewitter; Liane; others] Pearl ▲ PEA 9155 [ADD]

Hall, Rodney (bass)
Offenbach, J.:Les Contes d'Hoffmann, w. Beverly Sills (sop—Olympia/Giulietta/Antonia/Stella), Edith Evans (mez—Nicklausse/Mother's Voice), Michael Devlin (ten—Spalanzani), André Turp (ten—Hoffmann), Luigi Vellucci (ten—Andrès/Cochenille/Pitichinaccio/Frantz), Donald Bernard (bar—Luther/Schlemil), Norman Treigle (bass—Lindorf/Coppélius/Dapertutto/Dr. Miracle), John West (bass—Crespel), Alton Brim (sgr—Nathanaël), Rodney Hall (sgr—Hermann), K. Andersson (cnd), New Orleans Opera Orch, New Orleans Opera Chorus *(rec Feb 27, 1964)* VAI Audio 2-▲ VAIA 1121-2 [ADD]
Puccini, G.:Madama Butterfly, w. Dorothy Kirsten (sop—Madama Butterfly), Rosalind Nadell (mez—Suzuki), Eileen Ireland (mez—Kate), Daniele Barioni (ten—Pinkerton), Thomas Carter (ten—Goro), Arthur Cosenza (ten—Yamadori), Richard Torigi (bar—Sharpless), Rodney Hall (bass—The Bronze), Harold Crane (bass—Commissioner), R. Cellini (cnd), New Orleans Opera Orch, New Orleans Opera Chorus *(rec live, Mar 1960)* VAI Audio 2-▲ VAIA 1054-2

Halland, Edward (bass)
Mussorgsky, M.:Boris Godunov (sels), w. Walter Widdop (ten), Robert Gwynne (sgr), Franklin Kelsey (sgr), A. Coates (cnd), *(orch unknown)*—Revolutionary Scene, Act. IV *(rec Hayes, Studio B, Nov. 3, 1925)* Claremont ▲ GSE 785061
Wagner, R.:Tannhäuser (sels), w. Lauritz Melchior (ten), Walter Widdop (ten), Friedrich Schorr (b–bar), A. Coates (cnd), London SO, New SO—Ov; Venusberg Bacchanale; 1st Pilgrims' Chorus; Wolfram's Cavatina; Prelude; Pilgrims' Return; Rome Narration *(rec 1925–30)* Claremont ▲ GSE 78 50 54

Hälldin, Kaysa (alt)
Nilsson, T.:Out of Earthly Night, w. Gudrun Bruna (sop), Marianne Mellnäs (sop), Lars Sjögren (ten), Göran Swartz (bass), Sture Hedin (sgr), Ola Kyhlberg (sgr), Lars Ljungman (sgr), Nils Philipson (sgr), Ulrik Quale (sgr), Nils Spangenberg (sgr), Britta Therén (sgr), Karl-Erik Welin (org), Torsten Nilsson (cnd), Oscar's Motet Choir *(rec Oscar's Church, Stockholm, Sweden, Apr 26-27, 1978)* BIS ▲ CD 138 [AAD]

Halldórsdóttir, Marta Guthrún (sop)
Cello, w. Bryndís Halla Gylfadóttir (vc), Snorri Sigfús Birgisson (pno) Music from Iceland ▲ ITM 804

Halley (sgr)
Falla, M. de:Atlántida, w. T. Stratas (sop), G. Simionato (mez), R. Browne (sgr), T. Schippers (cnd), La Scala Orch, La Scala Chorus *(rec live, Milan 6/18/62)* Memories 2-▲ HR 4464/65 [ADD]

Hallin, Margareta (sop)
Verdi, G.:Rigoletto, w. B. Nordin (sop), K. Meyer (mez), B. Ericson (mez), Kjellgren (mez), N. Gedda (ten), O. Sivall (ten), H. Hasslo (bar), I. Wixell (bar), B. Alstergård (bar), A. Tyrén (bass), S. Ehrling (cnd), Stockholm Royal Opera House Orch, Stockholm Royal Opera Chorus *(rec live Jan. 18, 1959)* BIS ▲ CD 296 [AAD]

Hallstein, Ingeborg (sop)
Beethoven, L. van:Fidelio, w. C. Ludwig (mez), J. Vickers (ten), G. Unger (ten), W. Berry (bass), G. Frick (bass), O. Klemperer (cnd), Philharmonia Orch, Philharmonia Chorus [G]; w. minimal dialog EMI Classics ("Studio" series) 2-▲ CDMB 69324 [ADD]
Beethoven, L. van:Fidelio, w. Ingeborg Hallstein (sop—Marzelline), Christa Ludwig (mez—Leonore/Fidelio), Gerhard Unger (ten—Jaquino), Jon Vickers (ten—Florestan), Walter Berry (bass—Pizarro), Franz Crass (bass—Don Fernando), Gottlob Frick (bass—Rocco), O. Klemperer (cnd), Philharmonia Orch, Philharmonia Chorus EMI Classics 2-▲ CDCB 55170
Handel, G.F.:Serse, w. Fritz Wunderlich (ten), et al., R. Kubelik (cnd), Bavarian RSO, Bavarian Radio Chorus [G] *(rec 10/22-28/62)* Verona 3-▲ 27032/34 (m) [AAD]
Lehár, F.:Das Land des Lächelns (sels), w. Renate Holm (sop), Heinz Hoppe (ten), Alexander (sgr), Marszalek (cnd), Operretta Orch, Operetta Chorus [G] Acanta ▲ CD 43494 [DDD]
Lehár, F.:Die lustige Witwe (sels), w. L. Popp (sop), H. Hoppe (ten), Alexander (bar), B. Kusche (bar), Marszalek (cnd), Operretta Orch, Operetta Chorus [G] Acanta ▲ CD 43455 [DDD]
Lincke, P.:Frau Luna (sels), w. Renata Tebaldi (sop), Willi Brokmeier (ten), W. Schmidt-Boelcke (cnd), Bavarian RSO, Bavarian Radio Chorus [G] Acanta ▲ CD 42484 [DDD]
Mozart, W.A.:Arias, w. Arleen Augér (sop), Kathleen Battle (sop), Irma Beilke (sop), Helena Braun (sop), Lisa Della Casa (sop), Maria Cebotari (sop), Ileana Cotrubas (sop), Helen Donath (sop), Mirella Freni (sop), Reri Grist (sop), Edita Gruberova (sop), Elisabeth Grümmer (sop), Hilde Güden (sop), Luise Helletsgruber (sop), Gundula Janowitz (sop), Sena Jurinac (sop), Erika Köth (sop), Evelyn Lear (sop), Wilma Lipp (sop), Margaret Marshall (sop), Edith Mathis (sop), Jarmila Novotna (sop), Margherita Perras (sop), Lucia Popp (sop), Elisabeth Rethberg (sop), Anneliese Rothenberger (sop), Elisabeth Schumann (sop), Elisabeth Schwarzkopf (sop), Graziella Sciutti (sop), Irmgard Seefried (sop), Graziella Sciutti (sop), Julia Varady (sop), Agnes Baltsa (mez), Margit Bokor (mez), Brigitte Fassbaender (mez), Christa Ludwig (mez), Ann Murray (mez), Francisco Araiza (ten), Anton Dermota (ten), Helge Rosvaenge (ten), Rudolf Schock (ten), Peter Schreier (ten), Leopold Simoneau (ten), Eric Tappy (ten), Richard Tauber (ten), Gösta Winbergh (ten), Josef Witt (ten), Fritz Wunderlich (ten), Christian Boesch (bar), Willy Domgraf-Fassbaender (bar), Karl Dönch (bar), Dietrich Fischer-Dieskau (bar), Erich Kunz (bar), Eberhard Wächter (bar), Hans Hotter (b–bar), Paul Schöffler (b–bar), Cesare Siepi (b–bar), José Van Dam (b–bar), Walter Berry (bass), Geraint Evans (bass), Nicolai Ghiaurov (bass), Alexander Kipnis (bass), Richard Mayr (bass), Kurt Moll (bass), James Morris (bass), Ezio Pinza (bass), Martti Talvela (bass), Giorgio Tozzi (bass), Hans Duhan (sgr), Res Fischer (sgr), Marie Gerhart (sgr), *(various orchs & cnds)*—sels from Idomeneo, Die Entführung aus der Serail, Le nozze di Figaro, Don Giovanni, Così fan tutte, Die Zauberflöte & various arias Orfeo d'or ("Festspiel Dokumente" series) 5-▲ 408955

Halmai, Katalin (mez)
From Schubert to Strauss with French Horn, w. Friedrich, Ádám (hn), Ingrid Kertesi (sop), Sándor Falvai (pno) Hungaroton ▲ HCD 31585 [DDD]

Halvorson, Carl (ten)
Bowles, P.:The Wind Remains, w. Lucy Schaufer (mez), J. Sheffer (cnd), Eos Ensemble *(rec Manhattan Center Studios, New York, Sept 22 & 23, 1995)* Catalyst ▲ 09026-68409-2 [DDD]
Hindemith, P.:Hin und zurück, w. Jeanne Ommerlé (sop—Helene), Carl Halvorson (ten—Robert), Austin Wright Moore (ten—Sage), Richard Holmes (bar—Doctor), Robert Osborne (b–bar—Orderly), S. R. Radcliffe (cnd), New York Chamber Ensemble *(rec LeFrak Concert Hall, Queens College, Flushing, NY, May 30 & 31, 1994)* Albany ▲ TROY 173 [DDD]
Moore, D.:Gallantry, w. Margaret Bishop (sop—Lola Markham), Julia Parks (mez—Announcer), Carl Halvorson (ten—Donald Hopewell), Richard Holmes (bar—Doctor Gregg), S. R. Radcliffe (cnd), New York Chamber Ensemble *(rec LeFrak Concert Hall, Queens College, Flushing, NY, May 30 & 31, 1994)* Albany ▲ TROY 173 [DDD]

Hamari, Júlia (mez)
Bach, J.S.:Cant 35, w. H. Rilling (cnd), Stuttgart Bach Collegium Hänssler Classic ▲ 98.811 [AAD]
Bach, J.S.:Cant 43, w. A. Augér (sop), L.-M. Harder (ten), P. Huttenlocher (bar), H. Rilling (cnd), Stuttgart Bach Collegium, Gächinger Kantorei [G] *(rec 1981–82)* Hänssler Classic ▲ 98.885 [AAD]
Bach, J.S.:Cant 54, w. H. Rilling (cnd), Stuttgart Bach Collegium Hänssler Classic ▲ 98.805 [ADD]

▲ = CD ♦ = Enhanced CD Δ = MD ▮ = Cassette Tape □ = DCC

Hamari, Júlia (mez) (cont.)

Bach, J.S.:Cant 63, w. A. Augér (sop), H. Laurich (cta), A. Kraus (ten), W. Heldwein (bass), W. Schöne (bass), H. Rilling (cnd), Stuttgart Bach Collegium, Gächinger Kantorei [G] *(rec Feb 1971 & Feb 1981)* Hänssler Classic ▲ 98.823 [AAD]

Bach, J.S.:Cant 69, w. H. Donath (sop), A. Kraus (ten), W. Schöne (bass), H. Rilling (cnd), Bach Ensemble *(rec Mar–Apr 1973)* Hänssler Classic ▲ 98.829 [AAD]

Bach, J.S.:Cant 75, w. I. Reichelt, V. Gohl (mez), A. Baldin (ten), A. Kraus (ten), H.–F. Kunz (bass), H. Rilling (cnd), Stuttgart Bach Collegium, Frankfurt Kantorei [G] *(rec 1970)* Hänssler Classic ▲ 98.891 [AAD]

Bach, J.S.:Cant 77, w. H. Donath (sop), A. Kraus (ten), W. Schöne (bar), H. Rilling (cnd), Stuttgart Bach Collegium, Gächinger Kantorei Hänssler Classic ▲ 98.809 [AAD]

Bach, J.S.:Cant 81, w. A. Kraus (ten), S. Nimsgern (b–bar), H. Rilling (cnd), Bach Ensemble [G] *(rec 1984)* Hänssler Classic ▲ 98.876 [AAD]

Bach, J.S.:Cant 87, w. A. Baldin (ten), W. Heldwein (bass), H. Rilling (cnd), Stuttgart Bach Collegium, Gächinger Kantorei [G] *(rec 1980–81)* Hänssler Classic ▲ 98.885 [AAD]

Bach, J.S.:Cant 98, w. A. Augér (sop), L.–M. Harder (ten), W. Heldwein (bass), H. Rilling (cnd), Stuttgart Bach Collegium, Gächinger Kantorei [G] *(rec Oct 1982 & July 1983)* Hänssler Classic ▲ 98.817 [AAD]

Bach, J.S.:Cant 100, w. A. Augér (sop), A. Kraus (ten), P. Huttenlocher (bar), H. Rilling (cnd), Württemberg CO, Gächinger Kantorei [G] *(rec 1983–84)* Hänssler Classic 5–▲ 98.976

Bach, J.S.:Cant 114, w. G. Schnaut (mez), K. Equiluz (ten), W. Schöne (bass), H. Rilling (cnd), Stuttgart Bach Collegium, Frankfurt Kantorei, Gächinger Kantorei [G] *(rec 1974)* Hänssler Classic ▲ 98.814 [AAD]

Bach, J.S.:Cant 159, w. A. Baldin (ten), P. Huttenlocher (bar), H. Rilling (cnd), Stuttgart Bach Collegium, Gächinger Kantorei [G] *(rec 1983)* Hänssler Classic ▲ 98.879 [AAD]

Bach, J.S.:Cant 164, w. E. Wiens (sop), L.–M. Harder (ten), W. Heldwein (bass), H. Rilling (cnd), Stuttgart Bach Collegium, Gächinger Kantorei Hänssler Classic ▲ 98.811 [AAD]

Bach, J.S.:Cant 171, w. A. Augér (sop), A. Badin (ten), W. Heldwein (bass), H. Rilling (cnd), Württemberg CO, Gächinger Kantorei [G] Hänssler Classic ▲ 98.871 [AAD]

Bach, J.S.:Cant 177, w. A. Augér (sop), P. Schreier (ten), H. Rilling (cnd), Stuttgart Bach Collegium, Gächinger Kantorei Hänssler Classic ▲ 98.803 [AAD]

Bach, J.S.:Cant 183, w. A. Augér (sop), P. Schreier (ten), W. Heldwein (bass), H. Rilling (cnd), Stuttgart Bach Collegium, Gächinger Kantorei Hänssler Classic ▲ 98.801 [AAD]

Bach, J.S.:Cant 188, w. A. Augér (sop), A. Baldin (ten), W. Heldwein (bass), H. Rilling (cnd), Württemberg CO, Gächinger Kantorei [G] *(rec June & Sept 1983)* Hänssler Classic ▲ 98.817 [AAD]

Bach, J.S.:Cant 193, w. A. Augér (sop), H. Rilling (cnd), Bach Ensemble *(rec July 1983)* Hänssler Classic ▲ 98.829 [AAD]

Bach, J.S.:Cant 205, w. Edith Mathis (sop), Carolyn Watkinson (alt), Peter Schreier (ten), Siegfreid Lorenz (bass), P. Schreier (cnd), Berlin CO, Berlin Soloists Berlin Classics ▲ BER 9224

Bach, J.S.:Cant 207, w. Edith Mathis (sop), Carolyn Watkinson (alt), Peter Schreier (ten), Siegfreid Lorenz (bass), P. Schreier (cnd), Berlin CO, Berlin Soloists Berlin Classics ▲ BER 9224

Bach, J.S.:Christmas Oratorio, w. A. Augér (sop), P. Schreier (ten), W. Schöne (bass), H. Rilling (cnd), Stuttgart Bach Collegium Hänssler Classic 3–▲ 98.854 [DDD]

Bach, J.S.:Christmas Oratorio, w. A. Augér (sop), P. Schreier (ten), W. Schöne (bass), H. Rilling (cnd), Stuttgart Bach Collegium, Gächinger Kantorei [G] *(rec 1984)* Hänssler Classic 5–▲ 98.976

Bach, J.S.:Easter Oratorio, w. A. Augér (sop), A. Kraus (ten), P. Huttenlocher (bar), H. Rilling (cnd), Stuttgart Bach Collegium, Gächinger Kantorei [G] *(rec 1980–81)* Hänssler Classic 5–▲ 98.976

Bartók, B.:Songs, w. I. Prunyi (pno), J. Kovács (cnd), Hungarian State Orch—5 Songs, Op. 15 [Sz.61] [orchd. by Zltán Kodály]; 5 Songs, Op. 16 [Sz.63]; 5 Songs [from 8 Hungarian Folksongs, Sz.64]; Songs for Voice & Orch.; 5 Songs for Voice & Orch., Sz.101 [Hun] Hungaroton ▲ HCD 31535 [DDD]

Gluck, C.W.:Orfeo ed Euridice, w. V. Kincses (sop), M. Zempleni (sop), E. Lukács (cnd), Hungarian State Opera Orch, Hungarian State Opera Chorus LaserLight ▲ 14113 [DDD]

Haydn, J.:Stabat Mater, w. Krisztina Láki (sop), Claes Hakan Ahnsjö (ten), Richard Anlauf (bass), F. Bernius (cnd), Württemberg CO, Stuttgart Chamber Choir *(rec 1978)* Vox Box 2–▲ CDX 5081 [ADD]

Humperdinck, E.:Hänsel und Gretel, w. L. Popp (sop), B. Fassbaender (mez), A. Schlemm (mez), W. Berry (bass), G. Solti (cnd), Vienna PO London 2–▲ 421111–2 [ADD]

Leoncavallo, R.:Pagliacci, w. M. Caballé (sop), R. Scotto (sop), A. Varnay (mez), J. Carreras (ten), M. Manuguerra (bar), T. Allen (bar), K. Nurmela (bar), U. Benelli (bar), R. Muti (cnd), Philharmonia Orch, Ambrosian Opera Chorus EMI Classics 2–▲ CDMB 63650

Mahler, G.:Sym 2, w. F. Lott (sop), M. Jansons (cnd), Oslo PO, Oslo Phil Chorus Chandos ("Collect" series) 2–▲ CHAN 6595/96 [DDD]

Mozart, W.A.:Requiem, w. E. Mathis (sop), W. Ochman (ten), K. Ridderbusch (bass), K. Böhm (cnd), Vienna PO, Vienna State Opera Chorus [L] Deutsche Grammophon ▲ 413553–2 [ADD]

Pergolesi, G.B.:Stabat mater, w. M. Kalmár (sop), L. Gardelli (cnd), Franz Liszt CO [L] Hungaroton ▲ HCD 12201

Rossini, G.:La donna del lago, w. M. Caballé (sop), F. Bonisolli (ten), R. Bottazzo (ten), P. Bellugi (cnd), Turin RAI Orch, Turin RAI Chorus [I] *(rec live 5/19/70)* Melodram 2–▲ MEL 27074 (m) [AAD]

Rossini, G.:La donna del lago, w. M. Caballé (sop), F. Bonisolli (ten), R. Bottazzo (ten), P. Bellugi (cnd), Turin Radio Orch, Turin RAI Chorus [I] *(rec live 5/19/70)* Standing Room Only 2–▲ SRO 803–2 (m) [ADD]

Rossini, G.:La donna del lago, w. A. Balboni (sop), M. Caballé (sop), F. Bonisolli (ten), R. Bottazzo (ten), G. Sinimberghi (ten), P. Washington (bass), P. Bellugi (cnd), Turin RAI Orch, Turin RAI Chorus *(rec live, Torino, 1970)* Foyer 2–▲ FOY 2028 [AAD]

Strauss (II), Joh.:Der Zigeunerbaron, w. Pamela Coburn (sop), Christiane Oelze (sop), Elisabeth von Magnus (alt), Herbert Lippert (ten), Rudolf Schasching (ten), Wolfgang Holzmair (bar), Jurgen Flimm (sgr), Robert Florianschutz (sgr), Hans–Jurgen Lazar (sgr), N. Harnoncourt (cnd), Vienna SO, Arnold Schoenberg Choir *(rec Vienna, 1994)* Teldec 2–▲ 94555–2

Wagner, R.:Die Meistersinger von Nürnberg, w. H. Bode (sop), A. Kollo (ten), N. Bailey (bar), B. Weikl (bar), K. Moll (bass), G. Solti (cnd), Vienna PO, Vienna State Opera Chorus [G] London 4–▲ 417497–2 [ADD]

Weber, C.M. von:Oberon, w. B. Nilsson (sop), A. Augér (sop), P. Domingo (ten), H. Prey (bar), R. Kubelik (cnd), Bavarian RSO Deutsche Grammophon 2–▲ 419038–2 [ADD]

Weber, C.M. von:Oberon, w. B. Nilsson (sop), A. Augér (sop), P. Domingo (ten), H. Prey (bar), R. Kubelik (cnd), Bavarian RSO Deutsche Grammophon ("Domingo Edition" series) ▲ 435406–2 [ADD]

Hamel, Michel (ten)

Gounod, C.:Le Médecin malgré lui, w. Lina Dachary (sop), Monique Stiot (mez), Joseph Peyron (ten), Christophe Benoit (bar), Janine Capderou (sgr), Jean–Louis Soumagnas (sgr), J.–C. Hartemann (cnd), ORTF Lyric Orch Musidisc ▲ MUS 202322 [AAD]

Hahn, R.:O mon del inconnu!, w. Christiane Château (sop), Lina Dachary (sop), Monique Stiot (mez), Joseph Peyron (ten), Aimé Doniat (bar), Dominique Tirmont (bar), Philippe Gaudin (sgr), Jacques Provins (sgr), J. Brebion (cnd), ORTF Lyric Orch Musidisc 2–▲ MUS 202562 [AAD]

Ravel, M.:L'Heure espagnole, w. S. Danco (mez—Concepcion), J. Giraudeau (ten—Gonzalve), M. Hamel (ten—Torquemada), J. Cameron (bar—Ramiro), A. Vessières (bass—Gomez), B. Maderna (cnd), BBC SO *(rec Nov. 1960)* Stradivarius ▲ STR 10062 [ADD]

Hameleers, Frank (ten)

Einhorn, R.:Voices of Light, w. Susan Narucki (sop), Corrie Pronk (alt), Henk van Heijnsbergen (b–bar), Ronald Hoogeveen (vn), Harm Bakker (vl), Michael Feves (vl), Naomi Hirschfeld (vl), S. Mercurio (cnd), Netherlands Radio PO, Martin Wright (cnd), Anonymous 4, Netherlands Radio Chorus *(rec Music Center of the Netherlands Radio & TV, Aug 23–25, 1995)* Sony Classical ▲ SK 62006 [DDD]

Hamelin, Rick (ten)

Rich, F.C.:The Hudson Oratorio, w. Kathryn Radcliffe (sop), Harold von Geldern (bar), F.C. Rich (cnd), Juilliard Orch members *(rec Church of the Epiphany, New York City, July 1996)* Albany ▲ TROY 217 [DDD]

Hamilton, David (ten)

Berlioz, H.:Requiem, "Grande Messe des Morts", w. J. Hopkins (cnd), Sydney Conservatorium for Music Orch, Sydney Conservatorium Choir, Willoughby Sym Chorus Walsingham Classics ▲ WAL 8000 [DDD]

Mozart, W.A.:Songs, w. J. Edwards (cta), P. Sharpe (sgr), D. Russell (sgr), M. Glasgow (sgr), C. Birch (sgr), P. Hooper (sgr), G. Lancaster (pno) *(rec July 1991)* Tall Poppies ▲ TP009 [DDD]

Hamilton, Katherine Mary (sgr)

Myers, G.:God's Trbn, w. Christine Helfrich (sop), Gordon Myers (bar), Richard Cragg (sgr), Matthew Gillis (sgr), Timothy Pehta (sgr), Paul Norman (sgr), Wendy Catlin (sgr) Sharon Hunter (sgr), Gloriae Dei Brass Ensemble Paraclete ▲ CDGD 017 [DDD]; ■ GDC 017

Hamilton, Lawrence (bar)

Lebaron, A.:The E. & O. Line (sels), w. Louise Cloutier (mez—Eurydice/Vendors), Hugh Panero (ten—Hermes), Lawrence Hamilton (bar—Orpheus/Men), Frank London (tpt), Marcus Rojas (tuba), Myra Melford (pno/kbd), Davey Williams (gtr), Fred Hopkins (elec bass), Thurman Barker (dr), A. LeBaron (cnd)—Juke Joint Jam Session; Eurydice Meets Hermes; Eurydice's Death [Funeral Band]; Eurydice's River Journey; Orpheus Laments [Looked Away] *(rec Coolidge Auditorium, Library of Congress, 1987)* Mode ▲ Mode 42

Hammes, Karl (bar)

Mozart, W.A.:Don Giovanni, w. Hedwig Jungkurth (sop—Elvira), Maria Reining (sop—Anna), Julius Patzak (ten—Ottavio), Karl Hammes (bar—Don Giovanni), Georg Hann (bass), Ludwig Weber (bass—Commandant), J. Keilberth (cnd), Stuttgart Reich RSO, Stuttgart Radio Chorus *(rec Mar, 1936)* Preiser 2–▲ PRE 90263

Strauss, R.:Ariadne auf Naxos, w. Erna Berger (sop), Viorica Ursuleac (sop), Helge Roswaenge (ten), C. Krauss (cnd), Berlin Reich RSO *(rec Berlin, 1935)* Preiser ▲ PRE 90259

Hammond–Stroud, Derek (bar)

Schubert, Franz:Songs (misc), w. G. Kirkwood (pno)—13 songs [G] *(rec 1988–89)* Symposium ▲ 1064

Wolf, H.:Italienische Liederbücher (sels), w. G. Kirkwood (pno)—8 songs [G] *(rec 1988–89)* Symposium ▲ 1064

Wolf, H.:Mörike–Lieder (sels), w. G. Kirkwood (pno), 8 songs [G] *(rec 1988–89)* Symposium ▲ 1064

Hammons, Thomas (bar)

Adams, J.:The Death of Klinghoffer, w. S. Friedman (mez), S. Sylvan (bar), J. Maddalena (bar), K. Nagano (cnd), Lyon Opera Orch, English Opera Group Chorus Elektra/Nonesuch 2–▲ 79281–2 2–■ 79281–4

Hamnøy, Kari (sop)

Schmidt, O.:The Öresund Sym, w. Anders Lundh (ten), O. Schmidt (cnd), Malmö SO, Ars Nova *(rec Malmö Concert Hall, Sweden, Apr. 11–13, 1994)* BIS ▲ CD 672 [DDD]

Hampe, Christiane (sop)

Zelenka, J.D.:Missa votiva, w. E. Graf (cta), J. Duske (ten), J. Gebhardt (bass), W. Wehnert (cnd), Hesse Bach Collegium, Marburg Bach Choir [L] Thorofon ▲ CTH 2172 [DDD]

Hampson, Thomas (bar)

American Dreamer:Songs of Stephen Foster Angel ▲ CDC 54621 ■ 4DS 54621

Bach, J.S.:Cant 152, w. C. Wegmann (trb), N. Harnoncourt (cnd), Vienna Concentus Musicus [G] Teldec 2–▲ 2292–42632–2 [DDD]

Bach, J.S.:Cant 153, w. S. Rampf (ct), K. Equiluz (ten), N. Harnoncourt (cnd), Vienna Concentus Musicus, Tölz Boys' Choir [G] Teldec 2–▲ 2292–42632–2 [DDD]

Bach, J.S.:Cant 154, w. P. Esswood (ct), K. Equiluz (ten), N. Harnoncourt (cnd), Vienna Concentus Musicus, Tölz Boys' Choir [G] Teldec 2–▲ 2292–42632–2 [DDD]

Bach, J.S.:Cant 155, w. A. Bergius (trb), P. Esswood (ct), K. Equiluz (ten), N. Harnoncourt (cnd), Vienna Concentus Musicus, Tölz Boys' Choir [G] Teldec 2–▲ 2292–42632–2 [DDD]

Bach, J.S.:Cant 156, w. P. Esswood (ct), K. Equiluz (ten), N. Harnoncourt (cnd), Vienna Concentus Musicus, Tölz Boys' Choir [G] Teldec 2–▲ 2292–42632–2 [DDD]

Bach, J.S.:Cant 185, w. H. Wittek (trb), P. Esswood (ct), K. Equiluz (ten), N. Harnoncourt (cnd), Vienna Concentus Musicus, Tölz Boys' Choir [G] Teldec 2–▲ 2292–44179–2 [DDD]

Barber, S.:Songs, w. C. Studer (sop), J. Browning (pno), Emerson String Quartet Deutsche Grammophon 2–▲ 435867–2 [DDD]

Beethoven, L. van:An die ferne Geliebte, w. Geoffrey Parsons (pno) *(rec live, Usher Hall, Edinburgh, Aug. 20–21, 1993)* EMI Classics ▲ CDC 55147 [DDD]

Bernstein, L.:Arias & Barcarolles, w. Frederica von Stade (mez), M. Tilson Thomas (cnd), London SO *(rec Henry Wood Hall, London, Sept 1993)* Deutsche Grammophon ▲ 439926–2 [DDD]

Bernstein, L.:Music of, w. J. Norman (sop), K. Te Kanawa (sop), J. Anderson (sop), F. von Stade (mez), C. Ludwig (mez), T. Troyanos (mez), J. Carreras (ten), D. Garrison (ten), J. Hadley (ten),T. Daly (sgr), G. Kremer (vn), M. Rostropovich (vc), M.T. Thomas (va), L. Bernstein (cnd), *(orch unknown)*—various popular works Deutsche Grammophon ▲ 439251–2 ■ 439251–4

Brahms, J.:Ein Deutsches Requiem, w. J. Williams (sop), D. Barenboim (cnd), Chicago SO, Chicago Sym Chorus [G] Erato ▲ 92856–2

Christmas with Thomas Hampson w. St. Paul CO [cnd:Hugh Wolff] Teldec ▲ 9031–73135–2 [DDD]

Copland, A.:Old American Songs, w. D. Upshaw (sop), H. Wolff (cnd), St. Paul CO Teldec ▲ 77310

Delius, F.:Sea Drift, w. C. Mackerras (cnd), Welsh National Opera Orch, Welsh National Opera Chorus Argo ▲ 430206–2 [DDD]

Duruflé, M.:Requiem, w. B. Bonney (soprano), J. Larmore (mezzo–soprano), Ambrosian Singers, M. Legrand (cnd), Philharmonia Orch Teldec ▲ 90879–2

Fauré, G.:Requiem, w. B. Bonney (sop), J. Larmore (mez), M. Legrand (cnd), Philharmonia Orch, Ambrosian Singers Teldec ▲ 90879–2

Foster, S.C.:Songs, w. Fiddle Fever EMI Classics ▲ CDC 54621 ■ 4DS 54621

Franz, R.:Songs, w. Geoffrey Parsons (pno)—Nun holt mir eine Kanne Wein; Ihr Auge; Die süsse Dirn' von Inverness *(rec live, Usher Hall, Edinburgh, Aug. 20–21, 1993)* EMI Classics ▲ CDC 55147 [DDD]

German Opera Arias, w. Fabio Luisi (cnd), Munich RSO, Pestalozzi School Children's Choir EMI Classics ▲ 55233–2

Gounod, C.:Faust, w. C. Studer (sop), R. Leech (ten), J. Van Dam (b–bar), M. Plasson (cnd), Toulouse Capitole Orch, Toulouse Capitole Chorus, *(highlights from the above)* EMI Classics ▲ CDC 54358 [DDD]

Gounod, C.:Faust, w. C. Studer (sop), R. Leech (ten), J. Van Dam (b–bar), M. Plasson (cnd), Toulouse Capitole Orch, Toulouse Capitole Chorus EMI Classics 3–▲ CDCC 54228 [DDD]

Great American Songwriter's, w. Bruce Hubbard (bar), Kiri Te Kanawa (sop), Frederica von Stade (mez) Angel ▲ CDM 64670

Grieg, E.:Lieder, Op. 48, w. Geoffrey Parsons (pno) *(rec live, Usher Hall, Edinburgh, Aug. 20–21, 1993)* EMI Classics ▲ CDC 55147 [DDD]

Griffes, C.T.:Songs, w. A. Guzelimian (pno)—17 songs—An den Wind; Am Kreuzweg wird begraben; Meeres Stille; Auf geheimem Waldespfade; Wohl lag ich einst in Gram und Schmerz; So halt' ich endlich dich umfangen; Mein Herz ist wie die dunkle Nacht; Der träumende See; Mit schwarzen Segeln; Das ist ein Brausen und Heulen; Wo ich bin, mich rings umdunkelt; Auf ihrem Grab; Das sterbende Kind; Elfe; Zwei Könige sassen auf Orkadal; Des Müden Abendlied; Nachtlied [G] Teldec ▲ 9031–72168–2 [DDD]

Hadley & Hampson, w. Jerry Hadley (ten), Welsh National Opera Orch [cnd:Carlo Rizzi] Teldec ▲ 73283–2

Handel, G.F.:Apollo e Dafne, w. R. Alexander (sop), N. Harnoncourt (cnd), Vienna Concentus Musicus Teldec ("Das alte Werk" series) ▲ 98645–2

Handel, G.F.:Giulio Cesare in Egitto (sels), w. Roberta Alexander (sop), N. Harnoncourt (cnd), Vienna Concentus Musicus Teldec ("Das alte Werk" series) ▲ 98645–2

Ives, C.:Songs, w. A. Guzelimian (pno)—Minnelied; Gruss; Frühlingslied; Du bist wie eine Blume; Ballad from Rosamunde; Ein Ton; Widmung; Marie; Rosenzweige; Wiegenlied; Feldeinsamkeit; Ich grolle nicht; Weil' auf mir; Ilmenau (Wanderers Nachtlied) [G] Teldec ▲ 9031–72168–2 [DDD]

Leading Man Angel ▲ CDC 55249 ■ 4DS 55249

Lehár, F.:Die lustige Witwe, w. F. Lott (sop), E. Szmytka (sop), J. Aler (ten), D. Bogarde (nar), F. Welser–Möst (cnd), London PO, Glyndebourne Festival Chorus EMI Classics ▲ CDCB 55152

Lieder aus "Des Knaben Wunderhorn", w. Geoffrey Parsons (pno) Teldec ▲ 2292–44923–2 [DDD]

Hampson, Thomas (bar) (cont.)

Loewe, C.:Songs, w. Geoffrey Parsons (pno)—Findlay *(rec live, Usher Hall, Edinburgh, Aug. 20–21, 1993)* EMI Classics ▲ CDC 55147 [DDD]

Macdowell, E.:Songs, w. A. Guzelimian (pno)—5 songs (Op. 11, Nos. 1–3 & Op. 12, Nos. 1 & 2)—Mein Liebchen, wir sassen beisammen; Du liebst mich nicht; Oben, wo die Sterne glühen; Nachtlied; Das Rosenband [G] Teldec ▲ 9031-72168-2 [DDD]

Mahler, G.:Kindertotenlieder, w. L. Bernstein (cnd), Vienna PO [G] Deutsche Grammophon 2-▲ 427697-2 [DDD]

Mahler, G.:Kindertotenlieder, w. L. Bernstein (cnd), Vienna PO Deutsche Grammophon ▲ 431682-2 [DDD]

Mahler, G.:Des Knaben Wunderhorn, w. G. Parsons (pno) Teldec ▲ 74726-2

Mahler, G.:Lieder eines fahrenden Gesellen, w. D. Lutz (pno) Teldec ▲ 74002

Mahler, G.:Songs, w. L. Berio (cnd), Philharmonia Orch—5 frühe Lieder; 6 frühe Lieder; Frühe Lieder [w. D. Lutz (piano)] Teldec ▲ 74002

Mahler, G.:Songs from Rückert, w. L. Bernstein (cnd), Vienna PO *(rec live, 2/90)* Deutsche Grammophon ▲ 431682-2 [DDD]

Massenet, J.:Hérodiade, w. Cheryl Studer (sop—Salomé), Nadine Denize (mez—Hérodiade), Ben Heppner (ten—Jean), José Van Dam (b-bar—Phanuel), Thomas Hampson (bass—Hérode), M. Plasson (cnd), Toulouse Capitole Orch, Toulouse Capitole Chorus EMI Classics 3-▲ CDCC 55378

Mendelssohn, F.:Elijah, w. Barbara Bonney (sop), Henriette Schellenberg (sop), Florence Quivar (mez), Marietta Simpson (mez), Reid Bartelme (trb), Jerry Hadley (ten), Richard Clement (ten), Thomas Paul (bar), R. Shaw (cnd), Atlanta SO, Atlanta Sym Chorus [E] *(rec Symphony Hall, Woodruff Arts Center, Atlanta, GA, Nov. 5–7, 1994)* Telarc 2-▲ CD 80389 [DDD]

Mendelssohn, F.:Die erste Walpurgisnacht, w. B. Remmert (alt), U. Heilman (ten), R. Pape (bass), N. Harnoncourt (cnd), CO of Europe Teldec ▲ 74882-2

Mendelssohn, F.:St. Paul, w. R. Yakar (sop), B. Baileys (mez), M. Schäfer (ten), M. Corboz (cnd), Lisbon Gulbenkian Foundation Orch, Lisbon Gulbenkian Foundation Chorus Erato 2-▲ 45279-2

Meyerbeer, G.:Songs EMI Classics ▲ CDC 54436

Monteverdi, C.:Vespro della Beata Vergine, w. M. Marshall (sop), F. Palmer (sop), P. Langridge (ten), K. Equiluz (ten), A. Korn (bass), N. Harnoncourt (cnd), Vienna Concentus Musicus, Hamburg Monteverdi Chorus, Vienna Boys' Chorus Teldec 2-▲ 92629-2

Monteverdi, C.:Vespro della Beata Vergine, w. L. Marshall (sop), F. Palmer (sop), P. Langridge (ten), K. Equiluz (ten), A. Korn (bass), N. Harnoncourt (cnd), Vienna Concentus Musicus, Hamburg Monteverdi Chorus, Vienna Boys' Chorus [L] Teldec 2-▲ 2292-42671-2

Mozart, W.A.:Ave verum corpus, w. Barbara Bonney (sop), Charlotte Margiono (sop), Sylvia McNair (sop), Elisabeth von Magnus (cta), Christoph Pregardien (ten), N. Harnoncourt (cnd), Vienna Concentus Musicus, Arnold Schoenberg Choir Teldec ▲ 98928 2

Mozart, W.A.:Così fan tutte, w. Kiri Te Kanawa (sop), Marie McLaughlin (sop), Ann Murray (mez), Hans-Peter Blochwitz (ten), G. Furlanetto (bar), J. Levine (cnd), Vienna PO, Vienna State Opera Chorus [I] Deutsche Grammophon 3-▲ 423897-2 [DDD]

Mozart, W.A.:Don Giovanni, w. E. Gruberova (sop), B. Bonney (sop), R. Alexander (sop), N. Harnoncourt (cnd), Royal Concertgebouw Orch [I] Teldec 3-▲ 2292-44184-2 [DDD]

Mozart, W.A.:Grabmusik, w. Barbara Bonney (sop), Charlotte Margiono (sop), Sylvia McNair (sop), Elisabeth von Magnus (cta), Christoph Pregardien (ten), N. Harnoncourt (cnd), Vienna Concentus Musicus, Arnold Schoenberg Choir Teldec ("Das alte Werk" series) ▲ 98928-2

Mozart, W.A.:Idomeneo, w. Heidi Grant-Murphy (sop—Ilia), Carol Vaness (sop—Elettra), Cecilia Bartoli (mez—Idamante), Plácido Domingo (ten—Idomeneo), Frank Lopardo (ten—High Priest), Thomas Hampson (bar—Arbace), Bryn Terfel (b-bar—The Voice), J. Levine (cnd), Metropolitan Opera Orch, Raymond Hughes (cnd), New York Metropolitan Opera Chorus *(rec Manhattan Center Studios, New York, Mar & Apr 1994)* Deutsche Grammophon 3-▲ 447 737-2 [DDD]

Mozart, W.A.:Idomeneo, w. Carol Vaness (sop—Elettra), Cecilia Bartoli (mez—Idamante), Heidi Grant Murphy (mez—Ilia), Plácido Domingo (ten— Idomeneo), Thomas Hampson (bar—Arbace), Bryn Terfel (bass-bar—La Voce), J. Levine (cnd), Metropolitan Opera Orch, New York Metropolitan Opera Chorus Deutsche Grammophon ▲ 447737-2

Mozart, W.A.:Nozze di Figaro, w. C. Margiono (sop), B. Bonney (sop), I. Rey (sop), A. Murray (mez), P.-L. Lang (mez), P. Langridge (ten), C. Späth (ten), K. Moll (bass), A. Scharinger (bass), K. Langan (bass), N. Harnoncourt (cnd), Royal Concertgebouw Orch, Netherlands Opera Chorus *(rec Amsterdam, May 1993)* Teldec 3-▲ 90861-2 [DDD]

Mozart, W.A.:Regina coeli, K.127, w. Barbara Bonney (sop), Charlotte Margiono (sop), Sylvia McNair (sop), Elisabeth von Magnus (cta), Christoph Pregardien (ten), N. Harnoncourt (cnd), Vienna Concentus Musicus, Arnold Schoenberg Choir Teldec ("Das alte Werk" series) ▲ 98928 2

Mozart, W.A.:Zauberflöte, w. E. Gruberova (sop), B. Bonney (sop), G. Schmid (sop), H.-P. Blochwitz (ten), M. Salminen (bass), A. Scharinger (bass), N. Harnoncourt (cnd), Zurich Opera Orch, Zurich Opera House Chorus [G] Teldec 2-▲ 2292-42716-2

Night & Day, w. John McGlinn (cnd), London SO, Ambrosian Chorus EMI Classics ▲ CDC 54203 [DDD] ■ 4DS 54203 (D)

An Old Song Re-sung, American Concert Songs, w. A. Guzelimian (pno) EMI Classics ▲ CDC 54051

Orff, C.:Carmina burana, w. E. Gruberova (sop), J. Aler (ten), S. Ozawa (cnd), Berlin PO, Berlin Cathedral Boys' Choir, Shin-Yuh Kai Chorus [G, L] Philips ▲ 422363-2 [DDD] □ 422363-5

Orff, C.:Carmina burana, w. Natalie Dessay (sop), Gérard Lesne (ct), M. Plasson (cnd), Toulouse Capitole Orch, Orféon Donostiarra, Midi-Pyrénées Children's Choir *(rec Halle-aux-Grains, Toulouse, Dec. 2, 4 & 6, 1994)* EMI Classics ▲ CDC 55392 [DDD]

Our Christmas Songs for You, w. Kiri Te Kanawa (sop), Roberto Alagna (ten), Jonathan Tunick (cnd), *(orch unknown)* EMI Classics ▲ CDC 56176

Puccini, G.:La Bohème, w. Leontina Vaduva (sop—Mimi), Ruth Ann Swenson (sop—Musetta), Roberto Alagna (ten—Rodolfo), Simon Keenlyside (bar—Schaunard), Thomas Hampson (bar—Marcello), Samuel Ramey (bass—Colline), Enrico Fissore (bass—Benoit), A. Pappano (cnd), Philharmonia Orch EMI Classics 2-♦ CDCB 56120

Rossini, G.:Il barbiere di Siviglia, w. A. Felle (sop), S. Mentzer (mez), J. Hadley (ten), S. Ramey (bass), G. Gelmetti (cnd), Tuscan Orch EMI ▲ 54863-2

Rossini, G.:Music of, w. M. Fortuna (sop), M. Lerner (sop), D. Voigt (sop), M. Horne (mez), K. Kuhlmann (mez), F. von Stade (mez), R. Blake (ten), C. Estep (ten), C. Merritt (ten), H. Runey (b-bar), J. Opalach (bass), S. Ramey (bass), R. Norrington (cnd), Orch of St. Luke's, New York Concert Chorale EMI Classics ▲ CDC 54643

Rossini, G.:Songs EMI Classics ▲ CDC 54436

Schubert, Franz:Fierrabras, w. K. Mattila (sop), C. Studer (sop), R. Gambill (ten), R. Holl (bass), L. Polgar (bass), C. Abbado (cnd), CO of Europe, Arnold Schoenberg Choir [G] *(rec live)* Deutsche Grammophon 2-▲ 427341-2 [DDD]

Schubert, Franz:Songs (comp), w. M. McLaughlin (sop), G. Johnson (pno)—soprano songs—D.312 & 542; baritone songs—D.166, 360, 396/383, 450, 540, 541, 548, 554, 677, 699, 700, 707, 737, 890 [G] Hyperion ▲ CDJ 33014 [DDD]

Schubert, Franz:Songs (comp), w. M. McLaughlin (sop), G. Johnson (pno), New Company Singers—soprano/piano songs—D.118, 564, 623, 658, 830, 831, 837, 838, 839, 846, 866/1, 866/3, 923; baritone/piano songs—D.293 & 923; baritone & chorus—Szene aus Faust, D.126 [G] Hyperion ▲ CDJ 33013 [DDD]

Schumann, R.:Dichterliebe, w. Geoffrey Parsons (pno) *(rec live, Usher Hall, Edinburgh, Aug. 20–21, 1993)* EMI Classics ▲ CDC 55147 [DDD]

Schumann, R.:Songs, w. G. Parsons (pno)—5 early Kerner-Lieder (1828); 12 Kerner-Lieder, Op. 35; Fünf Lieder, Op. 40 [G] Teldec ▲ 2292-44935-2 [DDD]

Schumann, R.:Songs, w. Geoffrey Parsons (pno)—Niemand; Dem roten Röslein gleicht mein Lieb *(rec live, Usher Hall, Edinburgh, Aug. 20–21, 1993)* EMI Classics ▲ CDC 55147 [DDD]

Tchaikovsky, P.:Eugene Onegin, w. K. Te Kanawa (sop—Tatiana), P. Bardon (mez—Olga), N. Rosenshein (ten—Lensky), T. Hampson (b-bar—Eugene Onegin), J. Connell (bass—Prince Gremin), C. Mackerras (cnd), Welsh National Opera Orch, Welsh National Opera Chorus [E] EMI Classics ▲ CDCB 55004

Thomas, A.:Hamlet, w. J. Anderson (sop—Ophelie), D. Graves (mez—Gertrude); G. Kunde (ten—Laerte), T. Hampson (bar—Hamlet), S. Ramey (bass—Claudius), A. de Almeida (cnd), London PO, Ambrosian Singers EMI Classics 3-▲ CDCC 54820

Wagner, R.:Götterdämmerung, w. E. Marton (sop), S. Jerusalem (ten), J. Tomlinson (bass), B. Haitink (cnd), Bavarian RSO [G] EMI Classics 4-▲ CDCD 54485

Hampson, Thomas (bar) (cont.)

Warren, E.R.:Abram in Egypt, w. B. Ferden (cnd), Cracow RSO, Cracow Radio Chorus *(rec Church of the Bernardines, Cracow, Poland, June 21–24, 1993)* Cambria ▲ CD 1095 [DDD]

Warren, E.R.:The Harp Weaver, w. B. Ferden (cnd), Cracow RSO, Cracow Radio Chorus *(rec Church of the Bernardines, Cracow, Poland, June 21–24, 1993)* Cambria ▲ CD 1095 [DDD]

Warren, E.R.:The Legend of King Arthur:A Choral Sym, w. L. Vincent (ten), S. Kawalla (cnd), Cracow Polish Radio-TV SO [E] Cambria ▲ CD 1043 [DDD]

Warren, E.R.:Singing Earth, w. B. Ferden (cnd), Cracow RSO *(rec Church of the Bernardines, Cracow, Poland, June 21–24, 1993)* Cambria ▲ CD 1095 [DDD]

Warren, E.R.:The Sleeping Beauty, w. Maria Venuti (mez—Princess), Thomas Hampson (bar—Prince), Gerd Nienstedt (b-bar—King), David Lutz (pno), B. Ferden (cnd), Cracow RSO, Cracow Radio Chorus *(rec Church of the Bernardines, Cracow, Poland, June 21–24, 1993)* Cambria ▲ CD 1095 [DDD]

Hamre, Knut (sgr)

Grieg, E.:Norwegian Folk Songs, Op. 66, w. H. Fiddle (sgr), R. Horvei (sgr), G. Botnen (pno) Simax ▲ PSC 1102

Grieg, E.:Norwegian Peasant Dances, Op. 72, w. H. Fiddle (sgr), R. Horvei (sgr), G. Botnen (pno) Simax ▲ PSC 1102

Hanák, Rado (bass)

Respighi, O.:Lucrezia, w. Adriana Kohútková (sop—Venilia), Michela Remor (sop—Lucrezia), Stefania Kaluza (mez—La Voce), Denisa Šlepkovská (mez—Servia), Ludovít Ludha (ten—Collatino), Igor Pasek (ten—Bruto), Ján Durčo (bar—Tito/Valerio), Richard Haan (bar—Tarquinio), Rado Hanák (bass—Arunte/Spurio Lucrezio) *(rec Concert Hall of the Slovak Radio, Bratislava, June 9–16, 1994)* Marco Polo ▲ 8.223717 [DDD]

Hanchard, Dana (sop)

Handel, G.F.:Radamisto, w. Monika Frimmer (sop), Juliana Gondek (sop), Lisa Saffer (sop), R. Popken (cta), Michael Dean (b-bar), Nicholas Cavallier (bass), N. McGegan (cnd), Freiburg Baroque Orch Harmonia Mundi USA 3-▲ HMU 907111/13

Monk, M.:Atlas, w. R. Een (sgr), S.-Z. Chen (sgr), S. Kalm (bar), M. Monk (cnd), *(orch unknown)* *(rec June 1992)* ECM New Series ▲ 78118-21491-2 [DDD]

Monteverdi, C.:Incoronazione, w. Constanze Backes (sop—Valletto), Catherine Bott (sop—Drusilla/Pallade/La Virtù), Dana Hanchard (sop—Nerone), Sylvia McNair (sop—Poppea), Marinella Pennicchi (sop—Amore/Damigella), Annie Sofie von Otter (mez—Ottavia/Venere/La Fortuna), Julian Clarkson (alt—Littore/Mercurio), Bernarda Fink (cta—Arnalta), Roberto Balconi (ct—Nutrice), Michael Chance (ct—Ottone), Nigel Robson (ten—Liberto/Soldato Secondo), Mark Tucker (ten—Lucano/Soldato Primo), Francesco Ellero d'Artegna (bass—Seneca), J. E. Gardiner (cnd), English Baroque Soloists *(rec Queen Elizabeth Hall, South Bank Ctr, London, Dec 1993)* Archiv 3-▲ 447088-2

Monteverdi, C.:Orfeo, w. Jennifer Lane (mez), Jeffrey Thomas (ten), Michael Brown (sgr), Timothy Leigh Evans (sgr), Paul Shipper (sgr), G. Toth (cnd), ARTEK Lyrichord 2-▲ LYR 9002 [DDD]

Hancock-Child, Nik (bar)

Gibbs, C.A.:Songs, w. R. Hancock-Child (pno)—The Bells; Araby; Ann's Cradle Song; Beggar's Song; Candlestick Maker's Song; 5 Eyes; As I Lay in the Early Sun; Silver; The Tiger Lily; The Sleeping Beauty; The Wanderer; Take Heed, Young Heart; Proud Maisie; Jenny Jones; The Ballad of Semmerwater; Padraic the Fiddler; Down in Yonder Meadow; Dream Song Midnight; A Ballad Maker; The Witch; The Splendour Falls; The Cherry Tree; Hypochondriacus; Dusk *(rec July 1990 & July 1991)* Marco Polo ▲ 8.223458 [DDD]

Hancorn, John (bass)

Program 3, w. Arnold Dolmetsch (vir), François (trb rcr), Jeanne Dolmetsch (trb rcr), Marguerite Dolmetsch (vl), Nigel Foster (hpd), Kathleen Livingstone (sop), Jennifer Bate (org), et al. IMP Allegro ▲ PCD 995 [DDD]

Handler, Karel (sgr)

Synagogue Chants, w. Marcel Lorand (sgr/harm), Jeno Kohn (sgr), Alexander Kovacs (sgr), Trio Lorand Supraphon ▲ SUP 3073

Handlos, Franz (bass)

Verdi, G.:I due Foscari, w. K. Ricciarelli (sop), E. Connell (sop), J. Carreras (ten), V. Bello (ten), M. Antoniak (ten), P. Cappuccilli (bar), S. Ramey (bass), L. Gardelli (cnd), Austrian RSO, Austrian Radio Chorus Philips 2-▲ 422426-2 [ADD]

Handt, Herbert (ten)

Bach, J.S.:Cant 106, "Actus tragicus", w. M. László (sop), J. Loomis (bass), H. Scherchen (cnd), Turin Radio Orch, Turin Radio Chorus [G] *(rec live, Jan 14, 1958)* Memories ▲ HR 4160 (m) [ADD]

Mussorgsky, M.:Khovanshchina, w. Jolanda Mancini (sop—Emma), Irene Companez (mez), Amedeo Berdini (ten—Prince Andrei Khovanski), Mirto Picchi (ten—Prince Vasili Golitsin), Herbert Handt (ten—Scribe), Andrea Mineo (bar—Kuzka), Giampiero Malaspina (bar—Shaklovity), Boris Christoff (bass—Dosifei), Mario Petri (bass—Prince Ivan Khovanski), Dimitri Lopatto (Varsonofiev/First Strelyets), Giorgio Conello (Second Strelyets), A. Rodzinski (cnd), *(orch unknown)* [I] *(rec Rome, 1958)* VAI Audio 2-▲ VAIA 1052-2

Mussorgsky, M.:Khovanshchina, w. Mietta Sighele (sop—Emma), Elena Souliotis (sop—Susanna), Fiorenza Cossotto (mez—Marfa), Herbert Handt (ten—Scribe), Veriano Luchetti (ten—Prince Andrey Khovansky), Ludovic Spiess (ten—Prince Vasily Golitsin), Claudio Strudthoff (ten—Streshnev), Angelo Marchiandi (bar—Kuz'ka), Teodoro Rovetta (bar—1st Strel'tsi), Siegmund Nimsgern (b-bar—Shaklovity), Cesare Siepi (b-bar—Dosifey), Carlo del Bosco (bass—2nd Strel'tsi), Ubaldo Carosi (bass—Varsonofiev), Nicolai Ghiaurov (bass—Prince Ivan Khovnasky), Giovanni Sciarpeletti (bass—Pastor), B. Leskovich (cnd), Rome RAI SO, Rome RAI Chorus—also includes bonus Act V [w Boris Christoff] (Rome, 1958) *(rec Rome, 1973)* Bella Voce 3-▲ BLV 107.402 [AAD]

Mussorgsky, M.:Khovanshchina, w. Irene Companez (cta), Mirto Picchi (ten), Boris Christoff (bass), Armedeo Berdini (sgr), Giorgio Canello (sgr), Dmitri Lopatto (sgr), Michele Malaspina (sgr), Jolanda Mancini (sgr), Mario Petri (sgr), A. Rodzinski (cnd), Rome RAI Radio-TV SO, Rome RAI Chorus Stradivarius 2-▲ STV DTM 12320 [ADD]

Hanft, Karl (sgr)

Orff, C.:Der Mond—Ein kleines Welttheater, w. Karl Erb (nar), Paul Kuen (ten—Lad 3), Josef Knapp (bar—Lad 2), Benno Kusche (bar—Lad 1), Georg Hann (bass—St. Peter), Georg Wieter (bass—Lad 4), Rudolf Wünzer (bass—The Farmer), Karl Hanft (sgr—Innkeeper), Willy Rösner (sgr—The Major), R. Alberth (cnd), Bavarian RSO, Bavarian Radio Chorus *(rec Studio 1, Bavarian Radio, Jan. 19–20, 1950)* Calig ▲ CAL 50948 (m) [ADD]

Haničinec, Petr (nar)

Martinů, B.:Hymn to St. James, w. N. Romanová (sop), D. Drobková (cta), R. Novák (ten), P. Kühn (cnd), Prague SO members, Prague Radio Chorus [Cz] *(rec 2–3/88)* Supraphon ▲ 11 0751-2 [DDD]

Martinů, B.:Mount of 3 Lights, w. V. Dolezal (ten), R. Novák (bass), J. Hora (org), P. Kühn (cnd), Prague Radio Men's Chorus, Kühn Chorus [Cz] *(rec 2–3/88)* Supraphon ▲ 11 0751-2 [DDD]

Hann, Georg (bass)

Haydn, J.:Die Jahreszeiten, w. Trude Eipperle (sop), Julius Patzak (ten), C. Krauss (cnd), Vienna PO, Vienna State Opera Chorus [G] *(rec live, June 1942)* Preiser 2-▲ PRE 93053 [AAD]

Haydn, J.:Die Schöpfung, w. Trude Eipperle (sop), Julius Patzak (ten), C. Krauss (cnd), Vienna PO, Vienna State Opera Chorus *(rec early 1940's)* Preiser 2-▲ PRE 90104 [AAD]

Lortzing, A.:Wildschütz (sels), w. H. Steinkopf (cnd), Berlin RSO—Fünftausend Taler *(rec 1943)* Myto 2-▲ MCD 943103

Lortzing, A.:Zar und Zimmermann, w. M. Gripekoven (sop—Marie), E. Mayer (cta—Widow Browe), H. Buchta (ten—Peter Ivonov), H. Schmid-Berikoven (ten—Marquis de Chateauneuf), G. Hann (b-bar—Tsar Peter I), W. Strienz (b-bar—Van Bett), B. Müller (bass) Myto 2-▲ MCD 943103

Lortzing, A.:Zar und Zimmermann (sels), w. H. Steinkopf (cnd), Berlin RSO—O cancta justitia!; Den hohen Herscher; Heil sei dem Tag *(rec 1943)* Myto 2-▲ MCD 943103

Mozart, W.A.:Don Giovanni, w. Hedwig Jungkurth (sop—Elvira), Maria Reining (sop—Anna), Julius Patzak (ten—Ottavio), Karl Hammes (bar—Don Giovanni), Ludwig Weber (bass—Commandant), J. Keilberth (cnd), Stuttgart Reich RSO, Stuttgart Radio Chorus *(rec Mar, 1936)* Preiser 2-▲ PRE 90263

Nicolai, O.:Lustigen Weiber, w. I. Bielke (sop), M. L. Schilp (mez), W. Ludwig (ten), W. Streinz (bass), A. Rother (cnd), Berlin RSO, Berlin State Opera Chorus *(rec May 2, 1943)* Preiser 2-▲ PRE 90208 [ADD]

▲ = CD ♦ = Enhanced CD Δ = MD ■ = Cassette Tape □ = DCC

Hann, Georg (bass) (cont.)

Orff, C.:Der Mond—Ein kleines Welttheater, w. Karl Erb (nar), Paul Kuen (ten—Lad 3), Josef Knapp (bar—Lad 2), Benno Kusche (bar—Lad 1), Georg Hann (bass—St. Peter), Georg Wieter (bass—Lad 4), Rudolf Wünzer (bass—The Farmer), Karl Hanft (sgr—Innkeeper), Willy Rösner (sgr—The Major), R. Alberth (cnd), Bavarian RSO, Bavarian Radio Chorus *(rec Studio 1, Bavarian Radio, Jan. 19–20, 1950)* Calig ▲ CAL 50948 (m) [ADD]

Puccini, G.:La Bohème, w. Trude Eipperle (sop), Hildegarde Ranczak (sop), Alfons Fügel (ten), Carl Kronenberg (bar), Georg Wieter (bass), Emil Graf (sgr), Otto Hillerbrandt (sgr), Karl Schmidt (sgr), C. Krauss (cnd), Bavarian State Opera Orch, Bavarian State Opera Chorus *(rec 1940)* Preiser 2–▲ PRE 90275

Puccini, G.:Tosca, w. H. Ranczak (sop), H. Roswaenge (ten), L. Ludwig (cnd), Berlin RSO *(rec Oct. 1944)* Preiser 2–▲ PRE 90210 [ADD]

Strauss (II), Joh.:Der Zigeunerbaron (sels), w. S. Jurinac (sop), W. Hollweg (ten), P. Anders (ten), K. Schmitt-Walter (bar), Schneider (sgr), Marszalek (cnd), Cologne RSO, Cologne Radio Chorus [G] Acanta ▲ CD 43807 [DDD]

Strauss, R.:Arabella, w. L. Della Casa (sop), M. Reining (sop), R. Anday (cta), H. Hotter (b–bar), J. Patzak (ten), K. Böhm (cnd), Vienna PO, Vienna State Opera Chorus *(rec live, Salzburg Festival, 8/12/47)* Melodram 3–▲ MEL 37077

Strauss, R.:Capriccio (sels), w. V. Ursuleac (sop—Die Gräfin), F. Klarwein (ten—Flamand), H. Hotter (b–bar—Olivier), G. Hann (b–bar—La Roche), G. Wieter (bass—Der Haushofmeister), C. Krauss (cnd), Bavarian State Opera Orch *(rec 1942)* Myto ▲ MCD 943104

Strauss, R.:Der Rosenkavalier, w. Adele Kern (sop), Viorica Ursuleac (sop), Georgine von Milinkovic (mez), Ludwig Weber (bass), C. Krauss (cnd), Bavarian State Opera Orch, Bavarian State Opera Chorus *(rec Munich, June 1942)* Preiser 3–▲ PRE 90218

Wagner, R.:Der fliegende Holländer, w. Viorica Ursuleac (sop), Luise Willer (mez), Karl Ostertag (ten), Hans Hotter (b–bar), C. Krauss (cnd), Bavarian State Opera Orch, Bavarian State Opera Chorus *(rec Mar 13–16, 1944)* Preiser 2–▲ PRE 90250 [ADD]

Wagner, R.:Die Meistersinger von Nürnberg (sels), w. K. Wessel (alt), E. Kunz (bar), A. Rother (cnd), Berlin RSO, Berlin Radio Chorus—Act 2 Preiser ▲ PRE 90168 [AAD]

Wolf, H.:Der Corregidor, w. M. Teschemacher (sop), M. Fuchs (sop), K. Erb (ten), J. Herrmann (bar), K. Böhme (b–bar), G. Frick (bass), K. Elmendorff (cnd), Saxon State Orch, Saxon State Chorus *(rec 1944)* Preiser 2–▲ PRE 90182 [AAD]

Hanna (sgr)

Kálmán, I.:Die Csárdásfürstin (sels), w. Erzsébet (sgr), György (sgr), Róbert (sgr), Tamás (cnd), Hungarian Radio–TV SO, Hungarian Radio–TV Chorus Hungaroton ▲ HCD 16780 [AAD]

Hannan, Eilene (sop)

Tchaikovsky, P.:Eugene Onegin (sels), w. S. Edwards (cnd), London PO—Tatiana's Letter Scene [Act I] Classics for Pleasure ("Eminence" series) ▲ CDEMX 2187 [DDD]

Hanner, Vivian (sgr)

Wagner, S.:Banadietrich, w. Beth Johanning (sop), Volker Horn (ten), André Wenhold (bar), Andreas Schmidt (bar), Adalbert Walker (bass), V. Gailis (cnd), Thuringian SO, Rudolstadt Festival Chorus *(rec Rudolstädt, June 1995)* Marco Polo 2–▲ 8.223895–6 [DDD]

Hannes, Arthur (nar)

Sousa, J.P.:Life & Music of, w. M. Diesenroth (cnd), Musikkorps des Wachtbataillons—narration with selected excerpts from Stars & Stripes Forever; The Crusader; The Belle of Chicago; The Gladiator; Semper Fidelis; Washington Post; High School Cadets; The Thunderer; Hands Across the Sea; El Capitan Vox Music Masters ("Music Masters" series) ▲ MMD 8515 [ADD] ■ MMC 8515

Hannula, Kaisa (sop)

Bergman, E.:The Singing Tree, w. C. Hellekant (cta), P. Lindroos (ten), P. Salomaa (bass), S. Tiilikainen (bar), M. Wallén (bass), U. Söderblom (cnd), Finnish National Opera Orch, Dominante Chamber Choir, Tapiola Chamber Choir Ondine 2–▲ ODE 794–2D [DDD]

Hansen, Eva Bruun (sop)

Schnittke, A.:Penitential Psalms, w. Elisabeth Rehling (sop), Annette Simonsen (alt), Maria Streijffert (alt), Karl–Gustav Andersson (ten), Poul Vejbo (ten), Stefan Parkman (cnd), Danish National Radio Choir Chandos ▲ CHAN 9480

Hansen, Kai (ten)

Liszt, F.:Missa choralis, w. Irene Graaner (sop), Else Paaske (alt), Michael Hansen (bar), Hans Christian Andersen (bass), Niels Henrik Nielsen (org), Tamás Vetö (cnd), Copenhagen Univ Choir Point ▲ PCD 5075 [ADD]

Hansen, Kurt (ten)

Mahler, G.:Sym 8, w. Oksana Krovytska (sop—Magna Peccatrix), Sheila Smith (sop—Una poenitentium), Shauna Southwick (sop—Mater gloriosa), Kristine Jepson (mez—Maria Aegyptiaca), Julie Simson (mez—Mulier Samaritana), Kurt Hansen (ten—Doctor Marianus), Brian Steele (bar—Pater ecstaticus), Eugene Green (b–bar—Pater profundus), R. Olson (cnd), Colorado MahlerFest Orch, Colorado MahlerFest Chorale, Colorado Mormon Chorale, Colorado Children's Chorale *(rec MahlerFest VIII, Boulder, CO, Jan 14–15, 1995)* MahlerFest 2–▲ MF8–1

Telemann, G.P.:Der Tag des Gerichts, w. Patrice Michaels Bell (sop), Sandra Walker (mez), Karen Brunssen (mez), Bruce Fowler (ten), William Stone (bar), Douglas Anderson (bar), T. Wikman (cnd), Music of the Baroque Orch, Baroque Music Chorus *(rec live, St. Paul's United Church of Christ, Feb 23, 1992)* Music of the Baroque 2–▲ MB 107

Hansen, Michael (bar)

Liszt, F.:Missa choralis, w. Irene Graaner (sop), Else Paaske (alt), Kai Hansen (ten), Hans Christian Andersen (bass), Niels Henrik Nielsen (org), Tamás Vetö (cnd), Copenhagen Univ Choir Point ▲ PCD 5075 [ADD]

Hansli, Asbjørn (bar)

Grieg, E.:Peer Gynt, w. C. Carlson (mez), V. Hanssen (mez), K. Bjørkøy (ten), P. Dreier (cnd), London SO, Oslo Phil Chorus [N] Unicorn–Kanchana 2–▲ UKCD 2003/04 [AAD]

Hansmann, Rotraud (sop)

Bach, J.S.:Cant 27, w. H. Watts (cta), K. Equiluz (ten), M. Van Egmond (b–bar), J. Jürgens (cnd), Concerto Amsterdam, Monteverdi Choir London Teldec (Das alte Werke) ▲ 93687

Bach, J.S.:Cant 158, w. H. Watts (cta), K. Equiluz (ten), M. Van Egmond (b–bar), J. Jürgens (cnd), Concerto Amsterdam, Monteverdi Choir London Teldec ("Das alte Werke" series) ▲ 93687

Bach, J.S.:Cant 198, w. H. Watts (cta), K. Equiluz (ten), M. Van Egmond (b–bar), J. Jürgens (cnd), Concerto Amsterdam, Monteverdi Choir London Teldec (Das alte Werke) ▲ 93687

Monteverdi, C.:Orfeo, w. C. Berberian (sop), L. Kozma (ten), K. Equiluz (bar), M. Van Egmond (bass), N. Harnoncourt (cnd), Vienna Concentus Musicus, Capella Antiqua München Teldec 2–▲ 42494–2

Schubert, Franz:Duetsche Messe, w. M. Lipovšek (mez), J. Reinprecht (ten), L. Spitzer (pno), F. Wolf (cnd), St. Augustin Orch, St. Augustin Chorus Preiser ▲ 93325

Schubert, Franz:Mass 3, w. M. Lipovšek (mez), J. Reinprecht (ten), Spitzer (bass), F. Wolf (cnd), St. Augustin Orch, St. Augustin Chorus Preiser ▲ 93325

Hanson, Suzan (sop)

Cage, J.:Europera 3, w. Ruby Hinds (mez), Patricia McAfee (mez), Michael Lyon (ten), Richard Powell (ten), Kevin Bell (bass), Brian Pezzone (pno), Vicki Ray (pno), Hannes Geiger (record players), Joseph Giri (record players), William Houston (record players), Dren McDonald (record players), Ronda Rindone (record players), Clarice Ross (record players), Scott Fraser (tape), A. Culver (cnd), Long Beach Opera Orch *(rec Center Theater, Long Beach, CA, Nov. 13, 1993)* Mode 2–▲ MODE 38/39

Hanssen, Vessa (mez)

Braein, E.F.:Anne Pedersdotter, w. K. Ekeberg (sop—Anne Pedersdotter), V. Hanssen (mez—Merete Beyer), R. Eriksen (alt—Herlofs–Marte), I. M. Brekke (alt—Bente), K. M. Sandve (ten—Martin Beyer), C. Ehrstedt (ten—Master Olaus), A. Helleland (ten—David), T. Gilje (ten—Jørund), S. A. Thorsen (bar—Master Johannes), S. Carlsen (bass—Absalon Pedersøn Beyer), T. Stensvold (bass—Master Laurentius), G. Oskarsson (bass—Jens Schelderup), P. Andersson (cnd), Norwegian National Opera Orch, Norwegian National Opera Chorus Simax 2–▲ PSC 3121

Grieg, E.:Peer Gynt, w. C. Carlson (mez), K. Bjørkøy (ten), A. Hansli (bar), P. Dreier (cnd), London SO, Oslo Phil Chorus [N] Unicorn–Kanchana 2–▲ UKCD 2003/04 [AAD]

Hanzelová, Elena (sgr)

Puccini, G.:Madama Butterfly (sels), w. Miriam Gauci (sop—Madama Butterfly), Nelly Boschkowa (mez—Suzuki), Yordi Ramiro (ten—F.B. Pinkerton), Jozef Abel (ten—Goro), Georg Tichy (bass—Sharpless), Anna Tomkovicová (sgr), Mária Stahelová (sgr) *(rec Concert Hall of the Czecho-Slovak Radio, Bratislava, May 2–10, 1991)* Naxos ▲ 8.553152 [DDD]

Harasimowicz, Bozena (sop)

Elsner, J.:Passio Domini Nostri Jesu Christi, w. Krzysztof Szmyt (ten), Czeslaw Galka (bar), Bogdan Sliwa (bar), Piotr Nowacki (bass), K. Kord (cnd), Warsaw PO, Henryk Wojnarowski (cnd), Ewa Marchwicka (cnd), Warsaw National Phil Chorus, E. Mlynarski State School of Music Children's Choir *(rec National Philharmonic, Warsaw, 1990)* Polskie Nagrania ▲ PNCD 078 [DDD]

Elsner, J.:Passio Domini Nostri Jesu Christi, w. K. Szmyt (ten), C. Galka (bar), P. Nowacki (bass), K. Kord (cnd), Warsaw National Philharmonic SO, Warsaw National Philharmonic Sym Chorus *(rec 1990)* Muza ▲ PNCD 078 [DDD]

Harasteanu, Pompei (bass)

Donizetti, G.:Lucia di Lammermoor, w. Silvia Voinea (sop—Lucia), Lucia Cicoara (mez—Alisa), Florin Georgescu (ten—Edgardo), Gabriel Nastase (ten—Arturo), Nicolae Herlea (bar—Lord Enrico), Pompei Harasteanu (bass—Raimondo), C. Petrovici (cnd), Romanian Opera Orch, Romanian Opera Chorus *(rec 1984)* Vox Box 2–▲ CDX 5164

Landowski, M.:Adagio Cantabile, w. Steliana Calos (sop), Dominique de Williencourt (vc), Jacques Taddei (org), R. Georgescu (cnd), Timisoara PO, Timisoara Chorus *(rec Mar. 16–18, 1993)* Chamade ▲ 5611 [DDD]

Landowski, M.:Leçons de Ténèbres, w. Steliana Calos (sop), Dominique de Williencourt (vc), Jacques Taddei (org), R. Georgescu (cnd), Timisoara PO, Timisoara Chorus *(rec Mar. 16–18, 1993)* Chamade ▲ 5611 [DDD]

Puccini, G.:La Bohème, w. Elvira Cirje–Druica (sop—Musetta), Eugenia Moldoveanu (sop—Mimi), Andrei Borsos (ten—Parpignol), Constantin Gabor (ten—Alcindoro), Ludovic Spiess (ten—Rodolfo), Lucian Marinescu (bar—Schaunard), David Ohanesian (bar—Marcello), Pompei Harasteanu (bass—Benoit), Dan Zancu (bass—Colline), C. Petrovici (cnd), Romanian Opera Orch, Romanian Opera Chorus *(rec 1982)* Vox Box 2–▲ CDX 5156

Puccini, G.:Tosca, w. Virginia Zeani (sop—Floria Tosca), Emilia Oprea (mez—Shepherd), Nicolae Andreescu (ten—Spoletta), Corneliu Fanateanu (ten—Mario Cavaradossi), Nicolae Herlea (bar—Baron Scarpia), Gheorghe Crasnaru (bass—Cesare Angelotti), Constantin Gabor (bass—Sacristan), Pompei Harasteanu (bass—Jailer), Adrian Stefanescu (bass—Sciarrone), C. Trailescu (cnd), Romanian Opera Orch, Romanian Opera Chorus *(rec Sept 1977)* Vox Box 2–▲ CDX 5153

Harbell, Christiane (sop)

Offenbach, J.:Le Fille du tambour–major, w. Christiane Harbell (sop—Stella), Monique de Pondeau (sop—Claudine), Germaine Light (mez—Duchess Della Volta), Marcelle Ranson–Hervé (ten—Duke Della Volta), André Mallabrera (ten—Griolet), Etienne Arnaud (bar—Robert), Louis Musy (bar—Monthabor), *(orch unknown)* Accord ▲ ACD 220692 [AAD]

Harbo, Erik (ten)

Bellman, C.M.:Songs—Hvila vid denna Källa; Opp Amaryllis; Nå, skruva fiolen; Joachim uti Babylon; Käraste bröder; En Potifars hustru; Fader Berg i hornet stöter; Ulla, min Ulla; Fjäriln vingad syns på Haga; Klang, mina flickor; Så lunka vi; Gubben Noach; Är jag född; Drick ur ditt glas; Märk hur vår skugga; Se svarta böljans hvita drägg; Träd fram, du nattens gud Danica ▲ DCD 8137

Kuhlau, F.:Lulu, w. T. Kiberg (sop), A. Frellesvig (sgr), K. von Binzer (ten), R. Saarman (ten), U. Cold (bass), M. Schønwandt (cnd), Danish National RSO, Danish National Radio Choir [Da] Kontrapunkt 3–▲ 32009/11 [DDD]

Harder, J. (sgr)

Porter, C.:Fifty Million Frenchmen, w. H. McGillin (sgr), K. Criswell (sop), K. McClelland (sgr), S. Powell (sgr), K. Ziemba (sgr), J. Graae (sgr), S. Waara (sgr), P. Cass (sgr), J. LeClerc (sgr) [1991 studio cast] New World ▲ 80417–2 [DDD]

Harder, Lutz–Michael (ten)

Bach, J.S.:Cant 38, w. A. Augér (sop), H. Watts (cta), P. Huttenlocher (bar), H. Rilling (cnd), Stuttgart Bach Collegium, Gächinger Kantorei [G] *(rec Feb & Apr 1980)* Hänssler Classic ▲ 98.818 [AAD]

Bach, J.S.:Cant 43, w. A. Augér (sop), J. Hamari (cta), P. Huttenlocher (bar), H. Rilling (cnd), Stuttgart Bach Collegium, Gächinger Kantorei [G] *(rec 1981–82)* Hänssler Classic ▲ 98.885 [AAD]

Bach, J.S.:Cant 80, w. A. Augér (sop), G. Schreckenbach (cta), P. Huttenlocher (bar), H. Rilling (cnd), Württemberg CO, Gächinger Kantorei [G] *(rec 1976 & 1983)* Hänssler Classic ▲ 98.819 [AAD]

Bach, J.S.:Cant 98, w. A. Augér (sop), J. Hamari (cta), W. Heldwein (bass), H. Rilling (cnd), Stuttgart Bach Collegium, Gächinger Kantorei [G] *(rec Oct 1982 & July 1983)* Hänssler Classic ▲ 98.817 [AAD]

Bach, J.S.:Cant 99, w. A. Augér (sop), H. Watts (cta), J. Bröcheler (bar), H. Rilling (cnd), Stuttgart Bach Collegium, Gächinger Kantorei [G] *(rec 1979)* Hänssler Classic ▲ 98.813 [AAD]

Bach, J.S.:Cant 115, w. A. Augér (sop), H. Watts (cta), W. Schöne (bass), H. Rilling (cnd), Stuttgart Bach Collegium, Gächinger Kantorei [G] *(rec 1980)* Hänssler Classic ▲ 98.819 [AAD]

Bach, J.S.:Cant 116, w. A. Augér (sop), H. Watts (cta), P. Huttenlocher (bar), H. Rilling (cnd), Stuttgart Bach Collegium, Gächinger Kantorei [G] *(rec 1980)* Hänssler Classic ▲ 98.820 [AAD]

Bach, J.S.:Cant 127, w. A. Augér (sop), W. Schöne (bass), H. Rilling (cnd), Stuttgart Bach Collegium, Gächinger Kantorei [G] *(rec 1980)* Hänssler Classic ▲ 98.878 [AAD]

Bach, J.S.:Cant 164, w. E. Wiens (sop), J. Hamari (cta), W. Heldwein (bass), H. Rilling (cnd), Stuttgart Bach Collegium, Gächinger Kantorei Hänssler Classic ▲ 98.811 [AAD]

Zimmermann, U.:Die weisse Rose (sels), w. G. Fontana (sop), U. Zimmermann (cnd), *(ensemble unknown)* [scenes for 2 solo voices & instrumental ensemble] [G] Orfeo ▲ 162871 [DDD]

Hardgrave, B. (sop)

Kupferman, M.:The Proscenium:...On the Demise of Gertrude, w. M. Kupferman (cnd), Music in the Mountains Festival Chamber Players Soundspells ▲ SP 107

Harding, Lola (sop)

Partch, H.:Settings (2) from "Finnegan's Wake", w. Dorothy Holden (fl), Hilmar Luckhardt (fl), Harry Partch (kithara) *(rec 1945)* Innova 4–▲ 401

Partch, H.:Yankee Doodle Fant, w. Hilmar Luckhardt (tin whistle), Don Thompson (tin whistle/ob), Lee Hoiby (flex–a–tones), Harry Partch (chromelodeon) *(rec 1945)* Innova 4–▲ 401

Hardy, Burwell (nar)

Balada, L.:Maria Sabina, w. América Dunham (nar—Maria Sabina), Burwell Hardy (nar—Town Crier), Guillermo Helguera (nar—Constable), Hector Cortés (nar—Executioner), J. Mester (cnd), Louisville Orch, Richard Spalding (cnd), Univ of Louisville Choir New World ▲ 804982

Balada, L.:Maria Sabina, w. Hector Cortés (nar—Executioner), Amèrica Dunham (nar—Maria Sabina), Burwell Hardy (nar—Town Crier), Guillermo Helguera (nar—Constable), J. Mester (cnd), Louisville Orch, Richard Spalding (cnd), Louisville Univ Chorus *(rec Feb 5, 1973)* New World ▲ 80498–2

Hardy, J. (sgr)

Argento, D.:Postcard from Morocco, w. S. Roche, B. Brandt, Y. Marshall, V. Sutton, B. Busse, M. Foreman, P. Brunelle (cnd), Minnesota Opera Orch CRI 2–▲ CD 614 [ADD]

Hardy, Janis (mez)

Smyth, E.:The Boatswain's Mate, w. E. Harrhy (sop), D. Dressen (ten), J. Bohn (bass), P. Brunelle (cnd), Plymouth Music Series Orch, Plymouth Music Series Chorus—Mrs. Water's Aria Virgin Classics ▲ CDC 59022

Smyth, E.:Mass in D, w. E. Harrhy (sop), D. Dressen (ten), J. Bohn (bass), P. Brunelle (cnd), Plymouth Music Series Orch, Plymouth Music Series Chorus Virgin Classics ▲ CDC 59022

Hardy, Rosemary (sop)

Birtwistle, H.:Nenia on the Death of Orpheus, w. J. Kalitzke (cnd), Musikfabrik NRW CPO ▲ CPO 999360 [DDD]

Knussen, O.:Where The Wild Things Are, w. M. King (mez), O. Knussen (cnd), London Sinfonietta [E] Arabesque ▲ Z 6535 [DDD]

Kurtág, G.:Messages of the Late Miss R.V. Troussova, w. P. Eötvös (cnd), Ensemble Modern *(rec June 14–16, 1990)* Sony Classical ▲ SK 53290 [DDD]

Ligeti, G.:The Ligeti Edition, w. Phyllis Bryn–Julson (sop), Christiane Oelze (sop), Rose Taylor (mez), Sibylle Ehlert (sgr), Omar Ebrahim (bar), Pierro–Laurent Aimard (pno), E.–P. Salonen (cnd), Philharmonia Orch, King's Singers—Vocal Works; Madrigals; Mysteries; Adventures; Songs; Nonsense Madrigals Sony Classical ▲ SK 62311

Hardy, Rosemary (sop) (cont.)

Purcell, H.:King Arthur, w. H. Sheppard (sop), J. Knibbs (cta), A. Deller (ct), M. Deller (alt), P. Elliott (ten), L. Nixon (ten), M. Bevan (bar), N. Beavan (bass), A. Deller (cnd), Deller Consort, King's Musick [E] Harmonia Mundi France 2-▲ HMC 90252/53

Weill, K.:Songs, w. H. Gruber (sgr), H. K. Gruber (cnd), Ensemble Modern—Berlin im Licht; Slow Fox and Algi-Song; Klopslied; Ach, wär mein Lieb ein brünnlein Kalt; Frauentanz, Op. 10; Bastille Musik; Ol-Musik; Suite panaméenne; Cowboy Song; Captain Valentine's Song; Die stille Stadt Largo ▲ 5114 [DDD]

Hargan, Alison (sop)

Beethoven, L. van:Sym 9, "Choral Sym", w. U. Walther (cta), E. Büchner (ten), K. Kováts (bass), H. Kegel (cnd), Dresden PO Capriccio ▲ 10 453 [DDD]

Beethoven, L. van:Sym 9, "Choral Sym", w. Della Jones (mez), David Rendall (ten), Gwynne Howell (b-bar), W. Morris (cnd), London SO, London Sym Chorus IMP ("LSO" series) ▲ IMP 6900032

Britten, H.:Praise We Great Men, w. M. King (alt), R. Tear (ten), W. White (bass), S. Rattle (cnd), City of Birmingham SO, City of Birmingham Sym Chorus [E] *(rec July, 1990)* EMI Classics 2-▲ ZDCB 54270 [DDD]

Elgar, E.:The Apostles, w. A. Hodgson (cta), D. Rendall (ten), S. Roberts (bar), B. Terfel (bass-bar), R. Lloyd (bass), R. Hickox (cnd), London SO, London Sym Chorus [E] Chandos 2-▲ CHAN 8875/76 [DDD]

Mahler, G.:Sym 4, w. S. Skrowaczewski (cnd), Hallé Orch [G] IMP Classics ▲ PCD 972 [DDD]

Hargis, Ellen (sop)

Canzonetta:16th Century Canzoni & Instrumental Dances, w. D. Douglass (cnd), King's Noyse, Paul O'Dette (lt) Harmonia Mundi USA ▲ HMU 907127

Purcell, H.:Musick's Hand-maid, w. Ian Honeyman (ten), Rodrigo del Pozo (ten), Harry van der Kamp (bass), Paul O'Dette (thb/cittern/lt), Andrew Lawrence-King (hps/org/hpd), A. Lawrence-King (cnd), Harp Consort Astrée ▲ E 8564

Rosenmüller, J.:Music of, w. Paul O'Dette (thb), Mary Springfels (va), D. Douglass (cnd), King's Noyse—Suite in C [from Studentenmusik]; Jubilent aethera; Son X à 5; Son VII à 4; In te, Domine, speravi; Son XI à 5; Son IV à 3; Ach Herr, strafe mich nicht in deinem Zorn; Son III à 2; Leiber Herre Gott, Wecke uns auf Harmonia Mundi ▲ HMU 907179

Tristan et Iseult:A Medieval Romance in Music & Poetry, w. Anne Azema (sop), Henri Ledroit (alt), William Hite (ten), Richard Morrison (bass), Andrea von Ramm (sgr), Boston Camerata [cnd:Joel Cohen] Erato ▲ 98482-2

Hargreaves, Matthew (bass)

Britten, H.:Curlew River, w. Hugo Ticciati (trb), Mark Milhofer (ten), Mark Evans (bar), Gwynn Hughes Jones (bar), D. Angus (cnd), Guildhall Chamber Ensemble Koch Schwann ▲ SCH 313972

Hargrove, Martin (bass)

Zuidam, R.:Freeze, w. Susan Narucki (sop—Patty Hearst), Gerrie de Vries (mez), Zeger Vandersteene (ten), Jaco Huijpen (bass), S. Asbury (cnd), Asko Ensemble NM Classics 2-▲ NM 92047

Harismendy, François (voc)

Lo Gai Saber:Troubadours and Minstrels, 1100-1300, w. J. Cohen (cnd), Camerata Mediterranea, Anne Azema (voc), Jean-Luc Madier (voc), Cheryl Ann Fulton (hp), Joel Cohen (instr), Shira Kammen (instr) Erato ▲ 2292-45647-2 [DDD]

Haroutunian, Vartan (bass)

Yekmalian, M.:Armenian Mass, w. Araxie Mansourian (sop), Levon Chabanian (cnd), St. Gayanée Chapel Armenian Liturgical Choir Arb ▲ 1416

Harper, Heather (sop)

Beethoven, L. van:Sym 9, "Choral Sym", w. A. Hodgson (cta), R. Tear (ten), G. Howell (bass), R. Hickox (cnd), Northern Sinfonia of England, London Sym Chorus members ASV Quicksilva ▲ ASQ 6069 [DDD]

Beethoven, L. van:Sym 9, "Choral Sym", w. Helen Watts (cta), Alexander Young (ten), Donald McIntyre (bass), L. Stokowski (cnd), London SO, London Sym Chorus *(rec London, Sept 23, 1967)* Music & Arts ▲ MUA CD 943

Brahms, J.:Gesang der Parzen, w. H. Prey (bar), P. Boulez (cnd), BBC SO, BBC Choral Society *(rec live July 20, 1973)* Memories 2-▲ HR 4493/94 [ADD]

Britten, H.:Chanson françaises (4), w. S. Bedford (cnd), English CO IMP ("BBC Radio Classics" series) ▲ IMP 5691582

Britten, H.:Les Illuminations, w. C. Groves (cnd), Royal PO IMP ("BBC Radio Classics" series) ▲ IMP 5691582

Britten, H.:Our Hunting Fathers, w. E. Downes (cnd), BBC PO IMP ("BBC Radio Classics" series) ▲ IMP 5691582

Britten, H.:Owen Wingrave, w. S. Fisher (Miss Wingrave), J. Vyvyan (Mrs. Julian), J. Baker (Kate), P. Pears (Sir P. Wingrave; Narrator), B. Luxon (Owen Wingrave), J. Shirley-Quirk (Coyle), B. Britten, Wandworth School Boys' Choir, English CO London 2-▲ 433200-2

Britten, H.:Peter Grimes, w. J. Vickers (ten), J. Summers (bar), C. Davis (cnd), Royal Opera House Orch, Royal Opera House Chorus Covent Garden [E] Philips 2-▲ 432578-2 [ADD]

Britten, H.:The Rape of Lucretia, w. J. Baker (mez), P. Pears (ten), B. Drake (bar), B. Luxon (bar), J. Shirley-Quirk (bar), B. Britten (cnd), English CO London 2-▲ 425666-2 [ADD]

Britten, H.:War Requiem, w. P. Langridge (ten), J. Shirley-Quirk (bar), R. Elms (org), R. Hickox (cnd), London SO, London Sym Chorus, St. Paul's Cathedral Choristers [E,L] Chandos 2-▲ CHAN 8983/84 [DDD]

Delius, F.:Requiem, w. T. Hemsley (bar), C. Groves (cnd), Royal Liverpool PO, Royal Liverpool Phil Choir *(rec live, Liverpool 1965)* Intaglio 2-▲ INCD 702-2 [ADD]

Handel, G.F.:Judas Maccabaeus, w. Helen Watts (cta), Alexander Young (ten), John Shirley-Quirk (bass), J. Somary (cnd), English CO, Amor Artis Chorale [E] *(rec 1979)* Vanguard Classics 2-▲ OVC 4071/72 [ADD]

Handel, G.F.:Judas Maccabaeus (sels), w. Helen Watts (cta), Alexander Young (ten), John Shirley-Quirk (bar), J. Somary (cnd), English CO, Amor Artis Chorale Vanguard Classics ▲ OVC 4073 [ADD]

Handel, G.F.:Messiah, w. Helen Watts (cta), John Wakefield (ten), John Shirley-Quirk (bar), C. Davis (cnd), London SO, London Sym Chorus Philips 2-▲ 438356-2

Handel, G.F.:Theodora, w. M. Lehane (mez), M. Forrester (cta), A. Young (ten), J. Lawrenson (bar), J. Somary (cnd), English CO, Amor Artis Chorale [E] *(rec 1968)* Vanguard Classics 2-▲ OVC 4074/5 [ADD]

Harty, H.:The Children of Lir w. B. Thomson (cnd), Ulster Orch Chandos ▲ CHAN 7033

Harty, H.:Ode to a Nightingale, w. B. Thomson (cnd), Ulster Orch Chandos ▲ CHAN 7033

Holst, G.:First Choral Sym, w. M. Sargent (cnd), BBC SO, BBC Sym Chorus *(rec Jan. 3, 1964)* Intaglio ▲ ING 740 [ADD]

Mahler, G.:Syms, w. E. Ameling (sop), M. Forrester (cta), H. Prey (bar), B. Haitink (cnd), Royal Concertgebouw Orch Philips 10-▲ 442050-2

Mahler, G.:Sym 2, w. H. Watts (cta), G. Solti (cnd), London SO, London Sym Chorus [G] London 2-▲ 425005-2 [ADD]

Mahler, G.:Sym 2, w. J. Baker (mez), O. Klemperer (cnd), Bavarian RSO *(rec 1965)* Enterprise ("Document" series) ▲ ENT LV 937 [DDD]

Mahler, G.:Sym 4, w. L. Maazel (cnd), Berlin RSO *(rec 1969; remastered 1994)* FNAC Music ▲ 642314

Mahler, G.:Sym 4, w. J. Barbirolli (cnd), BBC SO *(rec live, Prague, 1/16/67)* Intaglio ▲ INCD 7291 [ADD]

Mahler, G.:Sym 8, w. A. Augér (sop), L. Popp (sop), Y. Minton (mez), H. Watts (cta), A. Kollo (ten), J. Shirley-Quirk (bar), M. Talvela (bass), G. Solti (cnd), Chicago SO, Vienna State Opera Chorus, Vienna Boys' Choir, Vienna Singverein [G,L] London 2-▲ 414493-2 [ADD]

Mahler, G.:Sym 8, w. Hanneke van Bork (sop), Ileana Cotrubas (sop), Brigit Finnila (mez), Marianne Dieleman (cta), William Cochran (ten), Hermann Prey (bar), Hans Sotin (bass), B. Haitink (cnd), Royal Concertgebouw Orch Philips ("Solo" series) ▲ 446195-2

Mendelssohn, F.:A Midsummer Night's Dream (comp), w. J. Baker (mez), O. Klemperer (cnd), Philharmonia Orch, Philharmonia Chorus *(rec ca. 1961)* EMI Classics ▲ CDM 64144

Mozart, W.A.:Missa, K.427, w. Arleen Augér (sop), Horst Lubenthal (ten), Ulrik Cold (bass), S. Celibidache (cnd), Stuttgart RSO, Bavarian Radio Chorus, Southwest German Radio Chorus *(rec live, 1980's)* Topazio ▲ TOP 26045

Harper, Heather (sop) (cont.)

Mozart, W.A.:Nozze di Figaro, w. J. Blegen (sop), T. Berganza (mez), D. Fischer-Dieskau (bar), G. Evans (bar), D. Barenboim (cnd), English CO, John Alldis Choir [I] EMI Classics ("Studio" series) 3-▲ CDMC 63646 [ADD]

Offenbach, J.:Les Contes d'Hoffmann, w. Bakocevic (sgr), M. Mesplé (sop), S. Kónya (ten), G. Bacquier (bar), P. Maag (cnd), Buenos Aires Teatro Colón Orch, Buenos Aires Teatro Colón Chorus [F] *(rec live, Buenos Aires 8/3/70)* Melodram 2-▲ MEL 27090 [ADD]

Purcell, H.:Dido & Aeneas, w. Victoria de los Angeles (sop—Dido), Heather Harper (sop—Belinda), Patricia Johnson (mez—Sorceress), Peter Glossup (bar—Aeneas), J. Barbirolli (cnd), English CO, Ambrosian Singers EMI Classics 2-▲ ZDM 65664

Purcell, H.:Dido & Aeneas (sels), w. Victoria de los Angeles (sop—Dido), Heather Harper (sop—Belinda), Sibyl Michelow (sop), Elizabeth Robson (sop), Derek Simpson (vc), Colin Tilney (hpd), J. Barbirolli (cnd), English CO, Ambrosian Singers—Ov.; Shake the Cloud; Ah! Ah! Belinda; When Monarchs Unite; But Ere We This Perform; But Death, Alas! I Cannot Shun...When I am Laid in Earth; With Drooping Wings *(rec Abbey Road Studio 1, London, Aug. 1965)* EMI Classics ▲ CDK 65341 [ADD]

Ravel, M.:Shéhérazade Mez, w. P. Boulez (cnd), BBC SO [F] CBS ▲ MK 39023

Strauss, R.:4 Last Songs, w. N. del Mar (cnd), Royal PO IMP ("BBC Radio Classics" series) ▲ IMP 9138

Tippett, M.:The Ice Break, w. S. Sylvan (bar), D. Wilson-Johnson (bar), D. Atherton (cnd), London Sinfonietta, London Sym Chorus [E] Virgin Classics ▲ 59048 [DDD]

Tippett, M.:King Priam, w. Heather Harper (sop—Hecuba), Linda Hirst (sop—Serving Woman), Felicity Palmer (sop—Andromache), Julian Saipe (sop—Paris), Yvonne Minton (mez—Helen), Ann Murray (mez—Nurse), Kenneth Bowen (ten—Hermes), Peter Hall (ten—Young Guard), Philip Langridge (ten—Paris), Robert Tear (ten—Achilles), Thomas Allen (bar—Hector), Norman Bailey (bar—Priam), Stephen Roberts (bar—Patroclus), David Wilson-Johnson (bar—Old Man), D. Atherton (cnd), London Sinfonietta, London Sinfonietta Chorus Chandos ▲ CHAN 9406/7 [DDD]

Vaughan Williams, R.:Benedictine, w. D. Willcocks (cnd), London SO, London Sym Chorus EMI Classics ▲ CDM 64722

Vaughan Williams, R.:Sym 1, w. J. Shirley-Quirk (bar), A. Previn (cnd), London SO, London Sym Chorus [E] RCA Gold Seal ▲ 60580-2-RG [ADD] ■ 60580-4-RG (CrO2)

Vaughan Williams, R.:Sym 3, w. A. Previn (cnd), London SO RCA Gold Seal ▲ 60583-2-RG [ADD]

Vaughan Williams, R.:Sym 7, w. A. Previn (cnd), London SO RCA Gold Seal ▲ 60590-2-RG [ADD]

Vaughan Williams, R.:5 Tudor Portraits, w. D. Willcocks (cnd), London SO, *(chorus unknown)* EMI Classics ▲ CDM 64722

Vaughan Williams, R.:Variants of "Dives & Lazarus", w. D. Willcocks (cnd), London SO EMI Classics ▲ CDM 64722

Wagner, R.:Die Meistersinger von Nürnberg (sels), w. Helen Watts (cta), Alexander Young (ten), Donald McIntyre (bass), L. Stokowski (cnd), London SO, London Sym Chorus—Suite:Prelude Act III, Dance of the Apprentices, Entrance of the Mastersingers *(rec London, Sept 23, 1967)* Music & Arts ▲ MUA CD 943

Harper, Thomas (ten)

Famous Tenor Arias, w. Thomas Harper (ten), M. Halász (cnd), Czech-Slovak RSO Bratislava, Slovak Phil Chorus Naxos ▲ 8.550497 [DDD] Δ 7.550497 [DDD]

Mahler, G.:Das Lied von der Erde, w. Ruxandra Donose (sgr), M. Halász (cnd), Irish National SO *(rec National Concert Hall, Dublin, Apr 11-12, 1994)* Naxos ▲ 8.550933 [DDD]

Schreker, F.:Der ferne Klang, w. E. Grigorescu (sop), M. Halász (cnd), Hagen PO, Hagen Phil Chorus [G] Marco Polo 2-▲ 8.223270/271 [DDD]

Harrell, Mack (bar)

Bach, J.S.:St. Matthew Passion, w. Nadine Conner (sop), Jean Watson (cta), William Hain (ten), Herbert Janssen (bar), Lorenzo Alvary (bass), B. Walter (cnd), New York PO, New York Phil Chorus—Part I Minerva ▲ 20

Berg, A.:Wozzeck, w. E. Farrell (sop), F. Jagel (ten), R. Lloyd (bass), D. Mitropoulos (cnd), New York PO *(rec live 1950)* Andromeda ▲ ANR 2514 [ADD]

Harrhy, Eiddwen (sop)

Britten, H.:Spring Sym, w. Linda Finnie (cta), Robert Tear (ten), G. Rozhdestvensky (cnd), BBC SO, BBC Sym Chorus, London Voices, Southend Boys' Choir IMP ("BBC Radio Classics" series) ▲ IMP 5691752

Donizetti, G.:L'assedio di Calais, w. D. Jones (mez), R. Serbo (ten), J. Treleaven (ten), R. Smythe (bar), D. Parry (cnd), Philharmonia Orch, Geoffrey Mitchell Choir Opera Rara 2-▲ OR 9 [DDD]

Donizetti, G.:Ugo, conte di Parigi, w. Y. Kenny (sop), J. Price (sop), D. Jones (mez), M. Arthur (ten), C. du Plessis (bar), A. Francis (cnd), New Philharmonia Orch, Geoffrey Mitchell Choir Opera Rara 3-▲ ORC 1

Handel, G.F.:Amadigi di Gaula, w. E. Harrhy (sop—Melissa), J. Smith (sop—Oriana), P. Bertin (mez—Orgando), B. Fink (cta—Dardano), N. Stutzmann (cta—Amadigi), M. Minkowski (cnd), Louvre Musicians, Louvre Choir [I] Erato 2-▲ 2292-45490-2 [DDD]

Mendelssohn, F.:Psalm 42, w. H. Lamy (ten), P. Kooy (bass), P. Herreweghe (cnd), La Chapelle Royale Orch, Ghent Collegium Vocale [G] Harmonia Mundi France ▲ HMC 901272 [DDD]

Mendelssohn, F.:Psalm 115, w. P. Herreweghe (cnd), La Chapelle Royale Orch, Ghent Collegium Vocale [G] Harmonia Mundi France ▲ HMC 901272 [DDD]

Smyth, E.:The Boatswain's Mate, w. J. Hardy (alt), D. Dressen (ten), J. Bohn (bass), P. Brunelle (cnd), Plymouth Music Series Orch, Plymouth Music Series Chorus—Mrs. Water's Aria Virgin Classics ▲ CDC 59022

Smyth, E.:Mass in D, w. J. Hardy (alt), D. Dressen (ten), J. Bohn (bass), P. Brunelle (cnd), Plymouth Music Series Orch, Plymouth Music Series Chorus Virgin Classics ▲ CDC 59022

Harries, Kathryn (sop)

Chabrier, E.:Briséïs, ou Les Amants de Corinthe, w. Simon Keenlyside (trb), Mark Padmore (ten), Michael George (bass), Joan Rodgers (sgr), J. Y. Ossonce (cnd), BBC Scottish SO Hyperion ▲ CDA 66803

Massenet, J.:Cléopâtre, w. Daniéle Streiff (sop), M. Olmeda (sop), J. Maurette (ten), D. Henry (bar), M. Hacquard (bar), P. Fournillier (cnd), St.-Etienne Nouvel Orch, Saint-Etienne Nouvel Chorus [F] *(rec live, Massenet Festival in Saint-Etienne 1990)* Koch Schwann 2-▲ 3-1032-2 [DDD]

Harris (sgr)

Smith, Hale:The Valley Wind, w. Z. Carno (pno) CRI ■ C 301

Harris, Brenda (sop)

Handel, G.F.:Tolomeo, Rè di Egitto, w. Brenda Harris (sop—Seleuce), Andrea Matthews (sop—Elisa), Mary Ann Hart (mez—Alessandro), Jennifer Lane (mez—Tolomeo), Peter Castaldi (bar—King Araspe), Bradley Brookshire (hpd), R.A. Clark (cnd), Manhattan CO *(rec St. Jean Baptiste Church, NY, Mar 1995)* Vox Classics 3-▲ VOX 7530

Haydn, J.:La Cantarina, w. Brenda Harris (sop—Gasparina), Joyce Guyer (sop—Don Ettore), D'Anna Fortunato (mez—Apollonia), Jon Garrison (ten—Don Pelagio), R. Palmer (cnd), Palmer CO *(rec St. Michael's Church, New York City, Apr. 1994)* Newport Classic ▲ NPD 85595 [DDD]

Harris, Charles (trb)

Campra, A.:Messe de Requiem, w. J. Nelson (mez), J.-C. Orliac (ten), S. Roberts (bar), J. E. Gardiner (cnd), English Baroque Soloists, Monteverdi Choir London Erato ▲ 2292-45993-2

Scarlatti, D.:Salve regina, w. N. Clapton (alt), Bryam-Wigfield (org) Hyperion ▲ CDA 66182 [DDD]

Harris, Hilda (mez)

Burleigh, H.T.:Songs, w. Philip Creech (ten), Steven Cole (ten), Arthur Woodley (bass), Joseph Smith (pno)—Now Sleeps the Crimson Petal; Promis' Lan'; Ethiopia Saluting the Colors; Lovely Dark & Lonely One; Love Watches; Almona; O, Night of Dream & Wonder; His Helmet's Blaze; I Hear His Footsteps, Music Sweet; Thou Art Weary; This is Nirvana; Ahmed's Song of Farewell; Through Moanin' Pines; The Frolic; In de Col' Moonlight; A Jubilee; On Bended Knees; A New Hiding-Place; Worth While; The Jungle Flower; Kashmiri Song; Among the Fuchsias; Till I Wake; By an' By; Ev'ry Time I Feel de Spirit; Deep River; Oh, Didn't it Rain; Swing Low, Sweet Chariot; Wade in de Water; Heav'n, Heav'n Premier ▲ PRCD 1041 [DDD]

Davis, A.:X, The Life & Times of Malcolm X, w. Priscilla Baskerville (sop), Thomas J. Young (ten), Eugene Perry (bar—Malcolm), Herbert Perry (bass), W. H. Curry (cnd), Orch of St. Luke, Episteme [E] Gramavision 2-▲ R2-79470 [DDD]

Still, W.G.:Music of, w. William Warfield (nar), Yolanda Williams (sop), P. Brunelle (cnd), Plymouth Music Series Orch, Plymouth Music Series Chorus, Leigh Morris Chorale—Wailing Woman; Swanee River; And They Lynched Him on a Tree; Miss Sally's Party Collins Classics ▲ COL 1454

▲ = CD ♦ = Enhanced CD Δ = MD ■ = Cassette Tape ▯ = DCC

Harrison, F. (alt)
Vaughan Williams, R.:5 Tudor Portraits, w. P. Walker (sop), A. Boult (cnd), BBC SO, BBC Northern Singers Intaglio ▲ ING 757 [ADD]

Harrison, Lanny (nar)
Monk, M.:Key, w. Meredith Monk (sgr/elec org/jews hp), Daniel Sverdlik (sgr), Dick Higgins (sgr), Collin Walcott (sgr/mrdingam), Mark Berger (nar) *(rec live, Gary Weis' loft, Santa Monica, CA, Ace Gallery, Los Angeles, CA, The House, New York City, The Farm, Los Angeles, CA, July 1970–Jan 1971)* Lovely Music ▲ LCD 1051 [ADD]

Harrison, Rex (sgr)
Lerner, A.J.:My Fair Lady, w. J. Andrews (sgr), *(other artists unknown)* [1956 Broadway original cast] Legacy ("Mastersound" series) ▲ SK 66128
Lerner, A.J.:My Fair Lady, w. J. Andrews (sgr), S. Holloway (sgr), *(other artists unknown)* [1956 Broadway original cast] Columbia ▲ CK 05090 ■ JST 05090
Lerner, A.J.:My Fair Lady, w. J. Andrews (sgr) *(other artists unknown)* [1959 London cast] Columbia ▲ CK 02015 ■ JST 02015
Lerner, A.J.:My Fair Lady, w. *(other artists unknown) (rec 1964)* Sony Classical ▲ SK 66711 ■ ST 66711

Harrower, Peter (sgr)
Wagner, R.:Tannhäuser, w. Gré Brouwestijn (sop), Murray Dickie (ten), Karl Liebl (ten), Eberhard Waechter (bar), Alois Pernerstorfer (b-bar), Deszö Ernster (bass), Walter Brunelli (sgr), Rosl Schweiger (sgr), Herta Wilfert (sgr), A. Rodzinski (cnd), Rome RAI Radio-TV SO, Rome RAI Chorus Stradivarius 3-▲ STV 12318

Harsanyi, Janice (sop)
Orff, C.:Carmina burana, w. R. Petrak (ten), H. Presnell (bar), E. Ormandy (cnd), Philadelphia Orch, Rutgers Univ Choir Sony Classical ("Essential Classics" series) ▲ SBK 47668 ■ SBT 47668

Harshaw, Margareth (sop)
Wagner, R.:Tristan und Isolde (prelude & liebestod), w. B. Walter (cnd), Los Angeles PO *(rec live, 1952)* Historical Performers ▲ HPS 27
Wagner, R.:Tristan und Isolde (prelude & liebestod), w. B. Walter (cnd), Los Angeles PO *(rec live, 1950)* Legend ▲ LGD 119

Hart, Mary Ann (mez)
Handel, G.F.:Tolomeo, Rè di Egitto, w. Brenda Harris (sop—Seleuce), Andrea Matthews (sop—Elisa), Mary Ann Hart (mez—Alessandro), Jennifer Lane (mez—Tolomeo), Peter Castaldi (bar—King Araspe), Bradley Brookshire (hpd), R.A. Clark (cnd), Manhattan CO *(rec St. Jean Baptiste Church, NY, Mar 1995)* Vox Classics 3-▲ VOX 7530
Permit Me Voyage:Songs by American Composers, w. Mary Ann Hart (mez), D. Helmrich (pno) Albany ▲ TROY 118
Shostakovich, D.:From Jewish Folk Poetry, w. N. Pelle (sop), R. Nolan (ten), Y. Turovsky (cnd), Montreal Musici [R] Chandos ▲ CHAN 8800 [DDD]

Harten, Raphael (alt)
Bach, J.S.:Cant 106, "Actus tragicus", w. M. Klein (trb), M. van Altena (ten), M. van Egmond (b-bar), Leonhardt Consort, Collegium Vocale, Hanover Boys' Chorus [G] Teldec ▲ 2292-42602-2

Hartglass, C. (sop)
Benedict, J.:La Gitane et l'oiseau, w. Myriam Cabaud-Chiaparin (fl) *(rec Châteaugay Church, France, June 1995)* Ligia Digital ▲ 0201033 [DDD]
Bernstein, L.:I Hate Music, w. Bernard Leroy (pno) *(rec Châteaugay Church, France, June 1995)* Ligia Digital ▲ 0201033 [DDD]
Bernstein, L.:Mass (sels), w. Myriam Cabaud-Chiaparin (fl), Bernard Leroy (pno)—A Simple Song; I Go On *(rec Châteaugay Church, France, June 1995)* Ligia Digital ▲ 0201033 [DDD]
Longas, F.:Le Rossignol et l'Empereur, w. Myriam Cabaud-Chiaparin (fl) *(rec Châteaugay Church, France, June 1995)* Ligia Digital ▲ 0201033 [DDD]
Milhaud, D.:Chansons de Ronsard, w. Bernard Leroy (pno) *(rec Châteaugay Church, France, June 1995)* Ligia Digital ▲ 0201033 [DDD]
Saint-Saëns, C.:La Libellule, w. Bernard Leroy (pno) *(rec Châteaugay Church, France, June 1995)* Ligia Digital ▲ 0201033 [DDD]
Saint-Saëns, C.:Le Rossignol et la rose, w. Bernard Leroy (pno) *(rec Châteaugay Church, France, June 1995)* Ligia Digital ▲ 0201033 [DDD]
Strauss, R.:Songs, Op. 68, w. Bernard Leroy (pno) *(rec Châteaugay Church, France, June 1995)* Ligia Digital ▲ 0201033 [DDD]

Hartinger, Albert (bass)
Biber, H. von:Vesperae longiores ac breviores una cum litaniis Laurentanis, w. Kym Amps (sop), Christopher Robson (alt), Anton Rosner (ten), H. Arman (cnd), Salzburg Baroque Ensemble, Innsbruck Woodwind Circle, Salzburg Bach Choir, Salzburg St. Benedict College Schola Ars Musici ("Essence" series) ▲ AME 3022-2 [DDD]

Hartle, Enid (mez)
Donizetti, G.:Rosmonda d'Inghilterra, w. Yvonne Kenny (sop), Richard Greager (ten), Christian du Plessis (bar), Milla Andreaw (sgr), A. Francis (cnd), Ulster Orch, Opera Rara Chorus *(rec live, 1970's)* Italian Opera Rarities 2-▲ IOR 7730

Hartman, Vernon (bar)
Bernstein, L.:Songfest, w. Linda Hohenfeld (sop), Wendy White (mez), Patricia Spence (mez), Walter Plante (ten), John Cheek (bass), L. Slatkin (cnd), St. Louis SO RCA Red Seal ▲ 09026-61581-2

Hartmann, Carl (bar)
Wagner, R.:Parsifal (sels), w. E. Larcen (sop), H. Reimar (ten), L. Weber (bass), H. Knappertsbusch (cnd), Berlin German Opera Orch, Berlin German Opera Chorus—Act 3 *(rec 1943)* Enterprise ("Document" series) ▲ ENTLV 943 [ADD]
Wagner, R.:Parsifal (sels), w. Hans Reinmar (bar), Ludwig Weber (bass), Elsa Laren (sgr), H. Knappertsbusch (cnd), Berlin German Opera Orch, Berlin German Opera Chorus—complete Act 3 *(rec Berlin, March 31, 1942)* Grammofono 2000 ▲ GRM 78555

Hartmann, Roland (bar)
Wagner, S.:Der Bärenhäuter, w. B. Johanning (sop—Luise), K. Likic (sop—Lene), T. Koon (sop—Gunda), V. Horn (ten—Hans Kraft), A. Feilhaber (ten—Nikolaus Spitz), R. Hartmann (bar—Kaspar Wild), A. Wenhold (bar—Stranger), A. Waller (bass—Devil), H. Küchli (bass—Melchior Fröhlich), K. Bach (cnd), Thüringian SO, Thüringian State Theater Chorus *(rec Rudolstadt, July 25–31, 1993)* Marco Polo ("Opera Classics" series) 2-▲ 8.223713/4 [DDD]
Wagner, S.:Schwarzschwanenreich, w. Beth Johanning (sop—Linda), Kerstin Quandt (cta—Ursula), Walter Raffeiner (ten—Ludwig), Lucian Chioreanu (ten—A Boy), André Wenhold (bar—Oswald), Roland Hartmann (sgr—Tempter/Priest), Jutta Maria Schmitz (sgr—Ash-Woman), Ksenija Lukic (sgr—A Girl), K. Bach (cnd), Thüringian Saalfeld-Rudolstadt SO, Thüringian Landestheater Rudolstadt Chorus *(rec Thüringer Landestheater, Rudolstadt, June 1994)* Marco Polo 2-▲ 8.223777-8 [DDD]

Hartung (sgr)
Kálmán, I.:Gräfin Mariza, w. A. Görner (sop), F. Wunderlich (ten), B. Kusche (bar), Hofmann (sgr), Marszalek (cnd), Cologne Radio Orch, Cologne Radio Chorus [G] Acanta ▲ CD 42479 [DDD]

Harun, Steve (sgr)
Puccini, G.:La Bohème, w. Licia Albanese (sop—Mimi), Audrey Schuh (sop—Musetta), Giuseppe di Stefano (ten—Rodolfo), Arthur Cosenza (bar—Schaunard), Giuseppe Valdengo (bar—Marcello), Norman Treigle (bass—Colline), Warren Gadpaille (bass—Benoît/Alcindoro), Thomas Carter (sgr—Parpignol), Harold Crane (sgr—Custom House Official), Steve Harun (sgr—Sergeant), R. Cellini (cnd), New Orleans Opera Orch, New Orleans Opera Chorus *(rec Nov 1959)* VAI Audio 2-▲ VAIA 1119-2 [DDD]

Harvánek, Zdenek (bass)
Dvořák, A.:Armida, w. Joanna Borowska (sop—Armida), Monika Brychtová (sgr—Siren), Wieslaw Ochman (ten—Rinald), Richard Sporka (ten—Dudo), Jan Markvart (bar—Sven), Pavel Daniluk (bass—King), George Fortune (bass—Ismen), Zdenek Harvánek (bass—Ubald), Miloslav Podskalský (bass—Peter), Milan Bürger (sgr—Gernand), Roman Janál (sgr—Muezzin/Hlasatel), Vratislav Kříž (sgr—Gottfried), Vladimír Nacházel (sgr—Roger), G. Albrecht (cnd), Czech PO, Prague Chamber Choir *(rec 1995)* Orfeo 2-▲ 404962 [DDD]

Harvey, Frederick (bar)
Maunder, J.H.:From Olivet to Calvary, w. J. Mitchinson (ten), P. Moorse (org), Guildford Cathedral Choir [E] Classics for Pleasure ▲ CDCFP 4619 [ADD]

Harvey, Peter (bass)
Bach, C.P.E.:Auferstehung und Himmelfahrt Jesu, w. H. Martinpelto (sop), C. Prégardien (ten), P. Herreweghe (cnd), Orch of the Age of Enlightenment, Collegium Vocale Virgin Classics ▲ CDC 59069
Campra, A.:Messe de Requiem, w. D. Visse (ct), G. Ragon (ten), J. Malgoire (cnd), La Grande Écurie et la Chambre du Roy, Les Pages de la Chapelle *(rec Nov. 4–6, 1992)* FNAC Music ▲ 592223 [DDD]
Campra, A.:Messe de Requiem, w. Véronique Gens (sop), Anne Gotkovski (sop), Jean-Paul Fouchécourt (alt), Joseph Cornwell (ten), H. Niquet (cnd), Concert Spirituel Orch, Concert Spirituel Vocal Ensemble Adda ▲ ADD 241952 [DDD]
Campra, A.:Misere, w. D. Visse (ct), G. Ragon (ten), J. Malgoire (cnd), La Grande Écurie et la Chambre du Roy, Les Pages de la Chapelle *(rec Nov. 4–6, 1992)* FNAC Music ▲ 592223 [DDD]
Campra, A.:Motets, w. Véronique Gens (sop), Anne Gotkovski (sop), Jean-Paul Fouchécourt (alt), Douglas Nasrawi (ten), Marcos Loureiro de Sà (bar), Kevin Mallon (vn), H. Niquet (cnd), Concert Spirituel Orch, Concert Spirituel Vocal Ensemble—Te Deum; Notus in Judea Deus; Deus in Nomine Tuo Adda ▲ ADD 241942 [DDD]
Campra, A.:Motets, w. Véronique Gens (sop), Anne Gotkovsky (sop), Jean-Paul Fauchecourt (ct), Hervé Lamy (ten), H. Niquet (cnd), Concert Spirituel Orch, Concert Spirituel Vocal Ensemble—2 Noster Refugium; Cantate Domino; De Profundis Adda ▲ ADD 243912
Campra, A.:Motets, w. Véronique Gens (sop), Anne Gotkovski (sop), Jean-Paul Fouchécourt (alt), Joseph Cornwell (ten), H. Niquet (cnd), Concert Spirituel Orch, Concert Spirituel Vocal Ensemble—Benedictus Dominus Adda ▲ ADD 241952 [DDD]
du Mont, H.:Motets pour la chapelle du roy, w. H. Crook (cta), H. Lamy (ten), O. Schneebeli (cnd), Musica Aeterna, Les Pages de la Chapelle *(rec Sept. 1993)* FNAC Music ▲ 592054 [DDD]
Fauré, G.:Cantique de Jean Racine, w. M. Dami (sop), M. Corboz (cnd), Lausanne Instrumental Ensemble, Lausanne Vocal Ensemble [F] *(rec Feb. 14–16, 1992)* FNAC Music ▲ 592097 [DDD]
Fauré, G.:Motets, w. M. Dami (sop), M. Corboz (cnd), Lausanne Instrumental Ensemble, Lausanne Vocal Ensemble—Maria Mater Gratiae, Op. 47; Ave verum, Op. 65/1; Tantum ergo, Op. 65/2; Tu es Petrus; Tantum ergo [L] *(rec Feb. 14–16, 1992)* FNAC Music ▲ 592097 [DDD]
Fauré, G.:Requiem, w. M. Dami (sop), M. Corboz (cnd), Lausanne Instrumental Ensemble, Lausanne Vocal Ensemble [L] *(rec Feb. 14–16, 1992)* FNAC Music ▲ 592097 [DDD]
Lalande, M.-R. de:Dies Irae, w. P. Kwella (sop), L. Perillo (sop), H. Crook (ten), H. Lamy (ten), P. Herreweghe (cnd), La Chapelle Royale Orch, Chapelle Royale Choir [L] Harmonia Mundi France ▲ HMC 901352
Lalande, M.-R. de:Miserere mei, Deus, w. P. Kwella (sop), L. Perillo (sop), H. Crook (ten), H. Lamy (ten), P. Herreweghe (cnd), La Chapelle Royale Orch, Chapelle Royale Choir [L] Harmonia Mundi France ▲ HMC 901352
Lully, J.-B.:Motets, w. I. Desrochers (sop), D. Favat (sop), R. Duguay (ct), H. Lamy (ten), H. Niquet (cnd), Concert Spirituel Vocal Ensemble—Te Deum; Miserere; Plaude laetare Gallia *(rec Nov. 22–25, 1993)* FNAC Music ▲ 592308 [DDD]
Pousseur, H.:Traverser la forêt, w. Christian Crahay (nar), Marianne Pousseur (sop), J.-P. Peuvion (cnd), Liège New Music Ensemble, Gerhard Sporken (cnd), Vocal Ensemble Adda ▲ ADD 581295 [DDD]
Rameau, J.P.:Motets, w. I. Desrochers (sop), V. Gens (sop), J.-P. Fouchecourt (ct), H. Lamy (ten), M. Loureiro de Sà (bar), S. Imbodem (bass), *(orch unknown)*—Deus noster refugium; Quam dilecta; In convertendo [L] *(rec Apr. 13–18, 1992)* FNAC Music ▲ 592096 [DDD]
Walton, W.:The Twelve, w. P. Forbes (sop), R. Gleave (mez), S. Gay (alt), J. Oxley (ten), R. Hickox (cnd), City of London Sinfonia [E] Chandos ▲ CHAN 8824 [DDD]

Harvuot, Clifford (bar)
Puccini, G.:La Bohème, w. L. Albanese (sop), L. Hurley (sop), C. Bergonzi (ten), M. Sereni (bar), N. Scott (bass), E. Flagello (bass), T. Schippers (cnd), New York Metropolitan Opera Orch, New York Metropolitan Opera Chorus *(rec Feb. 15, 1958)* Golden Age of Opera 2-▲ GAO 139/40 [ADD]
Puccini, G.:Tosca, w. Leonie Rysanek (sop), Russell Christopher (ten), Andrea Velis (ten), Cornell MacNeil (bar), Fernando Corena (bass), Paul Plishka (bass), F. Molinari-Pradelli (cnd), San Francisco Opera Orch, San Francisco Opera Chorus Melodram 2-▲ CDM 27508

Harwood, Elizabeth (sop)
Britten, H.:A Midsummer Night's Dream, w. J. Veasey (mez), H. Watts (cta), A. Deller (ct), P. Pears (ten), J. Shirley-Quirk (bar), B. Britten (cnd), London SO, London Sym Chorus [E] London 2-▲ 425663-2 [ADD]
Handel, G.F.:Messiah, w. Janet Baker (mez), Paul Esswood (ct), Robert Tear (ten), Raimund Herincx (bass), C. Mackerras (cnd), English CO, Ambrosian Singers [E] Angel ("Studio" series) ▲ CDM 69040
Handel, G.F.:Messiah, w. Janet Baker (mez), Paul Esswood (ct), Robert Tear (ten), Raimund Herincx (bass), C. Mackerras (cnd), English CO, Ambrosian Singers [E] Angel ("Studio" series) 2-▲ CDMB 62748 [ADD]
Lehár, F.:Die lustige Witwe, w. T. Stratas (sop), W. Hollweg (ten), R. Kollo (ten), Z. Kelemen (bar), H. von Karajan (cnd), Berlin PO, German Opera Chorus [G] *(rec 1972)* Deutsche Grammophon 2-▲ 435712-2 [ADD]
Puccini, G.:La Bohème, w. M. Freni (sop), L. Pavarotti (ten), R. Panerai (bar), H. von Karajan (cnd), Berlin PO, German Opera Chorus [I] London 2-▲ 421049-2 [ADD] 2-■ 421049-4
Puccini, G.:La Bohème (sels), w. M. Freni (sop), L. Pavarotti (ten), R. Panerai (bar), H. von Karajan (cnd), Berlin PO, German Opera Chorus London ▲ 421245-2 [DDD] ■ 421245-4
Strauss, R.:Songs, w. N. del Mar (cnd), New Philharmonia Orch IMP ("BBC Radio Classics" series) ▲ IMP 9138
Sullivan, A.:Iolanthe (sels), w. S. Bevin (ten), D. Dowling (bar), E. Shilling (bar), J. Holmes (bass), A. Faris (cnd), Sadler's Wells Opera Orch, Sadler's Wells Opera Chorus Classics for Pleasure 2-▲ CDCFP 4730 [ADD]
Tippett, M.:The Midsummer Marriage, w. Joan Carlyle (sop—Joan), Elizabeth Harwood (sop—Beth), Elizabeth Bainbridge (mez), Helen Watts (cta—Sosostris), Stuart Burrows (ten—Jack), Alberto Remedios (ten—Mark), Stafford Dean (bass), Raimund Herincx (bass—King Fisher), C. Davis (cnd), Royal Opera House Orch, Royal Opera House Chorus Covent Garden Lyrita 2-▲ SRCD 2217

Hase, Susanna Moncayo von (cta)
Vivaldi, A.:Beatus vir, R.795, w. Caterina Calvi (sop), Vincenzo Manno (ten), Bonitatibus (sgr), Trogu (sgr) Agora Music ▲ 001
Vivaldi, A.:Gloria (& Intro), RV.588, w. Caterina Calvi (sop), Vincenzo Manno (ten), Bonitatibus (sgr), Trogu (sgr) Agora Music ▲ 001

Haseleu, Werner (bar)
Schoenberg, A.:Moses und Aaron, w. Renate Krahmer (sop), Gisela Pohl (cta), Reiner Goldberg (ten), H. Kegel (cnd), Leipzig RSO, Leipzig Radio Chorus Berlin Classics 2-▲ BER 1116 [ADD]

Haskin, Howard (ten)
Bowles, P.:Songs, w. Jo An Pickens (sop) *(rec live, Paris, May 8, 1994)* Koch Schwann ▲ SCH 315742
Dallapiccola, L.:Il Prigioniero, w. Phyllis Bryn-Julson (sop), Sven-Erik Alexandersson (ten), Jorma Hynninen (bar), Lage Wedin (bar), E.-P. Salonen (cnd), Swedish RSO, Eric Ericson Chamber Choir Sony Classical ▲ SK 68323
Massenet, J.:Thérèse, w. J. Piland (sop), C. van Tassel (bar), L. Vis (cnd), Netherlands PO, Netherlands Theater Chorus [F] Canal Grande ▲ CG 9220 [DDD]
Schnittke, A.:Life with an Idiot, w. T. Ringholz (sop), D. Duesing (bar), M. Rostropovich (cnd), Rotterdam PO, Rotterdam Vocal Ensemble *(rec Amsterdam, world premiere performance, April 13, 1992)* Sony Classical 2-▲ S2K 52495 [DDD]

Hasslo, Hugo (bar)
Verdi, G.:Rigoletto, w. M. Hallin (sop), B. Nordin (sop), K. Meyer (mez), B. Ericson (mez), Kjellgren (mez), N. Gedda (ten), O. Sivall (ten), I. Wixell (bar), B. Alstergård (bar), A. Tyrén (bass), S. Ehrling (cnd), Stockholm Royal Opera House Orch, Stockholm Royal Opera Chorus *(rec live Jan. 18, 1959)* BIS ▲ CD 296 [AAD]

Hasslo, Hugo (bar) (cont.)

Verdi, G.:Il trovatore (sels), w. Hjördis Schymberg (sop), Kerstin Meyer (mez), Jussi Björling (ten), Olle Sivall (ten), H. Sandberg (cnd), Royal Opera Orch, Royal Opera House Chorus Covent Garden—Non son tuo figlio?; Mal reggendo all'aspro assalto; Quale d'armi fragor; Ah! sì, ben mio, coll'essere; L'onda de' suoni mistici; Di quella pira l'orrendo foco; Miserere d'un'alma già vicina; Madre?...non dormi?; Se m'ami ancor; Ciel!...non m'inganna; Ti scosta... *(rec Royal Opera, Stockholm, Mar 6, 1960)* Myto ▲ MCD 953130

Hatano, Hitoshi (ten)

Mendelssohn, Fanny:Oratorio, w. I. Lippitz (sop), Annemarie Fischer-Kunz (cta), T. Thomaschke (bass), E.M. Blankenburg (cnd), Cologne Youth Orch, Cologne Youth Chorus CPO ▲ CPO 999009-2 [DDD]

Hatziano, Markella (mez)

Verdi, G.:Requiem Mass, w. Michèle Crider (sop), Gabriel Sadé (ten), Robert Lloyd (bass), R. Hickox (cnd), London SO, London Sym Chorus Chandos ▲ CHAN 9490

Haubold, Ingrid (sop)

Penderecki, K.:Polish Requiem, w. G. Winogrodska (mez), Z. Terzakis (ten), Smith (sgr), K. Penderecki (cnd), North German RSO, North German Radio Chorus [L] *(rec live, Lucerne, 1989)* Deutsche Grammophon 2-▲ 429720-2 [DDD]

Wagner, R.:Der fliegende Holländer, w. I. Haubold (sop—Senta), M. Schiml (mez—Nurse), P. Seiffert (ten—Erik), J. Hering (ten—Helsman), A. Muff (bar—The Dutchman), E. Knodt (bass—Sea Capt.), P. Steinberg (cnd), Vienna ORF SO, Budapest Radio Chorus [G] *(rec Sept. 1992)* Naxos 2-▲ 8.660025/26 [DDD]

Wagner, R.:Die Walküre (act 1/scene 3), w. R. Kollo (ten), C. Thielemann (cnd), German Opera Orch [G] EMI Classics ▲ CDC 54776

Haughton, Jane (sop)

Sui Palchi Delle Stelle:Sacred Music in the Neapolitan Conservatories at the Time of Francesco Provenzale, w. [cnd:Antonio Florio], Cappella Pietà de Turchini, Antonella Ippolito (sop), Daniela del Monaco (alt), Sebastiano Cassarà (vn), Rosario Di Meglio (vn), Antonella Bologna (va), Paolo Dionisio (vl), Antonio Florio (vc), Pierluigi Ciappareli (thb), Enrico Baiano (org/hpd) Symphonia ▲ SY 93S20 [DDD]

Haugland, Aage (bass)

Berg, A.:Wozzeck, w. H. Behrens (sop), P. Langridge (ten), H. Zednik (ten), F. Grundheber (bar), C. Abbado (cnd), Vienna PO, Vienna State Opera Chorus, Vienna Boys' Choir [G] *(rec live, 6/88)* Deutsche Grammophon 2-▲ 423587-2 [DDD]

Brorson, H.A.:Hymns, w. Jens Christensen (org)—Arise! All That God Hath Made; Here Come Your Little Poor Beings; The Loveliest Rose is Found; My Heart Always Abides; Oh, My Rose Withers Away; The One That God Hath Born & Bred; My Bridegroom, the Delicate, Handsome & Sweet; Peace is the Best Treasure of the Soul; others Kontrapunkt ▲ KPT 32214 [DDD]

Dørumsgaard, A.:Dusk in the Enchanted Wood, w. Poul Rosenbaum (pno) Point ▲ PCD 5088 [DDD]

Heise, P.:King & Marshall, w. P. Elming (ten), C. Christiansen (bass), M. Schønwandt (cnd), Danish National RSO, Danish National Choir Chandos 3-▲ CHAN 9143 [DDD]

Ibert, J.:Chansons de Don Quichotte, w. Poul Rosenbaum (pno) Point ▲ PCD 5088 [DDD]

Liebermann, R.:Medea, w. Françoise Pollet (sop—Medea), Yvi Jänicke (cta—Chalkiope), Zdena Furmančoková (sgr—Syrinx), Dagmar Hesse (sgr—Aiglaia), Hanne Krogen (sgr—Kore), Michaela Lucas (sgr—Oinone), Renate Spingler (sgr—Silene), Jochen Kowalski (ct—Kreon), Aage Haugland (bass—Jason), G. Albrecht (cnd), Hamburg State PO, Hamburg State Opera Chorus *(rec live, Hamburg, Germany, Sept 24, 1995)* Musiques Suisses ▲ 6126 [DDD]

Mussorgsky, M.:Boris Godunov, w. A. Haugland (bass—Boris, Pimen & Varlaam), D. Kitayenko (cnd), Danish Radio Concert Orch, Danish National Radio Choir [concert version based on Mussorgsky's original 1868–69 version] [R] *(rec live 2/27/86)* Kontrapunkt 2-▲ 32036/37 [DDD]

Mussorgsky, M.:Boris Godunov (sels)—all of the basso music from Boris Danacord 2-▲ DACOCD 304/05

Mussorgsky, M.:Khovanshchina, w. M. Lipovsek (mez), V. Atlantov (ten), P. Burchuladze (bass), C. Abbado (cnd), Vienna State Opera Orch, Slovak Phil Chorus [Shostakovich version] [R] Deutsche Grammophon 3-▲ 429758-2 [DDD]

Mussorgsky, M.:Nursery, w. Poul Rosenbaum (pno) Chandos 3-▲ CHAN 9336/38 [DDD]

Mussorgsky, M.:Nursery, w. Poul Rosenbaum (pno) Point ▲ PCD 5098 [DAD]

Mussorgsky, M.:Songs (comp), w. Poul Rosenbaum (pno) Chandos 3-▲ CHAN 9336/38 [DDD]

Mussorgsky, M.:Songs & Dances, w. Poul Rosenbaum (pno) Point ▲ PCD 5098 [DAD]

Mussorgsky, M.:Songs & Dances, w. Poul Rosenbaum (pno) Point ▲ PCD 5088 [DDD]

Mussorgsky, M.:Songs & Dances, w. Poul Rosenbaum (pno) Chandos 3-▲ CHAN 9336/38 [DDD]

Mussorgsky, M.:Songs (misc), w. Poul Rosenbaum (pno)—Master Haughty; The Classic; The Feast; Savishna; The Seminarist; The He-Goat; The Street-Urchin; Song of Mephistopheles; Evening Song Point ▲ PCD 5098 [DAD]

Mussorgsky, M.:Sunless, w. Poul Rosenbaum (pno) Chandos 3-▲ CHAN 9336/38 [DDD]

Nielsen, C.:Saul & David, w. T. Kiberg (sop), A. Gjevang (mez), P. Lindroos (ten), K. Westi (ten), C. Christiansen (bass), J. Klint (bass), N. Järvi (cnd), Danish National RSO, Danish National Radio Choir [Da] Chandos 2-▲ CHAN 8911/12 [DDD]

Schoenberg, A.:Moses und Aaron, w. B. Bonney (sop), M. Zakai (cta), P. Langridge (ten), F. Mazura (bar), G. Solti (cnd), Chicago SO, Chicago Sym Chorus, Glen Ellyn Children's Chorus [G] London 2-▲ 414264-2 [DDD]

Shostakovich, D.:Lady Macbeth of Mtsensk, w. M. Ewing (sop), E. Zaremba (mez), P. Langridge (ten), H. Zednik (ten), A. Kotcherga (bass), K. Moll (bass), S. Larin (bass), M.-W. Chung (cnd), Bastille Opera Orch, Bastille Opera Chorus Deutsche Grammophon 2-▲ 437511-2

Shostakovich, D.:Lady Macbeth of Mtsensk, w. G. Vishnevskaya (sop), B. Finnilä (mez), N. Gedda (ten), M. Rostropovich (cnd), London PO, Ambrosian Opera Chorus [R] EMI Classics 2-▲ CDCB 49955 [ADD]

Verdi, G.:Messa per Rossini, w. G. Benačková-Cápova (sop), F. Quivar (mez), J. Wagner (ten), A. Agache (bar), H. Rilling (cnd), Stuttgart RSO, Gächinger Kantorei, Prague Phil Chorus [L] Hänssler Classic 2-▲ CD 98.949 [DDD] 2-■ MC 96.949 (D)

Hauman, Constance (mez)

Puccini, G.:Madama Butterfly (sels), w. Ying Huang (sop—Cio-Cio-San), Constance Hauman (mez—Kate Pinkerton), Ning Liang (mez—Suzuki), Richard Troxell (ten—B. F. Pinkerton), Richard Cowan (sgr—Sharpless), Jing Ma Fan (sgr—Goro), Christopheren Nomura (sgr—Prince Yamadori), J. Conlon (cnd), Orch de Paris—Dovunque al Mondo; B. F. Pinkerton Giù; Bimba, Bimba, Non Piangere; Ah! Vien! Sei Mia!; Un Bel Dí; Ora a Noi; Petali d'Ogni Fior; Coro a Bocca Chiusa; Prelude; Io So Che Alle Sue Pene; Ah! Son Vil!; E Sia! A Lui Devo Obbedir; Butterfly! *(rec Olivier Messiaen Auditorium, Paris, 1996)* Sony Classical ▲ SK 61972 [DDD]

Haunstein, Rolf (bar)

Strauss, R.:Der Rosenkavalier (sels), w. A. Pusar-Jeric (sop), M. Stejskal (sop), A. Jahns (mez), U. Walther (cta), T. Adam (b-bar), H. Vonk (cnd), Dresden Staatskapelle, Dresden State Chorus [G] *(rec live 2/85)* Denon ▲ CO 8010 [DDD]

Hauptmann, Cornelius (bass)

Bach, J.S.:St. Matthew Passion, w. B. Bonney (sop), A. Monoyios (sop), A. S. von Otter (mez), M. Chance (ct), H. Crook (ten), A. Rolfe Johnson (ten), O. Bär (bar), A. Schmidt (bar), J. E. Gardiner (cnd), English Baroque Soloists, Monteverdi Choir London [G] Archiv 3-▲ 427648-2 [DDD]

Beethoven, L. van:Missa Solemnis, w. Rosa Mannion (sop), Birgit Remmert (alt), James Taylor (ten), P. Herreweghe (cnd), Champs Elysées Theater Orch, Chapelle Royale Choir, Collegium Vocale *(rec Auditorium Stravinski de Montreux, Feb. 20–21, 1995)* Harmonia Mundi France ▲ HMC 901557

Mozart, W.A.:Entführung, w. L. Orgonasova (sop), C. Sieden (sop), S. Olsen (ten), Uwe Peper (ten), Hans-Peter Minetti (nar), J. E. Gardiner (cnd), English Baroque Soloists, Monteverdi Choir London [G] Deutsche Grammophon 2-▲ 435857-2

Mozart, W.A.:Missa, K.427, w. A. Augér (sop), F. von Stade (mez), F. Lopardo (ten), L. Bernstein (cnd), Bavarian RSO, Bavarian Radio Chorus *(rec live April 1990)* Deutsche Grammophon ▲ 431791-2 [DDD] □ 431791-5

Mozart, W.A.:Missa, K.427, w. S. McNair (sop), D. Montague (mez), A. Rolfe Johnson (ten), J. E. Gardiner (cnd), English Baroque Soloists, Monteverdi Choir London [newly revised version, ed. Gardiner] [L] Philips ▲ 420210-2 [DDD]

Mozart, W.A.:Requiem, w. M. McLaughlin (sop), M. Ewing (sop), J. Hadley (ten), L. Bernstein (cnd), Bavarian RSO, Bavarian Radio Chorus [L] Deutsche Grammophon ▲ 427353-2 [DDD]

Hauptmann, Cornelius (bass) (cont.)

Schoenberg, A.:Die Jakobsleiter, w. Barbara Kilduff (sop—Seele 1), Jadwiga Rappé (cta—Sterbende), Wilfried Gahmlich (ten—Aufrührerischer), Cornelius Hauptmann (ten—Gabriel), Keith Lewis (ten—Berfener), Kurt Azesberger (bar—Mönch), Barbara Fuchs (sgr—Seele 2), Matteo de Monti (sgr—Ringender), Bjorn Waag (sgr—Auserwählter), E. Inbal (cnd), Frankfurt RSO, Robin Gritton (cnd), Berlin Radio Chorus *(rec Alte Oper, Frankfurt, Sept 6–9, 1994)* Denon ▲ CO 78977 [DDD]

Hausen, Sigrid (sgr)

Popp, M.:Ludus Danielis, w. T. Schlierf (spkr), A. Veljanov (spkr), P. Pöppel (sgr), M. Popp (cnd), Estampie *(rec Jan. 1–10, 1993)* Christophorus ▲ 77144 [DDD]

Hauser, L. (sop)

Perrin, J.:Cantosenhal, w. S. Imbodem (bass), H. Klopfenstein (cnd), Lausanne Conservatory Orch Gallo ▲ CD 630 [AAD]

Havenstein, Rolf (sgr)

Orff, C.:Carmina burana, w. Venceslava Hruba-Freiberger (sop), Piotr Kusiewicz (sgr), K. Penderecki (cnd), Karol Szymanowski State PO, Karol Szymanowski State Phil Choir *(rec Cracow, Poland, Jan 27–28, 1989)* Arts Music ▲ 47177-2 [DDD]

Haverinen, Margareta (sop)

Shostakovich, D.:Sym 14, w. Petteri Salomaa (bass), J. Swensen (cnd), Tapiola Sinfonietta Ondine ▲ ODE 845

Havlák, Lubomír (ten)

Martinů, B.:Bouquet, w. Libuše Domanínská (sop), Soňa Červená (alt), Ladislav Mráz (bass), K. Ančerl (cnd), Czech PO, Czech Phil Chorus *(rec 1967)* Praga ("Karel Ančerl Edition" series) ▲ PR 254061

Hawkins, Gordon (bar)

Gershwin, G.:Porgy & Bess (sels), w. Cynthia Clarey (sop—Serena), Cynthia Haymon (sop—Bess), Damon Evans (ten—Sportin' Life), Gordon Hawkins (bar—Porgy), Andrew Litton (pno), A. Litton (cnd), Dallas SO, Dallas Sym Chorus—Intro/Jasbo Brown; Summertime; A Woman Is a Sometime Thing; Gone, Gone, Gone; My Man's Gone Now; Leavin' for the Promise' Lan'; Oh I Got Plenty O' Nuttin'; Bess, You Is My Woman Now; Oh, I Can't Sit Down; I Ain't Got No Shame; It Ain't Necessarily So; Shame on All You Sinners; I Loves You, Porgy; Hurricane; There's a Boat Dat's Leavin' Soon for New York; Act 3, Scene 3 Orchestral Intro; Good Mornin', Sistuh; Oh Lawd, I'm on My Way! [concert suite arr A. Litton] *(rec Eugene McDermott Hall, Dallas, May 1995)* Dorian ▲ DOR 90223 [DDD]

Hawlata, Franz (bass)

Strauss, R.:Arabella (sels), w. P. Coburn (sop), R. Klepper (sop), M. Borst (mez), B. Skovhus (bar), M. Honeck (cnd), Munich RSO Capriccio ▲ 10481 [DDD]

Strauss, R.:Ariadne auf Naxos, w. P. Coburn (sop), R. Klepper (sop), M. Borst (mez), B. Skovhus (bar), M. Honeck (cnd), Munich RSO Capriccio ▲ 10481 [DDD]

Strauss, R.:Capriccio (sels), w. P. Coburn (sop), R. Klepper (sop), M. Borst (mez), B. Skovhus (bar), M. Honeck (cnd), Munich RSO Capriccio ▲ 10481 [DDD]

Strauss, R.:Der Rosenkavalier (sels), w. P. Coburn (sop), R. Klepper (sop), M. Borst (mez), B. Skovhus (bar), M. Honeck (cnd), Munich RSO Capriccio ▲ 10481 [DDD]

Haworth, Jill (sgr)

Broadway, w. Ethel Merman (sgr), Judy Holliday (sgr), Dick van Dyke (sgr), Doris Day (sgr), Topol (sgr), Mary Martin (sgr), William Warfield (sgr), et al. Sony Classical ("Greatest Hits" series) ▲ MLK 62365 ■ MLT 62365

Hawthorne, Nigel (nar)

Britten, H.:Night Mail, w. L. Friend (cnd), Nash Ensemble Hyperion ▲ CDA 66845

Lambert, C.:Poems by Li-Po, w. Philip Langridge (ten), Ian Brown (pno), L. Friend (cnd), Nash Ensemble Hyperion ▲ CDA 66754

Hayashi, Makoto (ten)

Mahler, G.:Lied von der Erde, w. Naoko Ihara (alt), T. Asahina (cnd), Osaka PO *(rec Symphony Hall, Osaka, Nov 11, 1995)* Canyon Classics ▲ 326

Hayashi, Yasuko (sop)

Halévy, F.:La Juive, w. M. Le Bris (sop), G. Tucker (ten), Sabate (sgr), A. Guadagno (cnd), *(orch & chorus unknown)* [F] *(rec live, London, 1973)* Legato Classics 2-▲ LCD 120-2 [AAD]

Hayden, M. (sgr)

Rodgers, R.:Carousel, w. S. Verrett (mez), *(other artists unknown)* [1994 Broadway cast] Angel ▲ CDQ 55199 ■ 4DQ 55199

Hayes, B. (sgr)

Rodgers, R.:Me & Juliet, w. I. Bigley (sgr), R. Walston (sgr), J. McCracken (sgr) [1953 Broadway cast] RCA ▲ 09026-61480-2 ■ 09026-61480-4

Hayes, Quentin (bass)

Wallace, V.:Maritana, w. Majella Cullagh (sop), Lynda Lee (mez), Paul Charles Clarke (ten), Ian Caddy (bar), Damien Smith (bar), P. O. Duinn (cnd), RTE Concert Orch, RTE Phil Choir *(rec O'Reilly Hall, Dublin, Sept 1995)* Marco Polo 2-▲ 8.223406-7 [DDD]

Hayes, Roland (sgr)

The Art of Roland Hayes, w. Reginald Boardman (pno) Smithsonian Collection ▲ SMI RD 041 (m)

Haymes, D. (sgr)

Rodgers, R.:State Fair, w. J. Crain (sgr), *(other artists unknown)* Classic Int'l Filmusicals ▲ CIFC 3009

Haymon, Cynthia (sop)

Gershwin, G.:Porgy & Bess, w. C. Haymon (sop—Bess), C. Clarey (sop—Serena), M. Simpson (sop—Maria), D. Evans (ten—Sporting Life), G. Baker (bar—Crown), W. White (bar—Porgy), S. Rattle (cnd), London PO, Glyndebourne Festival Chorus EMI Classics 3-▲ CDCC 49568

Gershwin, G.:Porgy & Bess (sels), w. Cynthia Clarey (sop—Serena), Cynthia Haymon (sop—Bess), Damon Evans (ten—Sportin' Life), Gordon Hawkins (bar—Porgy), Andrew Litton (pno), A. Litton (cnd), Dallas SO, Dallas Sym Chorus—Intro/Jasbo Brown; Summertime; A Woman Is a Sometime Thing; Gone, Gone, Gone; My Man's Gone Now; Leavin' for the Promise' Lan'; Oh I Got Plenty O' Nuttin'; Bess, You Is My Woman Now; Oh, I Can't Sit Down; I Ain't Got No Shame; It Ain't Necessarily So; Shame on All You Sinners; I Loves You, Porgy; Hurricane; There's a Boat Dat's Leavin' Soon for New York; Act 3, Scene 3 Orchestral Intro; Good Mornin', Sistuh; Oh Lawd, I'm on My Way! [concert suite arr A. Litton] *(rec Eugene McDermott Hall, Dallas, May 1995)* Dorian ▲ DOR 90223 [DDD]

Mendelssohn, F.:Sym 2, w. A. Hagley (sop), P. Straka (ten), W. Weller (cnd), Philharmonia Orch, Philharmonia Chorus [G] Chandos ▲ CHAN 8995 [DDD]

Hays, Debra (sop)

Sullivan, A.:HMS Pinafore, w. M. Rawlins (sgr), C. Freeman (ten), E. Schilling (sgr), E. Johnson (cta), M. Elder (cnd), Rochester PO, Eastman Chorale members—highlights *(rec 11/89)* Pro Arte ▲ CDd 480 [DDD]

Sullivan, A.:The Mikado, w. M. Rawlins (sgr), C. Freeman (ten), E. Schilling (sgr), E. Johnson (cta), M. Elder (cnd), Rochester PO, Eastman Chorale members—highlights *(rec 11/89)* Pro Arte ▲ CDd 480 [DDD]

Sullivan, A.:The Pirates of Penzance, w. M. Rawlins (sgr), C. Freeman (ten), E. Schilling (sgr), E. Johnson (cta), M. Elder (cnd), Rochester PO, Eastman Chorale members—highlights *(rec 11/89)* Pro Arte ▲ CDd 480 [DDD]

Hays, Sorrel (voc)

Hays, S.:Dreaming the World, w. Thomas Bruckner (bar), Sal Basile (voc), Jennifer López (voc), John Schaffer (voc), Joseph Kubera (pno), John Kennedy (perc), Charles Wood (perc), Maya Gunji (perc), Eric Kivnick (perc), Jai Smith (perc) New World ▲ 805202 [DDD]

Hayward, Robert (bar)

Beethoven, L. van:Sym 9, "Choral Sym", w. Gillian Webster (sop), Catherine Wyn-Rogers (cta), Martyn Hill (ten), R. Leppard (cnd), Royal PO, Ambrosian Singers Tring ("Royal Philharmonic Collection" series) ▲ TRP 51 [DDD]

Hayward, Thomas Tibbett (sgr)

Strauss (II), Joh.:Eine Nacht in Venedig, w. Nola Fairbanks (sgr—Ciboletta), Thomas Tibbett Hayward (sgr—Mario), Laurel Hurley (sgr—Nina), David Kurlan (sgr—Senator Bartoldi), Guen Omeron (sgr—Barbara), Jack Russell (sgr—Duke of Palobino), Kenneth Schon (sgr—Filippo Del Aqua), Norwood Smith (sgr—Caramello), Enzo Stuarti (sgr—Pappacoda) *(rec Belock Recording Studio, Bayside, NY)* Everest ▲ EVC 9036 [AAD]

Haywood, Lorna (sop)

Britten, H.:War Requiem, w. A. Rolfe-Johnson (ten), B. Luxon (bar), R. Shaw (cnd), Atlanta SO, Atlanta Sym Chorus [L] Telarc 2-▲ CD 80157 [DDD]

▲ = CD ♦ = Enhanced CD Δ = MD ■ = Cassette Tape □ = DCC

Haywood, Lorna (sop) (cont.)
Mozart, W.A.:Requiem, w. D'Anna Fortunado (mez), Partick Romero (ten), John Cheek (bass), J. Sommary (cnd), Amor Artis Orch, Amor Artis Chorale [period instrs] *(rec St. Jean Baptiste Church, New York City, Mar 1996)* Vox Classics ▲ VOX 7534 [DDD]

Házy, Erzsébet (sop)
Lehár, F.:Das Land des Lächelns (sels), w. Magda Kalmár (sop), Szimándy (sgr), Bende (sgr), G. Oberfrank (cnd), Budapest SO, Hungarian Radio–TV Chorus [Hun] Hungaroton ▲ HCD 16809 [ADD]
Szokolay, S.:Blood Wedding, w. O. Szőnyi (sop), E. Komlóssy (cta), Faragó (sgr), A. Kórodi (cnd), Hungarian State Opera Orch, Hungarian State Opera Chorus [Hun] Hungaroton 2-▲ HCD 11262/63 [ADD]

Heaney, Joe (sgr)
Cage, J.:Roaratorio:An Irish Circus on Finnegans Wake, w. J. Cage (voice), P. Glackin (fid), M. Mercier (bodrhan), P. Mercier (bodrhan), M. Mallory (fl), S. Ellis (uillean pipes) Wergo ▲ WER 6303-2
Cage, J.:Roaratorio:An Irish Circus on Finnegans Wake, w. J. Cage (voice), P. Glackin (fid), M. Mercier (bodrhan), P. Mercier (bodrhan), M. Mallory (fl), S. Ellis (uillean pipes) Mode 2-▲ mode 28/29

Hearn, George (sgr)
Lloyd Webber, A.:Sunset Boulevard, w. Glenn Close (sgr), A. Campbell (sgr), J. Kuhn (sgr)—highlights Polydor ▲ 31452-7241-2 ■ 31452-7241-4
Lloyd Webber, A.:Sunset Boulevard, w. Glenn Close (sgr), A. Campbell (sgr), J. Kuhn (sgr) [1994 cast] A&M ▲ 31452 3507-2 ■ 31452 3507-4

Heater, Claude (ten)
Still, W.G.:Tristan und Isolde, w. C. Ligendza (sop), S. Anderson (cta), A. Švorc (bass), M. Smith (bass), L. Toffolo (cnd), Trieste Teatro Comunale Giuseppe Verdi Orch, Trieste Teatro Comunale G. Verdi Chorus [G] *(rec live, Trieste, 12/13/69)* Melodram 3-▲ MEL 37072 (m) [AAD]
Wagner, R.:Der fliegende Holländer, w. L. Rysanek (sop), A.-M. Bessel (mez), F. Crass (bass), K. Ridderbusch (bass), W. Sawallisch (cnd), La Scala Orch, La Scala Chorus [G] *(rec live, Milan 2/2/66)* Memories 2-▲ HR 4281/82 (m) [ADD]

Hebert, T. (sgr)
Rodgers, R.:Flower Drum Song, w. K. Scott (sgr), I. Shepley (sgr), Y. S. Tung (sgr), Y. Saki (sgr) [1960 London cast] Angel ▲ ZDM 89953

Hechenberger, Herbert (ten)
Mozart, W.A.:Zauberflöte, w. Birgit Been (sop), Nathalie Boissy (sop), Marianne Seibel (sop), Renate Springer (sop), Elizabeth Vidal (sop), Eleanor James (mez), Salvador Guzman (ten), Wolfgang Newmann (ten), Klaus Häger (bass), Philip Langshaw (bass), Hans-Georg Moser (bass), P. Kuentz (cnd), Paul Kuentz Orch, Francis Bardot (cnd), Maitrise des Hauts-de-Seine members, Paul Kuentz Choirs Pierre Verany 2-▲ PVY 730055 [DDD]

Hecht, Joshua (bass)
Verdi, G.:Stiffelio, w. A. Gulin (sop—Lina), M. del Monaco (ten—Stiffelio), A. Marchiandi (ten—Raffaele), G. Fioravanti (bar—Stankar), J. Hecht (bass—Jorg), O. de Fabritiis (cnd), Naples Teatro San Carlo Orch, Naples Teatro San Carlo Chorus *(rec Dec. 26, 1972)* Standing Room Only 2-▲ SRO 169-2

Hechtel, F. (sop)
Singer, J.:Songs & Song Cycles, w. A. Miskell (ten), J. Singer (pno)—American Indian Song Suite; Arno is Deep; From Petrarch; Hannah; Memoria; Lost Garden; Old Wild Woman; Query to the Creator; Songs from Later Years (song cycle); Wry Rimes (song cycle) [E] Cambria ▲ CD 1051
Singer, J.:To Stir a Dream:American Poets in Song, w. A. Miskell (ten), Jeanne Singer (pno) Cambria ▲ CMB 1051 [DDD]

Hedegaard, Ole (ten)
Nielsen, C.:Springtime, w. J. Frandsen (cnd), South Jutland SO—Den milde dag er lys og lang *(rec "Musikhuset", DK-Sønderborg, 1982)* Paula ▲ PACD 18 [DAD]
Nielsen, C.:Tove, w. J. Frandsen (cnd), South Jutland SO, Vi sletternes sønner *(rec "Musikhuset", DK-Sønderborg, 1982)* Paula ▲ PACD 18 [DAD]

Hedin, Sture (sgr)
Nilsson, T.:Out of Earthly Night, w. Gudrun Bruna (sop), Marianne Mellnäs (sop), Kaysa Hälldin (alt), Lars Sjögren (ten), Göran Swartz (bass), Ola Kyhlberg (sgr), Lars Ljungman (sgr), Nils Philipson (sgr), Ulrik Quale (sgr), Nils Spangenberg (sgr), Britta Theren (sgr), Karl-Erik Welin (org), Torsten Nilsson (cnd), Oscar's Motet Choir *(rec Oscar's Church, Stockholm, Sweden, Apr 26-27, 1978)* BIS ▲ CD 138 [AAD]

Hedwein, W. (bass)
Bach, J.S.:Cant 176, w. I. Nielsen (sop), C. Watkinson (cta), H. Rilling (cnd), Stuttgart Bach Collegium, Gächinger Kantorei Hänssler Classic ▲ 98.801 [AAD]

Heidbüchel, Hein (ten)
Straus, O.:The Merry Nibelungs, w. Lisa Griffith (sop—Kriemhild), Gudrun Volkert (sop—Brunhilde), Daphne Evangelatos (cta—Ute), Gabriele Henkel (sgr—Giselher), Christine Mann (sgr—Vogel), Hein Heidbüchel (ten—Volker), Martin Gantner (sgr—Gunther), Gerd Grochowski (sgr—Dankwart), Michael Nowak (sgr—Siegfried), Josef Otten (sgr—Hagen), S. Köhler (cnd), Cologne RSO, Cologne Radio Chorus *(rec Cologne, Jan 31-Feb 17, 1995)* Capriccio ▲ 10752 [DDD]

Heidersbach, Käthe (sop)
Wagner, R.:Arias & Scenes, w. Maria Reining (sop), Hilde Scheppan (sop), Margarete Teschemacher (sop), Margarete Klose (mez), Max Lorenz (ten), Jaro Prohaska (bar), Karl Schmitt-Walter (bar), Kurt Böhme (bass), (orch unknown)—selections from Rienzi; Der Fliegende Holländer; Tannhäuser; Lohengrin; Tristan und Isolde; Die Meistersinger von Nürnberg; Die Walküre & Götterdämmerung *(rec 1927-1944)* Phonographe 2-▲ PHG 5016 [AAD]

Heijden, Francine van der (sop)
Meijering, Chiel:St. Louis Blues, w. Andrea van Beek (sop), Jeanette Huizinga (mez), Rein Kolpa (ten), Willem-Jan van Deuveren (ten), John Vredeveldt (ten), Gérard Bernts (bar), W. Megens (cnd), De Ereprijs Orch [I] *(rec Schouwburg Arnhem, Mar 10, 1995)* Donemus 2-▲ neos 01-02

Heijnsbergen, Henk van (b-bar)
Einhorn, R.:Voices of Light, w. Susan Narucki (sop), Corrie Pronk (alt), Frank Hameleers (ten), Ronald Hoogeveen (vn), Harm Bakker (vl), Michael Feves (vl), Naomi Hirschfeld (vl), S. Mercurio (cnd), Netherlands Radio PO, Martin Wright (cnd), Anonymous 4, Netherlands Radio Chorus *(rec Music Center of the Netherlands Radio & TV, Aug 23-25, 1995)* Sony Classical ▲ SK 62006 [DDD]

Heilmann, Uwe (ten)
Bach, J.S.:Magnificat, BWV 243, w. B. Hendricks (sop), J. Rigby (sop), A. Murray (mez), J. Hynninen (bar), N. Marriner (cnd), Academy of St. Martin in the Fields, *(chorus unknown)* EMI Classics ▲ CDC 54283-2
Beethoven, L van:Sym 9, "Choral Sym", w. S. McNair (sop), J. Van Nes (bar), B. Weikl (bar), K. Masur (cnd), Leipzig Gewandhaus Orch, London Radio Choir Philips ▲ 432995-2
Haydn, J.:L'Anima del filosofo, or Orfeo ed Euridice, w. Cecilia Bartoli (mez), Ildebrando d'Arcangelo (bass), C. Hogwood (cnd), Academy of Ancient Music, Academy of Ancient Music Chorus L'oiseau Lyre ▲ 452 668-2
Haydn, J.:The Seven Last Words of Christ on the Cross, w. Pamela Coburn (sop), Ingeborg Danz (mez), Andreas Schmidt (bar), H. Rilling (cnd), Stuttgart Bach Collegium, Gächinger Kantorei [oratorio version] [G] Hänssler Classic ▲ 98.977 [DDD]
Mendelssohn, F.:Die erste Walpurgisnacht, w. B. Remmert (alt), T. Hampson (bar), R. Pape (bass), N. Harnoncourt (cnd), CO of Europe Teldec ▲ 74882-2
Mozart, W.A.:Clemenza, w. Barbara Bonney (sop—Servilia), Cecilia Bartoli (mez—Sesto), Della Jones (mez—Vitellia), Diana Montague (mez—Annio), Uwe Heilman (ten—Tito), Giles Cachemaille (bar—Publio), C. Hogwood (cnd), Academy of Ancient Music, Academy of Ancient Music Chorus London ("Editions de l'oiseau-lyre" series) 2-▲ 444131-2 [DDD]
Mozart, W.A.:Finta giardiniera, w. E. Gruberova (sop), C. Margiono (sop), M. Bacelli (sop), D. Upshaw (sop), A. Scharinger (bass), N. Harnoncourt (cnd), Vienna Concentus Musicus Teldec 3-▲ 72309-2
Mozart, W.A.:Litaniae Lauretanae, K.195, w. B. Bonney (sop), E. von Magnus (cta), G. Cachemaille (bass), N. Harnoncourt (cnd), Vienna Concentus Musicus, Arnold Schoenberg Choir Teldec ("Das alte Werke" series) ▲ 93025
Mozart, W.A.:Requiem, w. A. M. Blasi (sop), M. Lipovšek (mez), J.-H. Rootering (bass), C. Davis (cnd), Bavarian RSO, Bavarian Radio Chorus [L] RCA Red Seal ▲ 09026-60599-2 [DDD] ■ 09026-60599-4 (CrO2) □ 09026-60599-5
Mozart, W.A.:Zauberflöte, w. S. Jo (sop), R. Ziesak (sop), A. Kraus (ten), K. Moll (bass), G. Solti (cnd), Vienna PO, Vienna State Opera Chorus London 2-▲ 433210-2 [DDD]

Heilmann, Uwe (ten) (cont.)
Mozart, W.A.:Zauberflöte (sels), w. S. Jo (sop), R. Ziesak (sop), A. Kraus (ten), K. Moll (bass), G. Solti (cnd), Vienna PO, Vienna State Opera Chorus London ▲ 433667-2 [DDD]
Strauss, R.:Capriccio, w. Kiri Te Kanawa (sop—Gräfin), Brigitte Fassbaender (mez—Clairon), Uwe Heilmann (ten—Flamand), Werner Hollweg (ten—Taupe), Olaf Bär (bar—Olivier), Håkan Hagegård (bar—Graf), Victor von Halem (b-bar—La Roche), U. Schirmer (cnd), Vienna PO [G] *(rec Vienna, Dec 1993)* London 2-▲ 444405-2 [DDD]
Vivaldi, A.:Gloria, RV.589, w. B. Hendricks (sop), A. Murray (mez), J. Rigby (mez), J. Hynninen (bar), N. Marriner (cnd), Academy of St. Martin in the Fields, Academy Chorus EMI Classics ▲ CDC 54283
Wagner, R.:Der fliegende Holländer, w. H. Beherns (sop—Senta), I. Vermillion (mez—Mary), U. Heilmann (ten—Helmsman), J. Protschka (ten—Erik), R. Hale (bar—The Dutchman), K. Rydl (bass—Daland), C. von Dohnányi (cnd), Vienna PO, Vienna State Opera Chorus London 2-▲ 436418-2 [DDD]

Heimes, Laura (sop)
Buxtehude, D.:Cants, w. Tamara Crout Matthews (sop), Steven Richards (ct), James Russell (ten), John Alston (bass), M. N. Johnson (cnd), Sarum Consort, St. Peter's in the Great Valley Chamber Choir—Wachet auf, ruft uns die Stimme!; Singet dem Herrn; Quemadmodum desiderat cervus; O fröhliche Stunden, o herrliche Zeit; Jubilate Domino omnis terra; Lobe den Herrn, meine Seele; Erfreue dich, Erde! *(rec St-Martin-in-the-Fields Church, Chestnut Hill, PA, Sept 7-9, 1994)* Pro gloria musicae ▲ PGM 102 [DDD]

Héja, Benedek (trb)
Puccini, G.:Tosca (sels), w. E. Marton (sop), J. Carreras (ten), F. Gerdesits (ten), J. Pons (bar), J. Nemeth (bar), J. Gregor (bass), M. Tilson Thomas (cnd), Hungarian State Orch, Hungarian Radio-TV Chorus *(rec Budapest, Dec. 14-22, 1988)* Sony Classical ("Opera Highlights" series) ▲ SMK 53500 [DDD]

Helder, Ruby (sgr)
The Girl Tenor *(rec 1908-1914)* Pearl ▲ PEA 9035 [AAD]

Heldwein, Walter (bass)
Bach, J.S.:Cant 2, w. H. Watts (cta), A. Baldin (ten), H. Rilling (cnd), Stuttgart Bach Collegium, Gächinger Kantorei Hänssler Classic ▲ 98.801 [AAD]
Bach, J.S.:Cant 24, w. A. Augér (sop), H. Watts (cta), K. Pugh (cta), A. Kraus (ten), W. Schöne (bass), H. Rilling (cnd), Stuttgart Bach Collegium, Gächinger Kantorei Hänssler Classic ▲ 98.803 [AAD]
Bach, J.S.:Cant 28, w. A. Augér (sop), G. Schreckenbach (cta), A. Kraus (ten), H. Rilling (cnd), Stuttgart Bach Collegium, Gächinger Kantorei [G] *(rec Nov 1981 & Feb 1982)* Hänssler Classic ▲ 98.827 [AAD]
Bach, J.S.:Cant 36, w. A. Augér (sop), G. Schreckenbach (cta), P. Schreier (ten), H. Rilling (cnd), Stuttgart Bach Collegium, Gächinger Kantorei [G] *(rec Oct 1980, Feb 1981 & Mar)* Hänssler Classic ▲ 98.823 [AAD]
Bach, J.S.:Cant 57, w. A. Augér (sop), H. Rilling (cnd), Stuttgart Bach Collegium, Gächinger Kantorei [G] *(rec Nov 1981 & Feb 1982)* Hänssler Classic ▲ 98.825 [AAD]
Bach, J.S.:Cant 63, w. A. Augér (sop), J. Hamari (mez), H. Laurich (cta), A. Kraus (ten), W. Schöne (bass), H. Rilling (cnd), Stuttgart Bach Collegium, Gächinger Kantorei [G] *(rec Feb 1971 & Feb 1981)* Hänssler Classic ▲ 98.823 [AAD]
Bach, J.S.:Cant 83, w. H. Watts (cta), A. Kraus (ten), H. Rilling (cnd), Bach Ensemble [G] *(rec 1979)* Hänssler Classic ▲ 98.875 [AAD]
Bach, J.S.:Cant 86, w. A. Augér (mez), H. Watts (cta), A. Kraus (ten), H. Rilling (cnd), Stuttgart Bach Collegium, Gächinger Kantorei [G] *(rec 1979)* Hänssler Classic ▲ 98.885 [AAD]
Bach, J.S.:Cant 87, w. J. Hamari (cta), A. Baldin (ten), H. Rilling (cnd), Stuttgart Bach Collegium, Gächinger Kantorei [G] *(rec 1980-81)* Hänssler Classic ▲ 98.885 [AAD]
Bach, J.S.:Cant 95, w. A. Augér (sop), A. Kraus (ten), H. Rilling (cnd), Stuttgart Bach Collegium, Württemberg CO, Gächinger Kantorei Hänssler Classic ▲ 98.812 [AAD]
Bach, J.S.:Cant 98, w. A. Augér (sop), J. Hamari (cta), L.-M. Harder (ten), H. Rilling (cnd), Stuttgart Bach Collegium, Gächinger Kantorei [G] *(rec Oct 1982 & July 1983)* Hänssler Classic ▲ 98.817 [AAD]
Bach, J.S.:Cant 153, w. A. Murray (mez), A. Kraus (ten), H. Rilling (cnd), Stuttgart Bach Collegium, Gächinger Kantorei [G] Hänssler Classic ▲ 98.871 [AAD]
Bach, J.S.:Cant 164, w. E. Wiens (sop), J. Hamari (cta), L.-M. Harder (ten), H. Rilling (cnd), Stuttgart Bach Collegium, Gächinger Kantorei Hänssler Classic ▲ 98.811 [AAD]
Bach, J.S.:Cant 171, w. A. Augér (sop), J. Hamari (cta), A. Badin (ten), H. Rilling (cnd), Württemberg CO, Gächinger Kantorei [G] Hänssler Classic ▲ 98.871 [AAD]
Bach, J.S.:Cant 180, w. A. Augér (sop), C. Watkinson (cta), A. Kraus (ten), H. Rilling (cnd), Stuttgart Bach Collegium, Gächinger Kantorei [G] *(rec Feb & Oct 1979)* Hänssler Classic ▲ 98.816 [AAD]
Bach, J.S.:Cant 183, w. A. Augér (sop), J. Hamari (cta), P. Schreier (ten), H. Rilling (cnd), Stuttgart Bach Collegium, Gächinger Kantorei Hänssler Classic ▲ 98.801 [AAD]
Bach, J.S.:Cant 188, w. A. Augér (sop), J. Hamari (cta), A. Baldin (ten), H. Rilling (cnd), Württemberg CO, Gächinger Kantorei [G] *(rec June & Sept 1983)* Hänssler Classic ▲ 98.817 [AAD]
Bach, J.S.:Cant 198, w. J. Beckmann (sop), A. Kraus (ten), H. Rilling (cnd), Stuttgart Bach Collegium, Gächinger Kantorei [G] *(rec Sept 1976 & Jan 1977)* Hänssler Classic ▲ 98.827 [AAD]

Helfrich, Christine (sop)
Myers, G.:God's Trbn, w. Gordon Myers (bar), Richard Cragg (sgr), Matthew Gillis (sgr), Timothy Pehta (sgr), Paul Norman (sgr), Wendy Catlin (sgr) Katherine Mary Hamilton (sgr), Sharon Hunter (sgr), Gloriae Dei Brass Ensemble Paraclete ▲ CDGD 017 [DDD]; ■ GDC 017

Helguera, Guillermo (nar)
Balada, L.:Maria Sabina, w. Hector Cortés (nar—Executioner), Amèrica Dunham (nar—Maria Sabina), Burwell Hardy (nar—Town Crier), Guillermo Helguera (nar—Constable), J. Mester (cnd), Louisville Orch, Richard Spalding (cnd), Louisville Univ Chorus *(rec Feb 5, 1973)* New World ▲ 80498-2
Balada, L.:Maria Sabina, w. América Dunham (nar—Maria Sabina), Burwell Hardy (nar—Town Crier), Guillermo Helguera (nar—Constable), Hector Cortés (nar—Executioner), J. Mester (cnd), Louisville Orch, Richard Spalding (cnd), Univ of Louisville Choir New World ▲ 804982

Helii, Michalis (sgr)
Glanville-Hicks, P.:Nausicaa (sels), w. Teresa Stratas (sop), Spiro Malas (bass), Michalis Heliots (sgr), George Moutsio (sgr), Edward Ruhl (sgr), Sophia Steffan (sop), George Tsantikos (sgr), C. Surinach (cnd), Athens SO, Athens Sym Chorus CRI ▲ CD 695 [ADD]

Heliotis, Michalis (ten)
Glanville-Hicks, P.:Nausicaa, w. Teresa Stratas (sop—Nausicaa), Sophia Steffan (cta—Queen Arete), Michalis Heliotis (ten—Antinous/Priest), George Moutsios (ten—Eurymachus), Edward Ruhl (ten—Phemius), George Tsantikos (ten—Clytoneus), Vassilis Koundouris (bar—Messenger), John Modenos (bar—Aethon), Spiro Malas (bass—King Alcinous), C. Surinach (cnd), Athens SO, Athens Sym Chorus *(rec Athens Festival, 1961)* CRI ▲ CD 695 [ADD]
Glanville-Hicks, P.:Nausicaa (sels), w. Teresa Stratas (sop), Spiro Malas (bass), Michalis Helii (sgr), George Moutsio (sgr), Edward Ruhl (sgr), Sophia Steffan (sop), George Tsantikos (sgr), C. Surinach (cnd), Athens SO, Athens Sym Chorus CRI ▲ CD 695 [ADD]

Hellekant, Charlotta (mez)
Bergman, E.:The Singing Tree, w. K. Hannula (sop), P. Lindroos (ten), P. Salomaa (bass), S. Tiilikainen (bar), M. Wallén (bass), U. Söderblom (cnd), Finnish National Opera Orch, Dominante Chamber Choir, Tapiola Chamber Choir Ondine 2-▲ ODE 794-2D [DDD]
Mahler, G.:Sym 2, w. R. Ziesak (sop), H. Blomstedt (cnd), San Francisco SO, San Francisco Sym Chorus London ▲ 443350-2

Helleland, Arild (ten)
Braein, E.F.:Anne Pedersdotter, w. K. Ekeberg (sop—Anne Pedersdotter), V. Hanssen (mez—Merete Beyer), R. Eriksen (alt—Herlofs-Marte), I. M. Brekke (alt—Bente), K. M. Sandve (ten—Martin Beyer), C. Ehrstedt (ten—Master Olaus), A. Helleland (ten—David), T. Gilje (ten—Jørund), S. A. Thorsen (bar—Master Johannes), S. Carlsen (bass—Absalon Pedersøn Beyer), T. Stensvold (bass—Master Laurentius), G. Oskarsson (bass—Jens Schelderup), P. Andersson (cnd), Norwegian National Opera Orch, Norwegian National Opera Chorus Simax 2-▲ PSC 3121

Heller, Joan (sop)
Babbitt, M.:Phonemena Sop & Tape Neuma ▲ 450-89
Bazelon, I.:Legends & Love Letters, w. F. Epstein (perc), C. Oldfather (pno), R. Annis (cl), J. Scolnik (fl), J. Moerchel (vc), C. Fussell (cnd), Collage New Music Ensemble Albany ▲ TROY 054 [DDD]
Berio, L.:Sequenza III Neuma ▲ 450-89

Heller, Joan (sop) (cont.)

Child, P.:Clare Cycle, w. D. Hoose (cnd), Collage New Music Ensemble [E] CRI ▲ CD 605 [DDD]
Cogan, R.:Polyutterances, w. T. Stumpf (pno) Neuma ▲ 450-89
Cogan, R.:Utterances Neuma ▲ 450-72 [DDD]
Fussell, C.C.:Songs, w. T. Stumpf (pno)—Goethe Lieder Neuma ▲ 450-89
Stumpf, T.:Lear's Daughters, w. T. Stumpf (pno) Neuma ▲ 450-89
Ung, C.:Tall Wind, w. Keith Underwood (fl), Robert Atherholt (ob), David Starobin (gtr), Chris Finckel (vc), A. Weisberg (cnd) *(rec Vanguard Recording Studio, New York, 1982)* CRI ▲ CRI 710 [DDD/ADD]

Heller, Marc (ten)

Sondheim, S.:Songs, w. Martin Ormandy (vc), Alfred Heller (pno)—The Hills of Tomorrow; Take Me to the World; Another 100 People; Not While I'm Around; You Must Meet My Wife; Send in the Clowns; Comedy Tonight; Love I Hear; Later; Anyone Can Whistle; Pretty Women; Losing My Mind; Johanna; Good Thing Going; Silly People; Ev'rybody Says Don't; Loving You; Green Finch & Linnet Bird; Being Alive; One More Kiss; Sunday Etcetera ▲ KTC 1185

Helletsgruber, Luise (sop)

Beethoven, L. van:Sym 9, "Choral Sym", w. Rosette Anday (cta), Georg Maikl (ten), Richard Mayr (bass), F. von Weingartner (cnd), Vienna PO, Vienna State Opera Chorus *(rec Feb. 2–5, 1935)* Preiser ▲ PRE 90193 [ADD]
Gounod, C.:Faust (sels), w. Luise Helletsgruber (sop—Marguerite), Helge Roswaenge (ten—Faust), Joel Berglund (ten—Mephistopheles), J. Krips (cnd), Vienna State Opera Orch *(rec Vienna, Nov. 10, 1936)* Koch Schwann 2–▲ SCH 314622 [ADD]
Mozart, W.A.:Arias, w. Arleen Augér (sop), Kathleen Battle (sop), Irma Beilke (sop), Helena Braun (sop), Lisa Della Casa (sop), Maria Cebotari (sop), Ileana Cotrubas (sop), Helen Donath (sop), Mirella Freni (sop), Reri Grist (sop), Edita Gruberova (sop), Elisabeth Grümmer (sop), Hilde Güden (sop), Ingeborg Hallstein (sop), Gundula Janowitz (sop), Sena Jurinac (sop), Erika Köth (sop), Evelyn Lear (sop), Wilma Lipp (sop), Margaret Marshall (sop), Edith Mathis (sop), Jarmila Novotna (sop), Margherita Perras (sop), Lucia Popp (sop), Elisabeth Rethberg (sop), Anneliese Rothenberger (sop), Elisabeth Schumann (sop), Elisabeth Schwarzkopf (sop), Graziella Sciutti (sop), Irmgard Seefried (sop), Graziella Sciutti (sop), Julia Varady (sop), Agnes Baltsa (mez), Margit Bokor (mez), Brigitte Fassbaender (mez), Christa Ludwig (mez), Ann Murray (mez), Francisco Araiza (ten), Anton Dermota (ten), Helge Rosvaenge (ten), Rudolf Schock (ten), Peter Schreier (ten), Leopold Simoneau (ten), Eric Tappy (ten), Richard Tauber (ten), Gösta Winbergh (ten), Josef Witt (ten), Fritz Wunderlich (ten), Christian Boesch (bar), Willy Domgraf–Fassbaender (bar), Karl Dönch (bar), Dietrich Fischer–Dieskau (bar), Erich Kunz (bar), Eberhard Wächter (bar), Hans Hotter (b–bar), Paul Schöffler (b–bar), Cesare Siepi (b–bar), José Van Dam (b–bar), Walter Berry (bass), Geraint Evans (bass), Nicolai Ghiaurov (bass), Alexander Kipnis (bass), Richard Mayr (bass), Kurt Moll (bass), James Morris (bass), Ezio Pinza (bass), Martti Talvela (bass), Giorgio Tozzi (bass), Hans Duhan (sgr), Res Fischer (sgr), Marie Gerhart (sgr), *(various orchs & cnds)*—sels from Idomeneo, Die Entführung aus der Serail, Le nozze di Figaro, Don Giovanni, Così fan tutte, Die Zauberflöte & various arias Orfeo d'or ("Festspiel Dokumente" series) 5–▲ 408955
Mozart, W.A.:Così fan tutte, w. I. Souez (sop), I. Eisinger (sop), H. Nash (ten), W. Domgraf–Fassbüander (bar), J. Brownlee (bar), F. Busch (cnd), Glyndebourne Festival Orch, Glyndebourne Festival Chorus [I] *(rec 1935)* Pearl 3–▲ PEAS 9406 (m) [AAD]
Mozart, W.A.:Così fan tutte, w. Irene Eisinger (sop—Despina), Luise Helletsgruber (sop—Dorabella), Ina Souez (sop—Fiordiligi), Heddle Nash (ten—Ferrando), John Brownlee (bass—Don Alfonso), Willi Domgraf–Fassbaender (bass—Guglielmo), F. Busch (cnd), Glyndebourne Festival Orch, Glyndebourne Festival Chorus *(rec June 25–28, 1935)* Arkadia ("The 78's" series) 2–▲ 78011 [ADD]
Mozart, W.A.:Don Giovanni, w. I. Souez (sop), A. Mildmay (sop), K. von Pataky (ten), J. Brownlee (bar), R. Henderson (bar), T. Franklin (bar), S. Baccaloni (bass), F. Busch (cnd), Glyndebourne Festival Orch, Glyndebourne Festival Chorus [I] *(rec 1936, orig. issued by HMV)* Pearl 3–▲ PEAS 9369 (m) [AAD]
Mozart, W.A.:Don Giovanni, w. E. Rethberg (sop), M. Bokor (mez), D. Borgioli (ten), A. Lazzari (ten), E. Pinza (bass), B. Walter (cnd), Salzburg Orch, Salzburg Mozarteum Chorus [I] *(rec live, Salzburg, Aug. 2, 1937)* Melodram ("Connaisseur" series) 3–▲ CD 37506 (m) [AAD]
Mozart, W.A.:Don Giovanni, w. E. Rethberg (sop), M. Bokor (mez), D. Borgioli (ten), K. Ettl (bass), E. Pinza (bass), B. Walter (cnd), Vienna PO, Vienna State Opera Chorus *(rec Salzburg, Aug. 2, 1937)* Melodram 3–▲ MLO 37506 [ADD]
Mozart, W.A.:Nozze di Figaro, w. Audrey Mildmay (sop), Aulikki Rautawaara (sop), Willi Domgraf–Fassbaender (bar), Roy Henderson (bar), F. Busch (cnd), Glyndebourne Festival Orch, Glyndebourne Festival Chorus *(rec 1934)* Grammofono 2000 2–▲ GRM 78624
Mozart, W.A.:Nozze di Figaro (sels), w. Audrey Mildmay (sop), Aulikki Rautawaara (sop), Constance Willis (mez), John Heddle Nash (ten), Willi Domgraf–Fassbaender (bar), Roy Henderson (bar), Norman Allin (bass), F. Busch (cnd), Glyndebourne Festival Orch Pearl ▲ PEA CD 9230

Helling, Hilke (cta)

Fux, J.J.:La Fede sacrilega nella morte del Precursor San Giovanni Battista, "Johannes der Täufer", w. J. Koslowsky (sop), M. Lins (sop), J. Calaminus (ten), G. Schwarz (bass), T. Reuber (cnd), Capella Piccola Neuss [period instrs] [I] Thorofon 2–▲ CTH 2071/72 [DDD]
Satie, E.:Socrate, w. D. Richards (pno) [composer's version for voice & piano] Wergo ▲ WER 6186–2 [DDD]
Weill, K.:Der Jasager, w. T. Schmeisser (treb), T. Bräutigam (ten), T. Fischer (ten), U. Schütte (bar), M. Knöppel (bass), W. Gundlach (cnd), Westphalia CO, Westphalia Kantorei Capriccio ▲ 60 020–1 [DDD]

Hellmann, Andrea (alt)

Bruckner, A.:Mass 3, w. M. Stader (sop), E. Haefliger (ten), K. Borg (bass), E. Jochum (cnd), Bavarian RSO, Bavarian Radio Chorus [L] Deutsche Grammophon 4–▲ 423127–2 [ADD]
Reger, M.:Cantatas, w. V. Schweizer (sop), R. Julius Koch (ob), R. Hellmann, U. Soldan (vn), B. Banz (va), C. Hellmann (vc), C. Fink (db), H. Bilgram (org), D. Hellmann (cnd), Mainz Bach Choir Entrée ▲ 0049 [ADD]

Hellmann, Claudia (mez)

Bruckner, A.:Mass 3, w. M. Stader (sop), E. Haefliger (ten), K. Borg (bass), E. Jochum (cnd), Bavarian RSO, Bavarian Radio Chorus Deutsche Grammophon ("The Originals" series) 2–▲ 447409–2

Helm, Hans (bar)

Schreker, F.:Der Schatzgräber, w. G. Schnaut (sop), J. Protschka (ten), H. Stamm (bass), G. Albrecht (cnd), Hamburg State Opera Orch, Hamburg State Opera Chorus [G] *(rec live 5/89)* Capriccio 2–▲ 60010–2 [DDD]
Wagner, R.:Lohengrin, w. Leonore Kirchstein (sop—Elsa von Brabant), Ruth Hesse (mez—Ortrud), Herbert Schachtschneider (ten—Lohengrin), Hans Helm (bar—Der Heerrufer des Königs), Otto von Rohr (bass—Heinrich der Vogler), Heinz Imdahl (sgr—Friedrich von Telramund), H. Swarowsky (cnd), Czech PO, Prague National Theater Orch, Vienna State Opera Chorus *(rec Aug 1968)* Weltbild Classics 3–▲ 703835 [ADD]

Helm, Karl (sgr)

Wagner, R.:Rienzi, der Letzte der Tribunen, w. Cheryl Studer (sop—Irene), René Kollo (ten—Rienzi), Friedrich Lenz (ten—Gesandte), Norbert Orth (ten—Baroncelli), Bodo Brinkmann (bar—Paolo Orsini), Keith Engen (bass—Cecco del Vecchio), Raimund Grumbach (bass—Gesandte), Jan–Hendrik Rootering (bass—Steffano Colonna), Carmen Anhorn (sgr—Ein Friedensbote), Karl Helm (sgr—Kardinal Orvieto), John Janssen (sgr—Adriano), Alfred Kuhn (sgr—Gesandte), Hans Wilbrink (sgr—Gesandte), W. Sawallisch (cnd), Bavarian State Opera Orch, Bavarian State Opera Chorus *(rec live, July 6, 1983)* Orfeo d'or 3–▲ 346953

Helmke, Erika (sop)

Weill, K.:The Threepenny Opera, w. L. Lenya (sop), K. Gerron (sgr), T. Mackeben (cnd), *(orch unknown)* [G] *(rec original German cast, 1930)* Mastersound ▲ DFCD1–110 (m) [ADD]
Weill, K.:The Threepenny Opera, w. L. Lenya (sop), K. Gerron (sgr), T. Mackeben (cnd), *(orch unknown)* [G] *(rec original German cast, 1930)* Teldec ▲ 9031–72025–2 [ADD]

Helmsey, Thomas (bar)

Wagner, R.:Die Meistersinger von Nürnberg, w. Gundula Janowitz (sop), Brigitte Fassbaender (mez), Sándor Kónya (ten), Gerhard Unger (ten), Thomas Stewart (bar), Franz Crass (bass), R. Kubelik (cnd), Bavarian RSO, Bavarian Radio Chorus *(rec 1967)* Calig 4–▲ 5097174 [ADD]

Heltau, Michael (nar)

Mozart, W.A.:Entführung, w. Reri Grist (sop—Blondchen), Anneliese Rothenberger (sop—Konstanze), Gerhard Unger (ten—Pedrillo), Fritz Wunderlich (ten—Belmonte), Fernando Corena (bass—Osmin), Michael Heltau (nar—Selim), Z. Mehta (cnd), Vienna PO, Vienna State Opera Chorus *(rec July 28, 1965)* Orfeo d'or ("Festspiel Dokumente" series) 2–▲ 392952 (m)
Mozart, W.A.:Entführung, w. C. Studer (sop), E. Szmytka (sop), K. Streit (ten), R. Gambill (ten), G. Missenhardt (bar), B. Weil (cnd), Vienna SO, Vienna State Opera Chorus Sony Classical 2–▲ S2K 48053

Hemm, Manfred (bar)

Alcalay, L.:fluchtpunktzeile, w. C. Ascher (mez), C. Kalmar (cnd), Vienna SO Vienna Modern Masters ▲ VMM 3020 [AAD]
Dvořák, A.:Biblical Songs, Op. 99, w. Z. Macal (cnd), New Jersey SO *(rec Apr. 9, 1994)* Delos 2–▲ DE 3161 [DDD]

Hemmings, David (trb)

Britten, H.:The Turn of the Screw, w. O. Dyer (sop), J. Vyvyan (sop), A. Mandikian (mez), G. Cross (ten), P. Pears (ten), B. Britten (cnd), English Opera Group Orch [E] London ▲ 425672–2 (m) [ADD]

Hempel, Frieda (sop)

Frieda Hempel *(rec between 1909 & 1925)* Pearl ▲ PEA 9032 [AAD]
Frieda Hempel Recordings from 1910–1935 Nimbus ▲ NI 7849
Pasquale Amato, w. Pasquale Amato (bar), Margarete Matzenauer (mez) *(rec by Victor & Fonotipia 1909–1914)* Preiser ("Lebendige Vergangenheit" series) ▲ PRE 89064 (m) [AAD]

Hemsley, Thomas (bar)

Bach, C.P.E.:Magnificat, w. Jennifer Vyvyan (sop), Helen Watts (cta), Wilfred Brown (ten), G. Jones (cnd), Geraint Jones Orch, Geraint Jones Singers EMI Classics ("Baroque" series) ▲ CDK 65737
Bach, J.S.:Magnificat, BWV 243, w. Anne Pashley (sop), Lucia Popp (sop), Janet Baker (mez), Robert Tear (ten), D. Barenboim (cnd), New Philharmonia Orch, New Philharmonia Chorus *(rec All Saints, Tooting, London, May 1968)* EMI Classics ▲ CDK 65334 [ADD]
Bliss, A.:The Olympians, w. R. Woodland (sop), S. Minty (mez), R. Herincx (bass), B. Fairfax (cnd), Polyphonia Orch, Ambrosian Singers *(rec 1972)* Intaglio 2–▲ ING 755 [ADD]
Delius, F.:Requiem, w. H. Harper (sop), C. Groves (cnd), Royal Liverpool PO, Royal Liverpool Phil Choir *(rec live, Liverpool 1965)* Intaglio 2–▲ INCD 702–2 [ADD]
Handel, G.F.:Alcina, w. J. Sutherland (sop), N. Procter (cta), N. Monti (ten), F. Wunderlich (ten), F. Leitner (cnd), Cappella Coloniensis, Cologne Radio Chorus Melodram 3–▲ CDM 37002
Wagner, R.:Die Meistersinger von Nürnberg, w. G. Janowitz (sop), B. Fassbaender (mez), S. Kónya (ten), G. Unger (ten), T. Stewart (bar), F. Crass (bass), R. Kubelik (cnd), Bavarian RSO, Bavarian Radio Chorus [G] *(rec live, Munich, Oct. 1967)* Myto 4–▲ 4 MCD 92569 [ADD]

Henderson, M. (sop)

Handel, D.:The Tyger, w. Sara Lambert Bloom (ob), Gabrielle Robinson (vn), Jina Lee (vn), Rebecca Boughton (va), Deborah Netanel (vc), Mark Butler (pno), C. Zimmerman (cnd) Vienna Modern Masters ▲ VMM 2019 [DDD]
Thome, D.:The Ruins of the Heart, w. G. Samuel (cnd), Cincinnati PO Centaur ▲ CRC 2144 [DDD]

Henderson, Roy (bar)

Gay, J.:The Beggar's Opera (sels), w. A. Mildmay (sop), M. Redgrave (sgr), *(orch & chorus unknown)*—ov; 37 songs [arr Frederic Austin, 1920] *(rec 1940 for HMV)* Pearl ▲ PEA 9917 (m) [AAD]
Mozart, W.A.:Don Giovanni, w. I. Souez (sop), L. Helletsgrüber (sop), A. Mildmay (sop), K. von Pataky (ten), J. Brownlee (bar), T. Franklin (bar), S. Baccaloni (bass), F. Busch (cnd), Glyndebourne Festival Orch, Glyndebourne Festival Chorus [I] *(rec 1936, orig. issued by HMV)* Pearl 3–▲ PEAS 9369 (m) [AAD]
Mozart, W.A.:Nozze di Figaro, w. Luise Helletsgrüber (sop), Audrey Mildmay (sop), Aulikki Rautawaara (sop), Willi Domgraf–Fassbaender (bar), F. Busch (cnd), Glyndebourne Festival Orch, Glyndebourne Festival Chorus *(rec 1934)* Grammofono 2000 2–▲ GRM 78624
Mozart, W.A.:Nozze di Figaro, w. Aulikki Rautawaara (sop), Audrey Mildmay (sop), Constance Willis (mez), John Heddle Nash (ten), Willi Domgraf–Fassbaender (bar), F. Busch (cnd), Glyndebourne Festival Orch, Glyndebourne Festival Chorus [I] *(rec 1934–35)* Pearl 2–▲ PEAS 9375 (m) [AAD]
Mozart, W.A.:Nozze di Figaro, w. Aulikki Rautawaara (sop), Audrey Mildmay (sop), Constance Willis (mez), John Heddle Nash (ten), Willi Domgraf–Fassbaender (bar), F. Busch (cnd), Glyndebourne Festival Orch *(rec 1934)* Legend 2–▲ LGD 132 [ADD]
Mozart, W.A.:Nozze di Figaro (sels), w. Luise Helletsgrüber (sop), Audrey Mildmay (sop), Aulikki Rautawaara (sop), Constance Willis (mez), John Heddle Nash (ten), Willi Domgraf–Fassbaender (bar), Norman Allin (bass), F. Busch (cnd), Glyndebourne Festival Orch Pearl ▲ PEA CD 9230
Stravinsky, I.:Les Noces, w. K. Winter (sop), L. Seymour (cta), P. Jones (ten), I. Stravinsky (cnd), *(orch & chorus unknown)* EMI Classics 2–▲ ZDCB 54607
Vaughan Williams, R.:Dona nobis pacem, w. R. Flynn (sop), R. Vaughan Williams (cnd), BBC SO, BBC Sym Chorus [E,L] *(rec 11/36, broadcast transcri)* Pearl ▲ GEMMCD 9342 (m) [AAD]
Vaughan Williams, R.:Serenade to Music, w. I. Baillie (sop), E. Suddaby (sop), S. Allen (sop), E. Turner (sop), M. Balfour (cta), A. Desmond (cta), M. Brunskill (cta), M. Jarred (cta), H. Nash (ten), W. Widdop (ten), P. Jones (ten), F. Titterton (ten), R. Henderson (bass), R. Easton (bass), H. Williams (bass), N. Allin (bass), H. J. Wood (cnd), BBC SO Dutton Laboratories ▲ CDAX 8004 [ADD]
Vaughan Williams, R.:Serenade to Music, w. I. Baillie (sop), E. Suddaby (sop), S. Allen (sop), E. Turner (sop), M. Balfour (cta), A. Desmond (cta), M. Brunskill (cta), M. Jarred (cta), H. Nash (ten), W. Widdop (ten), P. Jones (ten), F. Titterton (ten), R. Henderson (bass), R. Easton (bass), H. Williams (bass), N. Allin (bass), H. Wood (cnd), BBC SO [E] *(rec 10/15/38)* Pearl ▲ GEMMCD 9342 (m) [AAD]
Vaughan Williams, R.:Serenade to Music, w. Isobel Baillie (sop), Lilian Stiles–Allen (sop), Elsie Suddaby (sop), Eva Turner (sop), Margaret Balfour (cta), Muriel Brunskill (cta), Astra Desmond (cta), Mary Jarred (cta), Parry Jones (ten), Heddle Nash (ten), Frank Titterton (ten), Walter Widdop (ten), Roy Henderson (bar), Harold Williams (bar), Norman Allin (bass), Robert Easton (bass), H. Wood (cnd), BBC SO *(rec Abbey Road, Oct 15, 1938)* Claremont ▲ CDGSE 785066

Hendricks, Barbara (sop)

Bach, J.S.:Magnificat, BWV 243, w. J. Rigby (sop), A. Murray (mez), U. Heilmann (ten), J. Hynninen (bar), N. Marriner (cnd), Academy of St. Martin in the Fields, *(chorus unknown)* EMI Classics ▲ CDC 54283–2
Barber, S.:Knoxville:Summer of 1915, w. M. Tilson Thomas (cnd), London SO EMI Classics ▲ CDC 55358
Barber, S.:Songs, w. M. Tilson Thomas (cnd), London SO—Nocturne; Sure on This Shining Night EMI Classics ▲ CDC 55358
Basic 100, Vol. 60, w. John Aler (ten), Håkan Hagegård (bar), London SO [cnd:Eduardo Mata] RCA Victor ▲ 09026–68085–2 ■ 09026–68085–4
Bizet, G.:Les Pêcheurs de perles, w. J. Aler (ten), G. Quilico (bar), M. Plasson (cnd), Toulouse Capitole Orch, Toulouse Capitole Chorus [F] EMI Classics 2–▲ CDCB 49837 [DDD]
Brahms, J.:Ein Deutsches Requiem, w. J. Van Dam (bar), H. von Karajan (cnd), Vienna PO, Vienna Singverein [G] *(rec 1986)* Deutsche Grammophon ▲ 431651–2 [DDD]
Copland, A.:Poems (8) of Emily Dickinson, w. M. Tilson Thomas (cnd), London SO EMI Classics ▲ CDC 55358
Copland, A.:Quiet City, w. M. Tilson Thomas (cnd), London SO EMI Classics ▲ CDC 55358
Donizetti, G.:Don Pasquale, w. L. Canonici (ten), G. Bacquier (bar), L. Quilico (bar), R. Schirrer (bar), G. Ferro (cnd), Paris Lyon Opera Orch, Paris Lyon Opera Chorus [I] Erato 2–▲ 2292–45487–2–ZA [DDD]
Enescu, G.:Oedipe, w. B. Fassbaender (mez), M. Lipovšek (mez), J. Taillon (mez), N. Gedda (ten), J. Aler (ten), G. Bacquier (bar), Quilico (bar), J. Van Dam (bass–bar), L. Foster (cnd), Monte Carlo PO, Orféon Donostiarra, Petits Chanteurs de Monaco [F] EMI Classics 2–▲ CDCB 54011 [DDD]
Fauré, G.:La bonne chanson, w. M. Dalberto (pno) EMI Classics ▲ CDC 49841
Fauré, G.:Songs, w. M. Dalberto (pno)—Trois poèmes d'un jour & 16 (sels.) EMI Classics ▲ CDC 49841
Gershwin, G.:Songs, w. K. Labèque (pno), M. Labèque (pno) Philips ▲ 416460–2 [ADD]
Gounod, C.:Messe solennelle de St. Cécile, w. L. Dale (ten), J.–P. Lafont (bass), G. Prêtre (cnd), Radio France PO, French Radio Chorus [L] EMI Classics ▲ CDC 47094
Gounod, C.:Mors et vita, w. N. Denize (mez), J. Aler (ten), J. Van Dam (b–bar), M. Plasson (cnd), Toulouse Capitole Orch, Orféon Donostiarra [F] *(rec 1/92)* EMI Classics 2–▲ CDCB 54459

Hendricks, Barbara (sop) (cont.)

Great American Spirtuals, w. Kathleen Battle (sop), Florence Quivar (mez) Angel ▲ CDM 64669

Grieg, E.:Peer Gynt, w. E.–P. Salonen (cnd), Oslo PO, Oslo Phil Chorus CBS ▲ MK 44528 [DDD] □ MM 44528

Handel, G.F.:Serse, w. Barbara Hendricks (sop—Romilda), Anne–Marie Rodde (sop—Atalanta), Carolyn Watkinson (cta—Xerxes), Otrun Wenkel (cta—Amastre), Paul Esswood (ct—Arsamene), Ulrich Studer (bar—Elviro), Ulrik Cold (bass—Ariodate), J. Malgoire (cnd), La Grande Ecurie et la Chambre du Roy *(rec Paris, 1979)* Sony Classical 3–▲ SM3K 36941

Handel, G.F.:Solomon, w. Nancy Argenta (sop), Carolyn Watkinson (cta), Anthony Rolfe Johnson (ct), J. E. Gardiner (cnd), English Baroque Soloists, Monteverdi Choir London [E] Philips 2–▲ 412612–2 [DDD]

Humperdinck, E.:Hänsel und Gretel, w. B. Bonney (sop), E. Lind (sop), A.S. von Otter (mez), H. Schwarz (mez), M. Lipovšek (mez), Andreas Schmidt (bar), J. Tate (cnd), Bavarian RSO, Tölz Boys' Choir [G] EMI Classics 2–▲ CDCB 54022 [DDD]

Mahler, G.:Syms, w. J. Blegen (sop), M. Price (sop), G. Zeumer (sop), H. Wittek (trb), A. Baltsa (mez), C. Ludwig (mez), K. Riegel (ten), H. Prey (bar), A. Schmidt (bar), J. Van Dam (b–bar), L. Bernstein (cnd), New York PO, Royal Concertgebouw Orch, Vienna PO, Westminster Choir, New York Choral Artists, Brooklyn Boys' Choir, Vienna Boys' Choir, Vienna State Opera Chorus, Vienna Singverein Deutsche Grammophon 13–▲ 435162–2 [DDD]

Mahler, G.:Sym 4, w. E.–P. Salonen (cnd), Los Angeles PO [G] Sony Classical ▲ SK 48380 [DDD]

Mozart, W.A.:Arias, w. J. Sillman (org)., N. Marriner (cnd), Academy of St. Martin in the Fields, Academy Chorus EMI Classics ▲ CDC 49283

Mozart, W.A.:Complete Mozart Edition, w. J. Varady (sop), S. Mentzer (mez), F. Araiza (ten), T. Allen (bar), C. Davis (cnd), Bavarian RSO Philips 3–▲ 422537–2 [ADD]

Mozart, W.A.:Complete Mozart Edition, w. H.–P. Blochwitz (ten), P. Schreier (cnd), C.P.E. Bach CO Philips 2–▲ 422528–2 [ADD]

Mozart, W.A.:Missa, K.427, w. J. Perry (sop), P. Schreier (ten), B. Luxon (bar), H. von Karajan (cnd), Berlin PO Deutsche Grammophon ("Karajan Gold" series) ▲ 439012–2

Mozart, W.A.:Nozze di Figaro, w. L. Popp (sop), A. Baltsa (mez), G. Raimondi (ten), J. Van Dam (bar), N. Marriner (cnd), Academy of St. Martin in the Fields, Ambrosian Opera Chorus [I] Philips 3–▲ 416370–2 [DDD]

Mozart, W.A.:Nozze di Figaro (sels), w. L. Popp (sop), A. Baltsa (mez), G. Raimondi (ten), J. van Dam (b–bar), N. Marriner (cnd), Academy of St. Martin in the Fields, Ambrosian Opera Chorus [I] Philips ▲ 416870–2 [DDD]

Mozart, W.A.:Zauberflöte, w. B. Hendricks (sop—Pamina), J. Anderson (sop—Queen of the Night), U. Steinsky (sop—Papagena), J. Hadley (ten—Tamino), T. Allen (bar—Papageno), R. Lloyd (bass—Sarastro), C. Mackerras (cnd), Scottish CO, Scottish Chamber Chorus [G] Telarc 2–▲ CD 80302 [DDD]

Mozart, W.A.:Zauberflöte (sels), w. J. Hadley (sop), J. Anderson (sop), T. Allen (bar), R. Lloyd (b–bar), U. Steinsky (cnd), Scottish CO, Scottish Sym Chorus *(rec July 13–22, 1991)* Telarc ▲ CD 80345 [DDD]

Operetta Arias, w. Philharmonia Orch [cnd:Lawrence Foster] EMI Classics ▲ CDC 54626

Operetta Duets, w. Gino Quilico (bar), Lyon Opera Orch [cnd:Lawrence Foster] EMI Classics ▲ CDC 55151

Orff, C.:Carmina burana, w. John Aler (ten), Håakan Hagegård (bar), E. Mata (cnd), London SO, London Sym Chorus RCA Victor ▲ 09026–68085–2; ■ 09026–68085–4

Orff, C.:Carmina burana, w. M. Chance (ct), J. Black (bar), F. Welser–Möst (cnd), London PO, London Phil Chorus, St. Alban's Cathedral Choristers [G, L] EMI Classics ▲ CDC 54054 [DDD]

Plaisir d'Amour – Mélodies Françaises, w. Cherubini Quartet, Michel Dalberto (pno) EMI Classics ▲ CDC 55388

Puccini, G.:Turandot, w. K. Ricciarelli (sop), P. Domingo (ten), R. Raimondi (bass), H. von Karajan (cnd), Vienna PO, Vienna State Opera Chorus [I] Deutsche Grammophon 2–▲ 423855–2 [DDD]

Puccini, G.:Turandot (sels), w. K. Ricciarelli (sop), P. Domingo (ten), R. Raimondi (bass), H. von Karajan (cnd), Vienna PO, Vienna State Opera Chorus [I] Deutsche Grammophon ▲ 435409–2 [DDD]

Sacred Songs, w. Eric Ericson (cnd), Stockholm CO, Ericson's Chamber Choir EMI Classics ▲ CDC 54098 [DDD]

Schubert, Franz:Songs (comp), w. R. Lupu (pno), S. Meyer (cl), B. Schneider (hn)—Der Hirt auf dem Felsen; Lachen und weinen; Ständchen; Die Männer sind méchant, Auf dem Strom; Sehnsucht; Liebesbotschaft; Versunken; An den Mond; Du liebst mich nicht; Die Liebe hat gelogen; Die junge Nonne; Klaglied; Ellens Gesang III; Delphine; Heidenröslein [G] EMI Classics ▲ CDC 54239

Sings Spirituals, w. Dimitri Aklexeev (pno) EMI Classics ▲ CDC 47026 [DDD]

Strauss, R.:Die ägyptische Helena, w. G. Jones (sop), M. Kastu (ten), W. White (bass), C. Rayam (ten), B. Finnilä (mez), A. Dorati (cnd), Detroit SO London ("Grand Opera" series) 2–▲ 430381–2 [AAD]

Strauss, R.:4 Last Songs, w. Wolfgang Sawallisch (pno), W. Sawallisch (cnd), Philadelphia Orch EMI Classics ▲ CDC 55594

Strauss, R.:Der Rosenkavalier, w. K. Te Kanawa (sop), A. S. von Otter (mez), B. Haitink (cnd), Dresden Staatskapelle EMI Classics 3–▲ CDCC 54259

Strauss, R.:Der Rosenkavalier (sels), w. K. Te Kanawa (sop), A. S. von Otter (mez), R. Leech (ten), K. Rydl (bass), B. Haitink (cnd), Dresden Staatskapelle, Dresden State Opera Chorus EMI Classics ▲ ZDC 54493

Strauss, R.:Songs, w. Wolfgang Sawallisch (pno), W. Sawallisch (cnd), Philadelphia Orch—Ich wollt' ein Sträusslein binden; Säusle, liebe Myrthe; Kornblumen; Mohnblumen; Epheu; Wasserrose; Die Georgine; Die Zeitlose; Allerseelen; Ruhe, meine Seele!; Cäcilie; Heimliche Aufforderung; Morgen!; Das Rosenband; Heimkehr EMI Classics ▲ CDC 55594

Strauss, R.:Songs, w. R. Gothoni (pno)—22 songs EMI Classics ▲ CDC 54381

Vivaldi, A.:Gloria, RV.589, w. A. Murray (mez), J. Rigby (mez), U. Heilmann (ten), J. Hynninen (bar), N. Marriner (cnd), Academy of St. Martin in the Fields, Academy Chorus EMI Classics ▲ CDC 54283

When You Wish upon a Star, w. Jonathan Turick (cnd) Angel ▲ CDC 56177

Hendricks, Edward Scott (bar)

Vaughan Williams, R.:Epithalamion, w. R. Taylor (cnd), Chorus Civitas CO, Chorus Civitas *(rec The Stockade, Baton Rouge, Apr 24 & 27, 1995)* Centaur ▲ CRC 2299 [DDD]

Henius, Carla (alt)

Togni, C.:Gesang zur Nacht, w. Saschko Gawriloff (vn), Hans Damzel (cl), Werner Heider (pno), Mariolina de Robertis (pno) Stradivarius ▲ STV DTM 90002 [ADD]

Henkel, Gabriele (sgr)

Straus, O.:The Merry Nibelungs, w. Lisa Griffith (sop—Kriemhild), Gudrun Volkert (sop—Brunhilde), Daphne Evangelatos (cta—Ute), Gabriele Henkel (sgr—Giselher), Christine Mann (sgr—Vogel), Hein Heidbüchel (ten—Volker), Martin Gantner (sgr—Gunther), Gerd Grochowski (sgr—Dankwart), Michael Nowak (sgr—Siegfried), Josef Otten (sgr—Hagen), S. Köhler (cnd), Cologne RSO, Cologne Radio Chorus *(rec Cologne, Jan 31–Feb 17, 1995)* Capriccio ▲ 10752 [DDD]

Henneberger, J.–D. (nar)

Zbinden, J.–F.:Ethiopiques, w. A. Gerecz (cnd), Lausanne CO Grammont ▲ CTSP 3–2 [ADD]

Henneveux, Jean Guy (sgr)

Lehár, F.:Die lustige Witwe, w. Teresa Stich–Randall (mez—Missia Palmieri), Monique Stiot (mez—Manon), Germaine Duclos (sgr—Praskovia), Linda Felder (sgr—Olga), Christiane Jacquin (sgr—Nadia), Jeannette Levasseur (sgr—Sylviane), Henri Legay (ten—Camille de Coutançon), Joseph Peyron (ten—Kromsky), Robert Destain (sgr—Baron Popoff), Michel Fauche (sgr—Pristich), Gérard Friedmann (sgr—Lerida), Jacques Gilet (sgr—Bogdanowitch), Jean Guy Henneveux (sgr—Prince Danilo), Serge Klin (sgr—Figg), Jacques Villa (sgr—D'Estillac), A. Sibert (cnd), Belgian Radio–TV Orch, Belgian Radio–TV Chorus *(rec Grand Auditorium, Belgium, Apr 30, 1970)* Studio SM 2–▲ 2160 [AAD]

Hennig, Sebastian (trb)

Bach, J.S.:Cant 113, w. D. Bratschke (trb), R. Jacobs (ct), K. Equiluz (ten), M. van Egmond (b–bar), Leonhardt Consort, Collegium Vocale, Hanover Boys' Chorus [G] Teldec 2–▲ 2292–42606–2

Bach, J.S.:Cant 114, w. R. Jacobs (ct), K. Equiluz (ten), M. van Egmond (b–bar), Leonhardt Consort, Collegium Vocale, Hanover Boys' Chorus [G] Teldec 2–▲ 2292–42606–2

Hennig–Jensen, Gert (ten)

Gade, N.W.:Frühlings Fant, w. Anne Margrethe Dahl (sop), Kirsten Dolberg (cta), Sten Byriel (bass), Elisabeth Westenholz (pno), M. Schønwandt (cnd), Tivoli SO *(rec Tivoli Concert Hall, Apr 29–30, May 4, 1996)* Marco Polo/Dacapo ▲ 8.224051 [DDD]

Henning, S. (trb)

Pergolesi, G.B.:Stabat mater, w. R. Jacobs (alt), Concerto Vocale Harmonia Mundi ("Luxury Edition" series) ▲ HMX 2901119

Henreckson–Farnum, Elizabeth (sop)

Jane's Hand:The Jane Austen Songbooks, w. Julianne Baird (sop), Lorie Gratis (mez), Daniel Pincus (ten), Philip Anderson (ten), Martil Dillon (ten), Nancy Wilson (bar vn), Peter Segal (bar gtr), Mary Jane Newman (pno/hpd), Anthony Newman (pno) Vox Classics ▲ VOX 7537 [DDD]

Henri, Louie (sop)

Sullivan, A.:Iolanthe, w. H. Lytton (bar)—None Shall part us; H. Dearth—The sentry's song Symposium ▲ 1123

Henry, Clare (cta)

Handel, G.F.:Messiah (sels), w. Catherine Bott (sop), Gareth Roberts (ten), David Stephenson (bass), D. Jackson (cnd), London SO—Comfort Ye, My People, Saith Your God; Every Valley Shall Be Exalted; And the Glory of the Lord Shall Be Revealed; And He Shall Purify the Sons of Levi; For unto Us a Child Is Born; Pifa; Rejoice Greatly, O Daughter of Zion; Air:He Shall Feed His Flock Like a Shepherd; Behold the Lamb of God; He Was Despised and Rejected of Men; All We Like Sheep Have Gone Astray; The Trumpet Shall Sound; Chorus:Hallelujah! For the Lord God Omnipotent Reigneth Special Music Co. ▲ SCD 5102 [DDD]

Handel, G.F.:Messiah (sels), w. Catherine Bott (sop), Gareth Roberts (ten), David Stephenson (bass), D. Jackson (cnd), London SO—Comfort Ye, My People, Saith Your God; Every Valley Shall Be Exalted; And the Glory of the Lord Shall Be Revealed; And He Shall Purify the Sons of Levi; For unto Us a Child Is Born; Pifa; Rejoice Greatly, O Daughter of Zion; Air:He Shall Feed His Flock Like a Shepherd; Behold the Lamb of God; He Was Despised and Rejected of Men; All We Like Sheep Have Gone Astray; The Trumpet Shall Sound; Chorus:Hallelujah! For the Lord God Omnipotent Reigneth Special Music Co. 2–▲ S2D 5110 [DDD]

Henry, Didier (bar)

Chabrier, E.:Gwendoline, w. Adriana Kohútková (sop—Gwendoline), Gérard Garino (ten—Armel), Didier Henry (bar—Harald), J.–P. Pepin (cnd), Slovak PO, Czech Phil Chorus, Slovak Phil Chorus L'Empreinte Digitale 2–▲ ED 13059

Cras, J.:La Flûte de Pan, w. T. Prevost (fl), M.–C. Milliere (vn), J.–F. Benatar (va), P. Bary (vc)—[F] Quantum ▲ QM 6897 [DDD] ■ QM 1992 (D)

Debussy, C.:Pelléas et Mélisande, w. C. Alliot–Lugaz (sop), F. Golfier (sop), C. Carlson (mez), G. Cachemaille (bar), P. Thau (bass), C. Dutoit (cnd), Montreal SO, Montreal Sym Chorus [F] London 2–▲ 430502–2 [DDD]

Duruflé, M.:Mass, "Cum jubilo", w. M. Piquemal (cnd), Michel Piquemal Vocal Ensemble *(rec Eglise Saint Antoine des Quinze–Vingts Paris, June & Oct. 1994)* Naxos ▲ 8.553197 [DDD]

Leguerney, J.:Songs, w. Angéline Pondepeyre (pno)—7 poèmes de François Maynard; La nuit (3 songs); La solitude (3 songs); Le carnaval (3 songs) [all from St. Amand]; Je vous envoie; Genièvres hérissés; Bel Aubépin; Je me lamente; Au sommeil; Si mille oeillets; A la fontaine Bellerie; Chanson triste; Villanelle; Un voile obscur; Invocation; Comme un qui s'est perdu; Sérénade d'un Barbon; Le Paresseux; L'Insouciant *(rec July 1995)* Maguelone ("Mélodiste francais" series) ▲ MAG 519.232 [DDD]

Massenet, J.:Cléopâtre, w. B. Harries (sop), Daniéle Streiff (sop), M. Olmeda (sop), J. Maurette (ten), M. Hacquard (bar), P. Fournillier (cnd), St.–Etienne Nouvel Orch, Saint–Etienne Nouvel Chorus [F] *(rec live, Massenet Festival in Saint–Etienne 1990)* Koch Schwann 2–▲ 3–1032–2 [DDD]

Massenet, J.:Grisélidis, w. Michèle Command (sop), Brigitte Desnoues (sop), Jean–Luc Viala (ten), Maurice Sieyes (bar), Christian Treguier (bar), Jean–Philippe Courtis (bass), Claire Larcher (sgr), P. Fournillier (cnd), Franz Liszt SO, Budapest Lyon Chorus Koch Schwann 2–▲ SCH 312702 [DDD]

Massenet, J.:Songs, w. Angeline Pondepeyre (pno), Duo de Paris—Madrigal; Le sentier perdu; Nuit d'Espagne; Narcisse à la fontaine; Un adieu; Si les fleurs avaient des yeux; Sérénade de Zanetto; Puisqu'elle a pris ma vie; Vous aimerez demain; Elégie; A mignonne; La lettre; A colombine; Beaux yeux que j'Aime; Gavotte de Puyjoli; Fleurs cueillies; L'improvisateur; Poème du Souvenir *(rec 1868–1907)* Maguelone ▲ MAG 519.202 [DDD]

Ropartz, G.:Choral Music, w. Christian Papis (nar), Vincent Le Texier (b–bar), Christine Lajarrige (pno), Irène Brissot (hp), Eric Lebrun (org), M. Piquemal (cnd), Nancy SO, French Radio Chorus Soloists, Vittoria Regional French Choir—Psaume 136; Dimanche; Nocturne; Les Vêpres sonnent; Le Miracle de Saint Nicolas *(rec Salle Poirel, Nancy, Apr. 22–24, 1994)* Marco Polo ▲ 8.223774 [DDD]

Henry, R. (sgr)

Hoffmann, E.T.A.:Undine, w. Krisztina Láki (sop), Karl Ridderbusch (bass), R. Bader (cnd), Berlin RSO, St. Hedwig's Cathedral Choir *(rec Feb. 1982)* Koch Schwann 3–▲ SCH 310922 [DDD]

Henschel, Dieter (ten)

Schoeck, O.:Songs (comp), w. J. Banse (sop), W. Rieger (pno)—Wandsbecker Liederbuch, Op. 52; Im Nebel, Op. 45; 6 Lieder, Op. 51; 3 Lieder, Op. 35 *(rec May 1991)* Jecklin ▲ JD 677–2 [DDD]

Henschel, Dietrich (bar)

Gounod, C.:Messe solennelle de St. Cécile, w. Angela Maria Blasi (sop), Christian Elsner (ten), H.R. Zöbeley (cnd), Munich SO, Munich Motet Choir *(rec live, Herkulessaal, Munich, Mar 13 & 17, 1996)* Calig ▲ CAL 50956 [DDD]

Humperdinck, E.:Königskinder, w. Dagmar Schellenberger (sop—Goose girl), Marilyn Schmiege (cta—Witch), Thomas Moser (ten—King's Son), Heinrich Weber (ten—Broommaker), Dietrich Henschel (bar—Fiddler), Andreas Kohn (bass—Woodcutter), F. Luisi (cnd), Munich RSO, Michael Gläser (cnd), Bavarian Radio Chorus *(rec live, Munich Herkulessaal, Mar 22–24, 1996)* Calig 3–CAL 5096870 [DDD]

Korngold, E.W.:Der Ring des Polykrates, w. Beate Bilandzija (sop—Laura), Kirsten Blanck (sop—Lieschen), Endrik Wottrich (ten—Wilhelm), Jürgen Sacher (ten—Florian), Dietrich Henschel (bar—Peter), K. Seibel (cnd), German SO *(rec Jesus Christ Church, Dahlem, Sept 19–25, 1995)* CPO ▲ CPO 999402–2 [DDD]

Schoeck, O.:Songs (comp), w. Juliane Banse (sop), Wolfram Rieger (pno)—3 Songs, Op. 4; 4 Songs, Op. 8; Vorwurf, Op. 27; 3 Songs, Op. 10; 3 Songs, Op. 13; Lieder nach Gedichten von Goethe, Op. 19a; Lieder aus dem "Westöstlichen Divan" von Goethe, Op. 19b *(rec Feb 1994)* Jecklin ▲ JD 675

Wagner, S.:Das Märchen vom dicken fetten Pfannkuchen, w. W. A. Albert (cnd), Rhineland–Palatinate State PO *(rec Apr 1996)* CPO ▲ 999427–2 [DDD]

Hensel, Heinrich (sgr)

Wagner, R.:Arias & Scenes, w. Emmy Destinn (sop), Lilly Hafgren (sop), Frida Leider (sop), Emmi Leisner (cta), Ernst Kraus (ten), Lauritz Melchoir (ten), Leopold Demuth (bar), Friedrich Schorr (b–bar), Michael Bohynen (bass), Paul Knupfer (bass), Richard Mayr (bass), Heinrich Hensel (sgr), Walter Soomer (sgr) Iron Needle ▲ 1307 (m)

Henshaw, R. (sgr)

Gershwin, G.:Crazy for You, w. K. Ward (sgr) [1992 London cast] RCA ▲ 09026–61933–2 ■ 09026–61933–4

Hepburn, Audrey (nar)

Gardens of the World, w. I. Stupel (cnd), Artur Rubinstein PO Conifer Classics ▲ 74321–17841–2 ■ 74321–17841–4

Saint–Saëns, C.:Carnival of the Animals, w. M. Golabek (nar), R. Golabek (nar), F. Savage (nar), C. Heston (nar), J. E. Jones (nar), B. White (nar), L. Redgrave (nar), W. Shatner (nar), J. Rivers (nar), T. Danson (nar), L. Tomlin (nar), D. Raffin (nar), A. Hepburn (nar), D. Moore (nar), W. Matthau (nar), J. Smith (nar), L. Schifrin (cnd), Hollywood CO Dove Audio ▲ DOV 30700

Hepburn, Katharine (nar)

Copland, A.:Lincoln Portrait, w. E. Kunzel (cnd), Cincinnati Pops Orch [E] Telarc ▲ CD–80117 [DDD]

Heppe, Leo (ten)

Haydn, J.:Mass 7, "Kleine Orgelmesse", w. Eiko Katonosaka (sop), Elfriede Jahn (alt), Kurt Equiluz (ten), H. Gillesberger (cnd), Vienna State Opera Orch, Vienna Chamber Choir *(rec 1965)* Tuxedo ▲ TUXCD 1025

Krenek, E.:Jonny spielt auf, w. E. Lear (sop—Anita), L. Popp (sop—Yvonne), W. Blankenship (ten—Max), K. Equiluz (ten—Station Announcer), L. Heppe (ten—Manager), T. Stewart (bar—Daniello), G. Feldhof (bass—Jonny), H. Hollreiser (cnd), Vienna State Opera Orch [G] Vanguard Classics ▲ OVC 8048 [ADD]

Heppe, Leo (ten) (cont.)
Marschner, H.A.:Der Vampyr, w. L. Synek (sop), G. Oeggl (bar), Rathauscher (sgr), Skladal (sgr), Sperlbauer (sgr), Weise (sgr), K. Tenner (cnd), Vienna RSO, Vienna Radio Chorus [G] *(rec live, Vienna, 4/9/51)* Memories 2-▲ HR 4466/67 [ADD]

Heppner, Ben (ten)
Bach, J.S.:Cant 140, w. Rosemarie Landry (sop), Mark Pedrotti (bass), W. Riddell (cnd), CBC Vancouver SO, Tudor Singers of Montreal CBC ▲ 5163 [DDD]
Beethoven, L. van:Fidelio, w. Elizabeth Norberg-Schulz (sop—Marzelline), Deborah Voigt (sop—Lenore), Ben Heppner (ten—Florestan), Michael Schade (ten—Jaquino), Günter von Kannæen (b-bar—Don Pizarro), Matthias Hölle (bass—Rocco), Thomas Quasthoff (bass—Don Fernando), C. Davis (cnd), Bavarian RSO, Bavarian Radio Chorus, Bavarian State Opera Men's Chorus *(rec Herkulessaal der Residenz, Munich, May 15–25, 1995)* RCA Victor 2-▲ 09026-68344-2 [DDD]
Beethoven, L. van:Sym 9, "Choral Sym", w. Jane Eaglen (sop), Waltraud Meier (cta), Bryn Terfel (bar), C. Abbado (cnd), Berlin PO, Swedish Radio Chorus, Eric Ericson Chamber Choir *(rec Salzburg Easter Festival, 1996)* Sony Classical ▲ SK 62634 Δ SM 62634
Bizet, G.:Carmen (sels), w. R. Abbado (cnd), Munich RSO—La fleur que tu m'avais jetée *(rec Residenz Herkulesaal, Munich, Sept. 27–Oct. 3, 1993)* RCA Red Seal ▲ 09026-62504-2 [DDD]
Giordano, U.:Andrea Chénier (sels), w. R. Abbado (cnd), Munich RSO—Come un bel dì di maggio; Colpito qui m'avete ov'io geloso...Un dì all'azzurro spazio *(rec Residenz Herkulesaal, Munich, Sept. 27–Oct. 3, 1993)* RCA Red Seal ▲ 09026-62504-2 [DDD]
Leoncavallo, R.:La Bohème (sels), w. R. Abbado (cnd), Munich RSO—Musetta! O gioia della mia dimora!...Testa adorata *(rec Residenz Herkulesaal, Munich, Sept. 27–Oct. 3, 1993)* RCA Red Seal ▲ 09026-62504-2 [DDD]
Massenet, J.:Le Cid (sels), w. R. Abbado (cnd), Munich RSO—Ah! tout est bien fini...Ô souverain ô juge, ô père *(rec Residenz Herkulesaal, Munich, Sept. 27–Oct. 3, 1993)* RCA Red Seal ▲ 09026-62504-2 [DDD]
Massenet, J.:Hérodiade, w. Cheryl Studer (sop—Salomé), Nadine Denize (mez—Hérodiade), Ben Heppner (ten—Jean), José Van Dam (b-bar—Phanuel), Thomas Hampson (bass—Hérode), M. Plasson (cnd), Toulouse Capitole Orch, Toulouse Capitole Chorus EMI Classics 3-▲ CDCC 55378
Massenet, J.:Hérodiade (sels), w. R. Abbado (cnd), Munich RSO—Ne pouvant réprimer...Adieu donc, vains objets *(rec Residenz Herkulesaal, Munich, Sept. 27–Oct. 3, 1993)* RCA Red Seal ▲ 09026-62504-2 [DDD]
Meyerbeer, G.:L'Africaine (sels), w. R. Abbado (cnd), Munich RSO—Pays merveilleux...Ô Paradis *(rec Residenz Herkulesaal, Munich, Sept. 27–Oct. 3, 1993)* RCA Red Seal ▲ 09026-62504-2 [DDD]
Puccini, G.:La fanciulla del West (sels), w. R. Abbado (cnd), Munich RSO—Ch'ella mi creda libero e lontano *(rec Residenz Herkulesaal, Munich, Sept. 27–Oct. 3, 1993)* RCA Red Seal ▲ 09026-62504-2 [DDD]
Puccini, G.:Manon Lescaut (sels), w. R. Abbado (cnd), Munich RSO—Donna non vidi mai simile a questa! *(rec Residenz Herkulesaal, Munich, Sept. 27–Oct. 3, 1993)* RCA Red Seal ▲ 09026-62504-2 [DDD]
Puccini, G.:Turandot, w. E. Marton (sop—Turandot), M. Price (sop—Liù), B. Heppner (ten—Calaf), J.-H. Rootering (bass—Timur), R. Abbado (cnd), Munich RSO RCA Red Seal 2-▲ 09026-60898-2
Puccini, G.:Turandot (sels), w. R. Abbado (cnd), Munich RSO, Bavarian Radio Chorus—Nessun dorma *(rec Residenz Herkulesaal, Munich, Sept. 27–Oct. 3, 1993)* RCA Red Seal ▲ 09026-62504-2 [DDD]
Strauss, R.:Songs, w. A. Davis (cnd), Toronto SO—Ewig einsam; Wenn du einst die Gauen [both from Guntram]; Love Scene [from Feuersnot]; Act II scene change; Falke, Falke, du wiedergefundener [both from Die Frau ohne Schatten]; No. 10b, Träumerei am Kamin; No. 10d, Fröhlicher Beschluss [both from Intermezzo]; Orch intro. to Act III; In Syriens Glut... [both from Die Liebe der Danae]; Was erblicke ich? [from Daphne]; Potpourri [from Die schweigsame Frau]; Di rigori armato il seno [from Der Rosenkavalier] *(rec Roy Thomson Hall, Toronto, Nov. 16, 18 & 20, 1994)* CBC ▲ MVV 5142 [DDD]
Verdi, G.:Aida (sels), w. R. Abbado (cnd), Munich RSO—Se quel guerrier io fossi...Celeste Aida *(rec Residenz Herkulesaal, Munich, Sept. 27–Oct. 3, 1993)* RCA Red Seal ▲ 09026-62504-2 [DDD]
Verdi, G.:La forza del destino (sels), w. R. Abbado (cnd), Munich RSO—La vita è inferno all'infelice...Oh, tu che in seno agl'angeli [with Jürgen Musser (cl)] *(rec Residenz Herkulesaal, Munich, Sept. 27–Oct. 3, 1993)* RCA Red Seal ▲ 09026-62504-2 [DDD]
Verdi, G.:Luisa Miller (sels), w. R. Abbado (cnd), Munich RSO—Oh! fede negar potessi..Quando le sere al placido *(rec Residenz Herkulesaal, Munich, Sept. 27–Oct. 3, 1993)* RCA Red Seal ▲ 09026-62504-2 [DDD]
Verdi, G.:Il trovatore (sels), w. R. Abbado (cnd), Munich RSO—Ah sì, ben mio; Di quella pira [with Bavarian Radio Chorus (cnd:Michael Gläser)] *(rec Residenz Herkulesaal, Munich, Sept. 27–Oct. 3, 1993)* RCA Red Seal ▲ 09026-62504-2 [DDD]
Wagner, R.:Lohengrin, w. Sharon Sweet (sop—Elsa), Eva Marton (sop—Ortrud), Ben Heppner (ten—Lohengrin), Anton Rosner (ten—Nobleman), Heinrich Weber (ten—Nobleman), Jan-Hendrik Rootering (bar—Heinrich der Vögler), Sergei Leiferkus (bar—Friedrich von Telramund), Bryn Terfel (b-bar—King's Herald), Barbara Fleckenstein (sgr—Page), Atsuko Suzuki (sgr—Page), Gisela Ulmann (sgr—Page), Marion Rambausek (sgr—Page), Dankwart Siegele (sgr—Nobleman), Jürgen Weiss (sgr—Nobleman), C. Davis (cnd), Bavarian SO, Bavarian State Opera Chorus, Bavarian Radio Chorus *(rec Residenz Herkulesaal, Munich, May 14–28, 1994)* RCA Red Seal 3-▲ 09026-62646-2 [DDD]
Wagner, R.:Lohengrin (sels), w. Eva Marton (sop—Ortrud), Sharon Sweet (sop—Elsa von Brabant), Barbara Fleckenstein (sgr—Page), Marion Rambausek (sgr—Page), Atsuko Suzuki (sgr—Page), Gisela Ulmann (sgr—Page), Ben Heppner (ten—Lohengrin), Anton Rosner (ten—Nobleman), Heinrich Weber (ten—Nobleman), Sergei Leiferkus (bar—Friedrich von Telramund), Bryn Terfel (b-bar—King's Herald), Jan-Hendrik Rootering (bass—Henry the Fowler), Dankwart Siegele (sgr—Nobleman), Jürgen Weiss (sgr—Nobleman), C. Davis (cnd), Bavarian RSO, Michael Gläser (cnd), Udo Mehrpohl (cnd), Bavarian Radio Chorus, Bavarian State Opera Chorus—Seht! Seht! [from Act 1, Scene 2]; Nun sei bedankt, mein lieber Schwan!; Wenn ich im Kampfe für dich siege; Welch holde Wunder muss ich sehen?; Nun höret mich und achtet wohl; Durch Gottes Sieg ist jetzt dein Leben mein [all from Act 1, Scene 3]; Treulich geführt ziehet dahin [from Act 3, Scene 1]; Wie hehr erkenn' ich unsrer Liebe Wesen!; Höchstes Vertrau'n hast du mir schon zu danken; Weh' nun ist all' unser Glück dahin! [all from Act 3, Scene 2]; In fernem Land, unnahbar euren Schritten [from Act 3, Scene 3] *(rec Munich, Mar 14–28, 1994)* RCA Red Seal ▲ 09026-68239-2 [DDD]
Wagner, R.:Die Meistersinger von Nürnberg, w. C. Studer (sop—Eva), B. Heppner (ten—Walther von Stolzing), B. Weikl (bar—Hans Sachs), S. Lorenz (b-bar—Sixtus Beckmesser), K. Moll (bass—Veit Pogner), W. Sawallisch (cnd), Bavarian State Opera Orch, Bavarian State Opera Chorus EMI Classics ▲ CDCD 55142
Weber, C.M. von:Oberon, w. D. Voigt (sop), D. Ziegler (mez), G. Lakes (ten), J. Conlon (cnd), Cologne PO, Cologne Opera Chorus EMI Classics 2-▲ CDCB 54739

Héral, Pierre (bass)
Boieldieu, F.-A.:La Dame blanche, w. Michel Sénéchal (ten—Georges Brown), Aimé Doniat (bar—Dikson), Pierre Héral (bass—Mac-Irton), Adrien Legros (bass—Gaveston), P. Stoll (cnd), Paris SO, Paris Sym Chorus Accord 2-▲ ACD 220862 [AAD]

Herberich, Thomas (bass)
Monteverdi, C.:Vespers, w. Susanne Ryden (sop), Irena Troupova-Wilke (sop), Detlef Bratschke (alt), Erich Mentzel (ten), Hermann Oswald (ten), Manuel Warwitz (ten), Günther Schmidt (bass), H. Arman (cnd), Schütz Academy Capriccio ▲ CD 10521 [DDD]

Herbert, Lila (sop/mez)
Puccini, G.:Suor angelica, w. Elisabeth Carron (sop—Angelica), Joan Summers (sop—Genovieffa), Donna Owen (sop—Dolcina), Lou Ann Wyckoff (sop—Alms collector), Hanna Owen (sop—novice), Anthea De Forest (sop—novice), Charlotte Povia (mez—Abbess), Beverly Evans (mez—Monitress), Kay Creed (mez—Mistress), La Vergne Monette (sop/mez—lay sister), Joan August (sop/mez—lay sister), Pearle Goldsmith (sop/mez—other sister), Lila Herbert (sop/mez—other sister), Jodell Kenting (sop/mez—other sister), Ann Pretzat (sop/mez—other sister), Evelyn Sachs (cta—Princess), F. Patanè (cnd), *(orch unknown)* *(rec New York, Feb 23, 1967)* Legato Classics ▲ LCD 212-1 [ADD]

Herbert, William (ten)
Handel, G.F.:Sosarme, Rè di Media, w. Margaret Ritchie (sop—Elmira), Alfred Deller (mez—Sosarme), Nancy Evans (mez—Erenice), Helen Watts (cta—Melo), John Kentish (ct—Argone), William Herbert (ten—King Haliate), Ian Wallace (bass—Altomaro), A. Lewis (cnd), St. Cecilia Academy Orch Rome, St. Anthony Singers Theorema 2-▲ TH 121194/195

Herbillon, Jacques (bar)
Ravel, M.:Chansons madécasses, w. C. Lardé (fl), P. Degenne (vc), T. Paraskivesco (pno) [F] Calliope ▲ CAL 9893 [ADD]

Herdegen, Leszek (nar)
Penderecki, K.:The Passion & Death of Our Lord Jesus Christ According to St. Luke, w. Stefania Woytowicz (sop), Andrzej Hiolski (bar), Bernard Ladysz (bass), H. Czyz (cnd), Cracow PO, Cracow Phil Boys' Chorus, Cracow Phil Mixed Choir Polskie Nagrania 2-▲ PNCD 017 A/B

Herford, Henry (bar)
Britten, H.:A Midsummer Night's Dream, w. J. Gomez (sop), D. Jones (sop), J. Bowman (ct), N. Bailey (bar), R. Hickox (cnd), City of London Sinfonia Virgin Classics ▲ CDCB 59305
Gregson, E.:Missa Brevis Pacem, w. James Keenan (trb), E. Gregson (cnd), Royal Northern College of Music Wind Orch, Manchester Boy's Choir Doyen ▲ CD 043 [DDD]
Handel, G.F.:Messiah (sels), w. Felicity Lott (sop), Linda Finnie (mez), Glenn Winslade (ten), G. Malcolm (cnd), Scottish CO, Scottish Phil Singers IMP ("Classic" series) ▲ IMP 2031
Ives, C.:Songs, w. I. Metzmacher (cnd), Ensemble Modern—General W. Booth enters into heaven; On the antipodes; The Bells of Yale (Battell Chimes or Chapel Chimes); Aeschylus and Sophocles; Sunrise EMI Classics ▲ CDC 54552 [DDD]
Ives, C.:Songs, w. R. Bowman (pno)—In summer fields; In the alley; Religion; Luck & work; The Cage; Grantchester; Premonitions; Nov. 2, 1920; Duty; from "Lincoln, the Great Commoner"; Thoreau; Walt Whitman; The greatest man; So may it be! (The rainbow); Walking; August; September; December; Autumn; Afterglow; from the "Incantation"; Spring song; At sea; Tarrant moss; Waltz; Romanzo di Central Park; Canon; Mirage; Maple leaves; Charlie Rutlage; The camp-meeting Unicorn-Kanchana ▲ DKP CD 9112 [DDD]
Ives, C.:Songs, w. R. Bowman (pno)—General William Booth enters into Heaven; There is a certain garden; In Flanders Fields; etc. Unicorn-Kanchana ▲ DKP CD 9111 [DDD]
Lloyd, G.:Iernin, w. M. Hill Smith (sop), C. Powell (mez), G. Pogson (ten), M. Rivers (bar) Albany 3-▲ TROY 121/23 [DDD]

Herincx, Raimund (bar)
Handel, G.F.:Rodelinda, Regina de' Longobardi, w. Joan Sutherland (sop), Janet Baker (mez), C. Farncombe (cnd), Philomusica Orch, Chandos Choir *(rec 1959)* Memories 2-▲ MEM 4577 [ADD]

Herincx, Raimund (bass)
Bliss, A.:The Olympians, w. R. Woodland (sop), S. Minty (mez), T. Hemsley (bar), B. Fairfax (cnd), Polyphonia Orch, Ambrosian Singers *(rec 1972)* Intaglio 2-▲ ING 755 [ADD]
Handel, G.F.:Messiah, w. Elisabeth Harwood (sop), Janet Baker (mez), Paul Esswood (ct), Robert Tear (ten), C. Mackerras (cnd), English CO, Ambrosian Singers [E] Angel ("Studio" series) 2-▲ CDMB 62748 [ADD]
Handel, G.F.:Messiah, w. Elisabeth Harwood (sop), Janet Baker (mez), Paul Esswood (ct), Robert Tear (ten), C. Mackerras (cnd), English CO, Ambrosian Singers [E] Angel ("Studio" series) ▲ CDM 69040
Tippett, M.:The Midsummer Marriage, w. Joan Carlyle (sop—Joan), Elizabeth Harwood (sop—Beth), Elizabeth Bainbridge (mez), Helen Watts (cta—Sosostris), Stuart Burrows (ten—Jack), Alberto Remedios (ten—Mark), Stafford Dean (bass), Raimund Herincx (bass—King Fisher), C. Davis (cnd), Royal Opera House Orch, Royal Opera House Chorus Covent Garden Lyrita 2-▲ SRCD 2217

Hering, Jörg (ten)
Haydn, J.:Mass 9, "Heiligmesse", w. Matthias Ritter (sop), Simon Schnorr (alt), Benedikt Schillo (ten), Panito Iconomou (bass), B. Weil (cnd), Tölz Boys' Choir Sony Classical ("Vivarte" series) ▲ SK 66260
Haydn, J.:Mass 10, "Kriegsmesse", "Paukenmesse", w. Ann Monoyios (sop), Monica Groop (mez), Harry van der Kamp (bass), B. Weil (cnd), Tafelmusik, Tölz Boys' Choir Sony Classical ("Vivarte" series) ▲ SK 68255
Haydn, J.:Sacred Music, w. Matthias Ritter (sop), Simon Schnorr (alt), Benedikt Schillo (ten), Panito Iconomou (bass), B. Weil (cnd), Tölz Boys' Choir—Mare clausum (oratorio fragment), H.XXI-Va:9; Motetto Insanae et vanae curae, H.XXI:1; Motetti de Venerabili Sacramento I–IV, H.XXIIIc:5a–d; Te Deum, H.XXIIIc:2 Sony Classical ("Vivarte" series) ▲ SK 66260
Haydn, J.:Die Schöpfung, w. Ann Monoyios (sop—Gabriel/Eva), Jörg Hering (ten—Uriel), Harry van der Kamp (bass—Raphael/Adam), B. Weil (cnd), Tafelmusik, Tölz Boys' Choir *(rec Bad Tolz, Germany, Aug. 31–Sept. 4, 1993)* Sony Classical ("Vivarte" series) 2-▲ SX2K 57965 [DDD]
Schubert, Franz:Mass 1, w. Alexander Nader (sop), Thomas Puchegger (sop), Georg Leskovich (alto), Kurt Azesberger (ten), Harry van der Kamp (bass), Arno Hartmann (org), B. Weil (cnd), Orch of the Age of Enlightenment, Vienna Boys' Choir *(rec Vienna, Austria, Sept 1995)* Sony Classical ("Vivarte" series) ▲ SK 68247 [DDD]
Schubert, Franz:Mass 2, w. Thomas Puchegger (sop), Harry van der Kamp (bass), Arno Hartmann (org), B. Weil (cnd), Orch of the Age of Enlightenment, Vienna Boys' Choir *(rec Vienna, Austria, Sept 1995)* Sony Classical ("Vivarte" series) ▲ SK 68247 [DDD]
Schubert, Franz:Mass 3, w. Alexander Nader (sop), Thomas Puchegger (sop), Belá Fischer (alt), Georg Leskovich (alt), Harry Van der Kamp (bass), Arno Hartmann (org), B. Weil (cnd), Orch of the Age of Enlightenment, Chorus Viennensis, Vienna Boys' Choir Sony Classical ("Vivarte" series) ▲ SK 68248
Schubert, Franz:Mass 4, w. Alexander Nader (sop), Thomas Puchegger (sop), Belá Fischer (alt), Georg Leskovich (alt), Harry Van der Kamp (bass), Arno Hartmann (org), B. Weil (cnd), Orch of the Age of Enlightenment, Chorus Viennensis, Vienna Boys' Choir Sony Classical ("Vivarte" series) ▲ SK 68248
Schubert, Franz:Mass 6, w. Benjamin Schmidinger (sop), Albin Lenzer (alt), Kurt Azesberger (ten), Harry van der Kamp (bass), B. Weil (cnd), Orch of the Age of Enlightenment, Vienna Boys' Choir Sony Classical ▲ SK 66255
Wagner, R.:Der fliegende Holländer, w. I. Haubold (sop—Senta), M. Schiml (mez—Nurse), P. Seiffert (ten—Erik), J. Hering (ten—Helsman), A. Muff (bar—The Dutchman), E. Knodt (bass—Sea Capt.), P. Steinberg (cnd), Vienna ORF SO, Budapest Radio Chorus [G] *(rec Sept. 1992)* Naxos 2-▲ 8.660025/26 [DDD]

Hering, Sabine (alt)
Mauersberger, R.:Geh aus, mein Herz, und suche Freude, w. Sabine Dicke (sop), Dorothea Schmidt (sop), Friederike Urban (sop), Annette Bassenge (alt), Christiane Fischer (alt), Johannes Unger (org), Wolfgang Unger (dir), Thüringian Academic Sing Circle Thorofon ▲ CTH 2245 [DDD]

Herlea, Nicolae (bar)
Donizetti, G.:Lucia di Lammermoor, w. Silvia Voinea (sop—Lucia), Lucia Cicoara (mez—Alisa), Florin Georgescu (ten—Edgardo), Gabriel Nastase (ten—Arturo), Nicolae Herlea (bar—Lord Enrico), Pompei Harasteanu (bass—Raimondo), C. Petrovici (cnd), Romanian Opera Orch, Romanian Opera Chorus *(rec 1984)* Vox Box 2-▲ CDX 5164
Leoncavallo, R.:Pagliacci, w. Arta Florescu (sop—Nedda), Cornel Stavru (ten—Canio), Valentin Teodorian (ten—Beppe), Nicolae Herlea (bar—Tonio), Ladislau Konya (bar—Silvio), M. Popa (cnd), Bucharest Opera & Ballet Theater Orch, Bucharest Opera & Ballet Theater Chorus *(rec 1966)* Vox Box 2-▲ CDX 5161
Puccini, G.:Tosca, w. Virginia Zeani (sop—Floria Tosca), Emilia Oprea (mez—Shepherd), Nicolae Andreescu (ten—Spoletta), Corneliu Fanateanu (ten—Mario Cavaradossi), Nicolae Herlea (bar—Baron Scarpia), Gheorghe Crasnaru (bass—Cesare Angelotti), Constantin Gabor (bass—Sacristan), Pompei Harasteanu (bass—Jailer), Adrian Stefanescu (bass—Sciarrone), C. Trailescu (cnd), Romanian Opera Orch, Romanian Opera Chorus *(rec Sept 1977)* Vox Box 2-▲ CDX 5153
Rossini, G.:Il barbiere di Siviglia, w. Magda Ianculescu (sop—Rosina), Maria Sandulescu (mez—Berta), Valentin Teodorian (ten—Count Almaviva), Nicolae Herlea (bar—Figaro), Stefan Petrescu (bar—Fiorello), Constantin Gabor (bass—Don Bartolo), Valentin Loghin (bass—Don Basilio), M. Brediceanu (cnd), Romanian Opera Orch, Romanian Opera Chorus *(rec 1960–61)* Vox Box 2-▲ CDX 5159
Verdi, G.:La forza del destino, w. Maria Nistor-Slatinaru (sop—Donna Leonora), Mihaela Mariacineanu (mez—Curra), Zenaida Pally (mez—Preziosilla), Ludovic Speiss (ten—Don Alvaro), Ion Stoian (ten—Trabucco), Nicolae Herlea (bar—Don Carlo), Nicolae Florei (bass—Padre Guardiano) Constantin Gabor (bass—Fra Melitone), Dan Musetescu (bass—An Alcalde), Mihai Panghe (bass—Marquis of Calatrava), C. Litvin (cnd), Romanian Radio-TV Orch, Romanian Radio-TV Chorus *(rec Jan 1970)* Vox Box 3-▲ CD3X 3038

Herlea, Nicolae (bar) (cont.)

Verdi, G.:Rigoletto, w. Victoria Draganescu (sop—Countess Ceprano), Magda Ianculescu (sop—Gilda), Dorothea Palade (mez—Maddalena), Valeria Savu (mez—Giovanna), Ion Buzea (ten—Duke of Mantua), Dimitrie Scurtu (ten—Borsa), Nicolae Herlea (bar—Rigoletto), Stefan Petrescu (bar—Marullo), Jean Banescu (bass—Count Ceprano), Nicolae Florei (bass—Monterone), Nicolae Rafael (bass—Sparafucile), J. Bobescu (cnd), Romanian Opera Orch, Romanian Opera Chorus *(rec 1965)* Vox Box 2-▲ CDX 5162

Verdi, G.:La traviata, w. Elena Simionescu (sop—Annina), Virginia Zeani (sop—Violetta Valery), Elisabeta Neculce-Cartis (mez—Flora Bervoix), Ion Buzea (ten—Alfredo Germont), Vasile Moldoveanu (ten—Gastone/Viconte de Letorieres/Giuseppe), Teodor Panea (ten—Flora's Servant), Constantin Dumitru (bar—Commissioner/Baron Douphol), Nicolae Herlea (bar—Giorgio Germont), Valentin Loghin (bass—Marchese D'Obigny), Nicolae Rafael (bass—Doctor Grenvil), J. Bobescu (cnd), Romanian Opera Orch, Stelian Olariu (cnd), Romanian Opera Chorus *(rec 1968)* Vox Box 2-▲ CDX 5154

Verdi, G.:La traviata (sels), w. V. Zeani (sop), Buzea (sgr), J. Bobescu (cnd), Bucharest State Opera Orch [I] Allegretto ▲ ACD 8084 [ADD] ■ ACS 8084

Herlitzius, Evelyn (sop)

Beethoven, L. van:Fidelio (sels), w. Evelyn Herlitzius (sop—Leonore), Ruth Ziesak (sop—Marzelline), Stig Andersen (ten—Florestan), Herbert Lippert (ten—Jaquino), Albert Dohmen (bar—Don Pizarro), Andreas Kohn (bass—Don Fernando), Hans Tschammer (bass—Rocco), G. Solti (cnd), World Orch for Peace, London Voices—Finale Act II *(rec Victoria Hall, Geneva, July 5, 1995)* London ▲ 448901-2 [DDD]

Hermann, Dagmar (mez)

Bach, J.S.:Cant 78, w. T. Stich-Randall (sop), A. Dermota (ten), H. Braun (bar), F. Prohaska (cnd), Bach Guild Orch, Bach Guild Chorus [G] *(rec May 1954)* Vanguard Classics ("The Bach Guild" series) ▲ OVC 2009 [ADD]

Bach, J.S.:Cant 106, "Actus tragicus", w. T. Stich-Randall (sop), A. Dermota (ten), H. Braun (bar), F. Prohaska (cnd), Bach Guild Orch, Bach Guild Chorus [G] *(rec May 1954)* Vanguard Classics ("The Bach Guild" series) ▲ OVC 2009 [ADD]

Golden Operetta, Vol. 2:Operetta Melodies, w. F. Bauer-Theussl (cnd), Vienna Volksoper Orch, Vienna Volksoper Chorus, Renate Holm (sop), Lotte Rysanek (sop), Kurt Equiluz (ten), Horst Winter (ten), et al. Koch Präsent ▲ 399 224 [AAD]

Lehár, F.:Der Graf von Luxemburg (sels), w. Renate Holm (sop), Else Liebesberg (sop), Hilde Brauner (cta), Rudolf Christ (ten), Herbert Prikopa (bar), F. Bauer-Theussl (cnd), Vienna Volksoper Orch, Vienna Volksoper Chorus [G] Koch Präsent ▲ CD 399223 [AAD]

Smetana, B.:The Bartered Bride, w. Dorothea Siebert (sop), Maria von Ilosvay (mez), Hans Braun (bar), Kurt Böhme (bass), J. Keilberth (cnd), Bavarian RSO, Bavarian Radio Chorus *(rec 1958)* Pantheon 2-▲ PHE 6652 (m)

Straus, O.:Ein Walzertraum (sels), w. H. Brauner (cta), R. Holm (sop), E. Liebesberg (sop), R. Christ (ten), H. Prikopa (bar), F. Bauer-Theussl (cnd), Vienna Volksoper Orch, Vienna Volksoper Chorus [G] Koch Präsent ▲ CD 399223 [AAD]

Hermann, Roland (bar)

Bach, J.S.:Mass in b, BWV 232, w. Helen Donath (sop), Brigitte Fassbaender (cta), Claes H. Ahnsjö (ten), Robert Holl (bass), E. Jochum (cnd), Bavarian RSO, Bavarian Radio Chorus EMI Classics ("Doublefforte" series) 2-▲ CDFB 68640

Egk, W.:Peer Gynt, w. J. Perry (sop), N. Sharp (sop), C. Wulkopf (mez), H. Hopf (ten), H. Wallberg (cnd), Munich RSO, Bavarian Radio Chorus [G] Orfeo 2-▲ 005822 [DDD]

Hindemith, P.:Mathis der Maler, w. Josef Protschka (ten), Hermann Winkler (ten), Victor von Halem (bass), Harold Stamm (bass), G. Albrecht (cnd), Cologne RSO Wergo 3-▲ WER 6255-2

Kagel, M.:Sankt-Bach-Passion, w. Anne Sofie von Otter (mez), Hans Peter Blochowitz (ten), Peter Roggisch (narr), Gerd Zacher (org), M. Kagel (cnd), South German RSO, Limburg Cathedral Boys' Chorus, Hamburg North German Choir Montaigne ▲ MO 782044

Loewe, C.:Ballads, w. Geoffrey Parsons (pno)—includes Kaiser Karl V Historial Ballads (4), Op. 99; Gregor auf dem Stein, Legend in 5 Parts, Op. 38 Claves ▲ 50-8106

Mahler, G.:Des Knaben Wunderhorn, w. Janet Baker (mez), Geraint Evans (bar), W. Morris (cnd), London PO, London Symphonica IMP ▲ PCD 2020

Mahler, G.:Lieder eines fahrenden Gesellen, w. Janet Baker (mez), Geraint Evans (bar), W. Morris (cnd), London PO, London Symphonica IMP ▲ PCD 2020

Mahler, G.:Lieder und Gesänge aus der Jugendzeit, w. Geoffrey Parsons (pno) Claves ▲ 50-9011

Marschner, H.A.:Der Vampyr, w. Arleen Augér (sop), Donald Grobe (ten), Nikolas Hillebrand (bass), F. Rieger (cnd), Bavarian RSO, Bavarian Radio Chorus *(rec live, Munich, 1974)* Enterprise ("Documents" series) 2-▲ ENT 1009

Respighi, O.:Christus, w. C. Gaifa (ten), G. Sarti (bar), M. Balderi (cnd), Swiss-Italian Orch, Swiss-Italian Chorus [L] Claves ▲ CD 9203 [DDD]

Wagner, R.:Die Feen, w. L. E. Gray (sop), K. Lövaas (sop), K. Láki (sop), Anderson (sop), R. Alexander (sop), K. Moll (bass), W. Sawallisch (cnd), Bavarian RSO, Bavarian Radio Chorus [G] *(rec live, Munich Opera Fest. 1983)* Orfeo 3-▲ 062833 [DDD]

Wagner, R.:Die Meistersinger von Nürnberg, w. C. Ligendza (sop), C. Ludwig (mez), P. Domingo (ten), R. Laubenthal (ten), D. Fischer-Dieskau (bar), P. Lagger (bass), E. Jochum (cnd), German Opera Orch, German Opera Chorus [G] Deutsche Grammophon 4-▲ 415278-2 [ADD]

Wagner, R.:Die Meistersinger von Nürnberg, w. C. Ligendza (sop), C. Ludwig (mez), P. Domingo (ten), R. Laubenthal (ten), D. Fischer-Dieskau (bar), P. Lagger (bass), E. Jochum (cnd), German Opera Orch, German Opera Chorus Deutsche Grammophon ("Domingo Edition" series) ▲ 435406-2

Hermann, Roland (nar)

Schoenberg, A.:Ode to Napoleon, w. Rim Vogler (vn), Frank Reinecke (vn), Stefan Fehlandt (va), Michael Sanderling (vc), Frank-Immo Zichner (pno) *(rec Siemensvilla, Berlin-Lankwitz, Aug. 1994)* EDA ▲ EDA 008-2 [DDD]

Hermon, Michel (nar)

Milhaud, D.:Ani maamin, un chant perdu et retrouvé, w. Sharon Cooper (sop—la Voix), Anna Parus (mez), Bernard Freyd (nar—Isaac), Michel Hermon (nar—le Récitant), Michael Lonsdale (nar—Abraham), Jean Négroni (nar—Jacob), P. Méfano (cnd), Ensemble 2E2M, Madrigal de Bordeaux Arion ▲ ARN 68275 [DDD]

Hernandez (sgr)

Menotti, G.C.:Goya, w. Josie de Guzman (sgr), Daner (sgr), Wentzel (sgr), S. Mercurio (cnd), Spoleto Festival Orch, Westminster Choir [I] *(rec live 1991)* Nuova Era 2-▲ 7060/61 [DDD]

Hernàndez, Raúl (sgr)

Morales, M.:Ildegonda, w. Violeta Dávalos (sgr—Ildegonda), Grace Echauri (sgr—Idelbene), Raúl Hernàndez (sgr—Rizzardo), Ricardo Santin (sgr—Rolando), F. Lozano (cnd), Carlos Chávez SO, Escuola Nacional de Música Chorus Forlane 2-▲ FRL 16739 [DDD]

Herold, Vilhelm (ten)

Vilhelm Herold, w. Johanne Brun (sop), Emilie Ulrich (sop), Helge Nissen (b-bar) Nimbus ("Prima Voce" series) ▲ NI 7880 [ADD]

Herr, Martha (sop)

Cage, J.:Europera 5, w. G. Burgess (ten), Y. Mikhashoff (pno), J. Wiliams (victrola [78 rpm]), D. Metz (tape) *(rec Apr. 12, 1991)* Mode ▲ MOD 36 [DDD]

Thomson, V.:Portraits, w. Y. Mikhashoff (pno), J. Boudler (perc), D. Kuehn (tpt)—30 sels composed from 1926-1982 New Albion ▲ NA 034 [ADD]

Herrera, Gabriela (sop)

Orff, C.:Carmina burana, w. Frank Kelley (ten), Ben Holt (bar), H. de la Fuente (cnd), Mineria SO, Minería Sym Choir IMP ("Classic" series) ▲ IMP 2024

Herrmann, Anke (sgr)

Jommelli, N.:La Passione di Gesù Cristo, w. Debora Beronesi (sop), Jeffrey Francis (ten), Maurizio Picconi (sgr), A. de Marchi (cnd), Berlin Baroque Academy, Eufonia, Sigismondo D'India *(rec Mar 31-Apr 4, 1996)* K617 2-▲ 7063 [DDD]

Herrmann, B. (bass)

Wagner, R.:Der Ring des Nibelungen, w. K. Flagstad (sop), H. Konetzni (sop), E. Höngen (cta), G. Treptow (ten), S. Svanholm (ten), M. Lorenz (ten), F. Frantz (b-bar), L. Weber (bass), W. Furtwängler (cnd), La Scala Orch, La Scala Chorus *(rec live 1950)* Arkadia 12-▲ 351 [ADD]

Herrmann, Josef (bar)

Bizet, G.:Carmen, w. E. Weidlich (sop), E. Höngen (cta), T. Ralf (ten), K. Böhme (bass), K. Böhm (cnd), Dresden State Opera Orch, Dresden State Opera Chorus *(rec Dec. 4 & 5, 1942)* Preiser 2-▲ 90152 (m)

Josef Herrmann *(rec between 1941 & 1943)* Preiser ▲ PRE 89076 [AAD]

Strauss, R.:Die Frau ohne Schatten (sels), w. H. Konetzni (sop—Die Kaiserin), E. Schulz (sop—Die Färberin), T. RA. (ten—Der Kaiser), J. Herrmann (bar—Barak), K. Böhm (cnd), Vienna State Opera Orch, Vienna State Opera Chorus *(rec Nov. 23, 1943)* Koch Schwann 2-▲ SCH 314552 [ADD]

Verdi, G.:Otello (sels), w. Torsten Ralf (ten—Otello), Josef Hermann (ten—Iago), K Böhm (cnd), Saxon State Orch—Sì, pel ciel marmoreo giuro *(rec 1940)* Iron Needle ▲ IN 1311 [ADD]

Wagner, R.:Die Meistersinger von Nürnberg (sels), w. Maria Reining (sop—Eva), Peter Klein (ten—David), Max Lorenz (ten—Walther), Josef Hermann (bar—Hans Sachs), Erich Kunz (bar—Beckmesser), K. Böhm (cnd), Vienna State Opera Orch *(rec Vienna, Jan. 19, 1943)* Koch Schwann 2-▲ SCH 314732 [ADD]

Wagner, R.:Die Meistersinger von Nürnberg (sels), w. Maria Reining (sop—Eva), Torsten Ralf (ten—Walther), Josef Herrman (bar—Hans Sachs), Erich Kunz (bar—Beckmesser), Kurt Böhme (bass—Pogner), K. Böhm (cnd), Vienna State Opera Orch *(rec Vienna, 1944)* Koch Schwann 2-▲ SCH 314682 [ADD]

Wagner, R.:Der Ring des Nibelungen, w. Kirsten Flagstad (sop), Hilde Konetzni (sop), Elisabeth Höngen (cta), Max Lorenz (ten), Set Svanholm (ten), Günther Treptow (ten), Ludwig Weber (bass), Ferdinand Franz (sgr), W. Furtwängler (cnd), La Scala Orch, La Scala Chorus *(rec Milan, 1950)* Music & Arts 12-▲ CD 914

Wolf, H.:Der Corregidor, w. M. Teschemacher (sop), M. Fuchs (sop), K. Erb (ten), K. Böhme (b-bar), G. Hann (bass), G. Frick (bass), K. Elmendorff (cnd), Saxon State Orch, Saxon State Chorus *(rec 1944)* Preiser 2-▲ PRE 90182 [AAD]

Herrmann-Braun, Daagmar (cta)

Akademie Chamber Choir & Vienna SO, w. Akademie Chamber Choir [cnd:Ferdinand Grossmann], Vienna SO, Elisabeth Roon (sop), Laurence Dutoit (sop), Erich Majkut (ten), W. Berry (bass) Vox 90s ■ V9-9903

Herron (sgr)

Pergolesi, G.B.:San Guglielmo Duca d'Aquitania, w. K. Gamberucci (sop), Caldini (sgr), B. Lucarini (sop), R. Girolami (bass), G. Gatti (bar), F. Maestri (cnd), Terni CO [I] *(rec live, 12/18/86)* Bongiovanni 2-▲ GB 2060/61 [DDD]

Herseth, Freda (mez)

Crumb, G.:Lux Aeterna, w. Pamela Guidetti (b fl/sop rcr), James Freeman (sitar), Susan Jones (perc), William Kerrigan (perc) *(rec Lang Concert Hall, Swarthmore College)* CRI ▲ CD 723 [DDD]

Hert, Tamara (sop)

Boccherini, L.:Stabat Mater, w. K. Oshita (sop), J.-C. Orilac (ten), M. de la Fuente (cnd), La Follia Ensemble—2nd version—Op. 61 [L] *(rec 1979)* Arion ▲ ARN 68164 [ADD]

Herwig, Alfons (bar)

Wagner, R.:Der Ring des Nibelungen, w. Gré Brouwenstein (sop—Freia/Sieglinde), Ilse Hollweg (sop—Waldvogel), Gerda Lammers (sop—Ortlinde), Paula Lenchner (sop—Wellgunde/Gerhilde), Hilde Scheppan (sop—Helmwige), Astrid Varnay (sop—Brünnilde/3rd Norn), Lore Wissmann (sop—Woglinde), Maria von Ilosvay (mez—Flosshilde/Schwertleite/2nd Norn), Louise Charlotte Kamps (mez—Siegrune), Jean Madeira (mez—Erda/Rossweisse/1st Norn), Georgine van Milinkovic (mez—Fricka/Grimgerde), Elisabeth Schärtel (mez—Waltraute), Paul Kuën (ten—Mime), Ludwig Suthaus (ten—Loge), Josef Traxel (ten—Froh), Wolfgang Windgassen (ten—Siegmund/Siegfried), Alfons Herwig (bar—Donner), Hermann Uhde (bar—Gunther), Hans Hotter (b-bar—Wotan), Gustav Neidlinger (b-bar—Alberich), Josef Griendl (bass—Fasolt/Hunding/Hagen), Arnold van Mill (bass—Fafner), H. Knappertsbusch (cnd), Bayreuth Festival Orch, Bayreuth Festival Chorus *(rec live, Bayreuth, Aug 13-17, 1956)* Golden Melodram 14-▲ GM 1.001 [ADD]

Hesse, Dagmar (sgr)

Liebermann, R.:Medea, w. Françoise Pollet (sop—Medea), Yvi Jänicke (cta—Chalkiope), Zdena Furmančoková (sgr—Syrinx), Dagmar Hesse (sgr—Aiglaia), Hanne Krogen (sgr—Kore), Michaela Lucas (sgr—Oinone), Renate Spingler (sgr—Silene), Jochen Kowalski (ct—Kreon), Aage Haugland (bass—Jason), G. Albrecht (cnd), Hamburg State PO, Hamburg State Opera Chorus *(rec live, Hamburg, Germany, Sept 24, 1995)* Musiques Suisses ▲ 6126 [DDD]

Hesse, Ruth (mez)

Strauss, R.:Die Frau ohne Schatten, w. B. Nilsson (sop), L. Rysanek (sop), J. King (ten), W. Berry (bass), K. Böhm (cnd), Vienna SO Deutsche Grammophon 3-▲ 445325-2

Wagner, R.:Lohengrin, w. Leonore Kirchstein (sop—Elsa von Brabant), Ruth Hesse (mez—Ortrud), Herbert Schachtschneider (ten—Lohengrin), Hans Helm (bar—Der Heerrufer des Königs), Otto von Rohr (bass—Heinrich der Vogler), Heinz Imdahl (sgr—Friedrich von Telramund), H. Swarowsky (cnd), Czech PO, Prague National Theater Orch, Vienna State Opera Chorus *(rec Aug 1968)* Weltbild Classics 3-▲ 703835 [ADD]

Wagner, R.:Die Meistersinger von Nürnberg, w. H. Donath (sop), A. Kollo (ten), P. Schreier (ten), T. Adam (b-bar), R. Evans (bass), K. Ridderbusch (bass), H. von Karajan (cnd), Dresden Staatskapelle, Dresden State Chorus, Leipzig Radio Chorus [G] EMI Classics 4-▲ CDCD 49683 [ADD]

Wagner, R.:Der Ring des Nibelungen, w. Liselotte Becker-Egner (sop—Woglinde/Ortlinde/Wellgunde), Angelika Berger (sop—Wellgunde/Waltraute), Siw Ericsdotter (sop—Norn 3), Heidemaria Ferch (sop—Freia/Gerhilde), Bella Jasper (sop—Helmwige/Waldvogel/Woglinde), Ditha Sommer (sop—Sieglinde/Gutrune), Ursula Boese (mez—Erda), Ruth Hesse (mez—Fricka), Nadezda Kniplová (mez—Brünnhilde), Margit Kobeck (mez—Schwertleite/Norn 2), Hilde Rosner (mez—Flosshilde/Siegrunde), Erica Schubert (mez—Grimgerde/Flosshilde), Ingrid Göritz (cta—Rossweisse/Norn 1), Herbert Doussant (ten—Froh), Herold Kraus (ten—Mime), Gerald McKee (ten—Siegmund/Siegfried), Fritz Uhl (ten—Loge), Rudolf Knoll (bar—Gunther/Donner), Rolf Polke (bass-bar—Wotan/Wanderer), Rolf Kühne (bass—Alberich), Takao Okamura (bass—Fafner), Otto von Rohr (bass—Hagen/Fasolt/Hunding), H. Swarowsky (cnd), Czech PO, Prague National Theater Orch *(rec June 3 & 5, July 26-31, A)* Weltbild Classics 14-▲ 703769 [ADD]

Hesse, Ursula (mez)

Reimann, A.:Eingedunkelt *(rec Studio II, Radio Free Berlin, June 1995)* Orfeo ▲ C 412 961 [DDD]

Reimann, A.:Wie, die wie der Strandhafer wahren, w. Axel Bauni (pno) *(rec Studio II, Radio Free Berlin, June 1995)* Orfeo ▲ C 412 961 [DDD]

Heston, Charlton (nar)

Copland, A.:Lincoln Portrait, w. M. Abravanel (cnd), Utah SO *(rec 12/61)* Vanguard Classics ▲ OVC 4037 [ADD]

Saint-Saëns, C.:Carnival of the Animals, w. M. Golabek (nar), R. Golabek (nar), F. Savage (nar), C. Heston (nar), J. E. Jones (nar), B. White (nar), L. Redgrave (nar), W. Shatner (nar), J. Rivers (nar), T. Danson (nar), L. Tomlin (nar), D. Raffin (nar), A. Hepburn (nar), D. Moore (nar), W. Matthau (nar), J. Smith (nar), L. Schifrin (cnd), Hollywood CO Dove Audio ▲ DOV 30700

Heusser (sgr)

Kálmán, I.:Die Csárdásfürstin (sels), w. E. Köth (sop), F. Fehringer (ten), B. Kusche (bar), Hofmann (sgr), Marszalek (cnd), Cologne Radio Orch, Cologne Radio Chorus [G] Acanta ▲ CD 42435 [DDD]

Hewes (sgr)

Saint-Saëns, C.:Requiem, w. Weld (sgr), MacMaster (sgr), Watson (sgr), J. Somary (cnd), Amor Artis Orch, Amor Artis Chorale *(rec live)* Premier ▲ PRCD 1025 [DDD]

Heyde, Margrehte (sgr)

Heyde, O.:Songs, w. Ole Heyde (sgr/gtr), Kirstine Heyde Dias (vn), Knud Erik Jørgensen (va), Lars Gram (db)—44 songs from texts by Piet Hein Danica ▲ DCD 8175

Heyde, Ole (sgr/gtr)

Heyde, O.:Songs, w. Margrehte Heyde (sgr), Kirstine Heyde Dias (vn), Knud Erik Jørgensen (va), Lars Gram (db)—44 songs from texts by Piet Hein Danica ▲ DCD 8175

Heyner, Hubert (bar)

Elgar, E.:The Dream of Gerontius (sels), w. M. Balfour (cta), S. Wilson (ten), E. Elgar (cnd), Royal Albert Hall Orch, Royal Choral Society [E] *(rec 1927)* Opal ▲ CD 9810 (m) [AAD]

Heynis, Aafje (cta)
Brahms, J.:Choral Music, w. Wilma Lipp (sop), Franz Crass (bar), W. Sawallisch (cnd), Vienna SO, Vienna Singverein—Ein deutsches Requiem, Op. 45; Academic Festival Ov., Op. 80; Tragic Ov., Op. 81; Schicksalslied, Op. 54; Alto Rhap., Op. 53; Var. on a Theme of Haydn, Op. 56a
Philips ▲ 438760-2
Martin, F.:Le Mystère de la Nativité, w. Elly Ameling (sop), Hugues Cuénod (ten), Louis Devos (ten), Eric Tappy (ten), Pierre Bollet (bar), Derrik Olsen (bar), Charles Clavensy (b-bar), André Vessières (bass), E. Ansermet (cnd), Swiss Romande Orch, Jeunes de l'Eglise Chorus, Geneva Motet Chorus
Cascavelle 2-▲ CVL 2006 [ADD]

Hicks, H. (sgr)
Giordano, U.:Andrea Chénier, w. Montserrat Caballé (sop), Franco Corelli (ten), R. de Carlo (sgr), D. Dondi (sgr), G. Ellsworth (sgr), J. Fair (sgr), R. Falk (sgr), S. Felter (sgr), E. Green (sgr), H. Krauss (sgr), L. Miller (sgr), N. Riggins (sgr), H. Salerno (sgr), A. Guadagno (cnd), Academy of Music Orch, Academy of Music Chorus
Great Opera Performances 2-▲ GOP 766

Hidjov, Plamen (bass)
Bach, J.S.:Christmas Oratorio, w. Ludmila Hadjieva (sop), Roumiana Tzatcheva (alt), Lubomir Diacovski (ten), Tabakov, Kralev (cnd), Madrigal Chamber Ensemble, Sofia CO Soloists
Pentagon 3-▲ 302 [DDD]

Hiefinger, Maria (mez)
Hoffmann, E.T.A.:Undine, w. Barbara Baier (sop—Berthalda), Heidrun Plesch (sop—Undine), Corinna Tippe (sop—Die Herzogin), Maria Hiefinger (mez—Fisherman's Wife), Achim Schamberger (ten—Der Herzog), Johannes Beck (bar—Ritter Huldbrand von Ringstetten), Michael Albert (bass—Fisherman), Ulrich Bosch (bass—Heilmann), Bernd Hofmann (bass—Kühleborn), H. Dechant (cnd), Bamberg Youth Orch
Bayer 3-▲ 100256/58 [DDD]

Hiestermann, Horst (ten)
Berg, A.:Wozzeck, w. G. Schröter (mez), R. Goldberg (ten), T. Adam (b-bar), H. Kegel (cnd), Leipzig RSO *(rec Apr. 9, 1973)*
Berlin Classics ("Eterna" series) 2-▲ BER 2068 [ADD]
Einem, G. von:Dantons Tod, w. K. Laki (sop), I. Mayr (mez), W. Hollweg (ten), T. Adam (bass-bar), K. Rydl (bass), L. Zagrosek (cnd), Austrian RSO, Austrian Radio Chorus [G] *(rec live, Salzburg, 8/13/83)*
Orfeo 2-▲ 102842 [ADD]
Strauss, R.:Salome, w. C. Studer (sop), L. Rysanek (sop), B. Terfel (b-bar), G. Sinopoli (cnd), Berlin German Opera Orch
Deutsche Grammophon 2-▲ 431810-2 [DDD]
Weill, K.:Mahagonny, w. G. Ramm (sop), T. Schmidt (mez), J. Latham-König (cnd), König Ensemble
Capriccio ▲ 60028 [DDD]

Higgins, Dick (sgr)
Monk, M.:Key, w. Meredith Monk (sgr/elec org/jews hp), Daniel Sverdlik (sgr), Collin Walcott (sgr/mrdingam), Mark Berger (nar), Lanny Harrison (nar) *(rec live, Gary Weis' loft, Santa Monica, CA, Ace Gallery, Los Angeles, CA, The House, New York City, The Farm, Los Angeles, CA, July 1970–Jan 1971)*
Lovely Music ▲ LCD 1051 [ADD]

Higgins, Kimberly (alt)
Shewan, S.:Magnificat, w. Erin Stedman (sop), Robert Dingman (ten), Alexander Burgess (bar), Paul Shewan (tpt), Barbara Hull (tpt), Nanita Wilson (hn), Scott Emmons (trbn), Kirk Kettinger (tuba), Ann Musser Honeywell (org)
Albany ▲ TROY 149 [DDD]
Shewan, S.:The Voice of the Lord in the Storm, w. Erin Stedman (sop), Robert Dingman (ten), Alexander Burgess (bar), Paul Shewan (tpt), Barbara Hull (tpt), Nanita Wilson (hn), Scott Emmons (trbn), Kirk Kettinger (tuba), Ann Musser Honeywell (org)
Albany ▲ TROY 149 [DDD]

High, G. (sgr)
Soldier, D.:Apotheosis of John Brown, w. R. McCauley, R. A. Clark, M. L. Kortes, N. Davoy, J. White, L. Seaton, et al.
Newport Classic ▲ NPB 85549 [ADD]

Hildebrand, Helga (sop)
Lehár, F.:Der Graf von Luxemburg (sels), w. Erika Koth (sop), Manfred Schmidt (ten), Rudolf Schock (ten), Gustav Niedlinger (bass)
Emperor Operetta ▲ KO 86342

Hildmann, Hanslutz (spkr)
Corghi, A.:Divara—Wasser und Blut, w. Susanna von der Burg (sop—Divara), Suzanne McLeod (mez—Else Windscherer), Eva Lillian Thingboe (mez—Hille Feiken), Robert Schwarts (ten—Lame Man), Heinz Fitz (spkr—Bernd Knipperdollinck), Hanslutz Hildmann (spkr—Jan Matthys), Michael Holm (spkr—Bernhard Rothmann), Christopher Krieg (spkr—Jan van Leiden), W. Humburg (cnd), Münster SO, Münster City Theater Chorus [G] *(rec Grosses Haus, Münster State Theater, Nov. 27–29, 1993)*
Marco Polo 2-▲ 8.223706/07 [DDD]

Hill, Jenny (sop)
Massenet, J.:Sapho, w. Laura Sarti (mez), Bernard Dickerson (ten), Alexander Oliver (ten), Neilson Taylor (bar), George Macpherson (bass), Milla Andrew (sgr), B. Keefe (cnd), BBC SO, BBC Sym Chorus *(rec live, 1973)*
Memories 2-▲ MEM 4601 [AAD]

Hill, Martyn (ten)
Antheil, G.:Music of, w. Jagdish Mistry (vn), Hermann Kretzschmar (pno), H. K. Gruber (cnd), Ensemble Modern—Printemps I; Ballet mécanique; Fighting the Waves; A Jazz Symphony; Lithuanian Night; Jazz Sonata; Concerto for CO; Son 1 Vn; Printemps II *(rec Frankfurt, Germany, June 27–30 & Dec 20–23, 1)*
RCA Red Seal ▲ 09026-68066-2 [DDD]
Bax, A.:Fatherland, w. V. Handley (cnd), Royal PO, Brighton Festival Chorus [E]
Chandos ▲ CHAN 8625 [DDD]
Bax, A.:Songs, w. B. Thomson (cnd), London PO, Eternity; Glamour; A Lyke-Wake; Slumber Song
Chandos ▲ CHAN 8628 [DDD]
Bax, A.:Walsinghame, w. L. McWhirter (sop), V. Handley (cnd), Royal PO, Brighton Festival Chorus [E]
Chandos ▲ CHAN 8625 [DDD]
Beethoven, L. van:Sym 9, "Choral Sym", w. Gillian Webster (sop), Catherine Wyn-Rogers (cta), Robert Hayward (bar), R. Leppard (cnd), Royal PO, Ambrosian Singers
Tring ("Royal Philharmonic Collection" series) ▲ TRP 51 [DDD]
Boulanger, L.:Choral Music, w. A. Ball (pno), J. Wood (cnd), New London Chamber Choir—Les Sirènes; Soir sur la Plaine; Hymne au Soleil; Pour les funérailles d'un soldat
Hyperion ▲ CDA 66726
Boulanger, L.:Clairiès dans le ciel, w. A. Ball (pno)
Hyperion ▲ CDA 66726
Boulanger, L.:Renouveau, w. A. Ball (pno), J. Wood (cnd), New London Chamber Choir
Hyperion ▲ CDA 66726
Britten, H.:Ballad of Heroes, w. R. Hickox (cnd), London SO, London Sym Chorus [E]
Chandos 2-▲ CHAN 8983/84 [DDD]
Britten, H.:Gloriana (choral dances), w. H.D. Wetton (cnd), Holst Orch, Holst Singers [ver. for tenor, harp & chorus]
Hyperion ▲ CDA 66175
Britten, H.:Serenade, Op. 31, w. J. Bryant (hn), V. Ashkenazy (cnd), Royal PO *(rec live, Moscow, 11/89)*
RPO ▲ CDRPO 7015 [DDD]
Britten, H.:Spring Sym, w. E. Gale (sop), A. Hodgson (cta), R. Hickox (cnd), London SO, London Sym Chorus, Southend Boys' Choir [E]
Chandos ▲ CHAN 8855 [DDD]
British Music on Hyperion, w. Parley of Instruments, Roy Goodman (cnd), John Mark Ainsley (ten), Graham Johnson (pno), Salomon Quartet, BBC Scottish SO, Anthony Rolfe Johnson (ten), Royal PO, St. Paul's Cathedral Choir, Nash Ensemble, Suasan Gritton (sop), Sarah Wal
Hyperion ▲ HYP 15
Carter, E.:In Sleep, In Thunder, w. O. Knussen (cnd), London Sinfonietta [E]
Elektra/Nonesuch ■ 79110-4 (D)
Carter, E.:In Sleep, In Thunder, w. O. Knussen (cnd), London Sinfonietta
Wergo ▲ WER 6278-2
Dutilleux, H.:Prière pour nous autres charnels, w. Neal Davies (bar), Y. P. Tortelier (cnd), BBC PO
Chandos ▲ CHAN 9504
Finzi, G.:Song Cycles Ten, w. C. Benson (pno)—A Young Man's Exhortation, Op. 14; Till Earth Outwears, Op. 19a [E]
Hyperion 2-▲ CDA 66161/62
Hahn, R.:Chansons grises, w. G. Johnson (pno) [F]
Hyperion ▲ CDA 66045 [DDD]
Hahn, R.:Songs, w. Graham Johnson (pno)—15 early songs [F]
Hyperion ▲ CDA 66045 [DDD]
Handel, G.F.:Acis & Galatea, w. N. Burrowes (sop), A. R. Johnson (ten), W. White (bass), J. E. Gardiner (cnd), English Baroque Soloists [E]
Archiv ▲ 423406-2 [ADD]
Holloway, R.:Sea Surface Full of Clouds, w. P. Walmsley-Clark (sop), M. Cable (mez), C. Brett (alt), R. Hickox (cnd), City of London Sinfonia
Chandos ▲ CHAN 9228 [DDD]
Hovhaness, A.:Sym 24, w. John Wilbraham (tpt), Sax (vn), A. Hovhaness (cnd), National PO London, John Alldis Choir [E] *(rec 1974)*
Crystal ▲ CD 803 [ADD]

Hill, Martyn (ten) (cont.)
Howells, H.:Missa sabrinensis, w. Janice Watson (sop), Della Jones (cta), Donald Maxwell (bar), G. Rozhdestvensky (cnd), London SO, London Sym Chorus
Chandos ▲ CHAN 9348 [DDD]
Hughes, O.A.:Dewi Saint, w. Yvonne Kenny (sop), David Wilson-Johnson (bar), O. A. Hughes (cnd), BBC Welsh National SO, BBC Welsh National Chorus [E]
Chandos ▲ CHAN 8890 [DDD]
Martin, F.:In terra pax, w. Judith Howarth (sop), Della Jones (cta), Roderick Williams (bar), Stephen Roberts (bass), M. Bamert (cnd), London PO, Laszlo Heltay (cnd), Brighton Festival Chorus
Chandos ▲ CHAN 9465
Monteverdi, C.:Vespro della Beata Vergine, w. Elly Ameling (sop), Norma Burrowes (sop), Charles Brett (ct), Anthony Rolfe-Johnson (ten), Robert Tear (ten), Peter Knapp (bass), John Noble (bass), Francis Grier (org/hpd), James Lancelot (org/hpd), Andrew Leach (org/hpd), P. Ledger (cnd), London Early Music Consort, King's College Choir Cambridge—Nigra sum [con.]; Laudate pueri [psalm]; Sancta Maria [son. sopra]; Magnificat *(rec Chapel of King's College, Cambridge, July & Aug. 1975)*
EMI Classics ▲ CDK 65339 [ADD]
Monteverdi, C.:Vespro della Beata Vergine, w. Elly Ameling (sop), Norma Burrowes (sop), Charles Brett (ct), Robert Tear (ten), Anthony Rolfe Johnson (ten), Peter Knapp (bass), John Noble (bass), Munrow, Ledger (cnd), London Early Music Consort
EMI Classics ("Doublefforte" series) 2-▲ CDFB 68631
Mozart, W.A.:Music of, w. Gundula Janowitz (sop), Julia Bernheimer (mez), David Thomas (bass), Anthony Halstead (hn), Colin Lawson (b cl), Christopher Kite (pno), R. Goodman (cnd), Hanover Band—Cons for Hn, K.412, 417, 447, 494a & 495; Sym No. 40; Con for Cl; Eine kleine Nachtmusik; Requiem; Sym No. 41; Con No. 20 for Pno; Serenata Notturna
Nimbus 4-▲ NI 1791 [DDD]
Mozart, W.A.:Requiem, w. G. Janowitz (sop), J. Bernheimer (mez), D. Thomas (bass), R. Goodman (cnd), Hanover Band, Hanover Chorus [period instruments; H.C. Robbins Landon edition]
Nimbus 4-▲ NI 1791 [DDD]
Mozart, W.A.:Requiem, w. G. Janowitz (sop), J. Bernheimer (mez), D. Thomas (bass), R. Goodman (cnd), Hanover Band, Hanover Chorus [period instruments; H.C. Robbins Landon's edition; L]
Nimbus ▲ NI 5241-2 [DDD]
Mozart, W.A.:Requiem, w. Colette Alliot-Lugaz (sop), Dominique Vissé (ct), G. Reinhart (bar), J. Malgoire (cnd), La Grande Ecurie et la Chambre du Roy, Nord-Pas-de-Calais Choir [L]
CBS ▲ MDK 44904 [DDD]
Purcell, H.:Music for the Theater, w. E. Kirkby (sop), J. Nelson (sop), J. Bowman (ct), R. Covey-Crump (ten), C. Keyte (bass), D. Thomas (bass), C. Hogwood (cnd), Academy of Ancient Music
L'Oiseau-Lyre 6-▲ 425893-2 [ADD]
Schubert, Franz:Songs (comp), w. G. Johnson (pno)—16 songs—D.149, 151, 160, 161, 177, 197, 198, 201, 207, 211, 213, 214, 271, 302, 303, 325 [G]
Hyperion ▲ CDJ 33010
Sørensen, B.:The Echoing Garden, w. Åsa Bäverstam (sop), L. Segerstam (cnd), Danish National RSO, Danish National Radio Choir *(rec live, Danish Radio Concert Hall, 1992 & 1994)*
Marco Polo/Dacapo ▲ 8.224039 [DDD]
Stravinsky, I.:Pulcinella, w. A. Murray (mez), D. Thomas (bass), R. Hickox (cnd), City of London Sinfonia
Virgo ▲ CDZ 61107
Tippett, M.:Purcell Realizations, w. Andrew Ball (pno)—If music be the food of love; An Epithalamium; The Fatal hour comes on apace [w. Graig Ogden (gtr)]; Mad Bess; Sweeter than roses
Hyperion ▲ CDA 66700
Tippett, M.:Songs, w. Andrew Ball (pno)—Music; Songs for Ariel [Come unto these Yello sands/Full fathom five/Where the bee sucks]; Songs for Achilles [In the Tent/ Across the Plain/ By the Sea; w. Graig Ogden (gtr)]; Boyhood's End; The Heart's Assurance [Song/Compassion/The Dance/Remember Your Lovers]
Hyperion ▲ CDA 66700
Walton, W.:Anon in Love, w. R. Hickox (cnd), City of London Sinfonia [E]
Chandos ▲ CHAN 8824 [DDD]

Hill, Valerie (sop)
Vaughan Williams, R.:Sym 3, w. A. Boult (cnd), BBC SO
IMP ("BBC Radio Classics" series) ▲ IMP 5691642

Hill, Wendy (sop)
Handel, G.F.:Agrippina, w. S. Bradshaw (sop), L. Saffer (sop), G. Banditelli (cta), D. Minter (alt), R. Popken (alt), B. Szilágyi (bar), M. Dean (b-bar), N. Isherwood (bass), N. McGegan (cnd), Capella Savaria [period instrs] [I]
Harmonia Mundi USA 3-▲ HMU 907063/65 ■ HMU 407063/65
Werner, G.J.:Debora, w. G. Banditelli (mez), M. Klietmann (ten), K. Mertens (b-bar), P. Németh (cnd), Capella Savaria
Quintana ▲ QUI 903062

Hillary, Edmund (nar)
Lilburn, D.:Landfall in Unknown Seas, New Zealand CO
Koch International Classics ▲ KIC 7260 [DDD]

Hillebrand, Nikolas (bass)
Dittersdorf, K.D. von:Sacred Music, w. Hanna Farinelli (sop), Birgit Calm (alt), Heiner Hopfner (ten), G. Ratzinger (cnd), Munich Consortium Musicum, Regensburg Cathedral Choir—Requiem in c; Offertorium zu Ehren des Heiligen Johann von Nepomuk; Laurentanische Litanei
Ars Musici ▲ AM 1158-2 [DDD]
Marschner, H.A.:Der Vampyr, w. Arleen Augér (sop), Donald Grobe (ten), Roland Hermann (bar), F. Rieger (cnd), Bavarian RSO, Bavarian Radio Chorus *(rec live, Munich, 1974)*
Enterprise ("Documents" series) 2-▲ ENT 1009

Hillebrecht, Hildegard (sop)
Busoni, F.:Doktor Faust, w. W. Cochran (ten), D. Fischer-Dieskau (bar), K. C. Kohn (bass), F. Leitner (cnd), Bavarian RSO, Bavarian Radio Sym Chorus [G]
Deutsche Grammophon ("20th Century Classics" series) 3-▲ 427413-2 [ADD]
Cherubini, L.:Les Deux journées, w. F. Wunderlich (ten), M. Cordes (bar), R. Hoyem (sgr), H. Müller-Kray (cnd), Stockholm RSO, Stockholm Radio Chorus *(rec live, Stockholm 1960)*
Melodram ▲ CDM 19507 [ADD]
Janácek, L.:Jenůfa, w. A. Varnay (sop), W. Cochran (ten), Cox (sgr), R. Kubelik (cnd), Bavarian State Opera Orch, Bavarian State Opera Chorus [G] *(rec live in Munich, Mar. 17, 1970)*
Myto 2-▲ 2 MCD 90422 [ADD]
Strauss, R.:Elektra, w. A. Varnay (sop/mez), M. Mödl (sop/mez), J. King (ten), E. Wächter (bar), H. von Karajan (cnd), Vienna PO, Vienna State Opera Chorus [G] *(rec 1964)*
Melodram 2-▲ MEL 27044 [AAD]
Strauss, R.:Elektra (sels), w. A. Varnay (sop/mez), J. King (ten), H. von Karajan (cnd), Vienna PO, Vienna State Opera Chorus [G] *(rec live in Salzburg, 8/11/64)*
Arkadia 3-▲ 213 (m) [ADD]

Hillerbrandt, Otto (sgr)
Puccini, G.:La Bohème, w. Trude Eipperle (sop), Hildegarde Ranczak (sop), Alfons Fügel (ten), Carl Kronenberg (bar), Georg Hann (bass), Georg Wieter (bass), Emil Graf (sgr), Karl Schmidt (sgr), C. Krauss (cnd), Bavarian State Opera Orch, Bavarian State Opera Chorus *(rec 1940)*
Preiser 2-▲ PRE 90275

Hilley, R. (bar)
Rorem, N.:Hearing, w. R. Rees (sop), K. Wheeler (mez), M. Galloway (ten), R. Wagner (cl), J. Hamlin (tpt), D. Starobin (mand), D. Davidson (vn), K. Askew (va), J. Babich (db), P. Suits (pno), D. Druckman (perc), G. Smith (cnd)
Premier ▲ PRCD 1035 [ADD]

Hillier, Paul (bass)
The Age of Cathedrals, w. Theater of Voices [cnd:Paul Hillier], Paul Elliot (ten), Alan Bennett (ten)
Harmonia Mundi ▲ HMU 907157 ■ HMU 407157
Cavalieri, E. de:Rappresentatione di Anima et di Corpo, w. Judith Nelson (mez), W. Stewart (cnd), Whole Noyse
Koch International Classics ▲ KIC 7363
Mozart, W.A.:Vesperae de Dominica, w. L. Dawson (sop), E. James (mez), R. Covey-Crump (ten), S. Cleobury (cnd), Cambridge Classical Players, Hilliard Ensemble, King's College Choir [L]
EMI Classics ▲ CDC 49672 [DDD]
Mozart, W.A.:Vesperae solennes, w. L. Dawson (sop), E. James (mez), R. Covey-Crump (ten), S. Cleobury (cnd), Cambridge Classical Players, Hilliard Ensemble, King's College Choir [L]
EMI Classics ▲ CDC 49672 [DDD]
Proensa, w. Stephen Stubbs (lt/voc), Andrew Lawrence-King (hp/voc), Erin Headley (vielle)
ECM New Series ▲ 78118-21368-2 [DDD]
Songs for a Tudor King, w. P. Hillier (cnd), Hillard Ensemble, Judith Nelson (sop), David James (ct), Paul Elliott (ten), Leigh Nixon (ten)
Saga Classics ▲ 3378 [ADD]
Stockhausen, K.:Stimmung, w. K. Flowers (sop), P. Walmsley-Clark (sop), Long (sgr), R. Covey-Crump (ten), P. Rose (bass)
Hyperion ▲ CDA 66115

Hill Smith, Marilyn (sop)
Edwardian Echoes ▲ [DDD]
An Evening of Operetta, w. other soloists, various English orchs
Koch International ("Performance" series) ▲ KOC 322632 [DDD]
Lloyd, G.:Iernin, w. C. Powell (mez), G. Pogson (ten), H. Herford (bar), M. Rivers (bar)
Albany 3-▲ TROY 121/23 [DDD]
Pacini, G.:Maria Tudor, w. P. Walker (sop), K. Lewis (ten), C. Blades (bar), D. Parry (cnd), English SO *(rec 1983)* Italian Opera Rarities ▲ IOR 7714 [ADD]
Strauss (II), Joh.:Music of, w. C. Pollack (cnd), Slovak RSO Bratislava—Csárdás [from Fledermaus]; Goddess of Reason (quadrille); On the Banks of the Danube; First Love (romance); Clever Little Gretel (waltz); Take a Chance (gallop); Where the Lemon-Trees Blossom (waltz); New Csárdás [from Fledermaus]; If You Have a Sweet Beloved; Voices of Spring (waltz); The Slumbering Gables; First Thought; Odeon Waltz; A Verse for Dancing; Sweet Tears; Posthumous Waltz No. 4 *(rec Slovak Radio Concert Hall, Bratislava, May & Dec 1994)* Marco Polo ▲ 8.223276 [DDD]
Treasures of Operetta I, w. Peter Morrison (bar), Chandos Concert Orch [cnd:Stuart Barry]
Chandos ▲ CHAN 8362 [DDD]
Treasures of Operetta II, w. Peter Morrison (bar), Chandos Concert Orch [cnd:Stuart Barry], Ambrosian Singers Chandos ▲ CHAN 8561 [DDD]
Treasures of Operetta III, w. Peter Morrison (bar), Chandos Concert Orch [cnd:Stuart Barry], Chandos Singers Chandos ▲ CHAN 8759 [DDD]

Hilz, Christian (bass)
Bach, J.S.:Cant 36, w. Silke Wenzel (sop), Reiner Schneider-Waterburg (alt), Kobie van Rensburg (ten), W. Kelber (cnd), Munich Monteverdi Orch *(rec live, Dec 1995)* Calig ▲ 50963 [DDD]
Bach, J.S.:Cant 40, w. Silke Wenzel (sop), Reiner Schneider-Waterburg (alt), Kobie van Rensburg (ten), W. Kelber (cnd), Munich Monteverdi Orch *(rec live, Dec 1995)* Calig ▲ 50963 [DDD]
Bach, J.S.:Cant 91, w. Silke Wenzel (sop), Reiner Schneider-Waterburg (alt), Kobie van Rensburg (ten), W. Kelber (cnd), Munich Monteverdi Orch *(rec live, Dec 1995)* Calig ▲ 50963 [DDD]

Himmelheber, Liat (mez)
Ullmann, V.:Songs, w. Christine Schäfer (sop), Yaron Windmüller (bar), Axel Bauni (pno)—5 Liebeslieder, Op. 18; 6 Lieder, Op. 17; 3 Sonette, Op. 29; 6 Sonnets, Op. 34; Geistliche Lieder, Op. 20; Liederbuch des Hafis, op. 30; Der Mensch und sein Tag, Op. 47; Immer inmitten; Chinesische Lieder; 3 Lieder Orfeo 2-▲ 380952 [DDD]

Himmelmann, Friedrich (sgr)
Verdi, G.:Un ballo in maschera, w. Martha Mödl (sop—Ulrica), Walburga Wegner (sop—Amelia), Anny Schlemm (mez—Oscar), Lorenz Fehenberger (ten—Ricardo), Dietrich Fischer-Dieskau (bar—Renato), Wilhelm Schirp (bass—Samuel), Willy Schoneweib (bass—Tom), Gunther Wilhelms (bass—Silvan), Fritz Augustin (sgr—Ein Richter), Friedrich Himmelmann (sgr—Ein Diener Amelia), F. Busch (cnd), Cologne RSO, Bernhard Alois Zimmermann (cnd), Cologne Radio Chorus Calig 2-▲ 50946/47 (m) [ADD]

Hinds, Esther (sop)
Barber, S.:Antony & Cleopatra, w. J. Wells (bass), C. Badea (cnd), Spoleto Festival Orch, Westminster Choir [E] *(rec live at the Spoleto Festival in Spoleto, Italy, June 1983)*
New World 2-▲ 322/24-2 [AAD]
Sessions, R.:When Lilacs Last in the Dooryard Bloom'd, w. F. Quivar (mez), D. Cossa (bar), S. Ozawa (cnd), Boston SO, Tanglewood Festival Chorus [E] New World ▲ NW 296-2 [AAD]

Hinds, Ruby (mez)
Cage, J.:Europera 3, w. Suzan Hanson (sop), Ruby Hinds (mez), Patricia McAfee (mez), Michael Lyon (ten), Richard Powell (ten), Kevin Bell (bass), Brian Pezzone (pno), Vicki Ray (pno), Hannes Geiger (record players), Joseph Giri (record players), William Houston (record players), Dren McDonald (record players), Ronda Rindone (record players), Clarice Ross (record players), Scott Fraser (tape), A. Culver (cnd), Long Beach Opera Orch *(rec Center Theater, Long Beach, CA, Nov. 13, 1993)*
Mode 2-▲ MODE 38/39

Hines, Altonell (mez)
Thomson, V.:4 Saints in 3 Acts, w. Inez Matthews (sop—St Settlement), Beatrice Robinson-Wayne (sop—St Teresa I), Altonell Hines (mez—Commère), Ruby Greene (alt—St Teresa II), David Bethea (ten—St Stephen), Charles Holland (ten—St Chavez), Edward Matthews (bar—St Ignatius), Randolph Robinson (bar—St Plan), Abner Dorsey (bass—Compère), V. Thomson (cnd), *(orch unknown)* [abridged by Thompson] *(rec June 25, 1947)* RCA Gold Seal ▲ 09026-68163-2 [ADD]

Hines, Gregory (sgr)
The Gershwins in Hollywood, w. J. Mauceri (cnd), Hollywood Bowl SO, Patti Austin
Philips ▲ 434274-2 [DDD]

Hines, Jennifer (mez)
Starer, R.:Night Thoughts, w. Theresa Santiago (sop), Anthony Griffey (ten), Neil Michaels (bar), Adelaide Roberts (pno), Edgar Roberts (pno) Albany ▲ TROY 151 [DDD]

Hines, Jerome (bass)
Beethoven, L. van:Missa Solemnis, w. M. Marshall (sop), N. Merriman (mez), E. Conley (ten), A. Toscanini (cnd), NBC SO, Robert Shaw Chorale *(rec 1953)*
RCA Gold Seal ▲ 60272-2-RG [ADD] ■ 60272-4-RG
Handel, G.F.:Messiah, w. Elisabeth Schwarzkopf (sop), Grace Hoffman (cta), Nikolai Gedda (ten), O. Klemperer (cnd), Philharmonia Orch, Philharmonia Chorus EMI Classics 3-▲ ZDMC 63621
Meyerbeer, G.:Le Prophète, w. Renata Scotto (sop), Marilyn Horne (mez), James McCracken (ten), H. Lewis (cnd), Royal PO, Ambrosian Opera Chorus [F] CBS 3-▲ M3K 34340 [ADD]
Puccini, G.:La Bohème, w. R. Tebaldi (sop), Candida (sgr), F. Corelli (ten), F. Guarrera (bar), A. Guadagno (cnd), *(orch & chorus unknown)* [I] *(rec live, Philadelphia 12/2/69)*
Standing Room Only 2-▲ SRO 821-2 [ADD]
Verdi, G.:Macbeth, w. L. Rysanek (sop), C. Bergonzi (ten), L. Warren (bar), E. Leinsdorf (cnd), Metropolitan Opera Orch, New York Metropolitan Opera Chorus [I]
RCA Gold Seal 2-▲ 4516-2-RG [ADD]

Hintermeier, Margaretha (cta)
Haydn, J.:The Seven Last Words of Christ on the Cross, w. Inge Nielsen (sop), Anthony Rolfe Johnson (ten), Robert Holl (bass), N. Harnoncourt (cnd), Vienna Concentus Musicus, Arnold Schoenberg Choir [oratorio version] Teldec ▲ 2292-46458-2 ZK
Schmidt, F.:Das Buch mit sieben Siegeln, w. Gabriele Fontana (sop), Kurt Azesberger (ten), Eberhard Büchner (ten—Johannes), Robert Holl (bass—Voice of the Lord), Robert Holzer (bass), Martin Haselböck (org), H. Stein (cnd), Vienna SO, Vienna Sym Chorus *(rec live, Vienna Music Hall, May 1996)*
Calig 2-▲ CAL 50978/9 [DDD]
Schubert, Franz:Mass 2, w. B. Bonney (sop), B. Poschner (ten), J. A. Pita (ten), A. Schmidt (bar), C. Abbado (cnd), CO of Europe Deutsche Grammophon ▲ 435486-2
Schumann, R.:Requiem Mignon, w. B. Bonney (sop), B. Poschner (ten), J. A. Pita (ten), A. Schmidt (bar), C. Abbado (cnd), CO of Europe Deutsche Grammophon ▲ 435486-2
Wagner, R.:Das Rheingold, w. Gabriele Fontana (sop—Woglinde), Nancy Gustafson (sop—Freia), Ildiko Komlosi (mez—Wellgunde), Hanna Schwarz (mez—Fricka), Elena Zaremba (mez—Erda), Margareta Hintermeier (cta—Flosshilde), Kim Begley (ten—Loge), Peter Schreier (ten—Mime), Thomas Sunnegardh (ten—Froh), Robert Hale (bass-bar—Wotan), Walter Fink (bass—Fafner), Franz-Josef Kapellmann (bass—Alberich), Jan-Hendrik Rootering (bass—Fasolt), Eike Wilm Schulte (bass—Donner), C. von Dohnányi (cnd), Cleveland Orch *(rec Severance Hall, Cleveland, Ohio, Dec 1993)*
London 2-▲ 443690-2

Hintz, Gundula (sop)
Mozart, W.A.:Notturnos Sops, w. C. Schäfer (sop), D. Fischer-Dieskau (bar), Berlin PO Winds
Orfeo ▲ 218911 [DDD]
Mozart, W.A.:Più non si trovano, w. C. Schäfer (sop), D. Fischer-Dieskau (bar), Berlin PO Winds
Orfeo ▲ 218911 [DDD]

Hinz, Helle (sop)
Haeffner, J.C.F.:Electra, w. Hillevi Martinpelto (sop), Peter Mattei (bar), Mikael Samuelson (bar), Swedish Radio Choir, T. Schuback (cnd), Drottningholm Baroque Ensemble Caprice 2-▲ CAP 22030
Mozart, W.A.:Songs, w. H. Metz (pno)—Abendempfindung; An Chloë; Das Kinderspiel; Schlafe, mein Prinzchen; Trennungslied; Die Verschweigung; Warnung Kontrapunkt ▲ 32052 [DDD]

Hinz, Helle (sop) (cont.)
Schubert, Franz:Songs (misc), w. H. Metz (pno)—An die Musik; An die Nachtigall; An Sylvia; Fischerweise; Die Forelle; Fruhlingslaube; Ganymed; Im Frühling; Heidenröslein; Lachen und Weinen; Wiegenlied Kontrapunkt ▲ 32052 [DDD]

Hiolski, Andrzej (bar)
Bizet, G.:Carmen (sels), w. Krystyna Szczepanska (alt—Carmen), Bogdan Paprocki (ten—Don José), Andrzej Hiolski (bar—Escamillo), Alina Bolechowska (sgr—Micaela), J. Semkow (cnd), Warsaw PO, Warsaw National Phil Chorus Polskie Nagrania ▲ PNCD 213 [AAD]
Moniuszko, S.:Halka, w. Barbara Nieman (sop), Halina Sloniowska (sop), Jan Góralski (ten), Bogdan Paprocki (ten), Leslaw Pawluk (ten), Kazimierz Pustelak (ten), Edmund Kossowski (bass), Edward Pawlak (bass), Z. Gorzynski (cnd), Warsaw State Opera House Orch, Warsaw National Opera Chorus *(rec Warsaw, 1965)* Polskie Nagrania ▲ PNCD 092 [AAD]
Moniuszko, S.:Halka, w. B. Zagórzanka (sop), R. Racewicz (mez), W. Ochman (ten), J. Ostapuik (bass), R. Satanowski (cnd), Warsaw Teatr Wielki Orch, Warsaw Teatr Wielki Chorus *(rec live, 10/14/86)*
CPO 2-▲ CPO 999032-2 [DDD]
Moniuszko, S.:Haunted Manor, w. Bozena Betley-Siradzka (sop—Hanna), Anna Witkowska (sop—Marta/Stara Niewiasta), Wiera Baniewicz (mez—Jadwiga), Aleksandra Imalska (mez—Czesnikowa), Kazimierz Dluha (Grzes), Zdzislaw Nikodem (ten—Damazy), Wieslaw Ochman (ten—Stefan), Andrzej Hiolski (bar—Miecznik), Florian Skulski (bar—Maciej), Leonard Mróz (bass—Zbigniew), Andrzej Saciuk (bass—Skoluba), J. Krenz (cnd), Cracow Polish Radio-TV Orch, Cracow Polish Radio-TV Chorus *(rec Cracovia, 1978)* Agora Music ("Phoenix" series) 3-▲ 509 [ADD]
Moniuszko, S.:Haunted Manor, w. Halina Slonicka (sop), Bozena Brun-Baranska (mez), Barbara Lawcewicz (mez), Krystyna Szczepanska (mez), Zdzislaw Nikodem (ten), Bogdan Paprocki (ten), Edmund Kossowski (bass), Bernard Ladysz (bass), W. Rowicki (cnd), Warsaw State Opera House Orch, Warsaw National Opera Chorus *(rec Warsaw, 1965)* Polskie Nagrania ▲ PNCD 093 [AAD]
Penderecki, K.:The Passion & Death of Our Lord Jesus Christ According to St. Luke, w. Leszek Herdegen (nar), Stefania Woytowicz (sop), Bernard Ladysz (bass), H. Czyz (cnd), Cracow PO, Cracow Phil Boys' Chorus, Cracow Phil Mixed Choir Polskie Nagrania 2-▲ PNCD 017 A/B
Szymanowski, K.:King Roger, w. B. Zagórzanka (sop), A. Malewicz-Madey (cta), H. Grychnik (ten), W. Ochman (ten), L. A. Mróz (bass), K. Stryja (cnd), Polish State PO Katowice, Cracow Phil Boys' Chorus, Polish State Phil Chorus *(rec Apr. 7-9, 1990)*
Marco Polo ("Opera Classics" series) 2-▲ 8.223339/40 [DDD]
Szymanowski, K.:Stabat Mater, w. Stefania Woytowicz (sop), Krystyna Szczepanska (alt), W. Rowicki (cnd), Warsaw PO, Warsaw National Phil Chorus *(rec Concert Hall at the National PO, Warsaw, 1961)*
Polskie Nagrania ▲ PLN 063 [ADD]

Hirata, Kyoko (sop)
Ifukube, A.:Lullabies (3) Among the Native Tribes on the Island of Sakhalin, w. Yuko Umemura (pno)
Camerata ▲ 32CM 290

Hirayama, Michiko (sop)
Scelsi, G.:Khoom, w. Frank Lloyd (hn), Maurizio Ben Omar (perc), A. Brizzi (cnd), Arditti String Quartet
Salabert ▲ SCD 8904-5
Scelsi, G.:Music of, w. Maurizio Ben Omar (gtr/perc), Federico Mondelci (sax), A. Brizzi (cnd), Gruppo Musica Insieme, Nuovo Ensemble Italiano—Pranam I for Voice, 12 Instrs & Band; Ko-Tha [3 danses de Shiva] for Gtr; I presagi for 11 Instruments; Riti [I funerali di Alessandro Magno]; Trio for 3 Percussionists; Manto per quattro for Voice, Fl, Trbn & Vc; Kya for Sax & 7 Instruments; Entretiens avec Giacento Scelsi Memoire Vive ▲ CD 262009 [ADD/DDD]

Hirsch, Shelley (sgr)
Thorington, H.:Partial Perceptions, w. Joseph Celli (instrs), Helen Thorington (elec)
¿What Next? ▲ WN 0013

Hirst, Grayson (ten)
Britten, H.:Serenade, Op. 31, w. L. William Kuyper (hn), K. Klein (cnd), New York Virtuosi Chamber SO
Allegretto ▲ ACD 8203
Dvořák, A.:Songs, w. C. Ciesinski (mez), J. Ostendorf (bass-bar), R. Palmer (pno)—Serbian Songs, Op. 6; Folk Tunes, Op. 73; 4 Lieder, Op. 82; Love Songs, Op. 83; Russian Folk Duets
Erasmus ▲ WVH 084
Janácek, L.:The Diary of One Who Disappeared, w. S. Love (mez), Kubalek (pno), Columbia Pro Cantare Women's Ensemble [Cz] Arabesque ▲ Z 6513 [DDD]

Hirst, Linda (mez)
Handel, G.F.:Acis & Galatea, w. J. Baird (sop), S. Oosting (ten), J. Ostendorf (b-bar), J. Somary (cnd), Amor Artis Orch, Amor Artis Chorale [E] Newport Classic 2-▲ NC 60045 [DDD]
Lachenmann, H.:temA, w. Rechèrche Ensemble Montaigne ▲ MO 782023
Monteverdi, C.:Incoronazione, w. A. Augér (sop), S. Leonard (sop), D. Jones (mez), J. Bowman (ct), G. Reinhart (bass)., R. Hickox (cnd), City of London Baroque Sinfonia Virgin Classics 3-▲ CDCC 59524
Monteverdi, C.:Incoronazione, w. A. Augér (soprano—Poppea), D. Jones (mez—Nerone), L. Hirst (mez—Ottavia), J. Bowman (ct—Ottone), R. Hickox (cnd), City of London Baroque Sinfonia
Virgin Classics ▲ CDCC 45082
Tippett, M.:King Priam, w. Heather Harper (sop—Hecuba), Linda Hirst (sop—Serving Woman), Felicity Palmer (sop—Andromache), Julian Saipe (sop—Paris), Yvonne Minton (mez—Helen), Ann Murray (mez—Nurse), Kenneth Bowen (ten—Hermes), Peter Hall (ten—Young Guard), Philip Langridge (ten—Paris), Robert Tear (ten—Achilles), Thomas Allen (bar—Hector), Norman Bailey (bar—Priam), Stephen Roberts (bar—Patroclus), David Wilson-Johnson (bar—Old Man), D. Atherton (cnd), London Sinfonietta, London Sinfonietta Chorus Chandos ▲ CHAN 9406/7 [DDD]

Hirsti, Marianne (sop)
Beethoven, L. van:Missa Solemnis, w. C. Watkinson (cta), A. Murgatroyd (ten), M. George (bass), T. Kvam (cnd), Hanover Band, Oslo Cathedral Choir [period instrs] [L] Nimbus ▲ NI 5109 [DDD]
Grieg, E.:Songs, w. K. M. Sandve (ten), K. Skram (bar), R. Jansen (pno)—Four Songs, Op. 15; 3 Songs from Peer Gynt; 5 Songs by Vilhelm Krag, Op. 60; 6 Songs by Holger Drachmann, Op. 49 [N] *(rec March & Dec. 1991)* Victoria ▲ VCD 19038 [DDD]
Grieg, E.:Songs, w. K. M. Sandve (ten), K. Skram (bar), R. Jansen (pno)—Songs & Ballads by Munch, Op. 9; 5 Poems by Paulsen, Op. 26; Romances, Op. 39; 5 Songs by Benzon, Op. 69; 5 Songs by Benzon, Op. 70 Victoria ▲ VCD 19043
Grieg, E.:Songs, w. K. Skram (bar), R. Jansen (pno)—7 Children's Songs, Op. 61; Haugtussa, Op. 67; Songs from Haugtussa not included in Op. 67; Clara's Song; I Love You, Dear; The Princess; Sighs; Morning Prayer at School Victoria ▲ VCD 19040
Grieg, E.:Songs, w. C. Pfeiler (mez), K. M. Sandve (ten), K. Skram (bar), R. Jansen (pno)—Op. 4, Nos. 1, 2, 3, 4, 5 & 6; Op. 21, Nos. 1, 2, 3 & 4; Op. 44, Nos. 1, 2, 3, 4, 5 & 6; Op. 48, Nos. 1, 2, 3, 4, 5 & 6; Op. 58, Nos. 1, 2, 3, 4 & 5 [N, G] Victoria ▲ VCD 19041
Grieg, E.:Songs, w. C. Pfeiler (mez), K. M. Sandve (ten), K. Skram (bar), R. Jansen (pno)—4 Songs, Op. 2; 4 Songs by Christian Winther, Op. 10; 9 Songs, Op. 18; 6 Songs by Ibsen, Op. 25
Victoria ▲ VCD 19042
Grieg, E.:Songs, w. K. M. Sandve (ten), K. Skram (bar), R. Jansen (pno)—For L.M. Lindeman's Silver Wedding Anniversary; The Blueberry; Yuletide Cradle Song; Devoutest of Maidens; Little Lad; The Forgotten Maid; The White & Red, Red Roses Victoria ▲ VCD 19044
Thommessen, O.A.:Woven in Stems, w. A. Rasilainen (cnd), Aalborg SO Caprice ▲ CAP 21403

Hirte, Klaus (bar)
Wagner, R.:Die Meistersinger von Nürnberg, w. Hannelore Bode (sop), Jean Cox (ten), Karl Ridderbusch (bass), Hans Sotin (bass), S. Varviso (cnd), Bayreuth Festival Orch, Bayreuth Festival Chorus [1974] [G]
Philips 4-▲ 434611-2 [ADD]
Wagner, R.:Die Meistersinger von Nürnberg, w. Hannelore Bode (sop), Jean Cox (ten), Karl Ridderbusch (bass), Hans Sotin (bass), S. Varviso (cnd), Bayreuth Festival Orch, Bayreuth Festival Chorus [1974]
Philips 32-▲ 434420-2 [ADD/DDD]
Weill, K.:Aufstieg und Fall der Stadt Mahagonny, w. A. Silja (sop), A. Schlemm (mez), W. Neumann (ten), T. Lehrberger (ten), J. Latham-König (cnd), Cologne RSO, Cologne Radio Chorus [G]
Capriccio 2-▲ CD 10160/1 [DDD]

Hirtreiter, Bernhard (ten)
Brixi, F.X.:Missa di Gloria, w. F. Wagner (sop), R. Schneider-Waterberg (alt), M. Mantaj (bass), C. Hammer (org), W. Kelber (cnd), Munich Monteverdi Orch, Munich Concerto Vocale *(rec 1993)*
Calig ▲ CAL 50927 [ADD]

Hislop, Joseph (ten)
Joseph Hislop, w. Piero Coppola (cnd), John Barbirolli (cnd), Jacques Heuvel (cnd), et al., Percy Kahn (pno) *(rec HMV recordings, 1923–30)* Pearl ▲ PEA 9956 (m) [AAD]

Hitchen, Booth (ten)
Verdi, G.:La traviata, w. Maria Caniglia (sop—Violetta), Maria Huder (mez—Flora), Gladys Palmer (cta—Annina), Octave Dua (ten—Giuseppe), Beniamino Gigli (ten—Alfredo), Booth Hitchen (ten—D'Obigny), Adelio Zagonara (bar—Gastone), Aristide Baracchi (bar—Douphol), Mario Basiola (bar—Germont), Norman Walker (bass—Dr. Grenville), V. Gui (cnd), London PO, London Phil Chorus *(rec Royal Opera House, Covent Garden, May 22, 1939)* Minerva 2-▲ MN A28/29 (m) [ADD]

Hite, William (ten)
Angeli, Music of Angels, w. PAN Ensemble, Harlan B. Hokin (ten), Paul Cummings (bar), Tapestry *(rec Studio A, National Music Center, Lenox, MA, Sept 11–14, 1995)* Telarc ▲ CD 80448 [DDD]
Gilles, J.:Mess des morts, w. A. Azema (sop), J. Nirouët (alt), P. Mason (bar), J. Cohen (cnd), Boston Camerata, Ensemble de Tambours Provençaux, Aix-en-Provence Festival Chorus Erato ▲ 2292-45989-2
Mozart, W.A.:Laut verkünde unsre Freude, w. W. Bastian (ten), W. Sharp (bar), A. Parrott (cnd), Boston Early Music Festival Orch, Boston Early Music Festival Chorus [G] Denon ▲ CO 77152 [DDD]
Mozart, W.A.:Requiem, w. J. Bryden (sop), M. Westbrook-Geha (mez), S. Richardson (bar), A. Parrott (cnd), Boston Early Music Festival Orch, Boston Early Music Festival Chorus [L] Denon ▲ CO 77152 [DDD]
Tristan et Iseult:A Medieval Romance in Music & Poetry, w. Anne Azema (sop), Ellen Hargis (sop), Henri Ledroit (alt), Richard Morrison (bass), Andrea von Ramm (sgr), Boston Camerata [cnd:Joel Cohen] Erato ▲ 98482-2

Hlavenková, Anna (sop)
Zelenka, J.D.:Missa sanctissimae trinitatis, w. Magdalena Kožená (alt), Lubomir Moravec (alt), Stanislav Predota (ten), Richard Sporka (ten), Michal Pospí il (bass), M. Štryncl (cnd), Musica Florea Studio Matou ▲ MAT 17 [DDD]

Hlazmair, W. (bar)
Wolf, H.:Goethe-Lieder (sels), w. T. Palm (pno) Collins Classics ▲ COL 1402 [DDD]

Hloiski, A. (bar)
Szymanowski, K.:Stabat Mater, w. J. Gadulanka (sop), K. Szostek-Radkowa (mez), K. Stryja (cnd), Polish State PO, Polish State Phil Chorus Marco Polo ▲ 8.223293 [DDD]

Hoare, Peter (ten)
Sullivan, A.:The Yeomen of the Guard, w. Felicity Palmer (sop—Dame Carruthers), Pamela Helen Stephens (mez—Phoebe Meryll), Neill Archer (ten—Col Fairfax), Peter Hoare (ten—Leonard Meryll), Ralph Mason (ten—1st Yeoman), Donald Maxwell (bar—Wilfred Shadbolt), Peter Savidge (bar—Lieutenant Sir Richard Cholmondely), Donald Adams (bass—Sergeant Meryll), Richard Suart (bass—Jack Point), Peter Lloyd Evans (sgr—2nd Yeoman), Alwyn Mellor (sgr—Elsie Maynard), Clare O'Neill (sgr—Kate), C. Mackerras (cnd), Welsh National Opera Orch, Welsh National Opera Chorus *(rec Brangwyn Hall, Swasea, Wales, Apr 18–30 & May 1, 1995)* Telarc 2-▲ CD 80404 [DDD]

Hoch, Beverley (sop)
Handel, G.F.:Imeneo, w. Julianne Baird (sop—Rosmene), Beverly Hoch (sop—Clomiri), D'Anna Fortunato (cta—Tirinto), Jan Opalach (bass—Argenio), John Ostendorf (bass—Imeneo), Edward Brewer (hpd), R. Palmer (cnd), Brewer CO Vox Box 2-▲ CDX 5135 [DDD]
Mozart, W.A.:Zauberflöte, w. D. Upshaw (sop), A. Rolfe Johnson (ten), A. Schmidt (bar), R. Norrington (cnd), London Classical Players [period instrs] EMI Classics 2-▲ CDCB 54287
Mozart, W.A.:Zauberflöte (sels), w. D. Upshaw (sop), A. Rolfe Johnson (ten), A. Schmidt (bar), R. Norrington (cnd), London Classical Players [period instrs] EMI Classics ▲ CDC 54492
Summerdays:From the Musical Masterworks Festival at Old Lyme, w. Greenawald, Sheir (sop), John Koch (ten), Aloysia Friedman (vn), Michele Sidener (va), Norman Krieger (cnd), Norman Krieger (pno) Well-Tempered Productions ▲ WTP 5173 [DDD]
With Pipes & Voices, w. Burton Tidwell (org), Zion Evangelical Church Choir Wooster OH Arkay ▲ ARK 6150 [DDD]

Hodgson, Alfreda (cta)
Bach, J.S.:St. Matthew Passion, w. F. Lott (sop), R. Tear (ten), J. Shirley-Quirk (bar), S. Roberts (bar), D. Willcocks (cnd), Thames CO, Bach Choir [E] ASV Quicksilva 3-▲ ASQ 324 [ADD]
Beethoven, L. van:Sym 9, "Choral Sym", w. H. Harper (sop), R. Tear (ten), G. Howell (bass), R. Hickox (cnd), Northern Sinfonia of England, London Sym Chorus members ASV Quicksilva ▲ ASQ 6069 [DDD]
Brahms, J.:Alto Rhap, w. B. Haitink (cnd), Bavarian RSO, Bavarian Radio Chorus [G] Orfeo ▲ 025821 [DDD]
Britten, H.:Spring Sym, w. E. Gale (sop), M. Hill (ten), R. Hickox (cnd), London SO, London Sym Chorus, Southend Boys' Choir [E] Chandos ▲ CHAN 8855 [DDD]
Elgar, E.:The Apostles, w. A. Hargan (sop), D. Rendall (ten), S. Roberts (bar), B. Terfel (bass-bar), R. Lloyd (bass), R. Hickox (cnd), London SO, London Sym Chorus [E] Chandos 2-▲ CHAN 8875/76 [DDD]
Elgar, E.:The Dream of Gerontius, w. Robert Tear (ten), Benjamin Luxon (bar), A. Gibson (cnd), Scottish National Orch, Scottish National Chorus CRD 2-▲ 33267
Elgar, E.:The Kingdom, w. Y. Kenny (sop), C. Gillert (ten), B. Luxon (bass), L. Slatkin (cnd), London PO, London Phil Chorus RCA Red Seal 2-▲ 07863-57862-2
Handel, G.F.:Messiah, w. Kaaren Erickson (sop), Sylvia McNair (sop), Jon Humphrey (ten), Richard Stilwell (bar), R. Shaw (cnd), Atlanta SO, Atlanta Sym Chorus [E] Telarc 2-▲ CD 80093-2 [DDD]
Handel, G.F.:Messiah, w. Kaaren Erickson (sop), Sylvia McNair (sop), Jon Humphrey (ten), Richard Stilwell (bar), R. Shaw (cnd), Atlanta SO, Atlanta Sym Chorus [E] Telarc ▲ CD 80103 [DDD]; ▮ CS 30103 (D)
Haydn, J.:Salve regina, H.XXIIIb/2, w. Arleen Auger (sop), Anthony Rolfe Johnson (ten), Gwynne Howell (bass), John Birch (db), L. Heltay (cnd), Argo CO, London Chamber Choir *(rec St. Jude's, London, Feb 1979)* London 2-▲ 443027-2 [ADD]
Mahler, G.:Das Klagende Lied, w. H. Döse (sop), R. Tear (ten), S. Rae, S. Rattle (cnd), City of Birmingham SO, City of Birmingham Sym Chorus EMI ▲ CDC 47089
Mahler, G.:Das Lied von der Erde, w. J. Mitchinson (ten), J. Horenstein (cnd), BBC Northern SO *(rec live, Manchester, April 28, 1972)* Music & Arts ▲ CD 728-1 [AAD]
Mozart, W.A.:Requiem, w. Y. Kenny (sop), A. Davies (ten), G. Howell (bass), R. Hickox (cnd), Northern Sinfonia of England, London Sym Chorus Virgin Classics ▲ CDZ 59648
Pergolesi, G.B.:Stabat mater, w. M. Marshall (sop), G. Kehr (cnd), Mainz CO *(rec 1978)* Vox Box 2-▲ CDX 5081 [ADD]
Pergolesi, G.B.:Stabat mater, w. Felicity Palmer (sop), David Hill (org), G. Guest (cnd), Argo CO, St. John's College Choir Cambridge *(rec 1978)* London 2-▲ 443868-2 [ADD]
Tippett, M.:The Midsummer Marriage (dances), w. M. Tippett (cnd), English Northern Philharmonia, Opera North Chorus [E] Nimbus ▲ NI 5217 [DDD]

Hoeflin, Johannes (ten)
Schütz, H.:St. John Passion, w. Herta Flebbe (sop), Johannes Hoeflin (ten—Evangelist), Rolf Bössow (ten—Pilate), Gert Spierling (ten), Jakob Stämpfli (bass—Jesus), Teinhard Tuge (bass—soliloquies), W. Ehmann (cnd), Westphalia Kantorei *(rec Münster zu Herfor, Sept. 1961)* Cantate ▲ 57602 [ADD]

Hoekman, Guus (bass)
Bizet, G.:Les Pêcheurs de perles, w. E. Spoorenberg (sop), A. Vanzo (ten), J. Joris (bar), J. Fournet (cnd), Netherlands Radio PO [F] *(rec live, 1963)* Verona 2-▲ 2707/08 (m) [AAD]

Hoel, Lena (sop)
Kraus, J.M.:Soliman II, w. B. Ortendahl-Corin (sop), B.-O. Morgny (ten), T. Wallstrom (bass), P. Brunelle (cnd), Royal Swedish Opera Orch, Sweden Royal Opera Chorus Virgin Classics ▲ 59068 [DDD]
Sandström, S.-D.:The High Mass, w. Sara Olsson (sop), Siri Torjesen (sop), Marianne Eklöf (mez), Annika Skoglund (mez), Peter Bengtson (org), L. Segerstam (cnd), Swedish RSO, Eric Ericson Chamber Choir *(rec live, Berwald Hall, Stockholm, Nov. 25 & 26, 1994)* Caprice 2-▲ CAP 22036

Hoene, Barbara (sop)
Brahms, J.:Liebeslieder Waltzes SATB, w. Gisela Pohl (alt), Armin Ude (ten), Siegfried Lorenz (bar), Klaus Bässler (pno), Dieter Zechlin (pno), W.-D. Hauschild (cnd), Berlin RSO Berlin Classics ▲ BER 9269

Hoene, Barbara (sop) (cont.)
Brahms, J.:Neue Liebeslieder Waltzes, w. Gisela Pohl (alt), Armin Ude (ten), Siegfried Lorenz (bar), Klaus Bässler (pno), Dieter Zechlin (pno), W.-D. Hauschild (cnd), Berlin RSO Berlin Classics ▲ BER 9269

Hoff, B. (bass)
Grieg, E.:Lyric Pieces, w. G. Solum (hn), B. Fiskum (cnd), Trondheim Soloists—Op. 68/4 & 5 [arr Grieg for orch] Victoria ▲ VCD 19072

Höffgen, Marga (cta)
Bach, J.S.:Cant 41, w. H. Donath (sop), A. Kraus (ten), S. Nimsgern (b-bar), H. Rilling (cnd), Stuttgart Bach Collegium, Gächinger Kantorei [G] Hänssler Classic ▲ 98.870 [AAD]
Bach, J.S.:Cant 48, w. A. Baldin (ten), H. Rilling (cnd), Stuttgart Bach Collegium, Gächinger Kantorei [G] *(rec 1973)* Hänssler Classic ▲ 98.813 [AAD]
Bach, J.S.:Cant 54, w. Hermann Prey (bass), K. Thomas (cnd), Leipzig Gewandhaus Orch, Leipzig St. Thomas Church Choir Berlin Classics ▲ BER CD 9202
Bach, J.S.:Cant 56, w. Hermann Prey (bass), K. Thomas (cnd), Leipzig Gewandhaus Orch, Leipzig St. Thomas Church Choir Berlin Classics ▲ BER CD 9202
Bach, J.S.:Cant 82, w. Hermann Prey (bass), K. Thomas (cnd), Leipzig Gewandhaus Orch, Leipzig St. Thomas Church Choir Berlin Classics ▲ BER CD 9202
Bach, J.S.:Cant 96, w. H. Donath (sop), A. Kraus (ten), S. Nimsgern (b-bar), H. Rilling (cnd), Stuttgart Bach Collegium, Württemberg CO, Gächinger Kantorei [G] *(rec 1973)* Hänssler Classic ▲ 98.814 [AAD]
Bach, J.S.:Cant 108, w. H. Donath (sop), K. Equiluz (ten), H.-F. Kunz (bass), H. Rilling (cnd), Stuttgart Bach Collegium, Gächinger Kantorei [G] *(rec 1980–81)* Hänssler Classic ▲ 98.884 [AAD]
Bach, J.S.:Cant 125, w. K. Equiluz (ten), W. Schöne (bass), H. Rilling (cnd), Bach Ensemble [G] *(rec 1973)* Hänssler Classic ▲ 98.876 [AAD]
Beethoven, L. van:Missa Solemnis, w. E. Söderström (sop), W. Kmentt (ten), M. Talvela (bass), O. Klemperer (cnd), New Philharmonia Orch, New Philharmonia Chorus [L] EMI Classics ("Studio" series) 2-▲ CDMB 69538 [ADD]
Haydn, J.:Mass 3, "Cäcilienmesse", w. Maria Stader (sop), Richard Holm (ten), Josef Greindl (bass), E. Jochum (cnd), Bavarian RSO, Bavarian Radio Chorus Deutsche Grammophon 2-▲ 437383-2 [ADD]
Mahler, G.:Sym 2, w. M. Puetz (sop), C. Schuricht (cnd), Hessian RSO, Hesse Radio Chorus, Frankfurt Singakademie Choir *(rec 1960)* Originals 2-▲ ORISH 819 [ADD]
Verdi, G.:Requiem Mass, w. M. Stader (sop), F. Wunderlich (ten), G. Frick (bass), H. Müller-Kray (cnd), South German RSO, South German Radio Sym Chorus *(rec live, Stuttgart, 11/2/60)* Myto 2-▲ 2 MCD 91648 [ADD]
Wagner, R.:Die Meistersinger von Nürnberg, w. E. Grümmer (sop), R. Schock (ten), G. Unger (ten), H. Prey (bar), B. Kusche (bar), F. Frantz (b-bar), G. Frick (bass), R. Kempe (cnd), Berlin PO *(rec 1956)* EMI Classics 4-▲ CDMD 64154

Hoffman (sgr)
Strauss, R.:Die Frau ohne Schatten, w. L. Rysanek (sop), Thomas (sgr), H. von Karajan (cnd), Vienna State Opera Orch, Vienna State Opera Chorus [G] *(rec live, Vienna, 6/11/64)* Arkadia 3-▲ 207 (m) [ADD]

Hoffman, Cassandra (sop)
Purcell, H.:Dido & Aeneas, w. Cassandra Hoffman (sop—Belinda), Arlene Travis (sop—2nd Witch), Desirée Halac (mez—Sorceress/Spirit), Jennifer Lane (mez—Dido), Elizabeth Norman (alt), Thomas Bogdan (ten—A Sailor), Michael Brown (bar—Aeneas), Curtis Streetman (bar), Caitriona O'Leary (sgr—2nd Woman), Sarah Pillow (sgr—1st Witch), B. Brookshire (cnd), San Cassiano Musici *(rec St. Ignatius of Antioch Episcopal Church, New York City, Spring 1995)* Vox Classics ▲ VOX 7518

Hoffman, Grace (mez)
Cornelius, P.:Der Barbier von Bagdad, w. E. Schwarzkopf (sop), N. Gedda (ten), G. Unger (ten), O. Czerwenka (bass), E. Leinsdorf (cnd), Philharmonia Orch, Philharmonia Chorus EMI Classics ▲ CDMB 65284
Handel, G.F.:Messiah, w. Elisabeth Schwarzkopf (sop), Nikolai Gedda (ten), Jerome Hines (bass), O. Klemperer (cnd), Philharmonia Orch, Philharmonia Chorus EMI Classics 3-▲ ZDMC 63621
Humperdinck, E.:Hänsel und Gretel, w. Lislotte Maikl (sop—Sandman/Dew Fairy), Anneliese Rothenberger (sop—Gretel), Irmgard Seefried (sop—Hänsel), Grace Hoffman (mez—Gertrude), Elisabeth Höngen (cta—Witch), Walter Berry (bass—Peter), A. Cluytens (cnd), Vienna PO, Vienna Boys' Choir EMI Classics 2-▲ CDMB 65661
Mahler, G.:Das Klagende Lied, w. E. Lear (sop), E. Söderström (sop), S. Burrows (ten), E. Haefliger (ten), G. Nienstedt (bass), P. Boulez (cnd), London SO, London Sym Chorus Sony Classical ("Pierre Boulez Edition" series) ▲ SK 45841
Mahler, G.:Das Lied von der Erde, w. Ernst Haefliger (ten), H. Rosbaud (cnd), Cologne RSO *(rec live, Cologne, Germany, Apr 18, 1955)* Agorá Music ("Phoenix" series) ▲ 701 [ADD]
Strauss, R.:Ariadne auf Naxos, w. E. Schwarzkopf (sop), I. Seefried (sop), R. Streich (sop), L. Otto (sop), G. Hoffman (mez), R. Schock (ten), G. Unger (ten), H. Cuénod (ten), H. Prey (bar), F. Ollendorff (bass), H. von Karajan (cnd), Philharmonia Orch [G] *(rec 1954)* EMI Classics ("Studio" series) 2-▲ CDMB 69296 (m) [ADD]
Strauss, R.:Salome, w. B. Nilsson (sop), G. Stolze (ten), W. Kmentt (ten), E. Wächter (bar), G. Solti (cnd), Vienna PO [G] London 2-▲ 414414-2 [ADD]

Hoffman, Lore (sop)
Schumann, R.:Scenes from Goethe's "Faust", w. Walther Ludwig (ten), Karl Schmitt-Walter (bar), H. Schmidt-Isserstedt (cnd), Berlin German Opera Orch, Berlin German Opera Chorus Enterprise ("The Radio Years" series) 2-▲ ENT RY 66

Hoffman, Wendy (mez)
Mezzo-Soprano Arias Syrinx ▲ 94102 [DDD]

Hoffmann, Grace (alt)
Mahler, G.:Das Lied von der Erde, w. Helmut Melchert (ten), H. Rosbaud (cnd), Southwest German RSO Baden-Baden *(rec 1957)* Vox Box 2-▲ CDX2 5518

Hoffmann, Ludwig (bass)
Einem, G. von:Der Prozess, w. Lisa Della Casa (sop—Frl. Bürstner/Die Frau des Gerichtsdieners/Leni), Peter Klein (ten—Der Direktorstellvertreter/Der Student), Max Lorenz (ten—Josef K.), Erich Majkut (ten—Ein Bursche), László Szemere (ten—Titorelli), Alois Pernerstorfer (b-bar—Willem/Der Gerichtsdiener), Alfred Poell (b-bar—Der Advokat), Walter Berry (bass—Franz/Kanzleidirektor), Oskar Czerwenka (bass—Der Untersuchungsrichter/Der Prügler), Ludwig Hofmann (bass—Der Aufseher/Ein Passant/Der Geistliche/Der Fabrikant), Polly Batic (sgr—Frau Grubach), Endreh Koreh (sgr—Albert K.), Luise Leitner (sgr—Ein buckliges Mädchen), K. Böhm (cnd), Vienna PO, Vienna State Opera Chorus *(rec Aug 17, 1953)* Orfeo d'or ("Festspiel Dokumente" series) 2-▲ 392952 (m)
Wagner, R.:Der fliegende Holländer, w. Maria Müller (sop), Joel Berglund (ten), Franz Völker (ten), R. Kraus (cnd), Bayreuth Festival Orch, Bayreuth Festival Chorus *(rec live, Bayreuth, July 18, 1942)* Preiser 2-▲ PRE 90232 [ADD]
Wagner, R.:Der Ring des Nibelungen (sels), w. Adele Kern (sop), Anny Konetzni (sop), Hilde Konetzni (sop), Elisabeth Schumann (sop), Enid Szantho (cta), Josef Kalenberg (ten), Max Lorenz (ten), Set Svanholm (ten), Erich Zimmermann (ten), Hans Hotter (bar), Jaro Prohaska (bar), Emil Schipper (bar), Paul Schöffler (b-bar), H. Knappertsbusch (cnd), Vienna State Opera Orch *(rec Vienna, 1937–1943)* Koch Schwann 2-▲ SCH 314742 [ADD]
Wagner, R.:Siegfried (sels), w. E. Szantho (cta—Erda), M. Lorenz (ten—Siegfried), W. Wernigk (ten—Mime), L. Hoffmann (bass—Wanderer), H. Knappertsbusch (cnd), Vienna State Opera Orch, Vienna State Opera Chorus *(rec June 16, 1937)* Koch Schwann 2-▲ SCH 314602

Hoffmann, M. (nar)
Stravinsky, I.:L'Histoire du soldat, w. H. Schimmelpfennig (nar), A. Szerda (the Devil), P. Leiner (cnd), Contemporano Ensemble Bayer ▲ 100207 [DDD]

Hoffmeister, Frank (ten)
Bach, J.S.:Magnificat, BWV 243, w. J. Bryden (sop), J. Baird (sop), J Gall (ct), J. Opalach (bass), J. Rifkin (cnd), Bach Ensemble [L] Pro Arte ▲ CDD 185 [DDD]
Bach, J.S.:Mass in b, BWV 232, w. J. Baird (sop), J. Nelson (sop), J. Dooley (ct), J. Opalach (bass), J. Rifkin (cnd), Bach Ensemble [L] Elektra/Nonesuch 2-▲ 79036-2 [DDD]; 2-▮ 79036-4 (D)
Macbride, D.:Nocturnos de la Ventana, w. R. Black (cnd), Prism Orch [Sp] Owl ▲ OWL 34 [DDD]

▲ = CD ♦ = Enhanced CD Δ = MD ▮ = Cassette Tape ▯ = DCC

Hoffstedt, Gertrud (sop)

Haeffner, J.C.F.:Electra (sels), w. H. Martinpelto (sop), S. Dahlberg (ten), P.–A. Wahlgren (bar), T. Schuback (cnd), Drottningholm Baroque Ensemble—3 recitatives & arias [Sw] *(rec 1989–90)* Musica Sveciae ▲ MSCD 426 [DDD]

Naumann, J.G.:Arias, w. H. Martinpelto (sop), S. Dahlberg (ten), P. A. Wahlgren (bar), T. Schuback (cnd), Drottningholm Baroque Ensemble—sels. from Amphion & Cora och Alonzo [Sw] Musica Sveciae ▲ MSCD 426 [DDD]

Uttini, F.A.B.:Thetis och Pelée (sels), w. H. Martinpelto (sop), S. Dahlberg (ten), P.–A. Wahlgren (bar), T. Schuback (cnd), Drottningholm Baroque Ensemble [Sw] Musica Sveciae ▲ MSCD 426 [DDD]

Hofmann (sgr)

Jessel, L.:Schwarzwaldmädel (sels), w. E. Lind (sop), F. Fehringer (ten), B. Kusche (bar), Schörg (sgr), Schubart (sgr), Marszalek (cnd), Cologne RSO, Cologne Radio Chorus [G] Acanta ▲ CD 42552 [DDD]

Kálmán, I.:Die Csárdásfürstin (sels), w. E. Köth (sop), F. Fehringer (ten), B. Kusche (bar), Heusser (sgr), Marszalek (cnd), Cologne Radio Orch, Cologne Radio Chorus [G] Acanta ▲ CD 42435 [DDD]

Kálmán, I.:Gräfin Mariza, w. A. Görner (sop), F. Wunderlich (ten), B. Kusche (bar), Hartung (sgr), Marszalek (cnd), Cologne Radio Orch, Cologne Radio Chorus [G] Acanta ▲ CD 42479 [DDD]

Lehár, F.:Paganini (sels), w. A. Schlemm (mez), Lisolette Losch (sop), P. Anders (ten), Gehly (sgr), Schneider (sgr), Marszalek (cnd), Cologne RSO, Cologne Radio Chorus [G] Acanta ▲ CD 43810 [DDD]

Hofmann, Bernd (bass)

Hoffmann, E.T.A.:Undine, w. Barbara Baier (sop—Berthalda), Heidrun Plesch (sop—Undine), Corinna Tippe (sop—Die Herzogin), Maria Hiefinger (mez—Fisherman's Wife), Achim Schamberger (ten—Der Herzog), Johannes Beck (bar—Ritter Huldbrand von Ringstetten), Michael Albert (bass—Fisherman), Ulrich Bosch (bass—Heilmann), Bernd Hofmann (bass—Kühleborn), H. Dechant (cnd), Bamberg Youth Orch Bayer 3–▲ 100256/58 [DDD]

Hofmann, Ludwig (bass)

Nicolai, O.:Lustigen Weiber (sels), w. A. Jerger (b–bar—Herr Fluth), L. Hofmann (bass—Falstaff), F. von Weingartner (cnd), Vienna State Opera Orch *(rec Oct. 28, 1935)* Koch Schwann 2–▲ SCH 314602

Still, W.G.:Tristan und Isolde, w. Kirsten Flagstad (sop), Kerstin Thorborg (mez), Lauritz Melchoir (ten), Julius Huehn (sgr), A. Bodanzky (cnd), *(orch unknown)* *(rec Jan 2, 1937)* Enterprise ("The Fourties" series) 3–▲ ENT 304

Wagner, R.:Die Meistersinger von Nürnberg (sels), w. Lotte Lehmann (sop—Eva), Eyvind Laholm (ten—Walther), Ludwig Hofmann (bass—Hans Sachs), F. von Weingartner (cnd), Vienna State Opera Orch, Vienna State Opera Chorus *(rec Vienna, Sept. 20, 1935)* Koch Schwann 2–▲ SCH 314622 [ADD]

Wagner, R.:Parsifal, w. Gotthelf Pistor (ten), Cornelius Bronsgeest (bar), K. Muck (cnd), Berlin German Opera Orch, Berlin German Opera Chorus Preiser ▲ PRE 90270

Wagner, R.:Der Ring des Nibelungen, w. G. Jones (sop), H. Schwarz (mez), T. Altmeyer (ten), D. McIntyre (b–bar), P. Boulez (cnd), Bayreuth Festival Orch, Bayreuth Festival Chorus Philips 32–▲ 434420–2 [ADD/DDD]

Wagner, R.:Die Walküre (sels), w. A. Konetzni (sop—Brünhilde), L. Hofmann (bass—Wotan), H. Knappertsbusch (cnd), Vienna State Opera Orch, Vienna State Opera Chorus *(rec Oct. 28, 1942)* Koch Schwann 2–▲ SCH 314562 [ADD]

Wagner, R.:Die Walküre (sels), w. H. Konetzni (sop—Sieglinde), R. Merker (sop—Brünhilde), F. Völker (ten—Sigmund), L. Hofmann (bass—Wotan), B. Walter (cnd), Vienna State Opera Orch, Vienna State Opera Chorus *(rec Oct. 19, 1936)* Koch Schwann 2–▲ SCH 314592

Wagner, R.:Die Walküre (act 1), w. E. Martón (sop), M. Talvela (bass), Z. Mehta (cnd), New York PO [G] CBS ▲ MK 39745 [DDD]

Hofmann, Peter (ten)

Beethoven, L. van:Fidelio, w. H. Behrens (sop), S. Ghazarian (sop), T. Adam (b–bar), H. Sotin (bass), G. Solti (cnd), Chicago SO, Chicago Sym Chorus [G] London 2–▲ 410227–2 [DDD]

Duruflé, M.:Requiem, w. P. Mattei (bar), E. Lavotha (vc), M. Wager (org), St. Jacobs Chamber Choir *(rec Nov. 9–12, 1992)* BIS ▲ CD 602 [DDD]

Wagner, R.:Der fliegende Holländer, w. D. Vejzovic (sop), J. Van Dam (b–bar), Kurt Moll (bass), H. von Karajan (cnd), Berlin PO [G] EMI Classics 2–▲ CDMB 64650

Wagner, R.:Lohengrin, w. E. Connell (sop), N. Armstrong (sop), L. Roar (bass), B. Weikl (bass), S. Vogel (bass), W. Nelsson (cnd), Bayreuth Festival Orch, Bayreuth Festival Chorus CBS 3–▲ M3K 38594

Wagner, R.:Parsifal, w. D. Vejzovic (sop), J. Van Dam (b–bar), S. Nimsgern (b–bar), K. Moll (bass), H. von Karajan (cnd), Berlin PO, German Opera Chorus [G] Deutsche Grammophon 4–▲ 413347–2 [DDD]

Wagner, R.:Parsifal, w. W. Meier (mez), F. Mazura (bar), S. Estes (bass), H. Sotin (bass), M. Salminen (bass), J. Levine (cnd), Bayreuth Festival Orch, Bayreuth Festival Chorus [1985] [G] Philips 4–▲ 434616–2 [DDD]

Wagner, R.:Tristan und Isolde (sels), w. H. Behrens (sop), Y. Minton (mez), B. Weikl (bass), L. Bernstein (cnd), Bavarian RSO, Bavarian Radio Chorus Philips ▲ 438501–2

Hofmann, Rosemarie (sop)

Mendelssohn, F.:Die Hochzeit des Camacho, w. R. Hofman (sop—Quiteria), A. Ulbrich (mez—Lucinda), S. Weir (ten—Basilio), H. Rhys-Evans (ten—Vivaldo), N. van der Meel (ten—Camacho), W. Wild (bar—Carrasco), U. Malmberg (bass—Sancho Panza), U. Cold (bass—Don Quixote), J. van Immerseel (cnd), Anima Eterna Orch, Aachen Boys Choir, Chor Modus Novus [G] *(rec Sept. 19–22, 1992)* Channel Classics 2–▲ CCS 5593 [DDD]

Högman, Christina (sop)

Alfvén, H.:Sym 4, "Fran havsbandet [From the Seaward Skerries]", w. C.–H. Ahnsjö (ten), N. Järvi (cnd), Stockholm PO BIS ▲ CD 505 [DDD]

Bach, J.S.:Mass in b, BWV 232, w. M. Groop (mez), H. Crook (ten), P. Salomaa (bass), Drottningholm Baroque Ensemble, Mikaeli Chamber Choir Proprius 2–▲ PRCD 9070/71

Britten, H.:Les Illuminations, w. P. Csaba (cnd), New Stockholm CO [F] BIS ▲ CD 435 [DDD]

Campion, T.:Songs, w. J. Lindberg (lt)—5 songs BIS ▲ CD 257 [DDD]

Faire, Sweet & Cruell, w. Jakob Lindberg (lt) BIS ▲ CD 257 [DDD]

Handel, G.F.:Arias, w. I Quattro Temperamenti— HWV.202–210; "Hush, ye pretty warbling quire," from Acis & Galatea [E,G] BIS ▲ CD 403 [DDD]

Handel, G.F.:Cants, w. I Quattro Temperamenti [I] BIS ▲ CD 403 [DDD]

Kraus, J.M.:Funeral Music for Gustav III, w. H. Martinpelto (sop), C.–H. Ahnsjö (ten), T. Lander (bass), S. Parkman (cnd), Drottningholm Baroque Ensemble, Uppsala Univ Chamber Choir Musica Sveciae ▲ MSCD 416 [DDD]

Mendelssohn, Fanny:Songs, w. Roland Pöntinen (pno)—Die frühen Gräber; Die Mainacht; Italien; Fichtenbaum und Palme; Verlust; Warum sind denn die Rosen so blass; Dämmrung senkte sich von oben; Nach Süden; Vorwurf; Bergeslust *(rec Musikaliska Akademien, Stockholm, Sweden, May 24–27, 1995)* BIS ▲ CD 738 [DDD]

Monteverdi, C.:Ritorno d'Ulisse, w. L. Hunt (sop), B. Fink (cta), D. Vissé (ct), C. Prégardien (ten), G. Tucker (ten), D. Thomas (bass), R. Jacobs (cnd), Concerto Vocale [I] Harmonia Mundi France 3–▲ HMC 901427/29

Roman, J.H.:Bröllopsmusik, w. P. Mattei (b–bar), N.–E. Sparf (vn), E. Ericson (cnd), Drottningholm Baroque Ensemble *(rec 1992)* Musica Sveciae ▲ MSCD 413 [DDD]

Roman, J.H.:Funeral Music for Frederik I, w. E. Ericson (cnd), Drottningholm Baroque Ensemble, Eric Ericson Chamber Choir *(rec 1992)* Musica Sveciae ▲ MSCD 413 [DDD]

Roman, J.H.:Jubilate, w. P. Mattei (b–bar), E. Ericson (cnd), Drottningholm Baroque Ensemble, Eric Ericson Chamber Choir *(rec 1992)* Musica Sveciae ▲ MSCD 413 [DDD]

Schoenberg, A.:Qt 2 Strs, w. J.–J. Kantorow (cnd), Tapiola Sinfonietta BIS ▲ CD 703 [DDD]

Schumann, C.:Songs, w. Roland Pöntinen (pno)—Am Strande; Sie liebten sich beide; Beim Abschied; Er ist gekommen in Sturm und Regen; Liebst du um Schönheit; Warum willst du and're fragen; Die gute Nacht, die ich dir sage; Lorelei; Geheimes Flüstern hier und dort; O Lust, o Lust *(rec Musikaliska Akademien, Stockholm, Sweden, May 24–27, 1995)* BIS ▲ CD 738 [DDD]

Songs for the Guitar, w. Jakob Lindberg (gtr) BIS ▲ CD 293

Werfel, A.M.:Songs, w. Roland Pöntinen (pno)—Licht in der Nacht; Waldseligkeit; Ansturm; Erntelied; Laue Sommernacht; Ich wandle unter Blumen; Der Erkennende; Lobgesang *(rec Musikaliska Akademien, Stockholm, Sweden, May 24–27, 1995)* BIS ▲ CD 738 [DDD]

Högman, Nils (ten)

Schnittke, A.:Requiem, w. K. Salomonsson (sop), I. H. Sjöberg (sop), L. Lindholm (sop), A. F. Eker (cta), S. Parkman (cnd), Stockholm Sinfonietta, Uppsala Academic Chamber Choir [L] BIS ▲ CD 497 [DDD]

Hogset, Carl (ct)

Grieg, E.:Songs, w. *(various accompanists)*—5 sels Norway Music ▲ QCD 9304

Handel, G.F.:Alcina (sels), w. *(various accompanists)*—Verdi prati Norway Music ▲ QCD 9304

Handel, G.F.:Flavio, Rè di Longobardi (sels), w. *(various accompanists)*—Amor, nel mio penar Norway Music ▲ QCD 9304

Handel, G.F.:Giulio Cesare in Egitto (sels), w. *(various accompanists)*—Va tacito e nascosto Norway Music ▲ QCD 9304

Nordheim, A.:3 Unexpected Songs, w. *(various accompanists)* Norway Music ▲ QCD 9304

Purcell, H.:Songs, w. *(various accompanists)*—If musick be the food of love; An evening hymn; Musick for a while; others Norway Music ▲ QCD 9304

Hohenfeld, Linda (sop)

Bernstein, L.:Songfest, w. Wendy White (mez), Patricia Spence (mez), Walter Plante (ten), Vernon Hartman (bar), John Cheek (bass), L. Slatkin (cnd), St. Louis SO RCA Red Seal ▲ 09026–61581–2

Höher, Frank (trb)

Mozart, W.A.:Zauberflöte, w. M. Price (sop—Pamina), L. Serra (sop—Queen of the Night), M. Venuti (sop—Papagena), M. McLaughlin (sop—1st Lady), A. Murray (mez—2nd Lady), H. Schwarz (cta—3rd Lady), F. Höher (trb—1st Boy), M. Diedrich (trb—2nd Boy), F. Klos (trb—3rd Boy), P. Schreier (ten—Tamino), R. Tear (ten—Monostatos), R. Goldberg (ten—1st Armoured Man), K. Moll (bass—Sarastro), H. Rech (bass—2nd Armoured Man), C. Davis (cnd), Dresden Staatskapelle, Leipzig Radio Chorus Philips ("Duo" series) 2–▲ 442568–2

Höhn, Carola (sop)

Matthus, S.:Mirabeau, w. Carola Höhn (sop—Marie Antoinette), Carola Fischer (cta—Eveline Le Jay), Peter-Jürgend Schmidt (ten—Ludwig XVI), Jürgen Freier (bar—Honoré-Gabriel de Riqueti), Gerd Wolf (bass—Victor Riqueti), H. Fricke (cnd), Berlin State Opera Orch, Berlin State Opera Chorus *(rec Berlin, 1989)* Berlin Classics 2–▲ BER 1075 [DDD]

Schulhoff, E.:The Flames, w. Jane Eaglen (sop—Donna Anna, Nun, Woman, Marguerite), Carola Höhn (sop—Shadow), Celina Lindsley (sop—Shadow), Regina Schudel (sop—Shadow), Iris Vermillion (mez—La Morte), Christiane Berggold (alt—Shadow), Kaja Borris (alt—Shadow), Elvira Dressen (alt—Shadow), Kurt Westi (ten—Don Juan), Johann-Werner Prein (bass—Commendatore), Gerd Wolf (bass—Harlequin), J. Mauceri (cnd), Berlin German SO, Berlin RIAS Chamber Choir *(rec Jesus-Christus Church, Berlin Dahlem, Oct 1993/Apr 1994)* London 2–▲ 444630–2 [DDD]

Hokin, Harlan B. (ten)

Angeli, Music of Angels, w. PAN Ensemble, William Hite (ten), Paul Cummings (bar), Tapestry *(rec Studio A, National Music Center, Lenox, MA, Sept 11–14, 1995)* Telarc ▲ CD 80448 [DDD]

Holden, Poppy (sop)

Music for Mandolin, w. Alison Stephens (mand), Sue Mossop (mand), Richard Burnett (pno) Amon Ra ▲ CDSAR 53 [DDD]

Holecek, Heinz (bar)

Lehár, F.:Der Zarewitsch (sels), w. D. Koller (sop), G. di Stefano (ten), E.–G. Scherzer (cnd), Vienna Operetta Orch, Original Volga Cossacks Koch Schwann ▲ SCH 312732 [ADD]

Holecek, Heinz (bass)

Lehár, F.:Das Land des Lächelns, w. Dagmar Koller (sop), Valorie Goodall (sop), Guiseppe di Stefano (ten), H. Lambrecht (cnd), Vienna Volksoper Orch [G] *(rec 1967)* Preiser ▲ 93144 [ADD]

Holecek, Sebastian (sgr)

Schreker, F.:Irrelohe, w. Eva Randová (mez—Old Lola), Michael Pabst (ten—Count Heinrich), Monte Pederson (bar—Peter), Neven Belamaric (sgr—The Parson), Luana Devol (sgr—Eva), Sebastian Holecek (sgr—The Miller), Goran Smimic (sgr—The Forester) Sony Classical 2–▲ S2K 66850

Holiday, Billie (sgr)

Bernstein, L.:Fancy Free, w. L. Bernstein (cnd), New York City Ballet Orch—with jazz quintet in the Prologue MCA Classics ▲ MCAD 10280 (m) [AAD]

Holkmann, Loretta (mez)

Kupferman, M.:Challenger, w. R. Fink (sax), J. Domarkas (cnd), Lithuanian National PO Soundspells ▲ CD 104

Kupferman, M.:Jazz Sym, w. R. Fink (sax), J. Domarkas (cnd), Lithuanian National PO Soundspells ▲ CD 104

Holl, Robert (bass)

Bach, J.S.:Cant 186, w. N. Harnoncourt (cnd), Vienna Concentus Musicus, Tölz Boys' Choir [G] Teldec 2–▲ 2292–44179–2 [DDD]

Bach, J.S.:Cant 188, w. N. Harnoncourt (cnd), Vienna Concentus Musicus, Tölz Boys' Choir [G] Teldec 2–▲ 2292–44179–2 [DDD]

Bach, J.S.:Cant 208, "Hunting Cant", w. A. M. Blasi (sop), J. P. Kenny (alt), K. Equiluz (ten), N. Harnoncourt (cnd), Vienna Concentus Musicus, Arnold Schoenberg Choir [G] Teldec ▲ 2292–46151–2 [DDD]

Bach, J.S.:Cant 212, "Peasant Cant", w. A. M. Blasi (sop), N. Harnoncourt (cnd), Vienna Concentus Musicus, Arnold Schoenberg Choir [G] Teldec ▲ 2292–46151–2 [DDD]

Bach, J.S.:Mass in b, BWV 232, w. A. M. Blasi (sop), D. Ziegler (mez), J. Rappé (cta), K. Equiluz (ten), N. Harnoncourt (cnd), Vienna Concentus Musicus, Arnold Schoenberg Choir [L] Teldec 2–▲ 2292–42676–2 [DDD]

Bach, J.S.:Mass in b, BWV 232, w. Helen Donath (sop), Brigitte Fassbaender (cta), Claes H. Ahnsjö (ten), Roland Hermann (bar), E. Jochum (cnd), Bavarian RSO, Bavarian Radio Chorus EMI Classics ("Doublefforte" series) 2–▲ CDFB 68640

Beethoven, L. van:Missa Solemnis, w. M. Lipovsek (mez), N. Harnoncourt (cnd), CO of Europe, E. Ortner (cnd), Arnold Schoenberg Choir Teldec 2–▲ 9031–74884–2

Brahms, J.:Ernste Gesänge, w. Y. Talmi (cnd), Golders Orch [orchd. Erich Leinsdorf] [G] Ottavo ▲ OTR C98402 [DDD]

Diepenbrock, A.:Songs, w. Roberta Alexander (sop), Christa Pfeiler (mez), Jard Van Ness (mez), Daniel Esser (vc), Rudolf Jansen (pno)—Berceuse; Clair de lune; Mandoline; L'Invitation au voyage; Les Chats; Receuillement; Puisque l'aube grandit; Incantation; En Sourdine; La Chanson de l'hypertrophique NM Classics ▲ NM 92051

Haydn, J.:Die Jahreszeiten, w. Angela Marie Blasi (sop), Josef Protschka (ten), N. Harnoncourt (cnd), Vienna SO, Arnold Schoenberg Choir [G] Teldec 2–▲ 2292–42699–2

Haydn, J.:Die Schöpfung, w. Edita Gruberova (sop), Josef Protschka (ten), N. Harnoncourt (cnd), Vienna SO, Arnold Schoenberg Choir [G] Teldec 2–▲ 2292–42682–2

Haydn, J.:The Seven Last Words of Christ on the Cross, w. Inge Nielsen (sop), Margaretha Hintermeier (cta), Anthony Rolfe Johnson (ten), N. Harnoncourt (cnd), Vienna Concentus Musicus, Arnold Schoenberg Choir [oratorio version] Teldec ▲ 2292–46458–2 ZK

Mozart, W.A.:Finta semplice, w. Helen Donath (sop), Jutta-Renate Ihloff (sop), Teresa Berganza (mez), A. Rolfe Johnson (ten), Thomas Moser (ten), Robert Lloyd (b–bar), L. Hager (cnd), Salzburg Mozarteum Orch [I] Orfeo 3–▲ 085843 [DDD]

Mozart, W.A.:Missa, K.427, w. A. Augér (sop), B. Bonney (sop), H.–P. Blochwitz (ten), C. Abbado (cnd), Berlin PO, Berlin Radio Chorus [L] Sony Classical ▲ SK 46671 [DDD]

Mozart, W.A.:Missa, K.427, w. K. Láki (sop), Z. Dénes (sop), K. Equiluz (ten), N. Harnoncourt (cnd), Vienna Concentus Musicus, Vienna State Opera Chorus [L] Teldec ▲ 2292–43070–2

Mozart, W.A.:Requiem, w. Rachel Yakar (sop), Ortrun Wenkel (cta), Kurt Equiluz (ten), N. Harnoncourt (cnd), Vienna Concentus Musicus, Vienna State Opera Chorus [L] Teldec ▲ 2292–42911–2

Mozart, W.A.:Zaide, w. J. Blegen (sop), I. Hollweg (sop), T. Moser (ten), W. Schöne (bass), L. Hager (cnd), Salzburg Mozarteum Orch [G] Orfeo 2–▲ 055832 [DDD]

Schmidt, F.:Das Buch mit sieben Siegeln, w. Gabriele Fontana (sop), Margareta Hintermeier (alt), Kurt Azesberger (ten), Eberhard Büchner (ten—Johannes), Robert Holl (bass—Voice of the Lord), Robert Holzer (bass), Martin Haselböck (org), H. Stein (cnd), Vienna SO, Vienna Sym Chorus *(rec live, Vienna Music Hall, May 1996)* Calig 2–▲ CAL 50978/9 [DDD]

Schmidt, F.:Das Buch mit sieben Siegeln, w. Hertha Töpper (mez), Anton Dermota (ten), Thomas Moser (ten), A.J. Hochstrasser (cnd), Lower Austria Tonkünst Orch, Graezer Concert Choir *(rec 1975)* Preiser 2–▲ PRE 93263 [ADD]

Holl, Robert (bass) (cont.)
Schmidt, F.:Das Buch mit sieben Siegeln, w. Sylvia Greenberg (sop), Carolyn Watkinson (cta), Peter Schreier (ten), Thomas Moser (ten), Kurt Rydl (bass), L. Zagrosek (cnd), Austrian RSO, Vienna State Opera Chorus [G] Orfeo 2-▲ 143862 [DDD]
Schubert, Franz:Fierrabras, w. K. Mattila (sop), C. Studer (sop), R. Gambill (ten), T. Hampson (bar), L. Polgar (bass), C. Abbado (cnd), CO of Europe, Arnold Schoenberg Choir [G] *(rec live)* Deutsche Grammophon 2-▲ 427341-2 [DDD]
Schubert, Franz:Die Schöne Müllerin, w. D. Lutz (pno) [G] Preiser ▲ 93400
Shostakovich, D.:Sym 13, w. E. Inbal (cnd), Vienna SO, Chorus Viennensis *(rec May 13-17, 1993)* Denon/PCM Digital ▲ CO 75887 [DDD]
Verdi, G.:Ernani (sels), w. Felicia Weathers (sop—Elvira), Delia Wallis (mez—Giovanna), Placido Domingo (ten—Ernani), Wynford Evans (ten—Don Riccardo), Piero Francia (bar—Don Carlo), Agostino Ferrin (bass—Don Ruy Gomex de Silva), Robert Holl (bass—Iago), E. Downes (cnd), Omroep Orch, Omroep Chorus *(rec Amsterdam, Jan 15, 1972)* Bella Voce ▲ BLV 107.004 [AAD]

Holland, Ashley (bar)
Puccini, G.:Tosca, w. Jane Eaglen (sop—Floria Tosca), Charbel Michael (alt—Shepherd Boy), John Daszak (ten—Spoletta), Dennis O'Neill (ten—Mario Cavaradossi), Christopher Booth-Jones (bar—Sciarrone), Ashley Holland (bar—Jailor), Gregory Yurisich (bar—Baron Scarpia), Peter Rose (bass—Cesare Angelotti), Andrew Shore (bass—Sacristan), D. Parry (cnd), Philharmonia Orch, Geoffrey Mitchell Choir, Peter Kay Children's Chorus Chandos ("Opera in English" series) 2-▲ CHAN 3000

Holland, Charles (ten)
Thomson, V.:4 Saints in 3 Acts, w. Inez Matthews (sop—St Settlement), Beatrice Robinson-Wayne (sop—St Teresa I), Altonell Hines (mez—Commère), Ruby Greene (alt—St Teresa II), David Bethea (ten—St Stephen), Charles Holland (ten—St Chavez), Edward Matthews (bar—St Ignatius), Randolph Robinson (bar—St Plan), Abner Dorsey (bass—Compère), V. Thomson (cnd), *(orch unknown)* [abridged by Thompson] *(rec June 25, 1947)* RCA Gold Seal ▲ 09026-68163-2 [ADD]

Holland, John (reader)
Cerha, F.:Eine Art Chanson, w. H.C. Artmann (reader), HK Gruber (reader), M. Jones (reader), R. McGee (reader), G. Rühm (reader) *(rec live Apr. 30, 1993)* Largo ▲ 5126 [DDD]

Holloway, Michael (voc)
Martirano, S.:L's. G. A. Centaur ▲ CRC 2266 [DDD]

Hölle, Matthias (bass)
Beethoven, L. van:Fidelio, w. Elizabeth Norberg-Schulz (sop—Marzelline), Deborah Voigt (sop—Lenore), Ben Heppner (ten—Florestan), Michael Schade (ten—Jaquino), Günter von Kannaten (b-bar—Don Pizarro), Matthias Hölle (bass—Rocco), Thomas Quasthoff (bass—Don Fernando), C. Davis (cnd), Bavarian RSO, Bavarian Radio Chorus, Bavarian State Opera Men's Chorus *(rec Herkulessaal der Residenz, Munich, May 15-25, 1995)* RCA Victor 2-▲ 09026-68344-2 [DDD]
Dessau, P.:Haggada, w. Sabine Ritterbusch (sop), Renate Spingler (sop), Yvi Jänicke (alt), Peter Galliard (ten—Rabbi Tarfon/Jude/ten solo), Gabriel Sadé (ten—Pharaoh), Jochen Schmeckenbechier (bar—Rabbi Jehoschua), Bernd Weikl (bar—Moses), Matthias Hölle (bass—Speaker/Rabbi Akiwa), Alfred Muff (bass—Father/Rabbi Eleasar), Johann Tilli (bass—Rabbi Elieser/bass solo), G. Albrecht (cnd), Hamburg State PO, Berlin Carl Maria Von Weber Men's Choir, Hamburg Alsterspatzen, North German Radio Chorus [G] *(rec Musikhalle, Hamburg, Sept 4 & 5, 1994)* Capriccio 2-▲ 10590/91 [DDD]
Schumann, R.:Spanische Liebeslieder, w. M. Shirai (mez), M. Lipovsek (mez), J. Protschka (ten), N. Shetler (pno), N. Deutsch (pno) [G] Capriccio ▲ CDC 10079
Wagner, R.:Tannhäuser (sels), w. K. Te Kanawa (sop), R. Kollo (ten), Håkan Hagegård (bar), W. Meier (mez), M. Janowski (cnd), Philharmonia Orch, Ambrosian Singers; music from film soundtrack for Meeting Venus Teldec ▲ 2292 46336-2 [DDD] ▮ 2292 46336-4 ▯ 2292 46336-5
Weber, C.M. von:Der Freischütz, w. R. Ziesack (sop), S. Sweet (sop), A. Schmidt (bar), M. Janowski (cnd), German SO, Berlin Radio Chorus RCA Red Seal 2-▲ 09026-62538-2

Holleque, Elizabeth (sop)
Shostakovich, D.:Sym 14, w. N. Storojev (bass), Y. Turovsky (cnd), Montreal Musici Chandos ▲ CHAN 8607 [DDD]

Holliday, Jennifer (sgr)
Amen:A Gospel Celebration, w. Azusa Pacific Univ Choir, Central State Univ Chorus, Cincinnati Pops Chorale, Maureen McGovern (sgr), Lou Rawls (sgr), Cincinnati Pops Orch [cnd:Erich Kunzel] *(rec Feb. 28-Mar. 1, 1993)* Telarc ▲ CD 80315 [DDD] ▮ CD 80315
Broadway, w. Ethel Merman (sgr), Dick van Dyke (sgr), Doris Day (sgr), Topol (sgr), Mary Martin (sgr), Jill Haworth (sgr), William Warfield (sgr), et al. Sony Classical ("Greatest Hits" series) ▲ MLK 62365 ▮ MLT 62365

Holliday, Melanie (sop)
Strauss (II), Joh.:Die Fledermaus, w. M. Irosch (sop), D. Koller (sop), W. Kmentt (ten), R. Karczykowski (ten), H. Kraemmer (bar), R. Granzer (bar), E. Binder (cnd), Vienna Volksoper Orch, Vienna Volksoper Chorus [G] Denon 2-▲ CO 8101 [DDD]

Holloway, David (bar)
Delibes, L.:Lakmé, w. M. Spacagna (sop—Ellen), R. Welting (sop—Lakmé), A. Kraus (ten—Gérald), D. Holloway (bar—Frédéric), P. Plishka (bass—Nilakantha), N. Rescigno (cnd), Dallas Civic Opera Orch *(rec Nov. 1980)* Ornamenti 2-▲ FE 108 [ADD]

Holloway, Stanley (sgr)
Lerner, A.J.:My Fair Lady, w. R. Harrison (sgr), J. Andrews (sgr), *(other artists unknown)* [1956 Broadway original cast] Columbia ▲ CK 05090 ▮ JST 05090

Hollweg, Ilse (sop)
Handel, G.F.:Love In Bath, w. T. Beecham (cnd), Royal PO EMI Classics ▲ CDM 63374
Mozart, W.A.:Arias, w. L. Marshall (sop), L. Simoneau (ten), G. Unger (ten), G. Frick (bass), T. Beecham (cnd), Royal PO, Beecham Choral Society EMI Classics 2-▲ CDHB 63715
Mozart, W.A.:Entführung, w. L. Marshall (sop), L. Simoneau (ten), G. Unger (ten), G. Frick (bass), T. Beecham (cnd), Royal PO, Beecham Choral Society EMI Classics 2-▲ CDHB 63715
Mozart, W.A.:Zaide, w. J. Blegen (sop), T. Moser (ten), W. Schöne (bass), R. Holl (bass), L. Hager (cnd), Salzburg Mozarteum Orch [G] Orfeo 2-▲ 055832 [DDD]
Piccinni, N.:La cecchina (sels), w. M. Freni (sop), S. Bruscantini (bar), R. Panerai (bar), F. Caracciolo (cnd), Naples RAI Orch—13 arias *(rec live 11/25/69)* Arkadia 2-▲ 596 [ADD]
Wagner, R.:Der Ring des Nibelungen, w. Gré Brouwenstein (sop—Freia/Sieglinde), Ilse Hollweg (sop—Waldvogel), Gerda Lammers (sop—Ortlinde), Paula Lenchner (sop—Wellgunde/Gerhilde), Hilde Scheppan (sop—Helmwige), Astrid Varnay (sop—Brünnilde/3rd Norn), Lore Wissmann (sop—Woglinde), Maria von Ilosvay (mez—Flosshilde/Schwertleite/2nd Norn), Louise Charlotte Kamps (mez—Siegrune), Jean Madeira (mez—Erda/Rossweisse/1st Norn), Georgine van Milinkovic (mez—Fricka/Grimgerde), Elisabeth Schärtel (mez—Waltraute), Paul Kuen (ten—Mime), Ludwig Suthaus (ten—Loge), Josef Traxel (ten—Froh), Wolfgang Windgassen (ten—Siegmund/Siegfried), Alfons Herwig (bar—Donner), Hermann Uhde (bar—Gunther), Hans Hotter (b-bar—Wotan), Gustav Neidlinger (b-bar—Alberich), Josef Griendl (bass—Fasolt/Hunding/Hagen), Arnold van Mill (bass—Fafner), H. Knappertsbusch (cnd), Bayreuth Festival Orch, Bayreuth Festival Chorus *(rec live, Bayreuth, Aug 13-17, 1956)* Golden Melodram 14-▲ GM 1.001 [ADD]

Hollweg, Werner (ten)
Einem, G. von:Dantons Tod, w. K. Laki (sop), I. Mayr (mez), H. Hiestermann (ten), T. Adam (b-bar), K. Rydl (bass), L. Zagrosek (cnd), Austrian RSO, Austrian Radio Chorus [G] *(rec live, Salzburg, 8/13/83)* Orfeo 2-▲ 102842 [ADD]
Handel, G.F.:Messiah, w. Elizabeth Gale (sop), Marjana Lipovšek (mez), Roderick Kennedy (bass), N. Harnoncourt (cnd), Vienna Concentus Musicus Teldec 2-▲ 9031-77615-2
Handel, G.F.:Messiah (sels), w. Elizabeth Gale (sop), Marjana Lipovsek (mez), Roderick Kennedy (bass), N. Harnoncourt (cnd), Vienna Concentus Musicus, Stockholm Chamber Choir [E] Teldec ▲ 2292-42409-2
Haydn, J.:Die Schöpfung, w. Helena Döse (sop—Eva), Lucia Popp (sop—Gabriel), Werner Hollweg (ten—Uriel), Benjamin Luxon (bar—Adam), Kurt Moll (bass—Raphael), Jack McCormack (db), David Strange (vc), Antál Dorati (hpd), A. Dorati (cnd), Royal PO, Brighton Festival Chorus *(rec Kingsway Hall, London, Dec 1976)* London 2-▲ 443027-2 [ADD]
Lehár, F.:Die lustige Witwe, w. E. Harwood (sop), T. Stratas (sop), R. Kollo (ten), Z. Kelemen (bar), H. von Karajan (cnd), Berlin PO, German Opera Chorus [G] *(rec 1972)* Deutsche Grammophon 2-▲ 435712-2 [ADD]

Hollweg, Werner (ten) (cont.)
Monteverdi, C.:Combattimento, w. Joseph Schmidt (ten), Kurt Equiluz (ten), N. Harnoncourt (cnd), Vienna Concentus Musicus [I] Teldec ▲ 2292-43036-2
Monteverdi, C.:Lamento della ninfa, w. Schmidt (ten), K. Equiluz (ten), N. Harnoncourt (cnd), Vienna Concentus Musicus [I] Teldec ▲ 2292-43036-2
Mozart, W.A.:Complete Mozart Edition, w. A. Augér (sop), E. Gruberova (sop), I. Cotrubas (sop), A. Baltsa (mez), L. Hager (cnd), Salzburg Mozarteum Orch Philips 3-▲ 422529-2 [ADD]
Mozart, W.A.:Complete Mozart Edition, w. E. Mathis (sop), P. Schreier (ten), I. Wixell (bar), B. Klee (cnd), Berlin Staatskapelle Philips 2-▲ 422536-2 [ADD]
Mozart, W.A.:Complete Mozart Edition, w. Jessye Norman (sop), I. Cotrubas (sop), H. Donath (sop), T. Troyanos (mez), H. Prey (bar), H. Schmidt-Isserstedt (cnd), North German RSO Philips 3-▲ 422534-2 [ADD]
Mozart, W.A.:Missa solemnis, K.139, w. M. Lindsay (sop), G. Schreckenbach (mez), W. Grönroos (bar), M. Creed (cnd), Berlin RSO, Berlin RIAS Chamber Choir [L] Capriccio ▲ 10169 [DDD]
Mozart, W.A.:Missa solemnis, K.139, w. M. Lindsay (sop), G. Schreckenbach (mez), W. Grönroos (bar), M. Creed (cnd), Berlin RSO, Berlin RIAS Chamber Choir [L] LaserLight ▲ 15 883 [DDD]
Mozart, W.A.:Schuldigkeit, w. A. Augér (sop), K. Láki (sop), S. Geszty (sop), C. H. Ahnsjö (ten), R. Bader (cnd), Berlin Cathedral Choir [G] *(rec 1980)* Koch Schwann 2-▲ CD 313065 [ADD]
Puccini, G.:Mass, w. K. Lövaas (sop), B. McDaniel (bar), E. Inbal (cnd), Frankfurt RSO, West German Radio Chorus Philips ("Collector" series) ▲ 434170-2 [ADD]
Schubert, Franz:Lazarus, or Die Feier der Auferstehung, w. E. Mathis (sop), C. Wulkopf (mez), H. Schwarz (mez), H. Laubenthal (ten), H. Prey (bar), G. Chmura (cnd), Stuttgart RSO, Stuttgart Radio Chorus [G] Orfeo ▲ 011101 [DDD]
Strauss (II), Joh.:Die Fledermaus (sels), w. E. Gruberova (sop), B. Bonney (sop), M. Lipovšek (mez), W. Kmentt (ten), J. Protschka (ten), C. Boesch (bar), A. Scharinger (bass), N. Harnoncourt (cnd), Royal Concertgebouw Orch, Netherlands Opera Chorus Teldec ▲ 42427-2
Strauss (II), Joh.:Der Zigeunerbaron (sels), w. S. Jurinac (sop), P. Anders (ten), K. Schmitt-Walter (bar), Schneider (sgr), G. Hann (bass), Marszalek (cnd), Cologne RSO, Cologne Radio Chorus [G] Acanta ▲ CD 43807 [DDD]
Strauss, R.:Capriccio, w. Kiri Te Kanawa (sop—Gräfin), Brigitte Fassbaender (mez—Clairon), Uwe Heilmann (ten—Flamand), Werner Hollweg (ten—Taupe), Olaf Bär (bar—Olivier), Håkan Hagegård (bar—Graf), Victor von Halem (b-bar—La Roche), U. Schirmer (cnd), Vienna PO [G] *(rec Vienna, Dec 1993)* London 2-▲ 444405-2 [DDD]
Wolf, H.:Der Corregidor, w. H. Donath (sop), D. Soffel (mez), P. Maus (ten), K. Moll (bass), D. Fischer-Dieskau (bar), G. Albrecht (cnd), Berlin RSO [G] Koch Schwann 2-▲ CD 314 010

Holm, C. (sgr)
Rodgers, R.:Oklahoma!, w. A. Drake (sgr), L. Dixon (sgr), J. Roberts (sgr), H. da Silva (sgr), J. Blackton (cnd), *(orch unknown)* MCA Classics ▲ MCAD 10046 [AAD] ▮ MCAC 10046

Holm, Jörg (sgr)
Waits, T.:The Black Rider:The Casting of Magic Bullets, w. Angelika Thomas (sgr—Anne), Annette Paulmann (sgr—Kätchen), Sona Cervena (sgr—Bird/Messenger/Spoonwoman), Monika Tahal (sgr—Witness/Bird/Shrink/Wilhelm's Double/Skeleton), Susi Eisenkolb (sgr—Bridesmaid/Pegleg's Double), Heinz Vossbrink (sgr—Kuno), Dominique Horwitz (sgr—Pegleg), Gerd Kunath (sgr—Bertram), Stefan Kurt (sgr—Wilhelm), Klaus Schreiber (sgr—Robert/Man on Stag/Georg Schmid), Jörg Holm (Old Uncle/Duke), Jan Moritz Steffen (sgr—Young Kuno/Bird/Shrink/Skeleton), Tom Waits (vocals/coliope/organ/chamberlain/mar/emax/guitar/train whistle), Ralph Carney (saxophone/bass clarinet/baritone horn), Bill Douglas (bass instrument), Kenny Wollesen (perc) Island ▲ 314518559-2

Holm, Michael (spkr)
Corghi, A.:Divara—Wasser und Blut, w. Susanna von der Burg (sop—Divara), Suzanne McLeod (mez—Else Windscherer), Eva Lillian Thingboe (mez—Hille Feiken), Robert Schwarts (ten—Lame Man), Heinz Fitz (spkr—Bernd Knipperdollinck), Hanslutz Hildmann (spkr—Jan Matthys), Michael Holm (spkr—Bernhard Rothmann), Christopher Krieg (spkr—Jan van Leiden), W. Humburg (cnd), Münster SO, Münster City Theater Chorus [G] *(rec Grosses Haus, Münster State Theater, Nov. 27-29, 1993)* Marco Polo 2-▲ 8.223706/07 [DDD]

Holm, Renata (sop)
Golden Operetta, Vol. 2:Operetta Melodies, w. F. Bauer-Theussl (cnd), Vienna Volksoper Orch, Vienna Volksoper Chorus, Lotte Rysanek (sop), Dagmar Hermann (mez), Kurt Equiluz (ten), Horst Winter (ten), et al. Koch Präsent ▲ 399 224 [AAD]
Lehár, F.:Der Graf von Luxemburg (sels), w. Else Liebesberg (sop), Hilde Brauner (cta), Dagmar Hermann (mez), Rudolf Christ (ten), Herbert Prikopa (bar), F. Bauer-Theussl (cnd), Vienna Volksoper Orch, Vienna Volksoper Chorus [G] Koch Präsent ▲ CD 399223 [AAD]
Lehár, F.:Das Land des Lächelns (sels), w. Anneliese Rothenberger (sop), Nicolai Gedda (ten), W. Mattes (cnd), Graunke SO, Bavarian Radio Chorus Emperor Operetta ▲ KO 86341
Lehár, F.:Das Land des Lächelns (sels), w. I. Hallstein (sop), Heinz Hoppe (ten), Alexander (sgr), Marszalek (cnd), Operetta Orch, Operetta Chorus [G] Acanta ▲ CD 43494 [DDD]
Lehár, F.:Schön ist die Welt (sels), w. Rudolf Schock (ten), F. Fox (cnd), FFB Orch, Gunther Arndt Chorus Emperor Operetta ▲ KO 86344
Straus, O.:Ein Walzertraum (sels), w. H. Brauner (cta), E. Liebesberg (sop), D. Hermann (mez), R. Christ (ten), H. Prikopa (bar), F. Bauer-Theussl (cnd), Vienna Volksoper Orch, Vienna Volksoper Chorus [G] Koch Präsent ▲ CD 399223 [AAD]

Holm, Richard (ten)
Bruckner, A.:Motets, w. Eugen Jochum (cnd), Bavarian Radio Chorus—Locus iste; Ave Maria; Virga Jesse; Os justi; Pange lingua; Christus factus est pro nobis; Vexilla regis; Afferentur regi; Tota pulchra es Maria (w. Holm); Ecce sacerdos [L] Deutsche Grammophon 4-▲ 423127-2 [ADD]
Haydn, J.:Mass 3, "Cäcilienmesse", w. Maria Stader (sop), Marga Höffgen (cta), Josef Greindl (bass), E. Jochum (cnd), Bavarian RSO, Bavarian Radio Chorus Deutsche Grammophon 2-▲ 437383-2 [ADD]
Haydn, J.:Die Schöpfung, w. Irmgard Seefried (sop), Kim Borg (bass), I. Markevitch (cnd), Berlin PO, St. Hedwig's Cathedral Choir Deutsche Grammophon ("Double" series) 2-▲ 437380-2
Strauss, R.:Die ägyptische Helena, w. Annelies Kupper (sop—Aithra), Leonie Rysanek (sop—Helena), Ira Malaniuk (cta—Omniscient Seashell), Bernd Aldenhoff (ten—Menelas), Richard Holm (ten—Da-ud), Hermann Uhde (bar—Altair), J. Keilberth (cnd), Bavarian State Opera Orch, Bavarian State Opera Chorus *(rec Munich Opera Festival, Prince Regent Theater, Aug 10, 1956)* Orfeo d'or 2-▲ 424962
Weber, C.M. von:Der Freischütz, w. Irmgard Seefried (sop), Rita Streich (sop), Eberhard Wächter (bar), Kurt Böhme (b-bar), E. Jochum (cnd), Bavarian RSO, Bavarian Radio Chorus Deutsche Grammophon 2-▲ 439717-2 [ADD]

Holmer, Anna (voc)
Apple, J.:Voices in the Dark, w. David Moss (voc), Jacki Apple (elec) ¿What Next? ▲ WN 0014

Holmes, Jean (sgr)
Verdi, G.:Macbeth, w. Amy Shuard (sop—Lady Macbeth), Noreen Berry (mez—Lady-in-waiting), John Dobson (ten—Malcolm), André Turp (ten—Macduff), Tito Gobbi (bar—Macbeth), Edgar Boniface (bass—Servant), Rydderch Davies (bass—Doctor), Forbes Robinson (bass—Banco), Jean Holmes (sgr—Apparition), Celia Penny (sgr—Apparition), Glynne Thomas (sgr—Apparition), Brian Wrigt (sgr—Araldo), F. Molinari-Pradelli (cnd), Royal Opera House Orch, Royal Opera House Chorus Covent Garden *(rec London, Apr 8, 1960)* Bella Voce 2-▲ 7203 [AAD]

Holmes, John (bass)
Sullivan, A.:Iolanthe (sels), w. E. Harwood (sop), S. Bevin (ten), D. Dowling (bar), E. Shilling (bar), A. Faris (cnd), Sadler's Wells Opera Orch, Sadler's Wells Opera Chorus Classics for Pleasure 2-▲ CDCFP 4730 [ADD]
Sullivan, A.:The Mikado, w. M. Studholme (sop), J. Wakefield (ten), C. Revill (bar), D. Dowling (bar), A. Faris (cnd), Sadler's Wells Opera Orch, Sadler's Wells Opera Chorus Classics for Pleasure 2-▲ CDCFP 4730 [ADD]

Holmes, Richard (bar)
Hindemith, P.:Hin und zurück, w. Jeanne Ommerlé (sop—Helene), Carl Halvorson (ten—Robert), Austin Wright Moore (ten—Sage), Richard Holmes (bar—Doctor), Robert Osborne (b-bar—Orderly), S. R. Radcliffe (cnd), New York Chamber Ensemble *(rec LeFrak Concert Hall, Queens College, Flushing, NY, May 30 & 31, 1994)* Albany ▲ TROY 173 [DDD]

▲ = CD ♦ = Enhanced CD Δ = MD ▮ = Cassette Tape ▯ = DCC

Holmes, Richard (bar) (cont.)
Menotti, G.C.:The Telephone, w. Jeanne Ommerle (sop—Lucy), Richard Holmes (bar—Ben), S. R. Radcliffe (cnd), New York Chamber Ensemble *(rec LeFrak Concert Hall, Queens College, Flushing, NY, May 30 & 31, 1994)* Albany ▲ TROY 173 [DDD]
Moore, D.:Gallantry, w. Margaret Bishop (sop—Lola Markham), Julia Parks (mez—Announcer), Carl Halvorson (ten—Donald Hopewell), Richard Holmes (bar—Doctor Gregg), S. R. Radcliffe (cnd), New York Chamber Ensemble *(rec LeFrak Concert Hall, Queens College, Flushing, NY, May 30 & 31, 1994)* Albany ▲ TROY 173 [DDD]

Holroyd, Anna (mez)
Kaufmann, S.:Le Temps déchiré, w. B. Calmel (cnd), Bernard Calmel Orch *(rec Feb 1996)* Pavane ▲ ADW 7362 [DDD]

Holt, Anthony (bass)
Milhaud, D.:L'Homme et son désir, w. Marion Davies (sop), Yvonne Newman (mez), David Barrett (ten), D. Milhaud (cnd), BBC SO IMP ("BBC Radio Classics" series) ▲ IMP 5691512

Holt, Ben (bar)
Orff, C.:Carmina burana, w. Gabriela Herrera (sop), Frank Kelley (ten), H. de la Fuente (cnd), Mineria SO, Mineria Sym Choir IMP ("Classic" series) ▲ IMP 2024

Holton, Ruth (sop)
Adams, J.:Grand Pianola Music, w. Kym Amps (sop), Lyndsay Wagstaff (sop), Ellen Corver (pno), Sepp Grotenhuis (pno), S. Mosko (cnd), Netherlands Wind Ensemble Chandos ▲ CHAN 9363 [DDD]
Bach, J.S.:Cant 140, w. A. Rolfe Johnson (ten), S. Varcoe (b-bar), J. E. Gardiner (cnd), English Baroque Soloists, Monteverdi Choir London [G] Archiv ▲ 431809-2 [DDD]
Bach, J.S.:Cant 147, w. M. Chance (ct), A. Rolfe Johnson (ten), S. Varcoe (b-bar), J. E. Gardiner (cnd), English Baroque Soloists, Monteverdi Choir London [G] Archiv ▲ 431809-2 [DDD]
Clarke, J.:Come, Come Along for a Dance & a Song, w. C. Daniels (ten), S. Birchall (bass), R. Goodman (cnd), Parley of Instruments, Parley of Instruments Chorus Hyperion ▲ CDA 66578 [DDD]
Hall, H.:Yes, My Aminta, 'tis True, w. S. Birchall (bass), R. Goodman (cnd), Parley of Instruments, Parley of Instruments Chorus Hyperion ▲ CDA 66578 [DDD]
Handel, G.F.:Israel in Egypt, w. Elisabeth Friday (sgr), Michael Chance (alt), Philip Salmon (ten), Paul Tindall (sgr), J. E. Gardiner (cnd), English Baroque Soloists, Monteverdi Choir London Philips ▲ 432110-2
Handel, G.F.:Messiah, w. Vanessa Williamson (mez), James Griffett (ten), Lawrence Albert (bass), U. Walser (tpt), M. Brown (cnd), Gioia della Musica, Bmensky Akademicky Sbor Allegro 2-▲ ALGDPCD 1068 [DDD]
Handel, G.F.:Messiah (sels), w. Vanessa Williamson (mez), James Griffett (ten), L. Albert (bass), M. Brown (cnd), Gioia della Musica, Bmensky Akademicky Sbor Allegro ▲ ALG PCD 1078 [DDD]
Josquin Desprez:Missa, "Ave Maris Stella", w. D. Collot (sop), J.-L. Comoretto (ct), R. Le Chenadec (ct), T. Brehu (ten), H. Lamy (ten), B. Fabre-Garrus (bar), J. Gowings (bar) *(rec Jan. 1993)* Astrée ▲ E 8507 [DDD]
Josquin Desprez:Motets, w. D. Collot (sop), J.-L. Comoretto (ct), R. Le Chenadec (ct), T. Brehu (ten), H. Lamy (ten), B. Fabre-Garrus (bar), J. Gowings (bar)—Motets à la vierge *(rec Jan. 1993)* Astrée ▲ E 8507 [DDD]
Odes on the Death of Henry Purcell, w. Holman, Goodman (cnd), Parley of Instruments, Baroque Orch, Baroque Choir, R. Covey-Crump (ten), C. Daniels (ten), S. Birchall (bass) Hyperion ▲ CDA 66578 [DDD]
Purcell, H.:Dido & Aeneas, w. Ruth Holton (sop—Belinda), Elisabeth Priday (sop—2nd Woman), Donna Deam (sop—1st Witch), Shauna Beesley (sop—2nd Witch), Teresa Shaw (mez—Sorceress), Carolyn Watkinson (cta—Dido), Jonathan Peter Kenny (alt—Spirit), Paul Tindall (ten—Sailor), George Mosley (bass—Aeneas), J.E. Gardiner (cnd), English Baroque Soloists, Monteverdi Choir London *(rec Saint George's, Bristol, UK, July 12-14, 1990)* Philips ▲ 432114-2
Purcell, H.:Welcome to All the Pleasures, w. Nicola Jenkin (sop), Michael Chance (alt), Paul Tindall (ten), George Mosly (bass), J.E. Gardiner (cnd), English Baroque Soloists, Monteverdi Choir London *(rec Saint George's, Bristol, UK, July 12-14, 1990)* Philips ▲ 432114-2

Holvik, Karen (sop)
Blitzstein, M.:Songs, w. W. Sharp (bar), S. Blier (pno)—Monday morning blues; Croon-spoon; The new suit ("Zipperfly"); In the clear; Then; I wish it so; In twos; Penny candy; Emily (Ballad of the bombardier); Displaced; Four e e cummings Songs (o by the by; until and i heard; open your heart; jimmy's got a goil); What will it be for me; Rose song; Blues; Nickel under the foot; The cradle will rock; Bird upon the tree; Stay in my arms [E] Koch International Classics ▲ KIC 7050-2 [DDD]

Holzer, Robert (bass)
Schmidt, F.:Das Buch mit sieben Siegeln, w. Gabriele Fontana (sop), Margareta Hintermeier (alt), Kurt Azesberger (ten), Eberhard Büchner (ten—Johannes), Robert Holl (bass—Voice of the Lord), Martin Haselböck (org), H. Stein (cnd), Vienna SO, Vienna Sym Chorus *(rec live, Vienna Music Hall, May 1996)* Calig 2-▲ CAL 50978/9 [DDD]

Hölzl, Barbara (cta)
Kropfreiter, A.F.:Altdorfer-Passion, w. W. Pailer (bass), H. Geitner, *(ensemble unknown)* *(rec 3/88)* FSM ▲ FCD 97737 [DDD]

Holzmair, Wolfgang (bar)
Brahms, J.:Ein Deutsches Requiem, w. Elizabeth Norberg-Schulz (sop), H. Blomstedt (cnd), San Francisco SO London ▲ 443771-2
Brahms, J.:Romanzen aus Tieck's *Magelone*, w. G. Wyss (pno), W. Quadflieg (spkr) [G] Tudor 2-▲ 761 [DDD]
Braunfels, W.:Die Vögel, w. Helen Kwon (sop—Nightingale), Wolfgang Holzmair (bar—Hoopoe), Matthias Gorne (b-bar—Prometheus), Michael Krause (sgr—Loyal Friend), Endrik Wottrich (sgr—Good Hope), L. Zagrosek (cnd), Berlin German SO, Berlin Radio Chorus London ("Entartete Musik" series) ▲ 448 679-2
Duparc, H.:Chanson triste, w. Gerard Wyss (pno) Philips ▲ 446 686-2
Duparc, H.:Extase, w. Gerard Wyss (pno) Philips ▲ 446 686-2
Duparc, H.:L'Invitation au voyage, w. Gerard Wyss (pno) Philips ▲ 446 686-2
Duparc, H.:Le Manoir de Rosemonde, w. Gerard Wyss (pno) Philips ▲ 446 686-2
Duparc, H.:Sérénade, w. Gerard Wyss (pno) Philips ▲ 446 686-2
Duparc, H.:Soupir, w. Gerard Wyss (pno) Philips ▲ 446 686-2
Eisler, H.:Songs, w. Peter Stamm (pno)—sels from Eisler's Hollywood Songbook Koch Schwann ▲ SCH CD 313222
Fauré, G.:La bonne chanson, w. Gerard Wyss (pno) Philips ▲ 446 686-2
Fauré, G.:Mélodies 'de Venise', Op. 58, w. Gerard Wyss (pno)—4 sels Philips ▲ 446 686-2
Fauré, G.:Mirages, w. Gerard Wyss (pno) Philips ▲ 446 686-2
Fauré, G.:Poèmes d'un jour, w. Gerard Wyss (pno) Philips ▲ 446 686-2
Mendelssohn, F.:Songs, w. A. Wagner (pno)—21 songs (from Opp. 9, 19a, 34, 47, 57, 71, 86 & 99) [G] *(rec 1985)* Preiser ▲ 93368 [ADD]
Ravel, M.:Mélodies populaires grecques, w. Gerard Wyss (pno) Philips ▲ 446 686-2
Schubert, Franz:Die Schöne Müllerin, w. J. Demus (pno) [G] *(rec 1983)* Preiser ▲ 93337 [ADD]
Schubert, Franz:Schwanengesang, w. Imogen Cooper (pno) *(rec Vienna Konzerthaus, Austria, Jan. 10-12, 1994)* Philips ▲ 442460-2
Schubert, Franz:Songs (misc), w. G. Wyss (pno)—21 songs [G] Tudor ▲ 762 [DDD]
Schubert, Franz:Songs (misc), w. Imogen Cooper (pno)—Widerspruch; Der Wanderer an den Mond; Sehnsucht; Irdisches Glück; Lebensmut; Herbst *(rec Vienna Konzerthaus, Austria, Jan. 10-12, 1994)* Philips ▲ 442460-2
Schubert, Franz:Winterreise, w. Imogen Cooper (pno) Philips ▲ 446407-2
Strauss (II), Joh.:Der Zigeunerbaron, w. Pamela Coburn (sop), Christiane Oelze (sop), Julia Hamari (mez), Elisabeth von Magnus (alt), Herbert Lippert (ten), Rudolf Schasching (ten), Jurgen Flimm (sgr), Robert Florianschutz (sgr), Hans-Jurgen Lazar (sgr), N. Harnoncourt (cnd), Vienna SO, Arnold Schoenberg Choir *(rec Vienna, 1994)* Teldec 2-▲ 94555-2
Weill, K.:Berlin Requiem, w. J. Wagner (ten), H. Schmidt (cnd), Düsseldorf SO, Düsseldorf Sym Chorus [G] Koch Schwann ▲ CD 314 050 [DDD]
Weill, K.:Songs, w. M.-A. Schlingensiepen (cnd), Robert Schumann CO—Four Walt Whitman Songs (1943-47) [E] Koch Schwann ▲ CD 314 050 [DDD]

Homberger, Christophe (ten)
Schubert, Franz:Songs (misc), w. U. Koella (pno) Claves ▲ CD 9406

Homberger, Christophe (ten) (cont.)
Schubertiade:Rétrospective, w. Sine Nomine String Quartet, Lausanne Trio, S. Kanoff (pno), C. Favre (pno), Choeur des XVI de Fribourg, et al. Gallo ▲ CD 631 [AAD]

Homer, Louise (cta)
Caruso in Arias, Duets & Songs, w. Enrico Caruso (ten), Mario Ancona (bar), Titta Ruffo (bar), Antonio Scotti (bar) Supraphon Collection ▲ SUP 110618 (m) [ADD]
Scenes from Il Trovatore & Aida, w. Giovanni Martinelli (ten), Rosa Ponselle (sop), Giuseppe de Luca (bar), Ezio Pinza (bass), et al. Pearl ▲ PEA 9350 (m)

Honeyman, Ian (ten)
Biber, H. von:Requiem à 15, w. G. de Reyghere (sop), J. Feldman (sop), J. Bowman (ct), M. van Egmond (bass), Ricercar Consort, Erik Van Nevel (cnd), Capella Sancti Michaelis [L] *(rec 5/90)* Ricercar ▲ RIC 81063 [DDD]
Brossard, S. de:Motets, w. N. Rime (sop), J.-P. Fouchécourt (alt/ten), B. Deletré (bass), M. Gester (cnd), Parlement de Musique—Salve Rex Christe; Psallite Superi; Qui non diligit te; O Domine quia refugium; Templa nunc fument; Oratorio seu Dialogus Poenitentis animae cum Deo; Festis laeta sonent [L] *(rec 1992)* Opus 111 ▲ OPS 30-69 [DDD]
Bruhns, N.:Cants, w. Jill Feldman (sop), Greta de Reyghere (sop), James Bowman (ct), Guy de Mey (ten), Max Van Egmond (bass), Ricercar Consort—Hemmt eure Tränenflut; Jauchzet dem Herren alle Welt; Wohl dem, der den Herren fürchtet; De profundis; Paratum cor meum; O werter heil'ger Geis; Zeit meines Abschieds; Erstanden ist der heilige Christ; Herr hat seinem Stuhl im Himmel bereitet; Ich liege und schlafe; Mein Herz ist bereit; Muss nicht der Mensch auf dieser Erden in Stetem Streite sein Ricercar In Ecco 2-▲ REC8001/2
Capricornus, S.F.:Theatrum musicum quod per duodecim scenas seu sacras cantiones aperuit, w. D. Collot (sop), L. S. Norin (mez), K. Wessel (alt), S. Schreckenberger (bass), M. Gester (cnd), Parlement de Musique Opus 111 ▲ OPS 30-99
Hasse, J.A.:Miserere in e, w. Greta de Reyghere (sop), Dina Grossberger (mez), D Snellincks (bass), Il Fondamento Opus 111 ▲ OPS 3080
Hasse, J.A.:Requiem, w. Greta de Reyghere (sop), Dina Grossberger (mez), D. Snellincks (bass), Il Fondamento Ensemble Opus 111 ▲ OPS 3080
Kerll, J.C.:Missa pro defunctis, w. G. de Reyghere (sop), J. Bowman (alt), G. de Mey (ten), M. van Egmond (bass), E. van Nevel (cnd), Capella Sancti Michaelis, Ricercar Consort [L] *(rec 5/90)* Ricercar ▲ RIC 81063 [DDD]
Purcell, H.:Musick's Hand-maid, w. Ellen Hargis (sop), Rodrigo del Pozo (ten), Harry van der Kamp (bass), Paul O'Dette (thb/cittern/lt), Andrew Lawrence-King (hps/org/hpd), A. Lawrence-King (cnd), Harp Consort Astrée ▲ E 8564
Purcell, H.:Odes & Welcome Songs (misc), w. Jeni Bern (sop), Susan Bisatt (sop), William Purefoy (ct), Christopher Robson (ct), Thomas Guthrie (bass), R. Glenton (cnd), Orch of the Golden Age, Golden Age Choir—The noise of foreign wars (fragment) [ed. by Bruce Wood] *(rec Manchester Grammar School, England, May 13 & 14, 1995)* Naxos ▲ 8.553444 [DDD]
Purcell, H.:Raise, Raise the Voice, w. Jeni Bern (sop), Susan Bisatt (sop), William Purefoy (ct), Christopher Robson (ct), Thomas Guthrie (bass), R. Glenton (cnd), Orch of the Golden Age, Golden Age Choir *(rec Manchester Grammar School, England, May 13 & 14, 1995)* Naxos ▲ 8.553444 [DDD]
Purcell, H.:Te Deum & Jubilate, w. Jeni Bern (sop), Susan Bisatt (sop), William Purefoy (ct), Christopher Robson (ct), Thomas Guthrie (bass), David Staff (tpt), R. Glenton (cnd), Orch of the Golden Age, Golden Age Choir *(rec Manchester Grammar School, England, May 13 & 14, 1995)* Naxos ▲ 8.553444 [DDD]
Purcell, H.:Welcome to All the Pleasures, w. Jeni Bern (sop), Susan Bisatt (sop), William Purefoy (ct), Christopher Robson (ct), Thomas Guthrie (bass), R. Glenton (cnd), Orch of the Golden Age, Golden Age Choir *(rec Manchester Grammar School, England, May 13 & 14, 1995)* Naxos ▲ 8.553444 [DDD]

Hong, Hei-Kyung (sop)
James Levine's 25th Anniversary Metropolitan Opera Gala, w. J. Levine (cnd), Metropolitan Opera Orch, Ileana Cotrubas (sop), Renée Fleming (sop), Karita Mattila (sop), Birgit Nilsson (sop), Ruth Ann Swenson (sop), Kiri Te Kanawa (sop), Deborah Voigt (sop), Grace Bumbry (mez), Heidi Grant Murphy (mez), Anne Sofie von Otter (mez) *(rec live, Metropolitan Opera House, New York, Apr 27, 1996)* Deutsche Grammophon ▲ 449177-2 [DDD]

Höngen, Elisabeth (cta)
Beethoven, L. van:Syms (comp), w. E. Schwarzkopf (sop), H. Hopf (ten), O. Edelmann (bass), W. Furtwängler (cnd), Vienna PO, Bayreuth Festival Orch, Bayreuth Festival Chorus *(rec 1948-54)* EMI Classics 5-▲ CDHE 63606
Beethoven, L. van:Sym 9, "Choral Sym", w. Tilla Briem (sop), Peter Anders (ten), Rudolf Watzke (bass), W. Furtwängler (cnd), Berlin PO, Bruno Kittel Choir *(rec Mar 22, 1942)* Iron Needle 3-▲ IN 1348/50 [ADD]
Beethoven, L. van:Sym 9, "Choral Sym", w. Tilla Briem (sop), Peter Anders (ten), Rudolf Watzke (bass), W. Furtwängler (cnd), Berlin PO, Bruno Kittel Choir *(rec 1942)* Grammofono 2000 ▲ GRM 78581
Bizet, G.:Carmen, w. E. Weidlich (sop), T. Ralf (ten), J. Herrmann (bar), K. Böhme (bass), K. Böhm (cnd), Dresden State Opera Orch, Dresden State Opera Chorus *(rec Dec. 4 & 5, 1942)* Preiser 2-▲ 90152 (m)
Giordano, U.:Andrea Chénier, w. H. Konetzni (sop—Madelon), M. Sjöstedt (sop—Bersi), R. Tebaldi (sop—Maddalena de Coigny), E. Höngen (cta—La Contessa de Coigny), F. Corelli (ten—Andrea Chénier), E. Bastianini (bar—C. Gérard), K. Paskalis (bar—Pietro Fléville), L. Welter (bar—Fouquier Tinville), A. Pernerstorfer (b-bar—Mathieu), L. von Matačić (cnd), Vienna State Opera Orch, Vienna State Opera Chorus *(rec Vienna, June 26, 1960)* Fortissimo 2-▲ CDE 3003 [ADD]
Hindemith, P.:When Lilacs Last In The Dooryard Bloom'd, w. Hans Braun (bar), P. Hindemith (cnd), Vienna SO, Vienna State Opera Chorus *(rec 1956)* Tuxedo ▲ TUXCD 1061
Humperdinck, E.:Hänsel und Gretel, w. Lislotte Maikl (sop—Sandman/Dew Fairy), Anneliese Rothenberger (sop—Gretel), Irmgard Seefried (sop—Hänsel), Grace Hoffman (mez—Gertrude), Elisabeth Höngen (cta—Witch), Walter Berry (bass—Peter), A. Cluytens (cnd), Vienna PO, Vienna Boys' Choir EMI Classics 2-▲ CDMB 65661
Mozart, W.A.:Nozze di Figaro, w. E. Schwarzkopf (sop), I. Seefried (sop), S. Jurinac (sop), G. London (bar), E. Kunz (bar), H. von Karajan (cnd), Vienna PO, Vienna State Opera Chorus—omitting recitatives [I] *(rec 1950)* EMI Classics ("Studio" series) 2-▲ CDMB 69639 (m) [ADD]
Strauss, R.:Salome, w. Maria Cebotari (sop—Salome), Elisabeth Höngen (mez—Herodias), Karl Friedrich (ten—Narraboth), Julius Patzak (ten—Herod), Marko Rothmüller (bar—Jokanaan), C. Krauss (cnd), Vienna State Opera Orch, Vienna State Opera Chorus *(rec Covent Garden, London, Sept 30, 1947)* Legato 2-▲ LCD 211-2 [ADD]
Verdi, G.:Macbeth, w. J. Witt (ten), M. Ahlersmeyer (bar), H. Alsen (bass), K. Böhm (cnd), Vienna State Opera Orch, Vienna State Opera Chorus *(rec 1943)* Preiser 2-▲ PRE 90175 [AAD]
Wagner, R.:Parsifal, w. C. Ludwig (mez), H.-M. Uhle (ten), H. Hotter (b-bar), T. Franc (bass), W. Berry (bass), H. von Karajan (cnd), Vienna State Opera Orch, Vienna State Opera Chorus [G] *(rec live 4/1/61)* Arkadia 3-▲ 219 (m) [ADD]
Wagner, R.:Der Ring des Nibelungen, w. K. Flagstad (sop), H. Konetzni (sop), G. Treptow (ten), S. Svanholm (ten), M. Lorenz (ten), F. Frantz (b-bar), L. Weber (bass), B. Herrmann (bass), W. Furtwängler (cnd), La Scala Orch, La Scala Chorus *(rec live 1950)* Arkadia 12-▲ 351 [ADD]
Wagner, R.:Der Ring des Nibelungen, w. Kirsten Flagstad (sop), Hilde Konetzni (sop), Max Lorenz (ten), Set Svanholm (ten), Günther Treptow (ten), Josef Hermann (bar), Ludwig Weber (bass), Ferdinand Franz (sgr), W. Furtwängler (cnd), La Scala Orch, La Scala Chorus *(rec Milan, 1950)* Music & Arts 12-▲ CD 914

Honig, Dieter (b-bar)
Romberg, S.:The Student Prince (operetta), w. C. Jeffreys (sop), E. Geisen (ten), S. Gyártó (cnd), Hamburg State Opera Orch, Hamburg State Opera Chorus [G] Bayer ▲ 150004

Honoré, D. (ten)
Howells, H.:Requiem, w. J. Barton (trb), P. Flight (ct), T. Woody (bar), F. Burgomeister (cnd), Indianapolis Festival Orch, Christ Church Cathedral Men & Boys Choir Oxford Gothic ▲ G 49062 [DDD]

Hoogh, Hanke De (nar)
Honegger, A.:Le Roi David, w. Bernard Kruysen (bar), Sasja Hunnego (nar), A. Clement (cnd), Eindhovens Instrumental Ensemble, Eindhovens Chamber Choir [orig version] Emergo ▲ 3974

Hooper, P. (sgr)
Mozart, W.A.:Songs, w. J. Edwards (cta), P. Sharpe (sgr), D. Russell (sgr), D. Hamilton (ten), M. Glasgow (sgr), C. Birch (sgr), G. Lancaster (pno) *(rec July 1991)* Tall Poppies ▲ TP009 [DDD]

Hopf, H. (sgr)
Albert, E. d':Tiefland, w. G. Brouwenstijn, W. Kmentt, E. Wächter, P. Schöffler, O. Czerwenka, R. Moralt (cnd), Vienna SO *(rec 1957)* Philips 2-▲ 434781-2

Hopf, Hans (ten)
Beethoven, L. van:Syms (comp), w. E. Schwarzkopf (sop), E. Höngen (mez), O. Edelmann (bass), W. Furtwängler (cnd), Vienna PO, Bayreuth Festival Orch, Bayreuth Festival Chorus *(rec 1948-54)* EMI Classics 5-▲ CDHE 63606
Egk, W.:Peer Gynt, w. J. Perry (sop), N. Sharp (sop), C. Wulkopf (mez), R. Hermann (bar), H. Wallberg (cnd), Munich RSO, Bavarian Radio Chorus [G] Orfeo 2-▲ 005822 [DDD]
Mozart, W.A.:Don Giovanni, w. M. Schech (sop), M. Teschemacher (sop), M. Ahlersmeyer (bar), K. Böhme (bass), G. Frick (bass), K. Elmendorff (cnd), Saxon State Orch, Dresden State Opera Chorus [G] *(rec 1943)* Berlin Classics ("Dokumente" series) 3-▲ BER 2048 [ADD]
Mussorgsky, M.:Boris Godunov, w. Martha Mödl (sop—Marina Mniszek), Lotte Schädle (sop—Xenia), Dorothea Siebert (mez—Fyodor), Hertha Töpper (mez—Xenia's wet-nurs), Karl Hermann Bennert (Boyer Khrushchyov), Lorenz Fehenberger (ten—Prince Shuysky), Hans Hopf (ten—Grigory), Karl Ostertag (ten—Missail), Hans Hotter (b-bar—Boris Godunov), Hermann Uhde (bar—Andrey Shchelkalov), Kurt Böhme (bass—Varlaam), Kim Borg (bass—Pimen), Kieth Engen (bass—Lewicki), Adolf Keil (bass—Nikitich), Benno Kusche (bar—Rangoni), Heinz Maria Linz (bass—Czernikowski), E. Jochum (cnd), Bavarian RSO, Bavarian Radio Chorus *(rec Munich, May 1957)* Myto 3-▲ MCD 953131
Still, W.G.:Tristan und Isolde, w. C. Ligendza (sop), R. Baldani (mez), A. Dermota (ten), H. Sotin (bass), G. Neidlinger (bass), C. Kleiber (cnd), Vienna State Opera Orch, Vienna State Opera Chorus *(rec Oct. 7, 1973)* Exclusive 3-▲ EXL 18 [ADD]
Still, W.G.:Tristan und Isolde, w. Catarina Ligendza (sop), Ruša Baldani (mez), Hans Sotin (bass), C. Kleiber (cnd), Vienna PO, Vienna State Opera Chorus *(rec Vienna, Oct. 7, 1973)* Pantheon 3-▲ PHE 6601 (m)
Strauss, R.:Salome, w. Astrid Varnay (sop—Salome), Hertha Töpper (mez—Der Page der Herodias), Margarete Klose (cta—Herodias), Hans Hopf (ten—Narraboth), Karl Hoppe (ten—1st Nazarene), Karl Ostertag (ten—1st Jew), Julius Patzak (ten—Herodes), Hans Braun (bar—Jochanaan), Benno Kusche (bar—2nd Soldier), Adolf Keil (bass—1st Soldier), Hans Hermann Nissen (bass—Ein Kappadozier), Max Proebstl (bass—2nd Nazarene), Walter Carnotch (sgr—4th Jew), Emil Graf (sgr—3rd Jew), Paul Kaussen (sgr—2nd Jew), Hildegard Limmer (sgr—A slave), Georg Witter (sgr—5th Jew), H. Weigert (cnd), Bavarian RSO *(rec June 21-25, 1953)* Bella Voce 2-▲ BLV 7210 [AAD]
Wagner, R.:Die Meistersinger von Nürnberg, w. E. Schwarzkopf (sop), I. Malaniuk (cta), G. Unger (ten), E. Kunz (bar), O. Edelmann (b-bar), F. Dalberg (bass), H. von Karajan (cnd), Bayreuth Festival Orch, Bayreuth Festival Chorus [G] *(rec 1951)* EMI Classics ("Great Recordings of the Century" series) 4-▲ CDHD 63500 (m) [ADD]
Wagner, R.:Die Meistersinger von Nürnberg, w. L. Della Casa (sop), I. Malaniuk (cta), O. Edelmann (b-bar), K. Böhme (bass), H. Knappertsbusch (cnd), Bayreuth Festival Orch, Bayreuth Festival Chorus [G] *(rec live, 1952)* Arkadia 4-▲ 440 (m) [AAD]
Wagner, R.:Tannhäuser, w. E. Grümmer (sop), M. Schech (sop), F. Wunderlich (ten), D. Fischer-Dieskau (bar), G. Frick (bass), F. Konwitschny (cnd), Berlin State Opera Orch, Berlin State Opera Chorus [G] EMI Classics ("Studio" series) 3-▲ CDMC 63214 [ADD]
Wagner, R.:Tristan und Isolde (sels), w. Catarina Ligendza (sop), Ruša Baldani (mez), C. Kleiber (cnd), Vienna State Opera Orch *(rec live, 1973)* AS Disc ▲ ASD 2510

Hopferwieser, Josef (ten)
Strauss (II), Joh.:Die Fledermaus (sels), w. Ariane Calix (sop—Ida), Gabriele Fontana (sop—Rosalinde), Brigitte Karwautz (sop—Adele), Rohangiz Yachmi-Caucig (cta—Orlofsky), John Dickie (ten—Eisenstein), Josef Hopferwieser (ten—Alfred), Erich Wessner (ten—Dr. Blind), Andrea Martin (bar—Falke), Alfred Werner (bar—Frank), J. Wildner (cnd), Czech-Slovak RSO Bratislava, Bratislava City Chorus—Ov.; [Act I] Täubchen, das entflattert ist...; Ach, ich darf nicht hin zu dir; Nein, mit solchen Advokaten; Komm mit mir zum Souper; So muss allein ich bleiben; Trinke, Liebchen, trinke schnell; [Act II] Ein Souper heut' uns winkt; Ich lade gern mir Gäste ein; Mein Herr Marquis, ein Mann wie Sie; Dieser Anstand, so manierlich; Klänge der Heimat; Im Feuerstrom der Reben; Marianka komm und tanz me hier; [Act III] Entr'acte; Spiel' ich die Unschuld vom Lande; O Fledermaus, o Fledermaus *(rec Slovak Radio Concert Hall, Bratislava)* Naxos ▲ 8.553171 [DDD]

Hopfner, Heiner (ten)
Dittersdorf, K.D. von:Sacred Music, w. Hanna Farinelli (sop), Birgit Calm (alt), Nikolaus Hillebrand (bass), G. Ratzinger (cnd), Munich Consortium Musicum, Regensburg Cathedral Choir—Requiem in c; Offertorium zu Ehren des Heiligen Johann von Nepomuk; Laurentanische Litanei Ars Musici ▲ AM 1158-2 [DDD]
Romberg, A.:Der Lied von der Glocke, w. M. Friesenhausen (sop), R. Naber (alt), K. Ridderbusch (bass), G. Knüsel (cnd), Essen CO, Duisburg State Concert Chorus Calig ▲ CAL 50942

Hopkin, T. (sop)
Messiaen, O.:Poèmes pour Mi, w. D. Thoreson (pno) ACA Digital Recording ▲ CM 20024

Hopkins, Gerald (ten)
Gershwin, G.:Blue Monday Blues, w. A. Burton (sop), W. Sharp (bar), A. Woodley (b-bar), J. J. Offenbach (b-bar), M. Alsop (cnd), Concordia Orch EMI Classics ▲ CDC 54851

Hoppe, Heinz (ten)
Dostal, N.:Clivia (sels), w. Sari Barabas (sop), W. Schubert (cnd), Graunke SO, Bavarian Radio Chorus Emperor Operetta ▲ KO 86352
Fall, L.:Die Dollarprinzessin (sels), w. Sari Barabas (sop), Christine Gorner (sop), Harry Friedauer (ten), C. Michalski (cnd), Graunke SO, Botho Lucas Chorus Emperor Operetta ▲ KO 86353
Fall, L.:Der fidele Bauer (sels), w. Sonja Knittel (sop), Brigette Fassbaender (mez), Fritz Wunderlich (ten), Benno Kusche (bass), C. Michalski (cnd), Graunke SO, Rudolf Lamy Singers Emperor Operetta ▲ KO 86353
Fall, L.:Der liebe Augustin (sels), w. Sari Barabas (sop), Christine Gorner (sop), Benno Kusche (b-bar), C. Michalski (cnd), Graunke SO, Rudolf Lamy Singers Emperor Operetta ▲ KO 86352
Lehár, F.:Das Land des Lächelns (sels), w. I. Hallstein (sop), Renate Holm (sop), Alexander (sgr), Marszalek (cnd), Operretta Orch, Operetta Chorus [G] Acanta ▲ CD 43494 [DDD]
Lehár, F.:Die lustige Witwe (sels), w. I. Hallstein (sop), L. Popp (sop), Alexander (bar), B. Kusche (bar), Marszalek (cnd), Operetta Orch, Operetta Chorus [G] Acanta ▲ CD 43455 [DDD]
Lehár, F.:Zigeunerliebe (sels), w. Sari Barabas (sop), Christine Gorner (sop), Harry Friedauer (ten), C. Michalski (cnd), Graunke SO, Rudolf Lamy Singers Emperor Operetta ▲ KO 86342

Hoppe, Karl (bass)
Strauss, R.:Feuersnot, w. Maud Cunitz (sop—Diemut), Antonia Fahberg (sop—Elsbeth), Irmgard Barth (mez—Wigelis), Liselotte Nölser (sgr—Margret), Karl Ostertag (ten—Schweiker), Marcel Cordes (bar—Kunrad), Kieth Engen (bass—Kofel), Karl Hoppe (bass—Hämerlein), Max Proebstl (bass—Ortolf), Georg Wieter (bass—Jörg), R. Kempe (cnd), Bavarian State Opera Orch, Bavarian State Opera Chorus *(rec Munich Opera Festival, Prince Regent Theater, Aug 14, 1958)* Orfeo d'or 2-▲ 423962

Hoppe, Karl (ten)
Strauss, R.:Salome, w. Astrid Varnay (sop—Salome), Hertha Töpper (mez—Der Page der Herodias), Margarete Klose (cta—Herodias), Hans Hopf (ten—Narraboth), Karl Hoppe (ten—1st Nazarene), Karl Ostertag (ten—1st Jew), Julius Patzak (ten—Herodes), Hans Braun (bar—Jochanaan), Benno Kusche (bar—2nd Soldier), Adolf Keil (bass—1st Soldier), Hans Hermann Nissen (bass—Ein Kappadozier), Max Proebstl (bass—2nd Nazarene), Walter Carnotch (sgr—4th Jew), Emil Graf (sgr—3rd Jew), Paul Kaussen (sgr—2nd Jew), Hildegard Limmer (sgr—A slave), Georg Witter (sgr—5th Jew), H. Weigert (cnd), Bavarian RSO *(rec June 21-25, 1953)* Bella Voce 2-▲ BLV 7210 [AAD]

Horáček, Jaroslav (bass)
Janáček, L.:From the House of the Dead, w. M. Jirglova (sop), V. Pribyl (ten), R. Novák (bass), V. Neumann (cnd), Czech PO, Czech Phil Chorus [Cz] Supraphon 2-▲ SUP 10 2941 [ADD]
Smetana, B.:Choral Music, w. Miroslav Švejda (ten), Vratislav Jahna (bar), Z. Košler (cnd), Prague SO, Prague Radio Chorus, Czech Phil Chorus Supraphon ▲ SUP CD 3040

Horn, Volker (ten)
Mendelssohn, F.:Die Hochzeit des Camacho, w. R. Schudel (sop—Quiteria), C. Swanson (sop—Lucinda), C. Bieber (ten—Basilio), W. Mok (ten—Vivaldo), V. Horn (ten—Camacho), R. Lukas (bar—Carrasco), J. Becker (bass—Sancho Panza), W. Murray (bass—Don Quixote), B. Klee (cnd), Berlin RSO, Berlin Radio Chorus [G] Koch Schwann 2-▲ 314042 [DDD]
Wagner, S.:Banadietrich, w. Beth Johanning (sop), Vivian Hanner (sgr), André Wenhold (bar), Andreas Schmidt (bar), Adalbert Walker (bass), V. Gailis (cnd), Thuringian SO, Rudolstadt Festival Chorus *(rec Rudolstädt, June 1995)* Marco Polo 2-▲ 8.223895-6 [DDD]
Wagner, S.:Der Bärenhäuter, w. B. Johanning (sop—Luise), K. Likic (sop—Lene), T. Koon (sop—Gunda), V. Horn (ten—Hans Kraft), A. Feilhaber (ten—Nikolaus Spitz), R. Hartmann (bar—Kaspar Wild), A. Wenhold (bar—Stranger), A. Waller (bass—Devil), H. Kiichli (bass—Melchior Fröhlich), K. Bach (cnd), Thüringian SO, Thüringian State Theater Chorus *(rec Rudolstadt, July 25-31, 1993)* Marco Polo ("Opera Classics" series) 2-▲ 8.223713/4 [DDD]

Horna, Ruth (sop)
Weber, C.M. von:Oberon (sels), w. W. Mengelberg (cnd), Royal Concertgebouw Orch—Ozean du ungeheuer Archive Documents ("The Mengelberg Edition" series) ▲ ADCD 109

Horne, Marilyn (mez)
The Age of Bel Canto, w. Joan Sutherland (sop), Richard Conrad (bar), London SO [cnd:Richard Bonynge], London Sym Chorus London ("The Classic Sound" series) ▲ 448594-2
All through the Night:Lullabies RCA Victor ▲ 09026-61278-2 [DDD] ▮ 09026-61278-4 (CrO2) ▯ 09026-61278-5
The Art of Marilyn Horne Replay ("Butterfly" series) ▲ BMCD 032 [AAD]
Auber, D.-F.:Zerline (sels), w. L. Foster (cnd), Monte Carlo PO Erato ("Recital" series) ▲ 98501-2
Bellini, V.:Norma, w. J. Sutherland (sop), J. Alexander (ten), R. Cross (bass), R. Bonynge (cnd), London SO, London Sym Chorus [I] London 3-▲ 425488-2 [ADD]
Bellini, V.:Norma (sels), w. J. Sutherland (sop), J. Alexander (ten), R. Cross (bass), R. Bonynge (cnd), London SO, London Sym Chorus [I] London ("Opera Gala" series) ▲ 421886-2 [ADD]
Berlioz, H.:La Damnation de Faust, w. M. Horne (mez—Marguerite), N. Gedda (ten—Faust), R. Soyer (bass—Mephistofeles), D. Petkov (bass—Brander), G. Prêtre (cnd), Rome RAI SO, Rome RAI Chorus *(rec live 1/11/69)* Arkadia 4-▲ 461 [ADD]
Berlioz, H.:Les Troyens, w. S. Verrett (mez), N. Gedda (ten), V. Luchetti (ten), R. Massard (bar), G. Prêtre (cnd), Rome RAI SO, Rome RAI Chorus [F] *(rec live 5/30/69)* Melodram 3-▲ MEL 37060 [AAD]
Berlioz, H.:Les Troyens, w. S. Verrett (mez), N. Gedda (ten), V. Luchetti (ten), R. Massard (bar), G. Prêtre (cnd), Rome RAI SO, Rome RAI Chorus *(rec live 5/30/69)* Arkadia 4-▲ 461 [ADD]
Bizet, G.:Carmen, w. A. Maliponte (sop), J. McCracken (ten), T. Krause (bar), L. Bernstein (cnd), Metropolitan Opera Orch, Manhattan Opera Chorus [F] *(rec 1973)* Deutsche Grammophon 3-▲ 427440-2 [ADD]
Bizet, G.:Carmen (sels), w. M. Molese (sgr), M. Pellegrini (sgr), G. Griffiths (bar), D. Bowman (bar), F. Egerton (ten), H. Lewis (cnd), Royal PO, Royal Liverpool Phil Choir IMP Collectors Series ▲ IMPX 9016 [AAD]
Brahms, J.:Alto Rhap, w. R. Shaw (cnd), Atlanta SO, Atlanta Sym Chorus [G] Telarc ▲ CD 80176 [DDD]
Brahms, J.:Songs, Op. 91, w. P. Zukerman (va), M. Neikrug (pno) [G] RCA Red Seal ▲ 09026-61276-2
Copland, A.:Old American Songs, w. C. Davis (cnd), English CO—Set 1, Nos. 3-5; Set 2, Nos. 4 & 5 *(rec Walthamstow Assembly Hall, London, Aug 1985)* London 2-▲ 448261-2 [DDD]
Donizetti, G.:La favorita (sels), w. L. Foster (cnd), Monte Carlo PO Erato ("Recital" series) ▲ 98501-2
Donizetti, G.:Lucrezia Borgia, w. J. Sutherland (sop), G. Aragall (ten), I. Wixell (bar), R. Bonynge (cnd), National PO London [I] London 2-▲ 421497-2 [ADD]
Falla, M. de:El amor brujo, w. L. Bernstein (cnd), New York PO Odyssey ▲ MBK 44721 [ADD] ▮ YT 44721
Gluck, C.W.:Orfeo ed Euridice, w. H. Donath (sop), P. Lorengar (sop), G. Solti (cnd), Royal Opera House Orch, Royal Opera House Chorus Covent Garden London 2-▲ 417410-2 [ADD]
Godard, B.:La Vivandiere (sels), w. L. Foster (cnd), Monte Carlo PO Erato ("Recital" series) ▲ 98501-2
Gounod, C.:Sappho (sels), w. L. Foster (cnd), Monte Carlo PO Erato ("Recital" series) ▲ 98501-2
Handel, G.F.:Giulio Cesare in Egitto (sels), w. Joan Sutherland (sop), R. Bonynge (cnd), London New SO London ("Grand Opera" series) 3-▲ 433723-2 [ADD]
Handel, G.F.:Rinaldo, w. Cecelia Gasdia (sop), Christine Weidinger (sop), Ernesto Palacio (ten), J. Fisher (cnd), Venice Teatro La Fenice Orch *(rec live 1989)* Nuova Era 2-▲ 6813/14 [DDD]
Handel, G.F.:Semele, w. Kathleen Battle (sop), Sylvia McNair (sop), Michael Chance (ct), John Aler (ten), Samuel Ramey (bass), J. Nelson (cnd), English CO, Ambrosian Opera Chorus Deutsche Grammophon 3-▲ 435782-2 -
Live from Lincoln Center, w. Joan Sutherland
Live from Lincoln Center, w. Joan Sutherland (sop), Luciano Pavarotti (ten) London 2-▲ 417587-2 LH [DDD]
Mahler, G.:Songs from Rückert, w. H. Lewis (cnd), Milan RAI SO, Rome RAI SO *(rec live, Apr. 30 & June 18, 1971)* Arkadia ▲ 808
Mahler, G.:Sym 2, w. C .Neblett (sop), C. Abbado (cnd), Chicago SO, Chicago Sym Chorus [G] Deutsche Grammophon ("Galleria" series) 2-▲ 427262-2 [ADD]
Mahler, G.:Sym 2, w. K. Te Kanawa (sop), S. Ozawa (cnd), Boston SO, Tanglewood Festival Chorus [G] Philips 2-▲ 420824-2 [DDD]
Mahler, G.:Sym 3, w. J. Levine (cnd), Chicago SO [G] RCA Red Seal 2-▲ RCD2-1757
Marilyn Horne Memories ("Great Voices" series) 2-▲ MEM 4392 (m/s)
Marilyn Horne London ("Grandi Voici" series) ▲ 440415-2
Mendelssohn, F.:Songs, w. F. von Stade (mez), M. Katz (pno)—4 Duets RCA Red Seal ▲ 09026-61681-2
Meyerbeer, G.:Le Prophète, w. M. Rinaldi (sop), N. Gedda (ten), R. El Hage (bass), H. Lewis (cnd), Turin RSO, Turin Radio Chorus [F] *(rec live 7/11/70)* Foyer 3-▲ FOY 2035 [AAD]
Meyerbeer, G.:Le Prophète, w. Renata Scotto (sop), James McCracken (ten), Jerome Hines (bass), H. Lewis (cnd), Royal PO, Ambrosian Opera Chorus [F] CBS 3-▲ M3K 34340 [ADD]
Mozart, W.A.:Requiem, w. E. Ameling (sop), U. Benelli (bar), T. Franc (bass), I. Kertész (cnd), Vienna PO, Vienna State Opera Chorus London ("Weekend Classics" series) ▲ 417681-2 [ADD] ▮ 417681-4
Puccini, G.:Il trittico, w. R. Scotto (sop), I. Cotrubas (sop), P. Domingo (ten), T. Gobbi (bar), I. Wixell (bar), L. Maazel (cnd), London SO, Philharmonia Orch [I] CBS 3-▲ M3K 35912 [ADD]
Rarities from Her Repertoire Standing Room Only ▲ SRO 822-1 [ADD]
Rodgers, R.:The King & I, w. J. Andrews (sgr—Anna Leonowens), L. Salonga (sgr—Tuptim), B. Kingsley (sgr—The King), P. Bryson (sgr—Lun Tha), M. Horne (mez—Lady Thiang), M. Liufau (sgr—Prince Chulalongkorn), E. Kingsley (sgr—Louis Leonowens), R. Moore (sgr—Sir Edward Ramsay), M. Sheen (sgr—The Kralahome), J. Mauceri (cnd), Hollywood Bowl Orch, Los Angeles Master Chorale *(rec Culver City, CA, Apr 1992)* Philips ▲ 438007-2 [DDD]
Rossini Operas London ▲ 421306-2 LA [ADD]
Rossini, G.:Arias, w. A. Zedda (cnd), Turin RSO—arias from Il barbiere di Siviglia, La gazza ladra, Maometto II, Tancredi [F,I,S] CBS ▲ MK 44820 [DDD]
Rossini, G.:Arias, w. H. Lewis (cnd), Royal PO, Swiss Romande Orch, Ambrosian Opera Chorus [I] London ▲ 421306-2 [ADD]
Rossini, G.:Arias, w. H. Lewis (cnd), Milan RAI SO, Rome RAI SO—from Semiramide; Otello; La donna del lago; Tancredi; Cenerentola; L'Italiana in Algeri *(rec live, Apr. 30 & June 18, 1971)* Arkadia ▲ 808
Rossini, G.:Arias, w. Franci, Lewis, Schippers (cnd), La Scala Orch, Turin RAI SO—sels from Semiramide, Otello, La donna del Lago, Tancredi, La Cenerentola, L'Italiana in Algeri & L'Assedio di Dorinto *(rec live, 1968-71)* Enterprise ("Documents" series) ▲ ENT LV 979 (m)
Rossini, G.:Il barbiere di Siviglia, w. E. Dara (bar), L. Nucci (bar), S. Ramey (bass), R. Chailly (cnd), La Scala Orch, La Scala Chorus [I] CBS 3-▲ M3K 37862 [DDD]
Rossini, G.:Il barbiere di Siviglia (sels), w. R. Pierotti (mez), P. Barbacini (ten), E. Dara (bar), L. Nucci (bar), S. Ramey (bass), S. Sammaritano (bass), R. Chailly (cnd), La Scala Orch, La Scala Chorus *(rec Milan, Jan. 2-18, 1982)* Sony Classical ("Opera Highlights" series) ▲ SMK 53501 [DDD]

▲ = CD ♦ = Enhanced CD Δ = MD ▮ = Cassette Tape ▯ = DCC

Horne, Marilyn (mez) (cont.)

Rossini, G.:Bianca e Falliero, w. K. Ricciarelli (sop—Bianca), M. Horne (mez—Falliero), C. Merritt (ten—Contareno), G. Surjan (bass–Capellino), D. Renzetti (cnd), *(orch & chorus unknown) (rec live, 1986)* Legato Classics 3–▲ LCD 138–3 [ADD]

Rossini, G.:Giovanna d'Arco, w. M. Katz (pno) [I] CBS ▲ MK 44820 [DDD]

Rossini, G.:L'italiana in Algeri, w. K. Battle (sop), E. Palacio (ten), S. Ramey (bass), N. Zaccaria (bass), C. Scimone (cnd), Venice Solisti, Prague Phil Chorus [I] Erato ("Libretto" series) 2–▲ 2292–45404–2

Rossini, G.:Music of, w. M. Fortuna (sop), M. Lerner (sop), D. Voigt (sop), K. Kuhlmann (mez), F. von Stade (mez), R. Blake (ten), C. Estep (ten), C. Merritt (ten), T. Hampson (b–bar), H. Runey (b–bar), J. Opalach (bass), S. Ramey (bass), R. Norrington (cnd), Orch of St. Luke's, New York Concert Chorale EMI Classics ▲ CDC 54643

Rossini, G.:Semiramide, w. M. Caballé (sop), F. Araiza (ten), S. Ramey (bass), J. López–Cobos (cnd), *(orch unknown) (rec live, France, 1980)* HRE 2–▲ 1002–2 [ADD]

Rossini, G.:Semiramide, w. J. Sutherland (sop), J. Serge (ten), J. Rouleau (bass), S. Malas (bass), R. Bonynge (cnd), London SO, Ambrosian Singers [I] *(rec 1966)* London 3–▲ 425481–2 [ADD]

Rossini, G.:Semiramide, w. J. Sutherland (sop), Myers (sgr), Grant (sgr), R. Bonynge (cnd), New Philharmonia Orch, Ambrosian Opera Chorus [I] *(rec live at the Theatre Royal, Drury Lane, 2/9/69)* Arkadia 2–▲ 579 (m) [ADD]

Rossini, G.:The Siege of Corinth, w. B. Sills (sop), F. Bonisoli (ten), J. Diaz (bass), T. Schippers (cnd), La Scala Orch, La Scala Chorus [I] *(rec live 1969)* Melodram 2–▲ MEL 27043 [AAD]

Rossini, G.:Tancredi (sels), w. K. Ricciarelli (sop), *(orch unknown)*—4 solo arias & 2 duets *(rec live, 1983)* Legato Classics 3–▲ LCD 138–3 [ADD]

Saint–Saëns, C.:Samson et Dalila (sels), w. L. Foster (cnd), Monte Carlo PO Erato ("Recital" series) ▲ 98501–2

Schumann, R.:Frauenliebe und –leben, w. F. von Stade (mez), M. Katz (pno) [sung as duet] RCA Red Seal ▲ 09026–61681–2

Verdi, G.:Falstaff, w. S. Sweet (sop), F. Lopardo (ten), R. Panerai (bar), A. Titus (bar), C. Davis (cnd), Bavarian RSO, Bavarian Radio Chorus RCA Red Seal 2–▲ 09026–60705–2 [DDD]

Verdi, G.:Requiem Mass, w. J. Sutherland (sop), L. Pavarotti (ten), M. Talvela (bass), G. Solti (cnd), Vienna PO, Vienna State Opera Chorus [L] London 2–▲ 411944–2 [ADD]

Verdi, G.:Il trovatore, w. J. Sutherland (sop), L. Pavarotti (ten), I. Wixell (bar), N. Ghiaurov (bass), R. Bonynge (cnd), National PO London [I] London 2–▲ 417137–2 [ADD]

Verdi, G.:Il trovatore (sels), w. J. Sutherland (sop), L. Pavarotti (ten), R. Bonynge (cnd), National PO London London ▲ 421310–2 [ADD]

Vivaldi, A.:Orlando Furioso, w. V. de los Angeles (sop), L. Valentini–Terrani (mez), C. Gonzales (mez), Kosma (sgr), S. Bruscantini (bar), N. Zaccaria (bass), C. Scimone (cnd), Venice Solisti Erato 3–▲ 2292–45147–2 ZB

Hornik, Gottfried (bar)

Lortzing, A.:Der Wildschütz, oder Die Stimme der Natur, w. Edith Mathis (sop), Peter Schreier (ten), Hans Sotin (bass), B. Klee (cnd), Berlin State Chorus *(rec Berlin, 1982)* Berlin Classics 2–▲ BER 1143 [ADD]

Mozart:Missa Solemnis & Salieri:Te Deum (The Coronation Mass for Leopold II in Prague, September 1791), w. Vienna Academy, Ruth Ziesak (sop), E. von Magnus (mez), H. Wildahaber (ten), Hugo Distler Chorus, Vienna Hofburg Chapel Choir Novalis ▲ 150087 [DDD]

Mozart, W.A.:Masonic Music, w. C. Prégardien (ten), H. Wildhaber (ten), P. Schneyder (bass), M. Haselböck (cnd), Vienna Academy, Chorus Viennensis—Masonic Cants., K.429, 471, 619, 623 & Songs, K.148, 468, 483, 484 [G] Novalis ▲ 150081 [DDD]

Mozart, W.A.:Missa solemnis, K.337, w. R. Ziesak (sop), E. von Magnus (alt), H. Wildhaber (ten), H. Hüttler (cant), M. Jankowitsch (cant), P. Jelosits (cant), I. Rainer (org), M. Haselböck (cnd), Vienna Academy, Vienna Hofburg Chapel Choir [L] *(rec Apr. 1992)* Novalis ▲ 150087 [DDD]

Mozart, W.A.:Zauberflöte, w. Edith Mathis (sop), Karin Ott (sop), Janet Perry (sop), Anna Tomowa–Sintow (sop), Agnes Baltsa (mez), Hannah Schwarz (mez), Francisco Araiza (ten), José Van Dam (b–bar), H. von Karajan (cnd), Berlin PO, German Opera Chorus [G] Deutsche Grammophon 3–▲ 410967–2 [DDD]

Mozart, W.A.:Zauberflöte (sels), w. Edith Mathis (sop), Karin Ott (sop), Janet Perry (sop), Anna Tomowa–Sintow (sop), Agnes Baltsa (mez), Hannah Schwarz (mez), Francisco Araiza (ten), José Van Dam (b–bar), H. von Karajan (cnd), Berlin PO, German Opera Chorus [G] Deutsche Grammophon ▲ 415287–2 [DDD]

Hornik, Gottfried (nar)

Schoenberg, A.:A Survivor from Warsaw, w. C. Abbado (cnd), Vienna PO, Vienna State Opera Chorus Deutsche Grammophon ▲ 431774–2 [DDD]

Horská, Jaroslava (cta)

Mozart, W.A.:Requiem, w. M. Hajóssyová (sop), J. Kundlák (ten), P. Mikuláš (bass), Z. Košler (cnd), Slovak PO, Slovak Phil Chorus Naxos ▲ 8.550235 [DDD] △ 7.550235 [DDD]

Horsman, Leslie (bar)

Verdi, G.:Il trovatore, w. G. Cigna (sop—Leonora), G. Wettergren (mez—Azucena), M. Huder (mez—Ines), J. Björling (ten—Manrico), O. Dua (ten—Ruiz), C. Zambelli (ten—Ferrando), M. Basiola (bar—Count di Luna), L. Horsman (bar—Old Gypsy), V. Gui (cnd), Royal Opera Orch, Royal Opera House Chorus Covent Garden *(rec May 12, 1939)* Legato Classics 2–▲ LCD 173–2 [ADD]

Horton, Michael (ten)

Axelrod, L.:Songs, w. Louisa Ann Parks (sop), Nmon Ford–Livene (ten), Malcolm Mackenzie (bar), Richard Bernstein (bass), M. Beltrami (cnd)—sels w. lyrics by Burns, Browning, Byron, Keats, Morris, Poe, Rossetti, Shelley, Wordsworth & Yeats Marquis ▲ MAR 171

Horváth (sgr)

Vivaldi, A.:L'Olimpiade (sels), w. M. Zempléni (sop), T. Takács (mez), Káplán (sgr), L. Miller (bar), I. Gáti (bar), K. Kováts (bass), F. Szekeres (cnd), Hungarian State Orch, Budapest Madrigal Choir [I] White Label ▲ HRC 073 [ADD]

Horvath, Anka (sgr)

The Voice of Tino Pattiera:Arias, Duets & Songs, w. Tino Pattiera (ten), Meta Seinmeyer (sop), Michael Bohnen (bass) *(rec 1916–30)* Preiser 2–▲ PRE CD 89222

Horvei, Reidun (sgr)

Grieg, E.:Norwegian Folk Songs, Op. 66, w. K. Hamre (sgr), H. Fiddle (sgr), G. Botnen (pno) Simax ▲ PSC 1102

Grieg, E.:Norwegian Peasant Dances, Op. 72, w. K. Hamre (sgr), H. Fiddle (sgr), G. Botnen (pno) Simax ▲ PSC 1102

Horwitz, Dominique (sgr)

Waits, T.:The Black Rider:The Casting of Magic Bullets, w. Angelika Thomas (sgr—Anne), Annette Paulmann (sgr—Kätchen), Sona Cervena (sgr—Bird/Messenger/Spoonwoman), Monika Tahal (sgr—Witness/Bird/Shrink/Wilhelm's Double/Skeleton), Susi Eisenkolb (sgr—Bridesmaid/Pegleg's Double), Heinz Vossbrink (sgr—Kuno), Dominique Horwitz (sgr—Pegleg), Gerd Kunath (sgr—Bertram), Stefan Kurt (sgr—Wilhelm), Klaus Schreiber (sgr—Robert/Man on Stag/Georg Schmid), Jörg Holm (Old Uncle/Duke), Jan Moritz Steffen (sgr—Young Kuno/Bird/Shrink/Skeleton), Tom Waits (vocals/coliope/organ/chamberlain/mar/emax/guitar/train whistle), Ralph Carney (saxophone/bass clarinet/baritone horn), Bill Douglas (bass instrument), Kenny Wollesen (perc) Island ▲ 314518559–2

Hosking, Arthur (bar)

Sullivan, A.:Trial by Jury, w. W. Lawson (sop), D. Oldham (ten), G. Baker (bar), L. Sheffield (bar), H. Norris (cnd), D'Oyly Carte Opera Company Orch, D'Oyly Carte Opera Chorus *(rec 1928)* Pearl 2–▲ PEAS 9961 (m) [AAD]

Hoskins, Bob (sgr)

Gay, J.:The Beggar's Opera, w. S. Walker (mez), A. Thompson (ten), C. Daniels (ten), I. Caddy (b–bar), J. Barlow (cnd), Broadside Band [E] Hyperion 2–▲ CDA 66591/92

Hossfeld, Christianne (sgr)

Künneke, E.:The Alluring Flame, w. Birgit Fandrey (sgr—Dolores), Christianne Hossfeld (sgr—Lisbeth), Maria Mallé (sgr), Jürgen Sacher (ten—Master), Ralf Lukas (bar—Hoffman), Gerd Grochowski (sgr—1st Neighbor), Gerhard Peters (sgr—Friedrich), Zoran Todorovic (sgr—Jacinto), Theodor Weimer (sgr—2nd Neighbor), P. Falk (cnd), Cologne RSO, Cologne Radio Chorus *(rec Cologne, Nov 7–26, 1994)* Capriccio ▲ 10753 [DDD]

Hotter, Hans (b–bar)

Bach, J.S.:Cant 82, w. A. Bernard (cnd), Philharmonia Orch [G] *(rec 1950)* EMI Classics ("Great Recordings of the Century" series) ▲ CDH 63198–2 (m) [ADD]

Beethoven, L. van:Fidelio, w. S. Jurinac (sop), J. Vickers (ten), G. Frick (bass), O. Klemperer (cnd), Royal Opera House Orch, Royal Opera House Chorus Covent Garden [G] *(rec live, Covent Garden, 3/7/61)* Melodram 2–▲ MEL 27076 (m) [AAD]

Berg, A.:Lulu, w. P. Wise (sop—Lulu), B. Fassbaender (mez—Countess Geschwitz), H. Hotter (b–bar—Schigolch), J. Tate (cnd), French National Orch—Act 3 [G] *(rec live 9 & 10/91)* EMI Classics 3–▲ CDCC 54622 [DDD]

Berg, A.:Lulu, w. A. Silja (sop), B. Fassbaender (mez), W. Berry (b–bar), K. Moll (bass), A. Szramek (sgr), C. von Dohnányi (cnd), Vienna PO London 2–▲ 430415–2 [ADD]

Brahms, J.:Ein Deutsches Requiem, w. E. Schwarzkopf (sop), H. von Karajan (cnd), Vienna PO, Vienna Singverein [G] *(rec 10/47)* EMI Classics ("Great Recordings of the Century" series) ▲ CDH 61010 (m) [ADD]

Early Recordings *(rec 1939–43)* Preiser ▲ PRE 90200 [AAD]

Hans Hotter Sings Carl Lowe, w. Michael Raucheise (pno) *(rec 1943–45)* Preiser ▲ PRE CD 90301

Mozart, W.A.:Nozze di Figaro, w. Irma Beilke (sop), Helena Braun (sop), Gerda Sommerschuh (sop), Josef Witt (ten), Erich Kunz (bar), Gustav Neidlinger (b–bar), C. Krauss (cnd), Vienna PO, Vienna State Opera Chorus *(rec live, Salzburg Festival, Aug. 1942)* Preiser 3–▲ PRE 90203 [ADD]

Mussorgsky, M.:Boris Godunov, w. Martha Mödl (sop—Marina Mniszek), Lotte Schädle (sop—Xenia), Dorothea Siebert (mez—Fyodor), Hertha Töpper (mez—Xenia's wet–nurs), Karl Hermann Bennert (Boyer Khrushchyov), Lorenz Fehenberger (ten—Prince Shuysky), Hans Hopf (ten—Grigory), Karl Ostertag (ten—Missail), Hans Hotter (b–bar—Boris Godunov), Hermann Uhde (bar—Andrey Shchelkalov), Kurt Böhme (bass—Varlaam), Kim Borg (bass—Pimen), Kieth Engen (bass—Lewicki), Adolf Keil (bass—Nikitich), Benno Kusche (bar—Rangoni), Heinz Maria Linz (bass—Czernikowski), E. Jochum (cnd), Bavarian RSO, Bavarian Radio Chorus *(rec Munich, May 1957)* Myto 3–▲ MCD 953131

Orff, C.:Der Mond—Ein kleines Welttheater, w. R. Christ (ten), P. Kuén (ten), K. Schmitt–Walter (bar), H. Graml (bar), P. Lagger (bass), W. Sawallisch (cnd), Philharmonia Orch, Philharmonia Chorus [G] EMI Classics ("Studio" series) 2–▲ CDMB 63712 [ADD]

Schoenberg, A.:Gurrelieder, w. E. Martón (sop), F. Quivar (mez), G. Lakes (ten), Z. Mehta (cnd), New York PO, New York Choral Artists [G] Sony Classical 2–▲ S2K 48077 [DDD]

Schubert, Franz:Songs (misc), w. H. Altmann (pno)—10 songs—D.291, 530, 553, 583, 649, 674, 776, 778, 870, 933 [G] *(rec 1952 & 1959)* Preiser ▲ 93145 (m) [AAD]

Schubert, Franz:Winterreise, w. M. Raucheisen (pno) Deutsche Grammophon ▲ 437351–2

Schubert, Franz:Winterreise, w. G. Moore (pno) [G] EMI Classics ("Great Recordings of the Century" series) ▲ CDH 61002 (m)

Schumann, R.:Dichterliebe, w. H. Altmann (pno) [G] *(rec 1954)* Preiser ▲ 93145 (m) [AAD]

Sings Lieder, w. Hans Dokoupil (pno) *(rec 1968–69)* Preiser ▲ PRE 93390 [ADD]

Strauss, R.:Arabella, w. M. Reining (sop), L. Della Casa (sop), H. Taubmann (ten), K. Böhm (cnd), Vienna PO *(rec Salzburg Festival, 1947)* Deutsche Grammophon 3–▲ 445342–2 (m) [ADD]

Strauss, R.:Arabella, w. L. Della Casa (sop), M. Reining (sop), R. Anday (cta), G. Hann (bass), J. Patzak (ten), K. Böhm (cnd), Vienna PO, Vienna State Opera Chorus *(rec live, Salzburg Festival, 8/12/47)* Melodram 3–▲ MEL 37077

Strauss, R.:Capriccio, w. E. Schwarzkopf (sop), A. Moffo (sop), C. Ludwig (mez), N. Gedda (ten), D. Fischer–Dieskau (bar), E. Wächter (bar), W. Sawallisch (cnd), Philharmonia Orch [G] EMI Classics 2–▲ CDCB 49014 (m) [ADD]

Strauss, R.:Capriccio (sels), w. V. Ursuleac (sop—Die Gräfin), F. Klarwein (ten—Flamand), H. Hotter (b–bar—Olivier), G. Hann (b–bar—La Roche), G. Wieter (bass—Der Haushofmeister), C. Krauss (cnd), Bavarian State Opera Orch *(rec 1942)* Myto ▲ MCD 943104

Strauss, R.:Friedenstag, w. Viorica Ursuleac (sop—Maria), Anton Dermota (ten—Ein Piemonteser), Hans Hotter (b–bar—Kommandant), Herbert Alsen (bass—Wachtmeister), C. Krauss (cnd), Vienna State Opera Orch *(rec Vienna, Oct. 16, 1941)* Koch Schwann 2–▲ SCH 314625 [ADD]

Strauss, R.:Salome (sels), w. E. Schulz (sop—Salome), A. Dermota (ten—Narraboth), J. Witt (ten—Herodes), H. Hotter (bar—Jochanaan), P. Schöffler (b–bar—Jochanaan), R. Strauss (cnd), Vienna State Opera Orch, Vienna State Opera Chorus *(rec Feb. 15 & May 6, 1942)* Koch Schwann 2–▲ SCH 314532 [ADD]

Strauss, R.:Die Schweigsame Frau, w. G. von Milinkovic (mez), F. Wunderlich (ten), H. Prey (bar), K. Böhm (cnd), Vienna PO, Vienna State Opera Chorus *(rec live, Salzburg Festival, 8/8/59)* Melodram 2–▲ MEL 27071 (m) [AAD]

Strauss, R.:Die Schweigsame Frau, w. H. Güden (sop), F. Wunderlich (ten), H. Prey (bar), K. Böhm (cnd), Vienna PO *(rec Salzburg Festival, 1959)* Deutsche Grammophon 2–▲ 445335–2 (m) [ADD]

Strauss, R.:Songs, w. W. Klien (pno)—Die Nacht; Ruhe meine Seele; Mit deinen blauen Augen; etc. [G] *(rec 1967)* Preiser ▲ 93367 [ADD]

Strauss, R.:Taillefer, w. Maria Cebotari (sop), Walter Ludwig (ten), *(orch & chorus unknown) (rec 1943–44)* Preiser ▲ PRE 90222 [ADD]

Verdi, G.:Aida (sels), w. Hilde Scheppan (sop), Margarete Klose (cta), Helge Roswaenge (ten), A. Rother (cnd), Berlin Radio Orch, Berlin State Opera Chorus [G] *(rec Nov. 21, 1942)* Preiser ▲ PRE 90219 [ADD]

Wagner, R.:Arias & Scenes, w. K. Flagstad (sop), E. Rethberg (sop), B. Nilsson (sop), E. Schumann (sop), F. Leider (sop), L. Melchior (ten), G. Thill (ten), A. Pertile (ten), G. Hüsch (bar), F. Schorr (b–bar), A. Kipnis (bass), *(orch unknown)* EMI Classics ("Studio" series) 4–▲ CDMC 64008

Wagner, R.:Der fliegende Holländer, w. Viorica Ursuleac (sop), Luise Willer (mez), Karl Ostertag (ten), Georg Hann (bass), C. Krauss (cnd), Bavarian State Opera Orch, Bavarian State Opera Chorus *(rec Mar 13–16, 1944)* Preiser 2–▲ PRE 90250 [ADD]

Wagner, R.:Die Meistersinger von Nürnberg (sels), w. W. Windgassen (ten), A. Cluytens (cnd), Bayreuth Festival Orch, Bayreuth Festival Chorus—Monologue & Duet from Act 3 [G] *(rec live, 1957)* Arkadia 4–▲ 440 (m) [AAD]

Wagner, R.:Parsifal, w. C. Ludwig (mez), E. Höngen (cta), H.–M. Uhle (ten), T. Franc (bass), W. Berry (bass), H. von Karajan (cnd), Vienna State Opera Orch, Vienna State Opera Chorus [G] *(rec live 4/1/61)* Arkadia 3–▲ 219 (m) [ADD]

Wagner, R.:Parsifal, w. I. Dalis (mez), J. Thomas (ten), G. London (bar), G. Neidlinger (b–bar), H. Knappertsbusch (cnd), Bayreuth Festival Orch, Bayreuth Festival Chorus [1962] [G] Philips 4–▲ 416390–2 [ADD]

Wagner, R.:Das Rheingold, w. E. Grümmer (sop), R. Gorr (mez), A. Andersson (ten), S. Konya (ten), T. Adam (b–bar), J. Greindl (bass), H. Knappertsbusch (cnd), Bayreuth Festival Orch, Bayreuth Festival Chorus [G] *(rec live 1958)* Arkadia 2–▲ 441 [AAD]

Wagner, R.:Der Ring des Nibelungen, w. B. Nilsson (sop), K. Flagstad (sop), R. Crespin (sop), C. Watson (sop), C. Ludwig (mez), J. Madeira (mez), S. Svanholm (ten), J. King (ten), G. Stolze (ten), W. Windgassen (ten), G. London (bar), D. Fischer–Dieskau (bar), G. Neidlinger (b–bar), G. Frick (bass), G. Solti (cnd), Vienna PO [G] London 15–▲ 414100–2 [ADD]

Wagner, R.:Der Ring des Nibelungen, w. Gré Brouwenstein (sop—Freia/Sieglinde), Ilse Hollweg (sop—Waldvogel), Gerda Lammers (sop—Ortlinde), Paula Lenchner (sop—Wellgunde/Gerhilde), Hilde Scheppan (sop—Helmwige), Astrid Varnay (sop—Brünnilde/3rd Norn), Lore Wissmann (sop—Woglinde), Maria von Ilosvay (mez—Flosshilde/Schwertleite/2nd Norn), Louise Charlotte Kamps (mez—Siegrune), Jean Madeira (mez—Erda/Rossweisse/1st Norn), Georgine van Milinkovic (mez—Fricka/Grimgerde), Elisabeth Schärtel (mez—Waltraute), Paul Kuën (ten—Mime), Ludwig Suthaus (ten—Loge), Josef Traxel (ten—Froh), Wolfgang Windgassen (ten—Siegmund/Siegfried), Alfons Herwig (bar—Donner), Hermann Uhde (bar—Gunther), Hans Hotter (b–bar—Wotan), Gustav Neidlinger (b–bar—Alberich), Josef Griendl (bass—Fasolt/Hunding/Hagen), Arnold van Mill (bass—Fafner), H. Knappertsbusch (cnd), Bayreuth Festival Orch, Bayreuth Festival Chorus *(rec live, Bayreuth, Aug 13–17, 1956)* Golden Melodram 14–▲ GM 1.001 [ADD]

Wagner, R.:Der Ring des Nibelungen (sels), w. Adele Kern (sop), Anny Konetzni (sop), Hilde Konetzni (sop), Elisabeth Schumann (sop), Enid Szantho (cta), Josef Kalenberg (ten), Max Lorenz (ten), Set Svanholm (ten), Erich Zimmermann (ten), Jaro Prohaska (bar), Emil Schipper (bar), Paul Schöffler (b–bar), Ludwig Hoffmann (bass), H. Knappertsbusch (cnd), Vienna State Opera Orch *(rec Vienna, 1937–1943)* Koch Schwann 2–▲ SCH 314742 [ADD]

Wagner, R.:Der Ring des Nibelungen (sels), w. B. Nilsson (sop), W. Windgassen (ten), G. Solti (cnd), Vienna PO London ▲ 421313–2 [ADD]

Hotter, Hans (b–bar) (cont.)
Wagner, R.:Siegfried, w. B. Nilsson (sop), W. Windgassen (ten), G. Stolze (ten), G. Neidlinger (b–bar), G. Solti (cnd), Vienna PO [G] London 4–▲ 414110–2 [ADD]
Wagner, R.:Siegfried, w. A. Varnay (sop), W. Windgassen (ten), A. Andersson (ten), G. Stoltze (ten), J. Greindl (bass), H. Knappertsbusch (cnd), Bayreuth Festival Orch, Bayreuth Festival Chorus [G] *(rec live 1958)* Arkadia 4–▲ 443 [AAD]
Wagner, R.:Tristan und Isolde, w. M. Mödl (sop), R. Vinay (ten), H. von Karajan (cnd), Bayreuth Festival Orch, Bayreuth Festival Chorus *(rec 1955)* Arkadia 4–▲ 528 (m) [AAD]
Wagner, R.:Tristan und Isolde (sels), w. K. Flagstad (sop), V. Ursuleac (sop), S. Svanholm (ten), E. Kleiber (cnd), Buenos Aires Teatro Colón Orch, Buenos Aires Teatro Colón Chorus—highlights from Acts 1–3 [G] *(rec live, 1948)* Melodram 2–▲ MEL 25007 (m) [AAD]
Wagner, R.:Die Walküre, w. B. Nilsson (sop), R. Crespin (sop), C. Ludwig (mez), J. King (ten), G. Frick (bass), G. Solti (cnd), Vienna PO [G] London 4–▲ 414105–2 [ADD]
Wagner, R.:Die Walküre (act 2), w. M. Fuchs (sop), E. Flesch (sop), L. Lehmann (sop), M. Klose (cta), L. Melchior (ten), A. Jerger (b–bar), E. List (bass), B. Walter (cnd), Berlin State Opera Orch [G] *(rec 9/38 & 6/22/35)* EMI Classics ("References" series) ▲ CDH 64255
Wagner, R.:Die Walküre (act 2), w. M. Fuchs (sop), E. Flesch (sop), L. Lehmann (sop), M. Klose (cta), L. Melchior (ten), A. Jerger (b–bar), E. List (bass), B. Walter (cnd), Berlin State Opera Orch [G] *(rec 9/38 & 6/22/35)* Danacord 2–▲ DACOCD 317/18 (m)

Hotter, Hans (nar)
Schoenberg, A.:Gurrelieder, w. S. Dunn (sop), B. Fassbaender (mez), S. Jerusalem (ten), P. Haage (ten), H. Becht (bass), R. Chailly (cnd), Berlin RSO, St. Hedwig's Cathedral Choir, Düsseldorf Municipal Choral Society [G] London 2–▲ 430321–2 [DDD]

Houska, Eva Novšak (mez)
Dvořák, A.:Stabat Mater, w. A. P. Jeric (sop), J. Reja (ten), F. Petrusanec (bass), M. Munih (cnd), Ljubljana RSO, Ljubljana Radio Chorus [L] PMG ("Vienna Master" series) ▲ CD 160104 [DDD]
Dvořák, A.:Stabat Mater, w. A. Pusar–Jerik (sop), J. Reja (ten), F. Petrusanec (bass), M. Munih (cnd), Consortium Musicum Orch, Consortium Musicum Chorus [L] Vivace 2–▲ 140141 [ADD/DDD]

Hovencamp, Robert (sgr)
Rapchak, L.:The Lifework of Juan Diaz, w. C. Loverde (sop), R. Alderson (sgr), D. Rowader (sgr), L. Rapchak (cnd), Chicago Chamber Opera Albany ▲ TROY 091 [DDD]

Hovman, L. (alt)
Van De Vate, N.:An American Essay, w. C. Marstrand (sop), O. Støvring Larsen (ten), S. Kawalla (cnd), Koszalin State PO, Chorus Soranus Vienna Modern Masters ▲ VMM 3025 [DDD]

Howard, Jason (bar)
Classical Spectacular 2, w. Royal PO, Michael Reed (cnd), Gunnar Gudbjornsson (ten), Scots Guards Band, Welsh Guards Band, London Choral Society RPO Records ▲ CDRPO 5010 [DDD]

Howarth, Judith (sop)
Elgar, E.:Caractacus, w. A. Davies (ten), S. Roberts (bar), D. Wilson–Johnson (bar), A.R. Miles (bass), R. Hickox (cnd), London SO, London Sym Chorus [E] *(rec 1992)* Chandos 2–▲ CHAN 9156/57 [DDD]
Elgar, E.:The Light of Life, w. L. Finnie (mez), A. Davies (ten), J. Shirley–Quirk (bar), R. Hickox (cnd), London SO, London Sym Chorus Chandos ▲ CHAN 9208 [DDD]
Martin, F.:In terra pax, w. Della Jones (cta), Martyn Hill (ten), Roderick Williams (bar), Stephen Roberts (bass), M. Bamert (cnd), London PO, Laszlo Heltay (cnd), Brighton Festival Chorus Chandos ▲ CHAN 9465
Mendelssohn, F.:A Midsummer Night's Dream (comp), w. J. Rigby (mez), F. d' Avalos (cnd), Philharmonia Orch, Bach Choir—Op. 61 IMP Masters ▲ IMPMCD 78 [DDD]
Mendelssohn, F.:A Midsummer Night's Dream (comp), w. E. James (mez), J. Laredo (cnd), Scottish CO, Scottish Phil Singers [E] Nimbus 2–▲ NI 5041/42 [DDD]
Mendelssohn, F.:Sym 2, w. E. Wiens (sop), R. Tear (ten), F. d' Avalos (cnd), Philharmonia Orch, Bach Choir IMP Masters ▲ IMP MCD 83 [DDD]
Pastoral:Emma Johnson Plays British Clarinet Music, w. Emma Johnson (cl), M. Martineau (pno) ASV ▲ ASV 891 [DDD]
Smyth, E.:The Wreckers, w. Anne–Marie Owens (mez), Annemarie Sand (mez), Justin Lavender (ten), Anthony Roden (ten), Peter Sidhom (bar), David Wilson–Johnson (bar), Brian Bannatyne–Scott (bass), O. de la Martinez (cnd), BBC PO, Huddersfield Choral Society *(rec live, Royal Albert Hall, London, July 31, 1994)* Conifer Classics 2–▲ 75605–51250–2
Vaughan Williams, R.:Sacred Songs, w. J.M. Ainsley (ten), T. Allen (bar), M. Best (cnd), Corydon Orch, Corydon Singers—Towards the Unknown Region; Dona nobis pacem; O Clap your hands; Lord, Thou hast been our refuge; 4 Hymns Hyperion ▲ CDA 66655 [DDD]
Walton, W.:Troilus & Cressida, w. Judith Howarth (sop—Cressida), Arthur Davies (ten—Troilus), Nigel Robson (ten—Pandarus), Brian Cookson (ten—3rd Watchman), Peter Bodenham (ten—Priest), Keith Mills (ten—Soldier), Alan Opie (bar—Diomede), James Thornton (bar—Antenor), Clive Bayley (bass—Calkas), David Owen–Lewis (bass—Horaste), R. Hickox (cnd), English Northern Philharmonia, Opera North Chorus Chandos 2–▲ CHAN 9370/71 [DDD]

Howd, Janet (sop)
Proses Lyriques, w. Christopher Ross (pno) Duo Records ▲ DUOCD 89005

Howell, Gwynne (bass)
Bach, J.S.:Mass in b, BWV 232, w. F. Lott (sop), A. S. von Otter (mez), H. P. Blochwitz (ten), W. Shimell (bar), G. Solti (cnd), Chicago SO, Chicago Sym Chorus London 2–▲ 430353–2 [DDD]
Beethoven, L. van:Mass, Op. 86, w. Janice Watson (sop), Jean Rigby (mez), John Mark Ainsley (ten), M. Best (cnd), Corydon Orch, Corydon Singers Hyperion ▲ CDA 66830
Beethoven, L. van:Missa Solemnis, w. Ileana Cotrubas (sop), Kathleen Kuhlmann (mez), Robert Tear (ten), J. Pritchard (cnd), BBC SO, BBC Singers IMP ("BBC Radio Classics" series) ▲ IMP 5691552
Beethoven, L. van:Sym 9, "Choral Sym", w. H. Harper (sop), A. Hodgson (cta), R. Tear (ten), R. Hickox (cnd), Northern Sinfonia of England, London Sym Chorus members ASV Quicksilva ▲ ASQ 6069 [DDD]
Beethoven, L. van:Sym 9, "Choral Sym", w. Alison Hargen (sop), Della Jones (mez), David Rendall (ten), W. Morris (cnd), London SO, London Sym Chorus IMP ("LSO" series) ▲ IMP 6900032
Beethoven, L. van:Tremate, empi, tremate, w. Janice Watson (sop), M. Best (cnd), Corydon Orch Hyperion ▲ CDA 66830
Berlioz, H.:L'Enfance du Christ, w. Jean Rigby (mez), John Aler (ten), Gerald Finley (ten), Alastair Miles (bar), M. Best (cnd), Cordon Orch, Corydon Singers, St. Paul's Cathedral Choir Hyperion 2–▲ CDA 66991/2
Donizetti, G.:Caterina Cornaro, w. Montserrat Caballé (sop), Giacomo Aragall (ten), Ryan Edwards (sgr), G.–F. Masini (cnd), ORTF Orch *(rec Paris, Nov 25, 1973)* Agorá Music ("Phoenix" series) 2–▲ 505
Elgar, E.:Coronation Ode, w. T. Cahill (sop), A. Collins (cta), A. Rolfe Johnson (ten), A. Gibson (cnd), Scottish National Orch, Scottish National Chorus [E] *(rec 1976)* Chandos ("Collect" series) ▲ CHAN 6574 [ADD]
Elgar, E.:The Dream of Gerontius, w. F. Palmer (sop), A. Davies (ten), R. Hickox (cnd), London SO, London Sym Chorus [E] Chandos 2–▲ CHAN 8641/42 [DDD]
Handel, G.F.:Messiah, w. Elly Ameling (sop), Anna Reynolds (alt), Philip Langridge (ten), N. Marriner (cnd), Academy of St. Martin in the Fields, Academy of St. Martin in the Fields Chorus *(rec St John's, Smith Square, London, Jan & July 1976)* London ("Double Decker" series) 2–▲ 444824–2 [ADD]
Handel, G.F.:Messiah, w. Patricia Schuman (sop), Lucia Valentini Terrani (alt), Bruce Ford (ten), C. Scimone (cnd), Venice Solisti, John McCarthy (cnd), Ambrosian Singers *(rec Schio, Italy, June 23–30, 1989)* Arts 2–▲ 47105–2 [DDD]
Handel, G.F.:Messiah, w. Elly Ameling (sop), Anna Reynolds (mez), Philip Langridge (ten), N. Marriner (cnd), Academy of St. Martin in the Fields, Academy of St. Martin in the Fields Chorus [E] Argo ■ 421234–4
Handel, G.F.:Messiah, w. Patricia Schuman (sop), Lucia Valentini Terrani (alt), Bruce Ford (ten), Bernard Soustrot (tpt), C. Scimone (cnd), Venice Solisti, John McCarthy (cnd), Ambrosian Singers *(rec S. Francisco Church, Schio, Italy, June 23–30, 1989)* Arts 2–▲ 471052 [DDD]
Handel, G.F.:Messiah, w. Kiri Te Kanawa (sop), Anne Gjevang (mez), Richard Lewis (ten), G. Solti (cnd), Chicago SO, Chicago Sym Chorus [E] London 2–▲ 414396–2 [DDD]
Handel, G.F.:Messiah (sels), w. Kiri Te Kanawa (sop), Anne Gjevang (mez), Richard Lewis (ten), G. Solti (cnd), Chicago SO, Chicago Sym Chorus—arias & choruses London ▲ 430098–2 [DDD] ■ 430098–4

Howell, Gwynne (bass) (cont.)
Haydn, J.:Salve regina, H.XXIIIb/2, w. Arleen Auger (sop), Alfreda Hodgson (cta), Anthony Rolfe Johnson (ten), John Birch (db), L. Heltay (cnd), Argo CO, London Chamber Choir *(rec St. Jude's, London, Feb 1979)* London 2–▲ 443027–2 [ADD]
Haydn, J.:Die Schöpfung, w. Margaret Marshall (sop), Lucia Popp (sop), Vinson Cole (ten), Bernd Weikl (bar), R. Kubelik (cnd), Bavarian RSO, Bavarian Radio Chorus Orfeo 2–▲ 150852 [DDD] 2–■ 150852 (D)
Janácek, L.:The Cunning Little Vixen, w. L. Watson (sop), E. Bainbridge (mez), G. Knight (mez), D. Montague (mez), J. Dobson (ten), R. Tear (ten), T. Allen (bar), S. Rattle (cnd), Royal Opera House Orch [E] EMI Classics 2–▲ CDCB 54212
Mahler, G.:Das Klagende Lied, w. Teresa Cahill (sop), Janet Baker (mez), Robert Tear (ten), G. Rozhdestvensky (cnd), BBC SO, BBC Sym Chorus IMP ("BBC Radio" series) ▲ IMP 5691412
Mozart, W.A.:Kyrie, K.341, w. K. Te Kanawa (sop), E. Bainbridge (mez), A. Davies (ten), C. Davis (cnd), London SO, London Sym Chorus [L] Philips ▲ 412873–2
Mozart, W.A.:Missa, K.427, w. L. Marshall (sop), F. Palmer (sop), A. Rolfe Johnson (ten), N. Marriner (cnd), Academy of St. Martin in the Fields, Academy Chorus [L] Philips ▲ 420891–2 [ADD]
Mozart, W.A.:Requiem, w. Y. Kenny (sop), A. Hodgson (mez), A. Davies (ten), R. Hickox (cnd), Northern Sinfonia of England, London Sym Chorus Virgin Classics ▲ CDZ 59648
Mozart, W.A.:Vesperae solennes, w. K. Te Kanawa (sop), E. Bainbridge (mez), A. Davies (ten), C. Davis (cnd), London SO, London Sym Chorus [L] Philips ▲ 412873–2 [ADD]
Rossini, G.:Guillaume Tell, w. M. Caballé (sop), M. Mesplé (sop), C. Burles (ten), N. Gedda (ten), G. Bacquier (bar), L. Gardelli (cnd), Royal PO, Ambrosian Opera Chorus EMI Classics 4–▲ CDMD 69951
Schumann, R.:Scenes from Goethe's "Faust", w. E. Mathis (sop), B. Rayner Cook (bar), D. Fischer–Dieskau (bar), P. Boulez (cnd), BBC SO, BBC Sym Chorus *(rec live, London, March 7, 1973)* Memories 2–▲ HR 4489/90 [ADD]
Walton, W.:Belshazzar's Feast, w. D. Willcocks (cnd), Philharmonia Orch, Bach Choir [E] Chandos ▲ CHAN 8760 [DDD]

Howells, Anne (mez)
Donizetti, G.:Lucrezia Borgia, w. J. Sutherland (sop—Lucrezia Borgia), A. Howells (mez—Maffio Orsini), A. Kraus (ten—Gennaro), R. Leggate (ten—Liverotto), J. Summers (bar—Apostolo Gazella), P. Hudson (bass–bar—Gubetta), S. Dean (bass—Don Alfonso), R. Bonynge (cnd), Royal Opera House Orch *(rec London, Apr. 9, 1980)* Ornamenti 2–▲ FE 111 [ADD]
Sullivan, A.:The Mikado, w. M. McLaughlin (sop), J. Watson (sop), F. Palmer (sop/mez), D. Adams (bass), A. Rolfe Johnson (ten), R. Stuart (bar), R. Van Allan (bass), N. Folwell (bar), C. Mackerras (cnd), Welsh National Opera Orch, Welsh National Opera Chorus—Ov & dialogue omitted [E] Telarc ▲ CD 80284 [DDD]; ■ CS 30284 (D)

Howes, Sally Ann (sgr)
Loesser, F.:Hans Christian Andersen, w. Tommy Steele (sgr), et. al.—1977 revised stage version; London cast recording DRG ▲ 13116CD

Howitt, Barbara (sop)
Falla, M. de:El sombrero de tres picos, w. E. Jorda (cnd), London SO *(rec Apr. 1960)* Everest ▲ EVC 9000 [AAD]
Puccini, G.:Madama Butterfly, w. V. de los Angeles (sop—Madama Butterfly), B. Howitt (mez—Suzuki), J. Livingston (mez—Kate), J. Lanigan (ten—Pinkerton), D. Tree (ten—Goro), D. A. (ten—Yamadori), G. Evans (bar—Sharpless), M. Langdon (bass—Bonzo), R. Kempe (cnd), Royal Opera House Orch, Royal Opera House Chorus Covent Garden *(rec London, May 1957)* Ornamenti 2–▲ FE 112 [ADD]

Hoyde, Christopher de la (trb)
Purcell, H.:Timon of Athens, w. I. Davies (trb), J. Bowman (alt), J. M. Ainsley (ten), M. George (bass), R. Hickox (cnd), Collegium Musicum 90—Masque Chandos ("Chaconne" series) ▲ CHAN 0558 [DDD]

Hoyem, Robert (sgr)
Cherubini, L.:Les Deux journées, w. H. Hillebrecht (sop), F. Wunderlich (ten), M. Cordes (bar), H. Müller–Kray (cnd), Stockholm RSO, Stockholm Radio Chorus *(rec live, Stockholm 1960)* Melodram ▲ CDM 19507 [ADD]

Høyer, Per (bar)
Gade, N.W.:Gefion, w. F. Rasmussen (cnd), Aalborg SO Kontrapunkt ▲ KPT 32149 [DDD]
Gade, N.W.:Zion, w. F. Rasmussen (cnd), Aalborg SO Kontrapunkt ▲ KPT 32149 [DDD]
Koppel, H.D.:Moses, w. Elisabeth Meyer–Topsøe (sop), Kirsten Dolberg (mez), Kurt Westi (ten), Michael Kristensen (ten), Christian Christiansen (bass), O.A. Hughes (cnd), Danish National RSO, Jesper Grovw Jørgensen (cnd), Danish National Radio Choir *(rec Danish Radio Concert Hall, Mar 1996)* Marco Polo/Dacapo ▲ 8.224046 [DDD]
Nielsen, C.:Choral Music, w. Å. Bäverstam (sop), L. Ekdahl (girl sop), A. Thors (boy sop), K. M. Sandve (ten), E.–P. Salonen (cnd), Swedish RSO, Stockholm Boys' Choir, Swedish Radio Chorus—Springtime in Funen; The Blind Musician; The Old People; Dance Ballad *(rec Sept. 16–18, 1991)* Sony Classical ▲ SK 53276 [DDD]
Nielsen, C.:Hymnus Amoris, w. I. Nielsen (sop), A. Elkrog (ten), P. Elming (ten), J. Ditlevsen (bass), L. Segerstam (cnd), Danish National RSO, Copenhagen Boys' Choir, Danish National Radio Choir [L] Chandos ▲ CHAN 8853 [DDD]

Hruba–Freiberger, Venceslava (sop)
Bach, C.P.E.:Magnificat, w. B. Bornemann (alt), P. Schreier (ten), O. Bär (bar), H. Haenchen (cnd), C.P.E. Bach CO, Berlin Radio Chorus Berlin Classics ▲ BER 1011 [DDD]
Bach, J.S.:Cant 55, w. Peter Schreier (ten), M. Pommer (cnd), New Bach Collegium Musicum, Leipzig Univ Choir Berlin Classics ▲ BER 1066 [DDD]
Bach, J.S.:Cant 84, w. M. Pommer (cnd), Leipzig New Bach Collegium Musicum, Leipzig Univ Choir [G] Capriccio ▲ 10151 [DDD]
Bach, J.S.:Cant 84, w. Peter Schreier (ten), M. Pommer (cnd), Leipzig New Bach Collegium Musicum, Leipzig Univ Choir Berlin Classics ▲ BER 1066 [DDD]
Bach, J.S.:Cant 199, w. M. Pommer (cnd), Leipzig New Bach Collegium Musicum, Leipzig Univ Choir [G] Capriccio ▲ 10151 [DDD]
Bach, J.S.:Cant 199, w. Peter Schreier (ten), M. Pommer (cnd), Leipzig New Bach Collegium Musicum, Leipzig Univ Choir Berlin Classics ▲ BER 1066 [DDD]
Handel, G.F.:L'Allegro, Il Penseroso ed il Moderato, w. D. Schellenberger–Ernst (sop), J. Kowalski (alt), F. Kapellmann (bass), Rabsilber (sgr), R. Reuter (cnd), Berlin Comic Opera Orch, Berlin Radio Chorus Berlin Classics 2–▲ BER 1147 [DDD]
Handel, G.F.:The Choice of Hercules, w. Arleen Augér (sop), Eberhard Büchner (ten), Zäppfel (sgr), M. Pommer (cnd), Leipzig New Bach Collegium Musicum, Leipzig Univ Choir [E] Capriccio ▲ CDC 10019 [DDD]
Mozart, W.A.:Apollo et Hyacinthus, w. A. Raunig (alt), R. Popken (alt), J. Dickie (ten), M. Pommer (cnd), Leipzig RSO, Leipzig Radio Chorus Berlin Classics 2–▲ BER 1010 [DDD]
Orff, C.:Carmina burana, w. Rolf Havenstein (sgr), Piotr Kusiewicz (sgr), K. Penderecki (cnd), Karol Szymanowski State PO, Karol Szymanowski State Phil Choir *(rec Cracow, Poland, Jan 27–28, 1989)* Arts Music ▲ 47177–2 [DDD]
Reicha, A.:Requiem, w. A. Barová (mez), V. Dolezal (ten), L. Vele (bass), L. Mátl (cnd), Dvořák CO, Czech Phil Chorus [L] Supraphon ▲ 11 0332–2 [DDD]

Huang, Ying (sop)
Puccini, G.:Madama Butterfly, w. Richard Troxell (ten), J. Conlon (cnd), Orch de Paris—Original Motion Picture Soundtrack based on the opera by Puccini Sony Classical ▲ S2K 69258
Puccini, G.:Madama Butterfly (sels), w. Ying Huang (sop—Cio–Cio–San), Constance Hauman (mez—Kate Pinkerton), Ning Liang (mez—Suzuki), Richard Troxell (ten—B. F. Pinkerton), Richard Cowan (sgr—Sharpless), Jing Ma Fan (sgr—Goro), Christopheren Nomura (sgr—Prince Yamadori), J. Conlon (cnd), Orch de Paris—Dovunque al Mondo; B. F. Pinkerton Giù; Bimba, Bimba, Non Piangere; Ah! Vien! Sei Mia!; Un Bel Dí; Ora a Noi; Petali d'Ogni Fior; Coro a Bocca Chiusa; Prelude; Io So Che Alle Sue Pene; Ah! Son Vil!; E Sia! A Lui Devo Obbedir; Butterfly! *(rec Olivier Messiaen Auditorium, Paris, 1996)* Sony Classical ▲ SK 61972 [DDD]

Huarte, Lina (sop)
Carrion, M.R.:La Tempestad, w. D. Perez (sop), A. Kraus (ten), F. Kraus (bar), R. Alonso (bass), S. Ramalle (bass), E. Estella (cnd), Concierto Montilla Orch, Concierto Montilla Chorus Montilla ▲ MON 3011 [ADD]

Hubbard, Bruce (bar)
Copland, A.:Old American Songs, w. D. R. Davies (cnd), Orch of St. Luke [E]
EMI Classics ▲ CDC 54282
Great American Songwriter's, w. Kiri Te Kanawa (sop), Frederica von Stade (mez), Thomas Hampson (bar) Angel ▲ CDM 64670
Kern, J.:Show Boat, w. P. O'Hara (sop), T. Stratas (sop), K. Burns (mez), F. von Stade (mez), D. Garrison (ten), J. Hadley (ten), J. McGlinn (cnd), London Sinfonietta, Ambrosian Opera Chorus
EMI Classics ▲ ZDC 49847
Kern, J.:Show Boat, w. P. O'Hara (sop), T. Stratas (sop), K. Burns (mez), F. von Stade (mez), D. Garrison (ten), J. Hadley (ten), J. McGlinn (cnd), London Sinfonietta, Ambrosian Opera Chorus, Ambrosian Singers EMI Classics 3-▲ A23 49108
Kern, J.:Show Boat, w. F. von Stade (mez), T. Stratas (sop), J. Hadley (ten), P. O'Hara (sgr), K. Burns (mez), N. Kulp (sgr), J. McGlinn (cnd), London Sinfonietta, Ambrosian Chorus [original orchd Robert Russell Bennett]—also includes 45 minutes of music intended for the original performance but never included, plus music from revivals and films [1988 studio cast] Angel 3-▲ A23 49108 [DDD]

Huber, Hans (bass)
Weber, C.M. von:Missa sancta 1, w. Maria Taborsky (sop), Gerda Kink (cta), Hermann Pöllmann (ten), Gisela Schindler (org), E. Ehret (cnd), St. Michael Orch Munich, St. Michael Chorus Munich
Koch Schwann ▲ SCH CD 316372
Weber, C.M. von:Missa sancta 2, w. Maria Taborsky (sop), Gerda Kink (alt), Hermann Pöllmann (ten), Gisela Schindler (org), E. Ehret (cnd), Munich St. Michael's Orch, Munich St. Michael Choir
Studio SM ▲ D 2454 [ADD]

Huber, Kurt (ten)
Bach, J.S.:Cant 111, w. P. Esswood (ct), K. Equiluz (ten), M. van Egmond (b-bar), N. Harnoncourt (cnd), Vienna Concentus Musicus [G] Teldec 2-▲ 2292-42606-2
Bach, J.S.:Cant 112, w. P. Esswood (ct), K. Equiluz (ten), M. van Egmond (b-bar), N. Harnoncourt (cnd), Vienna Concentus Musicus [G] Teldec 2-▲ 2292-42606-2

Huberty, Lucien (bar)
Massé, V.:Les Noces de Jeannette, w. Renée Doria (sop), J. Allain (cnd), Pasdeloup Concerts Association Orch Accord ▲ ACD 201192 [AAD]

Huder, Maria (mez)
Giordano, U.:Andrea Chénier, w. Maria Caniglia (sop—Maddalena), Maria Huder (mez—Bersi), Vittoria Palombini (mez—Madelon), Giulietta Simionato (mez—Contessa), Beniamino Gigli (ten—Andrea), Adelio Zagonara (ten—Incroyable/Abbé), Gino Bechi (bar—Carlo), Leone Paci (bar—Mathieu), Giuseppe Taddei (b-bar—Pietro/Fouquier), Italo Tajo (b-bar—Roucher), Gino Conti (bass—Master/Schmidt), O. de Fabritiis (cnd), La Scala Orch, La Scala Chorus *(rec Nov 1941)*
Arkadia ("The 78's" series) 2-▲ 78012 [ADD]
Puccini, G.:Madama Butterfly, w. Toti dal Monte (sop—Madama Butterfly), Maria Huder (mez—Kate Pinkerton), Beniamino Gigli (ten—B.F. Pinkerton), Adelio Zagonara (ten—Goro), Mario Basiola (bar—Sharpless), Gino Conti (bass—Principe Yamadori), Ernesto Dominici (bass—Il Bonzo), Vittoria Paolombini (sgr—Suzuki), O. de Fabritiis (cnd), Rome Opera Orch, Giuseppe Conca (cnd), Rome Opera Chorus *(rec Aug 1939)* Arkadia 2-▲ CD 78004 (m) [ADD]
Verdi, G.:La traviata, w. Maria Caniglia (sop—Violetta), Maria Huder (mez—Flora), Gladys Palmer (cta—Annina), Octave Dua (ten—Giuseppe), Beniamino Gigli (ten—Alfredo), Booth Hitchen (ten—D'Obigny), Adelio Zagonara (bar—Gastone), Aristide Baracchi (bar—Douphol), Mario Basiola (bar—Germont), Norman Walker (bass—Dr. Grenville), V. Gui (cnd), London PO, London Phil Chorus *(rec Royal Opera House, Covent Garden, May 22, 1939)* Minerva 2-▲ MN A28/29 (m) [ADD]
Verdi, G.:Il trovatore, w. G. Cigna (sop—Leonora), G. Wettergren (mez—Azucena), M. Huder (mez—Ines), J. Björling (ten—Manrico), O. Dua (ten—Ruiz), C. Zambelli (ten—Ferrando), M. Basiola (bar—Count di Luna), L. Horsman (bar—Old Gypsy), V. Gui (cnd), Royal Opera Orch, Royal Opera House Chorus Covent Garden *(rec May 12, 1939)* Legato Classics 2-▲ LCD 173-2 [ADD]

Hudson, Paul (bass)
Donizetti, G.:Lucrezia Borgia, w. J. Sutherland (sop—Lucrezia Borgia), A. Howells (mez—Maffio Orsini), A. Kraus (ten—Gennaro), R. Leggate (ten—Liverotto), J. Summers (bar—Apostolo Gazella), P. Hudson (bass-bar—Gubetta), S. Dean (bass—Don Alfonso), R. Bonynge (cnd), Royal Opera House Orch *(rec London, Apr. 9, 1980)* Ornamenti 2-▲ FE 111 [ADD]
Haydn, J.:Mass 12, "Theresienmesse", w. Lucia Popp (sop), Rosalind Elias (mez), Robert Tear (ten), L. Bernstein (cnd), London SO, London Sym Chorus [L] Sony Classical 2-▲ SM2K 47522 [ADD]
Stravinsky, I.:Les Noces, w. A. Mory (sop), P. Parker (mez), J. Mitchinson (ten), M. Argerich (pno), H. Francesch (pno), K. Zimerman (pno), C. Katsaris (pno), L. Bernstein (cnd), English Bach Festival Orch, English Bach Festival Chorus [R]
Deutsche Grammophon ("20th Century Classics" series) ▲ 423251-2 [ADD]

Huehn, Julius (sgr)
Still, W.G.:Tristan und Isolde, w. Kirsten Flagstad (sop), Kerstin Thorborg (mez), Lauritz Melchior (ten), Ludwig Hofmann (bass), A. Bodanzky (cnd), *(orch unknown) (rec Jan 2, 1937)*
Enterprise ("The Fourties" series) 3-▲ ENT 304

Huemer, K. (bar)
Lehár, F.:Die lustige Witwe, w. D. Koller (sop), M. Irosch (sop), H. Papouschek (sop), P. Minich (ten), K. Ruzicka (ten), H. Prikopa (bar), R. Bibl (cnd), Vienna Volksoper Orch, Vienna Volksoper Chorus [G]
Denon 2-▲ CO 8103 [DDD]

Huffstodt, Karen (sop)
Spontini, G.:La vestale, w. Karen Huffstodt (sop—Julie), Denyce Graves (mez—La Grande Vestale), Patrick Raftery (ten—Cinna), Anthony Michaels-Moore (bar—Licinius), R. Muti (cnd), La Scala Orch, La Scala Chorus Sony Classical 3-▲ S3K 66357
Strauss, R.:Salome, w. H. Jossoud (mez), J. Dupouy (ten), J.L. Viala (ten), J. van Dam (bar), K. Nagano (cnd), Paris Lyon Opera Orch, Paris Lyon Opera Chorus Virgin Classics 2-▲ CDC 59054

Hughes, David (ten)
Mozart, W.A.:Idomeneo (sels), w. Gundula Janowitz (sop), Enriqueta Tarres (sop), Richard Lewis (ten), Luciano Pavarotti (ten), Neilson Taylor (bar), Dennis Wicks (bass), J. Pritchard (cnd), London PO, Glyndebourne Festival Chorus Budget ("The Greatest Voice in Opera" series) ▲ SYP 107

Hughes, Janet (mez)
Donizetti, G.:Il giovedì grasso, w. J. Gomez (sop), J. Peters (mez), U. Benelli (bar), B. Donlan (bar), F. Davià (bass), E. Esparza (sgr), D. Atherton (cnd), Eireann Radio-TV SO [I] *(rec live, 1970)*
Foyer ▲ FOY 2036 [AAD]
Donizetti, G.:Il giovedì grasso, w. J. Gomez (sop), J. Peters (mez), U. Benelli (bar), B. Donlan (bar), F. Davià (bass), E. Esparza (sgr), M. Williams (sgr), D. Atherton (cnd), Eireann Radio-TV SO [I] *(rec live, 1970)* Memories ▲ HR 4482 [ADD]

Hughes, Nan (mez)
Moss, L.:Songs of the Earth, w. Mark Steinberg (vn), David Krakauer (cl), Joel Sachs (pno), Cheryl Seltzer (pno) Capstone ▲ CPS 8619

Huguet, Josefina (sop)
Fernando de Lucia, w. Fernando de Lucia (ten), Antonio Pini-Corsi (bar), Maria Galvany (sop), Ernesto Badini (bar), Celestina Boninsegna (sop) Symposium ▲ SYM 1149
Leoncavallo, R.:Pagliacci, w. Josefina Huguet (sop—Nedda), Antonio Paoli (ten), Gaetano Pini-Corsi (ten—Beppe), Ernesto Badini (bar—Silvio), Francesco Cigada (bar—Tonio), Giuseppe Rosci (sgr—Un contadino), C. Sabajno (cnd), La Scala Orch, La Scala Chorus *(rec 1907)*
Bongiovanni ▲ GB 1120-2 [ADD]

Huh, Mi-Kyung (sop)
Stuart, P.:Kill Bear Comes Home, w. Elana Gizzi (sop—Hasty Girl), Mi-Kyung Huh (sop—Cold Feet), Therese Murray (sop—Song Bird), Cherie Pfeil (sop—1st Sister), Renia Shukis (sop—2nd Sister), Riki Connaughton (mez—4th Sister), Lucy Fee (mez—3rd Sister), David Averbach (ten—Song Leader), Mark Schmidt (ten—Kill Bear), Jason Smith (bar—Cheif Wife Hunter), P. Stuart (cnd), Rochester Opera Theater Orch, Rochester Opera Theater Chorus VM ▲ DRK 154 [DDD]

Huijpen, Jaco (bass)
Zuidam, R.:Freeze, w. Susan Narucki (sop—Patty Hearst), Gerrie de Vries (mez), Zeger Vandersteene (ten), Martin Hargrove (bass), S. Asbury (cnd), Asko Ensemble NM Classics 2-▲ NM 92047

Huijts, Frans (bar)
Biber, H. von:Requiem à 15, w. Marta Almajano (sop), Mieke van der Sluis (sop), John Elwes (ten), Mark Padmore (ten), Harry van der Kamp (bass), G. Leonhardt (cnd), Netherlands Bach Society Baroque Orch, Netherlands Bach Society Choir *(rec Utrecht, Germany, Oct 22-24, 1994)*
Deutsche Harmonia Mundi ▲ 05472-77344-2 [DDD]

Huizinga, Jeanette (mez)
Meijering, Chiel:St. Louis Blues, w. Andrea van Beek (sop), Francine van der Heijden (sop), Rein Kolpa (ten), Willem-Jan van Deuveren (ten), John Vredeveldt (ten), Gérard Bernts (bar), W. Megens (cnd), De Ereprijs Orch [I] *(rec Schouwburg Arnhem, Mar 10, 1995)* Donemus 2-▲ neos 01-02

Hulbert, C. (sgr)
Kern, J.:Sunny (sels), w. J. Buchanan (sgr), B. Hale (sgr), *(other artists unknown)*
Pearl ("Flapper" series) ▲ PEA CD 9105 [ADD]

Hulse, Eileen (sop)
Britten, H.:The Turn of the Screw, w. F. Lott (sop), N. Secunde (sop), P. Cannan (mez), P. Langridge (ten), S. Pay (bar), S. Bedford (cnd), Aldeburgh Festival Ensemble
Collins Classics ▲ COL 7030 [DDD]
Glière, R.:Con Coloratura Sop, w. R. Hickox (cnd), City of London Sinfonia
Chandos ▲ CHAN 9094 [DDD]
Schoenberg, A.:Herzgewächse, w. R. Craft (cnd), London SO
Koch International Classics ▲ KIC 7263-2 [DDD]
Strauss, R.:Songs, w. N. Järvi (cnd), Royal Scottish National Orch—6 Lieder, Op. 68
Chandos ▲ CHAN 9166 [DDD]

Humbert, Jacqueline (sgr)
Ashley, R.:eL/Aficionado, w. J. Humbert (sgr—Interrogator No. 2), T. Buckner (sgr—Agent), R. Ashley (sgr—Interrogator No. 1), S. Ashley (sgr—Interrogator No. 3), *(orch unknown)*
Lovely Music ▲ LCD 1004 [DDD]
Ashley, R.:Improvement, w. J. Humbert (sgr—Linda), J. La Barbara (sop—Now Eleanor), A. X. Neuburg (sgr—Mr. Payne's Mother), T. Buckner (sgr—Don/Mr. Payne/Linda's Companion), S. Ashley (sgr—Junior, Jr.), A. Klein (sgr—Doctor), R. Ashley (sgr—Narrator), *(cnd & orch unknown)* [E]
Elektra/Nonesuch 2-▲ 79289-2

Humphrey, Jon (ten)
Bach, J.S.:Cant 140, w. H. Schellenberg (sop), S. Sylvan (bar), B. H. Moyse (cnd), Orch of St. Luke
MusicMasters ▲ 7059-2-C [DDD]
Bach, J.S.:Magnificat, BWV 243, w. M. A. Kruger (sop), H. Schellenberg (sop), M. Westbrook-Geha (mez), S. Sylvan (bar), B. H. Moyse (cnd), Orch of St. Luke MusicMasters ▲ 7059-2-C [DDD]
Beethoven, L. van:Mass, Op. 86, w. H. Schellenberg (mez), M. Simpson (mez), M. Myers (ten), R. Shaw (cnd), Atlanta SO, Atlanta Sym Chorus [L] Telarc ▲ CD 80248 [DDD]
Handel, G.F.:Messiah, w. Kaaren Erickson (sop), Sylvia McNair (sop), Alfreda Hodgson (cta), Richard Stilwell (bar), R. Shaw (cnd), Atlanta SO, Atlanta Sym Chorus [E]
Telarc ▲ CD 80103 [DDD]; ■ CS 30103 (D)
Handel, G.F.:Messiah, w. Kaaren Erickson (sop), Sylvia McNair (sop), Alfreda Hodgson (cta), Richard Stilwell (bar), R. Shaw (cnd), Atlanta SO, Atlanta Sym Chorus [E] Telarc 2-▲ CD 80093-2 [DDD]
Haydn, J.:Die Schöpfung, w. Dawn Upshaw (sop), John Cheek (bass), R. Shaw (cnd), Atlanta SO, Atlanta Chamber Chorus [E] Telarc 2-▲ CD 80298 [DDD]
Haydn, J.:The Seven Last Words of Christ on the Cross, w. Benita Valente (sop), Jan DeGaetani (mez), Thomas Paul (bar), Juilliard String Quartet Sony Classical ▲ SK 44914 [DDD]
Schubert, Franz:Mass 6, w. B. Valente (sop), M. Simpson (mez), G. Siebert (ten), M. Myers (ten), R. Shaw (cnd), Atlanta SO, Atlanta Sym Chorus [L] Telarc ▲ CD 80212 [DDD]
Shostakovich, D.:From Jewish Folk Poetry, w. Benita Valente (sop), Jan de Gaetani (mez), Samuel Lipman (pno) *(rec live, Aspen Music Festival, 1980)* Bridge ▲ BCD 9048 [ADD]

Humphreys, Wendy (sop)
Bach, J.S.:Music of, w. Daniel Lichti (b-bar), Stuart Laughton (tpt/nat tpt/Renaissance cnt), William O'Meara (org), David Campion (timp/perc)—Prelude & Fugue in G; Grosser Herr [from Christmas Oratorio]; Mein gläubiges Herz [from Cant 68]; 3 Chorale Preludes; Prelude & Fugue in A
Doremi ▲ DHR 9303 [DDD]
Baroque Banquet, w. Daniel Lichti (b-bar), Stuart Laughton (tpt/nat tpt/cnt), William O'Meara (org), David Campion (timp/perc) Doremi ▲ 9303
Handel, G.F.:Samson (sels), w. Daniel Lichti (b-bar), Stuart Laughton (tpt/nat tpt/Renaissance cnt), William O'Meara (org), David Campion (timp/perc)—Let the Bright Seraphim
Doremi ▲ DHR 9303 [DDD]
Opening Day, w. Stuart Laughton (tpt), Wendy Humphreys (Celtic hp), Peter Tiefenbach (org/pno), William O'Meara (org) Doremi ▲ 9301 [DDD]
Scarlatti, A.:Endimione e Cintia, w. Daniel Lichti (b-bar), Stuart Laughton (tpt/nat tpt/Renaissance cnt), William O'Meara (org), David Campion (timp/perc)—Vaga Cintia Doremi ▲ DHR 9303 [DDD]

Humphries, Charles (ct)
Handel, G.F.:Messiah, w. Max Emanuel Cencic (sop), Ivan Sharpe (ten), Robert Torday (b-bar), P. Marschik (cnd), Academy of London Orch, Martin Schebesta (cnd), Vienna Boys' Choir *(rec Symphony Hall, Birmingham & Barbican Center, London, Nov 17 & 19, 1994)*
Capriccio 2-▲ 60068-2 [DDD]

Humphries, Jon (ten)
Stravinsky, I.:Cant Sop, w. Catherine Ciesinski (mez), R. Craft (cnd), Orch of St. Luke, Gregg Smith Singers MusicMasters ▲ 01612-67158-2
Stravinsky, I.:L'Histoire du soldat, w. Catherine Ciesinski (mez), David Evitts (bar), Mark Wait (pno), R. Craft (cnd), Orch of St. Luke, Gregg Smith Singers MusicMasters ▲ 01612-67152-2
Stravinsky, I.:In memoriam Dylan Thomas, w. R. Craft (cnd), Orch of St. Luke
MusicMasters ▲ 01612-67158-2

Hüni-Mišek, Felice (sop)
Wagner, R.:Die Walküre (sels), w. Maria Jeritza (sop—Brünnhilde), Felice Hüni-Mišek (sop—Sieglinde), Franz Völker (ten—Siegmund), Friedrich Schorr (b-bar—Wotan), C. Krauss (cnd), Vienna State Opera Orch *(rec June 11, 1933)* Koch Schwann 2-▲ SCH 314642 [ADD]

Hunnego, Sasja (nar)
Honegger, A.:Le Roi David, w. Bernard Kruysen (bar), Hanke De Hoogh (nar), A. Clement (cnd), Eindhovens Instrumental Ensemble, Eindhovens Chamber Choir (orig version) Emergo ▲ 3974

Hunt, Lorraine (sop)
Bach, J.S.:Anna Magdalena Bach Notebook, w. N. McGegan (hpd/clvd), D. Bowles (baroque vc)—French Suite No. 1, BWV 812; French Suite No. 2, BWV 813—first 3 sections; various minuets & other short pieces; 5 solo clavichord sels.; 4 Polonaises, in d,F,G & g; Prelude No. 1 from the Well-tempered Clavier Book 1; 5 Arias & Recitatives for Soprano & Continuo instruments *(Arias—Bist du bei mir, BWV 508; Willst du mein Herz mir schenken, BWV 518; Gedenke doch, mein Geist; Schlummert, ein; Recitative—Ich habe genug)* Harmonia Mundi USA ▲ HMU 907042
Charpentier, M.-A.:Médée, w. Isabelle Desrochers (sop—Cleone), Lorraine Hunt (sop—Medee), Noemi Rime (sop—Nerine), Monique Zanetti (sop—Creuse), Mark Padmore (ten—Jason), François Bazola (bar—Arcas), Jean-Marc Salzmann (bar—Oronte), Bernard Deletre (bass-Creon), W. Christie (cnd), Les Arts Florissants Erato 3-▲ 96558-2
Fauré, G.:Pelléas et Mélisande (suite), w. S. Ozawa (cnd), Boston SO
Deutsche Grammophon ▲ 423089-2 [DDD]
Handel, G.F.:Arias, w. Lisa Saffer (sop—Cuzzoni), Lorraine Hunt (mez—Durastanti), Drew Minter (ct—Senesino), David Thomas (bass—Montagnana), N. McGegan (cnd), Philharmonia Baroque Orch
Harmonia Mundi 4-▲ HMX 2907171.74
Handel, G.F.:Arias, w. N. McGegan (cnd), Philharmonia Baroque Orch—L'aure offeso; L'aure che spira; Cara speme; Dimmi, crudele Amore; La giustizia; Miriami; Ogni vento; Ombra cara; Pensieri; Qual leon; Qual nave; Svegliatevi; Vieni, o figlio [I] *(rec Oct. 1991)* Harmonia Mundi USA ▲ HMU 907056
Handel, G.F.:Arias, w. N. McGegan (cnd), Philharmonia Baroque Orch—opera & oratorio arias from Messiah, Theodora & Susanna Harmonia Mundi USA ▲ HMU 907149 [DDD]
Handel, G.F.:Ariodante, w. J. Gondek (sop), L. Saffer (sop), Jennifer Lane (mez), J. Lindemann (ten), R. Müller (ten), N. Cavallier (bass), N. McGegan (cnd), Freiburg Baroque Orch, Ralf Popken (cnd), Wilhelmshaven Vocal Ensemble [172-page libretto w. production photos]
Harmonia Mundi France 3-▲ HMC 907146.48

Hunt, Lorraine (sop) (cont.)
Handel, G.F.:Clori, Tirsi e Fileno, w. J. Feldman (sop), D. Minter (alt), N. McGegan (cnd), Philharmonia Baroque Orch [I] Harmonia Mundi USA ▲ HMU 907045
Handel, G.F.:Messiah, w. Janet Williams (sop), Patricia Spence (mez), Drew Minter (alt), Jeffery Thomas (ten), William Parker (bar), N. McGegan (cnd), Philharmonia Baroque Orch, Univ of California at Berkeley Chamber Chorus—standard version of Messiah *occupies the first sections of each of the three CDs, one part per disc. Each part is followed, after a significant pause, by alternative versions of certain sections of the preceding material, 13 altogether. [E]* Harmonia Mundi USA 3-▲ HMU 907050/52
Handel, G.F.:Messiah (sels), w. Janet Williams (sop), Patricia Spence (mez), Drew Minter (alt), Jeffery Thomas (ten), William Parker (bar), N. McGegan (cnd), Philharmonia Baroque Orch, Univ of California at Berkeley Chamber Chorus Harmonia Mundi USA ▲ HMU 907120
Handel, G.F.:Messiah (sels), w. Janet Williams (sop), Patricia Spence (mez), Drew Minter (alt), Jeffery Thomas (ten), William Parker (bar), N. McGegan (cnd), Philharmonia Baroque Orch, Univ of California at Berkeley Chamber Chorus [E] Harmonia Mundi USA ("Nightingale" series) ▲ HMN 907601
Handel, G.F.:Music of, w. Kenneth Gilbert (hpd), et al., D. Mintner (cnd), Philharmonia Baroque Orch, Ensemble 415, Concerto Vocale—sels. from Duetto "Tanti strali"; Flavio; Giulio Cesare; Harpsichord Suite No. 5; Nisi Dominus; Susanna; Water Music *(rec 1976–79)* Harmonia Mundi Plus ▲ HMP 390804
Handel, G.F.:Susanna, w. Jill Feldman (sop), Drew Minter (alt), Jeffery Thomas (ten), William Parker (bar), David Thomas (bass), N. McGegan (cnd), Philharmonia Baroque Orch, Univ of California at Berkeley Chamber Chorus [E] Harmonia Mundi USA 3-▲ HMU 907030/32
Handel, G.F.:Susanna (sels), w. Jill Feldman (sop), Drew Minter (alt), Jeffrey Thomas (ten), William Parker (bar), David Thomas (bass), N. McGegan (cnd), Philharmonia Baroque Orch Harmonia Mundi France ▲ HMU 907168
Handel, G.F.:Susanna (sels), w. Jill Feldman (sop), Drew Minter (alt), Jeffery Thomas (ten), William Parker (bar), David Thomas (bass), N. McGegan (cnd), Philharmonia Baroque Orch, Univ of California at Berkeley Chamber Chorus [E] Harmonia Mundi USA ("Nightingale" series) ▲ HMN 907601
Handel, G.F.:Theodora, w. Lorraine Hunt (sop—Theodora), Jennifer Lane (mez—Irene), Drew Minter (alt—Didymus), Jeffery Thomas (ten—Septimius), David Thomas (bass—Valens), N. McGegan (cnd), Philharmonia Baroque Orch, Univ of California at Berkeley Chamber Chorus [period instrs] [E] *(rec 9/91)* Harmonia Mundi USA 3-▲ HMU 907060/62 [DDD]
Handel, G.F.:Theodora (sels), w. Jennifer Lane (mez), Drew Minter (ct), Jeffrey Thomas (ten), David Thomas (bass), N. McGegan (cnd), Philharmonia Baroque Orch, Univ of California at Berkeley Chamber Chorus Harmonia Mundi France ▲ HMU 907188
Monteverdi, C.:Ritorno d'Ulisse, w. C. Högman (sop), B. Fink (cta), D. Vissé (ct), C. Prégardien (ten), G. Tucker (ten), D. Thomas (bass), R. Jacobs (cnd), Concerto Vocale [I] Harmonia Mundi France 3-▲ HMC 901427/29
Purcell, H.:Dido & Aeneas, w. L. Saffer (sop), D. Deam (sop), C. Brandes (sop), R. Rainero (sop), E. Rabiner (mez), P. Elliot (ten), M. Dean (bar), N. McGegan (cnd), Philharmonia Baroque Orch, Clare College Choir Cambridge Harmonia Mundi USA ▲ HMU 907110
Purcell, H.:The Fairy Queen, w. Susan Bickley (mez), Catherine Pierard (mez), Howard Crook (ten), Mark Padmore (ten), David Wilson-Johnson (bar), Richard Wistreich (bass), R. Norrington (cnd), London Classical Players, Schütz Choir London EMI Classics ▲ CDCB 55234

Hunter, Rita (sop)
Rita Hunter in Concert, w. V. Morris (pno) Tall Poppies ▲ TP 21
Wagner, R.:Götterdämmerung (sels), w. Rita Hunter (sop—Brünnhilde), Alberto Remedios (ten—Siegfried), C. Mackerras (cnd), London PO—Dawn; Brünnhilde & Siegfried's Entrance; Siegfried's Rhine Journey; Siegfried's Funeral Music; Brünnhilde's Immolation [Starke Scheite schichtet mir dort] Classics for Pleasure ▲ CDCFP 4670
Wagner, R.:Götterdämmerung (sels), w. M. Curphey (sop), A. Remedios (ten), N. Bailey (bar), C. Grant (bass), R. Goodall (cnd), Sadler's Wells Opera Orch, Sadler's Wells Opera Chorus—Act 3, Scenes 2 & 3 [E] Chandos ("Collect" series) ▲ CHAN 6593 [ADD]
Weber, C.M. von:Euryanthe, w. Jessye Norman (sop), Nicolai Gedda (ten), Tom Krause (bar), M. Janowski (cnd), Dresden Staatskapelle, Leipzig Radio Chorus Berlin Classics 3-▲ BER 1108 [ADD]

Hunter, Sharon (sgr)
Myers, G.:God's Trbn, w. Christine Helfrich (sop), Gordon Myers (bar), Richard Cragg (sgr), Matthew Gillis (sgr), Timothy Pehta (sgr), Paul Norman (sgr), Wendy Catlin (sgr) Katherine Mary Hamilton (sgr), Gloriae Dei Brass Ensemble Paraclete ▲ CDGD 017 [DDD]; ■ GDC 017

Hunziker, Bernhard (ten)
Wehrli, W.:Ein weltliches Requiem, w. R. Amsler (sop), D. Labusch (cta), R. Strebel (bass), K. Girod (cnd), Aargauer CO, Aargauer Chamber Choir *(rec live Jan. 12, 1992)* Jecklin ▲ JS 276-2 [DDD]

Hurley, Laurel (sop)
Bellini, V.:I Capuleti e i Montecchi, w. G. Simionato (mez), R. Cassily (ten), E. Flagello (bass), A. Gamson (cnd), American Opera Society Orch, American Opera Society Chorus [I] *(rec live, New York 10/14/58)* Melodram ("Connaisseur" series) 2-▲ CDM 27509 [ADD]
Puccini, G.:La Bohème, w. L. Albanese (sop), C. Bergonzi (ten), C. Harvuot (bar), M. Sereni (bar), N. Scott (bass), E. Flagello (bass), T. Schippers (cnd), New York Metropolitan Opera Orch, New York Metropolitan Opera Chorus *(rec Feb. 15, 1958)* Golden Age of Opera 2-▲ GAO 139/40 [ADD]
Strauss (II), Joh.:Eine Nacht in Venedig, w. Nola Fairbanks (sgr—Ciboletta), Thomas Tibbett Hayward (sgr—Mario), Laurel Hurley (sgr—Nina), David Kurlan (sgr—Senator Bartoldi), Guen Omeron (sgr—Barbara), Jack Russell (sgr—Duke of Palobino), Kenneth Schon (sgr—Filippo Del Aqua), Norwood Smith (sgr—Caramello), Enzo Stuarti (sgr—Pappacoda) *(rec Belock Recording Studio, Bayside, NY)* Everest ▲ EVC 9036 [AAD]

Hurney, Kate (sop)
Hovhaness, A.:Saturn, w. Lawrence Sobol (cl), Martin Berkovsky (pno) Crystal ▲ CD 808

Hüsch, Gerhard (bar)
Bach, J.S.:St. Matthew Passion, w. T. Lemnitz (sop), F. Beckmann (alt), K. Erb (ten), S. Schulze (bass), G. Ramin (cnd), Leipzig Gewandhaus Orch, St. Thomas Choir, *(abridged performance)* [G] *(rec Mar 1941)* Calig 2-▲ CAL 50 859/60 (m) [AAD]
Beethoven, L. van:An die ferne Geliebte, w. H. Udo Müller (pno) [G] *(rec Berlin 1936 for HMV)* Preiser ("Lebendige Vergangenheit" series) 2-▲ 89202 (m) [AAD]
Gerhard Hüsch *(rec between 1935–1939)* Preiser ▲ PRE 89071 [AAD]
Mozart, W.A.:Songs, w. M. Callas (sop), E. Grümmer (sop), E. Schwarzkopf (sop), R. Scotto (sop), T. Lemnitz (sop), E. Berger (sop), S. Jurinac (sop), E. Schumann (sop), I. Souez (sop), E. Rethberg (sop), L. Lehmann (sop), N. Gedda (ten), J. McCormack (ten), H. Roswenge (ten), H. Nash (ten), T. Gobbi (bar), G. Hüsch (bar), E. Kunz (bar), G. Frick (bass), E. Pinza (bass), A. Kipnis (bass) EMI Classics 4-▲ CDMD 63750
Mozart, W.A.:Zauberflöte, w. E. Berger (sop), T. Lemnitz (sop), I. Beilke (sop), H. Roswaenge (ten), W. Strienz (bass), T. Beecham (cnd), Berlin PO, Vereinigung Favres Soloists [G] *(rec Nov. 1937 & Feb.–Mar. 193)* Nimbus ("Prima Voce" series) 2-▲ NI 7827/8 (m) [ADD]
Mozart, W.A.:Zauberflöte, w. T. Lemnitz (sop), E. Berger (sop), I. Beilke (sop), H. Roswaenge (ten), H. Tessmer (ten), W. Strienz (bass), T. Beecham (cnd), Berlin PO, Favre Chorus [without dialog; G] *(rec 1937–38 for HMV)* Pearl 2-▲ PEAS 9371 (m) [AAD]
Mozart, W.A.:Zauberflöte, w. T. Lemnitz (sop), E. Berger (sop), I. Beilke (sop), H. Roswaenge (ten), H. Tessmer (ten), W. Strienz (bass), T. Beecham (cnd), Berlin PO, Favre Chorus [without dialog; G] *(rec 1937–38 for HMV)* Melodram 2-▲ MEL 27056 (m) [AAD]
Mozart, W.A.:Zauberflöte, w. T. Lemnitz (sop), E. Berger (sop), I. Beilke (sop), H. Roswaenge (ten), H. Tessmer (ten), W. Strienz (bass), T. Beecham (cnd), Berlin PO, Favre Chorus [without dialog; G] *(rec 1937–38 for HMV)* EMI Classics ("Great Recordings of the Century" series) 2-▲ CDHB 61034 (m) [ADD]
Pfitzner, H.:Songs, w. Hans Pfitzner (pno)—Hast du von den Fischerkindern, Op. 7/1; Zum Abschiede meiner Tochter, Op. 10/3; Der Gärtner, Op. 9/1; Die Einsame, Op. 9/2; Abbitte, Op. 29/1; In Danzig, Op. 22/1; Nachts, Op. 26/2; Michaelskirchplatz, Op. 19/2; Hussens Kerker, Op. 32/1; Säerspruch, Op. 32/2; Leuchtende Tage, Op. 40/1; Herbstgefühl, Op. 40/4 [G] Preiser ▲ 90029 (m) [AAD]
Schubert, Franz:Die Schöne Müllerin, w. H. Udo Müller (pno) [G] *(rec Berlin, 1935 for HMV)* Pearl ▲ PEA 9479 (m) [AAD]
Schubert, Franz:Die Schöne Müllerin, w. H. Udo Müller (pno) Preiser ("Lebendige Vergangenheit" series) 2-▲ 89202 (m) [AAD]

Hüsch, Gerhard (bar) (cont.)
Schubert, Franz:Schwanengesang, w. H.U. Müller (pno) [G]—6 selections—Nos. 4,7,10,12,13 & 14 *(rec 1937–39 HMV recordings, s)* Preiser ("Lebendige Vergangenheit" series) ▲ 89017 (m) [AAD]
Schubert, Franz:Songs (misc), w. H.U. Müller (pno)—5 songs—Der Wanderer; Widerschein; Lied eines Schiffers an die Dioskuren, D.360; Der Musensohn, D.764; Ständchen, D.957/4 [G] *(rec 1933–39 for HMV)* Pearl ▲ PEA 9479 (m) [AAD]
Schubert, Franz:Songs (misc), w. H.U. Müller (pno), et al.—11 songs—D.328, 360, 479–481, 547, 698, 764, 775, 949 [G] *(rec 1934–39)* Preiser ("Lebendige Vergangenheit" series) ▲ 89017 (m) [AAD]
Schubert, Franz:Winterreise, w. H. U. Müller (pno) [G] *(rec 1933 for HMV)* Pearl ▲ PEA 9469 (m) [AAD]
Schubert, Franz:Winterreise, w. H. U. Müller (pno) [G] *(rec 1933 for HMV)* Preiser ("Lebendige Vergangenheit" series) 2-▲ 89202 (m) [AAD]
Schumann, R.:Dichterliebe, w. Hans Udo Müller (pno) *(rec 1936)* Pearl ▲ PEA 9119 [ADD]
Wagner, R.:Arias & Scenes, w. K. Flagstad (sop), E. Rethberg (sop), B. Nilsson (sop), E. Schumann (sop), F. Leider (sop), L. Melchior (ten), G. Thill (ten), A. Pertile (ten), G. Hüsch (bar), F. Schorr (b-bar), H. Hotter (b-bar), A. Kipnis (bass), *(orch unknown)* EMI Classics ("Studio" series) 4-▲ CDMC 64008

Hüsch, Otto (sgr)
Schoeck, O.:Das Schloss Dürande (sels), w. Maria Cebotari (sop—Gabriele), Marta Fuchs (sop—Gräfin Morvaille), Brigitte Fassbaender (mez—Renald Willi Domgraf), Rut Berglund (cta—Priorin), Peter Anders (ten—Armand), Benno Arnold (ten—Jäger), Josef Greindl (bass—Nicole), Hans Wrana (bass—Jäger), Vasso Argyris (sgr—Volksredner), Otto Hüsch (sgr—Wildhüter), Leo Laschet (sgr—Jäger), Fritz Marcks (sgr—Jäger), Felix Schneider (sgr—Jäger), R. Heger (cnd)—Text; Ich kann es nicht glauben [from Act 1]; Text; Heil dir, du Feuerquelle [from Act 2]; Text; Gesucht und nicht gefunden [from Act 3]; Text; Der Jäger ist frei! [Act 3 Finale]; Text; Sie kommen mit Flinten und Stangen [Act 4]; Text; Du Narr des vermeintlichen Rechts [Act 4 finale]; Text *(rec live, Apr 1943)* Jecklin ▲ JD 692

Husen, Rainer van (ten)
Haydn, M.:German Masses, w. M. Flöth (bass), H.-G. Freimuth (cnd), Münster Wind Ensemble, Münster Cathedral Choir—No. 1 Calig ▲ CAL 50824 [ADD]
Schubert, Franz:Duetsche Messe, w. M. Flöth (bass), H.-G. Freimuth (cnd), Münster Wind Ensemble, Münster Cathedral Choir Calig ▲ CAL 50824 [ADD]

Husmann, Maria (sop)
Platz, R.H.:Dunkles Haus, w. Maria Husmann (sop—Woman), Michael Busch (bar—Man), Udo Zickwolf (nar—Child/Bird/Man), Carin Levine (a fl/b fl), R. Platz (cnd), Marstall Ensemble of the Bavarian State Opera *(rec 1991)* Thorofon ▲ CTH 2170

Hussu (sgr)
Donizetti, G.:Lucia di Lammermoor (sels), w. L. Gencer (sop), G. Prandelli (ten), N. Carta (bar), R. Botteghelli (bass), Sabatucci (sgr), O. de Fabritiis (cnd), Trieste Teatro Comunale Giuseppe Verdi Orch, Trieste Teatro Comunale G. Verdi Chorus *(rec live 12/13/57 & 2/10/58)* Melodram ▲ MEL 15003 (m) [AAD]

Hutin, M. (bass)
Mendelssohn, F.:Psalm 42, w. Y. Perrin (sop), M. Schwartz (mez), O. Dufour (ten), C. Traube (ten), P. Huttenlocher (bar), C. Ossola (bass), C. Liang-Sheng (cnd), Geneva SO, Geneva Univ Chorus Gallo ▲ CD 635 [AAD]
Mendelssohn, F.:Psalm 95, w. Y. Perrin (sop), M. Schwartz (mez), O. Dufour (ten), C. Traube (ten), P. Huttenlocher (bar), C. Ossola (bass), C. Liang-Sheng (cnd), Geneva SO, Geneva Univ Chorus Gallo ▲ CD 635 [AAD]
Mendelssohn, F.:Psalm 115, w. Y. Perrin (sop), M. Schwartz (mez), O. Dufour (ten), C. Traube (ten), P. Huttenlocher (bar), C. Ossola (bass), C. Liang-Sheng (cnd), Geneva SO, Geneva Univ Chorus Gallo ▲ CD 635 [AAD]

Hutt, Robert (ten)
Strauss, R.:Songs, w. R. Strauss (pno)—Breit über mein Haupt, Op. 19/2; Morgen, Op. 27/4 [G] *(rec 1921)* Pearl 2-▲ GEMMCDS 9365 (m) [AAD]
Wagner, R.:Die Meistersinger von Nürnberg (sels), w. E. Marherr-Wagner (mez), K. Jöken (bar), F. Schorr (b-bar), E. List (bass), L. Schützendorf (sgr), L. Blech (cnd), Berlin State Opera Orch, Berlin State Opera Chorus—Act 1:Hilf Gott! Will ich denn Schuster sein?; Das schöne Fest, Johannistag; Act 2:Johannistag! Johannistag!; Hab' ich heut' Singstund'?; Jerum! Jerum!; Act 3:Gleich, Meister! Hier!; Grüss' Gott, mein Evchen...Weilten die Stern' im lieblichen Tanz...O Sachs! Mein Freund!; Sankt Krispin, lobet ihn!; Silentium!...Wach' auf!; Verachtet mir die Meister nicht [G] *(rec Staatsoper unter den Linden, 5/22/28)* Pearl ▲ PEA 9340 (m) [AAD]
The Young Lotte Lehmann, w. Lehmann, Lotte (sop), Michael Böhnen (bass), Heinrich Schlusnus (bar) Preiser ("Lebendige Vergangenheit" series) 3-▲ PRE 89302 (m) [AAD]

Huttenlocher, Philippe (bar)
Bach, J.S.:Cant 8, w. A. Augér (sop), H. Watts (cta), A. Kraus (ten), H. Rilling (cnd), Stuttgart Bach Collegium, Gächinger Kantorei [G] *(rec 1979)* Hänssler Classic ▲ 98.813 [AAD]
Bach, J.S.:Cant 16, w. G. Schreckenbach (cta), P. Schreier (ten), H. Rilling (cnd), Stuttgart Bach Collegium, Gächinger Kantorei [G] Hänssler Classic ▲ 98.871 [AAD]
Bach, J.S.:Cant 25, w. A. Augér (sop), A. Kraus (ten), H. Rilling (cnd), Stuttgart Bach Collegium, Gächinger Kantorei Hänssler Classic ▲ 98.810 [ADD]
Bach, J.S.:Cant 26, w. A. Augér (sop), D. Soffel (sop), A. Kraus (ten), H. Rilling (cnd), Stuttgart Bach Collegium, Gächinger Kantorei [G] *(rec 1979 & 1980)* Hänssler Classic ▲ 98.821 [AAD]
Bach, J.S.:Cant 33, w. H. Watts (cta), F. Lang (ten), H. Rilling (cnd), Stuttgart Bach Collegium, Gächinger Kantorei Hänssler Classic ▲ 98.811 [AAD]
Bach, J.S.:Cant 37, w. A. Augér (sop), C. Watkinson (mez), A. Kraus (ten), H. Rilling (cnd), Stuttgart Bach Collegium, Gächinger Kantorei [G] *(rec 1979)* Hänssler Classic ▲ 98.886 [AAD]
Bach, J.S.:Cant 38, w. A. Augér (sop), H. Watts (cta), L.-M. Harder (ten), H. Rilling (cnd), Stuttgart Bach Collegium, Gächinger Kantorei [G] *(rec Feb & Apr 1980)* Hänssler Classic ▲ 98.818 [AAD]
Bach, J.S.:Cant 43, w. A. Augér (sop), J. Hamari (cta), L.-M. Harder (ten), H. Rilling (cnd), Stuttgart Bach Collegium, Gächinger Kantorei [G] *(rec 1981–82)* Hänssler Classic ▲ 98.885 [AAD]
Bach, J.S.:Cant 47, w. A. Augér (sop), H. Rilling (cnd), Stuttgart Bach Collegium, Gächinger Kantorei [G] *(rec 1982)* Hänssler Classic ▲ 98.815 [AAD]
Bach, J.S.:Cant 49, w. A. Augér (sop), H. Rilling (cnd), Stuttgart Bach Collegium [G] *(rec Oct 1982)* Hänssler Classic ▲ 98.817 [AAD]
Bach, J.S.:Cant 60, w. H. Watts (cta), A. Kraus (ten), H. Rilling (cnd), Stuttgart Bach Collegium, Gächinger Kantorei [G] *(rec 1977 & 1978)* Hänssler Classic ▲ 98.821 [AAD]
Bach, J.S.:Cant 62, w. I. Nielsen (sop), H. Watts (cta), A. Baldin (ten), H. Rilling (cnd), Stuttgart Bach Collegium, Gächinger Kantorei [G] *(rec Feb & Apr 1980)* Hänssler Classic ▲ 98.822 [AAD]
Bach, J.S.:Cant 64, w. A. Augér (sop), A. Murray (mez), H. Rilling (cnd), Stuttgart Bach Collegium, Gächinger Kantorei [G] *(rec Jan 1978 & Mar 1981)* Hänssler Classic ▲ 98.825 [AAD]
Bach, J.S.:Cant 66, w. G. Schreckenbach (cta), A. Kraus (ten), W. Schöne (bass), H. Rilling (cnd), Stuttgart Bach Collegium, Gächinger Kantorei [G] *(rec 1981)* Hänssler Classic ▲ 98.880 [AAD]
Bach, J.S.:Cant 68, w. A. Augér (sop), H. Rilling (cnd), Stuttgart Bach Collegium, Gächinger Kantorei [G] *(rec 1980–81)* Hänssler Classic ▲ 98.890 [AAD]
Bach, J.S.:Cant 74, w. H. Donath (sop), H. Laurich (cta), A. Kraus (ten), H. Rilling (cnd), Stuttgart Bach Collegium, Gächinger Kantorei Hänssler Classic ▲ 98.887 [AAD]
Bach, J.S.:Cant 80, w. A. Augér (sop), G. Schreckenbach (cta), L.-M. Harder (ten), H. Rilling (cnd), Württemberg CO, Gächinger Kantorei [G] *(rec 1976 & 1983)* Hänssler Classic ▲ 98.819 [AAD]
Bach, J.S.:Cant 82, w. N. Harnoncourt (cnd), Vienna Concentus Musicus [G] Teldec 2-▲ 2292-42577-2 [ADD]
Bach, J.S.:Cant 89, w. A. Augér (sop), H. Watts (cta), H. Rilling (cnd), Stuttgart Bach Collegium, Gächinger Kantorei [G] *(rec Sept & Dec 1977)* Hänssler Classic ▲ 98.818 [AAD]
Bach, J.S.:Cant 92, w. A. Augér (sop), G. Schreckenbach (cta), H. Watts (cta), A. Baldin (ten), H. Rilling (cnd), Bach Ensemble [G] *(rec 1980)* Hänssler Classic ▲ 98.877 [AAD]
Bach, J.S.:Cant 95, w. W. Wiedl (trb), K. Equiluz (ten), N. Harnoncourt (cnd), Vienna Concentus Musicus [G] Teldec ▲ 2292-42583-2 [ADD]
Bach, J.S.:Cant 96, w. W. Wiedl (trb), P. Esswood (ct), K. Equiluz (ten), N. Harnoncourt (cnd), Vienna Concentus Musicus [G] Teldec ▲ 2292-42583-2 [ADD]
Bach, J.S.:Cant 97, w. W. Wiedl (trb), P. Esswood (ct), K. Equiluz (ten), N. Harnoncourt (cnd), Vienna Concentus Musicus [G] Teldec ▲ 2292-42583-2 [ADD]

Huttenlocher, Phillippe (bar) (cont.)

Bach, J.S.:Cant 97, w. H. Donath (sop), H. Gardow (sop), A. Kraus (ten), H. Rilling (cnd), Bach Ensemble *(rec Jan–Feb 1974)* Hänssler Classic ▲ 98.835 [AAD]

Bach, J.S.:Cant 99, w. W. Wiedl (trb), P. Esswood (ct), K. Equiluz (ten), N. Harnoncourt (cnd), Vienna Concentus Musicus [G] Teldec ▲ 2292–42584–2

Bach, J.S.:Cant 100, w. A. Augér (sop), J. Hamari (cta), A. Kraus (ten), H. Rilling (cnd), Württemberg CO, Gächinger Kantorei [G] *(rec 1983–84)* Hänssler Classic 5–▲ 98.976

Bach, J.S.:Cant 101, w. W. Wiedl (trb), P. Esswood (ct), K. Equiluz (ten), N. Harnoncourt (cnd), Vienna Concentus Musicus [G] Teldec ▲ 2292–42584–2

Bach, J.S.:Cant 102, w. W. Wiedl (trb), P. Esswood (ct), K. Equiluz (ten), N. Harnoncourt (cnd), Vienna Concentus Musicus [G] Teldec ▲ 2292–42584–2

Bach, J.S.:Cant 103, w. P. Esswood (ct), K. Equiluz (ten), G. Leonhardt (cnd), Leonhardt Consort [G] Teldec ▲ 2292–42602–2

Bach, J.S.:Cant 104, w. K. Equiluz (ten), N. Harnoncourt (cnd), Vienna Concentus Musicus, Tölz Boys' Choir [G] Teldec ▲ 2292–42602–2

Bach, J.S.:Cant 116, w. A. Augér (sop), H. Watts (cta), L.–M. Harder (ten), H. Rilling (cnd), Stuttgart Bach Collegium, Gächinger Kantorei [G] *(rec 1980)* Hänssler Classic ▲ 98.820 [AAD]

Bach, J.S.:Cant 133, w. A. Augér (sop), D. Soffel (cta), A. Baldin (ten), H. Rilling (cnd), Stuttgart Bach Collegium, Gächinger Kantorei [G] *(rec Feb–Mar 1980)* Hänssler Classic ▲ 98.826 [AAD]

Bach, J.S.:Cant 135, w. H. Watts (cta), A. Kraus (ten), Stuttgart Bach Collegium, Gächinger Kantorei Hänssler Classic ▲ 98.802 [AAD]

Bach, J.S.:Cant 138, w. A. Augér (sop), R. Bollen (cta), A. Baldin (ten), H. Rilling (cnd), Stuttgart Bach Collegium, Gächinger Kantorei Hänssler Classic ▲ 98.812 [AAD]

Bach, J.S.:Cant 139, w. I. Nelson (sop), H. Watts (cta), A. Kraus (ten), H. Rilling (cnd), Stuttgart Bach Collegium, Gächinger Kantorei [G] *(rec 1979 & 1980)* Hänssler Classic ▲ 98.820 [AAD]

Bach, J.S.:Cant 140, w. A. Augér (sop), A. Baldin (ten), H. Rilling (cnd), Stuttgart Bach Collegium, Gächinger Kantorei [G] Novalis ▲ 150029 [DDD]

Bach, J.S.:Cant 146, w. C. Watkinson (cta), P. Schreier (ten), H. Rilling (cnd), Stuttgart Bach Collegium, Gächinger Kantorei [G] *(rec 1973)* Hänssler Classic ▲ 98.884 [AAD]

Bach, J.S.:Cant 149, w. A. Augér (sop), M. Georg (mez), A. Baldin (ten), H. Rilling (cnd), Stuttgart Bach Collegium, Gächinger Kantorei [G] *(rec 1984)* Hänssler Classic ▲ 98.815 [AAD]

Bach, J.S.:Cant 157, w. A. Kraus (ten), H. Rilling (cnd), Bach Ensemble *(rec Oct 1982, July 1983)* Hänssler Classic ▲ 98.835 [AAD]

Bach, J.S.:Cant 159, w. J. Hamari (cta), A. Baldin (ten), H. Rilling (cnd), Stuttgart Bach Collegium, Gächinger Kantorei [G] *(rec 1983)* Hänssler Classic ▲ 98.879 [AAD]

Bach, J.S.:Cant 182, w. D. Soffel (cta), A. Baldin (ten), H. Rilling (cnd), Stuttgart Bach Collegium, Gächinger Kantorei [G] *(rec 1975)* Hänssler Classic ▲ 98.880 [AAD]

Bach, J.S.:Cant 185, w. A. Augér (sop), H. Laurich (mez), A. Baldin (ten), H. Rilling (cnd), Stuttgart Bach Collegium, Frankfurt Kantorei Hänssler Classic ▲ 98.804 [AAD]

Bach, J.S.:Cant 197, w. C. Cuccaro (sop), M. Georg (mez), H. Rilling (cnd), Bach Ensemble *(rec Feb 1984)* Hänssler Classic ▲ 98.828 [AAD]

Bach, J.S.:Cant 198, w. A. Augér (sop), G. Schreckenbach (cta), A. Baldin (ten), H. Rilling (cnd), Bach Ensemble *(rec Sept 1983)* Hänssler Classic ▲ 98.830 [AAD]

Bach, J.S.:Easter Oratorio, w. A. Augér (sop), J. Hamari (cta), A. Kraus (ten), H. Rilling (cnd), Stuttgart Bach Collegium, Gächinger Kantorei [G] *(rec 1980–81)* Hänssler Classic 5–▲ 98.976

Bach, J.S.:Magnificat, BWV 243, w. A. Augér (sop), A. Murray (mez), H. Watts (cta), A. Kraus (ten), W. Schöne (bass), H. Rilling (cnd), Stuttgart Bach Collegium, Gächinger Kantorei *(rec 1979)* Sony Classical ("Essential Classics" series) ▲ SBK 48280 [ADD] ■ SBT 48280

Bach, J.S.:St. John Passion, w. F. Palmer (sop), B. Finnilä (cta), K. Equiluz (ten), W. Krenn (ten), R. van der Meer (bass), M. Corboz (cnd), Lausanne CO, Lausanne Vocal Ensemble Erato 2–▲ 2292–45406–2 FD

Bach, J.S.:St. Matthew Passion, w. M. Marshall (sop), C. Watkinson (cta), K. Equiluz (ten), G. Faulstisch (bar), R. Johnson (bar), M. Corboz (cnd), Lausanne CO, Lausanne Vocal Ensemble Erato 3–▲ 2292–45375–2 GX

Grétry, A.–E.–M.:La Caravane du Caire, w. I. Poulenard (sop), G. de Reyghere (sop), G. Ragon (ten), G. de Mey (ten), V. Le Téxier (bar), J. Bastin (bass), M. Minkowski (cnd), Ricercar Academy, Ricercar Academy Chorus [period instrs] [F] Ricercar 2–▲ RIC 100084/85 [DDD]

Haller, H.:Ed è subito sera, w. R. Tschupp (cnd), Basel SO [I] Grammont ▲ CTSP 10–2 [ADD]

Haydn, J.:Die Schöpfung, w. Krisztina Láki (sop), Neil Mackie (ten), S. Kuijken (cnd), La Petite Bande, Ghent Collegium Vocale Accent 2–▲ ACC 58228/29

Martin, F.:Die Weise von Liebe und Tod des Cornets Christoph Rilke, w. R. Dunand (cnd), Geneva Collegium Academicum *(rec Oct. 8, 1984)* Gallo ▲ CD 725 [ADD]

Mendelssohn, F.:Psalm 42, w. Y. Perrin (sop), M. Schwartz (mez), O. Dufour (ten), C. Traube (ten), C. Ossola (bass), M. Hutin (bass), C. Liang–Sheng (cnd), Geneva SO, Geneva Univ Chorus Gallo ▲ CD 635 [AAD]

Mendelssohn, F.:Psalm 95, w. Y. Perrin (sop), M. Schwartz (mez), O. Dufour (ten), C. Traube (ten), C. Ossola (bass), M. Hutin (bass), C. Liang–Sheng (cnd), Geneva SO, Geneva Univ Chorus Gallo ▲ CD 635 [AAD]

Mendelssohn, F.:Psalm 115, w. Y. Perrin (sop), M. Schwartz (mez), O. Dufour (ten), C. Traube (ten), C. Ossola (bass), M. Hutin (bass), C. Liang–Sheng (cnd), Geneva SO, Geneva Univ Chorus Gallo ▲ CD 635 [AAD]

Purcell, H.:Songs, w. J. E. Dähler (hpd)—18 songs [E] Claves ▲ CD 705 [ADD]

Rameau, J.P.:Castor et Pollux, w. P. Jeffes (ten), C. Farncombe (cnd), English Bach Festival Baroque Orch, English Bach Festival Singers Erato 2–▲ 95311–2

Rameau, J.P.:Les Indes galantes, w. L. Devos (ten), J. Elwes (ten), J.–F. Paillard (cnd), Jean–François Paillard CO Erato 3–▲ 95310–2

Ravel, M.:L'Enfant et les sortilèges, w. Arleen Augér (sop), Marilyn Richardson (sop), Jane Berbié (mez), Linda Finnie (mez), Jocelyne Taillon (mez), Davenny Wyner (mez), Philip Langridge (ten), Jules Bastin (bass), A. Previn (cnd), London SO, Ambrosian Opera Chorus Classics for Pleasure ("Eminence" series) ▲ CFP 2241

Schibler, A.:La Folie de Tristan, w. Audrey Michael (sop—Iseut), Arlette Chédel (mez—Brangien), Pierre–André Blaser (ten—Tristan), Philippe Huttenlocher (bar—Le roi Marc/Le pêcheur/Le portier), André Fauré (nar), William Jacques (nar), Snezana Zivojinovic (nar), J. Auberson (cnd), Lausanne CO, Romande Instrumental Group Rockband, Swiss Romande Radio Choir *(rec live, Festival de Montreux, Sept 15, 1980)* Jecklin ▲ JD 695

Uy, P.:Choral pour la Paix, w. Dinah Bryant (sop), Zeger Vandersteene (ten), Alain Carré (nar), Dominique Cornil (pno), G. Octors (cnd), Wallonie Royal CO, Denis Menier (cnd), Namur Chamber Choir *(rec Aulne, Belgium, 1995)* Cypres ▲ 2611 [DDD]

Hüttler, H. (cant)

Mozart, W.A.:Missa solemnis, K.337, w. R. Ziesak (sop), E. von Magnus (alt), H. Wildhaber (ten), G. Hornik (bar), M. Jankowitsch (cant), P. Jelosits (cant), I. Rainer (org), M. Haselböck (cnd), Vienna Academy, Vienna Hofburg Chapel Choir [L] *(rec Apr. 1992)* Novalis ▲ 150087 [DDD]

Hvorostovsky, Dmitri (bar)

Bellini, V.:Arias, w. I. Marin (cnd), Philharmonia Orch—Si, vincemmo [from Il Pirata]; Ah! per sempre io ti perdei [from Puritani] Philips ▲ 434912–2

Borodin, A.:Songs, w. Mikhail Arkadiev (pno)—For the shores of your distant homeland Philips ▲ 442536–2

Credo, w. St. Petersburg Russian Choir [cnd:Nikolai Korniev] Philips ▲ 446089–2

Dark Eyes:Russian Folk Songs, w. Ossipov Russian Folk Orch Philips ▲ 434080–2 PH [DDD] ■ 434080–4 PH (D)

Donizetti, G.:Arias, w. I. Marin (cnd), Philharmonia Orch—Vien, Leonora; A tanto amor, Leonora [both from La favorita]; Nei miei superbi gaudi [from Il duca d'Alba]; Di tua beltade immagine [from Poliuto]; Come Paride vezzoso [from L'elisir d'amore]; Bella siccome un angelo [from Don Pasquale]; O Lisbona, alfin ti miro [from Don Sebastiano]; Cruda, funesta smania [from Lucia di Lammermoor] Philips ▲ 434912–2

Mascagni, P.:Cavalleria rusticana, w. J. Norman (sop), M. Senn (mez), R. Laghezza (mez), G. Giacomini (ten), S. Bychkov (cnd), Orch de Paris Philips ▲ 432105–2 [DDD]

Hvorostovsky, Dmitri (bar) (cont.)

Rachmaninoff, S.:Songs, w. Mikhail Arkadiev (pno)—'Tis Pleasant Here; Everything Passes; Answer Was Given; Song for My Cornfield; Heed Me Not, Dear; I Wait for You; Night; Night Is Sad; I Am Alone Again Philips ▲ 446666–2

Rachmaninoff, S.:Songs, w. Mikhail Arkadiev (pno)—Morning; Child, you are beautiful like a flower; How I languish; Spring waters Philips ▲ 442536–2

Rimsky–Korsakov, N.:Songs, w. Mikhail Arkadiev (pno)—The clouds begin to scatter; The octave; The wave breaks into spray Philips ▲ 442536–2

Rossini, G.:Arias, w. I. Marin (cnd), Philharmonia Orch—Largo al Factotum [from Il barbiere di Siviglia]; Resta immobile [from Guilaume Tell] Philips ▲ 434912–2

Russian Romances Philips □ 432119–5

Songs & Dances of Death, w. Kirov Orch St. Petersburg [cnd:V. Gergiev] Philips ▲ 438872–2

Sviridov, G.:Russia Cast Adrift, w. Mikhail Arkadiev (pno)—Autumn; I Left My Home Behind; Open before Me, O My Guardian Angel; Silver Path; Russia Cast Adrift; Simon, Peter... Where Are You? Come to Me; Where Are You, O My Father's House; Beyond the Hills of the Milky Way; It Sounds, It Sounds, the Fateful Trumpet; An Owl Cries in Autumn; Oh I Believe, I Believe in Happiness!; O My Homeland, O Happy & Eternal Hour Philips ▲ 446666–2

Tchaikovsky, P.:Eugene Onegin, w. N. Focile (sop), I. Arkhipova (mez), S. Walker (mez), F. Egerton (ten), S. Bychkov (cnd), Orch de Paris Philips 2–▲ 438235–2

Tchaikovsky, P.:Iolanta, w. Galina Gorchakova (sop), Nikolai Gassiev (ten), Gegam Grigorian (ten), Dmitri Hvorostovsky (bar), Nikolai Putilin (bar), Sergei Alexashkin (bass), Gennady Bezzubenkov (bass), Larissa Diadkova (sgr), Olga Korzhenskaya (sgr), Tatyana Kravtsova (sgr), V. Gergiev (cnd), Kirov Opera Orch, Kirov Opera Chorus *(rec Mariinsky Theatre, St. Petersburg)* Philips 2–▲ 442796–2

Tchaikovsky, P.:Queen of Spades, w. M. Freni (sop), M. Forrester (cta), V. Atlantov (ten), S. Ozawa (cnd), Boston SO, Tanglewood Festival Chorus RCA Red Seal 3–▲ 09026–60992–2 [DDD]

Tchaikovsky, P.:Queen of Spades, w. M. Freni (sop), M. Forrester (cta), V. Atlantov (ten), S. Ozawa (cnd), Boston SO, Tanglewood Festival Chorus RCA Red Seal ▲ 09026–61227–2 [DDD] □ 09026–61227–5

Tchaikovsky, P.:Songs, w. O. Boshniakovich (pno)—9 songs—A tear trembles; None but the lonely heart; Reconciliation; The fearful minute; Don Juan's serenade; The nightingale; Exploit; I opened the window; Again, as before, alone Philips ▲ 432119–2 [DDD] □ 432119–5

Tchaikovsky, P.:Songs, w. Mikhail Arkadiev (pno)—Ah, if only you could for 1 moment; Amid the din of the ball; I should like in a single word; My protector, my angel, my friend; It happened in the early spring; I bless you, forests; Not a word, beloved; The love of a dead man; On the golden cornfields; Whether the day reigns; We sat together Philips ▲ 442536–2

Verdi, G.:Arias—arias from Don Carlos, Luisa Miller, Macbeth, Traviata, Trovatore [I] Philips ▲ 426740–2 [DDD]

Verdi, G.:La traviata, w. K. Te Kanawa (sop), A. Kraus (ten), Z. Mehta (cnd), Florence Maggio Musicale Orch, Florence Maggio Musicale Chorus [I] Philips 2–▲ 438238–2

Hyde, Philippa (sgr)

Arne, T.:Artaxerxes, w. Catherine Bott (sop), Patricia Spence (mez), Christopher Robson (alt), Richard Edgar–Wilson (ten), Ian Partridge (ten), R. Goodman (cnd), Parley of Instruments Hyperion ("The English Orpheus" series) 2–▲ CDA 67051/2

Hykes, David (sgr)

Earth to the Unknown Power, w. Harmonic Choir *(rec live, The Kitchen, New York, Nov 10 & 11, 1995)* Catalyst ▲ 09026–68347–2 [DDD]

Hynninen, Jorma (bar)

Bach, J.S.:Magnificat, BWV 243, w. B. Hendricks (sop), J. Rigby (sop), A. Murray (mez), U. Heilmann (ten), N. Marriner (cnd), Academy of St. Martin in the Fields, *(chorus unknown)* EMI Classics ▲ CDC 54283–2

Brahms, J.:Ernste Gesänge, w. R. Gothoni (pno) [G] Ondine ▲ ODE 738–2 [DDD]

Brahms, J.:Romanzen aus Tieck's *Magelone,* w. R. Gothoni (pno) [G] Ondine ▲ ODE 755–2 [DDD]

Collan, K.:Songs, w. Ralf Gothóni (pno), Pentti Koskimies (pno)—Ihr Bildnis; Erster Verlust; To Emma; At the Burn–beating; Old Man Hurtti; On the Shores of Lake Roine Finlandia ▲ FIN 500282 [ADD]

Dallapiccola, L.:Il Prigioniero, w. Phyllis Bryn–Julson (sop), Sven–Erik Alexandersson (ten), Howard Haskin (ten), Lage Wedin (bar), E.–P. Salonen (cnd), Swedish RSO, Eric Ericson Chamber Choir Sony Classical ▲ SK 68323

Gothoni, R.:The Bull & His Herdsman:A Zen Story from Ancient China, w. Soile Isokoski (sop), Jan Söderblom (vn), Ilari Angervo (va), Jan–Erik Kustafsson (vc), Heini Kärkkäinen (pno), R. Gothoni (cnd) Ondine ▲ ODE 832 [DDD]

Kilpinen, Y.:Songs, w. R. Gothoni (pno)—Hans Fritz von Zwehl Songs; Lakeus; Lieder un den Tod; Spielmannslieder [G] *(rec 1/91)* Ondine ▲ ODE 772–2 [DDD]

Kokkonen, J.:Requiem (in memoriam Maija Kokkonen), w. Satu Vihavainen (sop), U. Söderblom (cnd), Helsinki PO, Academic Choral Society Finlandia ▲ FIN 53353 [DDD]

Kuula, T.:Songs, w. Ralf Gothóni (pno), Pentti Koskimies (pno)—Beat, My Heart; Ave Maria, Op. 23/2; Fate; Night on the Moor Finlandia ▲ FIN 500282 [ADD]

Mahler, G.:Sym 8, w. Majken Bjerno (sop), Henriette Bonde–Hansen (sop), Inga Nielsen (sop), Kirsten Dolberg (alt), Anne Gjevang (alt), Raimo Sirkiä (ten), Carsten Stabell (bass), L. Segerstam (cnd), Danish National RSO, Copenhagen Boys' Choir, Berlin Phil Choir, Danish National Radio Choir Chandos 2–▲ CHAN 9305/06 [DDD]

Merikanto, A.:Juha, w. Eeva–Liisa Saarinen (mez), Raimo Sirkiä (ten), J.–P. Saraste (cnd), Finnish RSO Ondine 2–▲ ODE 872

Merikanto, O.:Music of, w. Eeva–Jiisa Saarinen (mez), Sauli Tiilikainen (bar), Kaija Saaikettu (vn), Erkki Rautio (vc), Pertti Eerola (pno), Ralf Gothoni (pno), Raija Kerppo (pno), Izumi Tateno (pno), Tauno Satomaa (cnd), Candomino Choir—Summer Evening (waltz); Valse lente; Romance; On the Highest Tree–Top; Annina; Bye, Bye Lullabye; The Weeping Flute; At Sea; Hey My Heart; Where Rustling Birches Bend; Play Softly, the Tune of Mourning; Fairy Tale by the Fireside; Idyll; Scherzo, Op. 6/4; O Dost Thou Remember That Hymn; Lade Ladoga; Why Do I Sing; The Thunderbird; The Happy Ones; Summer Evening's Idyll Finlandia ▲ FIN 500432 [AAD/DDD]

Mozart, W.A.:Nozze di Figaro, w. M. Price (sop), K. Battle (sop), M. Nicolesco (sop), A. Murray (mez), K. Rydl (bass), R. Muti (cnd), Vienna PO, Vienna State Opera Chorus [I] EMI Classics 3–▲ CDCC 47978 [DDD]

Mozart, W.A.:Nozze di Figaro (sels), w. M. Price (sop), K. Battle (sop), M. Nicolesco (sop), A. Murray (mez), K. Rydl (bass), R. Muti (cnd), Vienna PO, Vienna State Opera Chorus [I] EMI Classics ▲ CDC 54321

Nummi, S.:Wilderness, w. Ralf Gothóni (pno) *(rec Studio BIS, Djursholm, Sweden, May 18–19, 1984)* BIS ▲ CD 207 [AAD/DDD]

Opera Arias, w. Estonia SO [cnd:Eri Klas] Ondine ▲ ODE 731 [DDD]

Rachmaninoff, S.:The Bells, w. E. Ustinova (sop), K. Westi (ten), D. Kitayenko (cnd), Danish National RSO, Danish National Radio Choir Chandos ▲ CHAN 8966 [DDD]

Rachmaninoff, S.:Spring, w. D. Kitayenko (cnd), Danish National RSO, Danish National Radio Choir Chandos ▲ CHAN 8966 [DDD]

Sallinen, A.:Kullervo, w. G. Saarinen (pno), J. Silvasti (ten), M. Salminen (bass), U. Söderblom (cnd), Finnish National Opera Orch, Finnish National Opera Chorus [Fin] Ondine 3–▲ ODE 780–3T [DDD]

Sallinen, A.:Songs of Life & Death, w. O. Kamu (cnd), Helsinki PO, Helsinki Music Institute Choir Ondine ▲ ODE 844 [DDD]

Schubert, Franz:Die Schöne Müllerin, w. Ralf Gothoni (pno) Ondine ▲ ODE 719–2 [DDD]

Schumann, R.:Dichterliebe, w. R. Gothoni (pno) [G] Ondine ▲ ODE 738–2 [DDD]

Sibelius, J.:Kullervo, w. K. Mattila (sop), N. Järvi (cnd), Gothenburg SO, Laulun Ystävät Male Choir [Fin] BIS ▲ CD 313

Sibelius, J.:Kullervo, w. E.–L. Saarinen (mez), P. Berglund (cnd), Helsinki PO, Helsinki Univ Male Choir, Helsinki State Academy Male Choir EMI Classics ▲ CDM 65080

Sibelius, J.:Kullervo, w. M. Rorholm (mez), E.–P. Salonen (cnd), Los Angeles PO, Helsinki Univ Chorus [Fin] Sony Classical ▲ SK 52563

Sibelius, J.:The Maiden in the Tower, w. M. A. Häggander (sop), E. Hagegard (ten), T. Kruse (cta), N. Järvi (cnd), Gothenburg SO, Gothenburg Chorus [Fin] BIS ▲ CD 250 [DDD]

Sibelius, J.:The Rapid–Shooter's Brides, w. J. Panula (cnd), Gothenburg SO [Fin] BIS ▲ CD 270 [DDD]

Hynninen, Jorma (bar) (cont.)
Sibelius, J.:Songs, w. R. Gothóni (pno)—7 Songs, Op. 13; 6 Songs, Op. 50; 2 Songs from Shakespeare's *Twelth Night*, Op. 60; 8 Songs, Op. 57; Kaiutar; Norden
Finlandia ▲ 4509-95848-2 [ADD]
Sibelius, J.:Songs, w. L. Segerstam (cnd), Tampere PO Ondine ▲ ODE 823 [DDD]
Sibelius, J.:Songs, w. M. A. Häggander (sop), J. Panula (cnd), Gothenburg SO (for solo voice & orchestra) [Fin, Sw] BIS ▲ CD 270 [DDD]
Sibelius, J.:Syms (comp), w. K. Mattila (sop), N. Järvi (cnd), Gothenburg SO, Laulun Ystävät Male Choir
BIS 4-▲ CD 622/24 [ADD]
Sibelius, J.:The Tempest, w. R. Viljakainen (sop), M. Groop (mez), J. Silvasti (ten), S. Tiilikainen (bar), J.-P. Saraste (cnd), Finnish RSO, Finnish Opera Festival Chorus Ondine ▲ ODE 813 [DDD]
Sing Negro Spirituals, w. Osceola Davis (sgr) Ondine ▲ ODE 715
Vivaldi, A.:Gloria, RV.589, w. B. Hendricks (sop), A. Murray (mez), J. Rigby (mez), U. Heilmann (ten), N. Marriner (cnd), Academy of St. Martin in the Fields, Academy Chorus EMI Classics ▲ CDC 54283
Wolf, H.:Mörike-Lieder (sels), w. Ralf Gothóni (pno), Pentti Koskimies (pno)
Finlandia ▲ FIN 500282 [ADD]

Iancovich, Eleonora (cta)
Smareglia, A.:Nozze istrane, w. Maria Chiara (sop—Marussa), Eleonora Iancovich (cta—Luze), Ruggero Bondino (ten—Lorenzo), Alessandro Cassis (bar—Nicola), Alessandro Maddalena (bar—Biagio), Carlo Zardo (bass—Bara Menico), M. Wolf-Ferrari (cnd), Trieste Teatro Comunale Giuseppe Verdi Orch, Trieste Teatro Comunale G. Verdi Chorus *(rec Trieste, Feb 17, 1973)*
Bongiovanni ("Il Mito dell'Opera" series) 2-▲ 1133/34-2 [ADD]

Ianculescu, Magda (sop)
Rossini, G.:Il barbiere di Siviglia, w. Magda Ianculescu (sop—Rosina), Maria Sandulescu (mez—Berta), Valentin Teodorian (ten—Count Almaviva), Nicolae Herlea (bar—Figaro), Stefan Petrescu (bar—Fiorello), Constantin Gabor (bass—Don Bartolo), Valentin Loghin (bass—Don Basilio), M. Brediceanu (cnd), Romanian Opera Orch, Romanian Opera Chorus *(rec 1960-61)* Vox Box 2-▲ CDX 5159
Verdi, G.:Rigoletto, w. Victoria Draganescu (sop—Countess Ceprano), Magda Ianculescu (sop—Gilda), Dorothea Palade (mez—Maddalena), Valeria Savu (mez—Giovanna), Ion Buzea (ten—Duke of Mantua), Dimitrie Scurtu (ten—Borsa), Nicolae Herlea (bar—Rigoletto), Stefan Petrescu (bar—Marullo), Jean Banescu (bass—Count Ceprano), Nicolae Florei (bass—Monterone), Nicolae Rafael (bass—Sparafucile), J. Bobescu (cnd), Romanian Opera Orch, Romanian Opera Chorus *(rec 1965)*
Vox Box 2-▲ CDX 5162

Ichihara, Taro (ten)
Donizetti, G.:Arias, w. Lorenzo Bavaj (pno)—Una lacrima *(rec 1995)* Bongiovanni ▲ GB 2519 [DDD]
Gasparini, F.:Arias, w. Lorenzo Bavaj (pno)—Lasciar d'amarti *(rec 1995)*
Bongiovanni ▲ GB 2519 [DDD]
Giordani, G.:Arias, w. Lorenzo Bavaj (pno)—Caro mio ben *(rec 1995)* Bongiovanni ▲ GB 2519 [DDD]
Martini, J.P.A.:Arias, w. Lorenzo Bavaj (pno)—Piacer d'amor *(rec 1995)*
Bongiovanni ▲ GB 2519 [DDD]
Rossini, G.:Arias, w. Lorenzo Bavaj (pno)—L'orgia; La promessa; La partenza; L'esule; La gita in gondola *(rec 1995)* Bongiovanni ▲ GB 2519 [DDD]
Scarlatti, A.:Cants, w. Lorenzo Bavaj (pno)—Già il sole dal gange *(rec 1995)*
Bongiovanni ▲ GB 2519 [DDD]
Tosti, P.F.:Songs, w. Lorenzo Bavaj (pno)—La Serenata; Ideale; 'A vucchella; Marechiare; L'Ultima canzone *(rec 1995)* Bongiovanni ▲ GB 2519 [DDD]

Iconomou, Panito (bass)
Haydn, J.:Mass 9, "Heiligmesse", w. Matthias Ritter (sop), Simon Schnorr (alt), Jörg Hering (ten), Benedikt Schillo (ten), B. Weil (cnd), Tölz Boys' Choir Sony Classical ("Vivarte" series) ▲ SK 66260
Haydn, J.:Sacred Music, w. Matthias Ritter (sop), Simon Schnorr (alt), Jörg Hering (ten), Benedikt Schillo (ten), B. Weil (cnd), Tölz Boys' Choir—Mare clausum (oratorio fragment), H.XXI-Va:9; Motetto Insanae et vanae curae, H.XXI:1; Motetti de Venerabili Sacramento I-IV, H.XXIIIc:5a-d; Te Deum, H.XXIIIc:2
Sony Classical ("Vivarte" series) ▲ SK 66260

Idle, Eric (bar)
Sullivan, A.:The Mikado, w. L. Garrett (sop), J. Rigby (mez), S. Bullock (sop), F. Palmer (sop/mez), B. Bottone (ten), R. Angas (bass), R. Van Allan (bass), M. Richardson (bar), P. Robinson (cnd), English National Opera Orch, English Opera Group Chorus—sels [E]
MCA Classics ▲ MCAD 6215 [DDD]; ■ MCAC 6215 (D)

Iglesias, Franco (bass)
Verdi, G.:Simon Boccanegra, w. Renata Tebaldi (sop—Maria Boccanegra), Penelope Jensen (mez—Maria's Maidservant), Richard Tucker (ten—Gabriele Adorno), Rod MacWerter (ten—Paolo), Cornell MacNeil (bar—Simon Boccanegra), Ara Berberian (bar—Pietro), Ezio Flagello (bass—Jacopo Fiesco), Franco Iglesias (bass—Paolo), J. Levine (cnd), *(orch unknown) (rec live, Miami, 1970)*
Legato Classics 2-▲ LCD 189-2 [ADD]

Ignatowicz, Ewa (sop)
Gluck, C.W.:La Danza, w. K. Myrlak (ten), T. Bugaj (cnd), Warsaw Sinfonia [I]
Orfeo 2-▲ 135872 [DDD]

Ihara, Naoko (alt)
Mahler, G.:Lied von der Erde, w. Makoto Hayashi (ten), T. Asahina (cnd), Osaka PO *(rec Symphony Hall, Osaka, Nov 11, 1995)* Canyon Classics ▲ 326

Ihloff, Jutta-Renate (sop)
Mozart, W.A.:Finta semplice, w. Helen Donath (sop), Teresa Berganza (mez), A. Rolfe Johnson (ten), Thomas Moser (ten), Robert Lloyd (b-bar), Robert Holl (bass), L. Hager (cnd), Salzburg Mozarteum Orch [I] Orfeo 3-▲ 085843 [DDD]

Iktu, Mesut (bar)
Sinangil, A.D.:Mevlâna Oratorio (sels), w. Leyla Demiris (sop), Isin Güyer (mez), Mustafa Iktu (bass), Kâmil Sekerkaran (fl), A. D. Sinangil (cnd), Istanbul State Opera Orch, Istanbul State Opera Chorus—Récitatif I; Choral; Récitatif II; V[e] partie Gallo ▲ CD 836 [ADD]

Iktu, Mustafa (bass)
Sinangil, A.D.:Mevlâna Oratorio (sels), w. Leyla Demiris (sop), Isin Güyer (mez), Mesut Iktu (bar), Kâmil Sekerkaran (fl), A. D. Sinangil (cnd), Istanbul State Opera Orch, Istanbul State Opera Chorus—Récitatif I; Choral; Récitatif II; V[e] partie Gallo ▲ CD 836 [ADD]

Iliescu, Constantin (ten)
Verdi, G.:Il trovatore, w. Elena Dima (sop—Leonora), Victoria Draganescu (sop—Ines), Zenaida Pally (mez—Azucena), Ion Buzea (ten—Duke of Mantua), Constantin Iliescu (ten—Ruiz), Cornel Stavru (ten—Manrico), Octav Enigarescu (bar—Count di Luna), Constantin Dumitru (bass—Ferrando), E. Massini (cnd), Romanian Opera Orch, Romanian Opera Chorus *(rec 1960-61)*
Vox Box 2-▲ CDX 5163

Ilica, Luigi (nar)
Samaras, S.:La Martyre, w. B. Fidetzis (cnd), Pasardjik SO, Plovdiv Anghel Boukoreshtliev Choir
Orata ▲ ORAML 156

Illing, R. (sop)
Duparc, H.:Songs, w. David McSkimming (pno)—Chanson triste; Extase; Sérénade Florentine; Le manoir de Rosemonde; La vague et la cloche; Testament; Soupir; Elégie; Lamento; Au pays où se fait la guerre; Phidylé; L'invitation au voyage; La vie antérieure Chandos ▲ CHAN 9427
Herrmann, B.:Citizen Kane, w. T. Bremner (cnd), Australian PO Preamble ▲ PRCD 1788 [DDD]
Poulenc, F.:Songs, w. David McSkimming (pno)—Violon; Le pont; Métamorphoses; C
Chandos ▲ CHAN 9427

Illitsch, D. (sop)
Verdi, G.:Aida (sels), w. D. Illitsch (sop—Aida), E. Nikolaidi (cta), M. Lorenz (ten), L. Ludwig (cnd), Vienna State Opera Orch, Vienna State Opera Chorus *(rec Sept. 22, 1942)*
Koch Schwann 2-▲ SCH 314562 [ADD]

Ilosfalvy, Robert (ten)
Kacsóh, P.:János Vitéz, w. Mária Gyurkovics (sop), Anna Zentai (sop—Iluska), Tivadar Bilicsi (sgr), Hilda Gobbi (sgr), Sándor Pethes (sgr—Bartolo), Róbert Ilosfalvy (ten—Kukorica), György Melis (bar—Bagó), György Radnai (bar—Strázsamester), László Domahidy (bass—Csősz), E. Lukács (cnd), Hungarian State Opera Orch, Hungarian Radio-TV Chorus *(rec Budapest, 1961)*
Classical Diamonds 2-▲ CLD 4011-12 [AAD]

Ilosfalvy, Robert (ten) (cont.)
Lehár, F.:Die lustige Witwe (sels), w. Erika Koth (sop), Anneliese Rothenberger (sop), Nicolai Gedda (ten), W. Mattes (cnd), Graunke SO, Bavarian Radio Chorus Emperor Operetta ▲ KO 86343
Verdi, G.:La forza del destino (sels), w. Alexander Svéd (bar), Rubányi, Molinari-Pradelli (cnd), Hungarian State Opera Orch—Solenne in quest'ora; Urna fatale *(rec 1955)*
Hungaroton ("Great Hungarian Voices" series) ▲ HCD 31614 [ADD]

Ilosvay, Maria von (mez)
Humperdinck, E.:Hänsel und Gretel, w. E. Schwarzkopf (sop), E. Grümmer (sop), A. Felbermayer (sop), E. Schürhoff (mez), J. Metternich (bar), H. von Karajan (cnd), Philharmonia Orch, Loughton High School Chorus, Bancroft's School Chorus [G] *(rec 1953)*
EMI Classics ("Studio" series) 2-▲ CDMB 69293 (m) [ADD]
Rossini, G.:Stabat Mater, w. E. Grümmer (sop), C. Ludwig (mez), H. Fehn (bass), F. Fricsay (cnd), Cologne RSO, Cologne Radio Chorus [L] *(rec 1953)* Melodram ▲ CDM 16523 [AAD]
Smetana, B.:The Bartered Bride, w. Dorothea Siebert (sop), Dagmar Hermann (mez), Hans Braun (bar), Kurt Böhme (bass), J. Keilberth (cnd), Bavarian RSO, Bavarian Radio Chorus *(rec 1958)*
Pantheon 2-▲ PHE 6652 (m)
Wagner, R.:Der Ring des Nibelungen, w. Gré Brouwenstein (sop—Freia/Sieglinde), Ilse Hollweg (sop—Waldvogel), Gerda Lammers (sop—Ortlinde), Paula Lenchner (sop—Wellgunde/Gerhilde), Hilde Scheppan (sop—Helmwige), Astrid Varnay (sop—Brünnilde/3rd Norn), Lore Wissmann (sop—Woglinde), Maria von Ilosvay (mez—Flosshilde/Schwertleite/2nd Norn), Louise Charlotte Kamps (mez—Siegrune), Jean Madeira (mez—Erda/Rossweisse/1st Norn), Georgine von Milinkovic (mez—Fricka/Grimgerde), Elisabeth Schärtel (mez—Waltraute), Paul Kuën (ten—Mime), Ludwig Suthaus (ten—Loge), Josef Traxel (ten—Froh), Wolfgang Windgassen (ten—Siegmund/Siegfried), Alfons Herwig (bar—Donner), Hermann Uhde (bar—Gunther), Hans Hotter (b-bar—Wotan), Gustav Neidlinger (b-bar—Alberich), Josef Griendl (bass—Fasolt/Hunding/Hagen), Arnold van Mill (bass—Fafner), H. Knappertsbusch (cnd), Bayreuth Festival Orch, Bayreuth Festival Chorus *(rec live, Bayreuth, Aug 13-17, 1956)* Golden Melodram 14-▲ GM 1.001 [ADD]

Imalska, Aleksandra (mez)
Moniuszko, S.:Haunted Manor, w. Bozena Betley-Siradzka (sop—Hanna), Anna Witkowska (sop—Marta/Stara Niewiasta), Wiera Baniewicz (mez—Jadwiga), Aleksandra Imalska (mez—Czesnikowa), Kazimierz Dluha (Grzes), Zdzislaw Nikodem (ten—Damazy), Wieslaw Ochman (ten—Stefan), Andrzej Hiolski (bar—Miecznik), Florian Skulski (bar—Maciej), Leonard Mróz (bass—Zbigniew), Andrzej Saciuk (bass—Skoluba), J. Krenz (cnd), Cracow Polish Radio-TV Orch, Cracow Polish Radio-TV Chorus *(rec Cracovia, 1978)* Agorá Music ("Phoenix" series) 3-▲ 509 [ADD]

Imbodem, Stephan (bass)
Perrin, J.:Cantosenhal, w. L. Hauser (sop), H. Klopfenstein (cnd), Lausanne Conservatory Orch
Gallo ▲ CD 630 [AAD]
Rameau, J.P.:Motets, w. I. Desrochers (sop), V. Gens (sop), J.-P. Fouchecourt (ct), H. Lamy (ten), P. Harvey (bar), M. Loureiro de Sá (bar), *(orch unknown)*—Deus noster refugium; Quam dilecta; In convertendo [L] *(rec Apr. 13-18, 1992)* FNAC Music ▲ 592096 [DDD]

Imdahl, Heinz (sgr)
Wagner, R.:Das Liebesverbot, w. H. Zadek (cta), L. Sorell (mez), A. Dermota (ten), K. Equiluz (ten), L. Welter (bar), R. Heger (cnd), Austrian RSO, Austrian Radio Chorus *(rec live, Vienna, 1962)*
Melodram 2-▲ MEL 27052 [AAD]
Wagner, R.:Lohengrin, w. Leonore Kirchstein (sop—Elsa von Brabant), Ruth Hesse (mez—Ortrud), Herbert Schachtschneider (ten—Lohengrin), Hans Helm (bar—Der Heerrufer des Königs), Otto von Rohr (bass—Heinrich der Vogler), Heinz Imdahl (sgr—Friedrich von Telramund), H. Swarowsky (cnd), Czech PO, Prague National Theater Orch, Vienna State Opera Chorus *(rec Aug 1968)*
Weltbild Classics 3-▲ 703835 [ADD]

Infantino (sgr)
Borodin, A.:Prince Igor, w. Kalmus (sgr), G. Taddei (ten), B. Christoff (bass), O. Dominguez (mez), A. La Rosa Parodi (cnd), Rome RAI Orch, Rome RAI Chorus *(rec live 9/19/64)*
Melodram 2-▲ MEL 27028 (s)

Infantino, Luigi (ten)
Gencer & Infantino, w. Leyla Gencer (sop), Milan RAI SO [cnd:Alfredo Simonetto] *(rec Martini & Rossi Concert, 1958)* Incontri Memorabili ▲ CDMR 5017
Leoncavallo, R.:Edipo re, w. G. Fioravanti (bar), G. Malaspina (bar), R. Parodi (cnd), Naples Teatro San Carlo Orch, Naples Teatro San Carlo Chorus *(rec live, Naples, 1970)*
Italian Opera Rarities ▲ IOR 7723 [ADD]
Rossini, G.:Il barbiere di Siviglia, w. R. Broilo (sop—Berta), G. Simionato (mez—Rosina), L. Infantino (ten—Almaviva), G. Taddei (bar—Figaro), C. Badioli (bass—Bartolo), A. Cassinelli (bass—Basilio), F. Previtali (cnd), Milan RAI SO, Milan RAI Chorus *(rec 1950)* Cetra Classic 2-▲ CDO 6 [AAD]
Wagner, R.:Die Meistersinger von Nürnberg, w. Bruna Rizzoli (sop), Fernanda Cadoni (mez), Luigi Infantino (ten), Vito Tatone (ten), Renato Capecchi (bar), Giuseppe Taddei (bar), Boris Christoff (bass), Giovanni Ciavola (bass), James Loomis (bass), Silvo Maionica (bass), Vito Susca (bass), Raimondo Botteghelli (sgr), Walter Brunelli (sgr), Carlo Franzini (sgr), Ezio de Giorgi (sgr), Renzo Gonzales (sgr), L. von Matačić (cnd), Turin RAI Radio-TV SO, Turin RAI Chorus Stradivarius 4-▲ STV 12310

Ingham, Michael (sgr)
Ives, C.:Songs, w. H. Brant (pno)—Ann Street; His exaltation; The see'r; The last reader; General William Booth enters into heaven; The things our fathers loved; Walking; Luck and work; An election; Tom sails away; from "Paracelsus"; Walt Whitman; The camp meeting; 1,2,3; Grantchester; The new river; The cage; The Housatonic at Stockbridge; Charlie Rutledge; Requiem; Slugging a vampire; A sea dirge; Soliloquy; September; December; Majority; The swimmers; On the Antipodes *(rec Aug. 1991)*
AmCam ▲ ACR 10306CD [DDD]

Inghilleri, Giovanni (bar)
Puccini, G.:La Bohème, w. R. Tebaldi (sop), H. Gueden (sop), G. Prandelli (ten), F. Corena (bass), Raphäel Arié (bass), A. Erede (cnd), St. Cecilia Academy Orch Rome, St. Cecilia Academy Chorus Rome
London 2-▲ 440233-2 [ADD]
Verdi, G.:Aida, w. Dusolina Giannini (sop—Aida), Irene Minghini-Cattaneo (mez—Amneris), Giuseppe Nessi (ten—Messenger), Aureliano Pertile (ten—Radames), Giovanni Inghilleri (bar—Amonasro), Luigi Manfrini (bass—Ramfis), Guglielmo Masini (bass—King), C. Sabajno (cnd), La Scala Orch, Vittore Veneziani (cnd), La Scala Chorus *(rec 1928)* Arkadia ("The 78's" series) 2-▲ 78013 [ADD]
Verdi, G.:Aida, w. D. Giannini (sop), I. Minghini-Cattaneo (cta), A. Pertile (ten), L. Manfrini (bass), C. Sabajno (cnd), La Scala Orch, La Scala Chorus [I] *(rec 1928 for HMV)*
Pearl 2-▲ CDS 9402 (m) [AAD]

Ingram, Henry (ten)
Vivaldi, A.:Magnificat, RV.610, w. S. LeBlanc (sop), D. Forget (sop), R. Cunningham (alt), J. Lamon (cnd), Tafelmusik, Tafelmusik Chamber Choir [L] Hyperion ▲ CDA 66247 [DDD]

Ingram, James (sgr)
America, the Dream Goes on, w. J. Williams (cnd), Boston Pops Orch Philips ▲ 412627-2 [DDD]

Inou-Heller, Shihomi (sop)
Wolf, H.:Christnacht, w. M.-L. Wilke (mez), K. Thiem (bar), U. Gronostay (cnd), Berlin RSO, Berlin Radio Chorus [G] Koch Schwann ▲ CD 313013 [DDD]

Intino, Luciana d' (sop)
Rossini, G.:Aureliano in Palmira, w. N. Ciliento (mez), E. di Cesare (ten), Mazzola (sgr), G. Zani (cnd), Lucca Teatro Comunale Giglio Orch [I] *(rec live, Lucca, 10/28-11/2 1991)*
Nuova Era 2-▲ 7069/70 [DDD]

Invernizzi, Roberta (sop)
Gesualdo, D.C.:Madrigals, w. Elena Cecchi Fedi (sop), Daniela Del Monaco (cta), Roberto Balconi (ct), Gian Paolo Fagotto (ten), Giuseppe Zambon (ten), Giovanni Dagnino (bass), A. Curtis (cnd), I Fegi Armonici—Book 6 [Se la Mia Morte Brami; Beltà Poi Che T'Assenti; Tu Piangi O Fille Mia; Resta di Darmi Noia; Chiaro Risplender Suole; others] Symphonia ▲ SYM 94133
O Dolce Vita Mia, w. Accademia Strumentale Italiana [cnd:Alberto Rasi]
Stradivarius ▲ STV 33396 [DDD]
Porpora, N.A.:Cant per la notte di Natale, w. Rosita Frisani (sop—Dorindo), Roberta Invernizzi (sop—Angelo), Marco Lazzara (cta—Montano), E. Velardi (cnd), Alessandro Stradella Consort *(rec Genoa, Jan 29-30, 1995)* Bongiovanni 2-▲ GB 2181/2
Stradella, A.:Esule dalle sfere, w. Silvia Piccolo (sop), Marco Lazzara (alt), Mario Nuvoli (ten), Riccardo Ristori (bass), Carlo Lepore (bass), Alessandro Stradella Consort Bongiovanni ▲ GB 2165 [DDD]

▲ = CD ◆ = Enhanced CD Δ = MD ■ = Cassette Tape □ = DCC

Invernizzi, Roberta (sop) (cont.)
Stradella, A.:Locutus est Dominus de nube ignis, w. Alessandro Stradella Consort
Bongiovanni ▲ GB 2165 [DDD]
Stradella, A.:Il moro per amore, w. R. Invernizzi (sop—Eurinda), S. Piccollo (sop—Lucinda), M. Grazia Liguori (sop—Fiorino), M. Lazzara (cta—Lindora), V. Matacchini (cta—Feraspe/Floridoro), M. Beasley (ten—Filandro), R. Ristori (bass—Rodrigo), E. Velardi (cnd), Alessandro Stradella Consort [I] *(rec Oct. 31–Nov. 3, 1992)* Bongiovanni 3–▲ GB 2153/55
Stradella, A.:O di Cocito oscure deità, w. R. Invernizzi (sop—Proserpina), S. Piccollo (sop—Vendetta), M. Nuvoli (ten—Inganno), R. Ristori (bass—Plutone), E. Velardi (cnd), Alessandro Stradella Consort *(rec Oct. 25, 1993)* Bongiovanni ▲ GB 2164 [DDD]
Stradella, A.:Lo schiavo liberto, w. R. Invernizzi (sop—Armida), M. Lazzara (cta—Rinaldo), M. Nuvoli (ten—Carlo), R. Ristori (bass—Ubaldo), E. Velardi (cnd), Alessandro Stradella Consort *(rec Nov. 15, 1993)* Bongiovanni ▲ GB 2164 [DDD]
Vivaldi, A.:Gloria, RV.589, w. P. Vaccari (sop), R. Balconi (ct), L. Gariboldi (ten), C. Gubert (cnd), Padua Bach Academy CO, Padua Bach Academy Chamber Chorus Rivoalto ▲ RIV 9301 [DDD]
Vivaldi, A.:Magnificat, RV.610, w. P. Vaccari (sop), R. Balconi (ct), L. Gariboldi (ten), C. Gubert (cnd), Padua Bach Academy CO, Padua Bach Academy Chamber Chorus Rivoalto ▲ RIV 9301 [DDD]

Ioka, Junko (sop)
Mahler, G.:Sym 2, w. Setsuko Takemoto (mez), T. Asahina (cnd), Osaka PO, Hakaru Matsuoka (cnd), Yutaka Tomizawa (cnd), Musashino Chorus *(rec Suntory Hall, Tokyo, July 23, 1995)*
Canyon Classics 2–▲ 335

Ippolito, Antonella (sop)
Sui Palchi Delle Stelle:Sacred Music in the Neapolitan Conservatories at the Time of Francesco Provenzale, w. Cappella Pietà de Turchini [cnd:Antonio Florio], Jane Haughton (sop), Daniela del Monaco (alt), Sebastiano Cassarà (vn), Rosario Di Meglio (vn), Antonella Bologna (va), Paolo Dionisio (vl), Antonio Florio (vc), Pierluigi Ciapparelli (thb), Enrico Baiano (org/hpd)
Symphonia ▲ SY 93S20 [DDD]

Ireland, Eileen (mez)
Puccini, G.:Madama Butterfly, w. Dorothy Kirsten (sop—Madama Butterfly), Rosalind Nadell (mez—Suzuki), Eileen Ireland (mez—Kate), Daniele Barioni (ten—Pinkerton), Thomas Carter (ten—Goro), Arthur Cosenza (ten—Yamadori), Richard Torigi (bar—Sharpless), Rodney Hall (bass—The Bronze), Harold Crane (bass—Commissioner), R. Cellini (cnd), New Orleans Opera Orch, New Orleans Opera Chorus *(rec live, Mar 1960)* VAI Audio 2–▲ VAIA 1054–2

Irosch, Mirjana (sop)
Lehár, F.:Die lustige Witwe, w. D. Koller (sop), H. Papouschek (sop), P. Minich (ten), K. Ruzicka (ten), H. Prikopa (bar), K. Huemer (bar), R. Bibl (cnd), Vienna Volksoper Orch, Vienna Volksoper Chorus [G]
Denon 2–▲ CO 8103 [DDD]
Strauss (II), Joh.:Die Fledermaus, w. D. Koller (sop), M. Holliday (sop), W. Kmentt (ten), R. Karczykowski (ten), H. Kraemmer (bar), R. Granzer (bar), E. Binder (cnd), Vienna Volksoper Orch, Vienna Volksoper Chorus [G] Denon 2–▲ CO 8101 [DDD]

Irving, B. (nar)
Secunda, S.:Kol Nidre Service, w. S. Secunda (cantor)—Kol Nidre; Ya-Aleh; Koli Sh'ma; Ki Hine Kachomer; Elohai; Sh'ma Koleinu; Adonoy, Adonoy; Vaani, S'Filosi; B'rosh Hashono *(rec June 3–5, 1959)* Sony Classical ▲ MDK 35207 [ADD] ■ MGT 35207

Irwin, S. (b-bar)
Fauré, G.:Requiem, w. W. Reguson-Wagstaffe (trb), F. Burgomeister (cnd), Indianapolis Festival Orch, Christ Church Cathedral Men & Boys Choir Oxford Gothic ▲ G 49062 [DDD]

Isakov, Niko (sgr)
Tchaikovsky, P.:Eugene Onegin (sels), w. Alexandrina Pendachanska (sop), Nicolai Ghiaurov (bass), Lyubomir Diakovski (sgr), Dresden State Orch, Bulgarian National Chorus—Intro; Peasant's Chorus & Dance; Scene & Aria of Olga; Scene & Quartet; Letter Scene; plus others Laserlight ▲ 14210 [DDD]

Isakova, N. (sop)
Kabalevsky, D.:Colas Breugnon (ov), w. V. Kayevchenko (sop), L. Boldin (bar), N. Gutorovich (bar), G. Dudarev (bass), E. Maksimenko (sgr), G. Zhemchuzhin (cnd), Dantchenko Moscow Stanislavsky Music Theater Orch, Dantchenko Moscow Stanislavsky Music Theater Chorus
Olympia 2–▲ OLY 291 [ADD]

Isherwood, Nicholas (bass)
Handel, G.F.:Agrippina, w. S. Bradshaw (sop), W. Hill (sop), L. Saffer (sop), G. Banditelli (cta), D. Minter (alt), R. Popken (alt), B. Szilágyi (bar), M. Dean (b-bar), N. McGegan (cnd), Capella Savaria [period instrs] [I] Harmonia Mundi USA 3–▲ HMU 907063/65 ■ HMU 407063/65
Ives, C.:Songs, w. Marie-Noëlle André-Combes (pno), Eric Watson (pno)—Tom Sails Away; Ann Street; Thoreau; Maple Leaves; The Cage; 1, 2, 3; Evening; Serenity; A Unison Chant; The New River; The White Gulls; Slugging a Vampire; West London [A Sonnet]; From the Incantation; Charlie Rutlage; Slow March; The Indians; Walt Whitman [from 20th Stanza]; Afterglow; His Exaltation; At the River; In the Mornin'; The Camp Meeting; The Circus Band; From Paracelsus; Premonitions; On the Counter; A Sea Dirge; Like a Sick Eagle; Soliloquy [or A Study in 7th & Other Things]; Memories; The One Way; Remembrance; A Farewell to Land Accord ▲ ACD 201812 [DDD]
Scelsi, G.:Music of, w. Joëlle Léandre (sgr/db), Giancarlo Schiaffini (trbn/tuba), Frances-Marie Uitti (vc), Karin Schmeer (hp), Robyn Schulkowsky (tamtam)—Maknongan for Low-Registered Instrument (1976) [3 versions:bass, double bass, tuba]; Tre pezzi for Trombone (1956); Wo Ma for Bass (1960); C'est bien la nuit for Double Bass (1972); Le réveil profond for Double Bass (1977); Et Maintenant, c'est a vous a jouer for Cello & Double Bass (1974); Okanagon for Harp, Double Bass & Tamtam (1968); Mantram for Double Bass (1987) *(rec Sendesaal, Hessen Radio, Frankfurt, Feb. 8–9, May 18–21 & Aug)* Hat Hut ("NOW." series) ▲ hat ART CD 6124 [DDD]

Ishii, Kenzo (ten)
Bach, J.S.:St. John Passion, w. B. Schlick (sop), M. van Egmond (b-bar), C. de Wolff (cnd), Royal Concertgebouw Orch members, Holland Bach Choir [G] Sound 3–▲ CD 3488/90

Isokoski, Soile (sop)
Gothoni, R.:The Bull & His Herdsman:A Zen Story from Ancient China, w. Jorma Hynninen (bar), Jan Söderblom (vn), Ilari Angervo (va), Jan-Erik Kustafsson (vc), Heini Kärkkäinen (pno), R. Gothoni (cnd)
Ondine ▲ ODE 832 [DDD]
Kokkonen, J.:Requiem (in memoriam Maija Kokkonen), w. W. Grönroos (bar), U. Söderblom (cnd), Lahti SO, Savonlinna Opera Festival Chorus [L] BIS ▲ CD 508 [DDD]
Mendelssohn, F.:St. Paul, w. Peter Lika (bass), Rainer Trost (sgr), C. Spering (cnd), Das Neue Orch
Opus 111 2–▲ OPS 30–135/136
Mendelssohn, F.:Sym 2, w. M. Bach (sop), F. Lang (ten), C. Spering (cnd), Das Neue Orch, Cologne Chorus Musicus [period instrs] Opus 111 ▲ OPS 30–98
Mozart, W.A.:Così fan tutte, w. S. Isokoski (sop—Fiordiligi), N. Argenta (sop—Despina), M. Groop (mez—Dorabella), M. Schäfer (ten—Ferrando), P. Vollestad (bar—Guglielmo), H. Claessens (b-bar—Don Alfonso), S. Kuijken (cnd), La Petite Bande, La Petite Bande Chorus Accent 3–▲ ACC 9296/98
Schubert, Franz:Der Hirt auf dem Felsen, w. A.-M. Korsimaa (cl), M. Viitasalo (pno) *(rec Jan. 1993)*
Finlandia ▲ 4509–95878–2 [DDD]
Schubert, Franz:Songs (misc), w. M. Viitasalo (pno)—Sei mir gegrüsst, Op. 20/1; Nacht und Träume, Op. 43/2; Im Frühling; Gretchen am Spinnrade, Op. 2; Ganymed, Op.19/3; Du bist die Ruh, Op. 59/3; Die junge Nonne, Op. 43/1; Ave Maria, Op. 52/6; Lied der Mignon I, II & III, Op. 62/1–3; Mignons Gesang; Der Hirt auf dem Felsen, Op. 129 [w. A.-M. Korsimaa (clarinet)] *(rec Jan. 18–20, 1993)* Finlandia ▲ 4509–95877–2 [DDD]
Sibelius, J.:Kullervo, w. Raimo Laukka (bar), L. Segerstam (cnd), Danish National RSO, Danish National Radio Choir Chandos ▲ CHAN 9393 [DDD]
Zemlinsky, A. von:Der Geburtstag der Infantin, w. Iride Martinez (sgr), Andrew Collis (sgr), David Kuebler (ten), Juanita Lascarro (sgr), Machiko Obata (sgr), Anne Schwanewilms (sgr), Natalie Karl (sgr), Martina Rüping (sgr), Franfurter Kantorei (sgr), J. Conlon (cnd), Gürzenich Orch, Cologne PO *(rec Cologne, Feb 1996)* EMI Classics 2–▲ CDCB 56208

Itami, Naomi (sop)
Lehár, F.:Das Land des Lächelns, w. Nancy Gustafson (sop—Lisa), Naomi Itami (sop—Mi), Lynton Atkinson (ten—Gustl), Jerry Hadley (ten—Prince Sou Chong), R. Bonynge (cnd), English CO *(rec EMI Abbey Road, Studio One, London, England; Aug 2–25, 1995)* Telarc ▲ CD–80419 [DDD]

Itami, Naomi (sop) (cont.)
Lehár, F.:Der Zarewitsch, w. Nancy Gustafson (sop—Sonia), Naomi Itami (sop—Mascha), Lynton Atkinson (ten—Ivan), Jerry Hadley (ten—the Czarevitch), Jeffrey Carl (bar—Grand Duke/Soldier), R. Bonynge (cnd), English CO *(rec EMI Abbey Road, Studio One, London, England; Aug 25–27, 1995)*
Telarc ▲ CD–80395 [DDD]

Ito, Kyoko (sop)
Fauré, G.:Requiem, w. Ohga, K. Yamada (cnd), Tokyo Metropolitan SO, Tokyo Metropolitan Sym Chorus [L] *(rec 1973)* CBS ▲ MK 44738 [ADD]

Ivanov, Alexi (sgr)
Mussorgsky, M.:Boris Godunov, w. Irina Arkhipova (mez—Marina Mnishek), Evgenya Verbitskaya (mez—Nurse to Xenia), Valentina Klepatskaya (sgr—Fyodor), Tamara Sorokina (sgr—Xenia), Anton Grigoryev (ten—Simpleton), Vladimir Ivanovsky (ten—Grigory, the Pretender), Gyorgy Shulpin (bar—Prince Shuisky), Alexey Geleva (bass—Varlaam), Ivan Petrov (bass—Boris Godounov), Mark Reshetin (bass—Pimen), Alexi Ivanov (sgr—Andrei Shchelkalov), Evgeny Kibkalo (sgr—Rangoni), A. Melik-Pashayev (cnd), Bolshoi Theater Orch, Bolshoi Theater Chorus *(rec Moscow, 1962)*
Melodiya ("The Russian Opera" series) 3–▲ 74321–29349–2 [ADD]

Ivanov, Emil (ten)
Famous Opera Arias, w. Sofia SO [cnd:Stefan Linev] Gega ▲ 190

Ivanov, Nicolai (cant)
Hymns to the Mother of God at the Moleben, w. Trinity-St. Sergius Laura Monks' Choir [cnd:Archmandrite Matfei], Moscow Theological Academy Choir, Nicolai Zabelich (cant) *(rec Cathedral of the Dormition, Trinity-St. Sergiy Lavra, June 1987)* Russian Compact Disc ▲ RCD 15002 [AAD]

Ivanova, Assya (sop)
Schütz, H.:Motets (misc), w. V. Kissyova (sop), N. Pankova (sop), A. Bovarian (alt), V. Vassilev (ten), K. Mirinski (bass), S. Kralev (cnd), Sofia Madrigal—Christe Deus adjuva; Verbum caro factum est; Te Christe supplex invoco; Veni redemtor gentium; Veni sancte Spiritus Gega ▲ GD 174 [DDD]

Ivanovic, Aleksandra (mez)
Maric, L.:From the Darkness Chanting, w. Gordana Marjanovic (pno) Emergo ▲ EC 3951 [DDD]

Ivanovsky, Vladimir (ten)
Mussorgsky, M.:Boris Godunov, w. Irina Arkhipova (mez—Marina Mnishek), Evgenya Verbitskaya (mez—Nurse to Xenia), Valentina Klepatskaya (sgr—Fyodor), Tamara Sorokina (sgr—Xenia), Anton Grigoryev (ten—Simpleton), Vladimir Ivanovsky (ten—Grigory, the Pretender), Gyorgy Shulpin (bar—Prince Shuisky), Alexey Geleva (bass—Varlaam), Ivan Petrov (bass—Boris Godounov), Mark Reshetin (bass—Pimen), Alexi Ivanov (sgr—Andrei Shchelkalov), Evgeny Kibkalo (sgr—Rangoni), A. Melik-Pashayev (cnd), Bolshoi Theater Orch, Bolshoi Theater Chorus *(rec Moscow, 1962)*
Melodiya ("The Russian Opera" series) 3–▲ 74321–29349–2 [ADD]
Shostakovich, D.:Song of the Forest, w. I. Petrov (bass), A. Yulov (cnd), Moscow PO, Moscow State Boys' Choir, Yurlov Russian Choir Russian Disc ▲ RUS 11 048 [AAD]

Ives, Charles (voc)
Ives, C.:They Are There!, w. Kronos Quartet—using period recording apparatus, the Kronos String Quartet teams up with the composer in his voice & piano 1942 Columbia recording
Elektra/Nonesuch ▲ 79242–2–P ■ 79242–4–H

Ivogün, Maria (sop)
Maria Ivogün Preiser ("Lebendige Vergangenheit" series) ▲ PRE 89094 [ADD]
Maria Ivogün *(rec 1916–32)* Nimbus ("Prima Voce" series) ▲ NI 7832
Mozart, W.A.:Entführung (sels), w. Leo Slezak (ten), Richard Tauber (ten), K. Alwin (cnd), Vienna State Opera Orch—Hier soll ich dich; Konstanzel... wie ängstlich; Martern aller Arten *(rec 1905 - 1944)*
Minerva ▲ MN A14 [ADD]

Jackson (sgr)
Gershwin, G.:Porgy & Bess (sels), w. D. Brown (sop), A. Matthews (sop), Duncan (sgr), A. Smallens (cnd), *(orch unknown) (rec 1942 Broadway revival cas)* MCA ■ MCAC 1631 (m)

Jackson, H. (sgr)
Gershwin, G.:Porgy & Bess, w. A. Brown (sgr), E. Matthews (sgr), Todd Duncan (sgr), H. Dowdy (sgr), A. Long (sgr), Eva Jessye Choir [1940–1942 original cast]
MCA Classics ("Broadway Gold" series) ▲ MCAD 10520 ■ MCAC 10520

Jackson, Richard (bar)
Bach, J.S.:St. Matthew Passion, w. N. Argenta (sop), L. Lee (mez), J. Kenny (alt), J. MacDougall (ten), R. Müller (ten), S. Varcoe (b-bar), P. Goodwin (cnd), *(orch & chorus unknown)*
United 2–▲ UNI 89301 [DDD]
Bach, J.S.:St. Matthew Passion (sels), w. N. Argenta (sop), L. Lee (mez), J. Kenny (alt), J. MacDougall (ten), R. Müller (ten), S. Varcoe (b-bar), P. Goodwin (cnd), *(orch & chorus unknown) (rec St. George's Theater, London, Feb 24-27, 1994)* United ▲ UNI 88030 [DDD]
Britten, H.:Purcell Realizations, w. Susan Gritton (sop), Felicity Lott (sop), Sarah Walker (mez), James Bowman (alto), John Mark Ainsley (ten), Anthony Rolfe Johnson (ten), Simon Keenlyside (bass), Ian Bostridge (sgr), Graham Johnson (pno) Hyperion 2–▲ CDA 67061/62
Poulenc, F.:Songs, w. F. Lott (sop), A. Murray (mez), A. Rolfe-Johnson (ten), G. Johnson (pno) [F]
Hyperion ▲ CDA 66147
Schubert, Franz:Songs (comp), w. Christine Schäfer (sop), John Mark Ainsley (ten), Graham Johnson (pno), Stephen Layton (cnd), London Schubert Chorale—Der Einsame; Des Sängers Habe; Zwei Szenen aus dem Schauspiel Lacrimas (Lied der Delphine; Lied des Florio); Mondenschien (chorale); Gesänge Aus Wilhelm Meister (Nur wer die Sehnsucht kennt; Hwiss mich nicht reden; So lasst mich scheinen); Totengräberweise; Das Echo; An Silvia; Horch, horch die Lerch'; Trinklied; Wiegenlied; Widerspruch; Der Wanderer an den Mond; Grab und Mond (chorale); Nachthelle; Abschied von der Erde
Hyperion ▲ CDJ 33026

Jacob, I. (nar)
Stravinsky, I.:Perséphone, w. J. Aler (ten), R. Craft (cnd), Orch of St. Luke, Gregg Smith Singers, Newark Boys' Chorus MusicMasters ▲ 01612–67103–2

Jacobs, René (alt)
Amarilli, mia bella, w. Konrad Junghändel (lt) Harmonia Mundi ▲ HMA 190.1183
Bach, Joh. Christoph:Ach, dass ich Wassers genug hätte, w. Kuijken Consort Accent ▲ 77912 [DDD]
Bach, J.S.:Cant 21, w. G. de Reyghere (mez), C. Prégardien (ten), P. Lika (bass), S. Kuijken (vn), S. Kuijken (cnd), La Petite Bande, Netherlands Chamber Choir Virgin Classics ▲ CDC 59528
Bach, J.S.:Cant 33, w. M. van Altena (ten), G. Leonhardt (cnd), Leonhardt Consort, Hanover Boys' Choir Teldec 2–▲ 2292–42505–2 [AAD]
Bach, J.S.:Cant 35, w. C. Banchini (cnd), Ensemble 415 [G]
Harmonia Mundi France ▲ HMC 901273 [DDD]
Bach, J.S.:Cant 39, w. M. van Egmond (b-bar), G. Leonhardt (cnd), Leonhardt Consort, Hanover Boys' Choir [G] Teldec 2–▲ 2292–42556–2 [AAD]
Bach, J.S.:Cant 40, w. M. van Altena (ten), M. van Egmond (b-bar), Leonhardt Consort, Hanover Boys' Choir [G] Teldec 2–▲ 2292–42556–2 [AAD]
Bach, J.S.:Cant 53, w. C. Banchini (cnd), Ensemble 415 [G]
Harmonia Mundi France ▲ HMC 901273 [DDD]
Bach, J.S.:Cant 82, w. C. Banchini (cnd), Ensemble 415 [G]
Harmonia Mundi France ▲ HMC 901273 [DDD]
Bach, J.S.:Cant 113, w. S. Hennig (trb), D. Bratschke (trb), K. Equiluz (ten), M. van Egmond (b-bar), Leonhardt Consort, Collegium Vocale, Hanover Boys' Chorus [G] Teldec 2–▲ 2292–42606–2
Bach, J.S.:Cant 114, w. S. Hennig (trb), K. Equiluz (ten), M. van Egmond (b-bar), Leonhardt Consort, Collegium Vocale, Hanover Boys' Chorus [G] Teldec 2–▲ 2292–42606–2
Bach, J.S.:Cant 205, w. M. van der Sluis (sop), C. Prégardien (ten), D. Thomas (bass), G. Leonhardt (cnd), Orch of the Age of Enlightenment [G] Philips ▲ 432161–2 [DDD]
Bach, J.S.:Cant 214, w. M. van der Sluis (sop), C. Prégardien (ten), D. Thomas (bass), G. Leonhardt (cnd), Orch of the Age of Enlightenment [G] Philips ▲ 432161–2 [DDD]
Bach, J.S.:Magnificat, BWV 243, w. G. de Reyghere (sop), C. Prégardien (ten), P. Lika (bass), S. Kuijken (vn), S. Kuijken (cnd), La Petite Bande, Netherlands Chamber Choir
Veritas ▲ VC 7 90779–2 [DDD] ■ VC 7 90779–4 (D)
Bach, J.S.:Magnificat, BWV 243, w. G. de Reyghere (sop), C. Prégardien (ten), P. Lika (bass), S. Kuijken (vn), S. Kuijken (cnd), La Petite Bande, Netherlands Chamber Choir Virgin Classics ▲ CDC 59528

Jacobs, René (alt) (cont.)
Bach, J.S.:Music of, w. G. Murray (org), La Chapelle Royale Orch, Ensemble 415, Collegium Vocale—selections from Cantatas 35, 78 & 82, St. John Passion, St. Matthew Passion, & the Well–tempered Clavier; Chorale Prelude, BWV 622; Flute Sonata, BWV 1034; Toccata & Fugue in d *(rec 1969–88)* Harmonia Mundi Plus ▲ HMP 390801
Bach, J.S.:St. Matthew Passion, w. B. Schlick (sop), H. P. Blochwitz (ten), H. Crook (ten), U. Cold (bass), P. Kooy (bass), P. Herreweghe (cnd), La Chapelle Royale Orch, Ghent Collegium Vocale [G] Harmonia Mundi France 3–▲ HMC 901155/57
Buxtehude, D.:Jubilate Domino, omnis terra, w. Kuijken Consort Accent ▲ 77912 [DDD]
Buxtehude, D.:Muss der Tod denn nun doch trennen, w. Kuijken Consort Accent ▲ 77912 [DDD]
Campra, A.:L'Europe galante, w. M. Kweksilber (sop), R. Yakar (sop), S. Nimsgern (bar), G. Leonhardt (cnd), La Petite Bande Editio Classica 2–▲ 77059–2–RG [ADD]
Couperin, F.:Music of, w. Gérard Lesne (alt), Kenneth Gilbert (hpd), Christophe Rousset (hpd), W. Christie (cnd), Les Arts Florissants, Phillippe Herreweghe (cnd), Chapelle Royale Choir—Hpd pieces; Tenebeae Lessons [sels] Harmonia Mundi ("Great Baroque Composers" series) 3–▲ HMX 390870.72
Gluck, C.W.:Orfeo ed Euridice, w. M. Falewicz (sop), M. Kweksilber (sop), S. Kuijken (cnd), La Petite Bande, Collegium Vocale Accent 2–▲ 48223/24 [DDD]
Handel, G.F.:Partenope, w. Krisztina Laki (sop), Helga Müller–Molinari (mez), John York Skinner (alt), S. Kuijken (cnd), La Petite Bande Editio Classica 3–▲ 77109–2–RG [ADD]
Handel, G.F.:Tamerlano, w. Isabelle Poulenard (sop—Irene), Mieke van der Sluis (sop—Asteria), René Jacobs (alt—Andronico), Henri Ledroit (ct—Tamerlano), John Elwes (ten—Bajazet), Gregory Reinhart (bass—Leone), J. Malgoire (cnd), La Grande Écurie et la Chambre du Roy *(rec 1983)* Sony Classical 3–▲ SM3K 37893
Lully, J.–B.:Le Bourgeois gentilhomme, w. M. Kweksilber (sop), R. Yakar (sop), S. Nimsgern (bar), G. Leonhardt (cnd), La Petite Bande Editio Classica 2–▲ 77059–2–RG [ADD]
Lully, J.–B.:Music of, w. Gérard Lesne (alt), Kenneth Gilbert (hpd), Christophe Rousset (hpd), W. Christie (cnd), Les Arts Florissants, Phillippe Herreweghe (cnd), Chapelle Royale Choir—Hpd Pieces; 'Atys' excerpts; Dies Israe; Petits Motets Harmonia Mundi ("Great Baroque Composers" series) 3–▲ HMX 390870.72
Pergolesi, G.B.:Stabat mater, w. S. Henning (trb), Concerto Vocale Harmonia Mundi ("Luxury Edition" series) ▲ HMX 2901119
Purcell, H.:Music for Voc & Strs, w. W. Kuijken (vl), K. Junghanel (thb)—Tis Natures's voice; Musick for a while; Retir'd from any mortal's sight, Since from my dear Astrea's sight; Pious Celinda goes to prayers; Incassum, Lesbia; Ah! Cruel nymph; The fatal hour comes on a pace; As Amoret and Thirsis lay; Sweeter than Roses; I lov'd fair Celia; Young Thirsis' fate Accent ▲ 57802
Rameau, J.P.:Music of, w. Gérard Lesne (alt), Kenneth Gilbert (hpd), Christophe Rousset (hpd), W. Christie (cnd), Les Arts Florissants, Phillippe Herreweghe (cnd), Chapelle Royale Choir—Pieces; Les Indes Gallantes (sels) Harmonia Mundi ("Great Baroque Composers" series) 3–▲ HMX 390870.72
René Jacobs Recital, w. K. Junghänel (lt) *(rec 1985)* Musique d'Abord ▲ HMA 1901183
Telemann, G.P.:Cants, w. Berlin Academy for Early Music—Das Frauenzimmer verstimmt sich immer (aria); Vergiss dich selbst, mein schönster Engel (aria from the opera *Eginhard*); Meines bleibens ist nicht hier (cantata); Tirsis am Scheidewege (cantata); Nach Finsternis und Todesschatten (Cantata No. 27); An den Schlaf (The 5th Ode); Die Einsamkeit (for countertenor & harpsichord); Adagio in G (from Concerto grosso in e) Capriccio ▲ CD 10 338 [DDD]
Verdi, G.:Rigoletto, w. E. Berger (sop), H. Roswaenge (ten), H. Schlusnus (bass), J. Greindl (bass), R. Heger (cnd), Berlin State Opera Orch, Berlin State Opera Chorus [G] *(rec 11/20–22/44)* Preiser 2–▲ 90036 (m) [AAD]
Zelenka, J.D.:Lamentationes Jeremiae Prophetae, w. G. de Mey (ten), K. Widmer (bass), R. Jacobs (cnd), Schola Cantorum Basiliensis Instrumental Ensemble Editio Classica ▲ 77112–2–RG [ADD]

Jacobson, Ruth (sop)
Paulus, S.:All My Pretty Ones, w. P. Schoenfield (pno) [E] Albany ▲ TROY 036–2 [DDD]

Jacobsson, Kurt (sgr)
Hallén, A.:Harald der Wiking (act III, final scene), w. M. Meyerson (sgr—Berta), S. Lindström (sgr—Sigrun), A. Ljungholm (sgr—Harald), S. Sjöstedt (sgr—Sigleif), K. Jacobsson (sgr—Gudmund/Torgrim), S. Rybrant (cnd), Malmö SO, Malmö Radio Chorus [G] *(rec 6/6/74)* Musica Sveciae ▲ MSCD 621 [AAD]

Jacquelin, Marie–Françoise (sop)
Handel, G.F.:Rinaldo, w. Sophie Boulin (sop—Donna), Ileana Cotrubas (sop—Almirena), Marie–Françoise Jacquelin (sop—Sirene), Nicole Leport (sop—Sirene), Jeanette Scovotti (sop—Armida), Carolyn Watkinson (cta—Rinaldo), Charles Brett (ct—Eustazio), Paul Esswood (ct—Goffredo), Armand Arapian (ten—Mago Christiano/Araldo), Ulrik Cold (bass—Argante), J. Malgoire (cnd), La Grande Écurie et la Chambre du Roy *(rec Paris, 1977)* Sony Classical 3–▲ SM3K 34592

Jacques, William (nar)
Schibler, A.:La Folie de Tristan, w. Audrey Michael (sop—Iseut), Arlette Chédel (mez—Brangien), Pierre–André Blaser (ten—Tristan), Philippe Huttenlocher (bar—Le roi Marc/Le pêcheur/Le portier), André Fauré (nar), Snezana Zivojinovic (nar), J. Auberson (cnd), Lausanne CO, Romande Instrumental Group Rockband, Swiss Romande Radio Choir *(rec live, Festival de Montreux, Sept 15, 1980)* Jecklin ▲ JD 695
Stravinsky, I.:L'Histoire du soldat, w. J. V. Gilles (nar), F. Simon (the Soldier), E. Ansermet (cnd), Swiss Romande Orch members [F] *(rec 4/17/52)* Claves ▲ CD 8918 (m) [ADD]

Jacquin, Christiane (sgr)
Lehár, F.:Die lustige Witwe, w. Teresa Stich–Randall (mez—Missia Palmieri), Monique Stiot (mez—Manon), Germaine Duclos (sgr—Praskovia), Linda Felder (sgr—Olga), Christiane Jacquin (sgr—Nadia), Jeannette Levasseur (sgr—Sylviane), Henri Legay (ten—Camille de Coutançon), Joseph Peyron (ten—Kromsky), Robert Destain (sgr—Baron Popoff), Michel Fauche (sgr—Pristich), Gérard Friedmann (sgr—Lerida), Jacques Gilet (sgr—Bogdanowitch), Jean Guy Henneveux (sgr—Prince Danilo), Serge Klin (sgr—Figg), Jacques Villa (sgr—D'Estillac), A. Sibert (cnd), Belgian Radio–TV Orch, Belgian Radio–TV Chorus *(rec Grand Auditorium, Belgium, Apr 30, 1970)* Studio SM 2–▲ 2160 [AAD]

Jadan, Ivan (ten)
Ivan Jadan:Great Russian Tenor of the Century *(rec 1933–54)* Jadan ▲ DIDX 025756

Jadlowker, Hermann (ten)
Leoncavallo, R.:Pagliacci (sels), w. Enrico Caruso (ten), Antonio Paoli (ten), Giovanni Zenatello (ten), Amedeo Bassi (ten), Fernand Ansseau (ten), Hipolito Lazaro (ten), Nino (Filippo) Piccaluga (ten), Mario Chamlee (ten), Giacomo Lauri–Volpi (ten), Miguel Fleta (ten), Giovanni Martinelli (ten), Aureliano Pertile (ten), Georges Thill (ten), Alessandro Valente (ten), Francesco Merli (ten), Lauritz Melchior (ten), Marcel Wittrisch (ten), Joseph Schmidt (ten), Beniamino Gigli (ten), Giuseppe Lugo (ten), Helge Roswaenge (ten), Jussi Bjoerling (ten)—23 versions of the tenor aria "Vesti la giubba" *(rec 1907–1944)* Bongiovanni ▲ GB 1071 [ADD]
Mozart, W.A.:Idomeneo (sels) *(rec 1905 – 1944)* Minerva ▲ MN A14 [ADD]

Jagel, Frederick (ten)
Berg, A.:Wozzeck, w. E. Farrell (sop), M. Harrell (bar), R. Lloyd (bass), D. Mitropoulos (cnd), New York PO *(rec live 1950)* Andromeda ▲ ANR 2514 [ADD]
Carlo Tagliabue, w. Carlo Tagliabue (bar), Margherita Carosio (sop), Ettore Bergamaschi (ten), Zinka Milanov (sop), Bruna Castagna (cta), Norman Cordon (bass), Renata Tebaldi (sop), Alfredo Colella (bass) *(rec in studio and live, 1928–1951)* Bongiovanni ▲ GB 1070–2 [ADD]
Donizetti, G.:Lucia di Lammermoor, w. Lily Pons (sop—Lucia), Thelma Votipka (mez—Alisa), Frederick Jagel (ten—Edgardo), John Brownlee (bar—Enrico), Ezio Pinza (bass—Raimondo), G. Papi (cnd), *(orch unknown)* The Fourties 2–▲ ENT FT 1511
Verdi, G.:La forza del destino, w. Stella Roman (sop), Lawrence Tibbett (bar), Salvatore Baccaloni (bass), Ezio Pinza (bass), B. Walter (cnd), New York Metropolitan Opera Orch *(rec live, Jan 23, 1943)* The Fourties 2–▲ ENT 1503
Verdi, G.:La traviata, w. Rosa Ponselle (sop—Violetta), Henriette Wakefield (sop—Annina), Frederick Jagel (ten—Alfredo), Alfredo Gandolfi (bar—Baron), Lawrence Tibbett (bar—Giorgio), E. Panizza (cnd), *(orch unknown) (rec live, New York, Jan. 5, 1935)* The Fourties 2–▲ ENT FT 1513
Wagner, R.:Der Ring des Nibelungen, w. A. Davis (sop), L. Tibbett (bar), L. Stokowski (cnd), Philadelphia Orch *(rec 1933–1939)* Pearl 2–▲ CD 9076 [AAD]

Jäger, Brigitte (sop)
Kalitzke, J.:Bericht über den Tod des Musikers Jack Tiergarten, w. Werner Eggenhofer (nar), Till Krabbe (nar), Espen Fegran (bar), J. Kalitzke (cnd), North Rhine–Westphalia Musikfabrik *(rec live, Apr 29, 1994)* CPO ▲ 999358–2 [DDD]

Jahn, Elfriede (alt)
Haydn, J.:Mass 7, "Kleine Orgelmesse", w. Eiko Katonosaka (sop), Kurt Equiluz (ten), Leo Heppe (bass), H. Gillesberger (cnd), Vienna State Opera Orch, Vienna Chamber Choir *(rec 1965)* Tuxedo ▲ TUXCD 1025
Haydn, J.:Mass 10, "Kriegsmesse", "Paukenmesse", w. Elisabeth Thomann (sop), Stafford Wing (ten), Eishi Kawamura (bass), H. Gillesberger (cnd), Vienna State Opera Orch, Vienna Chamber Choir *(rec 1965)* Tuxedo ▲ TUXCD 1025

Jahn, Gertrud (mez)
Berg, A.:Wozzeck, w. A. Silja (sop), H. Laubenthal (ten), H. Zednik (ten), E. Waechter (bar), C. von Dohnányi (cnd), Vienna PO London 2–▲ 417348–2 [DDD]

Jahn, Gertrude (alt)
Schubert, Franz:Deutsche Messe, w. Elisabeth Thomann (sop), Stafford Wing (ten), Kunikazu Ohashi (bass), H. Gillesberger (cnd), Vienna SO, Vienna Chamber Choir Tuxedo ▲ TUXCD 1074 [ADD]
Schubert, Franz:Mass 3, w. Elisabeth Thomann (sop), Stafford Wing (ten), Kunikazu Ohashi (bass), H. Gillesberger (cnd), Vienna SO, Vienna Chamber Choir Tuxedo ▲ TUXCD 1074 [ADD]

Jahna, Vratislav (bar)
Smetana, B.:Choral Music, w. Miroslav Švejda (ten), Jaroslav Horáček (bass), Z. Košler (cnd), Prague SO, Prague Radio Chorus, Czech Phil Chorus Supraphon ▲ SUP CD 3040

Jahns, Annette (mez)
Strauss, R.:Der Rosenkavalier (sels), w. A. Pusar–Jeric (sop), M. Stejskal (sop), U. Walther (cta), R. Haunstein (bar), T. Adam (b–bar), H. Vonk (cnd), Dresden Staatskapelle, Dresden State Chorus [G] *(rec live 2/85)* Denon ▲ CO 8010 [DDD]

Jakubowski, Ireneusz (ten)
Cimarosa, D.:Requiem pro defunctis, w. K. Rymarczyk (sop), B. Krahel (mez), A. Niemierowicz (bar), S. Frontalini (cnd), Warmia National Orch, Olsztyn Academy Chorus [L] Bongiovanni ▲ GB 2088 [DDD]

Jalbert, Madeleine (alt)
Bach, J.S.:Magnificat, BWV 243, w. Hélène Obadia (sop), Brigitte Vinson (sop), Hervé Lamy (ten), Philip Langshaw (bass), P. Kuentz (cnd), Paul Kuentz Orch, Paul Kuentz Choir Pierre Verany ▲ PVY 730048
Bach, J.S.:Mass in b, BWV 232, w. Hélène Obadia (sop), Adrian Brand (ten), Paul Gay (bass), Eric Aubier (tpt), P. Kuentz (cnd), Paul Kuentz Orch, Paul Kuentz Choir Pierre Verany ▲ PVY 730060 [DDD]

Jalkéus, Margareta (sop)
Ellington, D.:Music of, w. Peder Pedersen's Big Band, Tritonus—Praise God [Introduction]; Heaven; Freedom–Suite; The Shepherd; The Majesty of God; Come Sunday; David Dances before the Lord; Almighty God; T.G.T.T.; Praise God & Dance [Final] *(rec Copenhagen, Jan 1996)* Classico ▲ CD 142

James (sgr)
Verdi, G.:Requiem Mass, w. Shafer (sgr), Farina (sgr), Crawford (sgr), D. Moe (cnd), Oberlin Musical Union Orch [L] Bainbridge 2–▲ BCD 2103 [DDD]

James, Carolyn (sop)
Lloyd, G.:The Vigil of Venus, w. Thomas Booth (ten), G. Lloyd (cnd), Welsh National Opera Orch, Welsh National Opera Chorus Albany ▲ TROY 170 [DDD]

James, David (alt)
Bach, J.S.:St. John Passion, w. P. Kwella (sop), W. Kendall (ten), I. Partridge (ten), M. George (bar), D. Wilson–Johnson (b–bar), H. Christophers (cnd), The Sixteen Orch, The Sixteen [G] Chandos ("Chaconne" series) 2–▲ CHAN 0507/08 [DDD]
Bryars, G.:Incipit Vita Nova, w. A. Dreyer (violin), U. Lachner (viola), R. Firth (cello) ECM New Series ▲ 78118–21533–2 [DDD]
Codex Speciálník, w. P. Hillier (cnd), Hillard Ensemble, R. Covey–Crump (ten), J. Potter (ten), G. Jones (bar) *(rec Gönningen City Church, Jan. 1993)* ECM New Series ▲ 78118–21504–2 [DDD]
Handel, G.F.:Messiah, w. Lynn Dawson (sop), Catherine Denley (mez), Arthur Davies (ten), Michael George (bass), H. Christophers (cnd), The Sixteen Orch, The Sixteen [20–member orchestra, 19–member chorus] [E] *(rec 1986)* Hyperion 2–▲ CDA 66251/52 [DDD]
Holliger, H.:Beiseit, w. Teodoro Anzellotti (acc), Elmar Schmid (cl), Johannes Nied (db), H. Holliger (cnd) ECM New Series ▲ 78118–21540–2 [ADD]
Kancheli, G.:Evening Prayers, w. Rogers Covey–Crump (ten), John Potter (ten), Gordon Jones (bar), D. R. Davies (cnd), Stuttgart CO *(rec Apr. 1994)* ECM New Series ▲ 78118–21510–2 [DDD]
Kancheli, G.:Sym 3, w. F. Welser–Möst (cnd), London PO EMI Classics ▲ CDC 55619
Officium, w. P. Hillier (cnd), Hillard Ensemble, R. Covey–Crump (ten), J. Potter (ten), G. Jones (bar), J. Gabarek (sop/ten saxs) *(rec Sept. 1993)* ECM New Series ▲ 78118–21525–2
Pärt, A.:Litany, w. Rogers Covey–Crump (ten), John Potter (ten), Gordon Jones (bass), T. Kaljuste (cnd), Tallinn CO, Estonian Phil Chamber Choir *(rec Niguliste Church, Tallinn, Sept 1995)* ECM New Series ▲ 78118–21592–2 [DDD] ▮ 78118–21592–4
Pärt, A.:Passio Domini nostri Jesu Christi secundum Joannem, w. L. Dawson (sop), R. Covey–Crump (ten), J. Potter (ten), G. Jones (bass), M. George (bass), P. Hillier (cnd), Hilliard Ensemble, Western Wind Chamber Chorus [L] ECM New Series ▲ 78118–21370–2 [DDD]; ▮ 78118–21370–4 (D)
Songs for a Tudor King, w. P. Hillier (cnd), Hillard Ensemble, Judith Nelson (sop), Paul Elliott (ten), Leigh Nixon (ten), P. Hillier (bar) Saga Classics ▲ 3378 [ADD]

James, Eirian (mez)
Handel, G.F.:Giulio Cesare in Egitto, w. Lynne Dawson (sop), Guillemette Laurens (mez), James Bowman (alt), Dominique Visse (alt), Nicolas Rivenq (bar), J. Malgoire (cnd), La Grande Écurie et la Chambre du Roy Astrée 3–▲ E 8558
Handel, G.F.:Teseo, w. Della Jones (mez), Derek Lee Ragin (ct), M. Minkowski (cnd), Louvre Musicians Erato 2–▲ 2292–45806–2 ZA
Mendelssohn, F.:A Midsummer Night's Dream (comp), w. J. Howarth (sop), J. Laredo (cnd), Scottish CO, Scottish Phil Singers [E] Nimbus 2–▲ NI 5041/42 [DDD]
Mozart, W.A.:Così fan tutte, w. A. Roocroft (sop), R. Gilfrey (bar), C. Feller (bass), J. E. Gardiner (cnd), English Baroque Soloists Archiv 3–▲ 437829–2 [DDD]
Mozart, W.A.:Don Giovanni, w. Charlotte Margiono (sop—Donna Elvira), Luba Orgonasova (sop—Donna Anna), Eirian James (mez—Zerlina), Julian Clarkson (alt—Masetto), Christoph Prégardien (ten—Don Ottavio), Rodney Gilfry (bar—Don Giovanni), Ildebrando d'Arcangelo (bass—Leporello), Andrea Silvestrelli (bass—Il Commendatore), J. E. Gardiner (cnd), English Baroque Soloists, Monteverdi Choir London Deutsche Grammophon ("4D Audio" series) 3–▲ 445870–2
Mozart, W.A.:Vesperae de Dominica, w. L. Dawson (sop), R. Covey–Crump (ten), P. Hillier (bass), S. Cleobury (cnd), Cambridge Classical Players, Hilliard Ensemble, King's College Choir [L] EMI Classics ▲ CDC 49672 [DDD]
Mozart, W.A.:Vesperae solennes, w. L. Dawson (sop), R. Covey–Crump (ten), P. Hillier (bass), S. Cleobury (cnd), Cambridge Classical Players, Hilliard Ensemble, King's College Choir [L] EMI Classics ▲ CDC 49672 [DDD]
Mozart, W.A.:Zauberflöte, w. Birgit Been (sop), Nathalie Boissy (sop), Marianne Seibel (sop), Renate Springer (sop), Elizabeth Vidal (sop), Eleanor James (mez), Salvador Guzman (ten), Herbert Hechenberger (ten), Wolfgang Newmann (ten), Klaus Häger (bass), Philip Langshaw (bass), Hans–Georg Moser (bass), P. Kuentz (cnd), Paul Kuentz Orch, Francis Bardot (cnd), Maitrise des Hauts–de–Seine members, Paul Kuentz Choirs Pierre Verany 2–▲ PVY 730055 [DDD]
Mussorgsky, M.:Boris Godunov, w. Wessela Zorova (mez), Samuel Ramey (bass), E. de Waart (cnd), Swiss Romande Orch *(rec live, 1993)* Serenissima 2–▲ SER 360109 [DDD]

Janál, Roman (sgr)
Dvořák, A.:Armida, w. Joanna Borowska (sop—Armida), Monika Brychtová (sgr—Siren), Wieslaw Ochman (ten—Rinald), Richard Sporka (ten—Dudo), Jan Markvart (bar—Sven), Pavel Daniluk (bass—King), George Fortune (bass—Ismen), Zdenek Harvánek (bass—Ubald), Miloslav Podskalský (bass—Peter), Milan Bürger (sgr—Gernand), Roman Janál (sgr—Muezzin/Hlasatel), Vratislav Kříz (sgr—Gottfried), Vladimír Nacházel (sgr—Roger), G. Albrecht (cnd), Czech PO, Prague Chamber Choir *(rec 1995)* Orfeo 2–▲ 404962 [DDD]

Janci, Stefan (bass)

Puccini, G.:La Bohème, w. Veronika Kinsces (sop—Mimi), Sidonia Haljakova (sop—Musette), Peter Dvorsky (ten—Rodolfo), Vijtech Scherenkel (ten—Parpingol), Ian Konsulov (bar—Marcello), Balazs Poka (bar—Schaunard), Stanislav Benacka (bass—Benoit), Dariusz Niemirowicz (bass—Colline), Stefan Janci (bass—Alcindoro), *(cnd & orch unknown)* Griffin ▲ GCD 2942

Jänicke, Yvi (cta)

Bach, J.S.:St. John Passion, w. C. Schäfer (sop), A. Kraus (ten), R. Hagen (bass), B. Possemeyer (bass), E. Weyand (cnd), Stuttgart Hymnus Orch, Stuttgart Hymnus Boys' Choir [G] *(rec 1990)* Hänssler Classic 2–▲ 98.968

Bizet, G.:Songs, w. T. Hans (pno)—Tarentelle; Ma vie a son secret; Guitare; Pastel; La coccinelle; Rose d'amour; Ouvre ton coeur; Rêve dala bien-aimée; A une fleur; Si vous aimezl; Pastorale; Vieille chanson; L'Esprit saint; Chanson d'avril; Adieux de l'hôtesse arabe; Absence; Douce mer; L'abandonnée; Vous ne priez pas!; Chant d'amour Orfeo ▲ 309931 [DDD]

Dessau, P.:Haggada, w. Sabine Ritterbusch (sop), Renate Spingler (sop), Peter Galliard (ten—Rabbi Tarfon/Jude/ten solo), Gabriel Sadé (ten—Pharaoh), Jochen Schmeckenbechier (bar—Rabbi Jehoschua), Bernd Weikl (bar—Moses), Matthias Hölle (bass—Speaker/Rabbi Akiwa), Alfred Muff (bass—Father/Rabbi Eleasar), Johann Tilli (bass—Rabbi Elieser/bass solo), G. Albrecht (cnd), Hamburg State PO, Berlin Carl Maria Von Weber Men's Choir, Hamburg Alsterspatzen, North German Radio Chorus [G] *(rec Musikhalle, Hamburg, Sept 4 & 5, 1994)* Capriccio 2–▲ 10590/91 [DDD]

Liebermann, R.:Medea, w. Françoise Pollet (sop—Medea), Yvi Jänicke (cta—Chalkiope), Zdena Furmančoková (sgr—Syrinx), Dagmar Hesse (sgr—Aiglaia), Hanne Krogen (sgr—Kore), Michaela Lucas (sgr—Oinone), Renate Spingler (sgr—Silene), Jochen Kowalski (ct—Kreon), Aage Haugland (bass—Jason), G. Albrecht (cnd), Hamburg State PO, Hamburg State Opera Chorus *(rec live, Hamburg, Germany, Sept 24, 1995)* Musiques Suisses ▲ 6126 [DDD]

Pfitzner, H.:Der blumen Rache, w. Yvonne Wiedstruck (sgr), Yaron Windmüller (voc), R. Reuter (cnd), Berlin RSO, Berlin Radio Chorus CPO ▲ CPO 999158 [DDD]

Pfitzner, H.:Das dunkle Reich, w. Yvonne Wiedstruck (voc), Yaron Windmüller (voc), R. Reuter (cnd), Berlin RSO, Berlin Radio Chorus CPO ▲ CPO 999158 [DDD]

Pfitzner, H.:Fons salutifer, w. Yvonne Wiedstruck (voc), Yaron Windmüller (voc), R. Reuter (cnd), Berlin RSO, Berlin Radio Chorus CPO ▲ CPO 999158 [DDD]

Wolf-Ferrari, E.:Italian Songbook, w. Bruno Canino (pno) CPO ▲ CPO 999270

Jankovic, Eleonora (mez)

Bellini, V.:I Puritani, w. Katia Ricciarelli (sop), Juan Luque Carmona (ten), Carlo Gaifa (ten), Chris Merritt (ten), Roberto Scandiuzzi (bass), G. Ferro (cnd), Sicilian SO, Bari Teatro Petruzzelli Chorus Fonit Cetra ("Digital Operas" series) 3–▲ FCT CDC 20

Bellini, V.:I Puritani, w. K. Ricciarelli (sop), C. Merritt (ten), C. Gaifa (ten), A. Riva (bass), R. Scandiuzzi (bass), G. Ferro (cnd), Sicilian SO, Bari Teatro Petruzzelli Chorus *(rec Apr. 10, 1986)* Cetra Classic ▲ CDC 20 [ADD]

Boito, A.:Mefistofele, w. Michèle Crider (sop—Margherita/Elena), Eleonora Jankovic (mez—Marta/Pantalis), Ernesto Gavazzi (ten—Wagner/Nereo), Vincenza La Scola (ten—Faust), Samuel Ramey (bass—Mefistofele), R. Muti (cnd), La Scala Orch, La Scala Chorus *(rec live Mar 3,5 & 8, 1995, Milan)* RCA Victor 2–▲ 09026–68284–2 [DDD]

Ferrero, L.:Mare nostro, w. A. Felle (sop—Candeggina), E. Jankovic (mez—Astradiva), C. Di Segni (ten—Rimestino), D. Serraiocco (bass-bar—Marchingello), A. Antoniozzi (bass—bar—Pigliatutto), G. Maisni (cnd), Venezze di Rovigo Conservatory of Music Orch, Venezze di Rovigo Conservatory of Music Chorus *(rec Oct. 21-24, 1991)* Ricordi 2–▲ RFCD 2016 [DDD]

Jankovsky, Zdenek (ten)

Honegger, A.:Jeanne d'Arc au bûcher, w. C. Château (sop), A.M. Rodde (sop), H. Brachet (mez), P. Proenza (ten), F. Loup (bass), S. Baudo (cnd), Czech PO, Czech PO Chorus *(rec 1974)* Supraphon 2–▲ 11 0557–2 [AAD]

Penderecki, K.:Dies Irae, w. O. Szwajgier (sop), L. Mróz (bass), S. Kawalla (cnd), Polish Radio–TV SO, Polish Radio–TV Chorus [L] Vienna Modern Masters ▲ VMM 3015 [DDD]

Jankowitsch, M. (cant)

Mozart, W.A.:Missa solemnis, K.337, w. R. Ziesak (sop), E. von Magnus (alt), H. Wildhaber (ten), G. Hornik (bar), H. Hüttler (cant), P. Jelosits (cant), I. Rainer (org), M. Haselböck (cnd), Vienna Academy, Vienna Hofburg Chapel Choir [L] *(rec Apr. 1992)* Novalis ▲ 150087 [DDD]

Janowitz, Gundula (sop)

Bach, J.S.:Mass in b, BWV 232, w. Christa Ludwig (mez), Peter Schreier (ten), Karl Ridderbusch (bass), Vienna Choral Academy, H. von Karajan (cnd), Berlin PO Deutsche Grammophon ("Double" series) 2–▲ 439696–2

Bach, J.S.:St. Matthew Passion, w. C. Ludwig (mez), H. Laubenthal (ten), P. Schreier (ten), W. Berry (bar), D. Fischer–Dieskau (bar), H. von Karajan (cnd), Berlin PO, Vienna Singverein, German Opera Chorus [G] Deutsche Grammophon 3–▲ 419789–2 [ADD]

Beethoven, L van:Fidelio, w. L. Popp (sop), R. Kollo (ten), H. Sotin (bass), D. Fischer–Dieskau (bar), L. Bernstein (cnd), Vienna PO, Vienna State Opera Chorus [G] Deutsche Grammophon 2–▲ 419436–2 [ADD]

Beethoven, L van:Missa Solemnis, w. C. Ludwig (mez), F. Wunderlich (ten), W. Berry (bass), H. von Karajan (cnd), Berlin PO, Vienna Singverein [L] Deutsche Grammophon ("Galleria" series) 2–▲ 423913–2 [ADD]

Beethoven, L van:Sym 9, "Choral Sym", w. H. Rössel–Majdan (alt), W. Kmentt (ten), W. Berry (bass), H. von Karajan (cnd), Berlin PO, Vienna Singverein Deutsche Grammophon ("The Originals" series) ▲ 447401–2

Brahms, J.:Ein Deutsches Requiem, w. E. Wächter (bar), H. von Karajan (cnd), Berlin PO, Vienna Singverein [G] Deutsche Grammophon ("Galleria" series) ▲ 427252–2 [ADD]

Handel, G.F.:Judas Maccabaeus, w. Hertha Töpper (alt), Peter Schreier (ten), Ernest Haefliger (ten), Theo Adam (bass), Siegfried Vogel (bass), H. Koch (cnd), Berlin RSO, Berlin Radio Chorus Berlin Classics 2–▲ BER 9112

Haydn, J.:Die Schöpfung, w. Fritz Wunderlich (ten), Dietrich Fischer–Dieskau (bass), H. von Karajan (cnd), Berlin PO, Vienna Singverein *(rec 1966 & 1968)* Deutsche Grammophon ("Galleria" series) 2–▲ 435077–2 [ADD]

Haydn, J.:Die Schöpfung, w. Gundula Janowitz (sop—Gabriel), Fritz Wunderlich (ten—Uriel), Kim Borg (bass—Raphael), H. von Karajan (cnd), Vienna PO, Vienna Singverein *(rec Salzburg, Aug 29, 1965)* Bella Voce 2–▲ 7204 [AAD]

Hindemith, P.:Das Marienleben, w. I. Gage (pno) [G] *(rec 1982)* Jecklin–Disco ▲ JD 574–2 [ADD]

Mozart, W.A.:Arias, w. Arleen Augér (sop), Kathleen Battle (sop), Irma Beilke (sop), Helena Braun (sop), Lisa Della Casa (sop), Maria Cebotari (sop), Ileana Cotrubas (sop), Helen Donath (sop), Mirella Freni (sop), Reri Grist (sop), Edita Gruberova (sop), Elisabeth Grümmer (sop), Hilde Güden (sop), Ingeborg Hallstein (sop), Luise Helletsgruber (sop), Sena Jurinac (sop), Erika Köth (sop), Evelyn Lear (sop), Wilma Lipp (sop), Margaret Marshall (sop), Edith Mathis (sop), Jarmila Novotna (sop), Margherita Perras (sop), Lucia Popp (sop), Elisabeth Rethberg (sop), Anneliese Rothenberger (sop), Elisabeth Schumann (sop), Elisabeth Schwarzkopf (sop), Graziella Sciutti (sop), Irmgard Seefried (sop), Graziella Sciutti (sop), Julia Varady (sop), Agnes Baltsa (mez), Margit Bokor (mez), Brigitte Fassbaender (mez), Christa Ludwig (mez), Ann Murray (mez), Francisco Araiza (ten), Anton Dermota (ten), Helge Rosvaenge (ten), Rudolf Schock (ten), Peter Schreier (ten), Leopold Simoneau (ten), Eric Tappy (ten), Richard Tauber (ten), Gösta Winbergh (ten), Josef Witt (ten), Fritz Wunderlich (ten), Christian Boesch (bar), Willy Domgraf–Fassbaender (bar), Karl Dönch (bar), Dietrich Fischer–Dieskau (bar), Erich Kunz (bar), Eberhard Wächter (bar), Hans Hotter (b-bar), Paul Schöffler (b-bar), Cesare Siepi (b-bar), José Van Dam (b-bar), Walter Berry (bass), Geraint Evans (bass), Nicolai Ghiaurov (bass), Alexander Kipnis (bass), Richard Mayr (bass), Kurt Moll (bass), James Morris (bass), Ezio Pinza (bass), Martti Talvela (bass), Giorgio Tozzi (bass), Hans Duhan (sgr), Res Fischer (sgr), Marie Gerhart (sgr), *(various orchs & cnds)*—sels from Idomeneo, Die Entführung aus der Serail, Le nozze di Figaro, Don Giovanni, Così fan tutte, Die Zauberflöte & various arias Orfeo d'or ("Festspiel Dokumente" series) 5–▲ 408955

Mozart, W.A.:Così fan tutte, w. R. Grist (sop), B. Fassbaender (mez), P. Schreier (ten), H. Prey (bar), D. Fischer–Dieskau (bar), K. Böhm (cnd), Vienna PO *(rec live, 1972)* Foyer 2–▲ FOY 2066 [ADD]

Mozart, W.A.:Così fan tutte (sels), w. R. Grist (sop), B. Fassbaender (mez), P. Schreier (ten), H. Prey (bar), R. Panerai (bar), K. Böhm (cnd), Vienna PO, Vienna State Opera Chorus—scenes & arias Deutsche Grammophon ▲ 429824–2 [ADD]

Janowitz, Gundula (sop) (cont.)

Mozart, W.A.:Don Giovanni, w. S. Jurinac (sop), G. von Milivkovic (mez), A. Kraus (ten), N. Ghiaurov (bass), C. M. Giulini (cnd), Rome RAI Orch, Rome RAI Chorus *(rec live, May 12, 1970)* Melodram 3–▲ MEL 37080

Mozart, W.A.:Don Giovanni, w. T. Zylis–Gara (sop), M. Freni (sop), A. Kraus (ten), R. Panerai (bar), V. von Halem (bass), N. Ghiaurov (bass), H. von Karajan (cnd), Vienna PO, Vienna State Opera Chorus [I] *(rec live, Salzburg, Aug. 1, 1969)* Memories 3–▲ HR 4362/64 (m) [ADD]

Mozart, W.A.:Idomeneo, w. Enriqueta Tarres (sop), Richard Lewis (ten), Luciano Pavarotti (ten), J. Pritchard (cnd), London PO, Glyndebourne Festival Chorus [I] *(rec live, Royal Albert Hall, London Aug. 17, 1964)* Melodram 2–▲ MEL 27003 (m)

Mozart, W.A.:Idomeneo, w. Enriqueta Tarres (sop), Richard Lewis (ten), Luciano Pavarotti (ten), J. Pritchard (cnd), London PO, Glyndebourne Festival Chorus [I] *(rec live at Royal Albert Hall, Aug. 17, 1964)* Verona 2–▲ 27038/39 (m) [AAD]

Mozart, W.A.:Idomeneo (sels), w. Enriqueta Tarres (sop), David Hughes (ten), Richard Lewis (ten), Luciano Pavarotti (ten), Neilson Taylor (bar), Dennis Wicks (bass), J. Pritchard (cnd), London PO, Glyndebourne Festival Chorus Budget ("The Greatest Voice in Opera" series) ▲ SYP 107

Mozart, W.A.:Music of, w. Julia Bernheimer (mez), Martyn Hill (ten), David Thomas (bass), Anthony Halstead (hn), Colin Lawson (b cl), Christopher Kite (pno), R. Goodman (cnd), Hanover Band—Cons for Hn, K.412, 417, 447, 494a & 495; Sym No. 40; Con for Cl; Eine kleine Nachtmusik; Requiem; Sym No. 41; Con No. 20 for Pno; Serenata Notturna Nimbus 4–▲ NI 1791 [DDD]

Mozart, W.A.:Nozze di Figaro, w. Mirella Freni (sop), Jane Berbié (mez), Frederica von Stade (mez), Michel Sénéchal (ten), José Van Dam (b-bar), Kurt Moll (bass), G. Solti (cnd), Paris Opera Orch, Paris Opera Chorus *(rec live, Paris, Apr 7, 1973)* Agora ("Phoenix" series) 3–▲ 515

Mozart, W.A.:Nozze di Figaro (sels), w. E. Mathis (sop), T. Troyanos (mez), D. Fischer–Dieskau (bar), H. Prey (bar), K. Böhm (cnd), Berlin German Opera Orch—Scenes & Arias Deutsche Grammophon ▲ 429822–2 [ADD]

Mozart, W.A.:Requiem, w. J. Bernheimer (mez), M. Hill (ten), D. Thomas (bass), R. Goodman (cnd), Hanover Band, Hanover Chorus [period instruments; H.C. Robbins Landon edition] Nimbus 4–▲ NI 1791 [DDD]

Mozart, W.A.:Requiem, w. J. Bernheimer (mez), M. Hill (ten), D. Thomas (bass), R. Goodman (cnd), Hanover Band, Hanover Chorus [period instruments; H.C. Robbins Landon's edition; L] Nimbus ▲ NI 5241–2 [DDD]

Mozart, W.A.:Zauberflöte, w. L. Popp (sop), R. Pütz (sop), N. Gedda (ten), W. Berry (bass), G. Frick (bass), O. Klemperer (cnd), Philharmonia Orch, Philharmonia Chorus [without dialog; G] EMI Classics ("Studio" series) 2–▲ CDMB 69971 [ADD]

Mozart, W.A.:Zauberflöte, w. Gundula Janowitz (sop—Pamina), Lucia Popp (sop—Queen of the Night), Nicolai Gedda (ten—Tamina), Walter Berry (bass—Papageno), Gottlob Frick (bass—Sarastro), O. Klemperer (cnd), Philharmonia Orch, Philharmonia Chorus EMI Classics 2–▲ CDCB 55173

Orff, C.:Carmina burana, w. G. Stolze (ten), D. Fischer–Dieskau (bar), G.L. Jochum (cnd), German Opera Orch, German Opera Chorus [G, L] Deutsche Grammophon ("Galleria" series) ▲ 423886–2 [ADD]

Orff, C.:Carmina burana, w. Gerhard Stolze (ten), Dietrich Fischer–Dieskau (bar), E. Jochum (cnd), Berlin German Opera Orch, Berlin German Opera Chorus *(rec Ufa–Studio, Berlin, Oct 1967)* Deutsche Grammophon ▲ 447437–2 [ADD]

Schubert, Franz:Songs (misc), w. Irwin Gage (pno) Deutsche Grammophon 2–▲ 437943–2 [ADD]

Schubert, Franz:Songs (misc), w. C. Spencer (pno)—15 songs—D.296, 297, 457, 491, 504, 514, 543, 547, 672, 833, 861, 866/2, 881, 917, 938 [G] Nuova Era ▲ 6860 [DDD]

Strauss, R.:Ariadne auf Naxos, w. R. Kempe (cnd), Dresden State Chorus EMI Classics 2–▲ CDMB 64159

Strauss, R.:4 Last Songs, w. S. Celibidache (cnd), Rome RAI SO *(rec Apr. 12, 1969)* Emozioni ▲ CDAR 2012 [ADD]

Strauss, R.:4 Last Songs, w. S. Celibidache (cnd), Rome Italian Radio–TV Orch *(rec 4/12/69)* Arkadia ▲ 570 [ADD]

Strauss, R.:4 Last Songs, w. H. von Karajan (cnd), Berlin PO Deutsche Grammophon ("The Originals" series) ▲ 447422–2

Strauss, R.:Songs, w. R. Stamp (cnd), Academy of London Orch Virgin Classics ▲ CDC 59538

Verdi, G.:Don Carlos, w. Shirley Verrett (mez), Franco Corelli (ten), Eberhard Waechter (bar), Nicolai Ghiaurov (bass), Martti Talvela (bass), H. Stein (cnd), Vienna PO, Vienna State Opera Chorus *(rec Vienna, Oct. 25, 1970)* Pantheon 2–▲ PHE 6614

Verdi, G.:La traviata, w. A. Moffo (sop), G. Zampieri (ten), E. Bastianini (bar), B. Klobucar (cnd), Vienna State Opera Orch, Vienna State Opera Chorus [I] *(rec live, Vienna, 1964)* Melodram (Connaisseur) 2–▲ CDM 27510 [ADD]

Wagner, R.:Die Meistersinger von Nürnberg, w. Brigitte Fassbaender (mez), Sándor Kónya (ten), Gerhard Unger (ten), Thomas Helmsey (bar), Thomas Stewart (bar), Franz Crass (bass), R. Kubelik (cnd), Bavarian RSO, Bavarian Radio Chorus *(rec 1967)* Calig 4–▲ 5097174 [ADD]

Wagner, R.:Die Meistersinger von Nürnberg, w. B. Fassbaender (mez), S. Kónya (ten), G. Unger (ten), T. Stewart (bar), F. Crass (bass), T. Hemsley (bass), R. Kubelik (cnd), Bavarian RSO, Bavarian Radio Chorus [G] *(rec live, Munich, Oct. 1967)* Myto 4–▲ 4 MCD 92569 [ADD]

Wagner, R.:Der Ring des Nibelungen, w. R. Crespin (sop), C. Ludwig (mez), H. Dernesch (mez), J. Vickers (ten), D. Fischer–Dieskau (bar), D. Thomas (bass), H. von Karajan (cnd), Berlin PO *(rec late 1960s)* Deutsche Grammophon 15–▲ 435211–2 [ADD]

Wagner, R.:Der Ring des Nibelungen, w. R. Crespin (sop), C. Ludwig (mez), H. Dernesch (mez), J. Vickers (ten), D. Fischer–Dieskau (bar), D. Thomas (bass), H. von Karajan (cnd), Berlin PO *(rec live at Salzburg Easter Festivals, 1967–1970)* Arkadia 12–▲ 223 (m) [ADD]

Janowski, Pavel (bass)

Catalani, A.:Mass, w. C. Basto (sop), A. Cipriani (cta), M. Frusoni (ten), G. Cosmi (cnd), Lucca Teatro Comunale Giglio Orch [L] *(rec 1985)* Bongiovanni ▲ GB 2027 [DDD]

Janssen, Herbert (bar)

Bach, J.S.:St. Matthew Passion, w. Nadine Conner (sop), Jean Watson (cta), William Hain (ten), Mack Harrell (bar), Lorenzo Alvary (bass), B. Walter (cnd), New York PO, New York Phil Chorus—Part I Minerva ▲ 20

Wagner, R.:Der fliegende Holländer (sels), w. K. Flagstad (sop), M. Lorenz (ten), L. Weber (bass), F. Reiner (cnd), Royal Opera House Orch, Royal Opera House Chorus Covent Garden *(rec live, Covent Garden, 6/11/37)* Standing Room Only ▲ SRO 808–1 (m) [ADD]

Wagner, R.:Götterdämmerung (sels), w. F. Leider (sop), Nezadál (sop), K. Thorborg (mez), L. Melchior (ten), L. Weber (bass), T. Beecham (cnd), London PO, Royal Opera House Chorus Covent Garden [G] *(rec from 1925 Polydor & 1929)* Legato Classics 2–▲ LCD 146–2 (m) [ADD]

Wagner, R.:Götterdämmerung (sels), w. Frida Leider (sop), Kerstin Thorborg (mez), Lauritz Melchior (ten), Emanuel List (bass), Maria Nezadál (sgr), T. Beecham (cnd), London PO, Royal Opera House Chorus Covent Garden *(rec Covent Garden, London, 1936)* Preiser ▲ PRE 90266

Wagner, R.:Götterdämmerung (sels), w. F. Leider (sop), A. von Stosch (sop), L. Melchior (ten), W. Schirp (bass), *(cnd & orch unknown)*—Act 2, Scenes 4 & 5 *(w. Furtwängler, Royal Opera House Orch. & Cho., 1938)*; Act 3, Schweigt eures Jammers *(Frida Leider & E. Marherr–Wagner, Blech, Berlin State Opera Orch., 1928)* Pearl ▲ PEA 9331 (m) [ADD]

Wagner, R.:Götterdämmerung (siegfried's funeral), w. Helen Traubel (sop), Doris Doré (sgr), A. Rodzinski (cnd), New York PO *(rec Carnegie Hall, New York City, Nov 25, 1945)* Enterprise ("The Radio Years" series) ▲ ENT RY 55

Wagner, R.:Lohengrin, w. H. Traubel (sop—Elsa), A. Varnay (sop—Ortrud), L. Melchior (ten—Lohengrin), F. Guerrera (bar—Herald), H. Janssen (bar—Telramund), D. Ernster (bass—King Heinrich), F. Stiedry (cnd), Metropolitan Opera Orch, New York Metropolitan Opera Chorus *(rec live Jan. 6, 1950)* Danacord 3–▲ DACOCD 322/24 [ADD]

Wagner, R.:Das Rheingold (sels), w. Helen Traubel (sop), Doris Doré (sgr), A. Rodzinski (cnd), New York PO—Entry of the Gods into Valhalla *(rec Carnegie Hall, New York City, Nov 25, 1945)* Enterprise ("The Radio Years" series) ▲ ENT RY 55

Wagner, R.:Siegfried (waldweben), w. Helen Traubel (sop), Doris Doré (sgr), A. Rodzinski (cnd), New York PO *(rec Carnegie Hall, New York City, Nov 25, 1945)* Enterprise ("The Radio Years" series) ▲ ENT RY 55

Wagner, R.:Tannhäuser, w. Helen Traubel (sop), Lauritz Melchior (ten/bar), Alexander Kipnis (bass), G. Szell (cnd), *(orch unknown)* Enterprise ("The Radio Years" series) 3–▲ ENT RY 26 (m)

Janssen, Herbert (bar) (cont.)
Wagner, R.:Tristan und Isolde, w. K. Flagstad (sop), S. Kalter (cta), L. Melchior (ten), E. List (bass), F. Reiner (cnd), Royal Opera House Orch, Royal Opera House Chorus Covent Garden [G] *(rec live, Covent Garden May/June 1936)* VAI Audio 3—▲ VAIA 1004-3 (m) [ADD]

Wagner, R.:Tristan und Isolde, w. Kirsten Flagstad (sop), Margarete Klose (mez), Lauritz Melchior (ten/bar), Sven Nilsson (bass), T. Beecham (cnd), Philharmonia Orch, Royal Opera House Chorus Covent Garden *(rec 1937)* Grammofono 2000 3—▲ GRM 78570 (m)

Wagner, R.:Tristan und Isolde, w. K. Flagstad (sop), M. Klose (cta), L. Melchior (ten), S. Nilsson (bass), Beecham, Reiner (cnd), *(orch unknown)*—a compilation of two 1937 live performance recordings, with some passages conducted by Beecham, others by Reiner [G]
EMI Classics ("Great Recordings of the Century" series) 3—▲ CDHC 64037

Wagner, R.:Tristan und Isolde, w. K. Flagstad (sop), L. Melchior (ten), P. Schoeffler (b-bar), T. Beecham (cnd), Royal Opera House Orch, Royal Opera House Chorus Covent Garden *(rec live, Covent Garden, 6/18 & 22/37)* Melodram 3—▲ MEL 37029 (m) [AAD]

Wagner, R.:Die Walküre (act 3), w. Helen Traubel (sop), Doris Doré (sgr), A. Rodzinski (cnd), New York PO *(rec Carnegie Hall, New York City, Nov 25, 1945)* Enterprise ("The Radio Years" series) ▲ ENT RY 55

Janssen, John (sgr)
Wagner, R.:Rienzi, der Letzte der Tribunen, w. Cheryl Studer (sop—Irene), René Kollo (ten—Rienzi), Friedrich Lenz (ten—Gesandte), Norbert Orth (ten—Baroncelli), Bodo Brinkmann (bar—Paolo Orsini), Keith Engen (bass—Cecco del Vecchio), Raimund Grumbach (bass—Steffano Colonna), Carmen Anhorn (sop—Ein Friedensbote), Karl Helm (bass—Kardinal Orvieto), John Janssen (sgr—Adriano), Alfred Kuhn (sgr—Gesandte), Hans Wilbrink (sgr—Gesandte), W. Sawallisch (cnd), Bavarian State Opera Orch, Bavarian State Opera Chorus *(rec live, July 6, 1983)* Orfeo d'or 3—▲ 346953

Janutas, Algridas (ten)
Beethoven, L. van:Syms (comp), w. Jean Glennon (sop), Dalia Schaechter (cta), Benno Schollum (bass), Y. Menuhin (cnd), Sinfonia Varsovia, Kuanas State Choir Lithuania
IMP ("IMG" series) 5—▲ IMP 6800025

Jaques, Josette (mez)
Rossini, G.:Stabat Mater, w. O. Liani (sop), M. Zamfir (ten), T. Krause (bar), P. Crispini (cnd), Geneva Elans Orch Ensemble, Geneva Elans Vocal Ensemble [L] Gallo ▲ CD 487

Jaresch, August (ten)
Strauss (II), Joh.:Die Fledermaus, w. H. Gueden (sop), J. Patzak (ten), A. Dermota (ten), A. Poell (b-bar), W. Lipp (sop), S. Wagner (ten), K. Preger (ten), C. Krauss (cnd), Vienna PO *(rec early 1950s)* London ("Historic" series) 2—▲ 425990-2 [AAD]

Jarred, Mary (cta)
Vaughan Williams, R.:Serenade to Music, w. I. Baillie (sop), E. Suddaby (sop), S. Allen (sop), E. Turner (sop), M. Balfour (cta), A. Desmond (cta), M. Brunskill (cta), H. Nash (ten), W. Widdop (ten), P. Jones (ten), F. Titterton (ten), R. Henderson (bass), R. Easton (bass), H. Williams (bass), N. Allin (bass), H. J. Wood (cnd), BBC SO Dutton Laboratories ▲ CDAX 8004 [ADD]

Vaughan Williams, R.:Serenade to Music, w. Isobel Baillie (sop), Lilian Stiles-Allen (sop), Elsie Suddaby (sop), Eva Turner (sop), Margaret Balfour (cta), Muriel Brunskill (cta), Astra Desmond (cta), Parry Jones (ten), Heddle Nash (ten), Frank Titterton (ten), Walter Widdop (ten), Roy Henderson (bar), Harold Williams (bar), Norman Allin (bass), Robert Easton (bass), H. Wood (cnd), BBC SO *(rec Abbey Road, Oct 15, 1938)* Claremont ▲ CDGSE 785066

Vaughan Williams, R.:Serenade to Music, w. I. Baillie (sop), E. Suddaby (sop), S. Allen (sop), E. Turner (sop), M. Balfour (cta), A. Desmond (cta), M. Brunskill (cta), H. Nash (ten), W. Widdop (ten), P. Jones (ten), F. Titterton (ten), R. Henderson (bass), R. Easton (bass), H. Williams (bass), N. Allin (bass), H. Wood (cnd), BBC SO [E] *(rec 10/15/38)* Pearl ▲ GEMMCD 9342 (m) [AAD]

Jaskulska, Benigna (sop)
Milwid, A.:Semper mi Iesu, w. Tutti e solo *(rec Grand Ballroom, Rydzyna Castle, Poland, Sept 1994)* Dorian Discovery ▲ DIS 80136 [DDD]

Sieprawski, P.:Justus germinavit, w. Tutti e solo *(rec Grand Ballroom, Rydzyna Castle, Poland, Sept 1994)* Dorian Discovery ▲ DIS 80136 [DDD]

Stachowicz, D.:Veni Consolator, w. Roman Gryn (tpt), Tutti e solo *(rec Grand Ballroom, Rydzyna Castle, Poland, Sept 1994)* Dorian Discovery ▲ DIS 80136 [DDD]

Szarzynski, S.S.:Veni Sancte Spiritus, w. Tutti e solo *(rec Grand Ballroom, Rydzyna Castle, Poland, Sept 1994)* Dorian Discovery ▲ DIS 80136 [DDD]

Jasper, Bella (sop)
Wagner, R.:Der Ring des Nibelungen, w. Liselotte Becker-Egner (sop—Woglinde/Ortlinde/Wellgunde), Angelika Berger (sop—Wellgunde/Waltraute), Siw Ericsdotter (sop—Norn 3), Heidemarie Ferch (sop—Freia/Gerhilde), Bella Jasper (sop—Helmwige/Waldvogel/Woglinde), Ditha Sommer (sop—Sieglinde/Gutrune), Ursula Boese (mez—Erda), Ruth Hesse (mez—Fricka), Nadezda Kniplová (mez—Brünnhilde), Margit Kobeck (mez—Schwertleite/Norn 2), Hilde Rosner (mez—Flosshilde/Siegrunde), Erica Schubert (mez—Grimgerde/Flosshilde), Ingrid Göritz (cta—Rossweisse/Norn 1), Herbert Doussant (ten—Froh), Herold Kraus (ten—Mime), Gerald McKee (ten—Siegmund/Siegfried), Fritz Uhl (ten—Loge), Rudolf Knoll (bar—Gunther/Donner), Rolf Polke (bass-bar—Wotan/Wanderer), Rolf Kühne (bass—Alberich), Takao Okamura (bass—Fafner), Otto von Rohr (bass—Hagen/Fasolt/Hunding), H. Swarowsky (cnd), Czech PO, Prague National Theater Orch *(rec June 3 & 5, July 26-31, A)* Weltbild Classics 14—▲ 703769 [ADD]

Jaszkowski, Bogumit (bass)
Bach, J.S.:St. Mark Passion, w. K. Myrlak (ten), et al., J. Bok (cnd), Warsaw SO, Warsaw Chamber Opera Chorus [L] Bongiovanni 2—▲ GB 2024/25 [ADD]

Jauquier, Charles (ten)
Pergolesi, G.B.:Mass in F, w. B. Retchizka (sop), G. Ferracini (sop), M. Minetto (cta), V. Gohl (cta), J. Loomis (bass), Milan Solisti, Plifonia Choir *(rec 1967)* Rivoalto ▲ RIV 8922 [ADD]

Jeannotte, J.-P. (ten)
Macmillan, E.:Bergerettes du Bas-Canada, w. R. Maheu (sop) *(rec July 8, 1961)*
Analekta ▲ AN 2 7804

Jedlička, Dalibor (bass)
Dvořák, A.:King & Charcoal Burner, w. Drahonira Drobkova (cta), Viktor Koci (ten), René Tucek (bar), J. Chaloupka (cnd), Prague National Theater Orch, Milan Maly (cnd), Prague National Theater Chorus *(final version) (rec 1989)* Supraphon ("Hidden Treasures from Prague" series) ▲ SUP CD 3078

Janáček, L.:The Cunning Little Vixen, w. L. Popp (sop), E. Randová (mez), C. Mackerras (cnd), Vienna PO [Cz] London 2—▲ 417129-2 [DDD]

Janáček, L.:From the House of the Dead, w. I. Zítek (sgr), V. Zítek (ten), C. Mackerras (cnd), Vienna PO, Vienna Opera Chorus London 2—▲ 430375-2 [DDD]

Janáček, L.:Káťa Kabanová, w. E. Söderström (sop), N. Kniplová (mez), P. Dvorský (ten), V. Krejčík (ten), Z. Svehla (ten), C. Mackerras (cnd), Vienna PO London 2—▲ 421852-2 [ADD]

Janáček, L.:The Makropulos Affair, w. E. Söderström (sop), V. Krejčík (ten), Z. Svehla (ten), V. Zítek (ten), C. Mackerras (cnd), Vienna PO, Vienna Opera Chorus London 2—▲ 430372-2 [ADD]

Jeffes, Peter (ten)
Rameau, J.P.:Castor et Pollux, w. P. Huttenlocher (bar), C. Farncombe (cnd), English Bach Festival Baroque Orch, English Bach Festival Singers Erato 2—▲ 95311-2

24 Aspects of an Amorous Nature, w. David Woodcock (pno) Symposium ▲ SYM 1183

Jeffreys, Anne (sgr)
Weill, K.:Street Scene, w. Polyna Stoska (sgr), M. Abravanel (cnd), Brian Sullivan Orch *(rec 1949)*
CBS ▲ MK 44668 (m) [ADD]

Jeffreys, Celia (sop)
Romberg, S.:The Student Prince (operetta), w. E. Geisen (ten), D. Honig (b-bar), S. Gyártó (ten), Hamburg State Opera Orch, Hamburg State Opera Chorus [G] Bayer ▲ 150004

Jehličková, Zora (sop)
Suk, J.:Epilogue, w. I. Kusnjer (bar), J. Galla (bass), V. Neumann (cnd), Czech PO, Czech Phil Chorus [Cz] Supraphon ▲ 11 0116-2 [DDD]

Suk, J.:Epilogue, w. Iván Kusnjer (bar), Ján Galla (bass), V. Neumann (cnd), Czech PO
Supraphon ▲ SUP 111962 [DDD]

Jelden, Georg (ten)
Furtwängler, W.:Te Deum, w. E. Mathis (sop), J. Dooley (alt), S. Wagner (cta), H. Chemin-Petit (cnd), Berlin PO *(rec live, 1967)* As Disc ▲ ASD 2506

Keiser, R.:Passions Oratorium, w. J. Bise (sop), M. Conrad (cta), U. Gilgen (bass), J.E. Dähler (cnd), Bernese Orch, Bernese Chorus [L] *(rec Feb. 1971)* Claves 2—▲ CD 9223/24 [ADD]

Schütz, H.:Die Geburt unsers Herren Jesu Christi, w. Edith Mathis (sop), Claus Ocker (bass), H. Thamm (cnd), *(ensemble unknown),* Windsbach Boys' Choir EMI Classics ("Baroque" series) ▲ CDK 65736

Jelosits, P. (cant)
Mozart, W.A.:Missa solemnis, K.337, w. E. Ziesak (sop), E. von Magnus (alt), H. Wildhaber (ten), G. Hornik (bar), H. Hüttler (cant), M. Jankowitsch (cant), I. Rainer (org), M. Haselböck (cnd), Vienna Academy, Vienna Hofburg Chapel Choir [L] *(rec Apr. 1992)* Novalis ▲ 150087 [DDD]

Jelosits, Peter (ten)
Bach, J.S.:Cant 62, w. P. Esswood (ct), K. Equiluz (ten), R. van der Meer (bass), N. Harnoncourt (cnd), Vienna Concentus Musicus, Vienna Concentus Musicus Chorus [G]
Teldec 2—▲ 2292-42565-2 [AAD]

Bach, J.S.:Cant 63, w. P. Esswood (ct), K. Equiluz (ten), R. van der Meer (bass), N. Harnoncourt (cnd), Vienna Concentus Musicus, Vienna Concentus Musicus Chorus [G]
Teldec 2—▲ 2292-42565-2 [AAD]

Bach, J.S.:Cant 64, w. P. Esswood (ct), R. van der Meer (bass), N. Harnoncourt (cnd), Vienna Concentus Musicus, Vienna Boys' Choir [G] Teldec 2—▲ 2292-42565-2 [AAD]

Jena, Else (mez)
Beethoven, L. van:Sym 9, "Choral Sym", w. Kerstin Lindberg-Torlind (sop), Erik Sjöberg (ten), Holger Byrding (bass), F. Busch (cnd), Danish National RSO, Danish National Radio Choir
Arlecchino ARL

Jenisová, Eva (sop)
Dvořák, A.:Stabat Mater, w. Hana Stolfova-Bandova (cta), Vladimir Dolezal (ten), Jiri Sulzenka (bass), L. Svárovsky (cnd), Czech PO, Petr Fiala (cnd), Brno Czech Phil Chorus Supraphon 2—▲ SUP CD 3093

Orff, C.:Carmina burana, w. V. Dolezal (ten), I. Kusnjer (bar), S. Gunzenhauser (cnd), Czech-Slovak RSO Bratislava, Slovak Phil Chorus Naxos ▲ 8.550196 [DDD] ▲ 7.550196 [DDD]

Jenkin, Nicola (sop)
Britten, B.:Hymn to St. Cecilia, w. R. Dean (sop), C. Trevor (alt), P. Daggett (ten), S. Birchall (bass), H. Christophers (cnd), The Sixteen *(rec 1 & 4/91)* Collins Classics ▲ 12862 [DDD]

Purcell, H.:Welcome to All the Pleasures, w. Ruth Holton (sop), Michael Chance (alt), Paul Tindall (ten), George Mosly (bass), J.E. Gardiner (cnd), English Baroque Soloists, Monteverdi Choir London *(rec Saint George's, Bristol, UK, July 12-14, 1990)* Philips ▲ 432114-2

Jenkins, Angela (sop)
Gay, J.:The Beggar's Opera (sels), w. P. Clark (sop), M. Cable (mez), E. Lane (mez), S. Minty (mez), E. Fleet (sgr), P. Hall (ten), V. Midgley (ten), N. Rogers (ten), J. Noble (bar), D. Stevens (cnd), Accademia Monteverdiana Orch, Accademia Monteverdiana Chorus—59 songs *(rec Aug. 1978)*
Koch Treasure ▲ 31621-2 [ADD]

Jenkins, Florence Foster (sop)
The Glory (????) of the Human Voice RCA Gold Seal ▲ 09026-61175-2

Jenkins, Neil (ten)
Byrd, W.:Mass in 3 Parts, w. A. Deller (ct), M. Bevan (bar), Deller Consort [L]
Musique d'Abord ▲ HMA 190211

Byrd, W.:Mass in 4 Parts, w. H. Sheppard (sop), A. Deller (ct), M. Bevan (bar), Deller Consort [L]
Musique d'Abord ▲ HMA 190211

Byrd, W.:Mass in 5 Parts, w. H. Sheppard (sop), A. Deller (ct), J. Buttrey (ten), M. Bevan (bar), Deller Consort [L] Musique d'Abord ▲ HMA 190211

Henze, H.-W.:Chamber Music, w. T. Walker (gtr), B. Jones (cnd), Scharoun Ensemble
Koch Schwann ▲ CD 310004 [DDD]

Vaughan Williams, R.:Hugh the Dover, w. R. Evans (sop), S. Walker (mez), B. Bottone (ten), A. Opie (bar), R. Van Allan (bass), M. Best (cnd), Corydon Orch, Corydon Singers, New London Children's Choir
Hyperion 2—▲ CDA 66901/02

Jensen, Penelope (sop)
Bach, J.S.:Magnificat, BWV 243, w. D. Upshaw (sop), M. Simpson (mez), D. Gordon (ten), W. Stone (bar), R. Shaw (cnd), Atlanta SO, Atlanta Chamber Chorus Telarc ▲ CD 80194 [DDD]

Verdi, G.:Simon Boccanegra, w. Renata Tebaldi (sop—Maria Boccanegra), Penelope Jensen (mez—Maria's Maidservant), Richard Tucker (ten—Gabriele Adorno), Rod MacWerter (ten—Paolo), Cornell MacNeil (bar—Simon Boccanegra), Ara Berberian (bar—Pietro), Ezio Flagello (bass—Jacopo Fiesco), Franco Iglesias (bass—Paolo), J. Levine (cnd), *(orch unknown) (rec live, Miami, 1970)*
Legato Classics 2—▲ LCD 189-2 [ADD]

Vivaldi, A.:Gloria, RV.589, w. D. Upshaw (sop), M. Simpson (mez), D. Gordon (ten), W. Stone (bar), R. Shaw (cnd), Atlanta SO, Atlanta Chamber Chorus Telarc ▲ CD 80194 [DDD]

Jepson, Helen (sop)
Verdi, G.:Otello (sels), w. G. Martinelli (ten), N. Massue (ten), L. Tibbett (bar), W. Pelletier (cnd), Metropolitan Opera Orch, New York Metropolitan Opera Chorus—eleven arias & scenes *(rec 1939)*
Pearl ▲ GEMMCD 9914 (m) [AAD]

Jepson, Kristine (mez)
Mahler, G.:Sym 8, w. Oksana Krovytska (sop—Magna Peccatrix), Sheila Smith (sop—Una poenitentium), Shauna Southwich (sop—Mater gloriosa), Kristine Jepson (mez—Maria Aegyptiaca), Julie Simson (mez—Mulier Samaritana), Kurt Hansen (ten—Doctor Marianus), Brian Steele (bar—Pater ecstaticus), Eugene Green (b-bar—Pater profundus), R. Olson (cnd), Colorado MahlerFest Orch, Colorado MahlerFest Chorale, Colorado Mormon Chorale, Colorado Children's Chorale *(rec MahlerFest VIII, Boulder, CO, Jan 14-15, 1995)* MahlerFest 2—▲ MF8-1

Jeranje, Tatiana (ten)
Gretchaninoff, A.:Missa Sancti Spiritus, w. V. Polianski (cnd), Russian State SO, Russian State Symphonic Cappella Chandos ▲ CHAN 9397 [DDD]

Jerger, Alfred (b-bar)
Mozart, W.A.:Nozze di Figaro (sels), w. Maria Reining (sop—Countess), Margherita Perras (sop—Susanna), Alfred Jerger (b-bar—Count), Paul Schöffler (b-bar—Figaro), W. Loibner (cnd), Vienna State Opera Orch *(rec May 24, 1938)* Koch Schwann 2—▲ SCH 314632 [ADD]

Nicolai, O.:Lustigen Weiber (sel), w. A. Jerger (b-bar—Herr Fluth), L. Hofmann (bass—Falstaff), F. von Weingartner (cnd), Vienna State Opera Orch *(rec Oct. 28, 1935)* Koch Schwann ▲ SCH 314602

Smetana, B.:Dalibor (sels), w. Hilde Konetzni (sop—Milada), Todor Mazaroff (ten—Dalibor), Alfred Jerger (bar—König), L. Ludwig (cnd), Vienna State Opera Orch *(rec Vienna, Nov. 21, 1942)*
Koch Schwann ▲ SCH 314692 [ADD]

Strauss (II), Joh.:Eine Nacht in Venedig, w. E. Réthy (sop), M. Schober (sop), R. Boesch (bar), K. Friedrich (ten), K. Preger (ten), A. Paulik (cnd), Vienna SO, Bregenz Festival Choir [G] *(rec 1951)*
Koch Schwann 3—▲ 3-1272-2 [ADD]

Strauss, R.:Arabella (sels), w. Margit Bokor (sop—Zdenka), Viorica Ursuleac (sop—Arabella), Alfred Jerger (bar—Mandryka), Richard Mayr (bass—Waldner), C. Krauss (cnd), Vienna State Opera Orch *(rec Vienna, Oct. 29, 1933)* Koch Schwann ▲ SCH 314625 [ADD]

Wagner, R.:Die Meistersinger von Nürnberg (sels), w. V. Ursuleac (sop—Eva), M. Lorenz (ten—Walther), E. Zimmermann (ten—David), A. Jerger (b-bar—Hans Sachs), C. Krauss (cnd), Vienna State Opera Orch, Vienna State Opera Chorus *(rec Feb. 26, 1933)* Koch Schwann 2—▲ SCH 314562 [ADD]

Wagner, R.:Die Meistersinger von Nürnberg (sels), w. V. Ursuleac (sop—Eva), F. Völker (ten—Walther), A. Jerger (b-bar—Hans Sachs), C. Krauss (cnd), Vienna State Opera Orch, Vienna State Opera Chorus *(rec Apr. 13, 1934)* Koch Schwann 2—▲ SCH 314602

Wagner, R.:Die Walküre (act 2), w. M. Fuchs (sop), E. Flesch (sop), L. Lehmann (sop), M. Klose (cta), L. Melchior (ten), H. Hotter (b-bar), E. List (bass), B. Walter (cnd), Berlin State Opera Orch [G] *(rec 9/38 & 6/22/35)* Danacord 2—▲ DACOCD 317/18 (m)

Wagner, R.:Die Walküre (act 2), w. M. Fuchs (sop), E. Flesch (sop), L. Lehmann (sop), M. Klose (cta), L. Melchior (ten), H. Hotter (b-bar), E. List (bass), B. Walter (cnd), Berlin State Opera Orch [G] *(rec 9/38 & 6/22/35)* EMI Classics ("References" series) ▲ CDH 64255

Jerger, Alfred (b-bar) (cont.)
Weill, K.:The Threepenny Opera, w. Liane (sop—Polly Peachum), A. Felbermayer (sop—Lucy), H. Fassler (sop—Jenny), R. Anday (cta—Mrs. Peachum), K. Preger (ten—Macheath), H. Roswaenge (ten—Street Crier), A. Jerger (bar—Peachum), F. Gutherie (bar), *(cnd & orch unknown)* Vanguard Classics ▲ OVC 8057 [ADD]

Jerič, Ana Pusar (sop)
Dvořák, A.:Stabat Mater, w. E. N. Houska (mez), J. Reja (ten), F. Petrusanec (bass), M. Munih (cnd), Ljubljana RSO, Ljubljana Radio Chorus [L] PMG (Vienna Master) ▲ CD 160104 [DDD]

Jerico, Santiago S. (bar)
Vives, A.:Doña Francisquita, w. R. Pierotti (sgr), A. R. Marbà (cnd), Tenerife SO Valois 2-▲ V 4710

Jeritza, Maria (sop)
Arias & Songs *(rec between 1914 & 1927)* Preiser ▲ PRE 89079 [AAD]
Joseph Schmidt, w. Joseph Schmidt (ten), Berlin RSO [cnd:Rudolf Hindemith, Bruno Seidler-Winkler, Hermann Scherchen, Fritz Stiedry, Max von Schillings], unknown orchestra [cnd:Idris Lewis], General Motors SO, General Motors Sym Chorus [cnd:Erno Rapee, José Iturbi, Oscar Straus], Helen Gleas Koch Schwann ▲ SCH 312572 [ADD]
Mascagni, P.:Cavalleria rusticana (sels), w. Maria Jeritza (sop—Santuzza), Helge Roswaenge (ten—Turiddu), H. Reichenberger (cnd), Vienna State Opera Orch *(rec Vienna, Sept. 26, 1933)* Koch Schwann 2-▲ SCH 314622 [ADD]
Wagner, R.:Die Walküre (sels), w. Maria Jeritza (sop—Brünnhilde), Felice Hüni-Mišek (sop—Sieglinde), Franz Völker (ten—Siegmund), Friedrich Schorr (b-bar—Wotan), C. Krauss (cnd), Vienna State Opera Orch *(rec June 11, 1933)* Koch Schwann 2-▲ SCH 314642 [ADD]
Wagner, R.:Die Walküre (sels), w. Lotte Lehmann (sop—Sieglinde), Maria Jeritza (sop—Brünnhilde), Franz Völker (ten—Siegmund), Friedrich Schorr (bass—Wotan), C. Krauss (cnd), Vienna State Opera Orch *(rec Vienna, Sept. 14, 1933)* Koch Schwann ▲ SCH 314622 [ADD]

Jerry, Mungo (bar)
Danova, R.:The Phantom of the Opera on Ice, w. Susannah Glanville (sop), Kathy Dooley (sop), Johnny Logan (ten), Stephen Lee Garden (ten), Nigel Paul (bar), P. Whitfield (cnd), Northern Light SO, Northern Light Choir, Russian Stars on Ice Chorus Plaza ▲ PZA 008

Jerusalem, Siegfried (ten)
Bach, J.S.:Cant 21, w. Arleen Augér (sop), Ortrun Wenkel (cta), Peter Schreier (ten), Theo Adam (b-bar), H.-J. Rotzsch (cnd), New Bach Collegium Musicum, Leipzig St. Thomas Church Choir Berlin Classics ▲ BER 2175 [ADD]
Bach, J.S.:Cant 137, w. Arleen Augér (sop), Ortrun Wenkel (cta), Peter Schreier (ten), Theo Adam (b-bar), H.-J. Rotzsch (cnd), New Bach Collegium Musicum, Leipzig St. Thomas Church Choir Berlin Classics ▲ BER 2175 [ADD]
Beethoven, L. van:Sym 9, "Choral Sym", w. A. Marc (sop), I. Vermillion (mez), F. Struckmann (bar), D. Barenboim (cnd), Berlin State Opera Orch, Berlin State Opera Chorus Erato ▲ 94353-2
Beethoven, L. van:Sym 9, "Choral Sym", w. H. Donath (sop), D. Soffel (mez), P. Lika (bass), S. Celibidache (cnd), Munich PO, Munich Phil Chorus *(rec Mar. 19, 1989)* Exclusive ▲ EXL 15 [AAD]
Haydn, J.:Die Jahreszeiten, w. Edith Mathis (sop), Dietrich Fischer-Dieskau (bar), N. Marriner (cnd), Academy of St. Martin in the Fields Philips ("Duo" series) 2-▲ 438715-2
Korngold, E.W.:Violanta, w. E. Martón (sop), W. Berry (bass), M. Janowski (cnd), Munich RSO, Bavarian Radio Chorus [G] CBS ▲ MK 35909 [ADD]
Liszt, F.:A Faust Sym, w. G. Solti (cnd), Chicago SO, Chicago Sym Chorus [G] London ▲ 417399-2 [DDD]
Mozart, W.A.:Arias, w. E. Steber (sop), I. Cotrubas (sop), K. Te Kanawa (sop), R. Stevens (mez), P. Domingo (ten), G. London (bar), E. Pinza (bass)—arias & duets from Don Giovanni, Le nozze di Figaro, Die Zauberflöte, etc. *(rec 1941-1978)* CBS Masterworks ▲ MDK 46579 [AAD] ■ MGT 46579
Mozart, W.A.:Requiem, w. A. Augér (sop), C. Watkinson (cta), S. Nimsgern (b-bar), H. Rilling (cnd), Stuttgart Bach Ensemble, Gächinger Kantorei [L] Odyssey ▲ MBK 42614 ■ YT 42614
Mozart, W.A.:Zauberflöte, w. L. Popp (sop), E. Gruberova (sop), W. Brendel (bar), R. Bracht (bass), B. Haitink (cnd), Bavarian RSO, Bavarian Radio Chorus [G] EMI Classics 3-▲ CDCC 47951 [DDD]
Mozart, W.A.:Zauberflöte (sels), w. L. Popp (sop), E. Gruberova (sop), W. Brendel (bar), R. Bracht (bass), B. Haitink (cnd), Bavarian RSO, Bavarian Radio Chorus [G] EMI Classics ▲ CDC 47008 [DDD]
Schoenberg, A.:Gurrelieder, w. S. Dunn (sop), B. Fassbaender (mez), P. Haage (ten), H. Becht (bass), H. Hotter (nar), R. Chailly (cnd), Berlin RSO, St. Hedwig's Cathedral Choir, Düsseldorf Municipal Choral Society [G] London 2-▲ 430321-2 [DDD]
Schumann, R.:Dichterliebe, w. E. Bashkirova (pno) Erato ▲ 2292-45740-2 ZK
Schumann, R.:Liederkreis, Op. 39, w. E. Bashkirova (pno) Erato ▲ 2292-45740-2 ZK
Wagner, R.:Götterdämmerung, w. E. Marton (sop), T. Hampson (bar), J. Tomlinson (bass), B. Haitink (cnd), Bavarian RSO [G] EMI Classics 4-▲ CDCD 54485
Wagner, R.:Lohengrin, w. Cheryl Studer (sop), Waltraud Meier (mez), Andreas Schmidt (bar), Harmut Welker (bar), Kurt Moll (bass), C. Abbado (cnd), Vienna PO Deutsche Grammophon 3-▲ 437808-2
Wagner, R.:Lohengrin (sels), w. C. Studer (sop), W. Meier (mez), B. Terfel (bar), C. Abbado (cnd), Berlin PO Deutsche Grammophon ▲ 439768-2
Wagner, R.:Die Meistersinger von Nürnberg (sels), w. C. Studer (sop), W. Meier (mez), B. Terfel (bar), C. Abbado (cnd), Berlin PO Deutsche Grammophon ▲ 439768-2
Wagner, R.:Das Rheingold, w. B. Svendén (sop), C. Ludwig (mez), H. Zednik (ten), E. Wlaschiha (bar), J. Morris (bass), J. Levine (cnd), Metropolitan Opera Orch [G] Deutsche Grammophon 3-▲ 427607-2 [DDD]
Wagner, R.:Der Ring des Nibelungen (sels), w. E. Marton (sop), C. Studer (sop), K. Te Kanawa (sop), M. Lipovšek (mez), R. Goldberg (ten), P. Haage (ten), J. Morris (bass), B. Haitink (cnd), Bayer RSO EMI Classics ▲ ZDC 54633
Wagner, R.:Der Ring des Nibelungen (sels), w. J. Norman (sop), H. Behrens (sop), K. Battle (sop), J. Morris (mez), C. Ludwig (mez), R. Goldberg (ten), E. Wlaschiha (bar), M. Salminen (bass), J. Levine (cnd), Metropolitan Opera Orch—The Compact Ring—Ride of the Valkyries Wotan's Farewell & Magic Fire Music, Forest Murmurs, Brünnhilde's Awakening, Siegfried's Funeral Music, Brünnhilde's Immolation, & others Deutsche Grammophon ▲ 437825-2
Wagner, R.:Der Ring des Nibelungen (sels), w. Jessye Norman (sop), Lucia Popp (sop), René Kollo (ten), Kurt Moll (bass), Matti Salminen (bass), M. Janowski (cnd), Dresden Staatskapelle RCA Victor ▲ 09026-68084-2; ■ 09026-68084-4
Wagner, R.:Siegfried, w. K. Te Kanawa (sop), E. Marton (sop), P. Haage (ten), J. Morris (bass), B. Haitink (cnd), Bavarian RSO [G] EMI Classics 4-▲ CDCD 54290
Wagner, R.:Siegfried, w. A. Evans (sop—Brünhilde), H. Leidland (sop—Waldvogel), B. Svendén (mez—Erda), S. Jerusalem (ten—Siegfried), G. Clark (ten—Mime), J. Tomlinson (bass—Der Wanderer), G. von Kannen (bass—Alberich), P. Kang (bass), *(cnd & orch unknown)* Teldec 4-▲ 4509-94193-2 [DDD]
Wagner, R.:Tannhäuser (sels), w. C. Studer (sop), W. Meier (mez), B. Terfel (bar), C. Abbado (cnd), Berlin PO Deutsche Grammophon ▲ 439768-2
Wagner, R.:Die Walküre (sels), w. C. Studer (sop), W. Meier (mez), B. Terfel (bar), C. Abbado (cnd), Berlin PO Deutsche Grammophon ▲ 439768-2
Weinberger, J.:Schwanda der Dudelsackpfeifer, w. L. Popp (sop), G. Killebrew (mez), H. Prey (bar), S. Nimsgern (bass), H. Wallberg (cnd), Munich RSO, Bavarian Radio Chorus [F] CBS 3-▲ M3K 36926 [ADD]

Jess, G. (bass)
Britten, H.:A Boy Was Born, w. S. Leonard (sop), N. Tibbels (sop), S. Bickley (mez), P. Hall (ten), T. Edwards (cnd), London Sinfonietta Chorus, St. Paul's Cathedral Choristers Virgin Classics ▲ CDC 59136
Britten, H.:Hymn to St. Cecilia, w. S. Leonard (sop), N. Tibbels (sop), S. Bickley (mez), P. Hall (ten), T. Edwards (cnd), London Sinfonietta Chorus, St. Paul's Cathedral Choir Virgin Classics ▲ CDC 59136
Britten, H.:Sonnets of Michelangelo, w. S. Leonard (sop), N. Tibbels (sop), S. Bickley (mez), P. Hall (ten), T. Edwards (cnd), London Sinfonietta Chorus, Choristers of St. Paul's Cathedral Virgin Classics ▲ CDC 59136

Jette, Maria (sop)
Argento, D.:Vars for Orch [The Mask of Night], w. P. Brunelle (cnd), Plymouth Festival Orch [E] Virgin Classics ▲ CDC 59009-2 [DDD]

Jetter, Margret (cta)
Bach, J.S.:Cant 150, w. M. Schreiber (sop), P. Maus (ten), H.-F. Kunz (bass), H. Rilling (cnd), Bach Ensemble *(rec June-July 1970)* Hänssler Classic ▲ 98.835 [AAD]

Jeun, S. (sop)
Rossini, G.:La cambiale di matrimonio, w. S. Jeun (sop—Fanny), M. Laurenza (sop—Clarina), L. Canonici (ten—Edoardo Milfort), R. Frontali (bar—Slook), E. Dara (bar—Tobia Mill), D. Renzetti (cnd), Turin RAI Orch *(rec Aug. 1991)* Ricordi ▲ RFCD 2011 [DDD]

Jevtovic, Phoebe (sgr)
Caccini, F.:La liberazione di Ruggiero dall'isola d'Alcina, w. Linda De Rungs (sop—Alcian/Vistola), Cecilia Amorocho (sgr—Melissa/Nunzia), Laura Lea Duckworth (sgr—Siren/Harpy), Eric Friedlander (sgr—Monster), L. Ernest Gross (sgr—Enchanted Cypress), Phoebe Jevtovic (sgr—Siren), James Rittenhouse (sgr—Ruggiero/Neptune), Sharon Sim (sgr—Siren), R. Burchard (cnd), Ars Femina Ensemble, TimeChange *(rec Louisville, KY, 1993)* Nannerl ▲ NR-ARS 003; ■ NR-ARS 003

Jezovšek, Vasiljka (sop)
Bach, J.S.:Cant 57, w. Sarah Connolly (cta), Mark Padmore (ten), Peter Kooy (bass), Phillippe Herreweghe (cnd), Collegium Vocale Harmonia Mundi ▲ HMC 901594
Bach, J.S.:Cant 110, w. Sarah Connolly (cta), Mark Padmore (ten), Peter Kooy (bass), Phillippe Herreweghe (cnd), Collegium Vocale Harmonia Mundi ▲ HMC 901594
Bach, J.S.:Cant 122, w. Sarah Connolly (cta), Mark Padmore (ten), Peter Kooy (bass), Phillippe Herreweghe (cnd), Collegium Vocale Harmonia Mundi ▲ HMC 901594

Jindrák, Jindřich (bar)
Dvořák, A.:Zigeunermelodien, Op. 55, w. Alfréd Holecek (pno) Supraphon ▲ SUP 0206 [AAD]
Roussel, A.:Evocations, w. Marie Mrázová (cta), Zdenek Svehla (ten), Z. Košler (cnd), Czech PO, Czech Phil Chorus Supraphon ▲ SUP 111823 [AAD]
Smetana, B.:Dalibor, w. N. Kniplova (mez), V. Pribyl (ten), J. Krombholc (cnd), Prague National Theater Orch, Prague National Theater Chorus [Cz] Supraphon 2-▲ 11 2185 [ADD]

Jirásek, Jan (voc/syn)
Jirásek, J.:Labyrinth, w. Irmela Nolte (fl), Pavel Skála (perc) *(rec Audiostudio of Czech Radio, Prague)* Arta ▲ 0054 [DDD]

Jirglova, Milada (sop)
Janácek, L.:From the House of the Dead, w. V. Pribyl (ten), J. Horacek (bass), R. Novák (bass), V. Neumann (cnd), Czech PO, Czech Phil Chorus [Cz] Supraphon 2-▲ SUP 10 2941 [AAD]

Jo, Sumi (sop)
Auber, D.-F.:Le Domino noir, w. Doris Lamprecht (sop), Martine Olmeda (sop), Isabelle Vernet (sop), Jocelyne Taillon (mez), Bruce Ford (ten), Patrick Power (ten), Gilles Cachemaille (bar), Jules Bastin (bass), R. Bonynge (cnd), English CO, London Voices London 2-▲ 440646-2
Carnaval:French Arias, w. Jo, Sumi (sop), English CO [cnd:R. Bonynge] London ▲ 440679-2 [DDD]
Mahler, G.:Sym 8, w. C. Studer (sop), W. Meier (mez), K. Lewis (ten), T. Allen (bar), H. Sotin (bass), G. Sinopoli (cnd), Philharmonia Orch, Philharmonia Chorus, Southend Boys' Choir [G] Deutsche Grammophon 2-▲ 435433-2
Mozart, W.A.:Zauberflöte, w. B. Bonney (sop—Pamina), S. Jo (sop—Queen of the Night), K. Streit (ten—Tamino), G. Cachemaille (b-bar—Papageno), K. Sigmundsson (bass—Sarastro), A. Östman (cnd), Drottningholm Court Theater Orch, Drottingholm Court Thea Chorus L'Oiseau-Lyre 2-▲ 440085-2 [DDD]
Mozart, W.A.:Zauberflöte, w. L. Orgonasova (sop), Martina Bovet (sop), G. Winbergh (ten), H. Hagegard (bar), A. Jordan (cnd), Paris Orchestral Ensemble, Romande Chamber Choir, Pro Arte Lausanne Erato 2-▲ 2292-45469-2 [DDD]
Mozart, W.A.:Zauberflöte, w. R. Ziesak (sop), U. Heilmann (ten), A. Kraus (ten), K. Moll (bass), G. Solti (cnd), Vienna PO, Vienna State Opera Chorus London 2-▲ 433210-2 [DDD]
Mozart, W.A.:Zauberflöte (sels), w. J. Protschka (ten), H. Prey (bar)—Ov., arias & choruses LaserLight ▲ 15 888 [DDD]
Mozart, W.A.:Zauberflöte (sels), w. R. Ziesak (sop), U. Heilmann (ten), A. Kraus (ten), K. Moll (bass), G. Solti (cnd), Vienna PO, Vienna State Opera Chorus London ▲ 433667-2 [DDD]
Orff, C.:Carmina burana, w. J. Kowalski (alt), B. Skovhus (bar), Z. Mehta (cnd), London PO, London Phil Choir, Southend Boys' Choir Teldec ▲ 74886-2
Rossini, G.:Tancredi, w. Sumi Jo (sop—Amenaide), Lucretia Lendi (mez—Roggiero), Anna Maria di Micco (mez—Isaura), Ewa Podles (cta—Tancredi), Stanford Olsen (ten—Argirio), Pietro Spagnoli (bar—Orbazzano), Ewald Demeyere (hpd), Lieven Baert (vc), Franck Coryn (db), A. Zedda (cnd), Collegium Instrumentale Brugense, Capella Brugensis *(rec Poissy Theatre & Centre Musical-Lyrique-Phonographique, Ile de France, Jan. 26-31, 1994)* Naxos ("Opera Classics" series) 2-▲ 8.660037/38 [DDD]
Verdi, G.:Un ballo in maschera, w. J. Barstow (sop), F. Quivar (mez), P. Domingo (ten), L. Nucci (bar), H. von Karajan (cnd), Vienna PO, Vienna State Opera Chorus [I] Deutsche Grammophon 2-▲ 427635-2 [DDD]
Virtuoso Arias, w. Monte Carlo PO [cnd:Paolo Olmi] *(rec Auditorium de l'Orchestre Philharmonique, Monte Carlo, June 1994)* Erato ▲ 97239-2 [DDD]

Jobin, Raoul (ten)
Bizet, G.:Carmen (sels), w. Risë Stevens (sop), N. Conner (sop), R. Woodo (bar), G. Sébastian (cnd), Metropolitan Opera Orch, New York Metropolitan Opera Chorus [F] Odyssey ■ YT 32102 (m)
Great Voices of Canada, Vol. 3 Analekta ▲ AN 27803
Her First Recordings, w. Eleanor Steber (sop), Armand Tokatyan (ten), Lucielle Browning (mez), Pino Bontempi (sgr), Annamary Dickey (sgr), George Cehanovsky (bar), Lorenzo Alvary ((bass), A. Kent (bar), Norman Cordon (bass) VAI Audio ▲ VAIA 1023 (m) [ADD]
Offenbach, J.:Les Contes d'Hoffmann, w. Patrice Munsel (sop), Jarmila Novotná (sop), Ezio Pinza (bass), T. Beecham (cnd), Metropolitan Opera Orch, New York Metropolitan Opera Chorus *(rec Feb 26, 1944)* Enterprise ("The Radio Years") 2-▲ ENT-19 (m)

Jochens, Wilfried (ten)
Bach, J.S.:St. Matthew Passion, w. Monika Frimmer (sop), Veronika Winter (sop), Lena Susanne Norin (alt), Christoph Prégardien (ten), Klaus Mertens (bass), Hans-Georg Wimmer (bass), H. Max (cnd), Das Kliene Konzert, Rhineland Kantorei Capriccio 2-▲ 60 046 [DDD]
Bach, W.F.:Cants (misc), w. B. Schlick (soprano), C. Schubert (contralto), J. Schreckenberger (bass), Rheinische Kantorei, H. Max (cnd), Das Kleine Konzert—Dies ist der Tag; Erzittert und fallet Capriccio ▲ 10 426 [DDD]
Bach, W.F.:Cants (misc), w. B. Schlick (soprano), C. Schubert (contralto), J. Schreckenberger (bass), Rheinische Kantorei, H. Max (cnd), Das Kleine Konzert—Lasset uns ablegen die Werke der Finsternis; Es ist eine Stimme eines Predigers in der Wüste Capriccio ▲ 10 425 [DDD]
Brassart, J.:Ave Maria, w. A. Teichert-Hailperin (sop), K. Smith (ct), M. Nitz (ten), Helga Weber Instrumental Circle Entrée ▲ 0041 [ADD]
Distler, H.:Choral-Passion, w. W. Jochens (ten—Evangelist), P. Kooy (bass—Jesus), G. Miehlke (bass—Pilatus), W. Gundlach (cnd), Dortmund Univ Chamber Choir *(rec Mar. 1993)* Thorofon ▲ CTH 2185 [DDD]
Dufay, G.:Magnificat, w. A. Teichert-Hailperin (sop), K. Smith (ct), Helga Weber Instrumental Circle—Octavi toni for 3 voices Entrée ▲ 0041 [ADD]
Dunstable, J.:Sacred Music, w. A. Teichert-Hailperin (sop), K. Smith (ct), M. Nitz (ten), H. Deutsch (bar), Helga Weber Instrumental Circle—Sancta Maria; Beata dei genetrix; Beata mater et innupta virgo; Speciosa facta es; Alma redemptoris mater Entrée ▲ 0041 [ADD]
Gabrieli, G.:Music of, w. David Cordier (alt), Rufus Müller (ten), Gerd Türk (ten), Harry van der Kamp (bass), R. Wilson (cnd), Musica Fiata, La Capella Ducale—Toccata [arr Wilson]; Buccinate in neomenia tuba à 19; Canzon XVII à 12; Dulcis Jesu patris imago [Son con voce à 20]; Timor et remor à 6; Son con 3 Vns; Son XIX à 15; In ecclesiis à 14; Canzon V à 7; Jubilate Deo à 10; Son XVIII à 14; Cantate Domino à 8; Canzon primi toni à 10; Misericordia tua Domine à 12; Canzon X à 8; Toccata primi toni; Magnificat à 33 [reconstructed by Wilson]; Benedictus es Dominus à 8 *(rec St. Osdag Church, Mandelsloh, Germany, June 11-15, 1994)* Sony Classical ("Vivarte" series) 2-▲ S2K 66254 [DDD]
Grandi, A.:Sacred Music, w. David Cordier (alt), Rufus Müller (ten), Gerd Türk (ten), Harry van der Kamp (bass), R. Wilson (cnd), Musica Fiata, La Capella Ducale—Heu mihi [Dialogo à 4]; O quam tu pulchra es; Cantemus Domino; Salvum me fac, Deus [Basso solo] *(rec St. Osdag Church, Mandelsloh, Germany, June 11-15, 1994)* Sony Classical ("Vivarte" series) 2-▲ S2K 66254 [DDD]

Jochens, Wilfried (ten) (cont.)
Hildegard Of Bingen:Sacred Songs, w. A. Teichert-Hailperin (sop), K. Smith (ct), M. Nitz (ten), H. Deutsch (bar), Helga Weber Instrumental Circle—Caritas abundat in omnia; O virtus sapientiae; O quam mirabilis; Hodie aperuit nobis clausa porta; Alleluia. O virga, mediatrix; O clarissima mater; O frondens virga Entrée ▲ 0041 [ADD]
Love Songs from the 14th & 15th Centuries, w. Almut Teichert-Hailperin (sop), Kevin Smith (ct), Martin Nitz (ten), Instrumentalkreis Helga Weber Entrée ▲ CHE 0042-2 [ADD]
Monteverdi, C.:Salve, o Regina, w. R. Wilson (cnd), Musica Fiata *(rec St. Osdag Church, Mandelsloh, Germany, June 11-15, 1994)* Sony Classical ("Vivarte" series) 2-▲ S2K 66254 [DDD]
Schelle, J.:Actus Musicus auf Weyh-Nachten, w. Mona Spägle (sop), H. Arman (cnd), Schütz Academy *(rec Dec 15-18, 1992)* Capriccio ▲ 10508 [DDD]
Schütz, H.:Weihnachtshistorie, w. Mona Spägle (sop), H. Arman (cnd), Schütz Academy *(rec Dec 15-18, 1992)* Capriccio ▲ 10508 [DDD]

Jochims, Wilfrid (nar)
Bach, J.S.:Cant 211, "Coffee Cant", w. Elisabeth Speiser (sop—Lieschen), Claus Ocker (bass—Schlendrian), R. Ewerhart (cnd), Württemberg CO *(rec 1966)* Vox Box 3-▲ CD3X 3039

Jochims, Wilfrid (ten)
Bach, J.S.:Cant 208, "Hunting Cant", w. Helen Donath (sop), Elisabeth Speiser (sop), Jakob Stämpfli (bass), H. Rilling (cnd), Stuttgart Bach Collegium, Stuttgart Memorial Church Figuralchor *(rec Southwest Sound Studio, Stuttgart-Bottnang, May 1965)* Musicaphon ▲ 51351 [AAD]

Jõgeva, Mare (mez)
Tubin, E.:Barbara von Tisenhusen, w. H. Raamat (sop), A. Kollo (ten), I. Kuusk (ten), V. Puura (bar), T. Sild (bar), H. Miilberg (bass), U. Kreen (bass), P. Lilje (cnd), Estonia Opera Co Orch [Estonian] Ondine 2-▲ ODE 776-2D [DDD]

Johanning, Beth (sop)
Wagner, S.:Banadietrich, w. Vivian Hanner (sgr), Volker Horn (ten), André Wenhold (bar), Andreas Schmidt (bar), Adalbert Walker (bass), V. Gailis (cnd), Thuringian SO, Rudolstadt Festival Chorus *(rec Rudolstädt, June 1995)* Marco Polo 2-▲ 8.223895-6 [DDD]
Wagner, S.:Der Bärenhäuter, w. B. Johanning (sop—Luise), K. Likic (sop—Lene), T. Koon (sop—Gunda), V. Horn (ten—Hans Kraft), A. Feilhaber (ten—Nikolaus Spitz), R. Hartmann (bar—Kaspar Wild), A. Wenhold (bar—Stranger), A. Waller (bass—Devil), H. Kiichli (bass—Melchior Fröhlich), K. Bach (cnd), Thüringian SO, Thüringian State Theater Chorus *(rec Rudolstadt, July 25-31, 1993)* Marco Polo ("Opera Classics" series) 2-▲ 8.223713/4 [DDD]
Wagner, S.:Schwarzschwanenreich, w. Beth Johanning (sop—Linda), Kerstin Quandt (cta—Ursula), Walter Raffeiner (ten—Ludwig), Lucian Chioreanu (ten—A Boy), André Wenhold (bar—Oswald), Roland Hartmann (sgr—Tempter/Priest), Jutta Maria Schmitz (sgr—Ash-Woman), Ksenija Lukie (sgr—A Girl), K. Bach (cnd), Thüringian Saalfeld-Rudolstadt SO, Thüringian Landestheater Rudolstadt Chorus *(rec Thüringer Landestheater, Rudolstadt, June 1994)* Marco Polo 2-▲ 8.223777-8 [DDD]

Johansen, Joanna (sop)
Rasmussen, S.:Landið, w. P. Vronský (cnd), Slovak RSO Bratislava *(rec Oct. 1993)* Tutl ▲ FKT 7
Sandagerðl Paulil:Gerandisdagurl Havn, w. P. Vronsky (cnd), Slovak RSO Bratislava *(rec Oct. 1993)* Tutl ▲ FKT 7

Johansen, Mogens Schmidt (bar)
Kuhlau, F.:Elverhøj, w. Bodil Gøbel (sop), Gurli Plesner (cta), J. Frandsen (cnd), Danish National RSO, Danish National Radio Choir *(rec Danish Radio Concert Hall, Aug 1974)* Marco Polo/Dacapo ▲ 8.224053 [AAD]

Johansen, Ronnie (sgr)
Cornelius, P.:Der Cid, w. Gertrud Ottenthal (sop), Robert Schunk (ten), Albert Dohmen (bar), Michael Schopper (bass), Endrik Wottrich (sgr), G. Kuhn (cnd), Berlin RSO, Berlin Radio Chorus Koch Schwann 2-▲ SCH 315222

Johansson, Eva (sop)
Gade, N.W.:Elverskud, w. A. Gjevang (cta), P. Elming (ten), D. Kitayenko (cnd), Danish National RSO, Danish National Radio Chamber Choir [Da] Chandos ▲ CHAN 9075 [DDD]

John, Elton (sgr)
Pavarotti & Friends for War Child, w. Luciano Pavarotti (ten), Eric Clapton (sgr), Sheryl Crow (sgr), Liza Minelli (sgr), Joan Osborne (sgr), Jon Secada (sgr), Eric Clapton (gtr), John McLaughlin (gtr), Marco Armiliato, Edoardo Bennato, José Molina, Al DiMeola, Kelly Family, Ligabue, Litfiba, P *(rec Modena, Italy, 1996)* London ▲ 452900-2 ■ 452900-4

Johns, William (ten)
Mercadante, S.:Il bravo, w. Miwako Matsumoto (sop—Violetta), Giovanna di Rocco (sop—Michelina), William Johns (ten—Il Bravo), Antonio Savastano (ten—Pisani), Gino Sinimberghi (ten—Cappello), Loris Gambelli (bass—Marco), Mario Machi (bass—Luigi), Paolo Washington (bass—Foscari), Maria Parazzini (sgr—Teodora), G. Ferro (cnd), Rome Opera Orch, Rome Opera Chorus *(rec Rome, Dec 30, 1976)* Italia 3-▲ CDC 94 [ADD]

Johnson (sgr)
Berlioz, H.:L'Enfance du Christ, w. A. S. von Otter (mez), G. Cachemaille (bar), J. Van Dam (b-bar), J. Bastin (bass), J.E. Gardiner (cnd), Lyon Opera Orch, Monteverdi Choir London [F] Erato 2-▲ 2292-45275-2 [DDD]

Johnson, C. (sgr)
Rodgers, R.:Carousel, w. J. Raitt (sgr), J. Clayton (sgr), J. Darling (sgr), E. Mattson (sgr), M. Vye (sgr), C. Baxter (sgr), J. Littau (cnd) [1945 cast] MCA Classics ▲ MCAD 10048 [AAD] ■ MCAC 10048

Johnson, David Wilson (bar)
Mussorgsky, M.:Sorochintsy Fair (sels), w. G. Rozhdestvensky (cnd), BBC SO, BBC Sym Chorus, BBC Singers [E] IMP ("BBC Radio Classics" series) ▲ IMP 9139

Johnson, Douglas (ten)
Gazzaniga, G.:Don Giovanni, w. L. Serra (sop), E. Szmytka (sop), E. Schmid-Lienbacher (sop), F. Furlanetto (bass), B. Weil (cnd), Tafelmusik Sony Classical ("Vivarte" series) ▲ SK 46693
Haydn, J.:Applausus:Jubilaeum virtutis Palatium, w. Rosemary Musoleno (sop—Temperantia), Kirsten Dolberg (mez—Prudentia), Douglas Johnson (ten—Justitia), Desmond Byrne (bass—Fortitudo), Jean-Philippe Courtis (bass—Theologia), P. Fournillier (cnd), Picardie Orch, Haydn Vocal Ensemble [L] *(rec 9/91)* Opus 111 2-▲ OPS 61-9207/8 [DDD]

Johnson, Edward (ten)
Great Voices of Canada, Vol. 2 Analekta ▲ AN 27802

Johnson, Elizabeth (cta)
Hovhaness, A.:Magnificat, w. Audrey Nossaman (sop), Thomas East (ten), Richard Dales (bar), R. Whitney (cnd), Louisville Orch, Univ of Louisville Choir Crystal ▲ CD 808
Sullivan, A.:HMS Pinafore, w. D. Hays (sop), M. Rawlins (sgr), C. Freeman (ten), E. Schilling (sgr), M. Elder (cnd), Rochester PO, Eastman Chorale members—highlights *(rec 11/89)* Pro Arte ▲ CDd 480 [DDD]
Sullivan, A.:The Mikado, w. D. Hays (sop), M. Rawlins (sgr), C. Freeman (ten), E. Schilling (sgr), M. Elder (cnd), Rochester PO, Eastman Chorale members—highlights *(rec 11/89)* Pro Arte ▲ CDd 480 [DDD]
Sullivan, A.:The Pirates of Penzance, w. D. Hays (sgr), M. Rawlins (sgr), C. Freeman (ten), E. Schilling (sgr), M. Elder (cnd), Rochester PO, Eastman Chorale members—highlights *(rec 11/89)* Pro Arte ▲ CDd 480 [DDD]

Johnson, Jay (voc)
Spasm, w. Michael Lowenstern (b cl), Heather Barringer (voc), Mark Gibbons (voc), Jerome Kitzke (voc), Matt Lambiase (voc), Tom Linker (voc), Ed Lowenstern (voc), Michael Lowenstern (voc) *(rec Creation Audio, Minneapolis, NYU Studios, New York City & Studio A, Stony Brook, Aug 1994-July 1996)* New World ▲ 80468-2

Johnson, Mimi (nar)
Ashley, R.:Automatic Writing, w. Robert Ashley (nar/elec/syn) Lovely Music ▲ LCD 1002 [AAD]

Johnson, Patricia (mez)
Berg, A.:Lulu, w. E. Lear (sop—Lulu), P. Johnson (mez—Countess Geschwitz), D. Grobe (ten—Alwa), Fischer-Dieskau (bar—Dr. Schön), K. Böhm (cnd), German Opera Orch, German Opera Chorus [G] *(rec 1968)* Deutsche Grammophon 3-▲ 435705-2 [ADD]
Purcell, H.:Dido & Aeneas, w. Victoria de los Angeles (sop—Dido), Heather Harper (sop—Belinda), Patricia Johnson (mez—Sorceress), Peter Glossup (bar—Aeneas), J. Barbirolli (cnd), English CO, Ambrosian Singers EMI Classics 2-▲ ZDM 65664

Johnson, Richard (bass)
Bach, J.S.:St. Matthew Passion, w. M. Marshall (sop), C. Watkinson (cta), K. Equiluz (ten), G. Faulstisch (bar), P. Huttenlocher (bar), M. Corboz (cnd), Lausanne CO, Lausanne Vocal Ensemble Erato 3-▲ 2292-45375-2 GX
Thomson, V.:Lord Byron, w. J. Ommerlé (sop), D. Fortunato (mez), M. Lord (ten), R. Zeller (bar), J. Bolle (cnd), Monadnock Music Festival Orch [E] *(rec live, Aug. 31 & Sept. 2, 1991)* Koch International Classics 2-▲ KIC 7124-2 [DDD]

Johnson, Robert (ten)
Puccini, G.:Turandot, w. Montserrat Caballé (sop—Turandot), Leona Mitchell (sop—Liu), Remy Corazza (ten—Pang), Joseph Franck (ten—Pong), Robert Johnson (ten—Prince of Persia), Raymond Manton (ten—Altoum), Luciano Pavarotti (ten—Calaf), Aldo Bramante (bar—a mandarin), Dale Duesing (bar—Ping), Giorgio Tozzi (bass—Timur), R. Chailly (cnd), *(orch unknown) (rec San Francisco, Nov. 4, 1977)* Legato Classics 2-▲ LCD 188-2

Johnson, Van (sgr)
Lerner, A.J.:Brigadoon, w. Gene Kelly (sgr), C. Charisse (sgr) *(rec 1954)* Sony Music Special Products ▲ AK 45440 ■ AT 45440

Johnson, W. (sgr)
Rodgers, R.:Pipe Dream, w. H. Traubel (sgr), J. Tyler (sgr) [1955 Broadway cast] RCA ▲ 09026-61481-2 ■ 09026-61481-4

Johnsson, Hillary (mez)
Fennimore, J.:Eventide, w. K. Williams (sop), P. Creech (ten), T. Rolek (cnd), Chelsea Chamber Ensemble [E] Albany ▲ TROY 023-2 [ADD]

Johnston, James (ten)
Mendelssohn, F.:Elijah, w. Isobel Baillie (sop), Gladys Ripley (cta), Harold Williams (b-bar), M. Sargent (cnd), Liverpool PO, Huddersfield Choral Society Dutton Laboratories 2-▲ DUT 2004 [ADD]

Johnston, Oliver (trb)
Handel, G.F.:Messiah, w. Rae Woodland (sop), Norma Proctor (cta), Paul Esswood (ct), Stephen Roberts (bar), J. Tobin (cnd), English SO, London Choral Society [Handel's original orchestration] [E] *(rec 1976)* Protone ■ CSPR 166/67
Lalande, M.-R. de:Confitebor tibi, Domine, w. G. Fisher (sop), C. Daniels (ct), A. Smith (ten), S. Varcoe (bass), E. Higginbottom (cnd), King's Consort, Oxford New College Choir [L] Erato (Musifrance) ▲ 2292-45014-2 [DDD]
Lalande, M.-R. de:De profundis solo Voices, Orch & Chorus, w. G. Fisher (sop), C. Daniels (ct), A. Smith (ten), S. Varcoe (bass), E. Higginbottom (cnd), King's Consort, New College Choir Oxford [L] Erato (Musifrance) ▲ 2292-45014-2 [DDD]
Lalande, M.-R. de:Miserere, w. G. Fisher (sop), C. Daniels (ct), A. Smith (ten), S. Varcoe (bass), E. Higginbottom (cnd), King's Consort, Oxford New College Choir [L] Erato (Musifrance) ▲ 2292-45014-2 [DDD]

Johnston, Robert (spkr)
Mozart, W.A.:Zauberflöte, w. Constanze Backes (sop—Papagena), Christiane Oelze (sop—Pamina), Susan Roberts (sop—First Lady), Cyndia Sieden (sop—Queen of the Night), Carola Guber (cta—Second Lady), Maria Jonas (cta—Third Lady), Andreas Dieterich (trb—First Boy), Jan Andreas Mendel (trb—Second Boy), Florian Wöller (trb—Third Boy), Uwe Peper (ten—Monostatos), Nicolas Robertson (ten—First Man in Armor), Michael Schade (ten—Tamino), Gerald Finley (bar—Papageno), Noel Mann (bass—Second Man in Armor), Harry Peeters (bass—Sarastro), Detlef Roth (bass—Speaker/First Priest), Robert Burt (speaker—Third Priest), Robert Johnston (speaker—Second Priest), Wolfgang Knauer (speaker—Fourth Priest), Douglas Welbat (speaker—Second Priest), J. E. Gardiner (cnd), English Baroque Soloists, Monteverdi Choir London *(rec Forum am Schlosspark, Ludwigsburg, July 1995)* Archiv 2-▲ 449166-2

Johnstone, Mark (ten)
Howells, H.:Requiem, w. Sally Barber (sop), Julia Field (alt), Andrew Angus (bar), Jeremy Backhouse (cnd), Vasari Singers *(rec All Hallows, Gospel Oak, Feb 18-20, 1994)* United ▲ CAL 88033 [DDD]

Jöken, K. (bar)
Wagner, R.:Die Meistersinger von Nürnberg (sels), w. E. Marherr-Wagner (mez), R. Hutt (ten), F. Schorr (b-bar), E. List (bass), L. Schützendorf (sgr), L. Blech (cnd), Berlin State Opera Orch, Berlin State Opera Chorus—Act 1:Hilf Gott! Will ich denn Schuster sein?; Das schöne Fest, Johannistag; Act 2:Johannistag! Johannistag!; Hab' ich heut' Singstund'?; Jerum! Jerum!; Act 3:Gleich, Meister! Hier!; Grüss' Gott, mein Evchen...Weilten die Stern' im lieblichen Tanz...O Sachs! Mein Freund!; Sankt Krispin, lobet ihn!; Silentium!...Wach' auf!; Verachtet mir die Meister nicht [G] *(rec Staatsoper unter den Linden, 5/22/28)* Pearl ▲ PEA 9340 (m) [AAD]

Joll, Philip (bass)
Wagner, R.:Parsifal, w. Waltraud Meier (mez—Kundry), Warren Ellsworth (ten—Parsifal), Nicholas Folwell (bar—Klingsor), Philip Joll (b-bar—Amfortas), Donald McIntyre (b-bar—Gurnemanz), R. Goodall (cnd), Welsh National Opera Orch, Welsh National Opera Chorus EMI Classics 2-▲ CDMD 65665

Joll, Phillip (b-bar)
Martinů, B.:The Greek Passion, w. Helen Field (sop), John Mitchinson (ten), John Tomlinson (bass), C. Mackerras (cnd), Brno State PO, Czech Phil Chorus [E] *(rec 1981)* Supraphon 2-▲ 10 3611-2 [DDD]

Jolson, Al (sgr)
Rodgers, R.:Music of, w. B. Crosby (sgr), R. Vallee (sgr), J. Macdonald (sgr), et al., Whiteman, Sinatra (cnd), Whiteman Orch, Sinatra Orch, Paramount Studio Orch—On Your Toes; Jumbo; Present Arms; One Dam Thing After Another; The Boys from Syracuse; Heads Up; Lido Lady; Peggy Ann; Love Me Tonight; Higher & Higher; Spring is Here; The Girl Friend; Simple Simon; Hallelujah; I'm a Bum Pearl ("Flapper" series) ▲ PAST CD 9794 [AAD]

Joly, Valérie (mez)
Aperghis, G.:L'origine des espèces, w. Françoise Degeorges (sop), Donatienne Michel-Dansac (sop), Emmanuelle Zoll (sop), Frédérique Wolf-Michaux (cta), Elena Andreyev (vc) Musique Française d'Aujourd'hui ▲ MFA 216004

Jona, A. (sgr)
Savinio, A.:Album 1914, w. L. Castellani (sop), B. Canino (pno/cel), D. Zaffaroni (bn) Stradivarius ▲ STR 33309 [DDD]

Jona, Alberto (bar)
Oyf'n Prip'chok:Jewish Melodies of the 20th Century, w. Oscar Alessi (pno) Nuova Era ▲ NUO 7261

Jonas, Maria (cta)
Mozart, W.A.:Zauberflöte, w. Constanze Backes (sop—Papagena), Christiane Oelze (sop—Pamina), Susan Roberts (sop—First Lady), Cyndia Sieden (sop—Queen of the Night), Carola Guber (cta—Second Lady), Maria Jonas (cta—Third Lady), Andreas Dieterich (trb—First Boy), Jan Andreas Mendel (trb—Second Boy), Florian Wöller (trb—Third Boy), Uwe Peper (ten—Monostatos), Nicolas Robertson (ten—First Man in Armour), Michael Schade (ten—Tamino), Gerald Finley (bar—Papageno), Noel Mann (bass—Second Man in Armour), Harry Peeters (bass—Sarastro), Detlef Roth (bass—Speaker/First Priest), Robert Burt (speaker—Third Priest), Robert Johnston (speaker—Second Priest), Wolfgang Knauer (speaker—Fourth Priest), Douglas Welbat (speaker—Second Priest), J. E. Gardiner (cnd), English Baroque Soloists, Monteverdi Choir London *(rec Forum am Schlosspark, Ludwigsburg, July 1995)* Archiv 2-▲ 449166-2

Jonášová, Jana (sop)
Janácek, L.:The Excursions of Mr. Brouček, w. Libuše Márová (mez), Vilém Přibyl (ten), Richard Novák (bass), Czech PO, Czech Phil Chorus Supraphon 2-▲ SUP 112153 [AAD]
Kabeláč, M.:Sym 8, w. V. Rabas (org), Strasbourg Theater Percussionists *(rec 1971)* Praga ▲ PR 255 004
Mozart, W.A.:Arias, w. Z. Lukás (cnd), Prague Chamber Soloists—Bella mia fiamma...Resta, o cara (concert aria), K.528 [I] Supraphon Collection ▲ 11 0621-2 [ADD]
Zelenka, J.D.:Missa Gratias agimus tibi, w. M. Mrázová (cta), V. Dolezal (ten), P. Mikuláš (bass), J. Belohlávek (cnd), Czech PO, Czech Phil Chorus [L] Supraphon ▲ 11 0816-2 [DDD]

Jones, Aled (nar)
Celebration:Christmas Fanfares & Carols, w BBC Welsh Chorus [cnd:John Hugh Thomas], Welsh Guards Fanfare Trumpeters, Huw Tregelles Williams (org) Nimbus ▲ NI 5310 [DDD]

Jones, Aled (trb)
Fauré, G.:Requiem, w. S. Roberts (bar), R. Hickox (cnd), Royal PO, London Sym Chorus [L] RPO ▲ RPO 7007 [DDD]
Fauré, G.:Requiem, w. S. Roberts (bar), R. Hickox (cnd), Royal PO, London Sym Chorus [L] MCA Classics ▲ MCAD 6199 [DDD]

Jones, Barney (nar)
Davies, S.:What Is the Matter in Amy Glennon?, w. Gregory Whitehead (nar—The Idea), Sheila Davies (nar—Amy Glennon/Chorus), Piers McKenzie (nar—Auctioneer), Fran Smith (sgr), Amy Newburg (sgr), Barney Jones (nar—The Fathers) ▲ WN 0013

Jones, Della (mez)
Beethoven, L. van:Sym 9, "Choral Sym", w. Alison Hargen (sop), David Rendall (ten), Gwynne Howell (b-bar), W. Morris (cnd), London SO, London Sym Chorus IMP ("LSO" series) ▲ IMP 6900032
Beethoven, L. van:Sym 9, "Choral Sym", w. Joan Rodgers (sop), Peter Bronder (ten), Bryn Terfel (bass), C. Mackerras (cnd), Royal Liverpool PO, Royal Liverpool Phil Choir Classics for Pleasure ("Eminence" series) ▲ CFP 2186 [DDD]
Bernstein, L.:Candide (restored), w. J. Anderson (sop), C. Ludwig (mez), J. Hadley (ten), N. Gedda (ten), A. Green (sgr), K. Ollmann (bar), L. Bernstein (cnd), London SO, London Sym Chorus *(rec 1989)* Deutsche Grammophon ▲ 429734–2 [DDD] ■ 429734–4
Bernstein, L.:Candide (restored), w. J. Anderson (sop), C. Ludwig (mez), J. Hadley (ten), N. Gedda (ten), A. Green (sgr), K. Ollmann (bar), L. Bernstein (cnd), London SO, London Sym Chorus Deutsche Grammophon ■ 437328–4
Bliss, A.:Pastoral, w. R. Hickox (cnd), Northern Sinfonia of England, Northern Sinfonia Chorus [E] Chandos ▲ CHAN 8886 [DDD]
Britten, H.:Gloriana, w. J. Barstow (sop—Queen Elizabeth I), D. Jones (mez—Lady Essex), P. Langridge (ten—Earl of Essex), J. M. Ainsley (ten—Spirit of the Masque), J. Summers (bar—Lord Mountjoy), J. Shirley-Quirk (bar—Recorder of Norwich), B. Terfel (b-bar—Henry Cuffe), C. Mackerras (cnd), Welsh National Opera Orch, Welsh National Opera Chorus Argo 2–▲ 440213–2 [DDD]
Britten, H.:A Midsummer Night's Dream, w. J. Gomez (sop), J. Bowman (ct), N. Bailey (bar), H. Herford (bar), R. Hickox (cnd), City of London Sinfonia Virgin Classics ▲ CDCB 59305
Debussy, C.:Proses lyriques, w. M. Martineau (pno) Chandos ▲ CHAN 9147 [DDD]
Donizetti, G.:L'assedio di Calais, w. E. Harrhy (sop), R. Serbo (ten), J. Treleaven (ten), R. Smythe (bar), D. Parry (cnd), Philharmonia Orch, Geoffrey Mitchell Choir Opera Rara 2–▲ OR 9 [DDD]
Donizetti, G.:Maria Padilla, w. L. McDonall (sop—Maria Padilla), D. Jones (mez—Ines Padilla), G. Clark (ten—Don Ruiz), C. du Plessis (bar—Don Pedro), A. Francis (cnd), London SO, Geoffrey Mitchell Choir [I] *(rec at Henry Wood Hall, London June 1980)* Opera Rara 3–▲ ORC 6
Donizetti, G.:Ugo, conte di Parigi, w. E. Harrhy (sop), Y. Kenny (sop), J. Price (sop), M. Arthur (ten), C. du Plessis (bar), A. Francis (cnd), New Philharmonia Orch, Geoffrey Mitchell Choir Opera Rara 3–▲ ORC 1
Duparc, H.:Songs, w. M. Martineau (pno)—L'Invitation au voyage; Extase; La vie anterieure [F] Chandos ▲ CHAN 9147 [DDD]
Falla, M. de:El sombrero de tres picos, w. G. Schwarz (cnd), London SO [Sp] Delos ▲ DCD 3060 [DDD]
Handel, G.F.:Messiah, w. Joan Rodgers (sop), Christopher Robson (ct), Philip Langridge (ten), Bryn Terfel (b-bar), R. Hickox (cnd), Collegium Musicum 90 [period instrs] [E] Chandos ("Chaconne" series) 2–▲ CHAN 0522/23 [DDD]
Handel, G.F.:Semele, w. Norma Burrowes (sop), Patrizia Kwella (sop), Elizabeth Priday (sop), Catherine Denley (mez), Timothy Penrose (alt), Anthony Rolfe-Johnson (ct), Maldwyn Davies (ten), Robert Lloyd (b-bar), David Thomas (bass), J. E. Gardiner (cnd), English Baroque Soloists, Monteverdi Choir London Erato 2–▲ 2292–45982–2
Handel, G.F.:Teseo, w. Eirian James (mez), Derek Lee Ragin (ct), M. Minkowski (cnd), Louvre Musicians Erato 2–▲ 2292–45806–2 ZA
Holst, G.:The Cloud Messenger, w. R. Hickox (cnd), London SO, London Sym Chorus [E] Chandos ▲ CHAN 8901 [DDD]
Howells, H.:Missa sabrinensis, w. Janice Watson (sop), Martyn Hill (ten), Donald Maxwell (bar), G. Rozhdestvensky (cnd), London SO, London Sym Chorus Chandos ▲ CHAN 9348 [DDD]
Martin, F.:In terra pax, w. Judith Howarth (sop), Martyn Hill (ten), Roderick Williams (bar), Stephen Roberts (bass), M. Bamert (cnd), London PO, Laszlo Heltay (cnd), Brighton Festival Chorus Chandos ▲ CHAN 9465
Meyerbeer, G.:Il crociato, w. Linda Kitchen (sop), Y. Kenny (sop), R. Platt (sop), D. Montague (mez), B. Ford (ten), U. Benelli (bar), D. Parry (cnd), Royal PO, Geoffrey Mitchell Choir [I] *(rec CTS Studios, Wembley, London, Dec. 1990–June 1991)* Opera Rara 4–▲ OR 10
Monteverdi, C.:Incoronazione, w. A. Augér (sop), S. Leonard (sop), L. Hirst (mez), J. Bowman (ct), G. Reinhart (bass), R. Hickox (cnd), City of London Baroque Sinfonia Virgin Classics 3–▲ CDCC 59524
Monteverdi, C.:Incoronazione, w. A. Augér (soprano—Poppea), D. Jones (mez—Nerone), L. Hirst (mez—Ottavia), J. Bowman (ct—Ottone), R. Hickox (cnd), City of London Baroque Sinfonia Virgin Classics ▲ CDCC 45082
Mozart, W.A.:Clemenza, w. Barbara Bonney (sop—Servilia), Cecilia Bartoli (mez—Sesto), Della Jones (mez—Vitellia), Diana Montague (mez—Annio), Uwe Heilman (ten—Tito), Giles Cachemaille (bar—Publio), C. Hogwood (cnd), Academy of Ancient Music, Academy of Ancient Music Chorus London ("Editions de l'oiseau-lyre" series) 2–▲ 444131–2 [DDD]
Mozart, W.A.:Requiem, w. Felicity Lott (sop), Keith Lewis (ten), Willard White (bass), David Bell (org), F. Welser-Möst (cnd), London PO, London Phil Choir Classics for Pleasure ("Eminence" series) ▲ CDEMX 2150 [DDD]
Mozart, W.A.:Requiem, w. F. Lott (sop), K. Lewis (ten), W. White (bar), F. Welser-Möst (cnd), London PO, London Phil Chorus EMI Classics ▲ CDM 63260
Parry, H.:The Lotus Eaters, w. M. Bamert (cnd), London PO, London Phil Chorus [E] Chandos ▲ CHAN 8990 [DDD]
Parry, H.:The Soul's Ransom, w. D. Wilson-Johnson (bar), M. Bamert (cnd), London PO, London Phil Chorus [E] Chandos ▲ CHAN 8990 [DDD]
Poulenc, F.:Songs, w. M. Martineau (pno)—3 songs—Banalities; La bestaire; La souris les Chemines de l'amour [F] Chandos ▲ CHAN 9147 [DDD]
Rossini, G.:Arias, w. R. Hickox (cnd), City of London Sinfonia, Richard Hickox Singers—nine arias, from Adelaide di Borgogna, Barbiere di Siviglia, Bianca e Falliero, Cenerentola, Donna del Lago, Italiana in Algeri, Otello, Signor Bruschino [I] Chandos ▲ CHAN 8865 [DDD]
Rossini, G.:Stabat Mater, w. H. Field (sop), A. Davies (ten), R. Earle (bass), R. Hickox (cnd), City of London Sinfonia, London Sym Chorus [L] Chandos ▲ CHAN 8780 [DDD]
Rubbra, E.:Sym 9, w. Lynne Dawson (sop), Stephen Roberts (bar), R. Hickox (cnd), BBC Welsh National SO, BBC Welsh National Chorus Chandos ▲ CHAN 9441
Satie, E.:Songs, w. M. Martineau (pno)—Trois melodies; La diva de l'empire; Ludions [F] Chandos ▲ CHAN 9147 [DDD]
Spanish Songs, w. M. Martineau (pno) Chandos ▲ CHAN 9277 [DDD]
Walton, W.:The Bear, w. J. Shirley-Quirk (bar), A. Opie (bass), R. Hickox (cnd), Northern Sinfonia of England Chandos ▲ CHAN 9245 [DDD]

Jones, Delyth (sop)
Vaughan Williams, R.:The Pilgrim's Progress, w. Elsa Kendal (cta), Charles Groves (ten), Robin Leggate (ten), V. Handley (cnd), BBC Northern SO, BBC Northern Singers IMP ("BBC Radio Classics" series) ▲ IMP 5691662

Jones, Gordon (bass)
Codex Speciálník, w. P. Hillier (cnd), Hillard Ensemble, D. James (ct), R. Covey-Crump (ten), J. Potter (ten) *(rec Gönningen City Church, Jan. 1993)* ECM New Series ▲ 78118–21504–2 [DDD]
The Essential Gregorian Chant, w. Pro Cantione Antiqua [cnd:James O'Donnell], James Griffett (ten), Ian Partridge (ten), Stephen Roberts (bar), Michael George (bass) Cala ▲ CAL CACD 88035 [DDD]
The Essential Gregorian Chant, w. James Griffett (ten), Ian Partridge (ten), Michael George (b-bar), Stephen Roberts (b-bar), Pro Cantione Antique [cnd:James O'Donnell] United ▲ UNI 88035 [DDD]
Gregorian Lent & Easter, w. Pro Cantione Antiqua [cnd:James O'Donnell], J. Griffett (ten), I. Partridge (ten), S. Roberts (bar), M. George (bass) *(rec All Saints, East Finchley, Dec 7–9, 1993)* United ▲ UNI 88016 [DDD]

Jones, Gordon (bass) (cont.)
Kancheli, G.:Evening Prayers, w. David James (ct), Rogers Covey-Crump (ten), John Potter (ten), D. R. Davies (cnd), Stuttgart CO *(rec Apr. 1994)* ECM New Series ▲ 78118–21510–2 [DDD]
Officium, w. P. Hillier (cnd), Hillard Ensemble, D. James (ct), R. Covey-Crump (ten), J. Potter (ten), J. Gabarek (sop/ten saxs) *(rec Sept. 1993)* ECM New Series ▲ 78118–21525–2
Pärt, A.:Litany, w. David James (ct), Rogers Covey-Crump (ten), John Potter (ten), T. Kaljuste (cnd), Tallinn CO, Estonian Phil Chamber Choir *(rec Niguliste Church, Tallinn, Sept 1995)* ECM New Series ▲ 78118–21592–2 [DDD] ■ 78118–21592–4
Pärt, A.:Passio Domini nostri Jesu Christi secundum Joannem, w. L. Dawson (sop), D. James (alt), R. Covey-Crump (ten), J. Potter (ten), M. George (bass), P. Hillier (cnd), Hilliard Ensemble, Western Wind Chamber Chorus [L] ECM New Series ▲ 78118–21370–2 [DDD]; ■ 78118–21370–4 (D)
10,000 Voices, w. D. O'Neill (ten), A. Sammons (vn), World Choir, Massed Guards Bands [cnd:O. Arwel Hughes] *(rec live May 23, 1992)* EMI Classics ▲ CDC 54628–2 [DDD]

Jones, Gwyneth (sop)
Beethoven, L. van:Sym 9, "Choral Sym", w. Tatiana Troyanos (mez), Jess Thomas (ten), Karl Ridderbusch (bass), K. Böhm (cnd), Vienna PO, Vienna State Opera Chorus Deutsche Grammophon ("Double" series) 2–▲ 437368–2
Humperdinck, E.:Hänsel und Gretel, w. E. Gruberova (sop), B. Bonney (sop), C. Oelze (sop), A. Murray (mez), C. Ludwig (mez), F. Grundheber (bar), C. Davis (cnd), Dresden Staatskapelle Philips 2–▲ 438013–2
Mendelssohn, F.:Elijah, w. Janet Baker (mez), Simon Woolf (trb), Nicolai Gedda (ten), Dietrich Fischer-Dieskau (bar), R. Frühbeck de Burgos (cnd), New Philharmonia Orch, New Philharmonia Chorus, Wandsworth School Boys' Choir *(rec 1968)* EMI Classics ("Doublefforte" series) 2–▲ CDFB 68601
Schmidt, F.:Notre Dame, w. J. King (ten), R. Laubenthal (ten), K. Moll (bass), C. Perick (cnd), Berlin RSO, St. Hedwig's Cathedral Choir, RIAS Chamber Chorus [G] Capriccio 2–▲ 10248/9 [DDD]
Sibelius, J.:Luonnotar, w. A. Dorati (cnd), London SO EMI Classics ▲ CDM 65182
Strauss, R.:Die ägyptische Helena, w. M. Kastu (ten), B. Hendricks (sop), W. White (bass), C. Rayam (ten), B. Finnilä (mez), A. Dorati (cnd), Detroit SO London ("Grand Opera" series) 2–▲ 430381–2 [AAD]
Strauss, R.:4 Last Songs, w. R. Paternostro (cnd), Tokyo SO [G] *(rec live, Suntory Hall, Tokyo, 5/29/91)* Koch Schwann ▲ CD 314081 [DDD]
Strauss, R.:Der Rosenkavalier, w. L. Popp (sop), C. Ludwig (mez), P. Domingo (ten), W. Berry (b-bar), L. Bernstein (cnd), Vienna PO [G] CBS 3–▲ M3K 42564 [ADD]
Strauss, R.:Salome, w. M. Dunn (mez), D. Fischer-Dieskau (bar), K. Böhm (cnd), Hamburg State Opera Orch *(rec live, 1970)* Deutsche Grammophon 2–▲ 445319–2 [ADD]
Strauss, R.:Songs, w. R. Paternostro (cnd), Tokyo SO—Opp. 10/1, 27/1, 27/2, 27/4, 41/1, 48/1, 56/5, 56/6 [G] *(rec live, Suntory Hall, Tokyo, 5/29/91)* Koch Schwann ▲ CD 314081 [DDD]
Verdi, G.:Aida, w. J. Vickers (ten), Dourian (sgr), Shaw (sgr), E. Downes (cnd), Royal Opera House Orch, Royal Opera House Chorus Covent Garden [I] *(rec live, Covent Garden, 1/27/68)* Melodram 2–▲ MEL 27019
Verdi, G.:Otello, w. G. Jones (sop—Desdemona), A. di Stasio (mez—Emilia), J. McCracken (ten—Otello), P. de Palma (ten—Cassio), D. Fischer-Dieskau (bar—Iago), J. Barbirolli (cnd), New Philharmonia Orch, Ambrosian Opera Chorus EMI Classics ▲ CDMB 65296
Wagner, R.:Arias & Scenes, w. R. Paternostro (cnd), Cologne SO—Götterdämmerung:Immolation Scene (Act 3); Lohengrin:Elsas Traumerzählung (Act 1); Tannhäuser:Hallenarie (Act 2); Gebet der Elisabeth (Act 3); Tristan und Isolde:Prelude & Liebestod [G] Chandos ▲ CHAN 8930 [DDD]
Wagner, R.:Götterdämmerung, w. H. Jung (mez), F. Mazura (bar), H. Becht (bar), P. Boulez (cnd), Bayreuth Festival Orch, Bayreuth Festival Chorus [G] Philips 4–▲ 434424–2 [DDD]
Wagner, R.:Götterdämmerung (immolation scene), w. R. Paternostro (cnd), Cologne SO [G] Chandos ▲ CHAN 8930 [DDD]
Wagner, R.:Parsifal, w. J. King (ten), T. Stewart (bar), D. McIntyre (b-bar), K. Ridderbusch (bass), F. Crass (bass), P. Boulez (cnd), Bayreuth Festival Orch, Bayreuth Festival Chorus [G] *(rec 1970)* Deutsche Grammophon 3–▲ 435718–2 [ADD]
Wagner, R.:Der Ring des Nibelungen, w. H. Schwarz (mez), T. Altmeyer (ten), L. Hofmann (bass), D. McIntyre (b-bar), P. Boulez (cnd), Bayreuth Festival Orch, Bayreuth Festival Chorus Philips 32–▲ 434420–2 [ADD/DDD]
Wagner, R.:Siegfried, w. H. Zednik (ten), H. Becht (bar), D. McIntyre (b-bar), P. Boulez (cnd), Bayreuth Festival Orch, Bayreuth Festival Chorus [G] Philips 3–▲ 434423–2 [DDD]

Jones, Gwynn Hughes (bar)
Britten, H.:Curlew River, w. Hugo Ticciati (trb), Mark Milhofer (ten), Mark Evans (bar), Matthew Hargreaves (bass), D. Angus (cnd), Guildhall Chamber Ensemble Koch Schwann ▲ SCH 313972

Jones, J. (sgr)
Rodgers, R.:Music of, w. S. Bass (sgr), J. Andrews (sgr), P. Como (sgr), D. Reese (sgr), N. Luboff (sgr), M. Gold (sgr), N. Walker (sgr), H. Bowen (sgr), V. Damone (sgr), P. Nero (pno), J. P. Morgan (sgr), E. Fisher (sgr), B. Goodman (cl), Ann-Margaret (sgr), Shorty Rogers (sgr), D. Shore (sgr), T. Martin (sgr), M. King (sgr), A. Newley (sgr) RCA ▲ 8590–2 R ■ 8590–4 R

Jones, James Earl (nar)
Copland, A.:Lincoln Portrait, w. G. Schwarz (cnd), Seattle SO [F] *(rec June 1992)* Delos ▲ DE 3140 [DDD]
Duffy, J.:A Time for Remembrance:A Peace Cant, w. Cynthia Clarey (mez), Z. Macal (cnd), Milwaukee SO *(rec Uihlein Hall, Milwaukee, WI, Nov. 22, 1993)* Koss Classics ▲ KC 1022 [DDD]
Hanson, H.:The Mystic Trumpeter, w. G. Schwarz (cnd), Seattle SO, Seattle Chorale *(rec June 6–7, 1994)* Delos ▲ DE 3160 [DDD]
Saint-Saëns, C.:Carnival of the Animals, w. M. Golabek (nar), R. Golabek (nar), F. Savage (nar), C. Heston (nar), J. E. Jones (nar), B. White (nar), L. Redgrave (nar), W. Shatner (nar), J. Rivers (nar), T. Danson (nar), L. Tomlin (nar), D. Raffin (nar), A. Hepburn (nar), D. Moore (nar), W. Matthau (nar), J. Smith (nar), L. Schifrin (cnd), Hollywood CO Dove Audio ▲ DOV 30700

Jones, Leah-Marian (mez)
Verdi, G.:La traviata, w. Angela Gheorghiu (sop—Violetta), Leah-Marian Jones (mez—Flora Bervoix), Gillian Knight (mez—Annina), Robin Leggate (ten—Gastone), Frank Lopardo (ten—Alfredo Germont), Rodney Gibson (ten—Servo di Flora), Neil Griffiths (ten—Giuseppe), Mark Beesley (bar—Dottore Grenvile), Leo Nucci (bar—Giorgio Germont), Richard Van Allan (bass—Barone Douphol), Roderick Earle (bass—Marquese d'Obigny), Bryan Secombe (bass—Commissionario), G. Solti (cnd), Royal Opera House Orch, Royal Opera House Chorus Covent Garden *(rec live, Royal Opera House, Covent Garden, Dec. 1994)* London 2–▲ 448119–2

Jones, M. (reader)
Cerha, F.:Eine Art Chanson, w. H.C. Artmann (reader), HK Gruber (reader), J. Holland (reader), R. McGee (reader), G. Rühm (reader) *(rec live Apr. 30, 1993)* Largo ▲ 5126 [DDD]

Jones, Nerys (sgr)
Weir, J.:Blond Eckbert, w. Anne-Marie Owens (mez), Nicholas Folwell (bar), Christopher Ventris (sgr), S. Edwards (cnd), English National Opera Orch Collins Classics ▲ COL 1461

Jones, Parry (ten)
Stravinsky, I.:Les Noces, w. K. Winter (sop), L. Seymour (cta), R. Henderson (bar), I. Stravinsky (cnd), *(orch & chorus unknown)* EMI Classics 2–▲ CDCB 54607
Vaughan Williams, R.:Serenade to Music, w. I. Baillie (sop), E. Suddaby (sop), S. Allen (sop), E. Turner (sop), M. Balfour (cta), A. Desmond (cta), M. Brunskill (cta), M. Jarred (cta), H. Nash (ten), W. Widdop (ten), F. Titterton (ten), R. Henderson (bass), R. Easton (bass), H. Williams (bass), N. Allin (bass), H. J. Wood (cnd), BBC SO Dutton Laboratories ▲ CDAX 8004 [ADD]
Vaughan Williams, R.:Serenade to Music, w. Isobel Baillie (sop), Lilian Stiles-Allen (sop), Elsie Suddaby (sop), Eva Turner (sop), Margaret Balfour (cta), Muriel Brunskill (cta), Astra Desmond (cta), Mary Jarred (cta), Heddle Nash (ten), Frank Titterton (ten), Walter Widdop (ten), Roy Henderson (bar), Harold Williams (bar), Norman Allin (bass), Robert Easton (bass), H. Wood (cnd), BBC SO *(rec Abbey Road, Oct 15, 1938)* Claremont ▲ CDGSE 785066
Vaughan Williams, R.:Serenade to Music, w. I. Baillie (sop), E. Suddaby (sop), S. Allen (sop), E. Turner (sop), M. Balfour (cta), A. Desmond (cta), M. Brunskill (cta), M. Jarred (cta), H. Nash (ten), W. Widdop (ten), F. Titterton (ten), R. Henderson (bass), R. Easton (bass), H. Williams (bass), N. Allin (bass), H. Wood (cnd), BBC SO [E] *(rec 10/15/38)* Pearl ▲ GEMMCD 9342 (m) [AAD]

Jones, Robert Harre (ct)
Dunstable, J.:Sacred Music, w. Charles Daniels (ten), Angus Smith (ten), D. Greig (cnd), Orlando Consort—Missa Rex Seculorum; Ave Maris Stella; Gloria in Canon; O Crux Gloriosa; Descendi in Ortum Meum; Speciosa Facta Es; Sub Tuam Portectionem; Veni Sancte Spiritus; Albanus Roseo Rutilat; Specialis Virgo; Preco Preheminencie; Salve Regina Metronome ▲ 1009

Jones, S. (sgr)
Rodgers, R.:Carousel, w. Gordon MacRae (sgr), C. Mitchell (sgr), B. Ruick (sgr), C. Turner (sgr), R. Rounseville (sgr) *(rec 1956)* Broadway Angel ▲ ZDM 64692 ■ EG 64692
Rodgers, R.:Oklahoma!, w. Gordon MacRae (sgr), R. Steiger (sgr), Gloria Grahame (sgr), Gene Nelson (sgr), C. Greenwood (sgr), J. Whitmore (sgr) *(rec 1955)* Broadway Angel ▲ ZDM 64691 ■ EG 64691

Jones-Hudson, Eleanor (sop)
Sullivan, A.:The Yeomen of the Guard (sels)—Were I thy bride Symposium ▲ 1123

Jonsson, Per (nar)
Larsson, L.-E.:God in Disguise, w. B. Nordin (sop), H. Hagegård (bar), S. Frykberg (cnd), Helsingborg SO, Helsingborg Sym Chorus [Sw] BIS ▲ CD 96 [AAD]

Jordacescu, Dan (bar)
Purcell, H.:Dido & Aeneas, w. Helen Donath (sop—Belinda), Shirley Verrett (sop—Dido), Oralia Dominguez (mez—Sorceress), Carmen Lavani (alt—A Spirit), Margaret Lensky (cta—2nd Witch), Carlo Gaifa (ten—A Sailor), Dan Jordacescu (bar—Aeneas), Rosina Cavicchioli (sgr—A Woman), Lilia Teresita Reyes (sgr—1st Witch), R. Leppard (cnd), Turin RAI SO, Ambrosian Chorus *(rec Torino, May 20, 1971)* Arkadia ▲ 619 [ADD]

Jordan, Irene (sop)
Milhaud, D.:Choëphores, w. Vera Zorina (nar), Virginia Babikian (sop), McHenry Boatwright (bar), L. Bernstein (cnd), New York PO, New York Schola Cantorum
Sony Classical ("Masterworks Heritage" series) ▲ MHK 62352

Jordan, Pamela (sop)
Morrill, D.:Just a Shape, w. Tremont String Quartet *(rec June 1991 & June 1992)* Centaur ▲ CRC 2143 [DDD]
Moss, L.:Songs to Poems, w. Nanette Butler Shannon (pno) Capstone ▲ CPS 8619

Jordis, Eelco von (bass)
Spohr, L.:Faust, w. C. Taha (sop), M. Vier (b-bar), G. Moull (cnd), Bielefeld PO, Bielefeld Opera Chorus [1852 version] *(rec live, June 1993)* CPO 2-▲ CPO 999247 [DDD]

Jørgensen, Palle Fuhr (nar)
Torstensson, K.:The Last Diary, w. R. de Leeuw (cnd), Asko Ensemble, Schoenberg Ensemble *(rec The Hague, Netherlands, Mar 6 1995)* Donemus ▲ CV 57 [DDD]

Joris, Jan (bar)
Bizet, G.:Les Pêcheurs de perles, w. E. Spoorenberg (sop), A. Vanzo (ten), G. Hoekman (bass), J. Fournet (cnd), Netherlands Radio PO [F] *(rec live, 1963)* Verona 2-▲ 2707/08 (m) [AAD]

Jörn, Karl (ten)
The Complete Destinn, w. Destinn, Emmy (sop), E. Caruso (ten), J. McCormack (ten), G. Martinelli (ten), G. Zenatello (ten), et al. Supraphon 12-▲ SUP 112136 [ADD]

Josey, Christopher (ten)
Mozart, W.A.:Zauberflöte, w. Natalie Dessay (sop—Queen of the Night), Linda Kitchen (sop—Papagena), Rosa Mannion (sop—Pamina), Anna-Maria Panzarella (sop—First Lady), Doris Lamprecht (mez—Second Lady), Delphine Haidan (cta—Third Lady), Hans Peter Blochwitz (ten—Tamino), Steven Cole (ten—Monostatos), Chrisopher Josey (ten—First Priest/First Armed Man), Anton Scharinger (bar—Papageno), Reinhard Hagen (bass—Sarastro), Laurent Naouri (bass—Second Priest/Second Armed Man), Willard White (bass—Speaker), W. Christie (cnd), Les Arts Florissants *(rec Paris Oct 2–9 1995)* Erato 2-▲ 12705-2 [DDD]

Joshua, Rosemary (sop)
Humperdinck, E.:Hänsel und Gretel, w. H. Behrens (sop—Gertrud, the Stepmother), R. Ziesak (sop—Gretel), R. Joshua (sop—Sandman), C. Schäfer (sop—Dew Fairy), J. Larmore (mez—Hänsel), H. Schwarz (cta—Nibblewitch), B. Weikl (bar—Peter, the Father), D. Runnicles (cnd), Bavarian RSO, Tölz Boys' Choir *(rec Munich, Feb. 1994)* Teldec 2-▲ 94549-2 [DDD]

Jossoud, Hélène (mez)
Chaynes, C.:Au-delà de l'espérance, w. Odette Chaynes-Decaux (pno) REM ▲ REM 311194 [DDD]
Donizetti, G.:Messa di Gloria e Credo, w. Danielle Borst (sop), Jean-Luc Viala (ten), Vincent Le Texier (bass-bar), M. Piquemal (cnd), Avignon-Provence Regional Lyric Orch, Provence-Alpes-Côte d'Azur Regional Choir Accord ▲ ACD 212142 [DDD]
Strauss, R.:Salome, w. K. Huffstodt (sop), J. Dupouy (ten), J.L. Viala (ten), J. van Dam (bar), K. Nagano (cnd), Paris Lyon Opera Orch, Paris Lyon Opera Chorus Virgin Classics 2-▲ CDCB 59054

Joswig, Margarete (sgr)
Durante, F.:Lamentationes Jeremiae Prophetae, w. Mechthild Bach (sop), Monika Frimmer (sop), P. Neumann (cnd), Collegium Cartusianum, Cologne Chamber Choir CPO ▲ CPO 999325

Jottini, Maria (sop)
Jottini & Volpi, w. Jottini, Maria (sop), Giacomo Lauri Volpi (ten), Florence Maggio Musicale Orch [cnd:Carlo Felice Cillario] *(rec Martini & Rossi Concert, 1957)* Incontri Memorabili ▲ CDMR 5021

Jourina, Irina (sop)
Rimsky-Korsakov, N.:Kaschei the Immortal, w. N. Terentieva (mez), A. Arkhipov (ten), V. Verestnikov (bar), V. Matorin (bass), A. Tchistiakov (cnd), Bolshoi Theater Orch, Yurloff Russian Choir [Russian] Russian Season ("Russian Season" series) ▲ LDC 288046 [DDD]

Journet, Marcel (bass)
Caruso, Ferrar & Journet:Highlights from Faust & French Opera, w. Caruso, Enrico (ten), Geraldine Farrar (sop) Nimbus ▲ NI 7859 [ADD]
The Complete Odéon & Victor Recordings, w. Clément, Edmond (ten), Geraldine Farrar (sop), Frank La Forge (pno), Rosario Bourdon (cnd) *(rec Odeon 1905; Victor 1911–1)* Romophone ▲ 82002-2
Gounod, C.:Faust, w. M. Berthon (sop—Marguerite), C. Vezzani (ten—Faust), L. Musy (b-bar—Valentin), M. Journet (bass—Mephistofeles), H. Busser (cnd), Paris Opera Orch, Paris Opera Chorus [F] *(rec 1930)* Music Memoria 2-▲ 30187
Gounod, C.:Faust, w. M. Berthon (sop), M. Coiffier (sop), J. Montfort (mez), C. Vezzani (ten), L. Musy (b-bar), M. Cozette (bar), H. Busser (cnd), Paris Opera Orch, Paris Opera Chorus [F] *(rec 1930)* Pearl 2-▲ PEA 9987 [AAD]
Gounod, C.:Roméo et Juliette, w. Yvonne Gall (sop—Juliette), Champell (sop—Stéphano), Jeanne Gouláncourt (mez—Gertrude), Agustarello Affre (ten—Roméo), Edmond Tirmont (ten—Tybalt), Alexis Boyer (bar—Mercutio), Pierre Dupré (bar—Paris), Hypolite Belhomme (bar—Grégorio), Marcel Journet (bass—Frère Laurent), Henri Albers (bass—Capulet), Valermont (bass—The Duke), F. Rühlmann (cnd), Paris Opéra-Comique Orch, Paris Opéra-Comique Chorus *(rec 1912)* VAI Audio ▲ VAIA 1064-3 F
The Italian Vocal Tradition, Vol. 1:The Voices of Toscanini, w. Toti dal Monte (sop), Claudio Muzio (sop), Rosetta Pampanini (sop), Biata Scacciati (sop), Giacomo Lauri-Volpi (ten), Francesco Merli (ten), Aureliano Pertile (ten), Carlo Galeffi (bar), Mariano Stabile (bar), Riccardo Stracciari (bar), Nazzareno de Angel *(rec 1921–35)* Iron Needle ▲ 1304
Opera Arias & Songs, w. Journet, Marcel (bass) Preiser ("Lebendige Vergangenheit" series) ▲ PRE 89021 (m) [AAD]

Julian, Conchita (sop)
Schifrin, L.:Cantos Aztecas, w. P. Domingo (ten), N. Storojev (bass), M. Felix (sgr), L. Schifrin (cnd), Mexican State SO, Mexico City Chorus [Sp] *(rec live 10/29/88)* Pro Arte ▲ CDD 494 [DDD]

Julicek, Petr (ten)
Janáček, L.:Music of, w. Zuzana Lapciková (sop), Pavla Dittmannová (cta), L. Svárovský (cnd), Brno State PO, Petr Fiala (cnd), Brno Czech Phil Chorus—Rákos Rákoczy (ballet); folk songs, choruses & dances Supraphon ▲ SUP CD 3129

Jung, Helene (mez)
Saint-Saëns, C.:Oratorio de Noël, w. V. Schweizer (sop), E. Wiens (sop), F. Melzer (ten), K. Widmer (bass), D. Hellmann (cnd), Mainz Bach Orch, Mainz Bach Choir *(rec 1976)* Calig ▲ CAL 50512 [AAD]
Wagner, R.:Götterdämmerung, w. G. Jones (sop), F. Mazura (bar), H. Becht (bar), P. Boulez (cnd), Bayreuth Festival Orch, Bayreuth Festival Chorus [G] Philips 4-▲ 434424-2 [DDD]

Jung, Helene (mez) (cont.)
Wagner, R.:Die Meistersinger von Nürnberg (sels), w. M. Teschemacher (sop), M. Kremer (ten), T. RA (ten), E. Fuchs (bar), H.-H. Nissen (bar), S. Nilsson (bass), K. Böhm (cnd), Saxon State Orch—Act. 3 *(rec 1939)* Pearl 2-▲ PEA 9121 [ADD]
Wagner, R.:Die Walküre (sels), w. M. Reining (sop), F. Krauss (ten), R. Bockelmann (bar), J. von Manowarda (bass), C. Leonhardt (cnd), Stuttgart Radio Orch—Act 2 (sels.); Act 3 (complete) *(rec Apr. 3, 1938)* Preiser 2-▲ PRE 90207 [ADD]

Junghanns, Egbert (bar)
Mendelssohn, F.:Vom Himmel hoch, w. Ute Selbig (sop), M. Flämig (cnd), Dresden PO, Dresden Kreuz Choir *(rec Dresden, Mar & Apr 1987)* Capriccio ▲ 10216 [DDD]
Saint-Saëns, C.:Oratorio de Noël, w. Ute Selbig (sop), Elisabeth Wilke (mez), Annette Markert (cta), Armin Ude (ten), Jutta Zoff (hp), Michael-Christfield Winkler (org), M. Flämig (cnd), Dresden PO, Dresden Kreuz Choir *(rec Dresden, Mar & Apr 1987)* Capriccio ▲ 10216 [DDD]

Jungkurth, Hedwig (sop)
Mozart, W.A.:Don Giovanni, w. Hedwig Jungkurth (sop—Elvira), Maria Reining (sop—Anna), Julius Patzak (ten—Ottavio), Karl Hammes (bar—Don Giovanni), Georg Hann (bass), Ludwig Weber (bass—Commandant), J. Keilberth (cnd), Stuttgart Reich RSO, Stuttgart Radio Chorus *(rec Mar. 1936)* Preiser 2-▲ PRE 90283

Jungwirth, Helena (sop)
Cherubini, L.:Masses, w. Monika Wiebe (sop), Rodrigo Orrego (ten), Wolf Matthias Friedrich (bass), H.R. Zöbeley (cnd), Munich SO, Munich Motet Choir—Missa Solemnis Calig ▲ CAL 50914
Weill, K.:Mahagonny, w. U. Lemper (sop), H. Wildhaber (ten), P. Haage (ten), T. Mohr (bar), S. Tremper (sgr), Jeffrey Cohen (pno), J. Mauceri (cnd), Berlin RIAS Chamber Ensemble [G] London ▲ 430168-2 [DDD]
Weill, K.:The Seven Deadly Sins, w. U. Lemper (sop), H. Wildhaber (ten), P. Haage (ten), T. Mohr (bar), S. Tremper (sgr), J. Mauceri (cnd), Berlin RIAS Chamber Ensemble [G] London ▲ 430168-2 [DDD]

Jungwirth, Manfred (bass)
Strauss, R.:Der Rosenkavalier, w. R. Crespin (sop), H. Donath (sop), Y. Minton (mez), G. Solti (cnd), Vienna PO [G] London 3-▲ 417493-2 [ADD]

Juon, Julia (mez)
Bertoni, F.:Orfeo ed Euridice, w. Jeannette Fischer (sop—Euridice), Julia Juon (mez—Orfeo), Steve Davislim (ten—Imeneo), R. Tschupp (cnd), Aargauer SO, Aarau New Canton School Choir *(rec Zurich Radio Studio, Oct 30–Nov 1, 1994)* Jecklin ▲ JEC 700

Jurado, Pilar (sgr)
Nebra, J.:Viento, w. Marta Almajano (sop), Maite Arruabarrena (sop), Raquel Pierotti (sop), Maria del Mar Doval (sgr), C. Coin (cnd), Limoges Baroque Ensemble Valois ▲ V 4752

Juranek, Lidia (sop)
Gluck, C.W.:La Corona, w. A. Slowakiewicz (sop), H. Gorzynska (sop), B. Nowicka (mez), T. Bugaj (cnd), Warsaw Sinfonia [I] Orfeo 2-▲ 135872 [DDD]

Jurecka, Antonin (ten)
Janácek, L.:Sárka, w. A. Nováková (sop), J. Válka (ten), K. Kunc (bass), B. Bakala (cnd), Brno RSO, Brno Radio Chorus *(rec live, 1953)* Multisonic ("Prague Spring Collection" series) ▲ 31 0154 [ADD]

Jurinac, Sena (sop)
Beethoven, L. van:Fidelio, w. C. Goltz (sop), G. Zampieri (ten), P. Schöffler (b-bar), O. Edelmann (bass), H. von Karajan (cnd), Vienna PO, Vienna State Opera Chorus [G] *(rec live, Salzburg Festival 7/27/57)* Claque 2-▲ CLQ 2007 (m)
Beethoven, L. van:Fidelio, w. M. Stader (sop), H. Peerce (ten), H. Knappertsbusch (cnd), Bavarian State Opera Orch, Bavarian State Opera Chorus [G] *(rec ca. 1961)* MCA Classics 2-▲ MCAD2-9809 [AAD]
Beethoven, L. van:Fidelio, w. J. Vickers (ten), H. Hotter (b-bar), G. Frick (bass), O. Klemperer (cnd), Royal Opera House Orch, Royal Opera House Chorus Covent Garden [G] *(rec live, Covent Garden, 3/7/61)* Melodram 2-▲ MEL 27076 (m) [ADD]
Beethoven, L. van:Fidelio, w. M. Mödl (sop), W. Windgassen (ten), A. Poell (bar), O. Edelmann (bass), G. Frick (bass), W. Furtwängler (cnd), Vienna PO *(rec Oct. 1953)* EMI Classics 2-▲ CDHB 64496
Cimarosa, D.:Giannina e Bernardone, w. D. De Cecco (sop), G. Sciutti (sop), M. Carlin (ten), M. Boriello (bar), S. Bruscantini (bar), C. De Antoni (sgr), N. Sanzogno (cnd), Milan RAI SO, Milan RAI Chorus [I] *(rec live, Milan July 26, 1953)* Melodram 2-▲ CDM 29505 [ADD]
Cornelius, P.:Der Barbier von Bagdad, w. H. Rössl-Majdan (mez), E. Majkut (ten), R. Schock (ten), A. Poell (bass-bar), G. Frick (bass), H. Hollreiser (cnd), Austrian RSO, Austrian Radio Chorus *(rec live Vienna 1952)* Melodram 2-▲ MEL 27050 (m) [AAD]
Cornelius, P.:Der Barbier von Bagdad, w. H. Rössl-Majdan (mez), E. Majkut (ten), R. Schock (ten), A. Poell (bass-bar), G. Frick (bass), H. Hollreiser (cnd), Austrian RSO, Austrian Radio Chorus [G] *(rec live Vienna, 1952)* Verona 2-▲ 27050/51 (m) [AA
Gluck, C.W.:Iphigénie en Tauride, w. F. Wunderlich (ten), H. Prey (bar), K. Engen (bass), R. Kubelik (cnd), Bavarian RSO, Bavarian Radio Chorus [1781 J.B. von Alxinger-Gluck German-language version] *(rec live, Munich 1965)* Myto 2-▲ 2 MCD 91544 [ADD]
Gluck, C.W.:Orfeo ed Euridice, w. G. Sciutti (sop), G. Simionato (mez), H. von Karajan (cnd), Vienna PO, Vienna State Opera Chorus *(rec live 1959)* Memories 2-▲ HR 4382/83 (m)
Humperdinck, E.:Hänsel und Gretel, w. Elisabeth Schwarzkopf (sop), Rita Streich (sop), Vittoria Palombini (mez), Rolando Panerai (bar), Bruna Ronshini (sgr), H. von Karajan (cnd), Milan Italian Radio-TV Orch, Milan RAI Chorus Stradivarius 2-▲ STV 12314
Humperdinck, E.:Hänsel und Gretel (sels), w. Sena Jurinac (sop—Hänsel), Elisabeth Schwarzkopf (sop—Gretel), Vittoria Palombini (mez—Witch), Rolando Panerai (sgr—Peter), Bruna Ronchini (sgr—Gertrude), H. Karajan (cnd), Milan RAI SO, Milan RAI Chorus—[Act 1] Suse, liebe Suse, was raschelt im Stroh; [Act 2] Ein Männlein steht im Walde ganz still und Stumm; Abends, will ich schlafen gehn; [Act 3] Wo bin ich? Wach' ich?; Und bist du dann drin...schwaps!; Die Englein haben's im Traum gesagt; Schunt, o schunt das Wunder an *(rec Milan, Dec. 25, 1954)* Legato Classics 3-▲ LCD 197-3
Mahler, G.:Songs from Rückert, w. I. Kertész (cnd), French National RSO—omitting Ich atmet' einen Linden Duft [G] *(rec live, Frankfurt, 3/25/62)* Melodram 3-▲ CDM 37091 [ADD]
Mozart, W.A.:Arias, w. Arleen Augér (sop), Kathleen Battle (sop), Irma Beilke (sop), Helena Braun (sop), Lisa Della Casa (sop), Maria Cebotari (sop), Ileana Cotrubas (sop), Helen Donath (sop), Mirella Freni (sop), Reri Grist (sop), Edita Gruberova (sop), Elisabeth Grümmer (sop), Hilde Güden (sop), Ingeborg Hallstein (sop), Luise Helletsgruber (sop), Gundula Janowitz (sop), Erika Köth (sop), Evelyn Lear (sop), Wilma Lipp (sop), Margaret Marshall (sop), Edith Mathis (sop), Jarmila Novotna (sop), Margherita Perras (sop), Lucia Popp (sop), Elisabeth Rethberg (sop), Anneliese Rothenberger (sop), Elisabeth Schumann (sop), Elisabeth Schwarzkopf (sop), Graziella Sciutti (sop), Irmgard Seefried (sop), Graziella Sciutti (sop), Julia Varady (sop), Agnes Baltsa (mez), Margit Bokor (mez), Brigitte Fassbaender (mez), Christa Ludwig (mez), Ann Murray (mez), Francisco Araiza (ten), Anton Dermota (ten), Helge Rosvaenge (ten), Rudolf Schock (ten), Peter Schreier (ten), Leopold Simoneau (ten), Eric Tappy (ten), Richard Tauber (ten), Gösta Winbergh (ten), Josef Witt (ten), Fritz Wunderlich (ten), Christian Boesch (bar), Willy Domgraf-Fassbaender (bar), Karl Dönch (bar), Dietrich Fischer-Dieskau (bar), Erich Kunz (bar), Eberhard Wächter (bar), Hans Hotter (b-bar), Paul Schöffler (b-bar), Cesare Siepi (b-bar), José Van Dam (b-bar), Walter Berry (bass), Geraint Evans (bass), Nicolai Ghiaurov (bass), Alexander Kipnis (bass), Richard Mayr (bass), Kurt Moll (bass), James Morris (bass), Ezio Pinza (bass), Martti Talvela (bass), Giorgio Tozzi (bass), Hans Duhan (sgr), Res Fischer (sgr), Marie Gerhart (sgr), *(various orchs & cnds)*—sels from Idomeneo, Die Entführung aus der Serail, Le nozze di Figaro, Don Giovanni, Così fan tutte, Die Zauberflöte & various arias Orfeo d'or ("Festspiel Dokumente" series) 5-▲ 408955
Mozart, W.A.:Così fan tutte (sels), w. A. Noni (sop), B. Thebom (mez), R. Lewis (ten), E. Kunz (bar), M. Borriello (bar), F. Busch (cnd), Glyndebourne Festival Orch *(rec Glyndebourne Festival, 1950)* Testament ▲ TES SBT 1040 [ADD]
Mozart, W.A.:Don Giovanni, w. I. Seefried (sop), M. Stader (sop), E. Haefliger (ten), D. Fischer-Dieskau (bar), K. C. Kohn (bass), F. Fricsay (cnd), Berlin RSO Deutsche Grammophon 3-▲ 437341-2
Mozart, W.A.:Don Giovanni, w. G. Janowitz (sop), G. von Milivkovic (mez), A. Kraus (ten), N. Ghiaurov (bass), C. M. Giulini (cnd), Rome RAI Orch, Rome RAI Chorus *(rec live, May 12, 1970)* Melodram 3-▲ MEL 37080
Mozart, W.A.:Nozze di Figaro, w. E. Schwarzkopf (sop), I. Seefried (sop), L. Villa (sop), R. Panerai (bar), H. von Karajan (cnd), La Scala Orch, La Scala Chorus [I] *(rec live Feb. 4, 1954)* Melodram 3-▲ MEL 37075 [AAD]

Jurinac, Sena (sop) (cont.)

Mozart, W.A.:Nozze di Figaro, w. E. Schwarzkopf (sop), I. Seefried (sop), E. Höngen (cta), G. London (bar), E. Kunz (bar), H. von Karajan (cnd), Vienna PO, Vienna State Opera Chorus—omitting recitatives [I] *(rec 1950)* EMI Classics ("Studio" series) 2-▲ CDMB 69639 (m) [ADD]

Mozart, W.A.:Nozze di Figaro, w. T. Stratas (sop), T. Berganza (mez), N. Condò (mez), A. Lazzari (ten), S. Bruscantini (bar), M. Petri (bass), G. Tadeo (bass), A. Mariotti (bass), Z. Mehta (cnd), *(orch unknown) (rec 1968)* Great Opera Performances 3-▲ GOP 712

Mozart, W.A.:Nozze di Figaro, w. G. Sciutti (sop), R. Stevens (mez), M. Sinclair (cta), D. McCoshan (ten), H. Counod (ten), G. Griffith (bar), S. Bruscantini (b-bar), F. Calabrese (bass), V. Gui (cnd), Glyndebourne Festival Orch, Glyndebourne Festival Chorus Classics for Pleasure ▲ CDCFP 4724 [ADD]

Mozart, W.A.:Requiem, w. L. West (alt), H. Loeffler (ten), F. Gutherie (bass), R. Leibowitz (cnd), Vienna State Opera Orch, Vienna State Opera Chorus [L] *(rec 1958)* MCA Classics 2-▲ MCAD2 9816 [AAD]

Mozart, W.A.:Requiem, w. L. West (alt), H. Loeffler (ten), F. Gutherie (bass), H. Scherchen (cnd), Vienna State Opera Orch, Vienna State Opera Chorus *(rec 1958)* Andromeda ▲ ANR 2525 [ADD]

Mozart, W.A.:Songs, w. M. Callas (sop), E. Grümmer (sop), E. Schwarzkopf (sop), R. Scotto (sop), T. Lemnitz (sop), E. Berger (sop), S. Jurinac (sop), E. Schumann (sop), I. Souez (sop), E. Rethberg (sop), L. Lehmann (sop), N. Gedda (ten), J. McCormack (ten), H. Roswenge (ten), H. Nash (ten), T. Gobbi (bar), G. Hüsch (bar), E. Kunz (bar), G. Frick (bass), E. Pinza (bass), A. Kipnis (bass) EMI Classics 4-▲ CDMD 63750

Mussorgsky, M.:Boris Godunov, w. N. Dobrianova (sop), D. Usunow (ten), N. Ghiaurov (bass), N. Ghiuselev (bass), A. Diakov (bass), H. von Karajan (cnd), Vienna PO, Vienna State Opera Chorus [R] *(rec live in Salzburg, 7/26/64)* Arkadia 2-▲ 210 (m) [ADD]

Pfitzner, H.:Palestrina, w. C. Ludwig (mez), F. Wunderlich (ten), G. Stolze (ten), O. Wiener (bar), G. Frick (bass), W. Berry (bass), R. Heger (cnd), Vienna State Opera Orch, Vienna State Opera Chorus *(rec live, Vienna 12/16/64)* Myto 3-▲ 3 MCD 92259 [ADD]

Strauss (II), Joh.:Der Zigeunerbaron (sels), w. W. Hollweg (ten), P. Anders (ten), K. Schmitt-Walter (bar), Schneider (sgr), G. Hann (bass), Marszalek (cnd), Cologne RSO, Cologne Radio Chorus [G] Acanta ▲ CD 43807 [DDD]

Strauss, R.:Der Rosenkavalier, w. Jarmila Barton (sop—Marianne), Lisa Della Casa (sop—Sophie), Sena Jurinac (sop—Octavian), Ilva Ligabue (sop—Orphan), Elisabeth Schwarzkopf (sop—Marschallin), Else Schürhoff (mez—Annina), Luisa Villa (mez—Milliner), Hugues Cuénod (ten—Marschallin's majordomo), Erich Majkut (ten—Valzacchi), Giuseppe Nessi (ten—Animal seller), Luciano Della Pergola (ten—Lackey/Faninal's majordomo), Antonio Pirino (ten—An Italian Singer), Gino Del Signore (ten—Lackey/Waiter), Erich Kunz (bar—Herr von Faninal), Paolo Pedani (bar—Lackey), Attilo Barbesi (bass—Lackey/Waiter), Enrico Campi (bass—Waiter), Otto Edelmann (bass—Baron Ochs), Bruno Fichtinger (bass—Notary), Franco Taino (bass—Waiter), Maria Amadini (sgr—Orphan), Pina Carrillo (sgr—Orphan), Joszi Trojan Regar (sgr—Innkeeper), H. von Karajan (cnd), La Scala Orch, La Scala Chorus *(rec La Scala Theater, Milan, Jan. 26, 1952)* Legato Classics 3-▲ LCD 197-3

Strauss, R.:Der Rosenkavalier, w. M. Reining (sop), H. Gueden (sop), L. Weber (bass), E. Kleiber (cnd), Vienna PO, Vienna State Opera Chorus [G] London ("Historic" series) ▲ 425950-2 (m) [ADD]

Strauss, R.:Der Rosenkavalier, w. E. Schwarzkopf (sop—Feldmarschallin), A. Rothenberger (sop—Sophie), S. Jurinac (sop—Octavian), O. Edelmann (bass—Baron Ochs), H. von Karajan (cnd), Vienna PO *(rec live, Salzburg, 8/1/64)* Arkadia 3-▲ 227 [ADD]

Strauss, R.:Der Rosenkavalier, w. L. Della Casa (sop), H. Gueden (sop), E. Kunz (bar), O. Edelmann (b-bar), H. von Karajan (cnd), Vienna PO, Vienna State Opera Chorus [G] *(rec live in Salzburg, 7/26/60)* Arkadia 3-▲ 213 [ADD]

Strauss, R.:Der Rosenkavalier (sels), w. L. Della Casa (sop—Feldmarschallin), S. Jurinac (sop—Octavian), H. von Karajan (cnd), Vienna PO *(rec live, Salzburg, 7/26/60)* Arkadia 3-▲ 227 [ADD]

Verdi, G.:Don Carlos, w. G. Simionato (mez), E. Fernandi (ten), E. Bastianini (bar), C. Siepi (b-bar), H. von Karajan (cnd), Vienna PO, Vienna State Opera Chorus [I] *(rec live, Salzburg 7/26/58)* Arkadia 2-▲ 220 [ADD]

Verdi, G.:Don Carlos, w. S. Jurinac (sop—Elisabetta), L. Rysanek (sop—Celestial Voice), F. Cossotto (mez—Princess Eboli), L. Dutoit (boy sop—Tebaldo), P. Domingo (ten—Don Carlo), E. Majkut (ten—Count of Lerma), M. Sereni (bar—Rodrigo), C. Siepi (bass—Philip II), I. Vinco (bass—Grand Inquisitor), T. Franc (bass—Friar), S. Varviso (cnd), Vienna State Opera Orch, Vienna State Opera Chorus Standing Room Only 2-▲ SRO 850 [ADD]

Wagner, R.:Der fliegende Holländer (sels), w. N. Bailey (bar), A. Van Mill (bass), F. Adam (cnd), Strasbourg Opera Orch, Strasbourg Opera Chorus—Senta's ballad (Jo-ho-hoe!...Traft ihr das Schiff) & Willst Du des Vaters Wahl [G] *(rec live, Strasbourg, 11/25/69)* Melodram 3-▲ CDM 37091 [ADD]

Wagner, R.:Tannhäuser, w. B. Martin (sop), H. Beirer (ten), H. Braun (bar), M. Talvela (bass), W. Sawallisch (cnd), La Scala Orch, La Scala Chorus [G] *(rec live, Milan 4/13/67)* Melodram 3-▲ CDM 37091 [ADD]

Jüten, Grit van (sop)

Künneke, E.:Der Vetter aus Dingsda (sels), w. Kollo (ten), B. Kusche (bar), Wolff (sgr), Breck (sgr), Geese, Künneke (cnd), Cologne RSO, Cologne Radio Chorus [G] Acanta ▲ CD 43460 [DDD]

Schultze, N.:Das kalte Herz, w. Elisabeth Steiner (mez), Heinz Kruse (ten), Detelf Zywietz (sgr), N. Schutze (cnd), Cologno RSO, Händel Collegium Koch Schwann 2-▲ SCH 318002 [DDD]

Kaarisola-Kulo, Satu (sop)

Vuori, H.:Songs of Dreams & Death, w. Heikki Kulo (vc) Finlandia ▲ FIN 12179 [DDD]

Kaasch, Donald (ten)

Rossini, G.:Armida, w. R. Fleming (sop), C. Bosi (ten), B. Fowler (ten), J. Francis (ten), G. Kunde (ten), I. Zennaro (ten), I. D'Arcangelo (bass), S. Zadvorny (bass), D. Gatti (cnd), Bologna Teatro Comunale Orch, Bologna Teatro Comunale Chorus *(rec Pesaro, Italy, Aug. 6-17, 1993)* Sony Classical 3-▲ S3K 58968 [DDD]

Stravinsky, I.:Oedipus Rex, w. F. Quivar (mez), P. Langridge (ten), J. Morris, J.-H. Rootering (bass), J. Bastin (bass), J. Levine (cnd), Chicago SO, Chicago Sym Chorus Deutsche Grammophon ▲ 435872-2

Kabaivanska, Raina (sop)

Basic 100, Vol. 78, w. Luciano Pavarotti (ten), Ingvar Wixell (bar), Rome Opera House Orch [cnd:Daniel Oren] RCA Victor ▲ 09026-68455-2 ■ 09026-68455-4

Boito, A.:Mefistofele (sels)—L'altra notte in fondo al mare Replay ("Butterfly" series) ▲ BMCD 033 [AAD]

Donizetti, G.:Fausta, w. G. Giacomini (ten), R. Bruson (bar), D. Oren (cnd), Rome Opera Orch, Rome Opera Chorus *(rec live, 1981)* Italian Opera Rarities 3-▲ IOR 7701 [ADD]

Magda Olivero & Flaviano Labò in Concert, w. Magda Olivero (sop), Flaviano Labò (ten), Jacques Bazire (cnd), Marsiglia Opera Orch, Gianpiero Matromei (bar), Carlo Meliciani (bar), Oliveiro de Fabritiis (cnd), La Scala Orch, Turin RAI Orch *(rec between 1969 & 1973)* Bongiovanni ▲ GB 1105 [ADD]

Massenet, J.:Thaïs, w. S. Bruscantini (bar), O. de Fabritiis (cnd), Catania Teatro Massimo Bellini Orch, Catania Teatro Massimo Bellini Chorus [I] *(rec live, 4/3/69)* Golden Age of Opera 2-▲ GAO 121/122 [ADD]

Puccini, G.:Madama Butterfly, w. Raina Kabaivanska (sop—Madama Butterfly), Alexandrina Milcheva (mez—Suzuki), Rossitza Troeva-Mircheva (cta—Kate Pinkerton), Nazzareno Antinori (ten—F.B. Pinkerton), Roumen Doikov (ten—Goro), Werther Vrachovski (ten—Il Principe Yamadori), Nelson Portella (bar—Sharpless), Kosta Dinkov (bass—Lo zio Bonzo), G. Bellini (cnd), Sofia PO, Svetoslav Obrenetov Bulgarian National Chorus *(rec Sophia, Bulgaria, Dec 1-13, 1982)* Arts Music 2-▲ 447161-2 [DDD]

Puccini, G.:Manon Lescaut, w. R. Kabaivanska (sop—Manon), R. Pallini (mez—Singer), P. Domingo (ten—des Grieux), E. Lorenzi (ten—Edmondo), F. Ricciardi (ten—Dancing Master), M. D'Anna (bar—Lescaut), A. Mariotti (bass—Geronte), F. Federici (bass—Innkeeper) Golden Age of Opera 2-▲ GAO 162/63 [ADD]

Puccini, G.:Tosca, w. Raina Kabaivanska (sop—Floria Tosca), Nazzareno Antinori (ten—Mario Cavaradossi), Roumen Doikov (ten—Spoletta), Enzo Dara (bar—Casare Angelotti/Il sagrestano), Nelson Portella (bar—Il Barone Scarpia), Stoyan Balabanov (bass—Sciarrone/Un carceriere), Borislav Peev (sgr—Un Pastore), G. Bellini (cnd), Sofia PO, Bulgarian National Radio Children's Choir, Svetoslav Obrenetov Bulgarian National Chorus *(rec Sophia, Bulgaria, Nov 14-27, 1982)* Arts Music ▲ 47158-2 [DDD]

Kabaivanska, Raina (sop) (cont.)

Puccini, G.:Tosca, w. Plácido Domingo (ten), Zanasi (sgr), F.M. Pradelli (cnd), La Scala Orch *(rec live, May 17, 1974)* Arkadia ("Historical Performances" series) 2-▲ 496

Puccini, G.:Tosca (sels)—Mario! Mario! Mario!; Vissi d'arte Replay ("Butterfly" series) ▲ BMCD 033 [AAD]

Puccini, G.:Tosca (sels), w. Luciano Pavarotti (ten), Ingvar Wixell (bar), D. Oren (cnd), Rome Opera Orch RCA ("Basic 100" series) ▲ 09026-68455-2 ■ 09026-68455-4

Verdi, G.:Don Carlos, w. O. Dominguez (mez), F. Corelli (ten), L. Quilico (bar), N. Ghiaurov (bass), N. Ghiuselev (bass), A. Guadagno (cnd), Hartford Opera Orch *(rec live 1966)* Melodram 2-▲ MEL 27511

Verdi, G.:Ernani, w. P. Domingo (ten), N. Ghiaurov (bass), Meliciani (sgr), A. Votto (cnd), La Scala Orch, La Scala Chorus *(rec live 12/7/69)* Melodram 2-▲ MEL 27064 (m) [AAD]

Verdi, G.:Ernani (sels)—Surta è la notte; Tu perfida Replay ("Butterfly" series) ▲ BMCD 033 [AAD]

Verdi, G.:Ernani (sels), w. P. Domingo (ten), La Scala Orch—six solo arias & one chorus *(rec live 12/4/69)* Melodram 2-▲ MEL 27064 (m) [AAD]

Verdi, G.:La forza del destino (sels), w. Giuseppe Giacomini (ten), Kurt Moll (bass), Norman Mittelmann (sgr), J. Rudel (cnd), *(orch unknown)*—Ah per sempre o mio bell'angiol; La vita è inferno all'infelice; Fuggir...ferito siete; Solenne in quest'ora; Fratello...Riconoscimi; Io muoio...confession *(rec Parigi, May 27, 1975)* Golden Age of Opera 2-▲ GAO 189/90 [ADD]

Verdi, G.:Otello, w. Mario del Monaco (ten), Tito Gobbi (bar), G. Solti (cnd), Royal Opera House Orch, Royal Opera House Chorus Covent Garden Pantheon 2-▲ PHE 6608

Verdi, G.:Otello, w. Josephine Veasey (mez), John Lanigan (ten), Mario del Monaco (ten), Tito Gobbi (bar), G. Solti (cnd), Royal Opera House Orch, Royal Opera House Covent Garden Chorus *(rec June 30, 1962)* Memories ▲ MEM 4583 [AAD]

Verdi, G.:Otello (sels)—Mia madre aveva una povera ancella Replay ("Butterfly" series) ▲ BMCD 033 [AAD]

Verdi, G.:Il trovatore, w. M. Cortez (ten), F. Bonisolli (ten), G. Zancanaro (bar), B. Bartoletti (cnd), Berlin State Opera Orch, Berlin State Opera Chorus [I] Acanta 2-▲ CD 43301 [DDD]

Wagner, R.:Rienzi, der Letzte der Tribunen (sels)—Finale dell'opera Replay ("Butterfly" series) ▲ BMCD 033 [AAD]

Zandonai, R.:Francesca da Rimini, w. P. Domingo (ten), M. Manuguerra (bar), N. Saetta (sgr), E. Queler (cnd), *(orch unknown) (rec live, March 22, 1973)* Standing Room Only 2-▲ SRO 840-2 [ADD]

Kabaivanska, Raina (sop)

Verdi, G.:La forza del destino (sels), w. Carlo Bergonzi (ten), I. Savini (cnd), Barcelona Teatro Liceo Orch, Barcelona Gran Teatro de Liceo Chorus *(rec live, Nov 13, 1972)* Arkadia ▲ 499

Kabat, J. (voc/glass hmc/saw/African dr/kalimba)

Kabat, J.:Child & the Moon-Tree, w. Neil B. Rolnick (elec) Centaur ▲ CRC 2047 [DDD]

Kabat, J.:Poems by H. D., w. B. Hudson (vn), M. Crispell (pno), A. Adzenyah (African drums/conga) [E] Leonarda ■ LE 319 (D)

Kachel, Jaroslav (ten)

Prokofiev, S.:They Are 7, w. K. Ančerl (cnd), Czech PO, Czech Phil Chorus Praga ▲ PR 254004

Kachlikova, Katerina (sop)

Brod, M.:Songs, Op. 32, w. Ivan Kusnjer (bar), Frantisek Kuda (pno) Supraphon ▲ SUP 112188 [DDD]

Kagel, Hans (bass)

Weber, C.M. von:Missa sancta 2, w. Gertrude Stoklassa (sop), Emmy Lisken (cta), Manfred Raucamp (ten), R. Bader (cnd), Stuttgart PO, Stuttgart Phil Chorus Koch Schwann ▲ SCH CD 316372

Kagel, M. (voice/glass tpt)

Kagel, M.:Blue's Blue:A Musico-Ethnological Reconstruction, w. M. Riessler (cl/sax), T. Ross (gtr), G. Wharton (vn) Montaigne ▲ MO 782003 [DDD]

Kahan, Bente (sgr)

Jiddischkeit:A Concert in the Jewish Spirit, w. Gjertrud's Gipsy Orch Victoria ▲ VCD 19064

Kaibaivanska, R. (sop)

Puccini, G.:Tosca, w. R. Kaibaivanska (sop—Floria), L. Pavarotti (ten—Mario), I. Wixell (bar—Scarpia), F. Federici (bass—Angelotti), D. Oren (cnd), Rome Opera Orch, Rome Opera Chorus RCA Red Seal ▲ 09026-61807-2; ■ 09026-61807-4

Puccini, G.:Tosca, w. R. Kaibaivanska (sop—Floria), L. Pavarotti (ten—Mario), I. Wixell (bar—Scarpia), F. Federici (bass—Angelotti), D. Oren (cnd), Rome Opera Orch, Rome Opera Chorus RCA Red Seal 2-▲ 09026-61806-2

Kalaš, Karel (bar)

Smetana, B.:The Brandenbergers in Bohemia, w. V. Soukupova (sop), A. Vetava (ten), J.H. Tichý (cnd), Prague National Theater Orch, Prague National Theater Chorus [G] Supraphon 2-▲ SUP 111802 [AAD]

Kalaš, Karel (bass)

Dvořák, A.:Stabat Mater, w. Drahomira Tikalova (sop), Marta Krasova (cta), Beno Blachut (ten), V. Talich (cnd), Czech PO, Czech Phil Chorus *(rec 1952)* Supraphon 2-▲ SUP 111902 [ADD]

Dvořák, A.:Vanda, w. Drahomira Tikalova (sop), Stefa Petrova (mez), Beno Blachut (ten), F. Dyk (cnd), Prague RSO, Jiri Pinkas (cnd), Prague Radio Chorus *(rec 1951)* Supraphon ("Hidden Treasures from Prague" series) 2-▲ SUP CD 3007 (m)

Kaldenberg, Keith (sgr)

Floyd, C.:Susannah, w. Phyllis Curtin (sop—Susannah Polk), Richard Cassilly (ten—Sam Polk), Norman Treigle (bass—Olin Blitch), Marietta Muhs Cosenza (sgr—Mrs. McLean), Marilyn Davidson (sgr—Mrs. Gleaton), Kay Long (sgr—Mrs. Hayes), Jean Young (sgr—Mrs. Ott), Alton Brim (sgr—Elder Hayes), Thomas Carter (sgr—Elder Gleaton), Jack Davis (sgr—Elder McLean), Keith Kaldenberg (sgr—Little Bat McLean), Burton Parker (sgr—Elder Ott), K. Andersson (cnd), New Orleans Opera Orch, New Orleans Opera Chorus *(rec Mar 31, 1962)* VAI Audio 2-▲ VAIA 1115-2 [ADD]

Kale, Stuart (ten)

Weill, K.:The Seven Deadly Sins, w. J. Migenes (sop), R. Tear (ten), A. Opie (bar), R. Kennedy (bass), M. Tilson Thomas (cnd), London SO CBS ▲ MK 44529 [DDD]

Kalenberg, Josef (ten)

Wagner, R.:Götterdämmerung (sels), w. G. Kappel (sop—Brünhilde), J. Kalenberg (ten—Siegfried), J. von Manowarda (bass—Mime), R. Heger (cnd), Vienna State Opera Orch, Vienna State Opera Chorus *(rec June 15, 1933)* Koch Schwann 2-▲ SCH 314592

Wagner, R.:Götterdämmerung (sels), w. Henny Trundt (sop—Brünnhilde), Josef Kalenberg (ten—Siegfried), Emil Schipper (bar—Gunther), Josef von Manowarda (bass—Hagen), C. Krauss (cnd), Vienna State Opera Orch *(rec Mar. 7, 1933)* Koch Schwann 2-▲ SCH 314642 [ADD]

Wagner, R.:Die Meistersinger von Nürnberg (sels), w. Viorica Ursuleac (sop—Eva), Rudolf Bockelmann (ten—Hans Sachs), Josef Kalenberg (ten—Walther), Hermann Wiedemann (bar—Beckmesser), C. Krauss (cnd), Vienna State Opera Orch, Vienna State Opera Chorus *(rec Jan. 20, 1933)* Koch Schwann 2-▲ SCH 314642 [ADD]

Wagner, R.:Der Ring des Nibelungen (sels), w. Adele Kern (sop), Anny Konetzni (sop), Hilde Konetzni (sop), Elisabeth Schumann (sop), Enid Szantho (cta), Josef Kalenberg (ten), Max Lorenz (ten), Set Svanholm (ten), Erich Zimmermann (ten), Hans Hotter (bar), Jaro Prohaska (bar), Emil Schipper (bar), Paul Schöffler (b-bar), Ludwig Hoffmann (bass), H. Knappertsbusch (cnd), Vienna State Opera Orch *(rec Vienna, 1937-1943)* Koch Schwann 2-▲ SCH 314742 [ADD]

Wagner, R.:Siegfried (sels), w. A. Konetzni (sop—Brünhilde), J. Kalenberg (ten—Siegfried), H. Knappertsbusch (cnd), Vienna State Opera Orch, Vienna State Opera Chorus *(rec Apr. 18, 1936)* Koch Schwann 2-▲ SCH 314562 [ADD]

Wagner, R.:Tannhäuser (sels), w. Lotte Lehmann (sop—Elisabeth), Josef Kalenberg (ten—Tannhäuser), Richard Mayr (bass—Landgraf), Friedrich Schorr (bass—Wolfram), R. Heger (cnd), Vienna State Opera Orch *(rec Vienna, Sept. 25, 1933)* Koch Schwann 2-▲ SCH 314622 [ADD]

Kales, Elisabeth (sop)

Strauss (II), Joh.:Wiener Blut, w. H. Papouschek (sop), S. Martikke (sop), A. Dallapozza (ten), K. Ruzicka (ten), E. Kuchar (ten), W. Kandutsch (bar), K. Dönch (bar), O. Kolmann (bass), R. Bibl (cnd), Vienna Volksoper Orch, Vienna Volksoper Chorus Denon 2-▲ CO 8105 [DDD]

Kállay, Gábor (ten)

Bengraf, J.:Sacred Music, w. Ingrid Kertesi (sop), Katalin Gémes (mez), Ákos Ambrus (bar), István Ella (org), Zsolt Kovács (vc), Balázs Arnóth (bn), Vilmos Buza (db), J. Dobra (cnd), Vienna-Szász CO, Tomkins Vocal Ensemble—Te Deum; O sacrum convivium; Libera me; Gloria [from Missa solemnis in D] Hungaroton ▲ HCD 31609 [DDD]

Kállay, Gábor (ten) (cont.)
Caldara, A.:Stabat Mater, w. I. Verebics (sop), É. Lax (mez), B. Szilágyi (bar), E. Kollár (cnd), Concerto Armonico Budapest, Monteverdi Chamber Choir [L] Hungaroton ▲ HCD 31273 [DDD]
Druschetzky, G.:Missa solemnis, w. Ingrid Kertesi (sop), Katalin Gémes (mez), Ákos Ambrus (bar), István Ella (org), Zsolt Kovács (vc), Balázs Árnóth (bn), Vilmos Buza (db), J. Dobra (cnd), Vienna–Szász CO, Tomkins Vocal Ensemble Hungaroton ▲ HCD 31609 [DDD]
Esterházy, P.:Harmonia caelestis, w. M. Fers (sop), M. Zádori (sop), K. Gémes (mez), K. Károlyi (cta), J. Moldvay (bass), P. Németh (cnd), Capella Savaria, Savaria Vocal Ensemble [period instrs] [L] Hungaroton 2-▲ HCD 31148/49 [DDD]
Liszt, F.:Septam sacramenta, w. T. Takács (mez), J. Bándi (ten), K. Kaváts (bar), Zsuzsa Elekes (org), I. Zámbó (cnd), Hungarian State Orch, Hungarian People's Army Male Chorus, Jeunesses Musicales Women's Chorus [L] Hungaroton ▲ HCD 12748 [DDD]

Kallen, Wendy (sop)
Vali, R.:Persian Folk Songs, w. R. Black (cnd), Slovak RSO Bratislava, Slovak Radio Chorus *(rec Slovak Radio & Television Studios)* Master Muscicians Collective ▲ MMC 2021 [DDD]

Kallisch, Cornelia (cta)
Bach, J.S.:Mass in b, BWV 232, w. A. Stumphius (sop), R. Wörle (ten), A. Schmidt (bass), H.-M. Schneidt (cnd), Munich Bach Orch, Munich Bach Choir *(rec Mar 21, 1992)* Calig 2-▲ CAL 5029/30 [ADD]
Bach, J.S.:Mass in b, BWV 232, w. M. Venuti (sop), C. Prégardien (ten), A. Scharinger (bass), E. Ortner (cnd), Salzburg Baroque Ensemble, Arnold Schoenberg Choir Koch Schwann 2-▲ SCH 312512 [DDD]
Handel, G.F.:Messiah, w. Donna Brown (sop), R. Sacca (ten), Alastair Miles (bass), H. Rilling (cnd), Stuttgart Bach Collegium, Stuttgart Gächinger Kantorei Hänssler Classic 2-▲ HAN 98975 [DDD]
Handel, G.F.:Messiah (reorchd Mozart), w. Donna Brown (sop), R. Saccà (ten), Alastair Miles (bass), H. Rilling (cnd), Stuttgart Bach Collegium, Gächinger Kantorei [G] Hänssler Classic 2-▲ 98.975 [DDD]
Hindemith, P.:Wie es wär', wenn's anders wär, w. Christiane Oelze (sop) Villa Musica Ensemble MD + G ▲ MDG 3040535 [DDD]
Schoeck, O.:Songs (comp), w. Till Körber (pno)—3 Songs, Op. 2; 4 Songs, Op. 3; Himmelstrauer [from Op. 5]; 4 Songs, Op. 14; 5 Songs [from Op. 15]; 4 Songs [from Op. 17]; 9 Songs [from Op. 20] *(rec May 1994)* Jecklin ▲ JD 674
Stravinsky, I.:Les Noces, w. U. Sonntag (sop), M. Schäfer (ten), P. Lika (bass), C. Rausch (bass), et al., W. Schäfer (cnd), Frankfurt Kantorei [G] Koch Schwann ▲ 314 021 [DDD]

Kalm, Stephen (bar)
Monk, M.:Atlas, w. D. Hanchard (sop), R. Een (sgr), S.-Z. Chen (sgr), M. Monk (cnd), *(orch unknown)* *(rec June 1992)* ECM New Series ▲ 78118-21491-2 [DDD]
Partch, H.:17 Lyrics by Li Po, w. Ted Mook (ten vn) Tzadik ▲ TZA 7012 [DDD]

Kálmándi, Mihály (bar)
Mascagni, P.:Lodoletta, w. M. Spacagna (sop), P. Kelen (ten), B. Szilágyi (bar), L. Polgár (bass), C. Rosekrans (cnd), Hungarian State Orch, Hungarian State Choruses [I] Hungaroton 2-▲ HCD 31307/08 [DDD]

Kalmár, Magda (sop)
Borodin, A.:Prince Igor, w. Infantino (sgr), G. Taddei (ten), B. Christoff (bass), O. Dominguez (mez), A. La Rosa Parodi (cnd), Rome RAI Orch, Rome RAI Chorus *(rec live 9/19/64)* Melodram 2-▲ MEL 27028 (s)
Cherubini, L.:Médée, w. S. Sass (sop), T. Takacs (mez), V. Luchetti (ten), K. Kovats (bass), L. Gardelli (cnd), Budapest SO, Hungarian Radio Chorus [I] Hungaroton 2-▲ HCD 11904/05
Erkel, F.:Hunyadi László, w. S. Sass (sop), D. Gulyás (ten), A. Molnar (ten), I. Gáti (bar), S. Sólyom-Nagy (bar), J. Kovács (cnd), Hungarian State Opera Orch, Hungarian State Opera Chorus [Hun] Hungaroton 3-▲ HCD 12581/83 [DDD]
Lehár, F.:Das Land des Lächelns (sels), w. Házy (sop), Szimándy (sgr), Bende (sgr), G. Oberfrank (cnd), Budapest SO, Hungarian Radio-TV Chorus [Hun] Hungaroton ▲ HCD 16809 [ADD]
Make Wonder:Songs from Operettas, w. Éva Köteles (sgr), Judit Takács (sgr), Bori Szita (sgr), Budapest SO [cnd:Tamás Bródy], Hungarian State Orch [cnd:András Sebestyén] Hungaroton ▲ HCD 16613 [AAD]
Mendelssohn, F.:A Midsummer Night's Dream (comp), w. M. Bokor (mez), A. Fischer (cnd), Hungarian State Orch [G] White Label ▲ HRC 049 [DDD]
Pergolesi, G.B.:Stabat mater, w. J. Hamari (mez), L. Gardelli (cnd), Franz Liszt CO [L] Hungaroton ▲ HCD 12201
Puccini, G.:Gianni Schicchi, w. C. Melis (sop), A. Ferencsik (cnd), Hungarian State Opera Orch [I] Hungaroton ▲ HCD 12541 [DDD]

Kalter, Sabine (cta)
Wagner, R.:Tristan und Isolde, w. K. Flagstad (sop), L. Melchior (ten), H. Janssen (bar), E. List (bass), F. Reiner (cnd), Royal Opera House Orch, Royal Opera House Chorus Covent Garden [G] *(rec live, Covent Garden May/June 1936)* VAI Audio 3-▲ VAIA 1004-3 (m) [ADD]
Wagner, R.:Tristan und Isolde, w. Kirsten Flagstad (sop), Lauritz Melchior (ten), Emmanuel List (bass), F. Reiner (cnd), London PO Enterprise ("The Radio Years" series) 3-▲ ENT 39 (m)

Kaludov, Kaludi (ten)
Janácek, L.:Slavonic Mass, w. N. Troitskaya (sop), E. Randova (cta), S. Leiferkas (bass), T. Trotter (org), C. Dutoit (cnd), Montreal SO, Montreal Sym Chorus London ▲ 436211-2
Mussorgsky, M.:Khovanshchina, w. A. Miltcheva (mez), M. Popov (ten), Z. Gadjev (bass), N. Ghiaurov (bass), N. Ghiuselev (bass), E. Tchakarov (cnd), Sofia National Opera Orch, Sofia National Opera Chorus Sony Classical 3-▲ S3K 45831
Orff, C.:Catulli Carmina, w. E. Stoyanova (sop), M. Milkov (cnd), Bulgarian Radio-TV SO, Bulgarian Radio-TV Chorus [L] *(rec live in Sofia, 1988)* Forlane ▲ FOR 16610 [DDD]
Rachmaninoff, S.:The Bells, w. A. Pendachanska (sop), S. Leiferkus (bar), C. Dutoit (cnd), Philadelphia Orch London ▲ 440355-2 [DDD]

Kaluza, Stefania (mez)
Respighi, O.:Lucrezia, w. Adriana Kohútková (sop—Venilia), Michela Remor (sop—Lucrezia), Stefania Kaluza (mez—La Voce), Denisa Šlepkovská (mez—Servia), Ludovít Ludha (ten—Collatino), Igor Pasek (ten—Bruto), Ján Durco (bar—Tito/Valerio), Richard Haan (bar—Tarquinio), Rado Hanák (bass—Arunte/Spurio Lucrezio) *(rec Concert Hall of the Slovak Radio, Bratislava, June 9-16, 1994)* Marco Polo ▲ 8.223717 [DDD]

Kamann, Karl (bar)
Wagner, R.:Die Meistersinger von Nürnberg (sels), w. Maria Reining (sop—Eva), Max Lorenz (ten—Walther), Erich Zimmermann (ten—David), Karl Kamann (bar—Hans Sachs), W. Furtwängler (cnd), Vienna State Opera Orch *(rec Vienna, Nov. 25, 1937)* Koch Schwann 2-▲ SCH 314702 [ADD]

Kamas, Pavel (bar)
Báchorek, M.:Hukvald Poem, w. Drahomíra Drobková (sop), Břetislav Vojkůvka (ten), Otakar Brousek (reciter), O. Trhlík (cnd), Prague SO, Ostrava Female Chamber Chorus, Permoník Children's Chorus *(rec Smetana Hall of Prague's Municipal House, Feb 10 & 11, 1988)* Panton ▲ 811338-2 [DDD]
Báchorek, M.:Music of, w. Osvald Albín (nar), Otakar Brousek (nar), Jan Vlassak (nar), Brigita Šulcová (sop), Drahomira Drobková (cta), Karel Průša (bass), Pavel Kamas (sgr), Jan Kyzlink (sgr), Jana Stuperkova-Majtnerova (sgr), Bretislav Vojkuvka (sgr), O. Trhlík (cnd), Ostrava Janáček PO, Prague SO, Ostrava Janáček Chorus, Ostrava Women's Chamber Chorus, Permoník Children's Chorus—Lidice; Stereofonietta; Hukvald Poem Panton ▲ PAN 811338 [AAD/DDD]

Kamenov, Hristo (ten)
Beethoven, L. van:Mass, Op. 86, w. E. Markova (sop), L. Parachikova (cta), I. Petrov (bass), C. Iliev (cnd), Sofia State PO, Sofia State Chorus [L] Musique d'Abord ▲ HMA 190109 [AAD]
Orff, C.:Carmina burana, w. R. Bareva (sop), Yanukov (bar), G. Robev (cnd), Sofia PO, Bulgarian choirs [G, L] Forlane ▲ FOR 16556 [DDD]
Orthodox Wedding Ceremony & New Year Service, w. M. Popsavov (cnd), Stefan Markov (bass) Gega ▲ GD 142 [DDD]
Orthodox Wedding Ceremony & New Year's Celebrations, w. Kamenov, Hristo (ten), S. Markov (bass), Bulgarian Mixed Choir [cnd:Miroslav Popsavov] *(rec 1993)* Jade ▲ JAD C 108
Schubert, Franz:Mass 2, w. E. Maksimova (sop), I. Dobrev (bass), V. Kazandjiev (cnd), Sofia Soloists CO, Rodina Chorus [L] Musique d'Abord ▲ HMA 190111 [AAD]

Kammer, Salome (nar)
Schoenberg, A.:Pierrot lunaire, w. H. Zender (cnd), Avantgarde Ensemble MD + G ▲ MDG 6130579 [DDD]

Kammer, Salome (voc)
Cage, J.:Aria MD + G ▲ MDG CD 6130701

Kammerloher, Katharina (alt)
Bach, J.S.:Cant 205, w. Efrat Ben-Nunn (sop), Christoph Prégardien (ten), Klaus Häger (bass), R. Jacobs (cnd), Berlin Academy for Early Music, Berlin Chamber Chorus Harmonia Mundi France 2-▲ HMC 901544.45

Kamp, Harry van der (bass)
Bach, Joh. Christoph:Motets & Cants, w. *(ensemble unknown)* Sony Classical ("Vivarte" series) ▲ SK 68264
Bach, J.S.:Cant 27, w. Markus Schäfer (ten), G. Leonhardt (cnd), Baroque Orch, Tölz Boys' Choir Sony Classical ("Vivarte" series) ▲ SK 68265
Bach, J.S.:Cant 34, w. Markus Schäfer (ten), G. Leonhardt (cnd), Baroque Orch, Tölz Boys' Choir Sony Classical ("Vivarte" series) ▲ SK 68265
Bach, J.S.:Cant 41, w. Markus Schäfer (ten), G. Leonhardt (cnd), Baroque Orch, Tölz Boys' Choir Sony Classical ("Vivarte" series) ▲ SK 68265
Bach, J.S.:Mass in b, BWV 232, w. J. Smith (sop), M. Chance (ct), N. van der Meel (ten), F. Brüggen (cnd), Orch of the 18th Century, Netherlands Chamber Choir [L] *(rec live)* Philips ("Digital Classics" series) 2-▲ 426238-2 [DDD]
Biber, H. von:Requiem à 15, w. Marta Almajano (sop), Mieke van der Sluis (sop), John Elwes (ten), Mark Padmore (ten), Frans Huijts (bar), G. Leonhardt (cnd), Netherlands Bach Society Baroque Orch, Netherlands Bach Society Choir *(rec Utrecht, Germany, Oct 22-24, 1994)* Deutsche Harmonia Mundi ▲ 05472-77344-2 [DDD]
Biber, H. von:Requiem à 15, w. S. Paiu (sgr), B. Lettinga (alt), G. Leonhardt (cnd), Netherlands Bach Society Baroque Orch, Netherlands Bach Society Choir Deutsche Harmonia Mundi ▲ 05472-77277-2
Bruhns, N.:Cants, w. *(ensemble unknown)* Sony Classical ("Vivarte" series) ▲ SK 68264
Buxtehude, D.:Cants, w. *(ensemble unknown)* Sony Classical ("Vivarte" series) ▲ SK 68264
Cavalli, P.F.:Vespero della beata Vergine Maria, w. Barbara Borden (sop), Emily van Evera (sop), Markus Brutscher (ten), Mark Padmore (ten), Rodrigo del Pozo (ten), Gerd Türk (ten), Harry van der Kamp (bass), Peter Zimpel (sgr), Bruce Dickey (sackbut), Charles Toet (sackbut), Concerto Palatino, Schola Cantorum Basiliensis Harmonia Mundi France ("Documenta" series) 2-▲ HMC 905219/20
Eybler, J.L.E. von:Requiem mit Libera, w. B. Schlick (sop), W. Helbich (cnd), Steintor Barock Bremen, Alsfeld Vocal Ensemble CPO ▲ CPO 999234 [DDD]
Gabrieli, G.:Music of, w. David Cordier (alt), Wilfried Jochens (ten), Rufus Müller (ten), Gerd Türk (ten), R. Wilson (cnd), Musica Fiata, La Capella Ducale—Toccata [arr Wilson]; Buccinate in neomenia tuba à 19; Canzon XVII à 12; Dulcis Jesu patris imago [Son con voce à 20]; Timor et remor à 6; Son con 3 Vns; Son XIX à 15; In ecclesiis à 14; Canzon V à 7; Jubilate Deo à 10; Son XVIII à 14; Cantate Domino à 8; Canzon primi toni à 10; Misericordia tua Domine à 12; Canzon X à 8; Toccata primi toni; Magnificat à 33 [reconstructed by Wilson]; Benedictus es Dominus à 8 *(rec St. Osdag Church, Mandelsloh, Germany, June 11-15, 1994)* Sony Classical ("Vivarte" series) 2-▲ S2K 66254 [DDD]
Grandi, A.:Sacred Music, w. David Cordier (alt), Wilfried Jochens (ten), Rufus Müller (ten), Gerd Türk (ten), R. Wilson (cnd), Musica Fiata, La Capella Ducale—Heu mihi [Dialogo à 4]; O quam tu pulchra es; Cantemus Domino; Salvum me fac, Deus [Basso solo] *(rec St. Osdag Church, Mandelsloh, Germany, June 11-15, 1994)* Sony Classical ("Vivarte" series) 2-▲ S2K 66254 [DDD]
Handel, G.F.:Te Deum, "Caroline", w. Mieke van der Sluis (sop), Graham Pushee (alt), Harry Van Berne (ten), W. Helbich (cnd), Bremen Baroque Orch, Alfelder Vocal Ensemble CPO ▲ CPO 999244 [DDD]
Handel, G.F.:The Ways of Zion Do Mourn, w. Mieke van der Sluis (sop), Graham Pushee (alt), Harry van Berne (ten), W. Helbich (cnd), Bremen Baroque Orch, Alfelder Vocal Ensemble CPO ▲ CPO 999244 [DDD]
Haydn, J.:Mass 10, "Kriegsmesse", "Paukenmesse", w. Ann Monoyios (sop), Monica Groop (mez), Jörg Hering (ten), B. Weil (cnd), Tafelmusik, Tölz Boys' Choir Sony Classical ("Vivarte" series) ▲ SK 68255
Haydn, J.:Die Schöpfung, w. Ann Monoyios (sop—Gabriel/Eva), Jörg Hering (ten—Uriel), Harry van der Kamp (bass—Raphael/Adam), B. Weil (cnd), Tafelmusik, Tölz Boys' Choir *(rec Bad Tolz, Germany, Aug. 31-Sept. 4, 1993)* Sony Classical ("Vivarte" series) 2-▲ SX2K 57965 [DDD]
Mozart, W.A.:Requiem, w. B. Schlick (sop), C. Watkinson (cta), C. Prégardien (ten), T. Koopman (cnd), Amsterdam Baroque Orch, Netherlands Bach Society Choir [L] Erato ▲ 2292-45472-2 [DDD] ■ 2292-45472-4
Purcell, H.:Anthems & Services, w. David Cordier (alt), John Elwes (ten), Peter Kooy (bass), Gustav Leonhardt (org), Tölz Boys' Choir—In thee, O Lord, do I put my trust; My beloved spake; O praise God in His holiness; Praise the Lord, O Jerusalem; Rejoice in the Lord always Sony Classical ("Vivarte" series) ▲ SK 53981
Purcell, H.:Musick's Hand-maid, w. Ellen Hargis (sop), Ian Honeyman (ten), Rodrigo del Pozo (ten), Paul O'Dette (thb/cittern/lt), Andrew Lawrence-King (hps/org/hpd), A. Lawrence-King (cnd), Harp Consort Astrée ▲ E 8564
Rosenmüller, J.:Cants, w. *(ensemble unknown)* Sony Classical ("Vivarte" series) ▲ SK 68264
Schubert, Franz:Mass 1, w. Alexander Nader (sop), Thomas Puchegger (sop), Georg Leskovich (alto), Jörg Hering (ten), Kurt Azesberger (ten), Arno Hartmann (org), B. Weil (cnd), Orch of the Age of Enlightenment, Vienna Boys' Choir *(rec Vienna, Austria, Sept 1995)* Sony Classical ("Vivarte" series) ▲ SK 68247 [DDD]
Schubert, Franz:Mass 2, w. Thomas Puchegger (sop), Jörg Hering (ten), Arno Hartmann (org), B. Weil (cnd), Orch of the Age of Enlightenment, Vienna Boys' Choir *(rec Vienna, Austria, Sept 1995)* Sony Classical ("Vivarte" series) ▲ SK 68247 [DDD]
Schubert, Franz:Mass 3, w. Alexander Nader (sop), Thomas Puchegger (sop), Belá Fischer (alt), Georg Leskovich (alt), Jörg Hering (ten), Arno Hartmann (org), B. Weil (cnd), Orch of the Age of Enlightenment, Chorus Viennensis, Vienna Boys' Choir Sony Classical ("Vivarte" series) ▲ SK 68248
Schubert, Franz:Mass 4, w. Alexander Nader (sop), Thomas Puchegger (sop), Belá Fischer (alt), Georg Leskovich (alt), Jörg Hering (ten), Arno Hartmann (org), B. Weil (cnd), Orch of the Age of Enlightenment, Chorus Viennensis, Vienna Boys' Choir Sony Classical ("Vivarte" series) ▲ SK 68248
Schubert, Franz:Mass 6, w. Benjamin Schmidinger (sop), Albin Lenzer (alt), Kurt Azesberger (ten), Jörg Hering (ten), B. Weil (cnd), Orch of the Age of Enlightenment, Vienna Boys' Choir Sony Classical ▲ SK 66255
Schütz, H.:Cants, w. *(ensemble unknown)* Sony Classical ("Vivarte" series) ▲ SK 68264
Schütz, H.:Symphoniae sacrae 1, w. Barbara Borden (sop), Nele Gramss (sop), Rogers Covey-Crump (ten), John Potter (ten), Douglas Nasrawi (ten), Concerto Palatino Choir Accent 2-▲ 9178/79 [DDD]
Steffani, A.:Stabat Mater, w. Marta Almajano (sop), Mieke van der Sluis (sop), John Elwes (ten), Mark Padmore (ten), G. Leonhardt (cnd), Netherlands Bach Society Baroque Orch, Netherlands Bach Society Choir *(rec Utrecht, Germany, Oct 22-24, 1994)* Deutsche Harmonia Mundi ▲ 05472-77344-2 [DDD]
Tunder, F.:Cants, w. *(ensemble unknown)* Sony Classical ("Vivarte" series) ▲ SK 68264
Valls, F.:Scala Arentina Mass, w. S. Paiu (sop), M. van der Sluis (sop), B. Lettinga (alt), D. Cordier (ct), J. Elwes (ten), G. Leonhardt (cnd), Netherlands Bach Society Baroque Orch, Netherlands Bach Society Choir Deutsche Harmonia Mundi ▲ 05472-77277-2
Weckmann, M.:Cants, w. *(ensemble unknown)* Sony Classical ("Vivarte" series) ▲ SK 68264

Kämpf, Bernd (bar)
Draeseke, F.:Mysterium:Christus, w. C. Bischoff (sop), A. Vogel (sop), E. Dersen (alt), K. Markus (ten), H.J. Ritzerfeld (ten), P. Langshaw (bar), J. Sonnenschmidt (org), U.-R. Follert (cnd), Breslau State PO, Evangelical Boys' Choir Palatine, Heilbronn Vocal Ensemble, Palatine Kurrende Bayer 5-▲ 100175/79
Duruflé, M.:Requiem, w. M. Palberg (mez), B. Kämpf (cnd), Neuwieder Chamber Chorus [L] Motette ▲ CD 50241 [DDD]

▲ = CD ♦ = Enhanced CD Δ = MD ■ = Cassette Tape □ = DCC

Kamps, Louise Charlotte (mez)
Wagner, R.:Der Ring des Nibelungen, w. Gré Brouwenstein (sop—Freia/Sieglinde), Ilse Hollweg (sop—Waldvogel), Gerda Lammers (sop—Ortlinde), Paula Lenchner (sop—Wellgunde/Gerhilde), Hilde Scheppan (sop—Helmwige), Astrid Varnay (sop—Brünnilde/3rd Norn), Lore Wissmann (sop—Woglinde), Maria von Ilosvay (mez—Flosshilde/Schwertleite/2nd Norn), Louise Charlotte Kamps (mez—Siegrune), Jean Madeira (mez—Erda/Rossweisse/1st Norn), Georgine van Milinkovic (mez—Fricka/Grimgerde), Elisabeth Schärtel (mez—Waltraute), Paul Kuën (ten—Mime), Ludwig Suthaus (ten—Loge), Josef Traxel (ten—Froh), Wolfgang Windgassen (ten—Siegmund/Siegfried), Alfons Herwig (bar—Donner), Hermann Uhde (bar—Gunther), Hans Hotter (b-bar—Wotan), Gustav Neidlinger (b-bar—Alberich), Josef Griendl (bass—Fasolt/Hunding/Hagen), Arnold van Mill (bass—Fafner), H. Knappertsbusch (cnd), Bayreuth Festival Orch, Bayreuth Festival Chorus *(rec live, Bayreuth, Aug 13–17, 1956)* Golden Melodram 14-▲ GM 1.001 [ADD]

Kanawa, Kiri Te (sop)—see Te Kanawa, Kiri

Kandutsch, W. (bar)
Strauss (II), Joh.:Wiener Blut, w. H. Papouschek (sop), S. Martikke (sop), E. Kales (sop), A. Dallapozza (ten), K. Ruzicka (ten), E. Kuchar (ten), K. Dönch (bar), O. Kolmann (bass), R. Bibl (cnd), Vienna Volksoper Orch, Vienna Volksoper Chorus Denon 2-▲ CO 8105 [DDD]

Kang, Eyvind (voc/vn/bass/hp/tuba/kpd/pno)
Kang, E.:Music of—Angel with Wings Torn Off; Earth; Thin; Rabid Pearly Tunnel; Inevitability; The Engagement; Winged Head over Troubled Waters; Invisible Man; Universal; Extra Cry; The Banishment; Living Corpses; and others Tzadik ("Composer" series) ▲ TZA 7013 [DDD]

Kang, Philip (bass)
Berlioz, H.:L'Enfance du Christ, w. M. Zimmermann (mez), J. Aler (ten), E. Wilm Schulte (bass), S. Dean (bass), E. Inbal (cnd), Frankfurt RSO, Cologne Radio Chorus [F] Denon 2-▲ CO 76863/4 [DDD]

Wagner, R.:Siegfried, w. A. Evans (sop—Brünhilde), H. Leidland (sop—Waldvogel), B. Svendén (mez—Erda), S. Jerusalem (ten—Siegfried), G. Clark (ten—Mime), J. Tomlinson (bass—Der Wanderer), G. von Kannen (bass—Alberich), *(cnd & orch unknown)* Teldec 4-▲ 4509-94193-2 [DDD]

Kannen, Günter von (bass)
Beethoven, L. van:Fidelio, w. Elizabeth Norberg-Schulz (sop—Marzelline), Deborah Voigt (sop—Lenore), Ben Heppner (ten—Florestan), Michael Schade (ten—Jaquino), Günter von Kanna‡en (b-bar—Don Pizarro), Matthias Hölle (bass—Rocco), Thomas Quasthoff (bass—Don Fernando), C. Davis (cnd), Bavarian RSO, Bavarian Radio Chorus, Bavarian State Opera Men's Chorus *(rec Herkulessaal der Residenz, Munich, May 15–25, 1995)* RCA Victor 2-▲ 09026-68344-2 [DDD]

Gazzaniga, G.:Don Giovanni, w. P. Coburn (sop), J. Kaufmann (sop), J. Aler (ten), R. Swensen (ten), J.-L. Chaignaud (bar), A. Scharinger (bass), S. Soltesz (cnd), Munich RSO, Munich Radio Chorus [I] Orfeo 2-▲ 214902 [DDD]

Wagner, R.:Siegfried, w. A. Evans (sop—Brünhilde), H. Leidland (sop—Waldvogel), B. Svendén (mez—Erda), S. Jerusalem (ten—Siegfried), G. Clark (ten—Mime), J. Tomlinson (bass—Der Wanderer), G. von Kannen (bass—Alberich), P. Kang (bass), *(cnd & orch unknown)* Teldec 4-▲ 4509-94193-2 [DDD]

Kapelle, Ingrid (sop)
Ryelandt, J.:Agnus Dei, w. Lucienne van Deyck (mez), Joseph Cornwell (ten), Huub Claessens (bass), Stephan Macleod (bass), G. Llewellyn (cnd), Royal Flanders PO, Altra Voce, Audite Nova *(rec live, Elisabeth Hall, Antwerp, Holland, Dec 9, 1994)* Marco Polo 2-▲ 8.223785/86 [DDD]

Kapellmann, Franz-Josef (bass)
Handel, G.F.:L'Allegro, Il Penseroso ed il Moderato, w. V. Hruba-Freiberger (sop), D. Schellenberger-Ernst (sop), J. Kowalski (alt), Rabsilber (sgr), R. Reuter (cnd), Berlin Comic Opera Orch, Berlin Radio Chorus Berlin Classics 2-▲ BER 1147 [DDD]

Wagner, R.:Das Rheingold, w. Gabriele Fontana (sop—Woglinde), Nancy Gustafson (sop—Freia), Ildiko Komlosi (mez—Wellgunde), Hanna Schwarz (mez—Fricka), Elena Zaremba (mez—Erda), Margareta Hintermeier (cta—Flosshilde), Kim Begley (ten—Loge), Peter Schreier (ten—Mime), Thomas Sunnegardh (ten—Froh), Robert Hale (bass-bar—Wotan), Walter Fink (bass—Fafner), Franz-Josef Kapellmann (bass—Alberich), Jan-Hendrik Rootering (bass—Fasolt), Eike Wilm Schulte (bass—Donner), C. von Dohnányi (cnd), Cleveland Orch *(rec Severance Hall, Cleveland, Ohio, Dec 1993)* London 2-▲ 443690-2

Káplán (sgr)
Vivaldi, A.:L'Olimpiade (sels), w. M. Zempléni (sop), T. Takács (mez), Horváth (sgr), L. Miller (bar), I. Gáti (bar), K. Kováts (bass), F. Szekeres (cnd), Hungarian State Orch, Budapest Madrigal Choir [I] White Label ▲ HRC 073 [ADD]

Kaposy, Andor (ten)
Mahler, G.:Das Klagende Lied, w. T. Zylis-Gara (sop), A. Reynolds (mez), W. Morris (cnd), New Philharmonia Orch, Ambrosian Singers [G] *(rec 1967)* Nimbus ▲ NI 5085 [AAD]

Mahler, G.:Das Klagende Lied, w. T. Zylis-Gara (sop), A. Reynolds (mez), W. Morris (cnd), New Philharmonia Orch, Ambrosian Singers IMP Classics ▲ IMPCD 1053 [DDD]

Kappel, Gertrude (sop)
Wagner, R.:Götterdämmerung (sels), w. G. Kappel (sop—Brünhilde), J. Kalenberg (ten—Siegfried), J. von Manowarda (bass—Mime), R. Heger (cnd), Vienna State Opera Orch, Vienna State Opera Chorus *(rec June 15, 1933)* Koch Schwann 2-▲ SCH 314592

Wagner, R.:Siegfried (sels), w. G. Kappel (sop—Brünhilde), R. Schubert (ten—Siegfried), E. Zimmermann (ten—Mime), R. Heger (cnd), Vienna State Opera Orch, Vienna State Opera Chorus *(rec June 13, 1933)* Koch Schwann 2-▲ SCH 314592

Karaindrou, Eleni (voc)
Karaindrou, E.:Film Music, w. Jan Garbarek (t sax), Vangelis Christopoulos (ob), Anthis Sokratis (tpt), Nikos Guinos (cl), Tassos Diakoyiorgis (santouri), Vangelis Skouras (hn), Petros Protopapas (fl), Andreas Tsekouras (acc), Christos Sfetsas (vc), L. Chalkiadakis (cnd), *(ensemble unknown)*—Farewell Theme; Scream; Improv. On Farewell & Waltz Theme; Farewell Theme II [all from The Beekeeper; w. Jan Garbarek (ten sax), Tassos Diakoyiorgis (satouri), Vassilis Dertilis (kbd), Eleni Karaindrou (pno), Lefteris Chalkiadakis (cnd)]; Elegy for Rosa; Rosa's Song (text:Christofis) [both from Rosa; w. Vangelis Skouras (Fr hn), Petros Protopapas (fl), Alekos Christidis (timp), Eleni Karaindrou (voc), Lefteis Chalkiadakis (cnd)]; Fairytale; Parade; Return; Song [all from Happy Homecoming, Comrade; w. Vangelis Skouras (Fr hn), Christos Sfetsas (vc), Aliki Krithari (hp), Andreas Tsekouras (acc), Eleni Karaindrou (pno), Nelli Semitekolo (pno), Anthis Sokratis (tpt), Lefteris Chalkiadakis (cnd)]; Wandering in Alexandria (2 vers) [both from Wandering; w. Tassos Diakoyiorgis (santouri), Nelli Semitekolo (prepared pno), Anthis Sokratis (tpt), Nikos Guinos (cl), Katerina Ktona (hpd), Christos Sfetsas (vc)]; The Journey [from Voyage to Cythera]; Adagio [from Landscape in the Mist] [both w. Vangelis Christopoulos (ob), str orch, Lefteris Chalkiadakis (cnd)] ECM ▲ 78118-21429-2 [AAD]

Karakaya, Anna (mez)
Aprikian, G.:Naissance de David de Sassoun, w. Fabienne Chanoyan (sop—Angel), Anna Karakaya (mez—Queen Taline), Armand Arapian (bar—King Mehèr/Priest), H. Sakssian (cnd), Bell'Arte Orch, Sipan-Komitas Choir Petit Chanteurs of Tebrotzassere School *(rec Ivry-sur-Seine, Jan 17–18, 1995)* Studio SM ▲ D2514

Karczykowski, Ryszard (ten)
Bizet, G.:Carmen (sels), w. Krystyna Szostek-Radkowa (mez), Monika Chabros (sgr) *(other artists unknown)* —Habanera z I aktu; Aris Don Jose z II aktu; Aria Micaeli z III aktu Polskie Nagrania ▲ PNCD 080 [AAD]

Shostakovich, D.:From Jewish Folk Poetry, w. E. Söderström (sop), O. Wenkel (cta), B. Haitink (cnd), Royal Concertgebouw Orch London ▲ 417581-2 [DDD/ADD]

Strauss (II), Joh.:Die Fledermaus, w. M. Irosch (sop), D. Koller (sop), M. Holliday (sop), W. Kmentt (ten), H. Kraemmer (bar), R. Granzer (bar), E. Binder (cnd), Vienna Volksoper Orch, Vienna Volksoper Chorus [G] Denon 2-▲ CO 8101 [DDD]

Karl, Natalie (sgr)
Zemlinsky, A. von:Der Geburtstag der Infantin, w. Soile Isokoski (sop), Iride Martinez (sgr), Andrew Collis (sgr), David Kuebler (ten), Juanita Lascarro (sgr), Machiko Obata (sgr), Anne Schwanewilms (sgr), Martina Rüping (sgr), Franfurter Kantorei (sgr), J. Conlon (cnd), Gürzenich Orch, Cologne PO *(rec Cologne, Feb 1996)* EMI Classics 2-▲ CDCB 56208

Karloff, Boris (nar)
Prokofiev, S.:Peter & the Wolf, w. M. Rossi (cnd), Vienna State Opera Orch *(rec 1957)* Vanguard Classics ("Everyman" series) ▲ OVC 5005 [ADD]

Karlsen, T. (sop)
Schlegel, L.:Songs Sop, w. F. van Ruth (pno) [G] Attacca ▲ 8951-4 [DDD]

Karnobatlova (sgr)
Rachmaninoff, S.:Aleko, w. Gyuselev (sgr), Kaychev (sgr), *(orch & chorus unknown)* [R] Monitor 2-■ 55004

Károlyi, Katalin (cta)
Esterházy, P.:Harmonia caelestis, w. M. Fers (sop), M. Zádori (sop), K. Gémes (mez), G. Kállay (ten), J. Moldvay (bass), P. Németh (cnd), Capella Savaria, Savaria Vocal Ensemble [period instrs] [L] Hungaroton 2-▲ HCD 31148/49 [DDD]

Karwautz, Brigitte (sop)
Strauss (II), Joh.:Die Fledermaus (sels), w. Ariane Calix (sop—Ida), Gabriele Fontana (sop—Rosalinde), Brigitte Karwautz (sop—Adele), Rohangiz Yachmi-Caucig (cta—Orlofsky), John Dickie (ten—Eisenstein), Josef Hopferwieser (ten—Alfred), Erich Wessner (ten—Dr. Blind), Andrea Martin (bar—Falke), Alfred Werner (bar—Frank), J. Wildner (cnd), Czech-Slovak RSO Bratislava, Bratislava City Chorus—Ov.; [Act I] Täubchen, das entflattert ist...; Ach, ich darf nicht hin zu dir; Nein, mit solchen Advokaten; Komm mit mir zum Souper; So muss allein ich bleiben; Trinke, Liebchen, trinke schnell; [Act II] Ein Souper heut' uns winkt; Ich lade gern mir Gäste ein; Mein Herr Marquis, ein Mann wie Sie; Dieser Anstand, so manierlich; Klänge der Heimat; Im Feuerstrom der Reben; Marianka komm und tanz me hier; [Act III] Entr'acte; Spiel' ich die Unschuld vom Lande; O Fledermaus, o Fledermaus Naxos ▲ 8.553171 [DDD]

Kasarova, Vasselina (mez)
Bellini, V.:Beatrice di Tenda, w. E. Gruberová (sop—Beatrice), V. Kasarova (mez—Agnese), D. Bernardini (ten—Orombello), B. Robinšak (ten—Anichino), I. Morosov (ten—Filippo Maria Visconti), D. Sumegi (bass—Rizzardo), P. Steinberg (cnd), Austrian RSO, Austrian Radio Chorus [I] *(rec live, Vienna Concert House 1/30 & 2/1/92)* Nightingale Classics 2-▲ NC 070560-2 [DDD]

Bellini, V.:I Capuleti e i Montecchi (sels), w. F. Haider (cnd), Munich RSO, Bavarian Radio Chorus—Se Romeo t'uccise un figlio RCA Red Seal ▲ 0902-668522-2 [DDD]

Berlioz, H.:Les Nuits d'été, w. P. Steinberg (cnd), ORF SO *(rec Vienna Concert House, June 12–24, 1994)* RCA Red Seal ▲ 09026-68008-2 [DDD]

Chausson, E.:Poème de l'amour et de la mer, w. P. Steinberg (cnd), ORF SO *(rec Vienna Concert House, June 12–24, 1994)* RCA Red Seal ▲ 09026-68008-2 [DDD]

Donizetti, G.:Arias, w. F. Haider (cnd), Munich RSO, Bavarian Radio Chorus—Sposa a Percy...per questa fiamma indomita [from Anna Bolena]; Fia dunque vero...O mio Fernando [from La Favorita] RCA Red Seal ▲ 0902-668522-2 [DDD]

Gluck, C.W.:Orfeo ed Euridice (sels), w. F. Haider (cnd), Munich RSO, Bavarian Radio Chorus—Che faró senza Euridice! RCA Red Seal ▲ 0902-668522-2 [DDD]

Handel, G.F.:Rinaldo (sels), w. F. Haider (cnd), Munich RSO, Bavarian Radio Chorus—Or la tromba in suon festante RCA Red Seal ▲ 0902-668522-2 [DDD]

Mozart, W.A.:Arias, w. F. Haider (cnd), Munich RSO, Bavarian Radio Chorus—Voi che sapete che cosa è amor [from Le nozze di Figaro]; Batti, batti, o bel Masetto [from Don Giovanni] RCA Red Seal ▲ 0902-668522-2 [DDD]

Ravel, M.:Shéhérazade Mez, w. P. Steinberg (cnd), ORF SO *(rec Vienna Concert House, June 12–24, 1994)* RCA Red Seal ▲ 09026-68008-2 [DDD]

Rossini, G.:Arias, w. F. Haider (cnd), Munich RSO, Bavarian Radio Chorus—Nacqui all'affanno e al pianto [from La cenerentola]; Una voce poco fa [from Il barbiere di Siviglia]; Amici in ogni evento...Pensa alla patria [from L'Italiana in Algeri] RCA Red Seal ▲ 0902-668522-2 [DDD]

Rossini, G.:Tancredi, w. Veronica Cangemi (sop—Roggiero), Eva Mei (sop—Amenaide), Vasselina Kasarova (mez—Tancredi), Melinda Paulsen (cta—Isaura), Ramón Vargas (ten—Argirio), Harry Peeters (bass—Orbazzano), Janos Maté (vn), Gottfried Greiner (vc), Ingo Nawra (db), David Syrus (hpd), R. Abbado (cnd), Munich RSO, Bavarian Radio Chorus *(rec Studio 1, Munich, July 17–30, 1995)* RCA Red Seal 3-▲ 09026-68349-2 [DDD]

Kasrashvili, Makvala (sop)
Shostakovich, D.:Sym 14, w. M. Krutikov (bass), A. Lazarev (cnd), Lausanne CO Virgin Classics ▲ CDC 59039

Kastu, Matti (ten)
Strauss, R.:Die ägyptische Helena, w. G. Jones (sop), B. Hendricks (sop), W. White (bass), C. Rayam (ten), B. Finnilä (mez), A. Dorati (cnd), Detroit SO London ("Grand Opera" series) 2-▲ 430381-2 [AAD]

Katano, Koki (ten)
Bach, J.S.:Cant 4, w. Yumiko Kurisu (sop), Akira Tachikawa (ct), Peter Kooy (bass), M. Suzuki (cnd), Japan Bach Collegium *(rec Kobe Shoin Women's University, Japan, June – July 1995)* BIS ▲ CD 751 [DDD]

Bach, J.S.:Cant 150, w. Yumiko Kurisu (sop), Akira Tachikawa (ct), Peter Kooy (bass), M. Suzuki (cnd), Japan Bach Collegium *(rec Kobe Shoin Women's University, Japan, June – July 1995)* BIS ▲ CD 751 [DDD]

Bach, J.S.:Cant 196, w. Yumiko Kurisu (sop), Akira Tachikawa (ct), Peter Kooy (bass), M. Suzuki (cnd), Japan Bach Collegium *(rec Kobe Shoin Women's University, Japan, June – July 1995)* BIS ▲ CD 751 [DDD]

Katchur, Swetlana (sop)
Shostakovich, D.:Alone, w. Wladimir Kazatchouk (ten), M. Jurowski (cnd), Berlin RSO, Berlin Radio Chorus *(rec Jesus Christ Church, Berlin-Dahlem, Sept 19–22, 1995)* Capriccio ▲ 10562 [DDD]

Katonosaka, Eiko (sop)
Haydn, J.:Mass 7, "Kleine Orgelmesse", w. Elfriede Jahn (alt), Kurt Equiluz (ten), Leo Heppe (bass), H. Gillesberger (cnd), Vienna State Opera Orch, Vienna Chamber Choir *(rec 1965)* Tuxedo ▲ TUXCD 1025

Katz, Florence (mez)
Emmanuel, M.:Songs, w. Marie-Catherine Girod (pno) Timpani ▲ 1030

Honegger, A.:Poésies, w. B. Desgraupes (cnd), Erwartung Ensemble *(rec L'Opéra Comique, Paris, Dec 1989 & May 1990)* Marco Polo ▲ 8.223788 [DDD]

Katz, Florence (sop)
Milhaud, D.:Machines agricoles, w. B. Desgraupes (cnd), Erwartung Ensemble *(rec L'Opéra Comique, Paris, Dec 1989 & May 1990)* Marco Polo ▲ 8.223788 [DDD]

Kaufman, Bel (nar)
Senator, R.:Holocaust Requiem Kaddish, w. J. Spiegelman (cnd), Moscow PO, Yurloff State Choir, Yekaterinburg Children's Chorus *(rec live Oct., 1992)* Delos ▲ DE 1032 [DDD]

Kaufman, Jolanta (sop)
Gloria Tibi Trinitas:Sacred Music of Slav Composers 18th–20th Centuries, w. [cnd:Andrzej Filaber], Warsaw Cathedral Choir, Anna Lubanska (alt), Ryszard Wróblewski (ten), Czeslaw Galka (bass), Maciej Piwowarski (org) Polskie Nagrania Edition ▲ ECD 057 [DDD]

Kaufmann, Julie (sop)
Beethoven, L. van:Songs, w. New Munich Piano Trio—4 Irish Songs; 7 Welsh Songs; 8 Scottish Songs Orfeo ▲ 378951

Brahms, J.:Ballads & Romances, Op. 75, w. Marilyn Schmeige (mez), Donald Sulzen (pno)—2 sels Orfeo ▲ 369961 [DDD]

Brahms, J.:Duets, Op. 20, w. Marilyn Schmeige (mez), Donald Sulzen (pno) Orfeo ▲ 369961 [DDD]

Brahms, J.:Duets, Op. 61, w. Marilyn Schmeige (mez), Donald Sulzen (pno) Orfeo ▲ 369961 [DDD]

Brahms, J.:Duets, Op. 66, w. Marilyn Schmeige (mez), Donald Sulzen (pno) Orfeo ▲ 369961 [DDD]

Brahms, J.:Romances & Songs, Op. 84, w. Marilyn Schmeige (mez), Donald Sulzen (pno)—3 sels Orfeo ▲ 369961 [DDD]

Brahms, J.:Songs, w. Marilyn Schmeige (mez), Donald Sulzen (pno) Orfeo ▲ 369961 [DDD]

Debussy, C.:Songs, w. I. Gage (pno)—Pantomime; Claire de lune; Pierrot; Apparition; Mandoline Orfeo ▲ 305931 [DDD]

Gazzaniga, G.:Don Giovanni, w. P. Coburn (sop), J. Aler (ten), R. Swensen (ten), J.-L. Chaignaud (bar), G. von Kannen (bass), A. Scharinger (bass), S. Soltesz (cnd), Munich RSO, Munich Radio Chorus [I] Orfeo 2-▲ 214902 [DDD]

Gluck, C.W.:La Recontre imprévue, w. J. Kaufmann (sop—Rezia), A. Stumphius (sop—Dardané), A.-M. Rodde (sop—Amine), I. Vermillion (mez—Balkis), R. Gambill (ten—Ali), C. H. Ahnsjö (ten—Osmin), J.-H. Rootering (bass—Un Calender), L. Hager (cnd), Munich RSO Orfeo 2-▲ 242912 [DDD]

Kaufmann, Julie (sop) (cont.)
Schoenberg, A.:Book of the Hanging Gardens, w. I. Gage (pno) Orfeo ▲ 305931 [DDD]
Strauss, R.:Songs, w. I. Gage (pno)—Ich wollt' ein Sträusslein binden, Op. 68/2; Wasserrose, Op. 22/4; Malven; Säusle, liebe Myrte, Op. 68/3; Wir beide wollen springen; Amor, Op. 68/5; Waldesfahrt, Op. 69/4; Das ist ein schlechtes Wetter, Op. 69/5; Als mir dein Lied erklang, Op. 68/4; Glückes genug Orfeo ▲ 305931 [DDD]

Kaufmann, Serge (nar)
Kaufmann, S.:Un Matin à varsovie, w. Béatrice Barbary (sop), Philippe Pennanguer (vc), B. Calmel (cnd), Bernard Calmel Orch *(rec Feb 1996)* Pavane ▲ ADW 7362 [DDD]

Kaussen, Paul (sgr)
Strauss, R.:Salome, w. Astrid Varnay (sop—Salome), Hertha Töpper (mez—Der Page der Herodias), Margarete Klose (cta—Herodias), Hans Hopf (ten—Narraboth), Karl Hoppe (ten—1st Nazarene), Karl Ostertag (ten—1st Jew), Julius Patzak (ten—Herodes), Hans Braun (bar—Jochanaan), Benno Kusche (bar—2nd Soldier), Adolf Keil (bass—1st Soldier), Hans Hermann Nissen (bass—Ein Kappadozier), Max Proebstl (bass—2nd Nazarene), Walter Carnotch (sgr—4th Jew), Emil Graf (sgr—3rd Jew), Paul Kaussen (sgr—2nd Jew), Hildegard Limmer (sgr—A slave), Georg Witter (sgr—5th Jew), H. Weigert (cnd), Bavarian RSO *(rec June 21–25, 1953)* Bella Voce 2-▲ BLV 7210 [AAD]

Kaváts, K. (bar)
Liszt, F.:Septam sacramenta, w. T. Takács (mez), J. Bándi (ten), G. Kallay (ten), Zsuzsa Elekes (org), I. Zámbó (cnd), Hungarian State Orch, Hungarian People's Army Male Chorus, Jeunesses Musicales Women's Chorus [L] Hungaroton ▲ HCD 12748 [DDD]

Kavrakos, Dmitri (bass)
Bellini, V.:Norma, w. Jane Eaglen (sop—Norma), Eva Mei (sop—Adalgisa), Vincenzo La Scola (ten—Pollione), Dmitri Kavrakos (bass—Oroveso), R. Muti (cnd), Florence Maggio Musicale Orch, Florence Maggio Musicale Chorus *(rec live, Alighieri Theater, Florence, July 1994)* EMI Classics 2-▲ CDCC 55471
Verdi, G.:Rigoletto, w. Andrea Rost (sop—Gilda), Mariana Pentcheva (cta—Maddalena), Roberto Alagna (ten—Il Duca di Mantova), Renato Bruson (bar—Rigoletto), Dmitri Kavrakos (bass—Sparafucile), R. Muti (cnd), La Scala Orch, La Scala Chorus Sony Classical 2-▲ S2K 66314

Kawamura, Eishi (bass)
Haydn, J.:Mass 10, "Kriegsmesse", "Paukenmesse", w. Elisabeth Thomann (sop), Elfriede Jahn (alt), Stafford Wing (ten), H. Gillesberger (cnd), Vienna State Opera Orch, Vienna Chamber Choir *(rec 1965)* Tuxedo ▲ TUXCD 1025

Kaychev (sgr)
Rachmaninoff, S.:Aleko, w. Karnobatlova (sgr), Gyuselev (sgr), *(orch & chorus unknown)* [R] Monitor 2-■ 55004

Kaye, Danny (ten)
Weill, K.:Songs, w. Mary Martin (sgr), *(orch unknown)*—Dreigroschenoper; Happy End; Mahagonny; Silbersee; Knickerbocker Holiday; Lady in the Dark; One Touch of Venus; and others Pearl 2-▲ PEA 9189

Kaye, Judy (sop)
Arlen, H.:Americanegro Suite, w. P. Howard (pno), Premierospel Quartet—plus ten Arlen songs from stage & screen Premier ▲ PRCD 1004 [DDD]
Bernstein, L.:Arias & Barcarolles, w. William Sharp (bar), Michael Barrett (pno), Steven Blier (pno) [E] Koch International Classics ▲ KIC 7000-2 [DDD] ■ 3-7000-4 (D)
Bernstein, L.:Songs & Duets, w. William Sharp (bar), M. Barrett (pno), S. Blier (pno), S. Sant'Ambrogio (vc)—sels. from On The Town, 1944 *(Some other time; Lonely town; Carried away; I can cook)*; Peter Pan, 1949 *(Dream with me)*; Wonderful Town, 1952 *(A little bit in love)*; Songfest, 1977 *(Storyette, H.M.; To what you said)* [E] Koch International Classics ▲ KIC 7000-2 [DDD] ■ 3-7000-4 (D)
Gershwin, G.:Songs, w. W. Sharp (bar), S. Blier (pno)—20 solo songs & duets Koch International Classics ▲ KIC 7028-2 [DDD] ■ 3-7028-4 (D)
Villa-Lobos, H.:Magdalena, w. et al. *(rec Lincoln Center cast, 1988)* CBS ▲ MK 44945 [DDD]

Kayevchenko, Valentina (sop)
Kabalevsky, D.:Colas Breugnon (ov), w. N. Isakova (sop), L. Boldin (bar), N. Gutorovich (bar), G. Dudarev (bass), E. Maksimenko (sgr), G. Zhemchuzhin (cnd), Dantchenko Moscow Stanislavsky Music Theater Orch, Dantchenko Moscow Stanislavsky Music Theater Chorus Olympia 2-▲ OLY 291 [ADD]

Kazaras, Peter (ten)
Janácek, L.:Jenůfa, w. G. Benačková (sop), L. Rysanek (sop), W. Ochman (ten), E. Queler (cnd), New York City Opera Orch [Cz] *(rec live at Carnegie Hall, Mar. 30, 1988)* BIS 2-▲ CD 449/50 [DDD]

Kazarnovskaya, Ljuba (sop)
Shostakovich, D.:Sym 14, w. S. Leiferkus (bar), N. Järvi (cnd), Gothenburg SO Deutsche Grammophon ▲ 437785-2

Kazatchouk, Wladimir (ten)
Shostakovich, D.:Alone, w. Swetlana Katchur (sop), M. Jurowski (cnd), Berlin RSO, Berlin Radio Chorus *(rec Jesus Christ Church, Berlin-Dahlem, Sept 19–22, 1995)* Capriccio ▲ 10562 [DDD]

Keel, Howard (sgr)
Berlin, I.:Annie Get Your Gun, w. J. Garland (sgr), K. Wynn (sgr), F. Morgan (sgr), *(other artists unknown) (rec 1949 soundtrack)* Sandy Hook ▲ CSH 2053
Kern, J.:Show Boat, w. K. Grayson (sgr), A. Gardner (sgr), *(other artists unknown) (rec 1951)* Sony Music Special Products ▲ AK 45436 ■ AT 45436
Kern, J.:Show Boat, w. K. Grayson (sgr), A. Gardner (sgr) *(rec 1951)* TCM ▲ R2 71998
Romberg, S.:Deep in My Heart, w. H. Traubel (sgr), J. Ferrer (sgr), R. Clooney (sgr), Gene Kelly (sgr), F. Kelly (sgr), V. Damone (sgr), J. Powell (sgr), A. Miller (sgr), W. Olvis (sgr), C. Richards (sgr), T. Martin (sgr), J. Weldon (sgr) Sony Music Special Products ▲ AK 47703

Keenan, James (trb)
Gregson, E.:Missa Brevis Pacem, w. Henry Herford (bar), E. Gregson (cnd), Royal Northern College of Music Wind Orch, Manchester Boy's Choir Doyen ▲ CD 043 [DDD]

Keenlyside, Simon (bar)
Britten, H.:Purcell Realizations, w. Susan Gritton (sop), Felicity Lott (sop), Sarah Walker (mez), James Bowman (alto), John Mark Ainsley (ten), Anthony Rolfe Johnson (ten), Richard Jackson (bass), Ian Bostridge (sgr), Graham Johnson (pno) Hyperion 2-▲ CDA 67061/62
Cavalli, P.F.:Calisto, w. Maria Bayo (sop), Graham Pushee (ct), Marcello Lippi (bar), René Jacobs (cnd), Concerto Vocale Harmonia Mundi France 3-▲ HMC 901515/17
Chabrier, E.:Briséïs, ou Les Amants de Corinthe, w. Kathryn Harries (sop), Mark Padmore (ten), Michael George (bass), Joan Rodgers (sgr), J. Y. Ossonce (cnd), BBC Scottish SO Hyperion ▲ CDA 66803
Duruflé, M.:Mass, "Cum jubilo", w. Aaron Webber (trb), Natalie Clein (vc), Iain Simcock (org), James O'Donnell (cnd), Westminster Cathedral Choir Hyperion ▲ CDA 66757
Duruflé, M.:Motets on Gregorian Chants, Op. 10, w. Aaron Webber (trb), Natalie Clein (vc), Iain Simcock (org), J. O'Donnell (cnd), Westminster Cathedral Choir Hyperion ▲ CDA 66757
Duruflé, M.:Notre Père, w. Aaron Webber (trb), Natalie Clein (vc), Iain Simcock (org), J. O'Donnell (cnd), Westminster Cathedral Choir Hyperion ▲ CDA 66757
Duruflé, M.:Requiem, w. Aaron Webber (trb), Natalie Clein (vc), Iain Simcock (org), J. O'Donnell (cnd), Westminster Cathedral Choir Hyperion ▲ CDA 66757
Puccini, G.:La Bohème, w. Leontina Vaduva (sop—Mimi), Ruth Ann Swenson (sop—Musetta), Roberto Alagna (ten—Rodolfo), Simon Keenlyside (bar—Schaunard), Thomas Hampson (bar—Marcello), Samuel Ramey (bass—Colline), Enrico Fissore (bass—Benoit), A. Pappano (cnd), Philharmonia Orch EMI Classics 2-♦ CDCB 56120
Schubert, Franz:Songs (comp), w. John Mark Ainsley (ten), Michael George (bass), Graham Schäfer (sgr), Graham Johnson (cnd), London Schubert Chorale—settings of Goethe's poetry Hyperion ▲ CDJ 33024
Schubert, Franz:Songs (misc), w. Malcolm Martineau (pno)—The Solitary; Serenade [from Cymbeline]; To Sylvia [from The 2 Gentlemen of Verona]; The Youth by the Spring; Sailor's Song to the Dioscuri; Group from Hades; The Gods of Greece; In the Forest; The Wanderer's Address to the Moon; Voluntary Oblivion; Intimations of Heaven; Prometheus; The Gondolier; The Stars; At Bruck; Wild Rose; In the Wood; Dame's Violets; With You Alone; You Are Repose Classics for Pleasure ("Eminence" series) ▲ CDEMX 2224 [DDD]

Keenlyside, Simon (bar) (cont.)
Schubert, Franz:Songs (misc), w. Lorna Anderson (sop), Catherine Wyn-Rogers (alt), Jamie McDougall (ten) Graham Johnson (pno), London Schubert Chorale—Das Leben ist ein Traum; Das Grab; Trinklied; Punschlied; Vaterlandslied; Selma und Selmar; Morgenlied; An die Sonne; Hermann und Thusnelda; Cora und die Sonne; Lorna; Genugsamkeit; Der Abend; Das Mädchen aus dem Fremde; Am Rosa (I); Am Rosa (II); An Sie; Gebet während der Schlacht; Das Abendroth; Die drei Sänger; Die Sterne; Cronnan; Furcht der Geliebten; Die Erscheinung; Stolie; Das Bild; Lob des Tokayers Hyperion ▲ CDJ 33022

Keil, Adolf (bass)
Mussorgsky, M.:Boris Godunov, w. Martha Mödl (sop—Marina Mniszek), Lotte Schädle (sop—Xenia), Dorothea Siebert (mez—Fyodor), Hertha Töpper (mez—Xenia's wet-nurs), Karl Hermann Bennert (Boyer Khrushchyov), Lorenz Fehenberger (ten—Prince Shuysky), Hans Hopf (ten—Grigory), Karl Ostertag (ten—Missail), Hans Hotter (b-bar—Boris Godunov), Hermann Uhde (bar—Andrey Shchelkalov), Kurt Böhme (bass—Varlaam), Kim Borg (bass—Pimen), Kieth Engen (bass—Lewicki), Adolf Keil (bass—Nikitich), Benno Kusche (bar—Rangoni), Heinz Maria Linz (bass—Czernikowski), E. Jochum (cnd), Bavarian RSO, Bavarian Radio Chorus *(rec Munich, May 1957)* Myto 3-▲ MCD 953131
Strauss, R.:Salome, w. Astrid Varnay (sop—Salome), Hertha Töpper (mez—Der Page der Herodias), Margarete Klose (cta—Herodias), Hans Hopf (ten—Narraboth), Karl Hoppe (ten—1st Nazarene), Karl Ostertag (ten—1st Jew), Julius Patzak (ten—Herodes), Hans Braun (bar—Jochanaan), Benno Kusche (bar—2nd Soldier), Adolf Keil (bass—1st Soldier), Hans Hermann Nissen (bass—Ein Kappadozier), Max Proebstl (bass—2nd Nazarene), Walter Carnotch (sgr—4th Jew), Emil Graf (sgr—3rd Jew), Paul Kaussen (sgr—2nd Jew), Hildegard Limmer (sgr—A slave), Georg Witter (sgr—5th Jew), H. Weigert (cnd), Bavarian RSO *(rec June 21–25, 1953)* Bella Voce 2-▲ BLV 7210 [AAD]

Keillor, Garrison (spkr)
Keillor, G.:Lake Woebegon Days-A Recital, w. P. Brunelle (cnd), Minnesota Orch Virgin Classics ▲ CDC 59583
Songs of the Cat, w. Frederica von Stade (mez) RCA Victor ▲ 09026-61161-2 [DDD] ■ 09026-61161-4 (CrO2)

Keith, Nancy (sop)
Bach, W.F.:Zerbrecht, zerreist, Aria, w. G. Hustis, S. Sargon [G] *(rec Mar-July 1991)* Crystal ▲ CD675
Berlioz, H.:Songs, w. G. Hustis (hn), S. Sargon (pno)—Le jeune pâtre breton [F] *(rec 3-7/91)* Crystal ▲ CD675
"Huntsman, What Quarry?", w. Gregory Hustis (hn), Simon Sargon (pno) Crystal ▲ CD675
Nicolai, O.:Variazioni concertanti, w. G. Hustis (hn), S. Sargon (pno) [I] Crystal ▲ CD675
Rutter, J.:Requiem, w. J. Martinson (org), T. Seelig (cnd), Dallas Women's Chorus, Turtle Creek Chorale *(rec July 28–29, 1993)* Reference ▲ RR 57 CD [DDD]
Schubert, Franz:Songs (misc), w. G. Hustis (hn), S. Sargon (pno)—Auf dem Strom, D.943 [G] Crystal ▲ CD675
Strauss, R.:Das Alphorn, w. G. Hustis (hn), S. Sargon (pno) [G] Crystal ▲ CD675

Kélémen, Zoltan (bar)
Lehár, F.:Die lustige Witwe, w. E. Harwood (sop), T. Stratas (sop), W. Hollweg (ten), R. Kollo (ten), H. von Karajan (cnd), Berlin PO, German Opera Chorus [G] *(rec 1972)* Deutsche Grammophon 2-▲ 435712-2 [ADD]
Wagner, R.:Parsifal, w. C. Ludwig (mez), A. Kollo (ten), D. Fischer-Dieskau (bar), G. Frick (bass), G. Solti (cnd), Vienna PO, Vienna State Opera Chorus, Vienna Boys' Choir [G] London 4-▲ 417143-2 [ADD]

Kelen, Péter (ten)
Cilea, F.:L'Arlesiana, w. M. Spacagna (sop), E. Zilio (mez), B. Póka (bar), T. Clementis (bass), C. Rosekrans (cnd), Hungarian State Orch, Hungarian State Chorus Quintana 2-▲ QUI 903067/68
Mascagni, P.:Lodoletta, w. M. Spacagna (sop), B. Szilágyi (bar), M. Kálmándi (bar), L. Polgár (bass), C. Rosekrans (cnd), Hungarian State Orch, Hungarian State Choruses [I] Hungaroton 2-▲ HCD 31307/08 [DDD]
Respighi, O.:La Fiamma, w. I. Tokody (sop), T. Takács (mez), S. Sólyom-Nagy (bar), L. Gardelli (cnd), Hungarian State Orch, Hungarian State Chorus [I] Hungaroton 3-▲ HCD 12591/93 [DDD]

Keller, J. (sgr)
Wyttenbach, J.:Encore!, w. T. Demenga (vc) [F] *(rec May 19–20, 1990)* Grammont ▲ CTSP 37-2 [ADD]

Keller, Marie-Thérèse (sop)
Massenet, J.:La Vierge, w. M. Command (sop), M. Castets (sop), M. Olmeda (sop), P. Salmon (ten), M. Hacquard (bar), P. Fournillier (cnd), Prague SO, Prague Sym Chorus Koch Schwann 2-▲ CD 313084 [DDD]

Keller, Peter (ten)
Janáček, L.:The Diary of One Who Disappeared, w. Clara Wirz (alt), Mario Venzago (pno), Mario Venzago (cnd), Lucerne Singers Accord ▲ ACD 220312 [DDD]

Kelley, Frank (ten)
Moore, T.:Irish Melodies, w. L. Shelton (sop), J. De Gaetani (mez), W. Sharp (bar), I. Kipnis (pno) [E] Elektra/Nonesuch ■ 79059-4 (D)
Mozart, W.A.:Missa, K.317, w. S. Baker (sop), J. Malafronte (mez), J. Maddalena (bar), M. Pearlman (cnd), Banchetto Musicale Harmonia Mundi USA ▲ HMU 907021
Mozart, W.A.:Vesperae solennes, w. S. Baker (sop), J. Malafronte (mez), J. Maddalena (bar), M. Pearlman (cnd), Banchetto Musicale Harmonia Mundi USA ▲ HMU 907021
Orff, C.:Carmina burana, w. Gabriela Herrera (sop), Ben Holt (bar), H. de la Fuente (cnd), Mineria SO, Mineria Sym Choir IMP ("Classic" series) ▲ IMP 2024
Paulus, S.:Voices, w. Martha Jane Weaver (mez), J. Alexander (cnd), Pacific SO, Pacific Chorale Albany ▲ TROY 182

Kelley, Paul Austin (ten)
Britten, H.:Songs, w. Michael Recchiuti (pno)—Holy Sonnets of John Donne; On This Island; plus others GM ▲ GM 2022CD
Quilter, R.:Songs, w. Michael Recchiuti (pno)—7 Elizabethan Lyrics; To Julia; plus others GM ▲ GM 2022CD

Kellock, Judith (sop)
Foss, L.:Airs (3) for Frank O'Hara's Angel, w. Lukas Foss (pno) Koch International Classics ▲ KIC 7209 [DDD]
Foss, L.:Songs (4), w. Lukas Foss (pno) Koch International Classics ▲ KIC 7209 [DDD]
Foss, L.:Thirteen Ways of Looking at a Blackbird, w. Lukas Foss (pno) Koch International Classics ▲ KIC 7209 [DDD]

Kelly, David (bass)
Herrmann, B.:Moby Dick, w. John Amis (ten), Robert Bowman (ten), Michael Rippon (bass), London PO, Aeolian Singers [E] Unicorn-Kanchana ▲ UKCD 2061
Herrmann, B.:Wuthering Heights, w. M. Beaton (sop—Catherine), P. Bowden (mez—Isabella), E. Bainbridge (mez—Nelly), M. Snashall (trb—Hareton), D. Bell (bar—Heathcliff), J. Kitchiner (bar—Hindley), J. Ward (bar—Edgar), M. Rippon (bass—Joseph), D. Kelly (bass—Mr. Lockwood), B. Herrmann (cnd), Pro Arte Orch *(rec 1965–66)* Unicorn-Kanchana 3-▲ UKCD 2050/51/52 [ADD]

Kelly, F. (sgr)
Romberg, S.:Deep in My Heart, w. H. Traubel (sgr), J. Ferrer (sgr), R. Clooney (sgr), Gene Kelly (sgr), V. Damone (sgr), J. Powell (sgr), A. Miller (sgr), W. Olvis (sgr), C. Richards (sgr), H. Keel (sgr), T. Martin (sgr), J. Weldon (sgr) Sony Music Special Products ▲ AK 47703

Kelly, Gene (sgr)
Kern, J.:Cover Girl, w. N. Wynn (sgr), P. Silvers (sgr) *(rec 1944)* Hollywood Soundstage ▲ HSCD 4005
Kern, J.:Cover Girl, w. N. Wynn (sgr), P. Silvers (sgr) *(rec 1944)* Curtain Calls ▲ CC 100/24
Lerner, A.J.:Brigadoon, w. V. Johnson (sgr), C. Charisse (sgr) *(rec 1954)* Sony Music Special Products ▲ AK 45440 ■ AT 45440
Porter, C.:The Pirate, w. J. Garland (sgr) Sony Music Special Products ▲ AK 48608
Romberg, S.:Deep in My Heart, w. H. Traubel (sgr), J. Ferrer (sgr), R. Clooney (sgr), F. Kelly (sgr), V. Damone (sgr), J. Powell (sgr), A. Miller (sgr), W. Olvis (sgr), C. Richards (sgr), H. Keel (sgr), T. Martin (sgr), J. Weldon (sgr) Sony Music Special Products ▲ AK 47703

1236 ▲ = CD ♦ = Enhanced CD ∆ = MD ■ = Cassette Tape ◻ = DCC

Kelly, J. (sgr)

Lloyd Webber, A.:Music of, w. C. Burt (sgr), Graham Bickly (sgr), C. D. Carroll (sgr), Yates (cnd), National SO, Munich SO—Song & Dance; The Phantom of the Opera; Starlight Express; Jeeves; Jesus Christ Superstar; Aspects of Love; Cats; The Requiem Mass Koch International ▲ KOCCD 340132 ■ KOCC 340134

Kelly, Paul Austin (ten)

Britten, H.:The Holy Sonnets of John Donne, w. Michael Recchiuti (pno) GM ▲ GM 2022 CD [DDD]

Britten, H.:The Holy Sonnets of John Donne, w. Michael Recchiuti (pno) GM Recordings ▲ GMR 2022

Britten, H.:On this Island, w. Michael Recchiuti (pno) GM Recordings ▲ GMR 2022

Britten, H.:On This Island, w. Michael Recchiuti (pno) GM ▲ GM 2022 CD [DDD]

Paine, J.K.:St. Peter, w. J. Ommerlé (sop), A. Fortunato (mez), D. Evitts (bar), G. Schuller (cnd), Boston Pro Arte CO, Back Bay Chorale [E] *(rec live in concert at Sanders Theater, Cambridge, Mass., 5/21/89)* GM 2–▲ 2027CD 2

Quilter, R.:Elizabethan Lyrics, w. Michael Recchiuti (pno) GM ▲ GM 2022 CD [DDD]

Quilter, R.:Elizabethan Lyrics, w. Michael Recchiuti (pno) GM Recordings ▲ GMR 2022

Quilter, R.:To Julia, w. Michael Recchiuti (pno) GM Recordings ▲ GMR 2022

Quilter, R.:To Julia, w. Michael Recchiuti (pno) GM ▲ GM 2022 CD [DDD]

Kelly, Sondra (cta)

Verdi, G.:Il trovatore, w. A. Millo (sop), D. Zajick (mez), P. Domingo (ten), T. Willson (ten), A. Laciura (ten), J. Morris (bass), G. Bater (bass), J. Levine (cnd), Metropolitan Opera Orch, New York Metropolitan Opera Chorus *(rec June 18, 1991)* Sony Classical 2–▲ S2K 48070 [DDD]

Kelm, Linda (sop)

Alfano, F.:Turandot, w. J. F. West (Calaf), C. Keene (cnd), *(orch unknown), (chorus unknown)*—6 arias & duets [I] *(rec live, New York 1985)* Standing Room Only 2–▲ SRO 839–2 [ADD]

Kelsey, Franklin (sgr)

Mussorgsky, M.:Boris Godunov (sels), w. Walter Widdop (ten), Edward Halland (bass), Robert Gwynne (sgr), A. Coates (cnd), *(orch unknown)*—Revolutionary Scene, Act. IV *(rec Hayes, Studio B, Nov. 3, 1925)* Claremont ▲ GSE 785061

Kelston, L. (sop)

Verdi, G.:Luisa Miller, w. L. Kelston (sop—Luisa), M.T. Pace (mez—Federica), G. Larui–Volpi (ten—Rodolfo), S. Colombo (bar—Miller), G. Vaghi (bar—Count Walter), D. Baronti (bass—Wurm), M. Rossi (cnd), Rome RAI Orch, Rome RAI Chorus *(rec 1951)* Cetra Classic 2–▲ CDO 17 [AAD]

Keman, D. (sgr)

Porter, C.:A Swell Party, w. A. Richards (sgr), N. Grace (sgr), A. Woods (sgr), M. Smith (sgr), *(other artists unknown)* [1992 London cast] Silva America ▲ SSD 1006 [DDD] ■ SSC 1006

Kemeny, Lynda (sop)

Krenek, E.:Der Sprüng über den Schatten, w. D. Amos (sop), S. MacLean (mez), J. Dürmüller (ten), U. Neuweiler (ten), J. Pflieger (bar), T. Brüning (sgr), D. de Villiers (cnd), Bielefeld PO, Bielefeld Phil Chorus [G] *(rec live, May 1989)* CPO 2–▲ CPO 999082–2 [DDD]

Kemmer, Mariette (sop)

Berlioz, H.:L'Enfance du Christ (sels), w. Claire Brua (mez), Gilles Ragon (ten), Nicolas Cavallier (bass), F. Quattrocchi (cnd), Lorraine PO—Toujours ce rêve *(rec June 1994)* Maguelone ▲ 350.509 [DDD]

Gluck, C.W.:Alceste (sels), w. Claire Brua (mez), Gilles Ragon (ten), Nicolas Cavallier (bass), F. Quattrocchi (cnd), Lorraine PO—Vivre sans toi *(rec June 1994)* Maguelone ▲ 350.509 [DDD]

Gounod, C.:Faust (sels), w. Claire Brua (mez), Gilles Ragon (ten), Nicolas Cavallier (bass), F. Quattrocchi (cnd), Lorraine PO—Faites lui mes aveux; La coupe du Roi de Thulé; Air des Bijoux *(rec June 1994)* Maguelone ▲ 350.509 [DDD]

Honegger, A.:Sémiramis, w. V. Ivanov (vn), L. Hager (cnd), RTL SO, Brussels Polyphonia Choir, Namur Belgium French Community Symphonic Choir *(rec Nov. 16–20, 1992)* Timpani ▲ 1C 1016 [DDD]

Mozart, W.A.:Così fan tutte (sels), w. Claire Brua (mez), Gilles Ragon (ten), Nicolas Cavallier (bass), F. Quattrocchi (cnd), Lorraine PO—Come scoglio *(rec June 1994)* Maguelone ▲ 350.509 [DDD]

Mozart, W.A.:Nozze di Figaro (sels), w. Claire Brua (mez), Gilles Ragon (ten), Nicolas Cavallier (bass), F. Quattrocchi (cnd), Lorraine PO—Ov; Voi che Sapete *(rec June 1994)* Maguelone ▲ 350.509 [DDD]

Rossini, G.:Le Comte Ory (sels), w. Claire Brua (mez), Gilles Ragon (ten), Nicolas Cavallier (bass), F. Quattrocchi (cnd), Lorraine PO—Ov; Que les destins prospères *(rec June 1994)* Maguelone ▲ 350.509 [DDD]

Kempe (ten)

Tubin, E.:The Parson of Reigi, w. M. Eensalu (sop), Maiste (bar), P. Mägi (cnd), Estonia Opera Co Orch, Estonia Opera Company Chorus Ondine 2–▲ ODE 783–2D [DDD]

Kempf, Kurt (sgr)

Mendelssohn, F.:Psalms, Op. 78, w. Christiane Buntschu (sgr), Natacha Casagrande (sgr), Pablo Pavon (sgr), M. Corboz (cnd), Lausanne Vocal Ensemble *(rec Lausanne Cathedral, Jan. 29–31, 1994)* FNAC Music ▲ 592298 [DDD]

Kendal, Elsa (cta)

Vaughan Williams, R.:The Pilgrim's Progress, w. Delyth Jones (sop), Charles Groves (ten), Robin Leggate (ten), V. Handley (cnd), BBC Northern SO, BBC Northern Singers IMP ("BBC Radio Classics" series) ▲ IMP 5691662

Kendall, William (ct)

Jommelli, N.:Didone abbandonata, w. Dorothea Röschmann (sop), Mechthild Bach (mez), Martina Borst (mez), Daniel Taylor (ct), Arno Raunig (ten), F. Bernius (cnd), Stuttgart CO—Didone; Enea; Iarba; Selene; Araspe; Osmida Orfeo 3–▲ CD 381953 [DDD]

Kendall, William (ten)

Bach, J.S.:Cant 131, w. S. Varcoe (b–bar), J. E. Gardiner (cnd), English Baroque Soloists, Monteverdi Choir London Erato ▲ 2292–45988–2

Bach, J.S.:St. John Passion, w. P. Kwella (sop), D. James (ct), I. Partridge (ten), M. George (bar), D. Wilson–Johnson (b–bar), H. Christophers (cnd), The Sixteen Orch, The Sixteen [G] Chandos ("Chaconne" series) 2–▲ CHAN 0507/08 [DDD]

Bach, J.S.:St. John Passion, w. B. Schlick (sop), C. Patriasz (cta), H. Crook (ten), P. Kooy (bass), P. Lika (bass), P. Herreweghe (cnd), La Chapelle Royale Orch, Ghent Collegium Vocale [G] Harmonia Mundi France 2–▲ HMC 901264/65 [DDD]

Beethoven, L. van:Mass, Op. 86, w. C. Margiono (sop), C. Robbin (mez), A. Miles (bass), J. E. Gardiner (cnd), Orch Révolutionnaire et Romantique, Monteverdi Choir London [period instrs] Archiv ▲ 435391–2 [DDD]

Beethoven, L. van:Missa Solemnis, w. C. Margiono (sop), C. Robbin (mez), A. Miles (bass), J. E. Gardiner (cnd), English Baroque Soloists, Monteverdi Choir London [L] Archiv ▲ 429779–2 [DDD] ▯ 429779–5

Haydn, J.:Mass 7, "Kleine Orgelmesse", w. Linda Russell (alto), Catherine Wyn–Rogers (alt), Michael George (bass), D. Hill (cnd), Brandenburg Orch, Winchester Cathedral Choir Hyperion ▲ CDA 66508 [DDD]

Haydn, J.:Mass 14, "Harmoniemesse", w. Linda Russell (alto), Catherine Wyn–Rogers (alt), Michael George (bass), D. Hill (cnd), Brandenburg Orch, Winchester Cathedral Choir Hyperion ▲ CDA 66508 [DDD]

Mozart, W.A.:Requiem, w. Y. Kenny (sop), S. Walker (mez), D. Wilson–Johnson (bar), G. Guest (cnd), English CO, St. John's College Choir Cambridge [L] Chandos ▲ CHAN 8574 [DDD]

Kendall–Smith, Belinda (bass)

Schultz, Andrew:Mephisto, w. Sonia Croucher (fl), Karen Schaupp (gtr), Michele Walsh (vn), G. Roberts (cnd), Perihelion Ensemble members *(rec Nickson Room, Music Dept, Univ of Queensland, Australia, Dec 1994)* Tall Poppies ▲ TP 065 [DDD]

Kenéz, Ernö (ten)

Verdi, G.:Rigoletto (sels), w. Mária Gyurkovics (sop), Olga Szönyi (mez), János Fodor (bar), Alexander Svéd (bar), József Bódy (bass), Kórodi, Molinari–Pradelli (cnd), Hungarian State Opera Orch—Pari siamo!; Figlia! Mio padre! A te dappresso; Cortigiani! Vil' razza dannata; Tutte le feste al tempio...Ah! solo per me!; Chi è mai... *(rec 1955–56)* Hungaroton ("Great Hungarian Voices" series) ▲ HCD 31614 [ADD]

Kennard, Julie (sop)

Howells, H.:Hymnus Paradisi, w. J. M. Ainsley (ten), V. Handley (cnd), Royal Liverpool PO, Royal Liverpool Phil Choir Hyperion ▲ CDA 66488

Kennard, Julie (sop) (cont.)

Scarlatti, D.:Stabat mater, w. P. Taylor (ten), J. Poole (cnd), BBC Singers *(rec 1976)* Sony Classical ("Essential Classics" series) ▲ SBK 48282 [AAD] ■ SBT 48282

Kennedy, D. James (nar)

Bish, D.:A Sym of Hymns, w. Sung Sook Lee (sop), D. Bish (org), R. McMurrin (cnd), Coral Ridge Orch, Coral Ridge Chorus [E] VQR Digital ▲ QR 2041 [DDD]

Bish, D.:A Sym of Hymns, w. Sung Sook Lee (sop), D. Bish (org), R. McMurrin (cnd), Coral Ridge Orch, Coral Ridge Chorus [E] VQR Digital ▲ QR 2041 [DDD]

Kennedy, Frederick (ten)

Art Song Heritage of the Americas, w. Henri Venazi (pno) CRS Master ▲ CRS 9662

Kennedy, Margaret (sop)

Pinkham, D.:Songs, w. William McMullen (ob), Paul Barnes (pno)—Carols & Cries; Music, Thou Soul of Heaven; Slow, Slow, Fresh Fount; The Hour Glass; Heaven–Haven/World Welter; The Moon Was But a Chin of Gold; To Make a Prairie; A Partridge in a Pear Tree; 3 Canticles from Luke; For Echo is the Soul of the Voice; When Love Was Gone; 3 Alleluias Arkay ▲ ARK 6153 [DDD]

Purcell, H.:Anthems & Services, w. S. Gritton (sop), E. O'Dwyer (trb), J. Goodman (trb), J. Bowman (ct), N. Short (ct), Rogers Covey–Crump (ten), C. Daniels (ten), M. Milhofer (ten), M. George (bass), R. Evans (bass), R. King (cnd), King's Consort—I Was Glad When They Said unto Me (coronation & verse anthem); O Consider My Adversity; Beati omnes qui timent Dominum; In the Black Dismal Dungeon of Dispair; Save Me, O God; Te Deum in B♭; Jubilant in B♭; Thy Way, O God, Is Holy Hyperion ▲ CDA 66677 [DDD]

Purcell, H.:Music for the Funeral of Queen Mary, w. S. Gritton (sop), E. O'Dwyer (trb), J. Goodman (trb), J. Bowman (ct), N. Short (ct), Rogers Covey–Crump (ten), C. Daniels (ten), M. Milhofer (ten), M. George (bass), R. Evans (bass), R. King (cnd), King's Consort Hyperion ▲ CDA 66677 [DDD]

Snyder, R.:Satirical Songs, w. Shirley Irek (pno) Coronet ▲ COR 400–9

Kennedy, Roderick (bass)

Boughton, R.:The Immortal Hour, w. A. Dawson (sop), D. Wilson–Johnson (bar), A. Melville (cnd), English CO, Geoffrey Mitchell Choir [E] Hyperion 2–▲ CDA 66101/02 [DDD]

Handel, G.F.:Messiah, w. Elizabeth Gale (sop), Marjana Lipovšek (mez), Werner Hollweg (ten), N. Harnoncourt (cnd), Vienna Concentus Musicus Teldec 2–▲ 9031–77615–2

Handel, G.F.:Messiah (sels), w. Elizabeth Gale (sop), Marjana Lipovsek (mez), Werner Hollweg (ten), N. Harnoncourt (cnd), Vienna Concentus Musicus, Stockholm Chamber Choir [E] Teldec ▲ 2292–42409–2

Massenet, J.:Hérodiade, w. M. Caballé (sop—Salomé), D. Vejzovic (mez—Hérodiade), J. Carreras (ten—Jean), J. Pons (bar—Hérode), E. Serra (bar—Vitellius), V. Esteve (bar—High Priest), R. Kennedy (bass—Phanuel), J. Delacôte (cnd), Barcelona Teatro Liceo Orch, Barcelona Gran Teatro de Liceo Chorus *(rec Jan. 6, 1984)* Legato Classics 2–▲ LCD 182 [ADD]

Verdi, G.:La forza del destino, w. Martina Arroyo (sop—Donna Leonora), Janet Coster (mez—Preziosilla), Kenneth Bowen (ten—Trabuco), Kenneth Collins (ten—Don Alvaro), Peter Glossop (bar—Don Carlo), Roderick Kennedy (bass—Marquis), J. Matheson (cnd), BBC Concert Orch, BBC Concert Chorus *(rec live, early 1980's)* Exclusive 2–▲ EXL 80 [ADD]

Weill, K.:The Seven Deadly Sins, w. J. Migenes (sop), R. Tear (ten), S. Kale (ten), A. Opie (bar), M. Tilson Thomas (cnd), London SO CBS ▲ MK 44529 [DDD]

Kenney, Yvonne (sop)

Handel, G.F.:Joseph & His Brethren, w. Catherine Denley (mez), Connor Burrowes (trb), James Bowman (ct), John Mark Ainsley (ten), Michael George (bass), R. King (cnd), King's Consort, New College Choir Oxford, King's Consort Choir Hyperion 3–▲ CDA 67171/3

Kenny, Jonathan Peter (alt)

Bach, J.S.:Cant 208, "Hunting Cant", w. A. M. Blasi (sop), K. Equiluz (ten), R. Holl (bass), N. Harnoncourt (cnd), Vienna Concentus Musicus, Arnold Schoenberg Choir [G] Teldec ▲ 2292–46151–2 [DDD]

Bach, J.S.:St. Matthew Passion, w. N. Argenta (sop), L. Lee (mez), J. MacDougall (ten), R. Müller (ten), R. Jackson (bar), S. Varcoe (b–bar), P. Goodwin (cnd), *(orch & chorus unknown)* United 2–▲ UNI 89301 [DDD]

Bach, J.S.:St. Matthew Passion (sels), w. N. Argenta (sop), L. Lee (mez), J. MacDougall (ten), R. Müller (ten), R. Jackson (bar), S. Varcoe (b–bar), P. Goodwin (cnd), *(orch & chorus unknown) (rec St. George's Theater, London, Feb 24–27, 1994)* United ▲ UNI 88030 [DDD]

Purcell, H.:Dido & Aeneas, w. Ruth Holton (sop—Belinda), Elisabeth Priday (sop—2nd Woman), Donna Deam (sop—1st Witch), Shauna Beesley (sop—2nd Witch), Teresa Shaw (mez—Sorceress), Carolyn Watkinson (cta—Dido), Jonathan Peter Kenny (alt—Spirit), Paul Tindall (ten—Sailor), George Mosley (bass—Aeneas), J.E. Gardiner (cnd), English Baroque Soloists, Monteverdi Choir London *(rec Saint George's, Bristol, UK, July 12–14, 1990)* Philips ▲ 432114–2

Kenny, Yvonne (sop)

Donizetti, G.:Emilia di Liverpool, w. A. Mason (sop), B. Mills (sop), C. Merritt (ten), S. Bruscantini (bar), G. Dolton (bar), C. Thornton–Holmes (bar), D. Parry (cnd), Philharmonia Orch, Geoffrey Mitchell Choir—complete opera, without dialogue Opera Rara 3–▲ OR 8

Donizetti, G.:L'Eremitaggio di Liverpool, w. A. Mason (sop), B. Mills (sop), C. Merritt (ten), S. Bruscantini (bar), G. Dolton (bar), C. Thornton–Holmes (bar), D. Parry (cnd), Philharmonia Orch, Geoffrey Mitchell Choir—complete opera, without dialogue Opera Rara 3–▲ OR 8

Donizetti, G.:Rosmonda d'Inghilterra, w. Enid Hartle (mez), Richard Greager (ten), Christian du Plessis (bar), Milla Andreaw (sgr), A. Francis (cnd), Ulster Orch, Opera Rara Chorus *(rec live, 1970's)* Italian Opera Rarities 2–▲ IOR 7730

Donizetti, G.:Ugo, conte di Parigi, w. E. Harrhy (sop), J. Price (sop), D. Jones (mez), M. Arthur (ten), C. du Plessis (bar), A. Francis (cnd), New Philharmonia Orch, Geoffrey Mitchell Choir Opera Rara 3–▲ ORC 1

Elgar, E.:The Kingdom, w. A. Hodgson (alt), C. Gillert (ten), B. Luxon (bass), L. Slatkin (cnd), London PO, London Phil Chorus RCA Red Seal 2–▲ 07863–57862–2

Handel, G.F.:Deborah, w. S. Gritton (sop), C. Denley (mez), J. Bowman (alt), M. George (bass), R. King (cnd), King's Consort, Oxford New College Choir Hyperion 2–▲ CDA 66841 [DDD]

Handel, G.F.:Messiah, w. Jean Rigby (cta), Thomas Randle (ten), Willard White (bass), O. A. Hughes (cnd), Royal PO, Royal Choral Society IMP Classics 2–▲ IMPDPCD 1106 [DDD]

Hughes, O.A.:Dewi Saint, w. Martyn Hill (ten), David Wilson–Johnson (bar), O. A. Hughes (cnd), BBC Welsh National SO, BBC Welsh National Chorus [E] Chandos ▲ CHAN 8890 [DDD]

Mahler, G.:Songs, w. C. Carlson (mez), G. Mahler (pno) [from 4 rolls for automatic piano Mahler created from his own music in 1905]—Ging heut' morgen übers Feld; Ich ging mit Lust durch einen grünen Wald IMP Classics ▲ IMPGLRS 101 [DDD]

Mahler, G.:Sym 4, w. M. Inoue (cnd), Royal PO RPO ▲ 5007 [DDD]

Mendelssohn, F.:Elijah, w. A.S. von Otter (mez), A. Rolfe Johnson (ten), T. Allen (bar), N. Marriner (cnd), Academy of St. Martin in the Fields Philips 2–▲ 432984–2 [DDD]

Meyerbeer, G.:Il crociato, w. Linda Kitchen (sop), R. Platt (sop), D. Montague (mez), D. Jones (mez), B. Ford (ten), U. Benelli (bar), D. Parry (cnd), Royal PO, Geoffrey Mitchell Choir [I] *(rec CTS Studios, Wembley, London, Dec. 1990–June 1991)* Opera Rara 4–▲ OR 10

Mozart, W.A.:Entführung, w. Carolyn Watson (cta), Peter Schreier (ten), Wilfried Gamlich (ten), Matti Salminen (bass), Wolfgang Reichmann (nar), N. Harnoncourt (cnd), Zurich Mozart Opera Orch, Zurich Mozart Opera Chorus [G] Teldec 2–▲ 2292–42643–2

Mozart, W.A.:Exsultate, w. C. P. Flor (cnd), Philharmonia Orch RCA Red Seal ▲ 09026–60812–2

Mozart, W.A.:Missa, K.317, w. K. Kuhlmann (mez), K. Lewis (ten), D. Wilson–Johnson (bar), C. P. Flor (cnd), Philharmonia Orch, London Voices RCA Red Seal ▲ 09026–60812–2

Mozart, W.A.:Requiem, w. S. Walker (mez), W. Kendall (ten), D. Wilson–Johnson (bar), G. Guest (cnd), English CO, St. John's College Choir Cambridge [L] Chandos ▲ CHAN 8574 [DDD]

Mozart, W.A.:Requiem, w. A. Hodgson (mez), A. Davies (ten), G. Howell (bass), R. Hickox (cnd), Northern Sinfonia of England, London Sym Chorus Virgin Classics ▲ CDZ 59648

Stravinsky, I.:Cant Sop, w. J. Aler (ten), E.–P. Salonen (cnd), London Sinfonietta, London Sinfonietta Chorus Sony Classical ▲ SK 46667

Stravinsky, I.:Pulcinella, w. J. Aler (ten), J. Tomlinson (bass), E.–P. Salonen (cnd), London Sinfonietta Sony Classical ▲ SK 45965

Vaughan Williams, R.:Dona nobis pacem, w. B. Terfel (b–bar), R. Hickox (cnd), London SO, London Sym Chorus, St. Paul's Cathedral Choristers EMI Classics ▲ CDC 54788

Kenny, Yvonne (sop) (cont.)

Vaughan Williams, R.:Sym 1, w. B. Rayner Cook (bar), B. Thomson (cnd), London SO, London Sym Chorus [E] Chandos ▲ CHAN 8764 [DDD]

Vaughan Williams, R.:Sym 3, w. B. Thomson (cnd), London SO Chandos ▲ CHAN 8594 [DDD]

Kent, Arthur (bar)

Her First Recordings, w. Eleanor Steber (sop), Armand Tokatyan (ten), Lucielle Browning (mez), Pino Bontempi (sgr), Annamary Dickey (sgr), George Cehanovsky (bar), Lorenzo Alvary ((bass), Raoul Jobin (ten), Norman Cordon (bass) VAI Audio ▲ VAIA 1023 (m) [ADD]

Verdi, G.:Un ballo in maschera, w. Stella Andreva (sop—Oscar), Zinka Milanov (sop—Amelia), Bruna Castagna (cta—Ulrica), Jussi Björling (ten—Riccardo), Lodovico Oliviero (ten—Un Servo D'Amelia), John Cartet (bar—Un Giudice), Arthur Kent (bar—Silvano), Alexander Sved (bar—Renato), Normann Cordon (bass—Samuel), Nicola Moscona (bass—Tom), E. Panizza (cnd), *(orch unknown)* *(rec live, New York, Dec. 14, 1940)* The Fourties 2-▲ ENT FT 1515

Kenting, Jodell (sop/mez)

Puccini, G.:Suor angelica, w. Elisabeth Carron (sop—Angelica), Joan Summers (sop—Genovieffa), Donna Owen (sop—Dolcina), Lou Ann Wyckoff (sop—Alms collector), Hanna Owen (sop—novice), Anthea De Forest (sop—novice), Charlotte Povia (mez—Abbess), Beverly Evans (mez—Monitress), Kay Creed (mez—Mistress), La Vergne Monette (sop/mez—lay sister), Joan August (sop/mez—lay sister), Pearle Goldsmith (sop/mez—other sister), Lila Herbert (sop/mez—other sister), Jodell Kenting (sop/mez—other sister), Ann Pretzat (sop/mez—other sister), Evelyn Sachs (cta—Princess), F. Patanè (cnd), *(orch unknown)* *(rec New York, Feb 23, 1967)* Legato Classics ▲ LCD 212-1 [ADD]

Kentish, John (ten)

Berlioz, H.:Benvenuto Cellini, w. J. Carlyle (sop), J. Veasey (mez), K. Lewis (ten), Cameron, Bushby, Garrard, Ward, A. Dorati (cnd), BBC SO, BBC Sym Chorus [E] *(rec live, Royal Festival Hall, 1964)* Music & Arts 2-▲ CD 618 (m) [AAD]

Handel, G.F.:Sosarme, Rè di Media, w. Margaret Ritchie (sop—Elmira), Alfred Deller (mez—Sosarme), Nancy Evans (mez—Erenice), Helen Watts (cta—Melo), John Kentish (ct—Argone), William Herbert (ten—King Haliate), Ian Wallace (bass—Altomaro), A. Lewis (cnd), St. Cecilia Academy Orch Rome, St. Anthony Singers Theorema 2-▲ TH 121194/195

Keönch, Boldizsar (ten)

Lickl, J.G.:Missa solemnis, w. Maria Zadori (sop), Judith Nemet (mez), Tamas Bator (bass), H. Williams (cnd), Pécs SO, Pécs Chamber Choir Koch Schwann ▲ SCH 312962

Lickl, J.G.:Requiem, w. Maria Zadori (sop), Judith Nemet (mez), Tamas Bator (bass), H. Williams (cnd), Pécs SO, Pécs Chamber Choir Koch Schwann ▲ SCH 312962

Kepros, N. (troubador)

Alfonso El Sabio:Cantigas de Santa Maria, w. J. DeGaetani (sop), C. Cassolas (ten), M. Jaffee (cnd), Waverly Consort [Port] *(rec 1972)* Vanguard Classics ("The Bach Guild" series) ▲ OVC 2013 [ADD]

Kerechanin, Ekaterina (sop)

Grieg, E.:Songs, w. R. Levina (sop), A. Martynov (ten), V. Katajev (cnd), Northern Crown Soloists Ensemble [arr. Tishchenko] MK ▲ MKA 417124 [DDD]

Kermoyan, M. (nar)

Kraft, William:Der Imagistes, w. E. Geer (nar), Los Angeles Percussion Ensemble [E] *(rec 1977)* CRI ▲ CD 639 [ADD/DDD]

Kern, Adele (sop)

Strauss, R.:Ariadne auf Naxos (sels), w. Adele Kern (sop—Zerbinetta), Anny Konetzni (sop—Ariadne), Set Svanholm (ten—Bacchus), Else Schulz (sgr—Composer), R. Moralt (cnd), Vienna State Opera Orch *(rec Vienna, Oct. 16, 1941)* Koch Schwann 2-▲ SCH 314625 [ADD]

Strauss, R.:Der Rosenkavalier, w. Viorica Ursuleac (sop), Georgine von Milinkovic (mez), Georg Hann (bass), Ludwig Weber (bass), C. Krauss (cnd), Bavarian State Opera Orch, Bavarian State Opera Chorus *(rec Munich, June 1942)* Preiser 3-▲ PRE 90218

Wagner, R.:Der Ring des Nibelungen (sels), w. Anny Konetzni (sop), Hilde Konetzni (sop), Elisabeth Schumann (sop), Enid Szantho (cta), Josef Kalenberg (ten), Max Lorenz (ten), Set Svanholm (ten), Erich Zimmermann (ten), Hans Hotter (bar), Jaro Prohaska (bar), Emil Schipper (bar), Paul Schöffler (b-bar), Ludwig Hoffmann (bass), H. Knappertsbusch (cnd), Vienna State Opera Orch *(rec Vienna, 1937–1943)* Koch Schwann 2-▲ SCH 314742 [ADD]

Kern, Patricia (mez)

Somers, H.:Limericks, w. E. Iseler (cnd), *(orch unknown)*, Elmer Iseler Singers *(rec Flora McRae Eaton Memorial Auditorium & St. Anne's Anglican Church, Toronto)* Centrediscs ▲ CMC 5495 [DDD]

Kerns, Robert (bar)

Puccini, G.:Madama Butterfly, w. M. Freni (sop), C. Ludwig (mez), L. Pavarotti (ten), H. von Karajan (cnd), Vienna PO [I] London 3-▲ 417577-2 [ADD]

Puccini, G.:Madama Butterfly (sels), w. M. Freni (sop), C. Ludwig (mez), L. Pavarotti (ten), H. von Karajan (cnd), Vienna PO [I] London ▲ 421247-2 [ADD] ■ 421247-4

Kert, Larry (sgr)

Bernstein, L.:West Side Story, w. C. Lawrence (sgr), C. Rivera (sgr) [1957 cast] Columbia ▲ CK 32603 ♦ CM 32603 ■ JST 32603

Gershwin, G.:Let 'Em Eat Cake, w. McGovern, J. Gilford (ten), M. Thomas (cnd), Orch of St. Luke, New York Choral Artists [E] CBS 2-▲ M2K 42522 [DDD]

Gershwin, G.:Of Thee I Sing, w. McGovern, J. Gilford (ten), M. Thomas (cnd), Orch of St. Luke, New York Choral Artists [E] CBS 2-▲ M2K 42522 [DDD]

Kertesi, Ingrid (sop)

Bach, J.S.:Cant 51, w. J. Pászthy (sop), J. Nemeth (mez), J. Mukk (ten), I. Gáti (bass), M. Antal (cnd), Failoni CO, Hungarian Radio Chorus Naxos ▲ 8.550643 [DDD]

Bach, J.S.:Cant 80, w. J. Nemeth (alt), J. Mukk (ten), I. Gáti (bass), M. Antal (cnd), Failoni CO, Hungarian Radio Chorus *(rec Jan 1992)* Naxos ▲ 8.550642 [DDD]

Bach, J.S.:Cant 147, w. J. Nemeth (alt), J. Mukk (ten), I. Gáti (bass), M. Antal (cnd), Failoni CO, Hungarian Radio Chorus *(rec Jan 1992)* Naxos ▲ 8.550642 [DDD]

Bach, J.S.:Cant 208, "Hunting Cant", w. J. Pászthy (sop), J. Nemeth (mez), J. Mukk (ten), I. Gáti (bass), M. Antal (cnd), Failoni CO, Hungarian Radio Chorus Naxos ▲ 8.550643 [DDD]

Bach, J.S.:Cant 211, "Coffee Cant", w. J. Mukk (ten), I. Gáti (bass), M. Antal (cnd), Failoni CO *(rec 1992)* Naxos ▲ 8.550641 [DDD]

Bach, J.S.:Cant 212, "Peasant Cant", w. J. Mukk (ten), I. Gáti (bass), M. Antal (cnd), Failoni CO *(rec 1992)* Naxos ▲ 8.550641 [DDD]

Bengraf, J.:Sacred Music, w. Katalin Gémes (mez), Gábor Kállay (ten), Ákos Ambrus (bar), István Ella (org), Zsolt Kovács (vc), Balázs Arnóth (bn), Vilmos Buza (db), J. Dobra (cnd), Vienna-Szász CO, Tomkins Vocal Ensemble—Te Deum; O sacrum convivium; Libera me; Gloria [from Missa solemnis in D] Hungaroton ▲ HCD 31609 [DDD]

Druschetzky, G.:Missa solemnis, w. Katalin Gémes (mez), Gábor Kállay (ten), Ákos Ambrus (bar), István Ella (org), Zsolt Kovács (vc), Balázs Arnóth (bn), Vilmos Buza (db), J. Dobra (cnd), Vienna-Szász CO, Tomkins Vocal Ensemble Hungaroton ▲ HCD 31609 [DDD]

From Schubert to Strauss with French Horn, w. Ádám Friedrich (hn), Katalin Halmai (mez), Sándor Falvai (pno) Hungaroton ▲ HCD 31585 [DDD]

Rossini, G.:Il barbiere di Siviglia, w. I. Kertesi (sop—Berta), S. Ganassi (mez—Rosina), R. Vargas (ten—Almaviva), A. Romero (bar—Dr. Bartolo), R. Servile (bar—Figaro), F. de Grandis (bass—Basilio), K. Sárkány (bass—Fiorello), A. Déri (pno), B. Sztankovits (gtr), W. Humburg (cnd), Failoni CO, Hungarian Radio Chorus *(rec Nov. 16–28, 1992)* Naxos 3-▲ 8.660027/29 [DDD]

Kessler, Martha (mez)

Bach, J.S.:Cant 20, w. V. Gohl (mez), T. Altmeyer (ten), A. Kraus (ten), W. Schöne (bass), H. Rilling (cnd), Stuttgart Bach Collegium, Frankfurt Kantorei Hänssler Classic ▲ 98.801 [AAD]

Constantinescu, P.:The Nativity, w. E. Petrescu (sop), V. Teodorian (ten), H. Bömches (bass), M. Basarab (cnd), Bucharest George Enescu PO, Bucharest George Enescu Phil Chorus *(rec 1977)* Olympia ▲ OCD 402 [AAD]

Kesteren, John van (ten)

Bach, J.S.:St. John Passion, w. P. Curtin (sop), E. Thomann (sop), E. Alberts (cta), W. Kmentt, R. Springer (bar), O. Wiener (bar), D. Smith (b-bar), F. Guthrie (bass), F. Lukasowsky (bass), H. Scherchen (cnd), Vienna State Opera Orch, Vienna Academy Chorus [G] *(rec ca 1960)* MCA Classics 2-▲ MCAD2-9804

Kesteren, John van (ten) (cont.)

Haydn, J.:The Seven Last Words of Christ on the Cross, w. Albert (sop), Otto Wiener (bar), Anatoli Babikian (bass), H. Scherchen (cnd), Vienna State Opera Orch, Vienna State Opera Chorus [oratorio version] [G] *(rec 1962)* MCA Classics 2-▲ MCAD2-9816 [AAD]

Orff, C.:Carmina burana, w. A. Augér (sop), J. Summers (bar), R. Muti (cnd), Philharmonia Orch, Philharmonia Chorus [G, L] EMI Classics ▲ CDC 47100

Orff, C.:Die Kluge, w. L. Popp (sop), T. Stewart (bar), F. Crass (bass), G. Frick (bass), K. Eichhorn (cnd), Munich RSO Eurodisc 2-▲ 69069-2-RG [ADD]

Orff, C.:Der Mond—Ein kleines Welttheater, w. T. Stewart (bar), F. Crass (bass), G. Frick (bass), K. Eichhorn (cnd), Munich RSO Eurodisc 2-▲ 69069-2-RG [ADD]

Ketchum, Anne-Marie (sop)

Cage, J.:Europera 4, w. Daisetta Kim (sop), Brian Pezzone (pno), Jerry Wheeler (victrola), Scott Fraser (tape), A. Culver (cnd), Long Beach Opera Orch *(rec Center Theater, Long Beach, CA, Nov. 13, 1993)* Mode 2-▲ MODE 38/39

Cordero, R.:Dodecaconcerto, w. C. Beavon (mez), M. Lifchitz (cnd), North/South Consonance Ensemble North/South Recordings ▲ NS 1003 [DDD]

Rands, B.:...in the receding mist Sop, w. C. Beavon (mez), M. Lifchitz (cnd), North/South Consonance Ensemble North/South Recordings ▲ NS 1003 [DDD]

Saylor, B.:See You in the Morning, w. C. Beavon (mez), M. Lifchitz (cnd), North/South Consonance Ensemble North/South Recordings ▲ NS 1003 [DDD]

Vega, A. de la:Testimonial, w. C. Beavon (mez), M. Lifchitz (cnd), North/South Consonance Ensemble North/South Recordings ▲ NS 1003 [DDD]

Ketchum, Hazel (sgr/saz-lt/perc)

Sonus Chanterai:Music of Medieval France, w. James Carrier (shm/rcrs/oud/hp/gemshn), J. Holenko (oud/chitarra/psaltery/saz-lt/perc), Will Mason (saz-lt/chitarra/vih/ham dlc/perc) *(rec St. John's Episcopal Church, Columbia, MD, Sept. 1993)* Dorian Discovery ▲ DIS 80123 [DDD]

Keyrouz, Sister Marie (sop)

Melchite Sacred Chant, w. Sister Marie Keyrouz (sgr), L'Ensemble de la Paix Harmonia Mundi France ▲ HMC 901497 ■ HMC 401497

Traditional Maronite Chant, w. Ensemble de la Paix Harmonia Mundi France ▲ HMC 901350

Keys, Miranda (sop)

Music for the Theatre, w. A. Reynolds (cnd), London Salon Ensemble, Donald Maxwell (bar) Meridian ▲ MER 84308 [DDD]

Keyte, Christopher (bass)

Bononcini, A.:Stabat Mater, w. Felicity Palmer (sop), Paul Esswood (ct), Philip Langridge (ten), John Scott (org), John Willison (vn), Chris Wellington (va), Don McVeigh (va), G. Guest (cnd), Philomusica Antiqua of London, St. John's College Choir Cambridge *(rec 1977)* London 2-▲ 443868-2 [ADD]

Caldara, A.:Crucifixus, w. Felicity Palmer (sop), Paul Esswood (ct), Philip Langridge (ten), John Scott (org), John Willison (vn), Chris Wellington (va), Don McVeigh (va), G. Guest (cnd), Philomusica Antiqua of London, St. John's College Choir Cambridge *(rec 1977)* London 2-▲ 443868-2 [ADD]

Davies, P.M.:The Lighthouse, w. Neil Mackie (ten), Ian Comboy (bass), P. M. Davies (cnd), BBC PO Collins Classics ▲ COL 1415 [DDD]

Lotti, A.:Crucifixus, w. Felicity Palmer (sop), Paul Esswood (ct), Philip Langridge (ten), John Scott (org), John Willison (vn), Chris Wellington (va), Don McVeigh (va), G. Guest (cnd), Philomusica Antiqua of London, St. John's College Choir Cambridge *(rec 1977)* London 2-▲ 443868-2 [ADD]

Pergolesi, G.B.:Magnificat in C, w. Elizabeth Vaughan (sop), Janet Baker (cta), Ian Partridge (ten), D. Willcocks (cnd), Academy of St. Martin in the Fields, King's College Choir Cambridge *(rec 1966)* London 2-▲ 443868-2 [ADD]

Purcell, H.:Music for the Theater, w. E. Kirkby (sop), J. Nelson (sop), J. Bowman (ct), M. Hill (ten), R. Covey-Crump (ten), D. Thomas (bass), C. Hogwood (cnd), Academy of Ancient Music L'Oiseau-Lyre 6-▲ 425893-2 [ADD]

Sir Cristemas, w. [cnd:Louis Halsey], Elizabethan Singers, Simon Preston (kbd/cnd), Ian Partridge (ten), Susan Longfield (sop) Boston Skyline ▲ BSD 124 [ADD]

Kharitonov, Dimitri (bass)

Shostakovich, D.:Songs, Op. 46, w. M. Elder (cnd), City of Birmingham SO [orchd Shostakovich, completed McBurney] *(rec Symphony Hall, Birmingham, England, Dec 16–18, 1992)* United ▲ CAL 88001 [DDD]

Kiberg, Tina (sop)

Beethoven, L. van:Missa Solemnis, w. R. Lang (cta), W. Cochran (ten), M. Krutikov (bass), A. Dorati (cnd), European SO, Univ of Maryland Chorus [L] *(rec live, Berlin Philharmonie, 7/3/88)* BIS 2-▲ CD 406/07 [DDD]

Janácek, L.:Slavonic Mass, w. R. Stene (cta), P. Svensson (ten), U. Cold (bass), C. Mackerras (cnd), Danish National RSO, Danish National Radio Choir, Copenhagen Boys' Choir Chandos ▲ CHAN 9310 [DDD]

Kuhlau, F.:Lulu, w. A. Frellesvig (sgr), K. von Binzer (ten), R. Saarman (ten), U. Cold (bass), E. Harbo (sgr), M. Schønwandt (cnd), Danish National RSO, Danish National Radio Choir [Da] Kontrapunkt 3-▲ 32009/11 [DDD]

Mahler, G.:Sym 2, w. Kirsten Dolberg (alt), L. Segerstam (cnd), Danish National RSO, Danish National Radio Choir Chandos 2-▲ CHAN 9266/67 [DDD]

Nielsen, C.:Saul & David, w. A. Gjevang (mez), P. Lindroos (ten), K. Westi (ten), C. Christiansen (bass), A. Haugland (bass), J. Klint (bass), N. Järvi (cnd), Danish National RSO, Danish National Radio Choir [Da] Chandos 2-▲ CHAN 8911/12 [DDD]

Kibkalo, Evgeny (sgr)

Mussorgsky, M.:Boris Godunov, w. Irina Arkhipova (mez—Marina Mnishek), Evgenya Verbitskaya (mez—Nurse to Xenia), Valentina Klepatskaya (sgr—Fyodor), Tamara Sorokina (sgr—Xenia), Anton Grigoryev (ten—Simpleton), Vladimir Ivanovsky (ten—Grigory, the Pretender), Gyorgy Shulpin (bar—Prince Shuisky), Alexey Geleva (bass—Varlaam), Ivan Petrov (bass—Boris Godounov), Mark Reshetin (bass—Pimen), Alexi Ivanov (sgr—Andrei Shchelkalov), Evgeny Kibkalo (sgr—Rangoni), A. Melik-Pashayev (cnd), Bolshoi Theater Orch, Bolshoi Theater Chorus *(rec Moscow, 1962)* Melodiya ("The Russian Opera" series) 3-▲ 74321-29349-2 [ADD]

Prokofiev, S.:War & Peace, w. Galina Vishnevskaya (sop—Natasha Rostovoa), Irina Arkhipova (mez—Hélène Bezukhova), Evgenya Verbitskaya (mez—Marya Akhrosimova), Alexi Maslennikov (ten—Anatole Kuragin), Vladimir Petrov (ten—Pierre Bezukhov), Pavel Lisitsian (bar—Napoleon), Alexi Krivchenya (bass—Field-Marshall Kutuzov), Evgeny Kibkalo (sgr—Prince Andrei Bolkonsky), A. Melik-Pashayev (cnd), Bolshoi Theater Orch, Bolshoi Theater Chorus *(rec Moscow, 1961)* Melodiya ("The Russian Opera" series) 3-▲ 74321-29350-2 [ADD]

Kiefer, Günter (bar)

Bach, J.S.:Cant 8, w. P. Esswood (ct), K. Equiluz (ten), M. van Egmond (b-bar), Leonhardt Consort, King's College Choir Cambridge [G] Teldec 2-▲ 2292-42498-2 [AAD]

Petrassi, G.:Beatitudes, w. A. Molino (cnd), Compania Stradivarius ▲ STR 33347

Kieffer, Deborah (mez)

Puccini, G.:Madama Butterfly (sels), w. Elisabeth Carron (sop—Cio-Cio-San), Deborah Kieffer (mez—Suzuki), Herman Malamood (ten—Pinkerton), David Clatworthy (bar—Sharpless), G. Morelli (cnd), *(orch unknown)*—Ancora un passo or via; Ieri son salita...Io seguo il mio destino; Adesso voi siete per me...Vogliatemi bene; Ti sero palpitante...Ah! Quanti occhi fisi, attenti!; Egli, col cuore grosso...Un bel di, vedremo; Ebbene, che fareste Madama Butterfly...Due cose potrei far; Sai cos'ebbe cuore di pensare...Che tua madre; Troppa luce e di fuor; Con onor muore...Tu? Tu? Piccolo Iddio *(rec New York, Oct 23, 1973)* Legato Classics ▲ LCD 212-1 [ADD]

Kiehr, Maria-Cristina (sop)

Bach, J.S.:Cant 201, w. Andreas Scholl (ct), James Taylor (ten), Kurt Azeberger (ten), Roman Trekel (bar), Peter Lika (bass), R. Jacobs (cnd), Berlin Academy for Early Music, Berlin Chamber Chorus Harmonia Mundi France 2-▲ HMC 901544.45

Caldara, A.:Maddalena ai Piedi di Cristo, w. Rosa Dominguez (sop), Bernarda Fink (cta), Andreas Scholl (ct), Gerd Türk (ten), Ulrich Messthaler (bass), R. Jacobs (cnd), Schola Cantorum Basiliensis Instrumental Ensemble Harmonia Mundi France 2-▲ HMC 905221.22

Giancelli, B.:Tastegiati, w. Concerto Soave L'Empreinte Digitale ▲ ED 13048

Handel, G.F.:Cants, w. Andreas Scholl (alt), A. de Marchi (cnd), Armonico Theater Ensemble—Il duello amoroso; Vendendo amor; La partenza; Nel dolce tempo; Sono liete, fortunate Accord ▲ ACD 204212 [DDD]

Kiehr, Maria-Cristina (sop) (cont.)

L'heritage de Monteverdi, Vol. 2, w. La Fenice, John Elwes (ten), Ulrich Messthaler (bar) *(rec Eglise de Mormont, Nov 1995)* Ricercar ▲ RIC 166148

Late 16th Century Venetian Harpsichord, w. Jean-Marc Aymes (hpd) L'Empreinte Digitale ▲ ED 13042

Marini, B.:Sons, Syms & Retornelli, w. Concerto Soave—Sinf secondo tuono L'Empreinte Digitale ▲ ED 13048

Merula, T.:Music of, w. Concerto Soave—Cappriccio cromatico; Canzon L'Empreinte Digitale ▲ ED 13048

Monteverdi, C.:Vespro della Beata Vergine, w. Barbara Borden (sop), Andreas Scholl (alt), John Bowen (ten), Andrew Murgatroyd (ten), Victor Torres (bar), Antonio Abete (bass), Jelle Draijer (bass), René Jacobs (cnd), Concerto Vocale, Netherlands Chamber Choir Harmonia Mundi 2-▲ 901566.67

Strozzi, B.:Sacred Music, w. Concerto Soave—Salve Regina; Erat Petrus; Mater Anna; Nascente Maria; Hodie oritur; Salve Sancta caro; O Maria L'Empreinte Digitale ▲ ED 13048

Kiel, Let (sgr)

Donizetti, G.:Il borgomastro di Saardam, w. Philipp Langridge (ten), Renato Capecchi (bar), J. Schaap (cnd), Zaanstad Opera Orch, Zaanstad Opera Chorus *(rec 1973)* Pantheon 2-▲ PHE 6630 (m)

Kiepura, Jan (ten)

Jan Kiepura, Vol. 1 Pearl ▲ PEA 9976 (m) [AAD]

Lotte Lehmann, w. Lotte Lehmann (sop), Richard Tauber (ten) Pearl ▲ PEA 9409 (m) [AAD]

Verdi, G.:Il trovatore (sels), w. J. Biel (ten), F. Tamagno (ten), L.-A. Escalaïs (ten), M. Gilion (ten), E. Caruso (ten), A. Paoli (ten), G. Zenatello (ten), J. Sembach (ten), L. Slezak (ten), F. Constantino (ten), G. Martinelli (ten), B. De Muro (ten), N. Fusati (ten), N. Piccaluga (ten), G. Lauri-Volpi (ten), A. Pertile (ten), E. Bergamaschi (ten), R. Tauber (ten), J. O'Sullivan (ten), H. Roswaenge (ten), G. Taccani (ten), V. Lois (ten), H. Lazaro (ten), A. Lindi (ten), A. Cortis (ten), F. Merli (ten), F. Völker (ten), J. Schmidt (ten), J. Bjoerling (ten), B. Gigli (ten), A. Salvarezza (ten), J. Soler (ten), M. Filippeschi (ten)—34 performances of the Act III tenor aria "Di quella pira!," *(rec from 1903-1956)* Bongiovanni ▲ GB 1051 [AAD]

Kiichli, Henry (bass)

Wagner, S.:Der Bärenhäuter, w. B. Johanning (sop—Luise), K. Likic (sop—Lene), T. Koon (sop—Gunda), V. Horn (ten—Hans Kraft), A. Feilhaber (ten—Nikolaus Spitz), R. Hartmann (bar—Kaspar Wild), A. Wenhold (bar—Stranger), A. Waller (bass—Devil), H. Kiichli (bass—Melchior Fröhlich), K. Bach (cnd), Thüringian SO, Thüringian State Theater Chorus *(rec Rudolstadt, July 25-31, 1993)* Marco Polo ("Opera Classics" series) 2-▲ 8.223713/4 [DDD]

Kilanowicz, Zofia (sop)

Chopin, F.:Songs Sop (comp), w. Katarzyna Jankowska (pno) *(rec Warsaw Philharmonic Hall, Jan 1993 & May 1994)* Canyon Classics ▲ CD 237

Górecki, H.-M.:Sym 3, "Sym of Sorrowful Songs", w. J. Kaspszyk (cnd), Karol Szymanowski State PO *(rec live, Breslau, Poland, Sept. 5, 1993)* EMI Classics ▲ CDC 55368 [DDD]

Górecki, H.-M.:Sym 3, "Sym of Sorrowful Songs", w. J. Swoboda (cnd), Polish State PO *(rec Symphony Hall, Katowice, Poland, 1993)* Vox Classics ▲ VOX 7511 [DDD]

Nicolai, O.:Te Deum, w. Bozena Betley (sop), Katarztna Suska (cta), Henryk Grychnik (ten), Czeslaw Galka (bar), Jerzy Gruszcynski (bass), R. Bader (cnd), Cracow PO, Cracow Phil Chorus Koch Schwann ▲ SCH CD 310872

Kilduff, Barbara (sop)

Schoenberg, A.:Die Jakobsleiter, w. Barbara Kilduff (sop—Seele 1), Jadwiga Rappé (cta—Sterbende), Wilfried Gahmlich (ten—Aufrührerischer), Cornelius Hauptmann (ten—Gabriel), Keith Lewis (ten—Berfener), Kurt Azesberger (bar—Mönch), Barbara Fuchs (sgr—Seele 2), Matteo de Monti (sgr—Ringender), Bjorn Waag (sgr—Auserwählter), E. Inbal (cnd), Frankfurt RSO, Robin Gritton (cnd), Berlin Radio Chorus *(rec Alte Oper, Frankfurt, Sept 6-9, 1994)* Denon ▲ CO 78977 [DDD]

Kiley, R. (sgr)

Rodgers, R.:No Strings, w. D. Carroll (sgr), *(artists unknown)* [1962 cast] Broadway Angel ▲ ZDM 64694 ■ EG 64694

Killebrew, Gerard (nar)

Vaughan Williams, R.:An Oxford Elegy, w. R. Taylor (cnd), Chorus Civitas CO, Chorus Civitas *(rec The Stockade, Baton Rouge, Apr 24 & 27, 1995)* Centaur ▲ CRC 2299 [DDD]

Killebrew, Gwendoline (mez)

Haydn, J.:Mass 10, "Kriegsmesse", "Paukenmesse", w. Patricia Wells (sop), Michael Devlin (b-bar), Alan Titus (bar), L. Bernstein (cnd), *(orch unknown)*, Norman Scribner Choir [L] *(rec 1973)* Sony Classical ("Bernstein:The Royal Edition" series) 2-▲ SM2K 47563 [ADD]

Haydn, J.:Mass 11, "Nelsonmesse", "Imperial Mass", "Coronation Mass", w. Judith Blegen (sop), Kenneth Riegel (ten), Simon Estes (bass), L. Bernstein (cnd), New York PO, Westminster Choir [L] *(rec 1976)* Sony Classical ("Bernstein:The Royal Edition" series) 2-▲ SM2K 47563 [ADD]

Nicolai, O.:Mass, w. G. Resick (sop), F. Lang (ten), H. C. Polster (bass), H. Hollreiser (cnd), North German RSO, North German Radio Chorus [L] Koch Schwann ▲ CD 313052 [ADD]

Puccini, G.:Edgar, w. R. Scotto (sop), C. Bergonzi (ten), V. Sardinero (bar), E. Queler (cnd), New York City Opera Orch, New York Schola Cantorum *(rec in concert at Carnegie Hall, 4/13/77)* CBS 2-▲ M2K 34584

Weinberger, J.:Schwanda der Dudelsackpfeifer, w. L. Popp (sop), S. Jerusalem (ten), H. Prey (bar), S. Nimsgern (bass), H. Wallberg (cnd), Munich RSO, Bavarian Radio Chorus [F] CBS 3-▲ M3K 36926 [ADD]

Killian, George (ten)

Demars, J.:An American Requiem, w. Joni Killian (sop), Linda Childs (mez), Robert La France (b-bar), James DeMars (cnd), Arizona State Univ Choirs *(rec Phoenix Symphony Hall, Jan 17, 1994)* Renaissance ▲ 94001 [DDD]

Killian, Joni (sop)

Demars, J.:An American Requiem, w. Linda Childs (mez), George Killian (ten), Robert La France (b-bar), James DeMars (cnd), Arizona State Univ Choirs *(rec Phoenix Symphony Hall, Jan 17, 1994)* Renaissance ▲ 94001 [DDD]

Kim, Daisetta (sop)

Cage, J.:Europera 4, w. Anne-Marie Ketchum (sop), Brian Pezzone (pno), Jerry Wheeler (victrola), Scott Fraser (tape), A. Culver (cnd), Long Beach Opera Orch *(rec Center Theater, Long Beach, CA, Nov. 13, 1993)* Mode 2-▲ MODE 38/39

Kim, Ettore (bar)

Bellini, V.:I Puritani, w. Edita Gruberova (sop), Katia Lytting (mez), Justin Lavender (ten), Carlo Tuand (ten), Francesco Ellero d'Artegna (bass), Dankwart Siegele (bass), F. Luisi (cnd), Munich RSO, Bavarian Radio Chorus Nightingale Classics 3-▲ NIG 70562

Donizetti, G.:Linda di Chamounix, w. Edita Gruberová (sop), Monica Groop (mez), Don Bernardini (sgr), F. Haider (cnd), Swedish RSO, Mikaeli Chamber Choir Nightingale Classics 3-▲ NIG 70561

Donizetti, G.:Roberto Devereux, w. Edita Gruberová (sop), Delores Ziegler (mez), Don Bernardini (sgr), F. Haider (cnd), Strasbourg PO, Rhine Opera Chorus Nightingale Classics 2-▲ NIG 70563

Kim, Hye Jin (cta)

Mysliveček, J.:Isacco figura, w. Ilona Czaková (sgr), Tatiana Korovina (sgr), Victoria Luchianez (sgr), Vladimir Dolezal (ten), Ivan Kusnjer (bar), I. Parik (cnd), Prague Sinfonietta, Pavel Kühn (cnd), Kühn Chorus Supraphon 2-▲ SUP 3209

Kimbrough, Matthew (bar)

Partch, H.:Revelation in the Courthouse Park, w. S. Costallos (sgr—Mom & Agave), C. Durham (ten—Sonny & Pentheus), M. Kimbrough (bar—Vendor & Herdsman), E. Earle (b-bar—Hobo & Tiresias), O. Babatunde (sgr—Dion & Dionysus), C. Roos (sgr—Mayor & Cadmus), O. Williams (sgr—Korypheus), R. Young (sgr—Cop & Guard), D. Mitchell (cnd), Partch Instrumentalists, marching band, *(chorus unknown)* [E] *(rec 10/87)* Tomato 2-▲ R2 70390 [DDD]

Rossini, G.:Arias, w. A. Aug(acu)er (sop), J. Larmore (mez), D. Baldwin (pno)—La Pesca (duet); Il Trovatore Arabesque ▲ Z 6623 [ADD]

Kimbrough, Steven (bar)

Korngold, E.W.:Songs, w. Dalton Baldwin (pno)—Six Songs, Op. 9, Nos. 1-6; Four Songs, Op. 14; Three Songs, Op. 18; Two Songs, Op. 41/3 & 4 [G] Acanta ▲ 43539 [DDD]

Korngold, E.W.:Songs, w. D. Baldwin (pno) Koch Schwann ▲ SCH 310942 [DDD]

Kimbrough, Steven (bar) (cont.)

Rossini, G.:Péchés de vieillesse (sels), w. A. Auger (sop), J. Larmore (mez), J. Aler (ten), D. Baldwin (pno)—Les Amants de Séville; Chanson de Zora; L'Esule; La Fioraia Fiorentina; La Lontananza; Musique Anodine; L'Orpheline du Tyrol; La Passegiata Quartettino; L'Ultimo Ricordo; Un Sou Complainte [I,F] Arabesque ▲ Z 6623 [ADD]

Schoenberg, A.:Songs, w. D. Baldwin (pno) Koch Schwann ▲ SCH 310942 [DDD]

Schreker, F.:Songs, w. D. Baldwin (pno) Koch Schwann ▲ SCH 310942 [DDD]

Weigl, K.:Songs, w. D. Baldwin (pno)—7 Songs, Op. 1 Koch Schwann ▲ SCH 310942 [DDD]

Weill, K.:Songs, w. D. Baldwin (pno) [E,G] Arabesque ▲ Z 6579

Weill, K.:Songs, w. V. Symonette (cnd), Cologne RSO—Songs from Firebrand of Florence; Love Life; One Touch of Venus; Knickerbocker Holiday; Johnny Johnson Koch Schwann ▲ SCH CD 314162

Zemlinsky, A. von:Songs (misc), w. C. Garben (pno)—(23) from Opp. 2, 5, 6, 7, 8, 10, 13, 22 & 27 [G] Acanta ▲ 43509 [DDD]

Kimm, Fiona (mez)

Turnage, M.-A.:Lament for a Hanging Man, w. O. Knussen (cnd), Nash Ensemble NMC ▲ NMC 24 [DDD]

Kincses, Veronika (mez)

Liszt, F.:Missa solemnis, w. T. Takács (mez), G. Korondy (ten), J. Gregor (bass), A. Ferencsik (cnd), Budapest SO, Budapest Sym Chorus [L] Hungaroton ▲ HCD 11861

Kincses, Veronika (sop)

Giordano, U.:Fedora, w. E. Martón (sop), J. Carreras (ten), J. Gregor (bass), G. Patanè (cnd), Hungarian Radio-TV SO, Hungarian Radio-TV Chorus [I] CBS 2-▲ M2K 42181 [DDD]

Gluck, C.W.:Orfeo ed Euridice, w. M. Zempleni (sop), J. Hamari (mez), E. Lukács (cnd), Hungarian State Opera Orch, Hungarian State Opera Chorus LaserLight ▲ 14113 [DDD]

Liszt, F.:Christus, w. Tamara Takács (mez), Robert Nagy (ten), Sándor Sólyom-Nagy (bar), László Polgár (bass), A. Dorati (cnd), Hungarian State Orch, Hungarian Radio-TV Chorus [L] Hungaroton 3-▲ HCD 12831/33 [DDD]

Liszt, F.:Hungarian Coronation Mass, w. T. Tákacs (mez), D. Gulyas (ten), L. Polgar (bass), G. Lehel (cnd), Budapest SO, Hungarian Radio Chorus [L] Hungaroton ▲ HCD 12148

Puccini, G.:La Bohème, w. Veronika Kinsces (sop—Mimi), Sidonia Haljakova (sop—Musette), Peter Dvorsky (ten—Rodolfo), Vijtech Scherenkel (ten—Parpingol), Ian Konsulov (bar—Marcello), Balazs Poka (bar—Schaunard), Stanislav Benacka (bass—Benoit), Dariusz Niemirowicz (bass—Colline), Stefan Janci (bass—Alcindoro), *(cnd & orch unknown)* Griffin ▲ GCD 2942

Puccini, G.:Madama Butterfly, w. T. Tákacs (mez), P. Dvorsky (ten), L. Miller (bar), G. Patanè (cnd), Hungarian State Opera Orch, Hungarian State Opera Chorus [I] Hungaroton 2-▲ HCD 12256/57

Respighi, O.:Semirama, w. E. Marton (sop), L. Bartolini (ten), L Miller (bar), L. Polgaar (bass), T. Clementis (bass), L. Gardelli (cnd), Hungarian State Orch, Hungarian Radio-TV Chorus [I] Hungaroton 2-▲ HCD 31197/98

King, James (ten)

Gluck, C.W.:Iphigénie en Aulide, w. Inge Borkh (sop—Klytämnestra), Christa Ludwig (mez—Iphigenie), Elisabeth Steiner (mez—Artemis), James King (ten—Achilles), Otto Edelmann (b-bar), Alois Pernerstorfer (b-bar), Walter Berry (bass), K. Böhm (cnd), Vienna PO, Salzburg Festival Chamber Choir, Vienna State Opera Chorus *(rec Salzburg, Aug 3, 1962)* Orfeo d'or ("Festspiel Dikumente" series) 2-▲ C 428962 (m) [ADD]

Hindemith, P.:Mathis der Maler, w. Urszula Koszut (sop), Trudeliese Schmidt (mez), Rose Wagemann (mez), William Cochran (ten), Donald Grobe (ten), Manfred Schmidt (ten), Dietrich Fischer-Dieskau (bar), Gerd Feldhoff (bass), Alexander Malta (bass), Peter Meven (bass), Karl Kreile (sgr), R. Kubelik (cnd), Bavarian RSO, Bavarian Radio Chorus EMI Classics 2-▲ CDCC 55237

Mahler, G.:Das Lied von der Erde, w. J. Baker (mez), B. Haitink (cnd), Royal Concertgebouw Orch Philips ("Silver Line" series) ▲ 432279-2 [ADD]

Monteverdi, C.:Combattimento, w. E. Kirkby (sop), P. Agnew (ct), A. Rooley (cnd), Consort of Musicke [I] Virgin Classics ▲ 59606 [DDD]

Schmidt, F.:Notre Dame, w. G. Jones (sop), R. Laubenthal (ten), K. Moll (bass), C. Perick (cnd), Berlin RSO, St. Hedwig's Cathedral Choir, RIAS Chamber Chorus [G] Capriccio 2-▲ 10248/9 [DDD]

Strauss, R.:Ariadne auf Naxos, w. L. Rysanek (sop), J. Scovotti (sop), T. Troyanos (mez), P. Schöffler (b-bar), K. Böhm (cnd), Vienna State Opera Orch, Vienna State Opera Chorus *(rec 1967)* Melodram 2-▲ MLO 270105 [ADD]

Strauss, R.:Daphne, w. H. Gueden (sop), F. Wunderlich (ten), P. Schöffler (bass), K. Böhm (cnd), Vienna SO, Vienna State Opera Chorus *(rec live 1963)* Deutsche Grammophon 2-▲ 445322-2

Strauss, R.:Elektra, w. A. Varnay (sop/mez), M. Mödl (sop/mez), H. Hillebrecht (sop), E. Wächter (bar), H. von Karajan (cnd), Vienna PO, Vienna State Opera Chorus [G] *(rec 1964)* Melodram 2-▲ MEL 27044 [AAD]

Strauss, R.:Elektra (sels), w. A. Varnay (sop/mez), H. Hillebrecht (sop), H. von Karajan (cnd), Vienna PO, Vienna State Opera Chorus [G] *(rec live in Salzburg, 8/11/64)* Arkadia 3-▲ 213 (m) [ADD]

Strauss, R.:Die Frau ohne Schatten, w. B. Nilsson (sop), L. Rysanek (sop), R. Hesse (mez), W. Berry (bass), K. Böhm (cnd), Vienna SO Deutsche Grammophon 3-▲ 445325-2

Wagner, R.:Parsifal, w. G. Jones (sop), T. Stewart (bar), D. McIntyre (b-bar), K. Ridderbusch (bass), F. Crass (bass), P. Boulez (cnd), Bayreuth Festival Orch, Bayreuth Festival Chorus [G] *(rec 1970)* Deutsche Grammophon 3-▲ 435718-2 [ADD]

Wagner, R.:Der Ring des Nibelungen, w. B. Nilsson (sop), K. Flagstad (sop), R. Crespin (sop), C. Watson (sop), C. Ludwig (mez), J. Madeira (mez), S. Svanholm (ten), G. Stolze (ten), W. Windgassen (ten), G. London (bar), D. Fischer-Dieskau (bar), H. Hotter (b-bar), G. Neidlinger (b-bar), G. Frick (bass), G. Solti (cnd), Vienna PO [G] London 15-▲ 414100-2 [ADD]

Wagner, R.:Der Ring des Nibelungen (sels), w. Birgit Nilsson (sop—Brünnhilde), Leonie Rysanek (sop—Sieglinde), James King (ten—Siegmund), Wolfgang Windgassen (ten), Theo Adam (b-bar—Wotan), Gustav Neidlinger (b-bar), Josef Greindl (bass), K. Böhm (cnd), Bayreuth Festival Orch *(rec Bayreuth, 1967)* Philips 2-▲ 454020-2

Wagner, R.:Die Walküre, w. B. Nilsson (sop), R. Crespin (sop), C. Ludwig (mez), H. Hotter (b-bar), G. Frick (bass), G. Solti (cnd), Vienna PO [G] London 4-▲ 414105-2 [ADD]

Wagner, R.:Die Walküre (act 1), w. Leonie Rysanek (sop), Gerd Nienstedt (bass), K. Böhm (cnd), Bayreuth Festival Orch *(rec live, Bayreuth Festival)* Philips ("Solo" series) ▲ 442640-2

King, Joslyn (mez)

Weisgall, H.:Six Characters in Search of an Author, w. E. Byrne (sop—Stepdaughter), S. Foster (sop—Prompter), E. Furtal (sop—Coloratura), J. King (mez—Mezzo), N. Maultsby (mez—Mother), P. LoVerne (cta—Madame Pace), D. Pritchett (alt—Wardrobe Mistress), B. Fowler (ten—Tenore Boffo), K. Anderson (ten—Director), A. Schroeder (bar—Accompanist), P. Zawisza (bar—Stage Manager), R. Orth (bar—Father), G. Lehman (bar—Son), M. Wadsworth (b-bar—Basso Cantante), L. Schaenen (cnd), Chicago Lyric Opera Orch, Lyric Opera Center Chorus *(rec Chicago, June 14 & 16, 1990)* New World 2-▲ 80454-2

King, M. (sgr)

Rodgers, R.:Music of, w. S. Bass (sgr), J. Andrews (sgr), P. Como (sgr), D. Reese (sgr), J. Jones (sgr), N. Luboff (sgr), M. Gold (sgr), N. Walker (sgr), H. Bowen (sgr), V. Damone (sgr), P. Nero (pno), J. P. Morgan (sgr), E. Fisher (sgr), B. Goodman (cl), Ann-Margaret (sgr), Shorty Rogers (sgr), D. Shore (sgr), T. Martin (sgr), A. Newley (sgr) RCA ▲ 8590-2 R ■ 8590-4 R

King, Malcolm (bass)

Stravinsky, I.:Pulcinella, w. J. Smith (sop), J. Fryatt (ten), S. Rattle (cnd), Northern Sinfonia of England EMI Classics ▲ CDM 64739

King, Mary (mez)

Birtwistle, H.:Meridan, w. O. Knussen (cnd), London Sinfonietta, London Sinfonietta Chorus NM Classics ▲ NMCD 009 [DDD]

Britten, H.:Praise We Great Men, w. A. Hargan (sop), R. Tear (ten), W. White (bass), S. Rattle (cnd), City of Birmingham SO, City of Birmingham Sym Chorus [E] *(rec July, 1990)* EMI Classics 2-▲ ZDCB 54270 [DDD]

Janácek, L.:Slavonic Mass, w. F. Palmer (sop), A. Gunson (mez), J. Mitchinson (ten), J. Parker-Smith (org), S. Rattle (cnd), City of Birmingham SO, City of Birmingham Sym Chorus EMI ▲ CDC 47504

Knussen, O.:Where The Wild Things Are, w. R. Hardy (sop), O. Knussen (cnd), London Sinfonietta [E] Arabesque ▲ Z 6535 [DDD]

Mahler, G.:Das Lied von der Erde, w. D. Fischer-Dieskau (bar), L. Bernstein (cnd), Vienna PO [G] London ▲ 417783-2 [ADD]

King, Robert (trb)

Couperin, F.:Leçons de ténèbres (for Ash Wednesday), w. J. Bowman (ct), M. Chance (ct), M. Caudle (bass vl) Hyperion ▲ CDA 66474

Kingsley, Ben (nar)

Prokofiev, S.:Peter & the Wolf, w. C. Mackerras (cnd), London SO Cala ▲ CAL 1022 [DDD]

Kingsley, Ben (sgr)

Rodgers, R.:The King & I, w. J. Andrews (sgr—Anna Leonowens), L. Salonga (sgr—Tuptim), B. Kingsley (sgr—The King), P. Bryson (sgr—Lun Tha), M. Horne (mez—Lady Thiang), M. Liufau (sgr—Prince Chulalongkorn), E. Kingsley (sgr—Louis Leonowens), R. Moore (sgr—Sir Edward Ramsay), M. Sheen (sgr—The Kralahome), J. Mauceri (cnd), Hollywood Bowl Orch, Los Angeles Master Chorale *(rec Culver City, CA, Apr 1992)* Philips ▲ 438007-2 [DDD]

Kingsley, E. (sgr)

Rodgers, R.:The King & I, w. J. Andrews (sgr—Anna Leonowens), L. Salonga (sgr—Tuptim), B. Kingsley (sgr—The King), P. Bryson (sgr—Lun Tha), M. Horne (mez—Lady Thiang), M. Liufau (sgr—Prince Chulalongkorn), E. Kingsley (sgr—Louis Leonowens), R. Moore (sgr—Sir Edward Ramsay), M. Sheen (sgr—The Kralahome), J. Mauceri (cnd), Hollywood Bowl Orch, Los Angeles Master Chorale *(rec Culver City, CA, Apr 1992)* Philips ▲ 438007-2 [DDD]

Kink, Gerda (cta)

Weber, C.M. von:Missa sancta 1, w. Maria Taborsky (sop), Hermann Pöllmann (ten), Hans Huber (bass), Gisela Schindler (org), E. Ehret (cnd), St. Michael Orch Munich, St. Michael Chorus Munich Koch Schwann ▲ SCH CD 316372

Weber, C.M. von:Missa sancta 2, w. Maria Taborsky (sop), Hermann Pöllmann (ten), Hans Huber (bass), Gisela Schindler (org), E. Ehret (cnd), Munich St. Michael's Orch, Munich St. Michael Choir Studio SM ▲ D 2454 [ADD]

Kipnis, Alexander (bass)

Alexander Kipnis RCA Gold Seal ▲ 60522-2-RG [ADD]

Alexander Kipnis in Opera & Song Phonographe 2-▲ PHG 5039 [ADD]

Alexander Kipnis Preiser ("Lebendige Vergangenheit" series) ▲ PRE 89019 (m) [AAD]

Alexander Kipnis, Vol. 2 *(rec 1916–26)* Preiser ("Lebendige Vergangenheit" series) ▲ PRE 89107 [ADD]

Beethoven, L. van:Missa Solemnis, w. Z. Milanov (sop), B. Castagna (mez), J. Björling, A. Toscanini (cnd), NBC SO, Westminster Choir [L] *(rec live 12/28/40)* Melodram 3-▲ MEL 38006

Beethoven, L. van:Missa Solemnis, w. Zinka Milanov (sop), Bruna Castagna (cta), Jussi Björling (ten), A. Toscanini (cnd), NBC SO, Westminster Choir *(rec 1940)* Grammofono 2000 ▲ GRM 78626

The Best of Alexander Kipnis Pearl ▲ PEA 9451 (m) [AAD]

Brahms, J.:Ernste Gesänge, w. G. Moore (pno) *(rec 1936)* Preiser 2-▲ 89204 (m) [AAD]

Brahms, J.:Ernste Gesänge, w. G. Moore (pno) *(rec 1936)* Music & Arts 2-▲ CD 661 (m) [AAD]

Brahms, J.:Songs, Vol. 1—Von ewiger Liebe, Op. 43/1; Die Mainacht, Op. 43/2; Erinnerung, Op. 63/2; O wüsst' ich doch den Weg zurück, Op. 63/8; Ein Sonett, Op. 14/4; Sonntag, Op. 47/3; Ständchen, Op. 106/1; Vergebliches Ständchen, Op. 84/4; Verrat, Op. 105/5; An die Nachtigall, Op. 46/4; Ernste Gesänge, Op. 121/1–4 [w. G. Moore (pno)]; Vol. 2—In stiller Nacht, Mein Mädel hat einen Rosenmund, Sandmännchen, Vor dem Fenster, Wiegenlied; Ruhe, Süssliebchen, im Schatten, Op. 33/9; Der Gang zum Liebchen, Op. 48/1; O kühler Wald, Op. 72/3; Dein blaues Auge, Op. 59/8; Mein Liebe ist grün, Op. 63/5; Geheimnis, Op. 71/3; Am Sonntag Morgen, Op. 49/1; In Waldeinsamkeit, Op. 85/6; Wir wandelten, Op. 96/2; Wie Melodien zieht es mir, Op. 105/1; Auf dem Kirchhofe, Op. 105/4; Die Überläufer, Op. 48/2; Ein Wanderer, Op. 106/5; Wie bist du, meine Königin, Op. 32/9; Blinde Kuh, Op. 58/1 [w. E. V. Wolff (pno)] Preiser 2-▲ 89204 (m) [AAD]

Brahms, J.:Songs—Von ewiger Liebe, Op. 43/1; Die Mainacht, Op. 43/2; Erinnerung, Op. 63/2; O wüsst' ich doch den Weg zurück, Op. 63/8; Ein Sonett, Op. 14/4; Sonntag, Op. 47/3; Ständchen, Op. 106/1; Vergebliches Ständchen, Op. 84/4; Verrat, Op. 105/5; An die Nachtigall, Op. 46/4; Ernste Gesänge, Op. 121/1–4 [w. Gerald Moore (pno); rec. June–July 1936, HMV DB 2994/99]; Sapphische Ode, Op. 94/4; Auf dem Kirchhofe, Op. 105/4; Immer leiser wird mein Schlummer, Op. 105/2; Feldeinsamkeit, Op. 86/2 [w. Arthur Bergh (pno); rec. New York City, 2/14/29; issued as American Columbia 2077M & 7204M] Music & Arts 2-▲ CD 661 (m) [AAD]

The Legendary Singers at Lindenoper Berlin (1927-1945)—, w. Gitta Alpar (sop), Erna Berger (sop), Tiana Lemnitz (sop), Maria Müller (sop), Margarete Klose (cta), Peter Anders (ten), Max Lorenz (ten), Walter Ludwig (ten), Lauritz Melchior (ten), Rudolf Schock (ten), Franz Völker (ten), Willi Domgraf-Fassb *(rec 1927; 1937; 1941–45)* Minerva ▲ MN A21 [ADD]

Mozart, W.A.:Don Giovanni, w. Rose Bampton (sop), Jarmila Novotna (sop), Bidú Sayão (sop), Charles Kullman (ten), Ezio Pinza (bass), B. Walter (cnd), *(orch unknown)* *(rec Mar 7, 1942)* Enterprise ("The Fourties" series) 3-▲ ENT 301

Mozart, W.A.:Requiem, w. E. Schumann (sop), K. Thorborg (mez), A. Dermota (ten), B. Walter (cnd), Vienna PO, Vienna State Opera Chorus EMI Classics ("Great Recordings of the Century" series) 3-▲ CDHC 63912

Mozart, W.A.:Songs, w. M. Callas (sop), E. Grümmer (sop), E. Schwarzkopf (sop), R. Scotto (sop), T. Lemnitz (sop), E. Berger (sop), S. Jurinac (sop), E. Schumann (sop), I. Souez (sop), E. Rethberg (sop), L. Lehmann (sop), N. Gedda (ten), J. McCormack (ten), H. Roswenge (ten), H. Nash (ten), T. Gobbi (bar), G. Hüsch (bar), E. Kunz (bar), G. Frick (bass), E. Pinza (bass) EMI Classics 4-▲ CDMD 63750

Mozart, W.A.:Zauberflöte, w. D. Komarek (sop), J. Novotna (sop), J. Osvath (sop), H. Roswaenge (ten), W. Domgraf-Fassbaender (bar), A. Toscanini (cnd), Vienna PO, Vienna Phil Chorus [G] *(rec live, Salzburg, July 30, 1937)* Melodram 3-▲ MEL 37040 (m) [AAD]

Mozart, W.A.:Zauberflöte, w. Jarmila Novotna (sop), Helge Roswaenge (ten), Julie Osvath (sgr), A. Toscanini (cnd), Vienna PO, Vienna State Opera Chorus Enterprise ("The 40's" series) 2-▲ ENT. 321

Mozart, W.A.:Zauberflöte (sels), w. Marcel Wittrisch (ten), Maria Galvany (sop), Eide Norena (sop), C. Schmalstich (cnd), Berlin State Opera Orch—Dies Bildnis (Act 1); O Isis und Osiris; Der Hölle Rache; Ach, ich fühl's *(rec 1905 - 1944)* Minerva ▲ MN A14 [ADD]

Mussorgsky, M.:Boris Godunov, w. Kerstin Thorborg (mez), René Maison (ten), G. Szell (cnd), New York Metropolitan Opera Orch, New York Metropolitan Opera Chorus *(rec live, Feb 13, 1943)* The Fourties 2-▲ ENT 1505

Mussorgsky, M.:Boris Godunov (sels), w. N. Berezowsky (cnd), RCA Victor SO—eight selections RCA Gold Seal ▲ 60522-2-RC [ADD] ■ 60522-4-RC (CrO2)

Mussorgsky, M.:Boris Godunov (sels), w. F. Reiner (cnd), New York PO *(rec live, 1944)* Legend ▲ LGD 122

Opera Arias & Songs, w. Arthur Bergh (pno), Frank Bibb (pno), Robert Hood Bowers (cnd) Sony Classical ("Masterworks Heritage" series) ▲ MHK 62354

Schumann, R.:Songs, w. Arthur Bergh (pno)—Wanderlied, Op. 35/3; Mondnacht, Op. 39/5 *(rec New York City, 10/24/29)* Music & Arts 2-▲ CD 661 (m) [AAD]

Strauss, R.:Songs, w. Arthur Bergh (pno)—Zueignung, Op. 10/1; Traum durch die Dämmerung, Op. 29/1 *(rec New York City, 10/23/29)* Music & Arts 2-▲ CD 661 (m) [AAD]

Verdi, G.:Aida (sels), w. Maria Nemeth (sop—Aida), Rosette Anday (cta—Amneris), Benjamino Gigli (ten—Radames), Alexander Kipnis (bass—Ramfis), K. Alwin (cnd), Vienna State Opera Orch *(rec May 23, 1937)* Koch Schwann 2-▲ SCH 314632 [ADD]

Verdi, G.:Don Carlos (sels), w. H. Konetzni (sop—Elisabetta), F. Völker (ten—Don Carlos), A. Kipnis (bass—Filippo), B. Walter (cnd), Vienna State Opera Orch, Vienna State Opera Chorus *(rec Dec. 16, 1936)* Koch Schwann 2-▲ SCH 314602

Wagner, R.:Arias & Scenes, w. K. Flagstad (sop), E. Rethberg (sop), B. Nilsson (sop), E. Schumann (sop), F. Leider (sop), L. Melchior (ten), G. Thill (ten), A. Pertile (ten), G. Hüsch (bar), F. Schorr (b-bar), H. Hotter (b-bar), *(orch unknown)* EMI Classics ("Studio" series) 4-▲ CDMC 64008

Wagner, R.:Der fliegende Holländer, w. M. Lawrence (sop), F. Destal (bar), F. Busch (cnd), Buenos Aires Teatro Colón Orch, Buenos Aires Teatro Colón Chorus [G] *(rec live broadcast 9/19/36)* Pearl 2-▲ PEAS 9910 (m) [ADD]

Wagner, R.:Parsifal (sels), w. Fritz Wolff (ten), Muck, Wagner (cnd), Bayreuth Festival Orch, Bayreuth Festival Chorus [1927]—Transformation Scene, Grail Scene, Flower Maidens Scene, Prelude to Act 3, Good Friday Music InSync ■ C 4137 (m)

Wagner, R.:Tannhäuser, w. Helen Traubel (sop), Lauritz Melchior (ten/bar), Herbert Janssen (bar), G. Szell (cnd), *(orch unknown)* Enterprise ("The Radio Years" series) 3-▲ ENT RY 26 (m)

Wolf, H.:Michelangelo-Lieder, w. Coenraad V. Bos (pno) *(rec 1933, "Hugo Wolf Society")* Music & Arts 2-▲ CD 661 (m) [AAD]

Kipnis, Alexander (bass) (cont.)

Wolf, H.:Michelangelo-Lieder, w. Coenraad V. Bos (pno) *(rec 1933, "Hugo Wolf Society")* Preiser 2-▲ 89204 (m) [AAD]

Wolf, H.:Songs (misc), w. Coenraad V. Bos (pno), Gerald Moore (pno), Ernst Victor Wolff (pno)—Grenzen der Menschheit; Um Mitternacht; Sterb' ich, so hüllt in Blumen meine Glieder; Michelangelo-Lieder I-III *[w. Bos, rec. 1933-4]*; Cophtisches Lied I; Der Musikant; Der Soldat I; Der Schreckenberger *[w. Moore, rec. 1935]*; Wie glänzt der helle Mond; Nun lasst uns Frieden schliessen; Wir haben beide lange Zeit geschwiegen; Geselle, woll'n wir uns in Kutten hüllen; Heb' auf dein blondes Haupt; Wie viele Zeit verlor ich; Was für ein Lied soll dir gesungen werden *[w. Wolff, rec. 1934] (rec "Hugo Wolf Society," 1933–35)* Music & Arts 2-▲ CD 661 (m) [AAD]

Wolf, H.:Songs (misc), w. Coenraad V. Bos (pno), Gerald Moore (pno), Ernst Victor Wolff (pno)—Grenzen der Menschheit; Um Mitternacht; Sterb' ich, so hüllt in Blumen meine Glieder; Michelangelo-Lieder I-III *[w. Bos, rec. 1933-4]*; Cophtisches Lied I; Der Musikant; Der Soldat I; Der Schreckenberger *[w. Moore, rec. 1935]*; Wie glänzt der helle Mond; Nun lasst uns Frieden schliessen; Wir haben beide lange Zeit geschwiegen; Geselle, woll'n wir uns in Kutten hüllen; Heb' auf dein blondes Haupt; Wie viele Zeit verlor ich; Was für ein Lied soll dir gesungen werden *[w. Wolff, rec. 1934] (rec 1933–35)* Preiser 2-▲ 89204 (m) [AAD]

Kirby, L. (sgr)

Rodgers, R.:Allegro, w. J. Battles (sgr) [1947 Broadway cast] RCA ▲ 07863-52758-2 ■ 07863-52758-4

Kirchner (sgr)

Mozart, W.A.:Bastien und Bastienne, w. Choy (sgr), Müller De Vries (sgr), R. Clemencic (cnd), Alpe Adria Ensemble [G] Nuova Era 2-▲ 7106/07 [DDD]

Rousseau, J.-J.:Le Devin du village, w. Choy (sgr), Müller de Vries (sgr), R. Clemencic (cnd), Alpe Adria Ensemble, Alpe Adria Chorus [F] Nuova Era 2-▲ 7106/07 [DDD]

Kirchschlager, Angelika (mez)

Mendelssohn, F.:Midsummer Night's Dream (ov & incidental), w. Kenneth Branagh (nar), Sylvia McNair (sop), C. Abbado (cnd), Berlin PO, Ernst Senff Chorus Women's Voices Sony Classical ▲ SK 62826

Kirchstein, Leonore (sop)

Wagner, R.:Lohengrin, w. Leonore Kirchstein (sop—Elsa von Brabant), Ruth Hesse (mez—Ortrud), Herbert Schachtschneider (ten—Lohengrin), Hans Helm (bar—Der Heerrufer des Königs), Otto von Rohr (bass—Heinrich der Vogler), Heinz Imdahl (sgr—Friedrich von Telramund), H. Swarowsky (cnd), Czech PO, Prague National Theater Orch, Vienna State Opera Chorus *(rec Aug 1968)* Weltbild Classics 3-▲ 703835 [ADD]

Kirk, Vernon (ten)

Szymanowski, K.:Kurpian Songs, w. Helen Miles (sop), Bo Holten (cnd), BBC Singers *(rec St Paul's Church, Knightsbridge, London, Nov 27, 1993)* United ▲ CAL 88021 [DDD]

Kirkby, Emma (sop)

Adeste Fideles! Christmas Down the Ages, w. English CO [cnd:Martin Neary], Westminster Abbey Consort, Westminster Abbey Ensemble, Westminster Abbey Choir Sony Classical ▲ SK 62688 ■ ST 62688

Adeste Fideles! Christmas down the Ages, w. Abbey Consort, Abbey Ensemble, Westminster Abbey Choir [cnd:MartinNeary], English CO [cnd:Paul Willey] Sony Classical ▲ SK 62688 ■ ST 62688

Arie Antiche Musica Oscura ("The Orpheus Circle" series) ▲ MOS 70988

Arne, T.:Songs, w. R. Morton (ten), R. Goodman (cnd), Parley of Instruments [E]—not advised of sels. Hyperion ▲ CDA 66237 [DDD]

Bach, J.S.:Cant 51, w. J. E. Gardiner (cnd), English Baroque Soloists [G] Philips ▲ 411458-2 [DDD]

Bach, J.S.:Cant 208, "Hunting Cant", w. J. Smith (sop), S. Davies (ten), M. George (b-bar), R. Goodman (cnd), Parley of Instruments [G] Hyperion ▲ CDA 66169

Bach, J.S.:Magnificat, BWV 243, w. J. E. Gardiner (cnd), English Baroque Soloists, Monteverdi Choir London [L] Philips ("Digital Classics" series) ▲ 411458-2 [DDD]

Bach, J.S.:Magnificat, BWV 243, w. T. Bonner (sop), M. Chance (ct), J. M. Ainsley (ten), S. Varcoe (b-bar), R. Hickox (cnd), Collegium Musicum 90 Chandos ("Chaconne" series) ▲ CHAN 0518 [DDD]

Bach, J.S.:Magnificat, BWV 243, w. J. Nelson (sop), C. Watkinson (cta), P. Elliott (ten), D. Thomas (bass), S. Preston (cnd), Academy of Ancient Music, Christ Church Cathedral Choir Oxford [E♭ version; L] L'Oiseau-Lyre ▲ 414678-2 [ADD]

Bach, J.S.:Mass in b, BWV 232, w. E. Van Evera (sop), R. Covey-Crump (ct), D. Thomas (bass), A. Parrott (cnd), Taverner Consort, Taverner Players, Tölz Boys' Choir [L] EMI Classics 2-▲ ZDCB 47292-2 [DDD]

Benda, G.A.:Cephalus & Aurora, w. R. Müller (ten), T. Roberts (pno)—includes Du kleine Blondine; Belise starb; Mein Geliebter hat versprochen; Faulheit, itzo will ich dir; Philint ist still und fleiht die Schonen; Cephalus & Aurore; Ein trunkner Dichter; Wir Arem, denn des Fieberes Kraft; Philint stand vor Babes Thür; Du fehlest mir, wie einsam und wie stille; Das Andenken; Von nonan, O liebe, lass ich dein Reich; Mein Thrysis!; Ich liebe nur Ismene; Liebe Amor Hyperion ▲ CDA 66649

Blow, J.:Songs, w. Michael Chance (ct), M. Neary (cnd), New London Consort, Westminster Abbey Choir—Whilst sullen years are past; The sullen years are past Sony Classical ▲ SK 66243

Bringing Light to the Unknown, w. Consort of Musicke, Evelyn Tubb (sop), et al. Musica Oscura ▲ OSC 280826 [DDD]

Couperin, F.:Leçons de ténèbres (for Good Friday), w. J. Nelson (mez), J. Ryan (vl), C. Hogwood (chamber org) L'Oiseau-Lyre ▲ 430283-2 [ADD]

Couperin, F.:Motets, w. J. Nelson (mez), J. Ryan (vl), C. Hogwood (chamber org) L'Oiseau-Lyre ▲ 430283-2 [ADD]

Dowland, J.:Ayres, w. A. Rooley (lt/orpharion)—17 sels., from all books Virgin Classics ▲ 59521 [DDD]

Dowland, J.:A Pilgrimes Solace, w. A. Rooley (lt/orpharion)—3 sels. Virgin Classics ▲ 59521 [DDD]

Elizabethan Songs, w. Anthony Rooley (lt) L'Oiseau-Lyre ▲ 425892-2 OH [ADD]

The Emma Kirkby Collection, w. various instrumental accompanists Hyperion ▲ CDA 66227

Emma Kirkby Sings Mrs. Arne, w. Academy of Ancient Music [cnd:C. Hogwood] L'Oiseau-Lyre ▲ 436132-2

Greene, M.:Songs, w. Lars Ulrik Mortensen (hpd), A. Rooley (cnd), Consort of Musicke Musica Oscura ("The Handel Circle" series) ▲ MOS 70978

Handel, G.F.:Arias, w. R. Goodman (cnd), Brandenburg Consort—Vedrai s'a tuo dispetto [from Almira]; Perché viva il caro sposo [from Rodrigo]; Vo' far guerra [from Rinaldo]; Ah! spietato; Desterò dall' empia Dite [both from Amadigi di Gaula]; Ombre, piante [from Rodelinda]; Sinfonia; V' adoro, pupille [both from Giulio Cesare]; Cor di padre [from Tamerlano]; Scoglio d'immota fronte [from Scipione] Hyperion ▲ CDA 66860

Handel, G.F.:Messiah, w. Emily Van Evera (sop), Margaret Cable (mez), James Bowman (ct), Joseph Cornwell (ten), David Thomas (bass), A. Parrott (cnd), Taverner Consort, Taverner Choir [E] EMI Classics 2-▲ CDCB 49801 [DDD]

Handel, G.F.:Messiah, w. Judith Nelson (mez), Carolyn Watkinson (cta), Paul Elliott (ten), David Thomas (bass), C. Hogwood (cnd), Academy of Ancient Music London 2-▲ 430488-2 [DDD]

Handel, G.F.:Messiah, w. Emily van Evera (sop), Margaret Cable (alt), James Bowman (ct), A. Parrott (cnd), Taverner Players, Taverner Choir Virgin Classics 2-▲ ZDMB 61330

Handel, G.F.:Orlando, w. Arleen Augér (sop), Catherine Robbin (mez), James Bowman (ct), David Thomas (bass), C. Hogwood (cnd), Academy of Ancient Music L'Oiseau-Lyre 3-▲ 430845-2 [DDD]

Handel, G.F.:The Triumph of Time & Truth, w. James Goodman (trb), Fisher (sop), Charles Brett (ct), Ian Partridge (ten), Stephen Varcoe (bar), D. Darlow (cnd), London Handel Orch, London Handel Chorus [E] Hyperion 2-▲ CDA 66071/72

Hasse, J.A.:Cleofide, w. Agnès Mellon (sop), Randall Wong (ct), Dominique Visse (ct), Derek Lee Ragin (ct), David Cordier (alt), W. Christie (cnd), Cappella Coloniensis [I] Capriccio 4-▲ 10193/96 [DDD]

Haydn, J.:Die Schöpfung, w. Anthony Rolfe Johnson (ten), Michael George (bass), C. Hogwood (cnd), Academy of Ancient Music, New College Choir Oxford [E] L'Oiseau-Lyre 2-▲ 430397-2 [DDD]

Hume, T.:Captain Humes Poeticall Musicke, w. Labyrinto *(rec Dec 1995)* Glossa ▲ GCD 920402 [DDD]

Hume, T.:The First Part of Ayres, w. Labyrinto *(rec Dec 1995)* Glossa ▲ GCD 920402 [DDD]

India, S. d':Laments, w. A. Rooley (chitarrone)—Lamento d'Olimpia; & other laments [I] Hyperion ▲ CDA 66106

India, S. d':Laments, w. A. Rooley (chitarrone)—Lamento d'Olimpia; & other laments [I] Elektra/Nonesuch ▲ 79125-2

▲ = CD ♦ = Enhanced CD Δ = MD ■ = Cassette Tape □ = DCC

Kirkby, Emma (sop) (cont.)

Johnson, Robert:Music for Shakespeare's Plays, w. D. Thomas (bass), A. Rooley (lt) Virgin Classics ▲ CDC 59321

Jones, Robert:The Muses Gardin for Delights, or the Fifth Book of Ayres, w. A. Rooley (lt) Virgin Classics ▲ CDC 59633

Monteverdi, C.:Ballo delle ingrate, w. Evelyn Tubb (sop), Barbara Nichols (sop), Maria Ewing (sop), A. Rooley (cnd), Consort of Musicke [I] Virgin Classics ▲ 59606 [DDD]

Monteverdi, C.:Combattimento, w. P. Agnew (ct), J. King (ten), A. Rooley (cnd), Consort of Musicke [I] Virgin Classics ▲ 59606 [DDD]

Monteverdi, C.:Lamento d'Olimpia, w. Rooley (chit) [I] Hyperion ▲ CDA 66106

Monteverdi, C.:Lamento d'Olimpia, w. Rooley (chit) [I] Elektra/Nonesuch ▲ 79125-2

Monteverdi, C.:Madrigals (book 2), Consort of Musicke Virgin Classics ▲ CDC 59282

Monteverdi, C.:Madrigals (book 3), Consort of Musicke Virgin Classics ▲ CDC 59283

Monteverdi, C.:Orfeo, w. P. Kwella (sop), J. Smith (sop), N. Rogers (ten), S. Varcoe (bar), D. Thomas (bass), N. Rogers (cnd), London Cornett & Sackbutt Ensemble, C. Medlam (cnd), London Baroque Chiaroscuro EMI Classics ▲ CDMB 64947

Monteverdi, C.:Selva morale et spirituale (sels), w. I. Partridge (ten), D. Thomas (bass), Parley of Instruments [L] Hyperion ▲ CDA 66021 [DDD]

Monteverdi, C.:Volgendo il ciel, w. S. LeBlanc (sop), M. Nichols (mez), P. Agnew (ct), Alan Ewing (bass), A. Rooley (cnd), Consort of Musicke [I] Virgin Classics ▲ 59606 [DDD]

Mozart, W.A.:Arias, w. C. Hogwood (cnd), Academy of Ancient Music—(opera arias) Il re pastore, K.208 *(Aer tranquillo e di sereni; L'amerò, sarò costante)*, Zaide, K.344 *(Ruhe sanft, mein holdes Leben; Trostlos schluchzet Philomele)*; (concert arias) Voi avete un cor fedele, K.217; Ah! lo previdi, K.272; Nehmt meinen Dank, ihr holden Gönner, K.383; Ch'io mi scordi di te, K.505 [G,I] L'Oiseau-Lyre ▲ 425835-2 [DDD]

Mozart, W.A.:Exsultate, w. C. Hogwood (cnd), Academy of Ancient Music, Westminster Cathedral Boys' Choir [L] L'Oiseau-Lyre ▲ 411832-2 [DDD]

Mozart, W.A.:Missa, K.317, w. C. Robbin (mez), J.M. Ainsley (ten), M. George (bass), C. Hogwood (cnd), Academy of Ancient Music, Winchester Cathedral Choir Argo ▲ 436585-2 [DDD]

Mozart, W.A.:Sacred Music, w. C. Hogwood (cnd), Academy of Ancient Music, Westminster Cathedral Boys' Choir—Regina coeli, K.108; Ergo interest, K.143; Regina coeli, K.127 [L] L'Oiseau-Lyre ▲ 411832-2 [DDD]

O Tuneful Voice:Songs & Duets from Late 18th Century England, w. Rufus Müller (ten), Timothy Roberts (pno/hpd), Frances Kelly (single-action hp) Hyperion ▲ CDA 66497 [DDD]

Pergolesi, G.B.:Salve regina in f, w. J. Bowman (ct), C. Hogwood (cnd), Academy of Ancient Music L'Oiseau-Lyre ▲ 425692-2 [DDD]

Pergolesi, G.B.:Stabat mater, w. J. Bowman (ct), C. Hogwood (cnd), Academy of Ancient Music L'Oiseau-Lyre ▲ 425692-2 [DDD]

Purcell, H.:Dido & Aeneas, w. J. Nelson (mez), D. Thomas (bass), A. Parrott (cnd), Taverner Players, Taverner Choir [E] Chandos ("Chaconne" series) ▲ CHAN 0521 [DDD]

Purcell, H.:Dido & Aeneas, w. Catherine Bott (sop—Dido), Emma Kirkby (sop—Belinda), Michael Chance (alt—Spirit), John Mark Ainsley (bar—Aeneas), David Thomas (bar—Sorceress), C. Hogwood (cnd), Academy of Ancient Music L'Oiseau-Lyre ▲ 436992-2 [DDD]

Purcell, H.:The Indian Queen, w. Catherine Bott (sop—Orazia/Married Woman), Emma Kirkby (sop—Indian Girl/Zempoalla/Cupid), John Mark Ainsley (ten—Indian Boy/Fame/Follower of Cupid/Aerial Spirits), Julian Podger (ten—Follower of Envy/Aerial Spirit), Gerald Finley (bar—Conjurer/Hymen/Follower of Cupid), Helen Parker (sgr—Aerial Spirits), David Thomas (bass—Envy/High Priest/Married Man/Follower of Cupid), Simon Berridge (sgr—Follower of Envy), Libby Crabtree (sgr—Follower of Hymen/Aerial Spirit), Tommy Williams (sgr—God of Dreams), C. Hogwood (cnd), Academy of Ancient Music *(rec Walthamstow Assembly Hall, London, July 1994)* L'Oiseau-Lyre ▲ 444339-2 [DDD]

Purcell, H.:Music for the Theater, w. J. Nelson (sop), J. Bowman (ct), M. Hill (ten), R. Covey-Crump (ten), C. Keyte (bass), D. Thomas (bass), C. Hogwood (cnd), Academy of Ancient Music L'Oiseau-Lyre 6-▲ 425893-2 [ADD]

Purcell, H.:Music of, w. Catherine Bott (sop), James Bowman (alt), Anthony Rooley (lt), Monica Huggett (vn), Catherine Mackintosh (vn), Christophe Coin (vc), Paula Chateauneuf (gtr), Hill, Hogwood (cnd), Brandenburg Consort, Academy of Ancient Music, Anthony Lewis (cnd), David Hill (cnd), St. Anthony Singers, Taverner Choir, Winchester Cathedral Choir—The Double Dealer; Come Ye Sons of Art; The Old Bachelor; Birthday Song for Queen Mary; Oedipus; King Arthur; Bonduca; The Fairy Queen; Son. No. 9 in F; Dido & Aeneas; Abdelazer; Bess of Bedlam; The Married Beau; Hear My Prayer, O Lord; Rejoice in the Lord Always L'Oiseau-Lyre ▲ 444620-2

Purcell, H.:Music of, w. Catherine Bott (sop), James Bowman (alt), Anthony Rooley (lt), Paula Chateauneuf (gtr), Monica Huggett (vn), Catherine Mackintosh (vn), Christophe Coin (vc), Hill, Hogwood (cnd), Academy of Ancient Music, Brandenburg Consort, David Hill (cnd), Anthony Lewis (cnd), St. Anthony Singers, Taverner Choir, Winchester Cathedral Choir—The Double Dealer; Come Ye Sons of Art; The Old Bachelor; Birthday Song for Queen Mary; Oedipus; King Arthur; Bonduca; The Fairy Queen; Son. No. 9 in F; Dido & Aeneas; Abdelazer; Bess of Bedlam; The Married Beau; Hear My Prayer, O Lord; Rejoice in the Lord Always London ("Editions de l'oiseau lyre" series) ▲ 444620-2

Purcell, H.:Songs, w. Michael Chance (ct), M. Neary (cnd), New London Consort, Westminster Abbey Choir—I was glad; Praise the Lord, O Jerusalem; Script for their green our groves appear; Ode for Queen Mary's Birthday; Elegy on the death of Queen Mary; The Queen's Epicedium; March; The Burial Service [composed w. Thomas Morley] Sony Classical ▲ SK 66243

Purcell, H.:Songs, w. D. Thomas (bass), A. Rooley (lt) Hyperion ▲ CDA 66056 [DDD]

The Spirits of England & France, Vol. 2, w. Robert White (bgp), Pavlo Beznosiuk (fid), Nick Bicat (perc), Gothic Voices [cnd:Christopher Page] Hyperion ▲ CDA 66773

Stradella, A.:L'anime del purgatorio, w. Evelyn Tubb (sop), David Thomas (bass), Richard Wistreich (bass), A. Rooley (cnd), Consort of Musicke Musica Oscura ("Favola in Musica" series) ▲ MOS 70984

Stradella, A.:L'anime del purgatorio, w. Evelyn Tubb (sop), Richard Wistreich (b-bar), David Thomas (bass), Consort of Musicke Musica Oscura ▲ OSC 70984 [DDD]

Tollett, T.:Music of, w. Michael Chance (ct), M. Neary (cnd), New London Consort, Westminster Abbey Choir—The Queen's Farewell (march) Sony Classical ▲ SK 66243

Venice Preserv'd, w. Judith Nelson (mez), Nigel Rogers (ten), Academy of Ancient Music [cnd:Christopher Hogwood] L'Oiseau-Lyre ▲ 425891-2 OH [ADD]

Vivaldi, A.:Arias, w. R. Goodman (cnd), Brandenburg Consort—Gelosia, tu gio rendi l'alma mia; Loombre, l'aure; Se mai senti spirati; Se in campo armato; Non mi lusinga vana speranza; Ferma Teodosiio; Ombre vane, Agitata da due venti; Non ti lusinghi, la credeltade Hyperion ▲ CDA 66745

Vivaldi, A.:Cants, w. J. Lamon (cnd), Tafelmusik, Tafelmusik Chamber Choir [period instrs]—Lungi dal vago volto, RV.680 [L] Hyperion ▲ CDA 66247 [DDD]

Vivaldi, A.:Gloria, RV.589, w. T. Bonner (sop), M. Chance (ct), R. Hickox (cnd), Collegium Musicum 90 Chandos ("Chaconne" series) ▲ CHAN 0518 [DDD]

Vivaldi, A.:Gloria, RV.589, w. J. Nelson (sop), C. Watkinson (cta), P. Elliott (ten), D. Thomas (bass), S. Preston (cnd), Academy of Ancient Music, Christ Church Cathedral Choir Oxford [L] L'Oiseau-Lyre ▲ 414678-2 [ADD]

Vivaldi, A.:Motets, w. J. Lamon (cnd), Tafelmusik, Tafelmusik Chamber Choir—"In turbata mare irato," RV.627 [L] Hyperion ▲ CDA 66247 [DDD]

Kirschstein, Leonore (sop)

Hindemith, P.:Cardillac, w. Donald Grobe (ten), Dietrich Fischer-Dieskau (bar), J. Keilberth (cnd), Cologne RSO [G] Deutsche Grammophon ("20th Century Classics" series) 2-▲ 431741-2 [ADD]

Strauss, R.:Ariadne auf Naxos, w. Lisa Della Casa (sop—Ariadne), Lisa Otto (sop—Najade), Rudolf Schock (ten—Bacchus), Leonore Kirschstein (sgr—Echo), Nada Puttar (sgr—Dryade), A. Erede (cnd), Berlin PO Testament ▲ SBT 1036 [ADD]

Kirsten, Dorothy (sop)

Dorothy Kirsten:Live Performances, 1944-75 VAI Audio ▲ VAIA 1087

Puccini, G.:La fanciulla del West, w. F. Corelli (ten), A. Colzani (bar), A. Guadagno (cnd), Philadelphia Lyric Opera Orch, Philadelphia Lyric Opera Chorus [I] *(rec live, 11/10/64)* Melodram 2-▲ MEL 27081 [AAD]

Kirsten, Dorothy (sop) (cont.)

Puccini, G.:Madama Butterfly, w. Dorothy Kirsten (sop—Madama Butterfly), Rosalind Nadell (mez—Suzuki), Eileen Ireland (mez—Kate), Daniele Barioni (ten—Pinkerton), Thomas Carter (ten—Goro), Arthur Cosenza (ten—Yamadori), Richard Torigi (bar—Sharpless), Rodney Hall (bass—The Bronze), Harold Crane (bass—Commissioner), R. Cellini (cnd), New Orleans Opera Orch, New Orleans Opera Chorus *(rec live, Mar 1960)* VAI Audio 2-▲ VAIA 1054-2

Romberg, S.:The Desert Song, w. Gordon MacRae (sgr) Sony ▲ BT 831

Romberg, S.:Music of (operetta sels), w. MacRae (sgr), Van Alexander (sgr), *(orch & chorus unknown)* —selections from *Desert Song, New Moon, Student Prince* EMI Classics ("Studio" series) ▲ CDM 69052

Kirtesi, Ingrid (sop)

Kálmán, I.:Gräfin Mariza (sels), w. Zsuzsa Csonka (sop), János Berkes (ten), L. Kovács (cnd), Hungarian Operetta Orch—Komm mit nach Varasadin *(rec Budapest, Oct 1995)* Naxos ▲ 8.550941 [DDD]

Kálmán, I.:Gräfin Mariza (sels), w. Zsuzsa Csonka (sop), János Berkes (ten), L. Kovács (cnd), Hungarian Operetta Orch—Auftrittsleid Mariza; Komm Zigány; Grüss mir die süssen *(rec Budapest, Jan 1996)* Naxos ▲ 8.550943 [DDD]

Lehár, F.:Operetta Arias, w. Zsuzsa Csonka (sop), János Berkes (ten), L. Kovács (cnd), Hungarian Operetta Orch—Freunde, das Leben ist lebenswert!; Meine Lippen, sie küssen si heiss [both from Giuditta]; O Mädchen, mein Mädchen [from Friedericke]; Dein ist mein ganzes Herz; Wer hat die Liebe uns ins Herz gesenkt?; Immer nur lächeln; Von Apfelblüten einen Kranz [all from Das Land des Lächlens]; Lippen schweigen [from Die lustige Witwe] *(rec Budapest, Oct 1995)* Naxos ▲ 8.550941 [DDD]

Lehár, F.:Paganini (sels), w. Zsuzsa Csonka (sop), János Berkes (ten), L. Kovács (cnd), Hungarian Operetta Orch—Liebe, du Himmel auf Erden *(rec Budapest, Jan 1996)* Naxos ▲ 8.550943 [DDD]

Stolz, R.:Arias, w. Zsuzsa Csonka (sop), János Berkes (ten), L. Kovács (cnd), Hungarian Operetta Orch—Ich liebe dich! [from Zauber der Bohème]; Zwei gerzen im Dreiviertaltakt; Du sollst der Kaiser meiner Seele sein [both from Der Favorit]; Adieu, mein kleiner Gardeoffizer [from Das Lied ist aus] *(rec Budapest, Jan 1996)* Naxos ▲ 8.550943 [DDD]

Strauss (II), Joh.:Arias, w. Zsuzsa Csonka (sop), János Berkes (ten), L. Kovács (cnd), Hungarian Operetta Orch—Ov; Klänge der Heimat; Trinke Liebchen! Trinke schnell!; Mein Herr Marquis [all from Die Fledermaus]; Laguenwaltzer [from Eine Nacht in Venedig] *(rec Budapest, Jan 1996)* Naxos ▲ 8.550943 [DDD]

Strauss (II), Joh.:Arias, w. Zsuzsa Csonka (sop), János Berkes (ten), L. Kovács (cnd), Hungarian Operetta Orch—Ov; Wer uns getraut; Als flotter Geist [both from Der Zigeunerbaron]; Frühlingstimmen (waltz); Komm in die Gondel [from Eine Nacht in Venedig] *(rec Budapest, Oct 1995)* Naxos ▲ 8.550941 [DDD]

Zeller, C.A.:Vogelhändler (sels), w. Zsuzsa Csonka (sop), János Berkes (ten), L. Kovács (cnd), Hungarian Operetta Orch—Wie mein Ahn'l zwanzig Jahr' *(rec Budapest, Jan 1996)* Naxos ▲ 8.550943 [DDD]

Kishegyi, Arpád (sgr)

Wayditch, G. von:The Caliph's Magician, w. Júlia Pászthi (sop—Eunuch), Sándor Palcso (ten—The Emir), István Rozsos (ten—Nawab), Zsolt Bende (bar—The Magician), Arpád Kishegyi (sgr—Djinn), András Nagy-Soljom (sgr—The Caliph), Csaba Ötvös (sgr—Djinn), Csilla Ötvös (sgr—Odalisk), A. Kórodi (cnd), Budapest National Opera Orch, Budapest National Opera Chorus *(rec 1975)* VAI Audio 2-▲ VAIA 1095-2 [ADD]

Kiss, Rózsa (sop)

Bach, J.S.:St. Matthew Passion, w. I. Verebics (sop), Á. Csenki (mez), J. Németh (mez), P. Cser (ten), J. Mukk (ten), I. Gati (bar), F. Korpás (bar), P. Köves (bass), G. Oberfrank (cnd), Hungarian State SO, Hungarian Festival Choir, Hungarian Radio Children's Choir [G] *(rec Feb 1993)* Naxos 3-▲ 8.550832/34 [DDD]

Kissel, Margarete (alt)

Mozart, W.A.:Vesperae, w. Christa Degler (sop), Desmond Clayton (ten), Hartmut Müller (bass), E. Hinreiner (cnd), Salzburg Mozarteum Camerata Academica Studio SM ▲ 2518

Kissyova, Vanilia (sop)

Gesualdo, D.C.:Madrigals, w. N. Pankova (sop), A. Bovarian (alt), V. Vassilev (ten), K. Mirinski (bass), S. Kralev (cnd), Sofia Madrigal—Io tacerò; Invan dunque o crudele; Moro lasso al mio duolo; Dolcissima mia vita Gega ▲ GD 174 [DDD]

Monteverdi, C.:Madrigals, w. N. Pankova (sop), A. Bovarian (alt), V. Vassilev (ten), K. Mirinski (bass), S. Kralev (cnd), Sofia Madrigal Ensemble—Psalmus 121, "Laetatus sum"; Batto qui pianse; Chiome d'oro; Amor che deggio far?; O come sei gentile; Psalmus 147, "Lauda Jerusalem" Gega ▲ GD 174 [DDD]

Schütz, H.:Motets (misc), w. A. Ivanova (sop), N. Pankova (sop), A. Bovarian (alt), V. Vassilev (ten), K. Mirinski (bass), S. Kralev (cnd), Sofia Madrigal—Christe Deus adjuva; Verbum caro factum est; Te Christe supplex invoco; Veni redemtor gentium; Veni sancte Spiritus Gega ▲ GD 174 [DDD]

Kit, Mikhail (bar)

Glinka, M.:Russlan & Ludmilla, w. Galina Gorchakova (sop), Larissa Diadkova (cta), Irinia Bogachova (sgr), Anna Netrebko (sgr), Yuri Masurin (ten), Konstantin Pluzhnikov (ten), Gennady Bezzubenkov (bass), Vladimir Ognovenko (bass), V. Gergiev (cnd), Kirov Opera Orch, Kirov Opera Chorus Philips ▲ 456 248-2

Kitchen, Linda (sop)

Meyerbeer, G.:Il crociato, w. Y. Kenny (sop), R. Platt (sop), D. Montague (mez), D. Jones (mez), B. Ford (ten), U. Benelli (bar), D. Parry (cnd), Royal PO, Geoffrey Mitchell Choir [I] *(rec CTS Studios, Wembley, London, Dec. 1990–June 1991)* Opera Rara 4-▲ OR 10

Mozart, W.A.:Zauberflöte, w. Natalie Dessay (sop—Queen of the Night), Linda Kitchen (sop—Papagena), Rosa Mannion (sop—Pamina), Anna-Maria Panzarella (sop—First Lady), Doris Lamprecht (mez—Second Lady), Delphine Haidan (cta—Third Lady), Hans Peter Blochwitz (ten—Tamino), Steven Cole (ten—Monostatos), Chrisopher Josey (ten—First Priest/First Armed Man), Anton Scharinger (bar—Papageno), Reinhard Hagen (bass—Sarastro), Laurent Naouri (bass—Second Priest/Second Armed Man), Willard White (bass—Speaker), W. Christie (cnd), Les Arts Florissants *(rec Paris Oct 2-9 1995)* Erato 2-▲ 12705-2 [DDD]

Vaughan Williams, R.:The Shepherds of the Delectable Mountains, w. J.-M. Ainsley (ten), A. Thompson (ten), A. Opie (bar), B. Terfel (b-bar), J. Best (bass), M. Best (cnd), City of London Sinfonia [E] Hyperion ▲ CDA 66569 [DDD]

Kitchiner, John (bar)

Herrmann, B.:Wuthering Heights, w. M. Beaton (sop—Catherine), P. Bowden (mez—Isabella), E. Bainbridge (mez—Nelly), M. Snashall (trb—Hareton), D. Bell (bar—Heathcliff), J. Kitchiner (bar—Hindley), J. Ward (bar—Edgar), M. Rippon (bass—Joseph), D. Kelly (bass—Mr. Lockwood), B. Herrmann (cnd), Pro Arte Orch *(rec 1965-66)* Unicorn-Kanchana 3-▲ UKCD 2050/51/52 [ADD]

Kittelson, Fay (mez)

Barber, S.:A Hand of Bridge, w. C. Aks (sop), W. Carney (ten), R. Muenz (bass), Adirondack CO, Gregg Smith Singers [E] Premier ▲ PRCD 1009 [ADD]

Kitzke, Jerome (voc)

Spasm, w. Michael Lowenstern (b cl), Heather Barringer (voc), Mark Gibbons (voc), Jay Johnson (voc), Matt Lambiase (voc), Tom Linker (voc), Ed Lowenstern (voc), Michael Lowenstern (voc) *(rec Creation Audio, Minneapolis, NYU Studios, New York City & Studio A, Stony Brook, Aug 1994–July 1996)* New World ▲ 80468-2

Kjellgren, Ingeborg (mez)

Verdi, G.:Rigoletto, w. M. Hallin (sop), B. Nordin (sop), K. Meyer (mez), B. Ericson (mez), N. Gedda (ten), O. Sivall (ten), H. Hasslo (bar), I. Wixell (bar), B. Alstergård (bar), A. Tyrén (bass), S. Ehrling (cnd), Stockholm Royal Opera House Orch, Stockholm Royal Opera Chorus *(rec live Jan. 18, 1959)* BIS ▲ CD 296 [AAD]

Kjølberg, Kristin (sop)

Habbestad, K.:Moster Suite, w. Njål Sparbo (bar), Odd Lund (goat's hn), T. Mikkelsen (cnd), Lithuanian National SO, Oslo Phil Women's Chamber Choir Norway Music ▲ 2912

Klare, Susanne (mez)

Huber, K.:Soliloquia, w. H. Lukomska (sop), D. Ahlstedt (ten), B. McDaniel (bar), H. G. Ahrens (b-bar), H. Zender (cnd), Munich Bavarian RSO, Munich Bavarian Radio Chorus [L] *(rec Dec. 17, 1979)* Grammont ▲ CTSP 24-2 [ADD]

Klare, Susanne (mez) (cont.)

Huber, K.:Soliloquia, Part II:Cuius legibus rotantur poli, w. H. Lukomska (sop), D. Ahlstedt (ten), B. McDaniel (bar), H. G. Ahrens (b–bar), H. Zender (cnd), Munich Bavarian RSO, Munich Bavarian Radio Chorus [L] *(rec Dec. 17, 1979)* Grammont ▲ CTSP 24-2 [ADD]

Klare, Susanne (sop)

Albinoni, T.:Il Nascimento de l'Aurora, w. June Anderson (sop), Margarita Zimmermann (sop), Sandra Browne (alt), Yoshihisa Yamaj (ten), C. Scimone (cnd), Venice Solisti Erato 2-▲ ERA SEL 96374 [DDD]

Klarwein, Franz (ten)

Strauss, R.:Capriccio (sels), w. V. Ursuleac (sop—Die Gräfin), F. Klarwein (ten—Flamand), H. Hotter (b–bar—Olivier), G. Hann (b–bar—La Roche), G. Wieter (bass—Der Haushofmeister), C. Krauss (cnd), Bavarian State Opera Orch *(rec 1942)* Myto ▲ MCD 943104

Klecker, Jiří (bass)

Mozart, W.A.:Ave verum corpus, w. E. Mirgova (sop), M. Kozená (cta), J. Griffett (ten), A. Kroper (cnd), Prague Concertino Nutturno Allegro ▲ ALG PCD 1022 [DDD]

Mozart, W.A.:Requiem, w. E. Mirgova (sop), M. Kozená (cta), J. Griffett (ten), A. Kroper (cnd), Prague Concertino Nutturno, Brnensky Academy Choir Allegro ▲ ALG PCD 1022 [DDD]

Klein, Adam (sgr)

Ashley, R.:Improvement, w. J. Humbert (sgr—Linda), J. La Barbara (sop—Now Eleanor), A. X. Neuburg (sgr—Mr. Payne's Mother), T. Buckner (sgr—Don/Mr. Payne/Linda's Companion), S. Ashley (sgr—Junior, Jr.), A. Klein (sgr—Doctor), R. Ashley (sgr—Narrator), *(cnd & orch unknown)* [E] Elektra/Nonesuch 2-▲ 79289-2

Klein, Markus (trb)

Bach, J.S.:Cant 88, w. P. Esswood (ct), K. Equiluz (ten), G. Leonhardt (cnd), Leonhardt Consort [G] Teldec 2-▲ 2292-42578-2 [ADD]

Bach, J.S.:Cant 89, w. P. Esswood (ct), M. van Egmond (b–bar), G. Leonhardt (cnd), Leonhardt Consort [G] Teldec 2-▲ 2292-42578-2 [ADD]

Bach, J.S.:Cant 106, "Actus tragicus", w. R. Harten (alt), M. van Altena (ten), M. van Egmond (b–bar), Leonhardt Consort, Collegium Vocale, Hanover Boys' Chorus [G] Teldec ▲ 2292-42602-2

Bach, J.S.:Cant 107, w. K. Equiluz (ten), M. van Egmond (b–bar), Leonhardt Consort, Collegium Vocale [G] Teldec 2-▲ 2292-42603-2

Klein, Peter (ten)

Beethoven, L. van:Fidelio, w. H. Konetzni (sop), I. Seefried (sop), T. Ralf (ten), P. Schöffler (b–bar), H. Alsen (bass), K. Böhm (cnd), Vienna State Opera Orch, Vienna State Opera Chorus *(rec Feb. 1944)* Preiser 2-▲ PRE 90195 [AAD]

Einem, G. von:Dantons Tod, w. M. Cebotari (sop—Lucille Desmoulins), R. Anday (cta—Frau des Simon), P. Klein (ten—de Séchelles), J. Patzak (ten—Camille Desmoulins), J. Witt (ten—Robspierre), P. Schöffler (bar—Danton), L. Weber (bass—Saint Just), F. Fricsay (cnd), Vienna PO, Vienna State Opera Chorus *(rec Aug. 6, 1947)* Stradivarius 2-▲ STR 10067 [ADD]

Einem, G. von:Der Prozess, w. Lisa Della Casa (sop—Frl. Bürstner/Die Frau des Gerichtsdieners/Leni), Peter Klein (ten—Der Direktorstellvertreter/Der Student), Max Lorenz (ten—Josef K.), Erich Majkut (ten—Ein Bursche), László Szemere (ten—Titorelli), Alois Pernerstorfer (b–bar—Willem/Der Gerichtsdiener), Alfred Poell (b–bar—Der Advokat), Walter Berry (bass—Franz/Kanzleidirektor), Oskar Czerwenka (bass—Der Untersuchungsrichter/Der Prügler), Ludwig Hofmann (bass—Der Aufseher/Ein Passant/Der Geistliche/Der Fabrikant), Polly Batic (sgr—Frau Grubach), Endreh Koreh (sgr—Albert K.), Luise Leitner (sgr—Ein buckliges Mädchen), K. Böhm (cnd), Vienna PO, Vienna State Opera Chorus *(rec Aug 17, 1953)* Orfeo d'or ("Festspiel Dokumente" series) 2-▲ 392952 (m)

Mozart, W.A.:Zauberflöte, w. Wilma Lipp (sop), Irmgard Seefried (sop), Walther Ludwig (ten), Karl Schmitt-Walter (bar), Josef Greindl (bass), Paul Schöffler (sgr), W. Furtwängler (cnd), Vienna PO, Vienna State Opera Chorus *(rec 1949)* Music & Arts 3-▲ CD 882 [AAD]

Wagner, R.:Die Meistersinger von Nürnberg, w. Irmgard Seefried (sop—Eva), Else Schürhoff (mez—Magdelene), Peter Klein (ten—David), August Seider (ten—Walther), Erich Kunz (bar—Beckmesser), Paul Schoeffler (b–bar—Hans Sachs), Herbert Alsen (bass—Pogner), K. Böhm (cnd), Vienna PO, Vienna State Opera Chorus *(rec Vienna, Nov. & Dec. 1944)* Preiser 4-▲ PRE 90234 [ADD]

Wagner, R.:Die Meistersinger von Nürnberg (sels), w. Maria Reining (sop—Eva), Peter Klein (ten—David), Max Lorenz (ten—Walther), Josef Hermann (bar—Hans Sachs), Erich Kunz (bar—Beckmesser), K. Böhm (cnd), Vienna State Opera Orch *(rec Vienna, Jan. 19, 1943)* Koch Schwann 2-▲ SCH 314732 [ADD]

Kleindienst, S. (sop)

Vlijmen, J. van:Un Malheureux vêtu de noir, w. Guy de Mey (ten), Pittman-Jennings (bar), Reinbert de Leeuw (cnd), Arnold Schoenberg Male Choir *(rec live, Flanders Opera, Antwerp, Dec 11, 1990)* Donemus ▲ CV 17/18

Kleinman, Marlena (cta)

Brahms, J.:Liebeslieder Waltzes SATB, w. B. Valente (sop), W. Conner (ten), M. Singher (bar), R. Serkin (pno), L. Fleisher (pno) [G] Sony Classical ("Essential Classics" series) ▲ SBK 48176 ▮ SBT 48176

Klemperer, Werner (nar)

Berlioz, H.:Lélio, "Le retourà la vie", w. G. Siebert (ten), W. Diana (bar), Z. Macal (cnd), Milwaukee Sym Chorus Koss Classics 2-▲ KC 1012 [DDD]

Berlioz, H.:Lélio, "Le retourà la vie", w. G. Siebert (ten), W. Diana (bar), Z. Macal (cnd), Milwaukee SO *(rec 1991)* Koss Classics ▲ KC 1017 [DDD]

Klemperer, Werner (spkr)

Kubik, G.:Gerald McBoing Boing, w. A. Stern (cnd), XTET Delos ▲ DE 6001 [DDD] ▮ CS 6001 (D)

Klepatskaya, Valentina (sgr)

Mussorgsky, M.:Boris Godunov, w. Irina Arkhipova (mez—Marina Mnishek), Evgenya Verbitskaya (mez—Nurse to Xenia), Valentina Klepatskaya (sgr—Fyodor), Tamara Sorokina (sgr—Xenia), Anton Grigoryev (ten—Simpleton), Vladimir Ivanovsky (ten—Grigory, the Pretender), Gyorgy Shulpin (bar—Prince Shuisky), Alexey Geleva (bass—Varlaam), Ivan Petrov (bass—Boris Godounov), Mark Reshetin (bass—Pimen), Alexi Ivanov (sgr—Andrei Shchelkalov), Evgeny Kibkalo (sgr—Rangoni), A. Melik-Pashayev (cnd), Bolshoi Theater Orch, Bolshoi Theater Chorus *(rec Moscow, 1962)* Melodiya ("The Russian Opera" series) 3-▲ 74321-29349-2 [ADD]

Klepper, Regina (sop)

Hiller, W.:Schulamit, w. Edeltraud Knabel (alt), Michael Schopper (bass), Elisabeth Woska (nar), Waltraut Mastrogiovanni-Kraxner (shofar), H.R. Zöbeley (cnd), Munich Residenz Orch, Munich Percussion Ensemble, Calw Aurelius Boys' Choir Soloists, Munich Motet Choir Wergo ▲ WER 6280-2

Kreutzer, C.:Das Nachtlager in Granada, w. M. Pabst (ten), H. Prey (bar), H. Froschauer (cnd), Cologne RSO, Cologne Radio Chorus Capriccio ▲ 60029 [DDD]

Strauss, R.:Arabella (sels), w. P. Coburn (sop), M. Borst (mez), B. Skovhus (bar), F. Hawlata (bass), M. Honeck (cnd), Munich RSO Capriccio ▲ 10481 [DDD]

Strauss, R.:Ariadne auf Naxos, w. P. Coburn (sop), M. Borst (mez), B. Skovhus (bar), F. Hawlata (bass), M. Honeck (cnd), Munich RSO Capriccio ▲ 10481 [DDD]

Strauss, R.:Capriccio (sels), w. P. Coburn (sop), M. Borst (mez), B. Skovhus (bar), F. Hawlata (bass), M. Honeck (cnd), Munich RSO Capriccio ▲ 10481 [DDD]

Strauss, R.:Der Rosenkavalier (sels), w. P. Coburn (sop), M. Borst (mez), B. Skovhus (bar), F. Hawlata (bass), M. Honeck (cnd), Munich RSO Capriccio ▲ 10481 [DDD]

Klietmann, Martin (ten)

Bruhns, N.:Jauchzet dem Herren alle Welt, "Psalm 100", w. P. Németh (cnd), Capella Savaria [period instrs]; [G] Hungaroton ▲ HCD 31134 [DDD]

Fux, J.J.:Dafne in Lauro, w. L. Akerlund (sop), S. Piccollo (sop), M. van der Sluis (sop), G. Lesne (alt), R. Clemencic (cnd), Clemencic Consort, La Cappella Vocal Ensemble [I] Nuova Era ("Ancient Music" series) 2-▲ 6930/31 [DDD]

Fux, J.J.:Plaudite, sonat tuba, w. E. H. Tarr (tpt), P. Németh (cnd), Capella Savaria [period instrs] [L] Hungaroton ▲ HCD 31134 [DDD]

Graun, K.H.:Der Tod Jesu, w. M. Zádori (sop), M. Fers (sop), K. Mertens (b–bar), P. Németh (cnd), Capella Savaria Musique d'Abord ▲ HMA 1903061

Handel, G.F.:Brockes-Passion, w. K. Farkas (sop), M. Zádori (sop), D. Minter (alt), J. Bándi (ten), G. de Mey (ten), I. Gáti (bar), N. McGegan (cnd), Capella Savaria, Hallé State Chorus [period instrs] [G] Hungaroton 3-▲ HCD 12734/36 [DDD]

Klietmann, Martin (ten) (cont.)

Handel, G.F.:St. John Passion, w. Mária Z(ádori (sop), Judit Németh (mez), Charles Brett (ct), Jósef Moldvay (bass), G. Németh (cnd), Capella Savaria, Capella Savaria Hungaroton ▲ HCD 12908 [DDD]

Haydn, J.:Mass 1a, Missa 'Rorate coeli desuper', w. G. Öhlinger (sop), M. Bayer (alt), A. Lebeda (bass), D. de Rooij an der Reil (org), Collegium Musicum Pragense Christophorus ▲ CD 74541 [DDD]

Haydn, J.:Mass 7, "Kleine Orgelmesse", w. G. Öhlinger (sop), M. Bayer (alt), A. Lebeda (bass), Collegium Musicum Pragense Christophorus ▲ CD 74541 [DDD]

Haydn, M.:Missa Pro Defuncto Archiepiscopo Sigismundo, w. Ibolya Verebics (sop), Judit Németh (mez), József Moldvay (bass), H. Rilling (cnd), Franz Liszt CO, Hungarian Radio-TV Chorus [L] Hungaroton ▲ HCD 31022 [DDD]

Haydn, M.:Missa Sancti Francisci, w. Ibolya Verebics (sop), Judit Németh (mez), József Moldvay (bass), H. Rilling (cnd), Franz Liszt CO, Hungarian Radio-TV Chorus [L] Hungaroton ▲ HCD 31022 [DDD]

Keiser, R.:Croesus, w. P. Grigorova (sop), S. Mizugushi (bass), R. Clemencic (cnd), Clemencic Consort, La Cappella Vocal Ensemble [G] Nuova Era ("Ancient Music" series) 2-▲ 6934/35 [DDD]

Monteverdi, C.:Salve, o Regina, w. P. Németh (cnd), Capella Savaria [period instrs] [L] Hungaroton ▲ HCD 31134 [DDD]

Schütz, H.:Kleine geistliche Konzerte (sels), w. P. Németh (cnd), Capella Savaria [period instrs]—5 selections—SWV.282, 285, 306, 308, 309 [G] Hungaroton ▲ HCD 31134 [DDD]

Schütz, H.:Symphoniae sacrae (sels), w. P. Németh (cnd), Capella Savaria [period instrs]—2 selections—Paratum cor meum, SWV.257; Singet dem Herren ein neues Lied, SWV.342 [G,L] Hungaroton ▲ HCD 31134 [DDD]

17th Century German Church Music Hungaroton ▲ HCD 31134 [DDD]

Telemann, G.P.:Brockes Passion, w. M. Zádori (sop), A. Markert (cta), G. De Mey (ten), I. Gáti (bar), N. McGegan (cnd), Capella Savaria, Hallé State Chorus [period instrs] Hungaroton 3-▲ HCD 31130/32 [DDD]

Werner, G.J.:Debora, w. W. Hill (sop), G. Banditelli (mez), K. Mertens (b–bar), P. Németh (cnd), Capella Savaria Quintana ▲ QUI 903062

Klin, Serge (sgr)

Lehár, F.:Die lustige Witwe, w. Teresa Stich-Randall (mez—Missia Palmieri), Monique Stiot (mez—Manon), Germaine Duclos (sgr—Praskovia), Linda Felder (sgr—Olga), Christiane Jacquin (sgr—Nadia), Jeannette Levasseur (sgr—Sylviane), Henri Legay (ten—Camille de Coutançon), Joseph Peyron (ten—Kromsky), Robert Destain (sgr—Baron Popoff), Michel Fauche (sgr—Pristich), Gérard Friedmann (sgr—Lerida), Jacques Gilet (sgr—Bogdanowitch), Jean Guy Henneveux (sgr—Prince Danilo), Serge Klin (sgr—Figg), Jacques Villa (sgr—D'Estillac), A. Sibert (cnd), Belgian Radio-TV Orch, Belgian Radio-TV Chorus *(rec Grand Auditorium, Belgium, Apr 30, 1970)* Studio SM 2-▲ 2160 [AAD]

Klint, Jørgen (bass)

Nielsen, C.:Saul & David, w. T. Kiberg (sop), A. Gjevang (mez), P. Lindroos (ten), K. Westi (ten), C. Christiansen (bass), A. Haugland (bass), N. Järvi (cnd), Danish National RSO, Danish National Radio Choir [Da] Chandos 2-▲ CHAN 8911/12 [DDD]

Nielsen, C.:Songs, w. Rosalind Bevan (pno)—Sang bag Ploven; I Aften; Balladen om Bjørnen; Den blinde Spillemand [w. Jens Schou (cl)]; Solnedgang; I Seraillets Have; Til Asali; Irmelin Rose; Har Dagen sanket al sin Sorg; Jeronimus Sang; Jeg baerer med Smil min Byrde; Jens Vejmand; Se dig ud en Sommerdag; Det bøodes der for; Det villeste; Nu lyser løov i Lunde; Min lille Fugl; Vi Sletternes Søonner; Jeg ved en Laerkerede; Den Danske Sang; Danmark i Tusind År; Forunderligt at sige *(rec Nov 1987)* Paula ▲ PACD 56

Nielsen, C.:Springtime, w. Inga Nielsen (sop), Kim von Binzer (ten), T. Vetö (cnd), Odense SO, Lille MUKO, St. Klemens School Children's Choir Unicorn-Kanchana ▲ DKPCD 9054

Klisans, Martins (ten)

Mozart, W.A.:Alma Dei creatoris, w. Dita Paëgle (sop), Antra Bìgaca (mez), S. Klava (cnd), Riga Musicians, Riga Radio Chorus Audiophile Classics ▲ 101.048 [DDD]

Mozart, W.A.:Litaniae Lauretanae, K.195, w. Dita Paëgle (sop), Antra Bìgaca (mez), Janis Màrkovs (bass), S. Klava (cnd), Riga Musicians, Riga Radio Chorus Audiophile Classics ▲ 101.048 [DDD]

Mozart, W.A.:Regina coeli, K.276, w. Dita Paëgle (sop), Antra Bìgaca (mez), Janis Màrkovs (bass), S. Klava (cnd), Riga Musicians, Riga Radio Chorus Audiophile Classics ▲ 101.048 [DDD]

Kliskic (sgr)

Mercadante, S.:La Vestale, w. G. Dimitrova (sop), D. Vejzovic (sop), G. Cecchele (ten), Romanò (sgr), Cepreaga (sgr), Sioli (sgr), Boldrini (sgr), V. Sutej (cnd), Spalato National Theater Orch, Spalato National Theater Chorus [I] *(rec 4/9/87)* Bongiovanni 2-▲ GB 2065/66 [DDD]

Klos, Friedemann (trb)

Mozart, W.A.:Zauberflöte, w. M. Price (sop—Pamina), L. Serra (sop—Queen of the Night), M. Venuti (sop—Papagena), M. McLaughlin (sop—1st Lady), A. Murray (mez—2nd Lady), H. Schwarz (cta—3rd Lady), F. Höher (trb—1st Boy), M. Diedrich (trb—2nd Boy), F. Klos (trb—3rd Boy), P. Schreier (ten—Tamino), R. Tear (ten—Monostatos), R. Goldberg (ten—1st Armoured Man), K. Moll (bass—Sarastro), H. Rech (bass—2nd Armoured Man), C. Davis (cnd), Dresden Staatskapelle, Leipzig Radio Chorus Philips ("Duo" series) 2-▲ 442568-2

Klose, Margarete (mez)

The Legendary Singers at Lindenoper Berlin (1927-1945)—, w. Gitta Alpar (sop), Erna Berger (sop), Tiana Lemnitz (sop), Maria Müller (sop), Peter Anders (ten), Max Lorenz (ten), Walter Ludwig (ten), Lauritz Melchior (ten), Rudolf Schock (ten), Franz Völker (ten), Willi Domgraf-Fassb *(rec 1927; 1937; 1941-45)* Minerva ▲ MN A21 [ADD]

Strauss, R.:Salome, w. I. Borkh (sop—Salome), M. Klose (mez—Herodias), C. Ludwig (mez—Page), M. Lorenz (ten—Herodes), F. Fehringer (ten—Narraboth), F. Frantz (bar—Jokanaan), K. Schröder (cnd), Hessian RSO *(rec 1952)* Myto 2-▲ 93592

Strauss, R.:Salome, w. Astrid Varnay (sop—Salome), Hertha Töpper (mez—Der Page der Herodias), Margarete Klose (cta—Herodias), Hans Hopf (ten—Narraboth), Karl Hoppe (ten—1st Nazarene), Karl Ostertag (ten—1st Jew), Julius Patzak (ten—Herodes), Hans Braun (bar—Jochanaan), Benno Kusche (bar—2nd Soldier), Adolf Keil (bass—1st Soldier), Hans Hermann Nissen (bass—Ein Kappadozier), Max Proebstl (bass—2nd Nazarene), Walter Carnotch (sgr—4th Jew), Emil Graf (sgr—3rd Jew), Paul Kaussen (sgr—2nd Jew), Hildegard Limmer (sgr—A slave), Georg Witter (sgr—5th Jew), H. Weigert (cnd), Bavarian RSO *(rec June 21-25, 1953)* Bella Voce 2-▲ BLV 7210 [AAD]

Verdi, G.:Aida (sels), w. Hilde Scheppan (sop), Helge Roswaenge (ten), Hans Hotter (bar), A. Rother (cnd), Berlin Radio Orch, Berlin State Opera Chorus [G] *(rec Nov. 21, 1942)* Preiser ▲ PRE 90219 [ADD]

Verdi, G.:Requiem Mass, w. Hilde Zadek (sop), Helge Roswaenge (ten), Boris Christoff (bass), H. von Karajan (cnd), Vienna PO, Vienna Singverein Stradivarius 2-▲ STV DTM 12323 [ADD]

Wagner, R.:Arias & Scenes, w. Kathe Heidersbach (sop), Maria Reining (sop), Hilde Scheppan (sop), Margarete Teschemacher (sop), Max Lorenz (ten), Jaro Prohaska (bar), Karl Schmitt-Walter (bar), Kurt Böhme (bass), *(orch unknown)*—selections from Rienzi; Der Fliegende Holländer; Tannhäuser; Lohengrin; Tristan und Isolde; Die Meistersinger von Nürnberg; Die Walküre & Götterdämmerung *(rec 1927-1944)* Phonographe 2-▲ PHG 5016 [AAD]

Wagner, R.:Lohengrin, w. Maud Cunitz (sop—Elsa), Margarete Klose (mez—Ortrud), Rudolf Schock (ten—Lohengrin), Josef Metternich (bar—Friedrich von Telramund), Gottlob Frick (bass—King Henry), W. Schüchter (cnd), North German RSO, North German Radio Chorus, West German Radio Men's Chorus *(rec 1953)* EMI Classics 2-▲ CDHC 65517

Wagner, R.:Lohengrin (sels), w. Maria Müller (sop), Franz Völker (ten), Joseph von Manowarda (bass), W. Furtwängler (cnd), Bayreuth Festival Orch, Bayreuth Festival Chorus—Prelude to Act III; Operatic sels. *(rec 1931)* Grammofono 2000 ▲ GRM 78515 [ADD]

Wagner, R.:Lohengrin (sels), w. Maria Müller (sop—Elsa), Margarete Klose (mez—Ortrud), Franz Völker (ten—Lohengrin), Jaro Prohaska (bar—Telramund), Josef von Manowarda (bass—King Heinrich), H. Tietjen (cnd), Vienna State Opera Orch *(rec Vienna, 1938)* Koch Schwann 2-▲ SCH 314682 [ADD]

Wagner, R.:Rienzi, der Letzte der Tribunen (sels), w. Hilde Scheppan (sop), Max Lorenz (ten), Jaro Prohaska (bar), A. Rother (cnd), Berlin State Opera Orch, Berlin State Opera Chorus *(rec 1941)* Preiser ▲ PRE 90223 [ADD]

Wagner, R.:Tristan und Isolde, w. Kirsten Flagstad (sop), Lauritz Melchior (ten/bar), Herbert Janssen (bar), Sven Nilsson (bass), T. Beecham (cnd), Philharmonia Orch, Royal Opera House Chorus Covent Garden *(rec 1937)* Grammofono 2000 3-▲ GRM 78570 (m)

Klose, Margarete (mez) (cont.)
Wagner, R.:Tristan und Isolde, w. K. Flagstad (sop), L. Melchior (ten), H. Janssen (bar), S. Nilsson (bass), Beecham, Reiner (cnd), *(orch unknown)*—a compilation of two 1937 live performance recordings, with some passages conducted by Beecham, others by Reiner [G]
EMI Classics ("Great Recordings of the Century" series) 3-▲ CDHC 64037
Wagner, R.:Tristan und Isolde, w. Helena Braun (sop—Isolde), Margarete Klose (mez—Brangäne), Günther Treptow (ten—Tristan), Paul Kuen (ten—Ein Hirte), Albrecht Peter (bar—Melot), Fritz Richard Bender (bar—Ein Steuermann), Ferdinand Frantz (b-bar—König Marke), Paul Schöffler (b-bar—Kurwenal), H. Knappertsbusch (cnd), Bavarian State Opera Orch, Bavarian State Opera Chorus *(rec live, Prinzregententheater, July 23, 1950)* Orfeo 3-▲ 355
Wagner, R.:Tristan und Isolde (sels), w. A. Konetzni (sop—Isolde), M. Klose (cta—Brangäne), M. Lorenz (ten—Tristan), W. Furtwängler (cnd), Vienna State Opera Orch, Vienna State Opera Chorus *(rec Dec. 25, 1941)* Koch Schwann 2-▲ SCH 314562 [ADD]
Wagner, R.:Tristan und Isolde (sels), w. Anny Konetzni (sop—Isolde), Margarete Klose (cta—Brangäne), Max Lorenz (ten—Tristan), Paul Schöffler (b-bar—Kurwenal), Herbert Alsen (bass—King Marke), W. Furtwängler (cnd), Vienna State Opera Orch, Vienna State Opera Chorus—extended excerpts from Acts 1 & 2; Act 3 (comp) Koch Schwann 2-▲ SCH 314612 [ADD]
Wagner, R.:Tristan und Isolde (acts 2 & 3), w. E. Schlüter (sop), L. Suthaus (ten), J. Prohaska (ten), G. Frick (bass), W. Furtwängler (cnd), Berlin State Opera Orch, Berlin State Opera Chorus [G] *(rec live, Berlin, 10/3/47)* Arkadia 2-▲ 358 [ADD]
Wagner, R.:Die Walküre (act 2), w. M. Fuchs (sop), E. Flesch (sop), L. Lehmann (sop), L. Melchior (ten), H. Hotter (b-bar), A. Jerger (b-bar), E. List (bass), B. Walter (cnd), Berlin State Opera Orch [G] *(rec 9/38 & 6/22/35)* EMI Classics ("References" series) ▲ CDH 64255
Wagner, R.:Die Walküre (act 2), w. M. Fuchs (sop), E. Flesch (sop), L. Lehmann (sop), L. Melchior (ten), H. Hotter (b-bar), A. Jerger (b-bar), E. List (bass), B. Walter (cnd), Berlin State Opera Orch [G] *(rec 9/38 & 6/22/35)* Danacord 2-▲ DACOCD 317/18 (m)

Kloubová, Zdena (sop)
Janácek, L.:Moravian Folk Poetry, w. Leo Vodička (ten), Radoslav Kvapil (pno)
Unicorn-Kanchana ▲ DKP CD 9154
Orff, C.:Carmina burana, w. Vladimir Dolezal (ten), Ivan Kusnjer (bar), G. Delogu (cnd), Prague SO, Bambini di Praga, Kühn Choir *(rec live, Prague, Dec 12, 1995)* Supraphon ▲ SUP 3160
Schnittke, A.:Requiem, w. Olga Štěpánová (alt), Vladimír Dolezal (ten), J. Belohlávek (cnd), Prague SO, Kühn Chorus *(rec live, Smetana Hall, Municipal House, Prague, Dec 19, 1990)*
Panton ("60 Years of the Prague SO" series) ▲ PAN 811374 [ADD]

Kmentt, Waldemar (ten)
Albert, E. d':Tiefland, w. G. Brouwenstijn, H. Hopf, E. Wächter, P. Schöffler, O. Czerwenka, R. Moralt (cnd), Vienna SO *(rec 1957)* Philips 2-▲ 434781-2
Bach, J.S.:St. John Passion, w. P. Curtin (sop), E. Thomann (sop), E. Alberts (cta), J. Van Kesteren (ten), R. Springer (bar), O. Wiener (bar), D. Smith (b-bar), F. Guthrie (bass), F. Lukasowsky (bass), H. Scherchen (cnd), Vienna State Opera Orch, Vienna Academy Chorus [G] *(rec ca 1960)*
MCA Classics 2-▲ MCAD2-9804
Bach, J.S.:St. John Passion, w. P. Curtin (sop), E. Alberts (cta), O. Weiner (ten), H. Scherchen (cnd), Vienna State Opera Orch, Vienna Academy Chorus *(rec 1962)*
Enterprise ("Documents" series) ▲ ENT LV 925
Beethoven, L. van:Missa Solemnis, w. E. Söderström (sop), M. Höffgen (cta), M. Talvela (bass), O. Klemperer (cnd), New Philharmonia Orch, New Philharmonia Chorus [L]
EMI Classics ("Studio" series) 2-▲ CDMB 69538 [ADD]
Beethoven, L. van:Sym 9, "Choral Sym", w. G. Janowitz (sop), H. Rössel-Majdan (alt), W. Berry (bass), H. von Karajan (cnd), Berlin PO, Vienna Singverein
Deutsche Grammophon ("The Originals" series) ▲ 447401-2
Haydn, J.:Mass 6, "Nikolai-messe", "6/4-Takt-Messe", w. Agnes Giebel (sop), Gottlob Frick (bass), E. Jochum (cnd), Bavarian RSO, Vienna Cathedral Choir, Vienna Boys' Choir
Philips ("Two-Fers" series) 2-▲ 446175-2
Haydn, J.:Mass 7, "Kleine Orgelmesse", w. Agnes Giebel (sop), Gottlob Frick (bass), E. Jochum (cnd), Bavarian RSO, Vienna Cathedral Choir, Vienna Boys' Choir
Philips ("Two-Fers" series) 2-▲ 446175-2
Haydn, J.:Die Schöpfung, w. Agnes Giebel (sop), Gottlob Frick (bass), E. Jochum (cnd), Bavarian RSO, Vienna Cathedral Choir, Vienna Boys' Choir Philips ("Two-Fers" series) 2-▲ 446175-2
Mahler, G.:Das Lied von der Erde, w. J. Baker (alt), R. Kubelik (cnd), Bavarian RSO *(rec 1975)*
Originals ▲ ORISH 806 [ADD]
Mahler, G.:Das Lied von der Erde, w. C. Ludwig (mez), C. Kleiber (cnd), Vienna SO
Exclusive ▲ EXL 53 [ADD]
Mahler, G.:Sym 9, w. J. Baker (alt), R. Kubelik (cnd), Bavarian RSO *(rec 1975)*
Originals ▲ ORISH 806 [ADD]
Mozart, W.A.:Così fan tutte, w. E. Schwarzkopf (sop—Fiordiligi), C. Ludwig (sop—Dorabella), G. Sciutti (sop—Despina), W. Kmentt (ten—Ferrando), H. Prey (bar—Gugliemo), K. Dönch (bar—D. Alfonso), K. Böhm (cnd), Vienna PO, Vienna State Opera Chorus [I] *(rec live, Salzburg, Aug. 8, 1962)*
Arkadia 2-▲ 455 [ADD]
Strauss (II), Joh.:Die Fledermaus, w. M. Irosch (sop), D. Koller (sop), M. Holliday (sop), R. Karczykowski (ten), H. Kraemmer (bar), R. Granzer (bar), E. Binder (cnd), Vienna Volksoper Orch, Vienna Volksoper Chorus [G] Denon 2-▲ CO 8101 [DDD]
Strauss (II), Joh.:Die Fledermaus, w. H. Gueden (sop), E. Köth (sop), R. Resnik (mez), G. Zampieri (ten), E. Wächter (bar), W. Berry (bass), E. Kunz (bar), H. von Karajan (cnd), Vienna PO, Vienna State Opera Chorus, with Gala Sequence [G] London 2-▲ 421046-2 [ADD]
Strauss (II), Joh.:Die Fledermaus (sels), w. E. Gruberova (sop), B. Bonney (sop), M. Lipovšek (mez), W. Hollweg (ten), J. Protschka (ten), C. Boesch (bar), A. Scharinger (bass), N. Harnoncourt (cnd), Royal Concertgebouw Orch, Netherlands Opera Chorus Teldec ▲ 42427-2
Strauss (II), Joh.:Der Zigeunerbaron, w. Emmy Loose (sop—Arsena), Gerda Scheyrer (sop—Saffi), Elisabeth Fez (cta—Mirabella), Hilde Rössl-Majdan (cta—Czipra), Waldemar Kmentt (ten—Barinkay), Paul Spani (ten—Ottokar), Erich Kunz (bar—Homonay), Kurt Preger (bar—Zsupan), Eberhard Wächter (bass—Carnero), A. Paulik (cnd), Vienna State Opera Orch, Vienna State Opera Chorus *(rec Brahmssaal, Vienna, Austria, June 1956)* Vanguard Classics 2-▲ OVC 8082/83 [ADD]
Strauss, R.:Arabella, w. L. Della Casa (sop), H. Gueden (sop), I. Malaniuk (cta), A. Dermota (ten), G. London (bar), O. Edelmann (bass), G. Solti (cnd), Vienna PO [G]
London ("Grand Opera" series) 2-▲ 430387-2 [ADD]
Strauss, R.:Salome, w. B. Nilsson (sop), G. Hoffman (mez), G. Stolze (ten), E. Wächter (bar), G. Solti (cnd), Vienna PO [G] London 2-▲ 414414-2 [ADD]

Knabel, Edeltraud (alt)
Hiller, W.:Schulamit, w. Regina Klepper (sop), Michael Schopper (bass), Elisabeth Woska (nar), Waltraut Mastrogiovanni-Kraxner (shofar), H.R. Zöbeley (cnd), Munich Residenz Orch, Munich Percussion Ensemble, Calw Aurelius Boys' Choir Soloists, Munich Motet Choir Wergo ▲ WER 6280-2

Knapp, Josef (bar)
Orff, C.:Der Mond—Ein kleines Welttheater, w. Karl Erb (nar), Paul Kuen (ten—Lad 3), Josef Knapp (bar—Lad 2), Benno Kusche (bar—Lad 1), Georg Hann (bass—St. Peter), Georg Wieter (bass—Lad 4), Rudolf Wünzer (bass—The Farmer), Karl Hanft (sgr—Innkeeper), Willy Rösner (sgr—The Major), R. Alberth (cnd), Bavarian RSO, Bavarian Radio Chorus *(rec Studio 1, Bavarian Radio, Jan. 19-20, 1950)*
Calig ▲ CAL 50948 (m) [ADD]

Knapp, Peter (bass)
Monteverdi, C.:Vespro della Beata Vergine, w. Elly Ameling (sop), Norma Burrowes (sop), Charles Brett (ct), Martyn Hill (ten), Anthony Rolfe-Johnson (ten), Robert Tear (ten), John Noble (bass), Francis Grier (org/hpd), James Lancelot (org/hpd), Andrew Leach (org/hpd), P. Ledger (cnd), London Early Music Consort, King's College Choir Cambridge—Nigra sum [con.]; Laudate pueri [psalm]; Sancta Maria [son. sopra]; Magnificat *(rec Chapel of King's College, Cambridge, July & Aug. 1975)*
EMI Classics ▲ CDK 65339 [ADD]
Monteverdi, C.:Vespro della Beata Vergine, w. Elly Ameling (sop), Norma Burrowes (sop), Charles Brett (ct), Robert Tear (ten), Anthony Rolfe Johnson (ten), Martyn Hill (ten), John Noble (bass), Munrow, Ledger (cnd), London Early Music Consort EMI Classics ("Doublefforte" series) 2-▲ CDFB 68631

Knappet (nar)
Dreyfus, G.:The Adventures of Sebastian the Fox, w. Dreyfus (bn) Move ▲ MD 3071

Knauer, Wolfgang (spkr)
Mozart, W.A.:Zauberflöte, w. Constanze Backes (sop—Papagena), Christiane Oelze (sop—Pamina), Susan Roberts (sop—First Lady), Cyndia Sieden (sop—Queen of the Night), Carola Guber (cta—Second Lady), Maria Jonas (cta—Third Lady), Andreas Dieterich (trb—First Boy), Jan Andreas Mendel (trb—Second Boy), Florian Wöller (trb—Third Boy), Uwe Peper (ten—Monostatos), Nicolas Robertson (ten—First Man in Armor), Michael Schade (ten—Tamino), Gerald Finley (bar—Papageno), Noel Mann (bass—Second Man in Armour), Harry Peeters (bass—Sarastro), Detlef Roth (bass—Speaker/First Priest), Robert Burt (speaker—Third Priest), Robert Johnston (speaker—Second Priest), Wolfgang Knauer (speaker—Fourth Priest), Douglas Welbat (speaker—Second Priest), J. E. Gardiner (cnd), English Baroque Soloists, Monteverdi Choir London *(rec Forum am Schlosspark, Ludwigsburg, July 1995)*
Archiv 2-▲ 449166-2

Knecht, E. (spkr)
Honegger, A.:Christophe Colomb, w. E. Knecht (speaker—Queen Isabella), S. Rawson (speaker—The Magician), N. Garvey (speaker—Christopher Columbus), A. Furnival (speaker—King Ferdinand), D. McCabe (bar), C. Peltz (cnd), Buffalo Opera Sacra Orch, Buffalo Opera Sacra Chorus [E] *(rec Buffalo, New York, Oct. 30-31, 1992)* Mode ▲ MOD 35 [DDD]

Kneihs, Hans Maria (spkr)
Kaufmann, D.:Heiligenlegende, w. G. König (rcr), E. Ortner (cnd), Austrian RSO, Austrian Radio Chorus
Vienna Modern Masters ▲ VMM 3020 [AAD]

Knetig, Jerzy (ten)
Maciejewski, R.:Missa pro defunctis, w. Zdzislawa Donat (sop), Jadwiga Rappé (alt), Janusz Niziolek (bass), T. Strugala (cnd), Warsaw PO, Henryk Wojnarowski (cnd), Warsaw National Phil Chorus *(rec National Philharmonic, Warsaw, May 2-15, 1989)* Polskie Nagrania 2-▲ PNCD 039 A/B
Suppé, F. von:Requiem, w. Aleksandra Baranska (sop), Katarzyna Suska (cta), Andrjez Hiolski (bass), R. Bader (cnd), Cracow PO, Cracow Phil Chorus Koch Schwann ▲ SCH CD 312482

Knezevic, Bojan (bar)
Mascagni, P.:Silvano, w. Rachel Sparer (sop—Matilde), Lorraine DiSimone (mez—Rosa), Joseph Wolverton (ten—Silvano), Bojan Knezevic (bar—Renzo), P. Tiboris (cnd), Bohuslav Martinů PO *(rec SUNY Performing Arts Center Theatre, Purchase, NY, May 23-25, 1995)*
Elysium ▲ GRK 707 [DDD]

Knibbs, Jean (cta)
Purcell, H.:King Arthur, w. R. Hardy (sop), H. Sheppard (sop), A. Deller (ct), M. Deller (alt), P. Elliott (ten), L. Nixon (ten), M. Bevan (bar), N. Beavan (bass), A. Deller (cnd), Deller Consort, King's Musick [E]
Harmonia Mundi France 2-▲ HMC 90252/53

Knight, Gillian (mez)
Janácek, L.:The Cunning Little Vixen, w. L. Watson (sop), E. Bainbridge (mez), D. Montague (mez), J. Dobson (ten), R. Tear (ten), T. Allen (bar), G. Howell (bass), S. Rattle (cnd), Royal Opera House Orch [E]
EMI Classics 2-▲ CDCB 54212
Sullivan, A.:The Pirates of Penzance, w. R. Evans (sop—Mabel), G. Knight (mez—Ruth), J. Gossage (mez—Edith), J. M. Ainsley (ten—Frederic), R. Suart (bar—Maj.-Gen. Stanley), N. Folwell (bar—Samuel), D. Adams (b-bar—Pirate King), R. Van Allan (bass—Sergeant of Police), C. Mackerras (cnd), Welsh National Opera Orch, Welsh National Opera Chorus *(rec May 4-6, 1993)*
Telarc ▲ CD 80353 [DDD]; ■ CS 30353
Verdi, G.:La traviata, w. Angela Gheorghiu (sop—Violetta), Leah-Marian Jones (mez—Flora Bervoix), Gillian Knight (mez—Annina), Robin Leggate (ten—Gastone), Frank Lopardo (ten—Alfredo Germont), Rodney Gibson (ten—Servo di Flora), Neil Griffiths (ten—Giuseppe), Mark Beesley (bar—Dottore Grenvile), Leo Nucci (bar—Giorgio Germont), Richard Van Allan (bass—Barone Douphol), Roderick Earle (bass—Marquese d'Obigny), Bryan Secombe (bass—Commissionario), G. Solti (cnd), Royal Opera House Orch, Royal Opera House Chorus Covent Garden *(rec live, Royal Opera House, Covent Garden, Dec. 1994)* London 2-▲ 448119-2

Knight, Joseph (bass)
Saint-Saëns, C.:Samson et Dalila, w. Risë Stevens (mez—Dalila), Ramón Vinay (ten—Samson), Thomas Carter (ten—1st Philistine), Tony Lopez (ten—Philistine Messenger), Joseph Mordino (bar—High Priest), Arthur Cosenza (bass—Abimélech), Joseph Knight (bass—2nd Philistine), Ara Berberian (bass—Old Hebrew), R. Cellini (cnd), New Orleans Opera Orch, New Orleans Opera Chorus *(rec live, Apr 2, 1960)*
VAI Audio 2-▲ VAIA 1055-2 [ADD]

Kniplová, Nadezda (sop)
Janácek, L.:Jenůfa, w. Libuse Domininská (sop—Jenufa), Nadeshda Kniplová (sop—Kostelnicka), Vilém Přibyl (ten—Laca), Ivo Zidek (ten—Steva), B. Gregor (cnd), Prague National Theater Orch, Prague National Theater Chorus EMI Classics 2-▲ CDMB 65476
Janácek, L.:Jenůfa, w. G. Beňačková (sop—Jenufa), N. Kniplová (mez—Kostelnička Buryja), V. Krejčík (ten—Steva Buryja), V. Přibyl (ten—Laca Klemen), F. Jílek (cnd), Brno Janáček Opera Orch, Brno Janáček Opera Chorus [Cz] Supraphon 2-▲ 10 2751-2 [AAD]
Janácek, L.:Káťa Kabanová, w. E. Söderström (sop), P. Dvorský (ten), V. Krejčík (ten), Z. Svehla (ten), D. Jedlička (bass), C. Mackerras (cnd), Vienna PO London 2-▲ 421852-2 [ADD]
Smetana, B.:Dalibor, w. V. Pribyl (ten), J. Jindrak (bar), J. Krombholc (cnd), Prague National Theater Orch, Prague National Theater Chorus [Cz] Supraphon 2-▲ 11 2185 [ADD]
Wagner, R.:Der Ring des Nibelungen, w. Liselotte Becker-Egner (sop—Woglinde/Ortlinde/Wellgunde), Angelika Berger (sop—Wellgunde/Waltraute), Siw Ericsdotter (sop—Norn 3), Heidemaria Ferch (sop—Freia/Gerhilde), Bella Jasper (sop—Helmwige/Waldvogel/Woglinde), Ditha Sommer (sop—Sieglinde/Gutrune), Ursula Boese (mez—Erda), Ruth Hesse (mez—Fricka), Nadezda Kniplová (mez—Brünnhilde), Margit Kobeck (mez—Schwertleite/Norn 2), Hilde Rosner (mez—Flosshilde/Siegrunde), Erica Schubert (mez—Grimgerde/Flosshilde), Ingrid Göritz (cta—Rossweisse/Norn 1), Herbert Doussant (ten—Froh), Herold Kraus (ten—Mime), Gerald McKee (ten—Siegmund/Siegfried), Fritz Uhl (ten—Loge), Rudolf Knoll (bar—Gunther/Donner), Rolf Polke (bass-bar—Wotan/Wanderer), Rolf Kühne (bass—Alberich), Takao Okamura (bass—Fafner), Otto von Rohr (bass—Hagen/Fasolt/Hunding), H. Swarowsky (cnd), Czech PO, Prague National Theater Orch *(rec June 3 & 5, July 26-31, A)* Weltbild Classics 14-▲ 703769 [ADD]

Knittel, Sonja (sop)
Fall, L.:Der fidele Bauer (sels), w. Brigette Fassbaender (mez), Heinz Hoppe (ten), Fritz Wunderlich (ten), Benno Kusche (bass), C. Michalski (cnd), Graunke SO, Rudolf Lamy Singers
Emperor Operetta ▲ KO 86353

Knodt, Erich (bass)
Wagner, R.:Der fliegende Holländer, w. I. Haubold (sop—Senta), M. Schiml (mez—Nurse), P. Seiffert (ten—Erik), J. Hering (ten—Helsman), A. Muff (bar—The Dutchman), E. Knodt (bass—Sea Capt.), P. Steinberg (cnd), Vienna ORF SO, Budapest Radio Chorus [G] *(rec Sept. 1992)*
Naxos 2-▲ 8.660025/26 [DDD]

Knoll, Rudolf (bar)
Wagner, R.:Der Ring des Nibelungen, w. Liselotte Becker-Egner (sop—Woglinde/Ortlinde/Wellgunde), Angelika Berger (sop—Wellgunde/Waltraute), Siw Ericsdotter (sop—Norn 3), Heidemaria Ferch (sop—Freia/Gerhilde), Bella Jasper (sop—Helmwige/Waldvogel/Woglinde), Ditha Sommer (sop—Sieglinde/Gutrune), Ursula Boese (mez—Erda), Ruth Hesse (mez—Fricka), Nadezda Kniplová (mez—Brünnhilde), Margit Kobeck (mez—Schwertleite/Norn 2), Hilde Rosner (mez—Flosshilde/Siegrunde), Erica Schubert (mez—Grimgerde/Flosshilde), Ingrid Göritz (cta—Rossweisse/Norn 1), Herbert Doussant (ten—Froh), Herold Kraus (ten—Mime), Gerald McKee (ten—Siegmund/Siegfried), Fritz Uhl (ten—Loge), Rudolf Knoll (bar—Gunther/Donner), Rolf Polke (bass-bar—Wotan/Wanderer), Rolf Kühne (bass—Alberich), Takao Okamura (bass—Fafner), Otto von Rohr (bass—Hagen/Fasolt/Hunding), H. Swarowsky (cnd), Czech PO, Prague National Theater Orch *(rec June 3 & 5, July 26-31, A)* Weltbild Classics 14-▲ 703769 [ADD]

Knöppel, Michael (bass)
Weill, K.:Der Jasager, w. H. Helling (cta), T. Schmeisser (treb), T. Bräutigam (ten), T. Fischer (ten), U. Schütte (bar), W. Gundlach (cnd), Westphalia CO, Westphalia Kantorei Capriccio ▲ 60 020-1 [DDD]

Knowles, Nancy (sop)
The Art of Flemish Song in the Courts of Europe, w. Live Oak, Frank Wallace (bar/fl/vih)
Centaur ▲ CRC 2109

Knupfer, Paul (bass)
Wagner, R.:Arias & Scenes, w. Emmy Destinn (sop), Lilly Hafgren (sop), Frida Leider (sop), Emmi Leisner (cta), Ernst Kraus (ten), Lauritz Melchoir (ten), Leopold Demuth (bar), Friedrich Schorr (b-bar), Michael Bohynen (bass), Richard Mayr (bass), Heinrich Hensel (sgr), Walter Soomer (sgr) Iron Needle ▲ 1307 (m)

Koban, Gisela (sop)
Mozart, W.A.:Davidde penitente, w. E. Csapo (sop), A. Baldin (ten), D. Kurz (cnd), Württemberg CO, Württemburg Choir *(rec 1978)* Allegretto ▲ ACD 8164 [ADD] ■ ACS 8164

Kobayashi, Marie (mez)
Folk Songs, w. Marie Kobayashi (mez), Jeff Cohen (pno) REM ▲ 311253
Reynolds, R.:Odyssey, w. Phillip Larson (b-bar), D. Robertson (cnd), Ensemble InterContemporain Neuma 2-▲ 450-91 [DDD]

Kobeck, Margit (mez)
Wagner, R.:Der Ring des Nibelungen, w. Liselotte Becker-Egner (sop—Woglinde/Ortlinde/Wellgunde), Angelika Berger (sop—Wellgunde/Waltraute), Siw Ericsdotter (sop—Norn 3), Heidemaria Ferch (sop—Freia/Gerhilde), Bella Jasper (sop—Helmwige/Waldvogel/Woglinde), Ditha Sommer (sop—Sieglinde/Gutrune), Ursula Boese (mez—Erda), Ruth Hesse (mez—Fricka), Nadezda Kniplová (mez—Brünnhilde), Margit Kobeck (mez—Schwertleite/Norn 2), Hilde Rosner (mez—Flosshilde/Siegrunde), Erica Schubert (mez—Grimgerde/Flosshilde), Ingrid Göritz (cta—Rossweisse/Norn 1), Herbert Doussant (ten—Froh), Herold Kraus (ten—Mime), Gerald McKee (ten—Siegmund/Siegfried), Fritz Uhl (ten—Loge), Rudolf Knoll (bar—Gunther/Donner), Rolf Polke (bass-bar—Wotan/Wanderer), Rolf Kühne (bass—Alberich), Takao Okamura (bass—Fafner), Otto von Rohr (bass—Hagen/Fasolt/Hunding), H. Swarowsky (cnd), Czech PO, Prague National Theater Orch *(rec June 3 & 5, July 26–31, A)* Weltbild Classics 14-▲ 703769 [ADD]

Köble, Joachim (alt)
Albrechtsberger, J.G.:Missa assumptionis beatae Mariae Virginis, w. F. Schmitt-Bohn (sop), C. Elsner (ten), U. Rausch (bass), R. Hug (cnd), Freiburg Baroque Soloists Ars Musici ▲ 0972-2 [DDD]
Haydn, M.:Missa Sancti Hieronymi, w. Florian Schmitt-Bohn (sop), Christian Elsner (ten), Ulrich Rausch (bass), R. Hug (cnd), Freiburg Baroque Soloists Ars Musici ▲ 0972-2 [DDD]

Koch (sgr)
Hoffmann, E.T.A.:Aurora, w. Thomas Rieger (trb), Maltraud Meier (mez), Siegfried Schulze (bass), Ohlmann (sgr), H. Dechant (cnd), Bamberg Youth Orch, Bamberg Oratorio Chorus Bayer 3-▲ 100276-78

Koch, Ferdinand (ten)
Liszt, F.:A Faust Sym, w. J. Horenstein (cnd), Southwest German RSO Baden-Baden, Southwest German Radio Chorus *(rec 1950s)* Vox Box ("Legends" series) 2-▲ CDX2 5504 [ADD]

Koch, John (ten)
Summerdays:From the Musical Masterworks Festival at Old Lyme, w. Sheir Greenawald (sop), Beverly Hoch (sop), Aloysia Friedman (vn), Michele Sidener (va), Norman Krieger (cnd), Norman Krieger (pno) Well-Tempered Productions ▲ WTP 5173 [DDD]

Koch, John M. (bar)
Schubert, Franz:Der Graf von Gleichen, w. Gwendolyn Coleman (sop), Karen Driscoll (sop), Tracy Thomas (sop), Brad Diamond (ten), G. Samuel (cnd), Cincinnati PO, CCM Chamber Choir *(rec Corbett Auditorium, Univ of Cincinnati, Mar 12–13, 1994)* Centaur 2-▲ 2281/2282 [DDD]

Koch, Katherin (alt)
Wolf, H.:Christnacht, w. Alison Browner (sop—Engel der Verkündigung), Katherin Koch (alt—Hirte), Christian Beller (ten), D. Kurz (cnd), Stuttgart Ensemble, Württemburg Choir *(rec live, Stuttgart, Feb 18, 1996)* Claves ▲ CD 509622 [DDD]

Koch, Matthias (alt)
Telemann, G.P.:Auferstehung und Himmelfahrt Jesu, w. Monika Frimmer (sop), Veronika Winter (sop), Nico Van der Meel (ten), Klaus Mertens (bass), H. Max (cnd), Das Kliene Konzert, Rhineland Kantorei Capriccio ▲ CD 10596 [DDD]

Koci, Viktor (ten)
Dvořák, A.:King & Charcoal Burner, w. Drahonira Drobkova (cta), René Tucek (bar), Dalibor Jedlicka (bass), J. Chaloupka (cnd), Prague National Theater Orch, Milan Maly (cnd), Prague National Theater Chorus [final version] *(rec 1989)* Supraphon ("Hidden Treasures from Prague" series) ▲ SUP CD 3078

Koeman, Greet (sop)
Gluck, C.W.:Orfeo ed Euridice, w. D. Duval (sop), K. Ferrier (cta), C. Bruck (cnd), Netherlands Opera Orch, Netherlands Opera Chorus *(rec live, 1951)* Verona 2-▲ 27016/17 (m) [AAD]

Kogermann, Tiit (ten)
Tüür, E.-S.:Requiem in memoriam Peeter Lilje, w. Kaia Urb (sop), T. Kaljuste (cnd), Tallinn CO, Estonian Phil Chamber Choir *(rec Estonia Concert Hall, Tallinn, 1994–95)* ECM ("ECM New" series) ▲ ECM 1590 [DDD]

Köhler, Axel (ct)
Handel, G.F.:Jephtha, w. Julia Gooding (sop), Christiane Oelze (sop), Catherine Denley (mez), John Mark Ainsley (ten), Michael George (bass), M. Creed (cnd), Berlin Academy for Early Music *(rec June 1992)* Berlin Classics 2-▲ BER 1057-2 [DDD]
Jubilate Domino, w. Lautten Compagney Capriccio ▲ 10 478 [DDD]
Monteverdi, C.:Arias & Duets, w. M. van der Sluis (sop), Lautten Compagney—Sancta Maria; Ego flos campi; O bone Jesu; Laudate Dominum; Venite, venite; Fugge, fugge anima mea; Ballo delle Ingrate; Vorrei baciarti; Ed è pur dunque vero; Di far sempre gioire; Eri già tutta mia; O rosetta che rosetta/Non cosi tosto io miro; Quel sguardo sdegnosetto; Sinfonia; Adagiati, Poppea, Pur ti miro Capriccio ▲ 10 470 [DDD]
Monteverdi, C.:Incoronazione, w. D. Borst (sop), Lootens (sop), G. Laurens (mez), J. Larmore (mez), M. Schopper (bass), R. Jacobs (cnd), Concerto Vocale [direction & new musical realization by René Jacobs] [I] Harmonia Mundi France 3-▲ HMC 901330/32

Köhler, Markus (bar)
Blacher, B.:Songs, w. Katharina Richter (sop), Cornella Wosnitza (sop), Horst Göbel (pno), Chatschatur Kanajan (vn), Piotr Prysiasnik (vn), Fred Günther (va), Ithay Khen (vc), Christian Peters (sax), Markus Weidmann (bn)—3 Chansons; Ungereimtes; 4 Lieder; Nebel; 13 Ways of Looking at a Blackbird; 5 Sinnsprüche Omars des Zeitmachers; 3 Psalmen; Aprèslude; Francesca da Rimini; Jazz-Koloraturen Signum ▲ SIG X73-00 [DDD]
Krenek, E.:Reisebuch aus den österreichischen Alpen, w. R. Schmiedel (pno) CPO ▲ CPO 999203 [DDD]

Kohn, Andreas (bass)
Beethoven, L. van:Fidelio (sels), w. Evelyn Herlitzius (sop—Leonore), Ruth Ziesak (sop—Marzelline), Stig Andersen (ten—Florestan), Herbert Lippert (ten—Jaquino), Albert Dohmen (bar—Don Pizarro), Andreas Kohn (bass—Don Fernando), Hans Tschammer (bass—Rocco), G. Solti (cnd), World Orch for Peace, London Voices—Finale Act II *(rec Victoria Hall, Geneva, July 5, 1995)* London ▲ 448901-2 [DDD]
Humperdinck, E.:Königskinder, w. Dagmar Schellenberger (sop—Goose girl), Marilyn Schmiege (cta—Witch), Thomas Moser (ten—King's Son), Heinrich Weber (ten—Broommaker), Dietrich Henschel (bar—Fiddler), Andreas Kohn (bass—Woodcutter), F. Luisi (cnd), Munich RSO, Michael Gläser (cnd), Bavarian Radio Chorus *(rec live, Munich Herkulessaal, Mar 22–24, 1996)* Calig 3-CAL 5096870 [DDD]

Kohn, Jeno (sgr)
Synagogue Chants, w. Marcel Lorand (sgr/harm), Karel Handler (sgr), Alexander Kovacs (sgr), Trio Lorand Supraphon ▲ SUP 3073

Kohn, Karl Christian (bass)
Busoni, F.:Doktor Faust, w. H. Hillebrecht (sop), W. Cochran (ten), D. Fischer-Dieskau (bar), F. Leitner (cnd), Bavarian RSO, Bavarian Radio Sym Chorus [G] Deutsche Grammophon ("20th Century Classics" series) 3-▲ 427413-2 [ADD]
Mozart, W.A.:Don Giovanni, w. I. Seefried (sop), S. Jurinac (sop), M. Stader (sop), E. Haefliger (ten), D. Fischer-Dieskau (bar), F. Fricsay (cnd), Berlin RSO Deutsche Grammophon 3-▲ 437341-2

Kohn, Ralph (bar)
Schubert, Franz:Songs (misc), w. Graham Johnson (pno)—Schwanengesang & Ausgewählte Lieder Priory ▲ PRI 571 [DDD]

Kohútková, Adriana (sop)
Chabrier, E.:Gwendoline, w. Adriana Kohútková (sop—Gwendoline), Gérard Garino (ten—Armel), Didier Henry (bar—Harald), J.-P. Pepin (cnd), Slovak PO, Czech Phil Chorus, Slovak Phil Chorus L'Empreinte Digitale 2-▲ ED 13059
Respighi, O.:La bella dormente nel bosco, w. Ivana Czaková (sop—Old Woman/Green Fairy), Adriana Kohútková (sop—Blue Fairy/Nightingale), Henrietta Lednárová (sop—Frog/Spindle), Jana Valásková (sop—Princess), Dagmar Pecková (mez—Cuckoo/Cat), Denisa Slepkovská (mez—Queen/Duchess), Karol Bernáth (ten—Doctor), Guillermo Dominguez (ten—Prince April), Igor Pasek (ten—Jester), Ján Durco (bar—Ambassador), Richard Haan (bar—King/Woodcutter), Stanislav Benacka (bass—Doctor), Anton Kúrnava (bass—Doctor), Marián Smolárik (bass—Doctor), M. Adriano (nar—Mr. Dollar Chèques), M. Adriano (cnd), Slovak RSO Bratislava, Ján Rozehnal (cnd), Slovak Phil Chorus *(rec Concert Hall of the Slovak Radio, Bratislava, June 8–20, 1994)* Marco Polo ("Opera Classics" series) ▲ 8.223742 [DDD]
Respighi, O.:Lucrezia, w. Adriana Kohútková (sop—Venilia), Michela Remor (sop—Lucrezia), Stefania Kaluza (mez—La Voce), Denisa Slepkovská (mez—Servia), Ludovít Ludha (ten—Collatino), Igor Pasek (ten—Bruto), Ján Durco (bar—Tito/Valerio), Richard Haan (bar—Tarquinio), Rado Hanák (bass—Arunte/Spurio Lucrezio) *(rec Concert Hall of the Slovak Radio, Bratislava, June 9–16, 1994)* Marco Polo ▲ 8.223717 [DDD]

Kokolios, Giorgio (sgr)
Verdi, G.:I vespri siciliani, w. Maria Callas (sop), Boris Christoff (bass), E. Kleiber (cnd), Florence Maggio Musicale Orch, Florence Maggio Musicale Chorus *(rec live, Florence, May 26, 1951)* Enterprise ("Documents" series) 3-▲ ENT LV 996

Kokolios-Bardi (sgr)
Verdi, G.:I vespri siciliani, w. M. Callas (sop), E. Mascherini (bar), E. Kleiber (cnd), Florence Teatro Comunale Orch, Florence Teatro Comunale Chorus [I] *(rec live 5/26/51)* Melodram 3-▲ MEL 36020 (m)

Kolassi, Irma (mez)
Debussy, C.:Songs—Beau soir; le son du cor [w. Marinette Gallay (pno)]; Le Promenoir des deux amants [w. André Collard (pno)] *(rec 1962 & 1959)* Mémoire Vive ▲ 262014 (m)
Fauré, G.:Songs—La chanson d'Eve, Op. 95 [w. André Collard (pno)]; Mirage, Op. 113 [w. Lily Bienvenu] *(rec 1961)* Mémoire Vive ▲ 262014 (m)
Honegger, A.:Songs, w. André Collard (pno)—La Douceur de tes yeux; Derrière Murcie en fleurs; Un grand sommeil noir; Trois Psaumes *(rec 1957)* Mémoire Vive ▲ 262014 (m)
Honegger, A.:Songs, w. André Collard (pno)—Un grand sommeil noir Mémoire Vive ▲ CD 262024
Ravel, M.:Songs, w. Lily Beinvenu (pno)—Sainte; Manteau de fleur; Les grands vents venus d'outremer; Trois poèmes de Stéphane Mallarmé *(rec 1961)* Mémoire Vive ▲ 262014 (m)

Kolb, Lauralyn (sop)
Beach, A.M.C.:Songs, w. D. McMahon (pno)—Nachts; Fairy Lullaby Far awa'i; Extase; Take, O Take Those Lips away; The Western Wind; Forgotten; Wir Drei Albany ▲ TROY 109
Mendelssohn, Fanny:Songs, w. A. Shrut (pno)—6 Lieder, Op. 1; 6 Lieder, Op. 7; 6 Lieder, Op. 9; 5 Lieder, Op. 10; Heimweh; Italien; Nonne; Sehnsucht; Verlust [G] Centaur ▲ CRC 2120 [DDD]
Poldowski:Songs, w. D. McMahon (pno)—Colombine; Bruxelles; Spleen; Dimanche d'Avril; Cythère; L'attente; Crépuscule du soir mystique; Dansons la Gigue, Op. 23 Albany ▲ TROY 109
Schumann, C.:Songs, w. D. McMahon (pno)—Ich stand in dunklen Träumen; Sie liebten sich Beide; Liebesgarten; Der Mond kommt still gegangen; Ich hab' in deinem Auge; Die stille Lotosblume Albany ▲ TROY 109

Kolk, Stanley (ten)
Donizetti, G.:Anna Bolena, w. R. Scotto (sop—Anna Bolena), K. Ciesinski (mez—Smeton), S. Marsee (mez—Giovanna Seymour), S. Kolk (ten—Riccardo Percy), S. Ramey (bass—Enrico VIII), J. Rudel (cnd), Philadelphia Opera Orch *(rec live, Dec. 16, 1975)* Legato Classics 2-▲ LCD 175 [ADD]
Orff, C.:Carmina burana, w. E. Mandac (sop), S. Milnes (bar), S. Ozawa (cnd), Boston SO, New England Conservatory Chorus [G, L] RCA Gold Seal ▲ 07863-56533-2 [ADD] ■ 07863-56533-4

Koller, Dagmar (sop)
Lehár, F.:Das Land des Lächelns, w. Valorie Goodall (sop), Guiseppe di Stefano (ten), Heinz Holecek (bass), H. Lambrecht (cnd), Vienna Volksoper Orch [G] *(rec 1967)* Preiser ▲ 93144 [ADD]
Lehár, F.:Die lustige Witwe, w. M. Irosch (sop), H. Papouschek (sop), P. Minich (ten), K. Ruzicka (ten), H. Prikopa (bar), K. Huemer (bar), R. Bibl (cnd), Vienna Volksoper Orch, Vienna Volksoper Chorus [G] Denon 2-▲ CO 8103 [DDD]
Lehár, F.:Der Zarewitsch (sels), w. G. di Stefano (ten), H. Holecek (bar), E.-G. Scherzer (cnd), Vienna Operetta Orch, Original Volga Cossacks Koch Schwann ▲ SCH 312732 [ADD]
Strauss (II), Joh.:Die Fledermaus, w. M. Irosch (sop), M. Holliday (sop), W. Kmentt (ten), R. Karczykowski (ten), H. Kraemmer (bar), R. Granzer (bar), E. Binder (cnd), Vienna Volksoper Orch, Vienna Volksoper Chorus [G] Denon 2-▲ CO 8101 [DDD]

Köller, Kurt (bar)
Gassmann, F.L.:La Contessina, w. Susanne Ganglberger (sop—Vespina), Elisabeth Mayer (sop—Contessina), Barbara Eisschiel (mez—Lindoro), Hermann Diller (ten—Gazzetta), Kurt Köller (bar—Pancrazio), Joseph Pichler (Graf Baccellone), H. Dechant (cnd), Collegium Aureum Bayer 2-▲ BR 100 252/3 [DDD]

Kollisch, Cornelia (mez)
Hindemith, P.:Die junge Magd, w. Villa Musica Ensemble MD + G ▲ MDG 3040535 [DDD]
Hindemith, P.:Melancholie, w. Villa Musica Ensemble MD + G ▲ MDG 3040535 [DDD]
Hindemith, P.:Des Todes Tod, w. Christiane Oelze (sop) or Cornelia Kollisch (mez), Villa Musica Ensemble MD + G ▲ MDG 3040535 [DDD]

Kollo (ten)
Künneke, E.:Der Vetter aus Dingsda (sels), w. G. Van Jüten (sop), B. Kusche (bar), Wolff (sgr), Breck (sgr), Geese, Künneke (cnd), Cologne RSO, Cologne Radio Chorus [G] Acanta ▲ CD 43460 [DDD]

Kollo, Ants (ten)
Beethoven, L. van:Missa Solemnis, w. E. Moser (sop), H. Schwarz (mez), K. Moll (bass), L. Bernstein (cnd), Royal Concertgebouw Orch, Hilversum Chorus [L] Deutsche Grammophon 2-▲ 413780-2 [ADD]
Mahler, G.:Sym 8, w. A. Augér (sop), H. Harper (sop), L. Popp (sop), Y. Minton (mez), H. Watts (cta), J. Shirley-Quirk (bar), M. Talvela (bass), G. Solti (cnd), Chicago SO, Vienna State Opera Chorus, Vienna Boys' Choir, Vienna Singverein [G,L] London 2-▲ 414493-2 [ADD]
Strauss (II), Joh.:Die Fledermaus, w. J. Varady (sop), L. Popp (sop), H. Prey (bar), I. Rebroff (bass), E. Kleiber (cnd), Bavarian State Opera Orch [G] Deutsche Grammophon 2-▲ 415646-2 [ADD]
Tubin, E.:Barbara von Tisenhusen, w. H. Raamat (sop), M. Jõgeva (mez), I. Kuusk (ten), V. Puura (bar), T. Sild (bar), H. Miilberg (bass), U. Kreen (bass), P. Lilje (cnd), Estonia Opera Co Orch [Estonian] Ondine 2-▲ ODE 776-2D [DDD]
Wagner, R.:Der fliegende Holländer, w. Martin (sop), N. Bailey (bar), M. Talvela (bass), G. Solti (cnd), Chicago SO, Chicago Sym Chorus [G] London 2-▲ 414551-2 [ADD]
Wagner, R.:Lohengrin, w. A. Tomowa-Sintow (sop), D. Vejzovic (sop), S. Nimsgern (b-bar), K. Ridderbusch (bass), H. von Karajan (cnd), Berlin PO, German Opera Chorus [G] EMI Classics ("Studio" series) 4-▲ CDMD 69314 [ADD]
Wagner, R.:Die Meistersinger von Nürnberg, w. H. Donath (sop), R. Hesse (mez), P. Schreier (ten), T. Adam (b-bar), R. Evans (bass), K. Ridderbusch (bass), H. von Karajan (cnd), Dresden Staatskapelle, Dresden State Chorus, Leipzig Radio Chorus [G] EMI Classics 4-▲ CDCD 49683 [ADD]
Wagner, R.:Die Meistersinger von Nürnberg, w. H. Bode (sop), J. Hamari (mez), N. Bailey (bar), B. Weikl (bar), K. Moll (bass), G. Solti (cnd), Vienna PO, Vienna State Opera Chorus [G] London 4-▲ 417497-2 [ADD]
Wagner, R.:Parsifal, w. C. Ludwig (mez), D. Fischer-Dieskau (bar), Z. Kelemen (bar), G. Frick (bass), G. Solti (cnd), Vienna PO, Vienna State Opera Chorus, Vienna Boys' Choir [G] London 4-▲ 417143-2 [ADD]
Wagner, R.:Rienzi, der Letzte der Tribunen, w. S. Wennberg (sop), Martin (sop), P. Schreier (ten), T. Adam (b-bar), H. Hollreiser (cnd), Dresden State Opera Orch, Dresden State Opera Chorus [G] EMI Classics ("Studio" series) 3-▲ CDMB 63980
Wagner, R.:Tannhäuser, w. H. Dernesch (sop), C. Ludwig (mez), H. Braun (bar), H. Sotin (bass), G. Solti (cnd), Vienna PO [Paris version] [G] London 3-▲ 414581-2 [ADD]

▲ = CD ♦ = Enhanced CD Δ = MD ■ = Cassette Tape □ = DCC

Kollo, Ants (ten) (cont.)

Wagner, R.:Tristan und Isolde, w. M. Price (sop), B. Fassbaender (mez), D. Fischer-Dieskau (bar), K. Moll (bass), C. Kleiber (cnd), Dresden State Opera Orch [G] Deutsche Grammophon 4-▲ 413315-2 [DDD]

World Stars Sing Operetta, w.Anna Moffo (sop), Lucia Popp (sop), José Carreras (ten), Thomas Moser (ten), Giuseppe Di Stefano (ten), Hermann Prey (bar), Karl Ridderbusch (bass), et al., various orchs *(rec 1968–1985)* Acanta ▲ 42941

Kollo, René (ten)

Beethoven, L. van:Fidelio, w. G. Janowitz (sop), L. Popp (sop), H. Sotin (bass), D. Fischer-Dieskau (bar), L. Bernstein (cnd), Vienna PO, Vienna State Opera Chorus [G] Deutsche Grammophon 2-▲ 419436-2 [ADD]

Lehár, F.:Arias—13 arias from Frasquita, Friederike, Giuditta, Land des Lächelns, Lustige Witwe, Paganini, Der Rastelbinder, Schön ist die Welt [G] Acanta ▲ 43261

Lehár, F.:Die lustige Witwe, w. E. Harwood (sop), T. Stratas (sop), W. Hollweg (ten), Z. Kelemen (bar), H. von Karajan (cnd), Berlin PO, German Opera Chorus [G] *(rec 1972)* Deutsche Grammophon 2-▲ 435712-2 [ADD]

Mahler, G.:Das Lied von der Erde, w. C. Ludwig (mez), L. Bernstein (cnd), Israel PO Sony Classical ▲ SMK 47589

Mozart, W.A.:Zauberflöte, w. Reri Grist (sop), Edita Gruberová (sop), Edith Mathis (sop), Gerhard Unger (ten), Hermann Prey (bar), José Van Dam (b-bar), Peter Meven (bass), H. von Karajan (cnd), Vienna PO, Vienna State Opera Chorus *(rec live, Salzburg, July 26, 1974)* Arkadia 2-▲ 233

Opera Gala Acanta ▲ CD 43458

Opera Gala II, w. various orchs Acanta ▲ 43265

Smetana, B.:The Bartered Bride, w. T. Stratas (sop), W. Berry (b-bar), A. Malta (bass), J. Krombholc (cnd), Munich RSO Eurodisc 2-▲ 7795-2-RG [ADD]

Strauss, E.:Songs, w. C. Thielemann (cnd), German Opera Orch—"Verführung," Op. 33/1 [G] EMI Classics ▲ CDC 54776

Strauss, R.:Ariadne auf Naxos, w. L. Price (sop), E. Gruberova (sop), G. Solti (cnd), London PO [G] London ("Grand Opera" series) 2-▲ 430384-2 [ADD]

Strauss, R.:4 Last Songs, w. C. Thielemann (cnd), German Opera Orch—Im Abendroth [G] EMI Classics ▲ CDC 54776

Strauss, R.:Die Frau ohne Schatten, w. C. Studer (sop), U. Vinzing (sop), H. Schwarz (mez), A. Muff (bass), Schmidt (sgr), W. Sawallisch (cnd), Bavarian RSO, Bavarian Radio Chorus [G] EMI Classics ▲ CDC 54494 [DDD]

Strauss, R.:Die Frau ohne Schatten, w. C. Studer (sop), U. Vinzing (sop), H. Schwarz (mez), A. Muff (bass), Schmidt (sgr), W. Sawallisch (cnd), Bavarian RSO, Bavarian Radio Chorus [uncut version] [G] EMI Classics 3-▲ CDCC 49074 [DDD]

Strauss, R.:Songs, w. C. Thielemann (cnd), German Opera Orch—Verführung, Op. 33/1 [G] EMI Classics ▲ CDC 54776

Der Tenor und seine Lieder:Am Brunnen vor dem Tore Acanta ▲ 43264

Der Tenor und seine Lieder:Du bist die Welt für mich Acanta ▲ 43262

Der Tenor und seine Lieder:Dunkelrote Rosen Acanta ▲ 43263

Wagner, R.:Arias & Scenes, w. C. Thielemann (cnd), German Opera Orch—from Tristan und Isolde *(Dünkt dich das?)*, Die Walküre (w. Ingride Haubold [soprano]) *(Ein Schwert verheiss mir der Vater; Die Männer Sippe; Winterstrme wiche dem Wonnemond)* [G] EMI Classics ▲ CDC 54776

Wagner, R.:Rienzi, der Letzte der Tribunen, w. Cheryl Studer (sop—Irene), René Kollo (ten—Rienzi), Friedrich Lenz (ten—Gesandte), Norbert Orth (ten—Baroncelli), Bodo Brinkmann (bar—Paolo Orsini), Keith Engen (bass—Cecco del Vecchio), Raimund Grumbach (bass—Gesandte), Jan-Hendrik Rootering (bass—Steffano Colonna), Carmen Anhorn (sgr—Ein Friedensbote), Karl Helm (sgr—Kardinal Orvieto), John Janssen (sgr—Adriano), Alfred Kuhn (sgr—Gesandte), Hans Wilbrink (sgr—Gesandte), W. Sawallisch (cnd), Bavarian State Opera Orch, Bavarian State Opera Chorus *(rec live, July 6, 1983)* Orfeo d'or 3-▲ 346953

Wagner, R.:Der Ring des Nibelungen (sels), w. Jessye Norman (sop), Lucia Popp (sop), Siegfried Jerusalem (ten), Kurt Moll (bass), Matti Salminen (bass), M. Janowski (cnd), Dresden Staatskapelle RCA Victor ▲ 09026-68084-2; ■ 09026-68084-4

Wagner, R.:Tannhäuser, w. Nadine Secunde (sop), Waltraude Meier (mez), Bernd Weikl (bar), Z. Mehta (cnd), Bavarian State Opera Orch, Bavarian State Opera Chorus *(rec live, Munich, 1994)* Serenissima 3-▲ SER 360166

Wagner, R.:Tannhäuser (sels), w. K. Te Kanawa (sop), W. Meier (mez), H. Hagegard (bar), M. Janowski (cnd), Philharmonia Orch, Ambrosian Singers Teldec ▲ 46336-2 ■ 46336-4

Wagner, R.:Tannhäuser (sels), w. K. Te Kanawa (sop), Håkan Hagegård (bar), W. Meier (mez), M. Holle (bass), M. Janowski (cnd), Philharmonia Orch, Ambrosian Singers; music from film soundtrack for Meeting Venus Teldec ▲ 2292 46336-2 [DDD] ■ 2292 46336-4 □ 2292 46336-5

Wagner, R.:Tristan und Isolde (sels), w. C. Thielemann (cnd), German Opera Orch—Act 3 (Wesendonck Lieder) [G] EMI Classics ▲ CDC 54776

Wagner, R.:Die Walküre (act 1/scene 3), w. I. Haubold (sop), C. Thielemann (cnd), German Opera Orch [G] EMI Classics ▲ CDC 54776

Weill, K.:The Threepenny Opera, w. U. Lemper (sop), Milva (sgr), S. Tremper (sgr), H. Dernesch (mez), M. Adorf (sgr), W. Reichmann (sgr), J. Mauceri (cnd), Berlin RIAS Sinfonietta, Berlin RIAS Chamber Choir [G] London ▲ 430075-2 [DDD]

Kolmann, Ossy (bass)

Strauss (II), Joh.:Wiener Blut, w. H. Papouschek (sop), S. Martikke (sop), E. Kales (sop), A. Dallapozza (ten), K. Ruzicka (ten), E. Kuchar (ten), W. Kandutsch (bar), K. Dönch (bar), R. Bibl (cnd), Vienna Volksoper Orch, Vienna Volksoper Chorus Denon 2-▲ CO 8105 [DDD]

Kolomyjec, Joanne (sop)

Heuberger, R.:Der Opernball (sels), w. M. DuBois (ten), R. Armenian (cnd), Kitchener-Waterloo SO—Im chambre séparée CBC ("SM 5000" series) ▲ SMCD 5126 [DDD]

Kálmán, I.:Die Csárdásfürstin (sels), w. M. DuBois (ten), R. Armenian (cnd), Kitchener-Waterloo SO—Machen wir's den Schwalben nach; Tanzen möcht' ich CBC ("SM 5000" series) ▲ SMCD 5126 [DDD]

Kálmán, I.:Gräfin Mariza, w. M. DuBois (ten), R. Armenian (cnd), Kitchener-Waterloo SO—Komm Zigany; Cxárdás CBC ("SM 5000" series) ▲ SMCD 5126 [DDD]

Lavallée, C.:The Widow (sels), w. M. DuBois (ten), R. Armenian (cnd), Kitchener-Waterloo SO—Oh! Trust My Love; Smiling Hope CBC ("SM 5000" series) ▲ SMCD 5126 [DDD]

Lehár, F.:Das Land des Lächelns (sels), w. M. DuBois (ten), R. Armenian (cnd), Kitchener-Waterloo SO—Dei einem Tee ā deux; Dein ist mein ganzes Herz; Ich möcht' wieder einmal die Heimat seh'n CBC ("SM 5000" series) ▲ SMCD 5126 [DDD]

Morawetz, O.:Sonnets, w. R. Kortgaard (pno) Centrediscs ▲ CDCCD 3589 [DDD]

Song to the Moon, w. Calgary PO [cnd:Mario Bernardi] *(rec Centre for Performing Arts, Calgary, AB, May 2–4, 1993)* CBC Records ("SM 5000" series) ▲ SMCD 5138 [DDD]

Strauss (II), Joh.:Eine Nacht in Venedig (sels), w. M. DuBois (ten), R. Armenian (cnd), Kitchener-Waterloo SO—Ov.; Sei mir gegrüsst, du holdes Venetia; Polka-Mazurka, Op. 415; Was mir der Zufall gab; Quadrille, Op. 416; Sie sagten meinem Liebesfleh'n; Lagunen-Walzer, Op. 411 CBC ("SM 5000" series) ▲ SMCD 5126 [DDD]

Kolpa, Rein (ten)

Meijering, Chiel:St. Louis Blues, w. Andrea van Beek (sop), Francine van der Heijden (sop), Jeanette Huizinga (mez), Willem-Jan van Deuveren (ten), John Vredeveldt (ten), Gérard Bernts (bar), W. Megens (cnd), De Ereprijs Orch [I] *(rec Schouwburg Arnhem, Mar 10, 1995)* Donemus 2-▲ neos 01-02

Komarek, Dora (sop)

Mozart, W.A.:Zauberflöte, w. J. Novotna (sop), J. Osvath (sop), H. Roswaenge (ten), W. Domgraf-Fassbaender (bar), A. Kipnis (bass), A. Toscanini (cnd), Vienna PO, Vienna Phil Chorus [G] *(rec live, Salzburg, July 30, 1937)* Melodram 3-▲ MEL 37040 (m) [AAD]

Komatsu, Hidenori (bar)

Cornelius, P.:Duets, Op. 6, w. Edith Mathis (sop), Cord Garben (pno) CPO ▲ CPO 999262 [DDD]

Cornelius, P.:Duets, Op. 16, w. Edith Mathis (sop), Cord Garben (pno) CPO ▲ CPO 999262 [DDD]

Schumann, R.:Songs, w. Edith Mathis (sop), Cord Garben (pno)—Duets from Opp. 37, 43, 74, 78 & 79 CPO ▲ CPO 999262 [DDD]

Komatsu, Hidenori (bass)

Weill, K.:The Seven Deadly Sins, w. B. Fassbaender (mez), K.-H. Brandt (ten), H. Sojer (ten), I. Urbas (bass), C. Garben (cnd), North German Radio PO Harmonia Mundi France ▲ HMC 901420

Komlosi, Ildiko (mez)

Wagner, R.:Das Rheingold, w. Gabriele Fontana (sop—Woglinde), Nancy Gustafson (sop—Freia), Ildiko Komlosi (mez—Wellgunde), Hanna Schwarz (mez—Fricka), Elena Zaremba (mez—Erda), Margareta Hintermeier (cta—Flosshilde), Kim Begley (ten—Loge), Peter Schreier (ten—Mime), Thomas Sunnegardh (ten—Froh), Robert Hale (bass-bar—Wotan), Walter Fink (bass—Fafner), Franz-Josef Kapellmann (bass—Alberich), Jan-Hendrik Rootering (bass—Fasolt), Eike Wilm Schulte (bass—Donner), C. von Dohnányi (cnd), Cleveland Orch *(rec Severance Hall, Cleveland, Ohio, Dec 1993)* London 2-▲ 443690-2

Komlóssy, Erszébet (cta)

Erkel, F.:Bánk Bán, w. K. Agay (sop), J. Réti (ten), J. Simándy (ten), S. Sólyom-Nagy (bar), J. Ferencsik (cnd), Budapest PO, Hungarian State Opera Chorus [Hun] *(rec 1969)* Hungaroton 2-▲ HCD 11376/77 [ADD]

Szokolay, S.:Blood Wedding, w. E. Házy (sop), O. Szönyi (sop), Faragó (sgr), A. Kórodi (cnd), Hungarian State Opera Orch, Hungarian State Opera Chorus [Hun] Hungaroton 2-▲ HCD 11262/63 [ADD]

Komsi, Anu (sop)

Kurtág, G.:Kafka Fragments, w. Sakari Oramo (vn) Ondine ▲ ODE CD 868

Kondo, Fusako (mez)

Honegger, A.:Chamber Music (comp), w. Ludwig String Quartet—String Quartets Nos. 1–3 (1916–17; 1934–36; 1936–37); Pâques à New York (Easter in New York) for Mezzo & String Quartet (1920) Timpani ▲ IC1011 [DDD]

Honegger, A.:Chamber Music (comp), w. D.-S. Kang (vn), P.-H. Xuereb (va), R. Wallfisch (vc), M. Arrignon (cl), A. Marion (fl), A. Haraldsdottir (fl), C. Moreaux (ob), T. Caens (tpt), M. Becquet (trbn), P. Zanlonghi (hp), P. Devoyon (pno), Ludwig String Quartet—Sonatine for Clarinet & Piano (1921–22); Rapsodie for 2 Flutes, Clarinet & Piano (1917); Danse de la Chêvre for Solo Flute (1921); Romance for Flute & Piano (1953); Petite Suite for 2 Flutes & Piano (1934); Trois Contrepoints for Piccolo, Oboe, Violin & Cello (1922); Intrada for Trumpet & Piano (1947); Hommage du trombone exprimant la tristesse de l'auteur absent for Trombone & Piano (1925); J'avais un fidèle amant for String Quartet (1929); Chanson de Ronsard & 3 Chansons de la petite Sirène for Mezzo, Flute & String Quartet (1924); Introduction et Danse for Flute, Harp & String Trio [undated]; Colloque for Flute, Celesta, Violin & Viola [undated] Timpani ▲ IC1010 [DDD]

Honegger, A.:Pâques à New York, w. Ludwig String Quartet Timpani ▲ IC1011 [DDD]

Konetzni, Anny (sop)

Mozart, W.A.:Idomeneo (sels), w. E. Réthy (sop—Idamante), A. Konetzni (sop—Ismene), J. Sabel (ten—Idomeneo), E. Kunz (bar—Arbace), R. Strauss (cnd), Vienna State Opera Orch, Vienna State Opera Chorus *(rec Dec. 3, 1941)* Koch Schwann 2-▲ SCH 314532 [ADD]

Strauss, R.:Ariadne auf Naxos (sels), w. Adele Kern (sop—Zerbinetta), Anny Konetzni (sop—Ariadne), Set Svanholm (ten—Bacchus), Else Schulz (sgr—Composer), R. Moralt (cnd), Vienna State Opera Orch *(rec Vienna, Oct. 16, 1941)* Koch Schwann 2-▲ SCH 314625 [ADD]

Wagner, R.:Parsifal, w. Anny Konetzni (sop—Kundry), Günther Treptow (ten—Parsifal), Paul Schöffler (bar—Amfortas), Hans Braun (bass—Titurel), Adolf Vogel (bass—Klingsor), Ludwig Weber (bass—Gurnemanz), R. Moralt (cnd), Vienna SO, Vienna State Opera Chorus *(rec Vienna)* Myto 4-▲ 4 MCD 954.136

Wagner, R.:Parsifal (sels), w. H. Grahl (ten), H. Weidemann (bar), H. Alsen (bass), H. Knappertsbusch (cnd), Vienna State Opera Orch, Vienna State Opera Chorus *(rec Apr. 6, 1939)* Koch Schwann 2-▲ SCH 314522 [ADD]

Wagner, R.:Das Rheingold (sels), w. A. Konetzni (sop—Fricka), J. Prohaska (bar—Wotan), N. Zec (b-bar—Fasolt), H. Alsen (bass—Fafner), J. Krips (cnd), Vienna State Opera Orch, Vienna State Opera Chorus *(rec Jan. 18, 1937)* Koch Schwann 2-▲ SCH 314592

Wagner, R.:Der Ring des Nibelungen (sels), w. Adele Kern (sop), Hilde Konetzni (sop), Elisabeth Schumann (sop), Enid Szantho (cta), Josef Kalenberg (ten), Max Lorenz (ten), Set Svanholm (ten), Erich Zimmermann (ten), Hans Hotter (bar), Jaro Prohaska (bar), Emil Schipper (bar), Paul Schöffler (b-bar), Ludwig Hoffmann (bass), H. Knappertsbusch (cnd), Vienna State Opera Orch *(rec Vienna, 1937–1943)* Koch Schwann 2-▲ SCH 314742 [ADD]

Wagner, R.:Siegfried (sels), w. A. Konetzni (sop—Brünhilde), J. Kalenberg (ten—Siegfried), H. Knappertsbusch (cnd), Vienna State Opera Orch, Vienna State Opera Chorus *(rec Apr. 18, 1936)* Koch Schwann 2-▲ SCH 314562 [ADD]

Wagner, R.:Tristan und Isolde (sels), w. Anny Konetzni (sop—Isolde), Margarete Klose (cta—Brangäne), Max Lorenz (ten—Tristan), Paul Schöffler (b-bar—Kurwenal), Herbert Alsen (bass—King Marke), W. Furtwängler (cnd), Vienna State Opera Orch, Vienna State Opera Chorus—extended excerpts from Acts 1 & 2; Act 3 (comp) Koch Schwann 2-▲ SCH 314612 [ADD]

Wagner, R.:Tristan und Isolde (sels), w. A. Konetzni (sop—Isolde), M. Klose (cta—Brangäne), M. Lorenz (ten—Tristan), W. Furtwängler (cnd), Vienna State Opera Orch, Vienna State Opera Chorus *(rec Dec. 25, 1941)* Koch Schwann 2-▲ SCH 314562 [ADD]

Wagner, R.:Die Walküre (sels), w. Anny Konetzni (sop—Brunnhilde), Maria Müller (sop—Sieglinde), Franz Völker (ten—Siegmund), Walter Grossmann (bass—Wotan), W. Furtwängler (cnd), Vienna State Opera Orch *(rec Vienna, Feb. 13–17, 1936)* Koch Schwann 2-▲ SCH 314702 [ADD]

Wagner, R.:Die Walküre (sels), w. A. Konetzni (sop—Brünhilde), L. Hofmann (bass—Wotan), H. Knappertsbusch (cnd), Vienna State Opera Orch, Vienna State Opera Chorus *(rec Oct. 28, 1942)* Koch Schwann 2-▲ SCH 314562 [ADD]

Konetzni, Hilde (sop)

Beethoven, L. van:Fidelio, w. I. Seefried (sop), P. Klein (ten), T. Ralf (ten), P. Schöffler (b-bar), H. Alsen (bass), K. Böhm (cnd), Vienna State Opera Orch, Vienna State Opera Chorus *(rec Feb. 1944)* Preiser 2-▲ PRE 90195 [AAD]

Giordano, U.:Andrea Chénier, w. H. Konetzni (sop—Madelon), M. Sjöstedt (sop—Bersi), R. Tebaldi (sop—Maddalena de Coigny), E. Höngen (cta—La Contessa de Coigny), F. Corelli (ten—Andrea Chénier), E. Bastianini (bar—C. Gérard), K. Paskalis (bar—Pietro Fléville), L. Welter (bar—Fouquier Tinville), A. Pernerstorfer (b-bar—Mathieu), L. von Matačič (cnd), Vienna State Opera Orch, Vienna State Opera Chorus *(rec Vienna, June 26, 1960)* Fortissimo 2-▲ CDE 3003 [ADD]

Gluck, C.W.:Iphigénie en Aulide (sels), w. Helena Braun (sop—Klytämnestra), Hilde Konetzni (sop—Iphigenie), Set Svanholm (bar—Achilles), Paul Schöffler (b-bar—Agamemnon), L. Ludwig (cnd), Vienna State Opera Orch *(rec Vienna, Oct. 29, 1942)* Koch Schwann ▲ SCH 314692 [ADD]

Mozart, W.A.:Don Giovanni, w. G. Grob-Prandl (sop), M. Stabile (bar), A. Pernerstorfer (b-bar), O. Czerwenka (bass), H. Swarowsky (cnd), Vienna SO, Vienna State Opera Chorus *(rec 1950)* Preiser 2-▲ PRE 90166 [AAD]

Mozart, W.A.:Don Giovanni (sels), w. Emmy Loose (sop), Irmgard Seefried (sop), Anton Dermota (ten), Erich Kunz (bar), Paul Schöffler (b-bar), Herbert Alsen (bass), Böhm, Moralt (cnd), Vienna PO *(rec 1944)* Preiser ▲ PRE 90249 [ADD]

Mozart, W.A.:Entführung (sels), w. Emmy Loose (sop), Irmgard Seefried (sop), Anton Dermota (ten), Erich Kunz (bar), Paul Schöffler (b-bar), Herbert Alsen (bass), Böhm, Moralt (cnd), Vienna PO *(rec 1944)* Preiser ▲ PRE 90249 [ADD]

Mozart, W.A.:Zauberflöte (sels), w. Emmy Loose (sop), Irmgard Seefried (sop), Anton Dermota (ten), Erich Kunz (bar), Paul Schöffler (b-bar), Herbert Alsen (bass), Böhm, Moralt (cnd), Vienna PO *(rec 1944)* Preiser ▲ PRE 90249 [ADD]

Smetana, B.:The Bartered Bride, w. R. Tauber (ten), F. Krenn (bass), T. Beecham (cnd), Royal Opera House Orch, Royal Opera House Chorus Covent Garden [G] *(rec live, Covent Garden, 5/1/39)* Standing Room Only 2-▲ SRO 830-2 [ADD]

Smetana, B.:Dalibor (sels), w. Hilde Konetzni (sop—Milada), Todor Mazaroff (ten—Dalibor), Alfred Jerger (bar—König), L. Ludwig (cnd), Vienna State Opera Orch *(rec Vienna, Nov. 21, 1942)* Koch Schwann 2-▲ SCH 314692 [ADD]

Strauss, R.:Elektra (sels), w. Hilde Konetzni (sop—Chrysothemis), Gertrude Rünger (cta/sop—Elektra), H. Knappertsbusch (cnd), Vienna State Opera Orch *(rec Vienna, Nov. 21, 1941)* Koch Schwann 2-▲ SCH 314662 [ADD]

Strauss, R.:Die Frau ohne Schatten (sels), w. H. Konetzni (sop—Die Kaiserin), E. Schulz (sop—Die Färberin), T. RA. (ten—Der Kaiser), J. Herrmann (bar—Barak), K. Böhm (cnd), Vienna State Opera Orch, Vienna State Opera Chorus *(rec Nov. 23, 1943)* Koch Schwann 2-▲ SCH 314552 [ADD]

Konetzni, Hilde (sop) (cont.)
Strauss, R.:Der Rosenkavalier (sels), w. Margit Bokor (sop—Octavian), Hilde Konetzni (sop—Marschallin), Elisabeth Schumann (sop—Sophie), H. Knappertsbusch (cnd), Vienna State Opera Orch *(rec Salzburg, June 13, 1937)* Koch Schwann 2-▲ SCH 314672 [ADD]
Strauss, R.:Songs, w. H. Konetzni (sop—4 solo songs), A. Dermota (ten—6 solo songs), A. Poell (bar—6 solo songs), Richard Strauss (pno)—Opp. 21/2, 21/3, 69/5, 88/2 *(Konetzni)*; Opp. 15/5, Op. 17/1, 21/1, 32/2, 37/1, 49/2 *(Dermota)*; Opp. 19/1, 21/4, 27/1, 27/3, 36/1, 48/5 *(Poell)* [G] *(rec 1943)* Preiser ▲ 93261 (m) [AAD]
Verdi, G.:Don Carlos (sels), w. H. Konetzni (sop—Elisabetta), F. Völker (ten—Don Carlos), A. Kipnis (bass—Filippo), B. Walter (cnd), Vienna State Opera Orch, Vienna State Opera Chorus *(rec Dec. 16, 1936)* Koch Schwann 2-▲ SCH 314602
Verdi, G.:Otello, w. Elena Nikolaidi (cta), Torsten Ralf (ten), Paul Schöffler (b-bar), K. Böhm (cnd), Vienna State Opera Orch, Vienna State Opera Chorus *(rec live, Aug. 1944)* Preiser 2-▲ PRE 90230 [ADD]
Wagner, R.:Der Ring des Nibelungen, w. K. Flagstad (sop), E. Höngen (cta), G. Treptow (ten), S. Svanholm (ten), M. Lorenz (ten), F. Frantz (b-bar), L. Weber (bass), B. Herrmann (bass), W. Furtwängler (cnd), La Scala Orch, La Scala Chorus *(rec live 1950)* Arkadia 12-▲ 351 [ADD]
Wagner, R.:Der Ring des Nibelungen, w. Kirsten Flagstad (sop), Elisabeth Höngen (cta), Max Lorenz (ten), Set Svanholm (ten), Günther Treptow (ten), Josef Hermann (bar), Ludwig Weber (bass), Ferdinand Franz (sgr), W. Furtwängler (cnd), La Scala Orch, La Scala Chorus *(rec Milan, 1950)* Music & Arts 12-▲ CD 914
Wagner, R.:Der Ring des Nibelungen (sels), w. Adele Kern (sop), Anny Konetzni (sop), Elisabeth Schumann (sop), Enid Szantho (cta), Josef Kalenberg (ten), Max Lorenz (ten), Set Svanholm (ten), Erich Zimmermann (ten), Hans Hotter (bar), Jaro Prohaska (bar), Emil Schipper (bar), Paul Schöffler (b-bar), Ludwig Hoffmann (bass), H. Knappertsbusch (cnd), Vienna State Opera Orch *(rec Vienna, 1937–1943)* Koch Schwann 2-▲ SCH 314742 [ADD]
Wagner, R.:Die Walküre (sels), w. Viorica Ursuleac (sop—Sieglinde), Hilde Konetzni (sop—Sieglinde), Gertrude Rünger (sop—Brünnhilde), Franz Völker (ten—Siegmund), Richard Mayr (bass—Hunding), Krauss, Knappertsbusch (cnd), Vienna State Opera Orch Koch Schwann 2-▲ SCH 314662 [ADD]
Wagner, R.:Die Walküre (sels), w. Hilde Konetzni (sop—Sieglinde), Günther Treptow (ten—Siegmund), Herbert Alsen (bass—Hunding), R. Moralt (cnd), Vienna SO—Act 1 Myto 4-▲ 4 MCD 954.136
Wagner, R.:Die Walküre (sels), w. Hilde Konetzni (sop—Sieglinde), Max Lorenz (ten—Siegmund), Julius Pölzer (ten—Siegmund), Set Svanholm (ten—Siegmund), Knappertsbusch, Martin (cnd), Vienna State Opera Orch Koch Schwann ▲ SCH 314692 [ADD]
Wagner, R.:Die Walküre (sels), w. H. Konetzni (sop—Sieglinde), R. Merker (sop—Brünhilde), F. Völker (ten—Sigmund), L. Hofmann (bass—Wotan), B. Walter (cnd), Vienna State Opera Orch, Vienna State Opera Chorus *(rec Oct. 19, 1936)* Koch Schwann 2-▲ SCH 314592

König, Klaus (ten)
Mahler, G.:Das Lied von der Erde, w. A. Baltsa (mez), K. Tennstedt (cnd), London PO EMI Classics ▲ CDC 54603
Suder, J.:Leider machen Leute, w. P. Coburn (sop), M. Morgan (bar), W. Probst (bar), U. Mund (cnd), Bamberg SO, Bavarian Radio Chorus [G] Orfeo 2-▲ 124862 [DDD]
Wagner, R.:Die Walküre (act 1), w. S. Dunn (sop), P. Meven (bass), L. Maazel (cnd), Pittsburgh SO [G] Telarc ▲ CD 80258 [DDD]

Koning, Kees-Jan de (bass)
Biber, H. von:Requiem à 15, w. E. Bongers (sop), A. Grimm (sop), K. Wessel (alt), P. de Groot (alt), M. Reyans (ten), S. Davies (ten), R. Steur (bass), T. Koopman (cnd), Amsterdam Baroque Orch, Amsterdam Baroque Choir Erato ▲ 91725
Biber, H. von:Vesperae longiores ac breviores una cum litaniis Laurentanis, w. E. Bongers (sop), A. Grimm (sop), K. Wessel (alt), P. de Groot (alt), M. Reyans (ten), S. Davies (ten), R. Steur (bass), T. Koopman (cnd), Amsterdam Baroque Orch, Amsterdam Baroque Choir Erato ▲ 91725

Konsulov, Ivan (bar)
Puccini, G.:La Bohème, w. Veronika Kinsces (sop—Mimi), Sidonia Haljakova (sop—Musette), Peter Dvorsky (ten—Rodolfo), Vijtech Scherenkel (ten—Parpingol), Ian Konsulov (bar—Marcello), Balazs Poka (bar—Schaunard), Stanislav Benacka (bass—Benoit), Dariusz Niemirowicz (bass—Colline), Stefan Janci (bass—Alcindoro), *(cnd & orch unknown)* Griffin ▲ GCD 2942
Tchaikovsky, P.:Queen of Spades, w. S. Evstatieva (sop), P. Dilova (mez), Mazulok (bass), E. Tchakarov (cnd), Sofia Festival Orch, Bulgarian National Chorus [R] Sony Classical 3-▲ S3K 45720

Konya, Dionisie (bar)
Puccini, G.:Turandot, w. Teodora Lucaciu (sop—Liù), Maria Slatinaru (sop—Princess Turandot), Corneliu Finateanu (ten—Pong), George Mircea (ten—Emperor Altoum), Ludovic Speiss (ten—Prince Calaf), Valentin Teodorian (ten—Pang), Octav Enigarescu (bar—Ping), Dionisie Konya (bar—A Mandarin), Mircea Stefanescu (bar—The Prince of Persia), Nicolae Florei (bass—Timur), C. Litvin (cnd), Romanian Radio-TV Orch, Romanian Radio-TV Chorus *(rec Jan 1970)* Vox Box 2-▲ CDX 5160

Konya, Ladislau (bar)
Leoncavallo, R.:Pagliacci, w. Arta Florescu (sop—Nedda), Cornel Stavru (ten—Canio), Valentin Teodorian (ten—Beppe), Nicolae Herlea (bar—Tonio), Ladislau Konya (bar—Silvio), M. Popa (cnd), Bucharest Opera & Ballet Theater Orch, Bucharest Opera & Ballet Theater Chorus *(rec 1966)* Vox Box 2-▲ CDX 5161

Kónya, Sándor (ten)
Offenbach, J.:Les Contes d'Hoffmann, w. H. Harper (sop), Bakocevic (sgr), M. Mesplé (sop), G. Bacquier (bar), P. Maag (cnd), Buenos Aires Teatro Colón Orch, Buenos Aires Teatro Colón Chorus [F] *(rec live, Buenos Aires 8/3/70)* Melodram 2-▲ MEL 27090 [ADD]
Opera Excerpts Melodram 2-▲ CDM 26518
Smetana, B.:Dalibor, w. Franz Crass (bass), Gerd Nienstedt (bass), R. Kubelik (cnd), Bavarian RSO, Bavarian Radio Chorus *(rec live, Munich, 1969)* Serenissima 2-▲ SER 360169
Smetana, B.:Dalibor (sels), w. F. Weathers (sop), G. Nienstedt (bass), R. Kubelik (cnd), Bavarian RSO, Bavarian Radio Chorus—nine solo, duet & trio arias featuring tenor Sandor Konya as Dalibor, from Acts 1–3 *(rec live, Munich, 1968)* Myto 2-▲ 2 MCD 92465 [ADD]
Wagner, R.:Lohengrin, w. L. Rysanek (sop), A. Varnay (sop), E. Blanc (bar), A. Cluytens (cnd), Bayreuth Festival Orch, Bayreuth Festival Chorus [G] *(rec live, 7/23/58)* Myto 3-▲ MCD 89002 (m) [ADD]
Wagner, R.:Lohengrin (sels), w. M. Pobbe (sop), A. Protti (bar), F. Leitner (cnd), Milan RAI SO [I] *(rec live 1959)* Melodram ▲ MEL 15004 (m) [AAD]
Wagner, R.:Die Meistersinger von Nürnberg, w. Gundula Janowitz (sop), Brigitte Fassbaender (mez), Gerhard Unger (ten), Thomas Helmsey (bar), Thomas Stewart (bar), Franz Crass (bass), R. Kubelik (cnd), Bavarian RSO, Bavarian Radio Chorus *(rec 1967)* Calig 4-▲ 5097174 [ADD]
Wagner, R.:Die Meistersinger von Nürnberg, w. G. Janowitz (sop), B. Fassbaender (mez), G. Unger (ten), T. Stewart (bar), F. Crass (bass), T. Hemsley (bass), R. Kubelik (cnd), Bavarian RSO, Bavarian Radio Chorus [G] *(rec live, Munich, Oct. 1967)* Myto 4-▲ 4 MCD 92569 [ADD]
Wagner, R.:Das Rheingold, w. E. Grümmer (sop), R. Gorr (mez), A. Andersson (ten), T. Adam (b-bar), H. Hotter (b-bar), J. Greindl (bass), H. Knappertsbusch (cnd), Bayreuth Festival Orch, Bayreuth Festival Chorus [G] *(rec live 1958)* Arkadia 2-▲ 441 [AAD]

Koon, T. (sop)
Wagner, S.:Der Bärenhäuter, w. B. Johanning (sop—Luise), K. Likic (sop—Lene), T. Koon (sop—Gunda), V. Horn (ten—Hans Kraft), A. Feilhaber (ten—Nikolaus Spitz), R. Hartmann (bar—Kaspar Wild), A. Wenhold (bar—Stranger), A. Waller (bass—Devil), H. Kiichli (bass—Melchior Fröhlich), K. Bach (cnd), Thüringian SO, Thüringian State Theater Chorus *(rec Rudolstadt, July 25–31, 1993)* Marco Polo ("Opera Classics" series) 2-▲ 8.223713/4 [DDD]

Kooy, Peter (bass)
Bach, J.S.:Cant 4, w. Yumiko Kurisu (sop), Akira Tachikawa (ct), Koki Katano (ten), M. Suzuki (cnd), Japan Bach Collegium *(rec Kobe Shoin Women's University, Japan, June - July 1995)* BIS ▲ CD 751 [DDD]
Bach, J.S.:Cant 11, "Ascension Oratorio", w. B. Schlick (sop), C. Patriasz (cta), C. Prégardien (ten), P. Herreweghe (cnd), Collegium Vocale Orch Harmonia Mundi France ▲ HMC 901479
Bach, J.S.:Cants 12, w. Yumiko Kurisu (sop), Yoshikazu Mera (ct), Makoto Sakurada (ten), M. Suzuki (cnd), Japan Bach Collegium *(rec Kobe Shoin Women's Univ, Japan, Apr 11–14, 1996)* BIS ▲ CD 791 [DDD]
Bach, J.S.:Cant 43, w. B. Schlick (sop), C. Patriasz (cta), C. Prégardien (ten), P. Herreweghe (cnd), Collegium Vocale Harmonia Mundi France ▲ HMC 901479

Kooy, Peter (bass) (cont.)
Bach, J.S.:Cant 44, w. B. Schlick (sop), C. Patriasz (cta), C. Prégardien (ten), P. Herreweghe (cnd), Collegium Vocale Harmonia Mundi France ▲ HMC 901479
Bach, J.S.:Cant 54, w. Yumiko Kurisu (sop), Yoshikazu Mera (ct), Makoto Sakurada (ten), M. Suzuki (cnd), Japan Bach Collegium *(rec Kobe Shoin Women's Univ, Japan, Apr 11–14, 1996)* BIS ▲ CD 791 [DDD]
Bach, J.S.:Cant 56, w. P. Herreweghe (cnd), La Chapelle Royale Orch Harmonia Mundi France ▲ HMC 901365
Bach, J.S.:Cant 57, w. Vasiljka Jezovšek (sop), Sarah Connolly (cta), Mark Padmore (ten), Phillippe Herreweghe (cnd), Collegium Vocale Harmonia Mundi ▲ HMC 901594
Bach, J.S.:Cant 66, w. Barbara Schlick (sop), Kai Wessel (alt), James Taylor (ten), Phillippe Herreweghe (cnd), Collegium Vocale Harmonia Mundi France ▲ HMC 901513
Bach, J.S.:Cant 73, w. B. Schlick (sop), H. Crook (ten), P. Herreweghe (cnd), Collegium Vocale Orch, Collegium Vocale Virgin Classics ▲ CDC 59237-2
Bach, J.S.:Cant 80, w. Barbara Schlick (sop), Agnès Mellon (sop), Gérard Lesne (ct), Howard Crook (ten), P. Herreweghe (cnd), La Chapelle Royale Orch, Collegium Vocale Harmonia Mundi France Δ HMC 6901326
Bach, J.S.:Cant 82, w. P. Herreweghe (cnd), La Chapelle Royale Orch Harmonia Mundi France ▲ HMC 901365
Bach, J.S.:Cant 105, w. B. Schlick (sop), G. Lesne (mez), H. Crook (ten), P. Herreweghe (cnd), Collegium Vocale Orch, Collegium Vocale Virgin Classics ▲ CDC 59237-2
Bach, J.S.:Cant 110, w. Vasiljka Jezovšek (sop), Sarah Connolly (cta), Mark Padmore (ten), Phillippe Herreweghe (cnd), Collegium Vocale Harmonia Mundi ▲ HMC 901594
Bach, J.S.:Cant 122, w. Vasiljka Jezovšek (sop), Sarah Connolly (cta), Mark Padmore (ten), Phillippe Herreweghe (cnd), Collegium Vocale Harmonia Mundi ▲ HMC 901594
Bach, J.S.:Cant 131, w. B. Schlick (sop), G. Lesne (mez), H. Crook (ten), P. Herreweghe (cnd), Collegium Vocale Orch, Collegium Vocale Virgin Classics ▲ CDC 59237-2
Bach, J.S.:Cant 150, w. Yumiko Kurisu (sop), Akira Tachikawa (ct), Koki Katano (ten), M. Suzuki (cnd), Japan Bach Collegium *(rec Kobe Shoin Women's University, Japan, June - July 1995)* BIS ▲ CD 751 [DDD]
Bach, J.S.:Cant 158, w. P. Herreweghe (cnd), La Chapelle Royale Orch Harmonia Mundi France ▲ HMC 901365
Bach, J.S.:Cant 162, w. Yumiko Kurisu (sop), Yoshikazu Mera (ct), Makoto Sakurada (ten), M. Suzuki (cnd), Japan Bach Collegium *(rec Kobe Shoin Women's Univ, Japan, Apr 11–14, 1996)* BIS ▲ CD 791 [DDD]
Bach, J.S.:Cant 182, w. Yumiko Kurisu (sop), Yoshikazu Mera (ct), Makoto Sakurada (ten), M. Suzuki (cnd), Japan Bach Collegium *(rec Kobe Shoin Women's Univ, Japan, Apr 11–14, 1996)* BIS ▲ CD 791 [DDD]
Bach, J.S.:Cant 196, w. Yumiko Kurisu (sop), Akira Tachikawa (ct), Koki Katano (ten), M. Suzuki (cnd), Japan Bach Collegium *(rec Kobe Shoin Women's University, Japan, June - July 1995)* BIS ▲ CD 751 [DDD]
Bach, J.S.:Christmas Oratorio, w. B. Schlick (sop), M. Chance (ct), H. Crook (ten), P. Herreweghe (cnd), Ghent Collegium Vocale Orch, Ghent Collegium Vocale [G] Virgin Classics (Veritas) 2-▲ ZDCB 59530-2 [DDD]
Bach, J.S.:Easter Oratorio, w. Barbara Schlick (sop), Kai Wessel (alt), James Taylor (ten), Phillippe Herreweghe (cnd), Collegium Vocale Harmonia Mundi France ▲ HMC 901513
Bach, J.S.:Magnificat, BWV 243, w. A. Mellon (sop), B. Schlick (sop), G. Lesne (ct), H. Crook (ten), P. Herreweghe (cnd), La Chapelle Royale Orch, Collegium Vocale [L] Harmonia Mundi France ▲ HMC 901326
Bach, J.S.:Mass in b, BWV 232, w. B. Schlick (sop), C. Patriasz (cta), C. Brett (ct), H. Crook (ten), P. Herreweghe (cnd), Collegium Vocale Orch, Collegium Vocale [L] Virgin Classics ("Veritas" series) 2-▲ CDCB 59517-2 [DDD]
Bach, J.S.:Masses, BWV 233–36, "Lutheran Masses", w. A. Mellon (sop), G. Lesne (alto), C. Prégardien (ten), P. Herreweghe (cnd), Ghent Collegium Vocale Orch, Ghent Collegium Vocale—BWV 234 & 235 Virgin Classics ▲ CDC 59587
Bach, J.S.:Masses, BWV 233–36, "Lutheran Masses", w. A. Mellon (sop), G. Lesne (alto), C. Prégardien (ten), P. Herreweghe (cnd), Ghent Collegium Vocale Orch, Ghent Collegium Vocale—BWV 233 & 236 Virgin Classics ▲ CDC 59634
Bach, J.S.:St. John Passion, w. B. Schlick (sop), C. Patriasz (cta), H. Crook (ten), W. Kendall (ten), P. Lika (bass), P. Herreweghe (cnd), La Chapelle Royale Orch, Ghent Collegium Vocale [G] Harmonia Mundi France 2-▲ HMC 901264/65 [DDD]
Bach, J.S.:St. John Passion, w. B. Schlick (sop), K. Wessel (alto), G. de Mey (ten), G. Turk (ten), K. Mertens (b-bar), T. Koopman (cnd), Amsterdam Baroque Orch, Netherlands Bach Society Choir Erato 2-▲ 94675-2
Bach, J.S.:St. Matthew Passion, w. B. Schlick (sop), R. Jacobs (ct), H. P. Blochwitz (ten), H. Crook (ten), U. Cold (bass), P. Herreweghe (cnd), La Chapelle Royale Orch, Ghent Collegium Vocale [G] Harmonia Mundi France 3-▲ HMC 901155/57
Bach, J.S.:St. Matthew Passion, w. B. Schlick (sop), K. Wessel (alto), G. de Mey (ten), T. Koopman (cnd), Amsterdam Baroque Orch Erato 2-▲ 94676-2
Bach, J.S.:St. Matthew Passion, w. B. Schlick (sop), K. Wessel (alto), G. de Mey (ten), C. Pregardien (ten), T. Koopman (cnd), Amsterdam Baroque Orch, W. Cantryn (cnd), J. van Veldhoven (cnd), Breda Sacred Choir, Netherlands Bach Society Boys' Choir Erato ▲ 2292-45814-2
Bach, J.S.:St. Matthew Passion (sels), w. A. Mellon (sop), G. Lesne (alto), C. Prégardien (ten), P. Herreweghe (cnd), Ghent Collegium Vocale Orch, Ghent Collegium Vocale Virgin Classics ▲ CDC 59587
Charpentier, M.-A.:Motets for Double Choir, w. B. Schlick (sop), N. Zijlstra (sop), K. Wessel (alt), D. Visse (ct), H. van Berne (ten), C. Prégardien (ten), K. Martens (bass), T. Koopman (cnd), Amsterdam Baroque Orch—Canticum pro pace; Josué; Mors Saulis et Jonathae; Praelium Michaelis; Quam dilecta; 3 Leçons de Ténèbres Erato (Musifrance) ▲ 2292-45822-2 ZA
Distler, H.:Choral-Passion, w. W. Jochens (ten—Evangelist), P. Kooy (bass—Jesus), G. Miehlke (bass—Pilatus), W. Gundlach (cnd), Dortmund Univ Chamber Choir *(rec Mar. 1993)* Thorofon ▲ CTH 2185 [DDD]
Fauré, G.:Requiem, w. A. Mellon (sop), P. Herreweghe (cnd), Musique Oblique Ensemble, Chapelle Royale Choir [1893 version] [L] Harmonia Mundi France ▲ HMC 901292
Mendelssohn, F.:Psalm 42, w. E. Harrhy (sop), H. Lamy (ten), P. Herreweghe (cnd), La Chapelle Royale Orch, Ghent Collegium Vocale [G] Harmonia Mundi France ▲ HMC 901272 [DDD]
Mozart, W.A.:Missa, K.427, w. Jennifer Larmore (sop), Christiane Oelze (sop), Scot Weir (ten), P. Herreweghe (cnd), Champs Elysées Theater Orch, Chapelle Royale Choir, Collegium Vocale Harmonia Mundi France ▲ HMX 29001393
Mozart, W.A.:Missa, K.427, w. C. Oelze (sop), J. Larmore (mez), S. Weir (ten), P. Herreweghe (cnd), Champs Élysées Theater Orch, Chapelle Royale Choir, Collegium Vocale Harmonia Mundi France ▲ HMC 901393
Purcell, H.:Anthems & Services, w. David Cordier (alt), John Elwes (ten), Harry van der Kamp (bass), Gustav Leonhardt (org), Tölz Boys' Choir—In thee, O Lord, do I put my trust; My beloved spake; O praise God in His holiness; Praise the Lord, O Jerusalem; Rejoice in the Lord always Sony Classical ("Vivarte" series) ▲ SK 53981
Schütz, H.:Cantiones sacrae, w. Mona Spägele (sop), Ralf Popken (alt), Rogers Covey-Crump (ten), John Potter (ten), Thomas Ihlenfeldt (chit), Manfred Cordes (org)—complete 40 motets CPO 2-▲ 999405-2 [DDD]
Weill, K.:Berlin Requiem, w. A. Laiter (ten), P. Herreweghe (cnd), Musique Oblique Ensemble, Chapelle Royale Choir [G] *(rec May 1992)* Harmonia Mundi France ▲ HMC 901422
Weill, K.:Vom Tod im Wald, w. P. Herreweghe (cnd), Musique Oblique Ensemble [G] *(rec May 1992)* Harmonia Mundi France ▲ HMC 901422

Kopack, Sergej (bass)
Janácek, L.:Slavonic Mass, w. Gabriela Benackova (sop), Eva Randova (cta), Vilem Pribyl (ten), F. Jílek (cnd), Brno State PO, Josef Veselka (cnd), Czech Phil Chorus *(rec 1979)* Supraphon ▲ SUP CD 3045

Kopeczi, Alexandru (bass)

Puccini, G.:Madama Butterfly, w. Eugenia Moldoveanu (sop—Madama Butterfly), Mihaela Agachi (mez—Suzuki), Corina Circa (mez—Kate Pinkerton), Emil Gherman (ten—B.F. Pinkerton), Stefan Popescu (ten—Goro), Ioan Soanea (bar—The Bonze/Yakuside), Eduard Tumageanian (bar—Sharpless), Alexandru Kopeczi (bass—Prince Yamadori), Mircea Moisa (bass—Commissioner), P. Popescu (cnd), Satu Mare PO, Cluj–Napoca Phil Chorus *(rec 1979)* Vox Box 2-▲ CDX 5155

Kopleff, Florence (cta)

Beethoven, L. van:Sym 9, "Choral Sym", w. P. Curtin (sop), J. McCollum (ten), D. Gramm (bass), F. Reiner (cnd), Chicago SO RCA Gold Seal ▲ 09026-61795-2

Beethoven, L. van:Sym 9, "Choral Sym", w. B. Valente (sop), J. Hadley (ten), J. Cheek (bass), R. Shaw (cnd), Atlanta SO, Atlanta Sym Chorus Pro Arte ▲ CDD 245 [DDD]

Berlioz, H.:L'Enfance du Christ, w. C. Valletti (ten), G. Souzay (bar), G. Tozzi (bass), C. Munch (cnd), Boston SO, New England Conservatory Chorus RCA Gold Seal 2-▲ 09026-61234-2

Berlioz, H.:L'Enfance du Christ, w. Ceasare Valletti (ten), Gérard Souzay (bar), Lucien Oliver (bar), Giorgio Tozzi (bass), C. Munch (cnd), Boston SO, New England Conservatory Chorus *(rec Dec 1956)* RCA Victor Gold Seal 8-▲ 0902-668444-2 [ADD]

Mahler, G.:Sym 2, w. B. Sills (sop), M. Abravanel (cnd), Utah SO *(rec Salt Lake City, 1967)* Vanguard Classics ▲ SVC 2 [AAD]

Mahler, G.:Sym 2, w. B. Sills (sop), M. Abravanel (cnd), Utah SO [G] *(rec 1967)* Vanguard Classics ▲ OVC 4004 [ADD]

Milhaud, D.:L'Homme et son désir, w. L. Quilico (bar), M. Abravanel (cnd), Utah SO, Univ of Utah Chorus *(rec 1968)* Vanguard Classics ▲ OVC 8067 [ADD]

Milhaud, D.:Pacem in terris, w. L. Quilico (bar), M. Abravanel (cnd), Utah SO, Univ of Utah Chorus *(rec 1965)* Vanguard Classics ▲ OVC 8067 [ADD]

Kopp, Miroslav (ten)

Dvořák, A.:Arias & Scenes, w. Z. Košler (cnd), Czech PO, Czech Chorus—from The King of Charcoal Burner, The Stubborn L Panton ▲ PAN 811189

Martinů, B.:Špalíček, w. A. Kratochvilová (sop), R. Novák (bass), F. Jílek (cnd), Brno State PO, Kantiléna Children's Chorus [Cz] Supraphon 2-▲ 11 0752-2 [DDD]

Smetana, B.:The Bartered Bride (orch sels), w. Gabriela Benačková (sop), Peter Dvorský (ten), Z. Košler (cnd), Czech PO, Czech Phil Chorus Supraphon ▲ SUP 112251 [DDD]

Koppel, L. (sop)

Wagner, R.:Songs, w. B. Asker (bar), J. E. Frederiksen (pno), Hymnia Chamber Choir—Seven Faust–Lieder (1832); Der Tannenbaum; Geburtsangrüss an Cosima; Kraft–lied; Adieux de Marie Stuart; Dors mon enfant; Attente; Mignonne; Tout n'est qu'images fugitives; Les deux grenadiers *(rec 1988)* Classico ▲ CLASSCD 102

Koppelstetter, Marina (mez)

Orff, C.:Schulwerk (complete), w. Godela Orff (nar), Carolin Widmann (vn), Sabina Lehrmann (vc), Markus Zahnhausen (rcr), Karl Peinkofer Percussion Ensemble—4 Pieces for Xylophone; 5 Little Canons; 4 Dance Pieces; Songs & Instrumental Pieces; 3 Pieces for Fl & Perc; Songs & Dances; 2 Time Change Dances for Vn & Vc; 7 Folk Dances; Music for the Night *(rec Munich, 1994–95)* Celestial Harmonies ▲ 13104-2

Korbich, Eddie (sgr)

Bolcom, W.:Casino Paradise, w. J. Morris (sop), T. Nolen (bar), M. Barrett (cnd), *(ensemble unknown)* Koch International Classics ▲ KIC 7047-2 [DDD]

Koreh, Endreh (sgr)

Einem, G. von:Der Prozess, w. Lisa Della Casa (sop—Frl. Bürstner/Die Frau des Gerichtsdieners/Leni), Peter Klein (ten—Der Direktorstellvertreter/Der Student), Max Lorenz (ten—Josef K.), Erich Majkut (ten—Ein Bursche), László Szemere (ten—Titorelli), Alois Pernerstorfer (b–bar—Willem/Der Gerichtsdiener), Alfred Poell (b–bar—Der Advokat), Walter Berry (bass—Franz/Kanzleidirektor), Oskar Czerwenka (bass—Der Untersuchungsrichter/Der Prügler), Ludwig Hofmann (bass—Der Aufseher/Ein Passant/Der Geistliche/Der Fabrikant), Polly Batic (sgr—Frau Grubach), Endreh Koreh (sgr—Albert K.), Luise Leitner (sgr—Ein buckliges Mädchen), K. Böhm (cnd), Vienna PO, Vienna State Opera Chorus *(rec Aug 17, 1953)* Orfeo d'or ("Festspiel Dokumente" series) 2-▲ 392952 (m)

Korjus, Miliza (sop)

Great Love Duets, w. Erna Berger (sop), Lotte Lehmann (sop), Frida Leider (sop), Charles Kullman (ten), Lauritz Melchior (ten), Helge Roswaenge (ten), Tito Schipa (ten), Richard Tauber (ten), et al. Pearl ▲ PEA 9217

Helge Roswaenge, w. Helge Roswaenge (ten), Tiana Lemnitz (sop), Hans Reinmar (bar), Heinrich Schlusnus (bar), et al. Preiser 2-▲ PRE 89209 [AAD]

Miliza Korjus Pearl ▲ PEA 9186

Miliza Korjus Preiser ("Lebendige Vergangenheit" series) ▲ PRE 89054 (m) [AAD]

Strauss, R.:Ariadne auf Naxos, w. Erna Berger (sop), Viorica Ursuleac (sop), Helge Rosvaenge (ten), *(other soloists unknown)*, C. Krauss (cnd), Vienna State Opera Orch, Vienna State Opera Chorus *(rec 1935)* Arlecchino 3- ARL

Korn, Artur (bass)

Hindemith, P.:Das Unaufhörliche, w. Ulrike Sonntag (sop), Robert Wörle (ten), Siegfried Lorenz (bar), L. Zagrosek (cnd), Berlin RSO, Berlin Radio Chorus Wergo 2-▲ WER 66032

Monteverdi, C.:Vespro della Beata Vergine, w. M. Marshall (sop), F. Palmer (sop), P. Langridge (ten), K. Equiluz (ten), T. Hampson (bar), N. Harnoncourt (cnd), Vienna Concentus Musicus, Hamburg Monteverdi Chorus, Vienna Boys' Chorus Teldec 2-▲ 92629-2

Monteverdi, C.:Vespro della Beata Vergine, w. L. Marshall (sop), F. Palmer (sop), P. Langridge (ten), K. Equiluz (ten), T. Hampson (bar), N. Harnoncourt (cnd), Vienna Concentus Musicus, Hamburg Monteverdi Chorus, Vienna Boys' Chorus [L] Teldec 2-▲ 2292-42671-2

Kornewa, Natalia (sop)

Suder, J.:Festival Mass, w. Maria Neilau (alt), Vladimir Mostomoi (ten), Juri Dobrowolski (bass), Jessica Hartlieb (vn), Marlene Hinterberger (org), W.A. Albert (cnd), Bavarian State Youth Orch, St. Petersburg Chamber Choir Calig ▲ CAL 50945 [DDD]

Korondi (sgr)

Schumann, R.:Requiem, Op. 148, w. E. Andor (sop), Barlay (sgr), J. Gregor (bass), M. Forrai (cnd), Hungarian State Orch, Budapest Chorus [L] Hungaroton ▲ HCD 11809

Schumann, R.:Requiem Mignon, w. E. Andor (sop), Barlay (sgr), J. Gregor (bass), M. Forrai (cnd), Hungarian State Orch, Budapest Chorus [L] Hungaroton ▲ HCD 11809

Korondi, Anna (sop)

Brahms, J.:Choral Music, w. G. Mossyrsch (hp), J. Keiding (hn), J. Widihofer (hn), E. Ortner (cnd), Arnold Schoenberg Choir—Lieder und Romanzen, Op. 93a; 3 Gesänge, Op. 42; 7 Lieder, Op. 62; 5 Gesänge, Op. 104; 4 Gesänge, Op. 17 Teldec ▲ 4509-92058-2 [DDD]

Korondi, György (ten)

Beethoven, L. van:Syms (comp), w. Éva Andor (sop), Márta Szirmay (cta), Sándor Sólyom–Nagy (bar), J. Ferencsik (cnd), Hungarian State Orch, Miklós Forrai (cnd), Budapest Chorus *(rec 1969, 1971, 1974–76)* Classical Diamonds 6-▲ 4013-18 [ADD]

Beethoven, L. van:Sym 9, "Choral Sym", w. E. Andor (sop), H. Szirmay (cta), S. Solyom–Nagy (bar), J. Ferencsik (cnd), Hungarian PO, Budapest Phil Chorus Laserlight ▲ 15 905

Liszt, F.:Missa solemnis, w. V. Kincses (mez), T. Takács (mez), J. Gregor (bass), A. Ferencsik (cnd), Budapest SO, Budapest Sym Chorus [L] Hungaroton ▲ HCD 11861

Korovina, Tatiana (sgr)

Mysliveček, J.:Isacco figura, w. Ilona Czaková (sgr), Hye Jin Kim (sgr), Victoria Luchianez (sgr), Vladimir Dolezal (ten), Ivan Kusnjer (bar), I. Parik (cnd), Prague Sinfonietta, Pavel Kühn (cnd), Kühn Chorus Supraphon 2-▲ SUP 3209

Korpás, Ferenc (bar)

Bach, J.S.:St. Matthew Passion, w. R. Kiss (sop), I. Verebics (sop), Á. Csenki (mez), J. Németh (mez), P. Cser (ten), J. Mukk (ten), I. Gati (bar), P. Köves (bass), G. Oberfrank (cnd), Hungarian State SO, Hungarian Festival Choir, Hungarian Radio Children's Choir [G] *(rec Feb 1993)* Naxos 3-▲ 8.550832/34 [DDD]

Korzhenskaya, Olga (sgr)

Tchaikovsky, P.:Iolanta, w. Galina Gorchakova (sop), Nikolai Gassiev (ten), Gegam Grigorian (ten), Dmitri Hvorostovsky (bar), Nikolai Putilin (bar), Sergei Alexashkin (bass), Gennady Bezzubenkov (bass), Larissa Diadkova (sgr), Tatyana Kravtsova (sgr), V. Gergiev (cnd), Kirov Opera Orch, Kirov Opera Chorus *(rec Mariinsky Theatre, St. Petersburg)* Philips 2-▲ 442796-2

Koshetz, Nina (sop)

The World of Singing, Vol. 2:Singers of Imperial Russia, w. Evgenia Zbrueva (cta), Nicolai Figner (ten), Feodor Chaliapin (bass), Nina Friede (sgr), Maria Kouznetsova (sgr), Anastasia Vialtzeva (sgr) Enterprise ("Vocal Archives" series) 2-▲ ENT VA 2102

Koslowsky, Johanna (sop)

Fux, J.J.:La Fede sacrilega nella morte del Precursor San Giovanni Battista, "Johannes der Täufer", w. M. Lins (sop), H. Helling (cta), J. Calaminus (ten), G. Schwarz (bass), T. Reuber (cnd), Capella Piccola Neuss [period instrs] [I] Thorofon 2-▲ CTH 2071/72 [DDD]

Górecki, H.–M.:Sym 3, "Sym of Sorrowful Songs", w. K. Kord (cnd), Warsaw PO Philips ("Solo" series) ▲ 442411-2

Kosma (sgr)

Vivaldi, A.:Orlando Furioso, w. V. de los Angeles (sop), M. Horne (mez), L. Valentini–Terrani (mez), C. Gonzales (mez), S. Bruscantini (bar), N. Zaccaria (bass), C. Scimone (cnd), Venice Solisti Erato 3-▲ 2292-45147-2 ZB

Kossowski, Edmund (bass)

Moniuszko, S.:Halka, w. Barbara Nieman (sop), Halina Sloniowska (sop), Jan Góralski (ten), Bogdan Paprocki (ten), Leslaw Pawluk (ten), Kazimierz Pustelak (ten), Andrzej Hiolski (bar), Edward Pawlak (bass), Z. Gorzynski (cnd), Warsaw State Opera House Orch, Warsaw National Opera Chorus *(rec Warsaw, 1965)* Polskie Nagrania ▲ PNCD 092 [AAD]

Moniuszko, S.:Haunted Manor, w. Halina Slonicka (sop), Bozena Brun–Baranska (mez), Barbara Lawcewicz (mez), Krystyna Szczepanska (mez), Zdzislaw Nikodem (ten), Bogdan Paprocki (ten), Andrzej Hiolski (bar), Bernard Ladysz (bass), W. Rowicki (cnd), Warsaw State Opera House Orch, Warsaw National Opera Chorus *(rec Warsaw, 1965)* Polskie Nagrania ▲ PNCD 093 [AAD]

Kösters, Johannes M. (bar)

Rihm, W.:Hölderlin–Fragmente, w. C. Abbado (cnd), Berlin PO *(rec Philharmonie, Berlin, Feb. 26–28, 1993)* Sony Classical ▲ SK 53975 [DDD]

Kosugi, Takehisa (sgr)

Tudor, D.:Untitled, w. David Tudor (elec) Lovely Music ▲ LCD 1601 [ADD]

Koszut, Ursula (sop)

Hindemith, P.:Mathis der Maler, w. Trudeliese Schmidt (mez), Rose Wagemann (mez), William Cochran (ten), Donald Grobe (ten), James King (ten), Manfred Schmidt (ten), Dietrich Fischer–Dieskau (bar), Gerd Feldhoff (bass), Alexander Malta (bass), Peter Meven (bass), Karl Kreile (sgr), R. Kubelik (cnd), Bavarian RSO, Bavarian Radio Chorus EMI Classics 2-▲ CDCC 55237

Kotcherga, Anatoly (bass)

Janácek, L.:Slavonic Mass, w. G. Benačková (sop), F. Palmer (sop), G. Lakes (ten), M. Tilson Thomas (cnd), London SO, London Sym Chorus Sony Classical ▲ SK 47182

Mussorgsky, M.:Boris Godunov, w. V. Valente (sop—Xenia), E. Gorochovskaya (mez—Nurse), L. Nichiteanu (mez—Fyodor), E. Zarmeba (mez—Hostess), M. Lipovšek (cta—Marina), P. Langridge (ten—Prince Shuisky), H. Wildhaber (ten—Misail), A. Fedin (ten—Simpleton), S. Leiferkus (bar—Rangoni), A. Kotcherga (bass—B. Godounov), A. Shagidullin (bass—Shchelkalov), S. Ramey (bass—Pimen), S. Larin (bass—Girgory), G. Nikolsky (bass—Varlaam), C. Abbado (cnd), Berlin PO, Tölz Boys' Choir, Berlin Radio Chorus, Slovak Phil Chorus *(rec Nov. 7–30, 1993)* Sony Classical 3-▲ S3K 58977 [DDD]

Mussorgsky, M.:Songs & Dances, w. C. Abbado (cnd), Berlin PO—Nos. 1–4 *(rec Philharmonie, Berlin, Feb. 18–20, 1994)* Sony Classical ▲ SK 66276 [DDD]

Shostakovich, D.:Lady Macbeth of Mtsensk, w. M. Ewing (sop), E. Zaremba (mez), P. Langridge (ten), H. Zednik (ten), A. Haugland (bass), K. Moll (bass), S. Larin (bass), M.–W. Chung (cnd), Bastille Opera Orch, Bastille Opera Chorus Deutsche Grammophon 2-▲ 437511-2

Kotchinian, Arutiun (bass)

Tchaikovsky, P.:Iolanta, w. Michaela Gurevich (sop—Iolanta), Jaqueline Miura (sop—Brigitta), Tatjana Tabachuk (mez—Martha), Annette Kuhn (mez—Laura), Ian Denolfo (ten—Godefroy), Keith Alexander Bolves (ten—Alméric), Alexander Ben (bar—Robert), Georg Lehner (bar—Ibn–Hakia), Arutiun Kotchinian (bass—René), Kurt Geysen (bass—Bertrand), H. Rotman (cnd), Warsaw PO, ECOV Ensemble Members *(rec Vooruit Center of the Arts, Ghent, Belgium, Aug 28–29, 1993)* CPO 2-▲ CPO 999456-2 [DDD]

Köteles, Éva (sgr)

Make Wonder:Songs from Operettas, w. Magda Kalmár (sop), Judit Takács (sgr), Bori Szita (sgr), Budapest SO [cnd:Tamás Bródy], Hungarian State Orch [cnd:András Sebestyén] Hungaroton ▲ HCD 16613 [AAD]

Köth, Erika (sop)

Bach, J.S.:Cant 208, "Hunting Cant", w. Dietrich Fischer–Dieskau (bar), K. Forster (cnd), Berlin SO, St. Hedwig's Cathedral Choir EMI Classics ("Baroque" series) ▲ CDK 65729

Kálmán, I.:Die Csárdásfürstin (sels), w. F. Fehringer (ten), B. Kusche (bar), Heusser (sgr), Hofmann (sgr), Marszalek (cnd), Cologne Radio Orch, Cologne Radio Chorus [G] Acanta ▲ CD 42435 [DDD]

Lehár, F.:Der Graf von Luxemburg (sels), w. Helga Hildebrand (sop), Manfred Schmidt (ten), Rudolf Schock (ten), Gustav Niedlinger (bass) Emperor Operetta ▲ KO 86342

Lehár, F.:Die lustige Witwe (sels), w. Anneliese Rothenberger (sop), Nicolai Gedda (ten), Robert Ilosfalvy (ten), W. Mattes (cnd), Graunke SO, Bavarian Radio Chorus Emperor Operetta ▲ KO 86343

Mozart, W.A.:Arias, w. Arleen Augér (sop), Kathleen Battle (sop), Irma Beilke (sop), Helena Braun (sop), Lisa Della Casa (sop), Maria Cebotari (sop), Ileana Cotrubas (sop), Helen Donath (sop), Mirella Freni (sop), Reri Grist (sop), Edita Gruberova (sop), Elisabeth Grümmer (sop), Hilde Güden (sop), Ingeborg Hallstein (sop), Luise Helletsgruber (sop), Gundula Janowitz (sop), Sena Jurinac (sop), Evelyn Lear (sop), Wilma Lipp (sop), Margaret Marshall (sop), Edith Mathis (sop), Jarmila Novotna (sop), Margherita Perras (sop), Lucia Popp (sop), Elisabeth Rethberg (sop), Anneliese Rothenberger (sop), Elisabeth Schumann (sop), Elisabeth Schwarzkopf (sop), Graziella Sciutti (sop), Irmgard Seefried (sop), Graziella Sciutti (sop), Julia Varady (sop), Agnes Baltsa (mez), Margit Bokor (mez), Brigitte Fassbaender (mez), Christa Ludwig (mez), Ann Murray (mez), Francisco Araiza (ten), Anton Dermota (ten), Helge Rosvaenge (ten), Rudolf Schock (ten), Peter Schreier (ten), Leopold Simoneau (ten), Eric Tappy (ten), Richard Tauber (ten), Gösta Winbergh (ten), Josef Witt (ten), Fritz Wunderlich (ten), Christian Boesch (bar), Willy Domgraf–Fassbaender (bar), Karl Dönch (bar), Dietrich Fischer–Dieskau (bar), Erich Kunz (bar), Eberhard Wächter (bar), Hans Hotter (b–bar), Paul Schöffler (b–bar), Cesare Siepi (b–bar), José Van Dam (b–bar), Walter Berry (bass), Geraint Evans (bass), Nicolai Ghiaurov (bass), Alexander Kipnis (bass), Richard Mayr (bass), Kurt Moll (bass), James Morris (bass), Ezio Pinza (bass), Martti Talvela (bass), Giorgio Tozzi (bass), Hans Duhan (sgr), Res Fischer (sgr), Marie Gerhart (sgr), *(various orchs & cnds)*—sels from Idomeneo, Die Entführung aus der Serail, Le nozze di Figaro, Don Giovanni, Così fan tutte, Die Zauberflöte & various arias Orfeo d'or ("Festspiel Dokumente" series) 5-▲ 408955

Mozart, W.A.:Entführung (sels), w. Rudolf Schock (ten), G. Szell (cnd), Vienna PO—Welch' ein Geschick Orfeo d'or ("Festspiel Dokumente" series) ▲ 394201

Mozart, W.A.:Songs, w. Günter Weissenborn (pno) *(rec 1966)* Berlin Classics ▲ BER 9125

Mozart, W.A.:Zauberflöte, w. L. Della Casa (sop), G. Sciurri (sop), L. Simoneau (ten), W. Berry (bass), K. Böhme (bass), G. Szell (cnd), Vienna PO, Vienna State Opera Chorus [G] *(rec live at the Salzburg Festival, July 27, 1959)* Melodram ("Connaisseur" series) 2-▲ MEL 27505 (m) [AAD]

Nicolai, O.:Lustigen Weiber, w. Hertha Töpper (mez), Maria Rogner (sgr), Hans Günter Nöcker (b–bar), Kim Borg (bass), Naan Pödl (sgr), F. Rieger (cnd), Bavarian RSO, Bavarian Chorus *(rec 1960's)* Pantheon 2-▲ PHE 6660 (m)

Strauss (II), Joh.:Die Fledermaus, w. H. Gueden (sop), R. Resnik (mez), W. Kmentt (ten), G. Zampieri (ten), E. Wächter (bar), W. Berry (bass), E. Kunz (bar), H. von Karajan (cnd), Vienna PO, Vienna State Opera Chorus, with Gala Sequence [G] London 2-▲ 421046-2 [ADD]

Strauss, R.:Der Rosenkavalier, w. Erika Köth (sop—Sophie), Annelie Waas (sop—Marianne), Claire Watson (sop—Marschallin), Hertha Töpper (mez—Octavian), Brigitte Fassbaender (cta—Annina), Gerhard Stolze (ten—Valzacchi), Fritz Wunderlich (ten—Singer), Otto Wiener (bar—Faninal), Kurt Böhme (bass—Baron), J. Keilberth (cnd), Bavarian State Opera Orch, Bavarian State Opera Chorus *(rec Munich Opera Festival, National Theater, May 21, 1965)* Orfeo d'or 3-▲ 425963

Kotliarov, Mikhail (ten)
Shostakovich, D.:Song of the Forest, w. N. Storoyev (bass), V. Ashkenazy (cnd), Royal PO, Brighton Festival Chorus, New London Children's Choir London ▲ 436762-2 [DDD]

Kotoski, Dawn (sop)
Handel, G.F.:Acis & Galatea, w. D. Kotoski (sop—Galatea), D. Gordon (ten—Acis), G. Siebert (ten—Damon), J. Opalach (bass—Polyphemus), G. Schwarz (cnd), Seattle SO, Seattle Chorale [E] Delos 2-▲ DE 3107 [DDD]
Handel, G.F.:Giustino, w. Juliana Gondek (sop), Dorothea Röschmann (sop), Jennifer Lane (mez), Michael Chance (alt), Drew Minter (alt), Mark Padmore (ten), Dean Ely (sgr), N. McGegan (cnd), Freiburg Baroque Orch Harmonia Mundi France 3-▲ HMU 907130.32

Kotova, Raisa (sgr)
Taneyev, S.:At the Reading of a Psalm, w. Yuri Antonov (sgr), Yuri Belokrynkin (sgr), Adelina Kozlova (sgr), E. Svetlanov (cnd), USSR SO, Yurloff State Choir Russian Disc ▲ RUS 10044 [AAD]

Kotscherga, Anatoly (bass)
Rossini, G.:Stabat Mater, w. Daniela Dessi (sop), Lucia Mazzaria (sop), Gloria Scalchi (mez), Pietro Ballo (ten), Chris Merritt (ten), Roberto Scandiuzzi (bass), G. Gelmetti (cnd), Stuttgart RSO, North German Radio Chorus, Southwest German Radio Chorus Serenissima 2-▲ SER 360155 [DDD]
Tchaikovsky, P.:Mazeppa, w. Galina Gorchakoova (sop), Larissa Dyadkova (mez), Sergei Larin (ten), Sergei Leiferkus (bar), N. Järvi (cnd), Gothenburg SO, Stockholm Royal Opera Chorus Deutsche Grammophon 3-▲ 439906-2
Verdi, G.:Requiem Mass, w. Lucia Mazzaria (sop), Daniela Dessi (sop), Gloria Scalchi (mez), Pietro Ballo (ten), Chris Merritt (ten), Roberto Scandiuzzi (bass), G. Gelmetti (cnd), Stuttgart RSO, North German Radio Chorus, Southwest German Radio Chorus Serenissima 2-▲ SER 360155 [DDD]

Koudriavtchenko, Ekaterina (sop)
Rimsky-Korsakov, N.:Christmas Eve, w. Elena Zaremba (mez), Vladimir Bogtatchov (ten), Alexei Maslennikov (ten), Viatcheslav Voinarovski (ten), Viatcheslav Verestnikov (bar), Maxime Mikhailov (bass), Stanislav Souleimanov (bass), M. Yurovski (cnd), Moscow Forum Theater Orch, Yurloff Academic Choir Russian Season 4-▲ CMX 388054

Koudriavtsev, Boris (bar)
Karetnikov, N.:Till Eulenspiegel, w. E. Mazo (sop), L. Mkrtchian (cta), A. Proujanski (ten), P. Glouboky (bass), A. Motchalov (bass), A. Martinov (sgr), Polianski (cnd), Soviet Cinema Orch, Soviet Cinema Chorus *(rec Moscow, 1988)* Russian Season ("Russian Season" Series) 2-▲ LDC 288029/30 [DDD]

Koundouris, Vassilis (bar)
Glanville-Hicks, P.:Nausicaa, w. Teresa Stratas (sop—Nausicaa), Sophia Steffan (cta—Queen Arete), Michalis Heliotis (ten—Antinous/Priest), George Moutsios (ten—Eurymachus), Edward Ruhl (ten—Phemius), George Tsantikos (ten—Clytoneus), Vassilis Koundouris (bar—Messenger), John Modenos (bar—Aethon), Spiro Malas (bass—King Alcinous), C. Surinach (cnd), Athens SO, Athens Sym Chorus *(rec Athens Festival, 1961)* CRI ▲ CD 695 [ADD]

Kouznetsova, Maria (sgr)
The World of Singing, Vol. 2:Singers of Imperial Russia, w. Nina Koshetz (sop), Evgenia Zbrueva (cta), Nicolai Figner (ten), Feodor Chaliapin (bass), Nina Friede (sgr), Anastasia Vialtzeva (sgr) Enterprise ("Vocal Archives" series) 2-▲ ENT VA 2102

Kovács (sgr)
Vivaldi, A.:Magnificat, RV.611, w. T. Takács (mez), J. Németh (mez), Bátori (sgr), Szökefalvi-Nagy (sgr), F. Szekeres (cnd), Budapest Strings, Budapest Madrigal Choir [L] Hungaroton ▲ HCD 31259 [DDD]

Kovacs, Alexander (sgr)
Synagogue Chants, w. Marcel Lorand (sgr/harm), Karel Handler (sgr), Jeno Kohn (sgr), Trio Lorand Supraphon ▲ SUP 3073

Kovács, Pál (bar)
Liszt, F.:Requiem, w. Alfonz Bartha (ten), Sándor Palcsó (ten), Zsolt Bende (bar), A. Ferencsik (cnd), Hungarian State Orch, Hungarian People's Army Male Chorus [L] Hungaroton ▲ HCD 11267
Mahler, G.:Sym 8, w. Lyudmila Hadzhieva (sop), Maria Temeshi (sop), Darina Takova (sop), Tamara Takac (alt), Boryana Tabakova (alt), Janos Bandi (ten), Tamash Syule (bass), E. Tabakov (cnd), Sofia PO, Bulgarian National Chorus, Bulgarian National Radio Chorus, Bulgarian National Radio Children's Choir *(rec National Palace of Culture, Sofia, June 1991)* Capriccio 15-▲ 49043 [DDD]

Kovaleva, Anna (sop)
Rimsky-Korsakov, N.:Songs, w. Marianna Tarassova (mez), Konstantine Pluzhnikov (ten), Andrey Stavny (bar), Nikolai Okhotnikov (bass), Yury Serov (pno)—4 Romances, Op. 2; 4 Romances, Op. 3; 4 Romances, Op. 4; 4 Romances, Op. 7; 6 Romances, Op. 8; 2 Romances, Op. 25; 4 Romances, Op. 26; 4 Romances, Op. 27 *(rec St. Catherine's Lutheran Church, St. Petersburg, Sept-Dec 1993)* Russian Compact Disc ▲ RDCD 10051 [DDD]

Kováts, Kolos (bass)
Beethoven, L. van:Sym 9, "Choral Sym", w. A. Hargan (sop), U. Walther (cta), E. Büchner (ten), H. Kegel (cnd), Dresden PO Capriccio ▲ 10 453 [DDD]
Cherubini, L.:Médée, w. M. Kalmar (sop), S. Sass (sop), T. Takacs (mez), V. Luchetti (ten), L. Gardelli (cnd), Budapest SO, Hungarian Radio Chorus [I] Hungaroton 2-▲ HCD 11904/05
Verdi, G.:Arias, w. Sylvia Sass (sop), Giorgio Lamberti (ten), Oberfrank, Gardelli (cnd), Budapest MÁV SO, Hungarian State Opera Orch, Béla Pödör (cnd), Ferenc Sapszon (cnd), Ferenc Nagy (cnd), Hungarian People's Army Male Chorus, Hungarian Radio-TV Chorus, Hungarian State Opera Chorus—Vieni, o Levita!...Tu sul labbro [from Nabucco]; Verginil...Il ciel per ora...Sciagurata! Hai tu creduto; Qui posa il fianco [both from I Lombardi]; Che mai vegg'io...Infelice! E tu credevi...; Vigili pure il ciel...Iddio n'ascolti [both from Ernani]; Mentre gonfiarsi l'anima [from Attila]; Studia il passo...Come dal ciel precipital [from Macbeth]; O patria, o cara patria...O tu, Palermo [from I vespri Siciliani]; A te l'estremo addio... [from Simon Boccanegra]; Ella giammai m'amò [from Don Carlo] Hungaroton ("Great Hungarian Voices" series) ▲ HCD 31650 [ADD/DDD]
Vivaldi, A.:L'Olimpiade (sels), w. M. Zempléni (sop), T. Takács (mez), Horváth (sgr), Káplán (sgr), L. Miller (bar), I. Gáti (bar), F. Szekeres (cnd), Hungarian State Orch, Budapest Madrigal Choir [I] White Label ▲ HRC 073 [ADD]

Köves, Péter (bass)
Bach, J.S.:St. Matthew Passion, w. R. Kiss (sop), I. Verebics (sop), Á. Csenki (mez), J. Németh (mez), P. Cser (ten), J. Mukk (ten), I. Gati (bar), F. Korpás (bar), G. Oberfrank (cnd), Hungarian State SO, Hungarian Festival Choir, Hungarian Radio Children's Choir [G] *(rec Feb 1993)* Naxos 3-▲ 8.550832/34 [DDD]

Kowalczyk, Stacy (sgr)
Catholic Classics, Vol. 1, w. Ann Alderson (sgr), Richard Alderson (sgr), Carey Lovett (sgr) Gia ▲ GIA 375

Kowalski, Jochen (alt)
Arias, w. Berlin RSO [cnd:Heinz Fricke] Capriccio ▲ CD 10 416 [DDD]
Bach, J.S.:Cant 35, w. H. Haenchen (cnd), C.P.E. Bach CO Berlin Classics ▲ BER 1132 [ADD]
Bach, J.S.:Cant 49, w. H. Haenchen (cnd), C.P.E. Bach CO Berlin Classics ▲ BER 1132 [ADD]
Bach, J.S.:Cant 169, w. H. Haenchen (cnd), C.P.E. Bach CO Berlin Classics ▲ BER 1132 [ADD]
Bach, J.S.:Mass in b, BWV 232, w. N. Marriner (cnd), Academy of St. Martin in the Fields—Qui sedes ad dextram patris; Agnus dei Capriccio ▲ 10 532 [DDD]
Bach, J.S.:St. Matthew Passion (sels), w. N. Marriner (cnd), Academy of St. Martin in the Fields—Du lieber Heiland du; Buss und Reu; Erbarme dich, erbarme dich, mein Gott; Erbarm' es Gott!; Können Tränen meiner Wangen Capriccio ▲ 10 532 [DDD]
Handel, G.F.:L'Allegro, Il Penseroso ed il Moderato, w. V. Hruba-Freiberger (sop), D. Schellenberger-Ernst (sop), F.Kapellmann (bass), Rabsilber (sgr), R. Reuter (cnd), Berlin Comic Opera Orch, Berlin Radio Chorus Berlin Classics 2-▲ BER 1147 [DDD]
Handel, G.F.:Arias, w. N. Marriner (cnd), Academy of St. Martin in the Fields—Behold a Virgin shall conceive; He was despised; O thou tellest good tidings to Zion [from *Messiah*]; Their land brought forth frogs [from *Israel in Egypt*]; Oh sacred oracles of truth [from *Belshazzar*]; May at last...[from *L'Allegro, il penseroso ed il Moderato*] Capriccio ▲ 10 532 [DDD]
Handel, G.F.:Samson, w. Roberta Alexander (sop), Maria Venuti (sop), Anthony Rolfe Johnson (ten), Aalstair Miles (bass), Anton Scharinger (bass), N. Harnoncourt (cnd), Vienna Concentus Musicus, Arnold Schoenberg Choir Teldec ▲ 74871-2

Kowalski, Jochen (alt) (cont.)
Handel, G.F.:Theodora, w. Roberta Alexander (sop), Jard van Nes (cta), Hans-Peter Blochwitz (ten), Anton Scharinger (bass), N. Harnoncourt (cnd), Vienna Concentus Musicus, Arnold Schoenberg Choir [E] Teldec 2-▲ 2292-46447-2 [DDD]
Jochen Kowalski, w. Berlin RSO Capriccio Δ 70416
Jochen Kowalski:Aria from Berlin's Operatic History, w. C. Schornsheim (hpd), R. Alpermann (hpd), H. Friedrich (vc), Markus Stauch (db), Berlin CO [cnd:M. Pommer] Berlin Classics ▲ BER 1050 [DDD]
Liebermann, R.:Medea, w. Françoise Pollet (sop—Medea), Yvi Jänicke (cta—Chalkiope), Zdena Furmančoková (sgr—Syrinx), Dagmar Hesse (sgr—Aiglaia), Hanne Krogen (sgr—Kore), Michaela Lucas (sgr—Oinone), Renate Spingler (sgr—Silene), Jochen Kowalski (ct—Kreon), Aage Haugland (bass—Jason), G. Albrecht (cnd), Hamburg State PO, Hamburg State Opera Chorus *(rec live, Hamburg, Germany, Sept 24, 1995)* Musiques Suisses ▲ 6126 [DDD]
Mozart, W.A.:Arias Capriccio Δ 80213 □ 70213
Orff, C.:Carmina burana, w. S. Jo (sop), B. Skovhus (bar), Z. Mehta (cnd), London PO, London Phil Choir, Southend Boys' Choir Teldec ▲ 74886-2
Pergolesi, G.B.:Salve regina in c, w. R. Alpemann (org), H. Haenchen (cnd), C.P.E. Bach CO *(rec Apr. 1994)* Berlin Classics ▲ BER 1047-2 [DDD]
Pergolesi, G.B.:Stabat mater, w. D. Naseband (trb), R. Alpemann (org), H. Haenchen (cnd), C.P.E. Bach CO *(rec Apr. 1992)* Berlin Classics ▲ BER 1047-2 [DDD]
Plaisir d'amour, w. Eclair Salon Orch Capriccio Δ 70324
Schütz, H.:Schwannengesang, w. W. Marschall (ten), D. Knothe (cnd), Berlin Soloists, Dreseden Capella Sagittariana, Berlin Radio Children's Choir Berlin Classics 2-▲ BER 1071 [DDD]
Vivaldi, A.:Sacred Choral Music, w. M. Marshall (sop), N. van der Meel (ten), V. Negri (cnd), Royal Concertgebouw CO—Deus tuorum militum, RV.612; Laudate pueri Dominum, RV.600; Sanctorum meritis, RV.620; Stabat mater, RV.621 [L] Philips ▲ 432091-2 [DDD]

Kowalski, Stanislaw (ten)
Szymanowski, K.:King Roger, w. B. Zagórzanka (sop—Roger), S. Kowalski (ten—Shepherd), Z. Nikodem (ten—Edrisi), F. Skulski (bar—Roger II), R. Satanowski (cnd), Warsaw Teatr Wielki Orch, Warsaw Teatr Wielki Chorus [Polish] Koch Schwann 2-▲ CD 314 014 [DDD]

Kozená, Magdaléna (cta)
Bach, J.S.:Christmas Oratorio, w. T. Hanuš (cnd), Prague Chamber PO—also includes Air for Violin & Orchestra Lotos ▲ CD 0031 [DDD]
Mozart, W.A.:Ave verum corpus, w. E. Mirgova (sop), J. Griffett (ten), J. Klecker (bass), A. Kroper (cnd), Prague Concertino Nutturno Allegro ▲ ALG PCD 1022 [DDD]
Mozart, W.A.:Requiem, w. E. Mirgova (sop), J. Griffett (ten), J. Klecker (bass), A. Kroper (cnd), Prague Concertino Nutturno, Brnensky Academy Choir Allegro ▲ ALG PCD 1022 [DDD]
Zelenka, J.D.:Missa sanctissimae trinitatis, w. Anna Hlavenková (sop), Lubomir Moravec (alt), Stanislav Predota (ten), Richard Sporka (ten), Michal Pospí il (bass), M. Štryncl (cnd), Musica Florea Studio Matou ▲ MAT 17 [DDD]
Zelenka, J.D.:Il penitenti al sepolchro del Redentore, w. Magdaléna Kozená (alt—Maddalena), Martin Prokeš (ten—Davidde), Michael Pospíšil (bass), Robert Hugo (cnd), Capella Regia Musicalis *(rec St Franciscus Church of the Convent of St Agnes of Bohemia, Prague, Nov 1994)* Panton ▲ 811389-2 [DDD]

Kozlova, Adelina (sgr)
Taneyev, S.:At the Reading of a Psalm, w. Yuri Antonov (sgr), Yuri Belokrynkin (sgr), Raisa Kotova (sgr), E. Svetlanov (cnd), USSR SO, Yurloff State Choir Russian Disc ▲ RUS 10044 [AAD]

Kozlovsky, Ivan (ten)
Ivan Kozlovsky:Russian Vocal School *(rec 1948-64)* Russian Compact Disc ▲ RCD 16002 [AAD]
Recital, w. USSR SO [cnd:S. Samosud, A. Orlov, A. Bron] Myto ▲ MCD 921.55 [ADD]
Vol. 2, w. USSR SO [cnd:S. Samosud, A. Orlov, A. Bron] Myto ▲ MCD 925.68 [ADD]

Kozma, Lajos (ten)
Beethoven, L. van:Christus am Ölberg, w. C. Deutekom (sop), F. Lindauer (sgr), R. Muti (cnd), Venice Teatro La Fenice Orch, Venice Teatro La Fenice Chorus [G] *(rec live, Venice 7/4/70)* Arkadia ▲ 743 [ADD]
Kodály, Z.:Psalmus hungaricus, w. I. Kertész (cnd), Brighton Festival Chorus London ("Enterprise" series) ▲ 433080-2 [ADD]
Monteverdi, C.:Orfeo, w. R. Hansmann (sop), C. Berberian (sop), K. Equiluz (bar), M. Van Egmond (bass), N. Harnoncourt (cnd), Vienna Concentus Musicus, Capella Antiqua München Teldec 2-▲ 42494-2

Kozub, Ernst (ten)
Wagner, R.:Der fliegende Holländer, w. A. Silja (sop), T. Adam (b-bar), M. Talvela (bass), O. Klemperer (cnd), New Philharmonia Orch, BBC Sym Chorus [G] EMI Classics ("Studio" series) 3-▲ CDMC 63344 [ADD]
Wagner, R.:Der fliegende Holländer, w. Anja Silja (sop—Senta), Anneliese Burmeister (mez—Mary), Ernst Kozub (ten—Erik), Gerhard Unger (ten—Steersman), Theo Adam (bass—Dutchman), Martti Talvela (bass—Daland), O. Klemperer (cnd), New Philharmonia Orch, BBC Sym Chorus EMI Classics 3-▲ CDCC 55179

Kozušník, Karel (ten)
Klein, G.:Madrigals, w. M. Čejková (sop), J. Suchánková (sop), H. Pracnové (alt), J. Belor (bar) *(rec Oct. 20 & 21, 1992)* Koch International Classics ▲ KIC 7230-2 [DDD]

Krabbe, Till (nar)
Kalitzke, J.:Bericht über den Tod des Musikers Jack Tiergarten, w. Werner Eggenhofer (nar), Brigitte Jäger (sop), Espen Fegran (bar), J. Kalitzke (cnd), North Rhine-Westphalia Musikfabrik *(rec live, Apr 29, 1994)* CPO ▲ 999358-2 [DDD]

Kraemmer, Hans (bar)
Strauss (II), Joh.:Die Fledermaus, w. M. Irosch (sop), D. Koller (sop), M. Holliday (sop), W. Kmentt (ten), R. Karczykowski (ten), R. Granzer (bar), E. Binder (cnd), Vienna Volksoper Orch, Vienna Volksoper Chorus [G] Denon 2-▲ CO 8101 [DDD]

Krafft, Brigitte (sgr)
Lehár, F.:Das Land des Lächelns (sels), w. Ana-Maria Miranda (sop), Bernard Sinclair (bar), J. Doussard (cnd), *(orch unknown)* [F] Forlane ▲ FOR 16715 [DDD]

Krahel, Barbara (mez)
Cimarosa, D.:Requiem pro defunctis, w. K. Rymarczyk (sop), I. Jakubowski (ten), A. Niemierowicz (bar), S. Frontalini (cnd), Warmia National Orch, Olsztyn Academy Chorus [L] Bongiovanni ▲ GB 2088 [DDD]

Krahmer, Renate (sop)
Bach, J.S.:Masses, BWV 233-36, "Lutheran Masses", w. Annelies Burmeister (alt), Peter Schreier (ten), Theo Adam (bass), M. Flämig (cnd), Dresden PO Berlin Classics 2-▲ BER 9130
Handel, G.F.:Imeneo, w. Sylvia Geszty (sop), Hans-Joachim Rotzsch (ten), Günther Leib (bass), Siegfried Vogel (bass), H.-T. Margraf (cnd), Halle Handel Festival Orch, Leipzig Radio Chorus *(rec 1966)* Berlin Classics ▲ BER 9110
Schoenberg, A.:Moses und Aaron, w. Gisela Pohl (cta), Reiner Goldberg (ten), Werner Haseleu (nar), H. Kegel (cnd), Leipzig RSO, Leipzig Radio Chorus Berlin Classics 2-▲ BER 1116 [ADD]

Krämer, Hans (bar)
Weber, C.M. von:Kampf und Sieg, w. L. Schmidt-Glänzel (sop), E. Fleischer (cta), G. Lutze (ten), H. Kegel (cnd), Leipzig RSO, Leipzig Radio Chorus [G] Forlane ▲ FOR 16572 (m) [AAD]

Krämer, Hans (bass)
Lortzing, A.:Der Waffenschmied, w. E. Ebert (sop—Marie), G. Prenzlow (mez—Mariens), H. Neukirch (ten—Georg), G. Leib (bar—Ritter), H. Krämer (bass—Hans), H. Fricke (cnd), Berlin State Opera Orch, Berlin State Opera Chorus Berlin Classics ("Eterna" series) ▲ BER 2036-2 [ADD]

Kramer, Joke (mez)
Verdi, G.:Requiem Mass, w. Mariana Slavova (sop), Alexander Stevenson (ten), Peter Lika (bass), P. Kuentz (cnd), Paul Kuentz Orch, Paul Kuentz Choir Pierre Verany 2-▲ PVY 730054 [DDD]

▲ = CD ♦ = Enhanced CD Δ = MD ■ = Cassette Tape □ = DCC

Krämer, Michaela (sop)

Mendelssohn, Fanny:Songs, w. Gerhild Romberger (alt), Alastair Thompson (ten), Gerrit Miehlke (bass), Richard Braun (pno), Willi Gundlach (cnd), Dortmund Univ Chamber Choir—Morgendämmerung; Im Herbste; Unter des Laubdachs Hut; Ich stand gelehnet an den Mast; Mitternacht; Abschied; Lockung; Abend; Aus meinen Tränen; Wenn ich in deine Augen seh'; Im wunderschönen Monat Mai; Schöne Fremde; Schweigend sinkt die Nacht hernieder; Nacht liegt auf den fremden Wegen; Hochzeitsbitter; Wandl' ich in dem Wald; Frühzeitiger Frühling; Blumengruss; O Herbst; Schilflied; Feldlied; März; Lichter Mai; Waldruhe; Nachtreigen *(rec Musikhochshule Detmold, Dortmund, Oct 1995)* Thorofon ▲ CTH 2299 [DDD]

Krasnaya, Nadexhda (sop)

Tchaikovsky, P.:Songs, w. V. Fedorovtsev (pno) Russian Disc ▲ RUS 11 078 [DDD]

Krasova, Marta (cta)

Dvořák, A.:Stabat Mater, w. Drahomira Tikalova (sop), Beno Blachut (ten), Karel Kalas (bass), V. Talich (cnd), Czech PO, Czech Phil Chorus *(rec 1952)* Supraphon 2-▲ SUP 111902 [ADD]

Krasteva, Svetla (sop)

Boccherini, L.:Credo, w. Fernanda Piccini (cta), Manuel Beltrand (ten), Duccio Dal Monte (bass), G. Cosmi (cnd), Lucca Teatro Comunale Giglio Orch *(rec Dec 18, 1993)* Bongiovanni ▲ GB 2178 [DDD]

Boccherini, L.:Kyrie & Gloria, w. Fernanda Piccini (cta), Manuel Beltrand (ten), Duccio Dal Monte (bass), G. Cosmi (cnd), Lucca Teatro Comunale Giglio Orch *(rec Dec 18, 1993)* Bongiovanni ▲ GB 2178 [DDD]

Boccherini, L.:Scene from Ines de Castro, w. G. Cosmi (cnd), Lucca Teatro Comunale Giglio Orch *(rec Dec 18, 1993)* Bongiovanni ▲ GB 2178 [DDD]

Traetta, T.:Litanies, w. I. Aramayo Sandivari (sgr), A. De Lucia (sgr), R. Gierlach (bar), I. Lo Vetere (cnd), Giovanile Ambrosiano Ensemble. Bongiovanni ▲ GB 2127 [DDD]

Traetta, T.:Stabat Mater, w. I. Aramayo Sandivari (sgr), A. De Lucia (sgr), R. Gierlach (bar), I. Lo Vetere (cnd), Giovanile Ambrosiano Ensemble, Piacenza Polifonico Farnesiano Chorus Bongiovanni ▲ GB 2127 [DDD]

Krátká, Jarmila (sop)

Martinů, B.:Alexandre bis, w. A. Barová (mez), R. Novák (ten), R. Tuček (bar), F. Jílek (cnd), Brno Janáček Opera Orch Supraphon ▲ SUP 11 2140 [AAD]

Martinů, B.:Comedy on the Bridge, w. A. Barová (mez), R. Novák (ten), R. Tuček (bar), F. Jílek (cnd), Brno Janáček Opera Orch Supraphon ▲ SUP 11 2140 [AAD]

Kratochvilová, Anna (sop)

Martinů, B.:Špaliček, w. M. Kopp (ten), R. Novák (bass), F. Jílek (cnd), Brno State PO, Kantiléna Children's Chorus [Cz] Supraphon 2-▲ 11 0752-2 [DDD]

Krattiger, Jurg (bass)

Fröhlich, F.T.:Choral Music, w. E. Speiser (sop), P. Steiner (ten), B. Billeter (pno), C. Spring (pno), Winterthur Vocal Ensemble [G] *(rec 1988)* Jecklin-Disco ▲ JD 627-2 [ADD]

Kraus, A. (ten)

Bellini, V.:I Puritani, w. A. Maliponte (sop—Elvira), A. di Stasio (sop—Enrichetta di Francia), A. Kraus (ten—Lord Arturo Talbo), A. Pedroni (ten—Bruno Roberton), P. Cappuccilli (bar—Sir Riccardo Forth), R. Raimondi (bass—Sir Giorgio), G. Gavazzeni (cnd), Catania Teatro Massimo Bellini Orch, Catania Teatro Massimo Bellini Chorus *(rec Feb. 6, 1972)* Ornamenti 2-▲ FE 107 [ADD]

Bizet, G.:Les Pêcheurs de perles, w. A. Maliponte (sop—Leila), A. Kraus (ten—Nadir), S. Bruscantini (bar—Zurga), C. F. Cillario (cnd), Barcelona Teatro Liceo Orch, Barcelona Gran Teatro de Liceo Chorus Bongiovanni 2-▲ GB 516/17 [ADD]

Boito, A.:Mefistofele, w. R. Tebaldi (sop—Margheritta), E. Souliotis (sop—Elena), M. Mackenzie (mez—Marta), M. Ruggiero (mez—Pantalis), A. Kraus (ten—Faust), H. Kraus (ten—Wagner), N. Ghiaurov (bass—Mefistofele), N. Sanzogno (cnd), *(orch unknown)* Ornamenti 2-▲ FE 101

Delibes, L.:Lakmé, w. M. Spacagna (sop—Ellen), R. Welting (sop—Lakmé), A. Kraus (ten—Gérald), D. Holloway (bar—Frédéric), P. Plishka (bass—Nilakantha), N. Rescigno (cnd), Dallas Civic Opera Orch *(rec Nov. 1980)* Ornamenti 2-▲ FE 108 [ADD]

Lehár, F.:Eva, w. J. Granados (sop—Prunelles), A. M. Olaria (sop—Eva), A. Kraus (ten—Octavio Flaubert), L. de Cordoba (sgr—Gipsy), S. Ramalle (sgr—Dagoberto), J. Peromingo (sgr—Voisin), E. Estella (cnd), Madrid CO, Spanish National Radio Chorus [Sp] Montilla ▲ CDFM 2036

Kraus, Adalbert (ten)

Bach, J.S.:Cant 7, w. H. Watts (cta), W. Schöne (bass), H. Rilling (cnd), Stuttgart Bach Collegium, Gächinger Kantorei Hänssler Classic ▲ 98.802 [AAD]

Bach, J.S.:Cant 8, w. A. Augér (sop), H. Watts (cta), P. Huttenlocher (bar), H. Rilling (cnd), Stuttgart Bach Collegium, Gächinger Kantorei [G] *(rec 1979)* Hänssler Classic ▲ 98.813 [AAD]

Bach, J.S.:Cant 11, "Ascension Oratorio", w. C. Cuccaro (sop), M. Georg (alt), A. Schmidt (bass), H. Rilling (cnd), Württemberg CO, Gächinger Kantorei [G] Novalis ▲ 150028 [DDD]

Bach, J.S.:Cant 11, "Ascension Oratorio", w. C. Cuccaro (sop), M. Georg (alt), A. Schmidt (bass), H. Rilling (cnd), Württemberg CO, Gächinger Kantorei [G] *(rec 1984)* Hänssler Classic 5-▲ 98.976

Bach, J.S.:Cant 18, w. E. Csapò (sop), G. Schnaut (mez), W. Schöne (bass), H. Rilling (cnd), Bach Ensemble [G] *(rec 1975)* Hänssler Classic ▲ 98.877 [AAD]

Bach, J.S.:Cant 20, w. V. Gohl (mez), M. Kessler (mez), T. Altmeyer (ten), W. Schöne (bass), H. Rilling (cnd), Stuttgart Bach Collegium, Frankfurt Kantorei Hänssler Classic ▲ 98.801 [AAD]

Bach, J.S.:Cant 24, w. A. Augér (sop), H. Watts (cta), K. Pugh (cta), W. Heldwein (bass), W. Schöne (bass), H. Rilling (cnd), Stuttgart Bach Collegium, Gächinger Kantorei Hänssler Classic ▲ 98.803 [AAD]

Bach, J.S.:Cant 25, w. A. Augér (sop), P. Huttenlocher (bar), H. Rilling (cnd), Stuttgart Bach Collegium, Gächinger Kantorei Hänssler Classic ▲ 98.810 [ADD]

Bach, J.S.:Cant 26, w. A. Augér (sop), D. Soffel (sop), P. Huttenlocher (bar), H. Rilling (cnd), Stuttgart Bach Collegium, Gächinger Kantorei [G] *(rec 1979 & 1980)* Hänssler Classic ▲ 98.821 [AAD]

Bach, J.S.:Cant 28, w. A. Augér (sop), G. Schreckenbach (cta), W. Heldwein (bass), H. Rilling (cnd), Stuttgart Bach Collegium, Gächinger Kantorei [G] *(rec Nov 1981 & Feb 1982)* Hänssler Classic ▲ 98.827 [AAD]

Bach, J.S.:Cant 34, w. H. Watts (cta), W. Schöne (bass), Stuttgart Bach Collegium, Gächinger Kantorei Hänssler Classic ▲ 98.887 [AAD]

Bach, J.S.:Cant 37, w. A. Augér (sop), C. Watkinson (mez), P. Huttenlocher (bar), H. Rilling (cnd), Stuttgart Bach Collegium, Gächinger Kantorei [G] *(rec 1979)* Hänssler Classic ▲ 98.886 [AAD]

Bach, J.S.:Cant 40, w. V. Gohl (mez), S. Nimsgern (b-bar), H. Rilling (cnd), Stuttgart Bach Collegium, Stuttgart Gedächtnis Figural Choir [G] *(rec June-July 1970)* Hänssler Classic ▲ 98.824 [AAD]

Bach, J.S.:Cant 41, w. H. Donath (sop), M. Höffgen (mez), S. Nimsgern (b-bar), H. Rilling (cnd), Stuttgart Bach Collegium, Gächinger Kantorei [G] Hänssler Classic ▲ 98.870 [AAD]

Bach, J.S.:Cant 46, w. H. Watts (cta), W. Schöne (bass), H. Rilling (cnd), Stuttgart Bach Collegium, Gächinger Kantorei Hänssler Classic ▲ 98.808 [AAD]

Bach, J.S.:Cant 55, w. H. Rilling (cnd), Stuttgart Bach Collegium, Gächinger Kantorei [G] *(rec 1982)* Hänssler Classic ▲ 98.819 [AAD]

Bach, J.S.:Cant 60, w. H. Watts (cta), P. Huttenlocher (bar), H. Rilling (cnd), Stuttgart Bach Collegium, Gächinger Kantorei [G] *(rec 1977 & 1978)* Hänssler Classic ▲ 98.821 [AAD]

Bach, J.S.:Cant 63, w. A. Augér (sop), J. Hamarī (mez), H. Laurich (cta), W. Heldwein (bass), W. Schöne (bass), H. Rilling (cnd), Stuttgart Bach Collegium, Gächinger Kantorei [G] *(rec Feb 1971 & Feb 1981)* Hänssler Classic ▲ 98.823 [AAD]

Bach, J.S.:Cant 66, w. G. Schreckenbach (cta), P. Huttenlocher (bar), W. Schöne (bass), H. Rilling (cnd), Stuttgart Bach Collegium, Gächinger Kantorei [G] *(rec 1981)* Hänssler Classic ▲ 98.880 [AAD]

Bach, J.S.:Cant 69, w. H. Donath (sop), J. Hamari (b-bar), W. Schöne (bass), H. Rilling (cnd), Bach Ensemble *(rec Mar-Apr 1973)* Hänssler Classic ▲ 98.829 [AAD]

Bach, J.S.:Cant 74, w. H. Donath (sop), H. Laurich (cta), P. Huttenlocher (bar), H. Rilling (cnd), Stuttgart Bach Collegium, Gächinger Kantorei Hänssler Classic ▲ 98.887 [AAD]

Bach, J.S.:Cant 75, w. I. Reichelt, V. Gohl (mez), J. Hamari (cta), A. Baldin (ten), H.-F. Kunz (bass), H. Rilling (cnd), Stuttgart Bach Collegium, Frankfurt Kantorei [G] *(rec 1970)* Hänssler Classic ▲ 98.891 [AAD]

Bach, J.S.:Cant 77, w. P. Esswood (ct), M. van Egmond (b-bar), G. Leonhardt (cnd), Leonhardt Consort [G] Teldec 2-▲ 2292-42576-2 [ADD]

Kraus, Adalbert (ten) (cont.)

Bach, J.S.:Cant 77, w. H. Donath (sop), J. Hamari (mez), W. Schöne (bar), H. Rilling (cnd), Stuttgart Bach Collegium, Gächinger Kantorei Hänssler Classic ▲ 98.809 [AAD]

Bach, J.S.:Cant 81, w. J. Hamari (mez), S. Nimsgern (b-bar), H. Rilling (cnd), Bach Ensemble [G] *(rec 1984)* Hänssler Classic ▲ 98.876 [AAD]

Bach, J.S.:Cant 83, w. H. Watts (cta), W. Heldwein (bass), H. Rilling (cnd), Bach Ensemble [G] *(rec 1979)* Hänssler Classic ▲ 98.875 [AAD]

Bach, J.S.:Cant 86, w. A. Augér (mez), H. Watts (cta), W. Heldwein (bass), H. Rilling (cnd), Stuttgart Bach Collegium, Gächinger Kantorei [G] *(rec 1979)* Hänssler Classic ▲ 98.885 [AAD]

Bach, J.S.:Cant 88, w. I. Reichelt (sop), V. Gohl (mez), W. Schöne (bass), H. Rilling (cnd), Stuttgart Bach Collegium, Remembrance Florid Church Chorus Hänssler Classic ▲ 98.804 [AAD]

Bach, J.S.:Cant 90, w. H. Watts (cta), H. Rilling (cnd), Stuttgart Bach Collegium, Gächinger Kantorei [G] *(rec 1977 & 1978)* Hänssler Classic ▲ 98.821 [AAD]

Bach, J.S.:Cant 91, w. H. Donath (sop), H. Watts (cta), W. Schöne (bass), H. Rilling (cnd), Stuttgart Bach Collegium, Württemberg CO, Gächinger Kantorei, Frankfurt Choir [G] *(rec Feb 1972)* Hänssler Classic ▲ 98.822 [AAD]

Bach, J.S.:Cant 95, w. A. Augér (sop), W. Heldwein (bass), H. Rilling (cnd), Stuttgart Bach Collegium, Württemberg CO, Gächinger Kantorei Hänssler Classic ▲ 98.812 [AAD]

Bach, J.S.:Cant 96, w. H. Donath (sop), M. Höffgen (mez), S. Nimsgern (b-bar), H. Rilling (cnd), Stuttgart Bach Collegium, Württemberg CO, Gächinger Kantorei [G] *(rec 1973)* Hänssler Classic ▲ 98.814 [AAD]

Bach, J.S.:Cant 97, w. H. Donath (sop), H. Gardow (sop), P. Huttenlocher (bar), H. Rilling (cnd), Bach Ensemble *(rec Jan-Feb 1974)* Hänssler Classic ▲ 98.835 [AAD]

Bach, J.S.:Cant 100, w. A. Augér (sop), J. Hamari (cta), P. Huttenlocher (bar), H. Rilling (cnd), Württemberg CO, Gächinger Kantorei [G] *(rec 1983-84)* Hänssler Classic 5-▲ 98.976

Bach, J.S.:Cant 106, "Actus tragicus", w. E. Csapò (sop), H. Schwarz (cta), W. Schöne (bass), H. Rilling (cnd), Bach Ensemble *(rec Jan 1975)* Hänssler Classic ▲ 98.830 [AAD]

Bach, J.S.:Cant 113, w. A. Augér (sop), G. Schreckenbach (cta), N. Tüller (bass), H. Rilling (cnd), Stuttgart Bach Collegium, Gächinger Kantorei Hänssler Classic ▲ 98.810 [ADD]

Bach, J.S.:Cant 117, w. M. Georg (mez), A. Schmidt (bar), H. Rilling (cnd), Stuttgart Bach Collegium, Gächinger Kantorei [G] Novalis ▲ 150028 [DDD]

Bach, J.S.:Cant 119, w. A. Augér (sop), A. Murray (mez), W. Schöne (bass), H. Rilling (cnd), Bach Ensemble *(rec Sept & Dec 1977 & Jan 197)* Hänssler Classic ▲ 98.828 [AAD]

Bach, J.S.:Cant 120, w. H. Donath (sop), H. Laurich (cta), W. Schöne (bass), H. Rilling (cnd), Bach Ensemble *(rec Mar-Apr 1973)* Hänssler Classic ▲ 98.829 [AAD]

Bach, J.S.:Cant 121, w. A. Augér (sop), D. Soffel (cta), W. Schöne (bass), H. Rilling (cnd), Stuttgart Bach Collegium, Gächinger Kantorei [G] *(rec Feb & Apr 1980)* Hänssler Classic ▲ 98.824 [AAD]

Bach, J.S.:Cant 122, w. A. Augér (sop), G. Schreckenbach (cta), N. Tüller (bass), H. Rilling (cnd), Stuttgart Bach Collegium, Frankfurt Kantorei [G] *(rec Feb 1972)* Hänssler Classic ▲ 98.826 [AAD]

Bach, J.S.:Cant 126, w. H. Watts (cta), W. Schöne (bass), H. Rilling (cnd), Stuttgart Bach Collegium, Gächinger Kantorei [G] *(rec 1980)* Hänssler Classic ▲ 98.878 [AAD]

Bach, J.S.:Cant 135, w. H. Watts (cta), P. Huttenlocher (bar), Stuttgart Bach Collegium, Gächinger Kantorei Hänssler Classic ▲ 98.802 [AAD]

Bach, J.S.:Cant 139, w. I. Nelson (sop), H. Watts (cta), P. Huttenlocher (bar), H. Rilling (cnd), Stuttgart Bach Collegium, Gächinger Kantorei [G] *(rec 1979 & 1980)* Hänssler Classic ▲ 98.820 [AAD]

Bach, J.S.:Cant 143, w. E. Csapò (sop), W. Schöne (bass), H. Rilling (cnd), Stuttgart Bach Collegium [G] Hänssler Classic ▲ 98.870 [AAD]

Bach, J.S.:Cant 144, w. A. Augér (sop), H. Watts (cta), H. Rilling (cnd), Bach Ensemble [G] *(rec 1978)* Hänssler Classic ▲ 98.876 [AAD]

Bach, J.S.:Cant 145, w. C. Cuccaro (sop), A. Schmidt (bass), H. Rilling (cnd), Stuttgart Bach Collegium, Gächinger Kantorei [G] Novalis ▲ 150029 [DDD]

Bach, J.S.:Cant 151, w. N. Gamo-Yamamoto (sop), H. Laurich (cta), H.-F. Kunz (bass), H. Rilling (cnd), Stuttgart Bach Collegium, Frankfurt Kantorei [G] *(rec Feb 1971)* Hänssler Classic ▲ 98.825 [AAD]

Bach, J.S.:Cant 153, w. A. Murray (mez), W. Heldwein (bass), H. Rilling (cnd), Stuttgart Bach Collegium, Gächinger Kantorei [G] Hänssler Classic ▲ 98.871 [AAD]

Bach, J.S.:Cant 157, w. P. Huttenlocher (bar), H. Rilling (cnd), Bach Ensemble *(rec Oct 1982, July 1983)* Hänssler Classic ▲ 98.835 [AAD]

Bach, J.S.:Cant 161, w. H. Laurich (cta), H. Rilling (cnd), Stuttgart Bach Collegium, Gächinger Kantorei Hänssler Classic ▲ 98.812 [AAD]

Bach, J.S.:Cant 163, w. A. Augér (sop), H. Watts (cta), N. Tüller (bass), H. Rilling (cnd), Stuttgart Bach Collegium, Gächinger Kantorei [G] *(rec 1976 & 1977)* Hänssler Classic ▲ 98.820 [AAD]

Bach, J.S.:Cant 167, w. K. Graf (sop), H. Gardow (sop), N. Tüller (bass), H. Rilling (cnd), Stuttgart Bach Collegium, Remembrance Florid Church Chorus Hänssler Classic ▲ 98.803 [AAD]

Bach, J.S.:Cant 180, w. A. Augér (sop), C. Watkinson (cta), W. Heldwein (sop), H. Rilling (cnd), Stuttgart Bach Collegium, Gächinger Kantorei [G] *(rec Feb & Oct 1979)* Hänssler Classic ▲ 98.816 [AAD]

Bach, J.S.:Cant 198, w. J. Beckmann (sop), W. Heldwein (bass), H. Rilling (cnd), Stuttgart Bach Collegium, Gächinger Kantorei [G] *(rec Sept 1976 & Jan 1977)* Hänssler Classic ▲ 98.827 [AAD]

Bach, J.S.:Easter Oratorio, w. A. Augér (sop), J. Hamari (cta), P. Huttenlocher (bar), H. Rilling (cnd), Stuttgart Bach Collegium, Gächinger Kantorei [G] *(rec 1980-81)* Hänssler Classic 5-▲ 98.976

Bach, J.S.:Magnificat, BWV 243, w. A. Augér (sop), A. Murray (mez), H. Watts (cta), P. Huttenlocher (bar), W. Schöne (bass), H. Rilling (cnd), Stuttgart Bach Collegium, Gächinger Kantorei *(rec 1979)* Sony Classical ("Essential Classics" series) ▲ SBK 48280 [ADD] ■ SBT 48280

Bach, J.S.:St. John Passion, w. C. Schäfer (sop), Y. Jänicke (mez), R. Hagen (bass), B. Possemeyer (bass), E. Weyand (cnd), Stuttgart Hymnus Orch, Stuttgart Hymnus Boys' Choir [G] *(rec 1990)* Hänssler Classic 2-▲ 98.968

Bellini, V.:I Puritani (sels), w. J. Sutherland (sop), D. Cole (sop), R. Wolansky (bar), N. Ghiuselev (bass), R. Bonynge (cnd), San Francisco Opera Orch, San Francisco Opera Chorus *(rec live, San Francisco, 9/2/66)* Golden Age of Opera ▲ GAO 133 [ADD]

Bellini, V.:La sonnambula, w. R. Scotto (sop), I. Vinco (bass), N. Santi (cnd), Venice Teatro La Fenice Orch, Venice Teatro La Fenice Chorus [I] *(rec live, Venice 5/26/61)* Golden Age of Opera 2-▲ GAO 111/12 [ADD]

Carrion, M.R.:La Tempestad, w. L. Huarte (sop), D. Perez (sop), F. Kraus (bar), R. Alonso (bass), S. Ramalle (bass), E. Estella (cnd), Concierto Montilla Orch, Concierto Montilla Chorus Montilla ▲ MON 3011 [ADD]

Cherubini, L.:Ali Baba, ou Les Quarante voleurs, w. T. Stich-Randall (sop), V. Ganzarolli (bar), N. Sanzogno (cnd), La Scala Orch, La Scala Chorus *(rec 1963)* Memories 2-▲ MEM 4513 [ADD]

Donizetti, G.:Don Pasquale, w. G. D'Angelo (sop), R. Capecchi (bar), F. Corena (bass), U. d'Alessio (sgr), A. Erede (cnd), Naples Teatro San Carlo Orch, Naples Teatro San Carlo Chorus [I] *(rec live in Edinburgh, 9/7/63)* Verona 2-▲ 27023/24 (m) [AAD]

Donizetti, G.:La favorita (sels), w. M. Zotti (sop), F. Cossotto (mez), R. Raimondi (bass), O. de Fabritiis (cnd), NHK SO *(rec Sept. 13, 1971)* Myto 2-▲ MCD 93276

Donizetti, G.:La fille du régiment, w. J. Sutherland (sop), R. Resnik (mez), S. Maias (bass), R. Bonynge (cnd), Chicago Lyric Opera Orch, Chicago Lyric Opera Chorus [F] *(rec Nov. 20, 1973)* Myto 2-▲ MCD 93276

Donizetti, G.:Lucia di Lammermoor, w. R. Scotto (sop), P. Washington (bar), Sesto Bruscantini (bass-bar), B. Rigacci (cnd), *(orch unknown)* *(rec 1963)* Great Opera Performances 2-▲ GOP 747

Donizetti, G.:Lucia di Lammermoor, w. E. Gruberová (sop), D. Lloyd (ten), R. Bruson (bar), Royal PO, Ambrosian Opera Chorus *(rec 1983)* EMI Classics ▲ CDMB 64622

Donizetti, G.:Lucia di Lammermoor, w. B. Sills (sop), G. Mastromei (bar), V. de Narke (bass), J.E. Martini (cnd), Buenos Aires Teatro Colón Orch, Buenos Aires Teatro Colón Chorus *(rec 1968)* Arkadia 2-▲ 474

Gounod, C.:Faust, w. R. Scotto (sop), N. Ghiaurov (bass), P. Ethuin, *(orch unknown)* [F] *(rec live, Tokyo, 1973)* Standing Room Only 3-▲ SRO 811-3 [ADD]

Gounod, C.:Roméo et Juliette, w. C. Malfitano (sop), L. Quilico (bar), J. Van Dam (b-bar), G. Bacquier (bar), M. Plasson (cnd), Toulouse Capitole Orch, Toulouse Capitole Chorus [F] EMI Classics 3-▲ CDCC 47365

Haydn, J.:Die Jahreszeiten, w. Helen Donath (sop), Kurt Widmer (bass), W. Gönnenwein (cnd), Ludwigsburg Festival Orch, South German Madrigal Choir [G] Vox Box 2-▲ CDX 5045 [ADD]

Kraus, Adalbert (ten) (cont.)

Haydn, J.:Mass 14, "Harmoniemesse", w. Barbara Martig-Tüller (sop), Ria Bollen (alt), Kurt Widmer (bass), Melitta Veits (org), D. Hellmann (cnd), Southwest German RSO Baden-Baden Calig ▲ CAL 50490

Haydn, J.:Die Schöpfung, w. Helen Donath (sop), Scherr (alt), Kurt Widmer (bass), W. Gönnenwein (cnd), Ludwigsburg Festival Orch, South German Madrigal Choir [G] Vox Box 2-▲ CDX 5025 [ADD]

Lehár, F.:Die lustige Witwe, w. E. Schwarzkopf (sop), E. Loose (sop), N. Gedda (ten), E. Kunz (bar), O. Ackermann (cnd), Philharmonia Orch, Philharmonia Chorus [G] EMI Classics ("Studio" series) ▲ CDH 69520 (m) [ADD]

Lortzing, A.:Zar und Zimmermann (sels), w. Lucia Popp (sop), Hermann Prey (bar), Fritz Krenn (bass), Karl Ridderbusch (bass), H. Wallberg (cnd), Bavarian RSO, Bavarian Radio Chorus [G] Acanta 2-▲ CD 42424 [DDD]

Massenet, J.:Manon (sels), w. V. Zeani (sop), U. Rapalo (cnd), Naples Teatro San Carlo Orch—2 tenor arias & 2 soprano-tenor duets *(rec live, Naples 2/29/64)* Bongiovanni 2-▲ GB 550/51

Massenet, J.:Manon (sels), w. R. Scotto (sop)—three scenes for soprano-tenor duet [F] *(rec live, 1983)* Standing Room Only 3-▲ SRO 811-3 [ADD]

Massenet, J.:Werther, w. V. Zeani (sop), D. Trimarchi (bar), M. Basiola (bar), A. Votto (cnd), *(orch unknown)* *(rec Palermo, 1971)* Great Opera Performances 2-▲ GOP 749

Mozart, W.A.:Così fan tutte, w. E. Schwarzkopf (sop), H. Steffek (sop), C. Ludwig (mez), G. Taddei (bar), W. Berry (bass), K. Böhm (cnd), Philharmonia Orch, Philharmonia Chorus [I] EMI Classics ("Studio" series) 3-▲ CDMC 69330 [ADD]

Mozart, W.A.:Don Giovanni, w. G. Janowitz (sop), S. Jurinac (sop), G. von Milivkovic (mez), N. Ghiaurov (bass), C. M. Giulini (cnd), Rome RAI Orch, Rome RAI Chorus *(rec live, May 12, 1970)* Melodram 3-▲ MEL 37080

Mozart, W.A.:Don Giovanni, w. G. Janowitz (sop), T. Zylis-Gara (sop), M. Freni (sop), R. Panerai (bar), V. von Halem (bass), N. Ghiaurov (bass), H. von Karajan (cnd), Vienna PO, Vienna State Opera Chorus [I] *(rec live, Salzburg, Aug. 1, 1969)* Memories 3-▲ HR 4362/64 (m) [ADD]

Mozart, W.A.:Zauberflöte, w. S. Jo (sop), R. Ziesak (sop), U. Heilmann (ten), K. Moll (bass), G. Solti (cnd), Vienna PO, Vienna State Opera Chorus London 2-▲ 433210-2 [DDD]

Mozart, W.A.:Zauberflöte (sels), w. S. Jo (sop), R. Ziesak (sop), U. Heilmann (ten), K. Moll (bass), G. Solti (cnd), Vienna PO, Vienna State Opera Chorus London ▲ 433667-2 [DDD]

Puccini, G.:Tosca (sels), w. M. Callas (sop), R. Scotto (sop), C. Bergonzi (ten), T. Gobbi (bar), G. Prêtre (cnd), Orch de Paris EMI Classics ▲ ZDM 63087

Rossini, G.:Il barbiere di Siviglia (sels), w. R. Scotto (sop), A. di Stasio (mez), A. Protti (bar), C. Badioli (bass), E. Campi (bass), V. Bellezza (cnd), Naples Teatro San Carlo Orch, Naples Teatro San Carlo Chorus *(rec July 26, 1958)* Golden Age of Opera 2-▲ GAO 137/38 [ADD]

Verdi, G.:Rigoletto, w. A. Moffo (sop), R. Elias (mez), R. Merrill (bar), G. Solti (cnd), RCA Italian Opera Orch, RCA Italiana Opera Chorus [I] RCA Gold Seal ▲ 60203-2-RG ■ 60203-4-RG

Verdi, G.:Rigoletto, w. A. Moffo (sop), R. Elias (mez), R. Merrill (bar), G. Solti (cnd), RCA Italian Opera Orch, RCA Italiana Opera Chorus [I] RCA Gold Seal 2-▲ 6506-2-RG [ADD]

Verdi, G.:La traviata, w. B. Sills (sop), M. Zotti (sop), G. Borelli (mez), M. Zanasi (bar), A. Ceccato (cnd), Naples Teatro San Carlo Orch, Naples Teatro San Carlo Chorus *(rec live 1/17/70)* Melodram 2-▲ MEL 27063 (m) [AAD]

Verdi, G.:La traviata, w. M. Callas (sop), M. Sereni (bar), F. Ghione (cnd), Lisbon Teatro São Carlos Orch [I] *(rec live, Lisbon 3/27/58)* EMI Classics 2-▲ CDCB 49187

Verdi, G.:La traviata, w. K. Te Kanawa (sop), D. Hvorostovsky (bar), Z. Mehta (cnd), Florence Maggio Musicale Orch, Florence Maggio Musicale Chorus [I] Philips 2-▲ 438238-2

Kraus, Alfredo (ten)

Alfredo Kraus, w. Manuel de Falla Orch [cnd:Nicola Rescigno] Bongiovanni ▲ GB 535-2 [ADD]

Alfredo Kraus, w. Manuel de Falla Orch [cnd:Nicola Rescigno] Bongiovanni ▲ GB 536-2 [ADD]

Alfredo Kraus Memories ("Great Voices" series) 2-▲ MEM 4233 (m)

Alfredo Kraus, w. Manuel de Falla Orch [cnd:Nicola Rescigno] *(rec Spain, 1975)* Bongiovanni ▲ GB 534

Alfredo Kraus in Concerto, w. Italian Music Academy Orch [cnd:Franco Mannino], Felix Ayo (vn) *(rec live Apr. 3, 1989)* Fonit Cetra ▲ CDC 42 [DDD]

Arie Antiche, w. José Tordesillas (pno) Nimbus ▲ NI 5102 [DDD]

The Art of Alfredo Kraus, w. Canaria Grand PO [cnd:Gian Paolo Sanzogno], Edemiro Arnaltes (pno) RNE/Spanish Radio 3-▲ 65015/16/17

Bellini, V.:I Puritani, w. Mirella Freni (sop—Elvira), Rita Bezzi (mez—Enrichetta), Alfredo Kraus (ten—Arturo Talbot), Augusto Pedroni (ten—Sir Bruno Robertson), Attilio d'Orazi (bar—Sir Riccardo Forth), Raffaele Arié (bass—Sir Giorgio), Bruno Cioni (bass—Lord Gualtiero Walton), N. Verchi (cnd), Modena Teatro Comunale Orch, Modeno Teatro Comunale Chorus *(rec Modena Teatro Comunale, Dec. 26, 1962)* Legato Classics 2-▲ LCD 195-2 [ADD]

Canzoni Spagnole, w. Madrid CO *(rec 1960s)* Bongiovanni ▲ GB 510-2 [ADD]

Donizetti, G.:Don Pasquale, w. Ileana Cotrubas (sop), Wladimiro Ganzarolli (bar), Vincente Sardinero (bar), Sutliff (sgr), B. Bartoletti (cnd), Chicago Lyric Opera Orch, Chicago Lyric Opera Chorus *(rec live, Chicago, Nov. 2, 1974)* Arkadia 2-▲ 490

Donizetti, G.:Don Pasquale, w. Beverly Sills (sop), Alan Titus (bar), Donald Gramm (b-bar), S. Caldwell (cnd), London SO, Ambrosian Opera Chorus EMI Classics 2-▲ CDMB 66030

Donizetti, G.:Don Pasquale, w. Gianna D'Angelo (sop), Renato Capecchi (bar), Fernando Corena (bass), Ugo D'Alessio (sgr), A. Erede (cnd), Naples Teatro San Carlo Orch, Naples Teatro San Carlo Chorus Great Opera Performances 2-▲ GOP 763

Donizetti, G.:Don Pasquale, w. Margherita Guglielmi (sop—Norina), Alfredo Kraus (ten—Ernesto), Rolando Panerai (bar—Malatesta), Paolo Montarsolo (bass—Don Pasquale), P. Bellugi (cnd), La Scala Orch, La Scala Chorus *(rec Jan 13, 1974)* Golden Age of Opera 2-▲ GAO 202/203 [ADD]

Donizetti, G.:Lucrezia Borgia, w. J. Sutherland (sop—Lucrezia Borgia), A. Howells (mez—Maffio Orsini), A. Kraus (ten—Gennaro), R. Leggate (ten—Liverotto), J. Summers (bar—Apostolo Gazella), P. Hudson (bass-bar—Gubetta), S. Dean (bass—Don Alfonso), R. Bonynge (cnd), Royal Opera House Orch *(rec London, Apr. 9, 1980)* Ornamenti 2-▲ FE 111 [ADD]

Granada, w. Manuel de Falla Orch [cnd:Nicola Rescigno] *(rec 1960s)* Bongiovanni ▲ GB 533-2 [ADD]

The Incomparable Alfredo Kraus, w. Welsh National Opera Orch, Welsh National Opera Chorus [cnd:Carlo Rizzi] Philips ▲ 442785-2

James Levine's 25th Anniversary Metropolitan Opera Gala, w. J. Levine (cnd), Metropolitan Opera Orch, Ileana Cotrubas (sop), Renée Fleming (sop), Hei-Kyung Hong (sop), Karita Mattila (sop), Birgit Nilsson (sop), Ruth Ann Swenson (sop), Kiri Te Kanawa (sop), Deborah Voigt (sop), Grace Bumbry (mez), Heidi Grant Murphy (mez), Anne Sofie von Otter (mez) *(rec live, Metropolitan Opera House, New York, Apr 27, 1996)* Deutsche Grammophon ▲ 449177-2 [DDD]

Live at the Paris Opera, w. June Anderson (sop), Paris Opera Orch [cnd:Michelangelo Veltri] EMI Classics ▲ CDC 49067 [DDD]

Live at the Paris Opera

Las mejores arias, w. Madrid SO [cnd:Jose Olmendo] Montilla ▲ MNT 3035

Music from the film *Gayarre* Bongiovanni ▲ GB 501-2 [ADD]

A Singing Masterclass Bongiovanni 2-▲ GB 550/51-2 [DDD]

Verdi, G.:Rigoletto, w. Beverly Sills (sop), Sherill Milnes (bar), Samuel Ramey (bass), J. Rudel (cnd), Philharmonia Orch, Ambrosian Opera Chorus EMI Classics 2-▲ CDMB 724356603721

Kraus, Ernst (ten)

Wagner, R.:Arias & Scenes, w. Emmy Destinn (sop), Lilly Hafgren (sop), Frida Leider (sop), Emmi Leisner (cta), Lauritz Melchoir (ten), Leopold Demuth (bar), Friedrich Schorr (b-bar), Michael Bohynen (bass), Paul Knupfer (bass), Richard Mayr (bass), Heinrich Hensel (sgr), Walter Soomer (sgr) Iron Needle ▲ 1307 (m)

Kraus, Francisco (bar)

Carrion, M.R.:La Tempestad, w. L. Huarte (sop), D. Perez (sop), A. Kraus (ten), R. Alonso (bass), S. Ramalle (bass), E. Estella (cnd), Concierto Montilla Orch, Concierto Montilla Chorus Montilla ▲ MON 3011 [ADD]

Kraus, Herbert (ten)

Boito, A.:Mefistofele, w. R. Tebaldi (sop—Margheritta), E. Souliotis (sop—Elena), M. Mackenzie (mez—Marta), M. Ruggiero (mez—Pantalis), A. Kraus (ten—Faust), H. Kraus (ten—Wagner), N. Ghiaurov (bass—Mefistofele), N. Sanzogno (cnd), *(orch unknown)* Ornamenti 2-▲ FE 101

Kraus, Herbert (ten) (cont.)

Wagner, R.:Der Ring des Nibelungen, w. Liselotte Becker-Egner (sop—Woglinde/Ortlinde/Wellgunde), Angelika Berger (sop—Wellgunde/Waltraute), Siw Ericsdotter (sop—Norn 3), Heidemaria Ferch (sop—Freia/Gerhilde), Bella Jasper (sop—Helmwige/Waldvogel/Woglinde), Ditha Sommer (sop—Sieglinde/Gutrune), Ursula Boese (mez—Erda), Ruth Hesse (mez—Fricka), Nadezda Kniplová (mez—Brünnhilde), Margit Kobeck (mez—Schwertleite/Norn 2), Hilde Rosner (mez—Flosshilde/Siegrunde), Erica Schubert (mez—Grimgerde/Flosshilde), Ingrid Göritz (cta—Rossweisse/Norn 1), Herbert Doussant (ten—Froh), Herold Kraus (ten—Mime), Gerald McKee (ten—Siegmund/Siegfried), Fritz Uhl (ten—Loge), Rudolf Knoll (bar—Gunther/Donner), Rolf Polke (bass-bar—Wotan/Wanderer), Rolf Kühne (bass—Alberich), Takao Okamura (bass—Fafner), Otto von Rohr (bass—Hagen/Fasolt/Hunding), H. Swarowsky (cnd), Czech PO, Prague National Theater Orch *(rec June 3 & 5, July 26-31, A)* Weltbild Classics 14-▲ 703769 [ADD]

Kraus, Michael (ten)

Goldschmidt, B.:Der gewaltige Hahnrei, w. R. Alexander (sop), M. Posselt (sop), H. Lawrence (sop), R. Wörle (ten), M. Petzold (ten), C. Otelli (bar), L. Zagrosek (cnd), German SO, Berlin Radio Chorus London ▲ 440850-2 [DDD]

Goldschmidt, B.:Mediterranean Songs, w. R. Alexander (sop), M. Posselt (sop), H. Lawrence (sop), R. Wörle (ten), M. Petzold (ten), C. Otelli (bar), L. Zagrosek (cnd), German SO, Berlin Radio Chorus London ▲ 440850-2 [DDD]

Krenek, E.:Jonny spielt auf, w. A. Marc (sop), H. Kruse (ten), K. St. Hill (ten), L. Zagrosek (cnd), Leipzig Gewandhaus Orch [G] London 2-▲ 436631-2 [DDD]

Ullmann, V.:Kaiser von Atlantis, w. C. Oelze (sop—Bubikopf), I. Vermillion (mez—The Drummer), M. Petzold (ten—A Soldier), M. Kraus (ten—Kaiser Overall), H. Lippert (ten—Harlekin), F. Mazura (bar—The Loudspeaker), W. Berry (bass—Death), L. Zagrosek (cnd), Leipzig Gewandhaus Orch London ▲ 440854-2 [DDD]

Kraus, Otakar (sgr)

Britten, H.:The Rape of Lucretia (sels), w. Joan Cross (sop—Female Chorus), Kathleen Ferrier (cta—Lucretia), Peter Pears (ten—Male Chorus), Otakar Kraus (sgr—Tarquinius), B. Britten (cnd), English Opera Group Orch *(rec Oct 5, 1946)* Music & Arts ▲ CD 901 [ADD]

Krause, Anita (mez)

Rossini, G.:Mosè in Egitto (sels), w. Wendy Nielsen (sop—Elcia), Anita Krause (mez—Amenosi), Richard Margison (ten—Aronne), Gary Relyea (b-bar—Mosè), R. Bradshaw (cnd), Canadian Opera Company Orch, Canadian Opera Company Chorus—Scena, Coro & Preghiera [Dal tuo stellato soglio] *(rec George Weston Recital Hall, Ford Centre for the Performing Arts, North York, Ontario, Dec 20-23, 1994)* CBC ("SM 5000" series) ▲ SM5 5148 [DDD]

Krause, Michael (sgr)

Braunfels, W.:Die Vögel, w. Helen Kwon (sop—Nightingale), Wolfgang Holzmair (bar—Hoopoe), Matthias Gorne (b-bar—Prometheus), Michael Krause (sgr—Loyal Friend), Endrik Wottrich (sgr—Good Hope), L. Zagrosek (cnd), Berlin German SO, Berlin Radio Chorus London ("Entartete Musik" series) ▲ 448 679-2

Krause, Monika (sop)

Verdi, G.:La traviata (sels), w. Ivica Neshybová (sop), Rannveig Braga (mez), Yordy Ramiro (ten), Gerog Tichy (bar), Ladislav Neshyba (bass), Jozef Spaček (bass), A. Rahbari (cnd), Czech-Slovak RSO Bratislava, Jan Rozehnal (cnd), Slovak Phil Chorus—Prelude act I; Libiam ne'lieti calici; Un dí, felice; È strano! Ah, fors'e lui; Follie!...sempre libera; Lunge da lei...de'miei bollenti spiriti; O Mio rimoroso!; Pura si come un angelo...Dite alla giovine; Dammi tu forza; Di Provenza il mar; Noi siamo zingarelle; Prelude act III; Teneste la promessa...Addio del passato; Signora! Che t'accade?; Ah, Violetta! *(rec Bratislava Concert Hall, Dec 1990)* Naxos ▲ 8.553041 [DDD]

Krause, Richard (ten)

Handel, G.F.:Messiah, w. Edith Mathis (sop), James Bowman (alt), Claes Hakan Ahnsjö (ten), A. Dorati (cnd), Smithsonian Concerto Grosso, Univ of Maryland Choral Society [E] Pro Arte 2-▲ CDD 232 [DDD]; ■ PCD 232

Leoncavallo, R.:Pagliacci, w. P. Lorengar (sop), J. McCracken (ten), R. Merrill (bar), U. Benelli (bar), L. Gardelli (cnd), St. Cecilia Academy Orch Rome, St. Cecilia Academy Chorus Rome [I] IMP Collectors Series ▲ IMPX 9017 [AAD]

Verdi, G.:Falstaff, w. M. Freni (sop), I. Ligabue (sop), G. Simionato (mez), R. Elias (mez), G. Evans (bar), R. Merrill (bar), G. Solti (cnd), RCA Italian Opera Orch, RCA Italiana Opera Chorus [I] London 2-▲ 417168-2 [ADD]

Verdi, G.:La traviata, w. R. Braga (mez), Y. Ramiro (ten), A. Rahbari (cnd), Czech-Slovak RSO Bratislava, Slovak Phil Chorus [I] Naxos 2-▲ 8.660011/12 [DDD]

Wagner, R.:Tristan und Isolde, w. B. Nilsson (sop), R. Resnik (mez), H.-M. Uhle (ten), A. van Mill (bass), G. Solti (cnd), Vienna PO [G] London ("Grand Opera" series) 4-▲ 430234-2 [ADD]

Krause, Tom (bar)

Bach, J.S.:Cant 67, w. H. Watts (cta), W. Krenn (ten), E. Ansermet (cnd), Swiss Romande Orch, Lausanne Pro Arte Choir London ("Serenata" series) ▲ 433175-2 [ADD]

Bach, J.S.:Cant 130, w. E. Ameling (sop), H. Watts (cta), W. Krenn (ten), E. Ansermet (cnd), Swiss Romande Orch, Lausanne Pro Arte Choir London ("Serenata" series) ▲ 433175-2 [ADD]

Bach, J.S.:Magnificat, BWV 243, w. E. Ameling (sop), H. van Bork (sop), H. Watts (cta), W. Krenn (ten), K. Münchinger (cnd), Stuttgart CO, Vienna Academy Chorus London ("Serenata" series) ▲ 433175-2 [ADD]

Bach, J.S.:St. Matthew Passion, w. K. Te Kanawa (sop), A. S. von Otter (mez), H. P. Blochwitz (ten), A. Rolfe Johnson (ten), O. Bär (bar), G. Solti (cnd), Chicago SO, Chicago Sym Chorus, Glen Ellyn Children's Chorus [G] London 3-▲ 421177-2 [DDD]

Bach, J.S.:St. Matthew Passion (sels), w. K. Te Kanawa (sop), A. S. von Otter (mez), H. P. Blochwitz (ten), A. Rolfe Johnson (ten), O. Bär (bar), G. Solti (cnd), Chicago SO, Chicago Sym Chorus, Glen Ellyn Children's Chorus [G] London ▲ 425691-2 [DDD]

Beethoven, L. van:Fidelio, w. Birgit Nilsson (sop—Leonore), Graziella Sciutti (sop—Marzelline), Kurt Equiluz (ten—Erster Gefangener), Donald Grobe (ten—Jacquino), James McCracken (ten—Florestan), Tom Krause (bar—Don Pizarro), Hermann Prey (bar—Don Fernando), Kurt Böhme (bass—Rocco), Günther Adam (sgr—Zweiter Gefangener), L. Maazel (cnd), Vienna PO, Vienna State Opera Concert Association Chorus *(rec Sofiensaal, Vienna, Mar 1964)* London 2-▲ 448104-2 [ADD]

Beethoven, L. van:Missa Solemnis, w. S. McNair (sop), Janice Taylor (mez), J. Aler (ten), R. Shaw (cnd), Atlanta SO, Atlanta Sym Chorus [L] Telarc 2-▲ CD 80150 [DDD]

Bizet, G.:Carmen, w. R. Resnik (mez), J. Sutherland (sop), M. Del Monaco (ten), T. Schippers (cnd), Swiss Romande Orch London 2-▲ 411630-2 [ADD]

Bizet, G.:Carmen, w. A. Maliponte (sop), M. Horne (mez), J. McCracken (bar), L. Bernstein (cnd), Metropolitan Opera Orch, Manhattan Opera Chorus [F] *(rec 1973)* Deutsche Grammophon 3-▲ 427440-2 [ADD]

Brahms, J.:Songs, w. I. Gage (pno) *(rec Dec. 2-5, 1990)* Finlandia ▲ 4509-95862-2 [DDD]

Gluck, C.W.:Alceste, w. J. Norman (sop), N. Gedda (ten), B. Weikl (bar), S. Nimsgern (b-bar), S. Baudo (cnd), Bavarian RSO, Bavarian Radio Chorus [French version] Orfeo 3-▲ 027823 [DDD]

Gluck, C.W.:Alceste, w. J. Norman (sop), N. Gedda (ten), B. Weikl (bar), S. Nimsgern (b-bar), S. Baudo (cnd), Bavarian RSO, Bavarian Radio Chorus, *(highlights of above)* Orfeo ▲ 027901 [DDD]

Handel, G.F.:Messiah, w. Joan Sutherland (sop), Huguette Tourangeau (mez), Werner Krenn (ten), R. Bonynge (cnd), English CO, Ambrosian Singers [E] London ("Serenata" series) 2-▲ 433740-2 [ADD]

Mozart, W.A.:Requiem, w. A. Augér (sop), D. Ziegler (mez), J. Hadley (ten), R. Shaw (cnd), Atlanta SO, Atlanta Sym Chorus [L] Telarc ▲ CD 80128 [DDD]

Mussorgsky, M.:Songs & Dances, w. I. Gage (pno)—4 sels. *(rec Dec. 2-5, 1990)* Finlandia ▲ 4509-95862-2 [DDD]

Rossini, G.:Stabat Mater, w. O. Liani (sop), J. Jaques (mez), M. Zamfir (ten), P. Crispini (cnd), Geneva Elans Orch Ensemble, Geneva Elans Vocal Ensemble [L] Gallo ▲ CD 487

Schubert, Franz:Winterreise, w. G. Djupsjöbacka (pno) Finlandia ▲ 4509-95876-2 [DDD]

Schumann, R.:Dichterliebe, w. I. Gage (pno) *(rec Dec. 2-5, 1990)* Finlandia ▲ 4509-95862-2 [DDD]

Strauss (II), Joh.:Die Fledermaus, w. K. Te Kanawa (sop), E. Gruberová (sop), B. Fassbaender (mez), W. Brendel (bar), R. Leech (ten), O. Bär (bar), A. Previn (cnd), Vienna PO, Vienna State Opera Chorus [G] Philips 2-▲ 432157-2 [DDD]

Strauss, R.:Elektra, w. B. Nilsson (sop), M. Collier (sop), R. Resnik (mez), G. Stolze (ten), G. Solti (cnd), Vienna PO [G] London 2-▲ 417345-2 [ADD]

▲ = CD ♦ = Enhanced CD Δ = MD ■ = Cassette Tape ▯ = DCC

Krause, Tom (bar) (cont.)
Weber, C.M. von:Euryanthe, w. Jessye Norman (sop), Rita Hunter (sop), Nicolai Gedda (ten), M. Janowski (cnd), Dresden Staatskapelle, Leipzig Radio Chorus Berlin Classics 3-▲ BER 1108 [ADD]

Krauss, Fritz (ten)
Wagner, R.:Tannhäuser, w. T. Eipperle (sop), K. Schmitt-Walter (bar), S. Nilsson (bass), C. Leonhardt (cnd), Stuttgart Radio Orch, Stuttgart Radio Chorus [G] *(rec Oct. 24, 1937, mat. 39695)* Preiser 3-▲ 90133 (m) [AAD]
Wagner, R.:Die Walküre (sels), w. M. Reining (sop), H. Jung (mez), R. Bockelmann (bar), J. von Manowarda (bass), C. Leonhardt (cnd), Stuttgart Radio Orch—Act 2 (sels.); Act 3 (complete) *(rec Apr. 3, 1938)* Preiser 2-▲ PRE 90207 [ADD]
Wagner, R.:Die Walküre (sels), w. M. Reining (sop), C. Leonhardt (cnd), Stuttgart Radio Orch—4 solo arias from Act I Scene 3 *(Der Männer Sippe; Winterstürme wichen dem Wonnenmond; Du bist der Lenz; Siegmund heiss ich) [G] (rec April 3, 1938)* Preiser 3-▲ 90133 (m) [AAD]
Wagner, R.:Die Walküre (act 1), w. M. Reining (sop), J. von Manowarda (bass), C. Leonhardt (cnd), Stuttgart Reichssenders Orch *(rec April 28, 1940)* Preiser ▲ 90151 (m)

Krauss, H. (sgr)
Giordano, U.:Andrea Chénier, w. Montserrat Caballé (sop), Franco Corelli (ten), R. de Carlo (sgr), D. Dondi (sgr), G. Ellsworth (sgr), J. Fair (sgr), R. Falk (sgr), S. Felter (sgr), E. Green (sgr), H. Hicks (sgr), L. Miller (sgr), N. Riggins (sgr), H. Salerno (sgr), A. Guadagno (cnd), Academy of Music Orch, Academy of Music Chorus Great Opera Performances 2-▲ GOP 766

Kravtsova, Tatyana (sgr)
Tchaikovsky, P.:Iolanta, w. Galina Gorchakova (sop), Nikolai Gassiev (ten), Gegam Grigorian (ten), Dmitri Hvorostovsky (bar), Nikolai Putilin (bar), Sergei Alexashkin (bass), Gennady Bezzubenkov (bass), Larissa Diadkova (sgr), Olga Korzhenskaya (sgr), V. Gergiev (cnd), Kirov Opera Orch, Kirov Opera Chorus *(rec Mariinsky Theatre, St. Petersburg)* Philips 2-▲ 442796-2

Krebs, Helmut (ten)
Mahler, G.:Sym 3, w. D. Mitropoulos (cnd), New York PO *(rec live, Carnegie Hall, 4/15/56)* Arkadia ▲ 557 [AAD]
Mozart, W.A.:Entführung, w. S. Barabas (sop), R. Streich (sop), A. Dermota (ten), J. Greindl (bass), F. Fricsay (cnd), Berlin RSO, Berlin Radio Chorus [G] *(rec Jesus-Christuskirche, Berlin-Dahlem, Dec. 19-21, 1949)* Myto 2-▲ 2 MCD 92361 [ADD]
Mozart, W.A.:Missa, K.317, w. Maria Stader (sop), Sieglinde Wagner (mez), Josef Griendl (bass), I. Markevitch (cnd), Berlin PO, St. Hedwig's Cathedral Choir Deutsche Grammophon 2-▲ 437383-2
Strauss (II), Joh.:Die Fledermaus, w. E. Schwarzkopf (sop), R. Streich (sop), N. Gedda (ten), R. Christ (ten), E. Kunz (bar), K. Dönch (bar), H. von Karajan (cnd), Philharmonia Orch, Philharmonia Chorus [G] EMI Classics ("Studio" series) 2-▲ CDHB 69531 (m) [ADD]
Strauss (II), Joh.:Die Fledermaus, w. R. Streich (sop), A. Schlemm (mez), P. Anders (ten), F. Fricsay (cnd), Berlin RSO, Berlin Radio Chorus [G] *(rec live, Berlin, 11/8/49)* Melodram 2-▲ MEL 29001 (m) [AAD]
Verdi, G.:Requiem Mass, w. Maria Stader (sop), Marjana Radev (mez), Kim Borg (bass), F. Fricsay (cnd), Berlin RIAS SO, Berlin RIAS Chamber Choir, St. Hedwig Cathedral Choir *(rec Jesus-Christus Church, Berlin, Sept 1953)* Deutsche Grammophon ("The Originals" series) ▲ 447442-2 [ADD]

Kreen, Uno (bass)
Tubin, E.:Barbara von Tisenhusen, w. H. Raamat (sop), M. Jõgeva (mez), A. Kollo (ten), I. Kuusk (ten), V. Puura (bar), T. Sild (bar), H. Miilberg (bass), P. Lilje (cnd), Estonia Opera Co Orch [Estonian] Ondine 2-▲ ODE 776-2D [DDD]

Kreile, Karl (sgr)
Hindemith, P.:Mathis der Maler, w. Urszula Koszut (sop), Trudeliese Schmidt (mez), Rose Wagemann (mez), William Cochran (ten), Donald Grobe (ten), James King (ten), Manfred Schmidt (ten), Dietrich Fischer-Dieskau (bar), Gerd Feldhoff (bass), Alexander Malta (bass), Peter Meven (bass), R. Kubelik (cnd), Bavarian RSO, Bavarian Radio Chorus EMI Classics 2-▲ CDCC 55237

Kreis, Christiane (sop)
Distler, H.:Mörike-Chorliederbuch, w. Juliane Mechler (alt), Hendrik Ritter (ten), Bernd Stegmann (cnd), Berlin Vocal Ensemble *(rec Herrenberg, Jan 2-4, 1992)* Musicaphon ▲ BM 56820

Krejčík, Vladimír (ten)
Janáček, L.:Fate, w. Magdaléna Hajóssyová (sop), Vilém Přibyl (ten), F. Jílek (cnd), Brno Janáček Opera Orch, Brno Janáček Opera Chorus Supraphon ▲ SUP 0045 [AAD]
Janáček, L.:Jenůfa, w. G. Beňačková (sop—Jenufa), N. Kniplová (mez—Kostelnička Buryja), V. Krejčík (ten—Steva Buryja), V. Přibyl (ten—Laca Klemen), F. Jílek (cnd), Brno Janáček Opera Orch, Brno Janáček Opera Chorus [Cz] Supraphon 2-▲ 10 2751-2 [AAD]
Janáček, L.:Kát'a Kabanová, w. E. Söderström (sop), N. Kniplová (mez), P. Dvorsky (ten), Z. Svehla (ten), D. Jedlička (bass), C. Mackerras (cnd), Vienna PO London 2-▲ 421852-2 [ADD]
Janáček, L.:The Makropulos Affair, w. E. Söderström (sop), Z. Švehla (ten), V. Zítek (ten), D. Jedlička (bass), C. Mackerras (cnd), Vienna PO, Vienna Opera Chorus London 2-▲ 430372-2 [ADD]

Kremer, Gidon (nar)
Meschwitz, F.:Tier Gebete, w. E. Bashkirova (nar/pno) Philips ("Digital Classics" series) ▲ 416841-2 [DDD]
Ridout, A.:Little Sad Sound, w. E. Bashkirova (nar), A. Posch (db) Philips ("Digital Classics" series) ▲ 416841-2 [DDD]

Kremer, M. (ten)
Schumann, R.:Son 1 Vn, w. M. Argerich (pno) Deutsche Grammophon ▲ 419235-2 [DDD]
Schumann, R.:Son 2 Vn, w. M. Argerich (pno) Deutsche Grammophon ▲ 419235-2 [DDD]
Wagner, R.:Die Meistersinger von Nürnberg (sels), w. M. Teschemacher (sop), H. Jung (mez), T. RA. (ten), E. Fuchs (bar), H.-H. Nissen (bar), S. Nilsson (bass), K. Böhm (cnd), Saxon State Orch—Act. 3 *(rec 1939)* Pearl 2-▲ PEA 9121 [ADD]

Krenn, Fritz (bass)
Lortzing, A.:Zar und Zimmermann (sels), w. Lucia Popp (sop), Adalbert Kraus (ten), Hermann Prey (bar), Karl Ridderbusch (bass), H. Wallberg (cnd), Bavarian RSO, Bavarian Radio Chorus [G] Acanta 2-▲ CD 42424 [DDD]
Mozart, W.A.:Clemenza, w. M. Casula (sop), L. Popp (sop), T. Berganza (mez), B. Fassbaender (mez), T. Franc (bass), I. Kertész (cnd), Vienna State Opera Orch, Vienna State Opera Chorus London ("Grand Opera" series) 2-▲ 430105-2 [ADD]
Smetana, B.:The Bartered Bride, w. H. Konetzni (sop), R. Tauber (ten), T. Beecham (cnd), Royal Opera House Orch, Royal Opera House Chorus Covent Garden [G] *(rec live, Covent Garden, 5/1/39)* Standing Room Only 2-▲ SRO 830-2 [ADD]

Krenn, Werner (ten)
Bach, J.S.:Cant 67, w. H. Watts (cta), T. Krause, E. Ansermet (cnd), Swiss Romande Orch, Lausanne Pro Arte Choir London ("Serenata" series) ▲ 433175-2 [ADD]
Bach, J.S.:Cant 130, w. E. Ameling (sop), H. Watts (cta), T. Krause (bass), E. Ansermet (cnd), Swiss Romande Orch, Lausanne Pro Arte Choir London ("Serenata" series) ▲ 433175-2 [ADD]
Bach, J.S.:Magnificat, BWV 243, w. E. Ameling (sop), H. van Bork (sop), H. Watts (cta), T. Krause (bass), K. Münchinger (cnd), Stuttgart CO, Vienna Academy Chorus London ("Serenata" series) ▲ 433175-2 [ADD]
Bach, J.S.:St. John Passion, w. F. Palmer (sop), B. Finnilä (cta), K. Equiluz (ten), P. Huttenlocher (bar), R. van der Meer (bass), M. Corboz (cnd), Lausanne CO, Lausanne Vocal Ensemble Erato 2-▲ 2292-45406-2 FD
Handel, G.F.:Messiah, w. Joan Sutherland (sop), Huguette Tourangeau (mez), Tom Krause (bar), R. Bonynge (cnd), English CO, Ambrosian Singers [E] London ("Serenata" series) 2-▲ 433740-2 [ADD]
Lehár, F.:Die lustige Witwe (sels), w. J. Sutherland (sop), R. Resnik (mez), R. Bonynge (cnd), National PO London, Ambrosian Singers—overture & highlights from Acts 1 & 2 London ("Opera Gala" series) ▲ 421884-2 [ADD]
Mozart, W.A.:Missa, K.317, w. A. Tomowa-Sintow (sop), A. Baltsa (mez), J. van Dam (b-bar), H. von Karajan (cnd), Berlin PO, Vienna Singverein [L] Deutsche Grammophon ("Galleria" series) 2-▲ 423913-2 [ADD]
Mozart, W.A.:Missa, K.317, w. A. Tomowa-Sintow (sop), A. Baltsa (mez), J. van Dam (b-bar), H. von Karajan (cnd), Berlin PO, Vienna Singverein Deutsche Grammophon ▲ 429820-2 [ADD]
Mozart, W.A.:Missa, K.427, w. I. Cotrubas (sop), K. Te Kanawa (sop), H. Sotin (bass), R. Leppard (cnd), New Philharmonia Orch, John Alldis Choir [L] EMI Classics ▲ CDC 47385

Krenn, Werner (ten) (cont.)
Mozart, W.A.:Requiem, w. A. Tomowa-Sintow (sop), A. Baltsa (mez), J. van Dam (b-bar), H. von Karajan (cnd), Berlin PO, Vienna Singverein [L] Deutsche Grammophon ("Galleria" series) ▲ 419867-2 [ADD] ■ 419867-4
Mozart, W.A.:Requiem, w. A. Tomowa-Sintow (sop), A. Baltsa (mez), J. van Dam (b-bar), H. von Karajan (cnd), Berlin PO, Vienna Singverein Deutsche Grammophon ▲ 429821-2 [ADD] ■ 429821-4

Kretschmar, Helmut (ten)
Haydn, J.:Die Jahreszeiten, w. Teresa Stich-Randall (mez), Erik Wenk (bass), W. Goehr (cnd), North German RSO, Hamburg Chorus *(rec 1966)* FNAC Music 2-▲ 642325

Kreuger, Dana (mez)
Moore, D.:Ballad of Baby Doe, w. Jan Grissom (sop—Baby Doe), Dana Kreuger (mez—Augusta), Myrna Paris (cta—Mama), Brian Steele (bar—Horace), Mark Freiman (b-bar—W. J. Bryan), J. Moriarty (cnd), Central City Opera Orch, Central City Opera Chorus *(rec Central City, CO)* Newport Classic 2-▲ NPD 85593/2 [DDD]

Kreutzberger, Rudolf (sgr)
Schubert, Franz:Die Verschworenen, w. Ilona Steingruber (sop—Countess), Elizabeth Roon (mez—Helene), Laurence Dutoit (trb—Isella), Walter Anton (ten—Udolin), Walter Berry (bar—Count), Rudolf Kreutzberger (sgr—Astolf), F. Grossmann (cnd), Vienna SO, Vienna Academy Chamber Choir Theorema ▲ TH 121178

Krieg, Christopher (spkr)
Corghi, A.:Divara—Wasser und Blut, w. Susanna von der Burg (sop—Divara), Suzanne McLeod (mez—Else Windscherer), Eva Lillian Thingboe (mez—Hille Feiken), Robert Schwarts (ten—Lame Man), Heinz Fitz (spkr—Bernd Knipperdollinck), Hanslutz Hildmann (spkr—Jan Matthys), Michael Holm (spkr—Bernhard Rothmann), Christopher Krieg (spkr—Jan van Leiden), W. Humburg (cnd), Münster SO, Münster City Theater Chorus [G] *(rec Grosses Haus, Münster State Theater, Nov. 27-29, 1993)* Marco Polo 2-▲ 8.223706/07 [DDD]

Krieger, Jeanne (sop)
Ravel, M.:L'Heure espagnole, w. Jeanne Krieger (sop—Concepcion), Louis Arnoult (ten—Gonzalve), Raoul Gilles (ten—Torquemada), J. Aubert (bar—Ramiro), Hector Dufranne (bass—Don Inigo Gomez), G. Truc (cnd), *(orch unknown) (rec premiere recording, supervised by Ravel, 1929)* VAI Audio ▲ VAIA 1073

Krilovici, Marina (sop)
Mascagni, P.:Cavalleria rusticana, w. Marina Krilovici (sop—Santuzza), Viorica Cortez (mez—Lola), Milka Nistor (mez—Lucia), Cornel Stavru (ten—Turiddu), David Ohanesian (bar—Alfio), M. Popa (cnd), Bucharest Opera & Ballet Theater Orch, Bucharest Opera & Ballet Theater Chorus *(rec 1966)* Vox Box 2-▲ CDX 5161

Kringelborn, Solvieg (sop)
Grieg, E.:Songs, w. G. Rozhdestvensky (cnd), Royal Stockholm PO—Six Orchestral Songs (1894-5)—Solveigs Sang [Solveig's Song]; Solveigs Vuggevise [Solveig's Cradle Song]; Fra Monte Pincio [From Monte Pincio]; En Svane [A Swan]; Varen [Springtide]; Henrik Wergeland Chandos ▲ CHAN 9113 [DDD]

Kringleborn, Solvieg (sop)
Hall, P.:Four Tosserier, w. Bergen Wind Quintet [Nor] Simax ("Norway in Music" series) ▲ PSC 3105 [DDD]

Kringelborn, Solvieg (sop)
Sibelius, J.:Luonnotar, w. P. Järvi (cnd), Royal Stockholm PO Virgin Classics ▲ CDC 45213
Tavener, J.:Music of, w. D. Hill (cnd), Winchester Cathedral Choir—Thunder Entered Her; Angels; The Annunciation; Lament of the Mother of God; Hymns of Paradise; God Is with Us Virgin Classics ▲ CDC 45035

Kriska, Lucia (sgr)
Honegger, A.:Amphion, w. Olivier Lallouette (bar—Apollon), Laurent Manzoni (bar—Amphion), Iona Bentoiu (sgr—muse), Theodora Ciucur (sgr—muse), Lucia Kriska (sgr—muse), Adriana Mestes (sgr—muse), J.-F. Antonioli (cnd), Timisoara PO, Timisoara Banatul Phil Chorus, Timisoara Children's Chorus *(rec Salle Ion Vidu, Timisoara, Romania, Oct 28 & Nov 1, 1995)* Timpani ▲ 1035 [DDD]

Kristensen, Michael (ten)
Koppel, H.D.:Moses, w. Elisabeth Meyer-Topsøe (sop), Kirsten Dolberg (mez), Kurt Westi (ten), Per Høyer (bar), Christian Christiansen (bass), O.A. Hughes (cnd), Danish National RSO, Jesper Grovw Jørgensen (cnd), Danish National Radio Choir *(rec Danish Radio Concert Hall, Mar 1996)* Marco Polo/Dacapo ▲ 8.224046 [DDD]

Krivchenya, Alexi (bass)
Prokofiev, S.:War & Peace, w. Galina Vishnevskaya (sop—Natasha Rostovoa), Irina Arkhipova (mez—Hélène Bezukhova), Evgenya Verbitskaya (mez—Marya Akhrosimova), Alexi Maslennikov (ten—Anatole Kuragin), Vladimir Petrov (ten—Pierre Bezukhov), Pavel Lisitsian (bar—Napoleon), Alexi Krivchenya (bass—Field-Marshall Kutuzov), Evgeny Kibkalo (sgr—Prince Andrei Bolkonsky), A. Melik-Pashayev (cnd), Bolshoi Theater Orch, Bolshoi Theater Chorus *(rec Moscow, 1961)* Melodiya ("The Russian Opera" series) 3-▲ 74321-29350-2 [ADD]

Kříz, Vratislav (sgr)
Dvořák, A.:Armida, w. Joanna Borowska (sop—Armida), Monika Brychtová (sgr—Siren), Wieslaw Ochman (ten—Rinald), Richard Sporka (ten—Dudo), Jan Markvart (bar—Sven), Pavel Daniluk (bass—King), George Fortune (bass—Ismen), Zdenek Harvánek (bass—Ubald), Miloslav Podskalský (bass—Peter), Milan Bürger (sgr—Gernand), Roman Janál (sgr—Muezzin/Hlasatel), Vratislav Kříz (sgr—Gottfried), Vladimír Nacházel (sgr—Roger), G. Albrecht (cnd), Czech PO, Prague Chamber Choir *(rec 1995)* Orfeo 2-▲ 404962 [DDD]

Kroesen, J. (voc)
Ashley, R.:Perfect Lives [Private Parts], w. R. Ashley (nar), "Blue" G. Tyranny (kbds), D. Van Thiegem (voc), P. Gordon (pre-recorded orchestral beds) Lovely Music 3-▲ LCD 4917.3 [ADD] 2-■ LMC 4913/4947

Krogen, Hanne (sgr)
Liebermann, R.:Medea, w. Françoise Pollet (sop—Medea), Yvi Jänicke (cta—Chalkiope), Zdena Furmančoková (sgr—Syrinx), Dagmar Hesse (sgr—Aiglaia), Hanne Krogen (sgr—Kore), Michaela Lucas (sgr—Oinone), Renate Spingler (sgr—Silene), Jochen Kowalski (ct—Kreon), Aage Haugland (bass—Jason), G. Albrecht (cnd), Hamburg State PO, Hamburg State Opera Chorus *(rec live, Hamburg, Germany, Sept 24, 1995)* Musiques Suisses ▲ 6126 [DDD]

Krogh, Erling (ten)
Flanagan, W.:The Lady of Tearful Regret, w. D. Larsen (sop), W. Strickland (cnd), Oslo PO CRI ■ C 163

Kromm, Leroy (b-bar)
Handel, G.F.:Judas Maccabaeus, w. Linda Saffer (sop), Patricia Spence (mez), Brian Asawa (ct), Guy de Mey (ten), David Thomas (bass), N. McGegan (cnd), Philharmonia Baroque Orch, Univ of California at Berkeley Chamber Chorus [E] *(rec Nov. 15-18, 1992)* Harmonia Mundi USA 2-▲ HMU 907077/78

Kronenberg, Karl (bar)
Puccini, G.:La Bohème, w. Trude Eipperle (sop), Hildegarde Ranczak (sop), Alfons Fügel (ten), Georg Hann (bass), Georg Wieter (bass), Emil Graf (sgr), Otto Hillerbrandt (sgr), Karl Schmidt (sgr), C. Krauss (cnd), Bavarian State Opera Orch, Bavarian State Opera Chorus *(rec 1940)* Preiser 2-▲ PRE 90275
Wagner, R.:Lohengrin, w. H. Braun (sop—Ortrud), T. Epperle (sop—Elsa von Brabant), P. Anders (ten—Lohengrin), C. Kronenberg (bar—Frederich von Telramund), J. Greindl (bass—Heinrich der Vogler), R. Kraus (cnd), Cologne RSO, Cologne Radio Chorus *(rec Nov. 1951)* Myto 3-▲ MCD 93485

Kronwitter, Seppi (trb)
Bach, J.S.:Cant 52, w. Leonhardt Consort, Hanover Boys' Choir [G] Teldec 2-▲ 2292-42422-2 [AAD]
Bach, J.S.:Cant 61, w. K. Equiluz (ten), R. van der Meer (bass), N. Harnoncourt (cnd), Vienna Concentus Musicus, Vienna Boys' Choir [G] Teldec 2-▲ 2292-42565-2 [AAD]

Krooskos, Christiana (cta)
Mahler, G.:Sym 3, w. M. Abravanel (cnd), Utah SO, Utah Sym Chorus [G] *(rec 1969)* Vanguard Classics 2-▲ OVC 4005/06 [ADD]

Krovytska, Oksana (sop)
Mahler, G.:Sym 8, w. Oksana Krovytska (sop—Magna Peccatrix), Sheila Smith (sop—Una poenitentium), Shauna Southwick (sop—Mater gloriosa), Kristine Jepson (mez—Maria Aegyptiaca), Julie Simson (mez—Mulier Samaritana), Kurt Hansen (ten—Doctor Marianus), Brian Steele (bar—Pater ecstaticus), Eugene Green (b–bar—Pater profundus), R. Olson (cnd), Colorado MahlerFest Orch, Colorado MahlerFest Chorale, Colorado Mormon Chorale, Colorado Children's Chorale *(rec MahlerFest VIII, Boulder, CO, Jan 14–15, 1995)* MahlerFest 2–▲ MF8–1

Kruger, M. A. (sop)
Bach, J.S.:Magnificat, BWV 243, w. H. Schellenberg (sop), M. Westbrook–Geha (mez), I. Humphrey (ten), S. Sylvan (bar), B. H. Moyse (cnd), Orch of St. Luke MusicMasters ▲ 7059–2–C [DDD]

Krumbiegel, Ulrike (nar)
Nono, L.:Prometeo, w. I. Ade–Jesemann (sop), M. Bair–Ivenz (sop), S. Otto (alt), P. Hall (ten), M. Schadock (nar), C. Abbado (cnd), Berlin PO, Freiburg Soloists Choir *(rec May 23–25, 1993)* Sony Classical ▲ SK 53978 [DDD]

Kruse, Heinz (ten)
Krenek, E.:Jonny spielt auf, w. A. Marc (sop), M. Kraus (ten), K. St. Hill (ten), L. Zagrosek (cnd), Leipzig Gewandhaus Orch [G] London 2–▲ 436631–2 [DDD]
Schreker, F.:Die Gezeichneten, w. Elisabeth Connell (sop), Monte Pederson (bar), Alfred Muff (bass), László Polgar (bass), L. Zagrosek (cnd), Berlin German SO London 3–▲ 444442–2
Schultze, N.:Das kalte Herz, w. Grit van Jüten (sop), Elisabeth Steiner (mez), Detelf Zywietz (sgr), N. Schutze (cnd), Cologne RSO, Händel Collegium Koch Schwann 2–▲ SCH 318002 [DDD]
Zemlinsky, A. von:Der Traumgörge, w. P. Coburn (sop), J. Martin (sop), G. M. Ronge (sop), B. Calm (mez), P. Haage (ten), J. Protschka (ten), H. Welker (bar), M. Blasius (bass), V. von Halem (bass), G. Albrecht (cnd), Frankfurt RSO [G] Capriccio 2–▲ CD 10241/2 [DDD]

Kruse, T. (cta)
Sibelius, J.:The Maiden in the Tower, w. M. A. Häggander (sop), E. Hagegard (ten), J. Hynninen (bar), N. Järvi (cnd), Gothenburg SO, Gothenburg Chorus [Fin] BIS ▲ CD 250 [DDD]

Kruszelnicka, Salomea (sop)
Salomea Kruszelnicka Pearl ▲ PEA 9215

Krutikov, Mikhail (bass)
Beethoven, L. van:Missa Solemnis, w. T. Kiberg (sop), R. Lang (cta), W. Cochran (ten), A. Dorati (cnd), European SO, Univ of Maryland Chorus [L] *(rec live, Berlin Philharmonie, 7/3/88)* BIS 2–▲ CD 406/07 [DDD]
Shostakovich, D.:Sym 14, w. M. Kasrashvili (sop), A. Lazarev (cnd), Lausanne CO Virgin Classics ▲ CDC 59039

Krutikov, Mikhail (sgr)
Rachmaninoff, S.:The Miserly Knight, w. Vladimir Kudriashov (sgr), Alexander Arkhipov (sgr), Vladislav Verestnikov (sgr), Piotr Gluboky (sgr), A. Tchistiakov (cnd), Bolshoi Theater Orch, Russian State Choir Russian Season 3–▲ CMX 388053

Kruysen, Bernard (bar)
Debussy, C.:Songs, w. Francis Poulenc (pno), Jean–Charles Richard (pno)—Le Son du cor; L'èchelonnement des haies; Trois chansons de France; Fêtes galantes; Fête galantes; Trois poèmes de Mallarmé; Le promenoir des deux amants; Trois poèmes de Mallarmé Trois ballades de Villon; Trois chansons de France *(rec 1962–65)* Mémoire Vive ▲ 262010 (m)
Duparc, H.:Songs, w. N. Lee (pno)—L'Invitation au voyage; Sérénade Florentine; La Voyage et la Cloche; Extase; Chanson Triste; Lamento; Testament; Phidylé; Soupir; Le Manoir de Rosemonde; Elegie; La Vie Antérieure; Au Pays où se fait la Guerre Valois ▲ V 4703
Fauré, G.:Requiem, w. E. Ameling (sop), J. Fournet (cnd), Rotterdam PO [L] Philips ▲ 420707–2 [ADD]
Henkemans, H.:Villonerie, w. J. Fournet (cnd), Netherlands Radio PO Donemus ▲ CV 14
Honegger, A.:Le Roi David, w. Hanke De Hoogh (nar), Sasja Hunnego (nar), A. Clement (cnd), Eindhovens Instrumental Ensemble, Eindhovens Chamber Choir [orig version] Emergo ▲ 3974
Inghelbrecht, D.–E.:Requiem, w. Christiane Ede–Pierre (sop), J. Fournet (cnd), ORTF Lyric Orch, ORTF Choirs Studio SM ("Andre Charlin Collection" series) ▲ 2522
Inghelbrecht, D.–E.:Vézelay, w. Christiane Ede–Pierre (sop), J. Fournet (cnd), ORTF Lyric Orch, ORTF Choir Studio SM ("Andre Charlin Collection" series) ▲ 2522
Massenet, J.:Songs, w. N. Lee (pno)—11 songs [F] Arion ▲ ARN 68009 [AAD]
Poulenc, F.:Songs, w. Noël Lee (pno) Arion ▲ ARN 68258 [DDD]
Ravel, M.:Songs, w. N. Lee (pno)—Histoires naturelles; Un grand sommeil noir; Ronsard à son ame; Rêves; Cinq mélodies populaires grecques; Deux mélodies hébraïques; Sainte; Don Quichotte à Dulcinée Valois ▲ V4700

Kubiak, Teresa (sop)
Shostakovich, D.:Sym 14, w. I. Bushkin (bass), L. Bernstein (cnd), New York PO [R] *(rec Dec. 8, 1976)* Sony Classical ▲ SMK 47617 [ADD]

Kubik, Jiri (ten)
Dvořák, A.:The Spectre's Bride, Op. 69, w. Jitka Sobehartova (sop), Jan Markvart (bar), Bratislava Philharmonic Chorus, P. Tiboris (cnd), Bohuslav Martinů PO [Cz] *(rec Nov. 26–30, 1993)* Elysium ▲ GRK 700 [DDD]

Kubovčik, Vladimír (bass)
Respighi, O.:La Primavera, w. Henrietta Lednárová (sop—Prima fanciulla), Jana Valásková (sop—Sirvard), Beata Geriová (mez—Seconda fanciulla), Miroslav Dvorský (ten—Il giovine), Richard Haan (bar—L'orante), Vladimír Kubovčik (bass—Il vecchio), Vera Rasková (fl), M. Adriano (cnd), Slovak RSO Bratislava, Slovak Phil Chorus *(rec Slovak Radio Concert Hall, Bratislava, Jan. 4–9, Feb. 19 & June)* Marco Polo ▲ 8.223595 [DDD]

Kubrická, Daniela (sop)
Ibert, J.:Suite élisabéthaine, w. M. Adriano (cnd), Slovak RSO Bratislava, Slovak Phil Chorus *(rec Feb. 8–13, 1993)* Marco Polo ▲ 8.223508 [DDD]

Kuchar, Erich (ten)
Strauss (II), Joh.:Wiener Blut, w. H. Papouschek (sop), S. Martikke (sop), E. Kales (sop), A. Dallapozza (ten), K. Ruzicka (ten), W. Kandutsch (bar), K. Dönch (bar), O. Kolmann (bass), R. Bibl (cnd), Vienna Volksoper Orch, Vienna Volksoper Chorus Denon 2–▲ CO 8105 [DDD]

Kucharek, Helen (sop)
Handel, G.F.:Messiah, w. Jennifer Smith (sop), Linda Finnie (mez), Niel Mackie (ten), Rodney Macann (b–bar), T. Dean (cnd), Pro Christe Orch, Pro Christe Choir *(rec St. Augustine's Church, Kilburn, London, 1986)* Guild 2–▲ GMDD 7112/3 [ADD]

Kudriashov, Vladimir (ten)
Rachmaninoff, S.:The Miserly Knight, w. Mikhail Krutikov (sgr), Alexander Arkhipov (sgr), Vladislav Verestnikov (sgr), Piotr Gluboky (sgr), A. Tchistiakov (cnd), Bolshoi Theater Orch, Russian State Choir Russian Season 3–▲ CMX 388053

Kuebler, David (ten)
Zemlinsky, A. von:Der Geburtstag der Infantin, w. Soile Isokoski (sop), Iride Martinez (sgr), Andrew Collis (sgr), Juanita Lascarro (sgr), Machiko Obata (sgr), Anne Schwanewilms (sgr), Natalie Karl (sgr), Martina Rüping (sgr), Franfurter Kantorei (sgr), J. Conlon (cnd), Gürzenich Orch, Cologne PO *(rec Cologne, Feb 1996)* EMI Classics 2–▲ CDCB 56208

Kuen, Paul (ten)
Janácek, L.:The Excursions of Mr. Brouček, w. Antonie Fahberg (sop—Piccolo), Wilma Lipp (sop—Málinka), Lilian Benningsen (cta—Fanny Nowak), Paul Kuen (ten—Trambahn–Kondukteur), Karl Ostertag (ten—Vorsitzender des Hausbesitzerverbandes), Fritz Wunderlich (ten—Mazal), Kurt Böhme (b–bar—Sakristan von St. Veit), Kieth Engen (bass—Würfl), J. Keilberth (cnd), Bavarian SO *(rec live, Prinzregententheater, Nov. 19, 1959)* Orfeo 2–▲ 354942 (m)
Lortzing, A.:Die beiden Schützen, w. K. Nentwig (sop), B. Kusche (bar), K. Smitt–Walter (bar), M. Pröbstl (bass), J. Koetsier (cnd), Bavarian RSO *(rec 1950)* Memories 2–▲ MEM 4546 [ADD]
Orff, C.:Antigonae, w. Christel Goltz (sop), Karl Ostertag (ten), Benno Kusche (bar), Hermann Uhde (bar), N. Barth (bar), G. Solti (cnd), Bavarian State Opera Orch, Bavarian State Opera Chorus *(rec Prinzregententheater, Jan. 12, 1951)* Orfeo d'or 2–▲ 407952
Orff, C.:Die Kluge, w. E. Schwarzkopf (sop), R. Christ (ten), M. Cordes (bar), B. Kusche (bar), H. Prey (bar), G. Frick (bass), G. Wieter (bass), W. Sawallisch (cnd), Philharmonia Orch [G] EMI Classics ("Studio" series) 2–▲ CDMB 63712 [ADD]

Kuen, Paul (ten) (cont.)
Orff, C.:Der Mond—Ein kleines Welttheater, w. Karl Erb (nar), Paul Kuen (ten—Lad 3), Josef Knapp (bar—Lad 2), Benno Kusche (bar—Lad 1), Georg Hann (bass—St. Peter), Georg Wieter (bass—Lad 4), Rudolf Wünzer (bass—The Farmer), Karl Hanft (sgr—Innkeeper), Willy Rösner (sgr—The Major), R. Alberth (cnd), Bavarian RSO, Bavarian Radio Chorus *(rec Studio 1, Bavarian Radio, Jan. 19–20, 1950)* Calig ▲ CAL 50948 (m) [ADD]
Orff, C.:Der Mond—Ein kleines Welttheater, w. R. Christ (ten), K. Schmitt–Walter (bar), H. Graml (bar), H. Hotter (b–bar), P. Lagger (bass), W. Sawallisch (cnd), Philharmonia Orch, Philharmonia Chorus [G] EMI Classics ("Studio" series) 2–▲ CDMB 63712 [ADD]
Wagner, R.:Der Ring des Nibelungen, w. Gré Brouwenstein (sop—Freia/Sieglinde), Ilse Hollweg (sop—Waldvogel), Gerda Lammers (sop—Ortlinde), Paula Lenchner (sop—Wellgunde/Gerhilde), Hilde Scheppan (sop—Helmwige), Astrid Varnay (sop—Brünnilde/3rd Norn), Lore Wissmann (sop—Woglinde), Maria von Ilosvay (mez—Flosshilde/Schwertleite/2nd Norn), Louise Charlotte Kamps (mez—Siegrune), Jean Madeira (mez—Erda/Rossweisse/1st Norn), Georgine van Milinkovic (mez—Fricka/Grimgerde), Elisabeth Schärtel (mez—Waltraute), Paul Kuën (ten—Mime), Ludwig Suthaus (ten—Loge), Josef Traxel (ten—Froh), Wolfgang Windgassen (ten—Siegmund/Siegfried), Alfons Herwig (bar—Donner), Hermann Uhde (bar—Gunther), Hans Hotter (b–bar—Wotan), Gustav Neidlinger (b–bar—Alberich), Josef Griendl (bass—Fasolt/Hunding/Hagen), Arnold van Mill (bass—Fafner), H. Knappertsbusch (cnd), Bayreuth Festival Orch, Bayreuth Festival Chorus *(rec live, Bayreuth, Aug 13–17, 1956)* Golden Melodram 14–▲ GM 1.001 [ADD]
Wagner, R.:Siegfried, w. A. Varnay (sop), R. Siewert (cta), B. Aldenhoff (ten), S. Björling (bar), H. Pflanzl (bass), F. Dalberg (bass), H. von Karajan (cnd), Bayreuth Festival Orch, Bayreuth Festival Chorus [G] *(rec live 1951)* Melodram 4–▲ MEL 46106 (m) [AAD]
Wagner, R.:Tristan und Isolde, w. Helena Braun (sop—Isolde), Margarete Klose (mez—Brangäne), Günther Treptow (ten—Tristan), Paul Kuen (ten—Ein Hirte), Albrecht Peter (bar—Melot), Fritz Richard Bender (bar—Ein Steuermann), Ferdinand Frantz (b–bar—König Marke), Paul Schöffler (b–bar—Kurwenal), H. Knappertsbusch (cnd), Bavarian State Opera Orch, Bavarian State Opera Chorus *(rec live, Prinzregententheater, July 23, 1950)* Orfeo 3–▲ 355

Kuhlmann, Kathleen (mez)
Beethoven, L. van:Missa Solemnis, w. Ileana Cotrubas (sop), Robert Tear (ten), Gwynne Howell (bass), J. Pritchard (cnd), BBC SO, BBC Singers IMP ("BBC Radio Classics" series) ▲ IMP 5691552
Mozart, W.A.:Missa, K.317, w. Y. Kenny (sop), K. Lewis (ten), D. Wilson–Johnson (bar), C. P. Flor (cnd), Philharmonia Orch, London Voices RCA Red Seal ▲ 09026–60812–2
Rossini, G.:Music of, w. M. Fortuna (sop), M. Lerner (sop), D. Voigt (sop), M. Horne (mez), F. von Stade (mez), R. Blake (ten), C. Estep (ten), C. Merritt (ten), T. Hampson (b–bar), H. Runey (b–bar), J. Opalach (bass), S. Ramey (bass), R. Norrington (cnd), Orch of St. Luke's, New York Concert Chorale EMI Classics ▲ CDC 54643

Kuhn, Alfred (sgr)
Wagner, R.:Das Liebesverbot, w. Pamela Coburn (sop—Mariana), Friedrich Lenz (ten—Antonio), Hermann Prey (bar—Friedrich), Keith Engen (bass—Angelo), Raimund Grumbach (bass—Danieli/Wirt), Wolfgang Fassler (sgr—Luzio), Sabine Haas (sgr—Isabella/Claudios Schwester), Alfred Kuhn (sgr—Brighella/Chef der Sbirren), Hermann Sapell (sgr—Pontio Pilato), Robert Schunk (sgr—Claudio), Marianne Seibel (sgr—Dorella), W. Sawallisch (cnd), Bavarian State Orch, Bavarian State Chorus *(rec July 9, 1983)* Orfeo d'or 3–▲ 345953
Wagner, R.:Rienzi, der Letzte der Tribunen, w. Cheryl Studer (sop—Irene), René Kollo (ten—Rienzi), Friedrich Lenz (ten—Gesandte), Norbert Orth (ten—Baroncelli), Bodo Brinkmann (bar—Paolo Orsini), Keith Engen (bass—Cecco del Vecchio), Raimund Grumbach (bass—Gesandte), Jan–Hendrik Rootering (bass—Steffano Colonna), Carmen Anhorn (sgr—Ein Friedensbote), Karl Helm (sgr—Kardinal Orvieto), John Janssen (sgr—Adriano), Alfred Kuhn (sgr—Gesandte), Hans Wilbrink (sgr—Gesandte), W. Sawallisch (cnd), Bavarian State Opera Orch, Bavarian State Opera Chorus *(rec live, July 6, 1983)* Orfeo d'or 3–▲ 346953

Kuhn, Annette (mez)
Tchaikovsky, P.:Iolanta, w. Michaela Gurevich (sop—Iolanta), Jaqueline Miura (sop—Brigitta), Tatjana Tabachuk (mez—Martha), Annette Kuhn (mez—Laura), Ian Denolfo (ten—Godefroy), Keith Alexander Bolves (ten—Alméric), Alexander Ben (bar—Robert), Georg Lehner (bar—Ibn–Hakia), Arutiun Kotchinian (bass—René), Kurt Geysen (bass—Bertrand), H. Rotman (cnd), Warsaw PO, ECOV Ensemble Members *(rec Vooruit Center of the Arts, Ghent, Belgium, Aug 28–29, 1993)* CPO 2–▲ CPO 999456–2 [DDD]

Kuhn, Judy (sgr)
Lloyd Webber, A.:Sunset Boulevard, w. Glenn Close (sgr), A. Campbell (sgr), George Hearn (sgr)—highlights Polydor ▲ 31452–7241–2 ■ 31452–7241–4
Lloyd Webber, A.:Sunset Boulevard, w. Glenn Close (sgr), A. Campbell (sgr), George Hearn (sgr) [1994 cast] A&M ▲ 31452 3507–2 ■ 31452 3507–4

Kühne, Rolf (bass)
Wagner, R.:Der Ring des Nibelungen, w. Liselotte Becker–Egner (sop—Woglinde/Ortlinde/Wellgunde), Angelika Berger (sop—Wellgunde/Waltraute), Siw Ericsdotter (sop—Norn 3), Heidemaria Ferch (sop—Freia/Gerhilde), Bella Jasper (sop—Helmwige/Waldvogel/Woglinde), Ditha Sommer (sop—Sieglinde/Gutrune), Ursula Boese (mez—Erda), Ruth Hesse (mez—Fricka), Nadezda Kniplová (mez—Brünnhilde), Margit Kobeck (mez—Schwertleite/Norn 2), Hilde Rosner (mez—Flosshilde/Siegrunde), Erica Schubert (mez—Grimgerde/Flosshilde), Ingrid Göritz (cta—Rossweisse/Norn 1), Herbert Doussant (ten—Froh), Herold Kraus (ten—Mime), Gerald McKee (ten—Siegmund/Siegfried), Fritz Uhl (ten—Loge), Rudolf Knoll (bar—Gunther/Donner), Rolf Polke (bass-bar—Wotan/Wanderer), Rolf Kühne (bass—Alberich), Takao Okamura (bass—Fafner), Otto von Rohr (bass—Hagen/Fasolt/Hunding), H. Swarowsky (cnd), Czech PO, Prague National Theater Orch *(rec June 3 & 5, July 26–31, A)* Weltbild Classics 14–▲ 703769 [ADD]

Kühnle, Helmut (bass)
Hindemith, P.:Hin und zurück, w. Barbara Miller (sop), Claus Bock (ten), Ulrich Schaible (bar), A. Grüber (cnd), Berlin SO members *(rec 1971)* Allegretto ▲ ACD 8191

Kuhse, Hanne–Lore (sop)
Berg, A.:Lulu (sels), w. H. Kegel (cnd), Leipzig RSO—Adagio Berlin Classics ▲ BER 9020 [ADD]
Berg, A.:Wozzeck (sels), w. H. Kegel (cnd), Leipzig RSO Berlin Classics ▲ BER 9020 [ADD]
Mussorgsky, M.:Boris Godunov (sels), w. Peter Schreier (ten), Martin Ritzmann (ten), Theo Adam (b–bar), H. Kegel (cnd), Dresden State Orch, Leipzig Radio Chorus Berlin Classics ▲ BER 2032 [ADD]

Kuitse, Anda (sgr/perc)
Blak, K.:Drangar, w. Anders Hagberg (fl/s sax/perc), Tore Brunborg (s sax/t sax/perc), Lennart Kullgren (gtr/sgr), Kristian Blak (pno/sgr), Anders Jormin (bass instr/perc), Karin Korpelainen (dr/perc) *(rec Nordic House, Tórshavn, Jan. 1995)* Tutl ▲ HJF 33

Kulikova, S. (sgr)
Prokofiev, S.:Maddalena, w. N. Zagorinskaya (sgr), Y. Melnikova (sgr), S. Donets (sgr), S. Yakovlev (sgr), C. Tikhonov (cnd), Moscow Helikon Theater Chamber Ensemble [R] MK ▲ MKA 417056 [DDD]
Stravinsky, I.:Mavra, w. N. Zagorinskaya (sgr), Y. Melnikova (sgr), S. Donets (sgr), S. Yakovlev (bar), C. Tikhonov (cnd), Moscow Helikon Theater Chamber Ensemble MK ▲ MKA 417056 [DDD]

Kullman, Charles (ten)
Charles Kullmann Preiser ("Lebendige Vergangenheit" series) ▲ PRE 89057 (m) [AAD]
Great Love Duets, w. Erna Berger (sop), Miliza Korjus (sop), Lotte Lehmann (sop), Frida Leider (sop), Charles Kullman (ten), Lauritz Melchior (ten), Helge Roswaenge (ten), Tito Schipa (ten), Richard Tauber (ten), et al. Pearl ▲ PEA 9217
Mahler, G.:Das Lied von der Erde, w. Kerstin Thorborg (mez), B. Walter (cnd), Vienna PO *(rec Vienna, May 1936)* Grammofono 2000 ▲ GRM 78553
Mahler, G.:Das Lied von der Erde, w. K. Thorberg (mez), B. Walter (cnd), Vienna PO Enterprise ("Palladio" series) ▲ ENTPD 4172 [ADD]
Mozart, W.A.:Don Giovanni, w. Rose Bampton (sop), Jarmila Novotna (sop), Bidú Sayão (sop), Alexander Kipnis (bass), Ezio Pinza (bass), B. Walter (cnd), *(orch unknown)* *(rec Mar 7, 1942)* Enterprise ("The Fourties" series) 3–▲ ENT 301

Kulp, Nancy (sgr)
Kern, J.:Show Boat, w. F. von Stade (mez), T. Stratas (sop), J. Hadley (ten), B. Hubbard (bar), P. O'Hara (sgr), K. Burns (mez), J. McGlinn (cnd), London Sinfonietta, Ambrosian Chorus [original orchd Robert Russell Bennett]—also includes 45 minutes of music intended for the original performance but never included, plus music from revivals and films [1988 studio cast] Angel 3–▲ A23 49108 [DDD]

Kunath, Gerd (sgr)
Waits, T.:The Black Rider:The Casting of Magic Bullets, w. Angelika Thomas (sgr—Anne), Annette Paulmann (sgr—Kätchen), Sona Cervena (sgr—Bird/Messenger/Spoonwoman), Monika Tahal (sgr—Witness/Bird/Shrink/Wilhelm's Double/Skeleton), Susi Eisenkolb (sgr—Bridesmaid/Pegleg's Double), Heinz Vossbrink (sgr—Kuno), Dominique Horwitz (sgr—Pegleg), Gerd Kunath (sgr—Bertram), Stefan Kurt (sgr—Wilhelm), Klaus Schreiber (sgr—Robert/Man on Stag/Georg Schmid), Jörg Holm (Old Uncle/Duke), Jan Moritz Steffen (sgr—Young Kuno/Bird/Shrink/Skeleton), Tom Waits (vocals/coliope/organ/chamberlain/mar/emax/guitar/train whistle), Ralph Carney (saxophone/bass clarinet/baritone horn), Bill Douglas (bass instrument), Kenny Wollesen (perc) Island ▲ 314518559-2

Kunc, K. František (bass)
Janácek, L.:Sárka, w. A. Nováková (sop), A. Jurecka (ten), J. Válka (ten), B. Bakala (cnd), Brno RSO, Brno Radio Chorus *(rec live, 1953)* Multisonic ("Prague Spring Collection" series) ▲ 31 0154 [ADD]

Kunde, Gregory (ten)
Bellini, V.:Bianca e Fernando, w. Y. O. Shin (sop), W. Coppola (ten), A. Tomicich (bass), A. Licata (cnd), Catania Teatro Massimo Bellini Orch, Catania Teatro Massimo Bellini Chorus Nuova Era 2-▲ NUO 7076 [DDD]
Rossini, G.:Armida, w. R. Fleming (sop), C. Bosi (ten), B. Fowler (ten), J. Francis (ten), D. Kaasch (ten), I. Zennaro (ten), I. D'Arcangelo (bass), S. Zadvorny (bass), D. Gatti (cnd), Bologna Teatro Comunale Orch, Bologna Teatro Comunale Chorus *(rec Pesaro, Italy, Aug. 6–17, 1993)* Sony Classical 3-▲ S3K 58968 [DDD]
Thomas, A.:Hamlet, w. J. Anderson (sop—Ophelie), D. Graves (mez—Gertrude); G. Kunde (ten—Laerte), T. Hampson (bar—Hamlet), S. Ramey (bass—Claudius), A. de Almeida (cnd), London PO, Ambrosian Singers EMI Classics 3-▲ CDCC 54820

Kundlák, Jozef (ten)
Mozart, W.A.:Requiem, w. M. Hajóssyová (sop), J. Horská (cta), P. Mikuláš (bass), Z. Košler (cnd), Slovak PO, Slovak Phil Chorus Naxos ▲ 8.550235 [DDD] △ 7.550235 [DDD]

Kunz (sgr)
Rossini, G.:Il barbiere di Siviglia, w. R. Grist (sop), F. Wunderlich (ten), E. Wächter (bar), O. Czerwenka (bass), K. Böhm (cnd), Vienna State Opera Orch, Vienna State Opera Chorus *(rec live, Vienna 4/28/66)* Myto 2-▲ 2 MCD 91752 [ADD]

Kunz, Erich (bar)
German University Songs, w. Vienna State Opera Men's Chorus [cnd:Franz Litschauer], Vienna State Opera Orch Vanguard Classics ▲ OVC 6009 [ADD]
German University Songs, Vol. 2, w. Vienna State Opera Orch, Vienna State Opera Male Chorus [cnd:Anton Paulik] *(rec Brahmssaal, Musikverein, Vienna, June 1956)* Vanguard Classics ▲ OVC 6010 [ADD]
Lehár, F.:Die lustige Witwe, w. E. Schwarzkopf (sop), E. Loose (sop), N. Gedda (ten), A. Kraus (ten), O. Ackermann (cnd), Philharmonia Orch, Philharmonia Chorus [G] EMI Classics ("Studio" series) ▲ CDH 69520 (m) [ADD]
Lortzing, A.:Arias Testament ▲ SBT 1059
Mozart, W.A.:Arias Testament ▲ SBT 1059
Mozart, W.A.:Così fan tutte, w. L. della Casa (sop), E. Loose (sop), C. Ludwig (mez), A. Dermota (ten), P. Schoeffler (bass) London 2-▲ 417185-2 [ADD]
Mozart, W.A.:Così fan tutte (sels), w. S. Jurinac (sop), A. Noni (sop), B. Thebom (mez), R. Lewis (ten), M. Borriello (bar), F. Busch (cnd), Glyndebourne Festival Orch *(rec Glyndebourne Festival, 1950)* Testament ▲ TES SBT 1040 [ADD]
Mozart, W.A.:Così fan tutte (sels), w. Elisabeth Schwarzkopf (sop), Irmgard Seefried (sop), Christa Ludwig (mez), Anton Dermota (ten), Paul Schoeffler (b-bar), K. Böhm (cnd), Vienna PO—Sento, o Dio; Sorella, cosa dici?—Prenderò quel brunettino Orfeo d'or ("Festspiel Dokumente" series) ▲ 394201
Mozart, W.A.:Don Giovanni, w. L. Welitsch (sop), I. Seefried (sop), E. Schwarzkopf (sop), A. Dermota (ten), T. Gobbi (bar), A. Poell (b-bar), J. Greindl (bass), W. Furtwängler (cnd), Vienna PO, Vienna State Opera Chorus *(rec 1950)* Laudis 3-▲ LDS 4001 [AAD]
Mozart, W.A.:Don Giovanni, w. M. Caballé (sop), T. Stich-Randall (mez), E. Wächter (bar), M. Gielen (cnd), Naples Teatro San Carlo Orch, Naples Teatro San Carlo Chorus [I] *(rec live, Lisbon, 1960)* Standing Room Only 2-▲ SRO 813-2 [ADD]
Mozart, W.A.:Don Giovanni (sels), w. Hilde Konetzni (sop), Emmy Loose (sop), Irmgard Seefried (sop), Anton Dermota (ten), Paul Schöffler (b-bar), Herbert Alsen (bass), Böhm, Moralt (cnd), Vienna PO *(rec 1944)* Preiser ▲ PRE 90249 [ADD]
Mozart, W.A.:Entführung (sels), w. Hilde Konetzni (sop), Emmy Loose (sop), Irmgard Seefried (sop), Anton Dermota (ten), Paul Schöffler (b-bar), Herbert Alsen (bass), Böhm, Moralt (cnd), Vienna PO *(rec 1944)* Preiser ▲ PRE 90249 [ADD]
Mozart, W.A.:Idomeneo (sels), w. E. Réthy (sop—Idamante), A. Konetzni (sop—Ismene), J. Sabel (ten—Idomeneo), E. Kunz (bar—Arbace), R. Strauss (cnd), Vienna State Opera Orch, Vienna State Opera Chorus *(rec Dec. 3, 1941)* Koch Schwann 2-▲ SCH 314532 [ADD]
Mozart, W.A.:Nozze di Figaro, w. E. Schwarzkopf (sop), I. Seefried (sop), S. Jurinac (sop), E. Höngen (cta), G. London (bar), H. von Karajan (cnd), Vienna PO, Vienna State Opera Chorus—omitting recitatives [I] *(rec 1950)* EMI Classics ("Studio" series) 2-▲ CDMB 69639 (m) [ADD]
Mozart, W.A.:Nozze di Figaro, w. Irma Beilke (sop), Helena Braun (sop), Gerda Sommerschuh (sop), Josef Witt (ten), Hans Hotter (bar), Gustav Neidlinger (b-bar), C. Krauss (cnd), Vienna PO, Vienna State Opera Chorus *(rec live, Salzburg Festival, Aug. 1942)* Preiser 3-▲ PRE 90203 [ADD]
Mozart, W.A.:Nozze di Figaro, w. Elisabeth Schwarzkopf (sop—Countess), Irmgard Seefried (sop—Susanna), Hilde Güden (mez—Cherubino), Paul Schöffler (bar—Almaviva), Erich Kunz (bass—Figaro), W. Furtwängler (cnd), Vienna PO, Vienna State Opera Chorus *(rec Salzburg Festival, Aug 8, 1953)* EMI Classics 3-▲ CDHC 66080
Mozart, W.A.:Songs, w. M. Callas (sop), E. Grümmer (sop), E. Schwarzkopf (sop), R. Scotto (sop), T. Lemnitz (sop), E. Berger (sop), S. Jurinac (sop), E. Schumann (sop), I. Souez (sop), E. Rethberg (sop), L. Lehmann (sop), N. Gedda (ten), J. McCormack (ten), H. Roswenge (ten), H. Nash (ten), T. Gobbi (bar), G. Hüsch (bar), G. Frick (bass), E. Pinza (bass), A. Kipnis (bass) EMI Classics 4-▲ CDMD 63750
Mozart, W.A.:Zauberflöte, w. I. Seefried (sop-Pamina), W. Lipp (sop—Queen of the Night), A. Dermota (ten—Tamino), E. Kunz (bar—Papageno), J. Greindl (bass—Sarastro), W. Furtwängler (cnd), Vienna PO, Vienna State Opera Chorus [G] *(rec live, Salzburg, Aug. 6, 1951)* Arkadia 3-▲ 361 [ADD]
Mozart, W.A.:Zauberflöte, w. I. Seefried (sop-Pamina), W. Lipp (sop—Queen of the Night), A. Dermota (ten—Tamino), E. Kunz (bar—Papageno), J. Greindl (bass—Sarastro), W. Furtwängler (cnd), Vienna PO, Vienna State Opera Chorus [G] *(rec live, Salzburg, Aug. 6, 1951)* Foyer 3-▲ FOY 2003 [AAD]
Mozart, W.A.:Zauberflöte, w. I. Seefried (sop-Pamina), W. Lipp (sop—Queen of the Night), A. Dermota (ten—Tamino), E. Kunz (bar—Papageno), J. Greindl (bass—Sarastro), W. Furtwängler (cnd), Vienna PO, Vienna State Opera Chorus *(rec live 1951)* EMI Classics ▲ CDMC 65356
Mozart, W.A.:Zauberflöte, w. I. Seefried (sop-Pamina), W. Lipp (sop—Queen of the Night), A. Dermota (ten—Tamino), E. Kunz (bar—Papageno), J. Greindl (bass—Sarastro), H. von Karajan (cnd), Vienna PO, Musikfreunde Chorus [without dialogue; G] *(rec 1950)* EMI Classics ("Studio" series) 2-▲ CDHB 69631 (m)
Mozart, W.A.:Zauberflöte (sels), w. Hilde Konetzni (sop), Emmy Loose (sop), Irmgard Seefried (sop), Anton Dermota (ten), Paul Schöffler (b-bar), Herbert Alsen (bass), Böhm, Moralt (cnd), Vienna PO *(rec 1944)* Preiser ▲ PRE 90249 [ADD]
Strauss (II), Joh.:Arias Testament ▲ SBT 1059
Strauss (II), Joh.:Die Fledermaus, w. H. Gueden (sop), R. Streich (sop), G. Di Stefano (ten), G. Stolze (ten), G. Zampieri (ten), E. Wächter (bar), W. Berry (bass), H. von Karajan (cnd), Vienna State Opera Orch, Vienna State Opera Chorus [G] Arkadia 3-▲ 215 (m) [ADD]
Strauss (II), Joh.:Die Fledermaus, w. E. Schwarzkopf (sop), R. Streich (sop), N. Gedda (ten), H. Krebs (ten), R. Christ (ten), K. Dönch (bar), H. von Karajan (cnd), Philharmonia Orch, Philharmonia Chorus [G] EMI Classics ("Studio" series) 2-▲ CDHB 69531 (m) [ADD]
Strauss (II), Joh.:Die Fledermaus, w. H. Gueden (sop), E. Köth (sop), R. Resnik (mez), W. Kmentt (ten), G. Zampieri (ten), E. Wächter (bar), W. Berry (bass), H. von Karajan (cnd), Vienna PO, Vienna State Opera Chorus, with Gala Sequence [G] London 2-▲ 421046-2 [ADD]

Kunz, Erich (bar) (cont.)
Strauss (II), Joh.:Die Fledermaus (sels), w. Wilma Lipp (sop), Gerda Scheyer (sop), Christa Ludwig (mez), Anton Dermota (ten), Walter Berry (bar), Eberhard Wachter (bar), O. Ackermann (cnd), Philharmonia Orch, London Phil Chorus Emperor Operetta ▲ KO 86340
Strauss (II), Joh.:Der Zigeunerbaron, w. Emmy Loose (sop—Arsena), Gerda Scheyrer (sop—Saffi), Elisabeth Fez (cta—Mirabella), Hilde Rössl-Majdan (cta—Czipra), Waldemar Kmentt (ten—Barinkay), Paul Spani (ten—Ottokar), Erich Kunz (bar—Homonay), Kurt Preger (bar—Zsupan), Eberhard Wächter (bass—Carnero), A. Paulik (cnd), Vienna State Opera Orch, Vienna State Opera Chorus *(rec Brahmssaal, Vienna, Austria, June 1956)* Vanguard Classics 2-▲ OVC 8082/83 [ADD]
Strauss, R.:Die ägyptische Helena (sels), w. V. Ursuleac (sop—Helena), F. Völker (ten—Menelas), H. Roswaenge (ten—Da-Ud), E. Kunz (bar—Arbace), C. Krauss (cnd), Vienna State Opera Orch, Vienna State Opera Chorus *(rec Sept. 20, 1933)* Koch Schwann 2-▲ SCH 314552 [ADD]
Strauss, R.:Ariadne auf Naxos, w. M. Reining (sop), I. Seefried (sop), A. Noni (sop), M. Lorenz (ten), J. Witt (ten), P. Schöffler (bass), K. Böhm (cnd), Vienna State Opera Orch *(rec Strauss' 80th Birthday Festival, June 11, 1944)* Preiser 2-▲ PRE 90217 [ADD]
Strauss, R.:Der Rosenkavalier, w. L. Della Casa (sop), H. Gueden (sop), S. Jurinac (sop), O. Edelmann (b-bar), H. von Karajan (cnd), Vienna PO, Vienna State Opera Chorus [G] *(rec live in Salzburg, 7/26/60)* Arkadia 3-▲ 213 [ADD]
Strauss, R.:Der Rosenkavalier, w. Jarmila Barton (sop—Marianne), Lisa Della Casa (sop—Sophie), Sena Jurinac (sop—Octavian), Ilva Ligabue (sop—Orphan), Elisabeth Schwarzkopf (sop—Marschallin), Else Schürhoff (mez—Annina), Luisa Villa (mez—Milliner), Hugues Cuénod (ten—Marschallin's majordomo), Erich Majkut (ten—Valzacchi), Giuseppe Nessi (ten—Animal seller), Luciano Della Pergola (ten—Lackey/Faninal's majordomo), Antonio Pirino (ten—An Italian Singer), Gino Del Signore (ten—Lackey/Waiter), Erich Kunz (bar—Herr von Faninal), Paolo Pedani (bar—Lackey), Attilo Barbesi (bass—Lackey/Waiter), Enrico Campi (bass—Waiter), Otto Edelmann (bass—Baron Ochs), Bruno Fichtinger (bass—Notary), Franco Taino (bass—Waiter), Maria Amadini (sgr—Orphan), Pina Carrillo (sgr—Orphan), Joszi Trojan Regar (sgr—Innkeeper), H. von Karajan (cnd), La Scala Orch, La Scala Chorus *(rec La Scala Theater, Milan, Jan. 26, 1952)* Legato Classics 3-▲ LCD 197-3
Wagner, R.:Die Meistersinger von Nürnberg, w. E. Schwarzkopf (sop), I. Malaniuk (cta), H. Hopf (ten), G. Unger (ten), O. Edelmann (b-bar), F. Dalberg (bass), H. von Karajan (cnd), Bayreuth Festival Orch, Bayreuth Festival Chorus [G] *(rec 1951)* EMI Classics ("Great Recordings of the Century" series) 4-▲ CDHD 63500 (m) [ADD]
Wagner, R.:Die Meistersinger von Nürnberg, w. E. Schwarzkopf (sop), O. Edelmann (b-bar), H. von Karajan (cnd), Bayreuth Festival Orch, Bayreuth Festival Chorus *(rec 1951)* Arkadia 4-▲ 224
Wagner, R.:Die Meistersinger von Nürnberg, w. H. Scheppan (sop), L. Suthaus (ten), P. Schöffler (b-bar), H. Abendroth (cnd), Bayreuth Festival Orch, Bayreuth Festival Chorus *(rec 1943)* Preiser ▲ PRE 90174 [AAD]
Wagner, R.:Die Meistersinger von Nürnberg, w. Irmgard Seefried (sop—Eva), Else Schürhoff (mez—Magdelene), Peter Klein (ten—David), August Seider (ten—Walther), Erich Kunz (bar—Beckmesser), Paul Schoeffler (b-bar—Hans Sachs), Herbert Alsen (bass—Pogner), K. Böhm (cnd), Vienna PO, Vienna State Opera Chorus *(rec Vienna, Nov. & Dec. 1944)* Preiser 4-▲ PRE 90234 [ADD]
Wagner, R.:Die Meistersinger von Nürnberg (sels), w. K. Wessel (alt), G. Hann (bass), A. Rother (cnd), Berlin RSO, Berlin Radio Chorus—Act 2 Preiser ▲ PRE 90168 [AAD]
Wagner, R.:Die Meistersinger von Nürnberg (sels), w. Maria Reining (sop—Eva), Torsten Ralf (ten—Walther), Josef Herrman (bar—Hans Sachs), Erich Kunz (bar—Beckmesser), Kurt Böhme (bass—Pogner), K. Böhm (cnd), Vienna State Opera Orch *(rec Vienna, 1944)* Koch Schwann 2-▲ SCH 314682 [ADD]
Wagner, R.:Die Meistersinger von Nürnberg (sels), w. Maria Reining (sop—Eva), Peter Klein (ten—David), Max Lorenz (ten—Walther), Josef Hermann (bar—Hans Sachs), Erich Kunz (bar—Beckmesser), K. Böhm (cnd), Vienna State Opera Orch *(rec Vienna, Jan. 19, 1943)* Koch Schwann 2-▲ SCH 314732 [ADD]
Zeller, C.A.:Arias Testament ▲ SBT 1059

Kunz, Hanns-Friedrich (bass)
Bach, J.S.:Cant 75, w. I. Reichelt, V. Gohl (mez), J. Hamari (cta), A. Baldin (ten), A. Kraus (ten), H. Rilling (cnd), Stuttgart Bach Collegium, Frankfurt Kantorei [G] *(rec 1970)* Hänssler Classic ▲ 98.891 [AAD]
Bach, J.S.:Cant 94, w. H. Donath (sop), E. Paaske (cta), A. Baldin (ten), W. Schöne (bass), H. Rilling (cnd), Stuttgart Bach Collegium, Württemberg CO, Gächinger Kantorei Hänssler Classic ▲ 98.808 [AAD]
Bach, J.S.:Cant 108, w. H. Donath (sop), M. Höffgen (mez), K. Equiluz (ten), H. Rilling (cnd), Stuttgart Bach Collegium, Gächinger Kantorei [G] *(rec 1980–81)* Hänssler Classic ▲ 98.884 [AAD]
Bach, J.S.:Cant 150, w. M. Schreiber (sop), M. Jetter (cta), P. Maus (ten), H. Rilling (cnd), Bach Ensemble *(rec June-July 1970)* Hänssler Classic ▲ 98.835 [AAD]
Bach, J.S.:Cant 151, w. N. Gamo-Yamamoto (sop), H. Laurich (cta), A. Kraus (ten), H. Rilling (cnd), Stuttgart Bach Collegium, Frankfurt Kantorei [G] *(rec Feb 1971)* Hänssler Classic ▲ 98.825 [AAD]

Künzler, Barbara (sop)
Kraft, Walter:Christus, w. Anna Senn-Dähler (sop), Barbara Sutter (sop), Christine Guy (alt), Heidi Uhlmann (alt), Daniel Zellweger (alt), Matthias Senn (ten), Mikoto Usami (ten), Wolfgang Pailer (bass), Heinz Suter (bass), Klaus Knall (cnd), Evangelische Singgemeinde Choirs *(rec Ostdorf bei Balingen, Oct. 8–11, 1986)* Cantate 2-▲ 58004 [DDD]

Kupper, Anneliese (sop)
Strauss, R.:Die ägyptische Helena, w. Annelies Kupper (sop—Aithra), Leonie Rysanek (sop—Helena), Ira Malaniuk (cta—Omniscient Seashell), Bernd Aldenhoff (ten—Menelas), Richard Holm (ten—Da-ud), Hermann Uhde (bar—Altair), J. Keilberth (cnd), Bavarian State Opera Orch, Bavarian State Opera Chorus *(rec Munich Opera Festival, Prince Regent Theater, Aug 10, 1956)* Orfeo d'or 2-▲ 424962
Strauss, R.:Die ägyptische Helena, w. L. Rysanek (sop), B. Aldenhoff (ten), H. Uhde (bar), J. Keilberth (cnd), Bavarian State Opera Orch, Bavarian State Opera Chorus [G] *(rec live, Munich, 8/27/56)* Melodram 2-▲ MEL 27066 (m) [AAD]
Strauss, R.:Die Liebe der Danae, w. J. Traxel (ten), L. Szemere (ten), P. Schöffler (b-bar), C. Krauss (cnd), Vienna PO, Vienna State Opera Chorus [G] *(rec live, Salzburg, 8/14/52)* Melodram 3-▲ MEL 37061 (m) [AAD]
Wagner, R.:Der fliegende Holländer, w. Annelies Kupper (sop—Senta), Sieglinde Wagner (mez—Mary), Ernst Haefliger (ten—Steersman), Wolfgang Windgassen (ten—Erik), Josef Metternich (ten—Dutchman), Josef Greindl (bass—Daland), F. Fricsay (cnd), Berlin RIAS SO, Berlin RIAS Chamber Choir *(rec 1953)* Deutsche Grammophon 2-▲ 439714-2 (m) [ADD]

Kurenko, Maria (sop)
Rachmaninoff, S.:Songs, w. Vsevolod Pastukhoff (pno), Laurence Rosenthal (pno)—Melody; On the Death of a Linnet; Night Is Mournful; I Ask Mercy; Vocalise; Arion; I Remember That Day; Music; At Night in My Garden; To Her; Daisies; The Rat-Catcher; A Dream; A-ou; The Fountain; Yesterday We Met; The Changing Wind; Fragment from Alfred de Musset; It Is Pleasant Here; 2 Partings:A Dialogue (w. Vadim Gontzoff); What Happiness; Everything Is Taken from Me; The Ring; I Am Alone Again; We Will Rest; The Muse; Dissonance VAI Audio ▲ VAIA 1094 [ADD]

Kurisu, Yumiko (sop)
Bach, J.S.:Cant 4, w. Akira Tachikawa (ct), Koki Katano (ten), Peter Kooy (bass), M. Suzuki (cnd), Japan Bach Collegium *(rec Kobe Shoin Women's University, Japan, June – July 1995)* BIS ▲ CD 751 [DDD]
Bach, J.S.:Cants 12, w. Yoshikazu Mera (ct), Makoto Sakurada (ten), Peter Kooy (bass), M. Suzuki (cnd), Japan Bach Collegium *(rec Kobe Shoin Women's Univ, Japan, Apr 11–14, 1996)* BIS ▲ CD 791 [DDD]
Bach, J.S.:Cant 54, w. Yoshikazu Mera (ct), Makoto Sakurada (ten), Peter Kooy (bass), M. Suzuki (cnd), Japan Bach Collegium *(rec Kobe Shoin Women's Univ, Japan, Apr 11–14, 1996)* BIS ▲ CD 791 [DDD]
Bach, J.S.:Cant 150, w. Akira Tachikawa (ct), Koki Katano (ten), Peter Kooy (bass), M. Suzuki (cnd), Japan Bach Collegium *(rec Kobe Shoin Women's University, Japan, June – July 1995)* BIS ▲ CD 751 [DDD]

Kurisu, Yumiko (sop) (cont.)

Bach, J.S.:Cant 162, w. Yoshikazu Mera (ct), Makoto Sakurada (ten), Peter Kooy (bass), M. Suzuki (cnd), Japan Bach Collegium *(rec Kobe Shoin Women's Univ, Japan, Apr 11–14, 1996)* BIS ▲ CD 791 [DDD]

Bach, J.S.:Cant 182, w. Yoshikazu Mera (ct), Makoto Sakurada (ten), Peter Kooy (bass), M. Suzuki (cnd), Japan Bach Collegium *(rec Kobe Shoin Women's Univ, Japan, Apr 11–14, 1996)* BIS ▲ CD 791 [DDD]

Bach, J.S.:Cant 196, w. Akira Tachikawa (ct), Koki Katano (ten), Peter Kooy (bass), M. Suzuki (cnd), Japan Bach Collegium *(rec Kobe Shoin Women's University, Japan, June – July 1995)* BIS ▲ CD 751 [DDD]

Kurlan, David (sgr)

Strauss (II), Joh.:Eine Nacht in Venedig, w. Nola Fairbanks (sgr—Ciboletta), Thomas Tibbett Hayward (sgr—Mario), Laurel Hurley (sgr—Nina), David Kurlan (sgr—Senator Bartoldi), Guen Omeron (sgr—Barbara), Jack Russell (sgr—Duke of Palobino), Kenneth Schon (sgr—Filippo Del Aqua), Norwood Smith (sgr—Caramello), Enzo Stuarti (sgr—Pappacoda) *(rec Belock Recording Studio, Bayside, NY)* Everest ▲ EVC 9036 [AAD]

Kúrnava, Anton (bass)

Respighi, O.:La bella dormente nel bosco, w. Ivana Czaková (sop—Old Woman/Green Fairy), Adriana Kohútková (sop—Blue Fairy/Nightingale), Henrietta Lednárová (sop—Frog/Spindle), Jana Valásková (sop—Princess), Dagmar Pecková (mez—Cuckoo/Cat), Denisa Šlepkovská (mez—Queen/Duchess), Karol Bernáth (ten—Doctor), Guillermo Dominguez (ten—Prince April), Igor Pasek (ten—Jester), Ján Durčo (bar—Ambassador), Richard Haan (bar—King/Woodcutter), Stanislav Benačka (bass—Doctor), Anton Kúrnava (bass—Doctor), Marián Smolárik (bass—Doctor), M. Adriano (nar—Mr. Dollar Chèques), M. Adriano (cnd), Slovak RSO Bratislava, Ján Rozehnal (cnd), Slovak Phil Chorus *(rec Concert Hall of the Slovak Radio, Bratislava, June 8–20, 1994)* Marco Polo ("Opera Classics" series) ▲ 8.223742 [DDD]

Kurt, Stefan (sgr)

Waits, T.:The Black Rider:The Casting of Magic Bullets, w. Angelika Thomas (sgr—Anne), Annette Paulmann (sgr—Kätchen), Sona Cervena (sgr—Bird/Messenger/Spoonwoman), Monika Tahal (sgr—Witness/Bird/Shrink/Wilhelm's Double/Skeleton), Susi Eisenkolb (sgr—Bridesmaid/Pegleg's Double), Heinz Vossbrink (sgr—Kuno), Dominique Horwitz (sgr—Pegleg), Gerd Kunath (sgr—Bertram), Stefan Kurt (sgr—Wilhelm), Klaus Schreiber (sgr—Robert/Man on Stag/Georg Schmid), Jörg Holm (Old Uncle/Duke), Jan Moritz Steffen (sgr—Young Kuno/Bird/Shrink/Skeleton), Tom Waits (vocals/coliope/organ/chamberlain/mar/emax/guitar/train whistle), Ralph Carney (saxophone/bass clarinet/baritone horn), Bill Douglas (bass instrument), Kenny Wollesen (perc) Island ▲ 314518559–2

Kurz, Selma (sop)

Selma Kurz *(rec 1907–24)* Pearl ▲ PEA 9171 [ADD]

Kusche, Benno (bar)

Fall, L.:Der fidele Bauer (sels), w. Sonja Knittel (sop), Brigette Fassbaender (mez), Heinz Hoppe (ten), Fritz Wunderlich (ten), C. Michalski (cnd), Graunke SO, Rudolf Lamy Singers Emperor Operetta ▲ KO 86353

Fall, L.:Der liebe Augustin (sels), w. Sari Barabas (sop), Christine Gorner (sop), Heinz Hoppe (ten), C. Michalski (cnd), Graunke SO, Rudolf Lamy Singers Emperor Operetta ▲ KO 86352

Jessel, L.:Schwarzwaldmädel (sels), w. E. Lind (sop), F. Fehringer (ten), Hofmann (sgr), Schörg (sgr), Schubart (sgr), Marszalek (cnd), Cologne RSO, Cologne Radio Chorus [G] Acanta ▲ CD 42552 [DDD]

Kálmán, I.:Die Csárdásfürstin (sels), w. E. Köth (sop), F. Fehringer (ten), Heusser (sgr), Hofmann (sgr), Marszalek (cnd), Cologne Radio Orch, Cologne Radio Chorus [G] Acanta ▲ CD 42435 [DDD]

Kálmán, I.:Gräfin Mariza, w. A. Görner (sop), F. Wunderlich (ten), Hartung (sgr), Hofmann (sgr), Marszalek (cnd), Cologne Radio Orch, Cologne Radio Chorus [G] Acanta ▲ CD 42479 [DDD]

Künneke, E.:Der Vetter aus Dingsda (sels), w. G. Van Jüten (sop), Kollo (ten), Wolff (sgr), Breck (sgr), Geese, Künneke (cnd), Cologne RSO, Cologne Radio Chorus [G] Acanta ▲ CD 43460 [DDD]

Lehár, F.:Die lustige Witwe (sels), w. I. Hallstein (sop), L. Popp (sop), H. Hoppe (ten), Alexander (bar), Marszalek (cnd), Operretta Orch, Operetta Chorus [G] Acanta ▲ CD 43455 [DDD]

Lortzing, A.:Die beiden Schützen, w. K. Nentwig (sop), P. Kuen (ten), K. Smitt–Walter (bar), M. Pröbstl (bass), J. Koetsier (cnd), Bavarian RSO *(rec 1950)* Memories 2–▲ MEM 4546 [ADD]

Mussorgsky, M.:Boris Godunov, w. Martha Mödl (sop—Marina Mniszek), Lotte Schädle (sop—Xenia), Dorothea Siebert (mez—Fyodor), Hertha Töpper (mez—Xenia's wet–nurs), Karl Hermann Bennert (Boyer Khrushchyov), Lorenz Fehenberger (ten—Prince Shuysky), Hans Hopf (ten—Grigory), Karl Ostertag (ten—Missail), Hans Hotter (b–bar—Boris Godunov), Hermann Uhde (bar—Andrey Shchelkalov), Kurt Böhme (bass—Varlaam), Kim Borg (bass—Pimen), Kieth Engen (bass—Lewicki), Adolf Keil (bass—Nikitich), Benno Kusche (bar—Rangoni), Heinz Maria Linz (bass—Czernikowski), E. Jochum (cnd), Bavarian RSO, Bavarian Radio Chorus *(rec Munich, May 1957)* Myto 3–▲ MCD 953131

Orff, C.:Antigonae, w. Christel Goltz (sop), Paul Kuen (ten), Karl Ostertag (ten), Hermann Uhde (bar), N. Barth (bar), G. Solti (cnd), Bavarian State Opera Orch, Bavarian State Opera Chorus *(rec Prinzregententheater, Jan. 12, 1951)* Orfeo d'or 2–▲ 407952

Orff, C.:Die Kluge, w. E. Schwarzkopf (sop), R. Christ (ten), P. Kuén (ten), M. Cordes (bar), H. Prey (bar), G. Frick (bass), G. Wieter (bass), W. Sawallisch (cnd), Philharmonia Orch [G] EMI Classics ("Studio" series) 2–▲ CDMB 63712 [ADD]

Orff, C.:Der Mond—Ein kleines Welttheater, w. Karl Erb (nar), Paul Kuen (ten—Lad 3), Josef Knapp (bar—Lad 2), Benno Kusche (bar—Lad 1), Georg Hann (bass—St. Peter), Georg Wieter (bass—Lad 4), Rudolf Wünzer (bass—The Farmer), Karl Hanft (sgr—Innkeeper), Willy Rösner (sgr—The Major), R. Alberth (cnd), Bavarian RSO, Bavarian Radio Chorus *(rec Studio 1, Bavarian Radio, Jan. 19–20, 1950)* Calig ▲ CAL 50948 (m) [ADD]

Strauss (II), Joh.:Wiener Blut (sels), w. M. Schramm (sop), H. Gueden (sop), R. Schock (ten), R. Stolz (cnd), Vienna SO [G] Eurodisc ▲ 25–8370 [ADD]

Strauss, R.:Der Rosenkavalier, w. Claire Watson (sop—Feldmarschallin), Lucia Popp (sop—Sophie), Annelie Waas (sop—Marianne), Brigitte Fassbaender (mez—Octavian), Margaretthe Bence (ct—Annina), David Thaw (ten—Valzacchi), Karl Ridderbusch (bass—Baron Ochs), Benno Kusche (bass—Herr von Faninal), Albrecht Peter (bass—Police Inspector), C. Kleiber (cnd), Bavarian State Orch, Bavarian State Chorus *(rec live, Münchner Festspiele, July 20, 1974)* Arkadia 3–▲ 486 [ADD]

Strauss, R.:Salome, w. Astrid Varnay (sop—Salome), Hertha Töpper (mez—Der Page der Herodias), Margarete Klose (cta—Herodias), Hans Hopf (ten—Narraboth), Karl Hoppe (ten—1st Nazarene), Karl Ostertag (ten—1st Jew), Julius Patzak (ten—Herodes), Hans Braun (bar—Jochanaan), Benno Kusche (bar—2nd Soldier), Adolf Keil (bass—1st Soldier), Hans Hermann Nissen (bass—Ein Kappadozier), Max Proebstl (bass—2nd Nazarene), Walter Carnotch (sgr—4th Jew), Emil Graf (sgr—3rd Jew), Paul Kaussen (sgr—2nd Jew), Hildegard Limmer (sgr—A slave), Georg Witter (sgr—5th Jew), H. Weigert (cnd), Bavarian RSO *(rec June 21–25, 1953)* Bella Voce 2–▲ BLV 7210 [AAD]

Wagner, R.:Die Meistersinger von Nürnberg, w. E. Grümmer (sop), M. Höffgen (cta), R. Schock (ten), G. Unger (ten), H. Prey (bar), F. Frantz (b–bar), G. Frick (bass), R. Kempe (cnd), Berlin PO *(rec 1956)* EMI Classics 4–▲ CDMD 64154

Wagner, R.:Das Rheingold, w. L. Otto (sop), M. Muszely (sop), J. Blatter (mez), R. Stewart (mez), S. Wagner (mez), R. Schock (ten), H. Melchert (ten), F. Frantz (bass), B. Kusche (bass), J. Metternich (bass), R. Kempe (cnd), Berlin Staatskapelle *(rec Mar. 1959)* Berlin Classics ("Eterna" series) ▲ BER 2035 [ADD]

Kusiewicz, Piotr (sgr)

Orff, C.:Carmina burana, w. Venceslava Hruba–Freiberger (sop), Rolf Havenstein (sgr), K. Penderecki (cnd), Karol Szymanowski State PO, Karol Szymanowski State Phil Choir *(rec Cracow, Poland, Jan 27–28, 1989)* Arts Music ▲ 47177–2 [DDD]

Kusjner, Ivan (bar)

Live in Prague, w. Dagmar Pecková (mez), Prague National Theater Orch [cnd:Jan Stych] *(rec live, Jan 17, 1996)* Supraphon ▲ SUP 3180

Kusnjer, Iván (bar)

Brod, M.:Songs, Op. 32, w. Katerina Kachlikova (sop), Frantisek Kuda (pno) Supraphon ▲ SUP 112188 [DDD]

Dvořák, A.:The Spectre's Bride, Op. 69, w. L. Aghova (sop), J. Protschka (ten), G. Albrecht (cnd), Hamburg State PO, Prague Phil Chorus [Cz] *(rec live 1991)* Orfeo ▲ 259921 [DDD]

Kusnjer, Iván (bar) (cont.)

Dvořák, A.:The Spectre's Bride, Op. 110, w. Eva Urbanová (sop), Ludovit Ludha (ten), J. Belohlávek (cnd), Prague SO, Pavel Kühn (cnd), Prague Phil Chorus *(rec live, 1995)* Supraphon ▲ SUP 3091

Janácek, L.:Fate, w. Lívia Ághová (sop—Míla), Ludmila Nováková (sop—Frl. Stuhlá/Součková), Marta Benačková (cta—Mílas Mother), Štefan Margita (ten—Dr. Suda/Hrázda), Peter Straka (ten—Zivný), Ivan Kusnjer (bar—Konečný/Verva), Peter Mikuláš (bass—Lhotský), G. Albrecht (cnd), Czech PO, Prague Chamber Choir *(rec 1995)* Orfeo ▲ 384 951 [DDD]

Janácek, L.:Folk Ballads, w. Dagmar Peckova (sop), Marian Kaplansky (pno) Supraphon ▲ SUP 112225 [DDD]

Janácek, L.:Hukvaldy Folk Poetry, w. Dagmar Peckova (mez), Marian Kaplansky (pno) Supraphon ▲ SUP 112214 [DDD]

Janácek, L.:Moravian Folk Poetry, w. Dagmar Peckova (mez), Marian Kaplansky (pno) Supraphon ▲ SUP 112214 [DDD]

Janácek, L.:Silesian Songs, w. Dagmar Peckova (mez), Marian Kaplansky (pno) Supraphon ▲ SUP 112214 [DDD]

Mahler, G.:Lieder eines fahrenden Gesellen, w. J. Belohlávek (cnd), Czech PO Supraphon ▲ SUP 3026

Martinů, B.:Field Mass, w. M. Kejmar (tpt), B. Kotmel (cnd), Czech PO, Czech Phil Chorus [Cz] Chandos ▲ CHAN 9138 [DDD]

Mysliveček, J.:Isacco figura, w. Ilona Czaková (sgr), Hye Jin Kim (sgr), Tatiana Korovina (sgr), Victoria Luchianez (sgr), Vladimir Dolezal (ten), I. Parik (cnd), Prague Sinfonietta, Pavel Kühn (cnd), Kühn Chorus Supraphon 2–▲ SUP 3209

Orff, C.:Carmina burana, w. Zdena Kloubová (sop), Vladimir Dolezal (ten), G. Delogu (cnd), Prague SO, Bambini di Praga, Kühn Choir *(rec live, Prague, Dec 12, 1995)* Supraphon ▲ SUP 3160

Orff, C.:Carmina burana, w. E. Jenisová (sop), V. Dolezal (ten), S. Gunzenhauser (cnd), Czech–Slovak RSO Bratislava, Slovak Phil Chorus Naxos ▲ 8.550196 [DDD] Δ 7.550196 [DDD]

Smetana, B.:Dalibor, w. Eva Urbanová (sgr), Leo Maria Vodička (ten), Z. Košler (cnd), Prague National Theater Orch, Prague National Theater Chorus Supraphon 2–▲ SUP 0077 [DDD]

Suk, J.:Epilogue, w. Z. Jehličková (sop), J. Galla (bass), V. Neumann (cnd), Czech PO, Czech Phil Chorus [Cz] Supraphon ▲ 11 0116–2 [DDD]

Suk, J.:Epilogue, w. Zora Jehličková (sop), Ján Galla (bass), V. Neumann (cnd), Czech PO Supraphon 2–▲ SUP 111962 [DDD]

Zemlinsky, A. von:Lyric Sym, w. K. Armstrong (sop), B. Gregor (cnd), Czech PO Supraphon ▲ 11 0395–2 [DDD]

Zemlinsky, A. von:Lyric Sym, w. Jirina Markova (sop), V. Válek (cnd), Prague RSO *(rec live, Prague, 1993)* Praga ▲ PR 250092

Küttenbaum, Annette (mez)

Schoeck, O.:Massimilla Doni, w. E. Mathis (sop), H. Winkler (ten), H. Stamm (bass), G. Albrecht (cnd), Cologne RSO, Cologne Radio Chorus [G] Koch Schwann 2–▲ CD 314025 [DDD]

Wagner, R.:Götterdämmerung, w. A. Evans (sop—Brünnhilde), E.–M. Bundschuh (sop—Gutrune), H. Leidland (sop—Woglinde), A. Küttenbaum (sop—Wellgunde), W. Meier (mez—Waltraute), B. Svendén (mez—1st Norn), J. Turner (mez), *(cnd & orch unknown)* Teldec 4–▲ 4509–94194–2 [DDD]

Kuusk, Ivo (ten)

Tubin, E.:Barbara von Tisenhusen, w. H. Raamat (sop), M. Jôgeva (mez), A. Kollo (ten), V. Puura (bar), T. Sild (bar), H. Miilberg (bass), U. Kreen (bass), P. Lilje (cnd), Estonia Opera Co Orch [Estonian] Ondine 2–▲ ODE 776–2D [DDD]

Kuznetsova, Ludmila (mez)

Gretchaninoff, A.:Snowflakes, w. V. Polianski (cnd), Russian State SO [arr voice & orch] Chandos ▲ CHAN 9397 [DDD]

Kweksilber, Marjanne (sop)

Bach, J.S.:Cant 51, w. G. Leonhardt (cnd), Leonhardt Consort [G] Teldec 2–▲ 2292–42422–2 [AAD]

Beethoven, L. van:Folksong Arrs, w. S. Hoogland (pno), V. Beths (vn), A. Bijlsma (vc)—Irish Songs, WoO 152, Nos. 1,5,8 & 11; Scottish Songs, Op. 108, Nos. 2,3,5,7,8,17,20 & 24 [E] *(rec 6/90)* Channel Classics ▲ CCS 1491 [DDD]

Campra, A.:L'Europe galante, w. R. Yakar (sop), R. Jacobs (ct), S. Nimsgern (bar), G. Leonhardt (cnd), La Petite Bande Editio Classica 2–▲ 77059–2–RG [ADD]

Gluck, C.W.:Orfeo ed Euridice, w. M. Falewicz (sop), R. Jacobs (alt), S. Kuijken (cnd), La Petite Bande, Collegium Vocale Accent 2–▲ 48223/24 [DDD]

Handel, G.F.:Messiah, w. James Bowman (ct), Paul Elliot (ten), G. Reinhart (bar), T. Koopman (cnd), Amsterdam Baroque Orch, The Sixteen Erato 3–▲ 2292–45960–2

Lully, J.–B.:Le Bourgeois gentilhomme, w. R. Yakar (sop), R. Jacobs (ct), S. Nimsgern (bar), G. Leonhardt (cnd), La Petite Bande Editio Classica 2–▲ 77059–2–RG [ADD]

Kwella, Patrizia (sop)

Bach, J.S.:St. John Passion, w. D. James (ct), W. Kendall (ten), I. Partridge (ten), M. George (bar), D. Wilson–Johnson (b–bar), H. Christophers (cnd), The Sixteen Orch, The Sixteen [G] Chandos ("Chaconne" series) 2–▲ CHAN 0507/08 [DDD]

Gay, J.:The Beggar's Opera (sels), w. P. Elliott (ten), J. Barlow (cnd), Broadside Band—9 songs in 30 versions [E] Harmonia Mundi France ▲ HMC 901071

Handel, G.F.:L'Allegro, Il Penseroso ed il Moderato, w. Michael Ginn (trb), Marie McLaughlin (sop), J. E. Gardiner (cnd), English Baroque Soloists, Monteverdi Choir London Erato 2–▲ 2292–45377–2 ZA

Handel, G.F.:Aminta e Fillide, w. G. Fisher (sop), D. Darlow (cnd), London Handel Orch [I] Hyperion ▲ CDA 66118

Handel, G.F.:Chandos Anthems (11), w. L. Dawson (sop), J. Bowman (alt), I. Partridge (ten), M. George (bass), H. Christophers (cnd), The Sixteen Orch, The Sixteen Chandos ("Chaconne" series) 4–▲ CHAN 0554 [DDD]

Handel, G.F.:Chandos Anthems (11), w. J. Bowman (ct), I. Partridge (ten), M. George (bass), H. Christophers (cnd), The Sixteen Orch, The Sixteen—Anthem Nos. 7–9 [E] Chandos ("Chaconne" series) ▲ CHAN 0505 [DDD]

Handel, G.F.:Messiah (sels), w. Catherine Denley (mez), John Mark Ainsley (ten), Bryn Terfel (b–bar), M. Stephenson (cnd), London Musici, London Chamber Choir Conifer Classics ▲ 74321–15354–2

Handel, G.F.:Semele, w. Norma Burrowes (sop), Elizabeth Priday (sop), Catherine Denley (mez), Della Jones (mez), Timothy Penrose (alt), Anthony Rolfe–Johnson (ct), Maldwyn Davies (ten), Robert Lloyd (b–bar), David Thomas (bass), J. E. Gardiner (cnd), English Baroque Soloists, Monteverdi Choir London Erato 2–▲ 2292–45982–2

Holst, G.:The Dream–City, w. R. Hickox (cnd), City of London Sinfonia [E] Hyperion ▲ CDA 66099 [DDD]

Lalande, M.–R. de:Dies Irae, w. L. Perillo (sop), H. Crook (ten), H. Lamy (ten), P. Harvey (bar), P. Herreweghe (cnd), La Chapelle Royale Orch, Chapelle Royale Choir [L] Harmonia Mundi France ▲ HMC 901352

Lalande, M.–R. de:Miserere mei, Deus, w. L. Perillo (sop), H. Crook (ten), H. Lamy (ten), P. Harvey (bar), P. Herreweghe (cnd), La Chapelle Royale Orch, Chapelle Royale Choir [L] Harmonia Mundi France ▲ HMC 901352

Matthews, C.:Night's Mask, w. L. Friend (cnd), Nash Ensemble Virgin Classics ▲ CDC 59061

Monteverdi, C.:Orfeo, w. E. Kirkby (sop), J. Smith (sop), N. Rogers (ten), S. Varcoe (bar), D. Thomas (bass), N. Rogers (cnd), London Cornett & Sackbutt Ensemble, C. Medlam (cnd), London Baroque Chiaroscuro EMI Classics ▲ CDMB 64947

Telemann, G.P.:Cants, w. C. Denley (mez), S. Roberts (b–bar), M. George (bass), R. Hickox (cnd), Collegium Musicum 90—Die Donner Ode Chandos ("Chaconne" series) ▲ CHAN 0548 [DDD]

Telemann, G.P.:Motets, w. C. Denley (mez), S. Roberts (b–bar), M. George (bass), R. Hickox (cnd), Collegium Musicum 90—Deus judicium tuum Chandos ("Chaconne" series) ▲ CHAN 0548 [DDD]

Vivaldi, A.:Gloria, RV.589, w. E. Priday (sop), C. Wyn–Rogers (alt), A. Carwood (ten), S. Darlington (cnd), Hanover Band, Christ Church Cathedral Choir Oxford Nimbus ▲ NI 5278 [DDD]

Vivaldi, A.:Gloria (& Intro), RV.588, w. E. Priday (sop), C. Wyn–Rogers (alt), A. Carwood (ten), S. Darlington (cnd), Hanover Band, Christ Church Cathedral Choir Oxford Nimbus ▲ NI 5278 [DDD]

Kwon, Hellen (sop)

Braunfels, W.:Die Vögel, w. Helen Kwon (sop—Nightingale), Wolfgang Holzmair (bar—Hoopoe), Matthias Gorne (b–bar—Prometheus), Michael Krause (sgr—Loyal Friend), Endrik Wottrich (sgr—Good Hope), L. Zagrosek (cnd), Berlin German SO, Berlin Radio Chorus London ("Entartete Musik" series) ▲ 448 679–2

Kwon, Hellen (sop) (cont.)
Mendelssohn, Fanny:Io d'amor, oh Dio, mi moro, w. G. Albrecht (cnd), Hamburg State PO
Capriccio ▲ 10449 [DDD]
Mendelssohn, F.:Infelice, w. G. Albrecht (cnd), Hamburg State PO Capriccio ▲ 10449 [DDD]

Kyhlberg, Ola (sgr)
Nilsson, T.:Out of Earthly Night, w. Gudrun Bruna (sop), Marianne Mellnäs (sop), Kaysa Hälldin (alt), Lars Sjögren (ten), Göran Swartz (bass), Sture Hedin (sgr), Lars Ljungman (sgr), Nils Philipson (sgr), Ulrik Quale (sgr), Nils Spangenberg (sgr), Britta Therén (sgr), Karl-Erik Welin (org), Torsten Nilsson (cnd), Oscar's Motet Choir *(rec Oscar's Church, Stockholm, Sweden, Apr 26–27, 1978)*
BIS ▲ CD 138 [AAD]

Kyhle, Magnus (ten)
The Most Beloved Opera Choruses, w. Royal Swedish Opera Chorus [cnd:Sixten Ehrling], Carina Morling (mez), Ingrid Tobiasson (cta), Anders Lorentzon (bass) Caprice ▲ CAP 21520

Kyrkjebø, Sissel (sgr)
The Best of Christmas in Vienna, w. Plácido Domingo (ten), Vienna SO, Charles Aznavour (sgr), José Carreras (ten), Dionne Warwick (sgr) *(rec Vienna)* Sony Classical ▲ SK 62696 ■ ST 62696
Plácido Domingo:The Best of Christmas in Vienna, w. Plácido Domingo (ten), José Carreras (ten), Dionne Warwick (sgr), Charles Aznavour, Vienna SO [cnd:Vjekoslav Sutej]
Sony Classical ▲ SK 62696 ■ ST 62696

Kyzlink, Jan (bar)
Báchorek, M.:Music of, w. Osvald Albin (nar), Otakar Brousek (nar), Jan Vlassak (nar), Brigita Šulcová (sop), Drahomira Drobková (cta), Karel Průša (bass), Pavel Kamas (sgr), Jana Stuperkova-Majtnerova (sgr), Bretislav Vojkuvka (sgr), O. Trhlík (cnd), Ostrava Janáček PO, Prague SO, Ostrava Janáček Chorus, Ostrava Women's Chamber Chorus, Permoník Children's Chorus—Lidice; Stereofonietta; Hukvald Poem
Panton ▲ PAN 811338 [AAD/DDD]
Báchorek, M.:Stereofonietta, w. Brigita Šulcová (sop), O. Trhlík (cnd), Ostrava Janáček PO *(rec Smetana Hall of Prague's Municipal House, Feb 10 & 11, 1988)* Panton ▲ 811338-2 [AAD]

La Barbara, Joan (sop)
Ashley, R.:Improvement, w. J. Humbert (sgr—Linda), J. La Barbara (sop—Now Eleanor), A. X. Neuburg (sgr—Mr. Payne's Mother), T. Buckner (sgr—Don/Mr. Payne/Linda's Companion), S. Ashley (sgr—Junior, Jr.), A. Klein (sgr—Doctor), R. Ashley (sgr—Narrator), *(cnd & orch unknown)* [E]
Elektra/Nonesuch 2-▲ 79289-2
Cage, J.:Eight Whiskus Voice *(rec Central Park Summerstage, New York City, July 23, 1992)*
Music & Arts ▲ CD 875 [DDD]
Cage, J.:Four Walls, w. M. Leng Tan (pno) New Albion ▲ NA 037 [DDD]
Cage, J.:Music for..., w. William Winant (perc), Leonard Stein (pno) *(rec Central Park Summerstage, New York City, July 23, 1992)* Music & Arts ▲ CD 875 [DDD]
Cage, J.:Songs, w. L. Stein (pno), W. Winant (perc)—A Flower (1950); Mirakus (1984); Eight Whiskus (1984); The Wonderful Widow of Eighteen Springs (1942); Nowth upon Nacht (1984); Sonnekus (1985); Forever and Sunsmell (1942); Solos for Voice [from Songbooks] Nos. 49, 52 & 67 (1970); Music for Two (by One) (1984) New Albion ▲ NA 035 [DDD]
Dodge, C.:The Waves New Albion ▲ NA 043
Feldman, Morton:Only *(rec Fantasy Studios, Berkeley, CA, O'Henry Studios, Burbank, CA & Metamusic Productions, Los Angeles, CA, Jan 18, Aug 25–26 & Dec 1)* New Albion ▲ NA 085
Feldman, Morton:Pnos & Voices, w. Ralph Grierson (pno/cel) *(rec Fantasy Studios, Berkeley, CA, O'Henry Studios, Burbank, CA & Metamusic Productions, Los Angeles, CA, Jan 18, Aug 25–26 & Dec 1)*
New Albion ▲ NA 085
Feldman, Morton:Three Voices [E] New Albion ▲ NA 018
Feldman, Morton:Vertical Thoughts 5, w. S. Mosko (cnd), San Francisco Contemporary Music Players *(rec Fantasy Studios, Berkeley, CA, O'Henry Studios, Burbank, CA & Metamusic Productions, Los Angeles, CA, Jan 18, Aug 25–26 & Dec 1)* New Albion ▲ NA 085
Feldman, Morton:Voice, Vn & Pno, w. S. Mosko (cnd), San Francisco Contemporary Music Players *(rec Fantasy Studios, Berkeley, CA, O'Henry Studios, Burbank, CA & Metamusic Productions, Los Angeles, CA, Jan 18, Aug 25–26 & Dec 1)* New Albion ▲ NA 085
Feldman, Morton:Voices & Vc, w. Erika Duke Kirkpatrick (vc) *(rec Fantasy Studios, Berkeley, CA, O'Henry Studios, Burbank, CA & Metamusic Productions, Los Angeles, CA, Jan 18, Aug 25–26 & Dec 1)*
New Albion ▲ NA 085
Garcia, O.J.:Sitio sin Nombre O.O. Discs ▲ OO 6 [DDD]
La Barbara, J.:73 Poems Lovely Music ▲ LCD 3002 [DDD]
La Barbara, J.:Silent Scroll, w. Newband Mode ▲ 18
La Barbara, J.:"Sound Paintings"—Urban Tropics (1988); ShadowSong (1979); Time(d) Trials and Unscheduled Events (1984); Erin (1980); Klee Alee (1979); Berliner Träume (1983)
Lovely Music ▲ LCD 3001 [ADD]

La Barbara, Joan (sop/perc)
Cage, J.:Four [6], w. John Cage (voice/perc), Leonard Stein (pno/perc), William Winant (perc) *(rec Central Park Summerstage, New York City, July 23, 1992)* Music & Arts ▲ CD 875 [DDD]

La Barbara, Joan (voc)
Subotnick, M.:Trembling, w. R. Davidovici (vn), A. Wodnicki (pno), L. Austin ("Ghost" elec) *(rec Dec. 1992)* Centaur ▲ CRC 2170 [DDD]

Labbette, Dora (sop)
Delius, F.:Songs, w. T. Beecham (pno)—Cradle Song; The Nightingale; Twilight Fancies *(rec June 24 & July 10, 1929)* Dutton Laboratories ▲ CDLX 7011 [ADD]
Handel, G.F.:Messiah, w. Muriel Brunskill (cta), Hubert Eisdell (ten), Harold Williams (bar), T. Beecham (cnd), BBC SO, BBC Choir *(rec 1927)* Pearl 2-▲ PEA 9456 [DDD]

Labelle, Dominique (sop)
Mozart, W.A.:Missa, K.427, w. Nancy Armstrong (sop), Jeffery Thomas (ten), Richard Morrison (bass), A. Parrott (cnd), Boston Early Music Festival Orch, Handel & Haydn Society Chorus [L]
Denon ▲ CO 79573 [DDD]
Vaughan Williams, R.:Sym 7, w. R. Allam (nar), R. Leppard (cnd), Indianapolis SO, Indianapolis Symphonic Women's Choir Koss Classics ▲ KC 2214 [DDD]

Labò, Flaviano (ten)
Bellini, V.:Il pirata, w. Montserrat Caballé (sop—Imogene), Flora Raffanelli (sop—Adele), Flaviano Labó (ten—Gualtiero), Giuseppe Baratti (ten—Itulbo), Piero Cappuccilli (bar—Ernesto), E. Ghiglia (cnd), Florence Teatro Comunale Orch, Florence Teatro Comunale Chorus *(rec live, Florence, 1967)*
Melodram 2-▲ IMC 205002 [ADD]
Bellini, V.:Il pirata, w. M. Caballé (sop), P. Cappuccilli (bar), F. Capuana (cnd), Florence Maggio Musicale Orch, Florence Maggio Musicale Chorus [I] *(rec live, Florence 1967)*
Memories 2-▲ HR 4186/87 [ADD]
Bellini, V.:Il pirata, w. M. Caballè (sop), F. Raffanelli (sop), G. Baratti (ten), P. Cappuccilli (bar), U. Trama (bass), E. Ghiglia (cnd), *(orch unknown) (rec Florence, 1967)*
Great Opera Performances ▲ GOP 729
Bellini, V.:Il pirata, w. M. Caballé (sop), P. Cappuccilli (bar), F. Capuana (cnd), Florence Maggio Musicale Orch, Florence Maggio Musicale Chorus [I] *(rec live, Florence 1967)* Melodram 2-▲ MEL 27015
Cilea, F.:Gloria, w. M. Roberti (sop), A. M. Rota (cta), A. Albertini (bar), L. Testi (bar), E. Campi (bass), F. Mazzoli (bass), F. Previtali (cnd), Turin RAI Orch, Turin RAI Chorus [I] *(rec live, Turin July 8, 1969)*
Memories ▲ HR 4472 [ADD]
Flaviano Labò Bongiovanni ▲ GB 1068-2 [ADD]
Gounod, C.:Faust, w. Renata Scotto (sop—Margherita), Anna di Stasio (mez—Marta), Flaviano Labò (ten—Faust), Edoardo Gimenez (ten—Siebel), Piero Cappuccilli (bar—Valentino), Bruno Grella (bar—Wagner), Ruggero Raimondi (bass—Mefistofele), M. Gusella (cnd), Margherita Theater Orch, Margherita Theater Chorus *(rec Genova, 1970)* Golden Age of Opera 2-▲ GAO 170/71 [ADD]
Magda Olivero & Flaviano Labò in Concert, w. Magda Olivero (sop), Jacques Bazire (cnd), Marsiglia Opera Orch, Raina Kabaivanska (sop), Gianpiero Matromei (bar), Carlo Meliciani (bar), Oliveiro de Fabritiis (cnd), La Scala Orch, Turin RAI Orch *(rec between 1969 & 1973)*
Bongiovanni ▲ GB 1105 [ADD]
Verdi, G.:La traviata (sels), w. L. Gencer (sop), P. Cappuccilli (bar), N. Rescigno (cnd), Rio de Janeiro Teatro Municipale Orch, Rio de Janeiro Teatro Municipale Chorus *(rec live 8/8/64)*
Golden Age of Opera ▲ GAO 120 [ADD]

La Bruce, E. (mez)
Foss, L.:Thirteen Ways of Looking at a Blackbird, w. C. Meves (fl), A. Brovan (pno), M. Shadd (perc) [E] *(rec 1989–90)* Koss Classics ▲ KC 1006 [DDD]

Labusch, Dorothee (cta)
Wehrli, W.:Ein weltliches Requiem, w. R. Amsler (sop), B. Hunziker (ten), R. Strebel (bass), K. Girod (cnd), Aargauer CO, Aargauer Chamber Choir *(rec live Jan. 12, 1992)* Jecklin ▲ JS 276-2 [DDD]

Laciura, Anthony (ten)
Verdi, G.:Il trovatore, w. A. Millo (sop), D. Zajick (mez), S. Kelly (cta), P. Domingo (ten), T. Willson (ten), J. Morris (bass), G. Bater (bass), J. Levine (cnd), Metropolitan Opera Orch, New York Metropolitan Opera Chorus *(rec June 18, 1991)* Sony Classical 2-▲ S2K 48070 [DDD]

Lacoste, Mireille (sgr)
Varney, L.:Les Mousquetaires au couvent, w. Gabrielle Ristori (mez), Camille Rouquetty (ten), Gabriel Bacquier (bar), Louis Musy (b-bar), Pierre Blanc (sgr), Pauline Carton (sgr), Jacqueline Cauchard (sgr), Colette Riedinger (sgr), R. Benedetti (cnd) Musidisc 2-▲ MUS 202262 [AAD]

Lacy, Randolph (ten)
Rosner, A.:Nightstone, w. Timothy Hester (pno) *(rec Dudley Recital Hall, Univ of Houston)*
Albany ▲ TROY 163 [DDD]

Ladysz, Bernard (bass)
Donizetti, G.:Lucia di Lammermoor, w. M. Callas (sop), F. Tagliavini (ten), P. Cappuccilli (bar), T. Serafin (cnd), Philharmonia Orch [I] EMI Classics 2-▲ CDCB 47440
Moniuszko, S.:Haunted Manor, w. Halina Slonicka (sop), Bozena Brun-Baranska (mez), Barbara Lawcewicz (mez), Krystyna Szczepanska (mez), Zdzislaw Nikodem (ten), Bogdan Paprocki (ten), Andrzej Hiolski (bar), Edmund Kossowski (bass), W. Rowicki (cnd), Warsaw State Opera House Orch, Warsaw National Opera Chorus *(rec Warsaw, 1965)* Polskie Nagrania ▲ PNCD 093 [AAD]
Penderecki, K.:The Passion & Death of Our Lord Jesus Christ According to St. Luke, w. Leszek Herdegen (nar), Stefania Woytowicz (sop), Andrzej Hiolski (bar), H. Czyz (cnd), Cracow PO, Cracow Phil Boys' Chorus, Cracow Phil Mixed Choir Polskie Nagrania 2-▲ PNCD 017 A/B
Verdi, G.:I vespri siciliani, w. A. Stella (sop—Elena), M. Filippeschi (ten—Arrigo), G. Taddei (bar—Monforte), B. Ladysz (bass—Procida), T. Serafin (cnd), Palermo Teatro Massimo Orch, Palermo Teatro Massimo Chorus *(rec Jan. 18, 1957)* Golden Age of Opera 2-▲ GAO 145/46 [ADD]

Laethem, Katelijne van (sop)
Willaert, A.:Madrigals, w. Romanesque—Qual dolcezza giamai; Zoia zentil; Dessus le marché d'Arras; Allons, allons gay; Canzon di Adriano; Quante volte diss'io; Vecchie letrose; Chi la dira; Chi la dira Disminuita; Tiento IV sobre "Qui la dira"; E se per gelosia; Un giorno mi pregò; A la fontana; Cingari simo; O quando a quando havea; Joyssance vous donneray; Joyssance; Arousez vo violette; O bene mio famm'uno favore; Occhio non fu; Sempre mi ride sta Ricercar ▲ 151145
Willaert, A.:Ricercars, w. Romanesque—Ricercar X Ricercar ▲ 151145

Laferrière, Marie (sop)
Gratton, H.:Imagerie:Christmas Pastoral, w. M. Keable (actor), S. Léonard (actor), J.-L. Millette (actor), C. Rioux (mez), B. Levasseur (bar), N. Richard (b-bar), L. Lavigueur (cnd), Louis Lavigueur Instrumental Ensemble, Louis Lavigueur Vocal Ensemble [F] *(rec 5/91)*
CBC ("SM 5000" series) ▲ SMCD 5109 [DDD]

Lafont, Jean-Philippe (bar)
Debussy, C.:La Chute de la maison Usher, w. C. Barbaux (sop), G. Prêtre (cnd), Monte Carlo PO
EMI Classics ▲ CDM 64687
Gluck, C.W.:La Recontre imprévue, w. C. Le Coz (sop), L. Dawson (sop), C. Dubosc (sop), S. Marin-Degor (sop), G. Fletcher (sgr), F. Dudziak (ten), G. de Mey (ten), J.-L. Viala (ten), G. Cachémaille (bar), J. E. Gardiner (cnd), Paris Lyon Opera Orch, Paris Lyon Opera Chorus [F]
Erato 2-▲ 2292-45516-2 [DDD]
Gounod, C.:Messe solennelle de St. Cécile, w. B. Hendricks (sop), L. Dale (ten), G. Prêtre (cnd), Radio France PO, French Radio Chorus [L] EMI Classics ▲ CDC 47094
Schmitt, F.:Le palais hanté, w. C. Barbaux (sop), G. Prêtre (cnd), Monte Carlo PO
EMI Classics ▲ CDM 64687

La France, Robert (b-bar)
Demars, J.:An American Requiem, w. Joni Killian (sop), Linda Childs (mez), George Killian (ten), James DeMars (cnd), Arizona State Univ Choirs *(rec Phoenix Symphony Hall, Jan 17, 1994)*
Renaissance ▲ 94001 [DDD]

Lagger, Peter (bass)
Bruckner, A.:Te Deum, w. M. Stader (sop), S. Wagner (mez), E. Haefliger (ten), E. Jochum (cnd), Berlin PO, German Opera Chorus [L] Deutsche Grammophon 4-▲ 423127-2 [ADD]
Martin, F.:Requiem, w. E. Speiser (sop), R. Bollen (cta), E. Tappy (ten), A. Luy (org), F. Martin (cnd), Swiss-Italian Orch, Union Chorale, Choir of Our Lady of Lausanne, Ars Laeta Vocal Group *(rec live, May 4, 1973)* Jecklin-Disco ▲ JD 631-2 [ADD]
Orff, C.:Der Mond—Ein kleines Welttheater, w. R. Christ (ten), P. Kuén (ten), K. Schmitt-Walter (bar), H. Graml (bar), H. Hotter (b-bar), W. Sawallisch (cnd), Philharmonia Orch, Philharmonia Chorus [G]
EMI Classics ("Studio" series) 2-▲ CDMB 63712 [ADD]
Wagner, R.:Die Meistersinger von Nürnberg, w. C. Ligendza (sop), C. Ludwig (mez), P. Domingo (ten), R. Laubenthal (ten), D. Fischer-Dieskau (bar), R. Hermann (bar), E. Jochum (cnd), German Opera Orch, German Opera Chorus [G] Deutsche Grammophon 4-▲ 415278-2 [ADD]
Wagner, R.:Die Meistersinger von Nürnberg, w. C. Ligendza (sop), C. Ludwig (mez), P. Domingo (ten), R. Laubenthal (ten), D. Fischer-Dieskau (bar), R. Hermann (bar), E. Jochum (cnd), German Opera Orch, German Opera Chorus Deutsche Grammophon ("Domingo Edition" series) ▲ 435406-2

Laghezza, Rosa (mez)
Donizetti, G.:La fille du régiment, w. Edita Gruberová (sop), Deon van der Walt (sgr), Philippe Fourcade (bass), François Castel (sgr), M. Panni (cnd), Munich RSO, Bavarian Radio Chorus
Nightingale Classics 2-▲ NIG 70566
Mascagni, P.:Cavalleria rusticana, w. J. Norman (sop), M. Senn (mez), G. Giacomini (ten), D. Hvorostovsky (bar), S. Bychkov (cnd), Orch de Paris Philips ▲ 432105-2 [DDD]

Lagrange, Michèl (sop)
Berlioz, H.:Herminie, w. J.-C. Casadesus (cnd), Lille National Orch
Harmonia Mundi France ▲ HMC 901542
Lecocq, C.:Songs, w. Erwartung Ensemble—Le renard et les raisins; Le corbeau et le renard; La gernouille qui veut se faire plus grosse que le boeuf; Le loup et l'agneau; La cigale et la fourmi; Le savetier et le financier; La chauve-souris et les deux belettes Accord ▲ ACD 205222 [DDD]
Offenbach, J.:Songs, w. Erwartung Ensemble—Le berger et la mer; La laitière et le pot au lait; Le corbeau et le renard; La cigale et la fourmi; Le rat de ville et le rat des champs; Le savetier et le financier Accord ▲ ACD 205222 [DDD]
Poulenc, F.:Stabat mater, w. S. Baudo (cnd), Lyon National Orch, Lyon National Chorus [L]
Harmonia Mundi France ▲ HMC 905149
Ravel, M.:L'Enfant et les sortilèges, w. E. Vidal (sop), M. Damonte (mez), M. Mahé (mez), A. Chedel (cta), L. Pezzino (ten), M. Barrard (bar), V. le Texier (b-bar), A. Lombard (cnd), Bordeaux-Aquitaine National Orch, Bordeaux Grand Théâtre Municipal Chorus [F] Valois ▲ V 4670
Saint-Saëns, C.:Songs, w. Erwartung Ensemble—La cigale et la fourmi Accord ▲ ACD 205222 [DDD]

Laholm, Eyvind (ten)
Wagner, R.:Die Meistersinger von Nürnberg (sels), w. T. Lemnitz (sop), R. Bockelmann (bar), E. Fuchs (bar), W. Furtwängler (cnd), Vienna State Opera Orch, Vienna State Opera Chorus *(rec Sept. 5, 1938)*
Koch Schwann 2-▲ SCH 314522 [ADD]
Wagner, R.:Die Meistersinger von Nürnberg (sels), w. Lotte Lehmann (sop—Eva), Eyvind Laholm (ten—Walther), Ludwig Hofmann (bass—Hans Sachs), F. von Weingartner (cnd), Vienna State Opera Orch, Vienna State Opera Chorus *(rec Vienna, Sept. 20, 1935)*
Koch Schwann 2-▲ SCH 314622 [ADD]

Laine, Cleo (sgr)
Sometimes When We Touch, w. James Galway (fl) RCA Victor ▲ RCD1-3628 ■ ARK1-3628

Laiter, Alexandre (ten)
Weill, K.:Berlin Requiem, w. P. Kooy (bass), P. Herreweghe (cnd), Musique Oblique Ensemble, Chapelle Royale Choir [G] *(rec May 1992)* Harmonia Mundi France ▲ HMC 901422

Lakes, Gary (ten)
Albert, S.:Into Eclipse, w. G. Schwarz (cnd), Juilliard Orch [E] New World ▲ 80381-2 [DDD]

Lakes, Gary (ten) (cont.)
Beethoven, L. van:Sym 9, "Choral Sym", w. Roberta Alexander (sop), Florence Quivar (cta), Paul Plishka (bass), A. Previn (cnd), Royal PO RCA Red Seal ▲ 09026-60363-2
Berlioz, H.:Les Troyens, w. F. Pollet (sop—Dido), D. Voigt (sop—Cassandre), C. Dubosc (sop—Ascagne), H. Perraguin (cta—Anna), G. Lakes (ten—Aeneas), J.-L. Maurette (ten—Iopas), J. M. Ainsley (ten—Hylas), M. P. (ten—Panthee), G. Cross (ten—Sinon), G. Quilico (bar—Chorebe), J.-P. Courtis (b-bar—Narbal), M. Belleau (bass—Ghost of Hector), R. Schirrer (bass—Priam), C. Dutoit (cnd), Montreal SO, Montreal Sym Chorus London 4-▲ 443693-2 [DDD]
Janácek, L.:Slavonic Mass, w. G. Benačková (sop), F. Palmer (sop), A. Kotcherga (bass), M. Tilson Thomas (cnd), London SO, London Sym Chorus Sony Classical ▲ SK 47182
Schoenberg, A.:Gurrelieder, w. E. Marton (sop), F. Quivar (mez), H. Hotter (b-bar), Z. Mehta (cnd), New York PO, New York Choral Artists [G] Sony Classical 2-▲ S2K 48077 [DDD]
Strauss, R.:Ariadne auf Naxos, w. A. Tomowa-Sintow (sop), K. Battle (sop), A. Baltsa (mez), H. Prey (bar), J. Levine (cnd), Vienna PO Deutsche Grammophon 2-▲ 419225-2 [DDD]
Weber, C.M. von:Oberon, w. D. Voigt (sop), D. Ziegler (mez), B. Heppner (ten), J. Conlon (cnd), Cologne PO, Cologne Opera Chorus EMI Classics 2-▲ CDCB 54739

Láki, Krisztina (sop)
Einem, G. von:Dantons Tod, w. I. Mayr (mez), H. Hiestermann (ten), W. Hollweg (ten), T. Adam (bass-bar), K. Rydl (bass), L. Zagrosek (cnd), Austrian RSO, Austrian Radio Chorus [G] *(rec live, Salzburg, 8/13/83)* Orfeo 2-▲ 102842 [ADD]
Handel, G.F.:Partenope, w. Helga Müller-Molinari (mez), René Jacobs (alt), John York Skinner (alt), S. Kuijken (cnd), La Petite Bande Editio Classica 3-▲ 77109-2-RG [ADD]
Haydn, J.:Die Jahreszeiten, w. Helmut Wildhaber, Peter Lika (bass), S. Kuijken (cnd), La Petite Bande, Flanders Opera Choir Virgin Classics 2-▲ ZDCB 59268
Haydn, J.:Die Schöpfung, w. Neil Mackie (ten), Philippe Huttenlocher (bar), S. Kuijken (cnd), La Petite Bande, Ghent Collegium Vocale Accent 2-▲ ACC 58228/29
Haydn, J.:Stabat Mater, w. Júlia Hamari (mez), Claes Hakan Ahnsjö (ten), Richard Anlauf (bass), F. Bernius (cnd), Württemberg CO, Stuttgart Chamber Choir *(rec 1978)* Vox Box 2-▲ CDX 5081 [ADD]
Hoffmann, E.T.A.:Undine, w. R. Henry (sgr), Karl Ridderbusch (bass), R. Bader (cnd), Berlin RSO, St. Hedwig's Cathedral Choir *(rec Feb. 1982)* Koch Schwann 3-▲ SCH 310922 [DDD]
Mozart, W.A.:Missa, K.427, w. Z. Dénes (sop), K. Equiluz (ten), R. Holl (bass), N. Harnoncourt (cnd), Vienna Concentus Musicus, Vienna State Opera Chorus [L] Teldec ▲ 2292-43070-2
Mozart, W.A.:Schuldigkeit, w. A. Augér (sop), S. Geszty (sop), W. Hollweg (ten), C. H. Ahnsjö (ten), R. Bader (cnd), Berlin Cathedral Choir [G] *(rec 1980)* Koch Schwann 2-▲ CD 313065 [ADD]
Wagner, R.:Die Feen, w. L. E. Gray (sop), K. Lövaas (sop), Anderson (sop), R. Alexander (sop), R. Hermann (bar), K. Moll (bass), W. Sawallisch (cnd), Bavarian RSO, Bavarian Radio Chorus [G] *(rec live, Munich Opera Fest. 1983)* Orfeo 3-▲ 062833 [DDD]

Lakiová, K. (sop)
Mysliveček, J.:Belerofonte, w. C. Lindsleyová (sop), G. Mayová (sop), D. Ahlstedt (ten), R. Giménez (ten), S. Margita (ten), Z. Peskó (cnd), Prague CO, Czech Phil Chorus [I] *(rec 1987)* Supraphon 3-▲ 11 0006-2 [DDD]

Lallouette, Olivier (bass)
Handel, G.F.:Giulio Cesare in Egitto, w. Barbara Schlick (sop), Jennifer Larmore (mez), Marianne Rørholm (mez), Bernarda Fink (cta), Derek Lee Ragin (ct), Dominique Visse (ct), Furio Zanasi (bass), R. Jacobs (cnd), Concerto Cologne [period instrs] Harmonia Mundi France 3-▲ HMC 901385/87
Handel, G.F.:Riccardo Primo, w. Claire Brua (sop—Pulcheria), Sandrine Piau (sop—Costanza), Sara Mingardo (cta—Riccardo), Pascal Bertin (alt—Oronte), Roberto Scaltriti (bar—Isacio), Olivier Lallouette (bass—Berardo), C. Rousset (cnd), Les Talens Lyriques L'oiseau Lyre ▲ 452 201-2
Handel, G.F.:Scipione, w. Doris Lamprecht (sop), Sandrine Piau (sop), Vandaa Tabery (mez), Guy Flechter (ten), C. Rousset (cnd), Les Talens Lyriques [I] FNAC Music 3-▲ 592245 [DDD]
Honegger, A.:Amphion, w. Olivier Lallouette (bar—Apollon), Laurent Manzoni (bar—Amphion), Iona Bentoiu (sgr—muse), Theodora Ciucur (sgr—muse), Lucia Kriska (sgr—muse), Adriana Mestes (sgr—muse), J.-F. Antonioli (cnd), Timisoara PO, Timisoara Banatul Phil Chorus, Timisoara Children's Chorus *(rec Salle Ion Vidu, Timisoara, Romania, Oct 28 & Nov 1, 1995)* Timpani ▲ 1035 [DDD]

Lambert, Constant (nar)
Walton, W.:Façade, w. Edith Sitwell (nar), W. Walton (cnd), chamber orch Claremont ▲ CDGSE 785065

Lambert, Juliet (sgr)
Verdi, G.:Requiem Mass, w. O. Rovero (sop), J. Madeira (mez), G. Neri (bass), E. Kleiber (cnd), Vienna SO, Vienna Singverein *(rec live, Vienna 11/23/55)* Melodram 2-▲ CDM 28044 [ADD]

Lamberti, Giorgio (ten)
Bizet, G.:Carmen, w. D. Palade (sop), G. Alperyn (mez), A. Titus (bar), et al., A. Rahbari (cnd), Czech-Slovak RSO Bratislava, Slovak Phil Chorus, Bratislava Children's Choir [F] Naxos 3-▲ 8.660005/07 [DDD]
Bizet, G.:Carmen (sels), w. D. Palade (sop—Micaëla), A. Liebeck (sop—Frasquita), G. Alperyn (mez—Carmen), D. Schaechter (mez—Mercédès), G. Lamberti (ten—Don José), M. Dvorsky (ten—Remandado), J. Durco (ten—Cancairo), A. Titus (bar—Escamillo), V. Chmelo (bar—Morales), D. Rigosa (bass—Zuniga), A. Rahbari (cnd), Czech-Slovak RSO Bratislava, Slovak Phil Chorus, Bratislava Children's Choir *(rec July 1990)* Naxos ▲ 8.550727 [DDD]
Donizetti, G.:Gemma di Vergy, w. Montserrat Caballé (sop—Gemma di Vergy), Biancamaria Casoni (mez—Ida di Greville), Giorgio Lamberti (ten—Tamas), Renato Bruson (bar—Conte di Vergy), Mario Machi (bass—Rolando), Mario Rinaudo (bass—Guido), A. Gatto (cnd), Naples Teatro San Carlo Orch, Naples Teatro San Carlo Chorus *(rec Naples, Dec. 12, 1975)* Myto 2-▲ 952124
Puccini, G.:Il tabarro, w. I. Tokody (sop), S. Nimsgern (bar), G. Patanè (cnd), Munich RSO [I] Eurodisc ▲ 7775-2-RC [DDD]
Puccini, G.:Tosca, w. N. Miricioiu (sop), S. Carroli (bar), A. Rahbari (cnd), Czech-Slovak RSO Bratislava, Slovak Phil Chorus [I] Naxos 2-▲ 8.660001/02 [DDD]
Puccini, G.:Tosca (sels), w. Nelly Miricioiu (sop—Tosca), Giorgio Lamberti (ten—Cavaradossi), Miroslav Dvorsky (ten—Spoletta), Silvano Carroli (bar—Baron Scarpia), Jozef Spaček (bar—Sacristan), Jan Durco (bass—Sciarrone), Stanislav Benačka (bass—Gaoler), A. Rahbari (cnd), Czech-Slovak RSO Bratislava, Slovak Phil Chorus *(rec Concert Hall of the Slovak Radio, Bratislava, Apr. 7-14, 1990)* Naxos ▲ 8.553153 [DDD]
Respighi, O.:Belfagor, w. S. Sass (sop), T. Takács (mez), L. Miller (bar), L. Polgár (bass), L. Gardelli (cnd), Hungarian State Orch, Hungarian State Chorus [I] Hungaroton 2-▲ HCD 12850/51 [DDD]
Verdi, G.:Arias, w. Sylvia Sass (sop), Kolos Kováts (bass), Oberfrank, Gardelli (cnd), Budapest MÁV SO, Hungarian State Opera Orch, Béla Pödör (cnd), Ferenc Sapszon (cnd), Ferenc Nagy (cnd), Hungarian People's Army Male Chorus, Hungarian Radio-TV Chorus, Hungarian State Opera Chorus—Vieni, o Levital...Tu sul labbro [from Nabucco]; Verginil...Il ciel per ora...Sciaguratal Hai tu creduto; Qui posa il fianco [both from I Lombardi]; Che mai vegg'io...Infelice! E tu credevi...; Vigili pure il ciel...Iddio n'ascolti [both from Ernani]; Mentre gonfiarsi l'anima [from Attila]; Studia il passo...Come dal ciel precipita! [from Macbeth]; O patria, o cara patria...O tu, Palermo [from I vespri Siciliani]; A te l'estremo addio... [from Simon Boccanegra]; Ella giammai m'amò [from Don Carlo] Hungaroton ("Great Hungarian Voices" series) ▲ HCD 31650 [ADD/DDD]
Verdi, G.:Macbeth (sels), w. L. Gencer (sop), G. Guelfi (bar), G. Gavazzeni (cnd), Venice Teatro La Fenice Orch, Venice Teatro La Fenice Chorus [I] [highlights] *(rec live 4/9/68)* Melodram ▲ MEL 15002

Lambiase, Matt (voc)
Spasm, w. Michael Lowenstern (b cl), Heather Barringer (voc), Mark Gibbons (voc), Jay Johnson (voc), Jerome Kitzke (voc), Tom Linker (voc), Ed Lowenstern (voc), Michael Lowenstern (voc) *(rec Creation Audio, Minneapolis, NYU Studios, New York City & Studio A, Stony Brook, Aug 1994-July 1996)* New World ▲ 80468-2

Lammers, Gerda (sop)
Hindemith, P.:Das Marienleben, w. Gerhard Puchelt (pno)—new 1948 version *(rec Studio Thienhaus, Hamburg, Apr-June 1961)* Cantate ▲ C 57610 [ADD]

Lammers, Gerda (sop) (cont.)
Wagner, R.:Der Ring des Nibelungen, w. Gré Brouwenstein (sop—Freia/Sieglinde), Ilse Hollweg (sop—Waldvogel), Gerda Lammers (sop—Ortlinde), Paula Lenchner (sop—Wellgunde/Gerhilde), Hilde Scheppan (sop—Helmwige), Astrid Varnay (sop—Brünnilde/3rd Norn), Lore Wissmann (sop—Woglinde), Maria von Ilosvay (mez—Flosshilde/Schwertleite/2nd Norn), Louise Charlotte Kamps (mez—Siegrune), Jean Madeira (mez—Erda/Rossweisse/1st Norn), Georgine van Milinkovic (mez—Fricka/Grimgerde), Elisabeth Schärtel (mez—Waltraute), Paul Kuën (ten—Mime), Ludwig Suthaus (ten—Loge), Josef Traxel (ten—Froh), Wolfgang Windgassen (ten—Siegmund/Siegfried), Alfons Herwig (bar—Donner), Hermann Uhde (bar—Gunther), Hans Hotter (b-bar—Wotan), Gustav Neidlinger (b-bar—Alberich), Josef Griendl (bass—Fasolt/Hunding/Hagen), Arnold van Mill (bass—Fafner), H. Knappertsbusch (cnd), Bayreuth Festival Orch, Bayreuth Festival Chorus *(rec live, Bayreuth, Aug 13-17, 1956)* Golden Melodram 14-▲ GM 1.001 [ADD]

Lamoreaux, Rosa (sop)
Berlioz, H.:Messe solennelle Bar, w. Gene Tucker (ten), Terry Cook (bass), J. Reilly Lewis (cnd), Washington National Cathedral Choral Society Koch International Classics ▲ KIC 7204 [DDD]

Lamoree, Valarie (sop)
Boulez, P.:Improvisations sur Mallarmé I & II, w. J. Thome (cnd), Orch of Our Time—No. 2 Vox Box 2-▲ CDX 5144
Dallapiccola, L.:Concerto per la Notte di Natale dell'Anno, w. J. Thome (cnd), Orch of Our Time Vox Box 2-▲ CDX 5144
Pousseur, H.:Chants sacrés, w. Eric Rosenblith (vn), Jacob Glick (va), Michael Rudiakov (vc) Vox Box 2-▲ CDX 5144

Lamoree, Valerie (sop)
Westergaard, P.:Mr. & Mrs. Discobbolos, w. Jack Litten (ten), H. Sollberger (cnd), Group for Contemporary Music CRI ▲ CD 696 [ADD]

Lamos, Mark (nar)
Kaminsky, L.:And Trouble Came:An African AIDS Diary, w. Fidelio CRI ▲ CD 729 [DDD]

Lampe, Karl-Heinz (ten)
Haydn, M.:Missa in honorem Sanctae Ursulae, w. Mechthild Bach (sop), Gabriele Binder (cta), Joachim Gebhardt (bass), H.R. Zöbeley (cnd), Munich Residenz Orch, Munich Motet Choir Calig ▲ CAL 50901 [DDD]

Lampi, Mauro (sgr)
Donizetti, G.:Lucrezia Borgia, w. Montserrat Caballé (sop), Jane Berbié (mez), Alain Vanzo (ten), Kostas Paskalis (bar), Arnold Voketaitis (bass-bar), L. D. Clements (sgr), Adib Fazah (sgr), Vern Shinall (sgr), Jerold Siena (sgr), William Wiederanders (sgr), J. Perlea (cnd), New York City Opera Orch, New York City Chorus Great Opera Performances 2-▲ GOP 769

Lampo, Rosella (sop)
Haydn, J.:Stabat Mater, w. S. Zaramella (alt), V. Martino (ten), P. Turner (bass), D. Ferrari (cnd), Milan Sinfonietta, Concentus Musicae Antiquae Vocal Group Nuova Era ▲ NUO 7170 [DDD]

Lamprecht, Doris (mez)
Auber, D.-F.:Le Domino noir, w. Sumi Jo (sop), Martine Olmeda (sop), Isabelle Vernet (sop), Jocelyne Taillon (mez), Bruce Ford (ten), Patrick Power (ten), Gilles Cachemaille (bar), Jules Bastin (bass), R. Bonynge (cnd), English CO, London Voices London 2-▲ 440646-2
Handel, G.F.:Scipione, w. Sandrine Piau (sop), Vandaa Tabery (mez), Guy Flechter (ten), Oliver Lalouette (bass), C. Rousset (cnd), Les Talens Lyriques [I] FNAC Music 3-▲ 592245 [DDD]
Mozart, W.A.:Zauberflöte, w. Natalie Dessay (sop—Queen of the Night), Linda Kitchen (sop—Papagena), Rosa Mannion (sop—Pamina), Anna-Maria Panzarella (sop—First Lady), Doris Lamprecht (mez—Second Lady), Delphine Haidan (cta—Third Lady), Hans Peter Blochwitz (ten—Tamino), Steven Cole (ten—Monostatos), Chrisopher Josey (ten—First Priest/First Armed Man), Anton Scharinger (bar—Papageno), Reinhard Hagen (bass—Sarastro), Laurent Naouri (bass—Second Priest/Second Armed Man), Willard White (bass—Speaker), W. Christie (cnd), Les Arts Florissants *(rec Paris Oct 2-9 1995)* Erato 2-▲ 12705-2 [DDD]

Lamy, Hervé (ten)
Bach, J.S.:Magnificat, BWV 243, w. Hélène Obadia (sop), Brigitte Vinson (sop), Madeleine Jalabert (alt), Philip Langshaw (bass), P. Kuentz (cnd), Paul Kuentz Orch, Paul Kuentz Choir Pierre Verany ▲ PVY 730048
Campra, A.:Motets, w. Véronique Gens (sop), Anne Gotkovsky (sop), Jean-Paul Fouchecourt (ct), Peter Harvey (bass), H. Niquet (cnd), Concert Spirituel Orch, Concert Spirituel Vocal Ensemble—2 Noster Refugium; Cantate Domino; De Profundis Adda ▲ ADD 243912
du Mont, H.:Motets pour la chapelle du roy, w. H. Crook (cta), P. Harvey (bar), O. Schneebeli (cnd), Musica Aeterna, Les Pages de la Chapelle *(rec Sept. 1993)* FNAC Music ▲ 592054 [DDD]
Fauré, G.:Choral Music, w. Jean-François Hatton (org), F. Polgár (cnd), Paris Opera Soloists, Neuilly St-Croix Youth Chorus—Requiem, Op. 48 [1893 Version]; Salve Regina, Op. 67/1; Ave Maria, Op. 67/2; Tantum Ergo, Op. 65/2; Ave Verum, Op. 65/1; Cantique de Jean Racine, Op. 11 Adès ▲ ADE 202982
Josquin Desprez:Missa, "Ave Maris Stella", w. D. Collot (sop), R. Holton (sop), J.-L. Comoretto (ct), R. Le Chenadec (ct), T. Brehu (ten), B. Fabre-Garrus (bar), J. Gowings (bar) *(rec Jan. 1993)* Astrée ▲ E 8507 [DDD]
Josquin Desprez:Motets, w. D. Collot (sop), R. Holton (sop), J.-L. Comoretto (ct), R. Le Chenadec (ct), T. Brehu (ten), B. Fabre-Garrus (bar), J. Gowings (bar)—Motets à la vierge *(rec Jan. 1993)* Astrée ▲ E 8507 [DDD]
Lalande, M.-R. de:Dies Irae, w. P. Kwella (sop), L. Perillo (sop), H. Crook (ten), P. Harvey (bar), P. Herreweghe (cnd), La Chapelle Royale Orch, Chapelle Royale Choir [L] Harmonia Mundi France ▲ HMC 901352
Lalande, M.-R. de:Miserere mei, Deus, w. P. Kwella (sop), L. Perillo (sop), H. Crook (ten), P. Harvey (bar), P. Herreweghe (cnd), La Chapelle Royale Orch, Chapelle Royale Choir [L] Harmonia Mundi France ▲ HMC 901352
Lully, J.-B.:Motets, w. I. Desrochers (sop), D. Favat (sop), R. Duguay (ct), P. Harvey (bass), H. Niquet (cnd), Concert Spirituel Vocal Ensemble—Te Deum; Miserere; Plaude laetare Gallia *(rec Nov. 22-25, 1993)* FNAC Music ▲ 592308 [DDD]
Massenet, J.:Eve, w. Michèle Command (sop), Carolyn Sebron (mez), Jean-Philippe Courtis (bass), J.-P. Lore (cnd), French Oratorio Orch, French Oratorio Choir Erol 3-▲ 94002-04
Massenet, J.:Marie-Magdeleine, w. Michèle Command (sop), Carolyn Sebron (mez), Jean-Philippe Courtis (bass), J.-P. Lore (cnd), French Oratorio Orch, French Oratorio Choir Erol 3-▲ 94002-04
Mendelssohn, F.:Ave Maria, w. L. van Doeselaar (org), P. Herreweghe (cnd), Ghent Collegium Vocale Harmonia Mundi France ▲ HMC 901272 [DDD]
Mendelssohn, F.:Psalm 42, w. E. Harrhy (sop), P. Kooy (bass), P. Herreweghe (cnd), La Chapelle Royale Orch, Ghent Collegium Vocale [G] Harmonia Mundi France ▲ HMC 901272 [DDD]
Palestrina, G.:Officium tenebrarum, w. Olivier Opdebeeck (cnd), Cori Spezzati Vocal Ensemble Jade 2-▲ JADC 114
Rameau, J.P.:Motets, w. I. Desrochers (sop), V. Gens (sop), J.-P. Fouchecourt (ct), P. Harvey (bar), M. Loureiro de Sá (bar), S. Imbodem (bass), *(orch unknown)*—Deus noster refugium; Quam dilecta; In convertendo [L] *(rec Apr. 13-18, 1992)* FNAC Music ▲ 592096 [DDD]
Saint-Saëns, C.:Choral Music, w. J.-F. Hatton (org), Paris Opera Orch Soloists, F. Polgár (cnd), Neuilly St-Croix Youth Chorus—Pie Jesu; Ave Verum Adès ▲ ADE 202982
Sebastiani, J.:St. Matthew Passion, w. Greta de Reyghere (sop), Vincent Gregoire (ct), Stéphane van Dijck (ten), Hervé Lamy (ten—Evangéliste), Max van Egmond (bass—Christ), P. Pierlot (cnd), Ricercar Consort Ricercar ▲ 160144

Lancaster, B. (sgr)
York, W.:Songs on a Poem of Su Tung P'O, w. D. Ripley (bass), H. Weinberger (sgr) *(rec May 1987)* New World ▲ 80439-2

Lance, Albert (ten)
Massenet, J.:Werther, w. Mady Mesplé (sop—Sophie), Rita Gorr (mez—Charlotte), Robert Andreozzi (ten—Schmidt), Albert Lance (ten—Werther), Gabriel Bacquier (bar—Albert), Julien Giovannetti (bar—Le Bailli), Jacques Mars (bar—Johann), J. Etcheverry (cnd), *(orch unknown)* Adès 2-▲ ADE 140832 [AAD]

▲ = CD ♦ = Enhanced CD Δ = MD ▮ = Cassette Tape ▯ = DCC

Lance, Albert (ten) (cont.)

Offenbach, J.:Les Contes d'Hoffmann (sels), w. Andréa Guiot (sop—Antonia), Mady Mesplé (sop—Olympia), Suzanne Sarroca (sop—Giulietta), Albert Lance (ten—Hoffmann), Gabriel Bacquier (bar—Docteur Miracle), Robert Massard (bar—Dapertutto), J. Etcheverry (cnd), *(orch unknown)* —Prologue; Dans les rôles d'amoureux...; Il était une fois...; Allons! Courage et confiance...; C'est moi, coppélius!...; Les oiseaux dans la charmille; Barcarolle; Scintille, diamant...; Malheureux, tu ne comprends donc pas...; Hélas! Mon coeur s'égare encore...; Elle a fui, la touterelle...; Eh bien! Quoi! Toujours en colère!...; Tu ne chanteras plus?... Adès ▲ ADE 202702 [AAD]

Landauer, Bernhard (ct)

Dufay, G.:Songs, w. M. Posch (cnd), Unicorn Ensemble—J'ay mis mon cuer; Par droit je puis bien complaindre; Quel fronte signorille La dolce vista; Puisque vous estez campieur; Belle, que vous ay je mesfait; Vergene bella; Se la face ay pale; Donnes l'assault à la fortresse; Par le regard de vos beaux yeux; Resvelons nous; Ce jour de l'an; Mon chier amy; Pour l'amour de ma doulce amye; Helas mon dueil; Bon jour, bon mois; Resvelliés vous et faites chiere lye; Adieu ces bons vins de Lannoys *(rec Evangelische Kirche A.B., Vienna, Apr 15–18, 1995)* Naxos ▲ 8.553458 [DDD]

Lander, Thomas (bass)

Kraus, J.M.:Funeral Music for Gustav III, w. C. Högman (sop), H. Martinpelto (sop), C.–H. Ahnsjö (ten), S. Parkman (cnd), Drottningholm Baroque Ensemble, Uppsala Univ Chamber Choir Musica Sveciae ▲ MSCD 416 [DDD]

Peterson–Berger, W.:Songs, w. Gunnel Bohman (sop), Anders Kilström (pno) Musica Sveciae ▲ MSV 619 [DDD]

Landin, Ingmari (alt)

Nilsson, T.:Music of, w. Lars Sjögren (ten), Lage Wedin (bass), Jerker Halldén (fl), Nils–Erik Sparf (vn), Hans–Ola Ericsson (org), Anders Loguin (perc), Torsten Nilsson (cnd), Gustaf Sjökvist (cnd), Swedish Radio Chorus—Ordinarium Missae; Balthasar/Daniel; Drei Gedichte Phono Suecia ▲ PHN 40 [AAD]

Landry, Rosemarie (sop)

Bach, J.S.:Cant 140, w. Ben Heppner (ten), Mark Pedrotti (bass), W. Riddell (cnd), CBC Vancouver SO, Tudor Singers of Montreal CBC ▲ 5163 [DDD]

Chan Ka Nin:Everlasting Voices, w. Toronto Percussion Ensemble Centrediscs ▲ CD 3288

Tabachnik, M.:Le Pacte des Onzes, w. M. Tabachnik (cnd), Ensemble InterContemporain, New London Chamber Choir [F] *(rec March 30, 1987)* Grammont ▲ CTSP 26–2 [ADD]

Lane, Carys–Anne (sop)

Vivaldi, A.:Beatus vir, R.597, w. Jayne Whitaker (sop), Christine Swain (ob), Robert Glenton (vc), Christopher Stokes (org), N. Ward (cnd), Northern CO, Oxford Schola Cantorum *(rec St. Peter's Church, Hale, Cheshire, Mar. 14, 1994)* Naxos ▲ 8.550767 [DDD]

Lane, Elen (mez)

Gay, J.:The Beggar's Opera (sels), w. P. Clark (sop), A. Jenkins (sop), M. Cable (mez), S. Minty (mez), E. Fleet (sgr), P. Hall (ten), V. Midgley (ten), N. Rogers (ten), J. Noble (bar), D. Stevens (cnd), Accademia Monteverdiana Orch, Accademia Monteverdiana Chorus—59 songs *(rec Aug. 1978)* Koch Treasure ▲ 31621–2 [ADD]

Lane, Gloria (mez)

Verdi, G.:Nabucco, w. Gianni Raimondi (ten), Giangiacomo Guelfi (bar), Nicolai Ghiaurov (bass), Elena Saliotis (sgr), G. Gavazzeni (cnd), La Scala Orch, La Scala Chorus *(rec La Scala Theater, Milan, Dec. 7, 1966)* Pantheon 2–▲ PHE 6757 (m)

Lane, Jennifer (mez)

Bach, J.S.:Mass in b, BWV 232, w. J. Baird (sop), J. Nelson (sop), N. Zylstra, Z. Muñoz, S. Rickards, P. Romano, W. Sharp, J. Weaver (bass), J. Thomas (cnd), American Bach Soloists Koch International Classics 2–▲ KIC 7194–2 [DDD]

Bach, J.S.:St. John Passion, w. Tamara Matthews (sop), Mark Bleeke (ten—Evangelist), David Vanderwal (ten), Kevin Walsh (bar—Pilate), Nathaniel Watson (bass—Jesus), E. Milnes (cnd), Trinity Baroque Orch, Trinity Cathedral Choir *(rec Trinity Cathedral, Portland, OR, Mar 31, 1996)* PGM 2–▲ PGM 111

Caldara, A.:Vaticini di pace, w. Mary Enid Hains (sop), Linda Dayiantis–Straub (sop), David Arnot (ten), K. Mallon (cnd), Aradia Baroque Ensemble *(rec Toronto, Canada, Jan 1996)* Naxos ▲ 8.553772 [DDD]

Handel, G.F.:Ariodante, w. J. Gondek (sop), L. Saffer (sop), L. Hunt (mez), J. Lindemann (ten), R. Müller (ten), N. Cavallier (bass), N. McGegan (cnd), Freiburg Baroque Orch, Ralf Popken (cnd), Wilhelmshaven Vocal Ensemble [172–page libretto w. production photos] Harmonia Mundi France 3–▲ HMC 907146.48

Handel, G.F.:Berenice, w. Julianne Baird (sop—Berenice), Andrea Matthews (sop—Alessandro), D'Anna Fortunato (mez—Selene), Jennifer Lane (mez—Demetrio), Drew Minter (alt—Arsace), John McMaster (ten—Fabio), Jan Opalach (bass—Aristobolo), R. Palmer (cnd), Brewer CO Newport Classic 3–▲ NPD 85620/3 [DDD]

Handel, G.F.:Ezio, w. Julianne Baird (sop—Fulvia), Jennifer Lane (mez—Onoria), D'Anna Fortunato (cta—Ezio), Raymond Pellerin (alt—Emperor), Frederick Urrey (ten—Massimo), Nathaniel Watson (bar—Varo), Johannes Somary (org), R.A. Clark (cnd), Manhattan CO *(rec St. Jean Baptiste Church, New York, Mar. 1994)* Vox Classics 2–▲ VOX 27503 [DDD]

Handel, G.F.:Faramondo, w. Julianne Baird (sop—Clotilde), Mary Ellen Callahan (sop—Adolfo), D'Anna Fortunado (mez—Faramondo), Jennifer Lane (mez—Rosimonda), Drew Minter (alt—Gernando), Peter Castaldi (bar—Gustavo), Mark Singer (bar—Tebaldo), Edward Brewer (hpd), R. Palmer (cnd), Brewer CO [period instrs] Vox Classics 3–▲ VOX3 7536 [DDD]

Handel, G.F.:Giustino, w. Juliana Gondek (sop), Dawn Kotoski (sop), Dorothea Röschmann (sop), Michael Chance (alt), Drew Minter (alt), Mark Padmore (ten), Dean Ely (sgr), N. McGegan (cnd), Freiburg Baroque Orch Harmonia Mundi France 3–▲ HMU 907130.32

Handel, G.F.:Messiah, w. Julianne Baird (sop), David Price (ten), Kevin Deas (b–bar), V. Radu (cnd), Ama Deus Ensemble, Ama Deus Ensemble Chorus [period instruments; 1749 Covent Garden version] Vox Classics 2–▲ VOX2 7502 [DDD]

Handel, G.F.:Messiah (sels), w. Julianne Baird (sop), David Price (ten), Kevin Deas (b–bar), V. Radu (cnd), Ama Deus Ensemble—[Part 1] Sinf.; Comfort Ye My People; Every Valley Shall Be Exalted; And the Glory of the Lord; O Thou That Tellest Good Tidings to Zion; For Unto Us a Child is Born; Pifa; Rejoice Greatly o Daughter of Zion; He Shall Feed His Flock by Night; [Part 2] He was Despised and Rejected of Men; All We Like Sheep Have Gone Astray; Lift Up Your Heads, O Ye Gates; Why do the Nations So Furiously Rage Together; [Part 3]I Know That My Redeemer Liveth; Behold, I Tell You a Mystery; The Trumpet Shall Sound; Hallelujah Vox Classics ▲ VOX 7508 [DDD]

Handel, G.F.:Muzio Scevola, w. Julianne Baird (sop—Clelia), Andrea Matthews (sop—Fidalma), Erie Mills (sop—Orazio), D'Anna Fortunato (mez—Muzio), Jennifer Lane (mez—Irene), Frederick Urrey (ten—Tarquino), John Ostendorf (b–bar—Porsenna), R. Palmer (cnd), Brewer Baroque CO [period instrs] [I] *(rec 10/91)* Newport Classic 2–▲ NPD 85540/2 [DDD]

Handel, G.F.:Sosarme, Rè di Media, w. Julinne Baird (sop—Elmira), D'Anna Fortunato (mez—Sosarme), Jennifer Lane (mez—Erenice), Drew Minter (ct—Melo), Rarmond Pellerin (ct—Argone), John Aler (ten—King Haliate), Nathaniel Watson (bass—Varo), Edward Brewer (hpd) Newport Classic 2–▲ NPT 85575 [DDD]

Handel, G.F.:Theodora, w. Lorraine Hunt (sop—Theodora), Jennifer Lane (mez—Irene), Drew Minter (alt—Didymus), Jeffery Thomas (ten—Septimius), David Thomas (bass—Valens), N. McGegan (cnd), Philharmonia Baroque Orch, Univ of California at Berkeley Chamber Chorus [period instrs] [E] *(rec 9/91)* Harmonia Mundi USA 3–▲ HMU 907060/62 [DDD]

Handel, G.F.:Theodora (sels), w. Lorraine Hunt (sop), Drew Minter (ct), Jeffrey Thomas (ten), David Thomas (bass), N. McGegan (cnd), Philharmonia Baroque Orch, Univ of California at Berkeley Chamber Chorus Harmonia Mundi France ▲ HMU 907188

Handel, G.F.:Tolomeo, Rè di Egitto, w. Brenda Harris (sop—Seleuce), Andrea Matthews (sop—Elisa), Mary Ann Hart (mez—Alessandro), Jennifer Lane (mez—Tolomeo), Peter Castaldi (bar—King Araspe), Bradley Brookshire (hpd), R.A. Clark (cnd), Manhattan CO *(rec St. Jean Baptiste Church, NY, Mar 1995)* Vox Classics 3–▲ VOX 7530

Hasse, J.A.:Motets, w. Monique Zanetti (sop), M. Gester (cnd), Parlement de Musique—Gentes barbarae, Tartarae turbae; Alta nubes illustrata; Salva R. in A; Salva R. in G Opus 111 ▲ OPS 30–100

Monteverdi, C.:Orfeo, w. Jeffrey Thomas (ten), Michael Brown (sgr), Dana Hanchard (sgr), Timothy Leigh Evans (sgr), Paul Shipper (sgr), G. Toth (cnd), ARTEK Lyrichord 2–▲ LYR 9002 [DDD]

Lane, Jennifer (mez) (cont.)

Purcell, H.:Dido & Aeneas, w. Cassandra Hoffman (sop—Belinda), Arlene Travis (sop—2nd Witch), Desirée Halac (mez—Sorceress/Spirit), Jennifer Lane (mez—Dido), Elizabeth Norman (alt), Thomas Bogdan (ten—A Sailor), Michael Brown (bar—Aeneas), Curtis Streetman (bar), Caitriona O'Leary (sgr—2nd Woman), Sarah Pillow (sgr—1st Witch), B. Brookshire (cnd), San Cassiano Musici *(rec St. Ignatius of Antioch Episcopal Church, New York City, Spring 1995)* Vox Classics ▲ VOX 7518

Purcell, H.:Dido & Aeneas, w. Meredith Hall (sop—2nd Witch/Spirit), Ann Monoyios (sop—Belinda), Shari Saunders (sop—2nd Woman/1st Woman), Jennifer Lane (mez—Dido/Sorceress), Benjamin Butterfield (ten—Sailor), Russell Braun (bar—Aeneas), J. Lamon (cnd), Tafelmusik, Tafelmusik Chamber Choir *(rec Glenn Gould Studio, CBC Toronto, Apr 26–29, 1995)* CBC ▲ SM5 5147 [DDD]

Lane, Kenneth (ten)

Live at Carnegie Hall, w. Otto Herz (pno) Valhalla ▲ VRCD 1594

Verdi, G.:Otello (sels), w. Martin Kalmanoff (pno)—Dio! mi potevi; Niun mi tema Valhalla ▲ VRCD 1595 [ADD]

Wagner, R.:Arias & Scenes, w. Otto Herz (pno), Martin Kalmanoff (pno), Levering Rothfuss (pno)—Rienzi's Prayer [from Rienzi]; In fernem Land, Mein Liebe Schwan [from Lohengrin]; Siegmund heiss' ich! [from Die Walküre]; Nothung! Nothung!, Schmiede mein Hammer! [from Siegfried]; O König!, Die alte Weise, O diese Sonne! [from Tristan und Isolde]; Prize Song [from Die Meistersinger]; Siegfried's Narration, Brünnhilde! Heilige Braut! [from Götterdämmerung]; Amfortas! Die Wunde!, Nur eine Waffe taugt [from Parsifal] Valhalla VRCD 1595 [ADD]

Lang (sgr)

Bach, J.S.:Cant 31, w. Eberhard Büchner (ten), Siegfried Lorenz (bar), Hermann Christian Polster (bass), Termer (sgr), Weimann (sgr), H.–J. Rotzsch (cnd), Leipzig Gewandhaus Orch, St. Thomas Choir Berlin Classics ▲ BER 9025 [ADD]

Bach, J.S.:Cant 66, w. Eberhard Büchner (ten), Siegfried Lorenz (bar), Hermann Christian Polster (bass), Termer (sgr), Weimann (sgr), H.–J. Rotzsch (cnd), Leipzig Gewandhaus Orch, St. Thomas Choir Berlin Classics ▲ BER 9025 [ADD]

Bach, J.S.:Cant 106, "Actus tragicus", w. Eberhard Büchner (ten), Siegfried Lorenz (bar), Hermann Christian Polster (bass), Termer (sgr), Weimann (sgr), H.–J. Rotzsch (cnd), Leipzig Gewandhaus Orch, St. Thomas Choir Berlin Classics ▲ BER 9025 [ADD]

Lang, David (nar)

Lang, D.:Are You Experienced?, w. Hendrik Jan Renes (tuba), S. Mosko (cnd), Netherlands Wind Ensemble Chandos ▲ CHAN 9363 [DDD]

Lang, D.:Music of, w. J. Rozen (elec tuba), E. Niemann (pno), N. Tilles (pno), R. Schulte (vn), U. Oppens (pno), L. Vaillancourt (cnd), Le Nouvel Ensemble Moderne—Are You Experienced?; Orpheus Over & Under; Spud; Illumination Rounds CRI ▲ CD 625 [DDD]

Lang, Donald P. (sgr)

Weill, K.:Down in the Valley, w. I. Davidson (sop), M. Acito (ten), D. Collup (bar), J. Mabry (sgr), W. Gundlach (cnd), Westphalia CO, Westphalia Kantorei Capriccio ▲ 60 020–1 [DDD]

Lang, Frieder (ten)

Ave Maria, w. [cnd:Alphons von Aarburg], Zurich Boys' Choir, Daniel Perret (trb), Alain Clément (bass), Praxedis Rütti (hp), Daniel Winiger (org), Andrej Lütschg (vn) Tudor ▲ TUD 7029 [DDD]

Bach, J.S.:Cant 33, w. H. Watts (cta), P. Huttenlocher (bar), H. Rilling (cnd), Stuttgart Bach Collegium, Gächinger Kantorei Hänssler Classic ▲ 98.811 [AAD]

Dittersdorf, K.D. von:Doctor und Apotheker, w. Hildegard Uhrmacher (sop—Leonore), Donna Woodward (sop—Rosalia), Waltraud Meier (mez—Claudia), Martin Finke (ten—Sichel), Frieder Lang (ten—Gotthold), Alois Perl (ten—Gallus), Gerhard Unger (ten—Sturmwald), Thomas Pfeiffer (bar—Police Commisioner), Wolfgang Schöne (bar—Krautmann), Harald Stamm (bass—Stössel), J. Lockhart (cnd), Rhine State PO Bayer 2–▲ BR 100 238/39 [DDD]

Henze, H.–W.:Voices, w. G. Pelker (mez), J. Kalitzke (cnd), Musikfabrik NRW CPO ▲ CPO 999192 [DDD]

Mendelssohn, F.:Sym 2, w. S. Isokoski (sop), M. Bach (sop), C. Spering (cnd), Das Neue Orch, Cologne Chorus Musicus [period instrs] Opus 111 ▲ OPS 30–98

Moeschinger, A.:Cant, w. N. Tüller (bass), Bern Ad Hoc Ensemble—Prelude & Dialogue [F] Grammont ▲ CTSP 1–2 [ADD]

Nicolai, O.:Mass, w. G. Resick (sop), G. Killebrew (mez), H. C. Polster (bass), H. Hollreiser (cnd), North German RSO, North German Radio Chorus [L] Koch Schwann ▲ CD 313052 [ADD]

Romberg, A.:Der Lied von der Glocke, w. B. Schlick (sop), P. Lika (bass), C. Spering (cnd), Das Neue Orch, Cologne Chorus Musicus *(rec May 24–27, 1992)* Opus 111 ▲ OPS 30–67 [DDD]

Schoeck, O.:Der Sänger, w. R. Lang–Oester (pno) Koch Schwann ▲ SCH 310912 [DDD]

Stravinsky, I.:Canticum sacrum, w. Irene Friedli (alt), N. Järvi (cnd), Swiss Romande Orch, Lausanne Pro Arte Choir Chandos ▲ CHAN 9408 [DDD]

Stravinsky, I.:Chorale Variations on the German Christmas Carol "Vom Himmel hoch da komm' ich her", w. Irene Friedli (alt), N. Järvi (cnd), Swiss Romande Orch, Lausanne Pro Arte Choir Chandos ▲ CHAN 9408 [DDD]

Lang, H. (sgr)

Rodgers, R.:Pal Joey, w. V. Segal (sgr), *(other artists unknown)* [1950 revival cast] Columbia ▲ CK 04364 ■ JST 4364

Lang, Petra (mez)

Mozart, W.A.:Nozze di Figaro, w. C. Margiono (sop), B. Bonney (sop), I. Rey (sop), A. Murray (mez), P. Langridge (ten), C. Späth (ten), T. Hampson (bar), K. Moll (bass), A. Scharinger (bass), K. Langan (bass), N. Harnoncourt (cnd), Royal Concertgebouw Orch, Netherlands Opera Chorus *(rec Amsterdam, May 1993)* Teldec 3–▲ 90861–2 [DDD]

Lang, Rosemarie (cta)

Bach, J.S.:Cant 36, w. N. Argenta (sop), A. Rolfe Johnson (ten), O. Bär (bar), J. E. Gardiner (cnd), English Baroque Soloists, Monteverdi Choir London Archiv ▲ 437327–2

Bach, J.S.:Cant 61, w. N. Argenta (sop), A. Rolfe Johnson (ten), O. Bär (bar), J. E. Gardiner (cnd), English Baroque Soloists, Monteverdi Choir London Archiv ▲ 437327–2 [DDD]

Bach, J.S.:Cant 62, w. N. Argenta (sop), A. Rolfe Johnson (ten), O. Bär (bar), J. E. Gardiner (cnd), English Baroque Soloists, Monteverdi Choir London Archiv ▲ 437327–2 [DDD]

Beethoven, L. van:Missa Solemnis, w. T. Kiberg (sop), W. Cochran (ten), M. Krutikov (bass), A. Dorati (cnd), European SO, Univ of Maryland Chorus [L] *(rec live, Berlin Philharmonie, 7/3/88)* BIS 2–▲ CD 406/07 [DDD]

Elgar, E.:Sea Pictures, w. H.–P. Frank (cnd), Helsingborg SO [E] *(rec 1991)* BIS ▲ CD 530 [DDD]

Mahler, G.:Sym 8, w. Sylvia McNair (sop), Andrea Rost (sop), Cheryl Studer (sop), Anne Sofie von Otter (mez), Peter Seiffert (ten), Bryn Terfel (bar), Jan–Hendrik Rootering (bass), C. Abbado (cnd), Berlin PO, Berlin Radio Chorus, Prague Phil Chorus, Tölz Boys' Choir Deutsche Grammophon ("4D Audio" series) 2–▲ 445843–2

Nystroem, G.:Songs at the Sea, w. H.–P. Frank (cnd), Helsingborg SO [Sw] *(rec 1991)* BIS ▲ CD 530 [DDD]

Wagner, R.:Wesendonck Songs, w. H.–P. Frank (cnd), Helsingborg SO [G] *(rec 1991)* BIS ▲ CD 530 [DDD]

Langan, Kevin (bass)

Mozart, W.A.:Nozze di Figaro, w. C. Margiono (sop), B. Bonney (sop), I. Rey (sop), A. Murray (mez, P.–L. Lang (mez), P. Langridge (ten), C. Späth (ten), T. Hampson (bar), K. Moll (bass), A. Scharinger (bass), N. Harnoncourt (cnd), Royal Concertgebouw Orch, Netherlands Opera Chorus *(rec Amsterdam, May 1993)* Teldec 3–▲ 90861–2 [DDD]

Langdon, Michael (bass)

Beethoven, L. van:Cant on the Death of the Emperor Joseph II, w. K. Te Kanawa (sop), Y. Newman (mez), D. Barrett (bar), C. Davis (cnd), BBC SO, BBC Chorus, BBC Choral Society [G] *(rec live Oct. 7, 1970)* Intaglio ▲ INCD 7361 [ADD]

Britten, H.:Billy Budd, w. P. Pears (ten), P. Glossop (bar), J. Shirley–Quirk (bar), B. Luxon (bar), O. Brannigan (bass), B. Britten (cnd), London SO, Ambrosian Singers [E] London 3–▲ 417428–2 [ADD]

Puccini, G.:Madama Butterfly, w. V. de los Angeles (sop—Madama Butterfly), B. Howitt (mez—Suzuki), J. Livingston (mez—Kate), J. Lanigan (ten—Pinkerton), D. Tree (ten—Goro), D. A. (ten—Yamadori), G. Evans (bar—Sharpless), M. Langdon (bass—Bonzo), R. Kempe (cnd), Royal Opera House Orch, Royal Opera House Chorus Covent Garden *(rec London, May 1957)* Ornamenti 2–▲ FE 112 [ADD]

Langdon, Michael (bass) (cont.)

Verdi, G.:Aida, w. Maria Callas (sop—Aida), Joan Sutherland (sop—Priestess), Giulietta Simionato (cta—Amneris), Kurt Baum (ten—Radames), Hector Thomas (ten—Messenger), Jess Walters (bar—Amonasro), Michael Langdon (bass—King), Giulio Neri (bass—Ramfis), J. Barbirolli (cnd), Royal Opera House Orch, Royal Opera House Chorus Covent Garden *(rec Covent Garden, London, June 10, 1953)* Legato Classics 2-▲ LCD 187-2

Lange, Art (nar)

Feldman, Morton:Give My Regards to 8th Street *(rec Slee Concert Hall, Buffalo, New York, June 1-2, 1995)* Hat Hut ("Now" series) ▲ CD 6176 [DDD]

Lange, Michel ten Houte de (ten)

Beethoven, L. van:Music of, w. Anatol Karemacher (pno), Peter Kranen (pno)—Sketches for a Sym; 7 Early Songs; 4 Settings of Nur wer die; Sehnsucht kennt, WoO 134; Sketches for Pno Piece in C; 9 Short Sketchbook Frags Raptus ▲ 389.02.88

Neefe, C.G.:Vars Dittersdorf, w. Anatol Karemacher (pno), Peter Kranen (pno) Raptus ▲ 389.02.88

Neefe, C.G.:Vars Mozart, w. Anatol Karemacher (pno), Peter Kranen (pno) Raptus ▲ 389.02.88

Lange, Susanne (mez)

Schierbeck, P.:The Chinese Flute, w. M. Schønwandt (cnd), South Jutland SO Point ▲ PCD 5085 [ADD]

Schierbeck, P.:Sorceress, w. Jens Kaas (org), M. Schønwandt (cnd), South Jutland SO Point ▲ PCD 5085 [ADD]

Schoenberg, A.:Book of the Hanging Gardens, w. T. Lønskov (pno) [G] Kontrapunkt 3-▲ 32028/30 [DDD]

Schoenberg, A.:Songs, w. L. Thodberg Bertelsen (bar), T. Lonskov (pno)—Seven Early Songs; Two Songs, Op. 1; Four Songs, Op. 2; Six Songs, Op. 3; Gruss in die Ferne; Eight Songs, Op. 6; Two Ballads, Op. 12; Two Songs, Op. 14; The Book of the Hanging Gardens, Op. 15; Two Songs (Gedenken; Am Strande); Four Deutsche Volkslieder; Three Songs, Op. 48 [G] Kontrapunkt 3-▲ 32028/30 [DDD]

Thybo, L.:Aus dem Stundenbuch, w. E. Lundkvist (org) *(rec Vangede Church, Mar. 13, Apr. 11, 12 & 25)* Marco Polo/Dacapo ▲ 8.224009 [DDD]

Thybo, L.:Sonnengesang, w. G. Krogh (org) *(rec Vangede Church, Mar. 13, Apr. 11, 12 & 25)* Marco Polo/Dacapo ▲ 8.224009 [DDD]

Langebo, Karin (sop)

Jensen, L.I.:Japanischer Frühling, w. Ø. Fjeldstad (cnd), Oslo PO Simax ▲ PSC 3118

Langner, Elisabeth (nar)

Zender, H.:Hölderlin Lesen II, w. Eckart Schloifer (va) Pro Viva ▲ ISPV 163 [DDD]

Langridge, Philip (ten)

Au Jardin des Aveux, w. Ann Murray (mez), Roger Vignoles (pno) Virgin Classics ▲ CDC 59019

Bach, J.S.:Magnificat, BWV 243, w. F. Palmer (sop), M. Lipovšek (mez), N. Harnoncourt (cnd), Vienna Concentus Musicus, Arnold Schoenberg Choir [L] Teldec ▲ 2292-42984-2

Berg, A.:Wozzeck, w. H. Behrens (sop), H. Zednik (ten), F. Grundheber (bar), A. Haugland (bass), C. Abbado (cnd), Vienna PO, Vienna State Opera Chorus, Vienna Boys' Choir [G] *(rec live, 6/88)* Deutsche Grammophon 2-▲ 423587-2 [DDD]

Berlioz, H.:Roméo et Juliette, w. A. S. von Otter (sop), Morris (sgr), J. Levine (cnd), Berlin PO, Ernst Senff Chorus [F] Deutsche Grammophon 2-▲ 427665-2 [DDD]

Bononcini, A.:Stabat Mater, w. Felicity Palmer (sop), Paul Esswood (ct), Christopher Keyte (bass), John Scott (org), John Willison (vn), Chris Wellington (va), Don McVeigh (va), G. Guest (cnd), Philomusica Antiqua of London, St. John's College Choir Cambridge *(rec 1977)* London 2-▲ 443868-2 [ADD]

Britten, H.:The Beggar's Opera, w. A. Collins (sop—Mrs. Peachum), A. Murray (mez—Polly Peachum), P. Langridge (ten—MacHeath), R. Lloyd (b-bar—Peachum), *(not advised of orchestra & chorus)*, S. Bedford (cnd) Argo 2-▲ 436850-2 [DDD]

Britten, H.:Gloriana, w. J. Barstow (sop—Queen Elizabeth I), D. Jones (mez—Lady Essex), P. Langridge (ten—Earl of Essex), J. M. Ainsley (ten—Spirit of the Masque), J. Summers (bar—Lord Mountjoy), J. Shirley-Quirk (bar—Recorder of Norwich), B. Terfel (b-bar—Henry Cuffe), C. Mackerras (cnd), Welsh National Opera Orch, Welsh National Opera Chorus Argo 2-▲ 440213-2 [DDD]

Britten, H.:The Holy Sonnets of John Donne, w. Steuart Bedford (pno) Collins Classics ▲ COL 1468

Britten, H.:Sonnets of Michelangelo, w. Steuart Bedford (pno) Collins Classics ▲ COL 1468

Britten, H.:The Turn of the Screw, w. F. Lott (sop), N. Secunde (sop), E. Hulse (sop), P. Cannan (mez), S. Pay (bar), S. Bedford (cnd), Aldeburgh Festival Ensemble Collins Classics ▲ COL 7030 [DDD]

Britten, H.:War Requiem, w. H. Harper (sop), J. Shirley-Quirk (bar), R. Elms (org), R. Hickox (cnd), London SO, London Sym Chorus, St. Paul's Cathedral Choristers [E,L] Chandos 2-▲ CHAN 8983/84 [DDD]

Britten, H.:Winter Words, w. Steuart Bedford (pno) Collins Classics ▲ COL 1468

Caldara, A.:Crucifixus, w. Felicity Palmer (sop), Paul Esswood (ct), Christopher Keyte (bass), John Scott (org), John Willison (vn), Chris Wellington (va), Don McVeigh (va), G. Guest (cnd), Philomusica Antiqua of London, St. John's College Choir Cambridge *(rec 1977)* London 2-▲ 443868-2 [ADD]

Donizetti, G.:Betly, w. R. Capecchi (bar), P. Van den Berg (bass), J. Schaap (cnd), Zaanstad Opera Orch *(rec live, 1973)* Italian Opera Rarities ▲ IOR 7721 [ADD]

Donizetti, G.:Il borgomastro di Saardam, w. Renato Capecchi (bar), Let Kiel (sgr), J. Schaap (cnd), Zaanstad Opera Orch, Zaanstad Opera Chorus *(rec 1973)* Pantheon 2-▲ PHE 6630 (m)

Dvořák, A.:Songs, w. Graham Johnson (pno)—4 Songs, Op. 73; 2 Songs, Op. 82 Forlane ▲ FRL 16746 [DDD]

Dvořák, A.:Zigeunermelodien, Op. 55, w. Graham Johnson (pno) Forlane ▲ FRL 16746 [DDD]

Finzi, G.:Intimations of Immortality, w. R. Hickox (cnd), Royal Liverpool PO, Royal Liverpool Phil Choir EMI Classics ▲ CDM 64720

Handel, G.F.:Messiah, w. Joan Rodgers (sop), Della Jones (mez), Christopher Robson (ct), Bryn Terfel (b-bar), R. Hickox (cnd), Collegium Musicum 90 [period instrs] [E] Chandos ("Chaconne" series) 2-▲ CHAN 0522/23 [DDD]

Handel, G.F.:Messiah, w. Elly Ameling (sop), Anna Reynolds (mez), Gwynne Howell (bass), N. Marriner (cnd), Academy of St. Martin in the Fields, Academy of St. Martin in the Fields Chorus [E] Argo ■ 421234-4

Handel, G.F.:Messiah, w. Elly Ameling (sop), Anna Reynolds (alt), Gwynne Howell (bass), N. Marriner (cnd), Academy of St. Martin in the Fields, Academy of St. Martin in the Fields Chorus *(rec St John's, Smith Square, London, Jan & July 1976)* London ("Double Decker" series) 2-▲ 444824-2 [ADD]

Handel, G.F.:Messiah (reorchd Mozart), w. Felicity Lott (sop), Felicity Palmer (sop), Robert Lloyd (b-bar), C. Mackerras (cnd), Royal PO, Huddersfield Choral Society [E] ASV ▲ ASV CD 960

Handel, G.F.:Utrecht Te Deum & Jubilate, w. Felicity Palmer (sop), Marjana Lipovšek (mez), N. Harnoncourt (cnd), Vienna Concentus Musicus, Arnold Schoenberg Choir [L] Teldec ▲ 2292-42984-2

Haydn, J.:Die Schöpfung, w. Arleen Augér (sop), David Thomas (bass), S. Rattle (cnd), City of Birmingham SO, City of Birmingham Sym Chorus [E] EMI Classics 2-▲ CDCB 54159 [DDD]

Holst, G.:Savitri, w. F. Palmer (sop), S. Varcoe (bar), R. Hickox (cnd), City of London Sinfonia, Hickox Singers Hyperion ▲ CDA 66099 [DDD]

Janácek, L.:The Diary of One Who Disappeared, w. Graham Johnson (pno) Forlane ▲ FRL 16746 [DDD]

Lambert, C.:Poems by Li-Po, w. Ian Brown (pno), Nigel Hawthorne (nar), L. Friend (cnd), Nash Ensemble Hyperion ▲ CDA 66754

Liszt, F.:Songs, w. John Constable (pno)—Die Macht der Musik; Ihr Glocken von Marling; Im Rhein, im schönen Strome; Bist du!; Vergiftet sind meine Lieder; Jugendglück; Freudvoll und leidvoll; Der Fischerknabe; Der Hirt; Der Alpenjäger; Die drei Zigeuner; Der Glückliche; Kling leise, mein Lied; Wer nie sein Brot mit Tränen ass; Ich möchte hingehn; Die Vätergruft; Ich Scheide; Wanderers Nachtlied II Unicorn-Kanchana ▲ DKP CD 9162

Lotti, A.:Crucifixus, w. Felicity Palmer (sop), Paul Esswood (ct), Christopher Keyte (bass), John Scott (org), John Willison (vn), Chris Wellington (va), Don McVeigh (va), G. Guest (cnd), Philomusica Antiqua of London, St. John's College Choir Cambridge *(rec 1977)* London 2-▲ 443868-2 [ADD]

Monteverdi, C.:Vespro della Beata Vergine, w. M. Marshall (sop), F. Palmer (sop), K. Equiluz (ten), T. Hampson (bar), A. Korn (bass), N. Harnoncourt (cnd), Vienna Concentus Musicus, Hamburg Monteverdi Chorus, Vienna Boys' Chorus Teldec 2-▲ 92629-2

Langridge, Philip (ten) (cont.)

Monteverdi, C.:Vespro della Beata Vergine, w. L. Marshall (sop), F. Palmer (sop), K. Equiluz (ten), T. Hampson (bar), A. Korn (bass), N. Harnoncourt (cnd), Vienna Concentus Musicus, Hamburg Monteverdi Chorus, Vienna Boys' Chorus [L] Teldec 2-▲ 2292-42671-2

Mozart, W.A.:Clemenza, w. L. Popp (sop), R. Ziesack (sop), A. Murray (mez), D. Ziegler (mez), L. Polgar (bass), T. Grabowski (hpd), C. Hermann (vc), N. Harnoncourt (cnd), Zurich Opera Orch, Zurich Opera House Chorus Teldec 2-▲ 90857-2

Mozart, W.A.:Nozze di Figaro, w. C. Margiono (sop), B. Bonney (sop), I. Rey (sop), A. Murray (mez, P.-L. Lang (mez), P. Langridge (ten), C. Späth (ten), T. Hampson (bar), K. Moll (bass), A. Scharinger (bass), K. Langan (bass), N. Harnoncourt (cnd), Royal Concertgebouw Orch, Netherlands Opera Chorus *(rec Amsterdam, May 1993)* Teldec 3-▲ 90861-2 [DDD]

Mussorgsky, M.:Boris Godunov, w. V. Valente (sop—Xenia), E. Gorochovskaya (mez—Nurse), L. Nichiteanu (mez—Fyodor), E. Zarmeba (mez—Hostess), M. Lipovšek (cta—Marina), P. Langridge (ten—Prince Shuisky), H. Wildhaber (ten—Misail), A. Fedin (ten—Simpleton), S. Leiferkus (bar—Rangoni), A. Kotcherga (bass—B. Godounov), A. Shagidullin (bass—Shchelkalov), S. Ramey (bass—Pimen), S. Larin (bass—Girgory), G. Nikolsky (bass—Varlaam), C. Abbado (cnd), Berlin PO, Tölz Boys' Choir, Berlin Radio Chorus, Slovak Phil Chorus *(rec Nov. 7-30, 1993)* Sony Classical 3-▲ S3K 58977 [DDD]

Ravel, M.:L'Enfant et les sortilèges, w. Arleen Augér (sop), Marilyn Richardson (sop), Jane Berbié (mez), Linda Finnie (mez), Jocelyne Taillon (mez), Davenny Wyner (mez), Philippe Huttenlocher (bar), Jules Bastin (bass), A. Previn (cnd), London SO, Ambrosian Opera Chorus Classics for Pleasure ("Eminence" series) ▲ CFP 2241

Schoenberg, A.:Moses und Aaron, w. B. Bonney (sop), M. Zakai (cta), F. Mazura (bar), A. Haugland (bass), G. Solti (cnd), Chicago SO, Chicago Sym Chorus, Glen Ellyn Children's Chorus [G] London 2-▲ 414264-2 [DDD]

Schubert, Franz:Songs (comp), w. G. Johnson (pno)—14 songs—D.124, 163/165, 174, 179, 180, 206, 209, 309, 477, 539, 611, 672, 698, 749 [G] Hyperion ▲ CDJ 33004 [DDD]

Shostakovich, D.:Lady Macbeth of Mtsensk, w. M. Ewing (sop), E. Zaremba (mez), H. Zednik (ten), A. Haugland (bass), A. Kotcherga (bass), K. Moll (bass), S. Larin (bass), M.-W. Chung (cnd), Bastille Opera Orch, Bastille Opera Chorus Deutsche Grammophon 2-▲ 437511-2

Stravinsky, I.:Oedipus Rex, w. F. Quivar (mez), D. Kaasch (ten), J. Morris, J.-H. Rootering (bass), J. Bastin (bass), J. Levine (cnd), Chicago SO, Chicago Sym Chorus Deutsche Grammophon ▲ 435872-2

Stravinsky, I.:Oedipus Rex, w. J. Norman (sop), P. Schreier (ten), B. Terfel (b-bar), S. Ozawa (cnd), Saito Kinen Orch Philips ▲ 438865-2

Szymanowski, K.:Sym 3, w. A. Panufnik (cnd), BBC SO, BBC Singers, BBC Sym Chorus IMP ("BBC Radio Classics" series) ▲ IMP 9124

Tippett, M.:A Child Of Our Time, w. N. Armstrong (sop), F. Palmer (sop), J. Shirley-Quirk (bar), A. Previn (cnd), Royal PO, Brighton Festival Chorus [E] RPO ▲ RPO 7012 [DDD]

Tippett, M.:King Priam, w. Heather Harper (sop—Hecuba), Linda Hirst (sop—Serving Woman), Felicity Palmer (sop—Andromache), Julian Saipe (sop—Paris), Yvonne Minton (mez—Helen), Ann Murray (mez—Nurse), Kenneth Bowen (ten—Hermes), Peter Hall (ten—Young Guard), Philip Langridge (ten—Paris), Robert Tear (ten—Achilles), Thomas Allen (bar—Hector), Norman Bailey (bar—Priam), Stephen Roberts (bar—Patroclus), David Wilson-Johnson (bar—Old Man), D. Atherton (cnd), London Sinfonietta, London Sinfonietta Chorus Chandos ▲ CHAN 9406/7 [DDD]

Vaughan Williams, R.:Sancta civitas, w. B. Terfel (b-bar), R. Hickox (cnd), London SO, London Sym Chorus, St. Paul's Cathedral Choirsters EMI Classics ▲ CDC 54788

Langshaw, Philip (bass)

Bach, J.S.:Magnificat, BWV 243, w. Hélène Obadia (sop), Brigitte Vinson (sop), Madeleine Jalabert (alt), Hervé Lamy (ten), P. Kuentz (cnd), Paul Kuentz Orch, Paul Kuentz Choir Pierre Verany ▲ PVY 730048

Bach, J.S.:St. John Passion, w. Barbara Schlick (sop), Ingeborg Most (alt), Edrian Brand (ten), Alexander Stevenson (ten), Peter Lika (bass), P. Kuentz (cnd), Paul Kuentz Orch, Paul Kuentz Choir Pierre Verany 2-▲ PVY 730051 [DDD]

Draeseke, F.:Mysterium:Christus, w. C. Bischoff (sop), A. Vogel (sop), E. Dersen (alt), K. Markus (ten), H.J. Ritzerfeld (ten), B. Kämpff (bass), J. Sonnenschmidt (org), U.-R. Follert (cnd), Breslau State PO, Evangelical Boys' Choir Palatine, Heilbronn Vocal Ensemble, Palatine Kurrende Bayer 5-▲ 100175/79

Handel, G.F.:Messiah (sels), w. Barbara Schlick (sop), Jean Nirouet (ct), Alexander Stevenson (ten), P. Kuentz (cnd), Paul Kuentz Orch, Paul Kuentz Choir Pierre Verany ▲ PVY 730045

Mozart, W.A.:Missa, K.317, w. Mechtild Georg (sop), Barbara Schlick (sop), Alexander Stevenson (ten), P. Kuentz (cnd), Paul Kuentz Orch, Paul Kuentz Choir Pierre Verany ▲ PVY 730041

Mozart, W.A.:Zauberflöte, w. Birgit Been (sop), Nathalie Boissy (sop), Marianne Seibel (sop), Renate Springer (sop), Elizabeth Vidal (sop), Eleanor James (mez), Salvador Guzman (ten), Herbert Hechenberger (ten), Wolfgang Newmann (ten), Klaus Häger (bass), Hans-Georg Moser (bass), P. Kuentz (cnd), Paul Kuentz Orch, Francis Bardot (cnd), Maitrise des Hauts-de-Seine members, Paul Kuentz Choirs Pierre Verany 2-▲ PVY 730055 [DDD]

Langton, Sunny Joy (sop)

Women at an Exposition, w. Susanne Mentzer (mez), Elain Skorodin (vn), Kimberly Schmidt (pno) *(rec Nov. 1991)* Koch International Classics ▲ KIC 7240 [ADD]

Languirand, Jacques (nar)

Normandeau, R.:Petit Prince, w. Michel Dumont (nar—Aviator), Martin Pensa (nar—Little Prince), Christine Séguin (nar—Rose), Jean Marchand (nar—King), Luc Durand (nar—Conceited Man), Gilles Dupuis (nar—Drunkard), Guy Nadon (nar—Businessman), Jacques Languirand (nar—Lamplighter), Pierre Bourgault (nar—Geographer), Cynthia Dubois (nar—Snake), Monique Giroux (nar—Flower), Françoise Davoine (nar—Rose Garden), Jean-Louis Millette (nar—Fox), Gérard Poirier (nar—Railway Switchman), Claude Préfontaine (nar—Water Pill Salesman) *(rec Montreal, Aug 1994)* CBC 2-▲ 1091 [DDD]

Lanigan, John (ten)

Janácek, L.:Jenůfa (sels), w. M. Collier (sop), A. Varnay (sop), R. Cassilly (ten), R. Kubelik (cnd), Royal Opera House Orch, Royal Opera House Chorus Covent Garden—eight solo, duet & trio arias featuring Astrid Varnay [G] *(rec live at Covent Garden, Feb. 24, 1968)* Myto 2-▲ 2 MCD 90422 [ADD]

Puccini, G.:Madama Butterfly, w. V. de los Angeles (sop—Madama Butterfly), B. Howitt (mez—Suzuki), J. Livingston (mez—Kate), J. Lanigan (ten—Pinkerton), D. Tree (ten—Goro), D. A. (ten—Yamadori), G. Evans (bar—Sharpless), M. Langdon (bass—Bonzo), R. Kempe (cnd), Royal Opera House Orch, Royal Opera House Chorus Covent Garden *(rec London, May 1957)* Ornamenti 2-▲ FE 112 [ADD]

Verdi, G.:Otello, w. Raina Kabaivanska (sop), Josephine Veasey (mez), Mario del Monaco (ten), Tito Gobbi (bar), G. Solti (cnd), Royal Opera House Orch, Royal Opera House Covent Garden Chorus *(rec June 30, 1962)* Memories ▲ MEM 4583 [AAD]

Lankston (sgr)

Bernstein, L.:Candide, w. E. Mills (sop), D. Eisler (ten), J. Mauceri (cnd), New York City Opera Orch, New York Opera Chorus [E] *(rec 1985)* New World 2-▲ NW 340/41-2 2-■ NW 340/41-4

Lanman, Michael (bass)

Moore, D.:Devil & Daniel Webster, w. Joyce Guyer (sop—Mary Stone), Benjamin Bongers (ten—Walter Butler), Michael Philip Davis (ten—Simon Girty), Matthew Foerschler (ten—Miser Stephens), Darren Keith Woods (ten—Mr. Scratch), Michael Lanman (bass—Blackbeard Teach), David Soxman (bass—Clerk), Brian Steele (bass—Daniel Webster), John Stephens (bass—Jabez Stone), Andrew Stuckey (bass—King Philip), Robert Gibby Brand (actor), Cary Miller (actor), R. Patterson (cnd), Kansas City SO, Kansas City Lyric Opera Chorus *(rec Sept 1995)* Newport Classic ▲ NPD 85585 [DDD]

Lanskoy, Mikhail (bar)

Verdi, G.:I masnadieri, w. M. Rowland (sgr), M. Malagnini (sgr), T. Migliorini (sgr), R. Bruson (bar), C. Colombara (bass), W. Gönnenwein (cnd), Ludwigsburg Festival Orch, South German Madrigal Choir Bayer 2-▲ BR 500 001/2 [DDD]

Lantieri, Rita (sop)

Giordano, U.:La Cena delle beffe, w. Armiliato (sgr), M. Chingari (bar), N. Sanzogno (cnd), Piacenza SO [I] *(rec live, 12/14/88)* Bongiovanni 2-▲ GB 2068/69 [DDD]

Lantieri, Rita (sop) (cont.)
Smareglia, A.:La falena, w. Leyla Gencer (sop—La Falena), Rita Lantieri (sop—Albina, sua figlia), Ruggero Bondino (ten—Re Stellio), Dario Zerial (ten—Il ladro), Mario D'Anna (bar—Il vecchio Uberto), Aurio Tomicich (bass—Morio), Giuseppe Botta (sgr—Un marinaio), G. Gavazzeni (cnd), Trieste Teatro Comunale Giuseppe Verdi Orch, Trieste Teatro Comunale G. Verdi Chorus *(rec Trieste, Mar 18, 1876)* Bongiovanni 2-▲ GB 1131/32

Lanza, Mario (ten)
Ave Maria, w. Plácido Domingo (ten), Vienna Boys' Choir, Robert Shaw Chorale RCA Victor ▲ 09026-61838-2 ■ 09026-61838-4
Christmas' Greatest Voices, w. Leontyne Price (sop), Plácido Domingo (ten), et al. RCA ▲ 09026-68265-2; ■ 09026-68265-4
Christmas Treasures, w. Leontyne Price (sop), Marian Anderson (cta), Rosalind Elias (mez), Giorgio Tozzi (bass), Arthur Fiedler (cnd), Leopold Stokowski (cnd), Robert Shaw Chorale RCA Living Stereo ▲ 09026-61867-2 ■ 09026-61867-4
Golden Days, w. Jerry Hadley (ten), Tony Randall (sgr), American Theater Orch [cnd:Paul Gemignani], Harvard Glee Club RCA Victor ▲ 09026-62681-2 ■ 09026-62681-2
The Great Mario Lanza, w. Ray Sinatra Orch [cnd:Ray Sinatra] Goldies ▲ GLD 63201 [ADD]
Mario Lanza & Frances Yeend, w. Frances Yeend (sop), Hollywood Bowl Orch [cnd:Eugene Ormandy] *(rec live at the Hollywood Bowl, 8/27/47)* Melodram ▲ CDM 16512 (m) [AAD]
Mario Lanza at His Best RCA Living Stereo ("Living Stereo" series) ▲ 09026-68130-2 ■ 09026-68130-4
The Mario Lanza Collection RCA Victor 3-▲ 09026-60889-2 [ADD]
Mario Lanza Live from London *(rec 1958)* RCA Victor ▲ 09026-61884-2 ■ 09026-61884-4 (CrO2)
Three Tenors of the Golden Age, w. Jussi Björling (ten), Jan Peerce (ten), John Corigliano (vn), Constantine Callinicos (pno), Frederick Schauwecker (pno), RCA Victor Orch [cnd:Renato Cellini, Constantine Callinicos, Erich Leinsdorf, Sylvan Levin, Maximilian Pilzer, Frieder Weissmann], Rome Opera Orch, Rome Opera Chorus [cnd:Eri RCA Gold Seal ▲ 09026-68531-2 [ADD] ■ 09026-68531-4
Unforgettable Recitals:Mario Lanza & Frances Yeend, w. Frances Yeend (sop) *(rec Hollywood Bowl, 1947)* Melodram ▲ CDI 104001 [ADD]
The Voices of Living Stereo, Vol. 2, w. Eileen Farrell (sop), Birgit Nilsson (sop), Roberta Peters (sop), Leontyne Price (sop), Galina Vishnevskaya (sop), Rosalind Elias (mez), Shirley Verrett (mez), Marian Anderson (cta), Maureen Forrester (cta), Sergio Franchi (ten), Richard Lewis (ten), Jan Pee, Alexander Dedyukhin (pno), Franz Rupp (pno), Leo Taubman (pno), George Trovillo (pno), Charles Wadsworth (pno), Boston Pops Orch [cnd:Arthur Fiedler], Boston SO [cnd:Charles Munch], Chicago SO [cnd:Fritz Reiner], RCA Victor Orch, RCA Victor Chorus [cnd:Wa *(rec Boston & Chicago & New York & Rome, 1957–1964)* RCA Living Stereo ▲ 09026-68167-2 [ADD]

Lanzone, J. (bar)
Charpentier, G.:Songs, w. G. Féraldy (sop), J. Planel (ten), G. Charpentier (cnd), *(orch & chorus unknown)* —Chanson du chemin; Ronde des campagnons; A mules; Les chevaux de bois; Sérénade à Watteau; Les yeux de Berthe [F] *(rec 1934)* Music Memoria 3-▲ 30223

Lapciková, Zuzana (sop)
Janácek, L.:Music of, w. Pavla Dittmannová (cta), Petr Julícek (ten), L. Svárovský (cnd), Brno State PO, Petr Fiala (cnd), Brno Czech Phil Chorus—Rákos Rákoczy (ballet); folk songs, choruses & dances Supraphon ▲ SUP CD 3129

Lapina, Maria (sop)
Rachmaninoff, S.:Francesca da Rimini, w. Nilolaï Vassiliev (ten), Vitaly Tarastchenko (ten), Nikolaï Mechetniak (bar), Vladimir Matorin (bass), A. Tchistiakov (cnd), Bolshoi Theater Orch, Russian State Choir Russian Season 3-▲ CMX 388053
Rimsky-Korsakov, N.:A May Night, w. Natalia Erassova (mez), Elena Okolycheva (cta), Alexander Arkhipov (ten), Vitaly Tarastchenko (ten), Piotr Glouboky (bass), Viatcheslav Potchapski (bass), A. Tchistiakov (cnd), Bolshoi Theater Orch, Russian State Choir Russian Season 4-▲ CMX 388054

Lapins, Klaus (bar)
Liszt, F.:Legend of Saint Elizabeth, w. Maria Szechowska (sop), Doreen Millmann (mez), István Bercewy (bass), S. Heinrich (cnd), Warsaw RSO, Warsaw Radio Chorus [G] *(rec 1983)* Koch Schwann 2-▲ 3-1291-2 [ADD]

Laplante, Bruno (bar)
Gounod, C.:Songs, w. Janine Lachanee (pno)—O ma belle rebelle; Le premier jour de mai; Le vallon; Le lever; Venise; Chanson de printemps; L'absent; Sérénade; Au printemps; Les deux pigeons; Viens, les gazons sont verts; Où voulez-vous aller?; Ma belle amie est morte; Envoi de fleurs; Mignon; Prière Analekta ▲ AN 29404
Hahn, R.:Songs, w. Janine Lachanee (pno)—Si mes vers avaient des ailes; Paysage; LEnamouré; Infidélité; Le Rossignol des Lilas; Quand je fuspris au pavillon; Offrande; L'Incrédule; D'une prison; Fêtes Galantes; A Chloris; Études Latines Analekta ▲ AN 29402
Massenet, J.:Songs, w. France Duval (mez), Marc Durand (pno)—Poème d'octobre; Poème d'amour; Poème d'hiver; Poème d'un soir; Lui et Elle [all are song cycles] *(rec Chapelle historique du Bon Pasteur, Montréal, June 1992)* Analekta ▲ AN 2 9406 [DDD]
Massenet, J.:Songs, w. Janine Lachanee (pno)—Pensée d'Automne; Madrigal; Poème d'Avril; Ouvre tes yeux bleus; Elégie; A Colombine; Oh! si les fleus avaient des yeux; Sérénade de Zanetto; Automne; Roses d'octobre; Nuit d'Espagne; Si tu veux, mignonne; Fleuramye; Souvenir de Venise Analekta ▲ AN 29403
Satie, E.:Songs, w. M. Durand (pno)—30 sels. Analekta ▲ OPCD 1002
Words of Love, w. F. Duval (sop), C. Webster (pno) Analekta ▲ AN29401 [DDD] ■ AN4-9401

Lapointe, Jean-François (bar)
Caplet, A.:Myrrha, w. Sharon Coste (sop), Marc Duguay (ten), J. Grimbert (cnd), Paris Sorbonne Orch, Paris Sorbonne Chorus Marco Polo ▲ 8.223755 [DDD]

La Porta, Arturo (b-bar)
Giordano, U.:Andrea Chénier, w. Renata Tebaldi (sop—Maddalena), Anna di Stasio (mez—Bersi), Amalia Pini (mez—Madelon/Contessa), Mario Del Monaco (ten—Andrea Chenier), Antonio Pirino (ten—L'Incredibile/Abate), Aldo Protti (bar—Carlo Gerard), Arturo La Porta (bass/bar—Mathieu/Fleville), Silvano Pagliuca (bass/bar—Roucher/Fouquier-Tinville), Giorgio Onesti (bass—Dumas/Schmidt/Major-domo), F. Capuana (cnd), Italian Lyric Orch, Italian Lyric Chorus *(rec Tokyo, Oct 1, 1961)* Legato Classics 2-▲ LCD 214-2 [ADD]
Puccini, G.:La fanciulla del West (sels), w. Magda Olivero (sop—Minnie), Corinna Vozza (mez—Wowkle), Paolo Caroli (ten—Harry), Giacomo Lauri-Volpi (ten—Dick Johnson), Marco Rogani (ten—Pony Express Rider), Salvatore di Tommaso (ten—Trin), Adelio Zagonara (ten—Nick), Virgilio Ascorro (bar—Sid), Alfredo Colella (bar—Jake Wallace), Giuseppe Forgione (bar—Bello), Giancarlo Guelfi (bar—Jack Rance), Arturo la Porta (bar—Sonora), Gino Conti (bass—José Castro), Piere Passarotti (bass—Bill), Enzo Titta (bass—Larkens), Giulio Tomei (bass—Ashby), V. Bellezza (cnd), Rome Opera Orch, Rome Opera Chorus—Minnie, dalla mia casa son partito; Laggiù nel Soledad; Chi c'è per farmi i ricci; Oh! Mister Johnson, siete rimasto; Non so ben neppur io; Io non son che una povera fanciulla; No, Minnie, non piangete; Vorrei mettermi queste; Hallo!; Oh, se sapeste; Credo che abbiate torto; Ma ti giuro ch'io non ti lascio più; Vieni fuori!; Una parola sola!...Or son sei mesi; Che c'è di nuovo Jack?; È là; Siete pronto; Ch'ella mi creda; È Minnie!...È Minnie! *(rec Rome, Mar. 30, 1957)* Golden Age of Opera ▲ GAO 180 [ADD]

Larcen, Elsa (sop)
Wagner, R.:Parsifal (sels), w. H. Reimar (ten), C. Hartmann (bar), L. Weber (bass), H. Knappertsbusch (cnd), Berlin German Opera Orch, Berlin German Opera Chorus—Act 3 *(rec 1943)* Enterprise ("Document" series) ▲ ENTLV 943 [ADD]

Larcher, Claire (sgr)
Massenet, J.:Grisélidis, w. Michèle Command (sop), Brigitte Desnoues (sop), Jean-Luc Viala (ten), Didier Henry (bar), Maurice Sieyes (bar), Christian Treguier (bar), Jean-Philippe Courtis (bass), P. Fournillier (cnd), Franz Liszt SO, Budapest Lyon Chorus Koch Schwann 2-▲ SCH 312702 [DDD]

Laren, Elsa (sgr)
Wagner, R.:Parsifal (sels), w. Carl Hartmann (ten), Hans Reinmar (bar), Ludwig Weber (bass), H. Knappertsbusch (cnd), Berlin German Opera Orch, Berlin German Opera Chorus—complete Act 3 *(rec Berlin, March 31, 1942)* Grammofono 2000 ▲ GRM 78555

Larin, Sergei (bass)
Mussorgsky, M.:Boris Godunov, w. V. Valente (sop—Xenia), E. Gorochovskaya (mez—Nurse), L. Nichiteanu (mez—Fyodor), E. Zarmeba (mez—Hostess), M. Lipovšek (cta—Marina), P. Langridge (ten—Prince Shuisky), H. Wildhaber (ten—Misail), A. Fedin (ten—Simpleton), S. Leiferkus (bar—Rangoni), A. Kotcherga (bass—B. Godounov), A. Shagidullin (bass—Shchelkalov), S. Ramey (bass—Pimen), S. Larin (bass—Girgory), G. Nikolsky (bass—Varlaam), C. Abbado (cnd), Berlin PO, Tölz Boys' Choir, Berlin Radio Chorus, Slovak Phil Chorus *(rec Nov. 7–30, 1993)* Sony Classical 3-▲ S3K 58977 [DDD]
Shostakovich, D.:Lady Macbeth of Mtsensk, w. M. Ewing (sop), E. Zaremba (mez), P. Langridge (ten), H. Zednik (ten), A. Haugland (bass), A. Kotcherga (bass), K. Moll (bass), M.-W. Chung (cnd), Bastille Opera Orch, Bastille Opera Chorus Deutsche Grammophon 2-▲ 437511-2

Larin, Sergei (ten)
Tchaikovsky, P.:Mazeppa, w. Galina Gorchakoova (sop), Larissa Dyadkova (mez), Sergei Leiferkus (bar), Anatoly Kotscherga (bass), N. Järvi (cnd), Gothenburg SO, Stockholm Royal Opera Chorus Deutsche Grammophon 3-▲ 439906-2
Tchaikovsky, P.:Songs, w. Bekova Sisters—The Tender Stars Shone for Us, Op. 60/12; No, Only He Who's Known, Op. 6/6; Don Juan's Serenade, Op. 38/1; Amid the Noise of the Ball, Op. 38/3; Why Did I Dream of You, Op. 28/3; Mezza Notte; Night, Op. 60/9; Does the Day Reign?, Op. 47/6; To Forget So Soon; I Opened the Window, Op. 63/2; Rondel, Op. 65/6; This Moonlit Night, Op. 73/3; Disappointment, Op. 65/2; The Sun Has Set, Op. 73/4; I Shall Tell You Nothing, Op. 60/2; Amid Gloomy Days, Op. 73/5; Tell Me, of What in the Shade of the Branches, Op. 57/1; I Should Like a Single Word; Not a Word, O My Friend, Op. 6/2; It Was in Early Spring, Op. 38/2; A Tear Trembles, Op. 6/4; Why?, Op. 6/5; We Sat Together, Op. 73/1; O, If You Knew, Op. 60/3; Again I Am Alone, Op. 73/6 Chandos ▲ CHAN 9428 [DDD]

Larmore, Jennifer (mez)
Berlioz, H.:La Damnation de Faust, w. J. Larmor (mez—Marguerite), K. Olsen (ten—Faust), D. Wilson-Johnson (bar—Méphistophélès), H. Claessens (bar—Brander), G. Neuhold (cnd), Flanders Royal PO, Düsseldorf Municipal Choral Society Bayer 2-▲ 500017/18 [DDD]
Duruflé, M.:Requiem, w. B. Bonney (soprano), T. Hampson (bass-baritone), Ambrosian Singers, M. Legrand (cnd), Philharmonia Orch Teldec ▲ 90879-2
Falla, M. de:El amor brujo, w. H. Wolff (cnd), St. Paul CO *(rec Ordway Music Theatre, Saint Paul, MN, Feb. 1993)* Teldec ▲ 90852-2 [DDD]
Fauré, G.:Requiem, w. B. Bonney (sop), T. Hampson (bass-bar), M. Legrand (cnd), Philharmonia Orch, Ambrosian Singers Teldec ▲ 90879-2
Handel, G.F.:Giulio Cesare in Egitto, w. Barbara Schlick (sop), Marianne Rørholm (mez), Bernarda Fink (cta), Derek Lee Ragin (ct), Dominique Visse (ct), Oliver Lallouette (bass), Furio Zanasi (bass), R. Jacobs (cnd), Concerto Cologne [period instrs] Harmonia Mundi France 3-▲ HMC 901385/87
Handel, G.F.:Giulio Cesare in Egitto (sels), w. Barbara Schlick (sop), Marianne Rørholm (mez), Bernarda Fink (cta), Derek Lee Ragin (ct), R. Jacobs (cnd), Concerto Cologne Harmonia Mundi France ▲ HMC 901458
Handel, G.F.:Giulio Cesare in Egitto (sels)—Empio, dirò; Alma del gran pompeo; Va tacito; Al lampo del armi; Caro/Bello Harmonia Mundi ("Suite" series) ▲ HMT 7901575
Humperdinck, E.:Hänsel und Gretel, w. H. Behrens (sop—Gertrud, the Stepmother), R. Ziesak (sop—Gretel), R. Joshua (sop—Sandman), C. Schäfer (sop—Dew Fairy), J. Larmore (mez—Hänsel), H. Schwarz (cta—Nibblewitch), B. Weikl (bar—Peter, the Father), D. Runnicles (cnd), Bavarian RSO, Tölz Boys' Choir *(rec Munich, Feb. 1994)* Teldec 2-▲ 94549-2 [DDD]
Monteverdi, C.:Incoronazione, w. D. Borst (sop), Lootens (sop), G. Laurens (mez), A. Köhler (alt), M. Schopper (bass), R. Jacobs (cnd), Concerto Vocale [direction & new musical realization by René Jacobs] [I] Harmonia Mundi France 3-▲ HMC 901330/32
Monteverdi, C.:Incoronazione di Poppea (sels)—Disprezzata regina; Addio roma Harmonia Mundi ("Suite" series) ▲ HMT 7901575
Monteverdi, C.:Orfeo (sels)—In un fiorito prato; Ahi caso acerbo; Sinf Harmonia Mundi ("Suite" series) ▲ HMT 7901575
Mozart, W.A.:Missa, K.427, w. C. Oelze (sop), S. Weir (ten), P. Kooy (bass), P. Herreweghe (cnd), Champs Élysées Theater Orch, Chapelle Royale Choir, Collegium Vocale Harmonia Mundi France ▲ HMC 901393
Mozart, W.A.:Missa, K.427, w. Christiane Oelze (sop), Scot Weir (ten), Peter Kooy (bass), P. Herreweghe (cnd), Champs Élysées Theater Orch, Chapelle Royale Choir, Collegium Vocale Harmonia Mundi France ▲ HMX 29001393
Mozart, W.A.:Missa, K.139/47a—Laudamus te; Quoniam Harmonia Mundi ("Suite" series) ▲ HMT 7901575
Rossini, G.:Arias, w. A. Aug(acu)er (sop), M. Kimbrough (bar), D. Baldwin (pno)—La Pesca (duet); Il Trovatore Arabesque ▲ Z 6623 [ADD]
Rossini, G.:Il barbiere di Siviglia, w. A. Corbelli (bar), R. Gimeniz (bar), H. Hagegard (bar), S. Ramey (bass), J. López-Cobos (cnd), Lausanne CO, Geneva Grand Théâtre Chorus [I] Teldec 2-▲ 9031-74885-2
Rossini, G.:Il barbiere di Siviglia (sels), w. B. Frittoli (sop), R. Giménez (ten), Håkan Hagegård (bar), A. Corbelli (bar), S. Ramey (bass), J. López-Cobos (cnd), Lausanne CO, Geneva Grand Théâtre Chorus Teldec ▲ 93693-2
Rossini, G.:Péchés de vieillesse (sels), w. A. Auger (sop), J. Aler (ten), S. Kimbrough (bar), D. Baldwin (pno)—Les Amants de Séville; Chanson de Zora; L'Esule; La Fioraia Fiorentina; La Lontananza; Musique Anodine; L'Orpheline du Tyrol; La Passegiata Quartettino; L'Ultimo Ricordo; Un Sou Complainte [I,F] Arabesque ▲ Z 6623 [ADD]
Rossini, G.:Semiramide, w. C. Studer (sop), F. Lopardo (ten), S. Ramey (bass), I. Marin (cnd), London SO, Ambrosian Opera Chorus Deutsche Grammophon ▲ 437797-2
Verdi, G.:Rigoletto, w. L. Vaduva (sop), R. Leech (ten), A. Agache (bar), S. Ramey (bass), C. Rizzi (cnd), Welsh National Opera Orch Teldec ▲ 90851-2

Larrimore (sgr)
Verdi, G.:Un ballo in maschera (sels), w. A. Schuh (sgr), J. Björling (ten), M. Rothmüller (bar), N. Treigle (bass), J. Morris (bass), Feux (sgr), W. Herbert (cnd), *(orch unknown)* [I] *(rec live, New Orleans, 4/22/50)* Legato Classics ▲ LCD 154-1 (m) [ADD]

Larsen, Dorothy (sop)
Flanagan, W.:The Lady of Tearful Regret, w. E. Krogh (ten), W. Strickland (cnd), Oslo PO CRI ■ C 163

Larsen, O. Støvring (ten)
Van De Vate, N.:An American Essay, w. C. Marstrand (sop), L. Hovman (alt), S. Kawalla (cnd), Koszalin State PO, Chorus Soranus Vienna Modern Masters ▲ VMM 3025 [DDD]

Larson, Philip (bar)
Erickson, R.:Sierra, w. T. Nee (cnd), SONOR Ensemble of Univ of California San Diego *(rec 1987–91)* CRI ▲ CD 616 [DDD]
London, E.:Two A'Marvell's FOR WORDS, w. E. London (cnd), Cleveland Chamber SO GM ▲ GM 2045
Reynolds, R.:The Ivanov Suite, w. J. Fonville (pic), E. Harkins (tpt), J. Ngyesy (vn), R. Mushabec (vc), S. Schick (perc) New World ▲ 80431-2
Reynolds, R.:Odyssey, w. Marie Kobayashi (mez), D. Robertson (cnd), Ensemble InterContemporain Neuma 2-▲ 450-91 [DDD]
Reynolds, R.:The Vanity of Words Neuma ▲ 450-78 [DDD]
Reynolds, R.:Versions/Stages, w. J. Fonville (pic), E. Harkins (tpt), J. Ngyesy (vn), R. Mushabec (vc), S. Schick (perc) New World ▲ 80431-2
Reynolds, R.:Voicespace 1 Lovely Music ▲ LCD 1801 [ADD]
Reynolds, R.:Voicespace 3 Lovely Music ▲ LCD 1801 [ADD]
Reynolds, R.:Voicespace 4 Lovely Music ▲ LCD 1801 [ADD]
Xenakis, I.:Aïs, w. S. Schick (perc), T. Nee (cnd), La Jolla SO Neuma ▲ 450-86 [DDD]

Larson, Susan (mez)
Harbison, J.:Samuel Chapter, w. J. Harbison (cnd), Collage New Music Ensemble [E] Elektra/Nonesuch ▲ 79129-2 [DDD]

La Rue, Custer (sop)
The Daemon Lover:Traditional Ballads & Songs of England, Scotland & America, w. Baltimore Consort *(rec May 1992)* Dorian ▲ DOR 90174 [DDD]

La Rue, Custer (sop) (cont.)
The True Lover's Farewell:Appalachian Folk Balads, w. Baltimore Consort members [Mary Ann Ballard (vl), Mark Cudek (cittern/Renaissance gtr/baroque gtr/bass vl/lt/early wind instrs), Ronn McFarlane (lt)] *(rec Troy Savings Bank Music Hall, Troy, NY, Sept. 1994)* Dorian ▲ DOR 90213 [DDD]

Lascarro, Juanita (sgr)
Zemlinsky, A. von:Der Geburtstag der Infantin, w. Soile Isokoski (sop), Iride Martinez (sgr), Andrew Collis (sgr), David Kuebler (ten), Machiko Obata (sgr), Anne Schwanewilms (sgr), Natalie Karl (sgr), Martina Rüping (sgr), Franfurter Kantorei (sgr), J. Conlon (cnd), Gürzenich Orch, Cologne PO *(rec Cologne, Feb 1996)* EMI Classics 2-▲ CDCB 56208

Laschet, Leo (sgr)
Schoeck, O.:Das Schloss Dürande (sels), w. Maria Cebotari (sop—Gabriele), Marta Fuchs (sop—Gräfin Morvaille), Brigitte Fassbaender (mez—Renald Willi Domgraf), Rut Berglund (cta—Priorin), Peter Anders (ten—Armand), Benno Arnold (ten—Jäger), Josef Greindl (bass—Nicole), Hans Wrana (bass—Jäger), Vasso Argyris (sgr—Volksredner), Otto Hüsch (sgr—Wildhüter), Leo Laschet (sgr—Jäger), Fritz Marcks (sgr—Jäger), Felix Schneider (sgr—Jäger), R. Heger (cnd)—Text; Ich kann es nicht glauben [from Act 1]; Text; Heil dir, du Feuerquelle [from Act 2]; Text; Gesucht und nicht gefunden [from Act 3]; Text; Der Jäger ist frei! [Act 3 Finale]; Text; Sie kommen mit Flinten und Stangen [Act 4]; Text; Du Narr des vermeintlichen Rechts [Act 4 finale]; Text *(rec live, Apr 1943)* Jecklin ▲ JD 692

Laszczkowski, Jacek (sgr)
Mercadante, S.:Caritea, regina di Spagna, w. Nana Gordaze (sgr), Sonia Lee (sgr), Nicolas Rivenq (bar), Gregory Bonfatti (sgr), Ayhan Ustuk (sgr), G. Carella (cnd), Italian International Opera Orch, Bratislava Camera Chorus *(rec Italy, 1995)* Nuova Era 3-▲ NUO 7258

László, Magda (sop)
Bach, J.S.:Cant 106, "Actus tragicus", w. H. Handt (ten), J. Loomis (bass), H. Scherchen (cnd), Turin Radio Orch, Turin Radio Chorus [G] *(rec live, Jan 14, 1958)* Memories ▲ HR 4160 (m) [ADD]
Beethoven, L. van:Sym 9, "Choral Sym", w. P.-L. Munteanu (ten), H. Scherchen (cnd), Vienna State Opera Orch, Vienna Singakademie *(rec 1954)* Andromeda ▲ ANR 2533 [ADD]
Beethoven, L. van:Sym 9, "Choral Sym", w. Lucienne Devallier (cta), Petre Monteanu (ten), Raffaele Arié (bass), H. Scherchen (cnd), Swiss-Italian RSO, Swiss-Italian Radio-TV Chorus Accord ▲ ACD 201002 [AAD]
Giordano, U.:Madame Sans-Gêne, w. Magda László (sop—Caterina), Carlo Tagliabue (bar—Napoleone), Renato Berti (sgr—Despréaux), Irene Callaway (sgr—Toniotta/Carolina), Danilo Cestari (sgr—Neipperg/Vinaigre), Maria Luisa Malacchi (sgr—Giulia/Principessa Elisa), Carlo Perucci (sgr—Fouché), Danilo Vega (sgr—Lefebvre), Enzo Viaro (sgr—De Brigode/Gelsomino), A. Basile (cnd), Milan RAI SO, Milan RAI Chorus *(rec Milan, Aug 10, 1957)* Bongiovanni 2-▲ GB 1129/30
Stravinsky, I.:Oedipus Rex, w. M. Lazló (mez—Jocasta), N. Gedda (ten—Oedipus), A. Bertocci (ten—Shepherd), M. Petri (bar—Creon & Tireseus), N. Catalani (bar—Messenger), A. Foà (speaker), H. von Karajan (cnd), Rome RAI SO, Rome RAI Chorus *(rec Dec. 20, 1952)* Stradivarius ▲ DAT 12311 [ADD]

László, Margit (sop)
Vivaldi, A.:Juditha triumphans devicta Holofernes barbarie, w. Margit László (sop—Abra), Zsuzsa Barlay (cta—Juditha), József Réti (ten—Servo), Zsolt Bende (bar—Holofernes), József Dene (bar—Ozias), F. Szekeres (cnd), Hungarian State Orch, György Czigány (cnd), Budapest Madrigal Choir, 1968 Classical Diamonds ▲ CLD 4022-23 [ADD]

Latinucci, Pier Luigi (bass)
Bellini, V.:La sonnambula, w. L. Pagliughi (sop—Amina), W. Ruggeri (sop—Lisa), A. M. Anelli (mez—Teresa), F. Tagliavini (ten—Elvino), P. L. Latinucci (bass—Alessio), C. Siepi (bass—Conte Rodolfo), F. Capuana (cnd), Turin RSO, Turin Radio Chorus *(rec 1952)* Cetra Classics 2-▲ CDO 16 [AAD]
Mascagni, P.:L'amico Fritz, w. P. Tassinari (sop—Suzel), A. Pini (mez—Beppe), F. Tagliavini (ten—Fritz), A. Giannotti (ten—Frederico), S. Meletti (bar—David), P. L. Latinucci (bass—Hanezò), P. Mascagni (cnd), Turin RSO, Turin Radio Chorus *(rec 1941)* Cetra Classic 2-▲ CDO 18
Massenet, J.:Werther, w. F. Tagliavini (ten), M. Cortis (bar), F. Molinari-Pradelli (cnd), Turin RAI SO *(rec 1953)* Cetra Classic 2-▲ CDO 15 [AAD]
Puccini, G.:Tosca, w. R. Tebaldi (sop—Tosca), F. Corelli (ten—Cavaradossi), A. Colzani (bar—Scarpia), P. L. Latinucci (b-bar—Sacristan), G. Beloni (bass—Angelotti), M. Parenti (cnd), Livorno Teatro La Gran Guardia Orch, Livorno Teatro La Gran Guardia Chorus *(rec live Sept. 21, 1959)* Legato Classics 2-▲ LCD 171-2 [ADD]

Laubenthal (ten)
Orff, C.:Der Bernauerin, w. L. Popp (sop), Ostermayer (sgr), H. Lippert (ten), K. Eichhorn (cnd), Munich RSO, Munich Radio Chorus [G] Orfeo 2-▲ 255912 [DDD]

Laubenthal, Horst (ten)
Bach, J.S.:Christmas Oratorio, w. E. Ameling (sop), B. Fassbaender (mez), H. Prey (bar), E. Jochum (cnd), Tölz SO, Bavarian Radio Boys' Chorus—highlights Philips ("Silver Line" series) ▲ 422252-2 [ADD]
Bach, J.S.:St. Matthew Passion, w. G. Janowitz (sop), C. Ludwig (mez), P. Schreier (ten), W. Berry (bar), D. Fischer-Dieskau (bar), H. von Karajan (cnd), Berlin PO, Vienna Singverein, German Opera Chorus [G] Deutsche Grammophon 3-▲ 419789-2 [ADD]
Berg, A.:Wozzeck, w. A. Silja (sop), G. Jahn (mez), H. Zednik (ten), E. Waechter (bar), C. von Dohnányi (cnd), Vienna PO London 2-▲ 417348-2 [DDD]
Kiel, F.:Der Stern von Bethlehem, w. M. Schiml (sop), R. Bader (cnd), Berlin RSO, St. Hedwig's Cathedral Choir [G] Koch Schwann ▲ CD 313032 [DDD]
Mozart, L.:Missa solemnis, w. A. Augér (sop), G. Schreckenbach (mez), B. McDaniel (bar), R. Bader (cnd), Berlin Domkapelle Instrumental Ensemble, St. Hedwig's Cathedral Choir [L] Koch Schwann ▲ CD 313028 [ADD]
Mozart, W.A.:Missa brevis, K.220, w. E. Mathis (spo), T. Troyanos (mez), K. Engen (bass) Deutsche Grammophon ▲ 429820-2 [ADD]
Schubert, Franz:Lazarus, or Die Feier der Auferstehung, w. E. Mathis (sop), C. Wulkopf (mez), H. Schwarz (mez), W. Hollweg (ten), H. Prey (bar), G. Chmura (cnd), Stuttgart RSO, Stuttgart Radio Chorus [G] Orfeo ▲ 011101 [DDD]
Wagner, R.:Der Ring des Nibelungen (sels), w. Florence Austral (sop), Frieda Leider (sop), Elsie Suddaby (sop), Göta Ljunberg (sop), Walter Widdop (ten), Lauritz Melchoir (ten), Friedrich Schorr (bar), Rudolf Bockelmann (b-bar), Ivar Andresen (bass), Emmanuel List (bass), Collingwood, Blech, Coates, Barbirolli, Heger, Alwin, Muck (cnd), London SO—scenes from Siegriend & Götterdämmerung; 90 Motives from Der Ring [w. Collingwood & LSO] Pearl 7-▲ PEA 9137 [ADD]

Laubenthal, Rudolf (ten)
Haydn, J.:Mass 3, "Cäcilienmesse", w. Lucia Popp (sop), Doris Soffel (mez), Kurt Moll (bass), R. Kubelik (cnd), Bavarian RSO, Bavarian Radio Chorus [L] Orfeo 2-▲ 032822 [DDD]
Schmidt, F.:Notre Dame, w. G. Jones (sop), J. King (ten), K. Moll (bass), C. Perick (cnd), Berlin RSO, St. Hedwig's Cathedral Choir, RIAS Chamber Chorus [G] Capriccio 2-▲ 10248/9 [DDD]
Wagner, R.:Der fliegende Holländer (sels), w. Göta Ljungberg (sop), Elisabeth Rethberg (sop), Elisabeth Schumann (sop), Lauritz Melchior (ten), Friedrich Schorr (bar), *(cnd & orch unknown) (rec 1927-31)* Preiser 2-▲ PRE 89214 [AAD]
Wagner, R.:Götterdämmerung (sels), w. Göta Ljungberg (sop), Elisabeth Rethberg (sop), Elisabeth Schumann (sop), Lauritz Melchior (ten), Friedrich Schorr (bar), *(cnd & orch unknown) (rec 1927-31)* Preiser 2-▲ PRE 89214 [AAD]
Wagner, R.:Die Meistersinger von Nürnberg, w. C. Ligendza (sop), C. Ludwig (mez), P. Domingo (ten), D. Fischer-Dieskau (bar), R. Hermann (bar), P. Lagger (bass), E. Jochum (cnd), German Opera Orch, German Opera Chorus [G] Deutsche Grammophon 4-▲ 415278-2 [ADD]
Wagner, R.:Die Meistersinger von Nürnberg, w. C. Ligendza (sop), C. Ludwig (mez), P. Domingo (ten), D. Fischer-Dieskau (bar), R. Hermann (bar), P. Lagger (bass), E. Jochum (cnd), German Opera Orch, German Opera Chorus Deutsche Grammophon ("Domingo Edition" series) ▲ 435406-2
Wagner, R.:Die Meistersinger von Nürnberg (sels), w. Göta Ljungberg (sop), Elisabeth Rethberg (sop), Elisabeth Schumann (sop), Lauritz Melchior (ten), Friedrich Schorr (bar), *(cnd & orch unknown) (rec 1927-31)* Preiser 2-▲ PRE 89214 [AAD]
Wagner, R.:Das Rheingold (sels), w. Göta Ljungberg (sop), Elisabeth Rethberg (sop), Elisabeth Schumann (sop), Lauritz Melchior (ten), Friedrich Schorr (bar), *(cnd & orch unknown) (rec 1927-31)* Preiser 2-▲ PRE 89214 [AAD]

Laubenthal, Rudolf (ten) (cont.)
Wagner, R.:Tannhäuser (sels), w. Göta Ljungberg (sop), Elisabeth Rethberg (sop), Elisabeth Schumann (sop), Lauritz Melchior (ten), Friedrich Schorr (bar), *(cnd & orch unknown) (rec 1927-31)* Preiser 2-▲ PRE 89214 [AAD]
Wagner, R.:Die Walküre (sels), w. Göta Ljungberg (sop), Elisabeth Rethberg (sop), Elisabeth Schumann (sop), Lauritz Melchior (ten), Friedrich Schorr (bar), *(orch unknown) (rec 1927-31)* Preiser 2-▲ PRE 89214 [AAD]

Laukka, Raimo (bar)
Sibelius, J.:Kullervo, w. Siole Isokoski (sop), L. Segerstam (cnd), Danish National RSO, Danish National Radio Choir Chandos ▲ CHAN 9393 [DDD]
Tobias, R.:Des Jonah Sendung, w. Pille Lill (sop), Urve Tauts (mez), Peter Svensson (ten), Mati Palm (bass), Ines Maidre (org), N. Järvi (cnd), Estonian State SO, Oratorio Choir, Estonian Phil Chamber Choir, Tallinn Boys' Choir *(rec Estonia Concert Hall, Tallinn, Estonia, June 23-29, 1995)* BIS 2-▲ CD 731/732 [DDD]

Laurence, Elizabeth (mez)
Boulez, P.:Le Visage Nuptial, w. P. Bryn-Julson (sop), P. Boulez (cnd), BBC SO, BBC Singers [F] Erato ▲ 2292-45494-2 [DDD]

Laurens, Guillemette (mez)
Canto Mediterraneo, w. S. Sempé (cnd), Capriccio Stravagante Astrée ▲ 8548
Cererols, J.:Missa pro defunctis, w. E. van Nevel (cnd), Currende Instrumental Ensemble, Currende Vocal Ensemble *(rec May 1994)* Accent ▲ 94106 [DDD]
Cererols, J.:Vespers, w. E. van Nevel (cnd), Currende Instrumental Ensemble, Currende Vocal Ensemble *(rec May 1994)* Accent ▲ 94106 [DDD]
Charpentier, M.-A.:Les Arts florissants, w. C. Dussaut (sop), J. Feldman (sop), A. Mellon (sop), D. Visse (ct), P. Cantor (ten), G. Reinhart (bar), W. Christie (cnd), Les Arts Florissants [F] Musique d'Abord ▲ HMA 1901083
Couperin, F.:Leçons de ténèbres (for Good Friday), w. M. Van Der Sluis (sop), P. Monteilhet (lt), M. Muller (vl), L. Boulay (hpd/org)—[L] Erato (Musifrance) ▲ 2292-45012-2 [DDD]
Couperin, F.:Magnificat, w. M. Van Der Sluis (sop), P. Monteilhet (lt), M. Muller (vl), L. Boulay (hpd/org)—[L] Erato (Musifrance) ▲ 2292-45012-2 [DDD]
Handel, G.F.:Giulio Cesare in Egitto, w. Lynne Dawson (sop), Eirian James (mez), James Bowman (alt), Dominique Visse (alt), Nicolas Rivenq (bar), J. Malgoire (cnd), La Grande Écurie et la Chambre du Roy Astrée 3-▲ E 8558
Handel, G.F.:La Rezurrezione, w. Nancy Argenta (sop), Barbara Schlick (sop), Guy de Mey (ten), Klaus Mertens (bar), T. Koopman (cnd), Amsterdam Baroque Orch [I] Erato 2-▲ 2292-45617-2 [DDD]
Lully, J.-B.:Armide, w. V. Gens (sop), N. Rime (sop), H. Crook (ten), G. Ragon (ten), P. Herreweghe (cnd), La Chapelle Royale Orch, Collegium Vocale [F] Harmonia Mundi France 2-▲ HMC 901456/57
Lully, J.-B.:Atys, w. Agnès Mellon (sop), Guy de Mey (ten), Jean-François Gardeil (bar), W. Christie (cnd), Les Arts Florissants, Les Arts Florissants Chorus [F] Harmonia Mundi France 3-▲ HMC 901257/59 [DDD];
Lully, J.-B.:Divertissements, w. S. Sempé (cnd), Capriccio Stravagante Deutsche Harmonia Mundi ▲ 77218-2-RC [DDD]
Monteverdi & His Time, w. S. Sempé (cnd), Capriccio Stravagante Deutsche Harmonia Mundi ▲ 05472-77200-2 [DDD]
Monteverdi, C.:Incoronazione, w. D. Borst (sop), Lootens (sop), J. Larmore (mez), A. Köhler (alt), M. Schopper (bass), R. Jacobs (cnd), Concerto Vocale [direction & new musical realization by René Jacobs] [I] Harmonia Mundi France 3-▲ HMC 901330/32
Monteverdi, C.:Vespro della Beata Vergine, w. A. Mellon (sop), H. Crook (ten), D. Thomas (bass), P. Herreweghe (cnd), Toulouse Saqueboutiers, Chapelle Royale Choir, Collegium Vocale [L] Harmonia Mundi France 2-▲ HMC 901247/48 [DDD]
Purcell, H.:Dido & Aeneas, w. J. Feldman (sop), P. Cantor (ten), W. Christie (cnd), Les Arts Florissants [E] Harmonia Mundi France ▲ HMC 905173
Ravier, C.:Liturgie pour un Dieu mort, w. Gérard Iglesia (gtr), C. Ravier (cnd), *(ensemble unknown)*, Maurice Bourbon Male Chorus Ensemble Memoire Vive ▲ 262023

Laurenza, Mariena (sop)
Leo, L.:Amor vuol sofferenze, w. Vitalba Mosca (mez), Piero Guarnera (bar), Domenico Colaianni (sgr), Giovanna Donadini (sgr), Marilyne Fallot (sgr), Hyun Lee (sgr), D. Moles (cnd), Naples New Scarlatti Orch *(rec Martinafranca Festival, 1994)* Nuova Era 3-▲ NUO 7221
Rossini, G.:La cambiale di matrimonio, w. S. Jeun (sop—Fanny), M. Laurenza (sop—Clarina), L. Canonici (ten—Edoardo Milfort), R. Frontali (bar—Slook), E. Dara (bar—Tobia Mill), D. Renzetti (cnd), Turin RAI Orch *(rec Aug. 1991)* Ricordi ▲ RFCD 2011 [DDD]

Laurich, Hildegard (cta)
Bach, J.S.:Cant 63, w. A. Augér (sop), J. Hamarï (mez), A. Kraus (ten), W. Heldwein (bass), W. Schöne (bass), H. Rilling (cnd), Stuttgart Bach Collegium, Gächinger Kantorei [G] *(rec Feb 1971 & Feb 1981)* Hänssler Classic ▲ 98.823 [AAD]
Bach, J.S.:Cant 72, w. A. Augér (sop), W. Schöne (bass), H. Rilling (cnd), Bach Ensemble [G] *(rec 1983)* Hänssler Classic ▲ 98.875 [AAD]
Bach, J.S.:Cant 74, w. H. Donath (sop), A. Kraus (ten), P. Huttenlocher (bar), H. Rilling (cnd), Stuttgart Bach Collegium, Gächinger Kantorei Hänssler Classic ▲ 98.887 [AAD]
Bach, J.S.:Cant 120, w. H. Donath (sop), A. Kraus (ten), W. Schöne (bass), H. Rilling (cnd), Bach Ensemble *(rec Mar-Apr 1973)* Hänssler Classic ▲ 98.829 [AAD]
Bach, J.S.:Cant 151, w. N. Gamo-Yamamoto (sop), A. Kraus (ten), H.-F. Kunz (bass), H. Rilling (cnd), Stuttgart Bach Collegium, Frankfurt Kantorei [G] *(rec Feb 1971)* Hänssler Classic ▲ 98.825 [AAD]
Bach, J.S.:Cant 156, w. K. Equiluz (ten), W. Schöne (bass), H. Rilling (cnd), Bach Ensemble [G] *(rec 1973)* Hänssler Classic ▲ 98.875 [AAD]
Bach, J.S.:Cant 161, w. A. Kraus (ten), H. Rilling (cnd), Stuttgart Bach Collegium, Gächinger Kantorei Hänssler Classic ▲ 98.812 [AAD]
Bach, J.S.:Cant 185, w. A. Augér (sop), A. Baldin (ten), P. Huttenlocher (bar), H. Rilling (cnd), Stuttgart Bach Collegium, Frankfurt Kantorei Hänssler Classic ▲ 98.804 [AAD]
Bach, J.S.:Cant 187, w. M. Friesenhausen (sop), W. Schöne (bass), H. Rilling (cnd), Stuttgart Bach Collegium, Gächinger Kantorei Hänssler Classic ▲ 98.806 [AAD]

Lauridon, Gabin (bar)
Zinsstag, G.:Innanzi, w. Z. Peskó (cnd), French National Orch [F] *(rec Sept. 15, 1982)* Grammont ▲ CTSP 36-2 [ADD]

Laurikainen, Kauko (spkr)
Kortekangas, O.:Grand Hotel, w. E.-L. Saarinen (mez), S. Tiilikainen (bar), Pohjola, Söderström (cnd), Avanti! CO, Finnish Chamber Chorus, Tapiola Chorus [Fin] Ondine ▲ ODE 749-2 [ADD]

Lauri-Volpi, Giacomo (ten)
Giacomo Lauri-Volpi Vol. II *(rec 1941-46)* Preiser ▲ PRE CD 89133
Giacomo Lauri-Volpi Memories ("Great Voices" series) 2-▲ MEM 4195 (m)
Giacomo Lauri-Volpi, 1920-1934 *(rec 1920-34)* Pearl ▲ PEA 9010 [AAD]
Giacomo Lauri-Volpi Nimbus ("Prima Voce" series) ▲ NI 7845 [ADD]
Giacomo Lauri-Volpi:Non piagere Liù *(rec live between 1928 & 1955)* Foyer ▲ FOY 4002 [ADD]
Giacomo Lauri-Volpi Sings Verdi Nimbus ("Prima Voce" series) ▲ NI 7853 [ADD]
The Italian Vocal Tradition, Vol. 1:The Voices of Toscanini, w. Toti dal Monte (sop), Claudio Muzio (sop), Rosetta Pampanini (sop), Biata Scacciati (sop), Francesco Merli (ten), Aureliano Pertile (ten), Carlo Galeffi (bar), Mariano Stabile (bar), Riccardo Stracciari (bar), Nazzareno de Angel *(rec 1921-35)* Iron Needle ▲ 1304
Jottini & Volpi, w. Maria Jottini (sop), Florence Maggio Musicale Orch [cnd:Carlo Felice Cillario] *(rec Martini & Rossi Concert, 1957)* Incontri Memorabili ▲ CDMR 5021
Leoncavallo, R.:Pagliacci (sels), w. Enrico Caruso (ten), Antonio Paoli (ten), Giovanni Zenatello (ten), Amedeo Bassi (ten), Hermann Jadlowker (ten), Fernand Ansseau (ten), Hipolito Lazaro (ten), Nino (Filippo) Piccaluga (ten), Mario Chamlee (ten), Miguel Fleta (ten), Giovanni Martinelli (ten), Aureliano Pertile (ten), Georges Thill (ten), Alessandro Valente (ten), Francesco Merli (ten), Lauritz Melchior (ten), Marcel Wittrisch (ten), Joseph Schmidt (ten), Beniamino Gigli (ten), Giuseppe Lugo (ten), Helge Roswaenge (ten), Jussi Bjoerling (ten)—23 versions of the tenor aria "Vesti la giubba" *(rec 1907-1944)* Bongiovanni ▲ GB 1071 [ADD]

▲ = CD ♦ = Enhanced CD Δ = MD ■ = Cassette Tape □ = DCC

Lauri-Volpi, Giacomo (ten) (cont.)

Meyerbeer, G.:Les Huguenots, w. A. Pastori (sop), A. de Cavalieri (mez), G. Taddei (bar), G. Tozzi (bass), N. Zaccaria (bass), T. Serafin (cnd), Milan RAI SO, Milan RAI Chorus *(rec 1956)* Memories 3-▲ MEM 4566 [ADD]

Moffo & Volpi, w. Anna Moffo (sop), Milan RAI SO [cnd:Alfredo Simonetto], Rome RAI SO [cnd:Massimo Freccia] *(rec Martini & Rossi Concert, 1960)* Incontri Memorabili ▲ CDMR 5035

Opera Arias *(rec HMV & Victor 78 rpm discs 1928–34)* Preiser ("Lebendige Vergangenheit" series) ▲ PRE 89012 (m) [AAD]

Puccini, G.:La Bohème, w. Schimenti (sop), Micheluzi (sgr), G. Ciavola (bass), A. Paoletti (cnd), Rome Opera Orch, Rome Opera Chorus *(rec 1952)* Bongiovanni 2-▲ GB 1057/58 [ADD]

Puccini, G.:La Bohème, w. R. Tebaldi (sop), E. Ribetti (mez), E. Avolanti (ten), T. Gobbi (bar), S. Meletti (bar), C. Badioli (bass), G. Neri (bass), G. Santini (cnd), *(orch unknown)* *(rec 1951)* Great Opera Performances ▲ GOP 743

Puccini, G.:La fanciulla del West (sels), w. Magda Olivero (sop—Minnie), Corinna Vozza (mez—Wowkle), Paolo Caroli (ten—Harry), Giacomo Lauri-Volpi (ten—Dick Johnson), Marco Rogani (ten—Pony Express Rider), Salvatore di Tommaso (ten—Trin), Adelio Zagonara (ten—Nick), Virgilio Ascorro (bar—Sid), Alfredo Colella (bar—Jake Wallace), Giuseppe Forgione (bar—Bello), Giancarlo Guelfi (bar—Jack Rance), Arturo la Porta (bar—Sonora), Gino Conti (bass—José Castro), Piere Passarotti (bass—Bill), Enzo Titta (bass—Larkens), Giulio Tomei (bass—Ashby), V. Bellezza (cnd), Rome Opera Orch, Rome Opera Chorus—Minnie, dalla mia casa son partito; Laggiù nel Soledad; Chi c'è per farmi i ricci; Oh! Mister Johnson, siete rimasto; Non so ben neppur io; Io non son che una povera fanciulla; No, Minnie, non piangete; Vorrei mettermi queste; Hallo!; Oh, se sapeste; Credo che abbiate torto; Ma ti giuro ch'io non ti lascio più; Vieni fuori!; Una parola sola!...Or son sei mesi; Che c'è di nuovo Jack?; È là; Siete pronto; Ch'ella mi creda; È Minnie!...È Minnie! *(rec Rome, Mar. 30, 1957)* Golden Age of Opera ▲ GAO 180 [ADD]

Verdi, G.:Luisa Miller, w. L. Kelston (sop—Luisa), M.T. Pace (mez—Federica), G. Larui-Volpi (ten—Rodolfo), S. Colombo (bar—Miller), G. Vaghi (bar—Count Walter), D. Baronti (bass—Wurm), M. Rossi (cnd), Rome RAI Orch, Rome RAI Chorus *(rec 1951)* Cetra Classic 2-▲ CDO 17 [AAD]

Verdi, G.:Rigoletto (sels), w. L. Pagliughi (sop), T. Gobbi (bar), F. Previtali (cnd), Rome RAI Orch, Rome RAI Chorus [highlights] *(rec 1947)* Melodram ▲ MEL 15008

Verdi, G.:Il trovatore, w. Maria Callas (sop), Cloe Elmo (cta), Paolo Siveri (sgr), T. Serafin (cnd), Naples Teatro San Carlo Orch, Naples Teatro San Carlo Chorus *(rec Theatre of San Carlo, Naples, Jan. 27, 1951)* Pantheon 2-▲ PHE 6636 (m)

Verdi, G.:Il trovatore, w. M. Callas (sop), C. Elmo (mez), P. Silveri (bar), T. Serafin (cnd), Naples Teatro San Carlo Orch, Naples Teatro San Carlo Chorus [I] *(rec live, Naples, 1/27/51)* Melodram 2-▲ MEL 26001 (m) [AAD]

Verdi, G.:Il trovatore (sels), w. J. Biel (ten), F. Tamagno (ten), L.-A. Escalaïs (ten), M. Gilion (ten), E. Caruso (ten), A. Paoli (ten), G. Zenatello (ten), J. Sembach (ten), L. Slezak (ten), F. Constantino (ten), G. Martinelli (ten), B. De Muro (ten), N. Fusati (ten), N. Piccaluga (ten), A. Pertile (ten), E. Bergamaschi (ten), R. Tauber (ten), J. O'Sullivan (ten), H. Roswaenge (ten), G. Taccani (ten), V. Lois (ten), H. Lazaro (ten), A. Lindi (ten), A. Cortis (ten), F. Merli (ten), F. Völker (ten), J. Kiepura (ten), J. Schmidt (ten), J. Bjoerling (ten), B. Gigli (ten), A. Salvarezza (ten), J. Soler (ten), M. Filippeschi (ten)—34 performances of the Act III tenor aria "Di quella pira!," *(rec from 1903–1956)* Bongiovanni ▲ GB 1051 [AAD]

Laursen, John (ten)

Nielsen, C.:Songs, w. Eva Hess Thaysen (sop), Mette Ejsing (alt), Lars Thodberg Bertelsen (bar), Frode Stengaard (org), Tove Lønskov (pno)—Little Helle; Sir Oluf's Song; Dance-Song; Dawn [all from the play Sir Oluf He Rides]; The Storm Wages over the Dark Waters; My Girl Is as Fair as Amber; The Day the Eagle was Ready to Fly; A Mother was Told at the Feast; The Thistle Crop Looks Promising; Once When Death was Awaited; So Bitter was My Heart; Like a Venturous Fleet at Anchor [all from the play The Mother]; The Sign & the Word of the Cross; Of All the Flowers that Grow on Earth; As the Golden Sun Breaks Through; There is a Path; It Is No Great Struggle; Daffodil, Why Are You Here? [all from Hymns & Sacred Songs]; The Sun Springs Out Like a Rose [from the play Cosmus]; The Great Master Comes; See My Fragile Web; Our Eyes May Rejoice; When Summer's Song is Sung; Earth in Whose Embrace [all from 20 Popular Melodies]; Of What are You Singing? [The Lark]; Teach Me, O Stars of Night [both from 4 Popular Melodies]; Italian Shepherd's Song; We Love You, Our Lofty North!; Vocalise; The Power that Gave Me My Little Song [all from Amor & the Poet]; May Song [Merrily, with Joyful Song!] Rondo Grammofon ▲ RCD 8329

Lavani, Carmen (alt)

Purcell, H.:Dido & Aeneas, w. Helen Donath (sop—Belinda), Shirley Verrett (sop—Dido), Oralia Dominguez (mez—Sorceress), Carmen Lavani (alt—A Spirit), Margaret Lensky (cta—2nd Witch), Carlo Gaifa (ten—A Sailor), Dan Jordacescu (bar—Aeneas), Rosina Cavicchioli (sgr—A Woman), Lilia Teresita Reyes (sgr—1st Witch), R. Leppard (cnd), Turin RAI SO, Ambrosian Chorus *(rec Torino, May 20, 1971)* Arkadia ▲ 619 [ADD]

Lavender, Justin (ten)

Bellini, V.:I Puritani, w. Edita Gruberova (sop), Katia Lytting (mez), Carlo Tuand (ten), Ettore Kim (bar), Francesco Ellero d'Artegna (bass), Dankwart Siegele (bass), F. Luisi (cnd), Munich RSO, Bavarian Radio Chorus Nightingale Classics 3-▲ NIG 70562

Donizetti, G.:Arias, w. H. Williams (cnd), Bournemouth SO—Un Ange, une Femme Inconnue; Je Ne Meritais Pas...Oijt Ta Voix M'Inspire; La Maitresse du Roi?...Ange St Pur [all from La Favorita]; Ingemisco [from Requiem]; Si Compia il Sacrificio...Io l'Amai [from Gabriella di Vergy] IMP ("Classics" series) ▲ IMP 6700102

Rossini, G.:Arias, w. H. Williams (cnd), Bournemouth SO—Ch Ascolto?...Ah Come Mai Non Senti Pieta [from Otello]; Ne M'Abandonne Point...Asile Hereditaire [from Guillaume Tell]; Cujus Animam Gementem [Stabat Mater]; Languir per una Bella & Oh Come il Cor di Giubilo [from L'Italiana in Algeri]; Avanons...Grand Dieu Faut...Il Qu'un Peuple [from Le siege de Corinthe] IMP ("Classics" series) ▲ IMP 6700102

Smyth, E.:The Wreckers, w. Judith Howarth (sop), Anne-Marie Owens (mez), Annemarie Sand (mez), Anthony Roden (ten), Peter Sidhom (bar), David Wilson-Johnson (bar), Brian Bannatyne-Scott (bass), O. de la Martinez (cnd), BBC PO, Huddersfield Choral Society *(rec live, Royal Albert Hall, London, July 31, 1994)* Conifer Classics 2-▲ 75605-51250-2

Lavigren, P. (ten)

Falla, M. de:El retablo de maese Pedro, w. T. Tourne (sop), R. Cesari (bar), P. de Freitas Branco (cnd), Madrid Concert Orch EMI Classics 2-▲ ZDMB 64555

Lavrova, Tatyiana (sop)

Taneyev, S.:Duet for Romeo & Juliet, w. S. Lemeshev (ten), S. Samosud (cnd), All-Union RSO *(rec 1954)* Russian Disc ▲ RUS 15002 [AAD]

Law, Margot (sop)

Beach, A.M.C.:Mass, "Grand Mass", w. Martha Remington (mez), Ray Bauwens (ten), Joel Schneider (bar), B. Jones (cnd), Stow Festival Orch, Stow Festival Chorus *(rec Cathedral Church of St Paul, Tremont St, Boston, MA)* Albany ▲ TROY 179 [DDD]

Lawcewicz, Barbara (mez)

Moniuszko, S.:Haunted Manor, w. Halina Slonicka (sop), Bozena Brun-Baranska (mez), Krystyna Szczepanska (mez), Zdzislaw Nikodem (ten), Bogdan Paprocki (ten), Andrzej Hiolski (bar), Edmund Kossowski (bass), Bernard Ladysz (bass), W. Rowicki (cnd), Warsaw State Opera House Orch, Warsaw National Opera Chorus *(rec Warsaw, 1965)* Polskie Nagrania ▲ PNCD 093 [AAD]

Lawler, Emanuel (ten)

Sullivan, A.:Henry VIII, w. A. Penny (cnd), RTE Concert Orch *(rec Apr. 13–16, 1992)* Marco Polo ▲ 8.223461 [DDD]

Sullivan, A.:The Merchant of Venice, w. A. Penny (cnd), RTE Concert Orch *(rec Apr. 13–16, 1992)* Marco Polo ▲ 8.223461 [DDD]

Lawrence, C. (sgr)

Bernstein, L.:West Side Story, w. L. Kert (sgr), C. Rivera (sgr) [1957 cast] Columbia ▲ CK 32603 ♦ CM 32603 ■ JST 32603

Lawrence, Douglas (ten)

Britten, H.:War Requiem, w. Jeanine Altmeyer (sop), Michael Sells (bar), Ladd Thomas (org), W. Hall (cnd), William Hall Orch, William Hall Chorale, Columbus Boys' Choir Klavier ▲ KCD 11017 [ADD]

Lawrence, Gertrud (sgr)

Rodgers, R.:The King & I, w. Y. Brynner (sgr), *(other artists unknown)* [1951 Broadway cast] MCA Classics ▲ MCAD 10049 [AAD] ■ MCAC 10049

Lawrence, Helen (sop)

Goldschmidt, B.:Der gewaltige Hahnrei, w. R. Alexander (sop), M. Posselt (sop), R. Wörle (ten), M. Kraus (ten), M. Petzold (ten), C. Otelli (bar), L. Zagrosek (cnd), German SO, Berlin Radio Chorus London ▲ 440850-2 [DDD]

Goldschmidt, B.:Mediterranean Songs, w. R. Alexander (sop), M. Posselt (sop), R. Wörle (ten), M. Kraus (ten), M. Petzold (ten), C. Otelli (bar), L. Zagrosek (cnd), German SO, Berlin Radio Chorus London ▲ 440850-2 [DDD]

Lawrence, Marjorie (sop)

Opera Arias & Scenes, w. Piero Coppola (cnd), Pasdeloup Orch, Reyer Preiser ("Lebendige Vergangenheit" series) ▲ PRE 89011 (m) [AAD]

Wagner, R.:Der fliegende Holländer, w. F. Destal (bar), A. Kipnis (bass), F. Busch (cnd), Buenos Aires Teatro Colón Orch, Buenos Aires Teatro Colón Chorus [G] *(rec live broadcast 9/19/36)* Pearl 2-▲ PEAS 9910 (m) [ADD]

Lawrenson, John (bar)

Elgar, E.:The Starlight Express (suite), w. C. Glover (sop), G. Hurst (cnd), Bournemouth Sinfonietta Chandos ("Collect" series) ▲ CHAN 6582 [ADD]

Handel, G.F.:Theodora, w. H. Harper (sop), M. Lehane (mez), M. Forrester (cta), A. Young (ten), J. Somary (cnd), English CO, Amor Artis Chorale [E] *(rec 1968)* Vanguard Classics 2-▲ OVC 4074/5 [ADD]

Lawson, Mhairi (sop)

Haydn, J.:Songs, w. Oleg Kogan (vc), Rachel Podger (vn), Olga Tverskaya (pno) Opus 111 ▲ OPS 30-121

Lawson, Winifred (sop)

Sullivan, A.:The Gondoliers, w. A. Davies (ten), B. Lewis (cta), D. Oldham (ten), M. Bennett (sop), G. Baker (bar), L. Sheffield (bar), H. Lytton (bar), et al., H. Norris (cnd), D'Oyly Carte Opera Company Orch, D'Oyly Carte Opera Chorus—dialogue omitted *(rec 1927)* Pearl 2-▲ PEAS 9961 (m) [AAD]

Sullivan, A.:Trial by Jury, w. D. Oldham (ten), G. Baker (bar), L. Sheffield (bar), A. Hosking (bar), H. Norris (cnd), D'Oyly Carte Opera Company Orch, D'Oyly Carte Opera Chorus *(rec 1928)* Pearl 2-▲ PEAS 9961 (m) [AAD]

Lax, É. (mez)

Caldara, A.:Stabat Mater, w. I. Verebics (sop), G. Kállay (ten), B. Szilágyi (bar), E. Kollár (cnd), Concerto Armonico Budapest, Monteverdi Chamber Choir [L] Hungaroton ▲ HCD 31273 [DDD]

Echoes of Love:18th Century Italian Cantatas, w. Ensemble Barocco Padua Sans Souci, L. Serafini (sop) *(rec Apr. 1993)* Dynamic ▲ CDS 106 [DDD]

Laycock, Tim (sgr)

Old English Nursery Rhymes, w. Vivien Ellis (sop), Broadside Band [Jeremy Barlow (rcrs/perc), Sharon Lindo (vns/rcr), George Weigand (lt/mandore/cittern/gtr), Rosemary Thorndycraft (b vl/h-g), Ben Sansom (vn), Marilyn Sansom (vc)] *(rec Valley Recordings, Littleton-on-Severn, Feb 1996)* Saydisc ▲ CDSDL 419

Lazar, Hans-Jurgen (ten)

Strauss (II), Joh.:Der Zigeunerbaron, w. Pamela Coburn (sop), Christiane Oelze (sop), Julia Hamari (mez), Elisabeth von Magnus (alt), Herbert Lippert (ten), Rudolf Schasching (ten), Wolfgang Holzmair (bar), Jurgen Flimm (sgr), Robert Florianschutz (sgr), N. Harnoncourt (cnd), Vienna SO, Arnold Schoenberg Choir *(rec Vienna, 1994)* Teldec 2-▲ 94555-2

Lázaro, Hipolito (ten)

Leoncavallo, R.:Pagliacci (sels), w. Enrico Caruso (ten), Antonio Paoli (ten), Giovanni Zenatello (ten), Amedeo Bassi (ten), Hermann Jadlowker (ten), Fernand Ansseau (ten), Nino (Filippo) Piccaluga (ten), Mario Chamlee (ten), Giacomo Lauri-Volpi (ten), Miguel Fleta (ten), Giovanni Martinelli (ten), Aureliano Pertile (ten), Georges Thill (ten), Alessandro Valente (ten), Francesco Merli (ten), Lauritz Melchior (ten), Marcel Wittrisch (ten), Joseph Schmidt (ten), Beniamino Gigli (ten), Giuseppe Lugo (ten), Helge Roswaenge (ten), Jussi Bjoerling (ten)—23 versions of the tenor aria "Vesti la giubba" *(rec 1907–1944)* Bongiovanni ▲ GB 1071 [ADD]

Verdi, G.:Il trovatore (sels), w. J. Biel (ten), F. Tamagno (ten), L.-A. Escalaïs (ten), M. Gilion (ten), E. Caruso (ten), A. Paoli (ten), G. Zenatello (ten), J. Sembach (ten), L. Slezak (ten), F. Constantino (ten), G. Martinelli (ten), B. De Muro (ten), N. Fusati (ten), N. Piccaluga (ten), G. Lauri-Volpi (ten), A. Pertile (ten), E. Bergamaschi (ten), R. Tauber (ten), J. O'Sullivan (ten), H. Roswaenge (ten), G. Taccani (ten), V. Lois (ten), A. Lindi (ten), A. Cortis (ten), F. Merli (ten), F. Völker (ten), J. Kiepura (ten), J. Schmidt (ten), J. Bjoerling (ten), B. Gigli (ten), A. Salvarezza (ten), J. Soler (ten), M. Filippeschi (ten)—34 performances of the Act III tenor aria "Di quella pira!," *(rec from 1903–1956)* Bongiovanni ▲ GB 1051 [AAD]

Lazzara, Marco (ct)

Bellini, V.:Arias, w. A. Plotino (cnd), Genoa CO—Questa è la valle...Quando incise su quel marmo *(rec Dec 4, 1995)* Bongiovanni ▲ GB 2521 [DDD]

Berlioz, H.:Les Nuits d'été, w. A. Amoretti (pno) Bongiovanni ▲ GB 5540 [DDD]

Gluck, C.W.:Orfeo ed Euridice (sels), w. A. Plotino (cnd), Genoa CO—Ove trascorsi...Che farò senza Euridice *(rec Dec 4, 1995)* Bongiovanni ▲ GB 2521 [DDD]

Handel, G.F.:Arias, w. A. Plotino (cnd), Genoa CO—Va tacito e nascosto [from Giulio Cesare in Egitto]; Venti, turbini, prestate [from Rinaldo]; O Thou That Tellest Good Tidings to Zion [from Messiah] *(rec Dec 4, 1995)* Bongiovanni ▲ GB 2521 [DDD]

Pergolesi, G.B.:Stabat Mater (sels), w. A. Plotino (cnd), Genoa CO—Fac ut portem *(rec Dec 4, 1995)* Bongiovanni ▲ GB 2521 [DDD]

Porpora, N.A.:Cant per la notte di Natale, w. Rosita Frisani (sop—Dorindo), Roberta Invernizzi (sop—Angelo), Marco Lazzara (cta—Montano), E. Velardi (cnd), Alessandro Stradella Consort *(rec Genoa, Jan 29–30, 1995)* Bongiovanni 2-▲ GB 2181/2

Rossini, G.:Tancredi (sels), w. A. Plotino (cnd), Genoa CO—O patria...Di tanti palpiti *(rec Dec 4, 1995)* Bongiovanni ▲ GB 2521 [DDD]

Scarlatti, A.:Abramo, il tuo sembiante, w. S. Piccolo (sop), L. Bacchetta (sop), M. Nuvoli (ten), G. Dagnino (bass), E. Velardi (cnd), Alessandro Stradella Consort [period instrs] [I] Nuova Era ("Ancient Music" series) ▲ 7117 [DDD]

Stradella, A.:Esule dalle sfere, w. Roberta Invernizzi (sop), Silvia Piccolo (sop), Mario Nuvoli (ten), Riccardo Ristori (bass), Carlo Lepore (bass), Alessandro Stradella Consort Bongiovanni ▲ GB 2165 [DDD]

Stradella, A.:Il moro per amore, w. R. Invernizzi (sop—Eurinda), S. Piccollo (sop—Lucinda), M. Grazia Liguori (sop—Fiorino), M. Lazzara (cta—Lindora), V. Matacchini (cta—Feraspe/Floridoro), M. Beasley (ten—Filandro), R. Ristori (bass—Rodrigo), E. Velardi (cnd), Alessandro Stradella Consort [I] *(rec Oct. 31–Nov. 3, 1992)* Bongiovanni 3-▲ GB 2153/55

Stradella, A.:Lo schiavo liberto, w. R. Invernizzi (sop—Armida), M. Lazzara (cta—Rinaldo), M. Nuvoli (ten—Carlo), R. Ristori (bass—Ubaldo), E. Velardi (cnd), Alessandro Stradella Consort *(rec Nov. 15, 1993)* Bongiovanni ▲ GB 2164 [DDD]

Stradella, A.:Susanna, w. S. Piccollo (sop), L. Bertotti (sop), M. Nuvoli (ten), M. Perrella (bass), E. Velardi (cnd), Camerata Ligure [period instrs] [I] Bongiovanni 2-▲ GB 2121/22 [DDD]

Verdi, G.:Romances Voice, w. A. Amoretti (pno) Bongiovanni ▲ GB 5540 [DDD]

Lazzaretti, Bruno (ten)

Bizet, G.:Les Pêcheurs de perles (sels), w. W. Glashof (bar), H.-M. Schneidt (cnd), Berlin RSO—Act 1 duet, "Au fond du temple saint" Capriccio ▲ 10 380 [DDD]

Classics Go to the Movies, Vol. 2, w. Dresden PO, Budapest Festival Orch, Bulgarian TV-Radio SO, Bela Kovaks, Franz Liszt CO, Bruno Lazzaretti, Berlin RSO, Hungarian State Orch LaserLight ▲ 15 642

David, Felicien:Le Désert, w. O. Pascalin (nar), G.M. Guida (cnd), Berlin RSO, St. Hedwig's Cathedral Choir Capriccio ▲ 10 379 [DDD]

Lazzari, Agostino (ten)

Cilea, F.:Adriana Lecouvreur (sels), w. Margherita Carosio (sop), E. Piazza (cnd), Milan RAI SO, Milan RAI Chorus Fonit Cetra ("Martini & Rossi" series) ▲ FCT CDMR 5010

Cilea, F.:L'Arlesiana (sels), w. Margherita Carosio (sop), E. Piazza (cnd), Milan RAI SO, Milan RAI Chorus Fonit Cetra ("Martini & Rossi" series) ▲ FCT CDMR 5010

Donizetti, G.:Don Pasquale (sels), w. Margherita Carosio (sop), E. Piazza (cnd), Milan RAI SO, Milan RAI Chorus Fonit Cetra ("Martini & Rossi" series) ▲ FCT CDMR 5010

Donizetti, G.:Lucia di Lammermoor (sels), w. Margherita Carosio (sop), E. Piazza (cnd), Milan RAI SO, Milan RAI Chorus Fonit Cetra ("Martini & Rossi" series) ▲ FCT CDMR 5010

Lazzari, Agostino (ten) (cont.)
Giordano, U.:Il re (sels), w. Margherita Carosio (sop), E. Piazza (cnd), Milan RAI SO, Milan RAI Chorus Fonit Cetra ("Martini & Rossi" series) ▲ FCT CDMR 5010
Mascagni, P.:Nerone (sels), w. Margherita Carosio (sop), E. Piazza (cnd), Milan RAI SO, Milan RAI Chorus Fonit Cetra ("Martini & Rossi" series) ▲ FCT CDMR 5010
Massenet, J.:Werther, w. M. Olivero (sop), S. Meletti (bar), M. Rossi (cnd), Turin RSO, Turin Radio Chorus *(rec live, 6/12/63)* Melodram 2-▲ MEL 27065 (m) [AAD]
Mercadante, S.:Elisa e Claudio, w. Virginia Zeani (sop), Domenico Trimarchi (bar), Ugo Trama (bass), Fiorini (sgr), U. Rapalo (cnd), Naples Teatro San Carlo Orch, Naples Teatro San Carlo Chorus *(rec live, Naples, 1/31/71)* Melodram 2-▲ MEL 27099 [ADD]
Mozart, W.A.:Don Giovanni, w. E. Rethberg (sop), L. Helletsgruber (sop), M. Bokor (mez), D. Borgioli (ten), E. Pinza (bass), B. Walter (cnd), Salzburg Orch, Salzburg Mozarteum Chorus [I] *(rec live, Salzburg, Aug. 2, 1937)* Melodram ("Connaisseur" series) 3-▲ CD 37506 (m) [AAD]
Mozart, W.A.:Nozze di Figaro, w. Jarmila Novotna (sop), Aulikki Rautawaara (sop), Esther Réthy (sop), Mariano Stabile (bar), Ezio Pinza (bass), B. Walter (cnd), Vienna PO, Vienna State Opera Chorus *(rec live, 1937)* Melodram ▲ CDI 205003
Mozart, W.A.:Nozze di Figaro, w. S. Jurinac (sop), T. Stratas (sop), T. Berganza (mez), N. Condò (mez), S. Bruscantini (bar), M. Petri (bass), G. Tadeo (bass), A. Mariotti (bass), Z. Mehta (cnd), *(orch unknown) (rec 1968)* Great Opera Performances 3-▲ GOP 712
Paisiello, G.:Fedra, w. O. Beggiato (sop), R. Mattioli (sop), A. Tuccari (sop), L. Udovick (sop), A. Questa (cnd), Milan RAI SO, Milan RAI Chorus *(rec 1958)* Memories 2-▲ MEM 4502 [AAD]
Paisiello, G.:La Molinara, w. Graziella Sciutti (sop), Alvinio Misciano (ten), Sesto Bruscantini (bar), Franco Calabrese (bass), Leonardo Monreale (bass), F. Caracciolo (cnd), Alessandro Scarlatti CO Melodram 2-▲ CDM 29502
Pannain, G.:Beatrice Cenci (sels), w. Margherita Carosio (sop), E. Piazza (cnd), Milan RAI SO, Milan RAI Chorus Fonit Cetra ("Martini & Rossi" series) ▲ FCT CDMR 5010
Rossini, G.:Il turco in Italia, w. Graziella Sciurri (sop), Sesto Bruscantini (bar), Scipio Colombo (bar), N. Sanzogno (cnd), *(orch & chorus unknown) (rec Milan, Feb 25, 1958)* Pantheon 2-▲ PHE 6654 (m)
Verdi, G.:Nabucco (sels), w. Margherita Carosio (sop), E. Piazza (cnd), Milan RAI SO, Milan RAI Chorus Fonit Cetra ("Martini & Rossi" series) ▲ FCT CDMR 5010
Wagner, R.:Tannhäuser (sels), w. Margherita Carosio (sop), E. Piazza (cnd), Milan RAI SO, Milan RAI Chorus Fonit Cetra ("Martini & Rossi" series) ▲ FCT CDMR 5010

Lazzari, Virgilio (bass)
Verdi, G.:Falstaff, w. Augusta Ottrabella (sop—Nannetta), Franca Somigli (sop—Alice), Angelica Cravcenko (mez—Mrs. Quickly), Mita Vasari (mez—Meg), Dino Borgioli (ten—Fenton), Giuseppe Nessi (ten—Bardolfo), Alfredo Tedeschi (ten—Dr. Cajus), Piero Biasini (bar—Ford), Mariano Stabile (bar—Falstaff), Virgilio Lazzari (bass—Pistola), A. Toscanini (cnd), Vienna PO, Vienna State Opera Chorus *(rec Salzburg, Aug 23, 1937)* Minerva 2-▲ MN A36/37 (m) [ADD]

Lazzarini, Adriana (mez)
Cilea, F.:Adriana Lecouvreur, w. L. Gencer (sop—Adriana), A. Lazzarini (mez—Princess), F. Ricciardi (ten—Abbot), A. Zambon (ten—Maurizio), E. Sordello (bar—Michonnet), A. Zerbini (bass—Prince), O. de Fabritiis (cnd), Naples Teatro San Carlo Orch, Naples Teatro San Carlo Chorus *(rec Dec. 17, 1966)* Golden Age of Opera 2-▲ GAO 143/44 [ADD]
Donizetti, G.:Requiem Mass, w. G. Tucci (sop), G. Sinimberghi (ten), I. Sardi (bass), F. Maero (sgr), F. Molinari-Pradelli (cnd), Milan RAI SO, Milan RAI Chorus [L] *(rec live, Milan 3/21/61)* Memories ▲ HR 4131 [ADD]
Leo, L.:La Morte di Abele, w. Emilia Cundari (sop—Angelo), Giuliana Matteini (sop—Abele), Adriana Lazzarini (mez—Eva), Ferrando Ferrari (ten—Caino), Paolo Montarsolo (bass—Adamo), C. F. Cillario (cnd), Angelicum CO, Turin Polyphonic Chorus Dynamic 2-▲ CDL 144
Ricci, L.:Crispino e la comare, w. D. Lojarro (sop), Cossutta (ten), S. Alaimo (bar), R. Coviello (bar), A. Marani (bass), R. Ristori (bass), Benori (sgr), Siclari (sgr), P. Carignani (cnd), San Remo SO, San Remo Sym Chorus [I] *(rec live 11/89)* Bongiovanni 2-▲ GB 2095/96 [DDD]
Verdi, G.:Un ballo in maschera, w. R. Orlandi Malaspina (sop—Ameilia), D. Mazzucato (sop—Oscar), A. Lazzarini (mez—Ulrica), L. Pavarotti (ten—Riccardo), M. Zanasi (bar—Renato), A. Zerbini (bass—Samuel), G. Casarini (bass—Tom), G. Zecchillo (bass—Sil) Golden Age of Opera 2-▲ GAO 164/65 [ADD]
Verdi, G.:Un ballo in maschera, w. Leyla Gencer (sop), Carlo Bergonzi (ten), Mario Zanasi (bar), O. de Fabritiis (cnd), Bologna Teatro Comunale Orch, Bologna Teatro Comunale Chorus *(rec live, Nov 28, 1961)* Arkadia 2-▲ 622

Lazzarini, Serena (mez)
Delibes, L.:Lakmé, w. A. Ruffini (sop), G. Morino (ten), B. Praticò (bar), C. Piantini (cnd), Italian International Orch, Bratislava Chamber Chorus [F] Nuova Era 2-▲ 7096/97 [DDD]

Leanderson, Rolf (bar)
Bartók, B.:Songs, Op. 16, w. H. Leanderson (pno) [Hun] BIS ▲ CD 182 [ADD]
Hallnäs, H.:Songs, w. Marta Schele (sop), Birgit Finnila (cta), Elisef Lunden (pno)—3 sels BIS ▲ CD 38
Handel, G.F.:Alleluja & Amen, w. H. Fagius (org) *(rec Johannes Church, Stockholm, Sweden, May 16 & 17, Oct 20, 1978)* BIS ▲ CD 127 [AAD]
Handel, G.F.:Dolce pur d'amor l'affanno, w. Hans Fagius (org) *(rec Johannes Church, Stockholm, Sweden, May 16 & 17, Oct 20, 1978)* BIS ▲ CD 127 [AAD]
Kilpinen, Y.:Lieder der Liebe I–II, w. Helene Leanderson (pno) *(rec Nacka Aula, Nacka, Sweden, Jan 9–10, 1976)* BIS ▲ CD 43 [AAD]
Kilpinen, Y.:Lieder um den Tod, w. Helene Leanderson (pno) *(rec Nacka Aula, Nacka, Sweden, Jan 9–10, 1976)* BIS ▲ CD 43 [AAD]
Nystroem, G.:Songs, w. Marta Schele (sop), Birgit Finnila (cta), Elisef Lunden (pno)—3 sels BIS ▲ CD 38
Nystroem, G.:Songs at the Sea, w. Marta Schele (sop), Birgit Finnila (cta), Elisef Lunden (pno) BIS ▲ CD 38
Purcell, H.:Hail, Bright Cecilia, w. Hans Fagius (org)—'Tis Nature's Voice *(rec Johannes Church, Stockholm, Sweden, May 16 & 17, Oct 20, 1978)* BIS ▲ CD 127 [AAD]
Purcell, H.:Songs, w. Hans Fagius (org)—If Music be the Food of Love; How long, Great God; The Earth Trembled *(rec Johannes Church, Stockholm, Sweden, May 16 & 17, Oct 20, 1978)* BIS ▲ CD 127 [AAD]
Rameau, J.P.:Castor et Pollux, w. M. Schéle (sop), J. Scovotti (sop), G. Souzay (bar), J. Villisech (bass), N. Harnoncourt (cnd), Vienna Concentus Musicus Teldec ▲ 42510-2
Rosenberg, H.:Chinese Songs, w. Marta Schele (sop), Birgit Finnila (cta), Elisef Lunden (pno) BIS ▲ CD 38
Rosenberg, H.:Dagdrivaren, w. G.W. Nilson (cnd), Norrköping SO *(rec Hörsalen, Norrköping, Sweden, Nov. 27, 1981)* BIS ▲ CD 55 [AAD]
Telemann, G.P.:Cants, w. Gunilla von Bahr (fl), Hans Fagius (org)—Kleine Kantate von Wald und Au; Ew'ge Quelle, milder Strom *(rec Johannes Church, Stockholm, Sweden, May 16 & 17, Oct 20, 1978)* BIS ▲ CD 127 [AAD]
Werle, L.J.:Night Hunt, w. Marta Schele (sop), Birgit Finnila (cta), Elisef Lunden (pno) BIS ▲ CD 38

Léandre, Joëlle (sgr/db)
Scelsi, G.:Music of, w. Nicolas Isherwood (bass), Giancarlo Schiaffini (trbn/tuba), Fances-Marie Uitti (vc), Karin Schmeer (hp), Robyn Schulkowsky (tamtam)—Maknongan for Low-Registered Instrument (1976) [3 versions:bass, double bass, tuba]; Tre pezzi for Trombone (1956); Wo Ma for Bass (1960); C'est bien la nuit for Double Bass (1972); Le réveil profond for Double Bass (1977); Et Maintenant, c'est a vous a jouer for Cello & Double Bass (1974); Okanagon for Harp, Double Bass & Tamtam (1968); Mantram for Double Bass (1987) *(rec Sendesaal, Hessen Radio, Frankfurt, Feb. 8–9, May 18–21 & Aug)* Hat Hut ("NOW." series) ▲ hat ART CD 6124 [DDD]

Lear, Evelyn (sop)
Bach, J.S.:St. John Passion, w. Hertha Töpper (mez), Ernst Haefliger (ten), Hermann Prey (bar), Kieth Engen (bass), K. Richter (cnd), Munich Bach Orch, Munich Bach Choir Deutsche Grammophon ("2CD" series) 2-▲ 453 007-2
Barber, S.:Knoxville:Summer of 1915, *(orch unknown)* VAI Audio ▲ VAIA 1049
Berg, A.:Lulu, w. E. Lear (sop—Lulu), P. Johnson (mez—Countess Geschwitz), D. Grobe (ten—Alwa), Fischer-Dieskau (bar—Dr. Schön), K. Böhm (cnd), German Opera Orch, German Opera Chorus [G] *(rec 1968)* Deutsche Grammophon 3-▲ 435705-2 [ADD]

Lear, Evelyn (sop) (cont.)
Berg, A.:Wozzeck, w. E. Lear (sop—Marie), F. Wunderlich (ten—Andres), G. Stoltze (ten—The Captain), D. Fischer-Dieskau (bar—Wozzeck), K. Böhm (cnd), German Opera Orch, German Opera Chorus [G] *(rec 1965)* Deutsche Grammophon 3-▲ 435705-2 [ADD]
Krenek, E.:Jonny spielt auf, w. E. Lear (sop—Anita), L. Popp (sop—Yvonne), W. Blankenship (ten—Max), K. Equiluz (ten—Station Announcer), L. Heppe (ten—Manager), T. Stewart (bar—Daniello), G. Feldhof (bass—Jonny), H. Hollreiser (cnd), Vienna State Opera Orch [G] Vanguard Classics ▲ OVC 8048 [ADD]
Mahler, G.:Das Klagende Lied, w. E. Söderström (sop), G. Hoffman (mez), S. Burrows (ten), E. Haefliger (ten), G. Nienstedt (bass), P. Boulez (cnd), London SO, London Sym Chorus Sony Classical ("Pierre Boulez Edition" series) ▲ SK 45841
Mahler, G.:Des Knaben Wunderhorn, w. T. Stewart (bar), R. Kraus (cnd), Berlin PO *(rec 1962 & 1983)* VAI Audio ▲ VAIA 1061 (m) [ADD]
Mahler, G.:Songs, w. R. Weikert (cnd), Venice Teatro La Fenice Orch—Es sungen drei Engel [from Sym. 3]; Urlicht [from Sym. 2] *(rec 1978)* VAI Audio ▲ VAIA 1061 (m) [ADD]
Mozart, W.A.:Arias, w. Arleen Augér (sop), Kathleen Battle (sop), Irma Beilke (sop), Helena Braun (sop), Lisa Della Casa (sop), Maria Cebotari (sop), Ileana Cotrubas (sop), Helen Donath (sop), Mirella Freni (sop), Reri Grist (sop), Edita Gruberova (sop), Elisabeth Grümmer (sop), Hilde Güden (sop), Ingeborg Hallstein (sop), Luise Helletsgruber (sop), Gundula Janowitz (sop), Sena Jurinac (sop), Erika Köth (sop), Wilma Lipp (sop), Margaret Marshall (sop), Edith Mathis (sop), Jarmila Novotna (sop), Margherita Perras (sop), Lucia Popp (sop), Elisabeth Rethberg (sop), Anneliese Rothenberger (sop), Elisabeth Schumann (sop), Elisabeth Schwarzkopf (sop), Graziella Sciutti (sop), Irmgard Seefried (sop), Graziella Sciutti (sop), Julia Varady (sop), Agnes Baltsa (mez), Margit Bokor (mez), Brigitte Fassbaender (mez), Christa Ludwig (mez), Ann Murray (mez), Francisco Araiza (ten), Anton Dermota (ten), Helge Rosvaenge (ten), Rudolf Schock (ten), Peter Schreier (ten), Leopold Simoneau (ten), Eric Tappy (ten), Richard Tauber (ten), Gösta Winbergh (ten), Josef Witt (ten), Fritz Wunderlich (ten), Christian Boesch (bar), Willy Domgraf-Fassbaender (bar), Karl Dönch (bar), Dietrich Fischer-Dieskau (bar), Erich Kunz (bar), Eberhard Wächter (bar), Hans Hotter (b-bar), Paul Schöffler (b-bar), Cesare Siepi (b-bar), José Van Dam (b-bar), Walter Berry (bass), Geraint Evans (bass), Nicolai Ghiaurov (bass), Alexander Kipnis (bass), Richard Mayr (bass), Kurt Moll (bass), James Morris (bass), Ezio Pinza (bass), Martti Talvela (bass), Giorgio Tozzi (bass), Hans Duhan (sgr), Res Fischer (sgr), Marie Gerhart (sgr), *(various orchs & cnds)*—sels from Idomeneo, Die Entführung aus der Serail, Le nozze di Figaro, Don Giovanni, Così fan tutte, Die Zauberflöte & various arias Orfeo d'or ("Festspiel Dokumente" series) 5-▲ 408955
Mozart, W.A.:Missa, K.427, w. A. Giebel (sop), P. Munteanu (ten), F. Gutherie (bass), S. Celibidache (cnd), Rome RAI SO, Rome RAI Chorus *(rec Mar. 26, 1960)* Emozioni ▲ CDAR 2007 [ADD]
Mozart, W.A.:Zauberflöte (sels), w. R. Peters (sop), L. Otto (sop), F. Wunderlich (ten), F. Lenz (ten), D. Fischer-Dieskau (bar), F. Crass (bass), K. Böhm (cnd), Berlin PO, Berlin RIAS Chamber Choir—Scenes & Arias Deutsche Grammophon ▲ 429825-2 [ADD] ■ 429825-4
Ravel, M.:Shéhérazade Mez, *(cnd & orch unknown)* VAI Audio ▲ VAIA 1049
Strauss, R.:Arias, w. T. Stewart (bar), *(orch unknown)*—2 duets from Arabella—Sie wollen mich heiraten; Das war sehr gut *(rec live ca. 1970/1972)* VAI Audio ▲ VAIA 1011 (m/s) [ADD]
Strauss, R.:Songs, *(orch unknown)*—2 songs—Verführung, Op. 33/1; Gesang der Apollopriesteren, Op. 33/2 *(rec live ca. 1970/1972)* VAI Audio ▲ VAIA 1011 (m/s) [ADD]
Strauss, R.:Songs, w. Erik Werba (pno)—Ständchen, Op. 17; Morgen, Op. 27; Mein Herz ist stumm, Op. 19; Leises Lied, Op. 39; Allerseelen, Op. 10; Schlechtes Wetter, Op. 69; Ich wollt ein Sträusslein binden, Op. 68; An die Nacht, Op. 68; Säusle, liebe Myrtel, Op. 68; Wie erkenn' ich mein Treulieb, Op. 67; Guten Morgen, Op. 67; Sie trugen ihn, Op. 67; Wiegenlied, Op. 41; Ruhe, meine Seele, Op. 27, Befreit, Op. 39; Leise Lieder, Op. 41a; In der Campagna, Op. 41; Du meines Herzens Krönelein, Op. 21; Blindenklage, Op. 56; Die Georgine, Op. 10; Gefunden, Op. 56; Die Nacht; Op. 10; Schlagende Herzen, Op. 29; Wie sollten wir geheim sie halten, Op. 19; Meinem Kinde, Op. 37; Zueignung, Op. 10 *(rec Salzburg & Vienna, 1964–65)* VAI Audio ▲ VAIA 1080
Villa-Lobos, H.:Bachianas brasileira 5, w. *(orch. unknown)* [arr. for orch.] VAI Audio ▲ VAIA 1049
Wagner, R.:Arias & Scenes, w. T. Stewart (bar), *(orch unknown)*—soprano arias from Lohengrin, Tannhäuser; baritone arias from Fliegende Holländer, Tannhäuser, Walküre *(rec live ca. 1970/1972)* VAI Audio ▲ VAIA 1011 (m/s) [ADD]

Lebeda, Andreas (bass)
Haydn, J.:Mass 1a, Missa 'Rorate coeli desuper', w. G. Öhlinger (sop), M. Bayer (alt), M. Klietmann (ten), D. de Rooij an der Reil (org), Collegium Musicum Pragense Christophorus ▲ CD 74541 [DDD]
Haydn, J.:Mass 7, "Kleine Orgelmesse", w. G. Öhlinger (sop), M. Bayer (alt), M. Klietmann (ten), Collegium Musicum Pragense Christophorus ▲ CD 74541 [DDD]

Leblanc, Claudette (sop)
Debussy, C.:Songs, w. Valerie Tryon (pno)—Nuits d'toiles; Beau soir; Musique; Mandoline; Ariettes oubliées; Deux romances; Fêtes galantes Nos. 1 & 2; Proses lyriques; Noël des enfants qui n'ont plus de maisons Unicorn-Kanchana ▲ DKP 9133 [DDD]
Koechlin, C.:Chansons pour Gladys, w. B. Sharon (pno) Hyperion ▲ CDA 66243 [DDD]
Koechlin, C.:Rondels, w. B. Sharon (pno)—Op. 1/2–5 & Op. 8/2,4,5 [F] Hyperion ▲ CDA 66243 [DDD]
Koechlin, C.:Songs, w. B. Sharon (pno)—Si tu le veux, Op. 5/5; Aux temps des fées, Op. 7/4; Déclin d'amour, Op. 13/1; La Chanson des Ingénues, Op. 22/1; Le Cortège d'Amphitrite, Op. 31/2; Le repas préparé, Op. 31/5; Amphise et Melitta, Op. 31/6; Améthyste, Op. 35/2; Hymne à Vénus, Op. 68/1 [F] Hyperion ▲ CDA 66243 [DDD]

Leblanc, G. (sgr)
Lehár, F.:Giuditta (sels), w. Katalin Pitti (sop), G. Oberfrank (cnd), Budapest SO, Hungarian Radio-TV Chorus [Hun] Hungaroton ▲ HCD 16809 [DDD]

LeBlanc, M. C. (sop)
Mozart, W.A.:Missa, K.427, w. C. Pozderec (sop), F. Bardot (ten), L. Peintre (bar), F. Bardot (cnd), Altär SO, Paris Opera Children's Choir [L] Thésis ▲ THE11003

Le Blanc, Suzie (sop)
Blow, J.:The Glorious Day Is Come, w. Michael Chance (ct), Joseph Cornwell (ten), Richard Wistreich (bass), P. Holman (cnd), Parley of Instruments, Playford Consort Hyperion ▲ CDA 66770
Monteverdi, C.:Volgendo il ciel, w. E. Kirkby (sop), M. Nichols (mez), P. Agnew (ct), Alan Ewing (bass), A. Rooley (cnd), Consort of Musicke [I] Virgin Classics ▲ 59606 [DDD]
Moulinié, E.:Airs Lt, w. Stephen Stubbs (lt)—Book 1 *(rec Quebec, July 1995)* CBC ▲ 1095 [DDD]
Vivaldi, A.:Magnificat, RV.610, w. D. Forget (sop), R. Cunningham (alt), H. Ingram (ten), J. Lamon (cnd), Tafelmusik, Tafelmusik Chamber Choir [L] Hyperion ▲ CDA 66247 [DDD]

Le Bris, Michele (sop)
Halévy, F.:La Juive, w. Y. Hayashi (sop), G. Tucker (ten), Sabate (sgr), A. Guadagno (cnd), *(orch & chorus unknown)* [F] *(rec live, London, 1973)* Legato Classics 2-▲ LCD 120-2 [AAD]
Massenet, J.:Hérodiade (sels), w. Michele Le Bris (sop—Salomé), Denise Scharley (cta—Hérodiade), Guy Chauvet (ten—Jean), Robert Massard (bar—Hérode), J. Etcheverry (cnd), Paris Lyric Orch—Il est doux, Il est bon; Hérode, Ne me refuse pas; Jean, je le revois; Vision fugitive; Astres etincelants; Charme des jours passés; Salomé, laisse-moi t'aimer; Ne pouvant réprimer les élans de la foi; Quand nos jours s'éteindront...; Ballet Accord ▲ ACD 204272 [AAD]

Le Chenadec, R. (ct)
Josquin Desprez:Missa, "Ave Maris Stella", w. D. Collot (sop), R. Holton (sop), J.-L. Comoretto (ct), T. Brehu (ten), H. Lamy (ten), B. Fabre-Garrus (bar), J. Gowings (bar) *(rec Jan. 1993)* Astrée ▲ E 8507 [DDD]
Josquin Desprez:Motets, w. D. Collot (sop), R. Holton (sop), J.-L. Comoretto (ct), T. Brehu (ten), H. Lamy (ten), B. Fabre-Garrus (bar), J. Gowings (bar)—Motets à la vierge *(rec Jan. 1993)* Astrée ▲ E 8507 [DDD]

Lechner, Gabriele (sop)
Verdi, G.:Un ballo in maschera, w. Luciano Pavarotti (ten), Piero Cappuccilli (bar), C. Abbado (cnd), Vienna PO, Vienna State Opera Chorus *(rec live, 1986)* Serenissima 2-▲ SER 360118

LeClerc, J. (sgr)
Porter, C.:Fifty Million Frenchmen, w. H. McGillin (sgr), K. Criswell (sop), K. McClelland (sgr), S. Powell (sgr), K. Ziemba (sgr), J. Graae (sgr), J. Harder (sgr), S. Waara (sgr), P. Cass (sgr), [1991 studio cast] New World ▲ 80417-2 [DDD]

▲ = CD ♦ = Enhanced CD Δ = MD ■ = Cassette Tape □ = DCC

LeCocq, Michel (ten)

Hasse, J.A.:Piramo e Tisbe, w. Barbara Schlick (sop), Suzanne Gari (sop), H. Müller-Brühl (cnd), Capella Clementina Koch Schwann 2-▲ SCH 310882 [DDD]

Stravinsky, I.:Cant Sop, w. R. Yakar (sop), O.G. Blarr (cnd), Ensemble 1971 [E] Koch Schwann ▲ CD 313 050 [ADD]

Lecoq, Valérie (sgr)

Mozart, W.A.:Nozze di Figaro, w. Danielle Borst (sop—Countess Almaviva), Claudine Le Coz (sop—Marcellina), Sophie Marin-Degor (sop—Suzanna), Laura Polverelli (mez—Cherubino), Valérie Lecoq (sgr—Barberina), Philippe Cantor (ten—Antonio), Stuart Patterson (ten—Dons Basile & Curzio), Huub Claessens (bar—Figaro), Nicolas Revenq (bar—Count Almaviva), Patrick Donnelly (bass—Bartolo), J. Malgoire (cnd), La Grande Ecurie et la Chambre du Roy Astrée 8-▲ E 8606

Lecouvreur, Adriana (cta)

Charpentier, G.:Louise (abridged ed), w. N. Vallin (sop—Louise), C. Gaudel (mez—Irma), A. Lecouvreur (cta—La Mère), G. Thill (ten—Julien), A. Pernet (bass—La Père), E. Bigot (cnd), *(orch & chorus unknown)* [F] *(rec 1935 for Columbia Records)* Music Memoria 3-▲ 30223

Lecouvreur, Aimee (mez)

Charpentier, G.:Louise, w. N. Vallin (sop—Louise), C. Gaudel (sop—Irma), A. Lecouvreur (mez—Mother), G. Thill (ten—Julien), A. Pernet (bass—Father), E. Bigot (cnd), Raugel Orch, Raugel Chorus *(rec 1936)* Nimbus (Prima Voce) ▲ NI 7829 (m) [ADD]

Le Coz, Claudine (sop)

Gluck, C.W.:La Recontre imprévue, w. L. Dawson (sop), C. Dubosc (sop), S. Marin-Degor (sop), G. Fletcher (sgr), F. Dudziak (ten), G. de Mey (ten), J.-L. Viala (ten), G. Cachémaille (bar), J.-P. Lafont (bass), J. E. Gardiner (cnd), Paris Lyon Opera Orch, Paris Lyon Opera Chorus [F] Erato 2-▲ 2292-45516-2 [DDD]

Mozart, W.A.:Nozze di Figaro, w. Danielle Borst (sop—Countess Almaviva), Claudine Le Coz (sop—Marcellina), Sophie Marin-Degor (sop—Suzanna), Laura Polverelli (mez—Cherubino), Valérie Lecoq (sgr—Barberina), Philippe Cantor (ten—Antonio), Stuart Patterson (ten—Dons Basile & Curzio), Huub Claessens (bar—Figaro), Nicolas Revenq (bar—Count Almaviva), Patrick Donnelly (bass—Bartolo), J. Malgoire (cnd), La Grande Ecurie et la Chambre du Roy Astrée 8-▲ E 8606

Ledbetter, Victor (bar)

Handel, G.F.:Messiah, w. Karen Clift (sop), Catherine Robbin (mez), Bruce Fowler (ten), M. Pearlman (cnd), Boston Baroque Orch, Boston Baroque Chorus [E] Telarc 2-▲ CD 80322 [DDD]

Handel, G.F.:Messiah (sels), w. Karen Clift (sop), Catherine Robbin (mez), Bruce Fowler (ten), M. Pearlman (cnd), Boston Baroque Orch, Boston Baroque Chorus—Sinfonia; Comfort ye, my people; Every valley shall be exalted; And the glory of the Lord; And He shall purify; Behold, a virgin shall conceive; O thou that tellest good tidings to Zion; For unto us a Child is born; Rejoice greatly, O daughter of Zion; His yoke is easy; All we like sheep; Lift up your heads; The Lord gave the word; Their sound is gone out; Why do the nations?; Let us break their bonds asunder; He that dwelleth in heaven; Thou shalt break them; Hallelujah; I know that my Redeemer liveth; Since by man came death; Behold, I tell you a mystery; The trumpet shall sound; Then shall be brought to pass; O death, where is thy sting?; But thanks be to God; Worthy is the Lamb...Amen *(rec May 18–22, 1992)* Telarc ▲ CD 80348 [DDD]

Szymanowski, K.:Stabat Mater, w. C. Goerke (sop), M. Simpson (mez), R. Shaw (cnd), Atlanta SO, Atlanta Sym Chorus *(rec Atlanta, Nov. 7–8, 1993)* Telarc ▲ CD 80362 [DDD]

Ledbetter, William (sgr)

Puccini, G.:Tosca, w. Birgit Nilsson (sop—Floria Tosca), Puli Toro (mez—Shepherd), Jose Carreras (ten—Mario Cavaradossi), Joaquin Romaguera (ten—Spoleta), James Billings (bar—Sacristan), Richard Fredricks (bar—Baron Scarpa), Samuel Ramey (bass—Cesare Angelotti), William Ledbetter (sgr—Sciarrone), Richard Park (sgr—Cardinal), Don Yule (sgr—Jailer), J. Rudel (cnd), *(orch & chorus unknown)* *(rec Nov 13, 1974)* Legato Classics 2-▲ LCD-200-2

Lednárová, Henrietta (sop)

Respighi, O.:La bella dormente nel bosco, w. Ivana Czaková (sop—Old Woman/Green Fairy), Adriana Kohútková (sop—Blue Fairy/Nightingale), Henrietta Lednárová (sop—Frog/Spindle), Jana Valásková (sop—Princess), Dagmar Pecková (mez—Cuckoo/Cat), Denisa Šlepkovská (mez—Queen/Duchess), Karol Bernáth (ten—Doctor), Guillermo Dominguez (ten—Prince April), Igor Pasek (ten—Jester), Ján Durčo (bar—Ambassador), Richard Haan (bar—King/Woodcutter), Stanislav Benačka (bass—Doctor), Anton Kúrnava (bass—Doctor), Marián Smolárik (bass—Doctor), M. Adriano (nar—Mr. Dollar Chèques), M. Adriano (cnd), Slovak RSO Bratislava, Ján Rozehnal (cnd), Slovak Phil Chorus *(rec Concert Hall of the Slovak Radio, Bratislava, June 8–20, 1994)* Marco Polo ("Opera Classics" series) ▲ 8.223742 [DDD]

Respighi, O.:La Primavera, w. Henrietta Lednárová (sop—Prima fanciulla), Jana Valásková (sop—Sirvard), Beata Geriová (mez—Seconda fanciulla), Miroslav Dvorský (ten—Il giovine), Richard Haan (bar—L'orante), Vladimír Kubovčik (bass—Il vecchio), Vera Rasková (fl), M. Adriano (cnd), Slovak RSO Bratislava, Slovak Phil Chorus *(rec Slovak Radio Concert Hall, Bratislava, Jan. 4–9, Feb. 19 & June)* Marco Polo ▲ 8.223595 [DDD]

Ledroit, Henri (ct)

Handel, G.F.:Tamerlano, w. Isabelle Poulenard (sop—Irene), Mieke van der Sluis (sop—Asteria), René Jacobs (alt—Andronico), Henri Ledroit (ct—Tamerlano), John Elwes (ten—Bajazet), Gregory Reinhart (bass—Leone), J. Malgoire (cnd), La Grande Ecurie et la Chambre du Roy *(rec 1983)* Sony Classical 3-▲ SM3K 37893

Tristan et Iseult:A Medieval Romance in Music & Poetry, w. Anne Azema (sop), Ellen Hargis (sop), William Hite (ten), Richard Morrison (bass), Andrea von Ramm (sgr), Boston Camerata [cnd:Joel Cohen] Erato ▲ 98482-2

Lee, Christopher (nar)

Prokofiev, S.:Peter & the Wolf, w. Y. Menuhin (cnd), English String Orch Nimbus ▲ NI 5192 [DDD]

Stravinsky, I.:L'Histoire du soldat, w. L. Friend (cnd), Scottish CO members [E] Nimbus ▲ NI 5063 [DDD]

Lee, Howard (nar)

Eben, Petr:Job, w. D. Titterington (org) [E] Multisonic ▲ 31 0095-2 [DDD]

Lee, Hyun (sgr)

Leo, L.:Amor vuol sofferenze, w. Marilena Laurenza (sop), Vitalba Mosca (mez), Piero Guarnera (bar), Domenico Colaianni (sgr), Giovanna Donadini (sgr), Marilyne Fallot (sgr), D. Moles (cnd), Naples New Scarlatti Orch *(rec Martinafranca Festival, 1994)* Nuova Era 3-▲ NUO 7221

Lee, Lynda (mez)

Bach, J.S.:St. Matthew Passion, w. N. Argenta (sop), J. Kenny (alt), J. MacDougall (ten), R. Müller (ten), R. Jackson (bar), S. Varcoe (b-bar), P. Goodwin (cnd), *(orch & chorus unknown)* United 2-▲ UNI 89301 [DDD]

Bach, J.S.:St. Matthew Passion (sels), w. N. Argenta (sop), J. Kenny (alt), J. MacDougall (ten), R. Müller (ten), R. Jackson (bar), S. Varcoe (b-bar), P. Goodwin (cnd), *(orch & chorus unknown)* *(rec St. George's Theater, London, Feb 24–27, 1994)* United ▲ UNI 88030 [DDD]

Wallace, V.:Maritana, w. Majella Cullagh (sop), Paul Charles Clarke (ten), Ian Caddy (bar), Damien Smith (bar), Quentin Hayes (bass), P. O. Duinn (cnd), RTE Concert Orch, RTE Phil Choir *(rec O'Reilly Hall, Dublin, Sept 1995)* Marco Polo 2-▲ 8.223406-7 [DDD]

Lee, Nelli (sop)

Denisov, E.:Sun of the Incas, w. A. Lazarev (cnd), Bolshoi Theater SO Soloists Vox Box 2-▲ CDX 5121 [ADD]

Lee, Sandra (sop)

Lewandowksi, L.L.:Choral Music, w. Ann Sadan (alt), Don Carter (ten), Adam Cohn (b-bar), Michael Morris (bass), Carys Hughes (org), Robert Max (cnd), Zemel Choir—Ma Towu in F; Ma Towu in B♭; L'cho Dodi; Tow L'hodoss; Adoshem Moloch; W'hogen Ba'adenu [Uw'tsel]; W'schomru; L'icho Adoshem; J'Halahu [Hodo Al Erez]; Ladoshem Ho'orets; Uw'nucho Jomar; Adon Olom; Ki K'schimcho; Hajom Harass Olom; Kol Nidre; Schuwi Nafschi; Enosch, K'chozir Jomow; Halalujoh; Preise, Meine Seele Olympia ▲ OLY 347 [DDD]

Lee, Sonia (sgr)

Mercadante, S.:Caritea, regina di Spagna, w. Nana Gordaze (sgr), Jacek Laszczkowski (sgr), Nicolas Rivenq (bar), Gregory Bonfatti (sgr), Ayhan Ustuk (sgr), G. Carella (cnd), Italian International Opera Orch, Bratislava Camera Chorus *(rec Italy, 1995)* Nuova Era 3-▲ NUO 7258

Lee, Sung-Sook (sop)

Bish, D.:A Sym of Hymns, w. D. Bish (org), D. James Kennedy (nar), R. McMurrin (cnd), Coral Ridge Orch, Coral Ridge Chorus [E] VQR Digital ▲ QR 2041 [DDD]

Bish, D.:A Sym of Hymns, w. D. Bish (org), D. James Kennedy (nar), R. McMurrin (cnd), Coral Ridge Orch, Coral Ridge Chorus [E] VQR Digital ▲ QR 2041 [DDD]

Rossini, G.:Stabat Mater, w. Florence Quivar (mez), Kenneth Riegel (ten), Paul Plishka (bass), T. Schippers (cnd), Cincinnati SO, May Festival Chorus *(rec 1975)* Vox Box 2-▲ CDX 5141 [ADD]

Lee, W. L. (ten)

Camilo, M.:Batéy, w. P. E. Clark (sop), C.B. Rowe (sop), W. Zukof (ct), L. Bennett (ten), E. Levine (bar), Puntilla (sgr), New Generation Western Wind ▲ WW 2001

Darling, D.:Blessings:A Prayer for the Planet, w. P.E. Clark (sop), C.B. Rowe (sop), W. Zukof (ct), L. Bennett (ten), E. Levine (bar), D. Darling (acoustic & electric vc/syn/voice) Western Wind ▲ WW 2001

Darling, D.:Blessings (sels), w. P.E. Clark (sop), C.B. Rowe (sop), W. Zukof (ct), L. Bennett (ten), E. Levine (bar), D. Darling (acoustic & electric vc/syn/voice) Western Wind ▲ WW 2001

Lee, Wonjun (ten)

Mendelssohn, F.:Syms (comp), w. Gemma Bertagnolli (sop), Milena Rudiferia (mez), L. Jia (cnd), Trieste Teatro Comunale Giuseppe Verdi Orch, Ine Meisters (cnd), Trieste Teatro Comunale G. Verdi Chorus RS Prestige 3-▲ 953-0090 [DDD]

Mendelssohn, F.:Sym 2, w. Gemma Bertagnoli (sop), Milena Rudifera (sop), L. Jia (cnd), Trieste Teatro Comunale Giuseppe Verdi Orch, Trieste Teatro Comunale G. Verdi Chorus RS Applausi ▲ 6367-91

Leech, Richard (ten)

Berlioz, H.:Hymne des Marseillais, w. S. McNair (sop), D. Zinman (cnd), Baltimore SO, Baltimore Sym Chorus Telarc ▲ CD 80164 [DDD]

From the Heart:Italian Arias & Neopolitan Songs, w. London SO [cnd:John Fiore] *(rec Studio One, EMI Abbey Road, London, Dec 14–21, 1995)* Telarc ▲ CD 80432 [DDD]

Gounod, C.:Faust, w. C. Studer (sop), T. Hampson (bar), J. Van Dam (b-bar), M. Plasson (cnd), Toulouse Capitole Orch, Toulouse Capitole Chorus, *(highlights from the above)* EMI Classics ▲ CDC 54358 [DDD]

Gounod, C.:Faust, w. C. Studer (sop), T. Hampson (bar), J. Van Dam (b-bar), M. Plasson (cnd), Toulouse Capitole Orch, Toulouse Capitole Chorus EMI Classics 3-▲ CDCC 54228 [DDD]

Strauss (II), Joh.:Die Fledermaus, w. K. Te Kanawa (sop), E. Gruberová (sop), B. Fassbaender (mez), W. Brendel (bar), O. Bär (bar), T. Krause (bar), A. Previn (cnd), Vienna PO, Vienna State Opera Chorus [G] Philips 2-▲ 432157-2 [DDD]

Strauss (II), Joh.:Die Fledermaus (sels), w. K. Te Kanawa (sop), E. Gruberova (sop), B. Fassbaender (mez), W. Brendel (bar), O. Bär (bar), A. Previn (cnd), Vienna PO Philips ▲ 438503-2

Strauss, R.:Der Rosenkavalier (sels), w. B. Hendricks (sop), K. Te Kanawa (sop), A. S. von Otter (mez), K. Rydl (bass), B. Haitink (cnd), Dresden Staatskapelle, Dresden State Opera Chorus EMI Classics ▲ ZDC 54493

Strauss, R.:Salome, w. J. Norman (sop), K. Witt (mez), A. Markert (cta), W. Raffeiner (ten), J. Morris (bass), S. Ozawa (cnd), Dresden Staatskapelle Philips 2-▲ 432153-2

Verdi, G.:Rigoletto, w. L. Vaduva (sop), J. Larmore (mez), A. Agache (bar), S. Ramey (bass), C. Rizzi (cnd), Welsh National Opera Orch Teldec ▲ 90851-2

Leeson-Williams, Nigel (b-bar)

Cresswell, L.:A Modern Ecstacy, w. P. Boylan (sop), R. Bernas (cnd), CSR Bratislava SO *(rec 4/91)* Continuum ▲ CCD 1033

Lefèbvre, P. (ten)

Spontini, G.:La vestale, w. R. Plowright (sop), G. Pasino (mez), F. Araiza (ten), A. Cauli (bar), F. de Grandis (bass), G. Kuhn (cnd), Munich RSO, Munich Radio Chorus [F] Orfeo 2-▲ 256922 [DDD]

Lefebvre, Pierre (bass)

Catalani, A.:Edmea, w. M. Sokolinska Noto (sop), M. Frusoni (ten), M. Chingari (bar), A. Nosotti (bass), G. Pasella (bass), G. del Vivo (bass), M. de Bernart (cnd), Lucca Teatro Comunale Giglio Orch, Lucca Teatro Comunale del Giglio Chorus [I] *(rec live 9/89)* Bongiovanni 2-▲ GB 2093/94 [DDD]

Lefebvre, Pierre (ten)

Verdi, G.:Falstaff, w. E. Norberg-Schulz (sop—Nannetta), L. Serra (sop—Alice), S. Graham (mez—Meg Page), M. Lipovsek (cta—Miss Quickly), K. Begley (ten—Dr. Caius), P. Conti (ten—Ford), M. Luperi (ten—Pistol), J. Van Dam (b-bar—Falstaff), P. LeFebvre (bass—Bardolph), G. Solti (cnd), Berlin PO, Berlin Radio Chorus London ▲ 440650-2 [DDD]

Lefkowitz, D. (ten)

Gottlieb, J.:Sacred Music, w. M. Stone (sop), H. Reps (mez), H. Stahl (ten), R. Abelson (bar), R. Botton (bar), P. Newman (reader), S. Sturk (cnd), Metropolitan Brass Ensemble, New York Motet Choir Premier ("Composer" series) ▲ PRCD 1018 [DDD]

Legay, Henri (ten)

Bizet, G.:Ivan IV (sels), w. J. Micheau (sop), M. Sénéchal (ten), M. Roux (bar), G. Tzipine (cnd), French National RSO, French Radio Chorus [F] EMI Classics ("Studio" series) 2-▲ CDMB 69704 [ADD]

Lehár, F.:Die lustige Witwe, w. Teresa Stich-Randall (mez—Missia Palmieri), Monique Stiot (mez—Manon), Germaine Duclos (sgr—Praskovia), Linda Felder (sgr—Olga), Christiane Jacquin (sgr—Nadia), Jeannette Levasseur (sgr—Sylviane), Henri Legay (ten—Camille de Coutançon), Joseph Peyron (ten—Kromsky), Robert Destain (sgr—Baron Popoff), Michel Fauche (sgr—Pristich), Gérard Friedmann (sgr—Lerida), Jacques Gilet (sgr—Bogdanowitch), Jean Guy Henneveux (sgr—Prince Danilo), Serge Klin (sgr—Figg), Jacques Villa (sgr—D'Estillac), A. Sibert (cnd), Belgian Radio-TV Orch, Belgian Radio-TV Chorus *(rec Grand Auditorium, Belgium, Apr 30, 1970)* Studio SM 2-▲ 2160 [AAD]

Massenet, J.:Manon, w. V. De los Angeles (sop), M. Dens (bar), J. Borthayre (bass), P. Monteux (cnd), Paris Opéra-Comique Orch, Paris Opéra-Comique Chorus [F] EMI Classics 3-▲ CDMC 63549 (m) [ADD]

Offenbach, J.:Barbe-bleue, w. René Lenoty (ten), Aimé Doniat (bar), Rene Terrasson (sgr), J. Doussard (cnd), ORTF Lyric Orch, ORTF Lyric Chorale *(rec 1967)* Memories 2-▲ MEM 4591 [ADD]

Leggate, Robin (ten)

Donizetti, G.:Lucrezia Borgia, w. J. Sutherland (sop—Lucrezia Borgia), A. Howells (mez—Maffio Orsini), A. Kraus (ten—Gennaro), R. Leggate (ten—Liverotto), J. Summers (bar—Apostolo Gazella), P. Hudson (bass-bar—Gubetta), S. Dean (bass—Don Alfonso), R. Bonynge (cnd), Royal Opera House Orch *(rec London, Apr. 9, 1980)* Ornamenti 2-▲ FE 111 [ADD]

Vaughan Williams, R.:The Pilgrim's Progress, w. Delyth Jones (sop), Elsa Kendal (cta), Charles Groves (ten), V. Handley (cnd), BBC Northern SO, BBC Northern Singers IMP ("BBC Radio Classics" series) ▲ IMP 5691662

Verdi, G.:La traviata, w. Angela Gheorghiu (sop—Violetta), Leah-Marian Jones (mez—Flora Bervoix), Gillian Knight (mez—Annina), Robin Leggate (ten—Gastone), Frank Lopardo (ten—Alfredo Germont), Rodney Gibson (ten—Servo di Flora), Neil Griffiths (ten—Giuseppe), Mark Beesley (bar—Dottore Grenvile), Leo Nucci (bar—Giorgio Germont), Richard Van Allan (bass—Barone Douphol), Roderick Earle (bass—Marquese d'Obigny), Bryan Secombe (bass—Commissionario), G. Solti (cnd), Royal Opera House Orch, Royal Opera House Chorus Covent Garden *(rec live, Royal Opera House, Covent Garden, Dec. 1994)* London 2-▲ 448119-2

Legrand, Christiane (sop)

Berio, L.:Laborintus II, w. Sanguineti (nar), J. Baucomont (sop), C. Meunier (cta), L. Berio (cnd), Musique Vivante Ensemble, Chorale Experimentale [E,I] Musique d'Abord ▲ HMA 190764

Legros, Adrien (bass)

Boieldieu, F.-A.:La Dame blanche, w. Michel Sénéchal (ten—Georges Brown), Aimé Doniat (bar—Dikson), Pierre Héral (bass—Mac-Irton), Adrien Legros (bass—Gaveston), P. Stoll (cnd), Paris SO, Paris Sym Chorus Accord 2-▲ ACD 220862 [AAD]

Le Guin, Ursula (nar)

Armer, E.:Music of, w. Elinor Armer (nar), Women's Philharmonic, Elizabeth Appling (cnd), JoAnn Falletta (cnd), San Francisco Girls' Chorus, San Francisco Boys' Chorus, San Francisco Chamber Singers—The Great Instrument of the Geggerets; Anithaca; The Seasons of Oling; Eating with the Hoi; Open & Shut; Sailing Among the Pheromones; On the Antioriental Shores; Island Earth Koch International Classics 2-▲ KIC 7331 [DDD]

Lehane, Maureen (mez)

Handel, G.F.:Theodora, w. H. Harper (sop), M. Forrester (cta), A. Young (ten), J. Lawrenson (bar), J. Somary (cnd), English CO, Amor Artis Chorale [E] *(rec 1968)* Vanguard Classics 2-▲ OVC 4074/5 [ADD]

Lehman, Gary (bar)

Weisgall, H.:Six Characters in Search of an Author, w. E. Byrne (sop—Stepdaughter), S. Foster (sop—Prompter), E. Furtal (sop—Coloratura), J. King (mez—Mezzo), N. Maultsby (mez—Mother), P. LoVerne (cta—Madame Pace), D. Pritchett (alt—Wardrobe Mistress), B. Fowler (ten—Tenore Boffo), K. Anderson (ten—Director), A. Schroeder (bar—Accompanist), P. Zawisza (bar—Stage Manager), R. Orth (bar—Father), G. Lehman (bar—Son), M. Wadsworth (b-bar—Basso Cantante), L. Schaenen (cnd), Chicago Lyric Opera Orch, Lyric Opera Center Chorus *(rec Chicago, June 14 & 16, 1990)* New World 2-▲ 80454-2

Lehmann, Lotte (sop)

Arias & Duets, w. Richard Tauber (ten), Elisabeth Rethberg (sop), et al. *(rec 1919–26)* Preiser 2-▲ PRE 89219

Bach, J.S.:Songs, w. P. Ulanowsky (pno)—Bist du bei mir Claremont ▲ GSE78 50 57

Brahms, J.:Songs, w. P. Ulanowsky (pno)—Wie bist du, meine Königin; Wir wandelten; An die Nachtigall; Erlaube mir, fein's Mädchen; Da unten im Tale; Feinsliebchen, du sollst mir nicht barfuss geh'n; Die Mainacht; Sonntag; Ollebliche Wangen; Auf dem Kirchhofe Claremont ▲ GSE78 50 57

The Complete 1941 Radio Recital Cycle, w. Paul Ulanowsky (pno) *(rec Nov. & Dec. 1941)* Eklipse 2-▲ EKR 18

Great Love Duets, w. Erna Berger (sop), Miliza Korjus (sop), Frida Leider (sop), Charles Kullman (ten), Lauritz Melchior (ten), Helge Roswaenge (ten), Tito Schipa (ten), Richard Tauber (ten), et al. Pearl ▲ PEA 9217

Great Voices of the Century, w. Povla Frijsh (sop), Elena Gerhardt (sop), Gerald Moore (pno) *(rec 1929–1939)* Sanctus ▲ 001 [ADD]

The International Repertoire Grammofono 2000 ▲ GRM 78631

Lotte Lehmann RCA Gold Seal ▲ 7809-2-RG (m) [ADD]

Lotte Lehmann, w. Jan Kiepura (ten), Richard Tauber (ten) Pearl ▲ PEA 9409 (m) [AAD]

Lotte Lehmann in Concert *(rec 1943–50)* Eklipse 2-▲ EKR 20

Mozart, W.A.:Arias—Porgi Amor; Crudel, perchè finora [w. Heinrich Schulsnus (bar)]; Deh vieni, non tardar [all from Le nozze di Figaro]; La ci darem [from Don Giovanni; w. Heinrich Schulsnus (bar)] Nimbus ▲ NI 7873 [ADD]

Mozart, W.A.:Songs, w. M. Callas (sop), E. Grümmer (sop), E. Schwarzkopf (sop), R. Scotto (sop), T. Lemnitz (sop), E. Berger (sop), S. Jurinac (sop), E. Schumann (sop), I. Souez (sop), E. Rethberg (sop), L. Lehmann (sop), N. Gedda (ten), J. McCormack (ten), H. Roswenge (ten), H. Nash (ten), T. Gobbi (bar), G. Hüsch (bar), E. Kunz (bar), G. Frick (bass), E. Pinza (bass), A. Kipnis (bass) EMI Classics 4-▲ CDMD 63750

The New York Farewell Recital (1951), w. Paul Ulanowsky (pno) *(rec 1951)* VAI Audio ▲ VAIA 1038

Nicolai, O.:Lustigen Weiber (sels), w. *(other artists unknown)*—Non eilt herbei...Ha, ha, ha, er wird mir glauben Nimbus ▲ NI 7873 [ADD]

Opera & Lieder Pearl 2-▲ PEA 9234

Schubert, Franz:Songs (misc), w. P. Ulanowsky (pno)—Der Erlkönig Claremont ▲ GSE78 50 57

Schumann, R.:Songs, w. P. Ulanowsky (pno)—Der Nussbaum; Aufträge; Du bist wie eine Blume; Widmung Claremont ▲ GSE78 50 57

Sings Wagner, Richard Strauss, etc. Pearl ▲ PEA 9410 (m) [AAD]

Songs & Waltzes from Vienna, w. Paul Ulanowsky (pno) *(rec 1941)* Sony Masterworks (Portrait) ▲ MPK 47682 [ADD]

Strauss, R.:Der Rosenkavalier, w. E. Schumann (sop), M. Olczewska (mez), R. Mayr (bass), R. Heger (cnd), Vienna PO, Vienna State Opera Chorus—abridged performance [G] *(rec 1933 for HMV)* Pearl 2-▲ GEMMCDS 9365 (m) [AAD]

Strauss, R.:Der Rosenkavalier, w. E. Schumann (sop), R. Heger (cnd), Vienna PO EMI Classics 2-▲ CDHB 64487

Strauss, R.:Der Rosenkavalier (sels), w. Lotte Lehmann (sop—Feldmarschallin), Elisabeth Schumann (sop—Sophie), Eva Hadrabavá (sop—Octavian), H. Knappertsbusch (cnd), Vienna State Opera Orch *(rec Vienna, Apr. 22, 1936)* Koch Schwann 2-▲ SCH 314622 [ADD]

Strauss, R.:Songs, w. P. Ulanowsky (pno)—Ständchen; Morgen; Allerseelen; Zueignung Claremont ▲ GSE78 50 57

Strauss, R.:Songs, w. E. Schumann (sop), R. Mayr (bass), M. Olszewska (cnd), Vienna PO EMI Classics 2-▲ CDHB 64487

Tchaikovsky, P.:Eugene Onegin (sels)—Letter Scene Nimbus ▲ NI 7873 [ADD]

Thomas, A.:Mignon (sels)—Connais-tu le pays?; Elle est là près de lui Nimbus ▲ NI 7873 [ADD]

Wagner, R.:Arias & Scenes—Dich teure Halle; Allmächt'ge Jungfrau [both from Tannhäuse]; Du Armste kannst wohl nie ermessen [from Lohengrin]; Der Manner Sippe [from Die Walküre]; Gut'n Abend, Meister!...Doch starb eure Frau [w. Michael Bohnen (b-bar)]; O Sachs, mein Freund [both from Die Meistersinger] Nimbus ▲ NI 7873 [ADD]

Wagner, R.:Die Meistersinger von Nürnberg (sels), w. Lotte Lehmann (sop—Eva), Eyvind Laholm (ten—Walther), Ludwig Hofmann (bass—Hans Sachs), F. von Weingartner (cnd), Vienna State Opera Orch, Vienna State Opera Chorus *(rec Vienna, Sept. 20, 1935)* Koch Schwann 2-▲ SCH 314622 [ADD]

Wagner, R.:Tannhäuser (sels), w. Lotte Lehmann (sop—Elisabeth), Josef Kalenberg (ten—Tannhäuser), Richard Mayr (bass—Landgraf), Friedrich Schorr (bass—Wolfram), R. Heger (cnd), Vienna State Opera Orch *(rec Vienna, Sept. 25, 1933)* Koch Schwann 2-▲ SCH 314622 [ADD]

Wagner, R.:Die Walküre (sels), w. Lotte Lehmann (sop—Sieglinde), Maria Jeritza (sop—Brünnhilde), Franz Völker (ten—Siegmund), Friedrich Schorr (bass—Wotan), C. Krauss (cnd), Vienna State Opera Orch *(rec Vienna, Sept. 14, 1933)* Koch Schwann ▲ SCH 314622 [ADD]

Wagner, R.:Die Walküre (act 1), w. E. List (bass), B. Walter (cnd), Vienna PO [G] *(rec 6/20–22/35)* Danacord 2-▲ DACOCD 317/18 (m)

Wagner, R.:Die Walküre (act 1), w. L. Melchior (ten), E. List (bass), B. Walter (cnd), Vienna PO *(rec 1935)* EMI Classics ("Great Recordings of the Century" series) ▲ CDH 61020 (m) [ADD]

Wagner, R.:Die Walküre (act 2), w. M. Fuchs (sop), E. Flesch (sop), M. Klose (cta), L. Melchior (ten), H. Hotter (b-bar), A. Jerger (b-bar), E. List (bass), B. Walter (cnd), Berlin State Opera Orch [G] *(rec 9/38 & 6/22/35)* Danacord 2-▲ DACOCD 317/18 (m)

Wagner, R.:Die Walküre (act 2), w. K. Flagstad (sop), L. Melchior (ten), F. Schorr (b-bar), F. Reiner (cnd), *(orch unknown)* [G] *(rec 1936)* Legato Classics ▲ LCD 133-1 (m) [ADD]

Wagner, R.:Die Walküre (act 2), w. M. Fuchs (sop), E. Flesch (sop), M. Klose (cta), L. Melchior (ten), H. Hotter (b-bar), A. Jerger (b-bar), E. List (bass), B. Walter (cnd), Berlin State Opera Orch [G] *(rec 9/38 & 6/22/35)* EMI Classics ("References" series) ▲ CDH 64255

Weber, C.M. von:Der Freischütz (sels)—Wie nahte mir der Schlummer...Alles pflegt [from Act 2] Nimbus ▲ NI 7873 [ADD]

Weber, C.M. von:Oberon (sels)—Ozean du Ungeheuer [from Act 2] Nimbus ▲ NI 7873 [ADD]

Wolf, H.:Songs (misc), w. P. Ulanowsky (pno)—Frühling übers Jahr; In der Frühe; Auf ein altes bild; Heimweh; Auch kleine Dinge; Peregrina I Claremont ▲ GSE78 50 57

The Young Lotte Lehmann, w. Robert Hutt (ten), Michael Böhnen (bass), Heinrich Schlusnus (bar) Preiser ("Lebendige Vergangenheit" series) 3-▲ PRE 89302 (m) [AAD]

Lehner, Georg (bar)

Tchaikovsky, P.:Iolanta, w. Michaela Gurevich (sop—Iolanta), Jaqueline Miura (sop—Brigitta), Tatjana Tabachuk (mez—Martha), Annette Kuhn (mez—Laura), Ian Denolfo (ten—Godefroy), Keith Alexander Bolves (ten—Alméric), Alexander Ben (bar—Robert), Georg Lehner (bar—Ibn-Hakia), Arutiun Kotchinian (bass—René), Kurt Geysen (bass—Bertrand), H. Rotman (cnd), Warsaw PO, ECOV Ensemble Members *(rec Vooruit Center of the Arts, Ghent, Belgium, Aug 28–29, 1993)* CPO 2-▲ CPO 999456-2 [DDD]

Lehnert, Christa (sop)

Schumann, R.:Requiem Mignon, w. Edith Mathis (sop), Maura Moreira (cta), Margarete Witte-Waldbauer (alt), Robert Titze (bass), R. Wagner (cnd), Innsbruck SO, Innsbruck Chorus *(rec Innsbruck, 1963)* Allegretto ▲ ACD 8190

Lehrberger, Thomas (ten)

Weill, K.:Aufstieg und Fall der Stadt Mahagonny, w. A. Silja (sop), A. Schlemm (mez), W. Neumann (ten), K. Hirte (bar), J. Latham-König (cnd), Cologne RSO, Cologne Radio Chorus [G] Capriccio 2-▲ CD 10160/1 [DDD]

Lehtinen, M. (nar)

Aho, K.:Pergamon, w. L. Paasikivi (nar), E.-L. Saarinen (nar), T. Nyman (nar), P. Pietiläinen (org), O. Vänskä (cnd), Lahti SO *(rec Lahti, Finland, May 23–25, 1994)* BIS ▲ CD 646 [DDD]

Lehto, Petri (ten)

Sibelius, J.:Everyman, w. Lilli Paasikivi (mez), Sauli Tiilikainen (bar), Leena Saarenpää (pno), Pauli Pietiläinen (org), O. Vänskä (cnd), Lahti SO, Lahti Chamber Choir *(rec Church of the Cross, Lahti, Finland, Jan 11–13, 1995)* BIS ▲ CD-735 [DDD]

Leib, Günther (bar)

Lortzing, A.:Der Waffenschmied, w. E. Ebert (sop—Marie), G. Prenzlow (mez—Mariens), H. Neukirch (ten—Georg), G. Leib (bar—Ritter), H. Krämer (bass—Hans), H. Fricke (cnd), Berlin State Opera Orch, Berlin State Opera Chorus Berlin Classics ("Eterna" series) ▲ BER 2036-2 [ADD]

Leib, Günther (bass)

Handel, G.F.:Imeneo, w. Sylvia Geszty (sop), Renate Krahmer (sop), Hans-Joachim Rotzsch (ten), Siegfried Vogel (bass), H.-T. Margraf (cnd), Halle Handel Festival Orch, Leipzig Radio Chorus *(rec 1966)* Berlin Classics ▲ BER 9110

Mozart, W.A.:Zauberflöte, w. H. Donath (sop), S. Geszty (sop), P. Schreier (ten), T. Adam (bass), O. Suitner (cnd), Dresden Staatskapelle [I] RCA Gold Seal 3-▲ 6511-2 [ADD]

Leibundgut, Michael (bass)

Garcia, J.M.N.:Motets, w. Katharina Ott (sop), Luiz Alves da Silva (ct), Beat Mattmüller (ct), Andreas Schmidt (ct), Markus Schikora (ten), William Lombardi (ten), Peter Mächler (bass), L. A. da Silva (cnd), Turicum Ensemble *(rec Studio DRS, Zurich, Sept 26–29, 1994)* Claves ▲ CD 9521 [DDD]

Mesquita, J.J.E.L. de:Tercio, w. Luiz Alves da Silva (ct), Beat Mattmüller (ct), Markus Schikora (ten), L. A. da Silva (cnd), Turicum Ensemble *(rec Studio DRS, Zurich, Sept 26–29, 1994)* Claves ▲ CD 9521 [DDD]

Mesquita, J.J.E.L. de:Tractus (4) para o Sábado Santo, w. Luiz Alves da Silva (ct), Beat Mattmüller (ct), Markus Schikora (ten), L. A. da Silva (cnd), Turicum Ensemble *(rec Studio DRS, Zurich, Sept 26–29, 1994)* Claves ▲ CD 9521 [DDD]

Pinto, L.A.:Te Deum Laudamus, w. Katharina Ott (sop), Luiz Alves da Silva (ct), Beat Mattmüller (ct), Andreas Schmidt (ct), Markus Schikora (ten), William Lombardi (ten), Peter Mächler (bass), L. A. da Brooks (cnd), Turicum Ensemble *(rec Studio DRS, Zurich, Sept 26–29, 1994)* Claves ▲ CD 9521 [DDD]

Leider, Frida (sop)

The Art of Frida Leider Preiser ("Lebendige Vergangenheit" series) 3-▲ PRE 89301 (m) [AAD]

Frida Leider, Vol. 2 *(rec 1927–1942)* Preiser ("Lebendige Vergangenheit" series) ▲ PRE 89098 [AAD]

Great Love Duets, w. Erna Berger (sop), Miliza Korjus (sop), Lotte Lehmann (sop), Charles Kullman (ten), Lauritz Melchior (ten), Helge Roswaenge (ten), Tito Schipa (ten), Richard Tauber (ten), et al. Pearl ▲ PEA 9217

Opera Arias & Songs Preiser ("Lebendige Vergangenheit" series) ▲ PRE 89004 (m) [AAD]

Wagner, R.:Arias & Scenes, w. Emmy Destinn (sop), Lilly Hafgren (sop), Emmi Leisner (cta), Ernst Kraus (ten), Lauritz Melchoir (ten), Leopold Demuth (bar), Friedrich Schorr (b-bar), Michael Bohynen (bass), Paul Knupfer (bass), Richard Mayr (bass), Heinrich Hensel (sgr), Walter Soomer (sgr) Iron Needle ▲ 1307 (m)

Wagner, R.:Arias & Scenes, w. K. Flagstad (sop), E. Rethberg (sop), B. Nilsson (sop), E. Schumann (sop), L. Melchior (ten), G. Thill (ten), A. Pertile (ten), G. Hüsch (bar), F. Schorr (b-bar), H. Hotter (b-bar), A. Kipnis (bass), *(orch unknown)* EMI Classics ("Studio" series) 4-▲ CDMC 64008

Wagner, R.:Götterdämmerung (sels), w. Nezadál (sop), K. Thorborg (mez), L. Melchior (ten), H. Janssen (bar), L. Weber (bass), T. Beecham (cnd), London PO, Royal Opera House Chorus Covent Garden [G] *(rec from 1925 Polydor & 1929)* Legato Classics 2-▲ LCD 146-2 (m) [ADD]

Wagner, R.:Götterdämmerung (sels), w. Kerstin Thorborg (mez), Lauritz Melchior (ten), Herbert Janssen (bar), Emanuel List (bass), Maria Nezadál (sgr), T. Beecham (cnd), London PO, Royal Opera House Chorus Covent Garden *(rec Covent Garden, London, 1936)* Preiser ▲ PRE 90266

Wagner, R.:Götterdämmerung (sels), w. A. von Stosch (sop), L. Melchior (ten), H. Janssen (bar), W. Schirp (bass), *(cnd & orch unknown)*—Act 2, Scenes 4 & 5 *(w. Furtwängler, Royal Opera House Orch. & Cho., 1938)*; Act 3, Schweigt eures Jammers *(Frida Leider & E. Marherr-Wagner, Blech, Berlin State Opera Orch., 1928)* Pearl ▲ PEA 9331 (m) [AAD]

Wagner, R.:Parsifal (sels), w. J. Barbirolli (cnd), London SO—Act 2 *(Ich sah' das Kind) (rec 1931)* Pearl ▲ PEA 9331 (m) [AAD]

Wagner, R.:Der Ring des Nibelungen (sels), w. Florence Austral (sop), Elsie Suddaby (sop), Göta Ljungberg (sop), Walter Widdop (ten), Horst Laubenthal (ten), Lauritz Melchior (ten), Friedrich Schorr (bar), Rudolf Bockelmann (b-bar), Ivar Andresen (bass), Emmanuel List (bass), Collingwood, Blech, Coates, Barbirolli, Heger, Alwin, Muck (cnd), London SO—scenes from Siegriend & Götterdämmerung; 90 Motives from Der Ring [w. Collingwood & LSO] Pearl 7-▲ PEA 9137 [ADD]

Wagner, R.:Tristan und Isolde (sels)—Act 1 *(Doch nun von Tristan? [w. E. Marherr-Wagner, Leo Blech, Berlin State Opera Orch., rec. 1928])*; Act 3 *(Isoldes Liebestod [w. Barbirolli, London SO, rec. 1931])* Pearl ▲ PEA 9331 (m) [AAD]

Wagner, R.:Tristan und Isolde (sels), w. E. Marherr-Wagner (mez), L. Melchior (ten), L. Blech (cnd), A. Coates (cnd), J. Barbirolli (cnd), Berlin State Opera Orch, London SO—Act 1 *(Doch nun von Tristan [Leider, Marherr-Wagner])*, Act 2 *(Isolde! Geliebter; O sink hernieder [Leider, Melchior])*, Act 3 *(Mild und leise [Leider])* [G] *(rec late 1920s for HMV)* Legato Classics 2-▲ LCD 146-2 (m) [ADD]

Wagner, R.:Die Walküre (sels), w. G. Ljungberg (sop), E. Leisner (cta), F. Schorr (b-bar), L. Blech (cnd), Vienna State Opera Orch—nine selections from Acts 2 & 3 [G] Pearl ▲ PEA 9357 (m) [AAD]

Leidland, Hilde (sop)

Wagner, R.:Götterdämmerung, w. A. Evans (sop—Brünnhilde), E.-M. Bundschuh (sop—Gutrune), H. Leidland (sop—Woglinde), A. Küttenbaum (sop—Wellgunde), W. Meier (mez—Waltraute), B. Svendén (mez—1st Norn), J. Turner (mez), *(cnd & orch unknown)* Teldec 4-▲ 4509-94194-2 [DDD]

Wagner, R.:Siegfried, w. A. Evans (sop—Brünhilde), H. Leidland (sop—Waldvogel), B. Svendén (mez—Erda), S. Jerusalem (ten—Siegfried), G. Clark (ten—Mime), J. Tomlinson (bass—Der Wanderer), G. von Kannen (bass—Alberich), P. Kang (bass), *(cnd & orch unknown)* Teldec 4-▲ 4509-94193-2 [DDD]

Leiferkus, Sergei (bar)

Fleischmann, B.:Rothschild's Vn, w. Marina Shaguch (sop), Larissa Diadkova (mez), Ilya Levinsky (ten), Konstantin Pluzhnikov (ten), G. Rozhdestvensky (cnd), Rotterdam PO *(rec Rotterdam, Netherlands, Aug 24–31, 1995)* RCA Red Seal ▲ 09026-68434-2 [DDD]

Glinka, M.:Songs, w. Semion Skigin (pno)—A Farewell to St. Petersburg; Elegy; The Fire of Longing Burns in My Heart; I Recall a Wonderful Moment; Doubt; Mary; How Sweet It Is to Be with You; Say Not That It Grieves the Heart *(rec All Saints' Church, Petersham, Surrey, England, Apr 26–27, 1995)* Conifer Classics ▲ 75605-51264-2 [DDD]

Janácek, L.:Slavonic Mass, w. N. Troitskaya (sop), E. Randova (cta), K. Kaludov (ten), T. Trotter (org), C. Dutoit (cnd), Montreal SO, Montreal Sym Chorus London ▲ 436211-2

Mussorgsky, M.:Boris Godunov, w. V. Valente (sop—Xenia), E. Gorochovskaya (mez—Nurse), L. Nichiteanu (mez—Fyodor), E. Zarmeba (mez—Hostess), M. Lipovšek (cta—Marina), P. Langridge (ten—Prince Shuisky), H. Wildhaber (ten—Misail), A. Fedin (ten—Simpleton), S. Leiferkus (bar—Rangoni), A. Kotcherga (bass—B. Godounov), A. Shagidullin (bass—Shchelkalov), S. Ramey (bass—Pimen), S. Larin (bass—Girgory), G. Nikolsky (bass—Varlaam), C. Abbado (cnd), Berlin PO, Tölz Boys' Choir, Berlin Radio Chorus, Slovak Phil Chorus *(rec Nov. 7–30, 1993)* Sony Classical 3-▲ S3K 58977 [DDD]

Mussorgsky, M.:nursery, w. Semeon Skigin (pno) Conifer Classics ▲ 75605-51229-2 [DDD]

Mussorgsky, M.:Songs & Dances, w. Semeon Skigin (pno) Conifer Classics ▲ 75605-51229-2 [DDD]

Mussorgsky, M.:Songs & Dances, w. Y. Temirkanov (cnd), Royal PO RCA Red Seal ▲ 60195-2-RC [DDD]

Leiferkus, Sergei (bar) (cont.)
Mussorgsky, M.:Songs (misc), w. Semion Skigin (pno)—Cruel Death [Epitaph]; The Misunderstood One; Misfortune; The Spirit of Heaven; Pride; Is Spinning Man's Work?; Vision; Trouble; On the Dnieper; Yeryomushka's Cradle Song; The Feast; The Classicist; From My Tears *(rec All Saints' Church, Petersham, Surrey, Apr 26–29, 1995)* Conifer Classics ▲ 75605-51248-2 [DDD]
Mussorgsky, M.:Songs (misc), w. Semeon Skigin (pno)—The Puppet Show; Forgotten; The Seminarist; Savishna; The Billy-Goat; Song of Mephistopheles Conifer Classics ▲ 75605-51229-2 [DDD]
Mussorgsky, M.:Sunless, w. Semion Skigin (pno) *(rec All Saints' Church, Petersham, Surrey, Apr 26–29, 1995)* Conifer Classics ▲ 75605-51248-2 [DDD]
Rachmaninoff, S.:The Bells, w. A. Pendachanska (sop), K. Kaludov (ten), C. Dutoit (cnd), Philadelphia Orch London ▲ 440355-2 [DDD]
Rachmaninoff, S.:Songs, w. Joan Rodgers (sop), Maria Popescu (mez), Alexandre Naoumenko (ten), Howard Shelley (pno)—Letter to K. S. Stanislawsky; The Muse, Op. 34/1; In the Soul of Each of Us, Op. 34/2; The Storm, Op. 34/3; A Passing Breeze, Op. 34/4; Arion, Op. 35/5; The Raising of Lazarus, Op. 34/6; It Cannot Be, Op. 34/7; Music, Op. 34/8; You Knew Him, Op. 34/9; I Remember This Day, Op. 34/10; The Herald, Op. 34/11; What Happiness, Op. 34/12; Dissonance, Op. 34/13; Vocalise, Op. 34/14; From the Gospel of St. John; At Night in My Garden, Op. 38/1; To Her, Op. 38/2; Daisies, Op. 38/3; The Pied Piper, Op. 38/4; Sleep, Op. 38/5; A-oo, Op. 38/6; A Prayer; All Glory to God Chandos ▲ CHAN 9477
Rachmaninoff, S.:Songs, w. Joan Rodgers (sop), Maria Popescu (mez), Alexandre Naomenko (ten), Howard Shelley (pno)—At the Gates of the Holy Cloister; Nothing Shall I Say to You; Again You Are Bestirred, My Heart; April! A Festive Day in the Spring; Dusk Was Falling; Song of the Disenchanted; The Flower Died; Do You Remember the Evening?; O, No, I Beg You, Do Not Leave, Op. 4/1; Morning, Op. 4/2; In the Silence of the Secret Night, Op. 4/3; Sing not, O Lovely One, Op. 4/4; Oh, My Field, Op. 4/5; It Wasn't Long Ago, My Friend, Op. 4/6; Water Lily, Op. 8/1; My Child, Your Beauty Is That of a Flower, Op. 8/2; Thoughts, Reflection, Op. 8/3; I Fell in Love, to My Sorrow, Op. 8/4; A Dream, Op. 8/5; Prayer, Op. 8/6; I Await You, Op. 14/1; Small Island, Op. 14/2; How Fleeting Is Delight in Love, Op. 14/3; I Was with Her, Op. 14/4; Summer Nights, Op. 8/5; You Are so Loved by All, Op. 14/6; Do Not Believe Me, Friend, Op. 14/7; Oh, Do Not Grieve, Op. 14/8; She Is as Beautiful as Midday, Op. 14/9; In My Soul, Op. 14/10; Spring Torrents, Op. 14/11; It Is Time, Op. 14/12 Chandos ▲ CHAN 9405
Rachmaninoff, S.:Songs, w. Howard Shelley (pno)—At the Gates of the Holy Cloister; Nothing Shall I Say to You; Song of the Disenchanted; Do You Remember the Evening?; Were You Hiccoughing, Natasha?; O, No, I Beg You, Do Not Leave!, Op. 4/1; Morning, Op. 4/2; In the Silence of the Secret Night, Op. 4/3; Sing Not, O Lovely One, Op. 4/4; My Child, Your Beauty Is That of a Flower, Op. 8/2; Thoughts, Reflection, Op. 8/3; I Was with Her, Op. 14/4; You Are So Loved By All, Op. 14/6; She Is as Beautiful as Midday, Op. 14/9; Spring Torrents, Op. 14/11; It Is Time, Op. 14/12; Fate, Op. 21/1; By a Fresh Grave, Op. 21/2; Lilacs, Op. 21/5; Before the Icon, Op. 21/10; I Am No Prophet, Op. 21/11; All Was Taken from Me, Op. 26/2; We Shall Rest, Op. 26/3; Christ Is Risen, Op. 26/6; Yesterday We Met, Op. 26/13; All Passes, Op. 26/15; Letter to K.S. Stanislavsky; In the Soul of Each of Us, Op. 34/2; The Raising of Lazarus, Op. 34/6; You Knew Him, Op. 34/9; The Herald, Op. 34/11; From the Gospel of John *(rec St. Michael's Church, Highgate, London, Sept 19–20, 1994 & Jan 30)* Chandos ▲ CHAN 9374 [DDD]
Rachmaninoff, S.:Spring, w. C. Dutoit (cnd), Philadelphia Orch, *(chorus unknown)* London ▲ 440355-2 [DDD]
Shostakovich, D.:Sym 13, w. Y. Yevtushenko (reciter), K. Masur (cnd), New York PO, New York Choral Artists Men's Voices Teldec ▲ 90848
Shostakovich, D.:Sym 14, w. L. Kazarnovskaya (sop), N. Järvi (cnd), Gothenburg SO Deutsche Grammophon ▲ 437785-2
Tchaikovsky, P.:Mazeppa, w. Galina Gorchakoova (sop), Larissa Dyadkova (mez), Sergei Larin (ten), Anatoly Kotscherga (bass), N. Järvi (cnd), Gothenburg SO, Stockholm Royal Opera Chorus Deutsche Grammophon 3-▲ 439906-2
Tchaikovsky, P.:Songs, w. Semion Skigin (pno)—I Bless You, Forests; It Was in the Early Spring; Death; None But the Lonely Heart; Reconciliation; Sleep, Poor Friend; Dusk Fell on the Earth; The Love of a Dead Man; My Genius, My Angel, My Friend; Why?; A Tear Trembles; Frenzied Nights; Not a Word, O My Friend; I Should Like in a Single Word; Do Not Believe It, My Friend; On the Golden Cornfields; No Response, or Ord, or Greeting; Amid the Din of the Ball; Don Juan's Serenade *(rec All Saints' Church, Petersham, Surrey, Sept 4–10, 1995)* Conifer Classics ("The Complete Song Edition" series) ▲ 75605-51266-2 [DDD]
Wagner, R.:Lohengrin, w. Sharon Sweet (sop—Elsa), Eva Marton (sop—Ortrud), Ben Heppner (ten—Lohengrin), Anton Rosner (ten—Nobleman), Heinrich Weber (ten—Nobleman), Jan-Hendrik Rootering (bar—Heinrich der Vögler), Sergei Leiferkus (bar—Friedrich von Telramund), Bryn Terfel (b-bar—King's Herald), Barbara Fleckenstein (sgr—Page), Atsuko Suzuki (sgr—Page), Gisela Ulmann (sgr—Page), Marion Rambausek (sgr—Page), Dankwart Siegele (sgr—Nobleman), Jürgen Weiss (sgr—Nobleman), C. Davis (cnd), Bavarian SO, Bavarian State Opera Chorus, Bavarian Radio Chorus *(rec Residenz Herkulesaal, Munich, May 14–28, 1994)* RCA Red Seal 3-▲ 09026-62646-2 [DDD]
Wagner, R.:Lohengrin (sels), w. Eva Marton (sop—Ortrud), Sharon Sweet (sop—Elsa von Brabant), Barbara Fleckenstein (sgr—Page), Marion Rambausek (sgr—Page), Atsuko Suzuki (sgr—Page), Gisela Ulmann (sgr—Page), Ben Heppner (ten—Lohengrin), Anton Rosner (ten—Nobleman), Heinrich Weber (ten—Nobleman), Sergei Leiferkus (bar—Friedrich von Telramund), Bryn Terfel (b-bar—King's Herald), Jan-Hendrik Rootering (bass—Henry the Fowler), Dankwart Siegele (sgr—Nobleman), Jürgen Weiss (sgr—Nobleman), C. Davis (cnd), Bavarian RSO, Michael Gläser (cnd), Udo Mehrpohl (cnd), Bavarian Radio Chorus, Bavarian State Opera Chorus—Seht! Seht! [from Act 1, Scene 2]; Nun sei bedankt, mein lieber Schwan!; Wenn ich im Kampfe für dich siege; Welch holde Wunder muss ich sehen?; Nun höret mich und achtet wohl; Durch Gottes Sieg ist jetzt dein Leben mein [all from Act 1, Scene 3]; Treulich geführt ziehet dahin [from Act 3, Scene 1]; Wie hehr erkenn' ich unsrer Liebe Wesen!; Höchstes Vertrau'n hast du mir schon zu danken; Weh' nun ist all' unser Glück dahin! [all from Act 3, Scene 2]; In fernem Land, unnahbar euren Schritten [from Act 3, Scene 3] *(rec Munich, Mar 14–28, 1994)* RCA Red Seal ▲ 09026-68239-2 [DDD]

Leigh-Hunt, Barbara (nar)
Elgar, E.:Music of, w. Richard Pasco (nar), John Bingham (pno), Medici String Quartet—includes excerpts from Start of the Play; Qnt. for Pno; Qt. for Strs [slow movt.]; In the South; The Wand of Youth [suite]; Chanson de Matin; Salut d'Amour; Starlight Express; Son. for Vn; Son. for Vc; Adieu; others *(rec Gateway Studios, London)* Medici Quartet ▲ MQT 7001 [DDD]

Leisner, Emmi (cta)
The Art of Emmi Leisner *(rec 1913–1939)* Preiser ▲ PRE 89210 [AAD]
Mahler, G.:Sym 2, w. G. Bindernagel (sop), O. Fried (cnd), Berlin State Opera Orch, Berlin Cathedral Choir *(rec 1923 for Polydor)* Pearl 2-▲ PEAS 9929 (m) [AAD]
Wagner, R.:Arias & Scenes, w. Emmy Destinn (sop), Lilly Hafgren (sop), Frida Leider (sop), Ernst Kraus (ten), Lauritz Melchoir (ten), Leopold Demuth (bar), Friedrich Schorr (b-bar), Michael Bohynen (bass), Paul Knupfer (bass), Richard Mayr (bass), Heinrich Hensel (sgr), Walter Soomer (sgr) Iron Needle ▲ 1307 (m)
Wagner, R.:Die Walküre (sels), w. F. Leider (sop), G. Ljungberg (sop), F. Schorr (b-bar), L. Blech (cnd), Vienna State Opera Orch—nine selections from Acts 2 & 3 [G] *(rec 1927 [Blech] & 1932 [Barb])* Pearl ▲ PEA 9357 (m) [AAD]

Leitner, Luise (sgr)
Einem, G. von:Der Prozess, w. Lisa Della Casa (sop—Frl. Bürstner/Die Frau des Gerichtsdieners/Leni), Peter Klein (ten—Der Direktorstellvertreter/Der Student), Max Lorenz (ten—Josef K.), Erich Majkut (ten—Ein Bursche), László Szemere (ten—Titorelli), Alois Pernerstorfer (b-bar—Willem/Der Gerichtsdiener), Alfred Poell (b-bar—Der Advokat), Walter Berry (bass—Franz/Kanzleidirektor), Oskar Czerwenka (bass—Der Untersuchungsrichter/Der Prügler), Ludwig Hofmann (bass—Der Aufseher/Ein Passant/Der Geistliche/Der Fabrikant), Polly Batic (sgr—Frau Grubach), Endreh Koreh (sgr—Albert K.), Luise Leitner (sgr—Ein buckliges Mädchen), K. Böhm (cnd), Vienna PO, Vienna State Opera Chorus *(rec Aug 17, 1953)* Orfeo d'or ("Festspiel Dokumente" series) 2-▲ 392952 (m)

Lelio, Loretta di (sop)
Cilea, F.:L'Arlesiana, w. P. Tassinari (sop), F. Tagliavini (ten), G. Galli (bar), P. Silveri (bar), B. Carmassi (bass), A. Zerbini (bass), A. Basile (cnd), Turin RAI Orch, Turin RAI Chorus *(rec 1951)* Cetra Classics ▲ CDO 21 [AAD]

Leliwa, Tadeusz (ten)
The Harold Wayne Collection, Vol. 24 *(rec 1904–1909)* Symposium ▲ SYM 1185

Le Maigat, Pierre-Yves (b-bar)
Campra, A.:Tancrède, w. C. Alliot-Lugaz (sop), D. Evangelatos (cta), G. Reinhart (bar), F. le Roux (bar), Dubose (sgr), J. Malgoire (cnd), La Grande Ecurie et la Chambre du Roy Erato (Musifrance) 2-▲ 2292-45001-2 ZA [DDD]

Lemar, Jose (bass)
Puccini, G.:Madama Butterfly, w. Montserrat Caballé (sop—Cio-Cio-San), Carmen Rigai (mez—Suzuki), Bernabé Martí (ten—Pinkerton), Diego Monjo (ten—Goro), Juan Rico (ten—Yamadori), Manuel Ausensi (bar—Sharpless), Jose Lemar (bass—Bonze), Antonio Leval (bass—Imperial Commissioner), Alejandro Chiara (bass—Registrar), G. Rivoli (cnd), Madrid Radio-TV Orch, Madrid Radio-TV Chorus *(rec Madrid, June 12, 1968)* Legato Classics 2-▲ LCD 210-2 [ADD]

Lemeni, Nicola Rossi (bass)
Donizetti, G.:Anna Bolena, w. Maria Callas (sop), Gabriella Carturan (mez), Giulietta Simionato (mez), Gianni Raimondi (ten), Plinio Clabassi (bass), Luigi Rumo (sgr), G. Gavazzeni (cnd), La Scala Orch, La Scala Chorus Great Opera Performances 2-▲ GOP 768
Ebe Stignani, Nicola Lemeni, w. Ebe Stignani (mez), Milan RAI SO [cnd:Angelo Questa] *(rec Jan. 31, 1955)* Incontri Memorabili ("Martini & Rossi Concerts" series) ▲ 5013
Verdi, G.:Don Carlos, w. M. Caniglia (sop—Elisabeth de Valois), G. Sciutti (sop—Page), E. Stignani (mez—Princess Eboli), M. Picchi (ten—Don Carlos), M. Ponz de L. (ten—Count of Lerma), P. Silveri (bar—Rodrigue), N. Rossi Lemeni (bass—Philip II), G. Neri (bass—Grand Inquisitor), A. Gaggi (bass—Old Monk), F. Previtali (cnd), Rome RAI SO, Rome RAI Chorus *(rec Rome, 1951)* Cetra Classic 3-▲ CDO 25 [ADD]

Lemeshev, Sergei (ten)
Taneyev, S.:Duet for Romeo & Juliet, w. T. Lavrova (sop), S. Samosud (cnd), All-Union RSO *(rec 1954)* Russian Disc ▲ RUS 15002 [AAD]
Tchaikovsky, P.:Eugene Onegin, w. G. Vishnevskaya (sop), L. Avdeyeva (mez), Belov (sgr), Petrov (sgr), B. Khaikin (cnd), Bolshoi Theater Orch, Bolshoi Theater Chorus [R] *(rec ca. early '60s for Melodi)* Legato Classics 2-▲ LCD 163-2 (m) [ADD]

Lemmo, Antonio (ten)
Wolf-Ferrari, E.:I quatro rusteghi, w. A. P (Margarita), D. Lombardi (Lucieta), G. Merrino (Marina), M. Fratarcangeli (Felice) L. Belluso (Servant), A. Abete (Lunardo), M. Nicolini (Maurizio), G. Sorrentino (Filipeto), M. Peirone (Simon), D. Baronchelli (Cancian), A. Lemmo (Count Riccard) Arkadia-Akademia 2-▲ 139 [DDD]

Lemmon, Jack (nar)
Peter & the Wolf for Narrator & Orchestra, Op. 67 (1936), w. Prokofiev, Sergei, Prague Festival Orch [cnd:Pavel Urbanek] Laserlight ♦ 90035 [DDD]
Prokofiev, S.:Peter & the Wolf, w. P. Urbanek (cnd), Prague Festival Orch LaserLight ▲ 15386 [DDD]

Lemnitz, Tiana (sop)
Bach, J.S.:St. Matthew Passion, w. F. Beckmann (alt), K. Erb (ten), G. Hüsch (bar), S. Schulze (bass), G. Ramin (cnd), Leipzig Gewandhaus Orch, St. Thomas Choir, *(abridged performance)* [G] *(rec Mar 1941)* Calig 2-▲ CAL 50 859/60 (m) [AAD]
Cornelius, P.:Songs, w. T. Lemnitz (sop)—4 songs; W. Ludwig, tenor—An Bertha (set of 4 songs), Op. 15; Hanns-Heinz Nissen, baritone—5 songs; all with Michael Raucheisen, piano; [G] Melodram 2-▲ MEL 27050 (m) [AAD]
Helge Roswaenge, w. Helge Roswaenge (ten), Milizia Korjus (sop), Hans Reinmar (bar), Heinrich Schlusnus (bar), et al. Preiser 2-▲ PRE 89209 [AAD]
The Legendary Singers at Lindenoper Berlin (1927–1945)—, w. Gitta Alpar (sop), Erna Berger (sop), Maria Müller (sop), Margarete Klose (cta), Peter Anders (ten), Max Lorenz (ten), Walter Ludwig (ten), Lauritz Melchior (ten), Rudolf Schock (ten), Franz Völker (ten), Willi Domgraf-Fassb *(rec 1927; 1937; 1941–45)* Minerva ▲ MN A21 [ADD]
Mozart, W.A.:Songs, w. M. Callas (sop), E. Grümmer (sop), E. Schwarzkopf (sop), R. Scotto (sop), E. Berger (sop), S. Jurinac (sop), E. Schumann (sop), I. Souez (sop), E. Rethberg (sop), L. Lehmann (sop), N. Gedda (ten), J. McCormack (ten), H. Roswenge (ten), H. Nash (ten), T. Gobbi (bar), G. Hüsch (bar), E. Kunz (bar), G. Frick (bass), E. Pinza (bass), A. Kipnis (bass) EMI Classics 4-▲ CDMD 63750
Mozart, W.A.:Zauberflöte, w. E. Berger (sop), I. Beilke (sop), H. Roswaenge (ten), H. Tessmer (ten), G. Hüsch (bar), W. Strienz (bass), T. Beecham (cnd), Berlin PO, Favre Chorus [without dialog; G] *(rec 1937–38 for HMV)* Pearl 2-▲ PEAS 9371 (m) [AAD]
Mozart, W.A.:Zauberflöte, w. E. Berger (sop), I. Beilke (sop), H. Roswaenge (ten), G. Hüsch (bar), W. Strienz (bass), T. Beecham (cnd), Berlin PO, Vereinigung Favres Soloists [G] Nimbus ("Prima Voce" series) 2-▲ NI 7827/8 (m) [ADD]
Mozart, W.A.:Zauberflöte, w. E. Berger (sop), I. Beilke (sop), H. Roswaenge (ten), H. Tessmer (ten), G. Hüsch (bar), W. Strienz (bass), T. Beecham (cnd), Berlin PO, Favre Chorus [without dialog; G] *(rec 1937–38 for HMV)* Melodram 2-▲ MEL 27056 (m) [AAD]
Mozart, W.A.:Zauberflöte, w. E. Berger (sop), I. Beilke (sop), H. Roswaenge (ten), H. Tessmer (ten), G. Hüsch (bar), W. Strienz (bass), T. Beecham (cnd), Berlin PO, Favre Chorus [without dialog; G] *(rec 1937–38 for HMV)* EMI Classics ("Great Recordings of the Century" series) 2-▲ CDHB 61034 (m) [ADD]
Opera Arias Preiser ("Lebendige Vergangenheit" series) ▲ PRE 89025 (m) [AAD]
Strauss, R.:Feuersnot (sels), w. Maria Cebotari (sop), Paula Buchner (sop), Karl Schmitt-Walter (bar), A. Rother (cnd), Berlin Radio Orch *(rec 1943–44)* Preiser ▲ PRE 90222 [ADD]
Strauss, R.:Der Rosenkavalier (sels), w. Maria Cebotari (sop), Paula Buchner (sop), Karl Schmitt-Walter (bar), A. Rother (cnd), Berlin Radio Orch *(rec 1943–44)* Preiser ▲ PRE 90222 [ADD]
Strauss, R.:Salome (sels), w. Maria Cebotari (sop), Paula Buchner (sop), Karl Schmitt-Walter (bar), A. Rother (cnd), Berlin Radio Orch—Final Scene *(rec 1943–44)* Preiser ▲ PRE 90222 [ADD]
Tiana Lemnitz (rec. 1942–53) Berlin Classics ▲ BER 9014 [ADD]
Wagner, R.:Der fliegende Holländer (sels), w. Kirsten Flagstad (sop), Torsten Ralf (ten), Rudolf Bockelmann (b-bar), Ludwig Weber (bass), T. Beecham (cnd), Royal Opera House Orch, Royal Opera House Chorus Covent Garden Memories ("Golden" series) ▲ MEM 3003
Wagner, R.:Götterdämmerung (sels), w. Kirsten Flagstad (sop), Torsten Ralf (ten), Rudolf Bockelmann (b-bar), Ludwig Weber (bass), T. Beecham (cnd), Royal Opera House Orch, Royal Opera House Chorus Covent Garden Memories ("Golden" series) ▲ MEM 3003
Wagner, R.:Lohengrin (sels), w. Kirsten Flagstad (sop), Torsten Ralf (ten), Rudolf Bockelmann (b-bar), Ludwig Weber (bass), T. Beecham (cnd), Royal Opera House Orch, Royal Opera House Chorus Covent Garden Memories ("Golden" series) ▲ MEM 3003
Wagner, R.:Die Meistersinger von Nürnberg, w. Tiana Lemnitz (sop—Eva), Bernd Aldenhoff (ten—Walther von Stolzing), Gerhard Unger (ten—David), Ferdinand Frantz (b-bar—Hans Sachs), Kurt Boehme (bass—Veit Pogner), Heinrich Pflanzl (bass—Sixtus Beckmesser), R. Kempe (cnd), Saxon State Orch *(rec Dresden, 1951)* Myto 4-▲ MCD 961138
Wagner, R.:Die Meistersinger von Nürnberg (sels), w. Kirsten Flagstad (sop), Torsten Ralf (ten), Rudolf Bockelmann (b-bar), Ludwig Weber (bass), T. Beecham (cnd), Royal Opera House Orch, Royal Opera House Chorus Covent Garden Memories ("Golden" series) ▲ MEM 3003
Wagner, R.:Die Meistersinger von Nürnberg (sels), w. E. Laholm (ten), R. Bockelmann (bar), E. Fuchs (bar), W. Furtwängler (cnd), Vienna State Opera Orch, Vienna State Opera Chorus *(rec Sept. 5, 1938)* Koch Schwann 2-▲ SCH 314522 [ADD]
Wagner, R.:Tristan und Isolde (sels), w. Kirsten Flagstad (sop), Torsten Ralf (ten), Rudolf Bockelmann (b-bar), Ludwig Weber (bass), T. Beecham (cnd), Royal Opera House Orch, Royal Opera House Chorus Covent Garden Memories ("Golden" series) ▲ MEM 3003
Wagner, R.:Wesendonck Songs, w. R. Heger (cnd), Berlin Staatskapelle [G] *(rec 7/7/44)* Acanta ▲ 43275 (m)
Weber, C.M. von:Der Freischütz (sels), w. Tiana Lemnitz (sop—Agathe), Michael Bohnen (b-bar—Kaspar), H. Knappertsbusch (cnd), Vienna State Opera Orch *(rec Salzburg, Aug. 3, 1939)* Koch Schwann 2-▲ SCH 314672 [ADD]

Lemoye, Nathalie (sgr)
A European Christmas, w. Les Colibris [cnd:Bernard Gerard, Michel Wackenheim] Studio SM ("Traditionnels" series) ▲ 2481 [ADD]

Lemper, Ute (sop)
City of Strangers London ▲ 444400-2 [DDD]

Lemper, Ute (sop) (cont.)
Illusions:Songs of Dietrich & Piaf London ▲ 436720-2 LH [DDD]
Nyman, M.:Film Music London ▲ 4425227-2 [DDD]
Nyman, M.:Michael Nyman Songbook, w. M. Nyman (cnd), Michael Nyman Band [E,F,G] London ▲ 425227-2 [DDD]
Nyman, M.:Prospero's Books, w. S. Leonard (sop), D. Conway (sgr), M. Angel (ten), Michael Nyman Band London ▲ 425224-2 [DDD]
Weill, K.:Mahagonny, w. H. Jungwirth (sop), H. Wildhaber (ten), P. Haage (ten), T. Mohr (bar), S. Tremper (sgr), Jeffrey Cohen (pno), J. Mauceri (cnd), Berlin RIAS Chamber Ensemble [G] London ▲ 430168-2 [DDD]
Weill, K.:The Seven Deadly Sins, w. H. Jungwirth (sop), H. Wildhaber (ten), P. Haage (ten), T. Mohr (bar), S. Tremper (sgr), J. Mauceri (cnd), Berlin RIAS Chamber Ensemble [G] London ▲ 430168-2 [DDD]
Weill, K.:Songs, w. J. Mauceri (cnd), Berlin RSO—songs from Mahagonny, Three Penny Opera, Silverlake, One Touch of Venus, etc. London ▲ 425204-2 [DDD]
Weill, K.:Songs, w. J. Mauceri (cnd), Berlin RIAS Sinfonietta, London Voices—Bilbao Song; Surabaya Johnny; Was die Herren Matrosen sagen; Der Song von Mandelay; Das Lied vom Branntweinandler; Youkali; Les filles de Bordeaux; Le train du Ciel; Le grand Lustucru; Le roi d'Aquitaine; J'attends un navire; Tchaikovsky; One Life to Live; This Is New; A Song of Jenny; My Ship London ▲ 436417-2 [DDD]
Weill, K.:The Threepenny Opera, w. Milva (sgr), S. Tremper (sgr), H. Dernesch (mez), R. Kollo (ten), M. Adorf (sgr), W. Reichmann (sgr), J. Mauceri (cnd), Berlin RIAS Sinfonietta, Berlin RIAS Chamber Choir [G] London ▲ 430075-2 [DDD]

Lenchner, Paula (sop)
Wagner, R.:Der Ring des Nibelungen, w. Gré Brouwenstein (sop—Freia/Sieglinde), Ilse Hollweg (sop—Waldvogel), Gerda Lammers (sop—Ortlinde), Paula Lenchner (sop—Wellgunde/Gerhilde), Hilde Scheppan (sop—Helmwige), Astrid Varnay (sop—Brünnilde/3rd Norn), Lore Wissmann (sop—Woglinde), Maria von Ilosvay (mez—Flosshilde/Schwertleite/2nd Norn), Louise Charlotte Kamps (mez—Siegrune), Jean Madeira (mez—Erda/Rossweisse/1st Norn), Georgine von Milinkovic (mez—Fricka/Grimgerde), Elisabeth Schärtel (mez—Waltraute), Paul Kuën (ten—Mime), Ludwig Suthaus (ten—Loge), Josef Traxel (ten—Froh), Wolfgang Windgassen (ten—Siegmund/Siegfried), Alfons Herwig (bar—Donner), Hermann Uhde (bar—Gunther), Hans Hotter (b-bar—Wotan), Gustav Neidlinger (b-bar—Alberich), Josef Griendl (bass—Fasolt/Hunding/Hagen), Arnold van Mill (bass—Fafner), H. Knappertsbusch (cnd), Bayreuth Festival Orch, Bayreuth Festival Chorus *(rec live, Bayreuth, Aug 13-17, 1956)* Golden Melodram 14-▲ GM 1.001 [ADD]

Lendi, Lucretia (mez)
Rossini, G.:Tancredi, w. Sumi Jo (sop—Amenaide), Lucretia Lendi (mez—Roggiero), Anna Maria di Micco (mez—Isaura), Ewa Podles (cta—Tancredi), Stanford Olsen (ten—Argirio), Pietro Spagnoli (bar—Orbazzano), Ewald Demeyere (hpd), Lieven Baert (vc), Franck Coryn (db), A. Zedda (cnd), Collegium Instrumentale Brugense, Capella Brugensis *(rec Poissy Theatre & Centre Musical-Lyrique-Phonographique, Ile de France, Jan. 26-31, 1994)* Naxos ("Opera Classics" series) 2-▲ 8.660037/38 [DDD]
Vivaldi, A.:Catone in Utica, w. Cecilia Gasdia (sop), Susanna Rigacci (sop), Marilyn Schmiege (sop), Margarita Zimmerman (mez), C. Scimone (cnd), Venice Solisti Erato 2-▲ ERA SEL 11232 [DDD]

Lengert, Claus (trb)
Bach, J.S.:Cant 98, w. P. Esswood (ct), K. Equiluz (ten), M. van Egmond (b-bar), Leonhardt Consort [G] Teldec ▲ 2292-42583-2 [ADD]

Lenn, R. (sgr)
Berlin, I.:Annie Get Your Gun, w. E. Merman (sgr), R. Middleton (sgr), L. Bibb (sgr), K. Carnes (sgr), J. Garth (sgr), C. Turner (sgr), J. Blackton (cnd) [1946 cast] MCA Classics ▲ MCAD 10047 [AAD] ■ MCAC 10047

Lenoty, René (ten)
Offenbach, J.:Barbe-bleue, w. Henri Legay (ten), Aimé Doniat (bar), Rene Terrasson (sgr), J. Doussard (cnd), ORTF Lyric Orch, ORTF Lyric Chorale *(rec 1967)* Memories 2-▲ MEM 4591 [ADD]
Planquette, R.:Rip van Winkle, w. Claudine Collart (sop), Lina Dachary (sop), Freda Betti (cta), Joseph Peyron (ten), Charles Daguerressar (bar), Julien Giovannetti (bar), Jacques Pruvost (bar), Lucien Lovano (bass), Patrick Orladey (sgr), Joëlle Pierre (sgr), M. Cariven (cnd), ORTF Lyric Orch, ORTF Lyric Chorale Musidisc ▲ MUS 201602 [ADD]

Lensky, Margaret (cta)
Purcell, H.:Dido & Aeneas, w. Helen Donath (sop—Belinda), Shirley Verrett (sop—Dido), Oralia Dominguez (mez—Sorceress), Carmen Lavani (alt—A Spirit), Margaret Lensky (cta—2nd Witch), Carlo Gaifa (ten—A Sailor), Dan Jordacescu (bar—Aeneas), Rosina Cavicchioli (sgr—A Woman), Lilia Teresita Reyes (sgr—1st Witch), R. Leppard (cnd), Turin RAI SO, Ambrosian Chorus *(rec Torino, May 20, 1971)* Arkadia ▲ 619 [ADD]

Lenya, Lotte (sop)
Weill, K.:American & Berlin Theater Songs, *(orch unknown)*—20 songs *(rec mid-1950s)* CBS ▲ MK 42658 (m) [ADD]
Weill, K.:Aufstieg und Fall der Stadt Mahagonny, w. W. Brückner-Rüggeberg (cnd), North German RSO, North German Radio Chorus [G] *(rec 1956)* CBS 2-▲ M2K 37874 (m) [ADD]
Weill, K.:Songs—Wie man sich bettet & Alabama Song, from Mahagonny [G] *(rec 1930)* Teldec ▲ 9031-72025-2 [ADD]
Weill, K.:Songs—selections from Mahagonny *(Alabama Song; As you make your bed; etc.) & Happy End (Bilbao Song)*; Mme. Damia (with orchestra, rec. 1931, sung in French)—from Dreisgroschenoper *(Complainte de Mackie)* Mastersound ▲ DFCD1-110 (m) [ADD]
Weill, K.:The Threepenny Opera, w. W. Brückner-Rüggeberg (cnd), *(orch unknown)* [G] *(rec mid-1950s)* CBS ▲ MK 42637 (m) [ADD]
Weill, K.:The Threepenny Opera, w. E. Helmke (sop), K. Gerron (sgr), T. Mackeben (cnd), *(orch unknown)* [G] *(rec original German cast, 1930)* Teldec ▲ 9031-72025-2 [ADD]
Weill, K.:The Threepenny Opera, w. E. Helmke (sop), K. Gerron (sgr), T. Mackeben (cnd), *(orch unknown)* [G] *(rec original German cast, 1930)* Mastersound ▲ DFCD1-110 (m) [ADD]
Weill, K.:The Threepenny Opera, w. B. Arthur (sgr), C. Rae (sgr), *(orch unknown)* [E] Polydor ▲ 820260-2 ■ 820260-4E

Lenz, Friedrich (ten)
Beethoven, L. van:Fidelio (sels), w. L. Rysanek (sop), I. Seefried (sop), E. Haefliger (ten), D. Fischer-Dieskau (bar), K. Engen (bass), G. Frick (bass), F. Fricsay (cnd), Bavarian State Orch, Bavarian Opera Chorus—Overture, various arias & scenes, finale [G] IMP Collectors Series ▲ IMPX 9021 [AAD]
Mozart, W.A.:Zauberflöte (sels), w. E. Lear (sop), R. Peters (sop), L. Otto (sop), F. Wunderlich (ten), D. Fischer-Dieskau (bar), F. Crass (bass), K. Böhm (cnd), Berlin PO, Berlin RIAS Chamber Choir—Scenes & Arias Deutsche Grammophon ▲ 429825-2 [ADD] ■ 429825-4
Wagner, R.:Das Liebesverbot, w. Pamela Coburn (sop—Mariana), Friedrich Lenz (ten—Antonio), Hermann Prey (bar—Friedrich), Keith Engen (bass—Angelo), Raimund Grumbach (bass—Danieli/Wirt), Wolfgang Fassler (sgr—Luzio), Sabine Haas (sgr—Isabella/Claudios Schwester), Alfred Kuhn (sgr—Brighella/Chef der Sbirren), Hermann Sapell (sgr—Pontio Pilato), Robert Schunk (sgr—Claudio), Marianne Seibel (sgr—Dorella), W. Sawallisch (cnd), Bavarian State Orch, Bavarian State Chorus *(rec July 9, 1983)* Orfeo d'or 3-▲ 345953
Wagner, R.:Rienzi, der Letzte der Tribunen, w. Cheryl Studer (sop—Irene), René Kollo (ten—Rienzi), Friedrich Lenz (ten—Gesandte), Norbert Orth (ten—Baroncelli), Bodo Brinkmann (bar—Paolo Orsini), Keith Engen (bass—Cecco del Vecchio), Raimund Grumbach (bass—Gesandte), Jan-Hendrik Rootering (bass—Steffano Colonna), Carmen Anhorn (sgr—Ein Friedensbote), Karl Helm (sgr—Kardinal Orvieto), John Janssen (sgr—Adriano), Alfred Kuhn (sgr—Gesandte), Hans Wilbrink (sgr—Gesandte), W. Sawallisch (cnd), Bavarian State Opera Orch, Bavarian State Opera Chorus *(rec live, July 6, 1983)* Orfeo d'or 3-▲ 346953

Lenz, Wolfgang (ten)
Marschner, H.A.:Der Vampyr, w. Carole Farley (sop—Malwina), Nucci Condò (mez—Suse), Oslavio Di Credico (ten—George Dibdin), Josef Protschka (ten—Edgar Aubry), Romano Truffelli (ten—Richard Scrop), Martin Egel (bar—Sir Humphrey Davenaut), Andrea Snarski (bar—Toms Blunt), Siegmund Nimsgern (b-bar—Lord Ruthven), Armando Caforio (bass—Robert Green), Peter Boom (sgr—Il capo dei Vampiri), Carlo Di Giacomo (sgr—James Gadshill), Wolfgang Lenz (sgr—Sir Berkley), Galina Pisarenko (sgr—Janthe), Renzo Scorsoni (sgr—Un servitore di Berkley), Anastasia Tomaszewska Schepis (sgr—Emmy), G. Neuhold (cnd), Rome RAI SO, Rome RAI Chorus *(rec Rome, Jan 26, 1980)* Italia 2-▲ CDC 99 [ADD]

Lenzer, Albin (alt)
Schubert, Franz:Mass 6, w. Benjamin Schmidinger (sop), Kurt Azesberger (ten), Jörg Hering (ten), Harry van der Kamp (bass), B. Weil (cnd), Orch of the Age of Enlightenment, Vienna Boys' Choir Sony Classical ▲ SK 66255

Lenzi, Arnoldo (bar)
Verdi, G.:La traviata, w. Olga de Franco (sop—Flora Bervoix/Annina), Anna Rosza (sop—Violetta Valery), Giordano Callegari (ten—Gastone), Alessandro Ziliani (ten—Alfredo Germont), Luigi Borgonovo (bar—Giorgio Germont), Arnoldo Lenzi (bar—Barone Douphol), Antonio Gelli (bass—Marchese d'Obigny/Dottor Grenvil), C. Sabajno (cnd), La Scala Orch, Vittore Veneziani (cnd), La Scala Chorus *(rec Oct-Nov 1930)* Arkadia 2-▲ CD 78001 (m) [ADD]
Verdi, G.:La traviata, w. Olga de Franco (sop—Flora Bervoix/Annina), Anna Rosza (sop—Violetta Valéry), Giordano Callegari (ten—Gastone), Alessandro Ziliani (ten—Alfredo Germont), Luigi Borgonovo (bar—Giorgio Germont), Arnoldo Lenzi (bar—Baron Douphol), Antonio Gelli (bass—Marquis d'Obigny/Dr. Grenvil), C. Sabajno (cnd), La Scala Orch, La Scala Chorus *(rec La Scala Theatre, Milan, Oct.-Nov. 1930)* VAI Audio 2-▲ VAIA 1108-2

Leon, Manfredi Ponz de (sgr)
Verdi, G.:La battaglia di Legnano, w. Caterina Mancini (sop), Amedeo Berdini (bar), Rolando Panerai (bar), Albino Gaggi (bass), Edmea Limberti (sgr), F. Previtali (cnd), Rome RAI SO, Rome RAI Chorus *(rec 1951)* Cetra Classic 2-▲ CDON 40 [ADD]

Leonard, Sarah (sop)
Britten, H.:A Boy Was Born, w. N. Tibbels (sop), S. Bickley (mez), P. Hall (ten), G. Jess (bass), T. Edwards (cnd), London Sinfonietta Chorus, St. Paul's Cathedral Choristers Virgin Classics ▲ CDC 59136
Britten, H.:Hymn to St. Cecilia, w. N. Tibbels (sop), S. Bickley (mez), P. Hall (ten), G. Jess (bass), T. Edwards (cnd), London Sinfonietta Chorus, St. Paul's Cathedral Choir Virgin Classics ▲ CDC 59136
Britten, H.:Sonnets of Michelangelo, w. N. Tibbels (sop), S. Bickley (mez), P. Hall (ten), G. Jess (bass), T. Edwards (cnd), London Sinfonietta Chorus, Choristers of St. Paul's Cathedral Virgin Classics ▲ CDC 59136
Bryars, G.:The Black River, w. C. Bowers-Broadbent (org) ECM New Series ▲ 78118-21495-2
del Tredici, D.:Acrostic Song, w. H. Christophers (cnd), The Sixteen Chorus Collins Classics ▲ 12872 [DDD]
Desmarets, H.:Motets, w. Jean-Paul Fouchécourt (ten), Norman Richard (b-bar), C. Jackson (cnd), Montreal Ancient Music Ensemble, Les Violons du Roy—Domine ne in furore; Usquequo Domine Confitebor Tibi Domine; Lauda Jerusalem; Marche Lorraine K617 2-▲ 7053
Górecki, H.-M.:O Domina Nostra, w. C. Bowers-Broadbent (org) ECM New Series ("New" series) ▲ 78118-21495-2
Monteverdi, C.:Incoronazione, w. A. Augér (sop), D. Jones (mez), L. Hirst (mez), J. Bowman (ct), G. Reinhart (bass)., R. Hickox (cnd), City of London Baroque Sinfonia Virgin Classics 3-▲ CDCC 59524
Nyman, M.:Prospero's Books, w. U. Lemper (sop), D. Conway (sgr), M. Angel (ten), Michael Nyman Band London ▲ 425224-2 [DDD]
Satie, E.:Messe des pauvres, w. C. Bowers-Broadbent (org) ECM New Series ▲ 78118-21495-2
Schnittke, A.:Madrigals, w. Capricorn Hyperion ▲ CDA 66885

Leonardi, Mario (ten)
Coccia, C.:Caterina di Guisa, w. C. Apollonio (sop), N. Ciliento (mez), S. Antonucci (bar), M. de Bernart (cnd), Italian PO, Calabria Francesca Cilea Chorus *(rec Oct. 30 & Nov. 3, 1990)* Bongiovanni 2-▲ GB 2117/18 [DDD]

Leonhart, Jay (bass)
Clair de Lune & Sister Moon, w. Thomas Young (ten), Mike Renzi (pno), Grady Tate (dr) *(rec Nola Recording Studio, NYC, Oct 21 & 23, 1996)* Ocean ▲ OR 104

Le Paludier, Christophe (ten)
Boësset, A.:Music of, w. Marcel Bozonnet (nar), Véronique Dietschy (sop), Alain Zaepffel (ct), Jacques Bone (bass), Claire Antonini (lt), Marianne Muller (vl)—Madame de la fayette; Airs de cour; La princesse de cleves (sels) Adès ▲ ADE 204722

Lepejian, V. (nar)
Fleischer, T.:In the Mountains of Armenia, w. C. Maovsessian (cl), Armenian Church School Girls' Choir Old Jerusalem Opus One ▲ Cd 158 [DDD]

Lepore, Carlo (bass)
Bellini, V.:Mass in a, w. Leila Bersiani (sop), Valentina di Cola (sop), Stella Salvati (cta), José Antonio Campo (ten), E. Brizio (cnd), Prague SO, Czech Radio-TV Chorus *(rec Prague, June 1994)* Studio SM ▲ D 2444
Bellini, V.:Salve Regina in f, w. E. Brizio (cnd), Prague SO [orchd.] *(rec Prague, June 1994)* Studio SM ▲ D 2444
Generali, P.:Sacred Music, w. Leila Bersiani (sop), Valentina di Cola (sop), Emanuela Deffai (mez), Sella Salvati (cta), Paolo Macedonio (ten), Roberto Bencivenga (ten), E. Brizio (cnd), Czech Radio-TV Orch, Czech Radio-TV Chorus—Magnificat; Domine ad Adjuvandum; Virgam Virtutis; Ecce Virgo; Ave Maria Messe Pastorale; Te Deum *(rec FHS Studios, Prague, 1995)* Studio SM ▲ 2517 [DDD]
Monteverdi, C.:Ballo delle ingrate, w. Daniela Barcellona (sgr), Daniela Ciliberti (sgr), Andrea Concetti (sgr), Hans van Dijk (sgr), Remo Guerrini (sgr), Nadia Mantelli (sgr), Elena Marazzi (sgr), Humberto Orellana (sgr), Claudia Pallini (sgr), Luigi Polsini (sgr), Rosa Ricciotti (sgr), Alberto Rota (sgr), Ludovica Scoppola (sgr), *(orch unknown)* Nuova Era ▲ NUO 7224
Stradella, A.:Esule dalle sfere, w. Roberta Invernizzi (sop), Silvia Piccollo (sop), Marco Lazzara (alt), Mario Nuvoli (ten), Riccardo Ristori (bass), Alessandro Stradella Consort Bongiovanni ▲ GB 2165 [DDD]

Leport, Nicole (sop)
Handel, G.F.:Rinaldo, w. Sophie Boulin (sop—Donna), Ileana Cotrubas (sop—Almirena), Marie-Françoise Jacquelin (sop—Sirene), Nicole Leport (sop—Sirene), Jeanette Scovotti (sop—Armida), Carolyn Watkinson (cta—Rinaldo), Charles Brett (ct—Eustazio), Paul Esswood (ct—Goffredo), Armand Arapian (ten—Mago Christiano/Araldo), Ulrik Cold (bass—Argante), J. Malgoire (cnd), La Grande Écurie et la Chambre du Roy *(rec Paris, 1977)* Sony Classical 3-▲ SM3K 34592

Lerner, Mimi (mez)
Rossini, G.:Music of, w. M. Fortuna (sop), D. Voigt (sop), M. Horne (mez), K. Kuhlmann (mez), F. von Stade (mez), R. Blake (ten), C. Estep (ten), C. Merritt (ten), T. Hampson (b-bar), H. Runey (b-bar), J. Opalach (bass), S. Ramey (bass), R. Norrington (cnd), Orch of St. Luke's, New York Concert Chorale EMI Classics ▲ CDC 54643

Le Roi, Gaëlle (sop)
Fauré, G.:Requiem, w. F. Le Roux (bar), E. Krivine (cnd), Lyon National Orch, Lyon National Chorus [L] Denon ▲ CO 77527 [DDD]
Ravel, M.:La Nuit, w. J. Grimbert (cnd), Paris Sorbonne Orch, Paris Sorbonne Chorus Marco Polo ▲ 8.223755 [DDD]
Ravel, M.:Tout est lumière, w. J. Grimbert (cnd), Paris Sorbonne Orch, Paris Sorbonne Chorus Marco Polo ▲ 8.223755 [DDD]

Le Roux, François (bar)
Campra, A.:Tancrède, w. C. Alliot-Lugaz (sop), D. Evangelatos (cta), G. Reinhart (bar), P.-Y. le Maigat (bass-bar), Dubose (sgr), J. Malgoire (cnd), La Grande Écurie et la Chambre du Roy Erato (Musifrance) 2-▲ 2292-45001-2 ZA [DDD]
Debussy, C.:Pelléas et Mélisande, w. M. Ewing (sop), C. Ludwig (mez), J. Van Dam (bass-bar), J.-P. Courtis (bass), C. Abbado (cnd), Vienna PO, Vienna State Opera Chorus Deutsche Grammophon 2-▲ 435344-2 [DDD]
Duruflé, M.:Mass, "Cum jubilo", w. D. Keene (cnd), Voices of Ascension Orch, Voices of Ascension *(rec Church of the Ascension, New York City, May 13, 17 & 18, 1995)* Delos ▲ DE 3169 [DDD]

Le Roux, François (bar) (cont.)
Duruflé, M.:Requiem, w. Patricia Spence (mez), D. Keene (cnd), Voices of Ascension Orch, Voices of Ascension Chorus *(rec Church of the Ascension, New York City, June 5–6, 1994)* Delos ▲ DE 3169 [DDD]
Fauré, G.:Requiem, w. G. Le Roi (sop), E. Krivine (cnd), Lyon National Orch, Lyon National Chorus [L] Denon ▲ CO 77527 [DDD]
Fauré, G.:Songs, w. Natalie Dessay (sop), Béatrice Uria–Monzon (mez), Jean–Paul Fouchécourt (ten), Jeff Cohen (pno)—complete songs grouped by poets [Leconte de Lisle; Charles Baudelaire; Paul Verlaine; Jean de la Ville de Mirmont; Armand Silvestre; Victor Hugo; Théophile Gautier; 5 Melodies of Venice; Sully Prudhomme; Albert Samain; Louis Pommey; Paul de Chodens; Marc Monnier; Romain Bussine; Victor Wilder; Georgette Deblads; Villiers de l'Isle Adam; Charles Grandmougin; Henri de Régnier; Stéphan Bordèse; Charles Van Lerberghe; Baronne de Brimont; Maurice Maeterlinck; Edmond Haraucourt; Molière REM 4–▲ REM 311179 [DDD]
Mélodies Françaises en duo, w. Alliot–Lugaz, Colette (sop), Jeff Cohen (pno) *(rec 9/88)* REM ▲ 311086 [DDD]

Le Sage, S. (sop)
Purcell, H.:The Prophetess, or The History of Dioclesian, w. H. Sheppard (sop), A. Deller (ct), M. Worthley (ten), P. Todd (ten), M. Bevan (bar), A. Deller (cnd), Vienna Concentus Musicus—also includes incidental music from the play *(rec June 1965)* Vanguard Classics ("The Bach Guild" series) ▲ OVC 2517 [ADD]

Leskovich, Georg (alt)
Schubert, Franz:Mass 1, w. Alexander Nader (sop), Thomas Puchegger (sop), Jörg Hering (ten), Kurt Azesberger (ten), Harry van der Kamp (bass), Arno Hartmann (org), B. Weil (cnd), Orch of the Age of Enlightenment, Vienna Boys' Choir *(rec Vienna, Austria, Sept 1995)* Sony Classical ("Vivarte" series) ▲ SK 68247 [DDD]
Schubert, Franz:Mass 3, w. Alexander Nader (sop), Thomas Puchegger (sop), Belá Fischer (alt), Jörg Hering (ten), Harry Van der Kamp (bass), Arno Hartmann (org), B. Weil (cnd), Orch of the Age of Enlightenment, Chorus Viennensis, Vienna Boys' Choir Sony Classical ("Vivarte" series) ▲ SK 68248
Schubert, Franz:Mass 4, w. Alexander Nader (sop), Thomas Puchegger (sop), Belá Fischer (alt), Jörg Hering (ten), Harry Van der Kamp (bass), Arno Hartmann (org), B. Weil (cnd), Orch of the Age of Enlightenment, Chorus Viennensis, Vienna Boys' Choir Sony Classical ("Vivarte" series) ▲ SK 68248

Lesne, Brigitte (mez)
Monteverdi, C.:Motets, w. G. Lesne (ct), J. Benet (ten), J. Cabré (bar), Il Seminario Musicale—18 motets for 1, 2 & 3 voices [L] Virgin Classics ("Veritas" series) ▲ 59602 [DDD]

Lesne, Brigitte (sgr/hp/perc)
Ave Eva:Songs of Womanhood from the 12th & 13th Centuries Opus 111 ▲ OPS 30–134

Lesne, Gérard (ct)
Bach, J.S.:Cant 80, w. Barbara Schlick (sop), Agnès Mellon (sop), Howard Crook (ten), Peter Kooy (bass), P. Herreweghe (cnd), La Chapelle Royale Orch, Collegium Vocale Harmonia Mundi France ▲ HMC 6901326
Bach, J.S.:Cant 105, w. B. Schlick (sop), H. Crook (ten), P. Kooy (bass), P. Herreweghe (cnd), Collegium Vocale Orch, Collegium Vocale Virgin Classics ▲ CDC 59237–2
Bach, J.S.:Cant 131, w. B. Schlick (sop), H. Crook (ten), P. Kooy (bass), P. Herreweghe (cnd), Collegium Vocale Orch, Collegium Vocale Virgin Classics ▲ CDC 59237–2
Bach, J.S.:Magnificat, BWV 243, w. A. Mellon (sop), B. Schlick (sop), H. Crook (ten), P. Kooy (bass), P. Herreweghe (cnd), La Chapelle Royale Orch, Collegium Vocale [L] Harmonia Mundi France ▲ HMC 901326
Bach, J.S.:Masses, BWV 233–36, "Lutheran Masses", w. A. Mellon (sop), C. Prégardien (ten), P. Kooy (bass), P. Herreweghe (cnd), Ghent Collegium Vocale Orch, Ghent Collegium Vocale—BWV 233 & 236 Virgin Classics ▲ CDC 59634
Bach, J.S.:Masses, BWV 233–36, "Lutheran Masses", w. A. Mellon (sop), C. Prégardien (ten), P. Kooy (bass), P. Herreweghe (cnd), Ghent Collegium Vocale Orch, Ghent Collegium Vocale—BWV 234 & 235 Virgin Classics ▲ CDC 59587
Bach, J.S.:St. Matthew Passion (sels), w. A. Mellon (sop), C. Prégardien (ten), P. Kooy (bass), P. Herreweghe (cnd), Ghent Collegium Vocale Orch, Ghent Collegium Vocale Virgin Classics ▲ CDC 59587
Bononcini, G.:Cantate (12) e duetti, w. Il Seminario Musicale—Cants. for Alto Solo EMI Classics ▲ CDC 45000
Caldara, A.:Medea in Corinto, Il Seminario Musicale Virgin Classics ▲ CDC 59058
Charpentier, M.–A.:Leçons de ténèbres, H. 96–110, w. A. Mellon (cnd), Il Seminario Musicale—3 du jeudi Virgin Classics ▲ CDC 59295
Charpentier, M.–A.:Leçons de ténèbres, H. 96–110, w. A. Mellon (sop), I. Honeyman (cnd), Il Seminario Musicale—3 du jeudi Virgin Classics ▲ CDC 59278
Charpentier, M.–A.:Salve regina à 3 voix pareilles, w. John Elves (ten), Josep Cabré (bar), J. Savall (cnd), Concert des Nations Astrée ▲ E 8552 [DDD]
Couperin, F.:Music of, w. René Jacobs (alt), Kenneth Gilbert (hpd), Christophe Rousset (hpd), W. Christie (cnd), Les Arts Florissants, Phillippe Herreweghe (cnd), Chapelle Royale Choir—Hpd pieces; Tenebeae Lessons [sels] Harmonia Mundi ("Great Baroque Composers" series) 3–▲ HMX 390870.72
Fux, J.J.:Dafne in Lauro, w. L. Akerlund (sop), S. Piccollo (sop), M. van der Sluis (sop), M. Klietmann (ten), R. Clemencic (cnd), Clemencic Consort, La Cappella Vocal Ensemble [I] Nuova Era ("Ancient Music" series) 2–▲ 6930/31 [DDD]
Galuppi, B.:Motets, w. Il Seminario Musicale Virgin Classics ▲ CDC 45030
Handel, G.F.:Cants, w. Il Seminario Musicale—Carco sempre di gloria; La Lucrezia; Mi palpita il cor; Splenda l'alba in oriente [I] *(rec 10/90)* Virgin Classics ▲ 59059 [DDD]
Handel, G.F.:Poro, Rè dell'Indie, w. Rossana Bertini (sop), Gloria Banditelli (cta), Bernarda Fink (cta), F. Biondi (cnd), Europa Galante Opus 111 3–▲ OPS 30–113/15
Handel, G.F.:Trio Sons, w. Il Seminario Musicale—Sonata in G, Op. 5/4 *(rec 10/90)* Virgin Classics ▲ 59059 [DDD]
Lully, J.–B.:Music of, w. René Jacobs (alt), Kenneth Gilbert (hpd), Christophe Rousset (hpd), W. Christie (cnd), Les Arts Florissants, Phillippe Herreweghe (cnd), Chapelle Royale Choir—Hpd Pieces; 'Atys' excerpts; Dies Israe; Petits Motets Harmonia Mundi ("Great Baroque Composers" series) 3–▲ HMX 390870.72
Monteverdi, C.:Motets, w. B. Lesne (mez), J. Benet (ten), J. Cabré (bar), Il Seminario Musicale—18 motets for 1, 2 & 3 voices [L] Virgin Classics ("Veritas" series) ▲ 59602 [DDD]
O Lusitano:Portuguese Vilancetes, Cantigas & Romances, w. Circa 1500 Ensemble Virgin Classics ▲ 59071 [DDD]
Orff, C.:Carmina burana, w. Natalie Dessay (sop), Thomas Hampson (bar), M. Plasson (cnd), Toulouse Capitole Orch, Orféon Donostiarra, Midi–Pyrénées Children's Choir *(rec Halle–aux–Grains, Toulouse, Dec. 2, 4 & 6, 1994)* EMI Classics ▲ CDC 55392 [DDD]
Rameau, J.P.:Music of, w. René Jacobs (alt), Kenneth Gilbert (hpd), Christophe Rousset (hpd), W. Christie (cnd), Les Arts Florissants, Phillippe Herreweghe (cnd), Chapelle Royale Choir—Pieces; Les Indes Gallantes (sels) Harmonia Mundi ("Great Baroque Composers" series) 3–▲ HMX 390870.72
Vivaldi, A.:Cants, w. Il Seminario Musicale—Cessate omai cessate in A, R.684; Perfidissimo corl in A, R.674; Amor hai vinto in A, R.683; Qual per ignoto in A, R.677 Adda ▲ ADD 241872 [ADD]
Vivaldi, A.:L'Olimpiade, w. L. Meeuwsen (sop), M. van der Sluis (sop), E. von Magnus (alt), A. Christofelis (alt), W. Oberholtzer (bar), A. Walker Schultze (bass), R. Clemencic (cnd), Clemencic Consort, La Cappella Vocal Ensemble [I] *(rec live, Paris, 2/8–10/90)* Nuova Era ("Ancient Music" series) 2–▲ 6932/33 [DDD]
Vivaldi, A.:Salve regina, RV.616, Il Seminario Musicale Virgin Classics ▲ CDC 59232

Lestringant, Etienne (ten)
Charpentier, M.–A.:Messe de minuit pour Noël, w. G. Ragon (ten), J.–L. Bindi (bass), Piniec (sgr), P. Colléaux (cnd), Nantes Instrumental Ensemble [L] Arion ▲ ARN 68015 [AAD]

Letelier, Agustin (bar)
Bizet, G.:Carmen, w. Laura Bustamante (sop—Frasquita), Ximena Riveros (sop—Mercedes), Nancy Stokes (sop—Micaela), Regina Resnik (mez—Carmen), Plácido Domingo (ten—Don José), Ismildo Tedeschi (ten—Remendado), Ramon Vinay (ten—Escamillo), Juan Charles (ten/bar—Dancaire), Agustin Letelier (bar—Morles), Jorge Algorta (bass—Zuniga), A. Guadagno (cnd), Santiago Teatro Municipale Orch, Santiago Teatro Municipale Chorus *(rec Santiago Municipal Theater, Sept. 4, 1967)* Legato Classics 2–▲ LCD 194–2 [ADD]

Le Téxier, Vincent (b-bar)
Bizet, G.:Carmen (sels), w. Léontina Vaduva (sop), Béatrice Uria–Monzon (mez), Christian Papis (ten), A. Lombard (cnd), Bordeaux–Aquitaine National Orch—Toréador & other great arias Valois ▲ V 4769
Donizetti, G.:Messa di Gloria e Credo, w. Danielle Borst (sop), Hélène Jossoud (mez), Jean–Luc Viala (ten), M. Piquemal (cnd), Avignon–Provence Regional Lyric Orch, Provence–Alpes–Côte d'Azur Regional Choir Accord ▲ ACD 212142 [DDD]
Duparc, H.:Songs, w. M. Mahe (mez), N. Lee (pno) Pierre Verany ▲ PVY 793061 [DDD]
Fauré, G.:Songs, w. Philippe Biros (pno)—Les Roses d'Ispahan; Hymne; Chanson du pêcheur; Les matelots; Chant d'automne; L'absent; Fleur jetée; Le Voyageur; Chanson d'amour; Automne; Le Secret; Les Larmes; Au Cimetière; Les Berceaux; Tristesse; Chant d'automne; Nocturne; Nell; Poème d'un jour; L'absent; L'Horizon chimérique Valois ▲ V 4747
Grétry, A.–E.–M.:La Caravane du Caire, w. I. Poulenard (sop), G. de Reyghere (sop), G. Ragon (ten), G. de Mey (ten), P. Huttenlocher (bar), J. Bastin (bass), M. Minkowski (cnd), Ricercar Academy, Ricercar Academy Chorus [period instrs] [F] Ricercar 2–▲ RIC 100084/85 [DDD]
Ravel, M.:L'Enfant et les sortilèges, w. M. Lagrange (sop), E. Vidal (sop), M. Damonte (mez), M. Mahé (mez), A. Chedel (cta), L. Pezzino (ten), M. Barrard (bar), A. Lombard (cnd), Bordeaux–Aquitaine National Orch, Bordeaux Grand Théâtre Municipal Chorus [F] Valois ▲ V 4670
Ropartz, G.:Choral Music, w. Christian Papis (nar), Didier Henry (bar), Christine Lajarrige (pno), Irène Brissot (hp), Eric Lebrun (org), M. Piquemal (cnd), Nancy SO, French Radio Chorus Soloists, Vittoria Regional French Choir—Psaume 136; Dimanche; Nocturne; Les Vêpres sonnent; Le Miracle de Saint Nicolas *(rec Salle Poirel, Nancy, Apr. 22–24, 1994)* Marco Polo ▲ 8.223774 [DDD]
Ropartz, G.:Psalm 129, w. M. Piquemal (cnd), Jean–Walter Audoli Instrumental Ensemble, French Vittoria Regional Choir Accord ▲ ACD 205132 [DDD]
Ropartz, G.:Requiem, w. Catherine Dubosc (sop), Jacqueline Mayeur (mez), M. Piquemal (cnd), Jean–Walter Audoli Instrumental Ensemble, French Vittoria Regional Choir Accord ▲ ACD 205132 [DDD]
Ropartz, G.:Songs, w. P. Biros (pno)—Veilles de départ; Il pleut; En mai; Tout le long de la nuit; Chanson de bord; Le Temps des Saintes; Chant d'automne; Si j'étais roi; Quatre poèmes Valois ▲ V 4701 [DDD]

Lettinga, Bouke (alt)
Biber, H. von:Requiem à 15, w. S. Paiu (sgr), H. van der Kamp (bass), G. Leonhardt (cnd), Netherlands Bach Society Baroque Orch, Netherlands Bach Society Choir Deutsche Harmonia Mundi ▲ 05472–77277–2
Valls, F.:Scala Arentina Mass, w. S. Paiu (sop), M. van der Sluis (sop), D. Cordier (ct), J. Elwes (ten), H. van der Kamp (bass), G. Leonhardt (cnd), Netherlands Bach Society Baroque Orch, Netherlands Bach Society Choir Deutsche Harmonia Mundi ▲ 05472–77277–2

Leval, Antonio (bass)
Puccini, G.:Madama Butterfly, w. Montserrat Caballé (sop—Cio–Cio–San), Carmen Rigai (mez—Suzuki), Bernabé Martí (ten—Pinkerton), Diego Monjo (ten—Goro), Juan Rico (ten—Yamadori), Manuel Ausensi (bar—Sharpless), Jose Lemar (bass—Bonze), Antonio Leval (bass—Imperial Commissioner), Alejandro Chiara (bass—Registrar), G. Rivoli (cnd), Madrid Radio–TV Orch, Madrid Radio–TV Chorus *(rec Madrid, June 12, 1968)* Legato Classics 2–▲ LCD 210–2 [ADD]

Levasseur, Bernard (bar)
Gratton, H.:Imagerie:Christmas Pastoral, w. M. Keable (actor), S. Léonard (actor), J.–L. Millette (actor), M. Laferrière (sop), C. Rioux (mez), N. Richard (b-bar), L. Lavigueur (cnd), Louis Lavigueur Instrumental Ensemble, Louis Lavigueur Vocal Ensemble [F] *(rec 5/91)* CBC ("SM 5000" series) ▲ SMCD 5109 [DDD]

Levasseur, Jeannette (sgr)
Lehár, F.:Die lustige Witwe, w. Teresa Stich–Randall (mez—Missia Palmieri), Monique Stiot (mez—Manon), Germaine Duclos (sgr—Praskovia), Linda Felder (sgr—Olga), Christiane Jacquin (sgr—Nadia), Jeannette Levasseur (sgr—Sylviane), Henri Legay (ten—Camille de Coutançon), Joseph Peyron (ten—Kromsky), Robert Destain (sgr—Baron Popoff), Michel Fauche (sgr—Pristich), Gérard Friedmann (sgr—Lerida), Jacques Gilet (sgr—Bogdanowitch), Jean Guy Henneveux (sgr—Prince Danilo), Serge Klin (sgr—Figg), Jacques Villa (sgr—D'Estillac), A. Sibert (cnd), Belgian Radio–TV Orch, Belgian Radio–TV Chorus *(rec Grand Auditorium, Belgium, Apr 30, 1970)* Studio SM 2–▲ 2160 [AAD]

Levene, S. (sgr)
Loesser, F.:Guys and Dolls, w. R. Alda (sgr), V. Blaine (sgr) [1950 Broadway cast] MCA Classics ▲ MCAD 10301 [AAD] ■ MCAC 10301

Leverenz, Steffi (sgr)
Strauss (II), Joh.:Der Zigeunerbaron, w. Emmy Loose (sop), Hilde Zadek (sop), Rosette Anday (cta), Julius Patzak (ten), Karl Dönch (bar), Alfred Poell (bar), C. Krauss (cnd), Vienna PO, Vienna State Opera Chorus Phonographe 2–▲ PHG 5020 [AAD]

Levina, Raisa (sop)
Grieg, E.:Songs, w. E. Kerechanin (sop), A. Martynov (ten), V. Katajev (cnd), Northern Crown Soloists Ensemble [arr. Tishchenko] MK ▲ MKA 417124 [DDD]

Levine, Elliot (bar)
Camilo, M.:Batéy, w. P. E. Clark (sop), C.B. Rowe (sop), W. Zukof (ct), L. Bennett (ten), W. L. Lee (ten), Puntilla (sgr), New Generation Western Wind ▲ WW 2001
Darling, D.:Blessings:A Prayer for the Planet, w. P.E. Clark (sop), C.B. Rowe (sop), W. Zukof (ct), L. Bennett (ten), W.L. Lee (ten), D. Darling (acoustic & electric vc/syn/voice) Western Wind ▲ WW 2001
Darling, D.:Blessings (sels), w. P.E. Clark (sop), C.B. Rowe (sop), W. Zukof (ct), L. Bennett (ten), W.L. Lee (ten), D. Darling (acoustic & electric vc/syn/voice) Western Wind ▲ WW 2001

Levinsky, Ilya (ten)
Fleischmann, B.:Rothschild's Vn, w. Marina Shaguch (sop), Larissa Diadkova (mez), Konstantin Pluzhnikov (ten), Sergei Leiferkus (bar), G. Rozhdestvensky (cnd), Rotterdam PO *(rec Rotterdam, Netherlands, Aug 24–31, 1995)* RCA Red Seal ▲ 09026–68434–2 [DDD]

Levitt, Richard (ten)
Monteverdi, C.:Vespro della Beata Vergine, w. Gloria Prosper (sop), Adrienne Albert (mez), Melvin Brown (ten), Archi Drake (bass), R. Craft (cnd), Columbia Baroque Ensemble, Gregg Smith Singers, Texas Boys' Choir Sony Classical ("Essential Classics" series) 2–▲ SB2K 62656

Levko, Valentina (mez)
Tchaikovsky, P.:Queen of Spades, w. T. Milachkina (sop), V. Atlantov (ten), M. Ermler (cnd), Bolshoi Theater Orch, Bolshoi Theater Chorus [R] Philips 3–▲ 420375–2 [ADD]

Le Vot, Gérard (sgr)
Troubadours & Trouvères Studio SM ▲ 12 21.75

Levy, Emily (sgr)
Hildegard Of Bingen:Sacred Songs, w. Jocelyn West (sgr), Vivien Ellis (sgr), Stevie Wishart (sgr/h–g), Hester Briant (sgr), Fiona Cunningham (sgr), Tara Franks (sgr), Lucy Steele (sgr), Vickie Couperim (sgr), Julie Murphy (sgr), Oxford Girls' Choir—Honey & milk beneath her tongue; Ursula's virgins; The devil's virgins; Place of the ancient heart; Zeal of divinity; O fiery spirit; Red river falling; O orzchis ecclesia, Living–light angels; The clouds are grieving; The firstwoman; From their homeland; But the devil mocked; Song to Ecclesia *(rec Toddington, Gloucestershire, England, May 6–8, 1995)* Celestial Harmonies ▲ 13127–2

Lewis, Bertha (cta)
Sullivan, A.:The Gondoliers, w. W. Lawson (sop), A. Davies (ten), D. Oldham (ten), M. Bennett (sop), G. Baker (bar), L. Sheffield (bar), H. Lytton (bar), et al., H. Norris (cnd), D'Oyly Carte Opera Company Orch, D'Oyly Carte Opera Chorus—dialogue omitted *(rec 1927)* Pearl 2–▲ PEAS 9961 (m) [AAD]

Lewis, Brenda (sop)
Max Lorenz:Recital, 1933–1957, w. Max Lorenz (ten), Maria Reining (sop), Berlin RSO [cnd:Artur Rother], Bayreuth Festival Orch [cnd:Heinz Tietjen, Richard Strauss], German Large RSO [cnd:Rudolf Moralt, Max Schönherr, Anton Paulik], Hessen RSO [cnd:Kurt Schröder], Brenda Lewis (sop), Eberhard Wächter (ten), Wolfgang Zimmer (bar) *(rec 1933–57)* Myto ▲ MCD 934.88

Lewis, Keith (ten)
Berlioz, H.:Benvenuto Cellini, w. J. Carlyle (sop), J. Veasey (mez), Kentish, Cameron, Bushby, Garrard, Ward, A. Dorati (cnd), BBC SO, BBC Sym Chorus [E] *(rec live, Royal Festival Hall, 1964)* Music & Arts 2–▲ CD 618 (m) [AAD]
Berlioz, H.:Requiem, "Grande Messe des Morts", w. E. Inbal (cnd), Frankfurt RSO, Frankfurt Kantorei Denon 2–▲ CO 73205/06 [DDD]
Franck, C.:Les Béatitudes, w. D. Montague (mez), G. Cachemaille (bar), J. Cheek (bass), H. Rilling (cnd), Stuttgart RSO, Gächinger Kantorei [F] Hänssler Classic 2–▲ 98.964 [DDD]
Mahler, G.:Sym 8, w. S. Jo (sop), C. Studer (sop), W. Meier (mez), T. Allen (bar), H. Sotin (bass), G. Sinopoli (cnd), Philharmonia Orch, Philharmonia Chorus, Southend Boys' Choir [G] Deutsche Grammophon 2–▲ 435433–2
Mozart, W.A.:Don Giovanni, w. C. Vaness (sop), M. Ewing (sop), E. Gale (sop), T. Allen (bar), R. Van Allan (bass), B. Haitink (cnd), London PO, Glyndebourne Festival Chorus [I] EMI Classics 3–▲ CDCC 47036 [DDD]
Mozart, W.A.:Missa, K.317, w. Y. Kenny (sop), K. Kuhlmann (mez), D. Wilson–Johnson (bar), C. P. Flor (cnd), Philharmonia Orch, London Voices RCA Red Seal ▲ 09026–60812–2
Mozart, W.A.:Requiem, w. F. Lott (sop), D. Jones (mez), W. White (bar), F. Welser–Möst (cnd), London PO, London Phil Chorus EMI Classics ▲ CDM 63260
Mozart, W.A.:Requiem, w. Felicity Lott (sop), Cella Jones (mez), Willard White (bass), David Bell (org), F. Welser–Möst (cnd), London PO, London Phil Choir Classics for Pleasure ("Eminence" series) ▲ CDEMX 2150 [DDD]
Mozart, W.A.:Requiem, w. L. Dawson (sop), J. van Nes (cta), S. Estes (bass), C. M. Guilini (cnd), Philharmonia Orch, Philharmonia Chorus [L] Sony Classical ▲ SK 45577 [DDD]
Pacini, G.:Maria Tudor, w. M. Hill Smith (sop), P. Walker (sop), C. Blades (bar), D. Parry (cnd), English SO *(rec 1983)* Italian Opera Rarities ▲ IOR 7714 [ADD]
Rachmaninoff, S.:The Bells, w. S. Murphy (sop), D. Wilson–Johnson (bar), N. Järvi (cnd), Scottish National Orch, Scottish National Chorus [R] Chandos ▲ CHAN 8476 [DDD]
Schoenberg, A.:Die Jakobsleiter, w. Barbara Kilduff (sop—Seele 1), Jadwiga Rappé (cta—Sterbende), Wilfried Gahmlich (ten—Aufrührerischer), Cornelius Hauptmann (ten—Gabriel), Keith Lewis (ten—Berfener), Kurt Azesberger (bar—Mönch), Barbara Fuchs (sgr—Seele 2), Matteo de Monti (sgr—Ringender), Bjorn Waag (sgr—Auserwählter), E. Inbal (cnd), Frankfurt RSO, Robin Gritton (cnd), Berlin Radio Chorus *(rec Alte Oper, Frankfurt, Sept 6–9, 1994)* Denon ▲ CO 78977 [DDD]
Schumann, R.:Genoveva, w. J. Faulkner (sop—Genoveva), R. Behle (sop—Margaretha), K. Lewis (ten—Golo), A. Titus (bar—Siegfried), H. Stamm (bass—Hidulfus, Caspar), J. Tilli (bass—Balthasar), G. Albrecht (cnd), Hamburg State PO, Hamburg State Opera Chorus [G] *(rec 1992)* Orfeo 2–▲ 289932 [DDD]
Taneyev, S.:Duet for Romeo & Juliet, w. S. Murphy (sop), N. Järvi (cnd), Scottish National Orch [R] Chandos ▲ CHAN 8476 [DDD]

Lewis, Mary (sop)
Vaughan Williams, R.:Hugh the Dover (sels), w. Tudor Davis (ten), M. Sargent (cnd), *(orch unknown)*—Love Duet *(rec 1924–53)* Beulah ▲ 1PD13

Lewis, Richard (ten)
Bach, J.S.:Arias, w. Lois Marshall (sop), Maureen Forrester (alt), Norman Farrow (b–bar), Oscar Shumsky (vn), Brian Priestman (cnd), *(chorus unknown)*—Arias Nos. 32, 42, 120a, 132, & 182; Duet from Cant. 205 Vox Box 2–▲ CDX 5127 [ADD]
Bach, J.S.:Cant 3, w. Lois Marshall (sop), Maureen Forrester (alt), Norman Farrow (b–bar), B. Priestman (cnd), *(orch unknown)*, *(chorus unknown)* Vox Box 2–▲ CDX 5127 [ADD]
Bach, J.S.:Cant 102, w. Maureen Forrester (alt), Norman Farrow (b–bar), G. Leonhardt (cnd), Leonhardt Consort, Brian Priestman (cnd), *(chorus unknown)* Vox Box 2–▲ CDX 5127 [ADD]
Beethoven, L. van:Missa Solemnis, w. E. Farrell (sop), C. Smith (mez), K. Borg (bass), L. Bernstein (cnd), New York PO, Westminster Choir [L] Sony Classical 2–▲ SM2K 47522 [ADD]
Beethoven, L. van:Missa Solemnis, w. M. Arroyo (sop), M. Forrester (cta), C. Siepi (b–bar), E. Ormandy (cnd), Philadelphia Orch, Singing City Choir *(rec Mar. 29–30, 1967)* Sony Classical ("Essential Classics" series) ▲ SBK 53517 [ADD] ▮ SBT 53517
Beethoven, L. van:Sym 9, "Choral Sym", w. I. Borkh (sop), R. Siewert (cta), L. Weber (bass), R. Leibowitz (cnd), Royal PO, Beecham Choral Society [G] *(rec 6/61)* Chesky ▲ CD66 [ADD]
Coleridge–Taylor, S.:Scenes from *The Song of Hiawatha,* w. Malcolm Sargent (cnd), Royal Choral Society—Hiawatha's Wedding Feast Theorema ▲ TH 121224
Handel, G.F.:Messiah, w. Elsie Morison (sop), Marjorie Thomas (cta), James Milligan (bass), M. Sargent (cnd), Royal Liverpool PO, Huddersfield Choral Society Classics for Pleasure 2–▲ CDCFP 4718 [ADD]
Handel, G.F.:Messiah, w. Kiri Te Kanawa (sop), Anne Gjevang (mez), Gwynne Howell (bass), G. Solti (cnd), Chicago SO, Chicago Sym Chorus [E] London 2–▲ 414396–2 [DDD]
Handel, G.F.:Messiah (sels), w. Kiri Te Kanawa (sop), Anne Gjevang (mez), Gwynne Howell (bass), G. Solti (cnd), Chicago SO, Chicago Sym Chorus—arias & choruses London ▲ 430098–2 [DDD] ▮ 430098–4
Handel, G.F.:Messiah (sels), w. Elsie Morison (sop), Marjorie Thomas (cta), James Milligan (bass), Eric Chadwick (org), M. Sargent (cnd), Royal Liverpool PO, Huddersfield Choral Society Classics for Pleasure ▲ CDCFP 9007 [ADD]
Mahler, G.:Das Lied von der Erde, w. L. Chookasian (mez), E. Ormandy (cnd), Philadelphia Orch *(rec Feb. 9, 1966)* Sony Classical ("Essential Classics" series) ▲ SBK 53518 [ADD] ▮ SBT 53518
Mahler, G.:Das Lied von der Erde, w. M. Forrester (cta), F. Reiner (cnd), Chicago SO [G] RCA Gold Seal ▲ 60178–2–RG [ADD]
Mozart, W.A.:Così fan tutte (sels), w. S. Jurinac (sop), A. Noni (sop), B. Thebom (mez), E. Kunz (bar), M. Borriello (bar), F. Busch (cnd), Glyndebourne Festival Orch *(rec Glyndebourne Festival, 1950)* Testament ▲ TES SBT 1040 [ADD]
Mozart, W.A.:Idomeneo, w. Gundula Janowitz (sop), Enriqueta Tarres (sop), Luciano Pavarotti (ten), J. Pritchard (cnd), London PO, Glyndebourne Festival Chorus [I] *(rec live at Royal Albert Hall, Aug. 17, 1964)* Verona 2–▲ 27038/39 (m) [AAD]
Mozart, W.A.:Idomeneo, w. Gundula Janowitz (sop), Enriqueta Tarres (sop), Luciano Pavarotti (ten), J. Pritchard (cnd), London PO, Glyndebourne Festival Chorus [I] *(rec live, Royal Albert Hall, London Aug. 17, 1964)* Melodram 2–▲ MEL 27003 (m)
Mozart, W.A.:Idomeneo (sels), w. Gundula Janowitz (sop), Enriqueta Tarres (sop), David Hughes (ten), Luciano Pavarotti (ten), Neilson Taylor (bar), Dennis Wicks (bass), J. Pritchard (cnd), London PO, Glyndebourne Festival Chorus Budget ("The Greatest Voice in Opera" series) ▲ SYP 107
Strauss, R.:Salome, w. E. Martón (sop), B. Fassbaender (mez/sop), H. Zednik (ten), B. Weikl (bar), Z. Mehta (cnd), Berlin PO *(rec live)* Sony Classical 2–▲ S2K 46717
Strauss, R.:Salome, w. M. Caballé (sop), R. Resnik (mez), S. Milnes (bar), E. Leinsdorf (cnd), London SO RCA Gold Seal 2–▲ 6644–2–RG [ADD]
Sullivan, A.:The Gondoliers, w. G. Evans (bar), A. Young (ten), O. Brannigan (bass), M. Sargent (cnd), Pro Arte Orch, Glyndebourne Festival Chorus EMI Classics 2–▲ CDMB 64394
Sullivan, A.:HMS Pinafore, w. G. Baker (bar), J. Cameron (bar), M. Sargent (cnd), Pro Arte Orch, Glyndebourne Festival Chorus EMI Classics 2–▲ CDMB 64397
Sullivan, A.:The Mikado, w. O. Brannigan (bass), G. Evans (bar), I. Wallace (bass), M. Sargent (cnd), Pro Arte Orch, Glyndebourne Festival Chorus EMI Classics 2–▲ CDMB 64403
Sullivan, A.:The Pirates of Penzance, w. G. Baker (bar), J. Milligan (b–bar), J. Cameron (bar), M. Sargent (cnd), Pro Arte Orch, Glyndebourne Festival Chorus EMI Classics 2–▲ CDMB 64409
Sullivan, A.:The Sorcerer (sels), w. G. Baker (bar), E. Morison (sop), J. Cameron (bar), M. Sargent (cnd), Pro Arte Orch, Glyndebourne Festival Chorus EMI Classics 2–▲ CDMB 64397
Sullivan, A.:The Yeomen of the Guard, w. A. Young (ten), J. Cameron (bar), M. Sargent (cnd), Pro Arte Orch, Glyndebourne Festival Chorus EMI Classics 2–▲ CDMB 64415
Vaughan Williams, R.:On Wenlock Edge, w. A. Boulton (cnd), London PO [orch. version] *(rec Oct. 12, 1972)* Intaglio ▲ ING 741 [ADD]

Lewis, Richard (ten) (cont.)
The Voices of Living Stereo, Vol. 2, w. Eileen Farrell (sop), Birgit Nilsson (sop), Roberta Peters (sop), Leontyne Price (sop), Galina Vishnevskaya (sop), Rosalind Elias (mez), Shirley Verrett (mez), Marian Anderson (cta), Maureen Forrester (cta), Sergio Franchi (ten), Mario Lanza (ten), Jan Pee, Alexander Dedyukhin (pno), Franz Rupp (pno), Leo Taubman (pno), George Trovillo (pno), Charles Wadsworth (pno), Boston Pops Orch [cnd:Arthur Fiedler], Boston SO [cnd:Charles Munch], Chicago SO [cnd:Fritz Reiner], RCA Victor Orch, RCA Victor Chorus [cnd:Wa *(rec Boston & Chicago & New York & Rome, 1957–1964)* RCA Living Stereo ▲ 09026–68167–2 [ADD]
Walton, W.:Troilus & Cressida (sels), w. E. Schwarzkopf (sop), M. Sinclair (cta), P. Pears (ten), W. Walton (cnd), Philharmonia Orch—scenes EMI Classics ▲ ZDM 64199

Lewis, William (ten)
Barber, S.:A Hand of Bridge, w. P. Neway (sop), E. Alberts (mez), P. Maero (bass), V. Golschmann (cnd), Symphony of the Air [E] *(rec ca. 1960)* Vanguard Classics ▲ OVC 4016 [ADD]

Lewitová, J. (sgr)
Michna, A.V.:Sacred Music, w. M. Bornus–Szczycinski (sgr), M. Cechalová (sgr), M. Pospí il (sgr), M. Predota (sgr), R. Hugo (cnd), Capella Regis Musicalis—Missa V à 5 et à 7 si placet; Cantiones pro Defunctis; Missa VI pro Defunctis à 6 et à 10; Requiem Studio Matou ▲ MAT 1 [DDD]

L'Homme, F. (sgr)
"Le Patron" of the Saxophone, w. Marcel Mule (sax), Guy Chauvet (ten), G. Charon (sgr), P. Romby (sgr), Eugène Bozza (cnd), Francis Çebron (cnd), Phillipe Gaubert (cnd), *(orchs unknown),* Joseph Benvenutti (pno), Marcel Gaveau (pno), Marthe Pellas–Lenom (pno), François Combelle (sax) *(rec 1930–1940)* Clarinet Classics ▲ CC 0013 [AAD]

Liane (sop)
Weill, K.:The Threepenny Opera, w. Liane (sop—Polly Peachum), A. Felbermayer (sop—Lucy), H. Fassler (sop—Jenny), R. Anday (cta—Mrs. Peachum), K. Preger (ten—Macheath), H. Roswaenge (ten—Street Crier), A. Jerger (bar—Peachum), F. Gutherie (bar), *(cnd & orch unknown)* Vanguard Classics ▲ OVC 8057 [ADD]

Liang, Ning (mez)
Puccini, G.:Madama Butterfly (sels), w. Ying Huang (sop—Cio-Cio-San), Constance Hauman (mez—Kate Pinkerton), Ning Liang (mez—Suzuki), Richard Troxell (ten—B. F. Pinkerton), Richard Cowan (sgr—Sharpless), Jing Ma Fan (sgr—Goro), Christopheren Nomura (sgr—Prince Yamadori), J. Conlon (cnd), Orch de Paris—Dovunque al Mondo; B. F. Pinkerton Giù; Bimba, Bimba, Non Piangere; Ah! Vien! Sei Mia!; Un Bel Dí; Ora a Noi; Petali d'Ogni Fior; Coro a Bocca Chiusa; Prelude; Io So Che Alle Sue Pene; Ah! Son Vil!; E Sia! A Lui Devo Obbedir; Butterfly! *(rec Olivier Messiaen Auditorium, Paris, 1996)* Sony Classical ▲ SK 61972 [DDD]

Liani, Octavia (sop)
Rossini, G.:Stabat Mater, w. J. Jaques (mez), M. Zamfir (ten), T. Krause (bar), P. Crispini (cnd), Geneva Elans Orch Ensemble, Geneva Elans Vocal Ensemble [L] Gallo ▲ CD 487

Licette, Miriam (sop)
Gounod, C.:Faust, w. M. Licette (sop—Margarita), D. Vane (sop—Siebel), M. Brunskill (cta—Martha), H. Nash (ten—Faust), H. Williams (b–bar—Valentine), R. Easton (bass—Mephistopheles), R. Carr (bass—Wagner), T. Beecham (cnd), BBC SO, BBC Sym Chorus Dutton Laboratories 2–▲ CDAX 2001 [ADD]

Lichti, Daniel (b–bar)
Bach, J.S.:Cant 56, w. G. Funfgeld (cnd), Bach Festival Orch, Bethlehem Bach Choir [G] Dorian ▲ DOR 90127 [DDD]
Bach, J.S.:Cant 63, w. S. McNair (sop), J. Taylor (mez), D. Gordon (ten), G. Funfgeld (cnd), Bach Festival Orch, Bethlehem Bach Choir—plus Sanctus from Mass in b, BWV 232 [G] Dorian ▲ DOR 90113 [DDD]
Bach, J.S.:Cant 65, w. D. Gordon (ten), G. Funfgeld (cnd), Bach Festival Orch, Bethlehem Bach Choir [G] Dorian ▲ DOR 90113 [DDD]
Bach, J.S.:Cant 140, w. H. Schellenberg (sop), D. Gordon (ten), G. Funfgeld (cnd), Bach Festival Orch, Bethlehem Bach Choir [G] Dorian ▲ DOR 90127 [DDD]
Bach, J.S.:Music of, w. Wendy Humphreys (sop), Stuart Laughton (tpt/nat tpt/Renaissance cnt), William O'Meara (org), David Campion (timp/perc)—Prelude & Fugue in G; Grosser Herr [from Christmas Oratorio]; Mein gläubiges Herz [from Cant 68]; 3 Chorale Preludes; Prelude & Fugue in A Doremi ▲ DHR 9303 [DDD]
Baroque Banquet, w. Wendy Humphreys (sop), Stuart Laughton (tpt/nat tpt/cnt), William O'Meara (org), David Campion (timp/perc) Doremi ▲ 9303
Handel, G.F.:Samson (sels), w. Wendy Humphreys (sop), Stuart Laughton (tpt/nat tpt/Renaissance cnt), William O'Meara (org), David Campion (timp/perc)—Let the Bright Seraphim Doremi ▲ DHR 9303 [DDD]
Scarlatti, A.:Endimione e Cintia, w. Wendy Humphreys (sop), Stuart Laughton (tpt/nat tpt/Renaissance cnt), William O'Meara (org), David Campion (timp/perc)—Vaga Cintia Doremi ▲ DHR 9303 [DDD]
Schubert, Franz:Schwanngesang, w. Janina Fialkowska (pno) Doremi ▲ 9302
Schubert, Franz:Songs (misc), w. A. Shrut (pno)—Harfenspieler I–III, D.478–480 [G] Dorian ▲ DOR 90131 [DDD]
Schubert, Franz:Songs (misc), w. Janina Fialkowska (pno)—Frühlingsglaube; Heidenröslein; Die Forelle; Rastlose Liebe; Geheimes; Lachen und Weine; Nacht und Träume; Der Musensohn Doremi ▲ 9302
Schumann, R.:Songs, w. A. Shrut (pno)—Gesange des Harfners (3), Op. 98a, Nos. 4,6 & 8 [G] Dorian ▲ DOR 90131 [DDD]
Wolf, H.:Goethe–Lieder (sels), w. A. Shrut (pno)—Harfenspieler I–III; Cophtisches Lieder I–II; Der Rattenfänger; Prometheus; Anakreons Grab; Königlich Gebet [G] Dorian ▲ DOR 90131 [DDD]
Wolf, H.:Songs (misc), w. A. Shrut (pno)—Drei Gedichte von Michelangelo [G] Dorian ▲ DOR 90131 [DDD]

Liddell, Cynthia (nar)
Ashley, R.:Purposeful Lady Slow Afternoon, w. Mary Ashley (sgr), Barbara Lloyd (sgr), Mary Lucier (sgr) Lovely Music ▲ LCD 1002 [AAD]

Lidonni, Ferdinando (bar)
Puccini, G.:Manon Lescaut, w. Magda Olivero (sop—Manon), Tine Appelman (mez—Singer), Umberto Borso (ten—Chevalier), Mario Carlin (ten—Edmondo/Dancing Master/Lamplighter), Ferdinando Lidonni (bar—Lescaut), Giovanni Foiani (bass—Geronte/Sergeant/Captain), Joop Ruivenkamp (bass—Innkeeper), F. Vernizzi (cnd), Groot Omroep Orch, Groot Omroep Choir *(rec Amsterdam, Oct 31, 1964)* Bella Voce 2–▲ BLV 107.221 [AAD]

Liebeck, Ann (sop)
Bizet, G.:Carmen (sels), w. D. Palade (sop—Micaëla), A. Liebeck (sop—Frasquita), G. Alperyn (mez—Carmen), D. Schaechter (mez—Mercédès), G. Lamberti (ten—Don José), M. Dvorsky (ten—Remandado), J. Durco (ten—Cancairo), A. Titus (bar—Escamillo), V. Chmelo (bar—Morales), D. Rigosa (bass—Zuniga), A. Rahbari (cnd), Czech–Slovak RSO Bratislava, Slovak Phil Chorus, Bratislava Children's Choir *(rec July 1990)* Naxos ▲ 8.550727 [DDD]

Liebermann, Melinda (sop)
Scheidel–Austin, E.:Sonnets from the Portuguese, w. Cornelius Witthoeft (pno) Capstone ▲ CPS 8618
Les Vertige des Profondeurs, w. M. Burba (tpt/pno/didgeridoo/tools/eup/alphn) Thorofon ▲ CTH 2198 [AAD/DDD]

Liebesberg, Else (sop)
Kálmán, I.:Die Csárdásfürstin (sels), w. L. Rysanek (sop), R. Christ (ten), H. Prikopa (bar), F. Bauer–Theussl (cnd), Vienna Volksoper Orch, Vienna Volksoper Chorus [G] Koch Präsent ▲ CD 399226 [AAD]
Lehár, F.:Der Graf von Luxemburg (sels), w. Renate Holm (sop), Hilde Brauner (cta), Dagmar Hermann (mez), Rudolf Christ (ten), Herbert Prikopa (bar), F. Bauer–Theussl (cnd), Vienna Volksoper Orch, Vienna Volksoper Chorus [G] Koch Präsent ▲ CD 399223 [AAD]
Lehár, F.:Paganini (sels), w. E. Mechera (sop), Rudolf Christ (ten), K. Equiluz (ten), F. Bauer–Theussl (cnd), Vienna Volksoper Orch, Vienna Volksoper Chorus [G] Koch Präsent ▲ CD 399226 [AAD]
Straus, O.:Ein Walzertraum (sels), w. H. Brauner (cta), R. Holm (sop), D. Hermann (mez), R. Christ (ten), H. Prikopa (bar), F. Bauer–Theussl (cnd), Vienna Volksoper Orch, Vienna Volksoper Chorus [G] Koch Präsent ▲ CD 399223 [AAD]

Liebl, Karl (ten)

Wagner, R.:Der fliegende Holländer, w. L. Rysanek (sop), G. London (bar), G. Tozzi (bass), A. Dorati (cnd), Royal Opera House Orch, Royal Opera House Chorus Covent Garden [G] London 2-▲ 417319-2 [ADD]

Wagner, R.:Tannhäuser, w. Gré Brouwestijn (sop), Murray Dickie (ten), Eberhard Waechter (bar), Alois Pernerstorfer (b-bar), Deszö Ernster (bass), Walter Brunelli (sgr), Peter Harrower (sgr), Rosl Schweiger (sgr), Herta Wilfert (sgr), A. Rodzinski (cnd), Rome RAI Radio-TV SO, Rome RAI Chorus Stradivarius 3-▲ STV 12318

Wagner, R.:Tannhäuser (sels), w. G. Brouwenstijn (sop), H. Wilfert (sgr), E. Wächter (bar), A. Rodzinski (cnd), Rome RAI Orch, Rome RAI Chorus *(rec Nov. 21 1957)* Myto 3-▲ MCD 93277

Ligabue, Ilva (sop)

Boito, A.:Nerone, w. R. Baldani (mez), B. Prevedi (bar), A. Ferrin (bass), G. Gavazzeni (cnd), Turin RAI SO, Turin RAI Chorus *(rec live 1975)* Italian Opera Rarities 2-▲ IOR 7704 [ADD]

Cherubini, L.:Pimmalione, w. M. Adani (sop), G. Carturan (mez), U. Borghi (sgr), E. Gerelli (cnd), Milan RAI Orch, Milan RAI Chorus [I] *(rec live 1955)* Melodram ▲ CDM 19501 [AAD]

Cherubini, L.:Pimmalione, w. Mariella Adani (sop), Gabriella Carturan (mez), Umberto Borghi (sgr), E. Gerelli (cnd), Milan RAI SO, Milan RAI Chorus Melodram 2-▲ CDM 29501

Massenet, J.:Werther, w. D. Gatta (sop—Sofia), I. Ligabue (sop—Kaethlen), G. Simionato (mez—Charlotte), F. Tagliavini (ten—Werther), V. Pandano (ten—Schmidt), E. Campi (bass—Johann), S. Bruscantini (bass—Le Bailli), F. Capuana (cnd), La Scala Orch, La Scala Chorus *(rec Apr. 21, 1951)* Bongiovanni 2-▲ GB 1101/02 [ADD]

Pavarotti & Friends for War Child, w. Luciano Pavarotti (ten), Eric Clapton (sgr), Sheryl Crow (sgr), Elton John (sgr), Liza Minelli (sgr), Joan Osborne (sgr), Jon Secada (sgr), Eric Clapton (gtr), John McLaughlin (gtr), Marco Armiliato, Edoardo Bennato, José Molina, Al DiMeola, Kelly Family, Ligabue, Litfiba, P *(rec Modena, Italy, 1996)* London ▲ 452900-2 ■ 452900-4

Strauss, R.:Der Rosenkavalier, w. Jarmila Barton (sop—Marianne), Lisa Della Casa (sop—Sophie), Sena Jurinac (sop—Octavian), Ilva Ligabue (sop—Orphan), Elisabeth Schwarzkopf (sop—Marschallin), Else Schürhoff (mez—Annina), Luisa Villa (mez—Milliner), Hugues Cuénod (ten—Marschallin's majordomo), Erich Majkut (ten—Valzacchi), Giuseppe Nessi (ten—Animal seller), Luciano Della Pergola (ten—Lackey/Faninal's majordomo), Antonio Pirino (ten—An Italian Singer), Gino Del Signore (ten—Lackey/Waiter), Erich Kunz (bar—Herr von Faninal), Paolo Pedani (bar—Lackey), Attilo Barbesi (bass—Lackey/Waiter), Enrico Campi (bass—Waiter), Otto Edelmann (bass—Baron Ochs), Bruno Fichtinger (bass—Notary), Franco Taino (bass—Waiter), Maria Amadini (sgr—Orphan), Pina Carrillo (sgr—Orphan), Joszi Trojan Regar (sgr—Innkeeper), H. von Karajan (cnd), La Scala Orch, La Scala Chorus *(rec La Scala Theater, Milan, Jan. 26, 1952)* Legato Classics 3-▲ LCD 197-3

Verdi, G.:Ernani, w. F. Corelli (ten), P. Cappuccilli (bar), R. Raimondi (bass), O. de Fabritiis (cnd), Arena di Verona Orch, Arena di Verona Chorus *(rec live, Verona 7/15/72)* Golden Age of Opera 2-▲ GAO 131/32 [ADD]

Verdi, G.:Falstaff, w. M. Freni (sop), L. Alva (ten), R. Capecchi (bar), F. Corena (bass), C. M. Giulini (cnd), Royal Concertgebouw Orch, Netherlands Chamber Choir [I] *(rec live, The Hague 6/20/63)* Verona 2-▲ 27095/96

Verdi, G.:Falstaff, w. Oralia Dominguez (mez), Luigi Alva (ten), Geraint Evans (bar), Eberhardt Wächter (bar), F. Previtali (cnd), *(orch unknown)* *(rec Teatro Colon, Buenos Aires, Aug. 30, 1963)* Ornamenti ("Gala Evenings, Teatro Colon") 2-▲ 119

Verdi, G.:Falstaff, w. M. Freni (sop), G. Simionato (mez), R. Elias (mez), R. Krause (ten), G. Evans (bar), R. Merrill (bar), G. Solti (cnd), RCA Italian Opera Orch, RCA Italiana Opera Chorus [I] London 2-▲ 417168-2 [ADD]

Verdi, G.:La forza del destino (sels), w. C. Bergonzi (ten), Meliciani (sgr), G. Gavazzeni (cnd), La Scala Orch, La Scala Chorus [substantial highlights] *(rec live, Milan 12/7/65)* Myto 2-▲ 2 MCD 91750 [ADD]

Verdi, G.:I masnadieri, w. G. Raimondi (ten), R. Bruson (bar), B. Christoff (bass), G. Gavazzeni (cnd), Rome Opera Orch, Rome Opera Chorus [I] *(rec live, Rome, Nov. 25, 1972)* Golden Age of Opera 2-▲ GAO 135/36 [ADD]

Ligendza, Catarina (sop)

Still, W.G.:Tristan und Isolde, w. R. Baldani (mez), H. Hopf (ten), A. Dermota (ten), H. Sotin (bass), G. Neidlinger (bass), C. Kleiber (cnd), Vienna State Opera Orch, Vienna State Opera Chorus *(rec Oct. 7, 1973)* Exclusive 3-▲ EXL 18 [ADD]

Still, W.G.:Tristan und Isolde, w. S. Anderson (cta), C. Heater (ten), A. Švorc (bass), M. Smith (bass), L. Toffolo (cnd), Trieste Teatro Comunale Giuseppe Verdi Orch, Trieste Teatro Comunale G. Verdi Chorus [G] *(rec live, Trieste, 12/13/69)* Melodram 3-▲ MEL 37072 (m) [AAD]

Still, W.G.:Tristan und Isolde, w. Ruša Baldani (mez), Hans Hopf (ten), Hans Sotin (bass), C. Kleiber (cnd), Vienna PO, Vienna State Opera Chorus *(rec Vienna, Oct. 7, 1973)* Pantheon 3-▲ PHE 6601 (m)

Wagner, R.:Die Meistersinger von Nürnberg, w. C. Ludwig (mez), P. Domingo (ten), R. Laubenthal (ten), D. Fischer-Dieskau (bar), R. Hermann (bar), P. Lagger (bass), E. Jochum (cnd), German Opera Orch, German Opera Chorus Deutsche Grammophon ("Domingo Edition" series) ▲ 435406-2

Wagner, R.:Die Meistersinger von Nürnberg, w. C. Ludwig (mez), P. Domingo (ten), R. Laubenthal (ten), D. Fischer-Dieskau (bar), R. Hermann (bar), P. Lagger (bass), E. Jochum (cnd), German Opera Orch, German Opera Chorus [G] Deutsche Grammophon 4-▲ 415270-2 [ADD]

Wagner, R.:Tristan und Isolde, w. C. Ligendza (sop—Isolde), Y. Minton (mez—Brangäne), H. Brilioth (ten—Tristan), K. Moll (bass—King Mark), C. Kleiber (cnd), Bayreuth Festival Orch, Bayreuth Festival Chorus *(rec Bayreuth Festival, 1975)* Exclusive 3-▲ EXL 54 [ADD]

Wagner, R.:Tristan und Isolde (sels), w. Ruša Baldani (mez), Hans Hopf (ten), C. Kleiber (cnd), Vienna State Opera Orch *(rec live, 1973)* AS Disc ▲ ASD 2510

Light, Germaine (mez)

Offenbach, J.:Le Fille du tambour-major, w. Christiane Harbell (sop—Stella), Monique de Pondeau (sop—Claudine), Germaine Light (mez—Duchess Della Volta), Marcelle Ranson-Hervé (ten—Duke Della Volta), André Mallabrera (ten—Griolet), Etienne Arnaud (bar—Robert), Louis Musy (bar—Monthabor), *(orch unknown)* Accord ▲ ACD 220692 [AAD]

Ligot, Etienne (sgr)

Bellini, V.:La sonnambula, w. Maria Costanza Nocentini (sop), Vitalba Mosca (mez), Giuseppe Morino (ten), Giovanni Furlanetto (bar), Patrizia Ciofi (sgr), Walter Mikus (sgr), G. Carella (cnd), Italian International Orch Nuova Era 2-▲ NUO 7215 [DDD]

Liguori, Maria Grazia (sop)

Mascagni, P.:Sí, w. Vivian (sop), A. Felle (sop), Maria Gentile (sop), Nicoletti (sgr), Comas (sgr), S. Sanna (cnd), Montepulciano Arts Center Orch, Montepulciano Arts Center Chorus [I] *(rec live, 7/24/87)* Bongiovanni 2-▲ GB 2050/51 [DDD]

Stradella, A.:Il moro per amore, w. R. Invernizzi (sop—Eurinda), S. Piccollo (sop—Lucinda), M. Grazia Liguori (sop—Fiorino), M. Lazzara (cta—Lindora), V. Matacchini (cta—Feraspe/Floridoro), M. Beasley (ten—Filandro), R. Ristori (bass—Rodrigo), E. Velardi (cnd), Alessandro Stradella Consort [I] *(rec Oct. 31-Nov. 3, 1992)* Bongiovanni 3-▲ GB 2153/55

Lika, Peter (bass)

Adam, A.:Le Postillon de Lunjumeau, w. P. Coburn (sop), R. Swensen (ten), J. Linn (bar), K. Arp (cnd), Kaiserslauten Radio Orch, Stuttgart Chamber Choir [G] Capriccio 2-▲ 60040-2 [DDD]

Bach, J.S.:Cant 21, w. G. de Reyghere (mez), R. Jacobs (alt), C. Prégardien (ten), S. Kuijken (vn), S. Kuijken (cnd), La Petite Bande, Netherlands Chamber Choir Virgin Classics ▲ CDC 59528

Bach, J.S.:Cant 21, w. G. de Reyghere (mez), C. Prégardien (ten), S. Kuijken (cnd), La Petite Bande, Netherlands Chamber Choir [G] Veritas ▲ VC 7 90779-2 [DDD] ■ VC 7 90779-4 (D)

Bach, J.S.:Cant 201, w. Maria Cristina Kiehr (sop), Andreas Scholl (ct), James Taylor (ten), Kurt Azeberger (ten), Roman Trekel (bar), R. Jacobs (cnd), Berlin Academy for Early Music, Berlin Chamber Chorus Harmonia Mundi France 2-▲ HMC 901544.45

Bach, J.S.:Magnificat, BWV 243, w. G. de Reyghere (sop), R. Jacobs (alt), C. Prégardien (ten), S. Kuijken (vn), S. Kuijken (cnd), La Petite Bande, Netherlands Chamber Choir [L] Veritas ▲ VC 7 90779-2 [DDD] ■ VC 7 90779-4 (D)

Bach, J.S.:Magnificat, BWV 243, w. G. de Reyghere (sop), R. Jacobs (alt), C. Prégardien (ten), S. Kuijken (vn), S. Kuijken (cnd), La Petite Bande, Netherlands Chamber Choir Virgin Classics ▲ CDC 59528

Lika, Peter (bass) (cont.)

Bach, J.S.:St. John Passion, w. B. Schlick (sop), C. Patriasz (cta), H. Crook (ten), W. Kendall (ten), P. Kooy (bass), P. Herreweghe (cnd), La Chapelle Royale Orch, Ghent Collegium Vocale [G] Harmonia Mundi France 2-▲ HMC 901264/65 [DDD]

Bach, J.S.:St. John Passion, w. Barbara Schlick (sop), Ingeborg Most (alt), Edrian Brand (ten), Alexander Stevenson (ten), Philip Langshaw (bass), P. Kuentz (cnd), Paul Kuentz Orch, Paul Kuentz Choir Pierre Verany 2-▲ PVY 730051 [DDD]

Beethoven, L. van:Sym 9, "Choral Sym", w. H. Donath (sop), D. Soffel (mez), S. Jerusalem (ten), S. Celibidache (cnd), Munich PO, Munich Phil Chorus *(rec Mar. 19, 1989)* Exclusive ▲ EXL 15 [AAD]

Eisler, H.:Deutsche Sinfonie, w. Hendrikje Wangemann (sop), Annette Markert (alt), Matthias Görne (bar), Gert Gütschow (speaker), Volker Schwarz (speaker), L. Zagrosek (cnd), Leipzig Gewandhaus Orch, Ernst Senff Chorus *(rec Gewandhaus, Leipzig, May 1995)* London ("Entartet Musik" series) ▲ 448389-2 [DDD]

Haydn, J.:Die Jahreszeiten, w. Krisztina Láki (sop), Helmut Wildhaber, S. Kuijken (cnd), La Petite Bande, Flanders Opera Choir Virgin Classics 2-▲ ZDCB 59268

Mendelssohn, F.:St. Paul, w. Soile Isokoski (sop), Rainer Trost (sgr), C. Spering (cnd), Das Neue Orch Opus 111 2-▲ OPS 30-135/136

Romberg, A.:Der Lied von der Glocke, w. B. Schlick (sop), F. Lang (ten), C. Spering (cnd), Das Neue Orch, Cologne Chorus Musicus *(rec May 24-27, 1992)* Opus 111 ▲ OPS 30-67 [DDD]

Stravinsky, I.:Les Noces, w. U. Sonntag (sop), C. Kallisch (cta), M. Schäfer (ten), C. Rausch (bass), et al., W. Schäfer (cnd), Frankfurt Kantorei [G] Koch Schwann ▲ 314 021 [DDD]

Verdi, G.:Requiem Mass, w. Mariana Slavova (sop), Joke Kramer (mez), Alexander Stevenson (ten), P. Kuentz (cnd), Paul Kuentz Orch, Paul Kuentz Choir Pierre Verany 2-▲ PVY 730054 [DDD]

Likic, K. (sop)

Wagner, S.:Der Bärenhäuter, w. B. Johanning (sop—Luise), K. Likic (sop—Lene), T. Koon (sop—Gunda), V. Horn (ten—Hans Kraft), A. Feilhaber (ten—Nikolaus Spitz), R. Hartmann (bar—Kaspar Wild), A. Wenhold (bar—Stranger), A. Waller (bass—Devil), H. Kiichli (bass—Melchior Fröhlich), K. Bach (cnd), Thüringian SO, Thüringian State Theater Chorus *(rec Rudolstadt, July 25-31, 1993)* Marco Polo ("Opera Classics" series) 2-▲ 8.223713/4 [DDD]

Liley, Stephen (ten)

Essentially Christmas, w. East London Chorus, A. Doyle (sop), J. Lister (hp), P. Ayres (org), M. Kibbelwhite (cnd), Locke Brass Consort Koch International Classics ▲ KIC 7202 [DDD]

Purcell, H.:The Indian Queen, w. Tessa Bonner (sop), Sally Bruce-Payne (alt), Edward Caswell (bass), C. Mackintosh (cnd), Purcell Sinfony *(rec St. Bartholomew's Church, Orford, Suffolk, Sept 21-23, 1994)* Linn ▲ CKD 035

Liliani, Sergio (bass)

Verdi, G.:Il trovatore, w. Leyla Gencer (sop—Leonora), Laura Londi (sop—Ines), Fedora Barbieri (mez—Azucena), Mario del Monaco (ten—Manrico), Athos cesarini (ten—Ruiz), Walter Artioli (ten—Messanger) Ettore Bastianini (bar—Count Luna), Plinio Clabassi (bass—Ferrando), Sergio Liliani (bass—Gypsy), F. Previtali (cnd), Milan RAI SO, Milan RAI Chorus *(rec live, Milan, May 29, 1957)* Arkadia 2-▲ 483 [ADD]

Lill, Pille (sop)

Tobias, R.:Des Jonah Sendung, w. Urve Tauts (mez), Peter Svensson (ten), Raimo Laukka (bar), Mati Palm (bass), Ines Maidre (org), N. Järvi (cnd), Estonian State SO, Oratorio Choir, Estonian Phil Chamber Choir, Tallinn Boys' Choir *(rec Estonia Concert Hall, Tallinn, Estonia, June 23-29, 1995)* BIS 2-▲ CD 731/732 [DDD]

Lillie, Beatrice (nar)

Prokofiev, S.:Peter & the Wolf, w. S. Henderson (cnd), London SO [E] London ("Weekend Classics" series) ▲ 436105-2

Prokofiev, S.:Peter & the Wolf, w. S. Henderson (cnd), London SO [E] London ■ 411650-4

Saint-Saëns, C.:Carnival of the Animals, w. Katchen (pno), Graffman (pno), S. Henderson (cnd), London SO [E] London ■ 411650-4

Saint-Saëns, C.:Carnival of the Animals, w. S. Henderson (cnd), London SO [E] London ("Weekend Classics" series) ▲ 436105-2

Lilowa, Margarita (mez)

Cherubini, L.:Médée, w. L. Popp (sop), L. Rysanek (sop), B. Prevedi (ten), N. Ghiuselev (bass), H. Stein (cnd), Vienna State Opera Orch, Vienna State Opera Chorus *(rec live, Vienna 1/31/72)* Melodram 2-▲ CDM 27087 [ADD]

Lima, Luis (ten)

Donizetti, G.:Gemma di Vergy, w. Montserrat Caballe (sop—Gemma), Anna Ringart (mez—Ida), Luis Lima (ten—Tamas), Vicente Sardinero (bar—Il Conte), Juan Pons (bar—Guido), Francois Loup (b—Rolando), A. Gatto (cnd), Nouvel PO, Jean-Paul Kreder (cnd), French Radio Chorus *(rec live, Salle Pleyet, Paris, Apr 20, 1976)* Agorá Music ("Phoenix" series) 2-▲ 501 [ADD]

Massenet, J.:Le Roi de Lahore, w. J. Sutherland (sop), S. Milnes (bar), N. Ghiaurov (bass), R. Bonynge (cnd), National PO London, London Voices London ("Grand Opera" series) 2-▲ 433851-2 [DDD]

Vives, A.:Bohemios, w. M. Bayo (sop), C. Alvarez (bass), A. R. Marbà (cnd), Tenerife SO Valois ▲ V 4711

Limarilli, Gastone (ten)

Rossini, G.:Zelmira, w. Virginia Zeani (sop), Anna Maria Rota (cta), Enrico Campi (bass), Guido Mazzini (bass), Paolo Washington (bass), Giuseppe Moretti (sgr), Nicola Tagger (sgr), C. Francl (cnd), *(orch unknown)* Great Opera Performances 2-▲ GOP 780

Verdi, G.:Attila, w. M. Roberti (sop—Odabella), G. Limarilli (tenor—Foresto), G. Guelfi (baritone—Ezio), B. Christoff (bass—Attila), B. Bartoletti (cnd), Florence Teatro Comunale Orch, Florence Teatro Comunale Chorus *(rec Jan. 12, 1962)* Myto 2-▲ MCD 93589 [DDD]

Verdi, G.:Stiffelio, w. Gulin-Dominguez (sop), G. Guelfi (bar), G. Gavazzeni (cnd), Rome Opera Orch, Rome Opera Chorus *(rec live, Rome 1964)* Melodram 2-▲ MEL 27033

Verdi, G.:I vespri siciliani, w. Leyla Gencer (sop), Giangiacomo Guelfi (bar), Nicola Rossi-Lemeni (bass), G. Gavazzeni (cnd), Rome Opera Orch, Rome Opera Chorus *(rec Dec 5, 1964)* Pantheon 2-▲ PHE 6770

Verdi, G.:I vespri siciliani, w. L. Gencer (sop), G. Guelfi (bar), N. Rossi-Lemeni (bass), G. Gavazzeni (cnd), Rome Opera Orch, Rome Opera Chorus [I] *(rec live, Rome 1964)* Melodram 2-▲ MEL 27037 [ADD]

Limberti, Edmea (sgr)

Verdi, G.:La battaglia di Legnano, w. Caterina Mancini (sop), Amedeo Berdini (bar), Rolando Panerai (bar), Albino Gaggi (bass), Manfredi Ponz de Leon (sgr), F. Previtali (cnd), Rome RAI SO, Rome RAI Chorus *(rec 1951)* Cetra Classic 2-▲ CDON 40 [ADD]

Limmer, Hildegard (sgr)

Strauss, R.:Salome, w. Astrid Varnay (sop—Salome), Hertha Töpper (mez—Der Page der Herodias), Margarete Klose (cta—Herodias), Hans Hopf (ten—Narraboth), Karl Hoppe (ten—1st Nazarene), Karl Ostertag (ten—1st Jew), Julius Patzak (ten—Herodes), Hans Braun (bar—Jochanaan), Benno Kusche (bar—2nd Soldier), Adolf Keil (bass—1st Soldier), Hans Hermann Nissen (bass—Ein Kappadozier), Max Proebstl (bass—2nd Nazarene), Walter Carnotch (sgr—4th Jew), Emil Graf (sgr—3rd Jew), Paul Kaussen (sgr—2nd Jew), Hildegard Limmer (sgr—A slave), Georg Witter (sgr—5th Jew), H. Weigert (cnd), Bavarian RSO *(rec June 21-25, 1953)* Bella Voce 2-▲ BLV 7210 [AAD]

Lind, Eva (sop)

Humperdinck, E.:Hänsel und Gretel, w. B. Bonney (sop), B. Hendricks (sop), A.S. von Otter (mez), H. Schwarz (mez), M. Lipovšek (mez), Andreas Schmidt (bar), J. Tate (cnd), Bavarian RSO, Tölz Boys' Choir [G] EMI Classics 2-▲ CDCB 54022 [DDD]

Jessel, L.:Schwarzwaldmädel (sels), w. F. Fehringer (ten), B. Kusche (bar), Hofmann (sgr), Schörg (sgr), Schubart (sgr), Marszalek (cnd), Cologne RSO, Cologne Radio Chorus [G] Acanta ▲ CD 42552 [DDD]

Mozart, W.A.:Zauberflöte, w. K. Te Kanawa (sop), C. Studer (sop), F. Araiza (ten), O. Bär (bar), S. Ramey (bass), N. Marriner (cnd), Academy of St. Martin in the Fields, Ambrosian Opera Chorus [G] Philips 2-▲ 426276-2 [DDD]

Mozart, W.A.:Zauberflöte (sels), w. K. Te Kanawa (sop), C. Studer (sop), F. Araiza (ten), O. Bär (bar), S. Ramey (bass), N. Marriner (cnd), Academy of St. Martin in the Fields Philips ▲ 438495-2

Offenbach, J.:Les Contes d'Hoffmann, w. J. Norman (sop), C. Studer (sop), A. Sofie von Otter (mez), F. Araiza (ten), S. Ramey (bass), J. Tate (cnd), Dresden Staatskapelle Philips ▲ 438502-2

Lind, Eva (sop) (cont.)
Offenbach, J.:Les Contes d'Hoffmann, w. J. Norman (sop), C. Studer (sop), A. S. von Otter (mez), F. Araiza (ten), S. Ramey (bass), J. Tate (cnd), Dresden Staatskapelle — Philips 3-▲ 422374-2 [DDD]
Strauss (II), Joh.:Die Fledermaus, w. L. Popp (sop), A. Baltsa (mez), P. Domingo (ten), W. Brendel (bar), K. Rydl (bass), P. Domingo (cnd), Munich RSO, Bavarian Radio Chorus [G] — EMI Classics 2-▲ CDCB 47480
Weber, C.M. von:Der Freischütz (sels), w. K. Mattila (sop), F. Araiza (ten), K. Moll (bass), C. Davis (cnd), Dresden Staatskapelle — Philips ▲ 438497-2

Lindauer, Franz (sgr)
Beethoven, L. van:Christus am Ölberg, w. C. Deutekom (sop), L. Kozma (ten), R. Muti (cnd), Venice Teatro La Fenice Orch, Venice Teatro La Fenice Chorus [G] *(rec live, Venice 7/4/70)* — Arkadia ▲ 743 [ADD]

Lindauer, Oldřich (ten)
Reicha, A.:Te Deum, w. Marta Boháčová (sop), Karel Průša (bass), Ladislav Vachulka (org), V. Smetáček (cnd), Prague SO, Kühn Chorus *(rec Cathedral of the Ascension of the Virgin, Karlov, Prague, 1970)* — Panton ▲ PAN 800242 [AAD]

Lindberg-Torlind, Krestin (sop)
Beethoven, L. van:Sym 9, "Choral Sym", w. Else Jena (mez), Erik Sjöberg (ten), Holger Byrding (bass), F. Busch (cnd), Danish National RSO, Danish National Radio Choir — Arlecchino ARL
Brahms, J.:Ein Deutsches Requiem, w. B. Sonnerstedt (bar), W. Furtwängler (cnd), Stockholm PO *(rec 1948)* — Music & Arts 2-▲ CD 289 (m) [AAD]

Lindbloom, Christopher (sgr)
Wayditch, G. von:Jesus before Herod, w. Michael Best (ten—Jappeticus), Christopher Lindbloom (sgr—Philippo/Herod), Eileen Moss (sgr—Pabula), Vincent Russo (sgr—Pabo), Stephen A. Scot-Shepherd (sgr—Luke the Evangelist), Pauline Tweed (sgr—1st & 2nd girls), P. Erös (cnd), San Diego SO, San Diego Master Chorale *(rec 1979)* — VAI Audio 2-▲ VAIA 1095-2 [ADD]

Linde, Hans-Martin (bar)
Bach, J.S.:Anna Magdalena Bach Notebook, w. E. Ameling (sop), G. Leonhardt (hpd), J. Koch (va), A. May (vc)—sels. — Editio Classica ▲ 77150-2-RG [DDD]

Lindemann, Jörn (ten)
Handel, G.F.:Ariodante, w. J. Gondek (sop), L. Saffer (sop), L. Hunt (mez), Jennifer Lane (mez), R. Müller (ten), N. Cavallier (bass), N. McGegan (cnd), Freiburg Baroque Orch, Ralf Popken (cnd), Wilhelmshaven Vocal Ensemble [172-page libretto w. production photos] — Harmonia Mundi France 3-▲ HMC 907146.48

Linden, Hal (sgr)
Porter, C.:Anything Goes, w. E. Rodgers (sgr), *(other artists unknown)* [1962 cast] — Epic ▲ EK 15100 [DAD] ■ JST 15100

Linden, Sylvia (sop)
Diabelli, A.:Pastoralmesse, w. C. Degler (sop), S. Rauschkolb (cta), D. Clayton (ten), H. Müller (bass), E. Ehret (cnd), Munich St. Michael's Orch, Munich St. Michael Choir [L] — Koch Schwann ▲ CD 313015 [ADD]

Lindenstrand, Sylvia (mez)
Börtz, D.:Bacchanterna, w. Peter Mattei (bar), K. Ingebretsen (cnd), Kungliga Hovkapellet [soundtrack to the T.V. production] — Caprice 2-▲ CAP 22028

Lindermeier, Elisabeth (sop)
Wagner, R.:Götterdämmerung, w. Birgit Nilsson (sop—Brünnhilde), Leonie Rysanek (sop—Gutrune), Gerda Sommerschuh (sop—Woglinde), Elisabeth Lindermeier (sop—Wellgunde), Ruth Michaelis (sop—Flohilde), Marianne Schech (sop—Dritte Norne), Ira Malaniuk (mez—Waltraute), Irmgarth Barth (mez—Erste Norne), Hertha Töpper (mez—Zweite Norne), Bernd Aldenhoff (ten—Siegfried), Hermann Uhde (bar—Gunther), Gottlob Frick (bass—Hagen), H. Knappertsbusch (cnd), Bavarian State Opera Orch, Bavarian State Opera Chorus *(rec live, Prinzregententheater, Sept. 1, 1955)* — Orfeo 4-▲ 356944 (m)

Lindevald, April (mez)
Talma, L.:A Wreath of Blessings, w. Gina Scaggs (sop), Drew Martin (ten), Leslie Dorsey (bass), Gregg Smith (cnd), Gregg Smith Singers — Vox Box ("The American Composers" series) 3-▲ CDX 3037
Xenakis, I.:N'shima, w. Catherine Aks (sop), C. Z. Bornstein (cnd), ST-X Ensemble *(rec live, Thread Waxing Space, New York, June 21, 1995)* — Mode ▲ mode 53

Lindholm, Berit (sop)
Berlioz, H.:Les Troyens, w. J. Veasey (mez), J. Vickers (ten), P. Glossop (bar), R. Soyer (bass), C. Davis (cnd), Royal Opera House Orch [F] — Philips 4-▲ 416432-2 [ADD]

Lindholm, Lisbeth (sop)
Schnittke, A.:Requiem, w. K. Salomonsson (sop), I. H. Sjöberg (sop), A. F. Eker (cta), N. Högman (ten), S. Parkman (cnd), Stockholm Sinfonietta, Uppsala Academic Chamber Choir [L] — BIS ▲ CD 497 [DDD]

Lindi, Aroldo (ten)
Verdi, G.:Aida, w. Giannina Arangi-Lombardi (sop—Aida), Maria Capuana (mez—Amneris), Aroldo Lindi (ten—Radames), Giuseppe Nessi (ten—Messenger), Armando Borgioli (bar—Amonasro), Salvatore Baccaloni (bass—King), Tancredi Pasero (bass—Ramfis), L. Molajoli (cnd), La Scala Orch, La Scala Chorus *(rec Nov 1928)* — VAI Audio 2-▲ VAIA 1083-2
Verdi, G.:Il trovatore (sels), w. J. Biel (ten), F. Tamagno (ten), L.-A. Escalaïs (ten), M. Gilion (ten), E. Caruso (ten), A. Paoli (ten), G. Zenatello (ten), J. Sembach (ten), L. Slezak (ten), F. Constantino (ten), G. Martinelli (ten), B. De Muro (ten), N. Fusati (ten), N. Piccaluga (ten), G. Lauri-Volpi (ten), A. Pertile (ten), E. Bergamaschi (ten), R. Tauber (ten), J. O'Sullivan (ten), H. Roswaenge (ten), G. Taccani (ten), V. Lois (ten), H. Lazaro (ten), A. Cortis (ten), F. Merli (ten), F. Völker (ten), J. Kiepura (ten), J. Schmidt (ten), J. Bjoerling (ten), B. Gigli (ten), A. Salvarezza (ten), J. Soler (ten), M. Filippeschi (ten)—34 performances of the Act III tenor aria "Di quella pira!," *(rec from 1903–1956)* — Bongiovanni ▲ GB 1051 [AAD]

Lindroos, Peter (ten)
Bergman, E.:The Singing Tree, w. K. Hannula (sop), C. Hellekant (cta), P. Salomaa (bass), S. Tiilikainen (bar), M. Wallén (bass), U. Söderblom (cnd), Finnish National Opera Orch, Dominante Chamber Choir, Tapiola Chamber Choir — Ondine 2-▲ ODE 794-2D [DDD]
Nielsen, C.:Saul & David, w. T. Kiberg (sop), A. Gjevang (mez), K. Westi (ten), C. Christiansen (bass), A. Haugland (bass), J. Klint (bass), N. Järvi (cnd), Danish National RSO, Danish National Radio Choir [Da] — Chandos 2-▲ CHAN 8911/12 [DDD]

Lindroos, Petri (bar)
Klami, U.:In the Belly of Vipunen, w. S. Oramo (cnd), Finnish RSO, Polytech Men's Choir — Ondine ▲ ODE 859 [DDD]

Lindsay, M. (sop)
Mozart, W.A.:Missa solemnis, K.139, w. G. Schreckenbach (mez), W. Hollweg (ten), W. Grönroos (bar), M. Creed (cnd), Berlin RSO, Berlin RIAS Chamber Choir [L] — LaserLight ▲ 15 883 [DDD]
Mozart, W.A.:Missa solemnis, K.139, w. G. Schreckenbach (mez), W. Hollweg (ten), W. Grönroos (bar), M. Creed (cnd), Berlin RSO, Berlin RIAS Chamber Choir [L] — Capriccio ▲ 10169 [DDD]

Lindsey, Celina (sop)
Gershwin, G.:Porgy & Bess (sels), w. B. Matthews (bar), E. Stratta (cnd), Festival Orch—ten songs, most in concert arrs. by Robert Russell Bennett — Kem-Disc ▲ 1008 [DDD]

Lindskog, Per-Erik (ten)
Roman, J.H.:Te Deum, w. S. Rydén (sop), E. Ericson (cnd), Drottningholm Baroque Ensemble, Eric Ericson Chamber Choir *(rec 1992)* — Musica Sveciae ▲ MSCD 413 [DDD]
Schoenberg, A.:Moses und Aaron, w. David Pittman-Jennings (nar), Gabriele Fontana (sop—Young Girl), Yvonne Naef (cta—Sick Woman), John Graham-Hall (ten—Young Man/Naked Youth), Pår Lindskog (ten—Youth), Chris Merritt (ten—Aaron), Siegfried Lorenz (bar—Another Man), Michael Devlin (b-bar—Ephraimite), László Polgár (bass—Priest), P. Boulez (cnd), Royal Concertgebouw Orch, Winfried Maczewski (cnd), Netherlands Opera Chorus, Zaans Youth Choir, Waterland Music School *(rec Concertgebouw, Amsterdam, Oct 1995)* — Deutsche Grammophon 2-▲ 449 174-2 [DDD]

Lindsley, Celina (sop)
Busoni, F.:Turandot, w. J. Protschka (ten), R. Wörle (ten), R. Pape (bass), G. Albrecht (cnd), Berlin RSO, Berlin RIAS Chamber Choir — Capriccio ▲ 60039 [DDD]

Lindsley, Celina (sop) (cont.)
Martinů, B.:Ariadne, w. V. Dolezal (ten), R. Novák (ten), N. Phillips (bar), V. Neumann (cnd), Czech PO, Czech Phil Chorus [Cz] — Supraphon ▲ 10 4395-2 [DDD]
Schulhoff, E.:The Flames, w. Jane Eaglen (sop—Donna Anna, Nun, Woman, Marguerite), Carola Höhn (sop—Shadow), Celina Lindsley (sop—Shadow), Regina Schudel (sop—Shadow), Iris Vermillion (mez—La Morte), Christiane Berggold (alt—Shadow), Kaja Borris (alt—Shadow), Elvira Dressen (alt—Shadow), Kurt Westi (ten—Don Juan), Johann-Werner Prein (bass—Commendatore), Gerd Wolf (bass—Harlequin), J. Mauceri (cnd), Berlin German SO, Berlin RIAS Chamber Choir *(rec Jesus-Christus Church, Berlin Dahlem, Oct 1993/Apr 1994)* — London 2-▲ 444630-2 [DDD]
Wolf-Ferrari, E.:La vita nuova, w. George Fortune (bar), R. Bader (cnd), Berlin RSO, St. Hedwig's Cathedral Children's Choir — Koch Schwann ▲ SCH 312672 [DDD]

Lindsleyová, C. (sop)
Mysliveček, J.:Belerofonte, w. G. Mayová (sop), K. Lakiová (sop), D. Ahlstedt (ten), R. Gimenéz (ten), S. Margita (ten), Z. Peskó (cnd), Prague CO, Czech Phil Chorus [I] *(rec 1987)* — Supraphon 3-▲ 11 0006-2 [DDD]

Lindström, S. (sgr)
Hallén, A.:Harald der Wiking (act III, final scene), w. M. Meyerson (sgr—Berta), S. Lindström (sgr—Sigrun), A. Ljungholm (sgr—Harald), S. Sjöstedt (sgr—Sigleif), K. Jacobsson (sgr—Gudmund/Torgrim), S. Rybrant (cnd), Malmö SO, Malmö Radio Chorus [G] *(rec 6/6/74)* — Musica Sveciae ▲ MSCD 621 [AAD]

Linker, Tom (voc)
Spasm, w. Michael Lowenstern (b cl), Heather Barringer (voc), Mark Gibbons (voc), Jay Johnson (voc), Jerome Kitzke (voc), Matt Lambiase (voc), Ed Lowenstern (voc), Michael Lowenstern (voc) *(rec Creation Audio, Minneapolis, NYU Studios, New York City & Studio A, Stony Brook, Aug 1994–July 1996)* — New World ▲ 80468-2

Linn, Jürgen (bar)
Adam, A.:Le Postillon de Lunjumeau, w. P. Coburn (sop), R. Swensen (ten), P. Lika (bass), K. Arp (cnd), Kaiserslauten Radio Orch, Stuttgart Chamber Choir [G] — Capriccio 2-▲ 60040-2 [DDD]

Linos, Glenys (sop)
Zemlinsky, A. von:Songs to Poems by Maurice Maeterlinck, w. B. Klee (cnd), Berlin RSO [G] — Koch Schwann ▲ CD 311 053 [ADD]

Lins, Martina (sop)
Fux, J.J.:La Fede sacrilega nella morte del Precursor San Giovanni Battista, "Johannes der Täufer", w. J. Koslowsky (sop), H. Helling (cta), J. Calaminus (ten), G. Schwarz (bass), T. Reuber (cnd), Capella Piccola Neuss [period instrs] [I] — Thorofon 2-▲ CTH 2071/72 [DDD]
Scarlatti, A.:Lamentazioni par la Settimana Santa, w. N. Rime (sop), Parlement de Musique [I] — Opus 111 ▲ 30-66

Linsi, Otto (ten)
Donizetti, G.:Arias, w. Chris Walton (pno)—Eterno amore e fè; Me voglio fa' na casa; Il barcaiolo — Gallo ▲ CD 886 [ADD]
Puccini, G.:Arias, w. Chris Walton (pno)—Terra e mare; Storiella d'amore; Avanti Urania!; Sole e amore — Gallo ▲ CD 886 [ADD]
Rotoli, A.:Songs, w. Chris Walton (pno)—La gondola nera; Ho sognato; Il tuo pensiero — Gallo ▲ CD 886 [ADD]
Tosti, P.F.:Songs, w. Chris Walton (pno)—Io voglio amarti; L'ultima canzone; La serenata; Marechiare; Ideale; Non t'amo più; Rosa; April Serenata popolare — Gallo ▲ CD 886 [ADD]
Verdi, G.:Arias, w. Chris Walton (pno)—Stornello; Non t'accostare all'urna; Brindisi — Gallo ▲ CD 886 [ADD]

Linz, Heinz Maria (bass)
Mussorgsky, M.:Boris Godunov, w. Martha Mödl (sop—Marina Mniszek), Lotte Schädle (sop—Xenia), Dorothea Siebert (mez—Fyodor), Hertha Töpper (mez—Xenia's wet-nurs), Karl Hermann Bennert (Boyer Khrushchyov), Lorenz Fehenberger (ten—Prince Shuysky), Hans Hopf (ten—Grigory), Karl Ostertag (ten—Missail), Hans Hotter (b-bar—Boris Godunov), Hermann Uhde (bar—Andrey Shchelkalov), Kurt Böhme (bass—Varlaam), Kim Borg (bass—Pimen), Kieth Engen (bass—Lewicki), Adolf Keil (bass—Nikitich), Benno Kusche (bar—Rangoni), Heinz Maria Linz (bass—Czernikowski), E. Jochum (cnd), Bavarian RSO, Bavarian Radio Chorus *(rec Munich, May 1957)* — Myto 3-▲ MCD 953131

Lipnik, Lawrence (ct)
Byrd, W.:Songs, w. Tamara Crout (sop), Louis Bagger (hpd), New York Consort of Viols—Rejoice unto the Lord; Delight is dead; Farewell, false love; Who made thee, Hob, forsake the plough?; My mistress had a little dog; Browning (The leaves bee greene); Ye Sacred Muses *(rec Leverett, MA, May 24–26 & June 23, 1993)* — Lyrichord ▲ LEMS 8015 [DDD]

Lipovšek, Marjana (mez)
Bach, J.S.:Magnificat, BWV 243, w. F. Palmer (sop), P. Langridge (ten), N. Harnoncourt (cnd), Vienna Concentus Musicus, Arnold Schoenberg Choir [L] — Teldec ▲ 2292-42984-2
Beethoven, L. van:Missa Solemnis, w. R. Holl (bass), N. Harnoncourt (cnd), CO of Europe, E. Ortner (cnd), Arnold Schoenberg Choir — Teldec 2-▲ 9031-74884-2
Beethoven, L. van:Sym 9, "Choral Sym", w. M. Price (sop), P. Seifert (ten), J.-H. Rootering (bass), W. Sawallisch (cnd), Royal Concertgebouw Orch, Düsseldorf Municipal Choral Society — EMI Classics ▲ CDC 54505
Brahms, J.:Alto Rhap, w. C. Abbado (cnd), Berlin PO, Ernst Senff Chorus [G] — Deutsche Grammophon ▲ 427643-2 [DDD]
Brahms, J.:Alto Rhap, w. L. Hager (cnd), Luxembourg RSO — Forlane ▲ FOR 16671 [DDD]
Brahms, J.:Songs, w. C. Spencer (pno), D. Geringas (vc)—Gestillte Sehnsucht; Geistliches Wiegenlied; Wie Melodien zieht es; Immer leiser wird mein Schlummer; Klage; Auf den Kirchhofe; Der Tod, das ist die kühle Nacht; Wir wandelten; Es schauen die Blumen; Von ewiger Liebe; Die Mainacht; Wie bist du, mein Königin; Wenn du nur zuweilen lächelst; Es träumte mir; Unbewegte laue luft; Im Garten am Seegestade; Lerchengesang; Serenade; Abendregen; Dort in den Weiden steht ein Haus; Da unten im Tale; Och Moder, ich well en Ding han *(rec Apr. 29–May 1, 1992)* — Sony Classical ▲ SK 52490 [DDD]
Bruckner, A.:Mass 3, w. K. Mattila (sop), T. Moser (ten), K. Moll (bass), C. Davis (cnd), Bavarian RSO, Bavarian Radio Chorus [L] — Philips ▲ 422358-2 [DDD]
Enescu, G.:Oedipe, w. B. Hendricks (sop), B. Fassbaender (mez), J. Taillon (mez), N. Gedda (ten), J. Aler (ten), G. Bacquier (bar), Quilico (bar), J. Van Dam (bass-bar), L. Foster (cnd), Monte Carlo PO, Orféon Donostiarra, Petits Chanteurs de Monaco [F] — EMI Classics 2-▲ CDCB 54011 [DDD]
Famous Opera Arias, w. Munich Radio Orch [cnd:Giuseppe Patané] — Orfeo ▲ CD 179891 [DDD] ■ MC 179891 (D)
Handel, G.F.:Messiah, w. Elizabeth Gale (sop), Werner Hollweg (ten), Roderick Kennedy (bass), N. Harnoncourt (cnd), Vienna Concentus Musicus — Teldec 2-▲ 9031-77615-2
Handel, G.F.:Messiah (sels), w. Elizabeth Gale (sop), Werner Hollweg (ten), Roderick Kennedy (bass), N. Harnoncourt (cnd), Vienna Concentus Musicus, Stockholm Chamber Choir [E] — Teldec ▲ 2292-42409-2
Handel, G.F.:Utrecht Te Deum & Jubilate, w. Felicity Palmer (sop), Philip Langridge (ten), N. Harnoncourt (cnd), Vienna Concentus Musicus, Arnold Schoenberg Choir [L] — Teldec ▲ 2292-42984-2
Humperdinck, E.:Hänsel und Gretel, w. B. Bonney (sop), E. Lind (sop), B. Hendricks (sop), A.S. von Otter (mez), H. Schwarz (mez), Andreas Schmidt (bar), J. Tate (cnd), Bavarian RSO, Tölz Boys' Choir [G] — EMI Classics 2-▲ CDCB 54022 [DDD]
Mahler, G.:Kindertotenlieder, w. C. Abbado (cnd), Berlin PO *(rec Sept. 3–4, 1992)* — Sony Classical ▲ SK 53360 [DDD]
Mahler, G.:Das Lied von der Erde, w. T. Moser (ten), G. Solti (cnd), Royal Concertgebouw Orch *(rec live Dec. 1992)* — London ▲ 440314-2
Mahler, G.:Songs from Rückert, w. E. Werba (pno)—omitting "Blicke mir nicht" [G] — Orfeo ▲ 176891 [DDD]
Mahler, G.:Songs from Rückert, w. C. Abbado (cnd), Berlin PO—Ich bin der Welt abhanden gekommen *(rec Sept. 3–4, 1992)* — Sony Classical ▲ SK 53360 [DDD]
Martin, F.:Die Weise von Liebe und Tod des Cornets Christoph Rilke, w. L. Zagrosek (cnd), Austrian RSO [G] — Orfeo ▲ 164881 [DDD]

Lipovšek, Marjana (mez) (cont.)

Mozart, W.A.:Requiem, w. A. M. Blasi (sop), U. Heilmann (ten), J.-H. Rootering (bass), C. Davis (cnd), Bavarian RSO, Bavarian Radio Chorus [L] RCA Red Seal ▲ 09026-60599-2 [DDD] ■ 09026-60599-4 (CrO2) □ 09026-60599-5

Mussorgsky, M.:Boris Godunov, w. V. Valente (sop—Xenia), E. Gorochovskaya (mez—Nurse), L. Nichiteanu (mez—Fyodor), E. Zarmeba (mez—Hostess), M. Lipovšek (cta—Marina), P. Langridge (ten—Prince Shuisky), H. Wildhaber (ten—Misail), A. Fedin (ten—Simpleton), S. Leiferkus (bar—Rangoni), A. Kotcherga (bass—B. Godounov), A. Shagidullin (bass—Shchelkalov), S. Ramey (bass—Pimen), S. Larin (bass—Girgory), G. Nikolsky (bass—Varlaam), C. Abbado (cnd), Berlin PO, Tölz Boys' Choir, Berlin Radio Chorus, Slovak Phil Chorus *(rec Nov. 7-30, 1993)* Sony Classical 3-▲ S3K 58977 [DDD]

Mussorgsky, M.:Khovanshchina, w. V. Atlantov (ten), P. Burchuladze (bass), A. Haugland (bass), C. Abbado (cnd), Vienna State Opera Orch, Slovak Phil Chorus [Shostakovich version] [R] Deutsche Grammophon 3-▲ 429758-2 [DDD]

Mussorgsky, M.:Nursery, w. Graham Johnson (pno) Sony Classical ▲ SK 66858

Mussorgsky, M.:Songs & Dances, w. Graham Johnson (pno) Sony Classical ▲ SK 66858

Mussorgsky, M.:Songs (misc), w. Graham Johnson (pno)—Hebrew Song; Song of the Flea [from Song of Mephistopheles]; Hopak Sony Classical ▲ SK 66858

Mussorgsky, M.:Sunless, w. Graham Johnson (pno) Sony Classical ▲ SK 66858

Prokofiev, S.:Alexander Nevsky, w. S. Bychkov (cnd), Orch de Paris *(rec June 27-29, 1991 & Feb. 2)* Philips ▲ 434070-2

Prokofiev, S.:Cinderella (suites), w. S. Bychkov (cnd), Orch de Paris—No. 1 *(rec June 27-29, 1991 & Feb. 2)* Philips ▲ 434070-2

Puccini, G.:Suor angelica, w. L. Popp (sop), G. Patanè (cnd), Munich RSO, Munich Radio Chorus Eurodisc ▲ 7806-2-RC [DDD]

Schreker, F.:Songs, w. E. Werba (pno)—(5) Ich frag' nach dir; Dies aber kann mein Sehnen; Die Dunkelheit sinkt schwer; Sie sind so schön; Einst gibt ein Tag [G] Orfeo ▲ 176891 [DDD]

Schubert, Franz:Duetsche Messe, w. R. Hansmann (sop), J. Reinprecht (ten), L. Spitzer (pno), F. Wolf (cnd), St. Augustin Orch, St. Augustin Chorus Preiser ▲ 93325

Schubert, Franz:Mass 3, w. R. Hansmann (sop), J. Reinprecht (ten), Spitzer (bass), F. Wolf (cnd), St. Augustin Orch, St. Augustin Chorus Preiser ▲ 93325

Schubert, Franz:Songs (misc), w. G. Parsons (pno)—15 songs [G] Orfeo ▲ 159871 [DDD]

Schumann, R.:Frauenliebe und -leben, w. Graham Johnson (pno) *(rec Konzerthaus, Mozartsaal, Vienna, Oct. 4-6, 1993)* Sony Classical ▲ SK 57972 [DDD]

Schumann, R.:Liederkreis, Op. 39, w. Graham Johnson (pno) *(rec Konzerthaus, Mozartsaal, Vienna, Oct. 4-6, 1993)* Sony Classical ▲ SK 57972 [DDD]

Schumann, R.:Songs, w. Graham Johnson (pno)—Aus den hebräischen Gesängen; Der Nussbaum; Die Lotosblume [all from Myrthen, Op. 25/15, 3 & 7]; Er ist's; Mignon [both from Liederalbum für die Jugend, Op. 79/23 & 28]; Der Soldat [from Fünf Lieder, Op. 40/3]; Kennst du das Land?, Op. 98a/1 *(rec Konzerthaus, Mozartsaal, Vienna, Oct. 4-6, 1993)* Sony Classical ▲ SK 57972 [DDD]

Schumann, R.:Spanische Liebeslieder, w. M. Shirai (mez), J. Protschka (ten), M. Hölle (bass), N. Shetler (pno), N. Deutsch (pno) [G] Capriccio ▲ CDC 10079

Strauss (II), Joh.:Die Fledermaus (sels), w. E. Gruberova (sop), B. Bonney (sop), W. Kmentt (ten), W. Hollweg (ten), J. Protschka (ten), C. Boesch (bar), A. Scharinger (bass), N. Harnoncourt (cnd), Royal Concertgebouw Orch, Netherlands Opera Chorus Teldec ▲ 42427-2

Strauss, R.:Elektra, w. C. Studer (sop), E. Marton (sop), H. Winkler (ten), B. Weikl (bar), W. Sawallisch (cnd), Bavarian RSO, Bavarian Radio Chorus EMI Classics 2-▲ CDCB 54067

Strauss, R.:Songs, w. E. Werba (pno)—Op. 10, Nos. 1,3 & 4; Op. 27, Nos. 1 & 4 [G] Orfeo ▲ 176891 [DDD]

Stravinsky, I.:Oedipus Rex, w. A. Rolfe-Johnson (ten), J. Tomlinson (bass), F. Welser-Möst (cnd), London PO, London Phil Chorus EMI Classics ▲ CDC 54445

Verdi, G.:quattro pezzi sacri, w. C. Studer (sop), J. Carreras (ten), R. Riamondi (bass), C. Abbado (cnd), Vienna PO, Vienna State Opera Chorus Deutsche Grammophon 2-▲ 435884-2

Verdi, G.:Requiem Mass, w. C. Studer (sop), J. Carreras (ten), R. Riamondi (bass), C. Abbado (cnd), Vienna PO, Vienna State Opera Chorus Deutsche Grammophon 2-▲ 435884-2

Verdi, G.:Falstaff, w. E. Norberg-Schulz (sop—Nannetta), L. Serra (sop—Alice), S. Graham (mez—Meg Page), M. Lipovsek (cta—Miss Quickly), K. Begley (ten—Dr. Caius), P. Conti (ten—Ford), M. Luperi (ten—Pistol), J. Van Dam (b-bar—Falstaff), P. LeFebvre (bass—Bardolph), G. Solti (cnd), Berlin PO, Berlin Radio Chorus London ▲ 440650-2 [DDD]

Wagner, R.:Das Rheingold, w. J. Rappé (ten), H. Zednik (ten), P. Haage (ten), A. Schmidt (bar), T. Adam (b-bar), H. Tschammer (bass), K. Rydl (bass), J. Morris (bass), B. Haitink (cnd), Bavarian RSO [G] EMI Classics 2-▲ CDCB 49853 [DDD]

Wagner, R.:Der Ring des Nibelungen (sels), w. E. Marton (sop), C. Studer (sop), K. Te Kanawa (sop), S. Jerusalem (ten), R. Goldberg (ten), P. Haage (ten), J. Morris (bass), B. Haitink (cnd), Bayer RSO EMI Classics ▲ ZDC 54633

Wagner, R.:Wesendonck Songs, w. W. Sawallisch (cnd), Philadelphia Orch EMI Classics ▲ CDC 56165

Wolf, H.:Songs (misc), w. E. Werba (pno)—4 Mignon-Lieder [G] Orfeo ▲ 176891 [DDD]

Lipp, Wilma (sop)

Beethoven, L. van:Sym 9, "Choral Sym", w. F. Wunderlich (ten), F. Crass (bass), O. Klemperer (cnd), Philharmonia Orch, Vienna Singverein Arkadia ▲ 759

Brahms, J.:Choral Music, w. Aafje Heynis (cta), Franz Crass (bar), W. Sawallisch (cnd), Vienna SO, Vienna Singverein—Ein deutsches Requiem, Op. 45; Academic Festival Ov., Op. 80; Tragic Ov., Op. 81; Schicksalslied, Op. 54; Alto Rhap., Op. 53; Var. on a Theme of Haydn, Op. 56a Philips ▲ 438760-2

Janácek, L.:The Excursions of Mr. Brouček, w. Antonie Fahberg (sop—Piccolo), Wilma Lipp (sop—Málinka), Lilian Benningsen (cta—Fanny Nowak), Paul Kuen (ten—Trambahn-Kondukteur), Karl Ostertag (ten—Vorsitzender des Hausbesitzerverbandes), Fritz Wunderlich (ten—Mazal), Kurt Böhme (b-bar—Sakristan von St. Veit), Kieth Engen (bass—Würfl), J. Keilberth (cnd), Bavarian SO *(rec live, Prinzregententheater, Nov. 19, 1959)* Orfeo 2-▲ 354942 (m)

Millöcker, C.:Bettelstudent, w. Wilma Lipp (sop—Laura), Esther Rethy (sop—Bronislava), Rosette Anday (cta—Palmatica), Rudolf Christ (ten—Symon), Kurt Preger (ten—Ollendorf), Eberhard Waechter (bar—Jan), A. Paulik (cnd), Vienna Volksoper Orch, Vienna Volksoper Chorus *(rec Brahmssaal, Vienna, June 1995)* Omega 2-▲ OCD 1018/19 [ADD]

Mozart, W.A.:Arias, w. Arleen Augér (sop), Kathleen Battle (sop), Irma Beilke (sop), Helena Braun (sop), Lisa Della Casa (sop), Maria Cebotari (sop), Ileana Cotrubas (sop), Helen Donath (sop), Mirella Freni (sop), Reri Grist (sop), Edita Gruberova (sop), Elisabeth Grümmer (sop), Hilde Güden (sop), Ingeborg Hallstein (sop), Luise Helletsgruber (sop), Gundula Janowitz (sop), Sena Jurinac (sop), Erika Köth (sop), Evelyn Lear (sop), Margaret Marshall (sop), Edith Mathis (sop), Jarmila Novotna (sop), Margherita Perras (sop), Lucia Popp (sop), Elisabeth Rethberg (sop), Anneliese Rothenberger (sop), Elisabeth Schumann (sop), Elisabeth Schwarzkopf (sop), Graziella Sciutti (sop), Irmgard Seefried (sop), Graziella Sciutti (sop), Julia Varady (sop), Agnes Baltsa (mez), Margit Bokor (mez), Brigitte Fassbaender (mez), Christa Ludwig (mez), Ann Murray (mez), Francisco Araiza (ten), Anton Dermota (ten), Helge Rosvaenge (ten), Rudolf Schock (ten), Peter Schreier (ten), Leopold Simoneau (ten), Eric Tappy (ten), Richard Tauber (ten), Gösta Winbergh (ten), Josef Witt (ten), Fritz Wunderlich (ten), Christian Boesch (bar), Willy Domgraf-Fassbaender (bar), Karl Dönch (bar), Dietrich Fischer-Dieskau (bar), Erich Kunz (bar), Eberhard Wächter (bar), Hans Hotter (b-bar), Paul Schöffler (b-bar), Cesare Siepi (b-bar), José Van Dam (b-bar), Walter Berry (bass), Geraint Evans (bass), Nicolai Ghiaurov (bass), Alexander Kipnis (bass), Richard Mayr (bass), Kurt Moll (bass), James Morris (bass), Ezio Pinza (bass), Martti Talvela (bass), Giorgio Tozzi (bass), Hans Duhan (sgr), Res Fischer (sgr), Marie Gerhart (sgr), *(various orchs & cnds)*—sels from Idomeneo, Die Entführung aus der Serail, Le nozze di Figaro, Don Giovanni, Così fan tutte, Die Zauberflöte & various arias Orfeo d'or ("Festspiel Dokumente" series) 5-▲ 408955

Mozart, W.A.:Missa, K.317, w. Christa Ludwig (alt), Murray Dickie (ten), Walter Berry (bass), J. Horenstein (cnd), Vienna SO Vox Legends 2-▲ CDX 5524

Mozart, W.A.:Missa, K.427, w. C. Ludwig (sop), M. Dickie (ten), W. Berry (bass), F. Grossmann (cnd), Pro Musica Orch, Vienna Oratorio Chorus [L] *(rec stereo, 1958)* Preiser ▲ 90053 [AAD]

Mozart, W.A.:Requiem, w. H. Rössl-Majdan (mez), A. Dermota (ten), W. Berry (bass), H. von Karajan (cnd), Berlin PO, Vienna Singverein [L] *(rec 1961)* Deutsche Grammophon ("Resonance" series) ▲ 429160-2 [ADD] ■ 429160-4

Lipp, Wilma (sop) (cont.)

Mozart, W.A.:Vesperae solennes, w. Christa Ludwig (alt), Murray Dickie (ten), Walter Berry (bass), J. Horenstein (cnd), Vienna SO Vox Legends 2-▲ CDX 5524

Mozart, W.A.:Zauberflöte, w. I. Seefried (sop-Pamina), W. Lipp (sop—Queen of the Night), A. Dermota (ten—Tamino), E. Kunz (bar—Papageno), J. Greindl (bass—Sarastro), W. Furtwängler (cnd), Vienna PO, Vienna State Opera Chorus *(rec live 1951)* EMI Classics ▲ CDMC 65356

Mozart, W.A.:Zauberflöte, w. I. Seefried (sop-Pamina), W. Lipp (sop—Queen of the Night), A. Dermota (ten—Tamino), E. Kunz (bar—Papageno), J. Greindl (bass—Sarastro), H. von Karajan (cnd), Vienna PO, Musikfreunde Chorus [without dialogue; G] *(rec 1950)* EMI Classics ("Studio" series) 2-▲ CDHB 69631 (m)

Mozart, W.A.:Zauberflöte, w. Irmgard Seefried (sop), Peter Klein (ten), Walther Ludwig (ten), Karl Schmitt-Walter (bar), Josef Greindl (bass), Paul Schöffler (sgr), W. Furtwängler (cnd), Vienna PO, Vienna State Opera Chorus *(rec 1949)* Music & Arts 3-▲ CD 882 [AAD]

Mozart, W.A.:Zauberflöte, w. H. Gueden (sop), L. Simoneau (ten), W. Berry (bass), K. Bohme (bass), K. Böhm (cnd), Vienna PO, Vienna State Opera Chorus London ("Grand Opera" series) 2-▲ 414362-2 [ADD]

Mozart, W.A.:Zauberflöte, w. I. Seefried (sop-Pamina), W. Lipp (sop—Queen of the Night), A. Dermota (ten—Tamino), E. Kunz (bar—Papageno), J. Greindl (bass—Sarastro), W. Furtwängler (cnd), Vienna PO, Vienna State Opera Chorus [G] *(rec live, Salzburg, Aug. 6, 1951)* Foyer 3-▲ FOY 2003 [AAD]

Mozart, W.A.:Zauberflöte, w. I. Seefried (sop-Pamina), W. Lipp (sop—Queen of the Night), A. Dermota (ten—Tamino), E. Kunz (bar—Papageno), J. Greindl (bass—Sarastro), W. Furtwängler (cnd), Vienna PO, Vienna State Opera Chorus [G] *(rec live, Salzburg, Aug. 6, 1951)* Arkadia 3-▲ 361 [ADD]

Mozart, W.A.:Zauberflöte (sels), w. I. Seefried (sop), W. Ludwig (ten), K. Schmitt-Walter (bar), J. Greindl (bass), W. Furtwängler (cnd), Vienna PO, Vienna State Opera Chorus—Ov. & 11 arias *(rec live, Salzburg, July, 27, 1949)* Arkadia 3-▲ 361 [ADD]

Strauss (II), Joh.:Die Fledermaus, w. H. Gueden (sop), J. Patzak (ten), A. Dermota (ten), A. Jaresch (ten), A. Poell (b-bar), S. Wagner (mez), K. Preger (ten), C. Krauss (cnd), Vienna PO *(rec early 1950s)* London ("Historic" series) 2-▲ 425990-2 [ADD]

Strauss (II), Joh.:Die Fledermaus (sels), w. Gerda Scheyer (sop), Christa Ludwig (mez), Anton Dermota (ten), Walter Berry (bar), Erich Kunz (bar), Eberhard Wachter (bar), O. Ackermann (cnd), Philharmonia Orch, London Phil Chorus Emperor Operetta ▲ KO 86340

Strauss (II), Joh.:Die Fledermaus (sels), w. R. Schock (ten), O. Schenck (nar), W. Berry (bass), R. Stolz (cnd), Vienna SO [G] Eurodisc ▲ 25-8369 [ADD]

Lippert, Herbert (ten)

Beethoven, L. van:Fidelio (sels), w. Evelyn Herlitzius (sop—Leonore), Ruth Ziesak (sop—Marzelline), Stig Andersen (ten—Florestan), Herbert Lippert (ten—Jaquino), Albert Dohmen (bar—Don Pizarro), Andreas Kohn (bass—Don Fernando), Hans Tschammer (bass—Rocco), G. Solti (cnd), World Orch for Peace, London Voices—Finale Act II *(rec Victoria Hall, Geneva, July 5, 1995)* London ▲ 448901-2 [DDD]

Haydn, J.:Die Schöpfung, w. Ruth Ziesak (sop—Eve & Gabriel), Herbert Lippert (ten—Uriel), Rene Papé (bass—Raphael), Anton Scharinger (bass—Adam), G. Solti (cnd), Chicago SO, Chicago Sym Chorus London 2-▲ 443445-2 [DDD]

Orff, C.:Der Bernauerin, w. L. Popp (sop), Ostermayer (sgr), Laubenthal (ten), K. Eichhorn (cnd), Munich RSO, Munich Radio Chorus [G] Orfeo 2-▲ 255912 [DDD]

Strauss (II), Joh.:Der Zigeunerbaron, w. Pamela Coburn (sop), Christiane Oelze (sop), Julia Hamari (mez), Elisabeth von Magnus (alt), Rudolf Schasching (ten), Wolfgang Holzmair (bar), Jurgen Flimm (sgr), Robert Florianschutz (sgr), Hans-Jurgen Lazar (sgr), N. Harnoncourt (cnd), Vienna SO, Arnold Schoenberg Choir *(rec Vienna, 1994)* Teldec 2-▲ 94555-2

Ullmann, V.:Kaiser von Atlantis, w. C. Oelze (sop—Bubikopf), I. Vermillion (mez—The Drummer), M. Petzold (ten—A Soldier), M. Kraus (ten—Kaiser Overall), H. Lippert (ten—Harlekin), F. Mazura (bar—The Loudspeaker), W. Berry (bass—Death), L. Zagrosek (cnd), Leipzig Gewandhaus Orch London ▲ 440854-2 [DDD]

Lippi, Marcello (bass)

Bellini, V.:I Capuleti e i Montecchi, w. K. Ricciarelli (sop), D. Montague (mez), D. Raffanti (ten), B. Campanella (cnd), Venice Teatro La Fenice Orch, Venice Teatro La Fenice Chorus [I] *(rec 1991)* Nuova Era 2-▲ 7020/21 [DDD]

Cavalli, P.F.:Calisto, w. Maria Bayo (sop), Graham Pushee (ct), Simon Keenlyside (bar), René Jacobs (cnd), Concerto Vocale Harmonia Mundi France 3-▲ HMC 901515/17

Martin Y Soler, V.:Il Tutore Burlato, w. Liliana Marzano (sop—Menica), Maria Angeles Peters (sop—Violante), Juan Diego Florez (ten—Anselmo), Ernesto Palacio (ten—Il Cavaliere), Marcello Lippi (bar—Pippo), Giancarlo Tosi (bass—Don Fabrizio), Michela Forgione (hpd), M. Harth-Bedoya (cnd), Dianopolis Bulgarian CO *(rec VI Festival Internazionale di Gerace nella Chiesa di San Francesco, Aug 16, 1994)* Bongiovanni 2-▲ GB 2175/76-2 [DDD]

Rossini, G.:The Siege of Corinth, w. L. Serra (sop), M. Comencini (ten), D. Raffanti (ten), A. Caforio (bass), P. Olmi (cnd), Genoa Teatro Carlo Felice Orch, Genoa Teatro Carlo Felice Chorus, Prague Phil Chorus *(rec June 2 & 14, 1992)* Nuova Era 3-▲ 7140/42 [DDD]

Lippitz, Isabel (sop)

Mendelssohn, Fanny:Oratorio, w. Annemarie Fischer-Kunz (cta), H. Hatano (ten), T. Thomaschke (bass), E.M. Blankenburg (cnd), Cologne Youth Orch, Cologne Youth Chorus CPO ▲ CPO 999009-2 [DDD]

Mendelssohn, Fanny:Songs, w. Barbara Heller (pno)—23 songs in four groups:Op. 1, Op. 7, Op. 9 & Op. 10 [G] CPO ▲ CPO 999011-2 [DDD]

Schumann, C.:Songs, w. D. Richards (pno)—25 lieder (composed 1834-53)—Walzer; Am Strand; Volkslied; Er ist gekommen; Liebst du um Schönheit; Warum willst du and're fragen; Die gute Nacht; Ich stand in dunklen Träumen; Sie liebten sich beide; Liebeszauber; Der Mond kommt still gegangen; Ich hab' in deinem Auge; Die stille Lotosblume; Loreley; O weh des Scheidens; Beim Abschied; Mein Stern; Der Abendstern; Was weinst du, Blümlein; An einem lichten Morgen; Geheimes Flüstern; Auf einem grünen Hügel; Das ist ein Tag; O Lust, O Lust; Das Veilchen [G] Bayer ▲ 100206 [DDD]

Werfel, A.M.:Songs, w. B. Heller (pno)—Licht in der Nacht; Waldseligkeit; Ansturm; Erntelied; Hymne; Ekstase; Der Erkennende; Lobgesang; Hymne an die Nacht; Die stille Stadt; In meines Vaters Garten; Laue Sommernacht; Bei dir ist es traut; Ich wandle unter Blumen [G] CPO ▲ CPO 999018-2 [DDD]

Lipton, Martha (cta)

Brahms, J.:Alto Rhap, w. G. Cantelli (cnd), New York PO, Westminster Choir *(rec live, 1956)* Legend ▲ LGD 121

Handel, G.F.:Messiah, w. Eileen Farrell (sop), T. Cunningham (ten), William Warfield (bar), E. Ormandy (cnd), Philadelphia Orch, Mormon Tabernacle Choir [E] CBS 2-▲ M2K 00607 ■ M2T 00607

Mahler, G.:Sym 3, w. L. Bernstein (cnd), New York PO, New York Phil Chorus *(rec 1961)* Sony Classical ("Bernstein:The Royal Edition" series) 2-▲ SM2K 47576 [ADD]

Lishner, Leon (bass)

The Yiddish Art Song, w. Lazar Weiner (pno) *(rec mid-1970s)* Omega Classics ▲ OCD 3010 [ADD]

Lisi, Leonardo de (ten)

Castelnuovo-Tedesco, M.:Songs, w. Anna Toccafondi (pno)—Coplas, Op. 7/1; Chansons Grises; "1830", Op. 36; Poems de la Pléiade, Op. 79; Shakespeare Songs Op. 24/1; Poesia Svedese, Op. 189; Sera, Op. 23; Sonetto di Dante, Op. 101; Sonetti del Petrarca, Op. 74; L'infinito, Op. 22; Piccino Picciò, Op. 26 Vocalia ▲ VOC 001 [DDD]

Lisitsian, Pavel (bar)

Gounod, C.:Faust (sels), w. Pavel Lisitsian (bar—Valentin), V. Nebolsin (cnd), Bolshoi Theater Orch—Valentin's Cavatina; Terzetto [w. A. Pirogov (bass—Mephisto), I. Kozlovsky (ten—Faust)]; Valentin's Death Scene *(rec 1954)* Russian Compact Disc ("Talents of Russia" series) ▲ RCD 16025 [ADD]

The Great Armenian Baritone Pearl ▲ PEA 9036 [AAD]

Leoncavallo, R.:Pagliacci (sels), w. Pavel Lisitsian (bar—Silvio), A. Melik-Pashayev (cnd), Bolshoi Theater Orch—Prologue; Duet of Silvio & Nedda [w. N, Shpiller (sop—Nedda)] *(rec 1948)* Russian Compact Disc ("Talents of Russia" series) ▲ RCD 16025 [ADD]

Paval Lisitzian *(rec 1946-62)* Preiser ("Lebendige Vergangenheit" series) ▲ PRE 89061 [ADD]

VOCALISTS

Lisitsian, Pavel (bar) (cont.)
Prokofiev, S.:War & Peace, w. Galina Vishnevskaya (sop—Natasha Rostovoa), Irina Arkhipova (mez—Hélène Bezukhova), Evgenya Verbitskaya (mez—Marya Akhrosimova), Alexi Maslennikov (ten—Anatole Kuragin), Vladimir Petrov (ten—Pierre Bezukhov), Pavel Lisitsian (bar—Napoleon), Alexi Krivchenya (bass—Field-Marshall Kutuzov), Evgeny Kibkalo (sgr—Prince Andrei Bolkonsky), A. Melik-Pashayev (cnd), Bolshoi Theater Orch, Bolshoi Theater Chorus *(rec Moscow, 1961)* Melodiya ("The Russian Opera" series) 3-▲ 74321-29350-2 [ADD]
Puccini, G.:La Bohème (sels), w. Pavel Lisitsian (bar—Marseilles), S. Samosud (cnd), All-Union RSO—Duet of Roudolf & Marseilles [w. S. Lemeshev (ten—Roudolf)] *(rec 1954)* Russian Compact Disc ("Talents of Russia" series) ▲ RCD 16025 [ADD]
Tchaikovsky, P.:Queen of Spades, w. Elena Smolenskaya (sop), Evgenya Verbitskaya (mez), Georgi Nelepp (ten), A. Melik-Pashayev (cnd), Bolshoi Opera Orch, Bolshoi Theater Chorus Arlecchino 3- ARL
Verdi, G.:Arias—Germon's Aria; Duet of Violetta & Germon [both from Traviata; w. E. Shumskaya (sop—Violetta), A. Orlov (cnd), USSR Bolshoi Theatre Orch]; Renato's Ariozo; Renato's scene & aria [both from Masked Ball; w. O. Bron (cnd), Committee of Radioinformation SO]; Duet of Aida & Amonasro [from Aida; w. N. Sokolova (sop—Aida), A. Melik-Pashayev (cnd), USSR Bolshoi Theatre Orch] *(rec 1948, 1952, 1954)* Russian Compact Disc ("Talents of Russia" series) ▲ RCD 16025 [ADD]

Lisken, Emmy (cta)
Weber, C.M. von:Missa sancta 2, w. Gertrude Stoklassa (sop), Manfred Raucamp (ten), Hans Kagel (bass), R. Bader (cnd), Stuttgart PO, Stuttgart Phil Chorus Koch Schwann ▲ SCH CD 316372

Lisowska, Hanna (sop)
Mahler, G.:Sym 2, w. J. Rappé (ten), A. Wit (cnd), Polish National RSO Katowice, Cracow Polish Radio-TV Chorus *(rec Jan. 9-17, 1993)* Naxos 2-▲ 8.550523/24 [DDD]

List, Emanuel (bass)
Emanuel List *(rec 1927-51)* Preiser ("Lebendige Vergangenheit" series) ▲ PRE 89083 [AAD]
Wagner, R.:Götterdämmerung (sels), w. Frida Leider (sop), Kerstin Thorborg (mez), Lauritz Melchior (ten), Herbert Janssen (bar), Maria Nezadál (sgr), T. Beecham (cnd), London PO, Royal Opera House Chorus Covent Garden *(rec Covent Garden, London, 1936)* Preiser ▲ PRE 90266
Wagner, R.:Die Meistersinger von Nürnberg (sels), w. E. Marherr-Wagner (mez), R. Hutt (ten), K. Jöken (bar), F. Schorr (b-bar), L. Schützendorf (sgr), L. Blech (cnd), Berlin State Opera Orch, Berlin State Opera Chorus—Act 1:Hilf Gott! Will ich denn Schuster sein?; Das schöne Fest, Johannistag; Act 2:Johannistag! Johannistag!; Hab' ich heut' Singstund'?; Jerum! Jerum!; Act 3:Gleich, Meister! Hier!; Grüss' Gott, mein Evchen...Weilten die Stern' im lieblichen Tanz...O Sachs! Mein Freund!; Sankt Krispin, lobet ihn!; Silentium!...Wach' auf!; Verachtet mir die Meister nicht [G] *(rec Staatsoper unter den Linden, 5/22/28)* Pearl ▲ PEA 9340 (m) [AAD]
Wagner, R.:Der Ring des Nibelungen (sels), w. Florence Austral (sop), Frieda Leider (sop), Elsie Suddaby (sop), Göta Ljunberg (sop), Walter Widdop (ten), Horst Laubenthal (ten), Lauritz Melchoir (ten), Friedrich Schorr (bar), Rudolf Bockelmann (b-bar), Ivar Andresen (bass), Emmanuel List (bass), Collingwood, Blech, Coates, Barbirolli, Heger, Alwin, Muck (cnd), London SO—scenes from Siegriend & Götterdämmerung; 90 Motives from Der Ring [w. Collingwood & LSO] Pearl 7-▲ PEA 9137 [ADD]
Wagner, R.:Tristan und Isolde, w. Kirsten Flagstad (sop), Sabine Kalter (cta), Lauritz Melchoir (ten), F. Reiner (cnd), London PO Enterprise ("The Radio Years" series) 3-▲ ENT 39 (m)
Wagner, R.:Tristan und Isolde, w. K. Flagstad (sop), S. Kalter (cta), L. Melchior (ten), H. Janssen (bar), F. Reiner (cnd), Royal Opera House Orch, Royal Opera House Chorus Covent Garden [G] *(rec live, Covent Garden May/June 1936)* VAI Audio 3-▲ VAIA 1004-3 (m) [ADD]
Wagner, R.:Die Walküre (act 1), w. L. Lehmann (sop), B. Walter (cnd), Vienna PO [G] *(rec 6/20-22/35)* Danacord 2-▲ DACOCD 317/18 (m)
Wagner, R.:Die Walküre (act 1), w. L. Lehmann (sop), L. Melchior (ten), B. Walter (cnd), Vienna PO *(rec 1935)* EMI Classics ("Great Recordings of the Century" series) ▲ CDH 61020 (m) [ADD]
Wagner, R.:Die Walküre (act 2), w. M. Fuchs (sop), E. Flesch (sop), L. Lehmann (sop), M. Klose (cta), L. Melchior (ten), H. Hotter (b-bar), A. Jerger (b-bar), B. Walter (cnd), Berlin State Opera Orch [G] *(rec 9/38 & 6/22/35)* Danacord 2-▲ DACOCD 317/18 (m)
Wagner, R.:Die Walküre (act 2), w. M. Fuchs (sop), E. Flesch (sop), L. Lehmann (sop), M. Klose (cta), L. Melchior (ten), H. Hotter (b-bar), A. Jerger (b-bar), B. Walter (cnd), Berlin State Opera Orch [G] *(rec 9/38 & 6/22/35)* EMI Classics ("References" series) ▲ CDH 64255

List, Karyn (sop)
Rutter, J.:Requiem, w. Kathy Farmer (fl), Barbara Cook (ob), Julie Albertson (hp), Mary Alice Swope (vc), Tom Alderman (org), Jennifer Mautz (timp), Mike Del Campo (perc), Michael O'Neal (cnd), Michael O'Neal Singers *(rec Roswell United Methodist Church, Atlanta, GA, Mar 27, 1995)* ACA Digital Recording ▲ CM 20048 [DDD]

Litten, Jack (ten)
Westergaard, P.:Mr. & Mrs. Discobbolos, w. Valerie Lamoree (sop), H. Sollberger (cnd), Group for Contemporary Music CRI ▲ CD 696 [ADD]

Litz, Gisela (mez)
Bach, J.S.:Masses, BWV 233-36, "Lutheran Masses", w. A. Giebel (sop), H. Prey (bar), K. Redel (cnd), Pro Arte Orch, Pro Arte Chorale—BWV 233 in F Philips 2-▲ 438739-2
Strauss (II), Joh.:Der Zigeunerbaron (sels), w. Rita Streich (sop), Grace Bumbry (mez), Biserka Cvejic (mez), Nicolai Gedda (ten), Hermann Prey (bar), Kurt Bohme (bass), F. Allers (cnd), Munich Bavarian State Opera Orch, Munich Bavarian State Opera Chorus Emperor Operetta ▲ KO 86346

Liufau, M. (sgr)
Rodgers, R.:The King & I, w. J. Andrews (sgr—Anna Leonowens), L. Salonga (sgr—Tuptim), B. Kingsley (sgr—The King), P. Bryson (sgr—Lun Tha), M. Horne (mez—Lady Thiang), M. Liufau (sgr—Prince Chulalongkorn), E. Kingsley (sgr—Louis Leonowens), R. Moore (sgr—Sir Edward Ramsay), M. Sheen (sgr—The Kralahome), J. Mauceri (cnd), Hollywood Bowl Orch, Los Angeles Master Chorale *(rec Culver City, CA, Apr 1992)* Philips ▲ 438007-2 [DDD]

Liviabella, Sergio (sgr)
Verdi, G.:La forza del destino, w. Zinka Milanov (sop—Donna Leonora di Vargas), Rosalind Elias (mez—Preziosilla), Luisa Gioia (sgr—Curra), Angelo Mercuriali (ten—Trabuco), Giuseppe di Stefano (ten—Son Alvaro), Leonard Warren (bar—Don Carlos di Vargas), Giorgio Tozzi (b-bar—Padre guardiano), Dino Mantovani (bar—Fra Melitone), Paolo Washington (b-bar—Il marchese di Calatrava), Virgilio Carbonari (b-bar—un alcalde), Sergio Liviabella (sgr—un chirurgo), F. Previtali (cnd), St. Cecilia Academy Orch Rome, St. Cecilia Academy Chorus Rome [I] London ▲ 443678-2 [ADD]

Livingston, J. (mez)
Puccini, G.:Madama Butterfly, w. V. de los Angeles (sop—Madama Butterfly), B. Howitt (mez—Suzuki), J. Livingston (mez—Kate), J. Lanigan (ten—Pinkerton), D. Tree (ten—Goro), D. A. (ten—Yamadori), G. Evans (bar—Sharpless), M. Langdon (bass—Bonzo), R. Kempe (cnd), Royal Opera House Orch, Royal Opera House Chorus Covent Garden *(rec London, May 1957)* Ornamenti 2-▲ FE 112 [ADD]

Livingstone, Kathleen (sop)
Program 3, w. Arnold Dolmetsch (vlr), François (trb rcr), Jeanne Dolmetsch (trb rcr), Marguerite Dolmetsch (vl), Nigel Foster (hpd), John Hancorn (bass), Jennifer Bate (org), et al. IMP Allegro ▲ PCD 995 [DDD]

Livora, František (ten)
Janácek, L.:Slavonic Mass, w. Gabriela Benacková (sop), Vera Soukupová (cta), Karel Pruss (bass), V. Neumann (cnd), Czech PO, Czech Phil Chorus Panton ▲ PAN 811217
Janácek, L.:Slavonic Mass, w. Elisabeth Söderström (sop), Drahomira Drobkova (cta), Richard Novák (bass), C. Mackerras (cnd), Czech PO, Czech Phil Chorus Supraphon ▲ SUP 103575 [DDD]
Novák, V.:Storm, w. Jarmila Zilková (sop), Jarmila Smycková (sop), Z. Košler (cnd), Czech PO, Czech Phil Chorus Supraphon ▲ SUP CD 3088

Ljungberg, Göta (sop)
Wagner, R.:Der fliegende Holländer (sels), w. Elisabeth Rethberg (sop), Elisabeth Schumann (sop), Rudolf Laubenthal (ten), Lauritz Melchior (ten), Friedrich Schorr (bar), *(cnd & orch unknown) (rec 1927-31)* Preiser 2-▲ PRE 89214 [AAD]
Wagner, R.:Götterdämmerung (sels), w. Elisabeth Rethberg (sop), Elisabeth Schumann (sop), Rudolf Laubenthal (ten), Lauritz Melchior (ten), Friedrich Schorr (bar), *(cnd & orch unknown) (rec 1927-31)* Preiser 2-▲ PRE 89214 [AAD]

Ljungberg, Göta (sop) (cont.)
Wagner, R.:Die Meistersinger von Nürnberg (sels), w. Elisabeth Rethberg (sop), Elisabeth Schumann (sop), Rudolf Laubenthal (ten), Lauritz Melchior (ten), Friedrich Schorr (bar), *(cnd & orch unknown) (rec 1927-31)* Preiser 2-▲ PRE 89214 [AAD]
Wagner, R.:Das Rheingold (sels), w. Elisabeth Rethberg (sop), Elisabeth Schumann (sop), Rudolf Laubenthal (ten), Lauritz Melchior (ten), Friedrich Schorr (bar), *(cnd & orch unknown) (rec 1927-31)* Preiser 2-▲ PRE 89214 [AAD]
Wagner, R.:Der Ring des Nibelungen (sels), w. Florence Austral (sop), Frieda Leider (sop), Elsie Suddaby (sop), Walter Widdop (ten), Horst Laubenthal (ten), Lauritz Melchoir (ten), Friedrich Schorr (bar), Rudolf Bockelmann (b-bar), Ivar Andresen (bass), Emmanuel List (bass), Collingwood, Blech, Coates, Barbirolli, Heger, Alwin, Muck (cnd), London SO—scenes from Siegriend & Götterdämmerung; 90 Motives from Der Ring [w. Collingwood & LSO] Pearl 7-▲ PEA 9137 [ADD]
Wagner, R.:Tannhäuser (sels), w. Elisabeth Rethberg (sop), Elisabeth Schumann (sop), Rudolf Laubenthal (ten), Lauritz Melchior (ten), Friedrich Schorr (bar), *(cnd & orch unknown) (rec 1927-31)* Preiser 2-▲ PRE 89214 [AAD]
Wagner, R.:Die Walküre (sels), w. Elisabeth Rethberg (sop), Elisabeth Schumann (sop), Rudolf Laubenthal (ten), Lauritz Melchior (ten), Friedrich Schorr (bar), *(orch unknown) (rec 1927-31)* Preiser 2-▲ PRE 89214 [AAD]
Wagner, R.:Die Walküre (sels), w. F. Leider (sop), E. Leisner (cta), F. Schorr (b-bar), L. Blech (cnd), Vienna State Opera Orch—nine selections from Acts 2 & 3 [G] *(rec 1927 [Blech] & 1932 [Barb)* Pearl ▲ PEA 9357 (m) [AAD]

Ljungholm, A. (sgr)
Hallén, A.:Harald der Wiking (act III, final scene), w. M. Meyerson (sgr—Berta), S. Lindström (sgr—Sigrun), A. Ljungholm (sgr—Harald), S. Sjöstedt (sgr—Sigleif), K. Jacobsson (sgr—Gudmund/Torgrim), S. Rybrant (cnd), Malmö SO, Malmö Radio Chorus [G] *(rec 6/6/74)* Musica Sveciae ▲ MSCD 621 [AAD]

Ljungman, Lars (sgr)
Nilsson, T.:Out of Earthly Night, w. Gudrun Bruna (sop), Marianne Mellnäs (sop), Kaysa Hälldin (alt), Lars Sjögren (ten), Göran Swartz (bass), Sture Hedin (sgr), Ola Kyhlberg (sgr), Nils Philipson (sgr), Ulrik Quale (sgr), Nils Spangenberg (sgr), Britta Therén (sgr), Karl-Erik Welin (org), Torsten Nilsson (cnd), Oscar's Motet Choir *(rec Oscar's Church, Stockholm, Sweden, Apr 26-27, 1978)* BIS ▲ CD 138 [AAD]

Lloyd, Barbara (sgr)
Ashley, R.:Purposeful Lady Slow Afternoon, w. Cynthia Liddell (nar), Mary Ashley (sgr), Mary Lucier (sgr) Lovely Music ▲ LCD 1002 [AAD]

Lloyd, David (ten)
Donizetti, G.:Lucia di Lammermoor, w. E. Gruberová (sop), A. Kraus (ten), R. Bruson (bar), Royal PO, Ambrosian Opera Chorus *(rec 1983)* EMI Classics ▲ CDMB 64622

Lloyd, Edward (ten)
Handel, G.F.:Messiah (sels), w. Adele Addison (sop), Russell Oberlin (ct), William Warfield (bar), L. Bernstein (cnd), New York PO, Westminster Choir [E] CBS ▲ MYK 38481 ■ MYT 38481

Lloyd, Robert (bass)
Beethoven, L. van:Mass, Op. 86, w. A. Tomwa-Sintow (sop), P. Payne (mez), R. Tear (ten), C. Davis (cnd), London SO, London Sym Chorus [G] Philips 2-▲ 438362-2
Beethoven, L. van:Missa Solemnis, w. A. Tomwa-Sintow (sop), P. Payne (mez), R. Tear (ten), C. Davis (cnd), London SO, London Sym Chorus [G] Philips 2-▲ 438362-2
Berg, A.:Wozzeck, w. E. Farrell (sop), F. Jagel (ten), M. Harrell (bar), D. Mitropoulos (cnd), New York PO *(rec live 1950)* Andromeda ▲ ANR 2514 [ADD]
Berlioz, H.:Roméo et Juliette, w. N. Denize (mez), V. Cole (ten), E. Inbal (cnd), Frankfurt RSO, Frankfurt Radio Chorus Denon 2-▲ CO 73210/11 [DDD]
Britten, H.:The Beggar's Opera, w. A. Collins (sop—Mrs. Peachum), A. Murray (mez—Polly Peachum), P. Langridge (ten—MacHeath), R. Lloyd (b-bar—Peachum), *(not advised of orchestra & chorus)*, S. Bedford (cnd) Argo 2-▲ 436850-2 [DDD]
Britten, H.:A Midsummer Night's Dream, w. Sylvia McNair (sop—Tytania), Brian Asawa (ct—Oberon), C. Davis (cnd), London SO Philips 2-▲ 454 122-2
Elgar, E.:The Apostles, w. A. Hargan (sop), A. Hodgson (cta), D. Rendall (ten), S. Roberts (bar), B. Terfel (bass-bar), R. Hickox (cnd), London SO, London Sym Chorus [E] Chandos 2-▲ CHAN 8875/76 [DDD]
Handel, G.F.:Acis & Galatea [arr Mozart], w. E. Mathis (sop), R. Gambill (ten), A R. Johnson (ten), P. Schreier (cnd), Austrian RSO, Austrian Radio Chorus [E] Orfeo 2-▲ 133852 [DDD]
Handel, G.F.:Messiah, w. Sylvia McNair (sop), Anne Sofie von Otter (mez), Michael Chance (alt), Jerry Hadley (ten), N. Marriner (cnd), Academy of St. Martin in the Fields [E] *(rec live, Dublin 4/13/92)* Philips 2-▲ 434695-2 [DDD]
Handel, G.F.:Messiah (reorchd Mozart), w. Felicity Lott (sop), Felicity Palmer (sop), Phillip Langridge (ten), C. Mackerras (cnd), Royal PO, Huddersfield Choral Society [E] ASV ▲ ASV CD 960
Handel, G.F.:Semele, w. Norma Burrowes (sop), Patrizia Kwella (sop), Elizabeth Priday (sop), Catherine Denley (mez), Della Jones (mez), Timothy Penrose (alt), Anthony Rolfe-Johnson (ct), Maldwyn Davies (ten), David Thomas (bass), J. E. Gardiner (cnd), English Baroque Soloists, Monteverdi Choir London Erato 2-▲ 2292-45982-2
Massenet, J.:Werther, w. F. von Stade (mez), J. Carreras (ten), T. Allen (bar), C. Davis (cnd), Royal Opera House Orch Covent Garden, Royal Opera House Chorus Covent Garden [F] Philips 2-▲ 416654-2 [ADD]
Mozart, W.A.:Ave verum corpus, w. K. Te Kanawa (sop), A. Sofie von Otter (mez), A. R. Johnson (ten), N. Marriner (cnd), Academy of St. Martin in the Fields, Academy Chorus *(rec London, Mar. 10-12, 1993)* Philips ▲ 438999-2
Mozart, W.A.:Complete Mozart Edition, w. L. Popp (sop), J. Baker (mez), Y. Minton (mez), F. von Stade (mez), S. Burrows (ten), C. Davis (cnd), Royal Opera House Orch, Royal Opera House Chorus Covent Garden Philips 2-▲ 422544-2 [ADD]
Mozart, W.A.:Don Giovanni, w. S. Sweet (sop), K. Mattila (sop), M. McLaughlin (sop), F. Araiza (ten), T. Allen (bar), S. Alaimo (b-bar), N. Marriner (cnd), Academy of St. Martin in the Fields, Ambrosian Opera Chorus Philips 3-▲ 432129-2 [DDD]
Mozart, W.A.:Don Giovanni (sels), w. K. Mattila (sop), F. Araiza (ten), T. Allen (bar), N. Marriner (cnd), Academy of St. Martin in the Fields Philips ▲ 438494-2
Mozart, W.A.:Finta semplice, w. Helen Donath (sop), Jutta-Renate Ihloff (sop), Teresa Berganza (mez), A. Rolfe Johnson (ten), Thomas Moser (ten), Robert Holl (bass), L. Hager (cnd), Salzburg Mozarteum Orch [I] Orfeo 3-▲ 085843 [DDD]
Mozart, W.A.:Missa, K.427, w. K. Te Kanawa (sop), A. Sofie von Otter (mez), A. R. Johnson (ten), N. Marriner (cnd), Academy of St. Martin in the Fields, Academy of St. Martin in the Fields Chorus *(rec London, Mar. 10-12, 1993)* Philips ▲ 438999-2
Mozart, W.A.:Requiem, w. S. McNair (sop), C. Watkinson (cta), F. Araiza (ten), N. Marriner (cnd), Academy of St. Martin in the Fields, Academy Chorus [L] Philips ▲ 432087-2 [DDD]
Mozart, W.A.:Zauberflöte, w. B. Hendricks (sop—Pamina), J. Anderson (sop—Queen of the Night), U. Steinsky (sop—Papagena), J. Hadley (ten—Tamino), T. Allen (bar—Papageno), R. Lloyd (bass—Sarastro), C. Mackerras (cnd), Scottish CO, Scottish Chamber Chorus [G] Telarc 2-▲ CD 80302 [DDD]
Mozart, W.A.:Zauberflöte (sels), w. B. Hendricks (sop), J. Hadley (ten), J. Anderson (sop), T. Allen (bar), U. Steinsky (cnd), Scottish CO, Scottish Sym Chorus *(rec July 13-22, 1991)* Telarc ▲ CD 80345 [DDD]
Mussorgsky, M.:Songs & Dances, w. M. Jansons (cnd), Philadelphia Orch EMI Classics ▲ CDC 55232
Rossini, G.:Il barbiere di Siviglia (sels), w. A. Baltsa (mez), S. Burgess (mez), F. Araiza (ten), T. Allen (bar), D. Trimarchi (bar), N. Marriner (cnd), Academy of St. Martin in the Fields Philips ▲ 438498-2
Saint-Saëns, C.:Samson et Dalila, w. E. Obraztsova (mez), P. Domingo (ten), R. Bruson (bar), D. Barenboim (cnd), Orch de Paris Deutsche Grammophon 2-▲ 413297-2 [ADD]
Verdi, G.:Requiem Mass, w. Michèle Crider (sop), Markella Hatziano (mez), Gabriel Sadé (ten), R. Hickox (cnd), London SO, London Sym Chorus Chandos ▲ CHAN 9490
Verdi, G.:Rigoletto, w. E. Gruberova (sop), B. Fassbaender (mez), Schicoff (ten), R. Bruson (bar), G. Sinopoli (cnd), St. Cecilia Academy Orch Rome, St. Cecilia Academy Chorus Rome [I] Philips 2-▲ 412592-2 [DDD]

Lochak, Anatoly (sgr)

Rubinstein, A.:The Demon, w. Ludmilla Andrew (sop—Nanny), Marina Mescheriakova (sop—Tamara), Alison Browner (mez—Angel), Anatoly Lochak (sgr—Demon), Richard Robson (sgr—Old Servant), Valery Serkin (sgr—Prince Sinodal), Wjacheslav Weinorowski (sgr—Messenger), Leonid Zimnenko (sgr—Prince Gudal), A. Anissimov (cnd), Irish National SO, Gregory Rose (cnd), Wexford Festival Opera Chorus *(rec Wexford, Oct & Nov, 1994)* Marco Polo 2-▲ 8.223781-2 [DDD]

Lochner, A. (nar)

Debussy, C.:Chansons de Bilitis (recitation), w. A. Adorjan (fl), M. Larrieu (fl), S. Mildonian (hp), Y. Nagae (hp), E. Sun (cel) [F] Quantum ▲ QM 6912 [DDD]

Locke, Josef (ten)

Hear My Song EMI Classics ▲ CDC 54632

Loeffler, Hans (ten)

Mozart, W.A.:Requiem, w. S. Jurinac (sop), L. West (alt), F. Gutherie (bass), H. Scherchen (cnd), Vienna State Opera Orch, Vienna State Opera Chorus *(rec 1958)* Andromeda ▲ ANR 2525 [ADD]

Mozart, W.A.:Requiem, w. S. Jurinac (sop), L. West (alt), F. Gutherie (bass), R. Leibowitz (cnd), Vienna State Opera Orch, Vienna State Opera Chorus [L] *(rec 1958)* MCA Classics 2-▲ MCAD2 9816 [AAD]

LoForese, A. (ten)

Verdi, G.:Don Carlos, w. A. Cerquetti (sop), F. Barbieri (mez), E. Bastianini (bar), C. Siepi (b–bar), G. Neri (bass), A. Votto (cnd), Florence Maggio Musicale Orch, Florence Maggio Musicale Chorus *(rec July 16, 1956)* Melodram 3-▲ MLO 670104 [ADD]

Logan, Johnny (ten)

Danova, R.:The Phantom of the Opera on Ice, w. Susannah Glanville (sop), Kathy Dooley (sop), Stephen Lee Garden (ten), Mungo Jerry (bar), Nigel Paul (bar), P. Whitfield (cnd), Northern Light SO, Northern Light Choir, Russian Stars on Ice Chorus Plaza ▲ PZA 008

Loghin, Valentin (bass)

Rossini, G.:Il barbiere di Siviglia, w. Magda Ianculescu (sop—Rosina), Maria Sandulescu (mez—Berta), Valentin Teodorian (ten—Count Almaviva), Nicolae Herlea (bar—Figaro), Stefan Petrescu (bar—Fiorello), Constantin Gabor (bass—Don Bartolo), Valentin Loghin (bass—Don Basilio), M. Brediceanu (cnd), Romanian Opera Orch, Romanian Opera Chorus *(rec 1960-61)* Vox Box 2-▲ CDX 5159

Verdi, G.:La traviata, w. Elena Simionescu (sop—Annina), Virginia Zeani (sop—Violetta Valery), Elisabeta Neculce-Cartis (mez—Flora Bervoix), Ion Buzea (ten—Alfredo Germont), Vasile Moldoveanu (ten—Gastone/Viconte de Letorieres/Giuseppe), Teodor Panea (ten—Flora's Servant), Constantin Dumitru (bar—Commissioner/Baron Douphol), Nicolae Herlea (bar—Giorgio Germont), Valentin Loghin (bass—Marchese D'Obigny), Nicolae Rafael (bass—Doctor Grenvil), J. Bobescu (cnd), Romanian Opera Orch, Stelian Olariu (cnd), Romanian Opera Chorus *(rec 1968)* Vox Box 2-▲ CDX 5154

Logue, Joan (sop)

Dashow, J.:Some Dream Songs, w. M. Buffa (vn), G. Simonacci (pno)—[E] CRI ▲ CD 578 [DDD]

Lohnes, Nelson (bass)

Somers, H.:Kyrie, w. Roxolana Roslak (sop), Susan Cooper (mez), Robert Missen (ten), Timothy Cadan (bass), E. Iseler (cnd), *(orch unknown),* Elmer Iseler Singers *(rec Flora McRae Eaton Memorial Auditorium & St. Anne's Anglican Church, Toronto)* Centrediscs ▲ CMC 5495 [DDD]

Loibl, Josef (bar)

Ballads FSM ▲ 97216 [ADD]

Brahms, J.:Songs, w. N. Shelter (pno)—15 songs FSM ▲ FCD 97201 [DDD]

Schubert, Franz:Songs (misc), w. E. Werba (pno), N. Shelter (pno)—13 Goethe-Lieder FSM ▲ FCD 97202 [DDD]

Schumann, R.:Liederkreis, Op. 24, w. N. Shetler (pno) [G] FSM ▲ FCD 97719 [DDD]

Wolf, H.:Songs (misc), w. N. Shelter (pno)—14 Songs FSM ▲ FCD 97201 [DDD]

Wolf, H.:Songs (misc), w. E. Werba (pno), N. Shelter (pno)—10 Goethe-Lieder FSM ▲ FCD 97202 [DDD]

Lois, V. (ten)

Verdi, G.:Il trovatore (sels), w. J. Biel (ten), F. Tamagno (ten), L.-A. Escalaïs (ten), M. Gilion (ten), E. Caruso (ten), A. Paoli (ten), G. Zenatello (ten), J. Sembach (ten), L. Slezak (ten), F. Constantino (ten), G. Martinelli (ten), B. De Muro (ten), N. Fusati (ten), N. Piccaluga (ten), G. Lauri-Volpi (ten), A. Pertile (ten), E. Bergamaschi (ten), R. Tauber (ten), J. O'Sullivan (ten), H. Roswaenge (ten), G. Taccani (ten), H. Lazaro (ten), A. Lindi (ten), A. Cortis (ten), F. Merli (ten), F. Völker (ten), J. Kiepura (ten), J. Schmidt (ten), J. Bjoerling (ten), B. Gigli (ten), A. Salvarezza (ten), J. Soler (ten), M. Filippeschi (ten)—34 performances of the Act III tenor aria "Di quella pira!," *(rec from 1903-1956)* Bongiovanni ▲ GB 1051 [AAD]

Lojarro, Daniella (sop)

Ricci, L.:Crispino e la cornare, w. A. Lazzarini (mez), Cossutta (ten), S. Alaimo (bar), R. Coviello (bar), A. Marani (bass), R. Ristori (bass), Benori (sgr), Siclari (sgr), P. Carignani (cnd), San Remo SO, San Remo Sym Chorus [l] *(rec live 11/89)* Bongiovanni 2-▲ GB 2095/96 [DDD]

Verdi, G.:Rigoletto (sels), w. Elizabeth Carter (sgr), Roberto Serville (bar), Boiko Zvetanov (sgr)—Ov; Questa o quella; Pari siamo! Io la lingua—Figlia! Mio Padre; Giovanna, ho Dei rimorsi; Gualtier Maldé – Caro nome; Ella mi fu rapita!; Scorrendo uniti remota via; Cortigiani, vil razza danata; plus others Laserlight ▲ 14207 [DDD]

Lomanto, Enzo de Muro (ten)

Donizetti, G.:Lucia di Lammermoor, w. M. Capsir (sop—Lucia), E. de Muro Lomanto (ten—Sir Ravenswood), E. Venturini (ten—Lord Bucklaw), E. Molinari (bar—Lord Ashton), S. Baccaloni (bass—Bidebent), L. Molajoli (cnd), La Scala Orch, La Scala Chorus *(rec 1933)* Myto 2-▲ 2MCD 94299

Enzo De Muro Lomanto Bongiovanni ▲ GB 1047 [ADD]

Lombard, J. (sop)

Finney, R.L.:Chamber Music (36 songs), w. M. Norris (pno) Master Musicians Collective ▲ MMC 2012

Lombardi, G. A. (sop)

Mascagni, P.:Cavalleria rusticana, w. I. Mannarini (mez), M. Castagna (mez), A. Melandri (ten), G. Lulli (bar), L. Molajoli (cnd), La Scala Orch, La Scala Chorus *(rec 1930)* Preiser ▲ 90042 (m) [AAD]

Lombardi, William (ten)

Garcia, J.M.N.:Motets, w. Katharina Ott (sop), Luiz Alves da Silva (ct), Beat Mattmüller (ct), Andreas Schmidt (ct), Markus Schikora (ten), Peter Mächler (bass), Michael Leibundgut (bass), L. A. da Silva (cnd), Turicum Ensemble *(rec Studio DRS, Zurich, Sept 26-29, 1994)* Claves ▲ CD 9521 [DDD]

Pinto, L.A.:Te Deum Laudamus, w. Katharina Ott (sop), Luiz Alves da Silva (ct), Beat Mattmüller (ct), Andreas Schmidt (ct), Markus Schikora (ten), Peter Mächler (bass), Michael Leibundgut (bass), L. A. da Brooks (cnd), Turicum Ensemble *(rec Studio DRS, Zurich, Sept 26-29, 1994)* Claves ▲ CD 9521 [DDD]

Lombardo, Bernard (ten)

Cherubini, L.:Lodoïska, w. M. Devia (sop), F. Pedaci (sgr), T. Moser (ten), A. Corbelli (bar), W. Shimell (bar), R. Muti (cnd), La Scala Orch, La Scala Chorus Sony Classical 2-▲ SM2K 47290

Lombardo, Luca (sgr)

Cherubini, L.:Médée, w. Jano Tamar (sop), Patrizia Ciofi (sgr), Magali Damonte (sgr), Jean-Philippe Courtis (bass), P. Fournillier (cnd), Italian International Opera Orch, Sluk Chamber Chorus Bratislava *(rec Martina Franca Festival, 1995)* Nuova Era 2-▲ NUO 7253

Londi, Laura (sop)

Verdi, G.:Il trovatore, w. Leyla Gencer (sop—Leonora), Laura Londi (sop—Ines), Fedora Barbieri (mez—Azucena), Mario del Monaco (ten—Manrico), Athos cesarini (ten—Ruiz), Walter Artioli (ten—Messanger) Ettore Bastianini (bar—Count Luna), Plinio Clabassi (bass—Ferrando), Sergio Liliani (bass—Gypsy), F. Previtali (cnd), Milan RAI SO, Milan RAI Chorus *(rec live, Milan, May 29, 1957)* Arkadia 2-▲ 483 [ADD]

Verdi, G.:Il trovatore (sels), w. Leyla Gencer (sop—Leonora), Laura Londi (sop—Ines), Athos Cesarini (ten—Ruiz), Mario del Monaco (ten—Manrico), Ettore Bastianini (bar), F. Previtali (cnd), Milan RAI SO, Milan RAI Chorus *(rec Milan, May 18, 1957)* Agorá Music ("Phoenix" series) 3-▲ 510 [ADD]

London, George (b–bar)

Brahms, J.:Ein Deutsches Requiem, w. Irmgard Seefried (sop), B. Walter (cnd), New York PO, *(chorus unknown)* Melodram ▲ CDM 18004

London, George (b–bar) (cont.)

Brahms, J.:Ein Deutsches Requiem, w. Irmgard Seefried (sop), B. Walter (cnd), New York PO, Westminster Cathedral Choir *(rec New York City, Dec. 20-29, 1954)* Sony Classical ("Bruno Walter Edition, Vol. 2" series) ▲ SMK 64469 [ADD]

Brahms, J.:Ernste Gesänge [G] Sony Classical ("Essential Classics" series) ▲ SBK 48176 ■ SBT 48176

Mahler, G.:Kindertotenlieder, w. O. Klemperer (cnd), Cologne RSO [G] *(rec live, Cologne, 10/17/55)* Arkadia 2-▲ 578 (m) [ADD]

Mozart, W.A.:Arias, w. E. Steber (sop), I. Cotrubas (sop), K. Te Kanawa (sop), R. Stevens (mez), P. Domingo (ten), S. Jerusalem (ten), E. Pinza (bass)—arias & duets from Don Giovanni, Le nozze di Figaro, Die Zauberflöte, etc. *(rec 1941-1978)* CBS Masterworks ▲ MDK 46579 [AAD] ■ MGT 46579

Mozart, W.A.:Nozze di Figaro, w. E. Schwarzkopf (sop), I. Seefried (sop), S. Jurinac (sop), E. Höngen (cta), E. Kunz (bar), H. von Karajan (cnd), Vienna PO, Vienna State Opera Chorus—omitting recitatives [l] *(rec 1950)* EMI Classics ("Studio" series) 2-▲ CDMB 69639 (m) [ADD]

Of Gods & Demons, w. Vienna SO, Columbia SO, Metropolitan Opera Orch, Rudolf Moralt (cnd), Jean-Paul Moral (cnd), Kurt Adler (cnd) Sony Classical ("Masterworks Heritage" series) ▲ MHK 62758

Offenbach, J.:Les Contes d'Hoffmann, w. E. Schwarzkopf (sop), G. d'Angelo (sop), V. de los Angeles (sop), N. Gedda (ten), E. Blanc (bar), A. Cluytens (cnd), Paris Conservatory Societé des Concerts Orch, René DuClos Chorus [F] EMI Classics ("Studio" series) 2-▲ CDMB 63222 [ADD]

Recital, 1952-1955 Myto ▲ MCD 942.101

Strauss, R.:Arabella, w. L. Della Casa (sop), H. Gueden (sop), I. Malaniuk (cta), A. Dermota (ten), W. Kmentt (ten), O. Edelmann (bass), G. Solti (cnd), Vienna PO [G] London ("Grand Opera" series) 2-▲ 430387-2 [ADD]

Verdi, G.:Requiem Mass, w. L. Amara (sop), M. Forrester (cta), R. Tucker (ten), E. Ormandy (cnd), Philadelphia Orch, Westminster Choir Sony Classical ▲ SB2K 53252

Verdi, G.:Requiem Mass, w. L. Amara (sop), M. Forrester (cta), R. Tucker (ten), E. Ormandy (cnd), Philadelphia Orch, Westminster Choir [L] Odyssey ■ YT 35230

Wagner, R.:Der fliegende Holländer, w. L. Rysanek (sop), K. Liebl (ten), G. Tozzi (bass), A. Dorati (cnd), Royal Opera House Orch, Royal Opera House Chorus Covent Garden [G] London 2-▲ 417319-2 [ADD]

Wagner, R.:Der fliegende Holländer, w. A. Varnay (sop), J. Traxel (ten), A. van Mill (bass), J. Keilberth (cnd), Bayreuth Festival Orch, Bayreuth Festival Chorus [G] *(rec live, Bayreuth, 7/25/56)* Myto 2-▲ 2 MCD 93175

Wagner, R.:Der fliegende Holländer, w. L. Rysanek (sop), J. Greindl (bass), W. Sawallisch (cnd), Bayreuth Festival Orch, Bayreuth Festival Chorus [G] *(rec live, Bayreuth 1959)* Melodram 2-▲ MEL 26101

Wagner, R.:Parsifal, w. I. Dalis (mez), J. Thomas (ten), H. Hotter (b–bar), G. Neidlinger (b–bar), H. Knappertsbusch (cnd), Bayreuth Festival Orch, Bayreuth Festival Chorus [1962] [G] Philips 4-▲ 416390-2 [ADD]

Wagner, R.:Das Rheingold, w. K. Flagstad (sop), J. Madeira (mez), S. Svanholm (ten), G. Neidlinger (b–bar), K. Böhme (bass), G. Solti (cnd), Vienna PO [G] London 3-▲ 414101-2 [ADD]

Wagner, R.:Der Ring des Nibelungen, w. B. Nilsson (sop), K. Flagstad (sop), R. Crespin (sop), C. Watson (sop), C. Ludwig (mez), J. Madeira (mez), S. Svanholm (ten), J. King (ten), G. Stolze (ten), W. Windgassen (ten), G. London (bar), D. Fischer-Dieskau (bar), H. Hotter (b–bar), G. Neidlinger (b–bar), G. Frick (bass), G. Solti (cnd), Vienna PO [G] London 15-▲ 414100-2 [ADD]

Long (sgr)

Stockhausen, K.:Stimmung, w. K. Flowers (sop), P. Walmsley-Clark (sop), R. Covey-Crump (ten), P. Rose (bass), Hillier (sgr) Hyperion ▲ CDA 66115

Long, A. (sgr)

Gershwin, G.:Porgy & Bess, w. A. Brown (sgr), E. Matthews (sgr), H. Jackson (sgr), Todd Duncan (sgr), H. Dowdy (sgr), Eva Jessye Choir [1940-1942 original cast] MCA Classics ("Broadway Gold" series) ▲ MCAD 10520 ■ MCAC 10520

Long, Kay (sgr)

Floyd, C.:Susannah, w. Phyllis Curtin (sop—Susannah Polk), Richard Cassilly (ten—Sam Polk), Norman Treigle (bass—Olin Blitch), Marietta Muhs Cosenza (sgr—Mrs. McLean), Marilyn Davidson (sgr—Mrs. Gleaton), Kay Long (sgr—Mrs. Hayes), Jean Young (sgr—Mrs. Ott), Alton Brim (sgr—Elder Hayes), Thomas Carter (sgr—Elder Gleaton), Jack Davis (sgr—Elder McLean), Keith Kaldenberg (sgr—Little Bat McLean), Burton Parker (sgr—Elder Ott), K. Andersson (cnd), New Orleans Opera Orch, New Orleans Opera Chorus *(rec Mar 31, 1962)* VAI Audio 2-▲ VAIA 1115-2 [ADD]

Long, R. (mez)

Pfitzner, H.:Palestrina, w. C. Nossek (sop), P. Schreier (ten), S. Lorenz (bar), E. Wlaschiha (bass), O. Suitner (cnd), Berlin Staatskapelle, Berlin State Opera Chorus Berlin Classics ▲ BER 1001

Longfield, Susan (sop)

Sir Cristemas, w. [cnd:Louis Halsey], Elizabethan Singers, Simon Preston (kbd/cnd), Ian Partridge (ten), Christopher Keyte (bass) Boston Skyline ▲ BSD 124 [ADD]

Longhi, Daniela (sgr)

Verdi, G.:Simon Boccanegra, w. Alberto Cupido (ten), Ned Barth (bar), José Van Dam (b–bar), Manfred Schenk (bass), Dino Musio (sgr), M. Veltri (cnd), Marseille Opera Orch, Marseille Opera Chorus Lyrinx 3-▲ LYX 127 [DDD]

Longo, Anna Laura (sgr)

Rossini, G.:Demetrio e Polibio, w. Christine Weidinger (sop—Lisinga), Sara Mingardo (cta—Siveno), Anna Laura Longo (sgr—Olmira), Dalmacio Gonzales (ten—Demetrio/Eumene), Giorgio Surjan (bass—Polibio), Martino Fullone (sgr—Onao), M. Carraro (cnd), Graz SO, Bratislava Chamber Chorus *(rec live, Martina Franca Opera Festival, Italy, July 27, 1992)* Dynamic 2-▲ CDS 171/1-2 [DDD]

Lonsdale, Michaël (nar)

Gerhard, R.:La Peste, w. E. Colomer (cnd), Spanish National Youth Orch, BBC Sym Chorus Auvidis Montaigne ▲ MO 782101

Milhaud, D.:Ani maamin, un chant perdu et retrouvé, w. Sharon Cooper (sop—la Voix), Anna Parus (mez), Bernard Freyd (nar—Isaac), Michel Hermon (nar—le Récitant), Michael Lonsdale (nar—Abraham), Jean Négroni (nar—Jacob), P. Méfano (cnd), Ensemble 2E2M, Madrigal de Bordeaux Arion ▲ ARN 68275 [DDD]

Rebotier, J.:Plages, w. 2E2M Ensemble Adès ▲ ADE 204472 [DDD/AAD]

Loomis, James (bass)

Bach, J.S.:Cant 106, "Actus tragicus", w. M. László (sop), H. Handt (ten), H. Scherchen (cnd), Turin Radio Orch, Turin Radio Chorus [G] *(rec live, Jan 14, 1958)* Memories ▲ HR 4160 (m) [ADD]

Monteverdi, C.:Madrigals, w. Basia Retchitzka (sop), Eric Tappy (ten), Rodolfo Malacarne (ten), Laerte Malaguti (bar), E. Loehrer (cnd), Lugano Chamber Society Orch, Lugano Chamber Society Chorus—8 Madrigali Guerrieri e Amorosi Accord ▲ ACD 220872

Monteverdi, C.:Orfeo, w. Nuccia Focile (sop), Claudia Clarich (mez), Enrico Facini (ten), Paolo Coni (bar), H. Handt (cnd), Lucchese CO [orchd Respighi, 1934-35] *(rec live, VII Festival Internazionale di Marlia, 1984)* Claves ▲ CD 9419 [ADD]

Palestrina, G.:Sacred Music, w. Luciana Ticinelli-Fattori (sop), Maria Minetto (mez), Laerte Malaguti (bar), E. Loehrer (cnd), Lugano Chamber Society Instrumental Ensemble, Lugano Chamber Society Chorus—Vexilla Regis Prodeunt; Adoramus Te; Laudario Di Cortona Accord ▲ ACD 201562 [AAD]

Pergolesi, G.B.:Mass in F, w. B. Retchitzka (sop), G. Ferracini (sop), M. Minetto (cta), V. Gohl (cta), C. Jauquier (ten), Milan Solisti, Plifonia Choir *(rec 1967)* Rivoalto ▲ RIV 8922 [ADD]

Wagner, R.:Die Meistersinger von Nürnberg, w. Bruna Rizzoli (sop), Fernanda Cadoni (mez), Luigi Infantino (ten), Vito Tatone (ten), Renato Capecchi (bar), Giuseppe Taddei (bar), Boris Christoff (bass), Giovanni Ciavola (bass), Silvo Maionica (bass), Vito Susca (bass), Raimondo Botteghelli (sgr), Walter Brunelli (sgr), Carlo Franzini (sgr), Ezio de Giorgi (sgr), Renzo Gonzales (sgr), L. von Matačić (cnd), Turin RAI Radio-TV SO, Turin RAI Chorus Stradivarius 4-▲ STV 12310

Loonens, Bernard (ten)

Haydn, M.:Missa Pro Defuncto Archiepiscopo Sigismundo, w. Lena Lootens (sop), Cornelia Salje (alt), Dirk Snellings (b–bar), Philippe Benoit (cnd), Vivente Voce Choir *(rec Steurbaut Sound Recording Centre)* René Gailly ▲ CD 87125 [DDD]

Haydn, M.:Motets, w. Lena Lootens (sop), Cornelia Salje (alt), Dirk Snellings (b–bar), Philippe Benoit (cnd), Vivente Voce Choir—Aria de Passione Domini *(rec Steurbaut Sound Recording Centre)* René Gailly ▲ CD 87125 [DDD]

Loor, Friedl (sop)

Benatzky, R.:Im weissen Rössl (sels), w. H. Brauner (cta), K. Equiluz (ten), K. Terkal (ten), F. Bauer-Theussl (cnd), Vienna Volksoper Orch, Vienna Volksoper Chorus [G] Koch Präsent ▲ CD 399225 [AAD]

Loose, Emmy (sop)

Lehár, F.:Die lustige Witwe, w. E. Schwarzkopf (sop), N. Gedda (ten), E. Kunz (bar), A. Kraus (ten), O. Ackermann (cnd), Philharmonia Orch, Philharmonia Chorus [G] EMI Classics ("Studio" series) ▲ CDH 69520 (m) [ADD]

Mozart, W.A.:Così fan tutte, w. L. della Casa (sop), C. Ludwig (mez), A. Dermota (ten), E. Kunz (bar), P. Schoeffler (bass) London 2-▲ 417185-2 [ADD]

Mozart, W.A.:Don Giovanni (sels), w. Hilde Konetzni (sop), Irmgard Seefried (sop), Anton Dermota (ten), Erich Kunz (bar), Paul Schöffler (b-bar), Herbert Alsen (bass), Böhm, Moralt (cnd), Vienna PO *(rec 1944)* Preiser ▲ PRE 90249 [ADD]

Mozart, W.A.:Entführung (sels), w. Hilde Konetzni (sop), Irmgard Seefried (sop), Anton Dermota (ten), Erich Kunz (bar), Paul Schöffler (b-bar), Herbert Alsen (bass), Böhm, Moralt (cnd), Vienna PO *(rec 1944)* Preiser ▲ PRE 90249 [ADD]

Mozart, W.A.:Zauberflöte (sels), w. Hilde Konetzni (sop), Irmgard Seefried (sop), Anton Dermota (ten), Erich Kunz (bar), Paul Schöffler (b-bar), Herbert Alsen (bass), Böhm, Moralt (cnd), Vienna PO *(rec 1944)* Preiser ▲ PRE 90249 [ADD]

Strauss (II), Joh.:Der Zigeunerbaron, w. Emmy Loose (sop—Arsena), Gerda Scheyrer (sop—Saffi), Elisabeth Fez (cta—Mirabella), Hilde Rössl-Majdan (cta—Czipra), Waldemar Kmentt (ten—Barinkay), Paul Spani (ten—Ottokar), Erich Kunz (bar—Homonay), Kurt Preger (bar—Zsupan), Eberhard Wächter (bass—Carnero), A. Paulik (cnd), Vienna State Opera Orch, Vienna State Opera Chorus *(rec Brahmssaal, Vienna, Austria, June 1956)* Vanguard Classics 2-▲ OVC 8082/83 [ADD]

Strauss (II), Joh.:Der Zigeunerbaron, w. Hilde Zadek (sop), Rosette Anday (cta), Julius Patzak (ten), Karl Dönch (bar), Alfred Poell (bar), Steffi Leverenz (sgr), C. Krauss (cnd), Vienna PO, Vienna State Opera Chorus Phonographe 2-▲ PHG 5020 [AAD]

Strauss, R.:Arabella (sels), w. E. Schwarzkopf (sop), J. Metternich (bar), L. von Matačić (cnd), Philharmonia Orch [G] EMI Classics ("Great Recordings of the Century" series) ▲ CDH 61001 (m)

Loosli, Arthur (bass)

Schoeck, O.:Elegie, w. T. Hug (cnd), Bern Chamber Ensemble *(rec 1967)* Jecklin-Disco ▲ JD 510-2 [ADD]

Schoeck, O.:Nachhall, w. T. Loosli (cnd), Bern Radio Chamber Ensemble *(rec 1973)* Jecklin-Disco ▲ JD 535-2 [ADD]

Schoeck, O.:Songs (misc), w. K Grenacher (pno), T. Loosli (cnd), Bern Radio Chamber Ensemble—9 songs *(rec 1968)* Jecklin-Disco ▲ JD 535-2 [ADD]

Schubert, Franz:Winterreise, w. K. Grenacher (pno) [G] *(rec 1973)* Jecklin-Disco ▲ JS 268-2 [ADD]

Lootens, Lena (sop)

Bach, C.P.E.:Die Israeliten in der Wüste, w. B. Schlick (sop), H. Meens (ten), S. Barcoe (sgr), W. Christie (cnd), Cappella Coloniensis, Corona Musique d'Abord ▲ HMA 1901321

Haydn, M.:Missa Pro Defuncto Archiepiscopo Sigismundo, w. Cornelia Salje (alt), Bernard Loonens (ten), Dirk Snellings (b-bar), Philippe Benoit (cnd), Vivente Voce Choir *(rec Steurbaut Sound Recording Centre)* René Gailly ▲ CD 87125 [DDD]

Haydn, M.:Motets, w. Cornelia Salje (alt), Bernard Loonens (ten), Dirk Snellings (b-bar), Philippe Benoit (cnd), Vivente Voce Choir—Aria de Passione Domini *(rec Steurbaut Sound Recording Centre)* René Gailly ▲ CD 87125 [DDD]

Monteverdi, C.:Incoronazione, w. D. Borst (sop), G. Laurens (mez), J. Larmore (mez), A. Köhler (alt), M. Schopper (bass), R. Jacobs (cnd), Concerto Vocale [direction & new musical realization by René Jacobs] [I] Harmonia Mundi France 3-▲ HMC 901330/32

Lopardo, Frank (ten)

Mozart, W.A.:Così fan tutte, w. Renée Fleming (sop—Fiordiligi), Adelina Scarabelli (sop—Despina), Anne Sofie Von Otter (mez—Dorabella), Frank Lopardo (ten—Ferrando), Olaf Bar (bar—Guglielmo), Michele Pertusi (bass—Don Alfonso), G. Solti (cnd), CO of Europe London 3-▲ 444174-2

Mozart, W.A.:Idomeneo, w. Heidi Grant-Murphy (sop—Ilia), Carol Vaness (sop—Elettra), Cecilia Bartoli (mez—Idamante), Plácido Domingo (ten—Idomeneo), Frank Lopardo (ten—High Priest), Thomas Hampson (bar—Arbace), Bryn Terfel (b-bar—The Voice), J. Levine (cnd), Metropolitan Opera Orch, Raymond Hughes (cnd), New York Metropolitan Opera Chorus *(rec Manhattan Center Studios, New York, Mar & Apr 1994)* Deutsche Grammophon 3-▲ 447 737-2 [DDD]

Mozart, W.A.:Missa, K.427, w. A. Augér (sop), F. von Stade (mez), C. Hauptmann (bass), L. Bernstein (cnd), Bavarian RSO, Bavarian Radio Chorus *(rec live April 1990)* Deutsche Grammophon ▲ 431791-2 [DDD] □ 431791-5

Mozart, W.A.:Requiem, w. P. Pace (sop), W. Meier (mez), J. Morris (bass), R. Muti (cnd), Berlin PO, Swedish Radio Chorus [L] EMI Classics ▲ CDC 49640 [DDD]

Orff, C.:Carmina burana, w. B. Bonney (sop), A. Michaels-Moore (bar), A. Previn (cnd), Vienna PO, Arnold Schoenberg Choir, Vienna Boys' Choir Deutsche Grammophon ▲ 439950-2

Rossini, G.:Il barbiere di Siviglia, w. K. Battle (sop), P. Domingo (ten), L. Gallo (bar), R. Raimondi (bass), C. Abbado (cnd), CO of Europe [I] Deutsche Grammophon 2-▲ 435763-2

Rossini, G.:L'italiana in Algeri, w. A. Baltsa (mez), E. Dara (bar), R. Raimondi (bass), C. Abbado (cnd), Vienna PO, Vienna State Opera Chorus [I] Deutsche Grammophon 2-▲ 427331-2 [DDD]

Rossini, G.:Semiramide, w. C. Studer (sop), J. Larmore (mez), S. Ramey (bass), I. Marin (cnd), London SO, Ambrosian Opera Chorus Deutsche Grammophon ▲ 437797-2

Rossini, G.:Il Signor Bruschino, w. K. Battle (sop), C. Desderi (bar), S. Ramey (bass), I. Marin (cnd), English CO Deutsche Grammophon ▲ 435865-2

Verdi, G.:Falstaff, w. S. Sweet (sop), M. Horne (mez), R. Panerai (bar), A. Titus (bar), C. Davis (cnd), Bavarian RSO, Bavarian Radio Chorus RCA Red Seal 2-▲ 09026-60705-2 [DDD]

Verdi, G.:La traviata, w. Angela Gheorghiu (sop—Violetta), Leah-Marian Jones (mez—Flora Bervoix), Gillian Knight (mez—Annina), Robin Leggate (ten—Gastone), Frank Lopardo (ten—Alfredo Germont), Rodney Gibson (ten—Servo di Flora), Neil Griffiths (ten—Giuseppe), Mark Beesley (bar—Dottore Grenvile), Leo Nucci (bar—Giorgio Germont), Richard Van Allan (bass—Barone Douphol), Roderick Earle (bass—Marquese d'Obigny), Bryan Secombe (bass—Commissionario), G. Solti (cnd), Royal Opera House Orch, Royal Opera House Chorus Covent Garden *(rec live, Royal Opera House, Covent Garden, Dec. 1994)* London 2-▲ 448119-2

Lopatto, Dmitri (bar)

Mussorgsky, M.:Khovanshchina, w. Irene Companez (cta), Herbert Handt (ten), Mirto Picchi (ten), Boris Christoff (bass), Armedeo Berdini (sgr), Giorgio Canello (sgr), Michele Malaspina (sgr), Jolanda Mancini (sgr), Mario Petri (sgr), A. Rodzinski (cnd), Rome RAI Radio-TV SO, Rome RAI Chorus Stradivarius 2-▲ STV DTM 12320 [ADD]

Mussorgsky, M.:Khovanshchina, w. Jolanda Mancini (sop—Emma), Irene Companez (mez), Amedeo Berdini (ten—Prince Andrei Khovanski), Mirto Picchi (ten—Prince Vasili Golitsin), Herbert Handt (ten—Scribe), Andrea Mineo (bar—Kuzka), Giampiero Malaspina (bar—Shaklovity), Boris Christoff (bass—Dosifei), Mario Petri (bass—Prince Ivan Khovanski), Dimitri Lopatto (Varsonofiev/First Strelyets), Giorgio Conello (Second Strelyets), A. Rodzinski (cnd), *(orch unknown)* [I] *(rec Rome, 1958)* VAI Audio 2-▲ VAIA 1052-2

Wagner, R.:Parsifal, w. M. Callas (sop), Baldelli (sgr), R. Panerai (bar), B. Christoff (bass), V. Gui (cnd), Rome Radio-TV SO, Rome Radio-TV Chorus [I] *(rec in concert, 11/20-21/50)* Verona 3-▲ 27085/87

Wagner, R.:Parsifal, w. M. Callas (sop), Baldelli (sgr), R. Panerai (bar), B. Christoff (bass), V. Gui (cnd), Rome Radio-TV SO, Rome Radio-TV Chorus [I] *(rec 11/20-21/50)* Melodram 3-▲ MEL 36041 (m)

López, Jennifer (voc)

Hays, S.:Dreaming the World, w. Thomas Bruckner (bar), Sal Basile (voc), John Schaffer (voc), Sorrel Hays (voc), Joseph Kubera (pno), John Kennedy (perc), Charles Wood (perc), Maya Gunji (perc), Eric Kivnick (perc), Jai Smith (perc) New World ▲ 805202 [DDD]

Lopez, Tony (ten)

Saint-Saëns, C.:Samson et Dalila, w. Risë Stevens (mez—Dalila), Ramón Vinay (ten—Samson), Thomas Carter (ten—1st Philistine), Tony Lopez (ten—Philistine Messenger), Joseph Mordino (bar—High Priest), Arthur Cosenza (bass—Abimélech), Joseph Knight (bass—2nd Philistine), Ara Berberian (bass—Old Hebrew), R. Cellini (cnd), New Orleans Opera Orch, New Orleans Opera Chorus *(rec live, Apr 2, 1960)* VAI Audio 2-▲ VAIA 1055-2 [ADD]

Lorand, Marcel (sgr/harm)

Synagogue Chants, w. Karel Handler (sgr), Jeno Kohn (sgr), Alexander Kovacs (sgr), Trio Lorand Supraphon ▲ SUP 3073

Lord, Matthew (ten)

Thomson, V.:Lord Byron, w. J. Ommerlé (sop), D. Fortunato (mez), R. Zeller (bar), R. Johnson (bar), J. Bolle (cnd), Monadnock Music Festival Orch [E] *(rec live, Aug. 31 & Sept. 2, 1991)* Koch International Classics 2-▲ KIC 7124-2 [DDD]

Lorengar, Pilar (sop)

Gluck, C.W.:Iphigénie en Tauride, w. F. Bonisolli (ten), D. Fischer-Dieskau (bar), W. Grönroos (bar), L. Gardelli (cnd), Bavarian RSO, Bavarian Radio Chorus [F] Orfeo 2-▲ 052832 [DDD]

Gluck, C.W.:Orfeo ed Euridice, w. H. Donath (sop), M. Horne (mez), G. Solti (cnd), Royal Opera House Orch, Royal Opera House Chorus Covent Garden London 2-▲ 417410-2 [ADD]

Hindemith, P.:Mathis der Maler, w. D. Grobe (ten), D. Fischer-Dieskau (bar), L. Ludwig (cnd), Berlin RSO [G]—sels Deutsche Grammophon ("20th Century Classics" series) 2-▲ 431741-2 [ADD]

Leoncavallo, R.:Pagliacci, w. R. Krause (ten), J. McCracken (ten), R. Merrill (bar), U. Benelli (bar), L. Gardelli (cnd), St. Cecilia Academy Orch Rome, St. Cecilia Academy Chorus Rome [I] IMP Collectors Series ▲ IMPX 9017 [AAD]

Mozart, W.A.:Zauberflöte, w. C. Deutekom (sop), S. Burrows (ten), H. Prey (bar), D. Fischer-Dieskau (bar), M. Talvela (bass), G. Solti (cnd), Vienna PO [G] London 3-▲ 414568-2

Mozart, W.A.:Zauberflöte (sels), w. Cristina Deutekom (sop), Stuart Burrows (ten), Hermann Prey (bar), Martti Talvela (bass), G. Solti (cnd), Vienna PO London ▲ 421302-2 [ADD]

Rossini, G.:Arias, w. June Anderson (sop), Montserrat Caballé (sop), Maria Callas (sop), Edita Gruberova (sop), Mady Mesplé (sop), Nicolai Gedda (ten), Tito Gobbi (bar), Samuel Ramey (bass), *(orchs unknown)* —from Barbiere di Siviglia; La Cenerentola; La Gazza ladra; Petite messe solennelle; Semiramide; Stabat Mater *(rec 1958-89)* EMI Classics 2-▲ CZS 67440-2 [ADD/DDD]

Smetana, B.:The Bartered Bride, w. F. Wunderlich (ten), G. Frick (bass), R. Kempe (cnd), Bamberg SO, Bamberg RIAS Chorus [G] *(rec ca. 1963)* EMI Classics ("Studio" series) 2-▲ CDMB 64002

Verdi, G.:La traviata, w. S. Malagu (mez), G. Aragall (ten), D. Fischer-Dieskau (bar), L. Maazel (cnd), Berlin German Opera Orch, Berlin German Opera Chorus London ("Double Decker" series) 2-▲ 443000-2

Zarzuela Arias & Duets, w. Plácido Domingo (ten) *(rec live, 1981 Salzburg Festival)* CBS ▲ MK 39210 [DDD]

Lorentzon, Anders (bass)

The Most Beloved Opera Choruses, w. Royal Swedish Opera Chorus [cnd:Sixten Ehrling], Carina Morling (mez), Ingrid Tobiasson (cta), Magnus Kyhle (ten) Caprice ▲ CAP 21520

Lorentzon, Anders (sgr)

Berwald, F.:Estrella de Soria (sels), w. L. Nordin (sop), K. Dalayman (sgr), S. Smith (sgr), C. Sköld (sgr), S. Westerberg (cnd), Helsingborg SO, Malmö Chamber Choir Musica Sveciae ▲ MSV 523 [DDD]

Lorenz, Eberhard (sgr)

Schnittke, A.:Historia von D. Johann Fausten, w. Hanna Schwarz (mez—Fair Helen), Arno Raunig (alt—Mephostophiles), Eberhard Büchner (ten—Old Man), Jürgen Freier (bar—Dr. Johann Faustus), Jonathan Barreto-Ramos (sgr—Student), Jürgen Fersch (sgr—Student), Eberhard Lorenz (sgr—Erzähler), Christoph Johannes Wendel (sgr—Student), G. Albrecht (cnd), Hamburg State PO, Hamburg State Opera Chorus RCA Red Seal 2-▲ 09026-68413-2

Lorenz, G. (sop)

Mahler, G.:Sym 4, w. H. Swarowsky (cnd), Czech PO [G] *(rec 1972)* Supraphon Collection ▲ 11 0625-2 [ADD]

Lorenz, Max (ten)

Bach, J.S.:Cant 56, w. M. Pommer (cnd), Leipzig New Bach Collegium Musicum [G] Capriccio ▲ CDC 10028 [DDD]

Bach, J.S.:Cant 82, w. M. Pommer (cnd), Leipzig New Bach Collegium Musicum [G] Capriccio ▲ CDC 10028 [DDD]

Bach, J.S.:Music of, w. L. Güttler (tpt), A. Reiss (ten), P. Schreier (ten), H.-C. Polster (b-bar), M. Pommer (cnd), Leipzig New Bach Collegium Musicum, Leipzig Choirs—arias, choruses & chorales Capriccio ▲ CDC 10039 [DDD]

Brahms, J.:Ein Deutsches Requiem, w. M. A. Häggander (sop), H. Kegel (cnd), Leipzig RSO, Leipzig Radio Chorus [G] Capriccio ▲ 10095 [DDD]

Einem, G. von:Der Prozess, w. Lisa Della Casa (sop—Frl. Bürstner/Die Frau des Gerichtsdieners/Leni), Peter Klein (ten—Der Direktorstellvertreter/Der Student), Max Lorenz (ten—Josef K.), Erich Majkut (ten—Ein Bursche), László Szemere (ten—Titorelli), Alois Pernerstorfer (b-bar—Willem/Der Gerichtsdiener), Alfred Poell (b-bar—Der Advokat), Walter Berry (bass—Franz/Kanzleidirektor), Oskar Czerwenka (bass—Der Untersuchungsrichter/Der Prügler), Ludwig Hofmann (bass—Der Aufseher/Ein Passant/Der Geistliche/Der Fabrikant), Polly Batic (sgr—Frau Grubach), Endreh Koreh (sgr—Albert K.), Luise Leitner (sgr—Ein buckliges Mädchen), K. Böhm (cnd), Vienna PO, Vienna State Opera Chorus *(rec Aug 17, 1953)* Orfeo d'or ("Festspiel Dokumente" series) 2-▲ 392952 (m)

The Legendary Singers at Lindenoper Berlin (1927-1945)—, w. Gitta Alpar (sop), Erna Berger (sop), Tiana Lemnitz (sop), Maria Müller (sop), Margarete Klose (cta), Peter Anders (ten), Walter Ludwig (ten), Lauritz Melchior (ten), Rudolf Schock (ten), Franz Völker (ten), Willi Domgraf-Fassb *(rec 1927; 1937; 1941-45)* Minerva ▲ MN A21 [ADD]

Max Lorenz *(rec HMV, 1927-30)* Preiser ("Lebendige Vergangenheit" series) ▲ PRE 89053 (m) [AAD]

Max Lorenz:Recital, 1933-1957, w. Maria Reining (sop), Berlin RSO [cnd:Artur Rother], Bayreuth Festival Orch [cnd:Heinz Tietjen, Richard Strauss], German Large RSO [cnd:Rudolf Moralt, Max Schönherr, Anton Paulik], Hessen RSO [cnd:Kurt Schröder], Brenda Lewis (sop), Eberhard Wächter (ten), Wolfgang Zimmer (bar) *(rec 1933-57)* Myto ▲ MCD 934.88

Pfitzner, H.:Palestrina (sels), w. P. Schöffler (b-bar), R. Kempe (cnd), Vienna PO—solo tenor aria & one duet from Act I *(rec live, Salzburg, 8/1/55)* Myto 3-▲ 3 MCD 92259 [ADD]

Strauss, R.:Ariadne auf Naxos, w. M. Reining (sop), I. Seefried (sop), A. Noni (sop), J. Witt (ten), E. Kunz (bar), P. Schöffler (bass), K. Böhm (cnd), Vienna State Opera Orch *(rec Strauss' 80th Birthday Festival, June 11, 1944)* Preiser 2-▲ PRE 90217 [ADD]

Strauss, R.:Ariadne auf Naxos (sels), w. Alda Noni (sop—Zerbinetta), Maria Reining (sop—Ariadne), Irmgard Seefried (sop—Composer), Max Lorenz (ten—Bacchus), Paul Schöffler (b-bar—Musiklehrer), K. Böhm (cnd), Vienna State Opera Orch *(rec Vienna, June 11, 1944)* Koch Schwann 2-▲ SCH 314732 [ADD]

Strauss, R.:Salome, w. I. Borkh (sop—Salome), M. Klose (mez—Herodias), C. Ludwig (mez—Page), M. Lorenz (ten—Herodes), F. Fehringer (ten—Narraboth), F. Frantz (bar—Jokanaan), K. Schröder (cnd), Hessian RSO *(rec 1952)* Myto 2-▲ 93592

Verdi, G.:Aida (sels), w. D. Illitsch (sop—Aida), E. Nikolaidi (cta), L. Ludwig (cnd), Vienna State Opera Orch, Vienna State Opera Chorus *(rec Sept. 22, 1942)* Koch Schwann 2-▲ SCH 314562 [ADD]

Wagner, R.:Arias & Scenes, *(orch unknown)* Preiser ("Lebendige Vergangenheit" series) ▲ 89053 (m) [AAD]

Wagner, R.:Arias & Scenes, w. B. Siedler-Winkler (sgr), A. Rother (cnd), R. Moralt (cnd), *(orch unknown)* —arias & scenes from Rienzi, Tannhäuser, Tristan und Isolde, Die Walküre, Siegfried & Die Meistersinger von Nürnberg *(rec 1937-43)* Preiser ▲ PRE 90213 [ADD]

Wagner, R.:Arias & Scenes, w. Kathe Heidersbach (sop), Maria Reining (sop), Hilde Scheppan (sop), Margarete Teschemacher (sop), Margarete Klose (mez), Jaro Prohaska (bar), Karl Schmitt-Walter (bar), Kurt Böhme (bass), *(orch unknown)*—selections from Rienzi; Der Fliegende Holländer; Tannhäuser; Lohengrin; Tristan und Isolde; Die Meistersinger von Nürnberg; Die Walküre & Götterdämmerung *(rec 1927-1944)* Phonographe 2-▲ PHG 5016 [AAD]

Wagner, R.:Der fliegende Holländer (sels), w. K. Flagstad (sop), H. Janssen (bar), L. Weber (bass), F. Reiner (cnd), Royal Opera House Orch, Royal Opera House Chorus Covent Garden [G] *(rec live, Covent Garden, 6/11/37)* Standing Room Only ▲ SRO 808-1 (m) [ADD]

Lorenz, Max (ten) (cont.)

Wagner, R.:Götterdämmerung (sels), w. M. Lorenz (ten—Siegfried), P. Schöffler (b–bar—Gunther), J. von Manowarda (bass—Hagen), L. Reichwein (cnd), Vienna State Opera Orch, Vienna State Opera Chorus *(rec Sept. 10, 1942)* Koch Schwann 2–▲ SCH 314562 [ADD]

Wagner, R.:Die Meistersinger von Nürnberg, w. Maria Müller (sop), Jaro Prohaska (bar), Josef Greindl (bass), Bayreuth Festival Orch, Bayreuth Festival Chorus *(rec live, July–Aug 1943)* Grammofono 2000 4–▲ GRM 78602

Wagner, R.:Die Meistersinger von Nürnberg (sels), w. Maria Reining (sop—Eva), Peter Klein (ten—David), Max Lorenz (ten—Walther), Josef Hermann (bar—Hans Sachs), Erich Kunz (bar—Beckmesser), K. Böhm (cnd), Vienna State Opera Orch *(rec Vienna, Jan. 19, 1943)* Koch Schwann 2–▲ SCH 314732 [ADD]

Wagner, R.:Die Meistersinger von Nürnberg (sels), w. Maria Reining (sop—Eva), Max Lorenz (ten—Walther), Erich Zimmermann (ten—David), Karl Kamann (bar—Hans Sachs), W. Furtwängler (cnd), Vienna State Opera Orch *(rec Vienna, Nov. 25, 1937)* Koch Schwann 2–▲ SCH 314702 [ADD]

Wagner, R.:Die Meistersinger von Nürnberg (sels), w. V. Ursuleac (sop—Eva), M. Lorenz (ten—Walther), E. Zimmermann (ten—David), A. Jerger (b–bar—Hans Sachs), C. Krauss (cnd), Vienna State Opera Orch, Vienna State Opera Chorus *(rec Feb. 26, 1933)* Koch Schwann 2–▲ SCH 314562 [ADD]

Wagner, R.:Parsifal (sels), w. H. Braun (sop—Kundry), M. Lorenz (ten—Parsifal), P. Schöffler (b–bar—Amfortas), Reichwein, Knappertsbusch (cnd), Vienna State Opera Orch, Vienna State Opera Chorus Koch Schwann 2–▲ SCH 314562 [ADD]

Wagner, R.:Rienzi, der Letzte der Tribunen (sels), w. Hilde Scheppan (sop), Margarete Klose (cta), Jaro Prohaska (bar), A. Rother (cnd), Berlin State Opera Orch, Berlin State Opera Chorus *(rec 1941)* Preiser ▲ PRE 90223 [ADD]

Wagner, R.:Der Ring des Nibelungen, w. Kirsten Flagstad (sop), Hilde Konetzni (sop), Elisabeth Höngen (cta), Set Svanholm (ten), Günther Treptow (ten), Josef Hermann (bar), Ludwig Weber (bass), Ferdinand Franz (sgr), W. Furtwängler (cnd), La Scala Orch, La Scala Chorus *(rec Milan, 1950)* Music & Arts 12–▲ CD 914

Wagner, R.:Der Ring des Nibelungen, w. K. Flagstad (sop), H. Konetzni (sop), E. Höngen (cta), G. Treptow (ten), S. Svanholm (ten), F. Frantz (b–bar), L. Weber (bass), B. Herrmann (bass), W. Furtwängler (cnd), La Scala Orch, La Scala Chorus *(rec live 1950)* Arkadia 12–▲ 351 [ADD]

Wagner, R.:Der Ring des Nibelungen (sels), w. Adele Kern (sop), Anny Konetzni (sop), Hilde Konetzni (sop), Elisabeth Schumann (sop), Enid Szantho (cta), Josef Kalenberg (ten), Set Svanholm (ten), Erich Zimmermann (ten), Hans Hotter (bar), Jaro Prohaska (bar), Emil Schipper (bar), Paul Schöffler (b–bar), Ludwig Hoffmann (bass), H. Knappertsbusch (cnd), Vienna State Opera Orch *(rec Vienna, 1937–1943)* Koch Schwann 2–▲ SCH 314742 [ADD]

Wagner, R.:Siegfried (sels), w. E. Szantho (cta—Erda), M. Lorenz (ten—Siegfried), W. Wernigk (ten—Mime), L. Hoffmann (bass—Wanderer), H. Knappertsbusch (cnd), Vienna State Opera Orch, Vienna State Opera Chorus *(rec June 16, 1937)* Koch Schwann 2–▲ SCH 314602

Wagner, R.:Tannhäuser (sels), w. Maria Müller (sop), Anna Báthy (sop), W. Furtwängler (cnd), Vienna State Opera Orch Koch Schwann 2–▲ SCH 314702 [ADD]

Wagner, R.:Tannhäuser (sels), w. Maria Reining (sop—Elisabeth), Max Lorenz (ten—Tannhäuser), Arno Schellenberg (bar—Wolfram), H. Knappertsbusch (cnd), Vienna State Opera Orch *(rec Vienna, Nov. 20, 1937)* Koch Schwann 2–▲ SCH 314672 [ADD]

Wagner, R.:Tristan und Isolde (sels), w. A. Konetzni (sop—Isolde), M. Klose (cta—Brangäne), M. Lorenz (ten—Tristan), W. Furtwängler (cnd), Vienna State Opera Orch, Vienna State Opera Chorus *(rec Dec. 25, 1941)* Koch Schwann 2–▲ SCH 314562 [ADD]

Wagner, R.:Tristan und Isolde (sels), w. Anny Konetzni (sop—Isolde), Margarete Klose (cta—Brangäne), Max Lorenz (ten—Tristan), Paul Schöffler (b–bar—Kurwenal), Herbert Alsen (bass—King Marke), W. Furtwängler (cnd), Vienna State Opera Orch, Vienna State Opera Chorus—extended excerpts from Acts 1 & 2; Act 3 (comp) Koch Schwann 2–▲ SCH 314612 [ADD]

Wagner, R.:Die Walküre (sels), w. Hilde Konetzni (sop—Sieglinde), Max Lorenz (ten—Siegmund), Julius Pölzer (ten—Siegmund), Set Svanholm (ten—Siegmund), Knappertsbusch, Martin (cnd), Vienna State Opera Orch Koch Schwann ▲ SCH 314692 [ADD]

Wagner, R.:Die Walküre (act 1), w. M. Teschemacher (sop), K. Böhme (bass), K. Elmendorff (cnd), Saxon State Orch [G] *(rec 9/21/44)* Preiser ▲ 90015 (m) [AAD]

Lorenz, Siegfried (bar)

Bach, J.S.:Cants (misc), w. Edith Mathis (sop), Carolyn Watkinson (cta), Eberhard Büchner (ten), Peter Schreier (ten), Theo Adam (b–bar), P. Schreier (cnd), Berlin CO, Berlin Soloists Berlin Classics ▲ BER 9221

Bach, J.S.:Cant 31, w. Eberhard Büchner (ten), Hermann Christian Polster (bass), Lang (sgr), Termer (sgr), Weimann (sgr), H.–J. Rotzsch (cnd), Leipzig Gewandhaus Orch, St. Thomas Choir Berlin Classics ▲ BER 9025 [ADD]

Bach, J.S.:Cant 36, w. Edith Mathis (sop), Peter Schreier (ten), P. Schreier (cnd), Berlin CO, Berlin Soloists Berlin Classics ▲ BER 9220

Bach, J.S.:Cant 66, w. Eberhard Büchner (ten), Hermann Christian Polster (bass), Lang (sgr), Termer (sgr), Weimann (sgr), H.–J. Rotzsch (cnd), Leipzig Gewandhaus Orch, St. Thomas Choir Berlin Classics ▲ BER 9025 [ADD]

Bach, J.S.:Cant 106, "Actus tragicus", w. Eberhard Büchner (ten), Hermann Christian Polster (bass), Lang (sgr), Termer (sgr), Weimann (sgr), H.–J. Rotzsch (cnd), Leipzig Gewandhaus Orch, St. Thomas Choir Berlin Classics ▲ BER 9025 [ADD]

Bach, J.S.:Cant 110, w. W. Wiedl (trb), S. Frangoulis (trb), P. Esswood (ct), Stumpf (sgr), K. Equiluz (ten), M. van Egmond (b–bar), N. Harnoncourt (cnd), Vienna Concentus Musicus, Tölz Boys' Choir [G] Teldec 2–▲ 2292–42603–2

Bach, J.S.:Cant 203, w. Edith Mathis (sop), Peter Schreier (ten), P. Schreier (cnd), Berlin CO, Berlin Soloists Berlin Classics ▲ BER 9220

Bach, J.S.:Cant 205, w. Edith Mathis (sop), Carolyn Watkinson (alt), Julia Hamari (alt), Peter Schreier (ten), P. Schreier (cnd), Berlin CO, Berlin Soloists Berlin Classics ▲ BER 9224

Bach, J.S.:Cant 206, w. Edith Mathis (sop), Carolyn Watkinson (alt), Peter Schreier (ten), P. Schreier (cnd), Berlin CO, Berlin Soloists Berlin Classics ▲ BER CD 9225

Bach, J.S.:Cant 207, w. Edith Mathis (sop), Carolyn Watkinson (alt), Julia Hamari (alt), Peter Schreier (ten), P. Schreier (cnd), Berlin CO, Berlin Soloists Berlin Classics ▲ BER 9224

Bach, J.S.:Cant 209, w. Edith Mathis (sop), Peter Schreier (ten), P. Schreier (cnd), Berlin CO, Berlin Soloists Berlin Classics ▲ BER 9220

Bach, J.S.:Cant 215, w. Edith Mathis (sop), Carolyn Watkinson (alt), Peter Schreier (ten), P. Schreier (cnd), Berlin CO, Berlin Soloists Berlin Classics ▲ BER CD 9225

Brahms, J.:Liebeslieder Waltzes SATB, w. Barbara Hoene (sop), Gisela Pohl (alt), Armin Ude (ten), Klaus Bässler (pno), Dieter Zechlin (pno), W.–D. Hauschild (cnd), Berlin RSO Berlin Classics ▲ BER 9269

Brahms, J.:Neue Liebeslieder Waltzes, w. Barbara Hoene (sop), Gisela Pohl (alt), Armin Ude (ten), Klaus Bässler (pno), Dieter Zechlin (pno), W.–D. Hauschild (cnd), Berlin RSO Berlin Classics ▲ BER 9269

Hindemith, P.:Das Unaufhörliche, w. Ulrike Sonntag (sop), Robert Wörle (ten), Artur Korn (bass), L. Zagrosek (cnd), Berlin RSO, Berlin Radio Chorus Wergo 2–▲ WER 66032

Mendelssohn, F.:Die erste Walpurgisnacht, w. A. Burmeister (mez), E. Büchner (ten), K. Masur (cnd), Leipzig Gewandhaus Orch Berlin Classics ("Eterna" series) ▲ BER 2057 [ADD]

Mendelssohn, F.:Ov, Op. 101, w. A. Burmeister (mez), E. Büchner (ten), K. Masur (cnd), Leipzig Gewandhaus Orch Berlin Classics ("Eterna" series) ▲ BER 2057 [ADD]

Pfitzner, H.:Palestrina, w. C. Nossek (sop), R. Long (mez), P. Schreier (ten), E. Wlaschiha (bass), O. Suitner (cnd), Berlin Staatskapelle, Berlin State Opera Chorus Berlin Classics ▲ BER 1001

Prokofiev, S.:The Fiery Angel, w. N. Secunde (sop), R. Engert–Ely (mez), H. Zednik (ten), K. Moll (bass), N. Järvi (cnd), Gothenburg SO, Gothenburg Sym Chorus [R] Deutsche Grammophon 2–▲ 431669–2 [DDD]

Schoenberg, A.:Moses und Aaron, w. David Pittman–Jennings (nar), Gabriele Fontana (sop—Young Girl), Yvonne Naef (cta—Sick Woman), John Graham–Hall (ten—Young Man/Naked Youth), Pår Lindskog (ten—Youth), Chris Merritt (ten—Aaron), Siegfried Lorenz (bar—Another Man), Michael Devlin (b–bar—Ephraimite), László Polgár (bass—Priest), P. Boulez (cnd), Royal Concertgebouw Orch, Winfried Maczewski (cnd), Netherlands Opera Chorus, Zaans Youth Choir, Waterland Music School *(rec Concertgebouw, Amsterdam, Oct 1995)* Deutsche Grammophon 2–▲ 449 174–2 [DDD]

Schubert, Franz:Schwanengesang, w. N. Shetler (pno) [G] Capriccio ▲ 10097 [DDD]

Lorenz, Siegfried (bar) (cont.)

Schumann, R.:Genoveva, w. E. Moser (sop), P. Schreier (ten), D. Fischer–Dieskau (bar), K. Masur (cnd), Leipzig Gewandhaus Orch, Berlin Radio Chorus Berlin Classics ("Eterna" series) 2–▲ BER 2056 [ADD]

Wagner, R.:Die Meistersinger von Nürnberg, w. C. Studer (sop—Eva), B. Heppner (ten—Walther von Stolzing), B. Weikl (bar—Hans Sachs), S. Lorenz (b–bar—Sixtus Beckmesser), K. Moll (bass—Veit Pogner), W. Sawallisch (cnd), Bavarian State Opera Orch, Bavarian State Opera Chorus EMI Classics ▲ CDCD 55142

Lorenzi, Ermanno (ten)

Leoncavallo, R.:Pagliacci, w. M. Sighele (sop), R. Tucker (ten), K. Nurmela (bar), R. Muti (cnd), Florence Teatro Comunale Orch, Florence Teatro Comunale Chorus *(rec live, Florence, 1971)* Foyer ▲ FOY 2050 [AAD]

Puccini, G.:Manon Lescaut, w. R. Kabaivanska (sop—Manon), R. Pallini (mez—Singer), P. Domingo (ten—des Grieux), E. Lorenzi (ten—Edmondo), F. Ricciardi (ten—Dancing Master), M. D'Anna (bar—Lescaut), A. Mariotti (bass—Geronte), F. Federici (bass—Innkeeper) Golden Age of Opera 2–▲ GAO 162/63 [ADD]

Lortič, Janez (ten)

Bizet, G.:Les Pêcheurs de perles (sels), w. Igor Morozov (bar), J. Wildner (cnd), Slovak RSO Bratislava—Au fond du temple saint *(rec Slovak Radio Concert Hall, Bratislava, Feb. 15–24, 1994)* Naxos ▲ 8.553030 [DDD]

Donizetti, G.:Lucia di Lammermoor (sels), w. Igor Morozov (bar), J. Wildner (cnd), Slovak RSO Bratislava—Orrida è questa notte *(rec Slovak Radio Concert Hall, Bratislava, Feb. 15–24, 1994)* Naxos ▲ 8.553030 [DDD]

Rossini, G.:Guillaume Tell (sels), w. I. Morozov (bar), J. Wildner (cnd), Slovak RSO Bratislava—Arresta...Quali sguardi *(rec Bratislava, Feb. 15–24, 1994)* Naxos ▲ 8.553030 [DDD]

Verdi, G.:La forza del destino (sels), w. Igor Morozov (bar), J. Wildner (cnd), Slovak RSO Bratislava, Slovak Opera Chorus—Invano, Alvaro; Nè gustare m'è dato *(rec Slovak Radio Concert Hall, Bratislava, Feb. 15–24, 1994)* Naxos ▲ 8.553030 [DDD]

Verdi, G.:Otello (sels), w. Igor Morozov (bar), J. Wildner (cnd), Slovak RSO Bratislava—Desdemona rea, si, per ciel *(rec Slovak Radio Concert Hall, Bratislava, Feb. 15–24, 1994)* Naxos ▲ 8.553030 [DDD]

Verdi, G.:I vespri siciliani (sels), w. Igor Morozov (bar), J. Wildner (cnd), Slovak RSO Bratislava—Ebben? Non mi rispondi tu?; Quando al mio sen per te parlava *(rec Slovak Radio Concert Hall, Bratislava, Feb. 15–24, 1994)* Naxos ▲ 8.553030 [DDD]

Losch, Lisolette (sop)

Lehár, F.:Paganini (sels), w. A. Schlemm (mez), P. Anders (ten), Gehly (sgr), Hofmann (sgr), Schneider (sgr), Marszalek (cnd), Cologne RSO, Cologne Radio Chorus [G] Acanta ▲ CD 43810 [DDD]

Losova, Salome (sop)

Kozeluch, Joh. A.:Missa Pastoralis, w. Y. Škvárová (cta), M. Švejda (ten), M. Podskalský (bass), B. Kulínský (cnd), Prague PO, Prague Radio Chorus Multisonic ▲ 31 0003–2 [ADD]

Slavicky, K.:Psalmi, w. Dagmar Pecková (cta), Vladimir Dolezal (ten), Ludek Vele (bass), Jan Hora (org), P. Kühn (cnd), Kühn Chorus *(rec Dvorák Hall of Rudolfinum, Prague, Mar. 14–16, 1989)* Panton ("Protokol XX" series) ▲ PAN 811142 [DDD]

Lothar, Susanne (nar)

Nono, L.:Canto sospeso, w. B. Bonney (sop), S. Otto (alt), M. Torzewski (ten), B. Ganz (nar), Berlin Radio Chorus *(rec Dec. 9–11, 1992)* Sony Classical ▲ SK 53360 [DDD]

Lott, Felicity (sop)

Bach, J.S.:Mass in b, BWV 232, w. A. S. von Otter (mez), H. P. Blochwitz (ten), W. Shimell (bar), G. Howell (b–bar), G. Solti (cnd), Chicago SO, Chicago Sym Chorus London 2–▲ 430353–2 [DDD]

Bach, J.S.:St. Matthew Passion, w. A. Hodgson (cta), R. Tear (ten), J. Shirley–Quirk (bar), S. Roberts (bar), D. Willcocks (cnd), Thames CO, Bach Choir [E] ASV Quicksilva 3–▲ ASQ 324 [ADD]

Brahms, J.:Ein Deutsches Requiem, w. D. Wilson–Johnson (bar), R. Hickox (cnd), London SO, London Sym Chorus [G] Chandos ▲ CHAN 8942 [DDD]

Britten, H.:Chanson françaises (4), w. B. Thomson (cnd), Scottish National Orch [F] Chandos ▲ CHAN 8657 [DDD]

Britten, H.:Les Illuminations, w. B. Thomson (cnd), Scottish National Orch [F] Chandos ▲ CHAN 8657 [DDD]

Britten, H.:Peter Grimes, w. F. Lott (soprano—Ellen Orford), T. Allen (tenor—Captain Balstrode), A. R. Johnson (tenor—Peter Grimes), Covent Garden, B. Haitink (cnd), Royal Opera House Orch, Royal Opera House Chorus Covent Garden EMI Classics ▲ CDCB 54832

Britten, H.:Purcell Realizations, w. Susan Gritton (sop), Sarah Walker (mez), James Bowman (alto), John Mark Ainsley (ten), Anthony Rolfe Johnson (ten), Richard Jackson (bass), Simon Keenlyside (bass), Ian Bostridge (sgr), Graham Johnson (pno) Hyperion 2–▲ CDA 67061/62

Britten, H.:The Turn of the Screw, w. N. Secunde (sop), E. Hulse (sop), P. Cannan (mez), P. Langridge (ten), S. Pay (bar), S. Bedford (cnd), Aldeburgh Festival Ensemble Collins Classics ▲ COL 7030 [DDD]

Charpentier, M.–A.:Te Deum in C, w. I. Partridge (ten), S. Roberts (bar), P. Ledger (org), P. Ledger (cnd), Academy of St. Martin in the Fields, King's College Choir Cambridge EMI Classics ▲ CDM 63135

Chausson, E.:Songs, w. A. Jordan (cnd), Paris Chamber Ensemble FNAC Music ▲ 592300

Delage, M.:Songs, w. A. Jordan (cnd), Paris Chamber Ensemble FNAC Music ▲ 592300

Delius, F.:Songs, w. Sarah Walker (mez), Anthony Rolfe Johnson (ten), E. Fenby (cnd), Royal PO—Orchestral Songs; Songs w. Pno [Scandinavian, French & English] Unicorn–Kanchana ("Souvenir" series) ▲ UK 2075

Hahn, R.:Songs, w. Susan Bickley (mez), Ian Bostridge (ten), Stephen Varcoe (bar), Graham Johnson (pno), Stephen Layton (cnd), London Choral Society—[CD 1] Si mes vers avaient des ailes; Paysage; Rêverie; Offrande; Mai; Infidelité; Seule; Les Cygnes; Nocturne; 3 jours de vendange; D'une prison; Séraphine; L'Heure exquise; Fêtes galantes; 12 Rondels; [CD 2] Quand la nuit n'est pas étoilée; Le Plus beau présent; Sur l'eau; Le Rossignol des lilas; A Chloris; Ma jeunesse; Puisque j'ai mis ma lèvre; Etudes Latines; La Nymphe de la Source; Au Rossignol; Je me souviens; Air de la lettre; C'est très vilain d'être infidèle; C'est sa banlieue; Nous avons fait un beau voyage; La Dernière Valse Hyperion ("The Hyperion French Song Edition" series) 2–▲ CDA 67141/42

Handel, G.F.:Messiah (sels), w. Linda Finnie (mez), Glenn Winslade (ten), Henry Herford (bar), G. Malcolm (cnd), Scottish CO, Scottish Phil Singers IMP ("Classic" series) ▲ IMP 2031

Handel, G.F.:Messiah (reorchd Mozart), w. Felicity Palmer (sop), Phillip Langridge (ten), Robert Lloyd (b–bar), C. Mackerras (cnd), Royal PO, Huddersfield Choral Society [E] ASV ▲ ASV CD 960

Handel, G.F.:Ode for St. Cecilia's Day, w. Anthony Rolfe Johnson (ten), T. Pinnock (cnd), English CO, English Concert Choir [E] Archiv ▲ 419220–2 [DDD]

Haydn, J.:Mass 11, "Nelsonmesse", "Imperial Mass", "Coronation Mass", w. Carolyn Watkinson (cta), Maldwyn Davies (ten), David Wilson–Johnson (bar), T. Pinnock (cnd), English CO [L] Archiv ▲ 423097–2 [DDD]

Jaubert, M.:Songs, w. A. Jordan (cnd), Paris Chamber Ensemble FNAC Music ▲ 592300

Lehár, F.:Die lustige Witwe, w. E. Szmytka (sop), J. Aler (ten), T. Hampson (b–bar), D. Bogarde (nar), F. Welser–Möst (cnd), London PO, Glyndebourne Festival Chorus EMI Classics ▲ CDCB 55152

Mahler, G.:Sym 2, w. J. Hamari (mez), M. Jansons (cnd), Oslo PO, Oslo Phil Chorus Chandos ("Collect" series) 2–▲ CHAN 6595/96 [DDD]

Mozart, W.A.:Arias, w. J. Glover (cnd), London Mozart Players—(5 concert arias) K.217, 383, 528, 582, 583; (2 opera arias) Mitridate, Rè di Ponto *(Lungi da te*; Zaide *(Ruhe sanft, mein holdes Leben)* [G,I] ASV ▲ ASV 683 [DDD]

Mozart, W.A.:Così fan tutte (sels), w. Marie McLaughlin (sop), Nuccia Focile (sop), Jerry Hadley (ten), Alessandro Corbelli (bass), Gilles Cachemaille (bass) *(rec Usher Hall, Edinburgh, Scotland)* Telarc ▲ CD 80399 [DDD]

Mozart, W.A.:Don Giovanni, w. Christine Brewer (sop—Donna Anna), Nuccia Focile (sop—Zerlina), Felicity Lott (sop—Donna Elvira), Jerry Hadley (ten—Don Ottavio), Bo Skovhus (bar—Don Giovanni), Umberto Chiummo (bass—Masetto/Il Commendatore), Alessandro Corbelli (bass—Leporello), C. Mackerras (cnd), Scottish CO, Scottish Chamber Chorus *(rec Usher Hall, Edinburgh, Scotland, July 31–Aug 11, 1995)* Telarc 3–▲ CD 80420 [DDD]

Mozart, W.A.:Exsultate, w. J. Glover (cnd), London Mozart Players [L] ASV ▲ ASV 683 [DDD]

Mozart, W.A.:Requiem, w. D. Jones (mez), K. Lewis (ten), W. White (bar), F. Welser–Möst (cnd), London PO, London Phil Chorus EMI Classics ▲ CDM 63260

Lott, Felicity (sop) (cont.)
Mozart, W.A.:Requiem, w. Cella Jones (mez), Keith Lewis (ten), Willard White (bass), David Bell (org), F. Welser-Möst (cnd), London PO, London Phil Choir Classics for Pleasure ("Eminence" series) ▲ CDEMX 2150 [DDD]
Nocturnal Classics, w. B. Wilde (cnd), Serenata of London, J. Ogdon (pno), Cristina Ortiz (pno) Pickwick ("The Orchid" series) ▲ PICORCD 11007
On Wings of Song, w. Ann Murray (sgr), Graham Johnson (pno) *(rec June 1991)* EMI Classics ▲ CDC 54411-2 [DDD]
Poulenc, F.:Songs, w. Graham Johnson (pno)—34 Songs Forlane ▲ FOR 16730 [DDD]
Poulenc, F.:Songs, w. A. Murray (mez), A. Rolfe-Johnson (ten), R. Jackson (bass), G. Johnson (pno) [F] Hyperion ▲ CDA 66147
Schubert, Franz:Der Hirt auf dem Felsen, w. M. Collins (cl), I. Brown (pno) [G] IMP Classics ▲ PCD 868 [DDD]
Schubert, Franz:Songs (misc), w. Graham Johnson (pno)—Die Forelle, D.550; An Silvia, D.891; Heidenröslein, D.257; Du bist die Ruh, D.776; Der Musensohn, D.764; An die Musik, D.547; Auf dem Wasser zu singen, D.774; Sei mir gegrüsst, D.741; Litanei, D.343; Die junge Nonne, D.828; Ave Maria, D.839; Im Frühling, D.882; Gretchen am Spinnrade, D.118; Nacht und Träume, D.827; Ganymed, D.544; Lied der Mignon; Seligkeit, D.433 IMP ▲ PCD 2016
Songs on Poems by Victor Hugo, w. Graham Johnson (pno) Harmonia Mundi ▲ HMA 1901138
Strauss, R.:Capriccio (sels), w. N. Järvi (cnd), Scottish National Orch—Overture, Intermezzo & Closing Scene [G] Chandos ▲ CHAN 8758 [DDD]
Strauss, R.:4 Last Songs, w. N. Järvi (cnd), Scottish National Orch [G] Chandos ▲ CHAN 8518 [DDD]
Strauss, R.:4 Last Songs, w. N. Järvi (cnd), Scottish National Orch [G] Chandos ▲ CHAN 9054 [DDD]
Strauss, R.:Songs, w. N. Järvi (cnd), Scottish National Orch—Opp. 27/4, 37/3, 48/1, 88/1 [G] Chandos ▲ CHAN 8557 [DDD]
Strauss, R.:Songs, w. N. Järvi (cnd), Scottish National Orch—12 songs—Op. 27, Nos. 1,2 & 4; Op. 37, Nos. 3 & 4; Op. 39, No. 4; Op. 41, No. 1; Op. 43, No. 2; Op. 48, No. 1; Op. 49, No. 1; Op. 56, No. 6; Op. 88, No. 1 [G] Chandos ▲ CHAN 9054 [DDD]
Strauss, R.:Songs, w. N. Järvi (cnd), Scottish National Orch—Verführung; Winterliebe; Des Dichters Abendgang; Frühlingsfeier; Liebeshymnus; Winterweihe; Das Rosenband; Gesang der Apollopriesterin; Zueignung; Hymne an die Liebe; Rückkehr in die Heimat; Die Liebe [G] Chandos ▲ CHAN 9159 [DDD]
Strauss, R.:Songs, w. N. Järvi (cnd), Scottish National Orch—2 songs—Opp. 27/2 & 43/2 [G] Chandos ▲ CHAN 8538 [DDD]
Strauss, R.:Songs, w. N. Järvi (cnd), Scottish National Orch—Opp. 10/1 & 56/6 [G] Chandos ▲ CHAN 8572 [DDD]
Strauss, R.:Songs, w. N. Järvi (cnd), Scottish National Orch—Drei Hymnen, Op. 71 [G] Chandos ▲ CHAN 8734 [DDD]
Strauss, R.:Songs, w. N. Järvi (cnd), Scottish National Orch—Opp. 27/1 & 33/2 [G] Chandos ▲ CHAN 8631 [DDD]
Strauss, R.:Songs, w. N. Järvi (cnd), Scottish National Orch—Das Rosenband, Op. 36/1; Mein Auge, Op. 37/4; Befreit, Op. 39/4; Winterweihe, Op. 48/4 [G] Chandos ▲ CHAN 8744 [DDD]
Vaughan Williams, R.:Sym 1, w. J. Summers (bar), B. Haitink (cnd), London SO, London Sym Chorus [E] EMI Classics ▲ CDC 49911 [DDD]
Wolf, H.:Goethe-Lieder (sels), w. G. Parsons (pno)—9 songs [G] Chandos ▲ CHAN 8726 [DDD]
Wolf, H.:Italienische Liederbücher (sels), w. Peter Schreier (ten), Graham Johnson (pno) Hyperion ▲ CDA 66760
Wolf, H.:Mörike-Lieder (sels), w. Geoffrey Parsons (pno)—10 songs [G] Chandos ▲ CHAN 8726 [DDD]

Lotti, Roque (ten)
Gomes, A.C.:Il Guarany, w. Niza De Castro Tank (sop—Cecilia), Roque Lotti (ten—Ruy Bento), Manrico Patassini (ten—Pery), Paschoal Raymundo (ten—Don Alvaro), Paulo Fortes (bar—Gonzales), Juan Carlos Ortiz (b-bar—Il Cacico), Waldomiro Furlan (bass—Alonso), Josè Perrotta (bass—Don Antonio De Mariz), A. Belardi (cnd), Saõ Paulo Teatro Municipale Orch, Saõ Paulo Teatro Municipale Chorus *(rec Studios of the Teatro Municipal, Saõ Paulo, Brazil, 1959)* Arkadia 2-▲ HP 617.2 [ADD]

Lough, Ernest (trb)
Master Ernest Lough, w. George Thalben-Ball (pno/org), London Temple Church Choir Pearl ▲ PEA 9211 (m) [AAD]

Loup, François (bass)
Donizetti, G.:Gemma di Vergy, w. Montserrat Caballe (sop—Gemma), Anna Ringart (mez—Ida), Luis Lima (ten—Tamas), Vicente Sardinero (bar—Il Conte), Juan Pons (bar—Guido), Francois Loup (b—Rolando), A. Gatto (cnd), Nouvel PO, Jean-Paul Kreder (cnd), French Radio Chorus *(rec live, Salle Pleyet, Paris, Apr 20, 1976)* Agorá Music ("Phoenix" series) 2-▲ 501 [ADD]
Honegger, A.:Jeanne d'Arc au bûcher, w. C. Château (sop), A.M. Rodde (sop), H. Brachet (mez), P. Proenza (ten), Z. Jankovsky (ten), S. Baudo (cnd), Czech PO, Czech Chorus *(rec 1974)* Supraphon 2-▲ 11 0557-2 [AAD]

Lövaas, Kari (sop)
Grieg, E.:Songs, w. E. Marturet (cnd), Berlin SO Verdi Classics ▲ AU 32 116
Puccini, G.:Mass, w. W. Hollweg (ten), B. McDaniel (bar), E. Inbal (cnd), Frankfurt RSO, West German Radio Chorus Philips ("Collector" series) ▲ 434170-2 [ADD]
Sibelius, J.:Songs, w. E. Marturet (cnd), Berlin SO Verdi Classics ▲ AU 32 116
Strauss, R.:Songs, w. E. Marturet (cnd), Berlin SO Verdi Classics ▲ AU 32 116
Wagner, R.:Die Feen, w. L. E. Gray (sop), K. Láki (sop), Anderson (sop), R. Alexander (sop), R. Hermann (bar), K. Moll (bass), W. Sawallisch (cnd), Bavarian RSO, Bavarian Radio Chorus [G] *(rec live, Munich Opera Fest. 1983)* Orfeo 3-▲ 062833 [DDD]

Lovano, Lucien (bass)
Planquette, R.:Rip van Winkle, w. Claudine Collart (sop), Lina Dachary (sop), Freda Betti (cta), René Lenoty (ten), Joseph Peyron (ten), Charles Daguerressar (bar), Julien Giovannetti (bar), Jacques Pruvost (bar), Patrick Orladey (sgr), Joëlle Pierre (sgr), M. Cariven (cnd), ORTF Lyric Orch, ORTF Lyric Chorale Musidisc ▲ MUS 201602 [AAD]

Lovberg, Aase Nordmo (sgr)
Verdi, G.:Un ballo in maschera (sels), w. Ragnar Ulfung (ten), Erik Saeden (bar), C. Savina (cnd), Stockholm Royal Opera House Orch—Act III excerpts *(rec 1966)* Arkadia 2-▲ 488

Love, Shirley (mez)
Janácek, L.:The Diary of One Who Disappeared, w. G. Hirst (ten), Kubalek (pno), Columbia Pro Cantare Women's Ensemble [Cz] Arabesque ▲ Z 6513 [DDD]
Stravinsky, I.:The Rake's Progress, w. J. West (sop—Anne Trulove), S. Love (mez—Mother Goose), W. White (mez—Baba the Turk), J. Garrison (ten—Tome Rakewell), M. Lowrey (ten—Sellem), A. Woodley (bar—Father Truelove), J. Cheek (b-bar), *(orch unknown)* MusicMasters 2-▲ 01612-67131-2 [DDD]

Loverde, Carol (sop)
French & Italian Art Songs, w. J. Wustman (pno) Centaur ▲ CRC 2151
Rapchak, L.:The Lifework of Juan Diaz, w. R. Hovencamp (sgr), R. Alderson (sgr), D. Rowader (sgr), L. Rapchak (cnd), Chicago Chamber Opera Albany ▲ TROY 091 [DDD]

LoVerne, Paula (cta)
Weisgall, H.:Six Characters in Search of an Author, w. E. Byrne (sop—Stepdaughter), S. Foster (sop—Prompter), E. Furtal (sop—Coloratura), J. King (mez—Mezzo), N. Maultsby (mez—Mother), P. LoVerne (cta—Madame Pace), D. Pritchett (alt—Wardrobe Mistress), B. Fowler (ten—Tenore Boffo), K. Anderson (ten—Director), A. Schroeder (bar—Accompanist), P. Zawisza (bar—Stage Manager), R. Orth (bar—Father), G. Lehman (bar—Son), M. Wadsworth (b-bar—Basso Cantante), L. Schaenen (cnd), Chicago Lyric Opera Orch, Lyric Opera Center Chorus *(rec Chicago, June 14 & 16, 1990)* New World 2-▲ 80454-2

Lovett, Carey (sgr)
Catholic Classics, Vol. 1, w. Ann Alderson (sgr), Richard Alderson (sgr), Stacy Kowalczyk (sgr) Gia ▲ GIA 375

Lowe, J. (voc)
Lentz, D.:Missa Umbrarum, w. *(other artists unknown)* New Albion ▲ NA 006 [ADD]
Lentz, D.:O-Ke-Wa, w. *(other artists unknown)* New Albion ▲ NA 006 [ADD]
Lentz, D.:Postludium, w. *(other artists unknown)* New Albion ▲ NA 006 [ADD]

Lowe, Marion (sop)
Mendelssohn, F.:A Midsummer Night's Dream (sels), w. Jennifer Vyvyan (sop), P. Maag (cnd), London SO, Royal Opera House Women's Chorus Covent Garden—Op. 21; Op. 61, Nos 1, 3, 5, 7, 9, 11, 12 Classic Records ▲ CSCD 6001

Lowe, Stacey (sop)
Splendor of the High Holydays, w. Russell Ashley (bar), Lisa Rautenberg (vn), Mary Jane Newman (org/cnd) *(rec SUNY, Purchase, 1995)* Vox Classics ▲ VOX 7510 [DDD]

Lowenstern, Ed (voc)
Spasm, w. Michael Lowenstern (b cl), Heather Barringer (voc), Mark Gibbons (voc), Jay Johnson (voc), Jerome Kitzke (voc), Matt Lambiase (voc), Tom Linker (voc), Michael Lowenstern (voc) *(rec Creation Audio, Minneapolis, NYU Studios, New York City & Studio A, Stony Brook, Aug 1994–July 1996)* New World ▲ 80468-2

Lowenstern, Michael (voc)
Spasm, w. Michael Lowenstern (b cl), Heather Barringer (voc), Mark Gibbons (voc), Jay Johnson (voc), Jerome Kitzke (voc), Matt Lambiase (voc), Tom Linker (voc), Ed Lowenstern (voc) *(rec Creation Audio, Minneapolis, NYU Studios, New York City & Studio A, Stony Brook, Aug 1994–July 1996)* New World ▲ 80468-2

Lowenthal, Eugene (sgr)
Beethoven, L. van:Sym 9, "Choral Sym", w. Agnes Davis (sop), Robert Betts (sgr), Ruth Cathcart (sgr), L. Stokowski (cnd), Philadelphia Orch, Philadelphia Orch Chorus *(rec 1934)* Music & Arts ▲ CD 846 [ADD]
Beethoven, L. van:Sym 9, "Choral Sym", w. Agnes Davis (sop), Robert Betts (sgr), Ruth Cathcart (sgr), L. Stokowski (cnd), Philadelphia Orch Grammofono 2000 ▲ GRM 78577 (m)

Lower, C. Bray (sop)
Adams, J.L.:Night Peace, w. N. Rigel (hp), M. Cebulski (perc) *(rec Sept. 1992)* New Albion ▲ NA 061

Löwgren, Lennart (ct)
The Royal Court of the Vasa Kings, 1523–1611, w. Mikael Bellini (ct), Carl Unander-Scharin (ten), Lars Arvidson (bass), Sven-Anders Benktsson (bass), Sven Aberg (six-course Renaissance lt), Hortus Musicus, Tallinn [cnd:Andres Mustonen] Musica Sveciae ▲ MSV 202 [DDD]

Lowrey, Melvin (ten)
Stravinsky, I.:The Rake's Progress, w. J. West (sop—Anne Trulove), S. Love (mez—Mother Goose), W. White (mez—Baba the Turk), J. Garrison (ten—Tome Rakewell), M. Lowrey (ten—Sellem), A. Woodley (bar—Father Truelove), J. Cheek (b-bar), *(orch unknown)* MusicMasters 2-▲ 01612-67131-2 [DDD]

Lubanska, Anna (alt)
Gloria Tibi Trinitas:Sacred Music of Slav Composers 18th–20th Centuries, w. [cnd:Andrzej Filaber], Warsaw Cathedral Choir, Jolanta Kaufman (sop), Ryszard Wróblewski (ten), Czeslaw Galka (bass), Maciej Piwowarski (org) Polskie Nagrania Edition ▲ ECD 057 [DDD]

Lubaszenko, Edward (nar)
Penderecki, K.:St. Luke Passion, w. S. van Osten (sop), S. Roberts (bar), K. Rydl (bass), K. Penderecki (cnd), Polish National RSO Katowice, Cracow Boys Choir, Warsaw National Phil Chorus Argo ▲ 430328-2 [DDD]

Lubenthal, Horst (ten)
Mozart, W.A.:Missa, K.427, w. Arleen Augér (sop), Heather Harper (sop), Ulrik Cold (bass), S. Celibidache (cnd), Stuttgart RSO, Bavarian Radio Chorus, Southwest German Radio Chorus *(rec live, 1980's)* Topazio ▲ TOP 26045

Luboff, N. (sgr)
Rodgers, R.:Music of, w. S. Bass (sgr), J. Andrews (sgr), P. Como (sgr), D. Reese (sgr), J. Jones (sgr), M. Gold (sgr), N. Walker (sgr), H. Bowen (sgr), V. Damone (sgr), P. Nero (pno), J. P. Morgan (sgr), E. Fisher (sgr), B. Goodman (cl), Ann-Margaret (sgr), Shorty Rogers (sgr), D. Shore (sgr), T. Martin (sgr), M. King (sgr), A. Newley (sgr) RCA ▲ 8590-2 R ▮ 8590-4 R

Luca, Giuseppe De (bar)
Berlioz, H.:La Damnation de Faust (sels)—Canzone della pulce; Su queste rosa; E che fai tu *(rec Milan, 1905 & 1907)* Symposium ▲ SYM 1197
Bizet, G.:Les Pêcheurs de perles (sels), w. Beniamino Gigli (ten)—Del tempio al limitar *(rec 1927)* Minerva ▲ MN-A23 [ADD]
The De Luca Edition, Vol. 1:The Complete G & T, Fonotopia & Supplementary Victor Recordings *(rec 1902–30)* Pearl 3-▲ PEA 9159 [ADD]
The De Luca Edition, Vol. II:The Victor Recordings Pearl 3-▲ PEA 9160 [ADD]
Donizetti, G.:Don Pasquale (sels) *(other artists unknown)*—Bella siccome un angelo; Pronta io son...Convien far la semplicità [w. Aida Gonzaga (sop)]; Cheti, cheti...Aspetta, aspetta cara sposina [w. Ferruccio Corradetti (bar)] *(rec Milan, 1905 & 1907)* Symposium ▲ SYM 1197
Donizetti, G.:Don Pasquale (sels), w. Lucrezia Bori (sop)—Pronta io son *(rec 1921)* Minerva ▲ MN-A23 [ADD]
Donizetti, G.:La favorita (sels) *(other artists unknown)*—Giardini dell'Alcazar...Vien Leonora; A tanto amor *(rec Milan, 1905 & 1907)* Symposium ▲ SYM 1197
Donizetti, G.:Linda di Chamounix (sels)—Ambo nati in questa valle *(rec Milan, 1905 & 1907)* Symposium ▲ SYM 1197
Giuseppe de Luca *(rec 1907–1930)* Nimbus ("Prima Voce" series) ▲ NI 7815 [ADD]
Giuseppe de Luca On Radio:Broadcast Recordings of the Great Italian Baritone Unpublished on Disc (1941–44), w. Lily Pons (sop), Bidù Sayão (sop), Giovanni Martinelli (ten) *(rec 1941–44)* Enterprise ("The Radio Years" series) ▲ ENT RY 25 (m)
Giuseppe de Luca, Vol. 1 Pearl ▲ PEA 9967 (m) [AAD]
Giuseppe de Luca, Vol. 2 *(rec between 1927 & 1930)* Preiser ▲ PRE 89073 [AAD]
Greatist Hits on Records (1928–1939), w. Lily Pons (sop), Enrico di Mazzei (ten) *(rec 1928–1939)* Minerva ▲ MN A38 [ADD]
Meyerbeer, G.:Dinorah (sels), *(orch unknown)*—Sei vendicata assai *(rec Milan, 1905 & 1907)* Symposium ▲ SYM 1197
Mozart, W.A.:Don Giovanni (sels)—Deh, vieni alla finestra *(rec Milan, 1905 & 1907)* Symposium ▲ SYM 1197
Mozart, W.A.:Nozze di Figaro (sels)—Se vuol ballare?; Aprite un po' quel' occhi *(rec Milan, 1905 & 1907)* Symposium ▲ SYM 1197
The 1905 & 1907 Fonotipia Recordings Pearl 2-▲ PEA CD 9226
Opera Arias, w. Joseph Pasternack (cnd), Rosario Bourdon (cnd) *(rec 1917–24 from Victor 78s)* Preiser ("Lebendige Vergangenheit" series) ▲ PRE 89036 (m) [AAD]
Ponchielli, A.:La Gioconda (sels), w. Beniamino Gigli (ten)—Enzo Grimaldo *(rec 1927)* Minerva ▲ MN-A23 [ADD]
Puccini, G.:La Bohème (sels), w. Beniamino Gigli (ten)—Ah Mimì, tu più non torni *(rec 1927)* Minerva ▲ MN-A23 [ADD]
Rossini, G.:Il barbiere di Siviglia (sels)—Largo al factotum *(rec Milan, 1905 & 1907)* Symposium ▲ SYM 1197
Rossini, G.:Guillaume Tell (sels)—Resta immobile *(rec Milan, 1905 & 1907)* Symposium ▲ SYM 1197
Scenes from Il Trovatore & Aida, w. Giovanni Martinelli (ten), Rosa Ponselle (sop), Louise Homer (cta), Ezio Pinza (bass), et al. Pearl ▲ PEA 9350 (m)
Scenes from La forza del destino, w. Giovanni Martinelli (ten), R. Ponselle (sop), E. Pinza (bass) Pearl ▲ PEA 9351 (m)
Thomas, A.:Hamlet (sels)—Come il romito fior *(rec Milan, 1905 & 1907)* Symposium ▲ SYM 1197
Three Legendary Tenors:In Opera & Song, w. Jussi Björling (ten), Enrico Caruso (ten), Beniamino Gigli (ten) Nimbus ▲ NI 1434 [ADD]
Verdi, G.:Aida (sels), w. Elisabeth Rethberg (sop)—Ciel mio padre *(rec 1930)* Minerva ▲ MN-A23 [ADD]
Verdi, G.:Arias—O! de' verd' anni miei [from Ernani]; Pari siamo! [from Rigoletto]; Il balen [from Il Trovatore]; Di Provenza il mar [from La traviata]; Alla vita che t'arride; Eri tu, che macchiavi [both from Un ballo in maschera] *(rec Milan, 1905 & 1907)* Symposium ▲ SYM 1197
Verdi, G.:Ernani (sels), w. Grace Anthony (sop), Alfio Tedesco (ten)—O sommo Carlo *(rec 1928)* Minerva ▲ MN-A23 [ADD]
Verdi, G.:La forza del destino (sels), w. Beniamino Gigli (ten)—Solenne in quest'ora *(rec 1927)* Minerva ▲ MN-A23 [ADD]

Luca, Giuseppe De (bar) (cont.)

Verdi, G.:Rigoletto (sels), w. Amelita Galli–Curci (sop)—Ah, veglia o donna; Piangi, piangi, fanciulla; Oh mia Gilda, fanciulla *(rec 1927 & 1918)* Minerva ▲ MN–A23 [ADD]

Verdi, G.:La traviata (sels), w. Amelita Galli–Curci (sop)—Dite alla giovine *(rec 1927)* Minerva ▲ MN–A23 [ADD]

Lucaciu, Teodora (sop)

Puccini, G.:Turandot, w. Teodora Lucaciu (sop—Liù), Maria Slatinaru (sop—Princess Turandot), Corneliu Finateanu (ten—Pong), George Mircea (ten—Emperor Altoum), Ludovic Speiss (ten—Prince Calaf), Valentin Teodorian (ten—Pang), Octav Enigarescu (bar—Ping), Dionisie Konya (bar—A Mandarin), Mircea Stefanescu (bar—The Prince of Persia), Nicolae Florei (bass—Timur), C. Litvin (cnd), Romanian Radio–TV Orch, Romanian Radio–TV Chorus *(rec Jan 1970)* Vox Box 2–▲ CDX 5160

Lucarini, Bernadette (sop)

Gluck, C.W.:L'Innocenza giustificata, w. B. Lucarini (sop—Flaminia), A. Ruffini (sop—Claudia), A. R. de Simone (sop—Flavio), U. Benelli (bar—Valerio), G. Catalucci (cnd), In Canto di Terni Youth Orch [I] *(rec live 9/90)* Bongiovanni 2–▲ GB 2111/12 [DDD]

Hasse, J.A.:La Serva scaltra, w. Giorgio Gatti (bar), G. Catalucci (cnd), Sassari SO Ensemble [I] Bongiovanni ▲ GB 2101 [DDD]

Pergolesi, G.B.:San Guglielmo Duca d'Aquitania, w. K. Gamberucci (sop), Caldini (sgr), R. Girolami (bass), G. Gatti (bar), Herron (sgr), F. Maestri (cnd), Terni CO [I] *(rec live, 12/18/86)* Bongiovanni 2–▲ GB 2060/61 [DDD]

Lucas, Michaela (sgr)

Liebermann, R.:Medea, w. Françoise Pollet (sop—Medea), Yvi Jänicke (cta—Chalkiope), Zdena Furmančoková (sgr—Syrinx), Dagmar Hesse (sgr—Aiglaia), Hanne Krogen (sgr—Kore), Michaela Lucas (sgr—Oinone), Renate Spingler (sgr—Silene), Jochen Kowalski (ct—Kreon), Aage Haugland (bass—Jason), G. Albrecht (cnd), Hamburg State PO, Hamburg State Opera Chorus *(rec live, Hamburg, Germany, Sept 24, 1995)* Musiques Suisses ▲ 6126 [DDD]

Luccardi, Giancarlo (bass)

Massenet, J.:Thérèse, w. Agnes Baltsa (mez—Thèrése), Francisco Araiza (ten—Armand), Gino Sinimberghi (ten—Officer), George Fortune (bass—André), Giancarlo Luccardi (bass—Morel), Eftimios Michalopoulos (sgr—Officer/Municipal Officer), G. Albrecht (cnd), Rome RAI SO, Giuseppe Piccillo (cnd), Rome RAI Chorus Orfeo ▲ 387961 [DDD]

Luchetti, Veriano (ten)

Berlioz, H.:Les Troyens, w. M. Horne (mez), S. Verrett (mez), N. Gedda (ten), R. Massard (bar), G. Prêtre (cnd), Rome RAI SO, Rome RAI Chorus [F] *(rec live 5/30/69)* Melodram 3–▲ MEL 37060 [AAD]

Berlioz, H.:Les Troyens, w. M. Horne (mez), S. Verrett (mez), N. Gedda (ten), R. Massard (bar), G. Prêtre (cnd), Rome RAI SO, Rome RAI Chorus *(rec live 5/30/69)* Arkadia 4–▲ 461 [ADD]

Cherubini, L.:Médée, w. M. Kalmar (sop), S. Sass (sop), T. Takacs (mez), K. Kovats (bass), L. Gardelli (cnd), Budapest SO, Hungarian Radio Chorus [I] Hungaroton 2–▲ HCD 11904/05

Mussorgsky, M.:Khovanshchina, w. Mietta Sighele (sop—Emma), Elena Souliotis (sop—Susanna), Fiorenza Cossotto (mez—Marfa), Herbert Handt (ten—Scribe), Veriano Luchetti (ten—Prince Andrey Khovansky), Ludovic Spiess (ten—Prince Vasily Golitsin), Claudio Strudthoff (ten—Streshnev), Angelo Marchiandi (bar—Kuz'ka), Teodoro Rovetta (bar—1st Strel'tsi), Siegmund Nimsgern (b–bar—Shaklovity), Cesare Siepi (b–bar—Dosifey), Carlo del Bosco (bass—2nd Strel'tsi), Ubaldo Carosi (bass—Varsonofiev), Nicolai Ghiaurov (bass—Prince Ivan Khovnasky), Giovanni Sciarpeletti (bass—Pastor), B. Leskovich (cnd), Rome RAI SO, Rome RAI Chorus—also includes bonus Act V [w Boris Christoff] (Rome, 1958) *(rec Rome, 1973)* Bella Voce 3–▲ BLV 107.402 [AAD]

Scarlatti, A.:La Griselda, w. M. Freni (sop), L. Alva (ten), R. Panerai (bar), S. Bruscantini (bar), N. Sanzogno (cnd), Naples Alessandro Scarlatti RAI Orch, Naples Scarlatti Chorus [I] *(rec live 10/29/70)* Memories 2–▲ HR 4154/55 (m) [ADD]

Verdi, G.:Attila, w. Rita Orlandi Malaspina (sop—Odabella), Veriano Luchetti (ten—Foresto), Piero De Palma (ten—Uldino), Piero Cappuccilli (bar—Ezio), Nicolai Ghiaurov (bass—Attila), Luigi Roni (bass—Leone), G. Patanè (cnd), La Scala Orch, La Scala Chorus *(rec Milan, May 12, 1975)* Myto 2–▲ MCD 961140

Verdi, G.:Attila, w. Rita Orlandi Malaspina (sop—Odabella), Veriano Luchetti (ten—Foresto), Piero de Palma (ten—Uldino), Piero Cappuccilli (bar—Ezio), Nicolai Ghiaurov (bass—Attila), Luigi Roni (bass—Leone), G. Patanè (cnd), La Scala Orch, La Scala Chorus *(rec Milan, May 15, 1972)* Golden Age of Opera 2–▲ GAO 187/88 [ADD]

Verdi, G.:Don Carlos, w. Katia Ricciarelli (sop), Fiorenza Cossotto (mez), Guido Fabbris (ten), Piero Cappuccilli (bar), Gianfranco Casarini (bass), Nicolai Ghiaurov (bass), Alessandro Maddalena (bass), Aracelly Haengel (sgr), Marisa Salimbeni (sgr), Giorgio Zoranca (sgr), G. Prêtre (cnd), *(orch unknown)* Great Opera Performances 3–▲ GOP 777

Verdi, G.:Requiem Mass, w. Renata Scotto (sop), Agnes Baltsa (mez), Evgeny Nesterenko (bass), R. Muti (cnd), Philharmonia Orch, Ambrosian Chorus EMI Classics 2–▲ CDFB 68613

Luchianez, Victoria (sgr)

Myslivecek, J.:Isacco figura, w. Ilona Czaková (sgr), Hye Jin Kim (sgr), Tatiana Korovina (sgr), Vladimir Dolezal (ten), Ivan Kusnjer (bar), I. Parik (cnd), Prague Sinfonietta, Pavel Kühn (cnd), Kühn Chorus Supraphon 2–▲ SUP 3209

Lucia, A. De (sgr)

Traetta, T.:Litanies, w. S. Krasteva (sop), I. Aramayo Sandivari (sgr), R. Gierlach (bar), I. Lo Vetere (cnd), Giovanile Ambrosiano Ensemble Bongiovanni ▲ GB 2127 [DDD]

Traetta, T.:Stabat Mater, w. S. Krasteva (sop), I. Aramayo Sandivari (sgr), R. Gierlach (bar), I. Lo Vetere (cnd), Giovanile Ambrosiano Ensemble, Piacenza Polifonico Farnesiano Chorus Bongiovanni ▲ GB 2127 [DDD]

Lucia, Fernando de (ten)

Fernando de Lucia Bongiovanni 2–▲ GB 1064/65–2 [ADD]

Fernando de Lucia *(rec by G & T; four recordings, 1)* Opal 2–▲ CDS 9845 (m) [AAD]

Fernando de Lucia, w. Antonio Pini–Corsi (bar), Josefina Huguet (sop), Maria Galvany (sop), Ernesto Badini (bar), Celestina Boninsegna (sop) Symposium ▲ SYM 1149

Fernando de Lucia:Operatic Recordings 1902–21 Pearl 3–▲ PEA 9071 [AAD]

Rossini, G.:Il barbiere di Siviglia (sels), w. M. Resemba (sop), N. Sabatano (sop), F. Novelli (bar), G. Schottler (bass), A. di Tommaso (bass), S. Valentino (bass), S. Sassano (cnd), Naples Teatro San Carlo Orch, Naples Teatro San Carlo Chorus [I] *(rec 1918 for Phonotype)* Standing Room Only ▲ SRO 819–1 [ADD]

The World of Singing, Vol. 3:The Italian School, Part 1:The Italian Tenors Before World War I (1902–13), w. Antonio Aramburo (ten), Alessandro Bonci (ten), Giuseppe Borgatti (ten), Enrico Caruso (ten), Edoardo Garbin (ten), Fiorello Giraud (ten), Francesco Marconi (ten), Giovanni Battista de Negri (ten), Antonio Paoli (ten), Francesco T Enterprise ("Vocal Archives" series) 3–▲ ENT VA 2104

Lucier, Alvin (voc/elec)

Lucier, A.:I Am Sitting in a Room *(rec 1980)* Lovely Music ▲ LCD 1013 [ADD]

Lucier, Mary (sgr)

Ashley, R.:Purposeful Lady Slow Afternoon, w. Cynthia Liddell (nar), Mary Ashley (sgr), Barbara Lloyd (sgr) Lovely Music ▲ LCD 1002 [AAD]

Ludgin, Chester (bar)

Puccini, G.:Il tabarro, w. J. Crader (sop), P. Domingo (ten), J. Rudel (cnd), New York City Opera Orch, New York City Opera Chorus *(rec live 1968; stereo)* Melodram ▲ 17048

Ward, R.:The Crucible, w. P. Brooks (sop), F. Bible (mez), E. Buckley (cnd), New York City Opera Orch, New York City Opera Chorus [E] Albany 2–▲ TROY 025/26–2 [ADD]

Ludha, Ludovít (ten)

Dvořák, A.:The Spectre's Bride, Op. 110, w. Eva Urbanová (sop), Ivan Kusnjer (b–bar), J. Belohlávek (cnd), Prague SO, Pavel Kühn (cnd), Prague Phil Chorus *(rec live, 1995)* Supraphon ▲ SUP 3091

Respighi, O.:Lucrezia, w. Adriana Kohútková (sop—Venilia), Michela Remor (sop—Lucrezia), Stefania Kaluza (mez—La Voce), Denisa Šlepkovská (mez—Servia), Ludovít Ludha (ten—Collatino), Igor Pasek (ten—Bruto), Ján Durčo (bar—Tito/Valerio), Richard Haan (bar—Tarquinio), Rado Hanák (bass—Arunte/Spurio Lucrezio) *(rec Concert Hall of the Slovak Radio, Bratislava, June 9–16, 1994)* Marco Polo ▲ 8.223717 [DDD]

Ludlow, Lynn (spkr)

Partch, H.:Plectra & Percussion Dances (sels), w. Gate 5 Ensemble—Ring Around the Moon *(rec International House, KPFA–Berkeley, Nov 19, 1953)* Innova 4–▲ 401

Ludwig, Christa (mez)

Bach, J.S.:Mass in b, BWV 232, w. E. Schwarzkopf (sop), K. Ferrier (cta), A. Poell (b–bar), Schöffler (bass), H. von Karajan (cnd), Vienna SO [L] *(rec live at Vienna's International Bach Festival, June 15, 1950)* Verona 2–▲ 27073/74 (m) [AAD]

Bach, J.S.:Mass in b, BWV 232, w. E. Schwarzkopf (sop), K. Ferrier (cta), A. Poell (b–bar), Schöffler (bass), H. von Karajan (cnd), Vienna SO, Vienna Singverein—6 arias excerpted from the above rec'g Verona ▲ 27076 (m) [AAD]

Bach, J.S.:Mass in b, BWV 232, w. Gundula Janowitz (sop), Peter Schreier (ten), Karl Ridderbusch (bass), Vienna Choral Academy, H. von Karajan (cnd), Berlin PO Deutsche Grammophon ("Double" series) 2–▲ 439696–2

Bach, J.S.:St. Matthew Passion, w. G. Janowitz (sop), H. Laubenthal (ten), P. Schreier (ten), W. Berry (bar), D. Fischer–Dieskau (bar), H. von Karajan (cnd), Berlin PO, Vienna Singverein, German Opera Chorus [G] Deutsche Grammophon 3–▲ 419789–2 [ADD]

Bach, J.S.:St. Matthew Passion, w. I. Seefried (sop), K. Ferrier (cta), O. Edelmann (b–bar), P. Schoeffler (bass), H. von Karajan (cnd), Vienna SO, Vienna Singverein [G] *(rec live June 9, 1950)* Verona 3–▲ 27070/72 (m) [AAD]

Bach, J.S.:St. Matthew Passion, w. E. Schwarzkopf (sop), N. Gedda (ten), S. Fischer–Dieskau (bar), W. Berry (bass), O. Klemperer (cnd), Philharmonia Orch EMI Classics 3–▲ ZDMC 63058

Bach, J.S.:St. Matthew Passion (sels), w. I. Seefried (sop), K. Ferrier (cta), O. Edelmann (b–bar), P. Schöffler (bass), H. von Karajan (cnd), Vienna SO, Vienna Singverein Verona ▲ 27076 (m) [AAD]

Beethoven, L. van:Fidelio, w. Ingeborg Hallstein (sop—Marzelline), Christa Ludwig (mez—Leonore/Fidelio), Gerhard Unger (ten—Jaquino), Jon Vickers (ten—Florestan), Walter Berry (bass—Pizarro), Franz Crass (bass—Don Fernando), Gottlob Frick (bass—Rocco), O. Klemperer (cnd), Philharmonia Orch, Philharmonia Chorus EMI Classics 2–▲ CDCB 55170

Beethoven, L. van:Fidelio, w. I. Hallstein (sop), J. Vickers (ten), G. Unger (ten), W. Berry (bass), G. Frick (bass), O. Klemperer (cnd), Philharmonia Orch, Philharmonia Chorus [G]; w. minimal dialog EMI Classics ("Studio" series) 2–▲ CDMB 69324 [ADD]

Beethoven, L. van:Missa Solemnis, w. G. Janowitz (sop), F. Wunderlich (ten), W. Berry (bass), H. von Karajan (cnd), Berlin PO, Vienna Singverein [L] Deutsche Grammophon ("Galleria" series) 2–▲ 423913–2 [ADD]

Beethoven, L. van:Missa Solemnis, w. Margaret Price (sop), Wieslaw Ochman (ten), Martti Talvela (bass), K. Böhm (cnd), Vienna PO, Vienna State Opera Chorus *(rec 1957)* Deutsche Grammophon ("Double" series) 2–▲ 437386–2 [ADD]

Beethoven, L. van:Songs—In questa tomba oscura; Freudvoll und leidvoll; Die Trommel geruhret; Ich liebe dich RCA Red Seal ▲ 09026–62652–2

Bellini, V.:Norma, w. M. Callas (sop), F. Corelli (ten), N. Zaccaria (bass), T. Serafin (cnd), La Scala Orch, La Scala Chorus [I] EMI Classics ("Studio" series) 3–▲ CDMC 63000 [ADD]

Bellini, V.:Norma (sels), w. M. Callas (sop), F. Corelli (ten), N. Zaccaria (bass), T. Serafin (cnd), La Scala Orch, La Scala Chorus EMI Classics ▲ ZDM 63091

Bernstein, L.:Candide (restored), w. J. Anderson (sop), D. Jones (mez), J. Hadley (ten), N. Gedda (ten), A. Green (sgr), K. Ollmann (bar), L. Bernstein (cnd), London SO, London Sym Chorus Deutsche Grammophon ■ 437328–4

Bernstein, L.:Candide (restored), w. J. Anderson (sop), D. Jones (mez), J. Hadley (ten), N. Gedda (ten), A. Green (sgr), K. Ollmann (bar), L. Bernstein (cnd), London SO, London Sym Chorus *(rec 1989)* Deutsche Grammophon ▲ 429734–2 [DDD] ■ 429734–4

Bernstein, L.:Music of, w. J. Norman (sop), K. Te Kanawa (sop), J. Anderson (sop), F. von Stade (mez), T. Troyanos (mez), J. Carreras (ten), D. Garrison (ten), J. Hadley (ten), T. Hampson (bar), T. Daly (sgr), G. Kremer (vn), M. Rostropovich (vc), M.T. Thomas (va), L. Bernstein (cnd), *(orch unknown)*—various popular works Deutsche Grammophon ▲ 439251–2 ■ 439251–4

Bernstein, L.:Sym 1, "Jeremiah", w. L. Bernstein (cnd), Israel PO Deutsche Grammophon 2–▲ 445245–2 [ADD]

Brahms, J.:Alto Rhap, w. O. Klemperer (cnd), Philharmonia Orch, Philharmonia Chorus [G] EMI Classics ("Studio" series) ▲ CDM 69650 [ADD]

Debussy, C.:Pelléas et Mélisande, w. M. Ewing (sop), F. Le Roux (bar), J. Van Dam (bass–bar), J.–P. Courtis (bass), C. Abbado (cnd), Vienna PO, Vienna State Opera Chorus Deutsche Grammophon 2–▲ 435344–2 [DDD]

Gluck, C.W.:Iphigénie en Aulide, w. Inge Borkh (sop—Klytämnestra), Christa Ludwig (mez—Iphigenie), Elisabeth Steiner (mez—Artemis), James King (ten—Achilles), Otto Edelmann (b–bar), Alois Pernerstorfer (b–bar), Walter Berry (bass), K. Böhm (cnd), Vienna PO, Salzburg Festival Chamber Choir, Vienna State Opera Chorus *(rec Salzburg, Aug 3, 1962)* Orfeo d'or ("Festspiel Dikumente" series) 2–▲ C 428962 (m) [ADD]

Handel, G.F.:Giulio Cesare in Egitto, w. Lucia Popp (sop), Fritz Wunderlich (ten), Walter Berry (bass), F. Leitner (cnd), Munich PO, Bavarian Radio Chorus [G] *(rec live, Munich 7/1–5/65)* Verona 3–▲ 27035/37 [AAD]

Handel, G.F.:Giulio Cesare in Egitto, w. Lucia Popp (sop), Fritz Wunderlich (ten), Walter Berry (bass), F. Leitner (cnd), Munich PO, Bavarian Radio Chorus Melodram 3–▲ MEL 37059 [AAD]

Humperdinck, E.:Hänsel und Gretel, w. E. Gruberova (sop), G. Jones (sop), B. Bonney (sop), C. Oelze (sop), A. Murray (mez), F. Grundheber (bar), C. Davis (cnd), Dresden Staatskapelle Philips 2–▲ 438013–2

Humperdinck, E.:Hänsel und Gretel, w. I. Cotrubas (sop), E. Söderström (sop), F. von Stade (mez), S. Nimsgern (b–bar), J. Pritchard (cnd), Gürzenich Orch [G] CBS 2–▲ M2K 35898 [ADD]

Les Introuvables EMI Classics 4–▲ ZDMD 64074

Liebermann, R.:Die Schule der Frauen, w. Anneliese Rothenberger (sop—Agnes), Christa Ludwig (mez—Georgette), Nicolai Gedda (ten—Horace), Alois Pernerstorfer (b–bar—Gronte), Walter Berry (bass—Poquelin), Kurt Böhme (bass—Arnolphe), G. Szell (cnd), Vienna PO *(rec Salzburg, Aug 17, 1957)* Orfeo d'or ("Festspiel Dikumente" series) 2–▲ C 429962 (m) [ADD]

Mad About Angels, w. Cheryl Studer (sop), Anne Sofie von Otter (mez), José Carreras (ten), New York PO [cnd:Leonard Bernstein], English Baroque Soloists [cnd:John Eliot Gardiner], Philharmonia Orch, Philharmonia Chorus [cnd:Carlo Maria Giulini], Orp Deutsche Grammophon ▲ 449113–2 ■ 449113–4

Mahler, G.:Kindertotenlieder, w. H. von Karajan (cnd), Berlin PO Deutsche Grammophon ("Double" series) 2–▲ 439678–2

Mahler, G.:Kindertotenlieder, w. A. Vandernoot (cnd), Philharmonia Orch [G] EMI Classics ("Studio" series) ▲ CDM 69499 [ADD]

Mahler, G.:Das Lied von der Erde, w. R. Kollo (ten), L. Bernstein (cnd), Israel PO Sony Classical ▲ SMK 47589

Mahler, G.:Das Lied von der Erde, w. W. Kmentt (ten), C. Kleiber (cnd), Vienna SO Exclusive ▲ EXL 53 [ADD]

Mahler, G.:Das Lied von der Erde, w. F. Wunderlich (ten), O. Klemperer (cnd), Philharmonia Orch [G] EMI Classics ▲ CDC 47231

Mahler, G.:Das Lied von der Erde, w. T. Moser (ten), V. Neumann (cnd), Czech PO *(rec 1983)* Praga ▲ PR 254052

Mahler, G.:Songs—Ich ging mit lust; Phantasie; Frühlingsmorgen; Um schlimme Kinder artig zu machen; Scheiden und Meiden RCA Red Seal ▲ 09026–62652–2

Mahler, G.:Songs, w. O. Klemperer (cnd), Philharmonia Orch—Ich bin der Welt abhanden gekommen; Um Mitternacht; Das irdische Leben; Ich atmet' einen Lindenduft; Wo die schönen Trompeten blasen [G] EMI Classics ("Studio" series) ▲ CDM 69499 [ADD]

Mahler, G.:Songs from Rückert, w. H. von Karajan (cnd), Berlin PO *(rec 1975–81)* Deutsche Grammophon ("Double" series) 2–▲ 439678–2

Mahler, G.:Songs from Rückert, w. O. Klemperer (cnd), Philharmonia Orch—3 songs EMI Classics ("Studio" series) ▲ CDM 69499 [ADD]

Mahler, G.:Syms, w. J. Blegen (sop), B. Hendricks (sop), M. Price (sop), G. Zeumer (sop), H. Wittek (trb), A. Baltsa (mez), K. Riegel (ten), H. Prey (bar), A. Schmidt (bar), J. Van Dam (b–bar), L. Bernstein (cnd), New York PO, Royal Concertgebouw Orch, Vienna PO, Westminster Choir, New York Choral Artists, Brooklyn Boys' Choir, Vienna Boys' Choir, Vienna State Opera Chorus, Vienna Singverein Deutsche Grammophon 13–▲ 435162–2 [DDD]

Mahler, G.:Sym 2, w. Ileana Cotrubas (sop), Z. Mehta (cnd), Vienna PO, Vienna State Opera Chorus *(rec 1975)* London ("Double Decker" series) 2–▲ 440615–2 [ADD]

VOCALISTS 1277

Ludwig, Christa (mez) (cont.)

Mahler, G.:Sym 3, w. L. Bernstein (cnd), New York PO, Brooklyn Boys' Chorus, New York Choral Artists [G] Deutsche Grammophon 2-▲ 427328-2 [DDD]

Mahler, G.:Sym 3, w. V. Neumann (cnd), Czech PO, Czech Phil Chorus *(rec Dec. 16-19, 1981)* Supraphon 3-▲ 11 1972-2 [DDD]

Mozart, W.A.:Arias, w. Arleen Augér (sop), Kathleen Battle (sop), Irma Beilke (sop), Helena Braun (sop), Lisa Della Casa (sop), Maria Cebotari (sop), Ileana Cotrubas (sop), Helen Donath (sop), Mirella Freni (sop), Reri Grist (sop), Edita Gruberova (sop), Elisabeth Grümmer (sop), Hilde Güden (sop), Ingeborg Hallstein (sop), Luise Helletsgruber (sop), Gundula Janowitz (sop), Sena Jurinac (sop), Erika Köth (sop), Evelyn Lear (sop), Wilma Lipp (sop), Margaret Marshall (sop), Edith Mathis (sop), Jarmila Novotna (sop), Margherita Perras (sop), Lucia Popp (sop), Elisabeth Rethberg (sop), Anneliese Rothenberger (sop), Elisabeth Schumann (sop), Elisabeth Schwarzkopf (sop), Graziella Sciutti (sop), Irmgard Seefried (sop), Graziella Sciutti (sop), Julia Varady (sop), Agnes Baltsa (mez), Margit Bokor (mez), Brigitte Fassbaender (mez), Ann Murray (mez), Francisco Araiza (ten), Anton Dermota (ten), Helge Rosvaenge (ten), Rudolf Schock (ten), Peter Schreier (ten), Leopold Simoneau (ten), Eric Tappy (ten), Richard Tauber (ten), Gösta Winbergh (ten), Josef Witt (ten), Fritz Wunderlich (ten), Christian Boesch (bar), Willy Domgraf-Fassbaender (bar), Karl Dönch (bar), Dietrich Fischer-Dieskau (bar), Erich Kunz (bar), Eberhard Wächter (bar), Hans Hotter (b-bar), Paul Schöffler (b-bar), Cesare Siepi (b-bar), José Van Dam (b-bar), Walter Berry (bass), Geraint Evans (bass), Nicolai Ghiaurov (bass), Alexander Kipnis (bass), Richard Mayr (bass), Kurt Moll (bass), James Morris (bass), Ezio Pinza (bass), Martti Talvela (bass), Giorgio Tozzi (bass), Hans Duhan (sgr), Res Fischer (sgr), Marie Gerhart (sgr), *(various orchs & cnds)*—sels from Idomeneo, Die Entführung aus der Serail, Le nozze di Figaro, Don Giovanni, Così fan tutte, Die Zauberflöte & various arias Orfeo d'or ("Festspiel Dokumente" series) 5-▲ 408955

Mozart, W.A.:Così fan tutte, w. L. della Casa (sop), E. Loose (sop), A. Dermota (ten), E. Kunz (bar), P. Schoeffler (bass) London 2-▲ 417185-2 [ADD]

Mozart, W.A.:Così fan tutte, w. E. Schwarzkopf (sop—Fiordiligi), C. Ludwig (sop—Dorabella), G. Sciutti (sop—Despina), W. Kmentt (ten—Ferrando), H. Prey (bar—Gugliemo), K. Dönch (bar—D. Alfonso), K. Böhm (cnd), Vienna PO, Vienna State Opera Chorus [I] *(rec live, Salzburg, Aug. 8, 1962)* Arkadia 2-▲ 455 [ADD]

Mozart, W.A.:Così fan tutte, w. E. Schwarzkopf (sop), H. Steffek (sop), A. Kraus (ten), G. Taddei (bar), W. Berry (bass), K. Böhm (cnd), Philharmonia Orch, Philharmonia Chorus [I] EMI Classics ("Studio" series) 3-▲ CDMC 69330 [ADD]

Mozart, W.A.:Così fan tutte (sels), w. Elisabeth Schwarzkopf (sop), Irmgard Seefried (sop), Anton Dermota (ten), Erich Kunz (bar), Paul Schoeffler (b-bar), K. Böhm (cnd), Vienna PO—Sento, o Dio; Sorella, cosa dici?—Prenderò quel brunettino Orfeo d'or ("Festspiel Dokumente" series) ▲ 394201

Mozart, W.A.:Don Giovanni, w. C. Watson (sop), N. Gedda (ten), N. Ghiaurov (bass), O. Klemperer (cnd), New Philharmonia Orch, New Philharmonia Chorus EMI Classics 3-▲ CDMC 63841

Mozart, W.A.:Missa, K.317, w. Wilma Lipp (sop), Murray Dickie (ten), Walter Berry (bass), J. Horenstein (cnd), Vienna SO Vox Legends 2-▲ CDX 5524

Mozart, W.A.:Missa, K.427, w. W. Lipp (sop), M. Dickie (ten), W. Berry (bass), F. Grossmann (cnd), Pro Musica Orch, Vienna Oratorio Chorus [L] *(rec stereo, 1958)* Preiser ▲ 90053 [AAD]

Mozart, W.A.:Vesperae solennes, w. Wilma Lipp (sop), Murray Dickie (ten), Walter Berry (bass), J. Horenstein (cnd), Vienna SO Vox Legends 2-▲ CDX 5524

Orff, C.:De temporum fine comoedia, w. P. Schreier (ten), J. Greindl (bass), H. von Karajan (cnd), Cologne RSO, Cologne Radio Chorus [L] Deutsche Grammophon ("20th Century Classics" series) ▲ 429859-2 [ADD]

Pfitzner, H.:Palestrina, w. S. Jurinac (sop), F. Wunderlich (ten), G. Stolze (ten), O. Wiener (bar), G. Frick (bass), W. Berry (bass), R. Heger (cnd), Vienna State Opera Orch, Vienna State Opera Chorus *(rec live, Vienna 12/16/64)* Myto 3-▲ 3 MCD 92259 [ADD]

Puccini, G.:Madama Butterfly, w. M. Freni (sop), L. Pavarotti (ten), R. Kerns (bar), H. von Karajan (cnd), Vienna PO [I] London 3-▲ 417577-2 [ADD]

Puccini, G.:Madama Butterfly (sels), w. M. Freni (sop), L. Pavarotti (ten), R. Kerns (bar), H. von Karajan (cnd), Vienna PO [I] London ▲ 421247-2 [ADD] ■ 421247-4

Rossini, G.:Stabat Mater, w. E. Grümmer (sop), M. von Ilosvay (mez), H. Fehn (bass), F. Fricsay (cnd), Cologne RSO, Cologne Radio Chorus [L] *(rec 1953)* Melodram ▲ CDM 16523 [AAD]

Schubert, Franz:Songs (misc)—Geheimnis; Auf der Donau; Der Tod und das Mädchen; Frühlingsglaube; others RCA Red Seal ▲ 09026-62652-2

Schubert, Franz:Winterreise, w. James Levine (pno) Deutsche Grammophon ("Masters" series) ▲ 445521-2

Schumann, R.:Frauenliebe und -leben, w. G. Parsons (pno) *(rec 1966)* Praga ▲ PR 254052 (m)

Strauss (II), Joh.:Die Fledermaus (sels), w. Wilma Lipp (sop), Gerda Scheyer (sop), Anton Dermota (ten), Walter Berry (bar), Erich Kunz (bar), Eberhard Wachter (bar), O. Ackermann (cnd), Philharmonia Orch, London Phil Chorus Emperor Operetta ▲ KO 86340

Strauss, R.:Arias, w. W. Berry (b-bar), H. Hollreiser (cnd), German Opera Orch, German Opera Chorus—two of Ariadne's solo arias from Ariadne auf Naxos, duets from Elektra, Frau ohne Schatten, Rosenkavalier [G] *(rec Berlin, 1963-64)* Tessitura ▲ 0049-2 [ADD]

Strauss, R.:Capriccio, w. E. Schwarzkopf (sop), A. Moffo (sop), N. Gedda (ten), D. Fischer-Dieskau (bar), E. Wächter (bar), H. Hotter (b-bar), W. Sawallisch (cnd), Philharmonia Orch [G] EMI Classics 2-▲ CDCB 49014 (m) [ADD]

Strauss, R.:Der Rosenkavalier, w. Elisabeth Schwarzkopf (sop), Teresa Stich-Randall (mez), Otto Edelmann (b-bar), H. von Karajan (cnd), Philharmonia Orch, Philharmonia Chorus *(rec 1956)* EMI Classics ▲ CDCC 56113 (m)

Strauss, R.:Der Rosenkavalier, w. E. Mathis (sop), T. Troyanos (mez), O. Wiener (bar), T. Adam (b-bar), K. Böhm (cnd), Vienna PO *(rec Salzburg Festival, 1969)* Deutsche Grammophon 3-▲ 445338-2 [ADD]

Strauss, R.:Der Rosenkavalier, w. E. Schwarzkopf (sop), T. Stich-Randall (sop), O. Edelmann (bass), H. von Karajan (cnd), Philharmonia Orch [G] EMI Classics 3-▲ CDCC 49354 [ADD] 3-■ 3CDX 3970

Strauss, R.:Der Rosenkavalier, w. G. Jones (sop), L. Popp (sop), P. Domingo (ten), W. Berry (b-bar), L. Bernstein (cnd), Vienna PO [G] CBS 3-▲ M3K 42564 [ADD]

Strauss, R.:Der Rosenkavalier (sels), w. E. Schwarzkopf (sop), T. Stich-Randall (mez), O. Edelmann (bass), H. von Karajan (cnd), Philharmonia Orch, Philharmonia Chorus EMI Classics ▲ ZDM 63452

Strauss, R.:Der Rosenkavalier (sels), w. L. Rysanek (sop), et al.—selected scenes Melodram 2-▲ MEL 27098

Strauss, R.:Salome, w. I. Borkh (sop—Salome), M. Klose (mez—Herodias), C. Ludwig (mez—Page), M. Lorenz (ten—Herodes), F. Fehringer (ten—Narraboth), F. Frantz (bar—Jokanaan), K. Schröder (cnd), Hessian RSO *(rec 1952)* Myto 2-▲ 93592

Verdi, G.:Un ballo in maschera, w. M. Price (sop), K. Battle (sop), L. Pavarotti (ten), R. Bruson (bar), G. Solti (cnd), National PO London, National Phil London Chorus [I] London 2-▲ 410210-2 [DDD]

Verdi, G.:Un ballo in maschera, w. M. Price (sop), K. Battle (sop), L. Pavarotti (ten), R. Bruson (bar), G. Solti (cnd), National PO London, National Phil London Chorus [I] London ▲ 425529-2 [DDD]

Verdi, G.:Macbeth, w. C. Cossutta (ten), K. Ridderbusch (bass), S. Milnes (bass), K. Böhm (cnd), Vienna State Opera Orch, Vienna State Opera Chorus *(rec live 1970)* Legato Classics 2-▲ LCD 143-2 [ADD]

Verdi, G.:Requiem Mass, w. E. Schwarzkopf (sop), N. Gedda (ten), N. Ghiaurov (bass), C. M. Giulini (cnd), Philharmonia Orch, London Phil Choir [L] EMI Classics 2-▲ CDCB 47257 [ADD]

Wagner, R.:Götterdämmerung, w. B. Nilsson (sop), J. Watson (sop), W. Windgassen (ten), D. Fischer-Dieskau (bar), G. Frick (bass), G. Solti (cnd), Vienna PO [G] London 4-▲ 414115-2 [ADD]

Wagner, R.:Götterdämmerung (immolation scene), w. H. Knappertsbusch (cnd), North German RSO [G] *(rec live 3/24/63)* Arkadia ▲ 730 [ADD]

Wagner, R.:Götterdämmerung (immolation scene), w. H. Hollreiser (cnd), German Opera Orch [G] *(rec studio, Berlin, ca. 1963/64)* Tessitura ▲ 0049-2 [ADD]

Wagner, R.:Lohengrin, w. E. Grümmer (sop), J. Thomas (ten), D. Fischer-Dieskau (bar), G. Frick (bass), R. Kempe (cnd), Vienna PO, Vienna State Opera Chorus [G] EMI Classics 3-▲ CDCC 49017 [ADD]

Wagner, R.:Die Meistersinger von Nürnberg, w. C. Ligendza (sop), P. Domingo (ten), R. Laubenthal (ten), D. Fischer-Dieskau (bar), R. Hermann (bar), P. Lagger (bass), E. Jochum (cnd), German Opera Orch, German Opera Chorus Deutsche Grammophon ("Domingo Edition" series) ▲ 435406-2

Wagner, R.:Die Meistersinger von Nürnberg, w. C. Ligendza (sop), P. Domingo (ten), R. Laubenthal (ten), D. Fischer-Dieskau (bar), R. Hermann (bar), P. Lagger (bass), E. Jochum (cnd), German Opera Orch, German Opera Chorus [G] Deutsche Grammophon 4-▲ 415278-2 [ADD]

Ludwig, Christa (mez) (cont.)

Wagner, R.:Parsifal, w. E. Höngen (cta), H.-M. Uhle (ten), H. Hotter (b-bar), T. Franc (bass), W. Berry (bass), H. von Karajan (cnd), Vienna State Opera Orch, Vienna State Opera Chorus [G] *(rec live 4/1/61)* Arkadia 3-▲ 219 (m) [ADD]

Wagner, R.:Parsifal, w. A. Kollo (ten), D. Fischer-Dieskau (bar), Z. Kelemen (bar), G. Frick (bass), G. Solti (cnd), Vienna PO, Vienna State Opera Chorus, Vienna Boys' Choir [G] London 4-▲ 417143-2 [ADD]

Wagner, R.:Das Rheingold, w. B. Svendén (sop), S. Jerusalem (ten), H. Zednik (ten), E. Wlaschiha (bar), J. Morris (bass), J. Levine (cnd), Metropolitan Opera Orch [G] Deutsche Grammophon 3-▲ 427607-2 [DDD]

Wagner, R.:Rienzi, der Letzte der Tribunen, w. S. Svanholm (ten), P. Schoeffler (b-bar), J. Krips (cnd), *(orch unknown)* [G] *(rec live, Vienna, 1960)* Melodram 2-▲ MEL 27023

Wagner, R.:Der Ring des Nibelungen, w. B. Nilsson (sop), K. Flagstad (sop), R. Crespin (sop), C. Watson (sop), C. Ludwig (mez), J. Madeira (mez), S. Svanholm (ten), J. King (ten), G. Stolze (ten), W. Windgassen (ten), G. London (bar), D. Fischer-Dieskau (bar), H. Hotter (b-bar), G. Neidlinger (b-bar), G. Frick (bass), G. Solti (cnd), Vienna PO [G] London 15-▲ 414100-2 [ADD]

Wagner, R.:Der Ring des Nibelungen, w. R. Crespin (sop), G. Janowitz (sop), H. Dernesch (mez), J. Vickers (ten), D. Fischer-Dieskau (bar), D. Thomas (bass), H. von Karajan (cnd), Berlin PO *(rec late 1960s)* Deutsche Grammophon 15-▲ 435211-2 [ADD]

Wagner, R.:Der Ring des Nibelungen, w. R. Crespin (sop), G. Janowitz (sop), H. Dernesch (mez), J. Vickers (ten), D. Fischer-Dieskau (bar), D. Thomas (bass), H. von Karajan (cnd), Berlin PO *(rec live at Salzburg Easter Festivals, 1967-1970)* Arkadia 12-▲ 223 (m) [ADD]

Wagner, R.:Der Ring des Nibelungen (sels), w. J. Norman (sop), H. Behrens (sop), K. Battle (sop), J. Morris (mez), R. Goldberg (ten), S. Jerusalem (ten), E. Wlaschiha (bar), M. Salminen (bass), J. Levine (cnd), Metropolitan Opera Orch—The Compact Ring—Ride of the Valkyries Wotan's Farewell & Magic Fire Music, Forest Murmurs, Brünnhilde's Awakening, Siegfried's Funeral Music, Brünnhilde's Immolation, & others Deutsche Grammophon ▲ 437825-2

Wagner, R.:Tannhäuser, w. H. Dernesch (sop), A. Kollo (ten), H. Braun (bar), H. Sotin (bass), G. Solti (cnd), Vienna PO [Paris version] [G] London 3-▲ 414581-2 [ADD]

Wagner, R.:Tristan und Isolde, w. B. Nilsson (sop), W. Windgassen (ten), E. Wächter (bar), M. Talvela (bass), K. Böhm (cnd), Bayreuth Festival Orch, Bayreuth Festival Chorus [G] *(rec Bayreuth Festival, 1966)* Deutsche Grammophon 3-▲ 419889-2 [ADD]

Wagner, R.:Tristan und Isolde, w. B. Nilsson (sop), W. Windgassen (ten), E. Wächter (bar), M. Talvela (bass), K. Böhm (cnd), Bayreuth Festival Orch, Bayreuth Festival Chorus [G] Philips 3-▲ 434425-2 [ADD]

Wagner, R.:Tristan und Isolde, w. H. Dernesch (sop), J. Vickers (ten), P. Schreier (ten), B. Weikl (bar), W. Berry (bass), K. Ridderbusch (bass), H. von Karajan (cnd), Berlin PO, German Opera Chorus [G] EMI Classics ("Studio" series) 4-▲ CDMD 69319 [ADD]

Wagner, R.:Tristan und Isolde (prelude & liebestod), w. H. Knappertsbusch (cnd), North German RSO [G] *(rec live, 3/24/63)* Arkadia ▲ 730 [ADD]

Wagner, R.:Die Walküre, w. B. Nilsson (sop), R. Crespin (sop), J. King (ten), H. Hotter (b-bar), G. Frick (bass), G. Solti (cnd), Vienna PO [G] London 4-▲ 414105-2 [ADD]

Wolf, H.:Mörike-Lieder (sels) RCA Red Seal ▲ 09026-62652-2

Wolf, H.:Spanisches Liederbuch (sels) RCA Red Seal ▲ 09026-62652-2

Ludwig, Kurt (ten)

Nicolai, O.:Lustigen Weiber, w. H. Donath (sop), E. Mathis (sop), H. Schwarz (mez), K.-E. Mercker (ten), P. Schreier (ten), C. Dormoy (bar), B. Weikl (bar), K. Moll (bass), S. Vogel (bass), B. Klee (cnd), Berlin Staatskapelle, Berlin State Opera Chorus *(rec July 3, 1976)* Berlin Classics ("Eterna" series) ▲ BER 2046-2 [ADD]

Ludwig, Walther (ten)

Beethoven, L. van:Sym 9, "Choral Sym", w. Erna Berger (sop), Gertrude Pitzinger (cta), Rudolf Watzke (bass), W. Furtwängler (cnd), Berlin PO, Bruno Kittel Choir *(rec Queens Hall, London, May 1, 1937)* Music & Arts ▲ CD 818 [ADD]

Brahms, J.:Liebeslieder Waltzes SATB, w. E. Berger (sop), G. Pfitzinger (alt), E. Wenk (bass), E.-G. Scherzer (pno), G. Falbe (pno) *(rec 1959)* FNAC Music ▲ 642313

Brahms, J.:Neue Liebeslieder Waltzes, w. E. Berger (sop), G. Pfitzinger (alt), E. Wenk (bass), E.-G. Scherzer (pno), G. Falbe (pno) *(rec 1959)* FNAC Music ▲ 642313

The Legendary Singers at Lindenoper Berlin (1927-1945)—, w. Gitta Alpar (sop), Erna Berger (sop), Tiana Lemnitz (sop), Maria Müller (sop), Margarete Klose (cta), Peter Anders (ten), Max Lorenz (ten), Lauritz Melchior (ten), Rudolf Schock (ten), Franz Völker (ten), Willi Domgraf-Fassb *(rec 1927; 1937; 1941-45)* Minerva ▲ MN A21 [ADD]

Mozart, W.A.:Zauberflöte, w. Wilma Lipp (sop), Irmgard Seefried (sop), Peter Klein (ten), Karl Schmitt-Walter (bar), Josef Greindl (bass), Paul Schöffler (sgr), W. Furtwängler (cnd), Vienna PO, Vienna State Opera Chorus *(rec 1949)* Music & Arts 3-▲ CD 882 [AAD]

Mozart, W.A.:Zauberflöte (sels), w. I. Seefried (sop), W. Lipp (sop), K. Schmitt-Walter (bar), J. Greindl (bass), W. Furtwängler (cnd), Vienna PO, Vienna State Opera Chorus—Ov. & 11 arias *(rec live, Salzburg, July, 27, 1949)* Arkadia 3-▲ 361 [ADD]

Nicolai, O.:Lustigen Weiber, w. I. Bielke (sop), M. L. Schilp (mez), G. Hann (bass), W. Streinz (bass), A. Rother (cnd), Berlin RSO, Berlin State Opera Chorus *(rec May 2, 1943)* Preiser 2-▲ PRE 90208 [ADD]

Schubert, H.:Hymnisches Konzert, w. Erna Berger (sop), *(organist unknown)*, W. Furtwängler (cnd), Berlin PO Arkadia 2-▲ 365

Schumann, R.:Scenes from Goethe's "Faust", w. Lore Hoffman (sop), Karl Schmitt-Walter (bar), H. Schmidt-Isserstedt (cnd), Berlin German Opera Orch, Berlin German Opera Chorus Enterprise ("The Radio Years" series) 2-▲ ENT RY 66

Strauss, R.:Taillefer, w. Maria Cebotari (sop), Hans Hotter (bar), *(orch & chorus unknown)* *(rec 1943-44)* Preiser ▲ PRE 90222 [ADD]

Walther Ludwig *(rec 1932-37)* Preiser ("Lebendige Vergangenheit" series) ▲ PRE 89088 [AAD]

Luft, Lorna (sgr)

Gershwin, G.:Girl Crazy, w. J. Blazer (sop), D. Carroll (sgr), J. Mauceri (cnd), *(orch unknown)* Elektra/Nonesuch ▲ 9 79250-2

Luger, Suze (cta)

Beethoven, L. van:Sym 9, "Choral Sym", w. To de Sluys (sop), Louis van Tulder (ten), Willem Ravelli (bass), W. Mengelberg (cnd), Royal Concertgebouw Orch, Toonkunst Chorus *(rec 1938)* Music & Arts ▲ CD 918

Lugo, Giuseppe (ten)

Giuseppe Lugo Preiser ("Lebendige Vergangenheit" series) ▲ PRE 89034 (m) [AAD]

Leoncavallo, R.:Pagliacci (sels), w. Enrico Caruso (ten), Antonio Paoli (ten), Giovanni Zenatello (ten), Amedeo Bassi (ten), Hermann Jadlowker (ten), Fernand Ansseau (ten), Hipolito Lazaro (ten), Nino (Filippo) Piccaluga (ten), Mario Chamlee (ten), Giacomo Lauri-Volpi (ten), Miguel Fleta (ten), Giovanni Martinelli (ten), Aureliano Pertile (ten), Georges Thill (ten), Alessandro Valente (ten), Francesco Merli (ten), Lauritz Melchior (ten), Marcel Wittrisch (ten), Joseph Schmidt (ten), Beniamino Gigli (ten), Helge Roswaenge (ten), Jussi Bjoerling (ten)—23 versions of the tenor aria "Vesti la giubba" *(rec 1907-1944)* Bongiovanni ▲ GB 1071 [ADD]

Luise, Melchiorre (bass)

Puccini, G.:Tosca, w. Leyla Gencer (sop), Giuseppe Taddei (bar), Vittorio de Santis (sgr), V. Bellezza (cnd), *(orch & chorus unknown)* *(rec live, Naples, Mar. 21, 1955)* Great Opera Performances 2-▲ GOP 751

Lukas, Ralf (bar)

Künneke, E.:The Alluring Flame, w. Birgit Fandrey (sgr—Dolores), Christianne Hossfeld (sgr—Lisbeth), Maria Mallé (sgr), Jürgen Sacher (ten—Master), Ralf Lukas (bar—Hoffman), Gerd Grochowski (sgr—1st Neighbor), Gerhard Peters (sgr—Friedrich), Zoran Todorovic (sgr—Jacinto), Theodor Weimer (sgr—2nd Neighbor), P. Falk (cnd), Cologne RSO, Cologne Radio Chorus *(rec Cologne, Nov 7-26, 1994)* Capriccio ▲ 10753 [DDD]

Mendelssohn, F.:Die Hochzeit des Camacho, w. R. Schudel (sop—Quiteria), C. Swanson (sop—Lucinda), C. Bieber (ten—Basilio), W. Mok (ten—Vivaldo), V. Horn (ten—Camacho), R. Lukas (bar—Carrasco), J. Becker (bass—Sancho Panza), W. Murray (bass—Don Quixote), B. Klee (cnd), Berlin RSO, Berlin Radio Chorus [G] Koch Schwann 2-▲ 314042 [DDD]

Lukasowsky, Franz (bass)
Bach, J.S.:St. John Passion, w. P. Curtin (sop), E. Thomann (sop), E. Alberts (cta), W. Kmentt, J. Van Kesteren (ten), R. Springer (bar), O. Wiener (bar), D. Smith (b–bar), F. Guthrie (bass), H. Scherchen (cnd), Vienna State Opera Orch, Vienna Academy Chorus [G] *(rec ca 1960)* MCA Classics 2-▲ MCAD2-9804

Lukavsky, Radovan (nar)
Krček, J.:Sym 2, w. J. Belohlávek (cnd), Czech PO, Pavel Kühn (cnd), Kühn Chorus Supraphon ▲ SUP CD 3195

Luker, Rebecca (sgr)
Gershwin, G.:Strike up the Band, w. B. Barrett (sgr), D. Chastain (sgr), J. Mauceri (cnd), *(orch unknown)* [based on original Gershwin manuscripts] Elektra/Nonesuch 2-▲ 79273-2 2-■ 79273-4

Lukic, Ksenija (sop)
Dessau, P.:Les Voix, w. Horst Göbel (pno), N. Athinäos (cnd), Frankfurt State Orch Signum ▲ X65-00 [DDD]

Lukic, Ksenija (sgr)
Wagner, S.:Schwarzschwanenreich, w. Beth Johanning (sop—Linda), Kerstin Quandt (cta—Ursula), Walter Raffeiner (ten—Ludwig), Lucian Chioreanu (ten—A Boy), André Wenhold (bar—Oswald), Roland Hartmann (sgr—Tempter/Priest), Jutta Maria Schmitz (sgr—Ash-Woman), Ksenija Lukie (sgr—A Girl), K. Bach (cnd), Thüringian Saalfeld-Rudolstadt SO, Thüringian Landestheater Rudolstadt Chorus *(rec Thüringer Landestheater, Rudolstadt, June 1994)* Marco Polo 2-▲ 8.223777-8 [DDD]

Lukomska, Halina (sop)
Boulez, P.:Pli selon pli, Portrait de Mallarmé, w. P. Boulez (cnd), BBC SO Sony Classical ("Pierre Boulez Edition" series) ▲ SMK 68335
Huber, K.:Soliloquia, w. S. Klare (mez), D. Ahlstedt (ten), B. McDaniel (bar), H. G. Ahrens (b–bar), H. Zender (cnd), Munich Bavarian RSO, Munich Bavarian Radio Chorus [L] *(rec Dec. 17, 1979)* Grammont ▲ CTSP 24-2 [ADD]
Huber, K.:Soliloquia, Part II:Cuius legibus rotantur poli, w. S. Klare (mez), D. Ahlstedt (ten), B. McDaniel (bar), H. G. Ahrens (b–bar), H. Zender (cnd), Munich Bavarian RSO, Munich Bavarian Radio Chorus [L] *(rec Dec. 17, 1979)* Grammont ▲ CTSP 24-2 [ADD]

Lulli, Gino (bar)
Mascagni, P.:Cavalleria rusticana, w. G. Arangi-Lombardi (cta), A. Melandri (ten), L. Molajoli (cnd), Milan SO, La Scala Chorus [I] *(rec 1930 for Columbia Records)* Standing Room Only ▲ SRO 806-1 (m) [ADD]
Mascagni, P.:Cavalleria rusticana, w. G. A. Lombardi (sop), I. Mannarini (mez), M. Castagna (mez), A. Melandri (ten), L. Molajoli (cnd), La Scala Orch, La Scala Chorus *(rec 1930)* Preiser ▲ 90042 (m) [AAD]

Lund, Jan (ten)
Klit, L.:The Last Virtuoso, w. Hanne Andersen (sop), Edith Guillaume (mez), Jesper Buhl (bar), Jørgen Ole Børch (bass), S. A. Johansen (cnd), *(ensemble unknown)* Kontrapunkt ▲ KPT 32221

Lundberg, Mark (ten)
Wagner, R.:Die Walküre (act 1), w. Edda Moser (sop—Sieglinde), Mark Lundberg (ten—Siegmund), Frode Olsen (bass—Hunding), I. Törzs (cnd), Mecklenburg State Orch *(rec Mecklenburg State Theatre, Schwerin, June 29, 1994)* Calig ▲ CAL 50943 [DDD]

Lundh, Anders (ten)
Schmidt, O.:The Öresund Sym, w. Kari Hamnøy (sop), O. Schmidt (cnd), Malmö SO, Ars Nova *(rec Malmö Concert Hall, Sweden, Apr. 11-13, 1994)* BIS ▲ CD 672 [DDD]

Lundmark, A. (bar)
Söderman, A.:Poems & Songs, w. P.-M. Nilsson (sop), A. Kilström (pno), Eric Ericson Chamber Choir—13 songs for soprano/piano, choir, or baritone/piano [Sw] Musica Sveciae ▲ MSCD 525 [DDD]

Lundy, Carmen (mez)
Childs, B.:The Distant Land, w. Billy Childs (pno), Nana Yaw Asiedu (perc), Thomas Kelley (perc) *(rec Masonic Auditorium, Cleveland, OH, Feb 27, 1995)* Telarc ▲ CD 80409 [DDD]

Lundy, Nancy Allen (sop)
Kernis, A.J.:Nocturne, w. John Dent (tpt), Jeff Milarsky (glock), Benjamin Herman (glock), Leslie Stifelman (pno), Lisa Moore (pno), M. Barrett (cnd) *(rec Manhattan Center Studios, New York, May 31-June 3, 1995)* New Albion ♦ NA 083CD

Luperi, Mario (bass)
Verdi, G.:Falstaff, w. E. Norberg-Schulz (sop—Nannetta), L. Serra (sop—Alice), S. Graham (mez—Meg Page), M. Lipovsek (cta—Miss Quickly), K. Begley (ten—Dr. Caius), P. Conti (ten—Ford), M. Luperi (ten—Pistol), J. Van Dam (b–bar—Falstaff), P. LeFebvre (bass—Bardolph), G. Solti (cnd), Berlin PO, Berlin Radio Chorus London ▲ 440650-2 [DDD]

LuPone, P. (sgr)
Berlin, I.:Songs, w. J. Mauceri (cnd), Hollywood Bowl Orch—There's No Business Like Show Business; Heat Wave; No Strings; Let Yourself Go; Steppin' Out with My Baby; Hostess with the Mostes'; Best Thing for You; Lonely Heart; Always; I Got Lost in His Arms; Doin' What Comes Natur'lly; Count Your Blessings Instead of Sheep *(rec Culver City, CA, July 1994)* Philips ▲ 446406-2 [DDD]
Porter, C.:Anything Goes, w. H. McGillian (sgr), et al. [1987 revival cast] RCA ▲ 7769-2 RC [DDD] ■ 7769-4 RC

Lurtsema, Robert J. (nar)
Starer, R.:Remembering Felix, w. Harry Clark (vc), Sanda Schuldmann (pno) Albany ▲ TROY 151 [DDD]

Lustig, J. (sgr)
Wagner, R.:Tannhäuser, w. L. Rysanek (sop), M. Cordes (bar), G. Frick (bass), K. Böhm (cnd), Naples Teatro San Carlo Orch, Naples Teatro San Carlo Chorus [G] *(rec live, Naples, 3/17/56)* Melodram 3-▲ MEL 37073 (m) [AAD]

Lutze, Gert (ten)
Beethoven, L. van:Sym 9, "Choral Sym", w. Anny Schlemm (sop), Diana Eustrati (cta), Thomas Paul (bass), H. Abendroth (cnd), Leipzig RSO *(rec 1953)* Arlecchino ARL
Weber, C.M. von:Kampf und Sieg, w. L. Schmidt-Glänzel (sop), E. Fleischer (cta), H. Krämer (bar), H. Kegel (cnd), Leipzig RSO, Leipzig Radio Chorus [G] Forlane ▲ FOR 16572 (m) [AAD]

Luxon, Benjamin (bar)
Bach, J.S.:Anna Magdalena Bach Notebook, w. Blegen (sop), Kipnis (hpd/clvd), Meinis (vl) [G] Elektra/Nonesuch 2-▲ 79020-2 [DDD]
Bach, J.S.:St. Matthew Passion, w. E. Ameling (sop), B. Finnilä (cta), E. Haefliger (ten), S. McCoy (ten), B. McDaniel (bar), J. Somary (cnd), English CO, Ambrosian Singers *(rec 1977)* Vanguard Classics 3-▲ OVC 4060/62 [ADD]
Bach, J.S.:St. Matthew Passion (sels), w. E. Ameling (sop), B. Finnilä (cta), E. Haefliger (ten), S. McCoy (ten), B. McDaniel (bar), J. Somary (cnd), English CO, Ambrosian Singers Vanguard Classics ▲ OVC 4063 [ADD]
Beautiful Dreamer (& other Parlour Favorites), w. Benjamin Luxon (bar), David Willison (pno), Delmé String Quartet, et al. Omega Classics ▲ OCD 3005 [DDD]
Britten, H.:Billy Budd, w. P. Pears (ten), P. Glossop (bar), J. Shirley-Quirk (bar), M. Langdon (bass), O. Brannigan (bass), B. Britten (cnd), London SO, Ambrosian Singers [E] London 3-▲ 417428-2 [ADD]
Britten, H.:Owen Wingrave, w. S. Fisher (Miss Wingrave), J. Vyvyan (Mrs. Julian), H. Harper (Mrs. Coyle), J. Baker (Kate), P. Pears (Sir P. Wingrave; Narrator), J. Shirley-Quirk (Coyle), B. Britten, Wandworth School Boys' Choir, English CO London 2-▲ 433200-2
Britten, H.:The Rape of Lucretia, w. H. Harper (sop), J. Baker (mez), P. Pears (ten), B. Drake (bar), J. Shirley-Quirk (bar), B. Britten (cnd), English CO London 2-▲ 425666-2 [ADD]
Britten, H.:War Requiem, w. L. Haywood (sop), A. Rolfe-Johnson (ten), R. Shaw (cnd), Atlanta SO, Atlanta Sym Chorus [L] Telarc 2-▲ CD 80157 [DDD]
Butterworth, G.:Bredon Hill & Other Songs, w. D. Willison (pno) [E] Chandos ▲ CHAN 8831 [DDD]
Butterworth, G.:Songs (6) from *A Shropshire Lad*, w. D. Willison (pno) [E] Chandos ▲ CHAN 8831 [DDD]
Elgar, E.:The Apostles, w. S. Armstrong (sop), H. Watts (cta), R. Tear (ten), J. C. Case (bar), C. Grant (bass), A. Boult (cnd), London PO, London Phil Chorus, Downe House School Choir [E] EMI Classics ▲ CDMB 64206

Luxon, Benjamin (bar) (cont.)
Elgar, E.:The Dream of Gerontius, w. Alfreda Hodgson (cta), Robert Tear (ten), A. Gibson (cnd), Scottish National Orch, Scottish National Chorus CRD 2-▲ 33267
Elgar, E.:The Kingdom, w. Y. Kenny (sop), A. Hodgson (alt), C. Gillert (ten), L. Slatkin (cnd), London PO, London Phil Chorus RCA Red Seal 2-▲ 07863-57862-2
Fauré, G.:Requiem, w. Arleen Augér (sop), John Butt (org), English CO, King's College Choir Cambridge Classics for Pleasure ("Eminence" series) ▲ CDEMX 2166 [DDD]
Fauré, G.:Requiem, w. J. Bond (trb), G. Guest (cnd), Academy of St. Martin in the Fields, St. John's College Choir Cambridge [L] London ("Jubilee" series) ▲ 430360-2 [ADD]
Gurney, I.:Songs, w. D. Willison (pno)—20 songs:Carol of the Skiddaw Yowes; The apple orchard; The fields are full; The twa corbies; Severn Meadows; Desire in spring; Ha'nacker Mill; Down by the Salley Gardens; The scribe; Hawk & Buckle; On the Downs; The fiddler of Dooney; In Flanders; The folly of being comforted; I praise the tender flower; Black Stichel; An epitaph; By a bierside; Cranham Woods; Sleep [E] Chandos ▲ CHAN 8831 [DDD]
Handel, G.F.:Salve Regina, w. Janet Baker (mez), Helen Watts (cta), Robert Tear (ten), John Shirley-Quirk (bar), R. Leppard (cnd), English CO, London Voices Erato 3-▲ 2292-45994-2
Haydn, J.:Die Schöpfung, w. Helena Döse (sop—Eva), Lucia Popp (sop—Gabriel), Werner Hollweg (ten—Uriel), Benjamin Luxon (bar—Adam), Kurt Moll (bass—Raphael), Jack McCormack (db), David Strange (vc), Antál Dorati (hpd), A. Dorati (cnd), Royal PO, Brighton Festival Chorus *(rec Kingsway Hall, London, Dec 1976)* London 2-▲ 443027-2 [ADD]
Howells, H.:Songs, w. L. Dawson (sop), C. Pierard (mez), J.M. Ainsley (ten), J. Drake (pno)—7 various songs; 2 South African Settings; 3 Folksongs; A Garland for De la Mare; Peacock Pie, Op. 33; 4 French Chansons, Op. 29; In Green Ways, Op. 43; 12 various songs; 3 Children's Songs; 4 Songs, Op. 22 Chandos 2-▲ CHAN 9185/86 [DDD]
I Love My Love:A Collection of British Folk Songs, w. David Willison (pno) Chandos ▲ CHAN 8946 [DDD]
Mozart, W.A.:Missa, K.427, w. B. Hendricks (sop), J. Perry (sop), P. Schreier (ten), H. von Karajan (cnd), Berlin PO Deutsche Grammophon ("Karajan Gold" series) ▲ 439012-2
Quilter, R.:Songs, w. D. Willison (pno)—five song groups:Three Shakespeare Songs, Op. 6; To Julia, Op. 8; Seven Elizabethan Lyrics, Op. 12; Four Songs, Op. 14; Three Songs of William Blake, Op. 20; *eight individual songs*—Love's philosophy, Op. 3/1; Now sleeps the crimson petal, Op. 3/2; At close of day; Go, lovely rose, Op. 24/3; Arab love song, Op. 25/4; Music, when soft voices die, Op. 25/5; In the bud of the morninG o, Op. 25/6; I arise from dreams of thee, Op. 29 [E] Chandos ▲ CHAN 8782 [DDD]
Schubert, Franz:Die Schöne Müllerin, w. D. Willison (pno) [G] Chandos ▲ CHAN 8725 [DDD]
Schubert, Franz:Schwanengesang, w. D. Willison (pno) [G] Chandos ▲ CHAN 8721 [DDD]
Sing Folk Songs at Tanglewood, w. Bill Croft (sgr) Omega Classics ▲ OCD 3003 [DDD]
Sullivan, A.:Music, w. V. Masterson (sop), S. Armstrong (sop), R. Tear (ten), Alwyn, Hickox (cnd), Bournemouth Sinfonietta, Northern Sinfonietta of England—sels. from all operettas of Gilbert & Sullivan EMI Classics ▲ CDM 64393
A Ticket To Heaven (& other Parlour Favorites), w. David Willison (pno), Delmé String Quartet, et al. Omega Classics ▲ OCD 3006 [DDD]
Two Gentlemen Folk, w. Bill Crofut (sgr) Telarc ▲ CD 84401 [DDD] ■ CS 34401 (D)
Vaughan Williams, R.:The House of Life, w. D. Willison (pno) [E] Chandos ▲ CHAN 8475 [DDD]
Vaughan Williams, R.:In the Spring, w. D. Willison [E] Chandos ▲ CHAN 8475 [DDD]
Vaughan Williams, R.:Linden Lea, w. D. Willison (pno) [E] Chandos ▲ CHAN 8475 [DDD]
Vaughan Williams, R.:Poems by Fredegond Shove, w. D. Willison (pno) [E] Chandos ▲ CHAN 8475 [DDD]
Vaughan Williams, R.:Songs of Travel, w. D. Willison (pno) [E] Chandos ▲ CHAN 8475 [DDD]
Vaughan Williams, R.:Tired, w. D. Willison (pno) [E] Chandos ▲ CHAN 8475 [DDD]
Walton, W.:Belshazzar's Feast, w. A. Previn (cnd), Royal PO, London Collegium Musicum RPO ▲ RPO 7013 [DDD]
Warlock, P.:Songs Bar, w. D. Willison (pno)—32 songs [E] Chandos ▲ CHAN 8643 [DDD]

Luxon, Benjamin (nar)
Gorb, A.:Hymns Uproarious, w. S. Amit (nar), P. Gilbert-Dyson (cnd), Belmont Ensemble London Symposium ▲ SYM 1180
Walton, W.:Façade, w. S. Amit (nar), P. Gilbert-Dyson (cnd), Belmont Ensemble London Symposium ▲ SYM 1180
Watson, T.:Dick Whittington & His Cat, w. S. Amit (nar), P. Gilbert-Dyson (cnd), Belmont Ensemble London Symposium ▲ SYM 1180

Lyon, Michael (ten)
Cage, J.:Europera 3, w. Suzan Hanson (sop), Ruby Hinds (mez), Patricia McAfee (mez), Richard Powell (ten), Kevin Bell (bass), Brian Pezzone (pno), Vicki Ray (pno), Hannes Geiger (record players), Joseph Giri (record players), William Houston (record players), Dren McDonald (record players), Ronda Rindone (record players), Clarice Ross (record players), Scott Fraser (tape), A. Culver (cnd), Long Beach Opera Orch *(rec Center Theater, Long Beach, CA, Nov. 13, 1993)* Mode 2-▲ MODE 38/39

Lytting, Katia (mez)
Bellini, V.:I Puritani, w. Edita Gruberova (sop), Justin Lavender (ten), Carlo Tuand (ten), Ettore Kim (bar), Francesco Ellero d'Artegna (bass), Dankwart Siegele (bass), F. Luisi (cnd), Munich RSO, Bavarian Radio Chorus Nightingale Classics 3-▲ NIG 70562
Rossini, G.:Il Signor Bruschino, w. P. Orciani (sop), L. Canonici (ten), F. Massa (ten), B. Praticò (bar), P. Spagnoli (bar), N. de Carolis (b–bar), M. Viotti (cnd), Turin PO [I] Claves 8-▲ CD 9200 [DDD]
Rossini, G.:Il Signor Bruschino, w. Patrizia Orciani (sop), Luca Canonici (ten), Fulvio Massa (ten), Bruno Praticò (bar), Pietro Spagnoli (bar), Natale de Carolis (b–bar), M. Viotti (cnd), Turin PO Claves 2-▲ 50-8904/5

Lytton, Henry (bar)
Sullivan, A.:The Gondoliers, w. W. Lawson (sop), A. Davies (ten), B. Lewis (cta), D. Oldham (ten), M. Bennett (sop), G. Baker (bar), L. Sheffield (bar), et al., H. Norris (cnd), D'Oyly Carte Opera Company Orch, D'Oyly Carte Opera Chorus—dialogue omitted *(rec 1927)* Pearl 2-▲ PEAS 9961 (m) [AAD]
Sullivan, A.:Iolanthe, w. L. Henri (sop)—None Shall part us; H. Dearth—The sentry's song Symposium ▲ 1123

Maazel, Lorin (nar)
Prokofiev, S.:Peter & the Wolf, w. L. Maazel (cnd), French National Orch [E] Deutsche Grammophon ▲ 415921-2 [ADD] ■ 415921-4

Mabry, James (sgr)
Weill, K.:Down in the Valley, w. I. Davidson (sop), M. Acito (ten), D. Collup (bar), D. P. Lang (sgr), W. Gundlach (cnd), Westphalia CO, Westphalia Kantorei Capriccio ▲ 60 020-1 [DDD]

Mabry, Sharon (mez)
Barber, S.:Songs, w. P. Wade (pno)—O Boundless, Boundless; A Green Lowland; Now Have I Fed [E] Owl ▲ OWL 35 [DAD]
Goosen, F.:At Casterbridge Fair, w. P. Wade (pno)—three songs:After the Club-Dance; The Inquiry; A Wife Waits Owl ▲ OWL 35 [DAD]
Goosen, F.:Garland, w. P. Wade (pno) Owl ▲ OWL 35 [DAD]
Vercoe, E.:Herstory III, w. R. Platt (pno) [E] Owl ▲ OWL 35 [DAD]

McAdoo, Susan (mez)
Hummel, J.N.:Alma virgo, w. Amanda Halgrimson (sop), Helmut Wildhaber (ten), Petr Mikuláš (bass), Jan Engel (bass), M. Haselböck (cnd), Vienna Academy, Brünn Czech Phil Chorus Koch Schwann ▲ SCH CD 317792
Hummel, J.N.:Mass in E♭, Op. 80, w. Amanda Halgrimson (sop), Helmut Wildhaber (ten), Petr Mikuláš (bass), Jan Engel (bass), M. Haselböck (cnd), Vienna Academy, Brünn Czech Phil Chorus Koch Schwann ▲ SCH CD 317792
Hummel, J.N.:Quod quod in orbe, w. Amanda Halgrimson (sop), Helmut Wildhaber (ten), Petr Mikuláš (bass), Jan Engel (bass), M. Haselböck (cnd), Vienna Academy, Brünn Czech Phil Chorus Koch Schwann ▲ SCH CD 317792

McAfee, Patricia (mez)
Cage, J.:Europera 3, w. Suzan Hanson (sop), Ruby Hinds (mez), Michael Lyon (ten), Richard Powell (ten), Kevin Bell (bass), Brian Pezzone (pno), Vicki Ray (pno), Hannes Geiger (record players), Joseph Giri (record players), William Houston (record players), Oren McDonald (record players), Ronda Rindone (record players), Clarice Ross (record players), Scott Fraser (tape), A. Culver (cnd), Long Beach Opera Orch *(rec Center Theater, Long Beach, CA, Nov. 13, 1993)* Mode 2-▲ MODE 38/39

McAlpine, William (ten)
Donizetti, G.:Emilia di Liverpool (sels), w. A. Cantelo (sop), J. Sutherland (sop), D. Dowling (bar), H. Alan (bass), J. Pritchard (cnd), Royal Liverpool PO, Liverpool Music Group Singers—13 arias from Act 1, & 4 from Act 2 [I] *(rec live, Liverpool Sept. 1957)* Myto ▲ 1 MCD 91545 [ADD]

Macann, Rodney (b-bar)
Handel, G.F.:Messiah, w. Helen Kucharek (sop), Jennifer Smith (sop), Linda Finnie (mez), Niel Mackie (ten), T. Dean (cnd), Pro Christe Orch, Pro Christe Choir *(rec St. Augustine's Church, Kilburn, London, 1986)* Guild 2-▲ GMDD 7112/3 [ADD]

McCabe, Dan (bar)
Honegger, A.:Christophe Colomb, w. E. Knecht (speaker—Queen Isabella), S. Rawson (speaker—The Magician), N. Garvey (speaker—Christopher Columbus), A. Furnival (speaker—King Ferdinand), C. Peltz (cnd), Buffalo Opera Sacra Orch, Buffalo Opera Sacra Chorus [E] *(rec Buffalo, New York, Oct. 30-31, 1992)* Mode ▲ MOD 35 [DDD]

McCabe, Peter (ten)
French Sacred Music of the 14th Century, Vol. 1, w. Schola Discantus, Bradford Findell (ct), John Delorey (ct), Arthur Rawding (ten), Paul Guttry (bar), Kevin Moll (cnd) *(rec Emmanuel Church, Boston, 1994)* Lyrichord ("Early Music" series) ▲ LYR 8012 [DDD]

McCarthy, Michael (bass)
Schütz, H.:Weihnachtshistorie, w. Anna Crookes (sop—Angel), Paul Agnew (ct—Evangelist), Michael McCarthy (bass—Herod), Jeremy Summerly (cnd), Oxford Camerata *(rec Oxford, Aug 1995)* Naxos ▲ 8.553514 [DDD]

McCarty, M. (sgr)
Berlin, I.:Miss Liberty, w. E. Albert (sgr), A. McLerie (sgr), E. Griffies (sgr) [1949 Broadway cast] Sony Broadway ▲ SK 48015 ■ ST 48015

McClare, Stephen (ten)
Verdi, G.:Alzira (sels), w. Stephen McClare (ten—Otumbo), Richard Margison (ten—Zamoro), Gary Relyea (b-bar—Alvaro), R. Bradshaw (cnd), Canadian Opera Company Orch, Canadian Opera Company Chorus—Il prigioniero [prologue] *(rec George Weston Recital Hall, Ford Centre for the Performing Arts, North York, Ontario, Dec 20-23, 1994)* CBC ("SM 5000" series) ▲ SM5 5148 [DDD]

McClelland, K. (sgr)
Porter, C.:Fifty Million Frenchmen, w. H. McGillin (sgr), K. Criswell (sgr), S. Powell (sgr), K. Ziemba (sgr), J. Graae (sgr), J. Harder (sgr), S. Waara (sgr), P. Cass (sgr), J. LeClerc (sgr) [1991 studio cast] New World ▲ 80417-2 [DDD]

McCollum, John (ten)
Beethoven, L. van:Sym 9, "Choral Sym", w. P. Curtin (sop), F. Kopleff (cta), D. Gramm (bass), F. Reiner (cnd), Chicago SO RCA Gold Seal ▲ 09026-61795-2
Dittersdorf, K.D. von:Arcifanfano, King of Fools, or It's Always Too Late to Learn, w. P. Brooks (sop), A. Russell (sop), E. Steber (sop), J. Sopher (ten), H. Rehfuss (bar), D. Smith (bar), N. Jenkins (cnd), Clarion Music Society Orch, Clarion Music Society Chorus [E] *(rec live, New York 1965)* VAI Audio 2-▲ VAIA 1010-2 (m) [ADD]
Handel, G.F.:Judas Maccabaeus, w. Martina Arroyo (sop), Grace Bumbry (mez), Marvin Sorensen (ten), D. Watts (bass), M. Abravanel (cnd), Utah SO, Utah Sym Chorus [E] *(rec ca. 1959)* MCA Classics 3-▲ MCAD3-10515 [ADD]
Love's Secrets & Other Songs By American Composers, w. Eleanor Steber (sop), Mildred Miller (mez), Donald Gramm (bass-bar), Edwin Biltcliffe (pno), Richard Cumming (pno) Vox Box ("The American Composers" series) 2-▲ CDX 5129

McConnell, Regina (sop)
Burleigh, H.T.:Art Songs, w. Michael Cordovana (pno)—You Ask Me If I Love You?; The Prayer I Make for You; One Day; Elysium; The Prayer; And as the Gulls Soar; Heigh-Ho!; The Man in White; Now Sleeps the Crimson Petal; I Hear His Footstep, Music sweet; Just You; He Sent Me You; Were I a Star; Oh Love of a Day; Adoration; Tide; The Grey Wolf; The Dove and the Lily; Oh, My Lovel; Why Art Thou Not Near Me!; The Sailor's Wife; Carry Me Back to the Pine Wood; Lovely Dark and Lonely One *(rec Harmony Hall, Fort Washington, MD, Feb 23-24, 1995)* Centaur ▲ CRC 2252 [DDD]

McCord, Semenya (sgr)
Cage, J.:Apartment House 1776, w. Walter Buckingham (sgr—Protestant), Darrell Dunn (sgr—Native American), Semenya McCord (sgr—African American), Chiam Parchi (sgr—Sephardi), New England Conservatory Philharmonia *(rec New England Conservatory of Music, Boston, MA, Mar. 4 & 6, 1991)* Mode ▲ MODE 41

McCormack, John (ten)
A Christian Celebration Pearl ▲ PEA 9990 (m) [ADD]
The Complete Destinn, w. Emmy Destinn (sop), E. Caruso (ten), K. Jörn (ten), G. Martinelli (ten), G. Zenatello (ten), et al. Supraphon 12-▲ SUP 112136 [ADD]
The Complete Surviving Early Recordings Opal 2-▲ CDS 9847 (m) [AAD]
Count John McCormack, Vol. 1:Italian Opera Pearl ▲ PEA 9335 (m)
The Final Recordings *(rec 1941-42)* Pearl 2-▲ PEA 9188 [ADD]
The 1st Recordings, 1907-14 Enterprise ("Vocal Archives" series) ▲ ENT VA 1129
John McCormack Memoir Classics ("Great Voices of the Century" series) ▲ CDMOIR 418
John McCormack on Irish Song Pearl ▲ PEA 9338 (m) [AAD]
Legendary Three Tenors, w. Enrico Caruso (ten), Beniamino Gigli (ten), Ruggiero Leoncavallo (pno), Edwin Schneider (pno), Metropolitan Opera Orch, Metropolitan Opera Chorus [cnd:Giulio Setti], Philharmonia Orch, Philharmonia Chorus [cnd:Stanford Robinson] *(rec 1904-1950)* RCA Gold Seal ▲ 09026-68534-2 [ADD] ■ 09026-68534-4
Leider Singer, w. E. Schneider (sgr), Grace Moore (sop), F. Kreisler (vn), V. O'Brien (pno), L. Bori (sop), L. Kennedy (vc) Symposium ▲ 1164
McCormack & Kreisler in Recital, w. Fritz Kreisler (vn) Nimbus ▲ NI 7868 [ADD]
McCormack in American Song Pearl ▲ PEA 9971 (m) [ADD]
McCormack in Opera Nimbus ("Prima Voce" series) ▲ NI 7820 [ADD]
McCormack in Song *(rec between 1910 & 1941)* Nimbus ("Prima Voce" series) ▲ NI 7854 [ADD]
Mozart, W.A.:Don Giovanni (sels), w. Emilia Corsi (sop), Adelina Patti (sop), Mattia Battistini (bar), Ezio Pinza (bass), Landon Ronald (pno), C. Sabajno (cnd)—Alfin Siam liberati...Là ci darem la mano; Finch'han del vino; Batti, batti, o bel Masetto; Il mio tesoro; L'amerò, sarò costante *(rec 1905 - 1944)* Minerva ▲ MN A14 [ADD]
Mozart, W.A.:Songs, w. M. Callas (sop), E. Grümmer (sop), E. Schwarzkopf (sop), R. Scotto (sop), T. Lemnitz (sop), E. Berger (sop), S. Jurinac (sop), E. Schumann (sop), I. Souez (sop), E. Rethberg (sop), L. Lehmann (sop), N. Gedda (ten), H. Roswenge (ten), H. Nash (ten), T. Gobbi (bar), G. Hüsch (bar), E. Kunz (bar), G. Frick (bass), E. Pinza (bass), A. Kipnis (bass) EMI Classics 4-▲ CDMD 63750
The Victor & HMV Recordings *(rec 1910-11)* Romophone ▲ 82006-2 [ADD]
The Victor Recordings, w. Fritz Kreisler (vn), Carl Lamson (pno) *(rec 1921-25)* Biddulph 2-▲ LAB 068-69 [ADD]
When Irish Eyes Are Smiling ASV ("Living Era" series) ▲ ASL 5119 [ADD]

McCorvey, E. (ten)
Burleigh, H.T.:The Young Warrior, w. J.P. Williams (cnd), Bohuslav Martinů PO Albany ▲ TROY 104 [DDD]
Williams, Julius P.:Is It True?, w. J. P. Williams (cnd), Bohuslav Martinů PO Albany ▲ TROY 104 [DDD]

McCoshan, Daniel (ten)
Mozart, W.A.:Nozze di Figaro, w. S. Jurinac (sop), G. Sciutti (sop), R. Stevens (mez), M. Sinclair (cta), H. Cuenod (ten), G. Griffith (bar), S. Bruscantini (b-bar), F. Calabrese (bass), V. Gui (cnd), Glyndebourne Festival Orch, Glyndebourne Festival Chorus Classics for Pleasure ▲ CDCFP 4724 [ADD]

McCoy, Julie (sop)
Debussy, C.:Chansons (3) de Charles d'Orléans, w. Pam Elrod (mez), Nanette Soles (mez), Charles Bruffy (ten), Leonard Ratzlaff (bass), Robert Shaw (cnd), Robert Shaw Festival Singers *(rec Church of St. Pierre, Gramat, France, July 26-28, 1994)* Telarc ▲ CD 80408 [DDD]

McCoy, Seth (ten)
Bach, J.S.:St. Matthew Passion, w. E. Ameling (sop), B. Finnilä (cta), E. Haefliger (ten), B. Luxon (bar), B. McDaniel (bar), J. Somary (cnd), English CO, Ambrosian Singers *(rec 1977)* Vanguard Classics 3-▲ OVC 4060/62 [ADD]
Bach, J.S.:St. Matthew Passion (sels), w. E. Ameling (sop), B. Finnilä (cta), E. Haefliger (ten), B. Luxon (bar), B. McDaniel (bar), J. Somary (cnd), English CO, Ambrosian Singers Vanguard Classics ▲ OVC 4063 [ADD]
Rachmaninoff, S.:Monna Vanna, w. S. Milnes (bar), I. Buketoff (cnd), Iceland SO, Icelandic Opera Chorus Chandos ▲ CHAN 8987 [DDD]

McCracken, James (bar)
Beethoven, L. van:Fidelio, w. Birgit Nilsson (sop—Leonore), Graziella Sciutti (sop—Marzelline), Kurt Equiluz (ten—Erster Gefangener), Donald Grobe (ten—Jacquino), James McCracken (ten—Florestan), Tom Krause (bar—Don Pizarro), Hermann Prey (bar—Don Fernando), Kurt Böhme (bass—Rocco), Günther Adam (sgr—Zweiter Gefangener), L. Maazel (cnd), Vienna PO, Vienna State Opera Concert Association Chorus *(rec Sofiensaal, Vienna, Mar 1964)* London 2-▲ 448104-2 [ADD]
Bizet, G.:Carmen, w. A. Maliponte (sop), M. Horne (mez), T. Krause (bar), L. Bernstein (cnd), Metropolitan Opera Orch, Manhattan Opera Chorus [F] *(rec 1973)* Deutsche Grammophon 3-▲ 427440-2 [ADD]
Leoncavallo, R.:Pagliacci, w. P. Lorengar (sop), R. Krause (ten), R. Merrill (bar), U. Benelli (bar), L. Gardelli (cnd), St. Cecilia Academy Orch Rome, St. Cecilia Academy Chorus Rome [I] IMP Collectors Series ▲ IMPX 9017 [AAD]
Meyerbeer, G.:Le Prophète, w. Renata Scotto (sop), Marilyn Horne (mez), Jerome Hines (bass), H. Lewis (cnd), Royal PO, Ambrosian Opera Chorus [F] CBS 3-▲ M3K 34340 [ADD]
Rodgers, R.:Me & Juliet, w. I. Bigley (sgr), R. Walston (sgr), B. Hayes (sgr) [1953 Broadway cast] RCA ▲ 09026-61480-2 ■ 09026-61480-4
Schoenberg, A.:Gurrelieder, w. J. Norman (sop), T. Troyanos (mez), D. Arnold (bar), S. Ozawa (cnd), Boston SO, Tanglewood Festival Chorus Philips 2-▲ 412511-2
Verdi, G.:Otello, w. G. Jones (sop—Desdemona), A. di Stasio (mez—Emilia), J. McCracken (ten—Otello), P. de Palma (ten—Cassio), D. Fischer-Dieskau (bar—Iago), J. Barbirolli (cnd), New Philharmonia Orch, Ambrosian Opera Chorus EMI Classics ▲ CDMB 65296

McCulloch, Susan (sop)
Golden Melodies from Opera, w. R. Hickox (cnd), London SO, Royal PO [cnd:R. Stapelton], Josephine Barstow (sop), J. Oakman (ten), Edmund Barham (ten) Pickwick ("The Orchid" series) ▲ PICORCD 11005

McCutchan, A. (nar)
Welcher, D.:Haleakala:How Maui Snared the Sun, w. R. Chamberlain (nar), D. Johanos (cnd), Honolulu SO *(rec Jan. 10, 1992)* Marco Polo ▲ 8.223457 [DDD]

McDaniel, Barry (bar)
Bach, J.S.:Magnificat, BWV 243, w. Helen Donath (sop), Gundula Bernát-Klein (sop), Birgit Finnilä (alt), Peter Schreier (ten), W. Gönnenwein (cnd), German Bach Soloists, South German Madrigal Choir [E version] *(rec Stuttgart Radio, 1966)* Bayer ▲ 100081 [ADD]
Bach, J.S.:St. Matthew Passion, w. E. Ameling (sop), B. Finnilä (cta), E. Haefliger (ten), S. McCoy (ten), B. Luxon (bar), J. Somary (cnd), English CO, Ambrosian Singers *(rec 1977)* Vanguard Classics 3-▲ OVC 4060/62 [ADD]
Bach, J.S.:St. Matthew Passion (sels), w. E. Ameling (sop), B. Finnilä (cta), E. Haefliger (ten), S. McCoy (ten), B. Luxon (bar), J. Somary (cnd), English CO, Ambrosian Singers Vanguard Classics ▲ OVC 4063 [ADD]
Huber, K.:Soliloquia, w. H. Lukomska (sop), S. Klare (mez), D. Ahlstedt (ten), H. G. Ahrens (b-bar), H. Zender (cnd), Munich Bavarian RSO, Munich Bavarian Radio Chorus [L] *(rec Dec. 17, 1979)* Grammont ▲ CTSP 24-2 [ADD]
Huber, K.:Soliloquia, Part II:Cuius legibus rotantur poli, w. H. Lukomska (sop), S. Klare (mez), D. Ahlstedt (ten), H. G. Ahrens (b-bar), H. Zender (cnd), Munich Bavarian RSO, Munich Bavarian Radio Chorus [L] *(rec Dec. 17, 1979)* Grammont ▲ CTSP 24-2 [ADD]
Mozart, L.:Missa solemnis, w. A. Augér (sop), G. Schreckenbach (mez), H. Laubenthal (ten), R. Bader (cnd), Berlin Domkapelle Instrumental Ensemble, St. Hedwig's Cathedral Choir [L] Koch Schwann ▲ CD 313028 [ADD]
Mozart, W.A.:Complete Mozart Edition, w. B. Fassbaender (mez), T. Moser (ten), L. Hager (cnd), Salzburg Mozarteum Orch Philips 3-▲ 422533-2 [ADD]
Puccini, G.:Mass, w. K. Lövaas (sop), W. Hollweg (ten), E. Inbal (cnd), Frankfurt RSO, West German Radio Chorus Philips ("Collector" series) ▲ 434170-2 [ADD]
Schubert, Franz:Winterreise, w. J. Adler (pno) [G] Classic Studio Berlin ▲ CS 30208 [DDD]

Macdonald, J. (sgr)
Rodgers, R.:Music of, w. B. Crosby (sgr), R. Vallee (sgr), A. Jolson (sgr), et al., Whiteman, Sinatra (cnd), Whiteman Orch, Sinatra Orch, Paramount Studio Orch—On Your Toes; Jumbo; Present Arms; One Dam Thing After Another; The Boys from Syracuse; Heads Up; Lido Lady; Peggy Ann; Love Me Tonight; Higher & Higher; Spring is Here; The Girl Friend; Simple Simon; Hallelujah, I'm a Bum Pearl ("Flapper" series) ▲ PAST CD 9794 [AAD]

McDonald, James (ten)
Moss, L.:Miracles, w. Edward Walters (cl), Ruth Ann McDonald (pno) *(rec Peabody Conservatory of Music, Baltimore, MD)* Capstone ▲ CPS 8619
Moss, L.:Portals, w. Ruth Ann McDonald (pno) Capstone ▲ CPS 8619

MacDonald, Jeanette (sop)
Donizetti, G.:Lucia di Lammermoor, w. J. Sutherland (sop), M. Elkins (mez), J. Bowman (alt), J. Gibin (ten), J. Rouleau (bass), Shaw (sgr), T. Serafin (cnd), Royal Opera House Orch, Royal Opera House Chorus Covent Garden—3 duets from Act 1, & 3 soprano solo arias from Act 2 [I] Myto ▲ 1 MCD 91545 [ADD]
San Francisco & Other Favorites RCA Gold Seal ▲ 09026-60877-2 ■ 09026-60877-4

McDonall, Lois (sop)
Donizetti, G.:Maria Padilla, w. L. McDonall (sop—Maria Padilla), D. Jones (mez—Ines Padilla), G. Clark (ten—Don Ruiz), C. du Plessis (bar—Don Pedro), A. Francis (cnd), London SO, Geoffrey Mitchell Choir [I] *(rec at Henry Wood Hall, London June 1980)* Opera Rara 3-▲ ORC 6

McDonnell, Tom (bar)
Handel, G.F.:Israel in Egypt, w. Elizabeth Gale (sop), James Bowman (alt), Ian Partridge (ten), Alan Watt (bass), Watson (sgr), S. Preston (cnd), English CO, Christ Church Cathedral Choir Oxford London ("Jubilee" series) 2-▲ 421602-2 [ADD]
Handel, G.F.:Israel in Egypt, w. Elizabeth Gale (sop), Lillian Watson (sop), James Bowman (alt), Ian Partridge (ten), Alan Watt (bass), S. Preston (cnd), English CO, Christ Church Cathedral Choir Oxford *(rec Chapel of Merton College, Oxford, 1975)* London 2-▲ 443470-2 [ADD]

MacDougall, Jamie (ten)
Bach, J.S.:St. Matthew Passion, w. N. Argenta (sop), L. Lee (mez), J. Kenny (alt), R. Müller (ten), R. Jackson (bar), S. Varcoe (b-bar), P. Goodwin (cnd), *(orch & chorus unknown)* United 2-▲ UNI 89301 [DDD]
Bach, J.S.:St. Matthew Passion (sels), w. N. Argenta (sop), L. Lee (mez), J. Kenny (alt), R. Müller (ten), R. Jackson (bar), S. Varcoe (b-bar), P. Goodwin (cnd), *(orch & chorus unknown)* *(rec St. George's Theater, London, Feb 24-27, 1994)* United ▲ UNI 88030 [DDD]
Handel, G.F.:Acis & Galatea [arr Mozart], w. B. Bonney (sop), M. Schäfer (ten), J. Tomlinson (bass), T. Pinnock (cnd), English Concert, English Concert Choir London 2-▲ 425792-2
Maccunn, H.:The Dowie Dens o'Yarrow, w. Lisa Milne (sop), Janice Watson (sop), Peter Sidhom (bar), Stephen Gadd (bass), M. Brabbins (cnd), BBC Scottish SO, Scottish Opera Chorus Hyperion ▲ CDA 66815
Maccunn, H.:Jeanie Deans (sels), w. Lisa Milne (sop), Janice Watson (sop), Peter Sidhom (bar), Stephen Gadd (bass), M. Brabbins (cnd), BBC Scottish SO, Scottish Opera Chorus Hyperion ▲ CDA 66815
Maccunn, H.:Lay of Last Minstrel, w. Lisa Milne (sop), Janice Watson (sop), Peter Sidhom (bar), Stephen Gadd (bass), M. Brabbins (cnd), BBC Scottish SO, Scottish Opera Chorus Hyperion ▲ CDA 66815
Maccunn, H.:Ship o' the Fiend, w. Lisa Milne (sop), Janice Watson (sop), Peter Sidhom (bar), Stephen Gadd (bass), M. Brabbins (cnd), BBC Scottish SO, Scottish Opera Chorus Hyperion ▲ CDA 66815
Mozart, W.A.:Missa, K.317, w. Barbara Bonney (sop), Catherine Wyn-Rogers (cta), Stephen Gadd (bass), T. Pinnock (cnd), English CO, English Concert Choir Archive ▲ 445353-2

MacDougall, Jamie (ten) (cont.)
Mozart, W.A.:Vesperae solennes, w. Barbara Bonney (sop), Catherine Wyn-Rogers (cta), Stephen Gadd (bass), T. Pinnock (cnd), English CO, English Concert Choir Archive ▲ 445353-2
Purcell, H.:Dido & Aeneas, w. Rebecca Evans (sop—Belinda), Maria Ewing (sop—Dido), Mary Plazas (sop—1st witch), Patricia Rozario (sop—2nd woman), Sally Burgess (mez—Sorceress), Pamela Helen Stephens (mez—2nd witch), James Bowman (ct—Spirit), Jamie MacDougal (ten—Sailor), Karl Daymond (bar—Aeneas), R. Hickox (cnd), Collegium Musicum 90
Chandos ("Early Music" series) ▲ CHAN 0586 [DDD]
Purcell, H.:King Arthur, w. N. Argenta (sop), J. Gooding (sop), L. Perillo (sop), M. Tucker (ten), G. Finley (bar), B. Bannatyne-Scott (bass), T. Pinnock (cnd), English Concert, *(chorus unknown)*
Archiv 2-▲ 435490-2 [DDD]
Schubert, Franz:Songs (misc), w. Lorna Anderson (sop), Catherine Wyn-Rogers (alt) Simon Keenlyside (bar), Graham Johnson (pno), London Schubert Chorale—Das Leben ist ein Traum; Das Grab; Trinklied; Punschlied; Vaterlandslied; Selma und Selmar; Morgenlied; An die Sonne; Hermann und Thusnelda; Cora und die Sonne; Lorna; Genugsamkeit; Der Abend; Das Mädchen aus dem Fremde; Am Rosa (I); Am Rosa (II); An Sie; Gebet während der Schlacht; Das Abendroth; Die drei Sänger; Die Sterne; Cronnan; Furcht der Geliebten; Die Erscheinung; Stolie; Das Bild; Lob des Tokayers
Hyperion ▲ CDJ 33022

McEachern, Malcolm (bass)
Malcolm McEachern Pearl ▲ PEA 9455 (m) [AAD]

Macedonio, Paolo (ten)
Generali, P.:Sacred Music, w. Leila Bersiani (sop), Valentina di Cola (sop), Emanuela Deffai (mez), Sella Salvati (cta), Roberto Bencivenga (ten), Carlo Lepore (bass), E. Brizio (cnd), Czech Radio-TV Orch, Czech Radio-TV Chorus—Magnificat; Domine ad Adjuvandum; Virgam Virtutis; Ecce Virgo; Ave Maria Messe Pastorale; Te Deum *(rec FHS Studios, Prague, 1995)* Studio SM ▲ 2517 [DDD]

MacEwan, Sydney (bar)
Green, P.:Mass of St. Francis of Assisi, "Let Me Bring Love", w. Bernadette Greevy (mez), David Budway (pno), Cork Children's Choir Alanna ▲ ALA 5553

McFadden, Clara (sop)
Cello Octet Conjunto Ibérico, w. E. Arizcuren (cnd), Cello Octet Conjunto Ibérico *(rec 1992)*
Canal Grande ▲ CG 9323 [DDD]
Haydn, J.:L'Anima del filosofo, or Orfeo ed Euridice, w. Marylin Schmiege (mez), Christoph Prégardien, Gotthold Schwarz (bass), M. Schneider (cnd), La Stagione, La Stagione Choir
Deutsche Harmonia Mundi 2-▲ 05472-77229-2
Holzbauer, I.:Günther von Schwarzburg, w. Christoph Prégardien (ten), Robert Wörle (ten), Michael Schopper (bass), M. Schneider (cnd), La Stagione CPO 3-▲ CPO 999265
Janssen, G.:Noach, w. Clara McFadden (sop—Noach's Wife), Lieuwe Visser (bass—Noach), Huib Rooymans (nar), L. Vis (cnd), New Artis Orch, Mondriaan Quartet, Ay-Kherel Ensemble *(rec Amsterdam, June 20-21, 1994)* Donemus 2-▲ CV 42/43
Loevendie, T.:Gassir, the Hero, w. Claron McFadden (sop—Partridge/Priestess), Timothy Wilson (alt—Shamsi), Christopher Gillett (ten—Safi), Robert Poulton (bar—Gassir), Lieuwe Visser (bass—Yemni), Roger Smeets (sgr—Rafi), D. Porcelijn (cnd), Asko Ensemble *(rec live, Amsterdam Studios, June 14-15, 1993)* Donemus ▲ CV 35
Rameau, J.P.:Les Indes galantes, w. S. Piau (sop), I. Poulenard (sop), N. Rime (sop), M. Ruggeri (sop), H. Crook (ten), J.-P. Fouchecourt (ten), N. Rivenq (bar), J. Corréas (bass), B. Delétré (bass), W. Christie (cnd), Les Arts Florissants [F] Harmonia Mundi France 3-▲ HMC 901367/69
Villa-Lobos, H.:Bachiana brasileira 5, w. Conjunto Iberico Octet Canal Grande ▲ CG 9323 [DDD]

McFerrin, Bobby (sgr)
Hush, w. Ma, Yo-Yo (vc) Sony Classical ▲ SK 48177 ▲ SM 48177 ■ ST 48177
Mozart, W.A.:Con 20 Pno, w. Chick Corea (pno), B. McFerrin (cnd), St. Paul CO—Prelude [a capella voc & pno improvisation] Sony Classical ▲ SK 62601 [DDD] ■ ST 62601
Mozart, W.A.:Con 23 Pno, w. Chick Corea (pno), B. McFerrin (cnd), St. Paul CO—Prelude [a capella voc & pno improvisation] Sony Classical ▲ SK 62601 [DDD] ▲ SM 62601 ■ ST 62601
Mozart, W.A.:Son 2 Pno, w. Chick Corea (pno), B. McFerrin (cnd), St. Paul CO [Voc & Pno improvisation based on Adagio] Sony Classical ▲ SK 62601 [DDD] ■ ST 62601

McFerrin, B. (sgr)
Verdi, G.:Aida (sels), w. O. Rovere (sop), E. Stignani (mez), M. Filippeschi (ten), C. Cava (bass), V. Bellezza (cnd), Naples Teatro San Carlo Orch, Naples Teatro San Carlo Chorus [I] [highlights] *(rec live, Arena Flegrea, Naples, 7/15/56)* Golden Age of Opera ▲ GAO 130 [ADD]

McGee, R. (reader)
Cerha, F.:Eine Art Chanson, w. H.C. Artmann (reader), HK Gruber (reader), J. Holland (reader), M. Jones (reader), G. Rühm (reader) *(rec live Apr. 30, 1993)* Largo ▲ 5126 [DDD]

McGillian, H. (sgr)
Porter, C.:Anything Goes, w. P. LuPone (sgr), et al. [1987 revival cast]
RCA ▲ 7769-2 RC [DDD] ■ 7769-4 RC
Porter, C.:Fifty Million Frenchmen, w. K. Criswell (sop), K. McClelland (sgr), S. Powell (sgr), K. Ziemba (sgr), J. Graae (sgr), J. Harder (sgr), S. Waara (sgr), P. Cass (sgr), J. LeClerc (sgr) [1991 studio cast]
New World ▲ 80417-2 [DDD]

McGlinn, John (sgr)
Lerner, A.J.:Brigadoon, w. London Sinfonietta, Ambrosian Chorus [1992 studio cast]
Broadway Angel ▲ CDQ 54481 ■ 4DQ 54481
Porter, C.:Anything Goes, w. F. von Stade (mez), K. Criswell (sop), C. Groenendaal (sgr), J. Gilford (sgr), London SO, Ambrosian Chorus [original 1934 Broadway version w. original orchestration by Robert Russell Bennett & Hans Spialek] Angel ▲ CDC 49848-2 [DDD]

McGovern, Maureen (sgr)
Amen:A Gospel Celebration, w. Azusa Pacific Univ Choir, Central State Univ Chorus, Cincinnati Pops Chorale, Jennifer Holliday (sgr), Lou Rawls (sgr), Cincinnati Pops Orch [cnd:Erich Kunzel] *(rec Feb. 28-Mar. 1, 1993)* Telarc ▲ CD 80315 [DDD] ■ CD 80315
A Love until the End of Time:Domingo's Greatest Love Songs, w. Plácido Domingo (ten), Lee Holdridge (cnd), John Denver (sgr) CBS ▲ MK 42520 [ADD/DDD] ■ FMT 42520

Machado, Regina (sgr)
Chevalier, C.:Music of, w. Teca Calazans (sgr), Ze-Luis (sgr), Nigel Scragg (fl/a sax), Rosihna de Valenca (gtr), Jean-Yves Candela (pno), Wilson das Neves (perc), Regina Machado (perc), Silvano Michelino (perc)—Comme d'habitude; Couleur café; Une histoire d'amour; Les feuilles mortes; Les moulins de mon coeur; Syracuse; Je t'aimerai; Ces petits rien; La valse des lilas; L'absent; Que reste-il de nos amours; Un homme et une femme *(rec Studio Bastille)* Iris ▲ 010 [DDD]

Machi, Mario (bass)
Donizetti, G.:Gemma di Vergy, w. Montserrat Caballé (sop—Gemma di Vergy), Biancamaria Casoni (mez—Ida di Greville), Giorgio Lamberti (ten—Tamas), Renato Bruson (bar—Conte di Vergy), Mario Machì (bass—Rolando), Mario Rinaudo (bass—Guido), A. Gatto (cnd), Naples Teatro San Carlo Orch, Naples Teatro San Carlo Chorus *(rec Naples, Dec. 12, 1975)* Myto 2-▲ 952124
Donizetti, G.:Messa di Gloria e Credo, w. H. Mané (sop), G. Vighi (mez), P. Maus (ten), R. Bader (cnd), Berlin RSO, St. Hedwig's Cathedral Choir [L] Koch Schwann ▲ CD 313031 [ADD]
Mercadante, S.:Il bravo, w. Miwako Matsumoto (sop—Violetta), Giovanna di Rocco (sop—Michelina), William Johns (ten—Il Bravo), Antonio Savastano (ten—Pisani), Gino Sinimberghi (ten—Cappello), Loris Gambelli (bass—Marco), Mario Machì (bass—Luigi), Paolo Washington (bass—Foscari), Maria Parazzini (sgr—Teodora), G. Ferro (cnd), Rome Opera Orch, Rome Opera Chorus *(rec Rome, Dec 30, 1976)*
Italia 3-▲ CDC 94 [ADD]

Mächler, Peter (bass)
Coelho Neto, M.:Maria mater gratiae, w. Luiz Alves da Silva (ct), Beat Mattmüller (ct), Markus Schikora (ten), L. A. da Silva (cnd), Turicum Ensemble *(rec Studio DRS, Zurich, Sept 26-29, 1994)*
Claves ▲ CD 9521 [DDD]
Garcia, J.M.N.:Motets, w. Katharina Ott (sop), Luiz Alves da Silva (ct), Beat Mattmüller (ct), Andreas Schmidt (ct), Markus Schikora (ten), William Lombardi (ten), Michael Leibundgut (bass), L. A. da Silva (cnd), Turicum Ensemble *(rec Studio DRS, Zurich, Sept 26-29, 1994)* Claves ▲ CD 9521 [DDD]
Mesquita, J.J.E.L. de:Antiphona de Nossa Senhora, w. Luiz Alves da Silva (ct), Beat Mattmüller (ct), Markus Schikora (ten), L. A. da Silva (cnd), Turicum Ensemble *(rec Studio DRS, Zurich, Sept 26-29, 1994)* Claves ▲ CD 9521 [DDD]

Mächler, Peter (bass) (cont.)
Pinto, L.A.:Te Deum Laudamus, w. Katharina Ott (sop), Luiz Alves da Silva (ct), Beat Mattmüller (ct), Andreas Schmidt (ct), Markus Schikora (ten), William Lombardi (ten), Michael Leibundgut (bass), L. A. da Brooks (cnd), Turicum Ensemble *(rec Studio DRS, Zurich, Sept 26-29, 1994)*
Claves ▲ CD 9521 [DDD]

Machotková, Marcela (sop)
Dvořák, A.:The Jacobin (sels), w. Beno Blachut (ten), Vilém Přibyl (ten), J. Pinkas (cnd), Brno State PO
Supraphon ▲ SUP 112250 [AAD]
Martinů, B.:The Epic of Gilgamesh, w. J. Zaradníček (ten), V. Zítek (ten), K. Průša (bass), J. Belohlávek (cnd), Prague SO, Czech Phil Chorus Supraphon ▲ SUP 11 1824 [ADD]
Smetana, B.:The 2 Widows, w. N. Sormova (sop), J. Zahradnicek (ten), F. Jílek (cnd), Prague National Theater Orch, Prague National Theater Chorus [Cz] *(rec 1975)*
Supraphon 2-▲ SUP 11 2122 [AAD]

Macias, Reinaldo (ten)
Bomtempo, J.D.:Messe de requiem consacrée à...Camões, w. Angela Maria Blasi (sop), Liliana Bizineche-Eisinger (mez), Michel Brodard (bass), M. Corboz (cnd), Lisbon Gulbenkian Foundation Orch, Lisbon Gulbenkian Foundation Chorus *(rec Gulbenkian Foundation Grand Auditorium, June 14-16, 1994)* FNAC Music ▲ 592302 [DDD]

McIntyre, Donald (b-bar)
Beethoven, L. van:Sym 9, "Choral Sym", w. Heather Harper (sop), Helem Watts (cta), Alexander Young (ten), L. Stokowski (cnd), London SO, London Sym Chorus *(rec London, Sept 23, 1967)*
Music & Arts ▲ MUA CD 943
Debussy, C.:Pelléas et Mélisande, w. E. Söderström (sop), Y. Minton (mez), G. Shirley (ten), D. Ward (bass), P. Boulez (cnd), Royal Opera House Orch, Royal Opera House Chorus Covent Garden
Sony Classical (Pierre Boulez Edition) 3-▲ SM3K 47265
Wagner, R.:Die Meistersinger von Nürnberg (sels), w. Heather Harper (sop), Helem Watts (cta), Alexander Young (ten), L. Stokowski (cnd), London SO, London Sym Chorus—Suite:Prelude Act III, Dance of the Apprentices, Entrance of the Mastersingers *(rec London, Sept 23, 1967)*
Music & Arts ▲ MUA CD 943
Wagner, R.:Parsifal, w. G. Jones (sop), J. King (ten), T. Stewart (bar), K. Ridderbusch (bass), F. Crass (bass), P. Boulez (cnd), Bayreuth Festival Orch, Bayreuth Festival Chorus [G] *(rec 1970)*
Deutsche Grammophon 3-▲ 435718-2 [ADD]
Wagner, R.:Parsifal, w. Waltraud Meier (mez—Kundry), Warren Ellsworth (ten—Parsifal), Nicholas Folwell (bar—Klingsor), Philip Joll (b-bar—Amfortas), Donald McIntyre (b-bar—Gurnemanz), R. Goodall (cnd), Welsh National Opera Orch, Welsh National Opera Chorus EMI Classics 2-▲ CDMD 65665
Wagner, R.:Das Rheingold, w. H. Schwarz (mez), H. Zednik (ten), H. Becht (bar), P. Boulez (cnd), Bayreuth Festival Orch, Bayreuth Festival Chorus [G] Philips 2-▲ 434421-2 [DDD]
Wagner, R.:Der Ring des Nibelungen, w. G. Jones (sop), H. Schwarz (mez), T. Altmeyer (ten), L. Hofmann (bass), P. Boulez (cnd), Bayreuth Festival Orch, Bayreuth Festival Chorus
Philips 32-▲ 434420-2 [ADD/DDD]
Wagner, R.:Siegfried, w. G. Jones (sop), H. Zednik (ten), H. Becht (bar), P. Boulez (cnd), Bayreuth Festival Orch, Bayreuth Festival Chorus [G] Philips 3-▲ 434423-2 [DDD]

Mack, Jonathan (ten)
Biggs, J.:Songs of Laughter, Love, & Tears, w. D. Amos (cnd), Crystal CO [E] *(rec Feb. 16, 1992)*
Crystal ▲ CD501
Kraft, William:Contextures II:The Final Beast, w. M. Rawcliffe (sop), A. Previn (cnd), Los Angeles PO, New Albion Ensemble, Pasadena Boys' Choir [E,G,Gr,L]
Meet The Composer ▲ 79229-2 ■ 79229-4
Rachmaninoff, S.:All-Night Vigil, w. William Hall (cnd), Master Chorale of Orange County *(rec Santa Ana High School Auditorium, Santa Ana, CA)* Klavier ▲ KCD 11065 [DDD]

Mackay, Ann (sop)
Beethoven, L. van:Songs, w. English Piano Trio—The Sweetest Lad Was Jamie; O, How Can I Be Blithe & Glad; Cease Your Funning; Jeanie's Distress; Faithfu' Johnie; Dim, Dim is My Eye; Oh! Thou Art the Lad of My Heart, Willy [all Scottish Folk Songs] Meridian ▲ MER 84253 [DDD]
Handel, G.F.:Cants, w. E. Aadland (cnd), European Community CO—"Agrippina condotta a morire," HWV 110 [I] ASV ▲ ASV 766
Handel, G.F.:Silete Venti, w. E. Aadland (cnd), European Community CO [L] ASV ▲ ASV 766

MacKay, H. (nar)
Lansky, P.:Music for Computer-Processed Natural Sounds, w. J. Lansky (perc), C. Lansky (perc), P. Lansky (hands), J. Moses (hands)—Table's Clear (percussive kitchen paraphernalia); Night Traffic (traffic sounds); Now and Then (speech-music); Quakerbridge (people in a suburban shopping mall); The Sound of Two Hands Bridge ▲ BCD 9035 [DDD]

McKay, H. (sgr)
Lansky, P.:Smalltalk & August, w. P. Lansky (sgr/elec) New Albion ▲ NA 030 [DDD]

McKee, Gerald (ten)
Wagner, R.:Der Ring des Nibelungen, w. Liselotte Becker-Egner (sop—Woglinde/Ortlinde/Wellgunde), Angelika Berger (sop—Wellgunde/Waltraute), Siw Ericsdotter (sop—Norn 3), Heidemaria Ferch (sop—Freia/Gerhilde), Bella Jasper (sop—Helmwige/Waldvogel/Woglinde), Ditha Sommer (sop—Sieglinde/Gutrune), Ursula Boese (mez—Erda), Ruth Hesse (mez—Fricka), Nadezde Kniplová (mez—Brünnhilde), Margit Kobeck (mez—Schwertleite/Norn 2), Hilde Rosner (mez—Flosshilde/Siegrunde), Erica Schubert (mez—Grimgerde/Flosshilde), Ingrid Göritz (cta—Rossweisse/Norn 1), Herbert Doussant (ten—Froh), Herold Kraus (ten—Mime), Gerald McKee (ten—Siegmund/Siegfried), Fritz Uhl (ten—Loge), Rudolf Knoll (bar—Gunther/Donner), Rolf Polke (bass-bar—Wotan/Wanderer), Rolf Kühne (bass—Alberich), Takao Okamura (bass—Fafner), Otto von Rohr (bass—Hagen/Fasolt/Hunding), H. Swarowsky (cnd), Czech PO, Prague National Theater Orch *(rec June 3 & 5, July 26-31, A)* Weltbild Classics 14-▲ 703769 [ADD]

McKee, Joseph (bass)
Flowering of Vocal Music in America, 1767-1823, w. Susan Belling (sop), Cynthia Clarey (sop), Barbara Wallace (sop), Debra Vanderlinde (sop), D'Anna Fortunato (mez), Evelyn Petros (mez), Charles Bressler (ten), Richard Anderson (bar), James Tyeska (bar), Cynthia Otis (hp), Leonard Rav
New World ▲ 80467-2

McKeever, Jacquelyn (sgr)
Bernstein, L.:Wonderful Town, w. R. Russell (sgr), S. Chaplin (sgr), et al.
Sony Broadway ▲ SK 48021 ■ ST 48021

McKellar, Kenneth (ten)
Handel, G.F.:Messiah, w. George Malcolm (hpd), Ralph Downes (org), A. Boult (cnd), London SO, London Sym Chorus—And the glory of the Lord; And He shall purify; For unto us a Child is born; Glory to God in the highest; His yoke is easy; Behold the Lamb of God; Surely He hath borne our griefs; And with His stripes we are healed; All we like sheep have gone astray; All they that see Him...He trusted in God; Lift up your heads; The Lord gave the word; Their sound has gone out; Let us break the bonds asunder; Hallelujah; Since by man came death; Worthy is the Lamb...Amen London ▲ 436569-2
Handel, G.F.:Messiah, w. Joan Sutherland (sop), Grace Bumbry (mez), Joseph Ward (bar), A. Boult (cnd), London PO London 3-▲ 433003-2 [ADD]
Handel, G.F.:Messiah (sels), w. Joan Sutherland (sop), Grace Bumbry (mez), Joseph Ward (bar), A. Boult (cnd), London SO, London Sym Chorus—arias & choruses
London ("Weekend Classics" series) ▲ 417879-2 [AAD] ■ 417879-4

McKellen, Ian (nar)
Corigliano, J.:Creations (2), w. R. Werthen (cnd), I Fiamminghi CO *(rec Belgium, July 19-21, 1995)*
Telarc ▲ CD 80421 [DDD]

Mackenzie, Malcolm (bar)
Axelrod, L.:Songs, w. Louisa Ann Parks (sop), Michael Horton (ten), Nmon Ford-Livene (ten), Richard Bernstein (bass), M. Beltrami (cnd)—sels w. lyrics by Burns, Browning, Byron, Keats, Morris, Poe, Rossetti, Shelley, Wordsworth & Yeats Marquis ▲ MAR 171

Mackenzie, Mary (mez)
Boito, A.:Mefistofele, w. R. Tebaldi (sop—Margheritta), E. Souliotis (sop—Elena), M. Mackenzie (mez—Marta), M. Ruggiero (mez—Pantalis), A. Kraus (ten—Faust), H. Kraus (ten—Wagner), N. Ghiaurov (bass—Mefistofele), N. Sanzogno (cnd), *(orch unknown)* Ornamenti 2-▲ FE 101

McKenzie, Piers (nar)
Davies, S.:What Is the Matter in Amy Glennon?, w. Gregory Whitehead (nar—The Idea), Sheila Davies (nar—Amy Glennon/Chorus), Piers McKenzie (nar—Auctioneer), Fran Smith (sgr), Amy Newburg (sgr), Barney Jones (nar—The Fathers) ▲ WN 0013

Mackey, Hugh (bar)
Moeran, E.J.:Nocturne, w. V. Handley (cnd), Ulster Orch, Renaissance Singers [E] Chandos ▲ CHAN 8808 [DDD]

Mackie, Neil (ten)
Davies, P.M.:The Lighthouse, w. Ian Comboy (bass), Christopher Keyte (bass), P. M. Davies (cnd), BBC PO Collins Classics ▲ COL 1415 [DDD]
Handel, G.F.:Messiah, w. Helen Kucharek (sop), Jennifer Smith (sop), Linda Finnie (mez), Rodney Macann (b–bar), T. Dean (cnd), Pro Christe Orch, Pro Christe Choir *(rec St. Augustine's Church, Kilburn, London, 1986)* Guild 2–▲ GMDD 7112/3 [ADD]
Haydn, J.:Die Schöpfung, w. Krisztina Láki (sop), Philippe Huttenlocher (bar), S. Kuijken (cnd), La Petite Bande, Ghent Collegium Vocale Accent 2–▲ ACC 58228/29
Leighton, K.:Sym 3, w. B. Thomson (cnd), Scottish National Orch [E] Chandos ▲ CHAN 8741 [DDD]
Walton, W.:Gloria, w. A. Gunson (cta), S. Roberts (bar), D. Willcocks (cnd), Philharmonia Orch, Bach Choir [L] Chandos ▲ CHAN 8760 [DDD]

McKinney, W. (ten)
Righini, V.:Alcide al Bivio, w. L. Serra (sop), S. Browne (cta), R. El Hage (bass), M. Barta (ob), P. Molinari (hpd), T. Gotti (cnd), Swiss–Italian RSO, Swiss–Italian Radio Chorus *(rec 1979)* Bongiovanni 2–▲ GB 2157/58 [ADD]

McKnight, Anne (sop)
Puccini, G.:La Bohème, w. L. Albanese (sop), J. Peerce (ten), F. Valentino (bar), A. Toscanini (cnd), NBC SO, NBC Sym Chorus [I] RCA Gold Seal 2–▲ 60288–2–RG [ADD] 2–■ 60288–4–RG (CrO2)

McLaughlin, Marie (sop)
Fauré, G.:Requiem, w. G. Howell (bass–bar), S. Celibidache (cnd), London SO, London Sym Chorus *(rec Apr. 1982)* Exclusive ▲ EXL 52 [ADD]
Handel, G.F.:L'Allegro, Il Penseroso ed il Moderato, w. Michael Ginn (trb), Patrizia Kwella (sop), J. E. Gardiner (cnd), English Baroque Soloists, Monteverdi Choir London Erato 2–▲ 2292–45377–2 ZA
Mozart, W.A.:Così fan tutte, w. Kiri Te Kanawa (sop), Ann Murray (mez), Hans–Peter Blochwitz (ten), Thomas Hampson (bar), G. Furlanetto (bar), J. Levine (cnd), Vienna PO, Vienna State Opera Chorus [I] Deutsche Grammophon 3–▲ 423897–2 [DDD]
Mozart, W.A.:Così fan tutte (sels), w. Felicity Lott (sop), Nuccia Focile (sop), Jerry Hadley (ten), Alessandro Corbelli (bass), Gilles Cachemaille (bass) *(rec Usher Hall, Edinburgh, Scotland)* Telarc ▲ CD 80399 [DDD]
Mozart, W.A.:Don Giovanni, w. S. Sweet (sop), K. Mattila (sop), F. Araiza (ten), T. Allen (bar), S. Alaimo (b–bar), R. Lloyd (bass), N. Marriner (cnd), Academy of St. Martin in the Fields, Ambrosian Opera Chorus Philips 3–▲ 432129–2 [DDD]
Mozart, W.A.:Nozze di Figaro, w. L. Cherici (sop), K. Mattila (sop), M. Bacelli (mez), N. Curiel (mez), U. Benelli (ten), L. Gallo (bar), A. Nosotti (bass), M. Pertusi (bass), G. Tadeo (bass), Z. Mehta (cnd), Florence Maggio Musicale Orch, Florence Maggio Musicale Chorus Sony Classical ▲ SK 53286
Mozart, W.A.:Requiem, w. M. Ewing (sop), J. Hadley (ten), C. Hauptmann (bass), L. Bernstein (cnd), Bavarian RSO, Bavarian Radio Chorus [L] Deutsche Grammophon ▲ 427353–2 [DDD]
Mozart, W.A.:Zauberflöte, w. M. Price (sop—Pamina), L. Serra (sop—Queen of the Night), M. Venuti (sop—Papagena), M. McLaughlin (sop—1st Lady), A. Murray (mez—2nd Lady), H. Schwarz (cta—3rd Lady), F. Höher (trb—1st Boy), M. Diedrich (trb—2nd Boy), F. Klos (trb—3rd Boy), P. Schreier (ten—Tamino), R. Tear (ten—Monostatos), R. Goldberg (ten—1st Armoured Man), K. Moll (bass—Sarastro), H. Rech (bass—2nd Armoured Man), C. Davis (cnd), Dresden Staatskapelle, Leipzig Radio Chorus Philips ("Duo" series) 2–▲ 442568–2
Purcell, H.:Dido & Aeneas, w. J. Norman (sop), T. Allen (bar), R. Leppard (cnd), English CO, Ambrosian Singers [E] Philips ▲ 416299–2 [DDD]
Schubert, Franz:Songs (comp), w. T. Hampson (bar), G. Johnson (pno), New Company Singers—soprano/piano songs—D.118, 564, 623, 658, 830, 831, 837, 838, 839, 846, 866/1, 866/3, 923; baritone/piano songs—D.293 & 923; baritone & chorus—Szene aus Faust, D.126 [G] Hyperion ▲ CDJ 33013 [DDD]
Schubert, Franz:Songs (comp), w. T. Hampson (bar), G. Johnson (pno)—soprano songs—D.312 & 542; baritone songs—D.166, 360, 396/383, 450, 540, 541, 548, 554, 677, 699, 700, 707, 737, 890 [G] Hyperion ▲ CDJ 33014 [DDD]
Strauss, R.:Das Alphorn, w. B. Tuckwell (hn), V. Ashkenazy (pno) London ▲ 430370–2 [DDD]
Strauss, R.:songs, w. Graham Johnson (pno)—Die Drossel; Zueignung; Wie sollten wir geheim sie halten; In goldener Fülle; Wiegenlied; Weihnachtsgefühl; Abend–und Morgenrot; Nebel; Schlagende Herzen; Ruhe, meine Seele; Du meines Herzens Krönelein; Ach, was Kummer, Qual und Schmerzen; Das Bächlein; Las ruh'n die toten; In goldner Fülle; Nebel; Wiegenliedchen; Leises Lied; Weihnachtslied; Morgen! Wer lieben will, muss leiden; Ein Röslein zog ich mir im Garten; Die Nacht; Allerseelen; Gefunden; Ach Lieb, ich muss nun schneiden; All mein Gedanken...; Toten; Der müde Wanderer Hyperion ▲ CDA 66659
Sullivan, A.:The Mikado, w. A. Howells (mez), J. Watson (sop), F. Palmer (sop/mez), D. Adams (bass), A. Rolfe Johnson (ten), R. Stuart (bar), R. Van Allan (bass), N. Folwell (bar), C. Mackerras (cnd), Welsh National Opera Orch, Welsh National Opera Chorus—Ov & dialogue omitted [E] Telarc ▲ CD 80284 [DDD]; ■ CS 30284 (D)

McLean, James (ten)
Buechner, M.:Elizabeth, w. S. Anthony (sop), G. Schmöhe (cnd), Nuremberg SO [G] Nord–Disc 2–▲ NORD 2026 [DDD]

McLean, Priscilla (sgr)
McLean, P.:Wilderness, w. Barton McLean (perc) [w. animal, bird, insect, & surreal instrumental sounds on stereo tape] Capstone ▲ CPS 8622

McLean, Priscilla (sgr/perc/ocarinas/elec)
McLean, B.:Earth Music, w. Barton McLean (kbd/clariflute/syn/elec) Capstone ▲ CPS 8622

McLean, Priscilla (sgr/rcr/vn)
McLean, B.:Rainforest Images, w. Panaiotis (sgr), I. Troselj (sgr), K. Ryan (sgr), B. McLean (rcr/clariflute), B. Dickie (didgeridoo) Capstone ▲ CPS 8617n

MacLean, Susan (mez)
Krenek, E.:Der Sprung über den Schatten, w. D. Amos (sop), L. Kemeny (sop), J. Dürmüller (ten), U. Neuweiler (ten), J. Pflieger (bar), T. Brüning (sgr), D. de Villiers (cnd), Bielefeld PO, Bielefeld Phil Chorus [G] *(rec live, May 1989)* CPO 2–▲ CPO 999082–2 [DDD]

McLeod, Raymond (bass)
Rutenberg, P.:Ballad of the Buffalo Skinners, w. John Reyheim (ten), Peter Rutenberg (cnd), Los Angeles Chamber Singers [trad.; ed. & expanded Peter Rutenberg] Klavier ▲ KCD 11052 [DDD]

Macleod, Stephan (bass)
Ryelandt, J.:Agnus Dei, w. Ingrid Kapelle (sop), Lucienne van Deyck (mez), Joseph Cornwell (ten), Huub Claessens (bass), G. Llewellyn (cnd), Royal Flanders PO, Altra Voce, Audite Nova *(rec live, Elisabeth Hall, Antwerp, Holland, Dec 9, 1994)* Marco Polo 2–▲ 8.223785/86 [DDD]

McLeod, Suzanne (mez)
Corghi, A.:Divara—Wasser und Blut, w. Susanna von der Burg (sop—Divara), Suzanne McLeod (mez—Else Windscherer), Eva Lillian Thingboe (mez—Hille Feiken), Robert Schwarts (ten—Lame Man), Heinz Fitz (spkr—Bernd Knipperdollinck), Hanslutz Hildmann (spkr—Jan Matthys), Michael Holm (spkr—Bernhard Rothmann), Christopher Krieg (spkr—Jan van Leiden), W. Humburg (cnd), Münster SO, Münster City Theater Chorus [G] *(rec Grosses Haus, Münster State Theater, Nov. 27–29, 1993)* Marco Polo 2–▲ 8.223706/07 [DDD]

McLerie, A. (sgr)
Berlin, I.:Miss Liberty, w. E. Albert (sgr), M. McCarty (sgr), E. Griffies (sgr) [1949 Broadway cast] Sony Broadway ▲ SK 48015 ■ ST 48015

McLoughlin, Eileen (sop)
Monteverdi, C.:Ballo delle ingrate, w. April Cantelo (sop—Una dell' Ingrate), Eileen McLoughlin (sop—Amore), Alfred Deller (alt—Venere), David Ward (bass—Plutone), Julian Bream (lt), Desmond Dupre (vl), A. Deller (cnd), London Chamber Players *(rec Walthamstow Hall, London)* Vanguard Classics ▲ OVC 8100 [ADD]

MacMaster (sgr)
Saint-Saëns, C.:Requiem, w. Hewes (sgr), Weld (sgr), Watson (sgr), J. Somary (cnd), Amor Artis Orch, Amor Artis Chorale *(rec live)* Premier ▲ PRCD 1025 [DDD]

McMaster, John (ten)
Handel, G.F.:Berenice, w. Julianne Baird (sop—Berenice), Andrea Matthews (sop—Alessandro), D'Anna Fortunato (mez—Selene), Jennifer Lane (mez—Demetrio), Drew Minter (alt—Arsace), John McMaster (ten—Fabio), Jan Opalach (bass—Aristobolo), R. Palmer (cnd), Brewer CO Newport Classic 3–▲ NPD 85620/3 [DDD]

McMillan, Kevin (bar)
Bach, J.S.:Cant 173a, w. D. Röschmann (sop), H. Saint–Gelais (ten), B. Labadie (cnd), Les Violons du Roy *(rec Quebec City, Jan 1994)* Dorian ▲ DOR 90199 [DDD]
Bach, J.S.:Cant 211, "Coffee Cant", w. D. Röschmann (sop), H. Saint–Gelais (ten), B. Labadie (cnd), Les Violons du Roy *(rec Quebec City, Jan 1994)* Dorian ▲ DOR 90199 [DDD]
Bach, J.S.:Cant 212, "Peasant Cant", w. D. Röschmann (sop), H. Saint–Gelais (ten), B. Labadie (cnd), Les Violons du Roy *(rec Quebec City, Jan 1994)* Dorian ▲ DOR 90199 [DDD]
Brahms, J.:Ein Deutsches Requiem, w. Christiane Oelze (sop), H.M. Beuerle (cnd), Freiburg Bach Orch, Freiburg Bach Choir Ars Musici ▲ 1057 [DDD]
Brahms, J.:Songs, w. M. McMahon (pno)—Es schauen die Blumen; Meerfahrt; Der Tod, das ist die kühle Nacht [G] CBC ("Musica Viva" series) ▲ MVCD 1052 [DDD]
Britten, H.:Folksong Arrs, w. J. Greer (pno)—The Salley Gardens; The plough boy; Come you not from Newcastle?; The ash grove; The brisk young widow [E] Marquis ▲ ERAD 127 [DDD]
Britten, H.:Songs & Proverbs of William Blake, w. J. Greer (pno) [E] Marquis ▲ ERAD 127 [DDD]
Lieder on Poems of Heinrich Heine, w. Michael McMahon (pno) CBC Records ("Musica Viva" series) ▲ MVCD 1052 [DDD]
Liszt, F.:Songs, w. M. McMahon (pno)—Du bist wie eine Blume; Ein Fichtenbaum steht einsam; Im Rhein, im schönen Strome; Vergiftet sind meine Lieder [G] CBC ("Musica Viva" series) ▲ MVCD 1052 [DDD]
Mendelssohn, F.:Songs, w. M. McMahon (pno)—Allnächtlich im Traume seh' ich dich; Auf Flügeln des Gesanges; Gruss; Neue Liebe [G] CBC ("Musica Viva" series) ▲ MVCD 1052 [DDD]
Schoenberg, A.:Ode to Napoleon, w. M.–A. Hamelin (pno), Y. Turovsky (cnd), Montreal Musici [orchestral version] [G] Chandos ▲ CHAN 9116 [DDD]
Schubert, Franz:Die Schöne Müllerin, w. W. Jones (pno) [G] *(rec May 1991)* Dorian ▲ DOR 90162 [DDD]
Schubert, Franz:Schwanengesang, w. L. Natocherry (pno) Marquis ▲ MAR 151
Schubert, Franz:Songs (misc), w. M. McMahon (pno)—Der Atlas; Der Doppelgänger [G] CBC ("Musica Viva" series) ▲ MVCD 1052 [DDD]
Schubert, Franz:Songs (misc), w. L. Natocherry (pno) Marquis ▲ MAR 151
Schumann, R.:Dichterliebe, w. *(pno unknown)* CBC ("Musica Viva" series) ▲ MVCD 1052 [DDD]
Vaughan Williams, R.:Mystical Songs, w. St. James Cathedral Church Men & Boys' Choir Toronto [E] Marquis ▲ ERAD 127 [DDD]
Vaughan Williams, R.:Songs, w. J. Greer (pno), M. Hammer (vn)—Rolling in the dew; Searching for lambs; How cold the wind doth blow [E] Marquis ▲ ERAD 127 [DDD]

McNair, Sylvia (sop)
Bach, J.S.:Cant 63, w. J. Taylor (mez), D. Gordon (ten), D. Lichti (b–bar), G. Funfgeld (cnd), Bach Festival Orch, Bethlehem Bach Choir—plus Sanctus from Mass in b, BWV 232 [G] Dorian ▲ DOR 90113 [DDD]
Bach, J.S.:Mass in b, BWV 232, w. G. Simpson (mez), D. Ziegler (mez), J. Aler (ten), W. Stone (bar), T. Paul (bass), R. Shaw (cnd), Atlanta SO, Atlanta Chamber Chorus [L] Telarc 2–▲ CD 80233 [DDD]
Barber, S.:Knoxville:Summer of 1915, w. Y. Levi (cnd), Atlanta SO Telarc ▲ CD 80250 [DDD]
Beethoven, L. van:Leonore Prohaska, w. Karoline Eichhorn (narr), Marie–Pierre Langlamet (hp), Sascha Reckert (glass hmc), C. Abbado (cnd), Berlin PO, Berlin Radio Chorus *(rec Great Hall, Philharmonie, Berlin)* Deutsche Grammophon ▲ 447748–2 [DDD]
Beethoven, L. van:Missa Solemnis, w. Janice Taylor (mez), J. Aler (ten), T. Krause (bar), R. Shaw (cnd), Atlanta SO, Atlanta Sym Chorus [L] Telarc 2–▲ CD 80150 [DDD]
Beethoven, L. van:Sym 9, "Choral Sym", w. U. Heilmann (ten), J. Van Nes (bar), B. Weikl (bar), K. Masur (cnd), Leipzig Gewandhaus Orch, London Radio Choir Philips ▲ 432995–2
Beethoven, L. van:Die Weihe des Hauses (incidental music), w. Byrn Terfel (bar), Bruno Ganz (narr), C. Abbado (cnd), Berlin PO, Berlin Radio Chorus *(rec Great Hall, Philharmonie, Berlin)* Deutsche Grammophon ▲ 447748–2 [DDD]
Berlioz, H.:Hymne des Marseillais, w. R. Leech (ten), D. Zinman (cnd), Baltimore SO, Baltimore Sym Chorus Telarc ▲ CD 80164 [DDD]
Britten, H.:A Midsummer Night's Dream, w. Sylvia McNair (sop—Tytania), Brian Asawa (ct—Oberon), Robert Lloyd (bass), C. Davis (cnd), London SO Philips 2–▲ 454 122–2
Gluck, C.W.:Orfeo ed Euridice, w. C. Sieden (sop), D.L. Ragin (ct), J. E. Gardiner (cnd), English Baroque Soloists, Monteverdi Choir London Philips ▲ 434093–2
Handel, G.F.:Laudate pueri Dominum, w. J. E. Gardiner (cnd), English Baroque Soloists, Monteverdi Choir London [G] Philips ▲ 434920–2
Handel, G.F.:Messiah, w. Anne Sofie von Otter (mez), Michael Chance (alt), Jerry Hadley (ten), Robert Lloyd (b–bar), N. Marriner (cnd), Academy of St. Martin in the Fields [E] *(rec live, Dublin 4/13/92)* Philips 2–▲ 434695–2 [DDD]
Handel, G.F.:Messiah, w. Kaaren Erickson (sop), Alfreda Hodgson (cta), Jon Humphrey (ten), Richard Stilwell (bar), R. Shaw (cnd), Atlanta SO, Atlanta Sym Chorus [E] Telarc 2–▲ CD 80093–2 [DDD]
Handel, G.F.:Messiah, w. Kaaren Erickson (sop), Alfreda Hodgson (cta), Jon Humphrey (ten), Richard Stilwell (bar), R. Shaw (cnd), Atlanta SO, Atlanta Sym Chorus [E] Telarc ▲ CD 80103 [DDD]; ■ CS 30103 (D)
Handel, G.F.:Semele, w. Kathleen Battle (sop), Marylin Horne (mez), Michael Chance (ct), John Aler (ten), Samuel Ramey (bass), J. Nelson (cnd), English CO, Ambrosian Opera Chorus Deutsche Grammophon 3–▲ 435782–2 –
Haydn, J.:Mass 10, "Kriegsmesse", "Paukenmesse", w. Delores Ziegler (mez), Hans–Peter Blochwitz (ten), Andreas Schmidt (bar), J. Levine (cnd), Berlin SO, Berlin RIAS Chamber Choir Deutsche Grammophon ▲ 435853–2
Haydn, J.:Die Schöpfung, w. Donna Brown (sop), Michael Schade (ten), Gerald Finley (bar), Rodney Gilfry (bar), J. E. Gardiner (cnd), English Baroque Soloists, Monteverdi Choir London Archiv ▲ 449 217–2
Kern, J.:Songs, w. A. Previn (pno), D. Finck (db)—Land Where the Good Songs Go; I Won't Dance; Nobody Else but Me; The Folks Who Live on the Hill; A Fine Romance; Remind Me; You Couldn't Be Cuter; Why Was I Born?; I'm Old Fashioned; Al Philips ▲ 442129–2
Mahler, G.:Sym 2, w. J. van Nes (cta), B. Haitink (cnd), Berlin PO, Ernst Senff Chorus Philips ▲ 438935–2
Mahler, G.:Sym 2, w. J. van Nes (cta), E. Mata (cnd), Dallas SO, Dallas Sym Chorus [G] *(rec 9/89)* Pro Arte 2–▲ CDD 479 [DDD]
Mahler, G.:Sym 4, w. B. Haitink (cnd), Berlin PO Philips ▲ 434123–2
Mahler, G.:Sym 8, w. Andrea Rost (sop), Cheryl Studer (sop), Anne Sofie von Otter (mez), Rosemarie Lang (cta), Peter Seiffert (ten), Bryn Terfel (bar), Jan–Hendrik Rootering (bass), C. Abbado (cnd), Berlin PO, Berlin Radio Chorus, Prague Phil Chorus, Tölz Boys' Choir Deutsche Grammophon ("4D Audio" series) 2–▲ 445843–2
Mendelssohn, F.:Midsummer Night's Dream (ov & incidental), w. Kenneth Branagh (nar), Angelika Kirchschlager (mez), C. Abbado (cnd), Berlin PO, Ernst Senff Chorus Women's Voices Sony Classical ▲ SK 62826
Monteverdi, C.:Incoronazione, w. Constanze Backes (sop—Valletto), Catherine Bott (sop—Drusilla/Pallade/La Virtù), Dana Hanchard (sop—Nerone), Sylvia McNair (sop—Poppea), Marinella Pennicchi (sop—Amore/Damigella), Annie Sofie von Otter (mez—Ottavia/Venere/La Fortuna), Julian Clarkson (alt—Littore/Mercurio), Bernarda Fink (cta—Arnalta), Roberto Balconi (ct—Nutrice), Michael Chance (ct—Ottone), Nigel Robson (ten—Liberto/Soldato Secondo), Mark Tucker (ten—Lucano/Soldato Primo), Francesco Ellero d'Artegna (bass—Seneca), J. E. Gardiner (cnd), English Baroque Soloists *(rec Queen Elizabeth Hall, South Bank Ctr, London, Dec 1993)* Archiv 3–▲ 447088–2

McNair, Sylvia (sop) (cont.)

Mozart, W.A.:Ave verum corpus, w. Barbara Bonney (sop), Charlotte Margiono (sop), Elisabeth von Magnus (cta), Christoph Pregardien (ten), Thomas Hampson (bass), N. Harnoncourt (cnd), Vienna Concentus Musicus, Arnold Schoenberg Choir Teldec ▲ 98928 2

Mozart, W.A.:Complete Mozart Edition, w. A. M. Blasi (sop), I. Vermillion (mez), J. Hadley (ten), C. H. Ahnsjö (ten), N. Marriner (cnd), Academy of St. Martin in the Fields Philips 2-▲ 422535-2 [ADD]

Mozart, W.A.:Exsultate, w. J. E. Gardiner (cnd), English Baroque Soloists, Monteverdi Choir London [G] Philips ▲ 434920-2

Mozart, W.A.:Grabmusik, w. Barbara Bonney (sop), Charlotte Margiono (sop), Elisabeth von Magnus (cta), Christoph Pregardien (ten), Thomas Hampson (bass), N. Harnoncourt (cnd), Vienna Concentus Musicus, Arnold Schoenberg Choir Teldec ("Das alte Werk" series) ▲ 98928-2

Mozart, W.A.:Idomeneo, w. Hillevi Martinpelto (sop), Anne Sophie von Otter (mez), Anthony Rolfe Johnson (ten), J. E. Gardiner (cnd), English Baroque Soloists, Monteverdi Choir London Archiv 3-▲ 431674-2 [DDD]

Mozart, W.A.:Missa, K.317, w. D. Ziegler (mez), H.P. Blochwitz (ten), A. Schmidt (bar), J. Levine (cnd), Berlin SO, Berlin RIAS Chamber Choir Deutsche Grammophon ▲ 435853-2

Mozart, W.A.:Missa, K.427, w. D. Montague (mez), A. Rolfe Johnson (ten), C. Hauptmann (bass), J. E. Gardiner (cnd), English Baroque Soloists, Monteverdi Choir London [newly revised version, ed. Gardiner] [L] Philips ▲ 420210-2 [DDD]

Mozart, W.A.:Nozze di Figaro, w. Cecilia Bartoli (sop—Cherubino), Sylvia McNair (sop—Susanna), Cheryl Studer (sop—Countess Almaviva), Lucio Gallo (bar—Figaro), Boje Skovhus (bar—Count Almaviva), C. Abbado (cnd), Vienna PO, Vienna State Opera Chorus Deutsche Grammophon 3-▲ 445903-2

Mozart, W.A.:Regina coeli, K.127, w. Barbara Bonney (sop), Charlotte Margiono (sop), Elisabeth von Magnus (cta), Christoph Pregardien (ten), Thomas Hampson (bass), N. Harnoncourt (cnd), Vienna Concentus Musicus, Arnold Schoenberg Choir Teldec ("Das alte Werk" series) ▲ 98928 2

Mozart, W.A.:Requiem, w. C. Watkinson (cta), F. Araiza (ten), R. Lloyd (b–bar), N. Marriner (cnd), Academy of St. Martin in the Fields, Academy Chorus [L] Philips ▲ 432087-2 [DDD]

Orff, C.:Carmina burana, w. J. Aler (ten), Håkan Hagegård (bar), L. Slatkin (cnd), St. Louis SO RCA Red Seal ▲ 09026-61673-2; ■ 09026-61673-4

Rachmaninoff, S.:Vocalise, w. D. Zinman (cnd), Baltimore SO Telarc ▲ CD 80312 [DDD]

McNalley, Maureen (nar)

Schoenberg, A.:Pierrot lunaire, w. Dwight Peltzer (pno), Eric Rosenblith (vn/va), Chris Finckel (vc), Sue Ann Kahn (fl), Anand Devendra (cl/b cl), J. Thome (cnd), Orch of Our Time Vox Box 2-▲ CDX 5144

MacNeil, Cornell (bar)

Leoncavallo, R.:Pagliacci, w. Joan Carlyle (sop—Nedda), Jon Vickers (ten—Canio), José Noit (ten—Beppe), Cornell MacNeil (bar—Tonio), Bruno Tornasaetti (bar—Silvio), B. Bartoletti (cnd), *(orch unknown)* *(rec live, Buenos Aires, 1968)* VAI Audio ▲ VAIA 1014 [ADD]

Puccini, G.:La fanciulla del West, w. R. Tebaldi (sop), M. del Monaco (ten), G. Tozzi (bass), F. Capuana (cnd), St. Cecilia Academy Orch Rome, St. Cecilia Academy Chorus Rome [I] London 2-▲ 421595-2 [ADD]

Puccini, G.:Tosca, w. Leonie Rysanek (sop), Russell Christopher (ten), Andrea Velis (ten), Clifford Harvuot (bar), Fernando Corena (bass), Paul Plishka (bass), F. Molinari–Pradelli (cnd), San Francisco Opera Orch, San Francisco Opera Chorus Melodram 2-▲ CDM 27508

Verdi, G.:Aida, w. R. Tebaldi (sop) G. Simionato (mez), C. Bergonzi (ten), A. van Mill (bass), H. von Karajan (cnd), Vienna PO, Vienna State Opera Chorus [I] London 3-▲ 414087-2 [ADD]

Verdi, G.:Aida, w. R. Tebaldi (sop) G. Simionato (mez), C. Bergonzi (ten), A. van Mill (bass), H. von Karajan (cnd), Vienna PO, Vienna State Opera Chorus [I] London ("Jubilee" series) ▲ 417763-2 [ADD]

Verdi, G.:Alzira, w. V. Zeani (sop), G. Cecchele (ten), C. Cava (bass), F. Capuana (cnd), Rome Opera Orch, Rome Opera Chorus [I] *(rec live 3/16/67)* Melodram 2-▲ MEL 27013 (m) [AAD]

Verdi, G.:Alzira, w. V. Zeani (sop), G. Cecchele (ten), C. Cava (bass), F. Capuana (cnd), Rome Opera Orch, Rome Opera Chorus [I] *(rec live, 3/16/67)* Verona 2-▲ 27042/43 (m) [AAD]

Verdi, G.:Un ballo in maschera, w. B. Nilsson (sop), G. Simionato (mez), C. Bergonzi (ten), G. Solti (cnd), St. Cecilia Academy Orch Rome, St. Cecilia Academy Chorus Rome [I] London 2-▲ 425655-2 [ADD]

Verdi, G.:Un ballo in maschera, w. M. Caballé (sop—Amelia), T. Paniagua (sop—Oscar), L. Chookasian (cta—Ulrica), P. Domingo (ten—Riccardo), C. MacNeil (bar—Renato), J. Pons (bar—Tom), C. del Bosco (bass—Samuel), G. Patanè (cnd), *(orch unknown)* Ornamenti 2-▲ FE 103

Verdi, G.:Falstaff, w. Anna Moffo (sop—Nannetta), Renata Tebaldi (sop—Alice Ford), Anna Maria Canali (mez—Meg Page), Giulietta Simionato (mez—Dame Quickly), Mariano Caruso (ten—Doctor Caius), Alvinio Misciano (ten—Fenton), Luigi Vellucci (ten—Bardolfo), Tito Gobi (bar—Falstaff), Carnell MacNeil (bar—Ford), Kenneth Smith (bass–Pistola), T. Serafin (cnd), *(orch unknown)* *(rec Chicago, 1958)* Legato Classics 2-▲ LCD 206-2 [ADD]

Verdi, G.:Luisa Miller, w. A. Moffo (sop), S. Verrett (mez), C. Bergonzi (ten), G. Tozzi (bass), F. Cleva (cnd), RCA Italian Opera Orch [I] RCA Gold Seal 2-▲ 6646-2-RG [ADD]

Verdi, G.:Rigoletto, w. Renata Scotto (sop—Gilda), Stella Maris Silva (sop—Giovanna), Martha Carrizo (mez—Page), Carmen de la Mata (mez—Countess Ceprano), Noemi Souza (cta—Maddalena), Horacio Mastrango (ten—Borso), Richard Tucker (ten—Duke of Mantua), Cornell MacNeil (bar—Rigolotto), Riccardo Yost (bar—Marullo), Guerrino Boschetti (bass—Usher), Tulio Gogliardo (bass—Count Ceprano), Victor de Narké (bass—Monterone), William Wilderman (bass—Sparafucile), F. Previtali (cnd), Buenos Aires Teatro Colón Orch, Buenos Aires Teatro Colón Chorus *(rec Colon Theater, Buenos Aires, Aug. 22, 1967)* Legato Classics 2-▲ LCD 198-2

Verdi, G.:Rigoletto, w. Joan Sutherland (sop—Gilda), Renato Cioni (ten—Duke), Cornell MacNeil (bar—Rigoletto), N. Sanzogno (cnd), St. Cecilia Academy Orch Rome, St. Cecilia Academy Chorus Rome London ("Double Decca" series) 2-▲ 443853-2

Verdi, G.:Simon Boccanegra, w. Renata Tebaldi (sop—Maria Boccanegra), Penelope Jensen (mez—Maria's Maidservant), Richard Tucker (ten—Gabriele Adorno), Rod MacWerter (ten—Paolo), Cornell MacNeil (bar—Simon Boccanegra), Ara Berberian (bar—Pietro), Ezio Flagello (bass—Jacopo Fiesco), Franco Iglesias (bass—Paolo), J. Levine (cnd), *(orch unknown)* *(rec live, Miami, 1970)* Legato Classics 2-▲ LCD 189-2 [ADD]

Macpherson, George (bass)

Massenet, J.:Sapho, w. Jenny Hill (sop), Laura Sarti (mez), Bernard Dickerson (ten), Alexander Oliver (ten), Neilson Taylor (bar), Milla Andrew (sgr), B. Keefe (cnd), BBC SO, BBC Sym Chorus *(rec live, 1973)* Memories 2-▲ MEM 4601 [AAD]

MacRae, Gordon (sgr)

Rodgers, R.:Carousel, w. S. Jones (sgr), C. Mitchell (sgr), B. Ruick (sgr), C. Turner (sgr), R. Rounseville (sgr) *(rec 1956)* Broadway Angel ▲ ZDM 64692 ■ EG 64692

Rodgers, R.:Oklahoma!, w. S. Jones (sgr), R. Steiger (sgr), Gloria Grahame (sgr), Gene Nelson (sgr), C. Greenwood (sgr), J. Whitmore (sgr) *(rec 1955)* Broadway Angel ▲ ZDM 64691 ■ EG 64691

Romberg, S.:The Desert Song, w. D. Kirsten (sgr) Sony ▲ BT 831

Romberg, S.:Music of (operetta sels), w. D. Kirsten (sop), Van Alexander (sgr), *(orch & chorus unknown)* —selections from *Desert Song, New Moon, Student Prince* EMI Classics ("Studio" series) ▲ CDM 69052

Macurdy, John (bass)

Beethoven, L. van:Fidelio, w. Judith Blegen (sop), Leonie Rysanek (sop), Jon Vickers (ten), Walter Berry (bass), Giorgio Tozzi (bass), K. Böhm (cnd), San Francisco Opera Orch, San Francisco Opera Chorus Melodram 2-▲ CDM 27086

Mozart, W.A.:Don Giovanni, w. E. Moser (sop), K. Te Kanawa (sop), T. Berganza (mez), K. Riegel (ten), G. Raimondi (ten), J. Van Dam (b–bar), L. Maazel (cnd), Paris Opera Orch, Paris Opera Chorus [I] CBS 3-▲ M3K 35192

Mozart, W.A.:Don Giovanni (sels), w. E. Moser (sop), K. Te Kanawa (sop), T. Berganza (mez), K. Riegel (ten), G. Raimondi (ten), J. Van Dam (b–bar), L. Maazel (cnd), Paris Opera Orch CBS ■ MT 35859

MacWerter, Rod (ten)

Verdi, G.:Simon Boccanegra, w. Renata Tebaldi (sop—Maria Boccanegra), Penelope Jensen (mez—Maria's Maidservant), Richard Tucker (ten—Gabriele Adorno), Rod MacWerter (ten—Paolo), Cornell MacNeil (bar—Simon Boccanegra), Ara Berberian (bar—Pietro), Ezio Flagello (bass—Jacopo Fiesco), Franco Iglesias (bass—Paolo), J. Levine (cnd), *(orch unknown)* *(rec live, Miami, 1970)* Legato Classics 2-▲ LCD 189-2 [ADD]

McWhirter, Lynore (sop)

Bax, A.:Enchanted Summer, w. A. Williams–King (sop), V. Handley (cnd), Royal PO, Brighton Festival Chorus [E] Chandos ▲ CHAN 8625 [DDD]

Bax, A.:Walsinghame, w. M. Hill (ten), V. Handley (cnd), Royal PO, Brighton Festival Chorus [E] Chandos ▲ CHAN 8625 [DDD]

Madalin, Carol (mez)

Martucci, G.:La canzone dei ricordi, w. A. Bonavera (cnd), English CO Hyperion ▲ CDA 66290 [DDD]

Respighi, O.:Il Tramonto, w. A. Bonavera (cnd), English CO [I] Hyperion ▲ CDA 66290 [DDD]

Maddalena, Alessandro (bass)

Rossini, G.:Armida, w. C. Deutekom (sop), P. Bottazzo (ten), O. Garaventa (ten), E. Gimenez (ten), B. Trotta (sgr), G. Antonini (bass), C. Franci (cnd), Venice Teatro La Fenice Orch, Venice Teatro La Fenice Chorus *(rec live, Venice, 1970)* Foyer 2-▲ FOY 2030 [AAD]

Smareglia, A.:Nozze istrane, w. Maria Chiara (sop—Marussa), Eleonora Iancovich (cta—Luze), Ruggero Bondino (ten—Lorenzo), Alessandro Cassis (bar—Nicola), Alessandro Maddalena (bar—Biagio), Carlo Zardo (bass—Bara Menico), M. Wolf–Ferrari (cnd), Trieste Teatro Comunale Giuseppe Verdi Orch, Trieste Teatro Comunale G. Verdi Chorus *(rec Trieste, Feb 17, 1973)* Bongiovanni ("Il Mito dell'Opera" series) 2-▲ 1133/34-2 [ADD]

Verdi, G.:Don Carlos, w. Katia Ricciarelli (sop), Fiorenza Cossotto (mez), Guido Fabbris (ten), Veriano Luchetti (ten), Piero Cappuccilli (bar), Gianfranco Casarini (bass), Nicolai Ghiaurov (bass), Aracelly Haengel (sgr), Marisa Salimbeni (sgr), Giorgio Zoranca (sgr), G. Prêtre (cnd), *(orch unknown)* Great Opera Performances 3-▲ GOP 777

Maddalena, James (bar)

Adams, J.:The Death of Klinghoffer, w. S. Friedman (mez), S. Sylvan (bar), T. Hammons (bar), K. Nagano (cnd), Lyon Opera Orch, English Opera Group Chorus Elektra/Nonesuch 2-▲ 79281-2 2-■ 79281-4

Haydn, J.:Mass 11, "Nelsonmesse", "Imperial Mass", "Coronation Mass", w. Janet Baker (sop), Pamela Dellal (mez), Jeffery Thomas (ten), M. Pearlman (cnd), Banchetto Musicale [L] Arabesque ▲ Z 6560 [DDD]

Mozart, W.A.:Missa, K.317, w. S. Baker (sop), J. Malafronte (mez), F. Kelley (ten), M. Pearlman (cnd), Banchetto Musicale Harmonia Mundi USA ▲ HMU 907021

Mozart, W.A.:Vesperae solennes, w. S. Baker (sop), J. Malafronte (mez), F. Kelley (ten), M. Pearlman (cnd), Banchetto Musicale Harmonia Mundi USA ▲ HMU 907021

Madeira, Jean (mez)

Strauss, R.:Elektra, w. I. Borkh (sop), M. Schech (sop), D. Fischer–Dieskau (bar), K. Böhm (cnd), Dresden Staatskapelle [G] *(rec 1961)* Deutsche Grammophon 2-▲ 445329-2

Verdi, G.:Requiem Mass, w. O. Rovero (sop), J. Lambert (sgr), G. Neri (bass), E. Kleiber (cnd), Vienna SO, Vienna Singverein *(rec live, Vienna 11/23/55)* Melodram 2-▲ CDM 28044 [ADD]

Wagner, R.:Das Rheingold, w. K. Flagstad (sop), S. Svanholm (ten), G. London (bar), G. Neidlinger (b–bar), K. Böhme (bass), G. Solti (cnd), Vienna PO [G] London 3-▲ 414101-2 [ADD]

Wagner, R.:Der Ring des Nibelungen, w. B. Nilsson (sop), K. Flagstad (sop), R. Crespin (sop), C. Watson (sop), C. Ludwig (mez), S. Svanholm (ten), J. King (ten), G. Stolze (ten), W. Windgassen (ten), G. London (bar), D. Fischer–Dieskau (bar), H. Hotter (b–bar), G. Neidlinger (b–bar), G. Frick (bass), G. Solti (cnd), Vienna PO [G] London 15-▲ 414100-2 [ADD]

Wagner, R.:Der Ring des Nibelungen, w. Gré Brouwenstein (sop—Freia/Sieglinde), Ilse Hollweg (sop—Waldvogel), Gerda Lammers (sop—Ortlinde), Paula Lenchner (sop—Wellgunde/Gerhilde), Hilde Scheppan (sop—Helmwige), Astrid Varnay (sop—Brünnilde/3rd Norn), Lore Wissmann (sop—Woglinde), Maria von Ilosvay (mez—Flosshilde/Schwertleite/2nd Norn), Louise Charlotte Kamps (mez—Siegrune), Jean Madeira (mez—Erda/Rossweisse/1st Norn), Georgine van Milinkovic (mez—Fricka/Grimgerde), Elisabeth Schärtel (mez—Waltraute), Paul Kuĕn (ten—Mime), Ludwig Suthaus (ten—Loge), Josef Traxel (ten—Froh), Wolfgang Windgassen (ten—Siegmund/Siegfried), Alfons Herwig (bar—Donner), Hermann Uhde (bar—Gunther), Hans Hotter (b–bar—Wotan), Gustav Neidlinger (b–bar—Alberich), Josef Griendl (bass—Fasolt/Hunding/Hagen), Arnold van Mill (bass—Fafner), H. Knappertsbusch (cnd), Bayreuth Festival Orch, Bayreuth Festival Chorus *(rec live, Bayreuth, Aug 13–17, 1956)* Golden Melodram 14-▲ GM 1.001 [ADD]

Madier, Jean–Luc (voc)

Lo Gai Saber:Troubadours and Minstrels, 1100–1300, w. J. Cohen (cnd), Camerata Mediterranea, Anne Azema (voc), François Harismendy (voc), Cheryl Ann Fulton (hp), Joel Cohen (instr), Shira Kammen (instr) Erato ▲ 2292-45647-2 [DDD]

Madowarda, Josef von (sgr)

Josef von Madowara, w. *(rec between 1922–34)* Preiser ▲ PRE 89069 [AAD]

Maero, F. (sgr)

Donizetti, G.:Requiem Mass, w. G. Tucci (sop), A. Lazzarini (mez), G. Sinimberghi (ten), I. Sardi (bass), F. Molinari–Pradelli (cnd), Milan RAI SO, Milan RAI Chorus [L] *(rec live, Milan 3/21/61)* Memories ▲ HR 4131 [ADD]

Maero, Philip (bar)

Barber, S.:A Hand of Bridge, w. P. Neway (sop), E. Alberts (mez), W. Lewis (ten), V. Golschmann (cnd), Symphony of the Air [E] *(rec ca. 1960)* Vanguard Classics ▲ OVC 4016 [ADD]

Donizetti, G.:Lucia di Lammermoor, w. Roberta Peters (sop—Lucia), Miti Truccato Pace (mez—Alisa), Jan Peerce (ten—Edgardo), Piero de Palma (ten—Lord Arturo Bucklaw), Mario Carlin (ten—Normanno), Philip Maero (bar—Lord Enrico Ashton), Giorgio Tozzi (bass—Raimondo), E. Leinsdorf (cnd), Rome Opera Orch, Rome Opera Chorus *(rec Rome Opera House, Aug 5–14, 1957)* RCA Living Stereo 2-▲ 09026-68537-2 [ADD]

Puccini, G.:Madama Butterfly, w. L. Price (sop), R. Elias (mez), G. Tucker (ten), E. Leinsdorf (cnd), RCA Italian Opera Orch [I] RCA Red Seal 2-▲ 6160-2-RC [ADD]

Puccini, G.:Madama Butterfly (sels), w. Leontyne Price (sop), Rosalind Elias (mez), Piero De Palma (ten), Richard Tucker (ten), E. Leinsdorf (cnd), RCA Italian Opera Orch, RCA Italiana Opera Chorus RCA Victor ▲ 09026-68089-2; ■ 09026-68089-4

Puccini, G.:Madama Butterfly (sels), w. L. Price (sop), R. Elias (mez), G. Tucker (ten), E. Leinsdorf (cnd), RCA Italian Opera Orch [I] RCA ■ RK 1048

Maffeo, Gianni (bar)

Puccini, G.:La Bohème, w. Ileana Cotrubas (sop—Mimi), Margherita Guglielmi (sop—Musetta), José Carreras (ten—Rodolfo), Saverio Porzano (ten—Parpignol), Regolo Romani (ten—Vendor), Claudio Giombi (bar—Benoit), Gianni Maffeo (bar—Schaunard), Angelo Romero (bar—Marcello), Alfredo Giacomotti (bass—Alcindoro), Carlo Meliciani (bass—Customs Officer), Giuseppe Morresi (bass—Sergeant), Paolo Washington (bass—Colline), G. Prêtre (cnd), La Scala Orch, La Scala Chorus *(rec Washington D.C., Sept 8, 1976)* Legato Classics 2-▲ LCD 201-2

Maffezzoni, Gilberto (ten)

Verdi, G.:Nabucco, w. Monica Pick–Hieronimi (sop), Anna Schiatti (sop), Mina Blum (sop), Angelo Casertano (ten), Paolo Gavanelli (bass), Paata Burchuladze (bass), Franco Federici (bass), A. Guadagno (cnd), Arena di Verona Orch, Arena di Verona Chorus *(rec Berlin, Spring 1996)* Koch Schwann 2-▲ SCH CD 364272

Magdamo, Priscilla (alt)

Rorem, N.:Missa Brevis, w. Rosalind Rees (sop), Lin Garber (bar), Gregg Smith (cnd), Gregg Smith Singers Vox Box ("The American Composers" series) 3-▲ CDX 3037

Maginnis, Patrice (sop)

Tailleferre, G.:Chansons populaires françaises, w. John Fairweather (vn), David Ryther (vn), Jill Cohen (va), Karen Andrie (vc), Elizabeth Bodine (ob), Andy Connell (cl), Gordon Mumma (hn), June Orzel (bn), N. Paiement (cnd) *(rec UC, Santa Cruz, May 1992)* Helicon Classics ▲ HE 1008

Magnaghi, Vittorina (mez)

Bellini, V.:I Puritani (sels), w. Gabriella Tucci (sop—Elvira), Vittorina Magnaghi (mez—Enrichetta di Francia), Luciano Pavarotti (ten—Lord Arturo Talbo), Aldo Protti (bar—Sir Riccardo Forth), Ruggero Raimondi (bass—Sir Giorgio), A. Quadri (cnd), Vincenzo Bellini Theater Orch, Catania Teatro Massimo Bellini Chorus Budget ("The Greatest Voice in Opera" series) ▲ SYP 106

Magnus, Elisabeth von (cta)

Ashley, R.:Perfect Lives [Private Parts], w. R. Ashley (nar), J. Kroesen (voc), D. Van Thiegem (voc), P. Gordon (pre–recorded orchestral beds) Lovely Music 3-▲ LCD 4917.3 [ADD] 2-■ LMC 4913/4947

Magnus, Elisabeth von (cta) (cont.)
Handel, G.F.:Judas Maccabaeus, w. M. Meier-Schmid (sop), Jörg Dürmüller (ten), Robert Wörle (ten), Franz-Josef Selig (bass), T. Fey (cnd), Schlierbach CO, Munich Motet Choir [E] Christophorus 2-▲ 77128 [DDD]
Mozart:Missa Solemnis & Salieri:Te Deum (The Coronation Mass for Leopold II in Prague, September 1791), w. Vienna Academy, Ruth Ziesak (sop), H. Wildahaber (ten), G. Hornik (bass), Hugo Distler Chorus, Vienna Hofburg Chapel Choir Novalis ▲ 150087 [DDD]
Mozart, W.A.:Ave verum corpus, w. Barbara Bonney (sop), Charlotte Margiono (sop), Sylvia McNair (sop), Christoph Pregardien (ten), Thomas Hampson (bass), N. Harnoncourt (cnd), Vienna Concentus Musicus, Arnold Schoenberg Choir Teldec ▲ 98928 2
Mozart, W.A.:Dixit Dominus et Magnificat, w. E. Mei (sop), K. Azesberger (ten), G. Cachemaille (bass), N. Harnoncourt (cnd), Vienna Concentus Musicus, Arnold Schoenberg Choir Teldec ("Das alte Werke" series) ▲ 93025
Mozart, W.A.:Grabmusik, w. Barbara Bonney (sop), Charlotte Margiono (sop), Sylvia McNair (sop), Christoph Pregardien (ten), Thomas Hampson (bass), N. Harnoncourt (cnd), Vienna Concentus Musicus, Arnold Schoenberg Choir Teldec ("Das alte Werk" series) ▲ 98928-2
Mozart, W.A.:Litaniae de venerabili, w. A. Miles (bass), N. Harnoncourt (cnd), Vienna Concentus Musicus, Arnold Schoenberg Choir Teldec ▲ 72304-2
Mozart, W.A.:Litaniae Lauretanae, K.109, w. Eva Mei (sop), Kurt Azesberger (ten), Gilles Cachemaille (bass), N. Harnoncourt (cnd), Vienna Concentus Musicus, Arnold Schoenberg Choir *(rec Casino Zögernitz, Vienna, Dec. 1992)* Teldec ("Das alte Werke" series) ▲ 96147-2 [DDD]
Mozart, W.A.:Litaniae Lauretanae, K.195, w. B. Bonney (sop), U. Heilmann (tenor), G. Cachemaille (bass), N. Harnoncourt (cnd), Vienna Concentus Musicus, Arnold Schoenberg Choir Teldec ("Das alte Werke" series) ▲ 93025
Mozart, W.A.:Missa, K.257, w. A. Miles (bass), N. Harnoncourt (cnd), Vienna Concentus Musicus, Arnold Schoenberg Choir Teldec ▲ 72304-2
Mozart, W.A.:Missa, K.317, w. J. Rodgers (sop), J. Protschka (ten), L. Polgár (bass), N. Harnoncourt (cnd), Vienna Concentus Musicus, Arnold Schoenberg Choir [L] Teldec ▲ 2292-43354-2
Mozart, W.A.:Missa solemnis, K.337, w. R. Ziesak (sop), H. Wildhaber (ten), G. Hornik (bar), H. Hüttler (cant), M. Jankowitsch (cant), P. Jelosits (cant), I. Rainer (org), M. Haselböck (cnd), Vienna Academy, Vienna Hofburg Chapel Choir [L] *(rec Apr. 1992)* Novalis ▲ 150087 [DDD]
Mozart, W.A.:Missa brevis, K.275, w. E. Mei (sop), K. Azesberger (teno, G. Cachemaille (bass), N. Harnoncourt (cnd), Vienna Concentus Musicus, Arnold Schoenberg Choir Teldec ("Das alte Werke" series) ▲ 93025
Mozart, W.A.:Regina coeli, K.127, w. Barbara Bonney (sop), Charlotte Margiono (sop), Sylvia McNair (sop), Christoph Pregardien (ten), Thomas Hampson (bass), N. Harnoncourt (cnd), Vienna Concentus Musicus, Arnold Schoenberg Choir Teldec ("Das alte Werk" series) ▲ 98928 2
Mozart, W.A.:Vesperae solennes, w. J. Rodgers (sop), J. Protschka (ten), L. Polgár (bass), N. Harnoncourt (cnd), Vienna Concentus Musicus, Arnold Schoenberg Choir [L] Teldec ▲ 2292-43354-2
Strauss (II), Joh.:Der Zigeunerbaron, w. Pamela Coburn (sop), Christiane Oelze (sop), Julia Hamari (mez), Elisabeth von Magnus (alt), Herbert Lippert (ten), Rudolf Schasching (ten), Wolfgang Holzmair (bar), Jurgen Flimm (sgr), Robert Florianschutz (sgr), Hans-Jurgen Lazar (sgr), N. Harnoncourt (cnd), Vienna SO, Arnold Schoenberg Choir *(rec Vienna, 1994)* Teldec 2-▲ 94555-2
Vivaldi, A.:L'Olimpiade, w. L. Meeuwsen (sop), M. van der Sluis (sop), G. Lesne (alt), A. Christofelis (alt), W. Oberholtzer (bar), A. Walker Schultze (bass), R. Clemencic (cnd), Clemencic Consort, La Cappella Vocal Ensemble [I] *(rec live, Paris, 2/8–10/90)* Nuova Era ("Ancient Music" series) 2-▲ 6932/33 [DDD]

Magnus, Elisabeth von (cta/nar)
Mendelssohn, F.:A Midsummer Night's Dream (comp), w. P. Coburn (sop), C. Bantzer (nar), N. Harnoncourt (cnd), CO of Europe Teldec ▲ 74882-2

Magnúsdóttir, Sigridur Ella (mez)
Leifs, J.:Music of, w. Ólafur Vignir Albertsson (pno), Sólveig Anna Jónsdóttir (pno), Hjálmar Ragnarsson (pno), Edda Erlendsdóttir (pno), Marteinn Hunger Fridriksson (org), Hildigunnur Halldórsdóttir (vn), Gréta Gudnadóttir (vn), Gudmundur Kristmundsson (va), Sigurdur Halldórsson (vc), Richard Korn (db), Iceland SO, Icelandic Opera Chorus, Langholts Church Graduale Choir, Hamrahlid Choir—Icelandic Cant, Op. 13/4; Valse Lento, Op. 2/1; Icelandic Dance, Op. 11/2 [Tempo Giusto]; Requiem; Lullaby [After the Riots]; Fairy-Tale in the Wood [from Baldr, Op. 34]; Funeral March; Separation [from Elegy, Op. 53]; Galdra Loftur Ov, Op. 10; Funeral March, Op. 6; Reverie; Reunion [from Elegy, Op. 53]; Fine I, Op. 55; Andante [The Last Supper]; Preludia Organo, Op. 16/3 [In the Church]; The Tear of Stone [from Elegy, Op. 53] Music From Iceland ▲ ITM 605 [DDD]
Ragnarsson, H.:Music of, w. H. Halldórsdóttir (vn), G. Gudnadóttir (vn), G. Kristmundsson (va), S. Halldórsson (vc), R. Korn (db), Ó. V. Albertsson (pno), S. A. Jónsdóttir (pno), H. Ragnarsson (pno), E. Erlendsdóttir (pno), M. H. Fridriksson (org), Sakari, Wilkinson (cnd), Iceland SO, G. Cortes (cnd), J. Stefánsson (cnd), T. Ingólfsdóttir (cnd), Hamrahlid Choir, Icelandic Opera Chorus, Langholts Church Graduale Choir—Meine kleine Freundin [In the Ballroom]; Lovers Duet; After the concert; Meine kleine Freundin [Annie listens to the Radio]; Lif's Theme [On the Beach]; Lif's Theme II [Night Prayer]; Composing Ov [Vars I, II & III] Music From Iceland ▲ ITM 605 [DDD]

Magnusson, Lars (ten)
Scriabin, A.:Sym 1, w. I. Blom (cta), L. Segerstam (cnd), Stockholm PO, Stockholm Phil Chorus [R] BIS ▲ CD 534 [DDD]
Trojahn, M.:Enrico, w. T. Schmidt (sop), R. Salter (bar), D. R. Davies (cnd), Stuttgart RSO CPO 2-▲ CPO 999160 [DDD]

Maguire, Linda (mez)
Berlioz, H.:Les Nuits d'été, w. M. Bernardi (cnd), CBC Vancouver SO *(rec The Orpheum, Vancouver, B.C., Apr. 2, 5 & 6, 1993)* CBC ("SM 5000" series) ▲ SMCD 5137 [DDD]
Coulthard, J.:Songs, w. M. Bernardi (cnd), CBC Vancouver SO—The White Rose; Innocence; Cradle Song; Frolic *(rec The Orpheum, Vancouver, B.C., Apr. 2, 5 & 6, 1993)* CBC ("SM 5000" series) ▲ SMCD 5137 [DDD]
Handel, G.F.:Floridante (sels), w. Nancy Argenta (sop—Rossane), Ingrid Attrot (sop—Timante), Linda Maguire (mez—Elmira), Catherine Robbin (mez—Floridante), Mel Braun (bar—Coralbo/Orontes), A. Curtis (cnd), Tafelmusik [I] CBC ("SM 5000" series) ▲ SMCD 5110 [DDD]
Respighi, O.:Il Tramonto, w. M. Bernardi (cnd), CBC Vancouver SO *(rec The Orpheum, Vancouver, B.C., Apr. 2, 5 & 6, 1993)* CBC ("SM 5000" series) ▲ SMCD 5137 [DDD]
Wagner, R.:Wesendonck Songs, w. M. Bernardi (cnd), CBC Vancouver SO *(rec The Orpheum, Vancouver, B.C., Apr. 2, 5 & 6, 1993)* CBC ("SM 5000" series) ▲ SMCD 5137 [DDD]

Mahé, Martine (mez)
de Leeuw, T.:Antigone, w. R. de Leeuw (cnd), Netherlands Radio CO, Netherlands Radio Male Chamber Choir NM Classics ▲ NM 92036
Duparc, H.:Songs, w. V. Le Texier (bar), N. Lee (pno) Pierre Verany ▲ PVY 793061 [DDD]
Ravel, M.:L'Enfant et les sortilèges, w. M. Lagrange (sop), E. Vidal (sop), M. Damonte (mez), A. Chedel (cta), L. Pezzino (ten), M. Barrard (bar), V. le Texier (b-bar), A. Lombard (cnd), Bordeaux-Aquitaine National Orch, Bordeaux Grand Théâtre Municipal Chorus [F] Valois ▲ V 4670

Maher, Robert (bar)
Penn, W.:A Cornfield in July & the River, w. Steven Eldridge (pno) *(rec Carriage House, CT)* Capstone ▲ CPS 8618

Maheu, R. (sop)
Macmillan, E.:Bergerettes du Bas-Canada, w. J.-P. Jeannotte (ten) *(rec July 8, 1961)* Analekta ▲ AN 2 7804

Maias, S. (bass)
Donizetti, G.:La fille du régiment, w. J. Sutherland (sop), M. Sinclair (cta), L. Pavarotti (ten), R. Bonynge (cnd), Royal Opera House Orch [F] London 2-▲ 414520-2 [ADD]
Donizetti, G.:La fille du régiment, w. J. Sutherland (sop), R. Resnik (mez), A. Kraus (ten), R. Bonynge (cnd), Chicago Lyric Opera Orch, Chicago Lyric Opera Chorus [F] *(rec Nov. 20, 1973)* Myto 2-▲ MCD 93276

Maier, Theophil (ten)
Bach, J.S.:Cant 80, w. Antonia Fahberg (sop), Bargarete Bence (cta), Ulrich Schaible (bass), H. Rilling (cnd), Württemberg CO, Stuttgart Memorial Church Figuralchor *(rec 1964)* Vox Box 3-▲ CD3X 3039

Maikl, Georg (ten)
Beethoven, L. van:Sym 9, "Choral Sym", w. Luise Helletsgruber (sop), Rosette Anday (cta), Richard Mayr (bass), F. von Weingartner (cnd), Vienna PO, Vienna State Opera Chorus *(rec Feb. 2–5, 1935)* Preiser ▲ PRE 90193 [ADD]

Maikl, Liselotte (sop)
Humperdinck, E.:Hänsel und Gretel, w. Liselotte Maikl (sop—Sandman/Dew Fairy), Anneliese Rothenberger (sop—Gretel), Irmgard Seefried (sop—Hänsel), Grace Hoffman (mez—Gertrude), Elisabeth Höngen (cta—Witch), Walter Berry (bass—Peter), A. Cluytens (cnd), Vienna PO, Vienna Boys' Choir EMI Classics 2-▲ CDMB 65661

Mainardi, Michele (bar)
Massenet, J.:Manon (sels), w. M. Favero (sop), G. Di Stefano (ten), M. Borriello (bar), A. Guarnieri (cnd), La Scala Orch, La Scala Chorus *(rec live, Milan, 3/15/47)* Myto ▲ 1 MCD 90526 [ADD]

Maionica, Silvio (bass)
Catalani, A.:La Wally, w. R. Tebaldi (sop), G. Prandelli (ten), G. Santini (cnd), Rome RAI SO, Rome RAI Chorus *(rec 1960)* Enterprise (Palladio) 2-▲ ENTPD 4165 [ADD]
Gluck, C.W.:Alceste, w. M. Callas (sop), R. Gavarini (ten), R. Panerai (bar), C. M. Giulini (cnd), La Scala Orch, La Scala Chorus—plus "Callas Sings Gluck & Rossini" [French version] *(rec live, La Scala, 4/4/54)* Melodram 2-▲ MEL 26026
Verdi, G.:Aida, w. Antonietta Stella (sop—Aida), Mirella Parutto (sop—Priestess), Giulietta Simionato (mez—Amneris), Giuseppe DiStefano (ten—Radames), Giuseppe Zampiere (ten—Messenger), Giangiacomo Guelfi (bar—Amonasro), Silvio Maionica (bass—King of Egypt), Nicola Zaccaria (bass-Ramfis), A. Votto (cnd), La Scala Orch, La Scala Chorus *(rec Milan, Dec 7, 1956)* Legato Classics 2-▲ LCD 204-2 [ADD]
Wagner, R.:Die Meistersinger von Nürnberg, w. Bruna Rizzoli (sop), Fernanda Cadoni (mez), Luigi Infantino (ten), Vito Tatone (ten), Renato Capecchi (bar), Giuseppe Taddei (bar), Boris Christoff (bass), Giovanni Ciavola (bass), James Loomis (bass), Vito Susca (bass), Raimondo Botteghelli (sgr), Walter Brunelli (sgr), Carlo Franzini (sgr), Ezio de Giorgi (sgr), Renzo Gonzales (sgr), L. von Matačić (cnd), Turin RAI Radio-TV SO, Turin RAI Chorus Stradivarius 4-▲ STV 12310

Maison, René (ten)
Mussorgsky, M.:Boris Godunov, w. Kerstin Thorborg (mez), Alexander Kipnis (bass), G. Szell (cnd), New York Metropolitan Opera Orch, New York Metropolitan Opera Chorus *(rec live, Feb 13, 1943)* The Fourties 2-▲ ENT 1505

Maiste (bar)
Tubin, E.:The Parson of Reigi, w. M. Eensalu (sop), Kempe (ten), P. Mägi (cnd), Estonia Opera Co Orch, Estonia Opera Company Chorus Ondine 2-▲ ODE 783-2D [DDD]

Majkut, Erich (ten)
Akademie Chamber Choir & Vienna SO, w. [cnd:Ferdinand Grossmann], Akademie Chamber Choir, Vienna SO, Elisabeth Roon (sop), Laurence Dutoit (sop), Daagmar Herrmann-Braun (cta), W. Berry (bass) Vox 90s ■ V9-9903
Bach, J.S.:Christmas Oratorio, w. E. Roon (sop), D.H. Braun (mez), W. Berry (bass), L. Dutoit (echo), B. Seidlhofer (hpd), J. Nebois (org), F. Grossmann (cnd), Vienna SO, Akademie Chamber Choir Vox Box 2-▲ CDX 5096 [ADD]
Beethoven, L. van:Missa Solemnis, w. Ilona Steingruber (sop), Else Schuerhoff (alt), Otto Wiener (bass), O. Klemperer (cnd), Vienna SO, Akademie Chamber Choir *(rec Vienna, 1950)* Vox Legends 2-▲ CDX2 5527
Bruckner, A.:Te Deum, w. Hilde Güden (sop), Hilde Zadeck (cta), Gottlob Frick (bass), B. Walter (cnd), Vienna PO, Vienna State Opera Chorus *(rec live, 1955)* Enterprise ("Palladio" series) ▲ ENTPD 4209 [ADD]
Cornelius, P.:Der Barbier von Bagdad, w. S. Jurinac (sop), H. Rössl-Majdan (mez), R. Schock (ten), A. Poell (bass-bar), G. Frick (bass), H. Hollreiser (cnd), Austrian RSO, Austrian Radio Chorus *(rec live Vienna 1952)* Melodram 2-▲ MEL 27050 (m) [AAD]
Cornelius, P.:Der Barbier von Bagdad, w. S. Jurinac (sop), H. Rössl-Majdan (mez), R. Schock (ten), A. Poell (bass-bar), G. Frick (bass), H. Hollreiser (cnd), Austrian RSO, Austrian Radio Chorus [G] *(rec live Vienna, 1952)* Verona 2-▲ 27050/51 (m) [AA
Einem, G. von:Der Prozess, w. Lisa Della Casa (sop—Frl. Bürstner/Die Frau des Gerichtsdieners/Leni), Peter Klein (ten—Der Direktorstellvertreter/Der Student), Max Lorenz (ten—Josef K.), Erich Majkut (ten—Ein Bursche), László Szemere (ten—Titorelli), Alois Pernerstorfer (b-bar—Willem/Der Gerichtsdiener), Alfred Poell (b-bar—Der Advokat), Walter Berry (bass—Franz/Kanzleidirektor), Oskar Czerwenka (bass—Der Untersuchungsrichter/Der Prügler), Ludwig Hofmann (bass—Der Aufseher/Ein Passant/Der Geistliche/Der Fabrikant), Polly Batic (sgr—Frau Grubach), Endreh Koreh (sgr—Albert K.), Luise Leitner (sgr—Ein buckliges Mädchen), K. Böhm (cnd), Vienna PO, Vienna State Opera Chorus *(rec Aug 17, 1953)* Orfeo d'or ("Festspiel Dokumente" series) 2-▲ 392952 (m)
Strauss, R.:Der Rosenkavalier, w. Jarmila Barton (sop—Marianne), Lisa Della Casa (sop—Sophie), Sena Jurinac (sop—Octavian), Ilva Ligabue (sop—Orphan), Elisabeth Schwarzkopf (sop—Marschallin), Else Schürhoff (mez—Annina), Luisa Villa (mez—Milliner), Hugues Cuénod (ten—Marschallin's majordomo), Erich Majkut (ten—Valzacchi), Giuseppe Nessi (ten—Animal seller), Luciano Della Pergola (ten—Lackey/Faninal's majordomo), Antonio Pirino (ten—An Italian Singer), Gino Del Signore (ten—Lackey/Waiter), Erich Kunz (bar—Herr von Faninal), Paolo Pedani (bar—Lackey), Attilo Barbesi (bass—Lackey/Waiter), Enrico Campi (bass—Waiter), Otto Edelmann (bass—Baron Ochs), Bruno Fichtinger (bass—Notary), Franco Taino (bass—Waiter), Maria Amadini (sgr—Orphan), Pina Carrillo (sgr—Orphan), Joszi Trojan Regar (sgr—Innkeeper), H. von Karajan (cnd), La Scala Orch, La Scala Chorus *(rec La Scala Theater, Milan, Jan. 26, 1952)* Legato Classics 3-▲ LCD 197-3
Verdi, G.:Don Carlos, w. S. Jurinac (sop—Elisabetta), L. Rysanek (sop—Celestial Voice), F. Cossotto (mez—Princess Eboli), L. Dutoit (boy sop—Tebaldo), P. Domingo (ten—Don Carlo), E. Majkut (ten—Count of Lerma), M. Sereni (bar—Rodrigo), C. Siepi (bass—Philip II), I. Vinco (bass—Grand Inquisitor), T. Franc (bass—Friar), S. Varviso (cnd), Vienna State Opera Orch, Vienna State Opera Chorus Standing Room Only 2-▲ SRO 850 [ADD]

Majoram, Keith (bass)
Scarlatti, A.:Domine refugium factus, w. Marylin Sansom (vc), Charles Spinks (org), R. Norrington (cnd), Schütz Choir London *(rec 1973)* London 2-▲ 443868-2 [ADD]
Scarlatti, A.:O magnum mysterium, w. Marylin Sansom (vc), Charles Spinks (org), Roger Norrington (cnd), Schütz Choir London *(rec 1973)* London 2-▲ 443868-2 [ADD]
Scarlatti, D.:Stabat mater, w. Marylin Sansom (vc), Charles Spinks (org), R. Norrington (cnd), Schütz Choir London *(rec 1973)* London 2-▲ 443868-2 [ADD]

Makarova, Natalia (nar)
Prokofiev, S.:Music for Children, w. C. Rosenberger (pno)—includes the Russian fairy tale Prince Ivan & the Frog Princess [narr in E] Delos ▲ DE 6003 [DDD] ■ CS 6003 (D)
Tchaikovsky, P.:The Snow Maiden, w. C. Rosenberger (pno) Delos ▲ DE 6004 [DDD] ■ CS 6004 (D)

Maksimenko, E. (sgr)
Kabalevsky, D.:Colas Breugnon (ov), w. N. Isakova (sop), V. Kayevchenko (sop), L. Boldin (bar), N. Gutorovich (bar), G. Dudarev (bass), G. Zhemchuzhin (cnd), Dantchenko Moscow Stanislavsky Music Theater Orch, Dantchenko Moscow Stanislavsky Music Theater Chorus Olympia 2-▲ OLY 291 [ADD]

Maksimova, Emilia (sop)
Schubert, Franz:Mass 2, w. H. Kamenov (ten), I. Dobrev (bass), V. Kazandjiev (cnd), Sofia Soloists CO, Rodina Chorus [L] Musique d'Abord ▲ HMA 190111 [AAD]

Malacarne, Rodolfo (ten)
Cimarosa, D.:I Finti nobili (sels), w. C. Cadelo (sop), M.G. Ferracini (sop), R. Cassinelli (ten), G. Sarti (bar), B. Marinotti (cnd), RTSI Orch—Li sposi per accidente (Act 3) *(rec 1970)* Foyer ▲ FOY 2057 [AAD]
Monteverdi, C.:Madrigals, w. Basia Retchitzka (sop), Eric Tappy (ten), Laerte Malaguti (bar), James Loomis (bass), E. Loehrer (cnd), Lugano Chamber Society Orch, Lugano Chamber Society Chorus—8 Madrigali Guerrieri e Amorosi Accord ▲ ACD 220872
Rinaldo di Capua:La Zingara, w. Annalisa Monkewitz (sop—Nisa), Rodolfo Malacarne (ten—Tagliaborse), Laerte Malaguti (bass—Calcante), Josef Ulsamer (vl), Kurt-Heinz Stolze (hpd), G. Kehr (cnd), Mainz CO Dynamic ▲ CD 141 [ADD]

▲ = CD ♦ = Enhanced CD Δ = MD ■ = Cassette Tape □ = DCC

Malacchi, Maria Luisa (sop)
Giordano, U.:Madame Sans-Gêne, w. Magda László (sop—Caterina), Carlo Tagliabue (bar—Napoleone), Renato Berti (sgr—Despréaux), Irene Callaway (sgr—Toniotta/Carolina), Danilo Cestari (sgr—Neipperg/Vinaigre), Maria Luisa Malacchi (sgr—Giulia/Principessa Elisa), Carlo Perucci (sgr—Fouché), Danilo Vega (sgr—Lefebvre), Enzo Viaro (sgr—De Brigode/Gelsomino), A. Basile (cnd), Milan RAI SO, Milan RAI Chorus *(rec Milan, Aug 10, 1957)* Bongiovanni 2-▲ GB 1129/30

Malachovsky, Ondrej (bass)
Suchon, E.:The Whirlpool, w. G. Benačková (sop), P. Dvorsky (ten), O. Lenárd (cnd), Bratislava RSO Campion 2-▲ 1311/12 [DDD]

Malafronte, Judith (mez)
Bach, J.S.:Cant 198, w. J. Nelson (sop), J. Thomas (ten), W. Sharp (bar), J. Thomas (cnd), American Bach Soloists [G] Koch International Classics ▲ KIC 7163-2 [DDD]
Bach, J.S.:Psalms (4), w. Benita Valente (sop), J. Thomas (cnd), American Bach Soloists—Psalm 51:Tilge, Höchter, meine Sünden Koch International Classics ▲ KIC 7237 [DDD]
Mozart, W.A.:Missa, K.317, w. S. Baker (sop), F. Kelley (ten), J. Maddalena (bar), M. Pearlman (cnd), Banchetto Musicale Harmonia Mundi USA ▲ HMU 907021
Mozart, W.A.:Vesperae solennes, w. S. Baker (sop), F. Kelley (ten), J. Maddalena (bar), M. Pearlman (cnd), Banchetto Musicale Harmonia Mundi USA ▲ HMU 907021

Malagnini, Mario (sgr)
Leoncavallo, R.:La Bohème, w. L. Mazzaria (sop), M. Senn (mez), B. Praticò (sgr), J. Summers (bar), J. Latham-König (cnd), Venice Teatro La Fenice Orch, Venice Teatro La Fenice Chorus *(rec live, 1990)* Nuova Era 3-▲ 6917/19 [DDD]
Verdi, G.:I masnadieri, w. M. Rowland (sgr), T. Migliorini (sgr), R. Bruson (bar), M. Lanskoy (bar), C. Colombara (bass), W. Gönnenwein (cnd), Ludwigsburg Festival Orch, South German Madrigal Choir Bayer 2-▲ BR 500 001/2 [DDD]

Malagu, Stefania (mez)
Mascagni, P.:Cavalleria rusticana, w. E. Suliotis (sop), A. Di Stasio (mez), M. Del Monaco (ten), T. Gobbi (bar), S. Varviso (cnd), Rome Opera Orch, Rome Opera Chorus [I] IMP Collectors Series ▲ IMPX 9018 [AAD]
Verdi, G.:La traviata, w. P. Lorengar (sop), G. Aragall (ten), D. Fischer-Dieskau (bar), L. Maazel (cnd), Berlin German Opera Orch, Berlin German Opera Chorus London ("Double Decker" series) 2-▲ 443000-2

Malaguti, Laerte (bass)
Monteverdi, C.:Madrigals, w. Basia Retchitzka (sop), Eric Tappy (ten), Rodolfo Malacarne (ten), James Loomis (bass), E. Loehrer (cnd), Lugano Chamber Society Orch, Lugano Chamber Society Chorus—8 Madrigali Guerrieri e Amorosi Accord ▲ ACD 220872
Palestrina, G.:Sacred Music, w. Luciana Ticinelli-Fattori (sop), Maria Minetto (mez), James Loomis (bass), E. Loehrer (cnd), Lugano Chamber Society Instrumental Ensemble, Lugano Chamber Society Chorus—Vexilla Regis Prodeunt; Adoramus Te; Laudario Di Cortona Accord ▲ ACD 201562 [AAD]
Rinaldo di Capua:La Zingara, w. Annalisa Monkewitz (sop—Nisa), Rodolfo Malacarne (ten—Tagliaborse), Laerte Malaguti (bass—Calcante), Josef Ulsamer (vl), Kurt-Heinz Stolze (hpd), G. Kehr (cnd), Mainz CO Dynamic ▲ CD 141 [ADD]

Malakova, Petra (mez)
Vivaldi, A.:Il Farnace, w. M. Dupuy (mez), K. Angeloni (mez), D. Dessy (mez), L. Rizzi (cta), R. Garazioti (sgr), M. de Bernart (cnd), San Remo SO [I] *(rec live 12/1/82)* Arkadia-Akademia 2-▲ 110 [ADD]

Malamood, Herman (ten)
Puccini, G.:Madama Butterfly (sels), w. Elisabeth Carron (sop—Cio-Cio-San), Deborah Kieffer (mez—Suzuki), Herman Malamood (ten—Pinkerton), David Clatworthy (bar—Sharpless), G. Morelli (cnd), *(orch unknown)*—Ancora un passo or via; Ieri son salita...Io seguo il mio destino; Adesso voi siete per me...Vogliatemi bene; Ti sero palpitante...Ah! Quanti occhi fisi, attenti!; Egli, col cuore grosso...Un bel di, vedremo; Ebbene, che fareste Madama Butterfly...Due cose potrei far; Sai cos'ebbe cuore di pensare...Che tua madre; Troppa luce e di fuor; Con onor muore...Tu? Tu? Piccolo Iddio *(rec New York, Oct 23, 1973)* Legato Classics ▲ LCD 212-1 [ADD]

Malaniuk, Ira (cta)
Mozart, W.A.:Requiem, w. Lisa della Casa (sop), Anton Dermota (ten), Cesare Siepi (b-bar), B. Walter (cnd), Vienna PO, Vienna State Opera Chorus *(rec Salzburg, July 26, 1956)* Orfeo d'or ("Festspiel Dikumente" series) ▲ C 430961 (m) [ADD]
Schmidt, F.:Das Buch mit sieben Siegeln, w. Hilde Gueden (sop), Anton Dermota (ten), Fritz Wunderlich (ten), Walter Berry (bass), D. Mitropoulos (cnd), Vienna PO, Vienna Singverein Sony Classical ("Festspiel Dokumente:Salzburger Festspiele" series) 2-▲ SM2K 68442
Schmidt, F.:Das Buch mit sieben Siegeln, w. H. Gueden (sop), A. Dermota (ten), F. Wunderlich (ten), W. Berry (bass), D. Mitropoulos (cnd), Vienna PO, Vienna Singverein *(rec live, Salzburg Festival 1959)* Melodram 2-▲ MEL 27078
Strauss, R.:Die ägyptische Helena, w. Annelies Kupper (sop—Aithra), Leonie Rysanek (sop—Helena), Ira Malaniuk (cta—Omniscient Seashell), Bernd Aldenhoff (ten—Menelas), Richard Holm (ten—Da-ud), Hermann Uhde (bar—Altair), J. Keilberth (cnd), Bavarian State Opera Orch, Bavarian State Opera Chorus *(rec Munich Opera Festival, Prince Regent Theater, Aug 10, 1956)* Orfeo d'or 2-▲ 424962
Strauss, R.:Arabella, w. L. Della Casa (sop), H. Gueden (sop), A. Dermota (ten), W. Kmentt (ten), G. London (bar), O. Edelmann (bass), G. Solti (cnd), Vienna PO [G] London ("Grand Opera" series) 2-▲ 430387-2 [ADD]
Wagner, R.:Götterdämmerung, w. Birgit Nilsson (sop—Brünnhilde), Leonie Rysanek (sop—Gutrune), Gerda Sommerschuh (sop—Woglinde), Elisabeth Lindermeier (sop—Wellgunde), Ruth Michaelis (sop—Flohilde), Marianne Schech (sop—Dritte Norne), Ira Malaniuk (mez—Waltraute), Irmgarth Barth (mez—Erste Norne), Hertha Töpper (mez—Zweite Norne), Bernd Aldenhoff (ten—Siegfried), Hermann Uhde (bar—Gunther), Gottlob Frick (bass—Hagen), H. Knappertsbusch (cnd), Bavarian State Opera Orch, Bavarian State Opera Chorus *(rec live, Prinzregententheater, Sept. 1, 1955)* Orfeo 4-▲ 356944 (m)
Wagner, R.:Die Meistersinger von Nürnberg, w. E. Schwarzkopf (sop), H. Hopf (ten), G. Unger (ten), E. Kunz (bar), O. Edelmann (b-bar), F. Dalberg (bass), H. von Karajan (cnd), Bayreuth Festival Orch, Bayreuth Festival Chorus [G] *(rec 1951)* EMI Classics ("Great Recordings of the Century" series) 4-▲ CDHD 63500 (m) [ADD]
Wagner, R.:Die Meistersinger von Nürnberg, w. L. Della Casa (sop), H. Hopf (ten), O. Edelmann (b-bar), K. Böhme (bass), H. Knappertsbusch (cnd), Bayreuth Festival Orch, Bayreuth Festival Chorus [G] *(rec live, 1952)* Arkadia 4-▲ 440 (m) [AAD]
Wagner, R.:Das Rheingold, w. E. Schwarzkopf (sop), W. Windgassen (ten), S. Björling (bar), Pflanzl (sgr), H. von Karajan (cnd), Bayreuth Festival Orch, Bayreuth Festival Chorus [G] *(rec live, 1951)* Arkadia 2-▲ 216 (m) [ADD]
Wagner, R.:Das Rheingold, w. P. Brivkalne (sop), R. Siewert (cta), Fritz (sgr), Pflanzl (ten), S. Björling (bar), W. Faulhaber (bass), L. Weber (bass), F. Dalberg (bass), H. von Karajan (cnd), Bayreuth Festival Orch, Bayreuth Festival Chorus [G] *(rec live 8/1/51)* Melodram 2-▲ MEL 26107 (m) [AAD]

Malardenti (sgr)
Nivers, G.G.:Motets, w. Fanjat (sop), J. Nicolas (sop), Boraly (sgr), Maréchal (sgr), Houbart (org)—Motet a la Sainte Vierge pour le temps de Paques; Motet pour L'Élévation; Motet pour le Saint Sacrament; Motet du temps de carême pour le Saint Sacrement; Motet du temps de Noël pour le Saint Sacrement; Motet final du tout office pour le Roy [L] Pierre Verany ▲ PV.791101 [DDD]

Malas, Spiro (bass)
Donizetti, G.:L'elisir d'amore, w. J. Sutherland (sop); L. Pavarotti (ten), D. Cossa (bar), R. Bonynge (cnd), English CO [I] London 2-▲ 414461-2 [ADD]
Glanville-Hicks, P.:Nausicaa, w. Teresa Stratas (sop—Nausicaa), Sophia Steffan (cta—Queen Arete), Michalis Heliotis (ten—Antinous/Priest), George Moutsios (ten—Eurymachus), Edward Ruhl (ten—Phemius), George Tsantikos (ten—Clytoneus), Vassilis Koundouris (bar—Messenger), John Modenos (bar—Aethon), Spiro Malas (bass—King Alcinous), C. Surinach (cnd), Athens SO, Athens Sym Chorus *(rec Athens Festival, 1961)* CRI ▲ CD 695 [ADD]
Glanville-Hicks, P.:Nausicaa (sels), w. Teresa Stratas (sop), Michalis Helii (sgr), Michalis Heliots (sgr), George Moutsio (sgr), Edward Ruhl (sgr), Sophia Steffan (sop), George Tsantikos (sgr), C. Surinach (cnd), Athens SO, Athens Sym Chorus CRI ▲ CD 695 [ADD]

Malas, Spiro (bass) (cont.)
Handel, G.F.:Giulio Cesare in Egitto, w. Beverly Sills (sop), Maureen Forrester (cta), Fritz Wolff (ten), Norman Treigle (bass), J. Redel (cnd), New York City Opera Orch, New York City Opera Chorus RCA Gold Seal 2-▲ 6182-2-RG [ADD]
Rossini, G.:Semiramide, w. J. Sutherland (sop), M. Horne (mez), J. Serge (ten), J. Rouleau (bass), R. Bonynge (cnd), London SO, Ambrosian Singers [I] *(rec 1966)* London 3-▲ 425481-2 [ADD]

Malaspina, Giampiero (bar)
Leoncavallo, R.:Edipo re, w. L. Infantino (ten), G. Fioravanti (bar), R. Parodi (cnd), Naples Teatro San Carlo Orch, Naples Teatro San Carlo Chorus *(rec live, Naples, 1970)* Italian Opera Rarities ▲ IOR 7723 [ADD]
Mussorgsky, M.:Khovanshchina, w. Jolanda Mancini (sop—Emma), Irene Companez (mez), Amedeo Berdini (ten—Prince Andrei Khovanski), Mirto Picchi (ten—Prince Vasili Golitsin), Herbert Handt (ten—Scribe), Andrea Mineo (bar—Kuzka), Giampiero Malaspina (bar—Shaklovity), Boris Christoff (bass—Dosifei), Mario Petri (bass—Prince Ivan Khovanski), Dimitri Lopatto (Varsonofiev/First Strelyets), Giorgio Conello (Second Strelyets), A. Rodzinski (cnd), *(orch unknown)* [I] *(rec Rome, 1958)* VAI Audio 2-▲ VAIA 1052-2
Zandonai, R.:Francesca da Rimini, w. Lydia Marimpietri (sop—Biancofiore), Magda Olivero (sop—Francesca), Pinuccia Perotti (sop—Samaritana), Edda Vincenzi (sop—Garsenda), Gabriella Carturan (mez—Smaragdi), Biancamaria Casoni (mez—Altichiara), Anna Maria Rota (cta—Donella), Athos Cesarini (ten—Archer), Angelo Mercuriali (ten—Ser Toldo Berardengo), Mario del Monaco (ten—Paolo), Piero de Palma (ten—Malatestino), Rinaldo Pelizzoni (ten—Prisoner), Gianpiero Malaspina (bar—Gianciotto), Dino Mantovani (bar—Jester), Enrico Campi (bass—Ostasio), Giuseppe Morresi (bass—Tower warden), G. Gavazzeni (cnd), La Scala Orch, La Scala Chorus *(rec La Scala Theatre, Milan, June 4, 1959)* Legato Classics 2-▲ LCD 186-2

Malaspina, Massimiliano (bass)
Verdi, G.:Un ballo in maschera, w. Ghena Dimitrova (sop—Amelia), Isabella Stramaglia (sop—Oscar), Mirna Pecile (cta—Ulrica), Mario Carlin (ten—Un giudice), José Carreras (ten—Riccardo), Piero Cappuccilli (bar—Renato), Massimiliano Malaspina (bass—Samuel), Americo de Santis (bass—Silvano), Francesco Signor (bass—Tom), Ivan Del Manto (sgr—Un servo), G. Patanè (cnd), Parma Teatro Regio Orch *(rec Teatro Regio, Dec. 26, 1972)* Golden Age of Opera 2-▲ GAO 183/84

Malaspina, Michele (sgr)
Mussorgsky, M.:Khovanshchina, w. Irene Companez (cta), Herbert Handt (ten), Mirto Picchi (ten), Boris Christoff (bass), Armedeo Berdini (sgr), Giorgio Canello (sgr), Dmitri Lopatto (sgr), Jolanda Mancini (sgr), Mario Petri (sgr), A. Rodzinski (cnd), Rome RAI Radio-TV SO, Rome RAI Chorus Stradivarius 2-▲ STV DTM 12320 [ADD]

Malaspina, Rita Orlandi (sop)
Verdi, G.:Attila, w. Rita Orlandi Malaspina (sop—Odabella), Veriano Luchetti (ten—Foresto), Piero de Palma (ten—Uldino), Piero Cappuccilli (bar—Ezio), Nicolai Ghiaurov (bass—Attila), Luigi Roni (bass—Leone), G. Patanè (cnd), La Scala Orch, La Scala Chorus *(rec Milan, May 15, 1972)* Golden Age of Opera 2-▲ GAO 187/88 [ADD]
Verdi, G.:Attila, w. Rita Orlandi Malaspina (sop—Odabella), Veriano Luchetti (ten—Foresto), Piero De Palma (ten—Uldino), Piero Cappuccilli (bar—Ezio), Nicolai Ghiaurov (bass—Attila), Luigi Roni (bass—Leone), G. Patanè (cnd), La Scala Orch, La Scala Chorus *(rec Milan, May 12, 1975)* Myto 2-▲ MCD 961140
Verdi, G.:Un ballo in maschera, w. R. Orlandi Malaspina (sop—Ameilia), D. Mazzuccato (sop—Oscar), A. Lazzarini (mez—Ulrica), L. Pavarotti (ten—Riccardo), M. Zanasi (bar—Renato), A. Zerbini (bass—Samuel), G. Casarini (bass—Tom), G. Zecchillo (bass—Sil) Golden Age of Opera 2-▲ GAO 164/65 [ADD]

Malbin, Elaine (sop)
Busoni, F.:Arlecchino or Die Fenster, w. M. Dickie (ten), G. Evans (bar), I. Wallace (bar), F. Ollendorf (bass), Glyndeborne Festival Chorus, J. Pritchard (cnd), Glyndebourne Festival Orch EMI Classics ▲ CDMB 65284

Maletto, Giuseppe (ten)
Cavalieri, E. de:Rappresentatione di Anima et di Corpo, w. G. Bertagnolli (sop), C. Cavina (alt), B. Rossetti (sgr), R. Mattei (bar), A. Abete (sgr), M. Longhini (cnd), Verona Istitutioni Harmoniche Stradivarius ▲ STR 33339 [DDD]
Frescobaldi, G.:Arie musicali per cantarsi, w. G. Banditelli (mez), R. Bertini (sop), C. Cavina (alt), S. Naglia (ten), S. Foresti (bass), R. Alessandrini (cnd), Concerto Italiano Opus 111 2-▲ OPS 30-105/106

Malewicz-Madej, Anna (cta)
Moniuszko, S.:Mass in E♭, w. H. Slonicka (sop), W. Pilewski (bass), E. Kajdasz (cnd), Warsaw CO, Polish Radio Chorus Olympia ▲ OLY 395 [ADD]
Moniuszko, S.:Sacred Music, w. H. Slonicka (sop), W. Pilewski (bass), E. Kajdasz (cnd), Warsaw CO, Polish Radio Chorus—Ne memineris; Vide humilitatem meam; Litanie Ostrobramskie, No. 1 Olympia ▲ OLY 395 [ADD]
Szymanowski, K.:Demeter, w. K. Stryja (cnd), Polish State PO, Polish State Phil Chorus Marco Polo ▲ 8.223293 [DDD]
Szymanowski, K.:King Roger, w. B. Zagòrzanka (sop), H. Grychnik (ten), W. Ochman (ten), A. Hiolski (bar), L. A. Mròz (bass), K. Stryja (cnd), Polish State PO Katowice, Cracow Phil Boys' Chorus, Polish State Phil Chorus *(rec Apr. 7-9, 1990)* Marco Polo ("Opera Classics" series) 2-▲ 8.223339/40 [DDD]

Malfitano, Catherine (sop)
Gounod, C.:Roméo et Juliette, w. A. Kraus (ten), L. Quilico (bar), J. Van Dam (b-bar), G. Bacquier (bar), M. Plasson (cnd), Toulouse Capitole Orch, Toulouse Capitole Chorus [F] EMI Classics 3-▲ CDCC 47365
Strauss, R.:Salome, w. Hanna Schwarz (mez), Kenneth Riegel (ten), Bryn Terfel (b-bar), C. von Dohnányi (cnd), Vienna PO London 2-▲ 444178-2

Malgarini, Pina (mez)
Mascagni, P.:Zanetto, w. G. Arista (mez), T. Petralia (cnd), Milan RAI SO *(rec 1969)* Memories 2-▲ MEM 4519 [AAD]
Massenet, J.:Don Quichotte, w. Teresa Berganza (mez), Tommaso Frascati (ten), Carlo Badioli (bass), Boris Christoff (bass), A. Simonetto (cnd), Milan RAI SO, Milan RAI Chorus Melodram 2-▲ CDM 27027

Malinger, Ross (nar)
Prokofiev, S.:Peter & the Wolf, w. Kirstie Alley (nar), Lloyd Bridges (nar), G. Daugherty (cnd), RCA Victor SO—2 versions:1 with narration & 1 without *(rec Studio 1 & LA Studios East, Salt Lake City, Utah)* RCA Gold Seal ▲ 74321-31869-2 [DDD]

Malipiero, Giovanni (ten)
Donizetti, G.:Lucia di Lammermoor, w. Lina Pagliughi (sop—Lucia), Maria Vinciguerra (mez—Alisa), Armando Giannotti (ten—Normanno), Muzio Giovagnoli (ten—Arturo), Giovanni Malipiero (ten—Edgardo), Giuseppe Manacchini (bar—Enrico), Luciano Neroni (bass—Raimondo), U. Tansini (cnd), EIAR Orch, EIAR Chorus *(rec 1938)* Bongiovanni ("Il mito dell'opera" series) 2-▲ GB 1122-2 [ADD]
Donizetti, G.:Lucia di Lammermoor, w. Lina Pagliughi (sop—Lucia), Maria Vinciguerra (mez—Alisa), Armando Giannotti (ten—Normanno), Muzio Giovannoli (ten—Lord Arturo), Giovanni Malipiero (ten—Edgardo), Giuseppe Manacchini (bar—Lord Enrico), Luciano Neroni (bass—Raimondo), U. Tansini (cnd), EIAR Orch, EIAR Chorus *(rec Turin, 1942)* Melodram 2-▲ IMC 202004 [ADD]
Giovanni Malipiero Bongiovanni ▲ GB 1072-2 [ADD]
Puccini, G.:Manon Lescaut (sels), w. M. Favero (sop), R. Tebaldi (sop), J. Gardino (mez), G. Nessi (ten), M. Stabile (bar), T. Pasero (b-bar), C. Forti (bass), A. Toscanini (cnd), La Scala Orch, La Scala Chorus—Intermezzo; Act 3 *(rec live, Milan, May 18, 1946)* Arkadia ("Historical Performances" series) 2-▲ 604 (m)

Maliponte, Adriana (sop)
Bellini, V.:I Puritani, w. A. Maliponte (sop—Elvira), A. di Stasio (sop—Enrichetta di Francia), A. Kraus (ten—Lord Arturo Talbo), A. Pedroni (ten—Bruno Roberton), P. Cappuccilli (bar—Sir Riccardo Forth), R. Raimondi (bass—Sir Giorgio), G. Gavazzeni (cnd), Catania Teatro Massimo Bellini Orch, Catania Teatro Massimo Bellini Chorus *(rec Feb. 6, 1972)* Ornamenti 2-▲ FE 107 [ADD]
Bizet, G.:Carmen, w. M. Horne (mez), J. McCracken (bar), T. Krause (bar), L. Bernstein (cnd), Metropolitan Opera Orch, Manhattan Opera Chorus [F] *(rec 1973)* Deutsche Grammophon 3-▲ 427440-2 [ADD]

Maliponte, Adriana (sop) (cont.)
Bizet, G.:Les Pêcheurs de perles, w. A. Maliponte (sop—Leila), A. Kraus (ten—Nadir), S. Bruscantini (bar—Zurga), C. F. Cillario (cnd), Barcelona Teatro Liceo Orch, Barcelona Gran Teatro de Liceo Chorus Bongiovanni 2-▲ GB 516/17 [ADD]

Mallabrera, André (ten)
Charpentier, M.-A.:Magnificat, w. Martha Angelici (sop), Jocelyn Chamonin (sop), Rémy Corazza (ten), Georges Abdoun (bar), Jacques Mars (bass), Maurice André (tpt), Marie-Claire Alain (org), L. Martini (cnd), Jean-François Paillard CO, French Jeunesses Musicales Chorale *(rec Paris, Mar 15, 1963)* Vanguard Classics ▲ OVC 8075 [ADD]
Charpentier, M.-A.:Te Deum, H. 146, w. Martha Angelici (sop), Jocelyn Chamonin (sop), Rémy Corazza (ten), Georges Abdoun (bar), Jacques Mars (bass), Maurice André (tpt), Marie-Claire Alain (org), L. Martini (cnd), Jean-François Paillard CO, French Jeunesses Musicales Chorale *(rec Paris, Mar 15, 1963)* Vanguard Classics ▲ OVC 8075 [ADD]
Offenbach, J.:Le Fille du tambour-major, w. Christiane Harbell (sop—Stella), Monique de Pondeau (sop—Claudine), Germaine Light (mez—Duchess Della Volta), Marcelle Ranson-Hervé (ten—Duke Della Volta), André Mallabrera (ten—Griolet), Etienne Arnaud (bar—Robert), Louis Musy (bar—Monthabor), *(orch unknown)* Accord ▲ ACD 220692 [AAD]

Mallas-Godlewska, Ewa (sop)
Broschi, R.:Arias, w. Derek Lee Ragin (ct), C. Rousset (cnd), Les Talens Lyriques—Son qual nave ch'agitata; Se al labbro mio non credi; Ombra fedele anch'io Astrée ▲ E 8552 [DDD]
Broschi, R.:Arias, w. Derek Lee Ragin (ct), C. Rousset (cnd), Les Talens Lyriques—Son qual nave ch'agitata; Se al labbro mio non credi; Ombra fedele anch'io *(rec Metz, France, July 1993)* Travelling ▲ K 1005 Δ K 81005; ■ K 51005
Handel, G.F.:Arias, w. D. L. Ragin (ct), C. Rousset (cnd), Les Talens Lyriques—Handel Lascia ch'io pianga; Cara sposa *(rec Metz, France, July 1993)* Travelling ▲ K 1005 Δ K 81005; ■ K 51005
Hasse, J.A.:Arias, w. Derek Lee Ragin (ct), C. Rousset (cnd), Les Talens Lyriques—Generoso risvegliati o core *(rec Metz, France, July 1993)* Travelling ▲ K 1005 Δ K 81005; ■ K 51005
Pergolesi, G.B.:Salve regina in a, w. Derek Lee Ragin (ct), C. Rousset (cnd), Les Talens Lyriques *(rec Metz, France, July 1993)* Travelling ▲ K 1005; Δ K 81005; ■ K 51005;
Porpora, N.A.:Arias, w. Derek Lee Ragin (ct), C. Rousset (cnd), Les Talens Lyriques *(rec Metz, France, July 1993)* Travelling ▲ K 1005; Δ K 81005; ■ K 51005;

Mallé, Maria (sgr)
Künneke, E.:The Alluring Flame, w. Birgit Fandrey (sgr—Dolores), Christianne Hossfeld (sgr—Lisbeth), Jürgen Sacher (ten—Master), Ralf Lukas (bar—Hoffman), Gerd Grochowski (sgr—1st Neighbor), Gerhard Peters (sgr—Friedrich), Zoran Todorovic (sgr—Jacinto), Theodor Weimer (sgr—2nd Neighbor), P. Falk (cnd), Cologne RSO, Cologne Radio Chorus *(rec Cologne, Nov 7-26, 1994)* Capriccio ▲ 10753 [DDD]

Malmberg, Urban (bar)
Grieg, E.:Peer Gynt, w. B. Bonney (sop), M. Eklöf (mez), K. M. Sandve (ten), N. Järvi (cnd), Gothenburg SO, Gothenburg Sym Chorus [N] Deutsche Grammophon 2-▲ 423079-2 [DDD]
Grieg, E.:Peer Gynt, w. M. Häggander (sop), H. Blomstedt (cnd), San Francisco SO, *(chorus unknown)* [N] London ▲ 425448-2 [DDD]
Grieg, E.:Sigurd Jorsalfar, w. B. Bonney (sop), M. Eklöf (mez), K. M. Sandve (ten), N. Järvi (cnd), Gothenburg SO, Gothenburg Sym Chorus [N] Deutsche Grammophon 2-▲ 423079-2 [DDD]
Mendelssohn, F.:Die Hochzeit des Camacho, w. R. Hofman (sop—Quiteria), A. Ulbrich (mez—Lucinda), S. Weir (ten—Basilio), H. Rhys-Evans (ten—Vivaldo), N. van der Meel (ten—Camacho), W. Wild (bar—Carrasco), U. Malmberg (bass—Sancho Panza), U. Cold (bass—Don Quixote), J. van Immerseel (cnd), Anima Eterna Orch, Aachen Boys Choir, Chor Modus Novus [G] *(rec Sept. 19-22, 1992)* Channel Classics 2-▲ CCS 5593 [DDD]

Malone, Carol (sop)
Mozart, W.A.:Missa brevis, K.65, w. G. Schreckenbach (mez), K. Markus (ten), W. Grönroos (bar), R. Bader (cnd), Berlin RSO, St. Hedwig's Cathedral Choir [L] Koch Schwann ▲ SCH 313021 [ADD/DDD]
Rossini, G.:La Cenerentola, w. F. Palmer (sop), A. Baltsa (mez), F. Araiza (ten), S. Alaimo (bar), J. del Carlo (bass), R. Raimondi (bass), N. Marriner (cnd), Academy of St. Martin in the Fields, Ambrosian Chorus Philips ("Digital Classics" series) 3-▲ 420468-2 [DDD]

Malovany, Joseph (ten)
The Famous Cantor, w. Hungarian State Orch [cnd:Noam Sheriff] Hungaroton ▲ HCD 18178 [DDD]

Malta, Alexander (bass)
Hindemith, P.:Mathis der Maler, w. Urszula Koszut (sop), Trudeliese Schmidt (mez), Rose Wagemann (mez), William Cochran (ten), Donald Grobe (ten), James King (ten), Manfred Schmidt (ten), Dietrich Fischer-Dieskau (bar), Gerd Feldhoff (bass), Peter Meven (bass), Karl Kreile (sgr), R. Kubelík (cnd), Bavarian RSO, Bavarian Radio Chorus EMI Classics 2-▲ CDCC 55237
Smetana, B.:The Bartered Bride, w. T. Stratas (sop), R. Kollo (ten), W. Berry (b-bar), J. Krombholc (cnd), Munich RSO Eurodisc 2-▲ 7795-2-RG [ADD]

Malvisi, Desdemona (sop)
Verdi, G.:I lombardi alla prima crociata, w. C. Deutekom (sop), M. Aparici (sop), P. Domingo (ten), G. Raimondi (ten), M. Lo Monaco (ten), M. Dean (b-bar), C. Grant (bass), L. Gardelli (cnd), Royal PO, Ambrosian Singers Philips 2-▲ 422420-2 [ADD]

Manacchini, Giuseppe (bar)
Donizetti, G.:Lucia di Lammermoor, w. Lina Pagliughi (sop—Lucia), Maria Vinciguerra (mez—Alisa), Armando Giannotti (ten—Normanno), Muzio Giovagnoli (ten—Arturo), Giovanni Malipiero (ten—Edgardo), Giuseppe Manacchini (bar—Enrico), Luciano Neroni (bass—Raimondo), U. Tansini (cnd), EIAR Orch, EIAR Chorus *(rec 1938)* Bongiovanni ("Il mito dell'opera" series) 2-▲ GB 1122-2 [ADD]
Donizetti, G.:Lucia di Lammermoor, w. Lina Pagliughi (sop—Lucia), Maria Vinciguerra (mez—Alisa), Armando Giannotti (ten—Normanno), Muzio Giovannoli (ten—Lord Arturo), Giovanni Malipiero (ten—Edgardo), Giuseppe Manacchini (bar—Lord Enrico), Luciano Neroni (bass—Raimondo), U. Tansini (cnd), EIAR Orch, EIAR Chorus *(rec Turin, 1942)* Melodram 2-▲ IMC 202004 [ADD]

Manca di Nissa, Bernadette (cta)
Donizetti, G.:Anna Bolena, w. J. Sutherland (sop), S. Mentzer (mez), J. Hadley (ten), S. Ramey (bass), R. Bonynge (cnd), Welsh National Opera Orch [I] London 3-▲ 421096-2 [DDD]
Pergolesi, G.B.:Lo frate 'nnamorato, w. N. Focile (sop), A. Felle (sop), A. Corbelli (bar), R. Muti (cnd), La Scala Orch, La Scala Chorus EMI Classics 3-▲ CDCC 54240
Rossini, G.:Messa di gloria, w. A. C. Antonacci (sop), F. Araiza (ten), R. Gambill (ten), P. Spagnoli (bar), S. Accardo (cnd), St. Cecilia Academy Orch Rome, St. Cecilia Academy Chorus Rome *(rec Mar. 1-2, 1992)* Ricordi ▲ RFCD 2012 [DDD]
Verdi, G.:Falstaff, w. Maureen O'Flynn (sop), Daniela Dessi (sop), Delores Ziegler (mez), Ramon Vargas (ten), Ernesto Gavazzi (ten), Paolo Barbacini (ten), Juan Pons (bar), Roberto Frontali (bar), Luigi Roni (bass), R. Muti (cnd), La Scala Orch, La Scala Chorus *(rec Milan La Scala Theater, Italy, Mar. 29 & 31)* Sony Classical ▲ S2K 58961 [DDD]

Manchet, Éliane (sop)
Debussy, C.:Pelléas et Mélisande, w. E. Manchet (sop—Mélisande), M. Walker (bar—Pelléas), J. Carewe (cnd), Nice PO, Nice Opera Chorus—no texts [F] *(rec 6/88)* Pierre Verany 2-▲ PV.788093/4 [DDD]

Manci, G. (sop)
Fioravanti, V.:Le cantatrici villane, w. G. Manci (sop—Agata), M. Mauro (sop—Nunziella), M. A. Peters (sop—Rosa), F. Sovilla (mez—Giannetta), E. Palacio (ten—Carlino), G. Gatti (bar—Don Bucefalo), D. Serraiocco (bass—Don Marco), R. Tigani (cnd), Frosinone Licinio Refice Conservatory SO *(rec Oct. 22, 23 & 25, 1992)* Bongiovanni 2-▲ GB 2135/36 [DDD]

Mancini, Caterina (sop)
Verdi, G.:La battaglia di Legnano, w. Amedeo Berdini (bar), Rolando Panerai (bar), Albino Gaggi (bass), Edmea Limberti (sgr), Manfredi Ponz de Leon (sgr), F. Previtali (cnd), Rome RAI SO, Rome RAI Chorus *(rec 1951)* Cetra Classic 2-▲ CDON 40 [ADD]
Verdi, G.:Ernani, w. Vittorio Pandano (ten), Gino Penno (ten), Giuseppe Taddei (bar), Giacomo Vaghi (bar), Ezio Achilli (sgr), Licia Rossini (sgr), F. Previtali (cnd), Rome RAI SO, Rome RAI Chorus Cetra Classic 2-▲ CDON 39 [ADD]

Mancini, Caterina (sop) (cont.)
Verdi, G.:Nabucco, w. C. Mancini (sop—Abigaille), G. Gatti (sop—Fenena), B. Preziosa (sop—Anna), M. Binci (ten—Ismaele), L. Francardi (ten—Abdallo), P. Silveri (bar—Nabucodonosor), A. Cassinelli (bass—Zaccaria), A. Gaggi (bass—High Priest of Baal), F. Previtali (cnd), Rome RAI Orch, Rome RAI Chorus *(rec Rome, 1951)* Cetra Classic 2-▲ CDO 26 [ADD]

Mancini, Jolanda (sop)
Mussorgsky, M.:Khovanshchina, w. Irene Companez (cta), Herbert Handt (ten), Mirto Picchi (ten), Boris Christoff (bass), Armedeo Berdini (sgr), Giorgio Canello (sgr), Dmitri Lopatto (sgr), Michele Malaspina (sgr), Mario Petri (sgr), A. Rodzinski (cnd), Rome RAI Radio-TV SO, Rome RAI Chorus Stradivarius 2-▲ STV DTM 12320 [ADD]
Mussorgsky, M.:Khovanshchina, w. Jolanda Mancini (sop—Emma), Irene Companez (mez), Amedeo Berdini (ten—Prince Andrei Khovanski), Mirto Picchi (ten—Prince Vasili Golitsin), Herbert Handt (ten—Scribe), Andrea Mineo (bar—Kuzka), Giampiero Malaspina (bar—Shaklovity), Boris Christoff (bass—Dosifei), Mario Petri (bass—Prince Ivan Khovanski), Dimitri Lopatto (Varsonofiev/First Strelyets), Giorgio Conello (Second Strelyets), A. Rodzinski (cnd), *(orch unknown)* [I] *(rec Rome, 1958)* VAI Audio 2-▲ VAIA 1052-2

Mandac, Evelyn (sop)
Orff, C.:Carmina burana, w. S. Kolk (ten), S. Milnes (bar), S. Ozawa (cnd), Boston SO, New England Conservatory Chorus [G, L] RCA Gold Seal ▲ 07863-56533-2 [ADD] ■ 07863-56533-4

Mandelli, Luisa (sop)
Verdi, G.:La traviata, w. M. Callas (sop), A. Zanolli (sop), G. Raimondi (ten), E. Bastianini (bar), C. M. Giulini (cnd), La Scala Orch, La Scala Chorus *(rec live 1/19/56)* Myto 2-▲ MCD 89003 (m) [ADD]

Mandikian, Arda (mez)
Britten, H.:The Turn of the Screw, w. O. Dyer (sop), J. Vyvyan (sop), D. Hemmings (trb), G. Cross (ten), P. Pears (ten), B. Britten (cnd), English Opera Group Orch [E] London ▲ 425672-2 (m) [ADD]

Mané, Helen (sop)
Donizetti, G.:Messa di Gloria e Credo, w. G. Vighi (mez), P. Maus (ten), M. Machi (bass), R. Bader (cnd), Berlin RSO, St. Hedwig's Cathedral Choir [L] Koch Schwann ▲ CD 313031 [ADD]

Maneguzzer (sgr)
Puccini, G.:La Bohème (sels), w. R. Scotto (sop), G. Poggi (ten), T. Gobbi (bar), A. Votto (cnd), Florence Maggio Musicale IMP Collectors Series ▲ IMPX 9024 [AAD]

Manfrini, Luigi (bass)
Puccini, G.:La Bohème, w. Rosina Torri (sop—Mimi), Thea Vitulli (sop—Musetta), Aristodemo Giorgini (ten—Rodolfo), Giuseppe Nessi (ten—Parpignol), Ernesto Badini (bar—Marcello), Aristide Baracchi (bar—Schaunard), Luigi Manfrini (bass—Colline), Salvatore Baccaloni (bass—Benoit/Alcindoro), C. Sabajno (cnd), La Scala Orch, La Scala Chorus *(rec 1928)* VAI Audio 2-▲ VAIA 1078-2
Puccini, G.:La Bohème, w. R. Torri (sop), T. Vitulli (sop), A. Giorgini (ten), E. Badini (bar), C. Sabajno (cnd), La Scala Orch [I] *(rec 1927)* InSync 2-■ C 4131/2 (m)
Verdi, G.:Aida, w. Dusolina Giannini (sop—Aida), Irene Minghini-Cattaneo (mez—Amneris), Giuseppe Nessi (ten—Messenger), Aureliano Pertile (ten—Radames), Giovanni Inghilleri (bar—Amonasro), Luigi Manfrini (bass—Ramfis), Guglielmo Masini (bass—King), C. Sabajno (cnd), La Scala Orch, Vittore Veneziani (cnd), La Scala Chorus *(rec 1928)* Arkadia ("The 78's" series) 2-▲ 78013 [ADD]
Verdi, G.:Aida, w. D. Giannini (sop), I. Minghini-Cattaneo (cta), A. Pertile (ten), G. Inghilleri (bar), C. Sabajno (cnd), La Scala Orch, La Scala Chorus [I] *(rec 1928 for HMV)* Pearl 2-▲ CDS 9402 (m) [AAD]

Manga, Silvana (sgr)
Donizetti, G.:Gianni di Parigi, w. L. Serra (sop), E. Zilio (mez), G. Morino (ten), E. Fissore (bar), A. Romero (bar), C. F. Cillario (cnd), Milan RAI Orch, Milan RAI Chorus [I] *(rec live)* Nuova Era 2-▲ 6752/53 [DDD]

Mangin, Noel (bass)
Puccini, G.:Manon Lescaut, w. M. Caballé (sop—Manon Lescaut), P. Domingo (ten—Des Grieux), R. Tear (ten—Edmondo), V. Sardinero (bar—Lescaut), N. Mangin (bass—Geronte), B. Bartoletti (cnd), New Philharmonia Orch, Ambrosian Opera Chorus EMI Classics ▲ CDMB 64852

Manini, G. (sgr)
Donizetti, G.:Rita, or Le mari battu, w. U. Benelli (bar), S. Figacci (sgr), R. Franceschetto (sgr), F. Maestri (cnd), In Canto CO *(rec Sept. 1990)* Bongiovanni 2-▲ GB 2109/10 [DDD]

Mann, Chris (voc)
Chris Mann & the Impediments, w. Carolyn Connors (voc), Jeannie Marsch (voc), Rik Rue (voc) O.O. Discs ▲ CD 21 [ADD]

Mann, Christine (sgr)
Straus, O.:The Merry Nibelungs, w. Lisa Griffith (sop—Kriemhild), Gudrun Volkert (sop—Brunhilde), Daphne Evangelatos (cta—Ute), Gabriele Henkel (sgr—Giselher), Christine Mann (sgr—Vogel), Hein Heidbüchel (ten—Volker), Martin Gantner (sgr—Gunther), Gerd Grochowski (sgr—Dankwart), Michael Nowak (sgr—Siegfried), Josef Otten (sgr—Hagen), S. Köhler (cnd), Cologne RSO, Cologne Radio Chorus *(rec Cologne, Jan 31-Feb 17, 1995)* Capriccio ▲ 10752 [DDD]

Mann, Noel (bass)
Mozart, W.A.:Zauberflöte, w. Constanze Backes (sop—Papagena), Christiane Oelze (sop—Pamina), Susan Roberts (sop—First Lady), Cyndia Sieden (sop—Queen of the Night), Carola Guber (cta—Second Lady), Maria Jonas (cta—Third Lady), Andreas Dieterich (trb—First Boy), Jan Andreas Mendel (trb—Second Boy), Florian Wöller (trb—Third Boy), Uwe Peper (ten—Monostatos), Nicolas Robertson (ten—First Man in Armor), Michael Schade (ten—Tamino), Gerald Finley (bar—Papageno), Noel Mann (bass—Second Man in Armour), Harry Peeters (bass—Sarastro), Detlef Roth (bass—Speaker/First Priest), Robert Burt (speaker—Third Priest), Robert Johnston (speaker—Second Priest), Wolfgang Knauer (speaker—Fourth Priest), Douglas Welbat (speaker—Second Priest), J. E. Gardiner (cnd), English Baroque Soloists, Monteverdi Choir London *(rec Forum am Schlosspark, Ludwigsburg, July 1995)* Archiv 2-▲ 449166-2

Mannarini, Ida (mez)
Mascagni, P.:Cavalleria rusticana, w. G. A. Lombardi (sop), M. Castagna (mez), A. Melandri (ten), G. Lulli (bar), L. Molajoli (cnd), La Scala Orch, La Scala Chorus *(rec 1930)* Preiser ▲ 90042 (m) [AAD]
Puccini, G.:Madama Butterfly (sels), w. Margaret Sheridan (sop), Lionello Cecil (ten), Vittorio Wenberg (sgr), Carlo Sabajno (pno) *(rec La Scala, 1929-30)* Romophone ("Opera Magna" series) 2-▲ 89001-2

Manning, J. (spkr)
Schoenberg, A.:Pierrot lunaire, w. S. Rattle (cnd), Nash Ensemble [G] Chandos ("Collect" series) ▲ CHAN 6534 [ADD]

Manning, Jane (sop)
Bennett, Richard Rodney:Spells, w. D. Willcocks (cnd), Philharmonia Orch, Bach Choir [E] Continuum ▲ CCD 1030
Dallapiccola, L.:Divert in quattro esercizi, w. G. Hair (cnd), Australia Ensemble—[I] Entr'acte ▲ ESCD 6504 [DDD]
Dallapiccola, L.:Liriche greche, w. G. Hair (cnd), Australia Ensemble—[I] Entr'acte ▲ ESCD 6504 [DDD]
Jane Manning Sings Weir, Nash, Connolly, Bauld, Elias, Payne & Gilbert, w. Jane's Minstrels [cnd:Roger Montgomery] NMC ▲ NMC 25 [DDD]
Kraft, William:Settings from Pierrot Lunaire, w. Renee Krimsier (fl), Diane Heffner (cl), Nancy Cirillo (vn/va), Ronald Lowry (vc), Dean Anderson (perc), Hugh Hinton (pno) Albany ▲ TROY 218 [DDD]
Lumsdaine, D.:Aria for Edward John Eyre, w. J. Baddeley (nar), J. Rye (nar), E. Howarth (cnd), Gemini Ensemble NM Classics ▲ NMCD 007 [DDD]
McLeod, J.:Gokstad Ship, w. M. Skoczen-Staniszewska (hp), J. McLeod (cnd), Polish Radio-TV SO Vienna Modern Masters ▲ VMM 3026 [DDD]
Messiaen, O.:Harawi, w. David Miller (pno) Unicorn-Kanchana ("Souvenir" series) ▲ UKCD 2084
Satie, E.:Songs, w. Bojan Gorisek (pno) Audiophile Classics 10-▲ 101.391 [DDD]
Stravinsky, I.:Japanese Lyrics, w. S. Rattle (cnd), Nash Ensemble Chandos ("Collect" series) ▲ CHAN 6535 [ADD]

Mannion, Rosa (sop)
Beethoven, L. van:Missa Solemnis, w. Birgit Remmert (alt), James Taylor (ten), Cornelius Hauptmann (bass), P. Herreweghe (cnd), Champs Elysées Theater Orch, Chapelle Royale Choir, Collegium Vocale *(rec Auditorium Stravinski de Montreux, Feb. 20-21, 1995)* Harmonia Mundi France ▲ HMC 901557

▲ = CD ♦ = Enhanced CD Δ = MD ■ = Cassette Tape □ = DCC

Mannion, Rosa (sop) (cont.)
Mozart, W.A.:Zauberflöte, w. Natalie Dessay (sop—Queen of the Night), Linda Kitchen (sop—Papagena), Rosa Mannion (sop—Pamina), Anna-Maria Panzarella (sop—First Lady), Doris Lamprecht (mez—Second Lady), Delphine Haidan (cta—Third Lady), Hans Peter Blochwitz (ten—Tamino), Steven Cole (ten—Monostatos), Chrisopher Josey (ten—First Priest/First Armed Man), Anton Scharinger (bar—Papageno), Reinhard Hagen (bass—Sarastro), Laurent Naouri (bass—Second Priest/Second Armed Man), Willard White (bass—Speaker), W. Christie (cnd), Les Arts Florissants *(rec Paris Oct 2-9 1995)* Erato 2-▲ 12705-2 [DDD]

Manno, Vincenzo (ten)
Cavalli, P.F.:Ormindo, w. E. Zilio (mez), G. Gatti (bar), A. Rinaldi (bar), R. Fasano (cnd), Rome Virtuosi Stradivarius 2-▲ DAT 12307
Vivaldi, A.:Beatus vir, R.795, w. Caterina Calvi (sop), Susanna Moncayo Von Hase (cta), Bonitatibus (sgr), Trogu (sgr) Agora Music ▲ 001
Vivaldi, A.:Gloria (& Intro), RV.588, w. Caterina Calvi (sop), Susanna Moncayo Von Hase (cta), Bonitatibus (sgr), Trogu (sgr) Agora Music ▲ 001

Mannov, Johannes (bass)
Dvořák, A.:Mass, w. D. Röschmann (sop), I. Danz (alt), C. Elsner (ten), E. Krapp (org), W. Schäfer (cnd), Frankfurt Kantorei Ars Musici ▲ AM 1083-2 [DDD]
Rossini, G.:Petite messe solennelle, w. M. Musacchio (sop), C. Bandera (alt), G. Dominguez (ten), U. Koella (pno), N. Clayton (pno), F. Näf (cnd), *(chorus unknown)* Ars Musici ▲ AM 1091 [DDD]

Manowarda, Josef von (bass)
Mozart, W.A.:Zauberflöte (sels), w. Erna Berger (sop—Queen of the Night), Maria Reining (sop—Pamina), Josef von Manowarda (bass—Sarastro), H. Knappertsbusch (cnd), Vienna State Opera Orch *(rec Vienna, Dec. 4, 1941)* Koch Schwann 2-▲ SCH 314672 [ADD]
Verdi, G.:Don Carlos (sels), w. Viorica Ursuleac (sop—Elisabetta), Franz Völker (ten—Don Carlo), Josef von Manowarda (bass—Filippo), C. Krauss (cnd), Vienna State Opera Orch *(rec Vienna, Feb. 25, 1933)* Koch Schwann 2-▲ SCH 314662 [ADD]
Verdi, G.:Otello (sels), w. Viorica Ursuleac (sop—Desemona), Franz Völker (ten—Otello), Josef von Manowarda (bass—Iago), C. Krauss (cnd), Vienna State Opera Orch *(rec Vienna, Dec. 15, 1933)* Koch Schwann 2-▲ SCH 314662 [ADD]
Wagner, R.:Der fliegende Holländer (sels), w. Wilhelm Rode (bar—Holländer), Josef von Manowarda (bass—Daland), L. Reichwein (cnd), Vienna State Opera Orch *(rec Jan. 6, 1939)* Koch Schwann 2-▲ SCH 314632 [ADD]
Wagner, R.:Götterdämmerung (sels), w. M. Lorenz (ten—Siegfried), P. Schöffler (b-bar—Gunther), J. von Manowarda (bass—Hagen), L. Reichwein (cnd), Vienna State Opera Orch, Vienna State Opera Chorus *(rec Sept. 10, 1942)* Koch Schwann 2-▲ SCH 314562 [ADD]
Wagner, R.:Götterdämmerung (sels), w. Henny Trundt (sop—Brünnhilde), Josef Kalenberg (ten—Siegfried), Emil Schipper (bar—Gunther), Josef von Manowarda (bass—Hagen), C. Krauss (cnd), Vienna State Opera Orch *(rec Mar. 7, 1933)* Koch Schwann 2-▲ SCH 314642 [ADD]
Wagner, R.:Götterdämmerung (sels), w. G. Kappel (sop—Brünhilde), J. Kalenberg (ten—Siegfried), J. von Manowarda (bass—Mime), R. Heger (cnd), Vienna State Opera Orch, Vienna State Opera Chorus *(rec June 15, 1933)* Koch Schwann 2-▲ SCH 314592
Wagner, R.:Lohengrin (sels), w. Maria Müller (sop), Margarete Klose (mez), Franz Völker (ten), W. Furtwängler (cnd), Bayreuth Festival Orch, Bayreuth Festival Chorus—Prelude to Act III; Operatic sels. *(rec 1931)* Grammofono 2000 ▲ GRM 78515 [ADD]
Wagner, R.:Lohengrin (sels), w. Maria Müller (sop—Elsa), Margarete Klose (mez—Ortrud), Franz Völker (ten—Lohengrin), Jaro Prohaska (bar—Telramund), Josef von Manowarda (bass—King Heinrich), H. Tietjen (cnd), Vienna State Opera Orch *(rec Vienna, 1938)* Koch Schwann 2-▲ SCH 314682 [ADD]
Wagner, R.:Lohengrin (sels), w. Franz Völker (ten—Lohengrin), Josef von Manowarda (bass—King Henry), Zdenka Zika (sgr—Titurel), F. Rühlmann (cnd), Vienna State Opera Orch *(rec Vienna, June 3, 1933)* Koch Schwann 2-▲ SCH 314662 [ADD]
Wagner, R.:Parsifal (sels), w. Gertrude Fünger (cta—Kundry), Gunnar Graarud (ten—Parsifal), Emil Schipper (bar—Amfortas), Josef von Manowarda (bass—Gurnemanz), C. Krauss (cnd), Vienna State Opera Orch *(rec Apr. 13, 1933)* Koch Schwann 2-▲ SCH 314642 [ADD]
Wagner, R.:Das Rheingold (sels), w. Erich Zimmermann (ten—Mime), Herrmann Wiedemann (bar—Alberich), Josef von Manowarda (bass—Wotan), C. Krauss (cnd), Vienna State Opera Orch *(rec Feb. 28, 1933)* Koch Schwann 2-▲ SCH 314642 [ADD]
Wagner, R.:Die Walküre (sels), w. M. Reining (sop), H. Jung (mez), F. Krauss (ten), R. Bockelmann (bar), C. Leonhardt (cnd), Stuttgart Radio Orch—Act 2 (sels.); Act 3 (complete) *(rec Apr. 3, 1938)* Preiser 2-▲ PRE 90207 [ADD]
Wagner, R.:Die Walküre (act 1), w. M. Reining (sop), F. Krauss (ten), C. Leonhardt (cnd), Stuttgart Reichssenders Orch *(rec April 28, 1940)* Preiser ▲ 90151 (m)

Mansourian, Araxie (sop)
Yekmalian, M.:Armenian Mass, w. Vartan Haroutunian (bass), Levon Chabanian (cnd), St. Gayanée Chapel Armenian Liturgical Choir Arb ▲ 1416

Mantaj, Michael (bass)
Brixi, F.X.:Missa di Gloria, w. F. Wagner (sop), R. Schneider-Waterberg (alt), B. Hirtreiter (ten), C. Hammer (org), W. Kelber (cnd), Munich Monteverdi Orch, Munich Concorto Vocale *(rec 1993)* Calig ▲ CAL 50927 [ADD]

Mantelli, Nadia (sgr)
Monteverdi, C.:Ballo delle ingrate, w. Carlo Lepore (bass), Daniela Barcellona (sgr), Daniela Ciliberti (sgr), Andrea Concetti (sgr), Hans van Dijk (sgr), Remo Guerrini (sgr), Elena Marazzi (sgr), Humberto Orellana (sgr), Claudia Pallini (sgr), Luigi Polsini (sgr), Rosa Ricciotti (sgr), Alberto Rota (sgr), Ludovica Scoppola (sgr), *(orch unknown)* Nuova Era ▲ NUO 7224

Mantese, Cristina (sop)
Cimarosa, D.:Amor rende sagace, w. G. Bertagnolli (sop), D. Bruera (sop), M. Dalena (ten), E. Dara (bar), M. Nicolini (sgr), F. Neri (cnd), Bolzano Claudio Monteverdi Conservatory Youth Orch [I] *(rec live, Bolzano 7/25-27/91)* Bongiovanni 2-▲ GB 2126/27 [DDD]

Manton, Raymond (ten)
Puccini, G.:Turandot, w. Montserrat Caballé (sop—Turandot), Leona Mitchell (sop—Liu), Remy Corazza (ten—Pang), Joseph Franck (ten—Pong), Robert Johnson (ten—Prince of Persia), Raymond Manton (ten—Altoum), Luciano Pavarotti (ten—Calaf), Aldo Bramante (bar—a mandarin), Dale Duesing (bar—Ping), Giorgio Tozzi (bass—Timur), R. Chailly (cnd), *(orch unknown)* *(rec San Francisco, Nov. 4, 1977)* Legato Classics 2-▲ LCD 188-2

Mantovani, Dino (bar)
Bellini, V.:La sonnambula, w. Maria Callas (sop), Fiorenza Cossotto (mez), Nicola Monti (ten), Franco Ricciardi (ten), Nicola Zaccaria (bass), A. Votto (cnd), La Scala Orch, La Scala Chorus Melodram 2-▲ CDM 26037
Verdi, G.:La forza del destino, w. Zinka Milanov (sop—Donna Leonora di Vargas), Rosalind Elias (mez—Preziosilla), Luisa Gioia (sgr—Curra), Angelo Mercuriali (ten—Trabuco), Giuseppe di Stefano (ten—Son Alvaro), Leonard Warren (bar—Don Carlos di Vargas), Giorgio Tozzi (b-bar—Padre guardiano), Dino Mantovani (bar—Fra Melitone), Paolo Washington (b-bar—Il marchese di Calatrava), Virgilio Carbonari (b-bar—un alcalde), Sergio Liviabella (sgr—un chirurgo), F. Previtali (cnd), St. Cecilia Academy Orch Rome, St. Cecilia Academy Chorus Rome [I] London ▲ 443678-2 [ADD]
Zandonai, R.:Francesca da Rimini, w. Lydia Marimpietri (sop—Biancofiore), Magda Olivero (sop—Francesca), Pinuccia Perotti (sop—Samaritana), Edda Vincenzi (sop—Garsenda), Gabriella Carturan (mez—Smaragdi), Biancamaria Casoni (mez—Altichiara), Anna Maria Rota (cta—Donella), Athos Cesarini (ten—Archer), Angelo Mercuriali (ten—Ser Toldo Berardengo), Mario del Monaco (ten—Paolo), Piero de Palma (ten—Malatestino), Rinaldo Pelizzoni (ten—Prisoner), Gianpiero Malaspina (bar—Gianciotto), Dino Mantovani (bar—Jester), Enrico Campi (bass—Ostasio), Giuseppe Morresi (bass—Tower warden), G. Gavazzeni (cnd), La Scala Orch, La Scala Chorus *(rec La Scala Theatre, Milan, June 4, 1959)* Legato Classics 2-▲ LCD 186-2

Manuguerra, Matteo (bar)
Donizetti, G.:Lucia di Lammermoor (sels), w. Renata Scotto (sop—Lucia), Ruth Carron (mez—Alisa), Richard Tucker (ten—Edgardo), Matteo Manuguerra (bar—Enrico), Robert Hale (bass-bar—Raimondo), A. Guadagno (cnd), *(orch & chorus unknown)*—Lucia, perdona...Verranno a te; Sconsigliato! In queste porte; Il dolce suono; Non mi guardar si fiero...Spargi d'amaro pianto; Tombe degli avi miei...Fra poco a me ricovero; Tu che a Dio spiegasti l'ali *(rec Philadelphia, 1973)* Legato Classics 2-▲ LCD 198-2

Manuguerra, Matteo (bar) (cont.)
Leoncavallo, R.:Pagliacci, w. M. Caballé (sop), R. Scotto (sop), A. Varnay (mez), J. Hamari (mez), J. Carreras (ten), T. Allen (bar), K. Nurmela (bar), U. Benelli (bar), R. Muti (cnd), Philharmonia Orch, Ambrosian Opera Chorus EMI Classics 2-▲ CDMB 63650
Ponchielli, A.:La Gioconda, w. M. Caballé (sop—Gioconda), M. L. Nave (mez—Laura), P. Payne (mez—La Cieca), J. Carreras (ten—Enzo), M. Manuguerra (bar—Barnaba), B. Giaiotti (bass—Alvise), J. López-Cobos (cnd), *(orch unknown)* *(rec Dec. 6, 1979)* Legato Classics ▲ LCD 170-2 [ADD]
Verdi, G.:La battaglia di Legnano, w. K. Ricciarelli (sop), J. Carreras (ten), N. Ghiuselev (bass), L. Gardelli (cnd), ORF SO, ORTF Choir Philips 2-▲ 422435-2 [ADD]
Verdi, G.:I masnadieri, w. J. Sutherland (sop), F. Bonisolli (ten), S. Ramey (bass), R. Bonynge (cnd), Welsh National Opera Orch, Welsh National Opera Chorus London ("Grand Opera" series) 2-▲ 433854-2 [DDD]
Verdi, G.:La traviata, w. J. Sutherland (sop), L. Pavarotti (ten), R. Bonynge (cnd), National PO London, London Opera Chorus [I] London 2-▲ 430491-2 [DDD]
Verdi, G.:La traviata, w. J. Sutherland (sop), L. Pavarotti (ten), R. Bonynge (cnd), National PO London, London Opera Chorus [I] London ▲ 400057-2 [DDD] ■ 400057-4
Zandonai, R.:Francesca da Rimini, w. R. Kabaivanska (sop), P. Domingo (ten), N. Saetta (sgr), E. Queler (cnd), *(orch unknown)* *(rec live, March 22, 1973)* Standing Room Only 2-▲ SRO 840-2 [ADD]

Manz, Sue (bass)
Scelsi, G.:Anahit, w. Paul Zukofsky (vn), Julie Bogorad (fl), Peggy Russell (fl), Courtney Westcott (fl), Lawrence McDonald (cl), Joan Waryha (cl), Jean Hansen (b cl), Bill Suite (e hn), Nita VanPelt (sax), Bob Zobal (tpt), John Carter (trbn), Martin Lydecker (trbn), Stan Cortman (hn), Robert Ward (hn), William Curry (va), Jody Rowitsch (va), Irene Wade (va), Anne Fagerburg (vc), John Gockel (vc), Steven Stearman (bass) *(rec Oberlin Conservatory of Music, Oct 8, 1973)* CP² ▲ CP2 108 [AAD]

Manzoni, Laurent (bar)
Honegger, A.:Amphion, w. Olivier Lallouette (bar—Apollon), Laurent Manzoni (bar—Amphion), Iona Bentoiu (sgr—muse), Theodora Ciucur (sgr—muse), Lucia Kriska (sgr—muse), Adriana Mestes (sgr—muse), J.-F. Antonioli (cnd), Timisoara PO, Timisoara Banatul Phil Chorus, Timisoara Children's Chorus *(rec Salle Ion Vidu, Timisoara, Romania, Oct 28 & Nov 1, 1995)* Timpani ▲ 1035 [DDD]

Manzoni, Laurent (nar)
Stravinsky, I.:L'Histoire du soldat, w. A. Plotino (cnd), New Music Studium *(rec Torino, Italy, Jan 1995)* Arts ▲ 473572 [DDD]

Manzoni, Valeria (sgr)
Distel, H.:La Stazione, w. Teresita Fontana (sgr), Malwida Meysenbug (sgr), Federico Paternina (sgr), Arturo Schwarz (sgr) *(rec Milan, Italy & Bern, Switzerland, 1987 & May 1990)* Hat Hut ("NOW." series) ▲ hat ART CD 6060 [AAD]

Manzotti, Angelo (sop)
Broschi, R.:Arias, w. Maria Pia Jacoboni (clvd), Rome Solisti—Di costanza il core armato Bongiovanni ▲ GB 5564 [DDD]
Farinelli (Carlo Broschi):Aria for la Maestà de Ferdinando VI Re cattolico, w. Maria Pia Jacoboni (clvd), Rome Solisti Bongiovanni ▲ GB 5564 [DDD]
Giacomelli, G.:Merope (sels), w. Maria Pia Jacoboni (clvd), Rome Solisti—Quell'usignolo che innamorato canta; Sposa non mi conosci Bongiovanni ▲ GB 5564 [DDD]
Hasse, J.A.:Artaserse (sels), w. Maria Pia Jacoboni (clvd), Rome Solisti Bongiovanni ▲ GB 5564 [DDD]

Mapelli, Silvia (sop)
Astorga, E. d':Stabat Mater, w. Elisabetta Battaglia (sop), Narita (sgr), Zaramella (sgr), Concentus Musicae Antiqua Nuova Era ("Ancient Music" series) ▲ NUO 7198 [DDD]
Sammartini, G.B.:Cants for the Fridays in Lent, w. Caterina Calvi (cta), Vito Martino (ten), D. Ferrari (cnd), Capriccio Italiano Ensemble—Il pianto delle pie Donne; Pianto di Maddalena al Sepolcro Nuova Era ▲ NUO CD 7269
Sammartini, G.B.:Cants for the Fridays in Lent, w. Caterina Calvi (alt), Vito Martino (ten), D. Ferrari (cnd), Capriccio Italiano Ensemble—Il Pianto Delle Pie Donne, J.118; Pianto di Maddalena al Sepolcro, J.120 Enterprise ("Tiziano" series) ▲ ENT TZ 96007 [DDD]

Maragliano, Luisa (sop)
Giordano, U.:Andrea Chénier (sels), w. Angelo Lo Forese (ten), U. Rapalo (cnd), *(orch unknown)*—Vicino a te s'acqueta' *(rec Naples, 1969)* Golden Age of Opera ▲ GAO 204 [ADD]
Puccini, G.:Manon Lescaut (sels), w. Plácido Domingo (ten), B. Bartoletti (cnd), *(orch unknown)*—Sola, perduta abbandonata *(rec Chicago, 1968)* Golden Age of Opera ▲ GAO 204 [ADD]
Puccini, G.:Tosca (sels), w. Carlo Bergonzi (ten), F. Scaglia (cnd), *(orch unknown)*—Mario... Mario... son qui *(rec Naples, 1965)* Golden Age of Opera ▲ GAO 204 [ADD]
Verdi, G.:Aida (sels), w. Giangiacomo Guelfi (bar), G. Gavazzeni (cnd)—Ciel! Mio padre; Pur ti riveggo, mia dolce Aida; La fatal pietra *(rec 1960 & 72)* Golden Age of Opera ▲ GAO 204 [ADD]
Verdi, G.:Un ballo in maschera (sels), w. Piero Cappuccilli (bar), F. Mannino (cnd)—Morrò, ma prima in grazia *(rec Naples, 1964)* Golden Age of Opera ▲ GAO 204 [ADD]
Verdi, G.:Simon Boccanegra (sels), w. Piero Cappuccilli (bar), M. Rossi (cnd), *(orch unknown)*—Non sono una Grimaldi...; Figlia a tal nome io palpito' *(rec Naples, 1970)* Golden Age of Opera ▲ GAO 204 [ADD]

Maran, George (ten)
Mozart, W.A.:Missa, K.427, w. Annelohre Cahnbley (sop), Maria Stader (sop), Walter Raninger (bass), B. Paumgartner (cnd), Salzburg Mozarteum Orch, Salzburg Radio Chorus, Salzburg Mozarteum Chorus *(rec Aug 16, 1958)* Orfeo d'or ("Festspiel Dokumente" series) ▲ 397951 (m)

Marani, Antonio (bass)
Ricci, L.:Crispino e la cornare, w. D. Lojarro (sop), A. Lazzarini (mez), Cossutta (ten), S. Alaimo (bar), R. Coviello (bar), R. Ristori (bass), Benori (sgr), Siclari (sgr), P. Carignani (cnd), San Remo SO, San Remo Sym Chorus [I] *(rec live 11/89)* Bongiovanni 2-▲ GB 2095/96 [DDD]
Rossini, G.:Torvaldo e Dorliska, w. A. Buda (sop), F. Pediconi (sop), M. Ciliento (mez), E. Palacio (ten), S. Antonucci (bar), M. de Bernart (cnd), Swiss-Italian Orch, Cantemus, Swiss-Italian Radio-TV Chorus *(rec Jan. 11, 1992)* Arkadia-Akademia 2-▲ 123 [DDD]

Marazzi, Elena (sgr)
Monteverdi, C.:Ballo delle ingrate, w. Carlo Lepore (bass), Daniela Barcellona (sgr), Daniela Ciliberti (sgr), Andrea Concetti (sgr), Hans van Dijk (sgr), Remo Guerrini (sgr), Nadia Mantelli (sgr), Humberto Orellana (sgr), Claudia Pallini (sgr), Luigi Polsini (sgr), Rosa Ricciotti (sgr), Alberto Rota (sgr), Ludovica Scoppola (sgr), *(orch unknown)* Nuova Era ▲ NUO 7224

Marc, Alessandra (sop)
American Diva, w. New Zealand SO [cnd:Heinz Wallberg] Delos ▲ DE 3108 [DDD]
Beethoven, L. van:Sym 9, "Choral Sym", w. I. Vermillion (mez), S. Jerusalem (ten), F. Struckmann (bar), D. Barenboim (cnd), Berlin State Opera Orch, Berlin State Opera Chorus Erato ▲ 94353-2
Honegger, A.:Le Roi David, w. Sylvie Sullé (mez), Laurence Dale (ten), D. Mesguich (nar), J.-C. Casadesus (cnd), Lille National Orch EMI Classics ▲ CDC 54793
Krenek, E.:Jonny spielt auf, w. M. Kraus (ten), H. Kruse (ten), K. St. Hill (ten), L. Zagrosek (cnd), Leipzig Gewandhaus Orch [G] London 2-▲ 436631-2 [DDD]
Strauss, R.:Friedenstag, w. R. Roloff (bass), R. Bass (cnd), Collegiate Orch, Collegiate Chorale [G] *(rec in concert at Carnegie Hall, 11/19/89)* Koch International Classics ▲ KIC 7111-2 [DDD]
Verdi, G.:Requiem Mass, w. W. Meier (mez), P. Domingo (ten), F. Furlanetto (bass), D. Barenboim (cnd), Chicago SO, Chicago Sym Chorus Erato 2-▲ 96357-2
Wagner, R.:Lohengrin (sels), w. G. Schwarz (cnd), Seattle SO—Elsa's Dream (Einsam in trüben Tagen), Act I [G] *(rec Feb. 19-20, 1992)* Delos ▲ DE 3120 [DDD]
Zemlinsky, A. von:Lyric Sym, w. Hakan Hagegard (bar), R. Chailly (cnd), Royal Concertgebouw Orch London ("Entartete Musik" series) ▲ 443569-2 [DDD]

Marcella, Lou (ten)
Verdi, G.:La traviata (sels), w. Loretta di Franco (sop), Joan Sutherland (sop), Frederica von Stade (mez), Leo Goeke (ten), Luciano Pavarotti (ten), Gene Boucher (bar), Raymond Gibbs (bar), Sherrill Milnes (bar), Louis Sgarro (bar), John Trehy (bar) Budget ("The Greatest Voice in Opera" series) ▲ SYP 112

Marchand, Jean (nar)
Normandeau, R.:Petit Prince, w. Michel Dumont (nar—Aviator), Martin Pensa (nar—Little Prince), Christine Séguin (nar—Rose), Jean Marchand (nar—King), Luc Durand (nar—Conceited Man), Gilles Dupuis (nar—Drunkard), Guy Nadon (nar—Businessman), Jacques Languirand (nar—Lamplighter), Pierre Bourgault (nar—Geographer), Cynthia Dubois (nar—Snake), Monique Giroux (nar—Flower), Françoise Davoine (nar—Rose Garden), Jean-Louis Millette (nar—Fox), Gérard Poirier (nar—Railway Switchman), Claude Préfontaine (nar—Water Pill Salesman) *(rec Montreal, Aug 1994)* CBC 2-▲ 1091 [DDD]
Stravinsky, I.:L'Histoire du soldat, w. V. Davy (nar), J.-L. Millette (nar—Devil), J. Marchand (nar—soldier), A. Robert (cnd), Chambristes de Montreal CBC ("Musica Viva" series) ▲ MVCD 1049 [DDD]

Marchiandi, Angelo (ten)
Mussorgsky, M.:Khovanshchina, w. Mietta Sighele (sop—Emma), Elena Souliotis (sop—Susanna), Fiorenza Cossotto (mez—Marfa), Herbert Handt (ten—Scribe), Veriano Luchetti (ten—Prince Andrey Khovansky), Ludovic Spiess (ten—Prince Vasily Golitsin), Claudio Strudthoff (ten—Streshnev), Angelo Marchiandi (bar—Kuz'ka), Teodoro Rovetta (bar—1st Strel'tsi), Siegmund Nimsgern (b-bar—Shaklovity), Cesare Siepi (b-bar—Dosifey), Carlo del Bosco (bass—2nd Strel'tsi), Ubaldo Carosi (bass—Varsonofiev), Nicolai Ghiaurov (bass—Prince Ivan Khovnasky), Giovanni Sciarpeletti (bass—Pastor), B. Leskovich (cnd), Rome RAI SO, Rome RAI Chorus—also includes bonus Act V [w Boris Christoff] (Rome, 1958) *(rec Rome, 1973)* Bella Voce 3-▲ BLV 107.402 [AAD]
Verdi, G.:Stiffelio, w. A. Gulin (sop—Lina), M. del Monaco (ten—Stiffelio), A. Marchiandi (ten—Raffaele), G. Fioravanti (bar—Stankar), J. Hecht (bass—Jorg), O. de Fabritiis (cnd), Naples Teatro San Carlo Orch, Naples Teatro San Carlo Chorus *(rec Dec. 26, 1972)* Standing Room Only 2-▲ SRO 169-2

Marcks, Fritz (sgr)
Schoeck, O.:Das Schloss Dürande (sels), w. Maria Cebotari (sop—Gabriele), Marta Fuchs (sop—Gräfin Morvaille), Brigitte Fassbaender (mez—Renald Willi Domgraf), Rut Berglund (cta—Priorin), Peter Anders (ten—Armand), Benno Arnold (ten—Jäger), Josef Greindl (bass—Nicole), Hans Wrana (bass—Jäger), Vasso Argyris (sgr—Volksredner), Otto Hüsch (sgr—Wildhüter), Leo Laschet (sgr—Jäger), Fritz Marcks (sgr—Jäger), Felix Schneider (sgr—Jäger), R. Heger (cnd)—Text; Ich kann es nicht glauben [from Act 1]; Text; Heil dir, du Feuerquelle [from Act 2]; Text; Gesucht und nicht gefunden [from Act 3]; Text; Der Jäger ist frei! [Act 3 Finale]; Text; Sie kommen mit Flinten und Stangen [Act 4]; Text; Du Narr des vermeintlichen Rechts [Act 4 finale]; Text *(rec live, Apr 1943)* Jecklin ▲ JD 692

Marconi, Francesco (ten)
The World of Singing, Vol. 3:The Italian School, Part 1:The Italian Tenors Before World War I (1902–13), w. Antonio Aramburo (ten), Alessandro Bonci (ten), Giuseppe Borgatti (ten), Enrico Caruso (ten), Edoardo Garbin (ten), Fiorello Giraud (ten), Fernando de Lucia (ten), Giovanni Battista de Negri (ten), Antonio Paoli (ten), Francesco T Enterprise ("Vocal Archives" series) 3-▲ ENT VA 2104

Marcoulescou-Stern, Yolanda (sop)
Art Songs by American Composers, w. (sop), Katja Phillabaum (pno) Gasparo ▲ GSCD 287
French Art Songs, w. Katja Phillabaum (pno) Gasparo ▲ GSCD 293

Marcoux, Vanni (bar)
Vanni Marcoux Pearl ▲ PEA 9912

Mardones, José (bass)
The Great Spanish Bass *(rec 1910–30)* Pearl ▲ PEA 9127 [ADD]

Maréchal, Jaqueline (sgr)
Nivers, G.G.:Motets, w. Fanjat (sop), J. Nicolas (sop), Boraly (sgr), Malardenti (sgr), Houbart (org)—Motet a la Sainte Vierge pour le temps de Paques; Motet pour L'Élévation; Motet pour le Saint Sacrament; Motet du temps de carême pour le Saint Sacrement; Motet du temps de Noël pour le Saint Sacrement; Motet final du tout office pour le Roy [L] Pierre Verany ▲ PV.791101 [DDD]

Maresch, Jacques (ten)
Liszt, F.:Requiem, w. Daniel Galvez-Vallejo (ten), Lionel Peintre (bar), Bertrand Bontoux (bass), Francois-Henri Houbart (org), Y. Parmentier (cnd), Republican Guard Brass & Percussion, French Army Chorus Adès ▲ ADE 203032

Margiono, Charlotte (sop)
Beethoven, L. van:Ah, perfido!, w. J. E. Gardiner (cnd), Orch Révolutionnaire et Romantique, Monteverdi Choir London Archiv ▲ 435391-2 [DDD]
Beethoven, L. van:Mass, Op. 86, w. C. Robbin (mez), W. Kendall (ten), A. Miles (bass), J. E. Gardiner (cnd), Orch Révolutionnaire et Romantique, Monteverdi Choir London [period instrs] Archiv ▲ 435391-2 [DDD]
Beethoven, L. van:Missa Solemnis, w. C. Robbin (mez), W. Kendall (ten), A. Miles (bass), J. E. Gardiner (cnd), English Baroque Soloists, Monteverdi Choir London [L] Archiv ▲ 429779-2 [DDD] ▯ 429779-5
Brahms, J.:Ein Deutsches Requiem, w. R. Gilfry (bar), J. E. Gardiner (cnd), Orch Révolutionnaire et Romantique, Monteverdi Choir London [period instrs] Philips ▲ 432140-2 [DDD] ▯ 432140-5
Mozart, W.A.:Ave verum corpus, w. Barbara Bonney (sop), Sylvia McNair (sop), Elisabeth von Magnus (cta), Christoph Pregardien (ten), Thomas Hampson (bass), N. Harnoncourt (cnd), Vienna Concentus Musicus, Arnold Schoenberg Choir Teldec ▲ 98928 2
Mozart, W.A.:Così fan tutte (sels), w. van der Walt (sop), D. Ziegler (mez), G. Cachemaille (bar), N. Harnoncourt (cnd), Royal Concertgebouw Orch—sels. Teldec ▲ 9031-76455-2
Mozart, W.A.:Don Giovanni, w. Charlotte Margiono (sop—Donna Elvira), Luba Organosova (sop—Donna Anna), Eirian James (mez—Zerlina), Julian Clarkson (alt—Masetto), Christoph Prégardien (ten—Don Ottavio), Rodney Gilfry (bar—Don Giovanni), Ildebrando d'Arcangelo (bass—Leporello), Andrea Silvestrelli (bass—Il Commendatore), J. E. Gardiner (cnd), English Baroque Soloists, Monteverdi Choir London Deutsche Grammophon ("4D Audio" series) 3-▲ 445870-2
Mozart, W.A.:Finta giardiniera, w. E. Gruberova (sop), M. Bacelli (sop), D. Upshaw (sop), U. Heilmann (ten), A. Scharinger (bass), N. Harnoncourt (cnd), Vienna Concentus Musicus Teldec 3-▲ 72309-2
Mozart, W.A.:Grabmusik, w. Barbara Bonney (sop), Sylvia McNair (sop), Elisabeth von Magnus (cta), Christoph Pregardien (ten), Thomas Hampson (bass), N. Harnoncourt (cnd), Vienna Concentus Musicus, Arnold Schoenberg Choir Teldec ("Das alte Werk" series) ▲ 98928-2
Mozart, W.A.:Nozze di Figaro, w. B. Bonney (sop), I. Rey (sop), A. Murray (mez, P.-L. Lang (mez), P. Langridge (ten), C. Späth (ten), T. Hampson (bar), K. Moll (bass), A. Scharinger (bass), K. Langan (bass), N. Harnoncourt (cnd), Royal Concertgebouw Orch, Netherlands Opera Chorus *(rec Amsterdam, May 1993)* Teldec 3-▲ 90861-2 [DDD]
Mozart, W.A.:Regina coeli, K.108, w. N. Harnoncourt (cnd), Vienna Concentus Musicus, Arnold Schoenberg Choir *(rec Casino Zögernitz, Vienna, Dec. 1991)* Teldec ("Das alte Werke" series) ▲ 96147-2 [DDD]
Mozart, W.A.:Regina coeli, K.127, w. Barbara Bonney (sop), Sylvia McNair (sop), Elisabeth von Magnus (cta), Christoph Pregardien (ten), Thomas Hampson (bass), N. Harnoncourt (cnd), Vienna Concentus Musicus, Arnold Schoenberg Choir Teldec ("Das alte Werk" series) ▲ 98928 2

Margison, Richard (ten)
Rossini, G.:Mosè in Egitto (sels), w. Wendy Nielsen (sop—Elcia), Anita Krause (mez—Amenosi), Richard Margison (ten—Aronne), Gary Relyea (b-bar—Mosè), R. Bradshaw (cnd), Canadian Opera Company Orch, Canadian Opera Company Chorus—Scena, Coro & Preghiera [Dal tuo stellato soglio] *(rec George Weston Recital Hall, Ford Centre for the Performing Arts, North York, Ontario, Dec 20–23, 1994)* CBC ("SM 5000" series) ▲ SM5 5148 [DDD]
Verdi, G.:Alzira (sels), w. Stephen McClare (ten—Otumbo), Richard Margison (ten—Zamoro), Gary Relyea (b-bar—Alvaro), R. Bradshaw (cnd), Canadian Opera Company Orch, Canadian Opera Company Chorus—Il prigioniero [prologue] *(rec George Weston Recital Hall, Ford Centre for the Performing Arts, North York, Ontario, Dec 20–23, 1994)* CBC ("SM 5000" series) ▲ SM5 5148 [DDD]
Verdi, G.:Ernani (sels), w. Richard Margison (ten—Ernani), Gary Relyea (b-bar—Don Silva), R. Bradshaw (cnd), Canadian Opera Company Orch, Canadian Opera Company Chorus—Conspiracy [An alliance; Let the Lion of Castile Rise Again] *(rec George Weston Recital Hall, Ford Centre for the Performing Arts, North York, Ontario, Dec 20–23, 1994)* CBC ("SM 5000" series) ▲ SM5 5148 [DDD]
Verdi, G.:Inno delle nazioni, w. Richard Margison (ten—Bardo), R. Bradshaw (cnd), Canadian Opera Company Orch, Canadian Opera Company Chorus *(rec George Weston Recital Hall, Ford Centre for the Performing Arts, North York, Ontario, Dec 20–23, 1994)* CBC ("SM 5000" series) ▲ SM5 5148 [DDD]

Margita, Štefan (ten)
Janáček, L.:Fate, w. Lívia Ághová (sop—Míla), Ludmila Nováková (sop—Frl. Stuhlá/Součková), Marta Beňačková (cta—Mílas Mother), Štefan Margita (ten—Dr. Suda/Hrázda), Peter Straka (ten—Živný), Ivan Kusnjer (bar—Konečný/Verva), Peter Mikuláš (bass—Lhotský), G. Albrecht (cnd), Czech PO, Prague Chamber Choir *(rec 1995)* Orfeo ▲ 384 951 [DDD]
Mysliveček, J.:Belerofonte, w. C. Lindsleyová (sop), G. Mayová (sop), K. Lakiová (sop), D. Ahlstedt (ten), R. Gimenéz (ten), Z. Peskó (cnd), Prague CO, Czech Phil Chorus [I] *(rec 1987)* Supraphon 3-▲ 11 0006-2 [DDD]

Marherr-Wagner, Elfriede (mez)
Wagner, R.:Die Meistersinger von Nürnberg (sels), w. R. Hutt (ten), K. Jöken (bar), F. Schorr (b-bar), E. List (bass), L. Schützendorf (sgr), L. Blech (cnd), Berlin State Opera Orch, Berlin State Opera Chorus—Act 1:Hilf Gott! Will ich denn Schuster sein?; Das schöne Fest, Johannistag; Act 2:Johannistag! Johannistag!; Hab' ich heut' Singstund'?; Jerum! Jerum!; Act 3:Gleich, Meister! Hier!; Grüss' Gott, mein Evchen...Weilten die Stern' im lieblichen Tanz...O Sachs! Mein Freund!; Sankt Krispin, lobet ihn!; Silentium!...Wach' auf!; Verachtet mir die Meister nicht [G] *(rec Staatsoper unter den Linden, 5/22/28)* Pearl ▲ PEA 9340 (m) [AAD]
Wagner, R.:Tristan und Isolde (sels), w. F. Leider (sop), L. Melchior (ten), L. Blech (cnd), A. Coates (cnd), J. Barbirolli (cnd), Berlin State Opera Orch, London SO—Act 1 *(Doch nun von Tristan [Leider, Marherr-Wagner])*, Act 2 *(Isolde! Geliebter; O sink hernieder [Leider, Melchior])*, Act 3 *(Mild und leise [Leider])* [G] *(rec late 1920s for HMV)* Legato Classics 2-▲ LCD 146-2 (m) [ADD]

Mari (bar)
Scarlatti, D.:La Dirindina, w. K. Gamberucci (sop), G. Gatti (ten), F. Maestri (cnd), *(ensemble unknown)* [I] *(rec live, 1985)* Bongiovanni ▲ GB 2026 [DDD]

Mariacineanu, Mihaela (mez)
Verdi, G.:La forza del destino, w. Maria Nistor-Slatinaru (sop—Donna Leonora), Mihaela Mariacineanu (mez—Curra), Zenaida Pally (mez—Preziosilla), Ludovic Speiss (ten—Don Alvaro), Ion Stoian (ten—Trabucco), Nicolae Herlea (bar—Don Carlo), Nicolae Florei (bass—Padre Guardiano) Constantin Gabor (bass—Fra Melitone), Dan Musetescu (bass—An Alcalde), Mihai Panghe (bass—Marquis of Calatrava), C. Litvin (cnd), Romanian Radio-TV Orch, Romanian Radio-TV Chorus *(rec Jan 1970)* Vox Box 3-▲ CD3X 3038

Marimpietri, Lydia (sop)
Bach, J.S.:Magnificat, BWV 243, w. N. Panni (sop), A. Reynolds (mez), P. Munteanu (ten), B. Carmeli (bass), H. Scherchen (cnd), Milan RAI SO, Milan RAI Chorus [L] *(rec live, Apr 5, 1963)* Memories ▲ HR 4160 (m) [ADD]
Catalani, A.:La Wally, w. R. Tebaldi (sop), M. del Monaco (ten), P. Cappuccilli (bar), Justino Diaz (bass), F. Cleva (cnd), Monte Carlo Opera Orch, Turin Lyric Chorus [I] London 2-▲ 425417-2 [ADD]
Nono, L.:Epitaffio 1, w. M. Boriello (bar), B. Maderna (cnd), Rome RAI Orch, Rome RAI Chorus *(rec live, Rome 1/28/61)* Arkadia ▲ 027 [ADD]
Zandonai, R.:Francesca da Rimini, w. Lydia Marimpietri (sop—Biancofiore), Magda Olivero (sop—Francesca), Pinuccia Perotti (sop—Samaritana), Edda Vincenzi (sop—Garsenda), Gabriella Carturan (mez—Smaragdi), Biancamaria Casoni (mez—Altichiara), Anna Maria Rota (cta—Donella), Athos Cesarini (ten—Archer), Angelo Mercuriali (ten—Ser Toldo Berardengo), Mario del Monaco (ten—Paolo), Piero de Palma (ten—Malatestino), Rinaldo Pelizzoni (ten—Prisoner), Gianpiero Malaspina (bar—Gianciotto), Dino Mantovani (bar—Jester), Enrico Campi (bass—Ostasio), Giuseppe Morresi (bass—Tower warden), G. Gavazzeni (cnd), La Scala Orch, La Scala Chorus *(rec La Scala Theatre, Milan, June 4, 1959)* Legato Classics 2-▲ LCD 186-2

Marin-Degor, Sophie (sop)
Gluck, C.W.:La Recontre imprévue, w. C. Le Coz (sop), L. Dawson (sop), C. Dubosc (sop), G. Fletcher (sgr), F. Dudziak (ten), G. de Mey (ten), J.-L. Viala (ten), G. Cachémaille (bar), J.-P. Lafont (bass), J. E. Gardiner (cnd), Paris Lyon Opera Orch, Paris Lyon Opera Chorus [F] Erato 2-▲ 2292-45516-2 [DDD]
Mozart, W.A.:Così fan tutte, w. Sophie Marin-Degor (sop—Despina), Laura Polverelli (mez—Dorabella), Sophie Fournier (sgr—Fiordiligi), Nicolas Revenq (bar—Guglielmo), Patrick Donnelly (bass—Don Alfonso), Simon Edwards (sgr—Ferrando), J. Malgoire (cnd), La Grande Écurie et la Chambre du Roy Astrée 8-▲ E 8606
Mozart, W.A.:Don Giovanni, w. Danielle Borst (sop—Donna Anna), Véronique Gens (sop—Donna Elvira), Sophie Marin-Degor (sop—Zerlina), Huub Claessens (bar—Leporello), Nicolas Revenq (bar—Don Giovanni), Patrick Donnelly (bass—Commendatore), Simon Edwards (sgr—Don Ottavio), J. Malgoire (cnd), La Grande Écurie et la Chambre du Roy Astrée 8-▲ E 8606
Mozart, W.A.:Nozze di Figaro, w. Danielle Borst (sop—Countess Almaviva), Claudine Le Coz (sop—Marcellina), Sophie Marin-Degor (sop—Susanna), Laura Polverelli (mez—Cherubino), Valérie Lecoq (sgr—Barberina), Philippe Cantor (ten—Antonio), Stuart Patterson (ten—Dons Basile & Curzio), Huub Claessens (bar—Figaro), Nicolas Revenq (bar—Count Almaviva), Patrick Donnelly (bass—Bartolo), J. Malgoire (cnd), La Grande Écurie et la Chambre du Roy Astrée 8-▲ E 8606
Purcell, H.:Dido & Aeneas, w. Véronique Gens (sop—Dido), Sophie Marin-Degor (sop—Belinda), Sophie Daneman (sop—2nd woman/1st witch), Gaëlle Mechaly (sop—2nd witch), Claire Brua (mez—Sorceress), Steve Dugardin (alt—Chorus), Jean-Paul Fouchécourt (ten—Spirit/Sailor), Nathan Berg (b-bar—Aeneas), Jonathan Arnold (bass—Chorus), William Christie (hpd), W. Christie (cnd), Les Arts Florissants *(rec Massy Opera Theatre, Nov. 8–11, 1994)* Erato ▲ 98477-2 [DDD]

Marinescu, Lucian (bar)
Puccini, G.:La Bohème, w. Elvira Cirje-Druica (sop—Musetta), Eugenia Moldoveanu (sop—Mimi), Andrei Borsos (ten—Parpignol), Constantin Gabor (ten—Alcindoro), Ludovic Spiess (ten—Rodolfo), Lucian Marinescu (bar—Schaunard), David Ohanesian (bar—Marcello), Pompei Harasteanu (bass—Benoit), Dan Zancu (bass—Colline), C. Petrovici (cnd), Romanian Opera Orch, Romanian Opera Chorus *(rec 1982)* Vox Box 2-▲ CDX 5156

Marini, Luigi (ten)
Puccini, G.:La Bohème, w. Luba Mirella (sop—Musetta), Rosetta Pampanini (sop—Mimi), Luigi Marini (ten—Rodolfo), Giuseppe Nessi (ten—Alcindoro), Aristide Baracchi (bar—Schaunard), Gino Vanelli (bar—Marcello), Salvatore Baccaloni (bass—Benoit), Tancredi Pasero (bass—Colline), L. Molajoli (cnd), La Scala Orch, La Scala Chorus Bongiovanni 2-▲ 1125/26 [ADD]

Marinov, Pali (bass)
Stravinsky, I.:Les Noces, w. M. Quercia (sop), S. Cooper (mez), P. Capelle (ten), Vieuxtemps (pno), R. Conil (pno), Arzoumanian (pno), Raynaut (pno), R. Hayrabedian (cnd), Strasbourg Percussion Ensemble, Contemporary Choir Pierre Verany ▲ PV 787032 [DDD]

Mariotti, Alfredo (bass)
Mozart, W.A.:Nozze di Figaro, w. S. Jurinac (sop), T. Stratas (sop), T. Berganza (mez), N. Condò (mez), A. Lazzari (ten), S. Bruscantini (bar), M. Petri (bass), G. Tadeo (bass), Z. Mehta (cnd), *(orch unknown)* *(rec 1968)* Great Opera Performances 3-▲ GOP 712
Puccini, G.:La Bohème, w. Katia Ricciarelli (sop), Francisco Araiza (ten), Angelo Casertano (ten), Stefano Antonucci (bar), Claudio Giombi (bar), Paata Burchuladze (bass), Alberto Noli (bass), Andrea Piccinni (bass), Lauren Broglia (sgr), A. Guadagno (cnd), Arena di Verona Orch, Limburg Cathedral Boys' Chorus Koch Schwann 2-▲ SCH 315922
Puccini, G.:Manon Lescaut, w. R. Kabaivanska (sop—Manon), R. Pallini (mez—Singer), P. Domingo (ten—des Grieux), E. Lorenzi (ten—Edmondo), F. Ricciardi (ten—Dancing Master), M. D'Anna (bar—Lescaut), A. Mariotti (bass—Geronte), F. Federici (bass—Innkeeper) Golden Age of Opera 2-▲ GAO 162/63 [ADD]
Rossini, G.:La Cenerentola, w. B. Casoni (mez), U. Benelli (ten), S. Bruscantini (bar), P. Bellugi (cnd), Berlin RSO, Berlin Radio Chorus [I] Acanta 2-▲ CD 43271 [DDD]
Rossini, G.:L'italiana in Algeri, w. L. V. Terrani (mez), U. Benelli (ten), S. Bruscantini (bar), G. Bertini (cnd), Dresden State Orch [I] Acanta 2-▲ CD 42308 [DDD]

Markert, Annette (cta)
Eisler, H.:Deutsche Sinfonie, w. Hendrikje Wangemann (sop), Matthias Görne (bar), Peter Lika (bass), Gert Gütschow (speaker), Volker Schwarz (speaker), L. Zagrosek (cnd), Leipzig Gewandhaus Orch, Ernst Senff Chorus *(rec Gewandhaus, Leipzig, May 1995)* London ("Entartet Musik" series) ▲ 448389-2 [DDD]
Mendelssohn, F.:St. Paul, w. Melanie Diener (sop), James Taylor (ten), Matthias Görne (bass), P. Herreweghe (cnd), Champs Élysées Theater Orch, Chapelle Royale Choir, Collegium Vocale *(rec Stravinsky Auditorium, Montreaux)* Harmonia Mundi France 2-▲ HMC 901584.85

Markert, Annette (cta) (cont.)
Saint-Saëns, C.:Oratorio de Noël, w. Ute Selbig (sop), Elisabeth Wilke (mez), Armin Ude (ten), Egbert Junghans (bar), Jutta Zoff (hp), Michael-Christfield Winkler (org), M. Flämig (cnd), Dresden PO, Dresden Kreuz Choir *(rec Dresden, Mar & Apr 1987)* Capriccio ▲ 10216 [DDD]
Strauss, R.:Salome, w. J. Norman (sop), K. Witt (mez), W. Raffeiner (ten), R. Leech (ten), J. Morris (bass), S. Ozawa (cnd), Dresden Staatskapelle Philips 2-▲ 432153-2
Telemann, G.P.:Brockes Passion, w. M. Zádori (sop), M. Klietmann (ten), G. De Mey (ten), I. Gáti (bar), N. McGegan (cnd), Capella Savaria, Hallé State Chorus [period instrs] Hungaroton 3-▲ HCD 31130/32 [DDD]
Vivaldi, A.:Juditha triumphans devicta Holofernes barbarie, w. M. Zádori (sop), J. Németh (mez), K. Gémes (mez), G. Banditelli (cta), N. McGegan (cnd), Capella Savaria, Savaria Vocal Ensemble [L] Hungaroton 2-▲ HCD 31063/64 [DDD]

Markley, Richard (ten)
Puccini, G.:Madama Butterfly, w. Maria Spacagna (sop), Sharon Grahm (mez), Vivica Genaux (mez), Richard di Renzi (ten), Erich Parce (bar), James Butler (bass), C. Rosenkrans (cnd), Hungarian State Opera Orch, Anikó Katona (cnd), Hungarian State Opera Chorus—3 versions *(rec Italian Institute, Budapest, Sept 5-21, 1995)* Vox Classics 4-▲ VOX4 7525 [DDD]

Markov, Stefan (bass)
Orthodox Wedding Ceremony & New Year Service, w. M. Popsavov (cnd), Hristo Kamenov (ten) Gega ▲ GD 142 [DDD]
Orthodox Wedding Ceremony & New Year's Celebrations, w. Hristo Kamenov (ten), Bulgarian Mixed Choir [cnd:Miroslav Popsavov] *(rec 1993)* Jade ▲ JAD C 108

Markova, Emilia (sop)
Beethoven, L. van:Mass, Op. 86, w. L. Parachikova (cta), C. Kamenev (ten), I. Petrov (bass), C. Iliev (cnd), Sofia State PO, Sofia State Chorus [L] Musique d'Abord ▲ HMA 190109 [AAD]

Markova, Jirina (sop)
Zemlinsky, A. von:Lyric Sym, w. Ivan Kusnjer (bar), V. Válek (cnd), Prague RSO *(rec live, Prague, 1993)* Praga ▲ PR 250092

Màrkovs, Janis (bass)
Mozart, W.A.:Litaniae Lauretanae, K.195, w. Dita Paēgle (sop), Antra Bìgaca (mez), Martins Klisans (ten), S. Klava (cnd), Riga Musicians, Riga Radio Chorus Audiophile Classics ▲ 101.048 [DDD]
Mozart, W.A.:Regina coeli, K.276, w. Dita Paēgle (sop), Antra Bìgaca (mez), Martins Klisans (ten), S. Klava (cnd), Riga Musicians, Riga Radio Chorus Audiophile Classics ▲ 101.048 [DDD]

Markus, Karl (ten)
Draeseke, F.:Mysterium:Christus, w. C. Bischoff (sop), A. Vogel (sop), E. Dersen (alt), H.J. Ritzerfeld (ten), P. Langshaw (bar), B. Kämpff (bass), J. Sonnenschmidt (org), U.-R. Follert (cnd), Breslau State PO, Evangelical Boys' Choir Palatine, Heilbronn Vocal Ensemble, Palatine Kurrende Bayer 5-▲ 100175/79
Marschner, H.A.:Hans Heiling, w. M. Hajóssyová (sop), E. Seniglova (sop), M. Eklöf (mez), T. Mohr (bar), L. Neshyba (bass), E. Körner (cnd), Slovak PO, Slovak Phil Chorus [G] Marco Polo ("Opera Rara" series) 2-▲ 8.223306/07 [DDD]
Mozart, W.A.:Missa brevis, K.65, w. C. Malone (sop), G. Schreckenbach (mez), W. Grönroos (bar), R. Bader (cnd), Berlin RSO, St. Hedwig's Cathedral Choir [L] Koch Schwann ▲ SCH 313021 [ADD/DDD]
Schubert, Ferdinand:Requiem, w. D. Degos (trb), R. Soyer (bass), J. Galard (org), J.-P. Lore (cnd), French Oratorio Orch, J.-P. Lore Vocal Ensemble, Petits Chanteurs de Notre Dame de la Joie *(rec Nov. 9-11, 1980 & Jan. 25)* Esoldun ▲ MOS 1003 [ADD]
Schubert, Franz:Requiem, w. D. Degos (trb), R. Soyer (bass), J. Galard (org), J.-P. Lore (cnd), French Oratorio Orch, J.-P. Lore Vocal Ensemble, Petits Chanteurs de Notre Dame de la Joie *(rec Nov. 9-11, 1980 & Jan. 25)* Esoldun ▲ MOS 1003 [ADD]

Markvart, Jan (bar)
Dvořák, A.:Armida, w. Joanna Borowska (sop—Armida), Monika Brychtová (sgr—Siren), Wieslaw Ochman (ten—Rinald), Richard Sporka (ten—Dudo), Jan Markvart (bar—Sven), Pavel Daniluk (bass—King), George Fortune (bass—Ismen), Zdenek Harvánek (bass—Ubald), Miloslav Podskalský (bass—Peter), Milan Bürger (sgr—Gernand), Roman Janál (sgr—Muezzin/Hlasatel), Vratislav Kříz (sgr—Gottfried), Vladimír Nacházel (sgr—Roger), G. Albrecht (cnd), Czech PO, Prague Chamber Choir *(rec 1995)* Orfeo 2-▲ 404962 [DDD]
Dvořák, A.:The Spectre's Bride, Op. 69, w. Jitka Sobehartova (sop), Jiri Kubik (ten), Bratislava Philharmonic Chorus, P. Tiboris (cnd), Bohuslav Martinů PO [Cz] *(rec Nov. 26-30, 1993)* Elysium ▲ GRK 700 [DDD]

Maros, Ilona (sop)
Maros, M.:Music of, w. John-Edward Kelly (sax), Kangas, Maros (cnd), Budapest SO, Ostrobothnian CO, Prague Radio SO, Marosensemble—Sym No. 1; 4 Songs [from Gitanjali]; Sinf concertante [Sym No. 3]; Con for A Sax & Orch Phono Suecia ▲ PHN 23 [DDD]

Márová, Libuše (mez)
Fibich, Z.:The Bride of Messina, w. G. Benackova (sop), I. Zidek (ten), F. Jílek (cnd), Prague National Theater Orch, Prague National Theater Chorus Supraphon ▲ SUP 111492 [ADD]
Janácek, L.:The Excursions of Mr. Brouček, w. Janá Jonaová (sop), Vilém Přibyl (ten), Richard Novák (bass), Czech PO, Czech Phil Chorus Supraphon 2-▲ SUP 112153 [AAD]
Smetana, B.:The Kiss, w. Eva Deplotová (sop), Leo Marian Vodička (ten), F. Vajnar (cnd), Brno Janáček Opera Orch, Brno Janáček Opera Chorus Supraphon 2-▲ SUP 112180 [AAD]

Mars, Jacques (bar)
Bizet, G.:Les Pêcheurs de perles, w. J. Micheau (sop), N. Gedda (ten), E. Blanc (bar), P. Dervaux (cnd), Paris Opéra-Comique Orch, Paris Opéra-Comique Chorus [F] EMI Classics ("Studio" series) 2-▲ CDMB 69704 [ADD]
Charpentier, M.-A.:Magnificat, w. Martha Angelici (sop), Jocelyn Chamonin (sop), André Mallabrera (ct), Rémy Corazza (ten), Georges Abdoun (bar), Maurice André (tpt), Marie-Claire Alain (org), L. Martini (cnd), Jean-François Paillard CO, French Jeunesses Musicales Chorale *(rec Paris, Mar 15, 1963)* Vanguard Classics ▲ OVC 8075 [ADD]
Charpentier, M.-A.:Te Deum, H. 146, w. Martha Angelici (sop), Jocelyn Chamonin (sop), André Mallabrera (ct), Rémy Corazza (ten), Georges Abdoun (bar), Maurice André (tpt), Marie-Claire Alain (org), L. Martini (cnd), Jean-François Paillard CO, French Jeunesses Musicales Chorale *(rec Paris, Mar 15, 1963)* Vanguard Classics ▲ OVC 8075 [ADD]
Massenet, J.:Werther, w. Mady Mesplé (sop—Sophie), Rita Gorr (mez—Charlotte), Robert Andreozzi (ten—Schmidt), Albert Lance (ten—Werther), Gabriel Bacquier (bar—Albert), Julien Giovannetti (bar—Le Bailli), Jacques Mars (bar—Johann), J. Etcheverry (cnd), *(orch unknown)* Adès 2-▲ ADE 140832 [AAD]

Marsch, Jeannie (voc)
Chris Mann & the Impediments, w. Chris Mann (voc), Carolyn Connors (voc), Rik Rue (voc) O.O. Discs ▲ CD 21 [ADD]

Marschall, Werner (ten)
Schütz, H.:Schwannengesang, w. J. Kowalski (alt), D. Knothe (cnd), Berlin Soloists, Dreseden Capella Sagittariana, Berlin Radio Children's Choir Berlin Classics 2-▲ BER 1071 [DDD]

Marsee, Susanne (mez)
Donizetti, G.:Anna Bolena, w. R. Scotto (sop—Anna Bolena), K. Ciesinski (mez—Smeton), S. Marsee (mez—Giovanna Seymour), S. Kolk (ten—Riccardo Percy), S. Ramey (bass—Enrico VIII), J. Rudel (cnd), Philadelphia Opera Orch *(rec live, Dec. 16, 1975)* Legato Classics 2-▲ LCD 175 [ADD]
Donizetti, G.:Roberto Devereux, w. M. Caballé (sop), J. Carreras (ten), V. Sardinero (bar), J. Rudel (cnd), *(orch & chorus unknown)* [I] *(rec live, France 1977)* HRE 2-▲ 1004-2 [ADD]
Donizetti, G.:Roberto Devereux, w. B. Sills (sop), P. Domingo (ten), L. Quilico (bar), J. Rudel (cnd), New York City Opera Orch, New York City Opera Chorus *(rec 1970)* Melodram ▲ MLO 270107 [ADD]
Donizetti, G.:Roberto Devereux (sels), w. M. Caballé (sop), J. Carreras (ten), V. Sardinero (bar), J. Rudel (cnd), *(orch & chorus unknown)* [I] *(rec live, 1977)* Legato Classics ▲ LCD 108-1 [AAD]

Marsh, Calvin (bar)
Rossini, G.:Il barbiere di Siviglia, w. Roberta Peters (sop—Rosina), Margaret Roggero (mez—Berta), Cesare Valletti (ten—Count Almaviva), Calvin Marsh (bar—Fiorello/Sergeant), Robert Merrill (bar—Figaro), Fernando Corena (bass—Dr. Bartolo), Carlo Tomanelli (bass—Ambrogio), Giorgio Tozzi (bass—Don Basilio), E. Leinsdorf (cnd), Metropolitan Opera Orch, New York Metropolitan Opera Chorus *(rec Manhattan Center, New York, Sept 1-11, 1958)* RCA Living Stereo 3-▲ 09026-68552-2 [ADD]

Marshall (sop)
Gluck, C.W.:Orfeo ed Euridice, w. E. Gruberova (sop), A. Baltsa (mez), R. Muti (cnd), Philharmonia Orch, Ambrosian Opera Chorus Angel ("Studio" series) 2-▲ CDMB 63637 [DDD]

Marshall, Lois (sop)
Bach, J.S.:Arias, w. Maureen Forrester (alt), Richard Lewis (ten), Norman Farrow (b-bar), Oscar Shumsky (vn), Brian Priestman (cnd), *(chorus unknown)*—Arias Nos. 32, 42, 120a, 132, & 182; Duet from Cant. 205 Vox Box 2-▲ CDX 5127 [ADD]
Bach, J.S.:Cant 3, w. Maureen Forrester (alt), Richard Lewis (ten), Norman Farrow (b-bar), B. Priestman (cnd), *(orch unknown)*, *(chorus unknown)* Vox Box 2-▲ CDX 5127 [ADD]
Bach, J.S.:Mass in b, BWV 232, w. H. Töpper (mez), P. Pears (ten), K. Borg (bass), E. Jochum (cnd), Bavarian RSO, Bavarian Radio Chorus Philips 2-▲ 438739-2
Folksongs of the British Isles, w. Judy Loman (hp) *(rec 1976)* Marquis Classics ▲ MARD 102 [AAD]
Handel, Haydn & Mozart *(rec 1950s by EMI)* CBC Records ("Perspective" series) ▲ PSCD 2001 (m/s) [ADD]
Hindemith, P.:Das Marienleben, w. Roxolana Roslak (sop), Glenn Gould (pno) Sony Classical ("Glen Gould Edition" series) 2-▲ SM2K 52674
Monteverdi, C.:Vespro della Beata Vergine, w. F. Palmer (sop), P. Langridge (ten), K. Equiluz (ten), T. Hampson (bar), A. Korn (bass), N. Harnoncourt (cnd), Vienna Concentus Musicus, Hamburg Monteverdi Chorus, Vienna Boys' Chorus [L] Teldec 2-▲ 2292-42671-2
Mozart, W.A.:Arias, w. I. Hollweg (sop), L. Simoneau (ten), G. Unger (ten), G. Frick (bass), T. Beecham (cnd), Royal PO, Beecham Choral Society EMI Classics 2-▲ CDHB 63715
Mozart, W.A.:Entführung, w. I. Hollweg (sop), L. Simoneau (ten), G. Unger (ten), G. Frick (bass), T. Beecham (cnd), Royal PO, Beecham Choral Society EMI Classics 2-▲ CDHB 63715
Mozart, W.A.:Missa, K.317, w. A. Murray (mez), R. Covey-Crump (ten), D. Wilson-Johnson (bar), S. Cleobury (cnd), English CO, King's College Choir Cambridge [L] Argo ▲ 411904-2 [DDD]
Mozart, W.A.:Missa, K.427, w. F. Palmer (sop), A. Rolfe Johnson (ten), G. Howell (bass), N. Marriner (cnd), Academy of St. Martin in the Fields, Academy Chorus [L] Philips ▲ 420891-2 [ADD]
Mozart, W.A.:Missa solemnis, K.337, w. A. Murray (mez), R. Covey-Crump (ten), D. Wilson-Johnson (bar), S. Cleobury (cnd), English CO [L] Argo ▲ 411904-2 [DDD]
Schubert, Franz:Die Schöne Müllerin, w. Greta Kraus (pno) *(rec Hart House, Univ of Toronto, Ontario, Nov 1979)* CBC ("Perspective" series) ▲ PSCD 2010 [ADD]
Schubert, Franz:Winterreise, w. Anton Kuerti (pno) *(rec Hart House, Univ of Toronto, Ontario, Nov 1976)* CBC ("Perspective" series) ▲ PSCD 2011 [ADD]
Schubert, Franz:Winterreise, w. Anton Kuerti (pno) CBC ▲ CBC PSCD 2011 [ADD]
Strauss, R.:4 Last Songs, w. Roxolana Roslak (sop), Glenn Gould (pno)—Beim Schlafengehen Sony Classical ("Glen Gould Edition" series) 2-▲ SM2K 52674
Strauss, R.:Songs, w. Roxolana Roslak (sop), Glenn Gould (pno)—Songs for Orphelia, Op. 67/1-3 Sony Classical ("Glen Gould Edition" series) 2-▲ SM2K 52674

Marshall, Margaret (sop)
Bach, J.S.:Mass in b, BWV 232, w. J. Baker (mez), R. Tear (ten), S. Ramey (bass), N. Marriner (cnd), Academy of St. Martin in the Fields, *(chorus unknown)* [L] Philips 2-▲ 416415-2 [ADD]
Bach, J.S.:St. Matthew Passion, w. C. Watkinson (cta), K. Equiluz (ten), G. Faulstisch (bar), P. Huttenlocher (bar), R. Johnson (bar), M. Corboz (cnd), Lausanne CO, Lausanne Vocal Ensemble Erato 3-▲ 2292-45375-2 GX
Beethoven, L. van:Missa Solemnis, w. N. Merriman (mez), E. Conley (ten), J. Hines (bass), A. Toscanini (cnd), NBC SO, Robert Shaw Chorale *(rec 1953)* RCA Gold Seal ▲ 60272-2-RG [ADD] ■ 60272-4-RG
Elgar, E.:The Kingdom, w. F. Palmer (sop), Davies (ten), D. Wilson-Johnson (bar), R. Hickox (cnd), London SO, London Sym Chorus [E] Chandos 2-▲ CHAN 8788/89 [DDD]
Elgar, E.:The Light of Life, w. H. Watts (cta), J. Shirley-Quirk (bar), C. Groves (cnd), Royal Liverpool PO, Royal Liverpool Phil Choir EMI Classics ▲ CDM 64732
Elgar, E.:The Light of Life (sels), w. H. Watts (cta), J. Shirley-Quirk (bass), C. Groves (cnd), Royal Liverpool PO—Meditation EMI Classics ▲ CDM 64732
Handel, G.F.:Messiah, w. Saul Quirke (trb), Catherine Robbin (mez), Charles Brett (ct), Anthony Rolfe Johnson (ten), Robert Hale (b-bar), J. E. Gardiner (cnd), English Baroque Soloists, Monteverdi Choir London [E] Philips ▲ 412267-2 [DDD]
Handel, G.F.:Messiah, w. Saul Quirke (trb), Catherine Robbin (mez), Charles Brett (ct), Anthony Rolfe Johnson (ten), Robert Hale (b-bar), J. E. Gardiner (cnd), English Baroque Soloists, Monteverdi Choir London [E] Philips 3-▲ 411041-2 [DDD]
Haydn, J.:Die Schöpfung, w. Lucia Popp (sop), Vinson Cole (ten), Bernd Weikl (bar), Gwynne Howell (bass), R. Kubelik (cnd), Bavarian RSO, Bavarian Radio Chorus Orfeo 2-▲ 150852 [DDD] 2-■ 150852 (D)
Monteverdi, C.:Vespro della Beata Vergine, w. F. Palmer (sop), P. Langridge (ten), K. Equiluz (ten), T. Hampson (bar), A. Korn (bass), N. Harnoncourt (cnd), Vienna Concentus Musicus, Hamburg Monteverdi Chorus, Vienna Boys' Chorus Teldec 2-▲ 92629-2
Mozart, W.A.:Arias, w. Arleen Augér (sop), Kathleen Battle (sop), Irma Beilke (sop), Helena Braun (sop), Lisa Della Casa (sop), Maria Cebotari (sop), Ileana Cotrubas (sop), Helen Donath (sop), Mirella Freni (sop), Reri Grist (sop), Edita Gruberova (sop), Elisabeth Grümmer (sop), Hilde Güden (sop), Ingeborg Hallstein (sop), Luise Helletsgruber (sop), Gundula Janowitz (sop), Sena Jurinac (sop), Erika Köth (sop), Evelyn Lear (sop), Wilma Lipp (sop), Edith Mathis (sop), Jarmila Novotna (sop), Margherita Perras (sop), Lucia Popp (sop), Elisabeth Rethberg (sop), Anneliese Rothenberger (sop), Elisabeth Schumann (sop), Elisabeth Schwarzkopf (sop), Graziella Sciutti (sop), Irmgard Seefried (sop), Graziella Sciutti (sop), Julia Varady (sop), Agnes Baltsa (mez), Margit Bokor (mez), Brigitte Fassbaender (mez), Christa Ludwig (mez), Ann Murray (mez), Francisco Araiza (ten), Anton Dermota (ten), Helge Rosvaenge (ten), Rudolf Schock (ten), Peter Schreier (ten), Leopold Simoneau (ten), Eric Tappy (ten), Richard Tauber (ten), Gösta Winbergh (ten), Josef Witt (ten), Fritz Wunderlich (ten), Christian Boesch (bar), Willy Domgraf-Fassbaender (bar), Karl Dönch (bar), Dietrich Fischer-Dieskau (bar), Erich Kunz (bar), Eberhard Wächter (bar), Hans Hotter (b-bar), Paul Schöffler (b-bar), Cesare Siepi (b-bar), José Van Dam (b-bar), Walter Berry (bass), Geraint Evans (bass), Nicolai Ghiaurov (bass), Alexander Kipnis (bass), Richard Mayr (bass), Kurt Moll (bass), James Morris (bass), Ezio Pinza (bass), Martti Talvela (bass), Giorgio Tozzi (bass), Hans Duhan (sgr), Res Fischer (sgr), Marie Gerhart (sgr), *(various orchs & cnds)*—sels from Idomeneo, Die Entführung aus der Serail, Le nozze di Figaro, Don Giovanni, Così fan tutte, Die Zauberflöte & various arias Orfeo d'or ("Festspiel Dokumente" series) 5-▲ 408955
Pergolesi, G.B.:Stabat mater, w. L. Valentini-Terrani (mez), C. Abbado (cnd), London SO [L] Deutsche Grammophon ▲ 415103-2 [DDD]
Pergolesi, G.B.:Stabat mater, w. A. Hodgson (cta), G. Kehr (cnd), Mainz CO *(rec 1978)* Vox Box 2-▲ CDX 5081 [ADD]
Vivaldi, A.:Sacred Choral Music, w. J. Kowalski (ct), N. van der Meel (ten), V. Negri (cnd), Royal Concertgebouw CO—Deus tuorum militum, RV.612; Laudate pueri Dominum, RV.600; Sanctorum meritis, RV.620; Stabat mater, RV.621 [L] Philips ▲ 432091-2 [DDD]

Marstrand, Christine (sop)
Van De Vate, N.:An American Essay, w. L. Hovman (alt), O. Støvring Larsen (ten), S. Kawalla (cnd), Koszalin State PO, Chorus Soranus Vienna Modern Masters ▲ VMM 3025 [DDD]

Martens, Klaus (bass)
Charpentier, M.-A.:Motets for Double Choir, w. B. Schlick (sop), N. Zijlstra (sop), K. Wessel (alt), D. Visse (ct), H. van Berne (ten), C. Prégardien (ten), P. Kooy (bass), T. Koopman (cnd), Amsterdam Baroque Orch—Canticum pro pace; Josué; Mors Saulis et Jonathae; Praelium Michaelis; Quam dilecta; 3 Leçons de Ténèbres Erato (Musifrance) ▲ 2292-45822-2 ZA

Marti, Bernabé (ten)
Bellini, V.:Il pirata, w. M. Caballé (sop), F. Rafanelli (sop), Baratti, P. Cappuccilli (bar), R. Raimondi (bass), G. Gavazzeni (cnd), Rome Radio–TV Orch, Rome Radio–TV Chorus [I] *(rec Rome, 1973)* EMI Classics 2-▲ CDMB 64169
Puccini, G.:Madama Butterfly, w. Montserrat Caballé (sop—Cio-Cio-San), Carmen Rigai (mez—Suzuki), Bernabé Martí (ten—Pinkerton), Diego Monjo (ten—Goro), Juan Rico (ten—Yamadori), Manuel Ausensi (bar—Sharpless), Jose Lemar (bass—Bonze), Antonio Leval (bass—Imperial Commissioner), Alejandro Chiara (bass—Registrar), G. Rivoli (cnd), Madrid Radio–TV Orch, Madrid Radio–TV Chorus *(rec Madrid, June 12, 1968)* Legato Classics 2-▲ LCD 210-2 [ADD]

Martig-Müller, Barbara (sop)
Daetwyler, J.:Symphonie de la liberté, w. J. Daetwyler (cnd), Swiss-Italian Radio–TV Orch—[F] Grammont ▲ CTSP 15-2
Haydn, J.:Mass 14, "Harmoniemesse", w. Ria Bollen (alt), Adalbert Kraus (ten), Kurt Widmer (bass), Melitta Veits (org), D. Hellmann (cnd), Southwest German RSO Baden-Baden Calig ▲ CAL 50490

Martikke, S. (sop)
Strauss (II), Joh.:Wiener Blut, w. H. Papouschek (sop), E. Kales (sop), A. Dallapozza (ten), K. Ruzicka (ten), E. Kuchar (ten), W. Kandutsch (bar), K. Dönch (bar), O. Kolmann (bass), R. Bibl (cnd), Vienna Volksoper Orch, Vienna Volksoper Chorus Denon 2-▲ CO 8105 [DDD]

Martin (sop)
Argento, D.:Elizabethan Songs (6), w. A. Weisberg (cnd), *(ensemble unknown)* CRI ■ C 380
Wagner, R.:Der fliegende Holländer, w. A. Kollo (ten), N. Bailey (bar), M. Talvela (bass), G. Solti (cnd), Chicago SO, Chicago Sym Chorus [G] London 2-▲ 414551-2 [ADD]
Wagner, R.:Rienzi, der Letzte der Tribunen, w. S. Wennberg (sop), A. Kollo (ten), P. Schreier (ten), T. Adam (b-bar), H. Hollreiser (cnd), Dresden State Opera Orch, Dresden State Opera Chorus [G] EMI Classics ("Studio" series) 3-▲ CDMB 63980

Martin, Andrea (bar)
Donizetti, G.:Imelda de' Lambertazzi, w. D. D'Auria (sop), F. Sovilla (sop), F. Tenzi (ten), G. Sarti (bar), M. Andreae (cnd), Swiss-Italian Radio–TV Orch, Swiss-Italian Radio–TV Chorus [I] *(rec live)* Nuova Era 2-▲ 6778/79 [DDD]
Mozart, W.A.:Arias, w. D. Robin (cnd), Vienna Mozart Orch, Capella Istropolitana—arias & duets from Entführung aus dem Serail, Così fan tutte, Don Giovanni, Die Zauberflöte, Le nozze di Figaro [G,I] Naxos ▲ 8.550435 [DDD]
Mozart, W.A.:Così fan tutte, w. J. Borowska (sop—Fiordiligi), P. Coles (sop—Despina), R. Yachmi (mez—Dorabella), J. Dickie (ten—Ferrando), A. Martin (bar—Guglielmo), P. Mikuláš (b-bar—Don Alfonso), J. Wildner (cnd), Capella Istropolitana, Slovak Phil Chorus [I] *(rec Feb.–Mar. 1990)* Naxos 3-▲ 8.660008/10 [DDD]
Mozart, W.A.:Così fan tutte (sels), w. Joanna Borowska (sop—Fiordiligi), Priti Coles (sop—Despina), Rohangiz Yachmi (mez—Dorabella), John Dickie (ten—Ferrando), Andrea Martin (bar—Guglielmo), Peter Mikuláš (bass—Don Alfonso), Milada Synkova (hpd), J. Wildner (cnd), Capella Istropolitana, Slovak Phil Chorus—Ov.; [Act I] La mia Dorabella capace non è; È la fede della femmine; Una bella serenata; Ah guarda, sorella; Vorrei dir, e cor non ho; Sento, o Dio; Bella vita militar!; Soave sia il vento; Smanie implacabili; In uomini, in soldati; Alla bella Despinetta; Come Scoglio; Non siate ritrosi; Un'aura amorosa; [Act II] Una donna a quindici anni; Prenderò quel brunettino; La mano a me date; Ei parte...senti...ah no!; Donne mie la fate a tanti a tanti; Fra gle amplessi; Fortunato l'uom che prende *(rec Slovak Philharmonic Moyzes Hall, Bratislava, Feb.–Apr. 1990)* Naxos ▲ 8.553172 [DDD]
Mozart, W.A.:Music of, w. D. Robin (sop), G. Grünbacher (cl), K. Leitner (pno), K. Leitner (cnd), Vienna Mozart Orch—features selections from Die Entführung aus dem Serail, K.384; Don Giovanni, K.527; Serenade No. 13, K.525, "Eine kleine Nachtmusik"; Con. No. 21 in C for Piano & Orch., K.467; Symphony No. 41 in C, K.551, "Jupiter"; Con. No. 5 in A for Violin & Orch., K.219; Die Zauberflöte, K.620; Alla turca [arr. for orch.] *(rec Feb. 9–13, 1990)* Naxos ▲ 8.550866 [DDD]
Mozart, W.A.:Music of, w. D. Robin (sop), G. Grünbacher (cl), K. Leitner (pno), K. Leitner (cnd), Vienna Mozart Orch—features selections from Le nozze di Figaro, K.492; Con. No. 23 in A for Piano & Orch., K.488; Sym. No. 40 in g, K.550; Die Zauberflöte, K.620; Posthorn Serenade, K.320; Con. in A for Clarinet & Orch., K.622; Sym. No. 35 in in D, K.385 "Haffner" *(rec Feb. 9–13, 1990)* Naxos ▲ 8.550867 [DDD]
Salieri, A.:Axur, Re d'Ormus, w. E. Mei (sop), C. Rayam (ten), E. Nova (bass), A. Vespasiani (mez), M. Valenti (sop), R. Clemencic (cnd), Guido d'Arezzo Orch, Guido d'Arezzo Chorus [I] *(rec live 1989)* Nuova Era 3-▲ 6852/54 [DDD]
Strauss (II), Joh.:Die Fledermaus (sels), w. Ariane Calix (sop—Ida), Gabriele Fontana (sop—Rosalinde), Brigitte Karwautz (sop—Adele), Rohangiz Yachmi-Caucig (cta—Orlofsky), John Dickie (ten—Eisenstein), Josef Hopferwieser (ten—Alfred), Erich Wessner (ten—Dr. Blind), Andrea Martin (bar—Falke), Alfred Werner (bar—Frank), J. Wildner (cnd), Czech-Slovak RSO Bratislava, Bratislava City Chorus—Ov.; [Act I] Täubchen, das entflattert ist...; Ach, ich darf nicht hin zu dir; Nein, mit solchen Advokaten; Komm mit mir zum Souper; So muss allein ich bleiben; Trinke, Liebchen, trinke schnell; [Act II] Ein Souper heut' uns winkt; Ich lade gern mir Gäste ein; Mein Herr Marquis, ein Mann wie Sie; Dieser Anstand, so manierlich; Klänge der Heimat; Im Feuerstrom der Reben; Marianka komm und tanz me hier; [Act III] Entr'acte; Spiel' ich die Unschuld vom Lande; O Fledermaus, o Fledermaus *(rec Slovak Radio Concert Hall, Bratislava)* Naxos ▲ 8.553171 [DDD]
Torrejón Y Velasco, T. de:La purpura de la rosa, w. M. van der Sluis (sop), P. Mildenhall (sop), J. Benet (ten), R. Clemencic (cnd), Clemencic Consort, La Cappella Vocal Ensemble [Sp] Nuova Era ("Ancient Music" series) ▲ 6936 [DDD]

Martin, Barbara (sop)
Hovhaness, A.:O Lady Moon, w. Lawrence Sobol (cl), Elizabeth Rodgers (pno) Grenadilla ■ GSC 1073
Ung, C.:Mohori, w. A. Weisberg (cnd), Contemporary Chamber Ensemble *(rec National Edison Hotel, Feb 24, 1976)* CRI ▲ CRI 710 [DDD/ADD]
Wagner, R.:Tannhäuser, w. S. Jurinac (sop), H. Beirer (ten), H. Braun (bar), M. Talvela (bass), W. Sawallisch (cnd), La Scala Orch, La Scala Chorus [G] *(rec live, Milan 4/13/67)* Melodram 3-▲ CDM 37091 [ADD]

Martin, Barbara Ann (sop)
Husa, K.:Moravian Songs, w. Elizabeth Rodgers (pno) Grenadilla ■ GSC 1073
Husa, K.:Moravian Songs, w. Elizabeth Rodgers (pno) *(rec Sorcerer Sounds, NYC)* New World ▲ 80493-2

Martin, Drew (ten)
Loesser, F.:Guys and Dolls, w. Frank Sinatra (sgr), Bing Crosby (sgr), Dean Martin (sgr), J. Stafford (sgr), D. Shore (sgr), D. Reynolds (sgr), C. Dennis (sgr), A. Sherman (sgr), S. Davis Jr. (sgr), *(other artists unknown)* [studio cast] Reprise ▲ 45014-2 [AAD] ■ 45014-4
Talma, L.:A Wreath of Blessings, w. Gina Scaggs (sop), April Lindevald (alt), Leslie Dorsey (bass), Gregg Smith (cnd), Gregg Smith Singers Vox Box ("The American Composers" series) 3-▲ CDX 3037

Martin, Janis (mez/sop)
Janácek, L.:Slavonic Mass, w. H. Pilarczyk (sop), N. Gedda (ten), G. Gaynes (sgr), L. Bernstein (cnd), New York PO, Westminster Choir *(rec 1963)* Sony Classical ("Bernstein:The Royal Edition" series) ▲ SMK 47569 [ADD]
Schoenberg, A.:Erwartung, w. P. Boulez (cnd), BBC SO *(rec Apr. 14–15, 1977)* Sony Classical ▲ SMK 48466 [ADD]
Zemlinsky, A. von:Der Traumgörge, w. P. Coburn (sop), G. M. Ronge (sop), B. Calm (mez), P. Haage (ten), H. Kruse (ten), J. Protschka (ten), H. Welker (bar), M. Blasius (bass), V. von Halem (bass), G. Albrecht (cnd), Frankfurt RSO [G] Capriccio 2-▲ CD 10241/2 [DDD]

Martin, Marvis (sop)
Brahms, J.:Ein Deutsches Requiem, w. Kieth Spencer (bar), T.M. Sleeper (cnd), Univ of Miami SO, Univ of Miami Chorale Cane ▲ CR 1003
Canteloube, J.:Songs of Auvergne, w. J.-J. Kantorow (cnd), Auvergne CO [trans. Jean-Guy Bailly for orch.] Denon/PCM Digital ▲ DEN 75862 [DDD]

Martin, Mary (sgr)
Berlin, I.:Annie Get Your Gun, w. J. Raitt (sgr) *(rec 1957 TV broadcast)* Broadway Angel ▲ ZDM 64765 ■ EG 64765
Bernstein, L.:On the Town, w. N. Walker (sgr), B. Comden (sgr), A. Green (sgr), Tutti Camarata Orch, Leonard Joy Orch, Lynn Murray Orch, Lynn Murray Chorus MCA Classics ▲ MCAD 10280 (m) [AAD]

Martin, Mary (sgr) (cont.)
Bretón, T.:La Verbena de la paloma, w. Maria Bayo (sop), Raquel Pierotti (sop), Plácido Domingo (ten), Enrique Baquerizo (sgr), Rafael Castejon (sgr), Silva Tro (sgr), A. Ros-Marbá (cnd), Madrid SO Valois ("Zarauela" series) ▲ V 4725
Broadway, w. Ethel Merman (sgr), Judy Holliday (sgr), Dick van Dyke (sgr), Doris Day (sgr), Topol (sgr), Jill Haworth (sgr), William Warfield (sgr), et al. Sony Classical ("Greatest Hits" series) ▲ MLK 62365 ■ MLT 62365
Rodgers, R.:The Sound of Music, w. *(other artists unknown)* [1959 Broadway cast] CBS ▲ CK 32601 ■ JST 32601
Weill, K.:Songs, w. Danny Kaye (ten), *(orch unknown)*—Dreigroschenoper; Happy End; Mahagonny; Silbersee; Knickerbocker Holiday; Lady in the Dark; One Touch of Venus; and others Pearl 2-▲ PEA 9189

Martin, Tony (sgr)
Rodgers, R.:Music of, w. S. Bass (sgr), J. Andrews (sgr), P. Como (sgr), D. Reese (sgr), J. Jones (sgr), N. Luboff (sgr), M. Gold (sgr), N. Walker (sgr), H. Bowen (sgr), V. Damone (sgr), P. Nero (pno), J. P. Morgan (sgr), E. Fisher (sgr), B. Goodman (cl), Ann-Margaret (sgr), Shorty Rogers (sgr), D. Shore (sgr), M. King (sgr), A. Newley (sgr) RCA ▲ 8590-2 R ■ 8590-4 R
Romberg, S.:Deep in My Heart, w. H. Traubel (sgr), J. Ferrer (sgr), R. Clooney (sgr), Gene Kelly (sgr), F. Kelly (sgr), V. Damone (sgr), J. Powell (sgr), A. Miller (sgr), W. Olvis (sgr), C. Richards (sgr), H. Keel (sgr), J. Weldon (sgr) Sony Music Special Products ▲ AK 47703

Martinelli, Giovanni (ten)
The Acoustic Recordings *(rec 1913–23)* Preiser 2-▲ PRE 89213 [ADD]
Beethoven, L. van:Missa Solemnis, w. E. Rethberg (sop), M. Telva (mez), E. Pinza (bass), A. Toscanini (cnd), New York PO, Westminster Choir [L] *(rec live, New York 4/28/35)* Melodram 2-▲ CDM 28036 [ADD]
Bellini, V.:Norma, w. Gina Cigna (sop—Norma), Thelma Votipka (mez—Clotilde), Bruna Castagna (cta—Adalgisa), Giovanni Martinelli (ten—Pollione), Giodano Paltrinieri (ten—Flavio), Ezio Pinza (bass—Oroveso), E. Panizza (cnd), *(orch unknown)* *(rec live, New York, Feb. 20, 1937)* The Fourties 2-▲ ENT FT 1517
Bizet, G.:Carmen (sels), w. Geraldine Farrar (sop—Carmen), Giovanni Martinelli (ten—Don José), Pasquale Amato (bar—Escamillo), W. Rogers (cnd), *(orch unknown)*—L'amour est un oiseau rebelle; Près des remparts; Les tringles des sistres; Couplets du Toréador; Halte là! Qui va là?; Au quartier! pour l'appel!; La fleur que tu m'avais jetée; Non, tu ne m'aimes pas...Là-bas, dans la montagne; Voyons que j'essaie; Je dis que rien ne m'épouvante; Aragonaise [Prelude to Act 4; w. Arturo Toscanini (cnd), La Scala Orch]; Si tu m'aimes, Carmen; C'est toi! C'est moi!; Mais moi, Carmen, je t'aime encore Nimbus ▲ NI 7872 [ADD]
The Complete Destinn, w. Emmy Destinn (sop), E. Caruso (ten), J. McCormack (ten), K. Jörn (ten), G. Zenatello (ten), et al. Supraphon 12-▲ SUP 112136 [ADD]
Giovanni Martinelli:Operatic Arias Pearl ▲ PEA 9184
Giovanni Martinelli Nimbus ("Prima Voce" series) ▲ NI 7804 (m) [ADD]
Giovanni Martinelli, Vol. 2, w. Walter Rogers (cnd), Josef Pasternack (cnd), Nathaniel Shilkret (cnd) *(rec by Victor 1913–23)* Nimbus ("Prima Voce" series) ▲ NI 7826
Giuseppe de Luca On Radio:Broadcast Recordings of the Great Italian Baritone Unpublished on Disc (1941–44), w. Giuseppe de Luca (bar), Lily Pons (sop), Bidù Sayão (sop) *(rec 1941–44)* Enterprise ("The Radio Years" series) ▲ ENT RY 25 (m)
Halévy, F.:La Juive (sels), w. C. Boerner (sop—Eudoxie), E. Rethberg (sop—Rachel), G. Martinelli (ten—Éléazar), H. Clemens (ten—Léopold), Heller, Merola (cnd), *(orch unknown)*—Act 2 & Act 4 (sels.) *(rec Oct. 30, 1936 & 1926–27)* Standing Room Only ▲ SRO 848-1 [ADD]
The HMV & Victor Recordings, 1915–27 Enterprise ("Vocal Archives" series) ▲ ENT VA 1126
Leoncavallo, R.:Pagliacci (sels), w. Enrico Caruso (ten), Antonio Paoli (ten), Giovanni Zenatello (ten), Amedeo Bassi (ten), Hermann Jadlowker (ten), Fernand Ansseau (ten), Hipolito Lazaro (ten), Nino (Filippo) Piccaluga (ten), Mario Chamlee (ten), Giacomo Lauri-Volpi (ten), Miguel Fleta (ten), Aureliano Pertile (ten), Georges Thill (ten), Alessandro Valente (ten), Francesco Merli (ten), Lauritz Melchior (ten), Marcel Wittrisch (ten), Joseph Schmidt (ten), Beniamino Gigli (ten), Giuseppe Lugo (ten), Helge Roswaenge (ten), Jussi Bjoerling (ten)—23 versions of the tenor aria "Vesti la giubba" *(rec 1907–1944)* Bongiovanni ▲ GB 1071 [ADD]
Omaggio a Giovanni Martinelli Great Opera Performances 2-▲ GOP 788
Scenes from Il Trovatore & Aida, w. Rosa Ponselle (sop), Louise Homer (cta), Giuseppe de Luca (bar), Ezio Pinza (bass), et al. Pearl ▲ PEA 9350 (m)
Scenes from La forza del destino, w. R. Ponselle (sop), G. de Luca (bar), E. Pinza (bass) Pearl ▲ PEA 9351 (m)
Verdi, G.:Aida, w. Gina Cigna (sop), Bruna Castagna (mez), Ezio Pinza (bass), E. Panizza (cnd), New York Metropolitan Opera Orch, New York Metropolitan Opera Chorus *(rec live, Feb 6, 1937)* The Fourties 2-▲ ENT 1501
Verdi, G.:Otello, w. Elisabeth Rethberg (sop), Lawrence Tibbett (bar), E. Panizza (cnd), *(orch unknown)* *(rec Feb 12, 1938)* Enterprise ("The Fourties" series) 2-▲ ENT 309
Verdi, G.:Otello (sels), w. H. Jepson (sop), N. Massue (ten), L. Tibbett (bar), W. Pelletier (cnd), Metropolitan Opera Orch, New York Metropolitan Opera Chorus—eleven arias & scenes *(rec 1939)* Pearl ▲ GEMMCD 9914 (m) [AAD]
Verdi, G.:Il trovatore (sels), w. J. Biel (ten), F. Tamagno (ten), L.-A. Escalaïs (ten), M. Gilion (ten), E. Caruso (ten), A. Paoli (ten), G. Zenatello (ten), J. Sembach (ten), L. Slezak (ten), F. Constantino (ten), B. De Muro (ten), N. Fusati (ten), N. Piccaluga (ten), G. Lauri-Volpi (ten), A. Pertile (ten), E. Bergamaschi (ten), R. Tauber (ten), J. O'Sullivan (ten), H. Roswaenge (ten), G. Taccani (ten), V. Lois (ten), H. Lazaro (ten), A. Lindi (ten), A. Cortis (ten), F. Merli (ten), F. Völker (ten), J. Kiepura (ten), J. Schmidt (ten), J. Bjoerling (ten), B. Gigli (ten), A. Salvarezza (ten), J. Soler (ten), M. Filippeschi (ten)—34 performances of the Act III tenor aria "Di quella pira!," *(rec from 1903–1956)* Bongiovanni ▲ GB 1051 [AAD]

Martinez, Iride (sgr)
Zemlinsky, A. von:Der Geburtstag der Infantin, w. Soile Isokoski (sop), Andrew Collis (sgr), David Kuebler (ten), Juanita Lascarro (sgr), Machiko Obata (sgr), Anne Schwanewilms (sgr), Natalie Karl (sgr), Martina Rüping (sgr), Franfurter Kantorei (sgr), J. Conlon (cnd), Gürzenich Orch, Cologne PO *(rec Cologne, Feb 1996)* EMI Classics 2-▲ CDCB 56208

Martinez, Pura Maria (sop)
Schubert, Franz:Songs (misc), w. Nicolas Daza (gtr)—Nachtstück, D.672; Greisengesang, D.778; Hänflings Liebeswerbung, D.552; Meeres Stille, D.216; Heidenröslein, D.257; Jägers Abendlied, D.368; Schäfers Klagelied, D.121b; Frühlingsglaube, D.686b; Wehmut, D.772; Gesänge Des Harfners 1, D.478b RNE/Spanish National Radio ▲ 650001 [AAD]
Weber, C.M. von:Songs, w. Nicolas Daza (gtr)—5 Lieder, Op. 13; Lied, Op. 25; 3 Canzonette, Op. 29 RNE/Spanish National Radio ▲ 650001 [AAD]

Martini, Nino (sgr)
Rossini, G.:Il barbiere di Siviglia, w. Ira Petina (sop), Bidú Sayão (sop), John Brownlee (bar), Salvatore Baccaloni (bass), Ezio Pinza (bass), F. St. Leger (cnd), *(orch unknown)* *(rec Oct 4, 1943)* Enterprise ("The Fourties" series) 2-▲ ENT 307

Martinis, Carla (sop)
Verdi, G.:Otello, w. Carla Martinis (sop—Desdemona), Sieglinde Wagner (mez—Emilia), Anton Dermota (ten—Cassio), Paul Schöffler (ten—Iago), Ramon Vinay (ten—Otello), Josef Greindl (bass—Lodovico), W. Furtwängler (cnd), Vienna PO, Vienna State Opera Chorus *(rec live, Salzburg Festival, Aug 7, 1951)* EMI Classics ▲ CDMB 65751

Martino, Adriane (sop)
Debussy, C.:Pelléas et Mélisande, w. A. Reynolds (mez), G. Bacquier (bar), T. Rovetta (bar), N. Zaccaria (bass), L. Maazel (cnd), *(orch unknown)* *(rec 1969)* Great Opera Performances 3-▲ GOP 711
Szymanowski, K.:Stabat Mater, w. A. M. Rota (alt), R. Capecchi (bar), A. Rodzinski (cnd), Turin RAI SO, Turin RAI Chorus *(rec 1955)* Stradivarius 2-▲ DAT 12306 [ADD]

Martino, Vito (ten)
Haydn, J.:Stabat Mater, w. R. Lampo (sop), S. Zaramella (alt), P. Turner (bass), D. Ferrari (cnd), Milan Sinfonietta, Concentus Musicae Antiquae Vocal Group Nuova Era ▲ NUO 7170 [DDD]
Sammartini, G.B.:Cants for the Fridays in Lent, w. Silvia Mapelli (sop), Caterina Calvi (cta), D. Ferrari (cnd), Capriccio Italiano Ensemble—Il pianto delle pie Donne; Pianto di Maddalena al Sepolcro Nuova Era ▲ NUO CD 7269

1290 ▲ = CD ♦ = Enhanced CD Δ = MD ■ = Cassette Tape □ = DCC

Martino, Vito (ten) (cont.)
Sammartini, G.B.:Cants for the Fridays in Lent, w. Silvia Mapelli (sop), Caterina Calvi (alt), D. Ferrari (cnd), Capriccio Italiano Ensemble—Il Pianto Delle Pie Donne, J.118; Pianto di Maddalena al Sepolcro, J.120 Enterprise ("Tiziano" series) ▲ ENT TZ 96007 [DDD]

Martinov, A. (sgr)
Karetnikov, N.:Till Eulenspiegel, w. E. Mazo (sop), L. Mkrtchian (cta), A. Proujanski (ten), B. Koudriavtsev (bar), P. Glouboky (bass), A. Motchalov (bass), Polianski (cnd), Soviet Cinema Orch, Soviet Cinema Chorus *(rec Moscow, 1988)* Russian Season ("Russian Season" Series) 2-▲ LDC 288029/30 [DDD]

Martinovich, Boris (b-bar)
Borodin, A.:Prince Igor, w. S. Evstatieva (sop), A. Milcheva (mez), N. Ghiaurov (bass), N. Ghiuselev (bass), E. Tchakarov (cnd), Sofia Festival Orch, Sofia National Opera Chorus [R] Sony Classical 3-▲ S3K 44878 [DDD]
Glinka, M.:A Life for the Tsar, w. A. Pendachanska (sop), S. Toczyska (mez), C. Merritt (ten), E. Tchakarov (cnd), Sofia Festival Orch, Sofia National Opera Chorus [R] Sony Classical 3-▲ S3K 46487 [DDD]

Martinpelto, Hillevi (sop)
Bach, C.P.E.:Auferstehung und Himmelfahrt Jesu, w. C. Prégardien (ten), P. Harvey (bass), P. Herreweghe (cnd), Orch of the Age of Enlightenment, Collegium Vocale Virgin Classics ▲ CDC 59069
Haeffner, J.C.F.:Electra, w. Helle Hinz (sop), Peter Mattei (bar), Mikael Samuelson (bar), Swedish Radio Choir, T. Schuback (cnd), Drottningholm Baroque Ensemble Caprice 2-▲ CAP 22030
Haeffner, J.C.F.:Electra (sels), w. G. Hoffstedt (sop), S. Dahlberg (ten), P.-A. Wahlgren (bar), T. Schuback (cnd), Drottningholm Baroque Ensemble—3 recitatives & arias [Sw] *(rec 1989–90)* Musica Sveciae ▲ MSCD 426 [DDD]
Handel, G.F.:Dixit Dominus, w. Anne Sofie von Otter (mez), A. Öhrwall (cnd), Drottningholm Baroque Ensemble, Stockholm Bach Choir [L] BIS ▲ CD 322 [DDD]
Kraus, J.M.:Funeral Music for Gustav III, w. C. Högman (sop), C.-H. Ahnsjö (ten), T. Lander (bass), S. Parkman (cnd), Drottningholm Baroque Ensemble, Uppsala Univ Chamber Choir Musica Sveciae ▲ MSCD 416 [DDD]
Kraus, J.M.:Prosperin, w. Susanne Rydén (sop), Anna Eklund-Tarantino (sgr), Peter Mattei (bar), Lars Arvidson (bass), Stephen Smith (sgr), M. Tatlow (cnd), Stockholm CO, Stockholm Chamber Choir Musica Sveciae 2-▲ MSCD 422/23 [DDD]
Lehár, F.:Music of, w. Z. Terzakis (ten), E. Smola (cnd), BRTN PO—Die lustige Witwe *(Ov.)*, Paganini *(Gern hab' ich die Frau'n geküsst; Niemand liebt dich so wie ich)*, Der Graf von Luxemburg *(Es duftet nach Trèfle incarnat; Faschungsmarsch)*, Friederike *(O Mädchen, mein Mädchen)*, Zigeunerliebe *(Hör' ich Cymbalklänge; Zorika, Zorika)*, Schön ist die Welt *(Schön ist die Welt)*, Das Land des Lächelns *(Chinesischer Tanz; Dein ist mein ganzes Herz)*, Eva *(Fräulein Frau das klingt doch nicht gewöhnlich; Nur das eine Wort sprich es aus)*, Giuditta *(Intermezzo; Du bist meine Sonne; Herr Käpitan, der Weg ist weit; Schönste der Frau'n; Freunde, das Leben ist lebenswert)* Eufoda ▲ EUF 1188 [DDD]
Lidholm, I.:A Dream Play, w. Håkan Hagegård (bar), K. Ingebretsen (cnd), Royal Stockholm Orch Caprice 2-▲ CAP 22029
Mozart, W.A.:Idomeneo, w. Sylvia McNair (sop), Anne Sophie von Otter (mez), Anthony Rolfe Johnson (ten), J. E. Gardiner (cnd), English Baroque Soloists, Monteverdi Choir London Archiv 3-▲ 431674-2 [DDD]
Mozart, W.A.:Nozze di Figaro, w. A. Hagley (sop), R. Gilfrey (bar), B. Terfel (b-bar), J. E. Gardiner (cnd), English Baroque Soloists, Monteverdi Choir London [G] Archiv 3-▲ 439871-2 [DDD]
Naumann, J.G.:Arias, w. G. Hoffstedt (sop), S. Dahlberg (ten), P. A. Wahlgren (bar), T. Schuback (cnd), Drottningholm Baroque Ensemble—sels. from Amphion & Cora och Alonzo [Sw] Musica Sveciae ▲ MSCD 426 [DDD]
Roman, J.H.:The Sweedish Mass, w. A.-S. von Otter (sop), M. Samuelsson (bar), Drottningholm Baroque Ensemble, Adolf Fredrik Bach Choir Proprius ▲ PRCD 9920
Uttini, F.A.B.:Thetis och Pelée (sels), w. G. Hoffstedt (sop), S. Dahlberg (ten), P.-A. Wahlgren (bar), T. Schuback (cnd), Drottningholm Baroque Ensemble [Sw] Musica Sveciae ▲ MSCD 426 [DDD]

Martinucci, Nicola (ten)
Donizetti, G.:Poliuto, w. E. Connell (sop), R. Bruson (bar), J. Latham-König (cnd), Rome Opera Orch, Rome Opera Chorus [I] *(rec live, 1988)* Nuova Era 2-▲ 6776/77 [DDD]
Puccini, G.:Turandot, w. G. Dimitrova (sop), C. Gasdia (sop), R. Scandiuzzi (bass), D. Oren (cnd), Genoa Teatro Comunale Orch, Genoa Teatro Comunale Chorus [I] *(rec live, 1/20–27/89)* Nuova Era 2-▲ 6786/87 [DDD]
Puccini, G.:Turandot (sels), w. G. Dimitrova (sop), C. Gasdia (sop), R. Scandiuzzi (bass), D. Oren (cnd), Genoa Teatro Comunale Orch, Genoa Teatro Comunale Chorus [I] Nuova Era ▲ 6871 [DDD]

Martinucci, Pierluigi (bass)
Verdi, G.:Otello, w. Renata Tebaldi (sop—Desdemona), Luisa Ribacchi (mez—Emilia), Angelo Mercuriali (ten—Roderigo), Mario del Monaco (ten—Otello), Piero de Palma (ten—Cassio), Aldo Protti (bar—Iago), Dario Caselli (bass—A Herald), Fernando Corena (bass—Lodovico), Pierluigi Martinucci (bass—Montano), A. Erede (cnd), St. Cecilia Academy Orch Rome, St. Cecilia Academy Chorus Rome Theorema ▲ TH 121141/142

Marton, Éva (sop)
Bartók, B.:Bluebeard's Castle, w. S. Ramey (bass), A. Fischer (cnd), Hungarian State Orch, Hungarian State Chorus [Hun] CBS ▲ MK 44523 [DDD]
Boito, A.:Mefistofele, w. P. Domingo (ten), S. Ramey (bass), G. Patanè (cnd), Hungarian State SO, Hungarian State Opera Chorus [I] *(rec Budapest, 1988)* Sony Classical 2-▲ S2K 44983 [DDD]
Catalani, A.:La Wally, w. F. Araiza (ten), A. Titus (bar), F. Ellero d'Artegna (bass), P. Steinberg (cnd), Munich RSO, Bavarian Radio Chorus [I] Eurodisc 2-▲ 69073-2-RC [DDD] ■ 69073-4-RC (CrO2)
Giordano, U.:Andrea Chénier, w. J. Carreras (ten), G. Zancanaro (bar), G. Patanè (cnd), Hungarian State Orch, Hungarian State Chorus [I] CBS 2-▲ M2K 42369 [DDD]
Giordano, U.:Fedora, w. V. Kincses (sop), J. Carreras (ten), J. Gregor (bass), G. Patanè (cnd), Hungarian Radio-TV SO, Hungarian Radio-TV Chorus [I] CBS 2-▲ M2K 42181 [DDD]
Korngold, E.W.:Violanta, w. S. Jerusalem (ten), W. Berry (bass), M. Janowski (cnd), Munich RSO, Bavarian Radio Chorus [G] CBS ▲ MK 35909 [ADD]
Mahler, G.:Sym 2, w. J. Norman (sop), L. Maazel (cnd), Vienna PO, Vienna State Opera Chorus [G] CBS 2-▲ M2K 38667 [DDD]
Puccini, G.:Arias, w. G. Patanè (cnd), Munich RSO, 14 arias [I] CBS ▲ MK 42167 [DDD]
Puccini, G.:La fanciulla del West, w. Dennis O'Neill (ten), Walter Planté (ten), Alain Fondary (bar), L. Slatkin (cnd), Munich RSO RCA Red Seal ▲ 09026-60597-2
Puccini, G.:Music of, w. Kiri Te Kanawa (sop), José Carreras (ten), Luciano Pavarotti (ten), Richard Tucker (ten), *(other artists unknown)*—19 arias & duets from La bohème, Gianni Schicchi, Madama Butterfly, La Rondine, Tosca & Turandot *(six mono & 13 stereo recordings)* CBS ▲ MLK 45809 [AAD/ADD/D ■ MLT 45809
Puccini, G.:Tosca, w. J. Carreras (ten), J. Pons (bar), M. Tilson Thomas (cnd), Hungarian State Orch, Hungarian State Chorus Sony Classical 2-▲ S2K 45847
Puccini, G.:Tosca (sels), w. B. Heja (trb), J. Carreras (ten), F. Gerdesits (ten), J. Pons (bar), J. Nemeth (bar), J. Gregor (bass), M. Tilson Thomas (cnd), Hungarian State Orch, Hungarian Radio-TV Chorus *(rec Budapest, Dec. 14–22, 1988)* Sony Classical ("Opera Highlights" series) ▲ SMK 53500 [DDD]
Puccini, G.:Turandot, w. E. Marton (sop—Turandot), M. Price (sop—Liù), B. Heppner (ten—Calaf), J.-H. Rootering (bass—Timur), R. Abbado (cnd), Munich RSO RCA Red Seal 2-▲ 09026-60898-2
Puccini, G.:Turandot (sels), w. K. Ricciarelli (sop), J. Carreras (ten), L. Maazel (cnd), Vienna State Opera Orch, Vienna State Opera Chorus [I] CBS ▲ MK 42168 [DDD] ■ MT 42168 (D)
Respighi, O.:Semirama, w. V. Kincses (sop), L. Bartolini (ten), L. Miller (bar), L. Polgaar (bass), T. Clementis (bass), L. Gardelli (cnd), Hungarian State Orch, Hungarian Radio-TV Chorus [I] Hungaroton 2-▲ HCD 31197/98
Schoenberg, A.:Gurrelieder, w. F. Quivar (mez), G. Lakes (ten), H. Hotter (b-bar), Z. Mehta (cnd), New York PO, New York Choral Artists [G] Sony Classical 2-▲ S2K 48077 [DDD]
Strauss, R.:Elektra, w. C. Studer (sop), M. Lipovsek (mez), H. Winkler (ten), B. Weikl (bar), W. Sawallisch (cnd), Bavarian RSO, Bavarian Radio Chorus EMI Classics 2-▲ CDCB 54067
Strauss, R.:4 Last Songs, w. A. Davis (cnd), Toronto SO [G] CBS ▲ MDK 44910 [DDD]
Strauss, R.:Salome, w. B. Fassbaender (mez/sop), H. Zednik (ten), R. Lewis (ten), B. Weikl (bar), Z. Mehta (cnd), Berlin PO *(rec live)* Sony Classical 2-▲ S2K 46717

Marton, Éva (sop) (cont.)
Strauss, R.:Salome (final scene), w. A. Davis (cnd), Toronto SO [G] CBS ▲ MDK 45650 [DDD]
Wagner, R.:Götterdämmerung, w. S. Jerusalem (ten), T. Hampson (bar), J. Tomlinson (bass), B. Haitink (cnd), Bavarian RSO [G] EMI Classics 4-▲ CDCD 54485
Wagner, R.:Lohengrin, w. Sharon Sweet (sop—Elsa), Eva Marton (sop—Ortrud), Ben Heppner (ten—Lohengrin), Anton Rosner (ten—Nobleman), Heinrich Weber (ten—Nobleman), Jan-Hendrik Rootering (bar—Heinrich der Vögler), Sergei Leiferkus (bar—Friedrich von Telramund), Bryn Terfel (b-bar—King's Herald), Barbara Fleckenstein (sgr—Page), Atsuko Suzuki (sgr—Page), Gisela Ulmann (sgr—Page), Marion Rambausek (sgr—Page), Dankwart Siegele (sgr—Nobleman), Jürgen Weiss (sgr—Nobleman), C. Davis (cnd), Bavarian SO, Bavarian State Opera Chorus, Bavarian Radio Chorus *(rec Residenz Herkulesaal, Munich, May 14–28, 1994)* RCA Red Seal 3-▲ 09026-62646-2 [DDD]
Wagner, R.:Lohengrin (sels), w. Eva Marton (sop—Ortrud), Sharon Sweet (sop—Elsa von Brabant), Barbara Fleckenstein (sgr—Page), Marion Rambausek (sgr—Page), Atsuko Suzuki (sgr—Page), Gisela Ulmann (sgr—Page), Ben Heppner (ten—Lohengrin), Anton Rosner (ten—Nobleman), Heinrich Weber (ten—Nobleman), Sergei Leiferkus (bar—Friedrich von Telramund), Bryn Terfel (b-bar—King's Herald), Jan-Hendrik Rootering (bass—Henry the Fowler), Dankwart Siegele (sgr—Nobleman), Jürgen Weiss (sgr—Nobleman), C. Davis (cnd), Bavarian RSO, Michael Gläser (cnd), Udo Mehrpohl (cnd), Bavarian Radio Chorus, Bavarian State Opera Chorus—Seht! Seht! [from Act 1, Scene 2]; Nun sei bedankt, mein lieber Schwan!; Wenn ich im Kampfe für dich siege; Welch holde Wunder muss ich sehen?; Nun höret mich und achtet wohl; Durch Gottes Sieg ist jetzt dein Leben mein [all from Act 1, Scene 3]; Treulich geführt ziehet dahin [from Act 3, Scene 1]; Wie hehr erkenn' ich unsrer Liebe Wesen!; Höchstes Vertrau'n hast du mir schon zu danken; Weh' nun ist all' unser Glück dahin! [all from Act 3, Scene 2]; In fernem Land, unnahbar euren Schritten [from Act 3, Scene 3] *(rec Munich, Mar 14–28, 1994)* RCA Red Seal ▲ 09026-68239-2 [DDD]
Wagner, R.:Der Ring des Nibelungen (sels), w. C. Studer (sop), K. Te Kanawa (sop), M. Lipovšek (mez), S. Jerusalem (ten), R. Goldberg (ten), P. Haage (ten), J. Morris (bass), B. Haitink (cnd), Bayer RSO EMI Classics ▲ ZDC 54633
Wagner, R.:Siegfried, w. K. Te Kanawa (sop), S. Jerusalem (ten), P. Haage (ten), J. Morris (bass), B. Haitink (cnd), Bavarian RSO [G] EMI Classics 4-▲ CDCD 54290
Wagner, R.:Die Walküre (act 1), w. L. Hofmann (bass), M. Talvela (bass), Z. Mehta (cnd), New York PO [G] CBS ▲ MK 39745 [DDD]

Martynov, Alexei (ten)
Beethoven, L. van:Songs, w. A. Konstantinidi (pno)—Adelaide; Ich liebe dich; Neue Liebe, neues Leben; Wonne der Wehmut [G] *(rec 1991)* MK ▲ 417025 [DDD]
Grieg, E.:Songs, w. E. Kerechanin (sop), R. Levina (sop), V. Katajev (cnd), Northern Crown Soloists Ensemble [arr. Tishchenko] MK ▲ MKA 417124 [DDD]
Mendelssohn, F.:Songs, w. A. Konstantinidi (pno)—Auf Flügeln des Gesanges; Gruss; Der Mond; Nachtlied; Schlafloser Augen Leuchte; Venetianisches Gondellied [G] MK ▲ 417025 [DDD]
Schubert, Franz:Songs (misc), w. A. Konstantinidi (pno)—Auf dem See; Auf dem Wasser zu singen; Im Frühling; Der Schiffer; Ständchen [G] MK ▲ 417025 [DDD]
Schumann, R.:Songs, w. A. Konstantinidi (pno)—Aufträge; Er ist's; Geisternähe; Geständnis; Meine Rose; Schneeglöckchen [G] MK ▲ 417025 [DDD]
Strauss, R.:Songs, w. A. Konstantinidi (pno)—Morgen; Die Nacht; Ständchen; Zueignung [G] MK ▲ 417025 [DDD]
Tchaikovsky, P.:Songs, w. A. Konstantinidi (pno)—Absence; Ah! Si vous saviez; An dem schlummernden Strom; Attends!; Cradle Song During a Storm; Dawn of Spring; Don Juan's Serenade; In trüber Stund; Je voudrais mettre dans une seule parole; Nacht; New Hopes; No, Whom I Love I Will Not Name; La Nuit; O du mondhelle Nacht; L'Oublié; Le Rossignol; A Serenade; Le Soir et le matin; Sonne ging zur Ruhe; Summer Love Tale; The Tapers Were Flashing; La Tête blanche; Unsatisfied; Warum (Op. 6); Weil ich wie einstmals allein; What Matter!; Why? (Op. 28) [R] *(rec 1991)* MK ▲ 417054 [DDD]

Marucucci, M. (mez)
Mascagni, P.:Cavalleria rusticana, w. L.B. Rasa (sop), G. Simionato (mez), B. Gigli (ten), G. Bechi (bar), P. Mascagni (cnd), La Scala Orch, La Scala Chorus *(rec 1940)* Nimbus 2-▲ NI 7843/44 [ADD]

Maruna, Margarita (mez)
Haydn, J.:The Seven Last Words of Christ on the Cross, w. Elena Evseeva (sop), Arkady Mishenkin (ten), Boris Bezhko (bass), A. de Almeida (cnd), Moscow SO, Stanislav Gussev (cnd), Russian State Academy Chorus *(rec Mosfilm Studio, Moscow, Jan 27–28, 1995)* SOMM ▲ SOMMCD 203 [DDD]

Marzano, Liliana (sop)
Martin Y Soler, V.:Il Tutore Burlato, w. Liliana Marzano (sop—Menica), Maria Angeles Peters (sop—Violante), Juan Diego Florez (ten—Anselmo), Ernesto Palacio (ten—Il Cavaliere), Marcello Lippi (bar—Pippo), Giancarlo Tosi (bass—Don Fabrizio), Michela Forgione (hpd), M. Harth-Bedoya (cnd), Dianopolis Bulgarian CO *(rec VI Festival Internazionale di Gerace nella Chiesa di San Francesco, Aug 16, 1994)* Bongiovanni 2-▲ GB 2175/76-2 [DDD]

Masaki, Hiroko (sop)
Marc Grauwels & Friends, w. Marc Grauwels (fl), Marie-Noelle de Callataÿ (sop), Dennis James (glass hmc), Ingrid Procureur (hp), Yves Storms (gtr), Yvietta Matison (va), Mark Drobinsky (vc), Alain De Rijckere (bn), Daniel Blumenthal (pno), Frank Michiels (perc), Belgian RSO, W Syrinx 2-▲ 96101 [DDD]

Mascherini, Enzo (bar)
Donizetti, G.:La favorita, w. G. Simionato (mez), G. di Stefano (ten), C. Siepi (bass-bar), Rodriguez (sgr), R. Cellini (cnd), Palacio Bellas Artes Orch, Palacio Bellas Artes Chorus [I] *(rec live, Mexico City, 7/12/49)* Standing Room Only 2-▲ SRO 816-2 [ADD]
Puccini, G.:Tosca, w. R. Tebaldi (sop), G. Campora (ten), F. Corena (bass), A. Erede (cnd), St. Cecilia Academy Orch Rome, St. Cecilia Academy Chorus Rome Enterprise 2-▲ ENTPD 4106 [ADD]
Puccini, G.:Tosca, w. R. Tebaldi (sop), G. Campora (ten), F. Corena (bass), A. Erede (cnd), St. Cecilia Academy Orch Rome, St. Cecilia Academy Chorus Rome London 2-▲ 440236-2 [ADD]
Puccini, G.:Tosca, w. Ranata Tebaldi (sop), Gian Franco Volante (trb), Piero de Palma (ten), Giuseppe Campora (ten), Fernando Corena (bass), Dario Caselli (bass), Antonio Sacchetti (bass), A. Erede (cnd), St. Cecilia Academy Orch Rome, St. Cecilia Academy Chorus Rome *(rec 1952)* Andromeda 2-▲ ANR 2539 [ADD]
Verdi, G.:La forza del destino (sels), w. Barbato (sop), B. Gigli (ten), G. Neri (bass), A. Votto (cnd), Rio de Janeiro Teatro Municipale Orch, Rio de Janeiro Teatro Municipale Chorus [I] *(rec live 8/16/51)* Standing Room Only ▲ SRO 807-1 (m) [ADD]
Verdi, G.:Macbeth, w. M. Callas (sop), G. Penno (ten), I. Tajo (bass), V. de Sabata (cnd), *(orch unknown) (rec Milan, 1952)* Great Opera Performances 2-▲ GOP 750
Verdi, G.:I vespri siciliani, w. Maria Callas (sop—Duchess), Giorgio Kokolios Bardi (ten—Arrigo), Gino Sarri (ten—Danieli), Enzo Mascherini (bar—Guido di Monforte), Boris Christoff (bass—Giovanni da Procida), Mario Forsini (bass—Count Vaudemont), Bruneo Carmassi (bass—Bethune), E. Kleiber (cnd), Florence Teatro Comunale Orch, Florence Teatro Comunale Chorus *(rec live, Florence, 1951)* Melodram 3-▲ IMC 303016 [ADD]
Verdi, G.:I vespri siciliani, w. M. Callas (sop), Kokolios-Bardi (sgr), E. Kleiber (cnd), Florence Teatro Comunale Orch, Florence Teatro Comunale Chorus [I] *(rec live 5/26/51)* Melodram 3-▲ MEL 36020 (m)

Mascolo (sgr)
Giordano, U.:Fedora, w. Pia Tassinari (sop), Ferruccio Tagliavini (ten), Meletti (sgr), Micheluzzi (sgr), Jolanda Torriani (sgr), O.. Fabritiis (cnd), Milan RAI SO, Milan RAI Chorus *(rec live, July 10, 1954)* Arkadia 2-▲ 493

Masennikov, Alexander (ten)
Shostakovich, D.:From Jewish Folk Poetry, w. N. Doralik (sop), Z. Dolukhovna (mez), D. Shostakovich (pno) *(rec 1956)* Russian Disc ▲ RUS 15 015 [ADD]

Masetti-Bassi, Anna (mez)
Puccini, G.:Manon Lescaut, w. Maria Zamboni (sop—Manon), Anna Masetti-Bassi (mez—Singer), Francesco Merli (ten—Chevalier), Giuseppe Nessi (ten—Edmondo/Dancing Master/ Lamplighter), Lorenzo Conati (bar—Lescaut), Aristide Baracchi (bass—Innkeeper/Sergeant), Attilio Bordonali (bass—Geronte), Natale Villa (bass—Naval Captain), L. Molajoli (cnd), La Scala Orch, Vittore Veneziani (cnd), La Scala Chorus *(rec 1930)* Arkadia ("The 78's" series) 2-▲ 78014 [ADD]

Masini, Galliano (ten)
Galliano Massini Bongiovanni ▲ GB 1067-2 [ADD]

Masini, Galliano (ten)

Masini, Galliano (ten) (cont.)
Verdi, G.:La forza del destino, w. Maria Caniglia (sop), Ebe Stignani (mez), Carlo Tagliabue (bar), Tancredi Pasero (bass), G. Marinuzzi (cnd), EIAR Orch, EIAR Chorus *(rec 1941)*
Grammofono 2000 ▲ GRM 78567 (m)

Masini, Guglielmo (bass)
Verdi, G.:Aida, w. Dusolina Giannini (sop—Aida), Irene Minghini-Cattaneo (mez—Amneris), Giuseppe Nessi (ten—Messenger), Aureliano Pertile (ten—Radames), Giovanni Inghilleri (bar—Amonasro), Luigi Manfrini (bass—Ramfis), Guglielmo Masini (bass—King), C. Sabajno (cnd), La Scala Orch, Vittore Veneziani (cnd), La Scala Chorus *(rec 1928)*
Arkadia ("The 78's" series) 2-▲ 78013 [ADD]

Masini, Mafalda (mez)
Puccini, G.:Madama Butterfly, w. C. Petrella (sop—Madama Butterfly), M. Masini (mez—Suzuki), M. C. Foscale (sgr—Kate Pinkerton), F. Tagliavini (ten—Pinkerton), M. Caruso (ten—Goro), G. Taddei (bar—Sharpless), A. Albertini (bar—Yamadori), A. Biancardo (bass—Bonze), A. Questa (cnd), Turin RAI Orch, Cetra Chorus *(rec 1953)*
Cetra Classic 2-▲ CDO 10 [AAD]

Masková, Dagmar (sop)
Bruckner, A.:Mass 3, w. Vladimir Nacházel (sgr), Jiří Novotný (sgr), Jiří Seiler (sgr), Jiří Uherek (sgr), Eva Zbytovská (sgr), Jan Votava (trbn), Josef Ksica (org), Josef Pancík (cnd), Prague Chamber Choir
Orfeo ▲ 327 951 [DDD]

Bruckner, A.:Motets, w. Vladimir Nacházel (sgr), Jiří Novotný (sgr), Jiří Seiler (sgr), Jiří Uherek (sgr), Eva Zbytovská (sgr), Jan Votava (trbn), Josef Ksica (org), Josef Pancík (cnd), Prague Chamber Choir—Locus iste; Afferentur regi; Ave Maria (2); Pange lingua; Pange lingua (phrygisch); Tantum ergo (2); Libera me; Os iusti; Virga jesse; Vexilla regis; Christus factus est; Tota pulchra es Maria; Ecce sacerdos magnus
Orfeo ▲ 327 951 [DDD]

Dvořák, A.:Mass, w. Marta Benacková (alt), Walter Coppola (ten), Peter Mikuláš (bass), Josef Ksica (org), Josef Pancík (cnd), Prague Chamber Choir *(rec Dvořák Hall, Prague, Nov 1993)*
ECM New Series ▲ 78118-21539-2 [DDD]

Maslennikov, Alexei (ten)
Prokofiev, S.:War & Peace, w. Galina Vishnevskaya (sop—Natasha Rostovoa), Irina Arkhipova (mez—Hélène Bezukhova), Evgenya Verbitskaya (mez—Marya Akhrosimova), Alexi Maslennikov (ten—Anatole Kuragin), Vladimir Petrov (ten—Pierre Bezukhov), Pavel Lisitsian (bar—Napoleon), Alexi Krivchenya (bass—Field-Marshall Kutuzov), Evgeny Kibkalo (sgr—Prince Andrei Bolkonsky), A. Melik-Pashayev (cnd), Bolshoi Theater Orch, Bolshoi Theater Chorus *(rec Moscow, 1961)*
Melodiya ("The Russian Opera" series) 3-▲ 74321-29350-2 [ADD]

Rimsky-Korsakov, N.:Christmas Eve, w. Ekaterina Koudriavtchenko (sop), Elena Zaremba (mez), Vladimir Bogtatchov (ten), Viatcheslav Voinarovski (ten), Viatcheslav Verestnikov (bar), Maxime Mikhailov (bass), Stanislav Souleimanov (bass), M. Yurovski (cnd), Moscow Forum Theater Orch, Yurloff Academic Choir
Russian Season 4-▲ CMX 388054

Shchedrin, R.:Dead Souls, w. Larisa Avdeyeva (mez—Korobochka), Galina Borisova (mez—Plyushkin), Alexi Maslennikov (ten—Selifan), Vladislav Piavko (ten—Nozdryov), Vitali Vlasov (ten—Manilov), Boris Morozov (bass—Sabakevich), Alexander Voroshilo (sgr—Chichikov), Y. Temirkanov (cnd), Bolshoi Theater Orch, Bolshoi Theater Chorus, Moscow Chamber Choir *(rec Moscow, 1982)*
Melodiya ("The Russian Opera" series) 2-▲ 74321-29347-2 [ADD]

Mason, Anne (sop)
Donizetti, G.:Emilia di Liverpool, w. Y. Kenny (sop), B. Mills (sop), C. Merritt (ten), S. Bruscantini (bar), G. Dolton (bar), C. Thornton-Holmes (bar), D. Parry (cnd), Philharmonia Orch, Geoffrey Mitchell Choir—complete opera, without dialogue
Opera Rara 3-▲ OR 8

Donizetti, G.:L'Eremitaggio di Liverpool, w. Y. Kenny (sop), B. Mills (sop), C. Merritt (ten), S. Bruscantini (bar), G. Dolton (bar), C. Thornton-Holmes (bar), D. Parry (cnd), Philharmonia Orch, Geoffrey Mitchell Choir—complete opera, without dialogue
Opera Rara 3-▲ OR 8

Mason, Patrick (bar)
Carter, E.:Poems (3) of Robert Frost, w. D. Starobin (gtr), Speculum Musicae [E]
Bridge ▲ BCD 9014 [DDD]

Dutilleux, H.:Songs (4), w. Robert Spillman (pno)
Bridge ▲ BRI 9058 [DDD]

Fauré, G.:La bonne chanson, w. Robert Spillman (pno)
Bridge ▲ BRI 9058 [DDD]

Gilles, J.:Mess des morts, w. A. Azema (sop), J. Nirouët (alt), W. Hite (ten), J. Cohen (cnd), Boston Camerata, Ensemble de Tambours Provençaux, Aix-en-Provence Festival Chorus
Erato ▲ 2292-45989-2

Machover, T.:Valis, w. A. Azéma (sop), J. Felty (mez), T. Edwards (ten), T. Machover (elec), T. Machover (cnd), *(ensemble unknown)* [E]
Bridge ▲ BCD 9007 [DDD] ♦ BCS 7007 (D)

Poulenc, F.:La Fraîcheur et le feu, w. Robert Spillman (pno)
Bridge ▲ BRI 9058 [DDD]

Ravel, M.:Histoires naturelles, w. Robert Spillman (pno)
Bridge ▲ BRI 9058 [DDD]

Roxbury, R.:Songs of Walt Whitman, w. S. Palma (fl), D. Starobin (gtr) [E]
Bridge ▲ BCD 9022 [DDD]

Searle, H.:2 Practical Cats, w. S. Palma (fl), D. Starobin (gtr), T. Eddy (vc) [E]
Bridge ▲ BCD 9022 [DDD]

Mason, Ralph (ten)
Sullivan, A.:The Yeomen of the Guard, w. Felicity Palmer (sop—Dame Carruthers), Pamela Helen Stephens (mez—Phoebe Meryll), Neill Archer (ten—Col Fairfax), Peter Hoare (ten—Leonard Meryll), Ralph Mason (ten—1st Yeoman), Donald Maxwell (bar—Wilfred Shadbolt), Peter Sevidge (bar—Lieutenant Sir Richard Cholmondely), Donald Adams (bass—Sergeant Meryll), Richard Suart (bass—Jack Point), Peter Lloyd Evans (sgr—2nd Yeoman), Alwyn Mellor (sgr—Elsie Maynard), Clare O'Neill (sgr—Kate), C. Mackerras (cnd), Welsh National Opera Orch, Welsh National Opera Chorus *(rec Brangwyn Hall, Swasea, Wales, Apr 18-30 & May 1, 1995)*
Telarc 2-▲ CD 80404 [DDD]

Masquelin, Martine (sop)
Sauguet, H.:Neiges, w. D. Abramovitz (pno)
Sonpact ▲ SPT 93008 [DDD]

Massa, Fulvio (ten)
Rossini, G.:L'occassione fa il ladro, w. Maria Bayo (sop), Francesca Provvisionato (mez), Iorio Zennaro (ten), Fabio Previati (bar), Natale de Carolis (b-bar), M. Viotti (cnd), English CO
Claves 2-▲ 50-9208/9

Rossini, G.:L'occassione fa il ladro, w. M. Bayo (sop), F. Provvisionato (mez), I. Zennaro (ten), F. Previati (bar), N. de Carolis (b-bar), M. Viotti (cnd), English CO [I]
Claves 8-▲ CD 9200 [DDD]

Rossini, G.:La scala di seta, w. Teresa Ringholz (sop), Francesca Provvisionata (mez), Ramon Vargas (ten), Alessandro Corbelli (bar), Natale de Carolis (b-bar), M. Viotti (cnd), English CO
Claves 2-▲ 9219/20

Rossini, G.:Il Signor Bruschino, w. P. Orciani (sop), K. Lytting (mez), L. Canonici (ten), B. Praticò (bar), P. Spagnoli (bar), N. de Carolis (b-bar), M. Viotti (cnd), Turin PO [I]
Claves 8-▲ CD 9200 [DDD]

Rossini, G.:Il Signor Bruschino, w. Patrizia Orciani (sop), Katia Lytting (mez), Luca Canonici (ten), Bruno Praticò (bar), Pietro Spagnoli (bar), Natale de Carolis (b-bar), M. Viotti (cnd), Turin PO
Claves 2-▲ 50-8904/5

Massard, Robert (bar)
Berlioz, H.:Les Troyens, w. M. Horne (mez), S. Verrett (mez), N. Gedda (ten), V. Luchetti (ten), G. Prêtre (cnd), Rome RAI SO, Rome RAI Chorus *(rec live 5/30/69)*
Arkadia 4-▲ 461 [ADD]

Berlioz, H.:Les Troyens, w. M. Horne (mez), S. Verrett (mez), N. Gedda (ten), V. Luchetti (ten), G. Prêtre (cnd), Rome RAI SO, Rome RAI Chorus [F] *(rec live 5/30/69)*
Melodram 3-▲ MEL 37060 [AAD]

Bizet, G.:Carmen, w. M. Callas (sop), A. Guiot (sop), N. Gedda (ten), G. Prêtre (cnd), Paris Opera Orch, Paris Opera Chorus [F]
EMI Classics 2-▲ CDCB 54368

Bizet, G.:Carmen (sels), w. M. Callas (sop), A. Guiot (sop), N. Gedda (ten), G. Prêtre (cnd), Paris Opera Orch [F]
EMI Classics ▲ CDM 63075 ■ EG 63075

Massenet, J.:Hérodiade (sels), w. Michele Le Bris (sop—Salomé), Denise Scharley (cta—Hérodiade), Guy Chauvet (ten—Jean), Robert Massard (bar—Hérode), J. Etcheverry (cnd), Paris Lyric Orch—Il est doux, Il est bon; Hérode, Ne me refuse pas; Jean, je le revois; Vision fugitive; Astres entincelants; Charme des jours passés; Salomé, laisse-moi t'aimer; Ne pouvant reprimer les élans de la foi; Quand nos jours s'éteindront...; Ballet
Accord ▲ ACD 204272 [AAD]

Offenbach, J.:Les Contes d'Hoffmann (sels), w. Andréa Guiot (sop—Antonia), Mady Mesplé (sop—Olympia), Suzanne Sarroca (sop—Giulietta), Albert Lance (ten—Hoffmann), Gabriel Bacquier (bar—Docteur Miracle), Robert Massard (bar—Dapertutto), J. Etcheverry (cnd), *(orch unknown)*—Prologue; Dans les rôles d'amoureux...; Il était une fois...; Allons! Courage et confiance...; C'est moi, coppélius!...; Les oiseaux dans la charmille; Barcarolle; Scintille, diamant...; Malheureux, tu ne comprends donc pas...; Hélas! Mon coeur s'égare encore...; Elle a fui, la tourterelle...; Eh bien! Quoil Toujours en colère!...; Tu ne chanteras plus?...
Adès ▲ ADE 202702 [AAD]

Massard, Robert (bar) (cont.)
Saint-Saëns, C.:Samson et Dalila, w. Shirley Verrett (mez), Richard Cassilly (ten), G. Prêtre (cnd), La Scala Orch *(rec La Scala Theatre, May 30, 1969)*
Arkadia ("Historical Performances" series) 2-▲ 495

Massis, René (bar)
Catalani, A.:Dejanice, w. C. Basto (sop), M. L. Garbato (sop), O. Garaventa (ten), C. Zardo (bass), J. Latham-König (cnd), Lucca Teatro Comunale del Giglio Orch, Lucca Teatro Comunale del Giglio Chorus [I] *(rec 9/6/85)*
Bongiovanni 2-▲ GB 2031/32 [DDD]

Donizetti, G.:La favorita, w. Gloria Scalchi (mez), Luca Canonici (ten), Giorgio Surjan (bass), D. Renzetti (cnd), Milan RAI SO, Milan RAI Chorus
Fonit Cetra ("Ricordi" series) 3-▲ FCT RFCD 2015

Gluck, C.W.:Iphigénie en Tauride, w. D. Montague (mez), J. Aler (ten), T. Allen (bar), J.E. Gardiner (cnd), Lyon Opera Orch
Philips 2-▲ 416148-2 [DDD]

Massue, Nicholas (ten)
Verdi, G.:Otello (sels), w. H. Jepson (sop), G. Martinelli (ten), L. Tibbett (bar), W. Pelletier (cnd), Metropolitan Opera Orch, New York Metropolitan Opera Chorus—eleven arias & scenes *(rec 1939)*
Pearl ▲ GEMMCD 9914 (m) [AAD]

Masterson, Valerie (sop)
Song Recital, w. Roger Vignoles (pno), Richard Adeney (hp)
Pearl ▲ PEA 9590 [DDD]

Sullivan, A.:Music of, w. S. Armstrong (sop), R. Tear (ten), B. Luxon (bar), Alwyn, Hickox (cnd), Bournemouth Sinfonietta, Northern Sinfonietta of England—sels. from all operettas of Gilbert & Sullivan
EMI Classics ▲ CDM 64393

Sullivan, A.:The Pirates of Penzance (sels), w. D. Adams (bass), I. Godfrey (cnd), Royal PO, D'Oyly Carte Opera Chorus
London ("Weekend Classics" series) ▲ 436292-2

Mastrango, Horacio (ten)
Verdi, G.:Rigoletto, w. Renata Scotto (sop—Gilda), Stella Maris Silva (sop—Giovanna), Martha Carrizo (mez—Page), Carmen de la Mata (mez—Countess Ceprano), Noemi Souza (cta—Maddalena), Horacio Mastrango (ten—Borso), Richard Tucker (ten—Duke of Mantua), Cornell MacNeil (bar—Rigoletto), Riccardo Yost (bar—Marullo), Guerrino Boschetti (bass—Usher), Tulio Gagliardo (bass—Count Ceprano), Victor de Narké (bass—Monterone), William Wilderman (bass—Sparafucile), F. Previtali (cnd), Buenos Aires Teatro Colón Orch, Buenos Aires Teatro Colón Chorus *(rec Colon Theater, Buenos Aires, Aug. 22, 1967)*
Legato Classics 2-▲ LCD 198-2

Mastromei, Gianpietro (bar)
Donizetti, G.:Lucia di Lammermoor, w. B. Sills (sop), A. Kraus (ten), V. de Narke (bass), J.E. Martini (cnd), Buenos Aires Teatro Colón Orch, Buenos Aires Teatro Colón Chorus *(rec 1968)*
Arkadia 2-▲ 474

Masurin, Yuri (ten)
Glinka, M.:Russlan & Ludmilla, w. Galina Gorchakova (sop), Larissa Diadkova (cta), Irinia Bogachova (sgr), Anna Netrebko (sgr), Konstantin Pluzhnikov (ten), Mikhail Kit (bar), Gennady Bezzubenkov (bass), Vladimir Ognovenko (bass), V. Gergiev (cnd), Kirov Opera Orch, Kirov Opera Chorus
Philips ▲ 456 248-2

Mata, Carmen de la (mez)
Verdi, G.:Rigoletto, w. Renata Scotto (sop—Gilda), Stella Maris Silva (sop—Giovanna), Martha Carrizo (mez—Page), Carmen de la Mata (mez—Countess Ceprano), Noemi Souza (cta—Maddalena), Horacio Mastrango (ten—Borso), Richard Tucker (ten—Duke of Mantua), Cornell MacNeil (bar—Rigoletto), Riccardo Yost (bar—Marullo), Guerrino Boschetti (bass—Usher), Tulio Gagliardo (bass—Count Ceprano), Victor de Narké (bass—Monterone), William Wilderman (bass—Sparafucile), F. Previtali (cnd), Buenos Aires Teatro Colón Orch, Buenos Aires Teatro Colón Chorus *(rec Colon Theater, Buenos Aires, Aug. 22, 1967)*
Legato Classics 2-▲ LCD 198-2

Matacchini, Valeria (cta)
Stradella, A.:Il moro per amore, w. R. Invernizzi (sop—Eurinda), S. Piccolo (sop—Lucinda), M. Grazia Liguori (sop—Fiorino), M. Lazzara (cta—Lindora), V. Matacchini (cta—Feraspe/Floridoro), M. Beasley (ten—Filandro), R. Ristori (bass—Rodrigo), E. Velardi (cnd), Alessandro Stradella Consort [I] *(rec Oct. 31-Nov. 3, 1992)*
Bongiovanni 3-▲ GB 2153/55

Matheson, C. (ten)
Avshalomov, J.:Prophecy, w. L. Smith (org), J. Dexter (cnd), Mid-America Chorale
CRI ▲ CD 667 [ADD]

Mathis, Edith (sop)
Bach, J.S.:Cants (misc), w. Carolyn Watkinson (cta), Eberhard Büchner (ten), Peter Schreier (ten), Siegfried Lorenz (bar), Theo Adam (b-bar), P. Schreier (cnd), Berlin CO, Berlin Soloists
Berlin Classics ▲ BER 9221

Bach, J.S.:Cant 26, w. P. Schreier (ten), A. Schmidt (bar), D. Fischer-Dieskau (bar), K. Richter (cnd), Munich Bach Orch, Munich Bach Choir
Archiv ▲ 427130-2 [ADD]

Bach, J.S.:Cant 36, w. Peter Schreier (ten), Siegfried Lorenz (bar), P. Schreier (cnd), Berlin CO, Berlin Soloists
Berlin Classics ▲ BER 9220

Bach, J.S.:Cant 80, w. T. Schmidt (mez), P. Schreier (ten), D. Fischer-Dieskau (bar), K. Richter (cnd), Munich Bach Orch, Munich Bach Choir
Archiv ▲ 427130-2 [ADD]

Bach, J.S.:Cant 116, w. T. Schmidt (mez), P. Schreier (ten), D. Fischer-Dieskau (bar), K. Richter (cnd), Munich Bach Orch, Munich Bach Choir
Archiv ▲ 427130-2 [ADD]

Bach, J.S.:Cant 140, w. P. Schreier (ten), D. Fischer-Dieskau (bar), K. Richter (cnd), Munich Bach Orch, Munich Bach Choir [G]
Deutsche Grammophon ("Galleria" series) ▲ 419466-2 [ADD]

Bach, J.S.:Cant 202, "Wedding Cant", w. P. Schreier (cnd), Berlin CO
Berlin Classics ▲ BER 9222

Bach, J.S.:Cant 203, w. Peter Schreier (ten), Siegfried Lorenz (bar), P. Schreier (cnd), Berlin CO, Berlin Soloists
Berlin Classics ▲ BER 9220

Bach, J.S.:Cant 205, w. Carolyn Watkinson (alt), Julia Hamari (alt), Peter Schreier (ten), Siegfried Lorenz (bar), P. Schreier (cnd), Berlin CO, Berlin Soloists
Berlin Classics ▲ BER 9224

Bach, J.S.:Cant 206, w. Carolyn Watkinson (alt), Julia Hamari (alt), Peter Schreier (ten), Siegfried Lorenz (bar), P. Schreier (cnd), Berlin CO, Berlin Soloists
Berlin Classics ▲ BER CD 9225

Bach, J.S.:Cant 207, w. Carolyn Watkinson (alt), Julia Hamari (alt), Peter Schreier (ten), Siegfried Lorenz (bar), P. Schreier (cnd), Berlin CO, Berlin Soloists
Berlin Classics ▲ BER 9224

Bach, J.S.:Cant 209, w. Peter Schreier (ten), Siegfried Lorenz (bar), P. Schreier (cnd), Berlin CO, Berlin Soloists
Berlin Classics ▲ BER 9220

Bach, J.S.:Cant 211, "Coffee Cant", w. Peter Schreier (ten), Theo Adam (bass), P. Schreier (cnd), Berlin CO
Berlin Classics ▲ BER 9226

Bach, J.S.:Cant 212, "Peasant Cant", w. Peter Schreier (ten), Theo Adam (bass), P. Schreier (cnd), Berlin CO
Berlin Classics ▲ BER 9226

Bach, J.S.:Cant 215, w. Carolyn Watkinson (alt), Peter Schreier (ten), Siegfried Lorenz (bar), P. Schreier (cnd), Berlin CO, Berlin Soloists
Berlin Classics ▲ BER CD 9225

Bach, J.S.:Cant 249a, w. Hetty Plümacher (alt), Theo Altmeyer (ten), Jakob Stämpfli (bass), H. Rilling (cnd), Stuttgart Bach Collegium, Stuttgart Memorial Church Figuralchor *(rec Gedächtniskirche Stuttgart, Mar 1967)*
Musicaphon ▲ 51357 [AAD]

Brahms, J.:Liebeslieder Waltzes SATB, w. B. Fassbaender (mez), P. Schreier (ten), D. Fischer-Dieskau (bar), K. Engel (pno), W. Sawallisch (pno) [G]
Deutsche Grammophon ▲ 423133-2 [DDD]

Brahms, J.:Neue Liebeslieder Waltzes, w. B. Fassbaender (mez), P. Schreier (ten), D. Fischer-Dieskau (bar), K. Engel (pno), W. Sawallisch (pno) [G]
Deutsche Grammophon ▲ 423133-2 [DDD]

Brahms, J.:Songs, w. Gérard Wyss (pno)—Von ewiger Liebe, Op. 43; Dein blaues Aug, Op. 59; Meine Liebe ist grün, Op. 63/5; Anklänge, Op. 7/3; Volkslied, Op. 7/4; Die Trauernde, Op. 7/5; Klage, Op. 69/1; Das Mädchen, Op. 95/1; Spanisches Lied, Op. 6/1; Nachtwandler, Op. 86/3; Therese, Op. 86/1; Bei dir sind meine Gedanken, Op. 95/2; Sehnsucht, Op. 14/8; Gold überwiegt die Liebe, Op. 48/4; Schön war, das ich dir weihte, Op. 95/7; Klage, Op. 105/3; Regenlied; Mädchenlied, Op. 107/5; An die Nachtigall, Op. 46/4; Wie Melodien zieht es mir, Op. 105/1; Wiegenlied, Op. 49/4 *(rec Swiss Radio DRS, Studio Bern, May 20-22, 1994)*
Denon ▲ CO 78947 [DDD]

Bruckner, A.:Mass 1, w. M. Schiml (mez), W. Ochman (ten), K. Ridderbusch (bass), E. Jochum (cnd), Bavarian RSO, Bavarian Radio Chorus
Deutsche Grammophon ("The Originals" series) 2-▲ 447409-2

Bruckner, A.:Mass 1, w. M. Schiml (mez), W. Ochman (ten), K. Ridderbusch (bass), E. Jochum (cnd), Bavarian RSO, Bavarian Radio Chorus [L]
Deutsche Grammophon 4-▲ 423127-2 [ADD]

Cornelius, P.:Duets, Op. 6, w. Hidenori Komatsu (bar), Cord Garben (pno)
CPO ▲ CPO 999262 [DDD]

Cornelius, P.:Duets, Op. 16, w. Hidenori Komatsu (bar), Cord Garben (pno)
CPO ▲ CPO 999262 [DDD]

Mathis, Edith (sop) (cont.)

Fauré, G.:Requiem, w. K. Widmer (bass), J. Fournet (cnd), Swiss Festival Orch, Lucerne Festival Chorus *(rec 1984)* Koch Treasure ▲ 31619-2 [DDD]

Furtwängler, W.:Te Deum, w. J. Dooley (alt), S. Wagner (cta), G. Jelden (ten), H. Chemin–Petit (cnd), Berlin PO *(rec live, 1967)* As Disc ▲ ASD 2506

Handel, G.F.:Acis & Galatea [arr Mozart], w. R. Gambill (ten), A R. Johnson (ten), R. Lloyd (b–bar), P. Schreier (cnd), Austrian RSO, Austrian Radio Chorus [E] Orfeo 2-▲ 133852 [DDD]

Handel, G.F.:Messiah, w. James Bowman (alt), Claes Hakan Ahnsjö (ten), Richard Krause (ten), A. Dorati (cnd), Smithsonian Concerto Grosso, Univ of Maryland Choral Society [E] Pro Arte 2-▲ CDD 232 [DDD]; ■ PCD 232

Haydn, J.:Die Jahreszeiten, w. Sigfried Jerusalem (ten), Dietrich Fischer–Dieskau (bar), N. Marriner (cnd), Academy of St. Martin in the Fields Philips ("Duo" series) 2-▲ 438715-2

Haydn, J.:Die Schöpfung, w. Christoph Prégardien (ten), Harald Stamm (bass), M. Atzmon (cnd), World SO, Pécs Chamber Choir, Berlin Academy of Arts Chamber Choir, Shin–Yuh Kai Choir [G] *(rec Basilica San Francesco in Assisi, as part of the IPPNW "Hiroshima Concert 1990")* BIS 2-▲ CD 493/94 [DDD]

Loewe, C.:Songs, w. Cord Garben (pno)—Des Bettlers Tochter von Bednall Green; Der Freibeuter; Meine Ruh'ist hin; Szene aus Faust; Der Fischer; Gesang der Königin Maria Stuart auf den Tod Franz II; In die Ferne; Jephtas's Tochter; Die Zugvögel; Brautlied; Die engste Nähe; Frülingsweihe; Taubenpost; An den Wassern zu Babel; Die schlanke Wasserlilie *(rec Studio Villa Berg, Mar 1995)* CPO ▲ 999334-2 [DDD]

Lortzing, A.:Der Wildschütz, oder Die Stimme der Natur, w. Peter Schreier (ten), Gottfried Hornik (bar), Hans Sotin (bass), B. Klee (cnd), Berlin State Chorus *(rec Berlin, 1982)* Berlin Classics 2-▲ BER 1143 [ADD]

Martin, F.:Maria–Triptychon, w. W. Schneiderhan (vn), J. Fournet (cnd), Swiss Festival Orch *(rec 1984)* Koch Treasure ▲ 31619-2 [DDD]

Mendelssohn, F.:A Midsummer Night's Dream (comp), w. Brigitte Fassbaender (mez), O. Klemperer (cnd), Bavarian RSO, Bavarian Radio Chorus *(rec live, May 23, 1969)* Originals ▲ ORI SH 917

Mozart, W.A.:Arias, w. Arleen Augér (sop), Kathleen Battle (sop), Irma Beilke (sop), Helena Braun (sop), Lisa Della Casa (sop), Maria Cebotari (sop), Ileana Cotrubas (sop), Helen Donath (sop), Mirella Freni (sop), Reri Grist (sop), Edita Gruberova (sop), Elisabeth Grümmer (sop), Hilde Güden (sop), Ingeborg Hallstein (sop), Luise Helletsgruber (sop), Gundula Janowitz (sop), Sena Jurinac (sop), Erika Köth (sop), Evelyn Lear (sop), Wilma Lipp (sop), Margaret Marshall (sop), Jarmila Novotna (sop), Margherita Perras (sop), Lucia Popp (sop), Elisabeth Rethberg (sop), Anneliese Rothenberger (sop), Elisabeth Schumann (sop), Elisabeth Schwarzkopf (sop), Graziella Sciutti (sop), Irmgard Seefried (sop), Graziella Sciutti (sop), Julia Varady (sop), Agnes Baltsa (mez), Margit Bokor (mez), Brigitte Fassbaender (mez), Christa Ludwig (mez), Ann Murray (mez), Francisco Araiza (ten), Anton Dermota (ten), Helge Rosvaenge (ten), Rudolf Schock (ten), Peter Schreier (ten), Leopold Simoneau (ten), Eric Tappy (ten), Richard Tauber (ten), Gösta Winbergh (ten), Josef Witt (ten), Fritz Wunderlich (ten), Christian Boesch (bar), Willy Domgraf–Fassbaender (bar), Karl Dönch (bar), Dietrich Fischer–Dieskau (bar), Erich Kunz (bar), Eberhard Wächter (bar), Hans Hotter (b–bar), Paul Schöffler (b–bar), Cesare Siepi (b–bar), José Van Dam (b–bar), Walter Berry (bass), Geraint Evans (bass), Nicolai Ghiaurov (bass), Alexander Kipnis (bass), Richard Mayr (bass), Kurt Moll (bass), James Morris (bass), Ezio Pinza (bass), Martti Talvela (bass), Giorgio Tozzi (bass), Hans Duhan (sgr), Res Fischer (sgr), Marie Gerhart (sgr), *(various orchs & cnds)*—sels from Idomeneo, Die Entführung aus der Serail, Le nozze di Figaro, Don Giovanni, Così fan tutte, Die Zauberflöte & various arias Orfeo d'or ("Festspiel Dokumente" series) 5-▲ 408955

Mozart, W.A.:Complete Mozart Edition, w. E. Gruberova (sop), L. Popp (mez), F. Araiza (ten), P. Schreier (ten), W. Berry (bass), Salzburg Mozarteum Orch Philips 8-▲ 422523-2 [ADD]

Mozart, W.A.:Complete Mozart Edition, w. A. Augér (sop), A. Baltsa (mez), P. Schreier (ten), L. Hager (cnd), Salzburg Mozarteum Orch Philips 3-▲ 422530-2 [ADD]

Mozart, W.A.:Complete Mozart Edition, w. A. Augér (sop), H. Schwarz (mez), A. Rolfe Johnson (ten), L. Hager (cnd), Salzburg Mozarteum Orch, Salzburg Mozarteum Chorus Philips 2-▲ 422526-2 [ADD]

Mozart, W.A.:Complete Mozart Edition, w. E. Gruberova (sop), E. Moser (sop), L. Popp (mez), P. Schreier (ten), L. Hager (cnd), Salzburg Mozarteum Orch Philips 2-▲ 422531-2 [ADD]

Mozart, W.A.:Complete Mozart Edition, w. A. Augér (sop), J. Varady (sop), H. Donath (sop), P. Schreier (ten), L. Hager (cnd), Salzburg Mozarteum Orch Philips 3-▲ 422532-2 [ADD]

Mozart, W.A.:Complete Mozart Edition, w. P. Schreier (ten), W. Hollweg (bar), I. Wixell (bar), B. Klee (cnd), Berlin Staatskapelle Philips 2-▲ 422536-2 [ADD]

Mozart, W.A.:Don Giovanni, w. J. Varady (sop), A. Augér (sop), T. Moser (ten), A. Titus (bar), R. Panerai (bar), R. Scholze (bass), J.–H. Rootering (bass), R. Kubelik (cnd), Bavarian RSO, Bavarian Radio Chorus [I] Eurodisc 3-▲ 7798-2 [DDD]

Mozart, W.A.:Don Giovanni (sels), w. A. Tomowa–Sintow (sop), T. Zylis–Gara (sop), S. Milnes (bar), W. Berry (bass), K. Böhm (cnd), Vienna PO, Vienna State Opera Chorus—Scenes & Arias Deutsche Grammophon ▲ 429823-2 [ADD]

Mozart, W.A.:Exsultate, w. B. Klee (cnd), English CO [L] Novalis ▲ 150064 [DDD]

Mozart, W.A.:Missa, K.317, w. J. Rappé (ten), H. P. Blochwitz (ten), T. Quasthoff (bar), P. Schreier (cnd), Dresden Staatskapelle, Leipzig Radio Chorus Philips ▲ 426275-2

Mozart, W.A.:Missa brevis, K.220, w. T. Troyanos (mez), H. Laubenthal (ten), K. Engen (bass) Deutsche Grammophon ▲ 429820-2 [ADD]

Mozart, W.A.:Nozze di Figaro, w. Anneliese Rothenberger (sop), Hilde Gueden (sop), Peter Schreier (ten), Walter Berry (bar), Hermann Prey (bar), O. Suitner (cnd), Dresden Staatskapelle Berlin Classics 3-▲ BER 2096 [ADD]

Mozart, W.A.:Nozze di Figaro (sels), w. G. Janowitz (sop), T. Troyanos (mez), D. Fischer–Dieskau (bar), H. Prey (bar), K. Böhm (cnd), Berlin German Opera Orch—Scenes & Arias Deutsche Grammophon ▲ 429822-2 [ADD]

Mozart, W.A.:Requiem, w. J. Hamari (mez), W. Ochman (ten), K. Ridderbusch (bass), K. Böhm (cnd), Vienna PO, Vienna State Opera Chorus [L] Deutsche Grammophon ▲ 413553-2 [ADD]

Mozart, W.A.:Requiem, w. G. Bumbry (mez), G. Shirley (ten), M. Rintzler (bass), R. Frühbeck de Burgos (cnd), New Philharmonia Orch, New Philharmonia Chorus Classics for Pleasure ▲ CDCFP 4399 [ADD]

Mozart, W.A.:Sacred Music, w. B. Klee (cnd), English CO, Tallis Chamber Choir—Inter notos mulierum, K.72; Regina coeli, K.276; Laudate dominus from Vesperae solennes de confessore, K.339; Laudamus te (soprano aria) from Missa in c, K.427; Benedictus (soprano aria) from Missa brevis in B♭, K.275 [L] Novalis ▲ 150064 [DDD]

Mozart, W.A.:Schuldigkeit (sels), w. B. Klee (cnd), English CO—Sinf. & 2 arias [G] Novalis ▲ 150064 [DDD]

Mozart, W.A.:Songs, w. Karl Engel (pno) Novalis ▲ 150010 [DDD]

Mozart, W.A.:Zauberflöte, w. Reri Grist (sop), Edita Gruberová (sop), Rene Kollo (ten), Gerhard Unger (ten), Hermann Prey (bar), José Van Dam (b–bar), Peter Meven (bass), H. von Karajan (cnd), Vienna PO, Vienna State Opera Chorus *(rec live, Salzburg, July 26, 1974)* Arkadia 2-▲ 233

Mozart, W.A.:Zauberflöte, w. Karin Ott (sop), Janet Perry (sop), Anna Tomowa–Sintow (sop), Agnes Baltsa (mez), Hannah Schwarz (mez), Francisco Araiza (ten), Gottfried Hornik (bar), José Van Dam (b–bar), H. von Karajan (cnd), Berlin PO, German Opera Chorus [G] Deutsche Grammophon 3-▲ 410967-2 [DDD]

Mozart, W.A.:Zauberflöte (sels), w. Karin Ott (sop), Janet Perry (sop), Anna Tomowa–Sintow (sop), Agnes Baltsa (mez), Hannah Schwarz (mez), Francisco Araiza (ten), Gottfried Hornik (bar), José Van Dam (b–bar), H. von Karajan (cnd), Berlin PO, German Opera Chorus [G] Deutsche Grammophon ▲ 415287-2 [DDD]

Nicolai, O.:Lustigen Weiber, w. H. Donath (sop), H. Schwarz (mez), K. Ludwig (ten), K.–E. Mercker (ten), P. Schreier (ten), C. Dormoy (bar), B. Weikl (bar), K. Moll (bass), S. Vogel (bass), B. Klee (cnd), Berlin Staatskapelle, Berlin State Opera Chorus *(rec July 3, 1976)* Berlin Classics ("Eterna" series) ▲ BER 2046-2 [ADD]

Nicolai, O.:Lustigen Weiber, w. H. Donath (sop), H. Schwarz (cta), P. Schreier (ten), K. Moll (bass), B. Klee (cnd), Berlin Staatskapelle, Berlin State Opera Chorus Berlin Classics 2-▲ BER 2115 [ADD]

Schoeck, O.:Massimilla Doni, w. A. Küttenbaum (mez), H. Winkler (ten), H. Stamm (bass), G. Albrecht (cnd), Cologne RSO, Cologne Radio Chorus [G] Koch Schwann 2-▲ CD 314025 [DDD]

Schubert, Franz:Alfonso und Estrella, w. M. Falewicz (sop), P. Schreier (ten), H. Prey (bar), D. Fischer–Dieskau (bar), T. Adam (b–bar), O. Suitner (cnd), Berlin Staatskapelle, Berlin Radio Chorus Berlin Classics 3-▲ BER 2156 [ADD]

Mathis, Edith (sop) (cont.)

Schubert, Franz:Der Hirt auf dem Felsen, w. K. Weber (cl), K. Engel (pno) [G] Novalis ▲ 150026 [DDD]

Schubert, Franz:Lazarus, or Die Feier der Auferstehung, w. C. Wulkopf (mez), H. Schwarz (mez), W. Hollweg (ten), H. Laubenthal (ten), H. Prey (bar), G. Chmura (cnd), Stuttgart RSO, Stuttgart Radio Chorus [G] Orfeo ▲ 011101 [DDD]

Schubert, Franz:Songs (comp), w. G. Johnson (pno)—An die Musisk, D.547; Die Forelle, D.550; Schlaflied, D.527; Sehnsucht, D.516; Die Liebe, D.522; Impromptu, D.513a; Der Flug der Zeit, D.515; Trost, D.523; Die abgeblühte Linde, D514; Das Lied vom Reifen Hyperion ▲ CDJ 33021

Schubert, Franz:Songs (misc), w. K. Engel (pno)—18 songs [G] Novalis ▲ 150026 [DDD]

Schumann, R.:Liederkreis, Op. 39, w. Gérard Wyss (pno) *(rec Swiss Radio DRS, Studio Bern, May 20–22, 1994)* Denon ▲ CO 78947 [DDD]

Schumann, R.:Requiem Mignon, w. Christa Lehnert (sop), Maura Moreira (cta), Margarete Witte–Waldbauer (alt), Robert Titze (bass), R. Wagner (cnd), Innsbruck SO, Innsbruck Chorus *(rec Innsbruck, 1963)* Allegretto ▲ ACD 8190

Schumann, R.:Scenes from Goethe's "Faust", w. B. Rayner Cook (bar), D. Fischer–Dieskau (bar), G. Howell (bass), P. Boulez (cnd), BBC SO, BBC Sym Chorus *(rec live, London, March 7, 1973)* Memories 2-▲ HR 4489/90 [ADD]

Schumann, R.:Songs, w. Hidenori Komatsu (bar), Cord Garben (pno)—Duets from Opp. 37, 43, 74, 78 & 79 CPO ▲ CPO 999262 [DDD]

Schütz, H.:Die Geburt unsers Herren Jesu Christi, w. Georg Jelden (ten), Claus Ocker (bass), H. Thamm (cnd), *(ensemble unknown)*, Windsbach Boys' Choir EMI Classics ("Baroque" series) ▲ CDK 65736

Strauss, R.:Der Rosenkavalier, w. C. Ludwig (mez), T. Troyanos (mez), O. Wiener (bar), T. Adam (b–bar), K. Böhm (cnd), Vienna PO *(rec Salzburg Festival, 1969)* Deutsche Grammophon 3-▲ 445338-2 [ADD]

Zemlinsky, A. von:Kleider machen Leute, w. H. Winkler (ten), V. Vogel (ten), C. Otelli (bar), H. Franzen (bass), R. Scholze (bass), W. Slabbert (sgr), R. Weikert (cnd), Zurich Opera Orch, Zurich Opera House Chorus [G] *(rec live, Zurich Opera House, 6/29/90)* Koch Schwann 2-▲ CD 314 069 [DDD]

Mathis, Joyce (sop)

Mancini, H.:Film Music, w. A. Williams (sgr), L. Albright (sgr), B. Hackett (sgr), B. Greco (sgr), C. Byrd (sgr), P. Page (sgr), Mancini (cnd), Costa Orch, Conniff Orch, Mancini Orch—sels from Breakfast at Tiffany's; Peter Gunn; Mr. Lucky & others Columbia/Legacy ▲ CK 66505

Matorin, Vladimir (bass)

Rachmaninoff, S.:Aleko, w. Natalia Erassova (sop), Galina Borissova (cta), Vitaly Tarastchenko (ten), Viatcheslav Potchapski (bass), A. Tchistiakov (cnd), Bolshoi Theater Orch, Russian State Choir Russian Season 3-▲ CMX 388053

Rachmaninoff, S.:Francesca da Rimini, w. Maria Lapina (sop), Nilolaï Vassiliev (ten), Vitaly Tarastchenko (ten), Nikolaï Mechetniak (bar), A. Tchistiakov (cnd), Bolshoi Theater Orch, Russian State Choir Russian Season 3-▲ CMX 388053

Rachmaninoff, S.:Francesca da Rimini, w. V. Taraschenko (ten), N. Vasiliev (bar), A. Tchistiakov (cnd), Bolshoi Theater SO Soloists Russian Season ("Russian Season" series) ▲ LDC 288081

Rimsky–Korsakov, N.:Kaschei the Immortal, w. I. Jourina (sop), N. Terentieva (mez), A. Arkhipov (ten), V. Verestnikov (bar), A. Tchistiakov (cnd), Bolshoi Theater Orch, Yurloff Russian Choir [Russian] Russian Season ("Russian Season" series) ▲ LDC 288046 [DDD]

Matos, Eleni (mez)

Haydn, J.:Arianna a Naxos, w. P. Tiboris (cnd), Prague Virtuosi *(rec Studio Domovina, Prague, Mar 23–25, 1995)* Elysium ▲ GRK 706 [DDD]

Haydn, J.:Arias, w. Jeff Prillman (ten), P. Tiboris (cnd), Prague Virtuosi—L'anima del filosofo, H.XXVIII:13/3 [from Orfeo ed Euridice]; Scena di Berenice, H.XXIVa:10; Recitative & Aria of Oreste, H.XXIVa:10 [for Traetta's "Ifigenia in Tauride"] *(rec Studio Domovina, Prague, Mar 23–25, 1995)* Elysium ▲ GRK 706 [DDD]

Matromei, Gianpiero (bar)

Magda Olivero & Flaviano Labò in Concert, w. Magda Olivero (sop), Flaviano Labò (ten), Jacques Bazire (cnd), Marsiglia Opera Orch, Raina Kabaivanska (sop), Carlo Meliciani (bar), Oliveiro de Fabritiis (cnd), La Scala Orch, Turin RAI Orch *(rec between 1969 & 1973)* Bongiovanni ▲ GB 1105 [ADD]

Matrona, Pepe de la (voc)

Gough, O.:Saeta, w. Bruce Nockles (tpt), Michael Thompson (hn), John Pigneguy (hn), David Purser (trbn), Orlando Gough (kbd) *(rec London, 1995)* Catalyst ▲ 0902-668332-2 [DDD]

Matsumoto, Miwako (sop)

Mercadante, S.:Il bravo, w. Miwako Matsumoto (sop—Violetta), Giovanna di Rocco (sop—Michelina), William Johns (ten—Il Bravo), Antonio Savastano (ten—Pisani), Gino Sinimberghi (ten—Cappello), Loris Gambelli (bass—Marco), Mario Machì (bass—Luigi), Paolo Washington (bass—Foscari), Maria Parazzini (sgr—Teodora), G. Ferro (cnd), Rome Opera Orch, Rome Opera Chorus *(rec Rome, Dec 30, 1976)* Italia 3-▲ CDC 94 [ADD]

Mattei, Peter (bar)

Börtz, D.:Bacchanterna, w. Sylvia Lindenstrand (mez), K. Ingebretsen (cnd), Kungliga Hovkapellet [soundtrack to the T.V. production] Caprice 2-▲ CAP 22028

Duruflé, M.:Mass, "Cum jubilo", w. M. Wager (org), St. Jacobs Chamber Choir *(rec Nov. 9–12, 1992)* BIS ▲ CD 602 [DDD]

Duruflé, M.:Requiem, w. P. Hofman (ten), E. Lovotha (vc), M. Wager (org), St. Jacobs Chamber Choir *(rec Nov. 9–12, 1992)* BIS ▲ CD 602 [DDD]

Haeffner, J.C.F.:Electra, w. Hillevi Martinpelto (sop), Helle Hinz (sop), Mikael Samuelson (bar), Swedish Radio Choir, T. Schuback (cnd), Drottningholm Baroque Ensemble Caprice 2-▲ CAP 22030

Kraus, J.M.:Prosperin, w. Hillevi Martinpelto (sop), Susanne Rydén (sop), Anna Eklund–Tarantino (sgr), Lars Arvidson (bass), Stephen Smith (sgr), M. Tatlow (cnd), Stockholm CO, Stockholm Chamber Choir Musica Sveciae 2-▲ MSCD 422/23 [DDD]

Orff, C.:Carmina burana, w. Lena Nordin (sop), Hans Dornbusch (ten), Love Derwinger (pno), Roland Pöntinen (pno), Kroumata Percussion Ensemble, Cecilia Rydinger Alin (cnd), Allmänna Sången, Uppsala Choir School Children's Chorus [chamber version] *(rec Uppsala Univ Hall, Uppsala, Sweden, June 9–11, 1995)* BIS ▲ CD 734 [DDD]

Roman, J.H.:Bröllopsmusik, w. C. Högmann (sop), N.–E. Sparf (vn), E. Ericson (cnd), Drottningholm Baroque Ensemble *(rec 1992)* Musica Sveciae ▲ MSCD 413 [DDD]

Roman, J.H.:Jubilate, w. C. Högmann (sop), E. Ericson (cnd), Drottningholm Baroque Ensemble, Eric Ericson Chamber Choir *(rec 1992)* Musica Sveciae ▲ MSCD 413 [DDD]

Stenhammar, W.:Florez och Blanzefor, w. P. Järvi (cnd), Malmö SO [Sw] BIS ▲ CD 550 [DDD]

Mattei, Roberto (bar)

Cavalieri, E. de:Rappresentatione di Anima et di Corpo, w. G. Bertagnolli (sop), C. Cavina (alt), B. Rossetti (sgr), G. Maletto (ten), A. Abete (sgr), M. Longhini (cnd), Verona Istitutioni Harmoniche Stradivarius ▲ STR 33339 [DDD]

Matteini, Giuliana (sop)

Leo, L.:La Morte di Abele, w. Emilia Cundari (sop—Angelo), Giuliana Matteini (sop—Abele), Adriana Lazzarini (mez—Eva), Ferrando Ferrari (ten—Caino), Paolo Montarsolo (bass—Adamo), C. F. Cillario (cnd), Angelicum CO, Turin Polyphonic Chorus Dynamic 2-▲ CDL 144

Matteo, Vincenzo di (bar)

Rossini, G.:La pietra del paragone, w. M. C. Nocentini (sop), A. Trovarelli (mez), H. M. Molinari (cta), P. Barbacini (ten), R. Scaltriti (bar), A. Svab (bar), P. Rumetz (bass), C. Desderi (cnd), Camerata Musicale Orch, Modeno Teatro Comunale Chorus [I] *(rec 1992)* Nuova Era 2-▲ 7132/33 [DDD]

Matteuzzi, William (ten)

Cimarosa, D.:Il Matrimonio segreto, w. Susan Patterson (sop—Carolina), Janet Williams (mez—Elisseta), Gloria Banditelli (cta—Fidalma), William Matteuzzi (ten—Paolino), Alfonso Antoniozzi (bass—Geronimo), Petteri Salomaa (bass—Count Robinson), Hans Ludwig Hirsch (pno), G. Bellini (cnd), Eastern Netherlands Orch *(rec Muziekcentrum Enschede, Holland, Aug 26–Sept 8, 1991)* Arts 3-▲ 471172 [DDD]

Donizetti, G.:La fille du régiment, w. L. Serra (sop), M. Tagliasacchi (sop), E. Dara (bar), B. Campanella (cnd), Bologna Teatro Comunale Orch, Bologna Teatro Comunale Chorus [I] *(rec live, 2/16–26/89)* Nuova Era 2-▲ 6791/92 [DDD]

Opera Arias, w. Richard Bonynge (cnd), Bruno Campanella (cnd), Vittorio Parisi (cnd), various orchs & choruses Nuova Era ▲ NUO 6892 [DDD]

Matteuzzi, William (ten) (cont.)
Rossini, G.:Il barbiere di Siviglia, w. C. Bartoli (mez), L. Nucci (bar), P. Burchuladze (bass), G. Patanè (cnd), Bologna Teatro Comunale Orch, Bologna Teatro Comunale Chorus [I] London 3-▲ 425520-2 [DDD]
Rossini, G.:Il barbiere di Siviglia (sels), w. C. Bartoli (mez), L. Nucci (bar), P. Burchuladze (bass), G. Patanè (cnd), Bologna Teatro Comunale Orch, Bologna Teatro Comunale Chorus London ▲ 440289-2 [DDD]
Rossini, G.:La Cenerentola, w. C. Bartoli (mez—Cenerentola), F. Costa (mez—Clorinda), G. Banditelli (cta—Tisbe), W. Matteuzzi (ten—Don Ramiro), A. Corbelli (bar—Dandini), E. Dara (bar—Don Magnifico), M. Pertusi (bass—Alidoro), R. Chailly (cnd), Bologna Teatro Comunale Orch, Bologna Teatro Comunale Chorus *(rec June 22-July 2, 1992)* London 2-▲ 436902-2 [DDD]
Rossini, G.:La gazza ladra, w. K. Ricciarelli (sop), S. Ramey (bass), G. Gelmetti (cnd), Turin RSO *(rec live, Rossini Opera Festival in Pesaro, Italy, Aug. 1989)* Sony Classical 3-▲ S3K 45850 [DDD]
Rossini, G.:La pietra del paragone, w. Tiziana Carraro (sop—Fulvia), Elisabetta Gutierrez (mez—Baronessa Aspasia), Sara Mingardo (cta—Clarice), William Matteuzzi (ten—Giocondo), Marco Camastra (bar—Pacuvio), Pietro Spagnoli (bar—Conte Asdrubale), Gioacchino Zarrelli (bar—Fabrizio), José Fardilha (bass—Macrobio), B. Aprea (cnd), Graz SO, Sluk Chamber Chorus Bratislava *(rec 1993)* Bongiovanni 2-▲ GB 2179/80 [DDD]
Rossini, G.:La scala di seta, w. Luciana Serra (sop), Oslavio di Credico (ten), Roberto Coviello (bar), Natale de Carolis (b-bar), G. Ferro (cnd), Bologna Teatro Comunale Orch Fonit Cetra ("Ricordi" series) 2-▲ FCT RFCD 2003
Tosti, P.F.:Songs, w. P. Molinari (pno)—Chi sei tu; Van gli effluvi; O falce di luna calante; Ninna Nanna; That Day; Speak!; Pierrot's Lament; I Am Not Fair; Summer; Starlight; Lasciami; L'alba separa dalla luce l'ombra; In van preghi; Che dici Dynamic ▲ CD 109 [DDD]

Matthau, Walter (nar)
Saint-Saëns, C.:Carnival of the Animals, w. M. Golabek (nar), R. Golabek (nar), F. Savage (nar), C. Heston (nar), J. E. Jones (nar), B. White (nar), L. Redgrave (nar), W. Shatner (nar), J. Rivers (nar), T. Danson (nar), L. Tomlin (nar), D. Raffin (nar), A. Hepburn (nar), D. Moore (nar), J. Smith (nar), L. Schifrin (cnd), Hollywood CO Dove Audio ▲ DOV 30700

Matthews, Andrea (sop)
Gershwin, G.:Porgy & Bess (sels), w. D. Brown (sop), Jackson (sgr), Duncan (sgr), A. Smallens (cnd), *(orch unknown) (rec 1942 Broadway revival cas)* MCA ■ MCAC 1631 (m)
Handel, G.F.:Berenice, w. Julianne Baird (sop—Berenice), Andrea Matthews (sop—Alessandro), D'Anna Fortunato (mez—Selene), Jennifer Lane (mez—Demetrio), Drew Minter (alt—Arsace), John McMaster (ten—Fabio), Jan Opalach (bass—Aristobolo), R. Palmer (cnd), Brewer CO Newport Classic 3-▲ NPD 85620/3 [DDD]
Handel, G.F.:Muzio Scevola, w. Julianne Baird (sop—Clelia), Andrea Matthews (sop—Fidalma), Erie Mills (sop—Orazio), D'Anna Fortunato (mez—Muzio), Jennifer Lane (mez—Irene), Frederick Urrey (ten—Tarquino), John Ostendorf (b-bar—Porsenna), R. Palmer (cnd), Brewer Baroque CO [period instrs] [I] *(rec 10/91)* Newport Classic 2-▲ NPD 85540/2 [DDD]
Handel, G.F.:Siroe, Rè di Persia, w. Julianne Baird (mez), D'Anna Fortunato (mez), Steven Rickards (ct), Frederick Urrey (ten), John Ostendorf (b-bar), R. Palmer (cnd), Brewer Baroque CO [period instrs] [I] Newport Classic 3-▲ NCD 60125 [DDD]
Handel, G.F.:Tolomeo, Rè di Egitto, w. Brenda Harris (sop—Seleuce), Andrea Matthews (sop—Elisa), Mary Ann Hart (mez—Alessandro), Jennifer Lane (mez—Tolomeo), Peter Castaldi (bar—King Araspe), Bradley Brookshire (hpd), R.A. Clark (cnd), Manhattan CO *(rec St. Jean Baptiste Church, NY, Mar 1995)* Vox Classics 3-▲ VOX 7530
Herbert, V.:Music of, w. R.A. Clark (cnd), Manhattan CO Newport Classic ▲ NPT 85572
Rorem, N.:3 Sisters Who Are Not Sisters, w. Andrea Matthews (sop—Jenny), Carol Flamm (sgr—Helen), Madeline Tsingopoulos (sgr—Ellen), Frederick Urrey (ten—Samuel), Mark Singer (sgr—Sylvester), John Van Buskirk (pno) Newport Classic ▲ NPT 85594 [DDD]
Somary, J.:Songs of Innocence, w. Zheng Zhou (bar), J. Somary (cnd), Bronx Arts Ensemble Premier ▲ PRCD 1042 [DDD]

Matthews, Brian (bar)
Gershwin, G.:Porgy & Bess (sels), w. C. Lindsey (sop), E. Stratta (cnd), Festival Orch—ten songs, most in concert arrs. by Robert Russell Bennett Kem-Disc ▲ 1008 [DDD]

Matthews, Edward (bar)
Gershwin, G.:Porgy & Bess, w. A. Brown (sgr), H. Jackson (sgr), Todd Duncan (sgr), H. Dowdy (sgr), A. Long (sgr), Eva Jessye Choir [1940-1942 original cast] MCA Classics ("Broadway Gold" series) ▲ MCAD 10520 ■ MCAC 10520
Thomson, V.:4 Saints in 3 Acts, w. Inez Matthews (sop—St Settlement), Beatrice Robinson-Wayne (sop—St Teresa I), Altonell Hines (mez—Commère), Ruby Greene (alt—St Teresa II), David Bethea (ten—St Stephen), Charles Holland (ten—St Chavez), Edward Matthews (bar—St Ignatius), Randolph Robinson (bar—St Plan), Abner Dorsey (bass—Compère), V. Thomson (cnd), *(orch unknown)* [abridged by Thompson] *(rec June 25, 1947)* RCA Gold Seal ▲ 09026-68163-2 [ADD]

Matthews, Inez (sop)
Thomson, V.:4 Saints in 3 Acts, w. Inez Matthews (sop—St Settlement), Beatrice Robinson-Wayne (sop—St Teresa I), Altonell Hines (mez—Commère), Ruby Greene (alt—St Teresa II), David Bethea (ten—St Stephen), Charles Holland (ten—St Chavez), Edward Matthews (bar—St Ignatius), Randolph Robinson (bar—St Plan), Abner Dorsey (bass—Compère), V. Thomson (cnd), *(orch unknown)* [abridged by Thompson] *(rec June 25, 1947)* RCA Gold Seal ▲ 09026-68163-2 [ADD]

Matthews, Tamara (sop)
Bach, J.S.:St. John Passion, w. Jennifer Lane (alt), Mark Bleeke (ten—Evangelist), David Vanderwal (ten), Kevin Walsh (bar—Pilate), Nathaniel Watson (bass—Jesus), E. Milnes (cnd), Trinity Baroque Orch, Trinity Cathedral Choir *(rec Trinity Cathedral, Portland, OR, Mar 31, 1996)* PGM 2-▲ PGM 111
Buxtehude, D.:Cants, w. Laura Heimes (sop), Steven Richards (ct), James Russell (ten), John Alston (bass), M. N. Johnson (cnd), Sarum Consort, St. Peter's in the Great Valley Chamber Choir—Wachet auf, ruft uns die Stimme!; Singet dem Herrn; Quemadmodum desiderat cervus; O fröhliche Stunden, o herrliche Zeit; Jubilate Domino omnis terra; Lobe den Herrn, meine Seele; Erfreue dich, Erde! *(rec St-Martin-in-the-Fields Church, Chestnut Hill, PA, Sept 7-9, 1994)* Pro gloria musicae ▲ PGM 102 [DDD]

Mattila, Karita (sop)
Bruckner, A.:Mass 3, w. M. Lipovšek (mez), T. Moser (ten), K. Moll (bass), C. Davis (cnd), Bavarian RSO, Bavarian Radio Chorus [L] Philips ▲ 422358-2 [DDD]
Heiniö, M.:Vuelo de Alambre, w. J. Mercier (cnd), Turku PO Finlandia ▲ FIN 99403 [DDD]
Hindemith, P.:Das Marienleben, w. U. Söderblom (cnd), Lahti SO Finlandia ▲ FIN 99403 [DDD]
Hindemith, P.:Das Marienleben, w. U. Söderblom (cnd), Lahti SO, Savonlinna Opera Festival Chorus *(rec Dec. 1987 & May 1988)* Finlandia ▲ 4509-95857-2 [DDD]
James Levine's 25th Anniversary Metropolitan Opera Gala, w. J. Levine (cnd), Metropolitan Opera Orch, Ileana Cotrubas (sop), Renée Fleming (sop), Hei-Kyung Hong (sop), Birgit Nilsson (sop), Ruth Ann Swenson (sop), Kiri Te Kanawa (sop), Deborah Voigt (sop), Grace Bumbry (mez), Heidi Grant Murphy (mez), Anne Sofie von Otter (mez) *(rec live, Metropolitan Opera House, New York, Apr 27, 1996)* Deutsche Grammophon ▲ 449177-2 [DDD]
Kaipainen, J.:Starlit Night, w. O. Vänskä (cnd), Lahti Chamber Ensemble [Fin] Ondine ▲ ODE 792-2 [DDD]
Merikanto, A.:Genesis, w. U. Söderblom (cnd), Lahti SO, Savonlinna Opera Festival Chorus *(rec Dec. 1987 & May 1988)* Finlandia ▲ 4509-95857-2 [DDD]
Mozart, W.A.:Così fan tutte, w. E. Szmytka (sop), A. S. von Otter (mez), F. Araiza (ten), T. Allen (bar), J. van Dam (b-bar), N. Marriner (cnd), Academy of St. Martin in the Fields, Ambrosian Opera Chorus [I] Philips 3-▲ 422381-2 [DDD]
Mozart, W.A.:Don Giovanni, w. S. Sweet (sop), M. McLaughlin (sop), F. Araiza (ten), T. Allen (bar), S. Alaimo (b-bar), R. Lloyd (bass), N. Marriner (cnd), Academy of St. Martin in the Fields, Ambrosian Opera Chorus Philips 3-▲ 432129-2 [DDD]
Mozart, W.A.:Don Giovanni (sels), w. F. Araiza (ten), T. Allen (bar), R. Lloyd (bass), N. Marriner (cnd), Academy of St. Martin in the Fields Philips ▲ 438494-2
Mozart, W.A.:Nozze di Figaro, w. L. Cherici (sop), M. McLaughlin (sop), M. Bacelli (mez), N. Curiel (mez), U. Benelli (ten), L. Gallo (bar), A. Nosotti (bass), M. Pertusi (bass), G. Tadeo (bass), Z. Mehta (cnd), Florence Maggio Musicale Orch, Florence Maggio Musicale Chorus Sony Classical ▲ SK 53286

Mattila, Karita (sop) (cont.)
Reger, M.:An die Hoffnung, w. C. Abbado (cnd), Berlin PO *(rec Philharmonie, Berlin, Feb. 26-28, 1993)* Sony Classical ▲ SK 53975 [DDD]
Sallinen, A.:Dream Songs, w. U. Söderblom (cnd), Lahti SO, Savonlinna Opera Festival Chorus *(rec Dec. 1987 & May 1988)* Finlandia ▲ 4509-95857-2 [DDD]
Sallinen, A.:Dream Songs, w. U. Söderblom (cnd), Lahti SO Finlandia ▲ FIN 99403 [DDD]
Schubert, Franz:Fierrabras, w. C. Studer (sop), R. Gambill (ten), T. Hampson (bar), R. Holl (bass), L. Polgar (bass), C. Abbado (cnd), CO of Europe, Arnold Schoenberg Choir [G] *(rec live)* Deutsche Grammophon 2-▲ 427341-2 [DDD]
Sibelius, J.:Kullervo, w. J. Hynninen (bar), N. Järvi (cnd), Gothenburg SO, Laulun Ystävät Male Choir [Fin] BIS ▲ CD 313
Sibelius, J.:Songs, w. Ilmo Ranta (pno)—Svarta rosor; Flickan komifran sin äsklings möte; Var det en dröm; The Flower Songs Ondine ▲ ODE 856
Sibelius, J.:Syms (comp), w. J. Hynninen (bar), N. Järvi (cnd), Gothenburg SO, Laulun Ystävät Male Choir BIS 4-▲ CD 622/24 [ADD]
Strauss, R.:Hymnen von Friedrich Hölderlin, w. C. Abbado (cnd), Berlin PO *(rec Philharmonie, Berlin, Feb. 26-28, 1993)* Sony Classical ▲ SK 53975 [DDD]
Strauss, R.:Songs, w. M. Tilson Thomas (cnd), London SO—Zueignung, Op. 10/1; Muttertändelei, Op. 43/2; Meinem Kinde, Op. 37/3; Die heiligen drei Könige aus Morgenlied; Frühlingsfeier, Op. 56/5 *(rec Oct. 3-4, 1991)* Sony Classical ▲ SK 48242 [DDD]
Weber, C.M. von:Der Freischütz (sels), w. E. Lind (sop), F. Araiza (ten), K. Moll (bass), C. Davis (cnd), Dresden Staatskapelle Philips ▲ 438497-2

Mattioli, Renata (sop)
Mascagni, P.:Guglielmo Ratcliff, w. P.M. Ferraro (ten), F. Mazzoli (bass), A. La Rosa Parodi (cnd), RAI SO *(rec 1963)* Memories ▲ MEM 4515 [ADD]
Paisiello, G.:Fedra, w. O. Beggiato (sop), A. Tuccari (sop), L. Udovick (sop), A. Lazzari (ten), A. Questa (cnd), Milan RAI SO, Milan RAI Chorus *(rec 1958)* Memories 2-▲ MEM 4502 [AAD]
Puccini, G.:La Bohème (sels), w. P. Pellegrini (sgr), Bellesia (sgr), L. Pavarotti (ten), F. Molinari-Pradelli (cnd), Reggio Emilia Teatro Municipale Orch—sels from Pavarotti's debut performance *(rec live, Apr 29, 1961)* Melodram 2-▲ MEL 27031 [AAD]

Mattioli, Vito (bar)
Puccini, G.:La Bohème (sels), w. Bianco Bellisia (sop—Musetta), Alberto Pellegrini (sop—Mimi), Luciano Pavarotti (ten—Rodolfo), Walter de Ambrosis (bar—Schaunard), Vito Mattioli (bar—Marcello), Dmitri Nabokov (bass—Colline), Reggio Emilia Teatro Municipale Orch, Reggio Emilia Teatro Municipale Chorus Budget ("The Greatest Voice in Opera" series) ▲ SYP 105

Mattiucci, Franca (mez)
Pacini, G.:Saffo, w. L. Gencer (sop), T. del Bianco (ten), L. Quilico (bar), F. Capuana (cnd), Naples Teatro San Carlo Orch, Naples Teatro San Carlo Chorus [I] *(rec live, 4/7/67)* Arkadia 2-▲ 541 (m) [AAD]

Mattmann, Elisabeth (sop)
Balsons des Fleurs, w. Claude Chappuis (gtr) Gallo ▲ CD 751 [DDD]

Mattmüller, Beat (ct)
Coelho Neto, M.:Maria mater gratiae, w. Luiz Alves da Silva (ct), Markus Schikora (ten), Peter Mächler (b), L. A. da Silva (cnd), Turicum Ensemble *(rec Studio DRS, Zurich, Sept 26-29, 1994)* Claves ▲ CD 9521 [DDD]
Garcia, J.M.N.:Motets, w. Katharina Ott (sop), Luiz Alves da Silva (ct), Andreas Schmidt (ct), Markus Schikora (ten), William Lombardi (ten), Peter Mächler (bass), Michael Leibundgut (bass), L. A. da Silva (cnd), Turicum Ensemble *(rec Studio DRS, Zurich, Sept 26-29, 1994)* Claves ▲ CD 9521 [DDD]
Mesquita, J.J.E.L. de:Antiphona de Nossa Senhora, w. Luiz Alves da Silva (ct), Markus Schikora (ten), Peter Mächler (bass), L. A. da Silva (cnd), Turicum Ensemble *(rec Studio DRS, Zurich, Sept 26-29, 1994)* Claves ▲ CD 9521 [DDD]
Mesquita, J.J.E.L. de:Tercio, w. Luiz Alves da Silva (ct), Markus Schikora (ten), Michael Leibundgut (bass), L. A. da Silva (cnd), Turicum Ensemble *(rec Studio DRS, Zurich, Sept 26-29, 1994)* Claves ▲ CD 9521 [DDD]
Mesquita, J.J.E.L. de:Tractus (4) para o Sábado Santo, w. Luiz Alves da Silva (ct), Markus Schikora (ten), Michael Leibundgut (bass), L. A. da Silva (cnd), Turicum Ensemble *(rec Studio DRS, Zurich, Sept 26-29, 1994)* Claves ▲ CD 9521 [DDD]
Pinto, L.A.:Te Deum Laudamus, w. Katharina Ott (sop), Luiz Alves da Silva (ct), Andreas Schmidt (ct), Markus Schikora (ten), William Lombardi (ten), Peter Mächler (bass), Michael Leibundgut (bass), L. A. da Brooks (cnd), Turicum Ensemble *(rec Studio DRS, Zurich, Sept 26-29, 1994)* Claves ▲ CD 9521 [DDD]

Mattson, E. (sgr)
Rodgers, R.:Carousel, w. J. Raitt (sgr), J. Clayton (sgr), J. Darling (sgr), C. Johnson (sgr), M. Vye (sgr), C. Baxter (sgr), J. Littau (cnd) [1945 cast] MCA Classics ▲ MCAD 10048 [AAD] ■ MCAC 10048

Matzenauer, Margarete (mez)
Pasquale Amato, w. Pasquale Amato (bar), Frieda Hempel (sop) *(rec by Victor & Fonotipia 1909-1914)* Preiser ("Lebendige Vergangenheit" series) ▲ PRE 89064 (m) [AAD]

Maultsby, Nancy (mez)
Mozart, W.A.:Requiem, w. Ruth Ziesak (sop), Richard Croft (ten), David Arnold (bar), M. Pearlman (cnd), Boston Baroque Orch [completion by Robert Levin; performed on period instruments] *(rec Campion Center, Weston, MA, Nov 2-3, 1994)* Telarc ▲ CD 80410 [DDD]
Purcell, H.:Dido & Aeneas, w. Nancy Maultsby (sop—Dido), Susannah Waters (sop—Belinda), Margaret O'Keefe (sop—1st Witch), Sharon Baker (sop—2nd Woman), Laura Tucker (mez—Sorceress), Donna Ames (alt—Spirit), Richard Clement (ten—Sailor), Russell Braun (bar—Aeneas), M. Pearlman (cnd), Boston Baroque Orch Telarc ▲ CD 80424 [DDD]
Weisgall, H.:Six Characters in Search of an Author, w. E. Byrne (sop—Stepdaughter), S. Foster (sop—Prompter), E. Furtal (sop—Coloratura), J. King (mez—Mezzo), N. Maultsby (mez—Mother), P. LoVerne (cta—Madame Pace), D. Pritchett (alt—Wardrobe Mistress), B. Fowler (ten—Tenore Boffo), K. Anderson (ten—Director), A. Schroeder (bar—Accompanist), P. Zawisza (bar—Stage Manager), R. Orth (bar—Father), G. Lehman (bar—Son), M. Wadsworth (b-bar—Basso Cantante), L. Schaenen (cnd), Chicago Lyric Opera Orch, Lyric Opera Center Chorus *(rec Chicago, June 14 & 16, 1990)* New World 2-▲ 80454-2

Maurane, Camille (bar)
Debussy, C.:Pelléas et Mélisande, w. J. Micheau (sop), R. Gorr (mez), M. Roux (bar), X. Depraz (bass), J. Fournet (cnd), Lamoureux Orch *(rec 1953)* Philips 2-▲ 434783-2

Maurel, Victor (bar)
Verdi, G.:Otello (sels), w. C. Muzio (sop), R. Ponselle (sop), H. Spani (sop), E. Caruso (ten), N. Fusati (ten), L. Melchior (ten), F. Merli (ten), F. Tamagno (ten), B. Franci (bar), V. Maurel (bar), R. Stracciari (bar), T. Ruffo (bar) *(rec 1906-1933)* Music Memoria ▲ 30219
Victor Maurel:The Complete Recordings *(rec 1903-07)* Pearl ▲ PEA 9027 [AAD]

Maurette, Jean-Luc (ten)
Berlioz, H.:Les Troyens, w. F. Pollet (sop—Dido), D. Voigt (sop—Cassandre), C. Dubosc (sop—Ascagne), H. Perraguin (cta—Anna), G. Lakes (ten—Aeneas), J.-L. Maurette (ten—Iopas), J. M. Ainsley (ten—Hylas), M. P. (ten—Panthee), G. Cross (ten—Sinon), G. Quilico (bar—Chorebe), J.-P. Courtis (b-bar—Narbal), M. Belleau (bass—Ghost of Hector), R. Schirrer (bass—Priam), C. Dutoit (cnd), Montreal SO, Montreal Sym Chorus London 4-▲ 443693-2 [DDD]
Massenet, J.:Cléopâtre, w. B. Harries (sop), Danièle Streiff (sop), M. Olmeda (sop), D. Henry (bar), M. Hacquard (bar), P. Fournillier (cnd), St.-Etienne Nouvel Orch, Saint-Etienne Nouvel Choirs [F] *(rec live, Massenet Festival in Saint-Etienne 1990)* Koch Schwann 2-▲ 3-1032-2 [DDD]
Rossini, G.:Péchés de vieillesse (sels), w. M. Castets (sop), M. Georg (mez), M. Brodard (bar), R. Nolte (bass), E. Kalvelage (pno), C. Spering (org), M. Jorand (perc), Cologne Chorus Musicus—Toast pour le nouvel an, Roméo, La Grande Coquette, Un sou, Chanson de Zora, La Nuit de Noël, Le Dodo des enfants, Le Lazzarone, Adieux à la viel, Soupirs et sourire, L'Orpheline du Tyrol, Choeur de chasseurs démocrates; *Morceaux réservés*—Ave Maria, Les Amants de Séville, Le Chant des Titans, Chant funèbre [F] *(rec Aug. 1992)* Opus 111 ▲ OPS 30-70 [DDD]

Maurice, Glenda (mez)
Debussy, C.:La Damoiselle élue, w. I. Cotrubas (sop), G. Bertini (cnd), Stuttgart RSO, Stuttgart Radio Chorus [F] Orfeo ▲ 012821 [DDD]

Mauro, Ermanno (ten)
Bellini, V.:Norma, w. Margherita Rinaldi (sop—Adalgisa), Renata Scotto (sop—Norma), Giuseppina Arista (mez—Clotilde), Ermanno Mauro (ten—Pollione), Giancarlo Turati (ten—Flavio), Agostino Ferrin (bass—Oroveso), R. Muti (cnd), Florence Teatro Comunale Orch, Florence Teatro Comunale Chorus *(rec Florence, Dec 19, 1978)* Legato Classics 2-▲ LCD 203-2
Great Tenor Arias, w. Edmonton SO [cnd:Uri Mayer] CBC Records ("SM 5000" series) ▲ SMCD 5046 [DDD]

Mauro, M. (sop)
Fioravanti, V.:Le cantatrici villane, w. G. Manci (sop—Agata), M. Mauro (sop—Nunziella), M. A. Peters (sop—Rosa), F. Sovilla (mez—Giannetta), E. Palacio (ten—Carlino), G. Gatti (bar—Don Bucefalo), D. Serraiocco (bass—Don Marco), R. Tigani (cnd), Frosinone Licinio Refice Conservatory SO *(rec Oct. 22, 23 & 25, 1992)* Bongiovanni 2-▲ GB 2135/36 [DDD]

Maus, Peter (ten)
Bach, J.S.:Cant 150, w. M. Schreiber (sop), M. Jetter (cta), H.-F. Kunz (bass), H. Rilling (cnd), Bach Ensemble *(rec June-July 1970)* Hänssler Classic ▲ 98.835 [AAD]
Donizetti, G.:Messa di Gloria e Credo, w. H. Mané (sop), G. Vighi (mez), M. Machi (bass), R. Bader (cnd), Berlin RSO, St. Hedwig's Cathedral Choir [L] Koch Schwann ▲ CD 313031 [ADD]
Herzogenberg, H. von:Die Geburt Christi, w. R. Schudel (sop), A. Eggers (cta), E. Schramm (bass), C. Grube (cnd), Oriol Ensemble, *(various choruses)* [G] Hänssler Classic 2-▲ 98.574 [AAD]
Mozart, W.A.:Missa [longa], K.262, w. Regina Schudel (sop), Ulla Groenewold (cta), Berthold Possemeyer (bar), U. Gronostay (cnd), Berlin Radio Sinfonietta, Berlin Radio Chamber Choir [L] Koch Schwann ▲ CD 313 021 [ADD/DDD]
Mozart, W.A.:Missa brevis, K.258, w. Regina Schudel (sop), Ulla Groenewold (cta), Berthold Possemeyer (bar), U. Gronostay (cnd), Berlin Radio Sinfonietta, Berlin Chamber Chorus [L] Koch Schwann ▲ CD 313 021 [ADD/DDD]
Wolf, H.:Der Corregidor, w. H. Donath (sop), D. Soffel (mez), W. Hollweg (ten), K. Moll (bass), D. Fischer-Dieskau (bar), G. Albrecht (cnd), Berlin RSO [G] Koch Schwann 2-▲ CD 314 010

Maxwell, Donald (bar)
The Best of Richard Hickox, w. R. Hickox (cnd), London SO, London Sym Chorus, Penelope Walmsley-Clark (sop), John Graham-Hall (ten), Southend Boys' Choir, London Voices IMP Classics 3-▲ TCD 1073 [DDD]
Britten, H.:The Rape of Lucretia (sels), w. C. Pierard (sop), P. Rozario (sop), A. Gunson (mez), J. Rigby (cta), N. Robson (ten), A. Opie (bar), A. Miles (bass), R. Hickox (cnd), City of London Sinfonia Chandos 2-▲ CHAN 9254/55 [DDD]
Howells, H.:Missa sabrinensis, w. Janice Watson (sop), Della Jones (cta), Martyn Hill (ten), G. Rozhdestvensky (cnd), London SO, London Sym Chorus Chandos ▲ CHAN 9348 [DDD]
Music for the Theatre, w. A. Reynolds (cnd), London Salon Ensemble, Miranda Keys (sop) Meridian ▲ MER 84308 [DDD]
Orff, C.:Carmina burana, w. P. Walmsley-Clark (sop), J. Graham-Hall (ten), R. Hickox (cnd), London SO, London Sym Chorus [G, L] IMP Classics ▲ PCD 855
Sullivan, A.:The Yeomen of the Guard, w. Felicity Palmer (sop—Dame Carruthers), Pamela Helen Stephens (mez—Phoebe Meryll), Neill Archer (ten—Col Fairfax), Peter Hoare (ten—Leonard Meryll), Ralph Mason (ten—1st Yeoman), Donald Maxwell (bar—Wilfred Shadbolt), Peter Savidge (bar—Lieutenant Sir Richard Cholmondely), Donald Adams (bass—Sergeant Meryll), Richard Suart (bass—Jack Point), Peter Lloyd Evans (sgr—2nd Yeoman), Alwyn Mellor (sgr—Elsie Maynard), Clare O'Neill (sgr—Kate), C. Mackerras (cnd), Welsh National Opera Orch, Welsh National Opera Chorus *(rec Brangwyn Hall, Swasea, Wales, Apr 18-30 & May 1, 1995)* Telarc 2-▲ CD 80404 [DDD]

Maxwell, Linn (mez)
Argento, D.:From the Diary of V. Woolf, w. W. Huckaby (pno) [E] *(rec 1988)* Centaur ▲ CRC 2092 [DDD]
Pfitzner, H.:Songs, w. R. Benoit (pno)—12 songs—Op. 2, Nos. 2,4 & 6; Op. 9, Nos. 2,3 & 5; Opp. 11/4, 24/4 & 26/2 & 3 & 29/2; Folk song, "Untreu und Trost" [G] Centaur ▲ CRC 2070 [DDD]
Strauss, R.:Songs, w. R. Benoit (pno)—9 songs—Opp. 10/8, 21/1, 41b/2, 48/3-5, 49/5 & 69/5; Weinachtsgefühl (1899) [G] Centaur ▲ CRC 2070 [DDD]

May, Gisela (mez)
Weill, K.:Songs, w. H. Krtschil (pno) [G] Capriccio ▲ 10180 [DDD]

May, Jack (nar)
Vaughan Williams, R.:An Oxford Elegy, w. S. Darlington (cnd), English String Orch, Christ Church Cathedral Choir Oxford Nimbus ▲ NI 5166 [DDD]

May, Richard (bass)
Strauss, R.:Der Rosenkavalier (sels), w. Anni Andrassy (mez), B. Walter (cnd), *(orch unknown)*—Finale from Act 2 *(rec May 18, 1929)* Iron Needle ▲ IN 1312 [ADD]

May, Sylvie de (sop)
Lefébure-Wély, L.J.A.:Music of, w. Catherine Ravenne (alt), Xavier Bisaro (org), Vincent Genvrin (org), La Lyre Seraphique, L'Accent Grave Vocal Ensemble—Adoremus et procidamus; Marche en mib majeur; Adoro te [alterné]; Tantum ergo; Sacris solemnis; Elévation en la mineur; Marche en ut majeur; Noël varié, offertoire pour le jour de Noël; Sanctus; O Salutaris; Pastorale en sol majeur; Agnus Dei; Communion en fa majeur; Domine salvum; Missum redemptorem; Sortie en sib majeur et Cloches Media 7 ▲ 005 [DDD]
Lefébure-Wély, L.J.A.:Music of, w. Sophie Fournier (sop), Catherine Ravenne (alt), Antoine Espagno (db), Vincent Genvrin (org), La Lyre Seraphique, Pythagore Vocal Ensemble—Sainte cité, demeure permanente; Récit de Hautbois ou de Trompette harmonique; L'Encens divin; Offertoire [grand choeur]; Seigneur dès ma première enfance; Verset; Pleins de ferveur; Marche; Jour heureux, sainte allégresse; Esprit divin, Dieu de lumière; Andante, choeur de voix humaines; Afin d'être docile et sage; Mon fils, pour apprendre; Andante; Motet à la Sainte-Vierge; Andante; Du Roi des cieux tout célèbre la gloire; Scène pastorale; Andantino Media 7 ▲ 004 [DDD]

Mayer, Elisabeth (sop)
Gassmann, F.L.:La Contessina, w. Susanne Ganglberger (sop—Vespina), Elisabeth Mayer (sop—Contessina), Barbara Eisschiel (mez—Lindoro), Hermann Diller (ten—Gazzetta), Kurt Köller (bar—Pancrazio), Joseph Pichler (Graf Baccellone), H. Dechant (cnd), Collegium Aureum Bayer 2-▲ BR 100 252/3 [DDD]

Mayer, Emma (cta)
Lortzing, A.:Zar und Zimmermann, w. M. Gripekoven (sop—Marie), E. Mayer (cta—Widow Browe), H. Buchta (ten—Peter Ivonov), H. Schmid-Berikoven (ten—Marquis de Chateauneuf), G. Hann (b-bar—Tsar Peter I), W. Strienz (b-bar—Van Bett), B. Müller (bass) Myto 2-▲ MCD 943103

Mayer-Reinach, Ursula (mez)
Ben-Haim, P.:A Star Fell Down, w. P. Ben-Haim (pno) [He] Gallo ▲ CD 530 [AAD]
Bizet, G.:Songs, w. John Papaioannou (pno)—Adieux de l'Hotesse Arabe; Ouvre ton Coeur Gallo ▲ CD 605
Brandmüller, T.:Wie Du unsern Vätern geschworen hast, w. G. Augst (org), Mayence Brass Quartet [G] Gallo ▲ CD 604 [AAD]
David, Felicien:Songs, w. John Papaioannou (pno)—Le Tchibouk; Tristesse de l'Odalisque; Reverie Gallo ▲ CD 605
Garcia Lorca, F.:Canciones, w. John Papaioannou (pno)—La Morillas de Jaen; Nana de Sevilla Gallo ▲ CD 605
Gilboa, J.:Chagall sur la Bible, w. G. Augst (org), Mayence Brass Quartet Gallo ▲ CD 604 [AAD]
Hadjidakis, M.:Songs, w. John Papaioannou (pno)—Pera sto tholo potami; Kelomai se gongyla; Tassa alla Venise Gallo ▲ CD 605
Martin, F.:Sonnets à Cassandre, w. A. Sella (fl), G. Lewertoff (va), N. Enoch (vc) Gallo ▲ CD 633 [DDD]
Meyerbeer, G.:Songs, w. John Papaioannou (pno)—Sie und Uch; Scirocco Gallo ▲ CD 605
Offenbach, J.:Songs, w. John Papaioannou (pno)—Chanson Tzigane Gallo ▲ CD 605

Mayeur, Jacqueline (cta)
Cornelius, P.:Stabat Mater, w. D. Borst (sop), J.-L. Viala (ten), F. Vassar (bass-bar), M. Piquemal (cnd), Cannes-Provençe Alpes-Côte d'Azur Regional Orch, Cannes Regional Chorus Musique d'Abord ▲ HMA 1905206
Ropartz, G.:Requiem, w. Catherine Dubosc (sop), Vincent Le Texier (bar), M. Piquemal (cnd), Jean-Walter Audoli Instrumental Ensemble, French Vittoria Regional Choir Accord ▲ ACD 205132 [DDD]

Mayeur, Jacqueline (cta) (cont.)
Rossini, G.:Petite messe solennelle, w. Françoise Pollet (sop), Jean-Luc Viala (ten), Michel Piquemal (bar), Raymond Alessandrini (pno), Emmanuel Mandrin (harm), Michel Piquemal (cnd), Michel Piquemal Vocal Ensemble Accord 2-▲ ACD 203562 [DDD]

Mayhoff, M. (sgr)
Gounod, C.:Faust, w. V. de los Angeles (sop), C. Ward (sgr), R. Tucker (ten), H. Noel (sgr), N. Moscona (bass), D. Bernard (sgr), W. Herbert (cnd), New Orleans Opera Orch [F] *(rec Feb. 26, 1953)* Legato Classics 2-▲ LCD 167-2 [AAD]

Mayo, Lydia (sop)
Boieldieu, F.-A.:Le Calife de Bagdad, w. J. Michelini (sop), C. Cheriez (mez), L. Dale (ten), H. Rhys-Evans (ten), A. de Almeida (cnd), Camerata Provence Orch, Provence Camerata Chorus [F] Sonpact ▲ SPT 93007 [DDD]

Mayová, G. (sop)
Mysliveček, J.:Belerofonte, w. C. Lindsleyová (sop), K. Lakiová (sop), D. Ahlstedt (ten), R. Gimenéz (ten), S. Margita (ten), Z. Peskó (cnd), Prague CO, Czech Phil Chorus [I] *(rec 1987)* Supraphon 3-▲ 11 0006-2 [DDD]

Mayr, Ingrid (mez)
Einem, G. von:Dantons Tod, w. K. Laki (sop), H. Hiestermann (ten), W. Hollweg (ten), T. Adam (bass-bar), K. Rydl (bass), L. Zagrosek (cnd), Austrian RSO, Austrian Radio Chorus [G] *(rec live, Salzburg, 8/13/83)* Orfeo 2-▲ 102842 [ADD]

Mayr, Richard (bass)
Beethoven, L. van:Sym 9, "Choral Sym", w. Luise Helletsgruber (sop), Rosette Anday (cta), Georg Maikl (ten), F. von Weingartner (cnd), Vienna PO, Vienna State Opera Chorus *(rec Feb. 2-5, 1935)* Preiser ▲ PRE 90193 [ADD]
Mozart, W.A.:Requiem, w. Hanna Seebach-Ziegler (sop), Jella von Braun (alt), Hermann Gallos (ten), J. Messner (cnd), Cathedral Choral Society Orch, Salzburg Cathedral Choir *(rec Aug 9, 1931)* Orfeo d'or ("Festspiel Dokumente" series) ▲ 396951
Strauss, R.:Arabella (sels), w. Margit Bokor (sop—Zdenka), Viorica Ursuleac (sop—Arabella), Alfred Jerger (bar—Mandryka), Richard Mayr (bass—Waldner), C. Krauss (cnd), Vienna State Opera Orch *(rec Vienna, Oct. 29, 1933)* Koch Schwann 2-▲ SCH 314625 [ADD]
Strauss, R.:Der Rosenkavalier, w. L. Lehmann (sop), E. Schumann (sop), M. Olczewska (mez), R. Heger (cnd), Vienna PO, Vienna State Opera Chorus—abridged performance [G] *(rec 1933 for HMV)* Pearl 2-▲ GEMMCDS 9365 (m) [AAD]
Strauss, R.:Songs, w. L. Lehmann (sop), E. Schumann (sop), M. Olszewska (cnd), Vienna PO EMI Classics 2-▲ CDHB 64487
Wagner, R.:Arias & Scenes, w. Emmy Destinn (sop), Lilly Hafgren (sop), Frida Leider (sop), Emmi Leisner (cta), Ernst Kraus (ten), Lauritz Melchoir (ten), Leopold Demuth (bar), Friedrich Schorr (b-bar), Michael Bohynen (bass), Paul Knupfer (bass), Heinrich Hensel (sgr), Walter Soomer (sgr) Iron Needle ▲ 1307 (m)
Wagner, R.:Tannhäuser (sels), w. Lotte Lehmann (sop—Elisabeth), Josef Kalenberg (ten—Tannhäuser), Richard Mayr (bass—Landgraf), Friedrich Schorr (bass—Wolfram), R. Heger (cnd), Vienna State Opera Orch *(rec Vienna, Sept. 25, 1933)* Koch Schwann 2-▲ SCH 314622 [ADD]
Wagner, R.:Die Walküre (sels), w. Viorica Ursuleac (sop—Sieglinde), Hilde Konetzni (sop—Sieglinde), Gertrude Rünger (sop—Brünnhilde), Franz Völker (ten—Siegmund), Richard Mayr (bass—Hunding), Krauss, Knappertsbusch (cnd), Vienna State Opera Orch Koch Schwann 2-▲ SCH 314662 [ADD]

Mazaroff, Todor (ten)
Smetana, B.:Dalibor (sels), w. Hilde Konetzni (sop—Milada), Todor Mazaroff (ten—Dalibor), Alfred Jerger (bar—König), L. Ludwig (cnd), Vienna State Opera Orch *(rec Vienna, Nov. 21, 1942)* Koch Schwann 2-▲ SCH 314692 [ADD]

Mazeron, Liliane (sop)
Burgan, P.:Music of, w. Clara Novakova (fl), Michel Arrignon (cl), Alain Jacquon (pno), Henry Trio—Jeux de femmes [6 Erotic Poems of Verlaine]; Rondes Nocturnes; Bavardage; Berceuse Maguelone ▲ 350.529

Mazo, Ekaterina (sop)
Karetnikov, N.:Till Eulenspiegel, w. L. Mkrtchian (cta), A. Proujanski (ten), B. Koudriavtsev (bar), P. Glouboky (bass), A. Motchalov (bass), A. Martinov (sgr), Polianski (cnd), Soviet Cinema Orch, Soviet Cinema Chorus *(rec Moscow, 1988)* Russian Season ("Russian Season" Series) 2-▲ LDC 288029/30 [DDD]

Mazulok (bass)
Tchaikovsky, P.:Queen of Spades, w. S. Evstatieva (sop), P. Dilova (mez), I. Konsulov (bar), E. Tchakarov (cnd), Sofia Festival Orch, Bulgarian National Chorus [R] Sony Classical 3-▲ S3K 45720

Mazura, Franz (bar)
Berg, A.:Lulu, w. T. Stratas (sop), Y. Minton (mez), V. Schwarz (sop), K. Riegel (ten), P. Boulez (cnd), Paris Opera Orch—Act 3 [G] Deutsche Grammophon 3-▲ 415489-2 [ADD]
Schoenberg, A.:Moses und Aaron, w. B. Bonney (sop), M. Zakai (cta), P. Langridge (ten), A. Haugland (bass), G. Solti (cnd), Chicago SO, Chicago Sym Chorus, Glen Ellyn Children's Chorus [G] London 2-▲ 414264-2 [DDD]
Ullmann, V.:Kaiser von Atlantis, w. C. Oelze (sop—Bubikopf), I. Vermillion (mez—The Drummer), M. Petzold (ten—A Soldier), M. Kraus (ten—Kaisor Overall), H. Lippert (ten—Harlekin), F. Mazura (bar—The Loudspeaker), W. Berry (bass—Death), L. Zagrosek (cnd), Leipzig Gewandhaus Orch London ▲ 440854-2 [DDD]
Wagner, R.:Götterdämmerung, w. G. Jones (sop), H. Jung (mez), H. Becht (bar), P. Boulez (cnd), Bayreuth Festival Orch, Bayreuth Festival Chorus [G] Philips 4-▲ 434424-2 [DDD]
Wagner, R.:Parsifal, w. W. Meier (mez), P. Hofmann (ten), S. Estes (bass), H. Sotin (bass), M. Salminen (bass), J. Levine (cnd), Bayreuth Festival Orch, Bayreuth Festival Chorus [1985] [G] Philips 4-▲ 434616-2 [DDD]

Mazurok, Yuri (bar)
Bizet, G.:Carmen, w. E. Obraztsova (mez), P. Domingo (ten), C. Kleiber (cnd), Vienna State Opera Orch, Vienna State Opera Chorus Exclusive 2-▲ EXL 11 [ADD]
Tchaikovsky, P.:Eugene Onegin, w. A. Tomowa-Sintow (sop), R. Troava-Mircheva (cta), N. Gedda (ten), N. Ghiuselev (bass), E. Tchakarov (cnd), Sofia Festival Orch, Sofia National Opera Chorus [R] Sony Classical 2-▲ S2K 45539 [DDD]
Tchaikovsky, P.:Eugene Onegin, w. Lidiya Chernikh (sop), Tamara Sinyavskaya (mez), Alexander Vedernikov (bass), Alexander Fedin (sgr), V. Fedoseyev (cnd), USSR SO, Moscow SO, Fernseh SO Audiophile Classics ("Legacy Collection" series) 2-▲ 101.751
Verdi, G.:Il trovatore, w. Katia Ricciarelli (sop), Stefania Toczyska (mez), José Carreras (ten), C. Davis (cnd), Royal Opera House Orch, Royal Opera House Chorus Covent Garden Philips ("Two-Fers" series) 2-▲ 446151-2

Mazzara, M. (alt)
Steffani, A.:Vocal Music, w. S. Piccollo (sop), E. Velardi (cnd), Alessandro Stradella Consort—"Fileno Idolo Mio," Cantata for Soprano, 2 Violins & Continuo [attributed]; "Il Più Felice e Sfortunato Amante," Cantata for Alto, 2 Violins & Continuo [attributed]; "Porto L'Alma Incenerita," Chamber Duet for Soprano, Alto & Continuo [I] Bongiovanni ▲ GB 2123 [DDD]
Stradella, A.:Vocal Music, w. E. Smith (hpd), G. Dagnino (bass), S. Piccollo (sop), R. Balconi (ct), E. Velardi (cnd), Alessandro Stradella Consort—Sinfonia in E from the Cantata "Crudo Mar"; Toccata in a for Harpsichord; Exultate in Deo Fideles, Motet for Bass Solo & Violins; Si Apra al Riso Ogni Labbro, Cantata for 3 Voices & Strings [I,L] Bongiovanni ▲ GB 2123 [DDD]

Mazzaria, Lucia (sop)
Leoncavallo, R.:La Bohème, w. M. Senn (mez), B. Praticò (sgr), M. Malagnini (sgr), J. Summers (bar), J. Latham-König (cnd), Venice Teatro La Fenice Orch, Venice Teatro La Fenice Chorus *(rec live, 1990)* Nuova Era 3-▲ 6917/19 [DDD]
Pergolesi, G.B.:Adriano in Siria, w. D. Dessi (sop), J. Omilian (sop), S. Anselmi (sop), G. Banditelli (cta), E. di Cesare (ten), M. Panni (cnd), Rome Opera CO [I] *(rec live 12/20/86)* Bongiovanni 3-▲ GB 2078/80 [DDD]
Rossini, G.:Stabat Mater, w. Daniela Dessi (sop), Gloria Scalchi (mez), Pietro Ballo (ten), Chris Merritt (ten), Anatoli Kotscherga (bass), Roberto Scandiuzzi (bass), G. Gelmetti (cnd), Stuttgart RSO, North German Radio Chorus, Southwest German Radio Chorus Serenissima 2-▲ SER 360155 [DDD]

Mazzaria, Lucia (sop) (cont.)
Verdi, G.:Requiem Mass, w. Daniela Dessi (sop), Gloria Scalchi (mez), Pietro Ballo (ten), Chris Merritt (ten), Anatoli Kotscherga (bass), Roberto Scandiuzzi (bass), G. Gelmetti (cnd), Stuttgart RSO, North German Radio Chorus, Southwest German Radio Chorus Serenissima 2-▲ SER 360155 [DDD]

Mazzei, Enrico di (ten)
Greatist Hits on Records (1928-1939), w. Lily Pons (sop), Guiseppe De Luca (bar) *(rec 1928-1939)* Minerva ▲ MN A38 [ADD]
Puccini, G.:Tosca (sels), w. M.-C. Vallin (sop), P. Payen (bar), A. Endrèze (bar), G. Cloëz (cnd), Paris Opéra-Comique Orch, Paris Opéra-Comique Chorus [abridged version] [F] *(rec 1932)* Music Memoria ▲ 30376

Mazzetti, Sofia (sop)
Verdi, G.:I lombardi alla prima crociata (sels), w. Luciano Pavarotti (ten), G. Gavazzeni (cnd), Rome Opera Orch—O madre mia...La mia letizia infondere *(rec live, Nov. 20, 1969)* RCA Gold Seal ▲ 09026-68014-2 [ADD]

Mazzieri, Maurizo (bass)
Donizetti, G.:Maria Stuarda, w. M. Caballé (sop—Maria Stuarda), R. Bezinian (mez—Anna), M. V. Menendez (mez—Elisabetta), J. Carreras (ten—Roberto), M. Mazzieri (bass—Giorgio Talbot), E. Serra (bass—Lord Gugliemo Cecil), N. Santi (cnd), ORTF Lyric Orch, ORTF Lyric Chorale [I] *(rec live 3/26/72)* Memories 2-▲ HR4417/18 [ADD]
Donizetti, G.:Maria Stuarda (sels), w. José Carreras (ten), N. Santi (cnd), ORTF Lyric Orch—Ah!, rimiro il bel sembiante *(rec Paris, Mar 26, 1972)* Goldies ▲ GLD 63203 [ADD]

Mazzini, Guido (bass)
Puccini, G.:Manon Lescaut (sels), w. Carlo Gaifa (ten), Giuseppe Giacomini (ten), Giorgio Tadeo (bass), Angeles Gulin (sgr), M. Arena (cnd), *(orch unknown)*—Tra voi belle; Cortese damigella; Donna non vidi mai; Vedete, io son fedele; Tu, tu, amore; Ah! Manon, mi tradisce; Lescaut!; Ansia eterna crudel; No, pazzo son; Tutta su me ti posa; Manon...senti amor mio *(rec Treviso, Oct. 16, 1974)* Golden Age of Opera 2-▲ GAO 189/90 [ADD]
Rossini, G.:Zelmira, w. Virginia Zeani (sop), Anna Maria Rota (cta), Enrico Campi (bass), Paolo Washington (bass), Gastone Limarilli (sgr), Giuseppe Moretti (sgr), Nicola Tagger (sgr), C. Franci (cnd), *(orch unknown)* Great Opera Performances 2-▲ GOP 780

Mazzola (sgr)
Rossini, G.:Aureliano in Palmira, w. L. d' Intino (sop), N. Ciliento (mez), E. di Cesare (ten), G. Zani (cnd), Lucca Teatro Comunale Giglio Orch [I] *(rec live, Lucca, 10/28-11/2 1991)* Nuova Era 2-▲ 7069/70 [DDD]

Mazzola, Denia (sop)
Massenet, J.:Esclarmonde, w. José Sempere (ten), Christian Tréguier (bar), Hélène Parraguin (sgr), P. Fournillier (cnd), Franz Liszt SO, Massenet Festival Choir *(rec live, Massenet Festival, Saint-Etienne)* Koch Schwann 3-▲ SCH 312692 [DDD]

Mazzoli, Ferruccio (bass)
Cilea, F.:Gloria, w. M. Roberti (sop), A. M. Rota (cta), F. Labò (ten), A. Albertini (bar), L. Testi (bar), E. Campi (bass), F. Previtali (cnd), Turin RAI Orch, Turin RAI Chorus [I] *(rec live, Turin July 8, 1969)* Memories ▲ HR 4472 [ADD]
Gatta, Moffo, Rizzieri, Christoff & Mazzolli, w. Dora Gatta (sop), Anna Moffo (sop), Elena Rizzieri (sop), Boris Christoff (bass), Rome RAI SO, Turin RAI SO *(rec Martini & Rossi Concert)* Incontri Memorabili ▲ CDMR 5033
Mascagni, P.:Guglielmo Ratcliff, w. R. Mattioli (sop), P.M. Ferraro (ten), A. La Rosa Parodi (cnd), RAI SO *(rec 1963)* Memories ▲ MEM 4515 [ADD]
Verdi, G.:Macbeth, w. Leyla Gencer (sop), Mirto Picchi (ten), Giuseppe Taddei (bar), V. Gui (cnd), Palermo Teatro Massimo Orch, Palermo Teatro Massimo Chorus *(rec Palermo, Jan. 14, 1960)* Pantheon 2-▲ PHE 6604 (m)

Mazzoni, Silvia (mez)
Giordano, U.:Fedora, w. Mirella Freni (sop—Principessa Fedora), Adelina Scarabelli (sop—Contessa Olga), Silvia Mazzoni (mez—Dimitri), Monica Minarelli (sgr—Savoiardo), Placido Domingo (ten—Conte Loris), Ernesto Gavazzi (ten—Desiré), Aldo Bottion (ten—Barone Rouvel), Alessandro Corbelli (bar—Siriex), Luigi Roni (bass—Cirillo), Silvestro Sammaritano (bass—Baroff), Alfredo Giacomotti (bass—Gretch), Ernesto Panariello (bass—Lorek), Vincenzo Alaimo (sgr—Nicola), Arnold Bosman (sgr—Boleslao), Bruno Capisani (sgr—Sergio), Renato Zanchetta (sgr—Michele), G. Gavazzeni (cnd), La Scala Orch, La Scala Chorus *(rec La Scala, Apr 5, 1993)* Legato 2-▲ LCD 213-2 [ADD]
Mayr, S.:La rosa bianca e la rosa rossa, w. Susanna Anselmi (sop), Anna Caterina Antonacci (sop), Luca Canonici (ten), Francesco Facini (bass), Danilo Serraiocco (bass), T. Briccetti (cnd), Bergamo Stabile Orch Fonit Cetra ("Ricordi" series) 2-▲ FCT RFCD 2007

Mazzucato, Daniela (sop)
Cimarosa, D.:Il Matrimonio segreto, w. E. Dara (bar), B. de Simone (bar), A. Cavallaro (cnd), Marchigiana PO Nuova Era 2-▲ NUO 7014 [DDD]
Mozart, W.A.:Nozze di Figaro, w. Mirella Freni (sop), Teresa Berganza (mez), Mirto Picchi (ten), Hermann Prey (bar), José Van Dam (b-bar), Paolo Montarsolo (bass), C. Abbado (cnd), La Scala Orch, La Scala Chorus *(rec live, Apr 22, 1974)* Arkadia 3-▲ 614
Verdi, G.:Un ballo in maschera, w. R. Orlandi Malaspina (sop—Ameilia), D. Mazzuccato (sop—Oscar), A. Lazzarini (mez—Ulrica), L. Pavarotti (ten—Riccardo), M. Zanasi (bar—Renato), A. Zerbini (bass—Samuel), G. Casarini (bass—Tom), G. Zecchillo (bass—Sil) Golden Age of Opera 2-▲ GAO 164/65 [ADD]
Wolf-Ferrari, E.:Il campiello, w. D. Mazzucato (Gasparina), G. Devinu (Lucieta), M. Bolgan (Gnese), C. de Mola (Orsola), U. Benelli (Dona Cate Panciana), M. Rene Cosotti (Dona Pasqua Polegana), M. Comencini (Zorozeto), M. Biscotti (Astolfi), I. D'Arcangelo (Anzoleto), C. Striuli (Fabrizio del Ritorti), N. Bareza (cnd), Trieste Teatro Comunale Giuseppe Verdi Orch, Trieste Teatro Comunale G. Verdi Chorus *(rec Feb. 1992)* Ricordi 2-▲ RFCD 2014 [DDD]

Mdegley, V. (ten)
Ketèlbey, A.W.:Music of, w. J. Temperley (mez), L. Pearson (pno), J. Lanchbery (cnd), Philharmonia Orch, Ambrosian Singers—In a Persian Market; In a Monastery Garden; Chal Romano; In the Mystic Land of Egypt; The Clock and the Dresden Figures; Bells across the Meadows; In a Chinese Temple; In the Moonlight; Sanctuary of the Heart Classics for Pleasure ▲ CDCFP 4637 [ADD]

Mechaly, Gaëlle (sop)
Purcell, H.:Dido & Aeneas, w. Véronique Gens (sop—Dido), Sophie Marin-Degor (sop—Belinda), Sophie Daneman (sop—2nd woman/1st witch), Gaëlle Mechaly (sop—2nd witch), Claire Brua (mez—Sorceress), Steve Dugardin (alt—Chorus), Jean-Paul Fouchécourt (ten—Spirit/Sailor), Nathan Berg (b-bar—Aeneas), Jonathan Arnold (bass—Chorus), William Christie (hpd), W. Christie (cnd), Les Arts Florissants *(rec Massy Opera Theatre, Nov. 8-11, 1994)* Erato ▲ 98477-2 [DDD]

Mechera, Erika (sop)
Lehár, F.:Paganini (sels), w. E. Liebesberg (sop), Rudolf Christ (ten), K. Equiluz (ten), F. Bauer-Theussl (cnd), Vienna Volksoper Orch, Vienna Volksoper Chorus [G] Koch Präsent ▲ CD 399226 [AAD]

Mechetniak, Nikolaï (bar)
Rachmaninoff, S.:Francesca da Rimini, w. Maria Lapina (sop), Nikolaï Vassiliev (ten), Vitaly Tarastchenko (ten), Vladimir Matorin (bass), A. Tchistiakov (cnd), Bolshoi Theater Orch, Russian State Choir Russian Season 3-▲ CMX 388053

Mechler, Juliane (alt)
Distler, H.:Mörike-Chorliederbuch, w. Christiane Kreis (sop), Hendrik Ritter (ten), Bernd Stegmann (cnd), Berlin Vocal Ensemble *(rec Herrenberg, Jan 2-4, 1992)* Musicaphon ▲ BM 56820

Mechthild, Georg (mez)
Mangold, C.A.:Abraham, w. Monika Frimmer (sop), B Gärtner (ten), Gerd Türk (ten), Giles Cachemaille (bar), Philadelphia Orch, Darmstadt Concert Choir Christophorus 2-▲ 77172

Medgyaszay, Vilma (sop)
Bartók, B.:Pno Music, w. B. Bartók (pno), M. Basilides (cta), F. Székelyhidy (ten), J. Szigeti (vn), B. Goodman (cl), D. Bartók Pásztory (pno), H. J. Baker, E. J. Rubsam (perc)—studio, broadcast & piano roll recordings of music by Bartók, Kodály, Beethoven, Debussy, Liszt & Scarlatti, chronologically arranged from ca. 1920 through 1945—Sonatina; 6 Romanian Folk Dances; Evening in Transylvania; 8 sels. from 15 Hungarian Peasant Songs; Suite, Op. 14 (both the issued & test recordings); Allegro barbaro; 5 sels. from 2 Romanian Dances, 3 Burlesques, 10 Easy Pieces & 14 Bagatelles; & 4 Sons. by D. Scarlatti (test recordings); 8 sels. from 15 Hungarian Peasant Songs; 4 sels. from 9 Little Piano Pieces, Petite Suite & 3 Rondos on Folk Melodies; & "Sursum corda" from Liszt's Années de pèlerinage; 20 Hungarian Folk Songs; 5 Hungarian Folk Tunes; 8 Hungarian Folksongs; Hungarian Folk Tunes; 6 Romanian Folk Dances; Rhap. 1 Violin & Piano; Contrasts for Clarinet, Violin & Piano; 2 sels. from Mikrokosmos; 32 sels. from Mikrokosmos; Rhap. 1; Son. No. 2; Beethoven's "Kreutzer" Son.; Debussy's Son. 3; Son. 2 Pianos & Percussion; Petite Suite; 3 Hungarian Folk Tunes; 11 sels. from Improvs. on Hungarian Peasant Songs; Mikrokosmos; 3 Rondos on Folk Melodies; 9 Little Piano Pieces; 14 Bagatelles; 15 sels. from For Children & 2 sels. from 10 Easy Pieces Hungaroton 6-▲ HCD 12326/31 (m) [ADD]
Kodály, Z.:Hungarian Folk Music, w. M. Basilides (mez), F. Székelyhidy (ten), B. Bartók (pno) [arr. by Kodály for solo voice & piano]—20 Hungarian folk songs *(rec Budapest, 1928)* Hungaroton 6-▲ HCD 12326/31 (m) [ADD]

Meel, Nico van der (ten)
Bach, J.S.:Mass in b, BWV 232, w. J. Smith (sop), M. Chance (ct), H. van der Kamp (bass), F. Brüggen (cnd), Orch of the 18th Century, Netherlands Chamber Choir [L] *(rec live)* Philips ("Digital Classics" series) 2-▲ 426238-2 [DDD]
Mendelssohn, F.:Die Hochzeit des Camacho, w. R. Hofman (sop—Quiteria), A. Ulbrich (mez—Lucinda), S. Weir (ten—Basilio), H. Rhys-Evans (ten—Vivaldo), N. van der Meel (ten—Camacho), W. Wild (bar—Carrasco), U. Malmberg (bass—Sancho Panza), U. Cold (bass—Don Quixote), J. van Immerseel (cnd), Anima Eterna Orch, Aachen Boys Choir, Chor Modus Novus [G] *(rec Sept. 19-22, 1992)* Channel Classics 2-▲ CCS 5593 [DDD]
Schlegel, L.:Deutsche Liebeslieder, w. B. Pierik (sop), F. van Ruth (pno) [G] Attacca ▲ 8951-4 [DDD]
Telemann, G.P.:Auferstehung und Himmelfahrt Jesu, w. Monika Frimmer (sop), Veronika Winter (sop), Matthias Koch (alt), Klaus Mertens (bass), H. Max (cnd), Das Kliene Konzert, Rhineland Kantorei Capriccio ▲ CD 10596 [DDD]
Verhulst, J.:Songs, w. Annegeer Stumphius (sop), Leo Van Doeselaar (pno)—25 sels NM Classics ▲ NM 92029
Vivaldi, A.:Sacred Choral Music, w. M. Marshall (sop), J. Kowalski (ct), V. Negri (cnd), Royal Concertgebouw CO—Deus tuorum militum, RV.612; Laudate pueri Dominum, RV.600; Sanctorum meritis, RV.620; Stabat mater, RV.621 [L] Philips ▲ 432091-2 [DDD]
Wolf, H.:Songs (misc), w. Dido Keuning (pno)—An ***; Traurige Wege; Herbstentschluss; Sie haben heut' abend Gesellschaft; Ich stand in dunkeln Träumen; Das ist ein Brausen und Heulen; Aus meinen grossen Schmerzen; Mir traümte von eimen Königskind; Mein Liebchen, wir sassen beisammen; Es blasen die blauen Husaren; Ernst ist der Frühling; Spätherbstnebel; Wo ich bin, mich rings umdunkelt; Du bist wie eine Blume; In der Fremde; Rückkehr; Die Nacht; Erwartung; Nachruf; Wohin mit der Freud; Liebchen, wo bist du?; Nachtgruss; Frühlingsglocken; Ständchen; Liebesbotschaft *(rec Utrecht, Jan 1996)* Globe ▲ GLO 5149 [DDD]

Meens, Hein (ten)
Bach, C.P.E.:Die Israeliten in der Wüste, w. L. Lootens (sop), B. Schlick (sop), S. Barcoe (sgr), W. Christie (cnd), Cappella Coloniensis, Corona Musique d'Abord ▲ HMA 1901321
Zelenka, J.D.:Lamentationes Jeremiae Prophetae, w. U. Groenewold (cta), M. van Egmond (bass), R. Shaw (cnd), Academy of the Begynhof Amsterdam [L] Globe ▲ GLO 5050 [DDD]

Meer, Ruud van der (bass)
Bach, J.S.:Cant 36, w. P. Esswood (ct), K. Equiluz (ten), N. Harnoncourt (cnd), Vienna Concentus Musicus, Chorus Viennensis Teldec 2-▲ 2292-42506-2 [AAD]
Bach, J.S.:Cant 37, w. P. Esswood (ct), K. Equiluz (ten), N. Harnoncourt (cnd), Vienna Concentus Musicus, Chorus Viennensis [G] Teldec 2-▲ 2292-42506-2 [AAD]
Bach, J.S.:Cant 38, w. P. Esswood (ct), K. Equiluz (ten), N. Harnoncourt (cnd), Vienna Concentus Musicus, Chorus Viennensis [G] Teldec 2-▲ 2292-42506-2 [AAD]
Bach, J.S.:Cant 41, w. P. Esswood (ct), K. Equiluz (ten), N. Harnoncourt (cnd), Vienna Concentus Musicus, Vienna Concentus Musicus Chorus [G] Teldec 2-▲ 2292-42556-2 [AAD]
Bach, J.S.:Cant 42, w. P. Esswood (ct), K. Equiluz (ten), N. Harnoncourt (cnd), Vienna Concentus Musicus, Vienna Concentus Musicus Chorus [G] Teldec 2-▲ 2292-42556-2 [AAD]
Bach, J.S.:Cant 43, w. P. Esswood (ct), K. Equiluz (ten), N. Harnoncourt (cnd), Vienna Concentus Musicus, Vienna Concentus Musicus Chorus [G] Teldec 2-▲ 2292-42559-2 [AAD]
Bach, J.S.:Cant 44, w. P. Esswood (ct), K. Equiluz (ten), N. Harnoncourt (cnd), Vienna Concentus Musicus, Vienna Concentus Musicus Chorus [G] Teldec 2-▲ 2292-42559-2 [AAD]
Bach, J.S.:Cant 45, w. P. Esswood (ct), K. Equiluz (ten), Leonhardt Consort [G] Teldec 2-▲ 2292-42559-2 [AAD]
Bach, J.S.:Cant 46, w. P. Esswood (ct), K. Equiluz (ten), Leonhardt Consort [G] Teldec 2-▲ 2292-42559-2 [AAD]
Bach, J.S.:Cant 47, w. N. Harnoncourt (cnd), Vienna Concentus Musicus, Chorus Viennensis, Vienna Boys' Choir [G] Teldec 2-▲ 2292-42560-2 [AAD]
Bach, J.S.:Cant 49, w. N. Harnoncourt (cnd), Vienna Concentus Musicus, Chorus Viennensis, Vienna Boys' Choir [G] Teldec 2-▲ 2292-42560-2 [AAD]
Bach, J.S.:Cant 61, w. S. Kronwitter (trb), K. Equiluz (ten), N. Harnoncourt (cnd), Vienna Concentus Musicus, Vienna Boys' Choir [G] Teldec 2-▲ 2292-42565-2 [AAD]
Bach, J.S.:Cant 62, w. P. Esswood (ct), P. Jelosits (ten), K. Equiluz (ten), N. Harnoncourt (cnd), Vienna Concentus Musicus, Vienna Concentus Musicus Chorus [G] Teldec 2-▲ 2292-42565-2 [AAD]
Bach, J.S.:Cant 63, w. P. Esswood (ct), P. Jelosits (ten), K. Equiluz (ten), N. Harnoncourt (cnd), Vienna Concentus Musicus, Vienna Concentus Musicus Chorus [G] Teldec 2-▲ 2292-42565-2 [AAD]
Bach, J.S.:Cant 64, w. P. Esswood (ct), P. Jelosits (ten), N. Harnoncourt (cnd), Vienna Concentus Musicus, Vienna Boys' Choir [G] Teldec 2-▲ 2292-42565-2 [AAD]
Bach, J.S.:Cant 69, w. W. Wiedl (trb), P. Esswood (ct), K. Equiluz (ten), N. Harnoncourt (cnd), Vienna Concentus Musicus, Concentus Musicus [G] Teldec 2-▲ 2292-42572-2 [ADD]
Bach, J.S.:Cant 71, w. W. Wiedl (trb), P. Esswood (ct), K. Equiluz (ten), N. Harnoncourt (cnd), Vienna Concentus Musicus, Vienna Concentus Musicus Chorus [G] Teldec 2-▲ 2292-42572-2 [ADD]
Bach, J.S.:Cant 72, w. W. Wiedl (trb), P. Esswood (ct), N. Harnoncourt (cnd), Vienna Concentus Musicus, Tölz Boys' Choir [G] Teldec 2-▲ 2292-42572-2 [ADD]
Bach, J.S.:Cant 76, w. P. Esswood (ct), K. Equiluz (ten), N. Harnoncourt (cnd), Vienna Concentus Musicus, Vienna Concentus Musicus Chorus [G] Teldec 2-▲ 2292-42576-2 [ADD]
Bach, J.S.:Cant 78, w. P. Esswood (ct), K. Equiluz (ten), N. Harnoncourt (cnd), Vienna Concentus Musicus, Vienna Concentus Musicus Chorus [G] Teldec 2-▲ 2292-42576-2 [ADD]
Bach, J.S.:Cant 80, w. W. Wiedl (trb), P. Esswood (ct), K. Equiluz (ten), N. Harnoncourt (cnd), Vienna Concentus Musicus [G] Teldec 2-▲ 2292-42577-2 [ADD]
Bach, J.S.:Cant 81, w. P. Esswood (ct), K. Equiluz (ten), N. Harnoncourt (cnd), Vienna Concentus Musicus [G] Teldec 2-▲ 2292-42577-2 [ADD]
Bach, J.S.:St. John Passion, w. F. Palmer (sop), B. Finnilä (cta), K. Equiluz (ten), W. Krenn (ten), P. Huttenlocher (bar), M. Corboz (cnd), Lausanne CO, Lausanne Vocal Ensemble Erato 2-▲ 2292-45406-2 FD
Berlioz, H.:Choral Music, w. G. Garino (tenor), L. Visser (bass), J. Fournet (cnd), Dutch RSO, Dutch Radio Chorus—Le cinq mai, Op. 6; L'impériale, Op. 26; La mort d'Orphée; La révolution grecque, scène héroïque Denon ▲ CO 72886 [DDD]

Meeuwsen, Lucia (sop)
Kox, H.:L'Allegria, w. M. Margolis (cnd), Fine Arts CO [I] *(rec 1987)* Attacca ▲ Babel 9262-1 [ADD/DDD]
Schat, P.:Canto general, w. Frank de Groot (vn), Gerard Bouwhuis (pno) Donemus ▲ CV 19
Schat, P.:To You, w. L. Vis (cnd), Electronics Instrumental Ensemble Donemus ▲ CV 19

▲ = CD ♦ = Enhanced CD Δ = MD ■ = Cassette Tape □ = DCC

Meeuwsen, Lucia (sop) (cont.)

Vivaldi, A.:L'Olimpiade, w. M. van der Sluis (sop), E. von Magnus (alt), G. Lesne (alt), A. Christofelis (alt), W. Oberholtzer (bar), A. Walker Schultze (bass), R. Clemencic (cnd), Clemencic Consort, La Cappella Vocal Ensemble [I] *(rec live, Paris, 2/8–10/90)* Nuova Era ("Ancient Music" series) 2-▲ 6932/33 [DDD]

Meghnagi, Miriam (sgr)

Songs in Exile Fonè ▲ 89 F 08 CD [DDD]

Mehn, Christian (ten)

Chabrier, E.:Fisch-Ton-Kan, w. M. Delunsch (sop), B. Desnoues (sop), F. Dudziak (ten), J.-L. Georgel (bar), R. Delage (cnd), Strasbourg Collegium Musicum Orch Arion ▲ ARN 68252 [DDD]

Chabrier, E.:Vaucochard & Son I, w. M. Delunsch (sop), B. Desnoues (sop), F. Dudziak (ten), J.-L. Georgel (bar), R. Delage (cnd), Strasbourg Collegium Musicum Orch Arion ▲ ARN 68252 [DDD]

Chabrier, E.:A Wasted Education, w. M. Delunsch (sop), B. Desnoues (sop), F. Dudziak (ten), J.-L. Georgel (bar), R. Delage (cnd), Strasbourg Collegium Musicum Orch Arion ▲ ARN 68252 [DDD]

Mehta, Bejun (trb)

Songs & Arias, w. David Shifrin (cl), Carol Rosenberger (pno) Delos ▲ DCD 3019 [DDD]

Mei, Eva (sop)

Bellini, V.:Ariette da camera (6), w. Fabio Bidini (pno) *(rec Bavarian Radio, Munich, June 7–10, 1994)* RCA Red Seal ▲ 09026-68025-2 [DDD]

Bellini, V.:Norma, w. Jane Eaglen (sop—Norma), Eva Mei (sop—Adalgisa), Vincenzo La Scola (ten—Pollione), Dmitri Kavrakos (bass—Oroveso), R. Muti (cnd), Florence Maggio Musicale Orch, Florence Maggio Musicale Chorus *(rec live, Alighieri Theater, Florence, July 1994)* EMI Classics 2-▲ CDCC 55471

Donizetti, G.:Composizioni da camera, w. Fabio Bidini (pno) *(rec Bavarian Radio, Munich, June 7–10, 1994)* RCA Red Seal ▲ 09026-68025-2 [DDD]

Donizetti, G.:Don Pasquale, w. T. Allen (bar), R. Abbado (cnd), Munich RSO, Bavarian Radio Chorus RCA Red Seal 2-▲ 09026-61924-2

Mozart, W.A.:Dixit Dominus et Magnificat, w. E. von Magnus (cta), K. Azesberger (ten), G. Cachemaille (bass), N. Harnoncourt (cnd), Vienna Concentus Musicus, Arnold Schoenberg Choir Teldec ("Das alte Werke" series) ▲ 93025

Mozart, W.A.:Litaniae Lauretanae, K.109, w. Elisabeth von Magnus (alt), Kurt Azesberger (ten), Gilles Cachemaille (bass), N. Harnoncourt (cnd), Vienna Concentus Musicus, Arnold Schoenberg Choir *(rec Casino Zögernitz, Vienna, Dec. 1992)* Teldec ("Das alte Werke" series) ▲ 96147-2 [DDD]

Mozart, W.A.:Missa brevis, K.275, w. E. von Magnus (cta), K. Azesberger (teno, G. Cachemaille (bass), N. Harnoncourt (cnd), Vienna Concentus Musicus, Arnold Schoenberg Choir Teldec ("Das alte Werke" series) ▲ 93025

Rossini, G.:Les Soirées musicales, w. Fabio Bidini (pno)—La Promessa; Il Rimprovero; la Partenza; L'Orgia; L'Invito; La Pastorella delle alpi; La Gita in Gondola; La Danza *(rec Bavarian Radio, Munich, June 7–10, 1994)* RCA Red Seal ▲ 09026-68025-2 [DDD]

Rossini, G.:Tancredi, w. Veronica Cangemi (sop—Roggiero), Eva Mei (sop—Amenaide), Vasselina Kasarova (mez—Tancredi), Melinda Paulsen (cta—Isaura), Ramón Vargas (ten—Argirio), Harry Peeters (bass—Orbazzano), Janos Maté (vn), Gottfried Greiner (vc), Ingo Nawra (db), David Syrus (hpd), R. Abbado (cnd), Munich RSO, Bavarian Radio Chorus *(rec Studio 1, Munich, July 17–30, 1995)* RCA Red Seal 3-▲ 09026-68349-2 [DDD]

Salieri, A.:Axur, Re d'Ormus, w. A. Martin (bar), C. Rayam (ten), E. Nova (bass), A. Vespasiani (mez), M. Valenti (sop), R. Clemencic (cnd), Guido d'Arezzo Orch, Guido d'Arezzo Chorus [I] *(rec live 1989)* Nuova Era 3-▲ 6852/54 [DDD]

Meier, Waltraud (mez)

Beethoven, L. van:Missa Solemnis, w. C. Vaness (sop), H.-P. Blochwitz (ten), H. Tschammer (bass), J. Tate (cnd), English CO, Tallis Chamber Choir [L] EMI Classics ▲ CDC 49950 [DDD]

Beethoven, L. van:Sym 9, "Choral Sym", w. Jane Eaglen (sop), Ben Heppner (ten), Bryn Terfel (bar), C. Abbado (cnd), Berlin PO, Swedish Radio Chorus, Eric Ericson Chamber Choir *(rec Salzburg Easter Festival, 1996)* Sony Classical ▲ SK 62634 Δ SM 62634

Chausson, E.:Poème de l'amour et de la mer, w. R. Muti (cnd), Philadelphia Orch EMI Classics ▲ CDC 55120

Dittersdorf, K.D. von:Doctor und Apotheker, w. Hildegard Uhrmacher (sop—Leonore), Donna Woodward (sop—Rosalia), Waltraud Meier (mez—Claudia), Martin Finke (ten—Sichel), Frieder Lang (ten—Gotthold), Alois Perl (ten—Gallus), Gerhard Unger (ten—Sturmwald), Thomas Pfeiffer (bar—Police Commisioner), Wolfgang Schöne (bar—Krautmann), Harald Stamm (bass—Stössel), J. Lockhart (cnd), Rhine State PO Bayer 2-▲ BR 100 238/39 [DDD]

Hoffmann, E.T.A.:Aurora, w. Thomas Rieger (trb), Siegfried Schulze (bass), Koch (sgr), Ohlmann (sgr), H. Dechant (cnd), Bamberg Youth Orch, Bamberg Oratorio Chorus Bayer 3-▲ 100276-78

Mahler, G.:Kindertotenlieder, w. D. Barenboim (cnd), Orch de Paris [G] Erato ▲ 2292-45417-2 ZK [DDD]

Mahler, G.:Das Klagende Lied, w. C. Studer (sop), R. Goldberg (ten), T. Allen (bar), G. Sinopoli (cnd), Philharmonia Orch, Shin-Yuh Kai Chorus *(rec live, Japan 1990)* Deutsche Grammophon ▲ 435382-2 [DDD]

Mahler, G.:Sym 2, w. C. Studer (sop), C. Abbado (cnd), Vienna PO, Arnold Schoenberg Choir Deutsche Grammophon ▲ 439953-2

Mahler, G.:Sym 8, w. S. Jo (sop), C. Studer (sop), K. Lewis (ten), T. Allen (bar), H. Sotin (bass), G. Sinopoli (cnd), Philharmonia Orch, Philharmonia Chorus, Southend Boys' Choir [G] Deutsche Grammophon 2-▲ 435433-2

Mozart, W.A.:Requiem, w. P. Pace (sop), F. Lopardo (ten), J. Morris (bass), R. Muti (cnd), Berlin PO, Swedish Radio Chorus [L] EMI Classics ▲ CDC 49640 [DDD]

Saint-Saëns, C.:Samson et Dalila, w. P. Domingo (ten), S. Ramey (bass), A. Fondary (bar), M.-W. Chung (cnd), Bastille Opera Orch, Bastille Opera Chorus EMI Classics 2-▲ CDCB 54470

Verdi, G.:Requiem Mass, w. A. Marc (sop), P. Domingo (ten), F. Furlanetto (bass), D. Barenboim (cnd), Chicago SO, Chicago Sym Chorus Erato 2-▲ 96357-2

Wagner, R.:Götterdämmerung, w. A. Evans (sop—Brünnhilde), E.-M. Bundschuh (sop—Gutrune), H. Leidland (sop—Woglinde), A. Küttenbaum (sop—Wellgunde), W. Meier (mez—Waltraute), B. Svendén (mez—1st Norn), J. Turner (mez), *(cnd & orch unknown)* Teldec 4-▲ 4509-94194-2 [DDD]

Wagner, R.:Lohengrin, w. Cheryl Studer (sop), Siegfried Jerusalem (ten), Andreas Schmidt (bar), Harmut Welker (bar), Kurt Moll (bass), C. Abbado (cnd), Vienna PO Deutsche Grammophon 3-▲ 437808-2

Wagner, R.:Lohengrin (sels), w. C. Studer (sop), S. Jerusalem (ten), B. Terfel (bar), C. Abbado (cnd), Berlin PO Deutsche Grammophon ▲ 439768-2

Wagner, R.:Die Meistersinger von Nürnberg (sels), w. C. Studer (sop), S. Jerusalem (ten), B. Terfel (bar), C. Abbado (cnd), Berlin PO Deutsche Grammophon ▲ 439768-2

Wagner, R.:Parsifal, w. Waltraud Meier (mez—Kundry), Warren Ellsworth (ten—Parsifal), Nicholas Folwell (bar—Klingsor), Philip Joll (b-bar—Amfortas), Donald McIntyre (b-bar—Gurnemanz), R. Goodall (cnd), Welsh National Opera Orch, Welsh National Opera Chorus EMI Classics 2-▲ CDMD 65665

Wagner, R.:Parsifal, w. P. Hofmann (ten), F. Mazura (bar), S. Estes (bass), H. Sotin (bass), M. Salminen (bass), J. Levine (cnd), Bayreuth Festival Orch, Bayreuth Festival Chorus [1985] [G] Philips 4-▲ 434616-2 [DDD]

Wagner, R.:Tannhäuser, w. Nadine Secunde (sop), Rene Kollo (ten), Bernd Weikl (bar), Z. Mehta (cnd), Bavarian State Opera Orch, Bavarian State Opera Chorus *(rec live, Munich, 1994)* Serenissima 3-▲ SER 360166

Wagner, R.:Tannhäuser (sels), w. C. Studer (sop), S. Jerusalem (ten), B. Terfel (bar), C. Abbado (cnd), Berlin PO Deutsche Grammophon ▲ 439768-2

Wagner, R.:Tannhäuser (sels), w. K. Te Kanawa (sop), R. Kollo (ten), Håkan Hagegård (bar), M. Holle (bass), M. Janowski (cnd), Philharmonia Orch, Ambrosian Singers; music from film soundtrack for Meeting Venus Teldec ▲ 2292 46336-2 [DDD] ■ 2292 46336-4 □ 2292 46336-5

Wagner, R.:Tannhäuser (sels), w. K. Te Kanawa (sop), R. Kollo (ten), H. Hagegard (bar), M. Janowski (cnd), Philharmonia Orch, Ambrosian Singers Teldec ▲ 46336-2 ■ 46336-4

Wagner, R.:Die Walküre (sels), w. C. Studer (sop), S. Jerusalem (ten), B. Terfel (bar), C. Abbado (cnd), Berlin PO Deutsche Grammophon ▲ 439768-2

Wagner, R.:Wesendonck Songs, w. D. Barenboim (cnd), Orch de Paris [G] Erato ▲ 2292-45417-2 ZK [DDD]

Wolf, H.:Mörike-Lieder (sels), w. D. Barenboim (cnd), Orch de Paris—(3) In der Frühe; Denk'es, o Seele!; Wo find'ich Trost [G] Erato ▲ 2292-45417-2 ZK [DDD]

Meier-Schmid, M. (sop)

Handel, G.F.:Judas Maccabaeus, w. Elisabeth von Magnus (alt), Jörg Dürmüller (ten), Robert Wörle (ten), Franz-Josef Selig (bass), T. Fey (cnd), Schlierbach CO, Munich Motet Choir [E] Christophorus 2-▲ 77128 [DDD]

Meijer, Xenia (mez)

Biber, H. von:Chi la dura la vince, w. Barbara Schlick (sop), Gerd Türk (ten), Gotthold Schwarz (bass), W. Brunner (cnd), Salzburg Hofmusik CPO 3-▲ CPO 999258 [DDD]

Meinardus, Sylvia (sop)

Mozart, W.A.:Missa, K.427, w. H.-J. Möhring (fl), G. Passin (ob), F. Essmann (bn), H. Müller-Brühl (cnd), Cologne CO—Et incarnatus est [L] *(rec May 1968)* Koch Treasure ▲ 316182 [ADD]

Melandri, Antonio (ten)

Antonio Melandri *(rec 1929–31)* Preiser ▲ PRE CD 89134

Boito, A.:Mefistofele, w. Giannina Arangi-Lombardi (sop), Mafalda Favero (sop), Giuseppe Nessi (ten), Nazzareno de Angelis (bass), L. Molajoli (cnd), La Scala Orch, La Scala Chorus Grammofono 2000 2-▲ GRM 78606 (m)

Mascagni, P.:Cavalleria rusticana, w. L. Bruna Rasa (sop), M. Meloni (mez), R. Gallo Toscani (mez), A. Poli (bar), P. Mascagni (cnd), Holland Italian Opera Orch, Italian d'Olanda Opera Chorus [I] *(rec live at the Royal Theatre in the Hague, 11/7/38)* Bongiovanni ▲ GB 1050 (m) [AAD]

Mascagni, P.:Cavalleria rusticana, w. G. Arangi-Lombardi (cta), G. Lulli (bar), L. Molajoli (cnd), Milan SO, La Scala Chorus [I] *(rec 1930 for Columbia Records)* Standing Room Only ▲ SRO 806-1 (m) [ADD]

Mascagni, P.:Cavalleria rusticana, w. G. A. Lombardi (sop), I. Mannarini (mez), M. Castagna (mez), G. Lulli (bar), L. Molajoli (cnd), La Scala Orch, La Scala Chorus *(rec 1930)* Preiser ▲ 90042 (m) [AAD]

Melba, Nellie (sop)

Arias & Songs 1907–1926 Pearl ▲ PEA 9353 (m)

Hogarth-Melba Collection at Australia's National Film & Sound Archive Larrikin ▲ LRH221

Melba:The Last Recital & Other Famous Arias *(rec 1907–1913)* Phonographe ▲ PHG 5043 [ADD]

Nellie Melba:The Complete Victor Recordings, 1907–16 Romophone 3-▲ 81011-2

Nellie Melba Sings Verdi, Debussy, Gounod, Puccini & others RCA Gold Seal ▲ 09026-61412-2

"Un ange est venu":Melba in French Song & Opera Pearl ▲ PEA 9471 (m) [AAD]

Melbye, Mikael (bar)

Gade, N.W.:Elverskud, w. L. Balslev (sop), E. Guillaume (mez), F. Rasmussen (cnd), Collegium Musicum, Canzone Choir [Da] Kontrapunkt ▲ 32070 [DDD]

Melchert, Helmut (ten)

Dessau, P.:Die Verurteilung des Lukullus, w. Annelies Burmeister (mez—Das Fischweib), Helmut Melchert (ten—Lukullus), Hans-Joachim Rotzsch (ten—Der Kirschbaumträger), Peter Schreier (ten—Lukullus' Cook), Boris Carmeli (bass—King), H. Kegel (cnd), Leipzig RSO, Leipzig Radio Chorus Berlin Classics 2-▲ BER 1073 [ADD]

Mahler, G.:Das Lied von der Erde, w. Grace Hoffmann (alt), H. Rosbaud (cnd), Southwest German RSO Baden-Baden *(rec 1957)* Vox Box 2-▲ CDX2 5518

Strauss, R.:Salome, w. Christel Goltz (sop), Ernst Gutstein (bar), Siw Ericsdotter (sgr), O. Suitner (cnd), Dresden Staatskapelle *(rec 1963)* Berlin Classics 2-▲ BER 9101 [ADD]

Wagner, R.:Das Rheingold, w. L. Otto (sop), M. Muszely (sop), J. Blatter (mez), R. Stewart (mez), S. Wagner (mez), R. Schock (ten), H. Melchert (ten), F. Frantz (bass), B. Kusche (bass), J. Metternich (bass), R. Kempe (cnd), Berlin Staatskapelle *(rec Mar. 1959)* Berlin Classics ("Eterna" series) ▲ BER 2035 [ADD]

Melchior, Lauritz (ten)

Beethoven, L. van:Fidelio (sels), w. Kirsten Flagstad (sop) *(other artists unknown)*—Abscheulicher! Wo eilst du hin? Enterprise ("Vocal Archives" series) ▲ ENT VA 1128

Flagstad & Melchior Sing Wagner, w. Kirsten Flagstad (sop) *(rec 1935–40)* Pearl ▲ PEA 9049 [AAD]

The German & Italian Repertoire *(rec from 1923–39)* Grammofono 2000 ▲ GRM 78504 [ADD]

Great Love Duets, w. Erna Berger (sop), Miliza Korjus (sop), Lotte Lehmann (sop), Frida Leider (sop), Charles Kullman (ten), Helge Roswaenge (ten), Tito Schipa (ten), Richard Tauber (ten), et al. Pearl ▲ PEA 9217

The Great Operatic Recordings (1923–1940) Memories 2-▲ HR 4430 [ADD]

In Copenhagen *(rec 1939 & 1941)* Danacord ▲ DACOCD 325

Lauritz Melchior *(rec 1924–1939)* Nimbus ("Prima Voce" series) ▲ NI 7816 [ADD]

Lauritz Melchior *(rec. 1923–24)* Preiser ("Lebendige Vergangenheit" series) ▲ PRE 89032 (m) [AAD]

Lauritz Melchior II *(rec 1924–28)* Preiser ("Lebendige Vergangenheit" series) ▲ PRE 89068 [AAD]

The Lauritz Melchior Anthology, Vol. 1 ("The First Recordings") Danacord 2-▲ DACOCD 311/12 (m)

The Lauritz Melchior Anthology, Vol. 2 ("Red Polydors and Blue Parlophones, 1923–1926") Danacord 2-▲ DACOCD 313/14

The Lauritz Melchior Anthology, Vol. 3 ("Electrola & His Master's Voice, 1928–1931") Danacord 2-▲ DACOCD 315/16

The Lauritz Melchior Anthology, Vol. 4, Part 1 ("The Legendary Interpretations [Walküre], 1935–1938") Danacord 2-▲ DACOCD 317/18 (m)

The Lauritz Melchior Anthology, Vol. 4, Part 2 ("The Legendary Interpretations [Siegfried], 1927–1932; 70th Birthday Concert [Walküre, Act 1], 1960") Danacord 3-▲ DACOCD 319/21 (m)

Lauritz Melchior, Vol. 2, w. J. Barbirolli (cnd), L. Blech (cnd), A. Coates (cnd), R. Heger (cnd) *(rec 1929–30)* Preiser ("Lebendige Vergangenheit" series) ▲ PRE 89086 [ADD]

The Legendary Singers at Lindenoper Berlin (1927–1945)—, w. Gitta Alpar (sop), Erna Berger (sop), Tiana Lemnitz (sop), Maria Müller (sop), Margarete Klose (cta), Peter Anders (ten), Max Lorenz (ten), Walter Ludwig (ten), Rudolf Schock (ten), Franz Völker (ten), Willi Domgraf-Fassb *(rec 1927; 1937; 1941–45)* Minerva ▲ MN A21 [ADD]

Leoncavallo, R.:Pagliacci (sels), w. Enrico Caruso (ten), Antonio Paoli (ten), Giovanni Zenatello (ten), Amedeo Bassi (ten), Hermann Jadlowker (ten), Fernand Ansseau (ten), Hipolito Lazaro (ten), Nino (Filippo) Piccaluga (ten), Mario Chamlee (ten), Giacomo Lauri-Volpi (ten), Miguel Fleta (ten), Giovanni Martinelli (ten), Aureliano Pertile (ten), Georges Thill (ten), Alessandro Valente (ten), Francesco Merli (ten), Marcel Wittrisch (ten), Joseph Schmidt (ten), Beniamino Gigli (ten), Giuseppe Lugo (ten), Helge Roswaenge (ten), Jussi Bjoerling (ten)—23 versions of the tenor aria "Vesti la giubba" *(rec 1907–1944)* Bongiovanni ▲ GB 1071 [ADD]

Leoncavallo, R.:Pagliacci (sels) Enterprise ("Vocal Archives" series) ▲ ENT 1113

Opera Stars Sing on Radio, Vol. 1:Unpublished Broadcasts from the Fourties, w. Dusolina Giannini (sop), Helen Traubel (sop), Gladys Swarthout (cta), Richard Crooks (ten), Robert Merrill (bar), Lawrence Tibbett (bar), Ezio Pinza (bass) Enterprise ("The Radio Years" series) ▲ ENTRY 11

Still, W.G.:Tristan und Isolde, w. Kirsten Flagstad (sop), Kerstin Thorborg (mez), Ludwig Hofmann (bass), Julius Huehn (sgr), A. Bodanzky (cnd), *(orch unknown)* *(rec Jan 2, 1937)* Enterprise ("The Fourties" series) 3-▲ ENT 304

Studio & Live Performances 1923–1953, w. Kirsten Flagstad (sop) Memories 2-▲ MEM 4456 [ADD]

Verdi, G.:Aida (sels) *(cnd & orch unknown)* Enterprise ("Vocal Archives" series) ▲ ENT 1113

Verdi, G.:Otello (sels) *(cnd & orch unknown)* Enterprise ("Vocal Archives" series) ▲ ENT 1113

Verdi, G.:Otello (sels), w. C. Muzio (sop), R. Ponselle (sop), H. Spani (sop), E. Caruso (ten), N. Fusati (ten), F. Merli (ten), F. Tamagno (ten), B. Franci (bar), V. Maurel (bar), R. Stracciari (bar), T. Ruffo (bar) *(rec 1906–1933)* Music Memoria ▲ 30219

Wagner, R.:Arias & Scenes, w. K. Flagstad (sop), E. Rethberg (sop), B. Nilsson (sop), E. Schumann (sop), F. Leider (sop), G. Thill (ten), A. Pertile (ten), G. Hüsch (bar), F. Schorr (b-bar), H. Hotter (b-bar), A. Kipnis (bass), *(orch unknown)* EMI Classics ("Studio" series) 4-▲ CDMC 64008

Wagner, R.:Arias & Scenes, w. Kirsten Flagstad (sop) *(other artists unknown)*—Das süsse Lied verhallt [from Lohengrin]; O sink' hernieder [from Tristan und Isolde]; Zu neuen Taten [from Götterdämmerung]; Nur eine Waffe taugt [from Parsifal] Enterprise ("Vocal Archives" series) ▲ ENT VA 1128

Wagner, R.:Arias & Scenes, w. Kirsten Flagstad (sop), Ormandy, McArthur, Walter (cnd), Philadelphia Orch, San Francisco Opera Orch, RCA Victor SO, New York PO—arias & duets from Lohengrin, Tristan & Isolde, Götterdämmerung, Parsifal & Fidelio *(rec New York City, 1939–41)* Grammofono 2000 ▲ GRM 78526 (m)

Wagner, R.:Arias & Scenes, w. Emmy Destinn (sop), Lilly Hafgren (sop), Frida Leider (sop), Emmi Leisner (cta), Ernst Kraus (ten), Leopold Demuth (bar), Friedrich Schorr (b-bar), Michael Bohynen (bass), Paul Knupfer (bass), Richard Mayr (bass), Heinrich Hensel (sgr), Walter Soomer (sgr) Iron Needle ▲ 1307 (m)

Melchior, Lauritz (ten) (cont.)

Wagner, R.:Arias & Scenes, *(orch unknown)*—selections from Götterdämmering *(Prologue Duet—w. Flagstad, 1939)*, Lohengrin *(Mein lieber Schwan—1938; In fernem Land—1939; Das süsse Lied verhallt—w. Flagstad, 1940)*, Meistersinger *(Am stillen Herd—1939; Morgenlich leuchtend im rosigen Schein—1939)*, Parsifal *(Nur eine Waffe taugt—1938)*, Rienzi *(Allmächt'ger Vater, blick' herab—1923)*, Siegfried *(Notung! Notung!—1924)*, Tannhäuser *(Inbrunst im Herzen—1924; O Fürstin—1924; Dir töne lob—1929)*, Tristan *(Love Duet—w. Frida Leider, 1929 & w. Flagstad, 1939)*, Walküre *(Friedmund darf ich nicht heissen—1923; Ein Schwert verhiess mir der Vater—1923; Dich selige Frau—1935)* Memories 2-▲ HR 4430/31 [ADD]

Wagner, R.:Arias & Scenes, w. *(cnd & orch unknown)*—sels from Rienzi, Lohengrin, Die Walküre, Siegfried, Parsifal, Die Meistersinger von Nürnberg Enterprise ("Vocal Archives" series) ▲ ENT 1113

Wagner, R.:Arias & Scenes, w. Kirsten Flagstad (sop), E. McArthur (cnd), San Francisco Opera Orch, RCA Victor SO—duets from Lohengrin; Tristan und Isolde; Götterdämmerung; Parsifal Pearl ▲ PEA 9190

Wagner, R.:Arias & Scenes, w. K. Flagstad (sop), Walter, MacArthur, Sargent (cnd), New York PO, RCA Victor SO, San Francisco Opera Orch, BBC SO—selections from Götterdämering; Tristan & Isolde; Lohengrin Memories 2-▲ HR 4456/57 [ADD]

Wagner, R.:Der fliegende Holländer (sels), w. Göta Ljungberg (sop), Elisabeth Rethberg (sop), Elisabeth Schumann (sop), Rudolf Laubenthal (ten), Friedrich Schorr (bar), *(cnd & orch unknown) (rec 1927-31)* Preiser 2-▲ PRE 89214 [AAD]

Wagner, R.:Götterdämmerung (sels), w. Frida Leider (sop), Kerstin Thorborg (mez), Herbert Janssen (bar), Emanuel List (bass), Maria Nezadál (sgr), T. Beecham (cnd), London PO, Royal Opera House Chorus Covent Garden *(rec Covent Garden, London, 1936)* Preiser ▲ PRE 90266

Wagner, R.:Götterdämmerung (sels), w. Göta Ljungberg (sop), Elisabeth Rethberg (sop), Elisabeth Schumann (sop), Rudolf Laubenthal (ten), Friedrich Schorr (bar), *(cnd & orch unknown) (rec 1927-31)* Preiser 2-▲ PRE 89214 [AAD]

Wagner, R.:Götterdämmerung (sels), w. F. Leider (sop), Nezadál (sop), K. Thorborg (mez), H. Janssen (bar), L. Weber (bass), T. Beecham (cnd), London PO, Royal Opera House Chorus Covent Garden [G] *(rec from 1925 Polydor & 1929)* Legato Classics 2-▲ LCD 146-2 (m) [ADD]

Wagner, R.:Götterdämmerung (sels), w. F. Leider (sop), A. von Stosch (sop), H. Janssen (bar), W. Schirp (bass), *(cnd & orch unknown)*—Act 2, Scenes 4 & 5 *(w. Furtwängler, Royal Opera House Orch. & Cho., 1938)*; Act 3, Schweigt eures Jammers *(Frida Leider & E. Marherr-Wagner, Blech, Berlin State Opera Orch., 1928)* Pearl ▲ PEA 9331 (m) [AAD]

Wagner, R.:Götterdämmerung (sels), w. H. Traubel (sop), A. Toscanini (cnd), NBC SO—Dawn, Rhine Journey, Death & Funeral Music; Immolation Scene RCA Gold Seal ▲ 09026-60304-2 ■ 09026-60304-4

Wagner, R.:Lohengrin, w. H. Traubel (sop—Elsa), A. Varnay (sop—Ortrud), L. Melchior (ten—Lohengrin), F. Guerrera (bar—Herald), H. Janssen (bar—Telramund), D. Ernster (bass—King Heinrich), F. Stiedry (cnd), Metropolitan Opera Orch, New York Metropolitan Opera Chorus *(rec live Jan. 6, 1950)* Danacord 3-▲ DACOCD 322/24 [AAD]

Wagner, R.:Die Meistersinger von Nürnberg (sels), w. Göta Ljungberg (sop), Elisabeth Rethberg (sop), Elisabeth Schumann (sop), Rudolf Laubenthal (ten), Friedrich Schorr (bar), *(cnd & orch unknown) (rec 1927-31)* Preiser 2-▲ PRE 89214 [AAD]

Wagner, R.:Parsifal (sels), w. K. Flagstad (sop), E. McArthur (cnd), RCA Victor SO—Act 2 *(Dies alles hab' ich nun geträumt [Herzenleide Scene])* RCA Gold Seal ▲ 7915-2-RG (m) [ADD] ■ 7915-4-RG (CrO2)

Wagner, R.:Das Rheingold (sels), w. Göta Ljungberg (sop), Elisabeth Rethberg (sop), Elisabeth Schumann (sop), Rudolf Laubenthal (ten), Friedrich Schorr (bar), *(cnd & orch unknown) (rec 1927-31)* Preiser 2-▲ PRE 89214 [AAD]

Wagner, R.:Der Ring des Nibelungen (sels), w. Florence Austral (sop), Frieda Leider (sop), Elsie Suddaby (sop), Göta Ljunberg (sop), Walter Widdop (ten), Horst Laubenthal (ten), Friedrich Schorr (bar), Rudolf Bockelmann (b-bar), Ivar Andresen (bass), Emmanuel List (bass), Collingwood, Blech, Coates, Barbirolli, Heger, Alwin, Muck (cnd), London SO—scenes from Siegriend & Götterdämmerung; 90 Motives from Der Ring [w. Collingwood & LSO] Pearl 7-▲ PEA 9137 [ADD]

Wagner, R.:Der Ring des Nibelungen (sels), w. Helen Traubel (sop), A. Toscanini (cnd), NBC SO—Complete Scene III [from Act 1 of Die Walküre]; Dawn & Bruennhilde; Siegfried's Funeral Music; Brunnhilde Immolation [all from Götterdämmerung] *(rec 1941)* Grammofono 2000 ▲ GRM 78564

Wagner, R.:Tannhäuser (sels), w. Göta Ljungberg (sop), Elisabeth Rethberg (sop), Elisabeth Schumann (sop), Rudolf Laubenthal (ten), Friedrich Schorr (bar), *(cnd & orch unknown) (rec 1927-31)* Preiser 2-▲ PRE 89214 [AAD]

Wagner, R.:Tannhäuser (sels), w. Walter Widdop (ten), Friedrich Schorr (b-bar), Edward Halland (bass), A. Coates (cnd), London SO, New SO—Ov; Venusberg Bacchanale; 1st Pilgrims' Chorus; Wolfram's Cavatina; Prelude; Pilgrims' Return; Rome Narration *(rec 1925-30)* Claremont ▲ GSE 78 50 54

Wagner, R.:Tristan und Isolde, w. Kirsten Flagstad (sop), Sabine Kalter (cta), Emmanuel List (bass), F. Reiner (cnd), London PO Enterprise ("The Radio Years" series) 3-▲ ENT 39 (m)

Wagner, R.:Tannhäuser, w. Helen Traubel (sop), Herbert Janssen (bar), Alexander Kipnis (bass), G. Szell (cnd), *(orch unknown)* Enterprise ("The Radio Years" series) 3-▲ ENT RY 26 (m)

Wagner, R.:Tristan und Isolde, w. K. Flagstad (sop), S. Kalter (cta), H. Janssen (bar), E. List (bass), F. Reiner (cnd), Royal Opera House Orch, Royal Opera House Chorus Covent Garden [G] *(rec live, Covent Garden May/June 1936)* VAI Audio 3-▲ VAIA 1004-3 (m) [ADD]

Wagner, R.:Tristan und Isolde, w. Kirsten Flagstad (sop), Margarete Klose (mez), Herbert Janssen (bar), Sven Nilsson (bass), T. Beecham (cnd), Philharmonia Orch, Royal Opera House Chorus Covent Garden *(rec 1937)* Grammofono 2000 3-▲ GRM 78570 (m)

Wagner, R.:Tristan und Isolde, w. K. Flagstad (sop), M. Klose (cta), H. Janssen (bar), S. Nilsson (bass), Beecham, Reiner (cnd), *(orch unknown)*—a compilation of two 1937 live performance recordings, with some passages conducted by Beecham, others by Reiner [G] EMI Classics ("Great Recordings of the Century" series) 3-▲ CDHC 64037

Wagner, R.:Tristan und Isolde, w. K. Flagstad (sop), H. Janssen (bar), P. Schoeffler (b-bar), T. Beecham (cnd), Royal Opera House Orch, Royal Opera House Chorus Covent Garden *(rec live, Covent Garden, 6/18 & 22/37)* Melodram 3-▲ MEL 37029 (m) [AAD]

Wagner, R.:Tristan und Isolde (sels), w. F. Leider (sop), E. Marherr-Wagner (mez), L. Blech (cnd), A. Coates (cnd), J. Barbirolli (cnd), Berlin State Opera Orch, London SO—Act 1 *(Doch nun von Tristan [Leider, Marherr-Wagner])*, Act 2 *(Isolde! Geliebter; O sink hernieder [Leider, Melchior])*, Act 3 *(Mild und leise [Leider])* [G] *(rec late 1920s for HMV)* Legato Classics 2-▲ LCD 146-2 (m) [ADD]

Wagner, R.:Die Walküre, w. Helen Traubel (sop), Astrid Varnay (sop), Kerstin Throborg (cta), Friedrich Schorr (b-bar), E. Leinsdorf (cnd), *(orch unknown) (rec Dec 6, 1941)* Enterprise ("The Forties" series) 2-▲ ENT 318

Wagner, R.:Die Walküre (sels), w. Göta Ljungberg (sop), Elisabeth Rethberg (sop), Elisabeth Schumann (sop), Rudolf Laubenthal (ten), Friedrich Schorr (bar), *(orch unknown) (rec 1927-31)* Preiser 2-▲ PRE 89214 [AAD]

Wagner, R.:Die Walküre (sels), w. H. Traubel (sop), A. Toscanini (cnd), NBC SO—Act 1, Scene 3 [G] RCA Gold Seal ▲ 60264-2-RG [ADD] ■ 60264-4-RG (CrO2)

Wagner, R.:Die Walküre (act 1), w. L. Lehmann (sop), E. List (bass), B. Walter (cnd), Vienna PO *(rec 1935)* EMI Classics ("Great Recordings of the Century" series) ▲ CDH 61020 (m) [ADD]

Wagner, R.:Die Walküre (act 2), w. K. Flagstad (sop), L. Lehmann (sop), F. Schorr (b-bar), F. Reiner (cnd), *(orch unknown)* [G] *(rec 1936)* Legato Classics ▲ LCD 133-1 (m) [AAD]

Wagner, R.:Die Walküre (act 2), w. M. Fuchs (sop), E. Flesch (sop), L. Lehmann (sop), M. Klose (cta), H. Hotter (b-bar), A. Jerger (b-bar), E. List (bass), B. Walter (cnd), Berlin State Opera Orch [G] *(rec 9/38 & 6/22/35)* EMI Classics ("References" series) ▲ CDH 64255

Wagner, R.:Die Walküre (act 2), w. M. Fuchs (sop), E. Flesch (sop), L. Lehmann (sop), M. Klose (cta), H. Hotter (b-bar), A. Jerger (b-bar), E. List (bass), B. Walter (cnd), Berlin State Opera Orch [G] *(rec 9/38 & 6/22/35)* Danacord 2-▲ DACOCD 317/18 (m)

Meletti (sgr)

Giordano, U.:Fedora, w. Pia Tassinari (sop), Ferruccio Tagliavini (ten), Micheluzzi (sgr), Mascolo (sgr), Jolanda Torriani (sgr), O.. Fabritiis (cnd), Milan RAI SO, Milan RAI Chorus *(rec live, July 10, 1954)* Arkadia 2-▲ 493

Meletti, Saturno (bar)

Cilea, F.:Adriana Lecouvreur, w. Carla Gavazzi (sop), Miti Truccato Pace (mez), Giacinto Prandelli (ten), A. Simonetto (cnd), Milan RAI Lyric Orch, Milan RAI Chorus Fonit Cetra ("Classic Collection" series) 2-▲ FCT CDO 20

Mascagni, P.:L'amico Fritz, w. P. Tassinari (sop—Suzel), A. Pini (mez—Beppe), F. Tagliavini (ten—Fritz), A. Giannotti (ten—Frederico), S. Meletti (bar—David), P. L. Latinucci (bass—Hanezò), P. Mascagni (cnd), Turin RSO, Turin Radio Chorus *(rec 1941)* Cetra Classic 2-▲ CDO 18

Massenet, J.:Werther, w. M. Olivero (sop), A. Lazzari (ten), M. Rossi (cnd), Turin RSO, Turin Radio Chorus *(rec live, 6/12/63)* Melodram 2-▲ MEL 27065 (m) [AAD]

Puccini, G.:La Bohème, w. R. Tebaldi (sop), E. Ribetti (mez), E. Avolanti (ten), G. Lauri Volpi (ten), T. Gobbi (bar), C. Badioli (bass), G. Neri (bass), G. Santini (cnd), *(orch unknown) (rec 1951)* Great Opera Performances ▲ GOP 743

Rossini, G.:La Cenerentola, w. Ornella Rovero (sop), Miti Truccato Pace (mez), Giulietta Simionato (mez), Cesare Valletti (ten), Vito Susca (bass), Cristiano Dalamangas (sgr), M. Rossi (cnd), Turin RAI Orch, Bruno Erminero (cnd), Turin RAI Chorus Fonit Cetra ("Classic Collection" series) ▲ FCT CDON 34

Meliciani, Carlo (b-bar)

Donizetti, G.:Marino Faliero, w. M. Roberti (sop), O. Mori (bar), A. Ferrin (bass), A. Camozzo (cnd), *(orch & chorus unknown)* [I] *(rec live, Bergamo 1966)* Melodram 2-▲ MEL 27030

Janácek, L.:Jenůfa, w. Magda Olivero (sop—Kostelnicka), Bruna Baglioni (mez—La vecchia Buryja), Grace Bumbry (mez—Jenufa), Renato Cioni (ten—Steva Buryja), Robleto Merolla (bar—Laca Klemen), Carlo Meliciani (sgr—Vecchio compagno), J. Semkow (cnd), La Scala Orch, La Scala Chorus *(rec Milan, Apr 2, 1974)* Myto 2-▲ MCD 961142

Magda Olivero & Flaviano Labò in Concert, w. Magda Olivero (sop), Flaviano Labò (ten), Jacques Bazire (cnd), Marsiglia Opera Orch, Raina Kabaivanska (sop), Gianpiero Matromei (bar), Oliveiro de Fabritiis (cnd), La Scala Orch, Turin RAI Orch *(rec between 1969 & 1973)* Bongiovanni ▲ GB 1105 [ADD]

Puccini, G.:La Bohème, w. Ileana Cotrubas (sop—Mimi), Margherita Guglielmi (sop—Musetta), José Carreras (ten—Rodolfo), Saverio Porzano (ten—Parpignol), Regolo Romani (ten—Vendor), Claudio Giombi (bar—Benoit), Gianni Maffeo (bar—Schaunard), Angelo Romero (bar—Marcello), Alfredo Giacomotti (bass—Alcindoro), Carlo Meliciani (bass—Customs Officer), Giuseppe Morresi (bass—Sergeant), Paolo Washington (bass—Colline), G. Prêtre (cnd), La Scala Orch, La Scala Chorus *(rec Washington D.C., Sept 8, 1976)* Legato Classics 2-▲ LCD 201-2

Verdi, G.:Ernani, w. R. Kabaivanska (sop), P. Domingo (ten), N. Ghiaurov (bass), A. Votto (cnd), La Scala Orch, La Scala Chorus *(rec live 12/7/69)* Melodram 2-▲ MEL 27064 (m) [AAD]

Verdi, G.:La forza del destino (sels), w. I. Ligabue (sop), C. Bergonzi (ten), G. Gavazzeni (cnd), La Scala Orch, La Scala Chorus [substantial highlights] *(rec live, Milan 12/7/65)* Myto 2-▲ 2 MCD 91750 [ADD]

Verdi, G.:La forza del destino (sels), w. C. Bergonzi (ten), A. Votto (cnd), La Scala Orch—La vita è inferno all'infelice; O tu che in seno; Invano, Alvaro [I] *(rec live 12/7/65)* Melodram 2-▲ 27058 [AAD]

Melis, Carmen (sop)

Puccini, G.:Gianni Schicchi, w. M. Kalmár (sop), A. Ferencsik (cnd), Hungarian State Opera Orch [I] Hungaroton ▲ HCD 12541 [DDD]

Puccini, G.:Tosca, w. Carmen Melis (sop—Tosca), Nello Palai (ten—Spoletta), Piero Pauli (ten—Cavaradossi), Apollo Granforte (bar—Scarpia), Giovanni Azzimonti (bass—Angelotti/Sciarrone), Antonio Gelli (bass—Sagrestano), C. Sabajno (cnd), La Scala Orch, La Scala Chorus *(rec Nov 1929)* Arkadia 2-▲ CD 78002 (m) [ADD]

Puccini, G.:Tosca, w. C. Melis (sop—Tosca), P. Pauloi (ten—Cavarodossi), N. Palai (ten—Spoletta), A. Granforte (bar—Scarpia), G. Azzimonti (bass—Sciarrone/Angelotti), A. Gelli (bass—Sacristan), C. Sabajno (cnd), La Scala Orch, La Scala Chorus [I] *(rec Milan, Nov. 1929)* VAI Audio 2-▲ VAIA 1076-2 (m) [ADD]

Melis, György (bar)

Gounod, C.:Faust (sels), w. Alexandrina Pendachanska (sop—Margarethe), Giuseppe Sabbatini (ten—Faust), György Melis (bar—Valentin), Nicolai Ghiaurov (bass—Méphistophélès), Nikola Ghiuselev (bass—Méphistophélès), Berlin RSO, Vienna SO, Hungarian State Opera Orch, Bulgarian RSO, Sofia SO, Bulgarian National Chorus, Bulgarian National Chorus Radio Choir—Intro; Vien ou bière; O sainte médaille...Avant de quitter ces lieux; Le veau d'or [all from Act 2]; Quel trouble inconnu me pénètre!...Salut! demeure chaste et pure; Je voudrais bien savoir...Il était un roi de Thule; Un bouquet!...O Dieu! que de bijoux [both from Act 3]; Gloire immortelle de nos aieux; Vous qui faites l'endormie [both from Act 4]; Intermezzo; Walpurgis Night [both from Act 5] Laserlight ▲ 14209 [DDD]

Kacsóh, P.:János Vitéz, w. Mária Gyurkovics (sop), Anna Zentai (sop—Iluska), Tivadar Bilicsi (sgr), Hilda Gobbi (sgr), Sándor Pethes (sgr—Bartolo), Róbert Ilosfalvy (ten—Kukorica), György Melis (bar—Bagó), György Radnai (bar—Strázsamester), László Domahidy (bass—Csősz), E. Lukács (cnd), Hungarian State Opera Orch, Hungarian Radio-TV Chorus *(rec Budapest, 1961)* Classical Diamonds 2-▲ CLD 4011-12 [AAD]

Melinäs, Marianne (sop)

Nilsson, T.:Out of Earthly Night, w. Gudrun Bruna (sop), Kaysa Hälldin (alt), Lars Sjögren (ten), Göran Swartz (bass), Sture Hedin (sgr), Ola Kyhlberg (sgr), Lars Ljungman (sgr), Nils Philipson (sgr), Ulrik Quale (sgr), Nils Spangenberg (sgr), Britta Therén (sgr), Karl-Erik Welin (org), Torsten Nilsson (cnd), Oscar's Motet Choir *(rec Oscar's Church, Stockholm, Sweden, Apr 26-27, 1978)* BIS ▲ CD 138 [AAD]

Pettersson, G.A.:Vox Humana, w. Margot Rödin (alt), Sven-Erik Alexandersson (ten), Erland Hagegård (bar), S. Westerberg (cnd), Swedish RSO, Swedish Radio Chorus *(rec Royal Swedish Academy of Music, Stockholm, Sweden, Mar. 22 & May 24, 1976)* BIS ▲ CD 55 [AAD]

Mellon, Agnès (sop)

Bach, J.S.:Cant 80, w. Barbara Schlick (sop), Gérard Lesne (ct), Howard Crook (ten), Peter Kooy (bass), P. Herreweghe (cnd), La Chapelle Royale Orch, Collegium Vocale Harmonia Mundi France Δ HMC 6901326

Bach, J.S.:Magnificat, BWV 243, w. B. Schlick (sop), G. Lesne (ct), H. Crook (ten), P. Kooy (bass), P. Herreweghe (cnd), La Chapelle Royale Orch, Collegium Vocale [L] Harmonia Mundi France ▲ HMC 901326

Bach, J.S.:Masses, BWV 233-36, "Lutheran Masses", w. G. Lesne (alto), C. Prégardien (ten), P. Kooy (bass), P. Herreweghe (cnd), Ghent Collegium Vocale Orch, Ghent Collegium Vocale—BWV 233 & 236 Virgin Classics ▲ CDC 59634

Bach, J.S.:Masses, BWV 233-36, "Lutheran Masses", w. G. Lesne (alto), C. Prégardien (ten), P. Kooy (bass), P. Herreweghe (cnd), Ghent Collegium Vocale Orch, Ghent Collegium Vocale—BWV 234 & 235 Virgin Classics ▲ CDC 59587

Bach, J.S.:St. Matthew Passion (sels), w. G. Lesne (alto), C. Prégardien (ten), P. Kooy (bass), P. Herreweghe (cnd), Ghent Collegium Vocale Orch, Ghent Collegium Vocale Virgin Classics ▲ CDC 59587

Boccherini, L.:Stabat Mater, w. Ensemble 415 Harmonia Mundi France ▲ HMC 901378

Charpentier, M.-A.:Les Arts florissants, w. C. Dussaut (sop), J. Feldman (sop), G. Laurens (mez), D. Visse (ct), P. Cantor (ten), G. Reinhart (bar), W. Christie (cnd), Les Arts Florissants [F] Musique d'Abord ▲ HMA 1901083

Charpentier, M.-A.:Leçons de ténèbres, H. 96-110, w. G. Lesne (ct), I. Honeyman (cnd), Il Seminario Musicale—3 du jeudi Virgin Classics ▲ CDC 59278

Fauré, G.:Requiem, w. P. Kooy (bass), P. Herreweghe (cnd), Musique Oblique Ensemble, Chapelle Royale Choir [1893 version] [L] Harmonia Mundi France ▲ HMC 901292

Hasse, J.A.:Cleofide, w. Emma Kirkby (sop), Randall Wong (ct), Dominique Visse (ct), Derek Lee Ragin (ct), David Cordier (alt), W. Christie (cnd), Cappella Coloniensis [I] Capriccio 4-▲ 10193/96 [DDD]

Lully, J.-B.:Atys, w. Guillemette Laurens (mez), Guy de Mey (ten), Jean-François Gardeil (bar), W. Christie (cnd), Les Arts Florissants, Les Arts Florissants Chorus [F] Harmonia Mundi France 3-▲ HMC 901257/59 [DDD];

Monteverdi, C.:Vespro della Beata Vergine, w. G. Laurens (mez), H. Crook (ten), D. Thomas (bass), P. Herreweghe (cnd), Toulouse Saqueboutiers, Chapelle Royale Choir, Collegium Vocale [L] Harmonia Mundi France 2-▲ HMC 901247/48 [DDD]

Rameau, J.P.:Castor et Pollux, w. V. Gens (sop), H. Cook (ten), J. Corréas (bass), W. Christie (cnd), Les Arts Florissants Harmonia Mundi France 3-▲ HMC 901435/37

Mellon, Agnès (sop) (cont.)

Rameau, J.P.:Nélée et Myrthis, w. A. Mellon (sop—Myrthis), D. Michel-Dansac (sop—Maid), C. Pelon (sop—Maid), F. Semellaz (sop—Corinne), J. Corréas (bass—Nélée), W. Christie (cnd), Les Arts Florissants, Les Arts Florissants Chorus [F] *(rec 5/91)* Harmonia Mundi France ▲ HMC 901381

Rameau, J.P.:Pygmalion, w. A. Mellon (sop—Céphise), D. Michel-Dansac (sop—La Statue), S. Piau (sop—L'Amour), H. Crook (ten—Pygmalion), W. Christie (cnd), Les Arts Florissants, Les Arts Florissants Chorus [F] *(rec 5/91)* Harmonia Mundi France ▲ HMC 901381

Mellor, Alwyn (sop)

Sullivan, A.:The Yeomen of the Guard, w. Felicity Palmer (sop—Dame Carruthers), Pamela Helen Stephens (mez—Phoebe Meryll), Neill Archer (ten—Col Fairfax), Peter Hoare (ten—Leonard Meryll), Ralph Mason (ten—1st Yeoman), Donald Maxwell (bar—Wilfred Shadbolt), Peter Savidge (bar—Lieutenant Sir Richard Cholmondely), Donald Adams (bass—Sergeant Meryll), Richard Suart (bass—Jack Point), Peter Lloyd Evans (sgr—2nd Yeoman), Alwyn Mellor (sgr—Elsie Maynard), Clare O'Neill (sgr—Kate), C. Mackerras (cnd), Welsh National Opera Orch, Welsh National Opera Chorus *(rec Brangwyn Hall, Swasea, Wales, Apr 18–30 & May 1, 1995)* Telarc 2-▲ CD 80404 [DDD]

Melnikova, Y. (sgr)

Prokofiev, S.:Maddalena, w. S. Kulikova (sgr), N. Zagorinskaya (sgr), S. Donets (sgr), S. Yakovlev (sgr), C. Tikhonov (cnd), Moscow Helikon Theater Chamber Ensemble [R] MK ▲ MKA 417056 [DDD]

Stravinsky, I.:Mavra, w. S. Kulikova (sgr), N. Zagorinskaya (sgr), S. Donets (sgr), S. Yakovlev (bar), C. Tikhonov (cnd), Moscow Helikon Theater Chamber Ensemble MK ▲ MKA 417056 [DDD]

Meloni, Maria (mez)

Mascagni, P.:Cavalleria rusticana, w. L. Bruna Rasa (sop), R. Gallo Toscani (mez), A. Melandri (ten), A. Poli (bar), P. Mascagni (cnd), Holland Italian Opera Orch, Italian d'Olanda Opera Chorus [I] *(rec live at the Royal Theatre in the Hague, 11/7/38)* Bongiovanni ▲ GB 1050 (m) [AAD]

Melvin, Lee (ten)

Banfield, W.:Spiritual Songs, w. Timothy Holly (vc) Innova ▲ 510 [DDD]

Melzer, Friedrich (ten)

Saint-Saëns, C.:Oratorio de Noël, w. V. Schweizer (sop), E. Wiens (sop), H. Jung (mez), K. Widmer (bass), D. Hellmann (cnd), Mainz Bach Orch, Mainz Bach Choir *(rec 1976)* Calig ▲ CAL 50512 [AAD]

Mendel, Jan Andreas (trb)

Mozart, W.A.:Zauberflöte, w. Constanze Backes (sop—Papagena), Christiane Oelze (sop—Pamina), Susan Roberts (sop—First Lady), Cyndia Sieden (sop—Queen of the Night), Carola Guber (cta—Second Lady), Maria Jonas (cta—Third Lady), Andreas Dieterich (trb—First Boy), Jan Andreas Mendel (trb—Second Boy), Florian Wöller (trb—Third Boy), Uwe Peper (ten—Monostatos), Nicolas Robertson (ten—First Man in Armor), Michael Schade (ten—Tamino), Gerald Finley (bar—Papageno), Noel Mann (bass—Second Man in Armour), Harry Peeters (bass—Sarastro), Detlef Roth (bass—Speaker/First Priest), Robert Burt (speaker—Third Priest), Robert Johnston (speaker—Second Priest), Wolfgang Knauer (speaker—Fourth Priest), Douglas Welbat (speaker—Second Priest), J. E. Gardiner (cnd), English Baroque Soloists, Monteverdi Choir London *(rec Forum am Schlosspark, Ludwigsburg, July 1995)* Archiv 2-▲ 449166-2

Mendoza, Alfredo (ten)

Delgado, F.:Choral Music, w. Martha Molinar (sop), Luz Angélica Uribe (sop), Ana Paula Abitia (mez), Noé Colín (bass), B. J. Echenique (cnd), Mexico City CO, Alfredo Mendoza (cnd), Schola Cantorum—Te Deum al Sr. Felipe de Jesús Urtext ▲ URT 2001 [DDD]

Jerusalem, I.:Choral Music, w. Martha Molinar (sop), Luz Angélica Uribe (sop), Ana Paula Abitia (mez), Noé Colín (bass), B. J. Echenique (cnd), Mexico City CO, Alfredo Mendoza (cnd), Schola Cantorum—Magnificat a Dos Voces; Misa en Sol Mayor a 8 Voces Urtext ▲ URT 2001 [DDD]

Meneghel, Cinzia (alt)

Perti, G.A.:Liturgy for Good Friday, w. Patrizia Vaccari (sop), Maura Pederzoli (sop), Cristina Calzolari (sop), Alida Oliva (sop), Claudia Bugli (sop), Lucia Bagnoli (alt), Renzo Bez (alt), Alessandro Carmignani (alt), Michel van Goethem (alt), Mauro Collina (ten), Vincenzo Di Donato (ten), Paolo Fanciullacci (ten), Giovanni Caccamo (ten), Paolo Da Col (ten), Sergio Foresti (bass), Marco Scavazza (bass), Luca Ferracin (bass), Paride Montanari (bass), Liuwe Tamminga (org), Sergio Vartolo (org), S. Vartolo (cnd), Bologna San Petronio Capella Musicale Orch—Omnes amici mei; De lamentatione Jeremiae Prophetae:Heth. Cogitavit; Velum templi; Vinea mea; De lamentatione Jeremiae Prophetae:Lamed. Matribus suis; Tamquam ad latronem; Tenebrae factae sunt; Animam meam; Tradiderunt me; Jesum tradidit; De lamentatione Jeremiae Prophetae:Aleph. Ego vir; Caligaverunt *(rec St. Petronio Basilica, Bologna, Mar 28–31, 1995)* Naxos ▲ 8.553321 [DDD]

Menendez, Michèle Vilma (mez)

Donizetti, G.:Maria Stuarda, w. M. Caballé (sop—Maria Stuarda), R. Bezinian (mez—Anna), M. V. Menendez (mez—Elisabetta), J. Carreras (ten—Roberto), M. Mazzieri (bass—Giorgio Talbot), E. Serra (bass—Lord Gugliemo Cecil), N. Santi (cnd), ORTF Lyric Orch, ORTF Lyric Chorale [I] *(rec live 3/26/72)* Memories 2-▲ HR4417/18 [ADD]

Menni, Giuseppe (bass)

Verdi, G.:Rigoletto, w. Lina Pagliughi (sop—Gilda), Linda Brambilla (mez—Countess Ceprano), Vera De Cristoff (cta—Maddalena), Tino Folgar (ten—Duke of Mantua), Giuseppe Nessi (ten—Borsa), Luigi Piazza (bar—Rigolotto), Aristide Baracchi (b-bar—Monterone/Marullo), Salvatore Baccaloni (bass—Sparafucile), Giuseppe Menni (bass—Ceprano), C. Sabajno (cnd), La Scala Orch, La Scala Chorus *(rec La Scala Theatre, Milan, Nov.–Dec. 1927)* VAI Audio 2-▲ VAIA 1097-2

Verdi, G.:Rigoletto, w. Lina Pagliughi (sop—Gilda), Linda Brambilla (mez—Contessa di Ceprano), Vera de Cristoff (cta—Maddalena), Tino Folgar (ten—Duca di Mantova), Giuseppe Nessi (ten—Borsa), Aristide Baracchi (bar—Conte di Monterone/Marullo), Luigi Piazza (bar—Rigoletto), Salvatore Baccaloni (bass—Sparafucile), Giuseppe Menni (bass—Conte di Ceprano), C. Sabajno (cnd), La Scala Orch, La Scala Chorus *(rec 1927–28)* Arkadia 2-▲ CD 78003 (m) [ADD]

Menotti, Tatiana (sop)

Puccini, G.:La Bohème, w. L. Albanese (sop), B. Gigli (ten), A. Poli (bar), U. Berrettoni (cnd), La Scala Orch, La Scala Chorus [I] *(rec 1937)* EMI Classics ("Studio" series) 2-▲ CDHB 63335 (m) [ADD]

Puccini, G.:La Bohème, w. Licia Albanese (sop), Beniamino Gigli (ten), Afro Poli (bar), U. Berrettoni (cnd), La Scala Orch, La Scala Chorus *(rec Milan, 1938)* Phonographe 2-▲ PHG CD 5071

Puccini, G.:La Bohème, w. L. Albanese (sop—Mimì), T. Menotti (sop—Musetta), B. Gigli (ten—Rodolfo), N. Palai (ten—Parpignol), A. Poli (bar—Marcello), A. Baracchi (bar—Schaunard), D. Baronti (bass—Colline), C. Scattola (bass—Benoit/Alcindoro), U. Berrettoni (cnd), La Scala Orch, La Scala Chorus [I] *(rec Milan, May 1938)* Nimbus 2-▲ NI 7862/63 [ADD]

Puccini, G.:La Bohème, w. Licia Albanese (sop—Mimì), Tatiana Menotti (sop—Musetta), Beniamino Gigli (ten—Rodolfo), Nello Palai (ten—Parpignol), Aristide Baracchi (bar—Schaunard), Afro Poli (bar—Marcello), Duilio Baronti (bass—Colline), Carlo Scattola (bass—Benoit/Alcindoro), U. Berrettoni (cnd), La Scala Orch, Vittore Veneziani (cnd), La Scala Chorus *(rec Feb–Mar 1938)* Arkadia ("The 78's" series) 2-▲ 78009 [ADD]

Mentzel, Erich (ten)

Monteverdi, C.:Vespers, w. Susanne Ryden (sop), Irena Troupova-Wilke (sop), Detlef Bratschke (alt), Hermann Oswald (ten), Manuel Warwitz (ten), Thomas Herberich (bass), Günther Schmidt (bass), H. Arman (cnd), Schütz Academy Capriccio ▲ CD 10521 [DDD]

Mentzer, Susanne (mez)

Donizetti, G.:Anna Bolena, w. J. Sutherland (sop), B. Manca di Nissa (cta), J. Hadley (ten), S. Ramey (bass), R. Bonynge (cnd), Welsh National Opera Orch [I] London 3-▲ 421096-2 [DDD]

Gounod, C.:Faust, w. C. Gasdia (sop), B. Fassbaender (mez), J. Hadley (ten), A. Agache (bar), P. Fourcade (bass), C. Rizzi (cnd), Welsh National Opera Orch, Welsh National Opera Chorus Teldec 3-▲ 90872

Mascagni, P.:Cavalleria rusticana, w. A. Baltsa (mez), P. Domingo (ten), J. Pons (bar), G. Sinopoli (cnd), Philharmonia Orch, Royal Opera House Chorus Covent Garden [I] Deutsche Grammophon ▲ 429568-2 [DDD]

Mendelssohn, F.:A Midsummer Night's Dream (comp), w. L. Dawson (sop), J. Tate (cnd), Rotterdam PO, Toonkunst Chorus, Peter Hall Company EMI Classics 2-▲ CDCB 54348

Mozart, W.A.:Complete Mozart Edition, w. B. Hendricks (sop), J. Varady (sop), F. Araiza (ten), T. Allen (bar), C. Davis (cnd), Bavarian RSO Philips 3-▲ 422537-2 [ADD]

Mentzer, Susanne (mez) (cont.)

Mozart, W.A.:Nozze di Figaro, w. Rebecca Evans (sop—Barbarina), Nuccia Focile (sop—Susanna), Suzanne Murphy (sop—Marcellina), Carol Vaness (sop—Countess Almaviva), Susanne Mentzer (mez—Cherubino), Ryland Davies (ten—Don Basilio/Don Curzio), Alessandro Corbelli (bar—Count Almaviva), Alfonso Antoniozzi (bass—Doctor Bartolo/Antonio), Alastair Miles (bass—Figaro), C. Mackerras (cnd), Scottish CO, Scottish Chamber Chorus *(rec Usher Hall, Edingurgh, Scotland, July 31–Aug. 12, 1994)* Telarc 3-▲ CD 80388 [DDD]

Rossini, G.:Il barbiere di Siviglia, w. A. Felle (sop), J. Hadley (ten), T. Hampson (bass), S. Ramey (bass), G. Gelmetti (cnd), Tuscan Orch EMI ▲ 54863-2

Women at an Exposition, w. Sunny Joy Langton (sop), Elain Skorodin (vn), Kimberly Schmidt (pno) *(rec Nov. 1991)* Koch International Classics ▲ KIC 7240 [ADD]

Mera, Yoshikazu (ct)

Bach, J.S.:Cants 12, w. Yumiko Kurisu (sop), Makoto Sakurada (ten), Peter Kooy (bass), M. Suzuki (cnd), Japan Bach Collegium *(rec Kobe Shoin Women's Univ, Japan, Apr 11–14, 1996)* BIS ▲ CD 791 [DDD]

Bach, J.S.:Cant 54, w. Yumiko Kurisu (sop), Makoto Sakurada (ten), Peter Kooy (bass), M. Suzuki (cnd), Japan Bach Collegium *(rec Kobe Shoin Women's Univ, Japan, Apr 11–14, 1996)* BIS ▲ CD 791 [DDD]

Bach, J.S.:Cant 162, w. Yumiko Kurisu (sop), Makoto Sakurada (ten), Peter Kooy (bass), M. Suzuki (cnd), Japan Bach Collegium *(rec Kobe Shoin Women's Univ, Japan, Apr 11–14, 1996)* BIS ▲ CD 791 [DDD]

Bach, J.S.:Cant 182, w. Yumiko Kurisu (sop), Makoto Sakurada (ten), Peter Kooy (bass), M. Suzuki (cnd), Japan Bach Collegium *(rec Kobe Shoin Women's Univ, Japan, Apr 11–14, 1996)* BIS ▲ CD 791 [DDD]

Mercker, Karl-Ernst (ten)

Nicolai, O.:Lustigen Weiber, w. H. Donath (sop), E. Mathis (sop), H. Schwarz (mez), K. Ludwig (ten), P. Schreier (ten), C. Dormoy (bar), B. Weikl (bar), K. Moll (bass), S. Vogel (bass), B. Klee (cnd), Berlin Staatskapelle, Berlin State Opera Chorus *(rec July 3, 1976)* Berlin Classics ("Eterna" series) ▲ BER 2046-2 [ADD]

Mercuriali, Angelo (ten)

Donizetti, G.:La fille du régiment (sels), w. Mirella Freni (sop), Anna di Stasio (mez), Luciano Pavarotti (ten), Wladimiro Ganzarolli (bar), Walter Monachesi (bar), Giuseppe Morresi (bass), V. Gullino (sgr), Luisa Rezzadore (sgr), N. Sanzogno (cnd), La Scala Orch, La Scala Chorus Budget ("The Greatest Voice in Opera" series) ▲ SYP 108

Mozart, W.A.:Nozze di Figaro, w. G. Gatti (sop), A. Noni (sop), G. Sciurri (sop), J. Gardino (mez), M.T. Pace (mez), S. Bruscantini (bar), I. Tajo (bass), F. Corena (bass), F. Previtali (cnd), Rome RAI Orch [I] *(rec 1951)* Cetra Classic 2-▲ CDO 12

Verdi, G.:La forza del destino, w. Zinka Milanov (sop—Donna Leonora di Vargas), Rosalind Elias (mez—Preziosilla), Luisa Gioia (sgr—Curra), Angelo Mercuriali (ten—Trabuco), Giuseppe di Stefano (ten—Son Alvaro), Leonard Warren (bar—Don Carlos di Vargas), Giorgio Tozzi (b-bar—Padre guardiano), Dino Mantovani (bar—Fra Melitone), Paolo Washington (b-bar—Il marchese di Calatrava), Virgilio Carbonari (b-bar—un alcalde), Sergio Liviabella (sgr—un chirurgo), F. Previtali (cnd), St. Cecilia Academy Orch Rome, St. Cecilia Academy Chorus Rome [I] London ▲ 443678-2 [ADD]

Verdi, G.:Otello, w. Renata Tebaldi (sop—Desdemona), Luisa Ribacchi (mez—Emilia), Angelo Mercuriali (ten—Roderigo), Mario del Monaco (ten—Otello), Piero de Palma (ten—Cassio), Aldo Protti (bar—Iago), Dario Caselli (bass—A Herald), Fernando Corena (bass—Lodovico), Pierluigi Martinucci (bass—Montano), A. Erede (cnd), St. Cecilia Academy Orch Rome, St. Cecilia Academy Chorus Rome Theorema ▲ TH 121141/142

Zandonai, R.:Francesca da Rimini, w. Lydia Marimpietri (sop—Biancofiore), Magda Olivero (sop—Francesca), Pinuccia Perotti (sop—Samaritana), Edda Vincenzi (sop—Garsenda), Gabriella Carturan (mez—Smaragdi), Biancamaria Casoni (mez—Altichiara), Anna Maria Rota (cta—Donella), Athos Cesarini (ten—Archer), Angelo Mercuriali (ten—Ser Toldo Berardengo), Mario del Monaco (ten—Paolo), Piero de Palma (ten—Malatestino), Rinaldo Pelizzoni (ten—Prisoner), Gianpiero Malaspina (bar—Gianciotto), Dino Mantovani (bar—Jester), Enrico Campi (bass—Ostasio), Giuseppe Morresi (bass—Tower warden), G. Gavazzeni (cnd), La Scala Orch, La Scala Chorus *(rec La Scala Theatre, Milan, June 4, 1959)* Legato Classics 2-▲ LCD 186-2

Merighi, Giorgio (sgr)

Donizetti, G.:Maria di Rohan (sels), w. R. Scotto (sop), O. de Fabritiis (cnd), Lisbon Teatro São Carlos Orch, Lisbon Teatro São Carlos Chorus—1 soprano aria, "Cupo fatal mestizia" & 1 duet, "Ecco l'ora" [I] *(rec live, Lisbon 3/20/68)* Melodram (Connaisseur) 2-▲ CDM 27512 [ADD]

Meyerbeer, G.:Roberto il Diavolo, w. R. Scotto (sop), B. Christoff (bass), N. Sanzogno (cnd), Florence Maggio Musicale Orch, Florence Maggio Musicale Chorus [I] *(rec live, 4/7/68)* Arkadia 3-▲ 549 (m) [ADD]

Meyerbeer, G.:Roberto il Diavolo, w. R. Scotto (sop), B. Christoff (bass), N. Sanzogno (cnd), Florence Maggio Musicale Orch, Florence Maggio Musicale Chorus [I] *(rec live 4/7/68)* Melodram 3-▲ MEL 37024

Merker, Rose (sop)

Wagner, R.:Die Walküre (sels), w. H. Konetzni (sop—Sieglinde), R. Merker (sop—Brünhilde), F. Völker (ten—Sigmund), L. Hofmann (bass—Wotan), B. Walter (cnd), Vienna State Opera Orch, Vienna State Opera Chorus *(rec Oct. 19, 1936)* Koch Schwann 2-▲ SCH 314592

Merli, Francesco (ten)

Francesco Merli, Vol. 2 *(rec 1928–35)* Preiser ("Lebendige Vergangenheit" series) ▲ PRE 89091 [AAD]

The Italian Vocal Tradition, Vol. 1:The Voices of Toscanini, w. Toti dal Monte (sop), Claudio Muzio (sop), Rosetta Pampanini (sop), Biata Scacciati (sop), Giacomo Lauri-Volpi (ten), Aureliano Pertile (ten), Carlo Galeffi (bar), Mariano Stabile (bar), Riccardo Stracciari (bar), Nazzareno de Angel *(rec 1921–35)* Iron Needle ▲ 1304

Leoncavallo, R.:Pagliacci, w. Rosetta Pampanini (sop), Giuseppe Nessi (ten), Carlo Galeffi (bar), Gino Vanelli (bar), *(orch unknown)* *(rec Milan, 1930)* Melodram ▲ IMC 102003

Leoncavallo, R.:Pagliacci, w. Rosetta Pampanini (sop), Giuseppe Nessi (ten), Carlo Galeffi (bar), L. Molajoli (cnd), La Scala Orch, La Scala Chorus *(rec Milan, 1930)* Phonographe 2-▲ PHG CD 5066

Leoncavallo, R.:Pagliacci (sels), w. Enrico Caruso (ten), Antonio Paoli (ten), Giovanni Zenatello (ten), Amedeo Bassi (ten), Hermann Jadlowker (ten), Fernand Ansseau (ten), Hipolito Lazaro (ten), Nino (Filippo) Piccaluga (ten), Mario Chamlee (ten), Giacomo Lauri-Volpi (ten), Miguel Fleta (ten), Giovanni Martinelli (ten), Aureliano Pertile (ten), Georges Thill (ten), Alessandro Valente (ten), Lauritz Melchior (ten), Marcel Wittrisch (ten), Joseph Schmidt (ten), Beniamino Gigli (ten), Giuseppe Lugo (ten), Helge Roswaenge (ten), Jussi Bjoerling (ten)—23 versions of the tenor aria "Vesti la giubba" *(rec 1907–1944)* Bongiovanni ▲ GB 1071 [ADD]

Opera Arias Preiser ("Lebendige Vergangenheit" series) ▲ PRE 89026 (m) [AAD]

Puccini, G.:Manon Lescaut, w. Maria Zamboni (sop), Lorenzo Conati (sgr), L. Molajoli (cnd), La Scala Orch, La Scala Chorus *(rec Milan, 1930)* Melodram 2-▲ IMC 202001

Puccini, G.:Manon Lescaut, w. Maria Zamboni (sop), Lorenzo Conati (sgr), L. Molajoli (cnd), La Scala Orch, La Scala Chorus *(rec Milan, 1930)* Phonographie 2-▲ PHG 5006 [ADD]

Puccini, G.:Manon Lescaut, w. Maria Zamboni (sop—Manon), Anna Masetti-Bassi (mez—Singer), Francesco Merli (ten—Chevalier), Giuseppe Nessi (ten—Edmondo/Dancing Master/ Lamplighter), Lorenzo Conati (bar—Lescaut), Aristide Baracchi (bass—Innkeeper/Sergeant), Attilio Bordonali (bass—Geronte), Natale Villa (bass—Naval Captain), L. Molajoli (cnd), La Scala Orch, Vittore Veneziani (cnd), La Scala Chorus *(rec 1930)* Arkadia ("The 78's" series) 2-▲ 78014 [ADD]

Puccini, G.:Turandot, w. Gina Cigna (sop), Magda Olivero (sop), F. Ghione (cnd), Turin RAI SO *(rec 1938)* Phonographe 2-▲ PHG 5053

Verdi, G.:Otello (sels), w. C. Muzio (sop), R. Ponselle (sop), H. Spani (sop), E. Caruso (ten), N. Fusati (ten), L. Melchior (ten), F. Merli (ten), F. Tamagno (ten), B. Franci (bar), V. Maurel (bar), R. Stracciari (bar), T. Ruffo (bar) *(rec 1906–1933)* Music Memoria ▲ 30219

Verdi, G.:Il trovatore, w. Bianca Scacciati (sop), Giuseppina Zinetti (sop), Enrico Molinari (bar), L. Molajoli (cnd), Milan SO, La Scala Chorus *(rec live, 1930)* Melodram ▲ CDI 202002

Merli, Francesco (ten) (cont.)
Verdi, G.:Il trovatore (sels), w. J. Biel (ten), F. Tamagno (ten), L.-A. Escalaïs (ten), M. Gilion (ten), E. Caruso (ten), A. Paoli (ten), G. Zenatello (ten), J. Sembach (ten), L. Slezak (ten), F. Constantino (ten), G. Martinelli (ten), B. De Muro (ten), N. Fusati (ten), N. Piccaluga (ten), G. Lauri-Volpi (ten), A. Pertile (ten), E. Bergamaschi (ten), R. Tauber (ten), J. O'Sullivan (ten), H. Roswaenge (ten), G. Taccani (ten), V. Lois (ten), H. Lazaro (ten), A. Lindi (ten), A. Cortis (ten), F. Völker (ten), J. Kiepura (ten), J. Schmidt (ten), J. Bjoerling (ten), B. Gigli (ten), A. Salvarezza (ten), J. Soler (ten), M. Filippeschi (ten)—34 performances of the Act III tenor aria "Di quella pira!," *(rec from 1903–1956)* Bongiovanni ▲ GB 1051 [AAD]

Merman, Ethel (sgr)
Berlin, I.:Annie Get Your Gun, w. R. Middleton (sgr), L. Bibb (sgr), K. Carnes (sgr), J. Garth (sgr), R. Lenn (sgr), C. Turner (sgr), J. Blackton (cnd) [1946 cast] MCA Classics ▲ MCAD 10047 [AAD] ■ MCAC 10047
Berlin, I.:Annie Get Your Gun, w. B. Yarnell (sgr), *(other artists unknown)* [1966 Lincoln Center cast] RCA ▲ 1124 2 RC [ADD] ■ 1124 4 R
Broadway, w. Judy Holliday (sgr), Dick van Dyke (sgr), Doris Day (sgr), Topol (sgr), Mary Martin (sgr), Jill Haworth (sgr), William Warfield (sgr), et al. Sony Classical ("Greatest Hits" series) ▲ MLK 62365 ■ MLT 62365

Merolla, Robleto (bar)
Janáček, L.:Jenůfa, w. Magda Olivero (sop—Kostelnicka), Bruna Baglioni (mez—La vecchia Buryja), Grace Bumbry (mez—Jenufa), Renato Cioni (ten—Steva Buryja), Robleto Merolla (bar—Laca Klemen), Carlo Meliciani (sgr—Vecchio compagno), J. Semkow (cnd), La Scala Orch, La Scala Chorus *(rec Milan, Apr 2, 1974)* Myto 2-▲ MCD 961142

Merrill, Robert (bar)
America's Greatest Baritone Cantabile ("Biographies in Music") ▲ BIM 710-1
Bizet, G.:Carmen, w. L. Price (sop), M. Freni (sop), F. Corelli (ten), H. von Karajan (cnd), Vienna PO, Vienna State Opera Chorus [F] RCA Gold Seal 3-▲ 6199-2-RG [ADD] 2-■ 6199-4-RG
Bizet, G.:Carmen, w. L. Price (sop), M. Freni (sop), F. Corelli (ten), H. von Karajan (cnd), Vienna PO, Vienna State Opera Chorus [F] RCA Gold Seal ▲ 60190-2-RG [ADD] ■ 60190-4-RG
Bloch, E.:Avodath Hakodesh, w. L. Bernstein (cnd), New York PO [E,He] Sony Classical ▲ SMK 47533 [ADD]
Bock, J.:Fiddler on the Roof, w. Molly Picon (sgr), S. Black (cnd), London Festival Orch, London Festival Chorus London ("Phase 4 Stereo" series) ▲ 448 949-2
Donizetti, G.:Lucia di Lammermoor, w. J. Sutherland (sop), R. Cioni (ten), C. Siepi (bass-bar), J. Pritchard (cnd), St. Cecilia Academy Orch Rome, St. Cecilia Academy Chorus Rome [I] London 2-▲ 411622-2 [ADD]
Leoncavallo, R.:Pagliacci, w. V. de los Angeles (sop), J. Björling (ten), L. Warren (bar), R. Cellini (cnd), Columbus Orch, Robert Shaw Chorale EMI Classics ▲ ZDC 49503
Leoncavallo, R.:Pagliacci, w. P. Lorengar (sop), R. Krause (ten), J. McCracken (ten), U. Benelli (bar), L. Gardelli (cnd), St. Cecilia Academy Orch Rome, St. Cecilia Academy Chorus Rome [I] IMP Collectors Series ▲ IMPX 9017 [AAD]
Live from Carnegie Hall, Jan. 7, 1973, w. R. Tucker (ten) *(rec Carnegie Hall, NYC Jan. 7, 1973)* Teldec 2-▲ 93706-2
Mascagni, P.:Cavalleria rusticana, w. Z. Milanov (sop), Carol Smith (sop), J. Bjöerling (ten), R. Cellini (cnd), RCA Victor SO, Robert Shaw Chorale [I] RCA Gold Seal ▲ 6510-2-RG [ADD]
Opera Stars Sing on Radio, Vol. 1:Unpublished Broadcasts from the Fourties, w. Dusolina Giannini (sop), Helen Traubel (sop), Gladys Swarthout (cta), Richard Crooks (ten), Lauritz Melchior (ten), Lawrence Tibbett (bar), Ezio Pinza (bass) Enterprise ("The Radio Years" series) ▲ ENTRY 11
Operatic Duets, w. Jussi Björling (ten), Licia Albanese (sop), Zinka Milanov (sop), Renata Tebaldi (sop) RCA Gold Seal ▲ 7799-2-RG (m) [ADD] ■ 7799-4-RG (CrO2)
Puccini, G.:La Bohème, w. A. Moffo (sop), F. Costa (mez), G. Tucker (ten), G. Tozzi (bass), E. Leinsdorf (cnd), Rome Opera Orch, Rome Opera Chorus [I] RCA Gold Seal 2-▲ 3969-2-RG [ADD] 2-■ 3969-4-RG (CrO2)
Puccini, G.:La Bohème, w. V. de los Angeles (sop), J. Bjoerling (ten), T. Beecham (cnd), RCA Victor SO [I] EMI Classics 2-▲ CDCB 47235 (m) [ADD] 2-■ 4X2G 47235
Puccini, G.:La Bohème (sels), w. A. Moffo (sop), F. Costa (mez), G. Tucker (ten), G. Tozzi (bass), E. Leinsdorf (cnd), Rome Opera Orch, Rome Opera Chorus RCA Gold Seal ▲ 60189-2-RG [ADD] ■ 60189-4-RG (CrO2)
Puccini, G.:Manon Lescaut, w. L. Albanese (sop), J. Bjoerling (ten), J. Perlea (cnd), Rome Opera Orch, Rome Opera Chorus [I] RCA Gold Seal 2-▲ 60573-2-RG [ADD]
Robert Merrill on Radio, w. various orchs *(rec 1940 & 1946)* Enterprise ("The Radio Years" series) ▲ ENTRY 14
Rossini, G.:Il barbiere di Siviglia, w. R. Peters (sop), C. Valletti (ten), G. Tozzi (bass), F. Corena (bass), E. Leinsdorf (cnd), Metropolitan Opera Orch, New York Metropolitan Opera Chorus [I] RCA Gold Seal 3-▲ 6505-2-RG [ADD] 2-■ 6505-4-RG (CrO2)
Rossini, G.:Il barbiere di Siviglia, w. Roberta Peters (sop—Rosina), Margaret Roggero (mez—Berta), Cesare Valletti (ten—Count Almaviva), Calvin Marsh (bar—Fiorello/Sergeant), Robert Merrill (bar—Figaro), Fernando Corena (bass—Dr. Bartolo), Carlo Tomanelli (bass—Ambrogio), Giorgio Tozzi (bass—Don Basilio), E. Leinsdorf (cnd), Metropolitan Opera Orch, New York Metropolitan Opera Chorus *(rec Manhattan Center, New York, Sept 1-11, 1958)* RCA Living Stereo 3-▲ 09026-68552-2 [ADD]
Rossini, G.:Il barbiere di Siviglia (sels), w. R. Peters (sop), C. Valletti (ten), G. Tozzi (bass), F. Corena (bass), E. Leinsdorf (cnd), Metropolitan Opera Orch, New York Metropolitan Opera Chorus RCA Gold Seal ▲ 60188-2-RG [ADD] ■ 60188-4-RG (CrO2)
Rossini, G.:Il barbiere di Siviglia (sels), w. D. Mitropoulos (cnd), NBC SO—Largo al Factotum *(rec live, ca 1950)* Nickson 2-▲ NN 1008/1009 (m) [ADD]
Verdi, G.:Aida, w. L. Price (sop), R. Gorr (mez), J. Vickers (ten), G. Tozzi (bass), G. Solti (cnd), Rome Opera Orch, Rome Opera Chorus [I] London ▲ 421860-2 [ADD]
Verdi, G.:Aida, w. L. Price (sop), R. Gorr (mez), J. Vickers (ten), G. Tozzi (bass), G. Solti (cnd), Rome Opera Orch, Rome Opera Chorus [I] London 3-▲ 417416-2 [ADD]
Verdi, G.:Un ballo in maschera, w. L. Price (sop), C. Bergonzi (ten), E. Leinsdorf (cnd), RCA Italian Opera Orch [I] RCA Gold Seal 2-▲ 6645-2-RG [ADD]
Verdi, G.:Falstaff, w. M. Freni (sop), I. Ligabue (sop), G. Simionato (mez), R. Elias (mez), R. Krause (ten), G. Evans (bar), G. Solti (cnd), RCA Italian Opera Orch, RCA Italiana Opera Chorus [I] London 2-▲ 417168-2 [ADD]
Verdi, G.:Rigoletto, w. R. Peters (sop), J. Björling (ten), G. Tozzi (bass), J. Perlea (cnd), Rome Opera Orch, Rome Opera Chorus [I] RCA Gold Seal 2-▲ 60172-2-RG [ADD] 2-■ 60172-4-RG (CrO2)
Verdi, G.:Rigoletto, w. A. Moffo (sop), R. Elias (mez), A. Kraus (ten), G. Solti (cnd), RCA Italian Opera Orch, RCA Italiana Opera Chorus [I] RCA Gold Seal ▲ 60203-2-RG ■ 60203-4-RG
Verdi, G.:Rigoletto, w. A. Moffo (sop), R. Elias (mez), A. Kraus (ten), G. Solti (cnd), RCA Italian Opera Orch, RCA Italiana Opera Chorus [I] RCA Gold Seal 2-▲ 6506-2-RG [ADD]
Verdi, G.:La traviata, w. C. N. Albanese (sop), J. Peerce (ten), A. Toscanini (cnd), NBC SO [I] RCA Gold Seal 2-▲ 60303-2-RG [ADD] 2-■ 60303-4-RG (CrO2)
Verdi, G.:La traviata, w. C. N. Albanese (sop), J. Peerce (ten), A. Toscanini (cnd), NBC SO Music & Arts 2-▲ CD 271
Verdi, G.:La traviata, w. J. Sutherland (sop), C. Bergonzi (ten), J. Pritchard (cnd), Florence Maggio Musicale Orch, Florence Maggio Musicale Chorus [I] London 2-▲ 411877-2 [ADD]
Verdi, G.:La traviata, w. A. Moffo (sop), G. Tucker (ten), F. Previtali (cnd), Rome Opera Orch [I] RCA Gold Seal ▲ 60204-2-RG [ADD] ■ 60204-4-RG
Verdi, G.:La traviata, w. A. Moffo (sop), G. Tucker (ten), F. Previtali (cnd), Rome Opera Orch [I] RCA Gold Seal 2-▲ 4144-2-RG [ADD] 2-■ 4144-4-RG
Verdi, G.:La traviata (sels), w. J. Sutherland (sop), C. Bergonzi (ten), J. Pritchard (cnd), Florence Maggio Musicale Orch London ▲ 421325-2 [ADD]

Merriman, Nan (mez)
Bach, J.S.:Mass in b, BWV 232, w. P. Alarie (sop), L. Simoneau (ten), G. Neidlinger (bass), H. Scherchen (cnd), Vienna State Opera Orch, Vienna Academy Chorus [L] MCA Classics 2-▲ MCAD2-9821 [AAD]

Merriman, Nan (mez) (cont.)
Beethoven, L. van:Missa Solemnis, w. M. Marshall (sop), E. Conley (ten), J. Hines (bass), A. Toscanini (cnd), NBC SO, Robert Shaw Chorale *(rec 1953)* RCA Gold Seal ▲ 60272-2-RG [ADD] ■ 60272-4-RG
Bernstein, L.:Sym 1, "Jeremiah", w. L. Bernstein (cnd), St. Louis SO *(rec 1945)* RCA Red Seal ▲ 09026-61581-2
Gluck, C.W.:Orfeo ed Euridice (sels), w. B. Gibson (sop), A. Toscanini (cnd), NBC SO, Robert Shaw Chorale—Act 2 RCA Gold Seal ▲ 60280-2-RG; ■ 60280-4-RG
Mozart, W.A.:Così fan tutte, w. Elisabeth Schwarzkopf (sop), Graziella Sciutti (sop), Luigi Alva (ten), Rolando Panerai (bar), Franco Calabrese (bass), G. Cantelli (cnd), La Scala Orch, La Scala Chorus Stradivarius 2-▲ STV DTM 12304 [ADD]
Mozart, W.A.:Così fan tutte, w. E. Schwarzkopf (sop), L. Otto (sop), L. Simoneau (ten), R. Panerai (bar), S. Bruscantini (bar), H. von Karajan (cnd), Philharmonia Orch, Philharmonia Chorus [I] EMI Classics ("Studio" series) 3-▲ CDHC 69635 (m) [ADD]
Mozart, W.A.:Così fan tutte, w. E. Schwarzkopf (sop—Fiordiligi), G. Sciurri (sop—Despina), N. Merriman (mez—Dorabella), L. Alva (ten—Ferrando), R. Panerai (bar—Guglielmo), F. Clabrese (b-bar—Don Alfonso)., G. Cantelli (cnd), La Scala Orch, La Scala Chorus *(rec Jan. 27, 1956)* Datum 2-▲ DAT 12304 [ADD]
Mozart, W.A.:Così fan tutte (sels), w. Lisa Otto (sop), Elizabeth Schwarzkopf (sop), Rolando Panerai (bar), Leopold Simoneau (ten), Sesto Bruscantini (bass), H. von Karajan (cnd), Philharmonia Orch Classics for Pleasure ("Eminence" series) ▲ CDEMX 2211 [DDD]
Verdi, G.:Requiem Mass, w. L. Price (sop), R. Tucker (ten), G. Tozzi (bass), E. Ormandy (cnd), Philadelphia Orch *(rec live Apr. 6, 1957)* Standing Room Only ▲ SRO 842-1 [ADD]
Verdi, G.:Rigoletto (sels), w. Jan Peerce (ten), Frank Valentino (bar), Nicola Moscona (bass), G. Ribla (sgr), A. Toscanini (cnd), NBC SO—Act III (complete) Enterprise ("The Radio Years" series) ▲ ENT 48
Verdi, G.:Rigoletto (act 3), w. Jan Peerce (ten), Frank Valentino (bar), Nicola Moscona (bass), G. Ribla (sgr), A. Toscanini (cnd), NBC SO [I] *(rec New York, 7/25/43)* Melodram 2-▲ MEL 28022 (m) [AAD]
Verdi, G.:Rigoletto (act 4), w. Z. Milanov (sop), J. Peerce (ten), L. Warren (bar), A. Toscanini (cnd), NBC SO RCA Gold Seal ▲ 60276-2-RG [ADD] ■ 60276-4-RG (CrO2)

Merrino, G. (sgr)
Wolf-Ferrari, E.:I quatro rusteghi, w. A. P (Margarita), D. Lombardi (Lucieta), G. Merrino (Marina), M. Fratarcangeli (Felice) L. Belluso (Servant), A. Abete (Lunardo), M. Nicolini (Maurizio), G. Sorrentino (Filipeto), M. Peirone (Simon), D. Baronchelli (Cancian), A. Lemmo (Count Riccard) Arkadia-Akademia 2-▲ 139 [DDD]

Merritt, Chris (ten)
Bellini, V.:I Puritani, w. K. Ricciarelli (sop), E. Jankovic (mez), C. Gaifa (ten), A. Riva (bass), R. Scandiuzzi (bass), G. Ferro (cnd), Sicilian SO, Bari Teatro Petruzzelli Chorus *(rec Apr. 10, 1986)* Cetra Classic ▲ CDC 20 [ADD]
Bellini, V.:I Puritani, w. Katia Ricciarelli (sop), Eleonora Jankovic (mez), Juan Luque Carmona (ten), Carlo Gaifa (ten), Roberto Scandiuzzi (bass), G. Ferro (cnd), Sicilian SO, Bari Teatro Petruzzelli Chorus Fonit Cetra ("Digital Operas" series) 3-▲ FCT CDC 20
Donizetti, G.:arias, w. J. Fiore (cnd), Munich RSO—Io trar non volio [from Caterina Cornaro]; Deserto in terra [from Don Sebastiano]; Angelo casto e bel [from Il Duca d'Alba]; Fu macchiato l'onor mio [from Poliuto] Philips ▲ 434102-2
Donizetti, G.:Emilia di Liverpool, w. Y. Kenny (sop), A. Mason (sop), B. Mills (sop), S. Bruscantini (bar), G. Dolton (bar), C. Thornton-Holmes (bar), D. Parry (cnd), Philharmonia Orch, Geoffrey Mitchell Choir—complete opera, without dialogue Opera Rara 3-▲ OR 8
Donizetti, G.:L'Eremitaggio di Liverpool, w. Y. Kenny (sop), A. Mason (sop), B. Mills (sop), S. Bruscantini (bar), G. Dolton (bar), C. Thornton-Holmes (bar), D. Parry (cnd), Philharmonia Orch, Geoffrey Mitchell Choir—complete opera, without dialogue Opera Rara 3-▲ OR 8
Glinka, M.:A Life for the Tsar, w. A. Pendachanska (sop), S. Toczyska (mez), B. Martinovich (bass), E. Tchakarov (cnd), Sofia Festival Orch, Sofia National Opera Chorus [R] Sony Classical 3-▲ S3K 46487 [DDD]
Haydn, M.:Requiem in c, w. Siglinde Damisch (sop), Gabriele Schreckenbach (mez), Hans Udo Müller (pno), Gerhard Walterskirchen (org), E. Hinreiner (cnd), Salzburg RSO, Mozart Choir *(rec June 1981)* Koch Treasure ▲ 31608-2 [ADD]
Rossini, G.:Arias, w. J. Fiore (cnd), Munich RSO—La sua possente voce [from Cant. in onore del Sommo Pontefice Pio IX]; Ah! sì, per voi già sento [from Otello]; Balena in man del figlio [from Ermione]; Della cieca fortuna [from Elisabetta] Philips ▲ 434102-2
Rossini, G.:Bianca e Falliero, w. K. Ricciarelli (sop—Bianca), M. Horne (mez—Falliero), C. Merritt (ten—Contareno), G. Surjan (bass-Capellino), D. Renzetti (cnd), *(orch & chorus unknown) (rec live, 1986)* Legato Classics 3-▲ LCD 138-3 [ADD]
Rossini, G.:Guillaume Tell, w. C. Studer (sop), G. Zancanaro (bar), R. Muti (cnd), La Scala Orch, La Scala Chorus [I] *(rec live, 12/7/88)* Philips 4-▲ 422391-2 [DDD]
Rossini, G.:Music of, w. M. Fortuna (sop), M. Lerner (sop), D. Voigt (sop), M. Horne (mez), K. Kuhlmann (mez), F. von Stade (mez), R. Blake (ten), C. Estep (ten), T. Hampson (b-bar), H. Runey (b-bar), J. Opalach (bass), S. Ramey (bass), R. Norrington (cnd), Orch of St. Luke's, New York Concert Chorale EMI Classics ▲ CDG 54643
Rossini, G.:Stabat Mater, w. Daniela Dessi (sop), Lucia Mazzaria (sop), Gloria Scalchi (mez), Pietro Ballo (ten), Anatoli Kotscherga (bass), Roberto Scandiuzzi (bass), G. Gelmetti (cnd), Stuttgart RSO, North German Radio Chorus, Southwest German Radio Chorus Serenissima 2-▲ SER 360155 [DDD]
Schoenberg, A.:Moses und Aaron, w. David Pittman-Jennings (nar), Gabriele Fontana (sop—Young Girl), Yvonne Naef (cta—Sick Woman), John Graham-Hall (ten—Young Man/Naked Youth), Pår Lindskog (ten—Youth), Chris Merritt (ten—Aaron), Siegfried Lorenz (bar—Another Man), Michael Devlin (b-bar—Ephraimite), László Polgár (bass—Priest), P. Boulez (cnd), Royal Concertgebouw Orch, Winfried Maczewski (cnd), Netherlands Opera Chorus, Zaans Youth Choir, Waterland Music School *(rec Concertgebouw, Amsterdam, Oct 1995)* Deutsche Grammophon 2-▲ 449 174-2 [DDD]
Verdi, G.:Requiem Mass, w. Lucia Mazzaria (sop), Daniela Dessi (sop), Gloria Scalchi (mez), Pietro Ballo (ten), Anatoli Kotscherga (bass), Roberto Scandiuzzi (bass), G. Gelmetti (cnd), Stuttgart RSO, North German Radio Chorus, Southwest German Radio Chorus Serenissima 2-▲ SER 360155 [DDD]

Mertens, Klaus (bass)
Bach, J.S.:Cant 49, w. N. Argenta (sop), M. Ponseele (ob), S. Kuijken (vn), H. Suzuki (vc), P. Hantaï (org), La Petite Bande Accent ▲ ACC 9395 D [DDD]
Bach, J.S.:Cant 58, w. N. Argenta (sop), M. Ponseele (ob), S. Kuijken (vn), H. Suzuki (vc), P. Hantaï (org), La Petite Bande Accent ▲ ACC 9395 D [DDD]
Bach, J.S.:Cant 82, w. N. Argenta (sop), M. Ponseele (ob), S. Kuijken (vn), H. Suzuki (vc), P. Hantaï (org), La Petite Bande Accent ▲ ACC 9395 D [DDD]
Bach, J.S.:Christmas Oratorio, w. Ruth Ziesak (sop), Monica Groop (alt), Christoph Pregardien (ten), R. Otto (cnd), Concerto Cologne, Frankfurt Vocal Ensemble *(rec Festeburgkirche Frankfurt, Jan 9-16, 1991)* Capriccio 2-▲ 60025-2 [DDD]
Bach, J.S.:St. John Passion, w. B. Schlick (sop), K. Wessel (alto), G. de Mey (ten), G. Turk (ten), P. Kooy (bass), T. Koopman (cnd), Amsterdam Baroque Orch, Netherlands Bach Society Choir Erato 2-▲ 94675-2
Bach, J.S.:St. Matthew Passion, w. Monika Frimmer (sop), Veronika Winter (sop), Lena Susanne Norin (alt), Wilfried Jochens (ten), Christoph Prégardien (ten), Hans-Georg Wimmer (bass), H. Max (cnd), Das Kliene Konzert, Rhineland Kantorei Capriccio 2-▲ 60 046 [DDD]
Graun, K.H.:Der Tod Jesu, w. M. Zádori (sop), M. Fers (sop), M. Klietmann (ten), P. Németh (cnd), Capella Savaria Musique d'Abord ▲ HMA 1903061
Handel, G.F.:La Rezurrezione, w. Nancy Argenta (sop), Barbara Schlick (sop), Guillemette Laurens (mez), Guy de Mey (ten), T. Koopman (cnd), Amsterdam Baroque Orch [I] Erato 2-▲ 2292-45617-2 [DDD]
Haydn, J.:Mass 5, "Missa Sancti Josephi", "Grosse Orgelmesse", w. Dorthea Röschmann (sop), Bernarda Fink (cta), Helmut Wildhaber (ten), M. Haselböck (cnd), Vienna Academy, Hugo Distler Choir Novalis ▲ 150095 [DDD]
Haydn, J.:Mass 7, "Kleine Orgelmesse", w. Dorthea Röschmann (sop), Bernarda Fink (cta), Helmut Wildhaber (ten), M. Haselböck (cnd), Vienna Academy, Hugo Distler Choir Novalis ▲ 150095 [DDD]
Haydn, J.:Salve regina, H.XXIIIb/2, w. Dorthea Röschmann (sop), Bernarda Fink (cta), Helmut Wildhaber (ten), M. Haselböck (cnd), Vienna Academy, Hugo Distler Choir Novalis ▲ 150095 [DDD]

1300 ▲ = CD ♦ = Enhanced CD Δ = MD ■ = Cassette Tape □ = DCC

Mertens, Klaus (bass) (cont.)
Homilius, G.A.:St. Matthew Passion, w. A. Monoyios (sop), U. Groenwald (cta), G. Türk, C. Prégardien (ten), H.-G. Wimmer (bass), Berlin Academy for Early Music, Leverkusen Cappella Vocale
Berlin Classics 2-▲ BER 1046 [DDD]
Mozart, W.A.:Missa, K.427, w. Monika Frimmer (sop), Barbara Schlick (sop), Christoph Prégardien (ten), P. Neumann (cnd), Collegium Cartusianum, Cologne Chamber Choir Virgin Classics ▲ CDM 61167
Telemann, G.P.:Auferstehung und Himmelfahrt Jesu, w. Monika Frimmer (sop), Veronika Winter (sop), Matthias Koch (alt), Nico Van der Meel (ten), H. Max (cnd), Das Kliene Konzert, Rhineland Kantorei
Capriccio ▲ CD 10596 [DDD]
Telemann, G.P.:Cants, w. Constanze Backes (sop), Mechthild Georg (mez), Andreas Post (sgr), L. Rémy (cnd), Telemann CO, Helko Siede (cnd), Michaelstein Chamber Choir—Christmas cantatas, "Siehe, ich verkündige Euch" (1761) & "Der Herr hat offenbaret" (1762) *(rec Apr 28–May 2, 1996)*
CPO ▲ CPO 999419-2 [DDD]
Telemann, G.P.:Hamburger Admiralitätsmusik, w. Mieke van der Sluis (sop—Hammonia), Graham Pushee (ten—Themis), Rufus Müller (ten—Mercurius), Klaus Mertens (bass—Neptunius), David Thomas (bass—Mars), Michael Schopper (bass—Albis), W. Helbich (cnd), Bremen Baroque Orch, Alsfeld Vocal Ensemble *(rec Nov 9, 1995)* CPO 2-▲ CPO 999373-2 [DDD]
Telemann, G.P.:Hirten an der Krippe zu Bethlehem, w. Constanze Backes (sop), Mechthild Georg (mez), Andreas Post (sgr), L. Rémy (cnd), Telemann CO, Helko Siede (cnd), Michaelstein Chamber Choir *(rec Apr 28–May 2, 1996)* CPO ▲ CPO 999419-2 [DDD]
Werner, G.J.:Debora, w. W. Hill (sop), G. Banditelli (mez), M. Klietmann (ten), P. Németh (cnd), Capella Savaria Quintana ▲ QUI 903062

Mescheriakova, Marina (sop)
Rubinstein, A.:The Demon, w. Ludmilla Andrew (sop—Nanny), Marina Mescheriakova (sop—Tamara), Alison Browner (mez—Angel), Anatoly Lochak (sgr—Demon), Richard Robson (sgr—Old Servant), Valery Serkin (sgr—Prince Sinodal), Wjacheslav Weinorowski (sgr—Messenger), Leonid Zimnenko (sgr—Prince Gudal), A. Anissimov (cnd), Irish National SO, Gregory Rose (cnd), Wexford Festival Opera Chorus *(rec Wexford, Oct & Nov, 1994)* Marco Polo 2-▲ 8.223781-2 [DDD]

Mesguich, Daniel (nar)
Honegger, A.:Le Roi David, w. Christiane Eda-Pierre (sop), Martha Senn (mez), Tibere Raffalli (ten), A. Gaillard (nar), S. Baudo (cnd), Czech PO, Czech Chorus [F] Supraphon 2-▲ 11 0132 [DDD]
Honegger, A.:Le Roi David, w. Alessandra Marc (sop), Sylvie Sullé (mez), Laurence Dale (ten), J.-C. Casadesus (cnd), Lille National Orch EMI Classics ▲ CDC 54793

Mesplé, Mady (sop)
Adam, A.:Le toréador, ou l'accord parfait, w. Raymond Amade (ten), Charles Clavensy (b-bar), E. Bigot (cnd), ORTF Lyric Orch Musidisc ▲ MUS 201672 [AAD]
Auber, D.-F.:Fra Diavolo, w. M. Mesplé (sop—Zerline), J. Berbié (mez—Lady Pamela), N. Gedda (ten—Fra Diavolo), R. Corazza (ten—Lord Cockburn), T. Dran (ten—Lorenzo), J. Bastin (bass—Matheo), M. Soustrot (cnd), Monte Carlo PO, Jean LaForge Ensemble Choir EMI Classics ▲ CDCB 54810
Delibes, L.:Lakmé, w. D. Millet (sop), C. Burles (ten), R. Soyer (bass), A. Lombard (cnd), Paris Opéra-Comique Orch, Paris Opéra-Comique Chorus EMI Classics 2-▲ CDCB 49430
Delibes, L.:Lakmé (sels), w. D. Millet (sop), C. Burles (ten), R. Soyer (bass), A. Lombard (cnd), Paris Opéra-Comique Orch, Paris Opéra-Comique Chorus EMI Classics ▲ ZDM 63447
Massenet, J.:Werther, w. Mady Mesplé (sop—Sophie), Rita Gorr (mez—Charlotte), Robert Andreozzi (ten—Schmidt), Albert Lance (ten—Werther), Gabriel Bacquier (bar—Albert), Julien Giovannetti (bar—Le Bailli), Jacques Mars (bar—Johann), J. Etcheverry (cnd), *(orch unknown)*
Adès 2-▲ ADE 140832 [AAD]
Massenet, J.:Werther, w. V. De los Angeles (sop), N. Gedda (ten), G. Prêtre (cnd), Orch de Paris, Paris Chorus [F] EMI Classics ("Studio" series) 2-▲ CDMB 63973
Offenbach, J.:Les Contes d'Hoffmann, w. H. Harper (sop), Bakocevic (sgr), S. Kónya (ten), G. Bacquier (bar), P. Maag (cnd), Buenos Aires Teatro Colón Orch, Buenos Aires Teatro Colón Chorus [F] *(rec live, Buenos Aires 8/3/70)* Melodram 2-▲ MEL 27090 [ADD]
Offenbach, J.:Les Contes d'Hoffmann (sels), w. Andréa Guiot (sop—Antonia), Mady Mesplé (sop—Olympia), Suzanne Sarroca (sop—Giulietta), Albert Lance (ten—Hoffmann), Gabriel Bacquier (bar—Docteur Miracle), Robert Massard (bar—Dapertutto), J. Etcheverry (cnd), *(orch unknown)* —Prologue; Dans les rôles d'amoureux...; Il était une fois...; Allons! Courage et confiance...; C'est moi, coppélius!...; Les oiseaux dans la charmille; Barcarolle; Scintille, diamant...; Malheureux, tu ne comprends donc pas...; Hélas! Mon coeur s'égare encore...; Elle a fui, la tourterelle...; Eh bien! Quoi! Toujours en colère!...; Tu ne chanteras plus?... Adès ▲ ADE 202702 [AAD]
Rossini, G.:Arias, w. June Anderson (sop), Montserrat Caballé (sop), Maria Callas (sop), Edita Gruberova (sop), Pilar Lorengar (sop), Nicolai Gedda (ten), Tito Gobbi (bar), Samuel Ramey (bass), *(orchs unknown)* —from Barbiere di Siviglia; La Cenerentola; La Gazza ladra; Petite messe solennelle; Semiramide; Stabat Mater *(rec 1958–89)* EMI Classics 2-▲ CZS 67440-2 [ADD/DDD]
Rossini, G.:Guillaume Tell, w. M. Caballé (sop), C. Burles (ten), N. Gedda (ten), G. Bacquier (bar), G. Howell (bass), L. Gardelli (cnd), Royal PO, Ambrosian Opera Chorus EMI Classics 4-▲ CDMD 69951
Satie, E.:Geneviève de Brabant, w. A. Guiot (sop), D. Millet (sop), A. Esposito (sop), J.C. Benoit (bar), A. Ciccolini (pno), P. Dervaux (cnd), Orch de Paris, Paris Opera Chorus
Virgin Classics 2-▲ CDZB 62877
Satie, E.:Socrate, w. A. Guiot (sop), D. Millet (sop), A. Esposito (sop), J. C. Benoit (bar), P. Dervaux (cnd), Orch de Paris, Paris Opera Chorus Virgin Classics 2-▲ CDZB 62877
Villa-Lobos, H.:Bachiana brasileira 5, w. P. Capolongo (cnd), Orch de Paris [Port]
EMI Classics ▲ CDC 47357 [ADD]

Messerli, O. (alt)
Haydn, M.:Missa Sancti Leopoldi in festo Innocentium, w. R. Zela, A. Schram (sop), A. von Aarburg (cnd), Capella Concertante, Zurich Boys' Choir [L] *(rec 12/89)* Tudor ▲ 754 [DDD]
Haydn, M.:Vesperae pro festo Sanctorum Innocentium, w. L. Tsimitselis (sop), A. Schram (sop), A. von Aarburg (cnd), Capella Concertante, Zurich Boys' Choir [L] *(rec 12/89)* Tudor ▲ 754 [DDD]

Messier, Lise (sop)
Satoh, S.:Music of, w. Almond (vn), Leng Tan (pno), Pugliese (perc)—Birds in Warped Time II for Violin & Piano (1980); The Heavenly Spheres are Illuminated by Lights for Soprano, Piano & Percussion (1979); Incarnation II for solo Piano with tape delay (1970); Litania for 2 Pianos with tape delay (1973); A Gate into the Stars for solo Piano (1962) New Albion ▲ NA 008 [ADD]

Messthaler, Ulrich (bass)
Caldara, A.:Maddalena ai Piedi di Cristo, w. Maria Cristina Kiehr (sop), Rosa Dominguez (sop), Bernarda Fink (cta), Andreas Scholl (ct), Gerd Türk (ten), R. Jacobs (cnd), Schola Cantorum Basiliensis Instrumental Ensemble Harmonia Mundi France 2-▲ HMC 905221.22
L'heritage de Monteverdi, Vol. 2, w. La Fenice, Maria Cristina Kiehr (sop), John Elwes (ten) *(rec Eglise de Mormont, Nov 1995)* Ricercar ▲ RIC 166148

Mestes, Adriana (sgr)
Honegger, A.:Amphion, w. Olivier Lallouette (bar—Apollon), Laurent Manzoni (bar—Amphion), Iona Bentoiu (sgr—muse), Theodora Ciucur (sgr—muse), Lucia Kriska (sgr—muse), Adriana Mestes (sgr—muse), J.-F. Antonioli (cnd), Timisoara PO, Timisoara Banatul Phil Chorus, Timisoara Children's Chorus *(rec Salle Ion Vidu, Timisoara, Romania, Oct 28 & Nov 1, 1995)* Timpani ▲ 1035 [DDD]

Metcalf, William (bar)
Vaughan Williams, R.:Dona nobis pacem, w. Blanche Christensen (sop), M. Abravanel (cnd), Utah SO
Vanguard Classics ▲ SVC 7 [ADD]

Metternich, Josef (bar)
Humperdinck, E.:Hänsel und Gretel, w. E. Schwarzkopf (sop), E. Grümmer (sop), A. Felbermayer (sop), M. von Ilosvay (mez), E. Schürhoff (mez), H. von Karajan (cnd), Philharmonia Orch, Loughton High School Chorus, Bancroft's School Chorus [G] *(rec 1953)*
EMI Classics ("Studio" series) 2-▲ CDMB 69293 (m) [ADD]
Leoncavallo, R.:Pagliacci, w. Melitta Muszely (sop), Rudolf Schock (ten), H. Stein (cnd), Berlin State Opera Orch *(rec 1959)* Berlin Classics ▲ BER 9102 [ADD]
Strauss, R.:Arabella (sels), w. E. Schwarzkopf (sop), E. Loose (sop), L. von Matačić (cnd), Philharmonia Orch [G] EMI Classics ("Great Recordings of the Century" series) ▲ CDH 61001 (m)
Verdi, G.:Macbeth, w. Astrid Varnay (sop—Lady Macbeth), Trude Roesler (mez—Lady-in-waiting), Hasso Eschert (ten—Malcolm), Walter Geisler (ten—Macduff), Joseph Metternich (bar—Macbeth), Ludwig Weber (bass—Banquo), R. Kraus (cnd), West German Orch, West German Chorus *(rec Cologne, 1954)*
Myto 2-▲ 952128

Metternich, Josef (bar) (cont.)
Wagner, R.:Der fliegende Holländer, w. Annelies Kupper (sop—Senta), Sieglinde Wagner (mez—Mary), Ernst Haefliger (ten—Steersman), Wolfgang Windgassen (ten—Erik), Josef Metternich (bar—Dutchman), Josef Greindl (bass—Daland), F. Fricsay (cnd), Berlin RIAS SO, Berlin RIAS Chamber Choir *(rec 1953)*
Deutsche Grammophon 2-▲ 439714-2 (m) [ADD]
Wagner, R.:Lohengrin, w. Maud Cunitz (sop—Elsa), Margarete Klose (mez—Ortrud), Rudolf Schock (ten—Lohengrin), Josef Metternich (bar—Friedrich von Telramund), Gottlob Frick (bass—King Henry), W. Schüchter (cnd), North German RSO, North German Radio Chorus, West German Radio Men's Chorus *(rec 1953)* EMI Classics 2-▲ CDHC 65517
Wagner, R.:Das Rheingold, w. L. Otto (sop), M. Muszely (sop), J. Blatter (mez), R. Stewart (mez), S. Wagner (mez), R. Schock (ten), H. Melchert (ten), F. Frantz (bass), B. Kusche (bass), R. Kempe (cnd), Berlin Staatskapelle *(rec Mar. 1959)* Berlin Classics ("Eterna" series) ▲ BER 2035 [ADD]

Meulenaere, Luc de (ct)
Charpentier, M.-A.:Leçons de ténèbres, H. 96-110, w. Jan Caals (ten), Harry Ruyl (ten), Howard Crook (ct), Michel Verschaeve (bar), Kurt Widmer (bass), L. Devos (cnd), Musica Polyphonica
Erato 2-▲ ERA 96376 [DDD]

Meunier, Claudine (cta)
Berio, L.:Laborintus II, w. Sanguineti (nar), C. Legrand (sop), J. Baucomont (sop), L. Berio (cnd), Musique Vivante Ensemble, Chorale Experimentale [E,I] Musique d'Abord ▲ HMA 190764

Meven, Peter (bass)
Hindemith, P.:Mathis der Maler, w. Urszula Koszut (sop), Trudeliese Schmidt (mez), Rose Wagemann (mez), William Cochran (ten), Donald Grobe (ten), James King (ten), Manfred Schmidt (ten), Dietrich Fischer-Dieskau (bar), Gerd Feldhoff (bass), Alexander Malta (bass), Peter Meven (bass), Karl Kreile (sgr), R. Kubelik (cnd), Bavarian RSO, Bavarian Radio Chorus EMI Classics 2-▲ CDCC 55237
Mozart, W.A.:Zauberflöte, w. Reri Grist (sop), Edita Gruberová (sop), Edith Mathis (sop), Rene Kollo (ten), Gerhard Unger (ten), Hermann Prey (bar), José Van Dam (b-bar), H. von Karajan (cnd), Vienna PO, Vienna State Opera Chorus *(rec live, Salzburg, July 26, 1974)* Arkadia 2-▲ 233
Wagner, R.:Die Walküre (act 1), w. S. Dunn (sop), K. König (ten), L. Maazel (cnd), Pittsburgh SO [G]
Telarc ▲ CD 80258 [DDD]

Mey, Guy de (ten)
Bach, J.S.:St. John Passion, w. B. Schlick (sop), K. Wessel (alto), G. Turk (ten), K. Mertens (b-bar), P. Kooy (bass), T. Koopman (cnd), Amsterdam Baroque Orch, Netherlands Bach Society Choir
Erato 2-▲ 94675-2
Bach, J.S.:St. Matthew Passion, w. B. Schlick (sop), K. Wessel (alto), C. Pregardien (ten), P. Kooy (bass), T. Koopman (cnd), Amsterdam Baroque Orch, W. Cantryn (cnd), J. van Veldhoven (cnd), Breda Sacred Choir, Netherlands Bach Society Boys' Choir Erato ▲ 2292-45814-2
Bach, J.S.:St. Matthew Passion, w. B. Schlick (sop), K. Wessel (alto), P. Kooy (bass), T. Koopman (cnd), Amsterdam Baroque Orch Erato 2-▲ 94676-2
Brahms, J.:Liebeslieder Waltzes SATB, w. Greta De Reyghere (sop), Lucienne Van Deyck (mez), Huub Claessens (bass), Jean-Claude Vanden Eynden (pno), Luc Devos (pno) *(rec Consevatoire Royal, Liège, 1994)* Ricercar ▲ 153138
Brahms, J.:Neue Liebeslieder Waltzes, w. Greta De Reyghere (sop), Lucienne Van Deyck (mez), Huub Claessens (bass), Jean-Claude Vanden Eynden (pno), Luc Devos (pno) *(rec Consevatoire Royal, Liège, 1994)* Ricercar ▲ 153138
Bruhns, N.:Cants, w. Jill Feldman (sop), Greta de Reyghere (sop), James Bowman (ct), Ian Honeyman (ten), Max Van Egmond (bass), Ricercar Consort—Hemmt eure Tränenflut; Jauchzet dem Herren alle Welt; Wohl dem, der den Herren fürchtet; De profundis; Paratum cor meum; O werter heil'ger Geis; Zeit meines Abschieds; Erstanden ist der heilige Christ; Herr hat seinem Stuhl im Himmel bereitet; Ich liege und schlafe; Mein Herz ist bereit; Muss nicht der Mensch auf dieser Erden in Stetem Streite sein
Ricercar In Ecco 2-▲ REC8001/2
Gluck, C.W.:Le Cinesi, w. I. Poulenard (sop), A. S. von Otter (mez), G. Banditelli (cta), R. Jacobs (cnd), Schola Cantorum Basiliensis Instrumental Ensemble Editio Classica ▲ 77174-2-RG [DDD]
Gluck, C.W.:La Recontre imprévue, w. C. Le Coz (sop), L. Dawson (sop), C. Dubosc (sop), S. Marin-Degor (sop), G. Fletcher (sgr), F. Dudziak (ten), J.-L. Viala (ten), G. Cachémaille (bar), J.-P. Lafont (bass), J. E. Gardiner (cnd), Paris Lyon Opera Orch, Paris Lyon Opera Chorus [F]
Erato 2-▲ 2292-45516-2 [DDD]
Grétry, A.-E.-M.:La Caravane du Caire, w. I. Poulenard (sop), G. de Reyghere (sop), G. Ragon (ten), P. Huttenlocher (bar), V. Le Téxier (bar), J. Bastin (bass), M. Minkowski (cnd), Ricercar Academy, Ricercar Academy Chorus [period instrs] [F] Ricercar 2-▲ RIC 100084/85 [DDD]
Handel, G.F.:Brockes-Passion, w. K. Farkas (sop), M. Zádori (sop), D. Minter (alt), J. Bándi (ten), M. Klietmann (ten), I. Gáti (bar), N. McGegan (cnd), Capella Savaria, Hallé State Chorus [period instrs] [G]
Hungaroton 3-▲ HCD 12734/36 [DDD]
Handel, G.F.:Judas Maccabaeus, w. Linda Saffer (sop), Patricia Spence (mez), Brian Asawa (ct), Leroy Kromm (b-bar), David Thomas (bass), N. McGegan (cnd), Philharmonia Baroque Orch, Univ of California at Berkeley Chamber Chorus [E] *(rec Nov. 15–18, 1992)*
Harmonia Mundi USA 2-▲ HMU 907077/78
Handel, G.F.:La Rezurrezione, w. Nancy Argenta (sop), Barbara Schlick (sop), Guillemette Laurens (mez), Klaus Mertens (bar), T. Koopman (cnd), Amsterdam Baroque Orch [I]
Erato 2-▲ 2292-45617-2 [DDD]
Kerll, J.C.:Missa pro defunctis, w. G. de Reyghere (sop), J. Bowman (alt), I. Honeyman (ten), M. van Egmond (bass), E. van Nevel (cnd), Capella Sancti Michaelis, Ricercar Consort [L] *(rec 5/90)*
Ricercar ▲ RIC 81063 [DDD]
Lully, J.-B.:Atys, w. Agnès Mellon (sop), Guillemette Laurens (mez), Jean-François Gardeil (bar), W. Christie (cnd), Les Arts Florissants, Les Arts Florissants Chorus [F]
Harmonia Mundi France 3-▲ HMC 901257/59 [DDD];
Rameau, J.P.:Platée, w. J. Smith (sop), G. Ragon (ten), M. Minkowski (cnd), Louvre Musicians, Françoise Herr Vocal Ensemble [F] Erato ("Musifrance" series) 2-▲ 2292-45028-2 [DDD]
Telemann, G.P.:Brockes Passion, w. M. Zádori (sop), A. Markert (cta), M. Klietmann (ten), I. Gáti (bar), N. McGegan (cnd), Capella Savaria, Hallé State Chorus [period instrs]
Hungaroton 3-▲ HCD 31130/32 [DDD]
Vlijmen, J. van:Un Malheureux vêtu de noir, w. S. Kleindienst (sop), Pittman-Jennings (bar), Reinbert de Leeuw (cnd), Arnold Schoenberg Male Choir *(rec live, Flanders Opera, Antwerp, Dec 11, 1990)*
Donemus ▲ CV 17/18
Zelenka, J.D.:Lamentationes Jeremiae Prophetae, w. R. Jacobs (alt), K. Widmer (bass), R. Jacobs (cnd), Schola Cantorum Basiliensis Instrumental Ensemble Editio Classica ▲ 77112-2-RG [DDD]

Meyer, Kerstin (mez)
Elgar, E.:Sea Pictures, w. J. Barbirolli (cnd), Hallé Orch [E] *(rec live 7/24/70)*
Intaglio ▲ INCD 701-1 [ADD]
Elisabeth Söderström & Kerstin Meyer, w. Elisabeth Söderström (sop), Jan Eyron (pno) *(rec Nov. 1–3, 1974)* BIS ▲ CD 17 [AAD]
Verdi, G.:Rigoletto, w. M. Hallin (sop), B. Nordin (sop), B. Ericson (mez), Kjellgren (mez), N. Gedda (ten), O. Sivall (ten), H. Hasslo (bar), I. Wixell (bar), B. Alstergård (bar), A. Tyrén (bass), S. Ehrling (cnd), Stockholm Royal Opera House Orch, Stockholm Royal Opera Chorus *(rec live Jan. 18, 1959)*
BIS ▲ CD 296 [AAD]
Verdi, G.:Il trovatore (sels), w. Hjördis Schymberg (sop), Jussi Björling (ten), Olle Sivall (ten), Hugo Hasslo (bar), H. Sandberg (cnd), Royal Opera Orch, Royal Opera House Chorus Covent Garden—Non son tuo figlio?; Mal reggendo all'aspro assalto; Quale d'armi fragor; Ah! sì, ben mio, coll'essere; L'onda de' suoni mistici; Di quella pira l'orrendo foco; Miserere d'un'alma già vicina; Madre?...non dormi?; Se m'ami ancor; Ciel!...non m'inganna; Ti scosta... *(rec Royal Opera, Stockholm, Mar 6, 1960)*
Myto ▲ MCD 953130

Meyers, G. (bar)
Music of the Middle Ages, Vol. 6:English Polyphony of the 14th & Early 15th Centuries, w. Russell Oberlin (ct), C. Bressler (ten), R. Price (ten), M. Blackman (vl) Lyrichord ▲ LYR 8006 [ADD]
Music of the Middle Ages, Vol. 7, w. French Ars Antiqua, Russell Oberlin (ct), Charles Bressler (ten), R. Price (ten), M. Blackman (vl), P. Wolfe (org) Lyrichord ▲ LYR 8007 [ADD]

Meyerson, M. (sgr)
Hallén, A.:Harald der Wiking (act III, final scene), w. M. Meyerson (sgr—Berta), S. Lindström (sgr—Sigrun), A. Ljungholm (sgr—Harald), S. Sjöstedt (sgr—Sigleif), K. Jacobsson (sgr—Gudmund/Torgrim), S. Rybrant (cnd), Malmö SO, Malmö Radio Chorus [G] *(rec 6/6/74)* Musica Sveciae ▲ MSCD 621 [AAD]

Meyer-Topsøe, Elisabeth (sop)
Koppel, H.D.:Moses, w. Kirsten Dolberg (mez), Kurt Westi (ten), Michael Kristensen (ten), Per Høyer (bar), Christian Christiansen (bass), O.A. Hughes (cnd), Danish National RSO, Jesper Grovw Jørgensen (cnd), Danish National Radio Choir *(rec Danish Radio Concert Hall, Mar 1996)* Marco Polo/Dacapo ▲ 8.224046 [DDD]
Strauss, R.:4 Last Songs, w. H.N. Bihlmaier (cnd), Copenhagen PO Kontrapunkt ▲ KPT 32156 [DDD]
Wagner, R.:Wesendonck Songs, w. H. N. Bihlmaier (cnd), Copenhagen PO Kontrapunkt ▲ KPT 32156 [DDD]

Meysenbug, Malwida (sgr)
Distel, H.:La Stazione, w. Teresita Fontana (sgr), Valeria Manzoni (sgr), Federico Paternina (sgr), Arturo Schwarz (sgr) *(rec Milan, Italy & Bern, Switzerland, 1987 & May 1990)* Hat Hut ("NOW." series) ▲ hat ART CD 6060 [AAD]

Miatello, Cristina (sop)
Boccherini, L.:Arias, w. L'Arte dell'Arco, Ensemble Barocco Padovano Sans Souci—Se non ti moro allato; Numi se giusti siete; Mi dona, mi rende quell'alma pietosa; Di giudice severo; Per quel paterno amplesso; Tornate sereni; Caro, son tua così; Deh respirar lasciatemi *(rec Armonia Ca' Bianca Hall, Apr 12–14, 1995)* Dynamic ▲ CD 123 [DDD]
Bononcini, G.:Italian Cants, w. G. Morini (hpd), A. Fossà (vc)—Ah, non avesse, no, permesso il fato; Che tirannia di stelle; Cieco nume, tiranno spietato; Vidi in cimento due vaghi amori [I] Tactus ▲ TC 660002
Canzoni da Battello, w. Carlo Gaifa (ten), instr accompaniment Tactus ▲ TC 700001 [DDD]
Luzzaschi, L.:Madrigali, w. H. Alfonso (sop), M. Pennichi (sop), S. Vartolo (hpd) Musique d'Abord ▲ HMA 1901136
Scarlatti, A.:Cants, w. G. Morini (hpd), A. Fossà (vc)—Andante, o miei sospiri; Per un momento solo; Lascia più di tormentarmi; Lontan dalla sua Clori [I] Tactus ▲ TC 660002
Scarlatti, A.:Cants & Duets, w. C. Cavina (alt), G. Fagotto (ten), L. Scoppola (sgr), P. Pandolfo (ctb), R. Sensi (sgr), R. Alessandrini (cnd)—Clori mia, Clori bella (cantata for soprano, flute & bass continuo); Dimmi crudele, e quando (duet for soprano, alto & bass continuo); Son pur care le catene (duet for soprano, alto & bass continuo); Sovente Amor mi chiama (cantata for alto & bass continuo); Ammore, brutto figlio de pottana (cantata for tenor & bass continuo) [I] Tactus ▲ TC 661901
Scarlatti, A.:Lamentazioni par la Settimana Santa, w. G. P. Fagotto (ten), Aurora Ensemble Symphonia ▲ SYM 92D17 [DDD]
Stradella, A.:Cants, w. Gianpaolo Fagotto (ten), Antonio Abete (sgr), Roberto Balconi (sgr), Lavinia Bertotti (sgr), Roberta Giua (sgr), S. Balestracci (cnd), Santo Spirito Academy Orch, Santo Spirito Academy Chorus—for 5 w. vns [For Holy Christmas]; for 5 w. instruments [For the Souls in Purgatory] Stradivarius ▲ STV 33392 [DDD]

Micalucci, Carlo (sgr)
Donizetti, G.:Roberto Devereux, w. Montserrat Caballé (sop), Beverly Wolff (mez), Guido Fabbris (ten), Gianni Raimondi (ten), Walter Alberti (bar), Paolo Badoer (sgr), Carlo Padoan (sgr), B. Bartoletti (cnd), Venice Teatro La Fenice Orch, Venice Teatro La Fenice Chorus Great Opera Performances 2-▲ GOP 764

Micco, Anna Maria di (mez)
Rossini, G.:Tancredi, w. Sumi Jo (sop—Amenaide), Lucretia Lendi (mez—Roggiero), Anna Maria di Micco (mez—Isaura), Ewa Podles (cta—Tancredi), Stanford Olsen (ten—Argirio), Pietro Spagnoli (bar—Orbazzano), Ewald Demeyere (hpd), Lieven Baert (vc), Franck Coryn (db), A. Zedda (cnd), Collegium Instrumentale Brugense, Capella Brugensis *(rec Poissy Theatre & Centre Musical–Lyrique–Phonographique, Ile de France, Jan. 26–31, 1994)* Naxos ("Opera Classics" series) 2-▲ 8.660037/38 [DDD]

Michael, Audrey (sop)
Beethoven, L. van:Mass, Op. 86, w. L. Bizimeche-Eisinger (mez), M. Schaeffer (ten), M. Brodard (bar), M. Corboz (cnd), Lisbon Gulbenkian Foundation Orch, Lisbon Gulbenkian Foundation Chorus [L] Erato ▲ 2292-45461-2 ZK [DDD]
Handel, G.F.:Messiah (reorchd Mozart), w. Jard van Nes (cta), Hans-Peter Blochwitz (tenor), Marcus Fink (bass), M. Corboz (cnd), Lausanne Instrumental Ensemble, Lausanne Vocal Ensemble [G] Erato 2-▲ 2292-45497-2 [DDD]
Rameau, J.P.:Les Paladins, w. G. Raphanel (sop), B. Brewer (ten), D. Nasrawi (ten), G. Reinhart (bar), N. Rivenq (bar), J. Malgoire (cnd), La Grande Ecurie et la Chambre du Roy, Sagittarius Vocal Ensemble [F] Pierre Verany 2-▲ PV.790121/22 [DDD]
Schibler, A.:La Folie de Tristan, w. Audrey Michael (sop—Iseut), Arlette Chédel (mez—Brangien), Pierre-André Blaser (ten—Tristan), Philippe Huttenlocher (bar—Le roi Marc/Le pêcheur/Le portier), André Fauré (nar), William Jacques (nar), Snezana Zivojinovic (nar), J. Auberson (cnd), Lausanne CO, Romande Instrumental Group Rockband, Swiss Romande Radio Choir *(rec live, Festival de Montreux, Sept 15, 1980)* Jecklin ▲ JD 695
Suter, H.:Le Laudi di San Francesco d'Assisi, w. J. Winklet (alt), A. Baldin (ten), J. Will (bass), P. Laubschet (org), Bern SO, T. Loosli (cnd), Bern Bach Choir, Sekundar School Children's Choir Ars Musici ▲ AM 1015-2 [DDD]

Michael, Charbel (alt)
Puccini, G.:Tosca, w. Jane Eaglen (sop—Floria Tosca), Charbel Michael (alt—Shepherd Boy), John Daszak (ten—Spoletta), Dennis O'Neill (ten—Mario Cavaradossi), Christopher Booth-Jones (bar—Sciarrone), Ashley Holland (bar—Jailor), Gregory Yurisich (bar—Baron Scarpia), Peter Rose (bass—Cesare Angelotti), Andrew Shore (bass—Sacristan), D. Parry (cnd), Philharmonia Orch, Geoffrey Mitchell Choir, Peter Kay Children's Chorus Chandos ("Opera in English" series) 2-▲ CHAN 3000

Michael, Madelon (sop)
Oyens, T. de M.:Hymns, w. Tera de Marez Oyens (pno) Capstone ▲ CPS 8632

Michaelis, Ruth (sop)
Wagner, R.:Götterdämmerung, w. Birgit Nilsson (sop—Brünnhilde), Leonie Rysanek (sop—Gutrune), Gerda Sommerschuh (sop—Woglinde), Elisabeth Lindermeier (sop—Wellgunde), Ruth Michaelis (sop—Flohilde), Marianne Schech (sop—Dritte Norne), Ira Malaniuk (mez—Waltraute), Irmgarth Barth (mez—Erste Norne), Hertha Töpper (mez—Zweite Norne), Bernd Aldenhoff (ten—Siegfried), Hermann Uhde (bar—Gunther), Gottlob Frick (bass—Hagen), H. Knappertsbusch (cnd), Bavarian State Opera Orch, Bavarian State Opera Chorus *(rec live, Prinzregententheater, Sept. 1, 1955)* Orfeo 4-▲ 356944 (m)

Michaels, Neil (bar)
Starer, R.:Night Thoughts, w. Theresa Santiago (sop), Jennifer Hines (mez), Anthony Griffey (ten), Adelaide Roberts (pno), Edgar Roberts (pno) Albany ▲ TROY 151 [DDD]

Michaels-Moore, Anthony (bar)
Orff, C.:Carmina burana, w. B. Bonney (sop), F. Lopardo (ten), A. Previn (cnd), Vienna PO, Arnold Schoenberg Choir, Vienna Boys' Choir Deutsche Grammophon ▲ 439950-2
Puccini, G.:Arias, w. Angela Gheorghiu (sop), Nina Rautio (sop), Johan Botha (ten), E. Downes (cnd), Royal Opera House Orch, Royal Opera House Chorus Covent Garden—Se come voi piccina io fossi [from Le villi]; Addio mio dolce amor [from Edgar]; Donna non vidi mai; Sola, perduta, abbandonata [both from Manon Lescaut]; Donde lieta uscì [from La Bohème]; Act 1 Finale; E lucevan le stelle [both from Tosca]; Un tal baccano in chiesa; Or tutto è chiaro; Tre sbirri, una carozza; Un bel dì [from Madama Butterfly]; Ch'ella mi creda [from La fanciulla del West]; Chi il bel sogno di Doretta [from La rondine]; Nulla, silenzio [from Il tabarro]; Senza mamma [from Suor Angelica]; O mio babbino caro [from Gianni Schicchi]; Act I Finale; Nessun dorma [both from Turandot]; Signore, ascolta; Non piangere, Liù *(rec Henry Wood Hall, London, Feb 12–27 & Mar 5, 1995)* Conifer Classics ("Royal Opera House" series) ▲ 75605-55013-2 [DDD]
Spontini, G.:La vestale, w. Karen Huffstodt (sop—Julie), Denyce Graves (mez—La Grande Vestale), Patrick Raftery (ten—Cinna), Anthony Michaels-Moore (bar—Licinius), R. Muti (cnd), La Scala Orch, La Scala Chorus Sony Classical 3-▲ S3K 66357

Michalková, Alzbeta (mez)
Puccini, G.:Madama Butterfly, w. M. Gauci (sop), N. Boschkowá (mez), Y. Ramiro (ten), A. Rahbari (cnd), Czech-Slovak RSO Bratislava, Slovak Phil Chorus [I] Naxos 2-▲ 8.660015/16 [DDD]

Michalopoulos, Eftimios (sgr)
Massenet, J.:Thérèse, w. Agnes Baltsa (mez—Thérèse), Francisco Araiza (ten—Armand), Gino Sinimberghi (ten—Officer), George Fortune (bass—André), Giancarlo Luccardi (bass—Morel), Eftimios Michalopoulos (sgr—Officer/Municipal Officer), G. Albrecht (cnd), Rome RAI SO, Giuseppe Piccillo (cnd), Rome RAI Chorus Orfeo ▲ 387961 [DDD]

Micheau, Janine (sop)
Auber, D.-F.:Le Domino noir, w. J. Peyron (ten), G. Rey (bar), J. Gressier (cnd), French National RSO, French Radio Lyric Chorus Melodram 2-▲ MLO 270110 [ADD]
Bizet, G.:Carmen, w. V. de los Angeles (sop), N. Gedda (ten), E. Blanc (bar), T. Beecham (cnd), *(orch unknown)* [F] EMI Classics 3-▲ CDCC 49240 [ADD]
Bizet, G.:Ivan IV (sels), w. H. Legay (ten), M. Sénéchal (ten), M. Roux (bar), G. Tzipine (cnd), French National RSO, French Radio Chorus [F] EMI Classics ("Studio" series) 2-▲ CDMB 69704 [ADD]
Bizet, G.:Les Pêcheurs de perles, w. N. Gedda (ten), E. Blanc (bar), J. Mars (bar), P. Dervaux (cnd), Paris Opéra-Comique Orch, Paris Opéra-Comique Chorus [F] EMI Classics ("Studio" series) 2-▲ CDMB 69704 [ADD]
Cherubini, L.:Les Deux journées, w. M. Davies (ten), P. Gianotti (ten), E. Regnier (ten), C. Paul (bar), T. Beecham (cnd), Royal PO, BBC Theater Chorus *(rec live, London Dec. 19, 1947)* Intaglio 2-▲ INCD 7342 [ADD]
Debussy, C.:Pelléas et Mélisande, w. R. Gorr (mez), C. Maurane (bar), M. Roux (bar), X. Depraz (bass), J. Fournet (cnd), Lamoureux Orch *(rec 1953* Philips 2-▲ 434783-2

Michel, Solange (sop)
Vivaldi, A.:Gloria, RV.589, w. Andrée Esposito (sop), Janine Collard (cta), R. Wagner (cnd), Paris Conservatory Societé des Concerts Orch, Roger Wagner Chorale EMI Classics ("Baroque" series) ▲ CDK 65737

Michel-Dansac, Donatienne (sop)
Aperghis, G.:L'origine des espèces, w. Françoise Degeorges (sop), Emmanuelle Zoll (sop), Valérie Joly (mez), Frédérique Wolf-Michaux (cta), Elena Andreyev (vc) Musique Française d'Aujourd'hui ▲ MFA 216004
Bayer, F.:Music of, w. Alain Meunier (vc), Jean-Louis Haguenauer (pno), Renaud Francois, Francesca Paderni, Tetra Ensemble Pierre Verany ▲ PVY 796093
Pesson, G.:Music of, w. Sandra Roulx (mez), Stuart Patterson (ten), Paul-Alexandre Dubois (bar), Pascal Sausy (bar), Florence Millet (pno), D. My (cnd), Fa Ensemble, Paris String Quartet—Le gel, par jeu for Fl, Cl, Hn, Bass Mar, Vn & Vc; Qt for Strs; Non Sapremo Mai di Questo Mi for Fl, Vn & Pno; 5 Poèmes de Sandro Penna for Bar, B Cl, Hn, Vn & Vc; La lumière n'a pas de bras pour nous porter for Amplified Pno; La vita è come l'albero di natale for Vn & Pno; Nocturnes en quatuor for Cl, Pno, Vn & Vc; Les chants faëz for Pno & 10 Instrs; Sur-le-champ for 4 Voices & 9 Instrs [from a text by Pierre Alferi] Accord ▲ ACD 204682 [DDD]
Rameau, J.P.:Nélée et Myrthis, w. A. Mellon (sop—Myrthis), D. Michel-Dansac (sop—Maid), C. Pelon (sop—Maid), F. Semellaz (sop—Corinne), J. Corréas (bass—Nélée), W. Christie (cnd), Les Arts Florissants, Les Arts Florissants Chorus [F] *(rec 5/91)* Harmonia Mundi France ▲ HMC 901381
Rameau, J.P.:Pygmalion, w. A. Mellon (sop—Céphise), D. Michel-Dansac (sop—La Statue), S. Piau (sop—L'Amour), H. Crook (ten—Pygmalion), W. Christie (cnd), Les Arts Florissants, Les Arts Florissants Chorus [F] *(rec 5/91)* Harmonia Mundi France ▲ HMC 901381

Micheletti, Gaston (ten)
Bizet, G.:Carmen (sels), w. Conchita Supervia (mez), *(orch unknown)* Forlane ▲ FRL 16718 [ADD]
Bizet, G.:Carmen (sels), w. C. Supervia (mez), A. Vavon (sop), A. Bernadet (mez), A. Endreze (bar), G. Cloëz (cnd), Paris Opéra-Comique Orch, Paris Opéra-Comique Chorus—8 arias & scenes *(rec Paris 1930)* Nimbus ("Prima Voce" series) 2-▲ NI 7836/7 [ADD]
Bizet, G.:Carmen (sels), w. C. Supervia (mez), A. Vavon (sop), A. Bernadet (mez), J.-F. Delmas (b-bar), A. Endreze (bar), G. Cloëz (cnd), Paris Opéra-Comique Orch, Paris Opéra-Comique Chorus—14 arias & scenes [F] *(rec Paris, 1930)* The Classical Collector ▲ FDC 2002 (m) [AAD]

Michelini, Joëlle (sop)
Boieldieu, F.-A.:Le Calife de Bagdad, w. L. Mayo (sop), C. Cheriez (mez), L. Dale (ten), H. Rhys-Evans (ten), A. de Almeida (cnd), Camerata Provence Orch, Provence Camerata Chorus [F] Sonpact ▲ SPT 93007 [DDD]

Michelow, Sibyl (sop)
Purcell, H.:Dido & Aeneas (sels), w. Victoria de los Angeles (sop—Dido), Heather Harper (sop—Belinda), Elizabeth Robson (sop), Derek Simpson (vc), Colin Tilney (hpd), J. Barbirolli (cnd), English CO, Ambrosian Singers—Ov.; Shake the Cloud; Ah! Ah! Belinda; When Monarchs Unite; But Ere We This Perform; But Death, Alas! I Cannot Shun...When I am Laid in Earth; With Drooping Wings *(rec Abbey Road Studio 1, London, Aug. 1965)* EMI Classics ▲ CDK 65341 [ADD]

Micheluzzi, Mafalda (sop)
Giordano, U.:Fedora, w. Pia Tassinari (sop), Ferruccio Tagliavini (ten), Meletti (sgr), Mascolo (sgr), Jolanda Torriani (sgr), O.. Fabritiis (cnd), Milan RAI SO, Milan RAI Chorus *(rec live, July 10, 1954)* Arkadia 2-▲ 493
Leoncavallo, R.:Pagliacci, w. F. Corelli (ten), M. Carlin (ten), T. Gobbi (bar), L. Puglisi (bar), A. Simonetto (cnd), Milan RAI Orch, Milan RAI Chorus *(rec live 9/26/54 from RAI Milan)* HRE ▲ 1001-1 [ADD]
Puccini, G.:La Bohème, w. Schimenti (sop), G. Lauri-Volpi (ten), G. Ciavola (bass), A. Paoletti (cnd), Rome Opera Orch, Rome Opera Chorus *(rec 1952)* Bongiovanni 2-▲ GB 1057/58 [ADD]

Middleton, R. (sgr)
Berlin, I.:Annie Get Your Gun, w. E. Merman (sgr), L. Bibb (sgr), K. Carnes (sgr), J. Garth (sgr), R. Lenn (sgr), C. Turner (sgr), J. Blackton (cnd) [1946 cast] MCA Classics ▲ MCAD 10047 [AAD] ■ MCAC 10047

Midgley, Vernon (ten)
Gay, J.:The Beggar's Opera (sels), w. P. Clark (sop), A. Jenkins (sop), M. Cable (mez), E. Lane (mez), S. Minty (mez), E. Fleet (sgr), P. Hall (ten), N. Rogers (ten), J. Noble (bar), D. Stevens (cnd), Accademia Monteverdiana Orch, Accademia Monteverdiana Chorus—59 songs *(rec Aug. 1978)* Koch Treasure ▲ 31621-2 [ADD]

Miehlke, Gerrit (bass)
Distler, H.:Choral-Passion, w. W. Jochens (ten—Evangelist), P. Kooy (bass—Jesus), G. Miehlke (bass—Pilatus), W. Gundlach (cnd), Dortmund Univ Chamber Choir *(rec Mar. 1993)* Thorofon ▲ CTH 2185 [DDD]
Mendelssohn, Fanny:Songs, w. Michaela Krämer (sop), Gerhild Romberger (alt), Alastair Thompson (ten), Richard Braun (pno), Willi Gundlach (cnd), Dortmund Univ Chamber Choir—Morgendämmerung; Im Herbste; Unter des Laubdachs Hut; Ich stand gelehnet an den Mast; Mitternacht; Abschied; Lockung; Abend; Aus meinen Tränen; Wenn ich in deine Augen seh'; Im wunderschönen Monat Mai; Schöne Fremde; Schweigend sinkt die Nacht hernieder; Nacht liegt auf den fremden Wegen; Hochzeitsbitter; Wandl' ich in dem Wald; Frühzeitiger Frühling; Blumengruss; O Herbst; Schilflied; Feldlied; März; Lichter Mai; Waldruhe; Nachtreigen *(rec Musikhochschule Detmold, Dortmund, Oct 1995)* Thorofon ▲ CTH 2299 [DDD]

Mielsch, H.-U. (ten)
Mozart, W.A.:Requiem, w. U. Buckel (sop), M. Bence (cta), E. Wollitz (bass), R. Bader (cnd), Stuttgart PO, Böblingen Bach Choir Allegretto ▲ ACD 8060 [ADD] ■ ACS 8060

Migenes-Johnson, Julia (sop)
Bizet, G.:Carmen, w. F. Esham (sop), P. Domingo (ten), R. Raimondi (bass), L. Maazel (cnd), French National Orch [F] Erato ▲ 2292-45209-2 AW [DDD] ■ 2292-45209-4 AG (D)
Bizet, G.:Carmen, w. F. Esham (sop), P. Domingo (ten), R. Raimondi (bass), L. Maazel (cnd), French National Orch, French Radio Chorus [F] Erato 3-▲ 2292-45207-2 ZB [DDD]
Julia Migenes Acanta ▲ 43499
Julia Migenes Sings Preiser ▲ PRE 90047 [ADD]
Poulenc, F.:La Voix humaine, w. G. Prêtre (cnd), French National Orch [F] *(rec 1990)* Erato ▲ 2292-45651-2 [DDD]
Vienna, w. Vienna Volksoper Orch [cnd:Lalo Schifrin] Erato ▲ 4509-92875-2
Weill, K.:The Seven Deadly Sins, w. R. Tear (ten), S. Kale (ten), A. Opie (bar), R. Kennedy (bass), M. Tilson Thomas (cnd), London SO CBS ▲ MK 44529 [DDD]

Migliorini, Thierry (sgr)
Verdi, G.:I masnadieri, w. M. Rowland (sgr), M. Malagnini (sgr), R. Bruson (bar), M. Lanskoy (bar), C. Colombara (bass), W. Gönnenwein (cnd), Ludwigsburg Festival Orch, South German Madrigal Choir Bayer 2-▲ BR 500 001/2 [DDD]

Miháliková, Jarmila (sop)
Krček, J.:Testamenti, w. L. Vraspír (ten), J. Krček (cnd), Musica Bohemica, *(chorus unknown)* Panton ▲ 81 1030-2

Miilberg, Hans (bass)
Tubin, E.:Barbara von Tisenhusen, w. H. Raamat (sop), M. Jõgeva (mez), A. Kollo (ten), I. Kuusk (ten), V. Puura (bar), T. Sild (bar), U. Kreen (bass), P. Lilje (cnd), Estonia Opera Co Orch [Estonian] Ondine 2-▲ ODE 776-2D [DDD]

Mikhailov, Maxim (bass)
Mussorgsky, M.:Boris Godounov, w. Georgi Nelepp (ten), Mark Reizen (bass), *(other soloists unknown)*, N. Golovanov (cnd), Bolshoi Theater Orch, Bolshoi Theater Chorus *(rec 1948)* Arlecchino 3-▲ ARL121/23
Rimsky-Korsakov, N.:Christmas Eve, w. Ekaterina Koudriavtchenko (sop), Elena Zaremba (mez), Vladimir Bogtatchov (ten), Alexei Maslennikov (ten), Viatcheslav Voinarovski (ten), Viatcheslav Verestnikov (bar), Stanislav Souleimanov (bass), M. Yurovski (cnd), Moscow Forum Theater Orch, Yurloff Academic Choir Russian Season 4-▲ CMX 388054

Mikic, Vlado (bass)
Mokranjac, S.:Liturgy, w. M. Jagust (cnd), Belgrade Radio-TV Chorus Jade ▲ JAD C 021
Mokranjac, S.:Requiem, w. M. Jagust (cnd), Belgrade Radio-TV Chorus Jade ▲ JAD C 021

Mikuláš, Peter (bass)
Dvořák, A.:Mass, w. Dagmar Masková (sop), Marta Benacková (alt), Walter Coppola (ten), Josef Ksica (org), Josef Pancík (cnd), Prague Chamber Choir *(rec Dvořák Hall, Prague, Nov 1993)* ECM New Series ▲ 78118-21539-2 [DDD]
Hummel, J.N.:Alma virgo, w. Amanda Halgrimson (sop), Susan McAdoo (mez), Helmut Wildhaber (ten), Jan Engel (bass), M. Haselböck (cnd), Vienna Academy, Brünn Czech Phil Chorus Koch Schwann ▲ SCH CD 317792
Hummel, J.N.:Mass in E♭, Op. 80, w. Amanda Halgrimson (sop), Susan McAdoo (mez), Helmut Wildhaber (ten), Jan Engel (bass), M. Haselböck (cnd), Vienna Academy, Brünn Czech Phil Chorus Koch Schwann ▲ SCH CD 317792
Hummel, J.N.:Quod quod in orbe, w. Amanda Halgrimson (sop), Susan McAdoo (mez), Helmut Wildhaber (ten), Jan Engel (bass), M. Haselböck (cnd), Vienna Academy, Brünn Czech Phil Chorus Koch Schwann ▲ SCH CD 317792
Janácek, L.:Fate, w. Lívia Ághová (sop—Míla), Ludmila Nováková (sop—Frl. Stuhlá/Soucková), Marta Benacková (cta—Mílas Mother), Stefan Margita (ten—Dr. Suda/Hrázda), Peter Straka (ten—Zivný), Ivan Kusnjer (bar—Konečný/Verva), Peter Mikuláš (bass—Lhotský), G. Albrecht (cnd), Czech PO, Prague Chamber Choir *(rec 1995)* Orfeo ▲ 384 951 [DDD]
Mozart, W.A.:Così fan tutte, w. J. Borowska (sop—Fiordiligi), P. Coles (sop—Despina), R. Yachmi (mez—Dorabella), J. Dickie (ten—Ferrando), A. Martin (bar—Guglielmo), P. Mikulaš (b-bar—Don Alfonso), J. Wildner (cnd), Capella Istropolitana, Slovak Phil Chorus [I] *(rec Feb.-Mar. 1990)* Naxos 3-▲ 8.660008/10 [DDD]
Mozart, W.A.:Così fan tutte (sels), w. Joanna Borowska (sop—Fiordiligi), Priti Coles (sop—Despina), Rohangiz Yachmi (mez—Dorabella), John Dickie (ten—Ferrando), Andrea Martin (bar—Guglielmo), Peter Mikulaš (bass—Don Alfonso), Milada Synkova (hpd), J. Wildner (cnd), Capella Istropolitana, Slovak Phil Chorus—Ov.; [Act I] La mia Dorabella capace non è; È la fede della femmine; Una bella serenata; Ah guarda, sorella; Vorrei dir, e cor non ho; Sento, o Dio; Bella vita militar!; Soave sia il vento; Smanie implacabili; In uomini, in soldati; Alla bella Despinetta; Come Scoglio; Non siate ritrosi; Un'aura amorosa; [Act II] Una donna a quindici anni; Prenderò quel brunettino; La mano a me date; Ei parte...senti...ah no!; Donne mie la fate a tanti a tanti; Fra gle amplessi; Fortunato l'uom che prende *(rec Slovak Philharmonic Moyzes Hall, Bratislava, Feb.-Apr. 1990)* Naxos ▲ 8.553172 [DDD]
Mozart, W.A.:Requiem, w. M. Hajóssyová (sop), J. Horská (cta), J. Kundlák (ten), Z. Košler (cnd), Slovak PO, Slovak Phil Chorus Naxos ▲ 8.550235 [DDD] ▲ 7.550235 [DDD]
Rossini, G.:Petite messe solennelle, w. Livia Aghova (sop), Marta Benackova (mez), Gil Manuel Beltran (ten), Raphaele Cortesi (pno), Peter Toperczer (pno), Josef Ksica (harm), Romano Gandolfi (cnd), Prague Chamber Choir *(rec Domovina Studios, Prague, Sept. 10-12, 1994)* Discover International 2-▲ DI 920324-5 [DDD]
Shostakovich, D.:Sym 13, w. M. Shostakovich (cnd), Prague SO, Pavel Kühn (cnd), Prague Phil Chorus Supraphon ▲ SUP 0160 [DDD]
Shostakovich, D.:Sym 13, w. L. Slovák (cnd), Czech-Slovak RSO Bratislava, Slovak Phil Chorus Naxos ▲ 8.550630 [DDD]
Shostakovich, D.:Sym 14, w. M. Hajóssyová (sop), L. Slovák (cnd), Czech-Slovak RSO Bratislava *(rec Feb. 22-Mar. 4, 1991)* Naxos ▲ 8.550631 [ADD]
Zelenka, J.D.:Missa Gratias agimus tibi, w. J. Jonášová (sop), M. Mrázová (cta), V. Dolezal (ten), J. Belohlávek (cnd), Czech PO, Czech Phil Chorus [L] Supraphon ▲ 11 0816-2 [DDD]

Mikus, Walter (sgr)
Bellini, V.:La sonnambula, w. Maria Costanza Nocentini (sop), Vitalba Mosca (mez), Giuseppe Morino (ten), Giovanni Furlanetto (bar), Patrizia Ciofi (sgr), Etienne Ligot (sgr), G. Carella (cnd), Italian International Orch Nuova Era 2-▲ NUO 7215 [DDD]

Milachkina, T. (sop)
Tchaikovsky, P.:Queen of Spades, w. V. Levko (mez), V. Atlantov (ten), M. Ermler (cnd), Bolshoi Theater Orch, Bolshoi Theater Chorus [R] Philips 3-▲ 420375-2 [ADD]

Milanov, Zinka (sop)
Beethoven, L. van:Missa Solemnis, w. Bruna Castagna (cta), Jussi Björling (ten), Alexander Kipnis (bass), A. Toscanini (cnd), NBC SO, Westminster Choir *(rec 1940)* Grammofono 2000 ▲ GRM 78626
Beethoven, L. van:Missa Solemnis, w. B. Castagna (mez), J. Björling, A. Kipnis (bass), A. Toscanini (cnd), NBC SO, Westminster Choir [L] *(rec live 12/28/40)* Melodram 3-▲ MEL 38006
Carlo Tagliabue, w. Carlo Tagliabue (bar), Margherita Carosio (sop), Ettore Bergamaschi (ten), Bruna Castagna (cta), Frederick Jagel (ten), Norman Cordon (bass), Renata Tebaldi (sop), Alfredo Colella (bass) *(rec in studio and live, 1928-1951)* Bongiovanni ▲ GB 1070-2 [ADD]
In Memoriam *(rec 1976 & 1978)* Cantabile ("Biographies in Music" series) 2-▲ BIM 709-2
Mascagni, P.:Cavalleria rusticana, w. Zinka Milanov (sop—Santuzza), Jean Craft (mez—Lucia), Marietta Cosenza (mez—Lola), Giuseppe Gismondo (ten—Turiddu), Benjamin Rayson (bar—Alfio), R. Cellini (cnd), New Orleans Opera Orch, New Orleans Opera Chorus *(rec live, 1963)* VAI Audio ▲ VAIA 1053
Mascagni, P.:Cavalleria rusticana, w. Carol Smith (sop), J. Bjöerling (ten), R. Merrill (bar), R. Cellini (cnd), RCA Victor SO, Robert Shaw Chorale [I] RCA Gold Seal ▲ 6510-2-RG [ADD]
Mascagni, P.:Cavalleria rusticana (sels), Armed Forces Radio Orch *(rec 1938-1944)* Minerva ▲ MN A15 [ADD]
Mascagni, P.:Traditional Songs—Na Bembasi; Ukor; Daleko M'E Moj Split; Domovini Ljubavi; Gor' Cez Jezero; Ko Lani Sem *(rec 1938-1944)* Minerva ▲ MN A15 [ADD]
Mozart, W.A.:Don Giovanni (sels), Armed Forces Radio Orch—Don Ottavio, son morta...or sai che l'onore; Crudele...Non mi dir *(rec 1938-1944)* Minerva ▲ MN A15 [ADD]
Operatic Duets, w. Jussi Björling (ten), Licia Albanese (sop), Renata Tebaldi (sop), Robert Merrill (bar) RCA Gold Seal ▲ 7799-2-RG (m) [ADD] ■ 7799-4-RG (CrO2)
Ponchielli, A.:La Gioconda, w. Zinka Milanov (sop—La Gioconda), Rosalind Elias (mez—Laura), Belan Amparan (cta—La Cieca), Giacomo Cottino (ten—Isepo), Giuseppe Di Stefano (ten—Enzo Grimaldo), Fernando Valentini (bar—Zuane/Un Nocchiero), Leonard Warren (bar—Barnaba), Virgilio Carbonari (bass—Un Cantore), Plinio Clabassi (bass—Alvise Badoero), F. Previtali (cnd), St. Cecilia Academy Orch Rome, St. Cecilia Academy Chorus Rome Theorema 3-▲ TH 121182/184
Ponchielli, A.:La Gioconda (sels), w. C. Turner (mez), R. Turrini (sgr), C. Bardelli (bar), W. Herbert (cnd), *(orch & chorus unknown)*—abridged:the part of Goiconda [Milanov] is presented complete [I] *(rec live, New Orleans, 11/5/53)* Standing Room Only ▲ SRO 814-1 [ADD]
Puccini, G.:Tosca, w. J. Björling (ten), L. Warren (bar), E. Leinsdorf (cnd), Rome Opera Orch, Rome Opera Chorus [I] RCA Gold Seal 2-▲ 4514-2-RG [ADD] 2-■ 4514-2-RG
Puccini, G.:Tosca (sels), w. J. Björling (ten), L. Warren (bar), E. Leinsdorf (cnd), Rome Opera Orch, Rome Opera Chorus RCA Gold Seal ▲ 60192-2-RG [ADD] ■ 60192-4-RG (CrO2)

Milanov, Zinka (sop) (cont.)
Verdi, G.:Aida, w. F. Barbieri (mez), J. Björling (ten), L. Warren (bar), B. Christoff (bass), J. Perlea (cnd), Rome Opera Orch, Rome Opera Chorus [I] RCA Gold Seal 3-▲ 6652-2-RG (m) [ADD] 3-■ ALK3-5380 (m)
Verdi, G.:Aida, w. F. Barbieri (mez), J. Björling (ten), L. Warren (bar), B. Christoff (bass), J. Perlea (cnd), Rome Opera Orch, Rome Opera Chorus [I] RCA Gold Seal ▲ 60201-2-RG (m) [ADD] ■ 60201-4-RG (m)
Verdi, G.:Un ballo in maschera, w. Jan Peerce (ten), Leonard Warren (bar), B. Walter (cnd), *(orch unknown) (rec Jan 15, 1944)* Enterprise ("The Fourties" series) 2-▲ ENT 311
Verdi, G.:Un ballo in maschera, w. Stella Andreva (sop—Oscar), Zinka Milanov (sop—Amelia), Bruna Castagna (cta—Ulrica), Jussi Björling (ten—Riccardo), Lodovico Oliviero (ten—Un Servo D'Amelia), John Cartet (bar—Un Giudice), Alexander Sved (bar—Renato), Normann Cordon (bass—Samuel), Arthur Kent (bass—Silvano), Nicola Moscona (bass—Tom), E. Panizza (cnd), *(orch unknown) (rec live, New York, Dec. 14, 1940)* The Fourties 2-▲ ENT FT 1515
Verdi, G.:Un ballo in maschera (sels), w. E. Panizza (cnd), Armed Forces Radio Orch—Ecco l'orrido campo; Teco io sto; Morrò, ma prima in grazia *(rec 1938-1944)* Minerva ▲ MN A15 [ADD]
Verdi, G.:La forza del destino, w. M. Del Monaco (ten), L. Warren (bar), G. Pechner (bar), W. Wildermann (bass), W. Herbert (cnd), *(orch unknown) (rec live 1953)* Legato Classics 2-▲ LCD 118-2 (m) [AAD]
Verdi, G.:La forza del destino, w. Rosalind Elias (mez), Giuseppe Di Stefano (ten), Leonard Warren (bar), Giorgio Tozzi (bass), Paolo Washington (bass), F. Previtali (cnd), St. Cecilia Academy Orch Rome, St. Cecilia Academy Chorus Rome *(rec 1959)* Theorema 3-▲ TH 121157/59
Verdi, G.:La forza del destino, w. Zinka Milanov (sop—Donna Leonora di Vargas), Rosalind Elias (mez—Preziosilla), Luisa Gioia (sgr—Curra), Angelo Mercuriali (ten—Trabuco), Giuseppe di Stefano (ten—Son Alvaro), Leonard Warren (bar—Don Carlos di Vargas), Giorgio Tozzi (b-bar—Padre guardiano), Dino Mantovani (bar—Fra Melitone), Paolo Washington (b-bar—Il marchese di Calatrava), Virgilio Carbonari (b-bar—un alcalde), Sergio Liviabella (sgr—un chirurgo), F. Previtali (cnd), St. Cecilia Academy Orch Rome, St. Cecilia Academy Chorus Rome [I] London ▲ 443678-2 [ADD]
Verdi, G.:Requiem Mass, w. B. Castagna (cta), J. Björling (ten), N. Moscona (bass), A. Toscanini (cnd), NBC SO, Westminster Choir [L] *(rec 11/23/40)* Melodram 3-▲ MEL 38006
Verdi, G.:Requiem Mass, w. B. Castagna (cta), J. Björling (ten), N. Moscona (bass), A. Toscanini (cnd), NBC SO, Westminster Choir *(rec Mar. 4, 1938)* Legato Classics 2-▲ LCD 178-2
Verdi, G.:Requiem Mass, w. A. Toscanini (cnd), BBC SO, Libera me, Domine *(rec 1938-1944)* Minerva ▲ MN A15 [ADD]
Verdi, G.:Requiem Mass, w. Bruna Castagna (mez), Jussi Björling (ten), Nicola Moscona (bass), A. Toscanini (cnd), NBC SO, Westminster Choir *(rec Nov 23, 1940)* Music & Arts 2-▲ CD 240
Verdi, G.:Rigoletto (sels), w. A. Toscanini (cnd), NBC SO, Armed Forces Radio Chorus—V'ho ingannato *(rec 1938-1944)* Minerva ▲ MN A15 [ADD]
Verdi, G.:Rigoletto (act 4), w. N. Merriman (mez), J. Peerce (ten), L. Warren (bar), A. Toscanini (cnd), NBC SO RCA Gold Seal ▲ 60276-2-RG [ADD] ■ 60276-4-RG (CrO2)
Verdi, G.:Il trovatore, w. F. Barbieri (mez), J. Björling (ten), L. Warren (bar), R. Cellini (cnd), RCA Victor SO, Robert Shaw Chorale [I] RCA Gold Seal ▲ 60191-2-RG [ADD] ■ 60191-4-RG (CrO2)
Verdi, G.:Il trovatore, w. F. Barbieri (mez), J. Björling (ten), L. Warren (bar), R. Cellini (cnd), RCA Victor SO, Robert Shaw Chorale [I] RCA Gold Seal 2-▲ 6643-2-RG (m) [ADD] 2-■ CLK2-5377 (m)
Zinka Milanov RCA Gold Seal ▲ 60074-2-RG (m) [ADD] ■ 60074-4-RG

Milcheva-Nonova, Alexandrina (mez)
Borodin, A.:Prince Igor, w. S. Evstatieva (sop), B. Martinovich (b-bar), N. Ghiaurov (bass), N. Ghiuselev (bass), E. Tchakarov (cnd), Sofia Festival Orch, Sofia National Opera Chorus [R] Sony Classical 3-▲ S3K 44878 [DDD]
Gluck, C.W.:Le Cinesi, w. K. Erickson (sop), M. Schiml (sop), Moser (sgr), L. Gardelli (cnd), Munich RSO, Munich Radio Chorus [I] Orfeo ▲ 178891 [DDD] ■ MC 178891 (D)
Leoncavallo, R.:La Bohème, w. Lucia Popp (sop), Franco Bonisolli (ten), Bernd Weikl (bar), H. Wallberg (cnd), Munich RSO, Bavarian Radio Chorus [I] Orfeo 2-▲ 023822 [DDD]
Mussorgsky, M.:Nursery, w. S. Protich (pno) Pyramid ▲ PYR 13494
Mussorgsky, M.:Songs (misc), w. S. Protich (pno) Pyramid ▲ PYR 13494
Puccini, G.:Madama Butterfly, w. Raina Kabaivanska (sop—Madama Butterfly), Alexandrina Milcheva (mez—Suzuki), Rossitza Troeva-Mircheva (cta—Kate Pinkerton), Nazzareno Antinori (ten—F.B. Pinkerton), Roumen Doikov (ten—Goro), Werther Vrachovski (ten—Il Principe Yamadori), Nelson Portella (bar—Sharpless), Kosta Dinkov (bass—Lo zio Bonzo), G. Bellini (cnd), Sofia PO, Svetoslav Obrenetov Bulgarian National Chorus *(rec Sophia, Bulgaria, Dec 1-13, 1982)* Arts Music 2-▲ 447161-2 [DDD]
Rimsky-Korsakov, N.:Snow Maiden, w. Stefka Evstatieva (sop—Kupava), Elena Zemenkova (sop—Snow Maiden), Alexandrina Milcheva (mez—Spring Fairy), Vessela Zorova (mez—wife), Stefka Mineva (alt—Lehl), Avram Andreev (ten—Tsar), Lyubomir Dyakovski (ten—Cottager, Sprite), Lyubomir Videnov (bar—Misgir), Nicola Ghiuselev (bass—King), S. Angelov (cnd), Bulgarian RSO, Bulgarian National Chorus *(rec Sofia, 1985)* Capriccio 3-▲ 10749-51 [DDD]
Verdi, G.:Requiem Mass, w. Wiener-Chenisheva (sop), L. Bodourov (ten), N. Ghiuselev (bass), I. Marinov (cnd), Sofia State PO, Sofia State Chorus [L] Vivace 3-▲ E 326 [ADD]

Mildenhall, Pamela (sop)
Torrejón Y Velasco, T. de:La purpura de la rosa, w. M. van der Sluis (sop), J. Benet (ten), A. Martin (bar), R. Clemencic (cnd), Clemencic Consort, La Cappella Vocal Ensemble [Sp] Nuova Era ("Ancient Music" series) ▲ 6936 [DDD]

Mildmay, Audrey (sop)
Gay, J.:The Beggar's Opera (sels), w. R. Henderson (bar), M. Redgrave (sgr), *(orch & chorus unknown)*—ov; 37 songs [arr Frederic Austin, 1920] *(rec 1940 for HMV)* Pearl ▲ PEA 9917 (m) [AAD]
Mozart, W.A.:Don Giovanni, w. I. Souez (sop), L. Helletsgrüber (sop), K. von Pataky (ten), J. Brownlee (bar), R. Henderson (bar), T. Franklin (bar), S. Baccaloni (bass), F. Busch (cnd), Glyndebourne Festival Orch, Glyndebourne Festival Chorus [I] *(rec 1936, orig. issued by HMV)* Pearl 3-▲ PEAS 9369 (m) [AAD]
Mozart, W.A.:Nozze di Figaro, w. Aulikki Rautawaara (sop), Constance Willis (mez), John Heddle Nash (ten), Roy Henderson (bar), Willi Domgraf-Fassbaender (bar), F. Busch (cnd), Glyndebourne Festival Orch *(rec 1934)* Legend 2-▲ LGD 132 [ADD]
Mozart, W.A.:Nozze di Figaro, w. Luise Helletsgrüber (sop), Aulikki Rautawaara (sop), Willi Domgraf-Fassbaender (bar), Roy Henderson (bar), F. Busch (cnd), Glyndebourne Festival Orch, Glyndebourne Festival Chorus *(rec 1934)* Grammofono 2000 2-▲ GRM 78624
Mozart, W.A.:Nozze di Figaro, w. Aulikki Rautawaara (sop), Constance Willis (mez), John Heddle Nash (ten), Roy Henderson (bar), Willi Domgraf-Fassbaender (bar), F. Busch (cnd), Glyndebourne Festival Orch, Glyndebourne Festival Chorus [I] *(rec 1934-35)* Pearl 2-▲ PEAS 9375 (m) [AAD]
Mozart, W.A.:Nozze di Figaro (sels), w. Luise Helletsgrüber (sop), Aulikki Rautawaara (sop), Constance Willis (mez), John Heddle Nash (ten), Willi Domgraf-Fassbaender (bar), Roy Henderson (bar), Norman Allin (bass), F. Busch (cnd), Glyndebourne Festival Orch Pearl ▲ PEA CD 9230

Miles, Alastair (bass)
Beethoven, L. van:Mass, Op. 86, w. C. Margiono (sop), C. Robbin (mez), W. Kendall (ten), J. E. Gardiner (cnd), Orch Révolutionnaire et Romantique, Monteverdi Choir London [period instrs] Archiv ▲ 435391-2 [DDD]
Beethoven, L. van:Missa Solemnis, w. C. Margiono (sop), C. Robbin (mez), W. Kendall (ten), J. E. Gardiner (cnd), English Baroque Soloists, Monteverdi Choir London [L] Archiv ▲ 429779-2 [DDD] ▢ 429779-5
Berlioz, H.:L'Enfance du Christ, w. Jean Rigby (mez), John Aler (ten), Gerald Finley (ten), Gwynne Howell (bass), M. Best (cnd), Cordon Orch, Corydon Singers, St. Paul's Cathedral Choir Hyperion 2-▲ CDA 66991/2
Berlioz, H.:Roméo et Juliette, w. Olga Borodina (mez), Thomas Moser (ten), C. Davis (cnd), Vienna PO, Bavarian Radio Chorus Philips ▲ 442134-2
Britten, H.:The Rape of Lucretia (sels), w. C. Pierard (sop), P. Rozario (sop), A. Gunson (mez), J. Rigby (cta), N. Robson (ten), D. Maxwell (bar), A. Opie (bar), R. Hickox (cnd), City of London Sinfonia Chandos 2-▲ CHAN 9254/55 [DDD]
Donizetti, G.:Lucia di Lammermoor (sels), w. E. Gruberova (sop), A. Agache (ten), R. Bonynge (cnd), London SO, Ambrosian Singers—Oh giusto cielo...Il dolce suono; Ohimè! sorge il tremendo fantasma; S'avanza Enrico; Spargi d'amore pianto Teldec ▲ 4509-93691-2 [DDD]

Miles, Alastair (bass) (cont.)
Elgar, E.:Caractacus, w. J. Howarth (sop), A. Davies (ten), S. Roberts (bar), D. Wilson-Johnson (bar), R. Hickox (cnd), London SO, London Sym Chorus [E] *(rec 1992)*
Chandos 2-▲ CHAN 9156/57 [DDD]
Gounod, C.:Roméo et Juliette, w. Susan Graham (sop—Stephano), Ruth Ann Swenson (sop—Juliette), Sarah Walker (mez—Gertrude), Paul Charles Clarke (ten—Tybalt), Placido Domingo (ten—Roméo), Kurt Ollmann (bar—Mercutio), Alastair Miles (bass—Frère Laurent), David Pittman-Jennings (bass—Le Duc), Alain Vernhes (bass—Capulet), L. Slatkin (cnd), Munich RSO, Munich Radio Chorus *(rec Studio 1, Bavarian Radio, Munich, Nov 29 - Dec 10, 1995)* RCA Red Seal 2-▲ 09026-68440-2 [DDD]
Handel, G.F.:Messiah, w. Donna Brown (sop), Cornelia Kallisch (cta), R. Sacca (ten), H. Rilling (cnd), Stuttgart Bach Collegium, Stuttgart Gächinger Kantorei Hänssler Classic 2-▲ HAN 98975 [DDD]
Handel, G.F.:Messiah, w. Lynne Dawson (sop), Hilary Summers (cta), John Mark Ainsley (ten), R. Goodman (cnd), Brandenburg Consort, Stephen Cleobury (cnd), King's College Choir Cambridge [1752 version] Argo 2-▲ 440672-2 [DDD]
Handel, G.F.:Messiah (reorchd Mozart), w. Donna Brown (sop), Cornelia Kallisch (cta), R. Saccà (ten), H. Rilling (cnd), Stuttgart Bach Collegium, Gächinger Kantorei [G] Hänssler Classic 2-▲ 98.975 [DDD]
Handel, G.F.:Samson, w. Roberta Alexander (sop), Maria Venuti (sop), Jochen Kowalski (ct), Anthony Rolfe Johnson (ten), Anton Scharinger (bass), N. Harnoncourt (cnd), Vienna Concentus Musicus, Arnold Schoenberg Choir Teldec ▲ 74871-2
Handel, G.F.:Saul, w. D. Brown (sop), L. Dawson (sop), D. L. Ragin (ct), J. M. Ainsley (ten), J. E. Gardiner (cnd), English Baroque Soloists, Monteverdi Choir London Philips 3-▲ 426265-2 3PH [DDD]
Monteverdi, C.:Vespro della Beata Vergine, w. A. Monoyios (sop), M. Pennicchi (sop), M. Chance (ct), G. Tucker (ten), N. Robson (ten), S. Naglia (ten), B. Terfel (b-bar), J. E. Gardiner (cnd), English Baroque Soloists, His Majesties Sagbutts & Cornetts, London Monteverdi Choir Archiv 2-▲ 429565-2 [DDD]
Mozart, W.A.:Don Giovanni, w. N. Argenta (sop), A. Halgrimson (sop), L. Dawson (sop), J. M. Ainsley (ten), G. Finley (ten), A. Schmidt (bar), G. Yurisch (bar), R. Norrington (cnd), London Classical Players, Schütz Choir London EMI Classics ▲ CDCB 54859
Mozart, W.A.:Litaniae de venerabili, w. E. von Magnus (alt), N. Harnoncourt (cnd), Vienna Concentus Musicus, Arnold Schoenberg Choir Teldec ▲ 72304-2
Mozart, W.A.:Missa, K.257, w. E. von Magnus (alt), N. Harnoncourt (cnd), Vienna Concentus Musicus, Arnold Schoenberg Choir Teldec ▲ 72304-2
Mozart, W.A.:Nozze di Figaro, w. Rebecca Evans (sop—Barbarina), Nuccia Focile (sop—Susanna), Suzanne Murphy (sop—Marcellina), Carol Vaness (sop—Countess Almaviva), Susanne Mentzer (mez—Cherubino), Ryland Davies (ten—Don Basilio/Don Curzio), Alessandro Corbelli (bar—Count Almaviva), Alfonso Antoniozzi (bass—Doctor Bartolo/Antonio), Alastair Miles (bass—Figaro), C. Mackerras (cnd), Scottish CO, Scottish Chamber Chorus *(rec Usher Hall, Edingurgh, Scotland, July 31-Aug. 12, 1994)* Telarc 3-▲ CD 80388 [DDD]
Mozart, W.A.:Requiem, w. N. Argenta (sop), C. Robbin (mez), J.M. Ainsley (ten), R. Norrington (cnd), London Classical Players, Schütz Choir London [L] EMI Classics ▲ CDC 54525
Mozart, W.A.:Thamos, w. J. E. Gardiner (cnd), English Baroque Soloists, Monteverdi Choir London Archiv ▲ 437556-2 [DDD]
Verdi, G.:Requiem Mass, w. Donna Brown (sop), Luba Orgonasova (sop), Anne Sofie von Otter (mez), Luca Canonici (ten), J. E. Gardiner (cnd), Orch Révolutionnaire et Romantique, Monteverdi Choir London Philips 2-▲ 442142-2

Miles, Helen (sop)
Szymanowski, K.:Kurpian Songs, w. Vernon Kirk (ten), Bo Holten (cnd), BBC Singers *(rec St Paul's Church, Knightsbridge, London, Nov 27, 1993)* United ▲ CAL 88021 [DDD]

Miles-Kingston, Paul (trb)
Lloyd Webber, A.:Requiem for Soloists, Orch & Chorus, w. Sarah Brightman (sop), Placido Domingo (ten), L. Maazel (cnd), English CO, Winchester Cathedral Choir [L]
EMI Classics ▲ CDC 47146 [DDD] ■ 4DS 38218 (D)
Lloyd Webber, A.:Requiem for Soloists, Orch & Chorus, w. Sarah Brightman (sop), Placido Domingo (ten), L. Maazel (cnd), English CO, Winchester Cathedral Choir *(rec Studio 1, Abbey Road, London, Dec 20-22, 1984)* London ▲ 448616-2 ■ 48616

Milhaud, Madeleine (nar)
Honegger, A.:Judith, w. Netania Davrath (sop), Blanche Christensen (sop), M. Abravanel (cnd), Utah SO, Salt Lake City Symphonic Choir [F] *(rec Dec. 1964)* Vanguard Classics ▲ OVC 8088 [ADD]
Honegger, A.:Le Roi David, w. Netania Davrath (sop), Jean Preston (mez), Marvin Sorenson (ten), M. Singher (nar), M. Abravanel (cnd), Utah SO [F] Vanguard Classics ▲ OVC 4038 [ADD]
Stravinsky, I.:L'Histoire du soldat, w. J.-P. Aumont (the Soldier), M. Singher (the Devil), L. Stokowski (cnd), *(orch unknown)* [F] *(rec 1967)* Vanguard Classics ▲ OVC 8004 [ADD]

Milhofer, Mark (ten)
Britten, H.:Curlew River, w. Hugo Ticciati (trb), Mark Evans (bar), Gwynn Hughes Jones (bar), Matthew Hargreaves (bass), D. Angus (cnd), Guildhall Chamber Ensemble Koch Schwann ▲ SCH 313972
Purcell, H.:Anthems & Services, w. S. Gritton (sop), M. Kennedy (sop), E. O'Dwyer (trb), J. Goodman (trb), J. Bowman (ct), N. Short (ct), Rogers Covey-Crump (ten), C. Daniels (ten), M. George (bass), R. Evans (bass), R. King (cnd), King's Consort—I Was Glad When They Said unto Me (coronation & verse anthem); O Consider My Adversity; Beati omnes qui timent Dominum; In the Black Dismal Dungeon of Dispair; Save Me, O God; Te Deum in B♭; Jubilant in B♭; Thy Way, O God, Is Holy
Hyperion ▲ CDA 66677 [DDD]
Purcell, H.:Music for the Funeral of Queen Mary, w. S. Gritton (sop), M. Kennedy (sop), E. O'Dwyer (trb), J. Goodman (trb), J. Bowman (ct), N. Short (ct), Rogers Covey-Crump (ten), C. Daniels (ten), M. George (bass), R. Evans (bass), R. King (cnd), King's Consort Hyperion ▲ CDA 66677 [DDD]

Milinkovic, Georgine van (mez)
Mozart, W.A.:Don Giovanni, w. G. Janowitz (sop), S. Jurinac (sop), A. Kraus (ten), N. Ghiaurov (bass), C. M. Giulini (cnd), Rome RAI Orch, Rome RAI Chorus *(rec live, May 12, 1970)*
Melodram 3-▲ MEL 37080
Strauss, R.:Der Rosenkavalier, w. Adele Kern (sop), Viorica Ursuleac (sop), Georg Hann (bass), Ludwig Weber (bass), C. Krauss (cnd), Bavarian State Opera Orch, Bavarian State Opera Chorus *(rec Munich, June 1942)* Preiser 3-▲ PRE 90218
Strauss, R.:Die Schweigsame Frau, w. F. Wunderlich (ten), H. Hotter (b-bar), H. Prey (bar), K. Böhm (cnd), Vienna PO, Vienna State Opera Chorus *(rec live, Salzburg Festival, 8/8/59)*
Melodram 2-▲ MEL 27071 (m) [AAD]
Wagner, R.:Der Ring des Nibelungen, w. Gré Brouwenstein (sop—Freia/Sieglinde), Ilse Hollweg (sop—Waldvogel), Gerda Lammers (sop—Ortlinde), Paula Lenchner (sop—Wellgunde/Gerhilde), Hilde Scheppan (sop—Helmwige), Astrid Varnay (sop—Brünnilde/3rd Norn), Lore Wissmann (sop—Woglinde), Maria von Ilosvay (mez—Flosshilde/Schwertleite/2nd Norn), Louise Charlotte Kamps (mez—Siegrune), Jean Madeira (mez—Erda/Rossweisse/1st Norn), Georgine van Milinkovic (mez—Fricka/Grimgerde), Elisabeth Schärtel (mez—Waltraute), Paul Kuēn (ten—Mime), Ludwig Suthaus (ten—Loge), Josef Traxel (ten—Froh), Wolfgang Windgassen (ten—Siegmund/Siegfried), Alfons Herwig (bar—Donner), Hermann Uhde (bar—Gunther), Hans Hotter (b-bar—Wotan), Gustav Neidlinger (b-bar—Alberich), Josef Griendl (bass—Fasolt/Hunding/Hagen), Arnold van Mill (bass—Fafner), H. Knappertsbusch (cnd), Bayreuth Festival Orch, Bayreuth Festival Chorus *(rec live, Bayreuth, Aug 13-17, 1956)* Golden Melodram 14-▲ GM 1.001 [ADD]

Miller, A. (sgr)
Romberg, S.:Deep in My Heart, w. H. Traubel (sgr), J. Ferrer (sgr), R. Clooney (sgr), Gene Kelly (sgr), F. Kelly (sgr), V. Damone (sgr), J. Powell (sgr), W. Olvis (sgr), C. Richards (sgr), H. Keel (sgr), T. Martin (sgr), J. Weldon (sgr) Sony Music Special Products ▲ AK 47703

Miller, Barbara (sop)
Hindemith, P.:Hin und zurück, w. Claus Bock (ten), Ulrich Schaible (bar), Helmut Kühnle (bass), A. Grüber (cnd), Berlin SO members *(rec 1971)* Allegretto ▲ ACD 8191
Lutoslawski, W.:Die Strohkette, w. Oksana Sowiak (mez), Robert Dohn (fl), Willy Schnell (ob), Martin Klose (cl), Hartmut Stute (cl), Karl Steinbrecher (bn), A. Grüber (cnd) Vox Box 2-▲ CDX 5133

Miller, Jenny (sop)
Elgar, E.:Grania & Diarmid, w. B. Thomson (cnd), London PO Chandos ▲ CHAN 8610 [DDD]
Elgar, E.:Grania & Diarmid, w. B. Thomson (cnd), London PO *(rec All Saints' Church, Jan 18-19, 1988)*
Chandos ▲ CHAN 7038

Miller, Lajos (bar)
Giordano, U.:Andrea Chénier, w. Montserrat Caballé (sop), Franco Corelli (ten), R. de Carlo (sgr), D. Dondi (sgr), G. Ellsworth (sgr), J. Fair (sgr), R. Falk (sgr), S. Felter (sgr), E. Green (sgr), H. Hicks (sgr), H. Krauss (sgr), N. Riggins (sgr), H. Salerno (sgr), A. Guadagno (cnd), Academy of Music Orch, Academy of Music Chorus Great Opera Performances 2-▲ GOP 766
Puccini, G.:Madama Butterfly, w. V. Kincses (sop), T. Tákacs (mez), P. Dvorsky (ten), G. Patanè (cnd), Hungarian State Opera Orch, Hungarian State Opera Chorus [I] Hungaroton 2-▲ HCD 12256/57
Respighi, O.:Belfagor, w. S. Sass (sop), T. Takács (mez), G. Lamberti (ten), L. Polgár (bass), L. Gardelli (cnd), Hungarian State Orch, Hungarian State Chorus [I] Hungaroton 2-▲ HCD 12850/51 [DDD]
Respighi, O.:Semirama, w. E. Marton (sop), V. Kincses (sop), L. Bartolini (ten), L. Polgaar (bass), T. Clementis (bass), L. Gardelli (cnd), Hungarian State Orch, Hungarian Radio-TV Chorus [I]
Hungaroton 2-▲ HCD 31197/98
Vivaldi, A.:L'Olimpiade (sels), w. M. Zempléni (sop), T. Takács (mez), Horváth (sgr), Káplán (sgr), I. Gáti (bar), K. Kováts (bass), F. Szekeres (cnd), Hungarian State Orch, Budapest Madrigal Choir [I]
White Label ▲ HRC 073 [ADD]

Miller, Mildred (mez)
Bach, J.S.:Cant 202, "Wedding Cant", w. E. Schumann (sop), et al., B. Reibold (cnd), Stuyvesant String Quartet *(rec RCA Victor Studio No. 2, New York, Oct 10 & Nov 22, 1939)*
Pearl 2-▲ PEAS 9900 (m) [AAD]
Brahms, J.:Alto Rhap, w. B. Walter (cnd), Columbia SO, Occidental College Concert Choir *(rec Jan. 11, 1961)* Sony Classical ("Bruno Walter Edition, Vol. 2" series) ▲ SMK 64469 [ADD]
Love's Secrets & Other Songs By American Composers, w. Eleanor Steber (sop), John McCollum (ten), Donald Gramm (bass-bar), Edwin Biltcliffe (pno), Richard Cumming (pno)
Vox Box ("The American Composers" series) 2-▲ CDX 5129
Mahler, G.:Das Lied von der Erde, w. E. Haefliger (ten), B. Walter (cnd), New York PO [G]
CBS ▲ MK 42034

Miller, Patricia (sgr)
Cavalli, P.F.:Ercole armante, w. Felicity Palmer (sop—Jole), Yvonne Minton (mez—Giunone), Patricia Miller (sgr—Dejanira), Ulrik Cold (bass), M. Corboz (cnd), English Bach Baroque Orch, English Bach Festival Chorus Erato 3-▲ ERA SEL 12980 [ADD]

Millet, Danielle (sop)
Delibes, L.:Lakmé, w. M. Mesplé (sop), C. Burles (ten), R. Soyer (bass), A. Lombard (cnd), Paris Opéra-Comique Orch, Paris Opéra-Comique Chorus EMI Classics 2-▲ CDCB 49430
Delibes, L.:Lakmé (sels), w. M. Mesplé (sop), C. Burles (ten), R. Soyer (bass), A. Lombard (cnd), Paris Opéra-Comique Orch, Paris Opéra-Comique Chorus EMI Classics ▲ ZDM 63447
Satie, E.:Geneviéve de Brabant, w. A. Guiot (sop), M. Mesplé (sop), A. Esposito (sop), J.C. Benoit (bar), A. Ciccolini (pno), P. Dervaux (cnd), Orch de Paris, Paris Opera Chorus
Virgin Classics 2-▲ CDZB 62877
Satie, E.:Socrate, w. A. Guiot (sop), M. Mesplé (sop), A. Esposito (sop), J. C. Benoit (bar), P. Dervaux (cnd), Orch de Paris, Paris Opera Chorus Virgin Classics 2-▲ CDZB 62877

Millette, Jean-Louis (nar)
Normandeau, R.:Petit Prince, w. Michel Dumont (nar—Aviator), Martin Pensa (nar—Little Prince), Christine Séguin (nar—Rose), Jean Marchand (nar—King), Luc Durand (nar—Conceited Man), Gilles Dupuis (nar—Drunkard), Guy Nadon (nar—Businessman), Jacques Languirand (nar—Lamplighter), Pierre Bourgault (nar—Geographer), Cynthia Dubois (nar—Snake), Monique Giroux (nar—Flower), Françoise Davoine (nar—Rose Garden), Jean-Louis Millette (nar—Fox), Gérard Poirier (nar—Railway Switchman), Claude Préfontaine (nar—Water Pill Salesman) *(rec Montreal, Aug 1994)* CBC 2-▲ 1091 [DDD]
Stravinsky, I.:L'Histoire du soldat, w. V. Davy (nar), J.-L. Millette (nar—Devil), J. Marchand (nar—soldier), A. Robert (cnd), Chambristes de Montreal
CBC ("Musica Viva" series) ▲ MVCD 1049 [DDD]

Milligan, James (b-bar)
Handel, G.F.:Messiah, w. Elsie Morison (sop), Marjorie Thomas (cta), Richard Lewis (ten), M. Sargent (cnd), Royal Liverpool PO, Huddersfield Choral Society
Classics for Pleasure 2-▲ CDCFP 4718 [ADD]
Handel, G.F.:Messiah (sels), w. Elsie Morison (sop), Marjorie Thomas (cta), Richard Lewis (ten), Eric Chadwick (org), M. Sargent (cnd), Royal Liverpool PO, Huddersfield Choral Society
Classics for Pleasure ▲ CDCFP 9007 [ADD]
Sullivan, A.:The Pirates of Penzance, w. G. Baker (bar), J. Cameron (bar), R. Lewis (ten), M. Sargent (cnd), Pro Arte Orch, Glyndebourne Festival Chorus EMI Classics 2-▲ CDMB 64409

Millmann, Doreen (mez)
Liszt, F.:Legend of Saint Elizabeth, w. Maria Szechowska (sop), Klaus Lapins (bar), István Bercewy (bass), S. Heinrich (cnd), Warsaw RSO, Warsaw Radio Chorus [G] *(rec 1983)*
Koch Schwann 2-▲ 3-1291-2 [ADD]

Millo, Aprile (sop)
A Recital, w. Eugene Kohn (pno) *(rec live, 9/14/86)* Legato Classics ▲ LCD 126-1 [AAD]
Verdi, G.:Aida, w. D. Zajick (mez), P. Domingo (ten), J. Morris (bass), S. Ramey (bass), J. Levine (cnd), Metropolitan Opera Orch, New York Metropolitan Opera Chorus [I]
Sony Classical 3-▲ S3K 45973 [DDD] 3-■ S3T 45973 (D)
Verdi, G.:Aida (sels), w. D. Zajick (mez), P. Domingo (ten), J. Morris (bass), S. Ramey (bass), T. Cook (bass), J. Levine (cnd), Metropolitan Opera Orch, New York Metropolitan Opera Chorus *(rec New York, May 18-26, 1990)* Sony Classical ("Opera Highlights" series) ▲ SMK 53506 [DDD]
Verdi, G.:Don Carlos (sels), w. J. Bunnell (sop), D. Zajick (mez), M. Sylvester (ten), V. Chernov (bar), F. Furlanetto (bass), P. Plishka (bass), J. Levine (cnd), Metropolitan Opera Orch, New York Metropolitan Opera Chorus *(rec New York, Apr. 20-May 14, 1992)*
Sony Classical ("Opera Highlights" series) ▲ SMK 53507 [DDD]
Verdi, G.:I lombardi alla prima crociata (sels), w. A. Millo (sop—Giselda), C. Bergonzi (ten—Oronte), P. Plishka (bass—Pagano), E. Queler (cnd), *(orch unknown)*—4 acts abridged *(rec live 1986)*
Legato Classics ▲ LCD 105-1 [ADD]
Verdi, G.:Luisa Miller, w. F. Quivar (mez), P. Domingo (ten), V. Chernov (bar), J. Levine (cnd), Metropolitan Opera Orch, New York Metropolitan Opera Chorus Sony Classical 2-▲ S2K 48073
Verdi, G.:Luisa Miller (sels), w. W. White (mez), F. Quivar (cta), P. Domingo (ten), V. Chernov (bar), J.-H. Rootering (bass), P. Plishka (bass), J. Levine (cnd), Metropolitan Opera Orch, New York Metropolitan Opera Chorus *(rec New York, May 2-18, 1991)*
Sony Classical ("Opera Highlights" series) ▲ SMK 53508 [DDD]
Verdi, G.:Il trovatore, w. D. Zajick (mez), S. Kelly (cta), P. Domingo (ten), T. Willson (ten), A. Laciura (ten), J. Morris (bass), G. Bater (bass), J. Levine (cnd), Metropolitan Opera Orch, New York Metropolitan Opera Chorus *(rec June 18, 1991)* Sony Classical 2-▲ S2K 48070 [DDD]

Mills, Bronoven (sop)
Donizetti, G.:Emilia di Liverpool, w. Y. Kenny (sop), A. Mason (sop), C. Merritt (ten), S. Bruscantini (bar), G. Dolton (bar), C. Thornton-Holmes (bar), D. Parry (cnd), Philharmonia Orch, Geoffrey Mitchell Choir—complete opera, without dialogue Opera Rara 3-▲ OR 8
Donizetti, G.:L'Eremitaggio di Liverpool, w. Y. Kenny (sop), A. Mason (sop), C. Merritt (ten), S. Bruscantini (bar), G. Dolton (bar), C. Thornton-Holmes (bar), D. Parry (cnd), Philharmonia Orch, Geoffrey Mitchell Choir—complete opera, without dialogue Opera Rara 3-▲ OR 8

Mills, Erie (sop)
Bernstein, L.:Candide, w. D. Eisler (ten), Lankston (sgr), J. Mauceri (cnd), New York City Opera Orch, New York Opera Chorus [E] *(rec 1985)* New World 2-▲ NW 340/41-2 2-■ NW 340/41-4
Handel, G.F.:Muzio Scevola, w. Julianne Baird (sop—Clelia), Andrea Matthews (sop—Fidalma), Erie Mills (sop—Orazio), D'Anna Fortunato (mez—Muzio), Jennifer Lane (mez—Irene), Frederick Urrey (ten—Tarquino), John Ostendorf (b-bar—Porsenna), R. Palmer (cnd), Brewer Baroque CO [period instrs] [I] *(rec 10/91)* Newport Classic 2-▲ NPD 85540/2 [DDD]

Mills, Keith (ten)
Walton, W.:Troilus & Cressida, w. Judith Howarth (sop—Cressida), Arthur Davies (ten—Troilus), Nigel Robson (ten—Pandarus), Brian Cookson (ten—3rd Watchman), Peter Bodenham (ten—Priest), Keith Mills (ten—Soldier), Alan Opie (bar—Diomede), James Thornton (bar—Antenor), Clive Bayley (bass—Calkas), David Owen-Lewis (bass—Horaste), R. Hickox (cnd), English Northern Philharmonia, Opera North Chorus Chandos 2-▲ CHAN 9370/71 [DDD]

▲ = CD ◆ = Enhanced CD △ = MD ■ = Cassette Tape ◻ = DCC

Milne, Lisa (sop)

Handel, G.F.:Occasional Oratorio, w. Susan Gritton (sop), James Brown (ct), John Mark Ainsley (ten), Michael George (bass), R. King (cnd), King's Consort, New College Choir Oxford Hyperion 2–▲ CDA 66961/62

Maccunn, H.:The Dowie Dens o'Yarrow, w. Janice Watson (sop), Jamie MacDougall (ten), Peter Sidhom (bar), Stephen Gadd (bass), M. Brabbins (cnd), BBC Scottish SO, Scottish Opera Chorus Hyperion ▲ CDA 66815

Maccunn, H.:Jeanie Deans (sels), w. Janice Watson (sop), Jamie MacDougall (ten), Peter Sidhom (bar), Stephen Gadd (bass), M. Brabbins (cnd), BBC Scottish SO, Scottish Opera Chorus Hyperion ▲ CDA 66815

Maccunn, H.:Lay of Last Minstrel, w. Janice Watson (sop), Jamie MacDougall (ten), Peter Sidhom (bar), Stephen Gadd (bass), M. Brabbins (cnd), BBC Scottish SO, Scottish Opera Chorus Hyperion ▲ CDA 66815

Maccunn, H.:Ship o' the Fiend, w. Janice Watson (sop), Jamie MacDougall (ten), Peter Sidhom (bar), Stephen Gadd (bass), M. Brabbins (cnd), BBC Scottish SO, Scottish Opera Chorus Hyperion ▲ CDA 66815

Vivaldi, A.:Sacred Choral Music, w. Susan Gritton (sop), Catherine Denley (mez), Lynton Atkinson (trb), David Wilson–Johnson (bar), R. King (cnd), King's Consort—Magnificat; Lauda, Jerusalem; Kyrie eleison; Credo in unum Deum; Dixit Dominus Hyperion ▲ CDA 66769

Milnes, Sherrill (bar)

Bizet, G.:Carmen, w. I. Cotrubas (sop), T. Berganza (mez), P. Domingo (ten), C. Abbado (cnd), London SO, Ambrosian Opera Chorus [F] Deutsche Grammophon 3–▲ 419636–2 [ADD]

Bizet, G.:Carmen (sels), w. I. Cotrubas (sop), T. Berganza (mez), P. Domingo (ten), C. Abbado (cnd), London SO, Ambrosian Opera Chorus [F] Deutsche Grammophon ▲ 435401–2 [ADD]

Bravissimo, Domingo!, Vol. 1, w. Plácido Domingo (ten), Leontyne Price (sop) RCA Red Seal ▲ 07863–57020–2

Cilea, F.:Adriana Lecouvreur, w. R. Scotto (sop), E. Obraztsova (mez), P. Domingo (ten), J. Levine (cnd), Philharmonia Orch *(rec 1977)* CBS 2–▲ M2K 34588 [ADD]

Copland, A.:Old American Songs (set 1), w. E. Kunzel (cnd), Cincinnati Pops Orch [E] Telarc ▲ CD–80117 [DDD]

Copland, A.:The Tender Land (sels), w. E. Kunzel (cnd), Cincinnati Pops Orch—The Promise of Living [E] Telarc ▲ CD–80117 [DDD]

Donizetti, G.:Lucia di Lammermoor, w. J. Sutherland (sop), L. Pavarotti (ten), N. Ghiaurov (bass), R. Bonynge (cnd), Royal Opera House Orch [I] London 3–▲ 410193–2 [ADD]

Donizetti, G.:Lucia di Lammermoor (sels), w. J. Sutherland (sop), L. Pavarotti (ten), N. Ghiaurov (bass), R. Bonynge (cnd), Royal Opera House Orch, Royal Opera House Chorus Covent Garden [I] London ("Opera Gala" series) ▲ 421885–2 [ADD]

Fauré, G.:Requiem, w. K. Te Kanawa (sop), C. Dutoit (cnd), Montreal SO, Montreal Sym Chorus [L] London ▲ 421440–2 [DDD] □ 421440–5

Giordano, U.:Andrea Chénier, w. A. Gulin (sop—Maddalena), C. Bergonzi (ten—Andrea Chenier), S. Milnes (bar—Gérard), A. Guadagno (cnd), New Philharmonia Orch, Ambrosian Chorus *(rec live, London, 2/8/70)* Myto 2–▲ 2 MCD 91750 [ADD]

A Grand Night for Singing, w. Columbia SO, Mormon Tabernacle Choir CBS ■ MT 35170

Griffes, C.T.:Songs, w. J. Spong (pno)—An den Wind; Am Kreuzweg wird begraben; Meeres Stille; Auf geheimem Waldespfade; Song of the Dagger New World ▲ NW 273–2 [ADD]

Leoncavallo, R.:Pagliacci, w. M. Caballé (sop), P. Domingo (ten), N. Santi (cnd), London SO, John Alldis Choir RCA Gold Seal 2–▲ 09026–60865–2 [ADD]

Massenet, J.:Le Roi de Lahore, w. J. Sutherland (sop), L. Lima (ten), N. Ghiaurov (bass), R. Bonynge (cnd), National PO London, London Voices London ("Grand Opera" series) 2–▲ 433851–2 [DDD]

Massenet, J.:Thaïs, w. Beverly Sills (sop—Thaïs), Nicolai Gedda (ten—Nicias), Sherrill Milnes (bar—Athanaël), L. Maazel (cnd), New Philharmonia Orch, John Alldis Choir EMI Classics 2–▲ CDMB 65479

Mozart, W.A.:Arias, w. I. Cotrubas (sop), E. Gruberova (sop), L. Price (sop), J. Varady (sop), L. Popp (mez), F. Araiza (ten), P. Domingo (ten), P. de Palma (ten), P. Schreier (ten), F. Wunderlich (ten), A. Titus (bar), M. Talvela (bass)—sels. from Entführung aus dem Serail, Così fan tutte, Don Giovanni, Idomeneo, Die Zauberflöte, Le nozze di Figaro Eurodisc ▲ 69256–2–RG [ADD]

Mozart, W.A.:Così fan tutte, w. L. Price (sop), J. Raskin (sop), T. Troyanos (mez), G. Shirley (ten), E. Leinsdorf (cnd), New Philharmonia Orch, New Philharmonia Chorus [I] RCA Gold Seal 3–▲ 6677–2 [ADD]

Mozart, W.A.:Don Giovanni (sels), w. A. Tomowa–Sintow (sop), T. Zylis–Gara (sop), E. Mathis (sop), W. Berry (bass), K. Böhm (cnd), Vienna PO, Vienna State Opera Chorus—Scenes & Arias Deutsche Grammophon ▲ 429823–2 [ADD]

Orff, C.:Carmina burana, w. E. Mandac (sop), S. Kolk (ten), S. Ozawa (cnd), Boston SO, New England Conservatory Chorus [G, L] RCA Gold Seal ▲ 07863–56533–2 [ADD] ■ 07863–56533–4

Ponchielli, A.:La Gioconda, w. M. Caballé (sop), A. Baltsa (mez), L. Pavarotti (ten), N. Ghiaurov (bass), B. Bartoletti (cnd), National PO [I] London 3–▲ 414349–2 [DDD]

Ponchielli, A.:La Gioconda (sels), w. Placído Domingo (ten), A. Guadagno (cnd), London SO—Enzo Grimaldi, Principe di Santa Fior *(rec 1970)* RCA Gold Seal ▲ 09026–62595–2 [ADD]

Puccini, G.:Arias, w. M. Caballé (sop), M. Chiara (sop), M. Freni (sop), B. Nilsson (sop), J. Sutherland (sop), R. Tebaldi (sop), F. Corelli (ten), L. Pavarotti (ten) London ▲ 421315–2 [ADD]

Puccini, G.:La Bohème, w. M. Caballé (sop), J. Blegen (sop), P. Domingo (ten), R. Raimondi (bass), G. Solti (cnd), London PO, John Alldis Choir [I] RCA Red Seal 2–▲ RCD2–0371 2–■ ARK2–0371

Puccini, G.:La Bohème (sels), w. Plácido Domingo (ten), A. Guadagno (cnd), London SO—O Mimì, tu più non torni *(rec 1970)* RCA Gold Seal ▲ 09026–62595–2 [ADD]

Puccini, G.:La Bohème (sels), w. M. Cabballé (sop), J. Blegen (sop), P. Domingo (ten), G. Solti (cnd), London PO RCA Victor ▲ 09026–61725–2; ■ 09026–61725–4 (CrO2)

Puccini, G.:La fanciulla del West, w. C. Neblett (sop), P. Domingo (ten), Z. Mehta (cnd), Royal Opera House Orch Covent Garden, Royal Opera House Chorus Covent Garden [I] Deutsche Grammophon 2–▲ 419640–2 [ADD]

Puccini, G.:Il tabarro, w. L. Price (sop), P. Domingo (ten), E. Leinsdorf (cnd), New Philharmonia Orch, John Alldis Choir RCA Gold Seal 2–▲ 09026–60865–2 [ADD]

Puccini, G.:Tosca, w. L. Price (sop), P. Domingo (ten), Z. Mehta (cnd), New Philharmonia Orch, John Alldis Choir [I] RCA Victrola 2–▲ RCD2–0105

Puccini, G.:Tosca, w. M. Freni (sop), L. Pavarotti (ten), N. Rescigno (cnd), National PO London [I] London 2–▲ 414036–2 [ADD]

Rachmaninoff, S.:Monna Vanna, w. S. McCoy (ten), I. Buketoff (cnd), Iceland SO, Icelandic Opera Chorus Chandos ▲ CHAN 8987 [DDD]

Rossini, G.:Il barbiere di Siviglia, w. Beverly Sills (sop), Fedora Barbieri (mez), Nicolai Gedda (ten), Renato Capecchi (bar), Ruggero Raimondi (bass), J. Levine (cnd), London SO, John Alldis Choir EMI Classics 2–▲ CDMB 66040

Strauss, R.:Salome, w. M. Caballé (sop), R. Resnik (mez), R. Lewis (ten), E. Leinsdorf (cnd), London SO RCA Gold Seal 2–▲ 6644–2–RG [ADD]

Thomas, A.:Hamlet, w. J. Sutherland (sop), R. Bonynge (cnd), Welsh National Opera Orch, Welsh National Opera Chorus London ("Grand Opera" series) 3–▲ 433857–2 [DDD]

Verdi, G.:Aida, w. L. Price (sop), G. Bumbry (mez), P. Domingo (ten), R. Raimondi (bass), E. Leinsdorf (cnd), London SO [I] RCA ■ RK 1237

Verdi, G.:Aida, w. L. Price (sop), G. Bumbry (mez), P. Domingo (ten), R. Raimondi (bass), E. Leinsdorf (cnd), London SO [I] RCA Red Seal 3–▲ 6198–2–RC [ADD] 3–■ ARK3–2541

Verdi, G.:Aida (sels), w. L. Price (sop), G. Bumbry (mez), P. Domingo (ten), E. Leinsdorf (cnd), London SO RCA Victor ▲ 09026–62676–2 ■ 09026–62676–4

Verdi, G.:Attila, w. C. Deutekom (sop), G. Raimondi (ten), C. Bergonzi (ten), L. Gardelli (cnd), Royal PO, Ambrosian Singers Philips 2–▲ 426115–2

Verdi, G.:Un ballo in maschera, w. R. Tebaldi (sop), L. Pavarotti (ten), B. Bartoletti (cnd), St. Cecilia Academy Orch Rome, St. Cecilia Academy Chorus Rome London ▲ 440042–2

Verdi, G.:La forza del destino (sels), w. Placído Domingo (ten), A. Guadagno (cnd), London SO—Solenne in quest'ora; Invano, Alvaro, tu calaste al mondo *(rec 1970)* RCA Gold Seal ▲ 09026–62595–2 [ADD]

Milnes, Sherrill (bar) (cont.)

Verdi, G.:Macbeth, w. C. Ludwig (mez), C. Cossutta (ten), K. Ridderbusch (bass), K. Böhm (cnd), Vienna State Opera Orch, Vienna State Opera Chorus *(rec live 1970)* Legato Classics 2–▲ LCD 143–2 [ADD]

Verdi, G.:Otello, w. R. Scotto (sop), P. Domingo (ten), J. Levine (cnd), National PO London [I] RCA Red Seal 2–▲ RCD2–2951

Verdi, G.:Otello (sels), w. Placído Domingo (ten), A. Guadagno (cnd), London SO—Sì, pel ciel marmoreo giuro! *(rec 1970)* RCA Gold Seal ▲ 09026–62595–2 [ADD]

Verdi, G.:Rigoletto, w. Beverly Sills (sop), Alfredo Kraus (bar), Samuel Ramy (bass), J. Rudel (cnd), Philharmonia Orch, Ambrosian Opera Chorus EMI Classics 2–▲ CDMB 724356603721

Verdi, G.:Rigoletto, w. J. Sutherland (sop), H. Tourangeau (mez), L. Pavarotti (ten), M. Talvela (bass), R. Bonynge (cnd), London SO, London Sym Chorus [I] London 2–▲ 414269–2 [ADD]

Verdi, G.:La traviata, w. M. Caballé (sop), C. Bergonzi (ten), G. Prêtre (cnd), RCA Italian Opera Orch RCA Gold Seal 2–▲ 6180–2 RC [ADD]

Verdi, G.:La traviata (sels), w. Loretta di Franco (sop), Joan Sutherland (sop), Frederica von Stade (mez), Leo Goeke (ten), Lou Marcella (ten), Luciano Pavarotti (ten), Gene Boucher (bar), Raymond Gibbs (bar), Louis Sgarro (bar), John Trehy (bar) Budget ("The Greatest Voice in Opera" series) ▲ SYP 112

Verdi, G.:I vespri siciliani (sels), w. Placído Domingo (ten), A. Guadagno (cnd), London SO—Quando al mio sen *(rec 1970)* RCA Gold Seal ▲ 09026–62595–2 [ADD]

Walton, W.:Belshazzar's Feast, w. A. Gibson (cnd), Scottish National Orch, Scottish Festival Brass Bands, Scottish National Chorus *(rec 1977)* Chandos ("Collect" series) ▲ CHAN 6547 [ADD/DDD]

Milosevic (sgr)

Mussorgsky, M.:Boris Godunov, w. Cangalovic (sgr), Djokic (sgr), Petrovic (sgr), D. Miladinovic (cnd), Belgrade National Opera Orch, Belgrade National Opera Chorus *(rec live, La Fenice Theater, Venice, Jan. 3, 1967)* Arkadia 3–▲ 492

Miltcheva, Alexandrina (mez)

Mussorgsky, M.:Khovanshchina, w. M. Popov (ten), K. Kaludov (ten), Z. Gadjev (bass), N. Ghiaurov (bass), N. Ghiuselev (bass), E. Tchakarov (cnd), Sofia National Opera Orch, Sofia National Opera Chorus Sony Classical 3–▲ S3K 45831

Milva (sgr)

Weill, K.:The Threepenny Opera, w. U. Lemper (sop), S. Tremper (sgr), H. Dernesch (mez), R. Kollo (ten), M. Adorf (sgr), W. Reichmann (sgr), J. Mauceri (cnd), Berlin RIAS Sinfonietta, Berlin RIAS Chamber Choir [G] London ▲ 430075–2 [DDD]

Minarelli, Monica (sgr)

Giordano, U.:Fedora, w. Mirella Freni (sop—Principessa Fedora), Adelina Scarabelli (sop—Contessa Olga), Silvia Mazzoni (mez—Dimitri), Monica Minarelli (sgr—Savoiardo), Placido Domingo (ten—Conte Loris), Ernesto Gavazzi (ten—Desiré), Aldo Bottion (ten—Barone Rouvel), Alessandro Corbelli (bar—Siriex), Luigi Roni (bass—Cirillo), Silvestro Sammaritano (bass—Baroff), Alfredo Giacomotti (bass—Gretch), Ernesto Panariello (bass—Lorek), Vincenzo Alaimo (sgr—Nicola), Arnold Bosman (sgr—Boleslao), Bruno Capisani (sgr—Sergio), Renato Zanchetta (sgr—Michele), G. Gavazzeni (cnd), La Scala Orch, La Scala Chorus *(rec La Scala, Apr 5, 1993)* Legato 2–▲ LCD 213–2 [ADD]

Mascagni, P.:Amica, w. Katia Ricciarelli (sop), Elia Padovan (sgr), Fabio Armiliato (sgr), Walter Donati (sgr), M. Pace (cnd), Hungarian Radio–TV SO, Hungarian Radio–TV Chorus *(rec Budapest, Nov 1995)* Kicco Classic 2–▲ KC 00296 [DDD]

Minelli, Liza (sgr)

Pavarotti & Friends for War Child, w. Luciano Pavarotti (ten), Eric Clapton (sgr), Sheryl Crow (sgr), Elton John (sgr), Joan Osborne (sgr), Jon Secada (sgr), Eric Clapton (gtr), John McLaughlin (gtr), Marco Armiliato, Edoardo Bennato, José Molina, Al DiMeola, Kelly Family, Ligabue, Litfiba, P *(rec Modena, Italy, 1996)* London ▲ 452900–2 ■ 452900–4

Mineo, Andrea (bar)

Mussorgsky, M.:Khovanshchina, w. Jolanda Mancini (sop—Emma), Irene Companez (mez), Amedeo Berdini (ten—Prince Andrei Khovanski), Mirto Picchi (ten—Prince Vasili Golitsin), Herbert Handt (ten—Scribe), Andrea Mineo (bar—Kuzka), Giampiero Malaspina (bar—Shaklovity), Boris Christoff (bass—Dosifei), Mario Petri (bass—Prince Ivan Khovanski), Dimitri Lopatto (Varsonofiev/First Strelyets), Giorgio Conello (Second Strelyets), A. Rodzinski (cnd), *(orch unknown)* [I] *(rec Rome, 1958)* VAI Audio 2–▲ VAIA 1052–2

Minetti, Hans–Peter (nar)

Berlioz, H.:Lélio, "Le retourà la vie", w. M. Rabsilber (ten), B. Grabowski (bar), R. Reuter (cnd), Berlin Comic Opera Orch, Berlin Radio Chorus [F; narration G] Berlin Classics ▲ BER 2149 [DDD]

Mozart, W.A.:Entführung, w. L. Orgonasova (sop), C. Sieden (sop), S. Olsen (ten), Uwe Peper (ten), C. Hauptmann (bass), J. E. Gardiner (cnd), English Baroque Soloists, Monteverdi Choir London [G] Deutsche Grammophon 2–▲ 435857–2

Minetto, Maria (cta)

Caldara, A.:Il gioco del quadriglio, w. Maria–Grazia Ferraccini (sop), Basia Retchitzka (sop), Elana Rizzieri (sop), E. Loehrer (cnd), Lugano Chamber Society Orch, Minetto Chorus Dynamic ▲ CDL 140

Palestrina, G.:Sacred Music, w. Luciana Ticinelli–Fattori (sop), Laerte Malaguti (bar), James Loomis (bass), E. Loehrer (cnd), Lugano Chamber Society Instrumental Ensemble, Lugano Chamber Society Chorus—Vexilla Regis Prodeunt; Adoramus Te; Laudario Di Cortona Accord ▲ ACD 201562 [AAD]

Pergolesi, G.B.:Mass in F, w. B. Retchitzka (sop), G. Ferracini (sop), V. Gohl (cta), C. Jauquier (ten), J. Loomis (bass), Milan Solisti, Plifonia Choir *(rec 1967)* Rivoalto ▲ RIV 8922 [ADD]

Mineva, Stefka (mez)

Mussorgsky, M.:Boris Godunov, w. S. Mineva (mez—Marina), M. Svetlev (ten—Gregory), N. Ghiaurov (bass—Boris), N. Ghiuselev (bass—Pimen), E. Tchakarov (cnd), Sofia Festival Orch, Sofia National Opera Chorus [R] Sony Classical ("Russian Opera" series) 3–▲ S3K 45763

Rimsky–Korsakov, N.:Snow Maiden, w. Stefka Evstatieva (sop—Kupava), Elena Zemenkova (sop—Snow Maiden), Alexandrina Milcheva (mez—Spring Fairy), Vessela Zorova (mez—wife), Stefka Mineva (alt—Lehl), Avram Andreev (ten—Tsar), Lyubomir Dyakovski (ten—Cottager, Sprite), Lyubomir Videnov (bar—Misgir), Nicola Ghiuselev (bass—King), S. Angelov (cnd), Bulgarian RSO, Bulgarian National Chorus *(rec Sofia, 1985)* Capriccio 3–▲ 10749–51 [DDD]

Verdi, G.:Requiem Mass, w. Maria Belcheva (sop), Roumen Doykov (ten), Dimiter Petkov (bass), P. Tiboris (cnd), Sofia National Opera Orch, Sofia National Opera Chorus *(rec Bulgarian National Radio Studio, Mar 14–17, 1994)* Elysium ▲ GRK 708 [DDD]

Mingardo, Sara (cta)

Bellini, V.:La straniera, w. L. Alberti (sop—Alaide), S. Mingardo (mez—Isoletta), V. Bello (ten—Arturo), R. Frontale (bar—Il Barone di Valdeburgo), V. Sagona (bass—Il signore di Montalino), P. Zizich (bass—Osburgo), G. Masini (cnd), Trieste Teatro Comunale Giuseppe Verdi Orch, Trieste Teatro Comunale G. Verdi Chorus *(rec Dec. 1990)* Ricordi ▲ RFCD 2015 [DDD]

Handel, G.F.:Riccardo Primo, w. Claire Brua (sop—Pulcheria), Sandrine Piau (sop—Costanza), Sara Mingardo (cta—Riccardo), Pascal Bertin (alt—Oronte), Roberto Scaltriti (bar—Isacio), Olivier Lallouette (bass—Berardo), C. Rousset (cnd), Les Talens Lyriques L'oiseau Lyre ▲ 452 201–2

Rossini, G.:Demetrio e Polibio, w. Christine Weidinger (sop—Lisinga), Sara Mingardo (cta—Siveno), Anna Laura Longo (sgr—Olmira), Dalmacio Gonzales (ten—Demetrio/Eumene), Giorgio Surjan (bass—Polibio), Martino Fullone (sgr—Onao), M. Carraro (cnd), Graz SO, Bratislava Chamber Chorus *(rec live, Martina Franca Opera Festival, Italy, July 27, 1992)* Dynamic 2–▲ CDS 171/1–2 [DDD]

Rossini, G.:La pietra del paragone, w. Tiziana Carraro (sop—Fulvia), Elisabetta Gutierrez (mez—Baronessa Aspasia), Sara Mingardo (cta—Clarice), William Matteuzzi (ten—Giocondo), Marco Camastra (bar—Pacuvio), Pietro Spagnoli (bar—Conte Asdrubale), Gioacchino Zarrelli (bar—Fabrizio), Josè Fardilha (bass—Macrobio), B. Aprea (cnd), Graz SO, Sluk Chamber Chorus Bratislava *(rec 1993)* Bongiovanni 2–▲ GB 2179/80 [DDD]

Sarro, D.N.:Coronatemi il crine, w. G. Catalucci (cnd), In Canto CO *(rec Dec. 8, 1992)* Bongiovanni ▲ GB 2147 [DDD]

Sarro, D.N.:Dorina e Nibbio, w. S. Mingardo (cta—Dorina), G. Gatti (bar—Nibbio), G. Catalucci (cnd), In Canto CO *(rec Dec. 8, 1992)* Bongiovanni ▲ GB 2147 [DDD]

Minghini–Cattaneo, Irene (mez)

Verdi, G.:Aida, w. Dusolina Giannini (sop—Aida), Irene Minghini–Cattaneo (mez—Amneris), Giuseppe Nessi (ten—Messenger), Aureliano Pertile (ten—Radames), Giovanni Inghilleri (bar—Amonasro), Luigi Manfrini (bass—Ramfis), Guglielmo Masini (bass—King), C. Sabajno (cnd), La Scala Orch, Vittore Veneziani (cnd), La Scala Chorus *(rec 1928)* Arkadia ("The 78's" series) 2–▲ 78013 [ADD]

Minghini–Cattaneo, Irene (mez) (cont.)
Verdi, G.:Aida, w. D. Giannini (sop), A. Pertile (ten), G. Inghilleri (bar), L. Manfrini (bass), C. Sabajno (cnd), La Scala Orch, La Scala Chorus [I] *(rec 1928 for HMV)* Pearl 2-▲ CDS 9402 (m) [AAD]
Verdi, G.:Aida, w. Dusolina Giannini (sop), Aureliano Pertile (ten), C. Sabajno (cnd), La Scala Orch, La Scala Chorus *(rec Milan, 1928)* Phonographie 2-▲ PHG 5004 [ADD]
Verdi, G.:Requiem Mass, w. Maria Luisa Fanelli (sop), Fracno Lo Giudice (ten), E. Pinza (bass), C. Sabajno (cnd), La Scala Orch, La Scala Chorus *(rec 1927 for HMV)* Pearl ▲ GEMMCD 9374 (m) [AAD]

Minich, Peter (ten)
Lehár, F.:Die lustige Witwe, w. D. Koller (sop), M. Irosch (sop), H. Papouschek (sop), K. Ruzicka (ten), H. Prikopa (bar), K. Huemer (bar), R. Bibl (cnd), Vienna Volksoper Orch, Vienna Volksoper Chorus [G] Denon 2-▲ CO 8103 [DDD]

Minjelkiev, Bulat (bass)
Mussorgsky, M.:Khovanshchina, w. O. Borodina (mez), V. Galusin (ten), Ohotnikav (sgr), V. Gergiev (cnd), Kirov Opera Orch, Kirov Opera Chorus [R] Philips 3-▲ 432147-2 [DDD]

Minkiewicz, Ryszard (ten)
Zielenski, M.:Communiones totius anni, w. Kira Borescko (sop), Marcin Borus–Szczycinski (alt), Robert Hugo (org), M. Bornus–Szczycinski (cnd), Bornus Consort, Tallinn Linnamussikud Instrumental Ensemble, Tallin Linnamussikud Vocal Ensemble Urtext ▲ ACD 202662 [DDD]
Zielenski, M.:Offertoria totius anni, w. Kira Borescko (sop), Marcin Borus–Szczycinski (alt), Robert Hugo (org), M. Bornus–Szczycinski (cnd), Bornus Consort, Tallinn Linnamussikud Instrumental Ensemble, Tallin Linnamussikud Vocal Ensemble Urtext ▲ ACD 202662 [DDD]

Minter, Drew (ct)
Bach, J.S.:Cant 54, w. J. Thomas (cnd), American Bach Soloists [G] *(rec Apr & Oct 1990)* Koch International Classics ▲ KIC 7138-2 [DDD]
Bach, J.S.:Cant 106, "Actus tragicus", w. C. Brandes (sop), W. Sharp (bar), American Bach Soloists Koch International Classics ▲ KIC 7164 [DDD]
Handel, G.F.:Agrippina, w. S. Bradshaw (sop), W. Hill (sop), L. Saffer (sop), G. Banditelli (cta), R. Popken (alt), B. Szilágyi (bar), M. Dean (b-bar), N. Isherwood (bass), N. McGegan (cnd), Capella Savaria [period instrs] [I] Harmonia Mundi USA 3-▲ HMU 907063/65 ■ HMU 407063/65
Handel, G.F.:Arias, w. Lisa Saffer (sop—Cuzzoni), Lorraine Hunt (mez—Durastanti), Drew Minter (ct—Senesino), David Thomas (bass—Montagnana), N. McGegan (cnd), Philharmonia Baroque Orch Harmonia Mundi 4-▲ HMX 2907171.74
Handel, G.F.:Arias, w. N. McGegan (cnd), Philharmonia Baroque Orch—11 arias & scenes from Flavio, Giulio Cesare, Orlando, Riccardo Primo, Rodelinda, Tolomeo [all composed for the alto castrato Francesco Bernardi, stage name Senesino] [I] Harmonia Mundi France ▲ HMC 905183 [ADD]
Handel, G.F.:Berenice, w. Julianne Baird (sop—Berenice), Andrea Matthews (sop—Alessandro), D'Anna Fortunato (mez—Selene), Jennifer Lane (mez—Demetrio), Drew Minter (alt—Arsace), John McMaster (ten—Fabio), Jan Opalach (bass—Aristobolo), R. Palmer (cnd), Brewer CO Newport Classic 3-▲ NPD 85620/3 [DDD]
Handel, G.F.:Brockes–Passion, w. K. Farkas (sop), M. Zádori (sop), J. Bándi (ten), M. Klietmann (ten), G. de Mey (ten), I. Gáti (bar), N. McGegan (cnd), Capella Savaria, Hallé State Chorus [period instrs] [G] Hungaroton 3-▲ HCD 12734/36 [DDD]
Handel, G.F.:Clori, Tirsi e Fileno, w. J. Feldman (sop), L. Hunt (sop), N. McGegan (cnd), Philharmonia Baroque Orch [I] Harmonia Mundi USA ▲ HMU 907045
Handel, G.F.:Faramondo, w. Julianne Baird (sop—Clotilde), Mary Ellen Callahan (sop—Adolfo), D'Anna Fortunado (mez—Faramondo), Jennifer Lane (mez—Rosimonda), Drew Minter (alt—Gernando), Peter Castaldi (bar—Gustavo), Mark Singer (bar—Tebaldo), Edward Brewer (hpd), R. Palmer (cnd), Brewer CO [period instrs] Vox Classics 3-▲ VOX3 7536 [DDD]
Handel, G.F.:Giustino, w. Juliana Gondek (sop), Dawn Kotoski (sop), Dorothea Röschmann (sop), Jennifer Lane (mez), Michael Chance (alt), Mark Padmore (ten), Dean Ely (sgr), N. McGegan (cnd), Freiburg Baroque Orch Harmonia Mundi France 3-▲ HMU 907130.32
Handel, G.F.:Messiah, w. Lorraine Hunt (sop), Janet Williams (sop), Patricia Spence (mez), Jeffery Thomas (ten), William Parker (bar), N. McGegan (cnd), Philharmonia Baroque Orch, Univ of California at Berkeley Chamber Chorus—standard version of Messiah *occupies the first sections of each of the three CDs, one part per disc. Each part is followed, after a significant pause, by alternative versions of certain sections of the preceding material, 13 altogether. [E]* Harmonia Mundi USA 3-▲ HMU 907050/52
Handel, G.F.:Messiah (sels), w. Lorraine Hunt (sop), Janet Williams (sop), Patricia Spence (mez), Jeffery Thomas (ten), William Parker (bar), N. McGegan (cnd), Philharmonia Baroque Orch, Univ of California at Berkeley Chamber Chorus [E] Harmonia Mundi USA ("Nightingale" series) ▲ HMN 907601
Handel, G.F.:Messiah (sels), w. Lorraine Hunt (sop), Janet Williams (sop), Patricia Spence (mez), Jeffery Thomas (ten), William Parker (bar), N. McGegan (cnd), Philharmonia Baroque Orch, Univ of California at Berkeley Chamber Chorus Harmonia Mundi USA ▲ HMU 907120
Handel, G.F.:Ottone, Rè di Germania, w. Julianna Gondek (sop), Lisa Saffer (sop), Patricia Spence (mez), R. Popken (alt), Michael Dean (b-bar), N. McGegan (cnd), Freiburg Baroque Orch *(rec June 9-12, 1992)* Harmonia Mundi USA 3-▲ HMU 907073/75
Handel, G.F.:Sosarme, Rè di Media, w. Julinne Baird (sop—Elmira), D'Anna Fortunato (mez—Sosarme), Jennifer Lane (mez—Erenice), Drew Minter (ct—Melo), Rarmond Pellerin (ct—Argone), John Aler (ten—King Haliate), Nathaniel Watson (bass—Varo), Edward Brewer (hpd) Newport Classic 2-▲ NPT 85575 [DDD]
Handel, G.F.:Susanna, w. Jill Feldman (sop), Lorraine Hunt (sop), Jeffery Thomas (ten), William Parker (bar), David Thomas (bass), N. McGegan (cnd), Philharmonia Baroque Orch, Univ of California at Berkeley Chamber Chorus [E] Harmonia Mundi USA 3-▲ HMU 907030/32
Handel, G.F.:Susanna (sels), w. Jill Feldman (sop), Lorraine Hunt (sop), Jeffery Thomas (ten), William Parker (bar), David Thomas (bass), N. McGegan (cnd), Philharmonia Baroque Orch, Univ of California at Berkeley Chamber Chorus [E] Harmonia Mundi USA ("Nightingale" series) ▲ HMN 907601
Handel, G.F.:Susanna (sels), w. Jill Feldman (sop), Lorraine Hunt (sop), Jeffrey Thomas (ten), William Parker (bar), David Thomas (bass), N. McGegan (cnd), Philharmonia Baroque Orch Harmonia Mundi France ▲ HMU 907168
Handel, G.F.:Theodora, w. Lorraine Hunt (sop—Theodora), Jennifer Lane (mez—Irene), Drew Minter (alt—Didymus), Jeffery Thomas (ten—Septimius), David Thomas (bass—Valens), N. McGegan (cnd), Philharmonia Baroque Orch, Univ of California at Berkeley Chamber Chorus [period instrs] [E] *(rec 9/91)* Harmonia Mundi USA 3-▲ HMU 907060/62 [DDD]
Handel, G.F.:Theodora (sels), w. Lorraine Hunt (sop), Jennifer Lane (mez), Jeffrey Thomas (ten), David Thomas (bass), N. McGegan (cnd), Philharmonia Baroque Orch, Univ of California at Berkeley Chamber Chorus Harmonia Mundi France ▲ HMU 907188
Hungarian Baroque Songs & Dances, Budapest Collegium Musicum White Label ▲ HRC 183 [ADD]
Musick for Severall Friends, w. M. Springfels (cnd), Newberry Consort, David Douglass (vn), Kevin Mason (thb/lt) Harmonia Mundi France ("Musique d'abord" series) ▲ HMA 1907013
Purcell, H.:Songs, w. P. O'Dette (archlt), M. Springfels (vl), M. Meyerson (hpd/org)—Be Welcome Then, Great Sir; Celia Has a Thousand Charmes; Crown the Altar; The Fatal Hour Comes On Apace; From Silent Shades; Hark! How All Things; Hark! the Echoing Air; Here the Dieties Approve; I Attempt From Love's Sickness to Fly; If Musick be the Food of Love; Lord, What is Man; Musick For A While; Not All My Torments; Now That the Sun Hath Veil'd His Light; O Solitude; Sleep, Adam, Sleep; Sweeter Than Roses; Thrice Happy Lovers; 'Tis Nature's Voice [E] Harmonia Mundi USA ▲ HMU 907035

Minton, Yvonne (mez)
Berg, A.:Lulu, w. T. Stratas (sop), V. Schwarz (sop), K. Riegel (ten), F. Mazura (bar), P. Boulez (cnd), Paris Opera Orch—Act 3 [G] Deutsche Grammophon 3-▲ 415489-2 [ADD]
Cavalli, P.F.:Ercole armante, w. Felicity Palmer (sop—Jole), Yvonne Minton (mez—Giunone), Patricia Miller (sgr—Dejanira), Ulrik Cold (bass), M. Corboz (cnd), English Bach Baroque Orch, English Bach Festival Chorus Erato 3-▲ ERA SEL 12980 [ADD]
Debussy, C.:Pelléas et Mélisande, w. E. Söderström (sop), G. Shirley (ten), D. McIntyre (bass-bar), D. Ward (bass), P. Boulez (cnd), Royal Opera House Orch, Royal Opera House Chorus Covent Garden Sony Classical (Pierre Boulez Edition) 3-▲ SM3K 47265
Handel, G.F.:Messiah, w. Margaret Price (sop), Alexander Young (ten), Justino Diaz (bass), J. Somary (cnd), English CO, Amor Artis Chorale [E] *(rec 1970)* Vanguard Classics ▲ OVC 4020 [ADD]
Handel, G.F.:Messiah, w. Margaret Price (sop), Alexander Young (ten), Justino Diaz (bass), J. Somary (cnd), English CO, Amor Artis Chorale [E] *(rec 1970)* Vanguard Classics 2-▲ OVC 4018/19 [ADD]

Minton, Yvonne (mez) (cont.)
Mahler, G.:Songs from Rückert, w. P. Boulez (cnd), *(orch unknown)* Sony Classical ("Pierre Boulez Edition" series) ▲ SMK 68330
Mahler, G.:Sym 8, w. A. Augér (sop), H. Harper (sop), L. Popp (sop), H. Watts (cta), A. Kollo (ten), J. Shirley–Quirk (bar), M. Talvela (bass), G. Solti (cnd), Chicago SO, Vienna State Opera Chorus, Vienna Boys' Choir, Vienna Singverein [G,L] London 2-▲ 414493-2 [ADD]
Mozart, W.A.:Complete Mozart Edition, w. L. Popp (sop), J. Baker (mez), F. von Stade (mez), S. Burrows (ten), R. Lloyd (b-bar), C. Davis (cnd), Royal Opera House Orch, Royal Opera House Chorus Covent Garden Philips 2-▲ 422544-2 [ADD]
Mozart, W.A.:Complete Mozart Edition, w. J. Norman (sop), M. Freni (sop), I. Wixell (bar), C. Davis (cnd), BBC SO, BBC Sym Chorus Philips 3-▲ 422540-2 [ADD]
Mozart, W.A.:Così fan tutte, w. M. Price (sop), L. Popp (sop), L. Alva (ten), G. Evans (bar), H. Sotin (bass), O. Klemperer (cnd), New Philharmonia Orch, John Alldis Choir EMI Classics 3-▲ CDMC 63845
Mozart, W.A.:Requiem, w. H. Donath (sop), A. Davies (ten), G Nienstedt (bass), C. Davis (cnd), BBC SO, John Alldis Choir [L] Philips ▲ 420353-2 [ADD]
Schoenberg, A.:Gurrelieder, w. M. Napier (sop), J. Thomas (ten), K. Bowman (sgr), G. Reich (nar), S. Nimsgern (b-bar), P. Boulez (cnd), BBC SO *(rec Oct. 26–Dec. 06, 1974)* Sony Classical 2-▲ SM2K 48459 [ADD]
Schoenberg, A.:Orch Songs, Op. 22, w. P. Boulez (cnd), BBC SO *(rec Mar. 12, 1981)* Sony Classical 2-▲ SM2K 48459 [ADD]
Strauss, R.:Der Rosenkavalier, w. R. Crespin (sop), H. Donath (sop), M. Jungwirth (bass), G. Solti (cnd), Vienna PO [G] London 3-▲ 417493-2 [ADD]
Tippett, M.:King Priam, w. Heather Harper (sop—Hecuba), Linda Hirst (sop—Serving Woman), Felicity Palmer (sop—Andromache), Julian Saipe (sop—Paris), Yvonne Minton (mez—Helen), Ann Murray (mez—Nurse), Kenneth Bowen (ten—Hermes), Peter Hall (ten—Young Guard), Philip Langridge (ten—Paris), Robert Tear (ten—Achilles), Thomas Allen (bar—Hector), Norman Bailey (bar—Priam), Stephen Roberts (bar—Patroclus), David Wilson–Johnson (bar—Old Man), D. Atherton (cnd), London Sinfonietta, London Sinfonietta Chorus Chandos ▲ CHAN 9406/7 [DDD]
Verdi, G.:Pezzi sacri, w. Z. Mehta (cnd), Los Angeles PO, Los Angeles Master Chorale *(rec 1970)* London ("Double Decker" series) 2-▲ 444833-2 [ADD]
Wagner, R.:Das Liebesmahl der Apostel, w. P. Boulez (cnd), *(orch unknown)*, Westminster Choir Sony Classical ("Pierre Boulez Edition" series) ▲ SMK 68330
Wagner, R.:Tristan und Isolde, w. C. Ligendza (sop—Isolde), Y. Minton (mez—Brangäne), H. Brilioth (ten—Tristan), K. Moll (bass—King Mark), C. Kleiber (cnd), Bayreuth Festival Orch, Bayreuth Festival Chorus *(rec Bayreuth Festival, 1975)* Exclusive 3-▲ EXL 54 [ADD]
Wagner, R.:Tristan und Isolde (sels), w. H. Behrens (sop), P. Hofmann (ten), B. Weikl (bass), L. Bernstein (cnd), Bavarian RSO, Bavarian Radio Chorus Philips ▲ 438501-2
Wagner, R.:Wesendonck Songs, w. P. Boulez (cnd), *(orch unknown)* Sony Classical ("Pierre Boulez Edition" series) ▲ SMK 68330

Minton, Yvonne (spkr)
Schoenberg, A.:Pierrot lunaire, w. P. Zukerman (vn/va), L. Harrell (vc), D. Barenboim (pno), M. Debost (fl/pic), A. Pay (cl/b cl), P. Boulez (cnd) *(rec June 20–21, 1977)* Sony Classical ▲ SMK 48466 [ADD]

Minty, Shirley (mez)
Bliss, A.:The Olympians, w. R. Woodland (sop), T. Hemsley (bar), R. Herincx (bass), B. Fairfax (cnd), Polyphonia Orch, Ambrosian Singers *(rec 1972)* Intaglio 2-▲ ING 755 [ADD]
Bliss, A.:Pastoral, w. H.D. Wetton (cnd), Holst Orch, Holst Singers [E] Hyperion ▲ CDA 66175
Gay, J.:The Beggar's Opera (sels), w. P. Clark (sop), A. Jenkins (sop), M. Cable (mez), E. Lane (mez), S. Minty (mez), E. Fleet (sgr), P. Hall (ten), V. Midgley (ten), N. Rogers (ten), J. Noble (bar), D. Stevens (cnd), Accademia Monteverdiana Orch, Accademia Monteverdiana Chorus—59 songs *(rec Aug. 1978)* Koch Treasure ▲ 31621-2 [ADD]

Miraille, Dominique (bar)
Dupuy, B.A.:Sacred Music, w. Isabelle Poulenard (sop), Jean–Louis Comorette (ct), Erik Gruchet (ten), Jean–Louis Bindi (bass), A. Bourbon (cnd), Baroque Instrumental Ensemble, Toulouse Vocal Group—Noël; Motet; Magnificat Arion ▲ ARN 68330 [DDD]

Miranda, Ana–Maria (sop)
Galuppi, B.:Magnificat, w. J. E. Dähler (cnd), Southwest German CO Pforzheim, Bern Chamber Choir *(rec Berner Münster, Dec 1977)* Claves ▲ CD 50801 [ADD]
Lehár, F.:Das Land des Lächelns (sels), w. Brigitte Krafft (sgr), Bernard Sinclair (bar), J. Doussard (cnd), *(orch unknown)* [F] Forlane ▲ FOR 16715 [DDD]
Mozart, W.A.:Songs, w. C. Wirz (alt), M. Quillevéré (ten), U. Reinemann (bar), C. Ivaldi (pno)—K.152, 307, 308, 346, 351, 436–439, 441, 441b, 472, 473, 506, 510, 520, 523, 524, 532, 549, 561, 625, & K.Anh 5 *(rec 1979)* Arion ▲ ARN 68161 [ADD]
Vivaldi, A.:Gloria, RV.589, w. Ria Bollen (alt), J. E. Dähler (cnd), Southwest German CO Pforzheim, Bern Chamber Choir *(rec Berner Münster, Dec 1977)* Claves ▲ CD 50801 [ADD]

Mircea, George (ten)
Puccini, G.:Turandot, w. Teodora Lucaciu (sop—Liù), Maria Slatinaru (sop—Princess Turandot), Corneliu Fînateanu (ten—Pong), George Mircea (ten—Emperor Altoum), Ludovic Speiss (ten—Prince Calaf), Valentin Teodorian (ten—Pang), Octav Enigarescu (bar—Ping), Dionisie Konya (bar—A Mandarin), Mircea Stefanescu (bar—The Prince of Persia), Nicolae Florei (bass—Timur), C. Litvin (cnd), Romanian Radio–TV Orch, Romanian Radio–TV Chorus *(rec Jan 1970)* Vox Box 2-▲ CDX 5160

Mirella, Luba (sop)
Puccini, G.:La Bohème, w. Luba Mirella (sop—Musetta), Rosetta Pampanini (sop—Mimì), Luigi Marini (ten—Rodolfo), Giuseppe Nessi (ten—Alcindoro), Aristide Baracchi (bar—Schaunard), Gino Vanelli (bar—Marcello), Salvatore Baccaloni (bass—Benoit), Tancredi Pasero (bass—Colline), L. Molajoli (cnd), La Scala Orch, La Scala Chorus Bongiovanni 2-▲ 1125/26 [ADD]

Mirgova, E. (sop)
Mozart, W.A.:Ave verum corpus, w. M. Kozená (cta), J. Griffett (ten), J. Klecker (bass), A. Kroper (cnd), Prague Concertino Nutturno Allegro ▲ ALG PCD 1022 [DDD]
Mozart, W.A.:Requiem, w. M. Kozená (cta), J. Griffett (ten), J. Klecker (bass), A. Kroper (cnd), Prague Concertino Nutturno, Brnensky Academy Choir Allegro ▲ ALG PCD 1022 [DDD]

Miricioiu, Nelly (sop)
Puccini, G.:Tosca, w. G. Lamberti (ten), S. Carroli (bar), A. Rahbari (cnd), Czech–Slovak RSO Bratislava, Slovak Phil Chorus [I] Naxos 2-▲ 8.660001/02 [DDD]
Puccini, G.:Tosca (sels), w. Nelly Miricioiu (sop—Tosca), Giorgio Lamberti (ten—Cavaradossi), Miroslav Dvorsky (ten—Spoletta), Silvano Carroli (bar—Baron Scarpia), Jozef Spaček (bar—Sacristan), Jan Durco (bass—Sciarrone), Stanislav Benačka (bass—Gaoler), A. Rahbari (cnd), Czech–Slovak RSO Bratislava, Slovak Phil Chorus *(rec Concert Hall of the Slovak Radio, Bratislava, Apr. 7–14, 1990)* Naxos ▲ 8.553153 [DDD]

Mirinski, Konstantin (bass)
Gesualdo, D.C.:Madrigals, w. V. Kissyova (sop), N. Pankova (sop), A. Bovarian (alt), V. Vassilev (ten), S. Kralev (cnd), Sofia Madrigal—Io tacerò; Invan dunque o crudele; Moro lasso al mio duolo; Dolcissima mia vita Gega ▲ GD 174 [DDD]
Monteverdi, C.:Madrigals, w. V. Kissyova (sop), N. Pankova (sop), A. Bovarian (alt), V. Vassilev (ten), S. Kralev (cnd), Sofia Madrigal Ensemble—Psalmus 121, "Laetatus sum"; Batto qui pianse; Chiome d'oro; Amor che deggio far?; O come sei gentile; Psalmus 147, "Lauda Jerusalem" Gega ▲ GD 174 [DDD]
Schütz, H.:Motets (misc), w. V. Kissyova (sop), A. Ivanova (sop), N. Pankova (sop), A. Bovarian (alt), V. Vassilev (ten), S. Kralev (cnd), Sofia Madrigal—Christe Deus adjuva; Verbum caro factum est; Te Christe supplex invoco; Veni redemtor gentium; Veni sancte Spiritus Gega ▲ GD 174 [DDD]

Miroshnichenko, Evgenia (sop)
Glière, R.:Con Coloratura Sop, w. M. Ermler (cnd), Bolshoi Theater Orch *(rec 1974)* Consonance ▲ 81 3002 [AAD]

Misciano, Alvinio (ten)
Paisiello, G.:La Molinara, w. Graziella Sciutti (sop), Agostino Lazzari (ten), Sesto Bruscantini (bar), Franco Calabrese (bass), Leonardo Monreale (bass), F. Caracciolo (cnd), Alessandro Scarlatti CO Melodram 2-▲ CDM 29502
Puccini, G.:Tosca, w. M. Olivero (sop), Fioravanti (sgr), F. Vernizzi (cnd), Turin RAI Orch, Turin RAI Chorus *(rec live 1960)* Melodram 2-▲ MEL 27026

▲ = CD ◆ = Enhanced CD Δ = MD ■ = Cassette Tape □ = DCC

Misciano, Alvinio (ten) (cont.)
Puccini, G.:Tosca, w. Magda Olivero (sop), F. Vernizzi (cnd), Turin RAI Orch, Turin RAI Chorus Melodram 2-▲ CDM 27025
Puccini, G.:Tosca (sels), w. M. Olivero (sop), F. Vernizzi (cnd), Turin RAI Orch—3 duets [I] *(rec live, Turin, 3/7/60)* Myto 2-▲ 2 MCD 91136 [ADD]
Rossini, G.:L'italiana in Algeri, w. Teresa Berganza (mez), Sesto Bruscantini (bar), Mario Petri (sgr), N. Sanzogno (cnd), Milan RAI SO, Milan RAI Chorus *(rec June 28, 1957)* Pantheon 2-▲ PHE 6646 (m)
Verdi, G.:Falstaff, w. Anna Moffo (sop—Nannetta), Renata Tebaldi (sop—Alice Ford), Anna Maria Canali (mez—Meg Page), Giulietta Simionato (mez—Dame Quickly), Mariano Caruso (ten—Doctor Caius), Alvinio Misciano (ten—Fenton), Luigi Vellucci (ten—Bardolfo), Tito Gobi (bar—Falstaff), Carnell MacNeil (bar—Ford), Kenneth Smith (bass-Pistola), T. Serafin (cnd), *(orch unknown) (rec Chicago, 1958)* Legato Classics 2-▲ LCD 206-2 [ADD]

Mishenkin, Arkady (ten)
Haydn, J.:The Seven Last Words of Christ on the Cross, w. Elena Evseeva (sop), Margarita Maruna (mez), Boris Bezhko (bass), A. de Almeida (cnd), Moscow SO, Stanislav Gussev (cnd), Russian State Academy Chorus *(rec Mosfilm Studio, Moscow, Jan 27-28, 1995)* SOMM ▲ SOMMCD 203 [DDD]

Mishura-Lekhtman, Irina (mez)
Tchaikovsky, P.:The Snow Maiden, w. Vladimir Grishko (ten), N. Järvi (cnd), Detroit SO, Univ Musical Society Choral Union Chandos ▲ CHAN 9324 [DDD]

Miskell, Austin (ten)
A Musical Portrait *(rec 1952-82)* Cambria ▲ CD 1038 [ADD]
Pergolesi, G.B.:Vocal Music, w. M. Jaenike (cnd), Arte Antica—Laudate Pueri; Messa Solenne; Salve Regina for High Voice; Salve Regina for 2 High Voices & Orchestra; Ten Part Mass in G (sels.) Cambria ▲ 1039 [ADD]
Singer, J.:Songs & Song Cycles, w. F. Hechtel (sop), J. Singer (pno)—American Indian Song Suite; Arno is Deep; From Petrarch; Hannah; Memoria; Lost Garden; Old Wild Woman; Query to the Creator; Songs from Later Years (song cycle); Wry Rimes (song cycle) [E] Cambria ▲ CD 1051
Singer, J.:To Stir a Dream:American Poets in Song, w. F. Hechtel (sop), Jeanne Singer (pno) Cambria ▲ CMB 1051 [DDD]

Missen, Robert (ten)
Somers, H.:Kyrie, w. Roxolana Roslak (sop), Susan Cooper (mez), Nelson Lohnes (bass), Timothy Cadan (bass), E. Iseler (cnd), *(orch unknown)*, Elmer Iseler Singers *(rec Flora McRae Eaton Memorial Auditorium & St. Anne's Anglican Church, Toronto)* Centrediscs ▲ CMC 5495 [DDD]

Missenhardt, Günther (bar)
Mozart, W.A.:Entführung, w. C. Studer (sop), E. Szmytka (sop), K. Streit (ten), R. Gambill (ten), M. Heltau (nar), B. Weil (cnd), Vienna SO, Vienna State Opera Chorus Sony Classical 2-▲ S2K 48053
Mozart, W.A.:Entführung (sels), w. C. Studer (sop), E. Szmytka (sop), K. Streit (ten), R. Gambill (ten), B. Weil (cnd), Vienna SO, Vienna State Opera Chorus *(rec Vienna, Apr. 2-10, 1991)* Sony Classical ("Opera Highlights" series) ▲ SMK 53500 [DDD]

Mitchell, Brenda (sop)
Ferneyhough, B.:Qt 4 Strs, w. Arditti String Quartet Montaigne ▲ MO 782029

Mitchell, C. (sgr)
Rodgers, R.:Carousel, w. Gordon MacRae (sgr), S. Jones (sgr), B. Ruick (sgr), C. Turner (sgr), R. Rounseville (sgr) *(rec 1956)* Broadway Angel ▲ ZDM 64692 ■ EG 64692

Mitchell, Emily (sgr)
James Galway:Seasons, w. James Galway (fl), Chieftans RCA Victor ▲ 09026-61915-2 ■ 09026-61915-4 (CrO2)

Mitchell, Geoffrey (ct)
Purcell, H.:Songs, w. Jean Nibbs (sop), Peter Hall (ten), David Thomas (bass), Margaret Phillips (org), Michael Howard (cnd), Cantores in Ecclesia—Hear My Prayer, O Lord; Song of the 3 Children; Remember Not, Lord, Our Offences; Voluntary for Single Organ; Magnificat & Nunc Dimittis in g; Thy Work is a Lantern; Burial Sentences for Queen Mary [Man That is Born of a Woman; In the Midst of Life We Are in Death; Thou Knowest, Lord, the Secrets of Our Hearts]; O God, Thou Art My God; Magnificat & Nunc Dimittis in B♭; Voluntary on the 100th Psalm Tune; Turn Thou Us, O Good Lord; O Give Thanks Unto the Lord [Psalm 106] IMP ("BBC Radio Classics" series) ▲ IMP 9126

Mitchell, James (nar)
Stravinsky, I.:L'Histoire du soldat, w. M. Douglas (nar), Alvin Epstein (nar), E. Vardi (cnd), Kapp Sinfonietta [E] MCA Classics 2-▲ MCAD2-9820 [AAD]

Mitchell, Leona (sop)
Picker, T.:Sym 2, w. S. Comissiona (cnd), Houston SO Elektra/Nonesuch ▲ 79246-2-ZK
Puccini, G.:Turandot, w. Montserrat Caballé (sop—Turandot), Leona Mitchell (sop—Liu), Remy Corazza (ten—Pang), Joseph Franck (ten—Pong), Robert Johnson (ten—Prince of Persia), Raymond Manton (ten—Altoum), Luciano Pavarotti (ten—Calaf), Aldo Bramante (bar—a mandarin), Dale Duesing (bar—Ping), Giorgio Tozzi (bass—Timur), R. Chailly (cnd), *(orch unknown) (rec San Francisco, Nov. 4, 1977)* Legato Classics 2-▲ LCD 188-2

Mitchinson, John (ten)
Janácek, L.:Slavonic Mass, w. F. Palmer (sop), A. Gunson (mez), M. King (mez), J. Parker-Smith (org), S. Rattle (cnd), City of Birmingham SO, City of Birmingham Sym Chorus EMI ▲ CDC 47504
Liszt, F.:A Faust Sym, w. J. Horenstein (cnd), BBC Northern SO, BBC Northern Singers *(rec live)* Intaglio ▲ INCD 7141 [ADD]
Liszt, F.:A Faust Sym, w. J. Horenstein (cnd), BBC Northern SO, BBC Northern Singers *(rec live Apr. 1972)* Music & Arts ▲ CD 744 [AAD]
Mahler, G.:Das Lied von der Erde, w. A. Hodgson (cta), J. Horenstein (cnd), BBC Northern SO *(rec live, Manchester, April 28, 1972)* Music & Arts ▲ CD 728-1 [AAD]
Martinů, B.:The Greek Passion, w. Helen Field (sop), Phillip Joll (b-bar), John Tomlinson (bass), C. Mackerras (cnd), Brno State PO, Czech Phil Chorus [E] *(rec 1981)* Supraphon 2-▲ 10 3611-2 [DDD]
Maunder, J.H.:From Olivet to Calvary, w. F. Harvey (bar), P. Moorse (org), Guildford Cathedral Choir [E] Classics for Pleasure ▲ CDCFP 4619 [ADD]
Stravinsky, I.:Les Noces, w. A. Mory (sop), P. Parker (mez), P. Hudson (bass), M. Argerich (pno), H. Francesch (pno), K. Zimerman (pno), C. Katsaris (pno), L. Bernstein (cnd), English Bach Festival Orch, English Bach Festival Chorus [R] Deutsche Grammophon ("20th Century Classics" series) ▲ 423251-2 [ADD]

Mitic, N. (bar)
Tchaikovsky, P.:Mazeppa, w. Bakocevic (sgr), Cakarevic (sgr), Cangalovic (sgr), O. Danon (cnd), Belgrade National Opera Orch, Belgrade National Opera Chorus [R] *(rec live, Berlin, 9/27/69)* Myto 2-▲ 2 MCD 90527 [ADD]
Verdi, G.:La traviata, w. M. Caballé (sop), J. Carreras (ten), A. Guadagno (cnd), Philadelphia Lyric Opera Orch, Philadelphia Lyric Opera Chorus *(rec 1973)* Melodram 2-▲ MLO 270106 [ADD]

Mittelmann, Norman (sgr)
Verdi, G.:La forza del destino (sels), w. Raina Kabaivanska (sop), Giuseppe Giacomini (ten), Kurt Moll (bass), J. Rudel (cnd), *(orch unknown)*—Ah per sempre o mio bell'angiol; La vita è inferno all'infelice; Fuggir...ferito siete; Solenne in quest'ora; Fratello...Riconoscimi; Io muoio...confession *(rec Parigi, May 27, 1975)* Golden Age of Opera 2-▲ GAO 189/90 [ADD]

Mitzewa, E. (mez)
Dvořák, A.:Rusalka (sels), w. A. Burmeister (mez), T. Adam (bass-bar), A. Apelt (cnd), Berlin Staatskapelle Berlin Classics ("Eterna" series) ▲ BER 2033 [ADD]

Miura, Jaqueline (sop)
Tchaikovsky, P.:Iolanta, w. Michaela Gurevich (sop—Iolanta), Jaqueline Miura (sop—Brigitta), Tatjana Tabachuk (mez—Martha), Annette Kuhn (mez—Laura), Ian Denolfo (ten—Godefroy), Keith Alexander Bolves (ten—Alméric), Alexander Ben (bar—Robert), Georg Lehner (bar—Ibn-Hakia), Arutiun Kotchinian (bass—René), Kurt Geysen (bass—Bertrand), H. Rotman (cnd), Warsaw PO, ECOV Ensemble Members *(rec Voorruit Center of the Arts, Ghent, Belgium, Aug 28-29, 1993)* CPO 2-▲ CPO 999456-2 [DDD]

Miveloz, Christiane (alt)
Zbinden, J.-F.:Impératifs, w. K. Rosat (sop), Swiss-Italian Radio Chorus [F] Grammont ▲ CTSP 3-2 [ADD]

Mixová, Ivana (mez)
Smetana, B.:The Devil's Wall, w. Milada Šubrtová (sop), Vaclav Bednář (bass), Z. Chalabala (cnd), Prague National Theater Orch, Prague National Theater Chorus *(rec Prague, 1960)* Supraphon 2-▲ SUP 112201 [AAD]

Miyoshi, Akira (nar)
Miyoshi, A.:Poems of Animals, w. Y. Tanaka (pno), F. Kuyiyama (cnd), Chorale OMP Camerata ▲ 32CM-28
Miyoshi, A.:Symphonic Choral Poem, w. Y. Tanaka (pno), M. Asai (pno), F. Kuyiyama (cnd), Chorale OMP Camerata ▲ 32CM-28

Mizrahi, Alberto (ten)
Chants-Mystiques:Hidden Treasures of a Living Tradition, w. Chorale Mystique [cnd:Matthew Lazar] *(rec Jewish Theological Seminary, New York City, Mar & June 1995)* Polygram Classics ("Opus Magica" series) ▲ 314 520 340-2 [DDD]

Mizugushi, Satoshi (bass)
Keiser, R.:Croesus, w. P. Grigorova (sop), M. Klietmann (ten), R. Clemencic (cnd), Clemencic Consort, La Cappella Vocal Ensemble [G] Nuova Era ("Ancient Music" series) 2-▲ 6934/35 [DDD]

Mizzetti (sgr)
Giordano, U.:Fedora, w. R. Tebaldi (sop), G. di Stefano (ten), M. Sereni (bar), A. Basile (cnd), Naples Teatro San Carlo Orch, Naples Teatro San Carlo Chorus [I] *(rec live, 1961)* Legato Classics 2-▲ LCD 158-2 (m) [ADD]

Mkrtchian, Lina (cta)
And Life of the Future Century, w. Leningrad Chamber Choir, Evgeni Talisman (org) Multisonic ("Russian Stars on Classics" series) ▲ MUL 310053 [DDD]
Karetnikov, N.:Till Eulenspiegel, w. E. Mazo (sop), A. Proujanski (ten), B. Koudriavtsev (bar), P. Glouboky (bass), A. Motchalov (bass), A. Martinov (sgr), Polianski (cnd), Soviet Cinema Orch, Soviet Cinema Chorus *(rec Moscow, 1988)* Russian Season ("Russian Season" Series) 2-▲ LDC 288029/30 [DDD]

Mocchiutti, E. (bar)
Massenet, J.:Werther, w. L. Gencer (sop—Carlotta), G. Tavolaccini (sop—Sofia), F. Tagliavini (ten—Werther), M. Borriello (bar—Alberto), E. Mocchiutti (bar—Johann), V. Susca (bass—Il Podestà), R. Botteghelli (bass—Schmidt), C.F. Cillario (cnd), *(orch unknown)* Arkadia 2-▲ 599 [ADD]

Modenos, John (bar)
Glanville-Hicks, P.:Nausicaa, w. Teresa Stratas (sop—Nausicaa), Sophia Steffan (cta—Queen Arete), Michalis Heliotis (ten—Antinous/Priest), George Moutsios (ten—Eurymachus), Edward Ruhl (ten—Phemius), George Tsantikos (ten—Clytoneus), Vassilis Koundouris (bar—Messenger), John Modenos (bar—Aethon), Spiro Malas (bass—King Alcinous), C. Surinach (cnd), Athens SO, Athens Sym Chorus *(rec Athens Festival, 1961)* CRI ▲ CD 695 [ADD]

Modesti, Guiseppe (bass)
Bellini, V.:I Puritani (sels), w. J. Sutherland (sop), N. Filacuridi (sgr), E. Blanc (bar), *(orch unknown) (rec live, Edinburgh, Sept. 8, 1960)* Standing Room Only 2-▲ SRO 841-2 [ADD]
Bellini, V.:La sonnambula, w. M. Callas (sop), G. Carturan (mez), C. Valletti (ten), L. Bernstein (cnd), La Scala Orch, La Scala Chorus [I] *(rec live, 3/5/55)* Myto 2-▲ 2 MCD 89006 (m) [ADD]
Cherubini, L.:Médée, w. M. Callas (sop), F. Barbieri (mez), G. Penno (ten), Nache (sgr), L. Bernstein (cnd), La Scala Orch, La Scala Chorus [I] *(rec live, Milan 12/10/53)* Verona 2-▲ 27088/89
Cherubini, L.:Médée, w. M. Callas (sop), F. Barbieri (mez), G. Penno (ten), Nache (sgr), L. Bernstein (cnd), La Scala Orch, La Scala Chorus [I] *(rec live 12/10/53)* Melodram 2-▲ MEL 26022 (m) [AAD]
Donizetti, G.:Lucia di Lammermoor, w. Maria Callas (sop), Eugenio Fernandi (ten), Rolando Panerai (bar), T. Serafin (cnd), Rome RAI SO, Rome RAI Chorus *(rec live, Rome, 1957)* Enterprise ("Documents" series) 2-▲ ENTLV 973 [ADD]
Donizetti, G.:Lucia di Lammermoor, w. M. Callas (sop), G. di Stefano (ten), G. Zampieri (ten), R. Panerai (bar), H. von Karajan (cnd), La Scala Orch, La Scala Chorus *(rec 1954)* Melodram 2-▲ MLO 26040 [DDD]
Verdi, G.:Oberto, Conte di San Bonifacio, w. Elena Nicolai (mez), Gino Bonelli (sgr), Lydia Roan (sgr), Maria Vitale (sgr), A. Simonetto (cnd), Turin RAI Orch, Turin RAI Chorus Great Opera Performances 2-▲ GOP 774

Mödl, Martha (sop/mez)
Beethoven, L. van:Fidelio, w. S. Jurinac (sop), W. Windgassen (ten), A. Poell (bar), O. Edelmann (bass), G. Frick (bass), W. Furtwängler (cnd), Vienna PO *(rec Oct. 1953)* EMI Classics 2-▲ CDHB 64496
Martha Mödl Sings, w. Berlin State Opera Orch [cnd:Arthur Rother, Hans Löwlein] *(rec 1951-62)* Preiser ▲ PRE 90136 (m) [AAD]
Mussorgsky, M.:Boris Godunov, w. Martha Mödl (sop—Marina Mniszek), Lotte Schädle (sop—Xenia), Dorothea Siebert (mez—Fyodor), Hertha Töpper (mez—Xenia's wet-nurs), Karl Hermann Bennert (Boyer Khrushchyov), Lorenz Fehenberger (ten—Prince Shuysky), Hans Hopf (ten—Grigory), Karl Ostertag (ten—Missail), Hans Hotter (b-bar—Boris Godunov), Hermann Uhde (bar—Andrey Shchelkalov), Kurt Böhme (bass—Varlaam), Kim Borg (bass—Pimen), Kieth Engen (bass—Lewicki), Adolf Keil (bass—Nikitich), Benno Kusche (bar—Rangoni), Heinz Maria Linz (bass—Czernikowski), E. Jochum (cnd), Bavarian RSO, Bavarian Radio Chorus *(rec Munich, May 1957)* Myto 3-▲ MCD 953131
Strauss, R.:Elektra, w. A. Varnay (sop/mez), H. Hillebrecht (sop), J. King (ten), E. Wächter (bar), H. von Karajan (cnd), Vienna PO, Vienna State Opera Chorus [G] *(rec 1964)* Melodram 2-▲ MEL 27044 [AAD]
Verdi, G.:Un ballo in maschera, w. Martha Mödl (sop—Ulrica), Walburga Wegner (sop—Amelia), Anny Schlemm (mez—Oscar), Lorenz Fehenberger (ten—Ricardo), Dietrich Fischer-Dieskau (bar—Renato), Wilhelm Schirp (bass—Samuel), Willy Schoneweib (bass—Tom), Gunther Wilhelms (bass—Silvan), Fritz Augustin (sgr—Ein Richter), Friedrich Himmelmann (sgr—Ein Diener Amelia), F. Busch (cnd), Cologne RSO, Bernhard Alois Zimmermann (cnd), Cologne Radio Chorus Calig 2-▲ 50946/47 (m) [ADD]
Wagner, R.:Der Ring des Nibelungen, w. B. Nilsson (sop), L. Rysanek (sop), K. Dvořaková (sop), A. Burmeister (mez), V. Soukupova (mez), E. Wohlfahrt (ten), W. Windgassen (ten), T. Stewart (bar), T. Adam (b-bar), G. Neidlinger (b-bar), K. Böhme (bass), G. Nienstedt (bass), K. Böhm (cnd), Bayreuth Festival Orch, Bayreuth Festival Chorus [G] *(rec live, 1966-67)* Philips 14-▲ 420325-2 [ADD]
Wagner, R.:Tristan und Isolde, w. R. Vinay (ten), H. Hotter (b-bar), H. von Karajan (cnd), Bayreuth Festival Orch, Bayreuth Festival Chorus *(rec 1955)* Arkadia 4-▲ 528 (m) [AAD]
Wagner, R.:Tristan und Isolde (sels), w. Martha Mödl (sop—Isolde), Johanna Blatter (mez—Brangäne), Wolfgang Windgassen (ten—Tristan), A. Rother (cnd), Berlin City Opera Orch—Weh, ach wehe! dies zu dulden [rec. Nov 24., 1954]; Isolde!— Tristan! Geliebter! [rec. Oct. 24, 1954]; Lausch', Geliebter!— Lass mich sterben! [rec. Oct 24., 1954]; Mild und leise wie er lächelt [rec. Oct 22., 1952] Teldec ("Historic" series) ▲ 95516-2 [ADD]

Moffat, Julie (sop)
Dallapiccola, L.:choral music, w. H. Zender (cnd), Ensemble InterContemporain, James Wood (cnd), New London Chamber Choir—Canti di Prigionia; Cinque Frammenti di Saffo; Due Liriche di Anacreonte; Sex Carmina Alcaei; Tempus Destruendi; Tempus Aedificandi; Due Cori di Michelangelo Buonarroti il Giovane Erato ▲ ERA 98509 [DDD]
Zimmermann, B.A.:Omnia tempus habent, w. H. Zender (cnd), Ensemble Modern *(rec Frankfurt, May 1-4 & Oct 24-25, 1992)* RCA Red Seal ▲ 09026-61181-2 [DDD]

Moffo, Anna (sop)
Basic 100, Vol. 33, w. Artur Rubinstein (pno), Fritz Reiner (cnd), Leopold Stokowski (cnd) RCA Victor ▲ 09026-61851-2 ■ 09026-61851-4
"La Bellisima":Anna Moffo, the Debut Recordings, w. Philharmonia Orch, La Scala Orch [cnd:C. Davis, A. Galliera, A. Votto] *(rec 1956-59)* EMI Classics ▲ CDM 63413
Canteloube, J.:Songs of Auvergne (sels), w. L. Stokowski (cnd), American SO—7 songs RCA Gold Seal ▲ 7831-2-RG [ADD] ■ 7831-4-RG (CrO2)
Donizetti, G.:La fille du régiment, w. J. Gardino (mez), G. Campora (ten), G. Fioravanti (bar), F. Mannino (cnd), Milan RAI Orch, Milan RAI Chorus *(rec live Dec 2, 1960)* Melodram 2-▲ MEL 27018 [ADD]
Donizetti, G.:Lucia di Lammermoor, w. C. Bergonzi (ten), M. Sereni (bar), E. Flagello (bass), G. Prêtre (cnd), RCA Italian Opera Orch [I] RCA Gold Seal 2-▲ 6504-2-RG [ADD]
The Early Years:1956-1960 *(rec live in performance in Italy and Austria)* Legato Classics ("Biographies in Music" series) ▲ BIM 714-1

VOCALISTS

Moffo, Anna (sop) (cont.)
Gatta, Moffo, Rizzieri, Christoff & Mazzolli, w. Dora Gatta (sop), Elena Rizzieri (sop), Boris Christoff (bass), Ferruccio Mazzoli (bass), Rome RAI SO, Turin RAI SO *(rec Martini & Rossi Concert)* Incontri Memorabili ▲ CDMR 5033
Gluck, C.W.:Orfeo ed Euridice, w. J. Raskin (sop), S. Verrett (mez), R. Fasano (cnd), Collegium Musicum Italicum Instrumental Ensemble, Rome Virtuosi RCA Gold Seal 2-▲ 7896-2-RG [ADD]
Moffo & Volpi, w. Giacomo Lauri Volpi (ten), Milan RAI SO [cnd:Alfredo Simonetto], Rome RAI SO [cnd:Massimo Freccia] *(rec Martini & Rossi Concert, 1960)* Incontri Memorabili ▲ CDMR 5035
Mozart, W.A.:Nozze di Figaro, w. E. Schwarzkopf (sop), F. Cossotto (mez), G. Taddei (bar), E. Wächter (bar), C. M. Giulini (cnd), Philharmonia Orch, Philharmonia Chorus [I] EMI Classics ("Studio" series) 2-▲ CDMB 63266 [ADD]
Mozart, W.A.:Nozze di Figaro (sels), w. E. Schwarzkopf (sop), F. Cossotto (mez), G. Taddei (bar), E. Wächter (bar), C. M. Giulini (cnd), Philharmonia Orch, Philharmonia Chorus—sels. EMI Classics ("Studio" series) ▲ CDM 63409
Puccini, G.:La Bohème, w. M. Callas (sop), G. di Stefano (ten), R. Panerai (bar), A. Votto (cnd), La Scala Orch, La Scala Chorus [I] *(rec 1956)* EMI Classics 2-▲ CDCB 47475 (m) [ADD]
Puccini, G.:La Bohème, w. F. Costa (mez), G. Tucker (ten), R. Merrill (bar), G. Tozzi (bass), E. Leinsdorf (cnd), Rome Opera Orch, Rome Opera Chorus [I] RCA Gold Seal 2-▲ 3969-2-RG [ADD] 2-■ 3969-4-RG (CrO2)
Puccini, G.:La Bohème (sels), w. F. Costa (mez), G. Tucker (ten), R. Merrill (bar), G. Tozzi (bass), E. Leinsdorf (cnd), Rome Opera Orch, Rome Opera Chorus RCA Gold Seal ▲ 60189-2-RG [ADD] ■ 60189-4-RG (CrO2)
Puccini, G.:Madama Butterfly, w. R. Elias (mez), C. Valletti (ten), R. Cesari (bar), E. Leinsdorf (cnd), Rome Opera Orch, Rome Opera Chorus [I] RCA Gold Seal 2-▲ 4145-2-RG [ADD]
Puccini, G.:Madama Butterfly, w. R. Elias (mez), C. Valletti (ten), R. Cesari (bar), E. Leinsdorf (cnd), Rome Opera Orch, Rome Opera Chorus [I] RCA Gold Seal ▲ 60202-2-RG [ADD] ■ 60202-4-RG
Puccini, G.:Turandot, w. B. Nilsson (sop—Turnadot), A. Moffo (sop—Liù), F. Corelli (ten—Calaf), C. Anthony (ten—Pong), R. Nagy (ten—Pang), F. Guarrera (bar—Ping), B. Giaiotti (bass—Timur), L. Stokowski (cnd), Metropolitan Opera Orch, New York Metropolitan Opera Chorus *(rec Mar. 4, 1961)* Datum 2-▲ DAT 12301 [ADD]
Rachmaninoff, S.:Music of, w. Alexander Brailowsky (pno), Alexis Weissenberg (pno), Leonard Pennario (pno) (cnd) (cnd), *(orch unknown)* RCA ■ 5697-4-RV
Rachmaninoff, S.:Vocalise, w. L. Stokowski (cnd), American SO RCA Gold Seal ▲ 7831-2-RG [ADD] ■ 7831-4-RG (CrO2)
Strauss, R.:Capriccio, w. E. Schwarzkopf (sop), C. Ludwig (mez), N. Gedda (ten), D. Fischer-Dieskau (bar), E. Wächter (bar), H. Hotter (b-bar), W. Sawallisch (cnd), Philharmonia Orch [G] EMI Classics 2-▲ CDCB 49014 (m) [ADD]
Verdi, G.:Falstaff, w. Anna Moffo (sop—Nannetta), Renata Tebaldi (sop—Alice Ford), Anna Maria Canali (mez—Meg Page), Giulietta Simionato (mez—Dame Quickly), Mariano Caruso (ten—Doctor Caius), Alvinio Misciano (ten—Fenton), Luigi Vellucci (ten—Bardolfo), Tito Gobi (bar—Falstaff), Carnell MacNeil (bar—Ford), Kenneth Smith (bass-Pistola), T. Serafin (cnd), *(orch unknown)* *(rec Chicago, 1958)* Legato Classics 2-▲ LCD 206-2 [ADD]
Verdi, G.:Luisa Miller, w. S. Verrett (mez), C. Bergonzi (ten), C. MacNeil (bar), G. Tozzi (bass), F. Cleva (cnd), RCA Italian Opera Orch [I] RCA Gold Seal 2-▲ 6646-2-RG [ADD]
Verdi, G.:Rigoletto, w. R. Elias (mez), A. Kraus (ten), R. Merrill (bar), G. Solti (cnd), RCA Italian Opera Orch, RCA Italiana Opera Chorus [I] RCA Gold Seal 2-▲ 6506-2-RG [ADD]
Verdi, G.:Rigoletto, w. R. Elias (mez), A. Kraus (ten), R. Merrill (bar), G. Solti (cnd), RCA Italian Opera Orch, RCA Italiana Opera Chorus [I] RCA Gold Seal ▲ 60203-2-RG ■ 60203-4-RG
Verdi, G.:La traviata, w. G. Janowitz (sop), G. Zampieri (ten), E. Bastianini (bar), B. Klobucar (cnd), Vienna State Opera Orch, Vienna State Opera Chorus [I] *(rec live, Vienna, 1964)* Melodram (Connaisseur) 2-▲ CDM 27510 [ADD]
Verdi, G.:La traviata, w. G. Tucker (ten), R. Merrill (bar), F. Previtali (cnd), Rome Opera Orch [I] RCA Gold Seal ▲ 60204-2-RG [ADD] ■ 60204-4-RG
Verdi, G.:La traviata, w. G. Tucker (ten), R. Merrill (bar), F. Previtali (cnd), Rome Opera Orch [I] RCA Gold Seal 2-▲ 4144-2-RG [ADD] 2-■ 4144-4-RG
Villa-Lobos, H.:Bachiana brasileira 5, w. L. Stokowski (cnd), American SO RCA Gold Seal ▲ 7831-2-RG [ADD] ■ 7831-4-RG (CrO2)
Villa-Lobos, H.:Bachiana brasileira 5, w. L. Stokowski (cnd), American SO RCA Victor ▲ 09026-61724-2 ■ 09026-61724-4 (CrO2)
World Stars Sing Operetta, w. Lucia Popp (sop), José Carreras (ten), Ants Kollo (ten), Thomas Moser (ten), Giuseppe Di Stefano (ten), Hermann Prey (bar), Karl Ridderbusch (bass), et al., various orchs *(rec 1968-1985)* Acanta ▲ 42941

Mohr, Thomas (bar)
Marschner, H.A.:Hans Heiling, w. M. Hajóssyová (sop), E. Seniglova (sop), M. Eklöf (mez), K. Markus (ten), L. Neshyba (bass), E. Körner (cnd), Slovak PO, Slovak Phil Chorus [G] Marco Polo ("Opera Rara" series) 2-▲ 8.223306/07 [DDD]
Orff, C.:Carmina burana, w. Lisa Griffith (sop), Ulrich Ress (ten), M. Tang (cnd), Royal Flemish PO, Frankfurt Figuralchor, Frankfurt Children's Choir, Frankfurt Choral Society, Goethe Academy Children's Choir *(rec Oct. 1993)* Wergo ▲ WER 6602-2 [DDD]
Weill, K.:Mahagonny, w. U. Lemper (sop), H. Jungwirth (sop), H. Wildhaber (ten), P. Haage (ten), S. Tremper (sgr), Jeffrey Cohen (pno), J. Mauceri (cnd), Berlin RIAS Chamber Ensemble [G] London ▲ 430168-2 [DDD]
Weill, K.:The Seven Deadly Sins, w. U. Lemper (sop), H. Jungwirth (sop), H. Wildhaber (ten), P. Haage (ten), S. Tremper (sgr), J. Mauceri (cnd), Berlin RIAS Chamber Ensemble [G] London ▲ 430168-2 [DDD]

Moisa, Mircea (bass)
Puccini, G.:Madama Butterfly, w. Eugenia Moldoveanu (sop—Madama Butterfly), Mihaela Agachi (mez—Suzuki), Corina Circa (mez—Kate Pinkerton), Emil Gherman (ten—B.F. Pinkerton), Stefan Popescu (ten—Goro), Ioan Soanea (bar—The Bonze/Yakuside), Eduard Tumageanian (bar—Sharpless), Alexandru Kopeczi (bass—Prince Yamadori), Mircea Moisa (bass—Commissioner), P. Popescu (cnd), Satu Mare PO, Cluj-Napoca Phil Chorus *(rec 1979)* Vox Box 2-▲ CDX 5155

Mok, Judith (sop)
Hamburg, J.:Zey, w. L. Markiz (cnd), Amsterdam New Sinfonietta NM Classics ▲ NM 92041

Mok, Warren (ten)
Mendelssohn, F.:Die Hochzeit des Camacho, w. R. Schudel (sop—Quiteria), C. Swanson (sop—Lucinda), C. Bieber (ten—Basilio), W. Mok (ten—Vivaldo), V. Horn (ten—Camacho), R. Lukas (bar—Carrasco), J. Becker (bass—Sancho Panza), W. Murray (bass—Don Quixote), B. Klee (cnd), Berlin RSO, Berlin Radio Chorus [G] Koch Schwann 2-▲ 314042 [DDD]

Mola, Cinzia de (cta)
Wolf-Ferrari, E.:Il campiello, w. D. Mazzucato (Gasparina), G. Devinu (Lucieta), M. Bolgan (Gnese), C. de Mola (Orsola), U. Benelli (Dona Cate Panciana), M. Rene Cosotti (Dona Pasqua Polegana), M. Comencini (Zorozeto), M. Biscotti (Astolfi), I. D'Arcangelo (Anzoleto), C. Striuli (Fabrizio del Ritorti), N. Bareza (cnd), Trieste Teatro Comunale Giuseppe Verdi Orch, Trieste Teatro Comunale G. Verdi Chorus *(rec Feb. 1992)* Ricordi 2-▲ RFCD 2014 [DDD]

Moldoveanu, Eugenia (sop)
Puccini, G.:La Bohème, w. Elvira Cirje-Druica (sop—Musetta), Eugenia Moldoveanu (sop—Mimi), Andrei Borsos (ten—Parpignol), Constantin Gabor (ten—Alcindoro), Ludovic Spiess (ten—Rodolfo), Lucian Marinescu (bar—Schaunard), David Ohanesian (bar—Marcello), Pompei Harasteanu (bass—Benoit), Dan Zancu (bass—Colline), C. Petrovici (cnd), Romanian Opera Orch, Romanian Opera Chorus *(rec 1982)* Vox Box 2-▲ CDX 5156
Puccini, G.:Madama Butterfly, w. Eugenia Moldoveanu (sop—Madama Butterfly), Mihaela Agachi (mez—Suzuki), Corina Circa (mez—Kate Pinkerton), Emil Gherman (ten—B.F. Pinkerton), Stefan Popescu (ten—Goro), Ioan Soanea (bar—The Bonze/Yakuside), Eduard Tumageanian (bar—Sharpless), Alexandru Kopeczi (bass—Prince Yamadori), Mircea Moisa (bass—Commissioner), P. Popescu (cnd), Satu Mare PO, Cluj-Napoca Phil Chorus *(rec 1979)* Vox Box 2-▲ CDX 5155

Moldoveanu, Vasile (ten)
Verdi, G.:La traviata, w. Elena Simionescu (sop—Annina), Virginia Zeani (sop—Violetta Valery), Elisabeta Neculce-Cartis (mez—Flora Bervoix), Ion Buzea (ten—Alfredo Germont), Vasile Moldoveanu (ten—Gastone/Viconte de Letorieres/Giuseppe), Teodor Panea (ten—Flora's Servant), Constantin Dumitru (bar—Commissioner/Baron Douphol), Nicolae Herlea (bar—Giorgio Germont), Valentin Loghin (bass—Marchese D'Obigny), Nicolae Rafael (bass—Doctor Grenvil), J. Bobescu (cnd), Romanian Opera Orch, Stelian Olariu (cnd), Romanian Opera Chorus *(rec 1968)* Vox Box 2-▲ CDX 5154

Moldvay, József (bass)
Esterházy, P.:Harmonia caelestis, w. M. Fers (sop), M. Zádori (sop), K. Gémes (mez), K. Károlyi (cta), G. Kállay (ten), P. Németh (cnd), Capella Savaria, Savaria Vocal Ensemble [period instrs] [L] Hungaroton 2-▲ HCD 31148/49 [DDD]
Handel, G.F.:St. John Passion, w. Mária Z[ádori (sop), Judit Németh (mez), Charles Brett (ct), Martin Klietmann (ten), G. Németh (cnd), Capella Savaria, Capella Savaria Hungaroton ▲ HCD 12908 [DDD]
Haydn, M.:Missa Pro Defuncto Archiepiscopo Sigismundo, w. Ibolya Verebics (sop), Judit Németh (mez), Martin Klietmann (ten), H. Rilling (cnd), Franz Liszt CO, Hungarian Radio-TV Chorus [L] Hungaroton ▲ HCD 31022 [DDD]
Haydn, M.:Missa Sancti Francisci, w. Ibolya Verebics (sop), Judit Németh (mez), Martin Klietmann (ten), H. Rilling (cnd), Franz Liszt CO, Hungarian Radio-TV Chorus [L] Hungaroton ▲ HCD 31022 [DDD]
Liszt, F.:An die Künstler, w. A. Molnár (ten), T. Daróczi (ten), L. Domahidy Jr. (bass), I. Zámbó (cnd), Hungarian State Orch, Hungarian People's Army Male Chorus [G] Hungaroton ▲ HCD 12748 [DDD]
Mozart, W.A.:Alma Dei creatoris, w. Ibolya Verebics (sop), Judit Németh (cta), József Mukk (ten), Gábor Oláh (bar), István Ella (org), János Reményi (cnd), Hungarian Radio-TV Children's Chorus Girls' Voices, Hungarian Radio-TV Male Chamber Choir *(rec Hungaroton Studio, June 14-16, 1991)* Hungaroton ▲ HCD 4003 [DDD]
Mozart, W.A.:Ave verum corpus, w. Ibolya Verebics (sop), Judit Németh (cta), József Mukk (ten), Gábor Oláh (bar), István Ella (org), János Reményi (cnd), Hungarian Radio-TV Children's Chorus Girls' Voices, Hungarian Radio-TV Male Chamber Choir *(rec Hungaroton Studio, June 14-16, 1991)* Hungaroton ▲ HCD 4003 [DDD]
Mozart, W.A.:Miserere, w. Ibolya Verebics (sop), Judit Németh (cta), József Mukk (ten), Gábor Oláh (bar/Gregorian intonations), István Ella (org), János Reményi (cnd), Hungarian Radio-TV Children's Chorus Girls' Voices, Hungarian Radio-TV Male Chamber Choir *(rec Hungaroton Studio, June 14-16, 1991)* Hungaroton ▲ HCD 4003 [DDD]
Mozart, W.A.:Misericordias Domini, w. Ibolya Verebics (sop), Judit Németh (cta), József Mukk (ten), Gábor Oláh (bar/Gregorian intonations), István Ella (org), János Reményi (cnd), Hungarian Radio-TV Children's Chorus Girls' Voices, Hungarian Radio-TV Male Chamber Choir *(rec Hungaroton Studio, June 14-16, 1991)* Hungaroton ▲ HCD 4003 [DDD]
Mozart, W.A.:Missa brevis, K.65, w. Ibolya Verebics (sop), Judit Németh (cta), József Mukk (ten), Gábor Oláh (bar/Gregorian intonations), István Ella (org), János Reményi (cnd), Hungarian Radio-TV Children's Chorus Girls' Voices, Hungarian Radio-TV Male Chamber Choir *(rec Hungaroton Studio, June 14-16, 1991)* Hungaroton ▲ HCD 4003 [DDD]
Mozart, W.A.:Missa brevis, K.194, w. Ibolya Verebics (sop), Judit Németh (cta), József Mukk (ten), Gábor Oláh (bar/Gregorian intonations), István Ella (org), János Reményi (cnd), Hungarian Radio-TV Children's Chorus Girls' Voices, Hungarian Radio-TV Male Chamber Choir *(rec Hungaroton Studio, June 14-16, 1991)* Hungaroton ▲ HCD 4003 [DDD]
Mozart, W.A.:Sancta Maria, w. Ibolya Verebics (sop), Judit Németh (cta), József Mukk (ten), Gábor Oláh (bar/Gregorian intonations), István Ella (org), János Reményi (cnd), Hungarian Radio-TV Children's Chorus Girls' Voices, Hungarian Radio-TV Male Chamber Choir *(rec Hungaroton Studio, June 14-16, 1991)* Hungaroton ▲ HCD 4003 [DDD]

Molese, Michele (ten)
Bizet, G.:Carmen (sels), w. M. Horne (sop), M. Pellegrini (sgr), G. Griffiths (bar), D. Bowman (bar), F. Egerton (ten), H. Lewis (cnd), Royal PO, Royal Liverpool Phil Choir IMP Collectors Series ▲ IMPX 9016 [AAD]
Mercadante, S.:Il giuramento, w. P. Wells (sop), B. Wolff (mez), G. Colmagro (bar), T. Schippers (cnd), Juilliard Orch, Juilliard Chorus [I] *(rec live, Spoleto, 6/29/70)* Memories 2-▲ HR 4174/75 (m)
Mercadante, S.:Il giuramento, w. P. Wells (sop), B. Wolff (mez), G. Colmagro (bar), T. Schippers (cnd), Juilliard Orch, Juilliard Chorus [I] *(rec live, Spoleto, 6/29/70)* Myto 2-▲ 2 MCD 90632 [ADD]

Molin, Conny (sgr)
Verdi, G.:La traviata, w. Hjördis Schymberg (sop), Jussi Björling (ten), H. Sandberg (cnd), Stockholm Royal Opera House Orch, Stockholm Royal Opera Chorus Grammofono 2000 2-▲ GRM 78640
Verdi, G.:La traviata, w. Hjördis Schymberg (sop), Jussi Björling (ten), H. Sandberg (cnd), Stockholm Royal Opera House Orch, Stockholm Royal Theater Opera Chorus Enterprise ("The 40's" series) 2-▲ ENT 331
Verdi, G.:La traviata, w. H. Schymberg (sop), Alard (sgr), J. Björling (ten), H. Sandberg (cnd), *(orch unknown)* *(rec live 8/29/39)* Standing Room Only 2-▲ SRO 832-2 [ADD]

Molinar, Martha (sop)
Delgado, F.:Choral Music, w. Luz Angélica Uribe (sop), Ana Paula Abitia (mez), Alfredo Mendoza (ten), Noé Colín (bass), B. J. Echenique (cnd), Mexico City CO, Alfredo Mendoza (cnd), Schola Cantorum—Te Deum al Sr. Felipe de Jesús Urtext ▲ URT 2001 [DDD]
Jerusalem, I.:Choral Music, w. Luz Angélica Uribe (sop), Ana Paula Abitia (mez), Alfredo Mendoza (ten), Noé Colín (bass), B. J. Echenique (cnd), Mexico City CO, Alfredo Mendoza (cnd), Schola Cantorum—Magnificat a Dos Voces; Misa en Sol Mayor a 8 Voces Urtext ▲ URT 2001 [DDD]

Molinari, Enrico (bar)
Donizetti, G.:Lucia di Lammermoor, w. M. Capsir (sop—Lucia), E. de Muro Lomanto (ten—Sir Ravenswood), E. Venturini (ten—Lord Bucklaw), E. Molinari (bar—Lord Ashton), S. Baccaloni (bass—Bidebent), L. Molajoli (cnd), La Scala Orch, La Scala Chorus *(rec 1933)* Myto 2-▲ 2MCD 94299
Enrico Molinari *(rec 1924-30)* Preiser ("Lebendige Vergangenheit" series) ▲ PRE CD 89129
Verdi, G.:Il trovatore, w. Bianca Scacciati (sop), Giuseppina Zinetti (sop), Francesco Merli (ten), L. Molajoli (cnd), Milan SO, La Scala Chorus *(rec live, 1930)* Melodram ▲ CDI 202002

Moliner, N. (bar)
Gluck, C.W.:Alceste, w. K. Flagstad (sop—Alceste), A. Engeboll (ten—Admetus), N. Moliner (bar—High Priest) [French version] *(rec Apr. 14, 1957)* Eklipse 2-▲ EKR 24

Moliterno, Mark (bar)
Luening, O.:No Jerusalem But This, w. K. Sullivan (sop), Jacqueline Pierce (sop), Paul Sperry (ten), P. Wilder (sgr), S. Rosser (sgr), A. Goodman (cnd), Music Project CO, Goodman Chamber Choir [E] *(rec 6/6/90)* CRI ▲ CD 600 [DDD]

Moll, Kurt (bass)
Beethoven, L. van:Fidelio, w. J. Norman (sop), P. Coburn (sop), R. Goldberg (ten), H.-P. Blochwitz (ten), B. Haitink (cnd), Dresden Staatskapelle, Dresden State Chorus Philips ▲ 438496-2
Beethoven, L. van:Fidelio, w. J. Norman (sop), P. Coburn (sop), R. Goldberg (ten), H.-P. Blochwitz (ten), A. Schmidt (bar), E. Wlaschiha (bass), B. Haitink (cnd), Dresden Staatskapelle, Dresden State Chorus [G] Philips 2-▲ 426308-2 [DDD]
Beethoven, L. van:Missa Solemnis, w. C. Studer (sop), J. Norman (sop), P. Domingo (ten), J. Levine (cnd), Vienna PO, Leipzig Radio Chorus, Eric Ericson Chamber Chorus Deutsche Grammophon 2-▲ 435770-2 [DDD]
Beethoven, L. van:Missa Solemnis, w. E. Moser (sop), H. Schwarz (mez), A. Kollo (ten), L. Bernstein (cnd), Royal Concertgebouw Orch, Hilversum Chorus [L] Deutsche Grammophon 2-▲ 413780-2 [ADD]
Berg, A.:Lulu, w. A. Silja (sop), B. Fassbaender (mez), W. Berry (b-bar), H. Hotter (b-bar), A. Szramek (sgr), C. von Dohnányi (cnd), Vienna PO London 2-▲ 430415-2 [DDD]
Bruckner, A.:Mass 3, w. K. Mattila (sop), M. Lipovšek (mez), T. Moser (ten), C. Davis (cnd), Bavarian RSO, Bavarian Radio Chorus [L] Philips ▲ 422358-2 [DDD]
Charpentier, M.-A.:Magnificat, w. D. Upshaw (sop), A. Murray (mez), E. Robinson (mez), J. Aler (ten), N. Marriner (cnd), Academy of St. Martin in the Fields, Academy of St. Martin in the Fields Chorus EMI Classics ▲ CDC 54284

▲ = CD ♦ = Enhanced CD ∆ = MD ■ = Cassette Tape ◻ = DCC

Moll, Kurt (bass) (cont.)

Charpentier, M.-A.:Te Deum in C, w. D. Upshaw (sop), A. Murray (mez), E. Robinson (mez), J. Aler (ten), N. Marriner (cnd), Academy of St. Martin in the Fields, Academy of St. Martin in the Fields Chorus — EMI Classics ▲ CDC 54284

Famous Opera Arias, w. Munich Radio Orch [cnd:Kurt Eichhorn] — Orfeo ▲ C 009821 A [DDD]

Haydn, J.:Mass 3, "Cäcilienmesse", w. Lucia Popp (sop), Doris Soffel (mez), Rudolf Laubenthal (ten), R. Kubelik (cnd), Bavarian RSO, Bavarian Radio Chorus [L] — Orfeo 2-▲ 032822 [DDD]

Haydn, J.:Die Schöpfung, w. Kathleen Battle (sop), Gösta Winbergh (ten), J. Levine (cnd), Berlin PO, Stockholm Radio Chorus, Stockholm Chamber Choir — Deutsche Grammophon 2-▲ 427629-2 [DDD]

Haydn, J.:Die Schöpfung, w. Helena Döse (sop—Eva), Lucia Popp (sop—Gabriel), Werner Hollweg (ten—Uriel), Benjamin Luxon (bar—Adam), Kurt Moll (bass—Raphael), Jack McCormack (db), David Strange (vc), Antál Dorati (hpd), A. Dorati (cnd), Royal PO, Brighton Festival Chorus *(rec Kingsway Hall, London, Dec 1976)* — London 2-▲ 443027-2 [ADD]

Loewe, C.:Songs, w. Cord Garben (pno)—Kleiner Haushalt; Die Heinzalmännchen; Heinrich der Vogler; Das Vaterland; Der Nöck; Liederkranz for Bass, Op. 145; Prinz Eugen; Archibald Douglas *(rec Radio Berlin, Nov 1994)* — CPO ▲ 999306-2 [DDD]

Mozart, W.A.:Complete Mozart Edition, w. M. Price (sop), L. Serra (sop), R. Tear (ten), P. Schreier (ten), T. Adam (b-bar), C. Davis (cnd), Dresden Staatskapelle, Dresden State Chorus — Philips 3-▲ 422543-2 [ADD]

Mozart, W.A.:Don Giovanni, w. L. Price (sop), L. Popp (sop), S. Sass (sop), S. Burrows (ten), G. Bacquier (bar), B. Weikl (bar), A. Sramek (bar), G. Solti (cnd), London PO, London Opera Chorus — London ("Grand Opera" series) 3-▲ 425169-2 [ADD]

Mozart, W.A.:Missa, K.427, w. K. Battle (sop), L. Cuberli (sop), P. Seiffert (ten), J. Levine (cnd), Vienna PO, Vienna State Opera Chorus — Deutsche Grammophon ▲ 423664-2 [DDD]

Mozart, W.A.:Nozze di Figaro, w. K. Te Kanawa (sop), L. Popp (sop), F. von Stade (mez), T. Allen (bar), S. Ramey (bass), G. Solti (cnd), London PO [I] — London 3-▲ 410150-2 [DDD]

Mozart, W.A.:Nozze di Figaro, w. Mirella Freni (sop), Gundala Janowitz (sop), Jane Berbié (mez), Frederica von Stade (mez), Michel Sénéchal (ten), José Van Dam (b-bar), G. Solti (cnd), Paris Opera Orch, Paris Opera Chorus *(rec live, Paris, Apr 7, 1973)* — Agorá ("Phoenix" series) 3-▲ 515

Mozart, W.A.:Nozze di Figaro, w. C. Margiono (sop), B. Bonney (sop), I. Rey (sop), A. Murray (mez, P.-L. Lang (mez), P. Langridge (ten), C. Späth (ten), T. Hampson (bar), K. Moll (bass), A. Scharinger (bass), K. Langan (bass), N. Harnoncourt (cnd), Royal Concertgebouw Orch, Netherlands Opera Chorus *(rec Amsterdam, May 1993)* — Teldec 3-▲ 90861-2 [DDD]

Mozart, W.A.:Nozze di Figaro (sels), w. K. Te Kanawa (sop), L. Popp (sop), F. von Stade (mez), T. Allen (bar), S. Ramey (bass), G. Solti (cnd), London PO [I] — London ▲ 417395-2 [DDD] □ 417395-5

Mozart, W.A.:Zauberflöte, w. M. Price (sop—Pamina), L. Serra (sop—Queen of the Night), M. Venuti (sop—Papagena), M. McLaughlin (sop—1st Lady), A. Murray (mez—2nd Lady), H. Schwarz (cta—3rd Lady), F. Höher (trb—1st Boy), M. Diedrich (trb—2nd Boy), F. Klos (trb—3rd Boy), P. Schreier (ten—Tamino), R. Tear (ten—Monostatos), R. Goldberg (ten—1st Armoured Man), K. Moll (bass—Sarastro), H. Rech (bass—2nd Armoured Man), C. Davis (cnd), Dresden Staatskapelle, Leipzig Radio Chorus — Philips ("Duo" series) 2-▲ 442568-2

Mozart, W.A.:Zauberflöte, w. S. Jo (sop), R. Ziesak (sop), U. Heilmann (ten), A. Kraus (ten), G. Solti (cnd), Vienna PO, Vienna State Opera Chorus — London 2-▲ 433210-2 [DDD]

Mozart, W.A.:Zauberflöte (sels), w. S. Jo (sop), R. Ziesak (sop), U. Heilmann (ten), A. Kraus (ten), G. Solti (cnd), Vienna PO, Vienna State Opera Chorus — London ▲ 433667-2 [DDD]

Nicolai, O.:Lustigen Weiber, w. H. Donath (sop), E. Mathis (sop), H. Schwarz (cta), P. Schreier (ten), B. Klee (cnd), Berlin Staatskapelle, Berlin State Opera Chorus — Berlin Classics 2-▲ BER 2115 [ADD]

Nicolai, O.:Lustigen Weiber, w. H. Donath (sop), E. Mathis (sop), H. Schwarz (mez), K. Ludwig (ten), K.-E. Mercker (ten), P. Schreier (ten), C. Dormoy (bar), B. Weikl (bar), S. Vogel (bass), B. Klee (cnd), Berlin Staatskapelle, Berlin State Opera Chorus *(rec July 3, 1976)* — Berlin Classics ("Eterna" series) ▲ BER 2046-2 [ADD]

Prokofiev, S.:The Fiery Angel, w. N. Secunde (sop), R. Engert-Ely (mez), H. Zednik (ten), S. Lorenz (bar), N. Järvi (cnd), Gothenburg SO, Gothenburg Sym Chorus [R] — Deutsche Grammophon 2-▲ 431669-2 [DDD]

Schmidt, F.:Notre Dame, w. G. Jones (sop), J. King (ten), R. Laubenthal (ten), C. Perick (cnd), Berlin RSO, St. Hedwig's Cathedral Choir, RIAS Chamber Chorus [G] — Capriccio 2-▲ 10248/9 [DDD]

Schubert, Franz:Songs (misc), w. C. Garben (pno)—18 songs [G] — Orfeo ▲ 021821 [DDD]

Schubert, Franz:Winterreise, w. C. Garben (pno) [G] — Orfeo 2-▲ 042832 2-■ 042832

Shostakovich, D.:Lady Macbeth of Mtsensk, w. M. Ewing (sop), E. Zaremba (mez), P. Langridge (ten), H. Zednik (ten), A. Haugland (bass), A. Kotcherga (bass), S. Larin (bass), M.-W. Chung (cnd), Bastille Opera Orch, Bastille Opera Chorus — Deutsche Grammophon 2-▲ 437511-2

Spohr, L.:Jessonda, w. J. Varady (sop), R. Behle (sop), T. Moser (ten), D. Fischer-Dieskau (bar), G. Albrecht (cnd), Hamburg State PO, Hamburg State Opera Chorus [G] — Orfeo 2-▲ 240912 [DDD]

Strauss, R.:Der Rosenkavalier, w. A. Tomowa-Sintow (sop), J. Perry (sop), A. Baltsa (mez), H. von Karajan (cnd), Vienna PO, Vienna State Opera Chorus [G] — Deutsche Grammophon 3-▲ 423850-2 [DDD]

Verdi, G.:La forza del destino (sels), w. Raina Kabaivanska (sop), Giuseppe Giacomini (ten), Norman Mittelmann (sgr), J. Rudel (cnd), *(orch unknown)*—Ah per sempre o mio bell'anglol; La vita è inferno all'infelice; Fuggir...ferito siete; Solenne in quest'ora; Fratello...Riconoscimi; Io muoio...confession *(rec Parigi, May 27, 1975)* — Golden Age of Opera 2-▲ GAO 189/90 [ADD]

Wagner, R.:Die Feen, w. L. E. Gray (sop), K. Lövaas (sop), K. Láki (sop), Anderson (sop), R. Alexander (sop), R. Hermann (bar), W. Sawallisch (cnd), Bavarian RSO, Bavarian Radio Chorus [G] *(rec live, Munich Opera Fest. 1983)* — Orfeo 3-▲ 062833 [DDD]

Wagner, R.:Der fliegende Holländer, w. D. Vejzovic (sop), P. Hofmann (ten), J. Van Dam (b-bar), H. von Karajan (cnd), Berlin PO [G] — EMI Classics 2-▲ CDMB 64650

Wagner, R.:Lohengrin, w. Cheryl Studer (sop), Waltraud Meier (mez), Siegfried Jerusalem (ten), Andreas Schmidt (bar), Harmut Welker (bar), C. Abbado (cnd), Vienna PO — Deutsche Grammophon 3-▲ 437808-2

Wagner, R.:Die Meistersinger von Nürnberg, w. H. Bode (sop), J. Hamari (mez), A. Kollo (ten), N. Bailey (bar), B. Weikl (bar), G. Solti (cnd), Vienna PO, Vienna State Opera Chorus [G] — London 4-▲ 417497-2 [ADD]

Wagner, R.:Die Meistersinger von Nürnberg, w. C. Studer (sop—Eva), B. Heppner (ten—Walther von Stolzing), B. Weikl (bar—Hans Sachs), S. Lorenz (b-bar—Sixtus Beckmesser), K. Moll (bass—Veit Pogner), W. Sawallisch (cnd), Bavarian State Opera Orch, Bavarian State Opera Chorus — EMI Classics ▲ CDCD 55142

Wagner, R.:Parsifal, w. J. Norman (sop), P. Domingo (ten), E. Wlaschiha (bar), J. Morris (bass), J.-H. Rootering (bass), J. Levine (cnd), Metropolitan Opera Orch, New York Metropolitan Opera Chorus — Deutsche Grammophon 4-▲ 437501-2

Wagner, R.:Parsifal, w. D. Vejzovic (sop), P. Hofmann (ten), J. Van Dam (b-bar), S. Nimsgern (b-bar), H. von Karajan (cnd), Berlin PO, German Opera Chorus [G] — Deutsche Grammophon 4-▲ 413347-2 [DDD]

Wagner, R.:Der Ring des Nibelungen (sels), w. Jessye Norman (sop), Lucia Popp (sop), René Kollo (ten), Siegfried Jerusalem (ten), Matti Salminen (bass), M. Janowski (cnd), Dresden Staatskapelle — RCA Victor ▲ 09026-68084-2; ■ 09026-68084-4

Wagner, R.:Tristan und Isolde, w. M. Price (sop), B. Fassbaender (mez), A. Kollo (ten), D. Fischer-Dieskau (bar), C. Kleiber (cnd), Dresden State Opera Orch [G] — Deutsche Grammophon 4-▲ 413315-2 [DDD]

Wagner, R.:Tristan und Isolde, w. C. Ligendza (sop—Isolde), Y. Minton (mez—Brangäne), H. Brilioth (ten—Tristan), K. Moll (bass—King Mark), C. Kleiber (cnd), Bayreuth Festival Orch, Bayreuth Festival Chorus *(rec Bayreuth Festival, 1975)* — Exclusive 3-▲ EXL 54 [ADD]

Weber, C.M. von:Der Freischütz (sels), w. K. Mattila (sop), E. Lind (sop), F. Araiza (ten), C. Davis (cnd), Dresden Staatskapelle — Philips ▲ 438497-2

Wolf, H.:Der Corregidor, w. H. Donath (sop), D. Soffel (mez), W. Hollweg (ten), P. Maus (ten), D. Fischer-Dieskau (bar), G. Albrecht (cnd), Berlin RSO [G] — Koch Schwann 2-▲ CD 314 010

Möll, M. (nar)

Schillings, M. von:Hexenlied, w. J. Stulen (cnd), Cologne RSO — CPO ▲ CPO 999233 [DDD]

Mollet, Pierre (bar)

Berlioz, H.:La Damnation de Faust, w. Pierre Mollet (bar—Brandler), Michel Roux (bar—Méphistophélès), Consuelo Rubio (sgr—Marguerite), Richard Verreau (sgr—Faust) — Theorema 2-▲ TH 121170/171

Boulanger, L.:Psalm 129, w. I. Markevitch (cnd), Lamoureux Orch, Elisabeth Brasseur Chorale *(rec Salle Pleyel, Paris)* — Everest ▲ EVC 9034 [AAD]

Fauré, G.:La bonne chanson, w. Renée Doria (sop), Berthe Monmart (sop), Simone Gouat (pno) — Accord ▲ ACD 204262 [AAD]

Fauré, G.:La Chanson d'Eve, w. Renée Doria (sop), Berthe Monmart (sop), Simone Gouat (pno) — Accord ▲ ACD 204262 [AAD]

Fauré, G.:L'Horizon chimérique, w. Renée Doria (sop), Berthe Monmart (sop), Simone Gouat (pno) — Accord ▲ ACD 204262 [AAD]

Fauré, G.:Le Jardin clos, w. Renée Doria (sop), Berthe Monmart (sop), Simone Gouat (pno) — Accord ▲ ACD 204262 [AAD]

Fauré, G.:Songs, w. Renée Doria (sop), Berthe Monmart (sop), Simone Gouat (pno)—Chanson du pêcheur; Lydia; Tristesse; Au bord de l'eau; Puisqu'ici bas; Automne; Poème d'un jour; Les berceaux; Le secret; Aurore; Les roses d'ispahan; Nocturne; Clair de lune; Spleen; La rose; En prière; Mandoline; Green; En sourdine; A Clymène; C'est l'extase; Pleurs d'or; Arpège; Le parfum impérissable; Soir; Dans la forêt de septembre; Le don silencieux; Chanson — Accord ▲ ACD 204602 [AAD]

Molnár, András (ten)

Erkel, F.:Hunyadi László, w. M. Kalmár (sop), S. Sass (sop), D. Gulyás (ten), I. Gáti (bar), S. Sólyom-Nagy (bar), J. Kovács (cnd), Hungarian State Opera Orch, Hungarian State Opera Chorus [Hun] — Hungaroton 3-▲ HCD 12581/83 [DDD]

Liszt, F.:An die Künstler, w. T. Daróczi (ten), J. Molday (bar), L. Domahidy Jr. (bass), I. Zámbó (cnd), Hungarian State Orch, Hungarian People's Army Male Chorus [G] — Hungaroton ▲ HCD 12748 [DDD]

Liszt, F.:Choral Music, w. L. Révész (org), Gábor Ugrin (cnd), Hungarian State Chorus—Ave Maria I, S.20/1; Domine salvum fac regem, S.23; Te Deum laudamus, S.27; Ave maris stella, S.34/1; Inno a Maria Vergine, S.39; Rosario, S.56; In domum Domini ibimus, S.57; Chor der Engel, S.85 [G,I,L] — Hungaroton ▲ HCD 31103 [DDD]

Liszt, F.:Hungaria 1848, w. M. Temesi (sop), S. Sólyom-Nagy (bar), I. Zámbó (cnd), Hungarian State Orch, Hungarian People's Army Male Chorus—composed as a salute to the Hungarian revolution [G] — Hungaroton ▲ HCD 12748 [DDD]

Monachesi, Walter (bar)

Donizetti, G.:La fille du régiment, w. M. Freni (sop), A. di Stasio (mez), L. Pavarotti (ten), W. Ganzarolli (bar), N. Sanzogno (cnd), La Scala Orch, La Scala Chorus [I] *(rec live, 2/11/69)* — Verona 2-▲ 27046/47 (m) [AAD]

Donizetti, G.:La fille du régiment, w. M. Freni (sop), A. di Stasio (mez), L. Pavarotti (ten), W. Ganzarolli (bar), N. Sanzogno (cnd), La Scala Orch, La Scala Chorus [I] *(rec live, 2/11/69)* — Melodram 2-▲ MEL 27045

Donizetti, G.:La fille du régiment (sels), w. Mirella Freni (sop), Anna di Stasio (mez), Angelo Mercuriali (ten), Luciano Pavarotti (ten), Wladimiro Ganzarolli (bar), Giuseppe Morresi (bass), V. Gullino (sgr), Luisa Rezzadore (sgr), N. Sanzogno (cnd), La Scala Orch, La Scala Chorus — Budget ("The Greatest Voice in Opera" series) ▲ SYP 108

Verdi, G.:Simon Boccanegra, w. A. Stella (sop—Maria), C. Bergonzi (ten—Gabriele), G. Giorgetti (bar—Pietro), W. Monachesi (bar—Paolo), M. Petri (bar—Jacopo), P. Silveri (bar—Simon), F. Molinari-Pradelli (cnd), Rome Radio Orch, Rome RAI Chorus *(rec 1951)* — Cetra Classic ▲ CDO 23 [ADD]

Monaco, Daniela del (cta)

Gesualdo, D.C.:Madrigals, w. Elena Cecchi Fedi (sop), Roberta Invernizzi (sop), Roberto Balconi (ct), Gian Paolo Fagotto (ten), Giuseppe Zambon (ten), Giovanni Dagnino (bass), A. Curtis (cnd), I Fegi Armonici—Book 6 [Se la Mia Morte Brami; Beltà Poi Che T'Assenti; Tu Piangi O Fille Mia; Resta di Darmi Noia; Chiaro Risplender Suole; others] — Symphonia ▲ SYM 94133

Sui Palchi Delle Stelle:Sacred Music in the Neapolitan Conservatories at the Time of Francesco Provenzale, w. [cnd:Antonio Florio], Cappella Pietà de Turchini, Antonella Ippolito (sop), Jane Haughton (sop), Sebastiano Cassarà (vn), Rosario Di Meglio (vn), Antonella Bologna (va), Paolo Dionisio (vl), Antonio Florio (vc), Pierluigi Ciappareli (thb), Enrico Baiano (org/hpd) — Symphonia ▲ SY 93S20 [DDD]

Monaco, Mario del (ten)

Bellini, V.:Norma, w. M. Callas (sop), G. Simionato (mez), N. Zaccaria (bass), A. Votto (cnd), La Scala Orch, La Scala Chorus *(rec 12/7/55)* — HRE 2-▲ 1007-2

Bellini, V.:Norma, w. Maria Callas (sop), Gabriella Carturan (mez), Giulietta Simionato (mez), Giuseppe Zampieri (ten), Nicola Zaccaria (bass), A. Votto (cnd), La Scala Orch, La Scala Chorus — Melodram 2-▲ CDM 26036

Bellini, V.:Norma (sels), w. Athos Cesarini (ten), T. Serafin (cnd), Rome RAI SO—Svanir le voci; Meco all'altar di Venere; Me protegge, me difende *(rec Rome, June 29, 1955)* — Melodram ▲ CDI 104006 [ADD]

Berlioz, H.:Les Troyens (sels), w. N. Rankin (mez), G. Simionato (mez), R. Kubelik (cnd), La Scala Orch [I] *(rec May 27, 1960)* — VAI Audio ▲ VAIA 1026 [ADD]

Bizet, G.:Carmen, w. R. Resnik (mez), J. Sutherland (sop), T. Krause (bar), T. Schippers (cnd), Swiss Romande Orch — London 2-▲ 411630-2 [ADD]

Bizet, G.:Carmen, w. Joan Sutherland (sop), Regina Resnik (mez), T. Schippers (cnd), Swiss Romande Orch — London ("Double Decca" series) 2-▲ 443871-2

Bizet, G.:Carmen (sels), w. P. Maag (cnd), Naples Teatro San Carlo Orch—Il fior che avevi a me tu dato *(rec Naples, Dec. 14, 1960)* — Melodram ▲ CDI 104006 [ADD]

Boito, A.:Mefistofele, w. R. Tebaldi (sop), C. Siepi (bass), T. Serafin (cnd), St. Cecilia Academy Orch Rome, St. Cecilia Academy Chorus Rome *(rec 1958)* — London ▲ 440054-2

Catalani, A.:La Wally, w. R. Scotto (sop), R. Tebaldi (sop), G. Guelfi (bar), C.M. Giulini (cnd), *(orch unknown)* *(rec Milan, 1953)* — Great Opera Performances 2-▲ GOP 734

Catalani, A.:La Wally, w. L. Marimpietri (sop), R. Tebaldi (sop), P. Cappuccilli (bar), Justino Diaz (bass), F. Cleva (cnd), Monte Carlo Opera Orch, Turin Lyric Chorus [I] — London 2-▲ 425417-2 [ADD]

Catalani, A.:La Wally, w. R. Scotto (sop—Walter), R. Tebaldi (sop—Wally), J. Gardino (mez—Afra), M. Del Monaco (ten—Giuseppe Hagenbach), G.G. Guelfi (bar—Vincenzo Gellner), G. Tozzi (bass—Stromminger), C. M. Giulini (cnd), La Scala Orch, La Scala Chorus *(rec Dec. 7, 1953)* — Legato Classics 2-▲ LCD 177-2 [ADD]

Cilea, F.:Adriana Lecouvreur, w. R. Tebaldi (sop), F. Capuana (cnd), St. Cecilia Academy Orch Rome, St. Cecilia Academy Chorus Rome — London 2-▲ 430256-2 [ADD]

Famous Love Duets, Vol. 2, w. Gianna d'Angelo (sop), Montserrat Caballé (sop), Maria Callas (sop), Renata Scotto (sop), Beverly Sills (sop), Renata Tebaldi (sop), José Carreras (ten), Giuseppe Di Stefano (ten), Plácido Domingo (ten), Luciano Pava — Enterprise ("Documents" series) ▲ ENTLV 999

Giordano, U.:Andrea Chénier, w. M. Callas (sop), A. Protti (bar), A. Votto (cnd), La Scala Orch, La Scala Chorus *(rec live, Milan, 1/8/55)* — Melodram 2-▲ MEL 26002 [ADD]

Giordano, U.:Andrea Chénier, w. M. Callas (sop), A. Protti (bar), A. Votto (cnd), La Scala Orch, La Scala Chorus *(rec live)* — Verona 2-▲ VER 28020

Giordano, U.:Andrea Chénier, w. Renata Tebaldi (sop—Maddalena), Anna di Stasio (mez—Bersi), Amalia Pini (mez—Madelon/Contessa), Mario Del Monaco (ten—Andrea Chenier), Antonio Pirino (ten—L'Incredibile/Abate), Aldo Protti (bar—Carlo Gerard), Arturo La Porta (bass/bar—Mathieu/Fleville), Silvano Pagliuca (bass/bar—Roucher/Fouquier-Tinville), Giorgio Onesti (bass—Dumas/Schmidt/Major-domo), F. Capuana (cnd), Italian Lyric Orch, Italian Lyric Chorus *(rec Tokyo, Oct 1, 1961)* — Legato Classics 2-▲ LCD 214-2 [ADD]

Giordano, U.:Andrea Chénier (sels), w. R. Tebaldi (sop), F. Barbieri (mez), P. Silveri (bar), V. de Sabata (cnd), La Scala Orch, La Scala Chorus—14 arias from Acts 1-3 [I] *(rec live, Milan, 3/6/49)* — Myto ▲ 1 MCD 90634 [ADD]

Giordano, U.:Fedora, w. M. Olivero (sop), T. Gobbi (bar), L. Gardelli (cnd), Monte Carlo Opera Orch — London ("Grand Opera" series) 2-▲ 433033-2 [ADD]

Grandi Voci:Mario del Monaco *(rec 1954-59)* — London ▲ 440408-2 [ADD]

Leoncavallo, R.:Pagliacci (sels), w. F. Scaglia (cnd), Milan RAI SO—Recitar...Vesti la giubba *(rec Milan, May 22, 1957)* — Melodram ▲ CDI 104006 [ADD]

Monaco, Mario del (ten) (cont.)
Mario Del Monaco *(rec European and American, live & broadcast, 1950–1965)* Golden Age of Opera ▲ GAO 110 [ADD]
Mario Del Monaco Memories 2–▲ MEM 4541 [AAD]
Mascagni, P.:Cavalleria rusticana, w. E. Suliotis (sop), S. Malagu (mez), A. Di Stasio (mez), T. Gobbi (bar), S. Varviso (cnd), Rome Opera Orch, Rome Opera Chorus [I] IMP Collectors Series ▲ IMPX 9018 [AAD]
Puccini, G.:La fanciulla del West, w. R. Tebaldi (sop), C. MacNeil (bar), G. Tozzi (bass), F. Capuana (cnd), St. Cecilia Academy Orch Rome, St. Cecilia Academy Chorus Rome [I] London 2–▲ 421595–2 [ADD]
Puccini, G.:La fanciulla del West, w. E. Steber (sop), G. Guelfi (bar), D. Mitropoulos (cnd), Venice Teatro La Fenice Orch, Venice Teatro La Fenice Chorus *(rec live, 6/15/54)* Arkadia 2–▲ 565 (m)
Puccini, G.:Manon Lescaut, w. R. Tebaldi (sop), F. Molinari-Pradelli (cnd), St. Cecilia Academy Orch Rome, St. Cecilia Academy Chorus Rome London 2–▲ 430253–2 [ADD]
Puccini, G.:Manon Lescaut (sels), w. C. Petrella (sop) *(rec 1951)* Golden Age of Opera 2–▲ GAO 162/63 [ADD]
Puccini, G.:Tosca, w. R. Tebaldi (sop), F. Molinari-Pradelli (cnd), St. Cecilia Academy Orch Rome, St. Cecilia Academy Chorus Rome London 2–▲ 411871–2 [ADD]
Puccini, G.:Turandot, w. I. Borkh (sop), R. Tebaldi (sop), A. Erede (cnd), St. Cecilia Academy Orch Rome, St. Cecilia Academy Chorus Rome London 2–▲ 433761–2 [ADD]
Stella, Cossotto & Monaco, w. Antonietta Stella (sop), Fiorenza Cossotto (mez), Ferruccio Scaglia (cnd), Milan RAI SO, Rome RAI SO *(rec Martini & Rossi Concert, 1959 & 1960)* Incontri Memorabili ▲ CDMR 5031
Verdi, G.:Aida, w. Renata Tebaldi (sop—Aida), Ebe Stignani (mez—Amneris), Mario Del Monaco (ten—Radamès), Piero de Palma (ten—Messenger), Aldo Protti (bar—Amonasro), Fernando Corena (bass—King), Dario Caselli (bass—Ramfis), A. Erede (cnd), St. Cecilia Academy Orch Rome, St. Cecilia Academy Chorus Rome *(rec 1952)* Theorema 2–▲ TH 121133/34
Verdi, G.:Aida, w. M. Callas (sop), O. Dominguez (mez), G. Taddei (bar), O. de Fabritiis (cnd), Palacio Bellas Artes Orch, Palacio Bellas Artes Chorus *(rec live, Mexico City 7/3/51)* Melodram 2–▲ CDM 26015
Verdi, G.:Aida, w. R. Tebaldi (sop), E. Stignani (mez), A. Protti (bar), F. Corena (bass), A. Erede (cnd), St. Cecilia Academy Orch Rome, St. Cecilia Academy Chorus Rome London 2–▲ 440239–2 [ADD]
Verdi, G.:Aida (sels), w. A. Simonetto (cnd), Milan RAI SO—Se quel guerrier...Celeste Aida *(rec Milan, May 22, 1957)* IMC ▲ CDI 104006 [ADD]
Verdi, G.:Ernani, w. A. Cerquetti (sop), E. Bastianini (bar), B. Christoff (bass), D. Mitropoulos (cnd), Florence Maggio Musicale Orch [I] *(rec live 6/14/57)* Melodram 2–▲ MEL 27016
Verdi, G.:Ernani, w. Margherita Roberti (sop), Anna di Stasio (mez), Athos Cesarini (ten), Ettore Bastianini (bar), Mario Rinaudo (bass), Nicola Rossi-Lemeni (bass), F. Previtali (cnd), Naples Teatro San Carlo Orch, Naples Teatro San Carlo Chorus Melodram 2–▲ CDM 270100
Verdi, G.:Ernani (sels), w. D. Mitropoulos (cnd), Florence Maggio Musicale Orch, Florence Maggio Musicale Chorus—Merc, diletti amici..Come rugiada al cespite; Dell'esilio nel dolore...O tu che l'alma adora *(rec Firenze, June 14, 1957)* Melodram ▲ CDI 104006 [ADD]
Verdi, G.:La forza del destino, w. Z. Milanov (sop), L. Warren (bar), G. Pechner (bar), W. Wildermann (bass), W. Herbert (cnd), *(orch unknown)* *(rec live 1953)* Legato Classics 2–▲ LCD 118–2 (m) [AAD]
Verdi, G.:La forza del destino, w. R. Tebaldi (sop), G. Simionato (mez), E. Bastianini (bar), C. Siepi (b-bar), F. Molinari-Pradelli (cnd), St. Cecilia Academy Orch Rome, St. Cecilia Academy Chorus Rome [I] London 3–▲ 421598–2 [ADD]
Verdi, G.:La forza del destino (sels), w. D. Mitropoulos (cnd), Florence Maggio Musicale Orch, Florence Maggio Musicale Chorus—La vita è inferno all'infelice; O tu che in seno agli angeli *(rec Firenze, June 14, 1953)* Melodram ▲ CDI 104006 [ADD]
Verdi, G.:I lombardi alla prima crociata, w. C. Deutekom (sop), D. Malvisi (sop), M. Aparici (sop), P. Domingo (ten), G. Raimondi (ten), M. Dean (b-bar), C. Grant (bass), L. Gardelli (cnd), Royal PO, Ambrosian Singers Philips 2–▲ 422420–2 [ADD]
Verdi, G.:Macbeth (sels), w. A. Simonetto (cnd), Milan RAI SO—O Figli miei. Ah la paterna mano *(rec Milan, May 22, 1957)* Melodram ▲ CDI 104006 [ADD]
Verdi, G.:Otello, w. H. Gueden (sop), G. Simionato (mez), A. Protti (bar), C. Siepi (b-bar), A. Erede (cnd), St. Cecilia Academy Orch Rome, St. Cecilia Academy Chorus Rome London 2–▲ 440242–2 [ADD]
Verdi, G.:Otello, w. R. Tebaldi (sop), L. Warren (bar), A. Votto (cnd), La Scala Orch, La Scala Chorus *(rec July 1, 1954)* Melodram 2–▲ MLO 270101 [ADD]
Verdi, G.:Otello, w. Raina Kabaivanska (sop), Josephine Veasey (mez), John Lanigan (ten), Tito Gobbi (bar), G. Solti (cnd), Royal Opera House Orch, Royal Opera House Covent Garden Chorus *(rec June 30, 1962)* Memories ▲ MEM 4583 [AAD]
Verdi, G.:Otello, w. Renata Tebaldi (sop—Desdemona), Luisa Ribacchi (mez—Emilia), Angelo Mercuriali (ten—Roderigo), Mario del Monaco (ten—Otello), Piero de Palma (ten—Cassio), Aldo Protti (bar—Iago), Dario Caselli (bass—A Herald), Fernando Corena (bass—Lodovico), Pierluigi Martinucci (bass—Montano), A. Erede (cnd), St. Cecilia Academy Orch Rome, St. Cecilia Academy Chorus Rome Theorema ▲ TH 121141/142
Verdi, G.:Otello, w. Raina Kabaivanska (sop), Tito Gobbi (bar), G. Solti (cnd), Royal Opera House Orch, Royal Opera House Chorus Covent Garden Pantheon 2–▲ PHE 6608
Verdi, G.:Otello, w. R. Tebaldi (sop), A. Protti (bar), H. von Karajan (cnd), Vienna PO [I] London 2–▲ 411618–2 [ADD]
Verdi, G.:Otello (sels)—Esultate!; Qua, ragazzi, del vino!; Abbasso le spade; Già nella notte densa; Credo in un Dio crudel; Non pensateci più...tu? indietro! fuggi; Ora e per sempre addio sante memorie; Era la notte; Sì, pel ciel marmoreo giuro; Dio ti giocondi o sposo; Dio mi potevi scagliar; Vieni, l'aura è deserta; Messeri, il Doge mi richiama; Nium mi tema [all w. Antonietta Berdini (sop—Desdemona), Adriana Alinovi (mez—Emilia), Pierfrancesco Poli (ten—Cassio), Aldo Protti (bar—Iago), Franco Ferraris (cnd)]; Esultate!; Già nella notte densa; Atroce idea...non pensateci più; Ora e per sempre addio sante memorie; Era la notte; Sì, pel ciel marmoreo giuro; Dio ti giocondi o sposo; Dio mi potevi scagliar; Niun mi tema [all w. Irma Capece Minutolo (sop—Desdemona), Walter Brighi (ten—Cassio), Franco Bordoni (bar—Iago), Loris Gavarini (cnd)]; Esultate!; Già nella notte densa; Non pensateci più?..Tu? Indietro, fuggi; O mostruosa colpa; Dio ti giocondi o sposo; Dio mi potevi scagliar; Niun mi tema [all w. Stefania Moldovan (sop—Desdemona), Gyorgy Radnay (bar—Iago), Miklos Lukacs (cnd)] *(rec 1971)* Golden Age of Opera 2–▲ GAO 200/201 [ADD]
Verdi, G.:Otello (sels), w. K. Ricciarelli (sop), A. Protti (bar), F. Ferraris (cnd), Brussels Théâtre de la Monnaie Orch *(rec Nov. 9, 1972)* Standing Room Only 2–▲ SRO 169–2
Verdi, G.:Otello (sels), w. Tito Gobbi (bar—Iago), A. Erede (cnd), Japanese RSO—Esultate! L'orgoglio musulmano; Tu?! Indietro!...Ora e per sempre addio; Ah! Mille vite...Sì, pel ciel; Dio! mi potevi scagliar; Niun mi tema *(rec Tokyo, Feb. 4, 1952)* Melodram ▲ CDI 104006 [ADD]
Verdi, G.:Otello (sels), w. Mario Del Monaco (ten—Otello), Tito Gobbi (bar—Iago), N. Sanzogno (cnd), Palermo Teatro Massimo Orch *(rec Palermo, Jan 1, 1962)* Bella Voce 2–▲ 7203 [AAD]
Verdi, G.:Rigoletto, w. R. Tebaldi (sop), A. Protti (bar), P. de Palma (bass), F. Corena (bass), A. Erede (cnd), St. Cecilia Academy Orch Rome, St. Cecilia Academy Chorus Rome London 2–▲ 440245–2 [ADD]
Verdi, G.:Rigoletto, w. Hilde Gueden (sop—Gilda), Piero de Palma (ten—Borsa), Luisa Ribacchi (mez—Giovanna), Giulietta Simionato (mez—Maddalena), Mario del Monaco (ten—Duca de Mantova), Aldo Protti (bar—Rigoletto), Fernando Corena (bass—Conte Monterone), Cesare Siepi (bass—Sparafucile), A. Erede (cnd), St. Cecilia Academy Orch Rome, St. Cecilia Academy Chorus Rome Theorema ▲ TH 121179/180
Verdi, G.:Stiffelio, w. A. Gulin (sop—Lina), M. del Monaco (ten—Stiffelio), A. Marchiandi (ten—Raffaele), G. Fioravanti (bar—Stankar), J. Hecht (bass—Jorg), O. de Fabritiis (cnd), Naples Teatro San Carlo Orch, Naples Teatro San Carlo Chorus *(rec Dec. 26, 1972)* Standing Room Only 2–▲ SRO 169–2
Verdi, G.:Il trovatore, w. Leyla Gencer (sop—Leonora), Laura Londi (sop—Ines), Fedora Barbieri (mez—Azucena), Mario del Monaco (ten—Manrico), Athos cesarini (ten—Ruiz), Walter Artioli (ten—Messanger) Ettore Bastianini (bar—Count Luna), Plinio Clabassi (bass—Ferrando), Sergio Liliani (bass—Gypsy), F. Previtali (cnd), Milan RAI SO, Milan RAI Chorus *(rec live, Milan, May 29, 1957)* Arkadia 2–▲ 483 [ADD]
Verdi, G.:Il trovatore (sels), w. F. Previtali (cnd), Milan RAI SO, Milan RAI Chorus—Ah! sì, ben mio; Di quella pira *(rec Milan, Apr. 8, 1957)* Melodram ▲ CDI 104006 [ADD]

Monaco, Mario del (ten) (cont.)
Verdi, G.:Il trovatore (sels), w. Leyla Gencer (sop—Leonora), Laura Londi (sop—Ines), Athos Cesarini (ten—Ruiz), Mario del Monaco (ten—Manrico), Ettore Bastianini (bar), F. Previtali (cnd), Milan RAI SO, Milan RAI Chorus *(rec Milan, May 18, 1957)* Agorá Music ("Phoenix" series) 3–▲ 510 [ADD]
Wagner, R.:Lohengrin (sels), w. A. Simonetto (cnd), Milan RAI SO—In frenem Land *(rec Milan, May 22, 1957)* Melodram ▲ CDI 104006 [ADD]
Wagner, R.:Die Walküre (sels), w. F. Scaglia (cnd), Milan RAI SO—Ein Schwert verhiess mir der Vater; Winterstürme wichen dem Wonnemond *(rec Milan, May 22, 1957)* Melodram ▲ CDI 104006 [ADD]
Zandonai, R.:Francesca da Rimini, w. Lydia Marimpietri (sop—Biancofiore), Magda Olivero (sop—Francesca), Pinuccia Perotti (sop—Samaritana), Edda Vincenzi (sop—Garsenda), Gabriella Carturan (mez—Smaragdi), Biancamaria Casoni (mez—Altichiara), Anna Maria Rota (cta—Donella), Athos Cesarini (ten—Archer), Angelo Mercuriali (ten—Ser Toldo Berardengo), Mario del Monaco (ten—Paolo), Piero de Palma (ten—Malatestino), Rinaldo Pelizzoni (ten—Prisoner), Gianpiero Malaspina (bar—Gianciotto), Dino Mantovani (bar—Jester), Enrico Campi (bass—Ostasio), Giuseppe Morresi (bass—Tower warden), G. Gavazzeni (cnd), La Scala Orch, La Scala Chorus *(rec La Scala Theatre, Milan, June 4, 1959)* Legato Classics 2–▲ LCD 186–2
Zandonai, R.:Francesca da Rimini (sels), w. M. Olivero (sop), A. Gasparini (mez), A. Cesarini (ten), V. Carbonari (bass), N. Rescigno (cnd), Monte Carlo Opera Orch London ("Grand Opera" series) 2–▲ 433033–2 [ADD]

Moncloa, Catalina (sop)
Montsalvatge, X.:Sinf de requiem, w. A. Ros-Marbá (cnd), Madrid SO *(rec live, National Music Auditorium, Madrid, Nov. 23, 1993)* Marco Polo ▲ 8.223753 [DDD]

Mondelli, Massimo (bass)
Carissimi, G.:Oratorio della Santissima Vergine, w. P. Borri (sop), A. M. Ferrante (sop), P. Pace (sop), A. Christofellis (alt), L. Petroni (ten), F. Sclaverano (ten), R. Abbondanza (bass), P. Spagnoli (bass), F. Colusso (cnd), Seicentonovecento Ensemble [I] Bongiovanni ▲ GB 10011 [DDD]
Carissimi, G.:Oratorio di Daniele Profeta, w. P. Borri (sop), A. M. Ferrante (sop), P. Pace (sop), A. Christofellis (alt), L. Petroni (ten), F. Sclaverano (ten), R. Abbondanza (bass), P. Spagnoli (bass), F. Colusso (cnd), Seicentonovecento Ensemble [I] Bongiovanni ▲ GB 10011 [DDD]

Monestier, Nicole (sop)
Boieldieu, F.-A.:Le Calife de Bagdad, w. Ouaki (sgr), S. Elloir (sgr), Plantak (sgr), Fokenoy (sgr), B. Thomas (cnd), Bernard Thomas CO, Patrick Marco Vocal Ensemble [F] Thésis ▲ THC 82015 [DDD]

Monette, La Vergne (sop/mez)
Puccini, G.:Suor angelica, w. Elisabeth Carron (sop—Angelica), Joan Summers (sop—Genovieffa), Donna Owen (sop—Dolcina), Lou Ann Wyckoff (sop—Alms collector), Hanna Owen (sop—novice), Anthea De Forest (sop—novice), Charlotte Povia (mez—Abbess), Beverly Evans (mez—Monitress), Kay Creed (mez—Mistress), La Vergne Monette (sop/mez—lay sister), Joan August (sop/mez—lay sister), Pearle Goldsmith (sop/mez—other sister), Lila Herbert (sop/mez—other sister), Jodell Kenting (sop/mez—other sister), Ann Pretzat (sop/mez—other sister), Evelyn Sachs (cta—Princess), F. Patanè (cnd), *(orch unknown)* *(rec New York, Feb 23, 1967)* Legato Classics ▲ LCD 212–1 [ADD]

Mongelli, Andrea (bar)
Puccini, G.:La fanciulla del West, w. B. Nilsson (sop), J. Gibin (ten), L. von Matačić (cnd), La Scala Orch, La Scala Chorus [I] EMI Classics ("Studio" series) 2–▲ CDMB 63970

Monjo, Diego (ten)
Puccini, G.:Madama Butterfly, w. Montserrat Caballé (sop—Cio-Cio-San), Carmen Rigai (mez—Suzuki), Bernabé Martí (ten—Pinkerton), Diego Monjo (ten—Goro), Juan Rico (ten—Yamadori), Manuel Ausensi (bar—Sharpless), Jose Lemar (bass—Bonze), Antonio Leval (bass—Imperial Commissioner), Alejandro Chiara (bass—Registrar), G. Rivoli (cnd), Madrid Radio-TV Orch, Madrid Radio-TV Chorus *(rec Madrid, June 12, 1968)* Legato Classics 2–▲ LCD 210–2 [ADD]

Monk, Allan (bar)
Opera Arias, w. Calgary PO [cnd:Mario Bernardi] CBC Records ("SM 5000" series) ▲ SMCD 5102 [DDD] ■ SMC 5102 (D)

Monk, Meredith (sgr)
Monk, M.:Book of Days, w. Ensemble ECM New Series ▲ 78118–21399–2 [DDD]
Monk, M.:Do You Be, w. Ensemble ECM New Series ▲ 78118–21336–2 [DDD]
Monk, M.:Dolmen Music, w. Ensemble ECM New Series ▲ 78118–21197–2 [AAD]
Monk, M.:Turtle Dreams, w. Ensemble ECM New Series ▲ 78118–21240–2 [AAD]

Monkewitz, Annalisa (sop)
Rinaldo di Capua:La Zingara, w. Annalisa Monkewitz (sop—Nisa), Rodolfo Malacarne (ten—Tagliaborse), Laerte Malaguti (bass—Calcante), Josef Ulsamer (vl), Kurt-Heinz Stolze (hpd), G. Kehr (cnd), Mainz CO Dynamic ▲ CD 141 [ADD]

Monmart, Berthe (sop)
Fauré, G.:La bonne chanson, w. Renée Doria (sop), Pierre Mollet (bar), Simone Gouat (pno) Accord ▲ ACD 204262 [AAD]
Fauré, G.:La Chanson d'Eve, w. Renée Doria (sop), Pierre Mollet (bar), Simone Gouat (pno) Accord ▲ ACD 204262 [AAD]
Fauré, G.:L'Horizon chimérique, w. Renée Doria (sop), Pierre Mollet (bar), Simone Gouat (pno) Accord ▲ ACD 204262 [AAD]
Fauré, G.:Le Jardin clos, w. Renée Doria (sop), Pierre Mollet (bar), Simone Gouat (pno) Accord ▲ ACD 204262 [AAD]
Fauré, G.:Songs, w. Renée Doria (sop), Pierre Mollet (bar), Simone Gouat (pno)—Chanson du pêcheur; Lydia; Tristesse; Au bord de l'eau; Puisqu'ici bas; Automne; Poème d'un jour; Les berceaux; Le secret; Aurore; Les roses d'ispahan; Nocturne; Clair de lune; Spleen; La rose; En prière; Mandoline; Green; En sourdine; A Clymène; C'est l'extase; Pleurs d'or; Arpège; Le parfum impérissable; Soir; Dans la forêt de septembre; Le don silencieux; Chanson Accord ▲ ACD 204602 [AAD]

Monohan, Laurie (sgr)
An Empire Brass Christmas, w. Empire Brass Quintet, Kurt Wortman (perc), Brian Jones (perc) Telarc ▲ CD 80416 [DDD]
Passage, 138 B.C.–A.D. 1611, w. Empire Brass Quintet, M. Collver (sgr), Pete Maunu (acoustic/elec/12string gtr), Doug Lunn (fretless bass), D. Goldblatt (syn), K. Wortman (elec/acoustic perc) *(rec Lenox, MA & Los Angeles, CA May 27–29 & June 28–July)* Telarc ▲ CD 80355 [DDD]

Monoyios, Ann (sop)
Bach, J.S.:St. Matthew Passion, w. B. Bonney (sop), A. S. von Otter (mez), M. Chance (ct), H. Crook (ten), A. Rolfe Johnson (ten), O. Bär (bar), A. Schmidt (bar), C. Hauptmann (bass), J. E. Gardiner (cnd), English Baroque Soloists, Monteverdi Choir London [G] Archiv 3–▲ 427648–2 [DDD]
Clérambault, L.N.:La Musette, w. J. Richman (cnd), Concert Royal [F] Elektra/Nonesuch ▲ 71371–2 ■ 71371–4
Falla, M. de:Canciones populares españolas (7), w. M. Barrueco (gtr) EMI Classics ▲ CDC 54456
Haydn, J.:Mass 10, "Kriegsmesse", "Paukenmesse", w. Monica Groop (mez), Jörg Hering (ten), Harry van der Kamp (bass), B. Weil (cnd), Tafelmusik, Tölz Boys' Choir Sony Classical ("Vivarte" series) ▲ SK 68255
Haydn, J.:Salve regina, H.XXIIIb/1, w. B. Weil (cnd), Tafelmusik, Tölz Boys' Choir *(rec Bad Tolz, Germany, Sept. 5, 1993)* Sony Classical ("Vivarte" series) ▲ SK 53368 [DDD]
Haydn, J.:Die Schöpfung, w. Ann Monoyios (sop—Gabriel/Eva), Jörg Hering (ten—Uriel), Harry van der Kamp (bass—Raphael/Adam), B. Weil (cnd), Tafelmusik, Tölz Boys' Choir *(rec Bad Tolz, Germany, Aug. 31–Sept. 4, 1993)* Sony Classical ("Vivarte" series) 2–▲ SX2K 57965 [DDD]
Homilius, G.A.:St. Matthew Passion, w. U. Groenwald (cta), G. Türk, C. Prégardien (ten), K. Mertens (b-bar), H.-G. Wimmer (bass), Berlin Academy for Early Music, Leverkusen Cappella Vocale Berlin Classics 2–▲ BER 1046 [DDD]
Monteverdi, C.:Vespro della Beata Vergine, w. M. Pennicchi (sop), M. Chance (ct), G. Tucker (ten), N. Robson (ten), S. Naglia (ten), B. Terfel (b-bar), A. Miles (bass), J. E. Gardiner (cnd), English Baroque Soloists, His Majesties Sagbutts & Cornetts, London Monteverdi Choir Archiv 2–▲ 429565–2 [DDD]
Purcell, H.:Dido & Aeneas, w. Meredith Hall (sop—2nd Witch/Spirit), Ann Monoyios (sop—Belinda), Shari Saunders (sop—2nd Woman/1st Woman), Jennifer Lane (mez—Dido/Sorceress), Benjamin Butterfield (ten—Sailor), Russell Braun (bar—Aeneas), J. Lamon (cnd), Tafelmusik, Tafelmusik Chamber Choir *(rec Glenn Gould Studio, CBC Toronto, Apr 26–29, 1995)* CBC ▲ SM5 5147 [DDD]
Rameau, J.P.:Le Berger fidèle, w. Christine Brandes (sop), Howard Crook (ten), Nat Wilson (b-bar), Concert Royal Newport Classic ▲ NPT 85555

▲ = CD ♦ = Enhanced CD Δ = MD ■ = Cassette Tape □ = DCC

Monoyios, Ann (sop) (cont.)
Rameau, J.P.:L'Impatience, w. J. Richman (cnd), Concert Royal [F] Elektra/Nonesuch ▲ 71371-2 ■ 71371-4

Monreale, Leonardo (bass)
Donizetti, G.:I pazzi per progetto, w. S. Rigacci (sop), A. Cicogna (mez), G. Polidori (bar), G. Sarti (bar), V. M. Brunetti (bass), E. Fissore (bass), G. Micheli (cnd), Emilia Romagna Arturo Toscanini SO [I] *(rec live, 12/88)* Bongiovanni ▲ GB 2070 [DDD]
Paisiello, G.:La Molinara, w. Graziella Sciutti (sop), Agostino Lazzari (ten), Alvinio Misciano (ten), Sesto Bruscantini (bar), Franco Calabrese (bass), F. Caracciolo (cnd), Alessandro Scarlatti CO Melodram 2-▲ CDM 29502
Puccini, G.:Turandot, w. Birgit Nilsson (sop—Turandot), Renata Tebaldi (sop—Liù), Jussi Björling (ten—Calaf), Alessio De Paolis (ten—Emperor Altoum), Piero de Palma (ten—Pang), Mario Sereni (bar—Ping), Adelio Zagonara (bar—Prince of Persia), Giorgio Tozzi (bass—Timur), Tommaso Frascati (bass—Pong), Leonardo Monreale (bass—Mandarin), E. Leinsdorf (cnd), Rome Opera Orch, Rome Opera Chorus *(rec Rome Opera House, July 3-11, 1959)* RCA Living Stereo 2-▲ 09026-62687-2 [ADD]
Rossini, G.:La Cenerentola, w. Teresa Berganza (mez), Nicola Monti (ten), Sesto Bruscantini (bar), Mario Petri (bar), M. Rossi (cnd), Naples RAI SO, Naples Teatro San Carlo Chorus *(rec Oct 8, 1958)* Pantheon 2-▲ PHE 6656 (m)

Montague, Diana (mez)
Bellini, V.:I Capuleti e i Montecchi, w. K. Ricciarelli (sop), D. Raffanti (ten), M. Lippi (bass), B. Campanella (cnd), Venice Teatro La Fenice Orch, Venice Teatro La Fenice Chorus [I] *(rec 1991)* Nuova Era 2-▲ 7020/21 [DDD]
Bellini, V.:I Capuleti e i Montecchi (sels), w. Katia Ricciarelli (sop), Dano Raffanati (ten), B. Campanella (cnd), Venice Teatro La Fenice Orch, Venice Teatro La Fenice Chorus Nuova Era ▲ NUO 7183 [DDD]
Berlioz, H.:Les Nuits d'été, w. C. Robbin (mez), H. Crook (ten), G. Cachémaille (bar), J.E. Gardiner (cnd), Lyon Opera Orch [F] Erato ("Musifrance" series) ▲ 2292-45517-2 [DDD]
Berlioz, H.:Songs, w. B. Fournier (sop), C. Robbin (mez), H. Crook (ten), G. Cachémaille (bar), J.E. Gardiner (cnd), Lyon Opera Orch—Zaïde [Fournier]; La belle voyageuse [Montague]; La Captive [Robbin]; La mort d'Ophélie [Robbin]; Le jeune pâtre breton [Crook]; Aubade [Crook]; Le Chasseur danois [Cachémaille] [F] Erato ("Musifrance" series) ▲ 2292-45517-2 [DDD]
Franck, C.:Les Béatitudes, w. K. Lewis (ten), G. Cachemaille (bar), J. Cheek (bass), H. Rilling (cnd), Stuttgart RSO, Gächinger Kantorei [F] Hänssler Classic 2-▲ 98.964 [DDD]
Gluck, C.W.:Iphigénie en Tauride, w. J. Aler (ten), T. Allen (bar), R. Massis (bar), J.E. Gardiner (cnd), Lyon Opera Orch [F] Philips 2-▲ 416148-2 [DDD]
Handel, G.F.:Dixit Dominus, w. Arleen Augér (sop), Lynne Dawson (sop), Leigh Nixon (ten), Simon Birchall (bass), S. Preston (cnd), Westminster Abbey Orch, Westminster Abbey Choir [L] Archiv ▲ 423594-2 [DDD]
Handel, G.F.:Nisi Dominus, w. John Mark Ainsley (ten), Simon Birchall (bass), S. Preston (cnd), Westminster Abbey Orch, Westminster Abbey Choir [L] Archiv ▲ 423594-2 [DDD]
Janácek, L.:The Cunning Little Vixen, w. L. Watson (sop), E. Bainbridge (mez), G. Knight (mez), J. Dobson (ten), R. Tear (ten), T. Allen (bar), G. Howell (bass), S. Rattle (cnd), Royal Opera House Orch [E] EMI Classics 2-▲ CDCB 54212
Lloyd, G.:John Socman (sels), w. J. Watson (sop), T. Booth (ten), D. Wilson-Johnson (bar), M. Rivers (bar), M. George (bass), G. Lloyd (cnd), Philharmonia Orch, London Voices Albany ▲ TROY 131 [DDD]
Meyerbeer, G.:Il crociato, w. Linda Kitchen (sop), Y. Kenny (sop), R. Platt (sop), D. Jones (mez), B. Ford (ten), U. Benelli (bar), D. Parry (cnd), Royal PO, Geoffrey Mitchell Choir [I] *(rec CTS Studios, Wembley, London, Dec. 1990-June 1991)* Opera Rara 4-▲ OR 10
Mozart, W.A.:Clemenza, w. Barbara Bonney (sop—Servilia), Cecilia Bartoli (mez—Sesto), Della Jones (mez—Vitellia), Diana Montague (mez—Annio), Uwe Heilman (ten—Tito), Giles Cachemaille (bar—Publio), C. Hogwood (cnd), Academy of Ancient Music, Academy of Ancient Music Chorus London ("Editions de l'oiseau-lyre" series) 2-▲ 444131-2 [DDD]
Mozart, W.A.:Missa, K.427, w. S. McNair (sop), A. Rolfe Johnson (ten), C. Hauptmann (bass), J. E. Gardiner (cnd), English Baroque Soloists, Monteverdi Choir London [newly revised version, ed. Gardiner] [L] Philips ▲ 420210-2 [DDD]

Montaña, Elena (sop)
Falla, M. de:Psyché, w. Conchi Vacas (fl), Zoraida Avila (hp), Wen-Yu Ku (vn), Alison Montoya (va), Gloria Cuerda (vc) *(rec Madrid, Oct 1-3 1990)* RNE/Spanish National Radio ▲ M3/06 [DDD]
Ginastera, A.:Cantos del Tucumán, w. Conchi Vacas (fl), Wen-Yu Ku (vn), Zoraida Avila (hp), Conchi Sangregorio (perc) *(rec Madrid, Oct 1-3 1990)* RNE/Spanish National Radio ▲ M3/06 [DDD]
Guibert, A.:The Bath Tub, w. Conchi Vacas (fl), Wen-Yu Ku (vn), Alison Montoya (va), Gloria Cuerda (vc), Zoraida Avila (hp) *(rec Madrid, Oct 1-3 1990)* RNE/Spanish National Radio ▲ M3/06 [DDD]

Montanari, Paride (bass)
Perti, G.A.:Liturgy for Good Friday, w. Patrizia Vaccari (sop), Maura Pederzoli (sop), Cristina Calzolari (sop), Alida Oliva (sop), Claudia Bugli (sop), Lucia Bagnoli (alt), Cinzia Meneghel (alt), Renzo Bez (alt), Alessandro Carmignani (alt), Michel van Goethem (alt), Mauro Collina (ten), Vincenzo Di Donato (ten), Paolo Fanciullacci (ten), Giovanni Caccamo (ten), Paolo Da Col (ten), Sergio Foresti (bass), Marco Scavazza (bass), Luca Ferracin (bass), Liuwe Tamminga (org), Sergio Vartolo (org), S. Vartolo (cnd), Bologna San Petronio Capella Musicale Orch—Omnes amici mei; De lamentatione Jeremiae Prophetae:Heth. Cogitavit; Velum templi; Vinea mea; De lamentatione Jeremiae Prophetae:Lamed. Matribus suis; Tamquam ad latronem; Tenebrae factae sunt; Animam meam; Tradiderunt me; Jesum tradidit; De lamentatione Jeremiae Prophetae:Aleph. Ego vir; Caligaverunt *(rec St. Petronio Basilica, Bologna, Mar 28-31, 1995)* Naxos ▲ 8.553321 [DDD]

Montarsolo, Paolo (bass)
Donizetti, G.:Don Pasquale, w. Margherita Guglielmi (sop—Norina), Alfredo Kraus (ten—Ernesto), Rolando Panerai (bar—Malatesta), Paolo Montarsolo (bass—Don Pasquale), P. Bellugi (cnd), La Scala Orch, La Scala Chorus *(rec Jan 13, 1974)* Golden Age of Opera 2-▲ GAO 202/203 [ADD]
Leo, L.:La Morte di Abele, w. Emilia Cundari (sop—Angelo), Giuliana Matteini (sop—Abele), Adriana Lazzarini (mez—Eva), Ferrando Ferrari (ten—Caino), Paolo Montarsolo (bass—Adamo), C. F. Cillario (cnd), Angelicum CO, Turin Polyphonic Chorus Dynamic 2-▲ CDL 144
Mozart, W.A.:Nozze di Figaro, w. Mirella Freni (sop), Daniela Mazzucato (sop), Teresa Berganza (mez), Mirto Picchi (ten), Hermann Prey (bar), José Van Dam (b-bar), C. Abbado (cnd), La Scala Orch, La Scala Chorus *(rec live, Apr 22, 1974)* Arkadia 3-▲ 614
Rossini, G.:Il barbiere di Siviglia, w. T. Berganza (mez), L. Alva (ten), H. Prey (bar), C. Abbado (cnd), London SO, London Sym Chorus [I] Deutsche Grammophon 2-▲ 415695-2 [ADD]
Rossini, G.:La Cenerentola, w. Teresa Berganza (mez), Luigi Alva (ten), Renato Capecchi (bar), C. Abbado (cnd), Florence Maggio Musicale Orch, Florence Maggio Musicale Chorus *(rec Florence, May 1971)* Memories 2-▲ MEM 4283 [ADD]
Rossini, G.:L'italiana in Algeri, w. T. Berganza (sop), L. Zannini (mez), U. Benelli (ten), E. Dara (bar), A. Romero (bar), C. Abbado (cnd), Florence Teatro Comunale Orch, Florence Teatro Comunale Chorus *(rec 1973)* Great Opera Performances ▲ GOP 740

Monte, Duccio dal (bass)
Boccherini, L.:Credo, w. Svetla Krasteva (sop), Fernanda Piccini (cta), Manuel Beltrand (ten), G. Cosmi (cnd), Lucca Teatro Comunale Giglio Orch *(rec Dec 18, 1993)* Bongiovanni ▲ GB 2178 [DDD]
Boccherini, L.:Kyrie & Gloria, w. Svetla Krasteva (sop), Fernanda Piccini (cta), Manuel Beltrand (ten), G. Cosmi (cnd), Lucca Teatro Comunale Giglio Orch *(rec Dec 18, 1993)* Bongiovanni ▲ GB 2178 [DDD]

Monte, Toti dal (sop)
Gina Cigna & Toti Dal Monte, w. Gina Cigna (sop) Phonographe ("Great Voices" series) ▲ PHG 5057
The Italian Vocal Tradition, Vol. 1:The Voices of Toscanini, w. Toti dal Monte (sop), Claudio Muzio (sop), Rosetta Pampanini (sop), Biata Scacciati (sop), Giacomo Lauri-Volpi (ten), Francesco Merli (ten), Aureliano Pertile (ten), Carlo Galeffi (bar), Mariano Stabile (bar), Riccardo Stracciari (bar), Nazzareno de Angel *(rec 1921-35)* Iron Needle ▲ 1304
Opera Arias & Songs, w. Dal Monte, Toti (sop), La Scala Orch *(rec 1926-1929)* Preiser ("Lebendige Vergangenheit" series) ▲ PRE 89001 (m) [AAD]

Monte, Toti dal (sop) (cont.)
Puccini, G.:Madama Butterfly, w. Toti dal Monte (sop—Madama Butterfly), Maria Huder (mez—Kate Pinkerton), Beniamino Gigli (ten—B.F. Pinkerton), Adelio Zagonara (ten—Goro), Mario Basiola (bar—Sharpless), Gino Conti (bass—Principe Yamadori), Ernesto Dominici (bass—Il Bonzo), Vittoria Paolombini (sgr—Suzuki), O. de Fabritiis (cnd), Rome Opera Orch, Giuseppe Conca (cnd), Rome Opera Chorus *(rec Aug 1939)* Arkadia 2-▲ CD 78004 (m) [ADD]
Toti Dal Monte *(rec 1924-1939)* Pearl ▲ PEA 9493 (m) [AAD]

Monteanu, Petre (ten)
Beethoven, L. van:Sym 9, "Choral Sym", w. Magda Laszlo (sop), Lucienne Devallier (cta), Raffaele Arié (bass), H. Scherchen (cnd), Swiss-Italian RSO, Swiss-Italian Radio-TV Chorus Accord ▲ ACD 201002 [AAD]

Montefiore, David (cant)
Hazzan Rishon, Legendary Cantorial Recitativi, Opuses 1 & 2, w. C. Vineburg (pno), V. Zeltser (vn), A. Bacelar (vc), G. Lochner (vc), C. Morrison (va) Behar/Berg 2-▲ 001494

Monteil, Denise (sop)
Satie, E.:Socrate, w. M. Rosenthal (cnd), French National Orch—La mort de Socrate Adès ▲ ADE 203842 [AAD]

Monteyro, Lawrence (sop)
Music at the Time of Beaumarchais, w. Montserrat Figueras (sop), Raphel Oleg (vn), Miguel da Silva (va), Christophe Coin (vc), Marc Coppey (vc), José Miguel Moreno (gtr), Paul Badura-Skoda (pno), Philippe Cassard (pno), Eric Le Sage (pno), Bob Van Asperen (h Valois ▲ V 4767

Montfort, Jeanne (mez)
Gounod, C.:Faust, w. M. Berthon (sop), M. Coiffier (sop), C. Vezzani (ten), L. Musy (b-bar), M. Cozette (bar), M. Journet (bass), H. Busser (cnd), Paris Opera Orch, Paris Opera Chorus [F] *(rec 1930)* Pearl 2-▲ PEA 9987 [AAD]

Monti, Matteo de (sgr)
Schoenberg, A.:Die Jakobsleiter, w. Barbara Kilduff (sop—Seele 1), Jadwiga Rappé (cta—Sterbende), Wilfried Gahmlich (ten—Aufrührerischer), Cornelius Hauptmann (ten—Gabriel), Keith Lewis (ten—Berfener), Kurt Azesberger (bar—Mönch), Barbara Fuchs (sgr—Seele 2), Matteo de Monti (sgr—Ringender), Bjorn Waag (sgr—Auserwählter), E. Inbal (cnd), Frankfurt RSO, Robin Gritton (cnd), Berlin Radio Chorus *(rec Alte Oper, Frankfurt, Sept 6-9, 1994)* Denon ▲ CO 78977 [DDD]

Monti, Nicola (ten)
Bellini, V.:La sonnambula, w. M. Callas (sop), F. Cossotto (mez), N. Zaccaria (bass), A. Votto (cnd), La Scala Orch, La Scala Chorus [I] *(rec live 1957)* Melodram 2-▲ MEL 26003
Bellini, V.:La sonnambula, w. M. Callas (sop), F. Cossotto (mez), N. Zaccaria (bass), A. Votto (cnd), La Scala Orch, La Scala Chorus [I] *(rec live 1957)* Arkadia 2-▲ 503 (m) [AAD]
Bellini, V.:La sonnambula, w. M. Callas (sop), F. Cossotto (mez), N. Zaccaria (bass), A. Votto (cnd), La Scala Orch, La Scala Chorus [I] *(rec live 1957)* Verona 2-▲ 2704/05 (m) [AAD]
Bellini, V.:La sonnambula, w. M. Callas (sop), F. Cossotto (mez), N. Zaccaria (bass), A. Votto (cnd), La Scala Orch, La Scala Chorus [I] EMI Classics 2-▲ CDCB 47377 (m)
Bellini, V.:La sonnambula, w. Maria Callas (sop), Fiorenza Cossotto (mez), Franco Ricciardi (ten), Dino Mantovani (bar), Nicola Zaccaria (bass), A. Votto (cnd), La Scala Orch, La Scala Chorus Melodram 2-▲ CDM 26037
Bellini, V.:La sonnambula (sels), w. M. Callas (sop), F. Cossotto (mez), N. Zaccaria (bass), A. Votto (cnd), La Scala Orch, La Scala Chorus, from Act 2—Oh! se una volta sola rivederio; Ah, non creda mirarti [I] *(rec live, 7/4/57)* Myto 2-▲ 2 MCD 89006 (m) [ADD]
Handel, G.F.:Alcina, w. J. Sutherland (sop), N. Procter (cta), F. Wunderlich (ten), T. Hemsley (bar), F. Leitner (cnd), Cappella Coloniensis, Cologne Radio Chorus Melodram 3-▲ CDM 37002
Rossini, G.:Il barbiere di Siviglia (sels), w. G. d' Angelo (sop), G. Carturan (mez), R. Capecchi (bar), G. Giorgetti (bar), C. Cava (bass), G. Tadeo (bass), B. Bartoletti (cnd), Bavarian RSO IMP Collectors Series ▲ IMPX 9022 [AAD]
Rossini, G.:La Cenerentola, w. Teresa Berganza (mez), Sesto Bruscantini (bar), Mario Petri (bar), Leonardo Monreale (sgr), M. Rossi (cnd), Naples RAI SO, Naples Teatro San Carlo Chorus *(rec Oct 8, 1958)* Pantheon 2-▲ PHE 6656 (m)

Monticone, Rita (mez)
Verdi, G.:Falstaff, w. Pia Tassinari (sop—Alice Ford), Ines Alfani Tellini (sop—Nannetta), Aurora Buades (mez—Quickly), Rita Monticone (mez—Meg Page), Roberto D'Alessio (ten—Fenton), Giuseppe Nessi (ten—Bardolfo), Emilio Venturini (ten—Dr. Caius), Emilio Ghirardini (bar—Ford), Giacomo Rimini (bar—Sir John Falstaff), Salvatore Baccaloni (bass—Pistola), L. Molajoli (cnd), Milan SO, La Scala Chorus *(rec La Scala Theatre, Milan, Apr. 1932)* VAI Audio 2-▲ VAIA 1098-2

Moore, Austin Wright (ten)
Hindemith, P.:Hin und zurück, w. Jeanne Ommerlé (sop—Helene), Carl Halvorson (ten—Robert), Austin Wright Moore (ten—Sage), Richard Holmes (bar—Doctor), Robert Osborne (b-bar—Orderly), S. R. Radcliffe (cnd), New York Chamber Ensemble *(rec LeFrak Concert Hall, Queens College, Flushing, NY, May 30 & 31, 1994)* Albany ▲ TROY 173 [DDD]

Moore, C. (sgr)
Lloyd Webber, A.:Jesus Christ Superstar, w. P. Nicholas (sgr) [London cast] RCA ▲ 09026-61434-2 [DDD] ■ 09026-61434-4
Lloyd Webber, A.:Music of, w. M. Friedman (sgr), C. Carter (sgr), J. Barrowman (sgr), L. Robertson (sgr), J. Diedrich (sgr), Grania Renihan (sgr), J.O. Edwards (cnd), Munich SO—Cats; Joseph & the Amazing Technicolor Dreamcoat; Phantom of the Opera; Evita; Jesus Christ Superstar; Starlight Express; Song & Dance; Aspects of Love Koch International ▲ CD 340022 [DDD] ■ MC 340022

Moore, D. (nar)
Saint-Saëns, C.:Carnival of the Animals, w. M. Golabek (nar), R. Golabek (nar), F. Savage (nar), C. Heston (nar), J. E. Jones (nar), B. White (nar), L. Redgrave (nar), W. Shatner (nar), J. Rivers (nar), T. Danson (nar), L. Tomlin (nar), D. Raffin (nar), A. Hepburn (nar), D. Moore (nar), W. Matthau (nar), J. Smith (nar), L. Schifrin (cnd), Hollywood CO Dove Audio ▲ DOV 30700

Moore, Grace (sop)
Charpentier, M.-A.:Louise (sels), w. Josef Schmidt (ten), Robert Weede (bar), E. Rapée (cnd), Radio City Music Hall Orch, Radio City Music Hall Chorus—Depuis le jour Enterprise ("The Radio Years" series) ▲ ENT RY 58
Grace Moore & Josef Schmidt, w. Josef Schmidt (ten), Ernö Rapè (cnd) *(rec live Radio City Music Hall, NYC, 11/7/37)* Melodram ▲ CDM 18035 [ADD]
Joseph Schmidt, w. Joseph Schmidt (ten), Berlin RSO [cnd:Rudolf Hindemith, Bruno Seidler-Winkler, Hermann Scherchen, Fritz Stiedry, Max von Schillings], unknown orchestra [cnd:Idris Lewis], General Motors SO, General Motors Sym Chorus [cnd:Erno Rapee, José Iturbi, Oscar Straus], Helen Gleas Koch Schwann ▲ SCH 312572 [ADD]
Leider Singer, w. John McCormack (ten), E. Schneider (sgr), F. Kreisler (vn), V. O'Brien (pno), L. Bori (sop), L. Kennedy (vc) Symposium ▲ 1164
Leoncavallo, R.:Pagliacci (sels), w. Josef Schmidt (ten), Robert Weede (bar), E. Rapée (cnd), Radio City Music Hall Orch, Radio City Music Hall Chorus—Stridono lassù Enterprise ("The Radio Years" series) ▲ ENT RY 58
Love Me Forever *(rec 1925-42)* Pearl ▲ PEA 9116 [ADD]
Massenet, J.:Manon (sels), w. Josef Schmidt (ten), Robert Weede (bar), E. Rapée (cnd); Radio City Music Hall Orch, Radio City Music Hall Chorus—Obéissons quand leur voix appelle [Gavotte] Enterprise ("The Radio Years" series) ▲ ENT RY 58
Puccini, G.:La Bohème (sels), w. Josef Schmidt (ten), Robert Weede (bar), E. Rapée (cnd), Radio City Music Hall Orch, Radio City Music Hall Chorus—Che Gelida Manina; Sì, Mi Chiamano Mimì; O Soave Fanciulla Enterprise ("The Radio Years" series) ▲ ENT RY 58
Puccini, G.:Madama Butterfly (sels), w. Josef Schmidt (ten), Robert Weede (bar), E. Rapée (cnd), Radio City Music Hall Orch, Radio City Music Hall Chorus—Vogliatemi Bene Enterprise ("The Radio Years" series) ▲ ENT RY 58
Puccini, G.:Madama Butterfly (sels), w. W. Mengelberg (cnd), Royal Concertgebouw Orch—Un bel dí Archive Documents ("The Mengelberg Edition" series) ▲ ADCD 109
Puccini, G.:Tosca (sels), w. Josef Schmidt (ten), Robert Weede (bar), E. Rapée (cnd), Radio City Music Hall Orch, Radio City Music Hall Chorus—Recondita Armonia; Vissi d'Arte; E Lucevan le Stelle; Te Deum Enterprise ("The Radio Years" series) ▲ ENT RY 58

Moore, Roger (sgr)
Rodgers, R.:The King & I, w. J. Andrews (sgr—Anna Leonowens), L. Salonga (sgr—Tuptim), B. Kingsley (sgr—The King), P. Bryson (sgr—Lun Tha), M. Horne (mez—Lady Thiang), M. Liufau (sgr—Prince Chulalongkorn), E. Kingsley (sgr—Louis Leonowens), R. Moore (sgr—Sir Edward Ramsay), M. Sheen (sgr—The Kralahome), J. Mauceri (cnd), Hollywood Bowl Orch, Los Angeles Master Chorale *(rec Culver City, CA, Apr 1992)* Philips ▲ 438007-2 [DDD]

Mora, Fernando de la (ten)
The Artistry of Fernando de la Mora, w. Welsh National Opera Orch [cnd:Charles Mackerras] *(rec Brangwyn Hall, Swansea, Wales & Music Hall, Cincinnati, OH, Nov. 10-11, 1994 & Feb. 1)* Telarc ▲ CD 80411 [DDD]
Falla, M. de:La vida breve, w. C. Angell (mez), M. Senn (mez), E. Mata (cnd), Simón Bolívar SO [Sp] *(rec July 1993)* Dorian ▲ DOR 90192 [DDD]

Moran, John (sgr)
Moran, J.:Manson Family, w. T. Roache (sgr—Squeaky Fromme), J. Moran (sgr—Charles Manson) Iggy Pop (sgr—Jack Lord), *(orch unknown)* Point Music ▲ 432967-2 [DDD] ■ 432967-4

Moretta, Josette (nar)
Arma, P.:Music of, w. Fabrice Moretti (sax), Régis Poulain (bn), Jean-Marie Cottet (pno), Alain Béghin (perc), Francis Petit (perc), J.-L. Petit (cnd), Avray Atelier Musique—Phases contre phases for S Sax & Pno; Celui qui dort et dort for Nar, Bn, Xyl & Perc [after poems by Max Jacob]; 5 esquisses for Pno [from a Hungarian Theme]; Divertissement 1600 for Fls [w. Jean-Noël Catrice (fl), Béatrice Delpierre (fl), Pascale Haarscher (fl), Marie-Aude Menou (fl)]; 3 Regards for solo Ob [w. Jacques Vandeville (ob)]; Divert No. 6 for Cl & Pno [w. Dominique Vidal (cl)]; Parlando for solo Fl [w. Patrice Bocquillon (fl)] REM ▲ REM 311266 [DDD]

Morath, Hélène (cta)
Martin, F.:Le Vin herbé, w. B. Retchitzka (sop), O. de Nyzankowskyi (ten), H. Rehfuss (bar), D. Olsen (bass), F. Martin (pno), V. Desarzens (cnd), Winterthur State Orch members Jecklin-Disco 2-▲ JD 581/2-2 [ADD]

Moravec, Lubomir (alt)
Zelenka, J.D.:Missa sanctissimae trinitatis, w. Anna Hlavenková (sop), Magdalena Kozená (alt), Stanislav Predota (ten), Richard Sporka (ten), Michal Pospí il (bass), M. Stryncl (cnd), Musica Florea Studio Matou ▲ MAT 17 [DDD]

Mordino, Joseph (bar)
Saint-Saëns, C.:Samson et Dalila, w. Risë Stevens (mez—Dalila), Ramón Vinay (ten—Samson), Thomas Carter (ten—1st Philistine), Tony Lopez (ten—Philistine Messenger), Joseph Mordino (bar—High Priest), Arthur Cosenza (bass—Abimélech), Joseph Knight (bass—2nd Philistine), Ara Berberian (bass—Old Hebrew), R. Cellini (cnd), New Orleans Opera Orch, New Orleans Opera Chorus *(rec live, Apr 2, 1960)* VAI Audio 2-▲ VAIA 1055-2 [ADD]

Moreira, Maura (alt)
Bach, J.S.:St. Luke Passion, w. Christiane Sorell (sop), Kurt Equiluz (ten), Franz Wimer (bass), Josef Nebois (org), G. Barati (cnd), Vienna State Opera Orch, Akademie Chamber Choir Soloists Sarx 2-▲ SRX 2026 [ADD]
Brahms, J.:Alto Rhap, w. R. Wagner (cnd), Innsbruck SO, Innsbruck Chorus *(rec Innsbruck, 1963)* Allegretto ▲ ACD 8190
Haydn, J.:Mass 14, "Harmoniemesse", w. Christiane Sorell (sop), Elisabeth Thoman (sop), Rose Bahl (cta), Kurt Equiluz (ten), Gerhard Eder (bass), P. Wimburger (bass), G. Barati (cnd), Vienna State Opera Orch, Vienna Academy Chamber Choir *(rec 1964)* Tuxedo ▲ TUXCD 1055 [ADD]
Mahler, G.:Songs from Rückert, w. R. Wagner (cnd), Innsbruck SO *(rec Innsbruck, 1963)* Allegretto ▲ ACD 8190
Schumann, R.:Requiem Mignon, w. Christa Lehnert (sop), Edith Mathis (sop), Margarete Witte-Waldbauer (alt), Robert Titze (bass), R. Wagner (cnd), Innsbruck SO, Innsbruck Chorus *(rec Innsbruck, 1963)* Allegretto ▲ ACD 8190
Wagner, R.:Wesendonck Songs, w. R. Wagner (cnd), Innsbruck SO *(rec Innsbruck, 1963)* Allegretto ▲ ACD 8190

Morell, Adriana (sop)
Domingo at the Philharmonic, w. Plácido Domingo (ten), New York PO [cnd:Zubin Mehta] CBS ▲ MK 44942 [DDD] ■ MT 44942 (D)

Morelli, Carlo (bass)
Verdi, G.:Simon Boccanegra (sels), w. Celia Garcia (sop—Maria Boccanegra), Mario Filippeschi (ten—Gabriele Adorno), Ignacio Ruffino (ten—Pietro), Leonard Warren (bar—Simon Boccanegra), Roberto Silva (bass—Jacopo Fiesco), Carlo Morelli (bass—Paolo), R. Cellini (cnd), Mexican National Opera Orch, Mexican National Opera Chorus *(rec Palacio de las Bellas Artes, Mexico City, July 4, 1950)* Legato Classics ▲ LCD 185-1 [ADD]

Moreno, Rita (sgr)
Rodgers, R.:The King & I, w. Y. Brynner (sgr), M. Nixon (sgr), *(artists unknown)* *(rec 1956)* Broadway Angel ▲ ZDM 64693 ■ EG 64693

Moreschi, Alessandro (sgr)
The Last Castrato Opal ▲ CD 9823

Moresi, Giuseppe (bass)
Puccini, G.:Tosca, w. Renata Tebaldi (sop—Floria Tosca), Giuseppe di Stefano (ten—Mario Cavardossi), Rinaldo Pelizzoni (ten—Spoletta), Ettore Bastianini (bar—Baron Scarpia), Carlo Badioli (bass—Sacristan), Giuseppe Moresi (bass—Sciarrone), Franco Piva (bass—Jailer), Nicola Zaccaria (bass—Cesare Angelotti), G. Gavazzeni (cnd) *(rec Great Auditorium, Brussels World Fair, 1958)* Legato Classics 2-▲ LCD 2092 [ADD]

Moretti, Giuseppe (sgr)
Rossini, G.:Zelmira, w. Virginia Zeani (sop), Anna Maria Rota (cta), Enrico Campi (bass), Guido Mazzini (bass), Paolo Washington (bass), Gastone Limarilli (sgr), Nicola Tagger (sgr), C. Franci (cnd), *(orch unknown)* Great Opera Performances 2-▲ GOP 780

Moretto, M. (mez)
Cilea, F.:Adriana Lecouvreur (sels), w. M. Olivero (sop—Adriana), M. Moretto (mez—Princess di Bouillon), A. Cupido (ten—Maurizio), O. Mori (bar—Michonnet), C. Gandolfo (pno) *(rec Apr. 1993)* Bongiovanni ▲ GB 2515 [DDD]

Morgan, Beverly (mez)
Lerdahl, F.:Eros, w. F. Lerdahl (cnd), Collage New Music Ensemble [E] CRI ▲ CD 580 [ADD/DDD]

Morgan, F. (sgr)
Berlin, I.:Annie Get Your Gun, w. J. Garland (sgr), K. Wynn (sgr), H. Keel (sgr), *(other artists unknown)* *(rec 1949 soundtrack)* Sandy Hook ▲ CSH 2053

Morgan, J. P. (sgr)
Rodgers, R.:Music of, w. S. Bass (sgr), J. Andrews (sgr), P. Como (sgr), D. Reese (sgr), J. Jones (sgr), N. Luboff (sgr), M. Gold (sgr), N. Walker (sgr), H. Bowen (sgr), V. Damone (sgr), P. Nero (pno), E. Fisher (sgr), B. Goodman (cl), Ann-Margaret (sgr), Shorty Rogers (sgr), D. Shore (sgr), T. Martin (sgr), M. King (sgr), A. Newley (sgr) RCA ▲ 8590-2 R ■ 8590-4 R

Morgan, Leslie (sop)
Owen, J.:Songs, w. John Jenson (pno) *(rec July 7, 1989)* Centaur ▲ CRC 2233 [DDD]

Morgan, Mac (bar)
Strauss, R.:Enoch Arden, w. W. Ransom (pno) [E] *(rec June 1989)* ACA Digital Recording ▲ CM 20014
Suder, J.:Leider machen Leute, w. P. Coburn (sop), K. König (ten), W. Probst (bar), U. Mund (cnd), Bamberg SO, Bavarian Radio Chorus [G] Orfeo 2-▲ 124862 [DDD]

Morgan, Rachel Ann (mez)
Purcell, H.:Dido & Aeneas, w. C. Van Lunen (sop), D. Barick (bar), R. Shaw (cnd), Academy of the Begynhof Amsterdam [E] Globe ▲ GLO 5020 [DDD]

Morgan, Richard Lloyd (bass)
Henze, H.-W.:Elegy for Young Lovers, w. Regina Schudel (sop), Lawrence Richard (bass), Helmut Bernhofen (sgr), Bruno Fath (sgr), Aurelia Hajek (sgr), Silvia Weiss (sgr), B. Jones (cnd), Berlin Chamber Opera Orch *(rec Berlin)* Deutsche Schallplatten 2-▲ DS 1050

Morgny, B.-O. (ten)
Kraus, J.M.:Soliman II, w. L. Hoel (sop), B. Ortendahl-Corin (sop), T. Wallstrom (bass), P. Brunelle (cnd), Royal Swedish Opera Orch, Sweden Royal Opera Chorus Virgin Classics ▲ 59068 [DDD]

Mori, Orazio (bass)
Cilea, F.:Adriana Lecouvreur (sels), w. M. Olivero (sop—Adriana), M. Moretto (mez—Princess di Bouillon), A. Cupido (ten—Maurizio), O. Mori (bar—Michonnet), C. Gandolfo (pno) *(rec Apr. 1993)* Bongiovanni ▲ GB 2515 [DDD]
Donizetti, G.:Marino Faliero, w. M. Roberti (sop), A. Ferrin (bass), Meliciani (sgr), A. Camozzo (cnd), *(orch & chorus unknown)* [I] *(rec live, Bergamo 1966)* Melodram 2-▲ MEL 27030
Piccinni, N.:Didon, w. G. Tucci (sop), M. Petri (bass), M. Rossi (cnd), Naples RAI Orch, Naples RAI Chorus *(rec live 4/16/70)* Arkadia 2-▲ 596 [ADD]
Verdi, G.:La traviata, w. T. Fabbricini (sop—Violetta), A. Trevisan (mez—Annina), N. Curiel (mez—Flora), R. Alagna (ten—Alfredo), E. Cossutta (ten—Gastone), E. Gavazzi (ten—Giuseppe), O. Mori (bar—Douphol), E. Capuano (bass—d'Obigny), F. Musinu (bass—Grenvil), R. Muti (cnd), La Scala Orch, La Scala Chorus Sony Classical 2-▲ S2K 52486 [DDD]

Morino, Giuseppe (ten)
Bellini, V.:La sonnambula, w. Maria Costanza Nocentini (sop), Vitalba Mosca (mez), Giovanni Furlanetto (bar), Patrizia Ciofi (sgr), Etienne Ligot (sgr), Walter Mikus (sgr), G. Carella (cnd), Italian International Orch Nuova Era 2-▲ NUO 7215 [DDD]
Bizet, G.:Les Pêcheurs de perles, w. A. Ruffini (sop), B. Praticò (bar), C. Piantini (cnd), Italian International Orch, Slovak Phil Chorus [F] *(rec live 7/30–8/2/90)* Nuova Era 2-▲ 6944/45 [DDD]
Delibes, L.:Lakmé, w. A. Ruffini (sop), S. Lazzarini (mez), B. Praticò (bar), C. Piantini (cnd), Italian International Orch, Bratislava Chamber Chorus [F] Nuova Era 2-▲ 7096/97 [DDD]
Donizetti, G.:Gianni di Parigi, w. L. Serra (sop), E. Zilio (mez), E. Fissore (bar), A. Romero (bar), S. Manga (sgr), C. F. Cillario (cnd), Milan RAI Orch, Milan RAI Chorus [I] *(rec live)* Nuova Era 2-▲ 6752/53 [DDD]
Donizetti, G.:Maria di Rohan (sels), w. M. Nicolesco (sop), P. Coni (bar), M. de Bernart (cnd), Italian International Opera Orch, Slovak Phil Chorus [I] *(rec live)* Nuova Era 2-▲ 6732/33 [DDD]
Mercadante, S.:Il giuramento, w. M. Olmeda (sop), G. Carella (cnd), Loire PO Nuova Era 2-▲ NUO 7179 [DDD]
Opera Arias, w. Warmia National Orch [cnd:Bruno Amaducci] Nuova Era ▲ NUO 6851 [DDD]
Piccinni, N.:La cecchina, ossia la buona figliola, w. M. A. Peters (sop), A. Ruffini (sop), B. Praticò (bar), B. Campanella (cnd), Serenissima Pro Arte Orch [I] *(rec live 1990)* Memories 3-▲ DR 3101/03 [DDD]

Morison, Elsie (sop)
Handel, G.F.:Messiah, w. Marjorie Thomas (cta), Richard Lewis (ten), James Milligan (bass), M. Sargent (cnd), Royal Liverpool PO, Huddersfield Choral Society Classics for Pleasure 2-▲ CDCFP 4718 [ADD]
Handel, G.F.:Messiah (sels), w. Marjorie Thomas (cta), Richard Lewis (ten), James Milligan (bass), Eric Chadwick (org), M. Sargent (cnd), Royal Liverpool PO, Huddersfield Choral Society Classics for Pleasure ▲ CDCFP 9007 [ADD]
Mozart, W.A.:Requiem, w. Monica Sinclair (cta), Alexander Young (ten), Marian Nowakowski (bass), T. Beecham (cnd), Royal PO, BBC Sym Chorus *(rec 1958)* Theorema ▲ TH 121151
Sullivan, A.:The Sorcerer (sels), w. G. Baker (bar), J. Cameron (bar), R. Lewis (ten), M. Sargent (cnd), Pro Arte Orch, Glyndebourne Festival Chorus EMI Classics 2-▲ CDMB 64397

Morling, Carina (mez)
Donizetti, G.:Maria Stuarda (sels), w. Lena Nordin (sop), Ingus Petterssons (ten), Anders Bergström (bar), Tord Wallström (bar), Maria Wieslander (org), Sven Åberg (chit), Chrichan Larsson (vc), Nanette Nowels-Stenholm (pno), M. Guidarini (cnd), *(orch unknown)* Swedish Society ▲ SCD 1076
The Most Beloved Opera Choruses, w. [cnd:Sixten Ehrling], Royal Swedish Opera Chorus, Ingrid Tobiasson (cta), Magnus Kyhle (ten), Anders Lorentzon (bass) Caprice ▲ CAP 21520

Morozov, Boris (bass)
Glinka, M.:Russlan & Ludmilla, w. Nina Fomina (sop—Gorislava), Bela Rudenko (sop—Ludmilla), Tamara Sinyavskaya (mez—Ratmir), Boris Morozov (bass—Farlaf), Evgeny Nesterenko (bass—Russlan), Valeri Yaroslavtsev (bass—Svetozar), Y. Simonov (cnd), Bolshoi Theater Orch, Bolshoi Theater Chorus *(rec Moscow, 1978–1979)* Melodiya ("The Russian Opera" series) 3-▲ 74321-29348-2 [ADD]
Shchedrin, R.:Dead Souls, w. Larisa Avdeyeva (mez—Korobochka), Galina Borisova (mez—Plyushkin), Alexi Maslennikov (ten—Selifan), Vladislav Piavko (ten—Nozdryov), Vitali Vlasov (ten—Manilov), Boris Morozov (bass—Sobakevich), Alexander Voroshilo (sgr—Chichikov), Y. Temirkanov (cnd), Bolshoi Theater Orch, Bolshoi Theater Chorus, Moscow Chamber Choir *(rec Moscow, 1982)* Melodiya ("The Russian Opera" series) 2-▲ 74321-29347-2 [ADD]

Morozov, Igor (bar)
Bellini, V.:Beatrice di Tenda, w. E. Gruberová (sop—Beatrice), V. Kasarova (mez—Agnese), D. Bernardini (ten—Orombello), B. Robinšak (ten—Anichino), I. Morosov (ten—Filippo Maria Visconti), D. Sumegi (bass—Rizzardo), P. Steinberg (cnd), Austrian RSO, Austrian Radio Chorus [I] *(rec live, Vienna Concert House 1/30 & 2/1/92)* Nightingale Classics 2-▲ NC 070560-2 [DDD]
Bizet, G.:Les Pêcheurs de perles (sels), w. Janez Lotrič (ten), J. Wildner (cnd), Slovak RSO Bratislava—Au fond du temple saint *(rec Slovak Radio Concert Hall, Bratislava, Feb. 15–24, 1994)* Naxos ▲ 8.553030 [DDD]
Donizetti, G.:Lucia di Lammermoor (sels), w. Janez Lotrič (ten), J. Wildner (cnd), Slovak RSO Bratislava—Orrida è questa notte *(rec Slovak Radio Concert Hall, Bratislava, Feb. 15–24, 1994)* Naxos ▲ 8.553030 [DDD]
Rossini, G.:Guillaume Tell (sels), w. J. Lortič (ten), J. Wildner (cnd), Slovak RSO Bratislava—Arresta...Quali sguardi *(rec Bratislava, Feb. 15–24, 1994)* Naxos ▲ 8.553030 [DDD]
Verdi, G.:La forza del destino (sels), w. Janez Lotrič (ten), J. Wildner (cnd), Slovak RSO Bratislava, Slovak Opera Chorus—Invano, Alvaro; Nè gustare m'è dato *(rec Slovak Radio Concert Hall, Bratislava, Feb. 15–24, 1994)* Naxos ▲ 8.553030 [DDD]
Verdi, G.:Otello (sels), w. Janez Lotrič (ten), J. Wildner (cnd), Slovak RSO Bratislava—Desdemona rea, si, per ciel *(rec Slovak Radio Concert Hall, Bratislava, Feb. 15–24, 1994)* Naxos ▲ 8.553030 [DDD]
Verdi, G.:I vespri siciliani (sels), w. Janez Lotrič (ten), J. Wildner (cnd), Slovak RSO Bratislava—Ebben? Non mi rispondi tu?; Quando al mio sen per te parlava *(rec Slovak Radio Concert Hall, Bratislava, Feb. 15–24, 1994)* Naxos ▲ 8.553030 [DDD]

Morresi, Giuseppe (bass)
Bizet, G.:Carmen, w. Giovanna di Rocco (sop—Frasquita), Grace Bumbry (mez—Carmen), Anita Caminada (mez—Mercedes), Franco Corelli (ten—Don José), Mario Ferrara (ten—Dancario), Franco Bordoni (bar—Escamillo), Carlo Scaravelli (bar—Morales), Giuseppe Morresi (bass—Remendado), Francesco Signor (bass—Zuniga), O. de Fabritiis (cnd), *(orch unknown)* *(rec Macerata, July 21, 1974)* Golden Age of Opera 2-▲ GAO 181/82 [ADD]
Donizetti, G.:La fille du régiment (sels), w. Mirella Freni (sop), Anna di Stasio (mez), Angelo Mercuriali (ten), Luciano Pavarotti (ten), Wladimiro Ganzarolli (bar), Walter Monachesi (bar), V. Gullino (sgr), Luisa Rezzadore (sgr), N. Sanzogno (cnd), La Scala Orch, La Scala Chorus Budget ("The Greatest Voice in Opera" series) ▲ SYP 108
Leoncavallo, R.:Pagliacci, w. Joan Carlyle (sop—Nedda/Colombina), Carlo Bergonzi (ten—Canio/Pagliaccio), Franco Ricciardi (ten—Villager), Ugo Benelli (ten—Peppe/Arlecchino), Rolando Panerai (bar—Silvio), Giuseppe Taddei (bar—Tonio/Taddeo), Giuseppe Morresi (bass—Villager), H. von Karajan (cnd), La Scala Orch, La Scala Chorus *(rec La Scala, Milan, Oct 1965)* Deutsche Grammophon ("The Originals" series) ▲ 449727-2 [ADD]
Massenet, J.:Manon (sels), w. Mirella Freni (sop), Luciano Pavarotti (ten), Franco Ricciardi (ten), Wladimiro Ganzarolli (bar), Antonio Zerbini (bass), Ida Farina (sgr), P. Maag (cnd), La Scala Orch, La Scala Chorus *(rec live, Milan, 1969)* Budget ("The Greatest Voice in Opera" series) ▲ SYP 110
Puccini, G.:La Bohème, w. Ileana Cotrubas (sop—Mimi), Margherita Guglielmi (sop—Musetta), José Carreras (ten—Rodolfo), Saverio Porzano (ten—Parpignol), Regolo Romani (ten—Vendor), Claudio Giombi (bar—Benoit), Gianni Maffeo (bar—Schaunard), Angelo Romero (bar—Marcello), Alfredo Giacomotti (bass—Alcindoro), Carlo Meliciani (bass—Customs Officer), Giuseppe Morresi (bass—Sergeant), Paolo Washington (bass—Colline), G. Prêtre (cnd), La Scala Orch, La Scala Chorus *(rec Washington D.C., Sept 8, 1976)* Legato Classics 2-▲ LCD 201-2

Morresi, Giuseppe (bass) (cont.)
Zandonai, R.:Francesca da Rimini, w. Lydia Marimpietri (sop—Biancofiore), Magda Olivero (sop—Francesca), Pinuccia Perotti (sop—Samaritana), Edda Vincenzi (sop—Garsenda), Gabriella Carturan (mez—Smaragdi), Biancamaria Casoni (mez—Altichiara), Anna Maria Rota (cta—Donella), Athos Cesarini (ten—Archer), Angelo Mercuriali (ten—Ser Toldo Berardengo), Mario del Monaco (ten—Paolo), Piero de Palma (ten—Malatestino), Rinaldo Pelizzoni (ten—Prisoner), Gianpiero Malaspina (bar—Gianciotto), Dino Mantovani (bar—Jester), Enrico Campi (bass—Ostasio), Giuseppe Morresi (bass—Tower warden), G. Gavazzeni (cnd), La Scala Orch, La Scala Chorus *(rec La Scala Theatre, Milan, June 4, 1959)* Legato Classics 2–▲ LCD 186–2

Morris (sgr)
Berlioz, H.:Roméo et Juliette, w. A. S. von Otter (sop), P. Langridge (ten), J. Levine (cnd), Berlin PO, Ernst Senff Chorus [F] Deutsche Grammophon 2–▲ 427665–2 [DDD]

Morris, J. (bar)
Verdi, G.:Aida (sels), w. A. Millo (sop), D. Zajick (mez), P. Domingo (ten), S. Ramey (bass), T. Cook (bass), J. Levine (cnd), Metropolitan Opera Orch, New York Metropolitan Opera Chorus *(rec New York, May 18–26, 1990)* Sony Classical ("Opera Highlights" series) ▲ SMK 53506 [DDD]

Morris, James (bass)
Donizetti, G.:Maria Stuarda, w. J. Sutherland (sop), H. Tourangeau (mez), L. Pavarotti (ten), R. Soyer (bar), R. Bonynge (cnd), Bologna Teatro Comunale Orch, Bologna Teatro Comunale Chorus [I] London 2–▲ 425410–2 [ADD]
Donizetti, G.:Parisina, w. Montserrat Caballé (sop), Jérôme Pruett (ten), Louis Quilico (bar), E. Queler (cnd), New York City Opera Orch, New York Opera Chorus Pantheon 2–▲ PHE 6638
Donizetti, G.:Parisina, w. Montserrat Caballé (sop), Jérôme Pruett (ten), Louis Quilico (bar), E. Queler (cnd), New York City Opera Orch, New York Opera Chorus *(rec live, New York 1974)* Standing Room Only 2–▲ SRO 836–2 [ADD]
Fauré, G.:Requiem, w. J. Blegen (sop), R. Shaw (cnd), Atlanta SO, Atlanta Sym Chorus [L] Telarc ▲ CD 80135 [DDD]
Gershwin, G.:Songs, w. W. Bolcolm (pno) Elektra/Nonesuch ▲ 79151–2 [AAD]
Haydn, J.:Die Schöpfung, w. Norma Burrowes (sop), Rüdger Wohlers (ten), G. Solti (cnd), Chicago SO, Chicago Sym Chorus—sels. London ("Jubilee" series) ▲ 430739–2 [DDD]
Kern, J.:Songs, w. W. Bolcom (pno) Arabesque ▲ Z 6515 [DDD]
Mozart, W.A.:Requiem, w. P. Pace (sop), W. Meier (mez), F. Lopardo (ten), R. Muti (cnd), Berlin PO, Swedish Radio Chorus [L] EMI Classics ▲ CDC 49640 [DDD]
Offenbach, J.:Les Contes d'Hoffmann, w. E. Gruberova (sop), C. Eder (mez), P. Domingo (ten), M. Sénéchal (ten), Schmidt (sgr), G. Bacquier (bar), J. Diaz (bass), S. Ozawa (cnd), French National Orch, French Radio Chorus [F] Deutsche Grammophon 2–▲ 427682–2 [DDD]
Strauss, R.:Salome, w. J. Norman (sop), K. Witt (mez), A. Markert (cta), W. Raffeiner (ten), R. Leech (ten), S. Ozawa (cnd), Dresden Staatskapelle Philips 2–▲ 432153–2
Verdi, G.:Aida, w. A. Millo (sop), D. Zajick (mez), P. Domingo (ten), S. Ramey (bass), J. Levine (cnd), Metropolitan Opera Orch, New York Metropolitan Opera Chorus [I] Sony Classical 3–▲ S3K 45973 [DDD] 3–■ S3T 45973 (D)
Verdi, G.:Un ballo in maschera (sels), w. A. Schuh (sgr), Larrimore (sgr), J. Björling (ten), M. Rothmüller (bar), N. Treigle (bass), Feux (sgr), W. Herbert (cnd), *(orch unknown)* [I] *(rec live, New Orleans, 4/22/50)* Legato Classics ▲ LCD 154–1 (m) [ADD]
Verdi, G.:Il trovatore, w. A. Millo (sop), D. Zajick (mez), S. Kelly (cta), P. Domingo (ten), T. Willson (ten), A. Laciura (ten), G. Bater (bass), J. Levine (cnd), Metropolitan Opera Orch, New York Metropolitan Opera Chorus *(rec June 18, 1991)* Sony Classical 2–▲ S2K 48070 [DDD]
Wagner, R.:Parsifal, w. J. Norman (sop), P. Domingo (ten), E. Wlaschiha (bar), K. Moll (bass), J.-H. Rootering (bass), J. Levine (cnd), Metropolitan Opera Orch, New York Metropolitan Opera Chorus Deutsche Grammophon 4–▲ 437501–2
Wagner, R.:Das Rheingold, w. M. Lipovšek (mez), J. Rappé (ten), H. Zednik (ten), P. Haage (ten), A. Schmidt (bar), T. Adam (b-bar), H. Tschammer (bass), K. Rydl (bass), B. Haitink (cnd), Bavarian RSO [G] EMI Classics 2–▲ CDCB 49853 [DDD]
Wagner, R.:Das Rheingold, w. B. Svendén (sop), C. Ludwig (mez), S. Jerusalem (ten), H. Zednik (ten), E. Wlaschiha (bar), J. Levine (cnd), Metropolitan Opera Orch [G] Deutsche Grammophon 3–▲ 427607–2 [DDD]
Wagner, R.:Der Ring des Nibelungen (sels), w. E. Marton (sop), C. Studer (sop), K. Te Kanawa (sop), M. Lipovšek (mez), S. Jerusalem (ten), R. Goldberg (ten), P. Haage (ten), B. Haitink (cnd), Bayer RSO EMI Classics ▲ ZDC 54633
Wagner, R.:Siegfried, w. K. Te Kanawa (sop), E. Marton (sop), S. Jerusalem (ten), P. Haage (ten), B. Haitink (cnd), Bavarian RSO [G] EMI Classics 4–▲ CDCD 54290
Wagner, R.:Siegfried, w. H. Behrens (sop), B. Svenden (sop), R. Goldberg (ten), J. Levine (cnd), Metropolitan Opera Orch, New York Metropolitan Opera Chorus [G] Deutsche Grammophon 4–▲ 429407–2 [DDD]

Morris, Joan (mez)
After the Ball, w. William Bolcom (pno) Elektra/Nonesuch ▲ 79148–2
Blue Skies:Songs by Irving Berlin, w. William Bolcom (pno) Elektra/Nonesuch ▲ 79120–2 ■ 79120–4
Bolcom, W.:Casino Paradise, w. T. Nolen (bar), E. Korbich (sgr), M. Barrett (cnd), *(ensemble unknown)* Koch International Classics ▲ KIC 7047–2 [DDD]
Bolcom, W.:Sym 4, w. L. Slatkin (cnd), St. Louis SO [E] New World ▲ NW 356–2 [DDD]
Let's Do It:Bolcolm & Morris at Aspen, w. William Bolcom (pno) *(rec live in concert at the Aspen Music Festival, 7/22/89)* Omega Classics ▲ OCD 3004 [DDD]
Night & Day:The Cole Porter Album, w. William Bolcom (pno) Omega Classics ▲ OCD 3002 [DDD]
Silver Linings:Songs by Jerome Kern, w. William Bolcom (pno) Arabesque ▲ Z 6515
Wagner, R.:Der Ring des Nibelungen (sels), w. J. Norman (sop), H. Behrens (sop), K. Battle (sop), C. Ludwig (mez), R. Goldberg (ten), S. Jerusalem (ten), E. Wlaschiha (bar), M. Salminen (bass), J. Levine (cnd), Metropolitan Opera Orch—The Compact Ring—Ride of the Valkyries Wotan's Farewell & Magic Fire Music, Forest Murmurs, Brünnhilde's Awakening, Siegfried's Funeral Music, Brünnhilde's Immolation, & others Deutsche Grammophon ▲ 437825–2

Morris, Michael (bass)
Lewandowksi, L.L.:Choral Music, w. Sandra Lee (sop), Ann Sadan (alt), Don Carter (ten), Adam Cohn (b-bar), Carys Hughes (org), Robert Max (cnd), Zemel Choir—Ma Towu in F; Ma Towu in B♭; L'cho Dodi; Tow L'hodoss; Adoshem Moloch; W'hogen Ba'adenu [Uw'tsel]; W'schomru; L'icho Adoshem; J'Halahu [Hodo Al Erez]; Ladoshem Ho'orets; Uw'nucho Jomar; Adon Olom; Ki K'schimcho; Hajom Harass Olom; Kol Nidre; Schuwi Nafschi; Enosch, K'chozir Jomow; Halalujoh; Preise, Meine Seele Olympia ▲ OLY 347 [DDD]

Morris, Susan Rode (sop)
Burns, R.:Songs, w. Phebe Craig (hpd)—When rosy May comes wi' Flowers; Sweet are the Banks; Last May a braw Woaer; O saw ye bonie Lesley?; Oran gaoil; Thine am I; Weary fa' you Duncan Gray; My Harry was a gallant Gay; Lament for Abercairney; What shall I do with an auld Man?; Auld Lang Syne; Whare are ye gaun my bonie Lass?; I'll ay ca' in by yon Town; Her Daddie forbad; First when Maggie; O wha my Babie-Clouts will buy?; I hae a Wife o' my ain; Over the Water to Charlie; She's fair & fause; Peggy's Lament; Ae fond Kiss; Ye Banks & Braes o' bonie Doon; O whar gat ye that hauvermeal Bannock?; Now Nature hangs her Mantle green; Saw ye my Father?; Wae is my Heart?; Out over the Forth; O leave Novéls ye Mauchline Belles; My Love she's but a Lassie; Sir John Cope; McPherson's Rant; The Bairns gat out wi' an unco Shout; Corn Rigs; Jamie come try me *(rec Pony Tracks Ranch, Portola Valley, CA, Jan. 9–10, 1994)* Donsuemor ▲ DSM 40601 [DDD]
Burns, R.:Songs, w. Phebe Craig (hpd)—Dainty Davie; There Was a Lad; Ca' the Yowes; John Anderson; How Pleasant the Banks; Blew Bonnetts; Tam Glen; A Rosebud; Laddie Lie Near Me; Ettrick Banks; My Jo Janet; Willie Wastle; Lasly's March; Fareweel to a' our Scottish Fame [Parcel of Rogues]; Cauld Blaws the Wind; Turn Again Fair Eliza; The Birks of Aberfeldy; Roslin Castle; No Cold Approach, No Alter'd Mien; Castle Swien; The Winter it is Past; Peggie's Dream; Rattlin, Roarin Willie; A.A. Cameron Strathspey; I hae Been at Crookieden; By Yon Castle Wa'; Green Grow the Rashes O! *(rec Pony Tracks Ranch, Portola Valley, CA, Nov 27–28, 1994)* Donsuemor ▲ DSM 51201

Morris, Susan Rode (sop) (cont.)
Purcell, H.:Songs, w. Phebe Craig (hpd)—Prelude; Chacone; Minuet; Almand; Courante [all from Suite No. 8 in F]; Bess of Bedlam; I Lov'd Fair Celia; Who can from Joy Refrain; A Dialogue; The Fatal Hour; The Blessed Virgin's Expostulation; Ye Gentle Spirits of the Air; Dear Pritty Youth; We Sing to Him; Let Us Dance; Oh! Lead Me; On the Brow of Richmond Hill; Fairest Isle; Love in their Little Veins inspires; Hornpipe [from Suite No. 7]; The Rich Rival; Man is for the Woman made; A Mad Song [Beneath a Popular]; Musick for Awile *(rec Pony Tracks Rach, Portola Valley, CA, Nov. 2–4, 1997)* Donsuemor ▲ DSM 20601 [DDD]

Morrison, Peter (bar)
Porter, C.:Kiss Me, Kate, w. A. Drake (sgr), *(other artists unknown)* [1958 cast] Broadway Angel ▲ ZDM 64760 ■ EG 64760
Porter, C.:Kiss Me, Kate, w. A. Drake (sgr), *(other artists unknown)* [1948 Broadway cast] Columbia ▲ CK 04140 ■ JST 04140
Treasures of Operetta I, w. Marilyn Hill Smith (sop), Chandos Concert Orch [cnd:Stuart Barry] Chandos ▲ CHAN 8362 [DDD]
Treasures of Operetta II, w. Marilyn Hill Smith (sop), Chandos Concert Orch [cnd:Stuart Barry], Ambrosian Singers Chandos ▲ CHAN 8561 [DDD]
Treasures of Operetta III, w. Marilyn Hill Smith (sop), Chandos Concert Orch [cnd:Stuart Barry], Chandos Singers Chandos ▲ CHAN 8759 [DDD]

Morrison, Richard (bass)
Mozart, W.A.:Missa, K.427, w. Nancy Armstrong (sop), Dominique Labelle (sop), Jeffery Thomas (ten), A. Parrott (cnd), Boston Early Music Festival Orch, Handel & Haydn Society Chorus [L] Denon ▲ CO 79573 [DDD]
Tristan et Iseult:A Medieval Romance in Music & Poetry, w. Anne Azema (sop), Ellen Hargis (sop), Henri Ledroit (alt), William Hite (ten), Andrea von Ramm (sgr), Boston Camerata [cnd:Joel Cohen] Erato ▲ 98482–2

Morse, R. (sgr)
Loesser, F.:How to Succeed in Business without Really Trying, w. R. Vallee (sgr), *(other artists unknown)* [1961 Broadway cast] RCA ▲ 60352–2 RG [ADD] ■ 60352–4 RG

Mortagne, Christophe (ten)
Sauguet, H.:Les Pénitents en maillot roses, w. D. Abramovitz (pno) Sonpact ▲ SPT 93008 [DDD]

Morton, Richard (ten)
Arne, T.:Songs, w. E. Kirkby (sop), R. Goodman (cnd), Parley of Instruments [E]—not advised of sels. Hyperion ▲ CDA 66237 [DDD]

Morturier, Louis (sgr)
Berlioz, H.:La Damnation de Faust (sels), w. M. Berthon (sop), J. de Trévi (sgr), C. Panzéra (bar), P. Coppola (cnd), Pasdeloup Orch, St. Gervais Chorus [abridged vers] [F] *(rec 1931)* The Classical Collector 2–▲ FDC2 2006 [AAD]

Mory, Anny (sop)
Stravinsky, I.:Les Noces, w. P. Parker (mez), J. Mitchinson (ten), P. Hudson (bass), M. Argerich (pno), H. Francesch (pno), K. Zimerman (pno), C. Katsaris (pno), L. Bernstein (cnd), English Bach Festival Orch, English Bach Festival Chorus [R] Deutsche Grammophon ("20th Century Classics" series) ▲ 423251–2 [ADD]

Mosca, Vitalba (mez)
Bellini, V.:La sonnambula, w. Maria Costanza Nocentini (sop), Giuseppe Morino (ten), Giovanni Furlanetto (bar), Patrizia Ciofi (sgr), Etienne Ligot (sgr), Walter Mikus (sgr), G. Carella (cnd), Italian International Orch Nuova Era 2–▲ NUO 7215 [DDD]
Leo, L.:Amor vuol sofferenze, w. Marilena Laurenza (sop), Piero Guarnera (bar), Domenico Colaianni (sgr), Giovanna Donadini (sgr), Marilyne Fallot (sgr), Hyun Lee (sgr), D. Moles (cnd), Naples New Scarlatti Orch *(rec Martinafranca Festival, 1994)* Nuova Era 3–▲ NUO 7221

Moscona, Nicola (bass)
Beethoven, L. van:Sym 9, "Choral Sym", w. Jarmila Novotna (sop), Kerstin Thorborg (mez), Jan Pierce (ten), A. Toscanini (cnd), NBC SO, Westminster Choir *(rec 1939)* LYS ▲ LYS 128
Beethoven, L. van:Sym 9, "Choral Sym", w. Jarmila Novotná (sop), Kerstin Thorborg (mez), Jan Peerce (ten), A. Toscanini (cnd), NBC SO, Westminster Choir *(rec New York City, 1939)* Grammofono 2000 ▲ GRM 78524 (m)
Bellini, V.:Norma, w. M. Callas (sop), G. Simionato (mez), K. Baum (ten), G. Picco (cnd), Palacio Bellas Artes Orch, Palacio Bellas Artes Chorus *(rec live, Mexico City 5/23/50)* Melodram 2–▲ MEL 26018
Boito, A.:Mefistofele (sels), w. A. Toscanini (cnd), NBC SO, Robert Shaw Chorale, Columbus Boychoir—Prologue RCA Gold Seal ▲ 60276–2–RG [ADD] ■ 60276–4–RG
Gounod, C.:Faust, w. V. de los Angeles (sop), C. Ward (sgr), M. Mayhoff (sgr), R. Tucker (ten), H. Noel (sgr), D. Bernard (sgr), W. Herbert (cnd), New Orleans Opera Orch [F] *(rec Feb. 26, 1953)* Legato Classics 2–▲ LCD 167–2 [AAD]
Verdi, G.:Un ballo in maschera, w. Stella Andreva (sop—Oscar), Zinka Milanov (sop—Amelia), Bruna Castagna (cta—Ulrica), Jussi Björling (ten—Riccardo), Lodovico Oliviero (ten—Un Servo D'Amelia), John Cartet (bar—Un Giudice), Alexander Sved (bar—Renato), Normann Cordon (bass—Samuel), Arthur Kent (bass—Silvano), Nicola Moscona (bass—Tom), E. Panizza (cnd), *(orch unknown)* *(rec live, New York, Dec. 14, 1940)* The Fourties 2–▲ ENT FT 1515
Verdi, G.:I lombardi alla prima crociata (sels), w. V. Della Chiesa (sop), J. Peerce (ten), A. Toscanini (cnd), NBC SO—Act 3 Trio RCA Gold Seal ▲ 60276–2–RG [ADD] ■ 60276–4–RG (CrO2)
Verdi, G.:Requiem Mass, w. Z. Milanov (sop), B. Castagna (cta), J. Björling (ten), A. Toscanini (cnd), NBC SO, Westminster Choir [L] *(rec 11/23/40)* Melodram 3–▲ MEL 38006
Verdi, G.:Requiem Mass, w. Z. Milanov (sop), B. Castagna (cta), J. Björling (ten), A. Toscanini (cnd), NBC SO, Westminster Choir *(rec Mar. 4, 1938)* Legato Classics 2–▲ LCD 178–2
Verdi, G.:Requiem Mass, w. Zinka Milanov (sop), Bruna Castagna (mez), Jussi Björling (ten), A. Toscanini (cnd), NBC SO, Westminster Choir *(rec Nov 23, 1940)* Music & Arts 2–▲ CD 240
Verdi, G.:Rigoletto (sels), w. Nan Merriman (mez), Jan Peerce (ten), Frank Valentino (bar), G. Ribla (sgr), A. Toscanini (cnd), NBC SO—Act III (complete) Enterprise ("The Radio Years" series) ▲ ENT 48
Verdi, G.:Rigoletto (act 3), w. Nan Merriman (mez), Jan Peerce (ten), Frank Valentino (bar), G. Ribla (sgr), A. Toscanini (cnd), NBC SO [I] *(rec New York, 7/25/43)* Melodram 2–▲ MEL 28022 (m) [AAD]
Verdi, G.:Il trovatore, w. Norina Greco (sop), Bruna Castagna (mez), Jussi Björling (ten), Francesco Valentino (sgr), F. Calusio (cnd), *(orch & chorus unknown)* Enterprise ("The Radio Years" series) 2–▲ ENT 44 (m)
Verdi, G.:Il trovatore, w. Norina Greco (sop—Leonora), Bruna Castagna (cta—Azucena), Jussi Björling (ten—Manrico), Francesco Valentino (bar—Count di Luna), Nicola Moscona (bass—Ferrando), F. Calusio (cnd), *(orch unknown)* *(rec live, New York, Jan. 11, 1941)* The Fourties 2–▲ ENT FT 1507

Moscucci, Orietta (sop)
Boito, A.:Mefistofele, w. Orietta Moscucci (sop—Margherita), Amalia Pini (mez—Martha), Piero de Palma (ten—Wagner), Giacinto Prandelli (ten—Faust), Boris Christoff (bass—Mefistofele), V. Gui (cnd), Rome Opera Orch, Rome Opera Chorus EMI Classics 2–▲ CDMB 65655

Moser, Thomas (sgr)
Gluck, C.W.:Le Cinesi, w. K. Erickson (sop), M. Schiml (sop), A. Milcheva (mez), L. Gardelli (cnd), Munich RSO, Munich Radio Chorus [I] Orfeo ▲ 178891 [DDD] ■ MC 178891 (D)

Moser, Edda (sop)
Beethoven, L. van:Leonore (opera), w. Helen Donath (sop), Eberhard Büchner (ten), Richard Cassilly (ten), Theo Adam (b-bar), Hermann Christian Polster (bass), Karl Ridderbusch (bass), H. Blomstedt (cnd), Dresden Staatskapelle, Leipzig Radio Chorus Berlin Classics ▲ BER 1140
Beethoven, L. van:Missa Solemnis, w. H. Schwarz (mez), A. Kollo (ten), K. Moll (bass), L. Bernstein (cnd), Royal Concertgebouw Orch, Hilversum Chorus [L] Deutsche Grammophon 2–▲ 413780–2 [ADD]
Mozart, W.A.:Complete Mozart Edition, w. E. Mathis (sop), E. Gruberova (sop), L. Popp (mez), P. Schreier (ten), L. Hager (cnd), Salzburg Mozarteum Orch Philips 2–▲ 422531–2 [ADD]
Mozart, W.A.:Don Giovanni, w. K. Te Kanawa (sop), T. Berganza (mez), K. Riegel (ten), G. Raimondi (ten), J. Van Dam (b-bar), J. Macurdy (bass), L. Maazel (cnd), Paris Opera Orch, Paris Opera Chorus [I] CBS 3–▲ M3K 35192
Mozart, W.A.:Don Giovanni (sels), w. K. Te Kanawa (sop), T. Berganza (mez), K. Riegel (ten), G. Raimondi (ten), J. Van Dam (b-bar), J. Macurdy (bass), L. Maazel (cnd), Paris Opera Orch CBS ■ MT 35859

Moser, Edda (sop) (cont.)
Mozart, W.A.:Idomeneo, w. A. Rothenberger (sop), N. Gedda (ten), A. Dallapozza (ten), P. Schreier (ten), T. Adam (b-bar), H. Schmidt-Isserstedt (cnd), Dresden Staatskapelle, Leipzig Radio Chorus
EMI Classics ("Studio" series) 3-▲ CDMC 63990
Schumann, R.:Genoveva, w. P. Schreier (ten), D. Fischer-Dieskau (bar), S. Lorenz (b-bar), K. Masur (cnd), Leipzig Gewandhaus Orch, Berlin Radio Chorus
Berlin Classics ("Eterna" series) 2-▲ BER 2056 [ADD]
Wagner, R.:Arias & Scenes, w. A. Nanut (cnd), Ljubljana SO—Tristan und Isolde:Love-Death; Götterdämmerung:Brünnhilde's Immolation Stradivari Classics ▲ SCD 6064 [DDD]
Wagner, R.:Die Walküre (act 1), w. Edda Moser (sop—Sieglinde), Mark Lundberg (ten—Siegmund), Frode Olsen (bass—Hunding), I. Törzs (cnd), Mecklenburg State Orch *(rec Mecklenburg State Theatre, Schwerin, June 29, 1994)* Calig ▲ CAL 50943 [DDD]

Moser, Hans-Georg (bass)
Mozart, W.A.:Zauberflöte, w. Birgit Been (sop), Nathalie Boissy (sop), Marianne Seibel (sop), Renate Springer (sop), Elizabeth Vidal (sop), Eleanor James (mez), Salvador Guzman (ten), Herbert Hechenberger (ten), Wolfgang Newmann (ten), Klaus Häger (bass), Philip Langshaw (bass), P. Kuentz (cnd), Paul Kuentz Orch, Francis Bardot (cnd), Maitrise des Hauts-de-Seine members, Paul Kuentz Choirs Pierre Verany 2-▲ PVY 730055 [DDD]

Moser, Thomas (ten)
Berlioz, H.:Roméo et Juliette, w. Olga Borodina (mez), Alastair Miles (bass), C. Davis (cnd), Vienna PO, Bavarian Radio Chorus Philips ▲ 442134-2
Bruckner, A.:Mass 3, w. K. Mattila (sop), M. Lipovšek (mez), K. Moll (bass), C. Davis (cnd), Bavarian RSO, Bavarian Radio Chorus [L] Philips ▲ 422358-2 [DDD]
Cherubini, L.:Lodoïska, w. M. Devia (sop), F. Pedaci (sgr), B. Lombardo (ten), A. Corbelli (bar), W. Shimell (bar), R. Muti (cnd), La Scala Orch, La Scala Chorus Sony Classical 2-▲ SM2K 47290
Dvořák, A.:Requiem Mass, w. G. Beňačková (sop), B. Fassbaender (mez), J.-H. Rootering (bass), W. Sawallisch (cnd), Czech PO, Czech Chorus [L] Supraphon 2-▲ 10 4241 [DDD]
Humperdinck, E.:Königskinder, w. Dagmar Schellenberger (sop—Goose girl), Marilyn Schmiege (cta—Witch), Thomas Moser (ten—King's Son), Heinrich Weber (ten—Broommaker), Dietrich Henschel (bar—Fiddler), Andreas Kohn (bass—Woodcutter), F. Luisi (cnd), Munich RSO, Michael Gläser (cnd), Bavarian Radio Chorus *(rec live, Munich Herkulessaal, Mar 22-24, 1996)*
Calig 3-CAL 5096870 [DDD]
Mahler, G.:Das Lied von der Erde, w. C. Ludwig (mez), V. Neumann (cnd), Czech PO *(rec 1983)*
Praga ▲ PR 254052
Mahler, G.:Das Lied von der Erde, w. B. Fassbaender (mez), C. Katsaris (pno)—the first recording of Mahler's original piano/vocal score version [G] Teldec ▲ 2292-46276-2 ZK [DDD]
Mahler, G.:Das Lied von der Erde, w. M. Lipovšek (mez), G. Solti (cnd), Royal Concertgebouw Orch *(rec live Dec. 1992)* London ▲ 440314-2
Mozart, W.A.:Complete Mozart Edition, w. B. Fassbaender (mez), B. McDaniel (bar), L. Hager (cnd), Salzburg Mozarteum Orch Philips 3-▲ 422533-2 [ADD]
Mozart, W.A.:Don Giovanni, w. J. Varady (sop), A. Augér (sop), E. Mathis (sop), A. Titus (bar), R. Panerai (bar), R. Scholze (bass), J.-H. Rootering (bass), R. Kubelik (cnd), Bavarian RSO, Bavarian Radio Chorus [I] Eurodisc 3-▲ 7798-2 [DDD]
Mozart, W.A.:Finta semplice, w. Helen Donath (sop), Jutta-Renate Ihloff (sop), Teresa Berganza (mez), A. Rolfe Johnson (ten), Robert Lloyd (b-bar), Robert Holl (bass), L. Hager (cnd), Salzburg Mozarteum Orch [I] Orfeo 3-▲ 085843 [DDD]
Mozart, W.A.:Zaide, w. J. Blegen (sop), I. Hollweg (sop), W. Schöne (bass), R. Holl (bass), L. Hager (cnd), Salzburg Mozarteum Orch [G] Orfeo 2-▲ 055832 [DDD]
Schmidt, F.:Das Buch mit sieben Siegeln, w. Hertha Töpper (mez), Anton Dermota (ten), Robert Holl (bass), A.J. Hochstrasser (cnd), Lower Austria Tonkünst Orch, Graezer Concert Choir *(rec 1975)*
Preiser 2-▲ PRE 93263 [ADD]
Schmidt, F.:Das Buch mit sieben Siegeln, w. Sylvia Greenberg (sop), Carolyn Watkinson (cta), Peter Schreier (ten), Robert Holl (bass), Kurt Rydl (bass), L. Zagrosek (cnd), Austrian RSO, Vienna State Opera Chorus [G] Orfeo 2-▲ 143862 [DDD]
Spohr, L.:Jessonda, w. J. Varady (sop), R. Behle (sop), D. Fischer-Dieskau (bar), K. Moll (bass), G. Albrecht (cnd), Hamburg State PO, Hamburg State Opera Chorus [G] Orfeo 2-▲ 240912 [DDD]
Stravinsky, I.:Oedipus Rex, w. J. Norman (sop), S. Nimsgern (b-bar), R. Bracht (bass), C. Davis (cnd), Bavarian RSO, Bavarian Radio Chorus [L] Orfeo ▲ 071831 [DDD] ■ 071831 (D)
World Stars Sing Operetta, w. Moffo, Anna (sop), Lucia Popp (sop), José Carreras (ten), Ants Kollo (ten), Giuseppe Di Stefano (ten), Hermann Prey (bar), Karl Ridderbusch (bass), et al., various orchs *(rec 1968-1985)* Acanta ▲ 42941

Moses, Oral (b-bar)
Burleigh, H.T.:songs, w. Ann Sears (pno)—Deep River; Lovely Dark & Lonely One; Dry Bones; Wade in de Water; Ethiopia Saluting the Colors; The Dove & the Lily; Exile; Stan' Still, Jordan; Little Mother of Mine; Don't You Weep When I'm Gone; The Spring, My Dear, Is No Longer Spring; Oh! Rock Me, Julie; The Soldier; Mammy's Li'l Baby; Hear de Lambs A-Cryin'; The Trees Have Grown So; Thy Heart; Hard Trials; Didn't My Lord Deliver Daniel? Northeastern ▲ NR 252 [DDD]

Mosley, George (bass)
Purcell, H.:Dido & Aeneas, w. Ruth Holton (sop—Belinda), Elisabeth Priday (sop—2nd Woman), Donna Deam (sop—1st Witch), Shauna Beesley (sop—2nd Witch), Teresa Shaw (mez—Sorceress), Carolyn Watkinson (cta—Dido), Jonathan Peter Kenny (alt—Spirit), Paul Tindall (ten—Sailor), George Mosley (bass—Aeneas), J.E. Gardiner (cnd), English Baroque Soloists, Monteverdi Choir London *(rec Saint George's, Bristol, UK, July 12-14, 1990)* Philips ▲ 432114-2
Purcell, H.:Welcome to All the Pleasures, w. Ruth Holton (sop), Nicola Jenkin (sop), Michael Chance (alt), Paul Tindall (ten), J.E. Gardiner (cnd), English Baroque Soloists, Monteverdi Choir London *(rec Saint George's, Bristol, UK, July 12-14, 1990)* Philips ▲ 432114-2

Mosley, Robert (bar)
Black Christmas:Spirituals in the African-American Tradition, w. Vanessa Ayers (mez), Thomas Young (ten), Dinard Smith (pno), Ronald Isaac (cnd) ESS.A.Y ▲ ESS 1011 [DDD]

Moss, David (voc)
Apple, J.:Voices in the Dark, w. Anna Holmer (voc), Jacki Apple (elec) ¿What Next? ▲ WN 0014

Moss, Eileen (sgr)
Wayditch, G. von:Jesus before Herod, w. Michael Best (ten—Jappeticus), Christopher Lindbloom (sgr—Philippo/Herod), Eileen Moss (sgr—Pabula), Vincent Russo (sgr—Pabo), Stephen A. Scot-Shepherd (sgr—Luke the Evangelist), Pauline Tweed (sgr—1st & 2nd girls), P. Erős (cnd), San Diego SO, San Diego Master Chorale *(rec 1979)* VAI Audio 2-▲ VAIA 1095-2 [ADD]

Moss, Kurt (sgr)
Mozart, W.A.:Entführung, w. Mariella Devia (sop), Uwe Peper (ten), W. Sawallisch (cnd), La Scala Orch, La Scala Chorus *(rec live, 1994)* Serenissima 2-▲ SER 360161

Most, Ingeborg (alt)
Bach, J.S.:St. John Passion, w. Barbara Schlick (sop), Edrian Brand (ten), Alexander Stevenson (ten), Philip Langshaw (bass), Peter Lika (bass), P. Kuentz (cnd), Paul Kuentz Orch, Paul Kuentz Choir
Pierre Verany 2-▲ PVY 730051 [DDD]

Mostomoi, Vladimir (ten)
Suder, J.:Festival Mass, w. Natalia Kornewa (sop), Maria Neilau (alt), Juri Dobrowolski (bass), Jessica Hartlieb (vn), Marlene Hinterberger (org), W.A. Albert (cnd), Bavarian State Youth Orch, St. Petersburg Chamber Choir Calig ▲ CAL 50945 [DDD]

Mostowoy, Vladimir (ten)
Rachmaninoff, S.:All-Night Vigil, w. O. Borodina (mez), N. Korniev (cnd), St. Petersburg Chamber Choir *(rec St. Petersburg, Oct. 3-6, 1993)* Philips ▲ 442344-2

Motchalov, Alexei (bass)
Karetnikov, N.:Till Eulenspiegel, w. E. Mazo (sop), L. Mkrtchian (cta), A. Proujanski (ten), B. Koudriavtsev (bar), P. Glouboky (bass), A. Martinov (sgr), Polianski (cnd), Soviet Cinema Orch, Soviet Cinema Chorus *(rec Moscow, 1988)* Russian Season ("Russian Season" Series) 2-▲ LDC 288029/30 [DDD]

Mott, Charles (bar)
Elgar, E.:The Starlight Express (suite), w. A. Nicholls (sop), E. Elgar (cnd), *(orch unknown)* *(rec 1916)*
Pearl 5-▲ PEAS 9951/55 (m) [AAD]

Moubayed, Islen (sgr)
Verdi, G.:Un giorno di regno, w. Maria Casula (sop), Angelo Romero (bar), Enrico Fissore (bass), Franca Fabbri (sgr), Michele Guento (sgr), Ruggero Rado (sgr), Bernardino Trotta (sgr), A. Zedda (cnd), *(orch unknown)* Great Opera Performances 2-▲ GOP 782

Mouton, C. (bass)
Blanchard, P.:Music of, w. P. Blanchard (vn), V. Pagliarin (vn), C. Terranova (kbd), L. Robin (dr), M. Garay (perc)—Isidora; Koid'9; Perdoname; Folklores; Train de sables; Lithops; Marquesas Keys; Bodas de sangue *(rec Nov. 1992)* OMD ▲ CD 1538 [DDD]

Moutsios, George (ten)
Glanville-Hicks, P.:Nausicaa, w. Teresa Stratas (sop—Nausicaa), Sophia Steffan (cta—Queen Arete), Michalis Heliotis (ten—Antinous/Priest), George Moutsios (ten—Eurymachus), Edward Ruhl (ten—Phemius), George Tsantikos (ten—Clytoneus), Vassilis Koundouris (bar—Messenger), John Modenos (bar—Aethon), Spiro Malas (bass—King Alcinous), C. Surinach (cnd), Athens SO, Athens Sym Chorus *(rec Athens Festival, 1961)* CRI ▲ CD 695 [ADD]
Glanville-Hicks, P.:Nausicaa (sels), w. Teresa Stratas (sop), Spiro Malas (bass), Michalis Helii (sgr), Michalis Heliots (sgr), Edward Ruhl (sgr), Sophia Steffan (sop), George Tsantikos (sgr), C. Surinach (cnd), Athens SO, Athens Sym Chorus CRI ▲ CD 695 [ADD]

Möwes, T. (bass)
Weill, K.:Vom Tod im Wald, w. M. Pommer (cnd), Leipzig RSO Ondine ▲ ODE 771-2 [DDD]

Moyers, Bill (nar)
The Story of Percussion in the Orchestra, w. Nexus, Rochester PO Nexus ▲ 10306 [DDD]

Mráz, Ladislav (bar)
Martinů, B.:Bouquet, w. Libuše Domanínská (sop), Soňa Červená (alt), Lubomír Havlák (ten), K. Ančerl (cnd), Czech PO, Czech Phil Chorus *(rec 1967)* Praga ("Karel Ančerl Edition" series) ▲ PR 254061
Novák, V.:Storm, w. Maria Tauberová (sop), Drahomíra Tikalová (sop), Beno Blachut (ten), J. Krombholc (cnd), Czech PO, Czech Phil Chorus *(rec 1956)* Supraphon 2-▲ SUP 111982 (m) [DDD]

Mrázová, Marie (cta)
Roussel, A.:Evocations, w. Zdenek Svehla (ten), Jindřich Jindrák (bar), Z. Košler (cnd), Czech PO, Czech Phil Chorus Supraphon ▲ SUP 111823 [AAD]
Zelenka, J.D.:Missa Gratias agimus tibi, w. J. Jonášová (sop), V. Dolezal (ten), P. Mikuláš (bass), J. Belohlávek (cnd), Czech PO, Czech Phil Chorus [L] Supraphon ▲ 11 0816-2 [DDD]

Mróz, Leonard Andrzej (bass)
Ave Maria, w. Bozena Betley (sop), Wieslaw Ochman (ten), Marian Sawa (org)
Polskie Nagrania Edition ▲ ECD 049 [DDD]
Gade, N.W.:Kalanus, w. M. Rørholm (mez), N. Gedda (ten), F. Rasmussen (cnd), Collegium Musicum, Canzone Choir Kontrapunkt ▲ 32072 [DDD]
Moniuszko, S.:Haunted Manor, w. Bozena Betley-Siradzka (sop—Hanna), Anna Witkowska (sop—Marta/Stara Niewiasta), Wiera Baniewicz (mez—Jadwiga), Aleksandra Imalska (mez—Czesnikowa), Kazimierz Dluha (Grzes), Zdzislaw Nikodem (ten—Damazy), Wieslaw Ochman (ten—Stefan), Andrzej Hiolski (bar—Miecznik), Florian Skulski (bar—Maciej), Leonard Mróz (bass—Zbigniew), Andrzej Saciuk (bass—Skoluba), J. Krenz (cnd), Cracow Polish Radio-TV Orch, Cracow Polish Radio-TV Chorus *(rec Cracovia, 1978)* Agorá Music ("Phoenix" series) 3-▲ 509 [ADD]
Mozart, W.A.:Requiem, w. Barbara Nieman (sop), Krystyna Szostek-Radkowa (mez), Wieslaw Ochman (ten), K. Kord (cnd), Warsaw PO, Henryk Wojnarowski (cnd), Warsaw National Phil Chorus *(rec Warsaw, 1979)* Polskie Nagrania ▲ PNCD 135 [ADD]
Penderecki, K.:Dies Irae, w. O. Szwajgier (sop), Z. Jankovski (ten), S. Kawalla (cnd), Polish Radio-TV SO, Polish Radio-TV Chorus [L] Vienna Modern Masters ▲ VMM 3015 [DDD]

Mróz, Leonard Andrzej (bass)
Szymanowski, K.:King Roger, w. B. Zagòrzanka (sop), A. Malewicz-Madey (cta), H. Grychnik (ten), W. Ochman (ten), A. Hiolski (bar), K. Stryja (cnd), Polish State PO Katowice, Cracow Phil Boys' Chorus, Polish State Phil Chorus *(rec Apr. 7-9, 1990)*
Marco Polo ("Opera Classics" series) 2-▲ 8.223339/40 [DDD]

Muenz, Richard (b-bar)
Barber, S.:A Hand of Bridge, w. C. Aks (sop), F. Kittelson (mez), W. Carney (ten), Adirondack CO, Gregg Smith Singers [E] Premier ▲ PRCD 1009 [ADD]
Schuman, W.:The Mighty Casey, w. R. Rees (sop), T. Bogdan (ten), W. Schuman (cnd), Adirondack CO, Gregg Smith Singers, Long Island Choral Association [E] Premier ▲ PRCD 1009 [ADD]

Muff, Alfred (bass)
Dessau, P.:Haggada, w. Sabine Ritterbusch (sop), Renate Spingler (sop), Yvi Jänicke (alt), Peter Galliard (ten—Rabbi Tarfon/Jude/ten solo), Gabriel Sadé (ten—Pharaoh), Jochen Schmeckenbecher (bar—Rabbi Jehoschua), Bernd Weikl (bar—Moses), Matthias Hölle (bass—Speaker/Rabbi Akiwa), Alfred Muff (bass—Father/Rabbi Eleasar), Johann Tilli (bass—Rabbi Elieser/bass solo), G. Albrecht (cnd), Hamburg State PO, Berlin Carl Maria Von Weber Men's Choir, Hamburg Alsterspatzen, North German Radio Chorus [G] *(rec Musikhalle, Hamburg, Sept 4 & 5, 1994)* Capriccio 2-▲ 10590/91 [DDD]
Schreker, F.:Die Gezeichneten, w. Elisabeth Connell (sop), Heinz Kruse (ten), Monte Pederson (bar), László Polgar (bass), L. Zagrosek (cnd), Berlin German SO London 3-▲ 444442-2
Strauss, R.:Die Frau ohne Schatten, w. C. Studer (sop), U. Vinzing (sop), H. Schwarz (mez), R. Kollo (ten), Schmidt (sgr), W. Sawallisch (cnd), Bavarian RSO, Bavarian Radio Chorus [G]
EMI Classics ▲ CDC 54494 [DDD]
Strauss, R.:Die Frau ohne Schatten, w. C. Studer (sop), U. Vinzing (sop), H. Schwarz (mez), R. Kollo (ten), Schmidt (sgr), W. Sawallisch (cnd), Bavarian RSO, Bavarian Radio Chorus [uncut version] [G]
EMI Classics 3-▲ CDCC 49074 [DDD]
Wagner, R.:Der fliegende Holländer, w. I. Haubold (sop—Senta), M. Schiml (mez—Nurse), P. Seiffert (ten—Erik), J. Hering (ten—Helsman), A. Muff (bar—The Dutchman), E. Knodt (bass—Sea Capt.), P. Steinberg (cnd), Vienna ORF SO, Budapest Radio Chorus [G] *(rec Sept. 1992)*
Naxos 2-▲ 8.660025/26 [DDD]

Mühle, Anne-Marie (sop)
Crumb, G.:Madrigals (4 books), w. A.-M. Bergström (fl), S. Lüannerholm (hp), S. Röjder (db), S. Asikainen (perc)—[Sp] *(rec digital)* BIS ▲ CD 261

Mukk, Jozsef (ten)
Bach, J.S.:Cant 51, w. I. Kertesi (sop), J. Pászthy (sop), J. Nemeth (mez), I. Gáti (bass), M. Antal (cnd), Failoni CO, Hungarian Radio Chorus Naxos ▲ 8.550643 [DDD]
Bach, J.S.:Cant 80, w. I. Kertesi (sop), J. Nemeth (alt), I. Gáti (bass), M. Antal (cnd), Failoni CO, Hungarian Radio Chorus *(rec Jan 1992)* Naxos ▲ 8.550642
Bach, J.S.:Cant 147, w. I. Kertesi (sop), J. Nemeth (alt), I. Gáti (bass), M. Antal (cnd), Failoni CO, Hungarian Radio Chorus *(rec Jan 1992)* Naxos ▲ 8.550642 [DDD]
Bach, J.S.:Cant 208, "Hunting Cant", w. I. Kertesi (sop), J. Pászthy (sop), J. Nemeth (mez), I. Gáti (bass), M. Antal (cnd), Failoni CO, Hungarian Radio Chorus Naxos ▲ 8.550643 [DDD]
Bach, J.S.:Cant 211, "Coffee Cant", w. I. Kertesi (sop), I. Gáti (bass), M. Antal (cnd), Failoni CO *(rec 1992)* Naxos ▲ 8.550641 [DDD]
Bach, J.S.:Cant 212, "Peasant Cant", w. I. Kertesi (sop), I. Gáti (bass), M. Antal (cnd), Failoni CO *(rec 1992)* Naxos ▲ 8.550641 [DDD]
Bach, J.S.:St. Matthew Passion, w. R. Kiss (sop), I. Verebics (sop), Á. Csenki (mez), J. Németh (mez), P. Cser (ten), I. Gati (bar), F. Korpás (bar), P. Köves (bass), G. Oberfrank (cnd), Hungarian State SO, Hungarian Festival Choir, Hungarian Radio Children's Choir [G] *(rec Feb 1993)*
Naxos 3-▲ 8.550832/34 [DDD]
Mozart, W.A.:Alma Dei creatoris, w. Ibolya Verebics (sop), Judit Németh (cta), József Moldvay (bar), Gábor Oláh (bar), István Ella (org), János Reményi (cnd), Hungarian Radio-TV Children's Chorus Girls' Voices, Hungarian Radio-TV Male Chamber Choir *(rec Hungaroton Studio, June 14-16, 1991)*
Hungaroton ▲ HCD 4003 [DDD]
Mozart, W.A.:Ave verum corpus, w. Ibolya Verebics (sop), Judit Németh (cta), József Moldvay (bar), Gábor Oláh (bar), István Ella (org), János Reményi (cnd), Hungarian Radio-TV Children's Chorus Girls' Voices, Hungarian Radio-TV Male Chamber Choir *(rec Hungaroton Studio, June 14-16, 1991)*
Hungaroton ▲ HCD 4003 [DDD]
Mozart, W.A.:Miserere, w. Ibolya Verebics (sop), Judit Németh (cta), József Moldvay (bas), Gábor Oláh (bar/Gregorian intonations), István Ella (org), János Reményi (cnd), Hungarian Radio-TV Children's Chorus Girls' Voices, Hungarian Radio-TV Male Chamber Choir *(rec Hungaroton Studio, June 14-16, 1991)* Hungaroton ▲ HCD 4003 [DDD]

Mukk, Jozsef (ten) (cont.)
Mozart, W.A.:Misericordias Domini, w. Ibolya Verebics (sop), Judit Németh (cta), József Moldvay (bass), Gábor Oláh (bar/Gregorian intonations), István Ella (org), János Reményi (cnd), Hungarian Radio–TV Children's Chorus Girls' Voices, Hungarian Radio–TV Male Chamber Choir *(rec Hungaroton Studio, June 14–16, 1991)* Hungaroton ▲ HCD 4003 [DDD]
Mozart, W.A.:Missa brevis, K.65, w. Ibolya Verebics (sop), Judit Németh (cta), József Moldvay (bass), Gábor Oláh (bar/Gregorian intonations), István Ella (org), János Reményi (cnd), Hungarian Radio–TV Children's Chorus Girls' Voices, Hungarian Radio–TV Male Chamber Choir *(rec Hungaroton Studio, June 14–16, 1991)* Hungaroton ▲ HCD 4003 [DDD]
Mozart, W.A.:Missa brevis, K.194, w. Ibolya Verebics (sop), Judit Németh (cta), József Moldvay (b), Gábor Oláh (bar/Gregorian intonations), István Ella (org), János Reményi (cnd), Hungarian Radio–TV Children's Chorus Girls' Voices, Hungarian Radio–TV Male Chamber Choir *(rec Hungaroton Studio, June 14–16, 1991)* Hungaroton ▲ HCD 4003 [DDD]
Mozart, W.A.:Sancta Maria, w. Ibolya Verebics (sop), Judit Németh (cta), József Moldvay (bass), Gábor Oláh (bar/Gregorian intonations), István Ella (org), János Reményi (cnd), Hungarian Radio–TV Children's Chorus Girls' Voices, Hungarian Radio–TV Male Chamber Choir *(rec Hungaroton Studio, June 14–16, 1991)* Hungaroton ▲ HCD 4003 [DDD]

Mulder, Marisca (sop)
Verdi, G.:Macbeth (sels), w. Carol Vaness (sop), Ambrogio Riva (bass), R. Abbado (cnd), Munich RSO, Bavarian Radio Chorus—Grand Sleepwalking Scene [from Act IV] *(rec Studio 1, Bavaria, Apr 13–17, 1993)* RCA Red Seal ▲ 09026–61828–2 [DDD]

Müller, Bruno (bass)
Lortzing, A.:Zar und Zimmermann, w. M. Gripekoven (sop—Marie), E. Mayer (cta—Widow Browe), H. Buchta (ten—Peter Ivonov), H. Schmid-Berikoven (ten—Marquis de Chateauneuf), G. Hann (b-bar—Tsar Peter I), W. Strienz (b-bar—Van Bett) Myto 2–▲ MCD 943103

Müller, Hartmut (bass)
Diabelli, A.:Pastoralmesse, w. C. Degler (sop), S. Linden (sop), S. Rauschkolb (cta), D. Clayton (ten), E. Ehret (cnd), Munich St. Michael's Orch, Munich St. Michael Choir [L] Koch Schwann ▲ CD 313015 [ADD]
Mozart, W.A.:Missa, K.66, w. P. Wise (sop), M. Aoyama (cta), P. Baillie (ten), E. Hinreiner (cnd), Salzburg Camerata Academica, Salzburg RSO, Mozart Choir [L] *(rec May 1974)* Koch Treasure ▲ 316182 [ADD]
Mozart, W.A.:Missa, K.317, w. G. Fuchs (sop), Novak (alt), Sailer (ten), E. Hinreiner (cnd), Salzburg Mozarteum Orch, Salzburg Mozarteum Chorus [L] Pro Arte ▲ CDD 471 [DDD]
Mozart, W.A.:Vesperae, w. Christa Degler (sop), Margarete Kissel (alt), Desmond Clayton (ten), E. Hinreiner (cnd), Salzburg Mozarteum Camerata Academica Studio SM ▲ 2518

Müller, Maria (sop)
The Legendary Singers at Lindenoper Berlin (1927–1945)—, w. Gitta Alpar (sop), Erna Berger (sop), Tiana Lemnitz (sop), Margarete Klose (cta), Peter Anders (ten), Max Lorenz (ten), Walter Ludwig (ten), Lauritz Melchior (ten), Rudolf Schock (ten), Franz Völker (ten), Willi Domgraf-Fassb *(rec 1927; 1937; 1941–45)* Minerva ▲ MN A21 [ADD]
Wagner, R.:Der fliegende Holländer, w. Joel Berglund (ten), Franz Völker (ten), Ludwig Hoffmann (bass), R. Kraus (cnd), Bayreuth Festival Orch, Bayreuth Festival Chorus *(rec live, Bayreuth, July 18, 1942)* Preiser 2–▲ PRE 90232 [ADD]
Wagner, R.:Lohengrin, w. F. Volker (ten), J. Prohaska (bar), A. Rother (cnd), Berlin Staatskapelle [G] *(rec 1942)* Preiser 3–▲ 90043 (m) [AAD]
Wagner, R.:Lohengrin (sels), w. Maria Müller (sop—Elsa), Margarete Klose (mez—Ortrud), Franz Völker (ten—Lohengrin), Jaro Prohaska (bar—Telramund), Josef von Manowarda (bass—King Heinrich), H. Tietjen (cnd), Vienna State Opera Orch *(rec Vienna, 1938)* Koch Schwann 2–▲ SCH 314682 [ADD]
Wagner, R.:Lohengrin (sels), w. Margarete Klose (mez), Franz Völker (ten), Joseph von Manowarda (bass), W. Furtwängler (cnd), Bayreuth Festival Orch, Bayreuth Festival Chorus—Prelude to Act III; Operatic sels. *(rec 1931)* Grammofono 2000 ▲ GRM 78515 [ADD]
Wagner, R.:Die Meistersinger von Nürnberg, w. Max Lorenz (ten), Jaro Prohaska (bar), Josef Greindl (bass), Bayreuth Festival Orch, Bayreuth Festival Chorus *(rec live, July–Aug 1943)* Grammofono 2000 4–▲ GRM 78602
Wagner, R.:Tannhäuser (sels), w. Anna Báthy (sop), Max Lorenz (ten), W. Furtwängler (cnd), Vienna State Opera Orch Koch Schwann 2–▲ SCH 314702 [ADD]
Wagner, R.:Die Walküre (sels), w. Anny Konetzni (sop—Brunnhilde), Maria Müller (sop—Sieglinde), Franz Völker (ten—Siegmund), Walter Grossmann (bass—Wotan), W. Furtwängler (cnd), Vienna State Opera Orch *(rec Vienna, Feb. 13–17, 1936)* Koch Schwann 2–▲ SCH 314702 [ADD]
Wagner, R.:Die Walküre (act 3), w. K. Flagstad (sop—Brünnhilde), M. Müller (sop—Sieglinde), R. Bockelmann (b-bar—Wotan), W. Furtwängler (cnd), Royal Opera House Orch [G] *(rec Covent Garden, 5/26/37)* Myto ▲ 1 MCD 91443 [ADD]

Müller, Rufus (ten)
Bach, J.S.:St. Matthew Passion, w. N. Argenta (sop), L. Lee (mez), J. Kenny (alt), J. MacDougall (ten), R. Jackson (bar), S. Varcoe (b-bar), P. Goodwin (cnd), *(orch & chorus unknown)* United 2–▲ UNI 89301 [DDD]
Bach, J.S.:St. Matthew Passion (sels), w. N. Argenta (sop), L. Lee (mez), J. Kenny (alt), J. MacDougall (ten), R. Jackson (bar), S. Varcoe (b-bar), P. Goodwin (cnd), *(orch & chorus unknown) (rec St. George's Theater, London, Feb 24–27, 1994)* United ▲ UNI 88030 [DDD]
Benda, G.A.:Cephalus & Aurora, w. E. Kirby (sop), T. Roberts (pno)—includes Du kleine Blondine; Belise starb; Mein Geliebter hat versprochen; Faulheit, itzo will ich dir; Philint ist still und fleiht die Schonen; Cephalus & Aurore; Ein trunkner Dichter; Wir Arem, denn des Fieberes Kraft; Philint stand vor Babes Thür; Du fehlest mir, wie einsam und wie stille; Das Andenken; Von nonan, O liebe, lass ich dein Reich; Mein Thrysis!; Ich liebe nur Ismene; Liebe Amor Hyperion ▲ CDA 66649
Dowland, J.:The First Booke of Songs or Ayres, w. C. Wilson (lt) ASV ("Gaudeamus" series) ▲ CDGAU 135 [DDD]
Gabrieli, G.:Music of, w. David Cordier (alt), Wilfried Jochens (ten), Gerd Türk (ten), Harry van der Kamp (bass), R. Wilson (cnd), Musica Fiata, La Capella Ducale—Toccata [arr Wilson]; Buccinate in neomenia tuba à 19; Canzon XVII à 12; Dulcis Jesu patris imago [Son con voce à 20]; Timor et remor à 6; Son con 3 Vns; Son XIX à 15; In ecclesiis à 14; Canzon V à 7; Jubilate Deo à 10; Son XVIII à 14; Cantate Domino à 8; Canzon primi toni à 10; Misericordia tua Domine à 12; Canzon X à 8; Toccata primi toni; Magnificat à 33 [reconstructed by Wilson]; Benedictus es Dominus à 8 *(rec St. Osdag Church, Mandelsloh, Germany, June 11–15, 1994)* Sony Classical ("Vivarte" series) 2–▲ S2K 66254 [DDD]
Grandi, A.:Sacred Music, w. David Cordier (alt), Wilfried Jochens (ten), Gerd Türk (ten), Harry van der Kamp (bass), R. Wilson (cnd), Musica Fiata, La Capella Ducale—Heu mihi [Dialogo à 4]; O quam tu pulchra es; Cantemus Domino; Salvum me fac, Deus [Basso solo] *(rec St. Osdag Church, Mandelsloh, Germany, June 11–15, 1994)* Sony Classical ("Vivarte" series) 2–▲ S2K 66254 [DDD]
Handel, G.F.:Ariodante, w. J. Gondek (sop), L. Saffer (sop), L. Hunt (mez), Jennifer Lane (mez), J. Lindemann (ten), N. Cavallier (bass), N. McGegan (cnd), Freiburg Baroque Orch, Ralf Popken (cnd), Wilhelmshaven Vocal Ensemble [172-page libretto w. production photos] Harmonia Mundi France 3–▲ HMC 907146.48
O Tuneful Voice:Songs & Duets from Late 18th Century England, w. Emma Kirkby (sop), Timothy Roberts (pno/hpd), Frances Kelly (single-action hp) Hyperion ▲ CDA 66497 [DDD]
Purcell, H.:Sacred Choral & Vocal Music, w. E. Higginbottom (cnd), New College Choir Oxford [E, L] Meridian ▲ CDE 84112
Telemann, G.P.:Hamburger Admiralitätsmusik, w. Mieke van der Sluis (sop—Hammonia), Graham Pushee (ten—Themis), Rufus Müller (ten—Mercurius), Klaus Mertens (bass—Neptunius), David Thomas (bass—Mars), Michael Schopper (bass—Albis), W. Helbich (cnd), Bremen Baroque Orch, Alsfeld Vocal Ensemble *(rec Nov 9, 1995)* CPO 2–▲ CPO 999373–2 [DDD]

Müller-Molinari, Helga (mez)
Donizetti, G.:Requiem Mass, w. C. Studer (sop), A. Baldin (ten), J. P. Bogart (bass), J.-H. Rootering (bass), M. A. G. Martinez (cnd), Bamberg Sym Chorus [L] Orfeo ▲ 172881 [DDD]
Handel, G.F.:Partenope, w. Krisztina Laki (sop), René Jacobs (alt), John York Skinner (alt), S. Kuijken (cnd), La Petite Bande Editio Classica 3–▲ 77109–2–RG [ADD]
Mozart, W.A.:Requiem, w. A. Tomowa-Sintow (sop), V. Cole (ten), P. Burchuladze (bass), H. von Karajan (cnd), Vienna PO, Vienna Singverein [L] Deutsche Grammophon ("Karajan Gold" series) ▲ 439023–2 [DDD]

Müller-Molinari, Helga (mez) (cont.)
Rossini, G.:La pietra del paragone, w. M. C. Nocentini (sop), A. Trovarelli (mez), P. Barbacini (ten), V. Di Matteo (bar), R. Scaltriti (bar), A. Svab (bar), P. Rumetz (bass), C. Desderi (cnd), Camerata Musicale Orch, Modeno Teatro Comunale Chorus [I] *(rec 1992)* Nuova Era 2–▲ 7132/33 [DDD]
Vivaldi, A.:La Sena festeggiante, w. L Cuberli (sop), S. Nimsgern (b-bar), C. Scimone (cnd), Cappella Coloniensis Cetra Classic ▲ CDC 25 [AAD]

Mulligan, Mark (sgr)
Rorem, N.:Miss Julie, w. Theodora Fried (sgr—Miss Julie), Heather Sarris (sgr—Christine, the cook), Laurelyn Watson (sgr—Young Girl), David Blackburn (sgr—Mr. Niels), Mark Mulligan (sgr—Young Boy), Philip Torre (sgr—John, the valet), Judd Ernster (bass), D. Gilbert (cnd), Manhattan School of Music Opera Orch, Manhattan School of Music Opera Chorus Newport Classic 2–▲ NPT 85605 [DDD]

Munari, Gabriella (sop)
Bellafronte, R.:Era estate del '64, w. Adriano Paolini (pno) *(rec Villa Torano, Imola, Dec 1994)* Bongiovanni ▲ GB 5049–2 [DDD]

Munsel, Patrice (sop)
Offenbach, J.:Les Contes d'Hoffmann, w. Jarmila Novotná (sop), Raoul Jobin (ten), Ezio Pinza (bass), T. Beecham (cnd), Metropolitan Opera Orch, New York Metropolitan Opera Chorus *(rec Feb 26, 1944)* Enterprise ("The Radio Years") 2–▲ ENT–19 (m)

Munteanu, Petre (ten)
Bach, J.S.:Magnificat, BWV 243, w. L. Marimpietri (sop), N. Panni (sop), A. Reynolds (mez), B. Carmeli (bass), H. Scherchen (cnd), Milan RAI SO, Milan RAI Chorus [L] *(rec live, Apr 5, 1963)* Memories ▲ HR 4160 (m) [ADD]
Beethoven, L. van:Sym 9, "Choral Sym", w. M. László (sop), H. Scherchen (cnd), Vienna State Opera Orch, Vienna Singakademie *(rec 1954)* Andromeda ▲ ANR 2533 [ADD]
Mozart, W.A.:Missa, K.427, w. A. Giebel (sop), E. Lear (sop), F. Gutherie (bass), S. Celibidache (cnd), Rome RAI SO, Rome RAI Chorus *(rec Mar. 26, 1960)* Emozioni ▲ CDAR 2007 [ADD]

Murcell, Raymond (bar)
Rossini, G.:La pietra del paragone, w. A. Elgar (sop), B. Wolff (mez), E. Bonazzi (mez), J. Carreras (ten), J. Reardon (bar), A. Foldi (b-bar), J. Diaz (bass), N. Jenkins (cnd), Clarion Concerts Orch, Clarion Concerts Chorus [I] *(rec. ca. 1972)* Vanguard Classics 3–▲ OVC 8043/45 [ADD]

Murgatroyd, Andrew (ten)
Beethoven, L. van:Missa Solemnis, w. M. Hirsti (sop), C. Watkinson (cta), M. George (bass), T. Kvam (cnd), Hanover Band, Oslo Cathedral Choir [period instrs] [L] Nimbus ▲ NI 5109 [DDD]
Monteverdi, C.:Vespro della Beata Vergine, w. Barbara Borden (sop), Maria Cristina Kiehr (sop), Andreas Scholl (alt), John Bowen (ten), Victor Torres (bar), Antonio Abete (bass), Jelle Draijer (bass), René Jacobs (cnd), Concerto Vocale, Netherlands Chamber Choir Harmonia Mundi 2–▲ 901566.67
Tavener, J.:We Shall See Him As He Is, w. P. Rozario (sop), J. M. Ainsley (ten), R. Hickox (cnd), BBC Welsh National SO, BBC Welsh National Chorus [E] Chandos ▲ CHAN 9128 [DDD]

Murmela, Kari (bar)
Leoncavallo, R.:Pagliacci, w. Mietta Sighele (sop), Richard Tucker (ten), Walter Alberti (bar), R. Muti (cnd), Florence Maggio Musicale Orch, Florence Maggio Musicale Chorus *(rec Florence , 1971)* Memories ▲ MEM 4576 [ADD]

Muro, Bernardo de (ten)
Bernardo de Muro Bongiovanni 3–▲ 1028–1030
Verdi, G.:Il trovatore (sels), w. J. Biel (ten), F. Tamagno (ten), L.-A. Escalaïs (ten), M. Gilion (ten), E. Caruso (ten), A. Paoli (ten), G. Zenatello (ten), J. Sembach (ten), L. Slezak (ten), F. Constantino (ten), G. Martinelli (ten), N. Fusati (ten), N. Piccaluga (ten), G. Lauri-Volpi (ten), A. Pertile (ten), E. Bergamaschi (ten), R. Tauber (ten), J. O'Sullivan (ten), H. Roswaenge (ten), G. Taccani (ten), V. Lois (ten), H. Lazaro (ten), A. Lindi (ten), A. Cortis (ten), F. Merli (ten), F. Völker (ten), J. Kiepura (ten), J. Schmidt (ten), J. Bjoerling (ten), B. Gigli (ten), A. Salvarezza (ten), J. Soler (ten), M. Filippeschi (ten)—34 performances of the Act III tenor aria "Di quella pira!," *(rec from 1903–1956)* Bongiovanni ▲ GB 1051 [AAD]

Murphy, Andrew (b-bar)
Handel, G.F.:Messiah (reorchd Mozart), w. M. Altman (sgr), J. Davidson (sgr), Peter Elvin (sgr), P. Price (sgr), L. Woodside (cnd), Sinfonia Rubinstein, New York Oratorio Society [Sinfonia Rubinstein is made up from musicians from the Lodz Philharmonic Orchestra and the Lodz Opera of Poland] [E] Koch Schwann 2–▲ SC 100308 [DDD]

Murphy, Heidi Grant (mez)
James Levine's 25th Anniversary Metropolitan Opera Gala, w. J. Levine (cnd), Metropolitan Opera Orch, Ileana Cotrubas (sop), Renée Fleming (sop), Hei-Kyung Hong (sop), Karita Mattila (sop), Birgit Nilsson (sop), Ruth Ann Swenson (sop), Kiri Te Kanawa (sop), Deborah Voigt (sop), Grace Bumbry (mez), Anne Sofie von Otter (mez) *(rec live, Metropolitan Opera House, New York, Apr 27, 1996)* Deutsche Grammophon ▲ 449177–2 [DDD]
Mozart, W.A.:Idomeneo, w. Carol Vaness (sop—Elettra), Cecilia Bartoli (mez—Idamante), Heidi Grant Murphy (mez—Ilia), Plácido Domingo (ten— Idomeneo), Thomas Hampson (bar—Arbace), Bryn Terfel (bass-bar—La Voce), J. Levine (cnd), Metropolitan Opera Orch, New York Metropolitan Opera Chorus Deutsche Grammophon ▲ 447737–2

Murphy, Julie (sgr)
Hildegard Of Bingen:Sacred Songs, w. Jocelyn West (sgr), Vivien Ellis (sgr), Stevie Wishart (sgr/h-g), Hester Briant (sgr), Fiona Cunningham (sgr), Tara Franks (sgr), Emily Levy (sgr), Lucy Steele (sgr), Vickie Couperim (sgr), Julie Murphy (sgr), Oxford Girls' Choir—Honey & milk beneath her tongue; Ursula's virgins; The devil's virgins; Place of the ancient heart; Zeal of divinity; O fiery spirit; Red river falling; O orzchis ecclesia, Living-light angels; The clouds are grieving; The firstwoman; From their homeland; But the devil mocked; Song to Ecclesia *(rec Toddington, Gloucestershire, England, May 6–8, 1995)* Celestial Harmonies ▲ 13127–2

Murphy, Suzanne (sop)
Mozart, W.A.:Nozze di Figaro, w. Rebecca Evans (sop—Barbarina), Nuccia Focile (sop—Susanna), Suzanne Murphy (sop—Marcellina), Carol Vaness (sop—Countess Almaviva), Susanne Mentzer (mez—Cherubino), Ryland Davies (ten—Don Basilio/Don Curzio), Alessandro Corbelli (bar—Count Almaviva), Alfonso Antoniozzi (bass—Doctor Bartolo/Antonio), Alastair Miles (bass—Figaro), C. Mackerras (cnd), Scottish CO, Scottish Chamber Chorus *(rec Usher Hall, Edingurgh, Scotland, July 31–Aug. 12, 1994)* Telarc 3–▲ CD 80388 [DDD]
Rachmaninoff, S.:The Bells, w. K. Lewis (ten), D. Wilson-Johnson (bar), N. Järvi (cnd), Scottish National Orch, Scottish National Chorus [R] Chandos ▲ CHAN 8476 [DDD]
Rachmaninoff, S.:Vocalise, w. N. Järvi (cnd), Scottish National Orch Chandos ▲ CHAN 8476 [DDD]
Taneyev, S.:Duet for Romeo & Juliet, w. K. Lewis (ten), N. Järvi (cnd), Scottish National Orch [R] Chandos ▲ CHAN 8476 [DDD]

Murray, Ann (mez)
Au Jardin des Aveux, w. Philip Langridge (ten), Roger Vignoles (pno) Virgin Classics ▲ CDC 59019
Bach, J.S.:Cant 64, w. A. Augér (sop), P. Huttenlocher (bar), H. Rilling (cnd), Stuttgart Bach Collegium, Gächinger Kantorei [G] *(rec Jan 1978 & Mar 1981)* Hänssler Classic ▲ 98.825 [AAD]
Bach, J.S.:Cant 119, w. A. Augér (sop), A. Kraus (ten), W. Schöne (bass), H. Rilling (cnd), Bach Ensemble *(rec Sept & Dec 1977 & Jan 197)* Hänssler Classic ▲ 98.828 [AAD]
Bach, J.S.:Cant 153, w. A. Kraus (ten), W. Heldwein (bass), H. Rilling (cnd), Stuttgart Bach Collegium, Gächinger Kantorei [G] Hänssler Classic ▲ 98.871 [AAD]
Bach, J.S.:Magnificat, BWV 243, w. A. Augér (sop), H. Watts (cta), A. Kraus (ten), P. Huttenlocher (bar), W. Schöne (bass), H. Rilling (cnd), Stuttgart Bach Collegium, Gächinger Kantorei *(rec 1979)* Sony Classical ("Essential Classics" series) ▲ SBK 48280 [ADD] ■ SBT 48280
Bach, J.S.:Magnificat, BWV 243, w. B. Hendricks (sop), J. Rigby (sop), U. Heilmann (ten), J. Hynninen (bar), N. Marriner (cnd), Academy of St. Martin in the Fields, *(chorus unknown)* EMI Classics ▲ CDC 54283–2
Brahms, J.:Songs, w. Stephen Kovacevich (pno)—5 Lieder, Op. 105 EMI Classics ▲ CDC 55218
Britten, H.:The Beggar's Opera, w. A. Collins (sop—Mrs. Peachum), A. Murray (mez—Polly Peachum), P. Langridge (ten—MacHeath), R. Lloyd (b-bar—Peachum), *(not advised of orchestra & chorus)*, S. Bedford (cnd) Argo 2–▲ 436850–2 [DDD]
Charpentier, M.-A.:Magnificat, w. D. Upshaw (sop), E. Robinson (mez), J. Aler (ten), K. Moll (bass), N. Marriner (cnd), Academy of St. Martin in the Fields, Academy of St. Martin in the Fields Chorus EMI Classics ▲ CDC 54284

Murray, Ann (mez) (cont.)
Charpentier, M.-A.:Te Deum in C, w. D. Upshaw (sop), E. Robinson (mez), J. Aler (ten), K. Moll (bass), N. Marriner (cnd), Academy of St. Martin in the Fields, Academy of St. Martin in the Fields Chorus EMI Classics ▲ CDC 54284
Donizetti, G.:Lucia di Lammermoor, w. M. Caballé (sop), C. H. Ahnsjö (ten), V. Bello (ten), J. Carreras (ten), V. Sardinero (bar), S. Ramey (bass), J. López-Cobos (cnd), New Philharmonia Orch, Ambrosian Opera Chorus Philips 2-▲ 426563-2
Fauré, G.:Requiem, w. O. Bär (bar), S. Cleobury (cnd), English CO, King's College Choir Cambridge EMI Classics ▲ CDC 49880
Handel, G.F.:Alcina (sels), w. C. Mackerras (cnd), Orch of the Age of Enlightenment Forlane ▲ FRL 16738 [DDD]
Handel, G.F.:Ariodante (sels), w. C. Mackerras (cnd), Orch of the Age of Enlightenment Forlane ▲ FRL 16738 [DDD]
Handel, G.F.:Giulio Cesare in Egitto (sels), w. C. Mackerras (cnd), Orch of the Age of Enlightenment Forlane ▲ FRL 16738 [DDD]
Handel, G.F.:Serse (sels), w. C. Mackerras (cnd), Orch of the Age of Enlightenment Forlane ▲ FRL 16738 [DDD]
Humperdinck, E.:Hänsel und Gretel, w. E. Gruberova (sop), G. Jones (sop), B. Bonney (sop), C. Oelze (sop), C. Ludwig (mez), F. Grundheber (bar), C. Davis (cnd), Dresden Staatskapelle Philips 2-▲ 438013-2
Mahler, G.:Des Knaben Wunderhorn, w. T. Allen (bar), C. Mackerras (cnd), London PO Virgin Classics ▲ CDC 59037
Mahler, G.:Des Knaben Wunderhorn, w. Thomas Allen (bar), C. Mackerras (cnd), London PO Virgin Classics ("Ultraviolet" series) ▲ CUV 61202
Mendelssohn, F.:A Midsummer Night's Dream (comp), w. A. Augér (sop), N. Marriner (cnd), Philharmonia Orch, Ambrosian Singers [E] Philips ▲ 411106-2 [DDD]
Mozart, W.A.:Arias, w. Arleen Augér (sop), Kathleen Battle (sop), Irma Beilke (sop), Helena Braun (sop), Lisa Della Casa (sop), Maria Cebotari (sop), Ileana Cotrubas (sop), Helen Donath (sop), Mirella Freni (sop), Reri Grist (sop), Edita Gruberova (sop), Elisabeth Grümmer (sop), Hilde Güden (sop), Ingeborg Hallstein (sop), Luise Helletsgruber (sop), Gundula Janowitz (sop), Sena Jurinac (sop), Erika Köth (sop), Evelyn Lear (sop), Wilma Lipp (sop), Margaret Marshall (sop), Edith Mathis (sop), Jarmila Novotna (sop), Margherita Perras (sop), Lucia Popp (sop), Elisabeth Rethberg (sop), Anneliese Rothenberger (sop), Elisabeth Schumann (sop), Elisabeth Schwarzkopf (sop), Graziella Sciutti (sop), Irmgard Seefried (sop), Graziella Sciutti (sop), Julia Varady (sop), Agnes Baltsa (mez), Margit Bokor (mez), Brigitte Fassbaender (mez), Christa Ludwig (mez), Ann Murray (mez), Francisco Araiza (ten), Anton Dermota (ten), Helge Rosvaenge (ten), Rudolf Schock (ten), Peter Schreier (ten), Leopold Simoneau (ten), Eric Tappy (ten), Richard Tauber (ten), Gösta Winbergh (ten), Josef Witt (ten), Fritz Wunderlich (ten), Christian Boesch (bar), Willy Domgraf-Fassbaender (bar), Karl Dönch (bar), Dietrich Fischer-Dieskau (bar), Erich Kunz (bar), Eberhard Wächter (bar), Hans Hotter (b-bar), Paul Schöffler (b-bar), Cesare Siepi (b-bar), José Van Dam (b-bar), Walter Berry (bass), Geraint Evans (bass), Nicolai Ghiaurov (bass), Alexander Kipnis (bass), Richard Mayr (bass), Kurt Moll (bass), James Morris (bass), Ezio Pinza (bass), Martti Talvela (bass), Giorgio Tozzi (bass), Hans Duhan (sgr), Res Fischer (sgr), Marie Gerhart (sgr), *(various orchs & cnds)* —sels from Idomeneo, Die Entführung aus der Serail, Le nozze di Figaro, Don Giovanni, Così fan tutte, Die Zauberflöte & various arias Orfeo d'or ("Festspiel Dokumente" series) 5-▲ 408955
Mozart, W.A.:Clemenza, w. L. Popp (sop), R. Ziesack (sop), D. Ziegler (mez), P. Langridge (ten), L. Polgar (bass), T. Grabowski (hpd), C. Hermann (vc), N. Harnoncourt (cnd), Zurich Opera Orch, Zurich Opera House Chorus Teldec 2-▲ 90857-2
Mozart, W.A.:Così fan tutte, w. Kiri Te Kanawa (sop), Marie McLaughlin (sop), Hans-Peter Blochwitz (ten), Thomas Hampson (bar), G. Furlanetto (bar), J. Levine (cnd), Vienna PO, Vienna State Opera Chorus [I] Deutsche Grammophon 3-▲ 423897-2 [DDD]
Mozart, W.A.:Missa, K.317, w. L. Marshall (sop), R. Covey-Crump (ten), D. Wilson-Johnson (bar), S. Cleobury (cnd), English CO, King's College Choir Cambridge [L] Argo ▲ 411904-2 [DDD]
Mozart, W.A.:Missa solemnis, K.337, w. L. Marshall (sop), R. Covey-Crump (ten), D. Wilson-Johnson (bar), S. Cleobury (cnd), English CO [L] Argo ▲ 411904-2 [DDD]
Mozart, W.A.:Nozze di Figaro, w. C. Margiono (sop), B. Bonney (sop), I. Rey (sop), A. Murray (mez, P.-L. Lang (mez), P. Langridge (ten), C. Späth (ten), T. Hampson (bar), K. Moll (bass), A. Scharinger (bass), K. Langan (bass), N. Harnoncourt (cnd), Royal Concertgebouw Orch, Netherlands Opera Chorus *(rec Amsterdam, May 1993)* Teldec 3-▲ 90861-2 [DDD]
Mozart, W.A.:Nozze di Figaro, w. M. Price (sop), K. Battle (sop), M. Nicolesco (sop), J. Hynninen (bar), K. Rydl (bass), R. Muti (cnd), Vienna PO, Vienna State Opera Chorus [I] EMI Classics 3-▲ CDCC 47978 [DDD]
Mozart, W.A.:Nozze di Figaro (sels), w. M. Price (sop), K. Battle (sop), M. Nicolesco (sop), J. Hynninen (bar), K. Rydl (bass), R. Muti (cnd), Vienna PO, Vienna State Opera Chorus [I] EMI Classics ▲ CDC 54321
Mozart, W.A.:Requiem, w. K. Battle (sop), D. Rendall (ten), M. Salminen (bass), D. Barenboim (cnd), Orch de Paris, Paris Opera Chorus [L] EMI Classics ▲ CDC 47342 [DDD]
Mozart, W.A.:Zauberflöte, w. M. Price (sop—Pamina), L. Serra (sop—Queen of the Night), M. Venuti (sop—Papagena), M. McLaughlin (sop—1st Lady), A. Murray (mez—2nd Lady), H. Schwarz (cta—3rd Lady), F. Höher (trb—1st Boy), M. Diedrich (trb—2nd Boy), F. Klos (trb—3rd Boy), P. Schreier (ten—Tamino), R. Tear (ten—Monostatos), R. Goldberg (ten—1st Armoured Man), K. Moll (bass—Sarastro), H. Rech (bass—2nd Armoured Man), C. Davis (cnd), Dresden Staatskapelle, Leipzig Radio Chorus Philips ("Duo" series) 2-▲ 442568-2
Offenbach, J.:Les Contes d'Hoffmann, w. L. Serra (sop), R. Plowright (sop), J. Norman (sop), A. Murray (mez), J. Taillon (mez), N. Shicoff (ten), A. Oliver (ten), R. Tear (ten), J. Van Dam (b-bar), D. Duesing (bar), K. Rydl (bass), S. Cambreling (cnd), Brussels Théâtre de la Monnaie Orch [F] EMI Classics 3-▲ CDCC 49641 [DDD]
On Wings of Song, w. Lott, Felicity (sop), Graham Johnson (pno) *(rec June 1991)* EMI Classics ▲ CDC 54411-2 [DDD]
Poulenc, F.:Songs, w. F. Lott (sop), A. Rolfe-Johnson (ten), R. Jackson (bass), G. Johnson (pno) [F] Hyperion ▲ CDA 66147
Purcell, H.:Dido & Aeneas, w. R. Yakar (sop), A. Scharinger (bass), N. Harnoncourt (cnd), Vienna Concentus Musicus, Arnold Schoenberg Choir Teldec ("Das alte Werke" series) ▲ 93686
Purcell, H.:Dido & Aeneas, w. R. Yakar (sop), A. Scharinger (bass), N. Harnoncourt (cnd), Vienna Concentus Musicus [E] Teldec ▲ 2292-42959-2
Schubert, Franz:Songs (comp), w. G. Johnson (pno)—14 songs—D.222, 297, 473, 475, 476, 545, 546, 551, 573, 654, 695, 771, 786, 827 [G] Hyperion ▲ CDJ 33003 [DDD]
Stravinsky, I.:Pulcinella, w. M. Hill (ten), D. Thomas (bass), R. Hickox (cnd), City of London Sinfonia Virgo ▲ CDZ 61107
Tippett, M.:King Priam, w. Heather Harper (sop—Hecuba), Linda Hirst (sop—Serving Woman), Felicity Palmer (sop—Andromache), Julian Saipe (sop—Paris), Yvonne Minton (mez—Helen), Ann Murray (mez—Nurse), Kenneth Bowen (ten—Hermes), Peter Hall (ten—Young Guard), Philip Langridge (ten—Paris), Robert Tear (ten—Achilles), Thomas Allen (bar—Hector), Norman Bailey (bar—Priam), Stephen Roberts (bar—Patroclus), David Wilson-Johnson (bar—Old Man), D. Atherton (cnd), London Sinfonietta, London Sinfonietta Chorus Chandos ▲ CHAN 9406/7 [DDD]
Vivaldi, A.:Gloria, RV.589, w. B. Hendricks (sop), J. Rigby (mez), U. Heilmann (ten), J. Hynninen (bar), N. Marriner (cnd), Academy of St. Martin in the Fields, Academy Chorus EMI Classics ▲ CDC 54283

Murray, Carl (bar)
Horder, M.:Songs (40), w. Winifred Soutter (sop), Peter Allanson (bar), Stephen Betteridge (pno), Gordon Kirkwood (pno) Symposium ▲ 1039

Murray, David (bar)
Lovenstein, J.:Music of, w. Mary Brockenbrough (sop), Laura Sanders (sop), Barton Green (ten), Rockland Osgood (ten), David Murray (bar), Benjamin Sears (bar), Jonathan Lovenstein (pno), Heather O'Donnell (pno), James Silvers (pno), Rocy Reider (fl), Jason Horowitz (vn), Adrianna Hulscher (vn), James Johnston (vn), Mimi Ragson (vn), Peter Landeen (vc), Reinmar Seidler (vc)—Blake Songs; other works Titanic ▲ Ti 221 [DDD]

Murray, Therese (sop)
Stuart, P.:Kill Bear Comes Home, w. Elana Gizzi (sop—Hasty Girl), Mi-Kyung Huh (sop—Cold Feet), Therese Murray (sop—Song Bird), Cherie Pfeil (sop—1st Sister), Renia Shukis (sop—2nd Sister), Riki Connaughton (mez—4th Sister), Lucy Fee (mez—3rd Sister), David Averbach (ten—Song Leader), Mark Schmidt (ten—Kill Bear), Jason Smith (bar—Cheif Wife Hunter), P. Stuart (cnd), Rochester Opera Theater Orch, Rochester Opera Theater Chorus VM ▲ DRK 154 [DDD]

Murray, William (bass)
Mendelssohn, F.:Die Hochzeit des Camacho, w. R. Schudel (sop—Quiteria), C. Swanson (sop—Lucinda), C. Bieber (ten—Basilio), W. Mok (ten—Vivaldo), V. Horn (ten—Camacho), R. Lukas (bar—Carrasco), J. Becker (bass—Sancho Panza), W. Murray (bass—Don Quixote), B. Klee (cnd), Berlin RSO, Berlin Radio Chorus [G] Koch Schwann 2-▲ 314042 [DDD]

Musacchio, Martina (sop)
Rossini, G.:Petite messe solennelle, w. C. Bandera (alt), G. Dominguez (ten), J. Mannov (bass), U. Koella (pno), N. Clayton (pno), F. Näf (cnd), *(chorus unknown)* Ars Musici ▲ AM 1091 [DDD]

Muscente (sgr)
Bizet, G.:Don Procopio, w. M. Gentile (sop), Carmona (sgr), Barry (sgr), A. Antoniozzi (bar), S. Sanna (cnd), Berlin Radio Youth Orch, Symbolon Ensemble Chorus [I] *(rec live 5/25/86)* Bongiovanni 2-▲ GB 2043/44 [DDD]

Musetescu, Dan (bass)
Verdi, G.:La forza del destino, w. Maria Nistor-Slatinaru (sop—Donna Leonora), Mihaela Mariacineanu (mez—Curra), Zenaida Pally (mez—Preziosilla), Ludovic Speiss (ten—Don Alvaro), Ion Stoian (ten—Trabucco), Nicolae Herlea (bar—Don Carlo), Nicolae Florei (bass—Padre Guardiano) Constantin Gabor (bass—Fra Melitone), Dan Musetescu (bass—An Alcalde), Mihai Panghe (bass—Marquis of Calatrava), C. Litvin (cnd), Romanian Radio-TV Orch, Romanian Radio-TV Chorus *(rec Jan 1970)* Vox Box 3-▲ CD3X 3038

Musinowski, Sara (sgr)
Weill, K.:Songs, w. Hans-Joachim Tinnefeld (b gtr), Stefan Weinzierl (pno)—September Song; Listen to My Song; Mon Ami, My Friend; It Never Was You; One Life to Live; My Ship; I'm a Stranger Here Myself; Foolish Heart; Speak Low; Sing Me Not a Ballad; Lonely House; Trouble Man; Stay Well; Lost in the Stars Signum ▲ SIG X85-00 [DDD]

Musinu, Francesco (bass)
Paisiello, G.:Nina, o sia La pazza per amore, w. M. Bolgan (sop), F. Pediconi (sop), D. Bernardini (ten), G. Surian (bass), R. Bonynge (cnd), Catania Teatro Massimo Bellini Orch, Catania Teatro Massimo Bellini Chorus [I] *(rec live 1989)* Nuova Era 2-▲ 6872/73 [DDD]
Verdi, G.:La traviata, w. T. Fabbricini (sop—Violetta), A. Trevisan (mez—Annina), N. Curiel (mez—Flora), R. Alagna (ten—Alfredo), E. Cossutta (ten—Gastone), E. Gavazzi (ten—Giuseppe), O. Mori (bar—Douphol), E. Capuano (bass—d'Obigny), F. Musinu (bass—Grenvil), R. Muti (cnd), La Scala Orch, La Scala Chorus Sony Classical 2-▲ S2K 52486 [DDD]

Musio, Dino (sgr)
Verdi, G.:Simon Boccanegra, w. Alberto Cupido (ten), Ned Barth (bar), José Van Dam (b-bar), Manfred Schenk (bass), Daniela Longhi (sgr), M. Veltri (cnd), Marseille Opera Orch, Marseille Opera Chorus Lyrinx 3-▲ LYX 127 [DDD]

Musoleno, Rosemary (sop)
Haydn, J.:Applausus:Jubilaeum virtutis Palatium, w. Rosemary Musoleno (sop—Temperantia), Kirsten Dolberg (mez—Prudentia), Douglas Johnson (ten—Justitia), Desmond Byrne (bass—Fortitudo), Jean-Philippe Courtis (bass—Theologia), P. Fournillier (cnd), Picardie Orch, Haydn Vocal Ensemble [L] *(rec 9/91)* Opus 111 2-▲ OPS 61-9207/8 [DDD]

Musy, Louis (b-bar)
Gounod, C.:Faust, w. M. Berthon (sop), M. Coiffier (sop), J. Montfort (mez), C. Vezzani (ten), M. Cozette (bar), M. Journet (bass), H. Busser (cnd), Paris Opera Orch, Paris Opera Chorus [F] *(rec 1930)* Pearl 2-▲ PEA 9987 [AAD]
Gounod, C.:Faust, w. M. Berthon (sop—Marguerite), C. Vezzani (ten—Faust), L. Musy (b-bar—Valentin), M. Journet (bass—Mephistofeles), H. Busser (cnd), Paris Opera Orch, Paris Opera Chorus [F] *(rec 1930)* Music Memoria 2-▲ 30187
Offenbach, J.:Le Fille du tambour-major, w. Christiane Harbell (sop—Stella), Monique de Pondeau (sop—Claudine), Germaine Light (mez—Duchess Della Volta), Marcelle Ranson-Hervé (ten—Duke Della Volta), André Mallabrera (ten—Griolet), Etienne Arnaud (bar—Robert), Louis Musy (bar—Monthabor), *(orch unknown)* Accord ▲ ACD 220692 [AAD]
Varney, L.:Les Mousquetaires au couvent, w. Gabrielle Ristori (mez), Camille Rouquetty (ten), Gabriel Bacquier (bar), Pierre Blanc (sgr), Pauline Carton (sgr), Jacqueline Cauchard (sgr), Mireille Lacoste (sgr), Colette Riedinger (sgr), R. Benedetti (cnd) Musidisc 2-▲ MUS 202262 [AAD]

Muszely, Melitta (sop)
Fall, L.:Die Rose von Stambul (sels), w. Christine Gorner (sop), Fritz Wunderlich (ten), C. Michalski (cnd), Graunke SO Emperor Operetta ▲ KO 86353
Lehár, F.:Paganini (sels), w. Rudolf Schock (ten), Siegfried Borries (vn), W. Schmidt-Boelcke (cnd), FFB Orch, Gunther Arndt Chorus Emperor Operetta ▲ KO 86343
Lehár, F.:Der Zarewitsch (sels), w. Christine Gorner (sop), Fritz Wunderlich (ten), Willy Hagara (bar), C. Michalski (cnd), Bavarian SO Emperor Operetta ▲ KO 86341
Leoncavallo, R.:Pagliacci, w. Rudolf Schock (ten), Josef Metternich (bar), H. Stein (cnd), Berlin State Opera Orch *(rec 1959)* Berlin Classics ▲ BER 9102 [ADD]
Straus, O.:Ein Walzertraum (sels), w. Lisa Otto (sop), Rudolf Schock (ten), Bruno Fritz (bar), W. Schüchter (cnd), Berlin Orch, Berlin Chorus Emperor Operetta ▲ KO 86346
Wagner, R.:Das Rheingold, w. L. Otto (sop), J. Blatter (mez), R. Stewart (mez), S. Wagner (mez), R. Schock (ten), H. Melchert (ten), F. Frantz (bass), B. Kusche (bass), J. Metternich (bass), R. Kempe (cnd), Berlin Staatskapelle *(rec Mar. 1959)* Berlin Classics ("Eterna" series) ▲ BER 2035 [ADD]

Muzio, Claudia (sop)
Claudia Muzio Phonographe ("Great Voices" series) ▲ PHG CD 5065
Claudia Muzio *(rec 1934–1935)* Nimbus ("Prima Voce" series) ▲ NI 7814 (m) [ADD]
Claudia Muzio, Vol. 2 *(rec 1917–25)* Pearl ▲ PEA 9143 [ADD]
The Complete Columbia Recordings (1934–35) Romophone 2-▲ 81015-2 [ADD]
The Italian Vocal Tradition, Vol. 1:The Voices of Toscanini, w. Toti dal Monte (sop), Rosetta Pampanini (sop), Biata Scacciati (sop), Giacomo Lauri-Volpi (ten), Francesco Merli (ten), Aureliano Pertile (ten), Carlo Galeffi (bar), Mariano Stabile (bar), Riccardo Stracciari (bar), Nazzareno de Angel *(rec 1921–35)* Iron Needle ▲ 1304
The Legendary Recordings (1917–1925) *(rec 1917–25)* Enterprise ("Vocal Archives" series) ▲ ENT VA 1133
Rare Arias & Songs, 1920–25 Minerva ▲ MN A31 (m) ADD
A Selection of Her Finest Edison Recordings *(rec between 1920 & 1925)* Pearl 2-▲ PEA 9072 [AAD]
Verdi, G.:Otello (sels), w. R. Ponselle (sop), H. Spani (sop), E. Caruso (ten), N. Fusati (ten), L. Melchior (ten), F. Merli (ten), F. Tamagno (ten), B. Franci (bar), V. Maurel (bar), R. Stracciari (bar), T. Ruffo (bar) *(rec 1906–1933)* Music Memoria ▲ 30219

Myers (sgr)
Rossini, G.:Semiramide, w. J. Sutherland (sop), M. Horne (mez), Grant (sgr), R. Bonynge (cnd), New Philharmonia Orch, Ambrosian Opera Chorus [I] *(rec live at the Theatre Royal, Drury Lane, 2/9/69)* Arkadia 2-▲ 579 (m) [ADD]

Myers, Gordon (bar)
Myers, G.:God's Trbn, w. Christine Helfrich (sop), Richard Cragg (sgr), Matthew Gillis (sgr), Timothy Pehta (sgr), Paul Norman (sgr), Wendy Catlin (sgr) Katherine Mary Hamilton (sgr), Sharon Hunter (sgr), Gloriae Dei Brass Ensemble Paraclete ▲ CDGD 017 [DDD]; ■ GDC 017

Myers, K. (voc)
Rolnick, N.B.:Vocal Chords, w. N. B. Rolnick (elec) Centaur ▲ CRC 2047 [DDD]

Myers, Leah Anne (sop)
Mahler, G.:Beethoven's Sym 9, w. Ilene Sameth (mez), James Clark (ten), Richard Conant (bass), P. Tiboris (cnd), Brno State PO, Janáček Opera Chorus Bridge ▲ BCD 9033 [DDD]

Myers, Michael (ten)
Beethoven, L. van:Mass, Op. 86, w. H. Schellenberg (mez), M. Simpson (mez), J. Humphrey (ten), R. Shaw (cnd), Atlanta SO, Atlanta Sym Chorus [L] Telarc ▲ CD 80248 [DDD]

▲ = CD ♦ = Enhanced CD Δ = MD ■ = Cassette Tape □ = DCC

Myers, Michael (ten) (cont.)

Schubert, Franz:Mass 6, w. B. Valente (sop), M. Simpson (mez), J. Humphrey (ten), G. Siebert (ten), R. Shaw (cnd), Atlanta SO, Atlanta Sym Chorus [L] Telarc ▲ CD 80212 [DDD]

Scriabin, A.:Sym 1, w. S. Toczyska (mez), R. Muti (cnd), Philadelphia Orch, Philadelphia Choral Arts Society EMI Classics 3-▲ CDC 54251

Myrlak, Kazimierz (ten)

Bach, J.S.:St. Mark Passion, w. B. Jaszkowski (bar), et al., J. Bok (cnd), Warsaw SO, Warsaw Chamber Opera Chorus [G] Bongiovanni 2-▲ GB 2024/25 [ADD]

Gluck, C.W.:La Danza, w. E. Ignatowicz (sop), T. Bugaj (cnd), Warsaw Sinfonia [I] Orfeo 2-▲ 135872 [DDD]

Naber, R. (alt)

Romberg, A.:Der Lied von der Glocke, w. M. Friesenhausen (sop), H. Hopfner (ten), K. Ridderbusch (bass), G. Knüsel (cnd), Essen CO, Duisburg State Concert Chorus Calig ▲ CAL 50942

Nabokov, Dmitri (bass)

Puccini, G.:La Bohème (sels), w. Bianco Bellisia (sop—Musetta), Alberto Pellegrini (sop—Mimi), Luciano Pavarotti (ten—Rodolfo), Walter de Ambrosis (bar—Schaunard), Vito Mattioli (bar—Marcello), Dmitri Nabokov (bass—Colline), Reggio Emilia Teatro Municipale Orch, Reggio Emilia Teatro Municipale Chorus Budget ("The Greatest Voice in Opera" series) ▲ SYP 105

Nacházel, Vladimir (sgr)

Bruckner, A.:Mass 3, w. Dagmar Masková (sgr), Jiři Novotný (sgr), Jiři Seiler (sgr), Jiři Uherek (sgr), Eva Zbytovská (sgr), Jan Votava (trbn), Josef Ksica (org), Josef Pancík (cnd), Prague Chamber Choir Orfeo ▲ 327 951 [DDD]

Bruckner, A.:Motets, w. Dagmar Masková (sgr), Jiři Novotný (sgr), Jiři Seiler (sgr), Jiři Uherek (sgr), Eva Zbytovská (sgr), Jan Votava (trbn), Josef Ksica (org), Josef Pancík (cnd), Prague Chamber Choir—Locus iste; Afferentur regi; Ave Maria (2); Pange lingua; Pange lingua (phrygisch); Tantum ergo (2); Libera me; Os iusti; Virga jesse; Vexilla regis; Christus factus est; Tota pulchra es Maria; Ecce sacerdos magnus Orfeo ▲ 327 951 [DDD]

Dvořák, A.:Armida, w. Joanna Borowska (sop—Armida), Monika Brychtová (sgr—Siren), Wieslaw Ochman (ten—Rinald), Richard Sporka (ten—Dudo), Jan Markvart (bar—Sven), Pavel Daniluk (bass—King), George Fortune (bass—Ismen), Zdenek Harvánek (bass—Ubald), Miloslav Podskalský (bass—Peter), Milan Bürger (sgr—Gernand), Roman Janál (sgr—Muezzin/Hlasatel), Vratislav Kříz (sgr—Gottfried), Vladimír Nacházel (sgr—Roger), G. Albrecht (cnd), Czech PO, Prague Chamber Choir *(rec 1995)* Orfeo 2-▲ 404962 [DDD]

Nache (sgr)

Cherubini, L.:Médée, w. M. Callas (sop), F. Barbieri (mez), G. Penno (ten), G. Modesti (bass), L. Bernstein (cnd), La Scala Orch, La Scala Chorus [I] *(rec live 12/10/53)* Melodram 2-▲ MEL 26022 (m) [AAD]

Cherubini, L.:Médée, w. M. Callas (sop), F. Barbieri (mez), G. Penno (ten), G. Modesti (bass), L. Bernstein (cnd), La Scala Orch, La Scala Chorus [I] *(rec live, Milan 12/10/53)* Verona 2-▲ 27088/89

Nadell, Rosalind (mez)

Puccini, G.:Madama Butterfly, w. V. de los Angeles (sop), B. Faulkner (sgr), W. Fredericks (sgr), J. Thresh (sgr), D. Bernard (sgr), R. Torigi (sgr), A. Cosenza (bar), W. Herbert (cnd), New Orleans Opera Orch, New Orleans Opera Chorus *(rec live March 18, 1954)* Legato Classics 2-▲ LCD 168-2 [ADD]

Puccini, G.:Madama Butterfly, w. Dorothy Kirsten (sop—Madama Butterfly), Rosalind Nadell (mez—Suzuki), Eileen Ireland (mez—Kate), Daniele Barioni (ten—Pinkerton), Thomas Carter (ten—Goro), Arthur Cosenza (ten—Yamadori), Richard Torigi (bar—Sharpless), Rodney Hall (bass—The Bronze), Harold Crane (bass—Commissioner), R. Cellini (cnd), New Orleans Opera Orch, New Orleans Opera Chorus *(rec live, Mar 1960)* VAI Audio 2-▲ VAIA 1054-2

Nader, Alexander (sop)

Schubert, Franz:Mass 1, w. Thomas Puchegger (sop), Georg Leskovich (alto), Jörg Hering (ten), Kurt Azesberger (ten), Harry van der Kamp (bass), Arno Hartmann (org), B. Weil (cnd), Orch of the Age of Enlightenment, Vienna Boys' Choir *(rec Vienna, Austria, Sept 1995)* Sony Classical ("Vivarte" series) ▲ SK 68247 [DDD]

Schubert, Franz:Mass 3, w. Thomas Puchegger (sop), Belá Fischer (alt), Georg Leskovich (alt), Jörg Hering (ten), Harry Van der Kamp (bass), Arno Hartmann (org), B. Weil (cnd), Orch of the Age of Enlightenment, Chorus Viennensis, Vienna Boys' Choir Sony Classical ("Vivarte" series) ▲ SK 68248

Schubert, Franz:Mass 4, w. Thomas Puchegger (sop), Belá Fischer (alt), Georg Leskovich (alt), Jörg Hering (ten), Harry Van der Kamp (bass), Arno Hartmann (org), B. Weil (cnd), Orch of the Age of Enlightenment, Chorus Viennensis, Vienna Boys' Choir Sony Classical ("Vivarte" series) ▲ SK 68248

Nadon, Guy (nar)

Normandeau, R.:Petit Prince, w. Michel Dumont (nar—Aviator), Martin Pensa (nar—Little Prince), Christine Séguin (nar—Rose), Jean Marchand (nar—King), Luc Durand (nar—Conceited Man), Gilles Dupuis (nar—Drunkard), Guy Nadon (nar—Businessman), Jacques Languirand (nar—Lamplighter), Pierre Bourgault (nar—Geographer), Cynthia Dubois (nar—Snake), Monique Giroux (nar—Flower), Françoise Davoine (nar—Rose Garden), Jean-Louis Millette (nar—Fox), Gérard Poirier (nar—Railway Switchman), Claude Préfontaine (nar—Water Pill Salesman) *(rec Montreal, Aug 1994)* CBC 2-▲ 1091 [DDD]

Naef, Yvonne (cta)

Schoenberg, A.:Moses und Aaron, w. David Pittman-Jennings (nar), Gabriele Fontana (sop—Young Girl), Yvonne Naef (cta—Sick Woman), John Graham-Hall (ten—Young Man/Naked Youth), Pår Lindskog (ten—Youth), Chris Merritt (ten—Aaron), Siegfried Lorenz (bar—Another Man), Michael Devlin (b-bar—Ephraimite), László Polgár (bass—Priest), P. Boulez (cnd), Royal Concertgebouw Orch, Winfried Maczewski (cnd), Netherlands Opera Chorus, Zaans Youth Choir, Waterland Music School *(rec Concertgebouw, Amsterdam, Oct 1995)* Deutsche Grammophon 2-▲ 449 174-2 [DDD]

Nafé, Alicia (mez)

Bellini, V.:Adelson e Salvini, w. F. Previati (bar), A. Licata (cnd), Catania Teatro Massimo Bellini Orch, Catania Teatro Massimo Bellini Chorus Nuova Era 2-▲ NUO 7154 [DDD]

Falla, M. de:Canciones populares españolas (7), w. J. López-Cobos (cnd), Lausanne CO *(rec Mar. 25-27, 1992)* Denon ▲ CO 75339 [DDD]

Falla, M. de:La vida breve, w. A. Ordóñez (ten), J. López-Cobos (cnd), Cincinnati SO, May Festival Chorus [Sp] Telarc ▲ CD 80317 [DDD]

Mozart, W.A.:Nozze di Figaro, w. A. Augér (sop), B. Bonney (sop), H. Hagegard (bar), P. Salomaa (bass), A. Östman (cnd), Drottningholm Court Theater Orch, Drottingholm Court Thea Chorus [I] L'Oiseau-Lyre 3-▲ 421333-2 [DDD]

Nafé, Alicia (nar)

Falla, M. de:El amor brujo, w. S. Aguilar (nar), A.B. Egea (nar), J. López-Cobos (cnd), Lausanne CO *(rec Mar. 25-27, 1992)* Denon ▲ CO 75339 [DDD]

Nagano, Yonako (mez)

Takemitsu, T.:Music of, w. Tashi, w. H. Ibe (gtr), M. Nagasako (hp), K. Abe (vib), Y. Takahashi (pno), R. Noguchi (fl), M. Hamada (lt), T. Koizumi (picc), S. Ueki (vn), Y. Hattori (vc), R. Stoltzman (cl), P. Serkin (pno), Ozawa, Wakasugi (cnd), Boston SO—Quatrain; Stanza I; Sacrifice; Ring; Valeria; A Flock Descends into the Pentagonal Garden Deutsche Grammophon ("20th Century Classics" series) ▲ 423253-2 [ADD]

Naglia, Sandro (ten)

Frescobaldi, G.:Arie musicali per cantarsi, w. G. Banditelli (mez), R. Bertini (sop), C. Cavina (alt), G. Maletto (ten), S. Foresti (bass), R. Alessandrini (cnd), Concerto Italiano Opus 111 2-▲ OPS 30-105/106

Monteverdi, C.:Vespro della Beata Vergine, w. A. Monoyios (sop), M. Pennicchi (sop), M. Chance (ct), G. Tucker (ten), N. Robson (ten), B. Terfel (b-bar), A. Miles (bass), J. E. Gardiner (cnd), English Baroque Soloists, His Majesties Sagbutts & Cornetts, London Monteverdi Choir Archiv 2-▲ 429565-2 [DDD]

Nagy, Robert (ten)

Enescu, G.:Vox maris, w. H. Andreescu (cnd), Romanian National RSO, Romanian National Radio Chorus Olympia ▲ OLY 496

Liszt, F.:Christus, w. Veronika Kincses (sop), Tamara Takács (mez), Sándor Sólyom-Nagy (bar), László Polgár (bass), A. Dorati (cnd), Hungarian State Orch, Hungarian Radio-TV Chorus [L] Hungaroton 3-▲ HCD 12831/33 [DDD]

Nagy, Robert (ten) (cont.)

Puccini, G.:Turandot, w. B. Nilsson (sop—Turnadot), A. Moffo (sop—Liù), F. Corelli (ten—Calaf), C. Anthony (ten—Pong), R. Nagy (ten—Pang), F. Guarrera (bar—Ping), B. Giaiotti (bass—Timur), L. Stokowski (cnd), Metropolitan Opera Orch, New York Metropolitan Opera Chorus *(rec Mar. 4, 1961)* Datum 2-▲ DAT 12301 [ADD]

Nagy-Soljom, András (sgr)

Wayditch, G. von:The Caliph's Magician, w. Júlia Pászthi (sop—Eunuch), Sándor Palcso (ten—The Emir), István Rozsos (ten—Nawab), Zsolt Bende (bar—The Magician), Arpád Kishegyi (sgr—Djinn), András Nagy-Soljom (sgr—The Caliph), Csaba Ötvös (sgr—Djinn), Csilla Ötvös (sgr—Odalisk), A. Korodi (cnd), Budapest National Opera Orch, Budapest National Opera Chorus *(rec 1975)* VAI Audio 2-▲ VAIA 1095-2 [ADD]

Najera, Edmund (bar)

Blitzstein, M.:The Harpies, w. R. Rees (sop), T. Bogdan (ten), et al., G. Smith (cnd), Adirondack CO, Gregg Smith Singers [E] Premier ▲ PRCD 1009 [ADD]

Namchylak, Sainkho (voc)

Namchylak, S.:Amulet, w. Ned Rothenberg (alt sax/b cl/shak) *(rec 1992-95)* Leo ▲ LC 5417

Nancel, Nicky (sgr)

Offenbach, J.:Le Belle Hélène, w. G. Calvi (cnd), Théâtre Bouffes-Parisiens Orch & Ensemble Accord 2-▲ ACD 290002 [AAD]

Naoumenko, Alexandre (ten)

Rachmaninoff, S.:Songs, w. Joan Rodgers (sop), Maria Popescu (mez), Sergei Leiferkus (bass), Howard Shelley (pno)—Letter to K. S. Stanislawsky; The Muse, Op. 34/1; In the Soul of Each of Us, Op. 34/2; The Storm, Op. 34/3; A Passing Breeze, Op. 34/4; Arion, Op. 35/5; The Raising of Lazarus, Op. 34/6; It Cannot Be, Op. 34/7; Music, Op. 34/8; You Knew Him, Op. 34/9; I Remember This Day, Op. 34/10; The Herald, Op. 34/11; What Happiness, Op. 34/12; Dissonance, Op. 34/13; Vocalise, Op. 34/14; From the Gospel of St. John; At Night in My Garden, Op. 38/1; To Her, Op. 38/2; Daisies, Op. 38/3; The Pied Piper, Op. 38/4; Sleep, Op. 38/5; A-oo, Op. 38/6; A Prayer; All Glory to God Chandos ▲ CHAN 9477

Rachmaninoff, S.:Songs, w. Joan Rodgers (sop), Maria Popescu (mez), Sergei Leiferkus (bar), Howard Shelley (pno)—At the Gates of the Holy Cloister; Nothing Shall I Say to You; Again You Are Bestirred, My Heart; April! A Festive Day in the Spring; Dusk Was Falling; Song of the Disenchanted; The Flower Died; Do You Remember the Evening?; O, No, I Beg You, Do Not Leave, Op. 4/1; Morning, Op. 4/2; In the Silence of the Secret Night, Op. 4/3; Sing not, O Lovely One, Op. 4/4; Oh, My Field, Op. 4/5; It Wasn't Long Ago, My Friend, Op. 4/6; Water Lily, Op. 8/1; My Child, Your Beauty Is That of a Flower, Op. 8/2; Thoughts, Reflection, Op. 8/3; I Fell in Love, to My Sorrow, Op. 8/4; A Dream, Op. 8/5; Prayer, Op. 8/6; I Await You, Op. 14/1; Small Island, Op. 14/2; How Fleeting Is Delight in Love, Op. 14/3; I Was with Her, Op. 14/4; Summer Nights, Op. 8/5; You Are so Loved by All, Op. 14/6; Do Not Believe Me, Friend, Op. 14/7; Oh, Do Not Grieve, Op. 14/8; She Is as Beautiful as Midday, Op. 14/9; In My Soul, Op. 14/10; Spring Torrents, Op. 14/11; It Is Time, Op. 14/12 Chandos ▲ CHAN 9405

Naouri, Laurent (b-bar)

Bruneau, A.:Lazare, w. Françoise Pollet (sop), Mary Saint-Palais (sop), Sylvie Sullé (mez), Jean-Luc Viala (ten), J. Mercier (cnd), French National Orch, Maîtrise de Paris, Vittoria French Regional Choir Adès ▲ ADE 204512

Bruneau, A.:Requiem, w. Françoise Pollet (sop), Mary Saint-Palais (sop), Sylvie Sullé (mez), Jean-Luc Viala (ten), J. Mercier (cnd), French National Orch, Maîtrise de Paris, Vittoria French Regional Choir Adès ▲ ADE 204512

Mozart, W.A.:Zauberflöte, w. Natalie Dessay (sop—Queen of the Night), Linda Kitchen (sop—Papagena), Rosa Mannion (sop—Pamina), Anna-Maria Panzarella (sop—First Lady), Doris Lamprecht (mez—Second Lady), Delphine Haidan (cta—Third Lady), Hans Peter Blochwitz (ten—Tamino), Steven Cole (ten—Monostatos), Chrisopher Josey (ten—First Priest/First Armed Man), Anton Scharinger (bar—Papageno), Reinhard Hagen (bass—Sarastro), Laurent Naouri (bass—Second Priest/Second Armed Man), Willard White (bass—Speaker), W. Christie (cnd), Les Arts Florissants *(rec Paris Oct 2-9 1995)* Erato 2-▲ 12705-2 [DDD]

Rameau, J.P.:Hippolyte et Aricie, w. Véronique Gens (sop), Bernarda Fink (cta), Jean-Paul Fouchécourt (ten), Russell Smythe (bar), M. Minkowski (cnd), Louvre Musicians, Sagittarius Vocal Ensemble Archiv 3-▲ 445853-2

Napier, Marita (sop)

Schoenberg, A.:Gurrelieder, w. Y. Minton (mez), J. Thomas (ten), K. Bowman (sgr), G. Reich (nar), S. Nimsgern (b-bar), P. Boulez (cnd), BBC SO *(rec Oct. 26-Dec. 06, 1974)* Sony Classical 2-▲ SM2K 48459 [ADD]

Nara, Yumi (sop)

Chaynes, C.:Oginoha, "Lights from Japanese Poetry", w. P.-Y. Artaud (fl), D. Megévand (celtic hp), C. Giot (perc) REM ▲ REM 311194 [DDD]

Messiaen, O.:Harawi, w. Jay Gotilieb (pno) Adda ▲ ADD 581139 [DDD]

Schoenberg, A.:The Cabaret Songs, w. Izumi Okubo (vn/va), Machiko Takahashi (fl/pic), Vincent Jacquemin (cl/b cl), François Deppe (vc), Brigitte Foccroulle (pno), J.-P. Peuvion (cnd), Liège New Music Ensemble [arr Patrick Davin for Salon Orch] Adda ▲ ADD 581273 [DDD]

Schoenberg, A.:Pierrot lunaire, w. Izumi Okubo (vn/va), Machiko Takahashi (fl/pic), Vincent Jacquemin (cl/b cl), François Deppe (vc), Brigitte Foccroulle (pno), J.-P. Peuvion (cnd), Liège New Music Ensemble Adda ▲ ADD 581273 [DDD]

Narita (sgr)

Astorga, E. d':Stabat Mater, w. Elisabetta Battaglia (sop), Mapelli (sgr), Zaramella (sgr), Concentus Musicae Antiqua Nuova Era ("Ancient Music" series) ▲ NUO 7198 [DDD]

Narké, Victor de (bass)

Donizetti, G.:Lucia di Lammermoor, w. B. Sills (sop), A. Kraus (ten), G. Mastromei (bar), J.E. Martini (cnd), Buenos Aires Teatro Colón Orch, Buenos Aires Teatro Colón Chorus *(rec 1968)* Arkadia 2-▲ 474

Verdi, G.:Rigoletto, w. Renata Scotto (sop—Gilda), Stella Maris Silva (sop—Giovanna), Martha Carrizo (mez—Page), Carmen de la Mata (mez—Countess Ceprano), Noemi Souza (cta—Maddalena), Horacio Mastrango (ten—Borso), Richard Tucker (ten—Duke of Mantua), Cornell MacNeil (bar—Rigoletto), Riccardo Yost (bar—Marullo), Guerrino Boschetti (bass—Usher), Tulio Gagliardo (bass—Count Ceprano), Victor de Narké (bass—Monterone), William Wilderman (bass—Sparafucile), F. Previtali (cnd), Buenos Aires Teatro Colón Orch, Buenos Aires Teatro Colón Chorus *(rec Colon Theater, Buenos Aires, Aug. 22, 1967)* Legato Classics 2-▲ LCD 198-2

Narucki, Susan (sop)

Becker, J.J.:At Dieppe, w. Myron Romanul (pno) Koch International Classics ▲ KIC 7207 [DDD]

Crumb, G.:Federico's Little Songs, w. Speculum Musicae Bridge ▲ 9069

Crumb, G.:Night Music I, w. Speculum Musicae Bridge ▲ 9069

del Tredici, D.:Haddocks' Eyes, w. C. Bloom (nar), Z. Mehta (cnd), New York PO Ensemble New World ▲ 80390-2 [DDD]

Einhorn, R.:Voices of Light, w. Corrie Pronk (alt), Frank Hameleers (ten), Henk van Heijnsbergen (b-bar), Ronald Hoogeveen (vn), Harm Bakker (vl), Michael Feves (vl), Naomi Hirschfeld (vl), S. Mercurio (cnd), Netherlands Radio PO, Martin Wright (cnd), Anonymous 4, Netherlands Radio Chorus *(rec Music Center of the Netherlands Radio & TV, Aug 23-25, 1995)* Sony Classical ▲ SK 62006 [DDD]

Imbrie, A.W.:Roethke Songs, w. Martin Goldray (pno) *(rec SUNY Purchase, NY, Sept. 13, 1994)* New World ▲ 80441-2

Zuidam, R.:Freeze, w. Susan Narucki (sop—Patty Hearst), Gerrie de Vries (mez), Zeger Vandersteene (ten), Martin Hargrove (bass), Jaco Huijpen (bass), S. Asbury (cnd), Asko Ensemble NM Classics 2-▲ NM 92047

Naseband, Dennis (trb)

Pergolesi, G.B.:Stabat mater, w. J. Kowalski (alt), R. Alpemann (org), H. Haenchen (cnd), C.P.E. Bach CO *(rec Apr. 1992)* Berlin Classics ▲ BER 1047-2 [DDD]

Nash, Elizabeth (sop)

Leigh, W.:Songs, w. S. Down (pno)—9 Songs *(rec Aug. & Sept. 1991)* Tremula ▲ TREM 101-2

Nash, Heddle (ten)

Elgar, E.:The Dream of Gerontius, w. G. Ripley (cta), D. Noble (bar), N. Walker (bass), M. Sargent (cnd), Liverpool PO, Huddersfield Choral Society Testament ▲ TES SBT 2025 [ADD]

Nash, Heddle (ten) (cont.)
Gounod, C.:Faust, w. M. Licette (sop—Margarita), D. Vane (sop—Siebel), M. Brunskill (cta—Martha), H. Nash (ten—Faust), H. Williams (b-bar—Valentine), R. Easton (bass—Mephistopheles), R. Carr (bass—Wagner), T. Beecham (cnd), BBC SO, BBC Sym Chorus
Dutton Laboratories 2-▲ CDAX 2001 [ADD]
Mozart, W.A.:Così fan tutte, w. Irene Eisinger (sop—Despina), Luise Helletsgruber (sop—Dorabella), Ina Souez (sop—Fiordiligi), Heddle Nash (ten—Ferrando), John Brownlee (bass—Don Alfonso), Willi Domgraf-Fassbaender (bass—Guglielmo), F. Busch (cnd), Glyndebourne Festival Orch, Glyndebourne Festival Chorus *(rec June 25-28, 1935)* Arkadia ("The 78's" series) 2-▲ 78011 [ADD]
Mozart, W.A.:Così fan tutte, w. I. Souez (sop), L. Helletsgrüber (sop), I. Eisinger (sop), W. Domgraf-Fassbüander (bar), J. Brownlee (bar), F. Busch (cnd), Glyndebourne Festival Orch, Glyndebourne Festival Chorus [I] *(rec 1935)* Pearl 3-▲ PEAS 9406 (m) [AAD]
Mozart, W.A.:Così fan tutte (sels), w. Ina Suez (sop), C. Raybould (cnd), *(orch unknown)*—Hier soll ich dich; Konstanze!... wie ängstlich; Martern aller Arten *(rec 1905 - 1944)* Minerva ▲ MN A14 [ADD]
Mozart, W.A.:Nozze di Figaro, w. Aulikki Rautawaara (sop), Audrey Mildmay (sop), Constance Willis (mez), Roy Henderson (bar), Willi Domgraf-Fassbaender (bar), F. Busch (cnd), Glyndebourne Festival Orch, Glyndebourne Festival Chorus [I] *(rec 1934-35)* Pearl 2-▲ PEAS 9375 (m) [AAD]
Mozart, W.A.:Nozze di Figaro, w. Aulikki Rautawaara (sop), Audrey Mildmay (sop), Constance Willis (mez), Roy Henderson (bar), Willi Domgraf-Fassbaender (bar), F. Busch (cnd), Glyndebourne Festival Orch *(rec 1934)* Legend 2-▲ LGD 132 [ADD]
Mozart, W.A.:Nozze di Figaro (sels), w. Luise Helletsgrüber (sop), Audrey Mildmay (sop), Aulikki Rautawaara (sop), Constance Willis (mez), Willi Domgraf-Fassbaender (bar), Roy Henderson (bar), Norman Allin (bass), F. Busch (cnd), Glyndebourne Festival Orch Pearl ▲ PEA CD 9230
Mozart, W.A.:Songs, w. M. Callas (sop), E. Grümmer (sop), E. Schwarzkopf (sop), R. Scotto (sop), T. Lemnitz (sop), E. Berger (sop), S. Jurinac (sop), E. Schumann (sop), I. Souez (sop), E. Rethberg (sop), L. Lehmann (sop), N. Gedda (ten), J. McCormack (ten), H. Roswenge (ten), T. Gobbi (bar), G. Hüsch (bar), E. Kunz (bar), G. Frick (bass), E. Pinza (bass), A. Kipnis (bass) EMI Classics 4-▲ CDMD 63750
Serenade *(rec 1928-44)* Pearl ▲ PEA 9175 [ADD]
Vaughan Williams, R.:Serenade to Music, w. I. Baillie (sop), E. Suddaby (sop), S. Allen (sop), E. Turner (sop), M. Balfour (cta), A. Desmond (cta), M. Brunskill (cta), M. Jarred (cta), W. Widdop (ten), P. Jones (ten), F. Titterton (ten), R. Henderson (bass), R. Easton (bass), H. Williams (bass), N. Allin (bass), H. J. Wood (cnd), BBC SO Dutton Laboratories ▲ CDAX 8004 [ADD]
Vaughan Williams, R.:Serenade to Music, w. I. Baillie (sop), E. Suddaby (sop), S. Allen (sop), E. Turner (sop), M. Balfour (cta), A. Desmond (cta), M. Brunskill (cta), M. Jarred (cta), W. Widdop (ten), P. Jones (ten), F. Titterton (ten), R. Henderson (bass), R. Easton (bass), H. Williams (bass), N. Allin (bass), H. Wood (cnd), BBC SO [E] *(rec 10/15/38)* Pearl ▲ GEMMCD 9342 (m) [AAD]
Vaughan Williams, R.:Serenade to Music, w. Isobel Baillie (sop), Lilian Stiles-Allen (sop), Elsie Suddaby (sop), Eva Turner (sop), Margaret Balfour (cta), Muriel Brunskill (cta), Astra Desmond (cta), Mary Jarred (cta), Parry Jones (ten), Frank Titterton (ten), Walter Widdop (ten), Roy Henderson (bar), Harold Williams (bar), Norman Allin (bass), Robert Easton (bass), H. Wood (cnd), BBC SO *(rec Abbey Road, Oct 15, 1938)* Claremont ▲ CDGSE 785066

Nasrawi, Douglas (ten)
Campra, A.:Motets, w. Véronique Gens (sop), Anne Gotkovski (sop), Jean-Paul Fouchécourt (alt), Peter Harvey (bar), Marcos Loureiro de Sà (bar), Kevin Mallon (vn), H. Niquet (cnd), Concert Spirituel Orch, Concert Spirituel Vocal Ensemble—Te Deum; Notus in Judea Deus; Deus in Nomine Tuo
Adda ▲ ADD 241942 [DDD]
Rameau, J.P.:Les Paladins, w. A. Michael (sop), G. Raphanel (sop), B. Brewer (ten), G. Reinhart (bar), N. Rivenq (bar), J. Malgoire (cnd), La Grande Écurie et la Chambre du Roy, Sagittarius Vocal Ensemble [F]
Pierre Verany 2-▲ PV.790121/22 [DDD]
Schütz, H.:Symphoniae sacrae 1, w. Barbara Borden (sop), Nele Gramss (sop), Rogers Covey-Crump (ten), John Potter (ten), Harry van der Kamp (bass), Concerto Palatino Choir
Accent 2-▲ 9178/79 [DDD]

Nastase, Gabriel (ten)
Donizetti, G.:Lucia di Lammermoor, w. Silvia Voinea (sop—Lucia), Lucia Cicoara (mez—Alisa), Florin Georgescu (ten—Edgardo), Gabriel Nastase (ten—Arturo), Nicolae Herlea (bar—Lord Enrico), Pompei Harasteanu (bass—Raimondo), C. Petrovici (cnd), Romanian Opera Orch, Romanian Opera Chorus *(rec 1984)* Vox Box 2-▲ CDX 5164

Natech, Souad (sgr)
Mendelssohn, F.:Athalie, w. Danielle Borst (sop), Brigitte Desnoues (sop), Carolyn Watkinson (cta), Jean-Marc Avocat (sgr), B. Tetu (cnd), Lorraine PO, Lyon National Chorus
Koch Schwann ▲ SCH 314282 [DDD]

Navadic, Jacques (nar)
Debussy, C.:Martyre de Saint Sébastian (fragments), w. L. de Froment (cnd), Luxembourg RSO *(rec 1972)*
Vox Box 2-▲ CDX 5053 [ADD]

Navarro (sgr)
Falla, M. de:El retablo de maese Pedro, w. Seoane (sop), Gonzalo (sgr), E. Halffter (cnd), Champs Elysées Theater Orch *(rec ca. 1959)* MCA Classics ▲ MCAD 10481 (m/s) [ADD]

Nave, Maria Luisa (mez)
Cilea, F.:Adriana Lecouvreur, w. M. Olivero (sop), P. Domingo (ten), E. Sordello (bar), A. Silipigni (cnd), *(orch unknown)* [I] *(rec 1973)* Legato Classics 2-▲ LCD 140-2 [ADD]
Mascagni, P.:Cavalleria rusticana (sels), w. Giuseppe Giacomini (ten), Aldo Protti (bar), M. Gusella (cnd), *(orch unknown)*—O Lola ch'hai di latti la cammisa; Tu qui Santuzza; Intanto amici qua; Mamma, quel vino è generoso *(rec Parma, Feb. 6, 1969)* Golden Age of Opera 2-▲ GAO 189/90 [ADD]
Ponchielli, A.:La Gioconda, w. M. Caballé (sop—Gioconda), M. L. Nave (mez—Laura), P. Payne (mez—La Cieca), J. Carreras (ten—Enzo), M. Manuguerra (bar—Barnaba), B. Giaiotti (bass—Alvise), J. López-Cobos (cnd), *(orch unknown) (rec Dec. 6, 1979)* Legato Classics ▲ LCD 170-2 [ADD]

Neblett, Carol (sop)
Mahler, G.:Sym 2, w. M. Horne (mez), C. Abbado (cnd), Chicago SO, Chicago Sym Chorus [G]
Deutsche Grammophon ("Galleria" series) 2-▲ 427262-2 [ADD]
Puccini, G.:La fanciulla del West, w. P. Domingo (ten), S. Milnes (bar), Z. Mehta (cnd), Royal Opera House Orch Covent Garden, Royal Opera House Chorus Covent Garden [I]
Deutsche Grammophon 2-▲ 419640-2 [ADD]

Necheporenko, Y. (ten)
Rachmaninoff, S.:All-Night Vigil, w. A. Zlobin (ten), R. Sevostyanov (ten), O. Shepel (cnd), Voronezh Chamber Choir Globe ▲ GLO 5077 [DDD]

Necolescu, Antonio (ten)
Liszt, F.:A Faust Sym, w. F. d' Avalos (cnd), Hungarian State SO, Hungarian Radio Chorus
IMP Classics ▲ IMP PCD 1071 [DDD]

Neculce-Cartis, Elisabeta (mez)
Verdi, G.:La traviata, w. Elena Simionescu (sop—Annina), Virginia Zeani (sop—Violetta Valery), Elisabeta Neculce-Cartis (mez—Flora Bervoix), Ion Buzea (ten—Alfredo Germont), Vasile Moldoveanu (ten—Gastone/Viconte de Letorieres/Giuseppe), Teodor Panea (ten—Flora's Servant), Constantin Dumitru (bar—Commissioner/Baron Douphol), Nicolae Herlea (bar—Giorgio Germont), Valentin Loghin (bass—Marchese D'Obigny), Nicolae Rafael (bass—Doctor Grenvil), J. Bobescu (cnd), Romanian Opera Orch, Stelian Olariu (cnd), Romanian Opera Chorus *(rec 1968)* Vox Box 2-▲ CDX 5154

Neff, H. (sgr)
Porter, C.:Silk Stockings, w. D. Ameche (sgr) [1955 Broadway cast]
RCA ▲ 1102 RG [ADD] ■ 1102-4 RG

Negri, Adelaida (sop)
Adelaida Negri *(rec. between 1979 & 1991)* Ornamenti 2-▲ FE 002
"Da voi parto amate sponde..." *(rec Mar. 1993)* Ornamenti ▲ FE 105 [DDD]
Verdi, G.:Don Carlos (sels)—Tu che le vanità *(rec Buenos Aires, 1979)* Ornamenti 2-▲ FE 110 [ADD]

Negri, Giovanni Battista de (ten)
The World of Singing, Vol. 3:The Italian School, Part 1:The Italian Tenors Before World War I (1902-13), w. Antonio Aramburo (ten), Alessandro Bonci (ten), Giuseppe Borgatti (ten), Enrico Caruso (ten), Edoardo Garbin (ten), Fiorello Giraud (ten), Fernando de Lucia (ten), Francesco Marconi (ten), Antonio Paoli (ten), et al. Enterprise ("Vocal Archives" series) 3-▲ ENT VA 2104

Négroni, Jean (nar)
Milhaud, D.:Ani maamin, un chant perdu et retrouvé, w. Sharon Cooper (sop—la Voix), Anna Parus (mez), Bernard Freyd (nar—Isaac), Michel Hermon (nar—le Récitant), Michael Lonsdale (nar—Abraham), Jean Négroni (nar—Jacob), P. Méfano (cnd), Ensemble 2E2M, Madrigal de Bordeaux
Arion ▲ ARN 68275 [DDD]

Neidlinger, Gustav (b-bar)
Bach, J.S.:Mass in b, BWV 232, w. P. Alarie (sop), N. Merriman (cta), L. Simoneau (ten), H. Scherchen (cnd), Vienna State Opera Orch, Vienna Academy Chorus [L]
MCA Classics 2-▲ MCAD2-9821 [AAD]
Mozart, W.A.:Nozze di Figaro, w. Irma Beilke (sop), Helena Braun (sop), Gerda Sommerschuh (sop), Josef Witt (ten), Hans Hotter (bar), Erich Kunz (bar), C. Krauss (cnd), Vienna PO, Vienna State Opera Chorus *(rec live, Salzburg Festival, Aug. 1942)* Preiser 3-▲ PRE 90203 [ADD]
Still, W.G.:Tristan und Isolde, w. C. Ligendza (sop), R. Baldani (mez), H. Hopf (ten), A. Dermota (ten), H. Sotin (bass), C. Kleiber (cnd), Vienna State Opera Orch, Vienna State Opera Chorus *(rec Oct. 7, 1973)*
Exclusive 3-▲ EXL 18 [ADD]
Wagner, R.:Lohengrin, w. A. Varnay (sop), I. Bjoner (sop), J. Thomas (ten), W. Sawallisch (cnd), La Scala Orch, Prague Phil Chorus [G] *(rec live, Milan 1965)* Melodram 3-▲ MEL 37067 [AAD]
Wagner, R.:Parsifal, w. I. Dalis (mez), J. Thomas (ten), G. London (bar), H. Hotter (b-bar), H. Knappertsbusch (cnd), Bayreuth Festival Orch, Bayreuth Festival Chorus [1962] [G]
Philips 4-▲ 416390-2 [ADD]
Wagner, R.:Das Rheingold, w. K. Flagstad (sop), J. Madeira (mez), S. Svanholm (ten), G. London (bar), K. Böhme (bass), G. Solti (cnd), Vienna PO [G] London 3-▲ 414101-2 [ADD]
Wagner, R.:Der Ring des Nibelungen, w. B. Nilsson (sop), K. Flagstad (sop), R. Crespin (sop), C. Watson (sop), C. Ludwig (mez), J. Madeira (mez), S. Svanholm (ten), J. King (ten), G. Stolze (ten), W. Windgassen (ten), G. London (bar), D. Fischer-Dieskau (bar), H. Hotter (b-bar), G. Frick (bass), G. Solti (cnd), Vienna PO [G] London 15-▲ 414100-2 [ADD]
Wagner, R.:Der Ring des Nibelungen, w. Gré Brouwenstein (sop—Freia/Sieglinde), Ilse Hollweg (sop—Waldvogel), Gerda Lammers (sop—Ortlinde), Paula Lenchner (sop—Wellgunde/Gerhilde), Hilde Scheppan (sop—Helmwige), Astrid Varnay (sop—Brünnilde/3rd Norn), Lore Wissmann (sop—Woglinde), Maria von Ilosvay (mez—Flosshilde/Schwertleite/2nd Norn), Louise Charlotte Kamps (mez—Siegrune), Jean Madeira (mez—Erda/Rossweisse/1st Norn), Georgine van Milinkovic (mez—Fricka/Grimgerde), Elisabeth Schärtel (mez—Waltraute), Paul Kuën (ten—Mime), Ludwig Suthaus (ten—Loge), Josef Traxel (ten—Froh), Wolfgang Windgassen (ten—Siegmund/Siegfried), Alfons Herwig (bar—Donner), Hermann Uhde (bar—Gunther), Hans Hotter (b-bar—Wotan), Gustav Neidlinger (b-bar—Alberich), Josef Griendl (bass—Fasolt/Hunding/Hagen), Arnold van Mill (bass—Fafner), H. Knappertsbusch (cnd), Bayreuth Festival Orch, Bayreuth Festival Chorus *(rec live, Bayreuth, Aug 13-17, 1956)* Golden Melodram 14-▲ GM 1.001 [ADD]
Wagner, R.:Der Ring des Nibelungen, w. B. Nilsson (sop), L. Rysanek (sop), K. Dvořaková (sop), M. Mödl (sop), A. Burmeister (mez), V. Soukupova (mez), E. Wohlfahrt (ten), W. Windgassen (ten), T. Stewart (bar), T. Adam (b-bar), K. Böhme (bass), G. Nienstedt (bass), K. Böhm (cnd), Bayreuth Festival Orch, Bayreuth Festival Chorus [G] *(rec live, 1966-67)* Philips 14-▲ 420325-2 [ADD]
Wagner, R.:Der Ring des Nibelungen (sels), w. Birgit Nilsson (sop—Brünnhilde), Leonie Rysanek (sop—Sieglinde), James King (ten—Siegmund), Wolfgang Windgassen (ten), Theo Adam (b-bar—Wotan), Josef Greindl (bass), K. Böhm (cnd), Bayreuth Festival Orch *(rec Bayreuth, 1967)*
Philips 2-▲ 454020-2
Wagner, R.:Siegfried, w. B. Nilsson (sop), W. Windgassen (ten), G. Stolze (ten), H. Hotter (b-bar), G. Solti (cnd), Vienna PO [G] London 4-▲ 414110-2 [ADD]
Wagner, R.:Siegfried, w. B. Nilsson (sop), W. Windgassen (ten), E. Wohlfahrt (ten), T. Adam (b-bar), K. Böhm (cnd), Bayreuth Festival Orch, Bayreuth Festival Chorus [G] Philips 4-▲ 412483-2 [ADD]

Neilau, Maria (alt)
Suder, J.:Festival Mass, w. Natalia Kornewa (sop), Vladimir Mostomoi (ten), Juri Dobrowolski (bass), Jessica Hartlieb (vn), Marlene Hinterberger (org), W.A. Albert (cnd), Bavarian State Youth Orch, St. Petersburg Chamber Choir Calig ▲ CAL 50945 [DDD]

Neill, Stuart (sgr)
Bellini, V.:Il pirata, w. Lucia Aliberti (sop), Roberto Frontali (sgr), José Guadalupe Reyes (sgr), M. Viotti (cnd), Berlin German Opera Orch, Berlin German Opera Chorus
Berlin Classics 2-▲ BER 1115 [DDD]

Nelepp, Georgi (ten)
Mussorgsky, M.:Boris Godounov, w. Maxim Mikhailov (bass), Mark Reizen (bass), *(other soloists unknown)*, N. Golovanov (cnd), Bolshoi Theater Orch, Bolshoi Theater Chorus *(rec 1948)*
Arlecchino 3-▲ ARL121/23
Tchaikovsky, P.:Queen of Spades, w. Elena Smolenskaya (sop), Evgenya Verbitskaya (mez), Pavel Lisitsian (bar), A. Melik-Pashayev (cnd), Bolshoi Opera Orch, Bolshoi Theater Chorus
Arlecchino 3- ARL

Nell, Edward (voc)
Exquisite Corpses from P.S. 122, w. David Watson (shears/stick vn/gtr/tpt), Judy Dunaway (gtr/balloons), Anthony Coleman (sampler), Raissa St. Pierre (drums), Guy Yarden (vn/pno), Leslie Ross (bn), Linda Austin (gtr), Bruce Kaplan (gtr), Doug Henderson (peckhorn/bass/toy pno), Sue Ann Harkey (gtr), Cinnie Cole (sampler), et al. ¿What Next? ▲ WN 0002 [ADD]

Nelli, Herva (sop)
Verdi, G.:Aida, w. E. Gustavson (mez), G. Tucker (ten), G. Valdengo (bar), A. Toscanini (cnd), NBC SO, Robert Shaw Chorale [I] RCA Gold Seal 3-▲ 60251-2-RG (m) [ADD] 2-■ 60251-4-RG (CrO2)
Verdi, G.:Aida, w. E. Gustavson (mez), G. Tucker (ten), G. Valdengo (bar), A. Toscanini (cnd), NBC SO, Robert Shaw Chorale [I] RCA Gold Seal 7-▲ 60326-2-RG (m) [ADD] 6-■ 60326-4-RG (CrO2)
Verdi, G.:Falstaff, w. Teresa Stich-Randall (sop), Cloë Elmo (cta), Frank Guarrera (bar), Giuseppe Valdengo (bar), A. Toscanini (cnd), *(orch unknown) (rec 1950)* Music & Arts 2-▲ CD 248 [ADD]
Verdi, G.:Otello, w. R. Vinay (ten), G. Valdengo (bar), A. Toscanini (cnd), NBC SO [I]
RCA Gold Seal 2-▲ 60302-2-RG [ADD] 2-■ 60302-4-RG (CrO2)
Verdi, G.:Requiem Mass, w. F. Barbieri (mez), G. Di Stefano (Ten), C. Siepi (b-bar), A. Toscanini (cnd), NBC SO, Robert Shaw Chorale [L]
RCA Gold Seal 2-▲ 60299-2-RG (m) [ADD] 2-■ 60299-4-RG (CrO2)

Nelson (sop)
Scarlatti, A.:Arias Sop, w. Ferry (tpt), et al. [I] Musique d'Abord ▲ HMA 1905137

Nelson, Alice Marie (mez)
Lauer, E.:Songs on Poems of James Joyce, w. Elizabeth Lauer (pno) Capstone ▲ CPS 8632

Nelson, Daniel (ten)
Downey, J.:A Dolphin, w. Bourachoff (fl), B. Zaslav (va), B. Burda (perc), J. Downey (pno)
Gasparo ▲ GS 276 ■ GS 276C

Nelson, Gene (sgr)
Rodgers, R.:Oklahoma!, w. Gordon MacRae (sgr), S. Jones (sgr), R. Steiger (sgr), Gloria Grahame (sgr), C. Greenwood (sgr), J. Whitmore (sgr) *(rec 1955)* Broadway Angel ▲ ZDM 64691 ■ EG 64691

Nelson, I. (sop)
Bach, J.S.:Cant 139, w. H. Watts (cta), A. Kraus (ten), P. Huttenlocher (bar), H. Rilling (cnd), Stuttgart Bach Collegium, Gächinger Kantorei [G] *(rec 1979 & 1980)* Hänssler Classic ▲ 98.820 [AAD]

Nelson, J. (mez)
Campra, A.:Messe de Requiem, w. C. Harris (trb), J.-C. Orliac (ten), S. Roberts (bar), J. E. Gardiner (cnd), English Baroque Soloists, Monteverdi Choir London Erato ▲ 2292-45993-2
Charpentier, M.-A.:Leçons de ténèbres, H. 96-110, w. Verkinderen (sgr), R. Jacobs (cnd), Concerto Vocale—H.105, 106, 110 [L] Harmonia Mundi France ▲ HMC 901007
Couperin, F.:Leçons de ténèbres (for Good Friday), w. E. Kirkby (sop), J. Ryan (vl), C. Hogwood (chamber org) L'Oiseau-Lyre ▲ 430283-2 [ADD]
Couperin, F.:Motets, w. E. Kirkby (sop), J. Ryan (vl), C. Hogwood (chamber org)
L'Oiseau-Lyre ▲ 430283-2 [ADD]
Purcell, H.:Dido & Aeneas, w. E. Kirkby (sop), D. Thomas (bass), A. Parrott (cnd), Taverner Players, Taverner Choir [E] Chandos ("Chaconne" series) ▲ CHAN 0521 [DDD]

Nelson, Judith (mez)
Cavalieri, E. de:Rappresentatione di Anima et di Corpo, w. Paul Hillier (bass), W. Stewart (cnd), Whole Noyse Koch International Classics ▲ KIC 7363

▲ = CD ♦ = Enhanced CD Δ = MD ■ = Cassette Tape □ = DCC

Nelson, Judith (mez) (cont.)

Handel, G.F.:Messiah, w. Emma Kirkby (sop), Carolyn Watkinson (cta), Paul Elliott (ten), David Thomas (bass), C. Hogwood (cnd), Academy of Ancient Music London 2-▲ 430488-2 [DDD]

Handel, G.F.:La Rezurrezione, w. Linda Saffer (sop), Patricia Spence (mez), Jeffery Thomas (ten), Michael George (bass), N. McGegan (cnd), Philharmonia Baroque Orch [I] Harmonia Mundi USA 2-▲ HMU 907027/28

Venice Preserv'd, w. Emma Kirkby (sop), Nigel Rogers (ten), Academy of Ancient Music [cnd:Christopher Hogwood] L'Oiseau-Lyre ▲ 425891-2 OH [ADD]

Nelson, Judith (sop)

Bach, J.S.:Cant 198, w. J. Malafronte (mez), J. Thomas (ten), W. Sharp (bar), J. Thomas (cnd), American Bach Soloists [G] Koch International Classics ▲ KIC 7163-2 [DDD]

Bach, J.S.:Magnificat, BWV 243, w. E. Kirkby (sop), C. Watkinson (cta), P. Elliott (ten), D. Thomas (bass), S. Preston (cnd), Academy of Ancient Music, Christ Church Cathedral Choir Oxford [E♭ version; L] L'Oiseau-Lyre ▲ 414678-2 [ADD]

Bach, J.S.:Mass in b, BWV 232, w. J. Baird (sop), J. Dooley (ct), F. Hoffmeister (ten), J. Opalach (bass), J. Rifkin (cnd), Bach Ensemble [L] Elektra/Nonesuch 2-▲ 79036-2 [DDD] 2-■ 79036-4 (D)

Bach, J.S.:Mass in b, BWV 232, w. J. Baird (sop), N. Zylstra, J. Lane, Z. Muñoz, S. Rickards, P. Romano, W. Sharp, J. Weaver (bass), J. Thomas (cnd), American Bach Soloists Koch International Classics 2-▲ KIC 7194-2 [DDD]

Handel, G.F.:Apollo e Dafne, w. David Thomas (bass), N. McGegan (cnd), Philharmonia Baroque Orch Harmonia Mundi France ("Musique d'abord" series) ▲ HMA 1905157

Melani, A.:Cants, w. D. Ferry (tpt)—"All'armi, pensieri" for Soprano & Trumpet [I] Musique d'Abord ▲ HMA 1905137

Melani, A.:Sinf a 5, w. D. Ferry (tpt) [I] Musique d'Abord ▲ HMA 1905137

Purcell, H.:Music for the Theater, w. E. Kirkby (sop), J. Bowman (ct), M. Hill (ten), R. Covey-Crump (ten), C. Keyte (bass), D. Thomas (bass), C. Hogwood (cnd), Academy of Ancient Music L'Oiseau-Lyre 6-▲ 425893-2 [ADD]

Songs for a Tudor King, w. P. Hillier (cnd), Hillard Ensemble, David James (ct), Paul Elliott (ten), Leigh Nixon (ten), P. Hillier (bar) Saga Classics ▲ 3378 [ADD]

Vivaldi, A.:Gloria, RV.589, w. E. Kirkby (sop), C. Watkinson (cta), P. Elliott (ten), D. Thomas (bass), S. Preston (cnd), Academy of Ancient Music, Christ Church Cathedral Choir Oxford [L] L'Oiseau-Lyre ▲ 414678-2 [ADD]

Nelson, Nelda (sop)

Eaton, J.:Ars Poetica, w. Carole Morgan (fl), Daniel Rothmuller (vc), Beverly Wesner-Hoehn (hp), C. Colnot (cnd) *(rec Dec 18, 1986)* Indiana Univ School of Music ▲ 0-253-31842-4

Eaton, J.:The City of Clytæmnestra (sels), w. H. Sollberger (cnd), Indiana Univ New Music Ensemble—Aria & Scene *(rec Musical Arts Ctr, Bloomington, IN, Apr 4, 1985)* Indiana Univ School of Music ▲ 0-253-31842-4

Nemeckova, Kvetoslava (sop)

Janácek, L.:Amarus, w. Leo Marian Vodicka (ten), Vaclav Zitek (bar), Jan Hora (org), C. Mackerras (cnd), Czech PO, Lubomír Mátl (cnd), Czech Phil Chorus *(rec 1984)* Supraphon ▲ SUP CD 3045

Németh, József (bar)

Puccini, G.:Tosca (sels), w. E. Marton (sop), B. Heja (trb), J. Carreras (ten), F. Gerdesits (ten), J. Pons (bar), J. Gregor (bass), M. Tilson Thomas (cnd), Hungarian State Orch, Hungarian Radio-TV Chorus *(rec Budapest, Dec. 14-22, 1988)* Sony Classical ("Opera Highlights" series) ▲ SMK 53500 [DDD]

Németh, Judit (cta)

Mozart, W.A.:Alma Dei creatoris, w. Ibolya Verebics (sop), József Mukk (ten), József Moldvay (bar), Gábor Oláh (bar), István Ella (org), János Reményi (cnd), Hungarian Radio-TV Children's Chorus Girls' Voices, Hungarian Radio-TV Male Chamber Choir *(rec Hungaroton Studio, June 14-16, 1991)* Hungaroton ▲ HCD 4003 [DDD]

Mozart, W.A.:Ave verum corpus, w. Ibolya Verebics (sop), József Mukk (ten), József Moldvay (bar), Gábor Oláh (bar), István Ella (org), János Reményi (cnd), Hungarian Radio-TV Children's Chorus Girls' Voices, Hungarian Radio-TV Male Chamber Choir *(rec Hungaroton Studio, June 14-16, 1991)* Hungaroton ▲ HCD 4003 [DDD]

Mozart, W.A.:Miserere, w. Ibolya Verebics (sop), József Mukk (ten), József Moldvay (bass), Gábor Oláh (bar/Gregorian intonations), István Ella (org), János Reményi (cnd), Hungarian Radio-TV Children's Chorus Girls' Voices, Hungarian Radio-TV Male Chamber Choir *(rec Hungaroton Studio, June 14-16, 1991)* Hungaroton ▲ HCD 4003 [DDD]

Mozart, W.A.:Misericordias Domini, w. Ibolya Verebics (sop), József Mukk (ten), József Moldvay (bass), Gábor Oláh (bar/Gregorian intonations), István Ella (org), János Reményi (cnd), Hungarian Radio-TV Children's Chorus Girls' Voices, Hungarian Radio-TV Male Chamber Choir *(rec Hungaroton Studio, June 14-16, 1991)* Hungaroton ▲ HCD 4003 [DDD]

Mozart, W.A.:Missa brevis, K.65, w. Ibolya Verebics (sop), József Mukk (ten), József Moldvay (bass), Gábor Oláh (bar/Gregorian intonations), István Ella (org), János Reményi (cnd), Hungarian Radio-TV Children's Chorus Girls' Voices, Hungarian Radio-TV Male Chamber Choir *(rec Hungaroton Studio, June 14-16, 1991)* Hungaroton ▲ HCD 4003 [DDD]

Mozart, W.A.:Missa brevis, K.194, w. Ibolya Verebics (sop), József Mukk (ten), József Moldvay (b), Gábor Oláh (bar/Gregorian intonations), István Ella (org), János Reményi (cnd), Hungarian Radio-TV Children's Chorus Girls' Voices, Hungarian Radio-TV Male Chamber Choir *(rec Hungaroton Studio, June 14-16, 1991)* Hungaroton ▲ HCD 4003 [DDD]

Mozart, W.A.:Sancta Maria, w. Ibolya Verebics (sop), József Mukk (ten), József Moldvay (bass), Gábor Oláh (bar/Gregorian intonations), István Ella (org), János Reményi (cnd), Hungarian Radio-TV Children's Chorus Girls' Voices, Hungarian Radio-TV Male Chamber Choir *(rec Hungaroton Studio, June 14-16, 1991)* Hungaroton ▲ HCD 4003 [DDD]

Németh, Judit (mez)

Bach, J.S.:Cant 51, w. I. Kertesi (sop), J. Pászthy (sop), J. Mukk (ten), I. Gáti (bass), M. Antal (cnd), Failoni CO, Hungarian Radio Chorus Naxos ▲ 8.550643 [DDD]

Bach, J.S.:Cant 80, w. I. Kertesi (sop), J. Mukk (ten), I. Gáti (bass), M. Antal (cnd), Failoni CO, Hungarian Radio Chorus *(rec Jan 1992)* Naxos ▲ 8.550642 [DDD]

Bach, J.S.:Cant 147, w. I. Kertesi (sop), J. Mukk (ten), I. Gáti (bass), M. Antal (cnd), Failoni CO, Hungarian Radio Chorus *(rec Jan 1992)* Naxos ▲ 8.550642 [DDD]

Bach, J.S.:Cant 208, "Hunting Cant", w. I. Kertesi (sop), J. Pászthy (sop), J. Mukk (ten), I. Gáti (bass), M. Antal (cnd), Failoni CO, Hungarian Radio Chorus Naxos ▲ 8.550643 [DDD]

Bach, J.S.:St. Matthew Passion, w. R. Kiss (sop), I. Verebics (sop), Á. Csenki (mez), P. Cser (ten), J. Mukk (ten), I. Gati (bar), F. Korpás (bar), P. Köves (bass), G. Oberfrank (cnd), Hungarian State SO, Hungarian Festival Choir, Hungarian Radio Children's Choir [G] *(rec Feb 1993)* Naxos 3-▲ 8.550832/34 [DDD]

Handel, G.F.:St. John Passion, w. Mária Zládori (sop), Charles Brett (ct), Martin Klietmann (ten), Jósef Moldvay (bass), G. Németh (cnd), Capella Savaria, Capella Savaria Hungaroton ▲ HCD 12908 [DDD]

Haydn, M.:Missa Pro Defuncto Archiepiscopo Sigismundo, w. Ibolya Verebics (sop), Martin Klietmann (ten), József Moldvay (bass), H. Rilling (cnd), Franz Liszt CO, Hungarian Radio-TV Chorus [L] Hungaroton ▲ HCD 31022 [DDD]

Haydn, M.:Missa Sancti Francisci, w. Ibolya Verebics (sop), Martin Klietmann (ten), József Moldvay (bass), H. Rilling (cnd), Franz Liszt CO, Hungarian Radio-TV Chorus [L] Hungaroton ▲ HCD 31022 [DDD]

Lickl, J.G.:Missa solemnis, w. Maria Zadori (sop), Boldizsar Keönch (ten), Tamas Bator (bass), H. Williams (cnd), Pécs SO, Pécs Chamber Choir Koch Schwann ▲ SCH 312962

Lickl, J.G.:Requiem, w. Maria Zadori (sop), Boldizsar Keönch (ten), Tamas Bator (bass), H. Williams (cnd), Pécs SO, Pécs Chamber Choir Koch Schwann ▲ SCH 312962

Vivaldi, A.:Juditha triumphans devicta Holofernes barbarie, w. M. Zádori (sop), K. Gémes (mez), G. Banditelli (cta), A. Markert (cta), N. McGegan (cnd), Capella Savaria, Savaria Vocal Ensemble [L] Hungaroton 2-▲ HCD 31063/64 [DDD]

Vivaldi, A.:Magnificat, RV.611, w. T. Takács (mez), Bátori (sgr), Kovács (sgr), Szőkefalvi-Nagy (sgr), F. Szekeres (cnd), Budapest Strings, Budapest Madrigal Choir [L] Hungaroton ▲ HCD 31259 [DDD]

Nemeth, Maria (sop)

Goldmark, K.:Arias Pearl ▲ PEA 9197

Korngold, E.W.:Arias Pearl ▲ PEA 9197

Mozart, W.A.:Arias Pearl ▲ PEA 9197

Puccini, G.:Arias Pearl ▲ PEA 9197

Nemeth, Maria (sop) (cont.)

Verdi, G.:Aida (sels), w. Maria Nemeth (sop—Aida), Rosette Anday (cta—Amneris), Benjamino Gigli (ten—Radames), Alexander Kipnis (bass—Ramfis), K. Alwin (cnd), Vienna State Opera Orch *(rec May 23, 1937)* Koch Schwann 2-▲ SCH 314632 [ADD]

Verdi, G.:Arias Pearl ▲ PEA 9197

Wagner, R.:Arias & Scenes Pearl ▲ PEA 9197

Wagner, R.:Der fliegende Holländer (sels), w. Maria Nemeth (sop—Senta), Set Svanholm (ten—Erik), Joel Berglund (bar—Holländer), L. Reichwein (cnd), Vienna State Opera Orch *(rec Vienna, Sept. 28, 1942)* Koch Schwann ▲ SCH 314692 [ADD]

Weber, C.M. von:Arias Pearl ▲ PEA 9197

Nenci (ten)

Puccini, M.:Magnificat, w. M. Frusoni (ten), Di Benedetto (bass), G. Cosmi (cnd), Lucca Teatro Comunale del Giglio Orch, St. Cecilia Cappella Musicale [L] Bongiovanni ▲ GB 2047 [DDD]

Nentwig, Käthe (sop)

Lortzing, A.:Die beiden Schützen, w. P. Kuen (ten), B. Kusche (bar), K. Smitt-Walter (bar), M. Pröbstl (bass), J. Koetsier (cnd), Bavarian RSO *(rec 1950)* Memories 2-▲ MEM 4546 [ADD]

Néquecaur, Pierre (bar)

Gounod, C.:Philémon et Baucis, w. Anne-Marie Rodde (sop), Jean-Claude Orliac (ten), Félix Giband (bass), H. Gallois (cnd), French Radio Lyric Orch Musidisc ▲ MUS 202342 [AAD]

Neri, Giulio (bass)

Bellini, V.:Norma, w. A. Cerquetti (sop), G. Borelli, M. Pirazzini (mez), F. Corelli (ten), P. de Palma (ten), G. Santini (cnd), *(orch unknown)* *(rec Rome, 1958)* Great Opera Performances 2-▲ GOP 722

Boito, A.:Mefistofele, w. M. Pobbe (sop—Margherita), D. De Cecco (sop—Elena), E. Ticozzi (mez—Marta), F. Tagliavini (ten—Faust), G. Neri (bass—Mefistofele), A. Questa (cnd), Turin RSO, Turin Teatro Regio Chorus *(rec 1954)* Cetra Classic ▲ CDO 19

Boito, A.:Mefistofele, w. R. Noli (sop—Margherita), S. dall'Argine (sop—Elena), G. Poggi (ten—Faust), F. Capuana (cnd), La Scala Orch, La Scala Chorus [I] *(rec 1952)* Preiser 2-▲ 90122 (m) [AAD]

Boito, A.:Mefistofele, w. Marcella Pobbe (sop), Ebe Ticozzi (mez), Ferruccio Tagliavini (ten), A. Questa (cnd), Turin RAI SO, Turin Teatro Regio Chorus Fonit Cetra ("Classic Collection" series) 2-▲ FCT CDO 19

Ponchielli, A.:La Gioconda, w. M. Callas (sop), F. Barbieri (mez), G. Poggi (ten), P. Silveri (bar), A. Votto (cnd), Turin RAI SO, Turin RAI Chorus *(rec 1952)* Andromeda 3-▲ ANR 2528 [ADD]

Ponchielli, A.:La Gioconda, w. M. Callas (sop), F. Barbieri (mez), G. Poggi (ten), P. Silveri (bar), A. Votto (cnd), Turin RAI SO, Turin RAI Chorus *(rec 1952)* Enterprise ("Palladio" series) ▲ ENT PD 4152 [DDD]

Ponchielli, A.:La Gioconda, w. M. Callas (sop—Gioconda), F. Barbieri (mez—Laura), M. Amadini (sgr—La Cieca), G. Poggi (ten—Enzo), P. Silveri (bar—Barnaba), G. Neri (bass—Alvise), A. Votto (cnd), Turin RAI Orch, Turin RAI Chorus *(rec 1952)* Cetra Classic 3-▲ CDO 8

Puccini, G.:La Bohème, w. R. Tebaldi (sop), E. Ribetti (mez), E. Avolanti (ten), G. Lauri Volpi (ten), T. Gobbi (bar), S. Meletti (bar), C. Badioli (bass), G. Santini (cnd), *(orch unknown)* *(rec 1951)* Great Opera Performances ▲ GOP 743

Verdi, G.:Aida, w. Maria Callas (sop—Aida), Joan Sutherland (sop—Priestess), Giulietta Simionato (cta—Amneris), Kurt Baum (ten—Radames), Hector Thomas (ten—Messenger), Jess Walters (bar—Amonasro), Michael Langdon (bass—King), Giulio Neri (bass—Ramfis), J. Barbirolli (cnd), Royal Opera House Orch, Royal Opera House Chorus Covent Garden *(rec Covent Garden, London, June 10, 1953)* Legato Classics 2-▲ LCD 187-2

Verdi, G.:Aida, w. M. C. Verna (sop), M. Pirazzini (cta), F. Corelli (ten), G. Guelfi (bar), A. Questa (cnd), Turin RAI SO, Turin RAI Chorus *(rec 1956)* Enterprise ("Palladio") 2-▲ ENT PD 4184 [ADD]

Verdi, G.:Aida (sels), w. M. Callas (sop), E. Stignani (mez), M. Picchi (ten), R. De Falchi (bar), V. Bellezza (cnd), Rome Opera Orch—five arias with Callas (solo, three duets & quintet) *(rec live 10/2/50)* Melodram 2-▲ CDM 26019 [AAD]

Verdi, G.:Don Carlos, w. M. Caniglia (sop—Elisabeth de Valois), G. Sciutti (sop—Page), E. Stignani (mez—Princess Eboli), M. Picchi (ten—Don Carlos), M. Ponz de L. (ten—Count of Lerma), P. Silveri (bar—Rodrigue), N. Rossi Lemeni (bass—Philip II), G. Neri (bass—Grand Inquisitor), A. Gaggi (bass—Old Monk), F. Previtali (cnd), Rome RAI SO, Rome RAI Chorus *(rec Rome, 1951)* Cetra Classic 3-▲ CDO 25 [ADD]

Verdi, G.:Don Carlos, w. A. Cerquetti (sop), F. Barbieri (mez), A. LoForese (ten), E. Bastianini (bar), C. Siepi (b-bar), A. Votto (cnd), Florence Maggio Musicale Orch, Florence Maggio Musicale Chorus *(rec July 16, 1956)* Melodram 3-▲ MLO 670104 [ADD]

Verdi, G.:La forza del destino (sels), w. Barbato (sop), B. Gigli (ten), E. Mascherini (bar), A. Votto (cnd), Rio de Janeiro Teatro Municipale Orch, Rio de Janeiro Teatro Municipale Chorus [I] *(rec live 8/16/51)* Standing Room Only ▲ SRO 807-1 (m) [ADD]

Verdi, G.:Requiem Mass, w. O. Rovero (sop), J. Madeira (mez), J. Lambert (sgr), E. Kleiber (cnd), Vienna SO, Vienna Singverein *(rec live, Vienna 11/23/55)* Melodram 2-▲ CDM 28044 [ADD]

Verdi, G.:Rigoletto, w. L. Pagluighi (sop—Gilda), I. Colasanti (mez—Maddalena), F. Tagliavini (ten—Duca), A. Albertini (bar—Il Cavaliere Marullo), G. Taddei (bar—Rigoletto), G. Neri (bass—Sparafucile), A. Zerbini (bass—Conte di Monterone), A. Questa (cnd), Turin RSO, Turin Radio Chorus *(rec 1953)* Cetra Classics 2-▲ CDO 11 [AAD]

Wagner, R.:Lohengrin (sels), w. R. Tebaldi (sop—Elsa), E. Nicolai (mez—Ortrud), G. Penno (ten—Lohengrin), G. Guelfi (bar—Telramund), G. Neri (bass—Heinrich), G. Santini (cnd), Naples Teatro San Carlo Orch, Naples Teatro San Carlo Chorus—8 soprano duets/trio from Acts 1-3 [I] *(rec live, Naples, 12/26/54)* Standing Room Only ▲ SRO 834-1 [ADD]

Neroni, Luciano (bass)

Donizetti, G.:Lucia di Lammermoor, w. Lina Pagliughi (sop—Lucia), Maria Vinciguerra (mez—Alisa), Armando Giannotti (ten—Normanno), Muzio Giovagnoli (ten—Arturo), Giovanni Malipiero (ten—Edgardo), Giuseppe Manacchini (bar—Enrico), Luciano Neroni (bass—Raimondo), U. Tansini (cnd), EIAR Orch, EIAR Chorus *(rec 1938)* Bongiovanni ("Il mito dell'opera" series) 2-▲ GB 1122-2 [ADD]

Donizetti, G.:Lucia di Lammermoor, w. Lina Pagliughi (sop—Lucia), Maria Vinciguerra (mez—Alisa), Armando Giannotti (ten—Normanno), Muzio Giovannoli (ten—Lord Arturo), Giovanni Malipiero (ten—Edgardo), Giuseppe Manacchini (bar—Lord Enrico), Luciano Neroni (bass—Raimondo), U. Tansini (cnd), EIAR Orch, EIAR Chorus *(rec Turin, 1942)* Melodram 2-▲ IMC 202004 [ADD]

Verdi, G.:Nabucco, w. M. Callas (sop), G. Bechi (bar), V. Gui (cnd), Naples Teatro San Carlo Orch, Naples Teatro San Carlo Chorus [I] *(rec live 12/20/49)* Melodram 2-▲ MEL 26029 (m) [AAD]

Nes, Jard van (cta)

Beethoven, L. van:Syms (comp), w. Lynne Dawson (sop), Anthony Rolfe Johnson (ten), Eike Wilm Schulte (bass), F. Brüggen (cnd), Orch of the 18th Century, Lisbon Gulbenkian Foundation Chorus [on Sym. 9] Philips 5-▲ 442156-2

Beethoven, L. van:Sym 9, "Choral Sym", w. S. McNair (sop), U. Heilmann (ten), B. Weikl (bar), K. Masur (cnd), Leipzig Gewandhaus Orch, London Radio Choir Philips ▲ 432995-2

Brahms, J.:Alto Rhap, w. Boston SO, Tanglewood Festival Chorus Philips ▲ 442130-2

Brahms, J.:Alto Rhap, w. H. Blomstedt (cnd), San Francisco SO, San Francisco Sym Chorus [G] London ▲ 430281-2 [DDD]

Busoni, F.:Berceuse élégiaque, w. J. Bröcheler (bar), Schoenberg Ensemble Koch Schwann ▲ SCH 312632 [DDD]

Diepenbrock, A.:Songs, w. Roberta Alexander (sop), Christa Pfeiler (mez), Robert Holl (bass), Daniel Esser (vc), Rudolf Jansen (pno)—Berceuse; Clair de lune; Mandoline; L'Invitation au voyage; Les Chats; Receuillement; Puisque l'aube grandit; Incantation; En Sourdine; La Chanson de l'hypertrophique NM Classics ▲ NM 92051

Handel, G.F.:Messiah (reorchd Mozart), w. Audrey Michael (sop), Hans-Peter Blochwitz (tenor), Marcus Fink (bass), M. Corboz (cnd), Lausanne Instrumental Ensemble, Lausanne Vocal Ensemble [G] Erato 2-▲ 2292-45497-2 [DDD]

Handel, G.F.:Theodora, w. Roberta Alexander (sop), Jochen Kowalski (ct), Hans-Peter Blochwitz (ten), Anton Scharinger (bass), N. Harnoncourt (cnd), Vienna Concentus Musicus, Arnold Schoenberg Choir [E] Teldec 2-▲ 2292-46447-2 [DDD]

Laman, W.:Fleurs du Mal, w. H. Vonk (cnd), Residentie Orch The Hague [F] *(rec 1978-82)* Olympia ▲ OCD 506 [AAD]

Mahler, G.:Kindertotenlieder, w. J. Bröcheler (bar), Schoenberg Ensemble Koch Schwann ▲ SCH 312632 [DDD]

Nes, Jard van (cta) (cont.)
Mahler, G.:Des Knaben Wunderhorn, w. J. Bröcheler (bass), R. Benzi (cnd), Arnheim PO
Ottavo ▲ OTT 79238 [DDD]
Mahler, G.:Das Lied von der Erde, w. P. Schreier (ten), E. Inbal (cnd), Frankfurt RSO [G]
Denon ▲ CO 72605 [DDD]
Mahler, G.:Lieder eines fahrenden Gesellen, w. J. Bröcheler (bar), Schoenberg Ensemble
Koch Schwann ▲ SCH 312632 [DDD]
Mahler, G.:Songs from Rückert, w. Y. Talmi (cnd), Golders Orch [G] Ottavo ▲ OTR C98402 [DDD]
Mahler, G.:Sym 2, w. S. McNair (sop), E. Mata (cnd), Dallas SO, Dallas Sym Chorus [G] *(rec 9/89)*
Pro Arte 2-▲ CDD 479 [DDD]
Mahler, G.:Sym 2, w. S. McNair (sop), B. Haitink (cnd), Berlin PO, Ernst Senff Chorus
Philips ▲ 438935-2
Mozart, W.A.:Requiem, w. L. Dawson (sop), K. Lewis (ten), S. Estes (bass), C. M. Giulini (cnd), Philharmonia Orch, Philharmonia Chorus [L] Sony Classical ▲ SK 45577 [DDD]
Prokofiev, S.:Alexander Nevsky, w. C. Dutoit (cnd), Montreal SO, Montreal Sym Chorus
London ▲ 430506-2 [DDD]
Schumann, R.:Frauenliebe und -leben, w. R. Vignoles (pno) Ottavo ▲ PLY 89241 [DDD]
Strauss, R.:Ariadne auf Naxos, w. R. Hickox (cnd), Northern Sinfonia of England—Ov. (Andante); Dance Scene (Allegretto) Chandos ▲ CHAN 9354 [DDD]
Wagner, R.:Wesendonck Songs, w. R. Hickox (cnd), Northern Sinfonia of England
Chandos ▲ CHAN 9354 [DDD]
Wolf, H.:Mörike-Lieder (sels), w. R. Vignoles (pno) Ottavo ▲ PLY 89241 [DDD]

Neshyba, Ladislav (bass)
Marschner, H.A.:Hans Heiling, w. M. Hajóssyová (sop), E. Seniglova (sop), M. Eklöf (mez), K. Markus (ten), T. Mohr (bar), E. Körner (cnd), Slovak PO, Slovak Phil Chorus [G]
Marco Polo ("Opera Rara" series) 2-▲ 8.223306/07 [DDD]
Verdi, G.:La traviata (sels), w. Monika Krause (sop), Ivica Neshybová (sop), Rannveig Braga (mez), Yordy Ramiro (ten), Gerog Tichy (bar), Jozef Špaček (bass), A. Rahbari (cnd), Czech-Slovak RSO Bratislava, Jan Rozehnal (cnd), Slovak Phil Chorus—Prelude act I; Libiam ne'lieti calici; Un dí, felice; E strano! Ah, fors'e lui; Follie!...sempre libera; Lunge da lei...de'miei bollenti spiriti; O Mio rimorso!; Pura si come un angelo...Dite alla giovine; Dammi tu forza; Di Provenza il mar; Noi siamo zingarelle; Prelude act III; Teneste la promessa...Addio del passato; Signora! Che t'accade?; Ah, Violetta! *(rec Bratislava Concert Hall, Dec 1990)* Naxos ▲ 8.553041 [DDD]

Neshybová, Ivica (sop)
Verdi, G.:La traviata (sels), w. Monika Krause (sop), Rannveig Braga (mez), Yordy Ramiro (ten), Gerog Tichy (bar), Ladislav Neshyba (bass), Jozef Špaček (bass), A. Rahbari (cnd), Czech-Slovak RSO Bratislava, Jan Rozehnal (cnd), Slovak Phil Chorus—Prelude act I; Libiam ne'lieti calici; Un dí, felice; E strano! Ah, fors'e lui; Follie!...sempre libera; Lunge da lei...de'miei bollenti spiriti; O Mio rimorso!; Pura si come un angelo...Dite alla giovine; Dammi tu forza; Di Provenza il mar; Noi siamo zingarelle; Prelude act III; Teneste la promessa...Addio del passato; Signora! Che t'accade?; Ah, Violetta! *(rec Bratislava Concert Hall, Dec 1990)* Naxos ▲ 8.553041 [DDD]

Nessi, Giuseppe (ten)
Boito, A.:Mefistofele, w. Giannina Arangi-Lombardi (sop), Mafalda Favero (sop), Antonio Melandri (ten), Nazzareno de Angelis (bass), L. Molajoli (cnd), La Scala Orch, La Scala Chorus
Grammofono 2000 2-▲ GRM 78606 (m)
Leoncavallo, R.:Pagliacci, w. Rosetta Pampanini (sop), Francesco Merli (ten), Carlo Galeffi (bar), Gino Vanelli (bar), *(orch unknown) (rec Milan, 1930)* Melodram ▲ IMC 102003
Leoncavallo, R.:Pagliacci, w. Rosetta Pampanini (sop), Francesco Merli (ten), Carlo Galeffi (bar), L. Molajoli (cnd), La Scala Orch, La Scala Chorus *(rec Milan, 1930)* Phonographe 2-▲ PHG CD 5066
Leoncavallo, R.:Pagliacci, w. I. Pacetti (sop—Nedda), B. Gigli (ten—Canio), G. Nessi (ten—Peppe), M. Basiola (bar—Tonio), F. Ghione (cnd), La Scala Orch, La Scala Chorus [I] *(rec 1934 for HMV)*
Music Memoria ▲ 30275
Leoncavallo, R.:Pagliacci, w. I. Pacetti (sop—Nedda), B. Gigli (ten—Canio), G. Nessi (ten—Peppe), M. Basiola (bar—Tonio), F. Ghione (cnd), La Scala Orch, La Scala Chorus [I] *(rec July 1934)*
Nimbus 2-▲ NI 7843/44 [ADD]
Leoncavallo, R.:Pagliacci, w. I. Pacetti (sop—Nedda), B. Gigli (ten—Canio), G. Nessi (ten—Peppe), M. Basiola (bar—Tonio), F. Ghione (cnd), La Scala Orch, La Scala Chorus [I] *(rec 1934)*
EMI Classics ("Studio" series) ▲ CDH 63309 (m) [ADD]
Mascagni, P.:Cavalliera rusticana, w. Lina Bruna-Rasa (sop), Giulietta Simionato (mez), Benia Gigli (ten), Gino Bechi (bar), Carlo Galeffi (bar), P. Mascagni (cnd), La Scala Orch, La Scala Chorus *(rec Milan, 1940)* Phonographe 2-▲ PHG CD 5066
Puccini, G.:La Bohème, w. Luba Mirella (sop—Musetta), Rosetta Pampanini (sop—Mimi), Luigi Marini (ten—Rodolfo), Giuseppe Nessi (ten—Alcindoro), Aristide Baracchi (bar—Schaunard), Gino Vanelli (bar—Marcello), Salvatore Baccaloni (bass—Benoit), Tancredi Pasero (bass—Colline), L. Molajoli (cnd), La Scala Orch, La Scala Chorus Bongiovanni 2-▲ 1125/26 [ADD]
Puccini, G.:La Bohème, w. Rosina Torri (sop—Mimi), Thea Vitulli (sop—Musetta), Aristodemo Giorgini (ten—Rodolfo), Giuseppe Nessi (ten—Parpignol), Ernesto Badini (bar—Marcello), Aristide Baracchi (bar—Schaunard), Luigi Manfrini (bass—Colline), Salvatore Baccaloni (bass—Benoit/Alcindoro), C. Sabajno (cnd), La Scala Orch, La Scala Chorus *(rec 1928)* VAI Audio 2-▲ VAIA 1078-2
Puccini, G.:Madama Butterfly, w. Rosetta Pampanini (sop—Madama Butterfly), Conchita Velasquez (mez—Suzuki), Cesira Ferrari (mez—Kate Pinkerton), Alessandro Granda (ten—F. B. Pinkerton), Giuseppe Nessi (ten—Goro), Aristide Baracchi (bar—Il Principe Yamadori), Gino Vanelli (bar—Sharpless), Lino Bonardi (bass—Il Commissario Imperiale), Salvatore Baccaloni (bass—Lo zio Bonzo), L. Molajoli (cnd), La Scala Orch, La Scala Chorus Bongiovanni 2-▲ 1123/24 [ADD]
Puccini, G.:Madama Butterfly, w. R. Pampanini (sop), A. Granda (ten), G. Vanelli (bar), S. Baccaloni (bass), L. Malajoli (cnd), La Scala Orch, La Scala Chorus *(rec 1928)* Centaur 2-▲ CRC 2196/97
Puccini, G.:Manon Lescaut, w. Maria Zamboni (sop—Manon), Anna Masetti-Bassi (mez—Singer), Francesco Merli (ten—Chevalier), Giuseppe Nessi (ten—Edmondo/Dancing Master/ Lamplighter), Lorenzo Conati (bar—Lescaut), Aristide Baracchi (bass—Innkeeper/Sergeant), Attilio Bordonali (bass—Geronte), Natale Villa (bass—Naval Captain), L. Molajoli (cnd), La Scala Orch, Vittore Veneziani (cnd), La Scala Chorus *(rec 1930)* Arkadia ("The 78's" series) 2-▲ 78014 [ADD]
Puccini, G.:Manon Lescaut (sels), w. M. Favero (sop), R. Tebaldi (sop), J. Gardino (mez), G. Malipiero (ten), M. Stabile (bar), T. Pasero (b-bar), C. Forti (bass), A. Toscanini (cnd), La Scala Orch, La Scala Chorus—Intermezzo; Act 3 *(rec live, Milan, May 18, 1946)*
Arkadia ("Historical Performances" series) 2-▲ 604 (m)
Strauss, R.:Der Rosenkavalier, w. Jarmila Barton (sop—Marianne), Lisa Della Casa (sop—Sophie), Sena Jurinac (sop—Octavian), Ilva Ligabue (sop—Orphan), Elisabeth Schwarzkopf (sop—Marschallin), Else Schürhoff (mez—Annina), Luisa Villa (mez—Milliner), Hugues Cuénod (ten—Marschallin's majordomo), Erich Majkut (ten—Valzacchi), Giuseppe Nessi (ten—Animal seller), Luciano Della Pergola (ten—Lackey/Faninal's majordomo), Antonio Pirino (ten—An Italian Singer), Gino Del Signore (ten—Lackey/Waiter), Erich Kunz (bar—Herr von Faninal), Paolo Pedani (bar—Lackey), Attilio Barbesi (bass—Lackey/Waiter), Enrico Campi (bass—Waiter), Otto Edelmann (bass—Baron Ochs), Bruno Fichtinger (bass—Notary), Franco Taino (bass—Waiter), Maria Amadini (sgr—Orphan), Pina Carrillo (sgr—Orphan), Joszi Trojan Regar (sgr—Innkeeper), H. von Karajan (cnd), La Scala Orch, La Scala Chorus *(rec La Scala Theater, Milan, Jan. 26, 1952)* Legato Classics 3-▲ LCD 197-3
Verdi, G.:Aida, w. Dusolina Giannini (sop—Aida), Irene Minghini-Cattaneo (mez—Amneris), Giuseppe Nessi (ten—Messenger), Aureliano Pertile (ten—Radames), Giovanni Inghilleri (bar—Amonasro), Luigi Manfrini (bass—Ramfis), Guglielmo Masini (bass—King), C. Sabajno (cnd), La Scala Orch, Vittore Veneziani (cnd), La Scala Chorus *(rec 1928)* Arkadia ("The 78's" series) 2-▲ 78013 [ADD]
Verdi, G.:Aida, w. Giannina Arangi-Lombardi (sop—Aida), Maria Capuana (mez—Amneris), Aroldo Lindi (ten—Radames), Giuseppe Nessi (ten—Messenger), Armando Borgioli (bar—Amonasro), Salvatore Baccaloni (bass—King), Tancredi Pasero (bass—Ramfis), L. Molajoli (cnd), La Scala Orch, La Scala Chorus *(rec Nov 1928)* VAI Audio 2-▲ VAIA 1083-2
Verdi, G.:Falstaff, w. Augusta Ottrabella (sop—Nannetta), Franca Somigli (sop—Alice), Angelica Cravcenko (mez—Mrs. Quickly), Mita Vasari (mez—Meg), Dino Borgioli (ten—Fenton), Giuseppe Nessi (ten—Bardolfo), Alfredo Tedeschi (ten—Dr. Cajus), Piero Biasini (bar—Ford), Mariano Stabile (bar—Falstaff), Virgilio Lazzari (bass—Pistola), A. Toscanini (cnd), Vienna PO, Vienna State Opera Chorus *(rec Salzburg, Aug 23, 1937)* Minerva 2-▲ MN A36/37 (m) [ADD]

Nessi, Giuseppe (ten) (cont.)
Verdi, G.:Falstaff, w. Pia Tassinari (sop—Alice Ford), Ines Alfani Tellini (sop—Nannetta), Aurora Buades (mez—Quickly), Rita Monticone (mez—Meg Page), Roberto D'Alessio (ten—Fenton), Giuseppe Nessi (ten—Bardolfo), Emilio Venturini (ten—Dr. Caius), Emilio Ghirardini (bar—Ford), Giacomo Rimini (bar—Sir John Falstaff), Salvatore Baccaloni (bass—Pistola), L. Molajoli (cnd), Milan SO, La Scala Chorus *(rec La Scala Theatre, Milan, Apr. 1932)* VAI Audio 2-▲ VAIA 1098-2
Verdi, G.:Rigoletto, w. Lina Pagliughi (sop—Gilda), Linda Brambilla (mez—Countess Ceprano), Vera De Cristoff (cta—Maddalena), Tino Folgar (ten—Duke of Mantua), Giuseppe Nessi (ten—Borsa), Luigi Piazza (bar—Rigoletto), Aristide Baracchi (b-bar—Monterone/Marullo), Salvatore Baccaloni (bass—Sparafucile), Giuseppe Menni (bass—Ceprano), C. Sabajno (cnd), La Scala Orch, La Scala Chorus *(rec La Scala Theatre, Milan, Nov.-Dec. 1927 & Feb. 192)* VAI Audio 2-▲ VAIA 1097-2
Verdi, G.:Rigoletto, w. Lina Pagliughi (sop—Gilda), Linda Brambilla (mez—Contessa di Ceprano), Vera de Cristoff (cta—Maddalena), Tino Folgar (ten—Duca di Mantova), Giuseppe Nessi (ten—Borsa), Aristide Baracchi (bar—Conte di Monterone/Marullo), Luigi Piazza (bar—Rigoletto), Salvatore Baccaloni (bass—Sparafucile), Giuseppe Menni (bass—Conte di Ceprano), C. Sabajno (cnd), La Scala Orch, La Scala Chorus *(rec 1927-28)* Arkadia 2-▲ CD 78003 (m) [ADD]

Nesterenko, Evgeny (bass)
Glinka, M.:Russlan & Ludmilla, w. Nina Fomina (sop—Gorislava), Bela Rudenko (sop—Ludmilla), Tamara Sinyavskaya (mez—Ratmir), Boris Morozov (bass—Farlaf), Evgeny Nesterenko (bass—Russlan), Valeri Yaroslavtsev (bass—Svetozar), Y. Simonov (cnd), Bolshoi Theater Orch, Bolshoi Theater Chorus *(rec Moscow, 1978-1979)* Melodiya ("The Russian Opera" series) 3-▲ 74321-29348-2 [ADD]
Gounod, C.:Faust, w. K. Te Kanawa (sop), F. Araiza (ten), C. Davis (cnd), Bavarian RSO, Bavarian Radio Chorus [F] Philips 3-▲ 420164-2 [DDD]
Rachmaninoff, S.:Aleko (sels), w. E. Shenderovich (pno)—1 aria Russian Disc ▲ RUS 11 372 [DDD]
Rachmaninoff, S.:Songs, w. E. Shenderovich (pno)—5 songs Russian Disc ▲ RUS 11 372 [DDD]
Sviridov, G.:Songs, w. E. Shenderovich (pno)—Approaching Izhory Russian Disc ▲ RUS 11 372 [DDD]
Tchaikovsky, P.:Songs, w. E. Shenderovich (pno)—17 songs Russian Disc ▲ RUS 11 372 [DDD]
Verdi, G.:Nabucco, w. G. Dimitrova (sop), L. V. Terrani (mez), P. Domingo (ten), P. Cappuccilli (bar), G. Sinopoli (cnd), German Opera Orch, German Opera Chorus [I]
Deutsche Grammophon 2-▲ 410512-2 [DDD]
Verdi, G.:Requiem Mass, w. Renata Scotto (sop), Agnes Baltsa (mez), Veriano Luchetti (ten), R. Muti (cnd), Philharmonia Orch, Ambrosian Chorus EMI Classics 2-▲ CDFB 68613

Netrebko, Anna (sgr)
Glinka, M.:Russlan & Ludmilla, w. Galina Gorchakova (sop), Larissa Diadkova (cta), Irinia Bogachova (sgr), Yuri Masurin (ten), Konstantin Pluzhnikov (ten), Mikhail Kit (bar), Gennady Bezzubenkov (bass), Vladimir Ognovenko (bass), V. Gergiev (cnd), Kirov Opera Orch, Kirov Opera Chorus
Philips ▲ 456 248-2

Neuburg, Amy X. (sgr)
Ashley, R.:Improvement, w. J. Humbert (sgr—Linda), J. La Barbara (sop—Now Eleanor), A. X. Neuburg (sgr—Mr. Payne's Mother), T. Buckner (sgr—Don/Mr. Payne/Linda's Companion), S. Ashley (sgr—Junior, Jr.), A. Klein (sgr—Doctor), R. Ashley (sgr—Narrator), *(cnd & orch unknown)* [E]
Elektra/Nonesuch 2-▲ 79289-2

Neukirch, Harald (ten)
Lortzing, A.:Der Waffenschmied, w. E. Ebert (sop—Marie), G. Prenzlow (mez—Mariens), H. Neukirch (ten—Georg), G. Leib (bar—Ritter), H. Krämer (bass—Hans), H. Fricke (cnd), Berlin State Opera Orch, Berlin State Opera Chorus Berlin Classics ("Eterna" series) ▲ BER 2036-2 [ADD]

Neumann, Günther (ten)
Auber, D.-F.:Fra Diavolo, w. H. Termer (sop), E. Büchner (bar), W.-D. Hauschild (cnd), Berlin RSO
Berlin Classics ▲ BER 2140 [ADD]

Neumann, Wolfgang (ten)
Weill, K.:Aufstieg und Fall der Stadt Mahagonny, w. A. Silja (sop), A. Schlemm (mez), T. Lehrberger (ten), K. Hirte (bar), J. Latham-König (cnd), Cologne RSO, Cologne Radio Chorus [G]
Capriccio 2-▲ CD 10160/1 [DDD]

Neuweiler, Ulrich (ten)
Krenek, E.:Der Sprung über den Schatten, w. D. Amos (sop), L. Kemeny (sop), S. MacLean (mez), J. Dürmüller (ten), J. Pflieger (bar), T. Brüning (sgr), D. de Villiers (cnd), Bielefeld PO, Bielefeld Phil Chorus [G] *(rec live, May 1989)* CPO 2-▲ CPO 999082-2 [DDD]

Neves, Susan (sop)
Mascagni, P.:Il piccolo Marat, w. S. Neves (sop—Mariella), C. Pfeiler (mez—Principessa di Fleury), D. Galvez-Vallejo (ten—Marat), S. Cowan (bar—Soldier), M. Dirks (bar—Il Ladro), F. Vassar (bass—L'Orco), H. Claessens (bass—Spy), K. Bakels (cnd), Netherlands RSO, Netherlands Radio Chorus *(rec Feb. 9, 1992)* Bongiovanni 2-▲ GB 2168/69 [DDD]

Neway, Patricia (sop)
Barber, S.:A Hand of Bridge, w. E. Alberts (mez), W. Lewis (ten), P. Maero (bass), V. Golschmann (cnd), Symphony of the Air [E] *(rec ca. 1960)* Vanguard Classics ▲ OVC 4016 [ADD]

Newburg, Amy (sgr)
Davies, S.:What Is the Matter in Amy Glennon?, w. Gregory Whitehead (nar—The Idea), Sheila Davies (nar—Amy Glennon/Chorus), Piers McKenzie (nar—Auctioneer), Fran Smith (sgr), Barney Jones (nar—The Fathers) ▲ WN 0013

Newley, Anthony (sgr)
Rodgers, R.:Music of, w. S. Bass (sgr), J. Andrews (sgr), P. Como (sgr), D. Reese (sgr), J. Jones (sgr), N. Luboff (sgr), M. Gold (sgr), N. Walker (sgr), H. Bowen (sgr), V. Damone (sgr), P. Nero (pno), J. P. Morgan (sgr), E. Fisher (sgr), B. Goodman (cl), Ann-Margaret (sgr), Shorty Rogers (sgr), D. Shore (sgr), T. Martin (sgr), M. King (sgr) RCA ▲ 8590-2 R ■ 8590-4 R

Newman, Daisy (sop)
Gershwin, G.:Porgy & Bess (sels), w. A. Woodley (bar), H. de la Fuente (cnd), Mineria SO, New Philharmonia Orch, Oklahoma City Ambassors Choir IMP Classics ▲ IMPPCD 1057 [DDD]

Newman, Paul (nar)
Stravinsky, I.:Oedipus Rex, w. R. Craft (cnd), Orch of St. Luke MusicMasters 2-▲ 01612-67078-2

Newman, Paul (reader)
Gottlieb, J.:Sacred Music, w. M. Stone (sop), H. Reps (mez), D. Lefkowitz (ten), H. Stahl (ten), R. Abelson (bar), R. Botton (bar), S. Sturk (cnd), Metropolitan Brass Ensemble, New York Motet Choir
Premier ("Composer" series) ▲ PRCD 1018 [DDD]

Newman, Randy (nar)
Newman, M.:Music of, w. Maria Newman (vn)—The Selfish Giant for Vn & Nar; The Nightingale & the Rose for Vn & Nar Raptoria Caam ▲ RCD 1003
Newman, M.:Music of, w. Viklarbo Chamber Ensemble—On a Pincushion; A Guide to Chamber Music; The Happy Prince for Vn & Nar Raptoria Caam ▲ RCD 1002

Newman, Yvonne (mez)
Beethoven, L. van:Cant on the Death of the Emperor Joseph II, w. K. Te Kanawa (sop), D. Barrett (bar), M. Langdon (bass), C. Davis (cnd), BBC SO, BBC Chorus, BBC Choral Society [G] *(rec live Oct. 7, 1970)*
Intaglio ▲ INCD 7361 [ADD]
Milhaud, D.:L'Homme et son désir, w. Marion Davies (sop), David Barrett (ten), Anthony Holt (bass), D. Milhaud (cnd), BBC SO IMP ("BBC Radio Classics" series) ▲ IMP 5691512

Newmann, Wolfgang (ten)
Mozart, W.A.:Zauberflöte, w. Birgit Been (sop), Nathalie Boissy (sop), Marianne Seibel (sop), Renate Springer (sop), Elizabeth Vidal (sop), Eleanor James (mez), Salvador Guzman (ten), Herbert Hechenberger (ten), Klaus Häger (bass), Philip Langshaw (bass), Hans-Georg Moser (bass), P. Kuentz (cnd), Paul Kuentz Orch, Francis Bardot (cnd), Maitrise des Hauts-de-Seine members, Paul Kuentz Choirs Pierre Verany 2-▲ PVY 730055 [DDD]

Newton, Lauren (sgr)
Newton, L.:Vexations 1611, w. Woody Schabata (vib) *(rec Vienna, Sept. 22, 1983)*
Hat Hut ("NOW." series) ▲ hat ART CD 6024 [ADD]
Rüegg, M.:Music of, w. Wolfgang Puschnig (fl/s sax), Harry Sokal (s sax), Roman Schwaller (t sax), Karl Fian (tpt), Christian Radovan (trbn), Woody Schabata (vib)—Reflections on Aubade; Reflections on Méditation; Reflections on Sévère Réprimande; Reflections on Idylle; Reflections on Gnossiennes Nos. 1 & 2; Satie ist mir im traum 3x nicht erschienen *(rec Vienna, Sept. 20-22, 1983 & Mar.)*
Hat Hut ("NOW." series) ▲ hat ART CD 6024 [ADD]

▲ = CD ♦ = Enhanced CD Δ = MD ■ = Cassette Tape □ = DCC

Newton, Lauren (sgr) (cont.)
Satie, E.:Gnossiennes Pno, w. Harry Sokal (sax)—No. 3 [arr. voice & instruments] *(rec Vienna, Sept. 21, 1983)* Hat Hut ("NOW." series) ▲ hat ART CD 6024 [ADD]

Nezadál, Maria (sop)
Wagner, R.:Götterdämmerung (sels), w. F. Leider (sop), K. Thorborg (mez), L. Melchior (ten), H. Janssen (bar), L. Weber (bass), T. Beecham (cnd), London PO, Royal Opera House Chorus Covent Garden [G] *(rec from 1925 Polydor & 1929)* Legato Classics 2-▲ LCD 146-2 (m) [ADD]
Wagner, R.:Götterdämmerung (sels), w. Frida Leider (sop), Kerstin Thorborg (mez), Lauritz Melchior (ten), Herbert Janssen (bar), Emanuel List (bass), T. Beecham (cnd), London PO, Royal Opera House Chorus Covent Garden *(rec Covent Garden, London, 1936)* Preiser ▲ PRE 90266

Nezhdanova, Antonina (sop)
Antonina Nezhdanova:Recordings from 1906–1940 Pearl ▲ PEA 9995 [AAD]

Nezhyba, Ladislav (bass)
Mozart, W.A.:Missa, K.317, w. Ludmila Vernerova (sop), Marta Benackova (mez), Richard Sporka (ten), G. Delogu (cnd), Prague Virtuosi, Prague Chamber Choir *(rec Domovina Studio, Prague, June 4–6, 1994)* Discover International ▲ DI 920260 [DDD]
Mozart, W.A.:Vesperae solennes, w. Ludmila Vernerova (sop), Marta Benackova (mez), Richard Sporka (ten), G. Delogu (cnd), Prague Virtuosi, Prague Chamber Choir *(rec Domovina Studio, Prague, June 4–6, 1994)* Discover International ▲ DI 920260 [DDD]

Nibbs, Jean (sop)
Purcell, H.:Songs, w. Geoffrey Mitchell (ct), Peter Hall (ten), David Thomas (bass), Margaret Phillips (org), Michael Howard (cnd), Cantores in Ecclesia—Hear My Prayer, O Lord; Song of the 3 Children; Remember Not, Lord, Our Offences; Voluntary for Single Organ; Magnificat & Nunc Dimittis in g; Thy Work is a Lantern; Burial Sentences for Queen Mary [Man That is Born of a Woman; In the Midst of Life We Are in Death; Thou Knowest, Lord, the Secrets of Our Hearts]; O God, Thou Art My God; Magnificat & Nunc Dimittis in B♭; Voluntary on the 100th Psalm Tune; Turn Thou Us, O Good Lord; O Give Thanks Unto the Lord [Psalm 106] IMP ("BBC Radio Classics" series) ▲ IMP 9126

Niccolini, Nicola (sgr)
Verdi, G.:Un ballo in maschera, w. Maria Caniglia (sop—Amelia), Fedora Barbieri (mez—Ulrica), Beniamino Gigli (ten—Riccardo), Gino Bechi (bar—Renato), Tancredi Pasero (bass—Samuel), Blando Giusti (sgr—Un Giudice), Nicola Niccolini (sgr—Silvano), Ugo Novelli (sgr—Tom), Elda Ribetti (sgr—Oscar), T. Serafin (cnd), Rome Opera Orch, Giuseppe Conca (cnd), Rome Opera Chorus *(rec 1943)* Arkadia 2-▲ CD 78005 (m) [ADD]

Nichiteanu, Liliana (mez)
Mussorgsky, M.:Boris Godunov, w. V. Valente (sop—Xenia), E. Gorochovskaya (mez—Nurse), L. Nichiteanu (mez—Fyodor), E. Zarmeba (mez—Hostess), M. Lipovšek (cta—Marina), P. Langridge (ten—Prince Shuisky), H. Wildhaber (ten—Misail), A. Fedin (ten—Simpleton), S. Leiferkus (bar—Rangoni), A. Kotcherga (bass—B. Godounov), A. Shagidullin (bass—Shchelkalov), S. Ramey (bass—Pimen), S. Larin (bass—Girgory), G. Nikolsky (bass—Varlaam), C. Abbado (cnd), Berlin PO, Tölz Boys' Choir, Berlin Radio Chorus, Slovak Phil Chorus *(rec Nov. 7–30, 1993)* Sony Classical 3-▲ S3K 58977 [DDD]

Nicholas, Jeremy (nar)
Prokofiev, S.:Peter & the Wolf, w. O. Lenárd (cnd), Czech–Slovak RSO Bratislava Naxos ▲ 8.550499 [DDD]

Nicholas, Paul (sgr)
Lloyd Webber, A.:Jesus Christ Superstar, w. C. Moore (sgr) [London cast] RCA ▲ 09026-61434-2 [DDD] ■ 09026-61434-4

Nicholls, Agnes (sop)
Elgar, E.:The Starlight Express (suite), w. C. Mott (bar), E. Elgar (cnd), *(orch unknown)* *(rec 1916)* Pearl 5-▲ PEAS 9951/55 (m) [AAD]

Nichols, Barbara (sop)
Monteverdi, C.:Ballo delle ingrate, w. Evelyn Tubb (sop), Emma Kirkby (sop), Maria Ewing (sop), A. Rooley (cnd), Consort of Musicke [I] Virgin Classics ▲ 59606 [DDD]

Nichols, Mary (mez)
Monteverdi, C.:Volgendo il ciel, w. E. Kirkby (sop), S. LeBlanc (sop), P. Agnew (ct), Alan Ewing (bass), A. Rooley (cnd), Consort of Musicke [I] Virgin Classics ▲ 59606 [DDD]

Nicolai, Claudio (bar)
Hindemith, P.:Neues vom Tage, w. Elisabeth Werres (sop), R. Ries (sgr), J. Latham–König (cnd), Cologne RSO [G] Wergo 2-▲ WER 6192/93-2

Nicolai, Elena (mez)
Bellini, V.:Norma, w. M. Callas (sop), F. Corelli (ten), B. Christoff (bass), A. Votto (cnd), Trieste Teatro Comunale Giuseppe Verdi Orch, Trieste Teatro Comunale G. Verdi Chorus *(rec live 11/19/53)* Melodram 2-▲ CDM 26031 [ADD]
Bellini, V.:Norma (sels), w. M. Callas (sop), F. Corelli (ten), B. Christoff (bass), A. Votto (cnd), Trieste Teatro Comunale Giuseppe Verdi Orch, Trieste Teatro Comunale G. Verdi Chorus—13 arias [I] *(rec live 11/19/53)* Myto 2-▲ 2 MCD 91340 [ADD]
Verdi, G.:Aida (sels), w. A. Cerquetti (sop), G. Penno (ten), G. Guelfi (bar), B. Christoff (bass), G. Santini (cnd), Naples Teatro San Carlo Orch, Naples Teatro San Carlo Chorus [I] [highlights] *(rec live, Naples, July 24, 1954)* Golden Age of Opera ▲ GAO 134 [ADD]
Verdi, G.:Oberto, Conte di San Bonifacio, w. Giuseppe Modesti (bass), Gino Bonelli (sgr), Lydia Roan (sgr), Maria Vitale (sgr), A. Simonetto (cnd), Turin RAI Orch, Turin RAI Chorus Great Opera Performances 2-▲ GOP 774
Wagner, R.:Lohengrin (sels), w. R. Tebaldi (sop—Elsa), E. Nicolai (mez—Ortrud), G. Penno (ten—Lohengrin), G. Guelfi (bar—Telramund), G. Neri (bass—Heinrich), G. Santini (cnd), Naples Teatro San Carlo Orch, Naples Teatro San Carlo Chorus—8 soprano duets/trio from Acts 1–3 [I] *(rec live, Naples, 12/26/54)* Standing Room Only ▲ SRO 834-1 [ADD]

Nicolas, Jacqueline (sop)
Campra, A.:Motets, w. A.–M. Lasla (bass vl), W. Christie (org)—O Dulcis amor; Salve Regina; Quemadmodum desiderat cervus; Ubi es, deus meus; O Sacrum convivium; Jubilate deo Pierre Verany ▲ PV.784093 [DDD]
Nivers, G.G.:Motets, w. Fanjat (sop), Boraly (sgr), Malardenti (sgr), Maréchal (sgr), Houbart (org)—Motet a la Sainte Vierge pour le temps de Paques; Motet pour L'Elévation; Motet pour le Saint Sacrament; Motet du temps de carême pour le Saint Sacrement; Motet du temps de Noël pour le Saint Sacrement; Motet final du tout office pour le Roy [L] Pierre Verany ▲ PV.791101 [DDD]
Scarlatti, A.:Cants, w. A. Aubin (ct)—Diana & Endimione; Ero & Leandro; Correa nel sen Amato [I; w. strs & hpd ensemble] Pierre Verany ▲ PV.790013 [DDD]

Nicolesco, Mariana (sop)
Donizetti, G.:Maria di Rohan (sels), w. G. Morino (ten), P. Coni (bar), M. de Bernart (cnd), Italian International Opera Orch, Slovak Phil Chorus [I] *(rec live)* Nuova Era 2-▲ 6732/33 [DDD]
Mozart, W.A.:Nozze di Figaro, w. M. Price (sop), K. Battle (sop), A. Murray (mez), J. Hynninen (bar), K. Rydl (bass), R. Muti (cnd), Vienna PO, Vienna State Opera Chorus [I] EMI Classics 3-▲ CDCC 47978 [DDD]
Mozart, W.A.:Nozze di Figaro (sels), w. M. Price (sop), K. Battle (sop), A. Murray (mez), J. Hynninen (bar), K. Rydl (bass), R. Muti (cnd), Vienna PO, Vienna State Opera Chorus [I] EMI Classics ▲ CDC 54321
Puccini, G.:La Rondine, w. K. Te Kanawa (sop), P. Domingo (ten), D. Rendall (ten), L. Nucci (bar), L. Maazel (cnd), London SO, Ambrosian Opera Chorus [I] CBS 2-▲ M2K 37852 [DDD]
Verdi, G.:Simon Boccanegra, w. G. Sabbatini (ten), R. Bruson (bar), S. Rinaldi–Miliani (bar), R. Scandiuzzi (bass), N. de Angelis (bass), R. Paternostro (cnd), Tokyo SO, Nikikai Chorus *(rec live 2/90)* Capriccio 2-▲ 60018-2 [DDD]

Nicoletti (sgr)
Mascagni, P.:Sí, w. Vivian (sop), A. Felle (sop), Maria Gentile (sop), M.G. Liguori (sop), Comas (sgr), S. Sanna (cnd), Montepulciano Arts Center Orch, Montepulciano Arts Center Chorus [I] *(rec live, 7/24/87)* Bongiovanni 2-▲ GB 2050/51 [DDD]

Nicolini, Mattia (sgr)
Cimarosa, D.:Amor rende sagace, w. G. Bertagnolli (sop), D. Bruera (sop), C. Mantese (sop), M. Dalena (ten), E. Dara (bar), F. Neri (cnd), Bolzano Claudio Monteverdi Conservatory Youth Orch [I] *(rec live, Bolzano 7/25–27/91)* Bongiovanni 2-▲ GB 2126/27 [DDD]

Nicolini, Mattia (sgr) (cont.)
Paisiello, G.:Il mondo della luna, w. Gemma Bertagnolli (sop—Clarice), Enzo Dara (bar—Buonafede), Riccardo Ristori (bass—Cecco), Carla Di Censo (sgr—Flaminia), Daniele Gaspari (sgr—Ecclittico), Mattia Nicolini (sgr—Ernesto), F. Neri (cnd), Bolzano Monteverdi Orch *(rec Aug 4–6, 1993)* Bongiovanni 2-▲ GB 2173/74 [DDD]

Nicosia, J. (sop)
Ran, S.:Apprehensions, w. L. Flax (cl), A. Feinberg (pno) *(rec 1979–91)* CRI ▲ CD 609 [ADD/DDD]

Niedlinger, Gustav (bass)
Lehár, F.:Der Graf von Luxemburg (sels), w. Helga Hildebrand (sop), Erika Koth (sop), Manfred Schmidt (ten), Rudolf Schock (ten) Emperor Operetta ▲ KO 86342

Nielsen, Inge (sop)
Bach, J.S.:Cant 62, w. H. Watts (cta), A. Baldin (ten), P. Huttenlocher (bar), H. Rilling (cnd), Stuttgart Bach Collegium, Gächinger Kantorei [G] *(rec Feb & Apr 1980)* Hänssler Classic ▲ 98.822 [AAD]
Bach, J.S.:Cant 176, w. C. Watkinson (cta), W. Hedwein (bass), H. Rilling (cnd), Stuttgart Bach Collegium, Gächinger Kantorei Hänssler Classic ▲ 98.801 [AAD]
Haydn, J.:The Seven Last Words of Christ on the Cross, w. Margaretha Hintermeier (cta), Anthony Rolfe Johnson (ten), Robert Holl (bass), N. Harnoncourt (cnd), Vienna Concentus Musicus, Arnold Schoenberg Choir [oratorio version] Teldec ▲ 2292-46458-2 ZK
Mahler, G.:Sym 8, w. Majken Bjerno (sop), Henriette Bonde–Hansen (sop), Kirsten Dolberg (alt), Anne Gjevang (alt), Raimo Sirkiä (ten), Jorma Hynninen (bar), Carsten Stabell (bass), L. Segerstam (cnd), Danish National RSO, Copenhagen Boys' Choir, Berlin Phil Choir, Danish National Radio Choir Chandos 2-▲ CHAN 9305/06 [DDD]
Nielsen, C.:Hymnus Amoris, w. A. Elkrog (ten), P. Elming (ten), P. Høyer (bar), J. Ditlevsen (bass), L. Segerstam (cnd), Danish National RSO, Copenhagen Boys' Choir, Danish National Radio Choir [L] Chandos ▲ CHAN 8853 [DDD]
Nielsen, C.:Springtime, w. Kim von Binzer (ten), Jørgen Klint (bass), T. Vető (cnd), Odense SO, Lille MUKO, St. Klemens School Children's Choir Unicorn–Kanchana ▲ DKPCD 9054
Nielsen, C.:Springtime, w. P. Gronlund (ten), S. Byriel (b–bar), L. Segerstam (cnd), Danish National RSO, Danish National Radio Choir, Danish National Radio Children's Choir [Da] Chandos ▲ CHAN 8853 [DDD]
Zemlinsky, A. von:Der Geburtstag der Infantin, w. B. Haldas (sop), K. Riegel (ten), D. Weller (bass), G. Albrecht (cnd), Berlin RSO, Berlin RIAS Women's Chamber Choir [G] Koch Schwann ▲ CD 314 013 [DDD]

Nielsen, Lise–Lotte (sop)
Pape, A.:I've Never Seen A Butterfly Here, w. Søren Kaas Claesson (vn), Geir Draugsvoll (acc) *(rec Oct 1995–Jan 1996)* Marco Polo/Dacapo ▲ 8.224028 [DDD]

Nielsen, Wendy (sop)
Rossini, G.:Giunone, w. Wendy Nielsen (sop—Giunone), R. Bradshaw (cnd), Canadian Opera Company Orch, Canadian Opera Company Chorus *(rec George Weston Recital Hall, Ford Centre for the Performing Arts, North York, Ontario, Dec 20–23, 1994)* CBC ("SM 5000" series) ▲ SM5 5148 [DDD]
Rossini, G.:Mosè in Egitto (sels), w. Wendy Nielsen (sop—Elcia), Anita Krause (mez—Amenosi), Richard Margison (ten—Aronne), Gary Relyea (b–bar—Mosè), R. Bradshaw (cnd), Canadian Opera Company Orch, Canadian Opera Company Chorus—Scena, Coro & Preghiera [Dal tuo stellato soglio] *(rec George Weston Recital Hall, Ford Centre for the Performing Arts, North York, Ontario, Dec 20–23, 1994)* CBC ("SM 5000" series) ▲ SM5 5148 [DDD]

Nieman, Barbara (sop)
Moniuszko, S.:Halka, w. Halina Sloniowska (sop), Jan Góralski (ten), Bogdan Paprocki (ten), Leslaw Pawluk (ten), Kazimierz Pustelak (ten), Andrzej Hiolski (bar), Edmund Kossowski (bass), Edward Pawlak (bass), Z. Gorzynski (cnd), Warsaw State Opera House Orch, Warsaw National Opera Chorus *(rec Warsaw, 1965)* Polskie Nagrania ▲ PNCD 092 [AAD]
Mozart, W.A.:Requiem, w. Krystyna Szostek–Radkowa (mez), Wieslaw Ochman (ten), Leonard Mróz (bass), K. Kord (cnd), Warsaw PO, Henryk Wojnarowski (cnd), Warsaw National Phil Chorus *(rec Warsaw, 1979)* Polskie Nagrania ▲ PNCD 135 [ADD]

Niemierowicz, Andrzej (bar)
Cimarosa, D.:Requiem pro defunctis, w. K. Rymarczyk (sop), B. Krahel (mez), I. Jakubowski (ten), S. Frontalini (cnd), Warmia National Orch, Olsztyn Academy Chorus [L] Bongiovanni ▲ GB 2088 [DDD]

Niemirowicz, Dariusz (bass)
Puccini, G.:La Bohème, w. Veronika Kinsces (sop—Mimi), Sidonia Haljakova (sop—Musette), Peter Dvorsky (ten—Rodolfo), Vijtech Scherenkel (ten—Parpingol), Ian Konsulov (bar—Marcello), Balazs Poka (bar—Schaunard), Stanislav Benacka (bass—Benoit), Dariusz Niemirowicz (bass—Colline), Stefan Janci (bass—Alcindoro), *(cnd & orch unknown)* Griffin ▲ GCD 2942

Nienstedt, Gerd (bass)
Mahler, G.:Das Klagende Lied, w. E. Lear (sop), E. Söderström (sop), G. Hoffman (mez), S. Burrows (ten), E. Haefliger (ten), P. Boulez (cnd), London SO, London Sym Chorus Sony Classical ("Pierre Boulez Edition" series) ▲ SK 45841
Mozart, W.A.:Requiem, w. H. Donath (sop), Y. Minton (mez), A. Davies (ten), C. Davis (cnd), BBC SO, John Alldis Choir [L] Philips ▲ 420353-2 [ADD]
Smetana, B.:Dalibor, w. Sándor Kónya (ten), Franz Crass (bass), R. Kubelik (cnd), Bavarian RSO, Bavarian Radio Chorus *(rec live, Munich, 1969)* Serenissima 2-▲ SER 360169
Smetana, B.:Dalibor (sels), w. F. Weathers (sop), S. Konya (ten), R. Kubelik (cnd), Bavarian RSO, Bavarian Radio Chorus—nine solo, duet & trio arias featuring tenor Sandor Konya as Dalibor, from Acts 1–3 *(rec live, Munich, 1968)* Myto 2-▲ 2 MCD 92465 [ADD]
Wagner, R.:Der Ring des Nibelungen, w. B. Nilsson (sop), L. Rysanek (sop), K. Dvořaková (sop), M. Mödl (sop), A. Burmeister (mez), V. Soukupova (mez), E. Wohlfahrt (ten), W. Windgassen (ten), T. Stewart (bar), T. Adam (b–bar), G. Neidlinger (b–bar), K. Böhme (bass), K. Böhm (cnd), Bayreuth Festival Orch, Bayreuth Festival Chorus [G] *(rec live, 1966–67)* Philips 14-▲ 420325-2 [ADD]
Wagner, R.:Die Walküre (act 1), w. Leonie Rysanek (sop), James King (ten), K. Böhm (cnd), Bayreuth Festival Orch *(rec live, Bayreuth Festival)* Philips ("Solo" series) ▲ 442640-2
Warren, E.R.:The Sleeping Beauty, w. Maria Venuti (mez—Princess), Thomas Hampson (bar—Prince), Gerd Nienstedt (b–bar—King), David Lutz (pno), B. Ferden (cnd), Cracow RSO, Cracow Radio Chorus *(rec Church of the Bernardines, Cracow, Poland, June 21–24, 1993)* Cambria ▲ CD 1095 [DDD]

Nienstedt, Tuula (mez)
Grondahl, A.:Songs, w. Uwe Wegner (pno)—Madonnas Svaner; Valborgsnat paa Havet; Der skreg en Fugi; Middelhavsnat; Storm *(rec Friedrich–Ebert Halle, Hamburg, Sept. 20–26, 1982)* Entrée ▲ 0068 [ADD]
Hamburg Baroque (Songs), w. Stephen Stubbs (lt), Andrew Lawrence–King (baroque hp) *(rec 1989)* Ambitus ▲ AMB 97837
Kinkel, J.:Songs, w. Uwe Wegner (pno)—An den Mond, Op. 7/5; Die Zigeuner, Op. 7/6; Die Lorelei, Op. 7/4; Die Geister haben's vernommen, Op. 6/3 *(rec Friedrich–Ebert Halle, Hamburg, Sept. 20–26, 1982)* Entrée ▲ 0068 [ADD]
Mendelssohn, Fanny:Songs, w. Uwe Wegner (pno)—Die frühen Gräber, Op. 9/4; Die Mainacht, Op. 9/6; Das Heimweh; Italien; Sehnsucht *(rec Friedrich–Ebert Halle, Hamburg, Sept. 20–26, 1982)* Entrée ▲ 0068 [ADD]
Schumann, C.:Songs, w. Uwe Wegner (pno)—Was weinst du, Blümlein, Op. 23/1; Liebst du um Schönheit, Op. 12; Sie liebten sich beide, Op. 13/2; Er ist gekommen in Sturm und Regen, Op. 12; Das ist ein Tag, der klingen mag, Op. 23/5 *(rec Friedrich–Ebert Halle, Hamburg, Sept. 20–26, 1982)* Entrée ▲ 0068 [ADD]

Nigoghossian, Sonia (mez)
Debussy, C.:Chansons de Bilitis, w. E. Sun (pno) [F] Quantum ▲ QM 6912 [DDD]

Nikodem, Zdzislaw (ten)
Moniuszko, S.:Haunted Manor, w. Halina Slonicka (sop), Bozena Brun–Baranska (mez), Barbara Lawcewicz (mez), Krystyna Szczepanska (mez), Bogdan Paprocki (ten), Andrzej Hiolski (bar), Edmund Kossowski (bass), Bernard Ladysz (bass), W. Rowicki (cnd), Warsaw State Opera House Orch, Warsaw National Opera Chorus *(rec Warsaw, 1965)* Polskie Nagrania ▲ PNCD 093 [AAD]

Nikodem, Zdzislaw (ten) (cont.)
Moniuszko, S.:Haunted Manor, w. Bozena Betley-Siradzka (sop—Hanna), Anna Witkowska (sop—Marta/Stara Niewiasta), Wiera Baniewicz (mez—Jadwiga), Aleksandra Imalska (mez—Czesnikowa), Kazimierz Dluha (Grzes), Zdzislaw Nikodem (ten—Damazy), Wieslaw Ochman (ten—Stefan), Andrzej Hiolski (bar—Miecznik), Florian Skulski (bar—Maciej), Leonard Mróz (bass—Zbigniew), Andrzej Saciuk (bass—Skoluba), J. Krenz (cnd), Cracow Polish Radio-TV Orch, Cracow Polish Radio-TV Chorus *(rec Cracovia, 1978)* Agora Music ("Phoenix" series) 3-▲ 509 [ADD]
Szymanowski, K.:King Roger, w. B. Zagórzanka (sop—Roger), S. Kowalski (ten—Shepherd), Z. Nikodem (ten—Edrisi), F. Skulski (bar—Roger II), R. Satanowski (cnd), Warsaw Teatr Wielki Orch, Warsaw Teatr Wielki Chorus [Polish] Koch Schwann 2-▲ CD 314 014 [DDD]

Nikolaidi, Elena (cta)
Verdi, G.:Aida (sels), w. D. Illitsch (sop—Aida), M. Lorenz (ten), L. Ludwig (cnd), Vienna State Opera Orch, Vienna State Opera Chorus *(rec Sept. 22, 1942)* Koch Schwann 2-▲ SCH 314562 [ADD]
Verdi, G.:Otello, w. Hilde Konetzni (sop), Torsten Ralf (ten), Paul Schöffler (b-bar), K. Böhm (cnd), Vienna State Opera Orch, Vienna State Opera Chorus *(rec live, Aug. 1944)* Preiser 2-▲ PRE 90230 [ADD]

Nikolsky, Gleb (bass)
Mussorgsky, M.:Boris Godunov, w. V. Valente (sop—Xenia), E. Gorochovskaya (mez—Nurse), L. Nichiteanu (mez—Fyodor), E. Zarmeba (mez—Hostess), M. Lipovšek (cta—Marina), P. Langridge (ten—Prince Shuisky), H. Wildhaber (ten—Misail), A. Fedin (ten—Simpleton), S. Leiferkus (bar—Rangoni), A. Kotcherga (bass—B. Godounov), A. Shagidullin (bass—Shchelkalov), S. Ramey (bass—Pimen), S. Larin (bass—Girgory), G. Nikolsky (bass—Varlaam), C. Abbado (cnd), Berlin PO, Tölz Boys' Choir, Berlin Radio Chorus, Slovak Phil Chorus *(rec Nov. 7–30, 1993)* Sony Classical 3-▲ S3K 58977 [DDD]

Nilsson, Birgit (sop)
Arias, w. Leontyne Price (sop), Giuseppe Di Stefano (ten) Legato Classics 2-▲ LCD 153-2 (m) [ADD]
Beethoven, L. van:Fidelio, w. Birgit Nilsson (sop—Leonore), Graziella Sciutti (sop—Marzelline), Kurt Equiluz (ten—Erster Gefangener), Donald Grobe (ten—Jacquino), James McCracken (ten—Florestan), Tom Krause (bar—Don Pizarro), Hermann Prey (bar—Don Fernando), Kurt Böhme (bass—Rocco), Günther Adam (sgr—Zweiter Gefangener), L. Maazel (cnd), Vienna PO, Vienna State Opera Concert Association Chorus *(rec Sofiensaal, Vienna, Mar 1964)* London 2-▲ 448104-2 [ADD]
Birgit Nillson:Swedish Radio Concerts *(rec 1947, 1959 & 1961)* Bluebell ▲ BLU 055 [ADD]
Birgit Nilsson Memories ("Great Voices" series) 2-▲ MEM 4275 (m) [ADD]
In Recital at Philharmonic Hall, w. John Wustman (pno) *(rec Lincoln Center, New York, 1967)* Melodram ▲ CDM 18027 (m) [AAD]
James Levine's 25th Anniversary Metropolitan Opera Gala, w. J. Levine (cnd), Metropolitan Opera Orch, Ileana Cotrubas (sop), Renée Fleming (sop), Hei-Kyung Hong (sop), Karita Mattila (sop), Ruth Ann Swenson (sop), Kiri Te Kanawa (sop), Deborah Voigt (sop), Grace Bumbry (mez), Heidi Grant Murphy (mez), Anne Sofie von Otter (mez) *(rec live, Metropolitan Opera House, New York, Apr 27, 1996)* Deutsche Grammophon ▲ 449177-2 [DDD]
Mozart, W.A.:Don Giovanni, w. Birgit Nilsson (sop—Donna Anna), Leontyne Price (sop—Donna Elvira), Eugenia Ratti (sop—Zerlina), Cesare Valletti (ten—Don Ottavio), Heinz Blankenburg (bar—Masetto), Fernando Corena (b-bar—Leporello), Arnold van Mill (b-bar—Il Commendatore), Cesare Siepi (b-bar—Don Giovanni), E. Leinsdorf (cnd), Vienna PO, Vienna State Opera Chorus [I] London 3-▲ 444594-2 [ADD]
Mozart, W.A.:Don Giovanni (sels), w. R. Grist (sop), M. Arroyo (sop), P. Schreier (ten), D. Fischer-Dieskau (bar), M. Talvela (bass), K. Böhm (cnd), Prague National Theater Orch IMP Collectors Series ▲ IMPX 9023 [AAD]
Puccini, G.:Arias, w. M. Caballé (sop), M. Chiara (sop), M. Freni (sop), J. Sutherland (sop), R. Tebaldi (sop), F. Corelli (ten), L. Pavarotti (ten), S. Milnes (bar) London ▲ 421315-2 [ADD]
Puccini, G.:La fanciulla del West, w. J. Gibin (ten), A. Mongelli (bar), L. von Matačić (cnd), La Scala Orch, La Scala Chorus [I] EMI Classics ("Studio" series) 2-▲ CDMB 63970
Puccini, G.:Tosca, w. Birgit Nilsson (sop—Floria Tosca), Puli Toro (mez—Shepherd), Jose Carreras (ten—Mario Cavaradossi), Joaquin Romaguera (ten—Spoleta), James Billings (bar—Sacristan), Richard Fredricks (bar—Baron Scarpa), Samuel Ramey (bass—Cesare Angelotti), William Ledbetter (sgr—Sciarrone), Richard Park (sgr—Cardinal), Don Yule (sgr—Jailer), J. Rudel (cnd), *(orch & chorus unknown) (rec Nov 13, 1974)* Legato Classics 2-▲ LCD-200-2
Puccini, G.:Tosca, w. F. Corelli (ten), D. Fischer-Dieskau (bar), L. Maazel (cnd), St. Cecilia Academy Orch Rome, St. Cecilia Academy Chorus Rome *(rec June 1966)* London ▲ 440051-2
Puccini, G.:Tosca, w. F. Tagliavini (ten), R. Vinay (ten), C. Maresco (cnd), Philadelphia Opera Orch, Philadelphia Opera Chorus *(rec Apr. 10, 1963)* Melodram 2-▲ MLO 270112 [ADD]
Puccini, G.:Turandot, w. Birgit Nilsson (sop—Turandot), Renata Tebaldi (sop—Liù), Jussi Björling (ten—Calaf), Alessio De Paolis (ten—Emperor Altoum), Piero de Palma (ten—Pang), Mario Sereni (bar—Ping), Adelio Zagonara (bar—Prince of Persia), Giorgio Tozzi (bass—Timur), Tommaso Frascati (bass—Pong), Leonardo Monreale (bass—Mandarin), E. Leinsdorf (cnd), Rome Opera Orch, Rome Opera Chorus *(rec Rome Opera House, July 3–11, 1959)* RCA Living Stereo 2-▲ 09026-62687-2 [ADD]
Puccini, G.:Turandot, w. R. Scotto (sop), F. Corelli (ten), B. Giaiotti (bass), F. Molinari-Pradelli (cnd), Rome Opera Orch, Rome Opera Chorus [I] EMI Classics ("Studio" series) 2-▲ CDMB 69327 [ADD]
Puccini, G.:Turandot, w. L. Price (sop), G. di Stefano (ten), T. Gobbi (bar), F. Molinari-Pradelli (cnd), Vienna State Opera Orch, Vienna State Opera Chorus [I] *(rec live, 6/22/61)* Legato Classics 2-▲ LCD 153-2 (m) [ADD]
Puccini, G.:Turandot, w. R. Tebaldi (sop), J. Bjoerling (ten), G. Tozzi (bass), E. Leinsdorf (cnd), Rome Opera Orch, Rome Opera Chorus [I] RCA Red Seal 2-▲ 5932-2-RC 3-■ AGK3-3970
Puccini, G.:Turandot, w. B. Nilsson (sop—Turnadot), A. Moffo (sop—Liù), F. Corelli (ten—Calaf), C. Anthony (ten—Pong), R. Nagy (ten—Pang), F. Guarrera (bar—Ping), B. Giaiotti (bass—Timur), L. Stokowski (cnd), Metropolitan Opera Orch, New York Metropolitan Opera Chorus *(rec Mar. 4, 1961)* Datum 2-▲ DAT 12301 [ADD]
Rossini, G.:Il barbiere di Siviglia (sels), w. Set Svanholm (ten), Sigurd Björling (bar), Ehrling, Grevillius, Larsson, Mann, Sandberg (cnd), Royal Stockholm PO, Swedish RSO—Largo al factotum Bluebell ▲ BLU 058 [ADD]
Sibelius, J.:Songs, w. J. Sólyom (pno)—Våren flyktar hastigt, Op. 13/4; Se'n har jag ej fragat mera, Op. 17/1; Illalle, Op. 17/6; Svarta rosor, Op. 36/1; Säf, säf, susa, Op. 36/4; Den första kyssen, Op. 37/1; Var det en dröm?, Op. 37/4; Flickan kom ifran sin älsklings möte, Op. 37/5; På verandan vid havet, Op. 38/2; Im Feld ein Mädchen singt, Op. 50/3 *(rec 1975)* BIS ▲ CD 15 [AAD]
Strauss, R.:Ariadne auf Naxos (sels), w. Set Svanholm (ten), Sigurd Björling (bar), *(orch unknown)*—Circe, Circe kannst du mich hören? Bluebell ▲ BLU 058 [ADD]
Strauss, R.:Elektra, w. M. Collier (sop), R. Resnik (mez), G. Stolze (ten), T. Krause (bar), G. Solti (cnd), Vienna PO [G] London 2-▲ 417345-2 [ADD]
Strauss, R.:Elektra, w. L. Rysanek (sop), R. Resnik (mez), W. Windgassen (ten), E. Wächter (bar), K. Böhm (cnd), *(orch unknown)* [G] *(rec live, Vienna 12/16/65)* Standing Room Only 2-▲ SRO 833-2 [ADD]
Strauss, R.:Die Frau ohne Schatten, w. L. Rysanek (sop), R. Hesse (mez), J. King (ten), W. Berry (bass), K. Böhm (cnd), Vienna SO Deutsche Grammophon 3-▲ 445325-2
Strauss, R.:Salome, w. G. Hoffman (mez), G. Stolze (ten), W. Kmentt (ten), E. Wächter (bar), G. Solti (cnd), Vienna PO [G] London 2-▲ 414414-2 [ADD]
Strauss, R.:Songs, w. J. Sólyom (pno)—Zueignung, Op. 10/1; Allerseelen, Op. 10/8; Ständchen, Op. 17/2; Ruhe, meine Seele, Op. 27/1; Cäcilie, Op. 27/2; Befreit, Op. 39/4; Wiegenlied, Op. 41/1 [G] *(rec 1975)* BIS ▲ CD 15 [AAD]
Verdi, G.:Aida (sels), w. G. Bumbry (mez), F. Corelli (ten), Z. Mehta (cnd), Rome Opera Orch [I] [highlights] EMI Classics (Classics for Pleasure) ▲ CDM 64035
Verdi, G.:Un ballo in maschera, w. G. Simionato (mez), C. Bergonzi (ten), C. MacNeil (bar), G. Solti (cnd), St. Cecilia Academy Orch Rome, St. Cecilia Academy Chorus Rome [I] London 2-▲ 425655-2 [ADD]
Verdi, G.:Macbeth, w. B. Prevedi (ten), G. Taddei (bar), T. Schippers (cnd), St. Cecilia Academy Orch Rome, St. Cecilia Academy Chorus Rome London ("Grand Opera" series) 2-▲ 433039-2 [ADD]
Verdi, G.:Otello (sels), w. Set Svanholm (ten), Sigurd Björling (bar), Ehrling, Grevillius, Larsson, Mann, Sandberg (cnd), Royal Stockholm PO, Swedish RSO—Desdemona rea!...Ora e per sempre adio...Si, pel ciel marmoreo giuro! Bluebell ▲ BLU 058 [ADD]

Nilsson, Birgit (sop) (cont.)
The Voices of Living Stereo, Vol. 2, w. Eileen Farrell (sop), Roberta Peters (sop), Leontyne Price (sop), Galina Vishnevskaya (sop), Rosalind Elias (mez), Shirley Verrett (mez), Marian Anderson (cta), Maureen Forrester (cta), Sergio Franchi (ten), Mario Lanza (ten), Richard Lewis (ten), Jan Pee, Alexander Dedyukhin (pno), Franz Rupp (pno), Leo Taubman (pno), George Trovillo (pno), Charles Wadsworth (pno), Boston Pops Orch [cnd:Arthur Fiedler], Boston SO [cnd:Charles Munch], Chicago SO [cnd:Fritz Reiner], RCA Victor Orch, RCA Victor Chorus [cnd:Wa *(rec Boston & Chicago & New York & Rome, 1957–1964)* RCA Living Stereo ▲ 09026-68167-2 [ADD]
Wagner, R.:Arias & Scenes, w. Set Svanholm (ten), Sigurd Björling (bar), Ehrling, Grevillius, Larsson, Mann, Sandberg (cnd), Royal Stockholm PO, Swedish RSO—Morgenlich leuchtend [from Die Meistersinger von Nürnberg]; Ein Schwert verhiess mir der Vater [from Die Walküre]; Mime hiess ein mürrischer Zwerg...Brünnhilde, heilige Braut [from Götterdämmerung] Bluebell ▲ BLU 058 [ADD]
Wagner, R.:Arias & Scenes, w. K. Flagstad (sop), E. Rethberg (sop), B. Nilsson (sop), E. Schumann (sop), F. Leider (sop), L. Melchior (ten), G. Thill (ten), A. Pertile (ten), G. Hüsch (bar), F. Schorr (b-bar), H. Hotter (b-bar), A. Kipnis (bass), *(orch unknown)* EMI Classics ("Studio" series) 4-▲ CDMC 64008
Wagner, R.:Götterdämmerung, w. Birgit Nilsson (sop—Brünnhilde), Leonie Rysanek (sop—Gutrune), Gerda Sommerschuh (sop—Woglinde), Elisabeth Lindermeier (sop—Wellgunde), Ruth Michaelis (sop—Flohilde), Marianne Schech (sop—Dritte Norne), Ira Malaniuk (mez—Waltraute), Irmgarth Barth (mez—Erste Norne), Hertha Töpper (mez—Zweite Norne), Bernd Aldenhoff (ten—Siegfried), Hermann Uhde (bar—Gunther), Gottlob Frick (bass—Hagen), H. Knappertsbusch (cnd), Bavarian State Opera Orch, Bavarian State Opera Chorus *(rec live, Prinzregententheater, Sept. 1, 1955)* Orfeo 4-▲ 356944 (m)
Wagner, R.:Götterdämmerung, w. J. Watson (sop), C. Ludwig (mez), W. Windgassen (ten), D. Fischer-Dieskau (bar), G. Frick (bass), G. Solti (cnd), Vienna PO [G] London 4-▲ 414115-2 [ADD]
Wagner, R.:Lohengrin, w. A. Varnay (sop), W. Windgassen (ten), H. Uhde (bar), E. Jochum (cnd), Bayreuth Festival Orch, Bayreuth Festival Chorus *(rec live, Bayreuth 1954)* Melodram 3-▲ MEL 36104
Wagner, R.:Der Ring des Nibelungen, w. L. Rysanek (sop), K. Dvořaková (sop), M. Mödl (sop), A. Burmeister (mez), V. Soukupova (mez), E. Wohlfahrt (ten), W. Windgassen (ten), T. Stewart (bar), T. Adam (b-bar), G. Neidlinger (b-bar), K. Böhme (bass), G. Nienstedt (bass), K. Böhm (cnd), Bayreuth Festival Orch, Bayreuth Festival Chorus [G] *(rec live, 1966–67)* Philips 14-▲ 420325-2 [ADD]
Wagner, R.:Der Ring des Nibelungen, w. K. Flagstad (sop), R. Crespin (sop), C. Watson (sop), C. Ludwig (mez), J. Madeira (mez), S. Svanholm (ten), J. King (ten), G. Stolze (ten), W. Windgassen (ten), G. London (bar), D. Fischer-Dieskau (bar), H. Hotter (b-bar), G. Neidlinger (b-bar), G. Frick (bass), G. Solti (cnd), Vienna PO [G] London 15-▲ 414100-2 [ADD]
Wagner, R.:Der Ring des Nibelungen (sels), w. W. Windgassen (ten), H. Hotter (b-bar), G. Solti (cnd), Vienna PO London ▲ 421313-2 [ADD]
Wagner, R.:Der Ring des Nibelungen (sels), w. Birgit Nilsson (sop—Brünnhilde), Leonie Rysanek (sop—Sieglinde), James King (ten—Siegmund), Wolfgang Windgassen (ten), Theo Adam (b-bar—Wotan), Gustav Neidlinger (b-bar), Josef Greindl (bass), K. Böhm (cnd), Bayreuth Festival Orch *(rec Bayreuth, 1967)* Philips 2-▲ 454020-2
Wagner, R.:Siegfried, w. W. Windgassen (ten), G. Stolze (ten), H. Hotter (b-bar), G. Neidlinger (b-bar), G. Solti (cnd), Vienna PO [G] London 4-▲ 414110-2 [ADD]
Wagner, R.:Siegfried, w. W. Windgassen (ten), E. Wohlfahrt (ten), T. Adam (b-bar), G. Neidlinger (b-bar), K. Böhm (cnd), Bayreuth Festival Orch, Bayreuth Festival Chorus [G] Philips 4-▲ 412483-2 [ADD]
Wagner, R.:Tristan und Isolde, w. R. Resnik (mez), H.-M. Uhle (ten), R. Krause (ten), A. van Mill (bass), G. Solti (cnd), Vienna PO [G] London ("Grand Opera" series) 4-▲ 430234-2 [ADD]
Wagner, R.:Tristan und Isolde, w. C. Ludwig (mez), W. Windgassen (ten), E. Wächter (bar), M. Talvela (bass), K. Böhm (cnd), Bayreuth Festival Orch, Bayreuth Festival Chorus [G] *(rec Bayreuth Festival, 1966)* Deutsche Grammophon 3-▲ 419889-2 [ADD]
Wagner, R.:Tristan und Isolde, w. C. Ludwig (mez), W. Windgassen (ten), E. Wächter (bar), M. Talvela (bass), K. Böhm (cnd), Bayreuth Festival Orch, Bayreuth Festival Chorus [G] Philips 3-▲ 434425-2 [ADD]
Wagner, R.:Tristan und Isolde (sels), w. W. Windgassen (ten), H. von Karajan (cnd), *(orch unknown)*—Love Duet *(rec 1959)* Arkadia 4-▲ 224
Wagner, R.:Die Walküre, w. R. Crespin (sop), C. Ludwig (mez), J. King (ten), H. Hotter (b-bar), G. Frick (bass), G. Solti (cnd), Vienna PO [G] London 4-▲ 414105-2 [ADD]
Wagner, R.:Die Walküre (sels), w. L. Rysanek (sop), L. Suthaus (ten), H. von Karajan (cnd), La Scala Orch—nine selections from Acts 1 & 2 *(rec live in Milan, 4/21/58)* Hunt Productions 12-▲ 12 CDKAR 223 (m) [ADD]
Weber, C.M. von:Der Freischütz (sels), w. Set Svanholm (ten), Sigurd Björling (bar), Ehrling, Grevillius, Larsson, Mann, Sandberg (cnd), Royal Stockholm PO, Swedish RSO—Durch die Wälder, durch die Auen Bluebell ▲ BLU 058 [ADD]
Weber, C.M. von:Oberon, w. A. Augér (sop), J. Hamari (mez), P. Domingo (ten), H. Prey (bar), R. Kubelik (cnd), Bavarian RSO Deutsche Grammophon 2-▲ 419038-2 [ADD]
Weber, C.M. von:Oberon, w. A. Augér (sop), J. Hamari (mez), P. Domingo (ten), H. Prey (bar), R. Kubelik (cnd), Bavarian RSO Deutsche Grammophon ("Domingo Edition" series) ▲ 435406-2 [ADD]

Nilsson, Ingegerd (sop)
Eirlksdottir, Karolina:Someone I Have Seen (act 2), w. P. Borin (cnd), Dies Caniculares Festival Orch Music from Iceland ▲ ITM 701 [ADD]

Nilsson, Pia-Maria (sop)
Roman, J.H.:Cantatas, w. C. Génetay (cnd), National Museum CO Proprius ▲ PRCD 9047
Söderman, A.:Poems & Songs, w. A. Kilström (pno), A. Lundmark (bar), Eric Ericson Chamber Choir—13 songs for soprano/piano, choir, or baritone/piano [Sw] Musica Sveciae ▲ MSCD 525 [DDD]

Nilsson, Raymond (ten)
Kodály, Z.:Psalmus hungaricus, w. J. Ferencsik (cnd), London PO, London Phil Chorus Everest ▲ EVC 9008 [AAD]

Nilsson, Sven (bass)
Wagner, R.:Die Meistersinger von Nürnberg (sels), w. M. Teschemacher (sop), H. Jung (mez), M. Kremer (ten), T. RA. (ten), E. Fuchs (bar), H.-H. Nissen (bar), K. Böhm (cnd), Saxon State Orch—Act. 3 *(rec 1939)* Pearl 2-▲ PEA 9121 [ADD]
Wagner, R.:Tannhäuser, w. T. Eipperle (sop), F. Krauss (bar), K. Schmitt-Walter (bar), C. Leonhardt (cnd), Stuttgart Radio Orch, Stuttgart Radio Chorus [G] *(rec Oct. 24, 1937, mat. 39695)* Preiser 3-▲ 90133 (m) [AAD]
Wagner, R.:Tristan und Isolde, w. Kirsten Flagstad (sop), Margarete Klose (mez), Lauritz Melchior (ten/bar), Herbert Janssen (bar), T. Beecham (cnd), Philharmonia Orch, Royal Opera House Chorus Covent Garden *(rec 1937)* Grammofono 2000 3-▲ GRM 78570 (m)
Wagner, R.:Tristan und Isolde, w. K. Flagstad (sop), M. Klose (cta), L. Melchior (ten), H. Janssen (bar), Beecham, Reiner (cnd), *(orch unknown)*—a compilation of two 1937 live performance recordings, with some passages conducted by Beecham, others by Reiner [G] EMI Classics ("Great Recordings of the Century" series) 3-▲ CDHC 64037

Nimoy, Leonard (nar)
The Birthday of the World:Music & Traditions of the High Holy Days, Part 1 [Rosh Hashanah], w. [cnd:Matthew Lazar], Western Wind *(rec West End Theater, NYC)* Western Wind ▲ 1854

Nimsgern, Siegmund (b-bar)
Bach, J.S.:Cant 26, w. P. Esswood (ct), K. Equiluz (ten), N. Harnoncourt (cnd), Vienna Concentus Musicus, Chorus Viennensis [G] Teldec 2-▲ 2292-42503-2 [AAD]
Bach, J.S.:Cant 27, w. P. Esswood (ct), K. Equiluz (ten), N. Harnoncourt (cnd), Vienna Concentus Musicus, Chorus Viennensis [G] Teldec 2-▲ 2292-42503-2 [AAD]
Bach, J.S.:Cant 28, w. P. Esswood (ct), K. Equiluz (ten), N. Harnoncourt (cnd), Vienna Concentus Musicus, Chorus Viennensis [G] Teldec 2-▲ 2292-42504-2 [AAD]
Bach, J.S.:Cant 31, w. K. Equiluz (ten), N. Harnoncourt (cnd), Vienna Concentus Musicus, Chorus Viennensis [G] Teldec 2-▲ 2292-42505-2 [AAD]
Bach, J.S.:Cant 34, w. P. Esswood (ct), K. Equiluz (ten), N. Harnoncourt (cnd), Vienna Concentus Musicus [G] Teldec 2-▲ 2292-42505-2 [AAD]
Bach, J.S.:Cant 40, w. V. Gohl (mez), A. Kraus (ten), H. Rilling (cnd), Stuttgart Bach Collegium, Stuttgart Gedächtnis Figural Choir [G] *(rec June–July 1970)* Hänssler Classic ▲ 98.824 [AAD]

Nimsgern, Siegmund (b-bar) (cont.)
Bach, J.S.:Cant 41, w. H. Donath (sop), M. Höffgen (mez), A. Kraus (ten), H. Rilling (cnd), Stuttgart Bach Collegium, Gächinger Kantorei [G] Hänssler Classic ▲ 98.870 [AAD]
Bach, J.S.:Cant 81, w. J. Hamari (mez), A. Kraus (ten), H. Rilling (cnd), Bach Ensemble [G] *(rec 1984)* Hänssler Classic ▲ 98.876 [AAD]
Bach, J.S.:Cant 96, w. H. Donath (sop), M. Höffgen (mez), A. Kraus (ten), H. Rilling (cnd), Stuttgart Bach Collegium, Württemberg CO, Gächinger Kantorei [G] *(rec 1973)* Hänssler Classic ▲ 98.814 [AAD]
Bach, J.S.:Cant 211, "Coffee Cant", w. E. Ameling (sop), G. English (ten), Collegium Aureum Editio Classica 2-▲ 77151-2-RG [ADD]
Bach, J.S.:Cant 212, "Peasant Cant", w. E. Ameling (sop), G. English (ten), Collegium Aureum Editio Classica 2-▲ 77151-2-RG [ADD]
Bach, J.S.:Christmas Oratorio, w. P. Esswood (ct), K. Equiluz (ten), N. Harnoncourt (cnd), Vienna Concentus Musicus, Vienna Boys' Choir [G] Teldec ▲ 9031-74893-2
Bach, J.S.:Christmas Oratorio, w. P. Esswood (ct), K. Equiluz (ten), N. Harnoncourt (cnd), Vienna Concentus Musicus Teldec 2-▲ 9031-77610-2
Campra, A.:L'Europe galante, w. M. Kweksilber (sop), R. Yakar (sop), R. Jacobs (ct), G. Leonhardt (cnd), La Petite Bande Editio Classica 2-▲ 77059-2-RG [ADD]
Cornelius, P.:Stabat Mater, w. B. Scherler (mez), M. Schmidt (ten), R. Didusch (sgr), H. Schernus (cnd), Cologne RSO, Cologne Radio Chorus [L] *(rec 1978)* Koch Schwann ▲ 3-1086-2 [ADD]
Gluck, C.W.:Alceste, w. J. Norman (sop), N. Gedda (ten), B. Weikl (bar), T. Krause (bar), S. Baudo (cnd), Bavarian RSO, Bavarian Radio Chorus [French version] Orfeo 3-▲ 027823 [DDD]
Gluck, C.W.:Alceste, w. J. Norman (sop), N. Gedda (ten), B. Weikl (bar), T. Krause (bar), S. Baudo (cnd), Bavarian RSO, Bavarian Radio Chorus, *(highlights of above)* Orfeo ▲ 027901 [DDD]
Humperdinck, E.:Hänsel und Gretel, w. I. Cotrubas (sop), E. Söderström (sop), F. von Stade (mez), C. Ludwig (mez), J. Pritchard (cnd), Gürzenich Orch [G] CBS 2-▲ M2K 35898 [ADD]
Lully, J.-B.:Le Bourgeois gentilhomme, w. M. Kweksilber (sop), R. Yakar (sop), R. Jacobs (ct), G. Leonhardt (cnd), La Petite Bande Editio Classica 2-▲ 77059-2-RG [ADD]
Marschner, H.A.:Der Vampyr, w. Carole Farley (sop—Malwina), Nucci Condò (mez—Suse), Oslavio Di Credico (ten—George Dibdin), Josef Protschka (ten—Edgar Aubry), Romano Truffelli (ten—Richard Scrop), Martin Egel (bar—Sir Humphrey Davenaut), Andréa Snarski (bar—Toms Blunt), Siegmund Nimsgern (b-bar—Lord Ruthven), Armando Caforio (bass—Robert Green), Peter Boom (sgr—Il capo dei Vampiri), Carlo Di Giacomo (sgr—James Gadshill), Wolfgang Lenz (sgr—Sir Berkley), Galina Pisarenko (sgr—Janthe), Renzo Scorsoni (sgr—Un servitore di Berkley), Anastasia Tomaszewska Schepis (sgr—Emmy), G. Neuhold (cnd), Rome RAI SO, Rome RAI Chorus *(rec Rome, Jan 26, 1980)* Italia 2-▲ CDC 99 [ADD]
Mendelssohn, F.:St. Paul, w. A. Giebel (sop), O. Dominguez (mez), Theo Altmeyer (ten), R. A. El Hage (bass), R. Muti (cnd), Milan RAI Orch, Milan RAI Chorus [G] *(rec live, Milan, 12/15/70)* Memories 2-▲ HR 4267/68 (m) [ADD]
Mozart, W.A.:Requiem, w. A. Augér (sop), C. Watkinson (cta), S. Jerusalem (ten), H. Rilling (cnd), Stuttgart Bach Ensemble, Gächinger Kantorei [L] Odyssey ▲ MBK 42614 ■ YT 42614
Mussorgsky, M.:Khovanshchina, w. Mietta Sighele (sop—Emma), Elena Souliotis (sop—Susanna), Fiorenza Cossotto (mez—Marfa), Herbert Handt (ten—Scribe), Veriano Luchetti (ten—Prince Andrey Khovansky), Ludovic Spiess (ten—Prince Vasily Golitsin), Claudio Strudthoff (ten—Streshnev), Angelo Marchiandi (bar—Kuz'ka), Teodoro Rovetta (bar—1st Strel'tsi), Siegmund Nimsgern (b-bar—Shaklovity), Cesare Siepi (b-bar—Dosifey), Carlo del Bosco (bass—2nd Strel'tsi), Ubaldo Carosi (bass—Varsonofiev), Nicolai Ghiaurov (bass—Prince Ivan Khovnasky), Giovanni Sciarpeletti (bass—Pastor), B. Leskovich (cnd), Rome RAI SO, Rome RAI Chorus—also includes bonus Act V [w Boris Christoff] (Rome, 1958) *(rec Rome, 1973)* Bella Voce 3-▲ BLV 107.402 [AAD]
Pergolesi, G.B.:La serva padrona, w. M. Bonifaccio (sop), Collegium Aureum [I] Deutsche Harmonia Mundi ▲ 77184-2-RC [DDD]
Pflüger, H.G.:Memento Mori, w. R. Bader (cnd), *(orch unknown)*, Capella Cracoviensis Bayer ▲ 800910
Puccini, G.:Il tabarro, w. I. Tokody (sop), G. Lamberti (ten), G. Patanè (cnd), Munich RSO [I] Eurodisc ▲ 7775-2-RC [DDD]
Rossini, G.:Mosè in Egitto, w. J. Anderson (sop), R. Raimondi (bass), C. Scimone (cnd), Philharmonia Orch, Ambrosian Opera Chorus [I] Philips 2-▲ 420109-2 [ADD]
Schoenberg, A.:Die glückliche Hand, w. P. Boulez (cnd), BBC SO, BBC Singers *(rec Mar. 12, 1981)* Sony Classical ▲ SMK 48464 [ADD]
Schoenberg, A.:Gurrelieder, w. M. Napier (sop), Y. Minton (mez), J. Thomas (ten), K. Bowman (sgr), G. Reich (nar), P. Boulez (cnd), BBC SO *(rec Oct. 26–Dec. 06, 1974)* Sony Classical 2-▲ SM2K 48459 [ADD]
Stravinsky, I.:Oedipus Rex, w. J. Norman (sop), T. Moser (ten), R. Bracht (bass), C. Davis (cnd), Bavarian RSO, Bavarian Radio Chorus [L] Orfeo ▲ 071831 [DDD] ■ 071831 (D)
Verdi, G.:Jérusalem, w. K. Ricciarelli (sop), J. Carreras (ten), G. Gavazzeni (cnd), Turin RAI Orch, Turin RAI Chorus [F] *(rec live 12/20/75)* Standing Room Only 2-▲ SRO 828-2 [ADD]
Vivaldi, A.:La Sena festeggiante, w. L Cuberli (sop), H. Müller-Molinari (mez), C. Scimone (cnd), Cappella Coloniensis Cetra Classic ▲ CDC 25 [AAD]
Wagner, R.:Lohengrin, w. A. Tomowa-Sintow (sop), D. Vejzovic (sop), A. Kollo (ten), K. Ridderbusch (bass), H. von Karajan (cnd), Berlin PO, German Opera Chorus [G] EMI Classics ("Studio" series) 4-▲ CDMD 69314 [ADD]
Wagner, R.:Lohengrin, w. J. Norman (sop), E. Randová (mez), P. Domingo (ten), D. Fischer-Dieskau (bar), H. Sotin (bass), G. Solti (cnd), Vienna PO, Vienna State Opera Chorus [G] London 4-▲ 421053-2 [DDD]
Wagner, R.:Lohengrin, w. J. Norman (sop), E. Randová (mez), P. Domingo (ten), D. Fischer-Dieskau (bar), H. Sotin (bass), G. Solti (cnd), Vienna PO, Vienna State Opera Chorus [G] London ▲ 425530-2 [DDD]
Wagner, R.:Parsifal, w. D. Vejzovic (sop), P. Hofmann (ten), J. Van Dam (b-bar), K. Moll (bass), H. von Karajan (cnd), Berlin PO, German Opera Chorus [G] Deutsche Grammophon 4-▲ 413347-2 [DDD]
Weinberger, J.:Schwanda der Dudelsackpfeifer, w. L. Popp (sop), G. Killebrew (mez), S. Jerusalem (ten), H. Prey (bar), H. Wallberg (cnd), Munich RSO, Bavarian Radio Chorus [F] CBS 3-▲ M3K 36926 [ADD]
Zimmermann, B.A.:Ich wandte mich und sah an alles Unrecht, das geschah unter der Sonne, w. C. Bantzer (nar), W. Quadflieg (nar), W. Humburg (cnd), Münster SO Stradivarius ▲ STR 33340

Nirouët, Jean (ct)
Gilles, J.:Mess des morts, w. A. Azema (sop), W. Hite (ten), P. Mason (bar), J. Cohen (cnd), Boston Camerata, Ensemble de Tambours Provençaux, Aix-en-Provence Festival Chorus Erato ▲ 2292-45989-2
Handel, G.F.:Messiah (sels), w. Barbara Schlick (sop), Alexander Stevenson (ten), Philip Langshaw (bass), P. Kuentz (cnd), Paul Kuentz Orch, Paul Kuentz Choir Pierre Verany ▲ PVY 730045
Vivaldi, A.:Nisi Dominus, w. P. Kuentz (cnd), Paul Kuentz Orch Pierre Verany ▲ PVY 730043
Vivaldi, A.:Stabat Mater Cta, w. P. Kuentz (cnd), Paul Kuentz Orch Pierre Verany ▲ PVY 730043

Nissen, Hans Hermann (bass)
Strauss, R.:Salome, w. Astrid Varnay (sop—Salome), Hertha Töpper (mez—Der Page der Herodias), Margarete Klose (cta—Herodias), Hans Hopf (ten—Narraboth), Karl Hoppe (ten—1st Nazarene), Karl Ostertag (ten—1st Jew), Julius Patzak (ten—Herodes), Hans Braun (bar—Jochanaan), Benno Kusche (bar—2nd Soldier), Adolf Keil (bass—1st Soldier), Hans Hermann Nissen (bass—Ein Kappadozier), Max Proebstl (bass—2nd Nazarene), Walter Carnotch (sgr—4th Jew), Emil Graf (sgr—3rd Jew), Paul Kaussen (sgr—2nd Jew), Hildegard Limmer (sgr—A slave), Georg Witter (sgr—5th Jew), H. Weigert (cnd), Bavarian RSO *(rec June 21-25, 1953)* Bella Voce 2-▲ BLV 7210 [AAD]
Wagner, R.:Die Meistersinger von Nürnberg, w. M. Reining (sop), H. Noort (ten), A. Dermota (ten), H. Alsen (bass), A. Toscanini (cnd), Vienna PO *(rec live, Salzburg, 1937)* Melodram 4-▲ MEL 47041
Wagner, R.:Die Meistersinger von Nürnberg (sels), w. M. Teschemacher (sop), H. Jung (mez), M. Kremer (ten), T. RA. (ten), E. Fuchs (bar), S. Nilsson (bass), K. Böhm (cnd), Saxon State Orch—Act. 3 *(rec 1939)* Pearl 2-▲ PEA 9121 [ADD]

Nissen, Helge (b-bar)
Vilhelm Herold, w. Vilhelm Herold (ten), Johanne Brun (sop), Emilie Ulrich (sop) Nimbus ("Prima Voce" series) ▲ NI 7880 [ADD]

Nistor, Milka (mez)
Mascagni, P.:Cavalleria rusticana, w. Marina Krilovici (sop—Santuzza), Viorica Cortez (mez—Lola), Milka Nistor (mez—Lucia), Cornel Stavru (ten—Turiddu), David Ohanesian (bar—Alfio), M. Popa (cnd), Bucharest Opera & Ballet Theater Orch, Bucharest Opera & Ballet Theater Chorus *(rec 1966)* Vox Box 2-▲ CDX 5161

Nistor-Slatinaru, Maria (sop)
Verdi, G.:La forza del destino, w. Maria Nistor-Slatinaru (sop—Donna Leonora), Mihaela Mariacineanu (mez—Curra), Zenaida Pally (mez—Preziosilla), Ludovic Speiss (ten—Don Alvaro), Ion Stoian (ten—Trabucco), Nicolae Herlea (bar—Don Carlo), Nicolae Florei (bass—Padre Guardiano) Constantin Gabor (bass—Fra Melitone), Dan Musetescu (bass—An Alcalde), Mihai Panghe (bass—Marquis of Calatrava), C. Litvin (cnd), Romanian Radio-TV Orch, Romanian Radio-TV Chorus *(rec Jan 1970)* Vox Box 3-▲ CD3X 3038

Nitz, Martin (ten)
Brassart, J.:Ave Maria, w. A. Teichert-Hailperin (sop), K. Smith (ct), W. Jochesn (ten), Helga Weber Instrumental Circle Entrée ▲ 0041 [ADD]
Dunstable, J.:Sacred Music, w. A. Teichert-Hailperin (sop), K. Smith (ct), W. Jochens (ten), H. Deutsch (bar), Helga Weber Instrumental Circle—Sancta Maria; Beata dei genetrix; Beata mater et innupta virgo; Speciosa facta es; Alma redemptoris mater Entrée ▲ 0041 [ADD]
Hildegard Of Bingen:Sacred Songs, w. A. Teichert-Hailperin (sop), K. Smith (ct), W. Jochens (ten), H. Deutsch (bar), Helga Weber Instrumental Circle—Caritas abundat in omnia; O virtus sapientiae; O quam mirabilis; Hodie aperuit nobis clausa porta; Alleluia. O virga, mediatrix; O clarissima mater; O frodens virga Entrée ▲ 0041 [ADD]
Love Songs from the 14th & 15th Centuries, w. Almut Teichert-Hailperin (sop), Kevin Smith (ct), Wilfried Jochens (ten), Instrumentalkreis Helga Weber Entrée ▲ CHE 0042-2 [ADD]

Nixon, Leigh (ten)
Handel, G.F.:Dixit Dominus, w. Arleen Augér (sop), Lynne Dawson (sop), Diana Montague (mez), Simon Birchall (bass), S. Preston (cnd), Westminster Abbey Orch, Westminster Abbey Choir [L] Archiv ▲ 423594-2 [DDD]
Purcell, H.:King Arthur, w. R. Hardy (sop), H. Sheppard (sop), J. Knibbs (cta), A. Deller (ct), M. Deller (alt), P. Elliott (ten), M. Bevan (bar), N. Beavan (bass), A. Deller (cnd), Deller Consort, King's Musick [E] Harmonia Mundi France 2-▲ HMC 90252/53
Songs for a Tudor King, w. P. Hillier (cnd), Hillard Ensemble, Judith Nelson (sop), David James (ct), Paul Elliott (ten), P. Hillier (bar) Saga Classics ▲ 3378 [ADD]
Tavener, J.:Innocence, w. Patricia Rozario (sop), Graham Titus (bass), Alice Neary (vc), Charles Fullbrook (bells), Martin Baker (org), Martin Neary (cnd), Westminster Abbey Choir *(rec Westminster Abbey, May 1-5, 1995)* Sony Classical ▲ SK 66613 [DDD]

Nixon, Marni (sop)
Bach, J.S.:Cant 198, w. Elaine Bonazzi (mez), Nico Castel (ten), Peter Binder (bar), R. Craft (cnd), Columbia SO, American Concert Choir Sony Classical ("Essential Classics" series) 2-▲ SB2K 62656
Castelnuovo-Tedesco, M.:Coplas, w. E. Gold (cnd), Vienna Volksoper Orch [Sp] *(rec Sept. 28-29, 1974)* Crystal ▲ CD501
Copland, A.:Poems (8) of Emily Dickinson, w. K. Clark (cnd), Pacific SO Reference ▲ RR 22CD [DDD]
Everybody's Favorite Wedding Music, w. Philharmonic Wedding Ensemble, Bert Lucarelli (cnd), John Cullum (bar) Essex Entertainment ▲ ESD 7050 ■ ESC 7050
Gershwin, G.:Songs, w. Lincoln Mayorga (pno) Reference ▲ RR 19CD [DDD]
Gold, E.:Songs of Love & Parting, w. E. Gold (cnd), Vienna Volksoper Orch [E] *(rec Sept. 28-29, 1974)* Crystal ▲ CD 501
Hovhaness, A.:Avak, the Healer, w. Thomas Stevens (tpt), E. Gold (cnd), Crystal CO Crystal ▲ CD 806
Hovhaness, A.:Avak, the Healer, w. Thomas Stevens (tpt), E. Gold (cnd), Crystal CO Crystal ■ C 800
Kern, J.:Songs, w. L. Mayorga (pno) Reference ▲ RR 28CD [DDD]

Nixon, Marnie (sgr)
Rodgers, R.:The King & I, w. Y. Brynner (sgr), R. Moreno (sgr), *(artists unknown)* *(rec 1956)* Broadway Angel ▲ ZDM 64693 ■ EG 64693

Niziolek, Janusz (bass)
Maciejewski, R.:Missa pro defunctis, w. Zdzislawa Donat (sop), Jadwiga Rappé (alt), Jerzy Knetig (ten), T. Strugala (cnd), Warsaw PO, Henryk Wojnarowski (cnd), Warsaw National Phil Chorus *(rec National Philharmonic, Warsaw, May 2-15, 1989)* Polskie Nagrania 2-▲ PNCD 039 A/B

Noble, Dennis (bar)
Elgar, E.:The Dream of Gerontius, w. G. Ripley (cta), H. Nash (ten), N. Walker (bass), M. Sargent (cnd), Liverpool PO, Huddersfield Choral Society Testament ▲ TES SBT 2025 [ADD]

Noble, John (bar)
Britten, H.:Albert Herring, w. S. Fisher (sop), A. Cantelo (sop), S. Rex (mez), P. Pears (ten), O. Brannigan (bass), B. Britten (cnd), English CO [E] London 2-▲ 421849-2 [ADD]
Delius, F.:Appalachia, w. C. Groves (cnd), London PO, BBC Chorus, BBC Choral Society, Goldsmith's Choral Union, London Phil Choir IMP ("BBC Radio Classics" series) ▲ IMP 9133
Gay, J.:The Beggar's Opera (sels), w. P. Clark (sop), A. Jenkins (sop), M. Cable (mez), E. Lane (mez), S. Minty (mez), E. Fleet (sgr), P. Hall (ten), V. Midgley (ten), N. Rogers (ten), D. Stevens (cnd), Accademia Monteverdiana Orch, Accademia Monteverdiana Chorus—59 songs *(rec Aug. 1978)* Koch Treasure ▲ 31021-2 [ADD]
Monteverdi, C.:Vespro della Beata Vergine, w. Elly Ameling (sop), Norma Burrowes (sop), Charles Brett (ct), Martyn Hill (ten), Anthony Rolfe-Johnson (ten), Robert Tear (ten), Peter Knapp (bass), Francis Grier (org/hpd), James Lancelot (org/hpd), Andrew Leach (org/hpd), P. Ledger (cnd), London Early Music Consort, King's College Choir Cambridge—Nigra sum [con.]; Laudate pueri [psalm]; Sancta Maria [son. sopra]; Magnificat *(rec Chapel of King's College, Cambridge, July & Aug. 1975)* EMI Classics ▲ CDK 65339 [ADD]
Monteverdi, C.:Vespro della Beata Vergine, w. Elly Ameling (sop), Norma Burrowes (sop), Charles Brett (ct), Robert Tear (ten), Anthony Rolfe Johnson (ten), Martyn Hill (ten), Peter Knapp (bass), Munrow, Ledger (cnd), London Early Music Consort EMI Classics ("Doublefforte" series) 2-▲ CDFB 68631
Orff, C.:Carmina burana, w. L. Popp (sop), G. Unger (ten), R. Wolansky (bar), R. Frühbeck de Burgos (cnd), New Philharmonia Orch, New Philharmonia Chorus EMI Classics ▲ CDM 64328
Vaughan Williams, R.:The Pilgrim's Progress, w. A. Boult (cnd), London PO, London Phil Chorus [E] EMI Classics ▲ CDMB 64212

Nocentini, Maria Costanza (sop)
Bellini, V.:La sonnambula, w. Vitalba Mosca (mez), Giuseppe Morino (ten), Giovanni Furlanetto (bar), Patrizia Ciofi (sgr), Etienne Ligot (sgr), Walter Mikus (sgr), G. Carella (cnd), Italian International Orch Nuova Era 2-▲ NUO 7215 [DDD]
Rossini, G.:La pietra del paragone, w. A. Trovarelli (mez), H. M. Molinari (cta), P. Barbacini (ten), V. Di Matteo (bar), R. Scaltriti (bar), A. Svab (bar), P. Rumetz (bass), C. Desderi (cnd), Camerata Musicale Orch, Modeno Teatro Comunale Chorus [I] *(rec 1992)* Nuova Era 2-▲ 7132/33 [DDD]

Nöcker, Hans Günter (b-bar)
Nicolai, O.:Lustigen Weiber, w. Erika Köth (sop), Hertha Töpper (mez), Maria Rogner (sgr), Kim Borg (bass), Naan Pödl (sgr), F. Rieger (cnd), Bavarian RSO, Bavarian Chorus *(rec 1960's)* Pantheon 2-▲ PHE 6660 (m)

Noel, H. (sgr)
Gounod, C.:Faust, w. V. de los Angeles (sop), C. Ward (sgr), M. Mayhoff (sgr), R. Tucker (ten), N. Moscona (bass), D. Bernard (sgr), W. Herbert (cnd), New Orleans Opera Orch [F] *(rec Feb. 26, 1953)* Legato Classics 2-▲ LCD 167-2 [AAD]

Noel, Rita (mez)
Britton, D.G.:Chinoiserie:Histoire d'un Amour Oriental, w. Portland String Quartet [F] *(rec Dec. 1991)* Arabesque ▲ Z 6632 [DDD]

Noit, José (ten)
Leoncavallo, R.:Pagliacci, w. Joan Carlyle (sop—Nedda), Jon Vickers (ten—Canio), José Noit (ten—Beppe), Cornell MacNeil (bar—Tonio), Bruno Tornasaetti (bar—Silvio), B. Bartoletti (cnd), *(orch unknown)* *(rec live, Buenos Aires, 1968)* VAI Audio ▲ VAIA 1014 [ADD]

Nolan, Rodney (ten)
Shostakovich, D.:From Jewish Folk Poetry, w. N. Pelle (sop), M. A. Hart (mez), Y. Turovsky (cnd), Montreal Musici [R] Chandos ▲ CHAN 8800 [DDD]

VOCALISTS

Nolen, Timothy (bar)
Bolcom, W.:Casino Paradise, w. J. Morris (sop), E. Korbich (sgr), M. Barrett (cnd), *(ensemble unknown)* Koch International Classics ▲ KIC 7047-2 [DDD]

Noli, Alberto (bass)
Puccini, G.:La Bohème, w. Katia Ricciarelli (sop), Francisco Araiza (ten), Angelo Casertano (ten), Stefano Antonucci (bar), Claudio Giombi (bar), Paata Burchuladze (bass), Alfredo Mariotti (bass), Andrea Piccinni (bass), Lauren Broglia (sgr), A. Guadagno (cnd), Arena di Verona Orch, Limburg Cathedral Boys' Chorus Koch Schwann 2-▲ SCH 315922

Noli, Rosetta (sop)
Boito, A.:Mefistofele, w. R. Noli (sop—Margherita), S. dall'Argine (sop—Elena), G. Poggi (ten—Faust), G. Neri (bass–Mefistofele), F. Capuana (cnd), La Scala Orch, La Scala Chorus [I] *(rec 1952)* Preiser 2-▲ 90122 (m) [AAD]

Nölser, Liselotte (sgr)
Strauss, R.:Feuersnot, w. Maud Cunitz (sop—Diemut), Antonia Fahberg (sop—Elsbeth), Irmgard Barth (mez—Wigelis), Liselotte Nölser (sgr—Margret), Karl Ostertag (ten—Schweiker), Marcel Cordes (bar—Kunrad), Kieth Engen (bass—Kofel), Karl Hoppe (bass—Hämerlein), Max Proebstl (bass—Ortolf), Georg Wieter (bass—Jörg), R. Kempe (cnd), Bavarian State Opera Orch, Bavarian State Opera Chorus *(rec Munich Opera Festival, Prince Regent Theater, Aug 14, 1958)* Orfeo d'or 2-▲ 423962

Nolte, Raimund (bass)
Rossini, G.:Péchés de vieillesse (sels), w. M. Castets (sop), M. Georg (mez), J.-L. Maurette (ten), M. Brodard (bar), E. Kalvelage (pno), C. Spering (org), M. Jorand (perc), Cologne Chorus Musicus—Toast pour le nouvel an, Roméo, La Grande Coquette, Un sou, Chanson de Zora, La Nuit de Noël, Le Dodo des enfants, Le Lazzarone, Adieux à la viel, Soupirs et sourire, L'Orpheline du Tyrol, Choeur de chasseurs démocrates; *Morceaux réservés*—Ave Maria, Les Amants de Séville, Le Chant des Titans, Chant funèbre [F] *(rec Aug. 1992)* Opus 111 ▲ OPS 30-70 [DDD]

Nomura, Christopheren (sgr)
Puccini, G.:Madama Butterfly (sels), w. Ying Huang (sop—Cio-Cio-San), Constance Hauman (mez—Kate Pinkerton), Ning Liang (mez—Suzuki), Richard Troxell (ten—B. F. Pinkerton), Richard Cowan (sgr—Sharpless), Jing Ma Fan (sgr—Goro), Christopheren Nomura (sgr—Prince Yamadori), J. Conlon (cnd), Orch de Paris—Dovunque al Mondo; B. F. Pinkerton Giù; Bimba, Bimba, Non Piangere; Ah! Vien! Sei Mia!; Un Bel Dí; Ora a Noi; Petali d'Ogni Fior; Coro a Bocca Chiusa; Prelude; Io So Che Alle Sue Pene; Ah! Son Vill; E Sia! A Lui Devo Obbedir; Butterfly! *(rec Olivier Messiaen Auditorium, Paris, 1996)* Sony Classical ▲ SK 61972 [DDD]

Noni, Alda (sop)
Alda Noni, Sesto Bruscantini, w. Sesto Bruscantini (bass), Turin RAI Orch [cnd:Nino Sanzogno] *(rec Dec. 3, 1951)* Incontri Memorabili ("Martini & Rossi Concerts" series) ▲ 5016
Cimarosa, D.:Il Matrimonio segreto, w. Giulietta Simionato (mez), Riccardo Cassinelli (ten), Cesare Valletti (ten), Sesto Bruscantini (bar), Rovero (sgr), M. Wolf-Ferrari (cnd), Florence Maggio Musicale Orch *(rec 1950)* Cetra Classic 2-▲ CDO 32
Cimarosa, D.:Il Matrimonio segreto (sels), w. H. Gueden (sop), F. Barbieri (mez), T. Schipa (ten), S. Bruscantini (bar), B. Christoff (bass), M. Rossi (cnd), La Scala Orch—Act I highlights [I] *(rec live, Milan March 22, 1949)* Melodram 2-▲ CDM 29505 [ADD]
Donizetti, G.:Don Pasquale, w. A. Noni (sop—Norina), C. Valletti (ten—Ernesto), M. Borriello (bar—Dr. Malatesta), S. Bruscantini (bass-bar—Pasquale), M. Rossi (cnd), Turin RAI SO, Turin RAI Chorus *(rec 1952)* Cetra Classic 2-▲ CDO 14 [AAD]
Donizetti, G.:L'elisir d'amore, w. B. Rizzoli (sop), C. Valletti (ten), S. Bruscantini (bar), A. Poli (bar), G. Gavazzeni (cnd), Rome RAI SO, Rome RAI Chorus *(rec 1952)* Cetra Classic ▲ CDO 5 [AAD]
Donizetti, G.:L'elisir d'amore, w. Cesare Valletti (ten), Sesto Bruscantini (bar), G. Gavazzeni (cnd), Rome RAI SO, Rome RAI Chorus Fonit Cetra ("Classic Collection" series) 2-▲ FCT CDO 5
Mozart, W.A.:Così fan tutte (sels), w. S. Jurinac (sop), B. Thebom (mez), R. Lewis (ten), E. Kunz (bar), M. Borriello (bar), F. Busch (cnd), Glyndebourne Festival Orch *(rec Glyndebourne Festival, 1950)* Testament ▲ TES SBT 1040 [ADD]
Mozart, W.A.:Nozze di Figaro, w. G. Gatti (sop), G. Sciurri (sop), J. Gardino (mez), M.T. Pace (mez), A. Mercuriali (ten), S. Bruscantini (bar), I. Tajo (bass), F. Corena (bass), F. Previtali (cnd), Rome RAI Orch [I] *(rec 1951)* Cetra Classic 2-▲ CDO 12
Mozart, W.A.:Zauberflöte, w. E. Schwarzkopf (sop), R. Streich (sop), N. Gedda (ten), G. Taddei (bar), M. Petri (bass), H. von Karajan (cnd), Rome Radio Orch, Rome RAI Chorus [I] *(rec live, Dec. 19, 1953)* Myto 2-▲ 2 MCD 89007 (m) [ADD]
Puccini, G.:La Bohème (sels), w. M. Carosio (sop), G. Poggi (ten), P. Silveri (bar), V. de Sabata (cnd), La Scala Orch, La Scala Chorus—6 arias from Acts 3 & 4 [I] *(rec live, Milan, 12/7/49)* Myto ▲ 1 MCD 90634 [ADD]
Rossini, G.:La Cenerentola, w. F. Cadoni (mez), M. de Gabarain (mez), H. Alan (bass), V. Gui (cnd), Glyndebourne Festival Orch, Glyndebourne Festival Chorus *(rec 1955)* EMI Classics 2-▲ CDMB 64183
Strauss, R.:Ariadne auf Naxos, w. M. Reining (sop), I. Seefried (sop), M. Lorenz (ten), J. Witt (ten), E. Kunz (bar), P. Schöffler (bass), K. Böhm (cnd), Vienna State Opera Orch *(rec Strauss' 80th Birthday Festival, June 11, 1944)* Preiser 2-▲ PRE 90217 [ADD]
Strauss, R.:Ariadne auf Naxos (sels), w. Alda Noni (sop—Zerbinetta), Maria Reining (sop—Ariadne), Irmgard Seefried (sop—Composer), Max Lorenz (ten—Bacchus), Paul Schöffler (b-bar—Musiklehrer), K. Böhm (cnd), Vienna State Opera Orch *(rec Vienna, June 11, 1944)* Koch Schwann 2-▲ SCH 314732 [ADD]

Noort, Henk (ten)
Wagner, R.:Die Meistersinger von Nürnberg, w. M. Reining (sop), A. Dermota (ten), H. H. Nissen (bar), H. Alsen (bass), A. Toscanini (cnd), Vienna PO *(rec live, Salzburg, 1937)* Melodram 4-▲ MEL 47041

Norberg-Schulz, Elizabeth (sop)
Beethoven, L. van:Fidelio, w. Elizabeth Norberg-Schulz (sop—Marzelline), Deborah Voigt (sop—Lenore), Ben Heppner (ten—Florestan), Michael Schade (ten—Jaquino), Günter von Kannațen (b-bar—Don Pizarro), Matthias Hölle (bass—Rocco), Thomas Quasthoff (bass—Don Fernando), C. Davis (cnd), Bavarian RSO, Bavarian Radio Chorus, Bavarian State Opera Men's Chorus *(rec Herkulessaal der Residenz, Munich, May 15-25, 1995)* RCA Victor 2-▲ 09026-68344-2 [DDD]
Brahms, J.:Ein Deutsches Requiem, w. Wolfgang Holzmair (bar), H. Blomstedt (cnd), San Francisco SO London ▲ 443771-2
Pergolesi, w. Nathalie Stutzmann (cta), Hanover Band, Ray Goodman (org) RCA Red Seal ▲ 09026-61215-2
Verdi, G.:Falstaff, w. E. Norberg-Schulz (sop—Nannetta), L. Serra (sop—Alice), S. Graham (mez—Meg Page), M. Lipovsek (cta—Miss Quickly), K. Begley (ten—Dr. Caius), P. Conti (ten—Ford), M. Luperi (ten—Pistol), J. Van Dam (b-bar—Falstaff), P. LeFebvre (bass—Bardolph), G. Solti (cnd), Berlin PO, Berlin Radio Chorus London ▲ 440650-2 [DDD]

Nørby, Einar (bar)
Delius, F.:Brigg Fair:An English Rhapsody, w. T. Beecham (cnd), Royal PO, BBC Sym Chorus *(rec 1955)* Sony Masterworks (Portrait) ▲ MPK 47680 [ADD]

Norden, Betsy (sop)
Bach, J.S.:Arias, w. Bob Haley (tpt), Donald Foster (org), Alexander String Quartet—(2) from Cantatas 21 & 36 [G] Crystal ▲ CD 952 [DDD] ■ C 952
Bach, J.S.:Cant 51, w. Bob Haley (tpt), Donald Foster (org), Alexander String Quartet [G] Crystal ▲ CD 952 [DDD] ■ C 952
Handel, G.F.:Arias, w. B. Haley (tpt), D. Foster (hpd), Alexander String Quartet—Destro dall' empia dite (from *Amadigi di Gaula*); Alle voci del bronzo guerriero (from Cantata No. 19, *O come chiare e belle*) [I] Crystal ▲ CD 952 [DDD] ■ C 952
Scarlatti, A.:Arias Sop, w. Bob Haley (tpt), Donald Foster (hpd), Alexander String Quartet—Con voce festiva; Mio tesoro [I] Crystal ▲ CD 952 [DDD] ■ C 952
Shepherd, A.:Triptych, w. Emerson String Quartet New World ▲ 80453-2

Norderval, Kirsten (sop)
Handel, G.F.:Semele, w. M. J. Newman (cnd), Collegium Brass—Where're You Walk *(rec Presbyterian Church, Mt. Kisco, NY, Aug 26-27, 1995)* Helicon ▲ HE 1006 [DDD]

Nordin, Birgit (sop)
Larsson, L.-E.:God in Disguise, w. H. Hagegård (bar), Jonsson (nar), S. Frykberg (cnd), Helsingborg SO, Helsingborg Sym Chorus [Sw] BIS ▲ CD 96 [AAD]
Verdi, G.:Rigoletto, w. M. Hallin (sop), K. Meyer (mez), B. Ericson (mez), Kjellgren (mez), N. Gedda (ten), O. Sivall (ten), H. Hasslo (bar), I. Wixell (bar), B. Alstergård (bar), A. Tyrén (bass), S. Ehrling (cnd), Stockholm Royal Opera House Orch, Stockholm Royal Opera Chorus *(rec live Jan. 18, 1959)* BIS ▲ CD 296 [AAD]

Nordin, Lena (sop)
Berwald, F.:Estrella de Soria (sels), w. K. Dalayman (sgr), S. Smith (sgr), A. Lorentzson (sgr), C. Sköld (sgr), S. Westerberg (cnd), Helsingborg SO, Malmö Chamber Choir Musica Sveciae ▲ MSV 523 [DDD]
Carissimi, G.:Ferma lascia ch'io parli, w. Maria Wieslander (org), Sven Åberg (chit), Chrichan Larsson (vc), Nanette Nowels-Stenholm (pno), M. Guidarini (cnd), *(orch unknown)* Swedish Society ▲ SCD 1076
Donizetti, G.:Maria Stuarda (sels), w. Carina Morling (mez), Ingus Petterssons (ten), Anders Bergström (bar), Tord Wallström (bar), Maria Wieslander (org), Sven Åberg (chit), Chrichan Larsson (vc), Nanette Nowels-Stenholm (pno), M. Guidarini (cnd), *(orch unknown)* Swedish Society ▲ SCD 1076
Orff, C.:Carmina burana, w. Hans Dornbusch (ten), Peter Mattei (bar), Love Derwinger (pno), Roland Pöntinen (pno), Kroumata Percussion Ensemble, Cecilia Rydinger Alin (cnd), Allmänna Sången, Uppsala Choir School Children's Chorus [chamber version] *(rec Uppsala Univ Hall, Uppsala, Sweden, June 9-11, 1995)* BIS ▲ CD 734 [DDD]
Schumann, R.:Gedichte, Op. 135, w. Nanette Nowels-Stenholm (pno) Swedish Society ▲ SCD 1076

Nordmo-Lövberg, Aase (sop)
Mascagni, P.:Cavalleria rusticana, w. A. Bjoerling (sop), M. Sehlmark (cta), J. Bjoerling (ten), G. Svedenbrandt (bass), K. Bendix (cnd), Stockholm Royal Opera House Orch, Stockholm Royal Opera Chorus [I, Sw] *(rec live, Stockholm, 12/8/54)* Legato Classics ▲ LCD 164-1 [ADD]

Norena, Eidé (sop)
Eidé Norena *(rec 1930-1937)* Nimbus ("Prima Voce" series) ▲ NI 7821 (m) [ADD]
Mozart, W.A.:Zauberflöte (sels), w. Marcel Wittrisch (ten), Alexander Kipnis (bass), Maria Galvany (sop), C. Schmalstich (cnd), Berlin State Opera Orch—Dies Bildnis (Act 1); O Isis und Osiris; Der Hölle Rache; Ach, ich fühl's *(rec 1905 - 1944)* Minerva ▲ MN A14 [ADD]
Opera & Oratorio Arias Preiser ("Lebendige Vergangenheit" series) ▲ PRE 89041 (m) [AAD]

Norin, Lena Susanne (mez)
Bach, J.S.:St. Matthew Passion, w. Monika Frimmer (sop), Veronika Winter (sop), Wilfried Jochens (ten), Christoph Prégardien (ten), Klaus Mertens (bass), Hans-Georg Wimmer (bass), H. Max (cnd), Das Kleine Konzert, Rhineland Kantorei Capriccio 2-▲ 60 046 [DDD]
Capricornus, S.F.:Theatrum musicum quod per duodecim scenas seu sacras cantiones aperuit, w. D. Collot (sop), K. Wessel (alt), I. Honeyman (ten), S. Schreckenberger (bass), M. Gester (cnd), Parlement de Musique Opus 111 ▲ OPS 30-99

Norman, Elizabeth (alt)
Purcell, H.:Dido & Aeneas, w. Cassandra Hoffman (sop—Belinda), Arlene Travis (sop—2nd Witch), Desirée Halac (mez—Sorceress/Spirit), Jennifer Lane (mez—Dido), Elizabeth Norman (alt), Thomas Bogdan (ten—A Sailor), Michael Brown (bar—Aeneas), Curtis Streetman (bar), Caitriona O'Leary (sgr—2nd Woman), Sarah Pillow (sgr—1st Witch), B. Brookshire (cnd), San Cassiano Music *(rec St. Ignatius of Antioch Episcopal Church, New York City, Spring 1995)* Vox Classics ▲ VOX 7518

Norman, Franz (bass)
Weber, C.M. von:Der Freischütz (sels), w. Set Svanholm (bar—Max), Franz Norman (bass—Kuno), Marjan Rus (bass—Kaspar), H. Knappertsbusch (cnd), Vienna State Opera Orch *(rec Vienna, June 18, 1941)* Koch Schwann ▲ SCH 314692 [ADD]

Norman, Jessye (sop)
Amazing Grace, w. Dalton Baldwin (pno), Geoffrey Parsons (pno), Christopher Bowers-Broadbent (org), Alexander Gibson (cnd), Willis Patterson (cnd), Royal PO, Ambrosian Singers Philips ▲ 432546-2 PH [DDD] ■ 432546-4 PH
Beethoven, L. van:Fidelio, w. P. Coburn (sop), R. Goldberg (ten), H.-P. Blochwitz (ten), K. Möll (bass), B. Haitink (cnd), Dresden Staatskapelle, Dresden State Chorus Philips ▲ 438496-2
Beethoven, L. van:Fidelio, w. P. Coburn (sop), R. Goldberg (ten), H.-P. Blochwitz (ten), A. Schmidt (bar), E. Wlaschiha (bass), K. Moll (bass), B. Haitink (cnd), Dresden Staatskapelle, Dresden State Chorus [G] Philips 2-▲ 426308-2 [DDD]
Beethoven, L. van:Missa Solemnis, w. C. Studer (sop), P. Domingo (ten), K. Moll (bass), J. Levine (cnd), Vienna PO, Leipzig Radio Chorus, Eric Ericson Chamber Chorus Deutsche Grammophon 2-▲ 435770-2 [DDD]
Beethoven, L. van:Sym 9, "Choral Sym", w. Brigitte Fassbaender (mez), Plácido Domingo (ten), Walter Berry (bass), K. Böhm (cnd), Vienna PO, Vienna State Opera Chorus Deutsche Grammophon ("Masters" series) ▲ 445503-2 [DDD]
Berg, A.:Early Songs, w. P. Boulez (cnd), London SO Sony Classical ▲ SK 66826
Berg, A.:Jugendlieder, w. Ann Schein (pno) Sony Classical ▲ SK 66826
Berg, A.:Lulu (suite), w. P. Boulez (cnd), New York PO Sony Classical ▲ SMK 45838 [DDD]
Berg, A.:Orchesterlieder (5) nach Ansichtskartentexten von Peter Altenberg, w. P. Boulez (cnd), London SO Sony Classical ▲ SK 66826
Berlioz, H.:Les Nuits d'été, w. C. Davis (cnd), London SO [F] Philips ▲ 412493-2 [ADD]
Bernstein, L.:Music of, w. K. Te Kanawa (sop), J. Anderson (sop), F. von Stade (mez), C. Ludwig (mez), T. Troyanos (mez), J. Carreras (ten), D. Garrison (ten), J. Hadley (ten), T. Hampson (bar), T. Daly (sgr), G. Kremer (vn), M. Rostropovich (vc), M.T. Thomas (va), L. Bernstein (cnd), *(orch unknown)*—various popular works Deutsche Grammophon ▲ 439251-2 ■ 439251-4
Bizet, G.:Carmen, w. M. Freni (sop), N. Shicoff (ten), S. Estes (bass), S. Ozawa (cnd), French National Orch, French Radio Chorus [F] Philips 3-▲ 422366-2 [DDD]
Bizet, G.:Carmen, w. M. Freni (sop), N. Shicoff (ten), S. Estes (bass), S. Ozawa (cnd), French National Orch, French Radio Chorus [F] Philips ▲ 426040-2 [DDD] ■ 426040-4 □ 426040-5
Brahms, J.:Alto Rhap, w. R. Muti (cnd), Philadelphia Orch Philips ("Digital Classics" series) ▲ 426253-2 [DDD] □ 426253-5
Brahms, J.:Songs, w. G. Parsons (pno) [G] Philips ▲ 416439-2 [ADD]
Brava, Jessye! Philips ▲ 442157-2 ■ 442157-4
Brava, Jessye!:The Olympic Edition Philips ▲ 454 693-2
Christmastide Philips ▲ 420180-2 PH [DDD]
Classics Philips ("Insignia" series) ▲ 434161-2 [ADD]
Debussy, C.:L'Enfant prodigue, w. J. Carreras (ten), D. Fischer-Dieskau (bar), G. Bertini (cnd), Stuttgart RSO, Stuttgart Radio Chorus [F] Orfeo ▲ 012821
Gluck, C.W.:Alceste, w. N. Gedda (ten), B. Weikl (bar), T. Krause (bar), S. Nimsgern (b-bar), S. Baudo (cnd), Bavarian RSO, Bavarian Radio Chorus [French version] Orfeo 3-▲ 027823 [DDD]
Gluck, C.W.:Alceste, w. N. Gedda (ten), B. Weikl (bar), T. Krause (bar), S. Nimsgern (b-bar), S. Baudo (cnd), Bavarian RSO, Bavarian Radio Chorus, *(highlights of above)* Orfeo ▲ 027901 [DDD]
In Recital, w. Geoffrey Parsons (pno) *(rec live at Hohenems, June 1987)* Philips ▲ 422048-2 PH [DDD]
In the Spirit:Sacred Music for Christmas, w. St. Luke's Orch [cnd:David Robertson], American Boys Choir, Riverside Church Choir, St. Barnabas Adult Choir, St. Thomas Men & Boys Choir Philips ▲ 454640-2 ■ 454640-4
The Incomparable Jessye Norman, Wesendonk Lieder EMI Classics ▲ CDM 69256
Jessye Norman EMI Classics ("Diva" series) ▲ CDM 65576
Jessye Norman at Notre Dame, w. Lyon Opera Orch [cnd:Lawrence Foster] Philips ▲ 432731-2 PH [DDD]
Lucky to Be Me, w. John Williams (pno) Philips ▲ 422401-2 PH ■ 422401-4 PH
Mahler, G.:Kindertotenlieder, w. S. Ozawa (cnd), Boston SO Philips 2-▲ 426249-2 [DDD]
Mahler, G.:Das Lied von der Erde, w. J. Vickers (ten), C. Davis (cnd), London SO [G] Philips ▲ 411474-2 [DDD]
Mahler, G.:Lieder eines fahrenden Gesellen, w. B. Haitink (cnd), Berlin PO Philips 2-▲ 426257-2 [DDD]
Mahler, G.:Sym 2, w. E. Marton (sop), L. Maazel (cnd), Vienna PO, Vienna State Opera Chorus [G] CBS 2-▲ M2K 38667 [DDD]

Norman, Jessye (sop) (cont.)
Mahler, G.:Sym 3, w. S. Ozawa (cnd), Boston SO, Tanglewood Festival Chorus, American Boychoir Philips ▲ 434909–2
Mahler, G.:Sym 3, w. C. Abbado (cnd), Vienna PO, Vienna State Opera Chorus, Vienna Boys' Choir [G] Deutsche Grammophon 2–▲ 410715–2 [DDD]
Mascagni, P.:Cavalleria rusticana, w. M. Senn (mez), R. Laghezza (mez), G. Giacomini (ten), D. Hvorostovsky (bar), S. Bychkov (cnd), Orch de Paris Philips ▲ 432105–2 [DDD]
Mozart, W.A.:Complete Mozart Edition, w. M. Freni (sop), Y. Minton (mez), I. Wixell (bar), C. Davis (cnd), BBC SO, BBC Sym Chorus Philips 3–▲ 422540–2 [ADD]
Mozart, W.A.:Complete Mozart Edition, w. I. Cotrubas (sop), H. Donath (sop), T. Troyanos (mez), W. Hollweg (ten), H. Prey (bar), H. Schmidt-Isserstedt (cnd), North German RSO Philips 3–▲ 422534–2 [ADD]
Offenbach, J.:Les Contes d'Hoffmann, w. C. Studer (sop), E. Lind (sop), A. S. von Otter (mez), F. Araiza (ten), S. Ramey (bass), J. Tate (cnd), Dresden Staatskapelle Philips 3–▲ 422374–2 [DDD]
Offenbach, J.:Les Contes d'Hoffmann, w. L. Serra (sop), R. Plowright (sop), J. Norman (sop), A. Murray (mez), J. Taillon (mez), N. Shicoff (ten), A. Oliver (ten), R. Tear (ten), J. Van Dam (b-bar), D. Duesing (bar), K. Rydl (bass), S. Cambreling (cnd), Brussels Théâtre de la Monnaie Orch [F] EMI Classics 3–▲ CDCC 49641 [DDD]
Offenbach, J.:Les Contes d'Hoffmann, w. E. Lind (sop), C. Studer (sop), A. Sofie von Otter (mez), F. Araiza (ten), S. Ramey (bass), J. Tate (cnd), Dresden Staatskapelle Philips ▲ 438502–2
Purcell, H.:Dido & Aeneas, w. M. McLaughlin (sop), T. Allen (bar), R. Leppard (cnd), English CO, Ambrosian Singers [E] Philips ▲ 416299–2 [DDD]
Ravel, M.:Chansons madécasses, w. P. Boulez (cnd), Ensemble InterContemporain [F] CBS ▲ MK 39023
Ravel, M.:Shéhérazade Mez, w. C. Davis (cnd), London SO [F] Philips ▲ 412493–2 [ADD]
Sacred Songs Philips ▲ 400019–2 PH [DDD] ■ 400019–4 PH (D)
Schoenberg, A.:Gurrelieder, w. P. Boulez (cnd), Ensemble InterContemporain—Lied der Waldtaube *(rec Sept. 15, 1979)* Sony Classical ▲ SMK 48466 [ADD]
Schoenberg, A.:Gurrelieder, w. T. Troyanos (mez), J. McCracken (ten), D. Arnold (bar), S. Ozawa (cnd), Boston SO, Tanglewood Festival Chorus Philips 2–▲ 412511–2
Schubert, Franz:Songs (misc), w. G. Parsons (pno) [G] Philips ▲ 422048–2 [DDD]
Schumann, R.:Frauenliebe und -leben, w. I. Gage (pno) [G] Philips ▲ 420784–2 [ADD]
Schumann, R.:Liederkreis, Op. 39, w. I. Gage (pno) [G] Philips ▲ 420784–2 [ADD]
Schumann, R.:Songs, w. G. Parsons (pno) [G] Philips ▲ 422048–2 [DDD]
Spirituals in Concert, w. Kathleen Battle (sop), James Levine (cnd) *(rec in Carnegie Hall)* Deutsche Grammophon ▲ 429790–2 GH [DDD] ■ 429790–4 GH (D) □ 429790–5
Strauss, R.:Ariadne auf Naxos, w. J. Varady (sop), E. Gruberova (sop), P. Frey (ten), O. Bär (bar), D. Fischer-Dieskau (bar), K. Masur (cnd), Leipzig Gewandhaus Orch [G] Philips 2–▲ 422084–2 [DDD]
Strauss, R.:4 Last Songs, w. K. Masur (cnd), Leipzig Gewandhaus Orch [G] Philips ▲ 411052–2 [DDD] □ 411052–5
Strauss, R.:Salome, w. K. Witt (mez), A. Markert (cta), W. Raffeiner (ten), R. Leech (ten), J. Morris (bass), S. Ozawa (cnd), Dresden Staatskapelle Philips 2–▲ 432153–2
Strauss, R.:Songs, w. G. Parsons (pno)—20 songs [G] Philips ▲ 416298–2 [DDD]
Strauss, R.:Songs, w. K. Masur (cnd), Leipzig Gewandhaus Orch—Cäcilie; Morgen; Wiegenlied; Ruhe, meine Seele; Meinem kinde; Zueignung [G] Philips ▲ 411052–2 [DDD] □ 411052–5
Stravinsky, I.:Oedipus Rex, w. T. Moser (ten), S. Nimsgern (b-bar), R. Bracht (bass), C. Davis (cnd), Bavarian RSO, Bavarian Radio Chorus [L] Orfeo ▲ 071831 [DDD] ■ 071831 (D)
Stravinsky, I.:Oedipus Rex, w. P. Langridge (ten), P. Schreier (ten), B. Terfel (b-bar), S. Ozawa (cnd), Saito Kinen Orch Philips ▲ 438865–2
Tchaikovsky, P.:Music of, w. I. Perlman (vn), Yo-Yo Ma (vc), Y. Temirkanov (cnd), Leningrad PO, Leningrad Military Orch—Waltz & Polonaise from Eugene Onegin; Sérénade mélancolique, Op. 26; Valse scherzo, Op. 34; Variations on a Rococo Theme, Op. 33; Overture 1812, Op. 49; Symphony No. 6 (3rd movt.); 3 Chansons française from Op. 65, for Voice & Piano; Aria (Adieu, forêts) from The Maid of Orleans *(rec live, Leningrad)* RCA Red Seal ▲ 60739–2-RC [DDD] ■ 09026-60739-4-RC (CrO2) □ 09026-60739-5
Verdi, G.:Aida, w. Yannula Pappas (mez), Walter Alberti (bar), Luigi Roni (b-bar), N. Sanzogno (cnd), Belgian Radio-TV Orch, Belgian Radio-TV Chorus *(rec live, Paris, May 4, 1973)* Agorá ("Phoenix" series) 2–▲ 507
Verdi, G.:Il corsaro, w. M. Caballé (sop), J. Carreras (ten), L. Gardelli (cnd), New Philharmonia Orch, Ambrosian Singers [I] Philips 2–▲ 426118–2 [ADD]
Verdi, G.:Un giorno di regno, w. F. Cossotto (mez), J. Carreras (ten), I. Wixell (bar), V. Sardinero (bar), W. Ganzarolli (bar), P. Elvin (bass), A. Cassinelli (bass), L. Gardelli (cnd), Royal PO, Ambrosian Singers Philips 2–▲ 422429–2 [ADD]
Wagner, R.:Lohengrin, w. E. Randová (mez), P. Domingo (ten), D. Fischer-Dieskau (bar), S. Nimsgern (b-bar), H. Sotin (bass), G. Solti (cnd), Vienna PO, Vienna State Opera Chorus [G] London ▲ 425530–2 [DDD]
Wagner, R.:Lohengrin, w. E. Randová (mez), P. Domingo (ten), D. Fischer-Dieskau (bar), S. Nimsgern (b-bar), H. Sotin (bass), G. Solti (cnd), Vienna PO, Vienna State Opera Chorus [G] London 4–▲ 421053–2 [DDD]
Wagner, R.:Parsifal, w. P. Domingo (ten), E. Wlaschiha (bar), K. Moll (bass), J. Morris (bass), J.-H. Rootering (bass), J. Levine (cnd), Metropolitan Opera Orch, New York Metropolitan Opera Chorus Deutsche Grammophon 4–▲ 437501–2
Wagner, R.:Der Ring des Nibelungen (sels), w. Lucia Popp (sop), René Kollo (ten), Siegfried Jerusalem (ten), Kurt Moll (bass), Matti Salminen (bass), M. Janowski (cnd), Dresden Staatskapelle RCA Victor ▲ 09026-68084-2; ■ 09026-68084-4
Wagner, R.:Der Ring des Nibelungen (sels), w. H. Behrens (sop), K. Battle (sop), J. Morris (mez), C. Ludwig (mez), R. Goldberg (ten), S. Jerusalem (ten), E. Wlaschiha (bar), M. Salminen (bass), J. Levine (cnd), Metropolitan Opera Orch—The Compact Ring—Ride of the Valkyries Wotan's Farewell & Magic Fire Music, Forest Murmurs, Brünnhilde's Awakening, Siegfried's Funeral Music, Brünnhilde's Immolation, & others Deutsche Grammophon ▲ 437825–2
Wagner, R.:Tristan und Isolde (prelude & liebestod), w. A. Davis (cnd), London SO [G] Philips ▲ 412655–2 [ADD]
Wagner, R.:Wesendonck Songs, w. A. Davis (cnd), London SO [G] Philips ▲ 412655–2 [ADD]
Weber, C.M. von:Euryanthe, w. Rita Hunter (sop), Nicolai Gedda (ten), Tom Krause (bar), M. Janowski (cnd), Dresden Staatskapelle, Leipzig Radio Chorus Berlin Classics 3–▲ BER 1108 [ADD]
With a Song in My Heart, w. Boston Pops Orch [cnd:John Williams] Philips ▲ 412625–2 PH [DDD]

Norman, Paul (bass)
Myers, G.:God's Trbn, w. Christine Helfrich (sop), Gordon Myers (bar), Richard Cragg (sgr), Matthew Gillis (sgr), Timothy Pehta (sgr), Wendy Catlin (sgr) Katherine Mary Hamilton (sgr), Sharon Hunter (sgr), Gloriae Dei Brass Ensemble Paraclete ▲ CDGD 017 [DDD]; ■ GDC 017

Northrop, P. (sgr)
Rodgers, R.:Pal Joey, w. H. Gallagher (sgr), E. Stritch (sgr) [1952 revival cast] Broadway Angel ▲ ZDM 64696 ■ EG 64696

Noska, B. (mez)
Epstein, P.A.:Songs (3) from "Home", w. Relâche Ensemble [E] Mode ▲ 22

Nosotti, Angelo (bass)
Catalani, A.:Edmea, w. M. Sokolinska Noto (sop), M. Frusoni (ten), M. Chingari (bar), P. Lefebvre (bass), G. Pasella (bass), G. del Vivo (bass), M. de Bernart (cnd), Lucca Teatro Comunale Giglio Orch, Lucca Teatro Comunale del Giglio Chorus [I] *(rec live 9/89)* Bongiovanni 2–▲ GB 2093/94 [DDD]
Mozart, W.A.:Nozze di Figaro, w. L. Cherici (sop), K. Mattila (sop), M. McLaughlin (sop), M. Bacelli (mez), N. Curiel (mez), U. Benelli (ten), L. Gallo (bar), M. Pertusi (bass), G. Tadeo (bass), Z. Mehta (cnd), Florence Maggio Musicale Orch, Florence Maggio Musicale Chorus Sony Classical ▲ SK 53286

Nossaman, Audrey (sop)
Hovhaness, A.:Magnificat, w. Elizabeth Johnson (cta), Thomas East (ten), Richard Dales (bar), R. Whitney (cnd), Louisville Orch, Univ of Louisville Choir Crystal ▲ CD 808

Nossek, Carola (sop)
Dessau, P.:Leonce & Lena, w. E. Büchner (bar), R. Süss (bar), O. Suitner (cnd), Berlin Staatskapelle Berlin Classics ▲ BER 1074 [ADD]

Nossek, Carola (sop) (cont.)
Pfitzner, H.:Palestrina, w. R. Long (mez), P. Schreier (ten), S. Lorenz (bar), E. Wlaschiha (bass), O. Suitner (cnd), Berlin Staatskapelle, Berlin State Opera Chorus Berlin Classics ▲ BER 1001

Noté, Jean (bar)
Historical Recordings, 1902–18 Cypres ▲ CYP 3603

Noto, Maria Sokolinska (sop)
Catalani, A.:Edmea, w. M. Frusoni (ten), M. Chingari (bar), P. Lefebvre (bass), A. Nosotti (bass), G. Pasella (bass), G. del Vivo (bass), M. de Bernart (cnd), Lucca Teatro Comunale Giglio Orch, Lucca Teatro Comunale del Giglio Chorus [I] *(rec live 9/89)* Bongiovanni 2–▲ GB 2093/94 [DDD]

Nova, Ettore (bass)
Salieri, A.:Axur, Re d'Ormus, w. A. Martin (bar), E. Mei (sop), C. Rayam (ten), A. Vespasiani (mez), M. Valenti (sop), R. Clemencic (cnd), Guido d'Arezzo Orch, Guido d'Arezzo Chorus [I] *(rec live 1989)* Nuova Era 3–▲ 6852/54 [DDD]

Novak (alt)
Mozart, W.A.:Missa, K.317, w. G. Fuchs (sop), Sailer (ten), H. Müller (bass), E. Hinreiner (cnd), Salzburg Mozarteum Orch, Salzburg Mozarteum Chorus [L] Pro Arte ▲ CDD 471 [DDD]

Novák, Richard (bass)
Dvořák, A.:Rusalka, w. G. Beňačková (sop), V. Soukupová (mez), W. Ochman (ten), V. Neumann (cnd), Czech PO, Prague Phil Chorus [Cz] Supraphon Collection ▲ 11 0617–2 [DDD]
Dvořák, A.:Rusalka, w. G. Beňačková (sop), V. Soukupová (mez), W. Ochman (ten), V. Neumann (cnd), Czech PO, Prague Phil Chorus [Cz] Supraphon 3–▲ 10 3641 [DDD]
Dvořák, A.:Rusalka (sels), w. Gabriela Beňačková (sop), Vera Soukupová (mez), V. Neumann (cnd), Czech PO, Czech Chorus Supraphon ▲ SUP 112252 [DDD]
Dvořák, A.:St Ludmilla, w. Vera Soukupová (mez), Eva Zikmundová (mez), Beno Blachut (ten), V. Smetáček (cnd), Prague SO, Czech Phil Chorus *(rec 1963)* Supraphon 2–▲ SUP 112141 [AAD]
Havelka, S.:Music of, w. Brigita Sulcova (sop), Anna Barova (cta), Vladimir Dolezal (ten), V. Neumann (cnd), Czech PO, Prague Phil Chorus—Epistola de M. Hieronymi De Praga Supplicio Panton ▲ PAN 810966
Janácek, L.:The Cunning Little Vixen, w. G. Beňačková (sop—Goldskin), M. Hajóssyová (sop—Cunning Little Vixen), R. Novák (bass—Forester), V. Neumann (cnd), Czech PO, Czech Phil Chorus, Kühn Children's Chorus [Cz] *(rec 1979–80)* Supraphon 2–▲ 10 3471–2 [AAD]
Janácek, L.:The Excursions of Mr. Brouček, w. Janá Jonaová (sop), Libuše Márová (mez), Vilém Přibyl (ten), Czech PO, Czech Phil Chorus Supraphon 2–▲ SUP 112153 [AAD]
Janácek, L.:From the House of the Dead, w. M. Jirglova (sop), V. Pribyl (ten), J. Horacek (bass), V. Neumann (cnd), Czech PO, Czech Phil Chorus [Cz] Supraphon 2–▲ SUP 10 2941 [AAD]
Janácek, L.:Slavonic Mass, w. Elisabeth Söderström (sop), Drahomira Drobkova (cta), František Livora (ten), C. Mackerras (cnd), Czech PO, Czech Phil Chorus Supraphon ▲ SUP 103575 [DDD]
Martinů, B.:Mount of 3 Lights, w. V. Dolezal (ten), P. Haničinec (nar), J. Hora (org), P. Kühn (cnd), Prague Radio Men's Chorus, Kühn Chorus [Cz] *(rec 2–3/88)* Supraphon ▲ 11 0751–2 [DDD]
Martinů, B.:The Prophecy of Isaiah, w. N. Romanová (sop), D. Drobková (alto), V. Kozderka (tpt), J. Peruška (va), I. Kiezlich (timp), S. Bogunia (pno), P. Kühn (cnd), Prague Radio Men's Chorus, Kühn Chorus [Cz] *(rec 2–3/88)* Supraphon ▲ 11 0751–2 [DDD]
Martinů, B.:Špalíček, w. A. Kratochvilová (sop), M. Kopp (ten), F. Jílek (cnd), Brno State PO, Kantiléna Children's Chorus [Cz] Supraphon 2–▲ 11 0752–2 [DDD]
Smetana, B.:The Bartered Bride, w. G. Beňačková (sop), P. Dvorsky (ten), Z. Košler (cnd), Czech PO, Czech Phil Chorus [Cz] Supraphon 3–▲ 10 3511–2 [DDD]

Novák, Richard (ten)
Martinů, B.:Alexandre bis, w. J. Krátká (sop), A. Barová (mez), R. Tuček (bar), F. Jílek (cnd), Brno Janáček Opera Orch Supraphon ▲ SUP 11 2140 [AAD]
Martinů, B.:Ariadne, w. C. Lindsley (sop), V. Dolezal (ten), N. Phillips (bar), V. Neumann (cnd), Czech PO, Czech Phil Chorus [Cz] Supraphon ▲ 10 4395–2 [DDD]
Martinů, B.:Comedy on the Bridge, w. J. Krátká (sop), A. Barová (mez), R. Tuček (bar), F. Jílek (cnd), Brno Janáček Opera Orch Supraphon ▲ SUP 11 2140 [AAD]
Martinů, B.:Hymn to St. James, w. N. Romanová (sop), D. Drobková (cta), P. Haničinec (nar), P. Kühn (cnd), Prague SO members, Prague Radio Chorus [Cz] *(rec 2–3/88)* Supraphon ▲ 11 0751–2 [DDD]
Ryba, J.J.:Czech Christmas Mass, w. L. Pešek (cnd), Dvořák CO, Kühn Chamber Choir Supraphon ▲ SUP 111007 [AAD]

Nováková, Alena (sop)
Janácek, L.:Šárka, w. A. Jurecka (ten), J. Válka (ten), K. Kunc (bass), B. Bakala (cnd), Brno RSO, Brno Radio Chorus *(rec live, 1953)* Multisonic ("Prague Spring Collection" series) ▲ 31 0154 [ADD]

Nováková, Ludmila (sop)
Janácek, L.:Fate, w. Lívia Ághová (sop—Míla), Ludmila Nováková (sop—Frl. Stuhlá/Součková), Marta Beňačková (cta—Mílas Mother), Štefan Margita (ten—Dr. Suda/Hrázda), Peter Straka (ten—Zivný), Ivan Kusnjer (bar—Konečný/Verva), Peter Mikuláš (bass—Lhotský), G. Albrecht (cnd), Czech PO, Prague Chamber Choir *(rec 1995)* Orfeo ▲ 384 951 [DDD]

Novelli, Francesco (bar)
Rossini, G.:Il barbiere di Siviglia (sels), w. M. Resemba (sop), N. Sabatano (sop), F. de Lucia (ten), G. Schottler (bass), A. di Tommaso (bass), S. Valentino (bass), S. Sassano (cnd), Naples Teatro San Carlo Orch, Naples Teatro San Carlo Chorus [I] *(rec 1918 for Phonotype)* Standing Room Only ▲ SRO 819–1 [ADD]
Verdi, G.:Aroldo, w. A. Stella (sop), G. Penno (ten), A. Protti (bar), T. Serafin (cnd), Florence Maggio Musicale Orch, Florence Maggio Musicale Chorus [I] *(rec live 6/3/53)* Melodram 2–▲ MEL 27014 (m) [AAD]

Novelli, Ugo (bass)
Verdi, G.:Un ballo in maschera, w. Maria Caniglia (sop—Amelia), Fedora Barbieri (mez—Ulrica), Beniamino Gigli (ten—Riccardo), Gino Bechi (bar—Renato), Tancredi Pasero (bass—Samuel), Blando Giusti (sgr—Un Giudice), Nicola Niccolini (sgr—Silvano), Ugo Novelli (sgr—Tom), Elda Ribetti (sgr—Oscar), T. Serafin (cnd), Rome Opera Orch, Giuseppe Conca (cnd), Rome Opera Chorus *(rec 1943)* Arkadia 2–▲ CD 78005 (m) [ADD]

Novotná, Jarmila (sop)
Beethoven, L. van:Sym 9, "Choral Sym", w. Kerstin Thorborg (mez), Jan Peerce (ten), Nicola Moscona (bass), A. Toscanini (cnd), NBC SO, Westminster Choir *(rec New York City, 1939)* Grammofono 2000 ▲ GRM 78524 (m)
Beethoven, L. van:Sym 9, "Choral Sym", w. Kerstin Thorborg (mez), Jan Pierce (ten), Nicola Moscona (bass), A. Toscanini (cnd), NBC SO, Westminster Choir *(rec 1939)* LYS ▲ LYS 128 Pearl ▲ PEA 9467 (m) [AAD]
Jarmila Novotna
Lehár, F.:Music of, w. E. Réthy (sop), M. Reining (sop), R. Tauber (ten), F. Lehár (cnd), Vienna SO, Vienna PO—6 orchestral sels. *(Musikalische Memorien I-IV; Die lustige Witwe—Overture; Eva—Prelude)*; 4 Arias from Giuditta *(Du bist meine Sonne—Tauber; Freunde, das Leben ist lebenswert—Tauber; Schön wie die blaue Sommernacht—Novotna & Tauber; Schönste der Frauen—Tauber)*; 1 Song & 5 Arias sung by Esther Rethy *(Wien, du bist das Herz der Welt; Giuditta—Meine Lippen, sie küssenso heiss; Paganini—Liebe, du Himmel auf Erden; Schön ist die Welt—Ich bin verliebt; Der Zarewitsch—Einer wird kommen; Zigeunerliebe—Hör ich Cymbalklänge)*; 2 Arias sung by Maria Reining *(Eva—Im heimlichen Dämmer der silbernen Ampel; Friederike—Warum hast du mich wachgeküsst?) (rec 1934–1942 Odeon & HMV rec)* Preiser ▲ 90150 (m) [AAD]

Novotná, Jarmila (sop) (cont.)
Mozart, W.A.:Arias, w. Arleen Augér (sop), Kathleen Battle (sop), Irma Beilke (sop), Helena Braun (sop), Lisa Della Casa (sop), Maria Cebotari (sop), Ileana Cotrubas (sop), Helen Donath (sop), Mirella Freni (sop), Reri Grist (sop), Edita Gruberova (sop), Elisabeth Grümmer (sop), Hilde Güden (sop), Ingeborg Hallstein (sop), Luise Helletsgruber (sop), Gundula Janowitz (sop), Sena Jurinac (sop), Erika Köth (sop), Evelyn Lear (sop), Wilma Lipp (sop), Margaret Marshall (sop), Edith Mathis (sop), Margherita Perras (sop), Lucia Popp (sop), Elisabeth Rethberg (sop), Anneliese Rothenberger (sop), Elisabeth Schumann (sop), Elisabeth Schwarzkopf (sop), Graziella Sciutti (sop), Irmgard Seefried (sop), Graziella Sciutti (sop), Julia Varady (sop), Agnes Baltsa (mez), Margit Bokor (mez), Brigitte Fassbaender (mez), Christa Ludwig (mez), Ann Murray (mez), Francisco Araiza (ten), Anton Dermota (ten), Helge Rosvaenge (ten), Rudolf Schock (ten), Peter Schreier (ten), Leopold Simoneau (ten), Eric Tappy (ten), Richard Tauber (ten), Gösta Winbergh (ten), Josef Witt (ten), Fritz Wunderlich (ten), Christian Boesch (bar), Willy Domgraf-Fassbaender (bar), Karl Dönch (bar), Dietrich Fischer-Dieskau (bar), Erich Kunz (bar), Eberhard Wächter (bar), Hans Hotter (b-bar), Paul Schöffler (b-bar), Cesare Siepi (b-bar), José Van Dam (b-bar), Walter Berry (bass), Geraint Evans (bass), Nicolai Ghiaurov (bass), Alexander Kipnis (bass), Richard Mayr (bass), Kurt Moll (bass), James Morris (bass), Ezio Pinza (bass), Martti Talvela (bass), Giorgio Tozzi (bass), Hans Duhan (sgr), Res Fischer (sgr), Marie Gerhart (sgr), *(various orchs & cnds)*—sels from Idomeneo, Die Entführung aus der Serail, Le nozze di Figaro, Don Giovanni, Così fan tutte, Die Zauberflöte & various arias — Orfeo d'or ("Festspiel Dokumente" series) 5-▲ 408955
Mozart, W.A.:Don Giovanni, w. Rose Bampton (sop), Bidú Sayão (sop), Charles Kullman (ten), Alexander Kipnis (bass), Ezio Pinza (bass), B. Walter (cnd), *(orch unknown)* *(rec Mar 7, 1942)* — Enterprise ("The Fourties" series) 3-▲ ENT 301
Mozart, W.A.:Nozze di Figaro, w. Bidu Sayao (sop—Susanna), Eleanor Steber (sop—Countess Almaviva), Jarmila Novotna (sop—Cherubino), Ira Petina (sop—Marcellina), John Brownlee (bar—Count Almaviva), Salvatore Baccaloni (bass—Bartolo), Ezio Pinza (bass—Figaro), B. Walter (cnd), *(orch unknown)* — The Fourties 2-▲ ENT FT 1509
Mozart, W.A.:Nozze di Figaro, w. Aulikki Rautawaara (sop), Esther Réthy (sop), Agostino Lazzari (ten), Mariano Stabile (bar), Ezio Pinza (bass), B. Walter (cnd), Vienna PO, Vienna State Opera Chorus *(rec live, 1937)* — Melodram ▲ CDI 205003
Mozart, W.A.:Zauberflöte, w. Helge Roswaenge (ten), Alexander Kipnis (bass), Julie Osvath (sgr), A. Toscanini (cnd), Vienna PO, Vienna State Opera Chorus — Enterprise ("The 40's" series) 2-▲ ENT 321
Mozart, W.A.:Zauberflöte, w. D. Komarek (sop), J. Osvath (sop), H. Roswaenge (ten), W. Domgraf-Fassbaender (bar), A. Kipnis (bass), A. Toscanini (cnd), Vienna PO, Vienna Phil Chorus [G] *(rec live, Salzburg, July 30, 1937)* — Melodram 3-▲ MEL 37040 (m) [AAD]
Offenbach, J.:Les Contes d'Hoffmann, w. Patrice Munsel (sop), Raoul Jobin (ten), Ezio Pinza (bass), T. Beecham (cnd), Metropolitan Opera Orch, New York Metropolitan Opera Chorus *(rec Feb 26, 1944)* — Enterprise ("The Radio Years") 2-▲ ENT-19 (m)

Novotný, Jiří (sgr)
Bruckner, A.:Mass 3, w. Dagmar Masková (sgr), Vladimír Nacházel (sgr), Jiří Seiler (sgr), Jiří Uherek (sgr), Eva Zbytovská (sgr), Jan Votava (trbn), Josef Kšica (org), Josef Pancík (cnd), Prague Chamber Choir — Orfeo ▲ 327 951 [DDD]
Bruckner, A.:Motets, w. Dagmar Masková (sgr), Vladimír Nacházel (sgr), Jiří Seiler (sgr), Jiří Uherek (sgr), Eva Zbytovská (sgr), Jan Votava (trbn), Josef Kšica (org), Josef Pancík (cnd), Prague Chamber Choir—Locus iste; Afferentur regi; Ave Maria (2); Pange lingua; Pange lingua (phrygisch); Tantum ergo (2); Libera me; Os iusti; Virga jesse; Vexilla regis; Christus factus est; Tota pulchra es Maria; Ecce sacerdos magnus — Orfeo ▲ 327 951 [DDD]

Nowacki, Piotr (bass)
Elsner, J.:Passio Domini Nostri Jesu Christi, w. Bozena Harasimowicz (sop), Krzysztof Szmyt (ten), Czeslaw Galka (bar), Bogdan Sliwa (bar), K. Kord (cnd), Warsaw PO, Henryk Wojnarowski (cnd), Ewa Marchwicka (cnd), Warsaw National Phil Chorus, E. Mlynarski State School of Music Children's Choir *(rec National Philharmonic, Warsaw, 1990)* — Polskie Nagrania ▲ PNCD 078 [DDD]
Elsner, J.:Passio Domini Nostri Jesu Christi, w. B. Harasimowicz (sop), K. Szmyt (ten), C. Galka (bar), K. Kord (cnd), Warsaw National Philharmonic SO, Warsaw National Philharmonic Sym Chorus *(rec 1990)* — Muza ▲ PNCD 078 [DDD]
Penderecki, K.:Als Jakob erwachte, w. Jadwiga Gadulanka (sop), Zahos Terzakis (ten), K. Penderecki (cnd), Royal Stockholm PO, Stockholm Royal Theater Opera Chorus — Chandos 2-▲ CHAN 9459
Penderecki, K.:Polish Requiem, w. Jadwiga Gadulanka (sop), Zahos Terzakis (ten), K. Penderecki (cnd), Royal Stockholm PO, Stockholm Royal Theater Opera Chorus — Chandos 2-▲ CHAN 9459

Nowak, Michael (sgr)
Míča, F.A.:L'origine di Jaromeriz in Moravia, w. Geraldine Cassidy (sgr), Manfred Equiluz (sgr), Geraldine Geister (sgr), Le Monde Classique [Cz] — Supraphon 2-▲ SUP 112192 [DDD]
Straus, O.:The Merry Nibelungs, w. Lisa Griffith (sop—Kriemhild), Gudrun Volkert (sop—Brunhilde), Daphne Evangelatos (cta—Ute), Gabriele Henkel (sgr—Giselher), Christine Mann (sgr—Vogel), Hein Heidbüchel (ten—Volker), Martin Gantner (sgr—Gunther), Gerd Grochowski (sgr—Dankwart), Michael Nowak (sgr—Siegfried), Josef Otten (sgr—Hagen), S. Köhler (cnd), Cologne RSO, Cologne Radio Chorus *(rec Cologne, Jan 31–Feb 17, 1995)* — Capriccio ▲ 10752 [DDD]

Nowicka, Barbara (mez)
Gluck, C.W.:La Corona, w. A. Slowakiewicz (sop), H. Gorzynska (sop), L. Juranek (sop), T. Bugaj (cnd), Warsaw Sinfonia [I] — Orfeo 2-▲ 135872 [DDD]

Nowkovski, Marian (bass)
Elgar, E.:The Dream of Gerontius, w. C. Shacklock (mez), J. Vickers (ten), J. Barbirolli (cnd), Rome Radio Orch, Rome RAI Chorus [E] *(rec live, Rome 11/20/57)* — Arkadia 2-▲ 584 [ADD]
Mozart, W.A.:Requiem, w. Elsie Morison (sop), Monica Sinclair (cta), Alexander Young (ten), T. Beecham (cnd), Royal PO, BBC Sym Chorus *(rec 1958)* — Theorema ▲ TH 121151

Nucci, Leo (bar)
Cecilia Gasdia, Leo Nucci & Ruggero Raimondi:In Concerto, w. Cecilia Gasdia (sop), Ruggero Raimondi (bass) — Bongiovanni ▲ GB 2516-2
Cilea, F.:Adriana Lecouvreur, w. J. Sutherland (sop), C. Bergonzi (ten), R. Bonynge (cnd), Welsh National Opera Orch, Welsh National Opera Chorus — London 2-▲ 425815-2 [DDD]
Donizetti, G.:Don Pasquale, w. M. Freni (sop), G. Winbergh (ten), S. Bruscantini (bar), R. Muti (cnd), Philharmonia Orch, Ambrosian Opera Chorus — EMI Classics 2-▲ CDCB 47068
Donizetti, G.:Don Pasquale (sels), w. M. Freni (sop), G. Winbergh (ten), S. Bruscantini (bar), R. Muti (cnd), Philharmonia Orch, Ambrosian Opera Chorus — EMI Classics ▲ CDC 54490
Donizetti, G.:L'elisir d'amore, w. K. Battle (sop), D. Upshaw (sop), L. Pavarotti (ten), E. Dara (bar), J. Levine (cnd), Metropolitan Orch, New York Metropolitan Opera Chorus — Deutsche Grammophon 2-▲ 429744-2 [DDD]
Donizetti, G.:Maria di Rudenz, w. Katia Ricciarelli (sop), Alberto Cupido (ten), E. Inbal (cnd), Venice Teatro La Fenice Orch, Venice Teatro La Fenice Chorus — Serenissima 2-▲ SER 360157 [DDD]
Giordano, U.:Andrea Chénier, w. M. Caballé (sop), L. Pavarotti (ten), R. Chailly (cnd), National PO London [I] — London 2-▲ 410117-2 [DDD]
Mozart, W.A.:Idomeneo, w. L. Popp (sop), E. Gruberova (sop), A. Baltsa (mez), L. Pavarotti (ten), J. Pritchard (cnd), Vienna PO, Vienna State Opera Chorus [I] — London 3-▲ 411805-2 [DDD]
Puccini, G.:La Rondine, w. M. Nicolesco (sop), K. Te Kanawa (sop), P. Domingo (ten), D. Rendall (ten), L. Maazel (cnd), London SO, Ambrosian Opera Chorus [I] — CBS 2-▲ M2K 37852 [DDD]
Puccini, G.:Tosca (sels), w. K. Te Kanawa (sop), J. Aragall (ten), G. Solti (cnd), National PO London, Welsh National Opera Chorus — London ▲ 421611-2 [DDD]
Puccini, G.:Il trittico, w. M. Freni (sop), E. Souliois (sop), G. Giacomini (ten), R. Alagna (ten), J. Pons (bar), B. Bartoletti (cnd), Florence Maggio Musicale Orch, Florence Maggio Musicale Chorus — London 3-▲ 436261-2 [DDD]
Puccini, G.:Le Villi, w. R. Scotto (sop), P. Domingo (ten), T. Gobbi (bar), L. Maazel (cnd), London National PO, Ambrosian Chorus [I] — CBS ▲ MK 36669 [ADD]
Rossini, G.:Il barbiere di Siviglia, w. M. Horne (mez), E. Dara (bar), S. Ramey (bass), R. Chailly (cnd), La Scala Orch, La Scala Chorus [I] — CBS 3-▲ M3K 37862 [DDD]
Rossini, G.:Il barbiere di Siviglia, w. C. Bartoli (mez), W. Matteuzzi (ten), P. Burchuladze (bass), G. Patanè (cnd), Bologna Teatro Comunale Orch, Bologna Teatro Comunale Chorus [I] — London 3-▲ 425520-2 [DDD]
Rossini, G.:Il barbiere di Siviglia (sels), w. C. Bartoli (mez), W. Matteuzzi (ten), P. Burchuladze (bass), G. Patanè (cnd), Bologna Teatro Comunale Orch, Bologna Teatro Comunale Chorus — London ▲ 440289-2 [DDD]

Nucci, Leo (bar) (cont.)
Rossini, G.:Il barbiere di Siviglia (sels), w. M. Horne (mez), R. Pierotti (mez), P. Barbacini (ten), E. Dara (bar), S. Ramey (bass), S. Sammaritano (bass), R. Chailly (cnd), La Scala Orch, La Scala Chorus *(rec Milan, Jan. 2–18, 1982)* — Sony Classical ("Opera Highlights" series) ▲ SMK 53501 [DDD]
Rossini, G.:Il turco in Italia, w. M. Caballé (sop), E. Dara (bar), S. Ramey (bass), R. Chailly (cnd), National PO London, Ambrosian Opera Chorus [I] — CBS 2-▲ M2K 37859 [DDD]
Verdi, G.:Aida, w. M. Chiara (sop), G. Dimitrova (sop), L. Pavarotti (ten), P. Burchuladze (bass), L. Maazel (cnd), La Scala Orch, La Scala Chorus [I] — London 3-▲ 417439-2 [DDD] 2-∎ 417439-4
Verdi, G.:Aida, w. K. Ricciarelli (sop), E. Obraztsova (mez), P. Domingo (ten), N. Ghiaurov (bass), C. Abbado (cnd), La Scala Orch, La Scala Chorus [I] — Deutsche Grammophon ▲ 435410-2 [DDD]
Verdi, G.:Aida, w. M. Chiara (sop), G. Dimitrova (sop), L. Pavarotti (ten), P. Burchuladze (bass), L. Maazel (cnd), La Scala Orch, La Scala Chorus [I] — London □ 433162-5
Verdi, G.:Aida, w. K. Ricciarelli (sop), E. Obraztsova (mez), P. Domingo (ten), N. Ghiaurov (bass), C. Abbado (cnd), La Scala Orch, La Scala Chorus [I] — Deutsche Grammophon 3-▲ 410092-2 [DDD]
Verdi, G.:Arias, w. K. Battle (sop), J. Sutherland (sop), J. Anderson (sop), M. Price (sop), L. Pavarotti (ten)—includes favorite arias from Aida, Ballo in maschera, Don Carlos, Nabucco, Rigoletto, Traviata, Trovatore — London ("Ovation" series) ▲ 430748-2 [DDD]
Verdi, G.:Un ballo in maschera, w. J. Barstow (sop), S. Jo (sop), F. Quivar (mez), P. Domingo (ten), H. von Karajan (cnd), Vienna PO, Vienna State Opera Chorus [I] — Deutsche Grammophon 2-▲ 427635-2 [DDD]
Verdi, G.:Otello, w. K. Te Kanawa (sop), L. Pavarotti (ten), G. Solti (cnd), Chicago SO, Chicago Sym Chorus [I] — London 2-▲ 433669-2 [DDD]
Verdi, G.:Rigoletto (sels), w. J. Anderson (sop), S. Verrett (mez), L. Pavarotti (ten), N. Ghiaurov (bass), R. Chailly (cnd), Bologna Teatro Comunale Orch, Bologna Teatro Comunale Chorus — London ▲ 436097-2 [DDD]
Verdi, G.:Simon Boccanegra, w. K. Te Kanawa (sop), J. Aragall (ten), P. Burchuladze (bass), G. Solti (cnd), La Scala Orch, La Scala Chorus [I] — London 2-▲ 425628-2 [DDD]
Verdi, G.:La traviata, w. Angela Gheorghiu (sop—Violetta), Leah-Marian Jones (mez—Flora Bervoix), Gillian Knight (mez—Annina), Robin Leggate (ten—Gastone), Frank Lopardo (ten—Alfredo Germont), Rodney Gibson (ten—Servo di Flora), Neil Griffiths (ten—Giuseppe), Mark Beesley (bar—Dottore Grenvile), Leo Nucci (bar—Giorgio Germont), Richard Van Allan (bass—Barone Douphol), Roderick Earle (bass—Marquese d'Obigny), Bryan Secombe (bass—Commissionario), G. Solti (cnd), Royal Opera House Orch, Royal Opera House Chorus Covent Garden *(rec live, Royal Opera House, Covent Garden, Dec. 1994)* — London 2-▲ 448119-2
Verdi, G.:Il trovatore, w. Antonella Banaudi (sop—Leonora), Barbara Frittoli (sop—Ines), Shirley Verrett (mez—Azucena), Enrico Facini (ten—Un messo), Piero de Palma (ten—Ruiz), Luciano Pavarotti (ten—Marico), Leo Nucci (bar—Il Conte di Luna), Roberto Scaltriti (bar—Un vecchio zingaro), Francesco Ellero d'Artegna (bass—Ferrando), Z. Mehta (cnd), Florence Maggio Musicale Orch, Florence Maggio Musicale Chorus *(rec Maggio Musicale Fiorentino Community Theater, June 18–July 2, 1990)* — London 2-▲ 430694-2

Nun, Efrat Ben (sop)
Monteverdi, C.:Orfeo, w. Efrat Ben Nun (sop—Euridice), Laurence Dale (ten—Orfeo), R. Jacobs (cnd), Concerto Vocale — Harmonia Mundi France ▲ HMC 901553.54

Nurmela, Karl (bar)
Leoncavallo, R.:Pagliacci, w. M. Caballé (sop), R. Scotto (sop), A. Varnay (mez), J. Hamari (mez), J. Carreras (ten), M. Manuguerra (bar), T. Allen (bar), U. Benelli (bar), R. Muti (cnd), Philharmonia Orch, Ambrosian Opera Chorus — EMI Classics 2-▲ CDMB 63650
Leoncavallo, R.:Pagliacci, w. M. Sighele (sop), R. Tucker (ten), E. Lorenzi (ten), R. Muti (cnd), Florence Teatro Comunale Orch, Florence Teatro Comunale Chorus *(rec live, Florence, 1971)* — Foyer ▲ FOY 2050 [AAD]
Leoncavallo, R.:Pagliacci (sels), w. R. Scotto (sop), J. Carreras (ten), R. Muti (cnd), Philharmonia Orch, Ambrosian Opera Chorus — EMI Classics ("Studio" series) ▲ CDM 63933 ∎ EG 63933

Nuvoli, Mario (ten)
Scarlatti, A.:Abramo, il tuo sembiante, w. S. Piccolo (sop), L. Bacchetta (sop), M. Lazzara (alt), G. Dagnino (bass), E. Velardi (cnd), Alessandro Stradella Consort [period instrs] [I] — Nuova Era ("Ancient Music" series) ▲ 7117 [DDD]
Stradella, A.:Esule dalle sfere, w. Roberta Invernizzi (sop), Silvia Piccolo (sop), Marco Lazzara (alt), Riccardo Ristori (bass), Carlo Lepore (bass), Alessandro Stradella Consort — Bongiovanni ▲ GB 2165 [DDD]
Stradella, A.:O di Cocito oscure deità, w. R. Invernizzi (sop—Proserpina), S. Piccolo (sop—Vendetta), M. Nuvoli (ten—Inganno), R. Ristori (bass—Plutone), E. Velardi (cnd), Alessandro Stradella Consort *(rec Oct. 25, 1993)* — Bongiovanni ▲ GB 2164 [DDD]
Stradella, A.:Lo schiavo liberto, w. R. Invernizzi (sop—Armida), M. Lazzara (cta—Rinaldo), M. Nuvoli (ten—Carlo), R. Ristori (bass—Ubaldo), E. Velardi (cnd), Alessandro Stradella Consort *(rec Nov. 15, 1993)* — Bongiovanni ▲ GB 2164 [DDD]
Stradella, A.:Susanna, w. S. Piccolo (sop), L. Bertotti (sop), M. Lazzara (cta), M. Perrella (bass), E. Velardi (cnd), Camerata Ligure [period instrs] [I] — Bongiovanni 2-▲ GB 2121/22 [DDD]

Nyborg, Anders (nar)
Nørholm, I.:Sym 2, w. E. Serov (cnd), Odense SO — Kontrapunkt ▲ KPT 32182 [DDD]

Nylund, Camilla (sop)
Heiniö, M.:Hermes, w. Juhani Lagerspetz (pno), J. Kangas (cnd), Ostrobothnian CO — Ondine ▲ ODE 870

Nyman, Tom (nar)
Aho, K.:Pergamon, w. L. Paasikivi (nar), E.-L. Saarinen (nar), M. Lehtinen (nar), P. Pietiläinen (org), O. Vänskä (cnd), Lahti SO *(rec Lahti, Finland, May 23–25, 1994)* — BIS ▲ CD 646 [DDD]

Nyzankowskyi, Oleg de (ten)
Martin, F.:Le Vin herbé, w. B. Retchitzka (sop), H. Morath (cta), H. Rehfuss (bar), D. Olsen (bass), F. Martin (pno), V. Desarzens (cnd), Winterthur State Orch members — Jecklin-Disco 2-▲ JD 581/2-2 [ADD]

Oak, Ellen (sgr)
Hildegard Of Bingen:Sacred Music—O frondens virga; Quia ergo femina; Hodie aperuit; O viridissima virga; O tu illustrata; Karitas; Ave generosa; O rubor sanguinis; O Ecclesia; Favus distillans; O pulcre facies; O choruscans lux stellarum; O virtus Sapientiae; Kyrie eleison; O gloriosissimi; Spiritus Sanctus vificans vita *(rec live, Benedictine Monastery, Clyde, MO)* — Bison Tales ▲ BT 0001 ∎ BT 0002

Oakman, John (ten)
Golden Melodies from Opera, w. R. Hickox (cnd), London SO, Royal PO [cnd:R. Stapelton], S. McCulloch (sop), Josephine Barstow (sop), Edmund Barham (ten) — Pickwick ("The Orchid" series) ▲ PICORCD 11005

Oancea, George (nar)
The Passion & Ressurrection of Jesus, w. [cnd:Marin Constantin], Madrigal Chamber Choir — Electrecord ▲ ELC 136 [DDD]

Obadia, Hélène (sop)
Bach, J.S.:Magnificat, BWV 243, w. Brigitte Vinson (sop), Madeleine Jalabert (alt), Hervé Lamy (ten), Philip Langshaw (bass), P. Kuentz (cnd), Paul Kuentz Orch, Paul Kuentz Choir — Pierre Verany ▲ PVY 730048
Bach, J.S.:Mass in b, BWV 232, w. Madeleine Jalbert (alt), Adrian Brand (ten), Paul Gay (bass), Eric Aubier (tpt), P. Kuentz (cnd), Paul Kuentz Orch, Paul Kuentz Choir — Pierre Verany ▲ PVY 730060 [DDD]

Obata, Machiko (sop)
Zemlinsky, A. von:Der Geburtstag der Infantin, w. Soile Isokoski (sop), Iride Martinez (sgr), Andrew Collis (sgr), David Kuebler (ten), Juanita Lascarro (sgr), Anne Schwanewilms (sgr), Natalie Karl (sgr), Martina Rüping (sgr), Franfurter Kantorei (sgr), J. Conlon (cnd), Gürzenich Orch, Cologne PO *(rec Cologne, Feb 1996)* — EMI Classics 2-▲ CDCB 56208

Oberholtzer, William (bar)
Vivaldi, A.:L'Olimpiade, w. L. Meeuwsen (sop), M. van der Sluis (sop), E. von Magnus (alt), G. Lesne (alt), A. Christofelis (alt), A. Walker Schultze (bass), R. Clemencic (cnd), Clemencic Consort, La Cappella Vocal Ensemble [I] *(rec live, Paris, 2/8–10/90)* — Nuova Era ("Ancient Music" series) 2-▲ 6932/33 [DDD]

▲ = CD ♦ = Enhanced CD Δ = MD ∎ = Cassette Tape □ = DCC

Oberlin, Russell (ct)
Byrd, W.:Songs, w. In Nomine Players—La Virginella; My Sweet Little Darling; What Pleasure Have Great Princes; Though Amaryllis Dance in Green; Blessed Is He That Fears the Lord; O Lord, How Long Wilt Thou Forget; The Man Is Blesst That God Doth Fear; Why Do I Use My Paper, Ink, and Pen Lyrichord ▲ LEMS 8014
Dowland, J.:Lt Songs, w. Joseph Iadone (lt)—Come Again! Sweet Love Doth Now Invite; Thou Mighty God; Can She Excuse My Wrongs?; Sempre Douland, Sempre Dolens; Flow So Fast, Ye Fountain; I Saw My Lady Weep; Weep You No More, Sad Fountains; Shall I Sue?; Flow My Tears; Lachrimae antiquae pavan; Far from Triumphing Court; Lady, If You So Spite Me; In Darkness Let Me Dwell Lyrichord ▲ LEM 8011
Handel, G.F.:Messiah (sels), w. Adele Addison (sop), Edward Lloyd (ten), William Warfield (bar), L. Bernstein (cnd), New York PO, Westminster Choir [E] CBS ▲ MYK 38481 ■ MYT 38481
Music of the Middle Ages, Vol. 3, w. J. Ladone (lt) Lyrichord ▲ LYR 8003 [ADD]
Music of the Middle Ages, Vol. 4:English Polyphony of the 13th & Early 14th Centuries, w. C. Bressler (ten), D. Perry (ten), S. Barab (vl), M. Blackman (vl) Lyrichord ▲ LYR 8004 [ADD]
Music of the Middle Ages, Vol. 5:English Medieval Songs of the 12th & 13th Centuries, w. S. Barab (vl) Lyrichord ▲ LYR 8005 [ADD]
Music of the Middle Ages, Vol. 6:English Polyphony of the 14th & Early 15th Centuries, w. C. Bressler (ten), R. Price (ten), G. Meyers (bar), M. Blackman (vl) Lyrichord ▲ LYR 8006 [ADD]
Music of the Middle Ages, Vol. 7, w. French Ars Antiqua, Charles Bressler (ten), R. Price (ten), G. Meyers (bar), M. Blackman (vl), P. Wolfe (org) Lyrichord ▲ LYR 8007 [ADD]
Notre Dame Organa Leonius & Perotinus Magister, w. C. Bressler (ten), D. Perry (ten), S. Barab (vl) Lyrichord ▲ LYR 8002 [ADD]
Troubadour & Trouvere Songs, w. S. Barab (vl) Lyrichord ▲ LYR 8001 [ADD]

Obraztsov, Anatoly (bass)
Gretchaninoff, A.:Mass "Et in terra pax", w. Ludmila Golub (org), Valéri Polianski (cnd), Russian State Symphonic Cappella Chandos ▲ CHAN 9486

Obraztsova, Elena (mez)
Bizet, G.:Carmen, w. P. Domingo (ten), J. Mazurok (bar), C. Kleiber (cnd), Vienna State Opera Orch, Vienna State Opera Chorus Exclusive 2-▲ EXL 11 [ADD]
Borodin, A.:Prince Igor, w. Elana Obraztsova (mez—Konchakovna), Tatiana Tugarinova (mez—Yaroslavna), Vladimir Atlantov (ten—Vladimir Igoryevich), Artur Eisen (bass—Vladimir Galitsky), Ivan Petrov (bass—Igor Svyatoslavich), Alexander Vedernikov (bass—Konchak), M. Ermler (cnd), Bolshoi Theater Orch, Bolshoi Theater Chorus *(rec Moscow, 1969)* Melodiya ("The Russian Opera" series) 3-▲ 74321-29346-2 [ADD]
Cilea, F.:Adriana Lecouvreur, w. R. Scotto (sop), P. Domingo (ten), S. Milnes (bar), J. Levine (cnd), Philharmonia Orch *(rec 1977)* CBS 2-▲ M2K 34588 [ADD]
Khachaturian, A.:Ode to Joy, w. A. Khachaturian (cnd), USSR Radio-TV Large SO, USSR Radio-TV Large Sym Chorus Russian Disc ▲ RUS 11 014 [AAD]
Mascagni, P.:Cavalleria rusticana, w. F. Barbieri (mez), P. Domingo (ten), R. Bruson (bar), G. Prêtre (cnd), La Scala Orch, La Scala Chorus [I] Philips ▲ 416137-2 [DDD]
Mascagni, P.:Cavalleria rusticana, w. Elena Obraztsova (mez—Santuzza), Placido Domingo (ten—Turridu), G. Prêtre (cnd), La Scala Orch, La Scala Chorus Philips ("Duo" series) 2-▲ 454 265-2
Prokofiev, S.:Alexander Nevsky, w. C. Abbado (cnd), London SO, London Sym Chorus Deutsche Grammophon ("The Originals" series) ▲ 447419-2
Prokofiev, S.:Alexander Nevsky, w. C. Abbado (cnd), London SO, London Sym Chorus [R] Deutsche Grammophon ▲ 419603-2 [DDD]
Prokofiev, S.:Alexander Nevsky, w. C. Abbado (cnd), London SO, London Sym Chorus [R] Deutsche Grammophon 3-▲ 435151-2
Saint-Saëns, C.:Samson et Dalila, w. P. Domingo (ten), R. Bruson (bar), R. Lloyd (b-bar), D. Barenboim (cnd), Orch de Paris Deutsche Grammophon 2-▲ 413297-2 [ADD]
Verdi, G.:Aida, w. K. Ricciarelli (sop), P. Domingo (ten), L. Nucci (bar), N. Ghiaurov (bass), C. Abbado (cnd), La Scala Orch, La Scala Chorus [I] Deutsche Grammophon 3-▲ 410092-2 [DDD]
Verdi, G.:Aida, w. K. Ricciarelli (sop), P. Domingo (ten), L. Nucci (bar), N. Ghiaurov (bass), C. Abbado (cnd), La Scala Orch, La Scala Chorus [I] Deutsche Grammophon ▲ 435410-2 [DDD]

Obukhova, Nadezhda (mez)
The Great Russian Mezzo-Soprano Pearl ▲ PEA CD 9200

Ocal, Bruhan (voc/perc)
Zawinul, J.:Stories of the Danube, w. Joe Zawinul (kbd), Walter Grassman (dr), C. Richter (cnd), Brno State PO Philips ▲ 454143-2

Ochman, Wieslaw (ten)
Ave Maria, w. Bozena Betley (sop), Leonard Mróz (bass), Marian Sawa (org) Polskie Nagrania Edition ▲ ECD 049 [DDD]
Beethoven, L. van:Missa Solemnis, w. Margaret Price (sop), Christa Ludwig (mez), Martti Talvela (bass), K. Böhm (cnd), Vienna PO, Vienna State Opera Chorus *(rec 1957)* Deutsche Grammophon ("Double" series) 2-▲ 437386-2 [ADD]
Bruckner, A.:Mass 1, w. E. Mathis (sop), M. Schiml (sop), K. Ridderbusch (bass), E. Jochum (cnd), Bavarian RSO, Bavarian Radio Chorus [L] Deutsche Grammophon 4-▲ 423127-2 [ADD]
Bruckner, A.:Mass 1, w. E. Mathis (sop), M. Schiml (mez), K. Ridderbusch (bass), E. Jochum (cnd), Bavarian RSO, Bavarian Radio Chorus Deutsche Grammophon ("The Originals" series) 2-▲ 447409-2
Dvořák, A.:Armida, w. Joanna Borowska (sop—Armida), Monika Brychtová (sgr—Siren), Wieslaw Ochman (ten—Rinald), Richard Sporka (ten—Dudo), Jan Markvart (bar—Sven), Pavel Daniluk (bass—King), George Fortune (bass—Ismen), Zdenek Harvánek (bass—Ubald), Miloslav Podskalský (bass—Peter), Milan Bürger (sgr—Gernand), Roman Janál (sgr—Muezzin/Hlasatel), Vratislav Kříz (sgr—Gottfried), Vladimír Nacházel (sgr—Roger), G. Albrecht (cnd), Czech PO, Prague Chamber Choir *(rec 1995)* Orfeo 2-▲ 404962 [DDD]
Dvořák, A.:Rusalka, w. G. Beňačkova (sop), V. Soukupová (mez), R. Novák (bass), V. Neumann (cnd), Czech PO, Prague Phil Chorus [Cz] Supraphon 3-▲ 10 3641 [DDD]
Dvořák, A.:Rusalka, w. G. Beňačkova (sop), V. Soukupová (mez), R. Novák (bass), V. Neumann (cnd), Czech PO, Prague Phil Chorus [Cz] Supraphon Collection ▲ 11 0617-2 [DDD]
Janácek, L.:Jenůfa, w. L. Popp (sop), E. Söderström (sop), E. Randová (mez), M. Dvorsky (ten), C. Mackerras (cnd), Vienna PO [Cz] London 2-▲ 414483-2 [DDD]
Janácek, L.:Jenůfa, w. G. Benačková (sop), L. Rysanek (sop), P. Kazaras (ten), E. Queler (cnd), New York City Opera Orch [Cz] *(rec live at Carnegie Hall, Mar. 30, 1988)* BIS 2-▲ CD 449/50 [DDD]
Moniuszko, S.:Halka, w. B. Zagòrzanka (sop), R. Racewicz (mez), A. Hiolski (bar), J. Ostapuik (bass), R. Satanowski (cnd), Warsaw Teatr Wielki Orch, Warsaw Teatr Wielki Chorus *(rec live, 10/14/86)* CPO 2-▲ CPO 999032-2 [DDD]
Moniuszko, S.:Haunted Manor, w. Bozena Betley-Siradzka (sop—Hanna), Anna Witkowska (sop—Marta/Stara Niewiasta), Wiera Baniewicz (mez—Jadwiga), Aleksandra Imalska (mez—Czesnikowa), Kazimierz Dluha (Grzes), Zdzislaw Nikodem (ten—Damazy), Wieslaw Ochman (ten—Stefan), Andrzej Hiolski (bar—Miecznik), Florian Skulski (bar—Maciej), Leonard Mróz (bass—Zbigniew), Andrzej Saciuk (bass—Skoluba), J. Krenz (cnd), Cracow Polish Radio-TV Orch, Cracow Polish Radio-TV Chorus *(rec Cracovia, 1978)* Agorá Music ("Phoenix" series) 3-▲ 509 [ADD]
Mozart, W.A.:Requiem, w. E. Mathis (sop), J. Hamari (mez), K. Ridderbusch (bass), K. Böhm (cnd), Vienna PO, Vienna State Opera Chorus [L] Deutsche Grammophon ▲ 413553-2 [ADD]
Mozart, W.A.:Requiem, w. Barbara Nieman (sop), Krystyna Szostek-Radkowa (mez), Leonard Mróz (bass), K. Kord (cnd), Warsaw PO, Henryk Wojnarowski (cnd), Warsaw National Phil Chorus *(rec Warsaw, 1979)* Polskie Nagrania ▲ PNCD 135 [ADD]
Polish Stars Sing the Carols, w. Zylis-Gara, Teresa (sop), Polish Radio-TV SO [cnd:Stefan Stuligrosz], Warsaw CO, Poznan State PO Men's & Boys' Choir Polskie Nagrania Edition ▲ ECD 025
Strauss, R.:Salome, w. H. Behrens (sop), A. Baltsa (mez), H. Angervo (alt), K.W. Böhm (ten), J. van Dam (bar), H. von Karajan (cnd), Vienna PO EMI Classics 2-▲ CDCB 49358
Szymanowski, K.:King Roger, w. B. Zagòrzanka (sop), A. Malewicz-Madey (cta), H. Grychnik (ten), A. Hiolski (bar), L. A. Mròz (bass), K. Stryja (cnd), Polish State PO Katowice, Cracow Phil Boys' Chorus, Polish State Phil Chorus *(rec Apr. 7-9, 1990)* Marco Polo ("Opera Classics" series) 2-▲ 8.223339/40 [DDD]

Ochman, Wieslaw (ten) (cont.)
Szymanowski, K.:Sym 3, w. J. Semkow (cnd), Polish National RSO Katowice, Polish Radio Chorus EMI Classics ▲ CDM 65082
Szymanowski, K.:Sym 3, w. K. Stryja (cnd), Polish State PO, Polish State Phil Chorus Marco Polo ▲ 8.223290 [DDD]

Ocker, Claus (bass)
Bach, J.S.:Cant 203, w. Dieter Messlinger (vc), Martin Galling (hpd), R. Ewerhart (cnd) *(rec 1966)* Vox Box 3-▲ CD3X 3039
Bach, J.S.:Cant 211, "Coffee Cant", w. Wilfrid Jochims (nar), Elisabeth Speiser (sop—Lieschen), Claus Ocker (bass—Schlendrian), R. Ewerhart (cnd), Württemberg CO *(rec 1966)* Vox Box 3-▲ CD3X 3039
Bach, J.S.:Cant 212, "Peasant Cant", w. Ursula Buckel (sop), Gabriele Zimmerman (fl), Peter Buck (vc), Martin Galling (hpd), R. Ewerhart (cnd), Württemberg CO *(rec 1965)* Vox Box 3-▲ CD3X 3039
Schütz, H.:Die Geburt unsers Herren Jesu Christi, w. Edith Mathis (sop), Georg Jelden (ten), H. Thamm (cnd), *(ensemble unknown)*, Windsbach Boys' Choir EMI Classics ("Baroque" series) ▲ CDK 65736

O'Connor, Caroline (sop)
Verdi, G.:Rigoletto (sels), w. O. Dominguez (mez), G. Di Stefano (ten), G. Valdengo (bar), I. Rufino (bass), R. Cellini (cnd), Palacio Bellas Artes Orch, Palacio Bellas Artes Chorus [abridged performance] *(rec live, Mexico City 6/22/48)* Golden Age of Opera 2-▲ GAO 128/29 [ADD]

O'Dwyer, Eamonn (trb)
Purcell, H.:Anthems & Services, w. S. Gritton (sop), M. Kennedy (sop), J. Goodman (trb), J. Bowman (ct), N. Short (ct), Rogers Covey-Crump (ten), C. Daniels (ten), M. Milhofer (ten), M. George (bass), R. Evans (bass), R. King (cnd), King's Consort—I Was Glad When They Said unto Me (coronation & verse anthem); O Consider My Adversity; Beati omnes qui timent Dominum; In the Black Dismal Dungeon of Dispair; Save Me, O God; Te Deum in B♭; Jubilant in B♭; Thy Way, O God, Is Holy Hyperion ▲ CDA 66677 [DDD]
Purcell, H.:Music for the Funeral of Queen Mary, w. S. Gritton (sop), M. Kennedy (sop), J. Goodman (trb), J. Bowman (ct), N. Short (ct), Rogers Covey-Crump (ten), C. Daniels (ten), M. Milhofer (ten), M. George (bass), R. Evans (bass), R. King (cnd), King's Consort Hyperion ▲ CDA 66677 [DDD]

Oeggl, Georg (bar)
Marschner, H.A.:Der Vampyr, w. L. Synek (sop), L. Heppe (ten), Rathauscher (sgr), Skladal (sgr), Sperlbauer (sgr), Weise (sgr), K. Tenner (cnd), Vienna RSO, Vienna Radio Chorus [G] *(rec live, Vienna, 4/9/51)* Memories 2-▲ HR 4466/67 [ADD]

Oelze, Christiane (sop)
Brahms, J.:Ein Deutsches Requiem, w. Kevin McMillan (bar), H.M. Beuerle (cnd), Freiburg Bach Orch, Freiburg Bach Choir Ars Musici ▲ 1057 [DDD]
Brahms, J.:Ein Deutsches Requiem, w. Gerald Finley (bar), P. Herreweghe (cnd), Champs Elysées Theater Orch, Chapelle Royale Choir, Collegium Vocale Harmonia Mundi ▲ HMC 901608 ■ HMC 401608
Bruckner, A.:Missa solemnis, w. C. Schubert (alt), J. Dümüller (ten), R. Hagen (bass), K. A. Rickenbacher (cnd), Bamberg SO, Bamberg Sym Chorus Virgin Classics ▲ CDC 59060
Bruckner, A.:Psalm 112, w. C. Schubert (alt), J. Dümüller (ten), R. Hagen (bass), K. A. Rickenbacher (cnd), Bamberg SO, Bamberg Sym Chorus Virgin Classics ▲ CDC 59060
Bruckner, A.:Psalm 114, w. C. Schubert (alt), J. Dümüller (ten), R. Hagen (bass), K. A. Richenbacher (cnd), Bamberg SO, Bamberg Sym Chorus Virgin Classics ▲ CDC 59060
Bruckner, A.:Psalm 150, w. C. Schubert (alt), J. Dümüller (ten), R. Hagen (bass), K. A. Rickenbacher (cnd), Bamberg SO, Bamberg Sym Chorus Virgin Classics ▲ CDC 59060
Handel, G.F.:Jephtha, w. Julia Gooding (sop), Catherine Denley (mez), Axel Köhler (ct), John Mark Ainsley (ten), Michael George (bass), M. Creed (cnd), Berlin Academy for Early Music *(rec June 1992)* Berlin Classics 2-▲ BER 1057-2 [DDD]
Hindemith, P.:Die Serenaden, w. Villa Musica Ensemble MD + G ▲ MDG 3040535 [DDD]
Hindemith, P.:Des Todes Tod, w. Cornelia Kollisch (mez), Villa Musica Ensemble MD + G ▲ MDG 3040535 [DDD]
Hindemith, P.:Wie es wär', wenn's anders wär, w. Cornelia Kallisch (mez), Villa Musica Ensemble MD + G ▲ MDG 3040535 [DDD]
Humperdinck, E.:Hänsel und Gretel, w. E. Gruberova (sop), G. Jones (sop), B. Bonney (sop), A. Murray (mez), C. Ludwig (mez), F. Grundheber (bar), C. Davis (cnd), Dresden Staatskapelle Philips 2-▲ 438013-2
Ligeti, G.:The Ligeti Edition, w. Phyllis Bryn-Julson (sop), Rosemary Hardy (sop), Rose Taylor (mez), Sibylle Ehlert (sgr), Omar Ebrahim (bar), Pierro-Laurent Aimard (pno), E.-P. Salonen (cnd), Philharmonia Orch, King's Singers—Vocal Works; Madrigals; Mysteries; Adventures; Songs; Nonsense Madrigals Sony Classical ▲ SK 62311
Mozart, W.A.:Arias, w. H. Haenchen (cnd), C.P.E. Bach CO—concert arias Berlin Classics ▲ BER 1094 [DDD]
Mozart, W.A.:Missa, K.427, w. Jennifer Larmore (sop), Scot Weir (ten), Peter Kooy (bass), P. Herreweghe (cnd), Champs Elysées Theater Orch, Chapelle Royale Choir, Collegium Vocale Harmonia Mundi France ▲ HMX 29001393
Mozart, W.A.:Missa, K.427, w. I. Verebics (sop), S. Weir (ten), O. Widmer (bass), H. Rilling (cnd), Stuttgart Bach Collegium, Gächinger Kantorei [L] Hänssler Classic 2-▲ 98.979 [DDD]
Mozart, W.A.:Requiem, w. I. Danz (mez), S. Weir (ten), A. Schmidt (bar), H. Rilling (cnd), Stuttgart Bach Collegium, Gächinger Kantorei [L] Hänssler Classic 2-▲ 98.979 [DDD]
Mozart, W.A.:Zauberflöte, w. Constanze Backes (sop—Papagena), Christiane Oelze (sop—Pamina), Susan Roberts (sop—First Lady), Cyndia Sieden (sop—Queen of the Night), Carola Guber (cta—Second Lady), Maria Jonas (cta—Third Lady), Andreas Dieterich (trb—First Boy), Jan Andreas Mendel (trb—Second Boy), Florian Wöller (trb—Third Boy), Uwe Peper (ten—Monostatos), Nicolas Robertson (ten—First Man in Armor), Michael Schade (ten—Tamino), Gerald Finley (bar—Papageno), Noel Mann (bass—Second Man in Armour), Harry Peeters (bass—Sarastro), Detlef Roth (bass—Speaker/First Priest), Robert Burt (speaker—Third Priest), Robert Johnston (speaker—Second Priest), Wolfgang Knauer (speaker—Fourth Priest), Douglas Welbat (speaker—Second Priest), J. E. Gardiner (cnd), English Baroque Soloists, Monteverdi Choir London *(rec Forum am Schlosspark, Ludwigsburg, July 1995)* Archiv 2-▲ 449166-2
Strauss (II), Joh.:Der Zigeunerbaron, w. Pamela Coburn (sop), Julia Hamari (mez), Elisabeth von Magnus (alt), Herbert Lippert (ten), Rudolf Schasching (ten), Wolfgang Holzmair (bar), Jurgen Flimm (sgr), Robert Florianschutz (sgr), Hans-Jurgen Lazar (sgr), N. Harnoncourt (cnd), Vienna SO, Arnold Schoenberg Choir *(rec Vienna, 1994)* Teldec 2-▲ 94555-2
Ullmann, V.:Kaiser von Atlantis, w. C. Oelze (sop—Bubikopf), I. Vermillion (mez—The Drummer), M. Petzold (ten—A Soldier), M. Kraus (ten—Kaiser Overall), H. Lippert (ten—Harlekin), F. Mazura (bar—The Loudspeaker), W. Berry (bass—Death), L. Zagrosek (cnd), Leipzig Gewandhaus Orch London ▲ 440854-2 [DDD]
Webern, A.:music of, w. Gerald Finley (bar), P. Boulez (cnd), Berlin PO, BBC Singers—Sym, Op. 21; Cants, Opp. 29 & 31; 3 Songs; Das Augenlicht; Vars, Op. 30; 5 Pieces Deutsche Grammophon ▲ 447 765-2

Offenbach, Jamie J. (b-bar)
Gershwin, G.:Blue Monday Blues, w. A. Burton (sop), G. Hopkins (ten), W. Sharp (bar), A. Woodley (b-bar), M. Alsop (cnd), Concordia Orch EMI Classics ▲ CDC 54851

O'Flynn, Maureen (sop)
Verdi, G.:Falstaff, w. Maureen O'Flynn (sop), Daniela Dessi (sop), Bernadette Manca di Nissa (mez), Delores Ziegler (mez), Ramon Vargas (ten), Ernesto Gavazzi (ten), Paolo Barbacini (ten), Juan Pons (bar), Roberto Frontali (bar), Luigi Roni (bass), R. Muti (cnd), La Scala Orch, La Scala Chorus *(rec Milan La Scala Theater, Italy, Mar. 29 & 31)* Sony Classical ▲ S2K 58961 [DDD]

Ogawa, A. (mez)
Shinohara, M.:Tabiyuki, w. M. Kakagawa (fl), I. Tsuji (ob), T. Takahashi (cl), K. Okazaki (fagotto), G. Kitamura (tpt), A. Murata (trbn), S. Eiso (perc), S. Ueki (vn), A. Naka4koji (va), S. Katsuta (vc), M. Komuro (contrabass), K. Komatsu (cnd) *(rec live Casals Hall, Tokyo, Mar. 5, 1994)* Camerata ▲ 30CM 375 [DDD]

Ognovenko, Vladimir (bass)
Glinka, M.:Russlan & Ludmilla, w. Galina Gorchakova (sop), Larissa Diadkova (cta), Irínia Bogachova (sgr), Anna Netrebko (sgr), Yuri Masurin (ten), Konstantin Pluzhnikov (ten), Mikhail Kit (bar), Gennady Bezzubenkov (bass), V. Gergiev (cnd), Kirov Opera Orch, Kirov Opera Chorus Philips ▲ 456 248-2

Ohanesian, David (bar)

Mascagni, P.:Cavalleria rusticana, w. Marina Krilovici (sop—Santuzza), Viorica Cortez (mez—Lola), Milka Nistor (mez—Lucia), Cornel Stavru (ten—Turiddu), David Ohanesian (bar—Alfio), M. Popa (cnd), Bucharest Opera & Ballet Theater Orch, Bucharest Opera & Ballet Theater Chorus *(rec 1966)* Vox Box 2-▲ CDX 5161

Puccini, G.:La Bohème, w. Elvira Cirje-Druica (sop—Musetta), Eugenia Moldoveanu (sop—Mimi), Andrei Borsos (ten—Parpignol), Constantin Gabor (ten—Alcindoro), Ludovic Spiess (ten—Rodolfo), Lucian Marinescu (bar—Schaunard), David Ohanesian (bar—Marcello), Pompei Harasteanu (bass—Benoit), Dan Zancu (bass—Colline), C. Petrovici (cnd), Romanian Opera Orch, Romanian Opera Chorus *(rec 1982)* Vox Box 2-▲ CDX 5156

O'Hara, Paige (sop)

Kern, J.:Show Boat, w. F. von Stade (mez), T. Stratas (sop), J. Hadley (ten), B. Hubbard (bar), K. Burns (mez), N. Kulp (sgr), J. McGlinn (cnd), London Sinfonietta, Ambrosian Chorus [original orchd Robert Russell Bennett]—also includes 45 minutes of music intended for the original performance but never included, plus music from revivals and films [1988 studio cast] Angel 3-▲ A23 49108 [DDD]

Kern, J.:Show Boat, w. T. Stratas (sop), K. Burns (mez), F. von Stade (mez), D. Garrison (ten), J. Hadley (ten), B. Hubbard (bar), J. McGlinn (cnd), London Sinfonietta, Ambrosian Opera Chorus, Ambrosian Singers EMI Classics 3-▲ A23 49108

Kern, J.:Show Boat, w. T. Stratas (sop), K. Burns (mez), F. von Stade (mez), D. Garrison (ten), J. Hadley (ten), B. Hubbard (bar), J. McGlinn (cnd), London Sinfonietta, Ambrosian Opera Chorus EMI Classics ▲ ZDC 49847

Ohashi, Kunikazu (bass)

Schubert, Franz:Deutsche Messe, w. Elisabeth Thomann (sop), Gertrude Jahn (alt), Stafford Wing (ten), H. Gillesberger (cnd), Vienna SO, Vienna Chamber Choir Tuxedo ▲ TUXCD 1074 [ADD]

Schubert, Franz:Mass 1, w. Laurence Dutoit (sop), Rose Bahl (alt), Kurt Equiluz (ten), Xaver Mayer (org), G. Barati (cnd), Vienna State Opera Orch, Vienna Academy Chamber Choir *(rec 1960)* Tuxedo ▲ TUXCD 1040 [ADD]

Schubert, Franz:Mass 3, w. Elisabeth Thomann (sop), Gertrude Jahn (alt), Stafford Wing (ten), H. Gillesberger (cnd), Vienna SO, Vienna Chamber Choir Tuxedo ▲ TUXCD 1074 [ADD]

Schubert, Franz:Mass 4, w. Laurence Dutoit (sop), Rose Bahl (alt), Kurt Equiluz (ten), Xaver Mayer (org), G. Barati (cnd), Vienna State Opera Orch, Vienna Academy Chamber Choir *(rec 1960)* Tuxedo ▲ TUXCD 1040 [ADD]

Öhlinger, G. (sop)

Haydn, J.:Mass 1a, Missa 'Rorate coeli desuper', w. M. Bayer (alt), M. Klietmann (ten), A. Lebeda (bass), D. de Rooij an der Reil (org), Collegium Musicum Pragense Christophorus ▲ CD 74541 [DDD]

Haydn, J.:Mass 7, "Kleine Orgelmesse", w. M. Bayer (alt), M. Klietmann (ten), A. Lebeda (bass), Collegium Musicum Pragense Christophorus ▲ CD 74541 [DDD]

Ohlmann (sgr)

Hoffmann, E.T.A.:Aurora, w. Thomas Rieger (trb), Maltraud Meier (mez), Siegfried Schulze (bass), Koch (sgr), H. Dechant (cnd), Bamberg Youth Orch, Bamberg Oratorio Chorus Bayer 3-▲ 100276-78

Öhmann, Carl Martin (ten)

Mahler, G.:Das Lied von der Erde, w. K. Thorborg (mez), C. Schuricht (cnd), Royal Concertgebouw Orch *(rec live, Amsterdam, Oct. 5, 1939)* Archipon ▲ ARCH 3.1 (m) [ADD]

Mahler, G.:Das Lied von der Erde, w. Kerstin Thorborg (alt), C. Schuricht (cnd), Royal Concertgebouw Orch *(rec live, Amsterdam, Oct 5, 1939)* Minerva ▲ MN A30 (m) [ADD]

Ohno, Kazumichi (ten)

Allusions in Moonlight:A Japanese Lieder Recital, w. Kyosuke, Kobayashi (pno) *(rec Mannheimer Reissmuseum, Sept 1994)* Thorofon ▲ CTH 2257 [DDD]

Ohotnikav (sgr)

Mussorgsky, M.:Khovanshchina, w. O. Borodina (mez), V. Galusin (ten), B. Minjelkiev (bass), V. Gergiev (cnd), Kirov Opera Orch, Kirov Opera Chorus [R] Philips 3-▲ 432147-2 [DDD]

Ohrenstein, Dora (sop)

Amato, B.:Two Together, w. J. Turk (b tuba) Dana Recording Project ▲ DRP 4 [ADD]

Bouchard, L.:Black Burned Wood, w. M. Rowell (vn/va), Phillip Bush (pno), J. Cirker (dr/perc), B. Ruyle (mar/xyl/perc) *(rec Feb. & Apr. 1993)* CRI ▲ CD 654 [DDD]

Brown, N.K.:Déjeuner sur l'herbe, w. J. Umble (a sax), K. Thomas Umble (fl), R. Fusco (pno) Dana Recording Project ▲ DRP 5 [DDD]

Childs, M.E.:Night, w. Phillip Bush (pno) XI Compact Discs ▲ XI 114

Davis, A.:Lost Moon Sisters, w. M. Rowell (vn), P. Bush (pno), J. Cirker (mar/vib) *(rec Feb. & Apr. 1993)* CRI ▲ CD 654 [DDD]

Johnson, S.:Confetti on Flesh, w. M. Rowell (vn), P. Bush (pno/syn), J. Cirker (mar/dr set) *(rec Feb. & Apr. 1993)* CRI ("Emergency Music" series) ▲ CD 654 [DDD]

Johnston, B.:Calamity Jane to Her Daughter, w. M. Rowell (vn), P. Bush (pno), B. Ruyle (perc) *(rec Feb. & Apr. 1993)* CRI ("Emergency Music" series) ▲ CD 654 [DDD]

Lebaron, A.:Dish, w. M. Rowell (vn), P. Bush (pno/syn), J. Thompson (elec bass), J. Cirker (dr), B. Ruyle (perc) *(rec Feb. & Apr. 1993)* CRI ("Emergency Music" series) ▲ CD 654 [DDD]

Okada, Naoko (sop)

Carvalho, J. de S.:Te Deum, w. Brigitte Fournier (sop), Elisabeth Graf (cta), John Elwes (ten), Michel Brodard (bar), M. Corboz (cnd), Lisbon Gulbenkian Foundation Orch, Lisbon Gulbenkian Foundation Chorus Cascavelle ▲ CVL 1016 [DDD]

Okamura, Takao (bass)

Wagner, R.:Der Ring des Nibelungen, w. Liselotte Becker-Egner (sop—Woglinde/Ortlinde/Wellgunde), Angelika Berger (sop—Wellgunde/Waltraute), Siw Ericsdotter (sop—Norn 3), Heidemaria Ferch (sop—Freia/Gerhilde), Bella Jasper (sop—Helmwige/Waldvogel/Woglinde), Ditha Sommer (sop—Sieglinde/Gutrune), Ursula Boese (mez—Erda), Ruth Hesse (mez—Fricka), Nadezda Kniplová (mez—Brünnhilde), Margit Kobeck (mez—Schwertleite/Norn 2), Hilde Rosner (mez—Flosshilde/Siegrunde), Erica Schubert (mez—Grimgerde/Flosshilde), Ingrid Göritz (cta—Rossweisse/Norn 1), Herbert Doussant (ten—Froh), Herold Kraus (ten—Mime), Gerald McKee (ten—Siegmund/Siegfried), Fritz Uhl (ten—Loge), Rudolf Knoll (bar—Gunther/Donner), Rolf Polke (bass-bar—Wotan/Wanderer), Rolf Kühne (bass—Alberich), Takao Okamura (bass—Fafner), Otto von Rohr (bass—Hagen/Fasolt/Hunding), H. Swarowsky (cnd), Czech PO, Prague National Theater Orch *(rec June 3 & 5, July 26–31, A)* Weltbild Classics 14-▲ 703769 [ADD]

Okazaki, K. L. (mez)

Schmid, E.:Suite From Poetry by Rainer Maria Rilke, w. E. Schmid (cnd), Basel SO [G] *(rec. April 6, 1989)* Grammont ▲ CTSP 33-2 [ADD]

O'Keefe, Margaret (sop)

Purcell, H.:Dido & Aeneas, w. Nancy Maultsby (sop—Dido), Susannah Waters (sop—Belinda), Margaret O'Keefe (sop—1st Witch), Sharon Baker (sop—2nd Woman), Laura Tucker (mez—Sorceress), Donna Ames (alt—Spirit), Richard Clement (ten—Sailor), Russell Braun (bar—Aeneas), M. Pearlman (cnd), Boston Baroque Orch Telarc ▲ CD 80424 [DDD]

Sérénade, w. Richard Schilling (gtr) Titanic ▲ Ti 212 [DDD]

Okhotnikov, Nikolai (bass)

Rimsky-Korsakov, N.:Songs, w. Anna Kovaleva (sop), Marianna Tarassova (mez), Konstantine Pluzhnikov (ten), Andrey Stavny (bar), Yury Serov (pno)—4 Romances, Op. 2; 4 Romances, Op. 3; 4 Romances, Op. 4; 4 Romances, Op. 7; 6 Romances, Op. 8; 2 Romances, Op. 25; 4 Romances, Op. 26; 4 Romances, Op. 27 *(rec St. Catherine's Lutheran Church, St. Petersburg, Sept–Dec 1993)* Russian Compact Disc ▲ RDCD 10051 [DDD]

Okolycheva, Elena (cta)

Rimsky-Korsakov, N.:A May Night, w. Maria Lapina (sop), Natalia Erassova (mez), Alexander Arkhipov (ten), Vitaly Tarastchenko (ten), Piotr Glouboky (bass), Viatcheslav Potchapski (bass), A. Tchistiakov (cnd), Bolshoi Theater Orch, Russian State Choir Russian Season 4-▲ CMX 388054

Oláh, Gábor (bar)

Mozart, W.A.:Alma Dei creatoris, w. Ibolya Verebics (sop), Judit Németh (cta), József Mukk (ten), József Moldvay (bar), István Ella (org), János Reményi (cnd), Hungarian Radio-TV Children's Chorus Girls' Voices, Hungarian Radio-TV Male Chamber Choir *(rec Hungaroton Studio, June 14–16, 1991)* Hungaroton ▲ HCD 4003 [DDD]

Oláh, Gábor (bar) (cont.)

Mozart, W.A.:Ave verum corpus, w. Ibolya Verebics (sop), Judit Németh (cta), József Mukk (ten), József Moldvay (bar), István Ella (org), János Reményi (cnd), Hungarian Radio-TV Children's Chorus Girls' Voices, Hungarian Radio-TV Male Chamber Choir *(rec Hungaroton Studio, June 14–16, 1991)* Hungaroton ▲ HCD 4003 [DDD]

Oláh, Gábor (bar/Gregorian intonations)

Mozart, W.A.:Miserere, w. Ibolya Verebics (sop), Judit Németh (cta), József Mukk (ten), József Moldvay (bass), István Ella (org), János Reményi (cnd), Hungarian Radio-TV Children's Chorus Girls' Voices, Hungarian Radio-TV Male Chamber Choir *(rec Hungaroton Studio, June 14–16, 1991)* Hungaroton ▲ HCD 4003 [DDD]

Mozart, W.A.:Misericordias Domini, w. Ibolya Verebics (sop), Judit Németh (cta), József Mukk (ten), József Moldvay (bass), István Ella (org), János Reményi (cnd), Hungarian Radio-TV Children's Chorus Girls' Voices, Hungarian Radio-TV Male Chamber Choir *(rec Hungaroton Studio, June 14–16, 1991)* Hungaroton ▲ HCD 4003 [DDD]

Mozart, W.A.:Missa brevis, K.65, w. Ibolya Verebics (sop), Judit Németh (cta), József Mukk (ten), József Moldvay (bass), István Ella (org), János Reményi (cnd), Hungarian Radio-TV Children's Chorus Girls' Voices, Hungarian Radio-TV Male Chamber Choir *(rec Hungaroton Studio, June 14–16, 1991)* Hungaroton ▲ HCD 4003 [DDD]

Mozart, W.A.:Missa brevis, K.194, w. Ibolya Verebics (sop), Judit Németh (cta), József Mukk (ten), József Moldvay (b), István Ella (org), János Reményi (cnd), Hungarian Radio-TV Children's Chorus Girls' Voices, Hungarian Radio-TV Male Chamber Choir *(rec Hungaroton Studio, June 14–16, 1991)* Hungaroton ▲ HCD 4003 [DDD]

Mozart, W.A.:Sancta Maria, w. Ibolya Verebics (sop), Judit Németh (cta), József Mukk (ten), József Moldvay (bass), István Ella (org), János Reményi (cnd), Hungarian Radio-TV Children's Chorus Girls' Voices, Hungarian Radio-TV Male Chamber Choir *(rec Hungaroton Studio, June 14–16, 1991)* Hungaroton ▲ HCD 4003 [DDD]

Olaria, A. M. (sop)

Lehár, F.:Eva, w. J. Granados (sop—Prunelles), A. M. Olaria (sop—Eva), A. Kraus (ten—Octavio Flaubert), L. de Cordoba (sgr—Gipsy), S. Ramalle (sgr—Dagoberto), J. Peromingo (sgr—Voisin), E. Estella (cnd), Madrid CO, Spanish National Radio Chorus [Sp] Montilla ▲ CDFM 2036

Olbrychski, Daniel (nar)

Schoenberg, A.:A Survivor from Warsaw, w. S. Kawalla (cnd), Polish Radio-TV SO, Polish Radio-TV Chorus [E] Vienna Modern Masters ▲ VMM 3015 [DDD]

Olczewska, Maria (mez)

Strauss, R.:Der Rosenkavalier, w. L. Lehmann (sop), E. Schumann (sop), R. Mayr (bass), R. Heger (cnd), Vienna PO, Vienna State Opera Chorus—abridged performance [G] *(rec 1933 for HMV)* Pearl 2-▲ GEMMCDS 9365 (m) [AAD]

Oldham, Derek (ten)

Friml, R.:Film Music, w. D. Vane (sop), H. Williams (bar), London Palladium Orch—The Vagabond King; The Blue Kitten; Rose Marie; The 3 Musketeers; The Firefly Pearl ("Flapper" series) ▲ PAST CD 9764 [AAD]

Sullivan, A.:The Gondoliers, w. W. Lawson (sop), A. Davies (ten), B. Lewis (cta), M. Bennett (sop), G. Baker (bar), L. Sheffield (bar), H. Lytton (bar), et al., H. Norris (cnd), D'Oyly Carte Opera Company Orch, D'Oyly Carte Opera Chorus—dialogue omitted *(rec 1927)* Pearl 2-▲ PEAS 9961 (m) [AAD]

Sullivan, A.:Trial by Jury, w. W. Lawson (sop), G. Baker (bar), L. Sheffield (bar), A. Hosking (bar), H. Norris (cnd), D'Oyly Carte Opera Company Orch, D'Oyly Carte Opera Chorus *(rec 1928)* Pearl 2-▲ PEAS 9961 (m) [AAD]

O'Leary, Caitriona (sgr)

Purcell, H.:Dido & Aeneas, w. Cassandra Hoffman (sop—Belinda), Arlene Travis (sop—2nd Witch), Desirée Halac (mez—Sorceress/Spirit), Jennifer Lane (mez—Dido), Elizabeth Norman (alt), Thomas Bogdan (ten—A Sailor), Michael Brown (bar—Aeneas), Curtis Streetman (bar), Caitriona O'Leary (sgr—2nd Woman), Sarah Pillow (sgr—1st Witch), B. Brookshire (cnd), San Cassiano Musici *(rec St. Ignatius of Antioch Episcopal Church, New York City, Spring 1995)* Vox Classics ▲ VOX 7518

Oliva, Alida (sop)

Perti, G.A.:Liturgy for Good Friday, w. Patrizia Vaccari (sop), Maura Pederzoli (sop), Cristina Calzolari (sop), Claudia Bugli (sop), Lucia Bagnoli (alt), Cinzia Meneghel (alt), Renzo Bez (alt), Alessandro Carmignani (alt), Michel van Goethem (alt), Mauro Collina (ten), Vincenzo Di Donato (ten), Paolo Fanciullacci (ten), Giovanni Caccamo (ten), Paolo Da Col (ten), Sergio Foresti (bass), Marco Scavazza (bass), Luca Ferracin (bass), Paride Montanari (bass), Liuwe Tamminga (org), Sergio Vartolo (org), S. Vartolo (cnd), Bologna San Petronio Capella Musicale Orch—Omnes amici mei; De lamentatione Jeremiae Prophetae:Heth. Cogitavit; Velum templi; Vinea mea; De lamentatione Jeremiae Prophetae:Lamed. Matribus suis; Tamquam ad latronem; Tenebrae factae sunt; Animam meam; Tradiderunt me; Jesum tradidit; De lamentatione Jeremiae Prophetae:Aleph. Ego vir; Caligaverunt *(rec St. Petronio Basilica, Bologna, Mar 28–31, 1995)* Naxos ▲ 8.553321 [DDD]

Oliver, Alexander (ten)

Gershwin, G.:Songs, w. S. Houben (sax), D. Duesing (pno)—He Loves and She Loves; Somebody Loves Me; Let's Do It; How Long Has This Been Going on; By Strauss; They All Laughed; Who Cares; But Not for Me; Love Walked in Ricercar ▲ RIC 135119 [DDD]

Massenet, J.:Sapho, w. Jenny Hill (sop), Laura Sarti (mez), Bernard Dickerson (ten), Neilson Taylor (bar), George Macpherson (bass), Milla Andrew (sgr), B. Keefe (cnd), BBC SO, BBC Sym Chorus *(rec live, 1973)* Memories 2-▲ MEM 4601 [AAD]

Offenbach, J.:Les Contes d'Hoffmann, w. L. Serra (sop), R. Plowright (sop), J. Norman (sop), A. Murray (mez), J. Taillon (mez), N. Shicoff (ten), R. Tear (ten), J. Van Dam (b-bar), D. Duesing (bar), K. Rydl (bass), S. Cambreling (cnd), Brussels Théâtre de la Monnaie Orch [F] EMI Classics 3-▲ CDCC 49641 [DDD]

Porter, C.:Songs, w. S. Houben (sax), D. Duesing (pno)—So in Love; Let's Do It; At Long Last Love; I Get A Kick Out of You; Every Time We Say Goodbye Ricercar ▲ RIC 135119 [DDD]

Oliver, Lucien (bar)

Berlioz, H.:L'Enfance du Christ, w. Florence Kopleff (cta), Ceasare Valletti (ten), Gérard Souzay (bar), Giorgio Tozzi (bass), C. Munch (cnd), Boston SO, New England Conservatory Chorus *(rec Dec 1956)* RCA Victor Gold Seal 8-▲ 0902-668444-2 [ADD]

Oliver, Robert (bass)

Bach, J.S.:Cant 131, w. Loren Driscoll (ten), Leonard Arner (ob), R. Craft (cnd), Columbia SO Sony Classical ("Essential Classics" series) 2-▲ SB2K 62656

Olivero, Magda (sop)

Alfano, F.:Risurrezione, w. A. Di Stasio (Matrena), Gismondo (Prince Dmitri), A. Boyer (Simonson), E. Boncompagni (cnd), Turin RAI Orch [I] *(rec live, Oct 22, 1971)* Standing Room Only 2-▲ SRO 839-2 [ADD]

Boito, A.:Mefistofele (sels), w. M. Olivero (sop—Margherita), M. Frusoni (ten—Faust), H. Smit (b-bar—Mefistofele), A. Kerjens (cnd), *(orch unknown)*—Act III *(rec live May 5, 1973)* VAI Audio 2-▲ VAIA 1062 [ADD]

Catalani, A.:La Wally (sels), w. M. Olivero (sop—Wally), M. Frusoni (ten—Hagenbach), A. Kerjens (cnd), *(orch unknown)*—Act IV *(rec live May 5, 1973)* VAI Audio 2-▲ VAIA 1062 [ADD]

Cherubini, L.:Médée, w. E. Baggiore (sgr), L. Ganbelli (bass), A. Lo Forese (sgr), N. Rescigno (cnd), Mantova Teatro Sociale Orch, Mantova Teatro Sociale Chorus [I] *(rec live, Mantova 1/23/71)* Myto 2-▲ 2 MCD 91136 [ADD]

Cilea, F.:Adriana Lecouvreur, w. Giulietta Simionato (mez), Franco Corelli (ten), Ettore Bastianini (bar), M. Rossi (cnd), Naples Teatro San Carlo Orch, Naples Teatro San Carlo Chorus *(rec Naples, Nov 28, 1959)* Agorá Music ("Phoenix" series) 2-▲ 502

Cilea, F.:Adriana Lecouvreur, w. G. Simionato (mez), F. Corelli (ten), E. Bastianini (bar), M. Rossi (cnd), Naples Teatro San Carlo Orch, Naples Teatro San Carlo Chorus [I] *(rec live 11/28/59)* Melodram 2-▲ MEL 27009 (m) [AAD]

Cilea, F.:Adriana Lecouvreur, w. M. L. Nave (mez), P. Domingo (ten), E. Sordello (bar), A. Silipigni (cnd), *(orch unknown)* [I] *(rec 1973)* Legato Classics 2-▲ LCD 140-2 [ADD]

Cilea, F.:Adriana Lecouvreur, w. M. Olivero (sop—Adriana), F. Ferrari (ten—Maurizio), R. Capecchi (bar—Michonnet), F. Vernizzi (cnd), *(orch unknown)* [I] *(rec live, Amsterdam 11/65)* Verona 2-▲ 27077/78

Olivero, Magda (sop) (cont.)

Cilea, F.:Adriana Lecouvreur (sels), w. M. Olivero (sop—Adriana), M. Frusoni (ten—Maurizio), H. Smit (bass-bar—Michonnet), A. Kerjens (cnd), *(orch unknown)*—Act IV *(rec live May 5, 1973)* VAI Audio 2-▲ VAIA 1062 [ADD]

Cilea, F.:Adriana Lecouvreur (sels), w. M. Olivero (sop—Adriana), M. Moretto (mez—Princess di Bouillon), A. Cupido (ten—Maurizio), O. Mori (bar—Michonnet), C. Gandolfo (pno) *(rec Apr. 1993)* Bongiovanni ▲ GB 2515 [DDD]

Concerti, w. U. Trama (bass), D. Antoioli (sgr), A. Protti (bar), K. Ostar (sgr), Fulvio Vernizzi (cnd) Great Opera Performances 2-▲ GOP 709

De Cavalieri, Fineschi, Olivero, Stignani, Tassinari, w. Cavalieri, Anna de (sop), Ornella Fineschi (sop), Ebe Stignani (mez), Pia Tassinari (mez), Rome RAI SO, Milan RAI SO *(rec 1953-58)* Incontri Memorabili ("Martini & Rossi Concerts" series) ▲ 5020

Giordano, U.:Fedora, w. M. del Monaco (ten), T. Gobbi (bar), L. Gardelli (cnd), Monte Carlo Opera Orch London ("Grand Opera" series) 2-▲ 433033-2 [ADD]

Giordano, U.:Fedora (sels), w. Giuseppe Giacomini (ten), Franco Piva (ten), Elena Baggiore (sgr), M. Braggio (cnd), *(orch unknown)*—Amor ti vieta; Loris Ipanoff, oggi lo Zar; Muta è mia madre, muto il fratello *(rec Piacenza, Jan. 9, 1972)* Golden Age of Opera 2-▲ GAO 189/90 [ADD]

In Recital, w. Ivan Davis (pno) *(rec Dallas, Dec 13, 1977)* Standing Room Only ▲ SRO 815-1 [ADD]

Janácek, L.:Jenůfa, w. Magda Olivero (sop—Kostelnicka), Bruna Baglioni (mez—La vecchia Buryja), Grace Bumbry (mez—Jenufa), Renato Cioni (ten—Steva Buryja), Robleto Merolla (bar—Laca Klemen), Carlo Meliciani (sgr—Vecchio compagno), J. Semkow (cnd), La Scala Orch, La Scala Chorus *(rec Milan, Apr 2, 1974)* Myto 2-▲ MCD 961142

Magda Olivero & Flaviano Labò in Concert, w. Flaviano Labò (ten), Jacques Bazire (cnd), Marsiglia Opera Orch, Raina Kabaivanska (sop), Gianpiero Matromei (bar), Carlo Meliciani (bar), Oliveiro de Fabritiis (cnd), La Scala Orch, Turin RAI Orch *(rec between 1969 & 1973)* Bongiovanni ▲ GB 1105 [ADD]

Mascagni, P.:Iris, w. L. Ottolini (ten), R. Capecchi (bar), P. Clabassi (bass), F. Vernizzi (cnd), Netherlands Radio Orch, Netherlands Radio Chorus *(rec Amsterdam, 1963)* Great Opera Performances ▲ GPO 708

Mascagni, P.:Iris, w. L. Ottolini (ten), R. Capecchi (bar), P. Clabassi (bass), F. Vernizzi (cnd), Netherlands Radio Orch, Netherlands Radio Chorus *(rec live, 1963)* Verona 2-▲ 27014/15 [AAD]

Mascagni, P.:Iris (sels), w. M. Olivero (sop—Iris), G. Gismondo (ten—Osaka), M. Basiola II (bar—Kyoto), O. de Fabritiis (cnd), *(orch unknown)*—scenes from Acts II & III *(rec live, June 3, 1966)* VAI Audio 2-▲ VAIA 1062 (m) [ADD]

Massenet, J.:Werther, w. A. Lazzari (ten), S. Meletti (bar), M. Rossi (cnd), Turin RSO, Turin Radio Chorus *(rec live, 6/12/63)* Melodram 2-▲ MEL 27065 (m) [AAD]

Mercadante, S.:Arias, w. R. Majone (cnd), Turin RAI Orch, Turin RAI Chorus—single arias from Virginia & Pelagio; Aria (La sette parole di nostro signore); Sinfonia from Rossini's Stabat Mater *(rec live, Turin, 11/23/70)* Melodram 2-▲ MEL 27099 [ADD]

Omaggio a Magda Olivero, w. Carmelina Gandolfo (pno), Marco Montanari (org) Great Opera Performances 2-▲ GOP 795

Puccini, G.:Arias, w. *(other soloists unknown)*, F. Vernizzi (cnd), Turin RSO—3 scenes from Tosca *(rec live, 3/7/60)* Melodram 2-▲ MEL 27065 (m) [AAD]

Puccini, G.:La Bohème (sels), w. J. Oncina (ten), S. Hubada (cnd), Zagreb Opera Orch—one solo soprano aria (Si, mi chiamano Mimi) & one duet (O soave fanciulla) [I] *(rec live 5/3/64)* Myto 2-▲ 2 MCD 91136 [ADD]

Puccini, G.:La fanciulla del West (sels), w. Magda Olivero (sop—Minnie), Corinna Vozza (mez—Wowkle), Paolo Caroli (ten—Harry), Giacomo Lauri-Volpi (ten—Dick Johnson), Marco Rogani (ten—Pony Express Rider), Salvatore di Tommaso (ten—Trin), Adelio Zagonara (ten—Nick), Virgilio Ascorro (bar—Sid), Alfredo Colella (bar—Jake Wallace), Giuseppe Forgione (bar—Bello), Giancarlo Guelfi (bar—Jack Rance), Arturo la Porta (bar—Sonora), Gino Conti (bass—José Castro), Piere Passarotti (bass—Bill), Enzo Titta (bass—Larkens), Giulio Tomei (bass—Ashby), V. Bellezza (cnd), Rome Opera Orch, Rome Opera Chorus—Minnie, dalla mia casa son partito; Laggiù nel Soledad; Chi c'è per farmi i ricci; Oh! Mister Johnson, siete rimasto; Non so ben neppur io; Io non son che una povera fanciulla; No, Minnie, non piangete; Vorrei mettermi queste; Hallo!; Oh, se sapeste; Credo che abbiate torto; Ma ti giuro ch'io non ti lascio più; Vieni fuori!; Una parola sola!...Or son sei mesi; Che c'è di nuovo Jack?; È là; Siete pronto; Ch'ella mi creda; È Minnie!...È Minnie! *(rec Rome, Mar. 30, 1957)* Golden Age of Opera ▲ GAO 180 [ADD]

Puccini, G.:Manon Lescaut, w. Magda Olivero (sop—Manon), Tine Appelman (mez—Singer), Umberto Borso (ten—Chevalier), Mario Carlin (ten—Edmondo/Dancing Master/Lamplighter), Ferdinando Lidonni (bar—Lescaut), Giovanni Foiani (bass—Geronte/Sergeant/Captain), Joop Ruivenkamp (bass—Innkeeper), F. Vernizzi (cnd), Groot Omroep Orch, Groot Omroep Choir *(rec Amsterdam, Oct 31, 1964)* Bella Voce 2-▲ BLV 107.221 [AAD]

Puccini, G.:Manon Lescaut (sels), w. Magda Olivero (sop—Manon), Giuseppe Venditelli (ten—Chevalier), P. Argento (cnd), Turin RAI SO—Oh, sarò la più bella! [Act 2] *(rec Turin, July 2, 1975)* Bella Voce 2-▲ BLV 107.221 [AAD]

Puccini, G.:Tosca, w. Alvinio Misciano (ten), F. Vernizzi (cnd), Turin RAI Orch, Turin RAI Chorus Melodram 2-▲ CDM 27025

Puccini, G.:Tosca, w. A. Misciano (ten), Fioravanti (sgr), F. Vernizzi (cnd), Turin RAI Orch, Turin RAI Chorus *(rec live 1900)* Melodram 2-▲ MEL 27026

Puccini, G.:Tosca (sels), w. A. Misciano (ten), F. Vernizzi (cnd), Turin RAI Orch—3 duets [I] *(rec live, Turin, 3/7/60)* Myto 2-▲ 2 MCD 91136 [ADD]

Puccini, G.:Turandot, w. Gina Cigna (sop), Francesco Merli (ten), F. Ghione (cnd), Turin RAI SO *(rec 1938)* Phonographe 2-▲ PHG 5053

Tchaikovsky, P.:Mazeppa, w. M. Radev (mez), D. Poleri (ten), E. Bastianini (bar), B. Christoff (bass), J. Perlea (cnd), Florence Maggio Musicale Orch, Florence Maggio Musicale Chorus [I] *(rec live 6/6/54)* Melodram 2-▲ MEL 27070 (m) [AAD]

Zandonai, R.:Francesca da Rimini, w. Lydia Marimpietri (sop—Biancofiore), Magda Olivero (sop—Francesca), Pinuccia Perotti (sop—Samaritana), Edda Vincenzi (sop—Garsenda), Gabriella Carturan (mez—Smaragdi), Biancamaria Casoni (mez—Altichiara), Anna Maria Rota (cta—Donella), Athos Cesarini (ten—Archer), Angelo Mercuriali (ten—Ser Toldo Berardengo), Mario del Monaco (ten—Paolo), Piero de Palma (ten—Malatestino), Rinaldo Pelizzoni (ten—Prisoner), Gianpiero Malaspina (bar—Gianciotto), Dino Mantovani (bar—Jester), Enrico Campi (bass—Ostasio), Giuseppe Morresi (bass—Tower warden), G. Gavazzeni (cnd), La Scala Orch, La Scala Chorus *(rec La Scala Theatre, Milan, June 4, 1959)* Legato Classics 2-▲ LCD 186-2

Zandonai, R.:Francesca da Rimini (sels), w. A. Gasparini (mez), A. Cesarini (ten), M. del Monaco (ten), V. Carbonari (bass), N. Rescigno (cnd), Monte Carlo Opera Orch London ("Grand Opera" series) 2-▲ 433033-2 [ADD]

Oliveros, Pauline (voc/acc)

Deep Listening Band:Deep Listening, w. S. Dempster (voc/trbn/didjeridu), Panaiotis (voc/whistling) New Albion ▲ NA 022 [DDD]

Oliveros, P.:In Memoriam Mr. Whitney, w. American Voices *(rec Connecticut, Mar. 10, 1991)* Mode ▲ MODE 40

Oliviero, Lodovico (ten)

Verdi, G.:Un ballo in maschera, w. Stella Andreva (sop—Oscar), Zinka Milanov (sop—Amelia), Bruna Castagna (cta—Ulrica), Jussi Björling (ten—Riccardo), Lodovico Oliviero (ten—Un Servo D'Amelia), John Cartet (bar—Un Giudice), Alexander Sved (bar—Renato), Normann Cordon (bass—Samuel), Arthur Kent (bass—Silvano), Nicola Moscona (bass—Tom), E. Panizza (cnd), *(orch unknown)* *(rec live, New York, Dec. 14, 1940)* The Fourties 2-▲ ENT FT 1515

Ollendorff, Fritz (bass)

Busoni, F.:Arlecchino or Die Fenster, w. E. Malbin (sop), M. Dickie (ten), G. Evans (bar), I. Wallace (bar), Glyndeborne Festival Chorus, J. Pritchard (cnd), Glyndebourne Festival Orch EMI Classics ▲ CDMB 65284

Rossini, G.:Il barbiere di Siviglia, w. M. Callas (sop), L. Alva (ten), T. Gobbi (bar), N. Zaccaria (bass), A. Galliera (cnd), Philharmonia Orch EMI Classics ▲ ZDM 63076

Rossini, G.:Il barbiere di Siviglia, w. Ruth-Margaret Pütz (sop), Annelies Burmeister (mez), Peter Schreier (ten), Hermann Prey (bar), Franz Crass (bass), O. Suitner (cnd), Berlin State Opera Orch Berlin Classics 2-▲ BER 9021 [ADD]

Ollendorff, Fritz (bass) (cont.)

Strauss, R.:Ariadne auf Naxos, w. E. Schwarzkopf (sop), I. Seefried (sop), R. Streich (sop), L. Otto (sop), G. Hoffman (mez), R. Schock (ten), G. Unger (ten), H. Cuénod (ten), H. Prey (bar), H. von Karajan (cnd), Philharmonia Orch [G] *(rec 1954)* EMI Classics ("Studio" series) 2-▲ CDMB 69296 (m) [ADD]

Ollmann, Kurt (bar)

Bernstein, L.:Candide (restored), w. J. Anderson (sop), C. Ludwig (mez), D. Jones (mez), J. Hadley (ten), N. Gedda (ten), A. Green (sgr), L. Bernstein (cnd), London SO, London Sym Chorus Deutsche Grammophon ■ 437328-4

Bernstein, L.:Candide (restored), w. J. Anderson (sop), C. Ludwig (mez), D. Jones (mez), J. Hadley (ten), N. Gedda (ten), A. Green (sgr), L. Bernstein (cnd), London SO, London Sym Chorus *(rec 1989)* Deutsche Grammophon ▲ 429734-2 [DDD] ■ 429734-4

Bernstein, L.:West Side Story, w. K. Te Kanawa (sop), T. Troyanos (mez), J. Carreras (ten), L. Bernstein (cnd), *(orch unknown)* [E] Deutsche Grammophon ▲ 415963-2 [DDD] ■ 415963-4 □ 415963-5

Bowles, P.:Secret Words, w. J. Sheffer (cnd), Eos Ensemble *(rec Manhattan Center Studios, New York, Sept 22 & 23, 1995)* Catalyst ▲ 09026-68409-2 [DDD]

Gershwin, G.:Oh, Kay!, w. Dawn Upshaw (sop—Kay), Kurt Ollmann (bar—Jimmy Winter), Adam Arkin (sgr—Shory McGee), E. Stern (cnd), *(orch unknown)* Elektra/Nonesuch ▲ 79361-2 ■ 79361-4

Gounod, C.:Roméo et Juliette, w. Susan Graham (sop—Stephano), Ruth Ann Swenson (sop—Juliette), Sarah Walker (mez—Gertrude), Paul Charles Clarke (ten—Tybalt), Placido Domingo (ten—Roméo), Kurt Ollmann (bar—Mercutio), Alastair Miles (bass—Frère Laurent), David Pittman-Jennings (bass—Le Duc), Alain Vernhes (bass—Capulet), L. Slatkin (cnd), Munich RSO, Munich Radio Chorus *(rec Studio 1, Bavarian Radio, Munich, Nov 29 - Dec 10, 1995)* RCA Red Seal 2-▲ 09026-68440-2 [DDD]

Rorem, N.:The Santa Fe Songs, w. Sheryl Staples (vn), Heiichiro Ohyama (va), Peter Rejto (vc), Lydia Artymiw (pno) *(rec live, Tucson Chamber Music Festival, Mar 12, 1995)* Arizona Friends of Chamber Music ▲ 1995 [DDD]

Ollu, Franck (nar)

Goebbels, H.:La Jalousie (Noises from a Novel), w. P. Rundel (cnd), Ensemble Modern *(rec May 1992)* ECM New Series ("New" series) ▲ 78118-21483-2 [DDD]

Olmeda, Martine (sop)

Auber, D.-F.:Le Domino noir, w. Sumi Jo (sop), Doris Lamprecht (sop), Isabelle Vernet (sop), Jocelyne Taillon (mez), Bruce Ford (ten), Patrick Power (ten), Gilles Cachemaille (bar), Jules Bastin (bass), R. Bonynge (cnd), English CO, London Voices London 2-▲ 440646-2

Massenet, J.:Cléopâtre, w. B. Harries (sop), Daniéle Streiff (sop), J. Maurette (ten), D. Henry (bar), M. Hacquard (bar), P. Fournillier (cnd), St.-Etienne Nouvel Orch, Saint-Etienne Nouvel Chorus [F] *(rec live, Massenet Festival in Saint-Etienne 1990)* Koch Schwann 2-▲ 3-1032-2 [DDD]

Massenet, J.:La Vierge, w. M. Command (sop), M. Castets (sop), M. Keller (sop), P. Salmon (ten), M. Hacquard (bar), P. Fournillier (cnd), Prague SO, Prague Sym Chorus Koch Schwann 2-▲ CD 313084 [DDD]

Mercadante, S.:Il giuramento, w. G. Morino (ten), G. Carella (cnd), Loire PO Nuova Era 2-▲ NUO 7179 [DDD]

Olsen, D. (bass)

Martin, F.:Le Vin herbé, w. B. Retchitzka (sop), H. Morath (cta), O. de Nyzankowskyi (ten), H. Rehfuss (bar), F. Martin (pno), V. Desarzens (cnd), Winterthur State Orch members Jecklin-Disco 2-▲ JD 581/2-2 [ADD]

Olsen, Derrik (bar)

Martin, F.:Le Mystère de la Nativité, w. Elly Ameling (sop), Aafje Heynis (cta), Hugues Cuénod (ten), Louis Devos (ten), Eric Tappy (ten), Pierre Bollet (bar), Charles Clavensy (b-bar), André Vessières (bass), E. Ansermet (cnd), Swiss Romande Orch, Jeunes de l'Eglise Chorus, Ceneva Motet Chorus Cascavelle 2-▲ CVL 2006 [ADD]

Martin, F.:Pilate, w. Ariette Chedel (cta), Eugenia Zareska (mez), Eric Tappy (ten), Jean-Christoph Benoit (bar), E. Ansermet (cnd), Swiss Romande Orch, Lausanne Pro Arte Choir Cascavelle 2-▲ CVL 2006 [ADD]

Olsen, Frode (bass)

Wagner, R.:Die Walküre (act 1), w. Edda Moser (sop—Sieglinde), Mark Lundberg (ten—Siegmund), Frode Olsen (bass—Hunding), I. Törzs (cnd), Mecklenburg State Orch *(rec Mecklenburg State Theatre, Schwerin, June 29, 1994)* Calig ▲ CAL 50943 [DDD]

Olsen, K. (ten)

Berlioz, H.:La Damnation de Faust, w. J. Larmor (mez—Marguerite), K. Olsen (ten—Faust), D. Wilson-Johnson (bar—Méphistophélès), H. Claessens (bar—Brander), G. Neuhold (cnd), Flanders Royal PO, Düsseldorf Municipal Choral Society Bayer 2-▲ 500017/18 [DDD]

Olsen, Stanford (ten)

Mozart, W.A.:Entführung, w. L. Orgonasova (sop), C. Sieden (sop), Uwe Peper (ten), C. Hauptmann (bass), Hans-Peter Minetti (nar), J. E. Gardiner (cnd), English Baroque Soloists, Monteverdi Choir London [G] Deutsche Grammophon 2-▲ 435857-2

Rossini, G.:Tancredi, w. Sumi Jo (sop—Amenaide), Lucretia Lendi (mez—Roggiero), Anna Maria di Micco (mez—Isaura), Ewa Podles (cta—Tancredi), Stanford Olsen (ten—Argirio), Pietro Spagnoli (bar—Orbazzano), Ewald Demeyere (hpd), Lieven Baert (vc), Franck Coryn (db), A. Zedda (cnd), Collegium Instrumentale Brugense, Capella Brugensis *(rec Poissy Theatre & Centre Musical-Lyrique-Phonographique, Ile de France, Jan. 20-31, 1994)* Naxos ("Opera Classics" series) 2-▲ 8.660037/38 [DDD]

Olsson, Catharina (mez)

Geijer, E.G.:Songs, w. Per-Arne Walhgren (bar), Thomas Schuback (pno) Musica Sveciae ▲ MSV 519 [ADD]

Olsson, Sara (sop)

Sandström, S.-D.:The High Mass, w. Lena Hoel (sop), Siri Torjesen (sop), Marianne Eklöf (mez), Annika Skoglund (mez), Peter Bengtson (org), L. Segerstam (cnd), Swedish RSO, Eric Ericson Chamber Choir *(rec live, Berwald Hall, Stockholm, Nov. 25 & 26, 1994)* Caprice 2-▲ CAP 22036

Olvis, William (ten)

Romberg, S.:Deep in My Heart, w. H. Traubel (sgr), J. Ferrer (sgr), R. Clooney (sgr), Gene Kelly (sgr), F. Kelly (sgr), V. Damone (sgr), J. Powell (sgr), A. Miller (sgr), C. Richards (sgr), H. Keel (sgr), T. Martin (sgr), J. Weldon (sgr) Sony Music Special Products ▲ AK 47703

Omaggio, Walter (ten)

Tosti, P.F.:Canti populari e romanze abruzzesi, w. C. Di Censo (sop), M. Gentile (mez), P. Speca (sgr), I. Crissante (pno) Nuova Era ▲ NUO 7166 [DDD]

O'Malley, Jeff (nar)

Gisberg:Music of, w. Gisburg (sgr/fl), Midori Seiler (vn), Ron Lawrence (va), Guy Tyler (db), Anthony Coleman (pno), Christine Bard (perc)—Low-End; Since You Have Left; The Woman Is Perfected; Sharks; Night & Wind; Saturnspacemonsters Walking on a Sandy Surface; Old Moon in Winter; Never Saw the Stars So Bright; Habe Die Liebe Verschlafen; W.A.L.S.H. Tzadik ▲ TZA CD 7019 [DDD]

Gisberg:Music of, w. Christine Bard (perc), Christina Sun (erhu), Jacqueline Leclair (ob), Quentin Chiappetta (sampler/pno/cpsr), Reuben Radding (bass instrument), Gisburg (voice/fl/cpsr)—Opening; No Stranger Not At All; Imaginary Movielandscape 1; Portrait; "Jowohl"; Mein Herz hat nicht vergessen [tango]; Ritual; Dying Takes Its Time; Fruits; Mic' N Drums Tzadik ("The Composers" series) ▲ TZA 7007 [DDD]

Omeron, Guen (sgr)

Strauss (II), Joh.:Eine Nacht in Venedig, w. Nola Fairbanks (sgr—Ciboletta), Thomas Tibbett Hayward (sgr—Mario), Laurel Hurley (sgr—Nina), David Kurlan (sgr—Senator Bartoldi), Guen Omeron (sgr—Barbara), Jack Russell (sgr—Duke of Palobino), Kenneth Schon (sgr—Filippo Del Aqua), Norwood Smith (sgr—Caramello), Enzo Stuarti (sgr—Pappacoda) *(rec Belock Recording Studio, Bayside, NY)* Everest ▲ EVC 9036 [AAD]

Omilian, Jolanta (sop)

Bellini, V.:Ariette da camera (6), w. S. Frontalini (cnd), Warmia National Orch [I] Bongiovanni ▲ GB 2098 [DDD]

Pergolesi, G.B.:Adriano in Siria, w. D. Dessi (sop), L. Mazzaria (sop), S. Anselmi (sop), G. Banditelli (cta), E. di Cesare (ten), M. Panni (cnd), Rome Opera CO [I] *(rec live 12/20/86)* Bongiovanni 3-▲ GB 2078/80 [DDD]

Ommerlé, Jeanne (sop)
Hindemith, P.:Hin und zurück, w. Jeanne Ommerlé (sop—Helene), Carl Halvorson (ten—Robert), Austin Wright Moore (ten—Sage), Richard Holmes (bar—Doctor), Robert Osborne (b-bar—Orderly), S. R. Radcliffe (cnd), New York Chamber Ensemble *(rec LeFrak Concert Hall, Queens College, Flushing, NY, May 30 & 31, 1994)* Albany ▲ TROY 173 [DDD]
Menotti, G.C.:The Telephone, w. Jeanne Ommerle (sop—Lucy), Richard Holmes (bar—Ben), S. R. Radcliffe (cnd), New York Chamber Ensemble *(rec LeFrak Concert Hall, Queens College, Flushing, NY, May 30 & 31, 1994)* Albany ▲ TROY 173 [DDD]
Paine, J.K.:St. Peter, w. A. Fortunato (mez), P. Kelly (ten), D. Evitts (bar), G. Schuller (cnd), Boston Pro Arte CO, Back Bay Chorale [E] *(rec live in concert at Sanders Theater, Cambridge, Mass., 5/21/89)* GM 2–▲ 2027CD 2
Thomson, V.:Lord Byron, w. D. Fortunato (mez), M. Lord (ten), R. Zeller (bar), R. Johnson (bar), J. Bolle (cnd), Monadnock Music Festival Orch [E] *(rec live, Aug. 31 & Sept. 2, 1991)* Koch International Classics 2–▲ KIC 7124-2 [DDD]

Oncina, Juan (ten)
Bellini, V.:Beatrice di Tenda, w. L. Gencer (sop), M. Zanasi (bar), V. Gui (cnd), Venice Teatro La Fenice Orch, Venice Teatro La Fenice Chorus *(rec 1964)* Memories 2–▲ MEM 4543 [ADD]
Donizetti, G.:Roberto Devereux (sels), w. M. Caballé (sop), L. Chookasian (mez), W. Alberti (bar), C.F. Cillario (cnd), *(orch & chorus unknown)*—9 arias from Acts 1 & 2 [I] *(rec live in Carnegie Hall, 12/16/65)* Standing Room Only 2–▲ SRO 801-2 (m) [ADD]
Puccini, G.:La Bohème (sels), w. M. Olivero (sop), S. Hubada (cnd), Zagreb Opera Orch—one solo soprano aria (Si, mi chiamano Mimi) & one duet (O soave fanciulla) [I] *(rec live 5/3/64)* Myto 2–▲ 2 MCD 91136 [ADD]
Rossini, G.:Le Comte Ory, w. J. Sinclair (sop), M. Sinclair (cta), M. Roux (bar), V. Gui (cnd), Glyndebourne Festival Orch, Glyndebourne Festival Chorus *(rec 1956)* EMI Classics 2–▲ CDMB 64180
Verdi, G.:Un giorno di regno, w. Lina Pagliughi (sop), Mario Carlin (ten), Sesto Bruscantini (bar), Renato Capecchi (bar), Laura Cozzi (sgr), Cristiano Dalamangas (sgr), A. Simonetto (cnd), Milan RAI Lyric Orch, Milan RAI Chorus *(rec 1951)* Cetra Classic 2–▲ CDON 37 [ADD]

Onegin, Sigrid (cta)
Brahms, J.:Alto Rhap, w. K. Singer (cnd), Berlin State Opera Orch, Berlin Doctors' Choir [G] *(rec 1929 from HMV 78 rpm discs)* Preiser ("Lebendige Vergangenheit" series) ▲ 89027 (m) [AAD]
Opera Arias Preiser ("Lebendige Vergangenheit" series) ▲ PRE 89027 (m) [AAD]

O'Neill, Clare (sop)
Sullivan, A.:The Yeomen of the Guard, w. Felicity Palmer (sop—Dame Carruthers), Pamela Helen Stephens (mez—Phoebe Meryll), Neill Archer (ten—Col Fairfax), Peter Hoare (ten—Leonard Meryll), Ralph Mason (ten—1st Yeoman), Donald Maxwell (bar—Wilfred Shadbolt), Peter Savidge (bar—Lieutenant Sir Richard Cholmondely), Donald Adams (bass—Sergeant Meryll), Richard Suart (bass—Jack Point), Peter Lloyd Evans (sgr—2nd Yeoman), Alwyn Mellor (sgr—Elsie Maynard), Clare O'Neill (sgr—Kate), C. Mackerras (cnd), Welsh National Opera Orch, Welsh National Opera Chorus *(rec Brangwyn Hall, Swasea, Wales, Apr 18–30 & May 1, 1995)* Telarc 2–▲ CD 80404 [DDD]

O'Neill, Dennis (ten)
Donizetti, G.:Anna Bolena (sels), w. Carol Vaness (sop), Melinda Paulsen (cta), Anton Rosner (ten), Ambrogio Riva (bass), R. Abbado (cnd), Munich RSO, Bavarian Radio Chorus—Final Scene & Aria [from Act II] *(rec Studio 1, Bavaria, Apr 13–17, 1993)* RCA Red Seal ▲ 09026-61828-2 [DDD]
Puccini, G.:La fanciulla del West, w. Eva Martón (sop), Walter Planté (ten), Alain Fondary (bar), L. Slatkin (cnd), Munich RSO RCA Red Seal ▲ 09026-60597-2
Puccini, G.:Tosca, w. Jane Eaglen (sop—Floria Tosca), Charbel Michael (alt—Shepherd Boy), John Daszak (ten—Spoletta), Dennis O'Neill (ten—Mario Cavaradossi), Christopher Booth-Jones (bar—Sciarrone), Ashley Holland (bar—Jailor), Gregory Yurisich (bar—Baron Scarpia), Peter Rose (bass—Cesare Angelotti), Andrew Shore (bass—Sacristan), D. Parry (cnd), Philharmonia Orch, Geoffrey Mitchell Choir, Peter Kay Children's Chorus Chandos ("Opera in English" series) 2–▲ CHAN 3000
10,000 Voices, w. G. Jones (bar), A. Sammons (vn), World Choir, Massed Guards Bands [cnd:O. Arwel Hughes] *(rec live May 23, 1992)* EMI Classics ▲ CDC 54628-2 [DDD]
Tosti, P.F.:Songs, w. R. Vignoles (pno)—15 songs Meridian ▲ CDE 84128
Verdi, G.:Requiem Mass, w. C. Vaness (sop), F. Quivar (mez), C. Colombara (bass), C. Davis (cnd), Bavarian RSO, Bavarian Radio Chorus RCA Red Seal 2–▲ 09026-60902-2
Verdi, G.:La traviata (sels), w. Carol Vaness (sop), R. Abbado (cnd), Munich RSO, Bavarian Radio Chorus—Final Scene & Aria [from Act I] *(rec Studio 1, Bavaria, Apr 13–17, 1993)* RCA Red Seal ▲ 09026-61828-2 [DDD]
Verdi, G.:Il trovatore (sels), w. Carol Vaness (sop), Anton Rosner (ten), R. Abbado (cnd), Munich RSO, Bavarian Radio Chorus—Scene, Aria & Miserere [from Act IV] *(rec Studio 1, Munich, Apr 13–17, 1993)* RCA Red Seal ▲ 09026-61828-2 [DDD]

Onesti, Giorgio (bass)
Giordano, U.:Andrea Chénier, w. Renata Tebaldi (sop—Maddalena), Anna di Stasio (mez—Bersi), Amalia Pini (mez—Madelon/Contessa), Mario Del Monaco (ten—Andrea Chenier), Antonio Pirino (ten—L'Incredibile/Abate), Aldo Protti (bar—Carlo Gerard), Arturo La Porta (bass/bar—Mathieu/Fleville), Silvano Pagliuca (bass/bar—Roucher/Fouquier-Tinville), Giorgio Onesti (bass—Dumas/Schmidt/Major-domo), F. Capuana (cnd), Italian Lyric Orch, Italian Lyric Chorus *(rec Tokyo, Oct 1, 1961)* Legato Classics 2–▲ LCD 214-2 [ADD]

Oosterkamp, Wout (bass)
Schreker, F.:Die Gezeichneten, w. M. Schmiege (mez), W. Cochran (ten), S. Cowan (bar), E. de Waart (cnd), Dutch Radio PO, Dutch Radio Phil Chorus Marco Polo 3–▲ 8.223328/30

Oosternrijk, Nienke (sgr)
Vaughan Williams, R.:Blake Songs, w. P. Oosternrijk (ob) Channel Classics ▲ CCS 9326 [DDD]

Oosting, Stephen (ten)
Albert, S.:Into Eclipse, w. S. Hodkinson (cnd), Eastman Musica Nova Ensemble *(rec Eastman Theater, Mar 26, 1983)* Albany ▲ TROY 192 [ADD]
Handel, G.F.:Acis & Galatea, w. J. Baird (sop), L. Hirst (mez), J. Ostendorf (b-bar), J. Somary (cnd), Amor Artis Orch, Amor Artis Chorale [E] Newport Classic 2–▲ NC 60045 [DDD]

Opalach, Jan (bass)
Bach, J.S.:Magnificat, BWV 243, w. J. Bryden (sop), J. Baird (sop), J Gall (ct), F. Hoffmeister (ten), J. Rifkin (cnd), Bach Ensemble [L] Pro Arte ▲ CDD 185 [DDD]
Bach, J.S.:Mass in b, BWV 232, w. J. Baird (sop), J. Nelson (sop), J. Dooley (ct), F. Hoffmeister (ten), J. Rifkin (cnd), Bach Ensemble [L] Elektra/Nonesuch 2–▲ 79036-2 [DDD] 2–■ 79036-4 (D)
Beaser, R.:The 7 Deadly Sins, w. D. R. Davies (cnd), American Composers Orch Argo ▲ 440337-2 [DDD]
Carter, E.:Syringa, w. K. Ciesinski (mez), W. Purvis (cnd), Speculum Musicae Bridge ▲ BCD 9014 [DDD]
Handel, G.F.:Acis & Galatea, w. D. Kotoski (sop—Galatea), D. Gordon (ten—Acis), G. Siebert (ten—Damon), J. Opalach (bass—Polyphemus), G. Schwarz (cnd), Seattle SO, Seattle Chorale [E] Delos 2–▲ DE 3107 [DDD]
Handel, G.F.:Berenice, w. Julianne Baird (sop—Berenice), Andrea Matthews (sop—Alessandro), D'Anna Fortunato (mez—Selene), Jennifer Lane (mez—Demetrio), Drew Minter (alt—Arsace), John McMaster (ten—Fabio), Jan Opalach (bass—Aristobolo), R. Palmer (cnd), Brewer CO Newport Classic 3–▲ NPD 85620/3 [DDD]
Handel, G.F.:Imeneo, w. Julianne Baird (sop—Rosmene), Beverly Hoch (sop—Clomiri), D'Anna Fortunato (cta—Tirinto), Jan Opalach (bass—Argenio), John Ostendorf (bass—Imeneo), Edward Brewer (hpd), R. Palmer (cnd), Brewer CO Vox Box 2–▲ CDX 5135 [DDD]
Rossini, G.:Music of, w. M. Fortuna (sop), M. Lerner (sop), D. Voigt (sop), M. Horne (mez), K. Kuhlmann (mez), F. von Stade (mez), R. Blake (ten), C. Estep (ten), C. Merritt (ten), T. Hampson (b-bar), H. Runey (b-bar), S. Ramey (bass), R. Norrington (cnd), Orch of St. Luke's, New York Concert Chorale EMI Classics ▲ CDC 54643
Stravinsky, I.:Pulcinella, w. J. Graham-Hall (ten), G. Wilson (ten), G. Schwarz (cnd), Seattle SO Delos ▲ DE 3100 [DDD]

Opie, A. (bass)
Walton, W.:The Bear, w. D. Jones (mez), J. Shirley-Quirk (bar), R. Hickox (cnd), Northern Sinfonia of England Chandos ▲ CHAN 9245 [DDD]

Opie, Alan (bar)
Britten, H.:Canticles I-V, w. M. Chance (ct), A. Rolfe-Johnson (ten), R. Vignoles (pno), S. Williams (hp), M. Thompson (hn) Hyperion ▲ CDA 66498
Britten, H.:Purcell Realizations, w. M. Chance (ct), A. Rolfe-Johnson (ten), R. Vignoles (pno)—3 Realizations (An evening hymn; Let the dreadful engines; In the black dismal dungeon of despair) Hyperion ▲ CDA 66498
Britten, H.:The Rape of Lucretia (sels), w. C. Pierard (sop), P. Rozario (sop), A. Gunson (mez), J. Rigby (cta), N. Robson (ten), D. Maxwell (bar), A. Miles (bass), R. Hickox (cnd), City of London Sinfonia Chandos 2–▲ CHAN 9254/55 [DDD]
Vaughan Williams, R.:Hugh the Dover, w. R. Evans (sop), S. Walker (mez), B. Bottone (ter), N. Jenkins (ten), R. Van Allan (bass), M. Best (cnd), Corydon Orch, Corydon Singers, New London Children's Choir Hyperion 2–▲ CDA 66901/02
Vaughan Williams, R.:The Shepherds of the Delectable Mountains, w. L. Kitchen (sop), J.-M. Ainsley (ten), A. Thompson (ten), B. Terfel (b-bar), J. Best (bass), M. Best (cnd), City of London Sinfonia [E] Hyperion ▲ CDA 66569 [DDD]
Walton, W.:Troilus & Cressida, w. Judith Howarth (sop—Cressida), Arthur Davies (ten—Troilus), Nigel Robson (ten—Pandarus), Brian Cookson (ten—3rd Watchman), Peter Bodenham (ten—Priest), Keith Mills (ten—Soldier), Alan Opie (bar—Diomede), James Thornton (bar—Antenor), Clive Bayley (bass—Calkas), David Owen-Lewis (bass—Horaste), R. Hickox (cnd), English Northern Philharmonia, Opera North Chorus Chandos 2–▲ CHAN 9370/71 [DDD]
Weill, K.:The Seven Deadly Sins, w. J. Migenes (sop), R. Tear (ten), S. Kale (ten), R. Kennedy (bass), M. Tilson Thomas (cnd), London SO CBS ▲ MK 44529 [DDD]

Oppleberg, Christian (bar)
Strauss (II), Joh.:Eine Nacht in Venedig (sels), w. Christine Gorner (sop), Rita Streich (sop), Cesare Curzi (ten), Nicolai Gedda (ten), F. Allers (cnd), Graunke SO, Graunke Chorus Emperor Operetta ▲ KO 86345

Oprea, Emilia (mez)
Puccini, G.:Tosca, w. Virginia Zeani (sop—Floria Tosca), Emilia Oprea (mez—Shepherd), Nicolae Andreescu (ten—Spoletta), Corneliu Fanateanu (ten—Mario Cavaradossi), Nicolae Herlea (bar—Baron Scarpia), Gheorghe Crasnaru (bass—Cesare Angelotti), Constantin Gabor (bass—Sacristan), Pompei Harasteanu (bass—Jailer), Adrian Stefanescu (bass—Sciarrone), C. Trailescu (cnd), Romanian Opera Orch, Romanian Opera Chorus *(rec Sept 1977)* Vox Box 2–▲ CDX 5153

Oprisanu, Carmen (mez)
Bizet, G.:Carmen (sels), w. Rob Haertel (perc), Daniel Speer Trombone Consort [arr Gerard de Krom] World Wind ▲ CD KK 9618 [DDD]

Orán, Maria (sop)
Vries, K. de:Music of, w. Ketting, Montgomery, Zinman (cnd), Netherlands Ballet Orch, Rotterdam PO—Areas; Bewegingen; Follia; Discantus; Phrases Donemus ▲ CV 25

Orazi, Attilio d' (bar)
Bellini, V.:I Puritani, w. Mirella Freni (sop—Elvira), Rita Bezzi (mez—Enrichetta), Alfredo Kraus (ten—Arturo Talbot), Augusto Pedroni (ten—Sir Bruno Robertson), Attilio d'Orazi (bar—Sir Riccardo Forth), Raffaele Arié (bass—Sir Giorgio), Bruno Cioni (bass—Lord Gualtiero Walton), N. Verchi (cnd), Modena Teatro Comunale Orch, Modeno Teatro Comunale Chorus *(rec Modena Teatro Comunale, Dec. 26, 1962)* Legato Classics 2–▲ LCD 195-2 [ADD]
Cilea, F.:Adriana Lecouvreur, w. M. Caballé (sop), F. Cossotto (mez), J. Carreras (ten), G.-F. Masini (cnd), *(orch unknown)* [I] *(rec 1976)* Legato Classics 2–▲ LCD 111-2 [AAD]

Orciani, Patrizia (sop)
Rossini, G.:Il Signor Bruschino, w. K. Lytting (mez), L. Canonici (ten), F. Massa (ten), B. Praticò (bar), P. Spagnoli (bar), N. de Carolis (b-bar), M. Viotti (cnd), Turin PO [I] Claves 8–▲ CD 9200 [DDD]
Rossini, G.:Il Signor Bruschino, w. Katia Lytting (mez), Luca Canonici (ten), Fulvio Massa (ten), Bruno Praticò (bar), Pietro Spagnoli (bar), Natale de Carolis (b-bar), M. Viotti (cnd), Turin PO Claves 2–▲ 50-8904/5

Orda, Alfred (bar)
Alfred Orda Operatic Recital, w. Polish RSO [cnd:S. Rachon, H. Debich, K. Missona] Symposium ▲ SYM 1117
A Recital of Russian & Polish Songs, w. Josephine Lee (pno), Ernest Lush (pno) Symposium ▲ SYM 1067

Ordassy, Carlotta (sop)
Verdi, G.:Ernani, w. L. Price (sop), F. Corelli (ten), C. Anthony (ten), M. Sereni (bar), C. Siepi (bass), C. Russel (bass), T. Schippers (cnd), *(orch unknown)* *(rec 1965)* Great Opera Performances ▲ GOP 702

Ordóñez, Antonio (ten)
Falla, M. de:La vida breve, w. A. Nafé (mez), J. López-Cobos (cnd), Cincinnati SO, May Festival Chorus [Sp] Telarc ▲ CD 80317 [DDD]

Orellana, Humberto (sgr)
Monteverdi, C.:Ballo delle ingrate, w. Carlo Lepore (bass), Daniela Barcellona (sgr), Daniela Ciliberti (sgr), Andrea Concetti (sgr), Hans van Dijk (sgr), Remo Guerrini (sgr), Nadia Mantelli (sgr), Elena Marazzi (sgr), Claudia Pallini (sgr), Luigi Polsini (sgr), Rosa Ricciotti (sgr), Alberto Rota (sgr), Ludovica Scoppola (sgr), *(orch unknown)* Nuova Era ▲ NUO 7224

Orff, Godela (nar)
Orff, C.:Schulwerk (complete), w. Marina Koppelstetter (mez), Carolin Widmann (vn), Sabina Lehrmann (vc), Markus Zahnhausen (rcr), Karl Peinkofer Percussion Ensemble—4 Pieces for Xylophone; 5 Little Canons; 4 Dance Pieces; Songs & Instrumental Pieces; 3 Pieces for Fl & Perc; Songs & Dances; 2 Time Change Dances for Vn & Vc; 7 Folk Dances; Music for the Night *(rec Munich, 1994–95)* Celestial Harmonies ▲ 13104-2
Orff, C.:Schulwerk (complete), w. Carolin Widmann (vn), Sonja Korkeala (vn), Markus Zahnhausen (rcr), Karl Peinkofer (perc), Andreas Schumacher (perc), Wilfried Hiller (perc/mar), Martin Ruhland (mar), Munich Hochschule Madrigal Choir—Wessobrun Prayer for a capella Choir; 2 Pieces for a capella Choir; 8 Pieces for 2 Vns; Mater et filia for women's a capella Choir; Devotional Yodel for male a capella Choir; 5 Pieces for Sop, Rcr & Perc; Death for Nar., Wood Bells, Bass Xyl & Tam-Tam; Omnia tempus habent for mixed Choir, Timp & Little Dr; Rubato, molto allegro, rubato; Abenlied for Nar, Bass Metallophon, Bass Xyl, Large Dr & Wine Glass; 5 Pieces for Fl & Perc; Devotional Yodel for male Choir [version 2]; 7 Pieces for 2 Xyl *(rec Munich, 1994–95)* Celestial Harmonies ▲ 13105-2

Orgonasova, Luba (sop)
Beethoven, L. van:Missa Solemnis, w. J. Rappé (ten), J.-H. Rootering (bass), C. Davis (cnd), Bavarian RSO, Bavarian Radio Chorus RCA Red Seal 2–▲ 09026-60967-2
Beethoven, L. van:Sym 9, "Choral Sym", w. Anne Sofie von Otter (mez), Anthony Rolfe Johnson (ten), Gilles Cachemaille (b-bar), J. E. Gardiner (cnd), Orch Révolutionnaire et Romantique [period instrs] *(rec All Saints' Church, London, Oct 1992)* Archiv ▲ 447074-2 [DDD]
Britten, H.:War Requiem, w. A. Rolfe-Johnson (ten), B. Skovhus (bar), J. E. Gardiner (cnd), North German RSO, Monteverdi Choir London, North German Radio Chorus, Tölz Boys' Choir Deutsche Grammophon 2–▲ 437801-2
Favorite Soprano Arias, w. Czech-Slovak RSO Bratislava [cnd:Will Humburg] *(rec 1990–91)* Naxos ▲ 8.550605 [DDD]
Mozart, W.A.:Don Giovanni, w. Charlotte Margiono (sop—Donna Elvira), Luba Orgonasova (sop—Donna Anna), Eirian James (mez—Zerlina), Julian Clarkson (alt—Masetto), Christoph Prégardien (ten—Don Ottavio), Rodney Gilfry (bar—Don Giovanni), Ildebrando d'Arcangelo (bass—Leporello), Andrea Silvestrelli (bass—Il Commendatore), J. E. Gardiner (cnd), English Baroque Soloists, Monteverdi Choir London Deutsche Grammophon ("4D Audio" series) 3–▲ 445870-2
Mozart, W.A.:Entführung, w. C. Sieden (sop), S. Olsen (ten), Uwe Peper (ten), C. Hauptmann (bass), Hans-Peter Minetti (nar), J. E. Gardiner (cnd), English Baroque Soloists, Monteverdi Choir London [G] Deutsche Grammophon 2–▲ 435857-2
Mozart, W.A.:Zauberflöte, w. S. Jo (sop), Martina Bovet (sop), G. Winbergh (ten), H. Hagegard (bar), A. Jordan (cnd), Paris Orchestral Ensemble, Romande Chamber Choir, Pro Arte Lausanne Erato 2–▲ 2292-45469-2 [DDD]
Puccini, G.:La Bohème, w. C. Gonzales (mez), J. Welch (ten), F. Previati (bar), W. Humburg (cnd), *(orch unknown)*, Bratislava Children's Choir [I] Naxos 2–▲ 8.660003/04 [DDD]

Orgonasova, Luba (sop) (cont.)
Puccini, G.:La Bohème (sels), w. Luba Orgonasova (sop—Mimi), Carmen Gonzales (sop—Musetta), Jonathan Welch (ten—Rudolfo), Fabio Previati (bar—Marcello), Boaz Senator (bar—Schaunard), Ivan Urbas (bass—Colline), Jiri Sulzenko (bass—Alcindoro), W. Humburg (cnd), Czech-Slovak RSO Bratislava, Bratislava Children's Choir, Slovak Phil Chorus *(rec Concert Hall, Czecho-Slovak Radio, Bratislava, Apr. 23–May 4, 1990)* Naxos ▲ 8.553151 [DDD]
Rossini, G.:Stabat Mater, w. Cecilia Bartoli (mez), Raul Gimenez (ten), Roberto Scandiuzzi (bass), M.-W. Chung (cnd), Vienna PO, Vienna State Opera Chorus Deutsche Grammophon ▲ 449 178-2
Verdi, G.:Requiem Mass, w. Donna Brown (sop), Anne Sofie von Otter (mez), Luca Canonici (ten), Alastair Miles (bass), J. E. Gardiner (cnd), Orch Révolutionnaire et Romantique, Monteverdi Choir London Philips 2-▲ 442142-2
Zemlinsky, A. von:Lyric Sym, w. Bo Skovhus (bar), C. P. Flor (cnd), North German RSO *(rec Musikhalle, Hamburg, Sept 8–10, 1994)* RCA Red Seal ▲ 09026-68111-2 [DDD]

Orladey, Patrick (sgr)
Planquette, R.:Rip van Winkle, w. Claudine Collart (sop), Lina Dachary (sop), Freda Betti (cta), René Lenoty (ten), Joseph Peyron (ten), Charles Daguerressar (bar), Julien Giovannetti (bar), Jacques Pruvost (bar), Lucien Lovano (bass), Joëlle Pierre (sgr), M. Cariven (cnd), ORTF Lyric Orch, ORTF Lyric Chorale Musidisc ▲ MUS 201602 [AAD]

Orlandini, Gino (bar)
Verdi, G.:La traviata, w. R. Tebaldi (sop), G. Prandelli (ten), C. M. Giulini (cnd), Milan RAI Orch, Milan RAI Chorus *(rec live 5/28/52)* Standing Room Only 2-▲ SRO 810-2 [ADD]

Orliac, Jean-Claude (ten)
Boccherini, L.:Stabat Mater, w. T. Hert (sop), K. Oshita (sop), M. de la Fuente (cnd), La Follia Ensemble—2nd version—Op. 61 [L] *(rec 1979)* Arion ▲ ARN 68164 [ADD]
Campra, A.:Messe de Requiem, w. J. Nelson (mez), C. Harris (trb), S. Roberts (bar), J. E. Gardiner (cnd), English Baroque Soloists, Monteverdi Choir London Erato ▲ 2292-45993-2
Gounod, C.:Philémon et Baucis, w. Anne-Marie Rodde (sop), Pierre Néquecaur (bar), Félix Giband (bass), H. Gallois (cnd), French Radio Lyric Orch Musidisc ▲ MUS 202342 [AAD]
Rameau, J.P.:La Danse, w. J. Gomez (sop), A.-M. Rodde (sop), J.E. Gardiner (cnd), Monteverdi Orch, Monteverdi Choir London Erato ▲ 45985-2

Orrego, Rodrigo (ten)
Cherubini, L.:Masses, w. Monika Wiebe (sop), Helena Jungwirth (alt), Wolf Matthias Friedrich (bass), H.R. Zöbeley (cnd), Munich SO, Munich Motet Choir—Missa Solemnis Calig ▲ CAL 50914

Ortega, Ginesa (mez)
Falla, M. de:El amor brujo, w. J. Pons (cnd), Barcelona Teatro Lliure CO [Sp] Harmonia Mundi France ▲ HMC 905213

Ortega, Gino (cantor)
Falla, M. de:El corregidor y la molinera, w. J. Pons (cnd), Barcelona's Free Theater CO Harmonia Mundi France ▲ HMC 901520
Falla, M. de:El retablo de maese Pedro, w. J. Pons (cnd), Barcelona Teatro Lliure CO [Sp] Harmonia Mundi France ▲ HMC 905213
Garcia Lorca, F.:Canciones, w. J. Pons (cnd), Barcelona's Free Theater CO Harmonia Mundi France ▲ HMC 901520

Ortendahl-Corin, Barbro (sop)
Kraus, J.M.:Soliman II, w. L. Hoel (sop), B.-O. Morgny (ten), T. Wallstrom (bass), P. Brunelle (cnd), Royal Swedish Opera Orch, Sweden Royal Opera Chorus Virgin Classics ▲ 59068 [DDD]

Orth, Norbert (ten)
Wagner, R.:Rienzi, der Letzte der Tribunen, w. Cheryl Studer (sop—Irene), René Kollo (ten—Rienzi), Friedrich Lenz (ten—Gesandte), Norbert Orth (ten—Baroncelli), Bodo Brinkmann (bar—Paolo Orsini), Keith Engen (bass—Cecco del Vecchio), Raimund Grumbach (bass—Gesandte), Jan-Hendrik Rootering (bass—Steffano Colonna), Carmen Anhorn (sgr—Ein Friedensbote), Karl Helm (sgr—Kardinal Orvieto), John Janssen (sgr—Adriano), Alfred Kuhn (sgr—Gesandte), Hans Wilbrink (sgr—Gesandte), W. Sawallisch (cnd), Bavarian State Opera Orch, Bavarian State Opera Chorus *(rec live, July 6, 1983)* Orfeo d'or 3-▲ 346953

Orth, Robert (bar)
Mozart, W.A.:Entführung, w. E. Gruberova (sop), F. Araiza (ten), R. Bracht (bass), H. Wallberg (cnd), Munich RSO Eurodisc 2-▲ 7792-2 [ADD]
Weisgall, H.:Six Characters in Search of an Author, w. E. Byrne (sop—Stepdaughter), S. Foster (sop—Prompter), E. Furtal (sop—Coloratura), J. King (mez—Mezzo), N. Maultsby (mez—Mother), P. LoVerne (cta—Madame Pace), D. Pritchett (alt—Wardrobe Mistress), B. Fowler (ten—Tenore Boffo), K. Anderson (ten—Director), A. Schroeder (bar—Accompanist), P. Zawisza (bar—Stage Manager), R. Orth (bar—Father), G. Lehman (bar—Son), M. Wadsworth (b-bar—Basso Cantante), L. Schaenen (cnd), Chicago Lyric Opera Orch, Lyric Opera Center Chorus *(rec Chicago, June 14 & 16, 1990)* New World 2-▲ 80454-2

Ortica (sgr)
Verdi, G.:I vespri siciliani, w. A. Cerquetti (sop), C. Tagliabue (bar), B. Christoff (bass), M. Rossi (cnd), Turin Radio Orch, Turin Radio Chorus [I] *(rec live, Turin, 11/16/55)* Claque 2-▲ CLQ 2017 (m)

Ortiz, Juan Carlos (bass)
Gomes, A.C.:Il Guarany, w. Niza De Castro Tank (sop—Cecilia), Roque Lotti (ten—Ruy Bento), Manrico Patassini (ten—Pery), Paschoal Raymundo (ten—Don Alvaro), Paulo Fortes (bar—Gonzales), Juan Carlos Ortiz (b-bar—Il Cacico), Waldomiro Furlan (bass—Alonso), Josè Perrotta (bass—Don Antonio De Mariz), A. Belardi (cnd), Saõ Paulo Teatro Municipale Orch, Saõ Paulo Teatro Municipale Chorus *(rec Studios of the Teatro Municipal, Saõ Paulo, Brazil, 1959)* Arkadia 2-▲ HP 617.2 [ADD]

Osborne, Joan (sgr)
Pavarotti & Friends for War Child, w. Luciano Pavarotti (ten), Eric Clapton (sgr), Sheryl Crow (sgr), Elton John (sgr), Liza Minelli (sgr) Jon Secada (sgr), Eric Clapton (gtr), John McLaughlin (gtr), Marco Armiliato, Edoardo Bennato, José Molina, Al DiMeola, Kelly Family, Ligabue, Litfiba, P *(rec Modena, Italy, 1996)* London ▲ 452900-2 ■ 452900-4

Osborne, Robert (b-bar)
Hoiby, L.:Choral Music, w. L. King (org), James A. Simms (cnd), Trinity Church Choir—Ascension (Holy Sonnet No. 7); At the Round Earth's Imagined Corners; Hear Us, O Hear Us Lord; Hymn to the New Age; Inherit the Kingdom; Let This Mind Be In You; Magnificat & Nunc Dimittis; The Offering Gothic ▲ G 49035 [DDD]
Sowerby, L.:Songs, w. Malcolm Halliday (pno)—Songs on Poems of John Masefield (3); Songs on Poems of John Galsworthy (3); American Folksong Arrs (3); Songs for Donna Harrison (3); British Folksong Arrs (2); Songs on Poems of Jeanne Delamarter (2); Late Songs; From the Hillcrest (2) *(rec Patrych Studios, NY, Mar 1995)* Albany ▲ TROY 196 [DDD]

Osgood, Rockland (ten)
Lovenstein, J.:Music of, w. Mary Brockenbrough (sop), Laura Sanders (sop), Barton Green (ten), David Murray (bar), Benjamin Sears (bar), Jonathan Lovenstein (pno), Heather O'Donnell (pno), James Silvers (pno), Rocy Reider (fl), Jason Horowitz (vn), Adrianna Hulscher (vn), James Johnston (vn), Mimi Ragson (vn), Peter Landeen (vc), Reinmar Seidler (vc)—Blake Songs; other works Titanic ▲ Ti 221 [DDD]

Oshita, Kumiko (sop)
Boccherini, L.:Stabat Mater, w. T. Hert (sop), J.-C. Orilac (ten), M. de la Fuente (cnd), La Follia Ensemble—2nd version—Op. 61 [L] *(rec 1979)* Arion ▲ ARN 68164 [ADD]

Oskarsson, Gudjon (bass)
Braein, E.F.:Anne Pedersdotter, w. K. Ekeberg (sop—Anne Pedersdotter), V. Hanssen (mez—Merete Beyer), R. Eriksen (alt—Herlofs-Marte), I. M. Brekke (alt—Bente), K. M. Sandve (ten—Martin Beyer), C. Ehrstedt (ten—Master Olaus), A. Helleland (ten—David), T. Gilje (ten—Jørund), S. A. Thorsen (bar—Master Johannes), S. Carlsen (bass—Absalon Pedersøn Beyer), T. Stensvold (bass—Master Laurentius), G. Oskarsson (bass—Jens Schelderup), P. Andersson (cnd), Norwegian National Opera Orch, Norwegian National Opera Chorus Simax 2-▲ PSC 3121

Ossola, Charles (bass)
Mendelssohn, F.:Psalm 42, w. Y. Perrin (sop), M. Schwartz (mez), O. Dufour (ten), C. Traube (ten), P. Huttenlocher (bar), M. Hutin (bass), C. Liang-Sheng (cnd), Geneva SO, Geneva Univ Chorus Gallo ▲ CD 635 [AAD]
Mendelssohn, F.:Psalm 95, w. Y. Perrin (sop), M. Schwartz (mez), O. Dufour (ten), C. Traube (ten), P. Huttenlocher (bar), M. Hutin (bass), C. Liang-Sheng (cnd), Geneva SO, Geneva Univ Chorus Gallo ▲ CD 635 [AAD]

Ossola, Charles (bass) (cont.)
Mendelssohn, F.:Psalm 115, w. Y. Perrin (sop), M. Schwartz (mez), O. Dufour (ten), C. Traube (ten), P. Huttenlocher (bar), M. Hutin (bass), C. Liang-Sheng (cnd), Geneva SO, Geneva Univ Chorus Gallo ▲ CD 635 [AAD]

Ostapuik, Jerzy (bass)
Moniuszko, S.:Halka, w. B. Zagòrzanka (sop), R. Racewicz (mez), W. Ochman (ten), A. Hiolski (bar), R. Satanowski (cnd), Warsaw Teatr Wielki Orch, Warsaw Teatr Wielki Chorus *(rec live, 10/14/86)* CPO 2-▲ CPO 999032-2 [DDD]

Ostar, K. (sgr)
Concerti, w. Magda Olivero (sop), U. Trama (bass), D. Antoioli (sgr), A. Protti (bar), Fulvio Vernizzi (cnd) Great Opera Performances 2-▲ GOP 709

Osten, Signue von (sop)
Penderecki, K.:St. Luke Passion, w. S. Roberts (bar), K. Rydl (bass), E. Lubaszenko (narr), K. Penderecki (cnd), Polish National RSO Katowice, Cracow Boys Choir, Warsaw National Phil Chorus Argo ▲ 430328-2 [DDD]

Ostendorf, John (bass)
Battistin, J.B.:Héraclitie et Démocrite, w. D. Fortunato (mez), E. Brewer (hpd), R. Palmer (cnd), Brewer CO [period instrs] *(rec 1985)* Erasmus ▲ WVH 071 [DDD]
Clérambault, L.N.:Cants, w. D. Fortunato (mez), E. Brewer (org), R. Palmer (cnd), Brewer CO—Le Soleil vainqueur (1721); Léandre et Héro [from Livre II (1713)] *(rec 1985)* Erasmus ▲ WVH 071 [DDD]
Dvořák, A.:Songs, w. C. Ciesinski (mez), G. Hirst (ten), R. Palmer (pno)—Serbian Songs, Op. 6; Folk Tunes, Op. 73; 4 Lieder, Op. 82; Love Songs, Op. 83; Russian Folk Duets Erasmus ▲ WVH 084
Handel, G.F.:Acis & Galatea, w. J. Baird (sop), L. Hirst (mez), S. Oosting (ten), J. Somary (cnd), Amor Artis Orch, Amor Artis Chorale [E] Newport Classic 2-▲ NC 60045 [DDD]
Handel, G.F.:Imeneo, w. Julianne Baird (sop—Rosmene), Beverly Hoch (sop—Clomiri), D'Anna Fortunato (cta—Tirinto), Jan Opalach (bass—Argenio), John Ostendorf (bass—Imeneo), Edward Brewer (hpd), R. Palmer (cnd), Brewer CO Vox Box 2-▲ CDX 5135 [DDD]
Handel, G.F.:Joshua, w. Julianne Baird (sop), D'Anna Fortunato (mez), John Aler (ten), R. Palmer (cnd), Brewer CO, Brewer Chorus [period instrs] Newport Classic 2-▲ NPD 85515/1-2 [DDD]
Handel, G.F.:Muzio Scevola, w. Julianne Baird (sop—Clelia), Andrea Matthews (sop—Fidalma), Erie Mills (sop—Orazio), D'Anna Fortunato (mez—Muzio), Jennifer Lane (mez—Irene), Frederick Urrey (ten—Tarquino), John Ostendorf (b-bar—Porsenna), R. Palmer (cnd), Brewer Baroque CO [period instrs] [I] *(rec 10/91)* Newport Classic 2-▲ NPD 85540/2 [DDD]
Handel, G.F.:Siroe, Rè di Persia, w. Andrea Matthews (sop), Julianne Baird (mez), D'Anna Fortunato (mez), Steven Rickards (ct), Frederick Urrey (ten), R. Palmer (cnd), Brewer Baroque CO [period instrs] [I] Newport Classic 3-▲ NCD 60125 [DDD]
Pergolesi, G.B.:La serva padrona, w. J. Baird (sop), R. Palmer (cnd), Philomel Baroque CO [I] Omega ▲ OCD 1016 [DDD]
Telemann, G.P.:Pimpinone, w. Julianne Baird (sop—Vespetta), John Ostendorf (bass—Pimpinone), R. Palmer (cnd), St. Luke's Baroque Orch Newport Classics ▲ NCD 60117 [DDD]

Ostermayer (sgr)
Orff, C.:Der Bernauerin, w. L. Popp (sop), Laubenthal (ten), H. Lippert (ten), K. Eichhorn (cnd), Munich RSO, Munich Radio Chorus [G] Orfeo 2-▲ 255912 [DDD]

Ostertag, Karl (ten)
Janácek, L.:The Excursions of Mr. Brouček, w. Antonie Fahberg (sop—Piccolo), Wilma Lipp (sop—Málinka), Lilian Benningsen (cta—Fanny Nowak), Paul Kuen (ten—Trambahn-Kondukteur), Karl Ostertag (ten—Vorsitzender des Hausbesitzerverbandes), Fritz Wunderlich (ten—Mazal), Kurt Böhme (b-bar—Sakristan von St. Veit), Kieth Engen (bass—Würfl), J. Keilberth (cnd), Bavarian SO *(rec live, Prinzregententheater, Nov. 19, 1959)* Orfeo 2-▲ 354942 (m)
Mussorgsky, M.:Boris Godunov, w. Martha Mödl (sop—Marina Mniszek), Lotte Schädle (sop—Xenia), Dorothea Siebert (mez—Fyodor), Hertha Töpper (mez—Xenia's wet-nurs), Karl Hermann Bennert (Boyer Khrushchyov), Lorenz Fehenberger (ten—Prince Shuysky), Hans Hopf (ten—Grigory), Karl Ostertag (ten—Missail), Hans Hotter (b-bar—Boris Godunov), Hermann Uhde (bar—Andrey Shchelkalov), Kurt Böhme (bass—Varlaam), Kim Borg (bass—Pimen), Kieth Engen (bass—Lewicki), Adolf Keil (bass—Nikitich), Benno Kusche (bar—Rangoni), Heinz Maria Linz (bass—Czernikowski), E. Jochum (cnd), Bavarian RSO, Bavarian Radio Chorus *(rec Munich, May 1957)* Myto 3-▲ MCD 953131
Orff, C.:Antigonae, w. Christel Goltz (sop), Paul Kuen (ten), Benno Kusche (bar), Hermann Uhde (bar), N. Barth (bar), G. Solti (cnd), Bavarian State Opera Orch, Bavarian State Opera Chorus *(rec Prinzregententheater, Jan. 12, 1951)* Orfeo d'or 2-▲ 407952
Strauss, R.:Feuersnot, w. Maud Cunitz (sop—Diemut), Antonia Fahberg (sop—Elsbeth), Irmgard Barth (mez—Wigelis), Liselotte Nölser (sgr—Margret), Karl Ostertag (ten—Schweiker), Marcel Cordes (bar—Kunrad), Kieth Engen (bass—Kofel), Karl Hoppe (bass—Hämerlein), Max Proebstl (bass—Ortolf), Georg Wieter (bass—Jörg), R. Kempe (cnd), Bavarian State Opera Orch, Bavarian State Opera Chorus *(rec Munich Opera Festival, Prince Regent Theater, Aug 14, 1958)* Orfeo d'or 2-▲ 423962
Strauss, R.:Salome, w. Astrid Varnay (sop—Salome), Hertha Töpper (mez—Der Page der Herodias), Margarete Klose (cta—Herodias), Hans Hopf (ten—Narraboth), Karl Hoppe (ten—1st Nazarene), Karl Ostertag (ten—1st Jew), Julius Patzak (ten—Herodes), Hans Braun (bar—Jochanaan), Benno Kusche (bar—2nd Soldier), Adolf Keil (bass—1st Soldier), Hans Hermann Nissen (bass—Ein Kappadozier), Max Proebstl (bass—2nd Nazarene), Walter Carnotch (sgr—4th Jew), Emil Graf (sgr—3rd Jew), Paul Kaussen (sgr—2nd Jew), Hildegard Limmer (sgr—A slave), Georg Wittor (sgr—5th Jew), H. Weigert (cnd), Bavarian RSO *(rec June 21–25, 1953)* Bella Voce 2-▲ BLV 7210 [AAD]
Wagner, R.:Der fliegende Holländer, w. Viorica Ursuleac (sop), Luise Willer (mez), Hans Hotter (b-bar), Georg Hann (bass), C. Krauss (cnd), Bavarian State Opera Orch, Bavarian State Opera Chorus *(rec Mar 13–16, 1944)* Preiser 2-▲ PRE 90250 [ADD]

Ostrowski, Janusz (nar)
Baird, T.:Tomorrow, w. K. Szostek-Radkowa (mez), J. Artysz (bar), E. Pawlak (bass), R. Czajkowski (cnd), Poznan Philharmonic SO [Pol] Olympia ▲ OCD 326 [AAD]

O'Sullivan, John (ten)
John O'Sullivan Symposium ▲ SYM 1152
Verdi, G.:Il trovatore (sels), w. J. Biel (ten), F. Tamagno (ten), L.-A. Escalaïs (ten), M. Gilion (ten), E. Caruso (ten), A. Paoli (ten), G. Zenatello (ten), J. Sembach (ten), L. Slezak (ten), F. Constantino (ten), G. Martinelli (ten), B. De Muro (ten), N. Fusati (ten), N. Piccaluga (ten), G. Lauri-Volpi (ten), A. Pertile (ten), E. Bergamaschi (ten), R. Tauber (ten), H. Roswaenge (ten), G. Taccani (ten), V. Lois (ten), H. Lazaro (ten), A. Lindi (ten), A. Cortis (ten), F. Merli (ten), F. Völker (ten), J. Kiepura (ten), J. Schmidt (ten), J. Bjoerling (ten), B. Gigli (ten), A. Salvarezza (ten), J. Soler (ten), M. Filippeschi (ten)—34 performances of the Act III tenor aria "Di quella pira!," *(rec from 1903–1956)* Bongiovanni ▲ GB 1051 [AAD]

Osvath, Julie (sop)
Mozart, W.A.:Zauberflöte, w. Jarmila Novotna (sop), Helge Roswaenge (ten), Alexander Kipnis (bass), A. Toscanini (cnd), Vienna PO, Vienna State Opera Chorus Enterprise ("The 40's" series) 2-▲ ENT 321
Mozart, W.A.:Zauberflöte, w. D. Komarek (sop), J. Novotna (sop), H. Roswaenge (ten), W. Domgraf-Fassbaender (bar), A. Kipnis (bass), A. Toscanini (cnd), Vienna PO, Vienna Phil Chorus [G] *(rec live, Salzburg, July 30, 1937)* Melodram 3-▲ MEL 37040 (m) [AAD]

Oswald, Hermann (ten)
Monteverdi, C.:Vespers, w. Susanne Ryden (sop), Irena Troupova-Wilke (sop), Detlef Bratschke (alt), Erich Mentzel (ten), Manuel Warwitz (ten), Thomas Herberich (bass), Günther Schmidt (bass), H. Arman (cnd), Schütz Academy Capriccio ▲ CD 10521 [DDD]

Otava, Zdenek (bar)
Skroup, F.:Columbus (sels), w. M. Subrtová (sop), B. Blachut (ten), F. Dyk (cnd), Prague RSO, Prague Radio Chorus *(rec 1962)* Multisonic ("Prague Opera Collection" series) ▲ 31 0153

Otelli, Claudio (bar)
Goldschmidt, B.:Der gewaltige Hahnrei, w. R. Alexander (sop), M. Posselt (sop), H. Lawrence (sop), R. Wörle (ten), M. Kraus (ten), M. Petzold (ten), L. Zagrosek (cnd), German SO, Berlin Radio Chorus London ▲ 440850-2 [DDD]
Goldschmidt, B.:Mediterranean Songs, w. R. Alexander (sop), M. Posselt (sop), H. Lawrence (sop), R. Wörle (ten), M. Kraus (ten), M. Petzold (ten), L. Zagrosek (cnd), German SO, Berlin Radio Chorus London ▲ 440850-2 [DDD]

Otelli, Claudio (bar) (cont.)
Zemlinsky, A. von:Kleider machen Leute, w. E. Mathis (sop), H. Winkler (ten), V. Vogel (ten), H. Franzen (bass), R. Scholze (bass), W. Slabbert (sgr), R. Weikert (cnd), Zurich Opera Orch, Zurich Opera House Chorus [G] *(rec live, Zurich Opera House, 6/29/90)* Koch Schwann 2-▲ CD 314 069 [DDD]

Ott, Elfriede (sgr)
Wiener Komödienlieder, w. Julius Patzak (ten) *(orch unknown) (rec 1963)* Preiser ▲ PRE 93060 [ADD]

Ott, Karin (sop)
Boulanger, L.:Songs, w. J. Lemaire (pno), Lugano String Quartet—Elle était descendue; Elle est gravement gaie; Parfois je suis triste; Un poète disait; Au pied de mon lit; Si tout ceci n'est qu'un pauvre rêve; Nous nous aimerons tant; Vous m'avez regardé avec toute votre; Les lilas qui avaient fleuri; Deux ancolies; Par ce que j'ai souffert; Je garde une médaille d'elle; Demain fera un an; Dans l'immense tristesse; Attente; Reflets; Le retour; Pie Jesu Signum ▲ X 39-00 [ADD]
Eisler, H.:Palmström, w. P. Antonini (cnd), Cremona Musica Insieme Group Nuova Era ("Icarus" series) ▲ NUO 7242
Garcia, J.M.N.:Motets, w. Luiz Alves da Silva (ct), Beat Mattmüller (ct), Andreas Schmidt (ct), Markus Schikora (ten), William Lombardi (ten), Peter Mächler (bass), Michael Leibundgut (bass), L. A. da Silva (cnd), Turicum Ensemble *(rec Studio DRS, Zurich, Sept 26-29, 1994)* Claves ▲ CD 9521 [DDD]
Mozart, W.A.:Zauberflöte, w. Edith Mathis (sop), Janet Perry (sop), Anna Tomowa-Sintow (sop), Agnes Baltsa (mez), Hannah Schwarz (mez), Francisco Araiza (ten), Gottfried Hornik (bar), José Van Dam (b-bar), H. von Karajan (cnd), Berlin PO, German Opera Chorus [G] Deutsche Grammophon 3-▲ 410967-2 [DDD]
Mozart, W.A.:Zauberflöte (sels), w. Edith Mathis (sop), Janet Perry (sop), Anna Tomowa-Sintow (sop), Agnes Baltsa (mez), Hannah Schwarz (mez), Francisco Araiza (ten), Gottfried Hornik (bar), José Van Dam (b-bar), H. von Karajan (cnd), Berlin PO, German Opera Chorus [G] Deutsche Grammophon ▲ 415287-2 [DDD]
Pinto, L.A.:Te Deum Laudamus, w. Luiz Alves da Silva (ct), Beat Mattmüller (ct), Andreas Schmidt (ct), Markus Schikora (ten), William Lombardi (ten), Peter Mächler (bass), Michael Leibundgut (bass), L. A. da Brooks (cnd), Turicum Ensemble *(rec Studio DRS, Zurich, Sept 26-29, 1994)* Claves ▲ CD 9521 [DDD]
Schoenberg, A.:Nachtwandler, w. Christoph Keller (pno) Nuova Era ▲ NUO 7242
Schoenberg, A.:Pierrot lunaire, w. P. Antonini (cnd), Cremona Musica Insieme Group Nuova Era ▲ NUO 7242
Viardot, P.G.:Songs, w. C. Keller (pno)—Madrid; Sérénade; Havanaise; Bonjour mon coeur; Grands oiseaux blancs; La petite chevrière; La chêne et le roseau; Chanson de la pluie; L'enfant et la mère; Désespoir; Adieu les beaux jours; Scène d'Hermione; Seize ans; La danse; L'oiselet; Aime-moi; La calandrina; L'espoir renait dans mon âme [F] CPO ▲ CPO 999044-2 [DDD]

Otten, Josef (sgr)
Straus, O.:The Merry Nibelungs, w. Lisa Griffith (sop—Kriemhild), Gudrun Volkert (sop—Brunhilde), Daphne Evangelatos (cta—Ute), Gabriele Henkel (sgr—Giselher), Christine Mann (sgr—Vogel), Hein Heidbüchel (ten—Volker), Martin Gantner (sgr—Gunther), Gerd Grochowski (sgr—Dankwart), Michael Nowak (sgr—Siegfried), Josef Otten (sgr—Hagen), S. Köhler (cnd), Cologne RSO, Cologne Radio Chorus *(rec Cologne, Jan 31-Feb 17, 1995)* Capriccio ▲ 10752 [DDD]

Ottenthal, Getrud (sop)
Cornelius, P.:Der Cid, w. Ronnie Johansen (sgr), Robert Schunk (ten), Albert Dohmen (bar), Michael Schopper (bass), Endrik Wottrich (sgr), G. Kuhn (cnd), Berlin RSO, Berlin Radio Chorus Koch Schwann 2-▲ SCH 315222
Mozart, W.A.:Don Giovanni, w. S. Ghazarian (sop), P. Pace (sop), G. Sabbatini (ten), R. Bruson (bar), A> Rinaldi-Miliani (bar), F. De Grandis (bass), N. Ghiuselev (bass), N. Järvi (cnd), Cologne RSO, Cologne Radio Chorus [I] Chandos 3-▲ CHAN 8920/22 [DDD]
Szymanowski, K.:Songs of the Infatuated Muezzin, w. G.M. Guida (cnd), Berlin RSO Capriccio ▲ 10 379 [DDD]

Otter, Annie Sofie von (mez)
Bach, J.S.:Christmas Oratorio, w. N. Argenta (sop), H.-P. Blochwitz (ten), O. Bär (bar), J. E. Gardiner (cnd), English Baroque Soloists, Monteverdi Choir London [G] Archiv 2-▲ 423232-2 [DDD]
Bach, J.S.:Christmas Oratorio (sels), w. N. Argenta (sop), H.-P. Blochwitz (ten), O. Bär (bar), J. E. Gardiner (cnd), English Baroque Soloists, Monteverdi Choir London [G] Archiv ▲ 427653-2 [DDD]
Bach, J.S.:Mass in b, BWV 232, w. F. Lott (sop), H. P. Blochwitz (ten), W. Shimell (bar), G. Howell (b-bar), G. Solti (cnd), Chicago SO, Chicago Sym Chorus London 2-▲ 430353-2 [DDD]
Bach, J.S.:St. Matthew Passion, w. B. Bonney (sop), A. Monoyios (sop), M. Chance (ct), H. Crook (ten), A. Rolfe Johnson (ten), O. Bär (bar), A. Schmidt (bar), C. Hauptmann (bass), J. E. Gardiner (cnd), English Baroque Soloists, Monteverdi Choir London [G] Archiv 3-▲ 427648-2 [DDD]
Bach, J.S.:St. Matthew Passion, w. K. Te Kanawa (sop), H. P. Blochwitz (ten), A. Rolfe Johnson (ten), O. Bär (bar), T. Krause (bass), G. Solti (cnd), Chicago SO, Chicago Sym Chorus, Glen Ellyn Children's Chorus [G] London 3-▲ 421177-2 [DDD]
Bach, J.S.:St. Matthew Passion (sels), w. K. Te Kanawa (sop), H. P. Blochwitz (ten), A. Rolfe Johnson (ten), O. Bär (bar), T. Krause (bass), G. Solti (cnd), Chicago SO, Chicago Sym Chorus, Glen Ellyn Children's Chorus [G] London ▲ 425691-2 [DDD]
Bartók, B.:Bluebeard's Castle, w. Anne Sofie von Otter (mez—Judith), John Tomlinson (bass—Duke Bluebeard), Sandor Eles (nar), B. Haitink (cnd), Berlin PO *(rec Berlin)* EMI Classics ▲ CDC 56162
Beethoven, L. van:Sym 9, "Choral Sym", w. Luba Orgonasova (sop), Anthony Rolfe Johnson (ten), Gilles Cachemaille (b-bar), J. E. Gardiner (cnd), Orch Révolutionnaire et Romantique [period instrs] *(rec All Saints' Church, London, Oct 1992)* Archiv ▲ 447074-2 [DDD]
Berlioz, H.:L'Enfance du Christ, w. Johnson (sgr), G. Cachemaille (bar), J. Van Dam (b-bar), J. Bastin (bass), J.E. Gardiner (cnd), Lyon Opera Orch, Monteverdi Choir London [F] Erato 2-▲ 2292-45275-2 [DDD]
Berlioz, H.:Les Nuits d'été, w. J. Levine (cnd), Berlin PO [F] Deutsche Grammophon 2-▲ 427665-2 [DDD]
Berlioz, H.:Roméo et Juliette, w. P. Langridge (ten), Morris (sgr), J. Levine (cnd), Berlin PO, Ernst Senff Chorus [F] Deutsche Grammophon 2-▲ 427665-2 [DDD]
Berlioz, H.:Songs, w. F. Pollet (sop), J. Aler (ten), T. Allen (bar), C. Garben (cnd), *(orch unknown)* Deutsche Grammophon 2-▲ 435860-2
Brahms, J.:Alto Rhap, w. J. Levine (cnd), Vienna PO, Arnold Schoenberg Choir Deutsche Grammophon ("4D Audio" series) ▲ 439887-2
Brahms, J.:Gypsy Songs (8), w. B. Forsberg (pno) [G] Deutsche Grammophon ▲ 429727-2 [DDD]
Brahms, J.:Liebeslieder Waltzes SATB, w. Barbara Bonney (sop), Kurt Streit (ten) Olaf Bär (bar), Bengt Forsberg (pno), Helmut Deutsch (pno) EMI Classics ▲ CDC 55430
Brahms, J.:Neue Liebeslieder Waltzes, w. Barbara Bonney (sop), Kurt Streit (ten) Olaf Bär (bar), Bengt Forsberg (pno), Helmut Deutsch (pno) EMI Classics ▲ CDC 55430
Brahms, J.:Songs, w. B. Forsberg (pno)—14 songs [G] Deutsche Grammophon ▲ 429727-2 [DDD]
Chausson, E.:Chanson perpétuelle, w. Nils-Erik Sparf (vn), Ulf Forsberg (vn), Matti Hirvikangas (va), Mats Lindström (vc), Bengt Forsberg (pno) *(rec Stockholm, Nov 1994)* Deutsche Grammophon ▲ 447 752-2 [DDD]
Delage, M.:Poèmes hindous, w. Andreas Alin (fl), Peter Rydström (fl/pic), Ulf Bjurenhed (ob/E hn), Lars Paulsson (cl), Per Billman (cl/b cl), Nils-Erik Sparf (vn), Ulf Forsberg (vn), Matti Hirvikangas (va), Mats Lindström (vc), Lisa Viguier (hp) *(rec Stockholm, Nov 1994)* Deutsche Grammophon ▲ 447 752-2 [DDD]
Fauré, G.:La bonne chanson, w. Nils-Erik Sparf (vn), Ulf Forsberg (vn), Matti Hirvikangas (va), Mats Lindström (vc), Tomas Gertonsson (db), Bengt Forsberg (pno) *(rec Stockhom, Nov 1994)* Deutsche Grammophon ▲ 447 752-2 [DDD]
Gluck, C.W.:Le Cinesi, w. I. Poulenard (sop), G. Banditelli (cta), G. de Mey (ten), R. Jacobs (cnd), Schola Cantorum Basiliensis Instrumental Ensemble Editio Classica ▲ 77174-2-RG [DDD]
Gluck, C.W.:Iphigénie en Aulide, w. L. Dawson (sop), J. Aler (ten), J. Van Dam (b-bar), Lyon Opera Orch, J. E. Gardiner (cnd), Monteverdi Choir London Erato ("Musifrance" series) 2-▲ 2292-45003-2-ZA [DDD]
Grieg, E.:Songs, w. B. Forsberg (pno)—features various sels. including Haugtussa Deutsche Grammophon ▲ 437521-2

Otter, Annie Sofie von (mez) (cont.)
Handel, G.F.:Cants, w. R. Goebel (cnd), Cologne Musica Antiqua—Haec est Regina virginum, HWV 235; Ah! che troppo ineguali, HWV 230; Donna, che in ciel di tanta luce splendi, HWV 233; Il pianto di Maria [Giunta l'ora fatal], HWV 234 *(rec Cologne, Mar & Aug 1993)* Archiv Produktion ▲ 439866-2 [DDD]
Handel, G.F.:Dixit Dominus, w. Hillevi Martinpelto (sop), A. Öhrwall (cnd), Drottningholm Baroque Ensemble, Stockholm Bach Choir [L] BIS ▲ CD 322 [DDD]
Handel, G.F.:Messiah, w. Sylvia McNair (sop), Michael Chance (alt), Jerry Hadley (ten), Robert Lloyd (b-bar), N. Marriner (cnd), Academy of St. Martin in the Fields [E] *(rec live, Dublin 4/13/92)* Philips 2-▲ 434695-2 [DDD]
Handel, G.F.:Messiah, w. Arleen Augér (sop), Michael Chance (ct), Howard Crook (ten), John Tomlinson (bass), T. Pinnock (cnd), English CO, English Concert Choir [E] Archiv 2-▲ 423630-2 [DDD]
Handel, G.F.:Messiah (sels), w. Arleen Augér (sop), Michael Chance (ct), Paul Crook (ten), John Tomlinson (bass), T. Pinnock (cnd), English CO, English Concert Choir [E] Archiv ▲ 427664-2 [DDD] ■ 427664-4
Humperdinck, E.:Hänsel und Gretel, w. B. Bonney (sop), E. Lind (sop), B. Hendricks (sop), H. Schwarz (mez), M. Lipovšek (mez), Andreas Schmidt (bar), J. Tate (cnd), Bavarian RSO, Tölz Boys' Choir [G] EMI Classics 2-▲ CDCB 54022 [DDD]
James Levine's 25th Anniversary Metropolitan Opera Gala, w. J. Levine (cnd), Metropolitan Opera Orch, Ileana Cotrubas (sop), Renée Fleming (sop), Hei-Kyung Hong (sop), Karita Mattila (sop), Birgit Nilsson (sop), Ruth Ann Swenson (sop), Kiri Te Kanawa (sop), Deborah Voigt (sop), Grace Bumbry (mez), Heidi Grant Murphy (mez), *(rec live, Metropolitan Opera House, New York, Apr 27, 1996)* Deutsche Grammophon ▲ 449177-2 [DDD]
Kagel, M.:Sankt-Bach-Passion, w. Hans Peter Blochowitz (ten), Roland Hermann (bar), Peter Roggisch (narr), Gerd Zacher (org), M. Kagel (cnd), South German RSO, Limburg Cathedral Boys' Chorus, Hamburg North German Choir Montaigne ▲ MO 782044
La Bonne Chanson:French Chamber Songs, w. Otter, Annie Sofie von (mez), Bengt Forsberg (pno), *(chamber ensemble unknown)* Deutsche Grammophon ▲ 447752-2
Love's Twilight:Late Romantic Songs, w. Otter, Anne Sofie von (mez) Deutsche Grammophon ▲ 437515-2
Mad About Angels, w. Cheryl Studer (sop), Christa Ludwig (mez), José Carreras (ten), New York PO [cnd:Leonard Bernstein], English Baroque Soloists [cnd:John Eliot Gardiner], Philharmonia Orch, Philharmonia Chorus [cnd:Carlo Maria Giulini], Orp Deutsche Grammophon ▲ 449113-2 ■ 449113-4
Mahler, G.:Sym 8, w. Sylvia McNair (sop), Andrea Rost (sop), Cheryl Studer (sop), Rosemarie Lang (cta), Peter Seiffert (ten), Bryn Terfel (bar), Jan-Hendrik Rootering (bass), C. Abbado (cnd), Berlin PO, Berlin Radio Chorus, Prague Phil Chorus, Tölz Boys' Choir Deutsche Grammophon ("4D Audio" series) 2-▲ 445843-2
Martin, F.:Chants de Noël, w. Andreas Alin (fl), Bengt Forsberg (pno) *(rec Stockholm, Nov 1994)* Deutsche Grammophon ▲ 447 752-2 [DDD]
Mendelssohn, F.:Elijah, w. Y. Kenny (sop), A. Rolfe Johnson (ten), T. Allen (bar), N. Marriner (cnd), Academy of St. Martin in the Fields Philips 2-▲ 432984-2 [DDD]
Monteverdi, C.:Incoronazione, w. Constanze Backes (sop—Valletto), Catherine Bott (sop—Drusilla/Pallade/La Virtù), Dana Hanchard (sop—Nerone), Sylvia McNair (sop—Poppea), Marinella Pennicchi (sop—Amore/Damigella), Annie Sofie von Otter (mez—Ottavia/Venere/La Fortuna), Julian Clarkson (alt—Littore/Mercurio), Bernarda Fink (cta—Arnalta), Roberto Balconi (ct—Nutrice), Michael Chance (ct—Ottone), Nigel Robson (ten—Liberto/Soldato Secondo), Mark Tucker (ten—Lucano/Soldato Primo), Francesco Ellero d'Artegna (bass—Seneca), J. E. Gardiner (cnd), English Baroque Soloists *(rec Queen Elizabeth Hall, South Bank Ctr, London, Dec 1993)* Archiv 3-▲ 447088-2
Mozart, W.A.:Ave verum corpus, w. K. Te Kanawa (sop), A. R. Johnson (ten), R. Lloyd (bass), N. Marriner (cnd), Academy of St. Martin in the Fields, Academy Chorus *(rec London, Mar. 10-12, 1993)* Philips ▲ 438999-2
Mozart, W.A.:Clemenza di Tito (sels), w. Anne Sofie von Otter (mez—Sesto), Leslie Schatzberger (bas cl), J. E. Gardiner (cnd), English Baroque Soloists—Parto, ma tu ben mio *(rec Queen Elizabeth Hall, South Bank Ctr, London, June 1990)* Archiv ▲ 449938-2 [DDD]
Mozart, W.A.:Così fan tutte, w. Renée Fleming (sop—Fiordiligi), Adelina Scarabelli (sop—Despina), Anne Sofie Von Otter (mez—Dorabella), Frank Lopardo (ten—Ferrando), Olaf Bar (bar—Guglielmo), Michele Pertusi (bass—Don Alfonso), G. Solti (cnd), CO of Europe London 3-▲ 444174-2
Mozart, W.A.:Così fan tutte, w. K. Mattila (sop), E. Szmytka (sop), F. Araiza (ten), T. Allen (bar), J. van Dam (b-bar), N. Marriner (cnd), Academy of St. Martin in the Fields, Ambrosian Opera Chorus [I] Philips 3-▲ 422381-2 [DDD]
Mozart, W.A.:Idomeneo, w. Sylvia McNair (sop), Hillevi Martinpelto (sop), Anthony Rolfe Johnson (ten), J. E. Gardiner (cnd), English Baroque Soloists, Monteverdi Choir London Archiv 3-▲ 431674-2 [DDD]
Mozart, W.A.:Missa, K.427, w. K. Te Kanawa (sop), A. R. Johnson (ten), R. Lloyd (bass), N. Marriner (cnd), Academy of St. Martin in the Fields, Academy of St. Martin in the Fields Chorus *(rec London, Mar. 10-12, 1993)* Philips ▲ 438999-2
Mozart, W.A.:Requiem, w. Barbara Bonney (sop), Hans-Peter Blochwitz (ten), Willard White (bass), J. E. Gardiner (cnd), English Baroque Soloists, Monteverdi Choir London [L] Philips ▲ 420197-2 [DDD]
Offenbach, J.:Les Contes d'Hoffmann, w. J. Norman (sop), C. Studer (sop), E. Lind (sop), F. Araiza (ten), S. Ramey (bass), J. Tate (cnd), Dresden Staatskapelle Philips 3-▲ 422374-2 [DDD]
Offenbach, J.:Les Contes d'Hoffmann, w. J. Norman (sop), E. Lind (sop), C. Studer (sop), F. Araiza (ten), S. Ramey (bass), J. Tate (cnd), Dresden Staatskapelle Philips ▲ 438502-2
Peterson-Berger, W.:Swedish Poetry, w. S. Köhler (cnd), Swedish RSO—Ask the East Wind, Ask the West Wind; Mumble Tumble Bumble Bee; Sift Sift Golden Grain; Did the East Wind See, Did the West Wind See; High Up on the Fern Thicket of the Slope [all from *Gullebarn's Lullabies*] [Sw] Musica Sveciae ▲ MSCD 630 [DDD]
Poulenc, F.:Rapsodie nègre, w. Andreas Alin (fl), Lars Paulsson (cl), Nils-Erik Sparf (vn), Ulf Forsberg (vn), Matti Hirvikangas (va), Mats Lindström (vc), Bengt Forsberg (pno) *(rec Stockhom, Nov 1994)* Deutsche Grammophon ▲ 447 752-2 [DDD]
Purcell, H.:Dido & Aeneas, w. L. Dawson (sop), N. Rogers (ten), S. Varcoe (bar), T. Pinnock (cnd), English Concert, *(chorus unknown)* [E] Archiv ▲ 427624-2 [DDD]
Ravel, M.:Trois poèmes de Stéphane Mallarmé, w. Peter Rydström (fl/pic), Andreas Alin (fl), Lars Paulsson (cl), Per Billman (cl/b cl), Nils-Erik Sparf (vn), Ulf Forsberg (vn), Matti Hirvikangas (va), Mats Lindström (vc), Bengt Forsberg (pno) *(rec Stockholm, Nov 1994)* Deutsche Grammophon ▲ 447 752-2 [DDD]
Roman, J.H.:The Swedish Mass, w. H. Martinpelto (sop), M. Samuelsson (bar), Drottningholm Baroque Ensemble, Adolf Fredrik Bach Choir Proprius ▲ PRCD 9920
Saint-Saëns, C.:Une Flûte invisible, w. Andreas Alin (fl), Bengt Forsberg (pno) *(rec Stockhom, Nov 1994)* Deutsche Grammophon ▲ 447 752-2 [DDD]
Schubert, Franz:Rosamunde, w. C. Abbado (cnd), CO of Europe, Ernst Senff Chorus Deutsche Grammophon ▲ 431655-2 [DDD]
Schumann, R.:Frauenliebe und -leben, w. Bengt Forsberg (pno) Deutsche Grammophon ▲ 445881-2
Schumann, R.:Spanisches Liederspiel, w. Barbara Bonney (sop), Kurt Streit (ten) Olaf Bär (bar), Bengt Forsberg (pno), Helmut Deutsch (pno) EMI Classics ▲ CDC 55430
Sibelius, J.:Songs, w. Bengt Forsberg (pno)—7 Songs, Op. 13; 6 Songs, Op. 50; 6 Songs, Op. 90; Skogsrået; Den judiska flickans sång; Likhet; En visa; Serenade; Tanken [w. Monica Groop (mez)] *(rec Musikaliska Akademien, Stockholm, Sweden, 1994-95)* BIS ▲ CD 757 [DDD]
Sibelius, J.:Songs, w. B. Forsberg (pno)— *four song groups*—Seven Songs, Op. 17; Six Songs, Op. 36; Five Songs, Op. 37; Six Songs, Op. 88; *four individual songs*—Arioso, Op. 3; Souda, souda, sinisorsa (1899); Les trois soeurs aveugles, Op. 46/4; Narciss (1918) [Fin,F,Sw] BIS ▲ CD 457 [DDD]
Stenhammar, W.:Sången, w. Iwa Sörenson (sop), Stefan Dahlberg (ten), Per-Arne Wahlgren (bar), H. Blomstedt (cnd), Swedish RSO, Swedish Radio Chorus, Stockholm State Academy of Music Chamber Choir, Adolf Fredrik Music School Children's Choir Caprice ▲ CAP 21358
Stenhammar, W.:Songs, w. H. Hagegard (bar), B. Forsberg (pno), T. Schuback (pno) Musica Sveciae ▲ MSCD 623
Strauss, R.:Der Rosenkavalier, w. K. Te Kanawa (sop), B. Hendricks (sop), B. Haitink (cnd), Dresden Staatskapelle EMI Classics 3-▲ CDCC 54259

1332

▲ = CD ♦ = Enhanced CD Δ = MD ■ = Cassette Tape □ = DCC

Otter, Annie Sofie von (mez) (cont.)

Strauss, R.:Der Rosenkavalier (sels), w. B. Hendricks (sop), K. Te Kanawa (sop), R. Leech (ten), K. Rydl (bass), B. Haitink (cnd), Dresden Staatskapelle, Dresden State Opera Chorus EMI Classics ▲ ZDC 54493

Stravinsky, I.:Oedipus Rex, w. V. Cole (ten), N. Gedda (ten), S. Estes (bass), H. Sotin (bass), P. Chéreau (nar), E.-P. Salonen (cnd), Swedish RSO, *(chorus unknown)* Sony Classical ▲ SK 48057

Verdi, G.:Requiem Mass, w. Donna Brown (sop), Luba Orgonasova (sop), Luca Canonici (ten), Alastair Miles (bass), J. E. Gardiner (cnd), Orch Révolutionnaire et Romantique, Monteverdi Choir London Philips 2-▲ 442142-2

Wolf, H.:Spanisches Liederbuch, w. Olaf Bar (bar), Geoffrey Parsons (pno) EMI Classics ▲ CDC 55325

Zemlinsky, A. von:Songs (misc), w. B. Bonney (sop), H.-P. Blochwitz (ten), A. Schmidt (bar), C. Garben (pno)—Lieder, Op. 2; Gesänge, Op. 5; Walzer-Gesänge nach toskanischen Volksliedern, Op. 6; Irmelin Rose und andere Gesänge, Op. 7; Turmwächterlied und andere Gesänge, Op. 8; Ehetanzlied und andere Gesänge, Op. 10; Schlummerlied; 6 Gesänge, Op. 13; 6 Lieder, Op. 22; Ahnung Beatricens; 12 Lieder, Op. 27 [G] Deutsche Grammophon 2-▲ 427348-2 [DDD]

Ottley, JoAnn (sop)

Gershwin, G.:Songs, w. David Power (bar), Duehlmeier-Gritton Duo—Fascinatin' Rhythm *(rec David Gardner Hall, University of Utah, Aug 16, 1994)* Centaur ▲ 2249 [DDD]

Otto, Lisa (sop)

Mozart, W.A.:Così fan tutte, w. E. Schwarzkopf (sop), N. Merriman (mez), L. Simoneau (ten), R. Panerai (bar), S. Bruscantini (bar), H. von Karajan (cnd), Philharmonia Orch, Philharmonia Chorus [I] EMI Classics ("Studio" series) 3-▲ CDHC 69635 (m) [ADD]

Mozart, W.A.:Così fan tutte (sels), w. Elizabeth Schwarzkopf (sop), Nan Merriman (mez), Rolando Panerai (bar), Leopold Simoneau (ten), Sesto Bruscantini (bass), H. von Karajan (cnd), Philharmonia Orch Classics for Pleasure ("Eminence" series) ▲ CDEMX 2211 [DDD]

Mozart, W.A.:Zauberflöte (sels), w. E. Lear (sop), R. Peters (sop), F. Wunderlich (ten), F. Lenz (ten), D. Fischer-Dieskau (bar), F. Crass (bass), K. Böhm (cnd), Berlin PO, Berlin RIAS Chamber Choir—Scenes & Arias Deutsche Grammophon ▲ 429825-2 [ADD] ■ 429825-4

Straus, O.:Ein Walzertraum (sels), w. Melita Muszely (sop), Rudolf Schock (ten), Bruno Fritz (bar), W. Schüchter (cnd), Berlin Orch, Berlin Chorus Emperor Operetta ▲ KO 86346

Strauss, R.:Ariadne auf Naxos, w. E. Schwarzkopf (sop), I. Seefried (sop), R. Streich (sop), G. Hoffman (mez), R. Schock (ten), G. Unger (ten), H. Cuénod (ten), H. Prey (bar), F. Ollendorff (bass), H. von Karajan (cnd), Philharmonia Orch [G] *(rec 1954)* EMI Classics ("Studio" series) 2-▲ CDMB 69296 (m) [ADD]

Strauss, R.:Ariadne auf Naxos, w. Lisa Della Casa (sop—Ariadne), Lisa Otto (sop—Najade), Rudolf Schock (ten—Bacchus), Leonore Kirschstein (sgr—Echo), Nada Puttar (sgr—Dryade), A. Erede (cnd), Berlin PO Testament ▲ SBT 1036 [ADD]

Wagner, R.:Das Rheingold, w. M. Muszely (sop), J. Blatter (mez), R. Stewart (mez), S. Wagner (mez), R. Schock (ten), H. Melchert (ten), F. Frantz (bass), B. Kusche (bass), J. Metternich (bass), R. Kempe (cnd), Berlin Staatskapelle *(rec Mar. 1959)* Berlin Classics ("Eterna" series) ▲ BER 2035 [ADD]

Otto, Susanne (cta)

Nono, L.:Canto sospeso, w. B. Bonney (sop), M. Torzewski (ten), S. Lothar (nar), B. Ganz (nar), Berlin Radio Chorus *(rec Dec. 9-11, 1992)* Sony Classical ▲ SK 53360 [DDD]

Nono, L.:guai ai gelidi mostri, w. Helena Rasker (alt), Klaus Burger (tuba/pic tpt), Stefano Scodanibbio (db), A. Richard (cnd), Rechêrche Ensemble Montaigne ▲ MO 782047

Nono, L.:Prometeo, w. I. Ade-Jesemann (sop), M. Bair-Ivenz (sop), P. Hall (ten), U. Krumbiegel (nar), M. Schadock (nar), C. Abbado (cnd), Berlin PO, Freiburg Soloists Choir *(rec May 23-25, 1993)* Sony Classical ▲ SK 53978 [DDD]

Ottolini, Luigi (ten)

Mascagni, P.:Iris, w. M. Olivero (sop), R. Capecchi (bar), P. Clabassi (bass), F. Vernizzi (cnd), Netherlands Radio Orch, Netherlands Radio Chorus *(rec live, 1963)* Verona 2-▲ 27014/15 [AAD]

Mascagni, P.:Iris, w. M. Olivero (sop), R. Capecchi (bar), P. Clabassi (bass), F. Vernizzi (cnd), Netherlands Radio Orch, Netherlands Radio Chorus *(rec Amsterdam, 1963)* Great Opera Performances ▲ GPO 708

Ottrabella, Augusta (sop)

Verdi, G.:Falstaff, w. Augusta Ottrabella (sop—Nannetta), Franca Somigli (sop—Alice), Angelica Cravcenko (mez—Mrs. Quickly), Mita Vasari (mez—Meg), Dino Borgioli (ten—Fenton), Giuseppe Nessi (ten—Bardolfo), Alfredo Tedeschi (ten—Dr. Cajus), Piero Biasini (bar—Ford), Mariano Stabile (bar—Falstaff), Virgilio Lazzari (bass—Pistola), A. Toscanini (cnd), Vienna PO, Vienna State Opera Chorus *(rec Salzburg, Aug 23, 1937)* Minerva 2-▲ MN A36/37 (m) [ADD]

Ötvös, Csaba (sgr)

Wayditch, G. von:The Caliph's Magician, w. Júlia Pászthi (sop—Eunuch), Sándor Palcso (ten—The Emir), István Rozsos (ten—Nawab), Zsolt Bende (bar—The Magician), Arpád Kishegyi (sgr—Djinn), András Nagy-Soljom (sgr—The Caliph), Csaba Ötvös (sgr—Djinn), Csilla Ötvös (sgr—Odalisk), A. Kórodi (cnd), Budapest National Opera Orch, Budapest National Opera Chorus *(rec 1975)* VAI Audio 2-▲ VAIA 1095-2 [ADD]

Ötvös, Csilla (sgr)

Wayditch, G. von:The Caliph's Magician, w. Júlia Pászthi (sop—Eunuch), Sándor Palcso (ten—The Emir), István Rozsos (ten—Nawab), Zsolt Bende (bar—The Magician), Arpád Kishegyi (sgr—Djinn), András Nagy-Soljom (sgr—The Caliph), Csaba Ötvös (sgr—Djinn), Csilla Ötvös (sgr—Odalisk), A. Kórodi (cnd), Budapest National Opera Orch, Budapest National Opera Chorus *(rec 1975)* VAI Audio 2-▲ VAIA 1095-2 [ADD]

Ouaki (sgr)

Boieldieu, F.-A.:Le Calife de Bagdad, w. N. Monestier (sop), S. Elloir (sgr), Plantak (sgr), Fokenoy (sgr), B. Thomas (cnd), Bernard Thomas CO, Patrick Marco Vocal Ensemble [F] Thésis ▲ THC 82015 [DDD]

Owen, Donna (sop)

Puccini, G.:Suor angelica, w. Elisabeth Carron (sop—Angelica), Joan Summers (sop—Genovieffa), Donna Owen (sop—Dolcina), Lou Ann Wyckoff (sop—Alms collector), Hanna Owen (sop—novice), Anthea De Forest (sop—novice), Charlotte Povia (mez—Abbess), Beverly Evans (mez—Monitress), Kay Creed (mez—Mistress), La Vergne Monette (sop/mez—lay sister), Joan August (sop/mez—lay sister), Pearle Goldsmith (sop/mez—other sister), Lila Herbert (sop/mez—other sister), Jodell Kenting (sop/mez—other sister), Ann Pretzat (sop/mez—other sister), Evelyn Sachs (cta—Princess), F. Patanè (cnd), *(orch unknown)* *(rec New York, Feb 23, 1967)* Legato Classics ▲ LCD 212-1 [ADD]

Owen, Hanna (sop)

Puccini, G.:Suor angelica, w. Elisabeth Carron (sop—Angelica), Joan Summers (sop—Genovieffa), Donna Owen (sop—Dolcina), Lou Ann Wyckoff (sop—Alms collector), Hanna Owen (sop—novice), Anthea De Forest (sop—novice), Charlotte Povia (mez—Abbess), Beverly Evans (mez—Monitress), Kay Creed (mez—Mistress), La Vergne Monette (sop/mez—lay sister), Joan August (sop/mez—lay sister), Pearle Goldsmith (sop/mez—other sister), Lila Herbert (sop/mez—other sister), Jodell Kenting (sop/mez—other sister), Ann Pretzat (sop/mez—other sister), Evelyn Sachs (cta—Princess), F. Patanè (cnd), *(orch unknown)* *(rec New York, Feb 23, 1967)* Legato Classics ▲ LCD 212-1 [ADD]

Owen-Lewis, David (bass)

Walton, W.:Troilus & Cressida, w. Judith Howarth (sop—Cressida), Arthur Davies (ten—Troilus), Nigel Robson (ten—Pandarus), Brian Cookson (ten—3rd Watchman), Peter Bodenham (ten—Priest), Keith Mills (ten—Soldier), Alan Opie (bar—Diomede), James Thornton (bar—Antenor), Clive Bayley (bass—Calkas), David Owen-Lewis (bass—Horaste), R. Hickox (cnd), English Northern Philharmonia, Opera North Chorus Chandos 2-▲ CHAN 9370/71 [DDD]

Owens, Anne-Marie (mez)

Smyth, E.:The Wreckers, w. Judith Howarth (sop), Annemarie Sand (mez), Justin Lavender (ten), Anthony Roden (ten), Peter Sidhom (bar), David Wilson-Johnson (bar), Brian Bannatyne-Scott (bass), O. de la Martinez (cnd), BBC PO, Huddersfield Choral Society *(rec live, Royal Albert Hall, London, July 31, 1994)* Conifer Classics 2-▲ 75605-51250-2

Weir, J.:Blond Eckbert, w. Nicholas Folwell (bar), Nerys Jones (sgr), Christopher Ventris (sgr), S. Edwards (cnd), English National Opera Orch Collins Classics ▲ COL 1461

Owstoska, R. (sop)

Szymanowski, K.:Penthesilea, w. K. Stryja (cnd), Polish State PO Marco Polo ▲ 8.223293 [DDD]

Oxley, James (ten)

Ireland, J.:Vexilla Regis, w. P. Bott (sop), T. Shaw (mez), B. Terfel (bass-bar), R. Hickox (cnd), London SO, London Sym Chorus [L] Chandos ▲ CHAN 8879 [DDD]

Walton, W.:The Twelve, w. P. Forbes (sop), R. Gleave (mez), S. Gay (alt), P. Harvey (bar), R. Hickox (cnd), City of London Sinfonia [E] Chandos ▲ CHAN 8824 [DDD]

Paasikivi, Lilli (mez)

Sibelius, J.:Belshazzar's Feast (incidental), w. O. Vänskä (cnd), Lahti SO *(rec Church of the Cross, Lahti, Finland, Jan 11-13, 1995)* BIS ▲ CD-735 [DDD]

Sibelius, J.:Everyman, w. Petri Lehto (ten), Sauli Tiilikainen (bar), Leena Saarenpää (pno), Pauli Pietiläinen (org), O. Vänskä (cnd), Lahti SO, Lahti Chamber Choir *(rec Church of the Cross, Lahti, Finland, Jan 11-13, 1995)* BIS ▲ CD-735 [DDD]

Paasikivi, Lilli (nar)

Aho, K.:Pergamon, w. E.-L. Saarinen (nar), T. Nyman (nar), M. Lehtinen (nar), P. Pietiläinen (org), O. Vänskä (cnd), Lahti SO *(rec Lahti, Finland, May 23-25, 1994)* BIS ▲ CD 646 [DDD]

Paaske, Else (cta)

Bach, J.S.:Cant 94, w. H. Donath (sop), A. Baldin (ten), H.-F. Kunz (bass), W. Schöne (bass), H. Rilling (cnd), Stuttgart Bach Collegium, Württemberg CO, Gächinger Kantorei Hänssler Classic ▲ 98.808 [AAD]

Liszt, F.:Missa choralis, w. Irene Graaner (sop), Kai Hansen (ten), Michael Hansen (bar), Hans Christian Andersen (bass), Niels Henrik Nielsen (org), Tamás Vetö (cnd), Copenhagen Univ Choir Point ▲ PCD 5075 [ADD]

Olsson, O.:Requiem, w. M. A. Häggander (sop), A. Andersson (ten), L. Wedin (bar), A. Öhrwall (cnd), Stockholm PO, Stockholm Phil Chorus Caprice ▲ CAP 21368 [DDD]

Pabst, Michael (ten)

Kreutzer, C.:Das Nachtlager in Granada, w. R. Klepper (sop), H. Prey (bar), H. Froschauer (cnd), Cologne RSO, Cologne Radio Chorus Capriccio ▲ 60029 [DDD]

Schreker, F.:Irrelohe, w. Eva Randová (mez—Old Lola), Michael Pabst (ten—Count Heinrich), Monte Pederson (bar—Peter), Neven Belamaric (sgr—The Parson), Luana Devol (sgr—Eva), Sebastian Holecek (sgr—The Miller), Goran Smimic (sgr—The Forester) Sony Classical 2-▲ S2K 66850

Pace, Miti Truccato (mez)

Cilea, F.:Adriana Lecouvreur, w. Carla Gavazzi (sop), Giacinto Prandelli (ten), Saturno Meletti (bar), A. Simonetto (cnd), Milan RAI Lyric Orch, Milan RAI Chorus Fonit Cetra ("Classic Collection" series) 2-▲ FCT CDO 20

Donizetti, G.:Lucia di Lammermoor, w. Roberta Peters (sop—Lucia), Mitì Truccato Pace (mez—Alisa), Jan Peerce (ten—Edgardo), Piero de Palma (ten—Lord Arturo Bucklaw), Mario Carlin (ten—Normanno), Philip Maero (bar—Lord Enrico Ashton), Giorgio Tozzi (bass—Raimondo), E. Leinsdorf (cnd), Rome Opera Orch, Rome Opera Chorus *(rec Rome Opera House, Aug 5-14, 1957)* RCA Living Stereo 2-▲ 09026-68537-2 [ADD]

Mozart, W.A.:Nozze di Figaro, w. G. Gatti (sop), A. Noni (sop), G. Sciurri (sop), J. Gardino (mez), A. Mercuriali (ten), S. Bruscantini (bar), I. Tajo (bass), F. Corena (bass), F. Previtali (cnd), Rome RAI Orch [I] *(rec 1951)* Cetra Classic 2-▲ CDO 12

Puccini, G.:Suor angelica, w. Gilda Capozzi (sgr), Rosanna Certeri (sgr), F. Previtali (cnd), *(orch & chorus unknown)* Cetra Classic 3-▲ 36

Rossini, G.:La Cenerentola, w. Ornella Rovero (sop), Giulietta Simionato (mez), Cesare Valletti (ten), Saturno Meletti (bar), Vito Susca (bass), Cristiano Dalamangas (sgr), M. Rossi (cnd), Turin RAI Orch, Bruno Erminero (cnd), Turin RAI Chorus Fonit Cetra ("Classic Collection" series) ▲ FCT CDON 34

Rossini, G.:L'occassione fa il ladro, w. C. Fusco (sop), G. Sinimberghi (ten), I. Tajo (bass), R. Gonzales (sgr), L. Colonna (cnd), Naples Alessandro Scarlatti RAI Orch [I] *(rec live, Naples, Sept. 29, 1963)* Arkadia ▲ 602 [ADD]

Verdi, G.:Luisa Miller, w. L. Kelston (sop—Luisa), M.T. Pace (mez—Federica), G. Larui-Volpi (ten—Rodolfo), S. Colombo (bar—Miller), G. Vaghi (bar—Count Walter), D. Baronti (bass—Wurm), M. Rossi (cnd), Rome RAI Orch, Rome RAI Chorus *(rec 1951)* Cetra Classic 2-▲ CDO 17 [AAD]

Pace, Patrizia (sop)

Carissimi, G.:Oratorio della Santissima Vergine, w. P. Borri (sop), A. M. Ferrante (sop), A. Christofellis (alt), L. Petroni (ten), F. Sclaverano (ten), R. Abbondanza (bass), M. Mondelli (bass), P. Spagnoli (bass), F. Colusso (cnd), Seicentonovecento Ensemble [I] Bongiovanni ▲ GB 10011 [DDD]

Carissimi, G.:Oratorio di Daniele Profeta, w. P. Borri (sop), A. M. Ferrante (sop), A. Christofellis (alt), L. Petroni (ten), F. Sclaverano (ten), R. Abbondanza (bass), M. Mondelli (bass), P. Spagnoli (bass), F. Colusso (cnd), Seicentonovecento Ensemble [I] Bongiovanni ▲ GB 10011 [DDD]

Mozart, W.A.:Don Giovanni, w. S. Ghazarian (sop), G. Ottenthal (sop), G. Sabbatini (ten), R. Bruson (bar), S. Rinaldi-Miliani (bar), F. De Grandis (bass), N. Ghiuselev (bass), N. Järvi (cnd), Cologne RSO, Cologne Radio Chorus [I] Chandos 3-▲ CHAN 8920/22 [DDD]

Mozart, W.A.:Requiem, w. W. Meier (mez), F. Lopardo (ten), J. Morris (bass), R. Muti (cnd), Berlin PO, Swedish Radio Chorus [L] EMI Classics ▲ CDC 49640 [DDD]

Paternoster, V.:Inzaffirio:Prayers (6) to the Virgin Mary, w. V. Paternoster (vc), F. Colusso (cnd), Seicentonovecento Ensemble Musicaimmagine ▲ MR 10006

Pacetti, Iva (sop)

Arias & Duets, w. Beniamino Gigli (ten), Giulio Tomei (bar) EMI Classics ▲ CDH 61052

Iva Pacetti, w. Pacetti, Iva (sop), Beniamino Gigli (ten), Mario Basiola (bar), Benvenuto Franci (bar) *(rec 1928-40)* Preiser ("Lebendige Vergangenheit" series) ▲ PRF 89124

Leoncavallo, R.:Pagliacci, w. I. Pacetti (sop—Nedda), B. Gigli (ten—Canio), G. Nessi (ten—Peppe), M. Basiola (bar—Tonio), F. Ghione (cnd), La Scala Orch, La Scala Chorus [I] *(rec 1934 for HMV)* Music Memoria ▲ 30275

Leoncavallo, R.:Pagliacci, w. I. Pacetti (sop—Nedda), B. Gigli (ten—Canio), G. Nessi (ten—Peppe), M. Basiola (bar—Tonio), F. Ghione (cnd), La Scala Orch, La Scala Chorus [I] *(rec July 1934)* Nimbus 2-▲ NI 7843/44 [ADD]

Leoncavallo, R.:Pagliacci, w. I. Pacetti (sop—Nedda), B. Gigli (ten—Canio), G. Nessi (ten—Peppe), M. Basiola (bar—Tonio), F. Ghione (cnd), La Scala Orch, La Scala Chorus [I] *(rec 1934)* EMI Classics ("Studio" series) ▲ CDH 63309 (m) [ADD]

Paci, Leone (bar)

Giordano, U.:Andrea Chénier, w. Maria Caniglia (sop—Maddalena), Maria Huder (mez—Bersi), Vittoria Palombini (mez—Madelon), Giulietta Simionato (mez—Contessa), Beniamino Gigli (ten—Andrea), Adelio Zagonara (ten—Incroyable/Abbé), Gino Bechi (bar—Carlo), Leone Paci (bar—Mathieu), Giuseppe Taddei (b-bar—Pietro/Fouquier), Italo Tajo (b-bar—Roucher), Gino Conti (bass—Master/Schmidt), O. de Fabritiis (cnd), La Scala Orch, La Scala Chorus *(rec Nov 1941)* Arkadia ("The 78's" series) 2-▲ 78012 [ADD]

Padmore, Mark (ten)

Bach, J.S.:Cant 57, w. Vasiljka Jezovšek (sop), Sarah Connolly (cta), Peter Kooy (bass), Phillippe Herreweghe (cnd), Collegium Vocale Harmonia Mundi ▲ HMC 901594

Bach, J.S.:Cant 110, w. Vasiljka Jezovšek (sop), Sarah Connolly (cta), Peter Kooy (bass), Phillippe Herreweghe (cnd), Collegium Vocale Harmonia Mundi ▲ HMC 901594

Bach, J.S.:Cant 122, w. Vasiljka Jezovšek (sop), Sarah Connolly (cta), Peter Kooy (bass), Phillippe Herreweghe (cnd), Collegium Vocale Harmonia Mundi ▲ HMC 901594

Biber, H. von:Requiem à 15, w. Marta Almajano (sop), Mieke van der Sluis (sop), John Elwes (ten), Frans Huijts (bar), Harry van der Kamp (bass), G. Leonhardt (cnd), Netherlands Bach Society Baroque Orch, Netherlands Bach Society Choir *(rec Utrecht, Germany, Oct 22-24, 1994)* Deutsche Harmonia Mundi ▲ 05472-77344-2 [DDD]

Cavalli, P.F.:Vespero della beata Vergine Maria, w. Barbara Borden (sop), Emily van Evera (sop), Markus Brutscher (ten), Rodrigo del Pozo (ten), Gerd Türk (ten), Harry van der Kamp (bass), Peter Zimpel (sgr), Bruce Dickey (sackbut), Charles Toet (sackbut), Concerto Palatino, Schola Cantorum Basiliensis Harmonia Mundi France ("Documenta" series) 2-▲ HMC 905219/20

Chabrier, E.:Briséïs, ou Les Amants de Corinthe, w. Kathryn Harries (sop), Simon Keenlyside (trb), Michael George (bass), Joan Rodgers (sgr), J. Y. Ossonce (cnd), BBC Scottish SO Hyperion ▲ CDA 66803

Charpentier, M.-A.:Médée, w. Isabelle Desrochers (sop—Cleone), Lorraine Hunt (sop—Medee), Noemi Rime (sop—Nerine), Monique Zanetti (sop—Creuse), Mark Padmore (ten—Jason), François Bazola (bar—Arcas), Jean-Marc Salzmann (bar—Oronte), Bernard Deletre (bass-Creon), W. Christie (cnd), Les Arts Florissants Erato 3-▲ 96558-2

Padmore, Mark (ten) (cont.)
Handel, G.F.:Giustino, w. Juliana Gondek (sop), Dawn Kotoski (sop), Dorothea Röschmann (sop), Jennifer Lane (mez), Michael Chance (alt), Drew Minter (alt), Dean Ely (sgr), N. McGegan (cnd), Freiburg Baroque Orch — Harmonia Mundi France 3-▲ HMU 907130.32
Handel, G.F.:Messiah, w. Sandrine Piau (sop), Barbara Schlick (sop), Andreas Scholl (alt), Nathan Berg (bass), W. Christie (cnd), Les Arts Florissants [1742 Dublin version] — Harmonia Mundi France 2-▲ HMC 901498/99
Haydn, J.:Mass 12, "Theresienmesse", w. Janine Watson (sop), Pamela Helen Stephen (mez), Stephen Varcoe (bass), R. Hickox (cnd), Collegium Musicum 90 — Chandos ▲ CHAN 0592
Lampe, J.F.:Pyramus & Thisbe, w. Susan Bisatt (sop), P. Holman (cnd), Opera Restor'd — Hyperion ▲ CDA 66759
Purcell, H.:The Fairy Queen, w. Lorraine Hunt (sop), Susan Bickley (mez), Catherine Pierard (mez), Howard Crook (ten), David Wilson-Johnson (bar), Richard Wistreich (bass), R. Norrington (cnd), London Classical Players, Schütz Choir London — EMI Classics ▲ CDCB 55234
Steffani, A.:Stabat Mater, w. Marta Almajano (sop), Mieke van der Sluis (sop), John Elwes (ten), Harry van der Kamp (bass), G. Leonhardt (cnd), Netherlands Bach Society Baroque Orch, Netherlands Bach Society Choir *(rec Utrecht, Germany, Oct 22–24, 1994)* — Deutsche Harmonia Mundi ▲ 05472-77344-2 [DDD]

Padoan, Carlo (sgr)
Donizetti, G.:Roberto Devereux, w. Montserrat Caballé (sop), Beverly Wolff (mez), Guido Fabbris (ten), Gianni Raimondi (ten), Walter Alberti (bar), Paolo Badoer (sgr), Carlo Micalucci (sgr), B. Bartoletti (cnd), Venice Teatro La Fenice Orch, Venice Teatro La Fenice Chorus — Great Opera Performances 2-▲ GOP 764

Padovan, Elia (sgr)
Mascagni, P.:Amica, w. Katia Ricciarelli (sop), Monica Minarelli (sgr), Fabio Armiliato (sgr), Walter Donati (sgr), M. Pace (cnd), Hungarian Radio-TV SO, Hungarian Radio-TV Chorus *(rec Budapest, Nov 1995)* — Kicco Classic 2-▲ KC 00296 [DDD]

Paēgle, Dita (sop)
Mozart, W.A.:Alma Dei creatoris, w. Antra Bīgaca (mez), Martins Klisans (ten), S. Klava (cnd), Riga Musicians, Riga Radio Chorus — Audiophile Classics ▲ 101.048 [DDD]
Mozart, W.A.:Litaniae Lauretanae, K.195, w. Antra Bīgaca (mez), Martins Klisans (ten), Janis Màrkovs (bass), S. Klava (cnd), Riga Musicians, Riga Radio Chorus — Audiophile Classics ▲ 101.048 [DDD]
Mozart, W.A.:Regina coeli, K.276, w. Antra Bīgaca (mez), Martins Klisans (ten), Janis Màrkovs (bass), S. Klava (cnd), Riga Musicians, Riga Radio Chorus — Audiophile Classics ▲ 101.048 [DDD]

Paēvatalu, Guido (bar)
Gade, N.W.:Elverskud, w. Susanne Elmark (sop–Elf–King's Daughter), Kirsten Dolberg (cta–Mother), M. Schønwandt (cnd), Tivoli SO, Tivoli Concert Choir *(rec Tivoli Concert Hall, Apr 29–30, May 4, 1996)* — Marco Polo/Dacapo ▲ 8.224051 [DDD]

Paevatalu, Guido (bar)
Horneman, C.F.E.:Music of, w. M. Schønwandt (cnd), Danish National RSO, Danish National Choir—Gurre; Helteliv; Alladin Ov. — Chandos ▲ CHAN 9373 [DDD]
Nielsen, C.:Aladdin, w. M. Ejsing (cta), G. Rozhdestvensky (cnd), Danish National RSO, Danish National Radio Chamber Choir — Chandos ▲ CHAN 9135 [DDD]

Páez, Fito (sgr)
Piazzolla, A.:Music of, w. Daniel Piazzolla Octet—Fuga y Misterio [composed with H. Ferrer]; Romance del Diablo; Verano Porteño; Tanti Anni Prima [all arr D. Piazzolla & S. Cosentino for octet]; Violentango; Libertango; Adiós Nonino *(rec Moebio Studios, Buenos Aires, Sept–Oct 1995)* — Milan ▲ 35782-2

Paganotti, Bernard (bass)
L'Ethique, w. Richard Pinhas (syns/gtr), Gilles Deleuze (voc), J. P. Goude (syn/perc), G. Grunblatt (syn), Patrick Gauthier (syn/bass), François Auger (drums), Clément Bailly (drums) — Cuneiform ▲ Rune 36X
Rhizosphere/Live, Paris 1982, w. Richard Pinhas (syns/gtr), Patrick Gauthier (syns), François Auger (perc), Clement Bailly (perc) — Cuneiform ▲ Rune 61

Page, Carolann (sop)
Foss, L.:Song of Songs, w. L. Foss (cnd), Milwaukee SO [E] *(rec 4/89)* — Koss Classics ▲ KC 1004 [DDD]

Page, Patti (sgr)
Mancini, H.:Film Music, w. A. Williams (sgr), J. Mathis (sgr), L. Albright (sgr), B. Hackett (sgr), B. Greco (sgr), C. Byrd (sgr), Mancini (cnd), Costa Orch, Conniff Orch, Mancini Orch—sels from Breakfast at Tiffany's; Peter Gunn; Mr. Lucky & others — Columbia/Legacy ▲ CK 66505

Pagliuca, Silvano (bass)
Donizetti, G.:Lucia di Lammermoor (sels), w. Christina Deutekom (sop—Lucia), Luciano Pavarotti (ten—Edgardo), Domenico Trimarchi (bar—Enrico Ashton), Silviano Pagliuca (bass—Raimondo Bidebent), C.M. Guilini (cnd), Naples Teatro San Carlo Orch, Naples Teatro San Carlo Chorus — Budget ("The Greatest Voice in Opera" series) ▲ SYP 103
Giordano, U.:Andrea Chénier, w. Renata Tebaldi (sop—Maddalena), Anna di Stasio (mez—Bersi), Amalia Pini (mez—Madelon/Contessa), Mario Del Monaco (ten—Andrea Chenier), Antonio Pirino (ten—L'Incredibile/Abate), Aldo Protti (bar—Carlo Gerard), Arturo La Porta (bass/bar—Mathieu/Fleville), Silvano Pagliuca (bass—Roucher/Fouquier-Tinville), Giorgio Onesti (bass—Dumas/Schmidt/Major-domo), F. Capuana (cnd), Italian Lyric Orch, Italian Lyric Chorus *(rec Tokyo, Oct 1, 1961)* — Legato Classics 2-▲ LCD 214-2 [ADD]
Pergolesi, G.B.:Il flaminio, w. D. Dessi (sop—Flaminio), F. Pediconi (sop—Agata), E. Zilio (mez—Giustina), M. Ferrugia (ten—Fernando), G. Sica (ten—Polidoro), V. Baiano (bass—Checa), S. Pagliuca (bass—Bastiano), M. Panni (cnd), Naples Teatro San Carlo Orch *(rec Nov. 12, 1983)* — Fonit Cetra 3-▲ CDC 39 [ADD]

Pagliughi, Lina (sop)
Bellini, V.:I Puritani, w. Mario Filippeschi (ten), Rolando Panerai (bar), Sesto Bruscantini (bass), F. Previtali (cnd), Rome RAI SO, Rome RAI Chorus *(rec Rome, Jan. 4 & 5, 1952)* — Pantheon 2-▲ PHE 6640 (m)
Bellini, V.:La sonnambula, w. L. Pagliughi (sop—Amina), W. Ruggeri (sop—Lisa), A. M. Anelli (mez—Teresa), F. Tagliavini (ten—Elvino), P. L. Latinucci (bass—Alessio), C. Siepi (bass—Conte Rodolfo), F. Capuana (cnd), Turin RSO, Turin Radio Chorus *(rec 1952)* — Cetra Classics 2-▲ CDO 16 [AAD]
Bellini, V.:La sonnambula, w. Anna Maria Anelli (sop), Ferruccio Tagliavini (ten), Cesare Siepi (b–bar), F. Capuana (cnd), Turin RAI SO — Fonit Cetra ("Classic Collection" series) 2-▲ FCT CDO 16
Donizetti, G.:La fille du régiment, w. Rina Corsi (mez), Cesare Valletti (ten), Sesto Bruscantini (bar), Eraldo Coda (bar), M. Rossi (cnd), Milan RAI Lyric Orch, Milan RAI Chorus *(rec 1950)* — Cetra Classic 2-▲ CDON 38 [ADD]
Donizetti, G.:Lucia di Lammermoor, w. Lina Pagliughi (sop—Lucia), Maria Vinciguerra (mez—Alisa), Armando Giannotti (ten—Normanno), Muzio Giovagnoli (ten—Arturo), Giovanni Malipiero (ten—Edgardo), Giuseppe Manacchini (bar—Enrico), Luciano Neroni (bass—Raimondo), U. Tansini (cnd), EIAR Orch, EIAR Chorus *(rec 1938)* — Bongiovanni ("Il mito dell'opera" series) 2-▲ GB 1122-2 [ADD]
Donizetti, G.:Lucia di Lammermoor, w. Lina Pagliughi (sop—Lucia), Maria Vinciguerra (mez—Alisa), Armando Giannotti (ten—Normanno), Muzio Giovannoli (ten—Lord Arturo), Giovanni Malipiero (ten—Edgardo), Giuseppe Manacchini (bar—Lord Enrico), Luciano Neroni (bass—Raimondo), U. Tansini (cnd), EIAR Orch, EIAR Chorus *(rec Turin, 1942)* — Melodram 2-▲ IMC 202004 [ADD]
Rossini, G.:Elisabetta, regina d'Inghilterra (sels), w. M. Vitale (sop), G. Campora (ten), Pinno (sgr), A. Simonetto (cnd), Milan RAI SO, Milan RAI Chorus—six arias [I] *(rec live, 4/27/53)* — Myto 2-▲ 2 MCD 90530 [ADD]
Verdi, G.:Un giorno di regno, w. Mario Carlin (ten), Juan Oncina (ten), Sesto Bruscantini (bar), Renato Capecchi (bar), Laura Cozzi (sgr), Cristiano Dalamangas (sgr), A. Simonetto (cnd), Milan RAI Lyric Orch, Milan RAI Chorus *(rec 1951)* — Cetra Classic 2-▲ CDON 37 [ADD]
Verdi, G.:Rigoletto, w. Salvatore Baccaloni (bass), Luigi Piazza (sgr), Tino Folgar (sgr), C. Sabajno (cnd), La Scala Orch, La Scala Chorus — Pearl 2-▲ PEA 9180 [ADD]
Verdi, G.:Rigoletto, w. L. Pagluighi (sop—Gilda), I. Colasanti (mez—Maddalena), F. Tagliavini (ten—Duca), A. Albertini (bar—Il Cavaliere Marullo), G. Taddei (bar—Rigoletto), G. Neri (bass—Sparafucile), A. Zerbini (bass—Conte di Monterone), A. Questa (cnd), Turin RSO, Turin Radio Chorus *(rec 1953)* — Cetra Classics 2-▲ CDO 11 [AAD]

Pagliughi, Lina (sop) (cont.)
Verdi, G.:Rigoletto, w. Lina Pagliughi (sop—Gilda), Linda Brambilla (mez—Contessa di Ceprano), Vera de Cristoff (cta—Maddalena), Tino Folgar (ten—Duca di Mantova), Giuseppe Nessi (ten—Borsa), Aristide Baracchi (bar—Conte di Monterone/Marullo), Luigi Piazza (bar—Rigoletto), Salvatore Baccaloni (bass—Sparafucile), Giuseppe Menni (bass—Conte di Ceprano), C. Sabajno (cnd), La Scala Orch, La Scala Chorus *(rec 1927–28)* — Arkadia 2-▲ CD 78003 (m) [ADD]
Verdi, G.:Rigoletto, w. Lina Pagliughi (sop—Gilda), Linda Brambilla (mez—Countess Ceprano), Vera De Cristoff (cta—Maddalena), Tino Folgar (ten—Duke of Mantua), Giuseppe Nessi (ten—Borsa), Luigi Piazza (bar—Rigoletto), Aristide Baracchi (b–bar—Monterone/Marullo), Salvatore Baccaloni (bass—Sparafucile), Giuseppe Menni (bass—Ceprano), C. Sabajno (cnd), La Scala Orch, La Scala Chorus *(rec La Scala Theatre, Milan, Nov.–Dec. 1927 & Feb. 192)* — VAI Audio 2-▲ VAIA 1097-2
Verdi, G.:Rigoletto (sels), w. G. Lauri-Volpi (ten), T. Gobbi (bar), F. Previtali (cnd), Rome RAI Orch, Rome RAI Chorus [highlights] *(rec 1947)* — Melodram ▲ MEL 15008

Pagowska, A. (alt)
Gorczycki, G.G.:Sacred Choral Music, w. R. Stacewicz (sop), I. Tkaczyk (alt), E. Sasiadek (ten), W. Brychcy (bass), Wroclaw Orch, S. Galonski (cnd), Edmund Kajdasz (cnd), Capella Bydgostiensis Pro Musica Antiqua, Madrigalists Choir, Polish Radio Chorus—Completorium; In virtute tua; Iudica me deus; Laetatus sum; Missa paschalis [L] *(rec 1966)* — Olympia ▲ OCD 320 [AAD]

Pailer, Wolfgang (bass)
Kraft, Walter:Christus, w. Anna Senn-Dähler (sop), Barbara Künzler (sop), Barbara Sutter (sop), Christine Guy (alt), Heidi Uhlmann (alt), Daniel Zellweger (alt), Matthias Senn (ten), Mikoto Usami (ten), Heinz Suter (bass), Klaus Knall (cnd), Evangelische Singgemeinde Choirs *(rec Ostdorf bei Balingen, Oct. 8–11, 1986)* — Cantate 2-▲ 58004 [DDD]
Kropfreiter, A.F.:Altdorfer-Passion, w. B. Hölzl (cta), H. Geitner, *(ensemble unknown)* *(rec 3/88)* — FSM ▲ FCD 97737 [DDD]
Marx, K.:When Jesus Left His Mother, w. F. Staehelin (sgr), C. Näf (cnd), Amarillis Instrumental Ensemble, Feld Evangelistic Kantorei, Amarillis Vocal Ensemble [G] *(rec 6/89)* — FSM ▲ FCD 97737 [DDD]

Paiu, S. (sop)
Biber, H. von:Requiem à 15, w. B. Lettinga (alt), H. van der Kamp (bass), G. Leonhardt (cnd), Netherlands Bach Society Baroque Orch, Netherlands Bach Society Choir — Deutsche Harmonia Mundi ▲ 05472-77277-2
Valls, F.:Scala Arentina Mass, w. M. van der Sluis (sop), B. Lettinga (alt), D. Cordier (ct), J. Elwes (ten), H. van der Kamp (bass), G. Leonhardt (cnd), Netherlands Bach Society Baroque Orch, Netherlands Bach Society Choir — Deutsche Harmonia Mundi ▲ 05472-77277-2

Palacio, Ernesto (ten)
Beethoven, L. van:Arias & Duets, w. Marisa Vitali (sop), M. de Bernart (cnd), I Pomeriggi Musicali Orch—Soll ein Schuh nicht drücken; O welch' ein Leben! ein ganzes Meer! [both from Die schöne Schusterin]; Primo amore piacer del ciel; Ne' giorni tuoi felici [from Olimpiade] *(rec Milano, Apr 1994)* — Arcadia ▲ 153 [DDD]
Donaudy, S.:Airs de style ancien, w. Samuele Pala (pno) *(rec Jungle Studios, Milan, July 26–28, 1995)* — Agorá ▲ 028 [DDD]
Donizetti, G.:L'Esule di Roma, w. C. Gasdia (sop), A. Ariostini (bar), S. Alaimo (bass–bar), M. de Bernart (cnd), Piacenza SO, Paris Opéra-Comique Chorus *(rec live, 10/14/86)* — Bongiovanni 2-▲ GB 2045/46 [DDD]
Donizetti, G.:Torquato Tasso, w. A. D'Auria (sop), L. Serra (sop), N. Ciliento (mez), R. Coviello (bar), S. Alaimo (bass–bar), A. Riva (bass), M.. Bernart (cnd), Genoa Teatro Comunale Orch, Genoa Teatro Comunale Chorus [I] *(rec live 10/16/85)* — Bongiovanni 3-▲ GB 2028/30 [DDD]
Fioravanti, V.:Le cantatrici villane, w. G. Manci (sop—Agata), M. Mauro (sop—Nunziella), M. A. Peters (sop—Rosa), F. Sovilla (mez—Giannetta), E. Palacio (ten—Carlino), G. Gatti (bar—Don Bucefalo), D. Serraiocco (bass—Don Marco), R. Tigani (cnd), Frosinone Licinio Refice Conservatory SO *(rec Oct. 22, 23 & 25, 1992;* ▯ — Bongiovanni 2-▲ GB 2135/36 [DDD]
Galuppi, B.:Adamo, w. Susanna Rigacci (sop—Angelo di Misericordia), Mara Zampieri (sop—Eva), Marilyn Schmiege (mez—Angelo di Giustizia), Ernesto Palacio (ten—Adamo), C. Scimone (cnd), Venice Solisti — Erato 2-▲ ERA SEL 12984 [ADD]
García, M.:Songs, w. Juan Carlos Rivera (gtr), Juan Jose Chuquisengo (pno)—Yo que soy contrabandista; Y otras canciones; I Who Am a Bandit; others — Almaviva ▲ 0114
Handel, G.F.:Rinaldo, w. Cecelia Gasdia (sop), Christine Weidinger (sop), Marylin Horne (mez), J. Fisher (cnd), Venice Teatro La Fenice Orch *(rec live 1989)* — Nuova Era 2-▲ 6813/14 [DDD]
Martin Y Soler, V.:Una Cosa rara, w. M. A. Peters (sop), M. Figueras (sop), G. Fabuel (sop), F. Belaza-Leoz (bar), S. Palatchi (bass), F. Garrigosa (bass), I. Fresán (sgr), J. Savall (cnd), Concert des Nations, La Capella Reial de Catalunya [I] *(rec 1991)* — Astrée 3-▲ E 8760 [DDD]
Martin Y Soler, V.:Il Tutore Burlato, w. Liliana Marzano (sop—Menica), Maria Angeles Peters (sop—Violante), Juan Diego Florez (ten—Anselmo), Ernesto Palacio (ten—Il Cavaliere), Marcello Lippi (bar—Pippo), Giancarlo Tosi (bass—Don Fabrizio), Michela Forgione (hpd), M. Harth-Bedoya (cnd), Dianopolis Bulgarian CO *(rec VI Festival Internazionale di Gerace nella Chiesa di San Francesco, Aug 16, 1994)* — Bongiovanni 2-▲ GB 2175/76-2 [DDD]
Mayr, S.:La Passione, w. Riccardo Ristori (bass), P. Pelucchi (cnd), Collegium Musicum — Agorá 2-▲ 005
Mozart, W.A.:Arias, w. T. Pál (cnd), Salieri CO—Misero! O sogno o son desto; Si mostra la sorte; Un aura amorosa [from Così fan tutte]; Dalla sua pace [from Don Giovanni]; Il mio tesoro [from Don Giovanni]; Se all'impero, amici Dei — Arkadia-Akademia ▲ 138 [DDD]
Pietro Metastasio's Kings & Heroes, w. Salieri CO [cnd:Tamás Pál] *(rec Nov. 23–24, 1993)* — Arkadia-Akademia ▲ 137 [DDD]
Rossini, G.:Arias, w. C. Rizzi (cnd), Bratislava RSO, Slovak Phil Chorus—8 Cantata Arias (1808–1824)—Pianto di Armonia sulla morte di Orfeo; Dolci aurette che spirate; La mia pace io già perdei; Se ostinata ancor non cedi; Giusto cielo i voti miei; Guidò Marte i nostri passi; Il pianto delle Muse in morte di Lord Byron [I] — Arkadia-Akademia ▲ 109 [DDD]
Rossini, G.:Ciro in Babilonia, w. C. Calvi (cta), Dessy-Ceriani (sgr), C. Rizzi (cnd), San Remo SO, San Remo Sym Chorus [I] *(rec live 10/30/88)* — Arkadia-Akademia 2-▲ 105 [DDD]
Rossini, G.:L'inganno felice, w. S. Rigacci (sop—Isabella), E. Palacio (ten—Duke Bertrando), G. Gatti (bar—Batone), R. Ripesi (bass—Tarabotto), G. Casali (bass—Ormondo), F. Maestri (cnd), In Canto CO *(rec Dec. 1992)* — Bongiovanni 2-▲ GB 2133/34 [DDD]
Rossini, G.:L'italiana in Algeri, w. K. Battle (sop), M. Horne (mez), S. Ramey (bass), N. Zaccaria (bass), C. Scimone (cnd), Venice Solisti, Prague Phil Chorus [I] — Erato ("Libretto" series) 2-▲ 2292-45404-2
Rossini, G.:Songs, w. M. A. Peters (sop), A. Cicogna (mez), F. Bettini (sgr), M. Carraro (cnd), *(orch unknown)*—Il carnevale di Venezia; L'Asia in Faville; Egle ed Irene; Un sou; Laus Deo; Dalle quete e pallid'ombre; Nella stagion di maggio; Hai la sottana; Ridiamo cantiamo; Les amants de Seville; La passeggiata; Le depart; Gli animali parlanti del giorno [I] — Bongiovanni ▲ GB 2125 [DDD]
Rossini, G.:Torvaldo e Dorliska, w. A. Buda (sop), F. Pediconi (sop), M. Ciliento (mez), S. Antonucci (bar), A. Marani (b–bar), M. de Bernart (cnd), Swiss-Italian Orch, Cantemus, Swiss-Italian Radio-TV Chorus *(rec Jan. 11, 1992)* — Arkadia-Akademia 2-▲ 123 [DDD]
Sacchini, A.:La contandina in corte, w. S. Rigacci (sop—Tancia), E. Palacio (ten—Ruggiero), G. Gatti (bar—Berto), C. Boersma (vc), M. Clavenna (db), M. T. Conti (hpd), G. Catalucci (cnd), Sassari SO *(rec Dec. 17–18, 1991)* — Bongiovanni 2-▲ GB 2145/46 [DDD]
Tosti, P.F.:Songs, w. M. Rapattoni (pno), H. Liviabella (vn), G. Scabbia (fl), B. Giuffredi (gtr), C. Passerini (hp), M. Decimo (vc) [arr. Massimo de Bernart for instrumental accompaniment]—La serenata; Sogno; 'A vucchella; Segreto; Ideale; 2ème Aubade; Anima mia; Donna, vorrei morir; Aprile; Ancora!; Mattinata; L'ultima canzone; Malìa; Non t'amo più; Il pescatore canta!; Tristezza; O falce di luna calante; L'abla separa dalla luce l'ombra; Mi guitarra dice "Te amo!"; Ricordati di me; Vuol note o banconote? — Arkadia-Akademia ▲ 125 [DDD]
Zingarelli, N.A.:Dante:Inferno, w. Samuele Pala (pno) *(rec S. Martino Church, Tirano, June 30, 1995)* — Agorá ▲ 018 [DDD]
Zingarelli, N.A.:La passione di Gesù Cristo, w. Simone Alaimo (b–bar), Juan Diego Florez (sgr), P. Pelucchi (cnd), Bergamo Collegium Musicum *(rec S. Martino Church, Tirano, June 30, 1995)* — Agorá ▲ 018 [DDD]

Palade, Doina (sop)
Bizet, G.:Carmen, w. G. Alperyn (mez), G. Lamberti (ten), A. Titus (bar), et al., A. Rahbari (cnd), Czech-Slovak RSO Bratislava, Slovak Phil Chorus, Bratislava Children's Choir [F] — Naxos 3-▲ 8.660005/07 [DDD]

1334

▲ = CD ♦ = Enhanced CD Δ = MD ■ = Cassette Tape ▯ = DCC

Palade, Doina (sop) (cont.)

Bizet, G.:Carmen (sels), w. D. Palade (sop—Micaëla), A. Liebeck (sop—Frasquita), G. Alperyn (mez—Carmen), D. Schaechter (mez—Mercédès), G. Lamberti (ten—Don José), M. Dvorsky (ten—Remandado), J. Durco (ten—Cancairo), A. Titus (bar—Escamillo), V. Chmelo (bar—Morales), D. Rigosa (bass—Zuniga), A. Rahbari (cnd), Czech-Slovak RSO Bratislava, Slovak Phil Chorus, Bratislava Children's Choir *(rec July 1990)* Naxos ▲ 8.550727 [DDD]

Palade, Dorothea (mez)

Verdi, G.:Rigoletto, w. Victoria Draganescu (sop—Countess Ceprano), Magda Ianculescu (sop—Gilda), Dorothea Palade (mez—Maddalena), Valeria Savu (mez—Giovanna), Ion Buzea (ten—Duke of Mantua), Dimitrie Scurtu (ten—Borsa), Nicolae Herlea (bar—Rigoletto), Stefan Petrescu (bar—Marullo), Jean Banescu (bass—Count Ceprano), Nicolae Florei (bass—Monterone), Nicolae Rafael (bass—Sparafucile), J. Bobescu (cnd), Romanian Opera Orch, Romanian Opera Chorus *(rec 1965)* Vox Box 2-▲ CDX 5162

Palai, Nello (ten)

Leoncavallo, R.:Pagliacci, w. Adelaide Saraceni (sop—Nedda), Alessandro Valente (ten—Canio), Nello Palai (ten—Beppe), Apollo Granforte (bar—Tonio), Leonildo Basi (bass—Silvio), C. Sabajno (cnd), La Scala Orch, La Scala Chorus *(rec Apr, Sept 1929 & Jan 1930)* VAI Audio 2-▲ VAIA 1082-2

Puccini, G.:La Bohème, w. Licia Albanese (sop—Mimì), Tatiana Menotti (sop—Musetta), Beniamino Gigli (ten—Rodolfo), Nello Palai (ten—Parpignol), Aristide Baracchi (bar—Schaunard), Afro Poli (bar—Marcello), Duilio Baronti (bass—Colline), Carlo Scattola (bass—Benoit/Alcindoro), U. Berrettoni (cnd), La Scala Orch, Vittore Veneziani (cnd), La Scala Chorus *(rec Feb-Mar 1938)* Arkadia ("The 78's" series) 2-▲ 78009 [ADD]

Puccini, G.:La Bohème, w. L. Albanese (sop—Mimì), T. Menotti (sop—Musetta), B. Gigli (ten—Rodolfo), N. Palai (ten—Parpignol), A. Poli (bar—Marcello), A. Baracchi (bar—Schaunard), D. Baronti (bass—Colline), C. Scattola (bass—Benoit/Alcindoro), U. Berrettoni (cnd), La Scala Orch, La Scala Chorus [I] *(rec Milan, May 1938)* Nimbus 2-▲ NI 7862/63 [ADD]

Puccini, G.:Tosca, w. C. Melis (sop—Tosca), P. Pauloi (ten—Cavarodossi), N. Palai (ten—Spoletta), A. Granforte (bar—Scarpia), G. Azzimonti (bass—Sciarrone/Angelotti), A. Gelli (bass—Sacristan), C. Sabajno (cnd), La Scala Orch, La Scala Chorus [I] *(rec Milan, Nov. 1929)* VAI Audio 2-▲ VAIA 1076-2 (m) [ADD]

Puccini, G.:Tosca, w. Carmen Melis (sop—Tosca), Nello Palai (ten—Spoletta), Piero Pauli (ten—Cavaradossi), Apollo Granforte (bar—Scarpia), Giovanni Azzimonti (bass—Angelotti/Sciarrone), Antonio Gelli (bass—Sagrestano), C. Sabajno (cnd), La Scala Orch, La Scala Chorus *(rec Nov 1929)* Arkadia 2-▲ CD 78002 (m) [ADD]

Palánkay, Klára (sop)

Bartók, B.:Bluebeard's Castle, w. M. Székely (bass), J. Ferencsik (cnd), Budapest PO [Hun] *(rec 1956)* Hungaroton ▲ HCD 11001 (m) [ADD]

Palatchi, Stefano (bass)

Donizetti, G.:Anna Bolena, w. Edita Gruberová (sop), Delores Ziegler (mez), E. Boncompagni (cnd), Hungarian RSO, Hungarian Radio Chorus Nightingale Classics 3-▲ NIG 70565

Martin Y Soler, V.:Una Cosa rara, w. M. A. Peters (sop), M. Figueras (sop), G. Fabuel (sop), E. Palacio (ten), F. Belaza-Leoz (bar), F. Garrigosa (bass), I. Fresán (sgr), J. Savall (cnd), Concert des Nations, La Capella Reial de Catalunya [I] *(rec 1991)* Astrée 3-▲ E 8760 [DDD]

Palberg, Mechthild (mez)

Duruflé, M.:Requiem, w. B. Kämpf (bar), B. Kämpf (cnd), Neuwieder Chamber Chorus [L] Motette ▲ CD 50241 [DDD]

Palcsó, Sándor (ten)

Liszt, F.:Requiem, w. Alfonz Bartha (ten), Zsolt Bende (bar), Pál Kovács (bar), A. Ferencsik (cnd), Hungarian State Orch, Hungarian People's Army Male Chorus [L] Hungaroton ▲ HCD 11267

Wayditch, G. von:The Caliph's Magician, w. Júlia Pászthi (sop—Eunuch), Sándor Palcso (ten—The Emir), István Rozsos (ten—Nawab), Zsolt Bende (bar—The Magician), Arpád Kishegyi (sgr—Djinn), András Nagy-Soljom (sgr—The Caliph), Csaba Ötvös (sgr—Djinn), Csilla Ötvös (sgr—Odalisk), A. Kórodi (cnd), Budapest National Opera Orch, Budapest National Opera Chorus *(rec 1975)* VAI Audio 2-▲ VAIA 1095-2 [ADD]

Pallini, Claudia (sgr)

Monteverdi, C.:Ballo delle ingrate, w. Carlo Lepore (bass), Daniela Barcellona (sgr), Daniela Ciliberti (sgr), Andrea Concetti (sgr), Hans van Dijk (sgr), Remo Guerrini (sgr), Nadia Mantelli (sgr), Elena Marazzi (sgr), Humberto Orellana (sgr), Luigi Polsini (sgr), Rosa Ricciotti (sgr), Alberto Rota (sgr), Ludovica Scoppola (sgr), *(orch unknown)* Nuova Era ▲ NUO 7224

Pallini, Rina (mez)

Puccini, G.:Manon Lescaut, w. R. Kabaivanska (sop—Manon), R. Pallini (mez—Singer), P. Domingo (ten—des Grieux), E. Lorenzi (ten—Edmondo), F. Ricciardi (ten—Dancing Master), M. D'Anna (bar—Lescaut), A. Mariotti (bass—Geronte), F. Federici (bass—Innkeeper) Golden Age of Opera 2-▲ GAO 162/63 [ADD]

Pally, Zenaida (mez)

Verdi, G.:La forza del destino, w. Maria Nistor-Slatinaru (sop—Donna Leonora), Mihaela Mariacineanu (mez—Curra), Zenaida Pally (mez—Preziosilla), Ludovic Speiss (ten—Don Alvaro), Ion Stoian (ten—Trabucco), Nicolae Herlea (bar—Don Carlo), Nicolae Florei (bass—Padre Guardiano) Conctantin Gabor (bass—Fra Melitone), Dan Musetescu (bass—An Alcalde), Mihai Pangho (bass—Marquis of Calatrava), C. Litvin (cnd), Romanian Radio-TV Orch, Romanian Radio-TV Chorus *(rec Jan 1970)* Vox Box 3-▲ CD3X 3038

Verdi, G.:Il trovatore, w. Elena Dima (sop—Leonora), Victoria Draganescu (sop—Ines), Zenaida Pally (mez—Azucena), Ion Buzea (ten—Duke of Mantua), Constantin Iliescu (ten—Ruiz), Cornel Stavru (ten—Manrico), Octav Enigarescu (bar—Count di Luna), Constantin Dumitru (bass—Ferrando), E. Massini (cnd), Romanian Opera Orch, Romanian Opera Chorus *(rec 1960-61)* Vox Box 2-▲ CDX 5163

Palm, Mati (bass)

Tobias, R.:Des Jonah Sendung, w. Pille Lill (sop), Urve Tauts (mez), Peter Svensson (ten), Raimo Laukka (bar), Ines Maidre (org), N. Järvi (cnd), Estonian State SO, Oratorio Choir, Estonian Phil Chamber Choir, Tallinn Boys' Choir *(rec Estonia Concert Hall, Tallinn, Estonia, June 23-29, 1995)* BIS 2-▲ CD 731/732 [DDD]

Palma, Piero de (ten)

Bellini, V.:Norma, w. A. Cerquetti (sop), G. Borelli, M. Pirazzini (mez), F. Corelli (ten), G. Neri (bass), G. Santini (cnd), *(orch unknown)* *(rec Rome, 1958)* Great Opera Performances 2-▲ GOP 722

Bellini, V.:Norma (sels), w. M. Callas (sop), M. Pirazzini (mez), F. Corelli (ten), G. Santini (cnd), Rome Opera Orch, Rome Opera Chorus [I] *(rec live 1/2/58)* Melodram ▲ MEL 16000 (m) [AAD]

Boito, A.:Mefistofele, w. Orietta Moscucci (sop—Margherita), Amalia Pini (mez—Martha), Piero de Palma (ten—Wagner), Giacinto Prandelli (ten—Faust), Boris Christoff (bass—Mefistofele), V. Gui (cnd), Rome Opera Orch, Rome Opera Chorus EMI Classics 2-▲ CDMB 65655

Cilea, F.:Adriana Lecouvreur (sels), w. Renata Tebaldi (sop—Adriana), Piero de Palma (ten—Abate), Gianni Poggi (ten—Mauriczio), Giuseppe Taddei (bar—Michonnet), Augusto Romani (bass—Prince), G. Santini (cnd), Naples Teatro San Carlo Orch, Naples Teatro San Carlo Chorus—Del sultano Amurate...Io son l'umile ancella; Giusto Cielo! che feci in tal giorno; Salvatemi! salvatemi!...Scostatevi, profani! *(rec San Carlo Theater, Naples, Dec. 26, 1952)* Legato Classics 2-▲ LCD 193-2 [ADD]

Donizetti, G.:Lucia di Lammermoor, w. Roberta Peters (sop—Lucia), Mitì Truccato Pace (mez—Alisa), Jan Peerce (ten—Edgardo), Piero de Palma (ten—Lord Arturo Bucklaw), Mario Carlin (ten—Normanno), Philip Maero (bar—Lord Enrico Ashton), Giorgio Tozzi (bass—Raimondo), E. Leinsdorf (cnd), Rome Opera Orch, Rome Opera Chorus *(rec Rome Opera House, Aug 5-14, 1957)* RCA Living Stereo 2-▲ 09026-68537-2 [ADD]

Mozart, W.A.:Arias, w. I. Cotrubas (sop), E. Gruberova (sop), L. Price (sop), J. Varady (sop), L. Popp (mez), F. Araiza (ten), P. Domingo (ten), P. Schreier (ten), F. Wunderlich (ten), S. Milnes (bar), A. Titus (bar), M. Talvela (bass)—sels. from Entführung aus dem Serail, Così fan tutte, Don Giovanni, Idomeneo, Die Zauberflöte, Le nozze di Figaro Eurodisc ▲ 69256-2-RG [ADD]

Puccini, G.:Madama Butterfly (sels), w. Leontyne Price (sop), Rosalind Elias (mez), Richard Tucker (ten), Phillip Maero (bar), E. Leinsdorf (cnd), RCA Italian Opera Orch, RCA Italiana Opera Chorus RCA Victor ▲ 09026-68089-2; ■ 09026-68089-4

Palma, Piero de (ten) (cont.)

Puccini, G.:Tosca, w. Ranata Tebaldi (sop), Gian Franco Volante (trb), Giuseppe Campora (ten), Enzo Mascherini (bar), Fernando Corena (bass), Dario Caselli (bass), Antonio Sacchetti (bass), A. Erede (cnd), St. Cecilia Academy Orch Rome, St. Cecilia Academy Chorus Rome *(rec 1952)* Andromeda 2-▲ ANR 2539 [ADD]

Puccini, G.:Turandot, w. Birgit Nilsson (sop—Turandot), Renata Tebaldi (sop—Liù), Jussi Björling (ten—Calaf), Alessio De Paolis (ten—Emperor Altoum), Piero de Palma (ten—Pang), Mario Sereni (bar—Ping), Adelio Zagonara (bar—Prince of Persia), Giorgio Tozzi (bass—Timur), Tommaso Frascati (bass—Pong), Leonardo Monreale (bass—Mandarin), E. Leinsdorf (cnd), Rome Opera Orch, Rome Opera Chorus *(rec Rome Opera House, July 3-11, 1959)* RCA Living Stereo 2-▲ 09026-62687-2 [ADD]

Verdi, G.:Aida, w. Renata Tebaldi (sop—Aida), Ebe Stignani (mez—Amneris), Mario Del Monaco (ten—Radamès), Piero de Palma (ten—Messenger), Aldo Protti (bar—Amonasro), Fernando Corena (bass—King), Dario Caselli (bass—Ramfis), A. Erede (cnd), St. Cecilia Academy Orch Rome, St. Cecilia Academy Chorus Rome *(rec 1952)* Theorema 2-▲ TH 121133/34

Verdi, G.:Attila, w. Rita Orlandi Malaspina (sop—Odabella), Veriano Luchetti (ten—Foresto), Piero De Palma (ten—Uldino), Piero Cappuccilli (bar—Ezio), Nicolai Ghiaurov (bass—Attila), Luigi Roni (bass—Leone), G. Patanè (cnd), La Scala Orch, La Scala Chorus *(rec Milan, May 12, 1975)* Myto 2-▲ MCD 961140

Verdi, G.:Attila, w. Rita Orlandi Malaspina (sop—Odabella), Veriano Luchetti (ten—Foresto), Piero de Palma (ten—Uldino), Piero Cappuccilli (bar—Ezio), Nicolai Ghiaurov (bass—Attila), Luigi Roni (bass—Leone), G. Patanè (cnd), La Scala Orch, La Scala Chorus *(rec Milan, May 15, 1972)* Golden Age of Opera 2-▲ GAO 187/88 [ADD]

Verdi, G.:Otello, w. Renata Tebaldi (sop—Desdemona), Luisa Ribacchi (mez—Emilia), Angelo Mercuriali (ten—Roderigo), Mario del Monaco (ten—Otello), Piero de Palma (ten—Cassio), Aldo Protti (bar—Iago), Dario Caselli (bass—A Herald), Fernando Corena (bass—Lodovico), Pierluigi Martinucci (bass—Montano), A. Erede (cnd), St. Cecilia Academy Orch Rome, St. Cecilia Academy Chorus Rome Theorema ▲ TH 121141/142

Verdi, G.:Otello, w. G. Jones (sop—Desdemona), A. di Stasio (mez—Emilia), J. McCracken (ten—Otello), P. de Palma (ten—Cassio), D. Fischer-Dieskau (bar—Iago), J. Barbirolli (cnd), New Philharmonia Orch, Ambrosian Opera Chorus EMI Classics ▲ CDMB 65296

Verdi, G.:Rigoletto, w. Hilde Gueden (sop—Gilda), Piero de Palma (ten—Borsa), Luisa Ribacchi (mez—Giovanna), Giulietta Simionato (mez—Maddalena), Mario del Monaco (ten—Duca de Mantova), Aldo Protti (bar—Rigoletto), Fernando Corena (bass—Conte Monterone), Cesare Siepi (bass—Sparafucile), A. Erede (cnd), St. Cecilia Academy Orch Rome, St. Cecilia Academy Chorus Rome Theorema ▲ TH 121179/180

Verdi, G.:Rigoletto, w. R. Tebaldi (sop), M. del Monaco (ten), A. Protti (bar), F. Corena (bass), A. Erede (cnd), St. Cecilia Academy Orch Rome, St. Cecilia Academy Chorus Rome London 2-▲ 440245-2 [ADD]

Verdi, G.:Il trovatore, w. Antonella Banaudi (sop—Leonora), Barbara Frittoli (sop—Ines), Shirley Verrett (mez—Azucena), Enrico Facini (ten—Un messo), Piero de Palma (ten—Ruiz), Luciano Pavarotti (ten—Marico), Leo Nucci (bar—Il Conte di Luna), Roberto Scaltriti (bar—Un vecchio zingaro), Francesco Ellero d'Artegna (bass—Ferrando), Z. Mehta (cnd), Florence Maggio Musicale Orch, Florence Maggio Musicale Chorus *(rec Maggio Musicale Fiorentino Community Theater, June 18-July 2, 1990)* London 2-▲ 430694-2

Zandonai, R.:Francesca da Rimini, w. Lydia Marimpietri (sop—Biancofiore), Magda Olivero (sop—Francesca), Pinuccia Perotti (sop—Samaritana), Edda Vincenzi (sop—Garsenda), Gabriella Carturan (mez—Smaragdi), Biancamaria Casoni (mez—Altichiara), Anna Maria Rota (cta—Donella), Athos Cesarini (ten—Archer), Angelo Mercuriali (ten—Ser Toldo Berardengo), Mario del Monaco (ten—Paolo), Piero de Palma (ten—Malatestino), Rinaldo Pelizzoni (ten—Prisoner), Gianpiero Malaspina (bar—Gianciotto), Dino Mantovani (bar—Jester), Enrico Campi (bass—Ostasio), Giuseppe Morresi (bass—Tower warden), G. Gavazzeni (cnd), La Scala Orch, La Scala Chorus *(rec La Scala Theatre, Milan, June 4, 1959)* Legato Classics 2-▲ LCD 186-2

Palmer, Felicity (sop/mez)

Bononcini, A.:Stabat Mater, w. Paul Esswood (ct), Philip Langridge (ten), Christopher Keyte (bass), John Scott (org), John Willison (vn), Chris Wellington (va), Don McVeigh (va), G. Guest (cnd), Philomusica Antiqua of London, St. John's College Choir Cambridge *(rec 1977)* London 2-▲ 443868-2 [ADD]

Caldara, A.:Crucifixus, w. Paul Esswood (ct), Philip Langridge (ten), Christopher Keyte (bass), John Scott (org), John Willison (vn), Chris Wellington (va), Don McVeigh (va), G. Guest (cnd), Philomusica Antiqua of London, St. John's College Choir Cambridge *(rec 1977)* London 2-▲ 443868-2 [ADD]

Cavalli, P.F.:Ercole armante, w. Felicity Palmer (sop—Jole), Yvonne Minton (mez—Giunone), Patricia Miller (sgr—Dejanira), Ulrik Cold (bass), M. Corboz (cnd), English Bach Baroque Orch, English Bach Festival Chorus Erato 3-▲ ERA SEL 12980 [ADD]

Handel, G.F.:Messiah (reorchd Mozart), w. Felicity Lott (sop), Phillip Langridge (ten), Robert Lloyd (b-bar), C. Mackerras (cnd), Royal PO, Huddersfield Choral Society [E] ASV ▲ ASV CD 960

Handel, G.F.:Utrecht Te Deum & Jubilate, w. Marjana Lipovšek (mez), Philip Langridge (ten), N. Harnoncourt (cnd), Vienna Concentus Musicus, Arnold Schoenberg Choir [L] Teldec ▲ 2292-42984-2

Lotti, A.:Crucifixus, w. Paul Esswood (ct), Philip Langridge (ten), Christopher Keyte (bass), John Scott (org), John Willison (vn), Chris Wellington (va), Don McVeigh (va), G. Guest (cnd), Philomusica Antiqua of London, St. John's College Choir Cambridge *(rec 1977)* London 2-▲ 443868-2 [ADD]

Mahler, G.:Sym 2, w. Tatiana Troyanos (mez), P. Boulez (cnd), BBC SO, Paris Conservatory Société des Concerts Orch, BBC Sym Chorus Originals 2-▲ ORISH 855

Pergolesi, G.B.:Stabat mater, w. Alfreda Hodgson (cta), David Hill (org), G. Guest (cnd), Argo CO, St. John's College Choir Cambridge *(rec 1978)* London 2-▲ 443868-2 [ADD]

Sullivan, A.:The Mikado, w. L. Garrett (sop), J. Rigby (mez), S. Bullock (sop), B. Bottone (ten), R. Angas (bass), E. Idle (bar), R. Van Allan (bass), M. Richardson (bar), P. Robinson (cnd), English National Opera Orch, English Opera Group Chorus—sels [E] MCA Classics ▲ MCAD 6215 [DDD]; ■ MCAC 6215 (D)

Sullivan, A.:The Mikado, w. M. McLaughlin (sop), A. Howells (mez), J. Watson (sop), D. Adams (bass), A. Rolfe Johnson (ten), R. Stuart (bar), R. Van Allan (bass), N. Folwell (bar), C. Mackerras (cnd), Welsh National Opera Orch, Welsh National Opera Chorus—Ov & dialogue omitted [E] Telarc ▲ CD 80284 [DDD]; ■ CS 30284 (D)

Sullivan, A.:The Yeomen of the Guard, w. Felicity Palmer (sop—Dame Carruthers), Pamela Helen Stephens (mez—Phoebe Meryll), Neill Archer (ten—Col Fairfax), Peter Hoare (ten—Leonard Meryll), Ralph Mason (ten—1st Yeoman), Donald Maxwell (bar—Wilfred Shadbolt), Peter Savidge (bar—Lieutenant Sir Richard Cholmondely), Donald Adams (bass—Sergeant Meryll), Richard Suart (bass—Jack Point), Peter Lloyd Evans (sgr—2nd Yeoman), Alwyn Mellor (sgr—Elsie Maynard), Clare O'Neill (sgr—Kate), C. Mackerras (cnd), Welsh National Opera Orch, Welsh National Opera Chorus *(rec Brangwyn Hall, Swasea, Wales, Apr 18-30 & May 1, 1995)* Telarc 2-▲ CD 80404 [DDD]

Tippett, M.:King Priam, w. Heather Harper (sop—Hecuba), Linda Hirst (sop—Serving Woman), Felicity Palmer (sop—Andromache), Julian Saipe (sop—Paris), Yvonne Minton (mez—Helen), Ann Murray (mez—Nurse), Kenneth Bowen (ten—Hermes), Peter Hall (ten—Young Guard), Philip Langridge (ten—Paris), Robert Tear (ten—Achilles), Thomas Allen (bar—Hector), Norman Bailey (bar—Priam), Stephen Roberts (bar—Patroclus), David Wilson-Johnson (bar—Old Man), D. Atherton (cnd), London Sinfonietta, London Sinfonietta Chorus Chandos ▲ CHAN 9406/7 [DDD]

Palmer, Gladys (cta)

Verdi, G.:La traviata, w. Maria Caniglia (sop—Violetta), Maria Huder (mez—Flora), Gladys Palmer (cta—Annina), Octave Dua (ten—Giuseppe), Beniamino Gigli (ten—Alfredo), Booth Hitchen (ten—D'Obigny), Adelio Zagonara (bar—Gastone), Aristide Baracchi (bar—Douphol), Mario Basiola (bar—Germont), Norman Walker (bass—Dr. Grenville), V. Gui (cnd), London PO, London Phil Chorus *(rec Royal Opera House, Covent Garden, May 22, 1939)* Minerva 2-▲ MN A28/29 (m) [ADD]

Palombi, A. (sgr)

Menichetti, D.:L'Epifania del Signore, w. K. Gamberucci (sop), F. Facini (bass), A. Della Santa (sgr), F. Esposito (sgr), H. Handt (cnd), Toscana Accademia Strumentale, Polifonica Lucchese Bongiovanni ▲ GB 5033 [DDD]

Palombini, Vittoria (mez)

Giordano, U.:Andrea Chénier, w. Maria Caniglia (sop—Maddalena), Maria Huder (mez—Bersi), Vittoria Palombini (mez—Madelon), Giulietta Simionato (mez—Contessa), Beniamino Gigli (ten—Andrea), Adelio Zagonara (ten—Incroyable/Abbé), Gino Bechi (bar—Carlo), Leone Paci (bar—Mathieu), Giuseppe Taddei (b-bar—Pietro/Fouquier), Italo Tajo (b-bar—Roucher), Gino Conti (bass—Master/Schmidt), O. de Fabritiis (cnd), La Scala Orch, La Scala Chorus *(rec Nov 1941)* Arkadia ("The 78's" series) 2-▲ 78012 [ADD]

Humperdinck, E.:Hänsel und Gretel, w. Sena Jurinac (sop), Elisabeth Schwarzkopf (sop), Rita Streich (sop), Rolando Panerai (bar), Bruna Ronshini (sgr), H. von Karajan (cnd), Milan Italian Radio-TV Orch, Milan RAI Chorus Stradivarius 2-▲ STV 12314

Humperdinck, E.:Hänsel und Gretel (sels), w. Sena Jurinac (sop—Hänsel), Elisabeth Schwarzkopf (sop—Gretel), Vittoria Palombini (mez—Witch), Rolando Panerai (sgr—Peter), Bruna Ronchini (sgr—Gertrude), H.. Karajan (cnd), Milan RAI SO, Milan RAI Chorus—[Act 1] Suse, liebe Suse, was raschelt im Stroh; [Act 2] Ein Männlein steht im Walde ganz still und Stumm; Abends, will ich schlafen gehn; [Act 3] Wo bin ich? Wach' ich?; Und bist du dann drin...schwaps!; Die Englein haben's im Traum gesagt; Schunt, o schunt das Wunder an *(rec Milan, Dec. 25, 1954)* Legato Classics 3-▲ LCD 197-3

Paltrinieri, Giodano (ten)

Bellini, V.:Norma, w. Gina Cigna (sop—Norma), Thelma Votipka (mez—Clotilde), Bruna Castagna (cta—Adalgisa), Giovanni Martinelli (ten—Pollione), Giodano Paltrinieri (ten—Flavio), Ezio Pinza (bass—Oroveso), E. Panizza (cnd), *(orch unknown)* *(rec live, New York, Feb. 20, 1937)* The Fourties 2-▲ ENT FT 1517

Pampanini, Rosetta (sop)

The Italian Vocal Tradition, Vol. 1:The Voices of Toscanini, w. Toti dal Monte (sop), Claudio Muzio (sop), Biata Scacciati (sop), Giacomo Lauri-Volpi (ten), Francesco Merli (ten), Aureliano Pertile (ten), Carlo Galeffi (bar), Mariano Stabile (bar), Riccardo Stracciari (bar), Nazzareno de Angel *(rec 1921-35)* Iron Needle ▲ 1304

Leoncavallo, R.:Pagliacci, w. Francesco Merli (ten), Giuseppe Nessi (ten), Carlo Galeffi (bar), Gino Vanelli (bar), *(orch unknown)* *(rec Milan, 1930)* Melodram ▲ IMC 102003

Leoncavallo, R.:Pagliacci, w. Francesco Merli (ten), Giuseppe Nessi (ten), Carlo Galeffi (bar), L. Molajoli (cnd), La Scala Orch, La Scala Chorus *(rec Milan, 1930)* Phonographe 2-▲ PHG CD 5066

Puccini, G.:La Bohème, w. Luba Mirella (sop—Musetta), Rosetta Pampanini (sop—Mimì), Luigi Marini (ten—Rodolfo), Giuseppe Nessi (ten—Alcindoro), Aristide Baracchi (bar—Schaunard), Gino Vanelli (bar—Marcello), Salvatore Baccaloni (bass—Benoit), Tancredi Pasero (bass—Colline), L. Molajoli (cnd), La Scala Orch, La Scala Chorus Bongiovanni 2-▲ 1125/26 [ADD]

Puccini, G.:Madama Butterfly, w. Rosetta Pampanini (sop—Madama Butterfly), Conchita Velasquez (mez—Suzuki), Cesira Ferrari (mez—Kate Pinkerton), Alessandro Granda (ten—F. B. Pinkerton), Giuseppe Nessi (ten—Goro), Aristide Baracchi (bar—Il Principe Yamadori), Gino Vanelli (bar—Sharpless), Lino Bonardi (bass—Il Commissario Imperiale), Salvatore Baccaloni (bass—Lo zio Bonzo), L. Molajoli (cnd), La Scala Orch, La Scala Chorus Bongiovanni 2-▲ 1123/24 [ADD]

Puccini, G.:Madama Butterfly, w. A. Granda (ten), G. Nessi (ten), G. Vanelli (bar), S. Baccaloni (bass), L. Malajoli (cnd), La Scala Orch, La Scala Chorus *(rec 1928)* Centaur 2-▲ CRC 2196/97

Rosetta Pampanini Preiser ("Lebendige Vergangenheit" series) ▲ PRE 89063 (m) [AAD]

Panaiotis (voc)

Deep Listening Band:Troglodyte's Delight, w. Pauline Oliveros (acc/voc/whistles), Stuart Dempster (trbn), Julie Lyon Balliett (voc), Fritz Hauser (perc) *(rec Tarpaper Cave, Rosendale, NY, June 1989)* ¿What Next? ▲ WN 003 ■ WN 0003

McLean, B.:Rainforest Images, w. I. Troselj (sgr), K. Ryan (sgr), P. McLean (sgr/rcr/vn), B. McLean (rcr/clariflute), B. Dickie (didgeridoo) Capstone ▲ CPS 8617n

Panaiotis (voc/whistling)

Deep Listening Band:Deep Listening, w. S. Dempster (voc/trbn/didjeridu), P. Oliveros (voc/acc) New Albion ▲ NA 022 [DDD]

Panariello, Ernesto (bass)

Giordano, U.:Fedora, w. Mirella Freni (sop—Principessa Fedora), Adelina Scarabelli (sop—Contessa Olga), Silvia Mazzoni (mez—Dimitri), Monica Minarelli (sgr—Savoiardo), Placido Domingo (ten—Conte Loris), Ernesto Gavazzi (ten—Desiré), Aldo Bottion (ten—Barone Rouvel), Alessandro Corbelli (bar—Siriex), Luigi Roni (bass—Cirillo), Silvestro Sammaritano (bass—Baroff), Alfredo Giacomotti (bass—Gretch), Ernesto Panariello (bass—Lorek), Vincenzo Alaimo (sgr—Nicola), Arnold Bosman (sgr—Boleslao), Bruno Capisani (sgr—Sergio), Renato Zanchetta (sgr—Michele), G. Gavazzeni (cnd), La Scala Orch, La Scala Chorus *(rec La Scala, Apr 5, 1993)* Legato 2-▲ LCD 213-2 [ADD]

Pandano, Vittorio (ten)

Massenet, J.:Werther, w. D. Gatta (sop—Sofia), I. Ligabue (sop—Kaethlen), G. Simionato (mez—Charlotte), F. Tagliavini (ten—Werther), V. Pandano (ten—Schmidt), E. Campi (bass—Johann), S. Bruscantini (bass—Le Bailli), F. Capuana (cnd), La Scala Orch, La Scala Chorus *(rec Apr. 21, 1951)* Bongiovanni 2-▲ GB 1101/02 [ADD]

Verdi, G.:Ernani, w. Caterina Mancini (sop), Gino Penno (ten), Giuseppe Taddei (bar), Giacomo Vaghi (bar), Ezio Achilli (sgr), Licia Rossini (sgr), F. Previtali (cnd), Rome RAI SO, Rome RAI Chorus Cetra Classic 2-▲ CDON 39 [ADD]

Panea, Teodor (ten)

Verdi, G.:La traviata, w. Elena Simionescu (sop—Annina), Virginia Zeani (sop—Violetta Valery), Elisabeta Neculce-Cartis (mez—Flora Bervoix), Ion Buzea (ten—Alfredo Germont), Vasile Moldoveanu (ten—Gastone/Viconte de Letorieres/Giuseppe), Teodor Panea (ten—Flora's Servant), Constantin Dumitru (bar—Commissioner/Baron Douphol), Nicolae Herlea (bar—Giorgio Germont), Valentin Loghin (bass—Marchese D'Obigny), Nicolae Rafael (bass—Doctor Grenvil), J. Bobescu (cnd), Romanian Opera Orch, Stelian Olariu (cnd), Romanian Opera Chorus *(rec 1968)* Vox Box 2-▲ CDX 5154

Panerai, Rolando (bar)

Bellini, V.:I Puritani, w. Lina Pagliughi (sop), Mario Filippeschi (ten), Sesto Bruscantini (bass), F. Previtali (cnd), Rome RAI SO, Rome RAI Chorus *(rec Rome, Jan. 4 & 5, 1952)* Pantheon 2-▲ PHE 6640 (m)

Bellini, V.:I Puritani, w. M. Callas (sop), G. di Stefano (ten), N. Rossi-Lemeni (bass), T. Serafin (cnd), La Scala Orch, La Scala Chorus [l] EMI Classics 2-▲ CDCB 47308 (m) [ADD]

Donizetti, G.:Don Pasquale, w. Margherita Guglielmi (sop—Norina), Alfredo Kraus (ten—Ernesto), Rolando Panerai (bar—Malatesta), Paolo Montarsolo (bass—Don Pasquale), P. Bellugi (cnd), La Scala Orch, La Scala Chorus *(rec Jan 13, 1974)* Golden Age of Opera 2-▲ GAO 202/203 [ADD]

Donizetti, G.:Don Pasquale, w. E. Ravaglia (sop), P. Bottazzo (ten), A. Frati (ten), F. Corena (bass), R. Muti (cnd), Vienna PO, Vienna State Opera Chorus [l] *(rec live, Salzburg, 8/11/71)* Melodram 2-▲ CDM 27094 [ADD]

Donizetti, G.:L'elisir d'amore, w. Rosanna Carteri (sop—Adina), Luigi Angela Vercelli (mez—Gianetta), Luigi Alva (ten—Nemorino), Rolando Panerai (bar—Belcore), Giuseppe Taddei (bar—Dulcamara), T. Serafin (cnd), La Scala Orch, La Scala Chorus EMI Classics 2-▲ CDMB 65658

Donizetti, G.:Lucia di Lammermoor, w. M. Callas (sop), G. di Stefano (ten), N. Zaccaria (bass), H. von Karajan (cnd), RIAS SO, La Scala Chorus [l] *(rec 9/29/55)* Verona 2-▲ 2709/10 (m) [AAD]

Donizetti, G.:Lucia di Lammermoor, w. Maria Callas (sop), Eugenio Fernandi (ten), Giuseppe Modesti (bass), T. Serafin (cnd), Rome RAI SO, Rome RAI Chorus *(rec live, Rome, 1957)* Enterprise ("Documents" series) 2-▲ ENTLV 973 [ADD]

Donizetti, G.:Lucia di Lammermoor, w. M. Callas (sop), G. Raimondi (ten), A. Zerbini (bass), F. Molinari-Pradelli (cnd), Naples Teatro San Carlo Orch, Naples Teatro San Carlo Chorus [l] *(rec live, 3/22/56)* Myto ▲ 2 MCD 90319 (m) [ADD]

Donizetti, G.:Lucia di Lammermoor, w. M. Callas (sop), G. di Stefano (ten), N. Zaccaria (bass), H. von Karajan (cnd), RIAS SO, La Scala Chorus [l] *(rec live, 1955)* EMI Classics (Studio) 2-▲ CDMB 63631 [ADD]

Donizetti, G.:Lucia di Lammermoor, w. M. Callas (sop), G. di Stefano (ten), H. von Karajan (cnd), La Scala Orch, La Scala Chorus [l] *(rec live, Milan 1/18/54)* Standing Room Only 2-▲ SRO 831-2 [ADD]

Donizetti, G.:Lucia di Lammermoor, w. M. Callas (sop), G. di Stefano (ten), N. Zaccaria (bass), H. von Karajan (cnd), RIAS SO, La Scala Chorus [l] *(rec 9/29/55)* Melodram 2-▲ MEL 26004

Panerai, Rolando (bar) (cont.)

Donizetti, G.:Lucia di Lammermoor, w. M. Callas (sop), G. di Stefano (ten), G. Zampieri (ten), G. Modesti (bass), H. von Karajan (cnd), La Scala Orch, La Scala Chorus *(rec 1954)* Melodram 2-▲ MLO 26040 [DDD]

Gluck, C.W.:Alceste, w. M. Callas (sop), R. Gavarini (ten), S. Maionica (bass), C. M. Giulini (cnd), La Scala Orch, La Scala Chorus—plus "Callas Sings Gluck & Rossini" [French version] *(rec live, La Scala, 4/4/54)* Melodram 2-▲ MEL 26026

Gounod, C.:Faust (sels), w. R. Tebaldi (sop), F. Cadoni (mez), M. Filippeschi (ten), I. Tajo (bass), F. Patanè (cnd), Naples Teatro San Carlo Orch, Naples Teatro San Carlo Chorus—Act IV, Scenes 1 & 2 & Act V, Scene 2 *(rec live, 4/26/51)* Standing Room Only 2-▲ SRO 810-2 [ADD]

Humperdinck, E.:Hänsel und Gretel (sels), w. Sena Jurinac (sop—Hänsel), Elisabeth Schwarzkopf (sop—Gretel), Vittoria Palombini (mez—Witch), Rolando Panerai (sgr—Peter), Bruna Ronchini (sgr—Gertrude), H.. Karajan (cnd), Milan RAI SO, Milan RAI Chorus—[Act 1] Suse, liebe Suse, was raschelt im Stroh; [Act 2] Ein Männlein steht im Walde ganz still und Stumm; Abends, will ich schlafen gehn; [Act 3] Wo bin ich? Wach' ich?; Und bist du dann drin...schwaps!; Die Englein haben's im Traum gesagt; Schunt, o schunt das Wunder an *(rec Milan, Dec. 25, 1954)* Legato Classics 3-▲ LCD 197-3

Humperdinck, E.:Hänsel und Gretel, w. Sena Jurinac (sop), Elisabeth Schwarzkopf (sop), Rita Streich (sop), Vittoria Palombini (mez), Bruna Ronshini (sgr), H. von Karajan (cnd), Milan Italian Radio-TV Orch, Milan RAI Chorus Stradivarius 2-▲ STV 12314

Leoncavallo, R.:Pagliacci, w. J. Carlyle (sop), C. Bergonzi (ten), U. Benelli (bar), G. Taddei (bar), H. von Karajan (cnd), La Scala Orch [l] Deutsche Grammophon 3-▲ 419257-2 [ADD]

Leoncavallo, R.:Pagliacci, w. M. Callas (sop), G. di Stefano (ten), T. Gobbi (bar), T. Serafin (cnd), La Scala Orch [l] EMI Classics 3-▲ CDCC 47981 [ADD]

Leoncavallo, R.:Pagliacci, w. Joan Carlyle (sop—Nedda/Colombina), Carlo Bergonzi (ten—Canio/Pagliaccio), Franco Ricciardi (ten—Villager), Ugo Benelli (bar—Peppe/Arlecchino), Rolando Panerai (bar—Silvio), Giuseppe Taddei (bar—Tonio/Taddeo), Giuseppe Morresi (bass—Villager), H. von Karajan (cnd), La Scala Orch, La Scala Chorus *(rec La Scala, Milan, Oct 1965)* Deutsche Grammophon ("The Originals" series) ▲ 449727-2 [ADD]

Mascagni, P.:Cavalleria rusticana, w. M. Callas (sop), E. Ticozzi (mez), G. di Stefano (ten), T. Serafin (cnd), La Scala Orch, La Scala Chorus [l] EMI Classics 3-▲ CDCC 47981 [ADD]

Massenet, J.:Manon, w. M. Freni (sop), L. Pavarotti (ten), P. Maag (cnd), La Scala Orch, La Scala Chorus [l] *(rec live, 6/3/69)* Melodram 2-▲ MEL 27046 [AAD]

Massenet, J.:Manon, w. M. Freni (sop), L. Pavarotti (ten), P. Maag (cnd), La Scala Orch, La Scala Chorus [l] *(rec live, 6/3/69)* Verona 2-▲ 27052/53 (m) [AAD]

Mercadante, S.:Il giuramento (sels), w. M. Vitale (sop), M. Pirazzini (mez), A. Berdini (bar), A. Simonetto (cnd), Milan RAI Orch, Milan RAI Chorus [l]—14 scenes & arias *(rec live, Milan, 4/5/51)* Myto 2-▲ 2 MCD 90632 [ADD]

Mozart, W.A.:Arias, w. S. Frontalini (cnd), Bacau PO—Le nozze di Figaro:Non più andrai; Don Giovanni:Madamina, il catalogo è questo Bongiovanni ▲ GB 2514 [DDD]

Mozart, W.A.:Così fan tutte, w. Elisabeth Schwarzkopf (sop), Graziella Sciutti (sop), Nan Merriman (mez), Luigi Alva (ten), Franco Calabrese (bass), G. Cantelli (cnd), La Scala Orch, La Scala Chorus Stradivarius 2-▲ STV DTM 12304 [ADD]

Mozart, W.A.:Così fan tutte, w. E. Schwarzkopf (sop—Fiordiligi), G. Sciurri (sop—Despina), N. Merriman (mez—Dorabella), L. Alva (ten—Ferrando), R. Panerai (bar—Guglielmo), F. Clabrese (b-bar—Don Alfonso)., G. Cantelli (cnd), La Scala Orch, La Scala Chorus *(rec Jan. 27, 1956)* Datum 2-▲ DAT 12304 [ADD]

Mozart, W.A.:Così fan tutte, w. M. Adani (sop), T. Stich-Randall (mez), T. Berganza (mez), L. Alva (ten), A. Cortis (ten), H. Rosbaud (cnd), Paris Conservatory Societé des Concerts Orch, Aix-en-Provence Festival Chorus [l] *(rec live, Aix-en-Provence, July 26, 1957)* Melodram 3-▲ MEL 37084 [AAD]

Mozart, W.A.:Così fan tutte, w. E. Schwarzkopf (sop), L. Otto (sop), N. Merriman (mez), L. Simoneau (ten), S. Bruscantini (bar), H. von Karajan (cnd), Philharmonia Orch, Philharmonia Chorus [l] EMI Classics ("Studio" series) 3-▲ CDHC 69635 (m) [ADD]

Mozart, W.A.:Così fan tutte (sels), w. Lisa Otto (sop), Elizabeth Schwarzkopf (sop), Nan Merriman (mez), Leopold Simoneau (ten), Sesto Bruscantini (bass), H. von Karajan (cnd), Philharmonia Orch Classics for Pleasure ("Eminence" series) ▲ CDEMX 2211 [DDD]

Mozart, W.A.:Così fan tutte (sels), w. G. Janowitz (sop), R. Grist (sop), B. Fassbaender (mez), P. Schreier (ten), H. Prey (bar), K. Böhm (cnd), Vienna PO, Vienna State Opera Chorus—scenes & arias Deutsche Grammophon ▲ 429824-2 [ADD]

Mozart, W.A.:Don Giovanni, w. J. Varady (sop), A. Augér (sop), E. Mathis (sop), T. Moser (ten), A. Titus (bar), R. Scholze (bass), J.-H. Rootering (bass), R. Kubelik (cnd), Bavarian RSO, Bavarian Radio Chorus [l] Eurodisc 3-▲ 7798-2 [DDD]

Mozart, W.A.:Don Giovanni, w. G. Janowitz (sop), T. Zylis-Gara (sop), M. Freni (sop), A. Kraus (ten), V. von Halem (bass), N. Ghiaurov (bass), H. von Karajan (cnd), Vienna PO, Vienna State Opera Chorus [l] *(rec live, Salzburg, Aug. 1, 1969)* Memories 3-▲ HR 4362/64 (m) [ADD]

Mozart, W.A.:Nozze di Figaro, w. E. Schwarzkopf (sop), I. Seefried (sop), S. Jurinac (sop), L. Villa (sop), H. von Karajan (cnd), La Scala Orch, La Scala Chorus [l] *(rec live Feb. 4, 1954)* Melodram 3-▲ MEL 37075 [AAD]

Piccinni, N.:La cecchina (sels), w. M. Freni (sop), I. Hollweg (sop), S. Bruscantini (bar), F. Caracciolo (cnd), Naples RAI Orch—13 arias *(rec live 11/25/69)* Arkadia 2-▲ 596 [ADD]

Puccini, G.:La Bohème, w. M. Freni (sop), E. Harwood (sop), L. Pavarotti (ten), H. von Karajan (cnd), Berlin PO, German Opera Chorus [l] London 2-▲ 421049-2 [ADD] 2-■ 421049-4

Puccini, G.:La Bohème, w. M. Callas (sop), A. Moffo (sop), G. di Stefano (ten), A. Votto (cnd), La Scala Orch, La Scala Chorus [l] *(rec 1956)* EMI Classics 2-▲ CDCB 47475 (m) [ADD]

Puccini, G.:La Bohème (sels), w. M. Freni (sop), H. Gueden (sop), G. Raimondi (ten), H. von Karajan (cnd), Vienna State Opera Orch—7 arias & scenes [l] *(rec live 11/9/63)* Verona 2-▲ 27079/80

Puccini, G.:La Bohème (sels), w. M. Freni (sop), E. Harwood (sop), L. Pavarotti (ten), H. von Karajan (cnd), Berlin PO, German Opera Chorus London ▲ 421245-2 [DDD] ■ 421245-4

Puccini, G.:Gianni Schicchi, w. H. Donath (sop), P. Seiffert (ten), G. Patanè (cnd), Munich RSO Eurodisc ▲ 7751-2-RC [DDD]

Puccini, G.:Madama Butterfly, w. R. Scotto (sop), C. Bergonzi (ten), J. Barbirolli (cnd), Rome Opera Orch, Rome Opera Chorus EMI Classics 2-▲ CDMB 69654

Puccini, G.:Madama Butterfly, w. R. Scotto (sop), A. di Stasio (mez), C. Bergonzi (ten), J. Barbirolli (cnd), Rome Opera Orch, Rome Opera Chorus [l] EMI Classics ("Studio" series) ▲ CDM 63411 ■ EG 63411

Rossini, G.:L'equivoco Stravagante, w. M. Guglielmi (sop), G. Baratti (ten), S. Bruscantini (b-bar), B. Rigacci (cnd), *(orch unknown)* [l] *(rec Naples, 1974)* Golden Age of Opera 2-▲ GAO 154/55

Scarlatti, A.:La Griselda, w. M. Freni (sop), L. Alva (ten), V. Luchetti (ten), S. Bruscantini (bar), N. Sanzogno (cnd), Naples Alessandro Scarlatti RAI Orch, Naples Scarlatti Chorus [l] *(rec live 10/29/70)* Memories 2-▲ HR 4154/55 (m) [ADD]

Verdi, G.:Arias, w. S. Frontalini (cnd), Bacau PO—Nabucco:Dioi di Giuda; Ernani:Gran Dio!...O de' verd'anni miei; Rigoletto:Cortigiani, vil razza dannata; Il trovatore:Il balen del suo sorriso; La traviata:Di Provenza; Un ballo in maschera:Alla vita che t'arride; Eri tu che macchiavi quell'anima; Don Carlo:Per me giunto è il dì supremo; Io morrò, ma lieto in dor; Otello:Credo in un Dio crudel; Falstaff:L'onore Bongiovanni ▲ GB 2514 [DDD]

Verdi, G.:La battaglia di Legnano, w. Caterina Mancini (sop), Amedeo Berdini (bar), Albino Gaggi (bass), Edmea Limberti (sgr), Manfredi Ponz de Leon (sgr), F. Previtali (cnd), Rome RAI SO, Rome RAI Chorus *(rec 1951)* Cetra Classic 2-▲ CDON 40 [ADD]

Verdi, G.:Falstaff, w. S. Sweet (sop), M. Horne (mez), F. Lopardo (ten), A. Titus (bar), C. Davis (cnd), Bavarian RSO, Bavarian Radio Chorus RCA Red Seal 2-▲ 09026-60705-2 [DDD]

Verdi, G.:Giovanna d'Arco, w. R. Tebaldi (sop), C. Bergonzi (ten), A. Simonetto (cnd), Milan RAI Orch, Milan RAI Chorus [l] *(rec live)* Melodram 2-▲ 27021

Verdi, G.:Giovanna d'Arco, w. Renata Tebaldi (sop), Carlo Bergonzi (ten), A. Simonetto (cnd), Milan RAI SO, Milan RAI Chorus *(rec Milan, May 26, 1951)* Pantheon 2-▲ PHE 6610 (m)

Verdi, G.:Oberto, Conte di San Bonifacio, w. G. Dimitrova (sop), R. Baldani (mez), A. Browner (mez), C. Bergonzi (ten), L. Gardelli (cnd), Munich RSO, Munich Radio Chorus [l] Orfeo ▲ 175881 [DDD]

Verdi, G.:Oberto, Conte di San Bonifacio, w. G. Dimitrova (sop), R. Baldani (mez), A. Browner (mez), C. Bergonzi (ten), L. Gardelli (cnd), Munich RSO, Munich Radio Chorus [l] Orfeo 2-▲ 105842 [DDD] 3-■ A 105843 F

Panerai, Rolando (bar) (cont.)
Verdi, G.:Rigoletto, w. M. Rinaldi (sop), V. Cortez (mez), F. Bonisolli (ten), B. Rundgren (b-bar), F. Molinari-Pradelli (cnd), Dresden State Orch, Dresden State Chorus [I] Acanta 2-▲ CD 41474 [DDD]
Verdi, G.:Simon Boccanegra, w. Leyla Gencer (sop), Glade Peterson (ten), Giuseppe Zampieri (ten), Tito Gobbi (bar), Vito Susca (bass), Giorgio Tozzi (bass), G. Gavazzeni (cnd), *(orch unknown)* Great Opera Performances 2-▲ GOP 767
Wagner, R.:Parsifal, w. M. Callas (sop), Baldelli (sgr), D. Lopatto (bar), B. Christoff (bass), V. Gui (cnd), Rome Radio-TV SO, Rome Radio-TV Chorus [I] *(rec 11/20-21/50)* Melodram 3-▲ MEL 36041 (m)
Wagner, R.:Parsifal, w. M. Callas (sop), Baldelli (sgr), D. Lopatto (bar), B. Christoff (bass), V. Gui (cnd), Rome Radio-TV SO, Rome Radio-TV Chorus [I] *(rec in concert, 11/20-21/50)* Verona 3-▲ 27085/87

Panero, Hugh (ten)
Lebaron, A.:The E. & O. Line (sels), w. Louise Cloutier (mez—Eurydice/Vendors), Hugh Panero (ten—Hermes), Lawrence Hamilton (bar—Orpheus/Men), Frank London (tpt), Marcus Rojas (tuba), Myra Melford (pno/kbd), Davey Williams (gtr), Fred Hopkins (elec bass), Thurman Barker (dr), A. LeBaron (cnd)—Juke Joint Jam Session; Eurydice Meets Hermes; Eurydice's Death [Funeral Band]; Eurydice's River Journey; Orpheus Laments [Looked Away] *(rec Coolidge Auditorium, Library of Congress, 1987)* Mode ▲ Mode 42

Panghe, Mihai (bass)
Verdi, G.:La forza del destino, w. Maria Nistor-Slatinaru (sop—Donna Leonora), Mihaela Mariacineanu (mez—Curra), Zenaida Pally (mez—Preziosilla), Ludovic Speiss (ten—Don Alvaro), Ion Stoian (ten—Trabucco), Nicolae Herlea (bar—Don Carlo), Nicolae Florei (bass—Padre Guardiano) Constantin Gabor (bass—Fra Melitone), Dan Musetescu (bass—An Alcalde), Mihai Panghe (bass—Marquis of Calatrava), C. Litvin (cnd), Romanian Radio-TV Orch, Romanian Radio-TV Chorus *(rec Jan 1970)* Vox Box 3-▲ CD3X 3038

Paniagua, Trinidad (sop)
Gottschalk, L.M.:Music of, w. José Alberto Esteves (ten), Pablo Garcia (bar), Eugene List (pno), Cary Lewis (pno), Brady Millican (pno), Adler, Buketoff (cnd), Berlin SO, Vienna State Opera Orch—Grande Tarantelle for Piano & Orchestra, Op. 67; Symphony No. 1, "La nuit des tropiques"; Symphony No. 2, "A Montevideo"; The Union (concert paraphrase on American national airs) for Piano & Orchestra, Op. 48; Variations on the Portuguese National Hymn for Piano & Orchestra, Op. 91; Grande fantaisie triomphale sur l'hymne national brésilien for Piano & Orchestra, Op. 69; Marche solennelle for Orchestra; Marcha triunfal y final de opera for Orchestra; Escenas campestres (opera in one act); Five Pieces for Piano Duet [Radieuse, Op. 72; Ses yeux, Op. 66; La Gallina, Op. 53; Ojos criollos, Op. 37; Pasquinade, Op. 59] Vox Box 2-▲ CDX 5009 [ADD]
Verdi, G.:Un ballo in maschera, w. M. Caballé (sop—Amelia), T. Paniagua (sop—Oscar), L. Chookasian (cta—Ulrica), P. Domingo (ten—Riccardo), C. MacNeil (bar—Renato), J. Pons (bar—Tom), C. del Bosco (bass—Samuel), G. Patanè (cnd), *(orch unknown)* Ornamenti 2-▲ FE 103

Pankova, Nikolina (sop)
Gesualdo, D.C.:Madrigals, w. V. Kissyova (sop), A. Bovarian (alt), V. Vassilev (ten), K. Mirinski (bass), S. Kralev (cnd), Sofia Madrigal—Io tacerò; Invan dunque o crudele; Moro lasso al mio duolo; Dolcissima mia vita Gega ▲ GD 174 [DDD]
Monteverdi, C.:Madrigals, w. V. Kissyova (sop), A. Bovarian (alt), V. Vassilev (ten), K. Mirinski (bass), S. Kralev (cnd), Sofia Madrigal Ensemble—Psalmus 121, "Laetatus sum"; Batto qui pianse; Chiome d'oro; Amor che deggio far?; O come sei gentile; Psalmus 147, "Lauda Jerusalem" Gega ▲ GD 174 [DDD]
Schütz, H.:Motets (misc), w. V. Kissyova (sop), A. Ivanova (sop), A. Bovarian (alt), V. Vassilev (ten), K. Mirinski (bass), S. Kralev (cnd), Sofia Madrigal—Christe Deus adjuva; Verbum caro factum est; Te Christe supplex invoco; Veni redemtor gentium; Veni sancte Spiritus Gega ▲ GD 174 [DDD]

Panni, Nicoletta (sop)
Bach, J.S.:Magnificat, BWV 243, w. L. Marimpietri (sop), A. Reynolds (mez), P. Munteanu (ten), B. Carmeli (bass), H. Scherchen (cnd), Milan RAI SO, Milan RAI Chorus [L] *(rec live, Apr 5, 1963)* Memories ▲ HR 4160 (m) [ADD]
Rimsky-Korsakov, N.:The Maid of Pskov, w. F. Cadoni (mez), A. Bertocci (ten), B. Christoff (bass), T. Schippers (cnd), *(orch unknown)* *(rec 1969)* Great Opera Performances 2-▲ GOP 720

Pantaleoni, Mimma (mez)
Mascagni, P.:Cavalleria rusticana, w. Delia Sanzio (sop—Santuzza), Mimma Pantaleoni (mez—Lola), Olga de Franco (cta—Lucia), Giovanni Breviario (ten—Turiddu), Piero Biasini (bar—Alfio), C. Sabajno (cnd), La Scala Orch, La Scala Chorus VAI Audio ▲ VAIA 1082-2

Panzarella, Anna-Maria (sop)
Mozart, W.A.:Zauberflöte, w. Natalie Dessay (sop—Queen of the Night), Linda Kitchen (sop—Papagena), Rosa Mannion (sop—Pamina), Anna-Maria Panzarella (sop—First Lady), Doris Lamprecht (mez—Second Lady), Delphine Haidan (cta—Third Lady), Hans Peter Blochwitz (ten—Tamino), Steven Cole (ten—Monostatos), Chrisopher Josey (ten—First Priest/First Armed Man), Anton Scharinger (bar—Papageno), Reinhard Hagen (bass—Sarastro), Laurent Naouri (bass—Second Priest/Second Armed Man), Willard White (bass—Speaker), W. Christie (cnd), Les Arts Florissants *(rec Paris Oct 2-9 1995)* Erato 2-▲ 12705-2 [DDD]

Panzéra, Charles (bar)
Berlioz, H.:La Damnation de Faust, w. M. Berthon (sop), J. de Trévi (ten), P. Coppola (cnd), Pasdeloup Concerts Association Orch, St. Gervais Chorus *(rec 1930)* Pearl ▲ PEA 9080 [ADD]
Berlioz, H.:La Damnation de Faust (sels), w. M. Berthon (sop), J. de Trévi (sgr), L. Morturier (sgr), P. Coppola (cnd), Pasdeloup Orch, St. Gervais Chorus [abridged vers] [F] *(rec 1931)* The Classical Collector 2-▲ FDC2 2006 [AAD]
Duparc, H.:Songs [w. M. Panzera-Baillot (pno accompaniment for 4 songs), P. Coppola (cnd for orchestral accompaniment for 2 songs]—Chanson triste; Soupir; L'invitation au voyage [piano & orchestral versions]; La vie antérieure [piano & orchestral versions] [F] *(rec 1931-34 HMV)* Pearl ▲ PEA 9919 (m) [AAD]
Fauré, G.:La bonne chanson, w. M. Panzera-Baillot (pno) [F] *(rec 1936 for HMV)* Pearl ▲ PEA 9919 (m) [AAD]
Fauré, G.:Songs, w. M. Panzera-Baillot (pno)—Les berceaux; La chanson du pêcheur [F] Pearl ▲ PEA 9919 (m) [AAD]
French Songs *(rec 1923-37)* EMI Classics ▲ CDH 64254
Schumann, R.:Dichterliebe, w. A. Cortot (pno) *(rec 1934 for HMV)* Pearl ▲ PEA 9919 (m) [AAD]
Schumann, R.:Dichterliebe, w. A. Cortot (pno) *(rec 1934 for HMV)* Biddulph ▲ LHW 005 [ADD]

Paoli, Antonio (ten)
Antonio Paoli *(rec for Gramophone 1907-11)* Preiser ("Lebendige Vergangenheit" series) ▲ PRE 89998 (m) [AAD]
Leoncavallo, R.:Pagliacci, w. Josefina Huguet (sop—Nedda), Gaetano Pini-Corsi (ten—Beppe), Ernesto Badini (bar—Silvio), Francesco Cigada (bar—Tonio), Giuseppe Rosci (sgr—Un contadino), C. Sabajno (cnd), La Scala Orch, La Scala Chorus *(rec 1907)* Bongiovanni 2-▲ GB 1120-2 [ADD]
Leoncavallo, R.:Pagliacci (sels), w. Enrico Caruso (ten), Giovanni Zenatello (ten), Amedeo Bassi (ten), Hermann Jadlowker (ten), Fernand Ansseau (ten), Hipolito Lazaro (ten), Nino (Filippo) Piccaluga (ten), Mario Chamlee (ten), Giacomo Lauri-Volpi (ten), Miguel Fleta (ten), Giovanni Martinelli (ten), Aureliano Pertile (ten), Georges Thill (ten), Alessandro Valente (ten), Francesco Merli (ten), Lauritz Melchior (ten), Marcel Wittrisch (ten), Joseph Schmidt (ten), Beniamino Gigli (ten), Giuseppe Lugo (ten), Helge Roswaenge (ten), Jussi Bjoerling (ten)—23 versions of the tenor aria "Vesti la giubba" *(rec 1907-1944)* Bongiovanni ▲ GB 1071 [ADD]
Verdi, G.:Arias Preiser ("Lebendige Vergangenheit" series) ▲ 89998 (m) [AAD]
Verdi, G.:Il trovatore (sels), w. J. Biel (ten), F. Tamagno (ten), L.-A. Escalaïs (ten), M. Gilion (ten), E. Caruso (ten), G. Zenatello (ten), J. Sembach (ten), L. Slezak (ten), F. Constantino (ten), G. Martinelli (ten), B. De Muro (ten), N. Fusati (ten), N. Piccaluga (ten), G. Lauri-Volpi (ten), A. Pertile (ten), E. Bergamaschi (ten), R. Tauber (ten), J. O'Sullivan (ten), H. Roswaenge (ten), G. Taccani (ten), V. Lois (ten), H. Lazaro (ten), A. Lindi (ten), A. Cortis (ten), F. Merli (ten), F. Völker (ten), J. Kiepura (ten), J. Schmidt (ten), J. Bjoerling (ten), B. Gigli (ten), A. Salvarezza (ten), J. Soler (ten), M. Filippeschi (ten)—34 performances of the Act III tenor aria "Di quella pira!," *(rec from 1903-1956)* Bongiovanni ▲ GB 1051 [AAD]

Paoli, Antonio (ten) (cont.)
The World of Singing, Vol. 3:The Italian School, Part 1:The Italian Tenors Before World War I (1902-13), w. Antonio Aramburo (ten), Alessandro Bonci (ten), Giuseppe Borgatti (ten), Enrico Caruso (ten), Edoardo Garbin (ten), Fiorello Giraud (ten), Fernando de Lucia (ten), Francesco Marconi (ten), Giovanni Battista de Negri (ten), et al. Enterprise ("Vocal Archives" series) 3-▲ ENT VA 2104
The World of Singing, Vol 4:The Italian School Part 1:Tenors before World War I, Book 2, w. Edoardo Garbin (ten), Fiorello Giraud (ten), Florencio Costantino (ten), Giuseppe Borgatti (ten), Carlo Albani (ten), Enrico Caruso (ten), Amedeo Bassi (ten), Piero Schivazzi (ten), Elvino Ventura (ten), Giovanni Zenatello (ten) Enterprise ("Vocal Archives" series) 3-▲ ENT VA 2107

Paolis, Alessio de (ten)
Puccini, G.:Turandot, w. Birgit Nilsson (sop—Turandot), Renata Tebaldi (sop—Liù), Jussi Björling (ten—Calaf), Alessio De Paolis (ten—Emperor Altoum), Piero de Palma (ten—Pang), Mario Sereni (bar—Ping), Adelio Zagonara (bar—Prince of Persia), Giorgio Tozzi (bass—Timur), Tommaso Frascati (bass—Pong), Leonardo Monreale (bass—Mandarin), E. Leinsdorf (cnd), Rome Opera Orch, Rome Opera Chorus *(rec Rome Opera House, July 3-11, 1959)* RCA Living Stereo 2-▲ 09026-62687-2 [ADD]

Paolombini, Vittoria (sgr)
Puccini, G.:Madama Butterfly, w. Toti dal Monte (sop—Madama Butterfly), Maria Huder (mez—Kate Pinkerton), Beniamino Gigli (ten—B.F. Pinkerton), Adelio Zagonara (ten—Goro), Mario Basiola (bar—Sharpless), Gino Conti (bass—Principe Yamadori), Ernesto Dominici (bass—Il Bonzo), Vittoria Paolombini (sgr—Suzuki), O. de Fabritiis (cnd), Rome Opera Orch, Giuseppe Conca (cnd), Rome Opera Chorus *(rec Aug 1939)* Arkadia 2-▲ CD 78004 (m) [ADD]

Papadjakou, Alexandra (cta)
Bellini, V.:Zaira, w. K. Ricciarelli (sop), R. Vargas (ten), S. Alaimo (ten), P. Olmi (cnd), Catania Teatro Massimo Bellini Orch, Catania Teatro Massimo Bellini Chorus [I] *(rec live 1990)* Nuova Era 2-▲ 6982/83 [DDD]

Pape, René (bass)
Beethoven, L. van:Missa Solemnis, w. Julia Varady (sop), Iris Vermillion (mez), Vinson Cole (ten), Kolja Blacher (vn), G. Solti (cnd), Berlin PO, Berlin Radio Chorus London ▲ 444337-2 [DDD]
Busoni, F.:Turandot, w. C. Lindsley (sop), J. Protschka (ten), R. Wörle (ten), G. Albrecht (cnd), Berlin RSO, Berlin RIAS Chamber Choir Capriccio ▲ 60039 [DDD]
Haydn, J.:Die Schöpfung, w. Ruth Ziesak (sop—Eve & Gabriel), Herbert Lippert (ten—Uriel), Rene Papé (bass—Raphael), Anton Scharinger (bass—Adam), G. Solti (cnd), Chicago SO, Chicago Sym Chorus London 2-▲ 443445-2 [DDD]
Korngold, E.W.:Das Wunder der Heliane, w. A. Tomowa-Sintow (sop), R. Runkel (cta), N. Gedda (ten), J. D. de Haan (ten), H. Welker (bar), J. Mauceri (cnd), Berlin RSO [G] London 3-▲ 436636-2 [DDD]
Mendelssohn, F.:Die erste Walpurgisnacht, w. B. Remmert (alt), U. Heilman (ten), T. Hampson (bar), N. Harnoncourt (cnd), CO of Europe Teldec ▲ 74882-2
Mozart, W.A.:Bastien und Bastienne, w. D. Schellenberger (sop), R. Eschrig (ten), M. Pommer (cnd), Leipzig RSO, Leipzig Radio Chorus Berlin Classics 2-▲ BER 1010 [DDD]
Mozart, W.A.:Requiem, w. A. Augér (sop), C. Bartoli (mez), V. Cole (ten), G. Solti (cnd), Vienna PO, Vienna Phil Chorus [L] *(rec live 12/5/91)* London ▲ 433688-2 [DDD] □ 433688-5

Papis, Christian (nar)
Ropartz, G.:Choral Music, w. Didier Henry (bar), Vincent Le Texier (b-bar), Christine Lajarrige (pno), Irène Brissot (hp), Eric Lebrun (org), M. Piquemal (cnd), Nancy SO, French Radio Chorus Soloists, Vittoria Regional French Choir—Psaume 136; Dimanche; Nocturne; Les Vêpres sonnent; Le Miracle de Saint Nicolas *(rec Salle Poirel, Nancy, Apr. 22-24, 1994)* Marco Polo ▲ 8.223774 [DDD]

Papis, Christian (ten)
Bizet, G.:Carmen (sels), w. Léontina Vaduva (sop), Béatrice Uria-Monzon (mez), Vincent Le Texier (bar), A. Lombard (cnd), Bordeaux-Aquitaine National Orch—Toréador & other great arias Valois ▲ V 4769

Papkov, Andre (bass)
Holy Radiant Light:The Sacred Song of Russia, w. [cnd:Elizabeth C. Patterson], Gloriae Dei Cantores Paraclete ▲ PCL 7 [DDD] ■ PCL 7

Papouschek, Helga (sop)
Lehár, F.:Die lustige Witwe, w. D. Koller (sop), M. Irosch (sop), P. Minich (ten), K. Ruzicka (ten), H. Prikopa (bar), K. Huemer (bar), R. Bibl (cnd), Vienna Volksoper Orch, Vienna Volksoper Chorus [G] Denon 2-▲ CO 8103 [DDD]
Strauss (II), Joh.:Wiener Blut, w. S. Martikke (sop), E. Kales (sop), A. Dallapozza (ten), K. Ruzicka (ten), E. Kuchar (ten), W. Kandutsch (bar), K. Dönch (bar), O. Kolmann (bass), R. Bibl (cnd), Vienna Volksoper Orch, Vienna Volksoper Chorus Denon 2-▲ CO 8105 [DDD]

Pappas, Yannula (mez)
Esplá, O.:Andalusian Folksongs (5), w. G. Stern (cnd), Israel SO—Rutas; Pregon; Las 12; El pescador; Coplilla [Sp] Meridian ▲ CDE 84134
Esplá, O.:Canciones playeras, w. G. Stern (cnd), Israel SO [Sp] Meridian ▲ CDE 84134
Granados, E.:Canciones amatorias (7), w. G. Stern (cnd), Israel SO—Mañanica era; Llorad corazon; Mira que soy; Iban al pinar [Sp] Meridian ▲ CDE 84134
Montsalvatge, X.:Canciones negras, w. G. Stern (cnd), Israel SO [Sp] Meridian ▲ CDE 84134
Turina, J.:Canto a Sevilla, w. G. Stern (cnd), Israel SO [Sp] Meridian ▲ CDE 84134
Verdi, G.:Aida, w. Jessye Norman (sop), Walter Alberti (bar), Luigi Roni (b-bar), N. Sanzogno (cnd), Belgian Radio-TV Orch, Belgian Radio-TV Chorus *(rec live, Paris, May 4, 1973)* Agorá ("Phoenix" series) 2-▲ 507

Paprocki, Bogdan (ten)
Bizet, G.:Carmen (sels), w. Krystyna Szczepanska (alt—Carmen), Bogdan Paprocki (ten—Don José), Andrzej Hiolski (bar—Escamillo), Alina Bolechowska (sgr—Micaela), J. Semkow (cnd), Warsaw PO, Warsaw National Phil Chorus Polskie Nagrania ▲ PNCD 213 [AAD]
Moniuszko, S.:Halka, w. Barbara Nieman (sop), Halina Sloniowska (sop), Jan Góralski (ten), Leslaw Pawluk (ten), Kazimierz Pustelak (ten), Andrzej Hiolski (bar), Edmund Kossowski (bass), Edward Pawlak (bass), Z. Gorzynski (cnd), Warsaw State Opera House Orch, Warsaw National Opera Chorus *(rec Warsaw, 1965)* Polskie Nagrania ▲ PNCD 092 [AAD]
Moniuszko, S.:Haunted Manor, w. Halina Slonicka (sop), Bozena Brun-Baranska (mez), Barbara Lawcewicz (mez), Krystyna Szczepanska (mez), Zdzislaw Nikodem (ten), Andrzej Hiolski (bar), Edmund Kossowski (bass), Bernard Ladysz (bass), W. Rowicki (cnd), Warsaw State Opera House Orch, Warsaw National Opera Chorus *(rec Warsaw, 1965)* Polskie Nagrania ▲ PNCD 093 [AAD]

Parachikova, Lilijana (cta)
Beethoven, L. van:Mass, Op. 86, w. E. Markova (sop), C. Kamenev (ten), I. Petrov (bass), C. Iliev (cnd), Sofia State PO, Sofia State Chorus [L] Musique d'Abord ▲ HMA 190109 [AAD]

Parazzini, Maria (sgr)
Mercadante, S.:Il bravo, w. Miwako Matsumoto (sop—Violetta), Giovanna di Rocco (sop—Michelina), William Johns (ten—Il Bravo), Antonio Savastano (ten—Pisani), Gino Sinimberghi (ten—Cappello), Loris Gambelli (bass—Marco), Mario Machi (bass—Luigi), Paolo Washington (bass—Foscari), Maria Parazzini (sgr—Teodora), G. Ferro (cnd), Rome Opera Orch, Rome Opera Chorus *(rec Rome, Dec 30, 1976)* Italia 3-▲ CDC 94 [ADD]

Parce, Erich (bar)
Diamond, D.:This Sacred Ground, w. G. Schwarz (cnd), Seattle SO, Seattle Chorale, Seattle Girls' Choir, Northwest Boychoir *(rec Feb. 13, 1994)* Delos ▲ DE 3141 [DDD]
Puccini, G.:Madama Butterfly, w. Maria Spacagna (sop), Sharon Graham (mez), Vivica Genaux (mez), Richard di Renzi (ten), Richard Markley (ten), James Butler (bass), C. Rosenkrans (cnd), Hungarian State Opera Orch, Anikó Katona (cnd), Hungarian State Opera Chorus—3 versions *(rec Italian Institute, Budapest, Sept 5-21, 1995)* Vox Classics 4-▲ VOX4 7525 [DDD]

Parcells, Elizabeth (sop)
A Jenny Lind Recital, w. James Winn (pno) Northeastern ("Classical Arts" series) ▲ NOR 237 ■ NR 237-C

Parchi, Chiam (sgr)
Cage, J.:Apartment House 1776, w. Walter Buckingham (sgr—Protestant), Darrell Dunn (sgr—Native American), Semenya McCord (sgr—African American), Chiam Parchi (sgr—Sephardi), New England Conservatory Philharmonia *(rec New England Conservatory of Music, Boston, MA, Mar. 4 & 6, 1991)* Mode ▲ MODE 41

VOCALISTS

Paré, Barbara (sop)
Gilmore, B.:Folksongs (5), w. E. Corporon (cnd), Cincinnati College Conservatory of Music Wind Sym *(rec Corbett Auditorium, May 30 & 31, 1992)* Klavier ▲ KCD 11066 [DDD]

Parent, Marie-Danielle (sop)
Geugeon, D.:Voix intimes, w. Yolande Parent (sop), L. Vaillancourt (cnd), Les Événements du Neuf *(rec Ottawa, 1983 & 1984)* Centrediscs ▲ CMC 5194 [DDD]
Vivier, C.:Kopernikus, "A Ritual Opera of Death", w. Y. Parent (sop), P. Vaillancourt (sop), J. Fleury (cta), D. Doane (ten), M. Ducharme (bar), Y. Saint-Amant (bass), F. Martel (cl), M. Bélanger (vn), L. Bouchard (tpt), L. Vaillancourt (cnd), *(orch unknown)* *(rec Feb. 1991)* CBC ("Musica Viva" series) ▲ MVCD 1047 [DDD]
Vivier, C.:Lonely Child, w. S. Garant (cnd), Quebec Society of Contemporary Music *(rec Ottawa, 1983 & 1984)* Centrediscs ▲ CMC 5194 [DDD]

Parent, Yolande (sop)
Geugeon, D.:Voix intimes, w. Marie-Danielle Parent (sop), L. Vaillancourt (cnd), Les Événements du Neuf *(rec Ottawa, 1983 & 1984)* Centrediscs ▲ CMC 5194 [DDD]
Vivier, C.:Kopernikus, "A Ritual Opera of Death", w. P. Vaillancourt (sop), M.-D. Parent (sop), J. Fleury (cta), D. Doane (ten), M. Ducharme (bar), Y. Saint-Amant (bass), F. Martel (cl), M. Bélanger (vn), L. Bouchard (tpt), L. Vaillancourt (cnd), *(orch unknown)* *(rec Feb. 1991)* CBC ("Musica Viva" series) ▲ MVCD 1047 [DDD]

Pares-Reyna, Margot (sop)
Clásicos de las Américas, w. Marcel Quillevéré (ten), Jesús Castro Balbi (gtr), Noël Lee (pno), Georges Rabol (pno), Erwartung Ensemble [cnd:Bernard Desgraupes], Jazzogène Orch [cnd:Jean-Luc Fillon] Opus 111 6-▲ 2000
Guastavino, C.:Songs, w. G. Rabol (pno)—Alegria de la soledad; Apegado a mi; Cantilena; Corderito; Cuando acaba de llover; Desde que te conocí; Dones sencillos; Deseo; Donde habite el olvido; En los surcos del armor; Encantamiento; Esta iglesia no tiene; Hallazgo; Jardin antiguo; Meciendo; Mi garganta; Pájaro muerto; La palomita; Piececitos; Prestame tu pañuelito; La primera pregunta; La puertas de la mañana; Riqueza; Rocío; Romance de José Cubas; La rosa e el sauce; El Sampedrino; Se equivocó la paloma; Severa Villafañe; Siesta; Violetas; Viniendo de Chilecito; Ya me voy a retirar [Sp] *(rec 5/90)* Opus 111 ▲ OPS 30-9002 [DDD]
Schubert, Franz:Mass 2, w. Fletcher (sgr), P. Fourcade (bass), M. Piquemal (cnd), Harmonia Nova Orch Ensemble, Michel Piquemal Vocal Ensemble [L] Gallo ▲ CD 584 [DDD]
Schubert, Franz:Mass 4, w. N. Stutzmann (alt), Fletcher (ten), P. Fourcade (bass), M. Piquemal (cnd), Harmonia Nova Orch Ensemble, Michel Piquemal Vocal Ensemble [L] Gallo ▲ CD 584 [DDD]

Pareto, Graziella (sop)
Great Recordings, 1906–27 Pearl ▲ PEA 9117 [ADD]

Paris, Myrna (cta)
Moore, D.:Ballad of Baby Doe, w. Jan Grissom (sop—Baby Doe), Dana Kreuger (mez—Augusta), Myrna Paris (cta—Mama), Brian Steele (bar—Horace), Mark Freiman (b-bar—W. J. Bryan), J. Moriarty (cnd), Central City Opera Orch, Central City Opera Chorus *(rec Central City, CO)* Newport Classic 2-▲ NPD 85593/2 [DDD]

Park, Richard (sgr)
Puccini, G.:Tosca, w. Birgit Nilsson (sop—Floria Tosca), Puli Toro (mez—Shepherd), Jose Carreras (ten—Mario Cavaradossi), Joaquin Romaguera (ten—Spoleta), James Billings (bar—Sacristan), Richard Fredricks (bar—Baron Scarpa), Samuel Ramey (bass—Cesare Angelotti), William Ledbetter (sgr—Sciarrone), Richard Park (sgr—Cardinal), Don Yule (sgr—Jailer), J. Rudel (cnd), *(orch & chorus unknown)* *(rec Nov 13, 1974)* Legato Classics 2-▲ LCD-200-2

Parker, Burton (sgr)
Floyd, C.:Susannah, w. Phyllis Curtin (sop—Susannah Polk), Richard Cassilly (ten—Sam Polk), Norman Treigle (bass—Olin Blitch), Marietta Muhs Cosenza (sgr—Mrs. McLean), Marilyn Davidson (sgr—Mrs. Gleaton), Kay Long (sgr—Mrs. Hayes), Jean Young (sgr—Mrs. Ott), Alton Brim (sgr—Elder Hayes), Thomas Carter (sgr—Elder Gleaton), Jack Davis (sgr—Elder McLean), Keith Kaldenberg (sgr—Little Bat McLean), Burton Parker (sgr—Elder Ott), K. Andersson (cnd), New Orleans Opera Orch, New Orleans Opera Chorus *(rec Mar 31, 1962)* VAI Audio 2-▲ VAIA 1115-2 [ADD]

Parker, Elinor (mez)
Leoncavallo, R.:Zazà, w. C. Petrella (sop), G. Campora (ten), A. Silipigni (cnd), Turin RAI SO *(rec 1969)* Memories 2-▲ MEM 4519 [AAD]

Parker, Helen (sgr)
Purcell, H.:The Indian Queen, w. Catherine Bott (sop—Orazia/Married Woman), Emma Kirkby (sop—Indian Girl/Zempoalla/Cupid), John Mark Ainsley (ten—Indian Boy/Fame/Follower of Cupid/Aerial Spirits), Julian Podger (ten—Follower of Envy/Aerial Spirit), Gerald Finley (bar—Conjurer/Hymen/Follower of Cupid), Helen Parker (sgr—Aerial Spirits), David Thomas (bass—Envy/High Priest/Married Man/Follower of Cupid), Simon Berridge (sgr—Follower of Envy), Libby Crabtree (sgr—Follower of Hymen/Aerial Spirit), Tommy Williams (sgr—God of Dreams), C. Hogwood (cnd), Academy of Ancient Music *(rec Walthamstow Assembly Hall, London, July 1994)* L'Oiseau-Lyre ▲ 444339-2 [DDD]

Parker, Patricia (mez)
Stravinsky, I.:Les Noces, w. A. Mory (sop), J. Mitchinson (ten), P. Hudson (bass), M. Argerich (pno), H. Francesch (pno), K. Zimerman (pno), C. Katsaris (pno), L. Bernstein (cnd), English Bach Festival Orch, English Bach Festival Chorus [R] Deutsche Grammophon ("20th Century Classics" series) ▲ 423251-2 [ADD]

Parker, W. (bass)
Bach, J.S.:Cant 56, w. N. McGegan (cnd), Arcadian Academy, Baroque Choral Guild [G] Harmonia Mundi USA ("Nightingale" series) ▲ HMN 907601

Parker, William (bar)
Argento, D.:The Andrée Expedition, w. W. Huckaby (pno) [E] *(rec 1988)* Centaur ▲ CRC 2092 [DDD]
Bach, J.S.:Cant 82, w. N. McGegan (cnd), Arcadian Academy, Baroque Choral Guild [G] Harmonia Mundi USA ("Nightingale" series) ▲ HMN 907601
Brahms, J.:Songs, w. Wm. Huckaby (pno)—8 songs [G] Centaur ▲ CRC 2022 [DAD]
Cadman, C.W.:American Indian Songs, w. William Huckaby (pno) *(rec Columbia Recording Studios, New York City)* New World ▲ 80463-2
Copland, A.:Songs (misc), w. Wm. Huckaby (pno)—8 songs [E] Centaur ▲ CRC 2022 [DAD]
Farwell, A.:Indian Songs (3), w. William Huckaby (pno) *(rec Columbia Recording Studios, New York City)* New World ▲ 80463-2
Griffes, C.T.:Songs, w. William Huckaby (pno)—Das ist ein Brausen und Heulen; Wo ich bin, mich rings umdunkelt; Des Müden Abendlied; Zwei Könige sassen auf Orkadel; The 1st Snowfall; An Old Song Re-sung *(rec Columbia Recording Studios, New York City)* New World ▲ 80463-2
Handel, G.F.:Messiah, w. Lorraine Hunt (sop), Janet Williams (sop), Patricia Spence (mez), Drew Minter (alt), Jeffery Thomas (ten), N. McGegan (cnd), Philharmonia Baroque Orch, Univ of California at Berkeley Chamber Chorus—standard version of Messiah *occupies the first sections of each of the three CDs, one part per disc. Each part is followed, after a significant pause, by alternative versions of certain sections of the preceding material, 13 altogether.* [E] Harmonia Mundi USA 3-▲ HMU 907050/52
Handel, G.F.:Messiah (sels), w. Lorraine Hunt (sop), Janet Williams (sop), Patricia Spence (mez), Drew Minter (alt), Jeffery Thomas (ten), N. McGegan (cnd), Philharmonia Baroque Orch, Univ of California at Berkeley Chamber Chorus Harmonia Mundi USA ▲ HMU 907120
Handel, G.F.:Messiah (sels), w. Lorraine Hunt (sop), Janet Williams (sop), Patricia Spence (mez), Drew Minter (alt), Jeffery Thomas (ten), N. McGegan (cnd), Philharmonia Baroque Orch, Univ of California at Berkeley Chamber Chorus [E] Harmonia Mundi USA ("Nightingale" series) ▲ HMN 907601
Handel, G.F.:Susanna, w. Jill Feldman (sop), Lorraine Hunt (sop), Drew Minter (alt), Jeffery Thomas (ten), David Thomas (bass), N. McGegan (cnd), Philharmonia Baroque Orch, Univ of California at Berkeley Chamber Chorus [E] Harmonia Mundi USA 3-▲ HMU 907030/32
Handel, G.F.:Susanna (sels), w. Jill Feldman (sop), Lorraine Hunt (sop), Drew Minter (alt), Jeffery Thomas (ten), David Thomas (bass), N. McGegan (cnd), Philharmonia Baroque Orch, Univ of California at Berkeley Chamber Chorus [E] Harmonia Mundi USA ("Nightingale" series) ▲ HMN 907601
Handel, G.F.:Susanna (sels), w. Jill Feldman (sop), Lorraine Hunt (sop), Drew Minter (alt), Jeffrey Thomas (ten), David Thomas (bass), N. McGegan (cnd), Philharmonia Baroque Orch Harmonia Mundi France ▲ HMU 907168

Parker, William (bar) (cont.)
Ives, C.:Songs, w. Dalton Baldwin (pno)—At the River; His Exaltation; Watchman!; The Camp Meeting; Sunrise [w. Ani Kavafian (vn)]; Chanson de Florian; Rosamunde; Qu'il m'irait bien; Élégie *(rec Columbia Recording Studios, New York City)* New World ▲ 80463-2
The Listeners *(rec Columbia Recording Studios, New York City)* New World ▲ 80475-2

Parkman, Stefan (ten)
Schnittke, A.:Sym 4, w. M. Bellini (alt), O. Kamu (cnd), Stockholm Sinfonietta, Uppsala Academic Chamber Choir [L] BIS ▲ CD 497 [DDD]

Parks, Julia (mez)
Moore, D.:Gallantry, w. Margaret Bishop (sop—Lola Markham), Julia Parks (mez—Announcer), Carl Halvorson (ten—Donald Hopewell), Richard Holmes (bar—Doctor Gregg), S. R. Radcliffe (cnd), New York Chamber Ensemble *(rec LeFrak Concert Hall, Queens College, Flushing, NY, May 30 & 31, 1994)* Albany ▲ TROY 173 [DDD]

Parks, Louisa Ann (sop)
Axelrod, L.:Songs, w. Michael Horton (ten), Nmon Ford-Livene (ten), Malcolm Mackenzie (bar), Richard Bernstein (bass), M. Beltrami (cnd)—sels w. lyrics by Burns, Browning, Byron, Keats, Morris, Poe, Rossetti, Shelley, Wordsworth & Yeats Marquis ▲ MAR 171

Parraguin, Hélène (sgr)
Massenet, J.:Esclarmonde, w. Denia Mazzola (sop), José Sempere (ten), Christian Tréguier (bar), P. Fournillier (cnd), Franz Liszt SO, Massenet Festival Choir *(rec live, Massenet Festival, Saint-Étienne)* Koch Schwann 3-▲ SCH 312692 [DDD]

Parramon, Virginia (sop)
Soler, J.:Mahler Lieder, w. Lluís Vidal (pno), J. Pons (cnd), Barcelona Teatro Lliure CO Harmonia Mundi France ▲ HMC 905231

Partch, Harry (nar)
Partch, H.:The Letter, w. *(ensemble unknown)* *(rec 1950, mono)* CRI ▲ CD 7000 (m/s) [AAD]

Partch, Harry (voc/adapted va)
Partch, H.:Bless This Home, w. Vincenzo Prockelo (ob), Danlee Mitchell (kithara/harmonic canon), Joseph Varhula (mazda mar), J. Garvey (cnd) *(rec Univ of Illinois, 1961)* Innova 4-▲ 401

Partch, Harry (voc/harmonic canon)
Partch, H.:The Mock Turtle Song & Jabberwocky, w. Danlee Mitchell (bass mar)—O Frabjous Day! *(rec Mill Valley Outdoor Club's Young People's Concert Series, Feb 13, 1954)* Innova 4-▲ 401

Partridge, Ian (ten)
Arne, T.:Artaxerxes, w. Catherine Bott (sop), Patricia Spence (mez), Philippa Hyde (sgr), Christopher Robson (alt), Richard Edgar-Wilson (ten), R. Goodman (cnd), Parley of Instruments Hyperion ("The English Orpheus" series) 2-▲ CDA 67051/2
Bach, J.S.:St. John Passion, w. P. Kwella (sop), D. James (ct), W. Kendall (ten), M. George (bar), D. Wilson-Johnson (b-bar), H. Christophers (cnd), The Sixteen Orch, The Sixteen [G] Chandos ("Chaconne" series) 2-▲ CHAN 0507/08 [DDD]
Berkeley, L.:Songs of the Half-Light, w. J. Savijoki (gtr) [E] Ondine ▲ ODE 779-2 [DDD]
Boulanger, L.:Du fond de l'abîme, w. B. Greevy (mez), N. Boulanger (cnd), BBC SO, BBC Sym Chorus *(rec live, London Nov. 1968)* Intaglio ▲ INCD 703-1 [ADD]
Britten, H.:Folksong Arrs, w. J. Savijoki (gtr)—The soldier and the sailor; The shooting of his dear; Bonny at morn; Master Kilby; I will give my love an apple; Sailor-boy [E] [arr. Tenor & Guitar] Ondine ▲ ODE 779-2 [DDD]
Britten, H.:Gloriana (choral dances), w. H. Tunstall (hp), H. Christophers (cnd), The Sixteen *(rec 1 & 4/91)* Collins Classics ▲ 12862 [DDD]
Britten, H.:Songs from the Chinese, w. J. Savijoki (gtr) Ondine ▲ ODE 779-2 [DDD]
Britten, H.:Winter Words ASV ("Quicksilva" series) ▲ ASQ 6172 [DDD]
Charpentier, M.-A.:Messe de minuit pour Noël, w. D. Willcocks (cnd), English CO, King's College Choir Cambridge EMI Classics ▲ CDM 63135
Charpentier, M.-A.:Te Deum in C, w. F. Lott (sop), S. Roberts (bar), P. Ledger (org), P. Ledger (cnd), Academy of St. Martin in the Fields, King's College Choir Cambridge EMI Classics ▲ CDM 63135
The Essential Gregorian Chant, w. [cnd:James O'Donnell], Pro Cantione Antiqua, James Griffett (ten), Stephen Roberts (bar), Michael George (bass), Gordon Jones (bass) Cala ▲ CAL CACD 88035 [DDD]
The Essential Gregorian Chant, w. Griffett, James (ten), Michael George (b-bar), Stephen Roberts (b-bar), Gordon Jones (bass), Pro Cantione Antique [cnd:James O'Donnell] United ▲ UNI 88035 [DDD]
Gregorian Lent & Easter, w. [cnd:James O'Donnell], Pro Cantione Antiqua, J. Griffett (ten), S. Roberts (bar), M. George (bass), G. Jones (bass) *(rec All Saints, East Finchley, Dec 7–9, 1993)* United ▲ UNI 88016 [DDD]
Handel, G.F.:Alexander's Feast (ode), w. N. Argenta (sop), M. George (bass), H. Christophers (cnd), The Sixteen Orch, The Sixteen Chorus Collins Classics 2-▲ COL 7016 [DDD]
Handel, G.F.:Chandos Anthems (11), w. L. Dawson (sop), H. Christophers (cnd), The Sixteen Orch, The Sixteen—Anthem Nos. 4–6 [E] Chandos ("Chaconne" series) ▲ CHAN 0504 [DDD]
Handel, G.F.:Chandos Anthems (11), w. L. Dawson (sop), P. Kwella (sop), J. Bowman (alt), M. George (bass), H. Christophers (cnd), The Sixteen Orch, The Sixteen Chandos ("Chaconne" series) 4-▲ CHAN 0554 [DDD]
Handel, G.F.:Chandos Anthems (11), w. L. Dawson (sop), M. George (bass), H. Christophers (cnd), The Sixteen Orch, The Sixteen—Nos. 1, 2 & 3 Chandos ("Chaconne" series) ▲ CHAN 0503 [DDD]
Handel, G.F.:Chandos Anthems (11), w. April Cantelo (sop), Andrew Davis (org), D. Willcocks (cnd), Academy of St. Martin in the Fields, King's College Choir Cambridge—No. 10 only *(rec Chapel of King's College, Cambridge, 1967)* London 2-▲ 443470-2 [ADD]
Handel, G.F.:Chandos Anthems (11), w. L. Dawson (sop), H. Christophers (cnd), The Sixteen Orch, The Sixteen—Anthem Nos. 10 & 11 [E] Chandos ("Chaconne" series) ▲ CHAN 0509 [DDD]
Handel, G.F.:Chandos Anthems (11), w. P. Kwella (sop), J. Bowman (ct), M. George (bass), H. Christophers (cnd), The Sixteen Orch, The Sixteen—Anthem Nos. 7–9 [E] Chandos ("Chaconne" series) ▲ CHAN 0505 [DDD]
Handel, G.F.:Dixit Dominus, w. Lynn Dawson (sop), Linda Russell (alt), Charles Brett (ct), Michael George (bass), H. Christophers (cnd), The Sixteen Orch, The Sixteen [L] Chandos ("Chaconne" series) ▲ CHAN 0517 [DDD]
Handel, G.F.:Israel in Egypt, w. Elizabeth Gale (sop), Lillian Watson (sop), James Bowman (alt), Tom McDonnell (bass), Alan Watt (bass), S. Preston (cnd), English CO, Christ Church Cathedral Choir Oxford *(rec Chapel of Merton College, Oxford, 1975)* London 2-▲ 443470-2 [ADD]
Handel, G.F.:Israel in Egypt, w. Elizabeth Gale (sop), James Bowman (alt), Tom McDonnell (bar), Alan Watt (bass), Watson (sgr), S. Preston (cnd), English CO, Christ Church Cathedral Choir Oxford London ("Jubilee" series) 2-▲ 421602-2 [ADD]
Handel, G.F.:Nisi Dominus, w. Charles Brett (ct), Michael George (bass), H. Christophers (cnd), The Sixteen Orch, The Sixteen [L] Chandos ("Chaconne" series) ▲ CHAN 0517 [DDD]
Handel, G.F.:The Triumph of Time & Truth, w. James Goodman (trb), Fisher (sop), Emma Kirkby (sop), Charles Brett (ct), Stephen Varcoe (bar), D. Darlow (cnd), London Handel Orch, London Handel Choir [E] Hyperion 2-▲ CDA 66071/72
Holst, G.:Psalms 86 & 148, w. R. Downes (org), I. Holst (cnd), English CO, Purcell Singers—Psalm 86 EMI Classics ▲ CDC 49784
Monteverdi, C.:Selva morale et spirituale (sels), w. E. Kirkby (sop), D. Thomas (bass), Parley of Instruments [L] Hyperion ▲ CDA 66021 [DDD]
Mozart, W.A.:Requiem, w. Jennifer Smith (sop), Helen Watts (cta), Stafford Dean (bass), M. Atzmon (cnd), BBC Welsh National SO, BBC Choral Society IMP ("BBC Radio" series) ▲ IMP 5691452
Pergolesi, G.B.:Magnificat in C, w. Elizabeth Vaughan (sop), Janet Baker (cta), Christopher Keyte (bass), D. Willcocks (cnd), Academy of St. Martin in the Fields, King's College Choir Cambridge *(rec 1966)* London 2-▲ 443868-2 [ADD]
Purcell, H.:Songs—Sweeter than Roses ASV ("Quicksilva" series) ▲ ASQ 6172 [DDD]
Schubert, Franz:Die Schöne Müllerin, w. Jennifer Partridge (pno) Classics for Pleasure ▲ CDCFP 4672
Schubert, Franz:Songs (misc), w. Jennifer Partridge (pno)—An Silvia; Auflösung; Fischerweise; Der Wanderer an den Mond; Wanderers Nachtlied II; Die Forelle; An die Laute; Der Einsame; Der Schiffer; An die Musik ASV Quicksilva ▲ ASQ 6171
Schumann, R.:Myrthen, w. Lynne Dawson (sop), Julius Drake (pno) Chandos ▲ CHAN 9307 [DDD]

▲ = CD ♦ = Enhanced CD Δ = MD ■ = Cassette Tape □ = DCC

Partridge, Ian (ten) (cont.)
Schumann, R.:Songs, w. Julius Drake (pno)—Sag an, o lieber Vogel mein, Op. 27/1; Dem roten Röslein gleicht mein Lieb, Op. 27/2; Was soll ich sagen?, Op. 27/3; Jasminenstrauch, Op. 27/4; Nur ein lächelnder Blick, Op. 27/5; Die Löwenbraut, Op. 31/1 Chandos ▲ CHAN 9307 [DDD]
Sir Cristemas, w. [cnd:Louis Halsey], Elizabethan Singers, Simon Preston (kbd/cnd), Susan Longfield (sop), Christopher Keyte (bass) Boston Skyline ▲ BSD 124 [ADD]

Partridge, J. (sop)
Trumpet & Soprano in Duet, w. James Watson (tpt) ASV ▲ ASV 2088 [DDD]

Parus, Anna (mez)
Milhaud, D.:Ani maamin, un chant perdu et retrouvé, w. Sharon Cooper (sop—la Voix), Bernard Freyd (nar—Isaac), Michel Hermon (nar—le Récitant), Michael Lonsdale (nar—Abraham), Jean Négroni (nar—Jacob), P. Méfano (cnd), Ensemble 2E2M, Madrigal de Bordeaux Arion ▲ ARN 68275 [DDD]

Parutto, Mirella (sop)
Verdi, G.:Aida, w. Antonietta Stella (sop—Aida), Mirella Parutto (sop—Priestess), Giulietta Simionato (mez—Amneris), Giuseppe DiStefano (ten—Radames), Giuseppe Zampiere (ten—Messenger), Giangiacomo Guelfi (bar—Amonasro), Silvio Maionica (bass—King of Egypt), Nicola Zaccaria (bass—Ramfis), A. Votto (cnd), La Scala Orch, La Scala Chorus *(rec Milan, Dec 7, 1956)* Legato Classics 2–▲ LCD 204–2 [ADD]
Verdi, G.:Nabucco, w. Ettore Bastianini (bar), Ivo Vinco (bass), B. Bartoletti (cnd), *(orch unknown)*, *(orch & chorus unknown)* *(rec live, Florence, Aug. 26, 1961)* Great Opera Performances 2–▲ GOP 751
Verdi, G.:Il trovatore, w. Fedora Barbieri (mez), Franco Corelli (ten), Ettore Bastianini (bar), Agostino Ferrin (bass), O. de Fabritiis (cnd), Rome Opera Orch, Rome Opera Chorus Stradivarius 2–▲ STV DTM 12313 [ADD]

Pascalin, Olivier (nar)
David, Felicien:Le Désert, w. B. Lazzaretti (ten), G.M. Guida (cnd), Berlin RSO, St. Hedwig's Cathedral Choir Capriccio ▲ 10 379 [DDD]

Pasco, Richard (nar)
Elgar, E.:Music of, w. Barbara Leigh-Hunt (nar), John Bingham (pno), Medici String Quartet—includes excerpts from Start of the Play: Qnt. for Pno; Qt. for Strs [slow movt.]; In the South; The Wand of Youth [suite]; Chanson de Matin; Salut d'Amour; Starlight Express; Son. for Vn; Son. for Vc; Adieu; others *(rec Gateway Studios, London)* Medici Quartet ▲ MQT 7001 [DDD]

Pasek, Igor (ten)
Respighi, O.:La bella dormente nel bosco, w. Ivana Czaková (sop—Old Woman/Green Fairy), Adriana Kohútková (sop—Blue Fairy/Nightingale), Henrietta Lednárová (sop—Frog/Spindle), Jana Valásková (sop—Princess), Dagmar Pecková (mez—Cuckoo/Cat), Denisa Slepkovská (mez—Queen/Duchess), Karol Bernáth (ten—Doctor), Guillermo Dominguez (ten—Prince April), Igor Pasek (ten—Jester), Ján Durčo (bar—Ambassador), Richard Haan (bar—King/Woodcutter), Stanislav Benačka (bass—Doctor), Anton Kúrnava (bass—Doctor), Marián Smolárik (bass—Doctor), M. Adriano (nar—Mr. Dollar Chèques), M. Adriano (cnd), Slovak RSO Bratislava, Ján Rozehnal (cnd), Slovak Phil Chorus *(rec Concert Hall of the Slovak Radio, Bratislava, June 8–20, 1994)* Marco Polo ("Opera Classics" series) ▲ 8.223742 [DDD]
Respighi, O.:Lucrezia, w. Adriana Kohútková (sop—Venilia), Michela Remor (sop—Lucrezia), Stefania Kaluza (mez—La Voce), Denisa Slepkovská (mez—Servia), Ludovít Ludha (ten—Collatino), Igor Pasek (ten—Bruto), Ján Durčo (bar—Tito/Valerio), Richard Haan (bar—Tarquinio), Rado Hanák (bass—Arunte/Spurio Lucrezio) *(rec Concert Hall of the Slovak Radio, Bratislava, June 9–16, 1994)* Marco Polo ▲ 8.223717 [DDD]

Pasella, Guido (bass)
Catalani, A.:Edmea, w. M. Sokolinska Noto (sop), M. Frusoni (ten), M. Chingari (bar), P. Lefebvre (bass), A. Nosotti (bass), G. del Vivo (bass), M. de Bernart (cnd), Lucca Teatro Comunale Giglio Orch, Lucca Teatro Comunale del Giglio Chorus [I] *(rec live 9/89)* Bongiovanni 2–▲ GB 2093/94 [DDD]

Pasero, Tancredi (bass)
Bellini, V.:Norma, w. Gina Signa (sop), Ebe Stignani (mez), Giovanni Breviario (ten), V. Gui (cnd), Turin EIAR SO, Turin EIAR Chorus *(rec 1937)* Grammofono 2000 2–▲ GRM 78583
Bellini, V.:Norma, w. Gina Cigna (sop—Norma), Ebe Stignani (sop—Adalgisa), Adriana Perris (mez—Clotilde), Giovanni Breviario (ten—Pollione), Emilio Renzi (ten—Flavio), Tancredi Pasero (bass—Oroveso), V. Gui (cnd), EIAR Orch, Achille Consoli (cnd), EIAR Chorus *(rec Aug/Sept 1937)* Arkadia ("The 78's" series) 2–▲ 78010 [ADD]
Bellini, V.:Norma, w. G. Cigna (sop), E. Stignani (mez), G. Breviario (ten), V. Gui (cnd), Turin EIAR SO, Turin EIAR Chorus *(rec 1937)* Memories 2–▲ MEM 4552 [ADD]
Bellini, V.:Norma (sels), w. *(other artists unknown)*—Ite sul Colle, o Druidi Enterprise ("Vocal Archives" series) ▲ ENT VA 1123
Bellini, V.:Norma (sels)—Ite sul colle, o Druidi *(rec 1927)* Minerva ▲ 4 (m) [ADD]
Bellini, V.:La sonnambula (sels), w. *(other artists unknown)*—Vi Ravviso, o Luoghi Ameni; Tu non Sai con Quei Begli Occhi; Oh Ciel! Che Tento? Enterprise ("Vocal Archives" series) ▲ ENT VA 1123
Bellini, V.:La sonnambula (sels)—Vi ravviso, o luoghi ameni; Oh ciel! che tento? [w. Gina Bernelli (sop)]; Tu non sai con quei begli occhi *(rec 1928 & 43)* Minerva ▲ 4 (m) [ADD]
Boito, A.:Mefistofele (sels)—Ave Signor; Son lo spirito che nega; Ecco il mondo *(rec 1927)* Minerva ▲ 4 (m) [ADD]
Boito, A.:Mefistofele (sels), w. *(other artists unknown)*—Ave Signor; Son lo Spirito Che Nega; Ecco il Mondo Enterprise ("Vocal Archives" series) ▲ ENT VA 1123
The Italian Vocal Tradition, Vol. 1:The Voices of Toscanini, w. Toti dal Monte (sop), Claudio Muzio (sop), Rosetta Pampanini (sop), Biata Scacciati (sop), Giacomo Lauri-Volpi (ten), Francesco Merli (ten), Aureliano Pertile (ten), Carlo Galeffi (bar), Mariano Stabile (bar), Riccardo Stracciari (bar), Nazzareno de Angel *(rec 1921–35)* Iron Needle ▲ 1304
Opera Arias & Scenes Preiser ("Lebendige Vergangenheit" series) ▲ PRE 89010 (m) [AAD]
Ponchielli, A.:La Gioconda (sels)—Si, morir ella de' *(rec 1928)* Minerva ▲ 4 (m) [ADD]
Ponchielli, A.:La Gioconda (sels), w. *(other artists unknown)*—Si, Morir Ella de' Enterprise ("Vocal Archives" series) ▲ ENT VA 1123
Puccini, G.:La Bohème, w. Luba Mirella (sop—Musetta), Rosetta Pampanini (sop—Mimì), Luigi Marini (ten—Rodolfo), Giuseppe Nessi (ten—Alcindoro), Aristide Baracchi (bar—Schaunard), Gino Vanelli (bar—Marcello), Salvatore Baccaloni (bass—Benoit), Tancredi Pasero (bass—Colline), L. Molajoli (cnd), La Scala Orch, La Scala Chorus Bongiovanni 2–▲ 1125/26 [ADD]
Puccini, G.:Manon Lescaut (sels), w. M. Favero (sop), R. Tebaldi (sop), J. Gardino (mez), G. Malipiero (ten), G. Nessi (ten), M. Stabile (bar), C. Forti (bass), A. Toscanini (cnd), La Scala Orch, La Scala Chorus—Intermezzo; Act 3 *(rec live, Milan, May 18, 1946)* Arkadia ("Historical Performances" series) 2–▲ 604 (m)
Rossini, G.:Arias, w. *(other artists unknown)*—La calunnia [from Il Barbiere di Siviglia]; Pietà Signore Enterprise ("Vocal Archives" series) ▲ ENT VA 1123
Rossini, G.:Arias, *(orch unknown)*—La calunnia [from Il barbiere di Siviglia]; Pietà Signore *(rec 1927 & 43)* Minerva ▲ 4 (m) [ADD]
Tancredi Pasero Preiser ▲ PRE 89704 [ADD]
Verdi, G.:Aida, w. Giannina Arangi-Lombardi (sop—Aida), Maria Capuana (mez—Amneris), Aroldo Lindi (ten—Radames), Giuseppe Nessi (ten—Messenger), Armando Borgioli (bar—Amonasro), Salvatore Baccaloni (bass—King), Tancredi Pasero (bass—Ramfis), L. Molajoli (cnd), La Scala Orch, La Scala Chorus *(rec Nov 1928)* VAI Audio 2–▲ VAIA 1083–2
Verdi, G.:Arias—Tu sul labbro de' veggenti [from Nabucco]; Infelice! e tuo credevi [from Ernani]; Il mio sangue, la vita darei [from Luisa Miller]; Quel vecchio maledivami [from Rigoletto]; Di due figli vivea, padre beato [from Il Trovatore]; Ella giammai m'amo...Dormirò sol [from Don Carlos]; Non imprecare, umiliati [from La forza del destino; w. Bianca Scacciati (sop), Francesco Merli (ten)]; Confutatis maledictis [from Messa da Requiem] *(rec 1927–44)* Minerva ▲ 4 (m) [ADD]
Verdi, G.:Arias, w. *(other artists unknown)*—Tu sul Labbro de' Veggenti [from Nabucco]; Il Mio Sangue, la Vita Darei [from Luisa Miller]; Quel Vecchio Maledivami [from Rigoletto]; Di Due Figli Vivea, Padre Beato [from Il Trovatore]; Ella Giammai M'amo...Dormirò Sol [from Don Carlos]; Non Imprecare, Umiliati [from La forza del destino]; Confutatis Maledictis [from Requiem] Enterprise ("Vocal Archives" series) ▲ ENT VA 1123

Pasero, Tancredi (bass) (cont.)
Verdi, G.:Un ballo in maschera, w. Maria Caniglia (sop—Amelia), Fedora Barbieri (mez—Ulrica), Beniamino Gigli (ten—Riccardo), Gino Bechi (bar—Renato), Tancredi Pasero (bass—Samuel), Blando Giusti (sgr—Un Giudice), Nicola Niccolini (sgr—Silvano), Ugo Novelli (sgr—Tom), Elda Ribetti (sgr—Oscar), T. Serafin (cnd), Rome Opera Orch, Giuseppe Conca (cnd), Rome Opera Chorus *(rec 1943)* Arkadia 2–▲ CD 78005 (m) [ADD]
Verdi, G.:La forza del destino, w. Maria Caniglia (sop), Ebe Stignani (mez), Galliano Masini (ten), Carlo Tagliabue (bar), G. Marinuzzi (cnd), EIAR Orch, EIAR Chorus *(rec 1941)* Grammofono 2000 ▲ GRM 78567 (m)
Verdi, G.:Requiem Mass (sels), w. M. Caniglia (sop), E. Stignani (mez), B. Gigli (ten), V. de Sabata (cnd), Rome CO, Rome RAI Chorus, Turin RAI Chorus—Dies irae; Sanctus; Libera me *(rec Dec. 14, 1940)* Legato Classics 2–▲ LCD 178–2

Pashley, Anne (sop)
Bach, J.S.:Magnificat, BWV 243, w. L. Popp (sop), J. Baker (mez), R. Tear (ten), D. Barenboim (cnd), New Philharmonia Orch, New Philharmonia Chorus EMI Classics ▲ CDM 64634–2
Bach, J.S.:Magnificat, BWV 243, w. Lucia Popp (sop), Janet Baker (mez), Robert Tear (ten), Thomas Hemsley (bar), D. Barenboim (cnd), New Philharmonia Orch, New Philharmonia Chorus *(rec All Saints, Tooting, London, May 1968)* EMI Classics ▲ CDK 65334 [ADD]

Pasino, Gisella (mez)
Franchetti, A.:Cristoforo Colombo, w. R. Ragatzu (sop—Isabella), G. Pasino (mez—Annacoana), M. Berti (ten—Ferdinand), R. Bruson (bar—Cristoforo Colombo), R. Scandiuzzi (bass—Don Roldano Ximenes), M. Viotti (cnd), Frankfurt RSO, Frankfurt Radio Chorus [I] *(rec live, Alte Oper Frankfurt, 8/30 & 9/2 1991)* Koch Schwann 3–▲ CD 3–1030–2 [DDD]
Ravel, M.:Shéhérazade Mez, w. H.–M. Schneidt (cnd), Berlin RSO LaserLight ▲ 14013 [DDD]
Ravel, M.:Shéhérazade Mez, w. H.–M. Schneidt (cnd), Berlin RSO Capriccio ▲ 10 381 [DDD]
Spontini, G.:La vestale, w. R. Plowright (sop), F. Araiza (ten), P. Lefèbvre (ten), A. Cauli (bar), F. de Grandis (bass), G. Kuhn (cnd), Munich RSO, Munich Radio Chorus [F] Orfeo 2–▲ 256922 [DDD]

Paskalis, Kostas (bar)
Bizet, G.:Carmen, w. M. Freni (sop), G. Bumbry (mez), J. Vickers (ten), R. Frühbeck de Burgos (cnd), Paris Opera Orch, Paris Opera Chorus [opéra comique version] [F] EMI Classics ("Studio" series) 2–▲ CDMB 63643 [ADD]
Donizetti, G.:Lucrezia Borgia, w. Montserrat Caballé (sop), Jane Berbié (mez), Alain Vanzo (ten), Arnold Voketaitis (b-bar), L. D. Clements (sgr), Adib Fazah (sgr), Mauro Lampi (sgr), Vern Shinall (sgr), Jerold Siena (sgr), William Wiederanders (sgr), J. Perlea (cnd), New York City Opera Orch, New York City Chorus Great Opera Performances 2–▲ GOP 769
Donizetti, G.:Lucrezia Borgia, w. M. Caballé (sop), J. Berbié (mez), A. Vanzo (ten), J. Perlea (cnd), *(orch & chorus unknown)* [I] *(rec live in New York, 4/20/65)* Standing Room Only 2–▲ SRO 801–2 (m) [ADD]
Giordano, U.:Andrea Chénier, w. H. Konetzni (sop—Madelon), M. Sjöstedt (sop—Bersi), R. Tebaldi (sop—Maddalena de Coigny), E. Höngen (cta—La Contessa de Coigny), F. Corelli (ten—Andrea Chénier), E. Bastianini (bar—C. Gérard), K. Paskalis (bar—Pietro Fléville), L. Welter (bar—Fouquier Tinville), A. Pernerstorfer (b-bar—Mathieu), L. von Matačić (cnd), Vienna State Opera Orch, Vienna State Opera Chorus *(rec Vienna, June 26, 1960)* Fortissimo 2–▲ CDE 3003 [ADD]
Verdi, G.:Rigoletto (sels), w. Renata Scotto (sop—Gilda), Corinna Vozza (mez—Giovanna), Bianca Vortoluzzi (cta—Maddalena), Luciano Pavarotti (ten—Duke of Mantua), Kostas Paskalis (bar—Rigoletto), Paolo Washington (bass—Sparafucile), C. M. Guilini (cnd), Rome Opera Orch, Rome Opera Chorus Budget ("The Greatest Voice in Opera" series) ▲ SYP 104

Pasquali, Renato (sgr)
Verdi, G.:I lombardi alla prima crociata, w. Renata Broilo (sop), Maria Vitale (sop), Miriam Pirazzini (mez), Aldo Bertocci (ten), Mario Frosini (sgr), Mario Petri (bass), Bruno Franchi (sgr), Gustavo Gallo (sgr), M. Wolf-Ferrari (cnd), Milan RAI Lyric Orch, Milan RAI Chorus *(rec 1954)* Cetra Classic 2–▲ CDON 41 [ADD]

Passarotti, Piero (bass)
Puccini, G.:La fanciulla del West (sels), w. Magda Olivero (sop—Minnie), Corinna Vozza (mez—Wowkle), Paolo Caroli (ten—Harry), Giacomo Lauri-Volpi (ten—Dick Johnson), Marco Rogani (ten—Pony Express Rider), Salvatore di Tommaso (ten—Trin), Adelio Zagonara (ten—Nick), Virgilio Ascorro (bar—Sid), Alfredo Colella (bar—Jake Wallace), Giuseppe Forgione (bar—Bello), Giancarlo Guelfi (bar—Jack Rance), Arturo la Porta (bar—Sonora), Gino Conti (bass—José Castro), Piere Passarotti (bass—Bill), Enzo Titta (bass—Larkens), Giulio Tomei (bass—Ashby), V. Bellezza (cnd), Rome Opera Orch, Rome Opera Chorus—Minnie, dalla mia casa son partito; Laggiù nel Soledad; Chi c'è per farmi i ricci; Oh! Mister Johnson, siete rimasto; Non so ben neppur io; Io non son che una povera fanciulla; No, Minnie, non piangete; Vorrei mettermi queste; Hallo!; Oh, se sapeste; Credo che abbiate torto; Ma ti giuro ch'io non ti lascio più; Vieni fuori!; Una parola sola!...Or son sei mesi; Che c'è di nuovo Jack?; È là; Siete pronto; Ch'ella mi creda; È Minnie!...È Minnie! *(rec Rome, Mar. 30, 1957)* Golden Age of Opera ▲ GAO 180 [ADD]

Passmore, Walter (bar)
Sullivan, A.:The Sorcerer (sels)—Mr. Well's song Symposium ▲ 1123

Pastorello, C. (sgr)
Morlacchi, F.:Poeta, w. P. Pellegrini (sgr), G. Catalucci (cnd), Orch Giovanile In Canto [I] Bongiovanni ▲ GB 2129 [DDD]

Pastori, A. (sop)
Meyerbeer, G.:Les Huguenots, w. A. de Cavalieri (mez), G. Lauri-Volpi (ten), G. Taddei (bar), G. Tozzi (bass), N. Zaccaria (bass), T. Serafin (cnd), Milan RAI SO, Milan RAI Chorus *(rec 1956)* Memories 3–▲ MEM 4566 [ADD]
Verdi, G.:Rigoletto (sels), w. Antonioli (ten), C. Tagliabue (bar), U. Rapalo (cnd), Naples Teatro San Carlo Orch, Naples Teatro San Carlo Chorus [I] *(rec live, Naples, 1/20/56)* The Golden Age of Opera ▲ GAO 115 [ADD]

Pászthy, Júlia (sop)
Bach, J.S.:Cant 51, w. I. Kertesi (sop), J. Nemeth (mez), J. Mukk (ten), I. Gáti (bass), M. Antal (cnd), Failoni CO, Hungarian Radio Chorus Naxos ▲ 8.550643 [DDD]
Bach, J.S.:Cant 208, "Hunting Cant", w. I. Kertesi (sop), J. Nemeth (mez), J. Mukk (ten), I. Gáti (bass), M. Antal (cnd), Failoni CO, Hungarian Radio Chorus Naxos ▲ 8.550643 [DDD]
Wayditch, G. von:The Caliph's Magician, w. Júlia Pászthi (sop—Eunuch), Sándor Palcso (ten—The Emir), István Rozsos (ten—Nawab), Zsolt Bende (bar—The Magician), Árpád Kishegyi (sgr—Djinn), András Nagy-Soljom (sgr—The Caliph), Csaba Ötvös (sgr—Djinn), Csilla Ötvös (sgr—Odalisk), A. Kórodi (cnd), Budapest National Opera Orch, Budapest National Opera Chorus *(rec 1975)* VAI Audio 2–▲ VAIA 1095–2 [ADD]

Pataky, Koloman von (ten)
Mozart, W.A.:Don Giovanni, w. I. Souez (sop), L. Helletsgrüber (sop), A. Mildmay (sop), J. Brownlee (bar), R. Henderson (bar), T. Franklin (bar), S. Baccaloni (bass), F. Busch (cnd), Glyndebourne Festival Orch, Glyndebourne Festival Chorus [I] *(rec 1936, orig. issued by HMV)* Pearl 3–▲ PEAS 9369 (m) [AAD]

Patassini, Manrico (ten)
Gomes, A.C.:Il Guarany, w. Niza De Castro Tank (sop—Cecilia), Roque Lotti (ten—Ruy Bento), Manrico Patassini (ten—Pery), Paschoal Raymundo (ten—Don Alvaro), Paulo Fortes (bar—Gonzales), Juan Carlos Ortiz (b-bar—Il Cacico), Waldomiro Furlan (bass—Alonso), José Perrotta (bass—Don Antonio De Mariz), A. Belardi (cnd), São Paulo Teatro Municipale Orch, São Paulo Teatro Municipale Chorus *(rec Studios of the Teatro Municipal, São Paulo, Brazil, 1959)* Arkadia 2–▲ HP 617.2 [ADD]

Patay, Péter (cta)
Werner, G.J.:Vesperae de Apostolis, w. Ágnes Dobszay (sop), Tamás Bubnó (ten), Péter Cser (bass), J. Mezei (cnd), Vienna–Szász CO, Budapest Schola Cantorum *(rec St. Columba's Presbyterian Church, Budapest, June 12–15, 1995)* Hungaroton ▲ HCD 31646 [DDD]

Paternina, Federico (sgr)
Distel, H.:La Stazione, w. Teresita Fontana (sgr), Valeria Manzoni (sgr), Malwida Meysenbug (sgr), Arturo Schwarz (sgr) *(rec Milan, Italy & Bern, Switzerland, 1987 & May 1990)* Hat Hut ("NOW." series) ▲ hat ART CD 6060 [AAD]

Patriasz, Catherine (cta)
Bach, J.S.:Cant 11, "Ascension Oratorio", w. B. Schlick (sop), C. Prégardien (ten), P. Kooy (bass), P. Herreweghe (cnd), Collegium Vocale Orch Harmonia Mundi France ▲ HMC 901479

Patriasz, Catherine (cta) (cont.)
Bach, J.S.:Cant 43, w. B. Schlick (sop), C. Prégardien (ten), P. Kooy (bass), P. Herreweghe (cnd), Collegium Vocale Harmonia Mundi France ▲ HMC 901479
Bach, J.S.:Cant 44, w. B. Schlick (sop), C. Prégardien (ten), P. Kooy (bass), P. Herreweghe (cnd), Collegium Vocale Harmonia Mundi France ▲ HMC 901479
Bach, J.S.:Mass in b, BWV 232, w. B. Schlick (sop), C. Brett (ct), H. Crook (ten), P. Kooy (bass), P. Herreweghe (cnd), Collegium Vocale Orch, Collegium Vocale [L] Virgin Classics ("Veritas" series) 2-▲ CDCB 59517-2 [DDD]
Bach, J.S.:St. John Passion, w. B. Schlick (sop), H. Crook (ten), W. Kendall (ten), P. Kooy (bass), P. Lika (bass), P. Herreweghe (cnd), La Chapelle Royale Orch, Ghent Collegium Vocale [G] Harmonia Mundi France 2-▲ HMC 901264/65 [DDD]

Patrick, Julian (bar)
Starer, R.:Ariel, Visions of Isaiah, w. R. Peters (sop), A. Kaplan (cnd), Camerata Singers, Camerata Singers *(rec 1972)* CRI ▲ CD 612 [ADD]

Patterson, Frank (ten)
Farewell My Derry Love Rego ▲ SH 8904-2 ■ SH 8904-4
Green, P.:The Man from Galilee, w. P. Green (cnd), Garda Siochana Choir Alanna ▲ ALA 5554 [DDD]
Ireland's Best Loved Ballads Rego ▲ RCD 7 ■ RC 7

Patterson, Marjorie (sop)
Spohr, L.:Songs (misc), w. Daniel Sarge (pno)—Lied des verlassenen Mädchens, WoO 90; Nachgefühl, WoO 91 *(rec Clara Wieck Auditorium, Sandhausen, July 24, 25 & 27, 1995)* Marco Polo ▲ 8.223869 [DDD]
Spohr, L.:Songs, Op. 25, w. Daniel Sarge (pno) *(rec Clara Wieck Auditorium, Sandhausen, July 24, 25 & 27, 1995)* Marco Polo ▲ 8.223869 [DDD]
Spohr, L.:Songs, Op. 37, w. Daniel Sarge (pno)—Nos. 1-5 *(rec Clara Wieck Auditorium, Sandhausen, July 24, 25 & 27, 1995)* Marco Polo ▲ 8.223869 [DDD]
Spohr, L.:Songs, Op. 41, w. Daniel Sarge (pno) *(rec Clara Wieck Auditorium, Sandhausen, July 24, 25 & 27, 1995)* Marco Polo ▲ 8.223869 [DDD]
Spohr, L.:Songs, Op. 72, w. Daniel Sarge (pno) *(rec Clara Wieck Auditorium, Sandhausen, July 24, 25 & 27, 1995)* Marco Polo ▲ 8.223869 [DDD]

Patterson, Stuart (ten)
Mozart, W.A.:Ave verum corpus, w. Noemi Rime (sop), Christine Batty (mez), Bernard Deletre (bass), G. Vashegyi (cnd), Budapest Orfeo Orch, Patrick Marco (cnd), Maitrise de Paris Pierre Verany ▲ PVY 730058 [DDD]
Mozart, W.A.:Missa, K.317, w. Noemi Rime (sop), Christine Batty (mez), Bernard Deletre (bass), G. Vashegyi (cnd), Budapest Orfeo Orch, Patrick Marco (cnd), Maitrise de Paris Pierre Verany ▲ PVY 730058 [DDD]
Mozart, W.A.:Nozze di Figaro, w. Danielle Borst (sop—Countess Almaviva), Claudine Le Coz (sop—Marcellina), Sophie Marin-Degor (sop—Suzanna), Laura Polverelli (mez—Cherubino), Valérie Lecoq (sgr—Barberina), Philippe Cantor (ten—Antonio), Stuart Patterson (ten—Dons Basile & Curzio), Huub Claessens (bar—Figaro), Nicolas Reveng (bar—Count Almaviva), Patrick Donnelly (bass—Bartolo), J. Malgoire (cnd), La Grande Ecurie et la Chambre du Roy Astrée 8-▲ E 8606
Mozart, W.A.:Vesperae solennes, w. Noemi Rime (sop), Christine Batty (mez), Bernard Deletre (bass), G. Vashegyi (cnd), Budapest Orfeo Orch, Patrick Marco (cnd), Maitrise de Paris Pierre Verany ▲ PVY 730058 [DDD]
Pesson, G.:Music of, w. Donatienne Michel-Dansac (sop), Sandra Roulx (mez), Paul-Alexandre Dubois (bar), Pascal Sausy (bar), Florence Millet (pno), D. My (cnd), Fa Ensemble, Paris String Quartet—Le gel, par jeu for Fl, Cl, Hn, Bass Mar, Vn & Vc; Qt for Strs; Non Sapremo Mai di Questo Mi for Fl, Vn & Pno; 5 Poèmes de Sandro Penna for Bar, B Cl, Hn, Vn & Vc; La lumière n'a pas de bras pour nous porter for Amplified Pno; La vita è come l'albero di natale for Vn & Pno; Nocturnes en quatuor for Cl, Pno, Vn & Vc; Les chants faëz for Pno & 10 Instrs; Sur-le-champ for 4 Voices & 9 Instrs [from a text by Pierre Alferi] Accord ▲ ACD 204682 [DDD]

Patterson, Susan (sop)
Cimarosa, D.:Il Matrimonio segreto, w. Susan Patterson (sop—Carolina), Janet Williams (mez—Elisetta), Gloria Banditelli (cta—Fidalma), William Matteuzzi (ten—Paolino), Alfonso Antoniozzi (bass—Geronimo), Petteri Salomaa (bass—Count Robinson), Hans Ludwig Hirsch (pno), G. Bellini (cnd), Eastern Netherlands Orch *(rec Muziekcentrum Enschede, Holland, Aug 26-Sept 8, 1991)* Arts 3-▲ 471172 [DDD]

Patti, Adelina (sop)
Mozart, W.A.:Don Giovanni (sels), w. Emilia Corsi (sop), John McCormack (ten), Mattia Battistini (bar), Ezio Pinza (bass), Landon Ronald (pno), C. Sabajno (cnd)—Alfin Siam liberati...Là ci darem la mano; Finch'han del vino; Batti, batti, o bel Masetto; Il mio tesoro; L'amerò, sarò costante *(rec 1905 - 1944)* Minerva ▲ MN A14 [ADD]

Pattiera, Tino (ten)
The Voice of Tino Pattiera:Arias, Duets & Songs, w. Anka Horvath (sgr), Meta Seinmeyer (sop), Michael Bohnen (bass) *(rec 1916-30)* Preiser 2-▲ PRE CD 89222

Patton, Mike (sgr)
Zorn, J.:Elegy, w. Barbara Chaffe (fl), David Abel (vn), Scummy (gtr), David Shea (turntables), David Slusser (sound effects), William Winant (perc) Tzadik ▲ TZA 7302 [ADD]

Patzak, Julius (ten)
Beethoven, L. van:Fidelio, w. K. Flagstad (sop), P. Schöffler (b-bar), J. Greindl (bass), W. Furtwängler (cnd), Vienna PO, Vienna State Opera Chorus [G] *(rec live, Salzburg 8/5/50)* Verona 2-▲ 27044/45 (m) [AAD]
Beethoven, L. van:Fidelio, w. K. Flagstad (sop), J. Griendl (bass), W. Furtwängler (cnd), Vienna PO, Vienna State Opera Chorus EMI Classics 2-▲ CDC 64901
Beethoven, L. van:Fidelio, w. K. Flagstad (sop), P. Schöffler (b-bar), J. Greindl (bass), W. Furtwängler (cnd), Vienna PO, Vienna State Opera Chorus [G] *(rec live 1950)* Arkadia 2-▲ 354
Beethoven, L. van:Fidelio (sels), w. E. Schlüte (sop), L. della Casa (sop), R. Schock (ten), F. Frantz (b-bar), H. Alsen (bass), W. Furtwängler (cnd), Vienna State Opera Orch, Vienna State Opera Chorus—Overture, 16 arias & choruses *(rec live, Salzburg Festspielhaus Aug. 3, 1948)* Melodram 2-▲ CDM 25009 [ADD]
Einem, G. von:Dantons Tod, w. M. Cebotari (sop—Lucille Desmoulins), R. Anday (cta—Frau des Simon), P. Klein (ten—de Séchelles), J. Patzak (ten—Camille Desmoulins), J. Witt (ten—Robspierre), P. Schöffler (bar—Danton), L. Weber (bass—Saint Just), F. Fricsay (cnd), Vienna PO, Vienna State Opera Chorus *(rec Aug. 6, 1947)* Stradivarius 2-▲ STR 10067 [ADD]
Haydn, J.:Die Jahreszeiten, w. Trude Eipperle (sop), Georg Hann (bass), C. Krauss (cnd), Vienna PO, Vienna State Opera Chorus [G] *(rec live, June 1942)* Preiser 2-▲ PRE 93053 [AAD]
Haydn, J.:Die Schöpfung, w. Trude Eipperle (sop), Georg Hann (bass), C. Krauss (cnd), Vienna PO, Vienna State Opera Chorus *(rec early 1940's)* Preiser 2-▲ PRE 90104 [AAD]
Julius Patzak *(rec between 1929 & 1937)* Preiser ("Lebendige Vergangenheit" series) ▲ PRE 89075 [AAD]
Mozart, W.A.:Don Giovanni, w. Hedwig Jungkurth (sop—Elvira), Maria Reining (sop—Anna), Julius Patzak (ten—Ottavio), Karl Hammes (bar—Don Giovanni), Georg Hann (bass), Ludwig Weber (bass—Commandant), J. Keilberth (cnd), Stuttgart Reich RSO, Stuttgart Radio Chorus *(rec Mar, 1936)* Preiser 2-▲ PRE 90263
Pfitzner, H.:Von deutscher Seele, w. Trude Eipperle (sop), Luise Willer (mez), Ludwig Weber (bass), C. Krauss (cnd), Vienna PO, Vienna State Opera Chorus *(rec Jan 1945)* Preiser 2-▲ PRE 90255 [ADD]
Schubert, Franz:Die Schöne Müllerin, w. M. Raucheisen (pno) *(rec 1943)* Preiser ▲ 93128 (m) [ADD]
Schubert, Franz:Winterreise, w. Jörg Demus (pno) *(rec 1964)* Preiser ▲ PRE 93067 [ADD]
Sings Opera & Operetta Pearl ▲ PEA 9383 (m) [AAD]
Strauss (II), Joh.:Die Fledermaus, w. H. Gueden (sop), A. Dermota (ten), A. Jaresch (ten), A. Poell (b-bar), W. Lipp (sop), S. Wagner (mez), K. Preger (ten), C. Krauss (cnd), Vienna PO *(rec early 1950s)* London ("Historic" series) 2-▲ 425990-2 [AAD]
Strauss (II), Joh.:Der Zigeunerbaron, w. Emmy Loose (sop), Hilde Zadek (sop), Rosette Anday (cta), Karl Dönch (bar), Alfred Poell (bar), Steffi Leverenz (sgr), C. Krauss (cnd), Vienna PO, Vienna State Opera Chorus Phonographe 2-▲ PHG 5020 [AAD]

Patzak, Julius (ten) (cont.)
Strauss, R.:Arabella, w. L. Della Casa (sop), M. Reining (sop), R. Anday (cta), H. Hotter (b-bar), G. Hann (bass), K. Böhm (cnd), Vienna PO, Vienna State Opera Chorus *(rec live, Salzburg Festival, 8/12/47)* Melodram 3-▲ MEL 37077
Strauss, R.:Salome, w. Maria Cebotari (sop—Salome), Elisabeth Höngen (mez—Herodias), Karl Friedrich (ten—Narraboth), Julius Patzak (ten—Herod), Marko Rothmüller (bar—Jokanaan), C. Krauss (cnd), Vienna State Opera Orch, Vienna State Opera Chorus *(rec Covent Garden, London, Sept 30, 1947)* Legato 2-▲ LCD 211-2 [ADD]
Strauss, R.:Salome, w. Astrid Varnay (sop—Salome), Hertha Töpper (mez—Der Page der Herodias), Margarete Klose (cta—Herodias), Hans Hopf (ten—Narraboth), Karl Hoppe (ten—1st Nazarene), Karl Ostertag (ten—1st Jew), Julius Patzak (ten—Herodes), Hans Braun (bar—Jochanaan), Benno Kusche (bar—2nd Soldier), Adolf Keil (bass—1st Soldier), Hans Hermann Nissen (bass—Ein Kappadozier), Max Proebstl (bass—2nd Nazarene), Walter Carnotch (sgr—4th Jew), Emil Graf (sgr—3rd Jew), Paul Kaussen (sgr—2nd Jew), Hildegard Limmer (sgr—A slave), Georg Witter (sgr—5th Jew), H. Weigert (cnd), Bavarian RSO *(rec June 21-25, 1953)* Bella Voce 2-▲ BLV 7210 [AAD]
Wiener Komödienlieder, w. Elfriede Ott (sgr) *(orch unknown) (rec 1963)* Preiser ▲ PRE 93060 [ADD]

Paul, Charles (bar)
Cherubini, L.:Les Deux journées, w. J. Micheau (sop), M. Davies (ten), P. Gianotti (ten), E. Regnier (ten), T. Beecham (cnd), Royal PO, BBC Theater Chorus *(rec live, London Dec. 19, 1947)* Intaglio 2-▲ INCD 7342 [ADD]

Paul, Nigel (bar)
Danova, R.:The Phantom of the Opera on Ice, w. Susannah Glanville (sop), Kathy Dooley (sop), Johnny Logan (ten), Stephen Lee Garden (ten), Mungo Jerry (bar), P. Whitfield (cnd), Northern Light SO, Northern Light Choir, Russian Stars on Ice Chorus Plaza ▲ PZA 008

Paul, Thomas (bass)
Bach, J.S.:Mass in b, BWV 232, w. S. McNair (sop), G. Simpson (mez), D. Ziegler (mez), J. Aler (ten), W. Stone (bar), R. Shaw (cnd), Atlanta SO, Atlanta Chamber Chorus [L] Telarc 2-▲ CD 80233 [DDD]
Beethoven, L. van:Sym 9, "Choral Sym", w. Anny Schlemm (sop), Diana Eustrati (cta), Gert Lutze (ten), H. Abendroth (cnd), Leipzig RSO *(rec 1953)* Arlecchino ARL
Bellini, V.:I Puritani, w. B. Sills (sop—Elvira), E. Shade (sop—Enrichetta), L. Pavarotti (ten—Arturo), L. Quilico (bar—Riccardo), P. Plishka (bass—Giorgio), T. Paul (bass—Walton), A. Guadagno (cnd), *(orch & chorus unknown) (rec live Jan. 18, 1972)* Legato Classics 2-▲ LCD 1762 [ADD]
Carter, E.:Syringa, w. J. DeGaetani (mez), H. Sollberger (cnd), Speculum Musicae, Group for Contemporary Music *(rec 5/81)* CRI ▲ CD 610 [ADD]
Carter, E.:Syringa, w. J. DeGaetani (mez), H. Sollberger (cnd), Speculum Musicae, Group for Contemporary Music [E] *(rec 5/81)* CRI ■ ACS 6003
Haydn, J.:The Seven Last Words of Christ on the Cross, w. Benita Valente (sop), Jan DeGaetani (mez), Jon Humphrey (ten), Juilliard String Quartet Sony Classical ▲ SK 44914 [DDD]
Mendelssohn, F.:Elijah, w. Barbara Bonney (sop), Henriette Schellenberg (sop), Florence Quivar (mez), Marietta Simpson (mez), Reid Bartelme (trb), Jerry Hadley (ten), Richard Clement (ten), Thomas Hampson (bar), R. Shaw (cnd), Atlanta SO, Atlanta Sym Chorus [E] *(rec Symphony Hall, Woodruff Arts Center, Atlanta, GA, Nov. 5-7, 1994)* Telarc 2-▲ CD 80389 [DDD]
Mozart, W.A.:Missa, K.317, w. C. Bogard (sop), J. de Gaetani (mez), R. White (ten), D. Zinman (cnd), Rochester PO, Roberts Wesleyan College Chorale *(rec 1978)* Allegretto ▲ ACD 8164 [ADD] ■ ACS 8164
Rands, B.:Canti dell'eclisse, w. G. Schwarz (cnd), Philadelphia Orch New World ▲ 803922

Pauley, Wilbur (bass)
Soldier, D.:War Prayer, w. Dionne Freeney (alt), Jason White (ten), R.A. Clark (cnd), Manhattan CO, Gospel Singers Newport Classic ▲ NPD 85589 [DDD]

Pauli, Piero (ten)
Puccini, G.:Tosca, w. Carmen Melis (sop—Tosca), Nello Palai (ten—Spoletta), Piero Pauli (ten—Cavaradossi), Apollo Granforte (bar—Scarpia), Giovanni Azzimonti (bass—Angelotti/Sciarrone), Antonio Gelli (bass—Sagrestano), C. Sabajno (cnd), La Scala Orch, La Scala Chorus *(rec Nov 1929)* Arkadia 2-▲ CD 78002 (m) [ADD]

Paulmann, Annette (sgr)
Waits, T.:The Black Rider:The Casting of Magic Bullets, w. Angelika Thomas (sgr—Anne), Annette Paulmann (sgr—Kätchen), Sona Cervena (sgr—Bird/Messenger/Spoonwoman), Monika Tahal (sgr—Witness/Bird/Shrink/Wilhelm's Double/Skeleton), Susi Eisenkolb (sgr—Bridesmaid/Pegleg's Double), Heinz Vossbrink (sgr—Kuno), Dominique Horwitz (sgr—Pegleg), Gerd Kunath (sgr—Bertram), Stefan Kurt (sgr—Wilhelm), Klaus Schreiber (sgr—Robert/Man on Stag/Georg Schmid), Jörg Holm (Old Uncle/Duke), Jan Moritz Steffen (sgr—Young Kuno/Bird/Shrink/Skeleton), Tom Waits (vocals/coliope/organ/chamberlain/mar/emax/guitar/train whistle), Ralph Carney (saxophone/bass clarinet/baritone horn), Bill Douglas (bass instrument), Kenny Wollesen (perc) Island ▲ 314518559-2

Pauloi, P. (ten)
Puccini, G.:Tosca, w. C. Melis (sop—Tosca), P. Pauloi (ten—Cavarodossi), N. Palai (ten—Spoletta), A. Granforte (bar—Scarpia), G. Azzimonti (bass—Sciarrone/Angelotti), A. Gelli (bass—Sacristan), C. Sabajno (cnd), La Scala Orch, La Scala Chorus [I] *(rec Milan, Nov. 1929)* VAI Audio 2-▲ VAIA 1076-2 (m) [ADD]

Paulsen, Melinda (mez)
Boulanger, N.:Songs, w. A. Gassenhuber (pno)—5 Songs; 7 Songs; Les heures claires Troubadisc ▲ TROCD 01407
Donizetti, G.:Anna Bolena (sels), w. Carol Vaness (sop), Dennis O'Neill (ten), Anton Rosner (ten), Ambrogio Riva (bass), R. Abbado (cnd), Munich RSO, Bavarian Radio Chorus—Final Scene & Aria [from Act II] *(rec Studio 1, Bavaria, Apr 13-17, 1993)* RCA Red Seal ▲ 09026-61828-2 [DDD]
Keiser, R.:Passions Oratorium, w. T. d'Althann (sop), P. Geitner (sop), J. Elbert (ten), H. Elbert (bass), C. Brembeck (cnd), Parthenia Baroque, Parthenia Vocal Christophorus ▲ 77143 [DDD]
Rossini, G.:Tancredi, w. Veronica Cangemi (sop—Roggiero), Eva Mei (sop—Amenaide), Vasselina Kasarova (mez—Tancredi), Melinda Paulsen (cta—Isaura), Ramón Vargas (ten—Argirio), Harry Peeters (bass—Orbazzano), Janos Maté (vn), Gottfried Greiner (vc), Ingo Nawra (db), David Syrus (hpd), R. Abbado (cnd), Munich RSO, Bavarian Radio Chorus *(rec Studio 1, Munich, July 17-30, 1995)* RCA Red Seal 3-▲ 09026-68349-2 [DDD]
Verdi, G.:Otello (sels), w. Carol Vaness (sop), R. Abbado (cnd), Munich RSO, Bavarian Radio Chorus—Canzone del salice; Ave Maria [both from Act IV] *(rec Studio 1, Bavaria, Apr 13-17, 1993)* RCA Red Seal ▲ 09026-61828-2 [DDD]

Pauly-Dreesen, Rose (sop)
Strauss, R.:Die ägyptische Helena (sels), w. F. Busch (cnd), Berlin State Opera Orch—from Act 1 (Helen's awakening; Bei jener Nacht); from Act 2 (Funeral march; Zweite Brautnacht! Zaubernacht!) [G] *(rec 10/2/28 for Parlophone)* Pearl 2-▲ GEMMCDS 9365 (m) [AAD]

Paunova, Mariana (cta)
Prokofiev, S.:Alexander Nevsky, w. E. Mata (cnd), Dallas SO, Dallas Sym Chorus *(rec 1992)* Dorian ▲ DOR 90169 [DDD]

Pavarotti, Luciano (ten)
Amore:Romantic Italian Love Songs London ▲ 436719-2 LH ■ 436719-4 LH
Anniversary London ▲ 417362-2 LH [DDD/ADD] ■ 417362-4
Arias & Duets, w. Mirella Freni (sop) London ▲ 421878-2 LA [ADD/DDD]
Arias & Duets (1974-1986), w. Giuseppe Taddei (bar), P. Domingo (ten), et al., Vienna State Opera Orch [var. cnd] Acanta ▲ 49402
Basic 100, Vol. 78, w. Raina Kabaivanska (sop), Ingvar Wixell (bar), Rome Opera House Orch [cnd:Daniel Oren] RCA Victor ▲ 09026-68455-2 ■ 09026-68455-4
Bellini, V.:Beatrice di Tenda, w. J. Sutherland (sop), R. Bonynge (cnd), London SO, Ambrosian Opera Chorus London ("Grand Opera" series) 3-▲ 433706-2 [ADD]
Bellini, V.:I Capuleti e i Montecchi, w. M. Rinaldi (sop—Giulietta), G. Aragall (ten—Romeo), L. Pavarotti (ten—Tebaldo), N. Zaccaria (bass—Capellio), C. Abbado (cnd), Residentie Orch The Hague, Bologna Chorus [I] *(rec live, Amsterdam 6/30/66)* Verona 2-▲ 28001/2

▲ = CD ♦ = Enhanced CD Δ = MD ■ = Cassette Tape □ = DCC

Pavarotti, Luciano (ten) (cont.)

Bellini, V.:I Capuleti e i Montecchi, w. R. Scotto (sop), G. Aragall (ten), A. Giacomotti (bass), A. Ferrin (bass), C. Abbado (cnd), La Scala Orch, La Scala Chorus *(rec live 1967)* Butterfly Music 2-▲ BMC 12 [AAD]

Bellini, V.:I Capuleti e i Montecchi, w. M. Rinaldi (sop), G. Aragall (ten), N. Zaccaria (bass), C. Abbado (cnd), Residentie Orch The Hague, Bologna Chorus *(rec live, Amsterdam 6/30/66)* Melodram 2-▲ MEL 27001

Bellini, V.:I Capuleti e i Montecchi, w. R. Scotto (sop), G. Aragall (ten), C. Abbado (cnd), La Scala Orch, La Scala Chorus [I] *(rec live, La Scala, 1/8/68)* Arkadia 2-▲ 550 (m) [AAD]

Bellini, V.:I Capuleti e i Montecchi (sels), w. Gaetano Ferrin (bass), Alfredo Giacomotti (bass), C. Abbado (cnd), La Scala Orch, La Scala Chorus—O di Cappelio generoso amici...E serbato a questo acciaro *(rec live, Nov. 20, 1969)* RCA Gold Seal ▲ 09026-68014-2 [ADD]

Bellini, V.:Norma, w. J. Sutherland (sop), M. Caballé (sop), S. Ramey (bass), R. Bonynge (cnd), Welsh National Opera Orch, Welsh National Opera Chorus [I] London 3-▲ 414476-2 [DDD]

Bellini, V.:I Puritani, w. J. Sutherland (sop), P. Cappuccilli (bar), N. Ghiaurov (bass), R. Bonynge (cnd), London SO [I] London 3-▲ 417588-2 [ADD]

Bellini, V.:I Puritani, w. Mirella Freni (sop), Sesto Bruscantini (b-bar), R. Muti (cnd), Rome RAI SO, Rome RAI Chorus *(rec Rome, 1969)* Enterprise ("Palladio" series) 3-▲ ENTPD 4205 [ADD]

Bellini, V.:I Puritani, w. Mirella Freni (sop), Mirelle Fiorentini (mez), Emilio Venturini (ten), Sesto Bruscantini (bar), Giovanni Antonini (bass), Bonaldo Giaiotti (bass), R. Muti (cnd), Rome RAI SO, Rome RAI Chorus Melodram 2-▲ CDM 27062

Bellini, V.:I Puritani, w. M. Freni (sop), S. Bruscantini (bar), B. Giaotti (bass), R. Muti (cnd), Rome RAI SO, Rome RAI Chorus [I] *(rec live, Rome 7/8/69)* Verona 3-▲ 27029/31

Bellini, V.:I Puritani, w. B. Sills (sop—Elvira), E. Shade (sop—Enrichetta), L. Pavarotti (ten—Arturo), L. Quilico (bar—Riccardo), P. Plishka (bass—Giorgio), T. Paul (bass—Walton), A. Guadagno (cnd), *(orch & chorus unknown)* *(rec live Jan. 18, 1972)* Legato Classics 2-▲ LCD 1762 [ADD]

Bellini, V.:I Puritani (sels), w. Gabriella Tucci (sop—Elvira), Vittorina Magnaghi (mez—Enrichetta di Francia), Luciano Pavarotti (ten—Lord Arturo Talbo), Aldo Protti (bar—Sir Riccardo Forth), Ruggero Raimondi (bass—Sir Giorgio), A. Quadri (cnd), Vincenzo Bellini Theater Orch, Catania Teatro Massimo Bellini Chorus Budget ("The Greatest Voice in Opera" series) ▲ SYP 106

Bellini, V.:I Puritani (sels), w. Mirella Freni (sop), Bonaldo Giaiotti (bass), R. Muti (cnd), Rome SO, Rome Sym Chorus—A te, o cara, amor talora *(rec live, Oct. 7, 1969)* RCA Gold Seal ▲ 09026-68014-2 [ADD]

Bellini, V.:I Puritani (sels), w. Mirella Freni (sop), Giovanni Antonini (bass), Bonaldo Giaiotti (bass), R. Muti (cnd), Rome RAI SO, Rome RAI Chorus—A te, o cara *(rec Rome, July 8, 1969)* Goldies ▲ GLD 63202 [ADD]

Bellini, V.:I Puritani (sels), w. G. Tucci (sop), A. Protti (bar), R. Raimondi (bass), A. Quadri (cnd), Catania Teatro Massimo Bellini Orch, Catania Teatro Massimo Bellini Chorus [I] *(rec live, Catania 3/22/68)* Verona 3-▲ 27029/31

Bellini, V.:I Puritani (sels), w. G. Tucci (sop), A. Protti (bar), R. Raimondi (bass), A. Quadri (cnd), Catania Teatro Massimo Bellini Orch, Catania Teatro Massimo Bellini Chorus [I] *(rec live, Catania 3/22/68)* Melodram ▲ MEL 15001

Bellini, V.:La sonnambula, w. J. Sutherland (sop), N. Ghiaurov (bass), R. Bonynge (cnd), National PO London [I] London 2-▲ 417424-2 [DDD]

Berlioz, H.:Requiem, "Grande Messe des Morts", w. J. Levine (cnd), Berlin PO, Ernst Senff Chorus Deutsche Grammophon 2-▲ 429724-2 [DDD]

Boito, A.:Mefistofele, w. M. Freni (sop), M. Caballé (sop), N. Ghiaurov (bass), O. de Fabritiis (cnd), National PO London [I] London 3-▲ 410175-2 [DDD]

Che gelida manina Foyer ▲ FOY 2043 [AAD]

Donizetti, G.:Arias—from La fille du régiment, L'elisir d'amore, La favorita, others [I] London ▲ 417638-2 [ADD]

Donizetti, G.:L'elisir d'amore, w. K. Battle (sop), D. Upshaw (sop), E. Dara (bar), L. Nucci (bar), J. Levine (cnd), Metropolitan Orch, New York Metropolitan Opera Chorus Deutsche Grammophon 2-▲ 429744-2 [DDD]

Donizetti, G.:L'elisir d'amore, w. J. Sutherland (sop), D. Cossa (bar), S. Malas (bass), R. Bonynge (cnd), English CO [I] London 2-▲ 414461-2 [ADD]

Donizetti, G.:L'elisir d'amore (sels), w. R. Bonynge (cnd), Adelaide Opera Orch—Quanto è bella; Una furtiva lacrima *(rec 1965)* Goldies ▲ GLD 63202 [ADD]

Donizetti, G.:L'elisir d'amore (sels), w. Reri Grist (sop), Sesto Bruscantini (bar), Ingvar Wixell (bar), Maria Ambrosio (sgr), G. Patanè (cnd), San Francisco War Memorial Opera House Orch, San Francisco War Memorial Opera House Chorus *(rec live, San Francisco, 1969)* Budget ("The Greatest Voice in Opera" series) ▲ SYP 109

Donizetti, G.:La favorita, w. F. Cossotto (mez), G. Bacquier (bar), N. Ghiaurov (bass), R. Bonynge (cnd), Bologna Teatro Comunale Orch, Bologna Teatro Comunale Chorus London 3-▲ 430038-2 [ADD]

Donizetti, G.:La fille du régiment, w. M. Freni (sop), A. di Stasio (mez), W. Ganzarolli (bar), W. Monachesi (bar), N. Sanzogno (cnd), La Scala Orch, La Scala Chorus [I] *(rec live, 2/11/69)* Verona 2-▲ 27046/47 (m) [AAD]

Donizetti, G.:La fille du régiment, w. M. Freni (sop), A. di Stasio (mez), W. Ganzarolli (bar), W. Monachesi (bar), N. Sanzogno (cnd), La Scala Orch, La Scala Chorus [I] *(rec live, 2/11/69)* Melodram 2-▲ MEL 27045

Donizetti, G.:La fille du régiment, w. J. Sutherland (sop), M. Sinclair (cta), S. Maias (bass), R. Bonynge (cnd), Royal Opera House Orch [F] London 2-▲ 414520-2 [ADD]

Donizetti, G.:La fille du régiment, w. M. Freni (sop), W. Ganzarolli (bar), N. Sanzogno (cnd), La Scala Orch, La Scala Chorus *(rec 1969)* Memories 2-▲ MEM 4507 [AAD]

Donizetti, G.:La fille du régiment (sels), w. Mirella Freni (sop), Anna di Stasio (mez), Angelo Mercuriali (ten), Wladimiro Ganzarolli (bar), Walter Monachesi (bar), Giuseppe Morresi (bass), V. Gullino (sgr), Luisa Rezzadore (sgr), N. Sanzogno (cnd), La Scala Orch, La Scala Chorus Budget ("The Greatest Voice in Opera" series) ▲ SYP 108

Donizetti, G.:Lucia di Lammermoor, w. R. Scotto (sop—Lucia), L. Pavarotti (ten—Edgardo), P. Cappuccilli (bar—Enrico), F. Molinari-Pradelli (cnd), Turin RAI Orch, Turin RAI Chorus [I] *(rec live, Turin 10/10/67)* Verona 2-▲ 27083/84

Donizetti, G.:Lucia di Lammermoor, w. J. Sutherland (sop), S. Milnes (bar), N. Ghiaurov (bass), R. Bonynge (cnd), Royal Opera House Orch [I] London 3-▲ 410193-2 [ADD]

Donizetti, G.:Lucia di Lammermoor, w. R. Scotto (sop), *(orch unknown)* Arkadia 2-▲ 540 [AAD]

Donizetti, G.:Lucia di Lammermoor (sels), w. Renato Scotto (sop), Anna Di Stazio (mez), F. Molinari-Pradelli (cnd), Turin RAI SO—Egli s'avanza; Sulla tomba che rinserra *(rec Torino, Oct 10, 1967)* Goldies ▲ GLD 63202 [ADD]

Donizetti, G.:Lucia di Lammermoor (sels), w. F. Molinari-Pradelli (cnd), Turin SO, Turin Sym Chorus—Tombe degl'avi miei *(rec live, June 30, 1967)* RCA Gold Seal ▲ 09026-68014-2 [ADD]

Donizetti, G.:Lucia di Lammermoor (sels), w. J. Sutherland (sop), S. Milnes (bar), N. Ghiaurov (bass), R. Bonynge (cnd), Royal Opera House Orch, Royal Opera House Chorus Covent Garden [I] London ("Opera Gala" series) ▲ 421885-2 [ADD]

Donizetti, G.:Lucia di Lammermoor (sels), w. Christina Deutekom (sop—Lucia), Luciano Pavarotti (ten—Edgardo), Domenico Trimarchi (bar—Enrico Ashton), Silviano Pagliuca (bass—Raimondo Bidebent), C.M. Guilini (cnd), Naples Teatro San Carlo Orch, Naples Teatro San Carlo Chorus Budget ("The Greatest Voice in Opera" series) ▲ SYP 103

Donizetti, G.:Maria Stuarda, w. J. Sutherland (sop), H. Tourangeau (mez), R. Soyer (bar), J. Morris (bass), R. Bonynge (cnd), Bologna Teatro Comunale Orch, Bologna Teatro Comunale Chorus [I] London 2-▲ 425410-2 [ADD]

Donizetti, G.:Requiem Mass, w. M. Cortez (ten), R. Bruson (bar), P. Washington (bass), G. Fackler (cnd), Arena di Verona Orch, Arena di Verona Chorus London ("Ovation" series) ▲ 425043-2 [ADD]

The Essential 3 Tenors, w. José Carreras (ten), Plácido Domingo (ten) RCA Gold Seal ▲ 74321-21273-2 [ADD]

Famous Love Duets, Vol. 2, w. Gianna d'Angelo (sop), Montserrat Caballé (sop), Maria Callas (sop), Renata Scotto (sop), Beverly Sills (sop), Renata Tebaldi (sop), José Carreras (ten), Mario Del Monaco (ten), Giuseppe Di Stefano (ten), Plácido Domingo (ten), et al. Enterprise ("Documents" series) ▲ ENTLV 999

Gala Concert at Royal Albert Hall London ("Jubilee" series) ▲ 430716-2 LM [DDD]

Pavarotti, Luciano (ten) (cont.)

Giordano, U.:Andrea Chénier, w. M. Caballé (sop), L. Nucci (bar), R. Chailly (cnd), National PO London [I] London 2-▲ 410117-2 [DDD]

Gounod, C.:Roméo et Juliette (sels), w. Renata Scotto (sop—Juliet), Giacomo Aragall (ten—Romeo), Luciano Pavarotti (ten—Tebaldo), Gaetano Ferrin (bass—Capellio), Alfredo Giacomotti (bass—Lorenzo), C. Abbado (cnd), La Scala Orch, La Scala Chorus Budget ("The Greatest Voice in Opera" series) ▲ SYP 111

Grandi Voci:Luciano Pavarotti, w. National PO [cnd:Ricardo Chailly, Oliveiro de Fabritis] *(rec 1979)* London ▲ 440400-2 [DDD]

Greatest Hits London 2-▲ 417011-2 LH2 2-■ 417011-4 LH2

Greatest Hits, Vol. 1 London ■ 417013-4 LH

Greatest Hits, Vol. 2 London ■ 417012-4 LH

Greatest Hits, Vol. 2 Butterfly Music ▲ BMC 19 [AAD]

In Concert London [ADD] ■ 417006-4 LH

King of the High C's London ▲ 421326-2 LA [ADD] ■ 417003-4 LH

Leoncavallo, R.:Pagliacci, w. D. Dessi (sop), P. Coni (bar), J. Pons (bar), R. Muti (cnd), Philadelphia Orch [I] Philips ▲ 438132-2

Leoncavallo, R.:Pagliacci, w. M. Freni (sop), I. Wixell (bar), G. Patanè (cnd), National PO London, National Phil London Chorus [I] London 2-▲ 414590-2 [ADD]

Leoncavallo, R.:Pagliacci (sels), w. J. Varady (sop), M. Freni (sop), P. Cappuccilli (bar), I. Wixell (bar), G. Gavazzeni (cnd), National PO London London ▲ 421870-2 [ADD]

Lincoln Center Hits London ■ 417007-4 LH

Live from Lincoln Center, w. Joan Sutherland (sop), Marilyn Horne (mez) London 2-▲ 417587-2 LH [DDD]

Live on Stage, w. Rome Opera Orch [cnd.:Carlo Maria Giulini], Royal Opera House Covent Garden Orch, Royal Opera House Covent Garden Chorus [cnd:Carlo Felice Cillario], et al. LaserLight ▲ 15104

Live Recordings, Vol. 1 (1964-67) LaserLight ▲ 15225

Live Recordings, Vol. 2 (1961-67) LaserLight ▲ 15226

London Records Great Studio Recordings of His Central Park Program, *(rec 1993)* London ▲ 443220-2 [DDD] ■ 443220-4

Luciano Pavarotti in Concert, w. Emilia Romagna Toscanini SO [cnd:Emerson Buckley] CBS ▲ MK 44816 [DDD] ■ MT 44816 (D)

Luciano Pavarotti in Recital *(rec New York, Oct 28, 1973)* Standing Room Only ("800" series) ▲ SRO 846-1 [ADD]

Mamma, w. Mancini Orch [cnd:Henry Mancini] London ▲ 411959-2 LH [DDD] ■ 411959-4 LH

Mascagni, P.:L'amico Fritz, w. M. Freni (sop), V. Sardinero (bar), G. Gavazzeni (cnd), Royal Opera House Orch Covent Garden, Royal Opera House Chorus Covent Garden [I] EMI Classics 2-▲ CDCB 47905 [ADD]

Mascagni, P.:Cavalleria rusticana, w. J. Varady (sop), P. Cappuccilli (bar), G. Gacazzeni (cnd), National PO London, National Phil London Chorus [I] London 2-▲ 414590-2 [ADD]

Mascagni, P.:Cavalleria rusticana (sels), w. Julia Varady (sop), Mirella Freni (sop), Piero Cappuccilli (bar), Ingvar Wixel (bar), G. Gavazzeni (cnd), National PO London London ▲ 421870-2 [ADD]

Massenet, J.:Manon, w. M. Freni (sop), R. Panerai (bar), P. Maag (cnd), La Scala Orch, La Scala Chorus [I] *(rec live, 6/3/69)* Verona 2-▲ 27052/53 (m) [AAD]

Massenet, J.:Manon, w. M. Freni (sop), R. Panerai (bar), P. Maag (cnd), La Scala Orch, La Scala Chorus [I] *(rec live, 6/3/69)* Melodram 2-▲ MEL 27046 [AAD]

Massenet, J.:Manon (sels), w. Mirella Freni (sop), Franco Ricciardi (ten), Wladimiro Ganzarolli (bar), Giuseppe Morresi (bass), Antonio Zerbini (bass), Ida Farina (sgr), P. Maag (cnd), La Scala Orch, La Scala Chorus *(rec live, Milan, 1969)* Budget ("The Greatest Voice in Opera" series) ▲ SYP 110

Mozart, W.A.:Idomeneo, w. L. Popp (sop), E. Gruberova (sop), A. Baltsa (mez), L. Nucci (bar), J. Pritchard (cnd), Vienna PO, Vienna State Opera Chorus [I] London 3-▲ 411805-2 [DDD]

Mozart, W.A.:Idomeneo, w. Gundula Janowitz (sop), Enriqueta Tarres (sop), Richard Lewis (ten), J. Pritchard (cnd), London PO, Glyndebourne Festival Chorus [I] *(rec live at Royal Albert Hall, Aug. 17, 1964)* Verona 2-▲ 27038/39 (m) [AAD]

Mozart, W.A.:Idomeneo, w. Gundula Janowitz (sop), Enriqueta Tarres (sop), Richard Lewis (ten), J. Pritchard (cnd), London PO, Glyndebourne Festival Chorus [I] *(rec live, Royal Albert Hall, London Aug. 17, 1964)* Melodram 2-▲ MEL 27003 (m)

Mozart, W.A.:Idomeneo (sels), w. Gundula Janowitz (sop), Enriqueta Tarres (sop), David Hughes (ten), Richard Lewis (ten), Neilson Taylor (bar), Dennis Wicks (bass), J. Pritchard (cnd), London PO, Glyndebourne Festival Chorus Budget ("The Greatest Voice in Opera" series) ▲ SYP 107

My Heart's Delight, w. N. Focile (sop), Royal PO [cnd:M. Benini] *(rec 1993)* London ▲ 433260-2 Δ 433260-4 ■ 433260-4

O Holy Night, w. National PO [cnd:Kurt Herbert Adler] London ▲ 414044-2 LH [ADD] ■ 414044-4

O sole mio London ▲ 410015-2 LH ■ 410015-4 LH

The Opera Collection Griffin 3-▲ MBSCD 307

Operatic Duets, w. Joan Sutherland (sop) London ▲ 400058-2 LH

Operatic Duets, w. Joan Sutherland (sop) London ("Opera Gala" series) ▲ 421894-2 LM [ADD]

Pavarotti & Friends London ▲ 440100-2 [ADD] ■ 440100-4

Pavarotti & Friends 2, w. Nancy Gustafson (sop), Bryan Adams (sgr), Andreas Vollenweider (kbd), Michael Kamen (cnd), Leone Mageira (cnd), Bologna Community Theater Orch London ▲ 444460-2 ■ 444460-4

Pavarotti & Friends for War Child, w. Eric Clapton (sgr), Sheryl Crow (sgr), Elton John (sgr), Liza Minelli (sgr), Joan Osborne (sgr), Jon Secada (sgr), Eric Clapton (gtr), John McLaughlin (gtr), Marco Armiliato, Edoardo Bennato, José Molina, Al DiMeola, Kelly Family, Ligabue, Litfiba, P *(rec Modena, Italy, 1996)* London ▲ 452900-2 ■ 452900-4

Pavarotti at Carnegie Hall, w. John Wustman (pno) London ▲ 421526-2 [DDD] ■ 421526-4 (D)

Pavarotti:The Early Years, Vol. 1 RCA Gold Seal ▲ 09026-62541-2

Pavarotti in Central Park, w. New York PO members, Harlem Boys Choir, Leone Magiera (cnd) London ▲ 444450-2 ■ 444450-4

Pavarotti in Hyde Park, w. Philharmonia Orch [cnd:Leone Magiera] *(rec live July 1991)* London ▲ 436320-2 [DDD]

Pavarotti Songbook London ▲ 433513-2 LH ■ 433513-4 LH

Ponchielli, A.:La Gioconda, w. M. Caballé (sop), A. Baltsa (mez), S. Milnes (bar), N. Ghiaurov (bass), B. Bartoletti (cnd), National PO [I] London 3-▲ 414349-2 [DDD]

Primo Tenore, w. Pavarotti, Luciano (ten) London ▲ 417713-2 LM

Puccini, G.:Arias, w. M. Caballé (sop), M. Chiara (sop), M. Freni (sop), B. Nilsson (sop), J. Sutherland (sop), R. Tebaldi (sop), F. Corelli (ten), S. Milnes (bar) London ▲ 421315-2 [ADD]

Puccini, G.:Arias—Nessun dorma; Non piangere, Lil...Ah! per l'ultima volta! [both from Turandot]; Che gelda manina; O soave faniculla [w. Mirella Freni (sop)]; In un coupé...O Mim tu non torni [all from La Bohème]; Récondita Armonia; Genta I dentro; Mario! Mario! Mario! [w. Mirella Freni (sop)]; E lucevan le stelle [all from Tosca]; Ch'ella mi creda [from La faniculla del West]; Addio Fiorito Asil; Viene la sera [w. Mirella Freni (sop); both from Madama Butterfly]; Ma se vi talenta...tra voi belle; Donna, non vidi mai [both from Manon Lescaut] London ▲ 425099-2

Puccini, G.:La Bohème, w. M. Freni (sop), M. Adani (sop), L. Saccomani (bar), M. Wolf-Ferrari (cnd), Genoa Teatro Comunale Orch, Genoa Teatro Comunale Chorus *(rec live, Apr 12, 1969)* Melodram 2-▲ MEL 27031 [AAD]

Puccini, G.:La Bohème, w. M. Freni (sop), E. Harwood (sop), R. Panerai (bar), H. von Karajan (cnd), Berlin PO, German Opera Chorus [I] London 2-▲ 421049-2 [ADD] 2-■ 421049-4

Puccini, G.:La Bohème, w. M. Freni (sop), M. Adani (sop), L. Saccomani (bar), M. Wolf-Ferrari (cnd), Genoa Teatro Comunale Orch, Genoa Teatro Comunale Chorus [I] *(rec live 4/12/69)* Verona 2-▲ 27079/80

Puccini, G.:La Bohème (sels), w. T. Schippers (cnd), Rome RAI SO—Che gelida manina *(rec Rome, Nov 19, 1966)* Goldies ▲ GLD 63202 [ADD]

Puccini, G.:La Bohème (sels), w. R. Mattioli (sop), P. Pellegrini (sgr), Bellesia (sgr), F. Molinari-Pradelli (cnd), Reggio Emilia Teatro Municipale Orch—sels from Pavarotti's debut performance *(rec live, Apr 29, 1961)* Melodram 2-▲ MEL 27031 [AAD]

Pavarotti, Luciano (ten) (cont.)
Puccini, G.:La Bohème (sels), w. Bianco Bellisia (sop—Musetta), Alberto Pellegrini (sop—Mimi), Luciano Pavarotti (ten—Rodolfo), Walter de Ambrosis (bar—Schaunard), Vito Mattioli (bar—Marcello), Dmitri Nabokov (bass—Colline), Reggio Emilia Teatro Municipale Orch, Reggio Emilia Teatro Municipale Chorus Budget ("The Greatest Voice in Opera" series) ▲ SYP 105
Puccini, G.:La Bohème (sels), w. M. Freni (sop), E. Harwood (sop), R. Panerai (bar), H. von Karajan (cnd), Berlin PO, German Opera Chorus London ▲ 421245–2 [DDD] ■ 421245–4
Puccini, G.:Madama Butterfly, w. M. Freni (sop), C. Ludwig (mez), R. Kerns (bar), H. von Karajan (cnd), Vienna PO [I] London 3–▲ 417577–2 [ADD]
Puccini, G.:Madama Butterfly (sels), w. M. Freni (sop), C. Ludwig (mez), R. Kerns (bar), H. von Karajan (cnd), Vienna PO [I] London ▲ 421247–2 [ADD] ■ 421247–4
Puccini, G.:Manon Lescaut, w. M. Freni (sop—Manon), C. Bartoli (mez—Musici I), L. Pavarotti (ten—Des Grieux), R. Vargas (ten—Edmondo), D. Croft (ten—Lescaut), G. Taddei (bar—Geronte), J. Levine (cnd), Metropolitan Opera Orch, New York Metropolitan Opera Chorus [I] *(rec 1992)* London ▲ 440200–2 [DDD]
Puccini, G.:Music of, w. Kiri Te Kanawa (sop), Eva Marton (sop), José Carreras (ten), Richard Tucker (ten), *(other artists unknown)*—19 arias & duets from La bohème, Gianni Schicchi, Madama Butterfly, La Rondine, Tosca & Turandot *(six mono & 13 stereo recordings)* CBS ▲ MLK 45809 [AAD/ADD/D ■ MLT 45809
Puccini, G.:Tosca, w. M. Freni (sop), S. Milnes (bar), N. Rescigno (cnd), National PO London [I] London 2–▲ 414036–2 [ADD]
Puccini, G.:Tosca, w. R. Kaibaivanska (sop—Floria), L. Pavarotti (ten—Mario), I. Wixell (bar—Scarpia), F. Federici (bass—Angelotti), D. Oren (cnd), Rome Opera Orch, Rome Opera Chorus RCA Red Seal 2–▲ 09026–61806–2
Puccini, G.:Tosca, w. R. Kaibaivanska (sop—Floria), L. Pavarotti (ten—Mario), I. Wixell (bar—Scarpia), F. Federici (bass—Angelotti), D. Oren (cnd), Rome Opera Orch, Rome Opera Chorus RCA Red Seal ▲ 09026–61807–2; ■ 09026–61807–4
Puccini, G.:Tosca (sels), w. Raina Kabaivanska (sop), Ingvar Wixell (bar), D. Oren (cnd), Rome Opera Orch RCA ("Basic 100" series) ▲ 09026–68455–2 ■ 09026–68455–4
Puccini, G.:Turandot, w. J. Sutherland (sop), M. Caballé (sop), N. Ghiaurov (bass), Z. Mehta (cnd), London PO, John Alldis Choir [I] London 2–▲ 414274–2 [ADD]
Puccini, G.:Turandot, w. Montserrat Caballé (sop—Turandot), Leona Mitchell (sop—Liu), Remy Corazza (ten—Pang), Joseph Franck (ten—Pong), Robert Johnson (ten—Prince of Persia), Raymond Manton (ten—Altoum), Luciano Pavarotti (ten—Calaf), Aldo Bramante (bar—a mandarin), Dale Duesing (bar—Ping), Giorgio Tozzi (bass—Timur), R. Chailly (cnd), *(orch unknown) (rec San Francisco, Nov. 4, 1977)* Legato Classics 2–▲ LCD 188–2
Puccini, G.:Turandot (sels), w. J. Sutherland (sop), M. Caballé (sop), N. Ghiaurov (bass), Z. Mehta (cnd), London PO London ▲ 421320–2 [ADD] ■ 421320–4
Puccini, G.:Turnadot (sels), w. G.–F. Masini (cnd), Grudgionz Festival Orch, Grudgionz Festival Chorus—Nessun dorma *(rec live, Apr. 23, 1964)* RCA Gold Seal ▲ 09026–68014–2 [ADD]
Puccini, G.:Turandot (sels), w. G.–F. Masini (cnd), Grudgionz Opera Theater Orch, Grudgionz Opera Theater Chorus—Nessun dorma *(rec Grudgionz, Apr 23, 1964)* Goldies ▲ GLD 63202 [ADD]
Recital, w. various orchs Melodram 2–▲ CDM 26507 (m) [AAD]
Rossini, G.:Stabat Mater, w. T. Zylis–Gara (sop), S. Verrett (mez), N. Zaccaria (bass), C.M. Giulini (cnd), Rome Radio Orch, Rome RAI Chorus [L] *(rec live 12/22/67)* Verona 2–▲ 27060/61 (m) [AAD]
Rossini, G.:Stabat Mater, w. T. Zylis–Gara (sop), S. Verrett (mez), N. Zaccaria (bass), C. M. Giulini (cnd), Rome RAI Orch, Rome RAI Chorus [L] *(rec live 12/22/67)* Melodram 2–▲ MEL 28012
Rossini, G.:Stabat Mater, w. C. M. Giulini (cnd), Rome RAI SO—Cuius aninam *(rec Rome, Dec 22, 1967)* Goldies ▲ GLD 63202 [ADD]
Rossini, G.:Stabat Mater, w. Teresa Zylis–Gara (sop), Shirley Verrett (mez), Nicola Zaccaria (bass), C. M. Giulini (cnd), Rome RAI Orch, Rome RAI Chorus *(rec Rome, Dec. 1967)* Emozioni ▲ ARCD 2041
Scenes & Arias Verona 2–▲ 28005/6
Tenorissimi, Mondiale 90, w. José Carreras (ten), Plácido Domingo (ten) EMI Classics ▲ CDC 54109
Tenors Greatest Hits, w. Placido Domingo (ten), José Carerras (ten) RCA Victor ▲ 09026–62709–2 ■ 09026–62709–4
The Three Tenors In Concert, w. José Carreras (ten), P. Domingo (ten), Zubin Mehta (cnd) *(rec Rome, July 7, 1990)* London ▲ 430433–2 ■ 430433–4 □ 430433–5
Tutto Pavarotti London 2–▲ 425681–2 LM2 [ADD/DDD] 2–■ 425681–4 LM2
Verdi, G.:Aida, w. M. Chiara (sop), G. Dimitrova (sop), L. Nucci (bar), P. Burchuladze (bass), L. Maazel (cnd), La Scala Orch, La Scala Chorus [I] London □ 433162–5
Verdi, G.:Aida, w. M. Chiara (sop), G. Dimitrova (sop), L. Nucci (bar), P. Burchuladze (bass), L. Maazel (cnd), La Scala Orch, La Scala Chorus [I] London 3–▲ 417439–2 [DDD] 2–■ 417439–4
Verdi, G.:Arias, w. K. Battle (sop), J. Sutherland (sop), J. Anderson (sop), M. Price (sop), L. Nucci (bar)—includes favorite arias from Aida, Ballo in maschera, Don Carlos, Nabucco, Rigoletto, Traviata, Trovatore London ("Ovation" series) ▲ 430748–2 [DDD]
Verdi, G.:Arias—Rigoletto, La boheme & La traviata Laserlight ▲ 15 104
Verdi, G.:Arias, w. C. Abbado (cnd), La Scala Orch [I] CBS ▲ MK 37228 ■ MT 37228
Verdi, G.:Arias, *(various cnds & orchs)*—arias from Aida, Ballo in maschera, Rigoletto, Traviata, Trovatore [I] London ▲ 417570–2 [DDD/ADD]
Verdi, G.:Un ballo in maschera, w. Gabriele Lechner (sop), Piero Cappuccilli (bar), C. Abbado (cnd), Vienna PO, Vienna State Opera Chorus *(rec live, 1986)* Serenissima 2–▲ SER 360118
Verdi, G.:Un ballo in maschera, w. R. Tebaldi (sop), S. Milnes (bar), B. Bartoletti (cnd), St. Cecilia Academy Orch Rome, St. Cecilia Academy Chorus Rome London ▲ 440042–2
Verdi, G.:Un ballo in maschera, w. M. Price (sop), K. Battle (sop), C. Ludwig (mez), R. Bruson (bar), G. Solti (cnd), National PO London, National Phil London Chorus [I] London 2–▲ 410210–2 [DDD]
Verdi, G.:Un ballo in maschera, w. R. Orlandi Malaspina (sop—Ameilia), D. Mazzuccato (sop—Oscar), A. Lazzarini (mez—Ulrica), L. Pavarotti (ten—Riccardo), M. Zanasi (bar—Renato), A. Zerbini (bass—Samuel), G. Casarini (bass—Tom), G. Zecchillo (bass—Sil) Golden Age of Opera 2–▲ GAO 164/65 [ADD]
Verdi, G.:Un ballo in maschera, w. M. Price (sop), K. Battle (sop), C. Ludwig (mez), R. Bruson (bar), G. Solti (cnd), National PO London, National Phil London Chorus [I] London ▲ 425529–2 [DDD]
Verdi, G.:Un ballo in maschera (sels), w. M. Arroyo (sop), C. Mackerras (cnd), San Francisco Opera Orch—Ma dall'arido stelo...Teco io sto *(rec Nov. 5, 1971)* Golden Age of Opera 2–▲ GAO 164/65 [ADD]
Verdi, G.:I lombardi alla prima crociata, w. R. Scotto (sop), R. Raimondi (bass), G. Gavazzeni (cnd), Rome Opera Orch, Rome Opera Chorus [I] *(rec live, Rome, 11/20/69)* Memories 2–▲ HR 4337/38 [ADD]
Verdi, G.:I lombardi alla prima crociata (sels), w. Sofia Mazzetti (sop), G. Gavazzeni (cnd), Rome Opera Orch—O madre mia...La mia letizia infondere *(rec live, Nov. 20, 1969)* RCA Gold Seal ▲ 09026–68014–2 [ADD]
Verdi, G.:Luisa Miller (sels), w. P. Maag (cnd), Turin RAI SO—Oh! fede negar potessi agl'occhi mieil; Quando le sere al placido *(rec Torino, 1969)* Goldies ▲ GLD 63202 [ADD]
Verdi, G.:Luisa Miller (sels), w. N. Bonavolontà (cnd), Rome SO—Oh! fede negar potessi...Quando le sere al placido *(rec live, Jan. 1, 1967)* RCA Gold Seal ▲ 09026–68014–2 [ADD]
Verdi, G.:Otello, w. K. Te Kanawa (sop), L. Nucci (bar), G. Solti (cnd), Chicago SO, Chicago Sym Chorus [I] London 2–▲ 433669–2 [DDD]
Verdi, G.:Requiem Mass, w. L. Price (sop), F. Cossotto (mez), N. Ghiaurov (bass), H. von Karajan (cnd), La Scala Orch, La Scala Chorus [L] *(rec live 1/16/67)* Verona 2–▲ 27060/61 (m) [AAD]
Verdi, G.:Requiem Mass, w. J. Sutherland (sop), M. Horne (mez), M. Talvela (bass), G. Solti (cnd), Vienna PO, Vienna State Opera Chorus [L] London 2–▲ 411944–2 [ADD]
Verdi, G.:Requiem Mass, w. L. Price (sop), F. Cossotto (mez), N. Ghiaurov (bass), H. von Karajan (cnd), La Scala Orch, La Scala Chorus [L] *(rec live 1/16/67)* Melodram 2–▲ MEL 28012
Verdi, G.:Rigoletto, w. J. Sutherland (sop), H. Tourangeau (mez), S. Milnes (bar), M. Talvela (bass), R. Bonynge (cnd), London SO, London Sym Chorus [I] London 2–▲ 414269–2 [ADD]
Verdi, G.:Rigoletto (sels), w. M. Rossi (cnd), Turin SO—Questa o quella; ella mi fu rapita...Parmi veder le lagrime; La donna è mobile *(rec live, Dec. 26, 1967)* RCA Gold Seal ▲ 09026–68014–2 [ADD]
Verdi, G.:Rigoletto (sels), w. Renata Scotto (sop—Gilda), Corinna Vozza (mez—Giovanna), Bianca Vortoluzzi (cta—Maddalena), Luciano Pavarotti (ten—Duke of Mantua), Kostas Paskalis (bar—Rigoletto), Paolo Washington (bass—Sparafucile), C. M. Guilini (cnd), Rome Opera Orch, Rome Opera Chorus Budget ("The Greatest Voice in Opera" series) ▲ SYP 104

Pavarotti, Luciano (ten) (cont.)
Verdi, G.:Rigoletto (sels), w. C. M. Giulini (cnd), Rome Opera Orch—La Donna è mobile Goldies ▲ GLD 63202 [ADD]
Verdi, G.:Rigoletto (sels), w. J. Anderson (sop), S. Verrett (mez), L. Nucci (bar), N. Ghiaurov (bass), R. Chailly (cnd), Bologna Teatro Comunale Orch, Bologna Teatro Comunale Chorus London ▲ 436097–2 [DDD]
Verdi, G.:La traviata, w. R. Scotto (sop), P. Glossop (bar), C. F. Cillario (cnd), Royal Opera House Orch, Royal Opera House Chorus Covent Garden *(rec live 1965)* Memories 2–▲ HR 4404/05 (m)
Verdi, G.:La traviata, w. J. Sutherland (sop), M. Manuguerra (bar), R. Bonynge (cnd), National PO London, London Opera Chorus [I] London ▲ 400057–2 [DDD] ■ 400057–4
Verdi, G.:La traviata, w. J. Sutherland (sop), M. Manuguerra (bar), R. Bonynge (cnd), National PO London, London Opera Chorus [I] London 2–▲ 430491–2 [DDD]
Verdi, G.:La traviata (sels), w. Loretta di Franco (sop), Joan Sutherland (sop), Frederica von Stade (mez), Leo Goeke (ten), Lou Marcella (ten), Luciano Pavarotti (ten), Gene Boucher (bar), Raymond Gibbs (bar), Sherrill Milnes (bar), Louis Sgarro (bar), John Trehy (bar) Budget ("The Greatest Voice in Opera" series) ▲ SYP 112
Verdi, G.:La traviata (sels), w. L. Magiera (cnd), Modena Teatro Comunale Orch—Lunge da lei...de' miei bollenti spiriti *(rec live, Feb. 7, 1965)* RCA Gold Seal ▲ 09026–68014–2 [ADD]
Verdi, G.:La traviata (sels), w. R. Scotto (sop), C. F. Cillario (cnd), Royal Opera House Orch, Royal Opera House Chorus Covent Garden—2 scenes [I] *(rec live, Covent Garden 3/19/65)* Verona 2–▲ 27081/82
Verdi, G.:La traviata (sels), w. R. Scotto (sop), C. F. Cillario (cnd), Royal Opera House Orch—4 arias *(rec live 3/25/65)* Legato Classics 2–▲ LCD 148–2 [ADD]
Verdi, G.:Il trovatore, w. J. Sutherland (sop), M. Horne (mez), I. Wixell (bar), N. Ghiaurov (bass), R. Bonynge (cnd), National PO London [I] London 2–▲ 417137–2 [ADD]
Verdi, G.:Il trovatore, w. Antonella Banaudi (sop—Leonora), Barbara Frittoli (sop—Ines), Shirley Verrett (mez—Azucena), Enrico Facini (ten—Un messo), Piero de Palma (ten—Ruiz), Luciano Pavarotti (ten—Marico), Leo Nucci (bar—Il Conte di Luna), Roberto Scaltriti (bar—Un vecchio zingaro), Francesco Ellero d'Artegna (bass—Ferrando), Z. Mehta (cnd), Florence Maggio Musicale Orch, Florence Maggio Musicale Chorus *(rec Maggio Musicale Fiorentino Community Theater, June 18–July 2, 1990)* London 2–▲ 430694–2
Verdi, G.:Il trovatore (sels), w. J. Sutherland (sop), M. Horne (mez), R. Bonynge (cnd), National PO London London ▲ 421310–2 [ADD]
Verismo Arias London ▲ 400083–2 LH [DDD]
Vincerò, w. Bologna CO [cnd:Loene Magiera] *(rec Milan, May 27, 1990)* Replay ▲ 8005
Volare, w. Mancini Orch [cnd:Henry Mancini] London ▲ 421052–2 LH [DDD] ■ 421052–4 LH (D) □ 421052–5
World's Favorite Tenor Arias London ▲ 400053–2 LH ■ 400053–4 LH

Pavlová, Jitka (sop)
Mozart, W.A.:Requiem, w. Polovecova (mez), Vorapajev (ten), Gennadi Bezzubenkov (bass), M. Glinka (cnd), Ljubljana SO, Leningrad Chorus [L] Stradivari Classics ▲ SCD 6003 [DDD] ■ SMC 6003 (D)

Pavon, Pablo (sgr)
Mendelssohn, F.:Psalms, Op. 78, w. Christiane Buntschu (sgr), Natacha Casagrande (sgr), Kurt Kempf (sgr), M. Corboz (cnd), Lausanne Vocal Ensemble *(rec Lausanne Cathedral, Jan. 29–31, 1994)* FNAC Music ▲ 592298 [DDD]

Pawlak, Edward (bass)
Baird, T.:Tomorrow, w. K. Szostek–Radkowa (mez), J. Artysz (bar), J. Ostrowski (nar), R. Czajkowski (cnd), Poznan Philharmonic SO [Pol] Olympia ▲ OCD 326 [AAD]
Moniuszko, S.:Halka, w. Barbara Nieman (sop), Halina Sloniowska (sop), Jan Góralski (ten), Bogdan Paprocki (ten), Leslaw Pawluk (ten), Kazimierz Pustelak (ten), Andrzej Hiolski (bar), Edmund Kossowski (bass), Z. Gorzynski (cnd), Warsaw State Opera House Orch, Warsaw National Opera Chorus *(rec Warsaw, 1965)* Polskie Nagrania ▲ PNCD 092 [AAD]

Pawluk, Leslaw (ten)
Moniuszko, S.:Halka, w. Barbara Nieman (sop), Halina Sloniowska (sop), Jan Góralski (ten), Bogdan Paprocki (ten), Kazimierz Pustelak (ten), Andrzej Hiolski (bar), Edmund Kossowski (bass), Edward Pawlak (bass), Z. Gorzynski (cnd), Warsaw State Opera House Orch, Warsaw National Opera Chorus *(rec Warsaw, 1965)* Polskie Nagrania ▲ PNCD 092 [AAD]

Pay, Sam (bar)
Britten, H.:The Turn of the Screw, w. F. Lott (sop), N. Secunde (sop), E. Hulse (sop), P. Cannan (mez), P. Langridge (ten), S. Bedford (cnd), Aldeburgh Festival Ensemble Collins Classics ▲ COL 7030 [DDD]

Payen, Paul (bar)
Puccini, G.:Tosca (sels), w. M.–C. Vallin (sop), E. di Mazzei (ten), A. Endrèze (bar), G. Cloëz (cnd), Paris Opéra–Comique Orch, Paris Opéra–Comique Chorus [abridged version] [F] *(rec 1932)* Music Memoria ▲ 30376

Payne, Patricia (mez)
Beethoven, L. van:Mass, Op. 86, w. A. Tomwa–Sintow (sop), R. Tear (ten), R. Lloyd (bass), C. Davis (cnd), London SO, London Sym Chorus [G] Philips 2–▲ 438362–2
Beethoven, L. van:Missa Solemnis, w. A. Tomwa–Sintow (sop), R. Tear (ten), R. Lloyd (bass), C. Davis (cnd), London SO, London Sym Chorus [G] Philips 2–▲ 438362–2
Ponchielli, A.:La Gioconda, w. M. Caballé (sop—Gioconda), M. L. Nave (mez—Laura), P. Payne (mez—La Cieca), J. Carreras (ten—Enzo), M. Manuguerra (bar—Barnaba), B. Giaiotti (bass—Alvise), J. López–Cobos (cnd), *(orch unknown) (rec Dec. 6, 1979)* Legato Classics ▲ LCD 170–2 [ADD]

Pearce, Judith (sgr)
Sings Classic Irish Songs, w. Neill (hp) Protone ■ CSPR 162

Pears, Peter (ten)
Bach, J.S.:Cant 67, w. K. Engen (bass), K. Richter (cnd), Munich Bach Orch, Munich Bach Choir Teldec ▲ 9031–77614–2
Bach, J.S.:Cant 108, w. K. Engen (bass), K. Richter (cnd), Munich Bach Orch, Munich Bach Choir Teldec ▲ 9031–77614–2
Bach, J.S.:Cant 127, w. K. Engen (bass), K. Richter (cnd), Munich Bach Orch, Munich Bach Choir Teldec ▲ 9031–77614–2
Bach, J.S.:Mass in b, BWV 232, w. L. Marshall (sop), H. Töpper (mez), K. Borg (bass), E. Jochum (cnd), Bavarian RSO, Bavarian Radio Chorus Philips 2–▲ 438739–2
Britten, H.:Albert Herring, w. S. Fisher (sop), A. Cantelo (sop), S. Rex (mez), J. Noble (bar), O. Brannigan (bass), B. Britten (cnd), English CO [E] London 2–▲ 421849–2 [ADD]
Britten, H.:Billy Budd, w. T. Uppman (bar), H. Alan (bar), G. Evans (b–bar), F. Dalberg (bass), B. Britten (cnd), Royal Opera House Orch, Royal Opera House Chorus Covent Garden *(rec Dec. 1, 1951)* VAI Audio 3–▲ VAIA 1034–3 [ADD]
Britten, H.:Billy Budd, w. P. Glossop (bar), J. Shirley–Quirk (bar), B. Luxon (bar), M. Langdon (bass), O. Brannigan (bass), B. Britten (cnd), London SO, Ambrosian Singers [E] London 3–▲ 417428–2 [ADD]
Britten, H.:Death in Venice, w. J. Bowman (ct), J. Shirley–Quirk (bar), S. Bedford (cnd), English CO, English Opera Group Chorus [E] London 2–▲ 425669–2 [ADD]
Britten, H.:Folksong Arrs, w. J. Cross (sop), B. Britten (pno) EMI Classics ▲ CDMB 64727
Britten, H.:Hölderlin–Fragmente, w. B. Britten (pno) London 2–▲ 433200–2
Britten, H.:The Holy Sonnets of John Donne, w. B. Britten (pno) EMI Classics ▲ CDC 54605
Britten, H.:The Holy Sonnets of John Donne, w. B. Britten (pno) [E] London 3–▲ 417428–2 [ADD]
Britten, H.:Les Illuminations, w. B. Britten (cnd), English CO [F] London ▲ 417153–2 [ADD]
Britten, H.:A Midsummer Night's Dream, w. E. Harwood (sop), J. Veasey (mez), H. Watts (cta), A. Deller (ct), J. Shirley–Quirk (bar), B. Britten (cnd), London SO, London Sym Chorus [E] London 2–▲ 425663–2 [ADD]
Britten, H.:Music of, w. Julian Bream (gtr) RCA Gold Seal ▲ 09026–61601–2
Britten, H.:Owen Wingrave, w. S. Fisher (Miss Wingrave), J. Vyvyan (Mrs. Julian), H. Harper (Mrs. Coyle), J. Baker (Kate), B. Luxon (Owen Wingrave), J. Shirley–Quirk (Coyle), B. Britten, Wandworth School Boys' Choir, English CO London 2–▲ 433200–2
Britten, H.:Peter Grimes, w. C. Watson (sop), G. Evans (bar), B. Britten (cnd), Royal Opera House Orch, Royal Opera House Chorus Covent Garden [E] London 3–▲ 414577–2 [ADD]
Britten, H.:Peter Grimes (sels), w. J. Cross (sop), R. Goodall (cnd), *(orch unknown)* EMI Classics ▲ CDMB 64727

1342

▲ = CD ♦ = Enhanced CD Δ = MD ■ = Cassette Tape □ = DCC

Pears, Peter (ten) (cont.)

Britten, H.:The Rape of Lucretia, w. H. Harper (sop), J. Baker (mez), B. Drake (bar), B. Luxon (bar), J. Shirley-Quirk (bar), B. Britten (cnd), English CO London 2-▲ 425666-2 [ADD]

Britten, H.:The Rape of Lucretia (sels), w. J. Cross (sop), R. Goodall (cnd), *(orch unknown)* EMI Classics ▲ CDMB 64727

Britten, H.:The Rape of Lucretia (sels), w. Joan Cross (sop—Female Chorus), Kathleen Ferrier (cta—Lucretia), Peter Pears (ten—Male Chorus), Otakar Kraus (sgr—Tarquinius), B. Britten (cnd), English Opera Group Orch *(rec Oct 5, 1946)* Music & Arts ▲ CD 901 [ADD]

Britten, H.:Serenade, Op. 31, w. Dennis Brain (hn), B. Britten (cnd), Boyd Neel String Orch Pearl ▲ PEA 9177 [ADD]

Britten, H.:Serenade, Op. 31, w. B. Britten (cnd), Boyd Neel String Orch *(rec 5/25/44)* London ("Historic" series) ▲ 425996-2 [ADD]

Britten, H.:Serenade, Op. 31, w. B. Tuckwell (hn), B. Britten (cnd), London SO [E] London ▲ 417153-2 [ADD]

Britten, H.:Songs & Proverbs of William Blake, w. D. Fischer-Dieskau (bar) [E] London 3-▲ 417428-2 [ADD]

Britten, H.:Sonnets of Michelangelo, w. B. Britten (cnd), Boyd Neel String Orch *(rec 7/54)* London ("Historic" series) ▲ 425996-2 [AAD]

Britten, H.:Sonnets of Michelangelo, w. Benjamin Britten (pno) *(rec 1941-44)* Pearl ▲ PEA 9177 [ADD]

Britten, H.:Sonnets of Michelangelo, w. B. Britten (pno) EMI Classics ▲ CDC 54605

Britten, H.:The Turn of the Screw, w. O. Dyer (sop), J. Vyvyan (sop), A. Mandikian (mez), D. Hemmings (trb), G. Cross (ten), B. Britten (cnd), English Opera Group Orch [E] London ▲ 425672-2 (m) [ADD]

Britten, H.:War Requiem, w. G. Vishnevskaya (sop), D. Fischer-Dieskau (bar), B. Britten (cnd), London SO, London Sym Chorus [E,L] London 2-▲ 414383-2 [ADD]

Seiber, M.:Music of, w. Julian Bream (gtr) RCA Gold Seal ▲ 09026-61601-2

Walton, W.:Music of, w. Julian Bream (gtr) RCA Gold Seal ▲ 09026-61601-2

Walton, W.:Troilus & Cressida (sels), w. E. Schwarzkopf (sop), M. Sinclair (cta), R. Lewis (ten), W. Walton (cnd), Philharmonia Orch—scenes EMI Classics ▲ ZDM 64199

Pearson (sgr)

Ligeti, G.:Aventures, w. Charlent (sgr), Cahn (sgr), B. Maderna (cnd), Darmstadt International Chamber Ensemble Wergo ▲ WER 60045-50 [ADD]

Ligeti, G.:Nouvelles aventures, w. Charlent (sgr), Cahn (sgr), B. Maderna (cnd), Darmstadt International Chamber Ensemble Wergo ▲ WER 60045-50 [ADD]

Pechan, Kornél (ten)

Werner, G.J.:Vesperae de Confessoris, w. Éva Bodrogi (sop), Regina Fülöp (cta), Péter Cser (bass), János Mezei (org), J. Mezei (cnd), Vienna-Szász CO, Budapest Schola Cantorum *(rec St. Columba's Presbyterian Church, Budapest, June 12-15, 1995)* Hungaroton ▲ HCD 31646 [DDD]

Pechner, Gerhard (bar)

Verdi, G.:La forza del destino, w. Z. Milanov (sop), M. Del Monaco (ten), L. Warren (bar), W. Wildermann (bass), W. Herbert (cnd), *(orch unknown)* *(rec live 1953)* Legato Classics 2-▲ LCD 118-2 (m) [AAD]

Pecile, Mirna (cta)

Donizetti, G.:Belisario, w. L. Gencer (sop), U. Grilli (ten), G. Taddei (bar), N. Zaccaria (bass), G. Gavazzeni (cnd), Venice Teatro La Fenice Orch, Venice Teatro La Fenice Chorus [I] *(rec live, Venice 5/14/69)* Melodram 2-▲ MEL 27051 [AAD]

Donizetti, G.:Belisario, w. L. Gencer (sop), U. Grilli (ten), G. Taddei (bar), N. Zaccaria (bass), G. Gavazzeni (cnd), Venice Teatro La Fenice Orch, Venice Teatro La Fenice Chorus [I] *(rec live in Venice, 5/14/69)* Verona 2-▲ 27048/49 (m) [AAD]

Verdi, G.:Un ballo in maschera, w. Ghena Dimitrova (sop—Amelia), Isabella Stramaglia (sop—Oscar), Mirna Pecile (cta—Ulrica), Mario Carlin (ten—Un giudice), José Carreras (ten—Riccardo), Piero Cappuccilli (bar—Renato), Massimiliano Malaspina (bass—Samuel), Americo de Santis (bass—Silvano), Francesco Signor (bass—Tom), Ivan Del Manto (sgr—Un servo), G. Patanè (cnd), Parma Teatro Regio Orch *(rec Teatro Regio, Dec. 26, 1972)* Golden Age of Opera 2-▲ GAO 183/84

Pecková, Dagmar (mez)

Dvořák, A.:Biblical Songs, Op. 99, w. J. Belohlávek (cnd), Czech PO—Nos. 1-5 *(rec House of Artists, Prague, Jan 4-7, 1996)* Canyon Classics 2-▲ 322

Janácek, L.:Folk Ballads, w. Ivan Kusnjer (bar), Marian Kaplansky (pno) Supraphon ▲ SUP 112225 [DDD]

Janácek, L.:Hukvaldy Folk Poetry, w. Ivan Kusnjer (bar), Marian Kaplansky (pno) Supraphon ▲ SUP 112214 [DDD]

Janácek, L.:Moravian Folk Poetry, w. Ivan Kusnjer (bar), Marian Kaplansky (pno) Supraphon ▲ SUP 112214 [DDD]

Janácek, L.:Silesian Songs, w. Ivan Kusnjer (bar), Marian Kaplansky (pno) Supraphon ▲ SUP 112214 [DDD]

Live in Prague, w. Ivan Kusjner (bar), Prague National Theater Orch [cnd:Jan Stych] *(rec live, Jan 17, 1996)* Supraphon ▲ SUP 3180

Mahler, G.:Kindertotenlieder, w. J. Belohlávek (cnd), Prague Chamber PO Supraphon ▲ SUP 3030

Mahler, G.:Lieder eines fahrenden Gesellen, w. J. Belohlávek (cnd), Prague Chamber PO Supraphon ▲ SUP 3030

Mahler, G.:Songs from Rückert, w. J. Belohlávek (cnd), Prague Chamber PO Supraphon ▲ SUP 3030

Respighi, O.:La bella dormente nel bosco, w. Ivana Czaková (sop—Old Woman/Green Fairy), Adriana Kohútková (sop—Blue Fairy/Nightingale), Henrietta Lednárová (sop—Frog/Spindle), Jana Valásková (sop—Princess), Dagmar Pecková (mez—Cuckoo/Cat), Denisa Slepkovská (mez—Queen/Duchess), Karol Bernáth (ten—Doctor), Guillermo Dominguez (ten—Prince April), Igor Pasek (ten—Jester), Ján Durčo (bar—Ambassador), Richard Haan (bar—King/Woodcutter), Stanislav Benačka (bass—Doctor), Anton Kúrnava (bass—Doctor), Marián Smolárik (bass—Doctor), M. Adriano (nar—Mr. Dollar Chèques), M. Adriano (cnd), Slovak RSO Bratislava, Ján Rozehnal (cnd), Slovak Phil Chorus *(rec Concert Hall of the Slovak Radio, Bratislava, June 8-20, 1994)* Marco Polo ("Opera Classics" series) ▲ 8.223742 [DDD]

Slavický, K.:Psalmi, w. Salome Losová (sop), Vladimir Dolezal (ten), Ludek Vele (bass), Jan Hora (org), P. Kühn (cnd), Kühn Chorus *(rec Dvořák Hall of Rudolfinum, Prague, Mar. 14-16, 1989)* Panton ("Protokol XX" series) ▲ PAN 811142 [DDD]

Pedaci, Francesca (sop)

Cherubini, L.:Lodoïska, w. M. Devia (sop), B. Lombardo (ten), T. Moser (ten), A. Corbelli (bar), W. Shimell (bar), R. Muti (cnd), La Scala Orch, La Scala Chorus Sony Classical 2-▲ SM2K 47290

Pacini, G.:Saffo, w. Francesca Pedaci (sop—Saffo), Gemma Bertagnolli (sop—Dirce), Mariana Pentcheva (mez—Climene), Carlo Ventre (ten—Faone), Aled Hall (ten—Ippia), Roberto de Candia (bar—Alcandro), Davide Baronchelli (bass—Lisimaco), M. Benini (cnd), Irish National SO, Lubomír Mátl (cnd), Wexford Festival Opera Chorus *(rec Wexford, Oct & Nov 1995)* Marco Polo 2-▲ 8.223883-4 [DDD]

Pedani, Paolo (bar)

Strauss, R.:Der Rosenkavalier, w. Jarmila Barton (sop—Marianne), Lisa Della Casa (sop—Sophie), Sena Jurinac (sop—Octavian), Ilva Ligabue (sop—Orphan), Elisabeth Schwarzkopf (sop—Marschallin), Else Schürhoff (mez—Annina), Luisa Villa (mez—Milliner), Hugues Cuénod (ten—Marschallin's majordomo), Erich Majkut (ten—Valzacchi), Giuseppe Nessi (ten—Animal seller), Luciano Della Pergola (ten—Lackey/Faninal's majordomo), Antonio Pirino (ten—An Italian Singer), Gino Del Signore (ten—Lackey/Waiter), Erich Kunz (bar—Herr von Faninal), Paolo Pedani (bar—Lackey), Attilo Barbesi (bass—Lackey/Waiter), Enrico Campi (bass—Waiter), Otto Edelmann (bass—Baron Ochs), Bruno Fichtinger (bass—Notary), Franco Taino (bass—Waiter), Maria Amadini (sgr—Orphan), Pina Carrillo (sgr—Orphan), Joszi Trojan Regar (sgr—Innkeeper), H. von Karajan (cnd), La Scala Orch, La Scala Chorus *(rec La Scala Theater, Milan, Jan. 26, 1952)* Legato Classics 3-▲ LCD 197-3

Pederson, Monte (bar)

Schreker, F.:Die Gezeichneten, w. Elisabeth Connell (sop), Heinz Kruse (ten), Alfred Muff (bass), László Polgar (bass), L. Zagrosek (cnd), Berlin German SO London 3-▲ 444442-2

Schreker, F.:Irrelohe, w. Eva Randová (mez—Old Lola), Michael Pabst (ten—Count Heinrich), Monte Pederson (bar—Peter), Neven Belamaric (sgr—The Parson), Luana Devol (sgr—Eva), Sebastian Holecek (sgr—The Miller), Goran Smimic (sgr—The Forester) Sony Classical 2-▲ S2K 66850

Pederzoli, Maura (sop)

Perti, G.A.:Liturgy for Good Friday, w. Patrizia Vaccari (sop), Cristina Calzolari (sop), Alida Oliva (sop), Claudia Bugli (sop), Lucia Bagnoli (alt), Cinzia Meneghel (alt), Renzo Bez (alt), Alessandro Carmignani (alt), Michel van Goethem (alt), Mauro Collina (ten), Vincenzo Di Donato (ten), Paolo Fanciullacci (ten), Giovanni Caccamo (ten), Paolo Da Col (ten), Sergio Foresti (bass), Marco Scavazza (bass), Luca Ferracin (bass), Paride Montanari (bass), Liuwe Tamminga (org), Sergio Vartolo (org), S. Vartolo (cnd), Bologna San Petronio Capella Musicale Orch—Omnes amici mei; De lamentatione Jeremiae Prophetae:Heth. Cogitavit; Velum templi; Vinea mea; De lamentatione Jeremiae Prophetae:Lamed. Matribus suis; Tamquam ad latronem; Tenebrae factae sunt; Animam meam; Tradiderunt me; Jesum tradidit; De lamentatione Jeremiae Prophetae:Aleph. Ego vir; Caligaverunt *(rec St. Petronio Basilica, Bologna, Mar 28-31, 1995)* Naxos ▲ 8.553321 [DDD]

Pediconi, Fiorella (sop)

Paisiello, G.:Nina, o sia La pazza per amore, w. M. Bolgan (sop), D. Bernardini (ten), F. Musinu (bass), G. Surian (bass), R. Bonynge (cnd), Catania Teatro Massimo Bellini Orch, Catania Teatro Massimo Bellini Chorus [I] *(rec live 1989)* Nuova Era 2-▲ 6872/73 [DDD]

Pergolesi, G.B.:Il flaminio, w. D. Dessi (sop—Flaminio), F. Pediconi (sop—Agata), E. Zilio (mez—Giustina), M. Ferrugia (ten—Fernando), G. Sica (ten—Polidoro), V. Baiano (bass-Checa), S. Pagliuca (bass—Bastiano), M. Panni (cnd), Naples Teatro San Carlo Orch *(rec Nov. 12, 1983)* Fonit Cetra 3-▲ CDC 39 [ADD]

Rossini, G.:Torvaldo e Dorliska, w. A. Buda (sop), M. Ciliento (mez), E. Palacio (ten), S. Antonucci (bar), A. Marani (b-bar), M. de Bernart (cnd), Swiss-Italian Orch, Cantemus, Swiss-Italian Radio-TV Chorus *(rec Jan. 11, 1992)* Arkadia-Akademia 2-▲ 123 [DDD]

Pedroni, Augusto (ten)

Bellini, V.:I Puritani, w. A. Maliponte (sop—Elvira), A. di Stasio (sop—Enrichetta di Francia), A. Kraus (ten—Lord Arturo Talbo), A. Pedroni (ten—Bruno Roberton), P. Cappuccilli (bar—Sir Riccardo Forth), R. Raimondi (bass—Sir Giorgio), G. Gavazzeni (cnd), Catania Teatro Massimo Bellini Orch, Catania Teatro Massimo Bellini Chorus *(rec Feb. 6, 1972)* Ornamenti 2-▲ FE 107 [ADD]

Bellini, V.:I Puritani, w. Mirella Freni (sop—Elvira), Rita Bezzi (mez—Enrichetta), Alfredo Kraus (ten—Arturo Talbot), Augusto Pedroni (ten—Sir Bruno Robertson), Attilio d'Orazi (bar—Sir Riccardo Forth), Raffaele Arié (bass—Sir Giorgio), Bruno Cioni (bass—Lord Gualtiero Walton), N. Verchi (cnd), Modena Teatro Comunale Orch, Modeno Teatro Comunale Chorus *(rec Modena Teatro Comunale, Dec. 26, 1962)* Legato Classics 2-▲ LCD 195-2 [ADD]

Pedrotti, Mark (bar)

Bach, J.S.:Cant 140, w. Rosemarie Landry (sop), Ben Heppner (ten), W. Riddell (cnd), CBC Vancouver SO, Tudor Singers of Montreal CBC ▲ 5163 [DDD]

Beethoven, L. van:Songs, w. S. Ralls (pno)—Adelaïde [G] CBC ("Musica Viva" series) ▲ MVCD 1051 [DDD]

Brahms, J.:Songs, w. S. Ralls (pno)—Alte Liebe; An die Nachtigall; Feldeinsamkeit; Immer leiser und wird mein Schlummer; Wie Melodien [G] CBC ("Musica Viva" series) ▲ MVCD 1051 [DDD]

Duparc, H.:Songs, w. S. Ralls (pno)—Chanson triste; L'invitation au voyage; Le manoir de Rosamonde; Phidylé [F] CBC ("Musica Viva" series) ▲ MVCD 1051 [DDD]

Morawetz, O.:Psalm 22, w. S. Ralls (pno) Centrediscs ▲ CDCCD 3589 [DDD]

Morawetz, O.:Songs, w. S. Ralls (pno)—Chimney-Sweeper; Grenadier; Mad Song [E] CBC ("Musica Viva" series) ▲ MVCD 1051 [DDD]

Morawetz, O.:Souvenirs, w. S. Ralls (pno) Centrediscs ▲ CDCCD 3589 [DDD]

Strauss, R.:Songs, w. S. Ralls (pno)—Befreit; Heimliche Aufforderung; Die Nacht; Nichts [G] CBC ("Musica Viva" series) ▲ MVCD 1051 [DDD]

Tchaikovsky, P.:Songs, w. S. Ralls (pno)—Blagoslavlyayu vas, lesa; Net, tol'ka tot, kto znal; Serenada Don Zhuana; Sleza drazhyt f tvajom rivnivom vzore [R] CBC ("Musica Viva" series) ▲ MVCD 1051 [DDD]

Peerce, Jan (ten)

Beethoven, L. van:Fidelio, w. S. Jurinac (sop), M. Stader (sop), H. Knappertsbusch (cnd), Bavarian State Opera Orch, Bavarian State Opera Chorus [G] *(rec ca. 1961)* MCA Classics 2-▲ MCAD2-9809 [AAD]

Beethoven, L. van:Sym 9, "Choral Sym", w. Jarmila Novotná (sop), Kerstin Thorborg (mez), Nicola Moscona (bass), A. Toscanini (cnd), NBC SO, Westminster Choir *(rec New York City, 1939)* Grammofono 2000 ▲ GRM 78524 (m)

Donizetti, G.:Lucia di Lammermoor, w. Roberta Peters (sop—Lucia), Mitì Truccato Pace (mez—Alisa), Jan Peerce (ten—Edgardo), Piero de Palma (ten—Lord Arturo Bucklaw), Mario Carlin (ten—Normanno), Philip Maero (bar—Lord Enrico Ashton), Giorgio Tozzi (bass—Raimondo), E. Leinsdorf (cnd), Rome Opera Orch, Rome Opera Chorus *(rec Rome Opera House, Aug 5-14, 1957)* RCA Living Stereo 2-▲ 09026-68537-2 [ADD]

Gounod, C.:Faust (sels)—Salut demeure Minerva ▲ MN-A19 [ADD]

Handel, G.F.:Judas Maccabaeus, w. Martina Arroyo (sop), Mary Davenport (mez), Lawrence Avery (ten), David Smith (bar), T. Scherman (cnd), Vienna State Opera Orch, Vienna Academy Chorus Vox Box 2-▲ CDX 5125 [ADD]

Jan Peerce Sings Hebrew Melodies, w. RCA SO RCA Living Stereo ▲ 09026-61687-2 ■ 09026-61687-4

Mozart, W.A.:Don Giovanni (sels)—Il mio tesoro intanto Minerva ▲ MN-A19 [ADD]

Puccini, G.:Arias—Nessun dorma [from Turandot]; Ch'ella mi creda [from La Fanciulla del West]; Recondita armonia; ...O dolci baci... [both from Tosca]; Che gelida manina; O soave fanclulla; O Mimì più tu non torni; Sono andati? [all from La Bohème] Minerva ▲ MN-A19 [ADD]

Puccini, G.:La Bohème, w. L. Albanese (sop), A. McKnight (sop), F. Valentino (bar), A. Toscanini (cnd), NBC SO, NBC Sym Chorus [I] RCA Gold Seal 2-▲ 60288-2-RG [ADD] 2-■ 60288-4-RG (CrO2)

Three Tenors of the Golden Age, w. Jussi Björling (ten), Mario Lanza (ten), John Corigliano (vn), Constantine Callinicos (pno), Frederick Schauwecker (pno), RCA Victor Orch [cnd:Renato Cellini, Constantine Callinicos, Erich Leinsdorf, Sylvan Levin, Maximilian Pilzer, Frieder Weissmann], Rome Opera Orch, Rome Opera Chorus [cnd:Eri RCA Gold Seal ▲ 09026-68531-2 [ADD] ■ 09026-68531-4

Verdi, G.:Arias, w. A. Toscanini (cnd), NBC SO, Westminster Choir—arias from Luisa Miller *(Oh! fede negar potessi; Quando le sere al placido)* & chorus from Nabucco *(Va pensiero sull'ali dorate)* [I] RCA Gold Seal 2-▲ 60299-2-RG (m) [ADD] 2-■ 60299-4-RG (CrO2)

Verdi, G.:Arias, w. A. Toscanini (cnd), NBC SO, Westminster Choir—arias from Luisa Miller *(Oh! fede negar potessi; Quando le sere al placido)* & chorus from Nabucco *(Va pensiero sull'ali dorate)* [I] RCA Gold Seal 7-▲ 60326-2-RG (m) [ADD] 6-■ 60326-4-RG (CrO2)

Verdi, G.:Un ballo in maschera, w. Zinka Milanov (sop), Leonard Warren (bar), B. Walter (cnd), *(orch unknown)* *(rec Jan 15, 1944)* Enterprise ("The Fourties" series) 2-▲ ENT 311

Verdi, G.:Inno delle nazioni, w. A. Toscanini (cnd), NBC SO, Westminster Choir RCA Gold Seal 7-▲ 60326-2-RG (m) [ADD] 6-■ 60326-4-RG (CrO2)

Verdi, G.:Inno delle nazioni, w. A. Toscanini (cnd), NBC SO, Westminster Choir RCA Gold Seal 2-▲ 60299-2-RG (m) [ADD] 2-■ 60299-4-RG (CrO2)

Verdi, G.:I lombardi alla prima crociata (sels), w. V. Della Chiesa (sop), N. Moscona (bass), A. Toscanini (cnd), NBC SO—Act 3 Trio RCA Gold Seal ▲ 60276-2-RG [ADD] ■ 60276-4-RG (CrO2)

Verdi, G.:Rigoletto (sels), w. Nan Merriman (mez), Frank Valentino (bar), Nicola Moscona (bass), G. Ribla (sgr), A. Toscanini (cnd), NBC SO—Act III (complete) Enterprise ("The Radio Years" series) ▲ ENT 48

Verdi, G.:Rigoletto (act 3), w. Nan Merriman (mez), Frank Valentino (bar), Nicola Moscona (bass), G. Ribla (sgr), A. Toscanini (cnd), NBC SO [I] *(rec New York, 7/25/43)* Melodram 2-▲ MEL 28022 (m) [AAD]

Verdi, G.:Rigoletto (act 4), w. Z. Milanov (sop), N. Merriman (mez), L. Warren (bar), A. Toscanini (cnd), NBC SO RCA Gold Seal ▲ 60276-2-RG [ADD] ■ 60276-4-RG (CrO2)

Verdi, G.:La traviata, w. C. N. Albanese (sop), R. Merrill (bar), A. Toscanini (cnd), NBC SO Music & Arts 2-▲ CD 271

Verdi, G.:La traviata, w. C. N. Albanese (sop), R. Merrill (bar), A. Toscanini (cnd), NBC SO [I] RCA Gold Seal 2-▲ 60303-2-RG [ADD] 2-■ 60303-4-RG (CrO2)

Verdi, G.:La traviata (sels)—Libiamo nei lieti calici; Un dì, felice, eterea; Parigi, o cara, noi lasceremo; Gran Dio! morir si giovine Minerva ▲ MN-A19 [ADD]

Verdi, G.:Il trovatore (sels)—Ah! si, ben mio; Di quella pira; Miserere Minerva ▲ MN-A19 [ADD]

Peerce, Jan (ten) (cont.)
The Voices of Living Stereo, Vol. 2, w. Eileen Farrell (sop), Birgit Nilsson (sop), Roberta Peters (sop), Leontyne Price (sop), Galina Vishnevskaya (sop), Rosalind Elias (mez), Shirley Verrett (mez), Marian Anderson (cta), Maureen Forrester (cta), Sergio Franchi (ten), Mario Lanza (ten), Richard Lewis (ten), Alexander Dedyukhin (pno), Franz Rupp (pno), Leo Taubman (pno), George Trovillo (pno), Charles Wadsworth (pno), Boston Pops Orch [cnd:Arthur Fiedler], Boston SO [cnd:Charles Munch], Chicago SO [cnd:Fritz Reiner], RCA Victor Orch, RCA Victor Chorus *(rec Boston & Chicago & New York & Rome, 1957–1964)* RCA Living Stereo ▲ 09026-68167-2 [ADD]

Peet, S. (sgr)
Celona, J.:Sum over Histories, w. B. Degazio (sgr), R. Sacks (sgr), A. Armin (elecs), R. Armin (elecs), J. Brownell (elecs), D. Hutton (elecs), G. Martynec (elecs), D. Mott (elecs), C. Sokol (elecs) Soundprints ▲ SP 9301

Peeters, Harry (bass)
Mascagni, P.:Nerone, w. R. Didonè (sop), D. Di Domenico (ten), S. Cowan (bar), M. Dirks (bar), Shapero (sgr), Strow-Piccolo (sgr), Tcholakov (sgr), K. Bakels (cnd), Hilversum RSO, Hilversum Chorus [I] Bongiovanni 2-▲ GB 2052/53 [DDD]
Mozart, W.A.:Zauberflöte, w. Constanze Backes (sop—Papagena), Christiane Oelze (sop—Pamina), Susan Roberts (sop—First Lady), Cyndia Sieden (sop—Queen of the Night), Carola Guber (cta—Second Lady), Maria Jonas (cta—Third Lady), Andreas Dieterich (trb—First Boy), Jan Andreas Mendel (trb—Second Boy), Florian Wöller (trb—Third Boy), Uwe Peper (ten—Monostatos), Nicolas Robertson (ten—First Man in Armor), Michael Schade (ten—Tamino), Gerald Finley (bar—Papageno), Noel Mann (bass—Second Man in Armour), Harry Peeters (bass—Sarastro), Detlef Roth (bass—Speaker/First Priest), Robert Burt (speaker—Third Priest), Robert Johnston (speaker—Second Priest), Wolfgang Knauer (speaker—Fourth Priest), Douglas Welbat (speaker—Second Priest), J. E. Gardiner (cnd), English Baroque Soloists, Monteverdi Choir London *(rec Forum am Schlosspark, Ludwigsburg, July 1995)* Archiv 2-▲ 449166-2
Rossini, G.:Tancredi, w. Veronica Cangemi (sop—Roggiero), Eva Mei (sop—Amenaide), Vasselina Kasarova (mez—Tancredi), Melinda Paulsen (cta—Isaura), Ramón Vargas (ten—Argirio), Harry Peeters (bass—Orbazzano), Janos Maté (vn), Gottfried Greiner (vc), Ingo Nawra (db), David Syrus (hpd), R. Abbado (cnd), Munich RSO, Bavarian Radio Chorus *(rec Studio 1, Munich, July 17–30, 1995)* RCA Red Seal 3-▲ 09026-68349-2 [DDD]

Peev, Borislav (sgr)
Puccini, G.:Tosca, w. Raina Kabaivanska (sop—Floria Tosca), Nazzareno Antinori (ten—Mario Cavaradossi), Roumen Doikov (ten—Spoletta), Enzo Dara (bar—Casare Angelotti/Il sagrestano), Nelson Portella (bar—Il Barone Scarpia), Stoyan Balabanov (bass—Sciarrone/Un carceriere), Borislav Peev (sgr—Un Pastore), G. Bellini (cnd), Sofia PO, Bulgarian National Radio Children's Choir, Svetoslav Obrenetov Bulgarian National Chorus *(rec Sophia, Bulgaria, Nov 14–27, 1982)* Arts Music ▲ 47158-2 [DDD]

Pehta, Timothy (sgr)
Myers, G.:God's Trbn, w. Christine Helfrich (sop), Gordon Myers (bar), Richard Cragg (sgr), Matthew Gillis (sgr), Paul Norman (sgr), Wendy Catlin (sgr) Katherine Mary Hamilton (sgr), Sharon Hunter (sgr), Gloriae Dei Brass Ensemble Paraclete ▲ CDGD 017 [DDD]; ■ GDC 017

Peintre, Lionel (bar)
Liszt, F.:Psalm 129, w. Francois-Henri Houbart (org), Yves Parmentier (cnd), French Army Chorus Adès ▲ ADE 203032
Liszt, F.:Requiem, w. Jacques Maresch (ten), Daniel Galvez-Vallejo (ten), Bertrand Bontoux (bass), Francois-Henri Houbart (org), Y. Parmentier (cnd), Republican Guard Brass & Percussion, French Army Chorus Adès ▲ ADE 203032
Mozart, W.A.:Missa, K.427, w. C. Pozderec (sop), M. C. LeBlanc (sop), F. Bardot (ten), F. Bardot (cnd), Altaïr SO, Paris Opera Children's Choir [L] Thésis ▲ THE11003
Shostakovich, D.:Sym 14, w. Marie Stéphane Bernard (sop), R. Hayrabedian (cnd), Musicatreize Opus 111 ▲ OPS 30165

Pelizzoni, Rinaldo (ten)
Puccini, G.:Tosca, w. Renata Tebaldi (sop—Floria Tosca), Guiseppe di Stefano (ten—Mario Cavardossi), Rinaldo Pelizzoni (ten—Spoletta), Ettore Bastianini (bar—Baron Scarpia), Carlo Badioli (bass—Sacristan), Guiseppe Moresi (bass—Sciarrone), Franco Piva (bass—Jailer), Nicola Zaccaria (bass—Cesare Angelotti), G. Gavazzeni (cnd) *(rec Great Auditorium, Brussels World Fair, 1958)* Legato Classics 2-▲ LCD 2092 [ADD]
Zandonai, R.:Francesca da Rimini, w. Lydia Marimpietri (sop—Biancofiore), Magda Olivero (sop—Francesca), Pinuccia Perotti (sop—Samaritana), Edda Vincenzi (sop—Garsenda), Gabriella Carturan (mez—Smaragdi), Biancamaria Casoni (mez—Altichiara), Anna Maria Rota (cta—Donella), Athos Cesarini (ten—Archer), Angelo Mercuriali (ten—Ser Toldo Berardengo), Mario del Monaco (ten—Paolo), Piero de Palma (ten—Malatestino), Rinaldo Pelizzoni (ten—Prisoner), Gianpiero Malaspina (bar—Gianciotto), Dino Mantovani (bar—Jester), Enrico Campi (bass—Ostasio), Giuseppe Morresi (bass—Tower warden), G. Gavazzeni (cnd), La Scala Orch, La Scala Chorus *(rec La Scala Theatre, Milan, June 4, 1959)* Legato Classics 2-▲ LCD 186-2

Pelker, Gudrun (mez)
Henze, H.-W.:Voices, w. F. Lang (ten), J. Kalitzke (cnd), Musikfabrik NRW CPO ▲ CPO 999192 [DDD]

Pellar, Rudolf (nar)
Slavicky, K.:Sinfonietta 4, w. Brigita Šulcová (sop), Václav Rabas (org), J. Belohlávek (cnd), Prague SO *(rec Dvořák Hall of Rudolfinum, Prague, Sept. 6 & 8, 1986)* Panton ("Protokol XX" series) ▲ PAN 811142 [DDD]

Pelle, Nadia (sop)
Lullabies, w. I Musici de Montreal [cnd:Yuli Turovsky] Chandos ▲ CHAN 9304 [DDD]
Schoenberg, A.:Qt 2 Strs, w. Y. Turovsky (cnd), Montreal Musici [orchestral version] [G] Chandos ▲ CHAN 9116 [DDD]
Shostakovich, D.:From Jewish Folk Poetry, w. M. A. Hart (mez), R. Nolan (ten), Y. Turovsky (cnd), Montreal Musici [R] Chandos ▲ CHAN 8800 [DDD]
Shostakovich, D.:Songs Sop, Op. 127, w. Borodin Trio Chandos ▲ CHAN 8924 [DDD]

Pellegrini, Alberta (sop)
Puccini, G.:La Bohème (sels), w. Bianco Bellisia (sop—Musetta), Alberta Pellegrini (sop—Mimi), Luciano Pavarotti (ten—Rodolfo), Walter de Ambrosis (bar—Schaunard), Vito Mattioli (bar—Marcello), Dmitri Nabokov (bass—Colline), Reggio Emilia Teatro Municipale Orch, Reggio Emilia Teatro Municipale Chorus Budget ("The Greatest Voice in Opera" series) ▲ SYP 105

Pellegrini, M. (sgr)
Bizet, G.:Carmen (sels), w. M. Horne (sop), M. Molese (sgr), G. Griffiths (bar), D. Bowman (bar), F. Egerton (ten), H. Lewis (cnd), Royal PO, Royal Liverpool Phil Choir IMP Collectors Series ▲ IMPX 9016 [AAD]

Pellegrini, Paolo (sgr)
Donizetti, G.:La bella prigioniera, w. S. Rigacci (sop), R. Franceschetto (sgr), F. Maestri (cnd), In Canto CO *(rec Apr. 1992)* Bongiovanni 2-▲ GB 2109/10 [DDD]
Donizetti, G.:Il Pigmalione, w. S. Rigacci (sop), F. Maestri (cnd), In Canto CO *(rec Sept. 1990)* Bongiovanni 2-▲ GB 2109/10 [DDD]
Haydn, J.:Lo Speziale, w. Gil Manuel Beltran (ten—Sempronio), Daniela Broganelli (sgr—Volpino), Cinzia Forte (sgr—Grilletta), Paolo Pellegrini (sgr—Mengone), Maurizio Gambini (vc), Marco Tinarelli (db), Gabriele Catalucci (hpd), F. Maestri (cnd), In Canto CO *(rec 1993)* Bongiovanni 2-▲ GB 2171/72 [DDD]
Morlacchi, F.:Poeta, w. C. Pastorello (sgr), G. Catalucci (cnd), Orch Giovanile In Canto [I] Bongiovanni ▲ GB 2129 [DDD]
Puccini, G.:La Bohème (sels), w. R. Mattioli (sop), Bellesia (sgr), L. Pavarotti (ten), F. Molinari-Pradelli (cnd), Reggio Emilia Teatro Municipale Orch—sels from Pavarotti's debut performance *(rec live, Apr 29, 1961)* Melodram 2-▲ MEL 27031 [AAD]
Salieri, A.:Arlecchinata, w. U. Benelli (bar), G. Gatti (bar), G. Catalucci (cnd), In Canto di Terni Youth Orch [I] *(rec live 9/90)* Bongiovanni 2-▲ GB 2111/12 [DDD]

Pellerin, Raymond (ct)
Handel, G.F.:Ezio, w. Julianne Baird (sop—Fulvia), Jennifer Lane (mez—Onoria), D'Anna Fortunato (cta—Ezio), Raymond Pellerin (ct—Emperor), Frederick Urrey (ten—Massimo), Nathaniel Watson (bar—Varo), Johannes Somary (org), R.A. Clark (cnd), Manhattan CO *(rec St. Jean Baptiste Church, New York, Mar. 1994)* Vox Classics 2-▲ VOX 27503 [DDD]

Pellerin, Raymond (ct) (cont.)
Handel, G.F.:Sosarme, Rè di Media, w. Julinne Baird (sop—Elmira), D'Anna Fortunato (mez—Sosarme), Jennifer Lane (mez—Erenice), Drew Minter (ct—Melo), Rarmond Pellerin (ct—Argone), John Aler (ten—King Haliate), Nathaniel Watson (bass—Varo), Edward Brewer (hpd) Newport Classic 2-▲ NPT 85575 [DDD]

Pellogrino, L. (cta)
Mascagni, P.:Cavalleria rusticana, w. G. Simionato (sop—Santuzza), F. Cadoni (mez—Lola), L. Pellogrino (cta—Lucia), A. Braschi (ten—Turiddu), C. Tagliabue (bar—Alfio), A. Basile (cnd), Italian Lyric Orch, Turin Cetra Chorus *(rec Turin, 1950)* Cetra Classic 2-▲ CDO 27 [ADD]

Pelon, Caroline (sop)
Couperin, F.:Motets, w. Sandrine Piau (sop), J.-P. Fouchécourt (ten), J. Corréas (bass), Les Talens Lyriques—Quatre versets d'un motet composé de l'ordre du Roy (1703); Verset du motet de l'année dernièr; Sept versets d'un motet composé de l'ordre du Roy (1704); Motet à Sainte Suzanne; Sept versets d'un motet composé de l'ordre du Roy (1705); Laudate Pueri Dominum rec. May 25–28, 1993 FNAC Music ▲ 592244 [DDD]
Rameau, J.P.:Nélée et Myrthis, w. A. Mellon (sop—Myrthis), D. Michel-Dansac (sop—Maid), C. Pelon (sop—Maid), F. Semellaz (sop—Corinne), J. Corréas (bass—Nélée), W. Christie (cnd), Les Arts Florissants, Les Arts Florissants Chorus [F] *(rec 5/91)* Harmonia Mundi France ▲ HMC 901381

Pelton, Carmen (sop)
Boziwick, G.:Beyond the Last Thought, w. G. Reuter (ob), C. Iverson (bn), K. Grossman (mar) Opus One ▲ CD 162

Pendachanska, Alexandrina (sop)
Glinka, M.:A Life for the Tsar, w. S. Toczyska (mez), C. Merritt (ten), B. Martinovich (bass), E. Tchakarov (cnd), Sofia Festival Orch, Sofia National Opera Chorus [R] Sony Classical 3-▲ S3K 46487 [DDD]
Gounod, C.:Faust (sels), w. Alexandrina Pendachanska (sop—Margarethe), Giuseppe Sabbatini (ten—Faust), György Melis (bar—Valentin), Nicolai Ghiaurov (bass—Méphistophélès), Nikola Ghiuselev (bass—Méphistophélès), Berlin RSO, Vienna SO, Hungarian State Opera Orch, Bulgarian RSO, Sofia SO, Bulgarian National Chorus, Bulgarian National Chorus Radio Choir—Intro; Vien ou bière; O sainte médaille...Avant de quitter ces lieux; Le veau d'or [all from Act 2]; Quel trouble inconnu me pénètre!...Salut! demeure chaste et pure; Je voudrais bien savoir...Il était un roi de Thule; Un bouquet!...O Dieu! que de bijoux [both from Act 3]; Gloire immortelle de nos aieux; Vous qui faites l'endormie [both from Act 4]; Intermezzo; Walpurgis Night [both from Act 5] Laserlight ▲ 14209 [DDD]
Rachmaninoff, S.:The Bells, w. K. Kaludov (ten), S. Leiferkus (bar), C. Dutoit (cnd), Philadelphia Orch London ▲ 440355-2 [DDD]
Tchaikovsky, P.:Eugene Onegin (sels), w. Nicolai Ghiaurov (bass), Lyubomir Diakovski (sgr), Niko Isakov (sgr), Dresden State Orch, Bulgarian National Chorus—Intro; Peasant's Chorus & Dance; Scene & Aria of Olga; Scene & Quartet; Letter Scene; plus others Laserlight ▲ 14210 [DDD]
Thomas, A.:Hamlet, w. Viorica Cortez (mez), Boje Skovhus (bar), R. Giovanetti (cnd), ORF SO, Arnold Schoenberg Choir *(rec live, 1994)* Serenissima 3-▲ SER 360147

Pennicchi, Marinella (sop)
Grétry, A.-E.-M.:Richard Coeur-de-lion, w. F. Neri (cnd), Balzano Claudio Monteverdi Conservatory Youth Orch Nuova Era 2-▲ NUO 7157 [DDD]
Luzzaschi, L.:Madrigali, w. H. Alfonso (sop), C. Miatello (sop), S. Vartolo (hpd) Musique d'Abord ▲ HMA 1901136
Monteverdi, C.:Incoronazione, w. Constanze Backes (sop—Valletto), Catherine Bott (sop—Drusilla/Pallade/La Virtù), Dana Hanchard (sop—Nerone), Sylvia McNair (sop—Poppea), Marinella Pennicchi (sop—Amore/Damigella), Annie Sofie von Otter (mez—Ottavia/Venere/La Fortuna), Julian Clarkson (alt—Littore/Mercurio), Bernarda Fink (cta—Arnalta), Roberto Balconi (ct—Nutrice), Michael Chance (ct—Ottone), Nigel Robson (ten—Liberto/Soldato Secondo), Mark Tucker (ten—Lucano/Soldato Primo), Francesco Ellero d'Artegna (bass—Seneca), J. E. Gardiner (cnd), English Baroque Soloists *(rec Queen Elizabeth Hall, South Bank Ctr, London, Dec 1993)* Archiv 3-▲ 447088-2
Monteverdi, C.:Vespro della Beata Vergine, w. A. Monoyios (sop), M. Chance (ct), G. Tucker (ten), N. Robson (ten), S. Naglia (ten), B. Terfel (b-bar), A. Miles (bass), J. E. Gardiner (cnd), English Baroque Soloists, His Majesties Sagbutts & Cornetts, London Monteverdi Choir Archiv 2-▲ 429565-2 [DDD]

Penning, Rick (ten)
Albright, W.:A Song to David, w. Melissa Semmes (nar), Charles Russell (nar), Deborah Carbaugh (sop), Susan Sacquitne-Druck (mez), James Bohn (bass), Dean Billmeyer (org), Howard Don Small (cnd), St. Mark's Cathedral Choir Minneapolis *(rec live, St. Mark's Cathedral, Minneapolis, MN, Apr. 28, 1991)* Gothic ▲ G 49066 [DDD]

Penno, Gino (ten)
Cherubini, L.:Médée, w. M. Callas (sop), F. Barbieri (mez), G. Modesti (bass), Nache (sgr), L. Bernstein (cnd), La Scala Orch, La Scala Chorus [I] *(rec live, Milan 12/10/53)* Verona 2-▲ 27088/89
Cherubini, L.:Médée, w. M. Callas (sop), F. Barbieri (mez), G. Modesti (bass), Nache (sgr), L. Bernstein (cnd), La Scala Orch, La Scala Chorus [I] *(rec live 12/10/53)* Melodram 2-▲ MEL 26022 (m) [AAD]
Verdi, G.:Aida (sels), w. A. Cerquetti (sop), E. Nicolai (mez), G. Guelfi (bar), B. Christoff (bass), G. Santini (cnd), Naples Teatro San Carlo Orch, Naples Teatro San Carlo Chorus [I] [highlights] *(rec live, Naples, July 24, 1954)* Golden Age of Opera ▲ GAO 134 [ADD]
Verdi, G.:Aroldo, w. A. Stella (sop), A. Protti (bar), F. Novelli (bar), T. Serafin (cnd), Florence Maggio Musicale Orch, Florence Maggio Musicale Chorus [I] *(rec live 6/3/53)* Melodram 2-▲ MEL 27014 (m) [AAD]
Verdi, G.:Ernani, w. Caterina Mancini (sop), Vittorio Pandano (ten), Giuseppe Taddei (bar), Giacomo Vaghi (bar), Ezio Achilli (sgr), Licia Rossini (sgr), F. Previtali (cnd), Rome RAI SO, Rome RAI Chorus Cetra Classic 2-▲ CDON 39 [ADD]
Verdi, G.:Giovanna d'Arco, w. Renata Tebaldi (sop—Giovanna), Gino Penno (ten—Carlo VII), Luciano Della Pergola (ten—Delil), Ugo Savarese (bar—Giacomo), Ignio Ricco (bass—Talbot), G. Santini (cnd), Naples Teatro San Carlo Orch, Naples Teatro San Carlo Chorus *(rec San Carlo Theater, Naples, Mar. 15, 1951)* Legato Classics 2-▲ LCD 193-2 [ADD]
Verdi, G.:Macbeth, w. M. Callas (sop), E. Mascherini (bar), I. Tajo (bass), V. de Sabata (cnd), (orch unknown) *(rec Milan, 1952)* Great Opera Performances 2-▲ GOP 750
Verdi, G.:Il trovatore, w. M. Callas (sop), E. Stignani (mez), C. Tagliabue (bar), A. Votto (cnd), La Scala Orch, La Scala Chorus [I] *(rec live 2/23/53)* Myto 2-▲ 2 MCD 90213 (m) [AAD]
Wagner, R.:Lohengrin (sels), w. R. Tebaldi (sop—Elsa), E. Nicolai (mez—Ortrud), G. Penno (ten—Lohengrin), G. Guelfi (bar—Telramund), G. Neri (bass—Heinrich), G. Santini (cnd), Naples Teatro San Carlo Orch, Naples Teatro San Carlo Chorus—8 soprano duets/trio from Acts 1–3 [I] *(rec live, Naples, 12/26/54)* Standing Room Only ▲ SRO 834-1 [ADD]

Penny, Celia (sgr)
Verdi, G.:Macbeth, w. Amy Shuard (sop—Lady Macbeth), Noreen Berry (mez—Lady-in-waiting), John Dobson (ten—Malcolm), André Turp (ten—Macduff), Tito Gobbi (bar—Macbeth), Edgar Boniface (bass—Servant), Rydderch Davies (bass—Doctor), Forbes Robinson (bass—Banco), Jean Holmes (sgr—Apparition), Celia Penny (sgr—Apparition), Glynne Thomas (sgr—Apparition), Brian Wrigt (sgr—Araldo), F. Molinari-Pradelli (cnd), Royal Opera House Orch, Royal Opera House Chorus Covent Garden *(rec London, Apr 8, 1960)* Bella Voce 2-▲ 7203 [AAD]

Penrose, Timothy (ct)
Blow, J.:Songs, w. J. Griffett (ten), M. Venhoda (cnd), Chamber Ensemble of Early Instruments—Welcome Ev'ry Guest; Ah, Heav'n! What Is't I Hear; Loving Above Himself; If I My Celia Could Persuade; The Fair Lover And His Black Mistress; Why Weeps Asteria?; The Spheres, Those Instruments Divine; Hark! How the Wakened Strings Resound Campion ▲ 1323 [DDD]
Handel, G.F.:Semele, w. Norma Burrowes (sop), Patrizia Kwella (sop), Elizabeth Priday (sop), Catherine Denley (mez), Della Jones (mez), Anthony Rolfe-Johnson (ct), Maldwyn Davies (ten), Robert Lloyd (b-bar), David Thomas (bass), J. E. Gardiner (cnd), English Baroque Soloists, Monteverdi Choir London Erato 2-▲ 2292-45982-2
Purcell, H.:Songs, w. J. Griffith (ten)—Ah, How Happy We Are; So! When the Glittering Queen of the Night; In Vain the Amorous Flute; Yes, Daphne; Crown the Altar; After War's Alarms Repeated Campion ▲ 1323 [DDD]

▲ = CD ♦ = Enhanced CD Δ = MD ■ = Cassette Tape □ = DCC

Pensa, Martin (nar)
Normandeau, R.:Petit Prince, w. Michel Dumont (nar—Aviator), Martin Pensa (nar—Little Prince), Christine Séguin (nar—Rose), Jean Marchand (nar—King), Luc Durand (nar—Conceited Man), Gilles Dupuis (nar—Drunkard), Guy Nadon (nar—Businessman), Jacques Languirand (nar—Lamplighter), Pierre Bourgault (nar—Geographer), Cynthia Dubois (nar—Snake), Monique Giroux (nar—Flower), Françoise Davoine (nar—Rose Garden), Jean-Louis Millette (nar—Fox), Gérard Poirier (nar—Railway Switchman), Claude Préfontaine (nar—Water Pill Salesman) *(rec Montreal, Aug 1994)* CBC 2-▲ 1091 [DDD]

Pentcheva, Mariana (cta)
Pacini, G.:Saffo, w. Francesca Pedaci (sop—Saffo), Gemma Bertagnolli (sop—Dirce), Mariana Pentcheva (cta—Climene), Carlo Ventre (ten—Faone), Aled Hall (ten—Ippia), Roberto de Candia (bar—Alcandro), Davide Baronchelli (bass—Lisimaco), M. Benini (cnd), Irish National SO, Lubomír Mátl (cnd), Wexford Festival Opera Chorus *(rec Wexford, Oct & Nov 1995)* Marco Polo 2-▲ 8.223883-4 [DDD]
Verdi, G.:Rigoletto, w. Andrea Rost (sop—Gilda), Mariana Pentcheva (cta—Maddalena), Roberto Alagna (ten—Il Duca di Mantova), Renato Bruson (bar—Rigoletto), Dmitri Kavrakos (bass—Sparafucile), R. Muti (cnd), La Scala Orch, La Scala Chorus Sony Classical 2-▲ S2K 66314

Peper, Uwe (ten)
Mozart, W.A.:Entführung, w. Mariella Devia (sop), Kurt Moss (sgr), W. Sawallisch (cnd), La Scala Orch, La Scala Chorus *(rec live, 1994)* Serenissima 2-▲ SER 360161
Mozart, W.A.:Entführung, w. L. Orgonasova (sop), C. Sieden (sop), S. Olsen (ten), C. Hauptmann (bass), Hans-Peter Minetti (nar), J. E. Gardiner (cnd), English Baroque Soloists, Monteverdi Choir London [G] Deutsche Grammophon 2-▲ 435857-2
Mozart, W.A.:Zauberflöte, w. Constanze Backes (sop—Papagena), Christiane Oelze (sop—Pamina), Susan Roberts (sop—First Lady), Cyndia Sieden (sop—Queen of the Night), Carola Guber (cta—Second Lady), Maria Jonas (cta—Third Lady), Andreas Dieterich (trb—First Boy), Jan Andreas Mendel (trb—Second Boy), Florian Wöller (trb—Third Boy), Uwe Peper (ten—Monostatos), Nicolas Robertson (ten—First Man in Armor), Michael Schade (ten—Tamino), Gerald Finley (bar—Papageno), Noel Mann (bass—Second Man in Armour), Harry Peeters (bass—Sarastro), Detlef Roth (bass—Speaker/First Priest), Robert Burt (speaker—Third Priest), Robert Johnston (speaker—Second Priest), Wolfgang Knauer (speaker—Fourth Priest), Douglas Welbat (speaker—Second Priest), J. E. Gardiner (cnd), English Baroque Soloists, Monteverdi Choir London *(rec Forum am Schlosspark, Ludwigsburg, July 1995)* Archiv 2-▲ 449166-2

Perez, Dolores (sop)
Carrion, M.R.:La Tempestad, w. L. Huarte (sop), A. Kraus (ten), F. Kraus (bar), R. Alonso (bass), S. Ramalle (bass), E. Estella (cnd), Concierto Montilla Orch, Concierto Montilla Chorus Montilla ▲ MON 3011 [ADD]

Pergola, Luciano della (ten)
Strauss, R.:Der Rosenkavalier, w. Jarmila Barton (sop—Marianne), Lisa Della Casa (sop—Sophie), Sena Jurinac (sop—Octavian), Ilva Ligabue (sop—Orphan), Elisabeth Schwarzkopf (sop—Marschallin), Else Schürhoff (mez—Annina), Luisa Villa (mez—Milliner), Hugues Cuénod (ten—Marschallin's majordomo), Erich Majkut (ten—Valzacchi), Giuseppe Nessi (ten—Animal seller), Luciano Della Pergola (ten—Lackey/Faninal's majordomo), Antonio Pirino (ten—An Italian Singer), Gino Del Signore (ten—Lackey/Waiter), Erich Kunz (bar—Herr von Faninal), Paolo Pedani (bar—Lackey), Attilo Barbesi (bass—Lackey/Waiter), Enrico Campi (bass—Waiter), Otto Edelmann (bass—Baron Ochs), Bruno Fichtinger (bass—Notary), Franco Taino (bass—Waiter), Maria Amadini (sgr—Orphan), Pina Carrillo (sgr—Orphan), Joszi Trojan Regar (sgr—Innkeeper), H. von Karajan (cnd), La Scala Orch, La Scala Chorus *(rec La Scala Theater, Milan, Jan. 26, 1952)* Legato Classics 3-▲ LCD 197-3
Verdi, G.:Giovanna d'Arco, w. Renata Tebaldi (sop—Giovanna), Gino Penno (ten—Carlo VII), Luciano Della Pergola (ten—Delil), Ugo Savarese (bar—Giacomo), Iginio Ricco (bass—Talbot), G. Santini (cnd), Naples Teatro San Carlo Orch, Naples Teatro San Carlo Chorus *(rec San Carlo Theater, Naples, Mar. 15, 1951)* Legato Classics 2-▲ LCD 193-2 [ADD]

Perillo, Linda (sop)
Lalande, M.-R. de:Dies Irae, w. P. Kwella (sop), H. Crook (ten), H. Lamy (ten), P. Harvey (bar), P. Herreweghe (cnd), La Chapelle Royale Orch, Chapelle Royale Choir [L] Harmonia Mundi France ▲ HMC 901352
Lalande, M.-R. de:Miserere mei, Deus, w. P. Kwella (sop), H. Crook (ten), H. Lamy (ten), P. Harvey (bar), P. Herreweghe (cnd), La Chapelle Royale Orch, Chapelle Royale Choir [L] Harmonia Mundi France ▲ HMC 901352
Mondonville, J.-J.C. de:Pièces de clavecin, Op. 5, w. Kenneth Weiss (hpd), Walter Reiter (vn) Meridian ▲ MER 84302 [DDD]
Purcell, H.:King Arthur, w. N. Argenta (sop), J. Gooding (sop), J. MacDougall (ten), M. Tucker (ten), G. Finley (bar), B. Bannatyne-Scott (bass), T. Pinnock (cnd), English Concert, *(chorus unknown)* Archiv 2-▲ 435490-2 [DDD]

Perl, Alois (ten)
Dittersdorf, K.D. von:Doctor und Apotheker, w. Hildegard Uhrmacher (sop—Leonore), Donna Woodward (sop—Rosalia), Waltraud Meier (mez—Claudia), Martin Finke (ten—Sichel), Frieder Lang (ten—Gotthold), Alois Perl (ten—Gallus), Gerhard Unger (ten—Sturmwald), Thomas Pfeiffer (bar—Police Commisioner), Wolfgang Schöne (bar—Krautmann), Harald Stamm (bass—Stössel), J. Lockhart (cnd), Rhine State PO Bayer 2-▲ BR 100 238/39 [DDD]

Perlman, Itzhak (nar)
Prokofiev, S.:Peter & the Wolf, w. Z. Mehta (cnd), Israel PO EMI Classics ▲ CDC 47067 [DDD]
Saint-Saëns, C.:Carnival of the Animals, w. K. Labèque (pno), M. Labèque (pno), Z. Mehta (cnd), Israel PO EMI Classics ▲ CDC 47067 [DDD]

Pernerstorfer, Alois (b-bar)
Einem, G. von:Der Prozess, w. Lisa Della Casa (sop—Frl. Bürstner/Die Frau des Gerichtsdieners/Leni), Peter Klein (ten—Der Direktorstellvertreter/Der Student), Max Lorenz (ten—Josef K.), Erich Majkut (ten—Ein Bursche), László Szemere (ten—Titorelli), Alois Pernerstorfer (b-bar—Willem/Der Gerichtsdiener), Alfred Poell (b-bar—Der Advokat), Walter Berry (bass—Franz/Kanzleidirektor), Oskar Czerwenka (bass—Der Untersuchungsrichter/Der Prügler), Ludwig Hofmann (bass—Der Aufseher/Ein Passant/Der Geistliche/Der Fabrikant), Polly Batic (sgr—Frau Grubach), Endreh Koreh (sgr—Albert K.), Luise Leitner (sgr—Ein buckliges Mädchen), K. Böhm (cnd), Vienna PO, Vienna State Opera Chorus *(rec Aug 17, 1953)* Orfeo d'or ("Festspiel Dokumente" series) 2-▲ 392952 (m) [ADD]
Giordano, U.:Andrea Chénier, w. H. Konetzni (sop—Madelon), M. Sjöstedt (sop—Bersi), R. Tebaldi (sop—Maddalena de Coigny), E. Heinzen (cta—La Contessa de Coigny), F. Corelli (ten—Andrea Chénier), E. Bastianini (bar—C. Gérard), K. Paskalis (bar—Pietro Fléville), L. Welter (bar—Fouquier Tinville), A. Pernerstorfer (b-bar—Mathieu), L. von Matačić (cnd), Vienna State Opera Orch, Vienna State Opera Chorus *(rec Vienna, June 26, 1960)* Fortissimo 2-▲ CDE 3003 [ADD]
Gluck, C.W.:Iphigénie en Aulide, w. Inge Borkh (sop—Klytämnestra), Christa Ludwig (mez—Iphigenie), Elisabeth Steiner (mez—Artemis), James King (ten—Achilles), Otto Edelmann (b-bar), Walter Berry (bass), K. Böhm (cnd), Vienna PO, Salzburg Festival Chamber Choir, Vienna State Opera Chorus *(rec Salzburg, Aug 3, 1962)* Orfeo d'or ("Festspiel Dikumente" series) 2-▲ C 428962 (m) [ADD]
Liebermann, R.:Die Schule der Frauen, w. Anneliese Rothenberger (sop—Agnes), Christa Ludwig (mez—Georgette), Nicolai Gedda (ten—Horace), Alois Pernerstorfer (b-bar—Gronte), Walter Berry (bass—Poquelin), Kurt Böhme (bass—Arnolphe), G. Szell (cnd), Vienna PO *(rec Salzburg, Aug 17, 1957)* Orfeo d'or ("Festspiel Dikumente" series) 2-▲ C 429962 (m) [ADD]
Mozart, W.A.:Don Giovanni, w. G. Grob-Prandl (sop), H. Konetzni (sop), M. Stabile (bar), O. Czerwenka (bass), H. Swarowsky (cnd), Vienna SO, Vienna State Opera Chorus *(rec 1950)* Preiser 2-▲ PRE 90166 [AAD]
Wagner, R.:Tannhäuser, w. Gré Brouwestijn (sop), Murray Dickie (ten), Karl Liebl (ten), Eberhard Waechter (bar), Alois Pernerstorfer (b-bar), Deszö Ernster (bass), Walter Brunelli (sgr), Peter Harrower (sgr), Rosl Schweiger (sgr), Herta Wilfert (sgr), A. Rodzinski (cnd), Rome RAI Radio-TV SO, Rome RAI Chorus Stradivarius 3-▲ STV 12318

Pernet, André (bass)
Charpentier, G.:Louise, w. N. Vallin (sop—Louise), C. Gaudel (sop—Irma), A. Lecouvreur (mez—Mother), G. Thill (ten—Julien), A. Pernet (bass—Father), E. Bigot (cnd), Raugel Orch, Raugel Chorus *(rec 1936)* Nimbus (Prima Voce) ▲ NI 7829 (m) [ADD]
Charpentier, G.:Louise (abridged ed), w. N. Vallin (sop—Louise), C. Gaudel (mez—Irma), A. Lecouvreur (cta—La Mère), G. Thill (ten—Julien), A. Pernet (bass—La Père), E. Bigot (cnd), *(orch & chorus unknown)* [F] *(rec 1935 for Columbia Records)* Music Memoria 3-▲ 30223

Peromingo, J. (sgr)
Lehár, F.:Eva, w. J. Granados (sop—Prunelles), A. M. Olaria (sop—Eva), A. Kraus (ten—Octavio Flaubert), L. de Cordoba (sgr—Gipsy), S. Ramalle (sgr—Dagoberto), J. Peromingo (sgr—Voisin), E. Estella (cnd), Madrid CO, Spanish National Radio Chorus [Sp] Montilla ▲ CDFM 2036

Perotti, Pinuccia (sop)
Zandonai, R.:Francesca da Rimini, w. Lydia Marimpietri (sop—Biancofiore), Magda Olivero (sop—Francesca), Pinuccia Perotti (sop—Samaritana), Edda Vincenzi (sop—Garsenda), Gabriella Carturan (mez—Smaragdi), Biancamaria Casoni (mez—Altichiara), Anna Maria Rota (cta—Donella), Athos Cesarini (ten—Archer), Angelo Mercuriali (ten—Ser Toldo Berardengo), Mario del Monaco (ten—Paolo), Piero de Palma (ten—Malatestino), Rinaldo Pelizzoni (ten—Prisoner), Gianpiero Malaspina (bar—Gianciotto), Dino Mantovani (bar—Jester), Enrico Campi (bass—Ostasio), Giuseppe Morresi (bass—Tower warden), G. Gavazzeni (cnd), La Scala Orch, La Scala Chorus *(rec La Scala Theater, Milan, June 4, 1959)* Legato Classics 2-▲ LCD 186-2

Perraguin, Hélène (cta)
Berlioz, H.:Les Troyens, w. F. Pollet (sop—Dido), D. Voigt (sop—Cassandre), C. Dubosc (sop—Ascagne), H. Perraguin (cta—Anna), G. Lakes (ten—Aeneas), J.-L. Maurette (ten—Iopas), J. M. Ainsley (ten—Hylas), M. P. (ten—Panthee), G. Cross (ten—Sinon), G. Quilico (bar—Chorebe), J.-P. Courtis (b-bar—Narbal), M. Belleau (bass—Ghost of Hector), R. Schirrer (bass—Priam), C. Dutoit (cnd), Montreal SO, Montreal Sym Chorus London 4-▲ 443693-2 [DDD]

Perras, Margherita (sop)
Mozart, W.A.:Arias, w. Arleen Augér (sop), Kathleen Battle (sop), Irma Beilke (sop), Helena Braun (sop), Lisa Della Casa (sop), Maria Cebotari (sop), Ileana Cotrubas (sop), Helen Donath (sop), Mirella Freni (sop), Reri Grist (sop), Edita Gruberova (sop), Elisabeth Grümmer (sop), Hilde Güden (sop), Ingeborg Hallstein (sop), Luise Helletsgruber (sop), Gundula Janowitz (sop), Sena Jurinac (sop), Erika Köth (sop), Evelyn Lear (sop), Wilma Lipp (sop), Margaret Marshall (sop), Edith Mathis (sop), Jarmila Novotna (sop), Lucia Popp (sop), Elisabeth Rethberg (sop), Anneliese Rothenberger (sop), Elisabeth Schumann (sop), Elisabeth Schwarzkopf (sop), Graziella Sciutti (sop), Irmgard Seefried (sop), Graziella Sciutti (sop), Julia Varady (sop), Agnes Baltsa (mez), Margit Bokor (mez), Brigitte Fassbaender (mez), Christa Ludwig (mez), Ann Murray (mez), Francisco Araiza (ten), Anton Dermota (ten), Helge Rosvaenge (ten), Rudolf Schock (ten), Peter Schreier (ten), Leopold Simoneau (ten), Eric Tappy (ten), Richard Tauber (ten), Gösta Winbergh (ten), Josef Witt (ten), Fritz Wunderlich (ten), Christian Boesch (bar), Willy Domgraf-Fassbaender (bar), Karl Dönch (bar), Dietrich Fischer-Dieskau (bar), Erich Kunz (bar), Eberhard Wächter (bar), Hans Hotter (b-bar), Paul Schöffler (b-bar), Cesare Siepi (b-bar), José Van Dam (b-bar), Walter Berry (bass), Geraint Evans (bass), Nicolai Ghiaurov (bass), Alexander Kipnis (bass), Richard Mayr (bass), Kurt Moll (bass), James Morris (bass), Ezio Pinza (bass), Martti Talvela (bass), Giorgio Tozzi (bass), Hans Duhan (sgr), Res Fischer (sgr), Marie Gerhart (sgr), *(various orchs & cnds)*—sels from Idomeneo, Die Entführung aus der Serail, Le nozze di Figaro, Don Giovanni, Così fan tutte, Die Zauberflöte & various arias Orfeo d'or ("Festspiel Dokumente" series) 5-▲ 408955
Mozart, W.A.:Entführung (sels), w. K. Alwin (cnd), Vienna PO—Welcher Kummer—Ach ich liebte Orfeo d'or ("Festspiel Dokumente" series) ▲ 394101
Mozart, W.A.:Nozze di Figaro (sels), w. Maria Reining (sop—Countess), Margherita Perras (sop—Susanna), Alfred Jerger (b-bar—Count), Paul Schöffler (b-bar—Figaro), W. Loibner (cnd), Vienna State Opera Orch *(rec May 24, 1938)* Koch Schwann 2-▲ SCH 314632 [ADD]

Perrella, Marco (bass)
Stradella, A.:Susanna, w. S. Piccollo (sop), L. Bertotti (sop), M. Lazzara (cta), M. Nuvoli (ten), E. Velardi (cnd), Camerata Ligure [period instrs] [I] Bongiovanni 2-▲ GB 2121/22 [DDD]

Perret, Daniel (trb)
Ave Maria, w. [cnd:Alphons von Aarburg], Zurich Boys' Choir, Frieder Lang (ten), Alain Clément (bass), Praxedis Rütti (hp), Daniel Winiger (org), Andrej Lütschg (vn) Tudor ▲ TUD 7029 [DDD]

Perrin, Yvonne (sop)
Mendelssohn, F.:Psalm 42, w. M. Schwartz (mez), O. Dufour (ten), C. Traube (ten), P. Huttenlocher (bar), C. Ossola (bass), M. Hutin (bass), C. Liang-Sheng (cnd), Geneva SO, Geneva Univ Chorus Gallo ▲ CD 635 [AAD]
Mendelssohn, F.:Psalm 95, w. M. Schwartz (mez), O. Dufour (ten), C. Traube (ten), P. Huttenlocher (bar), C. Ossola (bass), M. Hutin (bass), C. Liang-Sheng (cnd), Geneva SO, Geneva Univ Chorus Gallo ▲ CD 635 [AAD]
Mendelssohn, F.:Psalm 115, w. M. Schwartz (mez), O. Dufour (ten), C. Traube (ten), P. Huttenlocher (bar), C. Ossola (bass), M. Hutin (bass), C. Liang-Sheng (cnd), Geneva SO, Geneva Univ Chorus Gallo ▲ CD 635 [AAD]

Perris, Adriana (mez)
Bellini, V.:Norma, w. Gina Cigna (sop—Norma), Ebe Stignani (sop—Adalgisa), Adriana Perris (mez—Clotilde), Giovanni Breviario (ten—Pollione), Emilio Renzi (ten—Flavio), Tancredi Pasero (bass—Oroveso), V. Gui (cnd), EIAR Orch, Achille Consoli (cnd), EIAR Chorus *(rec Aug/Sept 1937)* Arkadia ("The 78's" series) 2-▲ 78010 [ADD]

Perrotta, José (bass)
Gomes, A.C.:Il Guarany, w. Niza De Castro Tank (sop—Cecilia), Roque Lotti (ten—Ruy Bento), Manrico Patassini (ten—Pery), Paschoal Raymundo (ten—Don Alvaro), Paulo Fortes (bar—Gonzales), Juan Carlos Ortiz (b-bar—Il Cacico), Waldomiro Furlan (bass—Alonso), José Perrotta (bass—Don Antonio De Mariz), A. Belardi (cnd), São Paulo Teatro Municipale Orch, São Paulo Teatro Municipale Chorus *(rec Studios of the Teatro Municipal, São Paulo, Brazil, 1959)* Arkadia 2-▲ HP 617.2 [ADD]

Perry, D. (ten)
Glass, Philip:Songs from the Trilogy, w. M. Vargas (sop), L. Childs (spkr), P. Esswood, Philip Glass Ensemble CBS ▲ MK 45580 ■ FMT 45580
Music of the Middle Ages, Vol. 4:English Polyphony of the 13th & Early 14th Centuries, w. Russell Oberlin (ct), C. Bressler (ten), S. Barab (vl), M. Blackman (vl) Lyrichord ▲ LYR 8004 [ADD]
Notre Dame Organa Leonius & Perotinus Magister, w. Russell Oberlin (ct), C. Bressler (ten), S. Barab (vl) Lyrichord ▲ LYR 8002 [ADD]

Perry, Eugene (bar)
Davis, A.:X, The Life & Times of Malcolm X, w. Priscilla Baskerville (sop), Hilda Harris (mez), Thomas J. Young (ten), Eugene Perry (bar—Malcolm), Herbert Perry (bass), W. H. Curry (cnd), Orch of St. Luke, Episteme [E] Gramavision 2-▲ R2-79470 [DDD]

Perry, Herbert (bass)
Davis, A.:X, The Life & Times of Malcolm X, w. Priscilla Baskerville (sop), Hilda Harris (mez), Thomas J. Young (ten), Eugene Perry (bar—Malcolm), W. H. Curry (cnd), Orch of St. Luke, Episteme [E] Gramavision 2-▲ R2-79470 [DDD]

Perry, Janet (sop)
Egk, W.:Peer Gynt, w. N. Sharp (sop), C. Wulkopf (mez), H. Hopf (ten), R. Hermann (bar), H. Wallberg (cnd), Munich RSO, Bavarian Radio Chorus [G] Orfeo 2-▲ 005822 [DDD]
Mercadante, S.:Il bravo, w. A. Tabiadon (mez), D. Di Domenico (ten), S. Bertocchi (ten), S. Antonucci (bar), B. Aprea (cnd), Italian International Orch, Slovak Phil Chorus [I] *(rec live 7/28-31/90)* Nuova Era 3-▲ 6971/73 [DDD]
Mozart, W.A.:Missa, K.427, w. B. Hendricks (sop), P. Schreier (ten), B. Luxon (bar), H. von Karajan (cnd), Berlin PO Deutsche Grammophon ("Karajan Gold" series) ▲ 439012-2
Mozart, W.A.:Zauberflöte, w. Edith Mathis (sop), Karin Ott (sop), Anna Tomowa-Sintow (sop), Agnes Baltsa (mez), Hannah Schwarz (mez), Francisco Araiza (ten), Gottfried Hornik (bar), José Van Dam (b-bar), H. von Karajan (cnd), Berlin PO, German Opera Chorus [G] Deutsche Grammophon 3-▲ 410967-2 [DDD]
Mozart, W.A.:Zauberflöte (sels), w. Edith Mathis (sop), Karin Ott (sop), Anna Tomowa-Sintow (sop), Agnes Baltsa (mez), Hannah Schwarz (mez), Francisco Araiza (ten), Gottfried Hornik (bar), José Van Dam (b-bar), H. von Karajan (cnd), Berlin PO, German Opera Chorus [G] Deutsche Grammophon ▲ 415287-2 [DDD]
Strauss, R.:Der Rosenkavalier, w. A. Tomowa-Sintow (sop), A. Baltsa (mez), K. Moll (bass), H. von Karajan (cnd), Vienna PO, Vienna State Opera Chorus [G] Deutsche Grammophon 3-▲ 423850-2 [DDD]
Telemann, G.P.:Harmonischer Gottes-Dienst, w. Ensemble Barocco Padua Sans Souci [period instrs]—Mit Sünden beleidigte Heiland; Ertrage nur das Joch der Mängel; Endlich wird die Stunde schlagen; Ach-Gott!; Deines neuen Bundesgnade; Jammerton *(rec Armonia Ca' Bianca Hall, July 19-21, 1995)* Dynamic ▲ CDS 146 [DDD]

Persson, Olle (bar)
Lundquist, I.T.:Sym 7, w. Anita Soldh (sop), S. Ehrling (cnd), Swedish RSO, Mikaeli Chamber Choir
Caprice ▲ CAP 21419 [DDD]

Pertile, Aureliano (ten)
Aureliano Pertile II *(rec 1927–1930)* Preiser ▲ PRE 89072 [AAD]
Aureliano Pertile, Vol. 1 *(rec 1922–32)* Pearl ▲ PEA 9209
Aureliano Pertile, Vol. 2 Pearl ▲ PEA 9229
Aureliano Pertile, Vol. 3 *(rec 1932–42)* Preiser ("Lebendige Vergangenheit" series) ▲ PRE 89116
The Best of His HMV Records (1927–1932) *(rec 1927–1932)* Iron Needle ▲ 1329 [ADD]
Bizet, G.:Carmen, w. Ines Alfani Tellini (sop), Aurora d'Alessio Buades (cta), Benvenuto Franci (bar), L. Molajoli (cnd), La Scala Orch, La Scala Chorus *(rec Milan, 1933)*
Phonographie 2-▲ PHG 5013 [ADD]
The 1st Legendary Acoustic Recordings, 1923–25
Enterprise ("Vocal Archives" series) ▲ ENT VA 1125
The Italian Vocal Tradition, Vol. 1:The Voices of Toscanini, w. Toti dal Monte (sop), Claudio Muzio (sop), Rosetta Pampanini (sop), Biata Scacciati (sop), Giacomo Lauri-Volpi (ten), Francesco Merli (ten), Carlo Galeffi (bar), Mariano Stabile (bar), Riccardo Stracciari (bar), Nazzareno de Angel *(rec 1921–35)*
Iron Needle ▲ 1304
Leoncavallo, R.:Pagliacci (sels), w. Enrico Caruso (ten), Antonio Paoli (ten), Giovanni Zenatello (ten), Amedeo Bassi (ten), Hermann Jadlowker (ten), Fernand Ansseau (ten), Hipolito Lazaro (ten), Nino (Filippo) Piccaluga (ten), Mario Chamlee (ten), Giacomo Lauri-Volpi (ten), Miguel Fleta (ten), Giovanni Martinelli (ten), Georges Thill (ten), Alessandro Valente (ten), Francesco Merli (ten), Lauritz Melchior (ten), Marcel Wittrisch (ten), Joseph Schmidt (ten), Beniamino Gigli (ten), Giuseppe Lugo (ten), Helge Roswaenge (ten), Jussi Bjoerling (ten)—23 versions of the tenor aria "Vesti la giubba" *(rec 1907–1944)*
Bongiovanni ▲ GB 1071 [ADD]
Opera Arias Preiser ("Lebendige Vergangenheit" series) ▲ PRE 89007 (m) [AAD]
Pertile Edition, Vol. 2:Il Tenore di Toscanini Grammofono 2000 ▲ GRM 78644
Rich & Rare:The Voice of Margaret Sheridan, w. Margaret Sheridan (sop), Renato Zanelli (ten), Hubert Greenslade (pno), Carlo Sabajno (cnd), La Scala Orch, Queens Hall Orch *(rec 1926–29)*
Time Machine ▲ 0100
Verdi, G.:Aida, w. Dusolina Giannini (sop—Aida), Irene Minghini-Cattaneo (mez—Amneris), Giuseppe Nessi (ten—Messenger), Aureliano Pertile (ten—Radames), Giovanni Inghilleri (bar—Amonasro), Luigi Manfrini (bass—Ramfis), Guglielmo Masini (bass—King), C. Sabajno (cnd), La Scala Orch, Vittore Veneziani (cnd), La Scala Chorus *(rec 1928)* Arkadia ("The 78's" series) 2-▲ 78013 [ADD]
Verdi, G.:Aida, w. Dusolina Giannini (sop), Irene Minghini-Cattaneo (cta), C. Sabajno (cnd), La Scala Orch, La Scala Chorus *(rec Milan, 1928)* Phonographie 2-▲ PHG 5004 [ADD]
Verdi, G.:Aida, w. D. Giannini (sop), I. Minghini-Cattaneo (cta), G. Inghilleri (bar), L. Manfrini (bass), C. Sabajno (cnd), La Scala Orch, La Scala Chorus [I] *(rec 1928 for HMV)*
Pearl 2-▲ CDS 9402 (m) [AAD]
Verdi, G.:Il trovatore, w. Maria Caniglia (sop), Apollo Granforte (bar), C. Sabajno (cnd), La Scala Orch, La Scala Chorus *(rec Milan, Sept–Oct. 1930)* Phonographie 2-▲ PHG 5002 [ADD]
Verdi, G.:Il trovatore, w. Maria Carena (sop—Leonora), Olga De Franco (sop—Ines), Irene Minghini Cattaneo (mez—Azucena), Aureliano Pertile (ten—Manrico), Giordano Callegari (ten—Ruiz/Messenger), Apollo Granforte (bar—Count), Bruno Carmassi (bass—Ferrando), Antonio Gelli (bass—Old Gypsy), C. Sabajno (cnd), La Scala Orch, Vittore Veneziani (cnd), La Scala Chorus *(rec 1930)*
Arkadia ("The 78's" series) 2-▲ 78007 [ADD]
Verdi, G.:Il trovatore (sels), w. J. Biel (ten), F. Tamagno (ten), L.-A. Escalaïs (ten), M. Gilion (ten), E. Caruso (ten), A. Paoli (ten), G. Zenatello (ten), J. Sembach (ten), L. Slezak (ten), F. Constantino (ten), G. Martinelli (ten), B. De Muro (ten), N. Fusati (ten), N. Piccaluga (ten), G. Lauri-Volpi (ten), E. Bergamaschi (ten), R. Tauber (ten), J. O'Sullivan (ten), H. Roswaenge (ten), G. Taccani (ten), V. Lois (ten), H. Lazaro (ten), A. Lindi (ten), A. Cortis (ten), F. Merli (ten), F. Völker (ten), J. Kiepura (ten), J. Schmidt (ten), J. Bjoerling (ten), B. Gigli (ten), A. Salvarezza (ten), J. Soler (ten), M. Filippeschi (ten)—34 performances of the Act III tenor aria "Di quella pira!," *(rec from 1903–1956)*
Bongiovanni ▲ GB 1051 [AAD]
Wagner, R.:Arias & Scenes, w. K. Flagstad (sop), E. Rethberg (sop), B. Nilsson (sop), E. Schumann (sop), F. Leider (sop), L. Melchior (ten), G. Thill (ten), G. Hüsch (bar), F. Schorr (b-bar), H. Hotter (b-bar), A. Kipnis (bass), *(orch unknown)* EMI Classics ("Studio" series) 4-▲ CDMC 64008

Pertusi, Michele (bass)
Bellini, V.:I Puritani (sels), w. Lucia Albert (sgr), Giuseppe Sabbatini (ten), Carlos Alvarez (bass)—All'erta! All'erta!; A te, o cara, amor talora; Son vergin vezzosa; Ah..Dolor! Ah Terror!; Cinta di fiori e col ben crin disciolto; O Rendetemi la speme—Vien, Diletto; Il Rival salvar tu dei—Suoni la tromba
Laserlight ▲ 14208 [DDD]
Mozart, W.A.:Così fan tutte, w. Renée Fleming (sop—Fiordiligi), Adelina Scarabelli (sop—Despina), Anne Sofie Von Otter (mez—Dorabella), Frank Lopardo (ten—Ferrando), Olaf Bar (bar—Guglielmo), Michele Pertusi (bass—Don Alfonso), G. Solti (cnd), CO of Europe London 3-▲ 444174-2
Mozart, W.A.:Nozze di Figaro, w. L. Cherici (sop), K. Mattila (sop), M. McLaughlin (sop), M. Bacelli (mez), N. Curiel (mez), U. Benelli (ten), L. Gallo (bar), A. Nosotti (bass), G. Tadeo (bass), Z. Mehta (cnd), Florence Maggio Musicale Orch, Florence Maggio Musicale Chorus Sony Classical ▲ SK 53286
Rossini, G.:La Cenerentola, w. C. Bartoli (mez—Cenerentola), F. Costa (mez—Clorinda), G. Banditelli (cta—Tisbe), W. Matteuzzi (ten—Don Ramiro), A. Corbelli (bar—Dandini), E. Dara (bar—Don Magnifico), M. Pertusi (bass—Alidoro), R. Chailly (cnd), Bologna Teatro Comunale Orch, Bologna Teatro Comunale Chorus *(rec June 22–July 2, 1992)* London 2-▲ 436902-2 [DDD]

Perucci, Carlo (sgr)
Giordano, U.:Madame Sans-Gêne, w. Magda László (sop—Caterina), Carlo Tagliabue (bar—Napoleone), Renato Berti (sgr—Despréaux), Irene Callaway (sgr—Toniotta/Carolina), Danilo Cestari (sgr—Neipperg/Vinaigre), Maria Luisa Malacchi (sgr—Giulia/Principessa Elisa), Carlo Perucci (sgr—Fouché), Danilo Vega (sgr—Lefebvre), Enzo Viaro (sgr—De Brigode/Gelsomino), A. Basile (cnd), Milan RAI SO, Milan RAI Chorus *(rec Milan, Aug 10, 1957)* Bongiovanni 2-▲ GB 1129/30

Peter, Albrecht (bar)
Strauss, R.:Der Rosenkavalier, w. Claire Watson (sop—Feldmarschallin), Lucia Popp (sop—Sophie), Annelie Waas (sop—Marianne), Brigitte Fassbaender (mez—Octavian), Margarethe Bence (ct—Annina), David Thaw (ten—Valzacchi), Karl Ridderbusch (bass—Baron Ochs), Benno Kusche (bass—Herr von Faninal), Albrecht Peter (bass—Police Inspector), C. Kleiber (cnd), Bavarian State Orch, Bavarian State Chorus *(rec live, Münchner Festspiele, July 20, 1974)* Arkadia 3-▲ 486 [ADD]
Wagner, R.:Tristan und Isolde, w. Helena Braun (sop—Isolde), Margarete Klose (mez—Brangäne), Günther Treptow (ten—Tristan), Paul Kuen (ten—Ein Hirte), Albrecht Peter (bar—Melot), Fritz Richard Bender (bar—Ein Steuermann), Ferdinand Frantz (b-bar—König Marke), Paul Schöffler (b-bar—Kurwenal), H. Knappertsbusch (cnd), Bavarian State Opera Orch, Bavarian State Opera Chorus *(rec live, Prinzregententheater, July 23, 1950)* Orfeo 3-▲ 355

Peter, P. (bar)
Gounod, C.:Roméo et Juliette, w. G. d'Angelo (sop—Juliette), F. Corelli (ten—Romeo), A. Ferrin (bar—Friar Lawrence), P. Gottlieb (bass—Mercutio), A. Guadagno (cnd), *(orch unknown)* *(rec live, Philadelphia, 4/14/64)*
HRE 2-▲ 1011-2 [ADD]

Peters, Brock (spkr)
Gould, M.:Fall River Legend, w. M. Rosenstock (cnd), National PO London—in addition to the 47-minute performance of the complete ballet score, this disc includes a 27-minute conversation recorded on 24 October 1990 between Morton Gould & Agnes de Mille concerning the creation of the Fall River Legend ballet Albany ▲ TROY 035-2 [DDD]

Peters, Gerhard (sgr)
Künneke, E.:The Alluring Flame, w. Birgit Fandrey (sgr—Dolores), Christianne Hossfeld (sgr—Lisbeth), Maria Mallé (sgr), Jürgen Sacher (ten—Master), Ralf Lukas (bar—Hoffman), Gerd Grochowski (sgr—1st Neighbor), Gerhard Peters (sgr—Friedrich), Zoran Todorovic (sgr—Jacinto), Theodor Weimer (sgr—2nd Neighbor), P. Falk (cnd), Cologne RSO, Cologne Radio Chorus *(rec Cologne, Nov 7–26, 1994)*
Capriccio ▲ 10753 [DDD]

Peters, Johanna (mez)
Donizetti, G.:Il giovedi grasso, w. J. Gomez (sop), J. Hughes (mez), U. Benelli (bar), B. Donlan (bar), F. Davià (bass), E. Esparza (sgr), D. Atherton (cnd), Eireann Radio-TV SO [I] *(rec live, 1970)*
Foyer ▲ FOY 2036 [AAD]

Peters, Johanna (mez) (cont.)
Donizetti, G.:Il giovedi grasso, w. J. Gomez (sop), J. Hughes (mez), U. Benelli (bar), B. Donlan (bar), F. Davià (bass), E. Esparza (sgr), M. Williams (sgr), D. Atherton (cnd), Eireann Radio-TV SO [I] *(rec live, 1970)* Memories ▲ HR 4482 [ADD]

Peters, Maria Angeles (sop)
Donizetti, G.:Le Convenienze Teatrali, w. A. Cicogna (mez), S. Tedesco (ten), R. Scaltriti (bar), B. Rigacci (cnd), Emilia Romagna Arturo Toscanini SO, Lugo Teatro Comunale Rossini Chorus [I] *(rec live, 6/90)*
Bongiovanni 2-▲ GB 2091/92 [DDD]
Fioravanti, V.:Le cantatrici villane, w. G. Manci (sop—Agata), M. Mauro (sop—Nunziella), M. A. Peters (sop—Rosa), F. Sovilla (mez—Giannetta), E. Palacio (ten—Carlino), G. Gatti (bar—Don Bucefalo), D. Serraiocco (bass—Don Marco), R. Tigani (cnd), Frosinone Licinio Refice Conservatory SO *(rec Oct. 22, 23 & 25, 1992;* ◻ Bongiovanni 2-▲ GB 2135/36 [DDD]
Martin Y Soler, V.:Una Cosa rara, w. M. Figueras (sop), G. Fabuel (sop), E. Palacio (ten), F. Belaza-Leoz (bar), S. Palatchi (bass), F. Garrigosa (bass), I. Fresán (sgr), J. Savall (cnd), Concert des Nations, La Capella Reial de Catalunya [I] *(rec 1991)* Astrée 3-▲ E 8760 [DDD]
Martin Y Soler, V.:Il Tutore Burlato, w. Liliana Marzano (sop—Menica), Maria Angeles Peters (sop—Violante), Juan Diego Florez (ten—Anselmo), Ernesto Palacio (ten—Il Cavaliere), Marcello Lippi (bar—Pippo), Giancarlo Tosi (bass—Don Fabrizio), Michela Forgione (hpd), M. Harth-Bedoya (cnd), Dianopolis Bulgarian CO *(rec VI Festival Internazionale di Gerace nella Chiesa di San Francesco, Aug 16, 1994)* Bongiovanni 2-▲ GB 2175/76-2 [DDD]
Piccinni, N.:La cecchinaLa cecchina, ossia la buona figliola, w. A. Ruffini (sop), G. Morino (ten), B. Praticò (bar), B. Campanella (cnd), Serenissima Pro Arte Orch [I] *(rec live 1990)*
Memories 3-▲ DR 3101/03 [DDD]
Rossini, G.:Songs, w. A. Cicogna (mez), E. Palacio (ten), F. Bettini (sgr), M. Carraro (cnd), *(orch unknown)* —Il carnevale di Venezia; L'Asia in Faville; Egle ed Irene; Un sou; Laus Deo; Dalle quete e pallid'ombre; Nella stagion di maggio; Hai la sottana; Ridiamo cantiamo; Les amants de Seville; La passeggiata; Le depart; Gli animali parlanti del giorno [I] Bongiovanni ▲ GB 2125 [DDD]
Vinci, L.:Arias, w. M. Carraro (cnd), Italian International Orch String Quartet—nine soprano arias from the operas La Caduta dei Decemviri, Catone in Utica, Lo Cecato Fauzo, Didone Abbandonata, La Festa de Bacco, & Semiramide Riconosciuta [I] *(rec live, Festival Internazionale di Gerace, 1990)*
Memories ▲ DR 3109 [DDD]

Peters, Roberta (sop)
Donizetti, G.:Lucia di Lammermoor, w. Roberta Peters (sop—Lucia), Mitì Truccato Pace (mez—Alisa), Jan Peerce (ten—Edgardo), Piero de Palma (ten—Lord Arturo Bucklaw), Mario Carlin (ten—Normanno), Philip Maero (bar—Lord Enricq Ashton), Giorgio Tozzi (bass—Raimondo), E. Leinsdorf (cnd), Rome Opera Orch, Rome Opera Chorus *(rec Rome Opera House, Aug 5–14, 1957)*
RCA Living Stereo 2-▲ 09026-68537-2 [ADD]
Mozart, W.A.:Zauberflöte (sels), w. E. Lear (sop), L. Otto (sop), F. Wunderlich (ten), F. Lenz (ten), D. Fischer-Dieskau (bar), F. Crass (bass), K. Böhm (cnd), Berlin PO, Berlin RIAS Chamber Choir—Scenes & Arias Deutsche Grammophon ▲ 429825-2 [ADD] ■ 429825-4
Offenbach, J.:Les Contes d'Hoffmann, w. L. Amara (sop), R. Stevens (mez), R. Tucker (ten), M. Singher (bar), P. Monteux (cnd), Metropolitan Opera Orch, New York Metropolitan Opera Chorus
Stradivarius 2-▲ DAT 12302
Opera Goes to the Movies, w. Plácido Domingo (ten), Leontyne Price (sop), et al.
RCA Victor ▲ 60841-2-RG ■ 60841-4-RG
Rossini, G.:Il barbiere di Siviglia, w. Roberta Peters (sop—Rosina), Margaret Roggero (mez—Berta), Cesare Valletti (ten—Count Almaviva), Calvin Marsh (bar—Fiorello/Sergeant), Robert Merrill (bar—Figaro), Fernando Corena (bass—Dr. Bartolo), Carlo Tomanelli (bass—Ambrogio), Giorgio Tozzi (bass—Don Basilio), E. Leinsdorf (cnd), Metropolitan Opera Orch, New York Metropolitan Opera Chorus *(rec Manhattan Center, New York, Sept 1–11, 1958)*
RCA Living Stereo 3-▲ 09026-68552-2 [ADD]
Rossini, G.:Il barbiere di Siviglia, w. C. Valletti (ten), R. Merrill (bar), G. Tozzi (bass), F. Corena (bass), E. Leinsdorf (cnd), Metropolitan Opera Orch, New York Metropolitan Opera Chorus [I]
RCA Gold Seal 3-▲ 6505-2-RG [ADD] 2-■ 6505-4-RG (CrO2)
Rossini, G.:Il barbiere di Siviglia (sels), w. C. Valletti (ten), R. Merrill (bar), G. Tozzi (bass), F. Corena (bass), E. Leinsdorf (cnd), Metropolitan Opera Orch, New York Metropolitan Opera Chorus
RCA Gold Seal ▲ 60188-2-RG [ADD] ■ 60188-4-RG (CrO2)
Starer, R.:Ariel, Visions of Isaiah, w. J. Patrick (bar), A. Kaplan (cnd), Camerata Singers, Camerata Singers *(rec 1972)* CRI ▲ CD 612 [ADD]
Verdi, G.:Rigoletto, w. J. Björling (ten), R. Merrill (bar), G. Tozzi (bass), J. Perlea (cnd), Rome Opera Orch, Rome Opera Chorus [I] RCA Gold Seal 2-▲ 60172-2-RG [ADD] 2-■ 60172-4-RG (CrO2)
The Voices of Living Stereo, Vol. 2, w. Eileen Farrell (sop), Birgit Nilsson (sop), Leontyne Price (sop), Galina Vishnevskaya (sop), Rosalind Elias (mez), Shirley Verrett (mez), Marian Anderson (cta), Maureen Forrester (cta), Sergio Franchi (ten), Mario Lanza (ten), Richard Lewis (ten), Jan Pee, Alexander Dedyukhin (pno), Franz Rupp (pno), Leo Taubman (pno), George Trovillo (pno), Charles Wadsworth (pno), Boston Pops Orch [cnd:Arthur Fiedler], Boston SO [cnd:Charles Munch], Chicago SO [cnd:Fritz Reiner], RCA Victor Orch, RCA Victor Chorus [cnd:Wa *(rec Boston & Chicago & New York & Rome, 1957–1964)* RCA Living Stereo ▲ 09026-68167-2 [ADD]

Petersen, M. (mez)
Smyth, E.:Songs (4) Mez, w. J. Schmeller (cnd), Ethel Smyth Ensemble *(rec 1992)*
Troubadisc ▲ TRO CD 01405 [DDD]
Smyth, E.:Songs (3) Mez, w. A. Gassenhuber (pno) *(rec 1992)* Troubadisc ▲ TRO CD 01405 [DDD]

Peterson, Glade (ten)
Verdi, G.:Simon Boccanegra, w. Leyla Gencer (sop), Giuseppe Zampieri (ten), Tito Gobbi (bar), Rolando Panerai (bar), Vito Susca (bass), Giorgio Tozzi (bass), G. Gavazzeni (cnd), *(orch unknown)*
Great Opera Performances 2-▲ GOP 767

Peterson, Joan (sop)
Imbrie, A.W.:Campion Songs, w. Nancy Wertsch (alt), Mark Bleeke (ten), Nathaniel Watson (bar), A. Korf (cnd), Parnassus *(rec Sept. 29, 1993)* New World ▲ 80441-2

Peterson, R. (bar)
Walton, W.:Belshazzar's Feast, w. M. Abravanel (cnd), Utah SO, Univ of Utah Civic Chorale
Allegretto ▲ ACD 8153 [ADD] ■ ACD 8153

Pethes, Sándor (sgr)
Kacsóh, P.:János Vitéz, w. Mária Gyurkovics (sop), Anna Zentai (sop—Iluska), Tivadar Bilicsi (sgr), Hilda Gobbi (sgr), Sándor Pethes (sgr—Bartolo), Róbert Ilosfalvy (ten—Kukorica), György Melis (bar—Bagó), György Radnai (bar—Strázsamester), László Domahidy (bass—Csősz), E. Lukács (cnd), Hungarian State Opera Orch, Hungarian Radio-TV Chorus *(rec Budapest, 1961)*
Classical Diamonds 2-▲ CLD 4011-12 [AAD]

Petina, Ira (sop)
Mozart, W.A.:Nozze di Figaro, w. Bidu Sayao (sop—Susanna), Eleanor Steber (sop—Countess Almaviva), Jarmila Novotna (sop—Cherubino), Ira Petina (sop—Marcellina), John Brownlee (bar—Count Almaviva), Salvatore Baccaloni (bass—Bartolo), Ezio Pinza (bass—Figaro), B. Walter (cnd), *(orch unknown)*
The Fourties 2-▲ ENT FT 1509
Rossini, G.:Il barbiere di Siviglia, w. Bidú Sayão (sop), John Brownlee (bar), Salvatore Baccaloni (bass), Ezio Pinza (bass), Nino Martini (ten), F. St. Leger (cnd), *(orch unknown)* *(rec Oct 4, 1943)*
Enterprise ("The Fourties" series) 2-▲ ENT 307

Petkov, Dimiter (bass)
Berlioz, H.:La Damnation de Faust, w. M. Horne (mez—Marguerite), N. Gedda (ten—Faust), R. Soyer (bass—Mephistofeles), D. Petkov (bass—Brander), G. Prêtre (cnd), Rome RAI SO, Rome RAI Chorus *(rec live 1/11/69)* Arkadia 4-▲ 461 [ADD]
Meyerbeer, G.:L'Africiane, w. Montserrat Caballe (sop—Selika), Christine Weidinger (sop—Inez), Miriam Ucelay (mez—Anna), Placido Domingo (ten—Vasco de Gama), Guillermo Sarabia (bar—Nelusko), Juan Thomas (b—bar—High Priest of Brahma), Dimiter Petkov (bass—Don Pedro), Juan Pons (bass—Don Diego), Eduardo Soto (bass—Grand Inquisitor), A. de Almeida (cnd), Barcelona Teatro Liceo Orch, Barcelona Gran Teatro de Liceo Chorus *(rec Barcelona, Nov 27, 1977)*
Legato Classics 2-▲ LCD 208-2 [ADD]

Petkov, Dimiter (bass) (cont.)

Meyerbeer, G.:Les Huguenots, w. Jeanette Scovotti (sop—Urbain), Rita Shane (sop—Marguerite de Valois), Enriqueta Tarrès (sop—Valentine), Nicolai Gedda (ten—Raoul de Nangis), Justino Diaz (bass—Marcel), Dimiter Petkov (bass—Le Comte de Saint-Bris), E. Märzendorfer (cnd), Austrian RSO, Austrian Radio Chorus *(rec Vienna, Feb 17, 1971)* Myto 2-▲ MCD 961141

Verdi, G.:Requiem Mass, w. Maria Belcheva (sop), Stefka Mineva (mez), Roumen Doykov (ten), P. Tiboris (cnd), Sofia National Opera Orch, Sofia National Opera Chorus *(rec Bulgarian National Radio Studio, Mar 14–17, 1994)* Elysium ▲ GRK 708 [DDD]

Petkov, Georgi (bar)

Verdi, G.:Don Carlos, w. M. Caballé (sop), F. Cossotto (mez), P. Domingo (ten), P. Cappuccilli (bar), E. Inbal (cnd), Arena di Verona Orch, Arena di Verona Chorus [I] *(rec live 7/2/69)* Melodram 3-▲ MEL 37057 (m) [AAD]

Petrak, Rudolf (ten)

Orff, C.:Carmina burana, w. J. Harsanyi (sop), H. Presnell (bar), E. Ormandy (cnd), Philadelphia Orch, Rutgers Univ Choir Sony Classical ("Essential Classics" series) ▲ SBK 47668 ■ SBT 47668

Petrella, Clara (sop)

Leoncavallo, R.:Zazà, w. E. Parker (mez), G. Campora (ten), A. Silipigni (cnd), Turin RAI SO *(rec 1969)* Memories 2-▲ MEM 4519 [AAD]

Puccini, G.:Madama Butterfly, w. C. Petrella (sop—Madama Butterfly), M. Masini (mez—Suzuki), M. C. Foscale (sgr—Kate Pinkerton), F. Tagliavini (ten—Pinkerton), M. Caruso (ten—Goro), G. Taddei (bar—Sharpless), A. Albertini (bar—Yamadori), A. Biancardo (bass—Bonze), A. Questa (cnd), Turin RAI Orch, Cetra Chorus *(rec 1953)* Cetra Classic 2-▲ CDO 10 [AAD]

Puccini, G.:Manon Lescaut (sels), w. M. del Monaco (ten) *(rec 1951)* Golden Age of Opera 2-▲ GAO 162/63 [ADD]

Puccini, G.:Il tabarro, w. Antenore Reali (sgr), Glauco Scarlini (sgr), G. Baroni (cnd), *(orch & chorus unknown)* Cetra Classic 3-▲ 36

Petrescu, Emilia (sop)

Constantinescu, P.:The Nativity, w. M. Kessler (mez), V. Teodorian (ten), H. Bömches (bass), M. Basarab (cnd), Bucharest George Enescu PO, Bucharest George Enescu Phil Chorus *(rec 1977)* Olympia ▲ OCD 402 [AAD]

Petrescu, Stefan (bar)

Rossini, G.:Il barbiere di Siviglia, w. Magda Ianculescu (sop—Rosina), Maria Sandulescu (mez—Berta), Valentin Teodorian (ten—Count Almaviva), Nicolae Herlea (bar—Figaro), Stefan Petrescu (bar—Fiorello), Constantin Gabor (bass—Don Bartolo), Valentin Loghin (bass—Don Basilio), M. Brediceanu (cnd), Romanian Opera Orch, Romanian Opera Chorus *(rec 1960–61)* Vox Box 2-▲ CDX 5159

Verdi, G.:Rigoletto, w. Victoria Draganescu (sop—Countess Ceprano), Magda Ianculescu (sop—Gilda), Dorothea Palade (mez—Maddalena), Valeria Savu (mez—Giovanna), Ion Buzea (ten—Duke of Mantua), Dimitrie Scurtu (ten—Borsa), Nicolae Herlea (bar—Rigoletto), Stefan Petrescu (bar—Marullo), Jean Banescu (bass—Count Ceprano), Nicolae Florei (bass—Monterone), Nicolae Rafael (bass—Sparafucile), J. Bobescu (cnd), Romanian Opera Orch, Romanian Opera Chorus *(rec 1965)* Vox Box 2-▲ CDX 5162

Petri, Mario (bar)

Cherubini, L.:Medée, w. M. Callas (sop), F. Barbieri (mez), V. Gui (cnd), Florence Maggio Musicale Orch, Florence Maggio Musicale Chorus [I] *(rec 1953)* Arkadia 2-▲ 516 (m) [AAD]

Debussy, C.:Pelléas et Mélisande, w. E. Schwarzkopf (sop), E. Haefliger (ten), M. Roux (bar), H. von Karajan (cnd), Rome Radio Orch, Rome RAI Chorus [F] *(rec live, 12/19/54)* Arkadia 2-▲ 218 (m) [ADD]

Mozart, W.A.:Don Giovanni, w. Leyla Gencer (sop—Donn'Elvra), Teresa Stich-Randall (mez—Donn'Anna), Sesto Bruscantini (bar—Leporello), Mario Petri (bar—Don Giovanni), F. Molinari-Pradelli (cnd), Milan RAI SO, Milan RAI Chorus Stradivarius 3-▲ STV DTM 12321 [ADD]

Mozart, W.A.:Nozze di Figaro, w. S. Jurinac (sop), T. Stratas (sop), T. Berganza (mez), N. Condò (mez), A. Lazzari (ten), S. Bruscantini (bar), G. Tadeo (bass), A. Mariotti (bass), Z. Mehta (cnd), *(orch unknown) (rec 1968)* Great Opera Performances 3-▲ GOP 712

Mozart, W.A.:Zauberflöte, w. E. Schwarzkopf (sop), R. Streich (sop), A. Noni (sop), N. Gedda (ten), G. Taddei (bar), H. von Karajan (cnd), Rome Radio Orch, Rome RAI Chorus [I] *(rec live, Dec. 19, 1953)* Myto 2-▲ 2 MCD 89007 (m) [ADD]

Mussorgsky, M.:Khovanshchina, w. Irene Companez (cta), Herbert Handt (ten), Mirto Picchi (ten), Boris Christoff (bass), Armedeo Berdini (sgr), Giorgio Canello (sgr), Dmitri Lopatto (sgr), Michele Malaspina (sgr), Jolanda Mancini (sgr), Mario Petri (sgr), A. Rodzinski (cnd), Rome RAI Radio-TV SO, Rome RAI Chorus Stradivarius 2-▲ STV DTM 12320 [ADD]

Mussorgsky, M.:Khovanshchina, w. Jolanda Mancini (sop—Emma), Irene Companez (mez), Amedeo Berdini (ten—Prince Andrei Khovanski), Mirto Picchi (ten—Prince Vasili Golitsin), Herbert Handt (ten—Scribe), Andrea Mineo (bar—Kuzka), Giampiero Malaspina (bar—Shaklovity), Boris Christoff (bass—Dosifei), Mario Petri (bass—Prince Ivan Khovanski), Dimitri Lopatto (Varsonofiev/First Strelyets), Giorgio Conello (Second Strelyets), A. Rodzinski (cnd), *(orch unknown)* [I] *(rec Rome, 1958)* VAI Audio 2-▲ VAIA 1052-2

Piccinni, N.:Didon, w. G. Tucci (sop), O. Mori (bass), M. Rossi (cnd), Naples RAI Orch, Naples RAI Chorus *(rec live 4/16/70)* Arkadia 2-▲ 596 [ADD]

Rossini, G.:La Cenerentola, w. Teresa Berganza (mez), Nicola Monti (ten), Sesto Bruscantini (bar), Leonardo Monreale (sgr), M. Rossi (cnd), Naples RAI SO, Naples Teatro San Carlo Chorus *(rec Oct 8, 1958)* Pantheon 2-▲ PHE 6656 (m)

Rossini, G.:L'italiana in Algeri, w. Teresa Berganza (mez), Alvino Misciano (ten), Sesto Bruscantini (bar), N. Sanzogno (cnd), Milan RAI SO, Milan RAI Chorus *(rec June 28, 1957)* Pantheon 2-▲ PHE 6646 (m)

Rossini, G.:Mosè in Egitto, w. Teresa Zylis-Gara (sop), Shirley Verrett (mez), Ottavio Garaventa (ten), Giampaolo Corradi (bass), Nicolai Ghiaurov (bass), W. Sawallisch (cnd), Rome RAI Orch, Rome RAI Chorus *(rec live, Rome, 1968)* Italian Opera Rarities 2-▲ IOR 7724 [ADD]

Stravinsky, I.:Oedipus Rex, w. M. Laszlò (mez—Jocasta), N. Gedda (ten—Oedipus), A. Bertocci (ten—Shepherd), M. Petri (bar—Creon & Tireseus), N. Catalani (bar—Messenger), A. Foà (speaker), H. von Karajan (cnd), Rome RAI SO, Rome RAI Chorus *(rec Dec. 20, 1952)* Stradivarius ▲ DAT 12311 [ADD]

Verdi, G.:Aida, w. A. Stella (sop), F. Barbieri (mez), F. Corelli (ten), A. Colzani (bar), V. Gui (cnd), Naples Teatro San Carlo Orch, Naples Teatro San Carlo Chorus [I] *(rec live, Naples 11/2/55)* Golden Age of Opera 2-▲ GAO 116/17 [ADD]

Verdi, G.:I lombardi alla prima crociata, w. Renata Broilo (sop), Maria Vitale (sop), Miriam Pirazzini (mez), Aldo Bertocci (ten), Mario Frosini (sgr), Bruno Franchi (sgr), Gustavo Gallo (sgr), Renato Pasquali (sgr), M. Wolf-Ferrari (cnd), Milan RAI Lyric Orch, Milan RAI Chorus *(rec 1954)* Cetra Classic 2-▲ CDON 41 [ADD]

Verdi, G.:Simon Boccanegra, w. A. Stella (sop—Maria), C. Bergonzi (ten—Gabriele), G. Giorgetti (bar—Pietro), W. Monachesi (bar—Paolo), M. Petri (bar—Jacopo), P. Silveri (bar—Simon), F. Molinari-Pradelli (cnd), Rome Radio Orch, Rome RAI Chorus *(rec 1951)* Cetra Classic ▲ CDO 23 [ADD]

Petroni, Luigi (ten)

Carissimi, G.:Oratorio della Santissima Vergine, w. P. Borri (sop), A. M. Ferrante (sop), P. Pace (sop), A. Christofellis (alt), F. Sclaverano (ten), R. Abbondanza (bass), M. Mondelli (bass), P. Spagnoli (bass), F. Colusso (cnd), Seicentonovecento Ensemble [I] Bongiovanni ▲ GB 10011 [DDD]

Carissimi, G.:Oratorio di Daniele Profeta, w. P. Borri (sop), A. M. Ferrante (sop), P. Pace (sop), A. Christofellis (alt), F. Sclaverano (ten), R. Abbondanza (bass), M. Mondelli (bass), P. Spagnoli (bass), F. Colusso (cnd), Seicentonovecento Ensemble [I] Bongiovanni ▲ GB 10011 [DDD]

Petros, Evelyn (sop)

Constantinides, D.:Vocal Music, w. Cynthia Dewey (nar), Angela DeVerger (sop), Susan Faust Straley (sop), Eugenia Epperson (fl), Richard Jernigan (cl), Kelly Smith Toney (vn), Hye-Yun Chung (hp), Stephen Brown (pno), John Raush (perc), D. Constantinides (cnd), Louisiana State Univ New Music Ensemble—Reflections IV for Sop, Fl, Hp & Pno; Intimations [1 Act Opera]; 4 Songs on Poems by Sappho; Mutability for Sop & Str Qt.; 4 Greek Songs Vestige ▲ 04

Flowering of Vocal Music in America, 1767-1823, w. Susan Belling (sop), Cynthia Clarey (sop), Barbara Wallace (sop), Debra Vanderlinde (sop), D'Anna Fortunato (mez), Charles Bressler (ten), Richard Anderson (bar), James Tyeska (bar), Joseph McKee (bass), Cynthia Otis (hp), Leonard Rav New World ▲ 80467-2

Petrov, Ivan (bass)

Beethoven, L. van:Mass, Op. 86, w. E. Markova (sop), L. Parachikova (cta), C. Kamenev (ten), C. Iliev (cnd), Sofia State PO, Sofia State Chorus [L] Musique d'Abord ▲ HMA 190109 [AAD]

Borodin, A.:Prince Igor, w. Elana Obraztsova (mez—Konchakovna), Tatiana Tugarinova (mez—Yaroslavna), Vladimir Atlantov (ten—Vladimir Igoryevich), Artur Eisen (bass—Vladimir Galitsky), Ivan Petrov (bass—Igor Svyatoslavich), Alexander Vedernikov (bass—Konchak), M. Ermler (cnd), Bolshoi Theater Orch, Bolshoi Theater Chorus *(rec Moscow, 1969)* Melodiya ("The Russian Opera" series) 3-▲ 74321-29346-2 [ADD]

Mussorgsky, M.:Boris Godunov, w. Irina Arkhipova (mez—Marina Mnishek), Evgenya Verbitskaya (mez—Nurse to Xenia), Valentina Klepatskaya (sgr—Fyodor), Tamara Sorokina (sgr—Xenia), Anton Grigoryev (ten—Simpleton), Vladimir Ivanovsky (ten—Grigory, the Pretender), Gyorgy Shulpin (bar—Prince Shuisky), Alexey Geleva (bass—Varlaam), Ivan Petrov (bass—Boris Godounov), Mark Reshetin (bass—Pimen), Alexi Ivanov (sgr—Andrei Shchelkalov), Evgeny Kibkalo (sgr—Rangoni), A. Melik-Pashayev (cnd), Bolshoi Theater Orch, Bolshoi Theater Chorus *(rec Moscow, 1962)* Melodiya ("The Russian Opera" series) 3-▲ 74321-29349-2 [ADD]

Shostakovich, D.:Song of the Forest, w. V. Ivanovsky (ten), A. Yulov (cnd), Moscow PO, Moscow State Boys' Choir, Yurlov Russian Choir Russian Disc ▲ RUS 11 048 [AAD]

Tchaikovsky, P.:Eugene Onegin, w. G. Vishnevskaya (sop), L. Avdeyeva (mez), S. Lemeshev (ten), Belov (sgr), B. Khaikin (cnd), Bolshoi Theater Orch, Bolshoi Theater Chorus [R] *(rec ca. early '60s for Melodi)* Legato Classics 2-▲ LCD 163-2 (m) [ADD]

Petrov, Vladimir (ten)

Prokofiev, S.:War & Peace, w. Galina Vishnevskaya (sop—Natasha Rostovoa), Irina Arkhipova (mez—Hélène Bezukhova), Evgenya Verbitskaya (mez—Marya Akhrosimova), Alexi Maslennikov (ten—Anatole Kuragin), Vladimir Petrov (ten—Pierre Bezukhov), Pavel Lisitsian (bar—Napoleon), Alexi Krivchenya (bass—Field-Marshall Kutuzov), Evgeny Kibkalo (sgr—Prince Andrei Bolkonsky), A. Melik-Pashayev (cnd), Bolshoi Theater Orch, Bolshoi Theater Chorus *(rec Moscow, 1961)* Melodiya ("The Russian Opera" series) 3-▲ 74321-29350-2 [ADD]

Petrova, Stefa (mez)

Dvořák, A.:Vanda, w. Drahomira Tikalova (sop), Beno Blachut (ten), Karel Kalas (bass), F. Dyk (cnd), Prague RSO, Jiri Pinkas (cnd), Prague Radio Chorus *(rec 1951)* Supraphon ("Hidden Treasures from Prague" series) 2-▲ SUP CD 3007 (m)

Petrovic (sgr)

Mussorgsky, M.:Boris Godunov, w. Cangalovic (sgr), Djokic (sgr), Milosevic (sgr), D. Miladinovic (cnd), Belgrade National Opera Orch, Belgrade National Opera Chorus *(rec live, La Fenice Theater, Venice, Jan. 3, 1967)* Arkadia 3-▲ 492

Petrusanec, Franjo (bass)

Dvořák, A.:Stabat Mater, w. A. P. Jeric (sop), E. N. Houska (mez), J. Reja (ten), M. Munih (cnd), Ljubljana RSO, Ljubljana Radio Chorus [L] PMG (Vienna Master) ▲ CD 160104 [DDD]

Dvořák, A.:Stabat Mater, w. A. Pusar-Jerik (sop), E. N. Houska (mez), J. Reja (ten), M. Munih (cnd), Consortium Musicum Orch, Consortium Musicum Chorus [L] Vivace 2-▲ 140141 [ADD/DDD]

Petterssons, Ingus (ten)

Donizetti, G.:Maria Stuarda (sels), w. Lena Nordin (sop), Carina Morling (mez), Anders Bergström (bar), Tord Wallström (bar), Maria Wieslander (org), Sven Åberg (chit), Chrichan Larsson (vc), Nanette Nowels-Stenholm (pno), M. Guidarini (cnd), *(orch unknown)* Swedish Society ▲ SCD 1076

Petzold, Martin (ten)

Goldschmidt, B.:Der gewaltige Hahnrei, w. R. Alexander (sop), M. Posselt (sop), H. Lawrence (sop), R. Wörle (ten), M. Kraus (ten), C. Otelli (bar), L. Zagrosek (cnd), German SO, Berlin Radio Chorus London ▲ 440850-2 [DDD]

Goldschmidt, B.:Mediterranean Songs, w. R. Alexander (sop), M. Posselt (sop), H. Lawrence (sop), R. Wörle (ten), M. Kraus (ten), C. Otelli (bar), L. Zagrosek (cnd), German SO, Berlin Radio Chorus London ▲ 440850-2 [DDD]

Ullmann, V.:Kaiser von Atlantis, w. C. Oelze (sop—Bubikopf), I. Vermillion (mez—The Drummer), M. Petzold (ten—A Soldier), M. Kraus (ten—Kaiser Overall), H. Lippert (ten—Harlekin), F. Mazura (bar—The Loudspeaker), W. Berry (bass—Death), L. Zagrosek (cnd), Leipzig Gewandhaus Orch London ▲ 440854-2 [DDD]

Peuypaoyen, Wimon (sgr)

Siamese Classical Music, Vol. 4:The Piphat Sepha, w. Fong Naam Marco Polo ▲ 8.223200 [DDD]

Peyron, Joseph (ten)

Adam, A.:Le Chalet, w. Denise Boursin (sop), Stanislas Staskiewicz (sgr), A. Wolff (cnd), ORTF Lyric Orch Musidisc ▲ MUS 201942 [AAD]

Adam, A.:Le Farfadet, w. Denise Boursin (sop), Stanislas Staskiewicz (sgr), A. Wolff (cnd), ORTF Lyric Orch Musidisc ▲ MUS 201942 [AAD]

Auber, D.-F.:Le Domino noir, w. J. Micheau (sop), G. Rey (bar), J. Gressier (cnd), French National RSO, French Radio Lyric Chorus Melodram 2-▲ MLO 270110 [ADD]

Gounod, C.:Le Médecin malgré lui, w. Lina Dachary (sop), Monique Stiot (mez), Michel Hamel (ten), Christophe Benoit (bar), Janine Capderou (sgr), Jean-Louis Soumagnas (sgr), J.-C. Hartemann (cnd), ORTF Lyric Orch Musidisc ▲ MUS 202322 [AAD]

Hahn, R.:O mon del inconnu!, w. Christiane Château (sop), Lina Dachary (sop), Monique Stiot (mez), Michel Hamel (ten), Aimé Doniat (bar), Dominique Tirmont (bar), Philippe Gaudin (sgr), Jacques Provins (sgr), J. Brebion (cnd), ORTF Lyric Orch Musidisc 2-▲ MUS 202562 [AAD]

Lehár, F.:Die lustige Witwe, w. Teresa Stich-Randall (mez—Missia Palmieri), Monique Stiot (mez—Manon), Germaine Duclos (sgr—Praskovia), Linda Felder (sgr—Olga), Christiane Jacquin (sgr—Nadia), Jeannette Levasseur (sgr—Sylviane), Henri Legay (ten—Camille de Coutançon), Joseph Peyron (ten—Kromsky), Robert Destain (sgr—Baron Popoff), Michel Fauche (sgr—Pristich), Gérard Friedmann (sgr—Lerida), Jacques Gilet (sgr—Bogdanowitch), Jean Guy Henneveux (sgr—Prince Danilo), Serge Klin (sgr—Figg), Jacques Villa (sgr—D'Estillac), A. Sibert (cnd), Belgian Radio-TV Orch, Belgian Radio-TV Chorus *(rec Grand Auditorium, Belgium, Apr 30, 1970)* Studio SM 2-▲ 2160 [AAD]

Planquette, R.:Rip van Winkle, w. Claudine Collart (sop), Lina Dachary (sop), Freda Betti (cta), René Lenoty (ten), Charles Daguerressar (bar), Julien Giovannetti (bar), Jacques Pruvost (bar), Lucien Lovano (bass), Patrick Orladey (sgr), Joëlle Pierre (sgr), M. Cariven (cnd), ORTF Lyric Orch, ORTF Lyric Chorale Musidisc ▲ MUS 201602 [AAD]

Pezzino, Léonardo (ten)

Ravel, M.:L'Enfant et les sortilèges, w. M. Lagrange (sop), E. Vidal (sop), M. Damonte (mez), M. Mahé (mez), A. Chedel (cta), M. Barrard (bar), V. le Texier (b-bar), A. Lombard (cnd), Bordeaux-Aquitaine National Orch, Bordeaux Grand Théâtre Municipal Chorus [F] Valois ▲ V 4670

Pfaff, Oly (ten)

Bruckner, A.:Motets, w. H. Zanotelli (cnd), Stuttgart Philharmonia Ensemble—12 Motets *(rec Apr. 6–7, 1979)* Calig ▲ CAL 50477 [ADD]

Pfeffer, Anneli (sop)

Weber, C.M. von:Peter Schmoll und seine Nachbarn, w. A. Pfeffer (sop—Minnette), J. Schmidt (ten—Martin Schmoll), S. Basa (ten—Karl Pirkner), H.-J. Schöpflin (ten—Niklas), R. Busching (bar—Peter Schmoll), H.J. Porcher (bass—Hans Bast), G. Markson (cnd), Hagen PO [G] *(rec Feb. 1–5, 1993)* Marco Polo 2-▲ 8.223592/93 [DDD]

Pfeiffer, Thomas (bar)

Dittersdorf, K.D. von:Doctor und Apotheker, w. Hildegard Uhrmacher (sop—Leonore), Donna Woodward (sop—Rosalia), Waltraud Meier (mez—Claudia), Martin Finke (ten—Sichel), Frieder Lang (ten—Gotthold), Alois Perl (ten—Gallus), Gerhard Unger (ten—Sturmwald), Thomas Pfeiffer (bar—Police Commisioner), Wolfgang Schöne (bar—Krautmann), Harald Stamm (bass—Stössel), J. Lockhart (cnd), Rhine State PO Bayer 2-▲ BR 100 238/39 [DDD]

Stavenhagen, B.:Songs, w. H. Spatzek (sop), H.-R. Förster (cnd), Vogtland PO Greiz/Reichenbach ebs ▲ ebs 6079 [DDD]

Pfeil, Cherie (sop)

Stuart, P.:Kill Bear Comes Home, w. Elana Gizzi (sop—Hasty Girl), Mi-Kyung Huh (sop—Cold Feet), Therese Murray (sop—Song Bird), Cherie Pfeil (sop—1st Sister), Renia Shukis (sop—2nd Sister), Riki Connaughton (mez—4th Sister), Lucy Fee (mez—3rd Sister), David Averbach (ten—Song Leader), Mark Schmidt (ten—Kill Bear), Jason Smith (bar—Cheif Wife Hunter), P. Stuart (cnd), Rochester Opera Theater Orch, Rochester Opera Theater Chorus VM ▲ DRK 154 [DDD]

Pfeiler, Christa (mez)

Diepenbrock, A.:Songs, w. Roberta Alexander (sop), Jard Van Ness (mez), Robert Holl (bass), Daniel Esser (vc), Rudolf Jansen (pno)—Berceuse; Clair de lune; Mandoline; L'Invitation au voyage; Les Chats; Receuillement; Puisque l'aube grandit; Incantation; En Sourdine; La Chanson de l'hypertrophique NM Classics ▲ NM 92051

Grieg, E.:Songs, w. M. Hirsti (sop), K. M. Sandve (ten), K. Skram (bar), R. Jansen (pno)—4 Songs, Op. 2; 4 Songs by Christian Winther, Op. 10; 9 Songs, Op. 18; 6 Songs by Ibsen, Op. 25 Victoria ▲ VCD 19042

Grieg, E.:Songs, w. M. Hirsti (sop), K. M. Sandve (ten), K. Skram (bar), R. Jansen (pno)—Op. 4, Nos. 1, 2, 3, 4, 5 & 6; Op. 21, Nos. 1, 2, 3 & 4; Op. 44, Nos. 1, 2, 3, 4, 5 & 6; Op. 48, Nos. 1, 2, 3, 4, 5 & 6; Op. 58, Nos. 1, 2, 3, 4 & 5 [N, G] Victoria ▲ VCD 19041

Mascagni, P.:Il piccolo Marat, w. S. Neves (sop—Mariella), C. Pfeiler (mez—Principessa di Fleury), D. Galvez-Vallejo (ten—Marat), S. Cowan (bar—Soldier), M. Dirks (bar—Il Ladro), F. Vassar (bass—L'Orco), H. Claessens (bass—Spy), K. Bakels (cnd), Netherlands RSO, Netherlands Radio Chorus *(rec Feb. 9, 1992)* Bongiovanni 2-▲ GB 2168/69 [DDD]

Pfitzinger, Gertrude (alt)

Brahms, J.:Liebeslieder Waltzes SATB, w. E. Berger (sop), W. Ludwig (ten), E. Wenk (bass), E.-G. Scherzer (pno), G. Falbe (pno) *(rec 1959)* FNAC Music ▲ 642313

Brahms, J.:Neue Liebeslieder Waltzes, w. E. Berger (sop), W. Ludwig (ten), E. Wenk (bass), E.-G. Scherzer (pno), G. Falbe (pno) *(rec 1959)* FNAC Music ▲ 642313

Pflanzl (ten)

Wagner, R.:Das Rheingold, w. E. Schwarzkopf (sop), I. Malaniuk (cta), W. Windgassen (ten), S. Björling (bar), H. von Karajan (cnd), Bayreuth Festival Orch, Bayreuth Festival Chorus [G] *(rec live, 1951)* Arkadia 2-▲ 216 (m) [ADD]

Wagner, R.:Das Rheingold, w. P. Brivkalne (sop), I. Malaniuk (cta), R. Siewert (cta), Fritz (sgr), S. Björling (bar), W. Faulhaber (bass), L. Weber (bass), F. Dalberg (bass), H. von Karajan (cnd), Bayreuth Festival Orch, Bayreuth Festival Chorus [G] *(rec live 8/1/51)* Melodram 2-▲ MEL 26107 (m) [AAD]

Pflanzl, Heinrich (bass)

Wagner, R.:Die Meistersinger von Nürnberg, w. Tiana Lemnitz (sop—Eva), Bernd Aldenhoff (ten—Walther von Stolzing), Gerhard Unger (ten—David), Ferdinand Frantz (b-bar—Hans Sachs), Kurt Boehme (bass—Veit Pogner), Heinrich Pflanzl (bass—Sixtus Beckmesser), R. Kempe (cnd), Saxon State Orch *(rec Dresden, 1951)* Myto 4-▲ MCD 961138

Wagner, R.:Siegfried, w. A. Varnay (sop), R. Siewert (cta), B. Aldenhoff (ten), P. Kuen (ten), S. Björling (bar), F. Dalberg (bass), H. von Karajan (cnd), Bayreuth Festival Orch, Bayreuth Festival Chorus [G] *(rec live 1951)* Melodram 4-▲ MEL 46106 (m) [AAD]

Pflieger, John (bar)

Krenek, E.:Der Sprüng über den Schatten, w. D. Amos (sop), L. Kemeny (sop), S. MacLean (mez), J. Dürmüller (ten), U. Neuweiler (ten), T. Brüning (sgr), D. de Villiers (cnd), Bielefeld PO, Bielefeld Phil Chorus [G] *(rec live, May 1989)* CPO 2-▲ CPO 999082-2 [DDD]

Philibosian, Nicole (sop)

Hurley, S.:Wind River Songs, w. Crispin Campbell (vc), Michael Coonrod (pno) *(rec Interlochen Center for the Arts)* Capstone ▲ CPS 8618

Philipson, Nils (sgr)

Nilsson, T.:Out of Earthly Night, w. Gudrun Bruna (sop), Marianne Mellnäs (sop), Kaysa Hälldin (alt), Lars Sjögren (ten), Göran Swartz (bass), Sture Hedin (sgr), Ola Kyhlberg (sgr), Lars Ljungman (sgr), Ulrik Quale (sgr), Nils Spangenberg (sgr), Britta Therén (sgr), Karl-Erik Welin (org), Torsten Nilsson (cnd), Oscar's Motet Choir *(rec Oscar's Church, Stockholm, Sweden, Apr 26–27, 1978)* BIS ▲ CD 138 [AAD]

Phillips, Norman (bar)

Martinů, B.:Ariadne, w. C. Lindsley (sop), V. Dolezal (ten), R. Novák (ten), V. Neumann (cnd), Czech PO, Czech Phil Chorus [Cz] Supraphon ▲ 10 4395-2 [DDD]

Philpot, Margaret (alt)

From a Spanish Palace Songbook:Music from the Time of Columbus, w. Shirley Rumsey (vihs/lts/gtrs), Christopher Wilson (vihs/lts/gtrs) Hyperion ▲ CDA 66454 [DDD]

Piaf, Edith (sgr)

Edith Piaf 30th Anniversary Anthology Angel 10-▲ CDMJ 79064

Piau, Sandrine (sop)

Chausson, E.:Mélodies (comp), w. Brigitte Balleys (mez), Jean François Gardeil (bar), Billy Eidi (pno), Ludwig String Quartet Timpani 2-▲ 2C 2028

Couperin, F.:Motets, w. C. Pelon (sop), J.-P. Fouchécourt (ten), J. Corréas (bass), Les Talens Lyriques—Quatre versets d'un motet composé de l'ordre du Roy (1703); Verset du motet de l'année dernièr; Sept versets d'un motet composé de l'ordre du Roy (1704); Motet à Sainte Suzanne; Sept versets d'un motet composé de l'ordre du Roy (1705); Laudate Pueri Dominum rec. May 25–28, 1993 FNAC Music ▲ 592244 [DDD]

Handel, G.F.:Messiah, w. Barbara Schlick (sop), Andreas Scholl (alt), Mark Padmore (ten), Nathan Berg (bass), W. Christie (cnd), Les Arts Florissants [1742 Dublin version] Harmonia Mundi France 2-▲ HMC 901498/99

Handel, G.F.:Riccardo Primo, w. Claire Brua (sop—Pulcheria), Sandrine Piau (sop—Costanza), Sara Mingardo (cta—Riccardo), Pascal Bertin (alt—Oronte), Roberto Scaltriti (bar—Isacio), Olivier Lallouette (bass—Berardo), C. Rousset (cnd), Les Talens Lyriques L'oiseau Lyre ▲ 452 201-2

Handel, G.F.:Scipione, w. Doris Lamprecht (sop), Vandaa Tabery (mez), Guy Flechter (ten), Oliver Lalouette (bass), C. Rousset (cnd), Les Talens Lyriques [I] FNAC Music 3-▲ 592245 [DDD]

Lalande, M.-R. de:Motets, w. V. Gens (sop), A. Steyer (sop), J.-P. Fouchécourt (ten), F. Piolino (ten), J. Corréas (bass), W. Christie (cnd), Les Arts Florissants [L] Harmonia Mundi France ▲ HMC 901351

Lalande, M.-R. de:Te Deum, w. V. Gens (sop), A. Steyer (sop), J.-P. Fouchécourt (ten), F. Piolino (ten), J. Corréas (bass), W. Christie (cnd), Les Arts Florissants [L] Harmonia Mundi France ▲ HMC 901351

Mendelssohn, F.:A Midsummer Night's Dream (comp), w. Delphine Collot (sop), P. Herreweghe (cnd), Champs Élysées Theater Orch Harmonia Mundi France ▲ HMC 901502

Rameau, J.P.:L'Impatience, w. Limoges Baroque Ensemble Soloists *(rec Sept 14–16, 1994)* FNAC Music ▲ CD 592333

Rameau, J.P.:Les Indes galantes, w. C. McFadden (sop), I. Poulenard (sop), N. Rime (sop), M. Ruggeri (sop), H. Crook (ten), J.-P. Fouchecourt (ten), N. Rivenq (bar), J. Corréas (bass), B. Delétré (bass), W. Christie (cnd), Les Arts Florissants [F] Harmonia Mundi France 3-▲ HMC 901367/69

Rameau, J.P.:Pygmalion, w. A. Mellon (sop—Céphise), D. Michel-Dansac (sop—La Statue), S. Piau (sop—L'Amour), H. Crook (ten—Pygmalion), W. Christie (cnd), Les Arts Florissants, Les Arts Florissants Chorus [F] *(rec 5/91)* Harmonia Mundi France ▲ HMC 901381

Piavko, Vladislav (ten)

Shchedrin, R.:Dead Souls, w. Larisa Avdeyeva (mez—Korobochka), Galina Borisova (mez—Plyushkin), Alexi Maslennikov (ten—Selifan), Vladislav Piavko (ten—Nozdryov), Vitali Vlasov (ten—Manilov), Boris Morozov (bass—Sobakevich), Alexander Voroshilo (sgr—Chichikov), Y. Temirkanov (cnd), Bolshoi Theater Orch, Bolshoi Theater Chorus, Moscow Chamber Choir *(rec Moscow, 1982)* Melodiya ("The Russian Opera" series) 2-▲ 74321-29347-2 [ADD]

Piazza, Luigi (bar)

Verdi, G.:Rigoletto, w. Lina Pagliughi (sop—Gilda), Linda Brambilla (mez—Contessa di Ceprano), Vera de Cristoff (cta—Maddalena), Tino Folgar (ten—Duca di Mantova), Giuseppe Nessi (ten—Borsa), Aristide Baracchi (bar—Conte di Monterone/Marullo), Luigi Piazza (bar—Rigoletto), Salvatore Baccaloni (bass—Sparafucile), Giuseppe Menni (bass—Conte di Ceprano), C. Sabajno (cnd), La Scala Orch, La Scala Chorus *(rec 1927–28)* Arkadia 2-▲ CD 78003 (m) [ADD]

Verdi, G.:Rigoletto, w. Lina Pagliughi (sop—Gilda), Linda Brambilla (mez—Countess Ceprano), Vera De Cristoff (cta—Maddalena), Tino Folgar (ten—Duke of Mantua), Giuseppe Nessi (ten—Borsa), Luigi Piazza (bar—Rigoletto), Aristide Baracchi (b-bar—Monterone/Marullo), Salvatore Baccaloni (bass—Sparafucile), Giuseppe Menni (bass—Ceprano), C. Sabajno (cnd), La Scala Orch, La Scala Chorus *(rec La Scala Theatre, Milan, Nov.-Dec. 1927 & Feb. 192)* VAI Audio 2-▲ VAIA 1097-2

Verdi, G.:Rigoletto, w. Lina Pagliughi (sop), Salvatore Baccaloni (bass), Tino Folgar (sgr), C. Sabajno (cnd), La Scala Orch, La Scala Chorus Pearl 2-▲ PEA 9180 [ADD]

Piccaluga, Nino (ten)

Leoncavallo, R.:Pagliacci (sels), w. Enrico Caruso (ten), Antonio Paoli (ten), Giovanni Zenatello (ten), Amedeo Bassi (ten), Hermann Jadlowker (ten), Fernand Ansseau (ten), Hipolito Lazaro (ten), Mario Chamlee (ten), Giacomo Lauri-Volpi (ten), Miguel Fleta (ten), Giovanni Martinelli (ten), Aureliano Pertile (ten), Georges Thill (ten), Alessandro Valente (ten), Francesco Merli (ten), Lauritz Melchior (ten), Marcel Wittrisch (ten), Joseph Schmidt (ten), Beniamino Gigli (ten), Giuseppe Lugo (ten), Helge Roswaenge (ten), Jussi Bjoerling (ten)—23 versions of the tenor aria "Vesti la giubba" *(rec 1907–1944)* Bongiovanni ▲ GB 1071 [ADD]

Nino Piccaluga Bongiovanni ▲ GB 1079 [ADD]

Verdi, G.:Il trovatore (sels), w. J. Biel (ten), F. Tamagno (ten), L.-A. Escalaïs (ten), M. Gilion (ten), E. Caruso (ten), A. Paoli (ten), G. Zenatello (ten), J. Sembach (ten), L. Slezak (ten), F. Constantino (ten), G. Martinelli (ten), B. De Muro (ten), N. Fusati (ten), G. Lauri-Volpi (ten), A. Pertile (ten), E. Bergamaschi (ten), R. Tauber (ten), J. O'Sullivan (ten), H. Roswaenge (ten), G. Taccani (ten), V. Lois (ten), H. Lazaro (ten), A. Lindi (ten), A. Cortis (ten), F. Merli (ten), F. Völker (ten), J. Kiepura (ten), J. Schmidt (ten), J. Bjoerling (ten), B. Gigli (ten), A. Salvarezza (ten), J. Soler (ten), M. Filippeschi (ten)—34 performances of the Act III tenor aria "Di quella pira!," *(rec from 1903–1956)* Bongiovanni ▲ GB 1051 [AAD]

Piccaver, Alfred (ten)

Alfred Piccaver Preiser ("Lebendige Vergangenheit" series) ▲ 89060 (m) [AAD]

Alfred Piccaver:The Complete Electric Recordings, 1928–30 Preiser 2-▲ PRE 89217 [ADD]

Mascagni, P.:Cavalleria rusticana (sels), w. Alfred Piccaver (ten—Turiddu), Emil Schipper (bar—Alfio), K. Alwin (cnd), Vienna State Opera Orch *(rec May 10, 1937)* Koch Schwann 2-▲ SCH 314632 [ADD]

Opera Arias(ten) (rec. 1928–30) Pearl ▲ PEA 9412 (m) [AAD]

Picchi, Mirto (ten)

Bellini, V.:Norma, w. M. Callas (sop), J. Sutherland (sop), E. Stignani (mez), G. Vaghi (bass), V. Gui (cnd), Royal Opera House Orch, Royal Opera House Chorus Covent Garden [I] *(rec live, Covent Garden 11/52)* Verona 3-▲ 27018/20 (m) [AAD]

Bellini, V.:Norma, w. J. Sutherland (sop), M. Callas (sop), E. Stignani (mez), G. Vaghi (bass), V. Gui (cnd), Royal Opera House Orch, Royal Opera House Chorus Covent Garden [I] *(rec live, Covent Garden 11/52)* Melodram 2-▲ MEL 26025

Bellini, V.:Norma, w. Maria Callas (sop), Joan Sutherland (sop), Ebe Stignani (cta), Paul Asciak (sgr), V. Gui (cnd), Royal Opera House Orch, Royal Opera House Chorus Covent Garden *(rec live, London, 1952)* Enterprise ("Documents" series) 3-▲ ENTLV 968 [ADD]

Bellini, V.:Norma, w. M. Callas (sop), J. Sutherland (sop), E. Stignani (mez), G. Vaghi (bass), V. Gui (cnd), Royal Opera House Orch, Royal Opera House Chorus Covent Garden [I] *(rec live, Covent Garden 11/52)* Legato Classics 2-▲ LCD 130-2 (m) [AAD]

Cherubini, L.:Médée, w. M. Callas (sop), R. Scotto (sop), M. Pirazzini (mez), T. Serafin (cnd), La Scala Orch, La Scala Chorus [I] *(rec live, 1953)* EMI Classics (Studio) 2-▲ CDMB 63625 [ADD]

Mozart, W.A.:Nozze di Figaro, w. Mirella Freni (sop), Daniela Mazzucato (sop), Teresa Berganza (mez), Hermann Prey (bar), José Van Dam (b-bar), Paolo Montarsolo (bass), C. Abbado (cnd), La Scala Orch, La Scala Chorus *(rec live, Apr 22, 1974)* Arkadia 3-▲ 614

Mussorgsky, M.:Khovanshchina, w. Irene Companez (cta), Herbert Handt (ten), Boris Christoff (bass), Armedeo Berdini (sgr), Giorgio Canello (sgr), Dmitri Lopatto (sgr), Michele Malaspina (sgr), Jolanda Mancini (sgr), Mario Petri (sgr), A. Rodzinski (cnd), Rome RAI Radio-TV SO, Rome RAI Chorus Stradivarius 2-▲ STV DTM 12320 [ADD]

Mussorgsky, M.:Khovanshchina, w. Jolanda Mancini (sop—Emma), Irene Companez (mez), Amedeo Berdini (ten—Prince Andrei Khovanski), Mirto Picchi (ten—Prince Vasili Golitsin), Herbert Handt (ten—Scribe), Andrea Mineo (bar—Kuzka), Giampiero Malaspina (bar—Shaklovity), Boris Christoff (bass—Dosifei), Mario Petri (bass—Prince Ivan Khovanski), Dimitri Lopatto (Varsonofiev/First Strelyets), Giorgio Conello (Second Strelyets), A. Rodzinski (cnd), *(orch unknown)* [I] *(rec Rome, 1958)* VAI Audio 2-▲ VAIA 1052-2

Spontini, G.:La vestale, w. R. Scotto (sop), O. Dominguez (mez), F. Tagliavini (ten), V. Gui (cnd), Florence Maggio Musicale Orch, Florence Maggio Musicale Chorus [I] *(rec live 5/5/70)* Melodram ("Connaisseur" series) 2-▲ CDM 27512 [ADD]

Verdi, G.:Aida (sels), w. M. Callas (sop), E. Stignani (mez), R. De Falchi (bar), G. Neri (bass), V. Bellezza (cnd), Rome Opera Orch—five arias with Callas (solo, three duets & quintet) *(rec live 10/2/50)* Melodram 2-▲ CDM 26019 [AAD]

Verdi, G.:Don Carlos, w. M. Caniglia (sop—Elisabeth de Valois), G. Sciutti (sop—Page), E. Stignani (mez—Princess Eboli), M. Picchi (ten—Don Carlos), M. Ponz de L. (ten—Count of Lerma), P. Silveri (bar—Rodrigue), N. Rossi Lemeni (bass—Philip II), G. Neri (bass—Grand Inquisitor), A. Gaggi (bass—Old Monk), F. Previtali (cnd), Rome RAI SO, Rome RAI Chorus *(rec Rome, 1951)* Cetra Classic 3-▲ CDO 25 [ADD]

Verdi, G.:Macbeth, w. Leyla Gencer (sop), Giuseppe Taddei (bar), Ferruccio Mazzoli (bass), V. Gui (cnd), Palermo Teatro Massimo Orch, Palermo Teatro Massimo Chorus *(rec Palermo, Jan. 14, 1960)* Pantheon 2-▲ PHE 6604 (m)

Piccini, Fernanda (cta)

Boccherini, L.:Credo, w. Svetla Krasteva (sop), Manuel Beltrand (ten), Duccio Dal Monte (bass), G. Cosmi (cnd), Lucca Teatro Comunale Giglio Orch *(rec Dec 18, 1993)* Bongiovanni ▲ GB 2178 [DDD]

Boccherini, L.:Kyrie & Gloria, w. Svetla Krasteva (sop), Manuel Beltrand (ten), Duccio Dal Monte (bass), G. Cosmi (cnd), Lucca Teatro Comunale Giglio Orch *(rec Dec 18, 1993)* Bongiovanni ▲ GB 2178 [DDD]

Piccinni, Andrea (bass)

Giordano, U.:Fedora, w. Maria Caniglia (sop), Aldo Bertocci (ten), Giacinto Prandelli (ten), Scipio Colombo (bar), Capozzi (sgr), M. Rossi (cnd), Turin RAI SO, Turin RAI Chorus *(rec 1950)* Cetra Classic 2-▲ Don 35

Puccini, G.:La Bohème, w. Katia Ricciarelli (sop), Francisco Araiza (ten), Angelo Casertano (ten), Stefano Antonucci (bar), Claudio Giombi (bar), Paata Burchuladze (bass), Alfredo Mariotti (bass), Alberto Noli (bass), Lauren Broglia (sgr), A. Guadagno (cnd), Arena di Verona Orch, Limburg Cathedral Boys' Chorus Koch Schwann 2-▲ SCH 315922

Piccoli, Francesco (ten)

Manfroce, N.A.:Ecuba, w. A. C. Antonacci (sop), D. di Domenico (ten), G. De Bellida (sgr), M. de Bernart (cnd), Italian PO, Italian Phil Chorus [I] *(rec live 1990)* Bongiovanni 2-▲ GB 2119/20 [DDD]

Piccollo, Silvia (sop)

Fux, J.J.:Dafne in Lauro, w. L. Akerlund (sop), M. van der Sluis (sop), G. Lesne (alt), M. Klietmann (ten), R. Clemencic (cnd), Clemencic Consort, La Cappella Vocal Ensemble [I] Nuova Era ("Ancient Music" series) 2-▲ 6930/31 [DDD]

Hasse, J.A.:Larinda e Vanesio, w. Silvia Piccollo (sop—Larinda), Giorgio Gatti (bar—Vanesio), S. Carchiolo (cnd), Catania Baroque Orch *(rec Sept. 29, 1992)* Bongiovanni ▲ GB 2137

Marcello, B.:Il pianto e il riso delle quattro stagioni, w. A. Carmignani (ct-Estate), M. Beasley (ten-Autunno), R. Franceschetto (bass-Inverno), F. Ghiglione (cnd), Don Milani Cultural Association Orch, G. B. Trofello Schola Cantorum *(rec Mar. 29, 1992)* Bongiovanni 2-▲ GB 2159/60 [DDD]

Scarlatti, A.:Abramo, il tuo sembiante, w. L. Bacchetta (sop), M. Lazzara (alt), M. Nuvoli (ten), G. Dagnino (bass), E. Velardi (cnd), Alessandro Stradella Consort [period instrs] [I] Nuova Era ("Ancient Music" series) ▲ 7117 [DDD]

Scarlatti, A.:Cants, w. R. Balconi (ten), S. Bagliano (rcr), Collegium Pro Musica—includes Clori mia, Clori bella; Filli che esprime la sua fede a Fileno; Ardo e ver per te d'amore; Tu sei quella che al nime sembri giusta, plus others Nuova Era ("Ancient Music" series) ▲ NUO 7162 [DDD]

Scarlatti, A.:Santa Maria Maddalena de'pazzi, w. R. Bertini (sop), G. Bandittelli (mez), F. Biondi (cnd), Europa Galante Opus 111 ▲ OPS 30-96

Steffani, A.:Vocal Music, w. M. Mazzara (alt), E. Velardi (cnd), Alessandro Stradella Consort—"Fileno Idolo Mio," Cantata for Soprano, 2 Violins & Continuo [attributed]; "Il Più Felice e Sfortunato Amante," Cantata for Alto, 2 Violins & Continuo [attributed]; "Porto L'Alma Incenerita," Chamber Duet for Soprano, Alto & Continuo [I] Bongiovanni ▲ GB 2123 [DDD]

Stradella, A.:Esule dalle sfere, w. Roberta Invernizzi (sop), Marco Lazzara (alt), Mario Nuvoli (ten), Riccardo Ristori (bass), Carlo Lepore (bass), Alessandro Stradella Consort Bongiovanni ▲ GB 2165 [DDD]

Piccollo, Silvia (sop) (cont.)
Stradella, A.:Il moro per amore, w. R. Invernizzi (sop—Eurinda), S. Piccollo (sop—Lucinda), M. Grazia Liguori (sop—Fiorino), M. Lazzara (cta—Lindora), V. Matacchini (cta—Feraspe/Floridoro), M. Beasley (ten—Filandro), R. Ristori (bass—Rodrigo), E. Velardi (cnd), Alessandro Stradella Consort [I] *(rec Oct. 31–Nov. 3, 1992)* Bongiovanni 3-▲ GB 2153/55
Stradella, A.:Ó di Cocito oscure deità, w. R. Invernizzi (sop—Proserpina), S. Piccollo (sop—Vendetta), M. Nuvoli (ten—Inganno), R. Ristori (bass—Plutone), E. Velardi (cnd), Alessandro Stradella Consort *(rec Oct. 25, 1993)* Bongiovanni ▲ GB 2164 [DDD]
Stradella, A.:Susanna, w. L. Bertotti (sop), M. Lazzara (cta), M. Nuvoli (ten), M. Perrella (bass), E. Velardi (cnd), Camerata Ligure [period instrs] [I] Bongiovanni 2-▲ GB 2121/22 [DDD]
Stradella, A.:Vocal Music, w. E. Smith (hpd), G. Dagnino (bass), M. Mazzara (alt), R. Balconi (ct), E. Velardi (cnd), Alessandro Stradella Consort—Sinfonia in E from the Cantata "Crudo Mar"; Toccata in a for Harpsichord; Exultate in Deo Fideles, Motet for Bass Solo & Violins; Si Apra al Riso Ogni Labbro, Cantata for 3 Voices & Strings [I,L] Bongiovanni ▲ GB 2123 [DDD]

Picconi, Maurizio (sgr)
Donizetti, G.:Il furioso all'isola di Santo Domingo, w. P. Antonucci (sop), L. Serra (sop), E. Tandura (mez), L. Canonici (ten), R. Coviello (bar), C. Rizzi (cnd), Piacenza SO, Piacenza Chorus [I] *(rec live, 11/10/87)* Bongiovanni 3-▲ GB 2056/58 [DDD]
Jommelli, N.:La Passione di Gesù Cristo, w. Debora Beronesi (sop), Anke Herrmann (sgr), Jeffrey Francis (ten), A. de Marchi (cnd), Berlin Baroque Academy, Eufonia, Sigismondo D'India *(rec Mar 31–Apr 4, 1996)* K617 2-▲ 7063 [DDD]

Pichler, Joseph (sgr)
Gassmann, F.L.:La Contessina, w. Susanne Ganglberger (sop—Vespina), Elisabeth Mayer (sop—Contessina), Barbara Eisschiel (mez—Lindoro), Hermann Diller (ten—Gazzetta), Kurt Köller (bar—Pancrazio), H. Dechant (cnd), Collegium Aureum Bayer 2-▲ BR 100 252/3 [DDD]

Picillo, Antonio (bass)
Verdi, G.:La traviata (sels), w. Anna de Santis (sop—Annina), Renata Tebaldi (sop—Violetta), Giuseppe Campora (ten—Alfredo), Gerardo Gaudioso (bar—Douphol), Giuseppe Taddei (bar—Germont), Antonio Picillo (bass—Grenvil), G. Santini (cnd), Naples Teatro San Carlo Orch, Naples Teatro San Carlo Chorus—E strano...Ah, fors'e lui; Follie!...Sempre libera; Pero l'attendo...Amami, Alfredo; Invitato a qui seguirmi; Alfredo, Alfredo, di questo core; Teneste la promessa...Addio del passato; Ma se tornando...Ah! Gran Dio! Morir si giovine; Se una pudica vergine *(rec San Carlo Theater, Naples, Jan. 17, 1952)* Legato Classics 2-▲ LCD 193-2 [ADD]

Pickens, Jo Ann (sop)
Bowles, P.:Songs, w. Howard Haskin (ten) *(rec live, Paris, May 8, 1994)* Koch Schwann ▲ SCH 315742
My Heritage, w. D. Sulzen (pno) Koch Schwann ▲ SCH 314472 [DDD]

Pick-Hieronimi, Monica (sop)
Beethoven, L. van:Christus am Ölberg, w. J. Anderson (sop), V. von Halem (bass), S. Baudo (cnd), Lyon National Orch, Lyon National Chorus [G] Harmonia Mundi France ▲ HMC 905181
Verdi, G.:Nabucco, w. Anna Schiatti (sop), Mina Blum (sop), Angelo Casertano (ten), Gilberto Maffezzoni (ten), Paolo Gavanelli (bass), Paata Burchuladze (bass), Franco Federici (bass), A. Guadagno (cnd), Arena di Verona Orch, Arena di Verona Chorus *(rec Berlin, Spring 1996)* Koch Schwann 2-▲ SCH CD 364272

Pickova, L. M. (sop)
Milesi, P.:Modi 2, w. Françoise Goddard (alt), M. Ferradini (ten), B. Andersen (bass), D. Cassamagnaghi (fl), S. Scanziani (ob), A. Bianchi (cl/b cl), E. Crisafulli (bn), C. Gazzola (hn), F. Gualandris (tuba), A. Girardi (celtic hp), R. Anedda (vn), E. Groppo (vn), M. Pagani (vn), M. Ravasio (va), S. Righini (vc), P. Rizzi (db), J. Scully (perc), P. Milesi (cnd) Cuneiform ▲ RUNE 63

Picon, Molly (sgr)
Bock, J.:Fiddler on the Roof, w. Robert Merrill (bar), S. Black (cnd), London Festival Orch, London Festival Chorus London ("Phase 4 Stereo" series) ▲ 448 949-2

Pierard, Catherine (sop/mez)
Britten, H.:The Rape of Lucretia (sels), w. P. Rozario (sop), A. Gunson (mez), J. Rigby (cta), N. Robson (ten), D. Maxwell (bar), A. Opie (bar), A. Miles (bass), R. Hickox (cnd), City of London Sinfonia Chandos 2-▲ CHAN 9254/55 [DDD]
Howells, H.:Songs, w. L. Dawson (sop), J.M. Ainsley (ten), B. Luxon (bar), J. Drake (pno)—7 various songs; 2 South African Settings; 3 Folksongs; A Garland for De la Mare; Peacock Pie, Op. 33; 4 French Chansons, Op. 29; In Green Ways, Op. 43; 12 various songs; 3 Children's Songs; 4 Songs, Op. 22 Chandos 2-▲ CHAN 9185/86 [DDD]
Purcell, H.:The Fairy Queen, w. Lorraine Hunt (sop), Susan Bickley (mez), Howard Crook (ten), Mark Padmore (ten), David Wilson-Johnson (bar), Richard Wistreich (bass), R. Norrington (cnd), London Classical Players, Schütz Choir London EMI Classics ▲ CDCB 55234
Purcell, H.:The Prophetess, or The History of Dioclesian, w. J. Bowman (alt), J. M. Ainsley (ten), I. Bostridge (ten), M. George (bass), R. Hickox (cnd), Collegium Musicum 90—Masque Chandos ("Chaconne" series) ▲ CHAN 0558 [DDD]
Purcell, H.:The Prophetess, or The History of Dioclesian, w. James Bowman (alt), John Mark Ainsley (ten), Michael George (bass), R. Hickox (cnd), Collegium Musicum 90 Chandos ▲ CHAN 0569/70 [DDD]

Pierce, Jacqueline (sop)
Luening, O.:No Jerusalem But This, w. K. Sullivan (sop), Paul Sperry (ten), M. Moliterno (bar), P. Wilder (sgr), S. Rosser (sgr), A. Goodman (cnd), Music Project CO, Goodman Chamber Choir [E] *(rec 6/6/90)* CRI ▲ CD 600 [DDD]

Pieres, Josep (alt)
Britten, H.:A Ceremony of Carols, w. S. Bardolet (trb), X. Canadell (trb), F. Gasa (alt), M. L. Ibañez (hp), G. Estrada (org), Escolania de Montserrat, I. Segarra (cnd) *(rec 1978?)* Koch Treasure ▲ 31624-2 [ADD]
Mendelssohn, F.:Motets, Op. 39, w. S. Bardolet (trb), X. Canadell (trb), F. Gasa (alt), M. L. Ibañez (hp), G. Estrada (org), I. Segarra (cnd), Montserrat Escolania *(rec 1978?)* Koch Treasure ▲ 31624-2 [ADD]

Pierik, B. (sop)
Schlegel, L.:Deutsche Liebeslieder, w. N. van der Meel (ten), F. van Ruth (pno) [G] Attacca ▲ 8951-4 [DDD]

Pierotti, Raquel (mez)
Bretón, T.:La Verbena de la paloma, w. Maria Bayo (sop), Plácido Domingo (ten), Enrique Baquerizo (sgr), Rafael Castejon (sgr), Milagros Martin (sgr), Silva Tro (sgr), A. Ros-Marbá (cnd), Madrid SO Valois ("Zarauela" series) ▲ V 4725
Nebra, J.:Viento, w. Marta Almajano (sop), Maite Arruabarrena (sop), Pilar Jurado (sop), Maria del Mar Doval (sgr), C. Coin (cnd), Limoges Baroque Ensemble Valois ▲ V 4752
Rossini, G.:Il barbiere di Siviglia (sels), w. M. Horne (mez), P. Barbacini (ten), E. Dara (bar), L. Nucci (bar), S. Ramey (bass), S. Sammaritano (bass), R. Chailly (cnd), La Scala Orch, La Scala Chorus *(rec Milan, Jan. 2–18, 1982)* Sony Classical ("Opera Highlights" series) ▲ SMK 53501 [DDD]
Vives, A.:Doña Francisquita, w. S. S. Jerico (sgr), A. R. Marbá (cnd), Tenerife SO Valois 2-▲ V 4710

Pierre, Joëlle (sgr)
Planquette, R.:Rip van Winkle, w. Claudine Collart (sop), Lina Dachary (sop), Freda Betti (cta), René Lenoty (ten), Joseph Peyron (ten), Charles Daguerressar (bar), Julien Giovannetti (bar), Jacques Pruvost (bar), Lucien Lovano (bass), Patrick Orladey (sgr), M. Carivèn (cnd), ORTF Lyric Orch, ORTF Lyric Chorale Musidisc ▲ MUS 201602 [AAD]

Pieweck, Katja (sop)
Haydn, M.:Missa Sancti Aloysii, w. Erdmann (sgr), Wegrzyn (cnd), Hanover Chamber Academy Ars Musici ▲ 1113
Kaleidoscope, w. Hannover Girls' Choir, Andrea Schnaus (pno) *(rec 1982 & 1993)* Thorofon ▲ CTH 2174 [ADD/DDD]

Pikal, Guido (ten)
Furtwängler, W.:Religiöser Hymnus, w. *(sop unknown)*, A. Walter (cnd), Frankfurt on the Oder PO, Frankfurt on the Oder Phil Chorus *(rec Konzarthalle C.P.E. Bach, Frankfurt on the Oder, June 22–25 1993)* Marco Polo ▲ 8.223546 [DDD]

Pikal, Guido (ten) (cont.)
Furtwängler, W.:Songs, w. Alfred Walter (pno), A. Walter (cnd), Frankfurt on the Oder PO, Frankfurt on the Oder Phil Chorus—Der traurige Jäger; Der Schatzgräber; Geduld; Auf dem See; Du sendest, Freund, mir Lieder; Erinnerung; Das Vaterland; Möwenflug; Lied; Erinnerung; Der Soldat *(rec Maison de la Radio Bruxelles, Oct. 7–8, 1993)* Marco Polo ▲ 8.223546 [DDD]

Pike, Julian (ten)
Klein, G.:Original Sin, w. Sotto Voce Vocal Ensemble Arion ▲ ARN 68272 [DDD]

Piland, J. (sop)
Massenet, J.:Thérèse, w. H. Haskin (ten), C. van Tassel (bar), L. Vis (cnd), Netherlands PO, Netherlands Theater Chorus [F] Canal Grande ▲ CG 9220 [DDD]

Pilarczyk, Helga (sop)
Berg, A.:Lulu (suite), w. A. Dorati (cnd), London SO Mercury Living Presence ▲ 432006-2 [ADD]
Berg, A.:Wozzeck (sels), w. A. Dorati (cnd), London SO—3 sels. [G] Mercury Living Presence ▲ 434325-2 [ADD]
Janácek, L.:Slavonic Mass, w. J. Martin (mez), N. Gedda (ten), G. Gaynes (sgr), L. Bernstein (cnd), New York PO, Westminster Choir *(rec 1963)* Sony Classical ("Bernstein:The Royal Edition" series) ▲ SMK 47569 [ADD]
Schoenberg, A.:Pierrot lunaire, w. *(other artists unknown)*, P. Boulez (cnd) Adès ▲ ADE 202912 [AAD]

Pilarczyk, Olga (sop)
Schoenberg, A.:Erwartung, w. V. Neumann (cnd), Czech PO *(rec 1964)* Praga ▲ PR 250082

Pilewski, Witold (bass)
Moniuszko, S.:Mass in E♭, w. H. Slonicka (sop), A. Malewicz (mez), E. Kajdasz (cnd), Warsaw CO, Polish Radio Chorus Olympia ▲ OLY 395 [ADD]
Moniuszko, S.:Sacred Music, w. H. Slonicka (sop), A. Malewicz (mez), E. Kajdasz (cnd), Warsaw CO, Polish Radio Chorus—Ne memineris; Vide humilitatem meam; Litanie Ostrobramskie, No. 1 Olympia ▲ OLY 395 [ADD]

Pilgrim, Neva (sop)
Caltabiano, R.:Torched Liberty, w. V. Pritsker (vn), G. Macero (vc), L. Greene (pic/fl/alt fl), K. Schempf (E♭/A/B♭ cl), G. Coble (tpt), S. Heyman (pno), L. Luttinger (perc), R. Caltabiano (cnd) Opus One ▲ CD 168 [DDD]
Ziffrin, M.:Sym, "Letters", w. R. Black (cnd), Slovak RSO Bratislava *(rec Slovak Radio & TV Studios, Slovak National Republic, June & Sept 1993)* MMC ▲ MMC 2015 [DDD]

Pillow, Sarah (sgr)
Purcell, H.:Dido & Aeneas, w. Cassandra Hoffman (sop—Belinda), Arlene Travis (sop—2nd Witch), Desirée Halac (mez—Sorceress/Spirit), Jennifer Lane (mez—Dido), Elizabeth Norman (alt), Thomas Bogdan (ten—A Sailor), Michael Brown (bar—Aeneas), Curtis Streetman (bar), Caitriona O'Leary (sgr—2nd Woman), Sarah Pillow (sgr—1st Witch), B. Brookshire (cnd), San Cassiano Musici *(rec St. Ignatius of Antioch Episcopal Church, New York City, Spring 1995)* Vox Classics ▲ VOX 7518

Pilou, J. (sop)
Gounod, C.:Roméo et Juliette (sels), w. J. Pilou (sop—Juliette), F. Corelli (ten—Romeo), A. Guadagno (cnd), *(orch unknown)*—8 arias & scenes *(rec live, Philadelphia, 10/24/67)* HRE 2-▲ 1011-2 [ADD]

Piltti, Lea (sop)
Strauss, R.:Songs, w. M. Reining (sop—6 solo songs), L. Piltti (sop—7 solo songs), A. Dermota (ten—8 solo songs), R. Strauss (pno)—Opp. 10/1, 27/2, 29/1, 37/3, 41/1, 48/1 *(Reining)*; Opp. 15/5, 17/2, 21/1, 29/2, 48/2, 48/3, 49/1 *(Piltti)*; Opp. 10/1, 10/3, 17/1, 19/2, 21/2, 27/3, 32/1, 37/2 *(Dermota)* [G] *(rec Vienna, Apr. 1942)* Preiser ▲ 93262 (m) [AAD]

Pinchik, Pierre (cant)
Echoes of the Temple:Cantors in Prayer & Folksong, w. Gershon Sirota (cant), Samuel Vigoda (cant), Joseph Rosenblatt (cant), Arthur Tracy (cant), et al. *(rec 1914–36)* Pearl ▲ PEA 9126 [ADD]

Pincus, Daniel (ten)
Jane's Hand:The Jane Austen Songbooks, w. Julianne Baird (sop), Elizabeth Henreckson-Farnum (sop), Lorie Gratis (mez), Philip Anderson (ten), Martil Dillon (ten), Nancy Wilson (bar vn), Peter Segal (bar gtr), Mary Jane Newman (pno/hpd), Anthony Newman (pno) Vox Classics ▲ VOX 7537 [DDD]

Pinheiro, Reginaldo (ten)
Mozart, W.A.:Music of, w. Philip Defrancq (ten), Jan Van Der Crabben (bar), Jan Vermeulen (pno), Guy Penson (org), P. Peire (cnd), Collegium Instrumentale Brugense, Capella Brugensis—Zerfliesset heut', geliebte Brüder [song]; Dir Seele des Weltalls [cant]; O heiliges Band der Freundschaft [song]; Die ihr einem Neuen Grade [Maurer-Geselienlied]; Die Maurerfreude [cant]; Maurerische Trauermusik; Die ihr der unermesslichen Weltalls Schöpfer ehrt [Kleine deutsche Kantate]; Laut verkünde unsre Freude [Eine kleine Freimaurerkantate]; Lasst uns mit geschlugnen Händen [hymn]; Ihr unsre neuen Leiter [song] *(rec Studio Steurbaut, Gent, Dec 1992)* René Gailly ▲ 92013 [DDD]

Pini, Amalia (mez)
Boito, A.:Mefistofele, w. Orietta Moscucci (sop—Margherita), Amalia Pini (mez—Martha), Piero de Palma (ten—Wagner), Giacinto Prandelli (ten—Faust), Boris Christoff (bass—Mefistofele), V. Gui (cnd), Rome Opera Orch, Rome Opera Chorus EMI Classics 2-▲ CDMB 65655
Giordano, U.:Andrea Chénier, w. Renata Tebaldi (sop—Maddalena), Anna di Stasio (mez—Bersi), Amalia Pini (mez—Madelon/Contessa), Mario Del Monaco (ten—Andrea Chenier), Antonio Pirino (ten—L'Incredibile/Abate), Aldo Protti (bar—Carlo Gerard), Arturo La Porta (bass/bar—Mathieu/Fleville), Silvano Pagliuca (bass/bar—Roucher/Fouquier-Tinville), Giorgio Onesti (bass—Dumas/Schmidt/Major-domo), F. Capuana (cnd), Italian Lyric Orch, Italian Lyric Chorus *(rec Tokyo, Oct 1, 1961)* Legato Classics 2-▲ LCD 214-2 [ADD]
Mascagni, P.:L'amico Fritz, w. P. Tassinari (sop—Suzel), A. Pini (mez—Beppe), F. Tagliavini (ten—Fritz), A. Giannotti (ten—Frederico), S. Meletti (bar—David), P. L. Latinucci (bass—Hanezò), P. Mascagni (cnd), Turin RSO, Turin Radio Chorus *(rec 1941)* Cetra Classic 2-▲ CDO 18

Pini-Corsi, Antonio (bar)
Fernando de Lucia, w. Lucia, Fernando de (ten), Josefina Huguet (sop), Maria Galvany (sop), Ernesto Badini (bar), Celestina Boninsegna (sop) Symposium ▲ SYM 1149

Pini-Corsi, Gaetano (ten)
Leoncavallo, R.:Pagliacci, w. Josefina Huguet (sop—Nedda), Antonio Paoli (ten), Gaetano Pini-Corsi (ten—Beppe), Ernesto Badini (bar—Silvio), Francesco Cigada (bar—Tonio), Giuseppe Rosci (sgr—Un contadino), C. Sabajno (cnd), La Scala Orch, La Scala Chorus *(rec 1907)* Bongiovanni ▲ GB 1120-2 [ADD]

Piniec (sgr)
Charpentier, M.-A.:Messe de minuit pour Noël, w. E. Lestringant (ten), G. Ragon (ten), J.-L. Bindi (bass), P. Colléaux (cnd), Nantes Instrumental Ensemble [L] Arion ▲ ARN 68015 [AAD]

Pinkasovitch, Salomo (cant)
Cantor Salomo Pinkasovitch:His Great Recordings 1920–1930 Pearl ▲ PEA 9015 [AAD]

Pinno (sgr)
Rossini, G.:Elisabetta, regina d'Inghilterra (sels), w. M. Vitale (sop), L. Pagliughi (sop), G. Campora (ten), A. Simonetto (cnd), Milan RAI SO, Milan RAI Chorus—six arias [I] *(rec live, 4/27/53)* Myto 2-▲ 2 MCD 90530 [ADD]

Pinza, Ezio (bass)
Beethoven, L. van:Missa Solemnis, w. E. Rethberg (sop), M. Telva (mez), G. Martinelli (ten), A. Toscanini (cnd), New York PO, Westminster Choir [L] *(rec live, New York 4/28/35)* Melodram 2-▲ CDM 28036 [ADD]
Bellini, V.:Norma, w. Gina Cigna (sop—Norma), Thelma Votipka (mez—Clotilde), Bruna Castagna (cta—Adalgisa), Giovanni Martinelli (ten—Pollione), Giodano Paltrinieri (ten—Flavio), Ezio Pinza (bass—Oroveso), E. Panizza (cnd), *(orch unknown)* *(rec live, New York, Feb. 20, 1937)* The Fourties 2-▲ ENT FT 1517
Bellini, V.:Norma (sels), w. *(other artists unknown)*—Ite sul Colle o Druidi; Ah del Tebro al Giogo Indegno; Deh non Volerli Vittime Enterprise ("Vocal Archives" series) ▲ ENT VA 1132
Bellini, V.:I Puritani (sels)—Cinta di Fiori Enterprise ("Vocal Archives" series) ▲ ENT VA 1132
Boito, A.:Mefistofele (sels), w. *(other artists unknown)*—Ave Signor!; Son lo Spirito Che Nega Enterprise ("Vocal Archives" series) ▲ ENT VA 1132
Donizetti, G.:La favorita (sels), w. *(other artists unknown)*—Non Sai Tu; Spendon Più Belle in Ciel le Stelle Enterprise ("Vocal Archives" series) ▲ ENT VA 1132

Pinza, Ezio (bass) (cont.)

Donizetti, G.:Lucia di Lammermoor, w. Lily Pons (sop—Lucia), Thelma Votipka (mez—Alisa), Frederick Jagel (ten—Edgardo), John Brownlee (bar—Enrico), Ezio Pinza (bass—Raimondo), G. Papi (cnd), *(orch unknown)* The Fourties 2–▲ ENT FT 1511

Donizetti, G.:Lucia di Lammermoor (sels), w. Beniamino Gigli (ten), *(orch unknown)* Forlane ▲ FRL 16718 [ADD]

Donizetti, G.:Lucia di Lammermoor (sels), w. *(other artists unknown)*—Dalle Stanze Ove Lucia Enterprise ("Vocal Archives" series) ▲ ENT VA 1132

Ezio Pinza Memoir Classics ("Great Voices of the Century" series) ▲ CDMOIR 404 [AAD]

Ezio Pinza Phonographe ("Great Voices" series) 2–▲ PHG CD 5061

Ezio Pinza Preiser ("Lebendige Vergangenheit" series) ▲ PRE 89050 (m) [AAD]

Ezio Pinza II *(rec 1923–39)* Preiser ("Lebendige Vergangenheit" series) ▲ PRE 89085 [ADD]

Ezio Pinza Sings Verdi, Mozart, Monteverdi, Puccini And Others RCA Gold Seal ▲ 09026-61245-2

Ezio Pinza, Vol. III w. Metropolitan Opera Orch [cnd:Bruno Walter] *(rec 1944 & 46)* Preiser ▲ PRE CD 89132

Great Voices series *(rec live 1923–46)* Memories 2–▲ MEM 4411 [ADD]

His First Recordings Italian Opera, 1923–1930 Iron Needle ▲ 1323

The Italian Vocal Tradition, Vol. 1:The Voices of Toscanini, w. Toti dal Monte (sop), Claudio Muzio (sop), Rosetta Pampanini (sop), Biata Scacciati (sop), Giacomo Lauri–Volpi (ten), Francesco Merli (ten), Aureliano Pertile (ten), Carlo Galeffi (bar), Mariano Stabile (bar), Riccardo Stracciari (bar), Nazzareno de Angel *(rec 1921–35)* Iron Needle ▲ 1304

Mozart, W.A.:Arias, w. E. Steber (sop), I. Cotrubas (sop), K. Te Kanawa (sop), R. Stevens (mez), P. Domingo (ten), S. Jerusalem (ten), G. London (bar)—arias & duets from Don Giovanni, Le nozze di Figaro, Die Zauberflöte, etc. *(rec 1941–1978)* CBS Masterworks ▲ MDK 46579 [AAD] ■ MGT 46579

Mozart, W.A.:Don Giovanni, w. L. Helletsgruber (sop), E. Rethberg (sop), M. Bokor (mez), D. Borgioli (ten), K. Ettl (bass), B. Walter (cnd), Vienna PO, Vienna State Opera Chorus *(rec Salzburg, Aug. 2, 1937)* Melodram 3–▲ MLO 37506 [ADD]

Mozart, W.A.:Don Giovanni, w. E. Rethberg (sop), L. Helletsgruber (sop), M. Bokor (mez), D. Borgioli (ten), A. Lazzari (ten), B. Walter (cnd), Salzburg Orch, Salzburg Mozarteum Chorus [I] *(rec live, Salzburg, Aug. 2, 1937)* Melodram ("Connaisseur" series) 3–▲ CD 37506 (m) [AAD]

Mozart, W.A.:Don Giovanni, w. Rose Bampton (sop), Jarmila Novotna (sop), Bidú Sayão (sop), Charles Kullman (ten), Alexander Kipnis (bass), B. Walter (cnd), *(orch unknown)* *(rec Mar 7, 1942)* Enterprise ("The Fourties" series) 3–▲ ENT 301

Mozart, W.A.:Don Giovanni (sels), w. Emilia Corsi (sop), Adelina Patti (sop), John McCormack (ten), Mattia Battistini (bar), Landon Ronald (pno), C. Sabajno (cnd)—Alfin Siam liberati...Là ci darem la mano; Finch'han del vino; Batti, batti, o bel Masetto; Il mio tesoro; L'amerò, sarò costante *(rec 1905 – 1944)* Minerva ▲ MN A14 [ADD]

Mozart, W.A.:Nozze di Figaro, w. Bidu Sayao (sop—Susanna), Eleanor Steber (sop—Countess Almaviva), Jarmila Novotna (sop—Cherubino), Ira Petina (sop—Marcellina), John Brownlee (bar—Count Almaviva), Salvatore Baccaloni (bass—Bartolo), Ezio Pinza (bass—Figaro), B. Walter (cnd), *(orch unknown)* The Fourties 2–▲ ENT FT 1509

Mozart, W.A.:Nozze di Figaro, w. Jarmila Novotna (sop), Aulikki Rautawaara (sop), Esther Réthy (sop), Agostino Lazzari (ten), Mariano Stabile (bar), B. Walter (cnd), Vienna PO, Vienna State Opera Chorus *(rec live, 1937)* Melodram ▲ CDI 205003

Mozart, W.A.:Songs, w. M. Callas (sop), E. Grümmer (sop), E. Schwarzkopf (sop), R. Scotto (sop), T. Lemnitz (sop), E. Berger (sop), S. Jurinac (sop), E. Schumann (sop), I. Souez (sop), E. Rethberg (sop), L. Lehmann (sop), N. Gedda (ten), J. McCormack (ten), H. Roswenge (ten), H. Nash (ten), T. Gobbi (bar), G. Hüsch (bar), E. Kunz (bar), G. Frick (bass), A. Kipnis (bass) EMI Classics 4–▲ CDMD 63750

Offenbach, J.:Les Contes d'Hoffmann, w. Patrice Munsel (sop), Jarmila Novotná (sop), Raoul Jobin (ten), T. Beecham (cnd), Metropolitan Opera Orch, New York Metropolitan Opera Chorus *(rec Feb 26, 1944)* Enterprise ("The Radio Years") 2–▲ ENT–19 (m)

Omaggio a Ezio Pinza Great Opera Performances 2–▲ GOP 793

Opera Arias EMI Classics ("References" series) ▲ CDH 64253

Opera Stars Sing on Radio, Vol. 1:Unpublished Broadcasts from the Fourties, w. Dusolina Giannini (sop), Helen Traubel (sop), Gladys Swarthout (cta), Richard Crooks (ten), Lauritz Melchoir (ten), Robert Merrill (bar), Lawrence Tibbett (bar) Enterprise ("The Radio Years" series) ▲ ENTRY 11

Puccini, G.:La Bohème (sels), w. *(other artists unknown)*—Vecchia Zimarra Enterprise ("Vocal Archives" series) ▲ ENT VA 1132

Recital Sony Masterworks ("Portrait" series) ▲ MPK 45693 [ADD]

Rossini, G.:Il barbiere di Siviglia, w. Ira Petina (sop), Bidú Sayão (sop), John Brownlee (bar), Salvatore Baccaloni (bass), Nino Martini (sgr), F. St. Leger (cnd), *(orch unknown)* *(rec Oct 4, 1943)* Enterprise ("The Fourties" series) 2–▲ ENT 307

Rossini, G.:Mosè in Egitto (sels), w. Ezio Pinza (bass) *(other artists unknown)*—Dal Tuo Stellato Soglio Enterprise ("Vocal Archives" series) ▲ ENT VA 1132

Scenes from Il Trovatore & Aida, w. Giovanni Martinelli (ten), Rosa Ponselle (sop), Louise Homer (cta), Giuseppe de Luca (bar), et al. Pearl ▲ PEA 9350 (m)

Scenes from La forza del destino, w. Giovanni Martinelli (ten), R. Ponselle (sop), G. de Luca (bar) Pearl ▲ PEA 9351 (m)

Verdi, G.:Aida, w. Gina Cigna (sop), Bruna Castagna (mez), Giovanni Martinelli (ten), E. Panizza (cnd), New York Metropolitan Opera Orch, New York Metropolitan Opera Chorus *(rec live, Feb 6, 1937)* The Fourties 2–▲ ENT 1501

Verdi, G.:Arias, w. *(other artists unknown)*—Che Mai Vegg'io...Infelice! [from Ernani]; Di Due Figli...Abbietta Zingara; Giorni Poveri Vivea [both from Il Trovatore]; O Tu Palermo [from I vespri siciliani]; Il Santo Speco [from La forza del destino]; A Te l'Estremo Addio...Il Lacerato Spirito [from Simon Boccanegra]; Dormirò Sol nel Manto Mio Regal [from Don Carlo] Enterprise ("Vocal Archives" series) ▲ ENT VA 1132

Verdi, G.:La forza del destino, w. Stella Roman (sop), Frederick Jagel (ten), Lawrence Tibbett (bar), Salvatore Baccaloni (bass), B. Walter (cnd), New York Metropolitan Opera Orch *(rec live, Jan 23, 1943)* The Fourties 2–▲ ENT 1503

Verdi, G.:Requiem Mass, w. Maria Luisa Fanelli (sop), Irene Minghini–Cattaneo (mez), Fracno Lo Giudice (ten), C. Sabajno (cnd), La Scala Orch, La Scala Chorus *(rec 1927 for HMV)* Pearl ▲ GEMMCD 9374 (m) [AAD]

Verdi, G.:Requiem Mass, w. Maria Caniglia (sop), Ebe Stignani (cta), Beniamino Gigli (ten), T. Serafin (cnd), La Scala Orch, La Scala Chorus *(rec 1939)* Phonographie ▲ PHG 5012 [ADD]

Verdi, G.:Requiem Mass, w. Maria Caniglia (sop), Ebe Stignani (cta), Benjamino Gigli (ten), T. Serafin (cnd), Rome Opera Orch, Rome Opera Chorus *(rec 1939)* Pearl ▲ PEA 9162 [ADD]

Piolatto, M. G. (mez)

Verdi, G.:Luisa Miller, w. K. Ricciarelli (sop—Luisa), M. G. Piolatto (mez—Laura), S. Silva (cta—Federica), J. Carreras (ten—Rodolfo), E. Pranod (ten—A Peasant), R. Bruson (bar—Miller), G. Casarini (bar—Wurm) M. Rinaudo (bass—Count Walter), F. Previtali (cnd), Turin Teatro Regio Orch, Turin Teatro Regio Chorus *(rec May 9, 1976)* Legato Classics 2–▲ LCD 180 [ADD]

Piolino, Francois (ten)

Lalande, M.–R. de:Motets, w. V. Gens (sop), S. Piau (sop), A. Steyer (sop), J.–P. Fouchécourt (ten), J. Corréas (bass), W. Christie (cnd), Les Arts Florissants [L] Harmonia Mundi France ▲ HMC 901351

Lalande, M.–R. de:Te Deum, w. V. Gens (sop), S. Piau (sop), A. Steyer (sop), J.–P. Fouchécourt (ten), J. Corréas (bass), W. Christie (cnd), Les Arts Florissants [L] Harmonia Mundi France ▲ HMC 901351

Piquemal, Michel (bar)

Rossini, G.:Petite messe solennelle, w. Françoise Pollet (sop), Jacqueline Mayeur (mez), Jean–Luc Viala (ten), Raymond Alessandrini (pno), Emmanuel Mandrin (harm), Michel Piquemal (cnd), Michel Piquemal Vocal Ensemble Accord 2–▲ ACD 203562 [DDD]

Rossini, G.:Sacred Music, w. Evelyne Razimowsky (sop), Jean–Claude Pennetier (pno), Myriam Richardot (org), Michel Piquemal (cnd), Michel Piquemal Vocal Ensemble—La passegiata; Ave Marie; Inno Alla Pace; Ave Maria; Toast pour le nouvel an; Duetto Buffo di Due Batti; La fede; La speranza; La carita; Cantemus Domino; La notte del Santo Natalie; Preghiera; I Gondolieri Adès ▲ ADE 204192 [AAD]

Pirazzini, Miriam (mez)

Bellini, V.:Norma, w. A. Cerquetti (sop), G. Borelli, F. Corelli (ten), P. de Palma (ten), G. Neri (bass), G. Santini (cnd), *(orch unknown)* *(rec Rome, 1958)* Great Opera Performances 2–▲ GOP 722

Pirazzini, Miriam (mez) (cont.)

Bellini, V.:Norma (sels), w. M. Callas (sop), F. Corelli (ten), P. De Palma (ten), G. Santini (cnd), Rome Opera Orch, Rome Opera Chorus [I] *(rec live 1/2/58)* Melodram ▲ MEL 16000 (m) [AAD]

Cherubini, L.:Médée, w. M. Callas (sop), R. Scotto (sop), M. Picchi (ten), T. Serafin (cnd), La Scala Orch, La Scala Chorus [I] *(rec live, 1953)* EMI Classics (Studio) 2–▲ CDMB 63625 [ADD]

Mercadante, S.:Il giuramento (sels), w. M. Vitale (sop), R. Panerai (bar), A. Berdini (bar), A. Simonetto (cnd), Milan RAI Orch, Milan RAI Chorus [I]—14 scenes & arias *(rec live, Milan, 4/5/51)* Myto 2–▲ 2 MCD 90632 [ADD]

Puccini, G.:Madama Butterfly, w. V. de los Angeles (sop), J. Bjoerling (ten), M. Sereni (bar), G. Santini (cnd), Rome Opera Orch, Rome Opera Chorus [I] EMI Classics ("Studio" series) 2–▲ CDMB 63634 [ADD]

Verdi, G.:Aida, w. M. C. Verna (sop), F. Corelli (ten), G. Guelfi (bar), G. Neri (bass), A. Questa (cnd), Turin RAI SO, Turin RAI Chorus *(rec 1956)* Enterprise ("Palladio") 2–▲ ENT PD 4184 [ADD]

Verdi, G.:I lombardi alla prima crociata, w. Renata Broilo (sop), Maria Vitale (sop), Aldo Bertocci (ten), Mario Frosini (sgr), Mario Petri (bass), Bruno Franchi (sgr), Gustavo Gallo (sgr), Renato Pasquali (sgr), M. Wolf–Ferrari (cnd), Milan RAI Lyric Orch, Milan RAI Chorus *(rec 1954)* Cetra Classic 2–▲ CDON 41 [ADD]

Pirino, Antonio (ten)

Giordano, U.:Andrea Chénier, w. Renata Tebaldi (sop—Maddalena), Anna di Stasio (mez—Bersi), Amalia Pini (mez—Madelon/Contessa), Mario Del Monaco (ten—Andrea Chenier), Antonio Pirino (ten—L'Incredibile/Abate), Aldo Protti (bar—Carlo Gerard), Arturo La Porta (bass/bar—Mathieu/Fleville), Silvano Pagliuca (bass/bar—Roucher/Fouquier–Tinville), Giorgio Onesti (bass—Dumas/Schmidt/Major–domo), F. Capuana (cnd), Italian Lyric Orch, Italian Lyric Chorus *(rec Tokyo, Oct 1, 1961)* Legato Classics 2–▲ LCD 214–2 [ADD]

Strauss, R.:Der Rosenkavalier, w. Jarmila Barton (sop—Marianne), Lisa Della Casa (sop—Sophie), Sena Jurinac (sop—Octavian), Ilva Ligabue (sop—Orphan), Elisabeth Schwarzkopf (sop—Marschallin), Else Schürhoff (mez—Annina), Luisa Villa (mez—Milliner), Hugues Cuénod (ten—Marschallin's majordomo), Erich Majkut (ten—Valzacchi), Giuseppe Nessi (ten—Animal seller), Luciano Della Pergola (ten—Lackey/Faninal's majordomo), Antonio Pirino (ten—An Italian Singer), Gino Del Signore (ten—Lackey/Waiter), Erich Kunz (bar—Herr von Faninal), Paolo Pedani (bar—Lackey), Attilo Barbesi (bass—Lackey/Waiter), Enrico Campi (bass—Waiter), Otto Edelmann (bass—Baron Ochs), Bruno Fichtinger (bass—Notary), Franco Taino (bass—Waiter), Maria Amadini (sgr—Orphan), Pina Carrillo (sgr—Orphan), Joszi Trojan Regar (sgr—Innkeeper), H. von Karajan (cnd), La Scala Orch, La Scala Chorus *(rec La Scala Theater, Milan, Jan. 26, 1952)* Legato Classics 3–▲ LCD 197–3

Pisarenko, Galina (sgr)

Marschner, H.A.:Der Vampyr, w. Carole Farley (sop—Malwina), Nucci Condò (mez—Suse), Oslavio Di Credico (ten—George Dibdin), Josef Protschka (ten—Edgar Aubry), Romano Truffelli (ten—Richard Scrop), Martin Egel (bar—Sir Humphrey Davenaut), Andréa Snarski (bar—Toms Blunt), Siegmund Nimsgern (b–bar—Lord Ruthven), Armando Caforio (bass—Robert Green), Peter Boom (sgr—Il capo dei Vampiri), Carlo Di Giacomo (sgr—James Gadshill), Wolfgang Lenz (sgr—Sir Berkley), Galina Pisarenko (sgr—Janthe), Renzo Scorsoni (sgr—Un servitore di Berkley), Anastasia Tomaszewska Schepis (sgr—Emmy), G. Neuhold (cnd), Rome RAI SO, Rome RAI Chorus *(rec Rome, Jan 26, 1980)* Italia 2–▲ CDC 99 [ADD]

Pistor, Gotthelf (ten)

Wagner, R.:Parsifal, w. Cornelius Bronsgeest (bar), Ludwig Hofmann (bass), K. Muck (cnd), Berlin German Opera Orch, Berlin German Opera Chorus Preiser ▲ PRE 90270

Pita, J. A. (ten)

Schubert, Franz:Mass 2, w. B. Bonney (sop), B. Poschner (ten), M. Hintermeier (cta), A. Schmidt (bar), C. Abbado (cnd), CO of Europe Deutsche Grammophon ▲ 435486–2

Schumann, R.:Requiem Mignon, w. B. Bonney (sop), B. Poschner (ten), M. Hintermeier (cta), A. Schmidt (bar), C. Abbado (cnd), CO of Europe Deutsche Grammophon ▲ 435486–2

Pitti, Katalin (sop)

Lehár, F.:Giuditta (sels), w. Gyózó Leblanc (sgr), G. Oberfrank (cnd), Budapest SO, Hungarian Radio–TV Chorus [Hun] Hungaroton ▲ HCD 16809 [ADD]

Pittman, Matthew (ten)

Britten, H.:Hymn to St. Cecilia, w. Christine Goerke (sop), Nanette Soles (mez), Leonard Ratzlaff (bass), Robert Shaw (cnd), Robert Shaw Festival Singers *(rec Church of St. Pierre, Gramat, France, July 26–28, 1994)* Telarc ▲ CD 80408 [DDD]

Pittman–Jennings, David (bass)

Gounod, C.:Roméo et Juliette, w. Susan Graham (sop—Stephano), Ruth Ann Swenson (sop—Juliette), Sarah Walker (mez—Gertrude), Paul Charles Clarke (ten—Tybalt), Placido Domingo (ten—Roméo), Kurt Ollmann (bar—Mercutio), Alastair Miles (bass—Frère Laurent), David Pittman–Jennings (bass—Le Duc), Alain Vernhes (bass—Capulet), L. Slatkin (cnd), Munich RSO, Munich Radio Chorus *(rec Studio 1, Bavarian Radio, Munich, Nov 29 - Dec 10, 1995)* RCA Red Seal 2–▲ 09026–68440–2 [DDD]

Vlijmen, J. van:Un Malheureux vêtu de noir, w. S. Kleindienst (sop), Guy de Mey (ten), Reinbert de Leeuw (cnd), Arnold Schoenberg Male Choir *(rec live, Flanders Opera, Antwerp, Dec 11, 1990)* Donemus ▲ CV 17/18

Pittman–Jennings, David (nar)

Schoenberg, A.:Moses und Aaron, w. Gabriele Fontana (sop—Young Girl), Yvonne Naef (cta—Sick Woman), John Graham–Hall (ten—Young Man/Naked Youth), Pår Lindskog (ten—Youth), Chris Merritt (ten—Aaron), Siegfried Lorenz (bar—Another Man), Michael Devlin (b–bar—Ephraimite), László Polgár (bass—Priest), P. Boulez (cnd), Royal Concertgebouw Orch, Winfried Maczewski (cnd), Netherlands Opera Chorus, Zaans Youth Choir, Waterland Music School *(rec Concertgebouw, Amsterdam, Oct 1995)* Deutsche Grammophon 2–▲ 449 174–2 [DDD]

Pitzinger, Gertrude (cta)

Beethoven, L. van:Sym 9, "Choral Sym", w. Erna Berger (sop), Walther Ludwig (ten), Rudolf Watzke (bass), W. Furtwängler (cnd), Berlin PO, Bruno Kittel Choir *(rec Queens Hall, London, May 1, 1937)* Music & Arts ▲ CD 818 [ADD]

Piva, Franco (bass)

Giordano, U.:Fedora (sels), w. Magda Olivero (sop), Giuseppe Giacomini (ten), Elena Baggiore (sgr), M. Braggio (cnd), *(orch unknown)*—Amor ti vieta; Loris Ipanoff, oggi lo Zar; Muta è mia madre, muto il fratello *(rec Piacenza, Jan. 9, 1972)* Golden Age of Opera 2–▲ GAO 189/90 [ADD]

Puccini, G.:Tosca, w. Renata Tebaldi (sop—Floria Tosca), Guiseppe di Stefano (ten—Mario Cavardossi), Rinaldo Pelizzoni (ten—Spoletta), Ettore Bastianini (bar—Baron Scarpia), Carlo Badioli (bass—Sacristan), Guiseppe Moresi (bass—Sciarrone), Franco Piva (bass—Jailer), Nicola Zaccaria (bass—Cesare Angelotti), G. Gavazzeni (cnd) *(rec Great Auditorium, Brussels World Fair, 1958)* Legato Classics 2–▲ LCD 2092 [ADD]

Plançon, Pol (bass)

Eames & Plançon Nimbus ▲ NI 7860 [ADD]

Pol Plançon Pearl ▲ PEA 9497 (m) [AAD]

Planel, Jean (ten)

Charpentier, G.:Songs, w. G. Féraldy (sop), J. Lanzone (bar), G. Charpentier (cnd), *(orch & chorus unknown)*—Chanson du chemin; Ronde des campagnons; A mules; Les chevaux de bois; Sérénade à Watteau; Les yeux de Berthe [F] *(rec 1934)* Music Memoria 3–▲ 30223

Plantak (sgr)

Boieldieu, F.–A.:Le Calife de Bagdad, w. N. Monestier (sop), Ouaki (sgr), S. Elloir (sgr), Fokenoy (sgr), B. Thomas (cnd), Bernard Thomas CO, Patrick Marco Vocal Ensemble [F] Thésis ▲ THC 82015 [DDD]

Plantamura, Carol (sop)

Erickson, R.:Postcards, w. J. Hübscher (lt) *(rec 1987–91)* CRI ▲ CD 616 [DDD]

Rands, B.:Canti del Sole, w. P. Sperry (ten), B. Rands (cnd), SONOR Ensemble of Univ of California San Diego CRI ▲ CD 591 [ADD]

Reynolds, R.:Not only Night, w. H. Sollberger (cnd), SONOR Ensemble of Univ of California San Diego members *(rec Dec. 1–2, 1992)* CRI ▲ CD 652 [DDD]

Yuasa, J.:Mutterings, w. H. Sollberger (cnd), SONOR Ensemble of Univ of California San Diego members *(rec Oct. 13–14, 1992)* CRI ▲ CD 652 [DDD]

Planté, Walter (ten)

Bernstein, L.:Songfest, w. Linda Hohenfeld (sop), Wendy White (mez), Patricia Spence (mez), Vernon Hartman (bar), John Cheek (bass), L. Slatkin (cnd), St. Louis SO RCA Red Seal ▲ 09026–61581–2

▲ = CD ♦ = Enhanced CD Δ = MD ■ = Cassette Tape □ = DCC

Planté, Walter (ten) (cont.)

Puccini, G.:La fanciulla del West, w. Eva Martón (sop), Dennis O'Neill (ten), Alain Fondary (bar), L. Slatkin (cnd), Munich RSO RCA Red Seal ▲ 09026-60597-2

Rachmaninoff, S.:The Bells, w. Christos (sop), Arnold Voketaitis (bar), L. Slatkin (cnd), St. Louis SO, St. Louis Sym Chorus *(rec 1980)* Vox Box 3-▲ CD3X 3002 [ADD]

Plantey, Bernard (ten)

Tournemire, C.:Sagesse, w. H. Puig-Roget (pno) *(rec 1973)* Memoire Vive ▲ 262006 [ADD]

Tournemire, C.:Sagesse, w. Henriette Puig-Roget (pno) Memoire Vive ▲ CD 262024

Platt, Rachel (sop)

Meyerbeer, G.:Il crociato, w. Linda Kitchen (sop), Y. Kenny (sop), D. Montague (mez), D. Jones (mez), B. Ford (ten), U. Benelli (bar), D. Parry (cnd), Royal PO, Geoffrey Mitchell Choir [I] *(rec CTS Studios, Wembley, London, Dec. 1990–June 1991)* Opera Rara 4-▲ OR 10

Plazas, Mary (sop)

Purcell, H.:Dido & Aeneas, w. Rebecca Evans (sop—Belinda), Maria Ewing (sop—Dido), Mary Plazas (sop—1st witch), Patricia Rozario (sop—2nd woman), Sally Burgess (mez—Sorceress), Pamela Helen Stephens (mez—2nd witch), James Bowman (ct—Spirit), Jamie MacDougal (ten—Sailor), Karl Daymond (bar—Aeneas), R. Hickox (cnd), Collegium Musicum 90 Chandos ("Early Music" series) ▲ CHAN 0586 [DDD]

Plesch, Heidrun (sop)

Hoffmann, E.T.A.:Undine, w. Barbara Baier (sop—Berthalda), Heidrun Plesch (sop—Undine), Corinna Tippe (sop—Die Herzogin), Maria Hiefinger (mez—Fisherman's Wife), Achim Schamberger (ten—Der Herzog), Johannes Beck (bar—Ritter Huldbrand von Ringstetten), Michael Albert (bass—Fisherman), Ulrich Bosch (bass—Heilmann), Bernd Hofmann (bass—Kühleborn), H. Dechant (cnd), Bamberg Youth Orch Bayer 3-▲ 100256/58 [DDD]

Plesner, Gurli (cta)

Kuhlau, F.:Elverhøj, w. Bodil Gøbel (sop), Mogens Schmidt Johansen (bar), J. Frandsen (cnd), Danish National RSO, Danish National Radio Choir *(rec Danish Radio Concert Hall, Aug 1974)* Marco Polo/Dacapo ▲ 8.224053 [AAD]

Plishka, Paul (bass)

Beethoven, L. van:Sym 9, "Choral Sym", w. Roberta Alexander (sop), Florence Quivar (cta), Gary Lakes (ten), A. Previn (cnd), Royal PO RCA Red Seal ▲ 09026-60363-2

Bellini, V.:I Puritani, w. B. Sills (sop—Elvira), E. Shade (sop—Enrichetta), L. Pavarotti (ten—Arturo), L. Quilico (bar—Riccardo), P. Plishka (bass—Giorgio), T. Paul (bass—Walton), A. Guadagno (cnd), *(orch & chorus unknown)* *(rec live Jan. 18, 1972)* Legato Classics 2-▲ LCD 1762 [ADD]

Delibes, L.:Lakmé, w. M. Spacagna (sop—Ellen), R. Welting (sop—Lakmé), A. Kraus (ten—Gérald), D. Holloway (bar—Frédéric), P. Plishka (bass—Nilakantha), N. Rescigno (cnd), Dallas Civic Opera Orch *(rec Nov. 1980)* Ornamenti 2-▲ FE 108 [ADD]

Massenet, J.:Le Cid, w. G. Bumbry (mez), P. Domingo (ten), E. Queler (cnd), New York Opera Orch *(rec 1976)* CBS 2-▲ M2K 34211 [ADD]

Mussorgsky, M.:Boris Godunov (sels), w. A. Lombard (cnd), Bordeaux-Aquitaine National Orch—Coronation Scene, Monologue & Prayer & Death of Boris [R] Forlane ▲ FOR 16613 [DDD]

Puccini, G.:Tosca, w. Leonie Rysanek (sop), Russell Christopher (ten), Andrea Velis (ten), Clifford Harvuot (bar), Cornell MacNeil (bar), Fernando Corena (bass), F. Molinari-Pradelli (cnd), San Francisco Opera Orch, San Francisco Opera Chorus Melodram 2-▲ CDM 27508

Puccini, G.:Turandot, w. M. Caballé (sop—Turnadot), M. Freni (sop—Liu), J. Carreras (ten—Calaf), M. Sénéchal (ten—Emperor Altoum), V. Sardinero (bar—Ping), P. Plishka (bass—Timur), A. Lombard (cnd), Strasbourg PO, Maîtrise de la Cathédrale, Rhine Opera Chorus EMI Classics ▲ CDMB 65293

Rossini, G.:Stabat Mater, w. Sung-Sook Lee (sop), Florence Quivar (mez), Kenneth Riegel (ten), T. Schippers (cnd), Cincinnati SO, May Festival Chorus *(rec 1975)* Vox Box 2-▲ CDX 5141 [ADD]

Sings Songs of Ukraine, w. Thomas Hrynkiv (pno) Forlane ▲ FOR 16645 [DDD]

Verdi, G.:Arias, w. A. Lombard (cnd), Bordeaux-Aquitaine National Orch—five arias from Don Carlos, Macbeth, Nabucco, Vespri Siciliani [I] Forlane ▲ FOR 16613 [DDD]

Verdi, G.:Don Carlos (sels), w. J. Bunnell (sop), A. Millo (sop), D. Zajick (mez), M. Sylvester (ten), V. Chernov (bar), F. Furlanetto (bass), J. Levine (cnd), Metropolitan Opera Orch, New York Metropolitan Opera Chorus *(rec New York, Apr. 20–May 14, 1992)* Sony Classical ("Opera Highlights" series) ▲ SMK 53507 [DDD]

Verdi, G.:I lombardi alla prima crociata (sels), w. A. Millo (sop—Giselda), C. Bergonzi (ten—Oronte), P. Plishka (bass—Pagano), E. Queler (cnd), *(orch unknown)*—4 acts abridged *(rec live 1986)* Legato Classics ▲ LCD 105-1 [ADD]

Verdi, G.:Luisa Miller (sels), w. A. Millo (sop), W. White (mez), F. Quivar (cta), P. Domingo (ten), V. Chernov (bar), J.-H. Rootering (bass), J. Levine (cnd), Metropolitan Opera Orch, New York Metropolitan Opera Chorus *(rec New York, May 2–18, 1991)* Sony Classical ("Opera Highlights" series) ▲ SMK 53508 [DDD]

Verdi, G.:Requiem Mass, w. V. Dunn (sop), D. Curry (cta), J. Hadley (ten), R. Shaw (cnd), Atlanta SO, Atlanta Sym Chorus [L] Telarc 2-▲ CD 80152 [DDD] 2-■ CS 30152 (D)

Plowright, Rosalind (sop)

Berlioz, H.:Herminie, w. J.-P. Rouchon (cnd), Philharmonia Orch ASV ▲ ASV 895 [DDD]

Berlioz, H.:La Mort de Cléopâtre, w. J.-P. Rouchon (cnd), Philharmonia Orch ASV ▲ ASV 895 [DDD]

Mahler, G.:Sym 2, w. B. Fassbaender (mez), G. Sinopoli (cnd), Philharmonia Orch, Philharmonia Chorus [G] Deutsche Grammophon 2-▲ 415959-2 [DDD]

Mendelssohn, F.:Elijah, w. L. Finnie (mez), J. Budd (trb), A. Davies (ten), J. White (bass), R. Hickox (cnd), London SO, London Sym Chorus [E] Chandos 2-▲ CHAN 8774/75 [DDD]

Offenbach, J.:Les Contes d'Hoffmann, w. L. Serra (sop), J. Norman (sop), A. Murray (mez), J. Taillon (mez), N. Shicoff (ten), A. Oliver (ten), R. Tear (ten), J. Van Dam (b-bar), D. Duesing (bar), K. Rydl (bass), S. Cambreling (cnd), Brussels Théâtre de la Monnaie Orch [F] EMI Classics 3-▲ CDCC 49641 [DDD]

Spontini, G.:La vestale, w. G. Pasino (mez), F. Araiza (ten), P. Lefèbvre (ten), A. Cauli (bar), F. de Grandis (bass), G. Kuhn (cnd), Munich RSO, Munich Radio Chorus [F] Orfeo 2-▲ 256922 [DDD]

Pluhar, Erika (nar)

Ullmann, V.:Die Weise von Liebe und Tod, w. G. Albrecht (cnd), Czech PO [orchd Henning Brauel, 1994] *(rec live, 1994–95)* Orfeo ("Musica Rediviva" series) ▲ 366951 [DDD]

Plümacher, Hetty (cta)

Bach, J.S.:Cant 249a, w. Edith Mathis (sop), Theo Altmeyer (ten), Jakob Stämpfli (bass), H. Rilling (cnd), Stuttgart Bach Collegium, Stuttgart Memorial Church Figuralchor *(rec Gedächtniskirche Stuttgart, Mar 1967)* Musicaphon ▲ 51357 [AAD]

Schubert, Franz:Fierrabras, w. F. Wunderlich (ten), R. Wolansky (bar), O. von Rohr (bass), H. Müller-Kray (cnd), Bern State Orch, Berlin RIAS Chamber Choir, South Swiss Radio Chorus—abridged performance *(rec l959)* Myto ▲ MCD 89001 [ADD]

Plummer, Christopher (nar)

Walton, W.:Henry V (shakespeare senario), w. N. Marriner (cnd), Academy of St. Martin in the Fields, Academy Chorus [E] Chandos ▲ CHAN 8892 [DDD]

Walton, W.:Henry V (sels), w. N. Marriner (cnd), Academy of St. Martin in the Fields—Prologue; Passacaglia on the Death of Falstaff; Touch Her Soft Lips & Part; St. Crispins Day; Againcourt Chandos ("7000" series) ▲ CHAN 7041

Plummer, Christopher (sgr)

Rodgers, R.:The Sound of Music, w. J. Andrews (sgr), *(other artists unknown)* *(rec 1965)* RCA ▲ PCD 12005 ■ 2005-4 R

Pluzhnikov, Konstantin (ten)

Fleischmann, B.:Rothschild's Vn, w. Marina Shaguch (sop), Larissa Diadkova (mez), Ilya Levinsky (ten), Sergei Leiferkus (bar), G. Rozhdestvensky (cnd), Rotterdam PO *(rec Rotterdam, Netherlands, Aug 24–31, 1995)* RCA Red Seal ▲ 09026-68434-2 [DDD]

Glinka, M.:Russlan & Ludmilla, w. Galina Gorchakova (sop), Larissa Diadkova (cta), Irinia Bogachova (sgr), Anna Netrebko (sgr), Yuri Masurin (ten), Mikhail Kit (bar), Gennady Bezzubenkov (bass), Vladimir Ognovenko (bass), V. Gergiev (cnd), Kirov Opera Orch, Kirov Opera Chorus Philips ▲ 456 248-2

Rimsky-Korsakov, N.:Songs, w. Anna Kovaleva (sop), Marianna Tarassova (mez), Andrey Stavny (bar), Nikolai Okhotnikov (bass), Yury Serov (pno)—4 Romances, Op. 2; 4 Romances, Op. 3; 4 Romances, Op. 4; 4 Romances, Op. 7; 6 Romances, Op. 8; 2 Romances, Op. 25; 4 Romances, Op. 26; 4 Romances, Op. 27 *(rec St. Catherine's Lutheran Church, St. Petersburg, Sept–Dec 1993)* Russian Compact Disc ▲ RDCD 10051 [DDD]

Pluzhnikov, Konstantin (ten) (cont.)

Shostakovich, D.:From Jewish Folk Poetry, w. Marina Shaguch (sop), Larissa Diadkova (mez), G. Rozhdestvensky (cnd), Rotterdam PO *(rec Rotterdam, Netherlands, Aug 24–31, 1995)* RCA Red Seal ▲ 09026-68434-2 [DDD]

Pobbe, Marcella (sop)

Bizet, G.:Les Pêcheurs de perles, w. F. Tagliavini (ten), U. Savarese (bar), C. Cava (bass), O. de Fabritiis (cnd), Naples Teatro San Carlo Orch, Naples Teatro San Carlo Chorus [I] *(rec live 1/4/59)* Melodram 2-▲ MEL 27069 (m) [AAD]

Boito, A.:Mefistofele, w. M. Pobbe (sop—Margherita), D. De Cecco (sop—Elena), E. Ticozzi (mez—Marta), F. Tagliavini (ten—Faust), G. Neri (bass—Mefistofele), A. Questa (cnd), Turin RSO, Turin Teatro Regio Chorus *(rec 1954)* Cetra Classic ▲ CDO 19

Boito, A.:Mefistofele, w. Ebe Ticozzi (mez), Ferruccio Tagliavini (ten), Giulio Neri (bass), A. Questa (cnd), Turin RAI SO, Turin Teatro Regio Chorus Fonit Cetra ("Classic Collection" series) 2-▲ FCT CDO 19

Boito, A.:Mefistofele (sels), Turin RAI SO, San Remo SO *(rec Turin & San Remo, 1954–58)* Cetra Classic ▲ CDON 110

Cilea, F.:Adriana Lecouvreur (sels)—w. Torino RAI SO [cnd:Arturo Basile], Torino RAI SO [cnd:Ugo Cattini], Torino RAI SO [cnd:Andelo Questa], San Remo SO [cnd:Tullio Serafin]; sels unknown *(rec Torino & San Remo, 1954–58)* Cetra Classic ▲ CDON 110

Mascagni, P.:Isabeau, w. Marcella Pobbe (sop—Isabeau), Licia Galvano (mez—Giglietta), Pier Miranda Ferraro (ten—Folco), Orazio Gualtiero (bar—Cornelius), Rinaldo Rola (bass—Re Raimondo), Amelia Bazzini (sgr—Ermyngarde), Piero Benzi (sgr—L'araldo), Renata Davini (sgr—Ermynthrude), Piero Francia (sgr—Il Cavaliere), T. Serafin (cnd), San Remo SO *(rec Sanremo, Jan 13, 1962)* Bongiovanni ("Il Mito dell'Opera" series) 2-▲ GB 1135/36-2 [ADD]

Mascagni, P.:Isabeau (sels), Turin RAI SO, San Remo SO *(rec Torino & San Remo, 1954–58)* Cetra Classic ▲ CDON 110

Mascagni, P.:Isabeau (sels), w. Pier Miranda Ferraro (ten), Rinaldo Rosa (sgr), San Remo SO Cetra Classic ▲ CDON 44

Pobbe, Sciutti & Siepi, w. Graziella Sciutti (sop), Cesare Siepi (bass), Milan RAI SO [cnd:L. Toffolo], Turin RAI SO [cnd:Fulvio Vernizzi] *(rec Martini & Rossi Concert, 1959)* Incontri Memorabili ▲ CDMR 5032

Puccini, G.:Arias, w. Basile, Cattini, Questa, Serafin (cnd), San Remo SO, Turin RAI SO—from Suor Angelica, La Rondine, Tosca, Turandot, Manon Lescaut, La Bohème & Gianni Schicchi *(rec Torino & San Remo, 1954–58)* Cetra Classic ▲ CDON 110

Soprano Arias & Scenes, w. various orchs *(rec live in Italy, 1958–1964)* Melodram 2-▲ CDM 27069 (m) [AAD]

Wagner, R.:Lohengrin (sels), w. S. Kónya (ten), A. Protti (bar), F. Leitner (cnd), Milan RAI SO [I] *(rec live 1959)* Melodram ▲ MEL 15004 (m) [AAD]

Pochapsky, Vlatcheslav (b-bar)

Lokshin, A.:Sym 5, w. *(not advised of harp),* V. Katajev (cnd), Northern Crown Soloists Ensemble MK ▲ MKA 417124 [DDD]

Podenski, Daureen (sop)

Shore, C.:July Remembrances, w. R. Black (cnd), Prism Orch [E] Owl ▲ OWL 34 [DDD]

Podger, Julian (ten)

Purcell, H.:The Indian Queen, w. Catherine Bott (sop—Orazia/Married Woman), Emma Kirkby (sop—Indian Girl/Zempoalla/Cupid), John Mark Ainsley (ten—Indian Boy/Fame/Follower of Cupid/Aerial Spirits), Julian Podger (ten—Follower of Envy/Aerial Spirit), Gerald Finley (bar—Conjurer/Hymen/Follower of Cupid), Helen Parker (sgr—Aerial Spirits), David Thomas (bass—Envy/High Priest/Married Man/Follower of Cupid), Simon Berridge (sgr—Follower of Envy), Libby Crabtree (sgr—Follower of Hymen/Aerial Spirit), Tommy Williams (sgr—God of Dreams), C. Hogwood (cnd), Academy of Ancient Music *(rec Walthamstow Assembly Hall, London, July 1994)* L'Oiseau-Lyre ▲ 444339-2 [DDD]

Pödl, Naan (sgr)

Nicolai, O.:Lustigen Weiber, w. Erika Köth (sop), Hertha Töpper (mez), Maria Rogner (sgr), Hans Günter Nöcker (b-bar), Kim Borg (bass), F. Rieger (cnd), Bavarian RSO, Bavarian Chorus *(rec 1960's)* Pantheon 2-▲ PHE 6660 (m)

Podles, Ewa (cta)

Famous Arias, w. Collegium Instrumental de Bruges [cnd:Patrick Peire] Forlane ▲ FOR 16620 [DDD]

Gluck, C.W.:Arias, w. P. Peire (cnd), Collegium Instrumentale Brugense—sels from Orfeo ed Euridice & Iphegénie en Aulide Forlane ▲ FRL 16620 [DDD]

Gluck, C.W.:Orfeo ed Euridice, w. M.-N. de Callatay (sop), P. Peire (cnd), Collegium Instrumentale Brugense, Capella Brugensis [original instruments] Forlane 2-▲ FOR 16720 [DDD]

Handel, G.F.:Arias, w. P. Peire (cnd), Collegium Instrumentale Brugense—sels from Rinaldo Forlane ▲ FRL 16620 [DDD]

Mahler, G.:Sym 3, w. A. Wit (cnd), Polish National RSO Katowice, Jacek Mentel (cnd), Cracow Boys' Choir, Cracow Phil Choir *(rec Concert Hall of the Polish National Radio, Katowice, Nov 12–16, 1994)* Naxos 2-▲ 8.550525-6 [DDD]

Marcello, B.:Arias, w. P. Peire (cnd), Collegium Instrumentale Brugense—sels from Quella Fiamma Che M'Accende Forlane ▲ FRL 16620 [DDD]

Mussorgsky, M.:Nursery, w. Graham Johnson (pno) Forlane ▲ FRL 16683 [DDD]

Mussorgsky, M.:Songs & Dances, w. Graham Johnson (pno) Forlane ▲ FRL 16683 [DDD]

Ptaszynska, M.:Songs of Despair & Lonliness, w. Jerzy Marchwinski (pno) *(rec Polish Radio Studio S2, Oct. 9–11)* Polskle Nagrania ▲ PLN 075 [ADD]

Purcell, H.:Arias, w. P. Peire (cnd), Collegium Instrumentale Brugense—sels from Dido & Aeneas Forlane ▲ FRL 16620 [DDD]

Rachmaninoff, S.:Songs, w. Graham Johnson (pno)—Morning, Op. 14/2; Do Not Regret Me, Op. 14/8; I Am Waiting for You, Op. 14/1; In the Mysterious Night, Op. 4/3; Beautiful as the Day, Op. 14/9; Christ Has Risen, Op. 26/6; Springtime Waters, Op. 14/11 Forlane ▲ FRL 16683 [DDD]

Rossini, G.:Arias, w. P. G. Morandi (cnd), Hungarian State Opera Orch, Hungarian State Opera Chorus—Cruda sorte! Amor tiranno!; Amici, in ogni evento m'affido a voi...Pensa all patria [both from L'Italiana in Algeri]; Eccomi alfine in Babilonia...Ah! quel giorno ognor rammento [from Semiramide]; Oh patria...Di tanti palpiti [from Tancredi]; Non temer:d'un basso affto [from Maometto II]; Mura felici...Elena! oh tu, che chiamo! [from La donna del lago]; Una voce poco fa [from Il Barbiere di Siviglia]; Nacqui all'affanno, al pianto [from Cinderella] *(rec Italian Institute, Budapest, May 16–22, 1995)* Naxos ▲ 8.553543 [DDD]

Rossini, G.:Tancredi, w. Sumi Jo (sop—Amenaide), Lucretia Lendi (mez—Roggiero), Anna Maria di Micco (mez—Isaura), Ewa Podles (cta—Tancredi), Stanford Olsen (ten—Argirio), Pietro Spagnoli (bar—Orbazzano), Ewald Demeyere (hpd), Lieven Baert (vc), Franck Coryn (db), A. Zedda (cnd), Collegium Instrumentale Brugense, Capella Brugensis *(rec Poissy Theatre & Centre Musical-Lyrique-Phonographique, Ile de France, Jan. 26–31, 1994)* Naxos ("Opera Classics" series) 2-▲ 8.660037/38 [DDD]

Tchaikovsky, P.:Songs, w. Graham Johnson (pno)—Was I a Blade of Grass in a Field?; Zamphira's Song; If I Had Known; If the Day Shines Forlane ▲ FRL 16683 [DDD]

Vivaldi, A.:Arias, w. P. Peire (cnd), Collegium Instrumentale Brugense—sels from Orlando Furioso & Bajazet Forlane ▲ FRL 16620 [DDD]

Podskalsky, Miroslav (bass)

Dvořák, A.:Armida, w. Joanna Borowska (sop—Armida), Monika Brychtová (sgr—Siren), Wieslaw Ochman (ten—Rinald), Richard Sporka (ten—Dudo), Jan Markvart (bar—Sven), Pavel Daniluk (bass—King), George Fortune (bass—Ismen), Zdenek Harvánek (bass—Ubald), Miloslav Podskalský (bass—Peter), Milan Bürger (sgr—Gernand), Roman Janál (sgr—Muezzin/Hlasatel), Vratislav Kříz (sgr—Gottfried), Vladimír Nacházel (sgr—Roger), G. Albrecht (cnd), Czech PO, Prague Chamber Choir *(rec 1995)* Orfeo 2-▲ 404962 [DDD]

Kozeluch, Joh. A.:Missa Pastoralis, w. S. Losová (sop), Y. Škvárová (cta), M. Švejda (ten), B. Kulínský (cnd), Prague PO, Prague Radio Chorus Multisonic ▲ 31 0003-2 [ADD]

Poel, Karin van der (mez)

Bruynèl, T.:Le jardin, w. Harrie Starreveld (fl), Annelie de Man (hpd) Donemus ▲ NEAR 01 [DDD]

Hollander, H.:Sacred Music, w. S. van Grootel (sop), J. Boswinkel (bass), P. Rikkers (vn), J. van der Meer (db), T. van Eijk (org), Cappella Breda—Cantabant sancti; Domine Jesu Christe; Domine Deus; Ecce vicit leo; O nomen Jesu; Recipe me; Quem vidistis pastores; Sanctus Jacobus; Quid est hoc; O vos omnes; Ecce clamo; Ave Maria; O Beatum Virum; O bone Jesu; Te gloriosus Erasmus ▲ WVH 047 [DDD]

Poell, Alfred (bar)
Bach, J.S.:Mass in b, BWV 232, w. E. Schwarzkopf (sop), C. Ludwig (mez), K. Ferrier (cta), Schöffler (bass), H. von Karajan (cnd), Vienna SO, Vienna Singverein—6 arias excerpted from the above rec'g
Verona ▲ 27076 (m) [AAD]
Bach, J.S.:Mass in b, BWV 232, w. E. Schwarzkopf (sop), C. Ludwig (mez), K. Ferrier (cta), Schöffler (bass), H. von Karajan (cnd), Vienna SO [L] *(rec live at Vienna's International Bach Festival, June 15, 1950)*
Verona 2–▲ 27073/74 (m) [AAD]
Beethoven, L. van:Cant on the Death of the Emperor Joseph II, w. Ilona Steingruber (sop), C. Krauss (cnd), Vienna SO, Vienna Academy Chamber Choir *(rec live, 1953)* Originals ▲ ORISH 825 [ADD]
Beethoven, L. van:Fidelio, w. S. Jurinac (sop), M. Mödl (sop), W. Windgassen (ten), O. Edelmann (bass), G. Frick (bass), W. Furtwängler (cnd), Vienna PO *(rec Oct. 1953)* EMI Classics 2–▲ CDHB 64496
Cornelius, P.:Der Barbier von Bagdad, w. S. Jurinac (sop), H. Rössl–Majdan (mez), E. Majkut (ten), R. Schock (ten), G. Frick (bass), H. Hollreiser (cnd), Austrian RSO, Austrian Radio Chorus [G] *(rec live Vienna, 1952)*
Verona 2–▲ 27050/51 (m) [AA
Cornelius, P.:Der Barbier von Bagdad, w. S. Jurinac (sop), H. Rössl–Majdan (mez), E. Majkut (ten), R. Schock (ten), G. Frick (bass), H. Hollreiser (cnd), Austrian RSO, Austrian Radio Chorus *(rec live Vienna 1952)*
Melodram 2–▲ MEL 27050 (m) [AAD]
Einem, G. von:Der Prozess, w. Lisa Della Casa (sop—Frl. Bürstner/Die Frau des Gerichtsdieners/Leni), Peter Klein (ten—Der Direktorstellvertreter/Der Student), Max Lorenz (ten—Josef K.), Erich Majkut (ten—Ein Bursche), László Szemere (ten—Titorelli), Alois Pernerstorfer (b-bar—Willem/Der Gerichtsdiener), Alfred Poell (b-bar—Der Advokat), Walter Berry (bass—Franz/Kanzleidirektor), Oskar Czerwenka (bass—Der Untersuchungsrichter/Der Prügler), Ludwig Hofmann (bass—Der Aufseher/Ein Passant/Der Geistliche/Der Fabrikant), Polly Batic (sgr—Frau Grubach), Endreh Koreh (sgr—Albert K.), Luise Leitner (sgr—Ein buckliges Mädchen), K. Böhm (cnd), Vienna PO, Vienna State Opera Chorus *(rec Aug 17, 1953)* Orfeo d'or ("Festspiel Dokumente" series) 2–▲ 392952 (m)
Mozart, W.A.:Don Giovanni, w. L. Welitsch (sop), I. Seefried (sop), E. Schwarzkopf (sop), A. Dermota (ten), E. Kunz (bar), T. Gobbi (bar), J. Greindl (bass), W. Furtwängler (cnd), Vienna PO, Vienna State Opera Chorus *(rec 1950)*
Laudis 3–▲ LDS 4001 [AAD]
Strauss (II), Joh.:Die Fledermaus, w. H. Gueden (sop), J. Patzak (ten), A. Dermota (ten), A. Jaresch (ten), W. Lipp (sop), S. Wagner (mez), K. Preger (ten), C. Krauss (cnd), Vienna PO *(rec early 1950s)*
London ("Historic" series) 2–▲ 425990–2 [AAD]
Strauss (II), Joh.:Der Zigeunerbaron, w. Emmy Loose (sop), Hilde Zadek (sop), Rosette Anday (cta), Julius Patzak (ten), Karl Dönch (bar), Steffi Leverenz (sgr), C. Krauss (cnd), Vienna PO, Vienna State Opera Chorus Phonographe 2–▲ PHG 5020 [AAD]
Strauss, R.:Songs, w. H. Konetzni (sop—4 solo songs), A. Dermota (ten—6 solo songs), A. Poell (bar—6 solo songs), Richard Strauss (pno)—Opp. 21/2, 21/3, 69/5, 88/2 *(Konetzni)*; Opp. 15/5, Op. 17/1, 21/1, 32/2, 37/1, 49/2 *(Dermota)*; Opp. 19/1, 21/4, 27/1, 27/3, 36/1, 48/5 *(Poell)* [G] *(rec 1943)*
Preiser ▲ 93261 (m) [AAD]
Wagner, R.:Tannhäuser (sels), w. Set Svanholm (ten—Tannhäuser), Alfred Poell (bar—Wolfram), L. Reichwein (cnd), Vienna State Opera Orch *(rec Vienna, Oct. 11, 1942)*
Koch Schwann ▲ SCH 314692 [ADD]

Poggi, Gianni (ten)
Boito, A.:Mefistofele, w. R. Noli (sop—Margherita), S. dall'Argine (sop—Elena), G. Poggi (ten—Faust), G. Neri (bass–Mefistofele), F. Capuana (cnd), La Scala Orch, La Scala Chorus [I] *(rec 1952)*
Preiser 2–▲ 90122 (m) [AAD]
Cilea, F.:Adriana Lecouvreur (sels), w. Renata Tebaldi (sop—Adriana), Piero de Palma (ten—Abate), Gianni Poggi (ten—Mauricio), Giuseppe Taddei (bar—Michonnet), Augusto Romani (bass—Prince), G. Santini (cnd), Naples Teatro San Carlo Orch, Naples Teatro San Carlo Chorus—Del sultano Amurate...Io son l'umile ancella; Giusto Cielo! che feci in tal giorno; Salvatemi! salvatemi...Scostatevi, profani! *(rec San Carlo Theater, Naples, Dec. 26, 1952)* Legato Classics 2–▲ LCD 193–2 [ADD]
Il Mito dell'Opera:Gianni Poggi *(rec. 1957 & 1962)* Bongiovanni ▲ GB 1097 [ADD]
Ponchielli, A.:La Gioconda, w. M. Callas (sop), F. Barbieri (mez), P. Silveri (bar), G. Neri (bass), A. Votto (cnd), Turin RAI SO, Turin RAI Chorus *(rec 1952)* Andromeda 3–▲ ANR 2528 [ADD]
Ponchielli, A.:La Gioconda, w. M. Callas (sop), F. Barbieri (mez), P. Silveri (bar), G. Neri (bass), A. Votto (cnd), Turin RAI SO, Turin RAI Chorus *(rec 1952)*
Enterprise ("Palladio" series) ▲ ENT PD 4152 [DDD]
Ponchielli, A.:La Gioconda, w. M. Callas (sop—Gioconda), F. Barbieri (mez—Laura), M. Amadini (sgr—La Cieca), G. Poggi (ten—Enzo), P. Silveri (bar—Barnaba), G. Neri (bass—Alvise), A. Votto (cnd), Turin RAI Orch, Turin RAI Chorus *(rec 1952)* Cetra Classic 3–▲ CDO 8
Puccini, G.:La Bohème (sels), w. M. Carosio (sop), A. Noni (sop), P. Silveri (bar), V. de Sabata (cnd), La Scala Orch, La Scala Chorus—6 arias from Acts 3 & 4 [I] *(rec live, Milan, 12/7/49)*
Myto ▲ 1 MCD 90634 [ADD]
Puccini, G.:La Bohème (sels), w. R. Scotto (sop), T. Gobbi (bar), Maneguzzer (sgr), A. Votto (cnd), Florence Maggio Musicale IMP Collectors Series ▲ IMPX 9024 [AAD]
Verdi, G.:Un ballo in maschera, w. A. Cerquetti (sop), E. Stignani (mez), E. Bastianini (bar), E. Tieri (cnd), Florence Teatro Comunale Orch, Florence Teatro Comunale Chorus [I] *(rec live 1/6/57)*
Standing Room Only 2–▲ SRO 804–2 (m) [ADD]

Pogson, Geoffrey (ten)
Lloyd, G.:Iernin, w. M. Hill Smith (sop), C. Powell (mez), H. Herford (bar), M. Rivers (bar)
Albany 3–▲ TROY 121/23 [DDD]

Pohl, Albrecht (bass)
Luneburg 1647, w. Ensemble Lanterly, Mona Spagele (sop), Werner Buchin (alt)
MD + G ▲ MDG CD 6050647

Pohl, Gisela (cta)
Brahms, J.:Liebeslieder Waltzes SATB, w. Barbara Hoene (sop), Armin Ude (ten), Siegfried Lorenz (bar), Klaus Bässler (pno), Dieter Zechlin (pno), W.–D. Hauschild (cnd), Berlin RSO
Berlin Classics ▲ BER 9269
Brahms, J.:Neue Liebeslieder Waltzes, w. Barbara Hoene (sop), Armin Ude (ten), Siegfried Lorenz (bar), Klaus Bässler (pno), Dieter Zechlin (pno), W.–D. Hauschild (cnd), Berlin RSO
Berlin Classics ▲ BER 9269
Schoenberg, A.:Moses und Aaron, w. Renate Krahmer (sop), Reiner Goldberg (ten), Werner Haseleu (nar), H. Kegel (cnd), Leipzig RSO, Leipzig Radio Chorus Berlin Classics 2–▲ BER 1116 [ADD]

Poirier, Gérard (nar)
Normandeau, R.:Petit Prince, w. Michel Dumont (nar—Aviator), Martin Pensa (nar—Little Prince), Christine Séguin (nar—Rose), Jean Marchand (nar—King), Luc Durand (nar—Conceited Man), Gilles Dupuis (nar—Drunkard), Guy Nadon (nar—Businessman), Jacques Languirand (nar—Lamplighter), Pierre Bourgault (nar—Geographer), Cynthia Dubois (nar—Snake), Monique Giroux (nar—Flower), Françoise Davoine (nar—Rose Garden), Jean-Louis Millette (nar—Fox), Gérard Poirier (nar—Railway Switchman), Claude Préfontaine (nar—Water Pill Salesman) *(rec Montreal, Aug 1994)* CBC 2–▲ 1091 [DDD]

Pojar, Ioan (ten)
Bretan, N.:The Evening Star, w. Adriana Croitoru (sop—King's Daughter), Elena Casian (mez—Lady-in-Waiting), Marius Budoiu (ten—Mariner), Ioan Pojar (ten—Page), Ionel Voineag (ten—Evening Star), Bálint Szabó (bass—Michael the Archangel), B. Hary (cnd), Transylvania PO Cluj *(rec Cluj, Sept 1994)* Nimbus ▲ NI 5463 [DDD]

Póka, Balázs (bar)
Cilea, F.:L'Arlesiana, w. M. Spacagna (sop), E. Zilio (mez), P. Kelen (ten), T. Clementis (bass), C. Rosekrans (cnd), Hungarian State Orch, Hungarian State Chorus Quintana 2–▲ QUI 903067/68
Puccini, G.:La Bohème, w. Veronika Kincses (sop—Mimi), Sidonia Haljakova (sop—Musette), Peter Dvorsky (ten—Rodolfo), Vijtech Scherenkel (ten—Parpignol), Ian Konsulov (bar—Marcello), Balazs Poka (bar—Schaunard), Stanislav Benacka (bass—Benoit), Dariusz Niemirowicz (bass—Colline), Stefan Janci (bass—Alcindoro), *(cnd & orch unknown)* Griffin ▲ GCD 2942
Puccini, G.:Suor angelica, w. I. Tokody (sop), Barlay (sgr), L. Gardelli (cnd), Hungarian State Opera Orch, Hungarian State Opera Chorus [I] Hungaroton ▲ HCD 12490

Polatos, Chari (sgr)
Hatzis, C.:Crucifix, w. Exultate Chamber Singers *(rec 1993)* Centrediscs ▲ CMCCD 4693 [DDD]

Pöld (sgr)
Handel, G.F.:Judas Maccabaeus, w. Agnes Giebel (sop), Julianna Falk (cta), Fritz Wunderlich (ten), L. Welter (bar), R. Kubelik (cnd), Bavarian RSO, Bavarian Chorus [G] *(rec live 10/25/63)*
Melodram 2–▲ MEL 28026 [AAD]

Poleri, David (ten)
Berlioz, H.:La Damnation de Faust, w. S. Danco (sop), M. Singher (bar), D. Gramm (bass), C. Munch (cnd), Boston SO, Harvard Glee Club [F] RCA Gold Seal 2–▲ 7940–2–RG [ADD]
Berlioz, H.:La Damnation de Faust, w. Suzanne Danco (sop), Martial Singher (bar), Donald Gramm (bass), McHenry Boatwright (bass), Joseph de Pasquale (va), Louis Speyer (hn), C. Munch (cnd), Boston SO, Harvard Glee Club, Radcliffe Choral Society *(rec Feb 1954)*
RCA Victor Gold Seal 8–▲ 0902–668444–2 [ADD]
Tchaikovsky, P.:Mazeppa, w. M. Olivero (sop), M. Radev (mez), E. Bastianini (bar), B. Christoff (bass), J. Perlea (cnd), Florence Maggio Musicale Orch, Florence Maggio Musicale Chorus [I] *(rec live 6/6/54)*
Melodram 2–▲ MEL 27070 (m) [AAD]

Polgár, László (bass)
Liszt, F.:Christus, w. Veronika Kincses (sop), Tamara Takács (mez), Robert Nagy (ten), Sándor Sólyom-Nagy (bar), A. Dorati (cnd), Hungarian State Orch, Hungarian Radio–TV Chorus [L]
Hungaroton 3–▲ HCD 12831/33 [DDD]
Liszt, F.:Hungarian Coronation Mass, w. V. Kincses (sop), T. Tákacs (mez), D. Gulyas (ten), G. Lehel (cnd), Budapest SO, Hungarian Radio Chorus [L] Hungaroton ▲ HCD 12148
Mascagni, P.:Lodoletta, w. M. Spacagna (sop), P. Kelen (ten), B. Szilágyi (bar), M. Kálmándi (bar), C. Rosekrans (cnd), Hungarian State Orch, Hungarian State Choruses [I]
Hungaroton 2–▲ HCD 31307/08 [DDD]
Mozart, W.A.:Bastien und Bastienne, w. E. Gruberova (sop), V. Cole (ten), R. Leppard (cnd), Franz Liszt CO Sony Classical ▲ SK 45855
Mozart, W.A.:Clemenza, w. Christine Barbaux (sop—Servilia), Carol Vaness (sop—Viellia), Martha Senn (mez—Annio), Delores Ziegler (mez—Sesto), Gösta Winbergh (ten—Tito), László Polgár (bass—Publio), R. Muti (cnd), Vienna PO, Vienna State Opera Chorus *(rec live, Salzburg Festival, 1988)*
EMI Classics 2–▲ CDCB 55489
Mozart, W.A.:Clemenza, w. L. Popp (sop), R. Ziesack (sop), A. Murray (mez), D. Ziegler (mez), P. Langridge (ten), T. Grabowski (hpd), C. Hermann (vc), N. Harnoncourt (cnd), Zurich Opera Orch, Zurich Opera House Chorus Teldec 2–▲ 90857–2
Mozart, W.A.:Missa, K.317, w. J. Rodgers (sop), E. von Magnus (alt), J. Protschka (ten), N. Harnoncourt (cnd), Vienna Concentus Musicus, Arnold Schoenberg Choir [L] Teldec ▲ 2292–43354–2
Mozart, W.A.:Vesperae solennes, w. J. Rodgers (sop), E. von Magnus (alt), J. Protschka (ten), N. Harnoncourt (cnd), Vienna Concentus Musicus, Arnold Schoenberg Choir [L]
Teldec ▲ 2292–43354–2
Respighi, O.:Belfagor, w. S. Sass (sop), T. Takács (mez), G. Lamberti (ten), L. Miller (bar), L. Gardelli (cnd), Hungarian State Orch, Hungarian State Chorus [I] Hungaroton 2–▲ HCD 12850/51 [DDD]
Respighi, O.:Semirama, w. E. Marton (sop), V. Kincses (sop), L. Bartolini (ten), L Miller (bar), T. Clementis (bass), L. Gardelli (cnd), Hungarian State Orch, Hungarian Radio–TV Chorus [I]
Hungaroton 2–▲ HCD 31197/98
Schoenberg, A.:Moses and Aaron, w. David Pittman-Jennings (nar), Gabriele Fontana (sop—Young Girl), Yvonne Naef (cta—Sick Woman), John Graham-Hall (ten—Young Man/Naked Youth), Pår Lindskog (ten—Youth), Chris Merritt (ten—Aaron), Siegfried Lorenz (bar—Another Man), Michael Devlin (b-bar—Ephraimite), László Polgár (bass—Priest), P. Boulez (cnd), Royal Concertgebouw Orch, Winfried Maczewski (cnd), Netherlands Opera Chorus, Zaans Youth Choir, Waterland Music School *(rec Concertgebouw, Amsterdam, Oct 1995)* Deutsche Grammophon 2–▲ 449 174–2 [DDD]
Schreker, F.:Die Gezeichneten, w. Elisabeth Connell (sop), Heinz Kruse (ten), Monte Pederson (bar), Alfred Muff (bass), L. Zagrosek (cnd), Berlin German SO London 3–▲ 444442–2
Schubert, Franz:Fierrabras, w. K. Mattila (sop), C. Studer (sop), R. Gambill (ten), T. Hampson (bar), R. Holl (bass), C. Abbado (cnd), CO of Europe, Arnold Schoenberg Choir [G] *(rec live)*
Deutsche Grammophon 2–▲ 427341–2 [DDD]

Poli, Afro (bar)
Donizetti, G.:Don Pasquale, w. Adelaide Saraceni (sop), Tito Schipa (ten), Ernesto Badini (bar), C. Sabajno (cnd), La Scala Orch, La Scala Chorus *(rec 1932)*
Grammofono 2000 2–▲ GRM 78561 (m)
Donizetti, G.:L'elisir d'amore, w. A. Noni (sop), B. Rizzoli (sop), C. Valletti (ten), S. Bruscantini (bar), G. Gavazzeni (cnd), Rome RAI SO, Rome RAI Chorus *(rec 1952)* Cetra Classic ▲ CDO 5 [AAD]
Mascagni, P.:Cavalleria rusticana, w. L. Bruna Rasa (sop), M. Meloni (mez), R. Gallo Toscani (mez), A. Melandri (ten), P. Mascagni (cnd), Holland Italian Opera Orch, Italian d'Olanda Opera Chorus [I] *(rec live at the Royal Theatre in the Hague, 11/7/38)* Bongiovanni ▲ GB 1050 (m) [AAD]
Massenet, J.:Manon, w. V. De los Angeles (sop), F. Tagliavini (ten), N. Annovazzi (cnd), Rome Opera Orch, Rome Opera Chorus *(rec live 1957)* Melodram 2–▲ MEL 27082
Puccini, G.:La Bohème, w. L. Albanese (sop), T. Menotti (sop), B. Gigli (ten), U. Berrettoni (cnd), La Scala Orch, La Scala Chorus [I] *(rec 1937)*
EMI Classics ("Studio" series) 2–▲ CDHB 63335 (m) [ADD]
Puccini, G.:La Bohème, w. Licia Albanese (sop), Tatiana Menotti (sop), Beniamino Gigli (ten), U. Berrettoni (cnd), La Scala Orch, La Scala Chorus *(rec Milan, 1938)*
Phonographe 2–▲ PHG CD 5071
Puccini, G.:La Bohème, w. L. Albanese (sop—Mimi), T. Menotti (sop—Musetta), B. Gigli (ten—Rodolfo), N. Palai (ten—Parpignol), A. Poli (bar—Marcello), A. Baracchi (bar—Schaunard), D. Baronti (bass—Colline), C. Scattola (bass—Benoit/Alcindoro), U. Berrettoni (cnd), La Scala Orch, La Scala Chorus [I] *(rec Milan, May 1938)* Nimbus 2–▲ NI 7862/63 [ADD]
Puccini, G.:La Bohème, w. Licia Albanese (sop—Mimi), Tatiana Menotti (sop—Musetta), Beniamino Gigli (ten—Rodolfo), Nello Palai (ten—Parpignol), Aristide Baracchi (bar—Schaunard), Afro Poli (bar—Marcello), Duilio Baronti (bass—Colline), Carlo Scattola (bass—Benoit/Alcindoro), U. Berrettoni (cnd), La Scala Orch, Vittore Veneziani (cnd), La Scala Chorus *(rec Feb–Mar 1938)*
Arkadia ("The 78's" series) 2–▲ 78009 [ADD]

Poli, Liliana (sop)
Ligeti, G.:Requiem, w. Barbro Ericson (mez), M. Gielen (cnd), Hessian RSO, Hesse Radio Chorus [L]
Wergo ▲ WER 60045–50 [ADD]

Polidori, Graziano (bar)
Donizetti, G.:I pazzi per progetto, w. S. Rigacci (sop), A. Cicogna (mez), G. Sarti (bar), V. M. Brunetti (bass), E. Fissore (bass), L. Monreale (bass), G. Micheli (cnd), Emilia Romagna Arturo Toscanini SO [I] *(rec live, 12/88)* Bongiovanni ▲ GB 2070 [DDD]

Polke, Rolf (bass)
Wagner, R.:Der Ring des Nibelungen, w. Liselotte Becker-Egner (sop—Woglinde/Ortlinde/Wellgunde), Angelika Berger (sop—Wellgunde/Waltraute), Siw Ericsdotter (sop—Norn 3), Heidemaria Ferch (sop—Freia/Gerhilde), Bella Jasper (sop—Helmwige/Waldvogel/Woglinde), Ditha Sommer (sop—Sieglinde/Gutrune), Ursula Boese (mez—Erda), Ruth Hesse (mez—Fricka), Nadezda Kniplová (mez—Brünnhilde), Margit Kobeck (mez—Schwertleite/Norn 2), Hilde Rosner (mez—Flosshilde/Siegrunde), Erica Schubert (mez—Grimgerde/Flosshilde), Ingrid Göritz (cta—Rossweisse/Norn 1), Herbert Doussant (ten—Froh), Herold Kraus (ten—Mime), Gerald McKee (ten—Siegmund/Siegfried), Fritz Uhl (ten—Loge), Rudolf Knoll (bar—Gunther/Donner), Rolf Polke (bass-bar—Wotan/Wanderer), Rolf Kühne (bass—Alberich), Takao Okamura (bass—Fafner), Otto von Rohr (bass—Hagen/Fasolt/Hunding), H. Swarowsky (cnd), Czech PO, Prague National Theater Orch *(rec June 3 & 5, July 26–31, A)* Weltbild Classics 14–▲ 703769 [ADD]

Pollet, Françoise (sop)
Berlioz, H.:Les Nuits d'été, w. A. Jordan (cnd), Monte Carlo PO *(rec June 30–July 3, 1993)*
FNAC Music ▲ 592275 [DDD]
Berlioz, H.:Songs, w. A. S. von Otter (mez), J. Aler (ten), T. Allen (bar), C. Garben (cnd), *(orch unknown)*
Deutsche Grammophon 2–▲ 435860–2
Berlioz, H.:Les Troyens, w. F. Pollet (sop—Dido), D. Voigt (sop—Cassandre), C. Dubosc (sop—Ascagne), H. Perraguin (cta—Anna), G. Lakes (ten—Aeneas), J.–L. Maurette (ten—Iopas), J. M. Ainsley (ten—Hylas), M. P. (ten—Panthee), G. Cross (ten—Sinon), G. Quilico (bar—Chorebe), J.–P. Courtis (b-bar—Narbal), M. Belleau (bass—Ghost of Hector), R. Schirrer (bass—Priam), C. Dutoit (cnd), Montreal SO, Montreal Sym Chorus London 4–▲ 443693–2 [DDD]

▲ = CD ♦ = Enhanced CD Δ = MD ■ = Cassette Tape □ = DCC

Pollet, Françoise (sop) (cont.)

Bruneau, A.:Lazare, w. Mary Saint-Palais (sop), Sylvie Sullé (mez), Jean-Luc Viala (ten), Laurent Naouri (b-bar), J. Mercier (cnd), French National Orch, Maîtrise de Paris, Vittoria French Regional Choir Adès ▲ ADE 204512

Bruneau, A.:Requiem, w. Mary Saint-Palais (sop), Sylvie Sullé (mez), Jean-Luc Viala (ten), Laurent Naouri (b-bar), J. Mercier (cnd), French National Orch, Maîtrise de Paris, Vittoria French Regional Choir Adès ▲ ADE 204512

Chausson, E.:Poème de l'amour et de la mer, w. A. Jordan (cnd), Monte Carlo PO *(rec June 30–July 3, 1993)* FNAC Music ▲ 592275 [DDD]

Duparc, H.:Songs, w. J. Kaltenbach (cnd), Nancy SO—Le manoir de rosemonde; Chanson triste; L'invitation au voyage; La vie antérieure; Phydilé; Au pays où se fait la guerre; Testament; La vague et la cloche Accord ▲ ACD 202832

Liebermann, R.:Medea, w. Françoise Pollet (sop—Medea), Yvi Jänicke (cta—Chalkiope), Zdena Furmančoková (sgr—Syrinx), Dagmar Hesse (sgr—Aiglaia), Hanne Krogen (sgr—Kore), Michaela Lucas (sgr—Oinone), Renate Spingler (sgr—Silene), Jochen Kowalski (ct—Kreon), Aage Haugland (bass—Jason), G. Albrecht (cnd), Hamburg State PO, Hamburg State Opera Chorus *(rec live, Hamburg, Germany, Sept 24, 1995)* Musiques Suisses ▲ 6126 [DDD]

Quand on n'a que l'amour, w. Bruno Fontaine (pno), Lamoureux Concert Orch [cnd:Yutaka Sado] Accord ▲ ACD 205522 [DDD]

Ropartz, G.:Sym 3, w. N. Stutzmann (cta), T. Dran (ten), F. Vassar (b-bar), M. Plasson (cnd), Toulouse Capitole Orch, Orféon Donostiarra EMI Classics ▲ CDM 64689-2

Rossini, G.:Petite messe solennelle, w. Jacqueline Mayeur (mez), Jean-Luc Viala (ten), Michel Piquemal (bar), Raymond Alessandrini (pno), Emmanuel Mandrin (harm), Michel Piquemal (cnd), Michel Piquemal Vocal Ensemble Accord 2-▲ ACD 203562 [DDD]

Pöllmann, Hermann (ten)

Weber, C.M. von:Missa sancta 1, w. Maria Taborsky (sop), Gerda Kink (cta), Hans Huber (bass), Gisela Schindler (org), E. Ehret (cnd), St. Michael Orch Munich, St. Michael Chorus Munich Koch Schwann ▲ SCH CD 316372

Weber, C.M. von:Missa sancta 2, w. Maria Taborsky (sop), Gerda Kink (alt), Hans Huber (bass), Gisela Schindler (org), E. Ehret (cnd), Munich St. Michael's Orch, Munich St. Michael Choir Studio SM ▲ D 2454 [ADD]

Polovecova (mez)

Mozart, W.A.:Requiem, w. Jitka Pavlová (sop), Vorapajev (ten), Gennadi Bezzubenkov (bass), M. Glinka (cnd), Ljubljana SO, Leningrad Chorus [L] Stradivari Classics ▲ SCD 6003 [DDD] ■ SMC 6003 (D)

Polsini, Luigi (sgr)

Monteverdi, C.:Ballo delle ingrate, w. Carlo Lepore (bass), Daniela Barcellona (sgr), Daniela Ciliberti (sgr), Andrea Concetti (sgr), Hans van Dijk (sgr), Remo Guerrini (sgr), Nadia Mantelli (sgr), Elena Marazzi (sgr), Humberto Orellana (sgr), Claudia Pallini (sgr), Rosa Ricciotti (sgr), Alberto Rota (sgr), Ludovica Scoppola (sgr), *(orch unknown)* Nuova Era ▲ NUO 7224

Polster, Hermann Christian (bass)

Bach, J.S.:Cant 29, w. Regina Werner (sop), Heidi Riess (alt), Hans-Joachim Rotzsch (ten), H.-J. Rotzsch (cnd), Leipzig Gewandhaus Orch, Leipzig St. Thomas Church Choir Berlin Classics ▲ BER CD 9055

Bach, J.S.:Cant 31, w. Eberhard Büchner (ten), Siegfried Lorenz (bar), Lang (sgr), Termer (sgr), Weimann (sgr), H.-J. Rotzsch (cnd), Leipzig Gewandhaus Orch, St. Thomas Choir Berlin Classics ▲ BER 9025 [ADD]

Bach, J.S.:Cant 66, w. Eberhard Büchner (ten), Siegfried Lorenz (bar), Lang (sgr), Termer (sgr), Weimann (sgr), H.-J. Rotzsch (cnd), Leipzig Gewandhaus Orch, St. Thomas Choir Berlin Classics ▲ BER 9025 [ADD]

Bach, J.S.:Cant 106, "Actus tragicus", w. Eberhard Büchner (ten), Siegfried Lorenz (bar), Lang (sgr), Termer (sgr), Weimann (sgr), H.-J. Rotzsch (cnd), Leipzig Gewandhaus Orch, St. Thomas Choir Berlin Classics ▲ BER 9025 [ADD]

Bach, J.S.:Cant 119, w. Regina Werner (sop), Heidi Riess (alt), Hans-Joachim Rotzsch (ten), H.-J. Rotzsch (cnd), Leipzig Gewandhaus Orch, Leipzig St. Thomas Church Choir Berlin Classics ▲ BER CD 9055

Bach, J.S.:Music of, w. L. Güttler (tpt), M. Lorenz (ten), A. Reiss (ten), P. Schreier (ten), M. Pommer (cnd), Leipzig New Bach Collegium Musicum, Leipzig Choirs—arias, choruses & chorales Capriccio ▲ CDC 10039 [DDD]

Beethoven, L. van:Leonore (opera), w. Helen Donath (sop), Edda Moser (sop), Eberhard Büchner (ten), Richard Cassilly (ten), Theo Adam (b-bar), Karl Ridderbusch (bass), H. Blomstedt (cnd), Dresden Staatskapelle, Leipzig Radio Chorus Berlin Classics ▲ BER 1140

Beethoven, L. van:Missa Solemnis, w. Anna Tomowa-Sintow (sop), Annelies Burmeister (alt), Peter Schreier (ten), Gerhard Bosse (vn), Hannes Kastner (org), K. Masur (cnd), Leipzig Gewandhaus Orch, Leipzig Radio Chorus Berlin Classics ("Masur Edition" series) ▲ BER 9160

Beethoven, L. van:Music of, w. Sylvia Geszty (sop), Jozsef Reti (ten), Koch (cnd), Berlin RSO, Berlin State Orch, Berlin Soloists—Christ on the Mount of Olives (oratorio); Con in E♭ Pno; Irish Songs; Minuets; Canons; Epigrams; Joke Pieces; Incidental & Ballet Music Berlin Classics 3-▲ BER 9132

Mozart, W.A.:Schauspieldirektor, w. Sylvia Geszty (sop), Peter Schreier (ten), H. Koch (cnd), Berlin CO—features complete dialog *(rec 1908)* Berlin Classics ▲ BER 9136 [DDD]

Nicolai, O.:Mass, w. G. Resick (sop), C. Killebrew (mez), F. Lang (ten), H. Hollreiser (cnd), North German RSO, North German Radio Chorus [L] Koch Schwann ▲ CD 313052 [ADD]

Polverelli, Laura (mez)

Mozart, W.A.:Così fan tutte, w. Sophie Marin-Degor (sop—Despina), Laura Polverelli (mez—Dorabella), Sophie Fournier (sgr—Fiordiligi), Nicolas Revenq (bar—Guglielmo), Patrick Donnelly (bass—Don Alfonso), Simon Edwards (sgr—Ferrando), J. Malgoire (cnd), La Grande Écurie et la Chambre du Roy Astrée 8-▲ E 8606

Mozart, W.A.:Nozze di Figaro, w. Danielle Borst (sop—Countess Almaviva), Claudine Le Coz (sop—Marcellina), Sophie Marin-Degor (sop—Suzanna), Laura Polverelli (mez—Cherubino), Valérie Lecoq (sgr—Barberina), Philippe Cantor (ten—Antonio), Stuart Patterson (ten—Dons Basile & Curzio), Huub Claessens (bar—Figaro), Nicolas Revenq (bar—Count Almaviva), Patrick Donnelly (bass—Bartolo), J. Malgoire (cnd), La Grande Écurie et la Chambre du Roy Astrée 8-▲ E 8606

Pölzer, Julius (ten)

Wagner, R.:Götterdämmerung (sels), w. Gertrude Rünger (sop—Brünnhilde), Julius Pölzer (ten—Siegfried), H. Knappertsbusch (cnd), Vienna State Opera Orch *(rec Vienna, Sept. 25, 1938)* Koch Schwann 2-▲ SCH 314662 [ADD]

Wagner, R.:Die Walküre (sels), w. Hilde Konetzni (sop—Sieglinde), Max Lorenz (ten—Siegmund), Julius Pölzer (ten—Siegmund), Set Svanholm (ten—Siegmund), Knappertsbusch, Martin (cnd), Vienna State Opera Orch Koch Schwann ▲ SCH 314692 [ADD]

Weber, C.M. von:Der Freischütz (sels), w. Maria Reining (sop—Agathe), Elisabeth Rutgers (mez—Ännchen), Julius Pölzer (ten—Max), Herbert Alsen (bass—Kaspar), R. Moralt (cnd), Vienna State Opera Orch *(rec Jan. 1, 1939)* Koch Schwann 2-▲ SCH 314632 [ADD]

Pomerantz, L. (period dlc/voc)

Jewels of the Sephardim, Vol. 1:Songs from Medieval Spain, w. P. Maund (perc), K. Higginson (rcr) Songbird ▲ AEACD 1401

Jewels of the Sephardim, Vol. 2:Wings of Time—The Sephardic Legacy of Multi-Cultural Medieval Spain, w. P. Maund (perc), K. Higginson (rcr), S. Kammen (vielle/rebec) Songbird ▲ AEACD 1405

Pondeau, Monique de (sop)

Offenbach, J.:Le Fille du tambour-major, w. Christiane Harbell (sop—Stella), Monique de Pondeau (sop—Claudine), Germaine Light (mez—Duchess Della Volta), Marcelle Ranson-Hervé (ten—Duke Della Volta), André Mallabrera (ten—Griolet), Etienne Arnaud (bar—Robert), Louis Musy (bar—Monthabor), *(orch unknown)* Accord ▲ ACD 220692 [AAD]

Pons, Juan (bar)

Donizetti, G.:Gemma di Vergy, w. Montserrat Caballe (sop—Gemma), Anna Ringart (mez—Ida), Luis Lima (ten—Tamas), Vicente Sardinero (bar—Il Conte), Juan Pons (bar—Guido), Francois Loup (b—Rolando), A. Gatto (cnd), Nouvel PO, Jean-Paul Kreder (cnd), French Radio Chorus *(rec live, Salle Pleyel, Paris, Apr 20, 1976)* Agorá Music ("Phoenix" series) 2-▲ 501 [ADD]

Donizetti, G.:Lucia di Lammermoor, w. C. Studer (sop), P. Domingo (ten), S. Ramey (bass), I. Marin (cnd), London SO Deutsche Grammophon 2-▲ 435309-2

Pons, Juan (bar) (cont.)

Donizetti, G.:Poliuto, w. K. Ricciarelli (sop), J. Carreras (ten), O. Caetani (cnd), Vienna SO, Vienna Chorus CBS 2-▲ M2K 44821

From the Official Barcelona Games Ceremony, w. Domingo, Plácido (ten), José Carreras (ten), Montserrat Caballé (sop), Giacomo Aragall (ten), Teresa Berganza (mez) RCA Red Seal ▲ 09026-61204-2 ■ 09026-61204-4 □ 09026-61204-5

Leoncavallo, R.:Pagliacci, w. Teresa Stratas (sop—Nedda), Placido Domingo (ten—Canio), Juan Pons (bar—Tonio), G. Prêtre (cnd), La Scala Orch, La Scala Chorus Philips ("Duo" series) 2-▲ 454 265-2

Leoncavallo, R.:Pagliacci, w. D. Dessi (sop), L. Pavarotti (ten), P. Coni (bar), R. Muti (cnd), Philadelphia Orch [I] Philips ▲ 438132-2

Leoncavallo, R.:Pagliacci, w. T. Stratas (sop), P. Domingo (ten), G. Prêtre (cnd), La Scala Orch, La Scala Chorus [I] Philips 2-▲ 411484-2

Mascagni, P.:Cavalleria rusticana, w. A. Baltsa (mez), S. Mentzer (mez) P. Domingo (ten), G. Sinopoli (cnd), Philharmonia Orch, Royal Opera House Chorus Covent Garden [I] Deutsche Grammophon ▲ 429568-2 [DDD]

Mascagni, P.:Iris, w. I. Tokody (sop), P. Domingo (ten), G. Patanè (cnd), Munich RSO, Bavarian Radio Chorus CBS 2-▲ M2K 45526

Massenet, J.:Hérodiade, w. Renée Fleming (sop—Salome), Dolora Zajick (mez—Hérodiade), Plácido Domingo (ten—Jean), Juan Pons (bar—Erode), Kenneth Cox (bass—Phanuel), V. Gergiev (cnd), San Francisco Opera Orch, San Francisco Opera Chorus Sony Classical 2-▲ S2K 66847

Massenet, J.:Hérodiade, w. M. Caballé (sop—Salomé), D. Vejzovic (mez—Hérodiade), J. Carreras (ten—Jean), J. Pons (bar—Hérode), E. Serra (bar—Vitellius), V. Esteve (bar—High Priest), R. Kennedy (bass—Phanuel), J. Delacôte (cnd), Barcelona Teatro Liceo Orch, Barcelona Gran Teatro de Liceo Chorus *(rec Jan. 6, 1984)* Legato Classics 2-▲ LCD 182 [ADD]

Massenet, J.:Hérodiade (sels), w. Renée Fleming (sop—Salomé), Dolora Zajick (mez—Hérodiade), Plácido Domingo (ten—Jean), Juan Pons (bar—Hérode), Hector Vásquez (bar—Vitellius), Kenneth Cox (bass—Phanuel), V. Gergiev (cnd), San Francisco Opera Orch, San Francisco Opera Chorus Sony Classical ▲ SK 61965

Massenet, J.:Hérodiade (sels), w. Renée Fleming (sop), Dolora Zajick (mez), Kristin Clayton (sgr), Plácido Domingo (ten), Kenneth Cox (bass), Hector Vásquez (sgr), V. Gergiev (cnd), San Francisco Opera Orch, San Francisco Opera Chorus—highlights *(rec San Francisco Opera, Nov 1994)* Sony Classical ▲ SK 61965

Meyerbeer, G.:L'Africiane, w. Montserrat Caballe (sop—Selika), Christine Weidinger (sop—Inez), Miriam Ucelay (mez—Anna), Placido Domingo (ten—Vasco de Gama), Guillermo Sarabia (bar—Nelusko), Juan Thomas (b-bar—High Priest of Brahma), Dimiter Petkov (bass—Don Pedro), Juan Pons (bar—Don Diego), Eduardo Soto (bass—Grand Inquisitor), A. de Almeida (cnd), Barcelona Teatro Liceo Orch, Barcelona Gran Teatro de Liceo Chorus *(rec Barcelona, Nov 27, 1977)* Legato Classics 2-▲ LCD 208-2 [ADD]

Moreno Torroba, F.:Luisa Fernanda, w. Verónica Villaroel (sop), Ana Rodrigo (mez), Plácido Domingo (ten), A. Ros-Marbá (cnd), Madrid SO Valois 2-▲ V 4759

Penella, M.:El gato montés, w. V. Villarroel (sop), T. Berganza (mez), P. Domingo (ten), M. Roa (cnd), Madrid SO [Sp] Deutsche Grammophon 2-▲ 435776-2 [DDD]

Puccini, G.:Arias, w. Ilona Tokody (sop), E. Lukács (cnd), Hungarian State Opera Orch—O mio babbino caro [from Gianni Schicchi] *(rec live, Franz Liszt Music Academy, Budapest, Hungary, June 4, 1994)* VAI Audio ▲ VAIA 1089

Puccini, G.:La fanciulla del West, w. M. Zampieri (sop), P. Domingo (ten), L. Maazel (cnd), La Scala Orch, La Scala Chorus *(rec live 1991)* Sony Classical 2-▲ S2K 47189

Puccini, G.:Madama Butterfly, w. M. Freni (sop), T. Berganza (mez), J. Carreras (ten), G. Sinopoli (cnd), Philharmonia Orch, Ambrosian Opera Chorus [I] Deutsche Grammophon 3-▲ 423567-2 [DDD]

Puccini, G.:Tosca, w. E. Marton (sop), J. Carreras (ten), M. Tilson Thomas (cnd), Hungarian State Orch, Hungarian State Chorus Sony Classical 2-▲ S2K 45847

Puccini, G.:Tosca (sels), w. E. Marton (sop), B. Heja (trb), J. Carreras (ten), F. Gerdesits (ten), J. Nemeth (bar), J. Gregor (bass), M. Tilson Thomas (cnd), Hungarian State Orch, Hungarian Radio-TV Chorus *(rec Budapest, Dec. 14–22, 1988)* Sony Classical ("Opera Highlights" series) ▲ SMK 53500 [DDD]

Puccini, G.:Il trittico, w. M. Freni (sop), E. Souljois (sop), G. Giacomini (ten), R. Alagna (ten), L. Nucci (bar), B. Bartoletti (cnd), Florence Maggio Musicale Orch, Florence Maggio Musicale Chorus London 3-▲ 436261-2 [DDD]

Sorozábal, P.:La Tabernera del Puerto, w. María Bayo (sop), Plácido Domingo (ten), V.P. Pérez (cnd), Galicia SO Auvidis Valois ("Zarzuela Collection" series) ▲ V 4766

Tosti, P.F.:songs, w. Ilona Tokody (sop), E. Lukács (cnd), Hungarian State Opera Orch—'A Vucchella *(rec live, Franz Liszt Music Academy, Budapest, Hungary, June 4, 1994)* VAI Audio ▲ VAIA 1089

Verdi, G.:arias, w. Ilona Tokody (sop), E. Lukács (cnd), Hungarian State Opera Orch—Favella il Doge ad Amelia Grimaldi? [duet from Simon Boccanegra]; Di Provenza il mar; Un dì, quando le veneri...Dite alla giovine [both from La Traviata]; Pace, pace, mio Dio! [from La Forza del Destino]; Udiste? Come albeggi, la scure al figlio [duet from Il Trovatore]; Cortigiani, vil razza dannata; Mio padre! Dio! mia Gilda...Tutte le feste [both from Rigoletto]; Ciel! Mio padre! [from Aida] *(rec live, Franz Liszt Music Academy, Budapest, Hungary, June 4, 1994)* VAI Audio ▲ VAIA 1089

Verdi, G.:Aroldo, w. M. Caballé (sop), G. Cecchele (ten), E. Queler (cnd), New York Opera Orch, Westchester Choral Society, New York Oratorio Society [I] *(rec live, Carnegie Hall 4/8/79)* CBS 2-▲ M2K 35906 [ADD]

Verdi, G.:Un ballo in maschera, w. M. Caballé (sop—Amelia), T. Paniagua (sop—Oscar), L. Chookasian (cta—Ulrica), P. Domingo (ten—Riccardo), C. MacNeil (bar—Renato), J. Pons (bar—Tom), C. del Bosco (bass—Samuel), G. Patanè (cnd), *(orch unknown)* Ornamenti 2-▲ FE 103

Verdi, G.:Falstaff, w. Maureen O'Flynn (sop), Daniela Dessi (sop), Bernadette Manca di Nissa (mez), Delores Ziegler (mez), Ramon Vargas (ten), Ernesto Gavazzi (ten), Paolo Barbacini (ten), Roberto Frontali (bar), Luigi Roni (bass), R. Muti (cnd), La Scala Orch, La Scala Chorus *(rec Milan La Scala Theater, Italy, Mar. 29 & 31)* Sony Classical ▲ S2K 58961 [DDD]

Pons, Lilian (sop)

Donizetti, G.:Lucia di Lammermoor, w. Lily Pons (sop—Lucia), Thelma Votipka (mez—Alisa), Frederick Jagel (ten—Edgardo), John Brownlee (bar—Enrico), Ezio Pinza (bass—Raimondo), G. Papi (cnd), *(orch unknown)* The Fourties 2-▲ ENT FT 1511

Giuseppe de Luca On Radio:Broadcast Recordings of the Great Italian Baritone Unpublished on Disc (1941–44), w. Giuseppe de Luca (bar), Bidù Sayão (sop), Giovanni Martinelli (ten) *(rec 1941–44)* Enterprise ("The Radio Years" series) ▲ ENT RY 25 (m)

Pons, Lily (sop)

The Art Of The Coloratura Mastersound (Profile) ▲ DFCD1-111 (m) [ADD]

Greatist Hits on Records (1928–1939), w. Enrico di Mazzei (ten), Guiseppe De Luca (bar) *(rec 1928–1939)* Minerva ▲ MN A38 [ADD]

Lily Pons Phonographe ("Great Voices" series) ▲ PHG 5060

Lily Pons Sings Donizetti, Verdi, Debussy, Rossini & others RCA Gold Seal ▲ 09026-61411-2

Opera Arias & Songs Pearl ▲ PEA 9415 (m) [AAD]

Recital Sony Masterworks ("Portrait" series) ▲ MPK 45694 [ADD]

Ponselle, Rosa (sop)

Casta Diva Pearl ▲ PEA 9210

The Columbia Acoustic Recordings:1918–1924 Pearl 2-▲ PEA 9964 (m) [AAD]

The Cross-Over Album:Songs 1925–1950 Legato Classics ▲ LCD 179-1

In Opera & Song:Recordings from 1918–1939 Nimbus ("Prima Voce" series) 3-▲ NI 1777

The 1939 Victor & 1954 "Villa Pace" Recordings Romophone 3-▲ 81022-2

Ponselle:Volume 3 Nimbus ("Prima Voce" series) ▲ NI 7878 [ADD]

Rosa Ponselle RCA Gold Seal ▲ 7810-2-RG (m) [ADD]

Rosa Ponselle:The Best from Her Acoustic Recordings *(rec 1918–20)* Grammofono 2000 ▲ GRM 78576 (m)

Rosa Ponselle *(rec 1923–1939)* Nimbus ("Prima Voce" series) ▲ NI 7805 (m) [ADD]

Rosa Ponselle, Vol. 2 Nimbus ("Prima Voce" series) ▲ NI 7846 [ADD]

Scenes from Il Trovatore & Aida, w. Martinelli, Giovanni (ten), Louise Homer (cta), Giuseppe de Luca (bar), Ezio Pinza (bass), et al. Pearl ▲ PEA 9350 (m)

Scenes from La forza del destino, w. Martinelli, Giovanni (ten), G. de Luca (bar), E. Pinza (bass) Pearl ▲ PEA 9351 (m)

Ponselle, Rosa (sop) (cont.)

Verdi, G.:Otello (sels), w. C. Muzio (sop), H. Spani (sop), E. Caruso (ten), N. Fusati (ten), L. Melchior (ten), F. Merli (ten), F. Tamagno (ten), B. Franci (bar), V. Maurel (bar), R. Stracciari (bar), T. Ruffo (bar) *(rec 1906–1933)* Music Memoria ▲ 30219

Verdi, G.:La traviata, w. Rosa Ponselle (sop—Violetta), Henriette Wakefield (sop—Annina), Frederick Jagel (ten—Alfredo), Alfredo Gandolfi (bar—Baron), Lawrence Tibbett (bar—Giorgio), E. Panizza (cnd), *(orch unknown)* *(rec live, New York, Jan. 5, 1935)* The Fourties 2–▲ ENT FT 1513

When I Have Sung My Songs Cantabile ("Biographies in Music" series) 2–▲ BIM 701–2 (m)

Poole, Thomas (ten)

Constantinides, D.:Antigone, w. J. Yestadt (cnd), Louisiana State Univ SO Vestige ▲ 04

Handel, G.F.:Alessandro, w. L. Atkinson (trb), Watson (sop), A. Terzian (mez), B. J. Rieders (cta), D. Price (ten), Andersson (sgr), M. Nowakowski (cnd), Sinfonia Varsovia [I] *(rec live)* Koch Schwann 3–▲ CD SC 100 303 [DDD]

Pop, Iggy (sgr)

Moran, J.:Manson Family, w. T. Roache (sgr—Squeaky Fromme), J. Moran (sgr—Charles Manson) Iggy Pop (sgr—Jack Lord), *(orch unknown)* Point Music ▲ 432967–2 [DDD] ■ 432967–4

Popescu, Maria (mez)

Rachmaninoff, S.:Songs, w. Joan Rodgers (sop), Alexandre Naomenko (ten), Sergei Leiferkus (bar), Howard Shelley (pno)—At the Gates of the Holy Cloister; Nothing Shall I Say to You; Again You Are Bestirred, My Heart; April! A Festive Day in the Spring; Dusk Was Falling; Song of the Disenchanted; The Flower Died; Do You Remember the Evening?; O, No, I Beg You, Do Not Leave, Op. 4/1; Morning, Op. 4/2; In the Silence of the Secret Night, Op. 4/3; Sing not, O Lovely One, Op. 4/4; Oh, My Field, Op. 4/5; It Wasn't Long Ago, My Friend, Op. 4/6; Water Lily, Op. 8/1; My Child, Your Beauty Is That of a Flower, Op. 8/2; Thoughts, Reflection, Op. 8/3; I Fell in Love, to My Sorrow, Op. 8/4; A Dream, Op. 8/5; Prayer, Op. 8/6; I Await You, Op. 14/1; Small Island, Op. 14/2; How Fleeting Is Delight in Love, Op. 14/3; I Was with Her, Op. 14/4; Summer Nights, Op. 8/5; You Are so Loved by All, Op. 14/6; Do Not Believe Me, Friend, Op. 14/7; Oh, Do Not Grieve, Op. 14/8; She Is as Beautiful as Midday, Op. 14/9; In My Soul, Op. 14/10; Spring Torrents, Op. 14/11; It Is Time, Op. 14/12 Chandos ▲ CHAN 9405

Rachmaninoff, S.:Songs, w. Joan Rodgers (sop), Alexandre Naoumenko (ten), Sergei Leiferkus (bass), Howard Shelley (pno)—Letter to K. S. Stanislawsky; The Muse, Op. 34/1; In the Soul of Each of Us, Op. 34/2; The Storm, Op. 34/3; A Passing Breeze, Op. 34/4; Arion, Op. 35/5; The Raising of Lazarus, Op. 34/6; It Cannot Be, Op. 34/7; Music, Op. 34/8; You Knew Him, Op. 34/9; I Remember This Day, Op. 34/10; The Herald, Op. 34/11; What Happiness, Op. 34/12; Dissonance, Op. 34/13; Vocalise, Op. 34/14; From the Gospel of St. John; At Night in My Garden, Op. 38/1; To Her, Op. 38/2; Daisies, Op. 38/3; The Pied Piper, Op. 38/4; Sleep, Op. 38/5; A–oo, Op. 38/6; A Prayer; All Glory to God Chandos ▲ CHAN 9477

Popescu, Stefan (ten)

Puccini, G.:Madama Butterfly, w. Eugenia Moldoveanu (sop—Madama Butterfly), Mihaela Agachi (mez—Suzuki), Corina Circa (mez—Kate Pinkerton), Emil Gherman (ten—B.F. Pinkerton), Stefan Popescu (ten—Goro), Ioan Soanea (bar—The Bonze/Yakuside), Eduard Tumageanian (bar—Sharpless), Alexandru Kopeczi (bass—Prince Yamadori), Mircea Moisa (bass—Commissioner), P. Popescu (cnd), Satu Mare PO, Cluj–Napoca Phil Chorus *(rec 1979)* Vox Box 2–▲ CDX 5155

Popis, C. (ten)

Gounod, C.:Sappho, w. M. Command (sop), S. Coste (sop), E. Faury (bar), P. Fournillier (cnd), St.–Etienne Nouvel Orch Koch Schwann 2–▲ SCH 313112 [DDD]

Popken, Ralf (alt)

Handel, G.F.:Agrippina, w. S. Bradshaw (sop), W. Hill (sop), L. Saffer (sop), G. Banditelli (cta), D. Minter (alt), B. Szilágyi (bar), M. Dean (b–bar), N. Isherwood (bass), N. McGegan (cnd), Capella Savaria [period instrs] [I] Harmonia Mundi USA 3–▲ HMU 907063/65 ■ HMU 407063/65

Handel, G.F.:Ottone, Rè di Germania, w. Julianna Gondek (sop), Lisa Saffer (sop), Patricia Spence (mez), Drew Minter (alt), Michael Dean (b–bar), N. McGegan (cnd), Freiburg Baroque Orch *(rec June 9–12, 1992)* Harmonia Mundi USA 3–▲ HMU 907073/75

Handel, G.F.:Radamisto, w. Monika Frimmer (sop), Juliana Gondek (sop), Dana Hanchard (sop), Lisa Saffer (sop), Michael Dean (b–bar), Nicholas Cavallier (bass), N. McGegan (cnd), Freiburg Baroque Orch Harmonia Mundi USA 3–▲ HMU 907111/13

Mozart, W.A.:Apollo et Hyacinthus, w. V. Hruba–Frieberger (sop), A. Raunig (alt), J. Dickie (ten), M. Pommer (cnd), Leipzig RSO, Leipzig Radio Chorus Berlin Classics 2–▲ BER 1010 [DDD]

Schütz, H.:Cantiones sacrae, w. Mona Spägele (sop), Rogers Covey–Crump (ten), John Potter (ten), Peter Kooj (bass), Thomas Ihlenfeldt (chit), Manfred Cordes (org)—complete 40 motets CPO 2–▲ 999405–2 [DDD]

Steffani, A.:Enrico Leone, w. M. Frimmer (sop), S. Szameit (sop), N. Yoko (cta), C. Guber (cta), D. Diwiak (ten), G. Faulstich (bar), L. Rovatkay (cnd), Cappela Agostino Steffani [period instrs] [I] Calig ▲ CAL 50855 [DDD]

Popov, Mincho (ten)

Mussorgsky, M.:Khovanshchina, w. A. Miltcheva (mez), K. Kaludov (ten), Z. Gadjev (bass), N. Ghiaurov (bass), N. Ghiuselev (bass), E. Tchakarov (cnd), Sofia National Opera Orch, Sofia National Opera Chorus Sony Classical 3–▲ S3K 45831

Popp, Lucia (sop)

Bach, J.S.:Cant 210, w. P. Schreier (cnd), Berlin CO Berlin Classics ▲ BER 9222

Bach, J.S.:Magnificat, BWV 243, w. A. Pashley (sop), J. Baker (mez), R. Tear (ten), D. Barenboim (cnd), New Philharmonia Orch, New Philharmonia Chorus EMI Classics ▲ CDM 64634–2

Bach, J.S.:Magnificat, BWV 243, w. Anne Pashley (sop), Janet Baker (mez), Robert Tear (ten), Thomas Hemsley (bar), D. Barenboim (cnd), New Philharmonia Orch, New Philharmonia Chorus *(rec All Saints, Tooting, London, May 1968)* EMI Classics ▲ CDK 65334 [ADD]

Beethoven, L. van:Fidelio, w. G. Janowitz (sop), R. Kollo (ten), H. Sotin (bass), D. Fischer–Dieskau (bar), L. Bernstein (cnd), Vienna PO, Vienna State Opera Chorus [G] Deutsche Grammophon 2–▲ 419436–2 [ADD]

Berg, A.:Early Songs, w. I. Gage (pno) RCA Red Seal ▲ 09026–60950–2

Bizet, G.:Djamileh, w. F. Bonisolli (ten), L. Gardelli (cnd), Munich RSO [F] Orfeo ▲ 174881 [DDD]

Brahms, J.:Songs, w. Geoffrey Parsons (pno)—12 songs [G] Acanta ▲ 43510 [DDD]

Cherubini, L.:Médée, w. L. Rysanek (sop), M. Lilowa (mez), B. Prevedi (ten), N. Ghiuselev (bass), H. Stein (cnd), Vienna State Opera Orch, Vienna State Opera Chorus *(rec live, Vienna 1/31/72)* Melodram 2–▲ CDM 27087 [ADD]

German Children's Songs Orfeo ▲ 078831 [DDD]

Grieg, E.:Peer Gynt, w. N. Marriner (cnd), Academy of St. Martin in the Fields, Ambrosian Singers EMI Classics ▲ CDC 47003 [DDD]

Handel, G.F.:Giulio Cesare in Egitto, w. Christa Ludwig (mez), Fritz Wunderlich (ten), Walter Berry (bass), F. Leitner (cnd), Munich PO, Bavarian Radio Chorus [G] *(rec live, Munich 7/1–5/65)* Verona 3–▲ 27035/37 [AAD]

Handel, G.F.:Giulio Cesare in Egitto, w. Christa Ludwig (mez), Fritz Wunderlich (ten), Walter Berry (bass), F. Leitner (cnd), Munich PO, Bavarian Radio Chorus Melodram 3–▲ MEL 37059 [AAD]

Haydn, J.:Mass 3, "Cäcilienmesse", w. Doris Soffel (mez), Rudolf Laubenthal (ten), Kurt Moll (bass), R. Kubelik (cnd), Bavarian RSO, Bavarian Radio Chorus [L] Orfeo 2–▲ 032822 [DDD]

Haydn, J.:Mass 12, "Theresienmesse", w. Rosalind Elias (mez), Robert Tear (ten), Paul Hudson (bass), L. Bernstein (cnd), London SO, London Sym Chorus [L] Sony Classical 2–▲ SM2K 47522 [ADD]

Haydn, J.:Die Schöpfung, w. Margaret Marshall (sop), Vinson Cole (ten), Bernd Weikl (bar), Gwynne Howell (bass), R. Kubelik (cnd), Bavarian RSO, Bavarian Radio Chorus Orfeo 2–▲ 150852 [DDD] 2–■ 150852 (D)

Haydn, J.:Die Schöpfung, w. Helena Döse (sop—Eva), Lucia Popp (sop—Gabriel), Werner Hollweg (ten—Uriel), Benjamin Luxon (bar—Adam), Kurt Moll (bass—Raphael), Jack McCormack (db), David Strange (vc), Antál Dorati (hpd), A. Dorati (cnd), Royal PO, Brighton Festival Chorus *(rec Kingsway Hall, London, Dec 1976)* London 2–▲ 443027–2 [ADD]

Humperdinck, E.:Hänsel und Gretel, w. B. Fassbaender (mez), J. Hamari (mez), A. Schlemm (mez), W. Berry (bass), G. Solti (cnd), Vienna PO London 2–▲ 421111–2 [ADD]

Janácek, L.:The Cunning Little Vixen, w. E. Randová (mez), D. Jedlička (bass), C. Mackerras (cnd), Vienna PO [Cz] London 2–▲ 417129–2 [DDD]

Janácek, L.:Jenůfa, w. E. Söderström (sop), E. Randová (mez), M. Dvorsky (ten), W. Ochman (ten), C. Mackerras (cnd), Vienna PO [Cz] London 2–▲ 414483–2 [DDD]

Popp, Lucia (sop) (cont.)

Jugendstil:Lieder, w. Irwin Gage (pno) RCA Red Seal ▲ 09026–60950–2

Krenek, E.:Jonny spielt auf, w. E. Lear (sop—Anita), L. Popp (sop—Yvonne), W. Blankenship (ten—Max), K. Equiluz (ten—Station Announcer), L. Heppe (ten—Manager), T. Stewart (bar—Daniello), G. Feldhof (bass—Jonny), H. Hollreiser (cnd), Vienna State Opera Orch [G] Vanguard Classics ▲ OVC 8048 [ADD]

Lehár, F.:Die lustige Witwe (sels), w. I. Hallstein (sop), H. Hoppe (ten), Alexander (bar), B. Kusche (bar), Marszalek (cnd), Operretta Orch, Operetta Chorus [G] Acanta ▲ CD 43455 [DDD]

Leoncavallo, R.:La Bohème, w. Alexandrina Milcheva (mez), Franco Bonisolli (ten), Bernd Weikl (bar), H. Wallberg (cnd), Munich RSO, Bavarian Radio Chorus [I] Orfeo 2–▲ 023822 [DDD]

Lortzing, A.:Zar und Zimmermann (sels), w. Adalbert Kraus (ten), Hermann Prey (bar), Fritz Krenn (bass), Karl Ridderbusch (bass), H. Wallberg (cnd), Bavarian RSO, Bavarian Radio Chorus [G] Acanta 2–▲ CD 42424 [DDD]

Mahler, G.:Des Knaben Wunderhorn, w. A. Schmidt (bar), L. Bernstein (cnd), Royal Concertgebouw Orch [G] Deutsche Grammophon ▲ 427302–2 [DDD]

Mahler, G.:Des Knaben Wunderhorn, w. J. Baker (mez), M. Dickie (ten), D. Fischer–Dieskau (bar), B. Weikl (bar), K. Tennstedt (cnd), London PO EMI Classics ▲ CDZB 62707

Mahler, G.:Das Lied von der Erde, w. J. Baker (mez), M. Dickie (ten), D. Fischer–Dieskau (bar), B. Weikl (bar), P. Kletzki (cnd), Philharmonia Orch EMI Classics ▲ CDZB 62707

Mahler, G.:Songs, w. Geoffrey Parsons (pno)—9 songs [G] Acanta ▲ 43510 [DDD]

Mahler, G.:Syms, w. K. Tennstedt (cnd), London PO—Nos. 1–4 EMI Classics 4–▲ ZDMD 64471

Mahler, G.:Sym 8, w. A. Augér (sop), H. Harper (sop), Y. Minton (mez), H. Watts (cta), A. Kollo (ten), J. Shirley–Quirk (bar), M. Talvela (bass), G. Solti (cnd), Chicago SO, Vienna State Opera Chorus, Vienna Boys' Choir, Vienna Singverein [G,L] London 2–▲ 414493–2 [ADD]

Mozart, W.A.:Arias, w. I. Cotrubas (sop), E. Gruberova (sop), L. Price (sop), J. Varady (sop), F. Araiza (ten), P. Domingo (ten), P. de Palma (ten), P. Schreier (ten), F. Wunderlich (ten), S. Milnes (bar), A. Titus (bar), M. Talvela (bass)—sels. from Entführung aus dem Serail, Così fan tutte, Don Giovanni, Idomeneo, Die Zauberflöte, Le nozze di Figaro Eurodisc ▲ 69256–2–RG [ADD]

Mozart, W.A.:Arias, w. Arleen Augér (sop), Kathleen Battle (sop), Irma Beilke (sop), Helena Braun (sop), Lisa Della Casa (sop), Maria Cebotari (sop), Ileana Cotrubas (sop), Helen Donath (sop), Mirella Freni (sop), Reri Grist (sop), Edita Gruberova (sop), Elisabeth Grümmer (sop), Hilde Güden (sop), Ingeborg Hallstein (sop), Luise Helletsgruber (sop), Gundula Janowitz (sop), Sena Jurinac (sop), Erika Köth (sop), Evelyn Lear (sop), Wilma Lipp (sop), Margaret Marshall (sop), Edith Mathis (sop), Jarmila Novotna (sop), Margherita Perras (sop), Elisabeth Rethberg (sop), Anneliese Rothenberger (sop), Elisabeth Schumann (sop), Elisabeth Schwarzkopf (sop), Graziella Sciutti (sop), Irmgard Seefried (sop), Graziella Sciutti (sop), Julia Varady (sop), Agnes Baltsa (mez), Margit Bokor (mez), Brigitte Fassbaender (mez), Christa Ludwig (mez), Ann Murray (mez), Francisco Araiza (ten), Anton Dermota (ten), Helge Rosvaenge (ten), Rudolf Schock (ten), Peter Schreier (ten), Leopold Simoneau (ten), Eric Tappy (ten), Richard Tauber (ten), Gösta Winbergh (ten), Josef Witt (ten), Fritz Wunderlich (ten), Christian Boesch (bar), Willy Domgraf–Fassbaender (bar), Karl Dönch (bar), Dietrich Fischer–Dieskau (bar), Erich Kunz (bar), Eberhard Wächter (bar), Hans Hotter (b–bar), Paul Schöffler (b–bar), Cesare Siepi (b–bar), José Van Dam (b–bar), Walter Berry (bass), Geraint Evans (bass), Nicolai Ghiaurov (bass), Alexander Kipnis (bass), Richard Mayr (bass), Kurt Moll (bass), James Morris (bass), Ezio Pinza (bass), Martti Talvela (bass), Giorgio Tozzi (bass), Hans Duhan (sgr), Res Fischer (sgr), Marie Gerhart (sgr), *(various orchs & cnds)*—sels from Idomeneo, Die Entführung aus der Serail, Le nozze di Figaro, Don Giovanni, Così fan tutte, Die Zauberflöte & various arias Orfeo d'or ("Festspiel Dokumente" series) 5–▲ 408955

Mozart, W.A.:Clemenza, w. R. Ziesack (sop), A. Murray (mez), D. Ziegler (mez), P. Langridge (ten), L. Polgar (bass), T. Grabowski (hpd), C. Hermann (vc), N. Harnoncourt (cnd), Zurich Opera Orch, Zurich Opera House Chorus Teldec 2–▲ 90857–2

Mozart, W.A.:Clemenza, w. M. Casula (sop), T. Berganza (mez), B. Fassbaender (mez), T. Franc (bass), F. Krenn (bass), I. Kertész (cnd), Vienna State Opera Orch, Vienna State Opera Chorus London ("Grand Opera" series) 2–▲ 430105–2 [ADD]

Mozart, W.A.:Complete Mozart Edition, w. E. Mathis (sop), E. Gruberova (sop), E. Moser (sop), P. Schreier (ten), L. Hager (cnd), Salzburg Mozarteum Orch Philips 2–▲ 422531–2 [ADD]

Mozart, W.A.:Complete Mozart Edition, w. J. Baker (mez), Y. Minton (mez), F. von Stade (mez), S. Burrows (ten), R. Lloyd (b–bar), C. Davis (cnd), Royal Opera House Orch, Royal Opera House Chorus Covent Garden Philips 2–▲ 422544–2 [ADD]

Mozart, W.A.:Complete Mozart Edition, w. E. Gruberova (sop), E. Mathis (sop), F. Araiza (ten), P. Schreier (ten), W. Berry (bass), Salzburg Mozarteum Orch Philips 8–▲ 422523–2 [ADD]

Mozart, W.A.:Così fan tutte, w. M. Price (sop), Y. Minton (mez), L. Alva (ten), G. Evans (bar), H. Sotin (bass), O. Klemperer (cnd), New Philharmonia Orch, John Alldis Choir EMI Classics 3–▲ CDMC 63845

Mozart, W.A.:Don Giovanni, w. L. Price (sop), S. Sass (sop), S. Burrows (ten), G. Bacquier (bar), B. Weikl (bar), A. Sramek (bar), K. Moll (bass), G. Solti (cnd), London PO, London Opera Chorus London ("Grand Opera" series) 3–▲ 425169–2 [ADD]

Mozart, W.A.:Idomeneo, w. E. Gruberova (sop), A. Baltsa (mez), L. Pavarotti (ten), L. Nucci (bar), J. Pritchard (cnd), Vienna PO, Vienna State Opera Chorus [I] London 3–▲ 411805–2 [DDD]

Mozart, W.A.:Nozze di Figaro, w. K. Te Kanawa (sop), F. von Stade (mez), T. Allen (bar), S. Ramey (bass), K. Moll (bass), G. Solti (cnd), London PO [I] London 3–▲ 410150–2 [DDD]

Mozart, W.A.:Nozze di Figaro, w. B. Hendricks (sop), A. Baltsa (mez), G. Raimondi (ten), J. Van Dam (bar), N. Marriner (cnd), Academy of St. Martin in the Fields, Ambrosian Opera Chorus [I] Philips 3–▲ 416370–2 [DDD]

Mozart, W.A.:Nozze di Figaro (sels), w. K. Te Kanawa (sop), F. von Stade (mez), T. Allen (bar), S. Ramey (bass), K. Moll (bass), G. Solti (cnd), London PO [I] London ▲ 417395–2 [DDD] □ 417395–5

Mozart, W.A.:Nozze di Figaro (sels), w. B. Hendricks (sop), A. Baltsa (mez), G. Raimondi (ten), J. van Dam (b–bar), N. Marriner (cnd), Academy of St. Martin in the Fields, Ambrosian Opera Chorus [I] Philips ▲ 416870–2 [DDD]

Mozart, W.A.:Zauberflöte, w. Gundula Janowitz (sop—Pamina), Lucia Popp (sop—Queen of the Night), Nicolai Gedda (ten–Tamina), Walter Berry (bass—Papageno), Gottlob Frick (bass—Sarastro), O. Klemperer (cnd), Philharmonia Orch, Philharmonia Chorus EMI Classics 2–▲ CDCB 55173

Mozart, W.A.:Zauberflöte, w. G. Janowitz (sop), R. Pütz (sop), N. Gedda (ten), W. Berry (bass), G. Frick (bass), O. Klemperer (cnd), Philharmonia Orch, Philharmonia Chorus [without dialog; G] EMI Classics ("Studio" series) 2–▲ CDMB 69971 [ADD]

Mozart, W.A.:Zauberflöte, w. E. Gruberova (sop), S. Jerusalem (ten), W. Brendel (bar), R. Bracht (bass), B. Haitink (cnd), Bavarian RSO, Bavarian Radio Chorus [G] EMI Classics 3–▲ CDCC 47951 [DDD]

Mozart, W.A.:Zauberflöte (sels), w. E. Gruberova (sop), S. Jerusalem (ten), W. Brendel (bar), R. Bracht (bass), B. Haitink (cnd), Bavarian RSO, Bavarian Radio Chorus [G] EMI Classics ▲ CDC 47008 [DDD]

Opera Arias Acanta ▲ CD 43326

Orff, C.:Der Bernauerin, w. Ostermayer (sgr), Laubenthal (ten), H. Lippert (ten), K. Eichhorn (cnd), Munich RSO, Munich Radio Chorus [G] Orfeo 2–▲ 255912 [DDD]

Orff, C.:Carmina burana, w. G. Unger (ten), R. Wolansky (bar), J. Noble (bar), R. Frühbeck de Burgos (cnd), New Philharmonia Orch, New Philharmonia Chorus EMI Classics ▲ CDM 64328

Orff, C.:Die Kluge, w. J. Van Kesteren (ten), T. Stewart (bar), F. Crass (bass), G. Frick (bass), K. Eichhorn (cnd), Munich RSO Eurodisc 2–▲ 69069–2–RG [ADD]

Pfitzner, H.:Songs—4 songs RCA Red Seal ▲ 09026–60950–2

Puccini, G.:Suor angelica, w. M. Lipovšek (mez), G. Patanè (cnd), Munich RSO, Munich Radio Chorus Eurodisc ▲ 7806–2–RC [DDD]

Schoenberg, A.:Songs—4 songs RCA Red Seal ▲ 09026–60950–2

Schreker, F.:Songs—5 songs RCA Red Seal ▲ 09026–60950–2

Schubert, Franz:Mass 5, w. B. Fassbaender (mez), A. Dallapozza (ten), D. Fischer–Dieskau (bar), W. Sawallisch (cnd), Bavarian RSO, Bavarian Radio Chorus [L] EMI Classics ("Studio" series) ▲ CDM 69222

Schubert, Franz:Songs (comp), w. G. Johnson (pno)—24 songs from 1816, including Litanei, An mein Klavier, D.150, D.371, D.373, D.376, D.393, D.398, D.401, D.404, D.405, D.416, D.429, D.458, D.467, D.468 D.491, D.496, D.496a, D.497, D.500, D.502, D.504, D.508, D.509 [G] Hyperion ▲ CDJ 33017

Schubert, Franz:Tantum ergo, D.962, w. B. Fassbaender (mez), A. Dallapozza (ten), D. Fischer–Dieskau (bar), W. Sawallisch (cnd), Bavarian RSO, Bavarian Radio Chorus [L] EMI Classics ("Studio" series) ▲ CDM 69223

Popp, Lucia (sop) (cont.)

Strauss (II), Joh.:Die Fledermaus, w. E. Lind (sop), A. Baltsa (mez), P. Domingo (ten), W. Brendel (bar), K. Rydl (bass), P. Domingo (cnd), Munich RSO, Bavarian Radio Chorus [G] EMI Classics 2-▲ CDCB 47480

Strauss (II), Joh.:Die Fledermaus, w. J. Varady (sop), A. Kollo (ten), H. Prey (bar), I. Rebroff (bass), E. Kleiber (cnd), Bavarian State Opera Orch [G] Deutsche Grammophon 2-▲ 415646–2 [ADD]

Strauss, R.:4 Last Songs, w. M. Tilson Thomas (cnd), London SO *(rec May 21–22, 1993)* Sony Classical ▲ SK 48242 [DDD]

Strauss, R.:Der Rosenkavalier, w. G. Jones (sop), C. Ludwig (mez), P. Domingo (ten), W. Berry (b-bar), L. Bernstein (cnd), Vienna PO [G] CBS 3-▲ M3K 42564 [ADD]

Strauss, R.:Der Rosenkavalier, w. Claire Watson (sop—Feldmarschallin), Lucia Popp (sop—Sophie), Annelie Waas (sop—Marianne), Brigitte Fassbaender (mez—Octavian), Margaretthe Bence (ct—Annina), David Thaw (ten—Valzacchi), Karl Ridderbusch (bass—Baron Ochs), Benno Kusche (bass—Herr von Faninal), Albrecht Peter (bass—Police Inspector), C. Kleiber (cnd), Bavarian State Orch, Bavarian State Chorus *(rec live, Münchner Festspiele, July 20, 1974)* Arkadia 3-▲ 486 [ADD]

Strauss, R.:Songs RCA Red Seal ▲ 09026–60950–2

Wagner, R.:Der Ring des Nibelungen (sels), w. Jessye Norman (sop), René Kollo (ten), Siegfried Jerusalem (ten), Kurt Moll (bass), Matti Salminen (bass), M. Janowski (cnd), Dresden Staatskapelle RCA Victor ▲ 09026–68084–2; ■ 09026–68084–4

Weinberger, J.:Schwanda der Dudelsackpfeifer, w. G. Killebrew (mez), S. Jerusalem (ten), H. Prey (bar), S. Nimsgern (bass), H. Wallberg (cnd), Munich RSO, Bavarian Radio Chorus [F] CBS 3-▲ M3K 36926 [ADD]

World Stars Sing Operetta, w. Anna Moffo (sop), José Carreras (ten), Ants Kollo (ten), Thomas Moser (ten), Giuseppe Di Stefano (ten), Hermann Prey (bar), Karl Ridderbusch (bass), et al., various orchs *(rec 1968–1985)* Acanta ▲ 42941

Pöppel, Peter (sgr)

Popp, M.:Ludus Danielis, w. T. Schlierf (spkr), A. Veljanov (spkr), S. Hausen (sgr), M. Popp (cnd), Estampie *(rec Jan. 1–10, 1993)* Christophorus ▲ 77144 [DDD]

Porcher, Hans Joachim (bass)

Weber, C.M. von:Peter Schmoll und seine Nachbarn, w. A. Pfeffer (sop—Minnette), J. Schmidt (ten—Martin Schmoll), S. Basa (ten—Karl Pirkner), H.-J. Schöpflin (ten—Niklas), R. Busching (bar—Peter Schmoll), H.J. Porcher (bass—Hans Bast), G. Markson (cnd), Hagen PO [G] *(rec Feb. 1–5, 1993)* Marco Polo 2-▲ 8.223592/93 [DDD]

Portella, Nelson (bar)

Puccini, G.:Madama Butterfly, w. Raina Kabaivanska (sop—Madama Butterfly), Alexandrina Milcheva (mez—Suzuki), Rossitza Troeva-Mircheva (cta—Kate Pinkerton), Nazzareno Antinori (ten—F.B. Pinkerton), Roumen Doikov (ten—Goro), Werther Vrachovski (ten—Il Principe Yamadori), Nelson Portella (bar—Sharpless), Kosta Dinkov (bass—Lo zio Bonzo), G. Bellini (cnd), Sofia PO, Svetoslav Obrenetov Bulgarian National Chorus *(rec Sophia, Bulgaria, Dec 1–13, 1982)* Arts Music 2-▲ 447161–2 [DDD]

Puccini, G.:Tosca, w. Raina Kabaivanska (sop—Floria Tosca), Nazzareno Antinori (ten—Mario Cavaradossi), Roumen Doikov (ten—Spoletta), Enzo Dara (bar—Casare Angelotti/Il sagrestano), Nelson Portella (bar—Il Barone Scarpia), Stoyan Balabanov (bass—Sciarrone/Un carceriere), Borislav Peev (sgr—Un Pastore), G. Bellini (cnd), Sofia PO, Bulgarian National Radio Children's Choir, Svetoslav Obrenetov Bulgarian National Chorus *(rec Sophia, Bulgaria, Nov 14–27, 1982)* Arts Music ▲ 47158–2 [DDD]

Porzano, Saverio (ten)

Puccini, G.:La Bohème, w. Ileana Cotrubas (sop—Mimi), Margherita Guglielmi (sop—Musetta), José Carreras (ten—Rodolfo), Saverio Porzano (ten—Parpignol), Regolo Romani (ten—Vendor), Claudio Giombi (bar—Benoit), Gianni Maffeo (bar—Schaunard), Angelo Romero (bar—Marcello), Alfredo Giacomotti (bass—Alcindoro), Carlo Meliciani (bass—Customs Officer), Giuseppe Morresi (bass—Sergeant), Paolo Washington (bass—Colline), G. Prêtre (cnd), La Scala Orch, La Scala Chorus *(rec Washington D.C., Sept 8, 1976)* Legato Classics 2-▲ LCD 201–2

Poschner, B. (ten)

Schubert, Franz:Mass 2, w. B. Bonney (sop), M. Hintermeier (cta), J. A. Pita (ten), A. Schmidt (bar), C. Abbado (cnd), CO of Europe Deutsche Grammophon ▲ 435486–2

Schumann, R.:Requiem Mignon, w. B. Bonney (sop), M. Hintermeier (cta), J. A. Pita (ten), A. Schmidt (bar), C. Abbado (cnd), CO of Europe Deutsche Grammophon ▲ 435486–2

Pospi Il, Michal (bass)

Michna, A.V.:Sacred Music, w. M. Bornus-Szczycinski (sgr), M. Cechalová (sgr), J. Lewitová (sgr), M. Predota (sgr), R. Hugo (cnd), Capella Regis Musicalis—Missa V à 5 et à 7 si placet; Cantiones pro Defunctis; Missa VI pro Defunctis à 6 et à 10; Requiem Studio Matou ▲ MAT 1 [DDD]

Zelenka, J.D.:Missa sanctissimae trinitatis, w. Anna Hlavenková (sop), Magdalena Kozená (alt), Lubomir Moravec (alt), Stanislav Predota (ten), Richard Sporka (ten), M. Stryncl (cnd), Musica Florea Studio Matou ▲ MAT 17 [DDD]

Pospišil, Michael (bass)

Zelenka, J.D.:Il penitenti al sepolchro del Redentore, w. Magdaléna Kozená (alt—Maddalena), Martin Prokeš (ten—Davidde), Robert Hugo (cnd), Capella Regia Musicalis *(rec St Franciscus Church of the Convent of St Agnes of Bohemia, Prague, Nov 1994)* Panton ▲ 811380–2 [DDD]

Posselt, Martina (sop)

Goldschmidt, B.:Der gewaltige Hahnrei, w. R. Alexander (sop), H. Lawrence (sop), R. Wörle (ten), M. Kraus (ten), M. Petzold (ten), C. Otelli (bar), L. Zagrosek (cnd), German SO, Berlin Radio Chorus London ▲ 440850–2 [DDD]

Goldschmidt, B.:Mediterranean Songs, w. R. Alexander (sop), H. Lawrence (sop), R. Wörle (ten), M. Kraus (ten), M. Petzold (ten), C. Otelli (bar), L. Zagrosek (cnd), German SO, Berlin Radio Chorus London ▲ 440850–2 [DDD]

Possemeyer, Berthold (bar)

Bach, J.S.:St. John Passion, w. C. Schäfer (sop), Y. Jänicke (mez), A. Kraus (ten), R. Hagen (bass), E. Weyand (cnd), Stuttgart Hymnus Orch, Stuttgart Hymnus Boys' Choir [G] *(rec 1990)* Hänssler Classic 2-▲ 98.968

Mozart, W.A.:Missa [longa], K.262, w. Regina Schudel (sop), Ulla Groenewold (cta), Peter Maus (ten), U. Gronostay (cnd), Berlin Radio Sinfonietta, Berlin Radio Chamber Choir [L] Koch Schwann ▲ CD 313 021 [ADD/DDD]

Mozart, W.A.:Missa brevis, K.258, w. Regina Schudel (sop), Ulla Groenewold (cta), Peter Maus (ten), U. Gronostay (cnd), Berlin Radio Sinfonietta, Berlin Chamber Chorus [L] Koch Schwann ▲ CD 313 021 [ADD/DDD]

Pfitzner, H.:Heine-lieder, w. T. Palm (pno) Ars Produktion ▲ ARS 368326 [DDD]

Schubert, Franz:Schwanengesang, w. T. Palm (pno) Ars Produktion ▲ ARS 368326 [DDD]

Schumann, R.:Dichterliebe, w. T. Palm (pno) Ars Produktion ▲ ARS 368326 [DDD]

Post, Andreas (sgr)

Telemann, G.P.:Cants, w. Constanze Backes (sop), Mechthild Georg (mez), Klaus Mertens (bar), L. Rémy (cnd), Telemann CO, Helko Siede (cnd), Michaelstein Chamber Choir—Christmas cantatas, "Siehe, ich verkündige Euch" (1761) & "Der Herr hat offenbaret" (1762) *(rec Apr 28–May 2, 1996)* CPO ▲ CPO 999419–2 [DDD]

Telemann, G.P.:Hirten an der Krippe zu Bethlehem, w. Constanze Backes (sop), Mechthild Georg (mez), Klaus Mertens (bar), L. Rémy (cnd), Telemann CO, Helko Siede (cnd), Michaelstein Chamber Choir *(rec Apr 28–May 2, 1996)* CPO ▲ CPO 999419–2 [DDD]

Potchapski, Viatcheslav (bass)

Rachmaninoff, S.:Aleko, w. Natalia Erassova (sop), Galina Borissova (cta), Vitaly Tarastchenko (ten), Vladimir Matorin (bass), A. Tchistiakov (cnd), Bolshoi Theater Orch, Russian State Choir Russian Season 3-▲ CMX 388053

Rimsky-Korsakov, N.:A May Night, w. Maria Lapina (sop), Natalia Erassova (mez), Elena Okolycheva (cta), Alexander Arkhipov (ten), Vitaly Tarastchenko (ten), Piotr Glouboky (bass), A. Tchistiakov (cnd), Bolshoi Theater Orch, Russian State Choir Russian Season 4-▲ CMX 388054

Pott, Charles (bass)

Blow, J.:Songs, w. James Bowman (ct), John Mark Ainsley (ten), Michael George (bass), R. King (cnd), King's Consort—Sing unto the Lord, Oh ye Saints *(rec St Jude-on-the-Hill, London, Dec 20–21, 1968)* United ▲ CAL 88002 [DDD]

Pott, Charles (bass) (cont.)

Purcell, H.:Anthems & Services, w. Tom Seligman (trb), James Bowman (ct), Ashley Stafford (ct), John Mark Ainsley (ten), Andrew Gant (ten), Michael George (bass), R. King (cnd), King's Consort, King's Consort—O Sing unto the Lord; My beloved spake *(rec St Jude-on-the-Hill, London, Dec 20–21, 1968)* United ▲ CAL 88002 [DDD]

Potter, John (ten)

Codex Speciálník, w. P. Hillier (cnd), Hillard Ensemble, D. James (ct), R. Covey-Crump (ten), G. Jones (bar) *(rec Gönningen City Church, Jan. 1993)* ECM New Series ▲ 78118–21504–2 [DDD]

Kancheli, G.:Evening Prayers, w. David James (ct), Rogers Covey-Crump (ten), Gordon Jones (bar), D. R. Davies (cnd), Stuttgart CO *(rec Apr. 1994)* ECM New Series ▲ 78118–21510–2 [DDD]

Officium, w. P. Hillier (cnd), Hillard Ensemble, D. James (ct), R. Covey-Crump (ten), G. Jones (bar), J. Gabarek (sop/ten saxs) *(rec Sept. 1993)* ECM New Series ▲ 78118–21525–2

Pärt, A.:Litany, w. David James (ct), Rogers Covey-Crump (ten), Gordon Jones (bass), T. Kaljuste (cnd), Tallinn CO, Estonian Phil Chamber Choir *(rec Niguliste Church, Tallinn, Sept 1995)* ECM New Series ▲ 78118–21592–2 [DDD] ■ 78118–21592–4

Pärt, A.:Passio Domini nostri Jesu Christi secundum Joannem, w. L. Dawson (sop), D. James (alt), R. Covey-Crump (ten), G. Jones (bass), M. George (bass), P. Hillier (cnd), Hilliard Ensemble, Western Wind Chamber Chorus [L] ECM New Series ▲ 78118–21370–2 [DDD]; ■ 78118–21370–4 (D)

Schütz, H.:Cantiones sacrae, w. Mona Spägele (sop), Ralf Popken (alt), Rogers Covey-Crump (ten), Peter Kooj (bass), Thomas Ihlenfeldt (chit), Manfred Cordes (org)—complete 40 motets CPO 2-▲ 999405–2 [DDD]

Schütz, H.:Symphoniae sacrae 1, w. Barbara Borden (sop), Nele Gramss (sop), Rogers Covey-Crump (ten), Douglas Nasrawi (ten), Harry van der Kamp (bass), Concerto Palatino Choir Accent 2-▲ 9178/79 [DDD]

Potter, Thomas (bar)

Songs, Dances & Fantasy, w. Jerry Fuller (db), Frederick Ockwell (pno), Kenneth Dorsch (hpd), William Ferris (pno), Steve Hartman (hp), John Vorrasi (ten), Anne Waller (gtr) Musical Arts Society ▲ CD 41589 [AAD] ■ CS 41589

Potter, Thomas (bass)

Sowerby, L.:Forsaken of Man, w. Alicia Clark (sop), Judith Compton (alt), Paul Grizzell (bass), Matthew Greenberg (bass), Bruce Hall (sgr), John Vorassi (sgr), Thomas Weisflog (org), William Ferris (cnd), William Ferris Chorale *(rec St. Thomas the Apostle Church, Chicago, June 1990)* New World ▲ 803942 [AAD]

Pottier, Jacques (ten)

Honegger, A.:Le Roi David, w. Henri Doublier (nar), Jacqueline Brumaire (sop), Denise Scharley (alt), S. Baudo (cnd), Paris Opera Orch, Elisabeth Brasseur Chorale Accord ▲ ACD 200822 [AAD]

Poulenard, Isabelle (sop)

Charpentier, M.-A.:Le Malade imaginaire, w. J. Feldman (sop), M. Minkowski (cnd), Louvre Musicians Erato (Musifrance) ▲ 2292–45002–2 ZK

Clérambault, L.N.:Cants, w. G. Ragon (ten), Amalia Ensemble—Léandre et Héro (1713); Pirame et Tisbé (1713); L'Isle de Délos (1716); Apollon et Doris (1720) [F] *(rec 1/91)* Opus 111 ▲ OPS 39–9103 [DDD]

Couperin, F.:Motets, w. J. Feldman (sop), G. Reinhart (bass), J. ter Linden (bass vl), D. Moroney (hpd)—[L] Musique d'Abord ▲ HMA 1901150

Dupuy, B.A.:Sacred Music, w. Jean-Louis Comorette (ct), Erik Gruchet (ten), Dominique Miraille (bar), Jean-Louis Bindi (bass), A. Bourbon (cnd), Baroque Instrumental Ensemble, Toulouse Vocal Group—Noël; Motet; Magnificat Arion ▲ ARN 68330 [DDD]

Fauré, G.:Requiem, w. M. George (bass), M. Best (cnd), English CO, Corydon Singers [1893 version] Hyperion ▲ CDA 66292

Gluck, C.W.:Le Cinesi, w. A. S. von Otter (mez), G. Banditelli (cta), G. de Mey (ten), R. Jacobs (cnd), Schola Cantorum Basiliensis Instrumental Ensemble Editio Classica ▲ 77174–2–RG [DDD]

Grétry, A.-E.-M.:La Caravane du Caire, w. G. de Reyghere (sop), G. Ragon (ten), G. de Mey (ten), P. Huttenlocher (bar), V. Le Téxier (bar), J. Bastin (bass), M. Minkowski (cnd), Ricercar Academy, Ricercar Academy Chorus [period instrs] [F] Ricercar 2-▲ RIC 100084/85 [DDD]

Handel, G.F.:Cants, w. Jean-Louis Comoretto (ct), Il Divertimento—Menzognere speranze; Vedendo amor; Figli del mesto cor; Lungi dal mio bel nume Astrée ▲ E 8577

Handel, G.F.:Duets for Various Voices, w. Jean-Louis Comoretto (ct), Il Divertimento—No, di voi non vo' fidarmi; Troppo curda, troppo fiera; Tanti strali al sen mi scocchi Astrée ▲ E 8577

Handel, G.F.:Tamerlano, w. Isabelle Poulenard (sop—Irene), Mieke van der Sluis (sop—Asteria), René Jacobs (alt—Andronico), Henri Ledroit (ct—Tamerlano), John Elwes (ten—Bajazet), Gregory Reinhart (bass—Leone), J. Malgoire (cnd), La Grande Écurie et la Chambre du Roy *(rec 1983)* Sony Classical 3-▲ SM3K 37893

Handel, G.F.:Il Trionfo del Tempo e del Disinganno, w. Jennifer Smith (sop), Nathalie Stutzmann (cta), John Elwes (ten), M. Minkowski (cnd), Louvre Musicians Erato 2-▲ 2292–45351–2 ZA

Jacquet De La Guerre, E.:Le Raccomondement comique de Pierrot et de Nicole, w. M. Verschaeve (bass), G. Guillard (hpd), *(ensemble unknown)* [F] Arion 2-▲ ARN 268012 [AAD]

Pergolesi, G.B.:La serva padrona, w. Philippe Cantor (bar), G. Bezzina (cnd), Nice Baroque Ensemble Pierre Verany ▲ PVY 795111

Pergolesi, G.B.:Stabat mater, w. Jean-Louis Comoretto (ct), J. Malgoire (cnd), La Grande Écurie et la Chambre du Roy Astrée ▲ E 8556

Rameau, J.P.:Les Indes galantes, w. C. McFadden (sop), S. Piau (sop), N. Rime (sop), M. Ruggeri (sop), H. Crook (ten), J.-P. Fouchecourt (ten), N. Rivenq (bar), J. Corréas (bass), B. Delétré (bass), W. Christie (cnd), Les Arts Florissants [F] Harmonia Mundi France 3-▲ HMC 901367/69

Poulton, Robert (bar)

Loevendie, T.:Gassir, the Hero, w. Claron McFadden (sop—Partridge/Priestess), Timothy Wilson (alt—Shamsi), Christopher Gillett (ten—Safi), Robert Poulton (bar—Gassir), Lieuwe Visser (bass—Yemni), Roger Smeets (sgr—Rafi), D. Porcelijn (cnd), Asko Ensemble *(rec live, Amsterdam Studios, June 14–15, 1993)* Donemus ▲ CV 35

Pousseur, Marianne (sop)

Pousseur, H.:Traverser la forêt, w. Christian Crahay (nar), Peter Harvey (bar), J.-P. Peuvion (cnd), Liège New Music Ensemble, Gerhard Sporken (cnd), Vocal Ensemble Adda ▲ ADD 581295 [DDD]

Pousseur, Marianne (spkr)

Schoenberg, A.:Pierrot lunaire, w. P. Herreweghe (cnd), Musique Oblique Ensemble [G] Harmonia Mundi France ▲ HMC 901390

Povia, Charlotte (mez)

Puccini, G.:Suor angelica, w. Elisabeth Carron (sop—Angelica), Joan Summers (sop—Genovieffa), Donna Owen (sop—Dolcina), Lou Ann Wyckoff (sop—Alms collector), Hanna Owen (sop—novice), Anthea De Forest (sop—novice), Charlotte Povia (mez—Abbess), Beverly Evans (mez—Monitress), Kay Creed (mez—Mistress), La Vergne Monette (sop/mez—lay sister), Joan August (sop/mez—lay sister), Pearle Goldsmith (sop/mez—other sister), Lila Herbert (sop/mez—other sister), Jodell Kenting (sop/mez—other sister), Ann Pretzat (sop/mez—other sister), Evelyn Sachs (cta—Princess), F. Patanè (cnd), *(orch unknown)* *(rec New York, Feb 23, 1967)* Legato Classics ▲ LCD 212–1 [ADD]

Powell, Claire (mez)

Falla, M. de:El amor brujo, w. N. Cleobury (cnd), Aquarius Virgin Classics ("Ultraviolet" series) ▲ CUV 61138

Halffter, E.:Dominus pastor meus, w. Susan Chilcott (sop), Joan Cabero (ten), José Antonio Carril (bass), V. P. Pérez (cnd), Tenerife SO, La Laguna Univ Choir Discobi ▲ DIS 2009 [DDD]

Lloyd, G.:Iernin, w. M. Hill Smith (sop), G. Pogson (ten), H. Herford (bar), M. Rivers (bar) Albany 3-▲ TROY 121/23 [DDD]

Powell, Josef (sgr)

Romberg, S.:Deep in My Heart, w. H. Traubel (sgr), J. Ferrer (sgr), R. Clooney (sgr), Gene Kelly (sgr), F. Kelly (sgr), V. Damone (sgr), A. Miller (sgr), W. Olvis (sgr), C. Richards (sgr), H. Keel (sgr), T. Martin (sgr), J. Weldon (sgr) Sony Music Special Products ▲ AK 47703

Powell, Richard (ten)

Cage, J.:Europera 3, w. Suzan Hanson (sop), Ruby Hinds (mez), Patricia McAfee (mez), Michael Lyon (ten), Kevin Bell (bass), Brian Pezzone (pno), Vicki Ray (pno), Hannes Geiger (record players), Joseph Giri (record players), William Houston (record players), Dren McDonald (record players), Ronda Rindone (record players), Clarice Ross (record players), Scott Fraser (tape), A. Culver (cnd), Long Beach Opera Orch *(rec Center Theater, Long Beach, CA, Nov. 13, 1993)* Mode 2-▲ MODE 38/39

Powell, S. (sgr)
Porter, C.:Fifty Million Frenchmen, w. H. McGillin (sgr), K. Criswell (sop), K. McClelland (sgr), K. Ziemba (sgr), J. Graae (sgr), J. Harder (sgr), S. Waara (sgr), P. Cass (sgr), J. LeClerc (sgr) [1991 studio cast] New World ▲ 80417-2 [DDD]

Power, David (bar)
Gershwin, G.:Songs, w. JoAnn Ottley (sop), Duehlmeier-Gritton Duo—Fascinatin' Rhythm *(rec David Gardner Hall, University of Utah, Aug 16, 1994)* Centaur ▲ 2249 [DDD]

Power, Patrick (ten)
Auber, D.-F.:Le Domino noir, w. Sumi Jo (sop), Doris Lamprecht (sop), Martine Olmeda (sop), Isabelle Vernet (sop), Jocelyne Taillon (mez), Bruce Ford (ten), Gilles Cachemaille (bar), Jules Bastin (bass), R. Bonynge (cnd), English CO, London Voices London 2-▲ 440646-2
Balfe, M.W.:The Bohemian Girl, w. N. Thomas (sop), J. Summers (bar), R. Bonynge (cnd), Irish National SO, Ireland National Sym Chorus Argo 2-▲ 433324-2 [DDD]

Pöysti, Lasse (nar)
Sibelius, J.:The Lonely Ski Trail, w. O. Vänskä (cnd), Lahti SO *(rec Church of the Cross, Lahti, Finland, Jan 8-12, 1996)* BIS ▲ CD 815 [DDD]
Sibelius, J.:The Wood Nymph Nar, w. Harri Karri (pno), O. Vänskä (cnd), Lahti SO *(rec Church of the Cross, Lahti, Finland, Jan 8-12, 1996)* BIS ▲ CD 815 [DDD]

Pozderec, C. (sop)
Mozart, W.A.:Missa, K.427, w. M. C. LeBlanc (sop), F. Bardot (ten), L. Peintre (bar), F. Bardot (cnd), Altaïr SO, Paris Opera Children's Choir [L] Thésis ▲ THE11003

Pozo, Rodrigo del (ten)
Cavalli, P.F.:Vespero della beata Vergine Maria, w. Barbara Borden (sop), Emily van Evera (sop), Markus Brutscher (ten), Mark Padmore (ten), Gerd Türk (ten), Harry van der Kamp (bass), Peter Zimpel (sgr), Bruce Dickey (sackbut), Charles Toet (sackbut), Concerto Palatino, Schola Cantorum Basiliensis Harmonia Mundi France ("Documenta" series) 2-▲ HMC 905219/20
Purcell, H.:Musick's Hand-maid, w. Ellen Hargis (sop), Ian Honeyman (ten), Harry van der Kamp (bass), Paul O'Dette (thb/cittern/lt), Andrew Lawrence-King (hps/org/hpd), A. Lawrence-King (cnd), Harp Consort Astrée ▲ E 8564

Pozzer, Sylva (sop)
Caldara, A.:La costanza vince il rigore, w. Stefano Abarello (alt), Ensemble Barocco Padua Sans Souci *(rec Carrara Santo Stefano Church, Padua, May 3-7, 1996)* Dynamic ▲ CD 166 [DDD]
Caldara, A.:La lode premiata, w. Stefano Abarello (alt), Ensemble Barocco Padua Sans Souci *(rec Carrara Santo Stefano Church, Padua, May 3-7, 1996)* Dynamic ▲ CD 166 [DDD]
Viadana, L. da:Vespri per l'Assunzione, w. C. Calvino (alt), U. Müller Adam (ten), J. Clement (ten), S. Foresti (bass), L'Amaltea Ensemble, Vox Hesperia, St. Marco Capella Musicale Fonè ▲ FON 92F 08 [DDD]

Pracnové, H. (alt)
Klein, G.:Madrigals, w. M. Čejková (sop), J. Suchánková (sop), K. Kozunik (ten), J. Belor (bar) *(rec Oct. 20 & 21, 1992)* Koch International Classics ▲ KIC 7230-2 [DDD]

Prandelli, Giacinto (ten)
Boito, A.:Mefistofele, w. Orietta Moscucci (sop—Margherita), Amalia Pini (mez—Martha), Piero de Palma (ten—Wagner), Giacinto Prandelli (ten—Faust), Boris Christoff (bass—Mefistofele), V. Gui (cnd), Rome Opera Orch, Rome Opera Chorus EMI Classics 2-▲ CDMB 65655
Catalani, A.:La Wally, w. R. Tebaldi (sop), S. Majonica (bass), G. Santini (cnd), Rome RAI SO, Rome RAI Chorus *(rec 1960)* Enterprise (Palladio) 2-▲ ENTPD 4165 [ADD]
Cilea, F.:Adriana Lecouvreur, w. Carla Gavazzi (sop), Miti Truccato Pace (mez), Saturno Meletti (bar), A. Simonetto (cnd), Milan RAI Lyric Orch, Milan RAI Chorus Fonit Cetra ("Classic Collection" series) 2-▲ FCT CDO 20
Donizetti, G.:Lucia di Lammermoor (sels), w. L. Gencer (sop), N. Carta (bar), R. Botteghelli (bass), Hussu (sgr), Sabatucci (sgr), O. de Fabritiis (cnd), Trieste Teatro Comunale Giuseppe Verdi Orch, Trieste Teatro Comunale G. Verdi Chorus *(rec live 12/13/57 & 2/10/58)* Melodram ▲ MEL 15003 (m) [AAD]
Giacinto Prandelli, w. various Italian orchs *(rec live 1949-1956)* Bongiovanni ▲ GB 1066-2 [ADD]
Giordano, U.:Fedora, w. Maria Caniglia (sop), Aldo Bertocci (ten), Scipio Colombo (bar), Andrea Piccinni (bass), Capozzi (sgr), M. Rossi (cnd), Turin RAI SO, Turin RAI Chorus *(rec 1950)* Cetra Classic 2-▲ Don 35
Puccini, G.:La Bohème, w. R. Tebaldi (sop), H. Gueden (sop), G. Inghilleri (bar), F. Corena (bass), Raphaël Arié (bass), A. Erede (cnd), St. Cecilia Academy Orch Rome, St. Cecilia Academy Chorus Rome London 2-▲ 440233-2 [ADD]
Puccini, G.:Il trittico, w. V. de los Angeles (sop), F. Barbieri (mez), T. Gobbi (bar), *(other soloists unknown)*, Rome Opera Orch, Rome Opera Chorus *(rec Rome, 1950s)* EMI Classics 3-▲ CDMC 64165 (m)
Verdi, G.:La traviata, w. R. Tebaldi (sop), G. Orlandini (bar), C. M. Giulini (cnd), Milan RAI Orch, Milan RAI Chorus *(rec live 5/28/52)* Standing Room Only 2-▲ SRO 810-2 [ADD]
Verdi, G.:La traviata, w. Renata Tebaldi (sop—Violetta), Giacinto Prandelli (ten—Alfredo), Carlo Tagliabue (bar—Germont), T. Serafin (cnd), Naples Teatro San Carlo Orch, Naples Teatro San Carlo Chorus *(rec Arena Flegrea, Naples, July 3, 1954)* Golden Age of Opera 2-▲ GAO 191/192 [ADD]
Zandonai, R.:Francesca da Rimini, w. M. Caniglia (sop—Francesca), A. M. Canali (mez—Altichiara), A. Bertocci (ten—Ser Toldo Berardengo), M. Carlin (ten—Malatestino), G. Prandelli (ten—Paolo), C. Tagliabue (bar—Giovanni), E. Campi (bass—Il Giuliare/Il Torrigiano), A. Guarnieri (cnd), Rome RAI SO, Rome RAI Chorus *(rec 1952)* Cetra Classic ▲ CDO 22 [ADD]

Pranod, E. (ten)
Verdi, G.:Luisa Miller, w. K. Ricciarelli (sop—Luisa), M. G. Piolatto (mez—Laura), S. Silva (cta—Federica), J. Carreras (ten—Rodolfo), E. Pranod (ten—A Peasant), R. Bruson (bar—Miller), G. Casarini (bar—Wurm) M. Rinaudo (bass—Count Walter), F. Previtali (cnd), Turin Teatro Regio Orch, Turin Teatro Regio Chorus *(rec May 9, 1976)* Legato Classics 2-▲ LCD 180 [ADD]

Praticò, Bruno (bar)
Bizet, G.:Les Pêcheurs de perles, w. A. Ruffini (sop), G. Morino (ten), C. Piantini (cnd), Italian International Orch, Slovak Phil Chorus [F] *(rec live 7/30-8/2/90)* Nuova Era 2-▲ 6944/45 [DDD]
Delibes, L.:Lakmé, w. A. Ruffini (sop), S. Lazzarini (mez), G. Morino (ten), C. Piantini (cnd), Italian International Orch, Bratislava Chamber Chorus [F] Nuova Era 2-▲ 7096/97 [DDD]
Donizetti, G.:L'elisir d'amore, w. M. Devia (sop), P. Spagnoli (bar), M. Viotti (cnd), English CO, Tallis Chamber Choir Erato 2-▲ 4509-91701-2
Leoncavallo, R.:La Bohème, w. L. Mazzaria (sop), M. Senn (mez), M. Malagnini (sgr), J. Summers (bar), J. Latham-König (cnd), Venice Teatro La Fenice Orch, Venice Teatro La Fenice Chorus *(rec live, 1990)* Nuova Era 3-▲ 6917/19 [DDD]
Piccinni, N.:La cecchinaLa cecchina, ossia la buona figliola, w. M. A. Peters (sop), A. Ruffini (sop), G. Morino (ten), B. Campanella (cnd), Serenissima Pro Arte Orch [I] *(rec live 1990)* Memories 3-▲ DR 3101/03 [DDD]
Rossini, G.:La cambiale di matrimonio, w. A. Rossi (sop), M. Comencini (ten), B. de Simone (bar), M. Viotti (cnd), English CO [I] Claves 8-▲ CD 9200 [DDD]
Rossini, G.:La cambiale di matrimonio, w. Alessandra Rossi (sop), Maurizio Comencini (ten), Bruno De Simone (bar), Valeria Baiano (bass), Francesco Facini (bass), M. Viotti (cnd), English CO Claves ▲ 50-9101
Rossini, G.:Il Signor Bruschino, w. Patrizia Orciani (sop), Katia Lytting (mez), Luca Canonici (ten), Fulvio Massa (ten), Pietro Spagnoli (bar), Natale de Carolis (b-bar), M. Viotti (cnd), Turin PO Claves 2-▲ 50-8904/5
Rossini, G.:Il Signor Bruschino, w. P. Orciani (sop), K. Lytting (mez), L. Canonici (ten), F. Massa (ten), P. Spagnoli (bar), N. de Carolis (b-bar), M. Viotti (cnd), Turin PO [I] Claves 8-▲ CD 9200 [DDD]

Predota, Stanislav (ten)
Dvořák, A.:Songs, w. Milada Cechalová (sop), Adam Skoumal (pno)—Evening Songs, Opp. 3, 9 & 31; Songs, Op. 2; The Orphan, Op. 5; Rosemary; 2 Songs on Folk Poems, Op. posth.; 4 Songs, Op. 6; 3 Modern Greek Poems, Op. 50; 4 Songs, Op. 82 Studio Matous ▲ MAT 24 [DDD]
Janácek, L.:Moravian Folk Poetry, w. Eva Truplová (sop), Adam Skoumal (pno) Studio Matou ▲ MAT 15 [DDD]
Janácek, L.:Vocal Music, w. Eva Struplová (sop), Hanus Barton (pno), Adam Skoumal (pno), L. Cerny (cnd), *(ensemble unknown)*, Milan Uherek (cnd), Severácek Children's Choir—Little Queens; Folk Poetry from Hukvaldy; Folk Nocturnes; Nursery Rhymes Studio Matous ▲ MAT 16 [DDD]

Predota, Stanislav (ten) (cont.)
Michna, A.V.:Sacred Music, w. M. Bornus-Szczycinski (sgr), M. Cechalová (sgr), J. Lewitová (sgr), M. Pospí il (sgr), R. Hugo (cnd), Capella Regis Musicalis—Missa V à 5 et à 7 si placet; Cantiones pro Defunctis; Missa VI pro Defunctis à 6 et à 10; Requiem Studio Matou ▲ MAT 1 [DDD]
Zelenka, J.D.:Missa sanctissimae trinitatis, w. Anna Hlavenková (sop), Magdalena Kozená (alt), Lubomir Moravec (alt), Richard Sporka (ten), Michal Pospí il (bass), M. Stryncl (cnd), Musica Florea Studio Matou ▲ MAT 17 [DDD]

Préfontaine, Claude (nar)
Normandeau, R.:Petit Prince, w. Michel Dumont (nar—Aviator), Martin Pensa (nar—Little Prince), Christine Séguin (nar—Rose), Jean Marchand (nar—King), Luc Durand (nar—Conceited Man), Gilles Dupuis (nar—Drunkard), Guy Nadon (nar—Businessman), Jacques Languirand (nar—Lamplighter), Pierre Bourgault (nar—Geographer), Cynthia Dubois (nar—Snake), Monique Giroux (nar—Flower), Françoise Davoine (nar—Rose Garden), Jean-Louis Millette (nar—Fox), Gérard Poirier (nar—Railway Switchman), Claude Préfontaine (nar—Water Pill Salesman) *(rec Montreal, Aug 1994)* CBC 2-▲ 1091 [DDD]

Prégardien, Christoph (ten)
Bach, C.P.E.:Auferstehung und Himmelfahrt Jesu, w. H. Martinpelto (sop), P. Harvey (bass), P. Herreweghe (cnd), Orch of the Age of Enlightenment, Collegium Vocale Virgin Classics ▲ CDC 59069
Bach, J.S.:Cant 6, w. Barbara Schlick (sop), Andreas Scholl (ct), Gotthold Schwarz (bass), C. Coin (cnd), Limoges Baroque Ensemble, Accentus Chamber Choir Astrée ▲ E 8555
Bach, J.S.:Cant 11, "Ascension Oratorio", w. B. Schlick (sop), C. Patriasz (cta), P. Kooy (bass), P. Herreweghe (cnd), Collegium Vocale Orch Harmonia Mundi France ▲ HMC 901479
Bach, J.S.:Cant 21, w. G. de Reyghere (mez), P. Lika (bass), S. Kuijken (cnd), La Petite Bande, Netherlands Chamber Choir [G] Veritas ▲ VC 7 90779-2 [DDD] ■ VC 7 90779-4 (D)
Bach, J.S.:Cant 21, w. G. de Reyghere (mez), R. Jacobs (alt), P. Lika (bass), S. Kuijken (vn), S. Kuijken (cnd), La Petite Bande, Netherlands Chamber Choir Virgin Classics ▲ CDC 59528
Bach, J.S.:Cant 41, w. Barbara Schlick (sop), Andreas Scholl (ct), Gotthold Schwarz (bass), C. Coin (cnd), Limoges Baroque Ensemble, Accentus Chamber Choir Astrée ▲ E 8555
Bach, J.S.:Cant 43, w. B. Schlick (sop), C. Patriasz (cta), P. Kooy (bass), P. Herreweghe (cnd), Collegium Vocale Harmonia Mundi France ▲ HMC 901479
Bach, J.S.:Cant 44, w. B. Schlick (sop), C. Patriasz (cta), P. Kooy (bass), P. Herreweghe (cnd), Collegium Vocale Harmonia Mundi France ▲ HMC 901479
Bach, J.S.:Cant 49, w. Barbara Schlick (sop), Andreas Scholl (alt), Gotthold Schwarz (bass), C. Coin (cnd), Limoges Baroque Ensemble, Leipzig Concerto Vocale Astrée ▲ E 8530
Bach, J.S.:Cant 68, w. Barbara Schlick (sop), Andreas Scholl (ct), Gotthold Schwarz (bass), C. Coin (cnd), Limoges Baroque Ensemble, Accentus Chamber Choir Astrée ▲ E 8555
Bach, J.S.:Cant 85, w. Barbara Schlick (sop), Andreas Scholl (alt), Gotthold Schwarz (bass), Christophe Coin (piccolo vc/cnd), Leipzig Vocal Concerto, Limoges Baroque Ensemble Astrée ▲ E 8544
Bach, J.S.:Cant 115, w. Barbara Schlick (sop), Andreas Scholl (alt), Gotthold Schwarz (bass), C. Coin (cnd), Limoges Baroque Ensemble, Leipzig Concerto Vocale Astrée ▲ E 8530
Bach, J.S.:Cant 175, w. Barbara Schlick (sop), Andreas Scholl (alt), Gotthold Schwarz (bass), Christophe Coin (piccolo vc/cnd), Leipzig Vocal Concerto, Limoges Baroque Ensemble Astrée ▲ E 8544
Bach, J.S.:Cant 180, w. Barbara Schlick (sop), Andreas Scholl (alt), Gotthold Schwarz (bass), C. Coin (cnd), Limoges Baroque Ensemble, Leipzig Concerto Vocale Astrée ▲ E 8530
Bach, J.S.:Cant 183, w. Barbara Schlick (sop), Andreas Scholl (alt), Gotthold Schwarz (bass), Christophe Coin (piccolo vc/cnd), Leipzig Vocal Concerto, Limoges Baroque Ensemble Astrée ▲ E 8544
Bach, J.S.:Cant 199, w. Barbara Schlick (sop), Andreas Scholl (alt), Gotthold Schwarz (bass), Christophe Coin (piccolo vc/cnd), Leipzig Vocal Concerto, Limoges Baroque Ensemble Astrée ▲ E 8544
Bach, J.S.:Cant 205, w. Efrat Ben-Nunn (sop), Katharina Kammerloher (alt), Klaus Häger (bass), R. Jacobs (cnd), Berlin Academy for Early Music, Berlin Chamber Chorus Harmonia Mundi France 2-▲ HMC 901544.45
Bach, J.S.:Cant 205, w. M. van der Sluis (sop), R. Jacobs (ct), D. Thomas (bass), G. Leonhardt (cnd), Orch of the Age of Enlightenment [G] Philips ▲ 432161-2 [DDD]
Bach, J.S.:Cant 214, w. M. van der Sluis (sop), R. Jacobs (ct), D. Thomas (bass), G. Leonhardt (cnd), Orch of the Age of Enlightenment [G] Philips ▲ 432161-2 [DDD]
Bach, J.S.:Christmas Oratorio, w. Ruth Ziesak (sop), Monica Groop (alt), Klaus Mertens (bass), R. Otto (cnd), Concerto Cologne, Frankfurt Vocal Ensemble *(rec Festeburgkirche Frankfurt, Jan 9-16, 1991 & May 12-1)* Capriccio 2-▲ 60025-2 [DDD]
Bach, J.S.:Magnificat, BWV 243, w. G. de Reyghere (sop), R. Jacobs (alt), P. Lika (bass), S. Kuijken (vn), S. Kuijken (cnd), La Petite Bande, Netherlands Chamber Choir Virgin Classics ▲ CDC 59528
Bach, J.S.:Magnificat, BWV 243, w. G. de Reyghere (sop), R. Jacobs (alt), P. Lika (bass), S. Kuijken (vn), S. Kuijken (cnd), La Petite Bande, Netherlands Chamber Choir [L] Veritas ▲ VC 7 90779-2 [DDD] ■ VC 7 90779-4 (D)
Bach, J.S.:Mass in b, BWV 232, w. M. Venuti (sop), C. Kallisch (cta), A. Scharinger (bass), E. Ortner (cnd), Salzburg Baroque Ensemble, Arnold Schoenberg Choir Koch Schwann 2-▲ SCH 312512 [DDD]
Bach, J.S.:Masses, BWV 233-36, "Lutheran Masses", w. A. Mellon (sop), G. Lesne (alto), P. Kooy (bass), P. Herreweghe (cnd), Ghent Collegium Vocale Orch, Ghent Collegium Vocale—BWV 234 & 235 Virgin Classics ▲ CDC 59587
Bach, J.S.:Masses, BWV 233-36, "Lutheran Masses", w. A. Mellon (sop), G. Lesne (alto), P. Kooy (bass), P. Herreweghe (cnd), Ghent Collegium Vocale Orch, Ghent Collegium Vocale—BWV 233 & 236 Virgin Classics ▲ CDC 59634
Bach, J.S.:St. Matthew Passion, w. Monika Frimmer (sop), Veronika Winter (sop), Lena Susanne Norin (alt), Wilfried Jochens (ten), Klaus Mertens (bass), Hans-Georg Wimmer (bass), H. Max (cnd), Das Kliene Konzert, Rhineland Kantorei Capriccio 2-▲ 60 046 [DDD]
Bach, J.S.:St. Matthew Passion, w. B. Schlick (sop), K. Wessel (alto), G. de Mey (ten), P. Kooy (bass), T. Koopman (cnd), Amsterdam Baroque Orch, W. Cantryn (cnd), J. van Veldhoven (cnd), Breda Sacred Choir, Netherlands Bach Society Boys' Choir Erato ▲ 2292-45814-2
Bach, J.S.:St. Matthew Passion (sels), w. A. Mellon (sop), G. Lesne (alto), P. Kooy (bass), P. Herreweghe (cnd), Ghent Collegium Vocale Orch, Ghent Collegium Vocale Virgin Classics ▲ CDC 59587
Britten, H.:Nocturne, w. O. Vänskä (cnd), Tapiola Sinfonietta [E] *(rec 10-11/91)* BIS ▲ CD 540 [DDD]
Britten, H.:Now Sleeps the Crimson Petal, w. Ib Lanzky-Otto, O. Vänskä, Tapiola Sinfonietta [E] *(rec 10-11/91)* BIS ▲ CD 540 [DDD]
Britten, H.:Serenade, Op. 31, w. I. Lanzky-Otto (hn), O. Vänskä (cnd), Tapiola Sinfonietta [E] *(rec 10-11/91)* BIS ▲ CD 540 [DDD]
Charpentier, M.-A.:Motets for Double Choir, w. B. Schlick (sop), N. Zijlstra (sop), K. Wessel (alt), D. Visse (ct), H. van Berne (ten), P. Kooy (bass), K. Martens (bass), T. Koopman (cnd), Amsterdam Baroque Orch—Canticum pro pace; Josué; Mors Saulis et Jonathae; Praelium Michaelis; Quam dilecta; 3 Leçons de Ténèbres Erato (Musifrance) ▲ 2292-45822-2 ZA
Haydn, J.:L'Anima del filosofo, or Orfeo ed Euridice, w. Clara McFadden (sop), Marylin Schmiege (mez), Gotthold Schwarz (bass), M. Schneider (cnd), La Stagione, La Stagione Choir Deutsche Harmonia Mundi 2-▲ 05472-77229-2
Haydn, J.:Die Schöpfung, w. Edith Mathis (sop), Harald Stamm (bass), M. Atzmon (cnd), World SO, Pécs Chamber Choir, Berlin Academy of Arts Chamber Choir, Shin-Yuh Kai Choir [G] *(rec Basilica San Francesco in Assisi, as part of the IPPNW "Hiroshima Concert 1990")* BIS 2-▲ CD 493/94 [DDD]
Holzbauer, I.:Günther von Schwarzburg, w. Clara McFadden (sop), Robert Wörle (ten), Michael Schopper (bass), M. Schneider (cnd), La Stagione CPO 3-▲ CPO 999265
Homilius, G.A.:St. Matthew Passion, w. A. Monoyios (sop), U. Groenwald (cta), G. Türk, K. Mertens (b-bar), H.-G. Wimmer (bass), Berlin Academy for Early Music, Leverkusen Cappella Vocale Berlin Classics 2-▲ BER 1046 [DDD]
Mendelssohn, F.:Songs, w. Andreas Staier (pno)—6 Songs, including Auf Flügeln des Gesanges Deutsche Harmonia Mundi ▲ 05472-77319-2
Monteverdi, C.:Ritorno d'Ulisse, w. L. Hunt (sop), C. Högman (sop), B. Fink (cta), D. Vissé (ct), G. Tucker (ten), D. Thomas (bass), R. Jacobs (cnd), Concerto Vocale [I] Harmonia Mundi France 3-▲ HMC 901427/29
Mozart, W.A.:Ave verum corpus, w. Barbara Bonney (sop), Charlotte Margiono (sop), Sylvia McNair (sop), Elisabeth von Magnus (cta), Thomas Hampson (bass), N. Harnoncourt (cnd), Vienna Concentus Musicus, Arnold Schoenberg Choir Teldec ▲ 98928 2

▲ = CD ♦ = Enhanced CD Δ = MD ■ = Cassette Tape □ = DCC

Prégardien, Christoph (ten) (cont.)

Mozart, W.A.:Don Giovanni, w. Charlotte Margiono (sop—Donna Elvira), Luba Orgonasova (sop—Donna Anna), Eirian James (mez—Zerlina), Julian Clarkson (alt—Masetto), Christoph Prégardien (ten—Don Ottavio), Rodney Gilfry (bar—Don Giovanni), Ildebrando d'Arcangelo (bass—Leporello), Andrea Silvestrelli (bass—Il Commendatore), J. E. Gardiner (cnd), English Baroque Soloists, Monteverdi Choir London Deutsche Grammophon ("4D Audio" series) 3–▲ 445870–2

Mozart, W.A.:Grabmusik, w. Barbara Bonney (sop), Charlotte Margiono (sop), Sylvia McNair (sop), Elisabeth von Magnus (cta), Thomas Hampson (bass), N. Harnoncourt (cnd), Vienna Concentus Musicus, Arnold Schoenberg Choir Teldec ("Das alte Werk" series) ▲ 98928–2

Mozart, W.A.:Masonic Music, w. H. Wildhaber (ten), G. Hornik (bass), P. Schneyder (bass), M. Haselböck (cnd), Vienna Academy, Chorus Viennensis—Masonic Cants., K.429, 471, 619, 623 & Songs, K.148, 468, 483, 484 [G] Novalis ▲ 150081 [DDD]

Mozart, W.A.:Missa, K.427, w. Monika Frimmer (sop), Barbara Schlick (sop), Klaus Mertens (bass), P. Neumann (cnd), Collegium Cartusianum, Cologne Chamber Choir Virgin Classics ▲ CDM 61167

Mozart, W.A.:Regina coeli, K.127, w. Barbara Bonney (sop), Charlotte Margiono (sop), Sylvia McNair (sop), Elisabeth von Magnus (cta), Thomas Hampson (bass), N. Harnoncourt (cnd), Vienna Concentus Musicus, Arnold Schoenberg Choir Teldec ("Das alte Werk" series) ▲ 98928 2

Mozart, W.A.:Requiem, w. B. Schlick (sop), C. Watkinson (cta), H. van der Kamp (bass), T. Koopman (cnd), Amsterdam Baroque Orch, Netherlands Bach Society Choir [L] Erato ▲ 2292–45472–2 [DDD] ■ 2292–45472–4

Schubert, Franz:Die Schöne Müllerin, w. A. Staier (pno) Deutsche Harmonia Mundi ▲ 05472–77273–2

Schubert, Franz:Schwanengesang, w. Andreas Staier (pno) Deutsche Harmonia Mundi ▲ 05472–77319–2

Schubert, Franz:Songs (comp), w. Graham Johnson (pno)—Der Tod Oscars, D.375; Das Grab, D.377; Der Entfernten, D.350; Pflügerlied, D.39; Abschied von der Harfe, D.406; Der Jüngling an der Quelle, D.300; Abendlied, D.382; Stimme der Liebe, D.412; Romanze, D.144; Geist der Liebe, D.414; Klage, D.415; Julius an Theone, D.419; Der Leidende, D.432; Der Leidende, D.432b; Die frühe Liebe, D.430; Die Knabenzeit, D.400; Edone, D.445; Die Liebesgötter, D.446; An Chloen, D.363; Freude der Kinderjahre, D.455; Gesänge des Harfners aus Wilhelm Meister, D.478; Der Hirt, D.490; Am ersten Maimorgen, D.344; Bei dem Grabe meines Vaters, D.496; Mailied, D.503; Zufriedenheit, D.362; Skolie, D.507 Hyperion ▲ CDJ 33023

Schubert, Franz:Songs (misc), w. A. Staier (pno)—Songs of Schiller poems Deutsche Harmonia Mundi ▲ 05472–77296–2 [DDD]

Schubert, Franz:Songs (misc), w. Andreas Staier (hpd)—Am Flusse; Trost in Tränen; 4 Lieder, Op. 3; Sehnsucht; Die Liebe; Lieder, Op. 5; 3 Gesänge des Harfners; 3 Lieder, Op. 19; An die entferne; Versunken; An der Mond; 3 Lieder, Op. 32 [all after Goethe] Deutsche Harmonia Mundi ▲ 05472–77342–2 [DDD]

Schumann, R.:Dichterliebe, w. Andreas Staier (pno) Deutsche Harmonia Mundi ▲ 05472–77319–2

Preger, Kurt (ten)

Millöcker, C.:Bettelstudent, w. Wilma Lipp (sop—Laura), Esther Rethy (sop—Bronislava), Rosette Anday (cta—Palmatica), Rudolf Christ (ten—Symon), Kurt Preger (ten—Ollendorf), Eberhard Waechter (bar—Jan), A. Paulik (cnd), Vienna Volksoper Orch, Vienna Volksoper Chorus *(rec Brahmssaal, Vienna, June 1995)* Omega 2–▲ OCD 1018/19 [ADD]

Strauss (II), Joh.:Die Fledermaus, w. H. Gueden (sop), J. Patzak (ten), A. Dermota (ten), A. Jaresch (ten), A. Poell (b–bar), W. Lipp (sop), S. Wagner (mez), C. Krauss (cnd), Vienna PO *(rec early 1950s)* London ("Historic" series) 2–▲ 425990–2 [AAD]

Strauss (II), Joh.:Eine Nacht in Venedig, w. E. Réthy (sop), M. Schober (sop), R. Boesch (bar), K. Friedrich (ten), A. Jerger (b–bar), A. Paulik (cnd), Vienna SO, Bregenz Festival Choir [G] *(rec 1951)* Koch Schwann ▲ 3–1272–2 [ADD]

Strauss (II), Joh.:Der Zigeunerbaron, w. Emmy Loose (sop—Arsena), Gerda Scheyrer (sop—Saffi), Elisabeth Fez (cta—Mirabella), Hilde Rössl–Majdan (cta—Czipra), Waldemar Kmentt (ten—Barinkay), Paul Spani (ten—Ottokar), Erich Kunz (bar—Homonay), Kurt Preger (ten—Zsupan), Eberhard Wächter (bass—Carnero), A. Paulik (cnd), Vienna State Opera Orch, Vienna State Opera Chorus *(rec Brahmssaal, Vienna, Austria, June 1956)* Vanguard Classics 2–▲ OVC 8082/83 [ADD]

Weill, K.:The Threepenny Opera, w. Liane (sop—Polly Peachum), A. Felbermayer (sop—Lucy), H. Fassler (sop—Jenny), R. Anday (cta—Mrs. Peachum), K. Preger (ten—Macheath), H. Roswaenge (ten—Street Crier), A. Jerger (bar—Peachum), F. Gutherie (bar), *(cnd & orch unknown)* Vanguard Classics ▲ OVC 8057 [ADD]

Preid, Cynthia Vonn (mez)

Barber, G.:Songs of Destiny, w. Gail Barber (hp) Opus One ▲ CD 169

Prein, Johann-Werner (bass)

Schulhoff, E.:The Flames, w. Jane Eaglen (sop—Donna Anna, Nun, Woman, Marguerite), Carola Höhn (sop—Shadow), Celina Lindsley (sop—Shadow), Regina Schudel (sop—Shadow), Iris Vermillion (mez—La Morte), Christiane Berggold (alt—Shadow), Kaja Borris (alt—Shadow), Elvira Dressen (alt—Shadow), Kurt Westi (ten—Don Juan), Johann–Werner Prein (bass—Commendatore), Gerd Wolf (bass—Harlequin), J. Mauceri (cnd), Berlin German SO, Berlin RIAS Chamber Choir *(rec Jesus–Christus Church, Berlin Dahlem, Oct 1993/Apr 1994)* London 2–▲ 444630–2 [DDD]

Prenzlow, Gertraud (mez)

Dvořák, A.:Requiem Mass, w. Elisabeth Rose (sop), Peter Schreier (ten), Theo Adam (bass), K. Ančerl (cnd), Berlin RSO, Berlin Radio Chorus Forlane 2–▲ FRL 16636 [AAD]

Lortzing, A.:Der Waffenschmied, w. E. Ebert (sop—Marie), G. Prenzlow (mez—Mariens), H. Neukirch (ten—Georg), G. Leib (bar—Ritter), H. Krämer (bass—Hans), H. Fricke (cnd), Berlin State Opera Orch, Berlin State Opera Chorus Berlin Classics ("Eterna" series) ▲ BER 2036–2 [ADD]

Presnell, Harve (bar)

Orff, C.:Carmina burana, w. J. Harsanyi (sop), R. Petrak (ten), E. Ormandy (cnd), Philadelphia Orch, Rutgers Univ Choir Sony Classical ("Essential Classics" series) ▲ SBK 47668 ■ SBT 47668

Preston, Jean (mez)

Honegger, A.:Le Roi David, w. Netania Davrath (sop), Marvin Sorenson (ten), M. Singher (nar), M. Milhaud (nar), M. Abravanel (cnd), Utah SO [F] Vanguard Classics ▲ OVC 4038 [ADD]

Preston, Robert (sgr)

Mancini, H.:Victor/Victoria, w. J. Andrews (sgr), L. Ann Warren (sgr) GNP Crescendo ▲ GNPD 8038

Pretschner, Brigitte (alt)

Mahler, G.:Sym 3, w. E. Tabakov (cnd), Sofia PO, Bulgarian National Chorus, Bodra Smyana Children's Choir *(rec Bulgarian Concert Hall, Sofia, Apr 1990)* Capriccio 15–▲ 49043 [DDD]

Pretzat, Ann (sop/mez)

Puccini, G.:Suor angelica, w. Elisabeth Carron (sop—Angelica), Joan Summers (sop—Genovieffa), Donna Owen (sop—Dolcina), Lou Ann Wyckoff (sop—Alms collector), Hanna Owen (sop—novice), Anthea De Forest (sop—novice), Charlotte Povia (mez—Abbess), Beverly Evans (mez—Monitress), Kay Creed (mez—Mistress), La Vergne Monette (sop/mez—lay sister), Joan August (sop/mez—lay sister), Pearle Goldsmith (sop/mez—other sister), Lila Herbert (sop/mez—other sister), Jodell Kenting (sop/mez—other sister), Ann Pretzat (sop/mez—other sister), Evelyn Sachs (cta—Princess), F. Patanè (cnd), *(orch unknown)* *(rec New York, Feb 23, 1967)* Legato Classics ▲ LCD 212–1 [ADD]

Prevedi, Bruno (ten)

Bellini, V.:Norma, w. Caballé (soprano—Norma), F. Cossotto (mez), J. Carreras (ten), I. Vinco (bass), C. F. Cillario (cnd), Barcelona Teatro Liceo Orch, Barcelona Gran Teatro de Liceo Chorus [I] *(rec live, Barcelona 1/11/70)* Melodram 2–▲ CDM 27089 [ADD]

Boito, A.:Nerone, w. I. Ligabue (sop), R. Baldani (mez), A. Ferrin (bass), G. Gavazzeni (cnd), Turin RAI SO, Turin RAI Chorus *(rec live 1975)* Italian Opera Rarities 2–▲ IOR 7704 [ADD]

Cherubini, L.:Médée, w. L. Popp (sop), L. Rysanek (sop), M. Lilowa (mez), N. Ghiuselev (bass), H. Stein (cnd), Vienna State Opera Orch, Vienna State Opera Chorus *(rec live, Vienna 1/31/72)* Melodram 2–▲ CDM 27087 [ADD]

Spontini, G.:Agnes von Hohensauften, w. M. Caballé (sop), A. Stella (sop), G. Guelfi (bar), R. Muti (cnd), Rome Radio Orch, Rome RAI Chorus [I] *(rec live, 4/30/70)* Myto 2–▲ 2 MCD 90215 (m) [ADD]

Verdi, G.:Don Carlos, w. L. Gencer (sop), F. Cossotto (mez), S. Bruscantini (bar), N. Ghiaurov (bass), F. Previtali (cnd), Rome Opera Orch, Rome Opera Chorus *(rec live)* Melodram 3–▲ MEL 37022

Verdi, G.:Ernani, w. Montserrat Caballè (sop), Peter Glossop (bar), Boris Christoff (bass), G. Gavazzeni (cnd), Milan RAI SO, Milan RAI Chorus *(rec Milan, Mar. 25, 1969)* Pantheon 2–▲ PHE 6634 (m)

Prevedi, Bruno (ten) (cont.)

Verdi, G.:Macbeth, w. B. Nilsson (sop), G. Taddei (bar), T. Schippers (cnd), St. Cecilia Academy Orch Rome, St. Cecilia Academy Chorus Rome London ("Grand Opera" series) 2–▲ 433039–2 [ADD]

Verdi, G.:Nabucco, w. E. Suliotis (sop), T. Gobbi (ten), C. Cava (bass), L. Gardelli (cnd), Vienna State Opera Orch, Vienna State Opera Chorus [I] London 2–▲ 417407–2 [ADD]

Previati, Fabio (bar)

Bellini, V.:Adelson e Salvini, w. A. Nafé (mez), A. Licata (cnd), Catania Teatro Massimo Bellini Orch, Catania Teatro Massimo Bellini Chorus Nuova Era 2–▲ NUO 7154 [DDD]

Puccini, G.:La Bohème, w. L. Orgonasova (sop), C. Gonzales (mez), J. Welch (ten), W. Humburg (cnd), *(orch unknown)*, Bratislava Children's Choir [I] Naxos 2–▲ 8.660003/04 [DDD]

Puccini, G.:La Bohème (sels), w. Luba Orgonasova (sop—Mimi), Carmen Gonzales (sop—Musetta), Jonathan Welch (ten—Rudolfo), Fabio Previati (bar—Marcello), Boaz Senator (bar—Schaunard), Ivan Urbas (bass—Colline), Jiri Sulzenko (bass—Alcindoro), W. Humburg (cnd), Czech–Slovak RSO Bratislava, Bratislava Children's Choir, Slovak Phil Chorus *(rec Concert Hall, Czecho–Slovak Radio, Bratislava, Apr. 23–May 4, 1990)* Naxos ▲ 8.553151 [DDD]

Rossini, G.:L'inganno felice, w. A. Felle (sop), I. Zennaro (ten), N. de Carolis (b–bar), D. Serraiocco (b–bar), M. Viotti (cnd), English CO [I] Claves 8–▲ CD 9200 [DDD]

Rossini, G.:L'inganno felice, w. Amelia Felle (sop), Iorio Zennaro (ten), Natale de Carolis (b–bar), Danilo Serraiocco (bass), M. Viotti (cnd), English CO Claves ▲ 50–9211

Rossini, G.:L'occassione fa il ladro, w. M. Bayo (sop), F. Provvisionato (mez), F. Massa (ten), I. Zennaro (ten), N. de Carolis (b–bar), M. Viotti (cnd), English CO [I] Claves 8–▲ CD 9200 [DDD]

Rossini, G.:L'occassione fa il ladro, w. Maria Bayo (sop), Francesca Provvisionato (mez), Fulvio Massa (ten), Iorio Zennaro (ten), Natale de Carolis (b–bar), M. Viotti (cnd), English CO Claves 2–▲ 50–9208/9

Previn, André (nar)

Prokofiev, S.:Peter & the Wolf, w. A. Previn (cnd), Royal PO Telarc ▲ CD 80126 [DDD]

Prey, Annette (nar)

Brahms, J.:Romanzen aus Tieck's *Magelone*, w. H. Prey (bar), H. Deutsch (pno) [G] Orfeo 2–▲ 116842 [DDD]

Prey, Hermann (bar)

Bach, J.S.:Cant 54, w. Marga Hoffgen (sop), K. Thomas (cnd), Leipzig Gewandhaus Orch, Leipzig St. Thomas Church Choir Berlin Classics ▲ BER CD 9202

Bach, J.S.:Cant 56, w. Marga Hoffgen (sop), K. Thomas (cnd), Leipzig Gewandhaus Orch, Leipzig St. Thomas Church Choir Berlin Classics ▲ BER CD 9202

Bach, J.S.:Cant 82, w. Marga Hoffgen (sop), K. Thomas (cnd), Leipzig Gewandhaus Orch, Leipzig St. Thomas Church Choir Berlin Classics ▲ BER CD 9202

Bach, J.S.:Christmas Oratorio, w. E. Ameling (sop), B. Fassbaender (mez), H. Laubenthal (ten), E. Jochum (cnd), Tölz SO, Bavarian Radio Boys' Chorus—highlights Philips ("Silver Line" series) ▲ 422252–2 [ADD]

Bach, J.S.:Mass in b, BWV 232, w. A. Giebel (sop), J. Baker (mez), N. Gedda (ten), F. Crass (bass), O. Klemperer (cnd), New Philharmonia Orch, BBC Sym Chorus [L] EMI Classics ("Studio" series) 2–▲ ZDMB 63364–2 [ADD]

Bach, J.S.:Masses, BWV 233–36, "Lutheran Masses", w. A. Giebel (sop), G. Litz (mez), K. Redel (cnd), Pro Arte Orch, Pro Arte Chorale—BWV 233 in F Philips 2–▲ 438739–2

Bach, J.S.:St. John Passion, w. Evelyn Lear (sop), Hertha Töpper (mez), Ernst Haefliger (ten), Kieth Engen (bass), K. Richter (cnd), Munich Bach Orch, Munich Bach Choir Deutsche Grammophon ("2CD" series) 2–▲ 453 007–2

Beethoven, L. van:Fidelio, w. Birgit Nilsson (sop—Leonore), Graziella Sciutti (sop—Marzelline), Kurt Equiluz (ten—Erster Gefangener), Donald Grobe (ten—Jacquino), James McCracken (ten—Florestan), Tom Krause (bar—Don Pizarro), Hermann Prey (bar—Don Fernando), Kurt Böhme (bass—Rocco), Günther Adam (sgr—Zweiter Gefangener), L. Maazel (cnd), Vienna PO, Vienna State Opera Concert Association Chorus *(rec Sofiensaal, Vienna, Mar 1964)* London 2–▲ 448104–2 [ADD]

Brahms, J.:Ein Deutsches Requiem, w. I. Cotrubas (sop), L. Maazel (cnd), New Philharmonia Orch, New Philharmonia Chorus [G] *(rec 1976)* Sony Classical ▲ SK 45853 [ADD]

Brahms, J.:Ein Deutsches Requiem, w. M. Stader (sop), C. Schuricht (cnd), Stuttgart RSO, Stuttgart Radio Chorus, Frankfurt Radio Chorus *(rec Nov. 7, 1959)* Archipon ▲ ARCH 2.2CD (m) [ADD]

Brahms, J.:Gesang der Parzen, w. H. Harper (sop), P. Boulez (cnd), BBC SO, BBC Choral Society *(rec live July 20, 1973)* Memories 2–▲ HR 4493/94 [ADD]

Brahms, J.:Romanzen aus Tieck's *Magelone*, w. H. Deutsch (pno), Annette Prey (nar) [G] Orfeo 2–▲ 116842 [DDD]

Christmas with the Vienna Boys' Choir, w. Vienna Boys' Choir, Placido Domingo (ten) RCA Gold Seal ▲ 7930–2–RG [ADD] ■ 7930–4–RG

Gluck, C.W.:Iphigénie en Tauride, w. S. Jurinac (sop), F. Wunderlich (ten), K. Engen (bass), R. Kubelik (cnd), Bavarian RSO, Bavarian Radio Chorus [1781 J.B. von Alxinger–Gluck German–language version] *(rec live, Munich 1965)* Myto 2–▲ 2 MCD 91544 [ADD]

Kreutzer, C.:Das Nachtlager in Granada, w. R. Klepper (sop), M. Pabst (ten), H. Froschauer (cnd), Cologne RSO, Cologne Radio Chorus Capriccio ▲ 60029 [DDD]

Liebeslieder, w. Leonard Hokanson (pno) Denon ▲ CO 1254 [DDD]

Lortzing, A.:Zar und Zimmermann (sels), w. Lucia Popp (sop), Adalbert Kraus (ten), Fritz Krenn (bass), Karl Ridderbusch (bass), H. Wallberg (cnd), Bavarian RSO, Bavarian Radio Chorus [G] Acanta 2–▲ CD 42424 [DDD]

Mahler, G.:Syms, w. J. Blegen (sop), B. Hendricks (sop), M. Price (sop), G. Zeumer (sop), H. Wittek (trb), A. Baltsa (mez), C. Ludwig (mez), K. Riegel (ten), A. Schmidt (bar), J. Van Dam (b–bar), L. Bernstein (cnd), New York PO, Royal Concertgebouw Orch, Vienna PO, Westminster Choir, New York Choral Artists, Brooklyn Boys' Choir, Vienna Boys' Choir, Vienna State Opera Chorus, Vienna Singverein Deutsche Grammophon 13–▲ 435162–2 [DDD]

Mahler, G.:Syms, w. E. Ameling (sop), H. Harper (mez), M. Forrester (cta), B. Haitink (cnd), Royal Concertgebouw Orch Philips 10–▲ 442050–2

Mahler, G.:Sym 8, w. Hanneke van Bork (sop), Ileana Cotrubas (sop), Heather Harper (sop), Brigit Finnila (mez), Marianne Dieleman (cta), William Cochran (ten), Hans Sotin (bass), B. Haitink (cnd), Royal Concertgebouw Orch Philips ("Solo" series) ▲ 446195–2

Mahler, G.:Sym 8, w. J. Blegen (sop), M. Price (sop), G. Zeumer (sop), A. Baltsa (mez), K. Riegel (ten), A. Schmidt (bar), J. Van Dam (b–bar), L. Bernstein (cnd), Vienna PO, Vienna State Opera Chorus, Vienna Boys' Choir *(rec Salzburg Festival, 1975)* Deutsche Grammophon 2–▲ 435102–2 [ADD]

Mozart, W.A.:Complete Mozart Edition, w. Jessye Norman (sop), I. Cotrubas (sop), H. Donath (sop), T. Troyanos (mez), W. Hollweg (ten), H. Schmidt–Isserstedt (cnd), North German RSO Philips 3–▲ 422534–2 [ADD]

Mozart, W.A.:Così fan tutte, w. G. Janowitz (sop), R. Grist (sop), B. Fassbaender (mez), P. Schreier (ten), D. Fischer–Dieskau (bar), K. Böhm (cnd), Vienna PO *(rec live, 1972)* Foyer 2–▲ FOY 2066 [ADD]

Mozart, W.A.:Così fan tutte, w. E. Schwarzkopf (sop—Fiordiligi), C. Ludwig (sop—Dorabella), G. Sciutti (sop—Despina), W. Kmentt (ten—Ferrando), H. Prey (bar—Gugliemo), K. Dönch (bar—D. Alfonso), K. Böhm (cnd), Vienna PO, Vienna State Opera Chorus [I] *(rec live, Salzburg, Aug. 8, 1962)* Arkadia 2–▲ 455 [ADD]

Mozart, W.A.:Così fan tutte (sels), w. G. Janowitz (sop), R. Grist (sop), B. Fassbaender (mez), P. Schreier (ten), R. Panerai (bar), K. Böhm (cnd), Vienna PO, Vienna State Opera Chorus—scenes & arias Deutsche Grammophon ▲ 429824–2 [ADD]

Mozart, W.A.:Nozze di Figaro, w. Anneliese Rothenberger (sop), Hilde Gueden (sop), Edith Mathis (sop), Peter Schreier (ten), Walter Berry (bar), O. Suitner (cnd), Dresden Staatskapelle Berlin Classics 3–▲ BER 2096 [ADD]

Mozart, W.A.:Nozze di Figaro, w. Mirella Freni (sop), Daniela Mazzucato (sop), Teresa Berganza (mez), Mirto Picchi (ten), José Van Dam (b–bar), Paolo Montarsolo (bass), C. Abbado (cnd), La Scala Orch, La Scala Chorus *(rec live, Apr 22, 1974)* Arkadia 3–▲ 614

Mozart, W.A.:Nozze di Figaro, w. E. Schwarzkopf (sop), G. Sciurri (sop), G. Taddei (bar), C. M. Giulini (cnd), Residentie Orch The Hague, Netherlands Chamber Choir [I] *(rec live, Holland Festival, 1961)* Verona 3–▲ 27092/94

Mozart, W.A.:Nozze di Figaro (sels), w. Hilde Gueden (sop), Anneliese Rothenberger (sop), Walter Berry (bass), O. Suitner (cnd), Dresden Staatskapelle Berlin Classics ▲ BER 9079 [ADD]

Prey, Hermann (bar) (cont.)
Mozart, W.A.:Nozze di Figaro (sels), w. G. Janowitz (sop), E. Mathis (sop), T. Troyanos (mez), D. Fischer-Dieskau (bar), K. Böhm (cnd), Berlin German Opera Orch—Scenes & Arias
Deutsche Grammophon ▲ 429822-2 [ADD]
Mozart, W.A.:Zauberflöte, w. Reri Grist (sop), Edita Gruberová (sop), Edith Mathis (sop), Rene Kollo (ten), Gerhard Unger (ten), José Van Dam (b-bar), Peter Meven (bass), H. von Karajan (cnd), Vienna PO, Vienna State Opera Chorus *(rec live, Salzburg, July 26, 1974)* Arkadia 2-▲ 233
Mozart, W.A.:Zauberflöte, w. P. Lorengar (sop), C. Deutekom (sop), S. Burrows (ten), D. Fischer-Dieskau (bar), M. Talvela (bass), G. Solti (cnd), Vienna PO [G] London 3-▲ 414568-2
Mozart, W.A.:Zauberflöte (sels), w. S. Jo (sop), J. Protschka (ten)—Ov., arias & choruses
LaserLight ▲ 15 888 [DDD]
Mozart, W.A.:Zauberflöte (sels), w. Pilar Lorengar (sop), Cristina Deutekom (sop), Stuart Burrows (ten), Martti Talvela (bass), G. Solti (cnd), Vienna PO London ▲ 421302-2 [ADD]
Operatic Arias, w. Bratislava Phil, Bratislava Chorus [cnd:Kurt Wöss] Capriccio ▲ 10054 [DDD]
Orff, C.:Die Kluge, w. E. Schwarzkopf (sop), R. Christ (ten), P. Kuén (ten), M. Cordes (bar), B. Kusche (bar), G. Frick (bass), G. Wieter (bass), W. Sawallisch (cnd), Philharmonia Orch [G]
EMI Classics ("Studio" series) 2-▲ CDMB 63712 [ADD]
Puccini, G.:Mass, w. J. Carreras (ten), C. Scimone (cnd), *(orch unknown)*, Ambrosian Singers
Erato ▲ 96367-2
Rossini, G.:Il barbiere di Siviglia, w. Ruth-Margaret Pütz (sop), Annelies Burmeister (mez), Peter Schreier (ten), Franz Crass (bass), Fritz Ollendorff (bass), O. Suitner (cnd), Berlin State Opera Orch
Berlin Classics 2-▲ BER 9021 [ADD]
Rossini, G.:Il barbiere di Siviglia, w. T. Berganza (mez), L. Alva (ten), P. Montarsolo (bass), C. Abbado (cnd), London SO, London Sym Chorus [I] Deutsche Grammophon 2-▲ 415695-2 [ADD]
Schubert, Franz:Alfonso und Estrella, w. E. Mathis (sop), M. Falewicz (sop), P. Schreier (ten), D. Fischer-Dieskau (bar), T. Adam (b-bar), O. Suitner (cnd), Berlin Staatskapelle, Berlin Radio Chorus
Berlin Classics 3-▲ BER 2156 [ADD]
Schubert, Franz:Lazarus, or Die Feier der Auferstehung, w. E. Mathis (sop), C. Wulkopf (mez), H. Schwarz (mez), W. Hollweg (ten), H. Laubenthal (ten), G. Chmura (cnd), Stuttgart RSO, Stuttgart Radio Chorus [G] Orfeo ▲ 011101 [DDD]
Schubert, Franz:Die Schöne Müllerin, w. Bianconi (pno) [G] Denon ▲ CO 1072 [DDD]
Schumann, R.:Dichterliebe, w. L. Hokanson (pno) [G] Denon ▲ 7720 [DDD]
Schumann, R.:Liederkreis, Op. 39, w. L. Hokanson (pno) [G] Denon ▲ CO 1518 [DDD]
Strauss (II), Joh.:Die Fledermaus, w. J. Varady (sop), L. Popp (sop), A. Kollo (ten), I. Rebroff (bass), E. Kleiber (cnd), Bavarian State Opera Orch [G] Deutsche Grammophon 2-▲ 415646-2 [ADD]
Strauss (II), Joh.:Der Zigeunerbaron (sels), w. Rita Streich (sop), Grace Bumbry (mez), Biserka Cvejic (mez), Gisela Litz (alt), Nicolai Gedda (ten), Kurt Bohme (bass), F. Allers (cnd), Munich Bavarian State Opera Orch, Munich Bavarian State Opera Chorus Emperor Operetta ▲ KO 86346
Strauss, R.:Ariadne auf Naxos, w. E. Schwarzkopf (sop), I. Seefried (sop), R. Streich (sop), L. Otto (sop), G. Hoffman (mez), R. Schock (ten), G. Unger (ten), H. Cuénod (ten), F. Ollendorff (bass), H. von Karajan (cnd), Philharmonia Orch [G] *(rec 1954)*
EMI Classics ("Studio" series) 2-▲ CDMB 69296 (m) [ADD]
Strauss, R.:Ariadne auf Naxos, w. A. Tomowa-Sintow (sop), K. Battle (sop), A. Baltsa (mez), G. Lakes (ten), J. Levine (cnd), Vienna PO Deutsche Grammophon 2-▲ 419225-2 [DDD]
Strauss, R.:Die Schweigsame Frau, w. H. Güden (sop), F. Wunderlich (ten), H. Hotter (b-bar), K. Böhm (cnd), Vienna PO *(rec Salzburg Festival, 1959)* Deutsche Grammophon 2-▲ 445335-2 (m) [ADD]
Strauss, R.:Die Schweigsame Frau, w. G. von Milinkovic (mez), F. Wunderlich (ten), H. Hotter (b-bar), K. Böhm (cnd), Vienna PO, Vienna State Opera Chorus *(rec live, Salzburg Festival, 8/8/59)*
Melodram 2-▲ MEL 27071 (m) [AAD]
Verdi, G.:La forza del destino, w. G. Bumbry (sop—Leonora), H. Dernesch (sop—Preziosilla), N. Gedda (ten—Alvaro), H. Prey (bar—Don Carlos), G. Frick (bass—Pater Guardian), S. Vogel (bass—Marchese), G. Patanè (cnd), Dresden State Orch, Dresden State Opera Chorus *(rec Aug. 1965)*
Berlin Classics ("Eterna" series) ▲ BER 2025-2 [ADD]
Verdi, G.:La traviata (sels), w. T. Stratas (sop), F. Wunderlich (ten), G. Patanè (cnd), Bavarian State Opera Orch, Bavarian State Opera Chorus—substantial selections from Acts 1-3 *(rec live, Munich, 3/28/65)* Myto 2-▲ 2 MCD 91648 [ADD]
Wagner, R.:Das Liebesverbot, w. Pamela Coburn (sop—Mariana), Friedrich Lenz (ten—Antonio), Hermann Prey (bar—Friedrich), Keith Engen (bass—Angelo), Raimund Grumbach (bass—Danieli/Wirt), Wolfgang Fassler (sgr—Luzio), Sabine Haas (sgr—Isabella/Claudios Schwester), Alfred Kuhn (sgr—Brighella/Chef der Sbirren), Hermann Sapell (sgr—Pontio Pilato), Robert Schunk (sgr—Claudio), Marianne Seibel (sgr—Dorella), W. Sawallisch (cnd), Bavarian State Orch, Bavarian State Chorus *(rec July 9, 1983)* Orfeo d'or 3-▲ 345953
Wagner, R.:Die Meistersinger von Nürnberg, w. E. Grümmer (sop), M. Höffgen (cta), R. Schock (ten), G. Unger (ten), B. Kusche (bar), F. Frantz (b-bar), G. Frick (bass), R. Kempe (cnd), Berlin PO *(rec 1956)*
EMI Classics 4-▲ CDMD 64154
Wagner, R.:Tannhäuser (sels), w. Sylvia Sass (sop), Reiner Goldberg (ten), Bavarian State Opera Orch, Bavarian State Opera Chorus—Ov; Venusberg Bacchanal; Dich, teure halle, grüb' ich wieder; Freudig Begrüben wir die edle Halle; Intro; die Pilger sind's - Beglückt darf nun dich, o Heimat, ich schauen; plus others LaserLight ▲ 14211 [DDD]
Weber, C.M. von:Oberon, w. B. Nilsson (sop), A. Augér (sop), J. Hamari (mez), P. Domingo (ten), R. Kubelik (cnd), Bavarian RSO Deutsche Grammophon ("Domingo Edition" series) ▲ 435406-2 [ADD]
Weber, C.M. von:Oberon, w. B. Nilsson (sop), A. Augér (sop), J. Hamari (mez), P. Domingo (ten), R. Kubelik (cnd), Bavarian RSO Deutsche Grammophon 2-▲ 419038-2 [ADD]
Weinberger, J.:Schwanda der Dudelsackpfeifer, w. L. Popp (sop), G. Killebrew (mez), S. Jerusalem (ten), S. Nimsgern (bass), H. Wallberg (cnd), Munich RSO, Bavarian Radio Chorus [F]
CBS 3-▲ M3K 36926 [ADD]
World Stars Sing Operetta, w. Anna Moffo (sop), Lucia Popp (sop), José Carreras (ten), Ants Kollo (ten), Thomas Moser (ten), Giuseppe Di Stefano (ten), Karl Ridderbusch (bass), et al., various orchs *(rec 1968-1985)* Acanta ▲ 42941

Preziosa, B. (sop)
Verdi, G.:Nabucco, w. C. Mancini (sop—Abigaille), G. Gatti (sop—Fenena), B. Preziosa (sop—Anna), M. Binci (ten—Ismaele), L. Francardi (ten—Abdallo), P. Silveri (bar—Nabucodonosor), A. Cassinelli (bass—Zaccaria), A. Gaggi (bass—High Priest of Baal), F. Previtali (cnd), Rome RAI Orch, Rome RAI Chorus *(rec Rome, 1951)* Cetra Classic 2-▲ CDO 26 [ADD]

Přibyl, Vilém (ten)
Beethoven, L. van:Sym 9, "Choral Sym", w. Gabriela Benackova-Cápova (sop), Vera Soukupova (alt), Karel Prusa (bass), L. von Matačić (cnd), Czech PO Praga ▲ PR 250076
Dvořák, A.:The Jacobin, w. D. Šounová-Broukov (sop), K. Berman (bass), J. Pinkas (cnd), Brno State PO, Kühn Chorus Supraphon 2-▲ SUP 11 2190 [AAD]
Dvořák, A.:The Jacobin (sels), w. Marcela Machotková (sop), Beno Blachut (ten), J. Pinkas (cnd), Brno State PO Supraphon ▲ SUP 112250 [AAD]
Fibich, Z.:Šárka, w. Eva Depoltová (sop), Eva Randová (mez), Vaclav Zítek (bar), J. Štych (cnd), Brno State PO, J. Pancik (cnd), Janáček Opera Chorus *(rec 1978)* Supraphon 2-▲ SUP 0036
Janácek, L.:Amarus, w. Vera Soukupová (mez), F. Jílek (cnd), Czech PO, Josef Veselka (cnd), Prague Phil Chorus *(rec Czech Raio Broadcast, 1974)* Praga ▲ PR 250100
Janácek, L.:The Excursions of Mr. Brouček, w. Janá Jonaová (sop), Libuše Márová (mez), Richard Novák (bass), Czech PO, Czech Phil Chorus Supraphon 2-▲ SUP 112153 [AAD]
Janácek, L.:Fate, w. Magdaléna Hajóssyová (sop), Vladimír Krejčík (ten), F. Jílek (cnd), Brno Janáček Opera Orch, Brno Janáček Opera Chorus Supraphon ▲ SUP 0045 [AAD]
Janácek, L.:From the House of the Dead, w. M. Jirglova (sop), J. Horacek (bass), R. Novák (bass), V. Neumann (cnd), Czech PO, Czech Phil Chorus [Cz] Supraphon 2-▲ SUP 10 2941 [AAD]
Janácek, L.:Jenůfa, w. G. Benačková (sop—Jenufa), N. Kniplová (mez—Kostelnička Buryja), V. Krejčík (ten—Steva Buryja), V. Přibyl (ten—Laca Klemen), F. Jílek (cnd), Brno Janáček Opera Orch, Brno Janáček Opera Chorus [Cz] *(rec 1977-8)* Supraphon 2-▲ 10 2751-2 [AAD]
Janácek, L.:Jenůfa, w. Libuse Domininská (sop—Jenufa), Nadeshda Kniplová (sop—Kostelnicka), Vilém Príbyl (ten—Laca), Ivo Zidek (ten—Steva), B. Gregor (cnd), Prague National Theater Orch, Prague National Theater Chorus EMI Classics 2-▲ CDMB 65476

Přibyl, Vilém (ten) (cont.)
Janácek, L.:Slavonic Mass, w. Gabriela Benackova (sop), Eva Randova (cta), Sergej Kopack (bass), F. Jílek (cnd), Brno State PO, Josef Veselka (cnd), Czech Phil Chorus *(rec 1979)*
Supraphon ▲ SUP CD 3045
Smetana, B.:Dalibor, w. G. Abrahamová (sop), J. Krombholc (cnd), Prague RSO, Prague Radio Chorus [Cz] *(rec Sept. 1977)* Praga 2-▲ PR 250050/51
Smetana, B.:Dalibor, w. N. Kniplova (mez), J. Jindrak (bar), J. Krombholc (cnd), Prague National Theater Orch, Prague National Theater Chorus [Cz] Supraphon 2-▲ 11 2185 [ADD]

Price, Christina (sop)
Christina Price

Price, D. (ten)
Handel, G.F.:Alessandro, w. L. Atkinson (trb), Watson (sop), A. Terzian (mez), B. J. Rieders (cta), T. Poole (ten), Andersson (sgr), M. Nowakowski (cnd), Sinfonia Varsovia [I] *(rec live)*
Koch Schwann 3-▲ CD SC 100 303 [DDD]

Price, David (ten)
Bach, J.S.:Magnificat, BWV 243, w. Julianne Baird (sop), Lorie Gratis (mez), Kevin Deas (b-bar), Bronwyn Fix-Keller (hpd), V. Radu (cnd), Ama Deus Ensemble Vox Classics ▲ VOX 7531
Handel, G.F.:Messiah, w. Julianne Baird (sop), Jennifer Lane (mez), Kevin Deas (b-bar), V. Radu (cnd), Ama Deus Ensemble, Ama Deus Ensemble Chorus [period instruments; 1749 Covent Garden version]
Vox Classics 2-▲ VOX2 7502 [DDD]
Handel, G.F.:Messiah (sels), w. Julianne Baird (sop), Jennifer Lane (mez), Kevin Deas (b-bar), V. Radu (cnd), Ama Deus Ensemble—[Part 1] Sinf.; Comfort Ye My People; Every Valley Shall Be Exalted; And the Glory of the Lord; O Thou That Tellest Good Tidings to Zion; For Unto Us a Child is Born; Pifa; Rejoice Greatly o Daughter of Zion; He Shall Feed His Flock by Night; [Part 2] He was Despised and Rejected of Men; All We Like Sheep Have Gone Astray; Lift Up Your Heads, O Ye Gates; Why do the Nations So Furiously Rage Together; [Part 3]I Know That My Redeemer Liveth; Behold, I Tell You a Mystery; The Trumpet Shall Sound; Hallelujah Vox Classics ▲ VOX 7508 [DDD]

Price, Janet (sop)
Boulanger, L.:Choral Music, w. N. Boulanger (cnd), BBC SO, BBC Sym Chorus—Psalm 24 (1916); Pie Jesu (1918) *(rec live Nov. 1968, London)* Intaglio ▲ INCD 703-1 [ADD]
Donizetti, G.:Ugo, conte di Parigi, w. E. Harrhy (sop), Y. Kenny (sop), D. Jones (mez), M. Arthur (ten), C. du Plessis (bar), A. Francis (cnd), New Philharmonia Orch, Geoffrey Mitchell Choir
Opera Rara 3-▲ ORC 1
Fauré, G.:Requiem, w. J. Carol Case (bar), N. Boulanger (cnd), BBC SO, BBC Sym Chorus *(rec live, London Nov. 1968)* Intaglio ▲ INCD 703-1 [ADD]
Giannini, V.:Songs, w. C. Lewis (pno)—Songs on poems by Karl Flaster—Be Still My Heart; Far Above the Purple Hills; Heart Cry; I Did Not Know; I Only Know; I Shall Think of You; If I Had Known; It is a Spring Night; Little Girl in Blue; Longing; Love; Moonlight; My Love for You Has Grown; Parting; Sing to My Heart a Son; The Sun Had Set; Tell Me, Oh Blue, Blue Sky; There Were 2 Swans; 3 Oriental Chants; 3 Poems of the Sea [E] *(rec June 1991)* ACA Digital Recording ▲ CM 20011
Mathias, W.:Ave Rex, w. Kenneth Bowen (ten), Michael Rippon (bar), Geraint Evans (b-bar), Atherton, Willcocks (cnd), London SO, New Philharmonia Orch, Welsh National Opera Chorus, Windsor Bach Choir, St. George's Chapel Choristers Lyrita ▲ SRCD .324
Mathias, W.:This Worlde's Joie, w. Kenneth Bowen (ten), Michael Rippon (bar), Atherton, Willcocks (cnd), London SO, New Philharmonia Orch, Welsh National Opera Chorus, Windsor Bach Choir, St. George's Chapel Choristers Lyrita ▲ SRCD .324
Mozart, W.A.:Missa, K.317, w. Kevin Smith (ct), Anthony Rolfe-Johnson (ten), Graham Titus (bass), M. Davies (cnd), BBC Northern SO, Leeds Phil Chorus
IMP ("BBC Radio Classics" series) ▲ IMP 5691552
Williams, G.:Fairest of Stars, w. C. Groves (cnd), London SO Lyrita ▲ SRCD 327

Price Jones, Penelope (sop)
Martin, P.:Light Music, w. Philip Martin (pno) Altarus ▲ CD 9011
Martin, P.:Songs, w. P. Martin (pno) Altarus ▲ CD 9009
Martin, P.:Songs for the 4 Parts of the Night, w. Ruxandra Colan (vn) Altarus ▲ CD 9011

Price, Leontyne (sop)
Arias, w. Birgit Nilsson (sop), Giuseppe Di Stefano (ten) Legato Classics 2-▲ LCD 153-2 (m) [ADD]
Barber, S.:Antony & Cleopatra (sels), w. T. Schippers (cnd), New Philharmonia Orch—Give Me Some Music; Give Me My Robe *(rec 1953)* RCA Gold Seal ▲ 09026-61983-2
Barber, S.:Hermit Songs, w. S. Barber (pno) [E] *(rec 1954)*
Sony Masterworks ("Portrait" series) ▲ MPK 46727 [ADD]
Barber, S.:Hermit Songs, w. S. Barber (pno) *(rec 1953)* RCA Gold Seal ▲ 09026-61983-2
Barber, S.:Knoxville:Summer of 1915, w. T. Schippers (cnd), New Philharmonia Orch *(rec 1953)*
RCA Gold Seal ▲ 09026-61983-2
Berlioz, H.:Les Nuits d'été, w. F. Reiner (cnd), Chicago SO RCA Gold Seal 2-▲ 09026-61234-2
Bizet, G.:Carmen, w. M. Freni (sop), F. Corelli (ten), R. Merrill (bar), H. von Karajan (cnd), Vienna PO, Vienna State Opera Chorus [F] RCA Gold Seal 3-▲ 6199-2-RG [ADD] 2-■ 6199-4-RG
Bizet, G.:Carmen, w. M. Freni (sop), F. Corelli (ten), R. Merrill (bar), H. von Karajan (cnd), Vienna PO, Vienna State Opera Chorus [F] RCA Gold Seal ▲ 60190-2-RG [ADD] ■ 60190-4-RG
Bizet, G.:Carmen (sels), w. Mirella Freni (sop), Franco Corelli (ten), H. von Karajan (cnd), Vienna PO, Vienna State Opera Chorus RCA Victor ▲ 09026-68021-2; ■ 09026-68021-4
Bravissimo, Domingo!, Vol. 1, w. Plácido Domingo (ten), Sherrill Milnes (ten)
RCA Red Seal ▲ 07863-57020-2
Christmas' Greatest Voices, w. Plácido Domingo (ten), Mario Lanza (sop), et al.
RCA ▲ 09026-68265-2; ■ 09026-68265-4
A Christmas Offering, w. Vienna PO [cnd:Herbert von Karajan] London ■ 411614-4
Christmas Treasures, w. Marian Anderson (cta), Rosalind Elias (mez), Mario Lanza (ten), Giorgio Tozzi (bass), Arthur Fiedler (cnd), Leopold Stokowski (cnd), Robert Shaw Chorale
RCA Living Stereo ▲ 09026-61867-2 ■ 09026-61867-4
The Essential Leontyne Price *(rec 1958-95)* RCA Victor 11-▲ 09026-68153-2 [ADD/DDD]
Falla, M. de:El amor brujo, w. F. Reiner (cnd), Chicago SO *(rec Orchestral Hall, Chicago, Mar. 4, 1963)*
RCA Living Stereo ▲ 09026-62586-2 [ADD]; ■ 09026-62586-4
Falla, M. de:La vida breve (interlude & dance 1), w. F. Reiner (cnd), Chicago SO *(rec Orchestral Hall, Chicago, Apr. 26, 1958)* RCA Living Stereo ▲ 09026-62586-2 [ADD]; ■ 09026-62586-4
Gershwin, G.:Porgy & Bess (sels), w. H. Boatwright (sop), W. Warfield (bar), S. Henderson (cnd), RCA Victor SO, RCA Victor Chorus [E] RCA Gold Seal ▲ 5234-2-RG [ADD]
Gershwin, G.:Porgy & Bess (sels), *(orch unknown)*—Summertime London ▲ 436570-2 (m) [ADD]
God Bless America, w. National PO of London [cnd:Charles Gerhardt]
RCA Gold Seal ▲ 4421-2-RG [DDD] ■ 4421-4-RG
Grandi Voci:Leontyne Price *(rec. 1960-62 & 1977)* London ▲ 440402-2 [ADD]
Leontyne Price Memories ("Great Voices" series) 2-▲ MEM 4396 (m)
Live at Ordway Pro Arte ▲ CDD 231 [DDD]
Mozart, W.A.:Arias—arias from Don Giovanni, Idomeneo, Il re pastore, Le nozze di Figaro, etc.
RCA Gold Seal ▲ 09026-61357-2 ■ 09026-61357-4
Mozart, W.A.:Arias, w. I. Cotrubas (sop), E. Gruberova (sop), J. Varady (sop), L. Popp (mez), F. Araiza (ten), P. Domingo (ten), P. de Palma (ten), P. Schreier (ten), F. Wunderlich (ten), S. Milnes (bar), A. Titus (bar), M. Talvela (bass)—sels. from Entführung aus dem Serail, Così fan tutte, Don Giovanni, Idomeneo, Die Zauberflöte, Le nozze di Figaro Eurodisc ▲ 69256-2-RG [ADD]
Mozart, W.A.:Così fan tutte, w. J. Raskin (sop), T. Troyanos (mez), G. Shirley (ten), S. Milnes (bar), E. Leinsdorf (cnd), New Philharmonia Orch, New Philharmonia Chorus [I]
RCA Gold Seal 3-▲ 6677-2 [ADD]
Mozart, W.A.:Don Giovanni, w. H. Gueden (sop), G. Sciurri (sop), F. Wunderlich (ten), E. Wächter (bar), W. Berry (bass), H. von Karajan (cnd), Vienna PO, Vienna State Opera Chorus [I] *(rec live, 1963)*
Verona 3-▲ 27065/67 (m) [AAD]
Mozart, W.A.:Don Giovanni, w. L. Popp (sop), S. Sass (sop), S. Burrows (ten), G. Bacquier (bar), B. Weikl (bar), A. Sramek (bar), K. Moll (bass), G. Solti (cnd), London PO, London Opera Chorus
London ("Grand Opera" series) 3-▲ 425169-2 [ADD]

Price, Leontyne (sop) (cont.)

Mozart, W.A.:Don Giovanni, w. Birgit Nilsson (sop—Donna Anna), Leontyne Price (sop—Donna Elvira), Eugenia Ratti (sop—Zerlina), Cesare Valletti (ten—Don Ottavio), Heinz Blankenburg (bar—Masetto), Fernando Corena (b-bar—Leporello), Arnold van Mill (b-bar—Il Commendatore), Cesare Siepi (b-bar—Don Giovanni), E. Leinsdorf (cnd), Vienna PO, Vienna State Opera Chorus [I] London 3-▲ 444594-2 [ADD]

Mozart, W.A.:Requiem, w. H. Rössl-Majdan (mez), F. Wunderlich (ten), W. Berry (bass), H. von Karajan (cnd), Vienna PO, Vienna Singverein [L] *(rec live, Salzburg Festival, Aug. 24, 1960)* Melodram ▲ MEL 18003

Opera Goes to the Movies, w. Plácido Domingo (ten), Roberta Peters (sop), et al. RCA Victor ▲ 60841-2-RG ■ 60841-4-RG

The Prima Donna Collection RCA Gold Seal 4-▲ 09026-61236-2

The Prima Donna Collection Highlights, w. RCA Italiana Opera Orch, London SO, Philharmonia Orch, New Philharmonia Orch RCA Gold Seal ▲ 09026-62596-2

Primi Tenori:Carreras – Domingo – Pavarotti, w. Katia Ricciarelli (sop) *(rec 1969–1983)* Standing Room Only 2-▲ SRO 835-2

A Program of Song, w. D. Garvey (pno) *(rec 1959)* RCA Living Stereo ▲ 09026-61499-2 ■ 09026-61499-4

Puccini, G.:Arias, w. E. Downes (cnd), New Philharmonia Orch—15 arias [I] RCA Red Seal ▲ 5999-2-RC [ADD]

Puccini, G.:Madama Butterfly, w. R. Elias (mez), G. Tucker (ten), P. Maero (bar), E. Leinsdorf (cnd), RCA Italian Opera Orch [I] RCA Red Seal 2-▲ 6160-2-RC [ADD]

Puccini, G.:Madama Butterfly (sels), w. Rosalind Elias (mez), Piero De Palma (ten), Richard Tucker (ten), Phillip Maero (bar), E. Leinsdorf (cnd), RCA Italian Opera Orch, RCA Italiana Opera Chorus RCA Victor ▲ 09026-68089-2; ■ 09026-68089-4

Puccini, G.:Madama Butterfly (sels), w. P. Domingo (ten)—Bimba, bimba non piangere RCA Gold Seal ▲ 09026-61634-2

Puccini, G.:Madama Butterfly (sels), w. R. Elias (mez), G. Tucker (ten), P. Maero (bar), E. Leinsdorf (cnd), RCA Italian Opera Orch [I] RCA ■ RK 1048

Puccini, G.:Manon Lescaut (sels), w. P. Domingo (ten)—Oh saro la piu bella! RCA Gold Seal ▲ 09026-61634-2

Puccini, G.:Il tabarro, w. P. Domingo (ten), S. Milnes (bar), E. Leinsdorf (cnd), New Philharmonia Orch, John Alldis Choir RCA Gold Seal 2-▲ 09026-60865-2 [ADD]

Puccini, G.:Tosca, w. P. Domingo (ten), S. Milnes (bar), Z. Mehta (cnd), New Philharmonia Orch, John Alldis Choir [I] RCA Victrola 2-▲ RCD2-0105

Puccini, G.:Tosca, w. G. di Stefano (ten), G. Taddei (bar), H. von Karajan (cnd), Vienna PO, Vienna State Opera Chorus [I] London 2-▲ 421670-2 [ADD]

Puccini, G.:Tosca (sels), w. P. Domingo (ten)—Mario, Mario, Mario RCA Gold Seal ▲ 09026-61634-2

Puccini, G.:Turandot, w. B. Nilsson (sop), G. di Stefano (ten), T. Gobbi (bar), F. Molinari-Pradelli (cnd), Vienna State Opera Orch, Vienna State Opera Chorus [I] *(rec live, 6/22/61)* Legato Classics 2-▲ LCD 153-2 (m) [ADD]

Return to Carnegie Hall, w. David Garvey (pno) *(rec Carnegie Hall, New York, Jan 26, 1991)* RCA Red Seal ▲ 09026-68435-2 [DDD]

Right As the Rain, w. André Previn (pno) RCA Victor ▲ 2983-2-RG [ADD]

Strauss, R.:Ariadne auf Naxos, w. E. Gruberova (sop), R. Kollo (ten), G. Solti (cnd), London PO [G] London ("Grand Opera" series) 2-▲ 430384-2 [ADD]

Strauss, R.:Arias, w. E. Leinsdorf (cnd), Boston SO, London SO, New Philharmonia Orch—selections from Ägyptische Helena *(Awakening Scene)*, Ariadne auf Naxos *(Es gibt ein Reich)*, Frau ohne Schatten *(Empress's Awakening Scene)*, Guntram *(Fass ich sie bang)*, Rosenkavalier *(Marschallin's Monologue)*, Salome *(Interlude & Final Scene)* [G] RCA Gold Seal ▲ 60398-2-RG [ADD] ■ 60398-4-RG (CrO2)

Strauss, R.:4 Last Songs, w. E. Leinsdorf (cnd), New Philharmonia Orch [G] RCA Gold Seal ("Papillon Collection" series) ▲ 6722-2-RG [ADD]

Strauss, R.:Die Frau ohne Schatten (sels), w. E. Leinsdorf (cnd), New Philharmonia Orch—Empress's Awakening Scene [G] RCA Gold Seal ("Papillon Collection" series) ▲ 6722-2 RG [ADD]

Verdi, G.:Aida, w. G. Bumbry (mez), P. Domingo (ten), S. Milnes (bar), R. Raimondi (bass), E. Leinsdorf (cnd), London SO [I] RCA ■ RK 1237

Verdi, G.:Aida, w. G. Bumbry (mez), P. Domingo (ten), S. Milnes (bar), R. Raimondi (bass), E. Leinsdorf (cnd), London SO [I] RCA Red Seal 3-▲ 6198-2-RC [ADD] 3-■ ARK3-2541

Verdi, G.:Aida, w. R. Gorr (mez), J. Vickers (ten), R. Merrill (bar), G. Tozzi (bass), G. Solti (cnd), Rome Opera Orch, Rome Opera Chorus [I] London ▲ 421860-2 [ADD]

Verdi, G.:Aida, w. R. Gorr (mez), J. Vickers (ten), R. Merrill (bar), G. Tozzi (bass), G. Solti (cnd), Rome Opera Orch, Rome Opera Chorus [I] London 3-▲ 417416-2 [ADD]

Verdi, G.:Aida (sels), w. P. Domingo (ten)—Act IV, Scene 2 RCA Gold Seal ▲ 09026-61634-2

Verdi, G.:Aida (sels), w. G. Bumbry (mez), P. Domingo (ten), S. Milnes (bar), E. Leinsdorf (cnd), London SO RCA Victor ▲ 09026-62676-2 ■ 09026-62676-4

Verdi, G.:Arias [I] RCA Red Seal ▲ RCD1-7016

Verdi, G.:Un ballo in maschera, w. C. Bergonzi (ten), R. Merrill (bar), E. Leinsdorf (cnd), RCA Italian Opera Orch [I] RCA Gold Seal 2-▲ 6645-2-RG [ADD]

Verdi, G.:Un ballo in maschera (sels), w. P. Domingo (ten), *(cnd & orch unknown)*—Teco io sto! RCA Gold Seal ▲ 09026-61634-2

Verdi, G.:Ernani, w. C. Bergonzi (ten), M. Sereni (bar), E. Flagello (bass), T. Schippers (cnd), RCA Italian Opera Orch [I] RCA Gold Seal 2-▲ 6503-2-RG [ADD]

Verdi, G.:Ernani, w. C. Ordassy (sop), F. Corelli (ten), C. Anthony (ten), M. Sereni (bar), C. Siepi (bass), C. Russel (bass), T. Schippers (cnd), *(orch unknown)* *(rec 1965)* Great Opera Performances ▲ GOP 702

Verdi, G.:Otello (sels), w. P. Domingo (ten)—Gia nella notte RCA Gold Seal ▲ 09026-61634-2

Verdi, G.:Requiem Mass, w. F. Cossotto (mez), L. Pavarotti (ten), N. Ghiaurov (bass), H. von Karajan (cnd), La Scala Orch, La Scala Chorus [L] *(rec live 1/16/67)* Verona 2-▲ 27060/61 (m) [AAD]

Verdi, G.:Requiem Mass, w. F. Cossotto (mez), L. Pavarotti (ten), N. Ghiaurov (bass), H. von Karajan (cnd), La Scala Orch, La Scala Chorus [L] *(rec live 1/16/67)* Melodram 2-▲ MEL 28012

Verdi, G.:Requiem Mass, w. N. Merriman (mez), R. Tucker (ten), G. Tozzi (bass), E. Ormandy (cnd), Philadelphia Orch *(rec live Apr. 6, 1957)* Standing Room Only ▲ SRO 842-1 [ADD]

Verdi, G.:Requiem Mass, w. R. Elias (mez), J. Björling (ten), G. Tozzi (bass), F. Reiner (cnd), Vienna PO, Vienna Singverein [L] London 2-▲ 421608-2 [ADD]

Verdi, G.:Requiem Mass, w. Rosalind Elias (mez), Jussi Björling (ten), Giorgio Tozzi (bass), F. Reiner (cnd), Vienna PO, French Musical Society Vocal Group *(rec 1959)* London ("Double Decker" series) 2-▲ 444833-2 [ADD]

Verdi, G.:Il trovatore, w. R. Elias (mez), G. Tucker (ten), L. Warren (bar), G. Tozzi (bass), A. Basile (cnd), Rome Opera Orch RCA Gold Seal 2-▲ 60560-2-RG [ADD] 2-■ 60560-4-RG (CrO2)

The Voices of Living Stereo, Vol. 2, w. Eileen Farrell (sop), Birgit Nilsson (sop), Roberta Peters (sop), Galina Vishnevskaya (sop), Rosalind Elias (mez), Shirley Verrett (mez), Marian Anderson (cta), Maureen Forrester (cta), Sergio Franchi (ten), Mario Lanza (ten), Richard Lewis (ten), Jan Pee, Alexander Dedyukhin (pno), Franz Rupp (pno), Leo Taubman (pno), George Trovillo (pno), Charles Wadsworth (pno), Boston Pops Orch [cnd:Arthur Fiedler], Boston SO [cnd:Charles Munch], Chicago SO [cnd:Fritz Reiner], RCA Victor Orch, RCA Victor Chorus [cnd:Wa *(rec Boston & Chicago & New York & Rome, 1957–1964)* RCA Living Stereo ▲ 09026-68167-2 [ADD]

Price, Margaret (sop)

Beethoven, L. van:Missa Solemnis, w. Christa Ludwig (mez), Wieslaw Ochman (ten), Martti Talvela (bass), K. Böhm (cnd), Vienna PO, Vienna State Opera Chorus *(rec 1957)* Deutsche Grammophon ("Double" series) 2-▲ 437386-2 [ADD]

Beethoven, L. van:Sym 9, "Choral Sym", w. M. Lipovsk (alt), P. Seifert (ten), J.-H. Rootering (bass), W. Sawallisch (cnd), Royal Concertgebouw Orch, Düsseldorf Municipal Choral Society EMI Classics ▲ CDC 54505

Brahms, J.:Ein Deutsches Requiem, w. S. Ramey (bar), A. Previn (cnd), Royal PO, Ambrosian Singers [G] Teldec ("Digital Experience" series) ▲ 9031-75862-2 AW [DDD] ■ 9031-75862-4

Brahms, J.:Ein Deutsches Requiem, w. T. Allen (bar), W. Sawallisch (cnd), Bavarian RSO, Bavarian Radio Chorus [G] Orfeo ▲ 039101

Brahms, J.:Songs, w. J. Lochhart (pno)—19 songs [G] Orfeo ▲ 058831

Price, Margaret (sop) (cont.)

Brahms, J.:Songs—Volkslieder; Gypsy Songs, Op. 103/1-8; Meerfahrt, Op. 96/4; Es schauen die Blumen, Op. 96/3; Summerabend, Op. 85/1; Mondschein, Op. 85/2; Es liebt sich so lieblich im Lenze, Op. 71/1; Der Tod, das ist die kühle Nacht, Op. 96/1 RCA Red Seal ▲ 09026-60902-2

Cornelius, P.:Songs, w. Graham Johnson (pno)—Trauer und Trost, Op. 3 Forlane ▲ FRL 16728 [DDD]

Duparc, H.:Songs—3 songs Orfeo ▲ 038831 [DDD]

French & Spanish Songs Orfeo ▲ C 038831 A [DDD]

Granados, E.:Songs (4) Orfeo ▲ 038831 [DDD]

Handel, G.F.:Messiah, w. Yvonne Minton (mez), Alexander Young (ten), Justino Diaz (bass), J. Somary (cnd), English CO, Amor Artis Chorale [E] *(rec 1970)* Vanguard Classics ▲ OVC 4020 [ADD]

Handel, G.F.:Messiah, w. Yvonne Minton (mez), Alexander Young (ten), Justino Diaz (bass), J. Somary (cnd), English CO, Amor Artis Chorale [E] *(rec 1970)* Vanguard Classics 2-▲ OVC 4018/19 [ADD]

Liszt, F.:Sonetti di Petrarca Voice & Pno, w. *(pianist unknown)* RCA Gold Seal 2-▲ 09026-61635-2

Liszt, F.:Songs, w. James Lockhart (pno), Jack Brymer (cl)—O lieb', so lang du lieben kannst!; Die Lorelei; Die stille Wasserrose; Es muss ein Wunderbares sein; Kling leise, mein Lied Classics for Pleasure ▲ CFP 4669

Liszt, F.:Songs, w. Graham Johnson (pno)—Freudvoll und Leidvoll; Über Allen Gipfeln [Wanderers Nachtlied II]; Mignons Lied; Der du von Dem Himmel Bist [Wanderers Nachtlied I] Forlane ▲ FRL 16728 [DDD]

Liszt, F.:Songs, w. Graham Johnson (pno) Forlane ▲ FOR 16728 [DDD]

Mahler, G.:Des Knaben Wunderhorn, w. Thomas Dewey (pno)—Des Antonius von Padua Fischpredigt; Rheinlegendchen; Wo die schönen Trompeten blasen; Lob des hohen Verstandes; Das irdische Leben; Urlight Forlane ▲ FRL 16744 [DDD]

Mahler, G.:Lieder eines fahrenden Gesellen, w. Thomas Dewey (pno)—Wenn mein Schatz Hochzeit macht; Ging heut' Morgen über's Feld; Ich hab' ein glühend Messer; Die zwei blauen Augen Forlane ▲ FRL 16744 [DDD]

Mahler, G.:Songs from Rückert, w. Thomas Dewey (pno)—Blicke mir nicht in die Lieder; Ich atmet' einen linden Duft; Um Mitternacht; Liebst du um Schönheit; Ich bin der Welt abhanden gekommen Forlane ▲ FRL 16744 [DDD]

Mahler, G.:Syms, w. J. Blegen (sop), B. Hendricks (sop), G. Zeumer (sop), H. Wittek (trb), A. Baltsa (mez), C. Ludwig (mez), K. Riegel (ten), H. Prey (bar), A. Schmidt (bar), J. Van Dam (b-bar), L. Bernstein (cnd), New York PO, Royal Concertgebouw Orch, Vienna PO, Westminster Choir, New York Choral Artists, Brooklyn Boys' Choir, Vienna Boys' Choir, Vienna State Opera Chorus, Vienna Singverein Deutsche Grammophon 13-▲ 435162-2 [DDD]

Mahler, G.:Sym 4, w. J. Horenstein (cnd), London PO [G] Monitor ■ 55001

Mahler, G.:Sym 8, w. J. Blegen (sop), G. Zeumer (sop), A. Baltsa (mez), K. Riegel (ten), H. Prey (bar), A. Schmidt (bar), J. Van Dam (b-bar), L. Bernstein (cnd), Vienna PO, Vienna State Opera Chorus, Vienna Boys' Choir *(rec Salzburg Festival, 1975)* Deutsche Grammophon 2-▲ 435102-2 [ADD]

Mendelssohn, F.:Songs, w. G. Johnson (pno)—Frülingsglaube; Frage; Geständnis; Maienlied; Andreas Maienlied, 'Hexenlied"; Gruss; Neue Liebe; Auf Flügeln des Gesanges; Frühlingslied; Suleika:Ach, um deine feuchten Schwingen; Suleika:Was bedeutet die Bewegung?; Die Liebende schreibt; Erster Verlust; Volkslied; Minnelied; Schilflied; There Be None of Beauty's Daughter's; Sun of the Sleepless; Des Mädchens Klage; Der Mond; Das Waldschloss; Es weiss und rät es doch Keiner; Nachtlied; Wanderlied Hyperion ▲ CDA 66666 [DDD]

Mozart, W.A.:Arias—Parto parto [from La clemenza di Tito]; Deh vieni; Dove sons; Voi che sapete [all from Le nozze di Figaro]; Martern aller Arten [from Die Entfernung aus dem Serail]; 'Amero [from I Re pastore]; Mi tradi; Non mi dir [both from Don Giovanni]; Idol mio [from Idomeneo] RCA Gold Seal 2-▲ 09026-61635-2

Mozart, W.A.:Complete Mozart Edition, w. L. Serra (sop), R. Tear (ten), P. Schreier (ten), T. Adam (b-bar), K. Moll (bass), C. Davis (cnd), Dresden Staatskapelle, Dresden State Chorus Philips 3-▲ 422543-2 [ADD]

Mozart, W.A.:Così fan tutte, w. L. Popp (sop), Y. Minton (mez), L. Alva (ten), G. Evans (bar), H. Sotin (bass), O. Klemperer (cnd), New Philharmonia Orch, John Alldis Choir EMI Classics 3-▲ CDMC 63845

Mozart, W.A.:Nozze di Figaro, w. K. Battle (sop), M. Nicolesco (sop), A. Murray (mez), J. Hynninen (bar), K. Rydl (bass), R. Muti (cnd), Vienna PO, Vienna State Opera Chorus [I] EMI Classics 3-▲ CDCC 47978 [DDD]

Mozart, W.A.:Nozze di Figaro (sels), w. K. Battle (sop), M. Nicolesco (sop), A. Murray (mez), J. Hynninen (bar), K. Rydl (bass), R. Muti (cnd), Vienna PO, Vienna State Opera Chorus [I] EMI Classics ▲ CDC 54321

Mozart, W.A.:Zauberflöte, w. M. Price (sop—Pamina), L. Serra (sop—Queen of the Night), M. Venuti (sop—Papagena), M. McLaughlin (sop—1st Lady), A. Murray (mez—2nd Lady), H. Schwarz (cta—3rd Lady), F. Höher (trb—1st Boy), M. Diedrich (trb—2nd Boy), F. Klos (trb—3rd Boy), P. Schreier (ten—Tamino), R. Tear (ten—Monostatos), R. Goldberg (ten—1st Armoured Man), K. Moll (bass—Sarastro), H. Rech (bass—2nd Armoured Man), C. Davis (cnd), Dresden Staatskapelle, Leipzig Radio Chorus Philips ("Duo" series) 2-▲ 442568-2

Mussorgsky, M.:Nursery, w. *(pno unknown)* RCA Gold Seal 2-▲ 09026-61635-2

Puccini, G.:Turandot, w. E. Marton (sop—Turandot), M. Price (sop—Liù), B. Heppner (ten—Calaf), J.-H. Rootoring (bass—Timur), R. Abbado (cnd), Munich RSO RCA Red Seal 2-▲ 09026-60898-2

Ravel, M.:Mélodies populaires grecques *(pianist unknown)* Orfeo ▲ 038831 [DDD]

Ravel, M.:Shéhérazade Mez, w. M. Sargent (cnd), BBC SO IMP ("BBC Radio Classics" series) ▲ IMP 5691742

Schubert:21 Lieder Célèbres Forlane ▲ FOR 16698 [DDD]

Schubert, Franz:Der Hirt auf dem Felsen, w. H. Schöneberger (cl), W. Sawallisch (pno) [G] Orfeo ▲ 001811 [DDD]

Schubert, Franz:Songs (misc), w. James Lockhart (pno), Jack Brymer (cl)—Auf der Riesenkoppe, D.611; Der Hirt auf dem Felsen [The Shepherd on the Rock], D.965 Classics for Pleasure ▲ CFP 4669

Schubert, Franz:Songs (misc), w. W. Sawallisch (piano)—11 songs [G] Orfeo ▲ 001811 [DDD]

Schumann, R.:Frauenliebe und -leben, w. James Lockhart (pno) Classics for Pleasure ▲ CFP 4669

Schumann, R.:Frauenliebe und -leben, w. J. Lockhart (pno) [G] Orfeo ▲ 031821 [DDD]

Schumann, R.:Frauenliebe und -leben, w. T. Dewey (pno) Forlane ▲ FOR 16711 [DDD]

Schumann, R.:Gedichte, Op. 36, w. T. Dewey (pno) Forlane ▲ FOR 16711 [DDD]

Schumann, R.:Lieder-Album (sels), w. T. Dewey (pno) Forlane ▲ FOR 16711 [DDD]

Schumann, R.:Liederkreis, Op. 24, w. G. Johnson (pno) [G] Hyperion ▲ CDA 66596

Schumann, R.:Myrthen, w. T. Dewey (pno) Forlane ▲ FOR 16711 [DDD]

Schumann, R.:Songs, w. J. Lockhart (pno) [G] Orfeo ▲ 031821 [DDD]

Schumann, R.:Songs, w. G. Johnson (pno) [G] Hyperion ▲ CDA 66596

Schumann, R.:Songs, w. Thomas Dewey (pno)—Der Sandmann; Marienwörmchen; Zigeunerliedchen 1 & 2; Die wandelnde Glocke; Schneeglöckchen; Des Sennen Abschied; Er ist's [all from Liederalbum für die Jugend, Op. 79]; Widmung, Op. 25/1; Aus den östlichen Rosen, Op. 25/25; Volksliedchen, Op. 51/2; Rose, Meer und Sonne, Op. 37/9; Lied der Braut 1 & 2, Op. 25/11 & 12; Frauenliebe und Leben, Op. 42; Aus dem Liederbuch eines Malers, Op. 36 Forlane ▲ FRL 16711 [DDD]

Tchaikovsky, P.:Songs, w. James Lockhart (pno), Jack Brymer (cl)—None but the Weary Heart, Op. 6/6; Do Not Believe, My Friend, Op. 6/1; At the Ball, Op. 38/3 Classics for Pleasure ▲ CFP 4669

Vaughan Williams, R.:Sym 3, w. A. Boult (cnd), New Philharmonia Orch EMI Classics ▲ CDM 64018

Verdi, G.:Arias, w. K. Battle (sop), J. Sutherland (sop), J. Anderson (sop), L. Pavarotti (ten), L. Nucci (bar)—includes favorite arias from Aida, Ballo in maschera, Don Carlos, Nabucco, Rigoletto, Traviata, Trovatore London ("Ovation" series) ▲ 430748-2 [DDD]

Verdi, G.:Un ballo in maschera, w. K. Battle (sop), C. Ludwig (mez), L. Pavarotti (ten), R. Bruson (bar), G. Solti (cnd), National PO London, National Phil London Chorus [I] London 2-▲ 410210-2 [DDD]

Verdi, G.:Un ballo in maschera, w. K. Battle (sop), C. Ludwig (mez), L. Pavarotti (ten), R. Bruson (bar), G. Solti (cnd), National PO London, National Phil London Chorus [I] London ▲ 425529-2 [DDD]

Wagner, R.:Songs, w. Graham Johnson (pno) Forlane ▲ FOR 16728 [DDD]

Wagner, R.:Tristan und Isolde, w. B. Fassbaender (mez), A. Kollo (ten), D. Fischer-Dieskau (bar), K. Moll (bass), C. Kleiber (cnd), Dresden State Opera Orch [G] Deutsche Grammophon 4-▲ 413315-2 [DDD]

Wagner, R.:Wesendonck Songs, w. Graham Johnson (pno) Forlane ▲ FRL 16728 [DDD]

Wolf, H.:Songs (misc), w. Graham Johnson (pno)—Der Gärtner; Bei Einer Trauung; In der Frühe; Heimweh; Begegnung; Lebe Wohl; Gesang Weylas; Er ist's Forlane ▲ FRL 16728 [DDD]

Price, P. (sgr)
Handel, G.F.:Messiah (reorchd Mozart), w. Andrew Murphy (b–bar), M. Altman (sgr), J. Davidson (sgr), Peter Elvin (sgr), L. Woodside (cnd), Sinfonia Rubinstein, New York Oratorio Society [Sinfonia Rubinstein is made up from musicians from the Lodz Philharmonic Orchestra and the Lodz Opera of Poland] [E] Koch Schwann 2–▲ SC 100308 [DDD]

Price, R. (ten)
Music of the Middle Ages, Vol. 6:English Polyphony of the 14th & Early 15th Centuries, w. Russell Oberlin (ct), C. Bressler (ten), G. Meyers (bar), M. Blackman (vl) Lyrichord ▲ LYR 8006 [ADD]
Music of the Middle Ages, Vol. 7, w. French Ars Antiqua, Russell Oberlin (ct), Charles Bressler (ten), G. Meyers (bar), M. Blackman (vl), P. Wolfe (org) Lyrichord ▲ LYR 8007 [ADD]

Priday, Elizabeth (sop)
Handel, G.F.:Semele, w. Norma Burrowes (sop), Patrizia Kwella (sop), Catherine Denley (mez), Della Jones (mez), Timothy Penrose (alt), Anthony Rolfe-Johnson (ct), Maldwyn Davies (ten), Robert Lloyd (b-bar), David Thomas (bass), J. E. Gardiner (cnd), English Baroque Soloists, Monteverdi Choir London Erato 2–▲ 2292–45982–2
Purcell, H.:Dido & Aeneas, w. Ruth Holton (sop—Belinda), Elisabeth Priday (sop—2nd Woman), Donna Deam (sop—1st Witch), Shauna Beesley (sop—2nd Witch), Teresa Shaw (mez—Sorceress), Carolyn Watkinson (cta—Dido), Jonathan Peter Kenny (alt—Spirit), Paul Tindall (ten—Sailor), George Mosley (bass—Aeneas), J.E. Gardiner (cnd), English Baroque Soloists, Monteverdi Choir London *(rec Saint George's, Bristol, UK, July 12-14, 1990)* Philips ▲ 432114–2
Purcell, H.:King Arthur, w. J. Smith (sop), G. Fisher (sop), G. Ross (sop), A. Stafford (alt), P. Elliott (ten), S. Varcoe (bar), J.E. Gardiner (cnd), English Baroque Soloists, Monteverdi Choir London Erato 2–▲ 2292–45211–2 ZA
Purcell, H.:King Arthur, w. Gillian Fisher (sop), Gill Ross (sop), J. Smith (sop), A. Stafford (alt), P. Elliot (ten), S. Varcoe (bar), J.E. Gardiner (cnd), English Baroque Soloists, Monteverdi Choir London Erato ("Gardiner Purcell Collection" series) 2–▲ 96552–2
Purcell, H.:King Arthur (sels), w. J. Smith (sop), G. Fisher (sop), G. Ross (sop), J. E. Gardiner (cnd), English Baroque Soloists, Monteverdi Choir Erato ▲ 45919–2
Purcell, H.:Odes & Welcome Songs (misc), w. J. Smith (sop), K. Amps (sop), M. Chance (ct), Wilson (sgr), J. M. Ainsley (ten), S. Richardson (bar), T. Pinnock (cnd), English Concert, *(chorus unknown)* —Come ye Sons of Art; Welcome to All the Pleasures; Of Old, When Heroes Thought it Base Archiv ▲ 427663–2 [DDD]
Vivaldi, A.:Gloria, RV.589, w. P. Kwella (sop), C. Wyn-Rogers (alt), A. Carwood (ten), S. Darlington (cnd), Hanover Band, Christ Church Cathedral Choir Oxford Nimbus ▲ NI 5278 [DDD]
Vivaldi, A.:Gloria (& Intro), RV.588, w. P. Kwella (sop), C. Wyn-Rogers (alt), A. Carwood (ten), S. Darlington (cnd), Hanover Band, Christ Church Cathedral Choir Oxford Nimbus ▲ NI 5278 [DDD]

Prieto, Carmen (sgr)
Mozart, W.A.:Entführung, w. Teresa Stich-Randall (mez), Nicolai Gedda (ten), Michel Sénéchal (ten), H. Rosbaud (cnd), Paris Conservatory Societé des Concerts Orch, Elisabeth Brasseur Chorale *(rec Aix-en-Provence Festival, France, 1954)* Agorá ("Phoenix" series) 2–▲ 512

Prikopa, Herbert (bar)
Kálmán, I.:Die Csárdásfürstin (sels), w. E. Liebesberg (sop), L. Rysanek (sop), R. Christ (ten), F. Bauer-Theussl (cnd), Vienna Volksoper Orch, Vienna Volksoper Chorus [G] Koch Präsent ▲ CD 399226 [AAD]
Lehár, F.:Der Graf von Luxemburg (sels), w. Renate Holm (sop), Else Liebesberg (sop), Hilde Brauner (cta), Dagmar Hermann (mez), Rudolf Christ (ten), F. Bauer-Theussl (cnd), Vienna Volksoper Orch, Vienna Volksoper Chorus [G] Koch Präsent ▲ CD 399223 [AAD]
Lehár, F.:Die lustige Witwe, w. D. Koller (sop), M. Irosch (sop), H. Papouschek (sop), P. Minich (ten), K. Ruzicka (ten), K. Huemer (bar), R. Bibl (cnd), Vienna Volksoper Orch, Vienna Volksoper Chorus [G] Denon 2–▲ CO 8103 [DDD]
Straus, O.:Ein Walzertraum (sels), w. H. Brauner (cta), R. Holm (sop), E. Liebesberg (sop), D. Hermann (mez), R. Christ (ten), F. Bauer-Theussl (cnd), Vienna Volksoper Orch, Vienna Volksoper Chorus [G] Koch Präsent ▲ CD 399223 [AAD]

Prillman, Jeff (ten)
Haydn, J.:Arias, w. Eleni Matos (mez), P. Tiboris (cnd), Prague Virtuosi—L'anima del filosofo, H.XXVIII:13/3 [from Orfeo ed Euridice]; Scena di Berenice, H.XXIVa:10; Recitative & Aria of Oreste, H.XXIVa:10 [for Traetta's "Ifigenia in Tauride"] *(rec Studio Domovina, Prague, Mar 23–25, 1995)* Elysium ▲ GRK 706 [DDD]

Printemps, Yvonne (sop)
La Saison d'Amour *(rec 1929–40)* Pearl ▲ PEA 9158 [ADD]

Prior, Maddy (voc)
Sing Lustily & with Good Courage:Gallery Hymns of the 18th & Early 19th Centuries, w. Carnival Band Saydisc ▲ CDSDL 383 [DDD]
A Tapestry of Carols, w. Prior, Maddy (voc), Carnival Band Saydisc ▲ CDSDL 366 [DDD] ■ CSDL 366 (D)

Priotti, A. (bar)
Verdi, G.:La forza del destino, w. L. Gencer (sop), G. Carturan (mez), G. Di Stefano (ten), C. Siepi (b-bar), A. Votto (cnd), *(orch unknown) (rec live, Cologne 1957)* Melodram 3–▲ MEL 37010

Pritchett, Dianne (cta)
Weisgall, H.:Six Characters in Search of an Author, w. E. Byrne (sop—Stepdaughter), S. Foster (sop—Prompter), E. Furtal (sop—Coloratura), J. King (mez—Mezzo), N. Maultsby (mez—Mother), P. LoVerne (cta—Madame Pace), D. Pritchett (cta—Wardrobe Mistress), B. Fowler (ten—Tenore Boffo), K. Anderson (ten—Director), A. Schroeder (bar—Accompanist), P. Zawisza (bar—Stage Manager), R. Orth (bar—Father), G. Lehman (bar—Son), M. Wadsworth (b-bar—Basso Cantante), L. Schaenen (cnd), Chicago Lyric Opera Orch, Lyric Opera Center Chorus *(rec Chicago, June 14 & 16, 1990)* New World 2–▲ 80454–2

Pritchett, Lizabeth (mez)
Verdi, G.:Falstaff, w. Vivian Della Chiesa (sop—Alice), Audrey Schuh (sop—Nannetta), Lizabeth Pritchett (mez—Quickly), Evelyn Sachs (mez—Meg), André Turp (ten—Fenton), Virginio Assandri (ten—Caius), Luigi Vellucci (ten—Bardolfo), Leonard Warren (bar—Falstaff), Richard Torigi (bar—Ford), R. Cellini (cnd), New Orleans Opera Orch, New Orleans Opera Chorus *(rec live, May 5, 1956)* VAI Audio 2–▲ VAIA 1056–2

Probst, Wolfgang (bar)
Suder, J.:Leider machen Leute, w. P. Coburn (sop), K. König (ten), M. Morgan (bar), U. Mund (cnd), Bamberg SO, Bavarian Radio Chorus [G] Orfeo 2–▲ 124862 [DDD]

Pröbstl, Max (bass)
Lortzing, A.:Die beiden Schützen, w. K. Nentwig (sop), P. Kuen (ten), B. Kusche (bar), K. Smitt-Walter (bar), J. Koetsier (cnd), Bavarian RSO *(rec 1950)* Memories 2–▲ MEM 4546 [ADD]

Procter, Norma (cta)
Handel, G.F.:Alcina, w. J. Sutherland (sop), N. Monti (ten), F. Wunderlich (ten), T. Hemsley (bar), F. Leitner (cnd), Cappella Coloniensis, Cologne Radio Chorus Melodram 3–▲ CDM 37002
Handel, G.F.:Alcina, w. J. Sutherland (sop), van Dick (sgr), F. Leitner (cnd), Cappella Coloniensis, Cologne Radio Chorus [I] *(rec live, 1959)* Verona 3–▲ 27011/13 (m) [AAD]
Handel, G.F.:Messiah, w. Oliver Johnston (trb), Rae Woodland (sop), Paul Esswood (ct), Stephen Roberts (bar), J. Tobin (cnd), English SO, London Choral Society [Handel's original orchestration] [E] *(rec 1976)* Protone ■ CSPR 166/67
Handel, G.F.:Messiah (sels), w. Sheila. Armstrong (sop), Kenneth Bowen (ten), John Cameron (bar), L. Stokowski (cnd), London SO, London Sym Chorus [E] London ("Weekend Classics" series) ▲ 433874–2 [ADD] ■ 433874–4
Mahler, G.:Sym 3, w. J. Horenstein (cnd), London SO, Ambrosian Singers, Wandsworth School Boys' Choir [G] Unicorn-Kanchana ("Souvenir" series) 2–▲ UKCD 2006/07 [ADD]

Proebstl, Max (bass)
Bach, J.S.:St. Matthew Passion, w. I. Seefried (sop), A. Fahberg (sop), H. Töpper (alt), E. Haefliger (ten), D. Fischer-Dieskau (bar), K. Engen (bass), K. Richter (cnd), Munich Bach Orch, Munich Bach Choir Archiv ▲ 439338–2 [ADD]

Proebstl, Max (bass) (cont.)
Strauss, R.:Feuersnot, w. Maud Cunitz (sop—Diemut), Antonia Fahberg (sop—Elsbeth), Irmgard Barth (mez—Wigelis), Liselotte Nölser (sgr—Margret), Karl Ostertag (ten—Schweiker), Marcel Cordes (bar—Kunrad), Kieth Engen (bass—Kofel), Karl Hoppe (bass—Hämerlein), Max Proebstl (bass—Ortolf), Georg Wieter (bass—Jörg), R. Kempe (cnd), Bavarian State Opera Orch, Bavarian State Opera Chorus *(rec Munich Opera Festival, Prince Regent Theater, Aug 14, 1958)* Orfeo d'or 2–▲ 423962
Strauss, R.:Salome, w. Astrid Varnay (sop—Salome), Hertha Töpper (mez—Der Page der Herodias), Margarete Klose (cta—Herodias), Hans Hopf (ten—Narraboth), Karl Hoppe (ten—1st Nazarene), Karl Ostertag (ten—1st Jew), Julius Patzak (ten—Herodes), Hans Braun (bar—Jochanaan), Benno Kusche (bar—2nd Soldier), Adolf Keil (bass—1st Soldier), Hans Hermann Nissen (bass—Ein Kappadozier), Max Proebstl (bass—2nd Nazarene), Walter Carnotch (sgr—4th Jew), Emil Graf (sgr—3rd Jew), Paul Kaussen (sgr—2nd Jew), Hildegard Limmer (sgr—A slave), Georg Witter (sgr—5th Jew), H. Weigert (cnd), Bavarian RSO *(rec June 21–25, 1953)* Bella Voce 2–▲ BLV 7210 [AAD]

Proenza, Pedro (ten)
Honegger, A.:Jeanne d'Arc au bûcher, w. C. Château (sop), A.M. Rodde (sop), H. Brachet (mez), Z. Jankovsky (ten), F. Loup (bass), S. Baudo (cnd), Czech PO, Czech Chorus *(rec 1974)* Supraphon 2–▲ 11 0557–2 [AAD]

Prohaska, Jaro (bar)
Wagner, R.:Arias & Scenes, w. Kathe Heidersbach (sop), Maria Reining (sop), Hilde Scheppan (sop), Margarete Teschemacher (sop), Margarete Klose (mez), Max Lorenz (ten), Karl Schmitt-Walter (bar), Kurt Böhme (bass), *(orch unknown)*—selections from Rienzi; Der Fliegende Holländer; Tannhäuser; Lohengrin; Tristan und Isolde; Die Meistersinger von Nürnberg; Die Walküre & Götterdämmerung *(rec 1927–1944)* Phonographe 2–▲ PHG 5016 [AAD]
Wagner, R.:Lohengrin, w. M. Müller (sop), F. Volker (ten), A. Rother (cnd), Berlin Staatskapelle [G] *(rec 1942)* Preiser 3–▲ 90043 (m) [AAD]
Wagner, R.:Lohengrin (sels), w. Maria Müller (sop—Elsa), Margarete Klose (mez—Ortrud), Franz Völker (ten—Lohengrin), Jaro Prohaska (bar—Telramund), Josef von Manowarda (bass—King Heinrich), H. Tietjen (cnd), Vienna State Opera Orch *(rec Vienna, 1938)* Koch Schwann 2–▲ SCH 314682 [ADD]
Wagner, R.:Die Meistersinger von Nürnberg, w. Maria Müller (sop), Max Lorenz (ten), Josef Greindl (bass), Bayreuth Festival Orch, Bayreuth Festival Chorus *(rec live, July–Aug 1943)* Grammofono 2000 4–▲ GRM 78602
Wagner, R.:Das Rheingold (sels), w. A. Konetzni (sop—Fricka), J. Prohaska (bar—Wotan), N. Zec (b-bar—Fasolt), H. Alsen (bass—Fafner), J. Krips (cnd), Vienna State Opera Orch, Vienna State Opera Chorus *(rec Jan. 18, 1937)* Koch Schwann 2–▲ SCH 314592
Wagner, R.:Rienzi, der Letzte der Tribunen (sels), w. Hilde Scheppan (sop), Margarete Klose (cta), Max Lorenz (ten), A. Rother (cnd), Berlin State Opera Orch, Berlin State Opera Chorus *(rec 1941)* Preiser ▲ PRE 90223 [ADD]
Wagner, R.:Der Ring des Nibelungen (sels), w. Adele Kern (sop), Anny Konetzni (sop), Hilde Konetzni (sop), Elisabeth Schumann (sop), Enid Szantho (cta), Josef Kalenberg (ten), Max Lorenz (ten), Set Svanholm (ten), Erich Zimmermann (ten), Hans Hotter (bar), Emil Schipper (bar), Paul Schöffler (b-bar), Ludwig Hoffmann (bass), H. Knappertsbusch (cnd), Vienna State Opera Orch *(rec Vienna, 1937–1943)* Koch Schwann 2–▲ SCH 314742 [ADD]
Wagner, R.:Tristan und Isolde (acts 2 & 3), w. E. Schlüter (sop), M. Klose (cta), L. Suthaus (ten), G. Frick (bass), W. Furtwängler (cnd), Berlin State Opera Orch, Berlin State Opera Chorus [G] *(rec live, Berlin, 10/3/47)* Arkadia 2–▲ 358 [ADD]

Prokeš, Martin (ten)
Zelenka, J.D.:Il penitenti al sepolchro del Redentore, w. Magdaléna Kozená (alt—Maddalena), Martin Prokeš (ten—Davidde), Michael Pospíšil (bass), Robert Hugo (cnd), Capella Regia Musicalis *(rec St Franciscus Church of the Convent of St Agnes of Bohemia, Prague, Nov 1994)* Panton ▲ 811389–2 [DDD]

Prokina, Yelena (sop)
Prokofiev, S.:War & Peace, w. O. Borodina (mez), G. Gregoriam (ten), A. Gergalov (bar), V. Gergiev (cnd), Kirov Orch, Kirov Opera Chorus [R] Philips 3–▲ 434097–2
Shostakovich, D.:Sym 14, w. Sergei Aleksashkin (bass), Wilfried Rehm (vc), E. Inbal (cnd), Vienna SO *(rec Konzerthaus, Vienna, Apr 26–29, 1993)* Denon ▲ CO 78821 [DDD]

Prokofiev, Lina (nar)
Prokofiev, S.:Peter & the Wolf, w. N. Järvi (cnd), Scottish National Orch Chandos ▲ CHAN 8511 [DDD]

Pronk, Corrie (alt)
Einhorn, R.:Voices of Light, w. Susan Narucki (sop), Frank Hameleers (ten), Henk van Heijnsbergen (b-bar), Ronald Hoogeveen (vn), Harm Bakker (vl), Michael Feves (vl), Naomi Hirschfeld (vl), S. Mercurio (cnd), Netherlands Radio PO, Martin Wright (cnd), Anonymous 4, Netherlands Radio Chorus *(rec Music Center of the Netherlands Radio & TV, Aug 23–25, 1995)* Sony Classical ▲ SK 62006 [DDD]

Prosper, Gloria (sop)
Monteverdi, C.:Vespro della Beata Vergine, w. Adrienne Albert (mez), Melvin Brown (ten), Richard Levitt (ten), Archi Drake (bass), R. Craft (cnd), Columbia Baroque Ensemble, Gregg Smith Singers, Texas Boys' Choir Sony Classical ("Essential Classics" series) 2–▲ SB2K 62656

Protschka, Josef (ten)
Busoni, F.:Turandot, w. C. Lindsley (sop), R. Wörle (ten), R. Pape (bass), G. Albrecht (cnd), Berlin RSO, Berlin RIAS Chamber Choir Capriccio ▲ 60039 [DDD]
Dvořák, A.:The Spectre's Bride, Op. 69, w. L. Aghova (sop), I. Kusnjer (bar), G. Albrecht (cnd), Hamburg State PO, Prague Phil Chorus [Cz] *(rec live 1991)* Orfeo ▲ 259921 [DDD]
Haydn, J.:Die Jahreszeiten, w. Angela Marie Blasi (sop), Robert Holl (bass), N. Harnoncourt (cnd), Vienna SO, Arnold Schoenberg Choir [G] Teldec 2–▲ 2292–42699–2
Haydn, J.:Die Schöpfung, w. Edita Gruberova (sop), Robert Holl (bass), N. Harnoncourt (cnd), Vienna SO, Arnold Schoenberg Choir [G] Teldec 2–▲ 2292–42682–2
Hindemith, P.:Mathis der Maler, w. Hermann Winkler (ten), Roland Hermann (bar), Victor von Halem (bass), Harold Stamm (bass), G. Albrecht (cnd), Cologne RSO Wergo 3–▲ WER 6255–2
Marschner, H.A.:Der Vampyr, w. Carole Farley (sop—Malwina), Nucci Condò (mez—Suse), Oslavio Di Credico (ten—George Dibdin), Josef Protschka (ten—Edgar Aubry), Romano Truffelli (ten—Richard Scrop), Martin Egel (bar—Sir Humphrey Davenaut), Andrea Snarski (bar—Toms Blunt), Siegmund Nimsgern (b-bar—Lord Ruthven), Armando Caforio (bass—Robert Green), Peter Boom (sgr—Il capo dei Vampiri), Carlo Di Giacomo (sgr—James Gadshill), Wolfgang Lenz (sgr—Sir Berkley), Galina Pisarenko (sgr—Janthe), Renzo Scorsoni (sgr—Un servitore di Berkley), Anastasia Tomaszewska Schepis (sgr—Emmy), G. Neuhold (cnd), Rome RAI SO, Rome RAI Chorus *(rec Rome, Jan 26, 1980)* Italia 2–▲ CDC 99 [ADD]
Mendelssohn, F.:Songs, w. H. Deutsch (pno)—31 songs [G] Capriccio ▲ CD 10 363 [DDD]
Mozart, W.A.:Arias, w. K. Eichhorn (cnd), Munich RSO—arias from Le nozze di Figaro & Mitridate, re di Ponto LaserLight ▲ 15 889 [DDD]
Mozart, W.A.:Entführung (sels), Munich RSO—3 sels. LaserLight ▲ 15 890 [DDD]
Mozart, W.A.:Idomeneo (sels), w. G. Sabbatini (sop), S. Sass (sop)—4 arias & ballet music LaserLight ▲ 15 888 [DDD]
Mozart, W.A.:Missa, K.317, w. J. Rodgers (sop), E. von Magnus (alt), L. Polgár (bass), N. Harnoncourt (cnd), Vienna Concentus Musicus, Arnold Schoenberg Choir [L] Teldec ▲ 2292–43354–2
Mozart, W.A.:Missa solemnis, K.139, w. B. Bonney (sop), J. Rappé (ten), H. Hagegard (bar), N. Harnoncourt (cnd), Vienna Concentus Musicus, Arnold Schoenberg Choir [L] Teldec ▲ 2292–44180–2 [DDD]
Mozart, W.A.:Vesperae solennes, w. J. Rodgers (sop), E. von Magnus (alt), L. Polgár (bass), N. Harnoncourt (cnd), Vienna Concentus Musicus, Arnold Schoenberg Choir [L] Teldec ▲ 2292–43354–2
Mozart, W.A.:Zauberflöte (sels), w. S. Jo (sop), H. Prey (bar)—Ov., arias & choruses LaserLight ▲ 15 888 [DDD]
Schreker, F.:Der Schatzgräber, w. G. Schnaut (sop), H. Helm (bar), H. Stamm (bass), G. Albrecht (cnd), Hamburg State Opera Orch, Hamburg State Opera Chorus [G] *(rec live 5/89)* Capriccio 2–▲ 60010–2 [DDD]
Schubert, Franz:Die Schöne Müllerin, w. Helmut Deutsch (pno) [G] Capriccio ▲ 10082 [DDD]
Schumann, R.:Dichterliebe, w. Helmut Deutsch (pno) [G] Capriccio ▲ 10215 ■ 27215
Schumann, R.:Liederkreis, Op. 39, w. H. Deutsch (pno) [G] Capriccio ▲ 10215 ■ 27215

▲ = CD ♦ = Enhanced CD Δ = MD ■ = Cassette Tape □ = DCC

Protschka, Josef (ten) (cont.)
Schumann, R.:Spanische Liebeslieder, w. M. Shirai (mez), M. Lipovsek (mez), M. Hölle (bass), N. Shetler (pno), N. Deutsch (pno) [G] Capriccio ▲ CDC 10079
Strauss (II), Joh.:Die Fledermaus (sels), w. E. Gruberova (sop), B. Bonney (sop), M. Lipovšek (mez), W. Kmentt (ten), W. Hollweg (ten), C. Boesch (bar), A. Scharinger (bass), N. Harnoncourt (cnd), Royal Concertgebouw Orch, Netherlands Opera Chorus Teldec ▲ 42427-2
Wagner, R.:Der fliegende Holländer, w. H. Beherns (sop—Senta), I. Vermillion (mez—Mary), U. Heilmann (ten—Helmsman), J. Protschka (ten—Erik), R. Hale (bar—The Dutchman), K. Rydl (bass—Daland), C. von Dohnányi (cnd), Vienna PO, Vienna State Opera Chorus London 2-▲ 436418-2 [DDD]
Zemlinsky, A. von:Der Traumgörge, w. P. Coburn (sop), J. Martin (sop), G. M. Ronge (sop), B. Calm (mez), P. Haage (ten), H. Kruse (ten), H. Welker (bar), M. Blasius (bass), V. von Halem (bass), G. Albrecht (cnd), Frankfurt RSO [G] Capriccio 2-▲ CD 10241/2 [DDD]

Protti, Aldo (bar)
Bellini, V.:I Puritani (sels), w. G. Tucci (sop), L. Pavarotti (ten), R. Raimondi (bass), A. Quadri (cnd), Catania Teatro Massimo Bellini Orch, Catania Teatro Massimo Bellini Chorus [I] *(rec live, Catania 3/22/68)* Verona 3-▲ 27029/31
Bellini, V.:I Puritani (sels), w. G. Tucci (sop), L. Pavarotti (ten), R. Raimondi (bass), A. Quadri (cnd), Catania Teatro Massimo Bellini Orch, Catania Teatro Massimo Bellini Chorus [I] *(rec live, Catania 3/22/68)* Melodram ▲ MEL 15001
Bellini, V.:I Puritani (sels), w. Gabriella Tucci (sop—Elvira), Vittorina Magnaghi (mez—Enrichetta di Francia), Luciano Pavarotti (ten—Lord Arturo Talbo), Aldo Protti (bar—Sir Riccardo Forth), Ruggero Raimondi (bass—Sir Giorgio), A. Quadri (cnd), Vincenzo Bellini Theater Orch, Catania Teatro Massimo Bellini Chorus Budget ("The Greatest Voice in Opera" series) ▲ SYP 106
Concerti, w. Olivero, Magda (sop), U. Trama (bass), D. Antoioli (sgr), K. Ostar (sgr), Fulvio Vernizzi (cnd) Great Opera Performances 2-▲ GOP 709
Giordano, U.:Andrea Chénier, w. M. Callas (sop), M. del Monaco (ten), A. Votto (cnd), La Scala Orch, La Scala Chorus *(rec live, Milan, 1/8/55)* Melodram 2-▲ MEL 26002 [ADD]
Giordano, U.:Andrea Chénier, w. M. Callas (sop), M. del Monaco (ten), A. Votto (cnd), La Scala Orch, La Scala Chorus *(rec live)* Verona 2-▲ VER 28020
Giordano, U.:Andrea Chénier, w. Renata Tebaldi (sop—Maddalena), Anna di Stasio (mez—Bersi), Amalia Pini (mez—Madelon/Contessa), Mario Del Monaco (ten—Andrea Chenier), Antonio Pirino (ten—L'Incredibile/Abate), Aldo Protti (bar—Carlo Gerard), Arturo La Porta (bass/bar—Mathieu/Fleville), Silvano Pagliuca (bass/bar—Roucher/Fouquier-Tinville), Giorgio Onesti (bass—Dumas/Schmidt/Major-domo), F. Capuana (cnd), Italian Lyric Orch, Italian Lyric Chorus *(rec Tokyo, Oct 1, 1961)* Legato Classics 2-▲ LCD 214-2 [ADD]
Mascagni, P.:Cavalleria rusticana (sels), w. Giuseppe Giacomini (ten), Maria Luisa Nave (sgr), M. Gusella (cnd), *(orch unknown)*—O Lola ch'hai di latti la cammisa; Tu qui Santuzza; Intanto amici qua; Mamma, quel vino è generoso *(rec Parma, Feb. 6, 1969)* Golden Age of Opera 2-▲ GAO 189/90 [ADD]
Rossini, G.:Il barbiere di Siviglia (sels), w. R. Scotto (sop), A. di Stasio (mez), A. Kraus (ten), C. Badioli (bass), E. Campi (bass), V. Bellezza (cnd), Naples Teatro San Carlo Orch, Naples Teatro San Carlo Chorus *(rec July 26, 1958)* Golden Age of Opera 2-▲ GAO 137/38 [ADD]
Verdi, G.:Aida, w. Renata Tebaldi (sop—Aida), Ebe Stignani (mez—Amneris), Mario Del Monaco (ten—Radamès), Piero de Palma (ten—Messenger), Aldo Protti (bar—Amonasro), Fernando Corena (bass—King), Dario Caselli (bass—Ramfis), A. Erede (cnd), St. Cecilia Academy Orch Rome, St. Cecilia Academy Chorus Rome *(rec 1952)* Theorema 2-▲ TH 121133/34
Verdi, G.:Aida, w. R. Tebaldi (sop), E. Stignani (mez), M. del Monaco (ten), F. Corena (bass), A. Erede (cnd), St. Cecilia Academy Orch Rome, St. Cecilia Academy Chorus Rome London 2-▲ 440239-2 [ADD]
Verdi, G.:Aroldo, w. A. Stella (sop), G. Penno (ten), F. Novelli (bar), T. Serafin (cnd), Florence Maggio Musicale Orch, Florence Maggio Musicale Chorus [I] *(rec live 6/3/53)* Melodram 2-▲ MEL 27014 (m) [AAD]
Verdi, G.:La forza del destino, w. Leyla Gencer (sop—Leonora), Gabriella Carturan (mez—Preziosilla), Giuseppe di Stefano (ten—Don Alvaro), Aldo Protti (bar—Don Carlo), Cesare Siepi (b-bar), Franco Calabrese (bass—Marchese di Calatrava), Enrico Campi (bass—Fra Melitone), A. Votto (cnd), La Scala Orch, La Scala Chorus *(rec Bühnen der Stadt, Köln, July 5, 1957)* Agorá Music ("Phoenix" series) 3-▲ 510 [ADD]
Verdi, G.:La forza del destino, w. Leyla Gencer (sop), Giuseppe di Stefano (ten), Cesare Siepi (bass), A. Votto (cnd), La Scala Orch, La Scala Chorus *(rec La Scala Theatre, Milan, July 5, 1957)* Pantheon 3-▲ PHE 6627 (m)
Verdi, G.:Otello, w. Renata Tebaldi (sop—Desdemona), Luisa Ribacchi (mez—Emilia), Angelo Mercuriali (ten—Roderigo), Mario del Monaco (ten—Otello), Piero de Palma (ten—Cassio), Aldo Protti (bar—Iago), Dario Caselli (bass—A Herald), Fernando Corena (bass—Lodovico), Pierluigi Martinucci (bass—Montano), A. Erede (cnd), St. Cecilia Academy Orch Rome, St. Cecilia Academy Chorus Rome Theorema ▲ TH 121141/142
Verdi, G.:Otello, w. H. Gueden (sop), G. Simionato (mez), M. del Monaco (ten), C. Siepi (b-bar), A. Erede (cnd), St. Cecilia Academy Orch Rome, St. Cecilia Academy Chorus Rome London 2-▲ 440242-2 [ADD]
Verdi, G.:Otello, w. R. Tebaldi (sop), M. Del Monaco (ten), H. von Karajan (cnd), Vienna PO [I] London 2-▲ 411618-2 [ADD]
Verdi, G.:Otello (sels), w. K. Ricciarelli (sop), M. del Monaco (ten), F. Ferraris (cnd), Brussels Théâtre de la Monnaie Orch *(rec Nov. 9, 1972)* Standing Room Only 2-▲ SRO 169-2
Verdi, G.:Rigoletto, w. Hilde Gueden (sop—Gilda), Piero de Palma (ten—Borsa), Luisa Ribacchi (mez—Giovanna), Giulietta Simionato (mez—Maddalena), Mario del Monaco (ten—Duca de Mantova), Aldo Protti (bar—Rigoletto), Fernando Corena (bass—Conte Monterone), Cesare Siepi (bass—Sparafucile), A. Erede (cnd), St. Cecilia Academy Orch Rome, St. Cecilia Academy Chorus Rome Theorema ▲ TH 121179/180
Verdi, G.:Rigoletto, w. Gianna D'Angelo (sop), Vito Susca (bass), Giorgio Tadeo (bass), F. Molinari-Pradelli (cnd), Trieste Teatro Comunale Giuseppe Verdi Orch, Trieste Teatro Comunale G. Verdi Chorus Melodram 2-▲ CDM 27006
Verdi, G.:Rigoletto, w. R. Tebaldi (sop), M. del Monaco (ten), P. de Palma (bass), F. Corena (bass), A. Erede (cnd), St. Cecilia Academy Orch Rome, St. Cecilia Academy Chorus Rome London 2-▲ 440245-2 [ADD]
Wagner, R.:Lohengrin (sels), w. M. Pobbe (sop), S. Kónya (ten), F. Leitner (cnd), Milan RAI SO [I] *(rec live 1959)* Melodram ▲ MEL 15004 (m) [AAD]

Proujanski, Arkady (ten)
Karetnikov, N.:Till Eulenspiegel, w. E. Mazo (sop), L. Mkrtchian (cta), B. Koudriavtsev (bar), P. Glouboky (bass), A. Motchalov (bass), A. Martinov (sgr), Polianski (cnd), Soviet Cinema Orch, Soviet Cinema Chorus *(rec Moscow, 1988)* Russian Season ("Russian Season" Series) 2-▲ LDC 288029/30 [DDD]

Provins, Jacques (sgr)
Hahn, R.:O mon del inconnul, w. Christiane Château (sop), Lina Dachary (sop), Monique Stiot (mez), Michel Hamel (ten), Joseph Peyron (ten), Aimé Doniat (bar), Dominique Tirmont (bar), Philippe Gaudin (sgr), J. Brebion (cnd), ORTF Lyric Orch Musidisc 2-▲ MUS 202562 [AAD]

Provvisionato, Francesca (mez)
Donizetti, G.:Linda di Chamounix, w. Mariella Devia (sop—Linda), Sonia Ganassi (mez—Pierotto), Francesca Provvisionato (mez—Maddalena), Luca Canonici (ten—Carlo), Alfonso Antoniozzi (bass—Il Marchese di Boisfleury), Petteri Salomaa (bass—Antonio), Boguslaw Fiksinski (sgr—L'intendente), Donato Di Stefano (sgr—Il Prefetto), G. Bellini (cnd), Eastern Netherlands Orch, Andrew Wise (cnd), National Reisopera Choir *(rec Muziekcentrum Enschede, Holland, June 24–July 2, 1992)* Arts Music 3-▲ 47151-2 [DDD]
Rossini, G.:L'occassione fa il ladro, w. M. Bayo (sop), F. Massa (ten), I. Zennaro (ten), F. Previati (bar), N. de Carolis (b-bar), M. Viotti (cnd), English CO [I] Claves 8-▲ CD 9200 [DDD]
Rossini, G.:L'occassione fa il ladro, w. Maria Bayo (sop), Fulvio Massa (ten), Iorio Zennaro (ten), Fabio Previati (bar), Natale de Carolis (b-bar), M. Viotti (cnd), English CO Claves 2-▲ 50-9208/9
Rossini, G.:La scala di seta, w. Teresa Ringholz (sop), Fulvio Massa (ten), Ramon Vargas (ten), Alessandro Corbelli (bar), Natale de Carolis (b-bar), M. Viotti (cnd), English CO Claves 2-▲ 9219/20

Pruett, Jerome (ten)
Berlioz, H.:Les Nuits d'été, w. Josée Fabre (pno) Sonpact ▲ SPT 94013 [DDD]

Pruett, Jerome (ten) (cont.)
Donizetti, G.:Parisina, w. Montserrat Caballé (sop), Louis Quilico (bar), James Morris (bass), E. Queler (cnd), New York City Opera Orch, New York Opera Chorus *(rec live, New York 1974)* Standing Room Only 2-▲ SRO 836-2 [ADD]
Donizetti, G.:Parisina, w. Montserrat Caballé (sop), Louis Quilico (bar), James Morris (bass), E. Queler (cnd), New York City Opera Orch, New York Opera Chorus Pantheon 2-▲ PHE 6638
Massenet, J.:Songs, w. Josée Fabre (pno)—Voix Suprême; Poème du Souvenir; Plus Vite; Soleil Couchant; Les Alcyons; Elégie; Les Mains; Heure Vécue; Pensée d'Automne; Nuit d'Espagne; La Mort de la Cigale; Il Pleuvait; Sonnet; Soir de Rêve; Quelques Chansons Mauves Sonpact ▲ SPT 96018 [DDD]
Reyer, L.-E.-E.:Mélodies, w. Josée Fabre (pno)—Hylas; Sérénade; Douce harmonie; Vieille chanson du jeune temps; Comme à l'aube nouvelle; Il est un trésor plus rare que l'or; Fleur des nuits; Pourquoi ne m'aimez-vous?; Adieu, Suzon; Les larmes; J'ai dit à toute la nature; Aux étoiles Sonpact ▲ SPT 94013 [DDD]

Pruliére, Amperito Peris de (mez)
Falla, M. de:El amor brujo, w. M. Rosenthal (cnd), Paris Opera Orch *(rec ca. 1953)* MCA Classics ▲ MCAD 10481 (m/s) [ADD]

Průša, Karel (bass)
Báchorek, M.:Lidice, w. Jana Stupárkova-Majtnerová (sop), Osvald Albín (speaker), Jan Vlasák (speaker), O. Trhlík (cnd), Ostrava Janáček PO, Ostrava Janáček Mixed Chorus *(rec Smetana Hall of Prague's Municipal House, Feb 10 & 11, 1988)* Panton ▲ 811338-2 [AAD]
Báchorek, M.:Music of, w. Osvald Albin (nar), Otakar Brousek (nar), Jan Vlassak (nar), Brigita Šulcová (sop), Drahomira Drobková (cta), Pavel Kamas (sgr), Jan Kyzlink (sgr), Jana Stuperkova-Majtnerova (sgr), Bretislav Vojkuvka (sgr), O. Trhlík (cnd), Ostrava Janáček PO, Prague SO, Ostrava Janáček Chorus, Ostrava Women's Chamber Chorus, Permoník Children's Chorus—Lidice; Stereofonietta; Hukvald Poem Panton ▲ PAN 811338 [AAD/DDD]
Beethoven, L. van:Sym 9, "Choral Sym", w. Gabriela Benackova-Cápova (sop), Vera Soukupova (alt), Vilem Pribyl (ten), L. von Matačič (cnd), Czech PO Praga ▲ PR 250076
Fibich, Z.:The Romance of Spring, w. Nada Sormova (sop), F. Vajnar (cnd), Prague RSO, Prague Radio Chorus Supraphon ▲ SUP 3197
Janácek, L.:Slavonic Mass, w. Gabriela Benacková (sop), Vera Soukupová (cta), Frantisek Livora (ten), V. Neumann (cnd), Czech PO, Czech Phil Chorus Panton ▲ PAN 811217
Martinů, B.:The Epic of Gilgamesh, w. M. Machotková (sop), J. Zaradníček (ten), V. Zítek (ten), J. Belohlávek (cnd), Prague SO, Czech Phil Chorus Supraphon ▲ SUP 11 1824 [ADD]
Reicha, A.:Der neue Psalm, w. Magdaléna Hajóssyová (sop), Anna Barová (mez), Andreas Schmidt (bar), L. Mátl (cnd), Dvořák CO, Czech Phil Chorus Panton ▲ PAN 810758 [DDD]
Reicha, A.:Te Deum, w. Marta Boháčová (sop), Oldřich Lindauer (ten), Ladislav Vachulka (org), V. Smetáček (cnd), Prague SO, Kühn Chorus *(rec Cathedral of the Ascension of the Virgin, Karlov, Prague, 1970)* Panton ▲ PAN 800242 [AAD]

Pruvost, Jacques (bar)
Planquette, R.:Rip van Winkle, w. Claudine Collart (sop), Lina Dachary (sop), Freda Betti (cta), René Lenoty (ten), Joseph Peyron (ten), Charles Daguerressar (bar), Julien Giovannetti (bar), Lucien Lovano (bass), Patrick Orladey (sgr), Joëlle Pierre (sgr), M. Cariven (cnd), ORTF Lyric Orch, ORTF Lyric Chorale Musidisc ▲ MUS 201602 [AAD]

Prylova, Libuse (sop)
Janácek, L.:The Makropulos Affair, w. Helena Tattermuschová (sop), Rudolf Vanasek (ten), Ivo Zídek (ten), B. Gregor (cnd), Prague National Orch, Prague National Theater Chorus *(rec mid 1960's)* Supraphon 2-▲ SUP 108351 [AAD]

Puchegger, Thomas (sop)
Schubert, Franz:Mass 1, w. Alexander Nader (sop), Georg Leskovich (alto), Jörg Hering (ten), Kurt Azesberger (ten), Harry van der Kamp (bass), Arno Hartmann (org), B. Weil (cnd), Orch of the Age of Enlightenment, Vienna Boys' Choir *(rec Vienna, Austria, Sept 1995)* Sony Classical ("Vivarte" series) ▲ SK 68247 [DDD]
Schubert, Franz:Mass 2, w. Jörg Hering (ten), Harry van der Kamp (bass), Arno Hartmann (org), B. Weil (cnd), Orch of the Age of Enlightenment, Vienna Boys' Choir *(rec Vienna, Austria, Sept 1995)* Sony Classical ("Vivarte" series) ▲ SK 68247 [DDD]
Schubert, Franz:Mass 3, w. Alexander Nader (sop), Belá Fischer (alt), Georg Leskovich (alt), Jörg Hering (ten), Harry Van der Kamp (bass), Arno Hartmann (org), B. Weil (cnd), Orch of the Age of Enlightenment, Chorus Viennensis, Vienna Boys' Choir Sony Classical ("Vivarte" series) ▲ SK 68248
Schubert, Franz:Mass 4, w. Alexander Nader (sop), Belá Fischer (alt), Georg Leskovich (alt), Jörg Hering (ten), Harry Van der Kamp (bass), Arno Hartmann (org), B. Weil (cnd), Orch of the Age of Enlightenment, Chorus Viennensis, Vienna Boys' Choir Sony Classical ("Vivarte" series) ▲ SK 68248

Puetz, M. (sop)
Mahler, G.:Sym 2, w. M. Höffgen (cta), C. Schuricht (cnd), Hessian RSO, Hesse Radio Chorus, Frankfurt Singakademie Choir *(rec 1960)* Originals 2-▲ ORISH 819 [ADD]

Pugh, Katharina (cta)
Bach, J.S.:Cant 24, w. A. Augér (sop), H. Watts (cta), A. Kraus (ten), W. Heldwein (bass), W. Schöne (bass), H. Rilling (cnd), Stuttgart Bach Collegium, Gächinger Kantorei Hänssler Classic ▲ 98.803 [AAD]

Puglisi, Lino (bar)
Leoncavallo, R.:Pagliacci, w. M. Micheluzzi (sop), F. Corelli (ten), M. Carlin (ten), T. Gobbi (bar), A. Simonetto (cnd), Milan RAI Orch, Milan RAI Chorus *(rec live 9/26/54 from RAI Milan)* HRE ▲ 1001-1 [ADD]

Pullan, Bruce (bar)
Weisgarber, E.:Night, w. W. Fawcett (db), J. Washburn (cnd), Purcell Quartet, Vancouver Chamber Choir [E] Centrediscs ▲ CMCCD 3790 [DDD]

Puma, Salvatore (ten)
Puccini, G.:Il tabarro, w. N. De Rosa (sop—Giorgietta), S. Puma (ten—Luigi), E. Bastianini (bar—Michèle), M. Cordone (cnd), *(orch & chorus unknown)* [I] *(rec live, Hamburg Radio 1954)* Standing Room Only ▲ SRO 827-1

Puntilla (sgr)
Camilo, M.:Batéy, w. P. E. Clark (sop), C.B. Rowe (sop), W. Zukof (ct), L. Bennett (ten), W. L. Lee (ten), E. Levine (bar), New Generation Western Wind ▲ WW 2001

Purefoy, William (ct)
Purcell, H.:Odes & Welcome Songs (misc), w. Jeni Bern (sop), Susan Bisatt (sop), Christopher Robson (ct), Ian Honeyman (ten), Thomas Guthrie (bass), R. Glenton (cnd), Orch of the Golden Age, Golden Age Choir—The noise of foreign wars (fragment) [ed. by Bruce Wood] *(rec Manchester Grammar School, England, May 13 & 14, 1995)* Naxos ▲ 8.553444 [DDD]
Purcell, H.:Raise, Raise the Voice, w. Jeni Bern (sop), Susan Bisatt (sop), Christopher Robson (ct), Ian Honeyman (ten), Thomas Guthrie (bass), R. Glenton (cnd), Orch of the Golden Age, Golden Age Choir *(rec Manchester Grammar School, England, May 13 & 14, 1995)* Naxos ▲ 8.553444 [DDD]
Purcell, H.:Te Deum & Jubilate, w. Jeni Bern (sop), Susan Bisatt (sop), Christopher Robson (ct), Ian Honeyman (ten), Thomas Guthrie (bass), David Staff (tpt), R. Glenton (cnd), Orch of the Golden Age, Golden Age Choir *(rec Manchester Grammar School, England, May 13 & 14, 1995)* Naxos ▲ 8.553444 [DDD]
Purcell, H.:Welcome to All the Pleasures, w. Jeni Bern (sop), Susan Bisatt (sop), Christopher Robson (ct), Ian Honeyman (ten), Thomas Guthrie (bass), R. Glenton (cnd), Orch of the Golden Age, Golden Age Choir *(rec Manchester Grammar School, England, May 13 & 14, 1995)* Naxos ▲ 8.553444 [DDD]

Pusar–Jeric, Ana (sop)
Dvořák, A.:Stabat Mater, w. E. N. Houska (mez), J. Reja (ten), F. Petrusanec (bass), M. Munih (cnd), Consortium Musicum Orch, Consortium Musicum Chorus [L] Vivace 2-▲ 140141 [ADD/DDD]

Pusar–Jeric, Ana (sop) (cont.)

Rachmaninoff, S.:Songs, w. T. Hans (pno)—Oh, Never Sing to Me again, Op. 4/4; The Harvest of Sorrow, Op. 4/5; So Many Hours, So Many Fancies, Op. 4/6; For a Life of Pain I Have Giv'n My Love, Op. 8/4, Dream, Op. 8/5; A Prayer, Op. 8/6; I Wait for Thee, Op. 14/1; The Isle, Op. 14/2; Believe It Not!, Op. 14/7; Love's Flame, Op. 14/10; Twilight, Op. 21/3; The Answer, Op. 21/4; The Lilacs, Op. 21/5; Fragment from Musset, Op. 21/6; How Fair This Spot, Op. 21/7; Melody, Op. 21/9; No Prophet I, Op. 21/11; Sorrow in Springtime, Op. 21/12; To the Children, Op. 26/7; Before My Window, Op. 26/10; Day to Night Comparing, Op. 34/4; So Dread a Fate I'll Ne'er Believe!, Op. 34/7; The Morn of Life, Op. 34/10; In My Garden at Night, Op. 38/1; Daisies, Op. 38/3 [Cz] *(rec Nov. 12–15, 1992)* Orfeo ▲ 340941 [DDD]

Strauss, R.:Der Rosenkavalier (sels), w. M. Stejskal (sop), A. Jahns (mez), U. Walther (cta), R. Haunstein (bar), T. Adam (b–bar), H. Vonk (cnd), Dresden Staatskapelle, Dresden State Chorus [G] *(rec live 2/85)* Denon ▲ CO 8010 [DDD]

Pushee, Graham (ct)

Cavalli, P.F.:Calisto, w. Maria Bayo (sop), Simon Keenlyside (bar), Marcello Lippi (bar), René Jacobs (cnd), Concerto Vocale Harmonia Mundi France 3–▲ HMC 901515/17

Handel, G.F.:Te Deum, "Caroline", w. Mieke van der Sluis (sop), Harry Van Berne (ten), Harry van der Kamp (bass), W. Helbich (cnd), Bremen Baroque Orch, Alfelder Vocal Ensemble CPO ▲ CPO 999244 [DDD]

Handel, G.F.:The Ways of Zion Do Mourn, w. Mieke van der Sluis (sop), Harry van Berne (ten), Harry van der Kamp (bass), W. Helbich (cnd), Bremen Baroque Orch, Alfelder Vocal Ensemble CPO ▲ CPO 999244 [DDD]

Telemann, G.P.:Hamburger Admiralitätsmusik, w. Mieke van der Sluis (sop—Hammonia), Graham Pushee (ct—Themis), Rufus Müller (ten—Mercurius), Klaus Mertens (bass—Neptunius), David Thomas (bass—Mars), Michael Schopper (bass—Albis), W. Helbich (cnd), Bremen Baroque Orch, Alsfeld Vocal Ensemble *(rec Nov 9, 1995)* CPO 2–▲ CPO 999373–2 [DDD]

Pustelak, Kazimierz (ten)

Moniuszko, S.:Halka, w. Barbara Nieman (sop), Halina Sloniowska (sop), Jan Góralski (ten), Bogdan Paprocki (ten), Leslaw Pawluk (ten), Andrzej Hiolski (bar), Edmund Kossowski (bass), Edward Pawlak (bass), Z. Gorzynski (cnd), Warsaw State Opera House Orch, Warsaw National Opera Chorus *(rec Warsaw, 1965)* Polskie Nagrania ▲ PNCD 092 [AAD]

Penderecki, K.:Utrenia, w. Delfina Ambroziak (sop), Stefania Woytowicz (sop), Krystyna Szczepanska (mez), Boris Carmeli (bass), Wlodzimierz Denysenko (bass), A. Markowski (cnd), Warsaw PO, Józef Bok (cnd), Stanislaw Skoraczewski (cnd), Warsaw National Phil Chorus, Pioneer Choir *(rec Warsaw, 1973)* Polskie Nagrania ▲ PNCD 018

Szymanowski, K.:Harnasie, w. W. Rowicki (cnd), Warsaw PO, Antoni Szalinski (cnd), Warsaw National Phil Chorus Polskie Nagrania ▲ PNCD 242 [AAD]

Putilin, Nikolai (bar)

Tchaikovsky, P.:Iolanta, w. Galina Gorchakova (sop), Nikolai Gassiev (ten), Gegam Grigorian (ten), Dmitri Hvorostovsky (bar), Sergei Alexashkin (bass), Gennady Bezzubenkov (bass), Larissa Diadkova (sgr), Olga Korzhenskaya (sgr), Tatyana Kravtsova (sgr), V. Gergiev (cnd), Kirov Opera Orch, Kirov Opera Chorus *(rec Mariinsky Theatre, St. Petersburg)* Philips 2–▲ 442796–2

Putnam, Ashley (sop)

Puccini, G.:La Bohème, w. K. Ricciarelli (sop), J. Carreras (ten), I. Wixell (bar), C. Davis (cnd), Royal Opera House Orch [I] Philips 2–▲ 416492–2 [ADD]

Puttar, Nada (mez)

Strauss, R.:Ariadne auf Naxos, w. Lisa Della Casa (sop—Ariadne), Lisa Otto (sop—Najade), Rudolf Schock (ten—Bacchus), Leonore Kirschstein (sgr—Echo), Nada Puttar (sgr—Dryade), A. Erede (cnd), Berlin PO Testament ▲ SBT 1036 [ADD]

Pütz, Ruth–Margret (sop)

Gluck, C.W.:Orfeo ed Euridice, w. Elisabeth Söderström (sop), Dietrich Fischer–Dieskau (bar), F. Leitner (cnd), Cappella Coloniensis, Cologne Radio Chorus *(rec live, Cologne, Nov. 8, 1964)* Orfeo d'or 2–▲ 391952

Gluck, C.W.:Orfeo ed Euridice, w. Anneliese Rothenberger (sop), Grace Bumbry (mez), V. Neumann (cnd), Leipzig Opera Orch, Leipzig Radio Chorus *(rec Leipzig, 1967)* Berlin Classics 2–▲ BER 9033 [ADD]

Mozart, W.A.:Nozze di Figaro (sels), w. T. Stich–Randall (mez), T. Berganza (mez), A.–R. Johnson (ten), G. Bacquier (bar), F. Corena (bass), H. Wallberg (cnd), Swiss Romande Orch, Swiss Romande Chorus—Act IV Melodram 2–▲ CDM 27094 [ADD]

Mozart, W.A.:Zauberflöte, w. G. Janowitz (sop), L. Popp (sop), N. Gedda (ten), W. Berry (bass), G. Frick (bass), O. Klemperer (cnd), Philharmonia Orch, Philharmonia Chorus [without dialog; G] EMI Classics ("Studio" series) 2–▲ CDMB 69971 [ADD]

Rossini, G.:Il barbiere di Siviglia, w. Annelies Burmeister (mez), Peter Schreier (ten), Hermann Prey (bar), Franz Crass (bass), Fritz Ollendorff (bass), O. Suitner (cnd), Berlin State Opera Orch Berlin Classics 2–▲ BER 9021 [ADD]

Puura, Väino (bar)

Tubin, E.:Barbara von Tisenhusen, w. H. Raamat (sop), M. Jôgeva (mez), A. Kollo (ten), I. Kuusk (ten), T. Sild (bar), H. Miilberg (bass), U. Kreen (bass), P. Lilje (cnd), Estonia Opera Co Orch [Estonian] Ondine 2–▲ ODE 776–2D [DDD]

Quadflieg, Will (nar)

Doráti, A.:Jesus oder Barabbas?, w. M. Fischer–Dieskau (cnd), New Berlin CO, Czech PO members, Berlin HDK Chamber Choir [G] *(rec live 1992)* BIS ▲ CD 578 [DDD]

Mozart, W.A.:Entführung, w. E. Gruberova (sop), K. Battle (sop), G. Winbergh (ten), H. Zednik (ten), M. Talvela (bass), G. Solti (cnd), Vienna PO [G] London 2–▲ 417402–2 [DDD]

Zimmermann, B.A.:Ich wandte mich und sah an alles Unrecht, das geschah unter der Sonne, w. C. Bantzer (nar), S. Nimsgem (b–bar), W. Humburg (cnd), Münster SO Stradivarius ▲ STR 33340

Quadflieg, Will (spkr)

Brahms, J.:Romanzen aus Tieck's *Magelone,* w. W. Holzmair (bar), G. Wyss (pno) [G] Tudor 2–▲ 761 [DDD]

Quadlbauer, Brigitte (nar)

Benda, G.A.:Medea, w. Hertha Schell (nar), Peter Uray (nar), C. Benda (cnd), Prague CO *(rec Prague, Nov 1994)* Naxos ▲ 8.553346 [DDD]

Quaife, Merlyn (sop)

Lumsdaine, D.:Aria for Edward John Eyre, w. P. Gwynne (nar), J. Tong (nar), D. Stanhope (cnd), Seymour Group Vox Australis ▲ VAST 011

Merlyn Quaife, w. Jochen Schubert (pno) Move ▲ MD 3115

Quaille, Jacqueline van (sop)

Celis, F.:Preludio e Narrazione, w. F. Terby (cnd), BRTN PO Brussels *(rec BRTN–Concerthall, Dec 14, 1985)* Phaedra ▲ 92 003 [DDD]

Quale, Ulrik (sgr)

Nilsson, T.:Out of Earthly Night, w. Gudrun Bruna (sop), Marianne Mellnäs (sop), Kaysa Hälldin (alt), Lars Sjögren (ten), Göran Swartz (bass), Sture Hedin (sgr), Ola Kyhlberg (sgr), Lars Ljungman (sgr), Nils Philipson (sgr), Nils Spangenberg (sgr), Britta Therén (sgr), Karl–Erik Welin (org), Torsten Nilsson (cnd), Oscar's Motet Choir *(rec Oscar's Church, Stockholm, Sweden, Apr 26–27, 1978)* BIS ▲ CD 138 [AAD]

Quandt, Kerstin (cta)

Wagner, S.:Schwarzschwanenreich, w. Beth Johanning (sop—Linda), Kerstin Quandt (cta—Ursula), Walter Raffeiner (ten—Ludwig), Lucian Chioreanu (ten—A Boy), André Wenhold (bar—Oswald), Roland Hartmann (sgr—Tempter/Priest), Jutta Maria Schmitz (sgr—Ash–Woman), Ksenija Lukie (sgr—A Girl), K. Bach (cnd), Thüringian Saalfeld–Rudolstadt SO, Thüringian Landestheater Rudolstadt Chorus *(rec Thüringer Landestheater, Rudolstadt, June 1994)* Marco Polo 2–▲ 8.223777–8 [DDD]

Questhoff, Thomas (bar)

Mozart, W.A.:Missa, K.317, w. E. Mathis (sop), J. Rappé (ten), H. P. Blochwitz (ten), P. Schreier (cnd), Dresden Staatskapelle, Leipzig Radio Chorus Philips ▲ 426275–2

Reimann, A.:Entsorgt *(rec Studio II, Radio Free Berlin, Feb 1990)* Orfeo ▲ C 412 961 [DDD]

Quasthoff, Thomas (bar) (cont.)

Beethoven, L. van:Fidelio, w. Elizabeth Norberg–Schulz (sop—Marzelline), Deborah Voigt (sop—Lenore), Ben Heppner (ten—Florestan), Michael Schade (ten—Jaquino), Günter von Kannaten (b–bar—Don Pizarro), Matthias Hölle (bass—Rocco), Thomas Quasthoff (bar—Don Fernando), C. Davis (cnd), Bavarian RSO, Bavarian Radio Chorus, Bavarian State Opera Men's Chorus *(rec Herkulessaal der Residenz, Munich, May 15–25, 1995)* RCA Victor 2–▲ 09026–68344–2 [DDD]

Dvořák, A.:Stabat Mater, w. Marina Shaguch (sop), Ingeborg Danz (alt), James Taylor (ten), H. Rilling (cnd), Oregon Bach Festival Orch, Oregon Bach Festival Choir *(rec Silva Concert Hall, Hult Center for the Performing Arts, Eugene, Oregon, July 8–11, 1995)* Hänssler Classic ("Exclusive" series) 2–▲ CD 98.935 [DDD]

Schumann, R.:Dichterliebe, w. R. Szidon (pno) [G] RCA Red Seal ▲ 09026–61225–2

Schumann, R.:Liederkreis, Op. 39, w. R. Szidon (pno) [G] RCA Red Seal ▲ 09026–61225–2

Schumann, R.:Songs, w. R. Szidon (pno)—Die Fünf Lieder, Op. 53; Belsazar, Op. 57 [G] RCA Red Seal ▲ 09026–61225–2

Quercia, Mireille (sop)

Ohana, M.:Cantigas, w. F. Atlan (mez), R. Conil (pno), R. Hayrabedian (cnd), Strasbourg Percussion Ensemble, Choeur Contemporain [Sp] Pierre Verany ▲ PV 787032 [DDD]

Stravinsky, I.:Les Noces, w. S. Cooper (mez), P. Capelle (ten), P. Marinov (bass), Vieuxtemps (pno), R. Conil (pno), Arzoumanian (pno), Raynaut (pno), R. Hayrabedian (cnd), Strasbourg Percussion Ensemble, Contemporary Choir Pierre Verany ▲ PV 787032 [DDD]

Quilico, Gino (bar)

Adeste Fideles, w. Louis Quilico (bar), Judy Loman (hp), Toronto SO members [cnd:Jean Ashworth Bartle], Toronto Children's Chorus CBC Records ("SM 5000" series) ▲ SMCD 5119 [DDD]

Berlioz, H.:Les Troyens, w. F. Pollet (sop—Dido), D. Voigt (sop—Cassandre), C. Dubosc (sop—Ascagne), H. Perraguin (cta—Anna), G. Lakes (ten—Aeneas), J.–L. Maurette (ten—Iopas), J. M. Ainsley (ten—Hylas), M. P. (ten—Panthee), G. Cross (ten—Sinon), G. Quilico (bar—Chorebe), J.–P. Courtis (b–bar—Narbal), M. Belleau (bass—Ghost of Hector), R. Schirrer (bass—Priam), C. Dutoit (cnd), Montreal SO, Montreal Sym Chorus London 4–▲ 443693–2 [DDD]

Bizet, G.:Les Pêcheurs de perles, w. B. Hendricks (sop), J. Aler (ten), M. Plasson (cnd), Toulouse Capitole Orch, Toulouse Capitole Chorus [F] EMI Classics 2–▲ CDCB 49837 [DDD]

Enescu, G.:Oedipe, w. B. Hendricks (sop), B. Fassbaender (mez), M. Lipovšek (mez), J. Taillon (mez), N. Gedda (ten), J. Aler (ten), G. Bacquier (bar), J. Van Dam (bass–bar), L. Foster (cnd), Monte Carlo PO, Orféon Donostiarra, Petits Chanteurs de Monaco [F] EMI Classics 2–▲ CDCB 54011 [DDD]

Operetta Duets, w. Barbara Hendricks (sop), Lyon Opera Orch [cnd:Lawrence Foster] EMI Classics ▲ CDC 55151

Quilico, Louis (bar)

Adeste Fideles, w. Gino Quilico (bar), Judy Loman (hp), Toronto SO members [cnd:Jean Ashworth Bartle], Toronto Children's Chorus CBC Records ("SM 5000" series) ▲ SMCD 5119 [DDD]

Bellini, V.:I Puritani, w. B. Sills (sop—Elvira), E. Shade (sop—Enrichetta), L. Pavarotti (ten—Arturo), L. Quilico (bar—Riccardo), P. Plishka (bass—Giorgio), T. Paul (bass—Walton), A. Guadagno (cnd), *(orch & chorus unknown) (rec live Jan. 18, 1972)* Legato Classics 2–▲ LCD 1762 [ADD]

Donizetti, G.:Don Pasquale, w. B. Hendricks (sop), L. Canonici (ten), G. Bacquier (bar), R. Schirrer (bar), G. Ferro (cnd), Paris Lyon Opera Orch, Paris Lyon Opera Chorus [I] Erato 2–▲ 2292–45487–2–ZA [DDD]

Donizetti, G.:Il Duca d'Alba, w. Wladimiro Ganzarolli (bar), Enzo Tei (sgr), Ivana Tosini (sgr), T. Schippers (cnd), Trieste PO *(rec live at the Spoleto Festival, June 11, 1959)* Memories 2–▲ MEM 4579 [ADD]

Donizetti, G.:Parisina, w. Montserrat Caballé (sop), Jérôme Pruett (ten), James Morris (bass), E. Queler (cnd), New York City Opera Orch, New York Opera Chorus Pantheon 2–▲ PHE 6638

Donizetti, G.:Parisina, w. Montserrat Caballé (sop), Jérôme Pruett (ten), James Morris (bass), E. Queler (cnd), New York City Opera Orch, New York Opera Chorus *(rec live, New York 1974)* Standing Room Only 2–▲ SRO 836–2 [ADD]

Donizetti, G.:Roberto Devereux, w. B. Sills (sop), S. Marsee (mez), P. Domingo (ten), J. Rudel (cnd), New York City Opera Orch, New York City Opera Chorus *(rec 1970)* Melodram ▲ MLO 270107 [ADD]

Gounod, C.:Roméo et Juliette, w. C. Malfitano (sop), A. Kraus (ten), J. Van Dam (b–bar), G. Bacquier (bar), M. Plasson (cnd), Toulouse Capitole Orch, Toulouse Capitole Chorus [F] EMI Classics 3–▲ CDCC 47365

Milhaud, D.:L'Homme et son désir, w. F. Kopleff (cta), M. Abravanel (cnd), Utah SO, Univ of Utah Chorus *(rec 1968)* Vanguard Classics ▲ OVC 8067 [ADD]

Milhaud, D.:Pacem in terris, w. F. Kopleff (cta), M. Abravanel (cnd), Utah SO, Univ of Utah Chorus *(rec 1965)* Vanguard Classics ▲ OVC 8067 [ADD]

Pacini, G.:Saffo, w. L. Gencer (sop), F. Mattiucci (mez), T. del Bianco (ten), F. Capuana (cnd), Naples Teatro San Carlo Orch, Naples Teatro San Carlo Chorus [I] *(rec live, 4/7/67)* Arkadia 2–▲ 541 (m) [AAD]

Verdi, G.:Arias, w. U. Mayer (cnd), Edmonton SO [I] CBC ("SM 5000" series) ▲ SMCD 5043 [DDD]

Verdi, G.:Don Carlos, w. R. Kabaivanska (sop), O. Dominguez (mez), F. Corelli (ten), N. Ghiaurov (bass), N. Ghiuselev (bass), A. Guadagno (cnd), Hartford Opera Orch *(rec live 1966)* Melodram 2–▲ MEL 27511

Verdi, G.:Rigoletto, w. P. Wise (sop—Gilda), B. Evans (sop—Giovanna), M. Yauger (mez—Maddalena), J. Carreras (ten—Duke), L. Quilico (bar—Rigoletto), J. Rudel (cnd), *(orch unknown) (rec Apr. 22, 1973)* Standing Room Only 2–▲ SRO 843 [ADD]

Quillevéré, Marcel (ten)

Clásicos de las Américas, w. Margot Pares–Reyna (sop), Jesús Castro Balbi (gtr), Noël Lee (pno), Georges Rabol (pno), Erwartung Ensemble [cnd:Bernard Desgraupes], Jazzogène Orch [cnd:Jean–Luc Fillon] Opus 111 6–▲ 2000

Mozart, W.A.:Songs, w. A. M. Miranda (sop), C. Wirz (alt), U. Reinemann (bar), C. Ivaldi (pno)—K.152, 307, 308, 346, 351, 436–439, 441, 441b, 472, 473, 506, 510, 520, 523, 524, 532, 549, 561, 625, & K.Anh 5 *(rec 1979)* Arion ▲ ARN 68161 [ADD]

Quinn, Gerard (bar)

Verdi, G.:Il trovatore, w. S. Bisatt (sop), D. Hinnells (cnd), European Chamber Opera Orch, European Chamber Chorus ASV 2–▲ ASV 225 [DDD]

Quirke, Saul (trb)

Handel, G.F.:Messiah, w. Margaret Marshall (sop), Catherine Robbin (mez), Charles Brett (ct), Anthony Rolfe Johnson (ten), Robert Hale (b–bar), J. E. Gardiner (cnd), English Baroque Soloists, Monteverdi Choir London [E] Philips 3–▲ 411041–2 [DDD]

Handel, G.F.:Messiah, w. Margaret Marshall (sop), Catherine Robbin (mez), Charles Brett (ct), Anthony Rolfe Johnson (ten), Robert Hale (b–bar), J. E. Gardiner (cnd), English Baroque Soloists, Monteverdi Choir London [E] Philips ▲ 412267–2 [DDD]

Quivar, Florence (cta)

Beethoven, L. van:Missa Solemnis, w. P. Coburn (sop), A. Baldin (ten), A. Schmidt (bar), H. Rilling (cnd), Stuttgart Bach Collegium, Gächinger Kantorei [L] Hänssler Classic 2–▲ CD 98.956 [DDD] 2–■ MC 98.956 (D)

Beethoven, L. van:Sym 9, "Choral Sym", w. Roberta Alexander (sop), Gary Lakes (ten), Paul Plishka (bass), A. Previn (cnd), Royal PO RCA Red Seal ▲ 09026–60363–2

DDD Christmas, w. Kathleen Battle (sop), Taverner Consort, Taverner Choir, Taverner Players, New York Choral Artists, Toronto Mendelssohn Choir, King's Singers, Empire Brass Angel ▲ CDM 63666

Great American Spirtuals, w. Kathleen Battle (sop), Barbara Hendricks (sop) Angel ▲ CDM 64669

Handel, G.F.:Messiah, w. Kathleen Battle (sop), John Aler (ten), Samuel Ramey (bass), A. Davis (cnd), Toronto SO, Mendelssohn Club Chorus Philadelphia [E] EMI Classics 2–▲ CDCB 49027 [DDD]; ■ 4D2S 49027 (D)

Handel, G.F.:Messiah, w. Kathleen Battle (sop), John Aler (ten), Samuel Ramey (bass), A. Davis (cnd), Toronto SO, Mendelssohn Club Chorus Philadelphia [E] EMI Classics ▲ CDC 49407 [DDD]; ■ 4DS 49407 (D)

Mahler, G.:Sym 2, w. Nancy Gustafson (sop), Z. Mehta (cnd), Israel PO, Prague Phil Chorus *(rec Fredric R. Mann Auditorium, Tel Aviv, Jan–Feb. 1994)* Teldec ▲ 94545–2 [DDD]

Mahler, G.:Sym 3, w. Z. Mehta (cnd), Israel PO Sony Classical ▲ S2K 52579

Mahler, G.:Sym 3, w. B. Haitink (cnd), Berlin PO, Ernst Senff Chorus Women's Voices, Tölz Boys' Choir Philips ▲ 432162–2

▲ = CD ♦ = Enhanced CD Δ = MD ■ = Cassette Tape ▯ = DCC

Quivar, Florence (cta) (cont.)

Mendelssohn, F.:Elijah, w. Barbara Bonney (sop), Henriette Schellenberg (sop), Marietta Simpson (mez), Reid Bartelme (trb), Jerry Hadley (ten), Richard Clement (ten), Thomas Hampson (bar), Thomas Paul (bar), R. Shaw (cnd), Atlanta SO, Atlanta Sym Chorus [E] *(rec Symphony Hall, Woodruff Arts Center, Atlanta, GA, Nov. 5-7, 1994)* Telarc 2-▲ CD 80389 [DDD]

Rossini, G.:Stabat Mater, w. Sung-Sook Lee (sop), Kenneth Riegel (ten), Paul Plishka (bass), T. Schippers (cnd), Cincinnati SO, May Festival Chorus *(rec 1975)* Vox Box 2-▲ CDX 5141 [ADD]

Schoenberg, A.:Gurrelieder, w. E. Martón (sop), G. Lakes (ten), H. Hotter (b-bar), Z. Mehta (cnd), New York PO, New York Choral Artists [G] Sony Classical 2-▲ S2K 48077 [DDD]

Sessions, R.:When Lilacs Last in the Dooryard Bloom'd, w. E. Hinds (sop), D. Cossa (bar), S. Ozawa (cnd), Boston SO, Tanglewood Festival Chorus [E] New World ▲ NW 296-2 [AAD]

Stravinsky, I.:Oedipus Rex, w. P. Langridge (ten), D. Kaasch (ten), J. Morris, J.-H. Rootering (bass), J. Bastin (bass), J. Levine (cnd), Chicago SO, Chicago Sym Chorus Deutsche Grammophon ▲ 435872-2

Szymanowski, K.:Litany to the Virgin Mary, w. E. Szmytka (sop), J. Garrison (ten), J. Connell (bass), S. Rattle (cnd), City of Birmingham SO, City of Birmingham Sym Chorus EMI Classics ▲ CDC 55121

Szymanowski, K.:Stabat Mater, w. E. Szmytka (sop), J. Connell (bass), S. Rattle (cnd), City of Birmingham SO, City of Birmingham Sym Chorus EMI Classics ▲ CDC 55121

Verdi, G.:Un ballo in maschera, w. J. Barstow (sop), S. Jo (sop), P. Domingo (ten), L. Nucci (bar), H. von Karajan (cnd), Vienna PO, Vienna State Opera Chorus [I] Deutsche Grammophon 2-▲ 427635-2 [DDD]

Verdi, G.:Luisa Miller, w. A. Millo (sop), P. Domingo (ten), V. Chernov (bar), J. Levine (cnd), Metropolitan Opera Orch, New York Metropolitan Opera Chorus Sony Classical 2-▲ S2K 48073

Verdi, G.:Luisa Miller (sels), w. A. Millo (sop), W. White (mez), P. Domingo (ten), V. Chernov (bar), J.-H. Rootering (bass), P. Plishka (bass), J. Levine (cnd), Metropolitan Opera Orch, New York Metropolitan Opera Chorus *(rec New York, May 2-18, 1991)* Sony Classical ("Opera Highlights" series) ▲ SMK 53508 [DDD]

Verdi, G.:Messa per Rossini, w. G. Benačková-Čápova (sop), J. Wagner (ten), A. Agache (bar), A. Haugland (bass), H. Rilling (cnd), Stuttgart RSO, Gächinger Kantorei, Prague Phil Chorus [L] Hänssler Classic 2-▲ CD 98.949 [DDD] 2-■ MC 96.949 (D)

Verdi, G.:Requiem Mass, w. C. Vaness (sop), D. O'Neill (ten), C. Colombara (bass), C. Davis (cnd), Bavarian RSO, Bavarian Radio Chorus RCA Red Seal 2-▲ 09026-60902-2

Raamat, Helvi (sop)

Tubin, E.:Barbara von Tisenhusen, w. M. Jõgeva (mez), A. Kollo (ten), I. Kuusk (ten), V. Puura (bar), T. Sild (bar), H. Miilberg (bass), U. Kreen (bass), P. Lilje (cnd), Estonia Opera Co Orch [Estonian] Ondine 2-▲ ODE 776-2D [DDD]

Rabiner, Ellen (mez)

Purcell, H.:Dido & Aeneas, w. L. Hunt (sop), L. Saffer (sop), D. Deam (sop), C. Brandes (sop), R. Rainero (sop), P. Elliot (ten), M. Dean (bar), N. McGegan (cnd), Philharmonia Baroque Orch, Clare College Choir Cambridge Harmonia Mundi USA ▲ HMU 907110

Rabsilber, M. (ten)

Berlioz, H.:Lélio, "Le retourà la vie", w. B. Grabowski (bar), H.-P. Minetti (nar), R. Reuter (cnd), Berlin Comic Opera Orch, Berlin Radio Chorus [F; narration G] Berlin Classics ▲ BER 2149 [DDD]

Handel, G.F.:L'Allegro, Il Penseroso ed il Moderato, w. V. Hruba-Freiberger (sop), D. Schellenberger-Ernst (sop), J. Kowalski (alt), F.Kapellmann (bass), R. Reuter (cnd), Berlin Comic Opera Orch, Berlin Radio Chorus Berlin Classics 2-▲ BER 1147 [DDD]

Racewicz, Ryszarda (mez)

Moniuszko, S.:Halka, w. B. Zagòrzanka (sop), W. Ochman (ten), A. Hiolski (bar), J. Ostapuik (bass), R. Satanowski (cnd), Warsaw Teatr Wielki Orch, Warsaw Teatr Wielki Chorus *(rec live, 10/14/86)* CPO 2-▲ CPO 999032-2 [DDD]

Rácz, Istvan (bass)

Franck, C.:Choral Music, w. Mariann Bódi (sop), Attila Wendler (ten), Salomon Kamp (cnd), Debrecen Kodaly Choir—Quae est ista; Dextera Domini Hungaroton ▲ HCD 31579 [DDD]

Radcliffe, Kathryn (sop)

Rich, F.C.:The Hudson Oratorio, w. Rick Hamelin (ten), Harold von Geldern (bar), F.C. Rich (cnd), Juilliard Orch members *(rec Church of the Epiphany, New York City, July 1996)* Albany ▲ TROY 217 [DDD]

Radev, Mariana (mez)

Tchaikovsky, P.:Mazeppa, w. M. Olivero (sop), D. Poleri (ten), E. Bastianini (bar), B. Christoff (bass), J. Perlea (cnd), Florence Maggio Musicale Orch, Florence Maggio Musicale Chorus [I] *(rec live 6/6/54)* Melodram 2-▲ MEL 27070 (m) [AAD]

Verdi, G.:Requiem Mass, w. Maria Stader (sop), Helmut Krebs (ten), Kim Borg (bass), F. Fricsay (cnd), Berlin RIAS SO, Berlin RIAS Chamber Choir, St. Hedwig Cathedral Choir *(rec Jesus-Christus Church, Berlin, Sept 1953)* Deutsche Grammophon ("The Originals" series) ▲ 447442-2 [ADD]

Radnai, György (bar)

Kacsóh, P.:János Vitéz, w. Mária Gyurkovics (sop), Anna Zentai (sop—Iluska), Tivadar Bilicsi (sgr), Hilda Gobbi (sgr), Sándor Pethes (sgr—Bartolo), Róbert Ilosfalvy (ten—Kukorica), György Melis (bar—Bagó), György Radnai (bar—Strázsamester), László Domahidy (bass—Csősz), E. Lukács (cnd), Hungarian State Opera Orch, Hungarian Radio-TV Chorus *(rec Budapest, 1961)* Classical Diamonds 2-▲ CLD 4011-12 [AAD]

Rado, Ruggero (sgr)

Verdi, G.:Un giorno di regno, w. Maria Casula (sop), Angelo Romero (bar), Enrico Fissore (bass), Franca Fabbri (sgr), Michele Guento (sgr), Islen Moubayed (sgr), Bernardino Trotta (sgr), A. Zedda (cnd), *(orch unknown)* Great Opera Performances 2-▲ GOP 782

Rae, C. (sgr)

Weill, K.:The Threepenny Opera, w. L. Lenya (sop), B. Arthur (sgr), *(orch unknown)* [E] Polydor ▲ 820260-2 ■ 820260-4E

Rafael, Nicolae (bass)

Verdi, G.:Rigoletto, w. Victoria Draganescu (sop—Countess Ceprano), Magda Ianculescu (sop—Gilda), Dorothea Palade (mez—Maddalena), Valeria Savu (mez—Giovanna), Ion Buzea (ten—Duke of Mantua), Dimitrie Scurtu (ten—Borsa), Nicolae Herlea (bar—Rigoletto), Stefan Petrescu (bar—Marullo), Jean Banescu (bass—Count Ceprano), Nicolae Florei (bass—Monterone), Nicolae Rafael (bass—Sparafucile), J. Bobescu (cnd), Romanian Opera Orch, Romanian Opera Chorus *(rec 1965)* Vox Box 2-▲ CDX 5162

Verdi, G.:La traviata, w. Elena Simionescu (sop—Annina), Virginia Zeani (sop—Violetta Valery), Elisabeta Neculce-Cartis (mez—Flora Bervoix), Ion Buzea (ten—Alfredo Germont), Vasile Moldoveanu (ten—Gastone/Viconte de Letorieres/Giuseppe), Teodor Panea (ten—Flora's Servant), Constantin Dumitru (bar—Commissioner/Baron Douphol), Nicolae Herlea (bar—Giorgio Germont), Valentin Loghin (bass—Marchese D'Obigny), Nicolae Rafael (bass—Doctor Grenvil), J. Bobescu (cnd), Romanian Opera Orch, Stelian Olariu (cnd), Romanian Opera Chorus *(rec 1968)* Vox Box 2-▲ CDX 5154

Raffalli, Tibère (ten)

Honegger, A.:Le Roi David, w. Christiane Eda-Pierre (sop), Martha Senn (mez), D. Mesguich (nar), A. Gaillard (nar), S. Baudo (cnd), Czech PO, Czech Chorus [F] Supraphon 2-▲ 11 0132 [DDD]

Raffanati, Dano (ten)

Bellini, V.:I Capuleti e i Montecchi (sels), w. Katia Ricciarelli (sop), Diana Montague (mez), B. Campanella (cnd), Venice Teatro La Fenice Orch, Venice Teatro La Fenice Chorus Nuova Era ▲ NUO 7183 [DDD]

Raffanelli, Flora (sop)

Bellini, V.:Il pirata, w. M. Caballé (sop), B. Marti (ten), Baratti, P. Cappuccilli (bar), R. Raimondi (bass), G. Gavazzeni (cnd), Rome Radio-TV Orch, Rome Radio-TV Chorus [I] *(rec Rome, 1973)* EMI Classics 2-▲ CDMB 64169

Bellini, V.:Il pirata, w. M. Caballè (sop), G. Baratti (ten), F. Labò (ten), P. Cappuccilli (bar), U. Trama (bass), E. Ghiglia (cnd), *(orch unknown)* *(rec Florence, 1967)* Great Opera Performances ▲ GOP 729

Bellini, V.:Il pirata, w. Montserrat Caballé (sop—Imogene), Flora Raffanelli (sop—Adele), Flaviano Labó (ten—Gualtiero), Giuseppe Baratti (ten—Itulbo), Piero Cappuccilli (bar—Ernesto), E. Ghiglia (cnd), Florence Teatro Comunale Orch, Florence Teatro Comunale Chorus *(rec live, Florence, 1967)* Melodram 2-▲ IMC 205002 [ADD]

Raffanelli, Flora (sop) (cont.)

Bellini, V.:I Puritani, w. C. Deutekom (sop), N. Gedda (ten), S. Bruscantini (b-bar), A. Ferrin (bass), G. del Vivo (bass), R. Muti (cnd), *(orch unknown)* *(rec 1970)* Great Opera Performances ▲ GOP 735

Raffanti, Dano (ten)

Bellini, V.:I Capuleti e i Montecchi, w. E. Guberova (sop—Giulietta), A. Baltsa (mez—Romeo), D. Raffanti (ten—Tebaldo), R. Muti (cnd), Royal Opera House Orch, Royal Opera House Chorus Covent Garden EMI Classics ▲ CDMB 64846

Bellini, V.:I Capuleti e i Montecchi, w. K. Ricciarelli (sop), D. Montague (mez), M. Lippi (bass), B. Campanella (cnd), Venice Teatro La Fenice Orch, Venice Teatro La Fenice Chorus [I] *(rec 1991)* Nuova Era 2-▲ 7020/21 [DDD]

Rossini, G.:La donna del lago, w. K. Ricciarelli (sop), L. V. Terrani (mez), S. Ramey (bass), M. Pollini (cnd), CO of Europe, Prague Phil Chorus [I] CBS 2-▲ M2K 39311 [DDD]

Rossini, G.:The Siege of Corinth, w. L. Serra (sop), M. Comencini (ten), A. Caforio (bass), M. Lippi (bass), P. Olmi (cnd), Genoa Teatro Carlo Felice Orch, Genoa Teatro Carlo Felice Chorus, Prague Phil Choir *(rec June 2 & 14, 1992)* Nuova Era 3-▲ 7140/42 [DDD]

Raffeiner, Walter (ten)

Strauss, R.:Salome, w. J. Norman (sop), K. Witt (mez), A. Markert (cta), R. Leech (ten), J. Morris (bass), S. Ozawa (cnd), Dresden Staatskapelle Philips 2-▲ 432153-2

Wagner, S.:Schwarzschwanenreich, w. Beth Johanning (sop—Linda), Kerstin Quandt (cta—Ursula), Walter Raffeiner (ten—Ludwig), Lucian Chioreanu (ten—A Boy), André Wenhold (bar—Oswald), Roland Hartmann (sgr—Tempter/Priest), Jutta Maria Schmitz (sgr—Ash-Woman), Ksenija Lukie (sgr—A Girl), K. Bach (cnd), Thüringian Saalfeld-Rudolstadt SO, Thüringian Landestheater Rudolstadt Chorus *(rec Thüringer Landestheater, Rudolstadt, June 1994)* Marco Polo 2-▲ 8.223777-8 [DDD]

Raffin, Deborah (nar)

Saint-Saëns, C.:Carnival of the Animals, w. M. Golabek (nar), R. Golabek (nar), F. Savage (nar), C. Heston (nar), J. E. Jones (nar), B. White (nar), L. Redgrave (nar), W. Shatner (nar), J. Rivers (nar), T. Danson (nar), L. Tomlin (nar), A. Hepburn (nar), D. Moore (nar), W. Matthau (nar), J. Smith (nar), L. Schifrin (cnd), Hollywood CO Dove Audio ▲ DOV 30700

Raftery, Patrick (ten)

Spontini, G.:La vestale, w. Karen Huffstodt (sop—Julie), Denyce Graves (mez—La Grande Vestale), Patrick Raftery (ten—Cinna), Anthony Michaels-Moore (bar—Licinius), R. Muti (cnd), La Scala Orch, La Scala Chorus Sony Classical 3-▲ S3K 66357

Ragains (sop)

Peck, R.:Automobile, w. Middleton (fl), Calvetti (db), Johnson (perc) CRI ■ C 367

Ragatzu, Rosella (sop)

Franchetti, A.:Cristoforo Colombo, w. R. Ragatzu (sop—Isabella), G. Pasino (mez—Annacoana), M. Berti (ten—Ferdinand), R. Bruson (bar—Cristoforo Colombo), R. Scandiuzzi (bass—Don Roldano Ximenes), M. Viotti (cnd), Frankfurt RSO, Frankfurt Radio Chorus [I] *(rec live, Alte Oper Frankfurt, 8/30 & 9/2 1991)* Koch Schwann 3-▲ CD 3-1030-2 [DDD]

Ragin, Derek Lee (ct)

Bernstein, L.:Missa brevis, w. R. Shaw (cnd), Atlanta SO, Atlanta Sym Chorus [L] Telarc ▲ CD 80181 [DDD]

Broschi, R.:Arias, w. Ewa Mallas-Godlewska (sop), C. Rousset (cnd), Les Talens Lyriques—Son qual nave ch'agitata; Se al labbro mio non credi; Ombra fedele anch'io *(rec Metz, France, July 1993)* Travelling ▲ K 1005 △ K 81005; ■ K 51005

Broschi, R.:Arias, w. Ewa Mallas-Godlewska (sop), C. Rousset (cnd), Les Talens Lyriques—Son qual nave ch'agitata; Se al labbro mio non credi; Ombra fedele anch'io Astrée ▲ E 8552 [DDD]

Ev'ry Time I Feel the Spirit:Spirituals, w. Moses Hogan (pno), New World Ensemble, Chamber Choir New Orleans, Moses Hogan (cnd) Channel Classics ▲ CCS 2991 [DDD]

Gluck, C.W.:Orfeo ed Euridice, w. S. McNair (sop), C. Sieden (sop), J. E. Gardiner (cnd), English Baroque Soloists, Monteverdi Choir London Philips ▲ 434093-2

Handel, G.F.:Arias, w. E. Mallas-Godlewska (sop), C. Rousset (cnd), Les Talens Lyriques—Handel Lascia ch'io pianga; Cara sposa *(rec Metz, France, July 1993)* Travelling ▲ K 1005 △ K 81005; ■ K 51005

Handel, G.F.:Cants, w. Cologne Divitia Ensemble—4 cantatas—"Careo sempre di gloria"; "Lungi da me pensier tiranno"; Siete rose ruggiadose"; "Udite il mio consiglio" [I] Channel Classics ▲ CCS 0890 [DDD]

Handel, G.F.:Giulio Cesare in Egitto, w. Barbara Schlick (sop), Jennifer Larmore (mez), Marianne Rørholm (mez), Bernarda Fink (cta), Dominique Visse (ct), Oliver Lallouette (bass), Furio Zanasi (bass), R. Jacobs (cnd), Concerto Cologne [period instrs] Harmonia Mundi France 3-▲ HMC 901385/87

Handel, G.F.:Giulio Cesare in Egitto (sels), w. Barbara Schlick (sop), Jennifer Larmore (mez), Marianne Rørholm (mez), Bernarda Fink (cta), R. Jacobs (cnd), Concerto Cologne Harmonia Mundi France ▲ HMC 901458

Handel, G.F.:Saul, w. D. Brown (sop), L. Dawson (sop), J. M. Ainsley (ten), A. Miles (bar), J. E. Gardiner (cnd), English Baroque Soloists, Monteverdi Choir London Philips 3-▲ 426265-2 3PH [DDD]

Handel, G.F.:Teseo, w. Eirian James (mez), Della Jones (mez), M. Minkowski (cnd), Louvre Musicians Erato 2-▲ 2292-45806-2 ZA

Hasse, J.A.:Arias, w. Ewa Mallas-Godlewska (sop), C. Rousset (cnd), Les Talens Lyriques—Generoso risvegliati o core *(rec Metz, France, July 1993)* Travelling ▲ K 1005 △ K 81005; ■ K 51005

Hasse, J.A.:Cleofide, w. Emma Kirkby (sop), Agnès Mellon (sop), Randall Wong (ct), Dominique Visse (ct), David Cordier (alt), W. Christie (cnd), Cappella Coloniensis [I] Capriccio 4-▲ 10193/96 [DDD]

Italian Lute Songs, w. Peter Croton (lt) Channel Classics ▲ CCS 4092 [DDD]

Pergolesi, G.B.:Salve regina in a, w. Ewa Mallas-Godlewska (sop), C. Rousset (cnd), Les Talens Lyriques *(rec Metz, France, July 1993)* Travelling ▲ K 1005; △ K 81005; ■ K 51005;

Porpora, N.A.:Arias, w. Ewa Mallas-Godlewska (sop), C. Rousset (cnd), Les Talens Lyriques *(rec Metz, France, July 1993)* Travelling ▲ K 1005; △ K 81005; ■ K 51005;

Ragon, Gilles (ten)

Berlioz, H.:L'Enfance du Christ (sels), w. Mariette Kemmer (sop), Claire Brua (mez), Nicolas Cavallier (bass), F. Quattrocchi (cnd), Lorraine PO—Toujours ce rêve *(rec June 1994)* Maguelone ▲ 350.509 [DDD]

Campra, A.:Messe de Requiem, w. D. Visse (ct), P. Harvey (bar), J. Malgoire (cnd), La Grande Écurie et la Chambre du Roy, Les Pages de la Chapelle *(rec Nov. 4-6, 1992)* FNAC Music ▲ 592223 [DDD]

Campra, A.:Misere, w. D. Visse (ct), P. Harvey (bar), J. Malgoire (cnd), La Grande Écurie et la Chambre du Roy, Les Pages de la Chapelle *(rec Nov. 4-6, 1992)* FNAC Music ▲ 592223 [DDD]

Charpentier, M.-A.:In honorem Sancti Xaverii canticum, w. E. Baudry (sop), C. Dune (sop), P. Colléaux (cnd), Stradivaria Ensemble, Nantes Vocal Ensemble [L] Arion ▲ ARN 68037 [DDD]

Charpentier, M.-A.:Judicum Salomonis, w. A. Zaepffel (ct), J. Benet (ten), Elwes (ten), J. Cabré (bar), G. Reinhart (bar), P. Colléaux (cnd), Stradivaria Ensemble, Nantes Vocal Ensemble [L] Arion ▲ ARN 68037 [DDD]

Charpentier, M.-A.:Messe de minuit pour Noël, w. E. Lestringant (ten), J.-L. Bindi (bass), Piniec (sgr), P. Colléaux (cnd), Nantes Instrumental Ensemble [L] Arion ▲ ARN 68015 [AAD]

Clérambault, L.N.:Cants, w. I. Poulenard (sop), Amalia Ensemble—Léandre et Héro (1713); Pirame et Tisbé (1713); L'Isle de Délos (1716); Apollon et Doris (1720) [F] *(rec 1/91)* Opus 111 ▲ OPS 39-9103 [DDD]

Gluck, C.W.:Alceste (sels), w. Mariette Kemmer (sop), Claire Brua (mez), Nicolas Cavallier (bass), F. Quattrocchi (cnd), Lorraine PO—Vivre sans toi *(rec June 1994)* Maguelone ▲ 350.509 [DDD]

Gounod, C.:Faust (sels), w. Mariette Kemmer (sop), Claire Brua (mez), Nicolas Cavallier (bass), F. Quattrocchi (cnd), Lorraine PO—Faites lui mes aveux; La coupe du Roi de Thulé; Air des Bijoux *(rec June 1994)* Maguelone ▲ 350.509 [DDD]

Grétry, A.-E.-M.:La Caravane du Caire, w. I. Poulenard (sop), G. de Reyghere (sop), G. de Mey (ten), P. Huttenlocher (bar), V. Le Téxier (bar), J. Bastin (bass), M. Minkowski (cnd), Ricercar Academy, Ricercar Academy Chorus [period instrs] [F] Ricercar 2-▲ RIC 100084/85 [DDD]

Lully, J.-B.:Armide, w. V. Gens (sop), N. Rime (sop), G. Laurens (mez), H. Crook (ten), P. Herreweghe (cnd), La Chapelle Royale Orch, Collegium Vocale [F] Harmonia Mundi France 2-▲ HMC 901456/57

Mozart, W.A.:Così fan tutte (sels), w. Mariette Kemmer (sop), Claire Brua (mez), Nicolas Cavallier (bass), F. Quattrocchi (cnd), Lorraine PO—Come scoglio *(rec June 1994)* Maguelone ▲ 350.509 [DDD]

Ragon, Gilles (ten) (cont.)
Mozart, W.A.:Nozze di Figaro (sels), w. Mariette Kemmer (sop), Claire Brua (mez), Nicolas Cavallier (bass), F. Quattrocchi (cnd), Lorraine PO—Ov; Voi che Sapete *(rec June 1994)*
Maguelone ▲ 350.509 [DDD]
Rameau, J.P.:Platée, w. J. Smith (sop), G. de Mey (ten), M. Minkowski (cnd), Louvre Musicians, Françoise Herr Vocal Ensemble [F] Erato ("Musifrance" series) 2-▲ 2292-45028-2 [DDD]
Rossini, G.:Le Comte Ory (sels), w. Mariette Kemmer (sop), Claire Brua (mez), Nicolas Cavallier (bass), F. Quattrocchi (cnd), Lorraine PO—Ov; Que les destins prospères *(rec June 1994)*
Maguelone ▲ 350.509 [DDD]

Raimondi, Gianni (ten)
Debussy, C.:Pelléas et Mélisande, w. N. Denize (mez), F. von Stade (mez), R. Stilwell (bar), J. Van Dam (bass-bar), H. von Karajan (cnd), Berlin PO, German Opera Chorus [F]
EMI Classics 3-▲ CDCC 49350 [ADD]
Donizetti, G.:Anna Bolena, w. M. Callas (sop—Anna Bolena), G. Simionato (mez—Giovanna), G. Raimondi (ten—Percy), N. Rossi-Lemeni (bass—King), G. Gavazzeni (cnd), La Scala Orch, La Scala Chorus [I] *(rec live, Milan 4/14/57)* Verona 2-▲ 27090/91
Donizetti, G.:Anna Bolena, w. M. Callas (sop), G. Simionato (mez), G. Gavazzeni (cnd), La Scala Orch, La Scala Chorus [I] *(rec live, 4/17/57)* Melodram 2-▲ MEL 26010
Donizetti, G.:Anna Bolena, w. Maria Callas (sop), Gabriella Carturan (mez), Giulietta Simionato (mez), Plinio Clabassi (bass), Nicola Rossi Lemmeni (sgr), Luigi Rumo (sgr), G. Gavazzeni (cnd), La Scala Orch, La Scala Chorus Great Opera Performances 2-▲ GOP 768
Donizetti, G.:La favorita, w. S. Zanolli (sop), G. Simionato (mez), M. Zanasi (bar), N. Zaccaria (bass), F. Previtali (cnd), Naples Teatro San Carlo Orch, Naples Teatro San Carlo Chorus [I] *(rec live, Naples 5/12/63)* Golden Age of Opera 2-▲ GAO 105/06 [ADD]
Donizetti, G.:Lucia di Lammermoor, w. M. Callas (sop), R. Panerai (bar), A. Zerbini (bass), F. Molinari-Pradelli (cnd), Naples Teatro San Carlo Orch, Naples Teatro San Carlo Chorus [I] *(rec live, 3/22/56)* Myto ▲ 2 MCD 90319 (m) [ADD]
Donizetti, G.:Lucia di Lammermoor (sels), w. M. Callas (sop), *(orch unknown)* [I] *(rec live, 3/24/56)*
Myto ▲ 2 MCD 90319 (m) [ADD]
Donizetti, G.:Lucrezia Borgia, w. M. Caballé (sop), A. M. Rota (cta), E. Flagello (bass), E. Gracis (cnd), La Scala Orch, La Scala Chorus [I] *(rec live, 3/2/70)* Myto 2-▲ 2 MCD 90423 [ADD]
Donizetti, G.:Lucrezia Borgia (sels), w. L. Gencer (sop), L. Roni (bass-bar), E. Gracis (cnd), La Scala Orch, La Scala Chorus—8 scenes & arias [I] *(rec live, 3/12/70)* Myto 2-▲ 2 MCD 90423 [ADD]
Donizetti, G.:Roberto Devereux, w. Montserrat Caballé (sop), Beverly Wolff (mez), Guido Fabbris (ten), Walter Alberti (bar), Paolo Badoer (sgr), Carlo Micalucci (sgr), Carlo Padoan (sgr), B. Bartoletti (cnd), Venice Teatro La Fenice Orch, Venice Teatro La Fenice Chorus
Great Opera Performances 2-▲ GOP 764
Gounod, C.:Faust, w. M. Freni (sop), N. Ghiaurov (bass), G. Prêtre (cnd), La Scala Orch, La Scala Chorus *(rec live 1967)* Melodram 3-▲ MEL 37005
Maria Callas & Gianni Raimondi, w. Maria Callas (sop), Milan RAI SO, Milan RAI Chorus [cnd:A. Simonetto] *(rec Milan, Nov. 19, 1956)*
Incontri memorabili ("Martini & Rossi Concert" series) ▲ CDMR 5007 [ADD]
Meyerbeer, G.:L'Africaine (sels), w. A. Simonetto (cnd), Milan Italian Radio-TV Orch, Milan Italian Radio-TV Chorus—O Pardiso Fonit Cetra ("Martini & Rossi" series) ▲ FCT CDMR 5007
Mozart, W.A.:Don Giovanni, w. E. Moser (sop), K. Te Kanawa (sop), T. Berganza (mez), K. Riegel (ten), J. Van Dam (b-bar), J. Macurdy (bass), L. Maazel (cnd), Paris Opera Orch, Paris Opera Chorus [I]
CBS 3-▲ M3K 35192
Mozart, W.A.:Don Giovanni (sels), w. E. Moser (sop), K. Te Kanawa (sop), T. Berganza (mez), K. Riegel (ten), J. Van Dam (b-bar), J. Macurdy (bass), L. Maazel (cnd), Paris Opera Orch CBS ■ MT 35859
Mozart, W.A.:Nozze di Figaro, w. L. Popp (sop), B. Hendricks (sop), A. Baltsa (mez), J. Van Dam (bar), N. Marriner (cnd), Academy of St. Martin in the Fields, Ambrosian Opera Chorus [I]
Philips 3-▲ 416370-2 [DDD]
Mozart, W.A.:Nozze di Figaro (sels), w. L. Popp (sop), B. Hendricks (sop), A. Baltsa (mez), J. van Dam (b-bar), N. Marriner (cnd), Academy of St. Martin in the Fields, Ambrosian Opera Chorus [I]
Philips ▲ 416870-2 [DDD]
Mussorgsky, M.:Boris Godunov, w. G. Vishnevskaya (sop), N. Gedda (ten), M. Rostropovich (cnd), National SO Washington D.C., Washington Oratorio Society, Choral Arts Society [R]
Erato 3-▲ 2292-45418-2 ZB [DDD]
Ponchielli, A.:La Gioconda, w. Leyla Gencer (sop), Anna di Stasio (mez), Ruggero Raimondi (bass), B. Bartoletti (cnd), Rome Opera Orch, Rome Opera Chorus Melodram 3-▲ CDM 37092
Public Performances, 1953–71 *(rec 1953-1971)*
Memories ("Great Voices" series) ▲ MEM 4574 [ADD]
Puccini, G.:La Bohème, w. M. Freni (sop), H. Gueden (sop), G. Taddei (bar), H. von Karajan (cnd), Vienna State Opera Orch, Vienna State Opera Chorus [I] *(rec live 11/30/63)*
Melodram 2-▲ MELCD 27007
Puccini, G.:La Bohème (sels), w. M. Freni (sop), H. Gueden (sop), R. Panerai (bar), H. von Karajan (cnd), Vienna State Opera Orch—7 arias & scenes [I] *(rec live 11/9/63)* Verona 2-▲ 27079/80
Puccini, G.:Madama Butterfly, w. R. Tebaldi (sop), A. di Stasio (mez), G. Valdengo (bar), A. Questa (cnd), *(orch & chorus unknown)* [I] *(rec live, Arena Flegrea, Naples 8/9/58)*
Standing Room Only 2-▲ SRO 825-2 [ADD]
Rossini, G.:Armida, w. L. Albanese (sop), M. Callas (sop), M. Filippeschi (ten), T. Serafin (cnd), Florence Teatro Comunale Orch, Florence Teatro Comunale Chorus [I] *(rec live, Florence, 4/26/52)*
Melodram 2-▲ MEL 26024
Thomas, A.:Mignon (sels), w. A. Simonetto (cnd), Milan Italian Radio-TV Orch, Milan Italian Radio-TV Chorus—Ah! Non Credevi Tu Fonit Cetra ("Martini & Rossi" series) ▲ FCT CDMR 5007
Verdi, G.:Aida, w. L. Freni (sop), K. Ricciarelli (sop), A. Baltsa (mez), J. Carreras (ten), P. Cappuccilli (bar), J. Van Dam (b-bar), H. von Karajan (cnd), Vienna PO, Vienna State Opera Chorus [I]
EMI Classics (Studio) 3-▲ CDMC 69300 [ADD]
Verdi, G.:Attila, w. C. Deutekom (sop), C. Bergonzi (ten), S. Milnes (bar), L. Gardelli (cnd), Royal PO, Ambrosian Singers Philips 2-▲ 426115-2
Verdi, G.:I lombardi alla prima crociata, w. C. Deutekom (sop), D. Malvisi (sop), M. Aparici (sop), P. Domingo (ten), M. Lo Monaco (ten), M. Dean (b-bar), C. Grant (bass), L. Gardelli (cnd), Royal PO, Ambrosian Singers Philips 2-▲ 422420-2 [ADD]
Verdi, G.:Luisa Miller (sels), w. A. Simonetto (cnd), Milan Italian Radio-TV Orch, Milan Italian Radio-TV Chorus—Quando le Sere al Placido Fonit Cetra ("Martini & Rossi" series) ▲ FCT CDMR 5007
Verdi, G.:I masnadieri, w. I. Ligabue (sop), R. Bruson (bar), B. Christoff (bass), G. Gavazzeni (cnd), Rome Opera Orch, Rome Opera Chorus [I] *(rec live, Rome, Nov. 25, 1972)*
Golden Age of Opera 2-▲ GAO 135/36 [ADD]
Verdi, G.:Nabucco, w. Gloria Lane (mez), Giangiacomo Guelfi (bar), Nicolai Ghiaurov (bass), Elena Saliotis (sgr), G. Gavazzeni (cnd), La Scala Orch, La Scala Chorus *(rec La Scala Theater, Milan, Dec. 7, 1966)* Pantheon 2-▲ PHE 6757 (m)
Verdi, G.:La traviata, w. V. Zeani (sop), U. Savarese (bar), A. Questa (cnd), Naples Teatro San Carlo Orch, Naples Teatro San Carlo Chorus [I] *(rec live, Naples 8/11/57)*
Golden Age of Opera 2-▲ GAO 103/04 [ADD]
Verdi, G.:La traviata, w. Renata Scotto (sop—Violetta Valery), Giuliana Tavolaccini (sop—Flora Bervoix), Gianni Raimondi (ten—Alfredo Germont), Ettore Bastianini (bar—Giorgio Germont), A. Votto (cnd), La Scala Orch, La Scala Chorus *(rec La Scala Theatre, Milan, 1963)*
Deutsche Grammophon 2-▲ 439720-2 [ADD]
Verdi, G.:La traviata, w. M. Callas (sop), A. Zanolli (sop), L. Mandelli (sop), E. Bastianini (bar), C. M. Giulini (cnd), La Scala Orch, La Scala Chorus *(rec live 1/19/56)* Myto 2-▲ MCD 89003 (m) [ADD]
Verdi, G.:La traviata (sels), w. R. Scotto (sop), G. Tavolccini (sop), A. Bonato (sop), E. Bastianini (bar), A. Votto (cnd), La Scala Orch, La Scala Chorus IMP Collectors Series ▲ IMPX 9025 [AAD]
Verdi, G.:I vespri siciliani, w. R. Scotto (sop), P. Cappuccilli (bar), R. Raimondi (bass), G. Gavazzeni (cnd), La Scala Orch, La Scala Chorus [I] *(rec live, 12/4/70 [Acts 1–3], 12/10)*
Myto 2-▲ 2 MCD 90524 [ADD]

Raimondi, Ruggero (bass)
Bellini, V.:Norma, w. M. Caballé (sop), F. Cossotto (mez), P. Domingo (ten), C.F. Cillario (cnd), London PO, Ambrosian Opera Chorus [I] RCA Gold Seal 3-▲ 6502-2-RG [ADD]

Raimondi, Ruggero (bass) (cont.)
Bellini, V.:Il pirata, w. M. Caballé (sop), F. Rafanelli (sop), B. Marti (ten), G. Baratti (ten), P. Cappuccilli (bar), G. Gavazzeni (cnd), Rome Radio-TV Orch, Rome Radio-TV Chorus [I] *(rec Rome, 1973)*
EMI Classics 2-▲ CDMB 64169
Bellini, V.:I Puritani, w. A. Maliponte (sop—Elvira), A. di Stasio (sop—Enrichetta di Francia), A. Kraus (ten—Lord Arturo Talbo), A. Pedroni (ten—Bruno Roberton), P. Cappuccilli (bar—Sir Riccardo Forth), R. Raimondi (bass—Sir Giorgio), G. Gavazzeni (cnd), Catania Teatro Massimo Bellini Orch, Catania Teatro Massimo Bellini Chorus *(rec Feb. 6, 1972)* Ornamenti 2-▲ FE 107 [ADD]
Bellini, V.:I Puritani (sels), w. Gabriella Tucci (sop—Elvira), Vittorina Magnaghi (mez—Enrichetta di Francia), Luciano Pavarotti (ten—Lord Arturo Talbo), Aldo Protti (bar—Sir Riccardo Forth), Ruggero Raimondi (bass—Sir Giorgio), A. Quadri (cnd), Vincenzo Bellini Theater Orch, Catania Teatro Massimo Bellini Chorus Budget ("The Greatest Voice in Opera" series) ▲ SYP 106
Bellini, V.:I Puritani (sels), w. G. Tucci (sop), L. Pavarotti (ten), A. Protti (bar), A. Quadri (cnd), Catania Teatro Massimo Bellini Orch, Catania Teatro Massimo Bellini Chorus [I] *(rec live, Catania 3/22/68)*
Melodram ▲ MEL 15001
Bellini, V.:I Puritani (sels), w. G. Tucci (sop), L. Pavarotti (ten), A. Protti (bar), A. Quadri (cnd), Catania Teatro Massimo Bellini Orch, Catania Teatro Massimo Bellini Chorus [I] *(rec live, Catania 3/22/68)*
Verona 3-▲ 27029/31
Bizet, G.:Carmen, w. F. Esham (sop), J. Migenes-Johnson (sop), P. Domingo (ten), L. Maazel (cnd), French National Orch, French Radio Chorus [F] Erato 3-▲ 2292-45207-2 ZB [DDD]
Bizet, G.:Carmen, w. F. Esham (sop), J. Migenes-Johnson (sop), P. Domingo (ten), L. Maazel (cnd), French National Orch [F] Erato ▲ 2292-45209-2 AW [DDD] ■ 2292-45209-4 AG (D)
Cecilia Gasdia, Leo Nucci & Ruggero Raimondi:In Concerto, w. Cecilia Gasdia (sop), Leo Nucci (bar)
Bongiovanni ▲ GB 2516-2
Donizetti, G.:La favorita (sels), w. M. Zotti (sop), F. Cossotto (mez), A. Kraus (ten), O. de Fabritiis (cnd), NHK SO *(rec Sept. 13, 1971)* Myto 2-▲ MCD 93276
Gounod, C.:Faust, w. Renata Scotto (sop—Margherita), Anna di Stasio (mez—Marta), Flaviano Labò (ten—Faust), Edoardo Gimenez (ten—Siebel), Piero Cappuccilli (bar—Valentino), Bruno Grella (bar—Wagner), Ruggero Raimondi (bass—Mefistofele), M. Gusella (cnd), Margherita Theater Orch, Margherita Theater Chorus *(rec Genova, 1970)* Golden Age of Opera 2-▲ GAO 170/71 [ADD]
Mozart, W.A.:Don Giovanni (sels), w. Kiri Te Kanawa (sop), Teresa Berganza (mez), José Van Dam (bass-bar), L. Maazel (cnd), Paris Opera Orch, Paris Opera Chorus
Sony Classical ("Essential Classics" series) ▲ SBK 62663 ■ SBT 62663
Ponchielli, A.:La Gioconda, w. Leyla Gencer (sop), Anna di Stasio (mez), Gianni Raimondi (ten), B. Bartoletti (cnd), Rome Opera Orch, Rome Opera Chorus Melodram 3-▲ CDM 37092
Puccini, G.:La Bohème, w. M. Caballé (sop), J. Blegen (sop), P. Domingo (ten), S. Milnes (bar), G. Solti (cnd), London PO, John Alldis Choir [I] RCA Red Seal 2-▲ RCD2-0371 2-■ ARK2-0371
Puccini, G.:Tosca, w. K. Ricciarelli (sop), J. Carreras (ten), H. von Karajan (cnd), Berlin PO, German Opera Chorus [I] Deutsche Grammophon 2-▲ 413815-2 [ADD]
Puccini, G.:Turandot, w. K. Ricciarelli (sop), B. Hendricks (sop), P. Domingo (ten), H. von Karajan (cnd), Vienna PO, Vienna State Opera Chorus [I] Deutsche Grammophon 2-▲ 423855-2 [DDD]
Puccini, G.:Turandot (sels), w. K. Ricciarelli (sop), B. Hendricks (sop), P. Domingo (ten), H. von Karajan (cnd), Vienna PO, Vienna State Opera Chorus [I] Deutsche Grammophon ▲ 435409-2 [DDD]
Rossini, G.:Il barbiere di Siviglia, w. K. Battle (sop), P. Domingo (ten), F. Lopardo (ten), L. Gallo (bar), C. Abbado (cnd), CO of Europe [I] Deutsche Grammophon 2-▲ 435763-2
Rossini, G.:Il barbiere di Siviglia, w. Beverly Sills (sop), Fedora Barbieri (mez), Nicolai Gedda (ten), Renato Capecchi (bar), Sherill Milnes (bar), J. Levine (cnd), London SO, John Alldis Choir
EMI Classics 2-▲ CDMB 66040
Rossini, G.:La Cenerentola, w. C. Malone (sop), F. Palmer (sop), A. Baltsa (mez), F. Araiza (ten), S. Alaimo (bar), J. del Carlo (bass), N. Marriner (cnd), Academy of St. Martin in the Fields, Ambrosian Chorus Philips ("Digital Classics" series) 3-▲ 420468-2 [DDD]
Rossini, G.:L'italiana in Algeri, w. A. Baltsa (mez), F. Lopardo (ten), E. Dara (bar), C. Abbado (cnd), Vienna PO, Vienna State Opera Chorus [I] Deutsche Grammophon 2-▲ 427331-2 [DDD]
Rossini, G.:Mosè in Egitto, w. J. Anderson (sop), S. Nimsgern (b-bar), C. Scimone (cnd), Philharmonia Orch, Ambrosian Opera Chorus [I] Philips 2-▲ 420109-2 [ADD]
Verdi, G.:Aida, w. L. Price (sop), G. Bumbry (mez), P. Domingo (ten), S. Milnes (bar), E. Leinsdorf (cnd), London SO [I] RCA Red Seal 3-▲ 6198-2-RC [ADD] 3-■ ARK3-2541
Verdi, G.:Aida, w. L. Price (sop), G. Bumbry (mez), P. Domingo (ten), S. Milnes (bar), E. Leinsdorf (cnd), London SO [I] RCA ■ RK 1237
Verdi, G.:Attila, w. Antonietta Stella (sop), Gianfranco Cecchele (ten), Giangiacomo Guelfi (bar), R. Muti (cnd), Rome RAI Orch, Rome RAI Chorus *(rec live 1970)* Memories 2-▲ HR 4178/79 (m)
Verdi, G.:Attila, w. Antonietta Stella (sop), Gianfranco Cecchele (ten), Giangiacomo Guelfi (bar), R. Muti (cnd), Rome RAI SO, Rome RAI Chorus *(rec Rome, Nov. 21, 1970)* Pantheon 2-▲ PHE 6642 (m)
Verdi, G.:Ernani, w. I. Ligabue (sop), F. Corelli (ten), P. Cappuccilli (bar), O. de Fabritiis (cnd), Arena di Verona Orch, Arena di Verona Chorus *(rec live, Verona 7/15/72)*
Golden Age of Opera 2-▲ GAO 131/32 [ADD]
Verdi, G.:Ernani, w. Licia Galvano (sop—Giovanna), Leyla Gencer (sop—Elvira), Carlo Bergonzi (ten—Ernani), Nino Valori (ten—Don Riccardo), Piero Cappuccilli (bar—Don Carlo), Alessandro Cassis (bar—Jago), Ruggero Raimondi (bass—Don Ruy Gomez de Silva), G. Gavazzeni (cnd), Catania Teatro Massimo Bellini Orch, Catania Teatro Massimo Bellini Chorus *(rec live, Catania, Jan 15, 1972)*
Arkadia 2-▲ 621 [ADD]
Verdi, G.:I lombardi alla prima crociata, w. R. Scotto (sop), L. Pavarotti (ten), G. Gavazzeni (cnd), Rome Opera Orch, Rome Opera Chorus [I] *(rec live, Rome, 11/20/69)*
Memories 2-▲ HR 4337/38 [ADD]
Verdi, G.:Requiem Mass, w. C. Studer (sop), M. Lopivšek (cta), J. Carreras (ten), C. Abbado (cnd), Vienna PO, Vienna State Opera Chorus Deutsche Grammophon 2-▲ 435884-2
Verdi, G.:quattro pezzi sacri, w. C. Studer (sop), M. Lopivšek (cta), J. Carreras (ten), C. Abbado (cnd), Vienna PO, Vienna State Opera Chorus Deutsche Grammophon 2-▲ 435884-2
Verdi, G.:I vespri siciliani, w. R. Scotto (sop), G. Raimondi (ten), P. Cappuccilli (bar), G. Gavazzeni (cnd), La Scala Orch, La Scala Chorus [I] *(rec live, 12/4/70 [Acts 1–3], 12/10)*
Myto 2-▲ 2 MCD 90524 [ADD]

Rainero, Ruth (sop)
Purcell, H.:Dido & Aeneas, w. L. Hunt (sop), L. Saffer (sop), D. Deam (sop), C. Brandes (sop), E. Rabiner (mez), P. Elliot (ten), M. Dean (bar), N. McGegan (cnd), Philharmonia Baroque Orch, Clare College Choir Cambridge Harmonia Mundi USA ▲ HMU 907110

Rains, Claude (nar)
Strauss, R.:Enoch Arden, w. G. Gould (pno) *(rec 1961)*
Sony Classical ("Glenn Gould Edition" series) 2-▲ SM2K 52657 [ADD]

Raitt, John (sgr)
Berlin, I.:Annie Get Your Gun, w. M. Martin (sgr) *(rec 1957 TV broadcast)*
Broadway Angel ▲ ZDM 64765 ■ EG 64765
Kern, J.:Show Boat, w. B. Cook (sop), *(other artists unknown)* [1962 studio cast]
Columbia ▲ CK 02220 ■ JST 02220
Rodgers, R.:Carousel, w. J. Clayton (sgr), J. Darling (sgr), C. Johnson (sgr), E. Mattson (sgr), M. Vye (sgr), C. Baxter (sgr), J. Littau (cnd) [1945 cast]
MCA Classics ▲ MCAD 10048 [AAD] ■ MCAC 10048
Rodgers, R.:Music of, w. Y. Brynner (sgr)—The Sound of Music; Oklahoma!; The King & I; Carousel
RCA 4-▲ 60569-2 RG 4-■ 60569-4 RG

Ralf, Torsten (ten)
Beethoven, L. van:Fidelio, w. H. Konetzni (sop), I. Seefried (sop), P. Klein (ten), P. Schöffler (b-bar), H. Alsen (bass), K. Böhm (cnd), Vienna State Opera Orch, Vienna State Opera Chorus *(rec Feb. 1944)*
Preiser 2-▲ PRE 90195 [AAD]
Bizet, G.:Carmen, w. E. Weidlich (sop), E. Höngen (cta), J. Herrmann (bar), K. Böhme (bass), K. Böhm (cnd), Dresden State Opera Orch, Dresden State Opera Chorus *(rec Dec. 4 & 5, 1942)*
Preiser 2-▲ 90152 (m)
Torsten Ralf *(rec between 1938 & 1943)* Preiser ▲ PRE 89077 [AAD]
Verdi, G.:Otello, w. Hilde Konetzni (sop), Elena Nikolaidi (cta), Paul Schöffler (b-bar), K. Böhm (cnd), Vienna State Opera Orch, Vienna State Opera Chorus *(rec live, Aug. 1944)*
Preiser 2-▲ PRE 90230 [ADD]

▲ = CD ♦ = Enhanced CD ∆ = MD ■ = Cassette Tape □ = DCC

Ralf, Torsten (ten) (cont.)

Verdi, G.:Otello (sels), w. Torsten Ralf (ten—Otello), Josef Hermann (ten—Iago), K Böhm (cnd), Saxon State Orch—Sì, pel ciel marmoreo giuro *(rec 1940)* Iron Needle ▲ IN 1311 [ADD]

Wagner, R.:Der fliegende Holländer (sels), w. Kirsten Flagstad (sop), Tiana Lemnitz (sop), Rudolf Bockelmann (b-bar), Ludwig Weber (bass), T. Beecham (cnd), Royal Opera House Orch, Royal Opera House Chorus Covent Garden Memories ("Golden" series) ▲ MEM 3003

Wagner, R.:Götterdämmerung (sels), w. Kirsten Flagstad (sop), Tiana Lemnitz (sop), Rudolf Bockelmann (b-bar), Ludwig Weber (bass), T. Beecham (cnd), Royal Opera House Orch, Royal Opera House Chorus Covent Garden Memories ("Golden" series) ▲ MEM 3003

Wagner, R.:Lohengrin (sels), w. Kirsten Flagstad (sop), Tiana Lemnitz (sop), Rudolf Bockelmann (b-bar), Ludwig Weber (bass), T. Beecham (cnd), Royal Opera House Orch, Royal Opera House Chorus Covent Garden Memories ("Golden" series) ▲ MEM 3003

Wagner, R.:Die Meistersinger von Nürnberg (sels), w. Kirsten Flagstad (sop), Tiana Lemnitz (sop), Rudolf Bockelmann (b-bar), Ludwig Weber (bass), T. Beecham (cnd), Royal Opera House Orch, Royal Opera House Chorus Covent Garden Memories ("Golden" series) ▲ MEM 3003

Wagner, R.:Die Meistersinger von Nürnberg (sels), w. Maria Reining (sop—Eva), Torsten Ralf (ten—Walther), Josef Herrman (bar—Hans Sachs), Erich Kunz (bar—Beckmesser), Kurt Böhme (bass—Pogner), K. Böhm (cnd), Vienna State Opera Orch *(rec Vienna, 1944)* Koch Schwann 2-▲ SCH 314682 [ADD]

Wagner, R.:Tristan und Isolde (sels), w. Kirsten Flagstad (sop), Tiana Lemnitz (sop), Rudolf Bockelmann (b-bar), Ludwig Weber (bass), T. Beecham (cnd), Royal Opera House Orch, Royal Opera House Chorus Covent Garden Memories ("Golden" series) ▲ MEM 3003

Ramalle, Santiajo (bass)

Brahms, J.:Ein Deutsches Requiem, w. M. Price (sop), A. Previn (cnd), Royal PO, Ambrosian Singers [G] Teldec ("Digital Experience" series) ▲ 9031-75862-2 AW [DDD] ■ 9031-75862-4

Carrion, M.R.:La Tempestad, w. L. Huarte (sop), D. Perez (sop), A. Kraus (ten), F. Kraus (bar), R. Alonso (bass), E. Estella (cnd), Concierto Montilla Orch, Concierto Montilla Chorus Montilla ▲ MON 3011 [ADD]

Lehár, F.:Eva, w. J. Granados (sop—Prunelles), A. M. Olaria (sop—Eva), A. Kraus (ten—Octavio Flaubert), L. de Cordoba (sgr—Gipsy), S. Ramalle (bass—Dagoberto), J. Peromingo (sgr—Voisin), E. Estella (cnd), Madrid CO, Spanish National Radio Chorus [Sp] Montilla ▲ CDFM 2036

Rambausek, Marion (sgr)

Wagner, R.:Lohengrin, w. Sharon Sweet (sop—Elsa), Eva Marton (sop—Ortrud), Ben Heppner (ten—Lohengrin), Anton Rosner (ten—Nobleman), Heinrich Weber (ten—Nobleman), Jan-Hendrik Rootering (bar—Heinrich der Vögler), Sergei Leiferkus (bar—Friedrich von Telramund), Bryn Terfel (b-bar—King's Herald), Barbara Fleckenstein (sgr—Page), Atsuko Suzuki (sgr—Page), Gisela Ulmann (sgr—Page), Marion Rambausek (sgr—Page), Dankwart Siegele (sgr—Nobleman), Jürgen Weiss (sgr—Nobleman), C. Davis (cnd), Bavarian SO, Bavarian State Opera Chorus, Bavarian Radio Chorus *(rec Residenz Herkulesaal, Munich, May 14-28, 1994)* RCA Red Seal 3-▲ 09026-62646-2 [DDD]

Wagner, R.:Lohengrin (sels), w. Eva Marton (sop—Ortrud), Sharon Sweet (sop—Elsa von Brabant), Barbara Fleckenstein (sgr—Page), Marion Rambausek (sgr—Page), Atsuko Suzuki (sgr—Page), Gisela Ulmann (sgr—Page), Ben Heppner (ten—Lohengrin), Anton Rosner (ten—Nobleman), Heinrich Weber (ten—Nobleman), Sergei Leiferkus (bar—Friedrich von Telramund), Bryn Terfel (b-bar—King's Herald), Jan-Hendrik Rootering (bass—Henry the Fowler), Dankwart Siegele (sgr—Nobleman), Jürgen Weiss (sgr—Nobleman), C. Davis (cnd), Bavarian RSO, Michael Gläser (cnd), Udo Mehrpohl (cnd), Bavarian Radio Chorus, Bavarian State Opera Chorus—Seht! Seht! [from Act 1, Scene 2]; Nun sei bedankt, mein lieber Schwan!; Wenn ich im Kampfe für dich siege; Welch holde Wunder muss ich sehen?; Nun höret mich und achtet wohl; Durch Gottes Sieg ist jetzt dein Leben mein [all from Act 1, Scene 3]; Treulich geführt ziehet dahin [from Act 3, Scene 1]; Wie hehr erkenn' ich unsrer Liebe Wesen!; Höchstes Vertrau'n hast du mir schon zu danken; Weh' nun ist all' unser Glück dahin! [all from Act 3, Scene 2]; In fernem Land, unnahbar euren Schritten [from Act 3, Scene 3] *(rec Munich, Mar 14-28, 1994)* RCA Red Seal ▲ 09026-68239-2 [DDD]

Ramey, Samuel (bass)

Bach, J.S.:Mass in b, BWV 232, w. M. Marshall (sop), J. Baker (mez), R. Tear (ten), N. Marriner (cnd), Academy of St. Martin in the Fields, *(chorus unknown)* [L] Philips 2-▲ 416415-2 [ADD]

Bartók, B.:Bluebeard's Castle, w. E. Martón (sop), A. Fischer (cnd), Hungarian State Orch, Hungarian State Chorus [Hun] CBS ▲ MK 44523 [DDD]

Bellini, V.:Norma, w. J. Sutherland (sop), M. Caballé (sop), L. Pavarotti (sop), R. Bonynge (cnd), Welsh National Opera Orch, Welsh National Opera Chorus [I] London 3-▲ 414476-2 [DDD]

Blitzstein, M.:Regina, w. A. Réaux (sop), S. Greenawald (sop), K. Ciesinski (mez), J. Mauceri (cnd), Scottish Opera Orch, Scottish Opera Chorus [E] London 2-▲ 433812-2 [DDD]

Boito, A.:Mefistofele, w. Michèle Crider (sop—Margherita/Elena), Eleonora Jankovic (mez—Marta/Pantalis), Ernesto Gavazzi (ten—Wagner/Nereo), Vincenza La Scola (ten—Faust), Samuel Ramey (bass—Mefistofele), R. Muti (cnd), La Scala Orch, La Scala Chorus *(rec live Mar 3,5 & 8, 1995, Milan)* RCA Victor 2-▲ 09026-68284-2 [DDD]

Boito, A.:Mefistofele, w. Daniela Dessi (sop), Alberto Cupido (ten), B. Bartoletti (cnd), Florence Maggio Musicale Orch, Florence Maggio Musicale Chorus *(rec live, 1989)* Serenissima 2-▲ SER 360114

Boito, A.:Mefistofele, w. E. Marton (sop), P. Domingo (ten), G. Patanè (cnd), Hungarian State SO, Hungarian State Opera Chorus [I] *(rec Budapest, 1988)* Sony Classical 2-▲ S2K 44083 [DDD]

Copland, A.:Old American Songs, w. W. Jones (pno) [E] Argo ▲ 433027-2 [DDD]

Divas in Song:Marylin Horne, a 60th Birthday Celebration, w. Montserrat Caballé (sop), H. Donath (sop), R. A. Swenson (sop), F. von Stade (mez), R. Fleming (mez), J. Levine (cnd), M. Katz (pno), W. Jones (pno), K. Donath (pno), Manuel Burgueras (pno) RCA Red Seal ▲ 09026-62547-2

Donizetti, G.:Anna Bolena, w. J. Sutherland (sop), S. Mentzer (mez), B. Manca di Nissa (cta), J. Hadley (ten), R. Bonynge (cnd), Welsh National Opera Orch [I] London 3-▲ 421096-2 [DDD]

Donizetti, G.:Anna Bolena, w. R. Scotto (sop—Anna Bolena), K. Ciesinski (mez—Smeton), S. Marsee (mez—Giovanna Seymour), S. Kolk (ten—Riccardo Percy), S. Ramey (bass—Enrico VIII), J. Rudel (cnd), Philadelphia Opera Orch *(rec live, Dec. 16, 1975)* Legato Classics 2-▲ LCD 175 [ADD]

Donizetti, G.:Lucia di Lammermoor, w. C. Studer (sop), P. Domingo (ten), J. Pons (bar), I. Marin (cnd), London SO Deutsche Grammophon 2-▲ 435309-2

Donizetti, G.:Lucia di Lammermoor, w. M. Caballé (sop), A. Murray (mez), C. H. Ahnsjö (ten), V. Bello (ten), J. Carreras (ten), V. Sardinero (bar), J. López-Cobos (cnd), New Philharmonia Orch, Ambrosian Opera Chorus Philips 2-▲ 426563-2

Ev'ry Time We Say Goodbye, w. Warren Jones (pno) *(rec Champs-Elysées Theater, Paris)* Sony Classical ▲ SK 68339

Floyd, C.:Susannah, w. C. Studer (sop—Sussanah Polk), J. Hadley (ten—Sam Polk), S. Ramey (bass—Rev. Olin Blitch), K. Nagano (cnd), Paris Lyon Opera Orch, Paris Lyon Opera Chorus Virgin Classics ▲ CDCB 45039

French Opera Arias, w. London PO [cnd:Julius Rudel] Philips ▲ 432080-2 PH [DDD]

Handel, G.F.:Messiah, w. Kathleen Battle (sop), Florence Quivar (mez), John Aler (ten), A. Davis (cnd), Toronto SO, Mendelssohn Club Chorus Philadelphia [E] EMI Classics ▲ CDC 49407 [DDD]; ■ 4DS 49407 (D)

Handel, G.F.:Messiah, w. Kathleen Battle (sop), Florence Quivar (mez), John Aler (ten), A. Davis (cnd), Toronto SO, Mendelssohn Club Chorus Philadelphia [E] EMI Classics 2-▲ CDCB 49027 [DDD]; ■ 4D2S 49027 (D)

Handel, G.F.:Semele, w. Kathleen Battle (sop), Sylvia McNair (sop), Marylin Horne (mez), Michael Chance (ct), John Aler (ten), J. Nelson (cnd), English CO, Ambrosian Opera Chorus Deutsche Grammophon 3-▲ 435782-2 -

Ives, C.:Songs, w. W. Jones (pno)—Charles Rutledge; In the Alley; Slow March; An Old Flame; Circus Band; Romanza di Central Park; Night Song; Children's Hour; At the River; He is There [E] Argo ▲ 433027-2 [DDD]

James Levine's 25th Anniversary Metropolitan Opera Gala, w. J. Levine (cnd), Metropolitan Opera Orch, Ileana Cotrubas (sop), Renée Fleming (sop), Hei-Kyung Hong (sop), Karita Mattila (sop), Birgit Nilsson (sop), Ruth Ann Swenson (sop), Kiri Te Kanawa (sop), Deborah Voigt (sop), Grace Bumbry (mez), Heidi Grant Murphy (mez), Anne Sofie von Otter (mez) *(rec live, Metropolitan Opera House, New York, Apr 27, 1996)* Deutsche Grammophon ▲ 449177-2 [DDD]

Massenet, J.:Chérubin, w. D. Upshaw (sop), F. von Stade (mez), M. Anderson (cta), P. Steinberg (cnd), Munich RSO, Bavarian State Opera Chorus RCA Red Seal 2-▲ 09026-60593-2 [DDD]

Ramey, Samuel (bass) (cont.)

Mozart, W.A.:Don Giovanni, w. A. Tomowa-Sintow (sop), K. Battle (sop), A. Baltsa (mez), G. Winbergh (ten), F. Furlanetto (bass), P. Burchuladze (bass), H. von Karajan (cnd), Berlin PO, German Opera Chorus [I] Deutsche Grammophon 3-▲ 419179-2 [DDD]

Mozart, W.A.:Don Giovanni, w. S. Studer (sop), C. Vaness (sop), W. Shimell (bar), R. Muti (cnd), Vienna PO EMI Classics 3-▲ CDCC 54255

Mozart, W.A.:Don Giovanni (sels), w. A. Tomowa-Sintow (sop), K. Battle (sop), A. Baltsa (mez), G. Winbergh (ten), F. Furlanetto (bass), P. Burchuladze (bass), H. von Karajan (cnd), Berlin PO, German Opera Chorus [I] Deutsche Grammophon ▲ 419635-2 [DDD]

Mozart, W.A.:Nozze di Figaro, w. K. Te Kanawa (sop), L. Popp (sop), F. von Stade (mez), T. Allen (bar), K. Moll (bass), G. Solti (cnd), London PO [I] London 3-▲ 410150-2 [DDD]

Mozart, W.A.:Nozze di Figaro (sels), w. K. Te Kanawa (sop), L. Popp (sop), F. von Stade (mez), T. Allen (bar), K. Moll (bass), G. Solti (cnd), London PO [I] London ▲ 417395-2 [DDD] □ 417395-5

Mozart, W.A.:Zauberflöte, w. K. Te Kanawa (sop), C. Studer (sop), E. Lind (sop), F. Araiza (ten), O. Bär (bar), N. Marriner (cnd), Academy of St. Martin in the Fields, Ambrosian Opera Chorus [G] Philips 2-▲ 426276-2 [DDD]

Mozart, W.A.:Zauberflöte (sels), w. K. Te Kanawa (sop), C. Studer (sop), E. Lind (sop), F. Araiza (ten), O. Bär (bar), N. Marriner (cnd), Academy of St. Martin in the Fields Philips ▲ 438495-2

Mussorgsky, M.:Boris Godunov, w. Eirian James (mez), Wessela Zorova (mez), E. de Waart (cnd), Swiss Romande Orch *(rec live, 1993)* Serenissima 2-▲ SER 360109 [DDD]

Mussorgsky, M.:Boris Godunov, w. V. Valente (sop—Xenia), E. Gorochovskaya (mez—Nurse), L. Nichiteanu (mez—Fyodor), E. Zarmeba (mez—Hostess), M. Lipovšek (cta—Marina), P. Langridge (ten—Prince Shuisky), H. Wildhaber (ten—Misail), A. Fedin (ten—Simpleton), S. Leiferkus (bar—Rangoni), A. Kotcherga (bass—B. Godounov), A. Shagidullin (bass—Shchelkalov), S. Ramey (bass—Pimen), S. Larin (bass—Girgory), G. Nikolsky (bass—Varlaam), C. Abbado (cnd), Berlin PO, Tölz Boys' Choir, Berlin Radio Chorus, Slovak Phil Chorus *(rec Nov. 7-30, 1993)* Sony Classical 3-▲ S3K 58977 [DDD]

Offenbach, J.:Les Contes d'Hoffmann, w. J. Norman (sop), E. Lind (sop), C. Studer (sop), A. Sofie von Otter (mez), F. Araiza (ten), J. Tate (cnd), Dresden Staatskapelle Philips ▲ 438502-2

Offenbach, J.:Les Contes d'Hoffmann, w. J. Norman (sop), C. Studer (sop), E. Lind (sop), A. S. von Otter (mez), F. Araiza (ten), J. Tate (cnd), Dresden Staatskapelle Philips 3-▲ 422374-2 [DDD]

Opera Arias, w. D. Renzetti (cnd), Philharmonia Orch, Ambrosian Opera Chorus Philips ▲ 420184-2 PH [DDD] ■ 420184-4

Opera Arias, w. Munich Radio Orch [cnd:Jacques Delacôte] EMI Classics ▲ CDC 49582 [DDD]

Puccini, G.:La Bohème, w. Leontina Vaduva (sop—Mimi), Ruth Ann Swenson (sop—Musetta), Roberto Alagna (ten—Rodolfo), Simon Keenlyside (bar—Schaunard), Thomas Hampson (bar—Marcello), Samuel Ramey (bass—Colline), Enrico Fissore (bass—Benoit), A. Pappano (cnd), Philharmonia Orch EMI Classics 2-♦ CDCB 56120

Puccini, G.:Tosca, w. M. Freni (sop), P. Domingo (ten), G. Sinopoli (cnd), Philharmonia Orch, Royal Opera House Chorus Covent Garden [I] Deutsche Grammophon 2-▲ 431775-2 [DDD]

Puccini, G.:Tosca, w. Birgit Nilsson (sop—Floria Tosca), Puli Toro (mez—Shepherd), Jose Carreras (ten—Mario Cavaradossi), Joaquin Romaguera (ten—Spoleta), James Billings (bar—Sacristan), Richard Fredricks (bar—Baron Scarpa), Samuel Ramey (bass—Cesare Angelotti), William Ledbetter (sgr—Sciarrone), Richard Park (sgr—Cardinal), Don Yule (sgr—Jailer), J. Rudel (cnd), *(orch & chorus unknown)* *(rec Nov 13, 1974)* Legato Classics 2-▲ LCD-200-2

Rodgers, R.:Carousel, w. B. Cook (sop), S. Brightman (sop), M. Forrester (cta), et al., P. Geminiani (cnd), Royal PO, Ambrosian Singers [1987 studio cast] MCA Classics ▲ MCAD 6209 [DDD] ■ MCAC 6209

Rossini, G.:Arias, w. June Anderson (sop), Montserrat Caballé (sop), Maria Callas (sop), Edita Gruberova (sop), Pilar Lorengar (sop), Mady Mesplé (sop), Nicolai Gedda (ten), Tito Gobbi (bar), *(orchs unknown)* —from Barbiere di Siviglia; La Cenerentola; La Gazza ladra; Petite messe solennelle; Semiramide; Stabat Mater *(rec 1958-89)* EMI Classics 2-▲ CZS 67440-2 [ADD/DDD]

Rossini, G.:Il barbiere di Siviglia, w. A. Felle (sop), S. Mentzer (mez), J. Hadley (ten), T. Hampson (bass), G. Gelmetti (cnd), Tuscan Orch EMI ▲ 54863-2

Rossini, G.:Il barbiere di Siviglia, w. M. Horne (mez), E. Dara (bar), L. Nucci (bar), R. Chailly (cnd), La Scala Orch, La Scala Chorus [I] CBS 3-▲ M3K 37862 [DDD]

Rossini, G.:Il barbiere di Siviglia, w. J. Larmore (cta), A. Corbelli (bar), R. Gimeniz (bar), H. Hagegard (bar), J. López-Cobos (cnd), Lausanne CO, Geneva Grand Théâtre Chorus [I] Teldec 2-▲ 9031-74885-2

Rossini, G.:Il barbiere di Siviglia (sels), w. M. Horne (mez), R. Pierotti (mez), P. Barbacini (ten), E. Dara (bar), L. Nucci (bar), S. Sammaritano (bass), R. Chailly (cnd), La Scala Orch, La Scala Chorus *(rec Milan, Jan. 2-18, 1982)* Sony Classical ("Opera Highlights" series) ▲ SMK 53501 [DDD]

Rossini, G.:Il barbiere di Siviglia (sels), w. B. Frittoli (sop), J. Larmore (mez), R. Giménez (ten), Håkan Hagegård (bar), A. Corbelli (bar), J. López-Cobos (cnd), Lausanne CO, Geneva Grand Théâtre Chorus Teldec ▲ 93693-2

Rossini, G.:La donna del lago, w. K. Ricciarelli (sop), L. V. Terrani (mez), D. Raffanti (ten), M. Pollini (cnd), CO of Europe, Prague Phil Chorus [I] CBS 2-▲ M2K 39311 [DDD]

Rossini, G.:La gazza ladra, w. K. Ricciarelli (sop), W. Matteuzzi (ten), G. Gelmetti (cnd), Turin RSO *(rec live, Rossini Opera Festival in Pesaro, Italy, Aug. 1989)* Sony Classical 3-▲ S3K 45850 [DDD]

Rossini, G.:L'italiana in Algeri, w. K. Battle (sop), M. Horne (mez), E. Palacio (ten), N. Zaccaria (bass), C. Scimone (cnd), Venice Solisti, Prague Phil Chorus [I] Erato ("Libretto" series) 2-▲ 2292-45404-2

Rossini, G.:Music of, w. M. Fortuna (sop), M. Lerner (sop), D. Voigt (sop), M. Horne (mez), K. Kuhlmann (mez), F. von Stade (mez), R. Blake (ten), C. Estep (ten), C. Merritt (ten), T. Hampson (b-bar), H. Runey (b-bar), J. Opalach (bass), R. Norrington (cnd), Orch of St. Luke's, New York Concert Chorale EMI Classics ▲ CDC 54643

Rossini, G.:Otello, w. F. von Stade (mez), J. Carreras (ten), S. Fisichella (ten), J. López-Cobos (cnd), Philharmonia Orch, Ambrosian Opera Chorus [I] Philips 2-▲ 432456-2 [ADD]

Rossini, G.:Semiramide, w. C. Studer (sop), J. Larmore (mez), F. Lopardo (ten), I. Marin (cnd), London SO, Ambrosian Opera Chorus Deutsche Grammophon ▲ 437797-2

Rossini, G.:Semiramide, w. M. Caballé (sop), M. Horne (mez), F. Araiza (ten), J. López-Cobos (cnd), *(orch unknown)* *(rec live, France, 1980)* HRE 2-▲ 1002-2 [ADD]

Rossini, G.:Il Signor Bruschino, w. K. Battle (sop), F. Lopardo (ten), C. Desderi (bar), I. Marin (cnd), English CO Deutsche Grammophon ▲ 435865-2

Rossini, G.:Il turco in Italia, w. M. Caballé (sop), E. Dara (bar), L. Nucci (bar), R. Chailly (cnd), National PO London, Ambrosian Opera Chorus [I] CBS 2-▲ M2K 37859 [DDD]

Saint-Saëns, C.:Samson et Dalila, w. W. Meier (mez), P. Domingo (ten), A. Fondary (bar), M.-W. Chung (cnd), Bastille Opera Orch, Bastille Opera Chorus EMI Classics 2-▲ CDCB 54470

Thomas, A.:Hamlet, w. J. Anderson (sop—Ophelie), D. Graves (mez—Gertrude); G. Kunde (ten—Laerte), T. Hampson (bar—Hamlet), S. Ramey (bass—Claudius), A. de Almeida (cnd), London PO, Ambrosian Singers EMI Classics 3-▲ CDCC 54820

Verdi, G.:Aida, w. A. Millo (sop), D. Zajick (mez), P. Domingo (ten), J. Morris (bass), J. Levine (cnd), Metropolitan Opera Orch, New York Metropolitan Opera Chorus [I] Sony Classical 3-▲ S3K 45973 [DDD] 3-■ S3T 45973 (D)

Verdi, G.:Aida (sels), w. A. Millo (sop), D. Zajick (mez), P. Domingo (ten), J. Morris (bar), T. Cook (bass), J. Levine (cnd), Metropolitan Opera Orch, New York Metropolitan Opera Chorus *(rec New York, May 18-26, 1990)* Sony Classical ("Opera Highlights" series) ▲ SMK 53506 [DDD]

Verdi, G.:Attila, w. S. Studer (sop), N. Shicoff (ten), G. Zancanaro (bar), R. Muti (cnd), La Scala Orch, La Scala Chorus [I] EMI Classics 2-▲ CDCB 49952 [DDD]

Verdi, G.:I due Foscari, w. K. Ricciarelli (sop), E. Connell (sop), J. Carreras (ten), V. Bello (ten), M. Antoniak (ten), P. Cappuccilli (bar), F. Handlos (bass), L. Gardelli (cnd), Austrian RSO, Austrian Radio Chorus Philips 2-▲ 422426-2 [ADD]

Verdi, G.:I masnadieri, w. J. Sutherland (sop), F. Bonisolli (ten), M. Manugerra (bar), R. Bonynge (cnd), Welsh National Opera Orch, Welsh National Opera Chorus London ("Grand Opera" series) 2-▲ 433854-2 [DDD]

Verdi, G.:Rigoletto, w. L. Vaduva (sop), J. Larmore (mez), R. Leech (ten), A. Agache (bar), C. Rizzi (cnd), Welsh National Opera Orch Teldec ▲ 90851-2

Verdi, G.:Rigoletto, w. Beverly Sills (sop), Sherill Milnes (bar), Alfredo Kraus (bar), J. Rudel (cnd), Philharmonia Orch, Ambrosian Opera Chorus EMI Classics 2-▲ CDMB 724356603721

Ramey, Samuel (bass) (cont.)
Weill, K.:Street Scene, w. J. Barstow (sop), A. Réaux (sop), J. Hadley (ten), J. Mauceri (cnd), Scottish Opera Orch, Scottish Opera Chorus [E] London 2-▲ 433371-2 [DDD]

Ramiro, Yordi (ten)
Puccini, G.:Madama Butterfly, w. M. Gauci (sop), N. Boschkowá (mez), A. Michalková (mez), A. Rahbari (cnd), Czech-Slovak RSO Bratislava, Slovak Phil Chorus [I] Naxos 2-▲ 8.660015/16 [DDD]
Puccini, G.:Madama Butterfly (sels), w. Miriam Gauci (sop—Madama Butterfly), Nelly Boschkowa (mez—Suzuki), Yordi Ramiro (ten—F.B. Pinkerton), Jozef Abel (ten—Goro), Georg Tichy (bass—Sharpless), Anna Tomkovicová (sgr), Mária Stahelová (sgr), Elena Hanzelová (sgr) *(rec Concert Hall of the Czecho-Slovak Radio, Bratislava, May 2-10, 1991)* Naxos ▲ 8.553152 [DDD]
Verdi, G.:Rigoletto, w. A. Ferrarini (sop), E. Tumagian (bar), J. Spaček (bar), A. Rahbari (cnd), Czech-Slovak RSO Bratislava, Slovak Phil Chorus [I] Naxos 2-▲ 8.660013/14 [DDD]
Verdi, G.:La traviata, w. R. Braga (mez), R. Krause (ten), A. Rahbari (cnd), Czech-Slovak RSO Bratislava, Slovak Phil Chorus [I] Naxos 2-▲ 8.660011/12 [DDD]
Verdi, G.:La traviata (sels), w. Monika Krause (sop), Ivica Neshybová (sop), Rannveig Braga (mez), Gerog Tichy (bar), Ladislav Neshyba (bass), Jozef Spaček (bass), A. Rahbari (cnd), Czech-Slovak RSO Bratislava, Jan Rozehnal (cnd), Slovak Phil Chorus—Prelude act I; Libiam ne'lieti calici; Un dí, felice; E strano! Ah, fors'e lui; Follie!...sempre libera; Lunge da lei...de'miei bollenti spiriti; O Mio rimoroso!; Pura si come un angelo...Dite alla giovine; Dammi tu forza; Di Provenza il mar; Noi siamo zingarelle; Prelude act III; Teneste la promessa...Addio del passato; Signora! Che t'accade?; Ah, Violetta! *(rec Bratislava Concert Hall, Dec 1990)* Naxos ▲ 8.553041 [DDD]

Ramm, Andrea von (sgr)
Songs around Konrad von Würzburg, w. Sterling Jones (hp), Timothy C. Nelson (fl), Christian Schmid-Cadalbert (recitation) Christophorus ▲ CD 74542 [DDD]
Tristan et Iseult:A Medieval Romance in Music & Poetry, w. Anne Azema (sop), Ellen Hargis (sop), Henri Ledroit (alt), William Hite (ten), Richard Morrison (bass), Boston Camerata [cnd:Joel Cohen] Erato ▲ 98482-2

Ramm, Gabriele (sop)
Weill, K.:Mahagonny, w. T. Schmidt (mez), H. Hiestermann (ten), J. Latham-König (cnd), König Ensemble Capriccio ▲ 60028 [DDD]

Rampf, Stefan (ct)
Bach, J.S.:Cant 153, w. K. Equiluz (ten), T. Hampson (b-bar), N. Harnoncourt (cnd), Vienna Concentus Musicus, Tölz Boys' Choir [G] Teldec 2-▲ 2292-42632-2 [DDD]

Ramuz, Charles-Ferdinand (nar)
Stravinsky, I.:L'Histoire du soldat (sels), w. E. Ansermet (cnd), Swiss Romande Orch members [F] *(rec 2/25/40)* Claves ▲ CD 8918 (m) [ADD]

Ranczak, Hildegarde (sop)
Puccini, G.:La Bohème, w. P. A. (ten), M. Ahlersmeyer (bar), C. Krauss (cnd), Stuttgart RSO *(rec 1938)* Preiser 2-▲ PRE 90210 [ADD]
Puccini, G.:La Bohème, w. Trude Eipperle (sop), Alfons Fügel (ten), Carl Kronenberg (bar), Georg Hann (bass), Georg Wieter (bass), Emil Graf (sgr), Otto Hillerbrandt (sgr), Karl Schmidt (sgr), C. Krauss (cnd), Bavarian State Opera Orch, Bavarian State Opera Chorus *(rec 1940)* Preiser 2-▲ PRE 90275
Puccini, G.:Tosca, w. H. Roswaenge (ten), G. Hann (bass), L. Ludwig (cnd), Berlin RSO *(rec Oct. 1944)* Preiser 2-▲ PRE 90210 [ADD]

Rand, Lola (nar)
Debussy, C.:Chansons de Bilitis (recitation), w. Donald Peck (fl), Melody Lord (pno) [arr Peck] *(rec DePaul Concert Hall, Chicago, June 30, 1996)* Boston Records ▲ BR 1014 CD [DDD]

Randall, Tony (sgr)
Golden Days, w. Jerry Hadley (ten), Mario Lanza (ten), American Theater Orch [cnd:Paul Gemignani], Harvard Glee Club RCA Victor ▲ 09026-62681-2 ■ 09026-62681-2

Randle, Thomas (ten)
Handel, G.F.:Messiah, w. Yvonne Kenny (sop), Jean Rigby (cta), Willard White (bass), O. A. Hughes (cnd), Royal PO, Royal Choral Society IMP Classics 2-▲ IMPDPCD 1106 [DDD]

Randolph, David (nar)
A Demonstration of the Instruments of the Orchestra, w. Vienna State Opera Orch [cnd:Mario Rossi] *(rec Vienna, 1957)* Vanguard Classics 2-▲ OVC 8096/97 [ADD]

Randolph, M. (sop)
Flagello, N.:Lautrec, w. N. Flagello (cnd), Rome SO Phoenix ▲ PHCD 125 [ADD]

Randová, Eva (mez)
Bach, J.S.:Cant 102, w. K. Equiluz (ten), W. Schöne (bass), H. Rilling (cnd), Stuttgart Bach Collegium, Gächinger Kantorei Hänssler Classic ▲ 98.809 [AAD]
Dvořák, A.:Ave maris stella, w. Jaroslav Tvrzský (org) *(rec Dvořák Hall of Rudolfinum Prague, Sept. 4-6, 1989)* Panton ▲ PAN 811241 [DDD]
Dvořák, A.:Hymnus ad laudes in festo Sanctae Trinitatis, w. Jaroslav Tvrzský (org) *(rec Dvořák Hall of Rudolfinum Prague, Sept. 4-6, 1989)* Panton ▲ PAN 811241 [DDD]
Dvořák, A.:The Jacobin (sels), w. Z. Košler (cnd), Czech PO—Julia's lullaby [Act 3, Scene 5] *(rec Dvořák Hall of Rudolfinum Prague, Sept. 4-6, 1989)* Panton ▲ PAN 811241 [DDD]
Dvořák, A.:Kate & the Devil (sels), w. Z. Košler (cnd), Czech PO—The Princess [Act 3, Scene 1] *(rec Dvořák Hall of Rudolfinum Prague, Sept. 4-6, 1989)* Panton ▲ PAN 811241 [DDD]
Dvořák, A.:Rusalka (sels), w. Z. Košler (cnd), Czech PO—The Witch [Act 3]; Finale; The Strange Princess; The Prince & the Water Sprite [Act 2] *(rec Dvořák Hall of Rudolfinum Prague, Sept. 4-6, 1989)* Panton ▲ PAN 811241 [DDD]
Dvořák, A.:St Ludmilla, w. Z. Košler (cnd), Czech PO—Entrance, Svatava's recitative & aria *(rec Dvořák Hall of Rudolfinum Prague, Sept. 4-6, 1989)* Panton ▲ PAN 811241 [DDD]
Dvořák, A.:Stabat Mater, w. Z. Košler (cnd), Czech PO *(rec Dvořák Hall of Rudolfinum Prague, Sept. 4-6, 1989)* Panton ▲ PAN 811241 [DDD]
Dvořák, A.:Vanda (sels), w. Z. Košler (cnd), Czech PO, Kühn Chorus—Homena, priests & priestesses of the God of Darkness [Act 3, Scene 3]; Bozena, pagan Grand Priest & the people [Act 4, Scene 1] *(rec Dvořák Hall of Rudolfinum Prague, Sept. 4-6, 1989)* Panton ▲ PAN 811241 [DDD]
Famous Opera Arias, w. Brno State PO [cnd:Ondrej Lenárd] *(rec live 1992)* Supraphon ▲ SUP 1118546
Fibich, Z.:Šárka, w. Eva Deplotová (sop), Vilém Přibyl (ten), Vaclav Zítek (bar), J. Stych (cnd), Brno State PO, J. Pancik (cnd), Janáček Opera Chorus *(rec 1978)* Supraphon 2-▲ SUP 0036
Janácek, L.:The Cunning Little Vixen, w. L. Popp (sop), D. Jedlička (bass), C. Mackerras (cnd), Vienna PO [Cz] London 2-▲ 417129-2 [DDD]
Janácek, L.:Jenůfa, w. L. Popp (sop), E. Söderström (sop), M. Dvorsky (ten), W. Ochman (ten), C. Mackerras (cnd), Vienna PO [Cz] London 2-▲ 414483-2 [DDD]
Janácek, L.:Slavonic Mass, w. N. Troitskaya (sop), K. Kaludov (ten), S. Leiferkas (bass), T. Trotter (org), C. Dutoit (cnd), Montreal SO, Montreal Sym Chorus London ▲ 436211-2
Janácek, L.:Slavonic Mass, w. Gabriela Benackova (sop), Vilem Pribyl (ten), Sergej Kopack (bass), F. Jílek (cnd), Brno State PO, Josef Veselka (cnd), Czech Phil Chorus *(rec 1979)* Supraphon ▲ SUP CD 3045
Mahler, G.:Sym 2, w. G. Benačková (sop), V. Neumann (cnd), Czech PO, Czech Phil Chorus *(rec June 11-16, 1980)* Supraphon ▲ 11 1971-2 [AAD]
Schreker, F.:Irrelohe, w. Eva Randová (mez—Old Lola), Michael Pabst (ten—Count Heinrich), Monte Pederson (bar—Peter), Neven Belamaric (sgr—The Parson), Luana Devol (sgr—Eva), Sebastian Holecek (sgr—The Miller), Goran Smimic (sgr—The Forester) Sony Classical 2-▲ S2K 66850
Wagner, R.:Lohengrin, w. J. Norman (sop), P. Domingo (ten), D. Fischer-Dieskau (bar), S. Nimsgern (b-bar), H. Sotin (bass), G. Solti (cnd), Vienna PO, Vienna State Opera Chorus [G] London 4-▲ 421053-2 [DDD]
Wagner, R.:Lohengrin, w. J. Norman (sop), P. Domingo (ten), D. Fischer-Dieskau (bar), S. Nimsgern (b-bar), H. Sotin (bass), G. Solti (cnd), Vienna PO, Vienna State Opera Chorus [G] London ▲ 425530-2 [DDD]

Raninger, Walter (bass)
Mozart, W.A.:Missa, K.427, w. Annelohre Cahnbley (sop), Maria Stader (sop), George Maran (ten), B. Paumgartner (cnd), Salzburg Mozarteum Orch, Salzburg Radio Chorus, Salzburg Mozarteum Chorus *(rec Aug 16, 1958)* Orfeo d'or ("Festspiel Dokumente" series) ▲ 397951 (m)

Rankin, Nell (mez)
Beethoven, L. van:Sym 9, "Choral Sym", w. Emilia Cundari (sop), Albert Da Costa (ten), William Wilderman (bass), B. Walter (cnd), Columbia SO, Westminster Sym Choir *(rec American Legion Hall, Los Angeles, CA, Apr. 6, 1954)* Sony Classical ("Bruno Walter Edition, Vol. 2" series) ▲ SMK 64464 [ADD]
Berlioz, H.:Les Troyens (sels), w. G. Simionato (mez), M. del Monaco (ten), R. Kubelik (cnd), La Scala Orch [I] *(rec May 27, 1960)* VAI Audio ▲ VAIA 1026 [ADD]
Massenet, J.:Werther, w. J. Guido (sop—Sophie), N. Rankin (sop—Charlotte), C. Valletti (ten—Werther), A. Cosenza (bar—Albert), R. Cellini (cnd), New Orleans Opera Orch *(rec 1956)* Golden Age of Opera 2-▲ GAO 141/42 [ADD]

Ranson-Hervé, Marcelle (ten)
Offenbach, J.:Le Fille du tambour-major, w. Christiane Harbell (sop—Stella), Monique de Pondeau (sop—Claudine), Germaine Light (mez—Duchess Della Volta), Marcelle Ranson-Hervé (ten—Duke Della Volta), André Mallabrera (ten—Griolet), Etienne Arnaud (bar—Robert), Louis Musy (bar—Monthabor), *(orch unknown)* Accord ▲ ACD 220692 [AAD]

Raphanel, Ghyslaine (sop)
Rameau, J.P.:Les Paladins, w. A. Michael (sop), B. Brewer (ten), D. Nasrawi (ten), G. Reinhart (bar), N. Rivenq (bar), J. Malgoire (cnd), La Grande Ecurie et la Chambre du Roy, Sagittarius Vocal Ensemble [F] Pierre Verany 2-▲ PV.790121/22 [DDD]

Rapisardi, Grete (sop)
Puccini, G.:Gianni Schicchi, w. Giuseppe Savio (ten), Giuseppe Taddei (bar), A. Simonetto (cnd), *(orch & chorus unknown)* Cetra Classic 3-▲ 36
Puccini, G.:Gianni Schicchi, w. A. Dubbini (mez), G. Savio (ten), G. Taddei (bar), A. Simonetto (cnd), Turin RAI SO [I] *(rec 10/5/49)* Preiser ▲ 90074 (m) [AAD]
Puccini, G.:Gianni Schicchi, w. Giuseppe Savio (ten), Giuseppe Taddei (bar), A. Simonetto (cnd), *(orch & chorus unknown)* Cetra Classic ▲ 363

Rappé, Jadwiga (cta)
Bach, J.S.:Mass in b, BWV 232, w. A. M. Blasi (sop), D. Ziegler (mez), K. Equiluz (ten), R. Holl (bass), N. Harnoncourt (cnd), Vienna Concentus Musicus, Arnold Schoenberg Choir [L] Teldec 2-▲ 2292-42676-2 [DDD]
Maciejewski, R.:Missa pro defunctis, w. Zdzislawa Donat (sop), Jerzy Knetig (ten), Janusz Niziolek (bass), T. Strugala (cnd), Warsaw PO, Henryk Wojnarowski (cnd), Warsaw National Phil Chorus *(rec National Philharmonic, Warsaw, May 2-15, 1989)* Polskie Nagrania 2-▲ PNCD 039 A/B
Schoenberg, A.:Die Jakobsleiter, w. Barbara Kilduff (sop—Seele 1), Jadwiga Rappé (cta—Sterbende), Wilfried Gahmlich (ten—Aufrührerischer), Cornelius Hauptmann (ten—Gabriel), Keith Lewis (ten—Berfener), Kurt Azesberger (bar—Mönch), Barbara Fuchs (sgr—Seele 2), Matteo de Monti (sgr—Ringender), Bjorn Waag (sgr—Auserwählter), E. Inbal (cnd), Frankfurt RSO, Robin Gritton (cnd), Berlin Radio Chorus *(rec Alte Oper, Frankfurt, Sept 6-9, 1994)* Denon ▲ CO 78977 [DDD]

Rappé, Josef (ten)
Beethoven, L. van:Missa Solemnis, w. L. Orgonasova (sop), J.-H. Rootering (bass), C. Davis (cnd), Bavarian RSO, Bavarian Radio Chorus RCA Red Seal 2-▲ 09026-60967-2
Mahler, G.:Sym 2, w. H. Lisowska (sop), A. Wit (cnd), Polish National RSO Katowice, Cracow Polish Radio-TV Chorus *(rec Jan. 9-17, 1993)* Naxos 2-▲ 8.550523/24 [DDD]
Mozart, W.A.:Missa, K.317, w. E. Mathis (sop), H. P. Blochwitz (ten), T. Quasthoff (bar), P. Schreier (cnd), Dresden Staatskapelle, Leipzig Radio Chorus Philips ▲ 426275-2
Mozart, W.A.:Missa solemnis, K.139, w. B. Bonney (sop), J. Protschka (ten), H. Hagegard (bar), N. Harnoncourt (cnd), Vienna Concentus Musicus, Arnold Schoenberg Choir [L] Teldec ▲ 2292-44180-2 [DDD]
Wagner, R.:Das Rheingold, w. M. Lipovšek (mez), H. Zednik (ten), P. Haage (ten), A. Schmidt (bar), T. Adam (b-bar), H. Tschammer (bass), K. Rydl (bass), J. Morris (bass), B. Haitink (cnd), Bavarian RSO [G] EMI Classics 2-▲ CDCB 49853 [DDD]

Raptis, Paulos (ten)
Szymanowski, K.:Mandragora, w. R. Satanowski (cnd), Warsaw Opera Orch, Warsaw National Opera Chorus Koch Schwann ▲ CD 311064 [DDD]

Rasa, Lina Bruna (sop)
Mascagni, P.:Cavalleria rusticana, w. G. Simionato (mez), B. Gigli (ten), G. Bechi (bar), P. Mascagni (cnd), La Scala Orch, La Scala Chorus [I] *(rec 1940)* EMI Classics ("Studio" series) 2-▲ CDHB 69987 (m) [ADD]
Mascagni, P.:Cavalleria rusticana, w. M. Meloni (mez), R. Gallo Toscani (mez), A. Melandri (ten), A. Poli (bar), P. Mascagni (cnd), Holland Italian Opera Orch, Italian d'Olanda Opera Chorus [I] *(rec live at the Royal Theatre in the Hague, 11/7/38)* Bongiovanni ▲ GB 1050 (m) [AAD]
Mascagni, P.:Cavalleria rusticana, w. M. Marucucci (mez), G. Simionato (mez), B. Gigli (ten), G. Bechi (bar), P. Mascagni (cnd), La Scala Orch, La Scala Chorus *(rec 1940)* Nimbus 2-▲ NI 7843/44 [ADD]

Rasinowa, Lisa (sgr/gtr)
Russian Romances Koch Schwann ▲ SCH 310362 [DDD]

Rasker, Helena (alt)
Nono, L.:guai ai gelidi mostri, w. Susanne Otto (cta), Klaus Burger (tuba/pic tpt), Stefano Scodanibbio (db), A. Richard (cnd), Rechêrche Ensemble Montaigne ▲ MO 782047

Raskin, Judith (sop)
Gluck, C.W.:Orfeo ed Euridice, w. A. Moffo (sop), S. Verrett (mez), R. Fasano (cnd), Collegium Musicum Italicum Instrumental Ensemble, Rome Virtuosi RCA Gold Seal 2-▲ 7896-2-RG [ADD]
Haydn, J.:Die Schöpfung, w. Alexander Young (ten), John Reardon (bar), L. Bernstein (cnd), New York PO, Camerata Singers [G] *(rec 1966)* Sony Classical ("Bernstein:The Royal Edition" series) 2-▲ SM2K 47560 [ADD]
Mahler, G.:Sym 4, w. G. Szell (cnd), Cleveland Orch [G] CBS ▲ MK 42416 [ADD]
Mahler, G.:Sym 4, w. G. Szell (cnd), Cleveland Orch [G] CBS ▲ MYK 37225 [ADD] ■ MYT 37225
Mahler, G.:Sym 4, w. G. Szell (cnd), Cleveland Orch Sony Classical ("Essential Classics" series) ▲ SBK 46535 [ADD] ■ SBT 46535
Mozart, W.A.:Così fan tutte, w. L. Price (sop), T. Troyanos (mez), G. Shirley (ten), S. Milnes (bar), E. Leinsdorf (cnd), New Philharmonia Orch, New Philharmonia Chorus [I] RCA Gold Seal 3-▲ 6677-2 [ADD]
Mozart, W.A.:Exsultate, w. G. Szell (cnd), Cleveland Orch [L] *(rec 1964)* CBS ▲ MK 42416 [ADD]
Schubert, Franz:Songs (misc), w. Elly Ameling (sop), Judith Blegen (sop), Kiri Te Kanawa (sop)—Rastlose Liebe; Gretchen am Spinnrade; Trockne Blumen; Nur wer die Sehnsucht kennt Sony Classical ("Essential Classics" series) ▲ SBK 62422 ■ SBT 62422
Stravinsky, I.:The Rake's Progress, w. A. Young (ten), J. Reardon (bar), I. Stravinsky (cnd), Royal PO *(rec 1964)* Sony Classical 2-▲ SM2K 46299

Rasmussen, Paula (mez)
Debussy, C.:La Damoiselle élue, w. D. Upshaw (sop), E.-P. Salonen (cnd), Los Angeles PO, Los Angeles Master Chorale Women's Voices *(rec Feb. 22, 1993)* Sony Classical ▲ SK 58952 [DDD]

Rathauscher (sgr)
Marschner, H.A.:Der Vampyr, w. L. Synek (sop), L. Heppe (ten), G. Oeggl (bar), Skladal (sgr), Sperlbauer (sgr), Weise (sgr), K. Tenner (cnd), Vienna RSO, Vienna Radio Chorus [G] *(rec live, Vienna, 4/9/51)* Memories 2-▲ HR 4466/67 [ADD]

Ratti, Eugenia (sop)
Mozart, W.A.:Don Giovanni, w. Birgit Nilsson (sop—Donna Anna), Leontyne Price (sop—Donna Elvira), Eugenia Ratti (sop—Zerlina), Cesare Valletti (ten—Don Ottavio), Heinz Blankenburg (bar—Masetto), Fernando Corena (b-bar—Leporello), Arnold van Mill (b-bar—Il Commendatore), Cesare Siepi (b-bar—Don Giovanni), E. Leinsdorf (cnd), Vienna PO, Vienna State Opera Chorus [I] London 3-▲ 444594-2 [ADD]
Verdi, G.:Un ballo in maschera, w. M. Callas (sop), G. Simionato (mez), G. di Stefano (ten), E. Bastianini (bar), G. Gavazzeni (cnd), La Scala Orch, La Scala Chorus [I] *(rec live 12/7/57)* Arkadia 2-▲ 519 (m) [AAD]
Verdi, G.:Un ballo in maschera, w. M. Callas (sop), G. Simionato (mez), G. di Stefano (ten), E. Bastianini (bar), G. Gavazzeni (cnd), La Scala Orch, La Scala Chorus *(rec 1957)* Melodram ▲ MLO 26039 [ADD]

Ratti, Eugenia (sop) (cont.)

Verdi, G.:Un ballo in maschera, w. M. Callas (sop), F. Barbieri (mez), G. Di Stefano (ten), T. Gobbi (bar), A. Votto (cnd), La Scala Orch, La Scala Chorus [I] *(rec 1956)* EMI Classics 2-▲ CDCB 47498 (m)

Verdi, G.:Un ballo in maschera, w. G. Bouwenstijn (sop), A. Delori (cta), G. Zampieri (ten), F. Molinari-Pradelli (cnd), Netherlands Opera Orch, Netherlands Opera Chorus *(rec live 1958)* Globe 2-▲ GLO 5109

Ratzlaff, Leonard (bass)

Britten, H.:Hymn to St. Cecilia, w. Christine Goerke (sop), Nanette Soles (mez), Matthew Pittman (ten), Robert Shaw (cnd), Robert Shaw Festival Singers *(rec Church of St. Pierre, Gramat, France, July 26–28, 1994)* Telarc ▲ CD 80408 [DDD]

Debussy, C.:Chansons (3) de Charles d'Orléans, w. Julie McCoy (sop), Pam Elrod (mez), Nanette Soles (mez), Charles Bruffy (ten), Robert Shaw (cnd), Robert Shaw Festival Singers *(rec Church of St. Pierre, Gramat, France, July 26–28, 1994)* Telarc ▲ CD 80408 [DDD]

Rau (sgr)

Künneke, E.:Die grosse Sünderin (sels), w. M. Cunitz (sop), R. Schock (ten), Bajew (sgr), Gehly (sgr), Schröder (sgr), Weigelt (sgr), Marszalek (cnd), Cologne RSO, Cologne Radio Chorus [G] Acanta ▲ CD 42483 [DDD]

Raucamp, Manfred (ten)

Weber, C.M. von:Missa sancta 2, w. Gertrude Stoklassa (sop), Emmy Lisken (cta), Hans Kagel (bass), R. Bader (cnd), Stuttgart PO, Stuttgart Phil Chorus Koch Schwann ▲ SCH CD 316372

Raunig, Arno (ct)

Jommelli, N.:Didone abbandonata, w. Dorothea Röschmann (sop), Mechthild Bach (mez), Martina Borst (mez), William Kendall (ct), Daniel Taylor (ct), F. Bernius (cnd), Stuttgart CO—Didone; Enea; Iarba; Selene; Araspe; Osmida Orfeo 3-▲ CD 381953 [DDD]

Mozart, W.A.:Apollo et Hyacinthus, w. V. Hruba-Frieberger (sop), R. Popken (alt), J. Dickie (ten), M. Pommer (cnd), Leipzig RSO, Leipzig Radio Chorus Berlin Classics 2-▲ BER 1010 [DDD]

Mozart, W.A.:Arias, w. K. F. Schmid (cl), M. Dostal (org), W. Kobera (cnd), Vienna Amadeus Ensemble, Vienna Landstrasse Church Choir—Il padre adorato [from Idomneo]; Cara, lontano ancora [from Ascanio in Alba]; Parto, ma tu ben mio [from La clemenza di Tito] Divertimento ▲ DIV 31013 [DDD]

Mozart, W.A.:Exsultate, w. K. F. Schmid (cl), M. Dostal (org), W. Kobera (cnd), Vienna Amadeus Ensemble, Vienna Landstrasse Church Choir Divertimento ▲ DIV 31013 [DDD]

Salieri, A.:Arias, w. K. F. Schmid (cl), M. Dostal (org), W. Kobera (cnd), Vienna Amadeus Ensemble, Vienna Landstrasse Church Choir—Perdermi? [from Axur, Re d'ormus]; Lungi da te [from Armida]; A fulminas m'invita [from Anibale] Divertimento ▲ DIV 31013 [DDD]

Salieri, A.:Songs, w. K. F. Schmid (cl), M. Dostal (org), W. Kobera (cnd), Vienna Amadeus Ensemble, Vienna Landstrasse Church Choir—Fremat Thyrannus (motet) Divertimento ▲ DIV 31013 [DDD]

Schnittke, A.:Historia von D. Johann Fausten, w. Hanna Schwarz (mez—Fair Helen), Arno Raunig (ct—Mephostophiles), Eberhard Büchner (ten—Old Man), Jürgen Freier (bar—Dr. Johann Faustus), Jonathan Barreto-Ramos (sgr—Student), Jürgen Fersch (sgr—Student), Eberhard Lorenz (sgr—Erzähler), Christoph Johannes Wendel (sgr—Student), G. Albrecht (cnd), Hamburg State PO, Hamburg State Opera Chorus *(rec live, Hamburg, Germany)* RCA Red Seal 2-▲ 09026-68413-2

Rausch, Christoph (bass)

Stravinsky, I.:Les Noces, w. U. Sonntag (sop), C. Kallisch (cta), M. Schäfer (ten), P. Lika (bass), et al., W. Schäfer (cnd), Frankfurt Kantorei [G] Koch Schwann ▲ 314 021 [DDD]

Rausch, Ulrich (bass)

Albrechtsberger, J.G.:Missa assumptionis beatae Mariae Virginis, w. F. Schmitt-Bohn (sop), J. Köble (alt), C. Elsner (ten), R. Hug (cnd), Freiburg Baroque Soloists Ars Musici ▲ 0972-2 [DDD]

Haydn, M.:Missa Sancti Hieronymi, w. Florian Schmitt-Bohn (sop), Joachim Köble (alt), Christian Elsner (ten), R. Hug (cnd), Freiburg Baroque Soloists Ars Musici ▲ 0972-2 [DDD]

Rauschkolb, Sunhild (cta)

Diabelli, A.:Pastoralmesse, w. C. Degler (sop), S. Linden (sop), D. Clayton (ten), H. Müller (bass), E. Ehret (cnd), Munich St. Michael's Orch, Munich St. Michael Choir [L] Koch Schwann ▲ CD 313015 [ADD]

Rautawaara, Aulikki (sop)

Mozart, W.A.:Nozze di Figaro, w. Audrey Mildmay (sop), Constance Willis (mez), John Heddle Nash (ten), Roy Henderson (bar), Willi Domgraf-Fassbaender (bar), F. Busch (cnd), Glyndebourne Festival Orch *(rec 1934)* Legend 2-▲ LGD 132 [ADD]

Mozart, W.A.:Nozze di Figaro, w. Jarmila Novotna (sop), Esther Réthy (sop), Agostino Lazzari (ten), Mariano Stabile (bar), Ezio Pinza (bass), B. Walter (cnd), Vienna PO, Vienna State Opera Chorus *(rec live, 1937)* Melodram ▲ CDI 205003

Mozart, W.A.:Nozze di Figaro, w. Audrey Mildmay (sop), Constance Willis (mez), John Heddle Nash (ten), Roy Henderson (bar), Willi Domgraf-Fassbaender (bar), F. Busch (cnd), Glyndebourne Festival Orch, Glyndebourne Festival Chorus [I] *(rec 1934–35)* Pearl 2-▲ PEAS 9375 (m) [AAD]

Mozart, W.A.:Nozze di Figaro, w. Luise Helletsgrüber (sop), Audrey Mildmay (sop), Willi Domgraf-Fassbaender (bar), Roy Henderson (bar), F. Busch (cnd), Glyndebourne Festival Orch, Glyndebourne Festival Chorus *(rec 1934)* Grammofono 2000 2-▲ GRM 78624

Mozart, W.A.:Nozze di Figaro (sels), w. Luise Helletsgrüber (sop), Audrey Mildmay (sop), Constance Willis (mez), John Heddle Nash (ten), Willi Domgraf-Fassbaender (bar), Roy Hondorcon (bar), Norman Allin (bass), F. Busch (cnd), Glyndebourne Festival Orch Pearl ▲ PEA CD 9230

Rautio, Nina (sop)

Puccini, G.:Arias, w. Angela Gheorghiu (sop), Johan Botha (ten), Anthony Michaels-Moore (bar), E. Downes (cnd), Royal Opera House Orch, Royal Opera House Chorus Covent Garden—Se come voi piccina io fossi [from Le villi]; Addio mio dolce amor [from Edgar]; Donna non vidi mai; Sola, perduta, abbandonata [both from Manon Lescaut]; Donde lieta usci [from La Bohème]; Act 1 Finale; E lucevan le stelle [both from Tosca]; Un tal baccano in chiesa; Or tutto è chiaro; Tre sbirri, una carrozza; Un bel dì [from Madama Butterfly]; Ch'ella mi creda [from La fanciulla del West]; Chi il bel sogno di Doretta [from La rondine]; Nulla, silenzio [from Il tabarro]; Senza mamma [from Suor Angelica]; O mio babbino caro [from Gianni Schicchi]; Act I Finale; Nessun dorma [both from Turandot]; Signore, acolta; Non piangere, Liù *(rec Henry Wood Hall, London, Feb 12–27 & Mar 5, 1995)* Conifer Classics ("Royal Opera House" series) ▲ 75605-55013-2 [DDD]

Tchaikovsky, P.:Songs, w. Semion Skigin (pno)—If Only I Had Known; He Loved Me So Much; Do Not Leave Me; The Canary; Zemfira's Song; Gypsy's Song; The Fearful Minute; It Is Both Bitter & Sweet; To Forget So Soon; Was I Not a Little Blade of Grass?; Take My Heart Away; Cradle Song; Tell Me, What in the Shade of the Branches; Evening; The Mild Stars Shone for Us; Wait!; At Bedtime; Does the Day Reign? [R] *(rec All Saint's Church, Petersham, Surrey, Sept 1995 & Jan 1996)* Conifer Classics ▲ 51267 [DDD]

Ravaglia, Emilia (sop)

Donizetti, G.:Don Pasquale, w. P. Bottazzo (ten), A. Frati (ten), R. Panerai (bar), F. Corena (bass), R. Muti (cnd), Vienna PO, Vienna State Opera Chorus [I] *(rec live, Salzburg, 8/11/71)* Melodram 2-▲ CDM 27094 [ADD]

Massenet, J.:Werther, w. B. Casoni (mez), C. Bergonzi (ten), D. Trimarchi (bar), O. de Fabritiis (cnd), Naples Teatro San Carlo Orch, Naples Teatro San Carlo Chorus [I] *(rec live, Naples, 2/13/69)* Melodram 2-▲ 27058 [AAD]

Piccinni, N.:La cecchina, ossia la buona figliola, w. Lucia Alberti (sop—Il Cavaliere Armidoro), Emilia Ravaglia (sop—La Marchesa), Margherita Rinaldi (sop—Cecchina), Elena Zilio (mez—Paoluccia), Ugo Benelli (bar—Il Marchese della Conchiglia), Alessandro Corbelli (bar—Mengotto), Enzo Dara (bar—Tagliaferro), Renata Baldisseri (sgr—Sandrina), G. Gelmetti (cnd), Rome Opera Orch, Rome Opera Chorus *(rec Rome, Feb 4, 1981)* Italia 2-▲ CDC 95 [ADD]

Rossini, G.:La Cenerentola, w. L. V. Terrani (mez), F. Araiza (ten), E. Dara (bar), G. Ferro (cnd), Cappella Coloniensis, Cologne Radio Chorus [I] Sony Classical 2-▲ S2K 46433 [ADD]

Raveau, Alice (cta)

Gluck, C.W.:Orfeo ed Euridice, w. Jany Delille (sop), Germaine Féraldy (sop), H. Tomasi (cnd), Paris SO [1859 French version, edited by Berlioz & Saint-Saëns] *(rec Paris, 1935)* Pearl 2-▲ PEA 9169 [ADD]

Ravelli, Willem (bass)

Beethoven, L. van:Sym 9, "Choral Sym", w. To de Sluys (sop), Suze Luger (cta), Louis van Tulder (ten), W. Mengelberg (cnd), Royal Concertgebouw Orch, Toonkunst Chorus *(rec 1938)* Music & Arts ▲ CD 918

Ravenne, Catherine (alt)

Lefébure-Wély, L.J.A.:Music of, w. Sylvie de May (sop), Xavier Bisaro (org), Vincent Genvrin (org), La Lyre Seraphique, L'Accent Grave Vocal Ensemble—Adoremus et procidamus; Marche en mib majeur; Adoro te [alterné]; Tantum ergo; Sacris solemnis; Elévation en la mineur; Marche en ut majeur; Noël varié, offertoire pour le jour de Noël; Sanctus; O Salutaris; Pastorale en sol majeur; Agnus Dei; Communion en fa majeur; Domine salvum; Missum redemptorem; Sortie en sib majeur et Cloches Media 7 ▲ 005 [DDD]

Lefébure-Wély, L.J.A.:Music of, w. Sylvie de May (sop), Sophie Fournier (sop), Antoine Espagno (db), Vincent Genvrin (org), La Lyre Seraphique, Pythagore Vocal Ensemble—Sainte cité, demeure permanente; Récit de Hautbois ou de Trompette harmonique; L'Encens divin; Offertoire [grand choeur]; Seigneur dès ma première enfance; Verset; Pleins de ferveur; Marche; Jour heureux, sainte allégresse; Esprit divin, Dieu de lumière; Andante, choeur de voix humaines; Afin d'être docile et sage; Mon fils, pour apprendre; Andante; Motet à la Sainte-Vierge; Andante; Du Roi des cieux tout célèbre la gloire; Scène pastorale; Andantino Media 7 ▲ 004 [DDD]

Rawcliffe, Mary (sop)

Kraft, William:Contextures II:The Final Beast, w. J. Mack (ten), A. Previn (cnd), Los Angeles PO, New Albion Ensemble, Pasadena Boys' Choir [E,G,Gr,L] Meet The Composer ▲ 79229-2 ■ 79229-4

Rawding, Arthur (ten)

French Sacred Music of the 14th Century, Vol. 1, w. Schola Discantus, Bradford Findell (ct), John Delorey (ct), Peter McCabe (ten), Paul Guttry (bar), Kevin Moll (cnd) *(rec Emmanuel Church, Boston, 1994)* Lyrichord ("Early Music" series) ▲ LYR 8012 [DDD]

Rawlins, A. (nar)

Dreyfus, G.:Music of, w. F. Witt (cnd), Mandolin Orch, Melbourne Bassoon Quartet, J. Elton-Brown (cnd), Methodist Ladies' College Chorale—Germany Teddy (Symphony for Mandolin Orchestra); Auscapes for Women's Chorus; The Adventures of Sebastian the Fox for Narrator & Bassoon Quartet; Larino, Safe Haven (versions for 2 Oboes & English Horn & for Trumpet & Piano); Tender Mercies for Horn & Piano; There is Something of Don Quixote in All of Us for Solo Guitar Move ▲ MD 3129 [DDD]

Rawlins, Meredyth (sgr)

Sullivan, A.:HMS Pinafore, w. D. Hays (sop), C. Freeman (ten), E. Schilling (sgr), E. Johnson (cta), M. Elder (cnd), Rochester PO, Eastman Chorale members—highlights *(rec 11/89)* Pro Arte ▲ CDd 480 [DDD]

Sullivan, A.:The Mikado, w. D. Hays (sop), C. Freeman (ten), E. Schilling (sgr), E. Johnson (cta), M. Elder (cnd), Rochester PO, Eastman Chorale members—highlights *(rec 11/89)* Pro Arte ▲ CDd 480 [DDD]

Sullivan, A.:The Pirates of Penzance, w. D. Hays (sgr), C. Freeman (ten), E. Schilling (sgr), E. Johnson (cta), M. Elder (cnd), Rochester PO, Eastman Chorale members—highlights *(rec 11/89)* Pro Arte ▲ CDd 480 [DDD]

Rawls, Lou (sgr)

Amen:A Gospel Celebration, w. Azusa Pacific Univ Choir, Central State Univ Chorus, Cincinnati Pops Chorale, Jennifer Holliday (sgr), Maureen McGovern (sgr), Cincinnati Pops Orch [cnd:Erich Kunzel] *(rec Feb. 28–Mar. 1, 1993)* Telarc ▲ CD 80315 [DDD] ■ CD 80315

Rawn, Andy B. III (bass)

Italy's Love Songs, w. Adele Albani (pno) *(rec Alhambra, Sept 8, 1996)* Classic Digital ▲ B1996 [DDD]

Rawson, Stratton (nar)

Honegger, A.:Christophe Colomb, w. E. Knecht (speaker—Queen Isabella), S. Rawson (speaker—The Magician), N. Garvey (speaker—Christopher Columbus), A. Furnival (speaker—King Ferdinand), D. McCabe (bar), C. Peltz (cnd), Buffalo Opera Sacra Orch, Buffalo Opera Sacra Chorus [E] *(rec Buffalo, New York, Oct. 30–31, 1992)* Mode ▲ MOD 35 [DDD]

Rayam, Curtis (ten)

Graun, K.H.:Cesare e Cleopatra, w. Janet Williams (sop), Debora Beronesi (sop), Lynne Dawson (sop), R. Jacobs (cnd), Concerto Cologne, Berlin State Opera Chorus members Serenissima 3-▲ SER 360171 [DDD]

Salieri, A.:Axur, Re d'Ormus, w. A. Martin (bar), E. Mei (sop), E. Nova (bass), A. Vespasiani (mez), M. Valenti (sop), R. Clemencic (cnd), Guido d'Arezzo Orch, Guido d'Arezzo Chorus [I] *(rec live 1989)* Nuova Era 3-▲ 6852/54 [DDD]

Strauss, R.:Die ägyptische Helena, w. G. Jones (sop), M. Kastu (ten), B. Hendricks (sop), W. White (bass), B. Finnilä (mez), A. Dorati (cnd), Detroit SO London ("Grand Opera" series) 2-▲ 430381-2 [AAD]

Raymundo, Paschoal (ten)

Gomes, A.C.:Il Guarany, w. Niza De Castro Tank (sop—Cecilia), Roque Lotti (ten—Ruy Bento), Manrico Patassini (ten—Pery), Paschoal Raymundo (ten—Don Alvaro), Paulo Fortes (bar—Gonzales), Juan Carlos Ortiz (b-bar—Il Cacico), Waldomiro Furlan (bass—Alonso), Josè Perrotta (bass—Don Antonio De Mariz), A. Belardi (cnd), Saõ Paulo Teatro Municipale Orch, Saõ Paulo Teatro Municipale Chorus *(rec Studios of the Teatro Municipal, Saõ Paulo, Brazil, 1959)* Arkadia 2-▲ HP 617.2 [ADD]

Rayner, B. (bar)

Coates, E.:Songs, w. R. Terroni (pno)—I Heard You Singing; Bird Songs of Eventide; Homeward to You; and Today Ours ASV ("White Line" series) ▲ ASV 2081

Rayner Cook, Brian (bar)

Dvořák, A.:Biblical Songs, Op. 99, w. N. Järvi (cnd), Scottish National Orch Chandos ▲ CHAN 8608 [DDD]

Dvořák, A.:Biblical Songs, Op. 99, w. N. Järvi (cnd), Scottish National Orch [Cz] Chandos ▲ CHAN 9002 [DDD]

Ferguson, H.:Ballads (2), w. R. Hickox (cnd), London SO [E] Chandos ▲ CHAN 9082 [DDD]

Orff, C.:Carmina burana, w. S. Armstrong (sop), P. Hall (ten), M. Handford (cnd), Hallé Orch, Hallé State Chorus Classics for Pleasure ▲ CDCFP 9005 [ADD]

Parry, H.:Invocation, w. L. Dawson (sop), A. Davies (ten), M. Bamert (cnd), London PO, London Phil Chorus [E] Chandos ▲ CHAN 9025 [DDD]

Schumann, R.:Scenes from Goethe's "Faust", w. E. Mathis (sop), D. Fischer-Dieskau (bar), G. Howell (bass), P. Boulez (cnd), BBC SO, BBC Sym Chorus *(rec live, London, March 7, 1973)* Memories 2-▲ HR 4489/90 [ADD]

Vaughan Williams, R.:Dona nobis pacem, w. E. Wiens (sop), B. Thomson (cnd), London PO, London Phil Chorus [L] Chandos ▲ CHAN 8590 [DDD]

Vaughan Williams, R.:Mystical Songs, w. B. Thomson (cnd), London PO, London Phil Chorus [L] Chandos ▲ CHAN 8590 [DDD]

Vaughan Williams, R.:Sancta civitas, w. Gareth Roberts (ten), G. Rozhdestvensky (cnd), BBC SO, BBC Singers, BBC Sym Chorus IMP ("BBC Radio Classics" series) ▲ IMP 9125

Vaughan Williams, R.:Sym 1, w. Y. Kenny (sop), B. Thomson (cnd), London SO, London Sym Chorus [E] Chandos ▲ CHAN 8764 [DDD]

Walton, W.:Gloria, w. B. Robotham (sop), A. Rolfe Johnson (ten), L. Frémaux (cnd), City of Birmingham SO, Worcester Cathedral Choristers EMI Classics ▲ CDM 64201

Rayson, Benjamin (bar)

Mascagni, P.:Cavalleria rusticana, w. Zinka Milanov (sop—Santuzza), Jean Craft (mez—Lucia), Marietta Cosenza (mez—Lola), Giuseppe Gismondo (ten—Turiddu), Benjamin Rayson (bar—Alfio), R. Cellini (cnd), New Orleans Opera Orch, New Orleans Opera Chorus *(rec live, 1963)* VAI Audio ▲ VAIA 1053

Razimowsky, Evelyne (sop)

Rossini, G.:Sacred Music, w. Michel Piquemal (bar), Jean-Claude Pennetier (pno), Myriam Richardot (org), Michel Piquemal (cnd), Michel Piquemal Vocal Ensemble—La passegiata; Ave Marie; Inno Alla Pace; Ave Maria; Toast pour le nouvel an; Duetto Buffo di Due Batti; La fede; La speranza; La carita; Cantemus Domino; La notte del Santo Natalie; Preghiera; I Gondolieri Adès ▲ ADE 204192 [AAD]

Reali, Antenore (sgr)

Puccini, G.:Il tabarro, w. Clara Petrella (sop), Glauco Scarlini (sgr), G. Baroni (cnd), *(orch & chorus unknown)* Cetra Classic 3-▲ 36

Reardon, John (bar)

Bernstein, L.:Songfest, w. C. Dale (sop), R. Elias (mez), N. Williams (mez), N. Rosenshein (ten), D. Gramm (b-bar), L. Bernstein (cnd), National SO Washington D.C. [E] Deutsche Grammophon ▲ 415965-2 [ADD]

Reardon, John (bar) (cont.)
Haydn, J.:Die Schöpfung, w. Judith Raskin (sop), Alexander Young (ten), L. Bernstein (cnd), New York PO, Camerata Singers [G] *(rec 1966)*
Sony Classical ("Bernstein:The Royal Edition" series) 2-▲ SM2K 47560 [ADD]
Rossini, G.:La pietra del paragone, w. A. Elgar (sop), B. Wolff (mez), E. Bonazzi (mez), J. Carreras (ten), R. Murcell (bar), A. Foldi (b-bar), J. Diaz (bass), N. Jenkins (cnd), Clarion Concerts Orch, Clarion Concerts Chorus [I] *(rec. ca. 1972)* Vanguard Classics 3-▲ OVC 8043/45 [ADD]
Stravinsky, I.:The Rake's Progress, w. J. Raskin (sop), A. Young (ten), I. Stravinsky (cnd), Royal PO *(rec 1964)* Sony Classical 2-▲ SM2K 46299

Réaux, Angelina (sop)
Berg, A.:Lulu (suite), w. K. Masur (cnd), New York PO Teldec ▲ 95029-2
Blitzstein, M.:Regina, w. S. Greenawald (sop), K. Ciesinski (mez), S. Ramey (bass), J. Mauceri (cnd), Scottish Opera Orch, Scottish Opera Chorus [E] London 2-▲ 433812-2 [DDD]
Weill, K.:The Seven Deadly Sins, w. K. Masur (cnd), New York PO Teldec ▲ 95029-2
Weill, K.:Songs, w. R. Kapilow (pno), W. Schimmel (acc), B. Ruyle (perc)—conceived & first performed by Angelina Réaux for the 1988 New York Shakespeare Festival, this one-woman show features 21 songs composed from 1928-1946 [E,F,G] Koch International Classics 2-▲ KIC 7087-2 [DDD]
Weill, K.:Street Scene, w. J. Barstow (sop), J. Hadley (ten), S. Ramey (bass), J. Mauceri (cnd), Scottish Opera Orch, Scottish Opera Chorus [E] London 2-▲ 433371-2 [DDD]

Rebroff, Ivan (bass)
Strauss (II), Joh.:Die Fledermaus, w. J. Varady (sop), L. Popp (sop), A. Kollo (ten), H. Prey (bar), E. Kleiber (cnd), Bavarian State Opera Orch [G] Deutsche Grammophon 2-▲ 415646-2 [ADD]

Rech, H. (bass)
Mozart, W.A.:Zauberflöte, w. M. Price (sop—Pamina), L. Serra (sop—Queen of the Night), M. Venuti (sop—Papagena), M. McLaughlin (sop—1st Lady), A. Murray (mez—2nd Lady), H. Schwarz (cta—3rd Lady), F. Höher (trb—1st Boy), M. Diedrich (trb—2nd Boy), F. Klos (trb—3rd Boy), P. Schreier (ten—Tamino), R. Tear (ten—Monostatos), R. Goldberg (ten—1st Armoured Man), K. Moll (bass—Sarastro), H. Rech (bass—2nd Armoured Man), C. Davis (cnd), Dresden Staatskapelle, Leipzig Radio Chorus Philips ("Duo" series) 2-▲ 442568-2

Redgrave, Lynn (nar)
Saint-Saëns, C.:Carnival of the Animals, w. M. Golabek (nar), R. Golabek (nar), F. Savage (nar), C. Heston (nar), J. E. Jones (nar), B. White (nar), W. Shatner (nar), J. Rivers (nar), T. Danson (nar), L. Tomlin (nar), D. Raffin (nar), A. Hepburn (nar), D. Moore (nar), W. Matthau (nar), J. Smith (nar), L. Schifrin (cnd), Hollywood CO Dove Audio ▲ DOV 30700

Redgrave, Michael (bar)
Gay, J.:The Beggar's Opera (sels), w. R. Henderson (bar), A. Mildmay (sop), *(orch & chorus unknown)*—ov; 37 songs [arr Frederic Austin, 1920] *(rec 1940 for HMV)* Pearl ▲ PEA 9917 (m) [AAD]

Reed, A. (sgr)
Rodgers, R.:Music of, w. V. Clark (sgr), Gregg Edelman (sgr), J. Graae (sgr), L. Wintersteller (sgr)—Oklahoma; Carousel; The Sound of Music; South Pacific; Flower Drum Song; Cinderella & others Varèse Sarabande ▲ VSD 5516 ▮ VSC 5516

Rees, Déborah (sop)
Loussier, J.:Lumières, w. James Bowman (ct), André Arpino (perc), J.-P. Wallez (cnd), Harmonia Nova Orch, Patrick Marco Vocal Ensemble *(rec Studio de Miraval, 1957)* Media 7 ▲ CD 707 [DDD]

Rees, Rosiland (sop)
Blitzstein, M.:The Harpies, w. T. Bogdan (ten), E. Najera (bar), et al., G. Smith (cnd), Adirondack CO, Gregg Smith Singers [E] Premier ▲ PRCD 1009 [ADD]
Rorem, N.:Hearing, w. K. Wheeler (mez), M. Galloway (ten), R. Hilley (bar), R. Wagner (cl), J. Hamlin (tpt), D. Starobin (mand), D. Davidson (vn), K. Askew (va), J. Babich (db), P. Suits (pno), D. Druckman (perc), G. Smith (cnd) Premier ▲ PRCD 1035 [ADD]
Rorem, N.:Missa Brevis, w. Priscilla Magdamo (alt), Lin Garber (bar), Gregg Smith (cnd), Gregg Smith Singers Vox Box ("The American Composers" series) 3-▲ CDX 3037
Rorem, N.:Songs, w. N. Rorem (pno)—Alleluia; 2 Poems of Edith Sitwell; 3 Poems of Tennyson; 2 Poems of Elizabeth Bishop; 7 Poems of Paul Goodman; 2 Medieval Lyrics; 2 Poems of Whitman; I am Rose; A Journey; Let's Take a Walk; See How They Love Me; Early in the Morning
Premier ▲ PRCD 1035 [ADD]
Schuman, W.:Esses:Short Suite for Singers on Words Beginning with S, w. Leslie Dorsey (bass), Gregg Smith (cnd), Gregg Smith Singers Vox Box ("The American Composers" series) 3-▲ CDX 3037
Schuman, W.:The Mighty Casey, w. T. Bogdan (ten), R. Muenz (b-bar), W. Schuman (cnd), Adirondack CO, Gregg Smith Singers, Long Island Choral Association [E] Premier ▲ PRCD 1009 [ADD]
Schuman, W.:Orpheus & His Lute, w. Dwana Holroyd (pno), Gregg Smith (cnd), Gregg Smith Singers
Vox Box ("The American Composers" series) 3-▲ CDX 3037
Schuman, W.:Perceptions, w. Gregg Smith (cnd), Gregg Smith Singers
Vox Box ("The American Composers" series) 3-▲ CDX 3037
Schuman, W.:Prelude, w. Gregg Smith (cnd), Gregg Smith Singers
Vox Box ("The American Composers" series) 3-▲ CDX 3037
Smith, Gregg:Magnificat, w. G. Smith (cnd), Adirondack CO, Gregg Smith Singers, Adirondack Festival Chorus Premier ("Composer" series) ▲ PRCD 1020 [ADD/DDD]
Talma, L.:Voices of Peace, w. Scott Whittaker (ten), Charles Robert Stevens (bar), G. Smith (cnd), Adirondack CO, Gregg Smith Singers Vox Box ("The American Composers" series) 3-▲ CDX 3037

Reese, D. (sgr)
Rodgers, R.:Music of, w. S. Bass (sgr), J. Andrews (sgr), P. Como (sgr), J. Jones (sgr), N. Luboff (sgr), M. Gold (sgr), N. Walker (sgr), H. Bowen (sgr), V. Damone (sgr), P. Nero (pno), J. P. Morgan (sgr), E. Fisher (sgr), B. Goodman (cl), Ann-Margaret (sgr), Shorty Rogers (sgr), D. Shore (sgr), T. Martin (sgr), M. King (sgr), A. Newley (sgr) RCA ▲ 8590-2 R ▮ 8590-4 R

Reese, Sarah (sop)
Barber, S.:Prayers of Kierkegaard, w. A. Schenck (cnd), Chicago SO, Chicago Sym Chorus [E] 10/91)
Koch International Classics ▲ KIC 7125-2 [DDD]

Regar, Joszi Trojan (sgr)
Strauss, R.:Der Rosenkavalier, w. Jarmila Barton (sop—Marianne), Lisa Della Casa (sop—Sophie), Sena Jurinac (sop—Octavian), Ilva Ligabue (sop—Orphan), Elisabeth Schwarzkopf (sop—Marschallin), Else Schürhoff (mez—Annina), Luisa Villa (mez—Milliner), Hugues Cuénod (ten—Marschallin's majordomo), Erich Majkut (ten—Valzacchi), Giuseppe Nessi (ten—Animal seller), Luciano Della Pergola (ten—Lackey/Faninal's majordomo), Antonio Pirino (ten—An Italian Singer), Gino Del Signore (ten—Lackey/Waiter), Erich Kunz (bar—Herr von Faninal), Paolo Pedani (bar—Lackey), Attilo Barbesi (bass—Lackey/Waiter), Enrico Campi (bass—Waiter), Otto Edelmann (bass—Baron Ochs), Bruno Fichtinger (bass—Notary), Franco Taino (bass—Waiter), Maria Amadini (sgr—Orphan), Pina Carrillo (sgr—Orphan), Joszi Trojan Regar (sgr—Innkeeper), H. von Karajan (cnd), La Scala Orch, La Scala Chorus *(rec La Scala Theater, Milan, Jan. 26, 1952)* Legato Classics 3-▲ LCD 197-3

Regnier, Eugene (ten)
Cherubini, L.:Les Deux journées, w. J. Micheau (sop), M. Davies (ten), P. Gianotti (ten), C. Paul (bar), T. Beecham (cnd), Royal PO, BBC Theater Chorus *(rec live, London Dec. 19, 1947)*
Intaglio 2-▲ INCD 7342 [ADD]

Reguson-Wagstaffe, W. (trb)
Fauré, G.:Requiem, w. S. Irwin (b-bar), F. Burgomeister (cnd), Indianapolis Festival Orch, Christ Church Cathedral Men & Boys Choir Oxford Gothic ▲ G 49062 [DDD]

Rehfuss, Heinz (bar)
Bach, J.S.:Cant 57, w. Maria Stader (sop), J.-M. Auberson (cnd), Vienna Opera Orch
FNAC Music ("Via Classics" series) ▲ 642329
Beethoven, L. van:Missa Solemnis, w. M. Stader (sop), E. Cavalti (mez), E. Haefliger (ten), C. Schuricht (cnd), Hamburg SO, St. Hedwig's Cathedral Choir *(rec Sept. 15, 1957)*
Archipon 2-▲ ARCH 2.1CD (m) [ADD]
Brahms, J.:Songs, w. F. Martin (pno)—3 songs *(rec 1964)* FNAC Music ▲ 642313
Brahms, J.:Songs, w. F. Martin (pno)—Feldeinsamkeit; Vergebliches Ständchen; Mein Mädel hat einen Rosenmund Claves ▲ CD 9327 [ADD]
Dittersdorf, K.D. von:Arcifanfano, King of Fools, or It's Always Too Late to Learn, w. P. Brooks (sop), A. Russell (sop), E. Steber (sop), J. McCollum (ten), J. Sopher (ten), D. Smith (bar), N. Jenkins (cnd), Clarion Music Society Orch, Clarion Music Society Chorus [E] *(rec live, New York 1965)*
VAI Audio 2-▲ VAIA 1010-2 (m) [ADD]

Rehfuss, Heinz (bar) (cont.)
Falla, M. de:Atlántida, w. Montserrat Caballé (sop), E. Ansermet (cnd), Swiss Romande Orch, Lausanne Youth Chorus, Swiss Romande Red Chorus, Villamont College Little Chorus
Cascavelle ▲ CVL 2005 [ADD]
Mahler, G.:Des Knaben Wunderhorn, w. M. Forrester (cta), F. Prohaska (cnd), Vienna Festival Orch *(rec 5 & 6/63)* Vanguard Classics ▲ OVC 4045 [ADD]
Martin, F.:Monologe (6) aus "Jedermann", w. F. Martin (pno) Jecklin-Disco ▲ JD 563-2 [ADD]
Martin, F.:Le Vin herbé, w. B. Retchitzka (sop), H. Morath (cta), O. de Nyzankowskyi (ten), D. Olsen (bass), F. Martin (pno), V. Desarzens (cnd), Winterthur State Orch members
Jecklin-Disco 2-▲ JD 581/2-2 [ADD]
Milhaud, D.:Service sacré, w. D. Milhaud (cnd), Paris Opera Orch, French Radio-TV Chorus
Accord ▲ ACD 201892 [AAD]
Schubert, Franz:Songs (misc), w. F. Martin (pno)—Frühlingsglaube; Der Lindenbaum; Der Wanderer; Der Wanderer an den Mond; An die Laute; Der Doppelgänger Claves ▲ CD 9327 [ADD]
Schumann, R.:Songs, w. F. Martin (pno)—Widmung; Du bist wie eine Blume; Die Lotosblume; Die beiden Grendadiere Claves ▲ CD 9327 [ADD]
Wolf, H.:Songs (misc), w. F. Martin (pno)—Der Tambour; Der Rattenfänger Claves ▲ CD 9327 [ADD]

Rehkemper, Heinrich (bar)
Mahler, G.:Kindertotenlieder, w. J. Horenstein (cnd), Munich National Theatre Orch [G] *(rec 1928 for Polydor)* Pearl 2-▲ PEAS 9929 (m) [AAD]
Schubert, Franz:Songs (misc), w. Manfred Gurlitt (pno)—21 Lieder—fourteen song cycle selections *(Die schöne Müllerin—Nos. 2, 6, 11, 15, 17; Schwanengesang—Nos. 7 & 13; Winterreise—Nos. 1, 5, 7, 13, 15, 23, 24)*; seven individual songs—Das Rosenband, D.280; Erlkönig, D.328; Am, Bach im Frühling, D.361; Orpheus, D.474; Sei mir gegrüsst, D.741; Der Musensohn, D.764; Auf dem Wasser zu singen, D.774 *(rec 1924-28 for Grammophon)*
Preiser ("Lebendige Vergangenheit" series) ▲ 89058 (m) [AAD]

Rehling, Elisabeth (sop)
Nielsen, C.:Songs, w. Peder Severin (ten), Dorte Kirkeskov (pno), Jørgen Ernst Hansen (org)—Strange to Say...; Maria Sat on Hay & Straw; God's Angels Sing in Chorus; Now the Sun in the East...; Alas, My Rose...; Standing in Pain under the Cross...; It Is a Wonder...; Jesus Mine, Let My Heart Savour... [all from Hymns & Sacred Songs]; Jens the Road-Mender; The 1st Lark [both from Strophic Songs, Op. 21]; Vibeke's Song [I Came Upon a Song...]; Song of the Sea [The Sea Around Denmark] [both from the play Willemoes]; We Sons of the Plains; The Bird-Catcher's Song, The Tiny Forest Birds are Hiding...; Tove's Song [An Angel Stood Beside Me...]; The Hunter's Song [The Kite Swoops from the Mountain Crest...] [all from the play Tove]; Gulnare's Song [Zither, Let My Prayer Move You...]; Aladdin's Lullaby [Lullalullaby, Tiny Babe...]; Fatima's Song [The Moon is Already Risen...] [all from the play Aladdin]; Music to 5 Poems by J.P. Jacobsen, Op. 4; 10 Little Danish Songs *(rec West Jutland Academy of Music, Sept 1989)* Rondo Grammofon ▲ RCD 8327
Nielsen, C.:Songs, w. Peder Severin (ten), Dorte Kirkeskov (pno)—I Bear My Yoke with a Smile; Now the Day is Full of Song; How Sweetly on This Summer Evening; Often I'm Happy; Spring Has Come Now; Strangest Breeze of Twilight Hours; Harken to Its Gentle Wing-Beats; Sleep Sweetly, Little Baby Mine; In Shadow We Wander; Now Leaps the Spring from Its Bed; The Snow Queen [The Meadow Lies Buried in Snow So White]; There Lived a Man in Ribe Town [all from 20 Danish Songs]; Christmas Carol [Come Yule to Earth]; To the Queen of My Heart [Shall We Roam, My Love]; Angst [Hold Me Tighter]; The Guide Sings [To the Mountains Above the Village]; Flower Songs; In the Land of Dreams; Just Bow Your Head, O Flower; Song Behind the Plough; This Evening; Greeting; It Is Autumn; *(rec West Jutland Academy of Music, Apr 1988)* Rondo Grammofon ▲ RCD 8323
Schnittke, A.:Penitential Psalms, w. Eva Bruun Hansen (sop), Annette Simonsen (alt), Maria Streijffert (alt), Karl-Gustav Andersson (ten), Poul Vejbo (ten), Stefan Parkman (cnd), Danish National Radio Choir
Chandos ▲ CHAN 9480

Reich, A. (sgr)
Avni, T.:A Monk Observes a Skull, w. S. Magen (vc) Symposium ▲ 1110

Reich, Günter (nar)
Schoenberg, A.:Gurrelieder, w. M. Napier (sop), Y. Minton (mez), J. Thomas (ten), K. Bowman (sgr), S. Nimsgern (b-bar), P. Boulez (cnd), BBC SO *(rec Oct. 26-Dec. 06, 1974)*
Sony Classical 2-▲ SM2K 48459 [ADD]
Schoenberg, A.:Moses und Aaron, w. R. Cassilly (ten), P. Boulez (cnd), BBC SO, Ensemble InterContemporain, BBC Singers *(rec Nov. 30-Dec. 06, 1974)*
Sony Classical 2-▲ SM2K 48456 [ADD]
Schoenberg, A.:A Survivor from Warsaw, w. P. Boulez (cnd), BBC SO, BBC Sym Chorus *(rec 1976)*
Sony Classical 2-▲ S2K 44571 [ADD/DDD]

Reichelt, Ingeborg (sop)
Bach, J.S.:Cant 58, w. W. Schöne (bass), H. Rilling (cnd), Stuttgart Bach Collegium, Gächinger Kantorei [G] Hänssler Classic ▲ 98.871 [AAD]
Bach, J.S.:Cant 75, w. V. Gohl (mez), J. Hamari (cta), A. Baldin (ten), A. Kraus (ten), H.-F. Kunz (bass), H. Rilling (cnd), Stuttgart Bach Collegium, Frankfurt Kantorei [G] *(rec 1970)*
Hänssler Classic ▲ 98.891 [AAD]
Bach, J.S.:Cant 88, w. V. Gohl (mez), A. Kraus (ten), W. Schöne (bass), H. Rilling (cnd), Stuttgart Bach Collegium, Remembrance Florid Church Chorus Hänssler Classic ▲ 98.804 [AAD]

Reichmann, Wolfgang (nar)
Mozart, W.A.:Entführung, w. Yvonne Kenny (sop), Carolyn Watson (cta), Peter Schreier (ten), Wilfried Gamlich (ten), Matti Salminen (bass), N. Harnoncourt (cnd), Zurich Mozart Opera Orch, Zurich Mozart Opera Chorus [G] Teldec 2-▲ 2292-42643-2
Weill, K.:The Threepenny Opera, w. U. Lemper (sop), Milva (sgr), S. Tremper (sgr), H. Dernesch (mez), R. Kollo (ten), M. Adorf (sgr), J. Mauceri (cnd), Berlin RIAS Sinfonietta, Berlin RIAS Chamber Choir [G]
London ▲ 430075-2 [DDD]

Reid, Rufus (bass)
Previn, A.:Honey & Rue, w. Kathleen Battle (sop), Chris Gekker (tpt), James Pugh (trbn), Grady Tate (dr), A. Previn (cnd), Orch of St. Luke's Deutsche Grammophon ▲ 437787-2 ▮ 437 787-4

Reimar, Hans (ten)
Wagner, R.:Parsifal (sels), w. E. Larcen (sop), C. Hartmann (bar), L. Weber (bass), H. Knappertsbusch (cnd), Berlin German Opera Orch, Berlin German Opera Chorus—Act 3 *(rec 1943)*
Enterprise ("Document" series) ▲ ENTLV 943 [ADD]

Reimer, Eva-Christine (sgr)
Delius, F.:A Village Romeo & Juliet, w. Karsten Russ (sgr), Klaus Wallprecht (sgr), K. Seibel (cnd), Kiel PO CPO 2-▲ CPO 999328 [DDD]

Reinbold, Véronique (mez)
Essyad, A.:Le Collier des ruses, w. C. Bonnet (sop), F. Gonzalez (sop), P. Nahon (cnd), Ensemble Instrumental K617 2-▲ 7051

Reinemann, Udo (bar)
Mozart, W.A.:Songs, w. A. M. Miranda (sop), C. Wirz (alt), M. Quillevéré (ten), C. Ivaldi (pno)—K.152, 307, 308, 346, 351, 436-439, 441, 441b, 472, 473, 506, 510, 520, 523, 524, 532, 549, 561, 625, & K.Anh 5 *(rec 1979)* Arion ▲ ARN 68161 [ADD]

Reiner, Carl (nar)
Rogers, B.:The Musicians of Bremen, w. A. Stern (cnd), XTET Delos ▲ DE 6001 [DDD] ▮ CS 6001 (D)

Reinhardt, Doris (mez)
Boulanger, N.:Songs, w. I. Sabrié (sop), S. Robert (sop), E. Naoumoff (pno)—Lux aeterna [w. O. Charlier (violin) & R. Pidoux (cello)]; Le Couteau *(rec June 14-17, 1993)* Marco Polo ▲ 8.223636 [DDD]

Reinhardt, Ray (nar)
Kolb, B.:Chromatic Fant, w. G. Schwarz (cnd), Music Today Ensemble [E]
New World ▲ 80422-2 [DDD]

Reinhart, Gregory (bass)
Campra, A.:Tancrède, w. C. Alliot-Lugaz (sop), D. Evangelatos (cta), F. le Roux (bar), P.-Y. le Maigat (bass-bar), Dubose (sgr), J. Malgoire (cnd), La Grande Écurie et la Chambre du Roy
Erato (Musifrance) 2-▲ 2292-45001-2 ZA [DDD]
Charpentier, M.-A.:Les Arts florissants, w. C. Dussaut (sop), J. Feldman (sop), A. Mellon (sop), G. Laurens (mez), D. Visse (ct), P. Cantor (ten), W. Christie (cnd), Les Arts Florissants [F]
Musique d'Abord ▲ HMA 1901083

▲ = CD ♦ = Enhanced CD Δ = MD ▮ = Cassette Tape ◻ = DCC

Reinhart, Gregory (bass) (cont.)

Charpentier, M.-A.:Judicum Salomonis, w. A. Zaepffel (ct), J. Benet (ten), Elwes (ten), G. Ragon (ten), J. Cabré (bar), P. Colléaux (cnd), Stradivaria Ensemble, Nantes Vocal Ensemble [L] Arion ▲ ARN 68037 [DDD]

Couperin, F.:Motets, w. J. Feldman (sop), I. Poulenard (sop), J. ter Linden (bass vl), D. Moroney (hpd)—[L] Musique d'Abord ▲ HMA 1901150

Handel, G.F.:Messiah, w. Marjanne Kweksilber (sop), James Bowman (ct), Paul Elliot (ten), T. Koopman (cnd), Amsterdam Baroque Orch, The Sixteen Erato 3-▲ 2292-45960-2

Handel, G.F.:Tamerlano, w. Isabelle Poulenard (sop—Irene), Mieke van der Sluis (sop—Asteria), René Jacobs (alt—Andronico), Henri Ledroit (ct—Tamerlano), John Elwes (ten—Bajazet), Gregory Reinhart (bass—Leone), J. Malgoire (cnd), La Grande Écurie et la Chambre du Roy *(rec 1983)* Sony Classical 3-▲ SM3K 37893

Monteverdi, C.:Incoronazione, w. A. Augér (sop), S. Leonard (sop), D. Jones (mez), L. Hirst (mez), J. Bowman (ct), R. Hickox (cnd), City of London Baroque Sinfonia Virgin Classics 3-▲ CDCC 59524

Mozart, W.A.:Requiem, w. Colette Alliot-Lugaz (sop), Dominique Vissé (ct), Martyn Hill (ten), J. Malgoire (cnd), La Grande Écurie et la Chambre du Roy, Nord-Pas-de-Calais Choir [L] CBS ▲ MDK 44904 [DDD]

Rameau, J.P.:Les Paladins, w. A. Michael (sop), G. Raphanel (sop), B. Brewer (ten), D. Nasrawi (ten), N. Rivenq (bar), J. Malgoire (cnd), La Grande Écurie et la Chambre du Roy, Sagittarius Vocal Ensemble [F] Pierre Verany 2-▲ PV.790121/22 [DDD]

Reining, Maria (sop)

Lehár, F.:Music of, w. E. Réthy (sop), J. Novotna (sop), R. Tauber (ten), F. Lehár (cnd), Vienna SO, Vienna PO—6 orchestral sels. *(Musikalische Memorien I–IV; Die lustige Witwe—Overture; Eva—Prelude)*; 4 Arias from Giuditta *(Du bist meine Sonne—Tauber; Freunde, das Leben ist lebenswert—Tauber; Schön wie die blaue Sommernacht—Novotna & Tauber; Schönste der Frauen—Tauber)*; 1 Song & 5 Arias sung by Esther Rethy *(Wien, du bist das Herz der Welt; Giuditta—Meine Lippen, sie küssenso heiss; Paganini—Liebe, du Himmel auf Erden; Schön ist die Welt—Ich bin verliebt; Der Zarewitsch—Einer wird kommen; Zigeunerliebe—Hör ich Cymbalklänge)*; 2 Arias sung by Maria Reining *(Eva—Im heimlichen Dämmer der silbernen Ampel; Friederike—Warum hast du mich wachgeküsst?)* *(rec 1934–1942 Odeon & HMV rec)* Preiser ▲ 90150 (m) [AAD]

Maria Reining *(rec between 1942–43)* Preiser ▲ PRE 89065 [AAD]

Maria Reining Sings Preiser ▲ PRE 90083 (m) [AAD]

Max Lorenz:Recital, 1933-1957, w. Max Lorenz (ten), Berlin RSO [cnd:Artur Rother], Bayreuth Festival Orch [cnd:Heinz Tietjen, Richard Strauss], German Large RSO [cnd:Rudolf Moralt, Max Schönherr, Anton Paulik], Hessen RSO [cnd:Kurt Schröder], Brenda Lewis (sop), Eberhard Wächter (ten), Wolfgang Zimmer (bar) *(rec 1933–57)* Myto ▲ MCD 934.88

Mozart, W.A.:Don Giovanni, w. Hedwig Jungkurth (sop—Elvira), Maria Reining (sop—Anna), Julius Patzak (ten—Ottavio), Karl Hammes (bar—Don Giovanni), Georg Hann (bass), Ludwig Weber (bass—Commandant), J. Keilberth (cnd), Stuttgart Reich RSO, Stuttgart Radio Chorus *(rec Mar, 1936)* Preiser 2-▲ PRE 90263

Mozart, W.A.:Nozze di Figaro (sels), w. M. Reining (sop—Countess), M. Cebotari (sop—Susanna), M. Ahlersmeyer (bar—Count Almaviva), K. Böhm (cnd), Vienna State Opera Orch *(rec Nov. 7, 1941)* Koch Schwann 2-▲ SCH 314602

Mozart, W.A.:Nozze di Figaro (sels), w. Maria Reining (sop—Countess), Margherita Perras (sop—Susanna), Alfred Jerger (b-bar—Count), Paul Schöffler (b-bar—Figaro), W. Loibner (cnd), Vienna State Opera Orch *(rec May 24, 1938)* Koch Schwann 2-▲ SCH 314632 [ADD]

Mozart, W.A.:Zauberflöte (sels), w. Erna Berger (sop—Queen of the Night), Maria Reining (sop—Pamina), Josef von Manowarda (bass—Sarastro), H. Knappertsbusch (cnd), Vienna State Opera Orch *(rec Vienna, Dec. 4, 1941)* Koch Schwann 2-▲ SCH 314672 [ADD]

Strauss, R.:Arabella, w. L. Della Casa (sop), H. Taubmann (ten), H. Hotter (b-bar), K. Böhm (cnd), Vienna PO *(rec Salzburg Festival, 1947)* Deutsche Grammophon 3-▲ 445342-2 (m) [ADD]

Strauss, R.:Arabella, w. L. Della Casa (sop), R. Anday (cta), H. Hotter (b-bar), G. Hann (bass), J. Patzak (ten), K. Böhm (cnd), Vienna PO, Vienna State Opera Chorus *(rec live, Salzburg Festival, 8/12/47)* Melodram 3-▲ MEL 37077

Strauss, R.:Ariadne auf Naxos, w. I. Seefried (sop), A. Noni (sop), M. Lorenz (ten), J. Witt (ten), E. Kunz (bar), P. Schöffler (bass), K. Böhm (cnd), Vienna State Opera Orch *(rec Strauss' 80th Birthday Festival, June 11, 1944)* Preiser 2-▲ PRE 90217 [ADD]

Strauss, R.:Ariadne auf Naxos (sels), w. Alda Noni (sop—Zerbinetta), Maria Reining (sop—Ariadne), Irmgard Seefried (sop—Composer), Max Lorenz (ten—Bacchus), Paul Schöffler (b-bar—Musiklehrer), K. Böhm (cnd), Vienna State Opera Orch *(rec Vienna, June 11, 1944)* Koch Schwann 2-▲ SCH 314732 [ADD]

Strauss, R.:Daphne (sels), w. M. Reining (sop—Daphne), A. Dermota (ten—Leukippos), R. Moralt (cnd), Vienna State Opera Orch, Vienna State Opera Chorus *(rec May 8, 1942)* Koch Schwann 2-▲ SCH 314552 [ADD]

Strauss, R.:Der Rosenkavalier, w. H. Gueden (sop), S. Jurinac (sop), L. Weber (bass), E. Kleiber (cnd), Vienna PO, Vienna State Opera Chorus [G] London ("Historic" series) ▲ 425950-2 (m) [ADD]

Strauss, R.:Songs, w. M. Reining (sop—6 solo songs), L. Piltti (sop—7 solo songs), A. Dermota (ten—8 solo songs), R. Strauss (pno)—Opp. 10/1, 27/2, 29/1, 37/3, 41/1, 48/1 *(Reining)*; Opp. 15/5, 17/2, 21/1, 20/2, 48/2, 48/3, 49/1 *(Piltti)*; Opp. 10/1, 10/3, 17/1, 19/2, 21/2, 27/3, 32/1, 37/2 *(Dormota)* [G] *(rec Vienna, Apr. 1942)* Preiser ▲ 93262 (m) [AAD]

Wagner, R.:Arias & Scenes, w. Kathe Heidersbach (sop), Hilde Scheppan (sop), Margarete Teschemacher (sop), Margarete Klose (mez), Max Lorenz (ten), Jaro Prohaska (bar), Karl Schmitt-Walter (bar), Kurt Böhme (bass), *(orch unknown)*—selections from Rienzi; Der Fliegende Holländer; Tannhäuser; Lohengrin; Tristan und Isolde; Die Meistersinger von Nürnberg; Die Walküre & Götterdämmerung *(rec 1927–1944)* Phonographe 2-▲ PHG 5016 [AAD]

Wagner, R.:Die Meistersinger von Nürnberg, w. H. Noort (ten), A. Dermota (ten), H. H. Nissen (bar), H. Alsen (bass), A. Toscanini (cnd), Vienna PO *(rec live, Salzburg, 1937)* Melodram 4-▲ MEL 47041

Wagner, R.:Die Meistersinger von Nürnberg (sels), w. Maria Reining (sop—Eva), Peter Klein (ten—David), Max Lorenz (ten—Walther), Josef Hermann (bar—Hans Sachs), Erich Kunz (bar—Beckmesser), K. Böhm (cnd), Vienna State Opera Orch *(rec Vienna, Jan. 19, 1943)* Koch Schwann 2-▲ SCH 314732 [ADD]

Wagner, R.:Die Meistersinger von Nürnberg (sels), w. Maria Reining (sop—Eva), Torsten Ralf (ten—Walther), Josef Herrman (bar—Hans Sachs), Erich Kunz (bar—Beckmesser), Kurt Böhme (bass—Pogner), K. Böhm (cnd), Vienna State Opera Orch *(rec Vienna, 1944)* Koch Schwann 2-▲ SCH 314682 [ADD]

Wagner, R.:Die Meistersinger von Nürnberg (sels), w. Maria Reining (sop—Eva), Set Svanholm (ten—Walther), Paul Schöffler (b-bar—Hans Sachs), K. Böhm (cnd), Vienna State Opera Orch *(rec Vienna, Jan. 31, 1943)* Koch Schwann ▲ SCH 314692 [ADD]

Wagner, R.:Die Meistersinger von Nürnberg (sels), w. Maria Reining (sop—Eva), Max Lorenz (ten—Walther), Erich Zimmermann (ten—David), Karl Kamann (bar—Hans Sachs), W. Furtwängler (cnd), Vienna State Opera Orch *(rec Vienna, Nov. 25, 1937)* Koch Schwann 2-▲ SCH 314702 [ADD]

Wagner, R.:Tannhäuser (sels), w. Maria Reining (sop—Elisabeth), Max Lorenz (ten—Tannhäuser), Arno Schellenberg (bar—Wolfram), H. Knappertsbusch (cnd), Vienna State Opera Orch *(rec Vienna, Nov. 20, 1937)* Koch Schwann 2-▲ SCH 314672 [ADD]

Wagner, R.:Die Walküre (sels), w. F. Krauss (ten), C. Leonhardt (cnd), Stuttgart Radio Orch—4 solo arias from Act I Scene 3 *(Der Männer Sippe; Winterstürme wichen dem Wonnenmond; Du bist der Lenz; Siegmund heiss ich)* [G] *(rec April 3, 1938)* Preiser 3-▲ 90133 (m) [AAD]

Wagner, R.:Die Walküre (sels), w. H. Jung (mez), F. Krauss (ten), R. Bockelmann (bar), J. von Manowarda (bass), C. Leonhardt (cnd), Stuttgart Radio Orch—Act 2 (sels.); Act 3 (complete) *(rec Apr. 3, 1938)* Preiser 2-▲ PRE 90207 [ADD]

Wagner, R.:Die Walküre (act 1), w. F. Krauss (ten), J. von Manowarda (bass), C. Leonhardt (cnd), Stuttgart Reichssenders Orch *(rec April 28, 1940)* Preiser ▲ 90151 (m)

Weber, C.M. von:Der Freischütz (sels), w. Maria Reining (sop—Agathe), Elisabeth Rutgers (mez—Ännchen), Julius Pölzer (ten—Max), Herbert Alsen (bass—Kaspar), R. Moralt (cnd), Vienna State Opera Orch *(rec Jan. 1, 1939)* Koch Schwann 2-▲ SCH 314632 [ADD]

Reinmann, F. (bar)

Pfiffner, E.:Don Quijote, w. S. Burkhard (pno) *(rec May 1992)* Pro Viva ▲ ISPV 170 [DDD]

Pfiffner, E.:Monologue on Peace & War, w. J. Allen (vn), A. Rosenfeld (vn), C. Anderes (va), G. Pawlica (vc) *(rec May 1992)* Pro Viva ▲ ISPV 170 [DDD]

Reinmar, Hans (bar)

Helge Roswaenge, w. Helge Roswaenge (ten), Milizia Korjus (sop), Tiana Lemnitz (sop), Heinrich Schlusnus (bar), et al. Preiser 2-▲ PRE 89209 [AAD]

Wagner, R.:Parsifal (sels), w. Carl Hartmann (ten), Ludwig Weber (bass), Elsa Laren (sgr), H. Knappertsbusch (cnd), Berlin German Opera Orch, Berlin German Opera Chorus—complete Act 3 *(rec Berlin, March 31, 1942)* Grammofono 2000 ▲ GRM 78555

Reinprecht, Johann (ten)

Dvořák, A.:Mass, w. G. Schmid (sop), J. Bernheimer (mez), A. Sramek (bar), F. Wolf (cnd), St. Augustin Orch, St. Augustin Chorus [L] *(rec 1987)* Preiser ▲ 93378 [ADD]

Schubert, Franz:Duetsche Messe, w. R. Hansmann (sop), M. Lipovšek (mez), L. Spitzer (pno), F. Wolf (cnd), St. Augustin Orch, St. Augustin Chorus Preiser ▲ 93325

Schubert, Franz:Mass 3, w. R. Hansmann (sop), M. Lipovšek (mez), Spitzer (bass), F. Wolf (cnd), St. Augustin Orch, St. Augustin Chorus Preiser ▲ 93325

Reiss, Albert (ten)

Bach, J.S.:Music of, w. L. Güttler (tpt), M. Lorenz (ten), P. Schreier (ten), H.-C. Polster (b-bar), M. Pommer (cnd), Leipzig New Bach Collegium Musicum, Leipzig Choirs—arias, choruses & chorales Capriccio ▲ CDC 10039 [DDD]

Reizen, Mark (bass)

Mark Reizen Preiser ("Lebendige Vergangenheit" series) ▲ PRE 89059 (m) [AAD]

Mussorgsky, M.:Boris Godounov, w. Georgi Nelepp (ten), Maxim Mikhailov (bass), *(other soloists unknown)*, N. Golovanov (cnd), Bolshoi Theater Orch, Bolshoi Theater Chorus *(rec 1948)* Arlecchino 3-▲ ARL121/23

Mussorgsky, M.:Khovanshchina, w. *(other soloists unknown)*, B. Khaikin (cnd), Kirov Opera Orch, Kirov Opera Chorus *(rec 1947)* Arlecchino 3-▲ ARL103/05

Reja, Juri (ten)

Dvořák, A.:Stabat Mater, w. A. P. Jeric (sop), E. N. Houska (mez), F. Petrusanec (bass), M. Munih (cnd), Ljubljana RSO, Ljubljana Radio Chorus [L] PMG (Vienna Master) ▲ CD 160104 [DDD]

Dvořák, A.:Stabat Mater, w. A. Pusar-Jerik (sop), E. N. Houska (mez), F. Petrusanec (bass), M. Munih (cnd), Consortium Musicum Orch, Consortium Musicum Chorus [L] Vivace 2-▲ 140141 [ADD/DDD]

Relyea, Gary (bass)

Handel, G.F.:Messiah, w. Leslie Fagan (sop), Janis Taylor (mez), Mark Dubois (ten), G. Fagan (cnd), Concert Players Orch, Gerald Fagan Singers, London Fanshawe Symphonic Chorus Doremi 2-▲ 9306 [DDD]

Rossini, G.:Mosè in Egitto (sels), w. Wendy Nielsen (sop—Elcia), Anita Krause (mez—Amenosi), Richard Margison (ten—Aronne), Gary Relyea (bass—Mosè), R. Bradshaw (cnd), Canadian Opera Company Orch, Canadian Opera Company Chorus—Scena, Coro & Preghiera [Dal tuo stellato soglio] *(rec George Weston Recital Hall, Ford Centre for the Performing Arts, North York, Ontario, Dec 20–23, 1994)* CBC ("SM 5000" series) ▲ SM5 5148 [DDD]

Verdi, G.:Alzira (sels), w. Stephen McClare (ten—Otumbo), Richard Margison (ten—Zamoro), Gary Relyea (bass—Alvaro), R. Bradshaw (cnd), Canadian Opera Company Orch, Canadian Opera Company Chorus—Il prigioniero [prologue] *(rec George Weston Recital Hall, Ford Centre for the Performing Arts, North York, Ontario, Dec 20–23, 1994)* CBC ("SM 5000" series) ▲ SM5 5148 [DDD]

Verdi, G.:Ernani (sels), w. Richard Margison (ten—Ernani), Gary Relyea (bass—Don Silva), R. Bradshaw (cnd), Canadian Opera Company Orch, Canadian Opera Company Chorus—Conspiracy [An alliance; Let the Lion of Castile Rise Again] *(rec George Weston Recital Hall, Ford Centre for the Performing Arts, North York, Ontario, Dec 20–23, 1994)* CBC ("SM 5000" series) ▲ SM5 5148 [DDD]

Relyea, John (bass)

Berg, O.:Peter Quince at the Clavier, w. L. Freedman (E♭ & B♭ cl), J. Hess (pno), T. Tureski (perc) Centaur ▲ CRC 2167 [DDD]

Remedios, Alberto (ten)

Tippett, M.:The Midsummer Marriage, w. Joan Carlyle (sop—Joan), Elizabeth Harwood (sop—Beth), Elizabeth Bainbridge (mez), Helen Watts (cta—Sosostris), Stuart Burrows (ten—Jack), Alberto Remedios (ten—Mark), Stafford Dean (bass), Raimund Herincx (bass—King Fisher), C. Davis (cnd), Royal Opera House Orch, Royal Opera House Chorus Covent Garden Lyrita 2-▲ SRCD 2217

Wagner, R.:Götterdämmerung (sels), w. M. Curphey (sop), R. Hunter (sop), N. Bailey (bar), C. Grant (bass), R. Goodall (cnd), Sadler's Wells Opera Orch, Sadler's Wells Opera Chorus—Act 3, Scenes 2 & 3 [E] Chandos ("Collect" series) ▲ CHAN 6593 [ADD]

Wagner, R.:Götterdämmerung (sels), w. Rita Hunter (sop—Brünnhilde), Alberto Remedios (ten—Siegfried), C. Mackerras (cnd), London PO—Dawn; Brünnhilde & Siegfried's Entrance; Siegfried's Rhine Journey; Siegfried's Funeral Music; Brünnhilde's Immolation [Starke Scheite schichtet mir dort] Classics for Pleasure ▲ CDCFP 4670

Remington, Martha (mez)

Beach, A.M.C.:Mass, "Grand Mass", w. Margot Law (sop), Ray Bauwens (ten), Joel Schneider (bar), B. Jones (cnd), Stow Festival Orch, Stow Festival Chorus *(rec Cathedral Church of St Paul, Tremont St, Boston, MA)* Albany ▲ TROY 179 [DDD]

Remmert, Birgit (cta)

Beethoven, L. van:Missa Solemnis, w. Rosa Mannion (sop), James Taylor (ten), Cornelius Hauptmann (bass), P. Herreweghe (cnd), Champs Elysées Theater Orch, Chapelle Royale Choir, Collegium Vocale *(rec Auditorium Stravinski de Montreux, Feb. 20–21, 1995)* Harmonia Mundi France ▲ HMC 901557

Mahler, G.:Das Lied von der Erde, w. H.-P. Blochwitz (ten), P. Herreweghe (cnd), Musique Oblique Ensemble [arr. Schoenberg & Riehn for chamber orch.] Harmonia Mundi France ▲ HMC 901477

Mendelssohn, F.:Die erste Walpurgisnacht, w. U. Heilman (ten), T. Hampson (bar), R. Pape (bass), N. Harnoncourt (cnd), CO of Europe Teldec ▲ 74882-2

Remor, Michela (sop)

Respighi, O.:Lucrezia, w. Adriana Kohútková (sop—Venilia), Michela Remor (sop—Lucrezia), Stefania Kaluza (mez—La Voce), Denisa Šlepkovská (mez—Servia), Ludovít Ludha (ten—Collatino), Igor Pasek (ten—Bruto), Ján Durčo (bar—Tito/Valerio), Richard Haan (bar—Tarquinio), Rado Hanák (bass—Arunte/Spurio Lucrezio) *(rec Concert Hall of the Slovak Radio, Bratislava, June 9–16, 1994)* Marco Polo ▲ 8.223717 [DDD]

Rendall, David (ten)

Beethoven, L. van:Sym 9, "Choral Sym", w. Alison Hargen (sop), Della Jones (mez), Gwynne Howell (b-bar), W. Morris (cnd), London SO, London Sym Chorus IMP ("LSO" series) ▲ IMP 6900032

Elgar, E.:The Apostles, w. A. Hargan (sop), A. Hodgson (cta), S. Roberts (bar), B. Terfel (bass-bar), R. Lloyd (bass), R. Hickox (cnd), London SO, London Sym Chorus [E] Chandos 2-▲ CHAN 8875/76 [DDD]

Mozart, W.A.:Requiem, w. K. Battle (sop), A. Murray (mez), M. Salminen (bass), D. Barenboim (cnd), Orch de Paris, Paris Opera Chorus [L] EMI Classics ▲ CDC 47342 [DDD]

Puccini, G.:La Rondine, w. M. Nicolesco (sop), K. Te Kanawa (sop), P. Domingo (ten), L. Nucci (bar), L. Maazel (cnd), London SO, Ambrosian Opera Chorus [I] CBS 2-▲ M2K 37852 [DDD]

Renihan, Grania (sgr)

Lloyd Webber, A.:Music of, w. M. Friedman (sgr), C. Carter (sgr), C. Moore (sgr), J. Barrowman (sgr), L. Robertson (sgr), J. Diedrich (sgr), J.O. Edwards (cnd), Munich SO—Cats; Joseph & the Amazing Technicolor Dreamcoat; Phantom of the Opera; Evita; Jesus Christ Superstar; Starlight Express; Song & Dance; Aspects of Love Koch International ▲ CD 340022 [DDD] ■ MC 340022

Rensburg, Kobie van (ten)

Bach, J.S.:Cant 36, w. Silke Wenzel (sop), Reiner Schneider-Waterburg (alt), Christian Hilz (bass), W. Kelber (cnd), Munich Monteverdi Orch *(rec live, Dec 1995)* Calig ▲ 50963 [DDD]

Bach, J.S.:Cant 40, w. Silke Wenzel (sop), Reiner Schneider-Waterburg (alt), Christian Hilz (bass), W. Kelber (cnd), Munich Monteverdi Orch *(rec live, Dec 1995)* Calig ▲ 50963 [DDD]

Bach, J.S.:Cant 91, w. Silke Wenzel (sop), Reiner Schneider-Waterburg (alt), Christian Hilz (bass), W. Kelber (cnd), Munich Monteverdi Orch *(rec live, Dec 1995)* Calig ▲ 50963 [DDD]

Renzi, Emilio (ten)

Bellini, V.:Norma, w. Gina Cigna (sop—Norma), Ebe Stignani (sop—Adalgisa), Adriana Perris (mez—Clotilde), Giovanni Breviario (ten—Pollione), Emilio Renzi (ten—Flavio), Tancredi Pasero (bass—Oroveso), V. Gui (cnd), EIAR Orch, Achille Consoli (cnd), EIAR Chorus *(rec Aug/Sept 1937)* Arkadia ("The 78's" series) 2-▲ 78010 [ADD]

Renzi, Richard di (ten)
Puccini, G.:Madama Butterfly, w. Maria Spacagna (sop), Sharon Grahm (mez), Vivica Genaux (mez), Richard Markley (ten), Erich Parce (bar), James Butler (bass), C. Rosenkrans (cnd), Hungarian State Opera Orch, Anikó Katona (cnd), Hungarian State Opera Chorus—3 versions *(rec Italian Institute, Budapest, Sept 5-21, 1995)* Vox Classics 4-▲ VOX4 7525 [DDD]

Reps, H. (mez)
Gottlieb, J.:Sacred Music, w. M. Stone (sop), D. Lefkowitz (ten), H. Stahl (ten), R. Abelson (bar), R. Botton (bar), P. Newman (reader), S. Sturk (cnd), Metropolitan Brass Ensemble, New York Motet Choir Premier ("Composer" series) ▲ PRCD 1018 [DDD]

Resemba, Maria (sop)
Rossini, G.:Il barbiere di Siviglia (sels), w. N. Sabatano (sop), F. de Lucia (ten), F. Novelli (bar), G. Schottler (bass), A. di Tommaso (bass), S. Valentino (bass), S. Sassano (cnd), Naples Teatro San Carlo Orch, Naples Teatro San Carlo Chorus [I] *(rec 1918 for Phonotype)* Standing Room Only ▲ SRO 819-1 [ADD]

Reshetin, Mark (bass)
Mussorgsky, M.:Boris Godunov, w. Irina Arkhipova (mez—Marina Mnishek), Evgenya Verbitskaya (mez—Nurse to Xenia), Valentina Klepatskaya (sgr—Fyodor), Tamara Sorokina (sgr—Xenia), Anton Grigoryev (ten—Simpleton), Vladimir Ivanovsky (ten—Grigory, the Pretender), Gyorgy Shulpin (bar—Prince Shuisky), Alexey Geleva (bass—Varlaam), Ivan Petrov (bass—Boris Godounov), Mark Reshetin (bass—Pimen), Alexi Ivanov (sgr—Andrei Shchelkalov), Evgeny Kibkalo (sgr—Rangoni), A. Melik-Pashayev (cnd), Bolshoi Theater Orch, Bolshoi Theater Chorus *(rec Moscow, 1962)* Melodiya ("The Russian Opera" series) 3-▲ 74321-29349-2 [ADD]
Shostakovich, D.:Sym 14, w. G. Vishnevskaya (sop), R. Barshaï (cnd), Moscow CO *(rec Sept. 29, 1969)* Russian Disc ▲ RUS 11192 [AAD]

Resick, Georgine (sop)
Haimo, E.:Swenson Songs, w. Barry David Salwen (pno) *(rec Annenberg Audit., Snite Museum of Art, Univ. of Notre Dame)* Centaur ▲ CRC 2253 [DDD]
Nicolai, O.:Mass, w. G. Killebrew (mez), F. Lang (ten), H. C. Polster (bass), H. Hollreiser (cnd), North German RSO, North German Radio Chorus [L] Koch Schwann ▲ CD 313052 [ADD]
Righini, V.:Te Deum, w. M. Schiml (sop), R. Wohlers (ten), V. von Halem (bass), G. Albrecht (cnd), Berlin RSO, Berlin Radio Chorus [L] Koch Schwann ▲ CD 313052 [ADD]

Resnik, Regina (mez)
Barber, S.:Vanessa, w. E. Steber (sop), R. Elias (mez), N. Gedda (ten), G. Tozzi (bass), D. Mitropoulos (cnd), Metropolitan Opera Orch, Metropolitan Opera Chorus [E] RCA Gold Seal ▲ 7899-2-RG [ADD]
Berlioz, H.:Roméo et Juliette, w. A. Turp (ten), J. Ward (bar), P. Monteux (cnd), London SO, London Sym Chorus [F] MCA Classics 2-▲ MCAD2-9805
Berlioz, H.:Les Troyens, w. R. Resnik (mez—Dido), E. Steber (sop—Cassandra), R. Cassily (ten—Aeneas), R. Lawrence (cnd), American Opera Society Orch, American Opera Society Chorus *(rec live, Carnegie Hall, 12/29/59 & 1/12/60)* VAI Audio 3-▲ VAIA 1006-3 [ADD]
Bizet, G.:Carmen, w. J. Sutherland (sop), M. Del Monaco (ten), T. Krause (bar), T. Schippers (cnd), Swiss Romande Orch London 2-▲ 411630-2 [ADD]
Bizet, G.:Carmen, w. Joan Sutherland (sop), Mario del Monaco (ten), T. Schippers (cnd), Swiss Romande Orch London ("Double Decca" series) 2-▲ 443871-2
Bizet, G.:Carmen, w. Laura Bustamante (sop—Frasquita), Ximena Riveros (sop—Mercedes), Nancy Stokes (sop—Micaela), Regina Resnik (mez—Carmen), Plácido Domingo (ten—Don José), Ismildo Tedeschi (ten—Remendado), Ramon Vinay (ten—Escamillo), Juan Charles (ten/bar—Dancaire), Agustin Letelier (bar—Morles), Jorge Algorta (bass—Zuniga), A. Guadagno (cnd), Santiago Teatro Municipale Orch, Santiago Teatro Municipale Chorus *(rec Santiago Municipal Theater, Sept. 4, 1967)* Legato Classics 2-▲ LCD 194-2 [ADD]
Donizetti, G.:La fille du régiment, w. J. Sutherland (sop), A. Kraus (ten), S. Maias (bass), R. Bonynge (cnd), Chicago Lyric Opera Orch, Chicago Lyric Opera Chorus [F] *(rec Nov. 20, 1973)* Myto 2-▲ MCD 93276
Lehár, F.:Die lustige Witwe (sels), w. J. Sutherland (sop), W. Krenn (ten), R. Bonynge (cnd), National PO London, Ambrosian Singers—overture & highlights from Acts 1 & 2 London ("Opera Gala" series) ▲ 421884-2 [ADD]
Prokofiev, S.:The Ugly Duckling, w. L. Stokowski (cnd), New York Stadium SO *(rec Belock Recording Studio, Bayside, NY)* Everest ▲ EVC 9023 [AAD]
Regina in Opera:A 50th Anniversary Tribute Cantabile ("Biographies in Music") ▲ BIM 713-1
Strauss (II), Joh.:Die Fledermaus, w. H. Gueden (sop), E. Köth (sop), W. Kmentt (ten), G. Zampieri (ten), E. Wächter (bar), W. Berry (bass), E. Kunz (bar), H. von Karajan (cnd), Vienna PO, Vienna State Opera Chorus, with Gala Sequence [G] London 2-▲ 421046-2 [ADD]
Strauss, R.:Elektra, w. B. Nilsson (sop), L. Rysanek (sop), W. Windgassen (ten), E. Wächter (bar), K. Böhm (cnd), *(orch unknown)* [G] *(rec live, Vienna 12/16/65)* Standing Room Only 2-▲ SRO 833-2 [ADD]
Strauss, R.:Elektra, w. B. Nilsson (sop), M. Collier (sop), G. Stolze (ten), T. Krause (bar), G. Solti (cnd), Vienna PO [G] London 2-▲ 417345-2 [ADD]
Strauss, R.:Salome, w. M. Caballé (sop), R. Lewis (ten), S. Milnes (bar), E. Leinsdorf (cnd), London SO RCA Gold Seal 2-▲ 6644-2-RG [ADD]
Wagner, R.:Tristan und Isolde, w. B. Nilsson (sop), H.-M. Uhle (ten), R. Krause (ten), A. van Mill (bass), G. Solti (cnd), Vienna PO [G] London ("Grand Opera" series) 4-▲ 430234-2 [ADD]

Ress, Ulrich (ten)
Orff, C.:Carmina burana, w. Lisa Griffith (sop), Thomas Mohr (bar), M. Tang (cnd), Royal Flemish PO, Frankfurt Figuralchor, Frankfurt Children's Choir, Frankfurt Choral Society, Goethe Academy Children's Choir *(rec Oct. 1993)* Wergo ▲ WER 6602-2 [DDD]

Retchitzka, Basia (sop)
Caldara, A.:Il gioco del quadriglio, w. Maria-Grazia Ferraccini (sop), Elana Rizzieri (sop), Maria Minetto (cta), E. Loehrer (cnd), Lugano Chamber Society Orch, Minetto Chorus Dynamic ▲ CDL 140
Martin, F.:Le Vin herbé, w. H. Morath (cta), O. de Nyzankowskyi (ten), H. Rehfuss (bar), D. Olsen (bass), F. Martin (pno), V. Desarzens (cnd), Winterthur State Orch members Jecklin-Disco 2-▲ JD 581/2-2 [ADD]
Monteverdi, C.:Madrigals, w. Eric Tappy (ten), Rodolfo Malacarne (ten), Laerte Malaguti (bar), James Loomis (bass), E. Loehrer (cnd), Lugano Chamber Society Orch, Lugano Chamber Society Chorus—8 Madrigali Guerrieri e Amorosi Accord ▲ ACD 220872
Pergolesi, G.B.:Mass in F, w. G. Ferracini (sop), M. Minetto (cta), V. Gohl (cta), C. Jauquier (ten), J. Loomis (bass), Milan Solisti, Plifonia Choir *(rec 1967)* Rivoalto ▲ RIV 8922 [ADD]

Rethberg, Elisabeth (sop)
Arias & Duets, w. Richard Tauber (ten), Lotte Lehmann (sop), et al. *(rec 1919-26)* Preiser 2-▲ PRE 89219
Beethoven, L. van:Missa Solemnis, w. M. Telva (mez), G. Martinelli (ten), E. Pinza (bass), A. Toscanini (cnd), New York PO, Westminster Choir [L] *(rec live, New York 4/28/35)* Melodram 2-▲ CDM 28036 [ADD]
Elisabeth Rethberg:The Complete Brunswick Recordings, 1924-29 Romophone 2-▲ 81012-2
The Great Recordings Pearl ▲ PEA 9199
Halévy, F.:La Juive (sels), w. C. Boerner (sop—Eudoxie), E. Rethberg (sop—Rachel), G. Martinelli (ten—Éléazar), H. Clemens (ten—Léopold), Heller, Merola (cnd), *(orch unknown)*—Act 2 & Act 4 (sels.) *(rec Oct. 30, 1936 & 1926-27)* Standing Room Only ▲ SRO 848-1 [ADD]

Rethberg, Elisabeth (sop) (cont.)
Mozart, W.A.:Arias, w. Arleen Augér (sop), Kathleen Battle (sop), Irma Beilke (sop), Helena Braun (sop), Lisa Della Casa (sop), Maria Cebotari (sop), Ileana Cotrubas (sop), Helen Donath (sop), Mirella Freni (sop), Reri Grist (sop), Edita Gruberova (sop), Elisabeth Grümmer (sop), Hilde Güden (sop), Ingeborg Hallstein (sop), Luise Helletsgruber (sop), Gundula Janowitz (sop), Sena Jurinac (sop), Erika Köth (sop), Evelyn Lear (sop), Wilma Lipp (sop), Margaret Marshall (sop), Edith Mathis (sop), Jarmila Novotna (sop), Margherita Perras (sop), Lucia Popp (sop), Anneliese Rothenberger (sop), Elisabeth Schumann (sop), Elisabeth Schwarzkopf (sop), Graziella Sciutti (sop), Irmgard Seefried (sop), Graziella Sciutti (sop), Julia Varady (sop), Agnes Baltsa (mez), Margit Bokor (mez), Brigitte Fassbaender (mez), Christa Ludwig (mez), Ann Murray (mez), Francisco Araiza (ten), Anton Dermota (ten), Helge Rosvaenge (ten), Rudolf Schock (ten), Peter Schreier (ten), Leopold Simoneau (ten), Eric Tappy (ten), Richard Tauber (ten), Gösta Winbergh (ten), Josef Witt (ten), Fritz Wunderlich (ten), Christian Boesch (bar), Willy Domgraf-Fassbaender (bar), Karl Dönch (bar), Dietrich Fischer-Dieskau (bar), Erich Kunz (bar), Eberhard Wächter (bar), Hans Hotter (b-bar), Paul Schöffler (b-bar), Cesare Siepi (b-bar), José Van Dam (b-bar), Walter Berry (bass), Geraint Evans (bass), Nicolai Ghiaurov (bass), Alexander Kipnis (bass), Richard Mayr (bass), Kurt Moll (bass), James Morris (bass), Ezio Pinza (bass), Martti Talvela (bass), Giorgio Tozzi (bass), Hans Duhan (sgr), Res Fischer (sgr), Marie Gerhart (sgr), *(various orchs & cnds)*—sels from Idomeneo, Die Entführung aus der Serail, Le nozze di Figaro, Don Giovanni, Così fan tutte, Die Zauberflöte & various arias Orfeo d'or ("Festspiel Dokumente" series) 5-▲ 408955
Mozart, W.A.:Don Giovanni, w. L. Helletsgruber (sop), M. Bokor (mez), D. Borgioli (ten), K. Ettl (bass), E. Pinza (bass), B. Walter (cnd), Vienna PO, Vienna State Opera Chorus *(rec Salzburg, Aug. 2, 1937)* Melodram 3-▲ MLO 37506 [ADD]
Mozart, W.A.:Don Giovanni, w. L. Helletsgruber (sop), M. Bokor (mez), D. Borgioli (ten), A. Lazzari (ten), E. Pinza (bass), B. Walter (cnd), Salzburg Orch, Salzburg Mozarteum Chorus [I] *(rec live, Salzburg, Aug. 2, 1937)* Melodram ("Connaisseur" series) 3-▲ CD 37506 (m) [AAD]
Mozart, W.A.:Ridente la calma (sels) *(rec 1905 - 1944)* Minerva ▲ MN A14 [ADD]
Mozart, W.A.:Songs, w. M. Callas (sop), E. Grümmer (sop), E. Schwarzkopf (sop), R. Scotto (sop), T. Lemnitz (sop), E. Berger (sop), S. Jurinac (sop), E. Schumann (sop), I. Souez (sop), L. Lehmann (sop), N. Gedda (ten), J. McCormack (ten), H. Roswenge (ten), H. Nash (ten), T. Gobbi (bar), G. Hüsch (bar), E. Kunz (bar), G. Frick (bass), E. Pinza (bass), A. Kipnis (bass) EMI Classics 4-▲ CDMD 63750
Operatic Scenes & Arias Preiser ▲ PRE 89051 [ADD]
Verdi, G.:Aida (sels), w. Giuseppe De Luca (bar)—Ciel mio padre *(rec 1930)* Minerva ▲ MN-A23 [ADD]
Verdi, G.:Otello, w. Giovanni Martinelli (ten), Lawrence Tibbett (bar), E. Panizza (cnd), *(orch unknown) (rec Feb 12, 1938)* Enterprise ("The Fourties" series) 2-▲ ENT 309
Wagner, R.:Arias & Scenes, w. K. Flagstad (sop), B. Nilsson (sop), E. Schumann (sop), F. Leider (sop), L. Melchior (ten), G. Thill (ten), A. Pertile (ten), G. Hüsch (bar), F. Schorr (b-bar), H. Hotter (b-bar), A. Kipnis (bass), *(orch unknown)* EMI Classics ("Studio" series) 4-▲ CDMC 64008
Wagner, R.:Der fliegende Holländer (sels), w. Göta Ljungberg (sop), Elisabeth Schumann (sop), Rudolf Laubenthal (ten), Lauritz Melchior (ten), Friedrich Schorr (bar), *(cnd & orch unknown) (rec 1927-31)* Preiser 2-▲ PRE 89214 [AAD]
Wagner, R.:Götterdämmerung (sels), w. Göta Ljungberg (sop), Elisabeth Schumann (sop), Rudolf Laubenthal (ten), Lauritz Melchior (ten), Friedrich Schorr (bar), *(cnd & orch unknown) (rec 1927-31)* Preiser 2-▲ PRE 89214 [AAD]
Wagner, R.:Die Meistersinger von Nürnberg (sels), w. Göta Ljungberg (sop), Elisabeth Schumann (sop), Rudolf Laubenthal (ten), Lauritz Melchior (ten), Friedrich Schorr (bar), *(cnd & orch unknown) (rec 1927-31)* Preiser 2-▲ PRE 89214 [AAD]
Wagner, R.:Das Rheingold (sels), w. Göta Ljungberg (sop), Elisabeth Schumann (sop), Rudolf Laubenthal (ten), Lauritz Melchior (ten), Friedrich Schorr (bar), *(cnd & orch unknown) (rec 1927-31)* Preiser 2-▲ PRE 89214 [AAD]
Wagner, R.:Tannhäuser (sels), w. Göta Ljungberg (sop), Elisabeth Schumann (sop), Rudolf Laubenthal (ten), Lauritz Melchior (ten), Friedrich Schorr (bar), *(cnd & orch unknown) (rec 1927-31)* Preiser 2-▲ PRE 89214 [AAD]
Wagner, R.:Die Walküre (sels), w. Göta Ljungberg (sop), Elisabeth Schumann (sop), Rudolf Laubenthal (ten), Lauritz Melchior (ten), Friedrich Schorr (bar), *(orch unknown) (rec 1927-31)* Preiser 2-▲ PRE 89214 [AAD]

Réthy, Esther (sop)
Lehár, F.:Music of, w. M. Reining (sop), J. Novotna (sop), R. Tauber (ten), F. Lehár (cnd), Vienna SO, Vienna PO—6 orchestral sels. *(Musikalische Memorien I-IV; Die lustige Witwe—Overture; Eva—Prelude)*; 4 Arias from Giuditta *(Du bist meine Sonne—Tauber; Freunde, das Leben ist lebenswert—Tauber; Schön wie die blaue Sommernacht—Novotna & Tauber; Schönste der Frauen—Tauber)*; 1 Song & 5 Arias sung by Esther Réthy *(Wien, du bist das Herz der Welt; Giuditta—Meine Lippen, sie küssenso heiss; Paganini—Liebe, du Himmel auf Erden; Schön ist die Welt—Ich bin verliebt; Der Zarewitsch—Einer wird kommen; Zigeunerliebe—Hör ich Cymbalklänge)*; 2 Arias sung by Maria Reining *(Eva—Im heimlichen Dämmer der silbernen Ampel; Friederike—Warum hast du mich wachgeküsst?) (rec 1934-1942 Odeon & HMV rec)* Preiser ▲ 90150 (m) [AAD]
Millöcker, C.:Bettelstudent, w. Wilma Lipp (sop—Laura), Esther Réthy (sop—Bronislava), Rosette Anday (cta—Palmatica), Rudolf Christ (ten—Symon), Kurt Preger (ten—Ollendorf), Eberhard Waechter (bar—Jan), A. Paulik (cnd), Vienna Volksoper Orch, Vienna Volksoper Chorus *(rec Brahmssaal, Vienna, June 1995)* Omega 2-▲ OCD 1018/19 [ADD]
Mozart, W.A.:Idomeneo (sels), w. E. Réthy (sop—Idamante), A. Konetzni (sop—Ismene), J. Sabel (ten—Idomeneo), E. Kunz (bar—Arbace), R. Strauss (cnd), Vienna State Opera Orch, Vienna State Opera Chorus *(rec Dec. 3, 1941)* Koch Schwann 2-▲ SCH 314532 [ADD]
Mozart, W.A.:Nozze di Figaro, w. Jarmila Novotna (sop), Aulikki Rautawaara (sop), Agostino Lazzari (ten), Mariano Stabile (bar), Ezio Pinza (bass), B. Walter (cnd), Vienna PO, Vienna State Opera Chorus *(rec live, 1937)* Melodram ▲ CDI 205003
Strauss (II), Joh.:Eine Nacht in Venedig, w. M. Schober (sop), R. Boesch (bar), K. Friedrich (ten), A. Jerger (b-bar), K. Preger (ten), A. Paulik (cnd), Vienna SO, Bregenz Festival Choir [G] *(rec 1951)* Koch Schwann ▲ 3-1272-2 [ADD]

Réti, József (ten)
Bartók, B.:Cant Profana, "The Giant Stags", w. József Gregor (bass), A. Dorati (cnd), Budapest SO, Hungarian Radio-TV Chorus Hungaroton ▲ HCD 31503 [ADD]
Beethoven, L. van:Music of, w. Sylvia Geszty (sop), Hermann Christian Polster (bass), Koch (cnd), Berlin RSO, Berlin State Orch, Berlin Soloists—Christ on the Mount of Olives (oratorio); Con in E♭ Pno; Irish Songs; Minuets; Canons; Epigrams; Joke Pieces; Incidental & Ballet Music Berlin Classics 3-▲ BER 9132
Erkel, F.:Bánk Bán, w. K. Agay (sop), E. Komlóssy (cta), J. Simándy (ten), S. Sólyom-Nagy (bar), J. Ferencsik (cnd), Budapest PO, Hungarian State Opera Chorus [Hun] *(rec 1969)* Hungaroton 2-▲ HCD 11376/77 [ADD]
Vivaldi, A.:Juditha triumphans devicta Holofernes barbarie, w. Margit László (sop—Abra), Zsuzsa Barlay (cta—Juditha), József Réti (ten—Servo), Zsolt Bende (bar—Holofernes), József Dene (bar—Ozias), F. Szekeres (cnd), Hungarian State Orch, György Czigány (cnd), Budapest Madrigal Choir, 1968 Classical Diamonds ▲ CLD 4022-23 [ADD]

Revenq, Nicolas (bar)
Mozart, W.A.:Così fan tutte, w. Sophie Marin-Degor (sop—Despina), Laura Polverelli (mez—Dorabella), Sophie Fournier (sgr—Fiordiligi), Nicolas Revenq (bar—Guglielmo), Patrick Donnelly (bass—Don Alfonso), Simon Edwards (sgr—Ferrando), J. Malgoire (cnd), La Grande Écurie et la Chambre du Roy Astrée 8-▲ E 8606
Mozart, W.A.:Don Giovanni, w. Danielle Borst (sop—Donna Anna), Véronique Gens (sop—Donna Elvira), Sophie Marin-Degor (sop—Zerlina), Huub Claessens (bar—Leporello), Nicolas Revenq (bar—Don Giovanni), Patrick Donnelly (bass—Commendatore), Simon Edwards (sgr—Don Ottavio), J. Malgoire (cnd), La Grande Écurie et la Chambre du Roy Astrée 8-▲ E 8606
Mozart, W.A.:Nozze di Figaro, w. Danielle Borst (sop—Countess Almaviva), Claudine Le Coz (sop—Marcellina), Sophie Marin-Degor (sop—Suzanna), Laura Polverelli (mez—Cherubino), Valérie Lecoq (sgr—Barberina), Philippe Cantor (ten—Antonio), Stuart Patterson (ten—Dons Basile & Curzio), Huub Claessens (bar—Figaro), Nicolas Revenq (bar—Count Almaviva), Patrick Donnelly (bass—Bartolo), J. Malgoire (cnd), La Grande Écurie et la Chambre du Roy Astrée 8-▲ E 8606

Revill, Clive (bar)
Sullivan, A.:The Mikado, w. M. Studholme (sop), J. Wakefield (ten), D. Dowling (bar), J. Holmes (bass), A. Faris (cnd), Sadler's Wells Opera Orch, Sadler's Wells Opera Chorus
Classics for Pleasure 2–▲ CDCFP 4730 [ADD]

Rex, Sheila (mez)
Britten, H.:Albert Herring, w. S. Fisher (sop), A. Cantelo (sop), P. Pears (ten), J. Noble (bar), O. Brannigan (bass), B. Britten (cnd), English CO [E] London 2–▲ 421849–2 [ADD]

Rey, Gaston (bar)
Auber, D.–F.:Le Domino noir, w. J. Micheau (sop), J. Peyron (ten), J. Gressier (cnd), French National RSO, French Radio Lyric Chorus Melodram 2–▲ MLO 270110 [ADD]

Rey, Isabel (sop)
Mozart, W.A.:Nozze di Figaro, w. C. Margiono (sop), B. Bonney (sop), A. Murray (mez, P.–L. Lang (mez), P. Langridge (ten), C. Späth (ten), T. Hampson (bar), K. Moll (bass), A. Scharinger (bass), K. Langan (bass), N. Harnoncourt (cnd), Royal Concertgebouw Orch, Netherlands Opera Chorus *(rec Amsterdam, May 1993)* Teldec 3–▲ 90861–2 [DDD]
Zarzuelas, w. José Carreras (ten), English CO [cnd:E. Ricci] Erato ▲ 95789–2 ■ 95789–4

Reyans, Marcel (ten)
Biber, H. von:Requiem à 15, w. E. Bongers (sop), A. Grimm (sop), K. Wessel (alt), P. de Groot (alt), S. Davies (ten), R. Steur (bass), K.–J. de Koning (bass), T. Koopman (cnd), Amsterdam Baroque Orch, Amsterdam Baroque Choir Erato ▲ 91725
Biber, H. von:Vesperae longiores ac breviores una cum litaniis Laurentanis, w. E. Bongers (sop), A. Grimm (sop), K. Wessel (alt), P. de Groot (alt), S. Davies (ten), R. Steur (bass), K.–J. de Koning (bass), T. Koopman (cnd), Amsterdam Baroque Orch, Amsterdam Baroque Choir Erato ▲ 91725

Reyer, Walther (nar)
Beethoven, L. van:Egmont (incidental music), w. Netania Davrath (sop), M. Abravanel (cnd), Utah SO
Vanguard Classics 2–▲ OVC 8084/85 [ADD]
Opera Arias & Scenes, w. Lawrence, Marjorie (sop), Piero Coppola (cnd), Pasdeloup Orch, Reyer
Preiser ("Lebendige Vergangenheit" series) ▲ PRE 89011 (m) [AAD]

Reyes, José Guadalupe (sgr)
Bellini, V.:Il pirata, w. Lucia Aliberti (sop), Roberto Frontali (sgr), Stuart Neill (sgr), M. Viotti (cnd), Berlin German Opera Orch, Berlin German Opera Chorus Berlin Classics 2–▲ BER 1115 [DDD]

Reyes, Lilia Teresita (sgr)
Purcell, H.:Dido & Aeneas, w. Helen Donath (sop—Belinda), Shirley Verrett (sop—Dido), Oralia Dominguez (mez—Sorceress), Carmen Lavani (alt—A Spirit), Margaret Lensky (cta—2nd Witch), Carlo Gaifa (ten—A Sailor), Dan Jordacescu (bar—Aeneas), Rosina Cavicchioli (sgr—A Woman), Lilia Teresita Reyes (sgr—1st Witch), R. Leppard (cnd), Turin RAI SO, Ambrosian Chorus *(rec Torino, May 20, 1971)*
Arkadia ▲ 619 [ADD]

Reyghere, Greta de (sop)
Bach, J.S.:Cant 21, w. C. Prégardien (ten), P. Lika (bass), S. Kuijken (cnd), La Petite Bande, Netherlands Chamber Choir [G] Veritas ▲ VC 7 90779–2 [DDD] ■ VC 7 90779–4 (D)
Bach, J.S.:Cant 21, w. R. Jacobs (alt), C. Prégardien (ten), P. Lika (bass), S. Kuijken (vn), S. Kuijken (cnd), La Petite Bande, Netherlands Chamber Choir Virgin Classics ▲ CDC 59528
Bach, J.S.:Magnificat, BWV 243, w. R. Jacobs (alt), C. Prégardien (ten), P. Lika (bass), S. Kuijken (vn), S. Kuijken (cnd), La Petite Bande, Netherlands Chamber Choir [L]
Veritas ▲ VC 7 90779–2 [DDD] ■ VC 7 90779–4 (D)
Bach, J.S.:Magnificat, BWV 243, w. R. Jacobs (alt), C. Prégardien (ten), P. Lika (bass), S. Kuijken (vn), S. Kuijken (cnd), La Petite Bande, Netherlands Chamber Choir Virgin Classics ▲ CDC 59528
Biber, H. von:Requiem à 15, w. J. Feldman (sop), J. Bowman (ct), I. Honeyman (ten), M. van Egmond (bass), Ricercar Consort, Erik Van Nevel (cnd), Capella Sancti Michaelis [L] *(rec 5/90)*
Ricercar ▲ RIC 81063 [DDD]
Brahms, J.:Liebeslieder Waltzes SATB, w. Lucienne Van Deyck (mez), Guy De Mey (ten), Huub Claessens (bass), Jean-Claude Vanden Eynden (pno), Luc Devos (pno) *(rec Consevatoire Royal, Liège, 1994)* Ricercar ▲ 153138
Brahms, J.:Neue Liebeslieder Waltzes, w. Lucienne Van Deyck (mez), Guy De Mey (ten), Huub Claessens (bass), Jean-Claude Vanden Eynden (pno), Luc Devos (pno) *(rec Consevatoire Royal, Liège, 1994)* Ricercar ▲ 153138
Bruhns, N.:Cants, w. Jill Feldman (sop), James Bowman (ct), Ian Honeyman (ten), Guy de Mey (ten), Max Van Egmond (bass), Ricercar Consort—Hemmt eure Tränenflut; Jauchzet dem Herren alle Welt; Wohl dem, der den Herren fürchtet; De profundis; Paratum cor meum; O werter heil'ger Geis; Zeit meines Abschieds; Erstanden ist der heilige Christ; Herr hat seinem Stuhl im Himmel bereitet; Ich liege und schlafe; Mein Herz ist bereit; Muss nicht der Mensch auf dieser Erden in Stetem Streite sein
Ricercar In Ecco 2–▲ REC8001/2
Grétry, A.–E.–M.:La Caravane du Caire, w. I. Poulenard (sop), G. Ragon (ten), G. de Mey (ten), P. Huttenlocher (bar), V. Le Téxier (bar), J. Bastin (bass), M. Minkowski (cnd), Ricercar Academy, Ricercar Academy Chorus [period instrs] [F] Ricercar 2–▲ RIC 100084/85 [DDD]
Hasse, J.A.:Miserere in e, w. Dina Grossberger (mez), Ian Honeyman (ten), D Snellincks (bass), Il Fondamento Opus 111 ▲ OPS 3080
Hasse, J.A.:Requiem, w. Dina Grossberger (mez), Ian Honeyman (ten), D. Snellincks (bass), Il Fondamento Ensemble Opus 111 ▲ OPS 3080
Kerll, J.C.:Missa pro defunctis, w. J. Bowman (alt), I. Honeyman (ten), G. de Mey (ten), M. van Egmond (bass), E. van Nevel (cnd), Capella Sancti Michaelis, Ricercar Consort [L] *(rec 5/90)*
Ricercar ▲ RIC 81063 [DDD]
Sebastiani, J.:St. Matthew Passion, w. Vincent Gregoire (ct), Stéphane van Dijck (ten), Hervé Lamy (ten—Evangéliste), Max van Egmond (bass—Christ), P. Pierlot (cnd), Ricercar Consort
Ricercar ▲ 160144

Reyheim, John (ten)
Rutenberg, P.:Ballad of the Buffalo Skinners, w. Raymond McLeod (bass), Peter Rutenberg (cnd), Los Angeles Chamber Singers [trad.; ed. & expanded Peter Rutenberg] Klavier ▲ KCD 11052 [DDD]

Reynolds, Anna (mez)
Bach, J.S.:Magnificat, BWV 243, w. L. Marimpietri (sop), N. Panni (sop), P. Munteanu (ten), B. Carmeli (bass), H. Scherchen (cnd), Milan RAI SO, Milan RAI Chorus [L] *(rec live, Apr 5, 1963)*
Memories ▲ HR 4160 (m) [ADD]
Debussy, C.:Pelléas et Mélisande, w. A. Martino (sop), G. Bacquier (bar), T. Rovetta (bar), N. Zaccaria (bass), L. Maazel (cnd), *(orch unknown) (rec 1969* Great Opera Performances 3–▲ GOP 711
Handel, G.F.:Messiah, w. Elly Ameling (sop), Philip Langridge (ten), Gwynne Howell (bass), N. Marriner (cnd), Academy of St. Martin in the Fields, Academy of St. Martin in the Fields Chorus [E]
Argo ■ 421234–4
Handel, G.F.:Messiah, w. Elly Ameling (sop), Philip Langridge (ten), Gwynne Howell (bass), N. Marriner (cnd), Academy of St. Martin in the Fields, Academy of St. Martin in the Fields Chorus *(rec St John's, Smith Square, London, Jan & July 1976)* London ("Double Decker" series) 2–▲ 444824–2 [ADD]
Mahler, G.:Das Klagende Lied, w. T. Zylis-Gara (sop), A. Kaposy (ten), W. Morris (cnd), New Philharmonia Orch, Ambrosian Singers [G] *(rec 1967)* Nimbus ▲ NI 5085 [AAD]
Mahler, G.:Das Klagende Lied, w. T. Zylis-Gara (sop), A. Kaposy (ten), W. Morris (cnd), New Philharmonia Orch, Ambrosian Singers IMP Classics ▲ IMPCD 1053 [DDD]
Mahler, G.:Lieder und Gesänge aus der Jugendzeit, w. G. Parsons (pno)
IMP Classics ▲ IMPCD 1053 [DDD]

Reynolds, Debbie (sgr)
Loesser, F.:Guys and Dolls, w. F. Sinatra (sgr), B. Crosby (sgr), D. Martin (sgr), J. Stafford (sgr), D. Shore (sgr), C. Dennis (sgr), A. Sherman (sgr), S. Davis Jr. (sgr), *(other artists unknown)* [studio cast]
Reprise ▲ 45014–2 [AAD] ■ 45014–4

Reznikoff, Iégor (sgr)
Le Chant de Fontenay, w. Fontenay Abbey Monks' Choir Studio SM ▲ 12 16 40

Rezzadore, Luisa (sgr)
Donizetti, G.:La fille du régiment (sels), w. Mirella Freni (sop), Anna di Stasio (mez), Angelo Mercuriali (ten), Luciano Pavarotti (ten), Wladimiro Ganzarolli (bar), Walter Monachesi (bar), Giuseppe Morresi (bass), V. Gullino (sgr), N. Sanzogno (cnd), La Scala Orch, La Scala Chorus
Budget ("The Greatest Voice in Opera" series) ▲ SYP 108

Rhode, Chuck (ten)
Ron & Chuck Rhode at the Byrd Theatre, w. Ron Rhode (org)
Organ Historical Society ▲ VTOS 1001 [DDD]

Rhodes, Terry (sop)
Hoekman, T.:Margarets, w. Ellen Williams (mez), Timothy Hoekman (pno) Albany ▲ TROY 172 [DDD]
Hoiby, L.:Bermudas, w. Ellen Williams (mez), Hsiao-mei Ku (vn), Jonathan Bagg (va), Fred Raimi (vc), Thomas Warburton (pno) Albany ▲ TROY 172 [DDD]
Jaffe, S.:Fort Juniper Songs, w. Ellen Williams (mez), Stephen Jaffe (pno) Albany ▲ TROY 172 [DDD]
Kouneva, P.:Aeon, w. Ellen Williams (mez), Penka Kouneva (pno), Lynn Glasscock (perc), Robbie Link (gtr) Albany ▲ TROY 172 [DDD]
Ward, R.:Lady Kate (sels), w. Ellen Williams (mez), S. Tiley (cnd), *(orch unknown)*—Eve, I Can't Lie to an Old Friend Albany ▲ TROY 172 [DDD]
Ward, R.:Roman Fever (sels), w. Ellen Williams (mez), S. Tiley (cnd), *(orch unknown)*—It's Still the Most Beautiful View in the World Albany ▲ TROY 172 [DDD]

Rhys-Davies, Gareth (bar)
Sullivan, A.:Trial by Jury, w. Rebecca Evans (sop—Plaintiff), Barry Banks (ten—Defendant), Gareth Rhys-Davies (bar—Foreman of the Jury), Peter Savidge (bar—Counsel for the Plaintiff), Donald Adams (bass—Usher), Richard Suart (bass—The Learned Judge), C. Mackerras (cnd), Welsh National Opera Orch, Welsh National Opera Chorus *(rec Brangwyn Hall, Swasea, Wales, Apr 18–30 & May 1, 1995)*
Telarc 2–▲ CD 80404 [DDD]

Rhys-Evans, Huw (ten)
Boieldieu, F.–A.:Le Calife de Bagdad, w. L. Mayo (sop), J. Michelini (sop), C. Cheriez (mez), L. Dale (ten), A. de Almeida (cnd), Camerata Provence Orch, Provence Camerata Chorus [F]
Sonpact ▲ SPT 93007 [DDD]
Mendelssohn, F.:Die Hochzeit des Camacho, w. R. Hofman (sop—Quiteria), A. Ulbrich (mez—Lucinda), S. Weir (ten—Basilio), H. Rhys-Evans (ten—Vivaldo), N. van der Meel (ten—Camacho), W. Wild (bar—Carrasco), U. Malmberg (bass—Sancho Panza), U. Cold (bass—Don Quixote), J. van Immerseel (cnd), Anima Eterna Orch, Aachen Boys Choir, Chor Modus Novus [G] *(rec Sept. 19–22, 1992)*
Channel Classics 2–▲ CCS 5593 [DDD]

Riavez, José (ten)
Mascagni, P.:Cavalleria rusticana (sels), w. P. Mascagni (cnd), Berlin State Opera Orch—Prelude; O Lola, bianca come fior... *(rec 1927)* VAI Audio ▲ VAIA 1113 [ADD]

Ribacchi, Luisa (mez)
Verdi, G.:Otello, w. Renata Tebaldi (sop—Desdemona), Luisa Ribacchi (mez—Emilia), Angelo Mercuriali (ten—Roderigo), Mario del Monaco (ten—Otello), Piero de Palma (ten—Cassio), Aldo Protti (bar—Iago), Dario Caselli (bass—A Herald), Fernando Corena (bass—Lodovico), Pierluigi Martinucci (bass—Montano), A. Erede (cnd), St. Cecilia Academy Orch Rome, St. Cecilia Academy Chorus Rome
Theorema ▲ TH 121141/142
Verdi, G.:Rigoletto, w. Hilde Gueden (sop—Gilda), Piero de Palma (ten—Borsa), Luisa Ribacchi (mez—Giovanna), Giulietta Simionato (mez—Maddalena), Mario del Monaco (ten—Duca de Mantova), Aldo Protti (bar—Rigoletto), Fernando Corena (bass—Conte Monterone), Cesare Siepi (bass—Sparafucile), A. Erede (cnd), St. Cecilia Academy Orch Rome, St. Cecilia Academy Chorus Rome
Theorema ▲ TH 121179/180

Ribetti, Elda (mez)
Puccini, G.:La Bohème, w. R. Tebaldi (sop), E. Avolanti (ten), G. Lauri Volpi (ten), T. Gobbi (bar), S. Meletti (bar), C. Badioli (bass), G. Neri (bass), G. Santini (cnd), *(orch unknown) (rec 1951)*
Great Opera Performances ▲ GOP 743
Verdi, G.:Un ballo in maschera, w. Maria Caniglia (sop—Amelia), Fedora Barbieri (mez—Ulrica), Beniamino Gigli (ten—Riccardo), Gino Bechi (bar—Renato), Tancredi Pasero (bass—Samuel), Blando Giusti (sgr—Un Giudice), Nicola Niccolini (sgr—Silvano), Ugo Novelli (sgr—Tom), Elda Ribetti (mez—Oscar), T. Serafin (cnd), Rome Opera Orch, Giuseppe Conca (cnd), Rome Opera Chorus *(rec 1943)* Arkadia 2–▲ CD 78005 (m) [ADD]

Ribla, G. (sgr)
Verdi, G.:Rigoletto (sels), w. Nan Merriman (mez), Jan Peerce (ten), Frank Valentino (bar), Nicola Moscona (bass), A. Toscanini (cnd), NBC SO—Act III (complete)
Enterprise ("The Radio Years" series) ▲ ENT 48
Verdi, G.:Rigoletto (act 3), w. Nan Merriman (mez), Jan Peerce (ten), Frank Valentino (bar), Nicola Moscona (bass), A. Toscanini (cnd), NBC SO [I] *(rec New York, 7/25/43)*
Melodram 2–▲ MEL 28022 (m) [AAD]

Ricci, Anna (mez)
Casanovas, J.:Joan Miró, w. Àngel Soler (pno) *(rec Albert Moraleda Studio, 1993–95)*
Edicions Albert Moraleda 2–▲ 032D [DDD]
Cercós, J.:Songs, w. Àngel Soler (pno)—Sanglot, sanglot, pur sanglot! [from Les Fenêtres] *(rec Albert Moraleda Studio, 1993–95)* Edicions Albert Moraleda 2–▲ 032D [DDD]
Cerdà, A.:Tres letras asturianas, w. Àngel Soler (pno) *(rec Albert Moraleda Studio, 1993–95)*
Edicions Albert Moraleda 2–▲ 032D [DDD]
Giró, J.:Chansons françaises (3), w. Àngel Soler (pno)—Sérénade *(rec Albert Moraleda Studio, 1993–95)*
Edicions Albert Moraleda 2–▲ 032D [DDD]
Quadreny, J.M.M.:Cançons do broccol, w. Àngel Soler (pno) *(rec Albert Moraleda Studio, 1993–95)*
Edicions Albert Moraleda 2–▲ 032D [DDD]

Ricci, Gian Luca (bar)
Menotti, G.C.:The Telephone, w. A. V. Banks (mez), P. Vaglieri (cnd), Milan CO [E]
Nuova Era ▲ 7122 [DDD]
Paisiello, G.:La Serva padrona, w. A. V. Banks (mez—Serpina), G. L. Ricci (bar—Umberto), P. Vaglieri (cnd), Milan CO [I] Nuova Era ▲ 7043 [DDD]

Ricciardi, Franco (ten)
Bellini, V.:La sonnambula, w. Maria Callas (sop), Fiorenza Cossotto (mez), Nicola Monti (ten), Dino Mantovani (bar), Nicola Zaccaria (bass), A. Votto (cnd), La Scala Orch, La Scala Chorus
Melodram 2–▲ CDM 26037
Cilea, F.:Adriana Lecouvreur, w. L. Gencer (sop—Adriana), A. Lazzarini (mez—Princess), F. Ricciardi (ten—Abbot), A. Zambon (ten—Maurizio), E. Sordello (bar—Michonnet), A. Zerbini (bass—Prince), O. de Fabritiis (cnd), Naples Teatro San Carlo Orch, Naples Teatro San Carlo Chorus *(rec Dec. 17, 1966)*
Golden Age of Opera 2–▲ GAO 143/44 [ADD]
Leoncavallo, R.:Pagliacci, w. Joan Carlyle (sop—Nedda/Colombina), Carlo Bergonzi (ten—Canio/Pagliaccio), Franco Ricciardi (ten—Villager), Ugo Benelli (bar—Peppe/Arlecchino), Rolando Panerai (bar—Silvio), Giuseppe Taddei (bar—Tonio/Taddeo), Giuseppe Morresi (bass—Villager), H. von Karajan (cnd), La Scala Orch, La Scala Chorus *(rec La Scala, Milan, Oct 1965)*
Deutsche Grammophon ("The Originals" series) ▲ 449727–2 [ADD]
Massenet, J.:Manon (sels), w. Mirella Freni (sop), Luciano Pavarotti (ten), Wladimiro Ganzarolli (bar), Giuseppe Morresi (bass), Antonio Zerbini (bass), Ida Farina (sgr), P. Maag (cnd), La Scala Orch, La Scala Chorus *(rec live, Milan, 1969)* Budget ("The Greatest Voice in Opera" series) ▲ SYP 110
Puccini, G.:Manon Lescaut, w. R. Kabaivanska (sop—Manon), R. Pallini (mez—Singer), P. Domingo (ten—des Grieux), E. Lorenzi (ten—Edmondo), F. Ricciardi (ten—Dancing Master), M. D'Anna (bar—Lescaut), A. Mariotti (bass—Geronte), F. Federici (bass—Innkeeper)
Golden Age of Opera 2–▲ GAO 162/63 [ADD]

Ricciarelli, Katia (sop)
Bellini, V.:I Capuleti e i Montecchi, w. D. Montague (mez), D. Raffanti (ten), M. Lippi (bass), B. Campanella (cnd), Venice Teatro La Fenice Orch, Venice Teatro La Fenice Chorus [I] *(rec 1991)*
Nuova Era 2–▲ 7020/21 [DDD]
Bellini, V.:I Capuleti e i Montecchi (sels), w. Diana Montague (mez), Dano Raffanati (ten), B. Campanella (cnd), Venice Teatro La Fenice Orch, Venice Teatro La Fenice Chorus
Nuova Era ▲ NUO 7183 [DDD]
Bellini, V.:I Puritani, w. Eleonora Jankovic (mez), Juan Luque Carmona (ten), Carlo Gaifa (ten), Chris Merritt (ten), Roberto Scandiuzzi (bass), G. Ferro (cnd), Sicilian SO, Bari Teatro Petruzzelli Chorus
Fonit Cetra ("Digital Operas" series) 3–▲ FCT CDC 20
Bellini, V.:I Puritani, w. E. Jankovic (mez), C. Merritt (ten), C. Gaifa (ten), A. Riva (bass), R. Scandiuzzi (bass), G. Ferro (cnd), Sicilian SO, Bari Teatro Petruzzelli Chorus *(rec Apr. 10, 1986)*
Cetra Classic ▲ CDC 20 [ADD]

Ricciarelli, Katia (sop) (cont.)
Bellini, V.:Zaira, w. A. Papadjakou (cta), R. Vargas (ten), S. Alaimo (ten), P. Olmi (cnd), Catania Teatro Massimo Bellini Orch, Catania Teatro Massimo Bellini Chorus [I] *(rec live 1990)* Nuova Era 2–▲ 6982/83 [DDD]
Bellini, V.:Zaira (sels), w. R. Vargas (ten), P. Olmi (cnd), Catania Teatro Massimo Bellini Orch, Catania Teatro Massimo Bellini Chorus Nuova Era ▲ NUO 7187 [DDD]
Bizet, G.:Carmen (sels), w. A. Baltsa (mez), J. Carreras (ten), J. Van Dam (b–bar), H. von Karajan (cnd), Berlin PO, Paris Opera Chorus [F] Deutsche Grammophon ▲ 413322–2 [DDD]
Bizet, G.:Les Pêcheurs de perles (sels), w. Placído Domingo (ten), A. Guadagno (cnd), St. Cecilia Academy Orch Rome—Au fond du temple saint *(rec 1972)* RCA Gold Seal ▲ 09026–62595–2 [ADD]
Donizetti, G.:Anna Bolena, w. Doris Soffel (cta), Pietro Ballo (ten), Nicolai Ghiuselev (bass), E. Pidò (cnd), Palermo Teatro Massimo Orch, Palermo Teatro Massimo Chorus *(rec live, 1991)* Serenissima 3–▲ SER 360111
Donizetti, G.:Maria di Rudenz, w. Alberto Cupido (ten), Leo Nucci (bar), E. Inbal (cnd), Venice Teatro La Fenice Orch, Venice Teatro La Fenice Chorus Serenissima 2–▲ SER 360157 [DDD]
Donizetti, G.:Poliuto, w. J. Carreras (ten), J. Pons (bar), O. Caetani (cnd), Vienna SO, Vienna Chorus CBS 2–▲ M2K 44821
Mascagni, P.:Amica, w. Monica Minarelli (sgr), Elia Padovan (sgr), Fabio Armiliato (sgr), Walter Donati (sgr), M. Pace (cnd), Hungarian Radio–TV SO, Hungarian Radio–TV Chorus *(rec Budapest, Nov 1995)* Kicco Classic 2–▲ KC 00296 [DDD]
Nuttata 'e Sentimento—Neapolitan Songs, w. Italian Femminile Ensemble Kicco Classic ▲ 1695
Pavarotti & Ricciarelli Live, w. L. Pavarotti (ten)
Primi Tenori:Carreras – Domingo – Pavarotti, w. Leontyne Price (sop) *(rec 1969–1983)* Standing Room Only 2–▲ SRO 835–2
Puccini, G.:La Bohème, w. Francisco Araiza (ten), Angelo Casertano (ten), Stefano Antonucci (bar), Claudio Giombi (bar), Paata Burchuladze (bass), Alfredo Mariotti (bass), Alberto Noli (bass), Andrea Piccinni (bass), Lauren Broglia (sgr), A. Guadagno (cnd), Arena di Verona Orch, Limburg Cathedral Boys' Chorus Koch Schwann 2–▲ SCH 315922
Puccini, G.:La Bohème, w. J. Carreras (ten), C. Davis (cnd), Royal Opera House Orch Philips 2–▲ 442260–2
Puccini, G.:La Bohème, w. A. Putnam (sop), J. Carreras (ten), I. Wixell (bar), C. Davis (cnd), Royal Opera House Orch [I] Philips 2–▲ 416492–2 [ADD]
Puccini, G.:Madama Butterfly (sels), w. Plácido Domingo (ten), A. Guadagno (cnd), St. Cecilia Academy Orch Rome—Bimba dagli occhi pieni di malia *(rec 1972)* RCA Gold Seal ▲ 09026–62595–2 [ADD]
Puccini, G.:Tosca, w. J. Carreras (ten), R. Raimondi (bass), H. von Karajan (cnd), Berlin PO, German Opera Chorus [I] Deutsche Grammophon 2–▲ 413815–2 [ADD]
Puccini, G.:Turandot, w. B. Hendricks (sop), P. Domingo (ten), R. Raimondi (bass), H. von Karajan (cnd), Vienna PO, Vienna State Opera Chorus [I] Deutsche Grammophon 2–▲ 423855–2 [DDD]
Puccini, G.:Turandot (sels), w. E. Martón (sop), J. Carreras (ten), L. Maazel (cnd), Vienna State Opera Orch, Vienna State Opera Chorus [I] CBS ▲ MK 42168 [DDD] ■ MT 42168 (D)
Puccini, G.:Turandot (sels), w. B. Hendricks (sop), P. Domingo (ten), R. Raimondi (bass), H. von Karajan (cnd), Vienna PO, Vienna State Opera Chorus [I] Deutsche Grammophon ▲ 435409–2 [DDD]
Rossini, G.:Arias, w. G. Ferro (cnd), Paris Lyon Opera Orch, Paris Lyon Opera Chorus Virgin Classics ▲ CDC 59660
Rossini, G.:Bianca e Falliero, w. K. Ricciarelli (sop—Bianca), M. Horne (mez—Falliero), C. Merritt (ten—Contareno), G. Surjan (bass–Capellino), D. Renzetti (cnd), *(orch & chorus unknown)* *(rec live, 1986)* Legato Classics 3–▲ LCD 138–3 [ADD]
Rossini, G.:La donna del lago, w. L. V. Terrani (mez), D. Raffanti (ten), S. Ramey (bass), M. Pollini (cnd), CO of Europe, Prague Phil Chorus [I] CBS 2–▲ M2K 39311 [DDD]
Rossini, G.:La gazza ladra, w. W. Matteuzzi (ten), S. Ramey (bass), G. Gelmetti (cnd), Turin RSO *(rec live, Rossini Opera Festival in Pesaro, Italy, Aug. 1989)* Sony Classical 3–▲ S3K 45850 [DDD]
Rossini, G.:Tancredi (sels), w. M. Horne (mez), *(orch unknown)*—4 solo arias & 2 duets *(rec live, 1983)* Legato Classics 3–▲ LCD 138–3 [ADD]
Verdi, G.:Aida, w. E. Obraztsova (mez), P. Domingo (ten), L. Nucci (bar), N. Ghiaurov (bass), C. Abbado (cnd), La Scala Orch, La Scala Chorus [I] Deutsche Grammophon ▲ 435410–2 [DDD]
Verdi, G.:Aida, w. L. Freni (sop), A. Baltsa (mez), J. Carreras (ten), P. Cappuccilli (bar), G. Raimondi (ten), J. Van Dam (b–bar), H. von Karajan (cnd), Vienna PO, Vienna State Opera Chorus [I] EMI Classics (Studio) 3–▲ CDMC 69300 [ADD]
Verdi, G.:Aida, w. E. Obraztsova (mez), P. Domingo (ten), L. Nucci (bar), N. Ghiaurov (bass), C. Abbado (cnd), La Scala Orch, La Scala Chorus [I] Deutsche Grammophon 3–▲ 410092–2 [DDD]
Verdi, G.:Arias, w. P. Domingo (ten), Rome PO—arias & duets from Ballo in maschera, Il Corsaro, Don Carlos, Jerusalem, Giovanna d'Arco, I Masnadieri, Otello, Trovatore, I Vespri siciliani RCA Gold Seal ▲ 6534–2–RG [ADD] ■ 6534–4–RG (CrO2)
Verdi, G.:Un ballo in maschera, w. Reri Grist (sop), Elizabeth Bainbridge (mez), Plácido Domingo (ten), Piero Cappuccilli (bar), C. Abbado (cnd), Royal Opera House Orch, Royal Opera House Chorus Covent Garden *(rec 1975)* Arkadia 2–▲ 488
Verdi, G.:La battaglia di Legnano, w. J. Carreras (ten), M. Manuguerra (bar), N. Ghiuselev (bass), L. Gardelli (cnd), ORF SO, ORTF Choir Philips 2–▲ 422435–2 [ADD]
Verdi, G.:Don Carlos, w. Fiorenza Cossotto (mez), Guido Fabbris (ten), Veriano Luchetti (ten), Piero Cappuccilli (bar), Gianfranco Casarini (bass), Nicolai Ghiaurov (bass), Alessandro Maddalena (bass), Aracelly Haengel (sgr), Marisa Salimbeni (sgr), Giorgio Zoranca (sgr), G. Prêtre (cnd), *(orch unknown)* Great Opera Performances 3–▲ GOP 777
Verdi, G.:I due Foscari, w. E. Connell (sop), J. Carreras (ten), V. Bello (ten), M. Antoniak (ten), P. Cappuccilli (bar), S. Ramey (bass), F. Handlos (bass), L. Gardelli (cnd), Austrian RSO, Austrian Radio Chorus Philips 2–▲ 422426–2 [ADD]
Verdi, G.:Jérusalem, w. J. Carreras (ten), S. Nimsgern (b–bar), G. Gavazzeni (cnd), Turin RAI Orch, Turin RAI Chorus [F] *(rec live 12/20/75)* Standing Room Only 2–▲ SRO 828–2 [ADD]
Verdi, G.:I lombardi alla prima crociata (sels), w. J. Carreras (ten), *(pianist unknown)*—Act 3 duet, "Dove sola m'inoltro...Per dirupi e per foreste" *(rec live, New York, 1975)* Standing Room Only 2–▲ SRO 828–2 [ADD]
Verdi, G.:Luisa Miller, w. K. Ricciarelli (sop—Luisa), M. G. Piolatto (mez—Laura), S. Silva (cta—Federica), J. Carreras (ten—Rodolfo), E. Pranod (ten—A Peasant), R. Bruson (bar—Miller), G. Casarini (bar—Wurm) M. Rinaudo (bass—Count Walter), F. Previtali (cnd), Turin Teatro Regio Orch, Turin Teatro Regio Chorus *(rec May 9, 1976)* Legato Classics 2–▲ LCD 180 [ADD]
Verdi, G.:Otello (sels), w. M. del Monaco (ten), A. Protti (bar), F. Ferraris (cnd), Brussels Théâtre de la Monnaie Orch *(rec Nov. 9, 1972)* Standing Room Only 2–▲ SRO 169–2
Verdi, G.:Il trovatore, w. Richard Tucker (ten), Renato Bruson (bar), Zanibelli (sgr), A. Erede (cnd), Parma Teatro Regio Orch *(rec Parma, 1971)* Golden Age of Opera 2–▲ GAO 193/194
Verdi, G.:Il trovatore, w. Stefania Toczyska (mez), José Carreras (ten), Yuri Mazurok (bar), C. Davis (cnd), Royal Opera House Orch, Royal Opera House Chorus Covent Garden Philips ("Two–Fers" series) 2–▲ 446151–2
Zandonai, R.:Francesca da Rimini (sels), w. Placído Domingo (ten), A. Guadagno (cnd), St. Cecilia Academy Orch Rome—Benvenuto, signore mio cognato *(rec 1972)* RCA Gold Seal ▲ 09026–62595–2 [ADD]

Ricciotti, Rosa (sgr)
Monteverdi, C.:Ballo delle ingrate, w. Carlo Lepore (bass), Daniela Barcellona (sgr), Daniela Ciliberti (sgr), Andrea Concetti (sgr), Hans van Dijk (sgr), Remo Guerrini (sgr), Nadia Mantelli (sgr), Elena Marazzi (sgr), Humberto Orellana (sgr), Claudia Pallini (sgr), Luigi Polsini (sgr), Rosa Ricciotti (sgr), Alberto Rota (sgr), Ludovica Scoppola (sgr), *(orch unknown)* Nuova Era ▲ NUO 7224

Ricco, Iginio (bass)
Verdi, G.:Giovanna d'Arco, w. Renata Tebaldi (sop—Giovanna), Gino Penno (ten—Carlo VII), Luciano Della Pergola (ten—Delil), Ugo Savarese (bar—Giacomo), Iginio Ricco (bass—Talbot), G. Santini (cnd), Naples Teatro San Carlo Orch, Naples Teatro San Carlo Chorus *(rec San Carlo Theater, Naples, Mar. 15, 1951)* Legato Classics 2–▲ LCD 193–2 [ADD]

Richard, Lawrence (bass)
Henze, H.–W.:Elegy for Young Lovers, w. Regina Schudel (sop), Richard Lloyd Morgan (bass), Helmut Bernhofen (sgr), Bruno Fath (sgr), Aurelia Hajek (sgr), Silvia Weiss (sgr), B. Jones (cnd), Berlin Chamber Opera Orch *(rec Berlin)* Deutsche Schallplatten 2–▲ DS 1050

Richard, Norman (b–bar)
Desmarets, H.:Motets, w. Sarah Leonard (sop), Jean–Paul Fouchécourt (ten), C. Jackson (cnd), Montreal Ancient Music Ensemble, Les Violons du Roy—Domine ne in furore; Usquequo Domine Confitebor Tibi Domine; Lauda Jerusalem; Marche Lorraine K617 2–▲ 7053
Gratton, H.:Imagerie:Christmas Pastoral, w. M. Keable (actor), S. Léonard (actor), J.–L. Millette (actor), M. Laferrière (sop), C. Rioux (mez), B. Levasseur (bar), L. Lavigueur (cnd), Louis Lavigueur Instrumental Ensemble, Louis Lavigueur Vocal Ensemble [F] *(rec 5/91)* CBC ("SM 5000" series) ▲ SMCD 5109 [DDD]

Richards, A. (sgr)
Porter, C.:A Swell Party, w. N. Grace (sgr), A. Woods (sgr), D. Keman (sgr), M. Smith (sgr), *(other artists unknown)* [1992 London cast] Silva America ▲ SSD 1006 [DDD] ■ SSC 1006

Richards, C. (sgr)
Romberg, S.:Deep in My Heart, w. H. Traubel (sgr), J. Ferrer (sgr), R. Clooney (sgr), Gene Kelly (sgr), F. Kelly (sgr), V. Damone (sgr), J. Powell (sgr), A. Miller (sgr), W. Olvis (sgr), H. Keel (sgr), T. Martin (sgr), J. Weldon (sgr) Sony Music Special Products ▲ AK 47703

Richards, Stephen (bass)
Tavener, J.:Elis Thanaton, w. Patricia Rozario (sop), R. Hickox (cnd), City of London Sinfonia Chandos ▲ CHAN 9440

Richardson, Jill (sop)
Shewan, S.:A Feast of Carols, w. Alexander Burgess (bar), S. Shewan (cnd), Roberts Wesleyan College Brass Ensemble, Roberts Wesleyan College Chorale Albany ▲ TROY 149 [DDD]
Shewan, S.:The Widow's Lament in Springtime, w. Amy Anderson (ob), Rebecca Patterson (vc), Stephen Shewan (pno) Albany ▲ TROY 149 [DDD]

Richardson, Marilyn (sop)
Broadstock, B.:Eheu Fugaces, w. Christine Draeger (fl), Roslyn Dunlop (cl), Fiona Ziegler (vn), Susan Blake (vc), David Miller (pno), Daryl Pratt (perc) Vox Australis ▲ VAST018–2 [DDD]
Opera Arias, w. Queensland SO [cnd:Vladimir Kamirski] ABC Classics ▲ 434138–2 [DDD]
Ravel, M.:L'Enfant et les sortilèges, w. Arleen Augér (sop), Jane Berbié (mez), Linda Finnie (mez), Jocelyne Taillon (mez), Davenny Wyner (mez), Philip Langridge (ten), Philippe Huttenlocher (bar), Jules Bastin (bass), A. Previn (cnd), London SO, Ambrosian Opera Chorus Classics for Pleasure ("Eminence" series) ▲ CFP 2241
Sculthorpe, P.:Eliza Fraser Sings Vox Australis ▲ VAST018–2 [DDD]
Sculthorpe, P.:The Stars Turn, w. Susan Blake (vc), David Miller (pno) Vox Australis ▲ VAST018–2 [DDD]
Sitsky, L.:Deep in My Hidden Country, w. Christine Draeger (fl), Susan Blake (vc), David Miller (pno), Daryl Pratt (perc) Vox Australis ▲ VAST018–2 [DDD]

Richardson, Mark (bar)
Sullivan, A.:The Mikado, w. L. Garrett (sop), J. Rigby (mez), S. Bullock (sop), F. Palmer (sop/mez), B. Bottone (ten), R. Angas (bass), E. Idle (bar), R. Van Allan (bass), P. Robinson (cnd), English National Opera Orch, English Opera Group Chorus—sels [E] MCA Classics ▲ MCAD 6215 [DDD]; ■ MCAC 6215 (D)

Richardson, Nicholas (trb)
Ireland, J.:Songs, w. Stephen Ryde–Weller (trb), D. Hill (cnd), Bournemouth SO—The Holy Boy *(rec Winchester Cathedral, Jan 10–13, 1994)* London ▲ 444130–2 [DDD]

Richardson, Stephen (bar)
Mozart, W.A.:Requiem, w. J. Bryden (sop), M. Westbrook–Geha (mez), W. Hite (ten), A. Parrott (cnd), Boston Early Music Festival Orch, Boston Early Music Festival Chorus [L] Denon ▲ CO 77152 [DDD]
Purcell, H.:Odes & Welcome Songs (misc), w. J. Smith (sop), E. Priday (sop), K. Amps (sop), M. Chance (ct), Wilson (sgr), J. M. Ainsley (ten), T. Pinnock (cnd), English Concert, *(chorus unknown)*—Come ye Sons of Art; Welcome to All the Pleasures; Of Old, When Heroes Thought it Base Archiv ▲ 427663–2 [DDD]

Richter, Katharina (sop)
Blacher, B.:Songs, w. Cornella Wosnitza (sop), Markus Köhler (bar), Horst Göbel (pno), Chatschatur Kanajan (vn), Piotr Prysiasnik (vn), Fred Günther (va), Ithay Khen (vc), Christian Peters (sax), Markus Weidmann (bn)—3 Chansons; Ungereimtes; 4 Lieder; Nebel; 13 Ways of Looking at a Blackbird; 5 Sinnsprüche Omars des Zeitmachers; 3 Psalmen; Aprèslude; Francesca da Rimini; Jazz–Koloraturen Signum ▲ SIG X73–00 [DDD]

Rickards, Steven (ct)
Bach, J.S.:Cant 8, w. J. Baird (sop), J. Thomas (ten), J. Weaver (bass), J. Thomas (cnd), American Bach Soloists [G] Koch International Classics ▲ KIC 7163–2 [DDD]
Bach, J.S.:Cant 156, w. J. Thomas (ten), J. Weaver (bass), J. Thomas (cnd), American Bach Soloists [G] Koch International Classics ▲ KIC 7163–2 [DDD]
Bach, J.S.:Mass in b, BWV 232, w. J. Baird (sop), J. Nelson (sop), N. Zylstra, J. Lane, Z. Muñoz, S. Rickards, P. Romano, W. Sharp, J. Weaver (bass), J. Thomas (cnd), American Bach Soloists Koch International Classics 2–▲ KIC 7194–2 [DDD]
Buxtehude, D.:Cants, w. Laura Heimes (sop), Tamara Crout Matthews (sop), James Russell (ten), John Alston (bass), M. N. Johnson (cnd), Sarum Consort, St. Peter's in the Great Valley Chamber Choir—Wachet auf, ruft uns die Stimme!; Singet dem Herrn; Quemadmodum desiderat cervus; O fröhliche Stunden, o herrliche Zeit; Jubilate Domino omnis terra; Lobe den Herrn, meine Seele; Erfreue dich, Erde! *(rec St–Martin–in–the–Fields Church, Chestnut Hill, PA, Sept 7–9, 1994)* Pro gloria musicae ▲ PGM 102 [DDD]
Handel, G.F.:Siroe, Rè di Persia, w. Andrea Matthews (sop), Julianne Baird (mez), D'Anna Fortunato (mez), Frederick Urrey (ten), John Ostendorf (b–bar), R. Palmer (cnd), Brewer Baroque CO [period instrs] [I] Newport Classic 3–▲ NCD 60125 [DDD]
Purcell, H.:Pausanias, the Betrayer of His Country, w. Robert Houghton (pno)—Sweeter Than Roses [arr. Benjamin Britten] *(rec The Lodge, May & June 1995)* VAI Audio ▲ VAIA 1130 [DDD]

Rickenbacher, H.–J. (ten)
Mendelssohn, F.:Sacred Pieces, w. J–Ch. Geiser (org), Michel Corboz (cnd), Lausanne Vocal Ensemble *(rec Lausanne Cathedral, Jan. 29–31, 1994)* FNAC Music ▲ 592298 [DDD]

Rico, Juan (ten)
Puccini, G.:Madama Butterfly, w. Montserrat Caballé (sop—Cio–Cio–San), Carmen Rigai (mez—Suzuki), Bernabé Martí (ten—Pinkerton), Diego Monjo (ten—Goro), Juan Rico (ten—Yamadori), Manuel Ausensi (bar—Sharpless), Jose Lemar (bass—Bonze), Antonio Leval (bass—Imperial Commissioner), Alejandro Chiara (bass—Registrar), G. Rivoli (cnd), Madrid Radio–TV Orch, Madrid Radio–TV Chorus *(rec Madrid, June 12, 1968)* Legato Classics 2–▲ LCD 210–2 [ADD]

Ridderbusch, Karl (bass)
Bach, J.S.:Mass in b, BWV 232, w. Gundula Janowitz (sop), Christa Ludwig (mez), Peter Schreier (ten), Vienna Choral Academy, H. von Karajan (cnd), Berlin PO Deutsche Grammophon ("Double" series) 2–▲ 439696–2
Beethoven, L. van:Leonore (opera), w. Helen Donath (sop), Edda Moser (sop), Eberhard Büchner (ten), Richard Cassilly (ten), Theo Adam (b–bar), Hermann Christian Polster (bass), H. Blomstedt (cnd), Dresden Staatskapelle, Leipzig Radio Chorus Berlin Classics ▲ BER 1140
Beethoven, L. van:Sym 9, "Choral Sym", w. Gwyneth Jones (sop), Tatiana Troyanos (mez), Jess Thomas (ten), K. Böhm (cnd), Vienna PO, Vienna State Opera Chorus Deutsche Grammophon ("Double" series) 2–▲ 437368–2
Bruckner, A.:Mass 1, w. E. Mathis (sop), M. Schiml (mez), W. Ochman (ten), E. Jochum (cnd), Bavarian RSO, Bavarian Radio Chorus Deutsche Grammophon ("The Originals" series) 2–▲ 447409–2
Bruckner, A.:Mass 1, w. E. Mathis (sop), M. Schiml (sop), W. Ochman (ten), E. Jochum (cnd), Bavarian RSO, Bavarian Radio Chorus [L] Deutsche Grammophon 4–▲ 423127–2 [ADD]
Hoffmann, E.T.A.:Undine, w. Krisztina Láki (sop), R. Henry (sgr), R. Bader (cnd), Berlin RSO, St. Hedwig's Cathedral Choir *(rec Feb. 1982)* Koch Schwann 3–▲ SCH 310922 [DDD]
Lortzing, A.:Zar und Zimmermann (sels), w. Lucia Popp (sop), Adalbert Kraus (ten), Hermann Prey (bar), Fritz Krenn (bass), H. Wallberg (cnd), Bavarian RSO, Bavarian Radio Chorus [G] Acanta 2–▲ CD 42424 [DDD]

Ridderbusch, Karl (bass) (cont.)
Mozart, W.A.:Requiem, w. E. Mathis (sop), J. Hamari (mez), W. Ochman (ten), K. Böhm (cnd), Vienna PO, Vienna State Opera Chorus [L] Deutsche Grammophon ▲ 413553-2 [ADD]
Romberg, A.:Der Lied von der Glocke, w. M. Friesenhausen (sop), R. Naber (alt), H. Hopfner (ten), G. Knüsel (cnd), Essen CO, Duisburg State Concert Chorus Calig ▲ CAL 50942
Strauss, R.:Der Rosenkavalier, w. C. Watson (sop), B. Fassbaender (mez), C. Kleiber (cnd), Bavarian State Opera Orch *(rec 1977)* Exclusive 3-▲ EXL 49 [ADD]
Strauss, R.:Der Rosenkavalier, w. Claire Watson (sop—Feldmarschallin), Lucia Popp (sop—Sophie), Annelie Waas (sop—Marianne), Brigitte Fassbaender (mez—Octavian), Margaretthe Bence (ct—Annina), David Thaw (ten—Valzacchi), Karl Ridderbusch (bass—Baron Ochs), Benno Kusche (bass—Herr von Faninal), Albrecht Peter (bass—Police Inspector), C. Kleiber (cnd), Bavarian State Orch, Bavarian State Chorus *(rec live, Münchner Festspiele, July 20, 1974)* Arkadia 3-▲ 486 [ADD]
Verdi, G.:Macbeth, w. C. Ludwig (mez), C. Cossutta (ten), S. Milnes (bass), K. Böhm (cnd), Vienna State Opera Orch, Vienna State Opera Chorus *(rec live 1970)* Legato Classics 2-▲ LCD 143-2 [ADD]
Wagner, R.:Der fliegende Holländer, w. L. Rysanek (sop), A.-M. Bessel (mez), C. Heater (ten), F. Crass (bass), W. Sawallisch (cnd), La Scala Orch, La Scala Chorus [G] *(rec live, Milan 2/2/66)* Memories 2-▲ HR 4281/82 (m) [ADD]
Wagner, R.:Lohengrin, w. A. Tomowa-Sintow (sop), D. Vejzovic (sop), A. Kollo (ten), S. Nimsgern (b-bar), H. von Karajan (cnd), Berlin PO, German Opera Chorus [G] EMI Classics ("Studio" series) 4-▲ CDMD 69314 [ADD]
Wagner, R.:Die Meistersinger von Nürnberg, w. H. Donath (sop), R. Hesse (mez), A. Kollo (ten), P. Schreier (ten), T. Adam (b-bar), R. Evans (bass), H. von Karajan (cnd), Dresden Staatskapelle, Dresden State Chorus, Leipzig Radio Chorus [G] EMI Classics 4-▲ CDCD 49683 [ADD]
Wagner, R.:Die Meistersinger von Nürnberg, w. Hannelore Bode (sop), Jean Cox (ten), Klaus Hirte (bar), Hans Sotin (bass), S. Varviso (cnd), Bayreuth Festival Orch, Bayreuth Festival Chorus [1974] Philips 32-▲ 434420-2 [ADD/DDD]
Wagner, R.:Die Meistersinger von Nürnberg, w. Hannelore Bode (sop), Jean Cox (ten), Klaus Hirte (bar), Hans Sotin (bass), S. Varviso (cnd), Bayreuth Festival Orch, Bayreuth Festival Chorus [1974] [G] Philips 4-▲ 434611-2 [ADD]
Wagner, R.:Parsifal, w. G. Jones (sop), J. King (ten), T. Stewart (bar), D. McIntyre (b-bar), F. Crass (bass), P. Boulez (cnd), Bayreuth Festival Orch, Bayreuth Festival Chorus [G] *(rec 1970)* Deutsche Grammophon 3-▲ 435718-2 [ADD]
Wagner, R.:Tristan und Isolde, w. H. Dernesch (sop), C. Ludwig (mez), J. Vickers (ten), P. Schreier (ten), B. Weikl (bar), W. Berry (bass), H. von Karajan (cnd), Berlin PO, German Opera Chorus [G] EMI Classics ("Studio" series) 4-▲ CDMD 69319 [ADD]
World Stars Sing Operetta, w. Anna Moffo (sop), Lucia Popp (sop), José Carreras (ten), Ants Kollo (ten), Thomas Moser (ten), Giuseppe Di Stefano (ten), Hermann Prey (bar), et al., various orchs *(rec 1968-1985)* Acanta ▲ 42941

Rieders, B. J. (cta)
Handel, G.F.:Alessandro, w. L. Atkinson (trb), Watson (sop), A. Terzian (mez), T. Poole (ten), D. Price (ten), Andersson (sgr), M. Nowakowski (cnd), Sinfonia Varsovia [I] *(rec live)* Koch Schwann 3-▲ CD SC 100 303 [DDD]

Riedijk, Charlotte (nar)
Boogman, W.:La Disciplina Dei sentimenti, w. Jan Panis (sound projection), Hans Tutschku (sound projection), M. Foster (cnd), Asko Ensemble, Asko Choir *(rec Muziekcentrum Vredenburg Utrecht, Netherlands, Dec 17, 1993)* Donemus ▲ CV 57 [DDD]

Riedijk, Charlotte (sop)
Torstensson, K.:Urban Solo *(rec 1993 or 1994)* Donemus ▲ CV 32
Torstensson, K.:Urban Songs, w. S. Asbury (cnd), Asko Ensemble *(rec 1993 or 1994)* Donemus ▲ CV 32

Riedinger, Colette (sgr)
Varney, L.:Les Mousquetaires au couvent, w. Gabrielle Ristori (mez), Camille Rouquetty (ten), Gabriel Bacquier (bar), Louis Musy (b-bar), Pierre Blanc (sgr), Pauline Carton (sgr), Jacqueline Cauchard (sgr), Mireille Lacoste (sgr), R. Benedetti (cnd) Musidisc 2-▲ MUS 202262 [AAD]

Riegel, Kenneth (ten)
Berg, A.:Lulu, w. T. Stratas (sop), Y. Minton (mez), V. Schwarz (sop), F. Mazura (bar), P. Boulez (cnd), Paris Opera Orch—Act 3 [G] Deutsche Grammophon 3-▲ 415489-2 [ADD]
Berlioz, H.:La Damnation de Faust, w. F. von Stade (mez), J. Van Dam (b-bar), G. Solti (cnd), Chicago SO, Chicago Sym Chorus London 2-▲ 414680-2 [DDD]
Haydn, J.:Mass 11, "Nelsonmesse", "Imperial Mass", "Coronation Mass", w. Judith Blegen (sop), Gwendolen Killebrew (mez), Simon Estes (bass), L. Bernstein (cnd), New York PO, Westminster Choir [L] *(rec 1976)* Sony Classical ("Bernstein:The Royal Edition" series) 2-▲ SM2K 47563 [ADD]
Haydn, J.:Mass 14, "Harmoniemesse", w. Judith Blegen (sop), Fredrica von Stade (mez), Simon Estes (bass), L. Bernstein (cnd), New York PO, Westminster Choir [L] *(rec 1966)* Sony Classical 2-▲ SM2K 47560 [ADD]
Liszt, F.:A Faust Sym, w. L. Bernstein (cnd), Boston SO, Tanglewood Festival Chorus *(rec Symphony Hall, Boston, July 1976)* Deutsche Grammophon ("The Originals" series) 4-▲ 447449-2 [ADD]
Lourié, A.:Little Gidding, German Chamber PO Deutsche Grammophon ▲ 437788-2
Mahler, G.:Syms, w. J. Blegen (sop), B. Hendricks (sop), M. Price (sop), G. Zeumer (sop), H. Wittek (trb), A. Baltsa (mez), C. Ludwig (mez), H. Prey (bar), A. Schmidt (bar), J. Van Dam (b-bar), L. Bernstein (cnd), New York PO, Royal Concertgebouw Orch, Vienna PO, Westminster Choir, New York Choral Artists, Brooklyn Boys' Choir, Vienna Boys' Choir, Vienna State Opera Chorus, Vienna Singverein Deutsche Grammophon 13-▲ 435162-2 [DDD]
Mahler, G.:Sym 8, w. J. Blegen (sop), M. Price (sop), G. Zeumer (sop), A. Baltsa (mez), H. Prey (bar), A. Schmidt (bar), J. Van Dam (b-bar), L. Bernstein (cnd), Vienna PO, Vienna State Opera Chorus, Vienna Boys' Choir *(rec Salzburg Festival, 1975)* Deutsche Grammophon 2-▲ 435102-2 [ADD]
Mozart, W.A.:Don Giovanni, w. E. Moser (sop), K. Te Kanawa (sop), T. Berganza (mez), G. Raimondi (ten), J. Van Dam (b-bar), J. Macurdy (bass), L. Maazel (cnd), Paris Opera Orch, Paris Opera Chorus [I] CBS 3-▲ M3K 35192
Mozart, W.A.:Don Giovanni (sels), w. E. Moser (sop), K. Te Kanawa (sop), T. Berganza (mez), G. Raimondi (ten), J. Van Dam (b-bar), J. Macurdy (bass), L. Maazel (cnd), Paris Opera Orch CBS ■ MT 35859
Orff, C.:Carmina burana, w. J. Blegen (sop), P. Binder (bar), M. Tilson Thomas (cnd), Cleveland Orch, Cleveland Orch Chorus [G, L] CBS ▲ MK 33172 [ADD]
Rossini, G.:Stabat Mater, w. Sung-Sook Lee (sop), Florence Quivar (mez), Paul Plishka (bass), T. Schippers (cnd), Cincinnati SO, May Festival Chorus *(rec 1975)* Vox Box 2-▲ CDX 5141 [ADD]
Strauss, R.:Salome, w. Catherine Malfitano (sop), Hanna Schwarz (mez), Bryn Terfel (b-bar), C. von Dohnányi (cnd), Vienna PO London 2-▲ 444178-2
Zemlinsky, A. von:Eine florentinische Tragödie, w. D. Soffel (mez), G. Sarabia (bar), G. Albrecht (cnd), Berlin RSO [G] Koch Schwann ▲ CD 314012 [DDD]
Zemlinsky, A. von:Der Geburtstag der Infantin, w. B. Haldas (sop), I. Nielsen (sop), D. Weller (bass), G. Albrecht (cnd), Berlin RSO, Berlin RIAS Women's Chamber Choir [G] Koch Schwann ▲ CD 314 013 [DDD]

Rieger, Thomas (trb)
Hoffmann, E.T.A.:Aurora, w. Maltraud Meier (mez), Siegfried Schulze (bass), Koch (sgr), Ohlmann (sgr), H. Dechant (cnd), Bamberg Youth Orch, Bamberg Oratorio Chorus Bayer 3-▲ 100276-78

Ries, R. (sgr)
Hindemith, P.:Neues vom Tage, w. Elisabeth Werres (sop), Claudio Nicolai (bar), J. Latham-König (cnd), Cologne RSO [G] Wergo 2-▲ WER 6192/93-2

Riess, Heidi (alt)
Bach, J.S.:Cant 29, w. Regina Werner (sop), Hans-Joachim Rotzsch (ten), Hermann Christian Polster (bass), H.-J. Rotzsch (cnd), Leipzig Gewandhaus Orch, Leipzig St. Thomas Church Choir Berlin Classics ▲ BER CD 9055
Bach, J.S.:Cant 119, w. Regina Werner (sop), Hans-Joachim Rotzsch (ten), Hermann Christian Polster (bass), H.-J. Rotzsch (cnd), Leipzig Gewandhaus Orch, Leipzig St. Thomas Church Choir Berlin Classics ▲ BER CD 9055

Rigacci, Susanna (sop)
Donizetti, G.:La bella prigioniera, w. R. Franceschetto (sgr), P. Pellegrini (sgr), F. Maestri (cnd), In Canto CO *(rec Apr. 1992)* Bongiovanni 2-▲ GB 2109/10 [DDD]

Rigacci, Susanna (sop) (cont.)
Donizetti, G.:Betly, w. M. Comencini (ten), R. Scaltriti (bar), B. Rigacci (cnd), Emilia Romagna Arturo Toscanini SO, Lugo Teatro Comunale Rossini Chorus *(rec live, 6/90)* Bongiovanni 2-▲ GB 2091/92 [DDD]
Donizetti, G.:Olimpiade, w. D. Broganelli (sgr), F. Maestri (cnd), In Canto CO *(rec May 1991)* Bongiovanni 2-▲ GB 2109/10 [DDD]
Donizetti, G.:I pazzi per progetto, w. A. Cicogna (mez), G. Polidori (bar), G. Sarti (bar), V. M. Brunetti (bass), E. Fissore (bass), L. Monreale (bass), G. Micheli (cnd), Emilia Romagna Arturo Toscanini SO [I] *(rec live, 12/88)* Bongiovanni ▲ GB 2070 [DDD]
Donizetti, G.:Il Pigmalione, w. P. Pellegrini (sgr), F. Maestri (cnd), In Canto CO *(rec Sept. 1990)* Bongiovanni 2-▲ GB 2109/10 [DDD]
Galuppi, B.:Adamo, w. Susanna Rigacci (sop—Angelo di Misericordia), Mara Zampieri (sop—Eva), Marilyn Schmiege (mez—Angelo di Giustizia), Ernesto Palacio (ten—Adamo), C. Scimone (cnd), Venice Solisti Erato 2-▲ ERA SEL 12984 [ADD]
Hasse, J.A.:La Contadina, w. Romano Franceschetto (sgr), F. Maestri (cnd), In Canto CO [I] *(rec Oct. 5, 1991)* Bongiovanni ▲ GB 2128 [DDD]
Rossini, G.:L'inganno felice, w. S. Rigacci (sop—Isabella), E. Palacio (ten—Duke Bertrando), G. Gatti (bar—Batone), R. Ripesi (bass—Tarabotto), G. Casali (bass—Ormondo), F. Maestri (cnd), In Canto CO *(rec Dec. 1992)* Bongiovanni 2-▲ GB 2133/34 [DDD]
Sacchini, A.:La contandina in corte, w. S. Rigacci (sop—Tancia), E. Palacio (ten—Ruggiero), G. Gatti (bar—Berto), C. Boersma (vc), M. Clavenna (db), M. T. Conti (hpd), G. Catalucci (cnd), Sassari SO *(rec Dec. 17-18, 1991)* Bongiovanni 2-▲ GB 2145/46 [DDD]
Vivaldi, A.:Catone in Utica, w. Cecilia Gasdia (sop), Marilyn Schmiege (sop), Lucretia Lendi (mez), Margarita Zimmerman (mez), C. Scimone (cnd), Venice Solisti Erato 2-▲ ERA SEL 11232 [DDD]

Rigai, Carmen (mez)
Puccini, G.:Madama Butterfly, w. Montserrat Caballé (sop—Cio-Cio-San), Carmen Rigai (mez—Suzuki), Bernabé Martí (ten—Pinkerton), Diego Monjo (ten—Goro), Juan Rico (ten—Yamadori), Manuel Ausensi (bar—Sharpless), Jose Lemar (bass—Bonze), Antonio Leval (bass—Imperial Commissioner), Alejandro Chiara (bass—Registrar), G. Rivoli (cnd), Madrid Radio-TV Orch, Madrid Radio-TV Chorus *(rec Madrid, June 12, 1968)* Legato Classics 2-▲ LCD 210-2 [ADD]

Rigby, Jean (mez)
Bach, J.S.:Magnificat, BWV 243, w. B. Hendricks (sop), A. Murray (mez), U. Heilmann (ten), J. Hynninen (bar), N. Marriner (cnd), Academy of St. Martin in the Fields, *(chorus unknown)* EMI Classics ▲ CDC 54283-2
Beethoven, L van:Mass, Op. 86, w. Janice Watson (sop), John Mark Ainsley (ten), Gwynne Howell (bass), M. Best (cnd), Corydon Orch, Corydon Singers Hyperion ▲ CDA 66830
Berlioz, H.:L'Enfance du Christ, w. John Aler (ten), Gerald Finley (ten), Alastair Miles (bar), Gwynne Howell (bass), M. Best (cnd), Cordon Orch, Corydon Singers, St. Paul's Cathedral Choir Hyperion 2-▲ CDA 66991/2
Britten, H.:Phaedra, w. L. Friend (cnd), Nash Ensemble Hyperion ▲ CDA 66845
Britten, H.:The Rape of Lucretia (sels), w. C. Pierard (sop), P. Rozario (sop), A. Gunson (mez), N. Robson (ten), D. Maxwell (bar), A. Opie (bar), A. Miles (bass), R. Hickox (cnd), City of London Sinfonia Chandos 2-▲ CHAN 9254/55 [DDD]
Elgar, E.:The Music Makers, w. A. Davis (cnd), BBC SO, BBC Sym Chorus *(rec London, Aug. 1993)* Teldec ▲ 92374-2 [DDD]
Handel, G.F.:Messiah, w. Yvonne Kenny (sop), Thomas Randle (ten), Willard White (bass), O. A. Hughes (cnd), Royal PO, Royal Choral Society IMP Classics 2-▲ IMPDPCD 1106 [DDD]
Mahler, G.:Das Lied von der Erde, w. Robert Tear (ten), M. Wiggelsworth (cnd), Premiere Ensemble [arr. Schoenberg] RCA Red Seal ▲ 09026-68043-2
Mendelssohn, F.:A Midsummer Night's Dream (comp), w. J. Howarth (sop), F. d' Avalos (cnd), Philharmonia Orch, Bach Choir—Op. 61 IMP Masters ▲ IMPMCD 78 [DDD]
Sullivan, A.:The Mikado, w. L. Garrett (sop), S. Bullock (sop), F. Palmer (sop/mez), B. Bottone (ten), R. Angas (bass), E. Idle (bar), R. Van Allan (bass), M. Richardson (bar), P. Robinson (cnd), English National Opera Orch, English Opera Group Chorus—sels [E] MCA Classics ▲ MCAD 6215 [DDD]; ■ MCAC 6215 (D)
Vivaldi, A.:Gloria, RV.589, w. B. Hendricks (sop), A. Murray (mez), U. Heilmann (ten), J. Hynninen (bar), N. Marriner (cnd), Academy of St. Martin in the Fields, Academy Chorus EMI Classics ▲ CDC 54283

Riggins, N. (sgr)
Giordano, U.:Andrea Chénier, w. Montserrat Caballé (sop), Franco Corelli (ten), R. de Carlo (sgr), D. Dondi (sgr), G. Ellsworth (sgr), J. Fair (sgr), R. Falk (sgr), S. Felter (sgr), E. Green (sgr), H. Hicks (sgr), H. Krauss (sgr), L. Miller (sgr), H. Salerno (sgr), A. Guadagno (cnd), Academy of Music Orch, Academy of Music Chorus Great Opera Performances 2-▲ GOP 766

Righetti, R. (mez)
Verdi, G.:La traviata, w. M. Freni (sop), R. Cioni (ten), M. Sereni (bar), H. von Karajan (cnd), La Scala Orch, La Scala Chorus *(rec Milan, 1964)* Legend 2-▲ LGD 125 [ADD]

Rigosa, Danilo (bass)
Bizet, G.:Carmen (sels), w. D. Palade (sop—Micaëla), A. Liebeck (sop—Frasquita), G. Alperyn (mez—Carmen), D. Schaechter (mez—Mercédès), G. Lamberti (ten—Don José), M. Dvorsky (ton Romandado), J. Durco (ten—Cancairo), A. Titus (bar—Escamillo), V. Chmelo (bar—Morales), D. Rigosa (bass—Zuniga), A. Rahbari (cnd), Czech-Slovak RSO Bratislava, Slovak Phil Chorus, Bratislava Children's Choir *(rec July 1990)* Naxos ▲ 8.550727 [DDD]

Riley, Bill (sgr)
Chant, w. Gary Robison (sgr) Unison ■ V80134

Riley, Terry (voc)
Riley, T.:Songs for the 10 Voices of the 2 Prophets, w. T. Riley (syn) *(rec live, Munich, 5/10/82)* Kuckuck ■ 11067-4 (D)
Riley, T.:Songs for the 10 Voices of the 2 Prophets, w. T. Riley (syn) *(rec live, Munich, 5/10/82)* Kuckuck ▲ 12047-2

Rime, Noémi (sop)
Brossard, S. de:Motets, w. J.-P. Fouchécourt (alt/ten), I. Honeyman (ten), B. Deletré (bass), M. Gester (cnd), Parlement de Musique—Salve Rex Christe; Psallite Superi; Qui non diligit te; O Domine quia refugium; Templa nunc fument; Oratorio seu Dialogus Poenitentis animae cum Deo; Festis laeta sonent [L] *(rec 1992)* Opus 111 ▲ OPS 30-69 [DDD]
Charpentier, M.-A.:Le Malade imaginaire, w. C. Brua (sop), M. Zanetti (sop), D. Visse (ct), H. Crook (ten), J.-F. Gardeil (bar), W. Christie (cnd), Les Arts Florissants [F] Harmonia Mundi France ▲ HMC 901336
Charpentier, M.-A.:Médée, w. Isabelle Desrochers (sop—Cleone), Lorraine Hunt (sop—Medee), Noemi Rime (sop—Nerine), Monique Zanetti (sop—Creuse), Mark Padmore (ten—Jason), François Bazola (bar—Arcas), Jean-Marc Salzmann (bar—Oronte), Bernard Deletre (bass-Creon), W. Christie (cnd), Les Arts Florissants Erato 3-▲ 96558-2
Clérambault, L.N.:Cants, w. Jean-Paul Fouchécourt (ten), Nicolas Rivenq (bass), Hiro Kurosaki (vn), Ryo Terakado (vn), Marc Hantaï (fl), Eric Bellocq (thb), Elisabeth Matiffa (b vl), Bruno Croscet (basse de vn), W. Christie (cnd), Les Arts Florissants—Pyrame et Tisbé, La Muse de l'opéra ou les Caractères Lyriques, La Mort d'Hercule, Orphée Musique d'Abord ▲ HMA 1901329
Lully, J.-B.:Armide, w. V. Gens (sop), G. Laurens (mez), H. Crook (ten), G. Ragon (ten), P. Herreweghe (cnd), La Chapelle Royale Orch, Collegium Vocale [F] Harmonia Mundi France 2-▲ HMC 901456/57
Mozart, W.A.:Ave verum corpus, w. Christine Batty (mez), Stuart Patterson (ten), Bernard Deletre (bass), G. Vashegyi (cnd), Budapest Orfeo Orch, Patrick Marco (cnd), Maitrise de Paris Pierre Verany ▲ PVY 730058 [DDD]
Mozart, W.A.:Missa, K.317, w. Christine Batty (mez), Stuart Patterson (ten), Bernard Deletre (bass), G. Vashegyi (cnd), Budapest Orfeo Orch, Patrick Marco (cnd), Maitrise de Paris Pierre Verany ▲ PVY 730058 [DDD]
Mozart, W.A.:Vesperae solennes, w. Christine Batty (mez), Stuart Patterson (ten), Bernard Deletre (bass), G. Vashegyi (cnd), Budapest Orfeo Orch, Patrick Marco (cnd), Maitrise de Paris Pierre Verany ▲ PVY 730058 [DDD]
Rameau, J.P.:Les Indes galantes, w. C. McFadden (sop), S. Piau (sop), I. Poulenard (sop), M. Ruggeri (sop), H. Crook (ten), J.-P. Fouchecourt (ten), N. Rivenq (bar), J. Corréas (bass), B. Delétré (bass), W. Christie (cnd), Les Arts Florissants [F] Harmonia Mundi France 3-▲ HMC 901367/69

Rime, Noémi (sop) (cont.)
Rameau, J.P.:Motets, w. S. Daneman (sop), P. Agnew (ct), N. Rivenq (bar), N. Cavallier (bass), W. Christie (cnd), Les Arts Florissants—In convertendo, Quam dilecta, Deus noster refugium *(rec June 8-12, 1994)* Erato ▲ 96967-2 [DDD]
Scarlatti, A.:Lamentazioni par la Settimana Santa, w. M. Lins (sop), Parlement de Musique [I] Opus 111 ▲ 30-66

Rimini, Giacomo (bar)
Verdi, G.:Falstaff, w. Pia Tassinari (sop—Alice Ford), Ines Alfani Tellini (sop—Nannetta), Aurora Buades (mez—Quickly), Rita Monticone (mez—Meg Page), Roberto D'Alessio (ten—Fenton), Giuseppe Nessi (ten—Bardolfo), Emilio Venturini (ten—Dr. Caius), Emilio Ghirardini (bar—Ford), Giacomo Rimini (bar—Sir John Falstaff), Salvatore Baccaloni (bass—Pistola), L. Molajoli (cnd), Milan SO, La Scala Chorus *(rec La Scala Theatre, Milan, Apr. 1932)* VAI Audio 2-▲ VAIA 1098-2

Rinaldi, Alberto (bar)
Cavalli, P.F.:Ormindo, w. E. Zilio (mez), V. Manno (ten), G. Gatti (bar), R. Fasano (cnd), Rome Virtuosi Stradivarius 2-▲ DAT 12307

Rinaldi, Margherita (sop)
Bellini, V.:I Capuleti e i Montecchi, w. M. Rinaldi (sop—Giulietta), G. Aragall (ten—Romeo), L. Pavarotti (ten—Tebaldo), N. Zaccaria (bass—Capellio), C. Abbado (cnd), Residentie Orch The Hague, Bologna Chorus [I] *(rec live, Amsterdam 6/30/66)* Verona 2-▲ 28001/2
Bellini, V.:I Capuleti e i Montecchi, w. G. Aragall (ten), L. Pavarotti (ten), N. Zaccaria (bass), C. Abbado (cnd), Residentie Orch The Hague, Bologna Chorus *(rec live, Amsterdam 6/30/66)* Melodram 2-▲ MEL 27001
Bellini, V.:Norma, w. Margherita Rinaldi (sop—Adalgisa), Renata Scotto (sop—Norma), Giuseppina Arista (mez—Clotilde), Ermanno Mauro (ten—Pollione), Giancarlo Turati (ten—Flavio), Agostino Ferrin (bass—Oroveso), R. Muti (cnd), Florence Teatro Comunale Orch, Florence Teatro Comunale Chorus *(rec Florence, Dec 19, 1978)* Legato Classics 2-▲ LCD 203-2
Meyerbeer, G.:Le Prophète, w. M. Horne (mez), N. Gedda (ten), R. El Hage (bass), H. Lewis (cnd), Turin RSO, Turin Radio Chorus [F] *(rec live 7/11/70)* Foyer 3-▲ FOY 2035 [AAD]
Piccinni, N.:La cecchina, ossia la buona figliola, w. Lucia Alberti (sop—Il Cavaliere Armidoro), Emilia Ravaglia (sop—La Marchesa), Margherita Rinaldi (sop—Cecchina), Elena Zilio (mez—Paoluccia), Ugo Benelli (bar—Il Marchese della Conchiglia), Alessandro Corbelli (bar—Mengotto), Enzo Dara (bar—Tagliaferro), Renata Baldisseri (sgr—Sandrina), G. Gelmetti (cnd), Rome Opera Orch, Rome Opera Chorus *(rec Rome, Feb 4, 1981)* Italia 2-▲ CDC 95 [ADD]
Verdi, G.:Rigoletto, w. V. Cortez (mez), F. Bonisolli (ten), R. Panerai (bar), B. Rundgren (b-bar), F. Molinari-Pradelli (cnd), Dresden State Orch, Dresden State Chorus [I] Acanta 2-▲ CD 41474 [DDD]

Rinaldi-Miliani, Stefano (bar)
Mozart, W.A.:Don Giovanni, w. S. Ghazarian (sop), G. Ottenthal (sop), P. Pace (sop), G. Sabbatini (ten), R. Bruson (bar), F. De Grandis (bass), N. Ghiuselev (bass), N. Järvi (cnd), Cologne RSO, Cologne Radio Chorus [I] Chandos 3-▲ CHAN 8920/22 [DDD]
Verdi, G.:Simon Boccanegra, w. M. Nicolesco (sop), G. Sabbatini (ten), R. Bruson (bar), R. Scandiuzzi (bass), N. de Angelis (bass), R. Paternostro (cnd), Tokyo SO, Nikikai Chorus *(rec live 2/90)* Capriccio 2-▲ 60018-2 [DDD]

Rinaudo, Mario (bass)
Donizetti, G.:Gemma di Vergy, w. Montserrat Caballé (sop—Gemma di Vergy), Biancamaria Casoni (mez—Ida di Greville), Giorgio Lamberti (ten—Tamas), Renato Bruson (bar—Conte di Vergy), Mario Machì (bass—Rolando), Mario Rinaudo (bass—Guido), A. Gatto (cnd), Naples Teatro San Carlo Orch, Naples Teatro San Carlo Chorus *(rec Naples, Dec. 12, 1975)* Myto 2-▲ 952124
Verdi, G.:Ernani, w. Margherita Roberti (sop), Anna di Stasio (mez), Athos Cesarini (ten), Mario del Monaco (ten), Ettore Bastianini (bar), Nicola Rossi-Lemeni (bass), F. Previtali (cnd), Naples Teatro San Carlo Orch, Naples Teatro San Carlo Chorus Melodram 2-▲ CDM 270100
Verdi, G.:Luisa Miller, w. K. Ricciarelli (sop—Luisa), M. G. Piolatto (mez—Laura), S. Silva (cta—Federica), J. Carreras (ten—Rodolfo), E. Pranod (ten—A Peasant), R. Bruson (bar—Miller), G. Casarini (bar—Wurm) M. Rinaudo (bass—Count Walter), F. Previtali (cnd), Turin Teatro Regio Orch, Turin Teatro Regio Chorus *(rec May 9, 1976)* Legato Classics 2-▲ LCD 180 [ADD]

Ringart, Anna (mez)
Donizetti, G.:Gemma di Vergy, w. Montserrat Caballe (sop—Gemma), Anna Ringart (mez—Ida), Luis Lima (ten—Tamas), Vicente Sardinero (bar—Il Conte), Juan Pons (bar—Guido), Francois Loup (b—Rolando), A. Gatto (cnd), Nouvel PO, Jean-Paul Kreder (cnd), French Radio Chorus *(rec live, Salle Pleyel, Paris, Apr 20, 1976)* Agorá Music ("Phoenix" series) 2-▲ 501 [ADD]

Ringholz, Teresa (sop)
Friml, R.:Songs, w. D. Hunsberger (cnd), Eastman-Dryden Orch Arabesque ▲ Z 6562
Mozart, W.A.:Songs, w. R. Spillman (pno)—Abendempfindung; Als Luise die Briefe; An die Bescheidenheit; An die Einsamkeit; An die Freundschaft; An die Hoffnung; Die betrogene Welt; Geheime Liebe; Gesellenreise; Die kleine Spinnerin; Lied der Freiheit; Das Lied der Trennung; Das Traumbild; Das Veilchen; Die Verschweigung; Der Zauberer; Die Zufriedenheit [G] *(rec Sept. 1986)* Arabesque ▲ Z 6576 [DDD]
Romberg, S.:Music of (operetta sels), w. D. Hunsberger (cnd), Eastman-Dryden Orch—selections from The New Moon, Maytime, Desert Song, etc. [E] Arabesque ▲ Z 6540 [DDD]
Rossini, G.:La scala di seta, w. Francesca Provvisionata (mez), Fulvio Massa (ten), Ramon Vargas (ten), Alessandro Corbelli (bar), Natale de Carolis (b-bar), M. Viotti (cnd), English CO Claves 2-▲ 9219/20
Schnittke, A.:Life with an Idiot, w. H. Haskin (ten), D. Duesing (bar), M. Rostropovich (cnd), Rotterdam PO, Rotterdam Vocal Ensemble *(rec Amsterdam, world premiere performance, April 13, 1992)* Sony Classical 2-▲ S2K 52495 [DDD]

Rinpoche, Lama Kunga (sgr)
Radigue, E.:Mila's Journey Inspired By A Dream, w. Robert Ashley (sgr), Eliane Radigue (syn) Lovely Music ▲ LCD 2002 [AAD]

Rintzler, Marius (bass)
Mozart, W.A.:Requiem, w. E. Mathis (sop), G. Bumbry (mez), G. Shirley (ten), R. Frühbeck de Burgos (cnd), New Philharmonia Orch, New Philharmonia Chorus Classics for Pleasure ▲ CDCFP 4399 [ADD]

Rioux, Chantal (mez)
Gratton, H.:Imagerie:Christmas Pastoral, w. M. Keable (actor), S. Léonard (actor), J.-L. Millette (actor), M. Laferrière (sop), B. Levasseur (bar), N. Richard (b-bar), L. Lavigueur (cnd), Louis Lavigueur Instrumental Ensemble, Louis Lavigueur Vocal Ensemble [F] *(rec 5/91)* CBC ("SM 5000" series) ▲ SMCD 5109 [DDD]

Ripesi, R. (bass)
Rossini, G.:L'inganno felice, w. S. Rigacci (sop—Isabella), E. Palacio (ten—Duke Bertrando), G. Gatti (bar—Batone), R. Ripesi (bass—Tarabotto), G. Casali (bass—Ormondo), F. Maestri (cnd), In Canto CO *(rec Dec. 1992)* Bongiovanni 2-▲ GB 2133/34 [DDD]

Ripley, David (bass)
Bach, J.S.:St. John Passion, w. J. Baird (sop), J. Bryden (sop), J. Thomas (ten), J. Weaver (bass), K. Slowik (cnd), Smithsonian Chamber Players, Smithsonian Chamber Chorus [period instrs] [G] *(Slowik performs the original 1724 version, & includes the two choruses & three arias added to Bach's 1725 revision as appended tracks at the end of the discs, allowing the listener to either ignore the end tracks & hear the standard version or program the discs to play the 1725 sequence)* Smithsonian Collection 5-▲ ND 0380 [DDD]
York, W.:Songs on a Poem of Su Tung P'O, w. B. Lancaster (sgr), H. Weinberger (sgr) *(rec May 1987)* New World ▲ 80439-2

Ripley, Gladys (cta)
Elgar, E.:The Dream of Gerontius, w. H. Nash (ten), D. Noble (bar), N. Walker (bass), M. Sargent (cnd), Liverpool PO, Huddersfield Choral Society Testament ▲ TES SBT 2025 [ADD]
Mendelssohn, F.:Elijah, w. Isobel Baillie (sop), James Johnston (ten), Harold Williams (b-bar), M. Sargent (cnd), Liverpool PO, Huddersfield Choral Society Dutton Laboratories 2-▲ DUT 2004 [ADD]

Rippon, Angela (nar)
Prokofiev, S.:Peter & the Wolf, w. O.A. Hughes (cnd), Royal PO [E] ASV Quicksilva ▲ CD QS 6017 [ADD]

Rippon, Michael (bass)
Herrmann, B.:Moby Dick, w. John Amis (ten), Robert Bowman (ten), David Kelly (bass), London PO, Aeolian Singers [E] Unicorn-Kanchana ▲ UKCD 2061

Rippon, Michael (bass) (cont.)
Herrmann, B.:Wuthering Heights, w. M. Beaton (sop—Catherine), P. Bowden (mez—Isabella), E. Bainbridge (mez—Nelly), M. Snashall (trb—Hareton), D. Bell (bar—Heathcliff), J. Kitchiner (bar—Hindley), J. Ward (bar—Edgar), M. Rippon (bass—Joseph), D. Kelly (bass—Mr. Lockwood), B. Herrmann (cnd), Pro Arte Orch *(rec 1965-66)* Unicorn-Kanchana 3-▲ UKCD 2050/51/52 [ADD]
Mathias, W.:Ave Rex, w. Janet Price (sop), Kenneth Bowen (ten), Geraint Evans (b-bar), D. Atherton (cnd), D. Willcocks (cnd), London SO, New Philharmonia Orch, Welsh National Opera Chorus, Windsor Bach Choir, St. George's Chapel Choristers Lyrita ▲ SRCD .324
Mathias, W.:Elegy for a Prince, w. D. Atherton (cnd), D. Willcocks (cnd), London SO, New Philharmonia Orch Lyrita ▲ SRCD .324
Mathias, W.:This Worlde's Joie, w. Janet Price (sop), Kenneth Bowen (ten), D. Atherton (cnd), D. Willcocks (cnd), London SO, New Philharmonia Orch, Welsh National Opera Chorus, Windsor Bach Choir, St. George's Chapel Choristers Lyrita ▲ SRCD .324
Qu, X.:Mong Dong, w. *(other soloists unknown)*, K. Schermerhorn (cnd), Hong Kong PO *(rec Lyric Theatre of the Hong Kong Academy for Performing Arts, June 28, 1986)* Marco Polo ("Chinese Contemporary" series) ▲ 8.223915 [DDD]
Weill, K.:The Seven Deadly Sins, w. E. Ross (sop), A. R. Johnson (ten), I. Caley (ten), J. Tomlinson (bass), S. Rattle (cnd), City of Birmingham SO EMI Classics ▲ CDM 64739

Risani, Luigi (sgr)
Donizetti, G.:Caterina Cornaro, w. L. Gencer (sop), G. Aragall (ten), R. Bruson (bar), C.F. Cillario (cnd), Naples Teatro San Carlo Orch, Naples Teatro San Carlo Chorus *(rec live, 5/28/72)* Myto 2-▲ 2 MCD 92153 [ADD]

Ristori, Gabrielle (mez)
Varney, L.:Les Mousquetaires au couvent, w. Camille Rouquetty (ten), Gabriel Bacquier (bar), Louis Musy (b-bar), Pierre Blanc (sgr), Pauline Carton (sgr), Jacqueline Cauchard (sgr), Mireille Lacoste (sgr), Colette Riedinger (sgr), R. Benedetti (cnd) Musidisc 2-▲ MUS 202262 [AAD]

Ristori, Riccardo (bass)
Mayr, S.:La Passione, w. Ernesto Palacio (ten), P. Pelucchi (cnd), Collegium Musicum Agorá 2-▲ 005
Paisiello, G.:Il mondo della luna, w. Gemma Bertagnolli (sop—Clarice), Enzo Dara (bar—Buonafede), Riccardo Ristori (bass—Cecco), Carla Di Censo (sgr—Flaminia), Daniele Gaspari (sgr—Ecclittico), Mattia Nicolini (sgr—Ernesto), F. Neri (cnd), Bolzano Monteverdi Orch *(rec Aug 4-6, 1993)* Bongiovanni 2-▲ GB 2173/74 [DDD]
Ricci, L.:Crispino e la cornare, w. D. Lojarro (sop), A. Lazzarini (mez), Cossutta (ten), S. Alaimo (bar), R. Coviello (bar), A. Marani (bass), Benori (sgr), Siclari (sgr), P. Carignani (cnd), San Remo SO, San Remo Sym Chorus [I] *(rec live 11/89)* Bongiovanni 2-▲ GB 2095/96 [DDD]
Stradella, A.:Crudo mar di fiamme orribili, Alessandro Stradella Consort Bongiovanni ▲ GB 2165 [DDD]
Stradella, A.:Esule dalle sfere, w. Roberta Invernizzi (sop), Silvia Piccolo (sop), Marco Lazzara (alt), Mario Nuvoli (ten), Carlo Lepore (bass), Alessandro Stradella Consort Bongiovanni ▲ GB 2165 [DDD]
Stradella, A.:Il moro per amore, w. R. Invernizzi (sop—Eurinda), S. Piccollo (sop—Lucinda), M. Grazia Liguori (sop—Fiorino), M. Lazzara (cta—Lindora), V. Matacchini (cta—Feraspe/Floridoro), M. Beasley (ten—Filandro), R. Ristori (bass—Rodrigo), E. Velardi (cnd), Alessandro Stradella Consort [I] *(rec Oct. 31-Nov. 3, 1992)* Bongiovanni 3-▲ GB 2153/55
Stradella, A.:O di Cocito oscure deità, w. R. Invernizzi (sop—Proserpina), S. Piccollo (sop—Vendetta), M. Nuvoli (ten—Inganno), R. Ristori (bass—Plutone), E. Velardi (cnd), Alessandro Stradella Consort *(rec Oct. 25, 1993)* Bongiovanni ▲ GB 2164 [DDD]
Stradella, A.:Lo schiavo liberto, w. R. Invernizzi (sop—Armida), M. Lazzara (cta—Rinaldo), M. Nuvoli (ten—Carlo), R. Ristori (bass—Ubaldo), E. Velardi (cnd), Alessandro Stradella Consort *(rec Nov. 15, 1993)* Bongiovanni ▲ GB 2164 [DDD]

Ritchard, Cyril (nar)
Prokofiev, S.:Peter & the Wolf, w. E. Ormandy (cnd), Philadelphia Orch Odyssey ■ YT 34616
Prokofiev, S.:Peter & the Wolf, w. E. Ormandy (cnd), Philadelphia Orch Sony Classical ("Essential Classics" series) ▲ SBK 62638 ■ SBT 62638

Ritchie, Elizabeth (sop)
Baroque Beauties, w. J. Laredo (cnd), Scottish CO, City of London Sinfonia [cnd:R. Hickox], Bowman (ct), J. Purvis (pno) Pickwick ("The Orchid" series) ▲ PICORCD 11010
The Best of British Song IMP Classics ▲ PCD 1064 [DDD]
The Best of Classical Song, w. Jennifer Purvis (pno), Victoria Soames (cl) IMP Classics ▲ PCD 987 [DDD]
Paer, F.:Una voce al cor mi parta, w. V. Soames (cl), J. Purvis (pno) Clarinet Classics ▲ CC 0006 [ADD]
Spohr, L.:Faust (sels), w. V. Soames (cl), J. Purvis (pno)—Ich bin allein Clarinet Classics ▲ CC 0006 [ADD]
Spohr, L.:Songs (misc), w. V. Soames (cl), J. Purvis (pno)—6 deutsche Lieder, Op. 103 Clarinet Classics ▲ CC 0006 [ADD]

Ritchie, Margaret (sop)
Handel, G.F.:Sosarme, Rè di Media, w. Margaret Ritchie (sop—Elmira), Alfred Deller (mez—Sosarme), Nancy Evans (mez—Erenice), Helen Watts (cta—Melo), John Kentish (ct—Argone), William Herbert (ten—King Haliate), Ian Wallace (bass—Altomaro), A. Lewis (cnd), St. Cecilia Academy Orch Rome, St. Anthony Singers Theorema 2-▲ TH 121194/195

Rittenhouse, James (sgr)
Caccini, F.:La liberazione di Ruggiero dall'isola d'Alcina, w. Linda De Rungs (sop—Alcian/Vistola), Cecilia Amorocho (sgr—Melissa/Nunzia), Laura Lea Duckworth (sgr—Siren/Harpy), Eric Friedlander (sgr—Monster), L. Ernest Gross (sgr—Enchanted Cypress), Phoebe Jevtovic (sgr—Siren), James Rittenhouse (sgr—Ruggiero/Neptune), Sharon Sim (sgr—Siren), R. Burchard (cnd), Ars Femina Ensemble, TimeChange *(rec Louisville, KY, 1993)* Nannerl ▲ NR-ARS 003; ■ NR-ARS 003

Ritter, Hendrik (ten)
Distler, H.:Mörike-Chorliederbuch, w. Christiane Kreis (sop), Juliane Mechler (alt), Bernd Stegmann (cnd), Berlin Vocal Ensemble *(rec Herrenberg, Jan 2-4, 1992)* Musicaphon ▲ BM 56820

Ritter, Matthias (sop)
Haydn, J.:Mass 9, "Heiligmesse", w. Simon Schnorr (alt), Jörg Hering (ten), Benedikt Schillo (ten), Panito Iconomou (bass), B. Weil (cnd), Tölz Boys' Choir Sony Classical ("Vivarte" series) ▲ SK 66260
Haydn, J.:Sacred Music, w. Simon Schnorr (alt), Jörg Hering (ten), Benedikt Schillo (ten), Panito Iconomou (bass), B. Weil (cnd), Tölz Boys' Choir—Mare clausum (oratorio fragment), H.XXI-Va:9; Motetto Insanae et vanae curae, H.XXI:1; Motetti de Venerabili Sacramento I-IV, H.XXIIIc:5a-d; Te Deum, H.XXIIIc:2 Sony Classical ("Vivarte" series) ▲ SK 66260

Ritterbusch, Sabine (sop)
Dessau, P.:Haggada, w. Renate Spingler (sop), Yvi Jänicke (alt), Peter Galliard (ten—Rabbi Tarfon/Jude/ten solo), Gabriel Sadé (ten—Pharaoh), Jochen Schmeckenbecher (bar—Rabbi Jehoschua), Bernd Weikl (bar—Moses), Matthias Hölle (bass—Speaker/Rabbi Akiwa), Alfred Muff (bass—Father/Rabbi Eleasar), Johann Tilli (bass—Rabbi Elieser/bass solo), G. Albrecht (cnd), Hamburg State PO, Berlin Carl Maria Von Weber Men's Choir, Hamburg Alsterspatzen, North German Radio Chorus [G] *(rec Musikhalle, Hamburg, Sept 4 & 5, 1994)* Capriccio 2-▲ 10590/91 [DDD]

Ritzerfeld, H. J. (ten)
Draeseke, F.:Mysterium:Christus, w. C. Bischoff (sop), A. Vogel (sop), E. Dersen (alt), K. Markus (ten), P. Langshaw (bar), B. Kämpff (bass), J. Sonnenschmidt (org), U.-R. Follert (cnd), Breslau State PO, Evangelical Boys' Choir Palatine, Heilbronn Vocal Ensemble, Palatine Kurrende Bayer 5-▲ 100175/79

Ritzmann, Martin (ten)
Mussorgsky, M.:Boris Godunov (sels), w. Hanne-Lore Kuhse (sop), Peter Schreier (ten), Theo Adam (b-bar), H. Kegel (cnd), Dresden State Orch, Leipzig Radio Chorus Berlin Classics ▲ BER 2032 [ADD]

Riva, Ambrogio (bass)
Bellini, V.:I Puritani, w. K. Ricciarelli (sop), E. Jankovic (mez), C. Merritt (ten), C. Gaifa (ten), R. Scandiuzzi (bass), G. Ferro (cnd), Sicilian SO, Bari Teatro Petruzzelli Chorus *(rec Apr. 10, 1986)* Cetra Classic ▲ CDC 20 [ADD]
Donizetti, G.:Anna Bolena (sels), w. Carol Vaness (sop), Melinda Paulsen (cta), Dennis O'Neill (ten), Anton Rosner (ten), R. Abbado (cnd), Munich RSO, Bavarian Radio Chorus—Final Scene & Aria [from Act II] *(rec Studio 1, Bavaria, Apr 13-17, 1993)* RCA Red Seal ▲ 09026-61828-2 [DDD]

Riva, Ambrogio (bass) (cont.)
Donizetti, G.:Torquato Tasso, w. A. D'Auria (sop), L. Serra (sop), N. Ciliento (mez), E. Palacio (ten), R. Coviello (bar), S. Alaimo (b-bar), M.. Bernart (cnd), Genoa Teatro Comunale Orch, Genoa Teatro Comunale Chorus [I] *(rec live 10/16/85)* Bongiovanni 3-▲ GB 2028/30 [DDD]
Verdi, G.:Macbeth (sels), w. Carol Vaness (sop), Marisca Mulder (sop), R. Abbado (cnd), Munich RSO, Bavarian Radio Chorus—Grand Sleepwalking Scene [from Act IV] *(rec Studio 1, Bavaria, Apr 13-17, 1993)* RCA Red Seal ▲ 09026-61828-2 [DDD]

Rivadeneyra, Ines (mez)
Falla, M. de:El amor brujo, w. J. Arámbarri (cnd), Madrid Concert Orch *(rec 1959)* EMI Classics 2-▲ ZDMB 64555
Falla, M. de:El amor brujo, w. I. Markevitch (cnd), Spanish National Radio-TV SO *(rec 1966)* Philips ("Spanish" series) ▲ 432829-2 [ADD]
Falla, M. de:La vida breve, w. V. de los Angeles (sop), F. Cossutta (mez), R. Burgos (cnd), Spanish National Orch, Orféon Donostiarra [Sp] EMI Classics ▲ CDM 69590 [ADD]

Rivenq, Nicolas (bar)
Clérambault, L.N.:Cants, w. Noémi Rime (sop), Jean-Paul Fouchécourt (ten), Hiro Kurosaki (vn), Ryo Terakado (vn), Marc Hantaï (fl), Eric Bellocq (thb), Elisabeth Matiffa (b vl), Bruno Croscet (basse de vn), W. Christie (cnd), Les Arts Florissants—Pyrame et Tisbé, La Muse de l'opéra ou les Caractères Lyriques, La Mort d'Hercule, Orphée Musique d'Abord ▲ HMA 1901329
Handel, G.F.:Giulio Cesare in Egitto, w. Lynne Dawson (sop), Eirian James (mez), Guillemette Laurens (mez), James Bowman (alt), Dominique Visse (alt), J. Malgoire (cnd), La Grande Écurie et la Chambre du Roy Astrée 3-▲ E 8558
Mercadante, S.:Caritea, regina di Spagna, w. Nana Gordaze (sgr), Sonia Lee (sgr), Jacek Laszczkowski (sgr), Gregory Bonfatti (sgr), Ayhan Ustuk (sgr), G. Carella (cnd), Italian International Opera Orch, Bratislava Camera Chorus *(rec Italy, 1995)* Nuova Era 3-▲ NUO 7258
Rameau, J.P.:Les Indes galantes, w. C. McFadden (sop), S. Piau (sop), I. Poulenard (sop), N. Rime (sop), M. Ruggeri (sop), H. Crook (ten), J.-P. Fouchecourt (ten), J. Corréas (bass), B. Delétré (bass), W. Christie (cnd), Les Arts Florissants [F] Harmonia Mundi France 3-▲ HMC 901367/69
Rameau, J.P.:Motets, w. S. Daneman (sop), N. Rime (sop), P. Agnew (ct), N. Cavallier (bass), W. Christie (cnd), Les Arts Florissants—In convertendo, Quam dilecta, Deus noster refugium *(rec June 8-12, 1994)* Erato ▲ 96967-2 [DDD]
Rameau, J.P.:Les Paladins, w. A. Michael (sop), G. Raphanel (sop), B. Brewer (ten), D. Nasrawi (ten), G. Reinhart (bar), J. Malgoire (cnd), La Grande Écurie et la Chambre du Roy, Sagittarius Vocal Ensemble [F] Pierre Verany 2-▲ PV.790121/22 [DDD]

Rivera, Chita (sgr)
Bernstein, L.:West Side Story, w. C. Lawrence (sgr), L. Kert (sgr) [1957 cast] Columbia ▲ CK 32603 ♦ CM 32603 ■ JST 32603

Rivera, Madeline (sop)
Mendelssohn, F.:Sym 2, w. M. Chalker (sop), V. Cole (ten), G. Schwarz (cnd), Seattle SO, Seattle Chorale *(rec Apr. 22-23, 1991)* Delos ▲ DE 3112 [DDD]

Riveros, Ximena (sop)
Bizet, G.:Carmen, w. Laura Bustamante (sop—Frasquita), Ximena Riveros (sop—Mercedes), Nancy Stokes (sop—Micaela), Regina Resnik (mez—Carmen), Plácido Domingo (ten—Don José), Ismildo Tedeschi (ten—Remendado), Ramon Vinay (ten—Escamillo), Juan Charles (ten/bar—Dancaire), Agustin Letelier (bar—Morles), Jorge Algorta (bass—Zuniga), A. Guadagno (cnd), Santiago Teatro Municipale Orch, Santiago Teatro Municipale Chorus *(rec Santiago Municipal Theater, Sept. 4, 1967)* Legato Classics 2-▲ LCD 194-2 [ADD]

Rivers, Joan (nar)
Saint-Saëns, C.:Carnival of the Animals, w. M. Golabek (nar), R. Golabek (nar), F. Savage (nar), C. Heston (nar), J. E. Jones (nar), B. White (nar), L. Redgrave (nar), W. Shatner (nar), T. Danson (nar), L. Tomlin (nar), D. Raffin (nar), A. Hepburn (nar), D. Moore (nar), W. Matthau (nar), J. Smith (nar), L. Schifrin (cnd), Hollywood CO Dove Audio ▲ DOV 30700

Rivers, Malcolm (bar)
Lloyd, G.:Iernin, w. M. Hill Smith (sop), C. Powell (mez), G. Pogson (ten), H. Herford (bar) Albany 3-▲ TROY 121/23 [DDD]
Lloyd, G.:John Socman (sels), w. J. Watson (sop), D. Montague (mez), T. Booth (ten), D. Wilson-Johnson (bar), M. George (bass), G. Lloyd (cnd), Philharmonia Orch, London Voices Albany ▲ TROY 131 [DDD]

Rix, David (ct)
Vivaldi, A.:Cons Diverse Instrs, w. Joanna Graham (bn), Ruth McDowall (cl), Deborah Davis (fl), Duke Dobing (fl), Tim Caister (hn), Stephen Stirling (hn), Christopher Hooker (ob), Helen McQueen (ob), Michael Meekes (tpt), Crispian Steele-Perkins (tpt), Nicholas Kraemer (hpd), N. Kraemer (cnd), London Sinfonietta—Cons. in F, RV.539; in C, RV.533; in D, RV.122; in C, RV.537; in C, RV.560; in F, RV.538; in G, RV.545 *(rec All Saints Church, East Finchley, Oct. 1994 & Jan. 1995)* Naxos ("Vivaldi Collection" series) ▲ 8.553204 [DDD]

Rizzi, Lucia (cta)
Rossini, G.:L'italiana in Algeri, w. L. V. Terrani (mez), W. Ganzarolli (bar), E. Dara (bar), G. Ferro (cnd), Capella Coloniensis, Cologne Radio Chorus [period instrs] [I] CBS 2-▲ M2K 39048 [ADD]
Vivaldi, A.:Il Farnace, w. M. Dupuy (mez), K. Angeloni (mez), P. Malakova (mez), D. Dessy (mez), R. Garazioti (sgr), M. de Bernart (cnd), San Remo SO [I] *(rec live 12/1/82)* Arkadia-Akademia 2-▲ 110 [ADD]

Rizzieri, Elena (sop)
Caldara, A.:Il gioco del quadriglio, w. Maria-Grazia Ferraccini (sop), Basia Retchitzka (sop), Maria Minetto (cta), E. Loehrer (cnd), Lugano Chamber Society Orch, Minetto Chorus Dynamic ▲ CDL 140
Flotow, F. von:Martha, w. E. Rizzieri (sop—Lady Enrichetta), P. Tassinari (sop—Nancy), F. Tagliavini (ten—Lionello), C. Tagliabue (bar—Plumkett), B. Carmassi (bass—Sir Tristano), F. Molinari-Pradelli (cnd), Turin RAI Orch, Turin RAI Chorus *(rec 1953; Italian libretto)* Cetra Classic 2-▲ CDO 7 [AAD]
Gatta, Moffo, Rizzieri, Christoff & Mazzolli, w. Dora Gatta (sop), Anna Moffo (sop), Boris Christoff (bass), Ferruccio Mazzoli (bass), Rome RAI SO, Turin RAI SO *(rec Martini & Rossi Concert)* Incontri Memorabili ▲ CDMR 5033

Rizzoli, Bruna (sop)
Donizetti, G.:L'elisir d'amore, w. A. Noni (sop), C. Valletti (ten), S. Bruscantini (bar), A. Poli (bar), G. Gavazzeni (cnd), Rome RAI SO, Rome RAI Chorus *(rec 1952)* Cetra Classic ▲ CDO 5 [AAD]
Wagner, R.:Die Meistersinger von Nürnberg, w. Fernanda Cadoni (mez), Luigi Infantino (ten), Vito Tatone (ten), Renato Capecchi (bar), Giuseppe Taddei (bar), Boris Christoff (bass), Giovanni Ciavola (bass), James Loomis (bass), Silvo Maionica (bass), Vito Susca (bass), Raimondo Botteghelli (sgr), Walter Brunelli (sgr), Carlo Franzini (sgr), Ezio de Giorgi (sgr), Renzo Gonzales (sgr), L. von Matačić (cnd), Turin RAI Radio-TV SO, Turin RAI Chorus Stradivarius 4-▲ STV 12310

Roache, T. (sgr)
Moran, J.:Manson Family, w. T. Roache (sgr—Squeaky Fromme), J. Moran (sgr—Charles Manson) Iggy Pop (sgr—Jack Lord), *(orch unknown)* Point Music ▲ 432967-2 [DDD] ■ 432967-4

Roan, Lydia (sgr)
Verdi, G.:Oberto, Conte di San Bonifacio, w. Elena Nicolai (mez), Giuseppe Modesti (bass), Gino Bonelli (sgr), Maria Vitale (sgr), A. Simonetto (cnd), Turin RAI Orch, Turin RAI Chorus Great Opera Performances 2-▲ GOP 774

Roar, Leif (bass)
Wagner, R.:Lohengrin, w. E. Connell (sop), N. Armstrong (sop), P. Hofmann (ten), B. Weikl (bass), S. Vogel (bass), W. Nelsson (cnd), Bayreuth Festival Orch, Bayreuth Festival Chorus CBS 3-▲ M3K 38594

Robbin, Catherine (mez)
Beethoven, L. van:Mass, Op. 86, w. C. Margiono (sop), W. Kendall (ten), A. Miles (bass), J. E. Gardiner (cnd), Orch Révolutionnaire et Romantique, Monteverdi Choir London [period instrs] Archiv ▲ 435391-2 [DDD]
Beethoven, L. van:Missa Solemnis, w. C. Margiono (sop), W. Kendall (ten), A. Miles (bass), J. E. Gardiner (cnd), English Baroque Soloists, Monteverdi Choir London [L] Archiv ▲ 429779-2 [DDD] □ 429779-5
Berlioz, H.:Les Nuits d'été, w. D. Montague (mez), H. Crook (ten), G. Cachémaille (bar), J.E. Gardiner (cnd), Lyon Opera Orch [F] Erato ("Musifrance" series) ▲ 2292-45517-2 [DDD]

Robbin, Catherine (mez) (cont.)
Berlioz, H.:Songs, w. B. Fournier (sop), D. Montague (mez), H. Crook (ten), G. Cachémaille (bar), J.E. Gardiner (cnd), Lyon Opera Orch—Zaïde [Fournier]; La belle voyageuse [Montague]; La Captive [Robbin]; La mort d'Ophélie [Robbin]; Le jeune pâtre breton [Crook]; Aubade [Crook]; Le Chasseur danois [Cachémaille] [F] Erato ("Musifrance" series) ▲ 2292-45517-2 [DDD]
Brahms, J.:Liebeslieder Waltzes SATB, w. Kathleen Brett (sop), Benjamin Butterfield (ten), Russell Braun (bar), Stephen Ralls (pno), Bruce Ubukata (pno) *(rec Glenn Gould Studio, CBC Toronto, Dec. 7-9, 1993)* CBC ("Musica Viva" series) ▲ MVCD 1077 [DDD]
Brahms, J.:Songs, w. M. McMahon (pno)—Blinde Kuh; Die Mainacht; Sonntag; Von ewiger Liebe [G] Marquis ▲ ERAD113
Catherine Robbin, w. Michael McMahon (pno) *(rec 1985)* Marquis Classics ▲ ERAD113
Greer, J.:All Around the Circle, w. Kathleen Brett (sop), Benjamin Butterfield (ten), Russell Braun (bar), Stephen Ralls (pno), Bruce Ubukata (pno) CBC ▲ MVV 1077 [DDD]
Greer, J.:All Around the Circle, w. Kathleen Brett (sop), Benjamin Butterfield (ten), Russell Braun (bar), Stephen Ralls (pno), Bruce Ubukata (pno) *(rec Glenn Gould Studio, CBC Toronto, Dec. 7-9, 1993)* CBC ("Musica Viva" series) ▲ MVCD 1077 [DDD]
Handel, G.F.:Floridante (sels), w. Nancy Argenta (sop—Rossane), Ingrid Attrot (sop—Timante), Linda Maguire (mez—Elmira), Catherine Robbin (mez—Floridante), Mel Braun (bar—Coralbo/Orontes), A. Curtis (cnd), Tafelmusik [I] CBC ("SM 5000" series) ▲ SMCD 5110 [DDD]
Handel, G.F.:Messiah, w. Saul Quirke (trb), Margaret Marshall (sop), Charles Brett (ct), Anthony Rolfe Johnson (ten), Robert Hale (b-bar), J. E. Gardiner (cnd), English Baroque Soloists, Monteverdi Choir London [E] Philips 3-▲ 411041-2 [DDD]
Handel, G.F.:Messiah, w. Karen Clift (sop), Bruce Fowler (ten), Victor Ledbetter (bar), M. Pearlman (cnd), Boston Baroque Orch, Boston Baroque Chorus [E] Telarc 2-▲ CD 80322 [DDD]
Handel, G.F.:Messiah, w. Saul Quirke (trb), Margaret Marshall (sop), Charles Brett (ct), Anthony Rolfe Johnson (ten), Robert Hale (b-bar), J. E. Gardiner (cnd), English Baroque Soloists, Monteverdi Choir London [E] Philips ▲ 412267-2 [DDD]
Handel, G.F.:Messiah (sels), w. Karen Clift (sop), Bruce Fowler (ten), Victor Ledbetter (bar), M. Pearlman (cnd), Boston Baroque Orch, Boston Baroque Chorus—Sinfonia; Comfort ye, my people; Every valley shall be exalted; And the glory of the Lord; And He shall purify; Behold, a virgin shall conceive; O thou that tellest good tidings to Zion; For unto us a Child is born; Rejoice greatly, O daughter of Zion; His yoke is easy; All we like sheep; Lift up your heads; The Lord gave the word; Their sound is gone out; Why do the nations?; Let us break their bonds asunder; He that dwelleth in heaven; Thou shalt break them; Hallelujah; I know that my Redeemer liveth; Since by man came death; Behold, I tell you a mystery; The trumpet shall sound; Then shall be brought to pass; O death, where is thy sting?; But thanks be to God; Worthy is the Lamb...Amen *(rec May 18-22, 1992)* Telarc ▲ CD 80348 [DDD]
Handel, G.F.:Orlando, w. Arleen Augér (sop), Emma Kirkby (sop), James Bowman (ct), David Thomas (bass), C. Hogwood (cnd), Academy of Ancient Music L'Oiseau-Lyre 3-▲ 430845-2 [DDD]
Honegger, A.:Songs, w. M. McMahon (pno)—Saluste du Bartas [F] Marquis ▲ ERAD113
Mahler, G.:Kindertotenlieder, w. R. Armenian (cnd), Kitchener-Waterloo SO [G] CBC ("SM 5000" series) ▲ SMCD 5098 [DDD] ■ SMC 5098 (D)
Mahler, G.:Lieder eines fahrenden Gesellen, w. R. Armenian (cnd), Kitchener-Waterloo SO [G] CBC ("SM 5000" series) ▲ SMCD 5098 [DDD] ■ SMC 5098 (D)
Mahler, G.:Songs from Rückert, w. R. Armenian (cnd), Kitchener-Waterloo SO [G] CBC ("SM 5000" series) ▲ SMCD 5098 [DDD] ■ SMC 5098 (D)
Matson, S.:Range, w. Susan Greenberg (fl), Joseph Stone (fl), Glen Garrett (cl), Suren Karapetyan (hn), Peter Kent (vn), Kazi Pitelka (va), Sebastian Toettcher (vc), Don Ferrone (db), Doug Livingston (gtr/mand), John Schneider (gtr), Amy Shulman (hp), Terry Schoenig (perc), S. Matson (cnd) *(rec Schnee Studio, Universal City, CA, Mar 12, 1995)* New Albion ▲ NA 091
Mozart, W.A.:Missa, K.317, w. E. Kirkby (sop), J.M. Ainsley (ten), M. George (bass), C. Hogwood (cnd), Academy of Ancient Music, Winchester Cathedral Choir Argo ▲ 436585-2 [DDD]
Mozart, W.A.:Requiem, w. N. Argenta (sop), J.M. Ainsley (ten), A. Miles (bass), R. Norrington (cnd), London Classical Players, Schütz Choir London [L] EMI Classics ▲ CDC 54525
Pergolesi, G.B.:Stabat mater, w. D. Röschmann (sop), B. Labadie (cnd), Les Violons du Roy Dorian ▲ DOR 90196 [DDD]
Schubert, Franz:Songs (misc), w. M. McMahon (pno)—Der Fischer; Der König; Suleika [G] Marquis ▲ ERAD113
Schumann, R.:Frauenliebe und -leben, w. M. McMahon (pno) [G] CBC ("Musica Viva" series) ▲ MVCD 1050 [DDD]
Schumann, R.:Liederkreis, Op. 24, w. M. McMahon (pno) [G] CBC ("Musica Viva" series) ▲ MVCD 1050 [DDD]
Schumann, R.:Songs, w. M. McMahon (pno)—5 Maria Stuart Songs, Op. 135 [G] CBC ("Musica Viva" series) ▲ MVCD 1050 [DDD]
Schumann, R.:Spanische Liebeslieder, w. Kathleen Brett (sop), Benjamin Butterfield (ten), Russell Braun (bar), Stephen Ralls (pno), Bruce Ubukata (pno) CBC ("Musica Viva" series) ▲ MVCD 1077 [DDD]
Sweet Was the Song, w. Vancouver Chamber Choir Marquis Classics ▲ MAR 107
Vivaldi, A.:Motets, w. D. Röschmann (sop), B. Labadie (cnd), Les Violons du Roy Dorian ▲ DOR 90196 [DDD]
Vivaldi, A.:Stabat Mater Cta, w. B. Labadie (cnd), Les Violons du Roy Dorian ▲ DOR 90196 [DDD]

Robbins, Julien (bass)
James Levine's 25th Anniversary Metropolitan Opera Gala, w. J. Levine (cnd), Metropolitan Opera Orch, Ileana Cotrubas (sop), Renée Fleming (sop), Hei-Kyung Hong (sop), Karita Mattila (sop), Birgit Nilsson (sop), Ruth Ann Swenson (sop), Kiri Te Kanawa (sop), Deborah Voigt (sop), Grace Bumbry (mez), Heidi Grant Murphy (mez), Anne Sofie von Otter (mez) *(rec live, Metropolitan Opera House, New York, Apr 27, 1996)* Deutsche Grammophon ▲ 449177-2 [DDD]

Róbert (sgr)
Kálmán, I.:Die Csárdásfürstin (sels), w. Erzsébet (sgr), György (sgr), Hanna (sgr), Tamás (cnd), Hungarian Radio-TV SO, Hungarian Radio-TV Chorus Hungaroton ▲ HCD 16780 [AAD]

Robert, Sylvie (sop)
Boulanger, N.:Songs, w. I. Sabrié (sop), D. Reinhardt (mez), E. Naoumoff (pno)—Lux aeterna [w. O. Charlier (violin) & R. Pidoux (cello)]; Le Couteau *(rec June 14-17, 1993)* Marco Polo ▲ 8.223636 [DDD]

Roberti, Margherita (sop)
Cilea, F.:Gloria, w. A. M. Rota (cta), F. Labò (ten), A. Albertini (bar), L. Testi (bar), E. Campi (bass), F. Mazzoli (bass), F. Previtali (cnd), Turin RAI Orch, Turin RAI Chorus [I] *(rec live, Turin July 8, 1969)* Memories ▲ HR 4472 [ADD]
Donizetti, G.:Marino Faliero, w. O. Mori (bar), A. Ferrin (bass), Meliciani (sgr), A. Camozzo (cnd), *(orch & chorus unknown)* [I] *(rec live, Bergamo 1966)* Melodram 2-▲ MEL 27030
Verdi, G.:Attila, w. M. Roberti (sop—Odabella), G. Limarilli (tenor—Foresto), G. Guelfi (baritone—Ezio), B. Christoff (bass—Attila), B. Bartoletti (cnd), Florence Teatro Comunale Orch, Florence Teatro Comunale Chorus *(rec Jan. 12, 1962)* Myto 2-▲ MCD 93589 [DDD]
Verdi, G.:Ernani, w. Anna di Stasio (mez), Athos Cesarini (ten), Mario del Monaco (ten), Ettore Bastianini (bar), Mario Rinaudo (bass), Nicola Rossi-Lemeni (bass), F. Previtali (cnd), Naples Teatro San Carlo Orch, Naples Teatro San Carlo Chorus Melodram 2-▲ CDM 270100

Roberts, Gareth (ten)
Grainger, P.:Brigg Fair, w. Ashley Lawrence (cnd), BBC Singers IMP ("BBC Radio Classics" series) ▲ IMP 9128
Handel, G.F.:Messiah (sels), w. Catherine Bott (sop), Clare Henry (cta), David Stephenson (bass), D. Jackson (cnd), London SO—Comfort Ye, My People, Saith Your God; Every Valley Shall Be Exalted; And the Glory of the Lord Shall Be Revealed; And He Shall Purify the Sons of Levi; For unto Us a Child Is Born; Pifa; Rejoice Greatly, O Daughter of Zion; Air:He Shall Feed His Flock Like a Shepherd; Behold the Lamb of God; He Was Despised and Rejected of Men; All We Like Sheep Have Gone Astray; The Trumpet Shall Sound; Chorus:Hallelujah! For the Lord God Omnipotent Reigneth Special Music Co. ▲ SCD 5102 [DDD]

Roberts, Gareth (ten) (cont.)
Handel, G.F.:Messiah (sels), w. Catherine Bott (sop), Clare Henry (cta), David Stephenson (bass), D. Jackson (cnd), London SO—Comfort Ye, My People, Saith Your God; Every Valley Shall Be Exalted; And the Glory of the Lord Shall Be Revealed; And He Shall Purify the Sons of Levi; For unto Us a Child Is Born; Pifa; Rejoice Greatly, O Daughter of Zion; Air:He Shall Feed His Flock Like a Shepherd; Behold the Lamb of God; He Was Despised and Rejected of Men; All We Like Sheep Have Gone Astray; The Trumpet Shall Sound; Chorus:Hallelujah! For the Lord God Omnipotent Reigneth Special Music Co. 2-▲ S2D 5110 [DDD]
Vaughan Williams, R.:Sancta civitas, w. Brian Rayner Cook (bar), G. Rozhdestvensky (cnd), BBC SO, BBC Singers, BBC Sym Chorus IMP ("BBC Radio Classics" series) ▲ IMP 9125

Roberts, George (bar)
Bernhard, C.:Missa "Durch Adams Fall", w. Henriette Schellenberg (sop), Laverne G' Froerer (mez), Keith Boldt (ten), J. Washburn (cnd), CBC Vancouver SO, Vancouver Chamber Choir *(rec Ryerson United Church & The Orpheum, Vancouver, May 4–7, 1992)* CBC ▲ 5160 [DDD]
Fauré, G.:Messe basse, w. Henriette Schellenberg (sop), Laverne G' Froerer (mez), Keith Boldt (ten), J. Washburn (cnd), CBC Vancouver SO, Vancouver Chamber Choir [orchd J. Washburn] *(rec Ryerson United Church & The Orpheum, Vancouver, May 4–7, 1992)* CBC ▲ 5160 [DDD]
Haydn, J.:Mass 7, "Kleine Orgelmesse", w. Henriette Schellenberg (sop), Laverne G' Froerer (mez), Keith Boldt (ten), J. Washburn (cnd), CBC Vancouver SO, Vancouver Chamber Choir *(rec Ryerson United Church & The Orpheum, Vancouver, May 4–7, 1992)* CBC ▲ 5160 [DDD]
Weber, C.M. von:Missa sancta 2, w. Henriette Schellenberg (sop), Laverne G' Froerer (mez), Keith Boldt (ten), J. Washburn (cnd), CBC Vancouver SO, Vancouver Chamber Choir *(rec Ryerson United Church & The Orpheum, Vancouver, May 4–7, 1992)* CBC ▲ 5160 [DDD]

Roberts, J. (sgr)
Rodgers, R.:Oklahoma!, w. A. Drake (sgr), L. Dixon (sgr), C. Holm (sgr), H. da Silva (sgr), J. Blackton (cnd), *(orch unknown)* MCA Classics ▲ MCAD 10046 [AAD] ■ MCAC 10046

Roberts, Stephen (bar)
Bach, C.P.E.:Magnificat, w. F. Palmer (sop), H. Watts (cta), R. Tear (ten), P. Ledger (cnd), Academy of St. Martin in the Fields, King's College Choir Cambridge London ("Jubilee" series) ▲ 421148-2 [ADD]
Bach, J.S.:Magnificat, BWV 243, w. F. Palmer (sop), H. Watts (cta), R. Tear (ten), P. Ledger (cnd), Academy of St. Martin in the Fields, King's College Choir Cambridge London ("Jubilee" series) ▲ 421148-2 [ADD]
Bach, J.S.:St. Matthew Passion, w. F. Lott (sop), A. Hodgson (cta), R. Tear (ten), J. Shirley-Quirk (bar), D. Willcocks (cnd), Thames CO, Bach Choir [E] ASV Quicksilva 3-▲ ASQ 324 [ADD]
Campra, A.:Messe de Requiem, w. J. Nelson (mez), C. Harris (trb), J.-C. Orliac (ten), J. E. Gardiner (cnd), English Baroque Soloists, Monteverdi Choir London Erato ▲ 2292-45993-2
Charpentier, M.-A.:Te Deum in C, w. F. Lott (sop), I. Partridge (ten), P. Ledger (org), P. Ledger (cnd), Academy of St. Martin in the Fields, King's College Choir Cambridge EMI Classics ▲ CDM 63135
Elgar, E.:The Apostles, w. A. Hargan (sop), A. Hodgson (cta), D. Rendall (ten), B. Terfel (bass-bar), R. Lloyd (bass), R. Hickox (cnd), London SO, London Sym Chorus [E] Chandos 2-▲ CHAN 8875/76 [DDD]
Elgar, E.:Caractacus, w. J. Howarth (sop), A. Davies (ten), D. Wilson-Johnson (bar), A.R. Miles (bass), R. Hickox (cnd), London SO, London Sym Chorus [E] *(rec 1992)* Chandos 2-▲ CHAN 9156/57 [DDD]
The Essential Gregorian Chant, w. [cnd:James O'Donnell], Pro Cantione Antiqua, James Griffett (ten), Ian Partridge (ten), Michael George (bass), Gordon Jones (bass) Cala ▲ CAL CACD 88035 [DDD]
The Essential Gregorian Chant, w. James Griffett (ten), Ian Partridge (ten), Michael George (b-bar), Gordon Jones (bass), Pro Cantione Antique [cnd:James O'Donnell] United ▲ UNI 88035 [DDD]
Fauré, G.:Requiem, w. A. Jones (trb), R. Hickox (cnd), Royal PO, London Sym Chorus [L] RPO ▲ RPO 7007 [DDD]
Fauré, G.:Requiem, w. A. Jones (trb), R. Hickox (cnd), Royal PO, London Sym Chorus [L] MCA Classics ▲ MCAD 6199 [DDD]
Gregorian Lent & Easter, w. [cnd:James O'Donnell], Pro Cantione Antiqua, J. Griffett (ten), I. Partridge (ten), M. George (bass), G. Jones (bass) *(rec All Saints, East Finchley, Dec 7–9, 1993)* United ▲ UNI 88016 [DDD]
Handel, G.F.:Messiah, w. Oliver Johnston (trb), Rae Woodland (sop), Norma Proctor (cta), Paul Esswood (ct), J. Tobin (cnd), English SO, London Choral Society [Handel's original orchestration] [E] *(rec 1976)* Protone ■ CSPR 166/67
Martin, F.:In terra pax, w. Judith Howarth (sop), Della Jones (cta), Martyn Hill (ten), Roderick Williams (bar), M. Bamert (cnd), London PO, Laszlo Heltay (cnd), Brighton Festival Chorus Chandos ▲ CHAN 9465
Penderecki, K.:St. Luke Passion, w. S. van Osten (sop), K. Rydl (bass), E. Lubaszenko (nar), K. Penderecki (cnd), Polish National RSO Katowice, Cracow Boys Choir, Warsaw National Phil Chorus Argo ▲ 430328-2 [DDD]
Ravel, M.:Don Quichotte à Dulcinée, w. Y.P. Tortelier (cnd), Ulster Orch Chandos ▲ CHAN 8972 [DDD]
Rubbra, E.:Sym 9, w. Lynne Dawson (sop), Della Jones (alt), R. Hickox (cnd), BBC Welsh National SO, BBC Welsh National Chorus Chandos ▲ CHAN 9441
Stravinsky, I.:Canticum sacrum, w. J. M. Ainsley (ten), J. O'Donnell (cnd), City of London Sinfonia, Westminster Cathedral Choir Hyperion ▲ CDA 66437
Telemann, G.P.:Cants, w. P. Kwella (sop), C. Denley (mez), M. George (bass), R. Hickox (cnd), Collegium Musicum 90—Die Donner Ode Chandos ("Chaconne" series) ▲ CHAN 0548 [DDD]
Telemann, G.P.:Motets, w. P. Kwella (sop), C. Denley (mez), M. George (bass), R. Hickox (cnd), Collegium Musicum 90—Deus judicium tuum Chandos ("Chaconne" series) ▲ CHAN 0548 [DDD]
Tippett, M.:King Priam, w. Heather Harper (sop—Hecuba), Linda Hirst (sop—Serving Woman), Felicity Palmer (sop—Andromache), Julian Saipe (sop—Paris), Yvonne Minton (mez—Helen), Ann Murray (mez—Nurse), Kenneth Bowen (ten—Hermes), Peter Hall (ten—Young Guard), Philip Langridge (ten—Paris), Robert Tear (ten—Achilles), Thomas Allen (bar—Hector), Norman Bailey (bar—Priam), Stephen Roberts (bar—Patroclus), David Wilson-Johnson (bar—Old Man), D. Atherton (cnd), London Sinfonietta, London Sinfonietta Chorus Chandos ▲ CHAN 9406/7 [DDD]
Vaughan Williams, R.:Epithalamion, w. H. Shelley (pno), D. Willcocks (cnd), London PO, Bach Choir EMI Classics ▲ CDM 64730
Walton, W.:Belshazzar's Feast, w. C. Mackerras (cnd), English CO, Richard Cooke (cnd), John Pritchard (cnd), BBC Singers, BBC Sym Chorus, London Phil Choir IMP ("BBC Radio Classics" series) ▲ IMP 5691612
Walton, W.:Gloria, w. A. Gunson (cta), N. Mackie (ten), D. Willcocks (cnd), Philharmonia Orch, Bach Choir [L] Chandos ▲ CHAN 8760 [DDD]

Roberts, Susan (sop)
Mozart, W.A.:Zauberflöte, w. Constanze Backes (sop—Papagena), Christiane Oelze (sop—Pamina), Susan Roberts (sop—First Lady), Cyndia Sieden (sop—Queen of the Night), Carola Guber (cta—Second Lady), Maria Jonas (cta—Third Lady), Andreas Dieterich (trb—First Boy), Jan Andreas Mendel (trb—Second Boy), Florian Wöller (trb—Third Boy), Uwe Peper (ten—Monostatos), Nicolas Robertson (ten—First Man in Armor), Michael Schade (ten—Tamino), Gerald Finley (bar—Papageno), Noel Mann (bass—Second Man in Armour), Harry Peeters (bass—Sarastro), Detlef Roth (bass—Speaker/First Priest), Robert Burt (speaker—Third Priest), Robert Johnston (speaker—Second Priest), Wolfgang Knauer (speaker—Fourth Priest), Douglas Welbat (speaker—Second Priest), J. E. Gardiner (cnd), English Baroque Soloists, Monteverdi Choir London *(rec Forum am Schlosspark, Ludwigsburg, July 1995)* Archiv 2-▲ 449166-2
Orff, C.:Carmina burana, w. Lisa Griffith (sop), Frankfurt Kantorei, Frankfurt Singakademie Wergo 2-▲ WER 6275-2
Orff, C.:Catulli Carmina, w. Lisa Griffith (sop), Frankfurt Kantorei, Frankfurt Singakademie Wergo ▲ WER 6275-2
Orff, C.:Trionfo di Afrodite, w. Lisa Griffith (sop), Frankfurt Kantorei, Frankfurt Singakademie Wergo ▲ WER 6275-2

Robertson, L. (sgr)
Lloyd Webber, A.:Music of, w. M. Friedman (sgr), C. Carter (sgr), C. Moore (sgr), J. Barrowman (sgr), J. Diedrich (sgr), Grania Renihan (sgr), J.O. Edwards (cnd), Munich SO—Cats; Joseph & the Amazing Technicolor Dreamcoat; Phantom of the Opera; Evita; Jesus Christ Superstar; Starlight Express; Song & Dance; Aspects of Love Koch International ▲ CD 340022 [DDD] ■ MC 340022

Robertson, Nicolas (ten)
Bach, J.S.:Cant 211, "Coffee Cant", w. L. Dawson (sop), S. Adler (bar), Friends of Apollo [G] Meridian ▲ ECD 84110
Mozart, W.A.:Zauberflöte, w. Constanze Backes (sop—Papagena), Christiane Oelze (sop—Pamina), Susan Roberts (sop—First Lady), Cyndia Sieden (sop—Queen of the Night), Carola Guber (cta—Second Lady), Maria Jonas (cta—Third Lady), Andreas Dieterich (trb—First Boy), Jan Andreas Mendel (trb—Second Boy), Florian Wöller (trb—Third Boy), Uwe Peper (ten—Monostatos), Nicolas Robertson (ten—First Man in Armor), Michael Schade (ten—Tamino), Gerald Finley (bar—Papageno), Noel Mann (bass—Second Man in Armour), Harry Peeters (bass—Sarastro), Detlef Roth (bass—Speaker/First Priest), Robert Burt (speaker—Third Priest), Robert Johnston (speaker—Second Priest), Wolfgang Knauer (speaker—Fourth Priest), Douglas Welbat (speaker—Second Priest), J. E. Gardiner (cnd), English Baroque Soloists, Monteverdi Choir London *(rec Forum am Schlosspark, Ludwigsburg, July 1995)* Archiv 2-▲ 449166-2

Robeson, Paul (b-bar)
The Collector's Paul Robeson Monitor ▲ CD 61580
Favorite Songs, Vol. 1 Monitor ■ MFS 51580
Favorite Songs, Vol. 2 Monitor ■ MFS 51581
Kern, J.:Show Boat (sels), w. J. Bledsoe (sgr), M. Burke (sgr), E. Day (sgr), *(other artists unknown)* [original cast] Pearl ("Flapper" series) ▲ PEA CD 9105 [ADD]
The Odyssey Of Paul Robeson *(rec in studio and live, 1952–1958)* Omega Classics ▲ OCD 3007
Paul Robeson *(rec 1927–1939)* Memoir Classics ▲ CDMOIR 415 [AAD]
Paul Robeson *(rec 1927–36 for HMV)* Pearl ▲ PEA 9382 (m) [AAD]
Sings "Ol' Man River" & Other Favorites *(rec. 1928–1939)* Angel ▲ CDC 47839

Robin, Donna (sop)
Mozart, W.A.:Music of, w. A. Martin (bar), G. Grünbacher (cl), K. Leitner (pno), K. Leitner (cnd), Vienna Mozart Orch—features selections from Die Entführung aus dem Serail, K.384; Don Giovanni, K.527; Serenade No. 13, K.525, "Eine kleine Nachtmusik"; Con. No. 21 in C for Piano & Orch., K.467; Symphony No. 41 in C, K.551, "Jupiter"; Con. No. 5 in A for Violin & Orch., K.219; Die Zauberflöte, K.620; Alla turca [arr. for orch.] *(rec Feb. 9–13, 1990)* Naxos ▲ 8.550866 [DDD]
Mozart, W.A.:Music of, w. A. Martin (bar), G. Grünbacher (cl), K. Leitner (pno), K. Leitner (cnd), Vienna Mozart Orch—features selections from Le nozze di Fiagaro, K.492; Con. No. 23 in A for Piano & Orch., K.488; Sym. No. 40 in g, K.550; Die Zauberflöte, K.620; Posthorn Serenade, K.320; Con. in A for Clarinet & Orch., K.622; Sym. No. 35 in D, K.385 "Haffner" *(rec Feb. 9–13, 1990)* Naxos ▲ 8.550867 [DDD]

Robin, Mado (sgr)
Ses Plus Grands Rôles Laserlight ▲ 14265

Robinšak, Branko (ten)
Bellini, V.:Beatrice di Tenda, w. E. Gruberová (sop—Beatrice), V. Kasarova (mez—Agnese), D. Bernardini (ten—Orombello), B. Robinšak (ten—Anichino), I. Morosov (ten—Filippo Maria Visconti), D. Sumegi (bass—Rizzardo), P. Steinberg (cnd), Austrian RSO, Austrian Radio Chorus [I] *(rec live, Vienna Concert House 1/30 & 2/1/92)* Nightingale Classics 2-▲ NC 070560-2 [DDD]

Robinson, Allin (nar)
Foster, S.C.:Life & Music of, w. M. Diesenroth (cnd), Musikkorps des Wachtbataillons—narration & selected excerpts from Old Folks at Home; Oh! Susanna; Old Black Joe; Jeanie with the Light Brown Hair; My Old Kentucky Home; Camptown Races; Massa's in De Cold, Cold Ground; Come Where My Love Lies Dreaming; Beautiful Dreamer Vox Music Masters ("Music Masters" series) ▲ MMD 8515 [ADD] ■ MMC 8515

Robinson, Ethna (mez)
Charpentier, M.-A.:Magnificat, w. D. Upshaw (sop), A. Murray (mez), J. Aler (ten), K. Moll (bass), N. Marriner (cnd), Academy of St. Martin in the Fields, Academy of St. Martin in the Fields Chorus EMI Classics ▲ CDC 54284
Charpentier, M.-A.:Te Deum in C, w. D. Upshaw (sop), A. Murray (mez), J. Aler (ten), K. Moll (bass), N. Marriner (cnd), Academy of St. Martin in the Fields, Academy of St. Martin in the Fields Chorus EMI Classics ▲ CDC 54284

Robinson, Faye (sop)
Tippett, M.:Byzantium, w. G. Solti (cnd), Chicago SO London ▲ 433668-2 [DDD]
Tippett, M.:The Mask of Time, w. S. Walker (mez), R. Tear (ten), J. Cheek (bass), A. Davis (cnd), BBC SO, BBC Sym Chorus EMI Classics ▲ ZDMB 64111
Tippett, M.:Sym 3, w. R. Hickox (cnd), Bournemouth SO Chandos ▲ CHAN 9276 [DDD]

Robinson, Forbes (bass)
Verdi, G.:Macbeth, w. Amy Shuard (sop—Lady Macbeth), Noreen Berry (mez—Lady-in-waiting), John Dobson (ten—Malcolm), André Turp (ten—Macduff), Tito Gobbi (bar—Macbeth), Edgar Boniface (bass—Servant), Rydderch Davies (bass—Doctor), Forbes Robinson (bass—Banco), Jean Holmes (sgr—Apparition), Celia Penny (sgr—Apparition), Glynne Thomas (sgr—Apparition), Brian Wrigt (sgr—Araldo), F. Molinari-Pradelli (cnd), Royal Opera House Orch, Royal Opera House Chorus Covent Garden *(rec London, Apr 8, 1960)* Bella Voce 2-▲ 7203 [AAD]

Robinson, Randolph (bar)
Thomson, V.:4 Saints in 3 Acts, w. Inez Matthews (sop—St Settlement), Beatrice Robinson-Wayne (sop—St Teresa I), Altonell Hines (mez—Commère), Ruby Greene (alt—St Teresa II), David Bethea (ten—St Stephen), Charles Holland (ten—St Chavez), Edward Matthews (bar—St Ignatius), Randolph Robinson (bar—St Plan), Abner Dorsey (bass—Compère), V. Thomson (cnd), *(orch unknown)* [abridged by Thompson] *(rec June 25, 1947)* RCA Gold Seal ▲ 09026-68163-2 [ADD]

Robinson, Richard (ten)
Stravinsky, I.:In memoriam Dylan Thomas, w. I. Stravinsky (cnd), North German RSO *(rec live, Venice 9/23/58)* Arkadia 2-▲ 766 [ADD]

Robinson, Timothy (ten)
Bach, J.S.:Magnificat, BWV 243, w. Anna Crookes (sop), Jayne Whitaker (sop), Caroline Trevor (alt), Nicholas Gedge (b-bar), N. Ward (cnd), Northern CO, Oxford Schola Cantorum *(rec St. Peter's Church, Hale, Cheshire, Dec. 2, 1993)* Naxos ▲ 8.550763 [DDD]

Robinson-Wayne, Beatrice (sop)
Thomson, V.:4 Saints in 3 Acts, w. Inez Matthews (sop—St Settlement), Beatrice Robinson-Wayne (sop—St Teresa I), Altonell Hines (mez—Commère), Ruby Greene (alt—St Teresa II), David Bethea (ten—St Stephen), Charles Holland (ten—St Chavez), Edward Matthews (bar—St Ignatius), Randolph Robinson (bar—St Plan), Abner Dorsey (bass—Compère), V. Thomson (cnd), *(orch unknown)* [abridged by Thompson] *(rec June 25, 1947)* RCA Gold Seal ▲ 09026-68163-2 [ADD]

Robison, Gary (sgr)
Chant, w. Bill Riley (sgr) Unison ■ V80134

Robotham, Barbara (sop)
Walton, W.:Gloria, w. A. Rolfe Johnson (ten), B. Rayner Cook, L. Frémaux (cnd), City of Birmingham SO, Worcester Cathedral Choristers EMI Classics ▲ CDM 64201

Robson, Christopher (ct)
Arne, T.:Artaxerxes, w. Catherine Bott (sop), Patricia Spence (mez), Philippa Hyde (sgr), Richard Edgar-Wilson (ten), Ian Partridge (ten), R. Goodman (cnd), Parley of Instruments Hyperion ("The English Orpheus" series) 2-▲ CDA 67051/2
Biber, H. von:Vesperae longiores ac breviores una cum litaniis Laurentanis, w. Kym Amps (sop), Anton Rosner (ten), Albert Hartinger (bass), H. Arman (cnd), Salzburg Baroque Ensemble, Innsbruck Woodwind Circle, Salzburg Bach Choir, Salzburg St. Benedict College Schola Ars Musici ("Essence" series) ▲ AME 3022-2 [DDD]
Casken, J.:Golem, w. P. Rozario (sop), A. Clarke (bar), J. Hall (bar), R. Bernas (cnd), Music Projects London Virgin Classics 2-▲ CDC 59028
Handel, G.F.:Messiah, w. Joan Rodgers (sop), Della Jones (mez), Philip Langridge (ten), Bryn Terfel (b-bar), R. Hickox (cnd), Collegium Musicum 90 [period instrs] [E] Chandos ("Chaconne" series) 2-▲ CHAN 0522/23 [DDD]

Robson, Christopher (ct) (cont.)
Purcell, H.:Odes & Welcome Songs (misc), w. H. Cook (ten), J. Bowman (ct), D. Wilson-Johnson (bar), G. Leonhardt (hpd), G. Leonhardt (cnd), Orch of the Age of Enlightenment Virgin Classics ▲ CDC 59243
Purcell, H.:Odes & Welcome Songs (misc), w. Jeni Bern (sop), Susan Bisatt (sop), William Purefoy (ct), Ian Honeyman (ten), Thomas Guthrie (bass), R. Glenton (cnd), Orch of the Golden Age, Golden Age Choir—The noise of foreign wars (fragment) [ed. by Bruce Wood] *(rec Manchester Grammar School, England, May 13 & 14, 1995)* Naxos ▲ 8.553444 [DDD]
Purcell, H.:Raise, Raise the Voice, w. Jeni Bern (sop), Susan Bisatt (sop), William Purefoy (ct), Ian Honeyman (ten), Thomas Guthrie (bass), R. Glenton (cnd), Orch of the Golden Age, Golden Age Choir *(rec Manchester Grammar School, England, May 13 & 14, 1995)* Naxos ▲ 8.553444 [DDD]
Purcell, H.:Te Deum & Jubilate, w. Jeni Bern (sop), Susan Bisatt (sop), William Purefoy (ct), Ian Honeyman (ten), Thomas Guthrie (bass), David Staff (tpt), R. Glenton (cnd), Orch of the Golden Age, Golden Age Choir *(rec Manchester Grammar School, England, May 13 & 14, 1995)* Naxos ▲ 8.553444 [DDD]
Purcell, H.:Welcome to All the Pleasures, w. Jeni Bern (sop), Susan Bisatt (sop), William Purefoy (ct), Ian Honeyman (ten), Thomas Guthrie (bass), R. Glenton (cnd), Orch of the Golden Age, Golden Age Choir *(rec Manchester Grammar School, England, May 13 & 14, 1995)* Naxos ▲ 8.553444 [DDD]
Vivaldi, A.:Nisi Dominus, w. R. King (cnd), King's Consort [L] *(rec 4/86)* Meridian ▲ CDE 84129

Robson, Elizabeth (sop)
Purcell, H.:Dido & Aeneas (sels), w. Victoria de los Angeles (sop—Dido), Heather Harper (sop—Belinda), Sibyl Michelow (sop), Derek Simpson (vc), Colin Tilney (hpd), J. Barbirolli (cnd), English CO, Ambrosian Singers—Ov.; Shake the Cloud; Ah! Ah! Belinda; When Monarchs Unite; But Ere We This Perform; But Death, Alas! I Cannot Shun...When I am Laid in Earth; With Drooping Wings *(rec Abbey Road Studio 1, London, Aug. 1965)* EMI Classics ▲ CDK 65341 [ADD]

Robson, Nigel (ten)
Britten, B.:The Rape of Lucretia (sels), w. C. Pierard (sop), P. Rozario (sop), A. Gunson (mez), J. Rigby (cta), D. Maxwell (bar), A. Opie (bar), A. Miles (bass), R. Hickox (cnd), City of London Sinfonia Chandos 2-▲ CHAN 9254/55 [DDD]
Monteverdi, C.:Incoronazione, w. Constanze Backes (sop—Valletto), Catherine Bott (sop—Drusilla/Pallade/La Virtù), Dana Hanchard (sop—Nerone), Sylvia McNair (sop—Poppea), Marinella Pennicchi (sop—Amore/Damigella), Annie Sofie von Otter (mez—Ottavia/Venere/La Fortuna), Julian Clarkson (alt—Littore/Mercurio), Bernarda Fink (cta—Arnalta), Roberto Balconi (ct—Nutrice), Michael Chance (ct—Ottone), Nigel Robson (ten—Liberto/Soldato Secondo), Mark Tucker (ten—Lucano/Soldato Primo), Francesco Ellero d'Artegna (bass—Seneca), J. E. Gardiner (cnd), English Baroque Soloists *(rec Queen Elizabeth Hall, South Bank Ctr, London, Dec 1993)* Archiv 3-▲ 447088-2
Monteverdi, C.:Vespro della Beata Vergine, w. A. Monoyios (sop), M. Pennicchi (sop), M. Chance (ct), G. Tucker (ten), S. Naglia (ten), B. Terfel (b-bar), A. Miles (bass), J. E. Gardiner (cnd), English Baroque Soloists, His Majesties Sagbutts & Cornetts, London Monteverdi Choir Archiv 2-▲ 429565-2 [DDD]
Stravinsky, I.:Renard, w. J. Aler (ten), D. Wilson-Johnson (bar), J. Tomlinson (bass), E.-P. Salonen (cnd), London Sinfonietta Sony Classical ▲ SK 45965
Walton, W.:Troilus & Cressida, w. Judith Howarth (sop—Cressida), Arthur Davies (ten—Troilus), Nigel Robson (ten—Pandarus), Brian Cookson (ten—3rd Watchman), Peter Bodenham (ten—Priest), Keith Mills (ten—Soldier), Alan Opie (bar—Diomede), James Thornton (bar—Antenor), Clive Bayley (bass—Calkas), David Owen-Lewis (bass—Horaste), R. Hickox (cnd), English Northern Philharmonia, Opera North Chorus Chandos 2-▲ CHAN 9370/71 [DDD]

Robson, Richard (sgr)
Rubinstein, A.:The Demon, w. Ludmilla Andrew (sop—Nanny), Marina Mescheriakova (sop—Tamara), Alison Browner (mez—Angel), Anatoly Lochak (sgr—Demon), Richard Robson (sgr—Old Servant), Valery Serkin (sgr—Prince Sinodal), Wjacheslav Weinorowski (sgr—Messenger), Leonid Zimnenko (sgr—Prince Gudal), A. Anissimov (cnd), Irish National SO, Gregory Rose (cnd), Wexford Festival Opera Chorus *(rec Wexford, Oct & Nov, 1994)* Marco Polo 2-▲ 8.223781-2 [DDD]

Rocco, Giovanna di (sop)
Bizet, G.:Carmen, w. Giovanna di Rocco (sop—Frasquita), Grace Bumbry (mez—Carmen), Anita Caminada (mez—Mercedes), Franco Corelli (ten—Don José), Mario Ferrara (ten—Dancario), Franco Bordoni (bar—Escamillo), Carlo Scaravelli (bar—Morales), Giuseppe Morresi (bass—Remendado), Francesco Signor (bass—Zuniga), O. de Fabritiis (cnd), *(orch unknown)* *(rec Macerata, July 21, 1974)* Golden Age of Opera 2-▲ GAO 181/82 [ADD]
Mercadante, S.:Il bravo, w. Miwako Matsumoto (sop—Violetta), Giovanna di Rocco (sop—Michelina), William Johns (ten—Il Bravo), Antonio Savastano (ten—Pisani), Gino Sinimberghi (ten—Cappello), Loris Gambelli (bass—Marco), Mario Machì (bass—Luigi), Giuseppe Washington (bass—Foscari), Maria Parazzini (sgr—Teodora), G. Ferro (cnd), Rome Opera Orch, Rome Opera Chorus *(rec Rome, Dec 30, 1976)* Italia 3-▲ CDC 94 [ADD]

Rochaix, F. (nar)
Guyonnet, J.:La Cantate interrompue, w. S. Stenhammar (sop), S. Seban (pno), G. Calame (pno), E. Séjourne (perc), P. Geiss, E. Tarr (tpt), B. Nilsson (tpt), H. Ries (trbn), H. Rückert (trbn), J.-M. Collet, J. Guyonnet (cnd), Geneva Collegium Academicum [F] *(rec Nov. 15, 1986)* Grammont ▲ CTSP 30-2

Rocheleau, Daniel (trb)
Fauré, G.:Requiem, w. R. Perrin (org), M. L. de Rozel (cnd), Radio Canada Orch, Petits Chanteurs du Mont-Royal, Cap-de-la-Madeleine Choir, Petits Chanteurs de Trois-Rivières [L] *(rec 6/88)* REM ▲ 311096 XCD [DDD]

Rodde, Anne-Marie (sop)
Gluck, C.W.:La Recontre imprévue, w. J. Kaufmann (sop—Rezia), A. Stumphius (sop—Dardané), A.-M. Rodde (sop—Amine), I. Vermillion (mez—Balkis), R. Gambill (ten—Ali), C. H. Ahnsjö (ten—Osmin), J.-H. Rootering (bass—Un Calender), L. Hager (cnd), Munich RSO Orfeo 2-▲ 242912 [DDD]
Gounod, C.:Philémon et Baucis, w. Jean-Claude Orliac (ten), Pierre Néquecaur (bar), Félix Giband (bass), H. Gallois (cnd), French Radio Lyric Orch Musidisc ▲ MUS 202342 [AAD]
Handel, G.F.:Serse, w. Barbara Hendricks (sop—Romilda), Anne-Marie Rodde (sop—Atalanta), Carolyn Watkinson (cta—Xerxes), Otrun Wenkel (cta—Amastre), Paul Esswood (ct—Arsamene), Ulrich Studer (bar—Elviro), Ulrik Cold (bass—Ariodate), J. Malgoire (cnd), La Grande Ecurie et la Chambre du Roy *(rec Paris, 1979)* Sony Classical 3-▲ SM3K 36941
Honegger, A.:Jeanne d'Arc au bûcher, w. C. Château (sop), H. Brachet (mez), P. Proenza (ten), Z. Jankovsky (ten), F. Loup (bass), S. Baudo (cnd), Czech PO, Czech Chorus *(rec 1974)* Supraphon 2-▲ 11 0557-2 [AAD]
Rameau, J.P.:La Danse, w. J. Gomez (sop), J.-C. Orliac (ten), J.E. Gardiner (cnd), Monteverdi Orch, Monteverdi Choir London Erato ▲ 45985-2

Rode, Wilhelm (bar)
Wagner, R.:Der fliegende Holländer (sels), w. Wilhelm Rode (bar—Holländer), Josef von Manowarda (bass—Daland), L. Reichwein (cnd), Vienna State Opera Orch *(rec Jan. 6, 1939)* Koch Schwann 2-▲ SCH 314632 [ADD]
Wagner, R.:Die Walküre (sels), w. G. Rünger (sop), E. Friedrich (sop), K. Buschmann (ten), W. Brückner-Rüggeberg (cnd), Reich Radio Königsberg Large Orch—Act II, Scenes 2,3 & 4 & Act III, Scenes 1,2 & 3 [G] *(rec live 2/17 & 5/1 1938)* Preiser 2-▲ 90075 (m) [AAD]

Roden, Anthony (ten)
Smyth, E.:The Wreckers, w. Judith Howarth (sop), Anne-Marie Owens (mez), Annemarie Sand (mez), Justin Lavender (ten), Peter Sidhom (bar), David Wilson-Johnson (bar), Brian Bannatyne-Scott (bass), O. de la Martinez (cnd), BBC PO, Huddersfield Choral Society *(rec live, Royal Albert Hall, London, July 31, 1994)* Conifer Classics 2-▲ 75605-51250-2

Rodgers, E. (sgr)
Porter, C.:Anything Goes, w. Hal Linden (sgr), *(other artists unknown)* [1962 cast] Epic ▲ EK 15100 [DAD] ■ JST 15100

Rodgers, Joan (sop)
Beethoven, L. van:Sym 9, "Choral Sym", w. Della Jones (alt), Peter Bronder (ten), Bryn Terfel (bass), C. Mackerras (cnd), Royal Liverpool PO, Royal Liverpool Phil Choir Classics for Pleasure ("Eminence" series) ▲ CFP 2186 [DDD]
Bruckner, A.:Requiem, w. C. Denley (mez), M. Davies (ten), M. George (bass), Corydon Singers, M. Best (cnd), English CO Hyperion ▲ CDA 66245 [DDD]

Rodgers, Joan (sop) (cont.)
Chabrier, E.:Briséïs, ou Les Amants de Corinthe, w. Kathryn Harries (sop), Simon Keenlyside (trb), Mark Padmore (ten), Michael George (bass), J. Y. Ossonce (cnd), BBC Scottish SO Hyperion ▲ CDA 66803
Handel, G.F.:Messiah, w. Della Jones (mez), Christopher Robson (ct), Philip Langridge (ten), Bryn Terfel (b-bar), R. Hickox (cnd), Collegium Musicum 90 [period instrs] [E] Chandos ("Chaconne" series) 2-▲ CHAN 0522/23 [DDD]
Mahler, G.:Das Klagende Lied, w. L. Finnie (cta), H. P. Blochwitz (ten), R. Hickox (cnd), Bournemouth SO, Bath Festival Chorus, Waynflete Singers Chandos ▲ CHAN 9247 [DDD]
Mozart, W.A.:Così fan tutte (sels), w. L. Cuberli (sop), C. Bartoli (mez), J. Tomlinson (bass), D. Barenboim (cnd), Berlin PO, Berlin RIAS Chamber Choir Erato ▲ 94821
Mozart, W.A.:Don Giovanni (sels), w. L. Cuberli (sop), J. Tomlinson (bass), F. Furlanetto (bass), D. Barenboim (cnd), Berlin PO, Berlin RIAS Chamber Choir Erato ▲ 94823
Mozart, W.A.:Missa, K.317, w. E. von Magnus (alt), J. Protschka (ten), L. Polgár (bass), N. Harnoncourt (cnd), Vienna Concentus Musicus, Arnold Schoenberg Choir [L] Teldec ▲ 2292-43354-2
Mozart, W.A.:Nozze di Figaro (sels), w. L. Cuberli (sop), C. Bartoli (mez), A. Schmidt (bar), D. Barenboim (cnd), Berlin PO, Berlin RIAS Chamber Choir Erato ▲ 94822
Mozart, W.A.:Vesperae solennes, w. E. von Magnus (alt), J. Protschka (ten), L. Polgár (bass), N. Harnoncourt (cnd), Vienna Concentus Musicus, Arnold Schoenberg Choir [L] Teldec ▲ 2292-43354-2
Rachmaninoff, S.:Songs, w. Maria Popescu (mez), Alexandre Naomenko (ten), Sergei Leiferkus (bar), Howard Shelley (pno)—At the Gates of the Holy Cloister; Nothing Shall I Say to You; Again You Are Bestirred, My Heart; Aprill A Festive Day in the Spring; Dusk Was Falling; Song of the Disenchanted; The Flower Died; Do You Remember the Evening?; O, No, I Beg You, Do Not Leave, Op. 4/1; Morning, Op. 4/2; In the Silence of the Secret Night, Op. 4/3; Sing not, O Lovely One, Op. 4/4; Oh, My Field, Op. 4/5; It Wasn't Long Ago, My Friend, Op. 4/6; Water Lily, Op. 8/1; My Child, Your Beauty Is That of a Flower, Op. 8/2; Thoughts, Reflection, Op. 8/3; I Fell in Love, to My Sorrow, Op. 8/4; A Dream, Op. 8/5; Prayer, Op. 8/6; I Await You, Op. 14/1; Small Island, Op. 14/2; How Fleeting Is Delight in Love, Op. 14/3; I Was with Her, Op. 14/4; Summer Nights, Op. 8/5; You Are so Loved by All, Op. 14/6; Do Not Believe Me, Friend, Op. 14/7; Oh, Do Not Grieve, Op. 14/8; She Is as Beautiful as Midday, Op. 14/9; In My Soul, Op. 14/10; Spring Torrents, Op. 14/11; It Is Time, Op. 14/12 Chandos ▲ CHAN 9405
Rachmaninoff, S.:Songs, w. Maria Popescu (mez), Alexandre Naoumenko (ten), Sergei Leiferkus (bass), Howard Shelley (pno)—Letter to K. S. Stanislawsky; The Muse, Op. 34/1; In the Soul of Each of Us, Op. 34/2; The Storm, Op. 34/3; A Passing Breeze, Op. 34/4; Arion, Op. 35/5; The Raising of Lazarus, Op. 34/6; It Cannot Be, Op. 34/7; Music, Op. 34/8; You Knew Him, Op. 34/9; I Remember This Day, Op. 34/10; The Herald, Op. 34/11; What Happiness, Op. 34/12; Dissonance, Op. 34/13; Vocalise, Op. 34/14; From the Gospel of St. John; At Night in My Garden, Op. 38/1; To Her, Op. 38/2; Daisies, Op. 38/3; The Pied Piper, Op. 38/4; Sleep, Op. 38/5; A-oo, Op. 38/6; A Prayer; All Glory to God Chandos ▲ CHAN 9477
Vaughan Williams, R.:Sym 1, w. William Shimell (bar), V. Handley (cnd), Royal Liverpool PO Classics for Pleasure ("Eminence" series) ▲ CDEMX 2142 [DDD]

Rödin, Margot (mez)
Pettersson, G.A.:Barefoot Songs, w. A. Östman (pno) Swedish Society ▲ SCD 1033
Pettersson, G.A.:Vox Humana, w. Marianne Mellnäs (sop), Sven-Erik Alexandersson (ten), Erland Hagegård (bar), S. Westerberg (cnd), Swedish RSO, Swedish Radio Chorus *(rec Royal Swedish Academy of Music, Stockholm, Sweden, Mar. 22 & May 24, 1976)* BIS ▲ CD 55 [AAD]

Rodrigo, Ana (mez)
Moreno Torroba, F.:Luisa Fernanda, w. Verónica Villaroel (sop), Plácido Domingo (ten), Juan Pons (bar), A. Ros-Marbá (cnd), Madrid SO Valois 2-▲ V 4759

Rodriguez (sgr)
Donizetti, G.:La favorita, w. G. Simionato (mez), G. di Stefano (ten), E. Mascherini (bar), C. Siepi (b-bar), R. Cellini (cnd), Palacio Bellas Artes Orch, Palacio Bellas Artes Chorus [I] *(rec live, Mexico City, 7/12/49)* Standing Room Only 2-▲ SRO 816-2 [ADD]

Rodriguez, G. D. (boy alto)
Bernstein, L.:Chichester Psalms, w. G. Levine (cnd), Royal PO, Rome Phil Academy Chorus, St. Peter's Basilica Cappella Giulia Chorus Vatican City *(rec Apr. 7, 1994)* Justice ▲ JR 1801 [DDD]

Roe, Charles (bar)
Maslanka, D.:Mass, w. Lydia Catherine Easley (sop), Jane Smith (org), G.I. Hanson (cnd), Univ of Arizona Wind Orch, Univ of Arizona Sym Choir, Arizona Chamber Choir, Tuscon Boys' Chorus *(rec St. Thomas the Apostle Church, Tuscon, Arizona, Apr 29–30, 1996)* Albany 2-▲ TROY 221-22 [DDD]

Roesler, Trude (mez)
Verdi, G.:Macbeth, w. Astrid Varnay (sop—Lady Macbeth), Trude Roesler (mez—Lady-in-waiting), Hasso Eschert (ten—Malcolm), Walter Geisler (ten—Macduff), Joseph Metternich (bar—Macbeth), Ludwig Weber (bass—Banquo), R. Kraus (cnd), West German Orch, West German Chorus *(rec Cologne, 1954)* Myto 2-▲ 952128

Rogani, Marco (ten)
Puccini, G.:La fanciulla del West (sels), w. Magda Olivero (sop—Minnie), Corinna Vozza (mez—Wowkle), Paolo Caroli (ten—Harry), Giacomo Lauri-Volpi (ten—Dick Johnson), Marco Rogani (ten—Pony Express Rider), Salvatore di Tommaso (ten—Trin), Adelio Zagonara (ten—Nick), Virgilio Ascorro (bar—Sid), Alfredo Colella (bar—Jake Wallace), Giuseppe Forgione (bar—Bello), Giancarlo Guelfi (bar—Jack Rance), Arturo la Porta (bar—Sonora), Gino Conti (bass—José Castro), Piero Passarotti (bass—Bill), Enzo Titta (bass—Larkens), Giulio Tomei (bass—Ashby), V. Bellezza (cnd), Rome Opera Orch, Rome Opera Chorus—Minnie, dalla mia casa son partito; Laggiù nel Soledad; Chi c'è per farmi i ricci; Oh! Mister Johnson, siete rimasto; Non so ben neppur io; Io non son che una povera fanciulla; No, Minnie, non piangete; Vorrei mettermi queste; Hallo!; Oh, se sapeste; Credo che abbiate torto; Ma ti giuro ch'io non ti lascio più; Vieni fuori!; Una parola sola!...Or son sei mesi; Che c'è di nuovo Jack?; E là; Siete pronto; Ch'ella mi creda; E Minnie!...E Minnie! *(rec Rome, Mar. 30, 1957)* Golden Age of Opera ▲ GAO 180 [ADD]

Rogatchewsky, Joseph (ten)
Massenet, J.:Manon, w. G. Féraldy (sop), L. Guénot (bass), E. Cohen (cnd), Paris Opéra-Comique Orch, Paris Opéra-Comique Chorus [F] *(rec 1928–29 for Columbia)* Classical Collector 2-▲ FDC 2 2001 (m) [AAD]

Rogers, Alyce (mez)
Bach, J.S.:Cant 162, w. A. Augér (sop), K. Equiluz (ten), W. Schöne (bass), H. Rilling (cnd), Stuttgart Bach Collegium, Frankfurt Kantorei [G] *(rec Dec 1975 & Mar 1976)* Hänssler Classic ▲ 98.816 [AAD]

Rogers, Nigel (ten)
Gay, J.:The Beggar's Opera (sels), w. P. Clark (sop), A. Jenkins (sop), M. Cable (mez), E. Lane (mez), S. Minty (mez), E. Fleet (sgr), P. Hall (ten), V. Midgley (ten), J. Noble (bar), D. Stevens (cnd), Accademia Monteverdiana Orch, Accademia Monteverdiana Chorus—59 songs *(rec Aug. 1978)* Koch Treasure ▲ 31621-2 [ADD]
India, S. d':Laments—Lamento d'Orfeo Virgin Classics ▲ CDC 59231
Monteverdi, C.:Orfeo, w. P. Kwella (sop), E. Kirkby (sop), J. Smith (sop), S. Varcoe (bar), D. Thomas (bass), N. Rogers (cnd), London Cornett & Sackbutt Ensemble, C. Medlam (cnd), London Baroque Chiaroscuro EMI Classics ▲ CDMB 64947
Monteverdi, C.:Ritorno d'Ulisse, w. P. Esswood (ct), K. Equiluz (ten), M. Dickie (ten), M. Van Egmond (bass), N. Harnoncourt (cnd), Vienna Concentus Musicus Teldec ▲ 42496-2
Purcell, H.:Dido & Aeneas, w. L. Dawson (sop), A. S. von Otter (mez), S. Varcoe (bar), T. Pinnock (cnd), English Concert, *(chorus unknown)* [E] Archiv ▲ 427624-2 [DDD]
Venice Preserv'd, w. Emma Kirkby (sop), Judith Nelson (mez), Academy of Ancient Music [cnd:Christopher Hogwood] L'Oiseau-Lyre ▲ 425891-2 OH [ADD]

Rogers, Shorty (sgr)
Rodgers, R.:Music of, w. S. Bass (sgr), J. Andrews (sgr), P. Como (sgr), D. Reese (sgr), J. Jones (sgr), N. Luboff (sgr), M. Gold (sgr), N. Walker (sgr), H. Bowen (sgr), V. Damone (sgr), P. Nero (pno), J. P. Morgan (sgr), E. Fisher (sgr), B. Goodman (cl), Ann-Margaret (sgr), D. Shore (sgr), T. Martin (sgr), M. King (sgr), A. Newley (sgr) RCA ▲ 8590-2 R ■ 8590-4 R

Roggero, Margaret (mez)
Berlioz, H.:Les Nuits d'été, w. V. de los Angeles (sop), L. Chabay (ten), Y. Sze (bass), C. Munch (cnd), Boston SO RCA Gold Seal 2-▲ 09026-60681-2

Roggero, Margaret (mez) (cont.)
Berlioz, H.:Roméo et Juliette, w. L. Chabay (ten), Y. Sze (bass), C. Munch (cnd), Boston SO, Harvard Glee Club, Radcliffe Choral Society RCA Gold Seal 2-▲ 09026-60681-2
Berlioz, H.:Roméo et Juliette, w. Leslie Chabay (ten), Yi-Kwei Sze (bass), C. Munch (cnd), Boston SO, Harvard Glee Club, Radcliffe Choral Society *(rec Feb 1953)* RCA Victor Gold Seal 8-▲ 0902-668444-2 [ADD]
Rossini, G.:Il barbiere di Siviglia, w. Roberta Peters (sop—Rosina), Margaret Roggero (mez—Berta), Cesare Valletti (ten—Count Almaviva), Calvin Marsh (bar—Fiorello/Sergeant), Robert Merrill (bar—Figaro), Fernando Corena (bass—Dr. Bartolo), Carlo Tomanelli (bass—Ambrogio), Giorgio Tozzi (bass—Don Basilio), E. Leinsdorf (cnd), Metropolitan Opera Orch, New York Metropolitan Opera Chorus *(rec Manhattan Center, New York, Sept 1-11, 1958)* RCA Living Stereo 3-▲ 09026-68552-2 [ADD]

Roggisch, Peter (nar)
Kagel, M.:Sankt-Bach-Passion, w. Anne Sofie von Otter (mez), Hans Peter Blochowitz (ten), Roland Hermann (bar), Gerd Zacher (org), M. Kagel (cnd), South German RSO, Limburg Cathedral Boys' Chorus, Hamburg North German Choir Montaigne ▲ MO 782044

Rogner, Maria (sgr)
Nicolai, O.:Lustigen Weiber, w. Erika Köth (sop), Hertha Töpper (mez), Hans Günter Nöcker (b-bar), Kim Borg (bass), Naan Pödl (sgr), F. Rieger (cnd), Bavarian RSO, Bavarian Chorus *(rec 1960's)* Pantheon 2-▲ PHE 6660 (m)

Rohr, Otto von (bass)
Beethoven, L. van:Leonore (opera), w. H. Zadek (sop), A. Dermota (ten), P. Schöffler (b-bar), F. Leitner (cnd), Vienna SO, Vienna State Opera Chorus [G] *(rec live, Bregenz 1960)* Melodram 2-▲ CDM 27085 [AAD]
Schubert, Franz:Fierrabras, w. H. Plümacher (cta), F. Wunderlich (ten), R. Wolansky (bar), H. Müller-Kray (cnd), Bern State Orch, Berlin RIAS Chamber Choir, South Swiss Radio Chorus—abridged performance *(rec 1959)* Myto ▲ MCD 89001 [ADD]
Verdi, G.:I vespri siciliani, w. M. Cunitz (sop), H. Roswaenge (ten), H. Schlusnus (bar), K. Schröder (cnd), Hessian RSO, Hesse Radio Chorus *(rec 1951)* Myto 2-▲ MCD 93279
Wagner, R.:Lohengrin, w. Leonore Kirchstein (sop—Elsa von Brabant), Ruth Hesse (mez—Ortrud), Herbert Schachtschneider (ten—Lohengrin), Hans Helm (bar—Der Heerrufer des Königs), Otto von Rohr (bass—Heinrich der Vogler), Heinz Imdahl (sgr—Friedrich von Telramund), H. Swarowsky (cnd), Czech PO, Prague National Theater Orch, Vienna State Opera Chorus *(rec Aug 1968)* Weltbild Classics 3-▲ 703835 [ADD]
Wagner, R.:Der Ring des Nibelungen, w. Liselotte Becker-Egner (sop—Woglinde/Ortlinde/Wellgunde), Angelika Berger (sop—Wellgunde/Waltraute), Siw Ericsdotter (sop—Norn 3), Heidemaria Ferch (sop—Freia/Gerhilde), Bella Jasper (sop—Helmwige/Waldvogel/Woglinde), Ditha Sommer (sop—Sieglinde/Gutrune), Ursula Boese (mez—Erda), Ruth Hesse (mez—Fricka), Nadezda Kniplová (mez—Brünnhilde), Margit Kobeck (mez—Schwertleite/Norn 2), Hilde Rosner (mez—Flosshilde/Siegrunde), Erica Schubert (mez—Grimgerde/Flosshilde), Ingrid Göritz (cta—Rossweisse/Norn 1), Herbert Doussant (ten—Froh), Herold Kraus (ten—Mime), Gerald McKee (ten—Siegmund/Siegfried), Fritz Uhl (ten—Loge), Rudolf Knoll (bar—Gunther/Donner), Rolf Polke (bass-bar—Wotan/Wanderer), Rolf Kühne (bass—Alberich), Takao Okamura (bass—Fafner), Otto von Rohr (bass—Hagen/Fasolt/Hunding), H. Swarowsky (cnd), Czech PO, Prague National Theater Orch *(rec June 3 & 5, July 26-31, A)* Weltbild Classics 14-▲ 703769 [ADD]

Rola, Rinaldo (bass)
Mascagni, P.:Isabeau, w. Marcella Pobbe (sop—Isabeau), Licia Galvano (mez—Giglietta), Pier Miranda Ferraro (ten—Folco), Orazio Gualtiero (bar—Cornelius), Rinaldo Rola (bass—Re Raimondo), Amelia Bazzini (sgr—Ermyngarde), Piero Benzi (sgr—L'araldo), Renata Davini (sgr—Ermynthrude), Piero Francia (sgr—Il Cavaliere), T. Serafin (cnd), San Remo SO *(rec Sanremo, Jan 13, 1962)* Bongiovanni ("Il Mito dell'Opera" series) 2-▲ GB 1135/36-2 [ADD]

Rolfe Johnson, Anthony (ten)
Alwyn, W.:Invocations, w. J. Gomez (sop) *(rec Sept 1983)* Chandos ▲ CHAN 9220 [DDD]
Alwyn, W.:A Leave-Taking, w. J. Gomez (sop) *(rec Apr 1984)* Chandos ▲ CHAN 9220 [DDD]
Bach, J.S.:Cant 36, w. N. Argenta (sop), R. Lang (mez), O. Bär (bar), J. E. Gardiner (cnd), English Baroque Soloists, Monteverdi Choir London Archiv ▲ 437327-2
Bach, J.S.:Cant 61, w. N. Argenta (sop), R. Lang (mez), O. Bär (bar), J. E. Gardiner (cnd), English Baroque Soloists, Monteverdi Choir London Archiv ▲ 437327-2 [DDD]
Bach, J.S.:Cant 62, w. N. Argenta (sop), R. Lang (mez), O. Bär (bar), J. E. Gardiner (cnd), English Baroque Soloists, Monteverdi Choir London Archiv ▲ 437327-2 [DDD]
Bach, J.S.:Cant 106, "Actus tragicus", w. N. Argenta (sop), M. Chance (ct), S. Varcoe (b-bar), J. E. Gardiner (cnd), English Baroque Soloists, Monteverdi Choir London [G] Archiv ▲ 429782-2 [DDD]
Bach, J.S.:Cant 140, w. R. Holton (sop), S. Varcoe (b-bar), J. E. Gardiner (cnd), English Baroque Soloists, Monteverdi Choir London [G] Archiv ▲ 431809-2 [DDD]
Bach, J.S.:Cant 147, w. R. Holton (sop), M. Chance (ct), S. Varcoe (b-bar), J. E. Gardiner (cnd), English Baroque Soloists, Monteverdi Choir London [G] Archiv ▲ 431809-2 [DDD]
Bach, J.S.:Cant 198, w. N. Argenta (sop), M. Chance (ct), S. Varcoe (b-bar), J. E. Gardiner (cnd), English Baroque Soloists, Monteverdi Choir London [G] Archiv ▲ 429782-2 [DDD]
Bach, J.S.:St. Matthew Passion, w. K. Te Kanawa (sop), A. S. von Otter (mez), H. P. Blochwitz (ten), O. Bär (bar), T. Krause (bass), G. Solti (cnd), Chicago SO, Chicago Sym Chorus, Glen Ellyn Children's Chorus [G] London 3-▲ 421177-2 [DDD]
Bach, J.S.:St. Matthew Passion, w. B. Bonney (sop), A. Monoyios (sop), A. S. von Otter (mez), M. Chance (ct), H. Crook (ten), O. Bär (bar), A. Schmidt (bar), C. Hauptmann (bass), J. E. Gardiner (cnd), English Baroque Soloists, Monteverdi Choir London [G] Archiv 3-▲ 427648-2 [DDD]
Bach, J.S.:St. Matthew Passion (sels), w. K. Te Kanawa (sop), A. S. von Otter (mez), H. P. Blochwitz (ten), O. Bär (bar), T. Krause (bass), G. Solti (cnd), Chicago SO, Chicago Sym Chorus, Glen Ellyn Children's Chorus [G] London ▲ 425691-2 [DDD]
Beethoven, L. van:Syms (comp), w. Lynne Dawson (sop), Jard Van Nes (cta), Eike Wilm Schulte (bass), F. Brüggen (cnd), Orch of the 18th Century, Lisbon Gulbenkian Foundation Chorus [on Sym. 9] Philips 5-▲ 442156-2
Beethoven, L. van:Sym 9, "Choral Sym", w. Luba Orgonasova (sop), Anne Sofie von Otter (mez), Gilles Cachemaille (b-bar), J. E. Gardiner (cnd), Orch Révolutionnaire et Romantique [period instrs] *(rec All Saints' Church, London, Oct 1992)* Archiv ▲ 447074-2 [DDD]
British Music on Hyperion, w. Parley of Instruments, Roy Goodman (cnd), John Mark Ainsley (ten), Graham Johnson (pno), Salomon Quartet, BBC Scottish SO, Royal PO, St. Paul's Cathedral Choir, Nash Ensemble, Martyn Hill (ten), Suasan Gritton (sop), Sarah Wal Hyperion ▲ HYP 15
Britten, H.:Canticles I-V, w. M. Chance (ct), A. Opie (bar), R. Vignoles (pno), S. Williams (hp), M. Thompson (hn) Hyperion ▲ CDA 66498
Britten, H.:Canticles I-V, w. G. Johnson (pno)—Canticle I, "My beloved is mine" Hyperion ▲ CDA 66209
Britten, H.:Folksong Arrs, w. G. Johnson (pno)—O Waly Waly; Little Sir William; The Salley Gardens; The trees they grow so high [E] Hyperion ▲ CDA 66209
Britten, H.:Peter Grimes, w. F. Lott (sop—Ellen Orford), T. Allen (ten—Captain Balstrode), A. R. Johnson (ten—Peter Grimes), Covent Garden, B. Haitink (cnd), Royal Opera House Orch, Royal Opera House Chorus Covent Garden EMI Classics ▲ CDCB 54832
Britten, H.:Purcell Realizations, w. M. Chance (ct), A. Opie (bar), R. Vignoles (pno)—3 Realizations (An evening hymn; Let the dreadful engines; In the black dismal dungeon of despair) Hyperion ▲ CDA 66498
Britten, H.:Purcell Realizations, w. Susan Gritton (sop), Felicity Lott (sop), Sarah Walker (mez), James Bowman (ct), John Mark Ainsley (ten), Richard Jackson (bass), Simon Keenlyside (bass), Ian Bostridge (sgr), Graham Johnson (pno) Hyperion 2-▲ CDA 67061/62
Britten, H.:St. Nicolas, w. M. Best (cnd), English CO, Corydon Singers Hyperion ▲ CDA 66333
Britten, H.:Serenade, Op. 31, w. M. Thompson (hn), B. Thomson (cnd), Scottish National Orch [E] Chandos ▲ CHAN 8657 [DDD]
Britten, H.:Sonnets of Michelangelo, w. G. Johnson (pno) Hyperion ▲ CDA 66209
Britten, H.:War Requiem, w. L. Haywood (sop), B. Luxon (bar), R. Shaw (cnd), Atlanta SO, Atlanta Sym Chorus [L] Telarc 2-▲ CD 80157 [DDD]

Rolfe Johnson, Anthony (ten) (cont.)
Britten, H.:War Requiem, w. L. Orgonasova (sop), B. Skovhus (bar), J. E. Gardiner (cnd), North German RSO, Monteverdi Choir London, North German Radio Chorus, Tölz Boys' Choir Deutsche Grammophon 2-▲ 437801-2
Britten, H.:Winter Words, w. G. Johnson (pno) Hyperion ▲ CDA 66209
Butterworth, G.:Songs (6) from *A Shropshire Lad*, w. D. Willison (pno) IMP Classics ▲ IMPPCD 1065 [DDD]
Delius, F.:A Late Lark, w. E. Fenby (cnd), Royal PO Unicorn-Kanchana ("Souvenir" series) ▲ UK 2072
Delius, F.:Songs, w. Felicity Lott (sop), Sarah Walker (mez), E. Fenby (cnd), Royal PO—Orchestral Songs; Songs w. Pno [Scandinavian, French & English] Unicorn-Kanchana ("Souvenir" series) ▲ UK 2075
Elgar, E.:Coronation Ode, w. T. Cahill (sop), A. Collins (cta), G. Howell (bass), A. Gibson (cnd), Scottish National Orch, Scottish National Chorus [E] *(rec 1976)* Chandos ("Collect" series) ▲ CHAN 6574 [ADD]
Handel, G.F.:Acis & Galatea, w. N. Burrowes (sop), M. Hill (ten), W. White (bass), J. E. Gardiner (cnd), English Baroque Soloists [E] Archiv ▲ 423406-2 [ADD]
Handel, G.F.:Acis & Galatea [arr Mozart], w. E. Mathis (sop), R. Gambill (ten), R. Lloyd (b-bar), P. Schreier (cnd), Austrian RSO, Austrian Radio Chorus [E] Orfeo 2-▲ 133852 [DDD]
Handel, G.F.:Israel in Egypt, w. Nancy Argenta (sop), Emily Van Evera (sop), Jan Wilson (mez), Thomas (sgr), White (sgr), A. Parrott (cnd), Taverner Players, Taverner Choir [E] EMI Classics 2-▲ CDCB 54018 [DDD]
Handel, G.F.:Messiah, w. Saul Quirke (trb), Margaret Marshall (sop), Catherine Robbin (mez), Charles Brett (ct), Robert Hale (b-bar), J. E. Gardiner (cnd), English Baroque Soloists, Monteverdi Choir London [E] Philips 3-▲ 411041-2 [DDD]
Handel, G.F.:Messiah, w. Saul Quirke (trb), Margaret Marshall (sop), Catherine Robbin (mez), Charles Brett (ct), Robert Hale (b-bar), J. E. Gardiner (cnd), English Baroque Soloists, Monteverdi Choir London [E] Philips ▲ 412267-2 [DDD]
Handel, G.F.:Music of, w. Pauline Tinsley (sop), James Bowman (ct), David Wilson-Johnson (ten), Simon Preston (org), R. Leppard (cnd), English CO, London Phil Chorus—Zadok the Priest; Eternal Source of Light Divine; Tamerlano Ov; Dead March [from Saul]; When the Ear Heard Her; She Delivered the Poor That Cried; Their Bodies Are Buried in Peace; Glory Be to the Father; As It Was in the Beginning; Con a Due Cori in B♭; Waft Her Angels to the Skies; Con in g for Org, Op. 7/5; Hallelujah Chorus [from The Messiah] IMP ("BBC Radio Classics" series) ▲ IMP 5691522
Handel, G.F.:Ode for St. Cecilia's Day, w. Felicity Lott (sop), T. Pinnock (cnd), English CO, English Concert Choir [E] Archiv ▲ 419220-2 [DDD]
Handel, G.F.:Samson, w. Roberta Alexander (sop), Maria Venuti (sop), Jochen Kowalski (ct), Aalstair Miles (bass), Anton Scharinger (bass), N. Harnoncourt (cnd), Vienna Concentus Musicus, Arnold Schoenberg Choir Teldec ▲ 74871-2
Handel, G.F.:Semele, w. Norma Burrowes (sop), Patrizia Kwella (sop), Elizabeth Priday (sop), Catherine Denley (mez), Della Jones (mez), Timothy Penrose (alt), Maldwyn Davies (ten), Robert Lloyd (b-bar), David Thomas (bass), J. E. Gardiner (cnd), English Baroque Soloists, Monteverdi Choir London Erato 2-▲ 2292-45982-2
Handel, G.F.:Solomon, w. Nancy Argenta (sop), Barbara Hendricks (sop), Carolyn Watkinson (cta), J. E. Gardiner (cnd), English Baroque Soloists, Monteverdi Choir London [E] Philips 2-▲ 412612-2 [DDD]
Haydn, J.:Die Jahreszeiten, w. Barbara Bonney (sop), Andreas Schmidt (bar), J. E. Gardiner (cnd), English Baroque Soloists, Monteverdi Choir London [period instrs] Archiv 2-▲ 431818-2 [DDD]
Haydn, J.:Die Jahreszeiten (sels), w. Barbara Bonney (sop), Andreas Schmidt (bar), J. E. Gardiner (cnd), English Baroque Soloists, Monteverdi Choir London—arias & choruses Archiv ▲ 447282-2
Haydn, J.:Salve regina, H.XXIIIb/2, w. Arleen Auger (sop), Alfreda Hodgson (cta), Gwynne Howell (bass), John Birch (db), L. Heltay (cnd), Argo CO, London Chamber Choir *(rec St. Jude's, London, Feb 1979)* London 2-▲ 443027-2 [ADD]
Haydn, J.:Die Schöpfung, w. Emma Kirkby (sop), Michael George (bass), C. Hogwood (cnd), Academy of Ancient Music, New College Choir Oxford [E] L'Oiseau-Lyre 2-▲ 430397-2 [DDD]
Haydn, J.:The Seven Last Words of Christ on the Cross, w. Inge Nielsen (sop), Margaretha Hintermeier (cta), Robert Holl (bass), N. Harnoncourt (cnd), Vienna Concentus Musicus, Arnold Schoenberg Choir [oratorio version] Teldec ▲ 2292-46458-2 ZK
In Praise of Woman:150 Years of English Women Composers Hyperion ▲ CDA 66709
Ireland, J.:Songs, w. D. Willison (pno)—The Land of Lost Content & others IMP Classics ▲ IMPPCD 1065 [DDD]
Mendelssohn, F.:Elijah, w. Y. Kenny (sop), A.S. von Otter (mez), T. Allen (bar), N. Marriner (cnd), Academy of St. Martin in the Fields Philips 2-▲ 432984-2 [DDD]
Monteverdi, C.:Vespro della Beata Vergine, w. Elly Ameling (sop), Norma Burrowes (sop), Charles Brett (ct), Robert Tear (ten), Martyn Hill (ten), Peter Knapp (bass), John Noble (bass), Munrow, Ledger (cnd), London Early Music Consort EMI Classics ("Doubleforte" series) 2-▲ CDFB 68631
Monteverdi, C.:Vespro della Beata Vergine, w. Elly Ameling (sop), Norma Burrowes (sop), Charles Brett (ct), Martyn Hill (ten), Robert Tear (ten), Peter Knapp (bass), John Noble (bass), Francis Grier (org/hpd), James Lancelot (org/hpd), Andrew Leach (org/hpd), P. Ledger (cnd), London Early Music Consort, King's College Choir Cambridge—Nigra sum [con.]; Laudate pueri [psalm]; Sancta Maria [son. sopra]; Magnificat *(rec Chapel of King's College, Cambridge, July & Aug. 1975)* EMI Classics ▲ CDK 65339 [ADD]
Mozart, W.A.:Ave verum corpus, w. K. Te Kanawa (sop), A. Sofie von Otter (mez), R. Lloyd (bass), N. Marriner (cnd), Academy of St. Martin in the Fields, Academy Chorus *(rec London, Mar. 10-12, 1993)* Philips ▲ 438999-2
Mozart, W.A.:Complete Mozart Edition, w. A. Augér (sop), E. Mathis (sop), H. Schwarz (mez), L. Hager (cnd), Salzburg Mozarteum Orch, Salzburg Mozarteum Chorus Philips 2-▲ 422526-2 [ADD]
Mozart, W.A.:Finta semplice, w. Helen Donath (sop), Jutta-Renate Ihloff (sop), Teresa Berganza (mez), Thomas Moser (ten), Robert Lloyd (b-bar), Robert Holl (bass), L. Hager (cnd), Salzburg Mozarteum Orch [I] Orfeo 3-▲ 085843 [DDD]
Mozart, W.A.:Idomeneo, w. Sylvia McNair (sop), Hillevi Martinpelto (sop), Anne Sophie von Otter (mez), J. E. Gardiner (cnd), English Baroque Soloists, Monteverdi Choir London Archiv 3-▲ 431674-2 [DDD]
Mozart, W.A.:Missa, K.317, w. Janet Price (sop), Kevin Smith (ct), Graham Titus (bass), M. Davies (cnd), BBC Northern SO, Leeds Phil Chorus IMP ("BBC Radio Classics" series) ▲ IMP 5691552
Mozart, W.A.:Missa, K.427, w. L. Marshall (sop), F. Palmer (sop), G. Howell (bass), N. Marriner (cnd), Academy of St. Martin in the Fields, Academy Chorus [L] Philips ▲ 420891-2 [ADD]
Mozart, W.A.:Missa, K.427, w. K. Te Kanawa (sop), A. Sofie von Otter (mez), R. Lloyd (bass), N. Marriner (cnd), Academy of St. Martin in the Fields, Academy of St. Martin in the Fields Chorus *(rec London, Mar. 10-12, 1993)* Philips ▲ 438999-2
Mozart, W.A.:Missa, K.427, w. S. McNair (sop), D. Montague (mez), C. Hauptmann (bass), J. E. Gardiner (cnd), English Baroque Soloists, Monteverdi Choir London [newly revised version, ed. Gardiner] [L] Philips ▲ 420210-2 [DDD]
Mozart, W.A.:Nozze di Figaro (sels), w. R. Pütz (sop), T. Stich-Randall (mez), T. Berganza (mez), G. Bacquier (bar), F. Corena (bass), H. Wallberg (cnd), Swiss Romande Orch, Swiss Romande Chorus—Act IV Melodram 2-▲ CDM 27094 [ADD]
Mozart, W.A.:Zauberflöte, w. D. Upshaw (sop), B. Hoch (sop), A. Schmidt (bar), R. Norrington (cnd), London Classical Players [period instrs] EMI Classics 2-▲ CDCB 54287
Mozart, W.A.:Zauberflöte (sels), w. D. Upshaw (sop), B. Hoch (sop), A. Schmidt (bar), R. Norrington (cnd), London Classical Players [period instrs] EMI Classics ▲ CDC 54492
Poulenc, F.:Songs, w. F. Lott (sop), A. Murray (mez), R. Jackson (bass), G. Johnson (pno) [F] Hyperion ▲ CDA 66147
Schubert, Franz:Songs (comp), w. G. Johnson (pno)—15 songs—D.235, 237, 521, 534, 579, 767, 806, 856, 903, 904, 905, 906, 927, 933, 939 [G] Hyperion ▲ CDJ 33006 [DDD]
Songs to Shakespeare, w. Rolfe Johnson, Anthony (ten), Graham Johnson (pno) Hyperion ▲ CDA 66480 [DDD]
Stravinsky, I.:Oedipus Rex, w. M. Lipovsek (mez), J. Tomlinson (bass), F. Welser-Möst (cnd), London PO, London Phil Chorus EMI Classics ▲ CDC 54445
Stravinsky, I.:Perséphone, w. Anne Fournet (nar), K. Nagano (cnd), London PO Virgin Classics ▲ ZDMB 61249

Rolfe Johnson, Anthony (ten) (cont.)
Stravinsky, I.:Perséphone, w. A. Fournet (nar), K. Nagano (cnd), London PO, Tiffin Boys' School Choir, London Phil Chorus [F] Virgin Classics 2-▲ 59077 [DDD]
Sullivan, A.:The Mikado, w. M. McLaughlin (sop), A. Howells (mez), J. Watson (sop), F. Palmer (sop/mez), D. Adams (bass), R. Stuart (bar), R. Van Allan (bass), N. Folwell (bar), C. Mackerras (cnd), Welsh National Opera Orch, Welsh National Opera Chorus—Ov & dialogue omitted [E] Telarc ▲ CD 80284 [DDD]; ■ CS 30284 (D)
Vaughan Williams, R.:Songs of Travel, w. D. Willison (pno) IMP Classics ▲ IMPPCD 1065 [DDD]
Walton, W.:Gloria, w. B. Robotham (sop), B. Rayner Cook, L. Frémaux (cnd), City of Birmingham SO, Worcester Cathedral Choristers EMI Classics ▲ CDM 64201
Weill, K.:The Seven Deadly Sins, w. E. Ross (sop), I. Caley (ten), M. Rippon (bass), J. Tomlinson (bass), S. Rattle (cnd), City of Birmingham SO EMI Classics ▲ CDM 64739

Roloff, Roger (bass)
Janácek, L.:Slavonic Mass, w. C. Brewer (sop), M. Simpson (mez), K. Dent (ten), R. Shaw (cnd), Atlanta SO, Atlanta Sym Chorus [Sla] Telarc ▲ CD 80287 [DDD]
Strauss, R.:Friedenstag, w. A. Marc (sop), R. Bass (cnd), Collegiate Orch, Collegiate Chorale [G] *(rec in concert at Carnegie Hall, 11/19/89)* Koch International Classics ▲ KIC 7111-2 [DDD]

Romaguera, Joaquin (ten)
Puccini, G.:Tosca, w. Birgit Nilsson (sop—Floria Tosca), Puli Toro (mez—Shepherd), Jose Carreras (ten—Mario Cavaradossi), Joaquin Romaguera (ten—Spoleta), James Billings (bar—Sacristan), Richard Fredricks (bar—Baron Scarpa), Samuel Ramey (bass—Cesare Angelotti), William Ledbetter (sgr—Sciarrone), Richard Park (sgr—Cardinal), Don Yule (sgr—Jailer), J. Rudel (cnd), *(orch & chorus unknown) (rec Nov 13, 1974)* Legato Classics 2-▲ LCD-200-2

Roman, Stella (sop)
Verdi, G.:La forza del destino, w. Frederick Jagel (ten), Lawrence Tibbett (bar), Salvatore Baccaloni (bass), Ezio Pinza (bass), B. Walter (cnd), New York Metropolitan Opera Orch *(rec live, Jan 23, 1943)* The Fourties 2-▲ ENT 1503

Romani, Augusto (bass)
Cilea, F.:Adriana Lecouvreur (sels), w. Renata Tebaldi (sop—Adriana), Piero de Palma (ten—Abate), Gianni Poggi (ten—Maurizio), Giuseppe Taddei (bar—Michonnet), Augusto Romani (bass—Prince), G. Santini (cnd), Naples Teatro San Carlo Orch, Naples Teatro San Carlo Chorus—Del sultano Amurate...Io son l'umile ancella; Giusto Cielo! che feci in tal giorno; Salvatemi! salvatemi!...Scostatevi, profani! *(rec San Carlo Theater, Naples, Dec. 26, 1952)* Legato Classics 2-▲ LCD 193-2 [ADD]

Romani, Regolo (ten)
Puccini, G.:La Bohème, w. Ileana Cotrubas (sop—Mimi), Margherita Guglielmi (sop—Musetta), José Carreras (ten—Rodolfo), Saverio Porzano (ten—Parpignol), Regolo Romani (ten—Vendor), Claudio Giombi (bar—Benoit), Gianni Maffeo (bar—Schaunard), Angelo Romero (bar—Marcello), Alfredo Giacomotti (bass—Alcindoro), Carlo Meliciani (bass—Customs Officer), Giuseppe Morresi (bass—Sergeant), Paolo Washington (bass—Colline), G. Prêtre (cnd), La Scala Orch, La Scala Chorus *(rec Washington D.C., Sept 8, 1976)* Legato Classics 2-▲ LCD 201-2

Romanko, Olga (sop)
Stravinsky, I.:Songs, w. V. Samoilenki (pno), A. Golyshev (cnd), Bolshoi Theater Chamber Music Ensemble—The Cloud; 3 Songs; Cats' Lullabies; Lullaby; 2 Lyrics by K. Balmont; Pastorale; Pribautiki; 3 Stories for Children; 4 Russian Folk-Songs; Little Harmonic Ramuziana; In Memoriam Dylan T.; The Owl & the Pussy-cat; 3 Lyrics from Japanese Poetry; 3 Songs to Lyrics by Shakespeare; 2 Songs to Lyrics by S. Gorodestsky, Op. 6 MK ▲ MKA 417126 [DDD]

Romanò (sgr)
Mercadante, S.:La Vestale, w. G. Dimitrova (sop), D. Vejzovic (sop), G. Cecchele (ten), Cepreaga (sgr), Kliskic (sgr), Sioli (sgr), Boldrini (sgr), V. Sutej (cnd), Spalato National Theater Orch, Spalato National Theater Chorus [I] *(rec 4/9/87)* Bongiovanni 2-▲ GB 2065/66 [DDD]

Romano, Patrick (ten)
Bach, J.S.:Mass in b, BWV 232, w. J. Baird (sop), J. Nelson (sop), N. Zylstra, J. Lane, Z. Muñoz, S. Rickards, W. Sharp, J. Weaver (bass), J. Thomas (cnd), American Bach Soloists Koch International Classics 2-▲ KIC 7194-2 [DDD]
Mozart, W.A.:Requiem, w. Lorna Haywood (sop), D'Anna Fortunado (mez), John Cheek (bass), J. Sommary (cnd), Amor Artis Orch, Amor Artis Chorale [period instrs] *(rec St. Jean Baptiste Church, New York City, Mar 1996)* Vox Classics ▲ VOX 7534 [DDD]

Romanová, Natalia (sop)
Martinů, B.:Hymn to St. James, w. D. Drobková (cta), R. Novák (ten), P. Haničinec (nar), P. Kühn (cnd), Prague SO members, Prague Radio Chorus [Cz] *(rec 2-3/88)* Supraphon ▲ 11 0751-2 [DDD]
Martinů, B.:The Prophecy of Isaiah, w. D. Drobková (alto), R. Novák (bass), V. Kozderka (tpt), J. Peruška (va), I. Kiezlich (timp), S. Bogunia (pno), P. Kühn (cnd), Prague Radio Men's Chorus, Kühn Chorus [Cz] *(rec 2-3/88)* Supraphon ▲ 11 0751-2 [DDD]

Romay, L. (sgr)
Kern, J.:You Were Never Lovelier, w. F. Astaire (sgr), N. Wynn (sgr) *(rec 1942)* Hollywood Soundstage ▲ HSCD 4005

Romberger, Gerhild (alt)
Mendelssohn, Fanny:Songs, w. Michaela Krämer (sop), Alastair Thompson (ten), Gerrit Miehlke (bass), Richard Braun (pno), Willi Gundlach (cnd), Dortmund Univ Chamber Choir—Morgendämmerung; Im Herbste; Unter des Laubdachs Hut; Ich stand gelehnet an den Mast; Mitternacht; Abschied; Lockung; Abend; Aus meinen Tränen; Wenn ich in deine Augen seh'; Im wunderschönen Monat Mai; Schöne Fremde; Schweigend sinkt die Nacht hernieder; Nacht liegt auf den fremden Wegen; Hochzeitsbitter; Wandl' ich in dem Wald; Frühzeitiger Frühling; Blumengruss; O Herbst; Schilflied; Feldlied; März; Lichter Mai; Waldruhe; Nachtreigen *(rec Musikhochschule Detmold, Dortmund, Oct 1995)* Thorofon ▲ CTH 2299 [DDD]

Romby, P. (sgr)
"Le Patron" of the Saxophone, w. Mule, Marcel (sax), Guy Chauvet (ten), G. Charon (sgr), F. l'Homme (sgr), P. Romby (sgr), Eugène Bozza (cnd), Francis Çebron (cnd), Phillipe Gaubert (cnd), *(orchs unknown)*, Joseph Benvenutti (pno), Marcel Gaveau (pno), Marthe Pellas-Lenom (pno), François Combelle (sax) *(rec 1930-1940)* Clarinet Classics ▲ CC 0013 [AAD]

Romero, Angelo (bar)
Donizetti, G.:Gianni di Parigi, w. L. Serra (sop), E. Zilio (mez), G. Morino (ten), E. Fissore (bar), S. Manga (sgr), C. F. Cillario (cnd), Milan RAI Orch, Milan RAI Chorus [I] *(rec live)* Nuova Era 2-▲ 6752/53 [DDD]
Puccini, G.:La Bohème, w. Ileana Cotrubas (sop—Mimi), Margherita Guglielmi (sop—Musetta), José Carreras (ten—Rodolfo), Saverio Porzano (ten—Parpignol), Regolo Romani (ten—Vendor), Claudio Giombi (bar—Benoit), Gianni Maffeo (bar—Schaunard), Angelo Romero (bar—Marcello), Alfredo Giacomotti (bass—Alcindoro), Carlo Meliciani (bass—Customs Officer), Giuseppe Morresi (bass—Sergeant), Paolo Washington (bass—Colline), G. Prêtre (cnd), La Scala Orch, La Scala Chorus *(rec Washington D.C., Sept 8, 1976)* Legato Classics 2-▲ LCD 201-2
Rossini, G.:Il barbiere di Siviglia, w. I. Kertesi (sop—Berta), S. Ganassi (mez—Rosina), R. Vargas (ten—Almaviva), A. Romero (bar—Dr. Bartolo), R. Servile (bar—Figaro), F. de Grandis (bass—Basilio), K. Sárkány (bass—Fiorello), A. Déri (pno), B. Sztankovits (gtr), W. Humburg (cnd), Failoni CO, Hungarian Radio Chorus *(rec Nov. 16-28, 1992)* Naxos 3-▲ 8.660027/29 [DDD]
Rossini, G.:L'italiana in Algeri, w. T. Berganza (sop), L. Zannini (mez), U. Benelli (ten), E. Dara (bar), P. Montarsolo (bass), C. Abbado (cnd), Florence Teatro Comunale Orch, Florence Teatro Comunale Chorus *(rec 1973)* Great Opera Performances ▲ GOP 740
Verdi, G.:Un giorno di regno, w. Maria Casula (sop), Enrico Fissore (bass), Franca Fabbri (sgr), Michele Guento (sgr), Islen Moubayed (sgr), Ruggero Rado (sgr), Bernardino Trotta (sgr), A. Zedda (cnd), *(orch unknown)* Great Opera Performances 2-▲ GOP 782

Ronchini, Bruna (sgr)
Humperdinck, E.:Hänsel und Gretel (sels), w. Sena Jurinac (sop—Hänsel), Elisabeth Schwarzkopf (sop—Gretel), Vittoria Palombini (mez—Witch), Rolando Panerai (sgr—Peter), Bruna Ronchini (sgr—Gertrude), H.. Karajan (cnd), Milan RAI SO, Milan RAI Chorus—[Act 1] Suse, liebe Suse, was raschelt im Stroh; [Act 2] Ein Männlein steht im Walde ganz still und Stumm; Abends, will ich schlafen gehn; [Act 3] Wo bin ich? Wach' ich?; Und bist du dann drin...schwapsl; Die Englein haben's im Traum gesagt; Schunt, o schunt das Wunder an *(rec Milan, Dec. 25, 1954)* Legato Classics 3-▲ LCD 197-3

Ronge, Gabriele Maria (sop)
Zemlinsky, A. von:Der Traumgörge, w. P. Coburn (sop), J. Martin (sop), B. Calm (mez), P. Haage (ten), H. Kruse (ten), J. Protschka (ten), H. Welker (bar), M. Blasius (bass), V. von Halem (bass), G. Albrecht (cnd), Frankfurt RSO [G] Capriccio 2-▲ CD 10241/2 [DDD]

Roni, Luigi (bass)
Donizetti, G.:Lucrezia Borgia (sels), w. L. Gencer (sop), G. Raimondi (ten), E. Gracis (cnd), La Scala Orch, La Scala Chorus—8 scenes & arias [I] *(rec live, 3/12/70)* Myto 2-▲ 2 MCD 90423 [ADD]
Giordano, U.:Fedora, w. Mirella Freni (sop—Principessa Fedora), Adelina Scarabelli (sop—Contessa Olga), Silvia Mazzoni (mez—Dimitri), Monica Minarelli (sgr—Savoiardo), Placido Domingo (ten—Conte Loris), Ernesto Gavazzi (ten—Desiré), Aldo Bottion (ten—Barone Rouvel), Alessandro Corbelli (bar—Siriex), Luigi Roni (bass—Cirillo), Silvestro Sammaritano (bass—Baroff), Alfredo Giacomotti (bass—Gretch), Ernesto Panariello (bass—Lorek), Vincenzo Alaimo (sgr—Nicola), Arnold Bosman (sgr—Boleslao), Bruno Capisani (sgr—Sergio), Renato Zanchetta (sgr—Michele), G. Gavazzeni (cnd), La Scala Orch, La Scala Chorus *(rec La Scala, Apr 5, 1993)* Legato 2-▲ LCD 213-2 [ADD]
Verdi, G.:Aida, w. Jessye Norman (sop), Yannula Pappas (mez), Walter Alberti (bar), N. Sanzogno (cnd), Belgian Radio-TV Orch, Belgian Radio-TV Chorus *(rec live, Paris, May 4, 1973)* Agorá ("Phoenix" series) 2-▲ 507
Verdi, G.:Attila, w. Rita Orlandi Malaspina (sop—Odabella), Veriano Luchetti (ten—Foresto), Piero De Palma (ten—Uldino), Piero Cappuccilli (bar—Ezio), Nicolai Ghiaurov (bass—Attila), Luigi Roni (bass—Leone), G. Patanè (cnd), La Scala Orch, La Scala Chorus *(rec Milan, May 12, 1975)* Myto 2-▲ MCD 961140
Verdi, G.:Attila, w. Rita Orlandi Malaspina (sop—Odabella), Veriano Luchetti (ten—Foresto), Piero de Palma (ten—Uldino), Piero Cappuccilli (bar—Ezio), Nicolai Ghiaurov (bass—Attila), Luigi Roni (bass—Leone), G. Patanè (cnd), La Scala Orch, La Scala Chorus *(rec Milan, May 15, 1972)* Golden Age of Opera 2-▲ GAO 187/88 [ADD]
Verdi, G.:Falstaff, w. Maureen O'Flynn (sop), Daniela Dessi (sop), Bernadette Manca di Nissa (mez), Delores Ziegler (mez), Ramon Vargas (ten), Ernesto Gavazzi (ten), Paolo Barbacini (ten), Juan Pons (bar), Roberto Frontali (bar), R. Muti (cnd), La Scala Orch, La Scala Chorus *(rec Milan La Scala Theater, Italy, Mar. 29 & 31)* Sony Classical ▲ S2K 58961 [DDD]

Ronisch, Rosemarie (sop)
Mozart, W.A.:Entführung, w. Jutta Vulpius (sop), Rolf Apreck (ten), Jurgen Forster (ten), Arnold van Mill (bass), O. Suitner (cnd), Dresden State Opera Orch, Dresden State Opera Chorus Berlin Classics 2-▲ BER 9116

Ronshini, Bruna (sgr)
Humperdinck, E.:Hänsel und Gretel, w. Sena Jurinac (sop), Elisabeth Schwarzkopf (sop), Rita Streich (sop), Vittoria Palombini (mez), Rolando Panerai (bar), H. von Karajan (cnd), Milan Italian Radio-TV Orch, Milan RAI Chorus Stradivarius 2-▲ STV 12314

Roocroft, Amanda (sop)
Mozart, W.A.:Così fan tutte, w. E. James (mez), R. Gilfrey (bar), C. Feller (bass), J. E. Gardiner (cnd), English Baroque Soloists Archiv 3-▲ 437829-2 [DDD]
Operatic Arias, w. London PO [cnd:Franz Welser-Möst] EMI Classics ▲ CDC 55090

Roon, Elisabeth (sop)
Akademie Chamber Choir & Vienna SO, w. [cnd:Ferdinand Grossmann], Akademie Chamber Choir, Vienna SO, Laurence Dutoit (sop), Daagmar Herrmann-Braun (cta), Erich Majkut (ten), W. Berry (bass) Vox 90s ■ V9-9903
Bach, J.S.:Christmas Oratorio, w. D.H. Braun (mez), E. Majkut (ten), W. Berry (bass), L. Dutoit (echo), B. Seidlhofer (hpd), J. Nebois (org), F. Grossmann (cnd), Vienna SO, Akademie Chamber Choir Vox Box 2-▲ CDX 5096 [ADD]
Schubert, Franz:Die Verschworenen, w. Ilona Steingruber (sop—Countess), Elizabeth Roon (mez—Helene), Laurence Dutoit (trb—Isella), Walter Anton (ten—Udolin), Walter Berry (bar—Count), Rudolf Kreutzberger (sgr—Astolf), F. Grossmann (cnd), Vienna SO, Vienna Academy Chamber Choir Theorema ▲ TH 121178

Roos, Casper (sgr)
Partch, H.:Revelation in the Courthouse Park, w. S. Costallos (sgr—Mom & Agave), C. Durham (ten—Sonny & Pentheus), M. Kimbrough (bar—Vendor & Herdsman), E. Earle (b-bar—Hobo & Tiresias), O. Babatunde (sgr—Dion & Dionysus), C. Roos (sgr—Mayor & Cadmus), O. Williams (sgr—Korypheus), R. Young (sgr—Cop & Guard), D. Mitchell (cnd), Partch Instrumentalists, marching band, *(chorus unknown)* [E] *(rec 10/87)* Tomato 2-▲ R2 70390 [DDD]

Rootering, Jan-Hendrik (bass)
Beethoven, L van:Missa Solemnis, w. L. Orgonasova (sop), J. Rappé (ten), C. Davis (cnd), Bavarian RSO, Bavarian Radio Chorus RCA Red Seal 2-▲ 09026-60967-2
Beethoven, L van:Sym 9, "Choral Sym", w. M. Price (sop), M. Lipovsk (alt), P. Seifert (ten), W. Sawallisch (cnd), Royal Concertgebouw Orch, Düsseldorf Municipal Choral Society EMI Classics ▲ CDC 54505
Donizetti, G.:Requiem Mass, w. C. Studer (sop), H. Müller-Molinari (mez), A. Baldin (ten), J. P. Bogart (bass), M. A. G. Martínez (cnd), Bamberg SO, Bamberg Sym Chorus [L] Orfeo ▲ 172881 [DDD]
Dvořák, A.:Requiem Mass, w. G. Beňačková (sop), B. Fassbaender (mez), T. Moser (ten), W. Sawallisch (cnd), Czech PO, Czech Chorus [L] Supraphon 2-▲ 10 4241 [DDD]
Dvořák, A.:Stabat Mater, w. G. Beňačková (sop), O. Wenkel (cta), P. Dvorský (ten), W. Sawallisch (cnd), Czech PO, Czech Phil Chorus [L] Supraphon 2-▲ 10 3561-2 [DDD]
Gluck, C.W.:La Recontre imprévue, w. J. Kaufmann (sop—Rezia), A. Stumphius (sop—Dardané), A.-M. Rodde (sop—Amine), I. Vermillion (mez—Balkis), R. Gambill (ten—Ali), C. H. Ahnsjö (ten—Osmin), J.-H. Rootering (bass—Un Calender), L. Hager (cnd), Munich RSO Orfeo 2-▲ 242912 [DDD]
Haydn, J.:Die Schöpfung, w. Barbara Bonney (mez), Edith Wiens (sop), Hans-Peter Blochwitz (ten), Olaf Bär (bar), N. Marriner (cnd), Stuttgart Radio Orch, Stuttgart Radio Chorus [G] EMI Classics 2-▲ CDCB 54038 [DDD]
Loewe, C.:Ballads, w. H. Lechler (pno)—Herr Oluf, Op. 2/2; Elvershöh, Op. 3/2; Graf Eberstein, Op. 9/VI:5; Die wandelnde Glocke, Op. 20/3; Harald, Op. 45/1; Das Erkennen, Op. 65/2; Der Pilgrim vor St. Just, Op. 99/3; Die verfallene Mühle, Op. 109; Odins Meeresritt, Op. 118; Archibald Douglas, Op. 128; Der Nöck, Op. 129/2 [G] Calig ▲ CAL 50900 [DDD]
Mahler, G.:Sym 8, w. Sylvia McNair (sop), Andrea Rost (sop), Cheryl Studer (sop), Anne Sofie von Otter (mez), Rosemarie Lang (cta), Peter Seiffert (ten), Bryn Terfel (bar), C. Abbado (cnd), Berlin PO, Berlin Radio Chorus, Prague Phil Chorus, Tölz Boys' Choir Deutsche Grammophon ("4D Audio" series) 2-▲ 445843-2
Mozart, W.A.:Don Giovanni, w. J. Varady (sop), A. Augér (sop), E. Mathis (sop), T. Moser (ten), A. Titus (bar), R. Panerai (bar), R. Scholze (bass), R. Kubelik (cnd), Bavarian RSO, Bavarian Radio Chorus [I] Eurodisc 3-▲ 7798-2 [DDD]
Mozart, W.A.:Requiem, w. A. M. Blasi (sop), M. Lipovšek (mez), U. Heilmann (ten), C. Davis (cnd), Bavarian RSO, Bavarian Radio Chorus [L] RCA Red Seal ▲ 09026-60599-2 [DDD] ■ 09026-60599-4 (CrO2) □ 09026-60599-5
Puccini, G.:Turandot, w. E. Marton (sop—Turandot), M. Price (sop—Liù), B. Heppner (ten—Calaf), J.-H. Rootering (bass—Timur), R. Abbado (cnd), Munich RSO RCA Red Seal 2-▲ 09026-60898-2
Schumann, R.:Liederkreis, Op. 24, w. H. Lechler (pno) [G] Calig ▲ CAL 50892 [DDD]
Schumann, R.:Songs, w. H. Lechler (pno)—11 songs (Op. 89, Nos. 1-5 & Op. 98a, Nos. 3-6,8 & 9) [G] Calig ▲ CAL 50892 [DDD]
Strauss, R.:Songs, w. Hermann Lechler (pno)—18 songs (Opp. 10/1-5 & 8; 21/3; 27/1-4; 29/1-3; 32/1 & 2; 36/2; 47/5; 56/3) [G] Calig ▲ CAL 50863 [DDD]
Stravinsky, I.:Oedipus Rex, w. F. Quivar (mez), P. Langridge (ten), D. Kaasch (ten), J. Morris, J. Bastin (bass), J. Levine (cnd), Chicago SO, Chicago Sym Chorus Deutsche Grammophon ▲ 435872-2
Verdi, G.:Luisa Miller (sels), w. A. Millo (sop), W. White (mez), F. Quivar (cta), P. Domingo (ten), V. Chernov (bar), P. Plishka (bass), J. Levine (cnd), Metropolitan Opera Orch, New York Metropolitan Opera Chorus *(rec New York, May 2-18, 1991)* Sony Classical ("Opera Highlights" series) ▲ SMK 53508 [DDD]

Rootering, Jan-Hendrik (bass) (cont.)

Wagner, R.:Lohengrin, w. Sharon Sweet (sop—Elsa), Eva Marton (sop—Ortrud), Ben Heppner (ten—Lohengrin), Anton Rosner (ten—Nobleman), Heinrich Weber (ten—Nobleman), Jan-Hendrik Rootering (bar—Heinrich der Vögler), Sergei Leiferkus (bar—Friedrich von Telramund), Bryn Terfel (b-bar—King's Herald), Barbara Fleckenstein (sgr—Page), Atsuko Suzuki (sgr—Page), Gisela Ulmann (sgr—Page), Marion Rambausek (sgr—Page), Dankwart Siegele (sgr—Nobleman), Jürgen Weiss (sgr—Nobleman), C. Davis (cnd), Bavarian SO, Bavarian State Opera Chorus, Bavarian Radio Chorus *(rec Residenz Herkulesaal, Munich, May 14–28, 1994)* RCA Red Seal 3-▲ 09026-62646-2 [DDD]

Wagner, R.:Lohengrin (sels), w. Eva Marton (sop—Ortrud), Sharon Sweet (sop—Elsa von Brabant), Barbara Fleckenstein (sgr—Page), Marion Rambausek (sgr—Page), Atsuko Suzuki (sgr—Page), Gisela Ulmann (sgr—Page), Ben Heppner (ten—Lohengrin), Anton Rosner (ten—Nobleman), Heinrich Weber (ten—Nobleman), Sergei Leiferkus (bar—Friedrich von Telramund), Bryn Terfel (b-bar—King's Herald), Jan-Hendrik Rootering (bass—Henry the Fowler), Dankwart Siegele (sgr—Nobleman), Jürgen Weiss (sgr—Nobleman), C. Davis (cnd), Bavarian RSO, Michael Gläser (cnd), Udo Mehrpohl (cnd), Bavarian Radio Chorus, Bavarian State Opera Chorus—Seht! Seht! [from Act 1, Scene 2]; Nun sei bedankt, mein lieber Schwan!; Wenn ich im Kampfe für dich siege; Welch holde Wunder muss ich sehen?; Nun höret mich und achtet wohl; Durch Gottes Sieg ist jetzt dein Leben mein [all from Act 1, Scene 3]; Treulich geführt ziehet dahin [from Act 3, Scene 1]; Wie hehr erkenn' ich unsrer Liebe Wesen!; Höchstes Vertrau'n hast du mir schon zu danken; Weh' nun ist all' unser Glück dahin! [all from Act 3, Scene 2]; In fernem Land, unnahbar euren Schritten [from Act 3, Scene 3] *(rec Munich, Mar 14–28, 1994)* RCA Red Seal ▲ 09026-68239-2 [DDD]

Wagner, R.:Parsifal, w. J. Norman (sop), P. Domingo (ten), E. Wlaschiha (bar), K. Moll (bass), J. Morris (bass), J. Levine (cnd), Metropolitan Opera Orch, New York Metropolitan Opera Chorus Deutsche Grammophon 4-▲ 437501-2

Wagner, R.:Das Rheingold, w. Gabriele Fontana (sop—Woglinde), Nancy Gustafson (sop—Freia), Ildiko Komlosi (mez—Wellgunde), Hanna Schwarz (mez—Fricka), Elena Zaremba (mez—Erda), Margareta Hintermeier (cta—Flosshilde), Kim Begley (ten—Loge), Peter Schreier (ten—Mime), Thomas Sunnegardh (ten—Froh), Robert Hale (bass-bar—Wotan), Walter Fink (bass—Fafner), Franz-Josef Kapellmann (bass—Alberich), Jan-Hendrik Rootering (bass—Fasolt), Eike Wilm Schulte (bass—Donner), C. von Dohnányi (cnd), Cleveland Orch *(rec Severance Hall, Cleveland, Ohio, Dec 1993)* London 2-▲ 443690-2

Wagner, R.:Rienzi, der Letzte der Tribunen, w. Cheryl Studer (sop—Irene), René Kollo (ten—Rienzi), Friedrich Lenz (ten—Gesandte), Norbert Orth (ten—Baroncelli), Bodo Brinkmann (bar—Paolo Orsini), Keith Engen (bass—Cecco del Vecchio), Raimund Grumbach (bass—Gesandte), Jan-Hendrik Rootering (bass—Steffano Colonna), Carmen Anhorn (sgr—Ein Friedensbote), Karl Helm (sgr—Kardinal Orvieto), John Janssen (sgr—Adriano), Alfred Kuhn (sgr—Gesandte), Hans Wilbrink (sgr—Gesandte), W. Sawallisch (cnd), Bavarian State Opera Orch, Bavarian State Opera Chorus *(rec live, July 6, 1983)* Orfeo d'or 3-▲ 346953

Wolf, H.:Songs (misc), w. H. Lechler (pno)—Drei Gedichte von Michelangelo; 8 Eichendorff-Lieder; 8 Mörike-Lieder [G] Calig ▲ CAL 50870 [DDD]

Rooymans, Huib (nar)

Janssen, G.:Noach, w. Claron McFadden (sop—Noach's Wife), Lieuwe Visser (bass—Noach), L. Vis (cnd), New Artis Orch, Mondriaan Quartet, Ay-Kherel Ensemble *(rec Amsterdam, June 20–21, 1994)* Donemus 2-▲ CV 42/43

Rørholm, Marianne (mez)

Gade, N.W.:Kalanus, w. N. Gedda (ten), L. Mróz (bar), F. Rasmussen (cnd), Collegium Musicum, Canzone Choir Kontrapunkt ▲ 32072 [DDD]

Gade, N.W.:Korsfarerne, w. Westi (ten), Cold (bass), F. Rasmussen (cnd), Aarhus SO, Aarhus Sym Chorus [Da] BIS ▲ CD 465 [DDD]

Handel, G.F.:Giulio Cesare in Egitto, w. Barbara Schlick (sop), Jennifer Larmore (mez), Bernarda Fink (cta), Derek Lee Ragin (ct), Dominique Visse (ct), Oliver Lallouette (bass), Furio Zanasi (bass), R. Jacobs (cnd), Concerto Cologne [period instrs] Harmonia Mundi France 3-▲ HMC 901385/87

Handel, G.F.:Giulio Cesare in Egitto (sels), w. Barbara Schlick (sop), Jennifer Larmore (mez), Bernarda Fink (cta), Derek Lee Ragin (ct), R. Jacobs (cnd), Concerto Cologne Harmonia Mundi France ▲ HMC 901458

Norby, E.:Songs, w. P. Erős (cnd), Aalborg SO—Rilke Lieder Point ▲ PCD 5083 [ADD]

Sibelius, J.:Kullervo, w. J. Hynninen (bar), E.-P. Salonen (cnd), Los Angeles PO, Helsinki Univ Chorus [Fin] Sony Classical ▲ SK 52563

Rosa, Nora de (sop)

Arias, w. Arturo Basile (cnd) *(rec live, 1953 & 1955)* Standing Room Only ▲ SRO 827-1

Puccini, G.:Il tabarro, w. N. De Rosa (sop—Giorgietta), S. Puma (ten—Luigi), E. Bastianini (bar—Michèle), M. Cordone (cnd), *(orch & chorus unknown)* [I] *(rec live, Hamburg Radio 1954)* Standing Room Only ▲ SRO 827-1

Rosa, Rinaldo (sgr)

Mascagni, P.:Isabeau (sels), w. Marcella Pobbe (sop), Pier Miranda Ferraro (ten), San Remo SO Cetra Classic ▲ CDON 44

Rosales, Rachel (sop)

Dvorak, C.:Amandla Mandela!, w. L. Vardaman (sop), M. Lifchitz (cnd), North/South Consonance Ensemble North/South Recordings ▲ NS 1004 [DDD]

Greenberg, L.:This Man Was Your Brother, w. L. Vardaman (sop), M. Lifchitz (cnd), North/South Consonance Ensemble North/South Recordings ▲ NS 1004 [DDD]

Greenberg, L.:La Vida Es Sueño, w. L. Vardaman (sop), M. Lifchitz (cnd), North/South Consonance Ensemble North/South Recordings ▲ NS 1004 [DDD]

Lennon, J.A.:Translations, w. D. Krakauer (cl), M. Wu (vn), J. Sachs (pno) CRI ▲ CD 599 [ADD/DDD]

Lifchitz, M.:Of Bondage & Freedom, w. L. Vardaman (sop), M. Lifchitz (cnd), North/South Consonance Ensemble North/South Recordings ▲ NS 1004 [DDD]

Pleskow, R.:Arabesques, w. L. Vardaman (sop), M. Lifchitz (cnd), North/South Consonance Ensemble North/South Recordings ▲ NS 1004 [DDD]

Surinach, C.:Cantares, w. P. Zinger (cnd), Bronx Arts Ensemble [E] New World ▲ 80505-2

Surinach, C.:Songs of Spain, w. P. Zinger (cnd), Bronx Arts Ensemble New World ▲ 80505-2

Zyman, S.:Solamente Sola Antilles/New Directions ▲ 91055-2 ■ 91055-4

Rosat, Karine (sop)

Zbinden, J.-F.:Impératifs, w. C. Miveloz (alt), Swiss-Italian Radio Chorus [F] Grammont ▲ CTSP 3-2 [ADD]

Röschmann, Dorothea (sop)

Bach, J.S.:Cant 173a, w. H. Saint-Gelais (ten), K. McMillan (bar), B. Labadie (cnd), Les Violons du Roy *(rec Quebec City, Jan 1994)* Dorian ▲ DOR 90199 [DDD]

Bach, J.S.:Cant 204, w. B. Labadie (cnd), Les Violons du Roy *(rec Saint-Isidore Church, Québec, May 1994)* Dorian ▲ DOR 90207 [DDD]

Bach, J.S.:Cant 210, w. B. Labadie (cnd), Les Violons du Roy *(rec Saint-Isidore Church, Québec, May 1994)* Dorian ▲ DOR 90207 [DDD]

Bach, J.S.:Cant 211, "Coffee Cant", w. H. Saint-Gelais (ten), K. McMillan (bar), B. Labadie (cnd), Les Violons du Roy *(rec Quebec City, Jan 1994)* Dorian ▲ DOR 90199 [DDD]

Bach, J.S.:Cant 212, "Peasant Cant", w. H. Saint-Gelais (ten), K. McMillan (bar), B. Labadie (cnd), Les Violons du Roy *(rec Quebec City, Jan 1994)* Dorian ▲ DOR 90199 [DDD]

Dvořák, A.:Mass, w. I. Danz (alt), C. Elsner (ten), J. Mannov (bass), E. Krapp (org), W. Schäfer (cnd), Frankfurt Kantorei Ars Musici ▲ AM 1083-2 [DDD]

Handel, G.F.:Giustino, w. Juliana Gondek (sop), Dawn Kotoski (sop), Jennifer Lane (mez), Michael Chance (alt), Drew Minter (alt), Mark Padmore (ten), Dean Ely (sgr), N. McGegan (cnd), Freiburg Baroque Orch Harmonia Mundi France 3-▲ HMU 907130.32

Haydn, J.:Mass 5, "Missa Sancti Josephi", "Grosse Orgelmesse", w. Bernarda Fink (cta), Helmut Wildhaber (ten), Klaus Mertens (bar), M. Haselböck (cnd), Vienna Academy, Hugo Distler Choir Novalis ▲ 150095 [DDD]

Haydn, J.:Mass 7, "Kleine Orgelmesse", w. Bernarda Fink (cta), Helmut Wildhaber (ten), Klaus Mertens (bar), M. Haselböck (cnd), Vienna Academy, Hugo Distler Choir Novalis ▲ 150095 [DDD]

Haydn, J.:Salve regina, H.XXIIIb/2, w. Bernarda Fink (cta), Helmut Wildhaber (ten), Klaus Mertens (bar), M. Haselböck (cnd), Vienna Academy, Hugo Distler Choir Novalis ▲ 150095 [DDD]

Röschmann, Dorothea (sop) (cont.)

Jommelli, N.:Didone abbandonata, w. Mechthild Bach (mez), Martina Borst (mez), William Kendall (ct), Daniel Taylor (ct), Arno Raunig (ten), F. Bernius (cnd), Stuttgart CO—Didone; Enea; Iarba; Selene; Araspe; Osmida Orfeo 3-▲ CD 381953 [DDD]

Pergolesi, G.B.:Stabat mater, w. C. Robbin (mez), B. Labadie (cnd), Les Violons du Roy Dorian ▲ DOR 90196 [DDD]

Vivaldi, A.:Motets, w. C. Robbin (mez), B. Labadie (cnd), Les Violons du Roy Dorian ▲ DOR 90196 [DDD]

Rosci, Giuseppe (sgr)

Leoncavallo, R.:Pagliacci, w. Josefina Huguet (sop—Nedda), Antonio Paoli (ten), Gaetano Pini-Corsi (ten—Beppe), Ernesto Badini (bar—Silvio), Francesco Cigada (bar—Tonio), Giuseppe Rosci (sgr—Un contadino), C. Sabajno (cnd), La Scala Orch, La Scala Chorus *(rec 1907)* Bongiovanni ▲ GB 1120-2 [ADD]

Rose, Elisabeth (sop)

Dvořák, A.:Requiem Mass, w. Gertraud Prenzlow (cta), Peter Schreier (ten), Theo Adam (bass), K. Ančerl (cnd), Berlin RSO, Berlin Radio Chorus Forlane 2-▲ FRL 16636 [AAD]

Rose, Peter (bass)

Puccini, G.:Tosca, w. Jane Eaglen (sop—Floria Tosca), Charbel Michael (alt—Shepherd Boy), John Daszak (ten—Spoletta), Dennis O'Neill (ten—Mario Cavaradossi), Christopher Booth-Jones (bar—Sciarrone), Ashley Holland (bar—Jailor), Gregory Yurisich (bar—Baron Scarpia), Peter Rose (bass—Cesare Angelotti), Andrew Shore (bass—Sacristan), D. Parry (cnd), Philharmonia Orch, Geoffrey Mitchell Choir, Peter Kay Children's Chorus Chandos ("Opera in English" series) 2-▲ CHAN 3000

Stockhausen, K.:Stimmung, w. K. Flowers (sop), P. Walmsley-Clark (sop), Long (sgr), R. Covey-Crump (ten), Hillier (sgr) Hyperion ▲ CDA 66115

Rosen, Rudolf (bass)

Mozart, W.A.:Missa Solemnis, w. Christa Goetze (sop), Anna Schaffner (alt), Barnhard Gärtner (ten), Philippe Laubscher (org), F. Pantillon (cnd), Bieler SO, Pro Arte Chorale, Bern Vocal Ensemble Gallo ▲ CD 893 [DDD]

Rosen, Rudolf (nar)

Pantillon, F.:Bethlehem, w. Christa Goetze (sop), Philippe Laubscher (org), F. Pantillon (cnd), Bieler SO, Pro Arte Chorale, Bern Vocal Ensemble Gallo ▲ CD 893 [DDD]

Rosenberg, Berle Sanford (ten)

Live from Budapest, w. Budapest Concert Orch [cnd:Janos Acs] *(rec live in concert, 8/24/90)* Olympia ▲ OLY 370 [DDD]

O Sole Mio:Neapolitan Songs, w. Nemiga Wind Virtuosi [cnd:Arkady Berin, Lev Muranov] Olympia ▲ OLY 371 [DDD]

Rosenblatt, Joseph (cant)

Echoes of the Temple:Cantors in Prayer & Folksong, w. Gershon Sirota (cant), Pierre Pinchik (cant), Samuel Vigoda (cant), Arthur Tracy (cant), et al. *(rec 1914–36)* Pearl ▲ PEA 9126 [ADD]

Rosenblüth, Leo (bar)

Pergament, M.:Kol Nidre, w. M. Thyresson (org), E. Ericson (cnd), Stockholm Royal Conservatory Chamber Choir BIS ▲ CD 1 [AAD]

Rosenblüth, Leo (cant)

Ephros, G.:The Priestly Benediction, w. A. Vitolius (org) BIS ▲ CD 1 [AAD]

Rosenblüth, L.:Jewish Liturgical Music, w. G. von Bahr (fl), A. Vitolius (org), M. Thyresson (org), E. Ericson (cnd), Stockholm Royal Conservatory Chamber Choir—Psalms 93 & 155, plus 5 settings for High Holidays, Rosh Hashanah, Sabbath & Yom Kippur BIS ▲ CD 1 [AAD]

Rosenshein, Neil (ten)

Bernstein, L.:Songfest, w. C. Dale (sop), R. Elias (mez), N. Williams (mez), J. Reardon (bar), D. Gramm (b-bar), L. Bernstein (cnd), National SO Washington D.C. [E] Deutsche Grammophon ▲ 415965-2 [ADD]

Haydn, J.:Die Schöpfung, w. Lynn Dawson (sop), John Cheek (bass), J. Revzen (cnd), St. Paul CO, Minnesota Chorale Albany 2-▲ AR 005-6-2

Loeffler, C.M.:Irish Fants, w. J. Nelson (cnd), Indianapolis SO [E] New World ▲ NW 332-2 [DDD]

Tchaikovsky, P.:Eugene Onegin, w. K. Te Kanawa (sop—Tatiana), P. Bardon (mez—Olga), N. Rosenshein (ten—Lensky), T. Hampson (b-bar—Eugene Onegin), J. Connell (bass—Prince Gremin), C. Mackerras (cnd), Welsh National Opera Orch, Welsh National Opera Chorus [E] EMI Classics ▲ CDCB 55004

Rosing, Vladimir (ten)

Oda Slobodskaya & Vladimir Rosing in Russian Art Song, w. Oda Slobodskaya (sop) Pearl ▲ PEA 9021 [AAD]

Roslak, Roxolana (sop)

Hindemith, P.:Das Marienleben, w. Lois Marshall (sop), Glenn Gould (pno) Sony Classical ("Glen Gould Edition" series) 2-▲ SM2K 52674

Somers, H.:Kyrie, w. Susan Cooper (mez), Robert Missen (ten), Nelson Lohnes (bass), Timothy Cadan (bass), E. Iseler (cnd), *(orch unknown)*, Elmer Iseler Singers *(rec Flora McRae Eaton Memorial Auditorium & St. Anne's Anglican Church, Toronto)* Centrediscs ▲ CMC 5495 [DDD]

Strauss, R.:4 Last Songs, w. Lois Marshall (sop), Glenn Gould (pno)—Beim Schlafengehen Sony Classical ("Glen Gould Edition" series) 2-▲ SM2K 52674

Strauss, R.:Songs, w. Lois Marshall (sop), Glenn Gould (pno)—Songs for Orphelia, Op. 67/1-3 Sony Classical ("Glen Gould Edition" series) 2-▲ SM2K 52674

Rosner, Anton (ten)

Biber, H. von:Vesperae longiores ac breviores una cum litaniis Laurentanis, w. Kym Amps (sop), Christopher Robson (alt), Albert Hartinger (bass), H. Arman (cnd), Salzburg Baroque Ensemble, Innsbruck Woodwind Circle, Salzburg Bach Choir, Salzburg St. Benedict College Schola Ars Musici ("Essence" series) ▲ AME 3022-2 [DDD]

Donizetti, G.:Anna Bolena (sels), w. Carol Vaness (sop), Melinda Paulsen (cta), Dennis O'Neill (ten), Ambrogio Riva (bass), R. Abbado (cnd), Munich RSO, Bavarian Radio Chorus—Final Scene & Aria [from Act II] *(rec Studio 1, Bavaria, Apr 13–17, 1993)* RCA Red Seal ▲ 09026-61828-2 [DDD]

Verdi, G.:Il trovatore (sels), w. Carol Vaness (sop), Dennis O'Neill (ten), R. Abbado (cnd), Munich RSO, Bavarian Radio Chorus—Scene, Aria & Miserere [from Act IV] *(rec Studio 1, Munich, Apr 13–17, 1993)* RCA Red Seal ▲ 09026-61828-2 [DDD]

Wagner, R.:Lohengrin, w. Sharon Sweet (sop—Elsa), Eva Marton (sop—Ortrud), Ben Heppner (ten—Lohengrin), Anton Rosner (ten—Nobleman), Heinrich Weber (ten—Nobleman), Jan-Hendrik Rootering (bar—Heinrich der Vögler), Sergei Leiferkus (bar—Friedrich von Telramund), Bryn Terfel (b-bar—King's Herald), Barbara Fleckenstein (sgr—Page), Atsuko Suzuki (sgr—Page), Gisela Ulmann (sgr—Page), Marion Rambausek (sgr—Page), Dankwart Siegele (sgr—Nobleman), Jürgen Weiss (sgr—Nobleman), C. Davis (cnd), Bavarian SO, Bavarian State Opera Chorus, Bavarian Radio Chorus *(rec Residenz Herkulesaal, Munich, May 14–28, 1994)* RCA Red Seal 3-▲ 09026-62646-2 [DDD]

Wagner, R.:Lohengrin (sels), w. Eva Marton (sop—Ortrud), Sharon Sweet (sop—Elsa von Brabant), Barbara Fleckenstein (sgr—Page), Marion Rambausek (sgr—Page), Atsuko Suzuki (sgr—Page), Gisela Ulmann (sgr—Page), Ben Heppner (ten—Lohengrin), Anton Rosner (ten—Nobleman), Heinrich Weber (ten—Nobleman), Sergei Leiferkus (bar—Friedrich von Telramund), Bryn Terfel (b-bar—King's Herald), Jan-Hendrik Rootering (bass—Henry the Fowler), Dankwart Siegele (sgr—Nobleman), Jürgen Weiss (sgr—Nobleman), C. Davis (cnd), Bavarian RSO, Michael Gläser (cnd), Udo Mehrpohl (cnd), Bavarian Radio Chorus, Bavarian State Opera Chorus—Seht! Seht! [from Act 1, Scene 2]; Nun sei bedankt, mein lieber Schwan!; Wenn ich im Kampfe für dich siege; Welch holde Wunder muss ich sehen?; Nun höret mich und achtet wohl; Durch Gottes Sieg ist jetzt dein Leben mein [all from Act 1, Scene 3]; Treulich geführt ziehet dahin [from Act 3, Scene 1]; Wie hehr erkenn' ich unsrer Liebe Wesen!; Höchstes Vertrau'n hast du mir schon zu danken; Weh' nun ist all' unser Glück dahin! [all from Act 3, Scene 2]; In fernem Land, unnahbar euren Schritten [from Act 3, Scene 3] *(rec Munich, Mar 14–28, 1994)* RCA Red Seal ▲ 09026-68239-2 [DDD]

Rosner, Hilde (mez)
Wagner, R.:Der Ring des Nibelungen, w. Liselotte Becker-Egner (sop—Woglinde/Ortlinde/Wellgunde), Angelika Berger (sop—Wellgunde/Waltraute), Siw Ericsdotter (sop—Norn 3), Heidemaria Ferch (sop—Freia/Gerhilde), Bella Jasper (sop—Helmwige/Waldvogel/Woglinde), Ditha Sommer (sop—Sieglinde/Gutrune), Ursula Boese (mez—Erda), Ruth Hesse (mez—Fricka), Nadezda Kniplová (mez—Brünnhilde), Margit Kobeck (mez—Schwertleite/Norn 2), Hilde Rosner (mez—Flosshilde/Siegrunde), Erica Schubert (mez—Grimgerde/Flosshilde), Ingrid Göritz (cta—Rossweisse/Norn 1), Herbert Doussant (ten—Froh), Herold Kraus (ten—Mime), Gerald McKee (ten—Siegmund/Siegfried), Fritz Uhl (ten—Loge), Rudolf Knoll (bar—Gunther/Donner), Rolf Polke (bass-bar—Wotan/Wanderer), Rolf Kühne (bass—Alberich), Takao Okamura (bass—Fafner), Otto von Rohr (bass—Hagen/Fasolt/Hunding), H. Swarowsky (cnd), Czech PO, Prague National Theater Orch *(rec June 3 & 5, July 26–31, A)* Weltbild Classics 14-▲ 703769 [ADD]

Rösner, Willy (sgr)
Orff, C.:Der Mond—Ein kleines Welttheater, w. Karl Erb (nar), Paul Kuen (ten—Lad 3), Josef Knapp (bar—Lad 2), Benno Kusche (bar—Lad 1), Georg Hann (bass—St. Peter), Georg Wieter (bass—Lad 4), Rudolf Wünzer (bass—The Farmer), Karl Hanft (sgr—Innkeeper), Willy Rösner (sgr—The Major), R. Alberth (cnd), Bavarian RSO, Bavarian Radio Chorus *(rec Studio 1, Bavarian Radio, Jan. 19–20, 1950)* Calig ▲ CAL 50948 (m) [ADD]

Ross, Elise (sop)
Weill, K.:The Seven Deadly Sins, w. A. R. Johnson (ten), I. Caley (ten), M. Rippon (bass), J. Tomlinson (bass), S. Rattle (cnd), City of Birmingham SO EMI Classics ▲ CDM 64739

Ross, Gill (sop)
Purcell, H.:King Arthur, w. Gillian Fisher (sop), E. Priday (sop), J. Smith (sop), A. Stafford (alt), P. Elliot (ten), S. Varcoe (bar), J.E. Gardiner (cnd), English Baroque Soloists, Monteverdi Choir London Erato ("Gardiner Purcell Collection" series) 2-▲ 96552-2
Purcell, H.:King Arthur, w. J. Smith (sop), G. Fisher (sop), E. Priday (sop), A. Stafford (alt), P. Elliott (ten), S. Varcoe (bar), J.E. Gardiner (cnd), English Baroque Soloists, Monteverdi Choir London Erato 2-▲ 2292-45211-2 ZA
Purcell, H.:King Arthur (sels), w. J. Smith (sop), G. Fisher (sop), E. Priday (sop), J. E. Gardiner (cnd), English Baroque Soloists, Monteverdi Choir Erato ▲ 45919-2

Rosser, S. (sgr)
Luening, O.:No Jerusalem But This, w. K. Sullivan (sop), Jacqueline Pierce (sop), Paul Sperry (ten), M. Moliterno (bar), P. Wilder (sgr), A. Goodman (cnd), Music Project CO, Goodman Chamber Choir [E] *(rec 6/6/90)* CRI ▲ CD 600 [DDD]

Rossetti, Berta (sgr)
Cavalieri, E. de:Rappresentatione di Anima et di Corpo, w. G. Bertagnolli (sop), C. Cavina (alt), G. Maletto (ten), R. Mattei (bar), A. Abete (sgr), M. Longhini (cnd), Verona Istitutioni Harmoniche Stradivarius ▲ STR 33339 [DDD]

Rossi, Alessandra (sop)
Rossini, G.:La cambiale di matrimonio, w. M. Comencini (ten), B. de Simone (bar), B. Praticò (bar), M. Viotti (cnd), English CO [I] Claves 8-▲ CD 9200 [DDD]
Rossini, G.:La cambiale di matrimonio, w. Maurizio Comencini (ten), Bruno Praticò (bar), Bruno De Simone (bar), Valeria Baiano (bass), Francesco Facini (bass), M. Viotti (cnd), English CO Claves ▲ 50-9101
Scarlatti, D.:Cants, w. R. Girolami (bass), F. Maestri (cnd), *(ensemble unknown)*—"Amenissimi prati," for Bass & Instrumental Ensemble; "Se fedele tu m'adori," for Soprano & Ensemble [I] *(rec live, 1988)* Bongiovanni ▲ GB 2026 [DDD]

Rossi, M. (bar)
Leoncavallo, R.:Pagliacci, w. C. Gavazzi (sop—Nedda), C. Bergonzi (ten—Canio), S. Di Tommaso (ten—Beppe), C. Tagliabue (bar—Tonio), M. Rossi (bar—Silvio), A. Simonetto (cnd), Turin RAI SO, Turin RAI Chorus *(rec Turin, 1951)* Cetra Classic 2-▲ CDO 27 [ADD]

Rossi-Lemeni, Nicola (bass)
Bellini, V.:Norma, w. M. Callas (sop), E. Stignani (mez), M. Filippeschi (ten), T. Serafin (cnd), La Scala Orch, La Scala Chorus [I] EMI Classics 3-▲ CDC 47303 (m)
Bellini, V.:I Puritani, w. M. Callas (sop), G. di Stefano (ten), R. Panerai (bar), T. Serafin (cnd), La Scala Orch, La Scala Chorus [I] EMI Classics 2-▲ CDCB 47308 (m) [ADD]
Donizetti, G.:Anna Bolena, w. M. Callas (sop—Anna Bolena), G. Simionato (mez—Giovanna), G. Raimondi (ten—Percy), N. Rossi-Lemeni (bass—King), G. Gavazzeni (cnd), La Scala Orch, La Scala Chorus [I] *(rec live, Milan 4/14/57)* Verona 2-▲ 27090/91
Donizetti, G.:Anna Bolena, w. M. Callas (sop—Anna Bolena), G. Simionato (mez—Giovanna Seymour), N. Rossi-Lemeni (bass—Enrico VIII), G. Gavazzeni (cnd), Milan RAI SO, Milan RAI Chorus *(rec May 14, 1957)* EMI Classics ▲ CDMB 64941
Mascagni, P.:Il piccolo Marat, w. Virginia Zeani (sop), Clara Betner (mez), Umberto Borso (ten), O. de Fabritiis (cnd), Teatro La Gran Guardia Orch, Teatro La Gran Guardia Chorus [I] *(rec live, 10/26/61)* Fonè 2-▲ 88 F 17-37 [ADD]
Rossini, G.:Il barbiere di Siviglia, w. D. Gatta (sop), C. Valletti (ten), G. Bechi (bar), V. de Sabata (cnd), La Scala Orch, La Scala Chorus *(rec 1952)* Memories 2-▲ MEM 4525 [AAD]
Spontini, G.:La vestale, w. M. Callas (sop), F. Corelli (ten), E. Sordello (bar), V. Tatozzi (bar), N. Zaccaria (bass), A. Votto (cnd), La Scala Orch, La Scala Chorus Great Opera Performances ▲ GOP 741
Verdi, G.:Ernani, w. Margherita Roberti (sop), Anna di Stasio (mez), Athos Cesarini (ten), Mario del Monaco (ten), Ettore Bastianini (bar), Mario Rinaudo (bass), F. Previtali (cnd), Naples Teatro San Carlo Orch, Naples Teatro San Carlo Chorus Melodram 2-▲ CDM 270100
Verdi, G.:I vespri siciliani, w. L. Gencer (sop), G. Limarilli (ten), G. Guelfi (bar), G. Gavazzeni (cnd), Rome Opera Orch, Rome Opera Chorus [I] *(rec live, Rome 1964)* Melodram 2-▲ MEL 27037 [ADD]
Verdi, G.:I vespri siciliani, w. Leyla Gencer (sop), Giangiacomo Guelfi (bar), Gastone Limarilli (sgr), G. Gavazzeni (cnd), Rome Opera Orch, Rome Opera Chorus *(rec Dec 5, 1964)* Pantheon 2-▲ PHE 6770
Virginia Zeani, Soprano Arias, w. Virginia Zeani (sop), Turin Radio Orch [cnd:Fulvio Vernizzi] Melodram 2-▲ CDM 27013 (m) [AAD]

Rossini, Licia (sgr)
Verdi, G.:Ernani, w. Caterina Mancini (sop), Vittorio Pandano (ten), Gino Penno (ten), Giuseppe Taddei (bar), Giacomo Vaghi (bar), Ezio Achilli (sgr), F. Previtali (cnd), Rome RAI SO, Rome RAI Chorus Cetra Classic 2-▲ CDON 39 [ADD]

Rössl-Majdan, Hilde (alt)
Beethoven, L. van:Sym 9, "Choral Sym", w. G. Janowitz (sop), W. Kmentt (ten), W. Berry (bass), H. von Karajan (cnd), Berlin PO, Vienna Singverein Deutsche Grammophon ("The Originals" series) ▲ 447401-2
Haydn, J.:Mass 10, "Kriegsmesse", "Paukenmesse", w. Netania Davrath (sop), Anton Dermota (ten), W. Bery (bass), Anton Heiller (org), R. Harand (vc), M. Wöldike (cnd), Vienna State Opera Orch, Vienna State Opera Chorus *(rec May 14–16, 1960)* Vanguard Classics ("The Bach Guild" series) ▲ OVC 2518 [ADD]
Mahler, G.:Sym 2, w. Galina Vishnevskaya (sop), O. Klemperer (cnd), Vienna PO, Vienna Phil Chorus Music & Arts ▲ CD 881 [ADD]

Rössl-Majdan, Hilde (cta)
Strauss (II), Joh.:Der Zigeunerbaron, w. Emmy Loose (sop—Arsena), Gerda Scheyrer (sop—Saffi), Elisabeth Fez (cta—Mirabella), Hilde Rössl-Majdan (cta—Czipra), Waldemar Kmentt (ten—Barinkay), Paul Spani (ten—Ottokar), Erich Kunz (bar—Homonay), Kurt Preger (bar—Zsupan), Eberhard Wächter (bass—Carnero), A. Paulik (cnd), Vienna State Opera Orch, Vienna State Opera Chorus *(rec Brahmssaal, Vienna, Austria, June 1956)* Vanguard Classics 2-▲ OVC 8082/83 [ADD]

Rössl-Majdan, Hilde (mez)
Bach, J.S.:Magnificat, BWV 243, w. M. Coertse (sop), M. Sjöstedt (sop), A. Dermota (ten), F. Guthrie (bass), F. Prohaska (cnd), Vienna State Opera Orch, Vienna State Opera Chorus [L] *(rec June 1957)* Vanguard Classics ("The Bach Guild" series) ▲ OVC 2010 [ADD]
Cornelius, P.:Der Barbier von Bagdad, w. S. Jurinac (sop), E. Majkut (ten), R. Schock (ten), A. Poell (bass-bar), G. Frick (bass), H. Hollreiser (cnd), Austrian RSO, Austrian Radio Chorus *(rec live Vienna 1952)* Melodram 2-▲ MEL 27050 (m) [AAD]

Rössl-Majdan, Hilde (mez) (cont.)
Cornelius, P.:Der Barbier von Bagdad, w. S. Jurinac (sop), E. Majkut (ten), R. Schock (ten), A. Poell (bass-bar), G. Frick (bass), H. Hollreiser (cnd), Austrian RSO, Austrian Radio Chorus [G] *(rec live Vienna, 1952)* Verona 2-▲ 27050/51 (m) [AA
Mahler, G.:Sym 2, w. E. Schwarzkopf (sop), O. Klemperer (cnd), Philharmonia Orch, Philharmonia Chorus [G] EMI Classics ("Studio" series) ▲ CDM 69662 [ADD]
Mozart, W.A.:Requiem, w. W. Lipp (sop), A. Dermota (ten), W. Berry (bass), H. von Karajan (cnd), Berlin PO, Vienna Singverein [L] *(rec 1961)* Deutsche Grammophon ("Resonance" series) ▲ 429160-2 [ADD] ■ 429160-4
Mozart, W.A.:Requiem, w. L. Price (sop), F. Wunderlich (ten), W. Berry (bass), H. von Karajan (cnd), Vienna PO, Vienna Singverein [L] *(rec live, Salzburg Festival, Aug. 24, 1960)* Melodram ▲ MEL 18003

Rost, Andrea (sop)
Mahler, G.:Sym 8, w. Sylvia McNair (sop), Cheryl Studer (sop), Anne Sofie von Otter (mez), Rosemarie Lang (cta), Peter Seiffert (ten), Bryn Terfel (bar), Jan-Hendrik Rootering (bass), C. Abbado (cnd), Berlin PO, Berlin Radio Chorus, Prague Phil Chorus, Tölz Boys' Choir Deutsche Grammophon ("4D Audio" series) 2-▲ 445843-2
Verdi, G.:Rigoletto, w. Andrea Rost (sop—Gilda), Mariana Pentcheva (cta—Maddalena), Roberto Alagna (ten—Il Duca di Mantova), Renato Bruson (bar—Rigoletto), Dmitri Kavrakos (bass—Sparafucile), R. Muti (cnd), La Scala Orch, La Scala Chorus Sony Classical 2-▲ S2K 66314
Verdi, G.:Rigoletto (sels), w. Roberto Alagna (ten), Renato Bruson (bar), R. Muti (cnd), La Scala Orch Sony Classical ▲ SK 61966

Roswaenge, Helge (ten)
Beethoven, L. van:Fidelio (sels), w. *(other artists unknown)*—Gott, welch Dunkel hier *(rec 1938)* Minerva ▲ MN A35 (m) [ADD]
Cornelius, P.:Der Barbier von Bagdad (sels), w. *(other artists unknown)*—Ach das Lied hab ich getragen; O holdes Bild in Engelsschöne [w. Ilonka Rosvaenge (sop)] *(rec 1939)* Minerva ▲ MN A35 (m) [ADD]
The Early Recordings (1927–1929) Preiser 2-▲ PRE 89201 (m) [AAD]
Flotow, F. von:Martha (sels), w. *(other artists unknown)*—Mag der Himmel euch vergeben [w. Hedwig von Debicka (sop), Emmi Leisner (alt), Rudolf Watzke (bass)]; Letzte Rose; Ach so fromm *(rec 1928 & 1935)* Minerva ▲ MN A35 (m) [ADD]
Gounod, C.:Faust, w. H. Singstreu (sop—Margarete), H. Rosvaenge (ten—Faust), M. Bohnen (bass—Mephistopheles), H. Steiner (cnd), Berlin RSO, Berlin Radio Chorus *(rec 1938)* Myto 2-▲ MCD 94196
Gounod, C.:Faust (sels), w. Luise Helletsgruber (sop—Marguerite), Helge Roswaenge (ten—Faust), Joel Berglund (ten—Mephistopheles), J. Krips (cnd), Vienna State Opera Orch *(rec Vienna, Nov. 10, 1936)* Koch Schwann 2-▲ SCH 314622 [ADD]
Great Love Duets, w. Erna Berger (sop), Miliza Korjus (sop), Lotte Lehmann (sop), Frida Leider (sop), Charles Kullman (ten), Lauritz Melchior (ten), Tito Schipa (ten), Richard Tauber (ten), et al. Pearl ▲ PEA 9217
Helge Rosvaenge Sings Light Music *(rec 1927–37)* Preiser 2-▲ PRE CD 89225
Helge Roswaenge, w. Milizia Korjus (sop), Tiana Lemnitz (sop), Hans Reinmar (bar), Heinrich Schlusnus (bar), et al. Preiser 2-▲ PRE 89209 [AAD]
Helge Roswaenge, Vol. 3:1937–43 Preiser 2-▲ PRE 89211 [ADD]
Leoncavallo, R.:Pagliacci (sels), w. Enrico Caruso (ten), Antonio Paoli (ten), Giovanni Zenatello (ten), Amedeo Bassi (ten), Hermann Jadlowker (ten), Fernand Ansseau (ten), Hipolito Lazaro (ten), Nino (Filippo) Piccaluga (ten), Mario Chamlee (ten), Giacomo Lauri-Volpi (ten), Miguel Fleta (ten), Giovanni Martinelli (ten), Aureliano Pertile (ten), Georges Thill (ten), Alessandro Valente (ten), Francesco Merli (ten), Lauritz Melchior (ten), Marcel Wittrisch (ten), Joseph Schmidt (ten), Beniamino Gigli (ten), Giuseppe Lugo (ten), Jussi Bjoerling (ten)—23 versions of the tenor aria "Vesti la giubba" *(rec 1907–1944)* Bongiovanni ▲ GB 1071 [ADD]
Mascagni, P.:Cavalleria rusticana (sels), w. Maria Jeritza (sop—Santuzza), Helge Roswaenge (ten—Turiddu), H. Reichenberger (cnd), Vienna State Opera Orch *(rec Vienna, Sept. 26, 1933)* Koch Schwann 2-▲ SCH 314622 [ADD]
Mozart, W.A.:Arias, w. Arleen Augér (sop), Kathleen Battle (sop), Irma Beilke (sop), Helena Braun (sop), Lisa Della Casa (sop), Maria Cebotari (sop), Ileana Cotrubas (sop), Helen Donath (sop), Mirella Freni (sop), Reri Grist (sop), Edita Gruberova (sop), Elisabeth Grümmer (sop), Hilde Güden (sop), Ingeborg Hallstein (sop), Luise Helletsgruber (sop), Gundula Janowitz (sop), Sena Jurinac (sop), Erika Köth (sop), Evelyn Lear (sop), Wilma Lipp (sop), Margaret Marshall (sop), Edith Mathis (sop), Jarmila Novotna (sop), Margherita Perras (sop), Lucia Popp (sop), Elisabeth Rethberg (sop), Anneliese Rothenberger (sop), Elisabeth Schumann (sop), Elisabeth Schwarzkopf (sop), Graziella Sciutti (sop), Irmgard Seefried (sop), Graziella Sciutti (sop), Julia Varady (sop), Agnes Baltsa (mez), Margit Bokor (mez), Brigitte Fassbaender (mez), Christa Ludwig (mez), Ann Murray (mez), Francisco Araiza (ten), Anton Dermota (ten), Rudolf Schock (ten), Peter Schreier (ten), Leopold Simoneau (ten), Eric Tappy (ten), Richard Tauber (ten), Gösta Winbergh (ten), Josef Witt (ten), Fritz Wunderlich (ten), Christian Boesch (bar), Willy Domgraf-Fassbaender (bar), Karl Dönch (bar), Dietrich Fischer-Dieskau (bar), Erich Kunz (bar), Eberhard Wächter (bar), Hans Hotter (b-bar), Paul Schöffler (b-bar), Cesare Siepi (b-bar), José Van Dam (b-bar), Walter Berry (bass), Geraint Evans (bass), Nicolai Ghiaurov (bass), Alexander Kipnis (bass), Richard Mayr (bass), Kurt Moll (bass), James Morris (bass), Ezio Pinza (bass), Martti Talvela (bass), Giorgio Tozzi (bass), Hans Duhan (sgr), Res Fischer (sgr), Marie Gerhart (sgr), *(various orchs & cnds)*—sels from Idomeneo, Die Entführung aus der Serail, Le nozze di Figaro, Don Giovanni, Così fan tutte, Die Zauberflöte & various arias Orfeo d'or ("Festspiel Dokumente" series) 5-▲ 408955
Mozart, W.A.:Entführung (sels), w. *(other artists unknown)*—Hier soll ich dich denn sehen *(rec 1937)* Minerva ▲ MN A35 (m) [ADD]
Mozart, W.A.:Songs, w. M. Callas (sop), E. Grümmer (sop), E. Schwarzkopf (sop), R. Scotto (sop), T. Lemnitz (sop), E. Berger (sop), S. Jurinac (sop), E. Schumann (sop), I. Souez (sop), E. Rethberg (sop), L. Lehmann (sop), N. Gedda (ten), J. McCormack (ten), H. Nash (ten), T. Gobbi (bar), G. Hüsch (bar), E. Kunz (bar), G. Frick (bass), E. Pinza (bass), A. Kipnis (bass) EMI Classics 4-▲ CDMD 63750
Mozart, W.A.:Zauberflöte, w. Jarmila Novotna (sop), Alexander Kipnis (bass), Julie Osvath (sgr), A. Toscanini (cnd), Vienna PO, Vienna State Opera Chorus Enterprise ("The 40's" series) 2-▲ ENT 321
Mozart, W.A.:Zauberflöte, w. D. Komarek (sop), J. Novotna (sop), J. Osvath (sop), W. Domgraf-Fassbaender (bar), A. Kipnis (bass), A. Toscanini (cnd), Vienna PO, Vienna Phil Chorus [G] *(rec live, Salzburg, July 30, 1937)* Melodram 3-▲ MEL 37040 (m) [AAD]
Mozart, W.A.:Zauberflöte, w. E. Berger (sop), T. Lemnitz (sop), I. Beilke (sop), G. Hüsch (bar), W. Strienz (bass), T. Beecham (cnd), Berlin PO, Vereinigung Favres Soloists [G] *(rec Nov. 1937 & Feb.–Mar. 193)* Nimbus ("Prima Voce" series) 2-▲ NI 7827/8 (m) [ADD]
Mozart, W.A.:Zauberflöte, w. T. Lemnitz (sop), E. Berger (sop), I. Beilke (sop), H. Tessmer (ten), G. Hüsch (bar), W. Strienz (bass), T. Beecham (cnd), Berlin PO, Favre Chorus [without dialog; G] *(rec 1937–38 for HMV)* EMI Classics ("Great Recordings of the Century" series) 2-▲ CDHB 61034 (m) [ADD]
Mozart, W.A.:Zauberflöte, w. T. Lemnitz (sop), E. Berger (sop), I. Beilke (sop), H. Tessmer (ten), G. Hüsch (bar), W. Strienz (bass), T. Beecham (cnd), Berlin PO, Favre Chorus [without dialog; G] *(rec 1937–38 for HMV)* Melodram 2-▲ MEL 27056 (m) [AAD]
Mozart, W.A.:Zauberflöte, w. T. Lemnitz (sop), E. Berger (sop), I. Beilke (sop), H. Tessmer (ten), G. Hüsch (bar), W. Strienz (bass), T. Beecham (cnd), Berlin PO, Favre Chorus [without dialog; G] *(rec 1937–38 for HMV)* Pearl 2-▲ PEAS 9371 (m) [AAD]
Mozart, W.A.:Zauberflöte (sels), w. A. Toscanini (cnd), Vienna PO, Helge Roswaenge (ten) *(Dies Bildnis ist bezaubernd schön)*, Jarmila Novotna (sop), Willy Domgraf-Fassbaender (bar) *(Bei Männern, welche Liebe fühlen)*, Alexander Kipnis (bass) *(In diesen heil'gen Hallen)* Orfeo d'or ("Festspiel Dokumente" series) ▲ 394101
Mozart, W.A.:Zauberflöte (sels), w. *(other artists unknown)*—Dies Bildnis ist bezaubernd schön *(rec 1937)* Minerva ▲ MN A35 (m) [ADD]
1959 Concert, w. Philharmonia Hungarica [cnd:Zoltan Rozsnay] (rec. live, Grossen Musikvereinssaal, Vienna, 5/3/59) Preiser ▲ PRE 90103 (m) [ADD]
Opera Arias, w. Berlin State Opera Orch [cnd:Bruno Seidler-Winkler], rec. 1936–1942 for HMV Preiser ("Lebendige Vergangenheit" series) ▲ PRE 89018 (m) [AAD]
Operatic Arias & Duets *(rec 1928–1938 HMV, Odeon & Po)* Pearl ▲ PEA 9394 (m) [AAD]
Puccini, G.:Tosca, w. H. Ranczak (sop), G. Hann (bass), L. Ludwig (cnd), Berlin RSO *(rec Oct. 1944)* Preiser 2-▲ PRE 90210 [ADD]

Roswaenge, Helge (ten) (cont.)
Sings Select Lieder, w. Gerald Moore (pno), Bruno Seidler-Winkler (pno), Michael Raucheisen (pno) *(rec 1936-44)* Preiser ▲ PRE CD 89992
Strauss, R.:Die ägyptische Helena (sels), w. V. Ursuleac (sop—Helena), F. Völker (ten—Menelas), H. Roswaenge (ten—Da-Ud), E. Kunz (bar—Arbace), C. Krauss (cnd), Vienna State Opera Orch, Vienna State Opera Chorus *(rec Sept. 20, 1933)* Koch Schwann 2-▲ SCH 314552 [ADD]
Strauss, R.:Ariadne auf Naxos, w. Erna Berger (sop), Viorica Ursuleac (sop), Karl Hammes (bar), C. Krauss (cnd), Berlin Reich RSO *(rec Berlin, 1935)* Preiser ▲ PRE 90259
Strauss, R.:Ariadne auf Naxos, w. Erna Berger (sop), Miliza Korjus (sop), Viorica Ursuleac (sop), *(other soloists unknown)*, C. Krauss (cnd), Vienna State Opera Orch, Vienna State Opera Chorus *(rec 1935)* Arlecchino 3- ARL
Verdi, G.:Aida (sels), w. Hilde Scheppan (sop), Margarete Klose (cta), Hans Hotter (bar), A. Rother (cnd), Berlin Radio Orch, Berlin State Opera Chorus [G] *(rec Nov. 21, 1942)* Preiser ▲ PRE 90219 [ADD]
Verdi, G.:La forza del destino (sels), w. H. Schlusnus (bar), A. Rother (cnd), Berlin RSO *(rec 1942)* Myto 2-▲ MCD 93279
Verdi, G.:Requiem Mass, w. Hilde Zadek (sop), Margarete Klose (cta), Boris Christoff (bass), H. von Karajan (cnd), Vienna PO, Vienna Singverein Stradivarius 2-▲ STV DTM 12323 [ADD]
Verdi, G.:Rigoletto, w. E. Berger (sop), R. Jacobs (alt), H. Schlusnus (bass), J. Greindl (bass), R. Heger (cnd), Berlin State Opera Orch, Berlin State Opera Chorus [G] *(rec 11/20-22/44)* Preiser 2-▲ 90036 (m) [AAD]
Verdi, G.:Il trovatore (sels), w. J. Biel (ten), F. Tamagno (ten), L.-A. Escalaïs (ten), M. Gilion (ten), E. Caruso (ten), A. Paoli (ten), G. Zenatello (ten), J. Sembach (ten), L. Slezak (ten), F. Constantino (ten), G. Martinelli (ten), B. De Muro (ten), N. Fusati (ten), N. Piccaluga (ten), G. Lauri-Volpi (ten), A. Pertile (ten), E. Bergamaschi (ten), R. Tauber (ten), J. O'Sullivan (ten), G. Taccani (ten), V. Lois (ten), H. Lazaro (ten), A. Lindi (ten), A. Cortis (ten), F. Merli (ten), F. Völker (ten), J. Kiepura (ten), J. Schmidt (ten), J. Bjoerling (ten), B. Gigli (ten), A. Salvarezza (ten), J. Soler (ten), M. Filippeschi (ten)—34 performances of the Act III tenor aria "Di quella pira!," *(rec from 1903-1956)* Bongiovanni ▲ GB 1051 [AAD]
Verdi, G.:I vespri siciliani, w. M. Cunitz (sop), H. Schlusnus (bar), O. von Rohr (bass), K. Schröder (cnd), Hessian RSO, Hesse Radio Chorus *(rec 1951)* Myto 2-▲ MCD 93279
Wagner, R.:Lohengrin (sels), w. *(other artists unknown)*—Mein lieber Schwan; In fenem Land *(rec 1942)* Minerva ▲ MN A35 (m) [ADD]
Wagner, R.:Die Meistersinger von Nürnberg (sels), w. *(other artists unknown)*—Selig wie die Sonne [w. Pearl Yoder (sop), Lydia Kindermann (mez), Hans Reinmar (bar), Max Kuttner (bass)]; Am stillen Herd; Morgenlich leuchtend *(rec 1932)* Minerva ▲ MN A35 (m) [ADD]
Weber, C.M. von:Der Freischütz (sels), w. *(other artists unknown)*—Nein, länger trag ich nicht die Qualen *(rec 1936)* Minerva ▲ MN A35 (m) [ADD]
Weber, C.M. von:Oberon (sels), w. *(other artists unknown)*—Seit frühester Jugend im Kampf und Streit; Du der diese Prüfung schickt *(rec 1936)* Minerva ▲ MN A35 (m) [ADD]
Weill, K.:The Threepenny Opera, w. Liane (sop—Polly Peachum), A. Felbermayer (sop—Lucy), H. Fassler (sop—Jenny), R. Anday (cta—Mrs. Peachum), K. Preger (ten—Macheath), H. Roswaenge (ten—Street Crier), A. Jerger (bar—Peachum), F. Gutherie (bar), *(cnd & orch unknown)* Vanguard Classics ▲ OVC 8057 [ADD]

Rosza, Anna (sop)
Verdi, G.:La traviata, w. Olga de Franco (sop—Flora Bervoix/Annina), Anna Rosza (sop—Violetta Valery), Giordano Callegari (ten—Gastone), Alessandro Ziliani (ten—Alfredo Germont), Luigi Borgonovo (bar—Giorgio Germont), Arnoldo Lenzi (bar—Barone Douphol), Antonio Gelli (bass—Marchese d'Obigny/Dottor Grenvil), C. Sabajno (cnd), La Scala Orch, Vittore Veneziani (cnd), La Scala Chorus *(rec Oct-Nov 1930)* Arkadia 2-▲ CD 78001 (m) [ADD]
Verdi, G.:La traviata, w. Olga de Franco (sop—Flora Bervoix/Annina), Anna Rosza (sop—Violetta Valéry), Giordano Callegari (ten—Gastone), Alessandro Ziliani (ten—Alfredo Germont), Luigi Borgonovo (bar—Giorgio Germont), Arnoldo Lenzi (bar—Baron Douphol), Antonio Gelli (bass—Marquis d'Obigny/Dr. Grenvil), C. Sabajno (cnd), La Scala Orch, La Scala Chorus *(rec La Scala Theatre, Milan, Oct.-Nov. 1930)* VAI Audio 2-▲ VAIA 1108-2

Rota, Alberto (sgr)
Monteverdi, C.:Ballo delle ingrate, w. Carlo Lepore (bass), Daniela Barcellona (sgr), Daniela Ciliberti (sgr), Andrea Concetti (sgr), Hans van Dijk (sgr), Remo Guerrini (sgr), Nadia Mantelli (sgr), Elena Marazzi (sgr), Humberto Orellana (sgr), Claudia Pallini (sgr), Luigi Polsini (sgr), Rosa Ricciotti (sgr), Ludovica Scoppola (sgr), *(orch unknown)* Nuova Era ▲ NUO 7224

Rota, Anna Maria (cta)
Cilea, F.:Gloria, w. M. Roberti (sop), F. Labò (ten), A. Albertini (bar), L. Testi (bar), E. Campi (bass), F. Mazzoli (bass), F. Previtali (cnd), Turin RAI Orch, Turin RAI Chorus [I] *(rec live, Turin July 8, 1969)* Memories ▲ HR 4472 [ADD]
Donizetti, G.:Lucrezia Borgia, w. M. Caballé (sop), G. Raimondi (ten), E. Flagello (bass), E. Gracis (cnd), La Scala Orch, La Scala Chorus [I] *(rec live, 3/2/70)* Myto 2-▲ 2 MCD 90423 [ADD]
Rossini, G.:Zelmira, w. Virginia Zeani (sop), Enrico Campi (bass), Guido Mazzini (bass), Paolo Washington (bass), Gastone Limarilli (sgr), Giuseppe Moretti (sgr), Nicola Tagger (sgr), C. Franci (cnd), *(orch unknown)* Great Opera Performances 2-▲ GOP 780
Szymanowski, K.:Stabat Mater, w. A. Martino (sop), R. Capecchi (bar), A. Rodzinski (cnd), Turin RAI SO, Turin RAI Chorus *(rec 1955)* Stradivarius 2-▲ DAT 12306 [ADD]
Zandonai, R.:Francesca da Rimini, w. Lydia Marimpietri (sop—Biancofiore), Magda Olivero (sop—Francesca), Pinuccia Perotti (sop—Samaritana), Edda Vincenzi (sop—Garsenda), Gabriella Carturan (mez—Smaragdi), Biancamaria Casoni (mez—Altichiara), Anna Maria Rota (cta—Donella), Athos Cesarini (ten—Archer), Angelo Mercuriali (ten—Ser Toldo Berardengo), Mario del Monaco (ten—Paolo), Piero de Palma (ten—Malatestino), Rinaldo Pelizzoni (ten—Prisoner), Gianpiero Malaspina (bar—Gianciotto), Dino Mantovani (bar—Jester), Enrico Campi (bass—Ostasio), Giuseppe Morresi (bass—Tower warden), G. Gavazzeni (cnd), La Scala Orch, La Scala Chorus *(rec La Scala Theatre, Milan, June 4, 1959)* Legato Classics 2-▲ LCD 186-2

Roth, Detlef (bass)
Mozart, W.A.:Zauberflöte, w. Constanze Backes (sop—Papagena), Christiane Oelze (sop—Pamina), Susan Roberts (sop—First Lady), Cyndia Sieden (sop—Queen of the Night), Carola Guber (cta—Second Lady), Maria Jonas (cta—Third Lady), Andreas Dieterich (trb—First Boy), Jan Andreas Mendel (trb—Second Boy), Florian Wöller (trb—Third Boy), Uwe Peper (ten—Monostatos), Nicolas Robertson (ten—First Man in Armor), Michael Schade (ten—Tamino), Gerald Finley (bar—Papageno), Noel Mann (bass—Second Man in Armour), Harry Peeters (bass—Sarastro), Detlef Roth (bass—Speaker/First Priest), Robert Burt (speaker—Third Priest), Robert Johnston (speaker—Second Priest), Wolfgang Knauer (speaker—Fourth Priest), Douglas Welbat (speaker—Second Priest), J. E. Gardiner (cnd), English Baroque Soloists, Monteverdi Choir London *(rec Forum am Schlosspark, Ludwigsburg, July 1995)* Archiv 2-▲ 449166-2

Roth, Leo (ten)
Kol Nidre:Sacred Music of the Synagogue, w. Gloria Seipelt (alt), Rudolf Wiebel (bar), Werner Buschnakowski (org), Harry Foss (org), Leipzig RSO members, Jewish Congregation Choir Berlin, Leipzig Synagogue Choir EMI Classics ▲ CDM 65457

Rothenberger, Anneliese (sop)
Gluck, C.W.:Orfeo ed Euridice, w. Ruth-Margaret Pütz (sop), Grace Bumbry (mez), V. Neumann (cnd), Leipzig Opera Orch, Leipzig Radio Chorus *(rec Leipzig, 1967)* Berlin Classics 2-▲ BER 9033 [ADD]
Humperdinck, E.:Hänsel und Gretel, w. Lislotte Maikl (sop—Sandman/Dew Fairy), Anneliese Rothenberger (sop—Gretel), Irmgard Seefried (sop—Hänsel), Grace Hoffman (mez—Gertrude), Elisabeth Höngen (cta—Witch), Walter Berry (bass—Peter), A. Cluytens (cnd), Vienna PO, Vienna Boys' Choir EMI Classics 2-▲ CDMB 65661
Lehár, F.:Giuditta (sels), w. Nicolai Gedda (ten), W. Mattes (cnd), Graunke SO, Munich Theater Gartnerplatz Chorus Emperor Operetta ▲ KO 86342
Lehár, F.:Das Land des Lächelns (sels), w. Renate Holm (sop), Nicolai Gedda (ten), W. Mattes (cnd), Graunke SO, Bavarian Radio Chorus Emperor Operetta ▲ KO 86341
Lehár, F.:Die lustige Witwe (sels), w. Erika Koth (sop), Nicolai Gedda (ten), Robert Ilosfalvy (ten), W. Mattes (cnd), Graunke SO, Bavarian Radio Chorus Emperor Operetta ▲ KO 86343

Rothenberger, Anneliese (sop) (cont.)
Liebermann, R.:Die Schule der Frauen, w. Anneliese Rothenberger (sop—Agnes), Christa Ludwig (mez—Georgette), Nicolai Gedda (ten—Horace), Alois Pernerstorfer (b-bar—Gronte), Walter Berry (bass—Poquelin), Kurt Böhme (bass—Arnolphe), G. Szell (cnd), Vienna PO *(rec Salzburg, Aug 17, 1957)* Orfeo d'or ("Festspiel Dikumente" series) 2-▲ C 429962 (m) [ADD]
Mozart, W.A.:Arias, w. Arleen Augér (sop), Kathleen Battle (sop), Irma Beilke (sop), Helena Braun (sop), Lisa Della Casa (sop), Maria Cebotari (sop), Ileana Cotrubas (sop), Helen Donath (sop), Mirella Freni (sop), Reri Grist (sop), Edita Gruberova (sop), Elisabeth Grümmer (sop), Hilde Güden (sop), Ingeborg Hallstein (sop), Luise Helletsgruber (sop), Gundula Janowitz (sop), Sena Jurinac (sop), Erika Köth (sop), Evelyn Lear (sop), Wilma Lipp (sop), Margaret Marshall (sop), Edith Mathis (sop), Jarmila Novotna (sop), Margherita Perras (sop), Lucia Popp (sop), Elisabeth Rethberg (sop), Elisabeth Schumann (sop), Elisabeth Schwarzkopf (sop), Graziella Sciutti (sop), Irmgard Seefried (sop), Graziella Sciutti (sop), Julia Varady (sop), Agnes Baltsa (mez), Margit Bokor (mez), Brigitte Fassbaender (mez), Christa Ludwig (mez), Ann Murray (mez), Francisco Araiza (ten), Anton Dermota (ten), Helge Rosvaenge (ten), Rudolf Schock (ten), Peter Schreier (ten), Leopold Simoneau (ten), Eric Tappy (ten), Richard Tauber (ten), Gösta Winbergh (ten), Josef Witt (ten), Fritz Wunderlich (ten), Christian Boesch (bar), Willy Domgraf-Fassbaender (bar), Karl Dönch (bar), Dietrich Fischer-Dieskau (bar), Erich Kunz (bar), Eberhard Wächter (bar), Hans Hotter (b-bar), Paul Schöffler (b-bar), Cesare Siepi (b-bar), José Van Dam (b-bar), Walter Berry (bass), Geraint Evans (bass), Nicolai Ghiaurov (bass), Alexander Kipnis (bass), Richard Mayr (bass), Kurt Moll (bass), James Morris (bass), Ezio Pinza (bass), Martti Talvela (bass), Giorgio Tozzi (bass), Hans Duhan (sgr), Res Fischer (sgr), Marie Gerhart (sgr), *(various orchs & cnds)*—sels from Idomeneo, Die Entführung aus der Serail, Le nozze di Figaro, Don Giovanni, Così fan tutte, Die Zauberflöte & various arias Orfeo d'or ("Festspiel Dokumente" series) 5-▲ 408955
Mozart, W.A.:Entführung, w. Reri Grist (sop—Blondchen), Anneliese Rothenberger (sop—Konstanze), Gerhard Unger (ten—Pedrillo), Fritz Wunderlich (ten—Belmonte), Fernando Corena (bass—Osmin), Michael Heltau (nar—Selim), Z. Mehta (cnd), Vienna PO, Vienna State Opera Chorus *(rec July 28, 1965)* Orfeo d'or ("Festspiel Dokumente" series) 2-▲ 392952 (m)
Mozart, W.A.:Idomeneo, w. E. Moser (sop), N. Gedda (ten), A. Dallapozza (ten), P. Schreier (ten), T. Adam (b-bar), H. Schmidt-Isserstedt (cnd), Dresden Staatskapelle, Leipzig Radio Chorus EMI Classics ("Studio" series) 3-▲ CDMC 63990
Mozart, W.A.:Nozze di Figaro, w. Hilde Gueden (sop), Edith Mathis (sop), Peter Schreier (ten), Walter Berry (bar), Hermann Prey (bar), O. Suitner (cnd), Dresden Staatskapelle Berlin Classics 3-▲ BER 2096 [ADD]
Mozart, W.A.:Nozze di Figaro (sels), w. Hilde Gueden (sop), Hermann Prey (bar), Walter Berry (bass), O. Suitner (cnd), Dresden Staatskapelle Berlin Classics ▲ BER 9079 [ADD]
Strauss (II), Joh.:Wiener Blut (sels), w. Christine Gorner (sop), Nicolai Gedda (ten), W. Mattes (cnd), Graunke SO, Munich Theater Gartnerplatz Chorus Emperor Operetta ▲ KO 86345
Strauss, R.:Der Rosenkavalier, w. E. Schwarzkopf (sop—Feldmarschallin), A. Rothenberger (sop—Sophie), S. Jurinac (sop—Octavian), O. Edelmann (bass—Baron Ochs), H. von Karajan (cnd), Vienna PO *(rec live, Salzburg, 8/1/64)* Arkadia 3-▲ 227 [ADD]

Rothmüller, Marko (bar)
Schubert, Franz:Winterreise, w. S. Gyr (pno) *(rec 1954)* Symposium 2-▲ 1098-1099
Strauss, R.:Salome, w. Maria Cebotari (sop—Salome), Elisabeth Höngen (mez—Herodias), Karl Friedrich (ten—Narraboth), Julius Patzak (ten—Herod), Marko Rothmüller (bar—Jokanaan), C. Krauss (cnd), Vienna State Opera Orch, Vienna State Opera Chorus *(rec Covent Garden, London, Sept 30, 1947)* Legato 2-▲ LCD 211-2 [ADD]
Verdi, G.:Un ballo in maschera (sels), w. A. Schuh (sgr), Larrimore (sgr), J. Björling (ten), N. Treigle (bass), J. Morris (bass), Feux (sgr), W. Herbert (cnd), *(orch unknown)* [I] *(rec live, New Orleans, 4/22/50)* Legato Classics ▲ LCD 154-1 (m) [ADD]

Rotondo, Francesca (sop)
Mercadante, S.:Arias, w. Alberto Mondini (pno)—La rosa; La sposa de lo marenaro; La palomma; Lo zucchero d'amore; Il zeffiro; La primavera; Il Pastore svizzero; Il bolero; Il desiato ritorno; Il fiore e la lagrima; La prece Dell'Orfana; T'amo l'abbandonata; Salve Maria Stradivarius ▲ STV 1003 [DDD]
Mercadante, S.:Music of, w. Alberto Mondini (pno)—La rosa; La Sposa de lo Marenaro; La palomma; Lo Zucchero d'Ammore; Il Zeffiro; La primavera; Il pastore svizzero; Il bolero; Il desiato ritorno; Il fiore e la lagrima; La prece Dell'Orfana; T'Amo; L'Abbandonata; Salve Maria Stradivarius ▲ STV 1003 [DDD]

Rotzsch, Hans-Joachim (ten)
Bach, J.S.:Cant 29, w. Regina Werner (sop), Heidi Riess (alt), Hermann Christian Polster (bass), H.-J. Rotzsch (cnd), Leipzig Gewandhaus Orch, Leipzig St. Thomas Church Choir Berlin Classics ▲ BER CD 9055
Bach, J.S.:Cant 119, w. Regina Werner (sop), Heidi Riess (alt), Hermann Christian Polster (bass), H.-J. Rotzsch (cnd), Leipzig Gewandhaus Orch, Leipzig St. Thomas Church Choir Berlin Classics ▲ BER CD 9055
Beethoven, L. van:Syms (comp), w. I. Wenglor (sop), U. Zollenkopf (cta), T. Adam (bass-bar), F. Konwitschny (cnd), Leipzig Gewandhaus Orch, Leipzig Radio Chorus *(rec 1959-1961)* Berlin Classics ("Eterna" series) 6-▲ BER 2005 [ADD]
Beethoven, L. van:Sym 9, "Choral Sym", w. Ingeborg Wenglor (sop), Ursula Zollenkopf (alt), Theo Adam (bass), F. Konwitschny (cnd), Leipzig Gewandhaus Orch, Leipzig Radio Chorus Polskie Nagrania Edition ▲ ECD 028
Dessau, P.:Die Verurteilung des Lukullus, w. Annelies Burmeister (mez—Das Fischweib), Helmut Melchert (ten—Lukullus), Hans-Joachim Rotzsch (ten—Der Kirschbaumträger), Peter Schreier (ten—Lukullus' Cook), Boris Carmeli (bass—King), H. Kegel (cnd), Leipzig RSO, Leipzig Radio Chorus Berlin Classics 2-▲ BER 1073 [ADD]
Handel, G.F.:Imeneo, w. Sylvia Geszty (sop), Renate Krahmer (sop), Günther Leib (bass), Siegfried Vogel (bass), H.-T. Margraf (cnd), Halle Handel Festival Orch, Leipzig Radio Chorus *(rec 1966)* Berlin Classics ▲ BER 9110

Rouleau, Joseph (bass)
Donizetti, G.:Lucia di Lammermoor, w. J. McDonald (sop), J. Sutherland (sop), M. Elkins (mez), J. Bowman (alt), J. Gibin (ten), Shaw (sgr), T. Serafin (cnd), Royal Opera House Orch, Royal Opera House Chorus Covent Garden—3 duets from Act 1, & 3 soprano solo arias from Act 2 [I] Myto ▲ 1 MCD 91545 [ADD]
Leclerc, F.:Songs, w. G. Bellemare (cnd), Three Rivers SO *(rec 1990)* Analekta ▲ AN2-8601 [DDD] ■ AN4-8601
Rossini, G.:Semiramide, w. J. Sutherland (sop), M. Horne (mez), J. Serge (ten), S. Malas (bass), R. Bonynge (cnd), London SO, Ambrosian Singers [I] *(rec 1966)* London 3-▲ 425481-2 [ADD]

Roulx, Sandra (mez)
Pesson, G.:Music of, w. Donatienne Michel-Dansac (sop), Stuart Patterson (ten), Paul-Alexandre Dubois (bar), Pascal Sausy (bar), Florence Millet (pno), D. My (cnd), Fa Ensemble, Paris String Quartet—Le gel, par jeu for Fl, Cl, Hn, Bass Mar, Vn & Vc; Qt for Strs; Non Sapremo Mai di Questo Mi for Fl, Vn & Pno; 5 Poèmes de Sandro Penna for Bar, B Cl, Hn, Vn & Vc; La lumière n'a pas de bras pour nous porter for Amplified Pno; La vita è come l'albero di natale for Vn & Pno; Nocturnes en quatuor for Cl, Pno, Vn & Vc; Les chants faëz for Pno & 10 Instrs; Sur-le-champ for 4 Voices & 9 Instrs [from a text by Pierre Alferi] Accord ▲ ACD 204682 [DDD]

Rounseville, Robert (ten)
Bernstein, L.:Candide, w. Barbara Cook (sop), Max Adrian (sgr), et al. Sony Broadway ▲ SK 48017 ■ ST 48017
Rodgers, R.:Carousel, w. Gordon MacRae (sgr), S. Jones (sgr), C. Mitchell (sgr), B. Ruick (sgr), C. Turner (sgr) *(rec 1956)* Broadway Angel ▲ ZDM 64692 ■ EG 64692

Rouquetty, Camille (ten)
Varney, L.:Les Mousquetaires au couvent, w. Gabrielle Ristori (mez), Gabriel Bacquier (bar), Louis Musy (b-bar), Pierre Blanc (sgr), Pauline Carton (sgr), Jacqueline Cauchard (sgr), Mireille Lacoste (sgr), Colette Riedinger (sgr), R. Benedetti (cnd) Musidisc 2-▲ MUS 202262 [AAD]

Rouse, Mikel (sgr/elec)
Rouse, M.:Dennis Cleveland, w. *(other artists unknown)* New World ▲ 805062

Roux, Michel (bar)
Berlioz, H.:La Damnation de Faust, w. Pierre Mollet (bar—Brandler), Michel Roux (bar—Méphistophélès), Consuelo Rubio (sgr—Marguerite), Richard Verreau (sgr—Faust) Theorema 2-▲ TH 121170/171

Roux, Michel (bar) (cont.)
Berlioz, H.:La Damnation de Faust, w. Regine Crespin (sop), Andre Turp (ten), P. Monteux (cnd), London SO *(rec live, Mar 1962)* Music & Arts 2-▲ CD 928
Berlioz, H.:La Damnation de Faust, w. Régine Crespin (sop—Marguerite), Guy Fouché (ten—Faust), Michel Roux (bar—Méphistophélès), Peter van der Bilt (bass—Brander), J. Fournet (cnd), Amsterdam Radio PO, Groot Omroepkoor *(rec Amsterdam, Mar 23, 1963)* Bella Voce 2-▲ BLV 107.202 [AAD]
Bizet, G.:Ivan IV (sels), w. J. Micheau (sop), H. Legay (ten), M. Sénéchal (ten), G. Tzipine (cnd), French National RSO, French Radio Chorus [F] EMI Classics ("Studio" series) 2-▲ CDMB 69704 [ADD]
Debussy, C.:Pelléas et Mélisande, w. J. Micheau (sop), R. Gorr (mez), C. Maurane (bar), X. Depraz (bass), J. Fournet (cnd), Lamoureux Orch *(rec 1953* Philips 2-▲ 434783-2
Debussy, C.:Pelléas et Mélisande, w. E. Schwarzkopf (sop), E. Haefliger (ten), M. Petri (bass), H. von Karajan (cnd), Rome Radio Orch, Rome RAI Chorus [F] *(rec live, 12/19/54)* Arkadia 2-▲ 218 (m) [ADD]
Rossini, G.:Le Comte Ory, w. J. Sinclair (sop), M. Sinclair (cta), J. Oncina (ten), V. Gui (cnd), Glyndebourne Festival Orch, Glyndebourne Festival Chorus *(rec 1956)* EMI Classics 2-▲ CDMB 64180

Rovere, Ornella (sop)
Verdi, G.:Aida (sels), w. E. Stignani (mez), M. Filippeschi (ten), C. Cava (bass), B. McFerrin (sgr), V. Bellezza (cnd), Naples Teatro San Carlo Orch, Naples Teatro San Carlo Chorus [I] [highlights] *(rec live, Arena Flegrea, Naples, 7/15/56)* Golden Age of Opera ▲ GAO 130 [ADD]

Rovero, Ornella (sop)
Cimarosa, D.:Il Matrimonio segreto, w. Alda Noni (sop), Giulietta Simionato (mez), Riccardo Cassinelli (ten), Cesare Valletti (ten), Sesto Bruscantini (bar), M. Wolf-Ferrari (cnd), Florence Maggio Musicale Orch *(rec 1950)* Cetra Classic 2-▲ CDO 32
Rossini, G.:La Cenerentola, w. Miti Truccato Pace (mez), Giulietta Simionato (mez), Cesare Valletti (ten), Saturno Meletti (bar), Vito Susca (bass), Cristiano Dalamangas (sgr), M. Rossi (cnd), Turin RAI Orch, Bruno Erminero (cnd), Turin RAI Chorus Fonit Cetra ("Classic Collection" series) ▲ FCT CDON 34
Verdi, G.:Requiem Mass, w. J. Madeira (mez), J. Lambert (sgr), G. Neri (bass), E. Kleiber (cnd), Vienna SO, Vienna Singverein *(rec live, Vienna 11/23/55)* Melodram 2-▲ CDM 28044 [ADD]

Rovetta, Teodoro (bar)
Debussy, C.:Pelléas et Mélisande, w. A. Martino (soprano), A. Reynolds (mez), G. Bacquier (bar), N. Zaccaria (bass), L. Maazel (cnd), *(orch unknown) (rec 1969)* Great Opera Performances 3-▲ GOP 711
Mussorgsky, M.:Khovanshchina, w. Mietta Sighele (sop—Emma), Elena Souliotis (sop—Susanna), Fiorenza Cossotto (mez—Marfa), Herbert Handt (ten—Scribe), Veriano Luchetti (ten—Prince Andrey Khovansky), Ludovic Spiess (ten—Prince Vasily Golitsin), Claudio Strudthoff (ten—Streshnev), Angelo Marchiandi (bar—Kuz'ka), Teodoro Rovetta (bar—1st Strel'tsi), Siegmund Nimsgern (b-bar—Shaklovity), Cesare Siepi (b-bar—Dosifey), Carlo del Bosco (bass—2nd Strel'tsi), Ubaldo Carosi (bass—Varsonofiev), Nicolai Ghiaurov (bass—Prince Ivan Khovnasky), Giovanni Sciarpeletti (bass—Pastor), B. Leskovich (cnd), Rome RAI SO, Rome RAI Chorus—also includes bonus Act V [w Boris Christoff] (Rome, 1958) *(rec Rome, 1973)* Bella Voce 3-▲ BLV 107.402 [AAD]

Rowader, Darrell (sgr)
Rapchak, L.:The Lifework of Juan Diaz, w. C. Loverde (sop), R. Hovencamp (sgr), R. Alderson (sgr), L. Rapchak (cnd), Chicago Chamber Opera Albany ▲ TROY 091 [DDD]

Rowland, Martile (sop)
Verdi, G.:I masnadieri, w. M. Malagnini (sgr), T. Migliorini (sgr), R. Bruson (bar), M. Lanskoy (bar), C. Colombara (bass), W. Gönnenwein (cnd), Ludwigsburg Festival Orch, South German Madrigal Choir Bayer 2-▲ BR 500 001/2 [DDD]

Rozario, Patricia (sop)
Britten, H.:The Rape of Lucretia (sels), w. C. Pierard (sop), A. Gunson (mez), J. Rigby (cta), N. Robson (ten), D. Maxwell (bar), A. Opie (bar), A. Miles (bass), R. Hickox (cnd), City of London Sinfonia Chandos 2-▲ CHAN 9254/55 [DDD]
Canteloube, J.:Songs of Auvergne, w. J. Pritchard (cnd), Philharmonia Orch IMP Classics ▲ PCD 938 [DDD]
Casken, J.:Golem, w. C. Robson (ct), A. Clarke (bar), J. Hall (bar), R. Bernas (cnd), Music Projects London Virgin Classics 2-▲ CDC 59028
Purcell, H.:Dido & Aeneas, w. Rebecca Evans (sop—Belinda), Maria Ewing (sop—Dido), Mary Plazas (sop—1st witch), Patricia Rozario (sop—2nd woman), Sally Burgess (mez—Sorceress), Pamela Helen Stephens (mez—2nd witch), James Bowman (ct—Spirit), Jamie MacDougal (ten—Sailor), Karl Daymond (bar—Aeneas), R. Hickox (cnd), Collegium Musicum 90 Chandos ("Early Music" series) ▲ CHAN 0586 [DDD]
Schubert, Franz:Songs (comp), w. J.M. Ainsley (ten), I. Bostridge (ten), M. George (bass), G. Johnson (pno), S. Layton (cnd), London Schubert Chorale—Winterlied; Ossians Lied nach dem Falle Nathos; Das Mädchen von Inistore; Als ich sie erröten; Schwangesang; Totenkranz für ein Kind; Die Fröhlichkeit; Der Zufriedene; Alles um Liebe; Geist der Liebe; Dei erste Liebe; Die Täuschung; Liebesrausch; Huldigung; Heidenröslein; Nachtgesang; Der Morgenstern; Der Knappenlied; Trinklied vor der Schlacht; Schwertlied; Begräbnislied; Grablied; Osterlied; Hoffnung; Punschlied; Klage um Ali Bey; Abendständchen; Tische'rlied; Wiogonlied; Die Macht der Liebe; Trinklied, D.183; Trinklied, D.267 Hyperion ▲ CDJ 33020
Tavener, J.:Elis Thanaton, w. Stephen Richards (bass), R. Hickox (cnd), City of London Sinfonia Chandos ▲ CHAN 9440
Tavener, J.:Innocence, w. Leigh Nixon (ten), Graham Titus (bass), Alice Neary (vc), Charles Fullbrook (bells), Martin Baker (org), Martin Neary (cnd), Westminster Abbey Choir *(rec Westminster Abbey, May 1-5, 1995)* Sony Classical ▲ SK 66613 [DDD]
Tavener, J.:Lamentation, Last Prayer & Exultation, w. I. Simcock (org) Collins Classics ▲ COL 1428 [DDD]
Tavener, J.:Melina, w. J. Tavener (pno) Collins Classics ▲ COL 1428 [DDD]
Tavener, J.:Mini Song Cycle, w. J. Tavener (pno) Collins Classics ▲ COL 1428 [DDD]
Tavener, J.:To a Child Dancing in the Wind, w. K. Lukas (fl), S. Tees (va), H. Tunstall (hp) Collins Classics ▲ COL 1428 [DDD]
Tavener, J.:We Shall See Him As He Is, w. J. M. Ainsley (ten), A. Murgatroyd (ten), R. Hickox (cnd), BBC Welsh National Orch, BBC Welsh National Chorus [E] Chandos ▲ CHAN 9128 [DDD]
Vaughan Williams, R.:Sym 3, w. K. Bakels (cnd), Bournemouth SO *(rec Nov. 12, 1992)* Naxos ▲ 8.550733 [DDD]

Rozhdestvensky, Gennadi (nar)
Prokofiev, S.:Cantata for the 20th Aniversary of the October Revolution, w. N. Järvi (cnd), Philharmonia Orch, Philharmonia Chorus Chandos ▲ CHAN 9095 [DDD]

Rozsos, István (ten)
Wayditch, G. von:The Caliph's Magician, w. Júlia Pászthi (sop—Eunuch), Sándor Palcso (ten—The Emir), István Rozsos (ten—Nawab), Zsolt Bende (bar—The Magician), Arpád Kishegyi (sgr—Djinn), András Nagy-Soljom (sgr—The Caliph), Csaba Ötvös (sgr—Djinn), Csilla Ötvös (sgr—Odalisk), A. Kórodi (cnd), Budapest National Opera Orch, Budapest National Opera Chorus *(rec 1975)* VAI Audio 2-▲ VAIA 1095-2 [ADD]

Rubio, Consuelo (sop)
Berlioz, H.:La Damnation de Faust, w. Pierre Mollet (bar—Brandler), Michel Roux (bar—Méphistophélès), Consuelo Rubio (sgr—Marguerite), Richard Verreau (sgr—Faust) Theorema 2-▲ TH 121170/171

Rudenko, Bela (sop)
Glinka, M.:Russlan & Ludmilla, w. Nina Fomina (sop—Gorislava), Bela Rudenko (sop—Ludmilla), Tamara Sinyavskaya (mez—Ratmir), Boris Morozov (bass—Farlaf), Evgeny Nesterenko (bass—Russlan), Valeri Yaroslavtsev (bass—Svetozar), Y. Simonov (cnd), Bolshoi Theater Orch, Bolshoi Theater Chorus *(rec Moscow, 1978-1979)* Melodiya ("The Russian Opera" series) 3-▲ 74321-29348-2 [ADD]

Rudifera, Milena (sop/mez)
Mendelssohn, F.:Syms (comp), w. Gemma Bertagnolli (sop), Wonjun Lee (ten), L. Jia (cnd), Trieste Teatro Comunale Giuseppe Verdi Orch, Ine Meisters (cnd), Trieste Teatro Comunale G. Verdi Chorus RS Prestige 3-▲ 953-0090 [DDD]
Mendelssohn, F.:Sym 2, w. Gemma Bertagnolli (sop), Wonjun Lee (ten), L. Jia (cnd), Trieste Teatro Comunale Giuseppe Verdi Orch, Trieste Teatro Comunale G. Verdi Chorus RS Applausi ▲ 6367-91

Rudnjewa, Natalia (mez)
Benguerel, X.:Libre Vermell, w. L. Kramer (cnd), Belarus Minsk State PO, Belarus State Capella Chorus Minsk Koch Schwann 2-▲ SCH 314132

Rue, Rik (voc)
Chris Mann & the Impediments, w. Chris Mann (voc), Carolyn Connors (voc), Jeannie Marsch (voc) O.O. Discs ▲ CD 21 [ADD]

Ruffini, Alessandra (sop)
Bizet, G.:Les Pêcheurs de perles, w. G. Morino (ten), B. Praticò (bar), C. Piantini (cnd), Italian International Orch, Slovak Phil Chorus [F] *(rec live 7/30-8/2/90)* Nuova Era 2-▲ 6944/45 [DDD]
Delibes, L.:Lakmé, w. S. Lazzarini (mez), G. Morino (ten), B. Praticò (bar), C. Piantini (cnd), Italian International Orch, Bratislava Chamber Chorus [F] Nuova Era 2-▲ 7096/97 [DDD]
Donizetti, G.:L'elisir d'amore, w. Alessandra Ruffini (sop—Adina), Mariangela Spotorno (sop—Gianetta), Vincenzo La Scola (ten—Nemorino), Simone Alaimo (bar—Dulcamara), Roberto Frontali (bar—Belcore), P.G. Morandi (cnd), Hungarian State Opera Orch, Anikó Katona (cnd), Hungarian State Opera Chorus *(rec Budapest, July 1995)* Naxos 2-▲ 8.60045-6 [DDD]
Gluck, C.W.:L'Innocenza giustificata, w. B. Lucarini (sop—Flaminia), A. Ruffini (sop—Claudia), A. R. de Simone (sop—Flavio), U. Benelli (bar—Valerio), G. Catalucci (cnd), In Canto di Terni Youth Orch [I] *(rec live 9/90)* Bongiovanni 2-▲ GB 2111/12 [DDD]
Morlacchi, F.:Nuovo barbiere, w. G. Gatti (sop), M. Comencini (ten), A. Tomicich (bass), R. Franceschetto (sgr), G. Catalucci (cnd), Orch Giovanile In Canto [I] *(rec live 9/9/89)* Bongiovanni 2-▲ GB 2085/86 [DDD]
Piccinni, N.:La cecchinaLa cecchina, ossia la buona figliola, w. M. A. Peters (sop), G. Morino (ten), B. Praticò (bar), B. Campanella (cnd), Serenissima Pro Arte Orch [I] *(rec live 1990,* Memories 3-▲ DR 3101/03 [DDD]
Salieri, A.:La Locandiera, w. G. Sarti (bar), O. Di Credico (ten), P. Guarnera (bar), F. Luisi (cnd), Emilia Romagna Arturo Toscanini SO [I] *(rec live 1989)* Nuova Era 2-▲ 6888/89 [DDD]
Vivaldi, A.:Cants, w. C. Calvi (cta), R. Gini (cnd), Concerto Ensemble—(5 Cantatas) "Fonte del pianto," RV.656; "Sorge vermiglia in ciel," RV.667; "Lungi dal vago volto," RV.680; "Perfidissimo cor, iniquo fato," RV.674; "Piango, gemo, sospiro e peno," RV.675 [I] Nuova Era ("Ancient Music" series) ▲ 6859 [DDD]

Ruffino, Ignacio (bass)
Verdi, G.:Rigoletto (sels), w. C. O'Connor (sop), O. Dominguez (mez), G. Di Stefano (ten), G. Valdengo (bar), R. Cellini (cnd), Palacio Bellas Artes Orch, Palacio Bellas Artes Chorus [abridged performance] *(rec live, Mexico City 6/22/48)* Golden Age of Opera 2-▲ GAO 128/29 [ADD]
Verdi, G.:Simon Boccanegra (sels), w. Celia Garcia (sop—Maria Boccanegra), Mario Filippeschi (ten—Gabriele Adorno), Ignacio Ruffino (ten—Pietro), Leonard Warren (bar—Simon Boccanegra), Roberto Silva (bass—Jacopo Fiesco), Carlo Morelli (bass—Paolo), R. Cellini (cnd), Mexican National Opera Orch, Mexican National Opera Chorus *(rec Palacio de las Bellas Artes, Mexico City, July 4, 1950)* Legato Classics ▲ LCD 185-1 [ADD]

Ruffo, Titta (bar)
The Best of Titta Ruffo, w. various orchs *(rec 1912-1929)* Grammofono 2000 ▲ GRM 78518 [ADD]
Caruso in Arias, Duets & Songs, w. Enrico Caruso (ten), Louise Homer (cta), Mario Ancona (bar), Antonio Scotti (bar) Supraphon Collection ▲ SUP 110618 (m) [ADD]
Gigli:Arias, Duets & Songs, w. Beniamino Gigli (ten), Maria Caniglia (sop), Dusolina Giannini (sop), John Barbirolli (cnd), Eugene Goossens (cnd), Carlo Sabajno (cnd), et al. *(rec 1926-37)* Pearl 2-▲ PEA 9176 [ADD]
In His Vocal Prime, 1907-1922 Pearl ▲ PEA 9088 [ADD]
Ruffo Nimbus ("Prima Voce" series) ▲ NI 7810-2 (m) [ADD]
Titta Ruffo Edition (rec. 1912-1929 for Victor) Preiser ("Lebendige Vergangenheit" series) 3-▲ PRE 89303 (m) [AAD]
Titta Ruffo, Vol. 1 Pearl ("The Titta Ruffo Edition" series) 2-▲ PEA 9212
Titta Ruffo, Vol. 2 Pearl ("The Titta Ruffo Edition" series) 2-▲ PEA 9213
Titta Ruffo, Vol. 3 Pearl ("The Titta Ruffo Edition" series) 2-▲ PEA 9214
Verdi, G.:Otello (sels), w. C. Muzio (sop), R. Ponselle (sop), H. Spani (sop), E. Caruso (ten), N. Fusati (ten), L. Melchior (ten), F. Merli (ten), F. Tamagno (ten), B. Franci (bar), V. Maurel (bar), R. Stracciari (bar) *(rec 1906-1933)* Music Memoria ▲ 30219

Ruggeri, Gianpiero (sgr)
Rossini, G.:La gazetta, w. Teresa Verdera (sop), Kasimierz Sergiel (sgr), Ezio Maria Tisi (sgr), W. Keitel (cnd), Minsk Orch, Motet & Madrigal Posen Chamber Chorus Deutsche Schallplatten ▲ DS 1053

Ruggeri, Miriam (sop)
Bellini, V.:La sonnambula, w. L. Pagliughi (sop—Amina), W. Ruggeri (sop—Lisa), A. M. Anelli (mez—Teresa), F. Tagliavini (ten—Elvino), P. L. Latinucci (bass—Alessio), C. Siepi (bass—Conte Rodolfo), F. Capuana (cnd), Turin RSO, Turin Radio Chorus *(rec 1952)* Cetra Classics 2-▲ CDO 16 [AAD]
Rameau, J.P.:Les Indes galantes, w. C. McFadden (sop), S. Piau (sop), I. Poulenard (sop), N. Rime (sop), H. Crook (ten), J.-P. Fouchecourt (ten), N. Riveng (bar), J. Corréas (bass), B. Delétré (bass), W. Christie (cnd), Les Arts Florissants [F] Harmonia Mundi France 3-▲ HMC 901367/69

Ruhl, Edward (ten)
Glanville-Hicks, P.:Nausicaa, w. Teresa Stratas (sop—Nausicaa), Sophia Steffan (cta—Queen Arete), Michalis Heliotis (ten—Antinous/Priest), George Moutsios (ten—Eurymachus), Edward Ruhl (ten—Phemius), George Tsantikos (ten—Clytoneus), Vassilis Koundouris (bar—Messenger), John Modenos (bar—Aethon), Spiro Malas (bass—King Alcinous), C. Surinach (cnd), Athens SO, Athens Sym Chorus *(rec Athens Festival, 1961)* CRI ▲ CD 695 [ADD]
Glanville-Hicks, P.:Nausicaa (sels), w. Teresa Stratas (sop), Spiro Malas (bass), Michalis Helii (sgr), Michalis Heliots (sgr), George Moutsio (sgr), Sophia Steffan (sop), George Tsantikos (sgr), C. Surinach (cnd), Athens SO, Athens Sym Chorus CRI ▲ CD 695 [ADD]

Ruhland, G. (bass)
Dufay, G.:Choruses & Songs, w. Capella Antiqua Munich Elektra/Nonesuch ■ 71171-4
Dufay, G.:Hymns, w. Capella Antiqua Munich Elektra/Nonesuch ■ 71171-4
Dufay, G.:Sacred & Secular Music, w. Capella Antiqua Munich Elektra/Nonesuch ■ 71171-4

Rühm, Gerhard (reader)
Cerha, F.:Eine Art Chanson, w. H.C. Artmann (reader), HK Gruber (reader), J. Holland (reader), M. Jones (reader), R. McGee (reader) *(rec live Apr. 30, 1993)* Largo ▲ 5126 [DDD]

Ruick, B. (sgr)
Rodgers, R.:Carousel, w. Gordon MacRae (sgr), S. Jones (sgr), C. Mitchell (sgr), C. Turner (sgr), R. Rounseville (sgr) *(rec 1956)* Broadway Angel ▲ ZDM 64692 ■ EG 64692

Ruiter, Albert de (bass)
Christmas in the New World, w. Western Wind, Louise Schulman (vn), Wendy Gillespie (vl), Joseph Karpienia (gtr), Elaine Comparone (hpd) MusicMasters ▲ 01612-67176-2

Ruivenkamp, Joop (bass)
Puccini, G.:Manon Lescaut, w. Magda Olivero (sop—Manon), Tine Appelman (mez—Singer), Umberto Borso (ten—Chevalier), Mario Carlin (ten—Edmondo/Dancing Master/Lamplighter), Ferdinando Lidonni (bar—Lescaut), Giovanni Foiani (bass—Geronte/Sergeant/Captain), Joop Ruivenkamp (bass—Innkeeper), F. Vernizzi (cnd), Groot Omroep Orch, Groot Omroep Choir *(rec Amsterdam, Oct 31, 1964)* Bella Voce 2-▲ BLV 107.221 [AAD]

Rumetz, Paolo (bass)
Rossini, G.:La pietra del paragone, w. M. C. Nocentini (sop), A. Trovarelli (mez), H. M. Molinari (cta), P. Barbacini (ten), V. Di Matteo (bar), R. Scaltriti (bar), A. Svab (bar), C. Desderi (cnd), Camerata Musicale Orch, Modeno Teatro Comunale Chorus [I] *(rec 1992)* Nuova Era 2-▲ 7132/33 [DDD]

Rummel, Hedwig (alt)
Nørgård, P.:Sym 3, w. T. Vetö (cnd), Danish National RSO, Danish National Radio Choir *(rec live, Danish Radio Concert Hall, 1982)* Marco Polo/Dacapo ▲ 8.224041 [AAD]

Rumo, Luigi (sgr)
Donizetti, G.:Anna Bolena, w. Maria Callas (sop), Gabriella Carturan (mez), Giulietta Simionato (mez), Gianni Raimondi (ten), Plinio Clabassi (bass), Nicola Rossi Lemmeni (sgr), G. Gavazzeni (cnd), La Scala Orch, La Scala Chorus Great Opera Performances 2-▲ GOP 768

VOCALISTS

Rumowska-Machnikowska, Hanna (sop)
Moniuszko, S.:Songs & Arias, w. Anna Pawluk (pno), Wicherek (cnd), Polish Radio-TV SO, Polish RSO, Warsaw Theatr Wielk Orch—Do Faona; Przasniczka; Mogila; Nad Rzeka; Powiedzcie Mi; Czy Powroci; Gdyby Kto Mnie Kochal Szczerze; Przepioreczka; Nawrócona; Hola Ptaszki; O, Sama Nie Wiem; Oj, Polece Ja Daleko; Jako Od Wichru Krzew Polamany; O! Jakzebym Kleczec Juz Chciala Gdyby Rannym Slonkiem; Ha! Dzieciatko Nam Umiera O Mój Malenki
Polskie Nagrania ("Polskie Radio" series) ▲ PNCD 322

Rumsey, Shirley (voc/lt)
Music of the Spanish Renaissance *(rec Dec. 1-3, 1991)* Naxos ▲ 8.550614 [DDD]

Rundgren, Bengt (b-bar)
Verdi, G.:Rigoletto, w. M. Rinaldi (sop), V. Cortez (mez), F. Bonisolli (ten), R. Panerai (bar), F. Molinari-Pradelli (cnd), Dresden State Orch, Dresden State Chorus [I] Acanta 2-▲ CD 41474 [DDD]

Runey, Henry (b-bar)
Rossini, G.:Music of, w. M. Fortuna (sop), M. Lerner (sop), D. Voigt (sop), M. Horne (mez), K. Kuhlmann (mez), F. von Stade (mez), R. Blake (ten), C. Estep (ten), C. Merritt (ten), T. Hampson (b-bar), J. Opalach (bass), S. Ramey (bass), R. Norrington (cnd), Orch of St. Luke's, New York Concert Chorale
EMI Classics ▲ CDC 54643

Rünger, Gertrud (sop)
Strauss, R.:Elektra (sels), w. Hilde Konetzni (sop—Chrysothemis), Gertrude Rünger (cta/sop—Elektra), H. Knappertsbusch (cnd), Vienna State Opera Orch *(rec Vienna, Nov. 21, 1941)*
Koch Schwann 2-▲ SCH 314662 [ADD]
Strauss, R.:Die Frau ohne Schatten (sels), w. Viorica Ursuleac (sop—Die Kaiserin), Gertrude Rünger (cta/sop—Elisabetta), Franz Völker (ten—Der Kaiser), C. Krauss (cnd), Vienna State Opera Orch *(rec Vienna, June 1, 1933)* Koch Schwann 2-▲ SCH 314662 [ADD]
Wagner, R.:Götterdämmerung (sels), w. Gertrude Rünger (sop—Brünnhilde), Julius Pölzer (ten—Siegfried), H. Knappertsbusch (cnd), Vienna State Opera Orch *(rec Vienna, Sept. 25, 1938)*
Koch Schwann 2-▲ SCH 314662 [ADD]
Wagner, R.:Die Walküre (sels), w. E. Friedrich (sop), K. Buschmann (ten), W. Rode (bar), W. Brückner-Rüggeberg (cnd), Reich Radio Königsberg Large Orch—Act II, Scenes 2,3 & 4 & Act III, Scenes 1,2 & 3 [G] *(rec live 2/17 & 5/1 1938)* Preiser 2-▲ 90075 (m) [AAD]
Wagner, R.:Die Walküre (sels), w. Viorica Ursuleac (sop—Sieglinde), Hilde Konetzni (sop—Sieglinde), Gertrude Rünger (sop—Brünnhilde), Franz Völker (ten—Siegmund), Richard Mayr (bass—Hunding), Krauss, Knappertsbusch (cnd), Vienna State Opera Orch Koch Schwann 2-▲ SCH 314662 [ADD]

Rungs, Linda de (sop)
Caccini, F.:La liberazione di Ruggiero dall'isola d'Alcina, w. Linda De Rungs (sop—Alcian/Vistola), Cecilia Amorocho (sgr—Melissa/Nunzia), Laura Lea Duckworth (sgr—Siren/Harpy), Eric Friedlander (sgr—Monster), L. Ernest Gross (sgr—Enchanted Cypress), Phoebe Jevtovic (sgr—Siren), James Rittenhouse (sgr—Ruggiero/Neptune), Sharon Sim (sgr—Siren), R. Burchard (cnd), Ars Femina Ensemble, TimeChange *(rec Louisville, KY, 1993)* Nannerl ▲ NR-ARS 003; ■ NR-ARS 003

Runkel, Reinhild (cta)
Korngold, E.W.:Das Wunder der Heliane, w. A. Tomowa-Sintow (sop), N. Gedda (ten), J. D. de Haan (ten), H. Welker (bar), R. Pape (bass), J. Mauceri (cnd), Berlin RSO [G]
London 3-▲ 436636-2 [DDD]

Rüping, Martina (sgr)
Zemlinsky, A. von:Der Geburtstag der Infantin, w. Soile Isokoski (sop), Iride Martinez (sgr), Andrew Collis (sgr), David Kuebler (ten), Juanita Lascarro (sgr), Machiko Obata (sgr), Anne Schwanewilms (sgr), Natalie Karl (sgr), Franfurter Kantorei (sgr), J. Conlon (cnd), Gürzenich Orch, Cologne PO *(rec Cologne, Feb 1996)* EMI Classics 2-▲ CDCB 56208

Rürk, Gerd (ten)
Orff, C.:Songs & Hymns, w. Mechthild Bach (sop), Michael Schopper (bar), Wolfgang Brunner (pno)
Wergo ▲ WER 6279-2

Rus, Marjan (bass)
Weber, C.M. von:Der Freischütz (sels), w. Set Svanholm (bar—Max), Franz Norman (bass—Kuno), Marjan Rus (bass—Kaspar), H. Knappertsbusch (cnd), Vienna State Opera Orch *(rec Vienna, June 18, 1941)* Koch Schwann ▲ SCH 314692 [ADD]

Russ, Karsten (sgr)
Delius, F.:A Village Romeo & Juliet, w. Eva-Christine Reimer (sgr), Klaus Wallprecht (sgr), K. Seibel (cnd), Kiel PO CPO 2-▲ CPO 999328 [DDD]

Russel, Christofer (bass)
Verdi, G.:Ernani, w. L. Price (sop), C. Ordassy (sop), F. Corelli (ten), C. Anthony (ten), M. Sereni (bar), C. Siepi (bass), T. Schippers (cnd), *(orch unknown)* *(rec 1965)*
Great Opera Performances ▲ GOP 702

Russell, Anna (sop)
The Anna Russell Album Sony Masterworks ▲ MDK 47252 ■ MDT 47252
Dittersdorf, K.D. von:Arcifanfano, King of Fools, or It's Always Too Late to Learn, w. P. Brooks (sop), E. Steber (sop), J. McCollum (ten), J. Sopher (ten), H. Rehfuss (bar), D. Smith (bar), N. Jenkins (cnd), Clarion Music Society Orch, Clarion Music Society Chorus [E] *(rec live, New York 1965)*
VAI Audio 2-▲ VAIA 1010-2 (m) [ADD]

Russell, Charles (nar)
Albright, W.:A Song to David, w. Melissa Semmes (nar), Deborah Carbaugh (sop), Susan Sacquitne-Druck (mez), Rick Penning (ten), James Bohn (bass), Dean Billmeyer (org), Howard Don Small (cnd), St. Mark's Cathedral Choir Minneapolis *(rec live, St. Mark's Cathedral, Minneapolis, MN, Apr. 28, 1991)* Gothic ▲ G 49066 [DDD]

Russell, D. (sgr)
Mozart, W.A.:Songs, w. J. Edwards (cta), P. Sharpe (sgr), D. Hamilton (ten), M. Glasgow (sgr), C. Birch (sgr), P. Hooper (sgr), G. Lancaster (pno) *(rec July 1991)* Tall Poppies ▲ TP009 [DDD]

Russell, Jack (sgr)
Strauss (II), Joh.:Eine Nacht in Venedig, w. Nola Fairbanks (sgr—Ciboletta), Thomas Tibbett Hayward (sgr—Mario), Laurel Hurley (sgr—Nina), David Kurlan (sgr—Senator Bartoldi), Guen Omeron (sgr—Barbara), Jack Russell (sgr—Duke of Palobino), Kenneth Schon (sgr—Filippo Del Aqua), Norwood Smith (sgr—Caramello), Enzo Stuarti (sgr—Pappacoda) *(rec Belock Recording Studio, Bayside, NY)*
Everest ▲ EVC 9036 [AAD]

Russell, James (ten)
Buxtehude, D.:Cants, w. Laura Heimes (sop), Tamara Crout Matthews (sop), Steven Richards (ct), John Alston (bass), M. N. Johnson (cnd), Sarum Consort, St. Peter's in the Great Valley Chamber Choir—Wachet auf, ruft uns die Stimme!; Singet dem Herrn; Quemadmodum desiderat cervus; O fröhliche Stunden, o herrliche Zeit; Jubilate Domino omnis terra; Lobe den Herrn, meine Seele; Erfreue dich, Erde! *(rec St-Martin-in-the-Fields Church, Chestnut Hill, PA, Sept 7-9, 1994)*
Pro gloria musicae ▲ PGM 102 [DDD]

Russell, Linda (alt)
Handel, G.F.:Dixit Dominus, w. Lynn Dawson (sop), Charles Brett (ct), Ian Partridge (ten), Michael George (bass), H. Christophers (cnd), The Sixteen Orch, The Sixteen [L]
Chandos ("Chaconne" series) ▲ CHAN 0517 [DDD]
Haydn, J.:Mass 7, "Kleine Orgelmesse", w. Catherine Wyn-Rogers (alt), William Kendall (ten), Michael George (bass), D. Hill (cnd), Brandenburg Orch, Winchester Cathedral Choir
Hyperion ▲ CDA 66508 [DDD]
Haydn, J.:Mass 14, "Harmoniemesse", w. Catherine Wyn-Rogers (alt), William Kendall (ten), Michael George (bass), D. Hill (cnd), Brandenburg Orch, Winchester Cathedral Choir
Hyperion ▲ CDA 66508 [DDD]

Russell, Lynda (sop)
Mahler, G.:Sym 4, w. A. Wit (cnd), Polish National RSO Katowice Naxos ▲ 8.550527 [DDD]
Martin, F.:Maria-Triptychon, w. Duncan Riddell (vn), M. Bamert (cnd), London PO
Chandos ▲ CHAN 9411 [DDD]

Russell, Lynda (sop) (cont.)
Schubert, Franz:Songs (misc), w. David Campbell (cl), Peter Hill (pno)—Ganymed, D.544; Liebhaber in allen Gestalten, D.558; Nacht und Träume, D.827; Geheimes, D.719; Abendstern, D.806; Der Hirt auf dem Felsen, D.965; Suleika, D.720; Seligkeit, D.433; Wiegenlied, D.498; Gretchen am Spinnrade, D.118; An die Entfernte, D.765; Im Frühling, D.882; Suleikas zweiter Gesang, D.717; Du bist die Ruh, D.776; Lied der Mignon, D.877/4; Nachtviolen, D.752; Der Musensohn, D.764; Die Forelle, D.550 *(rec St. Martin's Church, East Woodhay, Hampshire, England, Nov 7-9, 1994)*
Naxos ▲ 8.553113 [DDD]

Russell, Rosalind (sgr)
Bernstein, L.:Music of, w. Barbara Cook (sop), Betty Comden (sgr), Adolph Green (sgr), et al—sels. from Candide, Mass, On the Town, Peter Pan, 1600 Pennsylvania Avenue, Trouble in Tahiti, West Side Story, Wonderful Town *(rec 1950-1973)* CBS ▲ MK 44760 [ADD]
Bernstein, L.:Wonderful Town, w. S. Chaplin (sgr), J. McKeever (sgr), et al.
Sony Broadway ▲ SK 48021 ■ ST 48021

Russo, Vincent (sgr)
Wayditch, G. von:Jesus before Herod, w. Michael Best (ten—Jappeticus), Christopher Lindbloom (sgr—Philippo/Herod), Eileen Moss (sgr—Pabula), Vincent Russo (sgr—Pabo), Stephen A. Scot-Shepherd (sgr—Luke the Evangelist), Pauline Tweed (sgr—1st & 2nd girls), P. Erös (cnd), San Diego SO, San Diego Master Chorale *(rec 1979)* VAI Audio 2-▲ VAIA 1095-2 [ADD]

Rutgers, Elisabeth (mez)
Weber, C.M. von:Der Freischütz (sels), w. Maria Reining (sop—Agathe), Elisabeth Rutgers (mez—Annchen), Julius Pölzer (ten—Max), Herbert Alsen (bass—Kaspar), R. Moralt (cnd), Vienna State Opera Orch *(rec Jan. 1, 1939)* Koch Schwann 2-▲ SCH 314632 [ADD]

Ruuttunen, Esa (bar)
Klami, U.:Song of Lake Küjärvi, w. O. Vänskä (cnd), Lahti SO *(rec Dec. 14-15, 1993)*
BIS ▲ CD 656 [DDD]

Ruyl, Harry (ten)
Charpentier, M.-A.:Leçons de ténèbres, H. 96-110, w. Jan Caals (ten), Howard Crook (ct), Luc de Meulenaere (ct), Michel Verschaeve (bar), Kurt Widmer (bass), L. Devos (cnd), Musica Polyphonica
Erato 2-▲ ERA 96376 [DDD]

Ruzicka, Kurt (ten)
Lehár, F.:Die lustige Witwe, w. D. Koller (sop), M. Irosch (sop), H. Papouschek (sop), P. Minich (ten), H. Prikopa (bar), K. Huemer (bar), R. Bibl (cnd), Vienna Volksoper Orch, Vienna Volksoper Chorus [G]
Denon 2-▲ CO 8103 [DDD]
Strauss (II), Joh.:Wiener Blut, w. H. Papouschek (sop), S. Martikke (sop), E. Kales (sop), A. Dallapozza (ten), E. Kuchar (ten), W. Kandutsch (bar), K. Dönch (bar), O. Kolmann (bass), R. Bibl (cnd), Vienna Volksoper Orch, Vienna Volksoper Chorus Denon 2-▲ CO 8105 [DDD]

Ryan, K. (sgr)
McLean, B.:Rainforest Images, w. Panaiotis (sgr), I. Troselj (sgr), P. McLean (sgr/rcr/vn), B. McLean (rcr/clariflute), B. Dickie (didgeridoo) Capstone ▲ CPS 8617n

Rydell, Roland (bar)
Tubin, E.:The Retreating Soldier's Song, w. JanÅke Larson (pno), N. Järvi (cnd), Lund's Student Choral Society BIS ▲ CD 269 [DDD]

Rydén, Susanne (sop)
Kraus, J.M.:Prosperin, w. Hillevi Martinpelto (sop), Anna Eklund-Tarantino (sgr), Peter Mattei (bar), Lars Arvidson (bass), Stephen Smith (sgr), M. Tatlow (cnd), Stockholm CO, Stockholm Chamber Choir
Musica Sveciae 2-▲ MSCD 422/23 [DDD]
Monteverdi, C.:Vespers, w. Irena Troupova-Wilke (sop), Detlef Bratschke (alt), Erich Mentzel (ten), Hermann Oswald (ten), Manuel Warwitz (ten), Thomas Herberich (bass), Günther Schmidt (bass), H. Arman (cnd), Schütz Academy Capriccio ▲ CD 10521 [DDD]
Roman, J.H.:Songs, w. N. E. Sparf (vn), K. Ottesen (vc), S. Åberg (thb/lt/gtr), B. Gäfvert (org/hpd)—Thet är en kostelig ting; 4 Songs from *Vårbetraktelser* [text by Jacob Freese]:Mit hierta rörs af frögd/I foglar, vilde djur/Min andagt/Gud, alla härars Gud; Ihr Augen worzu nutzt ihr mir [w. E. Nordenfelt (harpsichord)]; Sein eigen Hertze fressen [w. Nordenfelt]; Kom tysta enslighet; La Ragion gli affetti ascolta; The Happy Man; For the Few Hours; Herren lofver af Himlen hög [Ps. 148]; 5 Songs by Olof von Dalin:Ata litet, dricka vatten/At ju mången har idag/Födas, gråta dij och lindas/Ar det hela tidsfördrifvet/Den är lycklig född til Verlden; Herre när jag tig hafver; Jag förtröstar på Herran; Gud, jag will sjunga om din makt *(rec May 9-11 & July 10, 1994)* Swedish Society ▲ SCD 1066
Roman, J.H.:Te Deum, w. P.-E. Lindskog (ten), E. Ericson (cnd), Drottningholm Baroque Ensemble, Eric Ericson Chamber Choir *(rec 1992)* Musica Sveciae ▲ MSCD 413 [DDD]

Ryde-Weller, Stephen (trb)
Ireland, J.:Songs, w. Nicholas Richardson (trb), D. Hill (cnd), Bournemouth SO—The Holy Boy *(rec Winchester Cathedral, Jan 10-13, 1994)* London ▲ 444130-2 [DDD]

Rydl, Kurt (bass)
Einem, G. von:Dantons Tod, w. K. Laki (sop), I. Mayr (mez), H. Hiestermann (ten), W. Hollweg (ten), T. Adam (bass-bar), L. Zagrosek (cnd), Austrian RSO, Austrian Radio Chorus [G] *(rec live, Salzburg, 8/13/83)* Orfeo 2-▲ 102842 [ADD]
Mozart, W.A.:Entführung, w. S. Greenberg (sop), J. Thames (sop), J. Van Der Schaaf (ten), W. Gahmlich (ten), M. Viotti (cnd), Frankfurt RSO, Bamberg Sym Chorus LaserLight ▲ 14117 [DDD]
Mozart, W.A.:Entführung, w. S. Greenburg (sop), J. Thames (sop), J. van der Schaaf (ten), W. Gahmlich (ten), Trissenaar (sgr), M. Viotti (cnd), Frankfurt RSO, Bamberg Sym Chorus
Capriccio 2-▲ 10 403/04
Mozart, W.A.:Nozze di Figaro, w. M. Price (sop), K. Battle (sop), M. Nicolesco (sop), A. Murray (mez), J. Hynninen (bar), R. Muti (cnd), Vienna PO, Vienna State Opera Chorus [I]
EMI Classics 3-▲ CDCC 47978 [DDD]
Mozart, W.A.:Nozze di Figaro (sels), w. M. Price (sop), K. Battle (sop), M. Nicolesco (sop), A. Murray (mez), J. Hynninen (bar), R. Muti (cnd), Vienna PO, Vienna State Opera Chorus [I]
EMI Classics ▲ CDC 54321
Offenbach, J.:Les Contes d'Hoffmann, w. L. Serra (sop), R. Plowright (sop), J. Norman (sop), A. Murray (mez), J. Taillon (mez), N. Shicoff (ten), A. Oliver (ten), R. Tear (ten), J. Van Dam (b-bar), D. Duesing (bar), S. Cambreling (cnd), Brussels Théâtre de la Monnaie Orch [F]
EMI Classics 3-▲ CDCC 49641 [DDD]
Penderecki, K.:St. Luke Passion, w. S. van Osten (sop), S. Roberts (bar), E. Lubaszenko (narr), K. Penderecki (cnd), Polish National RSO Katowice, Cracow Boys Choir, Warsaw National Phil Chorus
Argo ▲ 430328-2 [DDD]
Schmidt, F.:Das Buch mit sieben Siegeln, w. Sylvia Greenberg (sop), Carolyn Watkinson (cta), Peter Schreier (ten), Thomas Moser (ten), Robert Holl (bass), L. Zagrosek (cnd), Austrian RSO, Vienna State Opera Chorus [G] Orfeo 2-▲ 143862 [DDD]
Strauss (II), Joh.:Die Fledermaus, w. L. Popp (sop), E. Lind (sop), A. Baltsa (mez), P. Domingo (ten), W. Brendel (bar), P. Domingo (cnd), Munich RSO, Bavarian Radio Chorus [G]
EMI Classics 2-▲ CDCB 47480
Strauss, R.:Der Rosenkavalier (sels), w. B. Hendricks (sop), K. Te Kanawa (sop), A. S. von Otter (mez), R. Leech (ten), B. Haitink (cnd), Dresden Staatskapelle, Dresden State Opera Chorus
EMI Classics ▲ ZDC 54493
Wagner, R.:Der fliegende Holländer, w. H. Beherns (sop—Senta), I. Vermillion (mez—Mary), U. Heilmann (ten—Helmsman), J. Protschka (ten—Erik), R. Hale (bar—The Dutchman), K. Rydl (bass—Daland), C. von Dohnányi (cnd), Vienna PO, Vienna State Opera Chorus
London 2-▲ 436418-2 [DDD]
Wagner, R.:Das Rheingold, w. M. Lipovšek (mez), J. Rappé (ten), H. Zednik (ten), P. Haage (ten), A. Schmidt (bar), T. Adam (b-bar), H. Tschammer (bass), J. Morris (bass), B. Haitink (cnd), Bavarian RSO [G] EMI Classics 2-▲ CDCB 49853 [DDD]

Rye, John (nar)
Lumsdaine, D.:Aria for Edward John Eyre, w. J. Manning (sop), J. Baddeley (nar), E. Howarth (cnd), Gemini Ensemble NM Classics ▲ NMCD 007 [DDD]

Ryhming, Gudrun (sop)
Roman, J.H.:Sacred Music, w. M. Spaeter (thb), K. Ottesen (vc), E. Nordenfelt (hpd/org)—Psalms 4, 5, 81, 103, 124 & 125; Mon coeur tressaille de joie; Oiseaux, animaux sauvages; Mes prères, hâtez-vous; Dieu, Dieu de to Gallo ▲ CD 764 [DDD]

Rymarczyk, Katarzyna (sop)
Cimarosa, D.:Requiem pro defunctis, w. B. Krahel (mez), I. Jakubowski (ten), A. Niemierowicz (bar), S. Frontalini (cnd), Warmia National Orch, Olsztyn Academy Chorus [L] Bongiovanni ▲ GB 2088 [DDD]

Rysanek, Leonie (sop)
Beethoven, L. van:Fidelio, w. Judith Blegen (sop), Jon Vickers (ten), Walter Berry (bass), John Macurdy (bass), Giorgio Tozzi (bass), K. Böhm (cnd), San Francisco Opera Orch, San Francisco Opera Chorus Melodram 2-▲ CDM 27086
Beethoven, L. van:Fidelio (sels), w. I. Seefried (sop), E. Haefliger (ten), F. Lenz (ten), D. Fischer-Dieskau (bar), K. Engen (bass), G. Frick (bass), F. Fricsay (cnd), Bavarian State Orch, Bavarian Opera Chorus—Overture, various arias & scenes, finale [G] IMP Collectors Series ▲ IMPX 9021 [AAD]
Cherubini, L.:Médée, w. L. Popp (sop), M. Lilowa (mez), B. Prevedi (ten), N. Ghiuselev (bass), H. Stein (cnd), Vienna State Opera Orch, Vienna State Opera Chorus *(rec live, Vienna 1/31/72)* Melodram 2-▲ CDM 27087 [ADD]
Janácek, L.:Jenůfa, w. G. Benačková (sop), P. Kazaras (ten), W. Ochman (ten), E. Queler (cnd), New York City Opera Orch [Cz] *(rec live at Carnegie Hall, Mar. 30, 1988)* BIS 2-▲ CD 449/50 [DDD]
Kálmán, I.:Die Csárdásfürstin (sels), w. E. Liebesberg (sop), R. Christ (ten), H. Prikopa (bar), F. Bauer-Theussl (cnd), Vienna Volksoper Orch, Vienna Volksoper Chorus [G] Koch Präsent ▲ CD 399226 [AAD]
Mascagni, P.:Cavalleria rusticana, w. Ruth Falcon (sop—Lola), Leonie Rysanek (sop—Santuzza), Astrid Varnay (sop—Mamma Lucia), Plácido Domingo (ten—Turiddu), Benito di Bella (bar—Alfio), N. Santi (cnd), Munich National Theater Orch, Munich National Theater Chorus *(rec Munich, Dec 25, 1978)* Legato Classics ▲ LCD 202-1
Puccini, G.:Tosca, w. Russell Christopher (ten), Andrea Velis (ten), Clifford Harvuot (bar), Cornell MacNeil (bar), Fernando Corena (bass), Paul Plishka (bass), F. Molinari-Pradelli (cnd), San Francisco Opera Orch, San Francisco Opera Chorus Melodram 2-▲ CDM 27508
Smetana, B.:Dalibor, w. L. Spiess (ten), E. Wächter (bar), J. Krips (cnd), Vienna State Opera Orch, Vienna State Opera Chorus *(rec live, Vienna, 10/19/69)* Myto 2-▲ 2 MCD 92465 [ADD]
Strauss, R.:Die ägyptische Helena, w. Annelies Kupper (sop—Aithra), Leonie Rysanek (sop—Helena), Ira Malaniuk (cta—Omniscient Seashell), Bernd Aldenhoff (ten—Menelas), Richard Holm (ten—Da-ud), Hermann Uhde (bar—Altair), J. Keilberth (cnd), Bavarian State Opera Orch, Bavarian State Opera Chorus *(rec Munich Opera Festival, Prince Regent Theater, Aug 10, 1956)* Orfeo d'or 2-▲ 424962
Strauss, R.:Die ägyptische Helena, w. A. Kupper (sop), B. Aldenhoff (ten), H. Uhde (bar), J. Keilberth (cnd), Bavarian State Opera Orch, Bavarian State Opera Chorus [G] *(rec live, Munich, 8/27/56)* Melodram 2-▲ MEL 27066 (m) [AAD]
Strauss, R.:Ariadne auf Naxos, w. J. Scovotti (sop), T. Troyanos (mez), J. King (ten), P. Schöffler (b-bar), K. Böhm (cnd), Vienna State Opera Orch, Vienna State Opera Chorus *(rec 1967)* Melodram 2-▲ MLO 270105 [ADD]
Strauss, R.:Arias—soprano arias from Ägyptische Helena *(Zweite Brauchnacht, from Act 2—Munich 1956, J. Keilberth cnd)*, Ariadne auf Naxos *(Ein schönes wär; Es gibt ein reich—Vienna 1967, K. Böhm cnd)*, Elektra *(Ich kann nicht zitzen—Vienna 1965, K. Böhm cnd)*, Rosenkavalier *(five arias from Acts 1 & 3, w. H. Schwarz (mez), C. Malone (sop)—Vienna 1978, R. Heger cnd)*, Salome *(Final Scene—Vienna 1971, F. Leitner cnd)* *(rec live 1956-1978)* HRE ▲ 1005-1 [ADD]
Strauss, R.:Arias—11 arias from Ägyptische Helena, Ariadne auf Naxos, Elektra, & Die Liebe der Danae [G] Arkadia 3-▲ 207 (m) [ADD]
Strauss, R.:Elektra, w. B. Nilsson (sop), R. Resnik (mez), W. Windgassen (ten), E. Wächter (bar), K. Böhm (cnd), *(orch unknown)* [G] *(rec live, Vienna 12/16/65)* Standing Room Only 2-▲ SRO 833-2 [ADD]
Strauss, R.:Die Frau ohne Schatten, w. B. Nilsson (sop), R. Hesse (mez), J. King (ten), W. Berry (bass), K. Böhm (cnd), Vienna SO Deutsche Grammophon 3-▲ 445325-2
Strauss, R.:Die Frau ohne Schatten, w. Hoffman (sgr), Thomas (sgr), H. von Karajan (cnd), Vienna State Opera Orch, Vienna State Opera Chorus [G] *(rec live, Vienna, 6/11/64)* Arkadia 3-▲ 207 (m) [ADD]
Strauss, R.:Die Liebe der Danae (sels), w. F. Frantz (b-bar), R. Kempe (cnd), Bavarian State Opera Orch—eleven arias from Acts 1,2 & 3 [G] *(rec 1953)* Melodram 3-▲ MEL 37061 (m) [AAD]
Strauss, R.:Der Rosenkavalier (sels), w. C. Ludwig (mez), et al.—selected scenes Melodram 2-▲ MEL 27098
Strauss, R.:Salome, w. C. Studer (sop), H. Hiestermann (ten), B. Terfel (b-bar), G. Sinopoli (cnd), Berlin German Opera Orch Deutsche Grammophon 2-▲ 431810-2 [DDD]
Strauss, R.:Salome, w. A. Varnay (sop/mez), G. Stolze (ten), D. Fischer-Dieskau (bar), F. Leitner (cnd), Bavarian State Opera Orch *(rec live, Monaco, 1971)* Melodram 2-▲ MEL 27098
Verdi, G.:Don Carlos, w. S. Jurinac (sop—Elisabetta), L. Rysanek (sop—Celestial Voice), F. Cossotto (mez—Princess Eboli), L. Dutoit (boy sop—Tebaldo), P. Domingo (ten—Don Carlo), E. Majkut (ten—Count of Lerma), M. Sereni (bar—Rodrigo), C. Siepi (bass—Philip II), I. Vinco (bass—Grand Inquisitor), T. Franc (bass—Friar), S. Varviso (cnd), Vienna State Opera Orch, Vienna State Opera Chorus Standing Room Only 2-▲ SRO 850 [ADD]
Verdi, G.:Macbeth, w. C. Bergonzi (ten), L. Warren (bar), J. Hines (bass), E. Leinsdorf (cnd), Metropolitan Opera Orch, New York Metropolitan Opera Chorus [I] RCA Gold Seal 2-▲ 4516-2-RG [ADD]
Wagner, R.:Arias & Scenes—arias from Fliegende Holländer: Traft ihr das Schiff *(Sawallisch, Bayreuth 1959)* & Walküre:Schläfst du Gast? (w. Jon Vickers); Der Männer Sippe *(Knappertsbusch, Bayreuth 1958)* Myto 3-▲ MCD 89002 (m) [ADD]
Wagner, R.:Arias & Scenes—from Fliegende Holländer *(Jo-ho-hoe!...Traft ihr das Schiff; w. Rudolf Michl, South German RSO, 1950)*, Lohengrin *(Euch Lüften, die mein Klagen; w. André Cluytens, Bayreuth 1958)*, Walküre *(Der Männer Sippe; w. Knappertsbusch, Bayreuth 1958)*, Rudolf Lustig (tenor)—from Rienzi *(Erstehe, hohe Roma, neu!; Kennt ihr mich nach? Es fordet Ruhe der Tribun; w. Herbert Kegel, Leipzig RSO, 1951)* Melodram 3-▲ MEL 37073 (m) [AAD]
Wagner, R.:Der fliegende Holländer, w. G. London (bar), J. Greindl (bass), W. Sawallisch (cnd), Bayreuth Festival Orch, Bayreuth Festival Chorus [G] *(rec live, Bayreuth 1959)* Melodram 2-▲ MEL 26101
Wagner, R.:Der fliegende Holländer, w. A.-M. Bessel (mez), C. Heater (ten), F. Crass (bass), K. Ridderbusch (bass), W. Sawallisch (cnd), La Scala Orch, La Scala Chorus [G] *(rec live, Milan 2/2/66)* Memories 2-▲ HR 4281/82 (m) [ADD]
Wagner, R.:Der fliegende Holländer, w. K. Liebl (ten), G. London (bar), G. Tozzi (bass), A. Dorati (cnd), Royal Opera House Orch, Royal Opera House Chorus Covent Garden [G] London 2-▲ 417319-2 [ADD]
Wagner, R.:Götterdämmerung, w. Birgit Nilsson (sop—Brünnhilde), Leonie Rysanek (sop—Gutrune), Gerda Sommerschuh (sop—Woglinde), Elisabeth Lindermeier (sop—Wellgunde), Ruth Michaelis (sop—Flohilde), Marianne Schech (sop—Dritte Norne), Ira Malaniuk (mez—Waltraute), Irmgarth Barth (mez—Erste Norne), Hertha Töpper (mez—Zweite Norne), Bernd Aldenhoff (ten—Siegfried), Hermann Uhde (bar—Gunther), Gottlob Frick (bass—Hagen), H. Knappertsbusch (cnd), Bavarian State Opera Orch, Bavarian State Opera Chorus *(rec live, Prinzregententheater, Sept. 1, 1955)* Orfeo 4-▲ 356944 (m)
Wagner, R.:Lohengrin, w. A. Varnay (sop), S. Kónya (ten), E. Blanc (bar), A. Cluytens (cnd), Bayreuth Festival Orch, Bayreuth Festival Chorus [G] *(rec live, 7/23/58)* Myto 3-▲ MCD 89002 (m) [ADD]
Wagner, R.:Der Ring des Nibelungen, w. B. Nilsson (sop), L. Rysanek (sop), K. Dvořaková (sop), M. Mödl (sop), A. Burmeister (mez), V. Soukupova (mez), E. Wohlfahrt (ten), W. Windgassen (ten), T. Stewart (bar), T. Adam (b-bar), G. Neidlinger (b-bar), K. Böhme (bass), G. Nienstedt (bass), K. Böhm (cnd), Bayreuth Festival Orch, Bayreuth Festival Chorus [G] *(rec live, 1966-67)* Philips 14-▲ 420325-2 [ADD]
Wagner, R.:Der Ring des Nibelungen (sels), w. Birgit Nilsson (sop—Brünnhilde), Leonie Rysanek (sop—Sieglinde), James King (ten—Siegmund), Wolfgang Windgassen (ten), Theo Adam (b-bar—Wotan), Gustav Neidlinger (b-bar), Josef Greindl (bass), K. Böhm (cnd), Bayreuth Festival Orch *(rec Bayreuth, 1967)* Philips 2-▲ 454020-2
Wagner, R.:Tannhäuser, w. J. Lustig (sgr), M. Cordes (bar), G. Frick (bass), K. Böhm (cnd), Naples Teatro San Carlo Orch, Naples Teatro San Carlo Chorus [G] *(rec live, Naples, 3/17/56)* Melodram 3-▲ MEL 37073 (m) [AAD]
Wagner, R.:Die Walküre (sels), w. B. Nilsson (sop), L. Suthaus (ten), H. von Karajan (cnd), La Scala Orch—nine selections from Acts 1 & 2 *(rec live in Milan, 4/21/58)* Hunt Productions 12-▲ 12 CDKAR 223 (m) [ADD]

Rysanek, Leonie (sop) (cont.)
Wagner, R.:Die Walküre (act 1), w. James King (ten), Gerd Nienstedt (bass), K. Böhm (cnd), Bayreuth Festival Orch *(rec live, Bayreuth Festival)* Philips ("Solo" series) ▲ 442640-2
Wagner, R.:Die Walküre (act 3), w. A. Varnay (sop—Brünhilde), L. Rysanek (sop—Sieglinde), S. Björling (bar—Wotan), H. von Karajan (cnd), Bayreuth Festival Orch *(rec Aug. 12, 1951)* EMI Classics ▲ ZDH 64704

Rysanek, Lotte (sop)
Golden Operetta, Vol. 2:Operetta Melodies, w. F. Bauer-Theussl (cnd), Vienna Volksoper Orch, Vienna Volksoper Chorus, Renate Holm (sop), Dagmar Hermann (mez), Kurt Equiluz (ten), Horst Winter (ten), et al. Koch Präsent ▲ 399 224 [AAD]

Sà, Marcos Loureiro de (bar)
Campra, A.:Motets, w. Véronique Gens (sop), Anne Gotkovski (sop), Jean-Paul Fouchécourt (alt), Douglas Nasrawi (ten), Peter Harvey (bar), Kevin Mallon (vn), H. Niquet (cnd), Concert Spirituel Orch, Concert Spirituel Vocal Ensemble—Te Deum; Notus in Judea Deus; Deus in Nomine Tuo Adda ▲ ADD 241942 [DDD]
Rameau, J.P.:Motets, w. I. Desrochers (sop), V. Gens (sop), J.-P. Fouchecourt (ct), H. Lamy (ten), P. Harvey (bar), S. Imbodem (bass), *(orch unknown)*—Deus noster refugium; Quam dilecta; In convertendo [L] *(rec Apr. 13-18, 1992)* FNAC Music ▲ 592096 [DDD]

Saarinen, Eeva-Jiisa (mez)
Kortekangas, O.:Grand Hotel, w. S. Tiilikainen (bar), K. Laurikainen (speaker), Pohjola, Söderström (cnd), Avanti! CO, Finnish Chamber Chorus, Tapiola Chorus [Fin] Ondine ▲ ODE 749-2 [ADD]
Merikanto, A.:Juha, w. Raimo Sirkiä (ten), Jorma Hynninen (bar), J.-P. Saraste (cnd), Finnish RSO Ondine 2-▲ ODE 872
Merikanto, O.:Music of, w. Jorma Hynninen (bar), Sauli Tiilikainen (bar), Kaija Saaikettu (vn), Erkki Rautio (vc), Pertti Eerola (pno), Ralf Gothoni (pno), Raija Kerppo (pno), Izumi Tateno (pno), Tauno Satomaa (cnd), Candomino Choir—Summer Evening (waltz); Valse lente; Romance; On the Highest Tree-Top; Annina; Bye, Bye Lullabye; The Weeping Flute; At Sea; Hey My Heart; Where Rustling Birches Bend; Play Softly, the Tune of Mourning; Fairy Tale by the Fireside; Idyll; Scherzo, Op. 6/4; O Dost Thou Remember That Hymn; Lade Ladoga; Why Do I Sing; The Thunderbird; The Happy Ones; Summer Evening's Idyll Finlandia ▲ FIN 500432 [AAD/DDD]
Sibelius, J.:Kullervo, w. J. Hynninen (bar), P. Berglund (cnd), Helsinki PO, Helsinki Univ Male Choir, Helsinki State Academy Male Choir EMI Classics ▲ CDM 65080

Saarinen, Eeva-Jiisa (nar)
Aho, K.:Pergamon, w. L. Paasikivi (nar), T. Nyman (nar), M. Lehtinen (nar), P. Pietiläinen (org), O. Vänskä (cnd), Lahti SO *(rec Lahti, Finland, May 23-25, 1994)* BIS ▲ CD 646 [DDD]

Saarman, Risto (ten)
Kuhlau, F.:Lulu, w. T. Kiberg (sop), A. Frellesvig (sgr), K. von Binzer (ten), U. Cold (bass), E. Harbo (sgr), M. Schønwandt (cnd), Danish National RSO, Danish National Radio Choir [Da] Kontrapunkt 3-▲ 32009/11 [DDD]

Sabatano, Nina (sop)
Rossini, G.:Il barbiere di Siviglia (sels), w. M. Resemba (sop), F. de Lucia (ten), F. Novelli (bar), G. Schottler (bass), A. di Tommaso (bass), S. Valentino (bass), S. Sassano (cnd), Naples Teatro San Carlo Orch, Naples Teatro San Carlo Chorus [I] *(rec 1918 for Phonotype)* Standing Room Only ▲ SRO 819-1 [ADD]

Sabate (sgr)
Halévy, F.:La Juive, w. M. Le Bris (sop), Y. Hayashi (sop), G. Tucker (ten), A. Guadagno (cnd), *(orch & chorus unknown)* [F] *(rec live, London, 1973)* Legato Classics 2-▲ LCD 120-2 [AAD]

Sabatucci (sgr)
Donizetti, G.:Lucia di Lammermoor (sels), w. L. Gencer (sop), G. Prandelli (ten), N. Carta (bar), R. Botteghelli (bass), Hussu (sgr), O. de Fabritiis (cnd), Trieste Teatro Comunale Giuseppe Verdi Orch, Trieste Teatro Comunale G. Verdi Chorus *(rec live 12/13/57 & 2/10/58)* Melodram ▲ MEL 15003 (m) [AAD]

Sabbatini, Giuseppe (ten)
Bellini, V.:I Puritani (sels), w. Lucia Albert (sgr), Carlos Alvarez (bass), Michele Pertusi (bass)—All'erta! All'erta!; A te, o cara, amor talora; Son vergin vezzosa; Ah..Dolor! Ah Terror!; Cinta di fiori e col ben crin disciolto; O Rendetemi la speme—Vien, Diletto; Il Rival salvar tu dei—Suoni la tromba Laserlight ▲ 14208 [DDD]
Gounod, C.:Faust (sels), w. Alexandrina Pendachanska (sop—Margarethe), Giuseppe Sabbatini (ten—Faust), György Melis (bar—Valentin), Nicolai Ghiaurov (bass—Méphistophélès), Nikola Ghiuselev (bass—Méphistophélès), Berlin RSO, Vienna SO, Hungarian State Opera Orch, Bulgarian RSO, Sofia SO, Bulgarian National Chorus, Bulgarian National Chorus Radio Choir—Intro; Vien ou bière; O sainte médaille...Avant de quitter ces lieux; Le veau d'or [all from Act 2]; Quel trouble inconnu me pénètre!...Salut! demeure chaste et pure; Je voudrais bien savoir...Il était un roi de Thule; Un bouquet!...O Dieu! que de bijoux [both from Act 3]; Gloire immortelle de nos aieux; Vous qui faites l'endormie [both from Act 4]; Intermezzo; Walpurgis Night [both from Act 5] Laserlight ▲ 14209 [DDD]
Mozart, W.A.:Clemenza (sels), w. R. Paternostro (cnd), NHK Chamber Soloists—Ah se foss intorno al trono LaserLight ▲ 15 890 [DDD]
Mozart, W.A.:Don Giovanni, w. S. Ghazarian (sop), G. Ottenthal (sop), P. Pace (sop), R. Bruson (bar), A> Rinaldi-Miliani (bar), F. De Grandis (bass), N. Ghiuselev (bass), N. Järvi (cnd), Cologne RSO, Cologne Radio Chorus [I] Chandos 3-▲ CHAN 8920/22 [DDD]
Verdi, G.:Simon Boccanegra, w. M. Nicolesco (sop), R. Bruson (bar), S. Rinaldi-Miliani (bar), R. Scandiuzzi (bass), N. de Angelis (bass), R. Paternostro (cnd), Tokyo SO, Nikikai Chorus *(rec live 2/90)* Capriccio 2-▲ 60018-2 [DDD]

Sabel, Jakob (ten)
Mozart, W.A.:Idomeneo (sels), w. E. Réthy (sop—Idamante), A. Konetzni (sop—Ismene), J. Sabel (ten—Idomeneo), E. Kunz (bar—Arbace), R. Strauss (cnd), Vienna State Opera Orch, Vienna State Opera Chorus *(rec Dec. 3, 1941)* Koch Schwann 2-▲ SCH 314532 [ADD]

Sabrié, Isabelle (sop)
Boulanger, N.:Songs, w. S. Robert (sop), D. Reinhardt (mez), E. Naoumoff (pno)—Lux aeterna [w. O. Charlier (violin) & R. Pidoux (cello)]; Le Couteau *(rec June 14-17, 1993)* Marco Polo ▲ 8.223636 [DDD]

Saccà, Roberto (ten)
Handel, G.F.:Messiah (reorchd Mozart), w. Donna Brown (sop), Cornelia Kallisch (cta), Alastair Miles (bass), H. Rilling (cnd), Stuttgart Bach Collegium, Gächinger Kantorei [G] Hänssler Classic 2-▲ 98.975 [DDD]

Sacchetti, Antonio (bass)
Puccini, G.:Tosca, w. Ranata Tebaldi (sop), Gian Franco Volante (trb), Piero de Palma (ten), Giuseppe Campora (ten), Enzo Mascherini (bar), Fernando Corena (bass), Dario Caselli (bass), A. Erede (cnd), St. Cecilia Academy Orch Rome, St. Cecilia Academy Chorus Rome *(rec 1952)* Andromeda 2-▲ ANR 2539 [ADD]

Saccomani, Lorenzo (bar)
Puccini, G.:La Bohème, w. M. Freni (sop), M. Adani (sop), L. Pavarotti (ten), M. Wolf-Ferrari (cnd), Genoa Teatro Comunale Orch, Genoa Teatro Comunale Chorus [I] *(rec live 4/12/69)* Verona 2-▲ 27079/80
Puccini, G.:La Bohème, w. M. Freni (sop), M. Adani (sop), L. Pavarotti (ten), M. Wolf-Ferrari (cnd), Genoa Teatro Comunale Orch, Genoa Teatro Comunale Chorus *(rec live, Apr 12, 1969)* Melodram 2-▲ MEL 27031 [AAD]

Sacher, Jürgen (ten)
Korngold, E.W.:Der Ring des Polykrates, w. Beate Bilandzija (sop—Laura), Kirsten Blanck (sop—Lieschen), Endrik Wottrich (ten—Wilhelm), Jürgen Sacher (ten—Florian), Dietrich Henschel (bar—Peter), K. Seibel (cnd), German SO *(rec Jesus Christ Church, Dahlem, Sept 19-25, 1995)* CPO ▲ CPO 999402-2 [DDD]
Künneke, E.:The Alluring Flame, w. Birgit Fandrey (sgr—Dolores), Christianne Hossfeld (sgr—Lisbeth), Maria Mallé (sgr), Jürgen Sacher (ten—Master), Ralf Lukas (bar—Hoffman), Gerd Grochowski (sgr—1st Neighbor), Gerhard Peters (sgr—Friedrich), Zoran Todorovic (sgr—Jacinto), Theodor Weimer (sgr—2nd Neighbor), P. Falk (cnd), Cologne RSO, Cologne Radio Chorus *(rec Cologne, Nov 7-26, 1994)* Capriccio ▲ 10753 [DDD]

Sachs, Evelyn (cta)
Puccini, G.:Suor angelica, w. Elisabeth Carron (sop—Angelica), Joan Summers (sop—Genovieffa), Donna Owen (sop—Dolcina), Lou Ann Wyckoff (sop—Alms collector), Hanna Owen (sop—novice), Anthea De Forest (sop—novice), Charlotte Povia (mez—Abbess), Beverly Evans (mez—Monitress), Kay Creed (mez—Mistress), La Vergne Monette (sop/mez—lay sister), Joan August (sop/mez—lay sister), Pearle Goldsmith (sop/mez—other sister), Lila Herbert (sop/mez—other sister), Jodell Kenting (sop/mez—other sister), Ann Pretzat (sop/mez—other sister), Evelyn Sachs (cta—Princess), F. Patanè (cnd), *(orch unknown) (rec New York, Feb 23, 1967)* Legato Classics ▲ LCD 212-1 [ADD]

Sachs, Evelyn (mez)
Verdi, G.:Falstaff, w. Vivian Della Chiesa (sop—Alice), Audrey Schuh (sop—Nannetta), Lizabeth Pritchett (mez—Quickly), Evelyn Sachs (mez—Meg), André Turp (ten—Fenton), Virginio Assandri (ten—Caius), Luigi Vellucci (ten—Bardolfo), Leonard Warren (bar—Falstaff), Richard Torigi (bar—Ford), R. Cellini (cnd), New Orleans Opera Orch, New Orleans Opera Chorus *(rec live, May 5, 1956)* VAI Audio 2-▲ VAIA 1056-2

Saciuk, Andrzej (bass)
Moniuszko, S.:Haunted Manor, w. Bozena Betley-Siradzka (sop—Hanna), Anna Witkowska (sop—Marta/Stara Niewiasta), Wiera Baniewicz (mez—Jadwiga), Aleksandra Imalska (mez—Czesnikowa), Kazimierz Dluha (Grzes), Zdzislaw Nikodem (ten—Damazy), Wieslaw Ochman (ten—Stefan), Andrzej Hiolski (bar—Miecznik), Florian Skulski (bar—Maciej), Leonard Mróz (bass—Zbigniew), Andrzej Saciuk (bass—Skoluba), J. Krenz (cnd), Cracow Polish Radio-TV Orch, Cracow Polish Radio-TV Chorus *(rec Cracovia, 1978)* Agorá Music ("Phoenix" series) 3-▲ 509 [ADD]

Sacks, R. (sgr)
Celona, J.:Sum over Histories, w. B. Degazio (sgr), S. Peet (sgr), R. Sacks (sgr), A. Armin (elecs), R. Armin (elecs), J. Brownell (elecs), D. Hutton (elecs), G. Martynec (elecs), D. Mott (elecs), C. Sokol (elecs) Soundprints ▲ SP 9301

Sacquitne-Druck, Susan (mez)
Albright, W.:A Song to David, w. Melissa Semmes (nar), Charles Russell (nar), Deborah Carbaugh (sop), Rick Penning (ten), James Bohn (bass), Dean Billmeyer (org), Howard Don Small (cnd), St. Mark's Cathedral Choir Minneapolis *(rec live, St. Mark's Cathedral, Minneapolis, MN, Apr. 28, 1991)* Gothic ▲ G 49066 [DDD]

Sadan, Ann (alt)
Lewandowksi, L.L.:Choral Music, w. Sandra Lee (sop), Don Carter (ten), Adam Cohn (b-bar), Michael Morris (bass), Carys Hughes (org), Robert Max (cnd), Zemel Choir—Ma Towu in F; Ma Towu in B♭; L'cho Dodi; Tow L'hodoss; Adoshem Moloch; W'hogen Ba'adenu [Uw'tsel]; W'schomru; L'icho Adoshem; J'Halahu [Hodo Al Erez]; Ladoshem Ho'orets; Uw'nucho Jomar; Adon Olom; Ki K'schimcho; Hajom Harass Olom; Kol Nidre; Schuwi Nafschi; Enosch, K'chozir Jomow; Halalujoh; Preise, Meine Seele Olympia ▲ OLY 347 [DDD]

Sadé, Gabriel (ten)
Dessau, P.:Haggada, w. Sabine Ritterbusch (sop), Renate Spingler (sop), Yvi Jänicke (alt), Peter Galliard (ten—Rabbi Tarfon/Jude/ten solo), Gabriel Sadé (ten—Pharaoh), Jochen Schmeckenbecher (bar—Rabbi Jehoschua), Bernd Weikl (bar—Moses), Matthias Hölle (bass—Speaker/Rabbi Akiwa), Alfred Muff (bass—Father/Rabbi Eleasar), Johann Tilli (bass—Rabbi Elieser/bass solo), G. Albrecht (cnd), Hamburg State PO, Berlin Carl Maria Von Weber Men's Choir, Hamburg Alsterspatzen, North German Radio Chorus [G] *(rec Musikhalle, Hamburg, Sept 4 & 5, 1994)* Capriccio 2-▲ 10590/91 [DDD]
Verdi, G.:Requiem Mass, w. Michèle Crider (sop), Markella Hatziano (mez), Robert Lloyd (bass), R. Hickox (cnd), London SO, London Sym Chorus Chandos ▲ CHAN 9490

Saedén, Erik (bar)
Alfvén, H.:A Boat with Flowers, w. S. Rybrant (cnd), Berlin PO Swedish Society ▲ SCD 1036
Alfvén, H.:Hanserlinagoransson, w. O. Höljer (pno) Swedish Society ▲ SCD 1036
Brahms, J.:Ernste Gesänge, w. H. Pålsson (pno) *(rec Nacka Aula, Nacka Sweden, July 26-27, 1976)* BIS ▲ CD 70 [AAD]
Dallapiccola, L.:Ulisse, w. C. Gayer (sop), V. von Halem (bass), A. Bernard (sgr), L. Maazel (cnd), Berlin German Opera Orch, Berlin German Opera Chorus *(rec live, Berlin 9/28/68)* Stradivarius 2-▲ STR 10063 [ADD]
Debussy, C.:Ballades (3) de François Villon, w. Hans Pålsson (pno) *(rec Nacka Aula, Nacka, Sweden, June 14, 1975)* BIS ▲ CD 28 [AAD]
Lindberg, O.:Requiem, w. I. Sörenson (sop), E. Thallang (alt), C. Solén (ten), O. Johansson (org), H. Kyhle (cnd), Stockholm Univ College of Music Orch, Englebrekt Church Oratory Choir *(rec Nov. 2, 1980)* Sterling ▲ CDS 1013
Mussorgsky, M.:Songs & Dances, w. Hans Palsson (pno) BIS ▲ CD 16 [AAD]
Pettersson, G.A.:Songs, w. A. Östman (pno) Swedish Society ▲ SCD 1033
Verdi, G.:Un ballo in maschera (sels), w. Ragnar Ulfung (ten), Lovberg (sgr), C. Savina (cnd), Stockholm Royal Opera House Orch—Act III excerpts *(rec 1966)* Arkadia 2-▲ 488
Wikström, I.:Den Brottsliga Modern, w. M. Tretom (sop), A. Häggstam (bass), Nordisk CO Proprius ▲ 9069

Saelens, Yves (ten)
Telemann, G.P.:Cants, w. Greetje Anthoni (sop), Stefan Geyer (bar), F. Heyerick (cnd), Le Mercure Galant Baroque Orch, Ex Tempore Vocal Ensemble—Der Tod Jesu *(rec Studio Steurbaut, Gent, June 1995)* René Gailly ▲ 92025 [DDD]

Saemundsdóttir, S. (sop)
Pálsson, P.P.:Music of, w. R. Bragadóttir (mez), Reykjavik CO—Gudis-Mana-Hasi; Crystals; Tomorro; August Sonnet; September Sonnet; Lantao; 6 Thoughtful Songs Music from Iceland ▲ ITM 807

Saetta, N. (sgr)
Zandonai, R.:Francesca da Rimini, w. R. Kabaivanska (sop), P. Domingo (ten), M. Manuguerra (bar), E. Queler (cnd), *(orch unknown) (rec live, March 22, 1973)* Standing Room Only 2-▲ SRO 840-2 [ADD]

Saffer, Lisa (sop)
Handel, G.F.:Agrippina, w. S. Bradshaw (sop), W. Hill (sop), G. Banditelli (cta), D. Minter (alt), R. Popken (alt), B. Szilágyi (bar), M. Dean (b-bar), N. Isherwood (bass), N. McGegan (cnd), Capella Savaria [period instrs] [I] Harmonia Mundi USA 3-▲ HMU 907063/65 ▮ HMU 407063/65
Handel, G.F.:Arias, w. Lisa Saffer (sop—Cuzzoni), Lorraine Hunt (mez—Durastanti), Drew Minter (ct—Senesino), David Thomas (bass—Montagnana), N. McGegan (cnd), Philharmonia Baroque Orch Harmonia Mundi 4-▲ HMX 2907171.74
Handel, G.F.:Arias, w. N. McGegan (cnd), Philharmonia Baroque Orch—12 arias from Alessandro, Flavio, Giulio Cesare, Ottone, Riccardo I, Rodelinda, Scipione, Tamerlano [composed for Italian soprano Francesca Cuzzoni] [I] Harmonia Mundi USA ▲ HMU 907036
Handel, G.F.:Ariodante, w. J. Gondek (sop), L. Hunt (mez), Jennifer Lane (mez), J. Lindemann (ten), R. Müller (ten), N. Cavallier (bass), N. McGegan (cnd), Freiburg Baroque Orch, Ralf Popken (cnd), Wilhelmshaven Vocal Ensemble [172-page libretto w. production photos] Harmonia Mundi France 3-▲ HMC 907146.48
Handel, G.F.:Judas Maccabaeus, w. Patricia Spence (mez), Brian Asawa (ct), Guy de Mey (ten), Leroy Kromm (b-bar), David Thomas (bass), N. McGegan (cnd), Philharmonia Baroque Orch, Univ of California at Berkeley Chamber Chorus [E] *(rec Nov. 15-18, 1992)* Harmonia Mundi USA 2-▲ HMU 907077/78
Handel, G.F.:Ottone, Rè di Germania, w. Julianna Gondek (sop), Patricia Spence (mez), Drew Minter (alt), R. Popken (alt), Michael Dean (b-bar), N. McGegan (cnd), Freiburg Baroque Orch *(rec June 9-12, 1992)* Harmonia Mundi USA 3-▲ HMU 907073/75
Handel, G.F.:Radamisto, w. Monika Frimmer (sop), Juliana Gondek (sop), Dana Hanchard (sop), R. Popken (cta), Michael Dean (b-bar), Nicholas Cavallier (bass), N. McGegan (cnd), Freiburg Baroque Orch Harmonia Mundi USA 3-▲ HMU 907111/13
Handel, G.F.:La Rezurrezione, w. Judith Nelson (mez), Patricia Spence (mez), Jeffery Thomas (ten), Michael George (bass), N. McGegan (cnd), Philharmonia Baroque Orch [I] Harmonia Mundi USA 2-▲ HMU 907027/28
Knussen, O.:Hums & Songs of Winnie-the-Pooh, w. O. Knussen (cnd), Lincoln Center Chamber Music Society Virgin Classics ▲ CDC 59308
Knussen, O.:Late Poems & an Epigram of Rainer Maria Rilke Virgin Classics ▲ CDC 59308

Saffer, Lisa (sop) (cont.)
Purcell, H.:Dido & Aeneas, w. L. Hunt (sop), D. Deam (sop), C. Brandes (sop), R. Rainero (sop), E. Rabiner (mez), P. Elliot (ten), M. Dean (bar), N. McGegan (cnd), Philharmonia Baroque Orch, Clare College Choir Cambridge Harmonia Mundi USA ▲ HMU 907110

Safiulin, Anatoly (bass)
Mussorgsky, M.:Nursery, w. Nikolai Demidenko (pno) Hyperion ▲ CDA 66775
Mussorgsky, M.:Peepshow, w. Nikolai Demidenko (pno) Hyperion ▲ CDA 66775
Mussorgsky, M.:Songs & Dances, w. Nikolai Demidenko (pno) Hyperion ▲ CDA 66775
Mussorgsky, M.:Sunless, w. Nikolai Demidenko (pno) Hyperion ▲ CDA 66775

Sagarminaga, Carlos (ten)
Puccini, G.:Tosca, w. Maria Callas (sop), Mario Filippeschi (ten), Robert Weede (bar), Ramon Alonso (bass), U. Mugnai (cnd), Palacio Bellas Artes Orch, Palacio Bellas Artes Chorus Melodram 3-▲ CDM 36032
Verdi, G.:Il trovatore (sels), w. M. Callas (sop), Feuss (sgr), K. Baum (ten), L. Warren (bar), G. Picco (cnd), Palacio Bellas Artes Orch, Palacio Bellas Artes Chorus—ten selections from Acts 1 & 4 [I] *(rec live, Mexico City 6/20/50)* Myto 2-▲ 2 MCD 90213 (m) [ADD]

Sagona, V. (bass)
Bellini, V.:La straniera, w. L. Alberti (sop—Alaide), S. Mingardo (mez—Isoletta), V. Bello (ten—Arturo), R. Frontale (bar—Il Barone di Valdeburgo), V. Sagona (bass—Il signore di Montalino), P. Zizich (bass—Osburgo), G. Masini (cnd), Trieste Teatro Comunale Giuseppe Verdi Orch, Trieste Teatro Comunale G. Verdi Chorus *(rec Dec. 1990)* Ricordi ▲ RFCD 2015 [DDD]

Sailer (ten)
Mozart, W.A.:Missa, K.317, w. G. Fuchs (sop), Novak (alt), H. Müller (bass), E. Hinreiner (cnd), Salzburg Mozarteum Orch, Salzburg Mozarteum Chorus [L] Pro Arte ▲ CDD 471 [DDD]

Sailer, Friederike (sop)
Vivaldi, A.:Gloria, RV.589, w. Margarethe Bence (alt), M. Couraud (cnd), Stuttgart Pro Musica Orch *(rec 1964)* Tuxedo ▲ TUXCD 1032 [ADD]
Vivaldi, A.:Motets, w. M. Couraud (cnd), Stuttgart Pro Musica Orch—O qui coeli terraeque *(rec 1964)* Tuxedo ▲ TUXCD 1032 [ADD]

St. Hill, Krister (ten)
Krenek, E.:Jonny spielt auf, w. A. Marc (sop), M. Kraus (ten), H. Kruse (ten), L. Zagrosek (cnd), Leipzig Gewandhaus Orch [G] London 2-▲ 436631-2 [DDD]

Saint-Amant, Yves (bass)
Vivier, C.:Kopernikus, "A Ritual Opera of Death", w. Y. Parent (sop), P. Vaillancourt (sop), M.-D. Parent (sop), J. Fleury (cta), D. Doane (ten), M. Ducharme (bar), F. Martel (cl), M. Bélanger (vn), L. Bouchard (tpt), L. Vaillancourt (cnd), *(orch unknown) (rec Feb. 1991)* CBC ("Musica Viva" series) ▲ MVCD 1047 [DDD]

Saint-Cricq, H. (ten)
Berlioz, H.:L'Enfance du Christ (sels), w. F. Rühlmann (cnd), *(orch unknown)*—Le repos de la Sainte Famille [F] *(rec 1930 for Pathé)* The Classical Collector 2-▲ FDC2 2006 [AAD]

Saint-Gelais, H. (ten)
Bach, J.S.:Cant 173a, w. D. Röschmann (sop), K. McMillan (bar), B. Labadie (cnd), Les Violons du Roy *(rec Quebec City, Jan 1994)* Dorian ▲ DOR 90199 [DDD]
Bach, J.S.:Cant 211, "Coffee Cant", w. D. Röschmann (sop), K. McMillan (bar), B. Labadie (cnd), Les Violons du Roy *(rec Quebec City, Jan 1994)* Dorian ▲ DOR 90199 [DDD]
Bach, J.S.:Cant 212, "Peasant Cant", w. D. Röschmann (sop), K. McMillan (bar), B. Labadie (cnd), Les Violons du Roy *(rec Quebec City, Jan 1994)* Dorian ▲ DOR 90199 [DDD]

Saint-Palais, Mary (sop)
Bruneau, A.:Lazare, w. Françoise Pollet (sop), Sylvie Sullé (mez), Jean-Luc Viala (ten), Laurent Naouri (b-bar), J. Mercier (cnd), French National Orch, Maîtrise de Paris, Vittoria French Regional Choir Adès ▲ ADE 204512
Bruneau, A.:Requiem, w. Françoise Pollet (sop), Sylvie Sullé (mez), Jean-Luc Viala (ten), Laurent Naouri (b-bar), J. Mercier (cnd), French National Orch, Maîtrise de Paris, Vittoria French Regional Choir Adès ▲ ADE 204512

Saipe, Julian (sop)
Tippett, M.:King Priam, w. Heather Harper (sop—Hecuba), Linda Hirst (sop—Serving Woman), Felicity Palmer (sop—Andromache), Julian Saipe (sop—Paris), Yvonne Minton (mez—Helen), Ann Murray (mez—Nurse), Kenneth Bowen (ten—Hermes), Peter Hall (ten—Young Guard), Philip Langridge (ten—Paris), Robert Tear (ten—Achilles), Thomas Allen (bar—Hector), Norman Bailey (bar—Priam), Stephen Roberts (bar—Patroclus), David Wilson-Johnson (bar—Old Man), D. Atherton (cnd), London Sinfonietta, London Sinfonietta Chorus Chandos ▲ CHAN 9406/7 [DDD]

Sakamoto, Akemi (mez)
Battiato, F.:Messa Arcaica, w. Franco Battiato (voc), Filippo Destrieri (kbd/cmpt), Carlo Guaitoli (pno), Angelo Privitera (kbd/cmpt), A. Ballista (cnd), Italian Virtuosi, Filippo Maria Bressan (cnd), Athestis Chorus Hemisphere ▲ 837234-2

Saki, Y. (sgr)
Rodgers, R.:Flower Drum Song, w. K. Scott (sgr), I. Shepley (sgr), Y. S. Tung (sgr), T. Hebert (sgr) [1960 London cast] Angel ▲ ZDM 89953

Sakkas, Spiros (bar)
Xenakis, I.:Oresteïa, w. Sylvio Gualda (perc), Strasbourg Univ Chorus Salabert ▲ SCD 8906

Sakurada, Makoto (ten)
Bach, J.S.:Cants 12, w. Yumiko Kurisu (sop), Yoshikazu Mera (ct), Peter Kooy (bass), M. Suzuki (cnd), Japan Bach Collegium *(rec Kobe Shoin Women's Univ, Japan, Apr 11-14, 1996)* BIS ▲ CD 791 [DDD]
Bach, J.S.:Cant 54, w. Yumiko Kurisu (sop), Yoshikazu Mera (ct), Peter Kooy (bass), M. Suzuki (cnd), Japan Bach Collegium *(rec Kobe Shoin Women's Univ, Japan, Apr 11-14, 1996)* BIS ▲ CD 791 [DDD]
Bach, J.S.:Cant 162, w. Yumiko Kurisu (sop), Yoshikazu Mera (ct), Peter Kooy (bass), M. Suzuki (cnd), Japan Bach Collegium *(rec Kobe Shoin Women's Univ, Japan, Apr 11-14, 1996)* BIS ▲ CD 791 [DDD]
Bach, J.S.:Cant 182, w. Yumiko Kurisu (sop), Yoshikazu Mera (ct), Peter Kooy (bass), M. Suzuki (cnd), Japan Bach Collegium *(rec Kobe Shoin Women's Univ, Japan, Apr 11-14, 1996)* BIS ▲ CD 791 [DDD]

Sakurai, Makiko (shomyo/Buddhist chant)
Fujieda, M.:Music of, w. Mamoru Fujueda (cmpt), Mineko Grimmer (audible sculptures), Kodo Uesugi (fukimono), Kazuko Takada (hikimono), Toshiyuki Matsukura (uchimono), Satoshi Sakai (uchimono), Koshin Ebihara (jumon)—The Night Chant III; Wind Chant; Cocoon Chant; Dust Chant; Falling Chant; The Night Chant I Tzadik ("The Composers" series) ▲ TZA 7003 [DDD]

Saldari, Luciano (ten)
Mascagni, P.:Lodoletta, w. Beltrami (sgr), G. Mucci (cnd), Teatro La Gran Guardia Orch, Teatro La Gran Guardia Chorus [I] *(rec live, 10/2/60)* Fonè 2-▲ 88 F 16-36 [ADD]
Verdi, G.:Macbeth, w. Grace Bumbry (mez—Lady Macbeth), Luciano Saldari (ten—Macduff), Paride Venturi (ten—Malcolm), Renato Bruson (bar—Macbeth), Agostino Ferrin (bass—Banquo), A. Gatto (cnd), Bologna Teatro Comunale Orch, Bologna Teatro Comunale Chorus *(rec Bologna, Mar. 18, 1975)* Golden Age of Opera 2-▲ GAO 185/86 [ADD]

Salerno, H. (sgr)
Giordano, U.:Andrea Chénier, w. Montserrat Caballé (sop), Franco Corelli (ten), R. de Carlo (sgr), D. Dondi (sgr), G. Ellsworth (sgr), J. Fair (sgr), R. Falk (sgr), S. Felter (sgr), E. Green (sgr), H. Hicks (sgr), H. Krauss (sgr), L. Miller (sgr), N. Riggins (sgr), A. Guadagno (cnd), Academy of Music Orch, Academy of Music Chorus Great Opera Performances 2-▲ GOP 766

Salimbeni, Marisa (sgr)
Verdi, G.:Don Carlos, w. Katia Ricciarelli (sop), Fiorenza Cossotto (mez), Guido Fabbris (ten), Veriano Luchetti (ten), Piero Cappuccilli (bar), Gianfranco Casarini (bass), Nicolai Ghiaurov (bass), Alessandro Maddalena (bass), Aracelly Haengel (sgr), Giorgio Zoranca (sgr), G. Prêtre (cnd), *(orch unknown)* Great Opera Performances 3-▲ GOP 777

Salinas, Hernán (sgr)
Piazzolla, D.H.:Los Amantes, w. Daniel Piazzolla Octet *(rec Moebio Studios, Buenos Aires, Sept-Oct 1995)* Milan ▲ 35782-2

1386 ▲ = CD ♦ = Enhanced CD Δ = MD ▮ = Cassette Tape ☐ = DCC

Salinas, Hernán (sgr) (cont.)
Piazzolla, D.H.:Mi Viejo Piazzolla, w. Daniel Piazzolla Octet *(rec Moebio Studios, Buenos Aires, Sept–Oct 1995)* Milan ▲ 35782-2

Salinas, Isaac (sgr)
Operatic Arias, w. Salinas, Isaac (sgr), Orquesta Sinfonietta [cnd:Laszlo Rooth] Montilla ▲ MNT 3038

Salinas, Maria Luisa (sop)
Falla, M. de:El sombrero de tres picos, w. E. Bátiz (cnd), Mexican State SO IMP ▲ PCD 2028

Saliotis, Elena (sgr)
Verdi, G.:Nabucco, w. Gloria Lane (mez), Gianni Raimondi (ten), Giangiacomo Guelfi (bar), Nicolai Ghiaurov (bass), G. Gavazzeni (cnd), La Scala Orch, La Scala Chorus *(rec La Scala Theater, Milan, Dec. 7, 1966)* Pantheon 2–▲ PHE 6757 (m)

Salje, Cornelia (alt)
Haydn, M.:Missa Pro Defuncto Archiepiscopo Sigismundo, w. Lena Lootens (sop), Bernard Loonens (ten), Dirk Snellings (b–bar), Philippe Benoit (cnd), Vivente Voce Choir *(rec Steurbaut Sound Recording Centre)* René Gailly ▲ CD 87125 [DDD]
Haydn, M.:Motets, w. Lena Lootens (sop), Bernard Loonens (ten), Dirk Snellings (b–bar), Philippe Benoit (cnd), Vivente Voce Choir—Aria de Passione Domini *(rec Steurbaut Sound Recording Centre)* René Gailly ▲ CD 87125 [DDD]

Salminen, Matti (bass)
Mozart, W.A.:Entführung, w. Yvonne Kenny (sop), Carolyn Watson (cta), Peter Schreier (ten), Wilfried Gamlich (ten), Wolfgang Reichmann (nar), N. Harnoncourt (cnd), Zurich Mozart Opera Orch, Zurich Mozart Opera Chorus [G] Teldec 2–▲ 2292–42643–2
Mozart, W.A.:Requiem, w. K. Battle (sop), A. Murray (mez), D. Rendall (ten), D. Barenboim (cnd), Orch de Paris, Paris Opera Chorus [L] EMI Classics ▲ CDC 47342 [DDD]
Mozart, W.A.:Zauberflöte, w. E. Gruberova (sop), B. Bonney (sop), G. Schmid (sop), H.–P. Blochwitz (ten), T. Hampson (bar), A. Scharinger (bass), N. Harnoncourt (cnd), Zurich Opera Orch, Zurich Opera House Chorus [G] Teldec 2–▲ 2292–42716–2
Opera Arias, w. Lahti SO [cnd:Eri Klas] BIS ▲ CD 520 [DDD]
Sallinen, A.:Kullervo, w. G. Saarinen (pno), J. Silvasti (ten), J. Hynninen (bar), U. Söderblom (cnd), Finnish National Opera Orch, Finnish National Opera Chorus [Fin] Ondine 3–▲ ODE 780–3T [DDD]
Wagner, R.:Der fliegende Holländer, w. L. Balsev (sop), R. Schunk (ten), S. Estes (bass), W. Nelsson (cnd), Bayreuth Festival Orch, Bayreuth Festival Chorus [G] Philips 2–▲ 434599–2 [DDD]
Wagner, R.:Götterdämmerung, w. H. Behrens (sop), C. Studer (sop), H. Schwarz (mez), R. Goldberg (ten), B. Weikl (bar), E. Wlaschiha (bar), J. Levine (cnd), Metropolitan Opera Orch, New York Metropolitan Opera Chorus Deutsche Grammophon 4–▲ 429385–2 [DDD]
Wagner, R.:Parsifal, w. W. Meier (mez), P. Hofmann (ten), F. Mazura (bar), S. Estes (bass), H. Sotin (bass), J. Levine (cnd), Bayreuth Festival Orch, Bayreuth Festival Chorus [1985] [G] Philips 4–▲ 434616–2 [DDD]
Wagner, R.:Der Ring des Nibelungen (sels), w. Jessye Norman (sop), Lucia Popp (sop), René Kollo (ten), Siegfried Jerusalem (ten), Kurt Moll (bass), M. Janowski (cnd), Dresden Staatskapelle RCA Victor ▲ 09026–68084–2; ▮ 09026–68084–4
Wagner, R.:Der Ring des Nibelungen (sels), w. J. Norman (sop), H. Behrens (sop), K. Battle (sop), J. Morris (mez), C. Ludwig (mez), R. Goldberg (ten), S. Jerusalem (ten), E. Wlaschiha (bar), J. Levine (cnd), Metropolitan Opera Orch—The Compact Ring—Ride of the Valkyries Wotan's Farewell & Magic Fire Music, Forest Murmurs, Brünnhilde's Awakening, Siegfried's Funeral Music, Brünnhilde's Immolation, & others Deutsche Grammophon ▲ 437825–2
Wagner, R.:Tannhäuser, w. C. Studer (sop), A. Baltsa (mez), P. Domingo (ten), A. Schmidt (bar), G. Sinopoli (cnd), Philharmonia Orch, Royal Opera House Chorus Covent Garden [G] Deutsche Grammophon 3–▲ 427625–2 [DDD]
Wagner, R.:Tannhäuser, w. C. Studer (sop), A. Baltsa (mez), P. Domingo (ten), A. Schmidt (bar), G. Sinopoli (cnd), Philharmonia Orch, Royal Opera House Chorus Covent Garden Deutsche Grammophon ▲ 435405–2 [DDD]

Salmon, Philip (ten)
Handel, G.F.:Israel in Egypt, w. Ruth Holton (sop), Elisabeth Friday (sgr), Michael Chance (alt), Paul Tindall (sgr), J. E. Gardiner (cnd), English Baroque Soloists, Monteverdi Choir London Philips ▲ 432110–2
Massenet, J.:La Vierge, w. M. Command (sop), M. Castets (sop), M. Olmeda (sop), M. Keller (sop), M. Hacquard (bar), P. Fournillier (cnd), Prague SO, Prague Sym Chorus Koch Schwann 2–▲ CD 313084 [DDD]

Salomaa, Petteri (bass)
Bach, J.S.:Mass in b, BWV 232, w. C. Högman (sop), M. Groop (mez), H. Crook (ten), Drottningholm Baroque Ensemble, Mikaeli Chamber Choir Proprius 2–▲ PRCD 9070/71
Bergman, E.:The Singing Tree, w. K. Hannula (sop), C. Hellekant (cta), P. Lindroos (ten), S. Tiilikainen (bar), M. Wallén (bass), U. Söderblom (cnd), Finnish National Opera Orch, Dominante Chamber Choir, Tapiola Chamber Choir Ondine 2–▲ ODE 794–2D [DDD]
Cimarosa, D.:Il Matrimonio segreto, w. Susan Patterson (sop—Carolina), Janet Williams (mez—Elisseta), Gloria Banditelli (cta—Fidalma), William Matteuzzi (ten—Paolino), Alfonso Antoniozzi (bass—Geronimo), Petteri Salomaa (bass—Count Robinson), Hans Ludwig Hirsch (pno), G. Bellini (cnd), Eastern Netherlands Orch *(rec Muziekcentrum Enschede, Holland, Aug 26–Sept 8, 1991)* Arts 3–▲ 471172 [DDD]
Donizetti, G.:Linda di Chamounix, w. Mariella Devia (sop—Linda), Sonia Ganassi (mez—Pierotto), Francesca Provvisionato (mez—Maddalena), Luca Canonici (ten—Carlo), Alfonso Antoniozzi (bass—Il Marchese di Boisfleury), Petteri Salomaa (bass—Antonio), Boguslaw Fiksinski (sgr—L'intendente), Donato Di Stefano (sgr—Il Prefetto), G. Bellini (cnd), Eastern Netherlands Orch, Andrew Wise (cnd), National Reisopera Choir *(rec Muziekcentrum Enschede, Holland, June 24–July 2, 1992)* Arts Music 3–▲ 47151–2 [DDD]
Mozart, W.A.:Nozze di Figaro, w. A. Augér (sop), B. Bonney (sop), A. Nafé (mez), H. Hagegard (bar), A. Östman (cnd), Drottningholm Court Theater Orch, Drottningholm Court Thea Chorus [I] L'Oiseau-Lyre 3–▲ 421333–2 [DDD]
Pergolesi, G.B.:La serva padrona, w. Jeanne Marie Bima (sop—Serpina); Petteri Salomaa (b–bar—Uberto);, H.L. Hirsch (cnd), Musica Poetica Freiberg *(rec Waldkirch, Germany, Nov 14–18, 1990)* Arts ▲ 47119–2 [DDD]
Shostakovich, D.:Sym 14, w. Margareta Haverinen (sop), J. Swensen (cnd), Tapiola Sinfonietta Ondine ▲ ODE 845

Salomonsson, Kristina (sop)
Schnittke, A.:Requiem, w. I. H. Sjöberg (sop), L. Lindholm (sop), A. F. Eker (cta), N. Högman (ten), S. Parkman (cnd), Stockholm Sinfonietta, Uppsala Academic Chamber Choir [L] BIS ▲ CD 497 [DDD]

Salonga, Lea (sgr)
Rodgers, R.:The King & I, w. J. Andrews (sgr—Anna Leonowens), L. Salonga (sgr—Tuptim), B. Kingsley (sgr—The King), P. Bryson (sgr—Lun Tha), M. Horne (mez—Lady Thiang), M. Liufau (sgr—Prince Chulalongkorn), E. Kingsley (sgr—Louis Leonowens), R. Moore (sgr—Sir Edward Ramsay), M. Sheen (sgr—The Kralahome), J. Mauceri (cnd), Hollywood Bowl Orch, Los Angeles Master Chorale *(rec Culver City, CA, Apr 1992)* Philips ▲ 438007–2 [DDD]

Salter, Richard (bar)
Rihm, W.:Die Eroberung von Mexico, w. R. Behle (sop), I. Metzmacher (cnd), Hamburg State PO, Hamburg State Opera Chorus [G] *(rec live Feb. 9, 1992)* CPO 2–▲ CPO 999185–2 [DDD]
Rihm, W.:Lieder, w. B. Wambach (pno), F. Lang (drum), M. Rosenthal (drum)—Vier Gedichte aus Atemwende [text by Paul Celan] for Voice & Piano (1973); Hölderlin–Fragmente for Voice & Piano (1976–7); Neue Alexanderlieder [5 poems by Ernst Herbeck] for Baritone & Piano 1979); Wölfli–Liederbuch for Baritone, Piano & 2 Drums (1980–81) [G] CPO ▲ CPO 999049–2 [ADD]
Trojahn, M.:Enrico, w. T. Schmidt (sop), L. Magnusson (ten), D. R. Davies (cnd), Stuttgart RSO CPO 2–▲ CPO 999160 [DDD]
Yun, I.:Sym 5, w. T. Ukigaya (cnd), Pomeranian PO CPO ▲ CPO 999148 [DDD]

Salvadori, Antonio (bar)
Marinuzzi, G.:Jacquerie, w. Ilaria Galgani (sop), Miro Solman (sgr), Martine Surais (sgr), A. Licata (cnd), Catania Teatro Massimo Bellini Orch, Catania Teatro Massimo Bellini Chorus *(rec Catania, 1994)* Nuova Era 2–▲ NUO 7200 [DDD]

Salvarezza, A. (ten)
Verdi, G.:Il trovatore (sels), w. J. Biel (ten), F. Tamagno (ten), L.–A. Escalaïs (ten), M. Gilion (ten), E. Caruso (ten), A. Paoli (ten), G. Zenatello (ten), J. Sembach (ten), L. Slezak (ten), F. Constantino (ten), G. Martinelli (ten), B. De Muro (ten), N. Fusati (ten), N. Piccaluga (ten), G. Lauri–Volpi (ten), A. Pertile (ten), E. Bergamaschi (ten), R. Tauber (ten), J. O'Sullivan (ten), H. Roswaenge (ten), G. Taccani (ten), V. Lois (ten), H. Lazaro (ten), A. Lindi (ten), A. Cortis (ten), F. Merli (ten), F. Völker (ten), J. Kiepura (ten), J. Schmidt (ten), J. Bjoerling (ten), B. Gigli (ten), J. Soler (ten), M. Filippeschi (ten)—34 performances of the Act III tenor aria "Di quella pira!," *(rec from 1903–1956)* Bongiovanni ▲ GB 1051 [AAD]

Salvati, Stella (cta)
Bellini, V.:Mass in a, w. Leila Bersiani (sop), Valentina di Cola (sop), José Antonio Campo (ten), Carlo Lepore (bass), E. Brizio (cnd), Prague SO, Czech Radio–TV Chorus *(rec Prague, June 1994)* Studio SM ▲ D 2444
Generali, P.:Sacred Music, w. Leila Bersiani (sop), Valentina di Cola (sop), Emanuela Deffai (mez), Paolo Macedonio (ten), Roberto Bencivenga (ten), Carlo Lepore (bass), E. Brizio (cnd), Czech Radio–TV Orch, Czech Radio–TV Chorus—Magnificat; Domine ad Adjuvandum; Virgam Virtutis; Ecce Virgo; Ave Maria Messe Pastorale; Te Deum *(rec FHS Studios, Prague, 1995)* Studio SM ▲ 2517 [DDD]

Salynikov, Andrei (ten)
Scriabin, A.:Sym 1, w. N. Gaponova (sop), E. Svetlanov (cnd), USSR SO, USSR Radio Chorus *(rec live, Moscow, April 14, 1990)* Russian Disc ▲ RC CD 11 056 [ADD]

Salzmann, Jean-Marc (bar)
Charpentier, M.–A.:Médée, w. Isabelle Desrochers (sop—Cleone), Lorraine Hunt (sop—Medee), Noemi Rime (sop—Nerine), Monique Zanetti (sop—Creuse), Mark Padmore (ten—Jason), François Bazola (bar—Arcas), Jean–Marc Salzmann (bar—Oronte), Bernard Deletre (bass–Creon), W. Christie (cnd), Les Arts Florissants Erato 3–▲ 96558–2

Sameth, Ilene (mez)
Mahler, G.:Beethoven's Sym 9, w. Leah Anne Myers (sop), James Clark (ten), Richard Conant (bass), P. Tiboris (cnd), Brno State PO, Janáček Opera Chorus Bridge ▲ BCD 9033 [DDD]

Sammarco, Mario (bar)
Mario Sammarco *(rec 1905–11)* Preiser ("Lebendige Vergangenheit" series) ▲ PRE 89100 [AAD]

Sammaritano, Silvestro (bass)
Giordano, U.:Fedora, w. Mirella Freni (sop—Principessa Fedora), Adelina Scarabelli (sop—Contessa Olga), Silvia Mazzoni (mez—Dimitri), Monica Minarelli (sgr—Savoiardo), Placido Domingo (ten—Conte Loris), Ernesto Gavazzi (ten—Desiré), Aldo Bottion (ten—Barone Rouvel), Alessandro Corbelli (bar—Siriex), Luigi Roni (bass—Cirillo), Silvestro Sammaritano (bass—Baroff), Alfredo Giacomotti (bass—Gretch), Ernesto Panariello (bass—Lorek), Vincenzo Alaimo (sgr—Nicola), Arnold Bosman (sgr—Boleslao), Bruno Capisani (sgr—Sergio), Renato Zanchetta (sgr—Michele), G. Gavazzeni (cnd), La Scala Orch, La Scala Chorus *(rec La Scala, Apr 5, 1993)* Legato 2–▲ LCD 213–2 [ADD]
Rossini, G.:Il barbiere di Siviglia (sels), w. M. Horne (mez), R. Pierotti (mez), P. Barbacini (ten), E. Dara (bar), L. Nucci (bar), S. Ramey (bass), R. Chailly (cnd), La Scala Orch, La Scala Chorus *(rec Milan, Jan. 2–18, 1982)* Sony Classical ("Opera Highlights" series) ▲ SMK 53501 [DDD]

Samuelson, Mikael (bar)
Haeffner, J.C.F.:Electra, w. Hillevi Martinpelto (sop), Helle Hinz (sop), Peter Mattei (bar), Swedish Radio Choir, T. Schuback (cnd), Drottningholm Baroque Ensemble Caprice 2–▲ CAP 22030
Lindblad, A.F.:Songs, w. MariAnne Häggander (sop), Thomas Schuback (pno), sels. unknown Caprice ▲ CAP 21425 [DDD]
Roman, J.H.:The Sweedish Mass, w. H. Martinpelto (sop), A.–S. von Otter (sop), Drottningholm Baroque Ensemble, Adolf Fredrik Bach Choir Proprius ▲ PRCD 9920
Segerstam, L.:Sym 14, w. L. Segerstam (cnd), Finnish RSO BIS ▲ CD 483 [DDD]

Sand, Annemarie (mez)
Smyth, E.:The Wreckers, w. Judith Howarth (sop), Anne–Marie Owens (mez), Justin Lavender (ten), Anthony Roden (ten), Peter Sidhom (bar), David Wilson–Johnson (bar), Brian Bannatyne–Scott (bass), O. de la Martinez (cnd), BBC PO, Huddersfield Choral Society *(rec live, Royal Albert Hall, London, July 31, 1994)* Conifer Classics 2–▲ 75605–51250–2

Sandaen, E. (bar)
Larsson, L.–E.:God in Disguise, w. E. Söderström (sop), L. Ekborg (nar), S. Westerberg (cnd), Swedish SO Swedish Society ▲ SCD 1020

Sanders, Laura (sop)
Lovenstein, J.:Music of, w. Mary Brockenbrough (sop), Barton Green (ten), Rockland Osgood (ten), David Murray (bar), Benjamin Sears (bar), Jonathan Lovenstein (pno), Heather O'Donnell (pno), James Silvers (pno), Rocy Reider (fl), Jason Horowitz (vn), Adrianna Hulscher (vn), James Johnston (vn), Mimi Ragson (vn), Peter Landeen (vc), Reinmar Seidler (vc)—Blake Songs; other works Titanic ▲ Ti 221 [DDD]

Sandivari, I. Aramayo (sgr)
Traetta, T.:Litanies, w. S. Krasteva (sop), A. De Lucia (sgr), R. Gierlach (bar), I. Lo Vetere (cnd), Giovanile Ambrosiano Ensemble Bongiovanni ▲ GB 2127 [DDD]
Traetta, T.:Stabat Mater, w. S. Krasteva (sop), A. De Lucia (sgr), R. Gierlach (bar), I. Lo Vetere (cnd), Giovanile Ambrosiano Ensemble, Piacenza Polifonico Farnesiano Chorus Bongiovanni ▲ GB 2127 [DDD]

Sandulescu, Maria (mez)
Rossini, G.:Il barbiere di Siviglia, w. Magda Ianculescu (sop—Rosina), Maria Sandulescu (mez—Berta), Valentin Teodorian (ten—Count Almaviva), Nicolae Herlea (bar—Figaro), Stefan Petrescu (bar—Fiorello), Constantin Gabor (bass—Don Bartolo), Valentin Loghin (bass—Don Basilio), M. Brediceanu (cnd), Romanian Opera Orch, Romanian Opera Chorus *(rec 1960–61)* Vox Box 2–▲ CDX 5159

Sandve, Kjell Magnus (ten)
Braein, E.F.:Anne Pedersdotter, w. K. Ekeberg (sop—Anne Pedersdotter), V. Hanssen (mez—Merete Beyer), R. Eriksen (alt—Herlofs–Marte), I. M. Brekke (alt—Bente), K. M. Sandve (ten—Martin Beyer), C. Ehrstedt (ten—Master Olaus), A. Helleland (ten—David), T. Gilje (ten—Jørund), S. A. Thorsen (bar—Master Johannes), S. Carlsen (bass—Absalon Pedersøn Beyer), T. Stensvold (bass—Master Laurentius), G. Oskarsson (bass—Jens Schelderup), P. Andersson (cnd), Norwegian National Opera Orch, Norwegian National Opera Chorus Simax 2–▲ PSC 3121
Grieg, E.:Peer Gynt, w. B. Bonney (sop), M. Eklöf (mez), U. Malmberg (bar), N. Järvi (cnd), Gothenburg SO, Gothenburg Sym Chorus [N] Deutsche Grammophon 2–▲ 423079–2 [DDD]
Grieg, E.:Sigurd Jorsalfar, w. B. Bonney (sop), M. Eklöf (mez), U. Malmberg (bar), N. Järvi (cnd), Gothenburg SO, Gothenburg Sym Chorus [N] Deutsche Grammophon 2–▲ 423079–2 [DDD]
Grieg, E.:Songs, w. M. Hirsti (sop), K. Skram (bar), R. Jansen (pno)—For L.M. Lindeman's Silver Wedding Anniversary; The Blueberry; Yuletide Cradle Song; Devoutest of Maidens; Little Lad; The Forgotten Maid; The White & Red, Red Roses Victoria ▲ VCD 19044
Grieg, E.:Songs, w. M. Hirsti (sop), K. Skram (bar), R. Jansen (pno)—Songs & Ballads by Munch, Op. 9; 5 Poems by Paulsen, Op. 26; Romances, Op. 39; 5 Songs by Benzon, Op. 69; 5 Songs by Benzon, Op. 70 Victoria ▲ VCD 19043
Grieg, E.:Songs, w. M. Hirsti (sop), C. Pfeiler (mez), K. Skram (bar), R. Jansen (pno)—Op. 4, Nos. 1, 2, 3, 4, 5 & 6; Op. 21, Nos. 1, 2, 3 & 4; Op. 44, Nos. 1, 2, 3, 4, 5 & 6; Op. 48, Nos. 1, 2, 3, 4, 5 & 6; Op. 58, Nos. 1, 2, 3, 4 & 5 [N, G] Victoria ▲ VCD 19041
Grieg, E.:Songs, w. M. Hirsti (sop), K. Skram (bar), R. Jansen (pno)—Four Songs, Op. 15; 3 Songs from Peer Gynt; 5 Songs by Vilhelm Krag, Op. 60; 6 Songs by Holger Drachmann, Op. 49 [N] *(rec March & Dec. 1991)* Victoria ▲ VCD 19038 [DDD]
Grieg, E.:Songs, w. M. Hirsti (sop), C. Pfeiler (mez), K. Skram (bar), R. Jansen (pno)—4 Songs, Op. 2; 4 Songs by Christian Winther, Op. 10; 9 Songs, Op. 18; 6 Songs by Ibsen, Op. 25 Victoria ▲ VCD 19042
Nielsen, C.:Choral Music, w. Å. Bäverstam (sop), L. Ekdahl (girl sop), A. Thors (boy sop), P. Hoyer (bar), E.–P. Salonen (cnd), Swedish RSO, Stockholm Boys' Choir, Swedish Radio Chorus—Springtime in Funen; The Blind Musician; The Old People; Dance Ballad *(rec Sept. 16–18, 1991)* Sony Classical ▲ SK 53276 [DDD]

Sanford, Sally (sop)
Purcell, H.:Songs, w. B. Wissick (vl/baroque vc), R. Erickson (hpd/org)—Tis Nature's Voice; Strike the Viol; Ye Gentle Spirits; Round O'; From Rosy Bowers; Hornpipe; Let Us Dance; Hard, the Echoing Air; Ah, How Sweet It Is Albany ▲ TROY 127

Sanguineti, Edoardo (nar)
Berio, L.:Laborintus II, w. C. Legrand (sop), J. Baucomont (sop), C. Meunier (cta), L. Berio (cnd), Musique Vivante Ensemble, Chorale Experimentale [E,I] Musique d'Abord ▲ HMA 190764

San Juan, O. (sgr)
Lerner, A.J.:Paint Your Wagon, w. J. Barton (sgr) [1951 Broadway original cast] RCA ▲ 60243-2 RG [ADD] ■ 60243-4 RG

Santa, A. Della (sgr)
Menichetti, D.:L'Epifania del Signore, w. K. Gamberucci (sop), F. Facini (bass), A. Palombi (sgr), F. Esposito (sgr), H. Handt (cnd), Toscana Accademia Strumentale, Polifonica Lucchese Bongiovanni ▲ GB 5033 [DDD]

Santiago, Theresa (sop)
Starer, R.:Night Thoughts, w. Jennifer Hines (mez), Anthony Griffey (ten), Neil Michaels (bar), Adelaide Roberts (pno), Edgar Roberts (pno) Albany ▲ TROY 151 [DDD]

Santin, Ricardo (sgr)
Morales, M.:Ildegonda, w. Violeta Dávalos (sgr—Ildegonda), Grace Echauri (sgr—Idelbene), Raúl Hernández (sgr—Rizzardo), Ricardo Santin (sgr—Rolando), F. Lozano (cnd), Carlos Chávez SO, Escuola Nacional de Música Chorus Forlane 2-▲ FRL 16739 [DDD]

Santis, Americo de (bass)
Verdi, G.:Un ballo in maschera, w. Ghena Dimitrova (sop—Amelia), Isabella Stramaglia (sop—Oscar), Mirna Pecile (cta—Ulrica), Mario Carlin (ten—Un giudice), José Carreras (ten—Riccardo), Piero Cappuccilli (bar—Renato), Massimiliano Malaspina (bass—Samuel), Americo de Santis (bass—Silvano), Francesco Signor (bass—Tom), Ivan Del Manto (sgr—Un servo), G. Patanè (cnd), Parma Teatro Regio Orch *(rec Teatro Regio, Dec. 26, 1972)* Golden Age of Opera 2-▲ GAO 183/84

Santis, Anna de (sop)
Verdi, G.:La traviata (sels), w. Anna de Santis (sop—Annina), Renata Tebaldi (sop—Violetta), Giuseppe Campora (ten—Alfredo), Gerardo Gaudioso (bar—Douphol), Giuseppe Taddei (bar—Germont), Antonio Picillo (bass—Grenvil), G. Santini (cnd), Naples Teatro San Carlo Orch, Naples Teatro San Carlo Chorus—E strano...Ah, fors'e lui; Follie!...Sempre libera; Pero l'attendo...Amami, Alfredo; Invitato a qui seguirmi; Alfredo, Alfredo, di questo core; Teneste la promessa...Addio del passato; Ma se tornando...Ah! Gran Dio! Morir si giovine; Se una pudica vergine *(rec San Carlo Theater, Naples, Jan. 17, 1952)* Legato Classics 2-▲ LCD 193-2 [ADD]

Santis, Vittorio de (sgr)
Puccini, G.:Tosca, w. Leyla Gencer (sop), Giuseppe Taddei (bar), Melchiorre Luise (bass), V. Bellezza (cnd), *(orch & chorus unknown) (rec live, Naples, Mar. 21, 1955)* Great Opera Performances 2-▲ GOP 751

Sanzio, Delia (sop)
Mascagni, P.:Cavalleria rusticana, w. Delia Sanzio (sop—Santuzza), Mimma Pantaleoni (mez—Lola), Olga de Franco (cta—Lucia), Giovanni Breviario (ten—Turiddu), Piero Biasini (bar—Alfio), C. Sabajno (cnd), La Scala Orch, La Scala Chorus VAI Audio ▲ VAIA 1082-2

Sapell, Hermann (sgr)
Wagner, R.:Das Liebesverbot, w. Pamela Coburn (sop—Mariana), Friedrich Lenz (ten—Antonio), Hermann Prey (bar—Friedrich), Keith Engen (bass—Angelo), Raimund Grumbach (bass—Danieli/Wirt), Wolfgang Fassler (sgr—Luzio), Sabine Haas (sgr—Isabella/Claudios Schwester), Alfred Kuhn (sgr—Brighella/Chef der Sbirren), Hermann Sapell (sgr—Pontio Pilato), Robert Schunk (sgr—Claudio), Marianne Seibel (sgr—Dorella), W. Sawallisch (cnd), Bavarian State Orch, Bavarian State Chorus *(rec July 9, 1983)* Orfeo d'or 3-▲ 345953

Sarabia, Guillermo (bar)
Bizet, G.:Les Pêcheurs de perles, w. I. Cotrubas (sop), A. Vanzo (ten), R. Soyer (bass), G. Prêtre (cnd), Paris Opera Orch, Paris Opera Chorus Classics for Pleasure ▲ CDCFP 4721 [ADD]
Meyerbeer, G.:L'Africiane, w. Montserrat Caballe (sop—Selika), Christine Weidinger (sop—Inez), Miriam Ucelay (mez—Anna), Placido Domingo (ten—Vasco de Gama), Guillermo Sarabia (bar—Nelusko), Juan Thomas (b-bar—High Priest of Brahma), Dimiter Petkov (bass—Don Pedro), Juan Pons (bass—Don Diego), Eduardo Soto (bass—Grand Inquisitor), A. de Almeida (cnd), Barcelona Teatro Liceo Orch, Barcelona Gran Teatro de Liceo Chorus *(rec Barcelona, Nov 27, 1977)* Legato Classics 2-▲ LCD 208-2 [ADD]
Zemlinsky, A. von:Eine florentinische Tragödie, w. D. Soffel (mez), K. Riegel (ten), G. Albrecht (cnd), Berlin RSO [G] Koch Schwann ▲ CD 314012 [DDD]

Saraceni, Adelaide (sop)
Donizetti, G.:Don Pasquale, w. Tito Schipa (ten), Ernesto Badini (bar), Afro Poli (bar), C. Sabajno (cnd), La Scala Orch, La Scala Chorus *(rec 1932)* Grammofono 2000 2-▲ GRM 78561 (m)
Leoncavallo, R.:Pagliacci, w. Adelaide Saraceni (sop—Nedda), Alessandro Valente (ten—Canio), Nello Palai (ten—Beppe), Apollo Granforte (bar—Tonio), Leonildo Basi (bass—Silvio), C. Sabajno (cnd), La Scala Orch, La Scala Chorus *(rec Apr, Sept 1929 & Jan 1930)* VAI Audio 2-▲ VAIA 1082-2

Sardi, Ivan (bass)
Albert, E. d':Tiefland, w. I. Strauss, Schock, Feldhoff, H. Zanotelli (cnd), Berlin SO Eurodisc 2-▲ 7797-2-RG [ADD]
Donizetti, G.:Requiem Mass, w. G. Tucci (sop), A. Lazzarini (mez), G. Sinimberghi (ten), F. Maero (sgr), F. Molinari-Pradelli (cnd), Milan RAI SO, Milan RAI Chorus [L] *(rec live, Milan 3/21/61)* Memories ▲ HR 4131 [ADD]
Mozart, W.A.:Nozze di Figaro, w. M. Stader (sop), I. Seefried (sop), H. Töpper (mez), D. Fischer-Dieskau (bar), R. Capecchi (bar), F. Fricsay (cnd), Berlin RSO [G] *(rec 1960)* Deutsche Grammophon 3-▲ 437671-2

Sardinero, Vincente (bar)
Donizetti, G.:Don Pasquale, w. Ileana Cotrubas (sop), Alfredo Kraus (ten), Wladimiro Ganzarolli (bar), Sutliff (sgr), B. Bartoletti (cnd), Chicago Lyric Opera Orch, Chicago Lyric Opera Chorus *(rec live, Chicago, Nov. 2, 1974)* Arkadia 2-▲ 490
Donizetti, G.:Gemma di Vergy, w. Montserrat Caballe (sop—Gemma), Anna Ringart (mez—Ida), Luis Lima (ten—Tamas), Vicente Sardinero (bar—Il Conte), Juan Pons (bar—Guido), Francois Loup (b—Rolando), A. Gatto (cnd), Nouvel PO, Jean-Paul Kreder (cnd), French Radio Chorus *(rec live, Salle Pleyel, Paris, Apr 20, 1976)* Agorá Music ("Phoenix" series) 2-▲ 501 [ADD]
Donizetti, G.:Lucia di Lammermoor, w. M. Caballé (sop), A. Murray (mez), C. H. Ahnsjö (ten), V. Bello (ten), J. Carreras (ten), S. Ramey (bass), J. López-Cobos (cnd), New Philharmonia Orch, Ambrosian Opera Chorus Philips 2-▲ 426563-2
Donizetti, G.:Roberto Devereux, w. M. Caballé (sop), S. Marsee (mez), J. Carreras (ten), J. Rudel (cnd), *(orch & chorus unknown)* [I] *(rec live, France 1977)* HRE 2-▲ 1004-2 [ADD]
Donizetti, G.:Roberto Devereux (sels), w. M. Caballé (sop), S. Marsee (mez), J. Carreras (ten), J. Rudel (cnd), *(orch & chorus unknown)* [I] *(rec live, 1977)* Legato Classics ▲ LCD 108-1 [AAD]
Mascagni, P.:L'amico Fritz, w. M. Freni (sop), L. Pavarotti (ten), G. Gavazzeni (cnd), Royal Opera House Orch Covent Garden, Royal Opera House Chorus Covent Garden [I] EMI Classics 2-▲ CDCB 47905 [ADD]
Puccini, G.:Edgar, w. R. Scotto (sop), G. Killebrew (mez), C. Bergonzi (ten), E. Queler (cnd), New York City Opera Orch, New York Schola Cantorum *(rec in concert at Carnegie Hall, 4/13/77)* CBS 2-▲ M2K 34584
Puccini, G.:Manon Lescaut, w. M. Caballé (sop—Manon Lescaut), P. Domingo (ten—Des Grieux), R. Tear (ten—Edmondo), V. Sardinero (bar—Lescaut), N. Mangin (bass—Geronte), B. Bartoletti (cnd), New Philharmonia Orch, Ambrosian Opera Chorus EMI Classics ▲ CDMB 64852
Puccini, G.:Turandot, w. M. Caballé (sop—Turnadot), M. Freni (sop—Liu), J. Carreras (ten—Calaf), M. Sénéchal (ten—Emperor Altoum), V. Sardinero (bar—Ping), P. Plishka (bass—Timur), A. Lombard (cnd), Strasbourg PO, Maîtrise de la Cathédrale, Rhine Opera Chorus EMI Classics ▲ CDMB 65293
Verdi, G.:Un giorno di regno, w. J. Norman (sop), F. Cossotto (mez), J. Carreras (ten), I. Wixell (bar), W. Ganzarolli (bar), P. Elvin (bass), A. Cassinelli (bass), L. Gardelli (cnd), Royal PO, Ambrosian Singers Philips 2-▲ 422429-2 [ADD]

Saretzki, Hans Dieter (ten)
Rossini, G.:Petite messe solennelle, w. G. de la Cruz (sop), M. L. Gilles (cta), H. G. Grimm (bass), W. A. Albert (cnd), Northwest German PO, Northwest German Phil Choir [orchestral version] [L] *(rec ca. 1970)* Koch Schwann ▲ 3-1345-2 [ADD]

Sarfaty, Regina (mez)
Beethoven, L. van:Sym 9, "Choral Sym", w. M. Arroy (sop), N. di Virgilio (ten), N. Scott (bass), L. Bernstein (cnd), New York PO, Juilliard Chorus *(rec New York, May 18, 1964)* Sony Classical ("Bernstein:The Royal Edition" series) Δ SM 47513 [ADD]

Sargon, Merja (sop)
Our Musical Past, Vol. 1:A Concert for Brass Band, Voice & Piano, w. Bernard Rose (pno) Library of Congress ▲ OMP 101/102 [ADD]

Sárkány, Kázmér (bass)
Rossini, G.:Il barbiere di Siviglia, w. I. Kertesi (sop—Berta), S. Ganassi (mez—Rosina), R. Vargas (ten—Almaviva), A. Romero (bar—Dr. Bartolo), R. Servile (bar—Figaro), F. de Grandis (bass—Basilio), K. Sárkány (bass—Fiorello), A. Déri (pno), B. Sztankovits (gtr), W. Humburg (cnd), Failoni CO, Hungarian Radio Chorus *(rec Nov. 16–28, 1992)* Naxos 3-▲ 8.660027/29 [DDD]

Sarragosse, Jean-Claude (bass)
Palestrina, G.:Sacred Music, w. Catherine Greuillet (sop), Thierry Gregoire (alt), Pierre Sciema (alt), Bruno Boterf (ten), Joel Suhubiette (ten), Jean-Luc Baudoin (ten), Laurent Stewart (org), Françoise Lasserre (cnd), Champagne-Ardenne Akademia Regional Vocal Ensemble—Ave maria; Salve regina; Vergine bella; Vergine saggia; Virgine pura; Virgine santa; Vergine sola; Vergine chiara; Vergine, quante lagrime; Vergine, tale è terra; Ave mundi spes; Ave regina coelorum; Alma redemptoris mater; Regina coieli laetare; Salve regina; Magnificat; others *(rec Convent of the Annunciation Dominican Church, Paris, Jan., 1994)* Pierre Verany ▲ PVY 794041 [DDD]

Sarri, Gino (ten)
Verdi, G.:I vespri siciliani, w. Maria Callas (sop—Duchess), Giorgio Kokolios Bardi (ten—Arrigo), Gino Sarri (ten—Danieli), Enzo Mascherini (bar—Guido di Monforte), Boris Christoff (bass—Giovanni da Procida), Mario Forsini (bass—Count Vaudemont), Bruneo Carmassi (bass—Bethune), E. Kleiber (cnd), Florence Teatro Comunale Orch, Florence Teatro Comunale Chorus *(rec live, Florence, 1951)* Melodram 3-▲ IMC 303016 [ADD]

Sarris, Heather (sgr)
Rorem, N.:Miss Julie, w. Theodora Fried (sgr—Miss Julie), Heather Sarris (sgr—Christine, the cook), Laurelyn Watson (sgr—Young Girl), David Blackburn (sgr—Mr. Niels), Mark Mulligan (sgr—Young Boy), Philip Torre (sgr—John, the valet), Judd Ernster (bass), D. Gilbert (cnd), Manhattan School of Music Opera Orch, Manhattan School of Music Opera Chorus Newport Classic 2-▲ NPT 85605 [DDD]

Sarroca, Suzanne (sop)
Offenbach, J.:Les Contes d'Hoffmann (sels), w. Andréa Guiot (sop—Antonia), Mady Mesplé (sop—Olympia), Suzanne Sarroca (sop—Giulietta), Albert Lance (ten—Hoffmann), Gabriel Bacquier (bar—Docteur Miracle), Robert Massard (bar—Dapertutto), J. Etcheverry (cnd), *(orch unknown)* —Prologue; Dans les rôles d'amoureux...; Il était une fois...; Allons! Courage et confiance...; C'est moi, coppélius!...; Les oiseaux dans la charmille; Barcarolle; Scintille, diamant...; Malheureux, tu ne comprends donc pas...; Hélas! Mon coeur s'égare encore...; Elle a fui, la tourterelle...; Eh bien! Quoi! Toujours en colère!...; Tu ne chanteras plus?... Adès ▲ ADE 202702 [AAD]

Sarti, Gastone (bar)
Cimarosa, D.:I Finti nobili (sels), w. C. Cadelo (sop), M.G. Ferracini (sop), R. Cassinelli (ten), R. Malacarne (ten), B. Marinotti (cnd), RTSI Orch—Li sposi per accidente (Act 3) *(rec 1970)* Foyer ▲ FOY 2057 [AAD]
Donizetti, G.:Imelda de' Lambertazzi, w. D. D'Auria (sop), F. Sovilla (sop), F. Tenzi (ten), A. Martin (bar), M. Andreae (cnd), Swiss-Italian Radio-TV Orch, Swiss-Italian Radio-TV Chorus [I] *(rec live)* Nuova Era 2-▲ 6778/79 [DDD]
Donizetti, G.:I pazzi per progetto, w. S. Rigacci (sop), A. Cicogna (mez), G. Polidori (bar), V. M. Brunetti (bass), E. Fissore (bass), L. Monreale (bass), G. Micheli (cnd), Emilia Romagna Arturo Toscanini SO [I] *(rec live, 12/88)* Bongiovanni ▲ GB 2070 [DDD]
Respighi, O.:Christus, w. C. Gaifa (ten), R. Hermann (bar), M. Balderi (cnd), Swiss-Italian Orch, Swiss-Italian Chorus [L] Claves ▲ CD 9203 [DDD]
Salieri, A.:La Locandiera, w. A. Ruffini (sop), O. Di Credico (ten), P. Guarnera (bar), F. Luisi (cnd), Emilia Romagna Arturo Toscanini SO [I] *(rec live 1989)* Nuova Era 2-▲ 6888/89 [DDD]

Sarti, Laura (mez)
Massenet, J.:Sapho, w. Jenny Hill (sop), Bernard Dickerson (ten), Alexander Oliver (ten), Neilson Taylor (bar), George Macpherson (bass), Milla Andrew (sgr), B. Keefe (cnd), BBC SO, BBC Sym Chorus *(rec live, 1973)* Memories 2-▲ MEM 4601 [AAD]

Sasiadek, E. (ten)
Gorczycki, G.G.:Sacred Choral Music, w. R. Stacewicz (sop), I. Tkaczyk (alt), A. Pagowska (alt), W. Brychcy (bass), Wroclaw Orch, S. Galonski (cnd), Edmund Kajdasz (cnd), Capella Bydgostiensis Pro Musica Antiqua, Madrigalists Choir, Polish Radio Chorus—Completorium; In virtute tua; Iudica me deus; Laetatus sum; Missa paschalis [L] *(rec 1966)* Olympia ▲ OCD 320 [AAD]

Sass, Sylvia (sop)
Cherubini, L.:Médée, w. M. Kalmar (sop), T. Takacs (mez), V. Luchetti (ten), K. Kovats (bass), L. Gardelli (cnd), Budapest SO, Hungarian Radio Chorus [I] Hungaroton 2-▲ HCD 11904/05
Erkel, F.:Hunyadi László, w. M. Kalmár (sop), D. Gulyás (ten), A. Molnar (ten), I. Gáti (bar), S. Sólyom-Nagy (bar), J. Kovács (cnd), Hungarian State Opera Orch, Hungarian State Opera Chorus [Hun] Hungaroton 3-▲ HCD 12581/83 [DDD]
Mozart, W.A.:Don Giovanni, w. L. Price (sop), L. Popp (sop), S. Burrows (ten), G. Bacquier (bar), B. Weikl (bar), A. Sramek (bar), K. Moll (bass), G. Solti (cnd), London PO, London Opera Chorus London ("Grand Opera" series) 3-▲ 425169-2 [ADD]
Mozart, W.A.:Idomeneo (sels), w. G. Sabbatini (sop), J. Protschka (ten)—4 arias & ballet music LaserLight ▲ 15 888 [DDD]
Mozart, W.A.:Sacred Music, w. G. Fuchs (sop), *(cnd & orch unknown)*—Ah, lo previdi...Ah, t'invola agl'occhi miei, K.272; Ave Verum Corpus, K.618; Exsultate, jubilate, K.165; Laudate Dominum, K.321 [L,I] LaserLight ▲ 15 884 [DDD]
Respighi, O.:Belfagor, w. T. Takács (mez), G. Lamberti (ten), L. Miller (bar), L. Polgár (bass), L. Gardelli (cnd), Hungarian State Orch, Hungarian State Chorus [I] Hungaroton 2-▲ HCD 12850/51 [DDD]
Verdi, G.:Arias, w. Giorgio Lamberti (ten), Kolos Kováts (bass), Oberfrank, Gardelli (cnd), Budapest MÁV SO, Hungarian State Opera Orch, Béla Pödör (cnd), Ferenc Sapszon (cnd), Ferenc Nagy (cnd), Hungarian People's Army Male Chorus, Hungarian Radio-TV Chorus, Hungarian State Opera Chorus—Vieni, o Levita!...Tu sul labbro [from Nabucco]; Verginil...Il ciel per ora...Sciagurata! Hai tu creduto; Qui posa il fianco [both from I Lombardi]; Che mai vegg'io...Infelice! E tu credevi...; Vigili pure il ciel...Iddio n'ascolti [both from Ernani]; Mentre gonfiarsi l'anima [from Attila]; Studia il passo...Come dal ciel precipita! [from Macbeth]; O patria, o cara patria...O tu, Palermo [from I vespri Siciliani]; A te l'estremo addio... [from Simon Boccanegra]; Ella giammai m'amò [from Don Carlo] Hungaroton ("Great Hungarian Voices" series) ▲ HCD 31650 [ADD/DDD]
Verdi, G.:Un ballo in maschera (sels), w. J. Carreras (ten), C. Mackerras (cnd), *(orch unknown)*—Act 2 duet, "Teco io sto" & Act 3 tenor aria, "Forse la soglia attinse...Ma se m'è forza perderti" [I] *(rec live, London, 1978)* Standing Room Only 2-▲ SRO 829-2 [ADD]
Verdi, G.:I lombardi alla prima crociata, w. J. Carreras (ten), N. Ghiuselev (bass), L. Gardelli (cnd), *(orch unknown)* [I] *(rec live, London, 1976)* Standing Room Only 2-▲ SRO 829-2 [ADD]
Wagner, R.:Tannhäuser (sels), w. Reiner Goldberg (ten), Hermann Prey (bar), Bavarian State Opera Orch, Bavarian State Opera Chorus—Ov; Venusberg Bacchanal; Dich, teure halle, grüb' ich wieder; Freudig Begrüben wir die edle Halle; Intro; die Pilger sind's - Beglückt darf nun dich, o Heimat, ich schauen; plus others Laserlight ▲ 14211 [DDD]

Saunders, Shari (sop)
Purcell, H.:Dido & Aeneas, w. Meredith Hall (sop—2nd Witch/Spirit), Ann Monoyios (sop—Belinda), Shari Saunders (sop—2nd Woman/1st Woman), Jennifer Lane (mez—Dido/Sorceress), Benjamin Butterfield (ten—Sailor), Russell Braun (bar—Aeneas), J. Lamon (cnd), Tafelmusik, Tafelmusik Chamber Choir *(rec Glenn Gould Studio, CBC Toronto, Apr 26–29, 1995)* CBC ▲ SM5 5147 [DDD]

Sausy, Pascal (bar)
Pesson, G.:Music of, w. Donatienne Michel-Dansac (sop), Sandra Roulx (mez), Stuart Patterson (ten), Paul-Alexandre Dubois (bar), Florence Millet (pno), D. My (cnd), Fa Ensemble, Paris String Quartet—Le gel, par jeu for Fl, Cl, Hn, Bass Mar, Vn & Vc; Qt for Strs; Non Sapremo Mai di Questo Mi for Fl, Vn & Pno; 5 Poèmes de Sandro Penna for Bar, B Cl, Hn, Vn & Vc; La lumière n'a pas de bras pour nous porter for Amplified Pno; La vita è come l'albero di natale for Vn & Pno; Nocturnes en quatuor for Cl, Pno, Vn & Vc; Les chants faëz for Pno & 10 Instrs; Sur-le-champ for 4 Voices & 9 Instrs [from a text by Pierre Alferi] Accord ▲ ACD 204682 [DDD]

Sautereau, Nadine (sop)
Landowski, M.:Music of, w. Jean-Christophe Benoit (bar), Xavier Depraz (bass), Michel Bouquet (spkr), Gilbert Audin (bn), Evelyne Aïello, Didier Bouture, Ludovic Chevalier, Laurent Decker, Françoise Deslogères, Landowski, Tzipine (cnd), Colonne Association des Concerts Orch, Boulogne-Billancourt Orch Conservatory, Paris Conservatory Société des Concerts Orch, L'Itinéraire Ensemble, Harmonia Nova Orch Ensemble—Con Bn; Con pour ondes Martenot; Femme sans passé; Hauts de Hurlevent; Horologe; Mouvement; Notes de Nuit; Souvenir d'un jardin d'enfance; Ventriloque Chamade 3-▲ 5639/40/41 [AAD/DDD]

Savage, Fred (nar)
Saint-Saëns, C.:Carnival of the Animals, w. M. Golabek (nar), R. Golabek (nar), C. Heston (nar), J. E. Jones (nar), B. White (nar), L. Redgrave (nar), W. Shatner (nar), J. Rivers (nar), T. Danson (nar), L. Tomlin (nar), D. Raffin (nar), A. Hepburn (nar), D. Moore (nar), W. Matthau (nar), J. Smith (nar), L. Schifrin (cnd), Hollywood CO Dove Audio ▲ DOV 30700

Savarese, Ugo (bar)
Bizet, G.:Les Pêcheurs de perles, w. M. Pobbe (sop), F. Tagliavini (ten), C. Cava (bass), O. de Fabritiis (cnd), Naples Teatro San Carlo Orch, Naples Teatro San Carlo Chorus [I] *(rec live 1/4/59)* Melodram 2-▲ MEL 27069 (m) [AAD]
Giordano, U.:Andrea Chénier, w. R. Tebaldi (sop), A. Basile (cnd), Turin RAI SO Cetra Classic 2-▲ CDO 24
Giordano, U.:Andrea Chénier, w. Renata Tebaldi (sop), José Soler (ten), A. Basile (cnd), Turin RAI SO Fonit Cetra ("Classic Collection" series) 2-▲ FCT CDO 24
Verdi, G.:La battaglia di Legnano (sels), w. L. Gencer (sop), J. Gibin (ten), F. Molinari-Pradelli (cnd), Trieste Teatro Comunale Giuseppe Verdi Orch, Trieste Teatro Comunale G. Verdi Chorus—extensive selections from Acts 1,3 & 4 [I] *(rec live 3/8/63)* Myto 2-▲ 2 MCD 89010 (m) [ADD]
Verdi, G.:Giovanna d'Arco, w. Renata Tebaldi (sop—Giovanna), Gino Penno (ten—Carlo VII), Luciano Della Pergola (ten—Delil), Ugo Savarese (bar—Giacomo), Iginio Ricco (bass—Talbot), G. Santini (cnd), Naples Teatro San Carlo Orch, Naples Teatro San Carlo Chorus *(rec San Carlo Theater, Naples, Mar. 15, 1951)* Legato Classics 2-▲ LCD 193-2 [ADD]
Verdi, G.:La traviata, w. V. Zeani (sop), G. Raimondi (ten), A. Questa (cnd), Naples Teatro San Carlo Orch, Naples Teatro San Carlo Chorus [I] *(rec live, Naples 8/11/57)* Golden Age of Opera 2-▲ GAO 103/04 [ADD]
Verdi, G.:La traviata, w. Maria Callas (sop), Francesco Albanese (ten), G. Santini (cnd), Turin RAI SO, Coro Cetra *(rec 1953)* Enterprise ("Documents" series) 2-▲ ENT 1002 (m)
Verdi, G.:La traviata (sels), w. R. Tebaldi (sop), N. Filacuridi (ten), T. Serafin (cnd), Florence Maggio Musicale Orch, Florence Maggio Musicale Chorus *(rec live, Florence 1956)* Melodram ▲ MEL 15006

Savastano, Antonio (ten)
Mercadante, S.:Il bravo, w. Miwako Matsumoto (sop—Violetta), Giovanna di Rocco (sop—Michelina), William Johns (ten—Il Bravo), Antonio Savastano (ten—Pisani), Gino Sinimberghi (ten—Cappello), Loris Gambelli (bass—Marco), Mario Machì (bass—Luigi), Paolo Washington (bass—Foscari), Maria Parazzini (sgr—Teodora), G. Ferro (cnd), Rome Opera Orch, Rome Opera Chorus *(rec Rome, Dec 30, 1976)* Italia 3-▲ CDC 94 [ADD]
Rossini, G.:Stabat Mater, w. Beatrice Haldas (sop), Lucia V. Terrani (mez), Raffaele Arié (bass), E. Loehrer (cnd), Swiss-Italian Radio-TV Orch, Swiss-Italian Radio-TV Chorus Accord ▲ ACD 201752 [AAD]

Savidge, Peter (bar)
Sullivan, A.:Trial by Jury, w. Rebecca Evans (sop—Plaintiff), Barry Banks (ten—Defendant), Gareth Rhys-Davies (bar—Foreman of the Jury), Peter Savidge (bar—Counsel for the Plaintiff), Donald Adams (bass—Usher), Richard Suart (bass—The Learned Judge), C. Mackerras (cnd), Welsh National Opera Orch, Welsh National Opera Chorus *(rec Brangwyn Hall, Swasea, Wales, Apr 18–30 & May 1, 1995)* Telarc 2-▲ CD 80404 [DDD]
Sullivan, A.:The Yeomen of the Guard, w. Felicity Palmer (sop—Dame Carruthers), Pamela Helen Stephens (mez—Phoebe Meryll), Neill Archer (ten—Col Fairfax), Peter Hoare (ten—Leonard Meryll), Ralph Mason (ten—1st Yeoman), Donald Maxwell (bar—Wilfred Shadbolt), Peter Savidge (bar—Lieutenant Sir Richard Cholmondely), Donald Adams (bass—Sergeant Meryll), Richard Suart (bass—Jack Point), Peter Lloyd Evans (sgr—2nd Yeoman), Alwyn Mellor (sgr—Elsie Maynard), Clare O'Neill (sgr—Kate), C. Mackerras (cnd), Welsh National Opera Orch, Welsh National Opera Chorus *(rec Brangwyn Hall, Swasea, Wales, Apr 18–30 & May 1, 1995)* Telarc 2-▲ CD 80404 [DDD]

Savio, Giuseppe (ten)
Puccini, G.:Gianni Schicchi, w. Grete Rapisardi (sop), Giuseppe Taddei (bar), A. Simonetto (cnd), *(orch & chorus unknown)* Cetra Classic ▲ 363
Puccini, G.:Gianni Schicchi, w. Grete Rapisardi (sop), Giuseppe Taddei (bar), A. Simonetto (cnd), *(orch & chorus unknown)* Cetra Classic 3-▲ 36
Puccini, G.:Gianni Schicchi, w. G. Rapisardi (sop), A. Dubbini (mez), G. Taddei (bar), A. Simonetto (cnd), Turin RAI SO [I] *(rec 10/5/49)* Preiser ▲ 90074 (m) [AAD]

Savu, Valeria (mez)
Verdi, G.:Rigoletto, w. Victoria Draganescu (sop—Countess Ceprano), Magda Ianculescu (sop—Gilda), Dorothea Palade (mez—Maddalena), Valeria Savu (mez—Giovanna), Ion Buzea (ten—Duke of Mantua), Dimitrie Scurtu (ten—Borsa), Nicolae Herlea (bar—Rigoletto), Stefan Petrescu (bar—Marullo), Jean Banescu (bass—Count Ceprano), Nicolae Florei (bass—Monterone), Nicolae Rafael (bass—Sparafucile), J. Bobescu (cnd), Romanian Opera Orch, Romanian Opera Chorus *(rec 1965)* Vox Box 2-▲ CDX 5162

Sayão, Bidù (sop)
Chicago 1950, w. Giuseppe Di Stefano (ten), Renata Tebaldi (sop), Chicago Radio Orch [cnd:Gaetano Merola] Myto ▲ MCD 924.67 [ADD]
Giuseppe de Luca On Radio:Broadcast Recordings of the Great Italian Baritone Unpublished on Disc (1941–44), w. Giuseppe de Luca (bar), Lily Pons (sop), Giovanni Martinelli (ten) *(rec 1941–44)* Enterprise ("The Radio Years" series) ▲ ENT RY 25 (m)
Mozart, W.A.:Don Giovanni, w. Rose Bampton (sop), Jarmila Novotna (sop), Charles Kullman (ten), Alexander Kipnis (bass), Ezio Pinza (bass), B. Walter (cnd), *(orch unknown)* *(rec Mar 7, 1942)* Enterprise ("The Fourties" series) 3-▲ ENT 301
Mozart, W.A.:Nozze di Figaro, w. Bidu Sayao (sop—Susanna), Eleanor Steber (sop—Countess Almaviva), Jarmila Novotna (sop—Cherubino), Ira Petina (sop—Marcellina), John Brownlee (bar—Count Almaviva), Salvatore Baccaloni (bass—Bartolo), Ezio Pinza (bass—Figaro), B. Walter (cnd), *(orch unknown)* The Fourties 2-▲ ENT FT 1509
Opera Arias & Brazilian Folk Songs *(rec 1941–1950)* Sony Classical ("Masterworks Heritage" series) ▲ MHK 62355
Rossini, G.:Il barbiere di Siviglia, w. Ira Petina (sop), John Brownlee (bar), Salvatore Baccaloni (bass), Ezio Pinza (bass), Nino Martini (sgr), F. St. Leger (cnd), *(orch unknown)* *(rec Oct 4, 1943)* Enterprise ("The Fourties" series) 2-▲ ENT 307

Scacciati, Bianca (sop)
The Italian Vocal Tradition, Vol. 1:The Voices of Toscanini, w. Toti dal Monte (sop), Claudio Muzio (sop), Rosetta Pampanini (sop), Giacomo Lauri-Volpi (ten), Francesco Merli (ten), Aureliano Pertile (ten), Carlo Galeffi (bar), Mariano Stabile (bar), Riccardo Stracciari (bar), Nazzareno de Angel *(rec 1921–35)* Iron Needle ▲ 1304
Verdi, G.:Il trovatore, w. Giuseppina Zinetti (sop), Francesco Merli (ten), Enrico Molinari (bar), L. Molajoli (cnd), Milan SO, La Scala Chorus *(rec live, 1930)* Melodram ▲ CDI 202002

Scaggs, Gina (sop)
Talma, L.:A Wreath of Blessings, w. April Lindevald (alt), Drew Martin (ten), Leslie Dorsey (bass), Gregg Smith (cnd), Gregg Smith Singers Vox Box ("The American Composers" series) 3-▲ CDX 3037

Scalchi, Gloria (mez)
Donizetti, G.:La favorita, w. Luca Canonici (ten), René Massis (bar), Giorgio Surjan (bass), D. Renzetti (cnd), Milan RAI SO, Milan RAI Chorus Fonit Cetra ("Ricordi" series) 3-▲ FCT RFCD 2015
Rossini, G.:Stabat Mater, w. Daniela Dessì (sop), Lucia Mazzaria (sop), Pietro Ballo (ten), Chris Merritt (ten), Anatoli Kotscherga (bass), Roberto Scandiuzzi (bass), G. Gelmetti (cnd), Stuttgart RSO, North German Radio Chorus, Southwest German Radio Chorus Serenissima 2-▲ SER 360155 [DDD]
Verdi, G.:Requiem Mass, w. Lucia Mazzaria (sop), Daniela Dessì (sop), Pietro Ballo (ten), Chris Merritt (ten), Anatoli Kotscherga (bass), Roberto Scandiuzzi (bass), G. Gelmetti (cnd), Stuttgart RSO, North German Radio Chorus, Southwest German Radio Chorus Serenissima 2-▲ SER 360155 [DDD]

Scales, Prunella (nar)
Walton, W.:Façade, w. Timothy West (nar), J. Glover (cnd), London Mozart Players [1951 version] [E] ASV ▲ ASV 679 [DDD/ADD]

Scaltriti, Roberto (bar)
Donizetti, G.:Betly, w. S. Rigacci (sop), M. Comencini (ten), B. Rigacci (cnd), Emilia Romagna Arturo Toscanini SO, Lugo Teatro Comunale Rossini Chorus *(rec live, 6/90)* Bongiovanni 2-▲ GB 2091/92 [DDD]
Donizetti, G.:Le Convenienze Teatrali, w. M.A. Peters (sop), A. Cicogna (mez), S. Tedesco (ten), B. Rigacci (cnd), Emilia Romagna Arturo Toscanini SO, Lugo Teatro Comunale Rossini Chorus [I] *(rec live, 6/90)* Bongiovanni 2-▲ GB 2091/92 [DDD]
Handel, G.F.:Riccardo Primo, w. Claire Brua (sop—Pulcheria), Sandrine Piau (sop—Costanza), Sara Mingardo (cta—Riccardo), Pascal Bertin (alt—Oronte), Roberto Scaltriti (bar—Isacio), Olivier Lallouette (bass—Berardo), C. Rousset (cnd), Les Talens Lyriques L'oiseau Lyre ▲ 452 201-2
Rossini, G.:La pietra del paragone, w. M. C. Nocentini (sop), A. Trovarelli (mez), H. M. Molinari (cta), P. Barbacini (ten), V. Di Matteo (bar), A. Svab (bar), P. Rumetz (bass), C. Desderi (cnd), Camerata Musicale Orch, Modeno Teatro Comunale Chorus [I] *(rec 1992)* Nuova Era 2-▲ 7132/33 [DDD]
Verdi, G.:Il trovatore, w. Antonella Banaudi (sop—Leonora), Barbara Frittoli (sop—Ines), Shirley Verrett (mez—Azucena), Enrico Facini (ten—Un messo), Piero de Palma (ten—Ruiz), Luciano Pavarotti (ten—Marico), Leo Nucci (bar—Il Conte di Luna), Roberto Scaltriti (bar—Un vecchio zingaro), Francesco Ellero d'Artegna (bass—Ferrando), Z. Mehta (cnd), Florence Maggio Musicale Orch, Florence Maggio Musicale Chorus *(rec Maggio Musicale Fiorentino Community Theater, June 18–July 2, 1990)* London 2-▲ 430694-2

Scandiuzzi, Roberto (bass)
Bellini, V.:I Puritani, w. K. Ricciarelli (sop), E. Jankovic (mez), C. Merritt (ten), C. Gaifa (ten), A. Riva (bass), G. Ferro (cnd), Sicilian SO, Bari Teatro Petruzzelli Chorus *(rec Apr. 10, 1986)* Cetra Classic ▲ CDC 20 [ADD]
Bellini, V.:I Puritani, w. Katia Ricciarelli (sop), Eleonora Jankovic (mez), Juan Luque Carmona (ten), Carlo Gaifa (ten), Chris Merritt (ten), G. Ferro (cnd), Sicilian SO, Bari Teatro Petruzzelli Chorus Fonit Cetra ("Digital Operas" series) 3-▲ FCT CDC 20
Franchetti, A.:Cristoforo Colombo, w. R. Ragatzu (sop—Isabella), G. Pasino (mez—Annacoana), M. Berti (ten—Ferdinand), R. Bruson (bar—Cristoforo Colombo), R. Scandiuzzi (bass—Don Roldano Ximenes), M. Viotti (cnd), Frankfurt RSO, Frankfurt Radio Chorus [I] *(rec live, Alte Oper Frankfurt, 8/30 & 9/2 1991)* Koch Schwann 3-▲ CD 3-1030-2 [DDD]
Puccini, G.:Turandot, w. G. Dimitrova (sop), C. Gasdia (sop), N. Martinucci (ten), D. Oren (cnd), Genoa Teatro Comunale Orch, Genoa Teatro Comunale Chorus [I] *(rec live, 1/20–27/89)* Nuova Era 2-▲ 6786/87 [DDD]
Puccini, G.:Turandot (sels), w. G. Dimitrova (sop), C. Gasdia (sop), N. Martinucci (ten), D. Oren (cnd), Genoa Teatro Comunale Orch, Genoa Teatro Comunale Chorus [I] Nuova Era ▲ 6871 [DDD]
Rossini, G.:Stabat Mater, w. Daniela Dessì (sop), Lucia Mazzaria (sop), Gloria Scalchi (mez), Pietro Ballo (ten), Chris Merritt (ten), Anatoli Kotscherga (bass), G. Gelmetti (cnd), Stuttgart RSO, North German Radio Chorus, Southwest German Radio Chorus Serenissima 2-▲ SER 360155 [DDD]
Rossini, G.:Stabat Mater, w. Luba Orgonasova (sop), Cecilia Bartoli (mez), Raul Gimenez (ten), M.-W. Chung (cnd), Vienna PO, Vienna State Opera Chorus Deutsche Grammophon ▲ 449 178-2
Verdi, G.:Requiem Mass, w. Lucia Mazzaria (sop), Daniela Dessì (sop), Gloria Scalchi (mez), Pietro Ballo (ten), Chris Merritt (ten), Anatoli Kotscherga (bass), G. Gelmetti (cnd), Stuttgart RSO, North German Radio Chorus, Southwest German Radio Chorus Serenissima 2-▲ SER 360155 [DDD]
Verdi, G.:Simon Boccanegra, w. M. Nicolesco (sop), G. Sabbatini (ten), R. Bruson (bar), S. Rinaldi-Miliani (bar), N. de Angelis (bass), R. Paternostro (cnd), Tokyo SO, Nikikai Chorus *(rec live 2/90)* Capriccio 2-▲ 60018-2 [DDD]

Scarabelli, Adelina (sop)
Donizetti, G.:Rita, or Le mari battu, w. P. Ballo (ten), A. Corbelli (bar), F. Amendola (cnd), Sicilian CO [I] *(rec live, Palermo 6/19–20/91)* Nuova Era ▲ 7045 [DDD]
Giordano, U.:Fedora, w. Mirella Freni (sop—Principessa Fedora), Adelina Scarabelli (sop—Contessa Olga), Silvia Mazzoni (mez—Dimitri), Monica Minarelli (sgr—Savoiardo), Placido Domingo (ten—Conte Loris), Ernesto Gavazzi (ten—Desiré), Aldo Bottion (ten—Barone Rouvel), Alessandro Corbelli (bar—Siriex), Luigi Roni (bass—Cirillo), Silvestro Sammaritano (bass—Baroff), Alfredo Giacomotti (bass—Gretch), Ernesto Panariello (bass—Lorek), Vincenzo Alaimo (sgr—Nicola), Arnold Bosman (sgr—Boleslao), Bruno Capicani (sgr—Sergio), Renato Zanchetta (sgr—Michele), G. Gavazzeni (cnd), La Scala Orch, La Scala Chorus *(rec La Scala, Apr 5, 1993)* Legato 2-▲ LCD 213-2 [ADD]
Mozart, W.A.:Così fan tutte, w. Renée Fleming (sop—Fiordiligi), Adelina Scarabelli (sop—Despina), Anne Sofie Von Otter (mez—Dorabella), Frank Lopardo (ten—Ferrando), Olaf Bar (bar—Guglielmo), Michele Pertusi (bass—Don Alfonso), G. Solti (cnd), CO of Europe London 3-▲ 444174-2

Scaravelli, Carlo (bar)
Bizet, G.:Carmen, w. Giovanna di Rocco (sop—Frasquita), Grace Bumbry (mez—Carmen), Anita Caminada (mez—Mercedes), Franco Corelli (ten—Don José), Mario Ferrara (ten—Dancario), Franco Bordoni (bar—Escamillo), Carlo Scaravelli (bar—Morales), Giuseppe Morresi (bass—Remendado), Francesco Signor (bass—Zuniga), O. de Fabritiis (cnd), *(orch unknown)* *(rec Macerata, July 21, 1974)* Golden Age of Opera 2-▲ GAO 181/82 [ADD]

Scardoni, Giovanna (voc)
Salieri, A.:La passione di Gesù Cristo, w. Daniela Citino (sop), Maria Teresa Toso (alt), Nikola Yovanovitch (ten), Mario Scardoni (bass), A. Turco (cnd), Verona Cathedral Cappella Musicale *(rec Verona Cathedral, Italy, Mar 30, 1995)* Bongiovanni ▲ GB 2190 [DDD]

Scardoni, Mario (bass)
Salieri, A.:La passione di Gesù Cristo, w. Daniela Citino (sop), Maria Teresa Toso (alt), Nikola Yovanovitch (ten), Giovanna Scardoni (voc), A. Turco (cnd), Verona Cathedral Cappella Musicale *(rec Verona Cathedral, Italy, Mar 30, 1995)* Bongiovanni ▲ GB 2190 [DDD]

Scarlini, Glauco (sgr)
Puccini, G.:Il tabarro, w. Clara Petrella (sop), Antenore Reali (sgr), G. Baroni (cnd), *(orch & chorus unknown)* Cetra Classic 3-▲ 36

Scarsoni, Renzo (sgr)
Leoncavallo, R.:Zingari, w. Aldo Bottion (ten), Gianna Galli (sgr), Guido Guarneri (sgr), E. Boncompagni (cnd), Turin RAI Orch, Turin RAI Chorus *(rec live, 1975)* Italian Opera Rarities ▲ IOR 7729 [ADD]

Scattola, Carlo (bass)
Puccini, G.:La Bohème, w. Licia Albanese (sop—Mimì), Tatiana Menotti (sop—Musetta), Beniamino Gigli (ten—Rodolfo), Nello Palai (ten—Parpignol), Aristide Baracchi (bar—Schaunard), Afro Poli (bar—Marcello), Duilio Baronti (bass—Colline), Carlo Scattola (bass—Benoit/Alcindoro), U. Berrettoni (cnd), La Scala Orch, Vittore Veneziani (cnd), La Scala Chorus *(rec Feb-Mar 1938)* Arkadia ("The 78's" series) 2-▲ 78009 [ADD]
Puccini, G.:La Bohème, w. L. Albanese (sop—Mimì), T. Menotti (sop—Musetta), B. Gigli (ten—Rodolfo), N. Palai (ten—Parpignol), A. Poli (bar—Marcello), A. Baracchi (bar—Schaunard), D. Baronti (bass—Colline), C. Scattola (bass—Benoit/Alcindoro), U. Berrettoni (cnd), La Scala Orch, La Scala Chorus [I] *(rec Milan, May 1938)* Nimbus 2-▲ NI 7862/63 [ADD]

Scavazza, Marco (bar)
Scarlatti, A.:Répons du Vendredi Saint, w. Nadi Caristi (sop), Paola Serno (mez), Giorgi Mazzucato (cnd), Rovigo City Chorus Studio SM ▲ 2515 [DDD]

Scavazza, Marco (bass)
Perti, G.A.:Liturgy for Good Friday, w. Patrizia Vaccari (sop), Maura Pederzoli (sop), Cristina Calzolari (sop), Alida Oliva (sop), Claudia Bugli (sop), Lucia Bagnoli (alt), Cinzia Meneghel (alt), Renzo Bez (alt), Alessandro Carmignani (alt), Michel van Goethem (alt), Mauro Collina (ten), Vincenzo Di Donato (ten), Paolo Fanciullacci (ten), Giovanni Caccamo (ten), Paolo Da Col (ten), Sergio Foresti (bass), Luca Ferracin (bass), Paride Montanari (bass), Liuwe Tamminga (org), Sergio Vartolo (org), S. Vartolo (cnd), Bologna San Petronio Capella Musicale Orch—Omnes amici mei; De lamentatione Jeremiae Prophetae:Heth. Cogitavit; Velum templi; Vinea mea; De lamentatione Jeremiae Prophetae:Lamed. Matribus suis; Tamquam ad latronem; Tenebrae factae sunt; Animam meam; Tradiderunt me; Jesum tradidit; De lamentatione Jeremiae Prophetae:Aleph. Ego vir; Caligaverunt *(rec St. Petronio Basilica, Bologna, Mar 28-31, 1995)* Naxos ▲ 8.553321 [DDD]

Schaaf, Jerrold van der (ten)
Mozart, W.A.:Entführung, w. S. Greenberg (sop), J. Thames (sop), W. Gahmlich (ten), K. Rydl (bass), M. Viotti (cnd), Frankfurt RSO, Bamberg Sym Chorus LaserLight ▲ 14117 [DDD]
Mozart, W.A.:Entführung, w. S. Greenburg (sop), J. Thames (sop), W. Gahmlich (ten), K. Rydl (bass), Trissenaar (sgr), M. Viotti (cnd), Frankfurt RSO, Bamberg Sym Chorus Capriccio 2-▲ 10 403/04

Schaarschmidt, Jo (nar)
Castelnuovo-Tedesco, M.:Platero y yo, w. Sonja Prunnbauer (gtr) Ars Musici ▲ 1138

Schachtschneider, Herbert (ten)
Schoenberg, A.:Gurrelieder, w. I. Borkh (sop), H. Töpper (mez), L. Fehenberger (ten), K. Engen (bass), R. Kubelik (cnd), Bavarian RSO—also includes songs by Berg, Schoenberg & Webern Deutsche Grammophon ("20th Century Classics" series) ▲ 431744-2 [ADD]
Wagner, R.:Lohengrin, w. Leonore Kirchstein (sop—Elsa von Brabant), Ruth Hesse (mez—Ortrud), Herbert Schachtschneider (ten—Lohengrin), Hans Helm (bar—Der Heerrufer des Königs), Otto von Rohr (bass—Heinrich der Vogler), Heinz Imdahl (sgr—Friedrich von Telramund), H. Swarowsky (cnd), Czech PO, Prague National Theater Orch, Vienna State Opera Chorus *(rec Aug 1968)* Weltbild Classics 3-▲ 703835 [ADD]

Schade, Michael (ten)
Beethoven, L. van:Fidelio, w. Elizabeth Norberg-Schulz (sop—Marzelline), Deborah Voigt (sop—Lenore), Ben Heppner (ten—Florestan), Michael Schade (ten—Jaquino), Günter von Kannaten (b-bar—Don Pizarro), Matthias Hölle (bass—Rocco), Thomas Quasthoff (bass—Don Fernando), C. Davis (cnd), Bavarian RSO, Bavarian Radio Chorus, Bavarian State Opera Men's Chorus *(rec Herkulessaal der Residenz, Munich, May 15-25, 1995)* RCA Victor 2-▲ 09026-68344-2 [DDD]
Haydn, J.:Die Schöpfung, w. Donna Brown (sop), Sylvia McNair (sop), Gerald Finley (bar), Rodney Gilfry (bar), J. E. Gardiner (cnd), English Baroque Soloists, Monteverdi Choir London Archiv ▲ 449 217-2
Mozart, W.A.:Zauberflöte, w. Constanze Backes (sop—Papagena), Christiane Oelze (sop—Pamina), Susan Roberts (sop—First Lady), Cyndia Sieden (sop—Queen of the Night), Carola Guber (cta—Second Lady), Maria Jonas (cta—Third Lady), Andreas Dieterich (trb—First Boy), Jan Andreas Mendel (trb—Second Boy), Florian Wöller (trb—Third Boy), Uwe Peper (ten—Monostatos), Nicolas Robertson (ten—First Man in Armor), Michael Schade (ten—Tamino), Gerald Finley (bar—Papageno), Noel Mann (bass—Second Man in Armour), Harry Peeters (bass—Sarastro), Detlef Roth (bass—Speaker/First Priest), Robert Burt (speaker—Third Priest), Robert Johnston (speaker—Second Priest), Wolfgang Knauer (speaker—Fourth Priest), Douglas Welbat (speaker—Second Priest), J. E. Gardiner (cnd), English Baroque Soloists, Monteverdi Choir London *(rec Forum am Schlosspark, Ludwigsburg, July 1995)* Archiv 2-▲ 449166-2
Sullivan, A.:HMS Pinafore, w. F. Palmer (sop—Little Buttercup), R. Evans (mez—Josephine), M. Schade (ten—Ralph Rackstraw), T. Allen (bar—Capt. Corcoran), R. Suart (bass—Rt. Hon. Sir Joseph Porter, K.C.B.), D. Adams (bass—Dick Deadeye), R. Van A. (bass—Bill Bobstay), C. Mackerras (cnd), Welsh National Opera Orch, Welsh National Opera Chorus *(rec Swansea, Wales, June 5-8, 1994)* Telarc ▲ CD 80374 [DDD]

Schadeberg, Christine (sop)
Berio, L.:Chamber Music, w. Musicians' Accord members *(rec St. Peter's Episcopal Church, New York, Apr 3, 1995)* Mode ▲ mode 48 [DDD]
Berio, L.:Circles, w. Musicians' Accord members *(rec Borden Hall, Manhattan School of Music, New York, June 17, 1995)* Mode ▲ mode 48
Berio, L.:Folk Songs Mez, w. T. Léon (cnd), Musicians' Accord members—Black Is the Color; I Wonder As I Wander; Loosin Yelav; Rossignolet du bois; A la femminisca; La donna ideale; Ballo; Motettu de tristura; Malurous qu'o uno fenno; Lo fiolairé; Azerbaijan Love Song *(rec St. Peter's Episcopal Church, New York, Jan 6, 1995)* Mode ▲ mode 48
Berio, L.:Folk Songs Sop, w. T. Léon (cnd), Musicians' Accord mode ▲ mode 48 [DDD]
Berio, L.:O King Voice, w. Musicians' Accord mode ▲ mode 48 [DDD]
Berio, L.:Sequenza III *(rec Sheppard Hall, City College of New York, July 7, 1995)* Mode ▲ mode 48 [DDD]
Blumenfeld, H.:Ange de flamme et de glaçe, w. Randall Gremillion (bass), G. Samuel (cnd), Cincinnati PO Centaur ▲ CRC 2277
Blumenfeld, H.:La Face cendrée, w. Randall Gremillion (bass), G. Samuel (cnd), Cincinnati PO Centaur ▲ CRC 2277
Blumenfeld, H.:Illuminations, w. Randall Gremillion (bass), G. Samuel (cnd), Cincinnati PO Centaur ▲ CRC 2277
Carter, E.:A Mirror on Which to Dwell, w. D. Palma (cnd), Speculum Musicae [E] Bridge ▲ BCD 9014 [DDD]
Dellaira, M.:Maud, w. electronically derived sounds Opus One ▲ 146
Feigin, J.:Music of, w. F. Cohen (cnd), Musicians' Accord—Ecstatic Poems of Kabir (5); Veränderungen; Poems of Linda Pastan (4); Fantasy Pieces; Poems of Wallace Stevens (4); Nexus; First Tradgedy; Echos from the Holocaust; Japanese Poems (8); Transience North/South Recordings 2-▲ N/S R 1011 [DDD]
Ibert, J.:Music of, w. Sue Ann Kahn (fl), E. Lawrence (fl), P. Schechter (fl), R. Schmidt (fl), David Krakauer (cl), L. Goldstein (bn), Curtis Macomber (vn), Susan Jolles (hp), Frederick Hand (gtr), Arthur Willis (pno)—Entr'acte; Jeux; Sonatine; 2 Movements; 2 Interludes; Aria; Pièce for solo Fl; Histoires; 2 Stèles orientées; Pastoral; Aria; Entr'acte Albany ▲ TROY 145
Ibert, J.:Stèles orientées, w. Sue Ann Kahn (fl) Albany ▲ TROY 145 [DDD]
Kassel, R.:Celebrating, w. T. Flanders (sop) Mode ▲ 23
Kassel, R.:Gathering, w. T. Flanders (sop) Mode ▲ 23
London, E.:Before the World Was Made, w. E. London (cnd), Cleveland Chamber SO Albany ▲ TROY 208 [DDD]

Schädle, Lotte (sop)
Mussorgsky, M.:Boris Godunov, w. Martha Mödl (sop—Marina Mniszek), Lotte Schädle (sop—Xenia), Dorothea Siebert (mez—Fyodor), Hertha Töpper (mez—Xenia's wet-nurs), Karl Hermann Bennert (Boyer Khrushchyov), Lorenz Fehenberger (ten—Prince Shuysky), Hans Hopf (ten—Grigory), Karl Ostertag (ten—Missail), Hans Hotter (b-bar—Boris Godunov), Hermann Uhde (bar—Andrey Shchelkalov), Kurt Böhme (bass—Varlaam), Kim Borg (bass—Pimen), Kieth Engen (bass—Lewicki), Adolf Keil (bass—Nikitich), Benno Kusche (bar—Rangoni), Heinz Maria Linz (bass—Czernikowski), E. Jochum (cnd), Bavarian RSO, Bavarian Radio Chorus *(rec Munich, May 1957)* Myto 3-▲ MCD 953131

Schadock, Mathias (nar)
Nono, L.:Prometeo, w. I. Ade-Jesemann (sop), M. Bair-Ivenz (sop), S. Otto (alt), P. Hall (ten), U. Krumbiegel (nar), C. Abbado (cnd), Berlin PO, Freiburg Soloists Choir *(rec May 23-25, 1993)* Sony Classical ▲ SK 53978 [DDD]

Schaechter, Dalia (cta)
Beethoven, L. van:Syms (comp), w. Jean Glennon (sop), Algridas Janutas (ten), Benno Schollum (bass), Y. Menuhin (cnd), Sinfonia Varsovia, Kuanas State Choir Lithuania IMP ("IMG" series) 5-▲ IMP 6800025

Schaechter, Dalia (mez)
Bizet, G.:Carmen (sels), w. D. Palade (sop—Micaëla), A. Liebeck (sop—Frasquita), G. Alperyn (mez—Carmen), D. Schaechter (mez—Mercédès), G. Lamberti (ten—Don José), M. Dvorsky (ten—Remandado), J. Durco (ten—Cancairo), A. Titus (bar—Escamillo), V. Chmelo (bar—Morales), D. Rigosa (bass—Zuniga), A. Rahbari (cnd), Czech-Slovak RSO Bratislava, Slovak Phil Chorus, Bratislava Children's Choir *(rec July 1990)* Naxos ▲ 8.550727 [DDD]

Schaeffer, M. (ten)
Beethoven, L. van:Mass, Op. 86, w. A. Michael (sop), L. Bizimeche-Eisinger (mez), M. Brodard (bar), M. Corboz (cnd), Lisbon Gulbenkian Foundation Orch, Lisbon Gulbenkian Foundation Chorus [L] Erato ▲ 2292-45461-2 ZK [DDD]

Schaer, Hanna (mez)
Mahler, G.:Songs, w. Françoise Tillard (pno)—Erinnurung; Frühlingsmorgen; Ablösung im sommer; Nicht wiedersehen; Ich ging mit lust; Hans und Grete; Starke einbildungskraft; Zu straburg auf der schanz'; Aus! Aus!; Scheiden und meiden; Das irdische Leben; Wer hat dies Liedlein erdacht?; Des Antonius von padua fischpredigt Adda ▲ ADD 581208
Werfel, A.M.:Songs, w. Françoise Tillard (pno)—Die stille Stadt; In meins Vaters Garten; Laue Sommernacht; Bei dir ist es traut; Ich wandle unter Blumen Adda ▲ ADD 581208

Schäfer, Christine (sop)
Bach, J.S.:St. John Passion, w. Y. Jänicke (mez), A. Kraus (ten), R. Hagen (bass), B. Possemeyer (bass), E. Weyand (cnd), Stuttgart Hymnus Orch, Stuttgart Hymnus Boys' Choir [G] *(rec 1990)* Hänssler Classic 2-▲ 98.968
Humperdinck, E.:Hänsel und Gretel, w. H. Behrens (sop—Gertrud, the Stepmother), R. Ziesak (sop—Gretel), R. Joshua (sop—Sandman), C. Schäfer (sop—Dew Fairy), J. Larmore (mez—Hänsel), H. Schwarz (cta—Nibblewitch), B. Weikl (bar—Peter, the Father), D. Runnicles (cnd), Bavarian RSO, Tölz Boys' Choir *(rec Munich, Feb. 1994)* Teldec 2-▲ 94549-2 [DDD]
Krenek, E.:Songs, w. Axel Bauni (pno)—O lacrymosa, Op. 48; Monolog der Stella, Op. 57; Die nachtigall, Op. 68; 5 Lieder, Op. 82; 4 Songs, Op. 112; The Flea, Op. 175; Wechselrahmen, Op. 189 *(rec Studio 3, Bavarian Radio)* Orfeo ▲ 373951 [DDD]
Mozart, W.A.:Notturnos Sops, w. G. Hintz (sop), D. Fischer-Dieskau (bar), Berlin PO Winds Orfeo ▲ 218911 [DDD]
Mozart, W.A.:Più non si trovano, w. G. Hintz (sop), D. Fischer-Dieskau (bar), Berlin PO Winds Orfeo ▲ 218911 [DDD]
Reimann, A.:Nightpiece, w. Axel Bauni (pno) *(rec Studio II, Radio Free Berlin, May 1995)* Orfeo ▲ C 412 961 [DDD]
Schoeck, O.:Songs (comp), w. Wolfram Rieger (pno)—Scheiden und Meiden; Auf den Tod eines Kindes [both from Op. 3]; An die Entfernte; Frühlingsblick [both from Op. 5]; In der Fremde; Erster Verlust [both from Op. 15]; Im Sommer; Gekommen ist der Maie; Erinnerung; Der frohe Wandersmann [all from Op. 17]; An einem heitern Morgen; Dichtersegen; Wein und Brot; Der Gärtner; Nachtlied [all from Op. 20]; 6 Lieder, Op. 6; 2 Lieder, Op. 12 *(rec Sept 1995)* Jecklin ▲ JD 671
Schubert, Franz:Songs (comp), w. John Mark Ainsley (ten), Richard Jackson (bar), Graham Johnson (pno), Stephen Layton (cnd), London Schubert Chorale—Der Einsame; Des Sängers Habe; Zwei Szenen aus dem Schauspiel Lacrimas (Lied der Delphine; Lied des Florio); Mondenschien (chorale); Gesänge Aus Wilhwlm Meister (Nur wer die Sehnsucht kennt; Hwiss mich nicht reden; So lasst mich scheinen); Totengräberweise; Das Echo; An Silvia; Horch, horch die Lerch'; Trinklied; Wiegenlied; Widerspruch; Der Wanderer an den Mond; Grab und Mond (chorale); Nachthelle; Abschied von der Erde Hyperion ▲ CDJ 33026
Schubert, Franz:Songs (comp), w. Matthias Görne (bar), Graham Johnson (pno)—22 songs including D.395, 410, 628-631, 633, 634, 646, 649, 652, 684, 690-694, 708, 711, 745, 854, 855 Hyperion ▲ 33027
Schumann, R.:Songs, w. Graham Johnson (pno)—Röselein, Röselein!; Mädchen-Schwermut; Die Blume der Ergebung; Melancholie; Zigeunerliedchen I; Zigeunerliedchen II; Die Meerfee; Herzeleid; Die Fensterscheibe; Der Gärtner; Die Spinnerin; Im Wald; Abendlied; Ihre Stimme; Nachtlied; Singet nicht in Trauertönen; Nur wer die Sehnsucht kennt; Heiss' mich nicht reden; So lasst mich scheinen; Mignon; Lied eines Schmiedes; Meine Rose; Kommen und Scheiden; Die Sennin; Einsamkeit; Der schwere Abend; Requiem; Das verlassene Mägdlein; Er ist's! Warnung; Sängers Trost; Aufträge Hyperion ▲ CDJ 33101
Ullmann, V.:Songs, w. Liat Himmelheber (mez), Yaron Windmüller (bar), Axel Bauni (pno)—5 Liebeslieder, Op. 18; 6 Lieder, Op. 17; 3 Sonette, Op. 29; 6 Sonnets, Op. 34; Geistliche Lieder, Op. 20; Liederbuch das Hafis, op. 30; Der Mensch und sein Tag, Op. 47; Immer inmitten; Chinesische Lieder; 3 Lieder Orfeo 2-▲ 380952 [DDD]

Schäfer, Graham (sgr)
Schubert, Franz:Songs (comp), w. John Mark Ainsley (ten), Michael George (bass), Simon Keenlyside (bass), Graham Johnson (cnd), London Schubert Chorale—settings of Goethe's poetry Hyperion ▲ CDJ 33024

Schäfer, Markus (ten)
Bach, J.S.:Cant 27, w. Harry van der Kamp (bass), G. Leonhardt (cnd), Baroque Orch, Tölz Boys' Choir Sony Classical ("Vivarte" series) ▲ SK 68265
Bach, J.S.:Cant 34, w. Harry van der Kamp (bass), G. Leonhardt (cnd), Baroque Orch, Tölz Boys' Choir Sony Classical ("Vivarte" series) ▲ SK 68265
Bach, J.S.:Cant 41, w. Harry van der Kamp (bass), G. Leonhardt (cnd), Baroque Orch, Tölz Boys' Choir Sony Classical ("Vivarte" series) ▲ SK 68265
Beethoven, L. van:Cant on the Death of the Emperor Joseph II, w. Alan Titus (bar), Bodil Arnesen (sgr), K.A. Rickenbacher (cnd), Berlin RSO, Berlin Radio Chorus Koch Schwann ▲ SCH 314352 [DDD]
Handel, G.F.:Acis & Galatea [arr Mozart], w. B. Bonney (sop), J. MacDougall (ten), J. Tomlinson (bass), T. Pinnock (cnd), English Concert, English Concert Choir London 2-▲ 425792-2
Mendelssohn, F.:St. Paul, w. R. Yakar (sop), B. Baileys (mez), T. Hampson (bar), M. Corboz (cnd), Lisbon Gulbenkian Foundation Orch, Lisbon Gulbenkian Foundation Chorus Erato 2-▲ 45279-2
Mozart, W.A.:Così fan tutte, w. S. Isokoski (sop—Fiordiligi), N. Argenta (sop—Despina), M. Groop (mez—Dorabella), M. Schäfer (ten—Ferrando), P. Vollestad (bar—Guglielmo), H. Claessens (b-bar—Don Alfonso)., S. Kuijken (cnd), La Petite Bande, La Petite Bande Chorus Accent 3-▲ ACC 9296/98
Orff, C.:Catulli Carmina, w. R. Ziesack (sop), *(other artists unknown)*, W. Schäfer (cnd), Frankfurt Kantorei [L] Koch Schwann ▲ 314 021 [DDD]
Stravinsky, I.:Les Noces, w. U. Sonntag (sop), C. Kallisch (cta), P. Lika (bass), C. Rausch (bass), et al., W. Schäfer (cnd), Frankfurt Kantorei [G] Koch Schwann ▲ 314 021 [DDD]

Schaffer, John (voc)
Hays, S.:Dreaming the World, w. Thomas Bruckner (bar), Sal Basile (voc), Jennifer López (voc), Sorrel Hays (voc), Joseph Kubera (pno), John Kennedy (perc), Charles Wood (perc), Maya Gunji (perc), Eric Kivnick (perc), Jai Smith (perc) New World ▲ 805202 [DDD]

Schaffner, Anna (alt)
Mozart, W.A.:Missa Solemnis, w. Christa Goetze (sop), Barnhard Gärtner (ten), Rudolf Rosen (bass), Philippe Laubscher (org), F. Pantillon (cnd), Bieler SO, Pro Arte Chorale, Bern Vocal Ensemble Gallo ▲ CD 893 [DDD]

Schaible, Ulrich (bar)
Hindemith, P.:Hin und zurück, w. Barbara Miller (sop), Claus Bock (ten), Helmut Kühnle (bass), A. Grüber (cnd), Berlin SO members *(rec 1971)* Allegretto ▲ ACD 8191

Schaible, Ulrich (bass)
Bach, J.S.:Cant 80, w. Antonia Fahberg (sop), Bargarete Bence (cta), Theophil Maier (ten), H. Rilling (cnd), Württemberg CO, Stuttgart Memorial Church Figuralchor *(rec 1964)* Vox Box 3-▲ CD3X 3039

Schamberger, Achim (ten)
Hoffmann, E.T.A.:Undine, w. Barbara Baier (sop—Berthalda), Heidrun Plesch (sop—Undine), Corinna Tippe (sop—Die Herzogin), Maria Hiefinger (mez—Fisherman's Wife), Achim Schamberger (ten—Der Herzog), Johannes Beck (bar—Ritter Huldbrand von Ringstetten), Michael Albert (bass—Fisherman), Ulrich Bosch (bass—Heilmann), Bernd Hofmann (bass—Kühleborn), H. Dechant (cnd), Bamberg Youth Orch Bayer 3-▲ 100256/58 [DDD]

Scharinger, Anton (bar)
Mozart, W.A.:Zauberflöte, w. Natalie Dessay (sop—Queen of the Night), Linda Kitchen (sop—Papagena), Rosa Mannion (sop—Pamina), Anna-Maria Panzarella (sop—First Lady), Doris Lamprecht (mez—Second Lady), Delphine Haidan (cta—Third Lady), Hans Peter Blochwitz (ten—Tamino), Steven Cole (ten—Monostatos), Chrisopher Josey (ten—First Priest/First Armed Man), Anton Scharinger (bar—Papageno), Reinhard Hagen (bass—Sarastro), Laurent Naouri (bass—Second Priest/Second Armed Man), Willard White (bass—Speaker), W. Christie (cnd), Les Arts Florissants *(rec Paris Oct 2-9 1995)* Erato 2-▲ 12705-2 [DDD]

▲ = CD ♦ = Enhanced CD Δ = MD ■ = Cassette Tape □ = DCC

Scharinger, Anton (bass)

Bach, J.S.:Mass in b, BWV 232, w. B. Bonney (sop), C. Wulkopf (mez), P. Schrier (ten), S. Celibidache (cnd), Munich PO, Munich Bach Choir — Exclusive ▲ EXL 33 [ADD]

Bach, J.S.:Mass in b, BWV 232, w. M. Venuti (sop), C. Kallisch (cta), C. Prégardien (ten), E. Ortner (cnd), Salzburg Baroque Ensemble, Arnold Schoenberg Choir — Koch Schwann 2-▲ SCH 312512 [DDD]

Gazzaniga, G.:Don Giovanni, w. P. Coburn (sop), J. Kaufmann (sop), J. Aler (ten), R. Swensen (ten), J.-L. Chaignaud (bar), G. von Kannen (bass), S. Soltesz (cnd), Munich RSO, Munich Radio Chorus [I] — Orfeo 2-▲ 214902 [DDD]

Handel, G.F.:Samson, w. Roberta Alexander (sop), Maria Venuti (sop), Jochen Kowalski (ct), Anthony Rolfe Johnson (ten), Aalstair Miles (bass), N. Harnoncourt (cnd), Vienna Concentus Musicus, Arnold Schoenberg Choir — Teldec ▲ 74871-2

Handel, G.F.:Theodora, w. Roberta Alexander (sop), Jard van Nes (cta), Jochen Kowalski (ct), Hans-Peter Blochwitz (ten), N. Harnoncourt (cnd), Vienna Concentus Musicus, Arnold Schoenberg Choir [E] — Teldec 2-▲ 2292-46447-2 [DDD]

Haydn, J.:Die Schöpfung, w. Ruth Ziesak (sop—Eve & Gabriel), Herbert Lippert (ten—Uriel), Rene Papé (bass—Raphael), Anton Scharinger (bass—Adam), G. Solti (cnd), Chicago SO, Chicago Sym Chorus — London 2-▲ 443445-2 [DDD]

Mozart, W.A.:Finta giardiniera, w. E. Gruberova (sop), C. Margiono (sop), M. Bacelli (sop), D. Upshaw (sop), U. Heilmann (ten), N. Harnoncourt (cnd), Vienna Concentus Musicus — Teldec 3-▲ 72309-2

Mozart, W.A.:Nozze di Figaro, w. C. Margiono (sop), B. Bonney (sop), I. Rey (sop), A. Murray (mez, P.-L. Lang (mez), P. Langridge (ten), C. Späth (ten), T. Hampson (bar), K. Moll (bass), A. Scharinger (bass), K. Langan (bass), N. Harnoncourt (cnd), Royal Concertgebouw Orch, Netherlands Opera Chorus *(rec Amsterdam, May 1993)* — Teldec 3-▲ 90861-2 [DDD]

Mozart, W.A.:Zauberflöte, w. E. Gruberova (sop), B. Bonney (sop), G. Schmid (sop), H.-P. Blochwitz (ten), T. Hampson (bar), M. Salminen (bass), N. Harnoncourt (cnd), Zurich Opera Orch, Zurich Opera House Chorus [G] — Teldec 2-▲ 2292-42716-2

Purcell, H.:Dido & Aeneas, w. R. Yakar (sop), A. Murray (mez), N. Harnoncourt (cnd), Vienna Concentus Musicus, Arnold Schoenberg Choir — Teldec ("Das alte Werke" series) ▲ 93686

Purcell, H.:Dido & Aeneas, w. R. Yakar (sop), A. Murray (mez), N. Harnoncourt (cnd), Vienna Concentus Musicus [E] — Teldec ▲ 2292-42959-2

Strauss (II), Joh.:Die Fledermaus (sels), w. E. Gruberova (sop), B. Bonney (sop), M. Lipovšek (mez), W. Kmentt (ten), W. Hollweg (ten), J. Protschka (ten), C. Boesch (bar), N. Harnoncourt (cnd), Royal Concertgebouw Orch, Netherlands Opera Chorus — Teldec ▲ 42427-2

Telemann, G.P.:St. Matthew Passion, w. M. Zedelius (sop), A. Browner (alt), H.P. Blochwitz (ten), W. Schmidt (bar), W. Seeliger (cnd), Darmstadt CO, Darmstadt Concert Choir — Christophorus ▲ 77149 [DDD]

Scharley, Denise (mez)

Honegger, A.:Le Roi David, w. Henri Doublier (nar), Jacqueline Brumaire (sop), Jacques Pottier (ten), S. Baudo (cnd), Paris Opera Orch, Elisabeth Brasseur Chorale — Accord ▲ ACD 200822 [AAD]

Massenet, J.:Hérodiade (sels), w. Michele Le Bris (sop—Salomé), Denise Scharley (cta—Hérodiade), Guy Chauvet (ten—Jean), Robert Massard (bar—Hérode), J. Etcheverry (cnd), Paris Lyric Orch—Il est doux, il est bon; Hérode, Ne me refuse pas; Jean, je le revois; Vision fugitive; Astres etincelants; Charme des jours passés; Salomé, laisse-moi t'aimer; Ne pouvant réprimer les élans de la foi; Quand nos jours s'éteindront...; Ballet — Accord ▲ ACD 204272 [AAD]

Poulenc, F.:Dialogues des Carmélites, w. D. Duval (sop), R. Crespin (sop), L. Berton (sop), R. Gorr (mez), P. Finel (ten), X. Depraz (bass), P. Dervaux (cnd), Paris Opera Orch [F] — EMI Classics 2-▲ CDCB 49331 (m) [ADD]

Schärtel, Elisabeth (mez)

Wagner, R.:Choruses, w. J. Greindl (bass), W. Pitz (cnd), Bayreuth Festival Orch, Bayreuth Festival Chorus—choruses from Lohengrin, Götterdämmerung, Parsifal, Fliegende Holländer, Tannhäuser, Meistersinger — Deutsche Grammophon ("Resonance" series) ▲ 429169-2 [ADD]

Wagner, R.:Der Ring des Nibelungen, w. Gré Brouwenstein (sop—Freia/Sieglinde), Ilse Hollweg (sop—Waldvogel), Gerda Lammers (sop—Ortlinde), Paula Lenchner (sop—Wellgunde/Gerhilde), Hilde Scheppan (sop—Helmwige), Astrid Varnay (sop—Brünnilde/3rd Norn), Lore Wissmann (sop—Woglinde), Maria von Ilosvay (mez—Flosshilde/Schwertleite/2nd Norn), Louise Charlotte Kamps (mez—Siegrune), Jean Madeira (mez—Erda/Rossweisse/1st Norn), Georgine van Milinkovic (mez—Fricka/Grimgerde), Elisabeth Schärtel (mez—Waltraute), Paul Kuën (ten—Mime), Ludwig Suthaus (ten—Loge), Josef Traxel (ten—Froh), Wolfgang Windgassen (ten—Siegmund/Siegfried), Alfons Herwig (bar—Donner), Hermann Uhde (bar—Gunther), Hans Hotter (b-bar—Wotan), Gustav Neidlinger (b-bar—Alberich), Josef Griendl (bass—Fasolt/Hunding/Hagen), Arnold van Mill (bass—Fafner), H. Knappertsbusch (cnd), Bayreuth Festival Orch, Bayreuth Festival Chorus *(rec live, Bayreuth, Aug 13-17, 1956)* — Golden Melodram 14-▲ GM 1.001 [ADD]

Schary, Elke (mez)

Strauss (II), Joh.:Eine Nacht in Venedig (sels), w. J. Scovotti (sop), E. Steiner (mez), C. Bini (ten), F. Stricker (ten), W. Brendel (bar), E. Märzendorfer (cnd), Hungarian State Orch, Hungarian State Chorus [G] — Acanta ▲ CD 43809 [DDD]

Schasching, Rudolf (ten)

Strauss (II), Joh.:Der Zigeunerbaron, w. Pamela Coburn (sop), Christiane Oelze (sop), Julia Hamari (moz), Elisabeth von Magnus (alt), Herbert Lippert (ten), Wolfgang Holzmair (bar), Jurgen Flimm (sgr), Robert Florianschutz (sgr), Hans-Jurgen Lazar (sgr), N. Harnoncourt (cnd), Vienna SO, Arnold Schoenberg Choir *(rec Vienna, 1994)* — Teldec 2-▲ 94555-2

Schaufer, Lucy (mez)

Bowles, P.:The Wind Remains, w. Carl Halvorson (ten), J. Sheffer (cnd), Eos Ensemble *(rec Manhattan Center Studios, New York, Sept 22 & 23, 1995)* — Catalyst ▲ 09026-68409-2 [DDD]

Schech, Marianne (sop)

Mozart, W.A.:Don Giovanni, w. M. Teschemacher (sop), H. Hopf (ten), M. Ahlersmeyer (bar), K. Böhme (bass), G. Frick (bass), K. Elmendorff (cnd), Saxon State Orch, Dresden State Opera Chorus [G] *(rec 1943)* — Berlin Classics ("Dokumente" series) 3-▲ BER 2048 [ADD]

Strauss, R.:Elektra, w. I. Borkh (sop), J. Madeira (mez), D. Fischer-Dieskau (bar), K. Böhm (cnd), Dresden Staatskapelle [G] *(rec 1961)* — Deutsche Grammophon 2-▲ 445329-2

Wagner, R.:Der fliegende Holländer, w. S. Wagner (mez), G. Frick (ten), F. Wunderlich (ten), R. Schock (ten), D. Fischer-Dieskau (bar), F. Konwitschny (cnd), Berlin Staatskapelle — Berlin Classics ("Eterna" series) 2-▲ BER 2097 [ADD]

Wagner, R.:Der fliegende Holländer (sels), w. Fritz Wunderlich (ten), Dietrich Fischer-Dieskau (bar), Gottlob Frick (bass), F. Konwitschny (cnd), Berlin Staatskapelle — Berlin Classics ▲ BER 9080 [ADD]

Wagner, R.:Götterdämmerung, w. Birgit Nilsson (sop—Brünnhilde), Leonie Rysanek (sop—Gutrune), Gerda Sommerschuh (sop—Woglinde), Elisabeth Lindermeier (sop—Wellgunde), Ruth Michaelis (sop—Flohilde), Marianne Schech (sop—Dritte Norne), Ira Malaniuk (mez—Waltraute), Irmgarth Barth (mez—Erste Norne), Hertha Töpper (mez—Zweite Norne), Bernd Aldenhoff (ten—Siegfried), Hermann Uhde (bar—Gunther), Gottlob Frick (bass—Hagen), H. Knappertsbusch (cnd), Bavarian State Opera Orch, Bavarian State Opera Chorus *(rec live, Prinzregententheater, Sept. 1, 1955)* — Orfeo 4-▲ 356944 (m)

Wagner, R.:Tannhäuser, w. E. Grümmer (sop), H. Hopf (ten), F. Wunderlich (ten), D. Fischer-Dieskau (bar), G. Frick (bass), F. Konwitschny (cnd), Berlin State Opera Orch, Berlin State Opera Chorus [G] — EMI Classics ("Studio" series) 3-▲ CDMC 63214 [ADD]

Scheff, Walter (bar)

Blitzstein, M.:The Airborne, w. R. Shaw (nar), L. Bernstein (cnd), New York City SO, RCA Victor Chorus — RCA Gold Seal ▲ 09026-62568-2

Scheibner, Andreas (bar)

Bach, J.S.:Cant 14, w. M. Frimmer (sop), E. Büchner (ten), M. Pommer (cnd), Leipzig New Bach Collegium Musicum, Leipzig St. Thomas Church Choir [G] — Capriccio ▲ CDC 10027

Bach, J.S.:Cant 143, w. M. Frimmer (sop), E. Büchner (ten), M. Pommer (cnd), Leipzig New Bach Collegium Musicum, Leipzig St. Thomas Church Choir [G] — Capriccio ▲ CDC 10027 [DDD]

Schéle, Märta (sop)

Argento, D.:From the Diary of V. Woolf, w. J. Ribera (pno), G. Schaub (fl) — Proprius ▲ PRCD 9982

Britten, H.:Songs from the Chinese, w. Josef Holeček (gtr) *(rec Castle Wik, Sweden, Sept 12 & 13, 1975)* — BIS ▲ CD 34 [AAD]

Schéle, Märta (sop) (cont.)

Britten, H.:Songs from the Chinese, w. J. Holeček (gtr) [E] — BIS ▲ CD 31 [AAD]

Castelnuovo-Tedesco, M.:Songs (6) from *The Divan of Moses-ibn-Ezra*, w. Josef Holeček (gtr) *(rec Castle Wik, Sweden, Oct 4 & 5, 1975)* — BIS ▲ CD 34 [AAD]

Debussy, C.:Chansons de Bilitis, w. Elisif Lundén (pno) *(rec Nacka Aula, Nacka, Sweden, Aug 13 & 14, 1975)* — BIS ▲ CD 34 [AAD]

Debussy, C.:Chansons de Bilitis, w. Elisif Lundén (pno) *(rec Nacka Aula, Nacka, Sweden, Aug. 14, 1975)* — BIS ▲ CD 28 [AAD]

Hallnäs, H.:Songs, w. Birgit Finnila (cta), Rolf Leanderson (bar), Elisef Lunden (pno)—3 sels — BIS ▲ CD 38

Milhaud, D.:Catalogue de fleurs, w. Elisif Lundén (pno) *(rec Nacka Aula, Nacka, Sweden, Aug 13 & 14, 1975)* — BIS ▲ CD 34 [AAD]

Nystroem, G.:Songs, w. Birgit Finnila (cta), Rolf Leanderson (bar), Elisef Lunden (pno)—3 sels — BIS ▲ CD 38

Nystroem, G.:Songs at the Sea, w. Birgit Finnila (cta), Rolf Leanderson (bar), Elisef Lunden (pno) — BIS ▲ CD 38

Rameau, J.P.:Castor et Pollux, w. J. Scovotti (sop), R. Leanderson (bar), G. Souzay (bar), J. Villisech (bass), N. Harnoncourt (cnd), Vienna Concentus Musicus — Teldec ▲ 42510-2

Ravel, M.:Mélodies populaires grecques, w. Elisif Lundén (pno) *(rec Nacka Aula, Nacka, Sweden, Aug 13 & 14, 1975)* — BIS ▲ CD 34 [AAD]

Rosenberg, H.:Chinese Songs, w. Birgit Finnila (cta), Rolf Leanderson (bar), Elisef Lunden (pno) — BIS ▲ CD 38

Schubert, Franz:Songs (misc), w. Albert Linder (hn), Ingemar Bergfelt (pno)—Auf dem Strome, Op. 119 *(rec Gothenburg Concert Hall, Sweden, May 8, 1976)* — BIS ▲ CD 34 [AAD]

Schumann, R.:Spanisches Liederspiel, w. Edith Thallaug (alt), Gösta Winbergh (ten), Erland Hagegard (bar), Lucia Negro (pno) *(rec Nacka Aula, Nacka, Sweden, 1976)* — BIS ▲ CD 77 [AAD]

Werle, L.J.:Chants for Dark Hours, w. J. Ribera (pno), G. Schaub (fl) — Proprius ▲ PRCD 9982

Werle, L.J.:Night Hunt, w. Birgit Finnila (cta), Rolf Leanderson (bar), Elisef Lunden (pno) — BIS ▲ CD 38

Schell, F. (voc)

Partch, H.:The Bewitched, w. J. Garvey (cnd), Univ of Illinois New Music Ensemble members — CRI ▲ CD 7001 [ADD]

Schell, Hertha (nar)

Benda, G.A.:Medea, w. Peter Uray (nar), Brigitte Quadlbauer (nar), C. Benda (cnd), Prague CO *(rec Prague, Nov 1994)* — Naxos ▲ 8.553346 [DDD]

Schellenberg, Arno (bar)

Wagner, R.:Tannhäuser (sels), w. Maria Reining (sop—Elisabeth), Max Lorenz (ten—Tannhäuser), Arno Schellenberg (bar—Wolfram), H. Knappertsbusch (cnd), Vienna State Opera Orch *(rec Vienna, Nov. 20, 1937)* — Koch Schwann 2-▲ SCH 314672 [ADD]

Schellenberg, Henriette (sop)

Bach, J.S.:Cant 140, w. J. Humphrey (ten), S. Sylvan (bar), B. H. Moyse (cnd), Orch of St. Luke — MusicMasters ▲ 7059-2-C [DDD]

Bach, J.S.:Cant 140, w. D. Gordon (ten), D. Lichti (b-bar), G. Funfgeld (cnd), Bach Festival Orch, Bethlehem Bach Choir [G] — Dorian ▲ DOR 90127 [DDD]

Bach, J.S.:Magnificat, BWV 243, w. M. A. Kruger (sop), M. Westbrook-Geha (mez), I. Humphrey (ten), S. Sylvan (bar), B. H. Moyse (cnd), Orch of St. Luke — MusicMasters ▲ 7059-2-C [DDD]

Beethoven, L. van:Mass, Op. 86, w. M. Simpson (mez), J. Humphrey (ten), M. Myers (ten), R. Shaw (cnd), Atlanta SO, Atlanta Sym Chorus [L] — Telarc ▲ CD 80248 [DDD]

Bernhard, C.:Missa "Durch Adams Fall", w. Laverne G' Froerer (mez), Keith Boldt (ten), George Roberts (bar), J. Washburn (cnd), CBC Vancouver SO, Vancouver Chamber Choir *(rec Ryerson United Church & The Orpheum, Vancouver, May 4-7, 1992)* — CBC ▲ 5160 [DDD]

Fauré, G.:Messe basse, w. Laverne G' Froerer (mez), Keith Boldt (ten), George Roberts (bar), J. Washburn (cnd), CBC Vancouver SO, Vancouver Chamber Choir [orchd J. Washburn] *(rec Ryerson United Church & The Orpheum, Vancouver, May 4-7, 1992)* — CBC ▲ 5160 [DDD]

Haydn, J.:Mass 7, "Kleine Orgelmesse", w. Laverne G' Froerer (mez), Keith Boldt (ten), George Roberts (bar), J. Washburn (cnd), CBC Vancouver SO, Vancouver Chamber Choir *(rec Ryerson United Church & The Orpheum, Vancouver, May 4-7, 1992)* — CBC ▲ 5160 [DDD]

Mendelssohn, F.:Elijah, w. Barbara Bonney (sop), Florence Quivar (mez), Marietta Simpson (mez), Reid Bartelme (trb), Jerry Hadley (ten), Richard Clement (ten), Thomas Hampson (bar), Thomas Paul (bar), R. Shaw (cnd), Atlanta SO, Atlanta Sym Chorus [E] *(rec Symphony Hall, Woodruff Arts Center, Atlanta, GA, Nov. 5-7, 1994)* — Telarc 2-▲ CD 80389 [DDD]

Weber, C.M. von:Missa sancta 2, w. Laverne G' Froerer (mez), Keith Boldt (ten), George Roberts (bar), J. Washburn (cnd), CBC Vancouver SO, Vancouver Chamber Choir *(rec Ryerson United Church & The Orpheum, Vancouver, May 4-7, 1992)* — CBC ▲ 5160 [DDD]

Schellenberger, Dagmar (sop)

Humperdinck, E.:Königskinder, w. Dagmar Schellenberger (sop—Goose girl), Marilyn Schmiege (cta—Witch), Thomas Moser (ten—King's Son), Heinrich Weber (ten—Broommaker), Dietrich Henschel (bar—Fiddler), Andreas Kohn (bass—Woodcutter), F. Luisi (cnd), Munich RSO, Michael Gläser (cnd), Bavarian Radio Chorus *(rec live, Munich Herkulessaal, Mar 22-24, 1996)* — Calig 3-CAL 5096870 [DDD]

Mozart, W.A.:Arias, w. R. Weikort (cnd), Berlin German Opera Orch—Alma grande e nobil core, K.578; Misera, dove son, K.369 — EMI Classics ▲ CDC 55008

Mozart, W.A.:Bastien und Bastienne, w. R. Eschrig (ten), R. Pape (bass), M. Pommer (cnd), Leipzig RSO, Leipzig Radio Chorus — Berlin Classics 2-▲ BER 1010 [DDD]

Mozart, W.A.:Clemenza (sels), w. R. Weikert (cnd), Berlin German Opera Orch—Non piu di fiori — EMI Classics ▲ CDC 55008

Mozart, W.A.:Così fan tutte (sels), w. R. Weikert (cnd), Berlin German Opera Orch—Per pieta, Come scoglio — EMI Classics ▲ CDC 55008

Mozart, W.A.:Don Giovanni (sels), w. R. Weikert (cnd), Berlin German Opera Orch—Mi tra di quel alma — EMI Classics ▲ CDC 55008

Mozart, W.A.:Idomeneo (sels), w. R. Weikert (cnd), Berlin German Opera Orch—Zeffiretti — EMI Classics ▲ CDC 55008

Mozart, W.A.:Nozze di Figaro (sels), w. R. Weikert (cnd), Berlin German Opera Orch—Porgi amor; Giunse alfin...Deh vieni non tardar — EMI Classics ▲ CDC 55008

Mozart, W.A.:Zauberflöte (sels), w. R. Weikert (cnd), Berlin German Opera Orch—Ach ich fhl's — EMI Classics ▲ CDC 55008

Schellenberger-Ernst, Dagmar (sop)

Handel, G.F.:L'Allegro, Il Penseroso ed il Moderato, w. V. Hruba-Freiberger (sop), J. Kowalski (alt), F.Kapellmann (bass), Rabsilber (sgr), R. Reuter (cnd), Berlin Comic Opera Orch, Berlin Radio Chorus — Berlin Classics 2-▲ BER 1147 [DDD]

Schemtchuk, Ludmilla (mez)

Prokofiev, S.:Alexander Nevsky, w. D. Kitayenko (cnd), Danish National RSO, Danish National Radio Choir [R] — Chandos ▲ CHAN 9001 [DDD]

Schenck, Otto (nar)

Strauss (II), Joh.:Die Fledermaus (sels), w. W. Lipp (sop), R. Schock (ten), W. Berry (bass), R. Stolz (cnd), Vienna SO [G] — Eurodisc ▲ 25-8369 [ADD]

Schenk, Manfred (bass)

Verdi, G.:Simon Boccanegra, w. Alberto Cupido (ten), Ned Barth (bar), José Van Dam (b-bar), Daniela Longhi (sgr), Dino Musio (sgr), M. Veltri (cnd), Marseille Opera Orch, Marseille Opera Chorus — Lyrinx 3-▲ LYX 127 [DDD]

Wagner, R.:Lohengrin, w. C. Studer (sop), P. Frey (ten), P. Schneider (cnd), Bayreuth Festival Orch, Bayreuth Festival Chorus — Philips 32-▲ 434420-2 [ADD/DDD]

Wagner, R.:Lohengrin, w. C. Studer (sop), P. Frey (ten), P. Schneider (cnd), Bayreuth Festival Orch, Bayreuth Festival Chorus [G] — Philips 4-▲ 434602-2 [DDD]

Wagner, R.:Lohengrin (sels), w. C. Studer (sop), G. Schnaut (sop), P. Frey (ten), P. Schneider (cnd), Bayreuth Festival Orch, Bayreuth Festival Chorus — Philips ▲ 438500-2

Scheppan, Hilde (sop)

Verdi, G.:Aida (sels), w. Margarete Klose (cta), Helge Roswaenge (ten), Hans Hotter (bar), A. Rother (cnd), Berlin Radio Orch, Berlin State Opera Chorus [G] *(rec Nov. 21, 1942)* — Preiser ▲ PRE 90219 [ADD]

Scheppan, Hilde (sop) (cont.)

Wagner, R.:Arias & Scenes, w. Kathe Heidersbach (sop), Maria Reining (sop), Margarete Teschemacher (sop), Margarete Klose (mez), Max Lorenz (ten), Jaro Prohaska (bar), Karl Schmitt-Walter (bar), Kurt Böhme (bass), *(orch unknown)*—selections from Rienzi; Der Fliegende Holländer; Tannhäuser; Lohengrin; Tristan und Isolde; Die Meistersinger von Nürnberg; Die Walküre & Götterdämmerung *(rec 1927–1944)* Phonographe 2–▲ PHG 5016 [AAD]

Wagner, R.:Götterdämmerung, w. M. Fuchs (sop), S. Svanholm (ten), R. Burg (bar), F. Dalberg (bass), K. Elmendorff (cnd), Bayreuth Festival Orch, Bayreuth Festival Chorus *(rec July 21, 1942)* Preiser 4–▲ PRE 90164 [AAD]

Wagner, R.:Die Meistersinger von Nürnberg, w. L. Suthaus (ten), E. Kunz (bar), P. Schöffler (b-bar), H. Abendroth (cnd), Bayreuth Festival Orch, Bayreuth Festival Chorus *(rec 1943)* Preiser ▲ PRE 90174 [AAD]

Wagner, R.:Rienzi, der Letzte der Tribunen (sels), w. Margarete Klose (cta), Max Lorenz (ten), Jaro Prohaska (bar), A. Rother (cnd), Berlin State Opera Orch, Berlin State Opera Chorus *(rec 1941)* Preiser ▲ PRE 90223 [ADD]

Wagner, R.:Der Ring des Nibelungen, w. Gré Brouwenstein (sop—Freia/Sieglinde), Ilse Hollweg (sop—Waldvogel), Gerda Lammers (sop—Ortlinde), Paula Lenchner (sop—Wellgunde/Gerhilde), Hilde Scheppan (sop—Helmwige), Astrid Varnay (sop—Brünnilde/3rd Norn), Lore Wissmann (sop—Woglinde), Maria von Ilosvay (mez—Flosshilde/Schwertleite/2nd Norn), Louise Charlotte Kamps (mez—Siegrune), Jean Madeira (mez—Erda/Rossweisse/1st Norn), Georgine van Milinkovic (mez—Fricka/Grimgerde), Elisabeth Schärtel (mez—Waltraute), Paul Kuën (ten—Mime), Ludwig Suthaus (ten—Loge), Josef Traxel (ten—Froh), Wolfgang Windgassen (ten—Siegmund/Siegfried), Alfons Herwig (bar—Donner), Hermann Uhde (bar—Gunther), Hans Hotter (b-bar—Wotan), Gustav Neidlinger (b-bar—Alberich), Josef Griendl (bass—Fasolt/Hunding/Hagen), Arnold van Mill (bass—Fafner), H. Knappertsbusch (cnd), Bayreuth Festival Orch, Bayreuth Festival Chorus *(rec live, Bayreuth, Aug 13–17, 1956)* Golden Melodram 14–▲ GM 1.001 [ADD]

Scherenkel, Vijtech (ten)

Puccini, G.:La Bohème, w. Veronika Kinsces (sop—Mimi), Sidonia Haljakova (sop—Musette), Peter Dvorsky (ten—Rodolfo), Vijtech Scherenkel (ten—Parpingol), Ian Konsulov (bar—Marcello), Balazs Poka (bar—Schaunard), Stanislav Benacka (bass—Benoit), Dariusz Niemirowicz (bass—Colline), Stefan Janci (bass—Alcindoro), *(cnd & orch unknown)* Griffin ▲ GCD 2942

Scherler, Barbara (mez)

Cornelius, P.:Stabat Mater, w. M. Schmidt (ten), S. Nimsgern (bass-bar), R. Didusch (sgr), H. Schernus (cnd), Cologne RSO, Cologne Radio Chorus [L] *(rec 1978)* Koch Schwann ▲ 3-1086-2 [ADD]

Scherr (alt)

Haydn, J.:Die Schöpfung, w. Helen Donath (sop), Adalbert Kraus (ten), Kurt Widmer (bass), W. Gönnenwein (cnd), Ludwigsburg Festival Orch, South German Madrigal Choir [G] Vox Box 2–▲ CDX 5025 [ADD]

Schey, Hermann (bar)

Mahler, G.:Lieder eines fahrenden Gesellen, w. O. Klemperer (cnd), Royal Concertgebouw Orch *(rec Nov. 24, 1948)* Archipon ▲ ARC 109 [ADD]

Verdi, G.:Requiem Mass, w. I. Auez (sop), L. Fischer (cta), L. van Tulder (ten), C. Schuricht (cnd), Royal Concertgebouw Orch, Amsterdam Toonkunst Choir *(rec live, Amsterdam, Nov. 2, 1939)* Archipon 2–▲ ARC 3.2/3 (m) [ADD]

Schey, Hermann (bass)

Beethoven, L. van:Christus am Ölberg, w. Erna Spoorenberg (sop—Seraph), Fritz Wunderlich (ten—Jesus), Hermann Schey (bass—Petrus), H. Spruit (cnd), Netherlands Radio PO, Groot Omroep Choir *(rec Mar 8, 1957)* Bella Voce ▲ 7003 [AAD]

Mahler, G.:Lieder eines fahrenden, w. W. Mengelberg (cnd), *(orch unknown)* Archive Documents ("The Mengelberg Edition" series) ▲ ADCD 116

Scheyer, Gerda (sop)

Strauss (II), Joh.:Die Fledermaus (sels), w. Wilma Lipp (sop), Christa Ludwig (mez), Anton Dermota (ten), Walter Berry (bar), Erich Kunz (bar), Eberhard Wachter (bar), O. Ackermann (cnd), Philharmonia Orch, London Phil Chorus Emperor Operetta ▲ KO 86340

Strauss (II), Joh.:Der Zigeunerbaron, w. Emmy Loose (sop—Arsena), Gerda Scheyrer (sop—Saffi), Elisabeth Fez (cta—Mirabella), Hilde Rössl-Majdan (cta—Czipra), Waldemar Kmentt (ten—Barinkay), Paul Spani (ten—Ottokar), Erich Kunz (bar—Homonay), Kurt Preger (bar—Zsupan), Eberhard Wächter (bass—Carnero), A. Paulik (cnd), Vienna State Opera Orch, Vienna State Opera Chorus *(rec Brahmssaal, Vienna, Austria, June 1956)* Vanguard Classics 2–▲ OVC 8082/83 [ADD]

Schiatti, Anna (sop)

Verdi, G.:Nabucco, w. Monica Pick-Hieronimi (sop), Mina Blum (sop), Angelo Casertano (ten), Gilberto Maffezzoni (ten), Paolo Gavanelli (bass), Paata Burchuladze (bass), Franco Federici (bass), A. Guadagno (cnd), Arena di Verona Orch, Arena di Verona Chorus *(rec Berlin, Spring 1996)* Koch Schwann 2–▲ SCH CD 364272

Schiavazzi, Piero (ten)

Donizetti, G.:Arias—O luce di quest'anima [from Linda di Chamounix; w. Rosina Storchio (sgr)]; Splendon le sacre faci [from Lucia di Lammermoor; w. Luisa Tetrazzini (sop)] Bongiovanni ("Il mito dell'opera" series) ▲ GB 1003-2 [ADD]

Leoncavallo, R.:Arias—Vesti la giubba; Un tal gioco; O Colombina [all ffrom Pagliacci]; Mai più Zazà; Dir che ci sono al mondo [both from Zazà] Bongiovanni ("Il mito dell'opera" series) ▲ GB 1003-2 [ADD]

Mascagni, P.:Arias—Orfani e senza pan; Perchè restar in silenzio così; Io passar tutti i dì la vedeva [all from Amica]; O amore [from L'amico Fritz]; O Lola; Mamma, quel vino è generoso; Brindisi [all from Cavalleria rusticana]; Avete altro a dirmi [from Cavalleria rusticana; w. Ferruccio Corradetti (sgr)]; Serenata [from Iris]; Un dì ero piccina [from Iris; w. Maria Farneti (sgr)] Bongiovanni ("Il mito dell'opera" series) ▲ GB 1003-2 [ADD]

Puccini, G.:Manon Lescaut (sels)—Ah! Manon, mi tradisce (2 versions); Donna non vidi mai (2 versions) Bongiovanni ("Il mito dell'opera" series) ▲ GB 1003-2 [ADD]

Verdi, G.:Arias—Ah, forse è lui [from La traviata; w. Gemma Bellincioni (sgr)]; O sommo Carlo [from Ernani; w. L. Pasini-Vitale, P. Amato e coro] Bongiovanni ("Il mito dell'opera" series) ▲ GB 1003-2 [ADD]

Schickele, Peter (nar)

Prokofiev, S.:Peter & the Wolf, w. Y. Levi (cnd), Atlanta SO [new text by Schickele] *(rec Mar. 20 & June 16, 1993)* Telarc ▲ CD 80350 [DDD] ■ CS 30350

Saint-Saëns, C.:Carnival of the Animals, w. R. Markham (pno), K. Broadway (pno), Y. Levi (cnd), Atlanta SO [poems by Schickele] *(rec Mar. 20 & June 16, 1993)* Telarc ▲ CD 80350 [DDD] ■ CS 30350

Schickele, P.:Bestiary:A Music Theater Piece, w. Calliope Vanguard Classics ▲ OVC 4066

Schicoff (ten)

Verdi, G.:Rigoletto, w. E. Gruberova (sop), B. Fassbaender (mez), R. Bruson (bar), R. Lloyd (b-bar), G. Sinopoli (cnd), St. Cecilia Academy Orch Rome, St. Cecilia Academy Chorus Rome [I] Philips 2–▲ 412592-2 [DDD]

Schikora, Markus (ten)

Coelho Neto, M.:Maria mater gratiae, w. Luiz Alves da Silva (ct), Beat Mattmüller (ct), Peter Mächler (b), L. A. da Silva (cnd), Turicum Ensemble *(rec Studio DRS, Zurich, Sept 26–29, 1994)* Claves ▲ CD 9521 [DDD]

Garcia, J.M.N.:Motets, w. Katharina Ott (sop), Luiz Alves da Silva (ct), Beat Mattmüller (ct), Andreas Schmidt (ct), William Lombardi (ten), Peter Mächler (bass), Michael Leibundgut (bass), L. A. da Silva (cnd), Turicum Ensemble *(rec Studio DRS, Zurich, Sept 26–29, 1994)* Claves ▲ CD 9521 [DDD]

Mesquita, J.J.E.L. de:Antiphona de Nossa Senhora, w. Luiz Alves da Silva (ct), Beat Mattmüller (ct), Peter Mächler (bass), L. A. da Silva (cnd), Turicum Ensemble *(rec Studio DRS, Zurich, Sept 26–29, 1994)* Claves ▲ CD 9521 [DDD]

Mesquita, J.J.E.L. de:Tercio, w. Luiz Alves da Silva (ct), Beat Mattmüller (ct), Michael Leibundgut (bass), L. A. da Silva (cnd), Turicum Ensemble *(rec Studio DRS, Zurich, Sept 26–29, 1994)* Claves ▲ CD 9521 [DDD]

Mesquita, J.J.E.L. de:Tractus (4) para o Sábado Santo, w. Luiz Alves da Silva (ct), Beat Mattmüller (ct), Michael Leibundgut (bass), L. A. da Silva (cnd), Turicum Ensemble *(rec Studio DRS, Zurich, Sept 26–29, 1994)* Claves ▲ CD 9521 [DDD]

Schikora, Markus (ten) (cont.)

Pinto, L.A.:Te Deum Laudamus, w. Katharina Ott (sop), Luiz Alves da Silva (ct), Beat Mattmüller (ct), Andreas Schmidt (ct), William Lombardi (ten), Peter Mächler (bass), Michael Leibundgut (bass), L. A. da Brooks (cnd), Turicum Ensemble *(rec Studio DRS, Zurich, Sept 26–29, 1994)* Claves ▲ CD 9521 [DDD]

Schiller, Frank (bar)

Zimmermann, U.:Die weisse Rose (sels), w. G. Szklarecka (sop), U. Zimmermann (cnd), Musica Viva Ensemble [scenes for 2 solo voices & instrumental ensemble] Berlin Classics ("Eterna" series) ▲ BER 2060 [DDD]

Schilling, E. (sgr)

Sullivan, A.:HMS Pinafore, w. D. Hays (sop), M. Rawlins (sgr), C. Freeman (ten), E. Johnson (cta), M. Elder (cnd), Rochester PO, Eastman Chorale members—highlights *(rec 11/89)* Pro Arte ▲ CDd 480 [DDD]

Sullivan, A.:The Mikado, w. D. Hays (sop), M. Rawlins (sgr), C. Freeman (ten), E. Johnson (cta), M. Elder (cnd), Rochester PO, Eastman Chorale members—highlights *(rec 11/89)* Pro Arte ▲ CDd 480 [DDD]

Sullivan, A.:The Pirates of Penzance, w. D. Hays (sgr), M. Rawlins (sgr), C. Freeman (ten), E. Johnson (cta), M. Elder (cnd), Rochester PO, Eastman Chorale members—highlights *(rec 11/89)* Pro Arte ▲ CDd 480 [DDD]

Schillo, Benedikt (ten)

Haydn, J.:Mass 9, "Heiligmesse", w. Matthias Ritter (sop), Simon Schnorr (alt), Jörg Hering (ten), Panito Iconomou (bass), B. Weil (cnd), Tölz Boys' Choir Sony Classical ("Vivarte" series) ▲ SK 66260

Haydn, J.:Sacred Music, w. Matthias Ritter (sop), Simon Schnorr (alt), Jörg Hering (ten), Panito Iconomou (bass), B. Weil (cnd), Tölz Boys' Choir—Mare clausum (oratorio fragment), H.XXI-Va:9; Motetto Insanae et vanae curae, H.XXI:1; Motetti de Venerabili Sacramento I–IV, H.XXIIIc:5a–d; Te Deum, H.XXIIIc:2 Sony Classical ("Vivarte" series) ▲ SK 66260

Schilp, Marie-Luise (mez)

Nicolai, O.:Lustigen Weiber, w. I. Bielke (sop), W. Ludwig (ten), G. Hann (bass), W. Streinz (bass), A. Rother (cnd), Berlin RSO, Berlin State Opera Chorus *(rec May 2, 1943)* Preiser 2–▲ PRE 90208 [ADD]

Schimenti (sop)

Puccini, G.:La Bohème, w. Micheluzi (sgr), G. Lauri-Volpi (ten), G. Ciavola (bass), A. Paoletti (cnd), Rome Opera Orch, Rome Opera Chorus *(rec 1952)* Bongiovanni 2–▲ GB 1057/58 [ADD]

Schiml, Marga (mez)

Beethoven, L. van:Syms (comp), w. Helena Doese (sop), Peter Schreier (ten), Theo Adam (bass), H. Blomstedt (cnd), Dresden Staatskapelle, Dresden State Opera Chorus, Leipzig Radio Choir *(rec Lukaskirche, Dresden, 1975–80)* Berlin Classics 5–▲ 0021942BC [ADD]

Beethoven, L. van:Syms (comp), w. Peter Schreier (ten), Theo Adam (b-bar), Helena Doese (sgr), H. Blomstedt (cnd), Dresden Staatskapelle, Dresden State Opera Chorus *(rec late 1970's–early 1980's)* Berlin Classics 5–▲ BER 2194 [DDD]

Bruckner, A.:Mass 1, w. E. Mathis (sop), W. Ochman (ten), K. Ridderbusch (bass), E. Jochum (cnd), Bavarian RSO, Bavarian Radio Chorus [L] Deutsche Grammophon 4–▲ 423127-2 [ADD]

Bruckner, A.:Mass 1, w. E. Mathis (sop), W. Ochman (ten), K. Ridderbusch (bass), E. Jochum (cnd), Bavarian RSO, Bavarian Radio Chorus Deutsche Grammophon ("The Originals" series) 2–▲ 447409-2

Dvořák, A.:Stabat Mater, w. L. Aghová (sop), A. Baldin (ten), L. Vele (bass), J. Belohlávek (cnd), Czech PO, Prague Phil Chorus [L] Chandos 2–▲ CHAN 8985/86 [DDD]

Gluck, C.W.:Le Cinesi, w. K. Erickson (sop), A. Milcheva (mez), Moser (sgr), L. Gardelli (cnd), Munich RSO, Munich Radio Chorus [I] Orfeo ▲ 178891 [DDD] ■ MC 178891 (D)

Kiel, F.:Der Stern von Bethlehem, w. H. Laubenthal (ten), R. Bader (cnd), Berlin RSO, St. Hedwig's Cathedral Choir [G] Koch Schwann ▲ CD 313032 [DDD]

Righini, V.:Te Deum, w. G. Resick (sop), R. Wohlers (ten), V. von Halem (bass), G. Albrecht (cnd), Berlin RSO, Berlin Radio Chorus [L] Koch Schwann ▲ CD 313052 [ADD]

Wagner, R.:Der fliegende Holländer, w. I. Haubold (sop—Senta), M. Schiml (mez—Nurse), P. Seiffert (ten—Erik), J. Hering (ten—Helsman), A. Muff (bar—The Dutchman), E. Knodt (bass—Sea Capt.), P. Steinberg (cnd), Vienna ORF SO, Budapest Radio Chorus [G] *(rec Sept. 1992)* Naxos 2–▲ 8.660025/26 [DDD]

Schimmelpfennig, Heinz (nar)

Stravinsky, I.:L'Histoire du soldat, w. A. Szerda (the Devil), M. Hoffmann (the Soldier), P. Leiner (cnd), Contemporano Ensemble Bayer ▲ 100207 [DDD]

Schindler, Margaret (sop)

Schultz, Andrew:Dead Songs, w. Perihelion Ensemble members *(rec Nickson Room, Music Dept, Univ of Queensland, Australia, Dec 1994)* Tall Poppies ▲ TP 065 [DDD]

Schiøtz, Aksel (ten)

Aksel Schiøtz Sings Nielsen, Reesen, Agerby, Heise *(rec 1938–41)* Pearl ▲ PEA 9140 [ADD]

Classic Schiøtz Pearl ▲ PEA CD 9254

Schubert, Franz:Die Schöne Müllerin, w. Gerald Moore (pno) *(rec London, Nov 1945)* Preiser ▲ PRE 90293

Schipa, Tito (ten)

Arias *(rec 1913–1938)* Memories ("Great Voices" series) 2–▲ MEM 4220 (m) [ADD]

Ave Schipa:Recordings of 1913–1942 Pearl ▲ PEA 9017 [AAD]

Cimarosa, D.:Il Matrimonio segreto (sels), w. H. Gueden (sop), A. Noni (sop), F. Barbieri (mez), S. Bruscantini (bar), B. Christoff (bass), M. Rossi (cnd), La Scala Orch—Act I highlights [I] *(rec live, Milan March 22, 1949)* Melodram 2–▲ CDM 29505 [ADD]

Donizetti, G.:Don Pasquale, w. Adelaide Saraceni (sop), Ernesto Badini (bar), Afro Poli (bar), C. Sabajno (cnd), La Scala Orch, La Scala Chorus *(rec 1932)* Grammofono 2000 2–▲ GRM 78561 (m)

The 1st Recordings, 1913–19 Enterprise ("Vocal Archives" series) ▲ ENT VA 1130

Great Love Duets, w. Erna Berger (sop), Miliza Korjus (sop), Lotte Lehmann (sop), Frida Leider (sop), Charles Kullman (ten), Lauritz Melchior (ten), Helge Roswaenge (ten), Richard Tauber (ten), et al. Pearl ▲ PEA 9217

New York Farewell Recital, w. Albert Carlo Amato (pno) *(rec Nov 1962)* Standing Room Only ▲ SRO 817-1 [ADD]

Rare Recordings 1918–1957 Pearl 2–▲ PEA 9988 (m) [AAD]

The Romance of Spain Pearl ▲ PEA CD 9183

Schipa in Song Nimbus ▲ NI 7870 [ADD]

Tito Schipa RCA Gold Seal ▲ 7969-2-RG (m) [ADD] ■ 7969-4-RG (CrO2)

Tito Schipa *(rec 1913–1937)* Nimbus ("Prima Voce" series) ▲ NI 7813 (m) [ADD]

Tito Schipa In Concert 1939–1959 Eklipse ▲ EKR CD 10

Tito Schipa, Vol. 1 Pearl ▲ PEA 9322 (m) [AAD]

Tito Schipa, Vol. 2 *(rec 1924–1934)* Pearl ▲ PEA 9364 (m) [AAD]

Verdi, G.:La traviata (sels), w. Amelita Galli-Curci (sop), *(orch unknown)* Forlane ▲ FRL 16718 [ADD]

Schipper, Emil (bar)

Mascagni, P.:Cavalleria rusticana (sels), w. Alfred Piccaver (ten—Turiddu), Emil Schipper (bar—Alfio), K. Alwin (cnd), Vienna State Opera Orch *(rec May 10, 1937)* Koch Schwann 2–▲ SCH 314632 [ADD]

Wagner, R.:Götterdämmerung (sels), w. Henny Trundt (sop—Brünnhilde), Josef Kalenberg (ten—Siegfried), Emil Schipper (bar—Gunther), Josef von Manowarda (bass—Hagen), C. Krauss (cnd), Vienna State Opera Orch *(rec Mar. 7, 1933)* Koch Schwann 2–▲ SCH 314642 [ADD]

Wagner, R.:Parsifal (sels), w. Gertrude Fünger (cta—Kundry), Gunnar Graarud (ten—Parsifal), Emil Schipper (bar—Amfortas), Josef von Manowarda (bass—Gurnemanz), C. Krauss (cnd), Vienna State Opera Orch *(rec Apr. 13, 1933)* Koch Schwann 2–▲ SCH 314642 [ADD]

Wagner, R.:Der Ring des Nibelungen (sels), w. Adele Kern (sop), Anny Konetzni (sop), Hilde Konetzni (sop), Elisabeth Schumann (sop), Enid Szantho (cta), Josef Kalenberg (ten), Max Lorenz (ten), Set Svanholm (ten), Erich Zimmermann (ten), Hans Hotter (bar), Jaro Prohaska (bar), Emil Schipper (bar), Paul Schöffler (b-bar), Ludwig Hoffmann (bass), H. Knappertsbusch (cnd), Vienna State Opera Orch *(rec Vienna, 1937–1943)* Koch Schwann 2–▲ SCH 314742 [ADD]

Schirp, Wilhelm (bass)
Verdi, G.:Un ballo in maschera, w. Martha Mödl (sop—Ulrica), Walburga Wegner (sop—Amelia), Anny Schlemm (mez—Oscar), Lorenz Fehenberger (ten—Ricardo), Dietrich Fischer-Dieskau (bar—Renato), Wilhelm Schirp (bass—Samuel), Willy Schoneweib (bass—Tom), Gunther Wilhelms (bass—Silvan), Fritz Augustin (sgr—Ein Richter), Friedrich Himmelmann (sgr—Ein Diener Amelia), F. Busch (cnd), Cologne RSO, Bernhard Alois Zimmermann (cnd), Cologne Radio Chorus Calig 2-▲ 50946/47 (m) [ADD]
Wagner, R.:Götterdämmerung (sels), w. F. Leider (sop), A. von Stosch (sop), L. Melchior (ten), H. Janssen (bar), *(cnd & orch unknown)*—Act 2, Scenes 4 & 5 *(w. Furtwängler, Royal Opera House Orch. & Cho., 1938)*; Act 3, Schweigt eures Jammers *(Frida Leider & E. Marherr-Wagner, Blech, Berlin State Opera Orch., 1928)* Pearl ▲ PEA 9331 (m) [AAD]
Schirrer, René (bar)
Berlioz, H.:Les Troyens, w. F. Pollet (sop—Dido), D. Voigt (sop—Cassandre), C. Dubosc (sop—Ascagne), H. Perraguin (cta—Anna), G. Lakes (ten—Aeneas), J.-L. Maurette (ten—Iopas), J. M. Ainsley (ten—Hylas), M. P. (ten—Panthee), G. Cross (ten—Sinon), G. Quilico (bar—Chorebe), J.-P. Courtis (b-bar—Narbal), M. Belleau (bass—Ghost of Hector), R. Schirrer (bass—Priam), C. Dutoit (cnd), Montreal SO, Montreal Sym Chorus London 4-▲ 443693-2 [DDD]
Donizetti, G.:Don Pasquale, w. B. Hendricks (sop), L. Canonici (ten), G. Bacquier (bar), L. Quilico (bar), G. Ferro (cnd), Paris Lyon Opera Orch, Paris Lyon Opera Chorus [I] Erato 2-▲ 2292-45487-2-ZA [DDD]
Messager, A.:Fortunio, w. C. Alliot-Lugaz (sop), T. Dran (ten), G. Cachémaille (bar), J. E. Gardiner (cnd), Paris Lyon Opera Orch, Paris Lyon Opera Chorus Erato 2-▲ 45983-2
Schirrer, René (nar)
Strauss, R.:Enoch Arden, w. Christian Ivaldi (pno) Adès ▲ ADE 141772
Strauss, R.:Das Schloss am Meere, w. Christian Ivaldi (pno) Adès ▲ ADE 141772
Schivazzi, Piero (ten)
The World of Singing, Vol 4:The Italian School Part 1:Tenors before World War I, Book 2, w. Edoardo Garbin (ten), Fiorello Giraud (ten), Florencio Costantino (ten), Antonio Paoli (ten), Giuseppe Borgatti (ten), Carlo Albani (ten), Enrico Caruso (ten), Amedeo Bassi (ten), Piero Schivazzi (ten), Elvino Ventura (ten), Giovanni Zenatello (ten) Enterprise ("Vocal Archives" series) 3-▲ ENT VA 2107
Schlanbusch, L. D. von (sgr)
Rodgers, R.:The Sound of Music, w. E. Farrell (sop), F. von Stade (mez), Håkan Hagegård (ten), B. Daniels (sgr), et al., E. Kunzel (cnd), Cincinnati Pops Orch, May Festival Chorus [1987 studio cast] Telarc ▲ CD 80162 [DDD] ■ CS 30162
Schlemm, Anny (mez)
Humperdinck, E.:Hänsel und Gretel, w. L. Popp (sop), B. Fassbaender (mez), J. Hamari (mez), W. Berry (bass), G. Solti (cnd), Vienna PO London 2-▲ 421111-2 [ADD]
Lehár, F.:Paganini (sels), w. Lisolette Losch (sop), P. Anders (ten), Gehly (sgr), Hofmann (sgr), Schneider (sgr), Marszalek (cnd), Cologne RSO, Cologne Radio Chorus [G] Acanta ▲ CD 43810 [DDD]
Mahler, G.:Sym 4, w. L. Ludwig (cnd), Dresden State Orch *(rec 1957)* Berlin Classics ("Dokumente" series) ▲ BER 2119 [ADD]
Strauss (II), Joh.:Die Fledermaus, w. R. Streich (sop), P. Anders (ten), H. Krebs (ten), F. Fricsay (cnd), Berlin RSO, Berlin Radio Chorus [G] *(rec live, Berlin, 11/8/49)* Melodram 2-▲ MEL 29001 (m) [AAD]
Verdi, G.:Un ballo in maschera, w. Martha Mödl (sop—Ulrica), Walburga Wegner (sop—Amelia), Anny Schlemm (mez—Oscar), Lorenz Fehenberger (ten—Ricardo), Dietrich Fischer-Dieskau (bar—Renato), Wilhelm Schirp (bass—Samuel), Willy Schoneweib (bass—Tom), Gunther Wilhelms (bass—Silvan), Fritz Augustin (sgr—Ein Richter), Friedrich Himmelmann (sgr—Ein Diener Amelia), F. Busch (cnd), Cologne RSO, Bernhard Alois Zimmermann (cnd), Cologne Radio Chorus Calig 2-▲ 50946/47 (m) [ADD]
Weill, K.:Aufstieg und Fall der Stadt Mahagonny, w. A. Silja (sop), W. Neumann (ten), T. Lehrberger (ten), K. Hirte (bar), J. Latham-König (cnd), Cologne RSO, Cologne Radio Chorus [G] Capriccio 2-▲ CD 10160/1 [DDD]
Schlemm, Anny (sop)
Beethoven, L. van:Sym 9, "Choral Sym", w. Diana Eustrati (cta), Gert Lutze (ten), Thomas Paul (bass), H. Abendroth (cnd), Leipzig RSO *(rec 1953)* Arlecchino ARL
Schlesser, André (sgr)
Ibert, J.:Chants—Romance Adès ▲ ADE 203462 [AAD]
Schlick, Barbara (sop)
Bach, C.P.E.:Die Israeliten in der Wüste, w. L. Lootens (sop), H. Meens (ten), S. Barcoe (sgr), W. Christie (cnd), Cappella Coloniensis, Corona Musique d'Abord ▲ HMA 1901321
Bach, J.S.:Cant 6, w. Andreas Scholl (ct), Christoph Prégardien (ten), Gotthold Schwarz (bass), C. Coin (cnd), Limoges Baroque Ensemble, Accentus Chamber Choir Astrée ▲ E 8555
Bach, J.S.:Cant 11, "Ascension Oratorio", w. C. Patriasz (cta), C. Prégardien (ten), P. Kooy (bass), P. Herreweghe (cnd), Collegium Vocale Orch Harmonia Mundi France ▲ HMC 901479
Bach, J.S.:Cant 41, w. Andreas Scholl (ct), Christoph Prégardien (ten), Gotthold Schwarz (bass), C. Coin (cnd), Limoges Baroque Ensemble, Accentus Chamber Choir Astrée ▲ E 8555
Bach, J.S.:Cant 43, w. C. Patriasz (cta), C. Prégardien (ten), P. Kooy (bass), P. Herreweghe (cnd), Collegium Vocale Harmonia Mundi France ▲ HMC 901479
Bach, J.S.:Cant 44, w. C. Patriasz (cta), C. Prégardien (ten), P. Kooy (bass), P. Herreweghe (cnd), Collegium Vocale Harmonia Mundi France ▲ HMC 901479
Bach, J.S.:Cant 49, w. Andreas Scholl (alt), Christophe Prégardien (ten), Gotthold Schwarz (bass), C. Coin (cnd), Limoges Baroque Ensemble, Leipzig Concerto Vocale Astrée ▲ E 8530
Bach, J.S.:Cant 66, w. Kai Wessel (alt), James Taylor (ten), Peter Kooy (bass), Phillippe Herreweghe (cnd), Collegium Vocale Harmonia Mundi France ▲ HMC 901513
Bach, J.S.:Cant 68, w. Andreas Scholl (ct), Christoph Prégardien (ten), Gotthold Schwarz (bass), C. Coin (cnd), Limoges Baroque Ensemble, Accentus Chamber Choir Astrée ▲ E 8555
Bach, J.S.:Cant 73, w. H. Crook (ten), P. Kooy (bass), P. Herreweghe (cnd), Collegium Vocale Orch, Collegium Vocale Virgin Classics ▲ CDC 59237-2
Bach, J.S.:Cant 80, w. Agnès Mellon (sop), Gérard Lesne (ct), Howard Crook (ten), Peter Kooy (bass), P. Herreweghe (cnd), La Chapelle Royale Orch, Collegium Vocale Harmonia Mundi France ∆ HMC 6901326
Bach, J.S.:Cant 85, w. Andreas Scholl (alt), Christoph Prégardien (ten), Gotthold Schwarz (bass), Christophe Coin (piccolo vc/cnd), Leipzig Vocal Concerto, Limoges Baroque Ensemble Astrée ▲ E 8544
Bach, J.S.:Cant 105, w. G. Lesne (mez), H. Crook (ten), P. Kooy (bass), P. Herreweghe (cnd), Collegium Vocale Orch, Collegium Vocale Virgin Classics ▲ CDC 59237-2
Bach, J.S.:Cant 115, w. Andreas Scholl (alt), Christophe Prégardien (ten), Gotthold Schwarz (bass), C. Coin (cnd), Limoges Baroque Ensemble, Leipzig Concerto Vocale Astrée ▲ E 8530
Bach, J.S.:Cant 131, w. G. Lesne (mez), H. Crook (ten), P. Kooy (bass), P. Herreweghe (cnd), Collegium Vocale Orch, Collegium Vocale Virgin Classics ▲ CDC 59237-2
Bach, J.S.:Cant 175, w. Andreas Scholl (alt), Christoph Prégardien (ten), Gotthold Schwarz (bass), Christophe Coin (piccolo vc/cnd), Leipzig Vocal Concerto, Limoges Baroque Ensemble Astrée ▲ E 8544
Bach, J.S.:Cant 180, w. Andreas Scholl (alt), Christophe Prégardien (ten), Gotthold Schwarz (bass), C. Coin (cnd), Limoges Baroque Ensemble, Leipzig Concerto Vocale Astrée ▲ E 8530
Bach, J.S.:Cant 183, w. Andreas Scholl (alt), Christoph Prégardien (ten), Gotthold Schwarz (bass), Christophe Coin (piccolo vc/cnd), Leipzig Vocal Concerto, Limoges Baroque Ensemble Astrée ▲ E 8544
Bach, J.S.:Cant 199, w. Andreas Scholl (alt), Christoph Prégardien (ten), Gotthold Schwarz (bass), Christophe Coin (piccolo vc/cnd), Leipzig Vocal Concerto, Limoges Baroque Ensemble Astrée ▲ E 8544
Bach, J.S.:Christmas Oratorio, w. M. Chance (ct), H. Crook (ten), P. Kooy (bass), P. Herreweghe (cnd), Ghent Collegium Vocale Orch, Ghent Collegium Vocale [G] Virgin Classics (Veritas) 2-▲ ZDCB 59530-2 [DDD]
Bach, J.S.:Christmas Oratorio, w. C. Watkinson (cta), K. Equiluz (ten), M. Brodard (bar), M. Corboz (cnd), Lausanne CO Erato ▲ 2292-45865-2
Bach, J.S.:Easter Oratorio, w. Kai Wessel (alt), James Taylor (ten), Peter Kooy (bass), Phillippe Herreweghe (cnd), Collegium Vocale Harmonia Mundi France ▲ HMC 901513

Schlick, Barbara (sop) (cont.)
Bach, J.S.:Magnificat, BWV 243, w. A. Mellon (sop), G. Lesne (ct), H. Crook (ten), P. Kooy (bass), P. Herreweghe (cnd), La Chapelle Royale Orch, Collegium Vocale [L] Harmonia Mundi France ▲ HMC 901326
Bach, J.S.:Mass in b, BWV 232, w. C. Patriasz (cta), C. Brett (ct), H. Crook (ten), P. Kooy (bass), P. Herreweghe (cnd), Collegium Vocale Orch, Collegium Vocale [L] Virgin Classics ("Veritas" series) 2-▲ CDCB 59517-2 [DDD]
Bach, J.S.:St. John Passion, w. K. Ishii (ten), M. van Egmond (b-bar), C. de Wolff (cnd), Royal Concertgebouw Orch members, Holland Bach Choir [G] Sound 3-▲ CD 3488/90
Bach, J.S.:St. John Passion, w. K. Wessel (alto), G. de Mey (ten), G. Turk (ten), K. Mertens (b-bar), P. Kooy (bass), T. Koopman (cnd), Amsterdam Baroque Orch, Netherlands Bach Society Choir Erato 2-▲ 94675-2
Bach, J.S.:St. John Passion, w. C. Patriasz (cta), H. Crook (ten), W. Kendall (ten), P. Kooy (bass), P. Lika (bass), P. Herreweghe (cnd), La Chapelle Royale Orch, Ghent Collegium Vocale [G] Harmonia Mundi France 2-▲ HMC 901264/65 [DDD]
Bach, J.S.:St. John Passion, w. Ingeborg Most (alt), Edrian Brand (ten), Alexander Stevenson (ten), Philip Langshaw (bass), Peter Lika (bass), P. Kuentz (cnd), Paul Kuentz Orch, Paul Kuentz Choir Pierre Verany 2-▲ PVY 730051 [DDD]
Bach, J.S.:St. Matthew Passion, w. R. Jacobs (ct), H. P. Blochwitz (ten), H. Crook (ten), U. Cold (bass), P. Kooy (bass), P. Herreweghe (cnd), La Chapelle Royale Orch, Ghent Collegium Vocale [G] Harmonia Mundi France 3-▲ HMC 901155/57
Bach, J.S.:St. Matthew Passion, w. K. Wessel (alto), G. de Mey (ten), C. Pregardien (ten), P. Kooy (bass), T. Koopman (cnd), Amsterdam Baroque Orch, W. Cantryn (cnd), J. van Veldhoven (cnd), Breda Sacred Choir, Netherlands Bach Society Boys' Choir Erato ▲ 2292-45814-2
Bach, J.S.:St. Matthew Passion, w. K. Wessel (alto), G. de Mey (ten), P. Kooy (bass), T. Koopman (cnd), Amsterdam Baroque Orch Erato 2-▲ 94676-2
Bach, W.F.:Cants (misc), w. C. Schubert (contralto), W. Jochens (tenor), J. Schreckenberger (bass), Rheinische Kantorei, H. Max (cnd), Das Kleine Konzert—Lasset uns ablegen die Werke der Finsternis; Es ist eine Stimme eines Predigers in der Wüste Capriccio ▲ 10 425 [DDD]
Bach, W.F.:Cants (misc), w. C. Schubert (contralto), W. Jochens (tenor), J. Schreckenberger (bass), Rheinische Kantorei, H. Max (cnd), Das Kleine Konzert—Dies ist der Tag; Erzittert und fallet Capriccio ▲ 10 426 [DDD]
Biber, H. von:Chi la dura la vince, w. Gerd Türk (ten), Gotthold Schwarz (bass), Xenia Meijer (sgr), W. Brunner (cnd), Salzburg Hofmusik CPO 3-▲ CPO 999258 [DDD]
Charpentier, M.-A.:Motets for Double Choir, w. N. Zijlstra (sop), K. Wessel (alt), D. Visse (ct), H. van Berne (ten), C. Prégardien (ten), P. Kooy (bass), K. Martens (bass), T. Koopman (cnd), Amsterdam Baroque Orch—Canticum pro pace; Josué; Mors Saulis et Jonathae; Praelium Michaelis; Quam dilecta; 3 Leçons de Ténèbres Erato (Musifrance) ▲ 2292-45822-2 ZA
Desmarets, H.:Sacred Music, w. Mieke Van der Sluis (sop), Harry Geraerts (ct), Fiori Musicali, New College Choir Oxford—Deux grands motets lorrains; Mystères de notre seigneur Jésus-Christ Erato ▲ ERA SEL 98529 [ADD]
Eybler, J.L.E. von:Requiem mit Libera, w. H. van der Kamp (bass), W. Helbich (cnd), Steintor Barock Bremen, Alsfeld Vocal Ensemble CPO ▲ CPO 999234 [DDD]
Festa Italiana, w. Fabio Biondi (vn), Pascal Monteilhet (va), Maurizio Naddeo (vc), Rinaldo Alessandrini (hpd), Concerto Italiano, Europa Galante Opus 111 5-▲ 2001
Handel, G.F.:Giulio Cesare in Egitto, w. Jennifer Larmore (mez), Marianne Rørholm (mez), Bernarda Fink (cta), Derek Lee Ragin (ct), Dominique Visse (ct), Oliver Lallouette (bass), Furio Zanasi (bass), R. Jacobs (cnd), Concerto Cologne [period instrs] Harmonia Mundi France 3-▲ HMC 901385/87
Handel, G.F.:Giulio Cesare in Egitto (sels), w. Jennifer Larmore (mez), Marianne Rørholm (mez), Bernarda Fink (cta), Derek Lee Ragin (ct), R. Jacobs (cnd), Concerto Cologne Harmonia Mundi France ▲ HMC 901458
Handel, G.F.:Messiah, w. Sandrine Piau (sop), Andreas Scholl (alt), Mark Padmore (ten), Nathan Berg (bass), W. Christie (cnd), Les Arts Florissants [1742 Dublin version] Harmonia Mundi France 2-▲ HMC 901498/99
Handel, G.F.:Messiah (sels), w. Jean Nirouet (ct), Alexander Stevenson (ten), Philip Langshaw (bass), P. Kuentz (cnd), Paul Kuentz Orch, Paul Kuentz Choir Pierre Verany ▲ PVY 730045
Handel, G.F.:La Rezurrezione, w. Nancy Argenta (sop), Guillemette Laurens (mez), Guy de Mey (ten), Klaus Mertens (bar), T. Koopman (cnd), Amsterdam Baroque Orch [I] Erato 2-▲ 2292-45617-2 [DDD]
Hasse, J.A.:Piramo e Tisbe, w. Suzanne Gari (sop), Michel LeCocq (ten), H. Müller-Brühl (cnd), Capella Clementina Koch Schwann 2-▲ SCH 310882 [DDD]
Leo, L.:Salve Regina, w. F. Biondi (cnd), Europa Galante Opus 111 ▲ OPS 30-88
Mozart, W.A.:Missa, K.317, w. Mechtild Georg (sop), Alexander Stevenson (ten), Philip Langshaw (bass), P. Kuentz (cnd), Paul Kuentz Orch, Paul Kuentz Choir Pierre Verany ▲ PVY 730041
Mozart, W.A.:Missa, K.427, w. Monika Frimmer (sop), Christoph Prégardien (ten), Klaus Mertens (bass), P. Neumann (cnd), Collegium Cartusianum, Cologne Chamber Choir Virgin Classics ▲ CDM 61167
Mozart, W.A.:Requiem, w. C. Watkinson (cta), C. Prégardien (ten), H. van der Kamp (bass), T. Koopman (cnd), Amsterdam Baroque Orch, Netherlands Bach Society Choir [L] Erato ▲ 2292-45472-2 [DDD] ■ 2292-45472-4
Pergolesi, G.B.:Salve regina in a, w. F. Biondi (cnd), Europa Galante Opus 111 ▲ OPS 30-88
Pergolesi, G.B.:Salve regina in d, w. F. Biondi (cnd), Europa Galante Opus 111 ▲ OPS 30-88
Romberg, A.:Der Lied von der Glocke, w. F. Lang (ten), P. Lika (bass), C. Spering (cnd), Das Neue Orch, Cologne Chorus Musicus *(rec May 24-27, 1992)* Opus 111 ▲ OPS 30-67 [DDD]
Telemann, G.P.:Cants, w. Manfred Harras (rcr), Ernst-Martin Eras (ob), Richard Gwilt (vn), Brian Franklin (vl), Sally Fortino (hpd)—Hemmet den Eifer, verbannet die Rache; Jauchzt, ihr Christen, seid vergnügt; Umschlinget uns, ihr sanften Freidensbande; Die Kinder des Höchsten sind rufende Stimmen; Lauter Wonne, lauter Freude Cantate ▲ 580003 [DDD]
Schlierf, T. (nar)
Popp, M.:Ludus Danielis, w. A. Veljanov (spkr), P. Pöppel (sgr), S. Hausen (sgr), M. Popp (cnd), Estampie *(rec Jan. 1-10, 1993)* Christophorus ▲ 77144 [DDD]
Schlusnus, Heinrich (bar)
Heinrich Schlusnus *(rec 1921-25)* Preiser ("Lebendige Vergangenheit" series) ▲ PRE 89110 [AAD]
Heinrich Schlusnus Lieder Album *(rec 1934-38)* Preiser 2-▲ PRE 89206 [AAD]
Heinrich Schlusnus:Opera Arias *(rec 1932-38)* Preiser ("Lebendige Vergangenheit" series) ▲ PRE 89006 (m) [AAD]
Heinrich Sclusnus Liederalbum, w. Franz Rupp (pno/org), Hermann Weigert (cnd), Alois Melichar (cnd), Berlin State Opera Orch *(rec between 1930-34)* Preiser 2-▲ PRE 89205 [ADD]
Heinrich Sclusnus Liederalbum, Vol. 2 *(rec 1934-1938)* Preiser 2-▲ PRE 89206 [ADD]
Helge Roswaenge, w. Helge Roswaenge (ten), Milizia Korjus (sop), Tiana Lemnitz (sop), Hans Reinmar (bar), et al. Preiser 2-▲ PRE 89209 [AAD]
Liederalbum, Vol. 2 *(rec 1925-31)* Preiser 2-▲ PRE 89216 [AAD]
Opera Arias & Scenes *(rec 1927-43)* Preiser 2-▲ PRE 89212 [AAD]
Verdi, G.:La forza del destino (sels), w. H. Roswaenge (ten), A. Rother (cnd), Berlin RSO *(rec 1942)* Myto 2-▲ MCD 93279
Verdi, G.:Rigoletto, w. E. Berger (sop), R. Jacobs (alt), H. Roswaenge (ten), J. Greindl (bass), R. Heger (cnd), Berlin State Opera Orch, Berlin State Opera Chorus [G] *(rec 11/20-22/44)* Preiser 2-▲ 90036 (m) [AAD]
Verdi, G.:I vespri siciliani, w. M. Cunitz (sop), H. Roswaenge (ten), O. von Rohr (bass), K. Schröder (cnd), Hessian RSO, Hesse Radio Chorus *(rec 1951)* Myto 2-▲ MCD 93279
The Young Lotte Lehmann, w. Lotte Lehmann (sop), Robert Hutt (ten), Michael Böhnen (bass) Preiser ("Lebendige Vergangenheit" series) 3-▲ PRE 89302 (m) [AAD]
Schlüter, Erna (sop)
Beethoven, L. van:Fidelio (sels), w. L. della Casa (sop), J. Patzak (ten), R. Schock (ten), F. Frantz (b-bar), H. Alsen (bass), W. Furtwängler (cnd), Vienna State Opera Orch, Vienna State Opera Chorus—Overture, 16 arias & choruses *(rec live, Salzburg Festspielhaus Aug. 3, 1948)* Melodram 2-▲ CDM 25009 [ADD]
Wagner, R.:Tristan und Isolde (acts 2 & 3), w. M. Klose (cta), L. Suthaus (ten), J. Prohaska (ten), G. Frick (bass), W. Furtwängler (cnd), Berlin State Opera Orch, Berlin State Opera Chorus [G] *(rec live, Berlin, 10/3/47)* Arkadia 2-▲ 358 [ADD]

Schmeckenbechier, Jochen (bar)
Dessau, P.:Haggada, w. Sabine Ritterbusch (sop), Renate Spingler (sop), Yvi Jänicke (alt), Peter Galliard (ten—Rabbi Tarfon/Jude/ten solo), Gabriel Sadé (ten—Pharaoh), Jochen Schmeckenbechier (bar—Rabbi Jehoschua), Bernd Weikl (bar—Moses), Matthias Hölle (bass—Speaker/Rabbi Akiwa), Alfred Muff (bass—Father/Rabbi Eleasar), Johann Tilli (bass—Rabbi Elieser/bass solo), G. Albrecht (cnd), Hamburg State PO, Berlin Carl Maria Von Weber Men's Choir, Hamburg Alsterspatzen, North German Radio Chorus [G] *(rec Musikhalle, Hamburg, Sept 4 & 5, 1994)* Capriccio 2-▲ 10590/91 [DDD]

Schmeige, Marilyn (mez)
Brahms, J.:Ballads & Romances, Op. 75, w. Julie Kaufmann (sop), Donald Sulzen (pno)—2 sels Orfeo ▲ 369961 [DDD]
Brahms, J.:Duets, Op. 20, w. Julie Kaufmann (sop), Donald Sulzen (pno) Orfeo ▲ 369961 [DDD]
Brahms, J.:Duets, Op. 61, w. Julie Kaufmann (sop), Donald Sulzen (pno) Orfeo ▲ 369961 [DDD]
Brahms, J.:Duets, Op. 66, w. Julie Kaufmann (sop), Donald Sulzen (pno) Orfeo ▲ 369961 [DDD]
Brahms, J.:Romances & Songs, Op. 84, w. Julie Kaufmann (sop), Donald Sulzen (pno)—3 sels Orfeo ▲ 369961 [DDD]
Brahms, J.:Songs, w. Julie Kaufmann (sop), Donald Sulzen (pno) Orfeo ▲ 369961 [DDD]

Schmeisser, Tobias (treb)
Weill, K.:Der Jasager, w. H. Helling (cta), T. Bräutigam (ten), T. Fischer (ten), U. Schütte (bar), M. Knöppel (bass), W. Gundlach (cnd), Westphalia CO, Westphalia Kantorei Capriccio ▲ 60 020-1 [DDD]

Schmid, G. (sop)
Dvořák, A.:Mass, w. J. Bernheimer (mez), J. Reinprecht (ten), A. Sramek (bar), F. Wolf (cnd), St. Augustin Orch, St. Augustin Chorus [L] *(rec 1987)* Preiser ▲ 93378 [ADD]
Mozart, W.A.:Zauberflöte, w. E. Gruberova (sop), B. Bonney (sop), H.-P. Blochwitz (ten), T. Hampson (bar), M. Salminen (bass), A. Scharinger (bass), N. Harnoncourt (cnd), Zurich Opera Orch, Zurich Opera House Chorus [G] Teldec 2-▲ 2292-42716-2

Schmid-Berikoven, Hermann (ten)
Lortzing, A.:Zar und Zimmermann, w. M. Gripekoven (sop—Marie), E. Mayer (cta—Widow Browe), H. Buchta (ten—Peter Ivonov), H. Schmid-Berikoven (ten—Marquis de Chateauneuf), G. Hann (b-bar—Tsar Peter I), W. Strienz (b-bar—Van Bett), B. Müller (bass) Myto 2-▲ MCD 943103

Schmid-Cadalbert, Christian (recitation)
Songs around Konrad von Würzburg, w. Andrea von Ramm, Sterling Jones (hp), Timothy C. Nelson (fl) Christophorus ▲ CD 74542 [DDD]

Schmidinger, Benjamin (sop)
Schubert, Franz:Mass 6, w. Albin Lenzer (alt), Kurt Azesberger (ten), Jörg Hering (ten), Harry van der Kamp (bass), B. Weil (cnd), Orch of the Age of Enlightenment, Vienna Boys' Choir Sony Classical ▲ SK 66255

Schmid-Lienbacher, Edith (sop)
Gazzaniga, G.:Don Giovanni, w. L. Serra (sop), E. Szmytka (sop), D. Johnson (sgr), F. Furlanetto (bass), B. Weil (cnd), Tafelmusik Sony Classical ("Vivarte" series) ▲ SK 46693

Schmidt (sgr)
Offenbach, J.:Les Contes d'Hoffmann, w. E. Gruberova (sop), C. Eder (mez), P. Domingo (ten), M. Sénéchal (ten), G. Bacquier (bar), J. Morris (bass), J. Diaz (bass), S. Ozawa (cnd), French National Orch, French Radio Chorus [F] Deutsche Grammophon 2-▲ 427682-2 [DDD]
Strauss, R.:Die Frau ohne Schatten, w. C. Studer (sop), U. Vinzing (sop), H. Schwarz (mez), R. Kollo (ten), A. Muff (bass), W. Sawallisch (cnd), Bavarian RSO, Bavarian Radio Chorus [G] EMI Classics ▲ CDC 54494 [DDD]
Strauss, R.:Die Frau ohne Schatten, w. C. Studer (sop), U. Vinzing (sop), H. Schwarz (mez), R. Kollo (ten), A. Muff (bass), W. Sawallisch (cnd), Bavarian RSO, Bavarian Radio Chorus [uncut version] [G] EMI Classics 3-▲ CDCC 49074 [DDD]

Schmidt (ten)
Monteverdi, C.:Lamento della ninfa, w. K. Equiluz (ten), W. Hollweg (ten), N. Harnoncourt (cnd), Vienna Concentus Musicus [I] Teldec ▲ 2292-43036-2

Schmidt, Andreas (bar)
Bach, J.S.:Cant 11, "Ascension Oratorio", w. C. Cuccaro (sop), M. Georg (alt), A. Kraus (ten), H. Rilling (cnd), Württemberg CO, Gächinger Kantorei [G] Novalis ▲ 150028 [DDD]
Bach, J.S.:Cant 11, "Ascension Oratorio", w. C. Cuccaro (sop), M. Georg (alt), A. Kraus (ten), H. Rilling (cnd), Württemberg CO, Gächinger Kantorei [G] *(rec 1984)* Hänssler Classic 5-▲ 98.976
Bach, J.S.:Cant 26, w. E. Mathis (sop), P. Schreier (ten), D. Fischer-Dieskau (bar), K. Richter (cnd), Munich Bach Orch, Munich Bach Choir Archiv ▲ 427130-2 [ADD]
Bach, J.S.:Cant 117, w. M. Georg (mez), A. Kraus (ten), H. Rilling (cnd), Stuttgart Bach Collegium, Gächinger Kantorei [G] Novalis ▲ 150028 [DDD]
Bach, J.S.:Cant 145, w. C. Cuccaro (sop), A. Kraus (ten), H. Rilling (cnd), Stuttgart Bach Collegium, Gächinger Kantorei [G] Novalis ▲ 150029 [DDD]
Bach, J.S.:Mass in b, BWV 232, w. A. Stumphius (sop), C. Kallisch (alto), R. Wörle (ten), H.-M. Schneidt (cnd), Munich Bach Orch, Munich Bach Choir *(rec Mar 21, 1992)* Calig 2-▲ CAL 5029/30 [ADD]
Bach, J.S.:St. Matthew Passion, w. B. Bonney (sop), A. Monoyios (sop), A. S. von Otter (mez), M. Chance (ct), H. Crook (ten), A. Rolfe Johnson (ten), O. Bär (bar), C. Hauptmann (bass), J. E. Gardiner (cnd), English Baroque Soloists, Monteverdi Choir London [G] Archiv 3-▲ 427648-2 [DDD]
Beethoven, L. van:Fidelio, w. J. Norman (sop), P. Coburn (sop), R. Goldberg (ten), H.-P. Blochwitz (ten), E. Wlaschiha (bass), K. Moll (bass), B. Haitink (cnd), Dresden Staatskapelle, Dresden State Chorus [G] Philips 2-▲ 426308-2 [DDD]
Beethoven, L. van:Missa Solemnis, w. P. Coburn (sop), F. Quivar (cta), A. Baldin (ten), H. Rilling (cnd), Stuttgart Bach Collegium, Gächinger Kantorei [L] Hänssler Classic 2-▲ CD 98.956 [DDD] 2-■ MC 98.956 (D)
Fauré, G.:Requiem, w. K. Battle (sop), C. M. Giulini (cnd), Philharmonia Orch, Philharmonia Chorus [L] Deutsche Grammophon ▲ 419243-2 [DDD]
Garcia, J.M.N.:Motets, w. Katharina Ott (sop), Luiz Alves da Silva (ct), Beat Mattmüller (ct), Markus Schikora (ten), William Lombardi (ten), Peter Mächler (bass), Michael Leibundgut (bass), L. A. da Silva (cnd), Turicum Ensemble *(rec Studio DRS, Zurich, Sept 26–29, 1994)* Claves ▲ CD 9521 [DDD]
Haydn, J.:Die Jahreszeiten, w. Barbara Bonney (sop), Anthony Rolfe Johnson (ct), J. E. Gardiner (cnd), English Baroque Soloists, Monteverdi Choir London [period instrs] Archiv 2-▲ 431818-2 [DDD]
Haydn, J.:Die Jahreszeiten (sels), w. Barbara Bonney (sop), Anthony Rolfe Johnson (ten), J. E. Gardiner (cnd), English Baroque Soloists, Monteverdi Choir London—arias & choruses Archiv ▲ 447282-2
Haydn, J.:Mass 10, "Kriegsmesse", "Paukenmesse", w. Sylvia McNair (sop), Delores Ziegler (mez), Hans-Peter Blochwitz (ten), J. Levine (cnd), Berlin SO, Berlin RIAS Chamber Choir Deutsche Grammophon ▲ 435853-2
Haydn, J.:The Seven Last Words of Christ on the Cross, w. Pamela Coburn (sop), Ingeborg Danz (mez), Uwe Heilmann (ten), H. Rilling (cnd), Stuttgart Bach Collegium, Gächinger Kantorei [oratorio version] [G] Hänssler Classic ▲ 98.977 [DDD]
Haydn, M.:Requiem in B♭, w. Pamela Coburn (sop), Ingeborg Danz (mez), H. Rilling (cnd), Stuttgart Bach Collegium, Gächinger Kantorei [L] Hänssler Classic ▲ 98.977 [DDD]
Humperdinck, E.:Hänsel und Gretel, w. B. Bonney (sop), E. Lind (sop), B. Hendricks (sop), A.S. von Otter (mez), H. Schwarz (mez), M. Lipovšek (mez), J. Tate (cnd), Bavarian RSO, Tölz Boys' Choir [G] EMI Classics 2-▲ CDCB 54022 [DDD]
Mahler, G.:Kindertotenlieder, w. J. López-Cobos (cnd), Cincinnati SO [G] Telarc ▲ CD 80269 [DDD]
Mahler, G.:Des Knaben Wunderhorn, w. L. Popp (sop), L. Bernstein (cnd), Royal Concertgebouw Orch [G] Deutsche Grammophon ▲ 427302-2 [DDD]
Mahler, G.:Lieder eines fahrenden Gesellen, w. J. López-Cobos (cnd), Cincinnati SO [G] Telarc ▲ CD 80269 [DDD]
Mahler, G.:Songs, w. C. Garben (cnd), Berlin RSO—Ablösung im Sommer; Zu Strasburg auf der Schanz'; Nicht Wiedersehen; Um schlimme Kinder artig zu machen; Hans und Grete; Ich ging mit Lust durch einen grünen Wald; Frühlingsmorgen; Scheiden und Meiden; Erinnerung RCA Red Seal ▲ 09026-61184-2
Mahler, G.:Songs from Rückert, w. J. López-Cobos (cnd), Cincinnati SO [G] Telarc ▲ CD 80269 [DDD]

Schmidt, Andreas (bar) (cont.)
Mahler, G.:Syms, w. J. Blegen (sop), B. Hendricks (sop), M. Price (sop), G. Zeumer (sop), H. Wittek (trb), A. Baltsa (mez), C. Ludwig (mez), K. Riegel (ten), H. Prey (bar), J. Van Dam (b-bar), L. Bernstein (cnd), New York PO, Royal Concertgebouw Orch, Vienna PO, Westminster Choir, New York Choral Artists, Brooklyn Boys' Choir, Vienna Boys' Choir, Vienna State Opera Chorus, Vienna Singverein Deutsche Grammophon 13-▲ 435162-2 [DDD]
Mahler, G.:Sym 8, w. J. Blegen (sop), M. Price (sop), G. Zeumer (sop), A. Baltsa (mez), K. Riegel (ten), H. Prey (bar), J. Van Dam (b-bar), L. Bernstein (cnd), Vienna PO, Vienna State Opera Chorus, Vienna Boys' Choir *(rec Salzburg Festival, 1975)* Deutsche Grammophon 2-▲ 435102-2 [ADD]
Mozart, W.A.:Don Giovanni, w. N. Argenta (sop), A. Halgrimson (sop), L. Dawson (sop), J. M. Ainsley (ten), G. Finley (ten), A. Miles (bar), G. Yurisch (bar), R. Norrington (cnd), London Classical Players, Schütz Choir London EMI Classics ▲ CDCB 54859
Mozart, W.A.:Missa, K.317, w. S. McNair (sop), D. Ziegler (mez), H.P. Blochwitz (ten), J. Levine (cnd), Berlin SO, Berlin RIAS Chamber Choir Deutsche Grammophon ▲ 435853-2
Mozart, W.A.:Nozze di Figaro (sels), w. L. Cuberli (sop), J. Rodgers (sop), C. Bartoli (mez), D. Barenboim (cnd), Berlin PO, Berlin RIAS Chamber Choir Erato ▲ 94822
Mozart, W.A.:Requiem, w. C. Oelze (sop), I. Danz (mez), S. Weir (ten), H. Rilling (cnd), Stuttgart Bach Collegium, Gächinger Kantorei [L] Hänssler Classic 2-▲ 98.979 [DDD]
Mozart, W.A.:Zauberflöte, w. D. Upshaw (sop), B. Hoch (sop), A. Rolfe Johnson (ten), R. Norrington (cnd), London Classical Players [period instrs] EMI Classics 2-▲ CDCB 54287
Mozart, W.A.:Zauberflöte (sels), w. D. Upshaw (sop), B. Hoch (sop), A. Rolfe Johnson (ten), R. Norrington (cnd), London Classical Players [period instrs] EMI Classics ▲ CDC 54492
Pinto, L.A.:Te Deum Laudamus, w. Katharina Ott (sop), Luiz Alves da Silva (ct), Beat Mattmüller (ct), Markus Schikora (ten), William Lombardi (ten), Peter Mächler (bass), Michael Leibundgut (bass), L. A. da Brooks (cnd), Turicum Ensemble *(rec Studio DRS, Zurich, Sept 26–29, 1994)* Claves ▲ CD 9521 [DDD]
Prokofiev, S.:Lt Kijé Suite, w. S. Ozawa (cnd), Berlin PO Deutsche Grammophon ▲ 435029-2 [DDD]
Reicha, A.:Der neue Psalm, w. Magdaléna Hajóssyová (sop), Anna Barová (mez), Karel Průša (bass), L. Mátl (cnd), Dvořák CO, Czech Phil Chorus Panton ▲ PAN 810758 [DDD]
Schubert, Franz:Mass 2, w. B. Bonney (sop), B. Poschner (ten), M. Hintermeier (cta), J. A. Pita (ten), C. Abbado (cnd), CO of Europe Deutsche Grammophon ▲ 435486-2
Schubert, Franz:Winterreise, w. R. Jansen (pno) [G] Deutsche Grammophon ▲ 435384-2 [DDD]
Schumann, R.:Requiem Mignon, w. B. Bonney (sop), B. Poschner (ten), M. Hintermeier (cta), J. A. Pita (ten), C. Abbado (cnd), CO of Europe Deutsche Grammophon ▲ 435486-2
Strauss, R.:Arabella, w. H. Donath (sop), J. Varady (sop), D. Fischer-Dieskau (bar), W. Berry (bass), W. Sawallisch (cnd), Bavarian State Orch Orfeo 2-▲ 169882 [DDD]
Strauss, R.:Der Rosenkavalier (sels), w. K. Battle (sop), R. Fleming (sop), F. von Stade (mez), C. Abbado (cnd), Berlin PO *(rec Dec. 31, 1992)* Sony Classical ▲ SK 52565
Strauss, R.:Songs, w. C. Garben (cnd), Berlin RSO—Hymnus und Pilgers Morgenlied, Op. 33; Das Thal und das Einsame, Op. 51; Notturno, Op. 44 RCA Red Seal ▲ 09026-61184-2
Wagner, R.:Lohengrin, w. Cheryl Studer (sop), Waltraud Meier (mez), Siegfried Jerusalem (ten), Harmut Welker (bar), Kurt Moll (bass), C. Abbado (cnd), Vienna PO Deutsche Grammophon 3-▲ 437808-2
Wagner, R.:Das Rheingold, w. M. Lipovšek (mez), J. Rappé (ten), H. Zednik (ten), P. Haage (ten), T. Adam (b-bar), H. Tschammer (bass), K. Rydl (bass), J. Morris (bass), B. Haitink (cnd), Bavarian RSO [G] EMI Classics 2-▲ CDCB 49853 [DDD]
Wagner, R.:Tannhäuser, w. C. Studer (sop), A. Baltsa (mez), P. Domingo (ten), M. Salminen (bass), G. Sinopoli (cnd), Philharmonia Orch, Royal Opera House Chorus Covent Garden Deutsche Grammophon ▲ 435405-2 [DDD]
Wagner, R.:Tannhäuser, w. C. Studer (sop), A. Baltsa (mez), P. Domingo (ten), M. Salminen (bass), G. Sinopoli (cnd), Philharmonia Orch, Royal Opera House Chorus Covent Garden [G] Deutsche Grammophon 3-▲ 427625-2 [DDD]
Wagner, S.:Banadietrich, w. Beth Johanning (sop), Vivian Hanner (sgr), Volker Horn (ten), André Wenhold (bar), Adalbert Walker (bass), V. Gailis (cnd), Thuringian SO, Rudolstadt Festival Chorus *(rec Rudolstadt, June 1995)* Marco Polo 2-▲ 8.223895-6 [DDD]
Weber, C.M. von:Der Freischütz, w. R. Ziesack (sop), S. Sweet (sop), M. Hölle (bass), M. Janowski (cnd), German SO, Berlin Radio Chorus RCA Red Seal 2-▲ 09026-62538-2
Zemlinsky, A. von:Songs (misc), w. B. Bonney (sop), A.-S. von Otter (mez), H.-P. Blochwitz (ten), C. Garben (pno)—Lieder, Op. 2; Gesänge, Op. 5; Walzer-Gesänge nach toskanischen Volksliedern, Op. 6; Irmelin Rose und andere Gesänge, Op. 7; Turmwächterlied und andere Gesänge, Op. 8; Ehetanzlied und andere Gesänge, Op. 10; Schlummerlied; 6 Gesänge, Op. 13; 6 Lieder, Op. 22; Ahnung Beatricens; 12 Lieder, Op. 27 [G] Deutsche Grammophon 2-▲ 427348-2 [DDD]
Zemlinsky, A. von:Songs (misc), w. Ruth Ziesak (sop), Iris Vermillion (mez), Hans Peter Blochwitz (ten), Cord Garben (pno)—Die schlanke Wasserlilie; Gute Nacht; Liebe und Frühling; Ich sah mein eigen Angesicht; In der Ferne; Waldgespräch; Der Rosenband; Abendstern; Des Mädchens Klage; Der Morgenstern; Wandl' ich im Wald des Abends; Orientalisches Sonett; Süsse, süsse Sommernacht; Herbsten; Nun schwillt der See so bang; In der Sonnengasse; Herr Bombardil; Es war ein alter König; Über eine Wiege; Mädel, kommst du mit zum Tanz?; Jane Grey; Der verlorene Haufen; Vorspiel; Ansturm; Auf See; Noch spür ich ihren Atem; Hörtest du denn nicht hinein; Die Beiden; Harmonie des Abends; Und einmal gehst du *(rec Stuttgart & Berlin, Germany, Mar. 30–June 8, 1993)* Sony Classical ▲ SK 57960

Schmidt, Dorothea (sop)
Mauersberger, R.:Geh aus, mein Herz, und suche Freude, w. Sabine Dicke (sop), Friederike Urban (sop), Annette Bassenge (alt), Christiane Fischer (alt), Sabine Hering (alt), Johannes Unger (org), Wolfgang Unger (dir), Thüringian Academic Sing Circle Thorofon ▲ CTH 2245 [DDD]

Schmidt, Günther (bass)
Monteverdi, C.:Vespers, w. Susanne Ryden (sop), Irena Troupova-Wilke (sop), Detlef Bratschke (alt), Erich Mentzel (ten), Hermann Oswald (ten), Manuel Warwitz (ten), Thomas Herberich (bass), H. Arman (cnd), Schütz Academy Capriccio ▲ CD 10521 [DDD]

Schmidt, Joseph (ten)
Charpentier, M.-A.:Louise (sels), w. Grace Moore (sop), Robert Weede (bar), E. Rapée (cnd), Radio City Music Hall Orch, Radio City Music Hall Chorus—Depuis le jour Enterprise ("The Radio Years" series) ▲ ENT RY 58
The Complete EMI Recordings, Vol. 1 EMI Classics ▲ ZDMB 64673
The Complete EMI Recordings, Vol. 2 *(rec 1932–37)* EMI Classics ▲ ZDMB 64676
Grace Moore & Josef Schmidt, w. Grace Moore (sop), Ernő Rapè (cnd) *(rec live Radio City Music Hall, NYC, 11/7/37)* Melodram ▲ CDM 18035 [ADD]
Joseph Schmidt, w. Berlin RSO [cnd:Rudolf Hindemith, Bruno Seidler-Winkler, Hermann Scherchen, Fritz Stiedry, Max von Schillings], unknown orchestra [cnd:Idris Lewis], General Motors SO, General Motors Sym Chorus [cnd:Erno Rapee, José Iturbi, Oscar Straus], et. al. Koch Schwann ▲ SCH 312572 [ADD]
Leoncavallo, R.:Pagliacci (sels), w. Enrico Caruso (ten), Antonio Paoli (ten), Giovanni Zenatello (ten), Amedeo Bassi (ten), Hermann Jadlowker (ten), Fernand Ansseau (ten), Hipolito Lazaro (ten), Nino (Filippo) Piccaluga (ten), Mario Chamlee (ten), Giacomo Lauri-Volpi (ten), Miguel Fleta (ten), Giovanni Martinelli (ten), Aureliano Pertile (ten), Georges Thill (ten), Alessandro Valente (ten), Francesco Merli (ten), Lauritz Melchior (ten), Marcel Wittrisch (ten), Beniamino Gigli (ten), Giuseppe Lugo (ten), Helge Roswaenge (ten), Jussi Bjoerling (ten)—23 versions of the tenor aria "Vesti la giubba" *(rec 1907–1944)* Bongiovanni ▲ GB 1071 [ADD]
Leoncavallo, R.:Pagliacci (sels), w. Grace Moore (sop), Robert Weede (bar), E. Rapée (cnd), Radio City Music Hall Orch, Radio City Music Hall Chorus—Stridono lassù Enterprise ("The Radio Years" series) ▲ ENT RY 58
Massenet, J.:Manon (sels), w. Grace Moore (sop), Robert Weede (bar), E. Rapée (cnd), Radio City Music Hall Orch, Radio City Music Hall Chorus—Obéissons quand leur voix appelle [Gavotte] Enterprise ("The Radio Years" series) ▲ ENT RY 58
Monteverdi, C.:Combattimento, w. Kurt Equiluz (ten), Werner Hollweg (ten), N. Harnoncourt (cnd), Vienna Concentus Musicus [I] Teldec ▲ 2292-43036-2
Opera Arias Bel Age ▲ 103.004 [ADD]
Puccini, G.:La Bohème (sels), w. Grace Moore (sop), Robert Weede (bar), E. Rapée (cnd), Radio City Music Hall Orch, Radio City Music Hall Chorus—Che Gelida Manina; Sì, Mi Chiamano Mimì; O Soave Fanciulla Enterprise ("The Radio Years" series) ▲ ENT RY 58

Schmidt, Joseph (ten) (cont.)

Puccini, G.:Madama Butterfly (sels), w. Grace Moore (sop), Robert Weede (bar), E. Rapée (cnd), Radio City Music Hall Orch, Radio City Music Hall Chorus—Vogliatemi Bene Enterprise ("The Radio Years" series) ▲ ENT RY 58

Puccini, G.:Tosca (sels), w. Grace Moore (sop), Robert Weede (bar), E. Rapée (cnd), Radio City Music Hall Orch, Radio City Music Hall Chorus—Recondita Armonia; Vissi d'Arte; E Lucevan le Stelle; Te Deum Enterprise ("The Radio Years" series) ▲ ENT RY 58

Religious Songs & Arias *(rec between 1929 & 1934)* Preiser ▲ PRE 90145 [AAD]

Verdi, G.:Il trovatore (sels), w. J. Biel (ten), F. Tamagno (ten), L.-A. Escalaïs (ten), M. Gilion (ten), E. Caruso (ten), A. Paoli (ten), G. Zenatello (ten), J. Sembach (ten), L. Slezak (ten), F. Constantino (ten), G. Martinelli (ten), B. De Muro (ten), N. Fusati (ten), N. Piccaluga (ten), G. Lauri-Volpi (ten), A. Pertile (ten), E. Bergamaschi (ten), R. Tauber (ten), J. O'Sullivan (ten), H. Roswaenge (ten), G. Taccani (ten), V. Lois (ten), H. Lazaro (ten), A. Lindi (ten), A. Cortis (ten), F. Merli (ten), F. Völker (ten), J. Kiepura (ten), J. Bjoerling (ten), B. Gigli (ten), A. Salvarezza (ten), J. Soler (ten), M. Filippeschi (ten)—34 performances of the Act III tenor aria "Di quella pira!," *(rec from 1903–1956)* Bongiovanni ▲ GB 1051 [AAD]

Weber, C.M. von:Peter Schmoll und seine Nachbarn, w. A. Pfeffer (sop—Minnette), J. Schmidt (ten—Martin Schmoll), S. Basa (ten—Karl Pirkner), H.-J. Schöpflin (ten—Niklas), R. Busching (bar—Peter Schmoll), H.J. Porcher (bass—Hans Bast), G. Markson (cnd), Hagen PO [G] *(rec Feb. 1–5, 1993)* Marco Polo 2-▲ 8.223592/93 [DDD]

Das Zauberlied *(rec 1929, 1930 & 1932)* Bel Age ▲ 103.001 [ADD]

Schmidt, Karl (sgr)

Puccini, G.:La Bohème, w. Trude Eipperle (sop), Hildegarde Ranczak (sop), Alfons Fügel (ten), Carl Kronenberg (bar), Georg Hann (bass), Georg Wieter (bass), Emil Graf (sgr), Otto Hillerbrandt (sgr), C. Krauss (cnd), Bavarian State Opera Orch, Bavarian State Opera Chorus *(rec 1940)* Preiser 2-▲ PRE 90275

Schmidt, Manfred (ten)

Cornelius, P.:Stabat Mater, w. B. Scherler (mez), S. Nimsgern (bass-bar), R. Didusch (sgr), H. Schernus (cnd), Cologne RSO, Cologne Radio Chorus [L] *(rec 1978)* Koch Schwann ▲ 3-1086-2 [ADD]

Hindemith, P.:Mathis der Maler, w. Urszula Koszut (sop), Trudeliese Schmidt (mez), Rose Wagemann (mez), William Cochran (ten), Donald Grobe (ten), James King (ten), Dietrich Fischer-Dieskau (bar), Gerd Feldhoff (bass), Alexander Malta (bass), Peter Meven (bass), Karl Kreile (sgr), R. Kubelik (cnd), Bavarian RSO, Bavarian Radio Chorus EMI Classics 2-▲ CDCC 55237

Lehár, F.:Der Graf von Luxemburg (sels), w. Helga Hildebrand (sop), Erika Koth (sop), Rudolf Schock (ten), Gustav Niedlinger (bass) Emperor Operetta ▲ KO 86342

Stuart, P.:Kill Bear Comes Home, w. Elana Gizzi (sop—Hasty Girl), Mi-Kyung Huh (sop—Cold Feet), Therese Murray (sop—Song Bird), Cherie Pfeil (sop—1st Sister), Renia Shukis (sop—2nd Sister), Riki Connaughton (mez—4th Sister), Lucy Fee (mez—3rd Sister), David Averbach (ten—Song Leader), Mark Schmidt (ten—Kill Bear), Jason Smith (bar—Cheif Wife Hunter), P. Stuart (cnd), Rochester Opera Theater Orch, Rochester Opera Theater Chorus VM ▲ DRK 154 [DDD]

Schmidt, Peter-Jürgend (ten)

Matthus, S.:Mirabeau, w. Carola Höhn (sop—Marie Antoinette), Carola Fischer (cta—Eveline Le Jay), Peter-Jürgend Schmidt (ten—Ludwig XVI), Jürgen Freier (bar—Honoré-Gabriel de Riqueti), Gerd Wolf (bass—Victor Riqueti), H. Fricke (cnd), Berlin State Opera Orch, Berlin State Opera Chorus *(rec Berlin, 1989)* Berlin Classics 2-▲ BER 1075 [DDD]

Schmidt, Trudeliese (mez)

Bach, J.S.:Cant 80, w. E. Mathis (sop), P. Schreier (ten), D. Fischer-Dieskau (bar), K. Richter (cnd), Munich Bach Orch, Munich Bach Choir Archiv ▲ 427130-2 [ADD]

Bach, J.S.:Cant 116, w. E. Mathis (sop), P. Schreier (ten), D. Fischer-Dieskau (bar), K. Richter (cnd), Munich Bach Orch, Munich Bach Choir Archiv ▲ 427130-2 [ADD]

Hindemith, P.:Mathis der Maler, w. Urszula Koszut (sop), Rose Wagemann (mez), William Cochran (ten), Donald Grobe (ten), James King (ten), Manfred Schmidt (ten), Dietrich Fischer-Dieskau (bar), Gerd Feldhoff (bass), Alexander Malta (bass), Peter Meven (bass), Karl Kreile (sgr), R. Kubelik (cnd), Bavarian RSO, Bavarian Radio Chorus EMI Classics 2-▲ CDCC 55237

Trojahn, M.:Enrico, w. L. Magnusson (ten), R. Salter (bar), D. R. Davies (cnd), Stuttgart RSO CPO 2-▲ CPO 999160 [DDD]

Weill, K.:Mahagonny, w. G. Ramm (sop), H. Hiestermann (ten), J. Latham-König (cnd), König Ensemble Capriccio ▲ 60028 [DDD]

Schmidt, Wolfgang (bar)

Telemann, G.P.:St. Matthew Passion, w. M. Zedelius (sop), A. Browner (alt), H.P. Blochwitz (ten), A. Scharinger (bass), W. Seeliger (cnd), Darmstadt CO, Darmstadt Concert Choir Christophorus ▲ 77149 [DDD]

Schmidt-Glänzel, L. (sop)

Weber, C.M. von:Kampf und Sieg, w. E. Fleischer (cta), G. Lutze (ten), H. Krämer (bar), H. Kegel (cnd), Leipzig RSO, Leipzig Radio Chorus [G] Forlane ▲ FOR 16572 (m) [AAD]

Schmiege, Marilyn (cta)

Humperdinck, E.:Königskinder, w. Dagmar Schellenberger (sop—Goose girl), Marilyn Schmiege (cta—Witch), Thomas Moser (ten—King's Son), Heinrich Weber (ten—Broommaker), Dietrich Henschel (bar—Fiddler), Andreas Kohn (bass—Woodcutter), F. Luisi (cnd), Munich RSO, Michael Gläser (cnd), Bavarian Radio Chorus *(rec live, Munich Herkulessaal, Mar 22–24, 1996)* Calig 3-CAL 5096870 [DDD]

Schmiege, Marilyn (mez)

Fauré, G.:La Chanson d'Eve, w. Donald Sulzen (pno) Orfeo ▲ 347941 [DDD]

Fauré, G.:Le Jardin clos, w. Donald Sulzen (pno) Orfeo ▲ 347941 [DDD]

Fauré, G.:Mélodies 'de Venise', Op. 58, w. Donald Sulzen (pno) Orfeo ▲ 347941 [DDD]

Galuppi, B.:Adamo, w. Susanna Rigacci (sop—Angelo di Misericordia), Mara Zampieri (sop—Eva), Marilyn Schmiege (mez—Angelo di Giustizia), Ernesto Palacio (ten—Adamo), C. Scimone (cnd), Venice Solisti Erato 2-▲ ERA SEL 12984 [ADD]

Haydn, J.:L'Anima del filosofo, or Orfeo ed Euridice, w. Clara McFadden (sop), Christoph Prégardien, Gotthold Schwarz (bass), M. Schneider (cnd), La Stagione, La Stagione Choir Deutsche Harmonia Mundi 2-▲ 05472-77229-2

Schreker, F.:Die Gezeichneten, w. W. Cochran (ten), S. Cowan (bar), W. Oosterkamp (bass), E. de Waart (cnd), Dutch Radio PO, Dutch Radio Phil Chorus Marco Polo 3-▲ 8.223328/30

Schmiege, Marilyn (sop)

Vivaldi, A.:Catone in Utica, w. Cecilia Gasdia (sop), Susanna Rigacci (sop), Lucretia Lendi (mez), Margarita Zimmerman (mez), C. Scimone (cnd), Venice Solisti Erato 2-▲ ERA SEL 11232 [DDD]

Schmitt, Edith (sop)

Rossini, G.:Petite messe solennelle, w. S. Gregoire (cta), R. Garin (ten), A. Golven (bass), F. Maciocchi (pno) J.-F. Hatton (harm), Paris Opéra-Comique Chorus IMP Masters ▲ IMP MCD61

Schmitt-Bohn, Florian (sop)

Albrechtsberger, J.G.:Missa assumptionis beatae Mariae Virginis, w. J. Köble (alt), C. Elsner (ten), U. Rausch (bass), R. Hug (cnd), Freiburg Baroque Soloists Ars Musici ▲ 0972-2 [DDD]

Haydn, M.:Missa Sancti Hieronymi, w. Joachim Köble (alt), Christian Elsner (ten), Ulrich Rausch (bass), R. Hug (cnd), Freiburg Baroque Soloists Ars Musici ▲ 0972-2 [DDD]

Schmitt-Walter, Karl (bar)

The Legendary Singers at Lindenoper Berlin (1927–1945)—, w. Gitta Alpar (sop), Erna Berger (sop), Tiana Lemnitz (sop), Maria Müller (sop), Margarete Klose (cta), Peter Anders (ten), Max Lorenz (ten), Walter Ludwig (ten), Lauritz Melchior (ten), Rudolf Schock (ten), Franz Völker (ten), et. al. *(rec 1927; 1937; 1941–45)* Minerva ▲ MN A21 [ADD]

Lortzing, A.:Hans Sachs, w. M. Weindl (sop), M. Loy (cnd), Frankenland State SO *(rec 1950)* Memories 2-▲ MEM 4550 [ADD]

Mozart, W.A.:Zauberflöte, w. Wilma Lipp (sop), Irmgard Seefried (sop), Peter Klein (ten), Walther Ludwig (ten), Josef Greindl (bass), Paul Schöffler (sgr), W. Furtwängler (cnd), Vienna PO, Vienna State Opera Chorus *(rec 1949)* Music & Arts 3-▲ CD 882 [AAD]

Mozart, W.A.:Zauberflöte (sels), w. I. Seefried (sop), W. Lipp (sop), W. Ludwig (ten), J. Greindl (bass), W. Furtwängler (cnd), Vienna PO, Vienna State Opera Chorus—Ov. & 11 arias *(rec live, Salzburg, July 27, 1949)* Arkadia 3-▲ 361 [ADD]

Orff, C.:Der Mond—Ein kleines Welttheater, w. R. Christ (ten), P. Kuën (ten), H. Graml (bar), H. Hotter (b-bar), P. Lagger (bass), W. Sawallisch (cnd), Philharmonia Orch, Philharmonia Chorus [G] EMI Classics ("Studio" series) 2-▲ CDMB 63712 [ADD]

Schmitt-Walter, Karl (bar) (cont.)

Schubert, Franz:Winterreise, w. Ferdinand Leitner (pno) *(rec 1940–43)* Preiser ▲ PRE 90288

Schumann, R.:Scenes from Goethe's "Faust", w. Lore Hoffman (sop), Walther Ludwig (ten), H. Schmidt-Isserstedt (cnd), Berlin German Opera Orch, Berlin German Opera Chorus Enterprise ("The Radio Years" series) 2-▲ ENT RY 66

Strauss (II), Joh.:Der Zigeunerbaron (sels), w. S. Jurinac (sop), W. Hollweg (ten), P. Anders (ten), Schneider (sgr), G. Hann (bass), Marszalek (cnd), Cologne RSO, Cologne Radio Chorus [G] Acanta ▲ CD 43807 [DDD]

Strauss, R.:Feuersnot (sels), w. Maria Cebotari (sop), Paula Buchner (sop), Tiana Lemnitz (sop), A. Rother (cnd), Berlin Radio Orch *(rec 1943–44)* Preiser ▲ PRE 90222 [ADD]

Strauss, R.:Der Rosenkavalier (sels), w. Maria Cebotari (sop), Paula Buchner (sop), Tiana Lemnitz (sop), A. Rother (cnd), Berlin Radio Orch *(rec 1943–44)* Preiser ▲ PRE 90222 [ADD]

Strauss, R.:Salome (sels), w. Maria Cebotari (sop), Paula Buchner (sop), Tiana Lemnitz (sop), A. Rother (cnd), Berlin Radio Orch—Final Scene *(rec 1943–44)* Preiser ▲ PRE 90222 [ADD]

Wagner, R.:Arias & Scenes, w. Kathe Heidersbach (sop), Maria Reining (sop), Hilde Scheppan (sop), Margarete Teschemacher (sop), Margarete Klose (mez), Max Lorenz (ten), Jaro Prohaska (bar), Kurt Böhme (bass), *(orch unknown)*—selections from Rienzi; Der Fliegende Holländer; Tannhäuser; Lohengrin; Tristan und Isolde; Die Meistersinger von Nürnberg; Die Walküre & Götterdämmerung *(rec 1927–1944)* Phonographe 2-▲ PHG 5016 [AAD]

Wagner, R.:Tannhäuser, w. T. Eipperle (sop), F. Krauss (bar), S. Nilsson (bass), C. Leonhardt (cnd), Stuttgart Radio Orch, Stuttgart Radio Chorus [G] *(rec Oct. 24, 1937, mat. 39695)* Preiser 3-▲ 90133 (m) [AAD]

Schmitz, G. (ten)

Rachmaninoff, S.:All-Night Vigil, w. H. Czaja (cta), Russian Papel College Choir [F. Jockwig (sgr), E. Lohneisen (sgr), P. Blitznetzow (sgr), J. Stojaspal (sgr)]—No. 2 Christophorus ▲ CHR 74609

Schmitz, Jutta Maria (sgr)

Wagner, S.:Schwarzschwanenreich, w. Beth Johanning (sop—Linda), Kerstin Quandt (cta—Ursula), Walter Raffeiner (ten—Ludwig), Lucian Chioreanu (ten—A Boy), André Wenhold (bar—Oswald), Roland Hartmann (sgr—Tempter/Priest), Jutta Maria Schmitz (sgr—Ash-Woman), Ksenija Lukie (sgr—A Girl), K. Bach (cnd), Thüringian Saalfeld-Rudolstadt SO, Thüringian Landestheater Rudolstadt Chorus *(rec Thüringer Landestheater, Rudolstadt, June 1994)* Marco Polo 2-▲ 8.223777-8 [DDD]

Schnaut, Gabriele (sop)

Bach, J.S.:Cant 18, w. E. Csapò (sop), A. Kraus (ten), W. Schöne (bass), H. Rilling (cnd), Bach Ensemble [G] *(rec 1975)* Hänssler Classic ▲ 98.877 [AAD]

Bach, J.S.:Cant 114, w. J. Hamari (cta), K. Equiluz (ten), W. Schöne (bass), H. Rilling (cnd), Stuttgart Bach Collegium, Frankfurt Kantorei, Gächinger Kantorei [G] *(rec 1974)* Hänssler Classic ▲ 98.814 [AAD]

Bach, J.S.:Cant 181, w. A. Augér (sop), G. Schreckenbach (cta), K. Equiluz (ten), N. Tütler (bass), H. Rilling (cnd), Stuttgart Bach Collegium, Gächinger Kantorei [G] *(rec 1981)* Hänssler Classic ▲ 98.878 [AAD]

Hindemith, P.:Mörder, Hoffnug der Frauen, w. Franz Grundheber (bar), G. Albrecht (cnd), Berlin RSO Wergo ▲ WER 60132-50 [DDD]

Schreker, F.:Der Schatzgräber, w. J. Protschka (ten), H. Helm (bar), H. Stamm (bass), G. Albrecht (cnd), Hamburg State Opera Orch, Hamburg State Opera Chorus [G] *(rec live 5/89)* Capriccio 2-▲ 60010-2 [DDD]

Wagner, R.:Lohengrin (sels), w. C. Studer (sop), P. Frey (ten), M. Schenk (bass), P. Schneider (cnd), Bayreuth Festival Orch, Bayreuth Festival Chorus Philips ▲ 438500-2

Schneider (sgr)

Lehár, F.:Paganini (sels), w. A. Schlemm (mez), Lisolette Losch (sop), P. Anders (ten), Gehly (sgr), Hofmann (sgr), Marszalek (cnd), Cologne RSO, Cologne Radio Chorus [G] Acanta ▲ CD 43810 [DDD]

Strauss (II), Joh.:Der Zigeunerbaron (sels), w. S. Jurinac (sop), W. Hollweg (ten), P. Anders (ten), K. Schmitt-Walter (bar), G. Hann (bass), Marszalek (cnd), Cologne RSO, Cologne Radio Chorus [G] Acanta ▲ CD 43807 [DDD]

Schneider, E. (sgr)

Leider Singer, w. McCormack, John (ten), Grace Moore (sop), F. Kreisler (vn), V. O'Brien (pno), L. Bori (sop), L. Kennedy (vc) Symposium ▲ 1164

Schneider, Felix (sgr)

Schoeck, O.:Das Schloss Dürande (sels), w. Maria Cebotari (sop—Gabriele), Marta Fuchs (sop—Gräfin Morvaille), Brigitte Fassbaender (mez—Renald Willi Domgraf), Rut Berglund (cta—Priorin), Peter Anders (ten—Armand), Benno Arnold (ten—Jäger), Josef Greindl (bass—Nicole), Hans Wrana (bass—Jäger), Vasso Argyris (sgr—Volksredner), Otto Hüsch (sgr—Wildhüter), Leo Laschet (sgr—Jäger), Fritz Marcks (sgr—Jäger), Felix Schneider (sgr—Jäger), R. Heger (cnd)—Text; Ich kann es nicht glauben [from Act 1]; Text; Heil dir, du Feuerquelle [from Act 2]; Text; Gesucht und nicht gefunden [from Act 3]; Text; Der Jäger ist frei! [Act 3 Finale]; Text; Sie kommen mit Flinten und Stangen [Act 4]; Text; Du Narr des vermeintlichen Rechts [Act 4 finale]; Text *(rec live, Apr 1943)* Jecklin ▲ JD 692

Schneider, Helen (sop)

Weill, K.:Songs, w. B. Coyle (pno), L. Fast (elec) CBS ▲ MK 45703 [DDD] ▮ FMT 45703 (D)

Schneider, Joel (bar)

Beach, A.M.C.:Mass, "Grand Mass", w. Margot Law (sop), Martha Remington (mez), Ray Bauwens (ten), B. Jones (cnd), Stow Festival Orch, Stow Festival Chorus *(rec Cathedral Church of St Paul, Tremont St, Boston, MA)* Albany ▲ TROY 179 [DDD]

Schneiderman, Helene (mez)

Copland, A.:Poems (8) of Emily Dickinson, w. D. R. Davies (cnd), Orch of St. Luke MusicMasters ▲ 01612-67101-2

Schneider-Waterberg, Reiner (alt)

Bach, J.S.:Cant 36, w. Silke Wenzel (sop), Kobie van Rensburg (ten), Christian Hilz (bass), W. Kelber (cnd), Munich Monteverdi Orch *(rec live, Dec 1995)* Calig ▲ 50963 [DDD]

Bach, J.S.:Cant 40, w. Silke Wenzel (sop), Kobie van Rensburg (ten), Christian Hilz (bass), W. Kelber (cnd), Munich Monteverdi Orch *(rec live, Dec 1995)* Calig ▲ 50963 [DDD]

Bach, J.S.:Cant 91, w. Silke Wenzel (sop), Kobie van Rensburg (ten), Christian Hilz (bass), W. Kelber (cnd), Munich Monteverdi Orch *(rec live, Dec 1995)* Calig ▲ 50963 [DDD]

Brixi, F.X.:Missa di Gloria, w. F. Wagner (sop), B. Hirtreiter (ten), M. Mantaj (bass), C. Hammer (org), W. Kelber (cnd), Munich Monteverdi Orch, Munich Concerto Vocale *(rec 1993)* Calig ▲ CAL 50927 [ADD]

Schnerring, Dieter (ten)

Serenade:Song & Aria Recital, w. Anton Illenberger (pno) Ars Musici ▲ 8003

Schneyder, Peter (bass)

Mozart, W.A.:Masonic Music, w. C. Prégardien (ten), H. Wildhaber (ten), G. Hornik (bass), M. Haselböck (cnd), Vienna Academy, Chorus Viennensis—Masonic Cants., K.429, 471, 619, 623 & Songs, K.148, 468, 483, 484 [G] Novalis ▲ 150081 [DDD]

Schnorr, Simon (alt)

Haydn, J.:Mass 9, "Heiligmesse", w. Matthias Ritter (sop), Jörg Hering (ten), Benedikt Schillo (ten), Panito Iconomou (bass), B. Weil (cnd), Tölz Boys' Choir Sony Classical ("Vivarte" series) ▲ SK 66260

Haydn, J.:Sacred Music, w. Matthias Ritter (sop), Jörg Hering (ten), Benedikt Schillo (ten), Panito Iconomou (bass), B. Weil (cnd), Tölz Boys' Choir—Mare clausum (oratorio fragment), H.XXI-Va:9; Motetto Insanae et vanae curae, H.XXI:1; Motetti de Venerabili Sacramento I-IV, H.XXIIIc:5a-d; Te Deum, H.XXIIIc:2 Sony Classical ("Vivarte" series) ▲ SK 66260

Schober, Maria (sop)

Strauss (II), Joh.:Eine Nacht in Venedig, w. E. Réthy (sop), R. Boesch (bar), K. Friedrich (ten), A. Jerger (b-bar), K. Preger (ten), A. Paulik (cnd), Vienna SO, Bregenz Festival Choir [G] *(rec 1951)* Koch Schwann ▲ 3-1272-2 [ADD]

Schock, Rudolf (ten)

Albert, E. d':Tiefland, w. I. Strauss, Feldhoff, Sardi, H. Zanotelli (cnd), Berlin SO Eurodisc 2-▲ 7797-2-RG [ADD]

Beethoven, L. van:Fidelio (sels), w. E. Schlüte (sop), L. della Casa (sop), J. Patzak (ten), F. Frantz (b-bar), H. Alsen (bass), W. Furtwängler (cnd), Vienna State Opera Orch, Vienna State Opera Chorus—Overture, 16 arias & choruses *(rec live, Salzburg Festspielhaus Aug. 3, 1948)* Melodram 2-▲ CDM 25009 [ADD]

Schock, Rudolf (ten) (cont.)

Cornelius, P.:Der Barbier von Bagdad, w. S. Jurinac (sop), H. Rössl–Majdan (mez), E. Majkut (ten), A. Poell (bass–bar), G. Frick (bass), H. Hollreiser (cnd), Austrian RSO, Austrian Radio Chorus *(rec live Vienna 1952)* Melodram 2-▲ MEL 27050 (m) [AAD]

Cornelius, P.:Der Barbier von Bagdad, w. S. Jurinac (sop), H. Rössl–Majdan (mez), E. Majkut (ten), A. Poell (bass–bar), G. Frick (bass), H. Hollreiser (cnd), Austrian RSO, Austrian Radio Chorus [G] *(rec live Vienna, 1952)* Verona 2-▲ 27050/51 (m) [AA

Künneke, E.:Die grosse Sünderin (sels), w. M. Cunitz (sop), Bajew (sgr), Gehly (sgr), Rau (sgr), Schröder (sgr), Weigelt (sgr), Marszalek (cnd), Cologne RSO, Cologne Radio Chorus [G] Acanta ▲ CD 42483 [DDD]

The Legendary Singers at Lindenoper Berlin (1927–1945)—, w. Gitta Alpar (sop), Erna Berger (sop), Tiana Lemnitz (sop), Maria Müller (sop), Margarete Klose (cta), Peter Anders (ten), Max Lorenz (ten), Walter Ludwig (ten), Lauritz Melchior (ten), Franz Völker (ten), Willi Domgraf-Fassb *(rec 1927; 1937; 1941–45)* Minerva ▲ MN A21 [ADD]

Lehár, F.:Der Graf von Luxemburg (sels), w. Helga Hildebrand (sop), Erika Koth (sop), Manfred Schmidt (ten), Gustav Niedlinger (bass) Emperor Operetta ▲ KO 86342

Lehár, F.:Paganini (sels), w. Melitta Muszely (sop), Siegfried Borries (vn), W. Schmidt-Boelcke (cnd), FFB Orch, Gunther Arndt Chorus Emperor Operetta ▲ KO 86343

Lehár, F.:Schön ist die Welt (sels), w. Renate Holm (sop), F. Fox (cnd), FFB Orch, Gunther Arndt Chorus Emperor Operetta ▲ KO 86344

Leoncavallo, R.:Pagliacci, w. Melitta Muszely (sop), Josef Metternich (bar), H. Stein (cnd), Berlin State Opera Orch *(rec 1959)* Berlin Classics ▲ BER 9102 [ADD]

Mozart, W.A.:Arias, w. Arleen Augér (sop), Kathleen Battle (sop), Irma Beilke (sop), Helena Braun (sop), Lisa Della Casa (sop), Maria Cebotari (sop), Ileana Cotrubas (sop), Helen Donath (sop), Mirella Freni (sop), Reri Grist (sop), Edita Gruberova (sop), Elisabeth Grümmer (sop), Hilde Güden (sop), Ingeborg Hallstein (sop), Luise Helletsgruber (sop), Gundula Janowitz (sop), Sena Jurinac (sop), Erika Köth (sop), Evelyn Lear (sop), Wilma Lipp (sop), Margaret Marshall (sop), Edith Mathis (sop), Jarmila Novotna (sop), Margherita Perras (sop), Lucia Popp (sop), Elisabeth Rethberg (sop), Anneliese Rothenberger (sop), Elisabeth Schumann (sop), Elisabeth Schwarzkopf (sop), Graziella Sciutti (sop), Irmgard Seefried (sop), Graziella Sciutti (sop), Julia Varady (sop), Agnes Baltsa (mez), Margit Bokor (mez), Brigitte Fassbaender (mez), Christa Ludwig (mez), Ann Murray (mez), Francisco Araiza (ten), Anton Dermota (ten), Helge Rosvaenge (ten), Peter Schreier (ten), Leopold Simoneau (ten), Eric Tappy (ten), Richard Tauber (ten), Gösta Winbergh (ten), Josef Witt (ten), Fritz Wunderlich (ten), Christian Boesch (bar), Willy Domgraf-Fassbaender (bar), Karl Dönch (bar), Dietrich Fischer-Dieskau (bar), Erich Kunz (bar), Eberhard Wächter (bar), Hans Hotter (b-bar), Paul Schöffler (b-bar), Cesare Siepi (b-bar), José Van Dam (b-bar), Walter Berry (bass), Geraint Evans (bass), Nicolai Ghiaurov (bass), Alexander Kipnis (bass), Richard Mayr (bass), Kurt Moll (bass), James Morris (bass), Ezio Pinza (bass), Martti Talvela (bass), Giorgio Tozzi (bass), Hans Duhan (sgr), Res Fischer (sgr), Marie Gerhart (sgr), *(various orchs & cnds)*—sels from Idomeneo, Die Entführung aus der Serail, Le nozze di Figaro, Don Giovanni, Così fan tutte, Die Zauberflöte & various arias Orfeo d'or ("Festspiel Dokumente" series) 5-▲ 408955

Mozart, W.A.:Entführung (sels), w. Erika Köth (sop), G. Szell (cnd), Vienna PO—Welch' ein Geschick Orfeo d'or ("Festspiel Dokumente" series) ▲ 394201

16 Operetta Arias Acanta ▲ 43480

Straus, O.:Ein Walzertraum (sels), w. Melita Muszely (sop), Lisa Otto (sop), Bruno Fritz (bar), W. Schüchter (cnd), Berlin Orch, Berlin Chorus Emperor Operetta ▲ KO 86346

Strauss (II), Joh.:Die Fledermaus (sels), w. W. Lipp (sop), O. Schenck (nar), W. Berry (bass), R. Stolz (cnd), Vienna SO [G] Eurodisc ▲ 25-8369 [ADD]

Strauss (II), Joh.:Wiener Blut (sels), w. M. Schramm (sop), H. Gueden (sop), B. Kusche (bar), R. Stolz (cnd), Vienna SO [G] Eurodisc ▲ 25-8370 [ADD]

Strauss, R.:Ariadne auf Naxos, w. L. Della Casa (sop), H. Güden (sop), I. Seefried (sop), P. Schöffler (bass), K. Böhm (cnd), Vienna PO *(rec Salzburg Festival, 1954)* Deutsche Grammophon 2-▲ 445332-2 (m) [ADD]

Strauss, R.:Ariadne auf Naxos, w. E. Schwarzkopf (sop), I. Seefried (sop), R. Streich (sop), L. Otto (sop), G. Hoffman (mez), R. Schock (ten), G. Unger (ten), H. Cuénod (ten), H. Prey (bar), F. Ollendorff (bass), H. von Karajan (cnd), Philharmonia Orch [G] *(rec 1954)* EMI Classics ("Studio" series) 2-▲ CDMB 69296 (m) [ADD]

Strauss, R.:Ariadne auf Naxos, w. Lisa Della Casa (sop—Ariadne), Lisa Otto (sop—Najade), Rudolf Schock (ten—Bacchus), Leonore Kirschstein (sgr—Echo), Nada Puttar (sgr—Dryade), A. Erede (cnd), Berlin PO Testament ▲ SBT 1036 [ADD]

Strauss, R.:Ariadne auf Naxos, w. Elisabeth Schwarzkopf (sop—Ariadne/Prima Donna), Irmgard Seefried (sop—Zerbinetta), Rita Streich (sop—The Composer), Rudolf Schock (ten—Bacchus), H. von Karajan (cnd), Philharmonia Orch EMI Classics 2-▲ CDCB 55176

12 Opera & Operetta Arias Acanta ▲ 13553

Wagner, R.:Der fliegende Holländer, w. M. Schech (sop), S. Wagner (mez), G. Frick (ten), F. Wunderlich (ten), D. Fischer-Dieskau (bar), F. Konwitschny (cnd), Berlin Staatskapelle Berlin Classics ("Eterna" series) 2-▲ BER 2097 [ADD]

Wagner, R.:Lohengrin, w. Maud Cunitz (sop—Elsa), Margarete Klose (mez—Ortrud), Rudolf Schock (ten—Lohengrin), Josef Metternich (bar—Friedrich von Telramund), Gottlob Frick (bass—King Henry), W. Schüchter (cnd), North German RSO, North German Radio Chorus, West German Radio Men's Chorus *(rec 1953)* EMI Classics 2-▲ CDHC 65517

Wagner, R.:Die Meistersinger von Nürnberg, w. E. Grümmer (sop), M. Höffgen (cta), G. Unger (ten), H. Prey (bar), B. Kusche (bar), F. Frantz (b-bar), G. Frick (bass), R. Kempe (cnd), Berlin PO *(rec 1956)* EMI Classics 4-▲ CDMD 64154

Wagner, R.:Das Rheingold, w. L. Otto (sop), M. Muszely (sop), J. Blatter (mez), R. Stewart (mez), S. Wagner (mez), H. Melchert (ten), F. Frantz (bass), B. Kusche (bass), J. Metternich (bass), R. Kempe (cnd), Berlin Staatskapelle *(rec Mar. 1959)* Berlin Classics ("Eterna" series) ▲ BER 2035 [ADD]

Schoeck, Hilde (sop)

Schoeck, O.:Das holde Bescheiden, w. Othmar Schoeck (pno)—Besuch in Urach [No. 36] *(rec live, Apr 1943)* Jecklin ▲ JD 692

Schöffler, Paul (b-bar)

Albert, E. d':Tiefland, w. G. Brouwenstijn, H. Hopf, W. Kmentt, E. Wächter, O. Czerwenka, R. Moralt (cnd), Vienna SO *(rec 1957)* Philips 2-▲ 434781-2

Bach, J.S.:Mass in b, BWV 232, w. E. Schwarzkopf (sop), C. Ludwig (mez), K. Ferrier (cta), A. Poell (b-bar), H. von Karajan (cnd), Vienna SO, Vienna Singverein—6 arias excerpted from the above rec'g Verona ▲ 27076 (m) [AAD]

Bach, J.S.:Mass in b, BWV 232, w. E. Schwarzkopf (sop), C. Ludwig (mez), K. Ferrier (cta), A. Poell (b-bar), H. von Karajan (cnd), Vienna SO [L] *(rec live at Vienna's International Bach Festival, June 15, 1950)* Verona 2-▲ 27073/74 (m) [AAD]

Bach, J.S.:St. Matthew Passion, w. I. Seefried (sop), C. Ludwig (mez), K. Ferrier (cta), O. Edelmann (b-bar), H. von Karajan (cnd), Vienna SO, Vienna Singverein [G] *(rec live June 9, 1950)* Verona 3-▲ 27070/72 (m) [AAD]

Bach, J.S.:St. Matthew Passion (sels), w. I. Seefried (sop), C. Ludwig (mez), K. Ferrier (cta), O. Edelmann (b-bar), H. von Karajan (cnd), Vienna SO, Vienna Singverein Verona ▲ 27076 (m) [AAD]

Beethoven, L. van:Fidelio, w. K. Flagstad (sop), J. Patzak (ten), J. Greindl (bass), W. Furtwängler (cnd), Vienna PO, Vienna State Opera Chorus [G] *(rec live 1950)* Arkadia 2-▲ 354

Beethoven, L. van:Fidelio, w. C. Goltz (sop), S. Jurinac (sop), G. Zampieri (ten), O. Edelmann (bass), H. von Karajan (cnd), Vienna PO, Vienna State Opera Chorus [G] *(rec live, Salzburg Festival 7/27/57)* Claque 2-▲ CLQ 2007 (m)

Beethoven, L. van:Fidelio, w. H. Konetzni (sop), I. Seefried (sop), P. Klein (ten), T. Ralf (ten), H. Alsen (bass), K. Böhm (cnd), Vienna State Opera Orch, Vienna State Opera Chorus *(rec Feb. 1944)* Preiser 2-▲ PRE 90195 [AAD]

Beethoven, L. van:Fidelio, w. K. Flagstad (sop), J. Patzak (ten), J. Greindl (bass), W. Furtwängler (cnd), Vienna PO, Vienna State Opera Chorus [G] *(rec live, Salzburg 8/5/50)* Verona 2-▲ 27044/45 (m) [AAD]

Beethoven, L. van:Leonore (opera), w. H. Zadek (sop), A. Dermota (ten), O. von Rohr (bass), F. Leitner (cnd), Vienna SO, Vienna State Opera Chorus [G] *(rec live, Bregenz 1960)* Melodram 2-▲ CDM 27085 [AAD]

Schöffler, Paul (b-bar) (cont.)

Einem, G. von:Dantons Tod, w. M. Cebotari (sop—Lucille Desmoulins), R. Anday (cta—Frau des Simon), P. Klein (ten—de Séchelles), J. Patzak (ten—Camille Desmoulins), J. Witt (ten—Robspierre), P. Schöffler (bar—Danton), L. Weber (bass—Saint Just), F. Fricsay (cnd), Vienna PO, Vienna State Opera Chorus *(rec Aug. 6, 1947)* Stradivarius 2-▲ STR 10067 [ADD]

Gluck, C.W.:Iphigénie en Aulide (sels), w. Helena Braun (sop—Klytämnestra), Hilde Konetzni (sop—Iphigenie), Set Svanholm (bar—Achilles), Paul Schöffler (b-bar—Agamemnon), L. Ludwig (cnd), Vienna State Opera Orch *(rec Vienna, Oct. 29, 1942)* Koch Schwann ▲ SCH 314692 [ADD]

Haydn, J.:Die Schöpfung, w. Anny Felbermayer (sop—Eve), Teresa Stich-Randall (sop—Gabriel), Anton Dermota (ten—Uriel), Paul Schöffler (b-bar—Adam), Frederick Guthrie (bass—Raphael), Franz Holletschek (cembalo), M. Wöldike (cnd), Vienna State Opera Orch, Vienna State Opera Chorus *(rec Musikverein, Vienna, Austria, May 1955)* Vanguard Classics 2-▲ SVC 34/35 [AAD]

Meyerbeer, G.:L'Africaine (sels), w. F. Prohaska (cnd), Vienna State Opera Orch—Figlia de Rè *(rec Musikverein, Vienna, Austria, May 1995)* Vanguard Classics ▲ OVC 8054 [ADD]

Mozart, W.A.:Così fan tutte, w. L. della Casa (sop), E. Loose (sop), C. Ludwig (mez), A. Dermota (ten), E. Kunz (bar) London 2-▲ 417185-2 [ADD]

Mozart, W.A.:Così fan tutte (sels), w. Elisabeth Schwarzkopf (sop), Irmgard Seefried (sop), Christa Ludwig (mez), Anton Dermota (ten), Erich Kunz (bar), K. Böhm (cnd), Vienna PO—Sento, o Dio; Sorella, cosa dici?—Prenderò quel brunettino Orfeo d'or ("Festspiel Dokumente" series) ▲ 394201

Mozart, W.A.:Don Giovanni (sels), w. Hilde Konetzni (sop), Emmy Loose (sop), Irmgard Seefried (sop), Anton Dermota (ten), Erich Kunz (bar), Herbert Alsen (bass), Böhm, Moralt (cnd), Vienna PO *(rec 1944)* Preiser ▲ PRE 90249 [ADD]

Mozart, W.A.:Entführung (sels), w. Hilde Konetzni (sop), Emmy Loose (sop), Irmgard Seefried (sop), Anton Dermota (ten), Erich Kunz (bar), Herbert Alsen (bass), Böhm, Moralt (cnd), Vienna PO *(rec 1944)* Preiser ▲ PRE 90249 [ADD]

Mozart, W.A.:Nozze di Figaro, w. Elisabeth Schwarzkopf (sop—Countess), Irmgard Seefried (sop—Susanna), Hilde Güden (mez—Cherubino), Paul Schöffler (bar—Almaviva), Erich Kunz (bass—Figaro), W. Furtwängler (cnd), Vienna PO, Vienna State Opera Chorus *(rec Salzburg Festival, Aug 8, 1953)* EMI Classics 3-▲ CDHC 66080

Mozart, W.A.:Nozze di Figaro (sels), w. Maria Reining (sop—Countess), Margherita Perras (sop—Susanna), Alfred Jerger (b-bar—Count), Paul Schöffler (b-bar—Figaro), W. Loibner (cnd), Vienna State Opera Orch *(rec May 24, 1938)* Koch Schwann 2-▲ SCH 314632 [ADD]

Mozart, W.A.:Zauberflöte, w. Wilma Lipp (sop), Irmgard Seefried (sop), Peter Klein (ten), Walther Ludwig (ten), Karl Schmitt-Walter (bar), Josef Greindl (bass), W. Furtwängler (cnd), Vienna PO, Vienna State Opera Chorus *(rec 1949)* Music & Arts 3-▲ CD 882 [AAD]

Mozart, W.A.:Zauberflöte (sels), w. Hilde Konetzni (sop), Emmy Loose (sop), Irmgard Seefried (sop), Anton Dermota (ten), Erich Kunz (bar), Herbert Alsen (bass), Böhm, Moralt (cnd), Vienna PO *(rec 1944)* Preiser ▲ PRE 90249 [ADD]

Pfitzner, H.:Palestrina (sels), w. M. Lorenz (ten), R. Kempe (cnd), Vienna PO—solo tenor aria & one duet from Act I *(rec live, Salzburg, 8/1/55)* Myto 3-▲ 3 MCD 92259 [ADD]

Strauss, R.:Ariadne auf Naxos, w. L. Rysanek (sop), J. Scovotti (sop), T. Troyanos (mez), J. King (ten), K. Böhm (cnd), Vienna State Opera Orch, Vienna State Opera Chorus *(rec 1967)* Melodram 2-▲ MLO 270105 [ADD]

Strauss, R.:Ariadne auf Naxos, w. L. Della Casa (sop), H. Güden (sop), I. Seefried (sop), R. Schock (ten), K. Böhm (cnd), Vienna PO *(rec Salzburg Festival, 1954)* Deutsche Grammophon 2-▲ 445332-2 (m) [ADD]

Strauss, R.:Ariadne auf Naxos, w. M. Reining (sop), I. Seefried (sop), A. Noni (sop), M. Lorenz (ten), J. Witt (ten), E. Kunz (bar), K. Böhm (cnd), Vienna State Opera Orch *(rec Strauss' 80th Birthday Festival, June 11, 1944)* Preiser 2-▲ PRE 90217 [ADD]

Strauss, R.:Ariadne auf Naxos (sels), w. Alda Noni (sop—Zerbinetta), Maria Reining (sop—Ariadne), Irmgard Seefried (sop—Composer), Max Lorenz (ten—Bacchus), Paul Schöffler (b-bar—Musiklehrer), K. Böhm (cnd), Vienna State Opera Orch *(rec Vienna, June 11, 1944)* Koch Schwann 2-▲ SCH 314732 [ADD]

Strauss, R.:Daphne, w. H. Gueden (sop), F. Wunderlich (ten), J. King (ten), K. Böhm (cnd), Vienna SO, Vienna State Opera Chorus *(rec live 1963)* Deutsche Grammophon 2-▲ 445322-2

Strauss, R.:Die Liebe der Danae, w. A. Kupper (sop), J. Traxel (ten), L. Szemere (ten), C. Krauss (cnd), Vienna PO, Vienna State Opera Chorus [G] *(rec live, Salzburg, 8/14/52)* Melodram 3-▲ MEL 37061 (m) [AAD]

Strauss, R.:Salome (sels), w. E. Schulz (sop—Salome), A. Dermota (ten—Narraboth), J. Witt (ten—Herodes), H. Hotter (bar—Jochanaan), P. Schöffler (b-bar—Jochanaan), R. Strauss (cnd), Vienna State Opera Orch, Vienna State Opera Chorus *(rec Feb. 15 & May 6, 1942)* Koch Schwann 2-▲ SCH 314532 [ADD]

Verdi, G.:Arias, w. F. Prohaska (cnd), Vienna State Opera Orch—M'ardon le tempia! [from Simon Boccanegra]; O tu Palermo [from I Vespri Siciliani] *(rec Musikverein, Vienna, Austria, May 1995)* Vanguard Classics ▲ OVC 8054 [ADD]

Verdi, G.:Otello, w. Hilde Konetzni (sop), Elena Nikolaidi (cta), Torsten Ralf (ten), K. Böhm (cnd), Vienna State Opera Orch, Vienna State Opera Chorus *(rec live, Aug. 1944)* Preiser 2-▲ PRE 90230 [ADD]

Verdi, G.:Otello, w. Carla Martinis (sop—Desdemona), Sieglinde Wagner (mez—Emilia), Anton Dermota (ten—Cassio), Paul Schöffler (ten—Iago), Ramon Vinay (ten—Otello), Josef Greindl (bass—Lodovico), W. Furtwängler (cnd), Vienna PO, Vienna State Opera Chorus *(rec live, Salzburg Festival, Aug 7, 1951)* EMI Classics ▲ CDMB 65751

Wagner, R.:Arias & Scenes, w. F. Prohaska (cnd), Vienna State Opera Orch—Wotan's Farewell & Magic Fire Music [from Die Walküre]; Hans Sachs' Fliedermonolog [from die Meistersinger]; Amfortas's Monologue [from Parsifal] *(rec Musikverein, Vienna, Austria, May 1995)* Vanguard Classics ▲ OVC 8054 [ADD]

Wagner, R.:Götterdämmerung (sels), w. Set Svanholm (ten—Siegfried), Paul Schöffler (b-bar—Gunther), Herbert Alsen (bass—Hagen), H. Knappertsbusch (cnd), Vienna State Opera Orch *(rec Vienna, June 27, 1941)* Koch Schwann ▲ SCH 314692 [ADD]

Wagner, R.:Götterdämmerung (sels), w. M. Lorenz (ten—Siegfried), P. Schöffler (b-bar—Gunther), J. von Manowarda (bass—Hagen), L. Reichwein (cnd), Vienna State Opera Orch, Vienna State Opera Chorus *(rec Sept. 10, 1942)* Koch Schwann 2-▲ SCH 314562 [ADD]

Wagner, R.:Die Meistersinger von Nürnberg, w. I. Seefried (sop), H. Beirer (ten), F. Reiner (cnd), Vienna PO, Vienna State Opera Chorus *(rec live, Vienna, 1955)* Melodram 4-▲ MEL 47083

Wagner, R.:Die Meistersinger von Nürnberg, w. H. Scheppan (sop), L. Suthaus (ten), E. Kunz (bar), H. Abendroth (cnd), Bayreuth Festival Orch, Bayreuth Festival Chorus *(rec 1943)* Preiser ▲ PRE 90174 [AAD]

Wagner, R.:Die Meistersinger von Nürnberg (sels), w. Maria Reining (sop—Eva), Set Svanholm (ten—Walther), Paul Schöffler (b-bar—Hans Sachs), K. Böhm (cnd), Vienna State Opera Orch *(rec Vienna, Jan. 31, 1943)* Koch Schwann ▲ SCH 314692 [ADD]

Wagner, R.:Parsifal, w. Anny Konetzni (sop—Kundry), Günther Treptow (ten—Parsifal), Paul Schöffler (bar—Amfortas), Hans Braun (bass—Titurel), Adolf Vogel (bass—Klingsor), Ludwig Weber (bass—Gurnemanz), R. Moralt (cnd), Vienna SO, Vienna State Opera Chorus *(rec Vienna)* Myto 4-▲ 4 MCD 954.136

Wagner, R.:Parsifal (sels), w. H. Braun (sop—Kundry), M. Lorenz (ten—Parsifal), P. Schöffler (b-bar—Amfortas), Reichwein, Knappertsbusch (cnd), Vienna State Opera Orch, Vienna State Opera Chorus *(rec Apr. 4, 1942 & Nov. 10, 1)* Koch Schwann 2-▲ SCH 314562 [ADD]

Wagner, R.:Rienzi, der Letzte der Tribunen, w. C. Ludwig (mez), S. Svanholm (ten), J. Krips (cnd), *(orch unknown)* [G] *(rec live, Vienna, 1960)* Melodram 2-▲ MEL 27023

Wagner, R.:Der Ring des Nibelungen (sels), w. Adele Kern (sop), Anny Konetzni (sop), Hilde Konetzni (sop), Elisabeth Schumann (sop), Enid Szantho (cta), Josef Kalenberg (ten), Max Lorenz (ten), Set Svanholm (ten), Erich Zimmermann (ten), Hans Hotter (bar), Jaro Prohaska (bar), Emil Schipper (bar), Ludwig Hoffmann (bass), H. Knappertsbusch (cnd), Vienna State Opera Orch *(rec Vienna, 1937–1943)* Koch Schwann 2-▲ SCH 314742 [ADD]

Wagner, R.:Tristan und Isolde, w. Helena Braun (sop—Isolde), Margarete Klose (mez—Brangäne), Günther Treptow (ten—Tristan), Paul Kuen (ten—Ein Hirte), Albrecht Peter (bar—Melot), Fritz Richard Bender (bar—Ein Steuermann), Ferdinand Frantz (b-bar—König Marke), Paul Schöffler (b-bar—Kurwenal), H. Knappertsbusch (cnd), Bavarian State Opera Orch, Bavarian State Opera Chorus *(rec live, Prinzregententheater, July 23, 1950)* Orfeo 3-▲ 355

Schöffler, Paul (b–bar) (cont.)
Wagner, R.:Tristan und Isolde, w. K. Flagstad (sop), L. Melchior (ten), H. Janssen (bar), T. Beecham (cnd), Royal Opera House Orch, Royal Opera House Chorus Covent Garden *(rec live, Covent Garden, 6/18 & 22/37)* Melodram 3–▲ MEL 37029 (m) [AAD]
Wagner, R.:Tristan und Isolde (sels), w. Anny Konetzni (sop—Isolde), Margarete Klose (cta—Brangäne), Max Lorenz (ten—Tristan), Paul Schöffler (b-bar—Kurwenal), Herbert Alsen (bass—King Marke), W. Furtwängler (cnd), Vienna State Opera Orch, Vienna State Opera Chorus—extended excerpts from Acts 1 & 2; Act 3 (comp.) *(rec Vienna, Jan. 2, 1943 & Dec. 25, 1)* Koch Schwann 2–▲ SCH 314612 [ADD]

Scholl, Andreas (alt)
Bach, J.S.:Cant 49, w. Barbara Schlick (sop), Christophe Prégardien (ten), Gotthold Schwarz (bass), C. Coin (cnd), Limoges Baroque Ensemble, Leipzig Concerto Vocale Astrée ▲ E 8530
Bach, J.S.:Cant 85, w. Barbara Schlick (sop), Christoph Prégardien (ten), Gotthold Schwarz (bass), Christophe Coin (piccolo vc/cnd), Leipzig Vocal Concerto, Limoges Baroque Ensemble Astrée ▲ E 8544
Bach, J.S.:Cant 115, w. Barbara Schlick (sop), Christophe Prégardien (ten), Gotthold Schwarz (bass), C. Coin (cnd), Limoges Baroque Ensemble, Leipzig Concerto Vocale Astrée ▲ E 8530
Bach, J.S.:Cant 175, w. Barbara Schlick (sop), Christoph Prégardien (ten), Gotthold Schwarz (bass), Christophe Coin (piccolo vc/cnd), Leipzig Vocal Concerto, Limoges Baroque Ensemble Astrée ▲ E 8544
Bach, J.S.:Cant 180, w. Barbara Schlick (sop), Christophe Prégardien (ten), Gotthold Schwarz (bass), C. Coin (cnd), Limoges Baroque Ensemble, Leipzig Concerto Vocale Astrée ▲ E 8530
Bach, J.S.:Cant 183, w. Barbara Schlick (sop), Christoph Prégardien (ten), Gotthold Schwarz (bass), Christophe Coin (piccolo vc/cnd), Leipzig Vocal Concerto, Limoges Baroque Ensemble Astrée ▲ E 8544
Bach, J.S.:Cant 199, w. Barbara Schlick (sop), Christoph Prégardien (ten), Gotthold Schwarz (bass), Christophe Coin (piccolo vc/cnd), Leipzig Vocal Concerto, Limoges Baroque Ensemble Astrée ▲ E 8544
Handel, G.F.:Cants, w. Maria Cristina Kiehr (sop), A. de Marchi (cnd), Armonico Theater Ensemble—Il duello amoroso; Vendendo amor; La partenza; Nel dolce tempo; Sono liete, fortunate Accord ▲ ACD 204212 [DDD]
Handel, G.F.:Messiah, w. Sandrine Piau (sop), Barbara Schlick (sop), Mark Padmore (ten), Nathan Berg (bass), W. Christie (cnd), Les Arts Florissants [1742 Dublin version] Harmonia Mundi France 2–▲ HMC 901498/99
Monteverdi, C.:Vespro della Beata Vergine, w. Barbara Borden (sop), Maria Cristina Kiehr (sop), John Bowen (ten), Andrew Murgatroyd (ten), Victor Torres (bar), Antonio Abete (bass), Jelle Draijer (bass), René Jacobs (cnd), Concerto Vocale, Netherlands Chamber Choir Harmonia Mundi 2–▲ 901566.67

Scholl, Andreas (ct)
Bach, J.S.:Cant 6, w. Barbara Schlick (sop), Christoph Prégardien (ten), Gotthold Schwarz (bass), C. Coin (cnd), Limoges Baroque Ensemble, Accentus Chamber Choir Astrée ▲ E 8555
Bach, J.S.:Cant 41, w. Barbara Schlick (sop), Christoph Prégardien (ten), Gotthold Schwarz (bass), C. Coin (cnd), Limoges Baroque Ensemble, Accentus Chamber Choir Astrée ▲ E 8555
Bach, J.S.:Cant 68, w. Barbara Schlick (sop), Christoph Prégardien (ten), Gotthold Schwarz (bass), C. Coin (cnd), Limoges Baroque Ensemble, Accentus Chamber Choir Astrée ▲ E 8555
Bach, J.S.:Cant 201, w. Maria Cristina Kiehr (sop), James Taylor (ten), Kurt Azeberger (ten), Roman Trekel (bar), Peter Lika (bass), R. Jacobs (cnd), Berlin Academy for Early Music, Berlin Chamber Chorus Harmonia Mundi France 2–▲ HMC 901544.45
Bach, J.S.:Cant 213, w. Efrat Ben-Nun (sop), James Taylor (ten), Klaus Häger (bass), R. Jacobs (cnd), Berlin Academy for Early Music, Berlin Chamber Chorus Harmonia Mundi France 2–▲ HMC 901544.45
Caldara, A.:Maddalena ai Piedi di Cristo, w. Maria Cristina Kiehr (sop), Rosa Dominguez (sop), Bernarda Fink (cta), Gerd Türk (ten), Ulrich Messthaler (bass), R. Jacobs (cnd), Schola Cantorum Basiliensis Instrumental Ensemble Harmonia Mundi France 2–▲ HMC 905221.22
Deutsche Barocklieder, w. Alix Verzier (vc), Markus Markl (hpd), Karl Ernst Schroder (lt), Friederike Heumann (va), Juan Manuel Quintana (va), Stephanie Pfister (vn), Pable Valetti (vn) Harmonia Mundi France ▲ HMC 901505
English Folksongs & Lute Songs, w. Andreas Martin (lt) Harmonia Mundi France ▲ HMC 901603

Schollum, Benno (bar)
Beethoven, L. van:Syms (comp), w. Jean Glennon (sop), Dalia Schaechter (cta), Algridas Janutas (ten), Y. Menuhin (cnd), Sinfonia Varsovia, Kuanas State Choir Lithuania IMP ("IMG" series) 5–▲ IMP 6300025
Schubert, Franz:Winterreise, w. Graham Johnson (pno) IMG/Pickwick ▲ PIC IMG 1616

Scholze, Rainer (bass)
Mozart, W.A.:Don Giovanni, w. J. Varady (sop), A. Augér (sop), E. Mathis (sop), T. Moser (ten), A. Titus (bar), R. Panerai (bar), J.-H. Rootering (bass), R. Kubelik (cnd), Bavarian RSO, Bavarian Radio Chorus [I] Eurodisc 3–▲ 7798–2 [DDD]
Zemlinsky, A. von:Kleider machen Leute, w. E. Mathis (sop), H. Winkler (ten), V. Vogel (ten), C. Otelli (bar), H. Franzen (bass), W. Slabbert (sgr), R. Weikert (cnd), Zurich Opera Orch, Zurich Opera House Chorus [G] *(rec live, Zurich Opera House, 6/29/90)* Koch Schwann 2–▲ CD 314 069 [DDD]

Schon, Kenneth (sgr)
Strauss (II), Joh.:Eine Nacht in Venedig, w. Nola Fairbanks (sgr—Ciboletta), Thomas Tibbett Hayward (sgr—Mario), Laurel Hurley (sgr—Nina), David Kurlan (sgr—Senator Bartoldi), Guen Omeron (sgr—Barbara), Jack Russell (sgr—Duke of Palobino), Kenneth Schon (sgr—Filippo Del Aqua), Norwood Smith (sgr—Caramello), Enzo Stuarti (sgr—Pappacoda) *(rec Belock Recording Studio, Bayside, NY)* Everest ▲ EVC 9036 [AAD]

Schöne, Lotte (sop)
Lotte Schöne & Richard Tauber In Operetta Nimbus ("Prima Voce" series) ▲ NI 7833 [ADD]
The Art of Lotta Sch(uml)one *(rec 1924–31)* Preiser 2–▲ PRE CD 89224

Schöne, Wolfgang (bar)
Bach, J.S.:Cant 77, w. H. Donath (sop), J. Hamari (mez), A. Kraus (ten), H. Rilling (cnd), Stuttgart Bach Collegium, Gächinger Kantorei Hänssler Classic ▲ 98.809 [AAD]
Dittersdorf, K.D. von:Doctor und Apotheker, w. Hildegard Uhrmacher (sop—Leonore), Donna Woodward (sop—Rosalia), Waltraud Meier (mez—Claudia), Martin Finke (ten—Sichel), Frieder Lang (ten—Gotthold), Alois Perl (ten—Gallus), Gerhard Unger (ten—Sturmwald), Thomas Pfeiffer (bar—Police Commisioner), Wolfgang Schöne (bar—Krautmann), Harald Stamm (bass—Stössel), J. Lockhart (cnd), Rhine State PO Bayer 2–▲ BR 100 238/39 [DDD]

Schöne, Wolfgang (bass)
Bach, J.S.:Cant 5, w. A. Augér (sop), C. Watkinson (alt), A. Baldin (ten), H. Rilling (cnd), Stuttgart Bach Collegium, Gächinger Kantorei [G] *(rec Feb & Oct 1979)* Hänssler Classic ▲ 98.816 [AAD]
Bach, J.S.:Cant 7, w. H. Watts (cta), A. Kraus (ten), H. Rilling (cnd), Stuttgart Bach Collegium, Gächinger Kantorei Hänssler Classic ▲ 98.802 [AAD]
Bach, J.S.:Cant 18, w. E. Csapò (sop), G. Schnaut (mez), A. Kraus (ten), H. Rilling (cnd), Bach Ensemble [G] *(rec 1975)* Hänssler Classic ▲ 98.877 [AAD]
Bach, J.S.:Cant 20, w. V. Gohl (mez), M. Kessler (mez), T. Altmeyer (ten), A. Kraus (ten), H. Rilling (cnd), Stuttgart Bach Collegium, Frankfurt Kantorei Hänssler Classic ▲ 98.801 [AAD]
Bach, J.S.:Cant 24, w. A. Augér (sop), H. Watts (cta), K. Pugh (cta), A. Kraus (ten), W. Heldwein (bass), H. Rilling (cnd), Stuttgart Bach Collegium, Gächinger Kantorei Hänssler Classic ▲ 98.803 [AAD]
Bach, J.S.:Cant 34, w. H. Watts (cta), A. Kraus (ten), Stuttgart Bach Collegium, Gächinger Kantorei Hänssler Classic ▲ 98.887 [AAD]
Bach, J.S.:Cant 44, w. A. Augér (sop), H. Watts (cta), A. Baldin (ten), H. Rilling (cnd), Stuttgart Bach Collegium, Gächinger Kantorei [G] *(rec 1979)* Hänssler Classic ▲ 98.886 [AAD]
Bach, J.S.:Cant 46, w. H. Watts (cta), A. Kraus (ten), H. Rilling (cnd), Stuttgart Bach Collegium, Gächinger Kantorei Hänssler Classic ▲ 98.808 [AAD]
Bach, J.S.:Cant 58, w. I. Reichelt (sop), H. Rilling (cnd), Stuttgart Bach Collegium, Gächinger Kantorei [G] Hänssler Classic ▲ 98.871 [AAD]
Bach, J.S.:Cant 63, w. A. Augér (sop), J. Hamari (mez), H. Laurich (cta), A. Kraus (ten), W. Heldwein (bass), H. Rilling (cnd), Stuttgart Bach Collegium, Gächinger Kantorei [G] *(rec Feb 1971 & Feb 1981)* Hänssler Classic ▲ 98.823 [AAD]

Schöne, Wolfgang (bass) (cont.)
Bach, J.S.:Cant 66, w. G. Schreckenbach (cta), A. Kraus (ten), P. Huttenlocher (bar), H. Rilling (cnd), Stuttgart Bach Collegium, Gächinger Kantorei [G] *(rec 1981)* Hänssler Classic ▲ 98.880 [AAD]
Bach, J.S.:Cant 69, w. H. Donath (sop), J. Hamari (b-bar), A. Kraus (ten), H. Rilling (cnd), Bach Ensemble *(rec Mar–Apr 1973)* Hänssler Classic ▲ 98.829 [AAD]
Bach, J.S.:Cant 72, w. A. Augér (sop), H. Laurich (cta), H. Rilling (cnd), Bach Ensemble [G] *(rec 1983)* Hänssler Classic ▲ 98.875 [AAD]
Bach, J.S.:Cant 88, w. I. Reichelt (sop), V. Gohl (mez), A. Kraus (ten), H. Rilling (cnd), Stuttgart Bach Collegium, Remembrance Florid Church Chorus Hänssler Classic ▲ 98.804 [AAD]
Bach, J.S.:Cant 91, w. H. Donath (sop), H. Watts (cta), A. Kraus (ten), H. Rilling (cnd), Stuttgart Bach Collegium, Württemberg CO, Gächinger Kantorei, Frankfurt Choir [G] *(rec Feb 1972)* Hänssler Classic ▲ 98.822 [AAD]
Bach, J.S.:Cant 94, w. H. Donath (sop), E. Paaske (cta), A. Baldin (ten), H.-F. Kunz (bass), H. Rilling (cnd), Stuttgart Bach Collegium, Württemberg CO, Gächinger Kantorei Hänssler Classic ▲ 98.808 [AAD]
Bach, J.S.:Cant 102, w. E. Randová (mez), K. Equiluz (ten), H. Rilling (cnd), Stuttgart Bach Collegium, Gächinger Kantorei Hänssler Classic ▲ 98.809 [AAD]
Bach, J.S.:Cant 106, "Actus tragicus", w. E. Csapò (sop), H. Schwarz (cta), A. Kraus (ten), H. Rilling (cnd), Bach Ensemble *(rec Jan 1975)* Hänssler Classic ▲ 98.830 [AAD]
Bach, J.S.:Cant 110, w. K. Graf (sop), H. Gardow (sop), A. Baldin (ten), H. Rilling (cnd), Stuttgart Bach Collegium, Gächinger Kantorei [G] *(rec Jan–Feb 1974)* Hänssler Classic ▲ 98.824 [AAD]
Bach, J.S.:Cant 114, w. G. Schnaut (mez), J. Hamari (cta), K. Equiluz (ten), H. Rilling (cnd), Stuttgart Bach Collegium, Frankfurt Kantorei, Gächinger Kantorei [G] *(rec 1974)* Hänssler Classic ▲ 98.814 [AAD]
Bach, J.S.:Cant 115, w. A. Augér (sop), H. Watts (cta), L.-M. Harder (ten), H. Rilling (cnd), Stuttgart Bach Collegium, Gächinger Kantorei [G] *(rec 1980)* Hänssler Classic ▲ 98.819 [AAD]
Bach, J.S.:Cant 119, w. A. Augér (sop), A. Murray (mez), A. Kraus (ten), H. Rilling (cnd), Bach Ensemble *(rec Sept & Dec 1977 & Jan 197)* Hänssler Classic ▲ 98.828 [AAD]
Bach, J.S.:Cant 120, w. H. Donath (sop), H. Laurich (cta), A. Kraus (ten), H. Rilling (cnd), Bach Ensemble *(rec Mar–Apr 1973)* Hänssler Classic ▲ 98.829 [AAD]
Bach, J.S.:Cant 121, w. A. Augér (sop), D. Soffel (cta), A. Kraus (ten), H. Rilling (cnd), Stuttgart Bach Collegium, Gächinger Kantorei [G] *(rec Feb & Apr 1980)* Hänssler Classic ▲ 98.824 [AAD]
Bach, J.S.:Cant 125, w. M. Höffgen (mez), K. Equiluz (ten), H. Rilling (cnd), Bach Ensemble [G] *(rec 1973)* Hänssler Classic ▲ 98.876 [AAD]
Bach, J.S.:Cant 126, w. H. Watts (cta), A. Kraus (ten), H. Rilling (cnd), Stuttgart Bach Collegium, Gächinger Kantorei [G] *(rec 1980)* Hänssler Classic ▲ 98.878 [AAD]
Bach, J.S.:Cant 127, w. A. Augér (sop), L.-M. Harder (ten), H. Rilling (cnd), Stuttgart Bach Collegium, Gächinger Kantorei [G] *(rec 1980)* Hänssler Classic ▲ 98.878 [AAD]
Bach, J.S.:Cant 128, w. G. Schreckenbach (cta), A. Baldin (ten), H. Rilling (cnd), Stuttgart Bach Collegium, Gächinger Kantorei [G] *(rec 1980–81)* Hänssler Classic ▲ 98.886 [AAD]
Bach, J.S.:Cant 132, w. A. Augér (sop), H. Watts (cta), K. Equiluz (ten), H. Rilling (cnd), Stuttgart Bach Collegium, Gächinger Kantorei [G] *(rec Sept 1976 & Jan & Apr 197)* Hänssler Classic ▲ 98.822 [AAD]
Bach, J.S.:Cant 143, w. E. Csapò (sop), A. Kraus (ten), H. Rilling (cnd), Stuttgart Bach Collegium [G] Hänssler Classic ▲ 98.870 [AAD]
Bach, J.S.:Cant 152, w. A. Augér (sop), H. Rilling (hpd), et al. [G] *(rec Mar–Apr 1976)* Hänssler Classic ▲ 98.826 [AAD]
Bach, J.S.:Cant 156, w. H. Laurich (cta), K. Equiluz (ten), H. Rilling (cnd), Bach Ensemble [G] *(rec 1973)* Hänssler Classic ▲ 98.875 [AAD]
Bach, J.S.:Cant 162, w. A. Augér (sop), A. Rogers (mez), K. Equiluz (ten), H. Rilling (cnd), Stuttgart Bach Collegium, Frankfurt Kantorei [G] *(rec Dec 1975 & Mar 1976)* Hänssler Classic ▲ 98.816 [AAD]
Bach, J.S.:Cant 178, w. G. Schreckenbach (cta), A. Baldin (ten), K. Equiluz (ten), H. Rilling (cnd), Stuttgart Bach Collegium, Gächinger Kantorei Hänssler Classic ▲ 98.806 [AAD]
Bach, J.S.:Cant 179, w. A. Augér (sop), K. Equiluz (ten), H. Rilling (cnd), Stuttgart Bach Collegium, Gächinger Kantorei Hänssler Classic ▲ 98.808 [AAD]
Bach, J.S.:Cant 187, w. M. Friesenhausen (sop), H. Laurich (mez), H. Rilling (cnd), Stuttgart Bach Collegium, Gächinger Kantorei Hänssler Classic ▲ 98.806 [AAD]
Bach, J.S.:Christmas Oratorio, w. A. Augér (sop), J. Hamari (cta), P. Schreier (ten), H. Rilling (cnd), Stuttgart Bach Collegium, Gächinger Kantorei [G] *(rec 1984)* Hänssler Classic 5–▲ 98.976
Bach, J.S.:Christmas Oratorio, w. A. Augér (sop), J. Hamari (cta), P. Schreier (ten), H. Rilling (cnd), Stuttgart Bach Collegium Stuttgart Classic 3–▲ 98.854 [DDD]
Bach, J.S.:Magnificat, BWV 243, w. A. Augér (sop), A. Murray (mez), H. Watts (cta), A. Kraus (ten), P. Huttenlocher (bar), H. Rilling (cnd), Stuttgart Bach Collegium, Gächinger Kantorei *(rec 1979)* Sony Classical ("Essential Classics" series) ▲ SBK 48280 [ADD] ■ SBT 48280
Mozart, W.A.:Zaide, w. J. Blegen (sop), I. Hollweg (sop), T. Moser (ten), R. Holl (bass), L. Hager (cnd), Salzburg Mozarteum Orch [G] Orfeo 2–▲ 055832 [DDD]

Schoneweib, Willy (bass)
Verdi, G.:Un ballo in maschera, w. Martha Mödl (sop—Ulrica), Walburga Wegner (sop—Amelia), Anny Schlemm (mez—Oscar), Lorenz Fehenberger (ten—Ricardo), Dietrich Fischer-Dieskau (bar—Renato), Wilhelm Schirp (bass—Samuel), Willy Schoneweib (bass—Tom), Gunther Wilhelms (bass—Silvan), Fritz Augustin (sgr—Ein Richter), Friedrich Himmelmann (sgr—Ein Diener Amelia), F. Busch (cnd), Cologne RSO, Bernhard Alois Zimmermann (cnd), Cologne Radio Chorus Calig 2–▲ 50946/47 (m) [ADD]

Schöpflin, Hans-Jürgen (ten)
Weber, C.M. von:Peter Schmoll und seine Nachbarn, w. A. Pfeffer (sop—Minnette), J. Schmidt (ten—Martin Schmoll), S. Basa (ten—Karl Pirkner), H.-J. Schöpflin (ten—Niklas), R. Busching (bar—Peter Schmoll), H.J. Porcher (bass—Hans Bast), G. Markson (cnd), Hagen PO [G] *(rec Feb. 1–5, 1993)* Marco Polo 2–▲ 8.223592/93 [DDD]

Schopper, Michael (bass)
Bach, J.S.:Cant 56, w. G. Leonhardt (cnd), Leonhardt Consort, Hanover Boys' Choir [G] Teldec 2–▲ 2292–42422–2 [AAD]
Cornelius, P.:Der Cid, w. Gertrud Ottenthal (sop), Ronnie Johansen (sgr), Robert Schunk (ten), Albert Dohmen (bar), Endrik Wottrich (sgr), G. Kuhn (cnd), Berlin RSO, Berlin Radio Chorus Koch Schwann 2–▲ SCH 315222
Hiller, W.:Schulamit, w. Regina Klepper (sop), Edeltraud Knabel (alt), Elisabeth Woska (nar), Waltraut Mastrogiovanni-Kraxner (shofar), H.R. Zöbeley (cnd), Munich Residenz Orch, Munich Percussion Ensemble, Calw Aurelius Boys' Choir Soloists, Munich Motet Choir Wergo ▲ WER 6280–2
Holzbauer, I.:Günther von Schwarzburg, w. Clara McFadden (sop), Christoph Prégardien (ten), Robert Wörle (ten), M. Schneider (cnd), La Stagione CPO 3–▲ CPO 999265
Monteverdi, C.:Incoronazione, w. D. Borst (sop), Lootens (sop), G. Laurens (mez), J. Larmore (mez), A. Köhler (alt), R. Jacobs (cnd), Concerto Vocale [direction & new musical realization by René Jacobs] [I] Harmonia Mundi France 3–▲ HMC 901330/32
Purcell, H.:The Fairy Queen, w. C. Bott (sop), J. Thomas (ten), T. Koopman (cnd), Amsterdam Baroque Orch, Amsterdam Baroque Choir Erato 2–▲ 98507–2
Telemann, G.P.:Hamburger Admiralitätsmusik, w. Mieke van der Sluis (sop—Hammonia), Graham Pushee (ten—Themis), Rufus Müller (ten—Mercurius), Klaus Mertens (bass—Neptunius), David Thomas (bass—Mars), Michael Schopper (bass—Albis), W. Helbich (cnd), Bremen Baroque Orch, Alsfeld Vocal Ensemble *(rec Nov 9, 1995)* CPO 2–▲ CPO 999373–2 [DDD]

Schörg (sgr)
Jessel, L.:Schwarzwaldmädel (sels), w. E. Lind (sop), F. Fehringer (ten), B. Kusche (bar), Hofmann (sgr), Schubart (sgr), Marszalek (cnd), Cologne RSO, Cologne Radio Chorus [G] Acanta ▲ CD 42552 [DDD]

Schorr, Friedrich (b–bar)
Bach, J.S.:Mass in b, BWV 232, w. E. Schumann (sop), M. Balfour (cta), W. Widdop (ten), A. Coates (cnd), London SO, London Phil Chorus [L] *(rec Kingsway Hall, London Mar–Apr 1929)* Pearl 2–▲ PEAS 9900 (m) [AAD]
Friedrich Schorr *(rec. 1921–1922 Grammophon)* Preiser ("Lebendige Vergangenheit" series) ▲ PRE 89052 (m) [AAD]
Friedrich Schorr Pearl ▲ PEA 9379 (m) [AAD]

Schorr, Friedrich (b–bar) (cont.)

The Legendary Singers at Lindenoper Berlin (1927–1945)—, w. Gitta Alpar (sop), Erna Berger (sop), Tiana Lemnitz (sop), Maria Müller (sop), Margarete Klose (cta), Peter Anders (ten), Max Lorenz (ten), Walter Ludwig (ten), Lauritz Melchior (ten), Rudolf Schock (ten), Franz Völker (ten), et. al. *(rec 1927; 1937; 1941–45)* Minerva ▲ MN A21 [ADD]

Wagner, R.:Arias & Scenes, w. K. Flagstad (sop), E. Rethberg (sop), B. Nilsson (sop), E. Schumann (sop), F. Leider (sop), L. Melchior (ten), G. Thill (ten), A. Pertile (ten), G. Hüsch (bar), H. Hotter (b–bar), A. Kipnis (bass), *(orch unknown)* EMI Classics ("Studio" series) 4–▲ CDMC 64008

Wagner, R.:Arias & Scenes Preiser ("Lebendige Vergangenheit" series) ▲ 89052 (m) [AAD]

Wagner, R.:Arias & Scenes, w. Emmy Destinn (sop), Lilly Hafgren (sop), Frida Leider (sop), Emmi Leisner (cta), Ernst Kraus (ten), Lauritz Melchoir (ten), Leopold Demuth (bar), Michael Bohynen (bass), Paul Knupfer (bass), Richard Mayr (bass), Heinrich Hensel (sgr), Walter Soomer (sgr) Iron Needle ▲ 1307 (m)

Wagner, R.:Der fliegende Holländer (sels), w. L. Blech (cnd), Berlin State Opera Orch—Die Frist ist um; Wie oft in Meeres *(rec 1929 HMV)* Pearl ▲ PEA 9944 (m) [AAD]

Wagner, R.:Der fliegende Holländer (sels), w. Göta Ljungberg (sop), Elisabeth Rethberg (sop), Elisabeth Schumann (sop), Rudolf Laubenthal (ten), Lauritz Melchior (ten), *(cnd & orch unknown) (rec 1927–31)* Preiser 2–▲ PRE 89214 [AAD]

Wagner, R.:Götterdämmerung (sels), w. Göta Ljungberg (sop), Elisabeth Rethberg (sop), Elisabeth Schumann (sop), Rudolf Laubenthal (ten), Lauritz Melchior (ten), *(cnd & orch unknown) (rec 1927–31)* Preiser 2–▲ PRE 89214 [AAD]

Wagner, R.:Die Meistersinger von Nürnberg (sels), w. Göta Ljungberg (sop), Elisabeth Rethberg (sop), Elisabeth Schumann (sop), Rudolf Laubenthal (ten), Lauritz Melchior (ten), *(cnd & orch unknown) (rec 1927–31)* Preiser 2–▲ PRE 89214 [AAD]

Wagner, R.:Die Meistersinger von Nürnberg (sels)—all of Schorr's issued electrical studio recordings in the role of Hans Sachs, with the exception of three duplicated sides *(rec 1927–31)* Pearl ▲ PEA 9944 (m) [AAD]

Wagner, R.:Die Meistersinger von Nürnberg (sels), w. E. Marherr–Wagner (mez), R. Hutt (ten), K. Jöken (bar), E. List (bass), L. Schützendorf (sgr), L. Blech (cnd), Berlin State Opera Orch, Berlin State Opera Chorus—Act 1:Hilf Gott! Will ich denn Schuster sein?; Das schöne Fest, Johannistag; Act 2:Johannistag! Johannistag!; Hab' ich heut' Singstund'?; Jerum! Jerum!; Act 3:Gleich, Meister! Hier!; Grüss' Gott, mein Evchen...Weilten die Stern' im lieblichen Tanz...O Sachs! Mein Freund!; Sankt Krispin, lobet ihn!; Silentium!...Wach' auf!; Verachtet mir die Meister nicht [G] *(rec Staatsoper unter den Linden, 5/22/28)* Pearl ▲ PEA 9340 (m) [AAD]

Wagner, R.:Das Rheingold (sels), w. Göta Ljungberg (sop), Elisabeth Rethberg (sop), Elisabeth Schumann (sop), Rudolf Laubenthal (ten), Lauritz Melchior (ten), *(cnd & orch unknown) (rec 1927–31)* Preiser 2–▲ PRE 89214 [AAD]

Wagner, R.:Der Ring des Nibelungen (sels), w. Florence Austral (sop), Frieda Leider (sop), Elsie Suddaby (sop), Göta Ljunberg (sop), Walter Widdop (ten), Horst Laubenthal (ten), Lauritz Melchoir (ten), Rudolf Bockelmann (b–bar), Ivar Andresen (bass), Emmanuel List (bass), Collingwood, Blech, Coates, Barbirolli, Heger, Alwin, Muck (cnd), London SO—scenes from Siegriend & Götterdämmerung; 90 Motives from Der Ring [w. Collingwood & LSO] Pearl 7–▲ PEA 9137 [ADD]

Wagner, R.:Tannhäuser (sels), w. Lotte Lehmann (sop—Elisabeth), Josef Kalenberg (ten—Tannhäuser), Richard Mayr (bass—Landgraf), Friedrich Schorr (bass—Wolfram), R. Heger (cnd), Vienna State Opera Orch *(rec Vienna, Sept. 25, 1933)* Koch Schwann 2–▲ SCH 314622 [ADD]

Wagner, R.:Tannhäuser (sels), w. Göta Ljungberg (sop), Elisabeth Rethberg (sop), Elisabeth Schumann (sop), Rudolf Laubenthal (ten), Lauritz Melchior (ten), *(cnd & orch unknown) (rec 1927–31)* Preiser 2–▲ PRE 89214 [AAD]

Wagner, R.:Tannhäuser (sels), w. Lauritz Melchior (ten), Walter Widdop (ten), Edward Halland (bass), A. Coates (cnd), London SO, New SO—Ov; Venusberg Bacchanale; 1st Pilgrims' Chorus; Wolfram's Cavatina; Prelude; Pilgrims' Return; Rome Narration *(rec 1925–30)* Claremont ▲ GSE 78 50 54

Wagner, R.:Die Walküre, w. Helen Traubel (sop), Astrid Varnay (sop), Kerstin Throborg (cta), Lauritz Melchoir (ten), E. Leinsdorf (cnd), *(orch unknown) (rec Dec 6, 1941)* Enterprise ("The Forties" series) 2–▲ ENT 318

Wagner, R.:Die Walküre (sels), w. Maria Jeritza (sop—Brünnhilde), Felice Hüni–Mišek (sop—Sieglinde), Franz Völker (ten—Siegmund), Friedrich Schorr (b–bar—Wotan), C. Krauss (cnd), Vienna State Opera Orch *(rec June 11, 1933)* Koch Schwann 2–▲ SCH 314642 [ADD]

Wagner, R.:Die Walküre (sels), w. Lotte Lehmann (sop—Sieglinde), Maria Jeritza (sop—Brünnhilde), Franz Völker (ten—Siegmund), Friedrich Schorr (bass—Wotan), C. Krauss (cnd), Vienna State Opera Orch *(rec Vienna, Sept. 14, 1933)* Koch Schwann ▲ SCH 314622 [ADD]

Wagner, R.:Die Walküre (sels), w. Göta Ljungberg (sop), Elisabeth Rethberg (sop), Elisabeth Schumann (sop), Rudolf Laubenthal (ten), Lauritz Melchior (ten), *(orch unknown) (rec 1927–31)* Preiser 2–▲ PRE 89214 [AAD]

Wagner, R.:Die Walküre (sels), w. F. Leider (sop), G. Ljungberg (sop), E. Leisner (cta), L. Blech (cnd), Vienna State Opera Orch—nine selections from Acts 2 & 3 [G] *(rec 1927 [Blech] & 1932 [Barb])* Pearl ▲ PEA 9357 (m) [AAD]

Wagner, R.:Die Walküre (act 2), w. K. Flagstad (sop), L. Lehmann (sop), L. Melchior (ten), F. Reiner (cnd), *(orch unknown)* [G] *(rec 1936)* Legato Classics ▲ LCD 133–1 (m) [AAD]

Weber, C.M. von:Der Freischütz (sels), w. A. Coates (cnd), London New SO—Hermit's Aria *(rec 1930)* GSE Claremont ▲ GSE 78 50 54

Schöter, Gisela (sop)

Humperdinck, E.:Hänsel und Gretel, w. I. Springer (mez), P. Schrier (ten), T. Adam (bar), O. Suitner (cnd), Dresden Staatskapelle, Dresden Kreuz Choir Berlin Classics ("Eterna" series) 2–▲ BER 2007 [ADD]

Schottler, Giorgio (bass)

Rossini, G.:Il barbiere di Siviglia (sels), w. M. Resemba (sop), N. Sabatano (sop), F. de Lucia (ten), F. Novelli (bar), A. di Tommaso (bass), S. Valentino (bass), S. Sassano (cnd), Naples Teatro San Carlo Orch, Naples Teatro San Carlo Chorus [I] *(rec 1918 for Phonotype)* Standing Room Only ▲ SRO 819–1 [ADD]

Schram, A. (sop)

Haydn, M.:Missa Sancti Leopoldi in festo Innocentium, w. R. Zela, O. Messerli (alto), A. von Aarburg (cnd), Capella Concertante, Zurich Boys' Choir [L] *(rec 12/89)* Tudor ▲ 754 [DDD]

Haydn, M.:Vesperae pro festo Sanctorum Innocentium, w. L. Tsimitselis (sop), O. Messerli (alt), A. von Aarburg (cnd), Capella Concertante, Zurich Boys' Choir [L] *(rec 12/89)* Tudor ▲ 754 [DDD]

Schramm, Ernst Gerold (bass)

Herzogenberg, H. von:Die Geburt Christi, w. R. Schudel (sop), A. Eggers (cta), P. Maus (ten), C. Grube (cnd), Oriol Ensemble, *(various choruses)* [G] Hänssler Classic 2–▲ 98.574 [AAD]

Schubert, Franz:Stabat mater, w. G. Zeumer (sop), D. Ellenbeck (ten), R. Bader (cnd), Berlin RSO, Berlin Radio Chorus Koch Schwann ▲ CD 313 055 [ADD]

Schramm, Margit (sop)

Strauss (II), Joh.:Wiener Blut (sels), w. H. Gueden (sop), R. Schock (ten), B. Kusche (bar), R. Stolz (cnd), Vienna SO [G] Eurodisc ▲ 25–8370 [ADD]

Schreckenbach, Gabriele (mez)

Bach, J.S.:Cant 16, w. P. Schreier (ten), P. Huttenlocher (bar), H. Rilling (cnd), Stuttgart Bach Collegium, Gächinger Kantorei [G] Hänssler Classic ▲ 98.871 [AAD]

Bach, J.S.:Cant 28, w. A. Augér (sop), A. Kraus (ten), W. Heldwein (bass), H. Rilling (cnd), Stuttgart Bach Collegium, Gächinger Kantorei [G] *(rec Nov 1981 & Feb 1982)* Hänssler Classic ▲ 98.827 [AAD]

Bach, J.S.:Cant 36, w. A. Augér (sop), P. Schreier (ten), W. Heldwein (bass), H. Rilling (cnd), Stuttgart Bach Collegium, Gächinger Kantorei [G] *(rec Oct 1980, Feb 1981 & Mar)* Hänssler Classic ▲ 98.823 [AAD]

Bach, J.S.:Cant 39, w. A. Augér (sop), F. Gerishen (bar), H. Rilling (cnd), Stuttgart Bach Collegium, Gächinger Kantorei Hänssler Classic ▲ 98.802 [AAD]

Bach, J.S.:Cant 66, w. A. Kraus (ten), P. Huttenlocher (bar), W. Schöne (bass), H. Rilling (cnd), Stuttgart Bach Collegium, Gächinger Kantorei [G] *(rec 1981)* Hänssler Classic ▲ 98.880 [AAD]

Bach, J.S.:Cant 80, w. A. Augér (sop), L.–M. Harder (ten), P. Huttenlocher (bar), H. Rilling (cnd), Württemberg CO, Gächinger Kantorei [G] *(rec 1976 & 1983)* Hänssler Classic ▲ 98.819 [AAD]

Bach, J.S.:Cant 92, w. A. Augér (sop), H. Watts (cta), A. Baldin (ten), P. Huttenlocher (bar), H. Rilling (cnd), Bach Ensemble [G] *(rec 1980)* Hänssler Classic ▲ 98.877 [AAD]

Schreckenbach, Gabriele (mez) (cont.)

Bach, J.S.:Cant 109, w. K. Equiluz (ten), H. Rilling (cnd), Stuttgart Bach Collegium, Gächinger Kantorei [G] *(rec Feb 1981)* Hänssler Classic ▲ 98.818 [AAD]

Bach, J.S.:Cant 113, w. A. Augér (sop), A. Kraus (ten), N. Tüller (bass), H. Rilling (cnd), Stuttgart Bach Collegium, Gächinger Kantorei Hänssler Classic ▲ 98.810 [ADD]

Bach, J.S.:Cant 122, w. A. Augér (sop), A. Kraus (ten), N. Tüller (bass), H. Rilling (cnd), Stuttgart Bach Collegium, Frankfurt Kantorei [G] *(rec Feb 1972)* Hänssler Classic ▲ 98.826 [AAD]

Bach, J.S.:Cant 128, w. A. Baldin (ten), W. Schöne (bass), H. Rilling (cnd), Stuttgart Bach Collegium, Gächinger Kantorei [G] *(rec 1980–81)* Hänssler Classic ▲ 98.886 [AAD]

Bach, J.S.:Cant 178, w. A. Baldin (ten), K. Equiluz (ten), W. Schöne (bass), H. Rilling (cnd), Stuttgart Bach Collegium, Gächinger Kantorei Hänssler Classic ▲ 98.806 [AAD]

Bach, J.S.:Cant 181, w. A. Augér (sop), G. Schnaut (mez), K. Equiluz (ten), N. Tütler (bass), H. Rilling (cnd), Stuttgart Bach Collegium, Gächinger Kantorei [G] *(rec 1981)* Hänssler Classic ▲ 98.878 [AAD]

Bach, J.S.:Cant 198, w. A. Augér (sop), A. Baldin (ten), P. Huttenlocher (bar), H. Rilling (cnd), Bach Ensemble *(rec Sept 1983)* Hänssler Classic ▲ 98.830 [AAD]

Bruch, M.:Gruss an die heilige Nacht, w. U. Gronostay (cnd), Berlin RSO, Berlin Radio Chorus [G] Koch Schwann ▲ CD 313013 [DDD]

Haydn, M.:Requiem in c, w. Siglinde Damisch (sop), Chris Merritt (ten), Hans Udo Müller (pno), Gerhard Walterskirchen (org), E. Hinreiner (cnd), Salzburg RSO, Mozart Choir *(rec June 1981)* Koch Treasure ▲ 31608–2 [ADD]

Mozart, L.:Missa solemnis, w. A. Augér (sop), H. Laubenthal (ten), B. McDaniel (bar), R. Bader (cnd), Berlin Domkapelle Instrumental Ensemble, St. Hedwig's Cathedral Choir [L] Koch Schwann ▲ CD 313028 [ADD]

Mozart, W.A.:Missa solemnis, K.139, w. M. Lindsay (sop), W. Hollweg (ten), W. Grönroos (bar), M. Creed (cnd), Berlin RSO, Berlin RIAS Chamber Choir [L] Capriccio ▲ 10169 [DDD]

Mozart, W.A.:Missa solemnis, K.139, w. M. Lindsay (sop), W. Hollweg (ten), W. Grönroos (bar), M. Creed (cnd), Berlin RSO, Berlin RIAS Chamber Choir [L] LaserLight ▲ 15 883 [DDD]

Mozart, W.A.:Missa brevis, K.65, w. C. Malone (sop), K. Markus (ten), W. Grönroos (bar), R. Bader (cnd), Berlin RSO, St. Hedwig's Cathedral Choir [L] Koch Schwann ▲ SCH 313021 [ADD/DDD]

Mozart, W.A.:Requiem, w. Edith Wiens (sop), Aldo Baldin (ten), Gerhard Faulstich (bar), U. Gronostay (cnd), Berlin RSO, Berlin RIAS Chamber Choir [L] LaserLight ▲ 15 882 [DDD]

Schreckenberger, Stephan (bass)

Bach, W.F.:Cants (misc), w. B. Schlick (soprano), C. Schubert (contralto), W. Jochens (tenor), Rheinische Kantorei, H. Max (cnd), Das Kleine Konzert—Lasset uns ablegen die Werke der Finsternis; Es ist eine Stimme eines Predigers in der Wüste Capriccio ▲ 10 425 [DDD]

Bach, W.F.:Cants (misc), w. B. Schlick (soprano), C. Schubert (contralto), W. Jochens (tenor), Rheinische Kantorei, H. Max (cnd), Das Kleine Konzert—Dies ist der Tag; Erzittert und fallet Capriccio ▲ 10 426 [DDD]

Capricornus, S.F.:Theatrum musicum quod per duodecim scenas seu sacras cantiones aperuit, w. D. Collot (sop), L. S. Norin (mez), K. Wessel (alt), I. Honeyman (ten), M. Gester (cnd), Parlement de Musique Opus 111 ▲ OPS 30–99

Mozart, W.A.:Requiem, w. M. Figueras (sop), C. Schubert (alt), G. Türk (ten), J. Savall (cnd), La Capella Reial de Catalunya, Le Concert des Nations Astrée ▲ E 8759

Schreiber, Klaus (sgr)

Waits, T.:The Black Rider:The Casting of Magic Bullets, w. Angelika Thomas (sgr—Anne), Annette Paulmann (sgr—Kätchen), Sona Cervena (sgr—Bird/Messenger/Spoonwoman), Monika Tahal (sgr—Witness/Bird/Shrink/Wilhelm's Double/Skeleton), Susi Eisenkolb (sgr—Bridesmaid/Pegleg's Double), Heinz Vossbrink (sgr—Kuno), Dominique Horwitz (sgr—Pegleg), Gerd Kunath (sgr—Bertram), Stefan Kurt (sgr—Wilhelm), Klaus Schreiber (sgr—Robert/Man on Stag/Georg Schmid), Jörg Holm (Old Uncle/Duke), Jan Moritz Steffen (sgr—Young Kuno/Bird/Shrink/Skeleton), Tom Waits (vocals/coliope/organ/chamberlain/mar/emax/guitar/train whistle), Ralph Carney (saxophone/bass clarinet/baritone horn), Bill Douglas (bass instrument), Kenny Wollesen (perc) Island ▲ 314518559–2

Schreiber, Magdalene (sop)

Bach, J.S.:Cant 150, w. M. Jetter (cta), P. Maus (ten), H.–F. Kunz (bass), H. Rilling (cnd), Bach Ensemble *(rec June–July 1970)* Hänssler Classic ▲ 98.835 [AAD]

Schreier, Peter (ten)

Ariosti, A.:Sacred Music, w. L. Güttler (cnd), Virtuosi Saxoniae—O quam suavis est Berlin Classics ▲ BER 1077 [DDD]

Bach, C.P.E.:Magnificat, w. V. Hruba–Freiberger (sop), B. Bornemann (alt), O. Bär (bar), H. Haenchen (cnd), C.P.E. Bach CO, Berlin Radio Chorus Berlin Classics ▲ BER 1011 [DDD]

Bach, J.S.:Cants (misc), w. Edith Mathis (sop), Carolyn Watkinson (cta), Eberhard Büchner (ten), Siegfried Lorenz (bar), Theo Adam (b–bar), P. Schreier (cnd), Berlin CO, Berlin Soloists Berlin Classics ▲ BER 9221

Bach, J.S.:Cant 4, w. Helga Terner (sop), Ortrun Wenkel (cta), Eberhard Büchner (ten), H.–J. Rotzsch (cnd), Leipzig Gewandhaus Orch, Leipzig St. Thomas Church Choir, Leipzig New Bach Collegium Musicum Berlin Classics ▲ BER 2067 [ADD]

Bach, J.S.:Cant 16, w. G. Schreckenbach (cta), P. Huttenlocher (bar), H. Rilling (cnd), Stuttgart Bach Collegium, Gächinger Kantorei [G] Hänssler Classic ▲ 98.871 [AAD]

Bach, J.S.:Cant 21, w. Arleen Augér (sop), Ortrun Wenkel (cta), Siegfried Jerusalem (ten), Theo Adam (b–bar), H.–J. Rotzsch (cnd), New Bach Collegium Musicum, Leipzig St. Thomas Church Choir Berlin Classics ▲ BER 2175 [ADD]

Bach, J.S.:Cant 26, w. E. Mathis (sop), A. Schmidt (bar), D. Fischer–Dieskau (bar), K. Richter (cnd), Munich Bach Orch, Munich Bach Choir Archiv ▲ 427130–2 [ADD]

Bach, J.S.:Cant 31, w. Helga Terner (sop), Ortrun Wenkel (cta), Eberhard Büchner (ten), H.–J. Rotzsch (cnd), Leipzig Gewandhaus Orch, Leipzig St. Thomas Church Choir, Leipzig New Bach Collegium Musicum Berlin Classics ▲ BER 2067 [ADD]

Bach, J.S.:Cant 36, w. A. Augér (sop), G. Schreckenbach (cta), W. Heldwein (bass), H. Rilling (cnd), Stuttgart Bach Collegium, Gächinger Kantorei [G] *(rec Oct 1980, Feb 1981 & Mar)* Hänssler Classic ▲ 98.823 [AAD]

Bach, J.S.:Cant 36, w. Edith Mathis (sop), Siegfried Lorenz (bar), P. Schreier (cnd), Berlin CO, Berlin Soloists Berlin Classics ▲ BER 9220

Bach, J.S.:Cant 50, w. Arleen Auger (sop), Ortrun Wenkel (cta), Theo Adam (b–bar), H.–J. Rotzsch (cnd), New Bach Collegium Musicum, Leipzig St. Thomas Church Choir Berlin Classics ▲ BER 2176 [ADD]

Bach, J.S.:Cant 55, w. Venceslava Hruba–Freiberger (sop), M. Pommer (cnd), New Bach Collegium Musicum, Leipzig Univ Choir Berlin Classics ▲ BER 1066 [DDD]

Bach, J.S.:Cant 55, w. M. Pommer (cnd), Leipzig New Bach Collegium Musicum, Leipzig Univ Choir [G] Capriccio ▲ 10151 [DDD]

Bach, J.S.:Cant 79, w. Arleen Augér (sop), Ortrun Wenkel (cta), Theo Adam (b–bar), H.–J. Rotzsch (cnd), New Bach Collegium Musicum, Leipzig St. Thomas Church Choir Berlin Classics ▲ BER 2176 [ADD]

Bach, J.S.:Cant 80, w. E. Mathis (sop), T. Schmidt (mez), D. Fischer–Dieskau (bar), K. Richter (cnd), Munich Bach Orch, Munich Bach Choir Archiv ▲ 427130–2 [ADD]

Bach, J.S.:Cant 80, w. Arleen Augér (sop), Ortrun Wenkel (cta), Theo Adam (b–bar), H.–J. Rotzsch (cnd), New Bach Collegium Musicum, Leipzig St. Thomas Church Choir Berlin Classics ▲ BER 2176 [ADD]

Bach, J.S.:Cant 84, w. Venceslava Hruba–Freiberger (sop), M. Pommer (cnd), Leipzig New Bach Collegium Musicum, Leipzig Univ Choir Berlin Classics ▲ BER 1066 [DDD]

Bach, J.S.:Cant 116, w. E. Mathis (sop), T. Schmidt (mez), D. Fischer–Dieskau (bar), K. Richter (cnd), Munich Bach Orch, Munich Bach Choir Archiv ▲ 427130–2 [ADD]

Bach, J.S.:Cant 134, w. Helga Terner (sop), Ortrun Wenkel (cta), Eberhard Büchner (ten), H.–J. Rotzsch (cnd), Leipzig Gewandhaus Orch, Leipzig New Bach Collegium Musicum, Leipzig St. Thomas Church Choir Berlin Classics ▲ BER 2067 [ADD]

Bach, J.S.:Cant 137, w. Arleen Augér (sop), Ortrun Wenkel (cta), Siegfried Jerusalem (ten), Theo Adam (b–bar), H.–J. Rotzsch (cnd), New Bach Collegium Musicum, Leipzig St. Thomas Church Choir Berlin Classics ▲ BER 2175 [ADD]

Schreier, Peter (ten) (cont.)
Bach, J.S.:Cant 140, w. E. Mathis (sop), D. Fischer-Dieskau (bar), K. Richter (cnd), Munich Bach Orch, Munich Bach Choir [G] Deutsche Grammophon ("Galleria" series) ▲ 419466-2 [ADD]
Bach, J.S.:Cant 146, w. C. Watkinson (cta), P. Huttenlocher (bass), H. Rilling (cnd), Stuttgart Bach Collegium, Gächinger Kantorei [G] *(rec 1973)* Hänssler Classic ▲ 98.884 [AAD]
Bach, J.S.:Cant 177, w. A. Augér (sop), J. Hamari (cta), H. Rilling (cnd), Stuttgart Bach Collegium, Gächinger Kantorei Hänssler Classic ▲ 98.803 [AAD]
Bach, J.S.:Cant 183, w. A. Augér (sop), J. Hamari (cta), W. Heldwein (bass), H. Rilling (cnd), Stuttgart Bach Collegium, Gächinger Kantorei Hänssler Classic ▲ 98.801 [AAD]
Bach, J.S.:Cant 192, w. Arleen Auger (sop), Ortrun Wenkel (cta), Theo Adam (b-bar), H.-J. Rotzsch (cnd), New Bach Collegium Musicum, Leipzig St. Thomas Church Choir Berlin Classics ▲ BER 2176 [ADD]
Bach, J.S.:Cant 199, w. Venceslava Hruba-Freiberger (sop), M. Pommer (cnd), Leipzig New Bach Collegium Musicum, Leipzig Univ Choir Berlin Classics ▲ BER 1066 [DDD]
Bach, J.S.:Cant 203, w. Edith Mathis (sop), Siegfried Lorenz (bar), P. Schreier (cnd), Berlin CO, Berlin Soloists Berlin Classics ▲ BER 9220
Bach, J.S.:Cant 205, w. Edith Mathis (sop), Carolyn Watkinson (alt), Julia Hamari (alt), Siegfreid Lorenz (bass), P. Schreier (cnd), Berlin CO, Berlin Soloists Berlin Classics ▲ BER 9224
Bach, J.S.:Cant 206, w. Edith Mathis (sop), Carolyn Watkinson (alt), Siegfried Lorenz (bass), P. Schreier (cnd), Berlin CO, Berlin Soloists Berlin Classics ▲ BER CD 9225
Bach, J.S.:Cant 207, w. Edith Mathis (sop), Carolyn Watkinson (alt), Julia Hamari (alt), Siegfreid Lorenz (bass), P. Schreier (cnd), Berlin CO, Berlin Soloists Berlin Classics ▲ BER 9224
Bach, J.S.:Cant 209, w. Edith Mathis (sop), Siegfried Lorenz (bar), P. Schreier (cnd), Berlin CO, Berlin Soloists Berlin Classics ▲ BER 9220
Bach, J.S.:Cant 211, "Coffee Cant", w. Edith Mathis (sop), Theo Adam (bass), P. Schreier (cnd), Berlin CO Berlin Classics ▲ BER 9226
Bach, J.S.:Cant 212, "Peasant Cant", w. Edith Mathis (sop), Theo Adam (bass), P. Schreier (cnd), Berlin CO Berlin Classics ▲ BER 9226
Bach, J.S.:Cant 215, w. Edith Mathis (sop), Carolyn Watkinson (alt), Siegfried Lorenz (bass), P. Schreier (cnd), Berlin CO, Berlin Soloists Berlin Classics ▲ BER CD 9225
Bach, J.S.:Christmas Oratorio, w. A. Augér (sop), J. Hamari (cta), W. Schöne (bass), H. Rilling (cnd), Stuttgart Bach Collegium Hänssler Classic 3-▲ 98.854 [DDD]
Bach, J.S.:Christmas Oratorio, w. A. Augér (sop), J. Hamari (cta), W. Schöne (bass), H. Rilling (cnd), Stuttgart Bach Collegium, Gächinger Kantorei [G] *(rec 1984)* Hänssler Classic 5-▲ 98.976
Bach, J.S.:Magnificat, BWV 243, w. Helen Donath (sop), Gundula Bernát-Klein (sop), Birgit Finnilä (alt), Barry McDaniel (bass), W. Gönnenwein (cnd), German Bach Soloists, South German Madrigal Choir [E♭ version] *(rec Stuttgart Radio, 1966)* Bayer ▲ 100081 [ADD]
Bach, J.S.:Mass in b, BWV 232, w. Gundula Janowitz (sop), Christa Ludwig (mez), Karl Ridderbusch (bass), Vienna Choral Academy, H. von Karajan (cnd), Berlin PO Deutsche Grammophon ("Double" series) 2-▲ 439696-2
Bach, J.S.:Mass in b, BWV 232, w. B. Bonney (sop), C. Wulkopf (mez), A. Scharinger (bass), S. Celibidache (cnd), Munich PO, Munich Bach Choir Exclusive ▲ EXL 33 [ADD]
Bach, J.S.:Masses, BWV 233-36, "Lutheran Masses", w. Renate Krahmer (sop), Annelies Burmeister (alt), Theo Adam (bass), M. Flämig (cnd), Dresden PO Berlin Classics 2-▲ BER 9130
Bach, J.S.:Music of, w. L. Güttler (tpt), M. Lorenz (ten), A. Reiss (ten), H.-C. Polster (b-bar), M. Pommer (cnd), Leipzig New Bach Collegium Musicum, Leipzig Choirs—arias, choruses & chorales Capriccio ▲ CDC 10039 [DDD]
Bach, J.S.:St. Matthew Passion, w. A. Burmeister (mez), T. Adam (bass), R. & E. Mauersberger (cnd), Leipzig Gewandhaus Orch, Dresden Kreuz Choir, St. Thomas Chorus *(rec 1970)* Berlin Classics 3-▲ BER 2144 [ADD]
Bach, J.S.:St. Matthew Passion, w. G. Janowitz (sop), C. Ludwig (mez), H. Laubenthal (ten), W. Berry (bar), D. Fischer-Dieskau (bar), H. von Karajan (cnd), Berlin PO, Vienna Singverein, German Opera Chorus [G] Deutsche Grammophon 3-▲ 419789-2 [ADD]
Beethoven, L. van:An die ferne Geliebte, w. Erik Werba (pno) *(rec Aug 12, 1979)* Orfeo d'or ("Festspiel Dokumente" series) ▲ 399951
Beethoven, L. van:Missa Solemnis, w. Anna Tomowa-Sintow (sop), Annelies Burmeister (alt), Hermann Christian Polster (bass), Gerhard Bosse (vn), Hannes Kastner (org), K. Masur (cnd), Leipzig Gewandhaus Orch, Leipzig Radio Chorus Berlin Classics ("Masur Edition" series) ▲ BER 9160
Beethoven, L. van:Songs, w. A. Stolte (sop), W. Olbertz (pno)—Scherlieder; Ariettas (4) & duet, Op. 82; Ernste Lieder Berlin Classics ▲ BER 2084 [DDD]
Beethoven, L. van:Songs, w. W. Olbertz (pno)—Liebeslieder Berlin Classics ▲ BER 2083 [ADD]
Beethoven, L. van:Songs, w. W. Olbertz (pno)—An die ferne Geliebte, Op. 98; Sechs Lieder, Op. 48; Lieder nach Goethe Berlin Classics ▲ BER 2082 [ADD]
Beethoven, L. van:Syms (comp), w. Marga Schiml (sop), Theo Adam (b-bar), Helena Doese (sgr), H. Blomstedt (cnd), Dresden Staatskapelle, Dresden State Opera Chorus *(rec late 1970's-early 1980's)* Berlin Classics 5-▲ BER 2194 [DDD]
Beethoven, L. van:Syms (comp), w. Helena Doese (sop), Marga Schiml (alt), Theo Adam (bass), H. Blomstedt (cnd), Dresden Staatskapelle, Dresden State Opera Chorus, Leipzig Radio Choir *(rec Lukaskirche, Dresden, 1975-80)* Berlin Classics 5-▲ 0021942BC [ADD]
Beethoven, L. van:Syms (comp), w. B. , C. Watkinson (cta), B. Haitink (cnd), Royal Concertgebouw Orch—[R. Holl (bass) in No. 9] Philips 5-▲ 442073-2
Brahms, J.:Liebeslieder Waltzes SATB, w. E. Mathis (sop), B. Fassbaender (mez), D. Fischer-Dieskau (bar), K. Engel (pno), W. Sawallisch (pno) [G] Deutsche Grammophon ▲ 423133-2 [DDD]
Brahms, J.:Neue Liebeslieder Waltzes, w. E. Mathis (sop), B. Fassbaender (mez), D. Fischer-Dieskau (bar), K. Engel (pno), W. Sawallisch (pno) [G] Deutsche Grammophon ▲ 423133-2 [DDD]
Britten, H.:Les Illuminations, w. H. Kegel (cnd), Leipzig RSO Berlin Classics ▲ BER 9035 [ADD]
Britten, H.:Serenade, Op. 31, w. P. Damm (cnd), Bohdan Warchal Slovak CO Campion ▲ 1313
Britten, H.:Serenade, Op. 31, w. Günther Opitz (hn), H. Kegel (cnd), Leipzig RSO Berlin Classics ▲ BER 9035 [ADD]
Christmas Lieder, w. Norman Shetler (pno) Eurodisc ▲ 69013-2-RG [ADD]
Dessau, P.:Einstein, w. Theo Adam (bass), Reiner Suss (bass), O. Suitner (cnd), Berlin Staatskapelle, Berlin State Opera Chorus Berlin Classics 2-▲ BER CD 9109
Dessau, P.:Die Verurteilung des Lukullus, w. Annelies Burmeister (mez—Das Fischweib), Helmut Melchert (ten—Lukullus), Hans-Joachim Rotzsch (ten—Der Kirschbaumträger), Peter Schreier (ten—Lukullus' Cook), Boris Carmeli (bass—King), H. Kegel (cnd), Leipzig RSO, Leipzig Radio Chorus Berlin Classics 2-▲ BER 1073 [ADD]
Dvořák, A.:Requiem Mass, w. Elisabeth Rose (sop), Gertraud Prenzlow (cta), Theo Adam (bass), K. Ančerl (cnd), Berlin RSO, Berlin Radio Chorus Forlane 2-▲ FRL 16636 [AAD]
Dvořák, A.:Songs, w. M. Lapsansky (pno)—Zigeunermelodien, Op. 55; Liebeslieder, Op. 83; Biblische Lieder, Op. 99 [G] Capriccio ▲ 10053 [DDD]
Dvořák, A.:Songs, w. M. Lapsansky (pno)—Liebeslieder, Op. 83/1-8; Biblical Songs, Op. 99/1-10 Berlin Classics ▲ BER 1080 [DDD]
Dvořák, A.:Zigeunermelodien, Op. 55, w. Erik Werba (pno) *(rec Aug 12, 1979)* Orfeo d'or ("Festspiel Dokumente" series) ▲ 399951
Dvořák, A.:Zigeunermelodien, Op. 55, w. M. Lapsansky (pno) Berlin Classics ▲ BER 1080 [DDD]
Fux, J.J.:Plaudite, sonat tuba, w. L. Güttler (cnd), Virtuosi Saxoniae Berlin Classics ▲ BER 1077 [DDD]
Handel, G.F.:Judas Maccabaeus, w. Gundula Janowitz (sop), Hertha Töpper (alt), Ernest Haefliger (ten), Theo Adam (bass), Siegfried Vogel (bass), H. Koch (cnd), Berlin RSO, Berlin Radio Chorus Berlin Classics 2-▲ BER 9112
Haydn, J.:Die Schöpfung, w. Jeannette van Dijck (sop), Theo Adam (bass), Hans Plumacher (vc), Heinz Detering (db), Fritz Lehan (hpd), G. Wand (cnd), Cologne Gürzenich Orch, Cologne Gürzenich Chorus Accord 2-▲ ACD 200422 [AAD]
Haydn, J.:Die Schöpfung, w. Regina Werner (sop), Theo Adam (bass), H. Koch (cnd), Berlin RSO, Berlin Radio Chorus Berlin Classics 2-▲ BER CD 9115
Heinichen, J.D.:Sacred Music, w. L. Güttler (cnd), Virtuosi Saxoniae—Lamentatio I Berlin Classics ▲ BER 1077 [DDD]
Humperdinck, E.:Hänsel und Gretel, w. G. Schöter (sop), I. Springer (mez), T. Adam (bar), O. Suitner (cnd), Dresden Staatskapelle, Dresden Kreuz Choir Berlin Classics ("Eterna" series) 2-▲ BER 2007 [ADD]

Schreier, Peter (ten) (cont.)
Killmayer, W.:Songs, w. B. Klee (cnd), Hanover Radio PO Wergo 2-▲ WER 6245 2
Lortzing, A.:Der Wildschütz, oder Die Stimme der Natur, w. Edith Mathis (sop), Gottfried Hornik (bar), Hans Sotin (bass), B. Klee (cnd), Berlin State Chorus *(rec Berlin, 1982)* Berlin Classics 2-▲ BER 1143 [ADD]
Mahler, G.:Das Lied von der Erde, w. J. Van Nes (cta), E. Inbal (cnd), Frankfurt RSO [G] Denon ▲ CO 72605 [DDD]
Mendelssohn, F.:Elijah, w. E. Ameling (sop), A. Burmeister (mez), T. Adam (b-bar), W. Sawallisch (cnd), Leipzig Gewandhaus Orch, Leipzig Radio Chorus Philips 2-▲ 438368-2
Mendelssohn, F.:Elijah, w. E. Ameling (sop), A. Burmeister (mez), T. Adam (b-bar), W. Sawallisch (cnd), Leipzig Gewandhaus Orch, Leipzig Radio Chorus [G] Philips 2-▲ 420106-2 [AAD]
Mendelssohn, F.:Songs, w. K. Engel (pno)—Auf Flügeln des Gesanges, Op. 34/2; Schilflied, Op. 71; Der Mond, Op. 86/5; Pagenlied; Im Frühling, Op. 9/4; Reiselied, Op. 34/6; Allnächtlich im Traume, Op. 86/4; Venezianisches Gondellied, Op. 57/5; An die Entfernte, Op. 71/3; Frühlingslied, Op. 19/1; Minnelied, Op. 34/1; Lieblingsplätzchen, Op. 99/3; Winterlied, Op. 19/3; Gruss, Op. 19/5; Das erste Veilchen, Op. 19/2; Da lieg ich unter den Bäumen, Op. 84/1; Minnelied, Op. 47/1; Morgengruss, Op. 47/2; Auf der Wanderschaft, Op. 71/5; Nachtlied, Op. 71/6; Hirtenlied, Op. 57/2; Frühlingslied, Op. 47/3; Neue Liebe, Op. 19/4; Andres Maienlied, Op. 8/8 *(rec Oct. 1993)* Berlin Classics ▲ BER 1107-2 [DDD]
Mendelssohn, F.:Sym 2, w. B. Bonney (sop), E. Wiens (sop), K. Masur (cnd), Leipzig Gewandhaus Orch, Leipzig Gewandhaus Chorus [G] Teldec ▲ 2292-44178-2 ZK [DDD]
Mozart, W.A.:Arias, w. H. Koch (cnd), Berlin CO—Per pietà, non ricerate, K.420; Misero! O sogno—Aura, che intorno, K.431 Berlin Classics ▲ BER 9129
Mozart, W.A.:Arias, w. I. Cotrubas (sop), E. Gruberova (sop), L. Price (sop), J. Varady (sop), L. Popp (mez), F. Araiza (ten), P. Domingo (ten), P. de Palma (ten), F. Wunderlich (ten), S. Milnes (bar), A. Titus (bar), M. Talvela (bass)—sels. from Entführung aus dem Serail, Così fan tutte, Don Giovanni, Idomeneo, Die Zauberflöte, Le nozze di Figaro Eurodisc ▲ 69256-2-RG [ADD]
Mozart, W.A.:Bastien und Bastienne, w. Adele Stolte (sop), Theo Adam (bass), H. Koch (cnd), Berlin CO Berlin Classics ▲ BER 9129
Mozart, W.A.:Complete Mozart Edition, w. M. Price (sop), L. Serra (sop), R. Tear (ten), T. Adam (b-bar), K. Moll (bass), C. Davis (cnd), Dresden Staatskapelle, Dresden State Chorus Philips 3-▲ 422543-2 [ADD]
Mozart, W.A.:Complete Mozart Edition, w. E. Mathis (sop), W. Hollweg (bar), I. Wixell (bar), B. Klee (cnd), Berlin Staatskapelle Philips 2-▲ 422536-2 [ADD]
Mozart, W.A.:Complete Mozart Edition, w. Kegel, Marriner (cnd) Philips 6-▲ 422522-2 [ADD]
Mozart, W.A.:Complete Mozart Edition, w. E. Mathis (sop), E. Gruberova (sop), E. Moser (sop), L. Popp (mez), L. Hager (cnd), Salzburg Mozarteum Orch Philips 2-▲ 422531-2 [ADD]
Mozart, W.A.:Complete Mozart Edition, w. A. Augér (sop), E. Mathis (sop), A. Baltsa (mez), L. Hager (cnd), Salzburg Mozarteum Orch Philips 3-▲ 422530-2 [ADD]
Mozart, W.A.:Complete Mozart Edition, w. E. Gruberova (sop), E. Mathis (sop), L. Popp (mez), F. Araiza (ten), W. Berry (bass), Salzburg Mozarteum Orch Philips 8-▲ 422523-2 [ADD]
Mozart, W.A.:Complete Mozart Edition, w. A. Augér (sop), E. Mathis (sop), J. Varady (sop), H. Donath (sop), L. Hager (cnd), Salzburg Mozarteum Orch Philips 3-▲ 422532-2 [ADD]
Mozart, W.A.:Così fan tutte, w. G. Janowitz (sop), R. Grist (sop), B. Fassbaender (mez), H. Prey (bar), D. Fischer-Dieskau (bar), K. Böhm (cnd), Vienna PO *(rec live, 1972)* Foyer 2-▲ FOY 2066 [ADD]
Mozart, W.A.:Così fan tutte (sels), w. G. Janowitz (sop), R. Grist (sop), B. Fassbaender (mez), H. Prey (bar), R. Panerai (bar), K. Böhm (cnd), Vienna PO, Vienna State Opera Chorus—scenes & arias Deutsche Grammophon ▲ 429824-2 [ADD]
Mozart, W.A.:Don Giovanni (sels), w. R. Grist (sop), B. Nilsson (sop), M. Arroyo (sop), D. Fischer-Dieskau (bar), M. Talvela (bass), K. Böhm (cnd), Prague National Theater Orch IMP Collectors Series ▲ IMPX 9023 [AAD]
Mozart, W.A.:Entführung, w. Yvonne Kenny (sop), Carolyn Watson (cta), Wilfried Gamlich (ten), Matti Salminen (bass), Wolfgang Reichmann (nar), N. Harnoncourt (cnd), Zurich Mozart Opera Orch, Zurich Mozart Opera Chorus [G] Teldec 2-▲ 2292-42643-2
Mozart, W.A.:Idomeneo, w. A. Rothenberger (sop), E. Moser (sop), N. Gedda (ten), A. Dallapozza (ten), T. Adam (b-bar), H. Schmidt-Isserstedt (cnd), Dresden Staatskapelle, Leipzig Radio Chorus EMI Classics ("Studio" series) 3-▲ CDMC 63990
Mozart, W.A.:Missa, K.427, w. B. Hendricks (sop), J. Perry (sop), B. Luxon (bar), H. von Karajan (cnd), Berlin PO Deutsche Grammophon ("Karajan Gold" series) ▲ 439012-2
Mozart, W.A.:Nozze di Figaro, w. Anneliese Rothenberger (sop), Hilde Gueden (sop), Edith Mathis (sop), Walter Berry (bar), Hermann Prey (bar), O. Suitner (cnd), Dresden Staatskapelle Berlin Classics 3-▲ BER 2096 [ADD]
Mozart, W.A.:Schauspieldirektor, w. Sylvia Geszty (sop), Hermann Christian Polster (bass), H. Koch (cnd), Berlin CO—features complete dialog *(rec 1968)* Berlin Classics ▲ BER 9136 [DDD]
Mozart, W.A.:Zauberflöte, w. H. Donath (sop), S. Geszty (sop), G. Leib (bass), T. Adam (bass), O. Suitner (cnd), Dresden Staatskapelle [I] RCA Gold Seal 3-▲ 6511-2 [ADD]
Mozart, W.A.:Zauberflöte, w. M. Price (sop—Pamina), L. Serra (sop—Queen of the Night), M. Venuti (sop—Papagena), M. McLaughlin (sop—1st Lady), A. Murray (mez—2nd Lady), H. Schwarz (cta—3rd Lady), F. Höher (trb—1st Boy), M. Diedrich (trb—2nd Boy), F. Klos (trb—3rd Boy), P. Schreier (ten—Tamino), R. Tear (ten—Monostatos), R. Goldberg (ten—1st Armoured Man), K. Moll (bass—Sarastro), H. Rech (bass—2nd Armoured Man), C. Davis (cnd), Dresden Staatskapelle, Leipzig Radio Chorus Philips ("Duo" series) 2-▲ 442568-2
Music for Tenor & Lute, w. Konrad Ragossnig (lt) Capriccio ▲ CDC 10047 [DDD]
Mussorgsky, M.:Boris Godunov (sels), w. Hanne-Lore Kuhse (sop), Martin Ritzmann (ten), Theo Adam (b-bar), H. Kegel (cnd), Dresden State Orch, Leipzig Radio Chorus Berlin Classics ▲ BER 2032 [ADD]
Nicolai, O.:Lustigen Weiber, w. H. Donath (sop), E. Mathis (sop), H. Schwarz (cta), K. Moll (bass), B. Klee (cnd), Berlin Staatskapelle, Berlin State Opera Chorus Berlin Classics 2-▲ BER 2115 [ADD]
Nicolai, O.:Lustigen Weiber, w. H. Donath (sop), E. Mathis (sop), H. Schwarz (mez), K. Ludwig (ten), K.-E. Mercker (ten), C. Dormoy (bar), B. Weikl (bar), K. Moll (bass), S. Vogel (bass), B. Klee (cnd), Berlin Staatskapelle, Berlin State Opera Chorus *(rec July 3, 1976)* Berlin Classics ("Eterna" series) ▲ BER 2046-2 [ADD]
Orff, C.:De temporum fine comoedia, w. C. Ludwig (mez), J. Greindl (bass), H. von Karajan (cnd), Cologne RSO, Cologne Radio Chorus [L] Deutsche Grammophon ("20th Century Classics" series) ▲ 429859-2 [ADD]
Peter Screier:From Boy Alto of the Dresden Kreuzchor to Lyric Tenor, w. Rudolf Mauersberger (pno/cnd), Walter Olbertz (pno), Norman Shetler (pno), various orchs *(rec ca. 1950)* Berlin Classics 4-▲ BER 9041 [ADD]
Pfitzner, H.:Palestrina, w. C. Nossek (sop), R. Long (mez), S. Lorenz (bar), E. Wlaschiha (bass), O. Suitner (cnd), Berlin Staatskapelle, Berlin State Opera Chorus Berlin Classics ▲ BER 1001
Rimsky-Korsakov, N.:Mozart & Salieri, w. T. Adam (b-bar), M. Janowski (cnd), Dresden Staatskapelle [G] Berlin Classics ("Eterna" series) ▲ BER 2089 [ADD]
Rossini, G.:Il barbiere di Siviglia, w. Ruth-Margaret Pütz (sop), Annelies Burmeister (mez), Hermann Prey (bar), Franz Crass (bass), Fritz Ollendorff (bass), O. Suitner (cnd), Berlin State Opera Orch Berlin Classics 2-▲ BER 9021 [ADD]
Scarlatti, A.:Su le sponde del Tebro, w. L. Güttler (cnd), Virtuosi Saxoniae Berlin Classics ▲ BER 1077 [DDD]
Schmidt, F.:Das Buch mit sieben Siegeln, w. Sylvia Greenberg (sop), Carolyn Watkinson (cta), Thomas Moser (ten), Robert Holl (bass), Kurt Rydl (bass), L. Zagrosek (cnd), Austrian RSO, Vienna State Opera Chorus [G] Orfeo 2-▲ 143862 [DDD]
Schubert, Franz:Alfonso und Estrella, w. E. Mathis (sop), M. Falewicz (sop), H. Prey (bar), D. Fischer-Dieskau (bar), T. Adam (b-bar), O. Suitner (cnd), Berlin Staatskapelle, Berlin Radio Chorus Berlin Classics 3-▲ BER 2156 [ADD]
Schubert, Franz:Offertorium, D.963, w. W. Sawallisch (cnd), Bavarian RSO, Bavarian Radio Chorus [L] EMI Classics ("Studio" series) ▲ CDM 69223
Schubert, Franz:Sacred Music, w. M. Hajossyova (sop), D. Knothe (cnd), Berlin RSO, Berlin Radio Chorus—Offertorium, D.963; Offertorium, D.223; Tantum ergo, D.962; Psalm 23, D.706; An die Sonne, D.439; Offertorium, D.136; Salve Regina, D.106; Salve Regina, D.386; Psalm 92, D.953; Chor der Engel, D.440 [G,L] Capriccio ▲ 10096 [DDD]

Schreier, Peter (ten) (cont.)

Schubert, Franz:Die Schöne Müllerin, w. Andras Schiff (pno) [G] London ▲ 430414-2 [DDD]

Schubert, Franz:Die Schöne Müllerin, w. Konrad Rogossnig (gtr) Berlin Classics ▲ BER 1123 [ADD]

Schubert, Franz:Songs (comp), w. G. Johnson (pno)—Das Finden, D.219; Die Nacht, D.358; An den Schlaf, D.447; Abendlied, D.499; Um Mitternacht, D.862; Der Liebliche Stern, D.861; Im Walde, D.834; Im Frühling, D.882; An mein Herz, D.860 [G] Hyperion ▲ CDJ 33018

Schubert, Franz:Winterreise, w. A. Schiff (pno) *(rec Aug. 10–12, 1991)* London ▲ 436122-2 [DDD]

Schumann, R.:Genoveva, w. E. Moser (sop), D. Fischer-Dieskau (bar), S. Lorenz (b-bar), K. Masur (cnd), Leipzig Gewandhaus Orch, Berlin Radio Chorus Berlin Classics ("Eterna" series) 2-▲ BER 2056 [ADD]

Schumann, R.:Songs, w. N. Shelter (pno)—Dichterliebe; Liederkreis, Op. 24; Lieder nach Heine Berlin Classics ▲ BER 2110 [ADD]

Schumann, R.:Songs, w. N. Shelter (pno)—Kerner Lieder, Op. 35; 6 Lieder, Op. 90 Berlin Classics ▲ BER 2113 [ADD]

Schumann, R.:Songs, w. N. Shelter (pno)—Lieder, Opp. 25, 37 & 40; other songs Berlin Classics ▲ BER 2112 [ADD]

Schumann, R.:Songs, w. N. Shelter (pno)—Liederkreis, Op. 39; 2 Gypsy Songs; other songs Berlin Classics ▲ BER 2111 [ADD]

Schütz, H.:Die Auferstehung unsres Herren Jesu Christi, w. H. Grüss (cnd), Capella Fidicinia Dresden, Dresden Church Choir Berlin Classics ▲ BER 9205

Shostakovich, D.:From Jewish Folk Poetry, w. Annelies Burmeister (mez), Maria Croonen (sgr), K. Sanderling (cnd), Berlin SO Berlin Classics ▲ BER 9016 [ADD]

Strauss, R.:Songs, w. Erik Werba (pno)—Die Georgine; Die Zeitlose; Ach weh, mir unglückhaftem Mann; Traum durch die Dämmerung; Du meines Herzens Krönelein; Wie sollten wir gemeinsam sie halten; Ruhe meine Seele; All' meine Gedanken; Nachtgang; Freundliche Vision; Heimliche Aufforderung; Morgen; Die Nacht; Ständchen *(rec Aug 12, 1979)* Orfeo d'or ("Festspiel Dokumente" series) ▲ 399951

Stravinsky, I.:Oedipus Rex, w. J. Norman (sop), P. Langridge (ten), B. Terfel (b-bar), S. Ozawa (cnd), Saito Kinen Orch Philips ▲ 438865-2

Wagner, R.:Die Meistersinger von Nürnberg, w. H. Donath (sop), R. Hesse (mez), A. Kollo (ten), T. Adam (b-bar), R. Evans (bass), K. Ridderbusch (bass), H. von Karajan (cnd), Dresden Staatskapelle, Dresden State Chorus, Leipzig Radio Chorus [G] EMI Classics 4-▲ CDCD 49683 [ADD]

Wagner, R.:Das Rheingold, w. Gabriele Fontana (sop—Woglinde), Nancy Gustafson (sop—Freia), Ildiko Komlosi (mez—Wellgunde), Hanna Schwarz (mez—Fricka), Elena Zaremba (mez—Erda), Margareta Hintermeier (cta—Flosshilde), Kim Begley (ten—Loge), Peter Schreier (ten—Mime), Thomas Sunnegardh (ten—Froh), Robert Hale (bass-bar—Wotan), Walter Fink (bass—Fafner), Franz-Josef Kapellmann (bass—Alberich), Jan-Hendrik Rootering (bass—Fasolt), Eike Wilm Schulte (bass—Donner), C. von Dohnányi (cnd), Cleveland Orch *(rec Severance Hall, Cleveland, Ohio, Dec 1993)* London 2-▲ 443690-2

Wagner, R.:Rienzi, der Letzte der Tribunen, w. S. Wennberg (sop), Martin (sop), A. Kollo (ten), T. Adam (b-bar), H. Hollreiser (cnd), Dresden State Opera Orch, Dresden State Opera Chorus [G] EMI Classics ("Studio" series) 3-▲ CDMB 63980

Wagner, R.:Tristan und Isolde, w. H. Dernesch (sop), C. Ludwig (mez), J. Vickers (ten), B. Weikl (bar), W. Berry (bass), K. Ridderbusch (bass), H. von Karajan (cnd), Berlin PO, German Opera Chorus [G] EMI Classics ("Studio" series) 4-▲ CDMD 69319 [ADD]

Walther (I), Joh.:Wittenberg Spiritual Songbook (sels), w. H. Grüss (cnd), Capella Fidicinia Leipzig [G] Capriccio ▲ CDC 11089

Wolf, H.:Italienische Liederbücher (sels), w. Felicity Lott (sop), Graham Johnson (pno) Hyperion ▲ CDA 66760

Zelenka, J.D.:Music of, w. L. Güttler (cnd), Virtuosi Saxoniae—Laudate pieri Berlin Classics ▲ BER 1077 [DDD]

Schröder (sgr)

Künneke, E.:Die grosse Sünderin (sels), w. M. Cunitz (sop), R. Schock (ten), Bajew (sgr), Gehly (sgr), Rau (sgr), Weigelt (sgr), Marszalek (cnd), Cologne RSO, Cologne Radio Chorus [G] Acanta ▲ CD 42483 [DDD]

Schroeder, A. (bar)

Weisgall, H.:Six Characters in Search of an Author, w. E. Byrne (sop—Stepdaughter), S. Foster (sop—Prompter), E. Furtal (sop—Coloratura), J. King (mez—Mezzo), N. Maultsby (mez—Mother), P. LoVerne (cta—Madame Pace), D. Pritchett (alt—Wardrobe Mistress), B. Fowler (ten—Tenore Boffo), K. Anderson (ten—Director), A. Schroeder (bar—Accompanist), P. Zawisza (bar—Stage Manager), R. Orth (bar—Father), G. Lehman (bar—Son), M. Wadsworth (b-bar—Basso Cantante), L. Schaenen (cnd), Chicago Lyric Opera Orch, Lyric Opera Center Chorus *(rec Chicago, June 14 & 16, 1990)* New World 2-▲ 80454-2

Schröter, Gisela (mez)

Berg, A.:Wozzeck, w. R. Goldberg (ten), H. Hiestermann (ten), T. Adam (b-bar), H. Kegel (cnd), Leipzig RSO *(rec Apr. 9, 1973)* Berlin Classics ("Eterna" series) 2-▲ BER 2068 [ADD]

Schubart (sgr)

Jessel, L.:Schwarzwaldmädel (sels), w. E. Lind (sop), F. Fehringer (ten), B. Kusche (bar), Hofmann (sgr), Schörg (sgr), Marszalek (cnd), Cologne RSO, Cologne Radio Chorus [G] Acanta ▲ CD 42552 [DDD]

Schubert, Claudia (cta)

Bach, W.F.:Cants (misc), w. B. Schlick (soprano), W. Jochens (tenor), J. Schreckenberger (bass), Rheinische Kantorei, H. Max (cnd), Das Kleine Konzert—Lasset uns ablegen die Werke der Finsternis; Es ist eine Stimme eines Predigers in der Wüste Capriccio ▲ 10 425 [DDD]

Bach, W.F.:Cants (misc), w. B. Schlick (soprano), W. Jochens (tenor), J. Schreckenberger (bass), Rheinische Kantorei, H. Max (cnd), Das Kleine Konzert—Dies ist der Tag; Erzittert und fallet Capriccio ▲ 10 426 [DDD]

Bruckner, A.:Missa solemnis, w. C. Oelze (sop), J. Dümüller (ten), R. Hagen (bass), K. A. Rickenbacher (cnd), Bamberg SO, Bamberg Sym Chorus Virgin Classics ▲ CDC 59060

Bruckner, A.:Psalm 112, w. C. Oelze (sop), J. Dümüller (ten), R. Hagen (bass), K. A. Rickenbacher (cnd), Bamberg SO, Bamberg Sym Chorus Virgin Classics ▲ CDC 59060

Bruckner, A.:Psalm 114, w. C. Oelze (sop), J. Dümüller (ten), R. Hagen (bass), K. A. Rickenbacher (cnd), Bamberg SO, Bamberg Sym Chorus Virgin Classics ▲ CDC 59060

Bruckner, A.:Psalm 150, w. C. Oelze (sop), J. Dümüller (ten), R. Hagen (bass), K. A. Rickenbacher (cnd), Bamberg SO, Bamberg Sym Chorus Virgin Classics ▲ CDC 59060

Mozart, W.A.:Requiem, w. M. Figueras (sop), G. Türk (ten), J. Schreckenberger (bass), J. Savall (cnd), La Capella Reial de Catalunya, Le Concert des Nations Astrée ▲ E 8759

Schubert, Erika (mez)

Wagner, R.:Der Ring des Nibelungen, w. Liselotte Becker-Egner (sop—Woglinde/Ortlinde/Wellgunde), Angelika Berger (sop—Wellgunde/Waltraute), Siw Ericsdotter (sop—Norn 3), Heidemaria Ferch (sop—Freia/Gerhilde), Bella Jasper (sop—Helmwige/Waldvogel/Woglinde), Ditha Sommer (sop—Sieglinde/Gutrune), Ursula Boese (mez—Erda), Ruth Hesse (mez—Fricka), Nadezda Kniplová (mez—Brünnhilde), Margit Kobeck (mez—Schwertleite/Norn 2), Hilde Rosner (mez—Flosshilde/Siegrunde), Erica Schubert (mez—Grimgerde/Flosshilde), Ingrid Göritz (cta—Rossweisse/Norn 1), Herbert Doussant (ten—Froh), Herold Kraus (ten—Mime), Gerald McKee (ten—Siegmund/Siegfried), Fritz Uhl (ten—Loge), Rudolf Knoll (bar—Gunther/Donner), Rolf Polke (bass-bar—Wotan/Wanderer), Rolf Kühne (bass—Alberich), Takao Okamura (bass—Fafner), Otto von Rohr (bass—Hagen/Fasolt/Hunding), H. Swarowsky (cnd), Czech PO, Prague National Theater Orch *(rec June 3 & 5, July 26–31, A)* Weltbild Classics 14-▲ 703769 [ADD]

Schubert, Richard (ten)

Wagner, R.:Siegfried (sels), w. G. Kappel (sop—Brünhilde), R. Schubert (ten—Siegfried), E. Zimmermann (ten—Mime), R. Heger (cnd), Vienna State Opera Orch, Vienna State Opera Chorus *(rec June 13, 1933)* Koch Schwann 2-▲ SCH 314592

Schudel, Regina (sop)

Henze, H.-W.:Elegy for Young Lovers, w. Richard Lloyd Morgan (bass), Lawrence Richard (bass), Helmut Bernhofen (sgr), Bruno Fath (sgr), Aurelia Hajek (sgr), Silvia Weiss (sgr), B. Jones (cnd), Berlin Chamber Opera Orch *(rec Berlin)* Deutsche Schallplatten 2-▲ DS 1050

Herzogenberg, H. von:Die Geburt Christi, w. A. Eggers (cta), P. Maus (ten), E. Schramm (bass), C. Grube (cnd), Oriol Ensemble, *(various choruses)* [G] Hänssler Classic 2-▲ 98.574 [AAD]

Schudel, Regina (sop) (cont.)

Mendelssohn, F.:Die Hochzeit des Camacho, w. R. Schudel (sop—Quiteria), C. Swanson (sop—Lucinda), C. Bieber (ten—Basilio), W. Mok (ten—Vivaldo), V. Horn (ten—Camacho), R. Lukas (bar—Carrasco), J. Becker (bass—Sancho Panza), W. Murray (bass—Don Quixote), B. Klee (cnd), Berlin RSO, Berlin Radio Chorus [G] Koch Schwann 2-▲ 314042 [DDD]

Mozart, W.A.:Missa [longa], K.262, w. Ulla Groenewold (cta), Peter Maus (ten), Berthold Possemeyer (bar), U. Gronostay (cnd), Berlin Radio Sinfonietta, Berlin Radio Chamber Choir [L] Koch Schwann ▲ CD 313 021 [ADD/DDD]

Mozart, W.A.:Missa brevis, K.258, w. Ulla Groenewold (cta), Peter Maus (ten), Berthold Possemeyer (bar), U. Gronostay (cnd), Berlin Radio Sinfonietta, Berlin Chamber Chorus [L] Koch Schwann ▲ CD 313 021 [ADD/DDD]

Schulhoff, E.:The Flames, w. Jane Eaglen (sop—Donna Anna, Nun, Woman, Marguerite), Carola Höhn (sop—Shadow), Celina Lindsley (sop—Shadow), Regina Schudel (sop—Shadow), Iris Vermillion (mez—La Morte), Christiane Berggold (alt—Shadow), Kaja Borris (alt—Shadow), Elvira Dressen (alt—Shadow), Kurt Westi (ten—Don Juan), Johann-Werner Prein (bass—Commendatore), Gerd Wolf (bass—Harlequin), J. Mauceri (cnd), Berlin German SO, Berlin RIAS Chamber Choir *(rec Jesus-Christus Church, Berlin Dahlem, Oct 1993/Apr 1994)* London 2-▲ 444630-2 [DDD]

Schuerhoff, Else (alt)

Beethoven, L. van:Missa Solemnis, w. Ilona Steingruber (sop), Ernst Majkut (ten), Otto Wiener (bass), O. Klemperer (cnd), Vienna SO, Akademie Chamber Choir *(rec Vienna, 1950)* Vox Legends 2-▲ CDX2 5527

Schuh, Audrey (sop)

Puccini, G.:La Bohème, w. Licia Albanese (sop—Mimi), Audrey Schuh (sop—Musetta), Giuseppe di Stefano (ten—Rodolfo), Arthur Cosenza (bar—Schaunard), Giuseppe Valdengo (bar—Marcello), Norman Treigle (bass—Colline), Warren Gadpaille (bass—Benoît/Alcindoro), Thomas Carter (sgr—Parpignol), Harold Crane (sgr—Custom House Official), Steve Harun (sgr—Sergeant), R. Cellini (cnd), New Orleans Opera Orch, New Orleans Opera Chorus *(rec Nov 1959)* VAI Audio 2-▲ VAIA 1119-2 [ADD]

Verdi, G.:Falstaff, w. Vivian Della Chiesa (sop—Alice), Audrey Schuh (sop—Nannetta), Lizabeth Pritchett (mez—Quickly), Evelyn Sachs (mez—Meg), André Turp (ten—Fenton), Virginio Assandri (ten—Caius), Luigi Vellucci (ten—Bardolfo), Leonard Warren (bar—Falstaff), Richard Torigi (bar—Ford), R. Cellini (cnd), New Orleans Opera Orch, New Orleans Opera Chorus *(rec live, May 5, 1956)* VAI Audio 2-▲ VAIA 1056-2

Schulte, Eike Wilm (bass)

Beethoven, L. van:Syms (comp), w. Lynne Dawson (sop), Jard Van Nes (cta), Anthony Rolfe Johnson (ten), F. Brüggen (cnd), Orch of the 18th Century, Lisbon Gulbenkian Foundation Chorus [on Sym. 9] Philips 5-▲ 442156-2

Berlioz, H.:L'Enfance du Christ, w. M. Zimmermann (mez), J. Aler (ten), S. Dean (bass), P. Kang (bass), E. Inbal (cnd), Frankfurt RSO, Cologne Radio Chorus [F] Denon 2-▲ CO 76863/4 [DDD]

Wagner, R.:Das Rheingold, w. Gabriele Fontana (sop—Woglinde), Nancy Gustafson (sop—Freia), Ildiko Komlosi (mez—Wellgunde), Hanna Schwarz (mez—Fricka), Elena Zaremba (mez—Erda), Margareta Hintermeier (cta—Flosshilde), Kim Begley (ten—Loge), Peter Schreier (ten—Mime), Thomas Sunnegardh (ten—Froh), Robert Hale (bass-bar—Wotan), Walter Fink (bass—Fafner), Franz-Josef Kapellmann (bass—Alberich), Jan-Hendrik Rootering (bass—Fasolt), Eike Wilm Schulte (bass—Donner), C. von Dohnányi (cnd), Cleveland Orch *(rec Severance Hall, Cleveland, Ohio, Dec 1993)* London 2-▲ 443690-2

Schultze, Andrew Walker (bass)

Perti, G.A.:Gesù al sepolcro, w. L. M. Åkerlund (sop), M. Zanetti (sop), C. Cavina (alt), M. Cecchetti (ten), S. Vartolo (cnd), San Petronio Cappella Musicale Orch [I] Tactus ▲ TC 661601

Vivaldi, A.:L'Olimpiade, w. L. Meeuwsen (sop), M. van der Sluis (sop), E. von Magnus (alt), G. Lesne (alt), A. Christofelis (alt), W. Oberholtzer (bar), R. Clemencic (cnd), Clemencic Consort, La Cappella Vocal Ensemble [I] *(rec live, Paris, 2/8–10/90)* Nuova Era ("Ancient Music" series) 2-▲ 6932/33 [DDD]

Schulz, Else (sop)

Strauss, R.:Ariadne auf Naxos (sels), w. Adele Kern (sop—Zerbinetta), Anny Konetzni (sop—Ariadne), Set Svanholm (ten—Bacchus), Else Schulz (sgr—Composer), R. Moralt (cnd), Vienna State Opera Orch *(rec Vienna, Oct. 16, 1941)* Koch Schwann 2-▲ SCH 314625 [ADD]

Strauss, R.:Die Frau ohne Schatten (sels), w. H. Konetzni (sop—Die Kaiserin), E. Schulz (sop—Die Färberin), T. RA. (ten—Der Kaiser), J. Herrmann (bar—Barak), K. Böhm (cnd), Vienna State Opera Orch, Vienna State Opera Chorus *(rec Nov. 23, 1943)* Koch Schwann 2-▲ SCH 314552 [ADD]

Strauss, R.:Salome (sels), w. E. Schulz (sop—Salome), A. Dermota (ten—Narraboth), J. Witt (ten—Herodes), H. Hotter (bar—Jochanaan), P. Schöffler (b-bar—Jochanaan), R. Strauss (cnd), Vienna State Opera Orch, Vienna State Opera Chorus *(rec Feb. 15 & May 6, 1942)* Koch Schwann 2-▲ SCH 314532 [ADD]

Schulze, Horst (nar)

Beethoven, L. van:Egmont (incidental music), w. Elisabeth Breul (sop), H. Bongartz (cnd), Berlin State Orch Berlin Classics ▲ BER 9106

Schulze, Siegfried (bass)

Bach, J.S.:St. Matthew Passion, w. T. Lemnitz (sop), F. Beckmann (alt), K. Erb (ten), G. Hüsch (bar), G. Ramin (cnd), Leipzig Gewandhaus Orch, St. Thomas Choir, *(abridged performance)* [G] *(rec Mar 1941)* Calig 2-▲ CAL 50 859/60 (m) [AAD]

Hoffmann, E.T.A.:Aurora, w. Thomas Rieger (trb), Maltraud Meier (mez), Koch (sgr), Ohlmann (sgr), H. Dechant (cnd), Bamberg Youth Orch, Bamberg Oratorio Chorus Bayer 3-▲ 100276-78

Schuman, Patricia (sop)

Handel, G.F.:Messiah, w. Lucia Valentini Terrani (alt), Bruce Ford (ten), Gwynne Howell (bass), Bernard Soustrot (tpt), C. Scimone (cnd), Venice Solisti, John McCarthy (cnd), Ambrosian Singers *(rec S. Francisco Church, Schio, Italy, June 23–30, 1989)* Arts 2-▲ 471052 [DDD]

Handel, G.F.:Messiah, w. Lucia Valentini Terrani (alt), Bruce Ford (ten), Gwynne Howell (bass), C. Scimone (cnd), Venice Solisti, John McCarthy (cnd), Ambrosian Singers *(rec Schio, Italy, June 23–30, 1989)* Arts 2-▲ 47105-2 [DDD]

Schumann, Elisabeth (sop)

Arias & Songs *(rec. 1926–30, from HMV 78 rpm)* Preiser ("Lebendige Vergangenheit" series) ▲ PRE 89031 (m) [AAD]

Bach, J.S.:Arias—Bist du bei mir (from the Anna Magdalena Notebook), BWV 508 *(w. orchestra cond. by L. Rosenek; from HMV DB 2291, rec. 6/23/34 in the Musikvereinsaal, Vienna)*; Aus Liebe will mein Heiland sterben (from the St Matthew Passion) & Es ist vollbracht from Cantata BWV 159 *(w. orchestra cond. by Karl Alwin; from HMV D 1410, rec. 11/11/27 in Small Queen's Hall, London)* Pearl 2-▲ PEAS 9900 (m) [AAD]

Bach, J.S.:Cant 202, "Wedding Cant", w. M. Miller (mez), et al., B. Reibold (cnd), Stuyvesant String Quartet *(rec RCA Victor Studio No. 2, New York, Oct 10 & Nov 22, 1939)* Pearl 2-▲ PEAS 9900 (m) [AAD]

Bach, J.S.:Mass in b, BWV 232, w. M. Balfour (cta), W. Widdop (ten), F. Schorr (bar), A. Coates (cnd), London SO, London Phil Chorus [L] *(rec Kingsway Hall, London Mar–Apr 1929)* Pearl 2-▲ PEAS 9900 (m) [AAD]

Elisabeth Schumann, w. orch (rec. 1927–1938 for HMV) Pearl ▲ PEA 9398 (m) [AAD]

Elisabeth Schumann, Vol. 2 *(rec 1920–1938)* Pearl ▲ PEA 9445 (m) [AAD]

1400

▲ = CD ♦ = Enhanced CD Δ = MD ■ = Cassette Tape □ = DCC

Schumann, Elisabeth (sop) (cont.)

Mozart, W.A.:Arias, w. Arleen Augér (sop), Kathleen Battle (sop), Irma Beilke (sop), Helena Braun (sop), Lisa Della Casa (sop), Maria Cebotari (sop), Ileana Cotrubas (sop), Helen Donath (sop), Mirella Freni (sop), Reri Grist (sop), Edita Gruberova (sop), Elisabeth Grümmer (sop), Hilde Güden (sop), Ingeborg Hallstein (sop), Luise Helletsgruber (sop), Gundula Janowitz (sop), Sena Jurinac (sop), Erika Köth (sop), Evelyn Lear (sop), Wilma Lipp (sop), Margaret Marshall (sop), Edith Mathis (sop), Jarmila Novotna (sop), Margherita Perras (sop), Lucia Popp (sop), Elisabeth Rethberg (sop), Anneliese Rothenberger (sop), Elisabeth Schwarzkopf (sop), Graziella Sciutti (sop), Irmgard Seefried (sop), Graziella Sciutti (sop), Julia Varady (sop), Agnes Baltsa (mez), Margit Bokor (mez), Brigitte Fassbaender (mez), Christa Ludwig (mez), Ann Murray (mez), Francisco Araiza (ten), Anton Dermota (ten), Helge Rosvaenge (ten), Rudolf Schock (ten), Peter Schreier (ten), Leopold Simoneau (ten), Eric Tappy (ten), Richard Tauber (ten), Gösta Winbergh (ten), Josef Witt (ten), Fritz Wunderlich (ten), Christian Boesch (bar), Willy Domgraf-Fassbaender (bar), Karl Dönch (bar), Dietrich Fischer-Dieskau (bar), Erich Kunz (bar), Eberhard Wächter (bar), Hans Hotter (b-bar), Paul Schöffler (b-bar), Cesare Siepi (b-bar), José Van Dam (b-bar), Walter Berry (bass), Geraint Evans (bass), Nicolai Ghiaurov (bass), Alexander Kipnis (bass), Richard Mayr (bass), Kurt Moll (bass), James Morris (bass), Ezio Pinza (bass), Martti Talvela (bass), Giorgio Tozzi (bass), Hans Duhan (sgr), Res Fischer (sgr), Marie Gerhart (sgr), *(various orchs & cnds)*—sels from Idomeneo, Die Entführung aus der Serail, Le nozze di Figaro, Don Giovanni, Così fan tutte, Die Zauberflöte & various arias Orfeo d'or ("Festspiel Dokumente" series) 5–▲ 408955

Mozart, W.A.:Exsultate, w. H. Wood (cnd), BBC SO Symposium ▲ SYM 1150

Mozart, W.A.:Nozze di Figaro (sels), w. Mariano Stabile (bar), Ninon Vallin (sop) *(rec 1905 - 1944)* Minerva ▲ MN A14 [ADD]

Mozart, W.A.:Requiem, w. K. Thorborg (mez), A. Dermota (ten), A. Kipnis (bass), B. Walter (cnd), Vienna PO, Vienna State Opera Chorus EMI Classics ("Great Recordings of the Century" series) 3–▲ CDHC 63912

Mozart, W.A.:Songs, w. M. Callas (sop), E. Grümmer (sop), E. Schwarzkopf (sop), R. Scotto (sop), T. Lemnitz (sop), E. Berger (sop), S. Jurinac (sop), I. Souez (sop), E. Rethberg (sop), L. Lehmann (sop), N. Gedda (ten), J. McCormack (ten), H. Roswenge (ten), H. Nash (ten), T. Gobbi (bar), G. Hüsch (bar), E. Kunz (bar), G. Frick (bass), E. Pinza (bass), A. Kipnis (bass) EMI Classics 4–▲ CDMD 63750

Schubert, Franz:Songs (misc), w. Gerald Moore (pno), Leo Rosenek (pno), Elizabeth Coleman (pno)—An die Nachtigall, D.497; Die Forelle, D.550; Ave Maria (Ellens Gesang III), D.839; An die Musik, D.547; Auf dem Wasser zu singen, D.774; Des Fischers Liebesglück, D.933; Der Musensohn, D.764; Fischerweise, D.881; Gretchen am Spinrade, D.118; Liebesbotschaft ("Schwanegesang" No. 1), D.957; Nacht und Träume, D.827; Seligkeit, D.433; Nähe des Geliebten, D.162; Lachen und Weinen, D.777; Frühlingstraum ("Winterreise" No. 11), D.911; Der Einsame, D.800; Nachtviolen, D.752; An die Geliebte, D.303; Wiegenlied (Schlafe, Schlafe), D.498; Der Schmetterling, D.633; Des Baches Wiegenlied (Die Schöne Müllerin" No. 20), D.957; Der Jüngling und der Tod, D.545; Das Heimweh, D.456; Dass sie hier gewesen, D.775; Der Vollmond strahlt ("Rosamunde" Romanze), D.797; Der Junge Nonne, D.828 *(rec 1933–1945)* Minerva ▲ MN–A22 [ADD]

Strauss, R.:Der Rosenkavalier, w. L. Lehmann (sop), R. Heger (cnd), Vienna PO EMI Classics 2–▲ CDHB 64487

Strauss, R.:Der Rosenkavalier, w. L. Lehmann (sop), M. Olczewska (mez), R. Mayr (bass), R. Heger (cnd), Vienna PO, Vienna State Opera Chorus—abridged performance [G] *(rec 1933 for HMV)* Pearl 2–▲ GEMMCDS 9365 (m) [AAD]

Strauss, R.:Der Rosenkavalier (sels), w. Margit Bokor (sop—Octavian), Hilde Konetzni (sop—Marschallin), Elisabeth Schumann (sop—Sophie), H. Knappertsbusch (cnd), Vienna State Opera Orch *(rec Salzburg, June 13, 1937)* Koch Schwann 2–▲ SCH 314672 [ADD]

Strauss, R.:Der Rosenkavalier (sels), w. Lotte Lehmann (sop—Feldmarschallin), Elisabeth Schumann (sop—Sophie), Eva Hadrabavá (sop—Octavian), H. Knappertsbusch (cnd), Vienna State Opera Orch *(rec Vienna, Apr. 22, 1936)* Koch Schwann 2–▲ SCH 314622 [ADD]

Strauss, R.:Songs, w. L. Lehmann (sop), R. Mayr (bass), M. Olszewska (cnd), Vienna PO EMI Classics 2–▲ CDHB 64487

Wagner, R.:Arias & Scenes, w. K. Flagstad (sop), E. Rethberg (sop), B. Nilsson (sop), F. Leider (sop), L. Melchior (ten), G. Thill (ten), A. Pertile (ten), G. Hüsch (bar), F. Schorr (b–bar), H. Hotter (b–bar), A. Kipnis (bass), *(orch unknown)* EMI Classics ("Studio" series) 4–▲ CDMC 64008

Wagner, R.:Der fliegende Holländer (sels), w. Göta Ljungberg (sop), Elisabeth Rethberg (sop), Rudolf Laubenthal (ten), Lauritz Melchior (ten), Friedrich Schorr (bar), *(cnd & orch unknown) (rec 1927–31)* Preiser 2–▲ PRE 89214 [AAD]

Wagner, R.:Götterdämmerung (sels), w. Göta Ljungberg (sop), Elisabeth Rethberg (sop), Rudolf Laubenthal (ten), Lauritz Melchior (ten), Friedrich Schorr (bar), *(cnd & orch unknown) (rec 1927–31)* Preiser 2–▲ PRE 89214 [AAD]

Wagner, R.:Die Meistersinger von Nürnberg (sels), w. Göta Ljungberg (sop), Elisabeth Rethberg (sop), Rudolf Laubenthal (ten), Lauritz Melchior (ten), Friedrich Schorr (bar), *(cnd & orch unknown) (rec 1927–31)* Preiser 2–▲ PRE 89214 [AAD]

Wagner, R.:Das Rheingold (sels), w. Göta Ljungberg (sop), Elisabeth Rethberg (sop), Rudolf Laubenthal (ten), Lauritz Melchior (ten), Friedrich Schorr (bar), *(cnd & orch unknown) (rec 1927–31)* Preiser 2–▲ PRE 89214 [AAD]

Wagner, R.:Der Ring des Nibelungen (sels), w. Adele Kern (sop), Anny Konetzni (sop), Hilde Konetzni (sop), Enid Szantho (cta), Josef Kalenberg (ten), Max Lorenz (ten), Set Svanholm (ten), Erich Zimmermann (ten), Hans Hotter (bar), Jaro Prohaska (bar), Emil Schipper (bar), Paul Schöffler (b–bar), Ludwig Hoffmann (bass), H. Knappertsbusch (cnd), Vienna State Opera Orch *(rec Vienna, 1937–1943)* Koch Schwann 2–▲ SCH 314742 [ADD]

Wagner, R.:Tannhäuser (sels), w. Göta Ljungberg (sop), Elisabeth Rethberg (sop), Rudolf Laubenthal (ten), Lauritz Melchior (ten), Friedrich Schorr (bar), *(cnd & orch unknown) (rec 1927–31)* Preiser 2–▲ PRE 89214 [AAD]

Wagner, R.:Die Walküre (sels), w. Göta Ljungberg (sop), Elisabeth Rethberg (sop), Rudolf Laubenthal (ten), Lauritz Melchior (ten), Friedrich Schorr (bar), *(orch unknown) (rec 1927–31)* Preiser 2–▲ PRE 89214 [AAD]

Schumann-Halley (sgr)

Handel, G.F.:Serse, w. L. Atkinson (trb), D. Cole (sop), A. Terzian (mez), A. Andersson (ten), T. Allen (bar), J. Teal (sgr), A. Duczmal (cnd), Amadeus CO [l] *(rec live recording produced by "Studios Classique Berlin")* Koch Schwann 3–▲ CD SC 100 300 [DDD]

Schumann-Heink, Ernestine (cta)

Schumann-Heink Nimbus ("Prima Voce" series) ▲ NI 7811–2 (m) [ADD]

Schunk, Robert (ten)

Cornelius, P.:Der Cid, w. Gertrud Ottenthal (sop), Ronnie Johansen (sgr), Albert Dohmen (bar), Michael Schopper (bass), Endrik Wottrich (sgr), G. Kuhn (cnd), Berlin RSO, Berlin Radio Chorus Koch Schwann 2–▲ SCH 315222

Wagner, R.:Der fliegende Holländer, w. L. Balsev (sop), S. Estes (bass), M. Salminen (bass), W. Nelsson (cnd), Bayreuth Festival Orch, Bayreuth Festival Chorus [G] Philips 2–▲ 434599–2 [DDD]

Wagner, R.:Das Liebesverbot, w. Pamela Coburn (sop—Mariana), Friedrich Lenz (ten—Antonio), Hermann Prey (bar—Friedrich), Keith Engen (bass—Angelo), Raimund Grumbach (bass—Danieli/Wirt), Wolfgang Fassler (sgr—Luzio), Sabine Haas (sgr—Isabella/Claudios Schwester), Alfred Kuhn (sgr—Brighella/Chef der Sbirren), Hermann Sapell (sgr—Pontio Pilato), Robert Schunk (sgr—Claudio), Marianne Seibel (sgr—Dorella), W. Sawallisch (cnd), Bavarian State Orch, Bavarian State Chorus *(rec July 9, 1983)* Orfeo d'or 3–▲ 345953

Schürhoff, Else (mez)

Humperdinck, E.:Hänsel und Gretel, w. E. Schwarzkopf (sop), E. Grümmer (sop), A. Felbermayer (sop), M. von Ilosvay (mez), J. Metternich (bar), H. von Karajan (cnd), Philharmonia Orch, Loughton High School Chorus, Bancroft's School Chorus [G] *(rec 1953)* EMI Classics ("Studio" series) 2–▲ CDMB 69293 (m) [ADD]

Schürhoff, Else (mez) (cont.)

Strauss, R.:Der Rosenkavalier, w. Jarmila Barton (sop—Marianne), Lisa Della Casa (sop—Sophie), Sena Jurinac (sop—Octavian), Ilva Ligabue (sop—Orphan), Elisabeth Schwarzkopf (sop—Marschallin), Else Schürhoff (mez—Annina), Luisa Villa (mez—Milliner), Hugues Cuénod (ten—Marschallin's majordomo), Erich Majkut (ten—Valzacchi), Giuseppe Nessi (ten—Animal seller), Luciano Della Pergola (ten—Lackey/Faninal's majordomo), Antonio Pirino (ten—An Italian Singer), Gino Del Signore (ten—Lackey/Waiter), Erich Kunz (bar—Herr von Faninal), Paolo Pedani (bar—Lackey), Attilo Barbesi (bass—Lackey/Waiter), Enrico Campi (bass—Waiter), Otto Edelmann (bass—Baron Ochs), Bruno Fichtinger (bass—Notary), Franco Taino (bass—Waiter), Maria Amadini (sgr—Orphan), Pina Carrillo (sgr—Orphan), Joszi Trojan Regar (sgr—Innkeeper), H. von Karajan (cnd), La Scala Orch, La Scala Chorus *(rec La Scala Theater, Milan, Jan. 26, 1952)* Legato Classics 3–▲ LCD 197–3

Wagner, R.:Die Meistersinger von Nürnberg, w. Irmgard Seefried (sop—Eva), Else Schürhoff (mez—Magdelene), Peter Klein (ten—David), August Seider (ten—Walther), Erich Kunz (bar—Beckmesser), Paul Schoeffler (b-bar—Hans Sachs), Herbert Alsen (bass—Pogner), K. Böhm (cnd), Vienna PO, Vienna State Opera Chorus *(rec Vienna, Nov. & Dec. 1944)* Preiser 4–▲ PRE 90234 [ADD]

Schütte, Ulrich (bar)

Weill, K.:Der Jasager, w. H. Helling (cta), T. Schmeisser (treb), T. Bräutigam (ten), T. Fischer (ten), M. Knöppel (bass), W. Gundlach (cnd), Westphalia CO, Westphalia Kantorei Capriccio ▲ 60 020–1 [DDD]

Schützendorf, L. (sgr)

Wagner, R.:Die Meistersinger von Nürnberg (sels), w. E. Marherr-Wagner (mez), R. Hutt (ten), K. Jöken (bar), F. Schorr (b–bar), E. List (bass), L. Blech (cnd), Berlin State Opera Orch, Berlin State Opera Chorus—Act 1:Hilf Gott! Will ich denn Schuster sein?; Das schöne Fest, Johannistag; Act 2:Johannistag! Johannistag!; Hab' ich heut' Singstund'?; Jerum! Jerum!; Act 3:Gleich, Meister! Hier!; Grüss' Gott, mein Evchen...Weilten die Stern' im lieblichen Tanz...O Sachs! Mein Freund!; Sankt Krispin, lobet ihn!; Silentium!...Wach' auf!; Verachtet mir die Meister nicht [G] *(rec Staatsoper unter den Linden, 5/22/28)* Pearl ▲ PEA 9340 (m) [AAD]

Schwanewilms, Anne (sgr)

Zemlinsky, A. von:Der Geburtstag der Infantin, w. Soile Isokoski (sop), Iride Martinez (sgr), Andrew Collis (sgr), David Kuebler (ten), Juanita Lascarro (sgr), Machiko Obata (sgr), Natalie Karl (sgr), Martina Rüping (sgr), Franfurter Kantorei (sgr), J. Conlon (cnd), Gürzenich Orch, Cologne PO *(rec Cologne, Feb 1996)* EMI Classics 2–▲ CDCB 56208

Schwarts, Robert (ten)

Corghi, A.:Divara—Wasser und Blut, w. Susanna von der Burg (sop—Divara), Suzanne McLeod (mez—Else Windscherer), Eva Lillian Thingboe (mez—Hille Feiken), Robert Schwarts (ten—Lame Man), Heinz Fitz (spkr—Bernd Knipperdollinck), Hanslutz Hildmann (spkr—Jan Matthys), Michael Holm (spkr—Bernhard Rothmann), Christopher Krieg (spkr—Jan van Leiden), W. Humburg (cnd), Münster SO, Münster City Theater Chorus [G] *(rec Grosses Haus, Münster State Theater, Nov. 27–29, 1993)* Marco Polo 2–▲ 8.223706/07 [DDD]

Schwartz, Magali (mez)

Demierre, J.:Songs—Bleu for solo Voice; Je deviendrai Médée for solo Voice; Désir d'azur:musique de danse (w. J. Demierre [piano & voice] *(rec Nov. 2 & 6–9, 1990)* Grammont ▲ CTSP 38–2 [DDD]

Mendelssohn, F.:Psalm 42, w. Y. Perrin (sop), O. Dufour (ten), C. Traube (ten), P. Huttenlocher (bar), C. Ossola (bass), M. Hutin (bass), C. Liang-Sheng (cnd), Geneva SO, Geneva Univ Chorus Gallo ▲ CD 635 [AAD]

Mendelssohn, F.:Psalm 95, w. Y. Perrin (sop), O. Dufour (ten), C. Traube (ten), P. Huttenlocher (bar), C. Ossola (bass), M. Hutin (bass), C. Liang-Sheng (cnd), Geneva SO, Geneva Univ Chorus Gallo ▲ CD 635 [AAD]

Mendelssohn, F.:Psalm 115, w. Y. Perrin (sop), O. Dufour (ten), C. Traube (ten), P. Huttenlocher (bar), C. Ossola (bass), M. Hutin (bass), C. Liang-Sheng (cnd), Geneva SO, Geneva Univ Chorus Gallo ▲ CD 635 [AAD]

Schwarz, Arturo (sgr)

Distel, H.:La Stazione, w. Teresita Fontana (sgr), Valeria Manzoni (sgr), Malwida Meysenbug (sgr), Federico Paternina (sgr) *(rec Milan, Italy & Bern, Switzerland, 1987 & May 1990)* Hat Hut ("NOW." series) ▲ hat ART CD 6060 [AAD]

Schwarz, Gotthold (bass)

Bach, J.S.:Cant 6, w. Barbara Schlick (sop), Andreas Scholl (ct), Christoph Prégardien (ten), C. Coin (cnd), Limoges Baroque Ensemble, Accentus Chamber Choir Astrée ▲ E 8555

Bach, J.S.:Cant 41, w. Barbara Schlick (sop), Andreas Scholl (ct), Christoph Prégardien (ten), C. Coin (cnd), Limoges Baroque Ensemble, Accentus Chamber Choir Astrée ▲ E 8555

Bach, J.S.:Cant 49, w. Barbara Schlick (sop), Andreas Scholl (alt), Christophe Prégardien (ten), C. Coin (cnd), Limoges Baroque Ensemble, Leipzig Concerto Vocale Astrée ▲ E 8530

Bach, J.S.:Cant 68, w. Barbara Schlick (sop), Andreas Scholl (ct), Christoph Prégardien (ten), C. Coin (cnd), Limoges Baroque Ensemble, Accentus Chamber Choir Astrée ▲ E 8555

Bach, J.S.:Cant 85, w. Barbara Schlick (sop), Andreas Scholl (alt), Christoph Prégardien (ten), Christophe Coin (piccolo vc/cnd), Leipzig Vocal Concerto, Limoges Baroque Ensemble Astrée ▲ E 8544

Bach, J.S.:Cant 115, w. Barbara Schlick (sop), Andreas Scholl (alt), Christophe Prégardien (ten), C. Coin (cnd), Limoges Baroque Ensemble, Leipzig Concerto Vocale Astrée ▲ E 8530

Bach, J.S.:Cant 175, w. Barbara Schlick (sop), Andreas Scholl (alt), Christoph Prégardien (ten), Christophe Coin (piccolo vc/cnd), Leipzig Vocal Concerto, Limoges Baroque Ensemble Astrée ▲ E 8544

Bach, J.S.:Cant 180, w. Barbara Schlick (sop), Andreas Scholl (alt), Christophe Prégardien (ten), C. Coin (cnd), Limoges Baroque Ensemble, Leipzig Concerto Vocale Astrée ▲ E 8530

Bach, J.S.:Cant 183, w. Barbara Schlick (sop), Andreas Scholl (alt), Christoph Prégardien (ten), Christophe Coin (piccolo vc/cnd), Leipzig Vocal Concerto, Limoges Baroque Ensemble Astrée ▲ E 8544

Bach, J.S.:Cant 199, w. Barbara Schlick (sop), Andreas Scholl (alt), Christoph Prégardien (ten), Christophe Coin (piccolo vc/cnd), Leipzig Vocal Concerto, Limoges Baroque Ensemble Astrée ▲ E 8544

Biber, H. von:Chi la dura la vince, w. Barbara Schlick (sop), Gerd Türk (ten), Xenia Meijer (sgr), W. Brunner (cnd), Salzburg Hofmusik CPO 3–▲ CPO 999258 [DDD]

Fux, J.J.:La Fede sacrilega nella morte del Precursor San Giovanni Battista, "Johannes der Täufer", w. J. Koslowsky (sop), M. Lins (sop), H. Helling (cta), J. Calaminus (ten), T. Reuber (cnd), Capella Piccola Neuss [period instrs] [l] Thorofon 2–▲ CTH 2071/72 [DDD]

Haydn, J.:L'Anima del filosofo, or Orfeo ed Euridice, w. Clara McFadden (sop), Marylin Schmiege (mez), Christoph Prégardien, M. Schneider (cnd), La Stagione, La Stagione Choir Deutsche Harmonia Mundi 2–▲ 05472–77229–2

Rheinberger, J.:Songs, w. Jürgen Sonnetheil (org)—Religious Songs (6), Op. 157; Elegaic Songs (2), Op. 128 *(rec Peine, May 1995–July 1996)* CPO ▲ 999351–2 [DDD]

Schubert, Franz:Mass 5, w. S. Chilcott (sop), R. Cyrille (alt), Vonk (ten), R. Delcroix (cnd), Basque Bayonne-Côte Orch, Ametsa D'Irun Choir [L] Forlane ▲ FOR 16649 [DDD]

Schwarz, Hanna (mez)

Bach, J.S.:Cant 106, "Actus tragicus", w. E. Csapó (sop), A. Kraus (ten), W. Schöne (bass), H. Rilling (cnd), Bach Ensemble *(rec Jan 1975)* Hänssler Classic ▲ 98.830 [AAD]

Beethoven, L. van:Missa Solemnis, w. E. Moser (sop), A. Kollo (ten), K. Moll (bass), L. Bernstein (cnd), Royal Concertgebouw Orch, Hilversum Chorus [L] Deutsche Grammophon 2–▲ 413780–2 [ADD]

Humperdinck, E.:Hänsel und Gretel, w. B. Bonney (sop), E. Lind (sop), B. Hendricks (sop), A.S. von Otter (mez), M. Lipovšek (mez), Andreas Schmidt (bar), J. Tate (cnd), Bavarian RSO, Tölz Boys' Choir [G] EMI Classics 2–▲ CDCB 54022 [DDD]

Humperdinck, E.:Hänsel und Gretel, w. H. Behrens (sop—Gertrud, the Stepmother), R. Ziesak (sop—Gretel), R. Joshua (sop—Sandman), C. Schäfer (sop—Dew Fairy), J. Larmore (mez—Hänsel), H. Schwarz (cta—Nibblewitch), B. Weikl (bar—Peter, the Father), D. Runnicles (cnd), Bavarian RSO, Tölz Boys' Choir *(rec Munich, Feb. 1994)* Teldec 2–▲ 94549–2 [DDD]

Mahler, G.:Songs from Rückert, w. C. Abbado (cnd), Chicago SO [G] Deutsche Grammophon ("Galleria" series) 2–▲ 423928–2 [ADD/DDD]

Mozart, W.A.:Complete Mozart Edition, w. A. Augér (sop), E. Mathis (sop), A. Rolfe Johnson (ten), L. Hager (cnd), Salzburg Mozarteum Orch, Salzburg Mozarteum Chorus Philips 2–▲ 422526–2 [ADD]

Schwarz, Hanna (mez) (cont.)
Mozart, W.A.:Zauberflöte, w. Edith Mathis (sop), Karin Ott (sop), Janet Perry (sop), Anna Tomowa-Sintow (sop), Agnes Baltsa (mez), Francisco Araiza (ten), Gottfried Hornik (bar), José Van Dam (b-bar), H. von Karajan (cnd), Berlin PO, German Opera Chorus [G] Deutsche Grammophon 3-▲ 410967-2 [DDD]
Mozart, W.A.:Zauberflöte, w. M. Price (sop—Pamina), L. Serra (sop—Queen of the Night), M. Venuti (sop—Papagena), M. McLaughlin (sop—1st Lady), A. Murray (mez—2nd Lady), H. Schwarz (cta—3rd Lady), F. Höher (trb—1st Boy), M. Diedrich (trb—2nd Boy), F. Klos (trb—3rd Boy), P. Schreier (ten—Tamino), R. Tear (ten—Monostatos), R. Goldberg (ten—1st Armoured Man), K. Moll (bass—Sarastro), H. Rech (bass—2nd Armoured Man), C. Davis (cnd), Dresden Staatskapelle, Leipzig Radio Chorus Philips ("Duo" series) 2-▲ 442568-2
Mozart, W.A.:Zauberflöte (sels), w. Edith Mathis (sop), Karin Ott (sop), Janet Perry (sop), Anna Tomowa-Sintow (sop), Agnes Baltsa (mez), Francisco Araiza (ten), Gottfried Hornik (bar), José Van Dam (b-bar), H. von Karajan (cnd), Berlin PO, German Opera Chorus [G] Deutsche Grammophon ▲ 415287-2 [DDD]
Nicolai, O.:Lustigen Weiber, w. H. Donath (sop), E. Mathis (sop), K. Ludwig (ten), K.-E. Mercker (ten), P. Schreier (ten), C. Dormoy (bar), B. Weikl (bar), K. Moll (bass), S. Vogel (bass), H. Klee (cnd), Berlin Staatskapelle, Berlin State Opera Chorus *(rec July 3, 1976)* Berlin Classics ("Eterna" series) ▲ BER 2046-2 [ADD]
Nicolai, O.:Lustigen Weiber, w. H. Donath (sop), E. Mathis (sop), P. Schreier (ten), K. Moll (bass), B. Klee (cnd), Berlin Staatskapelle, Berlin State Opera Chorus Berlin Classics 2-▲ BER 2115 [ADD]
Schnittke, A.:Historia von D. Johann Fausten, w. Hanna Schwarz (mez—Fair Helen), Arno Raunig (alt—Mephostophiles), Eberhard Büchner (ten—Old Man), Jürgen Freier (bar—Dr. Johann Faustus), Jonathan Barreto-Ramos (sgr—Student), Jürgen Fersch (sgr—Student), Eberhard Lorenz (sgr—Erzähler), Christoph Johannes Wendel (sgr—Student), G. Albrecht (cnd), Hamburg State PO, Hamburg State Opera Chorus *(rec live, Hamburg, Germany)* RCA Red Seal 2-▲ 09026-68413-2
Schubert, Franz:Lazarus, or Die Feier der Auferstehung, w. E. Mathis (sop), C. Wulkopf (mez), W. Hollweg (ten), H. Laubenthal (ten), H. Prey (bar), G. Chmura (cnd), Stuttgart RSO, Stuttgart Radio Chorus [G] Orfeo ▲ 011101 [DDD]
Strauss, R.:Die Frau ohne Schatten, w. C. Studer (sop), U. Vinzing (sop), R. Kollo (ten), A. Muff (bass), Schmidt (sgr), W. Sawallisch (cnd), Bavarian RSO, Bavarian Radio Chorus [uncut version] [G] EMI Classics 3-▲ CDCC 49074 [DDD]
Strauss, R.:Die Frau ohne Schatten, w. C. Studer (sop), U. Vinzing (sop), R. Kollo (ten), A. Muff (bass), Schmidt (sgr), W. Sawallisch (cnd), Bavarian RSO, Bavarian Radio Chorus [G] EMI Classics ▲ CDC 54494 [DDD]
Strauss, R.:Salome, w. Catherine Malfitano (sop), Kenneth Riegel (ten), Bryn Terfel (b-bar), C. von Dohnányi (cnd), Vienna PO London 2-▲ 444178-2
Wagner, R.:Götterdämmerung, w. H. Behrens (sop), C. Studer (sop), R. Goldberg (ten), B. Weikl (bar), E. Wlaschiha (bar), M. Salminen (bass), J. Levine (cnd), Metropolitan Opera Orch, New York Metropolitan Opera Chorus Deutsche Grammophon 4-▲ 429385-2 [DDD]
Wagner, R.:Das Rheingold, w. Gabriele Fontana (sop—Woglinde), Nancy Gustafson (sop—Freia), Ildiko Komlosi (mez—Wellgunde), Hanna Schwarz (mez—Fricka), Elena Zaremba (mez—Erda), Margareta Hintermeier (cta—Flosshilde), Kim Begley (ten—Loge), Peter Schreier (ten—Mime), Thomas Sunnegardh (ten—Froh), Robert Hale (bass-bar—Wotan), Walter Fink (bass—Fafner), Franz-Josef Kapellmann (bass—Alberich), Jan-Hendrik Rootering (bass—Fasolt), Eike Wilm Schulte (bass—Donner), C. von Dohnányi (cnd), Cleveland Orch *(rec Severance Hall, Cleveland, Ohio, Dec 1993)* London 2-▲ 443690-2
Wagner, R.:Das Rheingold, w. H. Zednik (ten), H. Becht (bar), D. McIntyre (b-bar), P. Boulez (cnd), Bayreuth Festival Orch, Bayreuth Festival Chorus [G] Philips 2-▲ 434421-2 [DDD]
Wagner, R.:Der Ring des Nibelungen, w. G. Jones (sop), T. Altmeyer (ten), L. Hofmann (bass), D. McIntyre (b-bar), P. Boulez (cnd), Bayreuth Festival Orch, Bayreuth Festival Chorus Philips 32-▲ 434420-2 [ADD/DDD]

Schwarz, Joseph (bar)
Joseph Schwarz *(rec. 1916-18 for Gramophone)* Preiser ("Lebendige Vergangenheit" series) ▲ PRE 89033 (m) [AAD]

Schwarz, Vera (sop)
Berg, A.:Lulu, w. T. Stratas (sop), Y. Minton (mez), K. Riegel (ten), F. Mazura (bar), P. Boulez (cnd), Paris Opera Orch—Act 3 [G] Deutsche Grammophon 3-▲ 415489-2 [ADD]

Schwarz, Volker (nar)
Eisler, H.:Deutsche Sinfonie, w. Hendrikje Wangemann (sop), Annette Markert (alt), Matthias Görne (bar), Peter Lika (bass), Gert Gütschow (speaker), L. Zagrosek (cnd), Leipzig Gewandhaus Orch, Ernst Senff Chorus *(rec Gewandhaus, Leipzig, May 1995)* London ("Entartet Musik" series) ▲ 448389-2 [DDD]

Schwarzkopf, Elisabeth (sop)
Bach & Mozart Arias, w. various Italian orchs *(rec live 1952-1961)* Melodram ▲ CDM 16529 [ADD]
Bach, J.S.:Cant 51, w. E. Jochum (cnd), Bavarian RSO *(rec Munich, 1951)* Bella Voce 2-▲ 107.201 [AAD]
Bach, J.S.:Cant 92, w. U. Rapalo (cnd), Naples Alessandro Scarlatti RAI Orch *(rec Naples, Apr 15, 1958)* Bella Voce 2-▲ 107.201 [AAD]
Bach, J.S.:Cant 202, "Wedding Cant", w. O. Klemperer (cnd), Royal Concertgebouw Orch *(rec 1957)* Legend ▲ LGD 103 [ADD]
Bach, J.S.:Cant 202, "Wedding Cant", w. O. Klemperer (cnd), Royal Concertgebouw Orch *(rec live, 1957)* As Disc ▲ ASD 2504 (m)
Bach, J.S.:Cant 202, "Wedding Cant", w. O. Klemperer (cnd), Royal Concertgebouw Orch *(rec Amsterdam, Feb 16, 1957)* Bella Voce 2-▲ 107.201 [AAD]
Bach, J.S.:Mass in b, BWV 232, w. K. Ferrier (cta), A. Galliera (cnd), Philharmonia Orch EMI Classics ▲ CDM 63655
Bach, J.S.:Mass in b, BWV 232, w. C. Ludwig (mez), K. Ferrier (cta), A. Poell (b-bar), Schöffler (bass), H. von Karajan (cnd), Vienna SO [L] *(rec live at Vienna's International Bach Festival, June 15, 1950)* Verona 2-▲ 27073/74 (m) [AAD]
Bach, J.S.:Mass in b, BWV 232, w. C. Ludwig (mez), K. Ferrier (cta), A. Poell (b-bar), Schöffler (bass), H. von Karajan (cnd), Vienna SO, Vienna Singverein—6 arias excerpted from the above rec'g Verona ▲ 27076 (m) [AAD]
Bach, J.S.:St. Matthew Passion, w. C. Ludwig (mez), N. Gedda (ten), S. Fischer-Dieskau (bar), W. Berry (bass), O. Klemperer (cnd), Philharmonia Orch EMI Classics 3-▲ ZDMC 63058
Beethoven, L. van:Syms (comp), w. E. Höngen (mez), H. Hopf (ten), O. Edelmann (bass), W. Furtwängler (cnd), Vienna PO, Bayreuth Festival Orch, Bayreuth Festival Chorus *(rec 1948-54)* EMI Classics 5-▲ CDHE 63606
Beethoven, L. van:Sym 9, "Choral Sym", w. Elsa Cavelti (mez), Ernst Haefliger (ten), Otto Edelmann (bass), W. Furtwängler (cnd), Philharmonia Orch, Lucerne Festival Chorus *(rec Aug 22, 1954)* Music & Arts ▲ CD 790 [ADD]
Brahms, J.:Ein Deutsches Requiem, w. D. Fischer-Dieskau (bar), O. Klemperer (cnd), Philharmonia Orch, Philharmonia Chorus [G] EMI Classics 2-▲ CDC 47238
Brahms, J.:Ein Deutsches Requiem, w. H. Hotter (bar), H. von Karajan (cnd), Vienna PO, Vienna Singverein [G] *(rec 10/47)* EMI Classics ("Great Recordings of the Century" series) ▲ CDH 61010 (m) [ADD]
Christmas Album, w. Charles Mackerras, Philharmonia Orch, Ambrosian Singers *(rec 1957)* EMI Classics ("Studio" series) ▲ CDM 63574 [ADD]
Cornelius, P.:Der Barbier von Bagdad, w. G. Hoffman (cta), N. Gedda (ten), G. Unger (ten), O. Czerwenka (bass), E. Leinsdorf (cnd), Philharmonia Orch, Philharmonia Chorus EMI Classics ▲ CDMB 65284
Debussy, C.:Pelléas et Mélisande, w. E. Haefliger (ten), M. Roux (bar), M. Petri (bass), H. von Karajan (cnd), Rome Radio Orch, Rome RAI Chorus [F] *(rec live, 12/19/54)* Arkadia 2-▲ 218 (m) [ADD]
Elisabeth Schwarzkopf EMI Classics ("Diva" series) ▲ CDM 65577
The Elisabeth Schwarzkopf Album Acanta ▲ 43801
Encores, w. Gerald Moore (pno), Geoffrey Parsons (pno) EMI Classics ▲ CDM 63654
Gieseking, W.:Kinderleider, w. W. Gieseking (pno)—Cantata 199, Mein Herze schwimmt in Blut *(rec 1955)* EMI Classics ▲ CDM 63655

Schwarzkopf, Elisabeth (sop) (cont.)
Great Sopranos of Our Time, w. Maria Callas (sop), Joan Sutherland (sop), Renata Scotto (sop), Montserrat Caballé (sop), Victoria de los Angeles (sop), Mirella Freni (sop), Ileana Cotrubas (sop), Edita Gruberova (sop) Classics for Pleasure ▲ CDEMX 9519 [ADD]
Handel, G.F.:Messiah, w. Grace Hoffman (cta), Nikolai Gedda (ten), Jerome Hines (bass), O. Klemperer (cnd), Philharmonia Orch, Philharmonia Chorus EMI Classics 3-▲ ZDMC 63621
Humperdinck, E.:Hänsel und Gretel, w. Sena Jurinac (sop), Rita Streich (sop), Vittoria Palombini (mez), Rolando Panerai (bar), Bruna Ronshini (sgr), H. von Karajan (cnd), Milan Italian Radio-TV Orch, Milan RAI Chorus Stradivarius 2-▲ STV 12314
Humperdinck, E.:Hänsel und Gretel, w. E. Grümmer (sop), A. Felbermayer (sop), M. von Ilosvay (mez), E. Schürhoff (mez), J. Metternich (bar), H. von Karajan (cnd), Philharmonia Orch, Loughton High School Chorus, Bancroft's School Chorus [G] *(rec 1953)* EMI Classics ("Studio" series) 2-▲ CDMB 69293 (m) [ADD]
Humperdinck, E.:Hänsel und Gretel (sels), w. Sena Jurinac (sop—Hänsel), Elisabeth Schwarzkopf (sop—Gretel), Vittoria Palombini (mez—Witch), Rolando Panerai (sgr—Peter), Bruna Ronchini (sgr—Gertrude), H.. Karajan (cnd), Milan RAI SO, Milan RAI Chorus—[Act 1] Suse, liebe Suse, was raschelt im Stroh; [Act 2] Ein Männlein steht im Walde ganz still und Stumm; Abends, will ich schlafen gehn; [Act 3] Wo bin ich? Wach' ich?; Und bist du dann drin...schwaps!; Die Englein haben's im Traum gesagt; Schunt, o schunt das Wunder an *(rec Milan, Dec. 25, 1954)* Legato Classics 3-▲ LCD 197-3
In Recital (1957 & 1962), w. Felix de Nobel (pno) Verona ▲ 27021 (m) [AAD]
Lehár, F.:Die lustige Witwe, w. E. Loose (sop), N. Gedda (ten), E. Kunz (bar), A. Kraus (ten), O. Ackermann (cnd), Philharmonia Orch, Philharmonia Chorus [G] EMI Classics ("Studio" series) ▲ CDH 69520 (m) [ADD]
Lehár, F.:Die lustige Witwe, w. H. Steffek (sop), N. Gedda (ten), E. Wächter (bar), L. von Matačić (cnd), Philharmonia Orch, Philharmonia Chorus [G] EMI Classics 2-▲ CDCB 47177
Lieder Recital, w. Gerald Moore (pno) *(rec Aug 7, 1956)* EMI Classics ▲ CDM 66084
Mahler, G.:Des Knaben Wunderhorn, w. D. Fischer-Dieskau (bar), G. Szell (cnd), London SO EMI Classics ▲ CDC 47277
Mahler, G.:Songs, w. B. Walter (cnd), Vienna PO *(rec May, 1960)* Arkadia ▲ 767 [ADD]
Mahler, G.:Songs, w. B. Walter (cnd), Vienna PO—Ich atmet' einen Linden Duft; Ich bin der Welt abhanden gekommen; Wo die schönen Trumpeten blasen [G] *(rec live, May 29, 1960)* Music & Arts 2-▲ CD 705-2 [AAD]
Mahler, G.:Sym 2, w. H. Rössl-Majdan (mez), O. Klemperer (cnd), Philharmonia Orch, Philharmonia Chorus [G] EMI Classics ("Studio" series) ▲ CDM 69662 [ADD]
Mahler, G.:Sym 4, w. O. Klemperer (cnd), Philharmonia Orch EMI Classics ▲ CDM 69667
Mahler, G.:Sym 4, w. B. Walter (cnd), Vienna PO *(rec May 1960)* Arkadia ▲ 767 [ADD]
Mahler, G.:Sym 4, w. B. Walter (cnd), Vienna PO *(rec live, May 29, 1960)* Music & Arts 2-▲ CD 705-2 [AAD]
Mozart, W.A.:Arias, w. Arleen Augér (sop), Kathleen Battle (sop), Irma Beilke (sop), Helena Braun (sop), Lisa Della Casa (sop), Maria Cebotari (sop), Ileana Cotrubas (sop), Helen Donath (sop), Mirella Freni (sop), Reri Grist (sop), Edita Gruberova (sop), Elisabeth Grümmer (sop), Hilde Güden (sop), Ingeborg Hallstein (sop), Luise Helletsgruber (sop), Gundula Janowitz (sop), Sena Jurinac (sop), Erika Köth (sop), Evelyn Lear (sop), Wilma Lipp (sop), Margaret Marshall (sop), Edith Mathis (sop), Jarmila Novotna (sop), Margherita Perras (sop), Lucia Popp (sop), Elisabeth Rethberg (sop), Anneliese Rothenberger (sop), Elisabeth Schumann (sop), Graziella Sciutti (sop), Irmgard Seefried (sop), Graziella Sciutti (sop), Julia Varady (sop), Agnes Baltsa (mez), Margit Bokor (mez), Brigitte Fassbaender (mez), Christa Ludwig (mez), Ann Murray (mez), Francisco Araiza (ten), Anton Dermota (ten), Helge Rosvaenge (ten), Rudolf Schock (ten), Peter Schreier (ten), Leopold Simoneau (ten), Eric Tappy (ten), Richard Tauber (ten), Gösta Winbergh (ten), Josef Witt (ten), Fritz Wunderlich (ten), Christian Boesch (bar), Willy Domgraf-Fassbaender (bar), Karl Dönch (bar), Dietrich Fischer-Dieskau (bar), Erich Kunz (bar), Eberhard Wächter (bar), Hans Hotter (b-bar), Paul Schöffler (b-bar), Cesare Siepi (b-bar), José Van Dam (b-bar), Walter Berry (bass), Geraint Evans (bass), Nicolai Ghiaurov (bass), Alexander Kipnis (bass), Richard Mayr (bass), Kurt Moll (bass), James Morris (bass), Ezio Pinza (bass), Martti Talvela (bass), Giorgio Tozzi (bass), Hans Duhan (sgr), Res Fischer (sgr), Marie Gerhart (sgr), *(various orchs & cnds)*—sels from Idomeneo, Die Entführung aus der Serail, Le nozze di Figaro, Don Giovanni, Così fan tutte, Die Zauberflöte & various arias Orfeo d'or ("Festspiel Dokumente" series) 5-▲ 408955
Mozart, W.A.:Arias, w. A. Brendel (pno), G. Szell (cnd), London SO—4 Concert arias EMI Classics ▲ CDH 63702
Mozart, W.A.:Così fan tutte, w. Graziella Sciutti (sop), Nan Merriman (mez), Luigi Alva (ten), Rolando Panerai (bar), Franco Calabrese (bass), G. Cantelli (cnd), La Scala Orch, La Scala Chorus Stradivarius 2-▲ STV DTM 12304 [ADD]
Mozart, W.A.:Così fan tutte, w. H. Steffek (sop), C. Ludwig (mez), A. Kraus (ten), G. Taddei (bar), W. Berry (bass), K. Böhm (cnd), Philharmonia Orch, Philharmonia Chorus [I] EMI Classics ("Studio" series) 3-▲ CDMC 69330 [ADD]
Mozart, W.A.:Così fan tutte, w. E. Schwarzkopf (sop—Fiordiligi), G. Sciurri (sop—Despina), N. Merriman (mez—Dorabella), L. Alva (ten—Ferrando), R. Panerai (bar—Guglielmo), F. Clabrese (b-bar—Don Alfonso)., G. Cantelli (cnd), La Scala Orch, La Scala Chorus *(rec Jan. 27, 1956)* Datum 2-▲ DAT 12304 [ADD]
Mozart, W.A.:Così fan tutte, w. L. Otto (sop), N. Merriman (mez), L. Simoneau (ten), R. Panerai (bar), S. Bruscantini (bar), H. von Karajan (cnd), Philharmonia Orch, Philharmonia Chorus [I] EMI Classics ("Studio" series) 3-▲ CDHC 69635 (m) [ADD]
Mozart, W.A.:Così fan tutte, w. E. Schwarzkopf (sop—Fiordiligi), C. Ludwig (sop—Dorabella), G. Sciutti (sop—Despina), W. Kmentt (ten—Ferrando), H. Prey (bar—Gugliemo), K. Dönch (bar—D. Alfonso), K. Böhm (cnd), Vienna PO, Vienna State Opera Chorus [I] *(rec live, Salzburg, Aug. 8, 1962)* Arkadia 2-▲ 455 [ADD]
Mozart, W.A.:Così fan tutte (sels), w. Lisa Otto (sop), Nan Merriman (mez), Rolando Panerai (bar), Leopold Simoneau (ten), Sesto Bruscantini (bass), H. von Karajan (cnd), Philharmonia Orch Classics for Pleasure ("Eminence" series) ▲ CDEMX 2211 [DDD]
Mozart, W.A.:Così fan tutte (sels), w. Irmgard Seefried (sop), Christa Ludwig (mez), Anton Dermota (ten), Erich Kunz (bar), Paul Schoeffler (b-bar), K. Böhm (cnd), Vienna PO—Sento, o Dio; Sorella, cosa dici?—Prenderò quel brunettino Orfeo d'or ("Festspiel Dokumente" series) ▲ 394201
Mozart, W.A.:Don Giovanni, w. E. Grümmer (sop), E. Berger (sop), A. Dermota (ten), C. Siepi (b-bar), O. Edelmann (b-bar), W. Berry (bass), W. Furtwängler (cnd), Vienna PO, Vienna State Opera Chorus *(rec Salzburg, Aug. 3, 1953)* EMI Classics ("Great Recordings of the Century" series) 2-▲ CDHB 63860
Mozart, W.A.:Don Giovanni, w. L. Welitsch (sop), I. Seefried (sop), A. Dermota (ten), E. Kunz (bar), T. Gobbi (bar), A. Poell (b-bar), J. Greindl (bass), W. Furtwängler (cnd), Vienna PO, Vienna State Opera Chorus *(rec 1950)* Laudis 3-▲ LDS 4001 [AAD]
Mozart, W.A.:Don Giovanni, w. E. Grümmer (sop), E. Berger (sop), A. Dermota (ten), C. Siepi (b-bar), O. Edelmann (b-bar), W. Berry (bass), W. Furtwängler (cnd), Vienna PO, Vienna State Opera Chorus *(rec 1953)* Arkadia 3-▲ 509 (m) [AAD]
Mozart, W.A.:Don Giovanni (sels), w. G. Sciutti (sop), J. Sutherland (sop), L. Alva (ten), E. Wächter (bar), C. M. Giulini (cnd), Philharmonia Orch EMI Classics ▲ ZDM 63078
Mozart, W.A.:Nehmt meninen Dank, w. A. Galliera (cnd), Philharmonia Orch EMI Classics ▲ CDM 63655
Mozart, W.A.:Nozze di Figaro, w. Elisabeth Schwarzkopf (sop—Countess), Irmgard Seefried (sop—Susanna), Hilde Güden (mez—Cherubino), Paul Schöffler (bar—Almaviva), Erich Kunz (bass—Figaro), W. Furtwängler (cnd), Vienna PO, Vienna State Opera Chorus *(rec Salzburg Festival, Aug 8, 1953)* EMI Classics 3-▲ CDHC 66080
Mozart, W.A.:Nozze di Figaro, w. A. Moffo (sop), F. Cossotto (mez), G. Taddei (bar), E. Wächter (bar), C. M. Giulini (cnd), Philharmonia Orch, Philharmonia Chorus [I] EMI Classics ("Studio" series) 2-▲ CDMB 63266 [ADD]
Mozart, W.A.:Nozze di Figaro, w. G. Sciurri (sop), G. Taddei (bar), H. Prey (bar), C. M. Giulini (cnd), Residentie Orch The Hague, Netherlands Chamber Choir [I] *(rec live, Holland Festival, 1961)* Verona 3-▲ 27092/94
Mozart, W.A.:Nozze di Figaro, w. I. Seefried (sop), S. Jurinac (sop), E. Höngen (cta), G. London (bar), E. Kunz (bar), H. von Karajan (cnd), Vienna PO, Vienna State Opera Chorus—omitting recitatives [I] *(rec 1950)* EMI Classics ("Studio" series) 2-▲ CDMB 69639 (m) [ADD]

1402
▲ = CD ♦ = Enhanced CD Δ = MD ■ = Cassette Tape ◻ = DCC

Schwarzkopf, Elisabeth (sop) (cont.)

Mozart, W.A.:Nozze di Figaro, w. I. Seefried (sop), S. Jurinac (sop), L. Villa (sop), R. Panerai (bar), H. von Karajan (cnd), La Scala Orch, La Scala Chorus [I] *(rec live Feb. 4, 1954)* Melodram 3–▲ MEL 37075 [AAD]

Mozart, W.A.:Nozze di Figaro (sels), w. A. Moffo (sop), F. Cossotto (mez), G. Taddei (bar), E. Wächter (bar), C. M. Giulini (cnd), Philharmonia Orch, Philharmonia Chorus—sels. EMI Classics ("Studio" series) ▲ CDM 63409

Mozart, W.A.:Songs, w. W. Gieseking (pno) EMI Classics ▲ CDH 63702

Mozart, W.A.:Songs, w. M. Callas (sop), E. Grümmer (sop), R. Scotto (sop), T. Lemnitz (sop), E. Berger (sop), S. Jurinac (sop), E. Schumann (sop), I. Souez (sop), E. Rethberg (sop), L. Lehmann (sop), N. Gedda (ten), J. McCormack (ten), H. Roswenge (ten), H. Nash (ten), T. Gobbi (bar), G. Hüsch (bar), E. Kunz (bar), G. Frick (bass), E. Pinza (bass), A. Kipnis (bass) EMI Classics 4–▲ CDMD 63750

Mozart, W.A.:Songs, w. F. de Nobel (pno)—Als Louise die Briefe; Un moto di gioia [G,I] *(rec in recital, 1957)* Verona ▲ 27021 (m) [AAD]

Mozart, W.A.:Zauberflöte, w. R. Streich (sop), A. Noni (sop), N. Gedda (ten), G. Taddei (bar), M. Petri (bass), H. von Karajan (cnd), Rome Radio Orch, Rome RAI Chorus [I] *(rec live, Dec. 19, 1953)* Myto 2–▲ 2 MCD 89007 (m) [ADD]

Offenbach, J.:Les Contes d'Hoffmann, w. G. d'Angelo (sop), V. de los Angeles (sop), N. Gedda (ten), G. London (bar), E. Blanc (bar), A. Cluytens (cnd), Paris Conservatory Societé des Concerts Orch, René DuClos Chorus [F] EMI Classics ("Studio" series) 2–▲ CDMB 63222 [ADD]

Opera Arias EMI Classics ▲ CDM 63657

Orff, C.:Die Kluge, w. R. Christ (ten), P. Kuén (ten), M. Cordes (bar), B. Kusche (bar), H. Prey (bar), G. Frick (bass), G. Wieter (bass), W. Sawallisch (cnd), Philharmonia Orch [G] EMI Classics ("Studio" series) 2–▲ CDMB 63712 [ADD]

Puccini, G.:Turandot, w. M. Callas (sop), E. Fernandi (ten), N. Zaccaria (bass), T. Serafin (cnd), La Scala Orch, La Scala Chorus [I] *(rec 1957)* EMI Classics 2–▲ CDCB 47971 (m) [ADD]

Recital, w. Hans Rosbaud (pno) (rec. live, Aix-en-Provence 7/29/54) Melodram 2–▲ CDM 26524 [ADD]

Recital, w. Geoffrey Parsons (pno) (rec. live, from a Swiss-Italian Radio 2 broadcast 10/6/67) Ermitage ▲ ERM 109 [ADD]

Recital, 29 June 1969, w. Aldo Ciccolini (pno) Arkadia ▲ 802 [ADD]

Recital I, w. various orchs *(rec. live from Salzburg, Vienna, Berlin & Hamburg, 1941–1960)* Melodram ▲ CDM 16501 [AAD]

Schubert, Franz:Songs (misc), w. E. Fischer (pno)—21 songs, including—An die Musik; An Sylvia; Ganymed; Gretchen am Spinnrade [G] *(rec 1952)* Angel ("Great Recordings of the Century" series) ▲ CDH 64026

Schubert, Franz:Songs (misc), w. F. de Nobel (pno)—5 songs—An Sylvia; Der Einsame; Romanze aus Rosamunde; Die Vögel; Gretchen am Spinnrade [G] *(rec in recital, 1957)* Verona ▲ 27021 (m) [AAD]

Schubert, Franz:Songs (misc), w. G. Moore (pno), G. Parsons (pno) EMI Classics ▲ CDM 63656

Schwarzkopf & Seefried, Duets, w. Irmgard Seefried (sop), Gerald Moore (pno), Philharmonia Orch [cnd:H. von Karajan] EMI Classics ▲ CDH 69793

Sings Operetta, w. Philharmonia Orch, Philharmonia Chorus [cnd:O. Ackermann] EMI Classics ▲ CDC 47284

Songs (rec. 1960–64) Verona ▲ 27075 [AAD]

Strauss (II), Joh.:Die Fledermaus, w. R. Streich (sop), N. Gedda (ten), H. Krebs (ten), R. Christ (ten), E. Kunz (bar), K. Dönch (bar), H. von Karajan (cnd), Philharmonia Orch, Philharmonia Chorus [G] EMI Classics ("Studio" series) 2–▲ CDHB 69531 (m) [ADD]

Strauss, R.:Arabella (sels), w. E. Loose (sop), J. Metternich (bar), L. von Matačić (cnd), Philharmonia Orch [G] EMI Classics ("Great Recordings of the Century" series) ▲ CDH 61001 (m)

Strauss, R.:Ariadne auf Naxos, w. I. Seefried (sop), R. Streich (sop), L. Otto (sop), G. Hoffman (mez), R. Schock (ten), G. Unger (ten), H. Cuénod (ten), H. Prey (bar), F. Ollendorff (bass), H. von Karajan (cnd), Philharmonia Orch [G] *(rec 1954)* EMI Classics ("Studio" series) 2–▲ CDMB 69296 (m) [ADD]

Strauss, R.:Ariadne auf Naxos, w. Elisabeth Schwarzkopf (sop—Ariadne/Prima Donna), Irmgard Seefried (sop—Zerbinetta), Rita Streich (sop—The Composer), Rudolf Schock (ten—Bacchus), H. von Karajan (cnd), Philharmonia Orch EMI Classics 2–▲ CDCB 55176

Strauss, R.:Capriccio, w. A. Moffo (sop), C. Ludwig (mez), N. Gedda (ten), D. Fischer-Dieskau (bar), E. Wächter (bar), H. Hotter (b-bar), W. Sawallisch (cnd), Philharmonia Orch [G] EMI Classics 2–▲ CDCB 49014 (m) [ADD]

Strauss, R.:Capriccio (sels), w. O. Ackermann (cnd), Philharmonia Orch—Closing Scene [G] EMI Classics ("Great Recordings of the Century" series) ▲ CDH 61001 (m)

Strauss, R.:4 Last Songs, w. G. Szell (cnd), Berlin RSO [G] EMI Classics ▲ CDC 47276

Strauss, R.:4 Last Songs, w. O. Ackermann (cnd), Philharmonia Orch [G] EMI Classics ("Great Recordings of the Century" series) ▲ CDH 61001 (m)

Strauss, R.:4 Last Songs, w. H. von Karajan (cnd), Philharmonia Orch EMI Classics ▲ CDM 63655

Strauss, R.:Der Rosenkavalier, w. Christa Ludwig (mez), Teresa Stich-Randall (mez), Otto Edelmann (b-bar), H. von Karajan (cnd), Philharmonia Orch, Philharmonia Chorus *(rec 1956)* EMI Classics ▲ CDCC 56113 (m)

Strauss, R.:Der Rosenkavalier, w. E. Schwarzkopt (sop—Feldmarschallin), A. Rothenberger (sop—Sophie), S. Jurinac (sop—Octavian), O. Edelmann (bass—Baron Ochs), H. von Karajan (cnd), Vienna PO *(rec live, Salzburg, 8/1/64)* Arkadia 3–▲ 227 [ADD]

Strauss, R.:Der Rosenkavalier, w. T. Stich-Randall (sop), C. Ludwig (mez), O. Edelmann (bass), H. von Karajan (cnd), Philharmonia Orch [G] EMI Classics 3–▲ CDCC 49354 [ADD] 3–■ 3CDX 3970

Strauss, R.:Der Rosenkavalier, w. Jarmila Barton (sop—Marianne), Lisa Della Casa (sop—Sophie), Sena Jurinac (sop—Octavian), Ilva Ligabue (sop—Orphan), Elisabeth Schwarzkopf (sop—Marschallin), Else Schürhoff (mez—Annina), Luisa Villa (mez—Milliner), Hugues Cuénod (ten—Marschallin's majordomo), Erich Majkut (ten—Valzacchi), Giuseppe Nessi (ten—Animal seller), Luciano Della Pergola (ten—Lackey/Faninal's majordomo), Antonio Pirino (ten—An Italian Singer), Gino Del Signore (ten—Lackey/Waiter), Erich Kunz (bar—Herr von Faninal), Paolo Pedani (bar—Lackey), Attilo Barbesi (bass—Lackey/Waiter), Enrico Campi (bass—Waiter), Otto Edelmann (bass—Baron Ochs), Bruno Fichtinger (bass—Notary), Franco Taino (bass—Waiter), Maria Amadini (sgr—Orphan), Pina Carrillo (sgr—Orphan), Joszi Trojan Regar (sgr—Innkeeper), H. von Karajan (cnd), La Scala Orch, La Scala Chorus *(rec La Scala Theater, Milan, Jan. 26, 1952)* Legato Classics 3–▲ LCD 197–3

Strauss, R.:Der Rosenkavalier (sels), w. T. Stich-Randall (mez), C. Ludwig (mez), O. Edelmann (bass), H. von Karajan (cnd), Philharmonia Orch, Philharmonia Chorus EMI Classics ▲ ZDM 63452

Strauss, R.:Songs, w. G. Gould (pno)—Ophelia Lieder [3 songs after Shakespeare], Op. 67, Nos. 1–3 [G] *(rec 1966)* Sony Classical ("Glenn Gould Edition" series) 2–▲ SM2K 52657 [ADD]

Strauss, R.:Songs, w. Felix de Nobel (pno)—3 songs—Ruhe meine Seele; Schlechtes Wetter; Hat gesagt:bleibt nicht dabei [G] *(rec in recital, 1957)* Verona ▲ 27021 (m) [AAD]

Verdi, G.:Requiem Mass, w. C. Ludwig (mez), N. Gedda (ten), N. Ghiaurov (bass), C. M. Giulini (cnd), Philharmonia Orch, London Phil Choir [L] EMI Classics 2–▲ CDCB 47257 [ADD]

Verdi, G.:Requiem Mass, w. Oralia Dominguez (mez), Giuseppe Di Stefano (ten), Cesare Siepi (b-bar), V. de Sabata (cnd), La Scala Orch, La Scala Chorus Theorema 2–▲ TH 121123/24

Verdi, G.:La traviata (sels), w. Oralia Dominguez (mez), Giuseppe DiStefano (ten), Cesare Siepi (b-bar), V. de Sabata (cnd), La Scala Orch, La Scala Chorus—Preludes to Acts I & III Theorema 2–▲ TH 121123/24

Wagner, R.:Die Meistersinger von Nürnberg, w. I. Malaniuk (cta), H. Hopf (ten), G. Unger (ten), E. Kunz (bar), O. Edelmann (b-bar), F. Dalberg (bass), H. von Karajan (cnd), Bayreuth Festival Orch, Bayreuth Festival Chorus [G] *(rec 1951)* EMI Classics ("Great Recordings of the Century" series) 4–▲ CDHD 63500 (m) [ADD]

Wagner, R.:Die Meistersinger von Nürnberg, w. E. Kunz (ten), O. Edelmann (b-bar), H. von Karajan (cnd), Bayreuth Festival Orch, Bayreuth Festival Chorus *(rec 1951)* Arkadia 4–▲ 224

Wagner, R.:Das Rheingold, w. I. Malaniuk (cta), W. Windgassen (ten), S. Björling (bar), Pflanzl (sgr), H. von Karajan (cnd), Bayreuth Festival Orch, Bayreuth Festival Chorus [G] *(rec live, 1951)* Arkadia 2–▲ 216 (m) [ADD]

Walton, W.:Troilus & Cressida (sels), w. M. Sinclair (cta), P. Pears (ten), R. Lewis (ten), W. Walton (cnd), Philharmonia Orch—scenes EMI Classics ▲ ZDM 64199

Weber, C.M. von:Abu Hassan, w. E. Witte (ten), M. Bohnen (bass), L. Ludwig (cnd), Berlin RSO, Berlin Radio Chorus [G] *(rec Germany 1941)* Forlane ▲ FOR 16572 (m) [AAD]

Schwarzkopf, Elisabeth (sop) (cont.)

Weber, C.M. von:Abu Hassan, w. Erich Witte (ten), Michael Bohnen (bass), L. Ludwig (cnd), Berlin RSO, Berlin Radio Chorus Grammofono 2000 ▲ GRM 78650

Wolf, H.:Italienische Liederbücher (sels), w. D. Fischer-Dieskau (bar), G. Moore (pno) EMI Classics ▲ CDM 63732

Wolf, H.:Songs (misc), w. G. Moore (pno), G. Parsons (pno)—Lieder EMI Classics ▲ CDM 63653

Wolf, H.:Songs (misc), w. F. de Nobel (pno)—13 songs [G] *(rec in recital, 1962)* Verona ▲ 27021 (m) [AAD]

Wolf, H.:Songs (misc), w. Wilhelm Furtwängler (pno) *(rec live, Salzburg Festival, 1954)* EMI Classics ▲ CDM 65749

Wolf, H.:Songs (misc), w. G. Moore (pno) *(rec live 1958)* EMI Classics ▲ CDC 64905

Schwarzkopf, H. Norman (nar)

Copland, A.:Lincoln Portrait, w. L. Slatkin (cnd), St. Louis SO [E] RCA Red Seal ▲ 09026-60983-2 [DDD] ■ 09026-60983-4 (CrO2)

Schweiger, Peter (nar)

Suter, R.:Die Ballade von des Cortez Leuten, w. R. Tschupp (cnd), Frankfurt RSO, Frankfurt Music School Chorus Jecklin ▲ JD 690

Schweiger, Rosl (sgr)

Wagner, R.:Tannhäuser, w. Gré Brouwestijn (sop), Murray Dickie (ten), Karl Liebl (ten), Eberhard Waechter (bar), Alois Pernerstorfer (b-bar), Deszö Ernster (bass), Walter Brunelli (sgr), Peter Harrower (sgr), Herta Wilfert (sgr), A. Rodzinski (cnd), Rome RAI Radio-TV SO, Rome RAI Chorus Stradivarius 3–▲ STV 12318

Schweigmann, M. (nar)

Bloch, A.:For the Light Is Come, w. P. Schwarz (org), North German RSO, North German Radio Chorus Pro Viva ▲ ISPV 169

Schweizer, Verena (sop)

Reger, M.:Cantatas, w. A. Hellmann (alt), R. Julius Koch (ob), R. Hellmann, U. Soldan (vn), B. Banz (va), C. Hellmann (vc), C. Fink (db), H. Bilgram (org), D. Hellmann (cnd), Mainz Bach Choir Entrée ▲ 0049 [ADD]

Saint-Saëns, C.:Oratorio de Noël, w. E. Wiens (sop), H. Jung (mez), F. Melzer (ten), K. Widmer (bass), D. Hellmann (cnd), Mainz Bach Orch, Mainz Bach Choir *(rec 1976)* Calig ▲ CAL 50512 [AAD]

Schwertsik, Christa (sgr)

Schwertsik, K.:Da uhu schaud me su draurech au.., w. K. Schwertsik (pno) *(rec May 1994)* Largo ▲ 5125 [DDD]

Schwertsik, K.:Gedichte an Ljuba, w. K. Schwertsik (pno) *(rec May 1994)* Largo ▲ 5125 [DDD]

Schwertsik, K.:Ich sein Blumenbein, w. K. Schwertsik (pno) *(rec May 1994)* Largo ▲ 5125 [DDD]

Schwertsik, K.:Späte Liebeslieder, w. C. van Kampen (vc) *(rec May 1994)* Largo ▲ 5125 [DDD]

Schwitters, K. (voc)

Schwitters, K.:Ursonate Wergo ▲ WER 6304-2

Schymberg, Hjördis (sop)

Beethoven, L. van:Sym 9, "Choral Sym", w. L. Tunell (cta), G. Bäckelin (ten), S. Björling (bar), W. Furtwängler (cnd), Stockholm Concert Society Orch *(rec Dec. 1, 1943)* Music & Arts ▲ CD 774 [AAD]

Jussi Bjorling:Recital, w. Jussi Björling (ten) *(rec 1941–51)* Myto ▲ MCD 934.86

Verdi, G.:La traviata, w. Jussi Björling (ten), Conny Molin (sgr), H. Sandberg (cnd), Stockholm Royal Opera House Orch, Stockholm Royal Opera Chorus Grammofono 2000 2–▲ GRM 78640

Verdi, G.:La traviata, w. Jussi Björling (ten), Conni Molin (sgr), H. Sandberg (cnd), Stockholm Royal Opera House Orch, Stockholm Royal Theater Opera Chorus Enterprise ("The 40's" series) 2–▲ ENT 331

Verdi, G.:La traviata, w. Alard (sgr), J. Björling (ten), Molin (sgr), H. Sandberg (cnd), *(orch unknown)* *(rec live 8/29/39)* Standing Room Only 2–▲ SRO 832-2 [ADD]

Verdi, G.:Il trovatore (sels), w. Kerstin Meyer (mez), Jussi Björling (ten), Olle Sivall (ten), Hugo Hasslo (bar), H. Sandberg (cnd), Royal Opera Orch, Royal Opera House Chorus Covent Garden—Non son tuo figlio?; Mal reggendo all'aspro assalto; Quale d'armi fragor; Ah! sì, ben mio, coll'essere; L'onda de' suoni mistici; Di quella pira l'orrendo foco; Miserere d'un'alma già vicina; Madre?...non dormi?; Se m'ami ancor; Ciel!...non m'inganna; Ti scosta... *(rec Royal Opera, Stockholm, Mar 6, 1960)* Myto ▲ MCD 953130

Sciannimanico, Lucia (mez)

Carulli, F.:Nocturnes (6) for 2 Voices & Gtr, w. Antonia E. Brown (sop), Adriano Sebastiani (gtr)—Dal di ch'io vi mirai; Di me chi vide mai; Quel cor che mi prometti; Io rivedrò sovente; V'è com'è bello il mar; Selve ombrose *(rec Florence, Sept 11–12, 1994)* Dynamic ▲ CDS 124 [DDD]

Sciarpeletti, Giovanni (bass)

Mussorgsky, M.:Khovanshchina, w. Mietta Sighele (sop—Emma), Elena Souliotis (sop—Susanna), Fiorenza Cossotto (mez—Marfa), Herbert Handt (ten—Scribe), Veriano Luchetti (ten—Prince Andrey Khovansky), Ludovic Spiess (ten—Prince Vasily Golitsin), Claudio Strudthoff (ten—Streshnev), Angelo Marchiandi (bar—Kuz'ka), Teodoro Rovetta (bar—1st Strel'tsi), Siegmund Nimsgern (b-bar—Shaklovity), Cesare Siepi (b-bar—Dosifey), Carlo del Bosco (bass—2nd Strel'tsi), Ubaldo Carosi (bass—Varsonofiev), Nicolai Ghiaurov (bass—Prince Ivan Khovnasky), Giovanni Sciarpeletti (bass—Pastor), B. Leskovich (cnd), Rome RAI SO, Rome RAI Chorus—also includes bonus Act V [w Boris Christoff] (Rome, 1958) *(rec Rome, 1973)* Bella Voce 3–▲ BLV 107.402 [AAD]

Sciema, Pierre (alt)

Palestrina, G.:Sacred Music, w. Catherine Greuillet (sop), Thierry Gregoire (alt), Bruno Boterf (ten), Joel Suhubiette (ten), Jean-Luc Baudoin (ten), Jean-Claude Sarragosse (bass), Laurent Stewart (org), Françoise Lasserre (cnd), Champagne-Ardenne Akademia Regional Vocal Ensemble—Ave maria; Salve regina; Vergine bella; Vergine saggia; Virgine pura; Virgine santa; Vergine sola; Vergine chiara; Vergine, quante lagrime; Vergine, tale è terra; Ave mundi spes; Ave regina coelorum; Alma redemptoris mater; Regina coieli laetare; Salve regina; Magnificat; others *(rec Convent of the Annunciation Dominican Church, Paris, Jan., 1994)* Pierre Verany ▲ PVY 794041 [DDD]

Sciurri, Graziella (sop)

Mozart, W.A.:Così fan tutte, w. E. Schwarzkopf (sop—Fiordiligi), G. Sciurri (sop—Despina), N. Merriman (mez—Dorabella), L. Alva (ten—Ferrando), R. Panerai (bar—Guglielmo), F. Clabrese (b-bar—Don Alfonso)., G. Cantelli (cnd), La Scala Orch, La Scala Chorus *(rec Jan. 27, 1956)* Datum 2–▲ DAT 12304 [ADD]

Mozart, W.A.:Don Giovanni, w. L. Price (sop), H. Gueden (sop), F. Wunderlich (ten), E. Wächter (bar), W. Berry (bass), H. von Karajan (cnd), Vienna PO, Vienna State Opera Chorus [I] *(rec live, 1963)* Verona 3–▲ 27065/67 (m) [AAD]

Mozart, W.A.:Nozze di Figaro, w. E. Schwarzkopf (sop), G. Taddei (bar), H. Prey (bar), C. M. Giulini (cnd), Residentie Orch The Hague, Netherlands Chamber Choir [I] *(rec live, Holland Festival, 1961)* Verona 3–▲ 27092/94

Mozart, W.A.:Nozze di Figaro, w. G. Gatti (sop), A. Noni (sop), J. Gardino (mez), M.T. Pace (mez), A. Mercuriali (ten), S. Bruscantini (bar), I. Tajo (bass), F. Corena (bass), F. Previtali (cnd), Rome RAI Orch [I] *(rec 1951)* Cetra Classic 2–▲ CDO 12

Mozart, W.A.:Zauberflöte, w. L. Della Casa (sop), E. Köth (sop), L. Simoneau (ten), W. Berry (bass), K. Böhme (bass), G. Szell (cnd), Vienna PO, Vienna State Opera Chorus [G] *(rec live at the Salzburg Festival, July 27, 1959)* Melodram ("Connaisseur" series) 2–▲ MEL 27505 (m) [AAD]

Rossini, G.:Il turco in Italia, w. Agostino Lazzari (ten), Sesto Bruscantini (bar), Scipio Colombo (bar), N. Sanzogno (cnd), *(orch & chorus unknown)* *(rec Milan, Feb 25, 1958)* Pantheon 2–▲ PHE 6654 (m)

Sciutti, Graziella (sop)

Beethoven, L. van:Fidelio, w. Birgit Nilsson (sop—Leonore), Graziella Sciutti (sop—Marzelline), Kurt Equiluz (ten—Erster Gefangener), Donald Grobe (ten—Jacquino), James McCracken (ten—Florestan), Tom Krause (bar—Don Pizarro), Hermann Prey (bar—Don Fernando), Kurt Böhme (bass—Rocco), Günther Adam (sgr—Zweiter Gefangener), L. Maazel (cnd), Vienna PO, Vienna State Opera Concert Association Chorus *(rec Sofiensaal, Vienna, Mar 1964)* London 2–▲ 448104-2 [ADD]

Cimarosa, D.:Giannina e Bernardone, w. D. De Cecco (sop), S. Jurinac (sop), M. Carlin (ten), M. Boriello (bar), S. Bruscantini (bar), C. De Antoni (sgr), N. Sanzogno (cnd), Milan RAI SO, Milan RAI Chorus [I] *(rec live, Milan July 26, 1953)* Melodram 2–▲ CDM 29505 [ADD]

Gluck, C.W.:Orfeo ed Euridice, w. S. Jurinac (sop), G. Simionato (mez), H. von Karajan (cnd), Vienna PO, Vienna State Opera Chorus *(rec live 1959)* Memories 2–▲ HR 4382/83 (m)

Sciutti, Graziella (sop) (cont.)
Mozart, W.A.:Arias, w. Arleen Augér (sop), Kathleen Battle (sop), Irma Beilke (sop), Helena Braun (sop), Lisa Della Casa (sop), Maria Cebotari (sop), Ileana Cotrubas (sop), Helen Donath (sop), Mirella Freni (sop), Reri Grist (sop), Edita Gruberova (sop), Elisabeth Grümmer (sop), Hilde Güden (sop), Ingeborg Hallstein (sop), Luise Helletsgruber (sop), Gundula Janowitz (sop), Sena Jurinac (sop), Erika Köth (sop), Evelyn Lear (sop), Wilma Lipp (sop), Margaret Marshall (sop), Edith Mathis (sop), Jarmila Novotna (sop), Margherita Perras (sop), Lucia Popp (sop), Elisabeth Rethberg (sop), Anneliese Rothenberger (sop), Elisabeth Schumann (sop), Elisabeth Schwarzkopf (sop), Irmgard Seefried (sop), Graziella Sciutti (sop), Julia Varady (sop), Agnes Baltsa (mez), Margit Bokor (mez), Brigitte Fassbaender (mez), Christa Ludwig (mez), Ann Murray (mez), Francisco Araiza (ten), Anton Dermota (ten), Helge Rosvaenge (ten), Rudolf Schock (ten), Peter Schreier (ten), Leopold Simoneau (ten), Eric Tappy (ten), Richard Tauber (ten), Gösta Winbergh (ten), Josef Witt (ten), Fritz Wunderlich (ten), Christian Boesch (bar), Willy Domgraf-Fassbaender (bar), Karl Dönch (bar), Dietrich Fischer-Dieskau (bar), Erich Kunz (bar), Eberhard Wächter (bar), Hans Hotter (b-bar), Paul Schöffler (b-bar), Cesare Siepi (b-bar), José Van Dam (b-bar), Walter Berry (bass), Geraint Evans (bass), Nicolai Ghiaurov (bass), Alexander Kipnis (bass), Richard Mayr (bass), Kurt Moll (bass), James Morris (bass), Ezio Pinza (bass), Martti Talvela (bass), Giorgio Tozzi (bass), Hans Duhan (sgr), Res Fischer (sgr), Marie Gerhart (sgr), *(various orchs & cnds)*—sels from Idomeneo, Die Entführung aus der Serail, Le nozze di Figaro, Don Giovanni, Così fan tutte, Die Zauberflöte & various arias — Orfeo d'or ("Festspiel Dokumente" series) 5-▲ 408955
Mozart, W.A.:Così fan tutte, w. Elisabeth Schwarzkopf (sop), Nan Merriman (mez), Luigi Alva (ten), Rolando Panerai (bar), Franco Calabrese (bass), G. Cantelli (cnd), La Scala Orch, La Scala Chorus — Stradivarius 2-▲ STV DTM 12304 [ADD]
Mozart, W.A.:Così fan tutte, w. E. Schwarzkopf (sop—Fiordiligi), C. Ludwig (sop—Dorabella), G. Sciutti (sop—Despina), W. Kmentt (ten—Ferrando), H. Prey (bar—Gugliemo), K. Dönch (bar—D. Alfonso), K. Böhm (cnd), Vienna PO, Vienna State Opera Chorus [l] *(rec live, Salzburg, Aug. 8, 1962)* — Arkadia 2-▲ 455 [ADD]
Mozart, W.A.:Don Giovanni (sels), w. E. Schwarzkopf (sop), J. Sutherland (sop), L. Alva (ten), E. Wächter (bar), C. M. Giulini (cnd), Philharmonia Orch — EMI Classics ▲ ZDM 63078
Mozart, W.A.:Nozze di Figaro, w. S. Jurinac (sop), R. Stevens (mez), M. Sinclair (cta), D. McCoshan (ten), H. Cuénod (ten), G. Griffith (bar), S. Bruscantini (b-bar), F. Calabrese (bass), V. Gui (cnd), Glyndebourne Festival Orch, Glyndebourne Festival Chorus — Classics for Pleasure ▲ CDCFP 4724 [ADD]
Paisiello, G.:La Molinara, w. Agostino Lazzari (ten), Alvinio Misciano (ten), Sesto Bruscantini (bar), Franco Calabrese (bass), Leonardo Monreale (bass), F. Caracciolo (cnd), Alessandro Scarlatti CO — Melodram 2-▲ CDM 29502
Pobbe, Sciutti & Siepi, w. Marcella Pobbe (sop), Cesare Siepi (bass), Milan RAI SO [cnd:L. Toffolo], Turin RAI SO [cnd:Fulvio Vernizzi] *(rec Martini & Rossi Concert, 1959)* — Incontri Memorabili ▲ CDMR 5032
Verdi, G.:Don Carlos, w. M. Caniglia (sop—Elisabeth de Valois), G. Sciutti (sop—Page), E. Stignani (mez—Princess Eboli), M. Picchi (ten—Don Carlos), M. Ponz de L. (ten—Count of Lerma), P. Silveri (bar—Rodrigue), N. Rossi Lemeni (bass—Philip II), G. Neri (bass—Grand Inquisitor), A. Gaggi (bass—Old Monk), F. Previtali (cnd), Rome RAI SO, Rome RAI Chorus *(rec Rome, 1951)* — Cetra Classic 3-▲ CDO 25 [ADD]

Sciaverano, Francesco (ten)
Carissimi, G.:Oratorio della Santissima Vergine, w. P. Borri (sop), A. M. Ferrante (sop), P. Pace (sop), A. Christofellis (alt), L. Petroni (ten), R. Abbondanza (bass), M. Mondelli (bass), P. Spagnoli (bass), F. Colusso (cnd), Seicentonovecento Ensemble [l] — Bongiovanni ▲ GB 10011 [DDD]
Carissimi, G.:Oratorio di Daniele Profeta, w. P. Borri (sop), A. M. Ferrante (sop), P. Pace (sop), A. Christofellis (alt), L. Petroni (ten), R. Abbondanza (bass), M. Mondelli (bass), P. Spagnoli (bass), F. Colusso (cnd), Seicentonovecento Ensemble [l] — Bongiovanni ▲ GB 10011 [DDD]

Scola, Vincenzo la (ten)
Bellini, V.:Norma, w. Jane Eaglen (sop—Norma), Eva Mei (sop—Adalgisa), Vincenzo La Scola (ten—Pollione), Dmitri Kavrakos (bass—Oroveso), R. Muti (cnd), Florence Maggio Musicale Orch, Florence Maggio Musicale Chorus *(rec live, Alighieri Theater, Florence, July 1994)* — EMI Classics 2-▲ CDCC 55471
Boito, A.:Mefistofele, w. Michèle Crider (sop—Margherita/Elena), Eleonora Jankovic (mez—Marta/Pantalis), Ernesto Gavazzi (ten—Wagner/Nereo), Vincenza La Scola (ten—Faust), Samuel Ramey (bass—Mefistofele), R. Muti (cnd), La Scala Orch, La Scala Chorus *(rec live Mar 3,5 & 8, 1995, Milan)* — RCA Victor 2-▲ 09026-68284-2 [DDD]
Donizetti, G.:L'elisir d'amore, w. Alessandra Ruffini (sop—Adina), Mariangela Spotorno (sop—Gianetta), Vincenzo La Scola (ten—Nemorino), Simone Alaimo (bar—Dulcamara), Roberto Frontali (bar—Belcore), P.G. Morandi (cnd), Hungarian State Opera Orch, Anikó Katona (cnd), Hungarian State Opera Chorus *(rec Budapest, July 1995)* — Naxos 2-▲ 8.60045-6 [DDD]
Donizetti, G.:Lucia di Lammermoor, w. Mariella Devia (sop), Renato Bruson (bar), S. Ranzani (cnd), La Scala Orch, La Scala Chorus — Serenissima 2-▲ SER 360153 [DDD]
Vincenzo La Scola, w. Paola Molinari (pno) *(rec Apr 15, 1996)* — Bongiovanni ▲ GB 2520 [DDD]

Scoppola, Ludovica (sgr)
Monteverdi, C.:Ballo delle ingrate, w. Carlo Lepore (bass), Daniela Barcellona (sgr), Daniela Ciliberti (sgr), Andrea Concetti (sgr), Hans van Dijk (sgr), Remo Guerrini (sgr), Nadia Mantelli (sgr), Elena Marazzi (sgr), Humberto Orellana (sgr), Claudia Pallini (sgr), Luigi Polsini (sgr), Rosa Ricciotti (sgr), Alberto Rota (sgr), *(orch unknown)* — Nuova Era ▲ NUO 7224
Scarlatti, A.:Cants & Duets, w. C. Miatello (sop), C. Cavina (alt), G. Fagotto (ten), P. Pandolfo (ctb), R. Sensi (sgr), R. Alessandrini (cnd)—Clori mia, Clori bella (cantata for soprano, flute & bass continuo); Dimmi crudele, e quando (duet for soprano, alto & bass continuo); Son pur care le catene (duet for soprano, alto & bass continuo); Sovente Amor mi chiama (cantata for alto & bass continuo); Ammore, brutto figlio de pottana (cantata for tenor & bass continuo) [l] — Tactus ▲ TC 661901

Scorsoni, Renzo (sgr)
Marschner, H.A.:Der Vampyr, w. Carole Farley (sop—Malwina), Nucci Condò (mez—Suse), Oslavio Di Credico (ten—George Dibdin), Josef Protschka (ten—Edgar Aubry), Romano Truffelli (ten—Richard Scrop), Martin Egel (bar—Sir Humphrey Davenaut), Andréa Snarski (bar—Toms Blunt), Siegmund Nimsgern (b-bar—Lord Ruthven), Armando Caforio (bass—Robert Green), Peter Boom (sgr—Il capo dei Vampiri), Carlo Di Giacomo (sgr—James Gadshill), Wolfgang Lenz (sgr—Sir Berkley), Galina Pisarenko (sgr—Janthe), Renzo Scorsoni (sgr—Un servitore di Berkley), Anastasia Tomaszewska Schepis (sgr—Emmy), G. Neuhold (cnd), Rome RAI SO, Rome RAI Chorus *(rec Rome, Jan 26, 1980)* — Italia 2-▲ CDC 99 [ADD]

Scot-Shepherd, Stephen A. (sgr)
Wayditch, G. von:Jesus before Herod, w. Michael Best (ten—Jappeticus), Christopher Lindbloom (sgr—Philippo/Herod), Eileen Moss (sgr—Pabula), Vincent Russo (sgr—Pabo), Stephen A. Scot-Shepherd (sgr—Luke the Evangelist), Pauline Tweed (sgr—1st & 2nd girls), P. Erös (cnd), San Diego SO, San Diego Master Chorale *(rec 1979)* — VAI Audio 2-▲ VAIA 1095-2 [ADD]

Scott, K. (sgr)
Rodgers, R.:Flower Drum Song, w. I. Shepley (sgr), Y. S. Tung (sgr), Y. Saki (sgr), T. Hebert (sgr) [1960 London cast] — Angel ▲ ZDM 89953

Scott, Norman (bass)
Beethoven, L. van:Sym 9, "Choral Sym", w. M. Arroy (sop), R. Sarfaty (mez), N. di Virgilio (ten), L. Bernstein (cnd), New York PO, Juilliard Chorus *(rec New York, May 18, 1964)* — Sony Classical ("Bernstein:The Royal Edition" series) Δ SM 47513 [ADD]
Puccini, G.:La Bohème, w. L. Albanese (sop), L. Hurley (sop), C. Bergonzi (ten), C. Harvuot (bar), M. Sereni (bar), E. Flagello (bass), T. Schippers (cnd), New York Metropolitan Opera Orch, New York Metropolitan Opera Chorus *(rec Feb. 15, 1958)* — Golden Age of Opera 2-▲ GAO 139/40 [ADD]

Scotti, Antonio (bar)
Caruso in Arias, Duets & Songs, w. Enrico Caruso (ten), Louise Homer (cta), Mario Ancona (bar), Titta Ruffo (bar) — Supraphon Collection ▲ SUP 110618 (m) [ADD]
Offenbach, J.:Les Contes d'Hoffmann (sels), w. Geraldine Farrar (sop), *(orch unknown)*—Belle nuit, ô nuit d'amour *(rec Oct. 6, 1909)* — Nimbus ▲ NI 7872 [ADD]

Scotto, Renata (sop)
Bellini, V.:I Capuleti e i Montecchi, w. G. Aragall (ten), L. Pavarotti (ten), C. Abbado (cnd), La Scala Orch, La Scala Chorus [l] *(rec live, La Scala, 1/8/68)* — Arkadia 2-▲ 550 (m) [AAD]

Scotto, Renata (sop) (cont.)
Bellini, V.:I Capuleti e i Montecchi, w. G. Aragall (ten), L. Pavarotti (ten), A. Giacomotti (bass), A. Ferrin (bass), C. Abbado (cnd), La Scala Orch, La Scala Chorus *(rec live 1967)* — Butterfly Music 2-▲ BMC 12 [AAD]
Bellini, V.:Norma, w. Margherita Rinaldi (sop—Adalgisa), Renata Scotto (sop—Norma), Giuseppina Arista (mez—Clotilde), Ermanno Mauro (ten—Pollione), Giancarlo Turati (ten—Flavio), Agostino Ferrin (bass—Oroveso), R. Muti (cnd), Florence Teatro Comunale Orch, Florence Teatro Comunale Chorus *(rec Florence, Dec 19, 1978)* — Legato Classics 2-▲ LCD 203-2
Bellini, V.:La sonnambula, w. A. Kraus (ten), I. Vinco (bass), N. Santi (cnd), Venice Teatro La Fenice Orch, Venice Teatro La Fenice Chorus [l] *(rec live, Venice 5/26/61)* — Golden Age of Opera 2-▲ GAO 111/12 [ADD]
Bellini, V.:La sonnambula (sels), Turin Lyric Orch—arias:sels. unknown — Cetra Classic ("Classics Collection" series) ▲ 111 [ADD]
Bellini, V.:La sonnambula (sels)—scenes — Melodram 2-▲ 27039
Bellini, V.:La straniera, w. E. Zilio (mez), R. Cioni (ten), D. Trimarchi (bar), E. Campi (bass), N. Sanzogno (cnd), Palermo Teatro Massimo Orch, Palermo Teatro Massimo Chorus [l] *(rec live, Palermo, 1968)* — Melodram 2-▲ 27039
Bellini, V.:La straniera, w. E. Zilio (mez), R. Cioni (ten), D. Trimarchi (bar), E. Campi (bass), N. Sanzogno (cnd), Palermo Teatro Massimo Orch, Palermo Teatro Massimo Chorus [l] *(rec live, Palermo, 1968)* — Verona 2-▲ 27097/98
Bizet, G.:Les Pêcheurs de perles (sels), Turin Lyric Orch—arias:sels. unknown — Cetra Classic ("Classics Collection" series) ▲ 111 [ADD]
Catalani, A.:La Wally, w. R. Tebaldi (sop), M. del Monaco (ten), G. Guelfi (bar), C.M. Giulini (cnd), *(orch unknown)* *(rec Milan, 1953)* — Great Opera Performances 2-▲ GOP 734
Catalani, A.:La Wally, w. R. Scotto (sop—Walter), R. Tebaldi (sop—Wally), J. Gardino (mez—Afra), M. Del Monaco (ten—Giuseppe Hagenbach), G.G. Guelfi (bar—Vincenzo Gellner), G. Tozzi (bass—Stromminger), C. M. Giulini (cnd), La Scala Orch, La Scala Chorus *(rec Dec. 7, 1953)* — Legato Classics 2-▲ LCD 177-2 [ADD]
Cherubini, L.:Médée, w. M. Callas (sop), M. Pirazzini (mez), M. Picchi (ten), T. Serafin (cnd), La Scala Orch, La Scala Chorus [l] *(rec live, 1953)* — EMI Classics (Studio) 2-▲ CDMB 63625 [ADD]
Christmas with Renata Scotto at St. Patrick's Cathedral, w. Lorenzo Anselmi (cnd), St. Patrick's Cathedral Choir, John Grady [org/cnd] *(rec St. Patrick's Cathedral, New York City, June 1981)* — VAI Audio ▲ VAIA 1013 [AAD]
Cilea, F.:Adriana Lecouvreur, w. E. Obraztsova (mez), P. Domingo (ten), S. Milnes (bar), J. Levine (cnd), Philharmonia Orch *(rec 1977)* — CBS 2-▲ M2K 34588 [ADD]
Donizetti, G.:Anna Bolena, w. R. Scotto (sop—Anna Bolena), K. Ciesinski (mez—Smeton), S. Marsee (mez—Giovanna Seymour), S. Kolk (ten—Riccardo Percy), S. Ramey (bass—Enrico VIII), J. Rudel (cnd), Philadelphia Opera Orch *(rec live, Dec. 16, 1975)* — Legato Classics 2-▲ LCD 175 [ADD]
Donizetti, G.:Don Pasquale, w. L. Alva (ten), W. Alberti (bar), F. Corena (bass), B. Rigacci (cnd), Florence Maggio Musicale Orch, Florence Maggio Musicale Chorus [l] *(rec live, Florence 3/1/67)* — Claque 2-▲ CLQ 2011 (m)
Donizetti, G.:Don Pasquale (sels), Turin Lyric Orch—arias:sels. unknown — Cetra Classic ("Classics Collection" series) ▲ 111 [ADD]
Donizetti, G.:L'elisir d'amore, w. C. Bergonzi (ten), P. Cava (ten), G. Taddei (bar), G. Gavazzeni (cnd), Florence Maggio Musicale Orch, Florence Maggio Musicale Chorus *(rec live 1967)* — Memories 2-▲ HR 4129/30 (s)
Donizetti, G.:L'elisir d'amore, w. Carlo Bergonzi (ten), Giuseppe Taddei (bar), Carlo Cava (bass), G. Gavazzeni (cnd), Florence Teatro Comunale Orch, Florence Teatro Comunale Chorus *(rec June 1967)* — Pantheon 2-▲ PHE 6612 (m)
Donizetti, G.:Lucia di Lammermoor, w. R. Scotto (sop—Lucia), L. Pavarotti (ten—Edgardo), P. Cappuccilli (bar—Enrico), F. Molinari-Pradelli (cnd), Turin RAI Orch, Turin RAI Chorus [l] *(rec live, Turin 10/10/67)* — Verona 2-▲ 27083/84
Donizetti, G.:Lucia di Lammermoor, w. L. Pavarotti (ten), *(orch unknown)* — Arkadia 2-▲ 540 [AAD]
Donizetti, G.:Lucia di Lammermoor, w. G. di Stefano (ten), E. Bastianini (bar), N. Sanzogno (cnd), La Scala Orch, La Scala Chorus *(rec 1959)* — Enterprise (Palladio) 2-▲ ENTPD 4117 [ADD]
Donizetti, G.:Lucia di Lammermoor, w. A. Kraus (ten), P. Washington (bar), Sesto Bruscantini (bass-bar), B. Rigacci (cnd), *(orch unknown)* *(rec 1963)* — Great Opera Performances 2-▲ GOP 747
Donizetti, G.:Lucia di Lammermoor (sels), w. Anna Di Stazio (mez), Luciano Pavarotti (ten), F. Molinari-Pradelli (cnd), Turin RAI SO—Egli s'avanza; Sulla tomba che rinserra *(rec Torino, Oct 10, 1967)* — Goldies ▲ GLD 63202 [ADD]
Donizetti, G.:Lucia di Lammermoor (sels), w. Renata Scotto (sop—Lucia), Ruth Carron (mez—Alisa), Richard Tucker (ten—Edgardo), Matteo Manuguerra (bar—Enrico), Robert Hale (bass-bar—Raimondo), A. Guadagno (cnd), *(orch & chorus unknown)*—Lucia, perdona...Verranno a te; Sconsigliato! In queste porte; Il dolce suono; Non mi guardar si fiero...Spargi d'amaro pianto; Tombe degli avi miei...Fra poco a me ricovero; Tu che a Dio spiegasti l'ali *(rec Philadelphia, 1973)* — Legato Classics 2-▲ LCD 198-2
Donizetti, G.:Maria di Rohan, w. R. Scotto (sop—Maria), E. Zilio (mez—Armando di Gondi), U. Grilli (ten—Riccardo), R. Bruson (bar—Enrico), G. Gavazzeni (cnd), Venice Teatro La Fenice Orch, Venice Teatro La Fenice Chorus *(rec live Mar. 26, 1974)* — Golden Age of Opera 2-▲ GAO 156/57 [ADD]
Donizetti, G.:Maria di Rohan (sels), w. G. Merighi (sgr), O. de Fabritiis (cnd), Lisbon Teatro São Carlos Orch, Lisbon Teatro São Carlos Chorus—1 soprano aria, "Cupo fatal mestizia" & 1 duet, "Ecco l'ora" [l] *(rec live, Lisbon 3/20/68)* — Melodram (Connaisseur) 2-▲ CDM 27512 [ADD]
Famous Love Duets, Vol. 2, w. Gianna d'Angelo (sop), Montserrat Caballé (sop), Maria Callas (sop), Beverly Sills (sop), Renata Tebaldi (sop), José Carreras (ten), Mario Del Monaco (ten), Giuseppe Di Stefano (ten), Plácido Domingo (ten), Luciano Pava — Enterprise ("Documents" series) ▲ ENTLV 999
Gounod, C.:Faust, w. Renata Scotto (sop—Margherita), Anna di Stasio (mez—Marta), Flaviano Labò (ten—Faust), Edoardo Gimenez (ten—Siebel), Piero Cappuccilli (bar—Valentino), Bruno Grella (bar—Wagner), Ruggero Raimondi (bass—Mefistofele), M. Gusella (cnd), Margherita Theater Orch, Margherita Theater Chorus *(rec Genova, 1970)* — Golden Age of Opera 2-▲ GAO 170/71 [ADD]
Gounod, C.:Faust, w. A. Kraus (ten), N. Ghiaurov (bass), P. Ethuin, *(orch unknown)* [F] *(rec live, Tokyo, 1973)* — Standing Room Only 3-▲ SRO 811-3 [ADD]
Gounod, C.:Roméo et Juliette (sels), w. Renata Scotto (sop—Juliet), Giacomo Aragall (ten—Romeo), Luciano Pavarotti (ten—Tebaldo), Gaetano Ferrin (bass—Capellio), Alfredo Giacomotti (bass—Lorenzo), C. Abbado (cnd), La Scala Orch, La Scala Chorus — Budget ("The Greatest Voice in Opera" series) ▲ SYP 111
Great Love Scenes, w. Plácido Domingo (ten), K. Te Kanawa (sop), I. Cotrubas (sop) — CBS ▲ MK 39030 ■ MT 39030
Great Operatic Scenes, w. José Carreras (ten) (rec. live 1973 & 1974) — Legato Classics ▲ LCD 150-1 (m) [AAD]
Great Sopranos of Our Time, w. Maria Callas (sop), Joan Sutherland (sop), Montserrat Caballé (sop), Elisabeth Schwarzkopf (sop), Victoria de los Angeles (sop), Mirella Freni (sop), Ileana Cotrubas (sop), Edita Gruberova (sop) — Classics for Pleasure ▲ CDEMX 9519 [ADD]
Leoncavallo, R.:Pagliacci, w. M. Caballé (sop), A. Varnay (mez), J. Hamari (mez), J. Carreras (ten), M. Manuguerra (bar), T. Allen (bar), K. Nurmela (bar), U. Benelli (bar), R. Muti (cnd), Philharmonia Orch, Ambrosian Opera Chorus — EMI Classics 2-▲ CDMB 63650
Leoncavallo, R.:Pagliacci (sels), w. J. Carreras (ten), K. Nurmela (bar), R. Muti (cnd), Philharmonia Orch, Ambrosian Opera Chorus — EMI Classics ("Studio" series) ▲ CDM 63933 ■ EG 63933
Mascagni, P.:Arias, w. Giulietta Simionato (mez), Turin Lyric Orch—arias from Lodoletta & Cavalleria Rusticana — Cetra Classic ("Classics Collection" series) ▲ 111 [ADD]
Massenet, J.:Manon (sels), w. A. Kraus (ten)—three scenes for soprano-tenor duet [F] *(rec live, 1983)* — Standing Room Only 3-▲ SRO 811-3 [ADD]
Meyerbeer, G.:Le Prophète, w. Marilyn Horne (mez), James McCracken (ten), Jerome Hines (bass), H. Lewis (cnd), Royal PO, Ambrosian Opera Chorus [F] — CBS 3-▲ M3K 34340 [ADD]
Meyerbeer, G.:Roberto il Diavolo, w. G. Merighi (sgr), B. Christoff (bass), N. Sanzogno (cnd), Florence Maggio Musicale Orch, Florence Maggio Musicale Chorus [l] *(rec live 4/7/68)* — Melodram 3-▲ MEL 37024
Meyerbeer, G.:Roberto il Diavolo, w. G. Merighi (sgr), B. Christoff (bass), N. Sanzogno (cnd), Florence Maggio Musicale Orch, Florence Maggio Musicale Chorus [l] *(rec live, 4/7/68)* — Arkadia 3-▲ 549 (m) [ADD]

Scotto, Renata (sop) (cont.)

Mozart, W.A.:Songs, w. M. Callas (sop), E. Grümmer (sop), E. Schwarzkopf (sop), T. Lemnitz (sop), E. Berger (sop), S. Jurinac (sop), E. Schumann (sop), I. Souez (sop), E. Rethberg (sop), L. Lehmann (sop), N. Gedda (ten), J. McCormack (ten), H. Roswenge (ten), H. Nash (ten), T. Gobbi (bar), G. Hüsch (bar), E. Kunz (bar), G. Frick (bass), E. Pinza (bass), A. Kipnis (bass) EMI Classics 4-▲ CDMD 63750

Puccini, G.:La Bohème (sels), w. G. Poggi (ten), T. Gobbi (bar), Maneguzzer (sgr), A. Votto (cnd), Florence Maggio Musicale IMP Collectors Series ▲ IMPX 9024 [AAD]

Puccini, G.:Edgar, w. G. Killebrew (mez), C. Bergonzi (ten), V. Sardinero (bar), E. Queler (cnd), New York City Opera Orch, New York Schola Cantorum *(rec in concert at Carnegie Hall, 4/13/77)* CBS 2-▲ M2K 34584

Puccini, G.:Madama Butterfly, w. P. Domingo (ten), I. Wixell (bar), L. Maazel (cnd), Philharmonia Orch, Ambrosian Singers [I] CBS 2-▲ M2K 35181 [AAD]

Puccini, G.:Madama Butterfly, w. A. di Stasio (mez), C. Bergonzi (ten), R. Panerai (bar), J. Barbirolli (cnd), Rome Opera Orch, Rome Opera Chorus [I] EMI Classics ("Studio" series) ▲ CDM 63411 ■ EG 63411

Puccini, G.:Madama Butterfly, w. C. Bergonzi (ten), R. Panerai (bar), J. Barbirolli (cnd), Rome Opera Orch, Rome Opera Chorus EMI Classics 2-▲ CDMB 69654

Puccini, G.:Madama Butterfly (sels), w. C. Bergonzi (ten), J. Barbirolli (cnd), Rome Opera Orch, Rome Opera Chorus EMI Classics ■ 4XS 36567

Puccini, G.:Tosca, w. P. Domingo (ten), R. Bruson (bar), J. Levine (cnd), Philharmonia Orch, Ambrosian Opera Chorus [I] EMI Classics 2-▲ CDCB 49364 [DDD]

Puccini, G.:Tosca (sels), w. M. Callas (sop), C. Bergonzi (ten), A. Kraus (ten), T. Gobbi (bar), G. Prêtre (cnd), Orch de Paris EMI Classics ▲ ZDM 63087

Puccini, G.:Tosca (sels), w. P. Domingo (ten), R. Bruson (bar), J. Levine (cnd), Philharmonia Orch, Ambrosian Opera Chorus EMI Classics ▲ CDC 54324

Puccini, G.:Il trittico, w. I. Cotrubas (sop), M. Horne (mez), P. Domingo (ten), T. Gobbi (bar), I. Wixell (bar), L. Maazel (cnd), London SO, Philharmonia Orch [I] CBS 3-▲ M3K 35912 [ADD]

Puccini, G.:Turandot, w. B. Nilsson (sop), F. Corelli (ten), B. Giaiotti (bass), F. Molinari-Pradelli (cnd), Rome Opera Orch, Rome Opera Chorus [I] EMI Classics ("Studio" series) 2-▲ CDMB 69327 [ADD]

Puccini, G.:Le Villi, w. P. Domingo (ten), T. Gobbi (bar), L. Nucci (bar), L. Maazel (cnd), London National PO, Ambrosian Chorus [I] CBS ▲ MK 36669 [ADD]

Refice, L.:Cecilia, w. H. Theyard (ten), G. Fourié (sgr), A. Campori (cnd), *(orch unknown)*—abriged version *(rec live 1976)* Vai Audio ▲ VAIA 1042 [ADD]

Renata Scotto Memories ("Great Voices" series) 2-▲ MEM 4291 (m) [ADD]

Rossini, G.:Il barbiere di Siviglia (sels), w. A. di Stasio (mez), A. Kraus (ten), A. Protti (bar), C. Badioli (bass), E. Campi (bass), V. Bellezza (cnd), Naples Teatro San Carlo Orch, Naples Teatro San Carlo Chorus *(rec July 26, 1958)* Golden Age of Opera 2-▲ GAO 137/38 [ADD]

Spontini, G.:La vestale, w. O. Dominguez (mez), F. Tagliavini (ten), M. Picchi (ten), V. Gui (cnd), Florence Maggio Musicale Orch, Florence Maggio Musicale Chorus [I] *(rec live 5/5/70)* Melodram ("Connaisseur" series) 2-▲ CDM 27512 [ADD]

Verdi, G.:Arias, w. Giuletta Simionato (mez), Turin Lyric Orch—arias from La Traviata & Aida Cetra Classic ("Classics Collection" series) ▲ 111 [ADD]

Verdi, G.:I lombardi alla prima crociata, w. L. Pavarotti (ten), R. Raimondi (bass), G. Gavazzeni (cnd), Rome Opera Orch, Rome Opera Chorus [I] *(rec live, Rome, 11/20/69)* Memories 2-▲ HR 4337/38 [ADD]

Verdi, G.:I lombardi alla prima crociata (sels), w. José Carreras (ten), E. Queler (cnd), *(orch unknown)*—La mia letizia infondere; Oh belle a questa misera; Al'armi!...Che ascolto! *(rec New York, Dec 7, 1972)* Goldies ▲ GLD 63203 [ADD]

Verdi, G.:Otello, w. P. Domingo (ten), S. Milnes (bass), J. Levine (cnd), National PO London [I] RCA Red Seal 2-▲ RCD2-2951

Verdi, G.:Requiem Mass, w. Agnes Baltsa (mez), Veriano Luchetti (ten), Evgeny Nesterenko (bass), R. Muti (cnd), Philharmonia Orch, Ambrosian Chorus EMI Classics 2-▲ CDFB 68613

Verdi, G.:Rigoletto, w. Renata Scotto (sop—Gilda), Stella Maris Silva (sop—Giovanna), Martha Carrizo (mez—Page), Carmen de la Mata (mez—Countess Ceprano), Noemi Souza (cta—Maddalena), Horacio Mastrango (ten—Borso), Richard Tucker (ten—Duke of Mantua), Cornell MacNeil (bar—Rigoletto), Riccardo Yost (bar—Marullo), Guerrino Boschetti (bass—Usher), Tulio Gagliardo (bass—Count Ceprano), Victor de Narké (bass—Monterone), William Wilderman (bass—Sparafucile), F. Previtali (cnd), Buenos Aires Teatro Colón Orch, Buenos Aires Teatro Colón Chorus *(rec Colon Theater, Buenos Aires, Aug. 22, 1967)* Legato Classics 2-▲ LCD 198-2

Verdi, G.:Rigoletto (sels), w. Renata Scotto (sop—Gilda), Corinna Vozza (mez—Giovanna), Bianca Vortoluzzi (cta—Maddalena), Luciano Pavarotti (ten—Duke of Mantua), Kostas Paskalis (bar—Rigoletto), Paolo Washington (bass—Sparafucile), C. M. Guilini (cnd), Rome Opera Orch, Rome Opera Chorus Budget ("The Greatest Voice in Opera" series) ▲ SYP 104

Verdi, G.:La traviata, w. L. Pavarotti (ten), P. Glossop (bar), C. F. Cillario (cnd), Royal Opera House Orch, Royal Opera House Chorus Covent Garden *(rec live 1965)* Memories 2-▲ HR 4404/05 (m)

Verdi, G.:La traviata, w. Renata Scotto (sop—Violetta Valery), Giuliana Tavolaccini (sop—Flora Borvoix), Gianni Raimondi (ten—Alfredo Germont), Ettore Bastianini (bar—Giorgio Germont), A. Votto (cnd), La Scala Orch, La Scala Chorus *(rec La Scala Theatre, Milan, 1963)* Deutsche Grammophon 2-▲ 439720-2 [ADD]

Verdi, G.:La traviata (sels), w. G. Tavolccini (sop), A. Bonato (sop), G. Raimondi (ten), E. Bastianini (bar), A. Votto (cnd), La Scala Orch, La Scala Chorus IMP Collectors Series ▲ IMPX 9025 [AAD]

Verdi, G.:La traviata (sels), w. L. Pavarotti (ten), C. F. Cillario (cnd), Royal Opera House Orch—4 arias *(rec live 3/25/65)* Legato Classics 2-▲ LCD 148-2 [ADD]

Verdi, G.:La traviata (sels), w. L. Pavarotti (ten), C. F. Cillario (cnd), Royal Opera House Orch, Royal Opera House Chorus Covent Garden—2 scenes [I] *(rec live, Covent Garden 3/19/65)* Verona 2-▲ 27081/82

Verdi, G.:I vespri siciliani, w. G. Raimondi (ten), P. Cappuccilli (bar), R. Raimondi (bass), G. Gavazzeni (cnd), La Scala Orch, La Scala Chorus [I] *(rec live, 12/4/70 [Acts 1-3], 12/10)* Myto 2-▲ 2 MCD 90524 [ADD]

Scovotti, Jeanette (sop)

Handel, G.F.:Rinaldo, w. Sophie Boulin (sop—Donna), Ileana Cotrubas (sop—Almirena), Marie-Françoise Jacquelin (sop—Sirene), Nicole Leport (sop—Sirene), Jeanette Scovotti (sop—Armida), Carolyn Watkinson (cta—Rinaldo), Charles Brett (ct—Eustazio), Paul Esswood (ct—Goffredo), Armand Arapian (ten—Mago Christiano/Araldo), Ulrik Cold (bass—Argante), J. Malgoire (cnd), La Grande Écurie et la Chambre du Roy *(rec Paris, 1977)* Sony Classical 3-▲ SM3K 34592

Meyerbeer, G.:Les Huguenots, w. Jeanette Scovotti (sop—Urbain), Rita Shane (sop—Marguerite de Valois), Enriqueta Tarrès (sop—Valentine), Nicolai Gedda (ten—Raoul de Nangis), Justino Diaz (bass—Marcel), Dimiter Petkov (bass—Le Comte de Saint-Bris), E. Märzendorfer (cnd), Austrian RSO, Austrian Radio Chorus *(rec Vienna, Feb 17, 1971)* Myto 2-▲ MCD 961141

Rameau, J.P.:Castor et Pollux, w. M. Schéle (sop), R. Leanderson (bar), G. Souzay (bar), J. Villisech (bass), N. Harnoncourt (cnd), Vienna Concentus Musicus Teldec ▲ 42510-2

Strauss (II), Joh.:Eine Nacht in Venedig (sels), w. E. Schary (mez), E. Steiner (mez), C. Bini (ten), F. Stricker (ten), W. Brendel (bar), E. Märzendorfer (cnd), Hungarian State Orch, Hungarian State Chorus [G] Acanta ▲ CD 43809 [DDD]

Strauss, R.:Ariadne auf Naxos, w. L. Rysanek (sop), T. Troyanos (mez), J. King (ten), P. Schöffler (b-bar), K. Böhm (cnd), Vienna State Opera Orch, Vienna State Opera Chorus *(rec 1967)* Melodram 2-▲ MLO 270105 [ADD]

Scurtu, Dimitrie (ten)

Verdi, G.:Rigoletto, w. Victoria Draganescu (sop—Countess Ceprano), Magda Ianculescu (sop—Gilda), Dorothea Palade (mez—Maddalena), Valeria Savu (mez—Giovanna), Ion Buzea (ten—Duke of Mantua), Dimitrie Scurtu (ten—Borsa), Nicolae Herlea (bar—Rigoletto), Stefan Petrescu (bar—Marullo), Jean Banescu (bass—Count Ceprano), Nicolae Florei (bass—Monterone), Nicolae Rafael (bass—Sparafucile), J. Bobescu (cnd), Romanian Opera Orch, Romanian Opera Chorus *(rec 1965)* Vox Box 2-▲ CDX 5162

Sears, Benjamin (bar)

Lovenstein, J.:Music of, w. Mary Brockenbrough (sop), Laura Sanders (sop), Barton Green (ten), Rockland Osgood (ten), David Murray (bar), Jonathan Lovenstein (pno), Heather O'Donnell (pno), James Silvers (pno), Rocy Reider (fl), Jason Horowitz (vn), Adrianna Hulscher (vn), James Johnston (vn), Mimi Ragson (vn), Peter Landeen (vc), Reinmar Seidler (vc)—Blake Songs; other works Titanic ▲ Ti 221 [DDD]

Sébastien, Marianne (alt)

Daetwyler, J.:Livre pour Toi seul, w. A. Demierre-Baruchet (pno)—[F] Gallo ▲ CD 578 [DAD]

Daetwyler, J.:Poèmes (3), w. C. Eisenhoffer (hp)—[F] Gallo ▲ CD 578 [DAD]

Sebron, Carolyn (mez)

Dunner, L.B.:Motherless Child Songs, w. J. Rubino (pno), L.B. Dunner (cl)—Motherless Child; I Gave My Love a Cherry; Nobody Knows the Trouble I've Seen; Deep River Innova ▲ MN 108

Massenet, J.:Eve, w. Michèle Command (sop), Hervé Lamy (ten), Jean-Philippe Courtis (bass), J.-P. Lore (cnd), French Oratorio Orch, French Oratorio Choir Erol 3-▲ 94002-04

Massenet, J.:Marie-Magdeleine, w. Michèle Command (sop), Hervé Lamy (ten), Jean-Philippe Courtis (bass), J.-P. Lore (cnd), French Oratorio Orch, French Oratorio Choir Erol 3-▲ 94002-04

Secada, Jon (sgr)

Pavarotti & Friends for War Child, w. Luciano Pavarotti (ten), Eric Clapton (sgr), Sheryl Crow (sgr), Elton John (sgr), Liza Minelli (sgr), Joan Osborne (sgr), Eric Clapton (gtr), John McLaughlin (gtr), Marco Armiliato, Edoardo Bennato, José Molina, Al DiMeola, Kelly Family, Ligabue, Litfiba, P *(rec Modena, Italy, 1996)* London ▲ 452900-2 ■ 452900-4

Secombe, Bryan (bass)

Verdi, G.:La traviata, w. Angela Gheorghiu (sop—Violetta), Leah-Marian Jones (mez—Flora Bervoix), Gillian Knight (mez—Annina), Robin Leggate (ten—Gastone), Frank Lopardo (ten—Alfredo Germont), Rodney Gibson (ten—Servo di Flora), Neil Griffiths (ten—Giuseppe), Mark Beesley (bar—Dottore Grenvile), Leo Nucci (bar—Giorgio Germont), Richard Van Allan (bass—Barone Douphol), Roderick Earle (bass—Marquese d'Obigny), Bryan Secombe (bass—Commissionario), G. Solti (cnd), Royal Opera House Orch, Royal Opera House Chorus Covent Garden *(rec live, Royal Opera House, Covent Garden, Dec. 1994)* London 2-▲ 448119-2

Secunda, S. (cantor)

Secunda, S.:Kol Nidre Service, w. B. Irving (nar)—Kol Nidre; Ya-Aleh; Koli Sh'ma; Ki Hine Kachomer; Elohai; Sh'ma Koleinu; Adonoy, Adonoy; Vaani, S'Filosi; B'rosh Hashono *(rec June 3-5, 1959)* Sony Classical ▲ MDK 35207 [ADD] ■ MGT 35207

Secunde, Nadine (sop)

Britten, H.:The Turn of the Screw, w. F. Lott (sop), E. Hulse (sop), P. Cannan (mez), P. Langridge (ten), S. Pay (bar), S. Bedford (cnd), Aldeburgh Festival Ensemble Collins Classics ▲ COL 7030 [DDD]

Prokofiev, S.:The Fiery Angel, w. R. Engert-Ely (mez), H. Zednik (ten), S. Lorenz (bar), K. Moll (bass), N. Järvi (cnd), Gothenburg SO, Gothenburg Sym Chorus [R] Deutsche Grammophon 2-▲ 431669-2 [DDD]

Wagner, R.:Tannhäuser, w. Waltraude Meier (mez), Rene Kollo (ten), Bernd Weikl (bar), Z. Mehta (cnd), Bavarian State Opera Orch, Bavarian State Opera Chorus *(rec live, Munich, 1994)* Serenissima 3-▲ SER 360166

Seebach, Maria (sop)

Mozart, W.A.:Grabmusik, w. Otto Wiener (bass), J. Messner (cnd), Salzburg Mozarteum Orch, Salzburg Cathedral Choir *(rec Aug 24, 1952)* Orfeo d'or ("Festspiel Dokumente" series) ▲ 396951

Seebach-Ziegler, Hanna (sop)

Mozart, W.A.:Requiem, w. Jella von Braun (alt), Hermann Gallos (ten), Richard Mayr (bass), J. Messner (cnd), Cathedral Choral Society Orch, Salzburg Cathedral Choir *(rec Aug 9, 1931)* Orfeo d'or ("Festspiel Dokumente" series) ▲ 396951

Seefried, Irmgard (sop)

Arias Deutsche Grammophon 2-▲ 437677-2

Arias & Songs, w. Gerald Moore (pno), Hermann von Nordberg (pno), Wilhelm Schmidt (pno), London Mozart Players [cnd:Harry Blech] Testament ▲ SBT 1026 [ADD]

Bach, J.S.:St. Matthew Passion, w. C. Ludwig (mez), K. Ferrier (cta), O. Edelmann (b-bar), P. Schoeffler (bass), H. von Karajan (cnd), Vienna SO, Vienna Singverein [G] *(rec live June 9, 1950)* Verona 3-▲ 27070/72 (m) [AAD]

Bach, J.S.:St. Matthew Passion, w. A. Fahberg (sop), H. Töpper (alt), E. Haefliger (ten), D. Fischer-Dieskau (bar), K. Engen (bass), M. Proebstl (bass), K. Richter (cnd), Munich Bach Orch, Munich Bach Choir Archiv ▲ 439338-2 [ADD]

Bach, J.S.:St. Matthew Passion (sels), w. C. Ludwig (mez), K. Ferrier (cta), O. Edelmann (b-bar), P. Schöffler (bass), H. von Karajan (cnd), Vienna SO, Vienna Singverein Verona ▲ 27076 (m) [AAD]

Beethoven, L. van:Fidelio, w. H. Konetzni (sop), P. Klein (ten), T. Ralf (ten), P. Schöffler (b-bar), H. Alsen (bass), K. Böhm (cnd), Vienna State Opera Orch, Vienna State Opera Chorus *(rec Feb. 1944)* Preiser 2-▲ PRE 90195 [AAD]

Beethoven, L. van:Fidelio (sels), w. L. Rysanek (sop), E. Haefliger (ten), F. Lenz (ten), D. Fischer-Dieskau (bar), K. Engen (bass), G. Frick (bass), F. Fricsay (cnd), Bavarian State Orch, Bavarian Opera Chorus—Overture, various arias & scenes, finale [G] IMP Collectors Series ▲ IMPX 9021 [AAD]

Brahms, J.:Ein Deutsches Requiem, w. George London (bar), B. Walter (cnd), New York PO, *(chorus unknown)* Melodram ▲ CDM 18004

Brahms, J.:Ein Deutsches Requiem, w. George London (bass), B. Walter (cnd), New York PO, Westminster Cathedral Choir *(rec New York City, Dec. 20-29, 1954)* Sony Classical ("Bruno Walter Edition, Vol. 2" series) ▲ SMK 64469 [ADD]

Brahms, J.:Songs, w. Erik Werba (pno)—Feinsliebchen; In stiller Nacht; Die Trauernde; Da unten im Tale *(rec Aug 18, 1960)* Orfeo d'or ("Festspiel Dokumente" series) ▲ 398951 (m)

Christmas Songs & Tales, w. Karl Scheit (gtr) Preiser ▲ PRE 90050

Haydn, J.:Die Schöpfung, w. Richard Holm (ten), Kim Borg (bass), I. Markevitch (cnd), Berlin PO, St. Hedwig's Cathedral Choir Deutsche Grammophon ("Double" series) 2-▲ 437380-2

Humperdinck, E.:Hänsel und Gretel, w. Lislotte Maikl (sop—Sandman/Dew Fairy), Anneliese Rothenberger (sop—Gretel), Irmgard Seefried (sop—Hänsel), Grace Hoffman (mez—Gertrude), Elisabeth Höngen (cta—Witch), Walter Berry (bass—Peter), A. Cluytens (cnd), Vienna PO, Vienna Boys' Choir EMI Classics 2-▲ CDMB 65661

Martin, F.:Maria-Triptychon, w. W. Schneiderhan (vn), F. Martin (cnd), Swiss-Italian Orch [L] *(rec Sept. 3, 1970)* Jecklin-Disco ▲ JD 645-2 [ADD]

Mozart, W.A.:Arias, w. Arleen Augér (sop), Kathleen Battle (sop), Irma Beilke (sop), Helena Braun (sop), Lisa Della Casa (sop), Maria Cebotari (sop), Ileana Cotrubas (sop), Helen Donath (sop), Mirella Freni (sop), Reri Grist (sop), Edita Gruberova (sop), Elisabeth Grümmer (sop), Hilde Güden (sop), Ingeborg Hallstein (sop), Luise Helletsgruber (sop), Gundula Janowitz (sop), Sena Jurinac (sop), Erika Köth (sop), Evelyn Lear (sop), Wilma Lipp (sop), Margaret Marshall (sop), Edith Mathis (sop), Jarmila Novotna (sop), Margherita Perras (sop), Lucia Popp (sop), Elisabeth Rethberg (sop), Anneliese Rothenberger (sop), Elisabeth Schumann (sop), Elisabeth Schwarzkopf (sop), Graziella Sciutti (sop), Graziella Sciutti (sop), Julia Varady (sop), Agnes Baltsa (mez), Margit Bokor (mez), Brigitte Fassbaender (mez), Christa Ludwig (mez), Ann Murray (mez), Francisco Araiza (ten), Anton Dermota (ten), Helge Rosvaenge (ten), Rudolf Schock (ten), Peter Schreier (ten), Leopold Simoneau (ten), Eric Tappy (ten), Richard Tauber (ten), Gösta Winbergh (ten), Josef Witt (ten), Fritz Wunderlich (ten), Christian Boesch (bar), Willy Domgraf-Fassbaender (bar), Karl Dönch (bar), Dietrich Fischer-Dieskau (bar), Erich Kunz (bar), Eberhard Wächter (bar), Hans Hotter (b-bar), Paul Schöffler (b-bar), Cesare Siepi (b-bar), José Van Dam (b-bar), Walter Berry (bass), Geraint Evans (bass), Nicolai Ghiaurov (bass), Alexander Kipnis (bass), Richard Mayr (bass), Kurt Moll (bass), James Morris (bass), Ezio Pinza (bass), Martti Talvela (bass), Giorgio Tozzi (bass), Hans Duhan (sgr), Res Fischer (sgr), Marie Gerhart (sgr), *(various orchs & cnds)*—sels from Idomeneo, Die Entführung aus der Serail, Le nozze di Figaro, Don Giovanni, Così fan tutte, Die Zauberflöte & various arias Orfeo d'or ("Festspiel Dokumente" series) 5-▲ 408955

Mozart, W.A.:Così fan tutte (sels), w. Elisabeth Schwarzkopf (sop), Christa Ludwig (mez), Anton Dermota (ten), Erich Kunz (bar), Paul Schoeffler (b-bar), K. Böhm (cnd), Vienna PO—Sento, o Dio; Sorella, cosa dici?—Prenderò quel brunettino Orfeo d'or ("Festspiel Dokumente" series) ▲ 394201

Mozart, W.A.:Don Giovanni, w. S. Jurinac (sop), M. Stader (sop), E. Haefliger (ten), D. Fischer-Dieskau (bar), K. C. Kohn (bass), F. Fricsay (cnd), Berlin RSO Deutsche Grammophon 3-▲ 437341-2

Seefried, Irmgard (sop) (cont.)

Mozart, W.A.:Don Giovanni, w. L. Welitsch (sop), E. Schwarzkopf (sop), A. Dermota (ten), E. Kunz (bar), T. Gobbi (bar), A. Poell (b-bar), J. Greindl (bass), W. Furtwängler (cnd), Vienna PO, Vienna State Opera Chorus *(rec 1950)* Laudis 3-▲ LDS 4001 [AAD]

Mozart, W.A.:Don Giovanni (sels), w. Hilde Konetzni (sop), Emmy Loose (sop), Anton Dermota (ten), Erich Kunz (bar), Paul Schöffler (b-bar), Herbert Alsen (bass), Böhm, Moralt (cnd), Vienna PO *(rec 1944)* Preiser ▲ PRE 90249 [ADD]

Mozart, W.A.:Entführung (sels), w. Hilde Konetzni (sop), Emmy Loose (sop), Anton Dermota (ten), Erich Kunz (bar), Paul Schöffler (b-bar), Herbert Alsen (bass), Böhm, Moralt (cnd), Vienna PO *(rec 1944)* Preiser ▲ PRE 90249 [ADD]

Mozart, W.A.:Nozze di Figaro, w. E. Schwarzkopf (sop), S. Jurinac (sop), L. Villa (sop), R. Panerai (bar), H. von Karajan (cnd), La Scala Orch, La Scala Chorus [I] *(rec live Feb. 4, 1954)* Melodram 3-▲ MEL 37075 [AAD]

Mozart, W.A.:Nozze di Figaro, w. Elisabeth Schwarzkopf (sop—Countess), Irmgard Seefried (sop—Susanna), Hilde Güden (mez—Cherubino), Paul Schöffler (bar—Almaviva), Erich Kunz (bass—Figaro), W. Furtwängler (cnd), Vienna PO, Vienna State Opera Chorus *(rec Salzburg Festival, Aug 8, 1953)* EMI Classics 3-▲ CDHC 66080

Mozart, W.A.:Nozze di Figaro, w. E. Schwarzkopf (sop), S. Jurinac (sop), E. Höngen (cta), G. London (bar), E. Kunz (bar), H. von Karajan (cnd), Vienna PO, Vienna State Opera Chorus—omitting recitatives [I] *(rec 1950)* EMI Classics ("Studio" series) 2-▲ CDMB 69639 (m) [ADD]

Mozart, W.A.:Nozze di Figaro, w. M. Stader (sop), H. Töpper (mez), D. Fischer-Dieskau (bar), R. Capecchi (bar), I. Sardi (bass), F. Fricsay (cnd), Berlin RSO [G] *(rec 1960)* Deutsche Grammophon 3-▲ 437671-2

Mozart, W.A.:Requiem, w. J. Tourel (mez), L. Simoneau (ten), W. Warfield (bar), B. Walter (cnd), New York PO *(rec 1956)* Historical Performers ▲ HPS 12 [ADD]

Mozart, W.A.:Zauberflöte, w. W. Lipp (sop—Queen of the Night), A. Dermota (ten—Tamino), E. Kunz (bar—Papageno), J. Greindl (bass—Sarastro), H. von Karajan (cnd), Vienna PO, Musikfreunde Chorus [without dialogue; G] *(rec 1950)* EMI Classics ("Studio" series) 2-▲ CDHB 69631 (m)

Mozart, W.A.:Zauberflöte, w. Wilma Lipp (sop), Peter Klein (ten), Walther Ludwig (ten), Karl Schmitt-Walter (bar), Josef Greindl (bass), Paul Schöffler (sgr), W. Furtwängler (cnd), Vienna PO, Vienna State Opera Chorus *(rec 1949)* Music & Arts 3-▲ CD 882 [AAD]

Mozart, W.A.:Zauberflöte, w. W. Lipp (sop—Queen of the Night), A. Dermota (ten—Tamino), E. Kunz (bar—Papageno), J. Greindl (bass—Sarastro), W. Furtwängler (cnd), Vienna PO, Vienna State Opera Chorus [G] *(rec live, Salzburg, Aug. 6, 1951)* Arkadia 3-▲ 361 [ADD]

Mozart, W.A.:Zauberflöte, w. W. Lipp (sop—Queen of the Night), A. Dermota (ten—Tamino), E. Kunz (bar—Papageno), J. Greindl (bass—Sarastro), W. Furtwängler (cnd), Vienna PO, Vienna State Opera Chorus [G] *(rec live, Salzburg, Aug. 6, 1951)* Foyer 3-▲ FOY 2003 [AAD]

Mozart, W.A.:Zauberflöte, w. W. Lipp (sop—Queen of the Night), A. Dermota (ten—Tamino), E. Kunz (bar—Papageno), J. Greindl (bass—Sarastro), W. Furtwängler (cnd), Vienna PO, Vienna State Opera Chorus *(rec live 1951)* EMI Classics ▲ CDMC 65356

Mozart, W.A.:Zauberflöte (sels), w. W. Lipp (sop), W. Ludwig (ten), K. Schmitt-Walter (bar), J. Greindl (bass), W. Furtwängler (cnd), Vienna PO, Vienna State Opera Chorus—Ov. & 11 arias *(rec live, Salzburg, July, 27, 1949)* Arkadia 3-▲ 361 [ADD]

Mozart, W.A.:Zauberflöte (sels), w. Hilde Konetzni (sop), Emmy Loose (sop), Anton Dermota (ten), Erich Kunz (bar), Paul Schöffler (b-bar), Herbert Alsen (bass), Böhm, Moralt (cnd), Vienna PO *(rec 1944)* Preiser ▲ PRE 90249 [ADD]

Schubert, Franz:Songs (misc), w. Erik Werba (pno)—Ganymed; Der König von Thule; Fretchen am Spinnrad; Gretchens Bitte; Szene aus Faust; Schäfers Klagelied; Wanderers Nachtlied; Liebhaber in allen Gestalten; Im Frühling; Fischerweise; Widerschein; Der Wanderer an den Mond; Der Tod und das Mädchen; Der Jüngling und der Tod; Das Lied im Grünen; Seligkeit Adès ▲ ADE 203102 [AAD]

Schumann, R.:Frauenliebe und -leben, w. Erik Werba (pno) *(rec Aug 18, 1960)* Orfeo d'or ("Festspiel Dokumente" series) ▲ 398951 (m)

Schumann, R.:Liederkreis, Op. 39, w. Erik Werba (pno)—In der Fremde; Waldesgespräch; Die Stille; Zwielicht; Frühlingsnacht *(rec Aug 18, 1960)* Orfeo d'or ("Festspiel Dokumente" series) ▲ 398951 (m)

Schumann, R.:Myrthen, w. Erik Werba (pno)—Widmung; Die Lotosblume; Lied der Suleika; Der Nussbaum *(rec Aug 18, 1960)* Orfeo d'or ("Festspiel Dokumente" series) ▲ 398951 (m)

Schumann, R.:Songs, w. Erik Werba (pno)—Lieder nach Gedichten der Königin Maria Stuart, Op. 135; Dein Angesicht aus, Op. 127; Meine Rose, Op. 90; Aufträge, Op. 77; Stille Tränen, Op. 35 *(rec Aug 18, 1960)* Orfeo d'or ("Festspiel Dokumente" series) ▲ 398951 (m)

Schwarzkopf & Seefried, Duets, w. Elisabeth Schwarzkopf (sop), Gerald Moore (pno), Philharmonia Orch [cnd:H. von Karajan] EMI Classics ▲ CDH 69793

Strauss, R.:Ariadne auf Naxos, w. L. Della Casa (sop), H. Güden (sop), R. Schock (ten), P. Schöffler (bass), K. Böhm (cnd), Vienna PO *(rec Salzburg Festival, 1954)* Deutsche Grammophon 2-▲ 445332-2 (m) [ADD]

Strauss, R.:Ariadne auf Naxos, w. M. Reining (sop), A. Noni (sop), M. Lorenz (ten), J. Witt (ten), E. Kunz (bar), P. Schöffler (bass), K. Böhm (cnd), Vienna State Opera Orch *(rec Strauss' 80th Birthday Festival, June 11, 1944)* Preiser 2-▲ PRE 90217 [ADD]

Strauss, R.:Ariadne auf Naxos, w. E. Schwarzkopf (sop), R. Streich (sop), L. Otto (sop), G. Hoffman (mez), R. Schock (ten), G. Unger (ten), H. Cuénod (ten), H. Prey (bar), F. Ollendorff (bass), H. von Karajan (cnd), Philharmonia Orch [G] *(rec 1954)* EMI Classics ("Studio" series) 2-▲ CDMB 69296 (m) [ADD]

Strauss, R.:Ariadne auf Naxos, w. Elisabeth Schwarzkopf (sop—Ariadne/Prima Donna), Irmgard Seefried (sop—Zerbinetta), Rita Streich (sop—The Composer), Rudolf Schock (ten—Bacchus), H. von Karajan (cnd), Philharmonia Orch EMI Classics 2-▲ CDCB 55176

Strauss, R.:Ariadne auf Naxos (sels), w. Alda Noni (sop—Zerbinetta), Maria Reining (sop—Ariadne), Irmgard Seefried (sop—Composer), Max Lorenz (ten—Bacchus), Paul Schöffler (b-bar—Musiklehrer), K. Böhm (cnd), Vienna State Opera Orch *(rec Vienna, June 11, 1944)* Koch Schwann 2-▲ SCH 314732 [ADD]

Wagner, R.:Die Meistersinger von Nürnberg, w. H. Beirer (ten), P. Schoeffler (b-bar), F. Reiner (cnd), Vienna PO, Vienna State Opera Chorus *(rec live, Vienna, 1955)* Melodram 4-▲ MEL 47083

Wagner, R.:Die Meistersinger von Nürnberg, w. Irmgard Seefried (sop—Eva), Else Schürhoff (mez—Magdelene), Peter Klein (ten—David), August Seider (ten—Walther), Erich Kunz (bar—Beckmesser), Paul Schoeffler (b-bar—Hans Sachs), Herbert Alsen (bass—Pogner), K. Böhm (cnd), Vienna PO, Vienna State Opera Chorus *(rec Vienna, Nov. & Dec. 1944)* Preiser 4-▲ PRE 90234 [ADD]

Weber, C.M. von:Der Freischütz, w. Rita Streich (sop), Richard Holm (ten), Eberhard Wächter (bar), Kurt Böhme (b-bar), E. Jochum (cnd), Bavarian RSO, Bavarian Radio Chorus Deutsche Grammophon 2-▲ 439717-2 [ADD]

Seers, Mary (sop)

Fauré, G.:Messe basse (in 3 movts), w. J. Scott (org), Matthew Best (cnd), Corydon Singers Hyperion ▲ CDA 66292

Sefcik, Peter (bar)

Duruflé, M.:Requiem, w. C. Guber (mezzo-soprano), C. O. Beyer (cello), T. Götting (organ), Kammerorchester, H. Hennig (cnd), H. Hennig (cnd), Hanover Youth Choir Ars Musici ▲ AM 1098-2 [DDD]

Vierne, L.:Messe solennelle, w. C. Guber (mez), T. Götting (org), H. Hennig (cnd), Hanover CO, Hanover Youth Choir Ars Musici ▲ AM 1098-2 [DDD]

Segal, Miriam Hayward (sop)

Ave Maria, w. Segal, Miriam Hayward (sop), K. Bower (pno), M. Keough (hp) Symposium ▲ SYM 1175 [DDD]

Segal, V. (sgr)

Rodgers, R.:Pal Joey, w. H. Lang (sgr), *(other artists unknown)* [1950 revival cast] Columbia ▲ CK 04364 ■ JST 4364

Segni, C. di (ten)

Ferrero, L.:Mare nostro, w. A. Felle (sop—Candeggina), E. Jankovic (mez—Astradiva), C. Di Segni (ten—Rimestino), D. Serraiocco (bass-bar—Marchingello), A. Antoniozzi (bass-bar—Pigliatutto), G. Maisni (cnd), Venezze di Rovigo Conservatory of Music Orch, Venezze di Rovigo Conservatory of Music Chorus *(rec Oct. 21-24, 1991)* Ricordi 2-▲ RFCD 2016 [DDD]

Segni, C. di (ten) (cont.)

Grétry, A.-E.-M.:Denys le tyran, w. S. Donzelli (sgr), R. Franceschetto (sgr), B. De Simone (bar), F. Vizioli (cnd), Italian International Orch, Ars Pulcherrima Artium Chorus [F] *(rec live, Fermo, Palazzo Sassatelli, 1989)* Memories ▲ DR 3106 [DDD]

Séguin, Christine (nar)

Normandeau, R.:Petit Prince, w. Michel Dumont (nar—Aviator), Martin Pensa (nar—Little Prince), Christine Séguin (nar—Rose), Jean Marchand (nar—King), Luc Durand (nar—Conceited Man), Gilles Dupuis (nar—Drunkard), Guy Nadon (nar—Businessman), Jacques Languirand (nar—Lamplighter), Pierre Bourgault (nar—Geographer), Cynthia Dubois (nar—Snake), Monique Giroux (nar—Flower), Françoise Davoine (nar—Rose Garden), Jean-Louis Millette (nar—Fox), Gérard Poirier (nar—Railway Switchman), Claude Préfontaine (nar—Water Pill Salesman) *(rec Montreal, Aug 1994)* CBC 2-▲ 1091 [DDD]

Sehlmark, Margit (cta)

Mascagni, P.:Cavalleria rusticana, w. A. Nordmo-Lövberg (sop), A. Bjoerling (sop), J. Bjoerling (ten), G. Svedenbrandt (bass), K. Bendix (cnd), Stockholm Royal Opera House Orch, Stockholm Royal Opera Chorus [I, Sw] *(rec live, Stockholm, 12/8/54)* Legato Classics ▲ LCD 164-1 [ADD]

Seibel, Marianne (sop)

Mozart, W.A.:Zauberflöte, w. Birgit Been (sop), Nathalie Boissy (sop), Marianne Seibel (sop), Renate Springer (sop), Elizabeth Vidal (sop), Eleanor James (mez), Salvador Guzman (ten), Herbert Hechenberger (ten), Wolfgang Newmann (ten), Klaus Häger (bass), Philip Langshaw (bass), Hans-Georg Moser (bass), P. Kuentz (cnd), Paul Kuentz Orch, Francis Bardot (cnd), Maitrise des Hauts-de-Seine members, Paul Kuentz Choirs Pierre Verany 2-▲ PVY 730055 [DDD]

Wagner, R.:Das Liebesverbot, w. Pamela Coburn (sop—Mariana), Friedrich Lenz (ten—Antonio), Hermann Prey (bar—Friedrich), Keith Engen (bass—Angelo), Raimund Grumbach (bass—Danieli/Wirt), Wolfgang Fassler (sgr—Luzio), Sabine Haas (sgr—Isabella/Claudios Schwester), Alfred Kuhn (sgr—Brighella/Chef der Sbirren), Hermann Sapell (sgr—Pontio Pilato), Robert Schunk (sgr—Claudio), Marianne Seibel (sgr—Dorella), W. Sawallisch (cnd), Bavarian State Orch, Bavarian State Chorus *(rec July 9, 1983)* Orfeo d'or 3-▲ 345953

Seider, August (ten)

Wagner, R.:Die Meistersinger von Nürnberg, w. Irmgard Seefried (sop—Eva), Else Schürhoff (mez—Magdelene), Peter Klein (ten—David), August Seider (ten—Walther), Erich Kunz (bar—Beckmesser), Paul Schoeffler (b-bar—Hans Sachs), Herbert Alsen (bass—Pogner), K. Böhm (cnd), Vienna PO, Vienna State Opera Chorus *(rec Vienna, Nov. & Dec. 1944)* Preiser 4-▲ PRE 90234 [ADD]

Seidler-Winkler, Bruno (sgr)

Wagner, R.:Arias & Scenes, w. M. Lorenz (ten), A. Rother (cnd), R. Moralt (cnd), *(orch unknown)*—arias & scenes from Rienzi, Tannhäuser, Tristan und Isolde, Die Walküre, Siegfried & Die Meistersinger von Nürnberg *(rec 1937-43)* Preiser ▲ PRE 90213 [ADD]

Seiffert, Peter (ten)

Beethoven, L. van:Sym 9, "Choral Sym", w. M. Price (sop), M. Lipovsk (alt), J.-H. Rootering (bass), W. Sawallisch (cnd), Royal Concertgebouw Orch, Düsseldorf Municipal Choral Society EMI Classics ▲ CDC 54505

Liszt, F.:A Faust Sym, w. S. Rattle (cnd), Berlin PO, Prague Phil Chorus EMI Classics ▲ CDC 55220

Magische Töne, w. Munich RSO [cnd:Jiri Kourt] RCA Red Seal ▲ 09026-61214-2

Mahler, G.:Sym 8, w. Sylvia McNair (sop), Andrea Rost (sop), Cheryl Studer (sop), Anne Sofie von Otter (mez), Rosemarie Lang (cta), Bryn Terfel (bar), Jan-Hendrik Rootering (bass), C. Abbado (cnd), Berlin PO, Berlin Radio Chorus, Prague Phil Chorus, Tölz Boys' Choir Deutsche Grammophon ("4D Audio" series) 2-▲ 445843-2

Mozart, W.A.:Missa, K.427, w. K. Battle (sop), L. Cuberli (sop), K. Moll (bass), J. Levine (cnd), Vienna PO, Vienna State Opera Chorus Deutsche Grammophon ▲ 423664-2 [DDD]

Peter Seiffert Sings Italian Arias, w. Berlin German Opera Orch [cnd:R. Weikert] EMI Classics ▲ CDC 55010

Puccini, G.:Gianni Schicchi, w. H. Donath (sop), R. Panerai (bar), G. Patanè (cnd), Munich RSO Eurodisc ▲ 7751-2-RC [DDD]

Wagner, R.:Arias & Scenes, w. Julia Varady (sop), D. Fischer-Dieskau (cnd), Bavarian State Orch, Bavarian State Chorus—Lohengrin:Ov; 'Wedding March & Chorus'; Tannhäuser:'Dich, teure Halle'; Ov Act 2; 'Gepriesen sei die Stunde'; Walküre:'Ein Schwert verhiess mir der Vater' EMI Classics ▲ CDC 56138

Wagner, R.:Der fliegende Holländer, w. I. Haubold (sop—Senta), M. Schiml (mez—Nurse), P. Seiffert (ten—Erik), J. Hering (ten—Helsman), A. Muff (bar—The Dutchman), E. Knodt (bass—Sea Capt.), P. Steinberg (cnd), Vienna ORF SO, Budapest Radio Chorus [G] *(rec Sept. 1992)* Naxos 2-▲ 8.660025/26 [DDD]

Seiler, Jiří (sgr)

Bruckner, A.:Mass 3, w. Dagmar Masková (sgr), Vladimír Nacházel (sgr), Jiří Novotný (sgr), Jiří Uherek (sgr), Eva Zbytovská (sgr), Jan Votava (trbn), Josef Kšica (org), Josef Pancík (cnd), Prague Chamber Choir Orfeo ▲ 327 951 [DDD]

Bruckner, A.:Motets, w. Dagmar Masková (sgr), Vladimír Nacházel (sgr), Jiří Novotný (sgr), Jiří Uherek (sgr), Eva Zbytovská (sgr), Jan Votava (trbn), Josef Kšica (org), Josef Pancík (cnd), Prague Chamber Choir—Locus iste; Afferentur regi; Ave Maria (2); Pange lingua; Pange lingua (phrygisch); Tantum ergo (2); Libera me; Os iusti; Virga jesse; Vexilla regis; Christus factus est; Tota pulchra es Maria; Ecce sacerdos magnus Orfeo ▲ 327 951 [DDD]

Seinemeyer, Meta (sop)

The Art of Meta Seinemeyer *(rec 1920-29)* Preiser 4-▲ PRE CD 89402

Opera Arias & Duets, w. Berlin State Opera Orch [cnd:Frieder Weissmann], rec. 1926-29, from Parlophon 7) Preiser ("Lebendige Vergangenheit" series) ▲ PRE 89029 (m) [AAD]

The Voice of Tino Pattiera:Arias, Duets & Songs, w. Tino Pattiera (ten), Anka Horvath (sgr), Michael Bohnen (bass) *(rec 1916-30)* Preiser 2-▲ PRE CD 89222

Seipelt, Gloria (alt)

Kol Nidre:Sacred Music of the Synagogue, w. Leo Roth (ten), Rudolf Wiebel (bar), Werner Buschnakowski (org), Harry Foss (org), Leipzig RSO members, Jewish Congregation Choir Berlin, Leipzig Synagogue Choir EMI Classics ▲ CDM 65457

Seitz, Alexander (trb)

Schubert, Franz:Deutsche Messe, w. Robert Wörle (ten), Ulrich Streckmann (bass), R. Kammler (cnd), Munich Residenz CO, Augsburg Cathedral Boys' Choir Calig ▲ CAL 50952 [DDD]

Schubert, Franz:Mass 2, w. Robert Wörle (ten), Ulrich Streckmann (bass), R. Kammler (cnd), Munich Residenz CO, Augsburg Cathedral Boys' Choir Calig ▲ CAL 50952 [DDD]

Seitz, Metchild (mez)

Schnebel, D.:Mit diesen Händen, w. Michael Bach (vc) *(rec Germany, Apr 21-22, 1994)* Mode ▲ mode 52 [DDD]

Selbig, Ute (sop)

Bruch, M.:Das Lied von der Glocke, w. Elisabeth Graf (alt), Matthias Bleidorn (ten), André Eckert (bass), Dresden PO *(rec Kreuzkirche Dresden, Jun 24, 1995)* Thorofon 2-▲ DCTH 2291/2 [DDD]

Mendelssohn, F.:Vom Himmel hoch, w. Egbert Junghanns (bar), M. Flämig (cnd), Dresden PO, Dresden Kreuz Choir *(rec Dresden, Mar & Apr 1987)* Capriccio ▲ 10216 [DDD]

Saint-Saëns, C.:Oratorio de Noël, w. Elisabeth Wilke (mez), Annette Markert (cta), Armin Ude (ten), Egbert Junghans (bar), Jutta Zoff (hp), Michael-Christfield Winkler (org), M. Flämig (cnd), Dresden PO, Dresden Kreuz Choir *(rec Dresden, Mar & Apr 1987)* Capriccio ▲ 10216 [DDD]

Selig, E. (sop)

Mahler, G.:Sym 2, w. E. Zareska (cta), C. Schuricht (cnd), Paris National Orch, Paris National Chorus [G] *(rec live, Paris 2/20/58)* Melodram ("Connaisseur" series) 2-▲ CD 27504 (m) [AAD]

Selig, Franz-Josef (bass)

Handel, G.F.:Judas Maccabaeus, w. M. Meier-Schmid (sop), Elisabeth von Magnus (alt), Jörg Dürmüller (ten), Robert Wörle (ten), T. Fey (cnd), Schlierbach CO, Munich Motet Choir [E] Christophorus 2-▲ 77128 [DDD]

Seligman, Tom (trb)

Purcell, H.:Anthems & Services, w. James Bowman (ct), Ashley Stafford (ct), John Mark Ainsley (ten), Andrew Gant (ten), Michael George (bass), Charles Pott (bass), R. King (cnd), King's Consort, King's Consort—O Sing unto the Lord; My beloved spake *(rec St Jude-on-the-Hill, London, Dec 20-21, 1968)* United ▲ CAL 88002 [DDD]

Sellheim, Judy May (mez)
Ung, C.:Spiral II, w. Daniel Perantoni (tuba), Robert Hamilton (pno), A. Weisberg (cnd) *(rec Kerr Center, Tempe, AZ, Jan 29, 1991)* CRI ▲ CRI 710 [DDD/ADD]

Sells, Michael (bar)
Britten, H.:War Requiem, w. Jeanine Altmeyer (sop), Douglas Lawrence (ten), Ladd Thomas (org), W. Hall (cnd), William Hall Orch, William Hall Chorale, Columbus Boys' Choir Klavier ▲ KCD 11017 [ADD]

Sembach, J. (ten)
Verdi, G.:Il trovatore (sels), w. J. Biel (ten), F. Tamagno (ten), L.-A. Escalaïs (ten), M. Gilion (ten), E. Caruso (ten), A. Paoli (ten), G. Zenatello (ten), L. Slezak (ten), F. Constantino (ten), G. Martinelli (ten), B. De Muro (ten), N. Fusati (ten), N. Piccaluga (ten), G. Lauri-Volpi (ten), A. Pertile (ten), E. Bergamaschi (ten), R. Tauber (ten), J. O'Sullivan (ten), H. Roswaenge (ten), G. Taccani (ten), V. Lois (ten), H. Lazaro (ten), A. Lindi (ten), A. Cortis (ten), F. Merli (ten), F. Völker (ten), J. Kiepura (ten), J. Schmidt (ten), J. Bjoerling (ten), B. Gigli (ten), A. Salvarezza (ten), J. Soler (ten), M. Filippeschi (ten)—34 performances of the Act III tenor aria "Di quella pira!," *(rec from 1903-1956)* Bongiovanni ▲ GB 1051 [AAD]

Semellaz, François (sop)
Rameau, J.P.:Nélée et Myrthis, w. A. Mellon (sop—Myrthis), D. Michel-Dansac (sop—Maid), C. Pelon (sop—Maid), F. Semellaz (sop—Corinne), J. Corréas (bass—Nélée), W. Christie (cnd), Les Arts Florissants, Les Arts Florissants Chorus [F] *(rec 5/91)* Harmonia Mundi France ▲ HMC 901381

Semmes, Melissa (nar)
Albright, W.:A Song to David, w. Charles Russell (nar), Deborah Carbaugh (sop), Susan Sacquitne-Druck (mez), Rick Penning (ten), James Bohn (bass), Dean Billmeyer (org), Howard Don Small (cnd), St. Mark's Cathedral Choir Minneapolis *(rec live, St. Mark's Cathedral, Minneapolis, MN, Apr. 28, 1991)* Gothic ▲ G 49066 [DDD]

Sempere, José (ten)
Massenet, J.:Esclarmonde, w. Denia Mazzola (sop), Christian Tréguier (bar), Hélène Parraguin (sgr), P. Fournillier (cnd), Franz Liszt SO, Massenet Festival Choir *(rec live, Massenet Festival, Saint-Étienne)* Koch Schwann 3-▲ SCH 312692 [DDD]

Senator, Boaz (bar)
Puccini, G.:La Bohème (sels), w. Luba Orgonasova (sop—Mimi), Carmen Gonzales (sop—Musetta), Jonathan Welch (ten—Rudolfo), Fabio Previati (bar—Marcello), Boaz Senator (bar—Schaunard), Ivan Urbas (bass—Colline), Jiri Sulzenko (bass—Alcindoro), W. Humburg (cnd), Czech-Slovak RSO Bratislava, Bratislava Children's Choir, Slovak Phil Chorus *(rec Concert Hall, Czecho-Slovak Radio, Bratislava, Apr. 23-May 4, 1990)* Naxos ▲ 8.553151 [DDD]

Sénéchal, Michel (ten)
Bizet, G.:Ivan IV (sels), w. J. Micheau (sop), H. Legay (ten), M. Roux (bar), G. Tzipine (cnd), French National RSO, French Radio Chorus [F] EMI Classics ("Studio" series) 2-▲ CDMB 69704 [ADD]
Boieldieu, F.-A.:La Dame blanche, w. Michel Sénéchal (ten—Georges Brown), Aimé Doniat (bar—Dikson), Pierre Héral (bass—Mac-Irton), Adrien Legros (bass—Gaveston), P. Stoll (cnd), Paris SO, Paris Sym Chorus Accord 2-▲ ACD 220862 [AAD]
Boulanger, L.:Vieille prière bouddhique, w. I. Markevitch (cnd), Lamoureux Orch, Elisabeth Brasseur Chorale *(rec Salle Pleyel, Paris)* Everest ▲ EVC 9034 [AAD]
Charpentier, G.:Louise, w. I. Cotrubas (sop), J. Berbié (mez), P. Domingo (ten), G. Bacquier (bar), G. Prêtre (cnd), New Philharmonia Orch, Ambrosian Opera Chorus [F] Sony Classical 3-▲ S3K 46429 [ADD]
Mozart, W.A.:Entführung, w. Teresa Stich-Randall (mez), Nicolai Gedda (ten), Carmen Prieto (sgr), H. Rosbaud (cnd), Paris Conservatory Societé des Concerts Orch, Elisabeth Brasseur Chorale *(rec Aix-en-Provence Festival, France, 1954)* Agorá ("Phoenix" series) 2-▲ 512
Mozart, W.A.:Nozze di Figaro, w. Mirella Freni (sop), Gundala Janowitz (sop), Jane Berbié (mez), Frederica von Stade (mez), José Van Dam (b-bar), Kurt Moll (bass), G. Solti (cnd), Paris Opera Orch, Paris Opera Chorus *(rec live, Paris, Apr 7, 1973)* Agorá ("Phoenix" series) 3-▲ 515
Offenbach, J.:Les Contes d'Hoffmann, w. E. Gruberova (sop), C. Eder (mez), P. Domingo (ten), Schmidt (sgr), G. Bacquier (bar), J. Morris (bass), J. Diaz (bass), S. Ozawa (cnd), French National Orch, French Radio Chorus [F] Deutsche Grammophon 2-▲ 427682-2 [DDD]
Puccini, G.:Turandot, w. M. Caballé (sop—Turnadot), M. Freni (sop—Liu), J. Carreras (ten—Calaf), M. Sénéchal (ten—Emperor Altoum), V. Sardinero (bar—Ping), P. Plishka (bass—Timur), A. Lombard (cnd), Strasbourg PO, Maîtrise de la Cathédrale, Rhine Opera Chorus EMI Classics ▲ CDMB 65293
Puccini, G.:Turandot (sels), w. M. Caballé (sop), M. Freni (sop), J. Carreras (ten), A. Lombard (cnd), Strasbourg PO, Rhine Opera Chorus EMI Classics ("Studio" series) ▲ CDM 63410

Seniglova, Eva (sop)
Marschner, H.A.:Hans Heiling, w. M. Hajóssyová (sop), M. Eklöf (mez), K. Markus (ten), T. Mohr (bar), L. Neshyba (bass), E. Körner (cnd), Slovak PO, Slovak Phil Chorus [G] Marco Polo ("Opera Rara" series) 2-▲ 8.223306/07 [DDD]

Senn, Martha (mez)
Falla, M. de:El amor brujo, w. E. Mata (cnd), Simón Bolívar SO *(rec Aula Magna of Venezuela Central Univ., Caracas, July 1994)* Dorian ▲ DOR 90210 [DDD]
Falla, M. de:El amor brujo, w. L. Izquierdo (cnd), Carme Ensemble [original ver.] [Sp] Nuova Era ▲ 6809 [DDD]
Falla, M. de:Canciones populares españolas (7), w. L. Izquierdo (cnd), Carme Ensemble [Sp] Nuova Era ▲ 6809 [DDD]
Falla, M. de:Canciones populares españolas (7), w. E. Mata (cnd), Simón Bolívar SO *(rec Aula Magna of Venezuela Central Univ., Caracas, July 1994)* Dorian ▲ DOR 90210 [DDD]
Falla, M. de:La vida breve, w. C. Angell (mez), F. de la Mora (ten), E. Mata (cnd), Simón Bolívar SO [Sp] *(rec July 1993)* Dorian ▲ DOR 90192 [DDD]
Honegger, A.:Le Roi David, w. Christiane Eda-Pierre (sop), Tibere Raffalli (ten), D. Mesguich (nar), A. Gaillard (nar), S. Baudo (cnd), Czech PO, Czech Chorus [F] Supraphon 2-▲ 11 0132 [DDD]
Leoncavallo, R.:La Bohème, w. L. Mazzaria (sop), B. Praticò (sgr), M. Malagnini (sgr), J. Summers (bar), J. Latham-König (cnd), Venice Teatro La Fenice Orch, Venice Teatro La Fenice Chorus *(rec live, 1990)* Nuova Era 3-▲ 6917/19 [DDD]
Mascagni, P.:Cavalleria rusticana, w. J. Norman (sop), R. Laghezza (mez), G. Giacomini (ten), D. Hvorostovsky (bar), S. Bychkov (cnd), Orch de Paris Philips ▲ 432105-2 [DDD]
Mozart, W.A.:Clemenza, w. Christine Barbaux (sop—Servilia), Carol Vaness (sop—Viellia), Martha Senn (mez—Annio), Delores Ziegler (mez—Sesto), Gösta Winbergh (ten—Tito), László Polgár (bass—Publio), R. Muti (cnd), Vienna PO, Vienna State Opera Chorus *(rec live, Salzburg Festival, 1988)* EMI Classics 2-▲ CDCB 55489

Senn, Matthias (ten)
Kraft, Walter:Christus, w. Anna Senn-Dähler (sop), Barbara Künzler (sop), Barbara Sutter (sop), Christine Guy (alt), Heidi Uhlmann (alt), Daniel Zellweger (alt), Mikoto Usami (ten), Wolfgang Pailer (bass), Heinz Suter (bass), Klaus Knall (cnd), Evangelische Singgemeinde Choirs *(rec Ostdorf bei Balingen, Oct. 8-11, 1986)* Cantate 2-▲ 58004 [DDD]

Senn-Dähler, Anna (sop)
Kraft, Walter:Christus, w. Barbara Künzler (sop), Barbara Sutter (sop), Christine Guy (alt), Heidi Uhlmann (alt), Daniel Zellweger (alt), Matthias Senn (ten), Mikoto Usami (ten), Wolfgang Pailer (bass), Heinz Suter (bass), Klaus Knall (cnd), Evangelische Singgemeinde Choirs *(rec Ostdorf bei Balingen, Oct. 8-11, 1986)* Cantate 2-▲ 58004 [DDD]

Sensi, R. (sgr)
Scarlatti, A.:Cants & Duets, w. C. Miatello (sop), C. Cavina (alt), G. Fagotto (ten), L. Scoppola (sgr), P. Pandolfo (ctb), R. Alessandrini (cnd)—Clori mia, Clori bella (cantata for soprano, flute & bass continuo); Dimmi crudele, e quando (duet for soprano, alto & bass continuo); Son pur care le catene (duet for soprano, alto & bass continuo); Sovente Amor mi chiama (cantata for alto & bass continuo); Ammore, brutto figlio de pottana (cantata for tenor & bass continuo) [I] Tactus ▲ TC 661901

Seoane (sop)
Falla, M. de:El retablo de maese Pedro, w. Gonzalo (sgr), Navarro (sgr), E. Halffter (cnd), Champs Elysées Theater Orch *(rec ca. 1959)* MCA Classics ▲ MCAD 10481 (m/s) [ADD]

Serafini, Lia (sop)
Echoes of Love:18th Century Italian Cantatas, w. Ensemble Barocco Padua Sans Souci, E. Lax (alt) *(rec Apr. 1993)* Dynamic ▲ CDS 106 [DDD]

Serbo, Rico (ten)
Donizetti, G.:L'assedio di Calais, w. E. Harrhy (sop), D. Jones (mez), J. Treleaven (ten), R. Smythe (bar), D. Parry (cnd), Philharmonia Orch, Geoffrey Mitchell Choir Opera Rara 2-▲ OR 9 [DDD]

Sereni, Mario (bar)
Donizetti, G.:L'elisir d'amore, w. M. Freni (sop), N. Gedda (ten), R. Capecchi (bar), F. Molinari-Pradelli (cnd), Rome Opera Orch [I] EMI Classics (Studio) 2-▲ CDMB 69897 [ADD]
Donizetti, G.:Lucia di Lammermoor, w. A. Moffo (sop), C. Bergonzi (ten), E. Flagello (bass), G. Prêtre (cnd), RCA Italian Opera Orch [I] RCA Gold Seal 2-▲ 6504-2-RG [ADD]
Giordano, U.:Andrea Chénier, w. A. Stella (sop—Maddalena), F. Corelli (ten—Andrea Chénier), M. Sereni (bar—Carlo Gerard), G. Santini (cnd), Rome Opera Orch, Rome Opera Chorus EMI Classics ▲ CDMB 65287
Giordano, U.:Fedora, w. R. Tebaldi (sop), Mizzetti (sgr), G. di Stefano (ten), A. Basile (cnd), Naples Teatro San Carlo Orch, Naples Teatro San Carlo Chorus [I] *(rec live, 1961)* Legato Classics 2-▲ LCD 158-2 (m) [ADD]
Puccini, G.:La Bohème, w. L. Albanese (sop), L. Hurley (sop), C. Bergonzi (ten), C. Harvuot (bar), N. Scott (bass), E. Flagello (bass), T. Schippers (cnd), New York Metropolitan Opera Orch, New York Metropolitan Opera Chorus *(rec Feb. 15, 1958)* Golden Age of Opera 2-▲ GAO 139/40 [ADD]
Puccini, G.:La Bohème, w. M. Freni (sop), N. Gedda (ten), T. Schippers (cnd), Rome Opera Orch, Rome Opera Chorus [I] EMI Classics ("Studio" series) 2-▲ CDMB 69657
Puccini, G.:La Bohème (sels), w. M. Freni (sop), N. Gedda (ten), T. Schippers (cnd), Rome Opera Orch, Rome Opera Chorus EMI Classics ("Studio" series) ▲ CDM 63932 ■ EG 63932
Puccini, G.:Madama Butterfly, w. V. de los Angeles (sop), M. Pirazzini (mez), J. Bjoerling (ten), G. Santini (cnd), Rome Opera Orch, Rome Opera Chorus [I] EMI Classics ("Studio" series) 2-▲ CDMB 63634 [ADD]
Puccini, G.:Turandot, w. Birgit Nilsson (sop—Turandot), Renata Tebaldi (sop—Liù), Jussi Björling (ten—Calaf), Alessio De Paolis (ten—Emperor Altoum), Piero de Palma (ten—Pang), Mario Sereni (bar—Ping), Adelio Zagonara (bar—Prince of Persia), Giorgio Tozzi (bass—Timur), Tommaso Frascati (bass—Pong), Leonardo Monreale (bass—Mandarin), E. Leinsdorf (cnd), Rome Opera Orch, Rome Opera Chorus *(rec Rome Opera House, July 3-11, 1959)* RCA Living Stereo 2-▲ 09026-62687-2 [ADD]
Verdi, G.:Don Carlos, w. S. Jurinac (sop—Elisabetta), L. Rysanek (sop—Celestial Voice), F. Cossotto (mez—Princess Eboli), L. Dutoit (boy sop—Tebaldo), P. Domingo (ten—Don Carlo), E. Majkut (ten—Count of Lerma), M. Sereni (bar—Rodrigo), C. Siepi (bass—Philip II), I. Vinco (bass—Grand Inquisitor), T. Franc (bass—Friar), S. Varviso (cnd), Vienna State Opera Orch, Vienna State Opera Chorus Standing Room Only 2-▲ SRO 850 [ADD]
Verdi, G.:Ernani, w. L. Price (sop), C. Bergonzi (ten), E. Flagello (bass), T. Schippers (cnd), RCA Italian Opera Orch [I] RCA Gold Seal 2-▲ 6503-2-RG [ADD]
Verdi, G.:Ernani, w. L. Price (sop), C. Ordassy (sop), F. Corelli (ten), C. Anthony (ten), C. Siepi (bass), C. Russel (bass), T. Schippers (cnd), *(orch unknown)* *(rec 1965)* Great Opera Performances ▲ GOP 702
Verdi, G.:La traviata, w. M. Callas (sop), A. Kraus (ten), F. Ghione (cnd), Lisbon Teatro São Carlos Orch [I] *(rec live, Lisbon 3/27/58)* EMI Classics 2-▲ CDCB 49187
Verdi, G.:La traviata, w. M. Freni (sop), R. Righetti (mez), R. Cioni (ten), H. von Karajan (cnd), La Scala Orch, La Scala Chorus *(rec Milan, 1964)* Legend 2-▲ LGD 125 [ADD]

Serge, John (ten)
Rossini, G.:Semiramide, w. J. Sutherland (sop), M. Horne (mez), J. Rouleau (bass), S. Malas (bass), R. Bonynge (cnd), London SO, Ambrosian Singers [I] *(rec 1966)* London 3-▲ 425481-2 [ADD]

Sergiel, Kasimierz (sgr)
Rossini, G.:La gazetta, w. Teresa Verdera (sop), Gianpiero Ruggeri (sgr), Ezio Maria Tisi (sgr), W. Keitel (cnd), Minsk Orch, Motet & Madrigal Posen Chamber Chorus Deutsche Schallplatten ▲ DS 1053

Serkin, Valery (sgr)
Rubinstein, A.:The Demon, w. Ludmilla Andrew (sop—Nanny), Marina Mescheriakova (sop—Tamara), Alison Browner (mez—Angel), Anatoly Lochak (sgr—Demon), Richard Robson (sgr—Old Servant), Valery Serkin (sgr—Prince Sinodal), Wjacheslav Weinorowski (sgr—Messenger), Leonid Zimnenko (sgr—Prince Gudal), A. Anissimov (cnd), Irish National SO, Gregory Rose (cnd), Wexford Festival Opera Chorus *(rec Wexford, Oct & Nov, 1994)* Marco Polo 2-▲ 8.223781-2 [DDD]

Serno, Paola (mez)
Scarlatti, A.:Répons du Vendredi Saint, w. Nadi Caristi (sop), Marco Scavazza (bar), Giorgi Mazzucato (cnd), Rovigo City Chorus Studio SM ▲ 2515 [DDD]

Serra, Enrique (bass)
Donizetti, G.:Maria Stuarda, w. M. Caballé (sop—Maria Stuarda), R. Bezinian (mez—Anna), M. V. Menendez (mez—Elisabetta), J. Carreras (ten—Roberto), M. Mazzieri (bass—Giorgio Talbot), E. Serra (bass—Lord Gugliemo Cecil), N. Santi (cnd), ORTF Lyric Orch, ORTF Lyric Chorale [I] *(rec live 3/26/72)* Memories 2-▲ HR4417/18 [ADD]
Massenet, J.:Hérodiade, w. M. Caballé (sop—Salomé), D. Vejzovic (mez—Hérodiade), J. Carreras (ten—Jean), J. Pons (bar—Hérode), E. Serra (bar—Vitellius), V. Esteve (bar—High Priest), R. Kennedy (bass—Phanuel), J. Delacôte (cnd), Barcelona Teatro Liceo Orch, Barcelona Gran Teatro de Liceo Chorus *(rec Jan. 6, 1984)* Legato Classics 2-▲ LCD 182 [ADD]

Serra, Luciana (sop)
Donizetti, G.:Don Pasquale, w. E. Dara (bar), A. Corbelli (bar), Bartolo (sgr), B. Campanella (cnd), Turin Teatro Regio Orch, Turin Teatro Regio Chorus [I] *(rec live)* Nuova Era 2-▲ 6715/16 [DDD]
Donizetti, G.:Don Pasquale, w. E. Dara (bar), A. Corbelli (bar), Bartolo (sgr), B. Campanella (cnd), Turin Teatro Regio Orch, Turin Teatro Regio Chorus [I] *(rec live)* Nuova Era ▲ 6766 [DDD]
Donizetti, G.:La fille du régiment, w. M. Tagliasacchi (sop), W. Matteuzzi (ten), E. Dara (bar), B. Campanella (cnd), Bologna Teatro Comunale Orch, Bologna Teatro Comunale Chorus [I] *(rec live, 2/16-26/89)* Nuova Era 2-▲ 6791/92 [DDD]
Donizetti, G.:Il furioso all'isola di Santo Domingo, w. P. Antonucci (sop), E. Tandura (mez), L. Canonici (ten), R. Coviello (bar), Picconi (sgr), C. Rizzi (cnd), Piacenza SO, Piacenza Chorus *(rec live, 11/10/87)* Bongiovanni 3-▲ GB 2056/58 [DDD]
Donizetti, G.:Gianni di Parigi, w. E. Zilio (mez), G. Morino (ten), E. Fissore (bar), A. Romero (bar), S. Manga (sgr), C. F. Cillario (cnd), Milan RAI Orch, Milan RAI Chorus [I] *(rec live)* Nuova Era 2-▲ 6752/53 [DDD]
Donizetti, G.:Torquato Tasso, w. A. D'Auria (sop), N. Ciliento (mez), E. Palacio (ten), R. Coviello (bar), S. Alaimo (bass-bar), A. Riva (bass), M.. Bernart (cnd), Genoa Teatro Comunale Orch, Genoa Teatro Comunale Chorus [I] *(rec live 10/16/85)* Bongiovanni 3-▲ GB 2028/30 [DDD]
Gazzaniga, G.:Don Giovanni, w. E. Szmytka (sop), E. Schmid-Lienbacher (sop), D. Johnson (sgr), F. Furlanetto (bass), B. Weil (cnd), Tafelmusik Sony Classical ("Vivarte" series) ▲ SK 46693
Luciana Serra *(rec. June 1993)* Fonit Cetra ▲ CDC 23 [DDD]
Mozart, W.A.:Complete Mozart Edition, w. M. Price (sop), R. Tear (ten), P. Schreier (ten), T. Adam (b-bar), K. Moll (bass), C. Davis (cnd), Dresden Staatskapelle, Dresden State Chorus Philips 3-▲ 422543-2 [ADD]
Mozart, W.A.:Zauberflöte, w. M. Price (sop—Pamina), L. Serra (sop—Queen of the Night), M. Venuti (sop—Papagena), M. McLaughlin (sop—1st Lady), A. Murray (mez—2nd Lady), H. Schwarz (cta—3rd Lady), F. Höher (trb—1st Boy), M. Diedrich (trb—2nd Boy), F. Klos (trb—3rd Boy), P. Schreier (ten—Tamino), R. Tear (ten—Monostatos), R. Goldberg (ten—1st Armoured Man), K. Moll (bass—Sarastro), H. Rech (bass—2nd Armoured Man), C. Davis (cnd), Dresden Staatskapelle, Leipzig Radio Chorus Philips ("Duo" series) 2-▲ 442568-2
Offenbach, J.:Les Contes d'Hoffmann, w. R. Plowright (sop), J. Norman (sop), A. Murray (mez), J. Taillon (mez), N. Shicoff (ten), A. Oliver (ten), R. Tear (ten), J. Van Dam (b-bar), D. Duesing (bar), K. Rydl (bass), S. Cambreling (cnd), Brussels Théâtre de la Monnaie Orch [F] EMI Classics 3-▲ CDCC 49641 [DDD]
Righini, V.:Alcide al Bivio, w. S. Browne (cta), W. McKinney (ten), R. El Hage (bass), M. Barta (ob), P. Molinari (hpd), T. Gotti (cnd), Swiss-Italian RSO, Swiss-Italian Radio Chorus *(rec 1979)* Bongiovanni 2-▲ GB 2157/58 [ADD]
Rossini, G.:La scala di seta, w. Oslavio di Credico (ten), William Matteuzzi (ten), Roberto Coviello (bar), Natale de Carolis (b-bar), G. Ferro (cnd), Bologna Teatro Comunale Orch Fonit Cetra ("Ricordi" series) 2-▲ FCT RFCD 2003

Serra, Luciana (sop) (cont.)
Rossini, G.:The Siege of Corinth, w. M. Comencini (ten), D. Raffanti (ten), A. Caforio (bass), M. Lippi (bass), P. Olmi (cnd), Genoa Teatro Carlo Felice Orch, Genoa Teatro Carlo Felice Chorus, Prague Phil Choir *(rec June 2 & 14, 1992)* Nuova Era 3-▲ 7140/42 [DDD]
Verdi, G.:Falstaff, w. E. Norberg-Schulz (sop—Nannetta), L. Serra (sop—Alice), S. Graham (mez—Meg Page), M. Lipovsek (cta—Miss Quickly), K. Begley (ten—Dr. Caius), P. Conti (ten—Ford), M. Luperi (ten—Pistol), J. Van Dam (b-bar—Falstaff), P. LeFebvre (bass—Bardolph), G. Solti (cnd), Berlin PO, Berlin Radio Chorus London ▲ 440650-2 [DDD]

Serraiocco, Danilo (bass)
Ferrero, L.:Mare nostro, w. A. Felle (sop—Candeggina), E. Jankovic (mez—Astradiva), C. Di Segni (ten—Rimestino), D. Serraiocco (bass-bar—Marchingello), A. Antoniozzi (bass-bar—Pigliatutto), G. Maisni (cnd), Venezze di Rovigo Conservatory of Music Orch, Venezze di Rovigo Conservatory of Music Chorus *(rec Oct. 21-24, 1991)* Ricordi 2-▲ RFCD 2016 [DDD]
Fioravanti, V.:Le cantatrici villane, w. G. Manci (sop—Agata), M. Mauro (sop—Nunziella), M. A. Peters (sop—Rosa), F. Sovilla (mez—Giannetta), E. Palacio (ten—Carlino), G. Gatti (bar—Don Bucefalo), D. Serraiocco (bass—Don Marco), R. Tigani (cnd), Frosinone Licinio Refice Conservatory SO *(rec Oct. 22, 23 & 25, 1992; D)* Bongiovanni 2-▲ GB 2135/36 [DDD]
Mayr, S.:La rosa bianca e la rosa rossa, w. Susanna Anselmi (sop), Anna Caterina Antonacci (sop), Silvia Mazzoni (mez), Luca Canonici (ten), Francesco Facini (bass), T. Briccetti (cnd), Bergamo Stabile Orch Fonit Cetra ("Ricordi" series) 2-▲ FCT RFCD 2007
Rossini, G.:L'inganno felice, w. A. Felle (sop), I. Zennaro (ten), F. Previati (bar), N. de Carolis (b-bar), M. Viotti (cnd), English CO [I] Claves 8-▲ CD 9200 [DDD]
Rossini, G.:L'inganno felice, w. Amelia Felle (sop), Iorio Zennaro (ten), Fabio Previati (bar), Natale de Carolis (b-bar), M. Viotti (cnd), English CO Claves ▲ 50-9211

Servile, Roberto (bar)
Lattuada, F.:Le Preziose ridicole, w. S. Valayre (sop—Madelon), A. Catarci (sop—Marotte), A. Cicogna (mez—Cathos), S. Tedesco (ten—La Grange), E. Di Cesare (ten—Mascarille), A. Veccia (bar—Croissy), R. Servile (bar—Jodelet), E. Fissore (bass—Gorgibus), E. Romagna (cnd), Toscanini SO, G. Masini (cnd), Rossini Teatro Comunale Chorus [I] *(rec live, 1991)* Ermitage ▲ ERM 404 [DDD]
Rossini, G.:Il barbiere di Siviglia, w. I. Kertesi (sop—Berta), S. Ganassi (mez—Rosina), R. Vargas (ten—Almaviva), A. Romero (bar—Dr. Bartolo), R. Servile (bar—Figaro), F. de Grandis (bass—Basilio), K. Sárkány (bass—Fiorello), A. Déri (pno), B. Sztankovits (gtr), W. Humburg (cnd), Failoni CO, Hungarian Radio Chorus *(rec Nov. 16-28, 1992)* Naxos 3-▲ 8.660027/29 [DDD]
Verdi, G.:Rigoletto (sels), w. Daniella Lojarro (sop), Elizabeth Carter (sgr), Boiko Zvetanov (sgr)—Ov; Questa o quella; Pari siamo! Io la lingua—Figlia! Mio Padre; Giovanna, ho Dei rimorsi; Gualtier Maldè - Caro nome; Ella mi fu rapita!; Scorrendo uniti remota via; Cortigiani, vil razza danata; plus others Laserlight ▲ 14207 [DDD]

Severin, Peder (ten)
Nielsen, C.:Songs, w. Elisabeth Rehling (sop), Dorte Kirkeskov (pno), Jørgen Ernst Hansen (org)—Strange to Say...; Maria Sat on Hay & Straw; God's Angels Sing in Chorus; Now the Sun in the East...; Alas, My Rose...; Standing in Pain under the Cross...; It Is a Wonder...; Jesus Mine, Let My Heart Savour... [all from Hymns & Sacred Songs]; Jens the Road-Mender; The 1st Lark [both from Strophic Songs, Op. 21]; Vibeke's Song [I Came Upon a Song...]; Song of the Sea [The Sea Around Denmark] [both from the play Willemoes]; We Sons of the Plains; The Bird-Catcher's Song, The Tiny Forest Birds are Hiding...; Tove's Song [An Angel Stood Beside Me...]; The Hunter's Song [The Kite Swoops from the Mountain Crest...] [all from the play Tove]; Gulnare's Song [Zither, Let My Prayer Move You...]; Aladdin's Lullaby [Lullalullaby, Tiny Babe...]; Fatima's Song [The Moon is Already Risen...] [all from the play Aladdin]; Music to 5 Poems by J.P. Jacobsen, Op. 4; 10 Little Danish Songs *(rec West Jutland Academy of Music, Sept 1989)* Rondo Grammofon ▲ RCD 8327
Nielsen, C.:Songs, w. Elisabeth Rehling (sop), Dorte Kirkeskov (pno)—I Bear My Yoke with a Smile; Now the Day is Full of Song; How Sweetly on This Summer Evening; Often I'm Happy; Spring Has Come Now; Strangest Breeze of Twilight Hours; Harken to Its Gentle Wing-Beats; Sleep Sweetly, Little Baby Mine; In Shadow We Wander; Now Leaps the Spring from Its Bed; The Snow Queen [The Meadow Lies Buried in Snow So White]; There Lived a Man in Ribe Town [all from 20 Danish Songs]; Christmas Carol [Come Yule to Earth]; To the Queen of My Heart [Shall We Roam, My Love]; Angst [Hold Me Tighter]; The Guide Sings [To the Mountains Above the Village]; Flower Songs; In the Land of Dreams; Just Bow Your Head, O Flower; Song Behind the Plough; This Evening; Greeting; It Is Autumn; *(rec West Jutland Academy of Music, Apr 1988)* Rondo Grammofon ▲ RCD 8323
Schubert, Franz:Die Schöne Müllerin, w. D. Kirkeskov (pno) *(rec Apr. 1992)* Danacord ▲ DACOCD 396 [DDD]

Sevostyanov, R. (ten)
Rachmaninoff, S.:All-Night Vigil, w. Y. Necheporenko (ten), A. Zlobin (ten), O. Shepel (cnd), Voronezh Chamber Choir Globe ▲ GLO 5077 [DDD]

Seymour, Linda (cta)
Stravinsky, I.:Les Noces, w. K. Winter (sop), P. Jones (ten), R. Henderson (bar), I. Stravinsky (cnd), *(orch & chorus unknown)* EMI Classics 2-▲ ZDCB 54607

Sgarro, Louis (bar)
Verdi, G.:La traviata (sels), w. Loretta di Franco (sop), Joan Sutherland (sop), Frederica von Stade (mez), Leo Goeke (ten), Lou Marcella (ten), Luciano Pavarotti (ten), Gene Boucher (bar), Raymond Gibbs (bar), Sherrill Milnes (bar), John Trehy (bar) Budget ("The Greatest Voice in Opera" series) ▲ SYP 112

Shackleton-Williams, Kay (sop)
Balada, L.:Escenas borrascosas, w. Kay Shackleton-Williams (sop—Isabel), Nancy Maria Balach (mez—Beatriz), Matthew Walley (ten—Colón), J.P. Izquierdo (cnd), Carnegie Mellon PO, Robert Page (cnd), Carnegie Mellon Concert Choir, Carnegie Mellon Repertory Chorus *(rec Carnegie Music Hall, Pittsburgh, PA, Apr 7-8, 1994)* New World ▲ 80498-2

Shacklock, Constance (mez)
Elgar, E.:The Dream of Gerontius, w. J. Vickers (ten), M. Nowkovski (bass), J. Barbirolli (cnd), Rome Radio Orch, Rome RAI Chorus [E] *(rec live, Rome 11/20/57)* Arkadia 2-▲ 584 [ADD]

Shade, Ellen (sop)
Bellini, V.:I Puritani, w. B. Sills (sop—Elvira), E. Shade (sop—Enrichetta), L. Pavarotti (ten—Arturo), L. Quilico (bar—Riccardo), P. Plishka (bass—Giorgio), T. Paul (bass—Walton), A. Guadagno (cnd), *(orch & chorus unknown) (rec live Jan. 18, 1972)* Legato Classics 2-▲ LCD 1762 [ADD]
Britten, H.:Canticle II, w. John Stewart (ten), Martin Katz (pno) Phoenix ▲ PHCD 129

Shafer (sgr)
Verdi, G.:Requiem Mass, w. James (sgr), Farina (sgr), Crawford (sgr), D. Moe (cnd), Oberlin Musical Union Orch [L] Bainbridge 2-▲ BCD 2103 [DDD]

Shaffran, James (bar)
Corigliano, J.:Of Rage & Remembrance, w. Michelle DeYoung (mez), Michael Accinno (boy sop), Robert Baker (ten), Michael Forest (ten), Jason Stearns (bar), L. Slatkin (cnd), National SO Washington D.C., Washington Oratorio Society Men's Chorus *(rec J. F. K. Center for the Performing Arts, Washington, D. C., Nov 9-11, 1995 & Apr 19 &)* RCA Red Seal ▲ 09026-68450-2 [DDD]

Shagidullin, Albert (bass)
Mussorgsky, M.:Boris Godunov, w. V. Valente (sop—Xenia), E. Gorochovskaya (mez—Nurse), L. Nichiteanu (mez—Fyodor), E. Zarmeba (mez—Hostess), M. Lipovšek (cta—Marina), P. Langridge (ten—Prince Shuisky), H. Wildhaber (ten—Misail), A. Fedin (ten—Simpleton), S. Leiferkus (bar—Rangoni), A. Kotcherga (bass—B. Godounov), A. Shagidullin (bass—Shchelkalov), S. Ramey (bass—Pimen), S. Larin (bass—Girgory), G. Nikolsky (bass—Varlaam), C. Abbado (cnd), Berlin PO, Tölz Boys' Choir, Berlin Radio Chorus, Slovak Phil Chorus *(rec Nov. 7-30, 1993)* Sony Classical 3-▲ S3K 58977 [DDD]

Shaguch, Marina (sop)
Dvořák, A.:Stabat Mater, w. Ingeborg Danz (alt), James Taylor (ten), Thomas Quasthoff (bass), H. Rilling (cnd), Oregon Bach Festival Orch, Oregon Bach Festival Choir *(rec Silva Concert Hall, Hult Center for the Performing Arts, Eugene, Oregon, July 8-11, 1995)* Hänssler Classic ("Exclusive" series) 2-▲ CD 98.935 [DDD]
Fleischmann, B.:Rothschild's Vn, w. Larissa Diadkova (mez), Ilya Levinsky (ten), Konstantin Pluzhnikov (ten), Sergei Leiferkus (bar), G. Rozhdestvensky (cnd), Rotterdam PO *(rec Rotterdam, Netherlands, Aug 24-31, 1995)* RCA Red Seal ▲ 09026-68434-2 [DDD]

Shaguch, Marina (sop) (cont.)
Shostakovich, D.:From Jewish Folk Poetry, w. Larissa Diadkova (mez), Konstantin Pluzhnikov (ten), G. Rozhdestvensky (cnd), Rotterdam PO *(rec Rotterdam, Netherlands, Aug 24-31, 1995)* RCA Red Seal ▲ 09026-68434-2 [DDD]

Shalyapin, Fiodor (bar)
Fiodor Shalyapin *(rec 1902-1934)* Russian Compact Disc ("Talents of Russia" series) ▲ RCD 16004 [ADD]
Russia & Fiodor Ivanovich Shalyapin *(rec 1910-34)* Russian Compact Disc ("Russian Vocal School" series) ▲ RCD 16003

Shane, Rita (sop)
Meyerbeer, G.:Les Huguenots, w. Jeanette Scovotti (sop—Urbain), Rita Shane (sop—Marguerite de Valois), Enriqueta Tarrès (sop—Valentine), Nicolai Gedda (ten—Raoul de Nangis), Justino Diaz (bass—Marcel), Dimiter Petkov (bass—Le Comte de Saint-Bris), E. Märzendorfer (cnd), Austrian RSO, Austrian Radio Chorus *(rec Vienna, Feb 17, 1971)* Myto 2-▲ MCD 961141

Shapero (sgr)
Mascagni, P.:Nerone, w. R. Didonè (sop), D. Di Domenico (ten), S. Cowan (bar), M. Dirks (bar), Harry Peeters (bass), Strow-Piccolo (sgr), Tcholakov (sgr), K. Bakels (cnd), Hilversum RSO, Hilversum Chorus [I] Bongiovanni 2-▲ GB 2052/53 [DDD]

Sharonova, Valentina (sop)
Cui, C.:Romances (16), w. V. Yurigin-Klevke (pno) Russian Disc ▲ RUS 11 021 [DDD]
Dargomyzhsky, A.:Romances (11), w. V. Yurigin-Klevke (pno) Russian Disc ▲ RUS 11021 [DDD]

Sharp, Norma (sop)
Egk, W.:Peer Gynt, w. J. Perry (sop), C. Wulkopf (mez), H. Hopf (ten), R. Hermann (bar), H. Wallberg (cnd), Munich RSO, Bavarian Radio Chorus [G] Orfeo 2-▲ 005822 [DDD]

Sharp, William (bar)
Bach, J.S.:Cant 82, w. J. Thomas (cnd), American Bach Soloists [G] *(rec Apr & Oct 1990)* Koch International Classics ▲ KIC 7138-2 [DDD]
Bach, J.S.:Cant 106, "Actus tragicus", w. C. Brandes (sop), D. Minter (alt), American Bach Soloists Koch International Classics ▲ KIC 7164 [DDD]
Bach, J.S.:Cant 198, w. J. Nelson (sop), J. Malafronte (mez), J. Thomas (ten), J. Thomas (cnd), American Bach Soloists [G] Koch International Classics ▲ KIC 7163-2 [DDD]
Bach, J.S.:Mass in b, BWV 232, w. J. Baird (sop), J. Nelson (sop), N. Zylstra, J. Lane, Z. Muñoz, S. Rickards, P. Romano, J. Weaver (bass), J. Thomas (cnd), American Bach Soloists Koch International Classics 2-▲ KIC 7194-2 [DDD]
Bach, J.S.:Mass in b, BWV 232, w. Jeffrey Thomas (cnd), American Bach Soloists Koch International Classics ▲ KIC 7610
Bernstein, L.:Arias & Barcarolles, w. Judy Kaye (mez), Michael Barrett (pno), Steven Blier (pno) [E] Koch International Classics ▲ KIC 7000-2 [DDD] ■ 3-7000-4 (D)
Bernstein, L.:Songs & Duets, w. Judy Kaye (sop), M. Barrett (pno), S. Blier (pno), S. Sant'Ambrogio (vc)—sels. from On The Town, 1944 *(Some other time; Lonely town; Carried away; I can cook)*; Peter Pan, 1949 *(Dream with me)*; Wonderful Town, 1952 *(A little bit in love)*; Songfest, 1977 *(Storyette, H.M.; To what you said)* [E] Koch International Classics ▲ KIC 7000-2 [DDD] ■ 3-7000-4 (D)
Blitzstein, M.:Songs, w. K. Holvik (sop), S. Blier (pno)—Monday morning blues; Croon-spoon; The new suit ("Zipperfly"); In the clear; Then; I wish it so; In twos; Penny candy; Emily (Ballad of the bombardier); Displaced; Four e e cummings Songs (o by the by; until and i heard; open your heart; jimmy's got a goil); What will it be for me; Rose song; Blues; Nickel under the foot; The cradle will rock; Bird upon the tree; Stay in my arms [E] Koch International Classics ▲ KIC 7050-2 [DDD]
Bowles, P.:Songs Bar, w. S. Blier (pno)—Four Blue Mountain Ballads; Sleeping song; April fool baby; A little closer, please; Three; Letter to Freddy; Secret words; My sister's hand in mine [E] New World ▲ NW 369-2 [DDD]
Divisions on an Ayre:Lute Songs & Instrumental Music circa 1600, w. Folger Consort Folger Consort ▲ BDCD1 9005 [DDD]
Ewazen, E.:"...to cast a shadow again", w. Chris Gekker (tpt), Colette Valentine (pno) *(rec Recital Hall, SUNY Purchase, 1993)* Well-Tempered Productions ▲ WTP 5172 [DDD]
Gershwin, G.:Blue Monday Blues, w. A. Burton (sop), G. Hopkins (ten), A. Woodley (b-bar), J. J. Offenbach (b-bar), M. Alsop (cnd), Concordia Orch EMI Classics ▲ CDC 54851
Gershwin, G.:Songs, w. J. Kaye (sop), S. Blier (pno)—20 solo songs & duets Koch International Classics ▲ KIC 7028-2 [DDD] ■ 3-7028-4 (D)
Liptak, D.:Songs Bar & Pno, w. A. Nel (pno) Gasparo ▲ GS 286
Moore, T.:Irish Melodies, w. L. Shelton (sop), J. De Gaetani (mez), F. Kelley (ten), I. Kipnis (pno) [E] Elektra/Nonesuch ■ 79059-4 (D)
Mozart, W.A.:Laut verkünde unsre Freude, w. W. Hite (ten), W. Bastian (ten), A. Parrott (cnd), Boston Early Music Festival Orch, Boston Early Music Festival Chorus [G] Denon ▲ CO 77152 [DDD]
Musto, J.:Recuerdo, w. S. Blier (pno) [E] New World ▲ NW 369-2 [DDD]
Thomson, V.:Songs Bar, w. S. Blier (pno)—Prayer to St. Catherine (1959); If thou a reason dost desire to know (1955); Two by Marianne Moore (1963); John Peel (1955); At the spring (1955) [E] New World ▲ NW 369-2 [DDD]

Sharpe, Ivan (ten)
Handel, G.F.:Messiah, w. Max Emanuel Cencic (sop), Charles Humphries (ct), Robert Torday (b-bar), P. Marschik (cnd), Academy of London Orch, Martin Schebesta (cnd), Vienna Boys' Choir *(rec Symphony Hall, Birmingham & Barbican Center, London, Nov 17 & 19, 1994)* Capriccio 2-▲ 60068-2 [DDD]

Sharpe, P. (sgr)
Mozart, W.A.:Songs, w. J. Edwards (cta), D. Russell (sgr), D. Hamilton (ten), M. Glasgow (sgr), C. Birch (sgr), P. Hooper (sgr), G. Lancaster (pno) *(rec July 1991)* Tall Poppies ▲ TP009 [DDD]

Sharubina, Nina (sop)
Russian Romances of the First Half of the 19th Century, w. Larissa Keda (pno) Erasmus ▲ WVH 161

Shatner, William (nar)
Saint-Saëns, C.:Carnival of the Animals, w. M. Golabek (nar), R. Golabek (nar), F. Savage (nar), C. Heston (nar), J. E. Jones (nar), B. White (nar), L. Redgrave (nar), J. Rivers (nar), T. Danson (nar), L. Tomlin (nar), D. Raffin (nar), A. Hepburn (nar), D. Moore (nar), W. Matthau (nar), J. Smith (nar), L. Schifrin (cnd), Hollywood CO Dove Audio ▲ DOV 30700

Shaw (sgr)
Donizetti, G.:Lucia di Lammermoor, w. J. McDonald (sop), J. Sutherland (sop), M. Elkins (mez), J. Bowman (alt), J. Gibin (ten), J. Rouleau (bass), T. Serafin (cnd), Royal Opera House Orch, Royal Opera House Chorus Covent Garden—3 duets from Act 1, & 3 soprano solo arias from Act 2 [I] Myto ▲ 1 MCD 91545 [ADD]
Verdi, G.:Aida, w. G. Jones (sop), J. Vickers (ten), Dourian (sgr), E. Downes (cnd), Royal Opera House Orch, Royal Opera House Chorus Covent Garden [I] *(rec live, Covent Garden, 1/27/68)* Melodram 2-▲ MEL 27019

Shaw, John (bar)
Sullivan, A.:Patience, w. T. Anthony (bass), A. Young (ten), G. Baker (bar), M. Sargent (cnd), Pro Arte Orch, Glyndebourne Festival Chorus EMI Classics 2-▲ CDMB 64406

Shaw, Robert (nar)
Blitzstein, M.:The Airborne, w. W. Scheff (bar), L. Bernstein (cnd), New York City SO, RCA Victor Chorus RCA Gold Seal ▲ 09026-62568-2

Shaw, Teresa (mez)
Ireland, J.:Vexilla Regis, w. P. Bott (sop), J. Oxley (ten), B. Terfel (bass-bar), R. Hickox (cnd), London SO, London Sym Chorus [L] Chandos ▲ CHAN 8879 [DDD]
Purcell, H.:Dido & Aeneas, w. Ruth Holton (sop—Belinda), Elisabeth Priday (sop—2nd Woman), Donna Deam (sop—1st Witch), Shauna Beesley (sop—2nd Witch), Teresa Shaw (mez—Sorceress), Carolyn Watkinson (cta—Dido), Jonathan Peter Kenny (alt—Spirit), Paul Tindall (ten—Sailor), George Mosley (bass—Aeneas), J.E. Gardiner (cnd), English Baroque Soloists, Monteverdi Choir London *(rec Saint George's, Bristol, UK, July 12-14, 1990)* Philips ▲ 432114-2

Shea, D. (voc)
Lebaron, A.:Con for Active Frogs, w. G. Cartwright (voc), J. Staley (voc), W. Trigg (perc), A. LeBaron (cnd), New Music Consort [E] Mode ▲ 30

▲ = CD ♦ = Enhanced CD Δ = MD ■ = Cassette Tape ◻ = DCC

Shearer, A. (sgr)
Lebaron, A.:Lamentation/Invocation, w. R. Yamins (sgr), M. Shapiro (vc), N. Kellman (perc), L. Bouchard (tpt), New Music Consort [E] Mode ▲ 30

Sheen, Martin (sgr)
Rodgers, R.:The King & I, w. J. Andrews (sgr—Anna Leonowens), L. Salonga (sgr—Tuptim), B. Kingsley (sgr—The King), P. Bryson (sgr—Lun Tha), M. Horne (mez—Lady Thiang), M. Liufau (sgr—Prince Chulalongkorn), E. Kingsley (sgr—Louis Leonowens), R. Moore (sgr—Sir Edward Ramsay), M. Sheen (sgr—The Kralahome), J. Mauceri (cnd), Hollywood Bowl Orch, Los Angeles Master Chorale *(rec Culver City, CA, Apr 1992)* Philips ▲ 438007-2 [DDD]

Sheffield, Leo (bar)
Sullivan, A.:The Gondoliers, w. W. Lawson (sop), A. Davies (ten), B. Lewis (cta), D. Oldham (ten), M. Bennett (sop), G. Baker (bar), H. Lytton (bar), et al., H. Norris (cnd), D'Oyly Carte Opera Company Orch, D'Oyly Carte Opera Chorus—dialogue omitted *(rec 1927)* Pearl 2-▲ PEAS 9961 (m) [AAD]
Sullivan, A.:Trial by Jury, w. W. Lawson (sop), D. Oldham (ten), G. Baker (bar), A. Hosking (bar), H. Norris (cnd), D'Oyly Carte Opera Company Orch, D'Oyly Carte Opera Chorus *(rec 1928)* Pearl 2-▲ PEAS 9961 (m) [AAD]

Shelton, Lucy (sop)
Albert, S.:To Wake the Dead, w. C. Kendall (cnd), 20th Century Consort [E] Delos ▲ DCD 1016 [DDD]
Albert, S.:TreeStone, w. G. Schwarz (cnd), New York Chamber SO [E] Delos ▲ DE 3059 [DDD]
Benson, W.:Moon Rain & Memory Jane, w. S. Doane (vc), S. Isserlis (vc) [E] Gasparo ▲ GS 261
Diamond, D.:Vocalises, w. Louise Schulman (va) *(rec RCA Studio A, New York City)* New World ▲ 80508-2
Knussen, O.:Océan de terre, w. O. Knussen (cnd), Lincoln Center Chamber Music Society Virgin Classics ▲ CDC 59308
Knussen, O.:Whitman Settings Sop & Pno, Op. 25, w. P. Serkin (pno) Virgin Classics ▲ CDC 59308
Knussen, O.:Whitman Settings Sop & Orch, Op. 25a, w. O. Knussen (cnd), London Sinfonietta *(rec Henry Wood Hall & All Hollows Gospel Oak, London, Oct & Dec 1995)* Deutsche Grammophon ▲ 449 572-2 [DDD]
Moore, T.:Irish Melodies, w. J. De Gaetani (mez), F. Kelley (ten), W. Sharp (bar), I. Kipnis (pno) [E] Elektra/Nonesuch ■ 79059-4 (D)
Ruders, P.:The Bells, w. D. Starobin (cnd), Speculum Musicae *(rec American Academy of Arts & Letters, New York City, Apr. 19–21, 1994)* Bridge ▲ BCD 9054 [DDD]
Ruders, P.:The Bells, w. D. Starobin (cnd), Speculum Musicae *(rec American Academy of Arts & Letters, Apr 21, 1994)* Bridge ▲ BCD 9057 [DDD]
Schoenberg, A.:Herzgewächse, w. O. Knussen (cnd), Da Capo Chamber Players Bridge ▲ BCD 9032 [DDD]
Schoenberg, A.:Pierrot lunaire, w. Da Capo Chamber Players—2 complete performances:in German & in Andrew Porter's English translation Bridge ▲ BCD 9032 [DDD]

Shepley, I. (sgr)
Rodgers, R.:Flower Drum Song, w. K. Scott (sgr), Y. S. Tung (sgr), Y. Saki (sgr), T. Hebert (sgr) [1960 London cast] Angel ▲ ZDM 89953

Sheppard, Honor (sop)
Byrd, W.:Mass in 4 Parts, w. A. Deller (ct), N. Jenkins (ten), M. Bevan (bar), Deller Consort [L] Musique d'Abord ▲ HMA 190211
Byrd, W.:Mass in 5 Parts, w. A. Deller (ct), J. Buttrey (ten), N. Jenkins (ten), M. Bevan (bar), Deller Consort [L] Musique d'Abord ▲ HMA 190211
Purcell, H.:King Arthur, w. R. Hardy (sop), J. Knibbs (cta), A. Deller (ct), M. Deller (alt), P. Elliott (ten), L. Nixon (ten), M. Bevan (bar), N. Beavan (bass), A. Deller (cnd), Deller Consort, King's Musick [E] Harmonia Mundi France 2-▲ HMC 90252/53
Purcell, H.:The Prophetess, or The History of Dioclesian, w. S. Le Sage (sop), A. Deller (ct), M. Worthley (ten), P. Todd (ten), M. Bevan (bar), A. Deller (cnd), Vienna Concentus Musicus—also includes incidental music from the play *(rec June 1965)* Vanguard Classics ("The Bach Guild" series) ▲ OVC 2517 [ADD]

Sheridan, Margaret (sop)
Puccini, G.:Madama Butterfly (sels), w. Ida Mannarini (mez), Lionello Cecil (ten), Vittorio Wenberg (sgr), Carlo Sabajno (pno) *(rec La Scala, 1929–30)* Romophone ("Opera Magna" series) 2-▲ 89001-2
Rich & Rare:The Voice of Margaret Sheridan, w. Aureliano Pertile (ten), Renato Zanelli (ten), Hubert Greenslade (pno), Carlo Sabajno (cnd), La Scala Orch, Queens Hall Orch *(rec 1926–29)* Time Machine ▲ 0100

Sherman, A. (sgr)
Loesser, F.:Guys and Dolls, w. F. Sinatra (sgr), B. Crosby (sgr), D. Martin (sgr), J. Stafford (sgr), D. Shore (sgr), D. Reynolds (sgr), C. Dennis (sgr), S. Davis Jr. (sgr), *(other artists unknown)* [studio cast] Reprise ▲ 45014-2 [AAD] ■ 45014-4

Shi, Ke-Long (voice)
Chen, Q.:Poème Lyrique II, w. J.-L. Petit (cnd), Ville d'Avray Instrumental Ensemble REM ▲ REM 311223 [DDD]

Shicoff, Neil (ten)
Bizet, G.:Carmen, w. J. Norman (sop), M. Freni (sop), S. Estes (bass), S. Ozawa (cnd), French National Orch, French Radio Chorus [F] Philips ▲ 426040-2 [DDD] ■ 426040-4 ◻ 426040-5
Bizet, G.:Carmen, w. J. Norman (sop), M. Freni (sop), S. Estes (bass), S. Ozawa (cnd), French National Orch, French Radio Chorus [F] Philips 3-▲ 422366-2 [DDD]
Offenbach, J.:Les Contes d'Hoffmann, w. L. Serra (sop), R. Plowright (sop), J. Norman (sop), A. Murray (mez), J. Taillon (mez), A. Oliver (ten), R. Tear (ten), J. Van Dam (b-bar), D. Duesing (bar), K. Rydl (bass), S. Cambreling (cnd), Brussels Théâtre de la Monnaie Orch [F] EMI Classics 3-▲ CDCC 49641 [DDD]
Verdi, G.:Attila, w. S. Studer (sop), G. Zancanaro (bar), S. Ramey (bass), R. Muti (cnd), La Scala Orch, La Scala Chorus [I] EMI Classics 2-▲ CDCB 49952 [DDD]
Verdi, G.:La traviata, w. E. Gruberova (sop), G. Zancanaro (bar), C. Rizzi (cnd), London SO, Ambrosian Singers Teldec 2-▲ 9031-76348-2 PL
Verdi, G.:La traviata (sels), w. E. Gruberova (sop), G. Zancanaro (bar), C. Rizzi (cnd), London SO [I] Teldec ▲ 4509-91975-2

Shields, A. (voc/elec)
Shields, A.:The Transformation of Ani CRI ▲ CD 611 [ADD]

Shields, A. (voc/kbd/syn)
Shields, A.:Apocalypse, w. A. Shields (voc/kbd/syn—The Woman, the Seaweed & Chorus), M. Willson (Shiva), J. Matus (elec gtr) CRI ▲ CD 647 [DDD]

Shilling, Eric (bar)
Sullivan, A.:Iolanthe (sels), w. E. Harwood (sop), S. Bevin (ten), D. Dowling (bar), J. Holmes (bass), A. Faris (cnd), Sadler's Wells Opera Orch, Sadler's Wells Opera Chorus Classics for Pleasure 2-▲ CDCFP 4730 [ADD]

Shilling, Eric (nar)
Britten, H.:The Young Person's Guide to the Orchestra, w. K. Ančerl (cnd), Czech PO *(rec 1963)* Supraphon ▲ 11 1945-2 [AAD]
Prokofiev, S.:Peter & the Wolf, w. K. Ančerl (cnd), Czech PO *(rec 1963)* Supraphon ▲ 11 1945-2 [AAD]

Shimada, T. (nar)
Levines, T.A.:Travel Journal:Books 1–3, w. Portland String Quartet [J] *(rec Dec. 1991 & July 1992)* Arabesque ▲ Z 6632 [DDD]

Shimell, William (bar)
Bach, J.S.:Mass in b, BWV 232, w. F. Lott (sop), A. S. von Otter (mez), H. P. Blochwitz (ten), G. Howell (b-bar), G. Solti (cnd), Chicago SO, Chicago Sym Chorus London 2-▲ 430353-2 [DDD]
Cherubini, L.:Lodoïska, w. M. Devia (sop), F. Pedaci (sgr), B. Lombardo (ten), T. Moser (ten), A. Corbelli (bar), R. Muti (cnd), La Scala Orch, La Scala Chorus Sony Classical 2-▲ SM2K 47290
Lambert, C.:Summer's Last Will & Testament, w. D. Lloyd-Jones (cnd), English Northern Philharmonia [E] Hyperion ▲ CDA 66565 [DDD]
Mozart, W.A.:Don Giovanni, w. S. Studer (sop), C. Vaness (sop), S. Ramey (bass), R. Muti (cnd), Vienna PO EMI Classics 3-▲ CDCC 54255

Shimell, William (bar) (cont.)
Vaughan Williams, R.:Sym 1, w. Joan Rodgers (sop), V. Handley (cnd), Royal Liverpool PO Classics for Pleasure ("Eminence" series) ▲ CDEMX 2142 [DDD]

Shin, Young Ok (sop)
Bellini, V.:Bianca e Fernando, w. G. Kunde (ten), W. Coppola (ten), A. Tomicich (bass), A. Licata (cnd), Catania Teatro Massimo Bellini Orch, Catania Teatro Massimo Bellini Chorus Nuova Era 2-▲ NUO 7076 [DDD]

Shinall, Vern (sgr)
Donizetti, G.:Lucrezia Borgia, w. Montserrat Caballé (sop), Jane Berbié (mez), Alain Vanzo (ten), Kostas Paskalis (bar), Arnold Voketaitis (bass-bar), L. D. Clements (sgr), Adib Fazah (sgr), Mauro Lampi (sgr), Jerold Siena (sgr), William Wiederanders (sgr), J. Perlea (cnd), New York City Opera Orch, New York City Chorus Great Opera Performances 2-▲ GOP 769

Shipper, Paul (sgr)
Monteverdi, C.:Orfeo, w. Jennifer Lane (mez), Jeffrey Thomas (ten), Michael Brown (sgr), Dana Hanchard (sgr), Timothy Leigh Evans (sgr), G. Toth (cnd), ARTEK Lyrichord 2-▲ LYR 9002 [DDD]

Shirai, Mitsuko (mez)
Boulanger, L.:Songs (4), w. H. Höll (pno)—Attente (1910); Reflets (1911); La Retour (1912); Dans l'immense Tristesse (1916) [F] Bayer ▲ 100041 [DDD]
Brahms, J.:Songs, w. H. Holl (pno)—21 songs Capriccio ▲ 10 204 [DDD]
Haydn, J.:Arianna a Naxos, w. H. Höll (pno) Camerata ▲ 32CM 123
Haydn, J.:Canzonettas, w. H. Höll (pno) Camerata ▲ 32CM 123
Mahler, G.:Des Knaben Wunderhorn, w. Hartmut Höll (pno)—9 sels Capriccio ▲ CD 10712 [DDD]
Mahler, G.:Lieder und Gesänge aus der Jugendzeit, w. Hartmut Höll (pno)—3 sels Capriccio ▲ CD 10712 [DDD]
Mahler, G.:Songs from Rückert, w. N. Marriner (cnd), Academy of St. Martin in the Fields Capriccio ▲ CD 10712 [DDD]
Mozart, W.A.:Songs, w. H. Höll (pno)—Abendempfindung, K.523; Als Luise die Briefe ihres ungetreuen Liebhabers verbrannte, K.520; An Chloe, K.524; Dans un bois solitaire, K.308; Einsam bin ich, meine Liebe, K.475a (fragment); Der Frühling, K.597; Ich würd' auf meinem Pfad, K.390; Die kleine Spinnerin, K.531; Komm, liebe Zither, komm, K.351; Das Lied der Trennung, K.519; Lied zur Gesellenreise, K.468; Oiseaux, si tous les ans, K.307; Ridente la calma, K.152; Sehnsucht nach dem Frühling, K.596; Sei du mein Trost, K.391; Das Traumbild, K.530; Das Veilchen, K.476; Die Verschweigung, K.518; Der Zauberer, K.472; Die Zufriedenheit, K.349; Die Zufriedenheit, K.473 [F,G,I] LaserLight ▲ 15 876 [DDD]
Mozart, W.A.:Songs, w. H. Höll (pno)—21 songs [F,G,I] Capriccio ▲ 10098 [DDD]
Schoeck, O.:Das holde Bescheiden, w. D. Fischer-Dieskau (bar), H. Höll (pno) *(rec Jan.–Feb. 1991; March 1992)* Claves 2-▲ CD 9308/9 [DDD]
Schumann, R.:Liederkreis, Op. 39, w. H. Höll (pno) [G] Capriccio ▲ 10099 [DDD]
Schumann, R.:Songs, w. H. Höll (pno)—4 Lieder der Mignon, Op. 98a; 5 Lieder der Maria Stuart, Op. 135; 5 Lieder nach Justinus Kerner, Op. 35 [G] Capriccio ▲ 10099 [DDD]
Schumann, R.:Spanische Liebeslieder, w. M. Lipovsek (mez), J. Protschka (ten), M. Hölle (bass), N. Shetler (pno), N. Deutsch (pno) [G] Capriccio ▲ CDC 10079
Wolf, H.:Songs (misc), w. D. Shallon (cnd), Berlin RSO—15 songs Capriccio ▲ CD 10 335 [DDD]

Shirley, George (nar)
Waxman, F.:Ruth, w. L. Foster (cnd), Berlin RSO *(rec Berlin, Nov 25–26, 1993)* Capriccio ▲ 10711 [DDD]
Waxman, F.:The Spirit of St. Louis, w. L. Foster (cnd), Berlin RSO *(rec Berlin, Nov 25–26, 1993)* Capriccio ▲ 10711 [DDD]

Shirley, George (ten)
Cherubini, L.:Mass in d, w. Patricia Wells (sop), Maureen Forrester (cta), Justino Diaz (bass), N. Jenkins (cnd), Clarion Concerts Orch, Clarion Concerts Chorus *(rec Vanguard's 23rd Street Recording Studio)* Vanguard Classics ▲ SVC-44 [AAD]
Debussy, C.:Pelléas et Mélisande, w. E. Söderström (sop), Y. Minton (mez), D. McIntyre (bass-bar), D. Ward (bass), P. Boulez (cnd), Royal Opera House Orch, Royal Opera House Chorus Covent Garden Sony Classical (Pierre Boulez Edition) 3-▲ SM3K 47265
Mozart, W.A.:Così fan tutte, w. L. Price (sop), J. Raskin (sop), T. Troyanos (mez), S. Milnes (bar), E. Leinsdorf (cnd), New Philharmonia Orch, New Philharmonia Chorus [I] RCA Gold Seal 3-▲ 6677-2 [ADD]
Mozart, W.A.:Requiem, w. E. Mathis (sop), G. Bumbry (mez), M. Rintzler (bass), R. Frühbeck de Burgos (cnd), New Philharmonia Orch, New Philharmonia Chorus Classics for Pleasure ▲ CDCFP 4399 [ADD]
Weigl, V.:Nature Moods, w. S. Drucker (cl), Gordon (vn) CRI ■ C 326

Shirley-Quirk, John (bar)
Bach, J.S.:Cant 82, w. J. Baker (sop), R. Tear (ten), N. Marriner (cnd), Academy of St. Martin in the Fields London ("Jubilee" series) ▲ 430260-2 [ADD]
Bach, J.S.:Cant 159, w. J. Baker (sop), R. Tear (ten), N. Marriner (cnd), Academy of St. Martin in the Fields London ("Jubilee" series) ▲ 430260-2 [ADD]
Bach, J.S.:Cant 170, w. J. Baker (sop), R. Tear (ten), N. Marriner (cnd), Academy of St. Martin in the Fields London ("Jubilee" series) ▲ 430260-2 [ADD]
Bach, J.S.:St. Matthew Passion, w. F. Lott (sop), A. Hodgson (cta), R. Tear (ten), S. Roberts (bar), D. Willcocks (cnd), Thames CO, Bach Choir [E] ASV Quicksilva 3-▲ ASQ 324 [ADD]
Berlioz, H.:Roméo et Juliette, w. B. Fassbaender (mez), N. Gedda (ten), L. Gardelli (cnd), ORF SO, Vienna State Opera Chorus [F] Orfeo 2-▲ 087842 [DDD]
Bliss, A.:Serenade, w. B. Priestman (cnd), London SO Lyrita ▲ SRCD 225 [ADD]
Britten, H.:Billy Budd, w. P. Pears (ten), P. Glossop (bar), B. Luxon (bar), M. Langdon (bass), O. Brannigan (bass), B. Britten (cnd), London SO, Ambrosian Singers [E] London 3-▲ 417428-2 [ADD]
Britten, H.:Death in Venice, w. J. Bowman (ct), P. Pears (ten), S. Bedford (cnd), English CO, English Opera Group Chorus [E] London 2-▲ 425669-2 [ADD]
Britten, H.:Folksong Arrs, w. O. Ellis (hp)—Bird scarers' song; Bonny at morn; Dafydd y Garreg en; Lemady; Lord! I married me a wife!; She's like the swallow Meridian ▲ 84119
Britten, H.:Gloriana, w. J. Barstow (sop—Queen Elizabeth I), D. Jones (mez—Lady Essex), P. Langridge (ten—Earl of Essex), J. M. Ainsley (ten—Spirit of the Masque), J. Summers (bar—Lord Mountjoy), J. Shirley-Quirk (bar—Recorder of Norwich), B. Terfel (b-bar—Henry Cuffe), C. Mackerras (cnd), Welsh National Opera Orch, Welsh National Opera Chorus Argo 2-▲ 440213-2 [DDD]
Britten, H.:A Midsummer Night's Dream, w. E. Harwood (sop), J. Veasey (mez), H. Watts (cta), A. Deller (ct), P. Pears (ten), B. Britten (cnd), London SO, London Sym Chorus [E] London 2-▲ 425663-2 [ADD]
Britten, H.:Owen Wingrave, w. S. Fisher (Miss Wingrave), J. Vyvyan (Mrs. Julian), H. Harper (Mrs. Coyle), J. Baker (Kate), P. Pears (Sir P. Wingrave; Narrator), B. Luxon (Owen Wingrave), B. Britten, Wandworth School Boys' Choir, English CO London 2-▲ 433200-2
Britten, H.:The Rape of Lucretia, w. H. Harper (sop), J. Baker (mez), P. Pears (ten), B. Drake (bar), B. Luxon (bar), B. Britten (cnd), English CO London 2-▲ 425666-2 [ADD]
Britten, H.:Tit for Tat, w. P. Ledger (pno) Meridian ▲ 84119
Britten, H.:War Requiem, w. H. Harper (sop), P. Langridge (ten), R. Elms (org), R. Hickox (cnd), London SO, London Sym Chorus, St. Paul's Cathedral Choristers [E,L] Chandos 2-▲ CHAN 8983/84 [DDD]
Butterworth, G.:Songs (6) from *A Shropshire Lad*, w. Nona Liddell (vn), Ivor McMahon (vn), Ambrose Gauntlett (vl), Martin Isepp (hpd/pno) Saga Classics ▲ EC 3336
Butterworth, G.:Songs (6) from *A Shropshire Lad*, w. M. Isepp (pno)—Loveliest of Trees Saga Classics ▲ 3353 [ADD]
Delius, F.:Brigg Fair:An English Rhapsody, w. C. Groves (cnd), Royal Liverpool PO, Royal Liverpool Phil Choir EMI Classics ▲ ZDMB 64218
Delius, F.:A Mass of Life, w. K. Te Kanawa (sop), P. Bowden (mez), R. Dowd (ten), N. del Mar (cnd), BBC SO, BBC Sym Chorus *(rec live, London 5/3/71)* Intaglio 2-▲ INCD 702-2 [ADD]
Elgar, E.:The Light of Life, w. M. Marshall (sop), H. Watts (cta), C. Groves (cnd), Royal Liverpool PO, Royal Liverpool Phil Choir EMI Classics ▲ CDM 64732
Elgar, E.:The Light of Life, w. J. Howarth (sop), L. Finnie (mez), A. Davies (ten), R. Hickox (cnd), London SO, London Sym Chorus Chandos ▲ CHAN 9208 [DDD]
Elgar, E.:The Light of Life (sels), w. M. Marshall (sop), H. Watts (cta), C. Groves (cnd), Royal Liverpool PO—Meditation EMI Classics ▲ CDM 64732

VOCALISTS

Shirley–Quirk, John (bar) (cont.)

Handel, G.F.:Judas Maccabaeus, w. Heather Harper (sop), Helen Watts (cta), Alexander Young (ten), J. Somary (cnd), English CO, Amor Artis Chorale [E] *(rec 1979)* Vanguard Classics 2-▲ OVC 4071/72 [ADD]

Handel, G.F.:Judas Maccabaeus (sels), w. Heather Harper (sop), Helen Watts (cta), Alexander Young (ten), J. Somary (cnd), English CO, Amor Artis Chorale Vanguard Classics ▲ OVC 4073 [ADD]

Handel, G.F.:Messiah, w. Heather Harper (sop), Helen Watts (cta), John Wakefield (ten), C. Davis (cnd), London SO, London Sym Chorus Philips 2-▲ 438356-2

Handel, G.F.:Salve Regina, w. Janet Baker (mez), Helen Watts (cta), Robert Tear (ten), Benjamin Luxon (bar), R. Leppard (cnd), English CO, London Voices Erato 3-▲ 2292-45994-2

Humfrey, P.:Anthems, w. Nona Liddell (vn), Ivor McMahon (vn), Ambrose Gauntlett (vl), Martin Isepp (hpd/pno)—A Hymne to God the Father Saga Classics ▲ EC 3336

Lutoslawski, W.:Les Espaces du sommeil, w. E.–P. Salonen (cnd), Los Angeles PO *(rec Nov. 29–Dec. 2, 1985)* Sony Classical ▲ SK 66280 [DDD]

Lutoslawski, W.:Les Espaces du sommeil, w. E.–P. Salonen (cnd), Los Angeles PO [F] CBS 2-▲ M2K 42271 [DDD]

Lutoslawski, W.:Les Espaces du sommeil, w. E.–P. Salonen (cnd), Los Angeles PO Sony Classical ▲ SMK 53473

Mahler, G.:Sym 8, w. A. Augér (sop), H. Harper (sop), L. Popp (sop), Y. Minton (mez), H. Watts (cta), A. Kollo (ten), M. Talvela (bass), G. Solti (cnd), Chicago SO, Vienna State Opera Chorus, Vienna Boys' Choir, Vienna Singverein [G,L] London 2-▲ 414493-2 [ADD]

Moeran, E.J.:Songs, w. Martin Isepp (hpd/pno), Nona Liddell (vn), Ivor McMahon (vn), Ambrose Gauntlett (vl)—When Smoke Stood Up from Ludlow; Say, Lad, Have You Things to Do?; Farewell to Barn & Stack & Trees [all from Ludlow Town] Saga Classics ▲ EC 3336

Mozart, W.A.:Requiem, w. I. Cotrubas (sop), H. Watts (cta), R. Tear (ten), N. Marriner (cnd), Academy of St. Martin in the Fields, Academy of St. Martin in the Fields Chorus [L] London ▲ 417746-2 [ADD]

Orff, C.:Carmina burana, w. N. Burrowes (sop), L. Devos (ten), A. Dorati (cnd), Royal PO, Brighton Festival Chorus [G,L] London ▲ 417714-2 [ADD]

Orff, C.:Carmina burana, w. Norma Burrowes (sop), Louis Devos (ten), A. Dorati (cnd), Royal PO, Brighton Festival Chorus, Southend Boys' Choir *(rec Kingsway Hall, London, Feb 1976)* London ("Phase 4 Stereo" series) ▲ 444105-2 [ADD]

Purcell, H.:Songs, w. Martin Isepp (hpd/pno), Nona Liddell (vn), Ivor McMahon (vn), Ambrose Gauntlett (vl)—Man Is for the Woman Made; Music for a While; Twas within a Furlong of Edinborough Town; When Night her Purple Veil Saga Classics ▲ EC 3336

Schoenberg, A.:Serenade Cl, w. P. Boulez (cnd), BBC SO, Ensemble InterContemporain *(rec Apr. 10, 1979)* Sony Classical ▲ SMK 48463 [ADD]

Schubert, Franz:Schwanengesang, w. Steuart Bedford (pno) ASV Quicksilva ▲ ASQ 6171

Tippett, M.:A Child Of Our Time, w. Jill Gomez (sop), Helen Watts (cta), Kenneth Wooliam (ten), G. Rozhdestvensky (cnd), BBC SO, BBC Sym Chorus IMP ("BBC Radio Classics" series) ▲ IMP 9130

Tippett, M.:A Child Of Our Time, w. N. Armstrong (sop), F. Palmer (sop), P. Langridge (ten), A. Previn (cnd), Royal PO, Brighton Festival Chorus [E] RPO ▲ RPO 7012 [DDD]

Vaughan Williams, R.:Songs, w. V. Turnnard (pno)—Linden Lea Saga Classics ▲ 3353 [ADD]

Vaughan Williams, R.:Sym 1, w. H. Harper (sop), A. Previn (cnd), London SO, London Sym Chorus [E] RCA Gold Seal ▲ 60580-2-RG [ADD] ■ 60580-4-RG (CrO2)

Walton, W.:The Bear, w. D. Jones (mez), A. Opie (bass), R. Hickox (cnd), Northern Sinfonia of England Chandos ▲ CHAN 9245 [DDD]

Walton, W.:Belshazzar's Feast, w. A. Previn (cnd), London SO, London Sym Chorus *(rec 1972)* EMI Classics ▲ CDM 64723

Shore, Andrew (bass)

Puccini, G.:Tosca, w. Jane Eaglen (sop—Floria Tosca), Charbel Michael (alt—Shepherd Boy), John Daszak (ten—Spoletta), Dennis O'Neill (ten—Mario Cavaradossi), Christopher Booth–Jones (bar—Sciarrone), Ashley Holland (bar—Jailor), Gregory Yurisich (bar—Baron Scarpia), Peter Rose (bass—Cesare Angelotti), Andrew Shore (bass—Sacristan), D. Parry (cnd), Philharmonia Orch, Geoffrey Mitchell Choir, Peter Kay Children's Chorus Chandos ("Opera in English" series) 2-▲ CHAN 3000

Shore, D. (sgr)

Loesser, F.:Guys and Dolls, w. F. Sinatra (sgr), B. Crosby (sgr), D. Martin (sgr), J. Stafford (sgr), D. Reynolds (sgr), C. Dennis (sgr), A. Sherman (sgr), S. Davis Jr. (sgr), *(other artists unknown)* [studio cast] Reprise ▲ 45014-2 [AAD] ■ 45014-4

Rodgers, R.:Music of, w. S. Bass (sgr), J. Andrews (sgr), P. Como (sgr), D. Reese (sgr), J. Jones (sgr), N. Luboff (sgr), M. Gold (sgr), N. Walker (sgr), H. Bowen (sgr), V. Damone (sgr), P. Nero (pno), J. P. Morgan (sgr), E. Fisher (sgr), B. Goodman (cl), Ann–Margaret (sgr), Shorty Rogers (sgr), T. Martin (sgr), M. King (sgr), A. Newley (sgr) RCA ▲ 8590-2 R ■ 8590-4 R

Short, Nigel (ct)

Danyel, J.:Songs, w. David Miller (lt)—Coy Daphne fled; Thou pretty bird; He whose desires are still abroad; Like as the lute delights; Dost thou withdraw thy grace?; Stay, cruel, stay!; The Passymeasures Galliard; Time, cruel, time; Grief keep within; Drop not, mine eyes; Let not Chloris think; Can doeful notes?; No, let chromatic tunes; Uncertain turns of thought; Eyes, look no more; Rosamund; If I could shut the gate; I die whenas I do not see; What delight they can enjoy; Now the earth, the skies, the air; Mistress Anne Grene Hyperion ▲ CDA 66714

Purcell, H.:Anthems & Services, w. S. Gritton (sop), M. Kennedy (sop), E. O'Dwyer (trb), J. Goodman (trb), J. Bowman (ct), Rogers Covey–Crump (ten), C. Daniels (ten), M. Milhofer (ten), M. George (bass), R. Evans (bass), R. King (cnd), King's Consort—I Was Glad When They Said unto Me (coronation & verse anthem); O Consider My Adversity; Beati omnes qui timent Dominum; In the Black Dismal Dungeon of Dispair; Save Me, O God; Te Deum in B♭; Jubilant in B♭; Thy Way, O God, Is Holy Hyperion ▲ CDA 66677 [DDD]

Purcell, H.:Music for the Funeral of Queen Mary, w. S. Gritton (sop), M. Kennedy (sop), E. O'Dwyer (trb), J. Goodman (trb), J. Bowman (ct), Rogers Covey–Crump (ten), C. Daniels (ten), M. Milhofer (ten), M. George (bass), R. Evans (bass), R. King (cnd), King's Consort Hyperion ▲ CDA 66677 [DDD]

Shuard, Amy (sop)

Verdi, G.:Macbeth, w. Amy Shuard (sop—Lady Macbeth), Noreen Berry (mez—Lady–in–waiting), John Dobson (ten—Malcolm), André Turp (ten—Macduff), Tito Gobbi (bar—Macbeth), Edgar Boniface (bass—Servant), Rydderch Davies (bass—Doctor), Forbes Robinson (bass—Banco), Jean Holmes (sgr—Apparition), Celia Penny (sgr—Apparition), Glynne Thomas (sgr—Apparition), Brian Wrigt (sgr—Araldo), F. Molinari–Pradelli (cnd), Royal Opera House Orch, Royal Opera House Chorus Covent Garden *(rec London, Apr 8, 1960)* Bella Voce 2-▲ 7203 [AAD]

Shukis, Renia (sop)

Stuart, P.:Kill Bear Comes Home, w. Elana Gizzi (sop—Hasty Girl), Mi–Kyung Huh (sop—Cold Feet), Therese Murray (sop—Song Bird), Cherie Pfeil (sop—1st Sister), Renia Shukis (sop—2nd Sister), Riki Connaughton (mez—4th Sister), Lucy Fee (mez—3rd Sister), David Averbach (ten—Song Leader), Mark Schmidt (ten—Kill Bear), Jason Smith (bar—Cheif Wife Hunter), P. Stuart (cnd), Rochester Opera Theater Orch, Rochester Opera Theater Chorus VM ▲ DRK 154 [DDD]

Shulpin, Gyorgy (bar)

Mussorgsky, M.:Boris Godunov, w. Irina Arkhipova (mez—Marina Mnishek), Evgenya Verbitskaya (mez—Nurse to Xenia), Valentina Klepatskaya (sgr—Fyodor), Tamara Sorokina (sgr—Xenia), Anton Grigoryev (ten—Simpleton), Vladimir Ivanovsky (ten—Grigory, the Pretender), Gyorgy Shulpin (bar—Prince Shuisky), Alexey Geleva (bass—Varlaam), Ivan Petrov (bass—Boris Godounov), Mark Reshetin (bass—Pimen), Alexi Ivanov (sgr—Andrei Shchelkalov), Evgeny Kibkalo (sgr—Rangoni), A. Melik–Pashayev (cnd), Bolshoi Theater Orch, Bolshoi Theater Chorus *(rec Moscow, 1962)* Melodiya ("The Russian Opera" series) 3-▲ 74321-29349-2 [ADD]

Shumskaya, Yelizaveta (sop)

Rachmaninoff, S.:The Bells, w. Mikhail Dovenman (ten), Alexei Bolshakov (bar), K. Kondrashin (cnd), Moscow PO, Alexander Yurlov (cnd), Russian Republican Capelle RCA Gold Seal ▲ 74321-32046-2 [ADD]

Yelizaveta Shumskaya:Russian Vocal School *(rec 1948–63)* Russian Compact Disc ▲ RCD 16005 [AAD]

Sica, Gennaro (ten)

Pergolesi, G.B.:Il flaminio, w. D. Dessi (sop—Flaminio), F. Pediconi (sop—Agata), E. Zilio (mez—Giustina), M. Ferrugia (ten—Fernando), G. Sica (ten—Polidoro), V. Baiano (bass–Checa), S. Pagliuca (bass—Bastiano), M. Panni (cnd), Naples Teatro San Carlo Orch *(rec Nov. 12, 1983)* Fonit Cetra 3-▲ CDC 39 [ADD]

Siclari (sgr)

Ricci, L.:Crispino e la cornare, w. D. Lojarro (sop), A. Lazzarini (mez), Cossutta (ten), S. Alaimo (bar), R. Coviello (bar), A. Marani (bass), R. Ristori (bass), Benori (sgr), P. Carignani (cnd), San Remo SO, San Remo Sym Chorus [I] *(rec live 11/89)* Bongiovanni 2-▲ GB 2095/96 [DDD]

Sidhom, Peter (bar)

Maccunn, H.:The Dowie Dens o'Yarrow, w. Lisa Milne (sop), Janice Watson (sop), Jamie MacDougall (ten), Stephen Gadd (bass), M. Brabbins (cnd), BBC Scottish SO, Scottish Opera Chorus Hyperion ▲ CDA 66815

Maccunn, H.:Jeanie Deans (sels), w. Lisa Milne (sop), Janice Watson (sop), Jamie MacDougall (ten), Stephen Gadd (bass), M. Brabbins (cnd), BBC Scottish SO, Scottish Opera Chorus Hyperion ▲ CDA 66815

Maccunn, H.:Lay of Last Minstrel, w. Lisa Milne (sop), Janice Watson (sop), Jamie MacDougall (ten), Stephen Gadd (bass), M. Brabbins (cnd), BBC Scottish SO, Scottish Opera Chorus Hyperion ▲ CDA 66815

Maccunn, H.:Ship o' the Fiend, w. Lisa Milne (sop), Janice Watson (sop), Jamie MacDougall (ten), Stephen Gadd (bass), M. Brabbins (cnd), BBC Scottish SO, Scottish Opera Chorus Hyperion ▲ CDA 66815

Poulenc, F.:Chamber Music, w. William Bennett (fl), David Campbell (cl), James Campbell (cl), Nicholas Daniel (ob), Richard Watkins (hn), Rachel Gough (bn), Peter Carter (vn), Chris West (db), Ieuan Jones (hp), Clifford Benson (pno), Julius Drake (pno), John York (pno)—Son for Ob; L'invitation au château; Villanelle; Son 2 Cls; Trio; Sxt; Son for Cl & Bn; Rapsodie nègre; Son for Cl; Mouvements perpétuels; Son for Fl *(rec All Saints' Church, East Finchley, London, Jan 12–20, 1994)* Cala ▲ CACD 1018 [DDD]

Smyth, E.:The Wreckers, w. Judith Howarth (sop), Anne–Marie Owens (mez), Annemarie Sand (mez), Justin Lavender (ten), Anthony Roden (ten), David Wilson–Johnson (bar), Brian Bannatyne–Scott (bass), O. de la Martinez (cnd), BBC PO, Huddersfield Choral Society *(rec live, Royal Albert Hall, London, July 31, 1994)* Conifer Classics 2-▲ 75605-51250-2

Siebert, Dorothea (mez)

Mussorgsky, M.:Boris Godunov, w. Martha Mödl (sop—Marina Mniszek), Lotte Schädle (sop—Xenia), Dorothea Siebert (mez—Fyodor), Hertha Töpper (mez—Xenia's wet–nurs), Karl Hermann Bennert (Boyer Khrushchyov), Lorenz Fehenberger (ten—Prince Shuysky), Hans Hopf (ten—Grigory), Karl Ostertag (ten—Missail), Hans Hotter (b-bar—Boris Godunov), Hermann Uhde (bar—Andrey Shchelkalov), Kurt Böhme (bass—Varlaam), Kim Borg (bass—Pimen), Kieth Engen (bass—Lewicki), Adolf Keil (bass—Nikitich), Benno Kusche (bar—Rangoni), Heinz Maria Linz (bass—Czernikowski), E. Jochum (cnd), Bavarian RSO, Bavarian Radio Chorus *(rec Munich, May 1957)* Myto 3-▲ MCD 953131

Siebert, Dorothea (sop)

Smetana, B.:The Bartered Bride, w. Dagmar Hermann (mez), Maria von Ilosvay (mez), Hans Braun (bar), Kurt Böhme (bass), J. Keilberth (cnd), Bavarian RSO, Bavarian Radio Chorus *(rec 1958)* Pantheon 2-▲ PHE 6652 (m)

Siebert, Glenn (ten)

Berlioz, H.:Lélio, "Le retourà la vie", w. W. Klemperer (nar), W. Diana (bar), Z. Macal (cnd), Milwaukee Sym Chorus Koss Classics 2-▲ KC 1012 [DDD]

Berlioz, H.:Lélio, "Le retourà la vie", w. W. Diana (bar), W. Klemperer (nar), Z. Macal (cnd), Milwaukee SO *(rec 1991)* Koss Classics ▲ KC 1017 [DDD]

Handel, G.F.:Acis & Galatea, w. D. Kotoski (sop—Galatea), D. Gordon (ten—Acis), G. Siebert (ten—Damon), J. Opalach (bass—Polyphemus), G. Schwarz (cnd), Seattle SO, Seattle Chorale [E] Delos 2-▲ DE 3107 [DDD]

Schubert, Franz:Mass 6, w. B. Valente (sop), M. Simpson (mez), J. Humphrey (ten), M. Myers (ten), R. Shaw (cnd), Atlanta SO, Atlanta Sym Chorus [L] Telarc ▲ CD 80212 [DDD]

Siebert, Isolde (sop)

Dvořák, A.:Biblical Songs, Op. 99, w. Joachim Krause (org) Entrée ▲ 0079 [ADD]

Lehmann, M.:A Prayer, w. Joachim Krause (org) Entrée ▲ 0079 [ADD]

Nilsson, T.:Consolamini popule meus, w. Joachim Krause (org) Entrée ▲ 0079 [ADD]

Virtuoso Operatic Arias for Soprano & Obbligato Clarinet, w. Dieter Klöcker (cl), Southwest German SO [cnd:Klaus Donath] Koch Schwann ▲ SCH 314018 [DDD]

Sieden, Cyndia (sop)

Gluck, C.W.:Orfeo ed Euridice, w. S. McNair (sop), D.L. Ragin (ct), J. E. Gardiner (cnd), English Baroque Soloists, Monteverdi Choir London Philips ▲ 434093-2

Mozart, W.A.:Entführung, w. L. Orgonasova (sop), S. Olsen (ten), Uwe Peper (ten), C. Hauptmann (bass), Hans–Peter Minetti (nar), J. E. Gardiner (cnd), English Baroque Soloists, Monteverdi Choir London [G] Deutsche Grammophon 2-▲ 435857-2

Mozart, W.A.:Zauberflöte, w. Constanze Backes (sop—Papagena), Christiane Oelze (sop—Pamina), Susan Roberts (sop—First Lady), Cyndia Sieden (sop—Queen of the Night), Carola Guber (cta—Second Lady), Maria Jonas (cta—Third Lady), Andreas Dieterich (trb—First Boy), Jan Andreas Mendel (trb—Second Boy), Florian Wöller (trb—Third Boy), Uwe Peper (ten—Monostatos), Nicolas Robertson (ten—First Man in Armor), Michael Schade (ten—Tamino), Gerald Finley (bar—Papageno), Noel Mann (bass—Second Man in Armour), Harry Peeters (bass—Sarastro), Detlef Roth (bass—Speaker/First Priest), Robert Burt (speaker—Third Priest), Robert Johnston (speaker—Second Priest), Wolfgang Knauer (speaker—Fourth Priest), Douglas Welbat (speaker—Second Priest), J. E. Gardiner (cnd), English Baroque Soloists, Monteverdi Choir London *(rec Forum am Schlosspark, Ludwigsburg, July 1995)* Archiv 2-▲ 449166-2

Siegele, Dankwart (bass)

Bellini, V.:I Puritani, w. Edita Gruberova (sop), Katia Lytting (mez), Justin Lavender (ten), Carlo Tuand (ten), Ettore Kim (bar); Francesco Ellero d'Artegna (bass), F. Luisi (cnd), Munich RSO, Bavarian Radio Chorus Nightingale Classics 3-▲ NIG 70562

Wagner, R.:Lohengrin, w. Sharon Sweet (sop—Elsa), Eva Marton (sop—Ortrud), Ben Heppner (ten—Lohengrin), Anton Rosner (ten—Nobleman), Heinrich Weber (ten—Nobleman), Jan–Hendrik Rootering (bar—Heinrich der Vögler), Sergei Leiferkus (bar—Friedrich von Telramund), Bryn Terfel (b-bar—King's Herald), Barbara Fleckenstein (sgr—Page), Atsuko Suzuki (sgr—Page), Gisela Ulmann (sgr—Page), Marion Rambausek (sgr—Page), Dankwart Siegele (sgr—Nobleman), Jürgen Weiss (sgr—Nobleman), C. Davis (cnd), Bavarian SO, Bavarian State Opera Chorus, Bavarian Radio Chorus *(rec Residenz Herkulesaal, Munich, May 14–28, 1994)* RCA Red Seal 3-▲ 09026-62646-2 [DDD]

Wagner, R.:Lohengrin (sels), w. Eva Marton (sop—Ortrud), Sharon Sweet (sop—Elsa von Brabant), Barbara Fleckenstein (sgr—Page), Marion Rambausek (sgr—Page), Atsuko Suzuki (sgr—Page), Gisela Ulmann (sgr—Page), Ben Heppner (ten—Lohengrin), Anton Rosner (ten—Nobleman), Heinrich Weber (ten—Nobleman), Sergei Leiferkus (bar—Friedrich von Telramund), Bryn Terfel (b-bar—King's Herald), Jan–Hendrik Rootering (bass—Henry the Fowler), Dankwart Siegele (sgr—Nobleman), Jürgen Weiss (sgr—Nobleman), C. Davis (cnd), Bavarian RSO, Michael Gläser (cnd), Udo Mehrpohl (cnd), Bavarian Radio Chorus, Bavarian State Opera Chorus—Seht! Seht! [from Act 1, Scene 2]; Nun sei bedankt, mein lieber Schwan!; Wenn ich im Kampfe für dich siege; Welch holde Wunder muss ich sehen?; Nun höret mich und achtet wohl; Durch Gottes Sieg ist jetzt dein Leben mein [all from Act 1, Scene 3]; Treulich geführt ziehet dahin [from Act 3, Scene 1]; Wie hehr erkenn' ich unsrer Liebe Wesen!; Höchstes Vertrau'n hast du mir schon zu danken; Weh' nun ist all' unser Glück dahin! [all from Act 3, Scene 2]; In fernem Land, unnahbar euren Schritten [from Act 3, Scene 3] *(rec Munich, Mar 14–28, 1994)* RCA Red Seal ▲ 09026-68239-2 [DDD]

Siena, Jerold (sgr)

Donizetti, G.:Lucrezia Borgia, w. Montserrat Caballé (sop), Jane Berbié (mez), Alain Vanzo (ten), Kostas Paskalis (bar), Arnold Voketaitis (bass–bar), L. D. Clements (sgr), Adib Fazah (sgr), Mauro Lampi (sgr), Vern Shinall (sgr), William Wiederanders (sgr), J. Perlea (cnd), New York City Opera Orch, New York City Chorus Great Opera Performances 2-▲ GOP 769

Siepi, Cesare (bass)
Beethoven, L. van:Missa Solemnis, w. M. Arroyo (sop), M. Forrester (cta), R. Lewis (ten), E. Ormandy (cnd), Philadelphia Orch, Singing City Choir *(rec Mar. 29–30, 1967)* Sony Classical ("Essential Classics" series) ▲ SBK 53517 [ADD] ■ SBT 53517
Bellini, V.:La sonnambula, w. L. Pagliughi (sop—Amina), W. Ruggeri (sop—Lisa), A. M. Anelli (mez—Teresa), F. Tagliavini (ten—Elvino), P. L. Latinucci (bass—Alessio), C. Siepi (bass—Conte Rodolfo), F. Capuana (cnd), Turin RSO, Turin Radio Chorus *(rec 1952)* Fonit Cetra ("Classic Collection" series) 2–▲ FCT CDO 16 [AAD]
Boito, A.:Mefistofele, w. R. Tebaldi (sop), M. del Monaco (ten), T. Serafin (cnd), St. Cecilia Academy Orch Rome, St. Cecilia Academy Chorus Rome *(rec 1958)* London ▲ 440054–2
Cesare Siepi, w. Arturo Basile (cnd), Alfredo Simonetto (cnd), Franco Capuano (cnd), Gabriele Santini (cnd), Turin RAI SO *(rec Torino, 1955)* Cetra Classics ("Classic Collections" series) ▲ CDON 107
Cesare Siepi:Recital (1947–1957) Myto ▲ MCD 935.91
Donizetti, G.:La favorita, w. G. Simionato (mez), G. di Stefano (ten), E. Mascherini (bar), Rodriguez (sgr), R. Cellini (cnd), Palacio Bellas Artes Orch, Palacio Bellas Artes Chorus [I] *(rec live, Mexico City, 7/12/49)* Standing Room Only 2–▲ SRO 816–2 [ADD]
Donizetti, G.:Lucia di Lammermoor, w. J. Sutherland (sop), R. Cioni (ten), R. Merrill (bar), J. Pritchard (cnd), St. Cecilia Academy Orch Rome, St. Cecilia Academy Chorus Rome [I] London 2–▲ 411622–2 [ADD]
Mozart, W.A.:Don Giovanni, w. E. Grümmer (sop), L. Della Casa (sop), R. Streich (sop), L. Simoneau (ten), G. Frick (bass), W. Berry (bass), F. Corena (bass), D. Mitropoulos (cnd), Vienna PO, Vienna State Opera Chorus [I] *(rec live, Salzburg, July 24, 1956)* Arkadia 3–▲ 552 (m) [ADD]
Mozart, W.A.:Don Giovanni, w. S. Danco (sop), L. della Casa (sop), A. Dermota (ten), F. Corena (bass), J. Krips (cnd), Vienna PO, Vienna State Opera Chorus London 3–▲ 411626–2 [ADD]
Mozart, W.A.:Don Giovanni, w. Birgit Nilsson (sop—Donna Anna), Leontyne Price (sop—Donna Elvira), Eugenia Ratti (sop—Zerlina), Cesare Valletti (ten—Don Ottavio), Heinz Blankenburg (bar—Masetto), Fernando Corena (b-bar—Leporello), Arnold van Mill (b-bar—Il Commendatore), Cesare Siepi (b-bar—Don Giovanni), E. Leinsdorf (cnd), Vienna PO, Vienna State Opera Chorus [I] London 3–▲ 444594–2 [ADD]
Mozart, W.A.:Don Giovanni, w. E. Grümmer (sop—D. Anna), R. Streich (sop—Zerlina), L. Della Casa (sop—D. Elvira), L. Simoneau (ten—Don Ottavio), C. Siepi (bass-baritone—Don Giovanni), W. Berry (bass—Masetto), G. Frick (bass—Il Commendatore), F. Corena (bass—Leporello), D. Mitropoulos (cnd), Vienna PO, Vienna State Opera Chorus *(rec Salzburg, July 24, 1956)* Sony Classical 3–▲ SM3K 64263 [ADD]
Mozart, W.A.:Don Giovanni, w. E. Schwarzkopf (sop), E. Grümmer (sop), E. Berger (sop), A. Dermota (ten), O. Edelmann (b-bar), W. Berry (bass), W. Furtwängler (cnd), Vienna PO, Vienna State Opera Chorus *(rec 1953)* Arkadia 3–▲ 509 (m) [AAD]
Mozart, W.A.:Don Giovanni, w. E. Schwarzkopf (sop), E. Grümmer (sop), E. Berger (sop), A. Dermota (ten), O. Edelmann (b-bar), W. Berry (bass), W. Furtwängler (cnd), Vienna PO, Vienna State Opera Chorus *(rec Salzburg, Aug. 3, 1953)* EMI Classics ("Great Recordings of the Century" series) 2–▲ CDHB 63860
Mozart, W.A.:Requiem, w. Lisa della Casa (sop), Ira Malaniuk (cta), Anton Dermota (ten), B. Walter (cnd), Vienna PO, Vienna State Opera Chorus *(rec Salzburg, July 26, 1956)* Orfeo d'or ("Festspiel Dikumente" series) ▲ C 430961 (m) [ADD]
Mussorgsky, M.:Khovanshchina, w. Mietta Sighele (sop—Emma), Elena Souliotis (sop—Susanna), Fiorenza Cossotto (mez—Marfa), Herbert Handt (ten—Scribe), Veriano Luchetti (ten—Prince Andrey Khovansky), Ludovic Spiess (ten—Prince Vasily Golitsin), Claudio Strudthoff (ten—Streshnev), Angelo Marchiandi (bar—Kuz'ka), Teodoro Rovetta (bar—1st Strel'tsi), Siegmund Nimsgern (b-bar—Shaklovity), Cesare Siepi (b-bar—Dosifey), Carlo del Bosco (bass—2nd Strel'tsi), Ubaldo Carosi (bass—Varsonofiev), Nicolai Ghiaurov (bass—Prince Ivan Khovnasky), Giovanni Sciarpeletti (bass—Pastor), B. Leskovich (cnd), Rome RAI SO, Rome RAI Chorus—also includes bonus Act V [w Boris Christoff] (Rome, 1958) *(rec Rome, 1973)* Bella Voce 3–▲ BLV 107.402 [AAD]
Pobbe, Sciutti & Siepi, w. Marcella Pobbe (sop), Graziella Sciutti (sop), Milan RAI SO [cnd:L. Toffolo], Turin RAI SO [cnd:Fulvio Vernizzi] *(rec Martini & Rossi Concert, 1959)* Incontri Memorabili ▲ CDMR 5032
Puccini, G.:La Bohème, w. R. Tebaldi (sop), C. Bergonzi (ten), E. Bastianini (bar), T. Serafin (cnd), St. Cecilia Academy Orch Rome, St. Cecilia Academy Chorus Rome Enterprise ("Flowers" series) 2–▲ ENTBL 15 [ADD]
Puccini, G.:La Bohème, w. R. Tebaldi (sop), G. d'Angelo (sop), C. Bergonzi (ten), E. Bastianini (bar), T. Serafin (cnd), St. Cecilia Academy Orch Rome, St. Cecilia Academy Chorus Rome [I] London 2–▲ 425534–2 [ADD]
Puccini, G.:La Bohème (sels), w. R. Tebaldi (sop), C. Bergonzi (ten), E. Bastianini (bar), T. Serafin (cnd), St. Cecilia Academy Orch Rome, St. Cecilia Academy Chorus Rome—scenes & arias London ▲ 421301–2 [ADD]
Recital Melodram ▲ CDM 16506
Thomas, A.:Mignon (sels), w. G. Simionato (mez), G. Di Stefano (ten), G. Picco (cnd), Palacio Bellas Artes Orch, Palacio Bellas Artes Chorus *(rec live, Mexico City, 6/20/49)* Golden Age of Opera 2–▲ GAO 128/29 [ADD]
Verdi, G.:Don Carlos, w. S. Jurinac (sop—Elisabetta), L. Rysanek (sop—Celestial Voice), F. Cossotto (mez—Princess Eboli), L. Dutoit (boy sop—Tebaldo), P. Domingo (ten—Don Carlo), E. Majkut (ten—Count of Lerma), M. Sereni (bar—Rodrigo), C. Siepi (bass—Philip II), I. Vinco (bass—Grand Inquisitor), T. Franc (bass—Friar), S. Varviso (cnd), Vienna State Opera Orch, Vienna State Opera Chorus Standing Room Only 2–▲ SRO 850 [ADD]
Verdi, G.:Don Carlos, w. S. Jurinac (sop), G. Simionato (mez), E. Fernandi (ten), E. Bastianini (bar), H. von Karajan (cnd), Vienna PO, Vienna State Opera Chorus [I] *(rec live, Salzburg 7/26/58)* Arkadia 2–▲ 220 [ADD]
Verdi, G.:Don Carlos, w. Anita Cerquetti (sop), Ettore Bastianini (bar), Gianni Barbieri (bass), A. Votto (cnd), Florence Maggio Musicale Orch, Florence Maggio Musicale Chorus Melodram 3–▲ CDM 370104
Verdi, G.:Don Carlos, w. A. Cerquetti (sop), F. Barbieri (mez), A. LoForese (ten), E. Bastianini (bar), G. Neri (bass), A. Votto (cnd), Florence Maggio Musicale Orch, Florence Maggio Musicale Chorus *(rec July 16, 1956)* Melodram 3–▲ MLO 670104 [ADD]
Verdi, G.:Ernani, w. L. Price (sop), C. Ordassy (sop), F. Corelli (ten), C. Anthony (ten), M. Sereni (bar), C. Russel (bass), T. Schippers (cnd), *(orch unknown)* *(rec 1965)* Great Opera Performances ▲ GOP 702
Verdi, G.:La forza del destino, w. L. Gencer (sop), G. Carturan (mez), G. Di Stefano (ten), A. Priotti (bar), A. Votto (cnd), *(orch unknown)* *(rec live, Cologne 1957)* Melodram 3–▲ MEL 37010
Verdi, G.:La forza del destino, w. Leyla Gencer (sop—Leonora), Gabriella Carturan (mez—Preziosilla), Giuseppe di Stefano (ten—Don Alvaro), Aldo Protti (bar—Don Carlo), Franco Calabrese (bass—Marchese di Calatrava), Enrico Campi (bass—Fra Melitone), A. Votto (cnd), La Scala Orch, La Scala Chorus *(rec Bühnen der Stadt, Köln, July 5, 1957)* Agorá Music ("Phoenix" series) 3–▲ 510 [ADD]
Verdi, G.:La forza del destino, w. R. Tebaldi (sop), G. Simionato (mez), M. del Monaco (ten), E. Bastianini (bar), F. Molinari-Pradelli (cnd), St. Cecilia Academy Orch Rome, St. Cecilia Academy Chorus Rome [I] London 3–▲ 421598–2 [ADD]
Verdi, G.:La forza del destino, w. Leyla Gencer (sop), Giuseppe di Stefano (ten), Aldo Protti (bar), A. Votto (cnd), La Scala Orch, La Scala Chorus *(rec La Scala Theatre, Milan, July 5, 1957)* Pantheon 3–▲ PHE 6627 (m)
Verdi, G.:Otello, w. H. Gueden (sop), G. Simionato (mez), M. del Monaco (ten), A. Protti (bar), A. Erede (cnd), St. Cecilia Academy Orch Rome, St. Cecilia Academy Chorus Rome London 2–▲ 440242–2 [ADD]
Verdi, G.:Requiem Mass, w. H. Nelli (sop), F. Barbieri (mez), G. Di Stefano (Ten), A. Toscanini (cnd), NBC SO, Robert Shaw Chorale [L] RCA Gold Seal 2–▲ 60299–2–RG (m) [ADD] 2–■ 60299–4–RG (CrO2)
Verdi, G.:Requiem Mass, w. Elizabeth Schwarzkopf (sop), Oralia Dominguez (mez), Giuseppe Di Stefano (ten), V. de Sabata (cnd), La Scala Orch, La Scala Chorus Theorema 2–▲ TH 121123/24

Siepi, Cesare (bass) (cont.)
Verdi, G.:Rigoletto, w. Hilde Gueden (sop—Gilda), Piero de Palma (ten—Borsa), Luisa Ribacchi (mez—Giovanna), Giulietta Simionato (mez—Maddalena), Mario del Monaco (ten—Duca de Mantova), Aldo Protti (bar—Rigoletto), Fernando Corena (bass—Conte Monterone), Cesare Siepi (bass—Sparafucile), A. Erede (cnd), St. Cecilia Academy Orch Rome, St. Cecilia Academy Chorus Rome Theorema ▲ TH 121179/180
Verdi, G.:La traviata (sels), w. Elizabeth Schwarzkopf (sop), Oralia Dominguez (mez), Giuseppe DiStefano (ten), V. de Sabata (cnd), La Scala Orch, La Scala Chorus—Preludes to Acts I & III Theorema 2–▲ TH 121123/24

Siewert, Ruth (cta)
Beethoven, L. van:Sym 9, "Choral Sym", w. I. Borkh (sop), R. Lewis (ten), L. Weber (bass), R. Leibowitz (cnd), Royal PO, Beecham Choral Society [G] *(rec 6/61)* Chesky ▲ CD66 [ADD]
Wagner, R.:Das Rheingold, w. P. Brivkalne (sop), I. Malaniuk (cta), Fritz (sgr), Pflanzl (ten), S. Björling (bar), W. Faulhaber (bass), L. Weber (bass), F. Dalberg (bass), H. von Karajan (cnd), Bayreuth Festival Orch, Bayreuth Festival Chorus [G] *(rec live 8/1/51)* Melodram 2–▲ MEL 26107 (m) [AAD]
Wagner, R.:Siegfried, w. A. Varnay (sop), B. Aldenhoff (ten), P. Kuen (ten), S. Björling (bar), H. Pflanzl (bass), F. Dalberg (bass), H. von Karajan (cnd), Bayreuth Festival Orch, Bayreuth Festival Chorus [G] *(rec live 1951)* Melodram 4–▲ MEL 46106 (m) [AAD]

Sieyes, Maurice (bar)
Massenet, J.:Grisélidis, w. Michèle Command (sop), Brigitte Desnoues (sop), Jean-Luc Viala (ten), Didier Henry (bar), Christian Treguier (bar), Jean-Philippe Courtis (bass), Claire Larcher (sgr), P. Fournillier (cnd), Franz Liszt SO, Budapest Lyon Chorus Koch Schwann 2–▲ SCH 312702 [DDD]

Sighele, Mietta (sop)
Leoncavallo, R.:Pagliacci, w. Richard Tucker (ten), Kari Murmela (bar), Walter Alberti (bar), R. Muti (cnd), Florence Maggio Musicale Orch, Florence Maggio Musicale Chorus *(rec Florence , 1971)* Memories ▲ MEM 4576 [ADD]
Leoncavallo, R.:Pagliacci, w. R. Tucker (ten), E. Lorenzi (ten), K. Nurmela (bar), R. Muti (cnd), Florence Teatro Comunale Orch, Florence Teatro Comunale Chorus *(rec live, Florence, 1971)* Foyer ▲ FOY 2050 [AAD]
Mussorgsky, M.:Khovanshchina, w. Mietta Sighele (sop—Emma), Elena Souliotis (sop—Susanna), Fiorenza Cossotto (mez—Marfa), Herbert Handt (ten—Scribe), Veriano Luchetti (ten—Prince Andrey Khovansky), Ludovic Spiess (ten—Prince Vasily Golitsin), Claudio Strudthoff (ten—Streshnev), Angelo Marchiandi (bar—Kuz'ka), Teodoro Rovetta (bar—1st Strel'tsi), Siegmund Nimsgern (b-bar—Shaklovity), Cesare Siepi (b-bar—Dosifey), Carlo del Bosco (bass—2nd Strel'tsi), Ubaldo Carosi (bass—Varsonofiev), Nicolai Ghiaurov (bass—Prince Ivan Khovnasky), Giovanni Sciarpeletti (bass—Pastor), B. Leskovich (cnd), Rome RAI SO, Rome RAI Chorus—also includes bonus Act V [w Boris Christoff] (Rome, 1958) *(rec Rome, 1973)* Bella Voce 3–▲ BLV 107.402 [AAD]

Sigmundsson, Kristinn (bar)
Eirlksdottlr, Karolina:Land Possessed by Poems, w. Gudridur St. Sigurdardóttir (pno) Music from Iceland ▲ ITM 701 [ADD]

Sigmundsson, Kristinn (bass)
Mozart, W.A.:Zauberflöte, w. B. Bonney (sop—Pamina), S. Jo (sop—Queen of the Night), K. Streit (ten—Tamino), G. Cachemaille (b-bar—Papageno), K. Sigmundsson (bass—Sarastro), A. Östman (cnd), Drottningholm Court Theater Orch, Drottingholm Court Thea Chorus L'Oiseau-Lyre 2–▲ 440085–2 [DDD]

Signa, Gina (sop)
Bellini, V.:Norma, w. Ebe Stignani (mez), Giovanni Breviario (ten), Tancredi Pasero (bass), V. Gui (cnd), Turin EIAR SO, Turin EIAR Chorus *(rec 1937)* Grammofono 2000 2–▲ GRM 78583

Signor, Francesco (bass)
Bizet, G.:Carmen, w. Giovanna di Rocco (sop—Frasquita), Grace Bumbry (mez—Carmen), Anita Caminada (mez—Mercedes), Franco Corelli (ten—Don José), Mario Ferrara (ten—Dancario), Franco Bordoni (bar—Escamillo), Carlo Scaravelli (bar—Morales), Giuseppe Morresi (bass—Remendado), Francesco Signor (bass—Zuniga), O. de Fabritiis (cnd), *(orch unknown)* *(rec Macerata, July 21, 1974)* Golden Age of Opera 2–▲ GAO 181/82 [ADD]
Verdi, G.:Un ballo in maschera, w. Ghena Dimitrova (sop—Amelia), Isabella Stramaglia (sop—Oscar), Mirna Pecile (cta—Ulrica), Mario Carlin (ten—Un giudice), José Carreras (ten—Riccardo), Piero Cappuccilli (bar—Renato), Massimiliano Malaspina (bass—Samuel), Americo de Santis (bass—Silvano), Francesco Signor (bass—Tom), Ivan Del Manto (sgr—Un servo), G. Patanè (cnd), Parma Teatro Regio Orch *(rec Teatro Regio, Dec. 26, 1972)* Golden Age of Opera 2–▲ GAO 183/84

Signore, Gino del (ten)
Cimarosa, D.:Gli Orazii e i Curiazzi, w. G. Simionato (mez), A. Vercelli (mez), T. Spataro (ten), C. M. Giulini (cnd), Milan RAI SO, Milan RAI Chorus [I] *(rec live 4/13/52)* Melodram 2–▲ CDM 29500 [AAD]
Strauss, R.:Der Rosenkavalier, w. Jarmila Barton (sop—Marianne), Lisa Della Casa (sop—Sophie), Sena Jurinac (sop—Octavian), Ilva Ligabue (sop—Orphan), Elisabeth Schwarzkopf (sop—Marschallin), Else Schürhoff (mez—Annina), Luisa Villa (mez—Milliner), Hugues Cuénod (ten—Marschallin's majordomo), Erich Majkut (ten—Valzacchi), Giuseppe Nessi (ten—Animal seller), Luciano Della Pergola (ten—Lackey/Faninal's majordomo), Antonio Pirino (ten—An Italian Singer), Gino Del Signore (ten—Lackey/Waiter), Erich Kunz (bar—Herr von Faninal), Paolo Pedani (bar—Lackey), Attilio Barbesi (bass—Lackey/Waiter), Enrico Campi (bass—Waiter), Otto Edelmann (bass—Baron Ochs), Bruno Fichtinger (bass—Notary), Franco Taino (bass—Waiter), Maria Amadini (sgr—Orphan), Pina Carrillo (sgr—Orphan), Joszi Trojan Regar (sgr—Innkeeper), H. von Karajan (cnd), La Scala Orch, La Scala Chorus *(rec La Scala Theater, Milan, Jan. 26, 1952)* Legato Classics 3–▲ LCD 197–3

Sigrist, Peter (ten)
Orff, C.:Carmina burana, w. Brigitte Fournier (sop), Michel Brodard (bar), Jean-Jacques Balet (pno), Mayumi Kameda (pno), Geneva Percussion Ensemble [version for 2 pnos & perc] Cascavelle ▲ CVL 1009 [DDD]

Sild, Tarmo (bar)
Tubin, E.:Barbara von Tisenhusen, w. H. Raamat (sop), M. Jõgeva (mez), A. Kollo (ten), I. Kuusk (ten), V. Puura (bar), H. Miilberg (bass), U. Kreen (bass), P. Lilje (cnd), Estonia Opera Co Orch [Estonian] Ondine 2–▲ ODE 776–2D [DDD]

Silja, Anja (sop)
Berg, A.:Lulu, w. B. Fassbaender (mez), W. Berry (b-bar), K. Moll (bass), H. Hotter (b-bar), A. Szramek (sgr), C. von Dohnányi (cnd), Vienna PO London 2–▲ 430415–2 [ADD]
Berg, A.:Wozzeck, w. G. Jahn (mez), H. Laubenthal (ten), H. Zednik (ten), E. Waechter (bar), C. von Dohnányi (cnd), Vienna PO London 2–▲ 417348–2 [DDD]
Schoenberg, A.:Erwartung, w. C. von Dohnányi (cnd), Vienna PO [G] London 2–▲ 417348–2 [DDD]
Wagner, R.:Der fliegende Holländer, w. E. Kozub (ten), T. Adam (b-bar), M. Talvela (bass), O. Klemperer (cnd), New Philharmonia Orch, BBC Sym Chorus [G] EMI Classics ("Studio" series) 3–▲ CDMC 63344 [ADD]
Wagner, R.:Der fliegende Holländer, w. Anja Silja (sop—Senta), Anneliese Burmeister (mez—Mary), Ernst Kozub (ten—Erik), Gerhard Unger (ten—Steersman), Theo Adam (bass—Dutchman), Martti Talvela (bass—Daland), O. Klemperer (cnd), New Philharmonia Orch, BBC Sym Chorus EMI Classics 3–▲ CDCC 55179
Wagner, R.:Tannhäuser, w. G. Bumbry (mez), W. Windgassen (ten), E. Wächter (bar), J. Greindl (bass), W. Sawallisch (cnd), Bayreuth Festival Orch, Bayreuth Festival Chorus [Dresden version with Paris Venusberg music] [G] Philips 3–▲ 434607–2 [ADD]
Weill, K.:Aufstieg und Fall der Stadt Mahagonny, w. A. Schlemm (mez), W. Neumann (ten), T. Lehrberger (ten), K. Hirte (bar), J. Latham-König (cnd), Cologne RSO, Cologne Radio Chorus [G] Capriccio 2–▲ CD 10160/1 [DDD]

Sills, Beverly (sop)
The Art of Beverly Sills EMI Classics ▲ CDM 64425
Bellini, V.:I Puritani, w. B. Sills (sop—Elvira), E. Shade (sop—Enrichetta), L. Pavarotti (ten—Arturo), L. Quilico (bar—Riccardo), P. Plishka (bass—Giorgio), T. Paul (bass—Walton), A. Guadagno (cnd), *(orch & chorus unknown)* *(rec live Jan. 18, 1972)* Legato Classics 2–▲ LCD 1762 [ADD]
Charpentier, G.:Louise, w. B. Sills (sop—Louise), M. Dunn (mez—Louise's Mother), N. Gedda (ten—Julien), J. Van Dam (bass-bar—Louise's Father), J. Rudel (cnd), Paris Opera Orch, Paris Opera Chorus EMI Classics ▲ CDMC 65299

VOCALISTS

Sills, Beverly (sop) (cont.)
Donizetti, G.:Don Pasquale, w. Alfredo Kraus (ten), Alan Titus (bar), Donald Gramm (b–bar), S. Caldwell (cnd), London SO, Ambrosian Opera Chorus EMI Classics 2-▲ CDMB 66030
Donizetti, G.:Lucia di Lammermoor, w. A. Kraus (ten), G. Mastromei (bar), V. de Narke (bass), J.E. Martini (cnd), Buenos Aires Teatro Colón Orch, Buenos Aires Teatro Colón Chorus *(rec 1968)* Arkadia 2-▲ 474
Donizetti, G.:Roberto Devereux, w. S. Marsee (mez), P. Domingo (ten), L. Quilico (bar), J. Rudel (cnd), New York City Opera Orch, New York City Opera Chorus *(rec 1970)* Melodram ▲ MLO 270107 [ADD]
Famous Love Duets, Vol. 2, w. Gianna d'Angelo (sop), Montserrat Caballé (sop), Maria Callas (sop), Renata Scotto (sop), Renata Tebaldi (sop), José Carreras (ten), Mario Del Monaco (ten), Giuseppe Di Stefano (ten), Plácido Domingo (ten), Luciano Pava Enterprise ("Documents" series) ▲ ENTLV 999
Great Scenes, w. Plácido Domingo (ten) (Rec. live, 1965-1971) Legato Classics ▲ LCD 142-1 [ADD]
Handel, G.F.:Giulio Cesare in Egitto, w. Maureen Forrester (cta), Fritz Wolff (ten), Spiro Malas (bass), Norman Treigle (bass), J. Redel (cnd), New York City Opera Orch, New York City Opera Chorus RCA Gold Seal 2-▲ 6182-2-RG [ADD]
Mahler, G.:Sym 2, w. F. Kopleff (cta), M. Abravanel (cnd), Utah SO [G] *(rec 1967)* Vanguard Classics ▲ OVC 4004 [ADD]
Mahler, G.:Sym 2, w. F. Kopleff (cta), M. Abravanel (cnd), Utah SO *(rec Salt Lake City, 1967)* Vanguard Classics ▲ SVC 2 [AAD]
Massenet, J.:Manon, w. N. Gedda (ten), G. Souzay (bar), G. Bacquier (bar), J. Rudel (cnd), New Philharmonia Orch, Ambrosian Opera Chorus [F] EMI Classics ("Studio" series) 3-▲ CDMC 69831 [ADD]
Massenet, J.:Manon, w. P. Domingo (ten), R. Fredricks (bar), J. Rudel (cnd), New York City Opera Orch, New York City Opera Chorus *(rec live, 1969)* Melodram 2-▲ MEL 27054
Massenet, J.:Manon, w. Beverly Sills (sop—Manon), Plácido Domingo (ten—Des Grieux), Nico Castel (ten—Guillot), Richard Fredricks (bar—Lescaut), Robert Hale (bar—De Brétigny), Malcom Smith (bass—Count de Grieux), J. Rudel (cnd), New York City Opera Orch, New York City Opera Chorus *(rec live, New York, 1969)* Melodram 2-▲ IMC 205008 [ADD]
Massenet, J.:Thaïs, w. Beverly Sills (sop—Thaïs), Nicolai Gedda (ten—Nicias), Sherrill Milnes (bar—Athanaël), L. Maazel (cnd), New Philharmonia Orch, John Alldis Choir EMI Classics 2-▲ CDMB 65479
Offenbach, J.:Les Contes d'Hoffmann, w. Beverly Sills (sop—Olympia/Giulietta/Antonia/Stella), Edith Evans (mez—Nicklausse/Mother's Voice), Michael Devlin (ten—Spalanzani), André Turp (ten—Hoffmann), Luigi Vellucci (ten—Andrès/Cochenille/Pitichinaccio/Frantz), Donald Bernard (bar—Luther/Schlemil), Norman Treigle (bass—Lindorf/Coppélius/Dapertutto/Dr. Miracle), John West (bass—Crespel), Alton Brim (sgr—Nathanaël), Rodney Hall (sgr—Hermann), K. Andersson (cnd), New Orleans Opera Orch, New Orleans Opera Chorus *(rec Feb 27, 1964)* VAI Audio 2-▲ VAIA 1121-2 [ADD]
Rossini, G.:Il barbiere di Siviglia, w. Fedora Barbieri (mez), Nicolai Gedda (ten), Renato Capecchi (bar), Sherill Milnes (bar), Ruggero Raimondi (bass), J. Levine (cnd), London SO, John Alldis Choir EMI Classics 2-▲ CDMB 66040
Rossini, G.:The Siege of Corinth, w. M. Horne (mez), F. Bonisoli (ten), J. Diaz (bass), T. Schippers (cnd), La Scala Orch, La Scala Chorus [I] *(rec live 1969)* Melodram 2-▲ MEL 27043 [AAD]
Rossini, G.:The Siege of Corinth, w. S. Verrett (mez), J. Diaz (bass), T. Schippers (cnd), London SO, Ambrosian Opera Chorus [I] *(rec London, 1974)* EMI Classics 3-▲ CDMC 64335
Verdi, G.:Rigoletto, w. Sherill Milnes (bar), Alfredo Kraus (bar), Samuel Ramy (bass), J. Rudel (cnd), Philharmonia Orch, Ambrosian Opera Chorus EMI Classics 2-▲ CDMB 724356603721
Verdi, G.:La traviata, w. M. Zotti (sop), G. Borelli (mez), A. Kraus (ten), M. Zanasi (bar), A. Ceccato (cnd), Naples Teatro San Carlo Orch, Naples Teatro San Carlo Chorus *(rec live 1/17/70)* Melodram 2-▲ MEL 27063 (m) [AAD]
Welcome to Vienna, w. London PO [cnd:Julius Rudel] EMI Classics ▲ CDM 64424

Silva, H. da (sgr)
Rodgers, R.:Oklahoma!, w. A. Drake (sgr), L. Dixon (sgr), C. Holm (sgr), J. Roberts (sgr), J. Blackton (cnd), *(orch unknown)* MCA Classics ▲ MCAD 10046 [AAD] ■ MCAC 10046

Silva, Luiz Alves da (ct)
Coelho Neto, M.:Maria mater gratiae, w. Beat Mattmüller (ct), Markus Schikora (ten), Peter Mächler (b), L. A. da Silva (cnd), Turicum Ensemble *(rec Studio DRS, Zurich, Sept 26-29, 1994)* Claves ▲ CD 9521 [DDD]
Garcia, J.M.N.:Motets, w. Katharina Ott (sop), Beat Mattmüller (ct), Andreas Schmidt (ct), Markus Schikora (ten), William Lombardi (ten), Peter Mächler (bass), Michael Leibundgut (bass), L. A. da Silva (cnd), Turicum Ensemble *(rec Studio DRS, Zurich, Sept 26-29, 1994)* Claves ▲ CD 9521 [DDD]
Mesquita, J.J.E.L. de:Antiphona de Nossa Senhora, w. Beat Mattmüller (ct), Markus Schikora (ten), Peter Mächler (bass), L. A. da Silva (cnd), Turicum Ensemble *(rec Studio DRS, Zurich, Sept 26-29, 1994)* Claves ▲ CD 9521 [DDD]
Mesquita, J.J.E.L. de:Tercio, w. Beat Mattmüller (ct), Markus Schikora (ten), Michael Leibundgut (bass), L. A. da Silva (cnd), Turicum Ensemble *(rec Studio DRS, Zurich, Sept 26-29, 1994)* Claves ▲ CD 9521 [DDD]
Mesquita, J.J.E.L. de:Tractus (4) para o Sábado Santo, w. Beat Mattmüller (ct), Markus Schikora (ten), Michael Leibundgut (bass), L. A. da Silva (cnd), Turicum Ensemble *(rec Studio DRS, Zurich, Sept 26-29, 1994)* Claves ▲ CD 9521 [DDD]
Pinto, L.A.:Te Deum Laudamus, w. Katharina Ott (sop), Beat Mattmüller (ct), Andreas Schmidt (ct), Markus Schikora (ten), William Lombardi (ten), Peter Mächler (bass), Michael Leibundgut (bass), L. A. da Brooks (cnd), Turicum Ensemble *(rec Studio DRS, Zurich, Sept 26-29, 1994)* Claves ▲ CD 9521 [DDD]

Silva, Roberto (bass)
Bellini, V.:I Puritani, w. M. Callas (sop), G. di Stefano (ten), Campolonghi (sgr), G. Picco (cnd), Palacio Bellas Artes Orch, Palacio Bellas Artes Chorus [I] *(rec live, Mexico City 5/29/52)* Melodram 2-▲ MEL 26027 (m) [AAD]
Verdi, G.:Simon Boccanegra (sels), w. Celia Garcia (sop—Maria Boccanegra), Mario Filippeschi (ten—Gabriele Adorno), Ignacio Ruffino (ten—Pietro), Leonard Warren (bar—Simon Boccanegra), Roberto Silva (bass—Jacopo Fiesco), Carlo Morelli (bass—Paolo), R. Cellini (cnd), Mexican National Opera Orch, Mexican National Opera Chorus *(rec Palacio de las Bellas Artes, Mexico City, July 4, 1950)* Legato Classics ▲ LCD 185-1 [ADD]

Silva, S. (cta)
Verdi, G.:Luisa Miller, w. K. Ricciarelli (sop—Luisa), M. G. Piolatto (mez—Laura), S. Silva (cta—Federica), J. Carreras (ten—Rodolfo), E. Pranod (ten—A Peasant), R. Bruson (bar—Miller), G. Casarini (bar—Wurm) M. Rinaudo (bass—Count Walter), F. Previtali (cnd), Turin Teatro Regio Orch, Turin Teatro Regio Chorus *(rec May 9, 1976)* Legato Classics 2-▲ LCD 180 [ADD]

Silva, Stella Maris (sop)
Verdi, G.:Rigoletto, w. Renata Scotto (sop—Gilda), Stella Maris Silva (sop—Giovanna), Martha Carrizo (mez—Page), Carmen de la Mata (mez—Countess Ceprano), Noemi Souza (cta—Maddalena), Horacio Mastrango (ten—Borso), Richard Tucker (ten—Duke of Mantua), Cornell MacNeil (bar—Rigoletto), Riccardo Yost (bar—Marullo), Guerrino Boschetti (bass—Usher), Tulio Gagliardo (bass—Count Ceprano), Victor de Narké (bass—Monterone), William Wilderman (bass—Sparafucile), F. Previtali (cnd), Buenos Aires Teatro Colón Orch, Buenos Aires Teatro Colón Chorus *(rec Colon Theater, Buenos Aires, Aug. 22, 1967)* Legato Classics 2-▲ LCD 198-2

Silvasti, Jorma (ten)
Sallinen, A.:Kullervo, w. G. Saarinen (pno), J. Hynninen (bar), M. Salminen (bass), U. Söderblom (cnd), Finnish National Opera Orch, Finnish National Opera Chorus [Fin] Ondine 3-▲ ODE 780-3T [DDD]
Sibelius, J.:The Tempest, w. R. Viljakainen (sop), M. Groop (mez), J. Hynninen (bar), S. Tiilikainen (bar), J.-P. Saraste (cnd), Finnish RSO, Finnish Opera Festival Chorus Ondine ▲ ODE 813 [DDD]

Silveri, Paolo (bar)
Cilea, F.:L'Arlesiana, w. L. di Lelio (sop), P. Tassinari (sop), F. Tagliavini (ten), G. Galli (bar), B. Carmassi (bass), A. Zerbini (bass), A. Basile (cnd), Turin RAI Orch, Turin RAI Chorus *(rec 1951)* Cetra Classics ▲ CDO 21 [AAD]
Giordano, U.:Andrea Chénier (sels), w. R. Tebaldi (sop), F. Barbieri (mez), M. del Monaco (ten), V. de Sabata (cnd), La Scala Orch, La Scala Chorus—14 arias from Acts 1-3 [I] *(rec live, Milan, 3/6/49)* Myto ▲ 1 MCD 90634 [ADD]

Silveri, Paolo (bar) (cont.)
Ponchielli, A.:La Gioconda, w. M. Callas (sop), F. Barbieri (mez), G. Poggi (ten), G. Neri (bass), A. Votto (cnd), Turin RAI SO, Turin RAI Chorus *(rec 1952)* Enterprise ("Palladio" series) ▲ ENT PD 4152 [DDD]
Ponchielli, A.:La Gioconda, w. M. Callas (sop), F. Barbieri (mez), G. Poggi (ten), G. Neri (bass), A. Votto (cnd), Turin RAI SO, Turin RAI Chorus *(rec 1952)* Andromeda 3-▲ ANR 2528 [ADD]
Ponchielli, A.:La Gioconda, w. M. Callas (sop—Gioconda), F. Barbieri (mez—Laura), M. Amadini (sgr—La Cieca), G. Poggi (ten—Enzo), P. Silveri (bar—Barnaba), G. Neri (bass—Alvise), A. Votto (cnd), Turin RAI Orch, Turin RAI Chorus *(rec 1952)* Cetra Classic 3-▲ CDO 8
Puccini, G.:La Bohème (sels), w. M. Carosio (sop), A. Noni (sop), G. Poggi (ten), V. de Sabata (cnd), La Scala Orch, La Scala Chorus—6 arias from Acts 3 & 4 [I] *(rec live, Milan, 12/7/49)* Myto ▲ 1 MCD 90634 [ADD]
Verdi, G.:Don Carlos, w. M. Caniglia (sop—Elisabeth de Valois), G. Sciutti (sop—Page), E. Stignani (mez—Princess Eboli), M. Picchi (ten—Don Carlos), M. Ponz de L. (ten—Count of Lerma), P. Silveri (bar—Rodrigue), N. Rossi Lemeni (bass—Philip II), G. Neri (bass—Grand Inquisitor), A. Gaggi (bass—Old Monk), F. Previtali (cnd), Rome RAI SO, Rome RAI Chorus *(rec Rome, 1951)* Cetra Classic 3-▲ CDO 25 [ADD]
Verdi, G.:Nabucco, w. C. Mancini (sop—Abigaille), G. Gatti (sop—Fenena), B. Preziosa (sop—Anna), M. Binci (ten—Ismaele), L. Francardi (ten—Abdallo), P. Silveri (bar—Nabucodonosor), A. Cassinelli (bass—Zaccaria), A. Gaggi (bass—High Priest of Baal), F. Previtali (cnd), Rome RAI Orch, Rome RAI Chorus *(rec Rome, 1951)* Cetra Classic 2-▲ CDO 26 [ADD]
Verdi, G.:Simon Boccanegra, w. A. Stella (sop—Maria), C. Bergonzi (ten—Gabriele), G. Giorgetti (bar—Pietro), W. Monachesi (bar—Paolo), M. Petri (bar—Jacopo), P. Silveri (bar—Simon), F. Molinari-Pradelli (cnd), Rome Radio Orch, Rome RAI Chorus *(rec 1951)* Cetra Classic ▲ CDO 23 [ADD]
Verdi, G.:Il trovatore, w. M. Callas (sop), C. Elmo (mez), G. Lauri-Volpi (ten), T. Serafin (cnd), Naples Teatro San Carlo Orch, Naples Teatro San Carlo Chorus [I] *(rec live, Naples, 1/27/51)* Melodram 2-▲ MEL 26001 (m) [AAD]

Silvers, Phil (sgr)
Kern, J.:Cover Girl, w. Gene Kelly (sgr), N. Wynn (sgr) *(rec 1944)* Hollywood Soundstage ▲ HSCD 4005
Kern, J.:Cover Girl, w. Gene Kelly (sgr), N. Wynn (sgr) *(rec 1944)* Curtain Calls ▲ CC 100/24

Silvestrelli, Andrea (bass)
Mozart, W.A.:Don Giovanni, w. Charlotte Margiono (sop—Donna Elvira), Luba Orgonasova (sop—Donna Anna), Eirian James (mez—Zerlina), Julian Clarkson (alt—Masetto), Christoph Prégardien (ten—Don Ottavio), Rodney Gilfry (bar—Don Giovanni), Ildebrando d'Arcangelo (bass—Leporello), Andrea Silvestrelli (bass—Il Commendatore), J. E. Gardiner (cnd), English Baroque Soloists, Monteverdi Choir London Deutsche Grammophon ("4D Audio" series) 3-▲ 445870-2

Sim, Sharon (sgr)
Caccini, F.:La liberazione di Ruggiero dall'isola d'Alcina, w. Linda De Rungs (sop—Alcian/Vistola), Cecilia Amorocho (sgr—Melissa/Nunzia), Laura Lea Duckworth (sgr—Siren/Harpy), Eric Friedlander (sgr—Monster), L. Ernest Gross (sgr—Enchanted Cypress), Phoebe Jevtovic (sgr—Siren), James Rittenhouse (sgr—Ruggiero/Neptune), Sharon Sim (sgr—Siren), R. Burchard (cnd), Ars Femina Ensemble, TimeChange *(rec Louisville, KY, 1993)* Nannerl ▲ NR-ARS 003; ■ NR-ARS 003

Simándy, József (ten)
Erkel, F.:Bánk Bán, w. K. Agay (sop), E. Komlóssy (cta), J. Réti (ten), S. Sólyom-Nagy (bar), J. Ferencsik (cnd), Budapest PO, Hungarian State Opera Chorus [Hun] *(rec 1969)* Hungaroton 2-▲ HCD 11376/77 [ADD]
Kodály, Z.:Psalmus hungaricus, w. A. Dorati (cnd), Hungarian State Orch, Budapest Chorus [Hun] Hungaroton ▲ HCD 11392
Kodály, Z.:Psalmus hungaricus, w. A. Dorati (cnd), Stockholm PO *(rec live, 12/16/67)* BIS 8-▲ CD 421/24 (m/s) [AAD]
Kodály, Z.:Psalmus hungaricus, w. A. Dorati (cnd), Hungarian State Orch, Budapest Chorus, Hungarian Radio-TV Children's Chorus Hungaroton ▲ HCD 31503 [ADD]

Simionato, Giulietta (mez)
Bellini, V.:I Capuleti e i Montecchi, w. L. Hurley (sop), R. Cassily (ten), E. Flagello (bass), A. Gamson (cnd), American Opera Society Orch, American Opera Society Chorus [I] *(rec live, New York 10/14/58)* Melodram ("Connaisseur" series) 2-▲ CDM 27509 [ADD]
Bellini, V.:I Capuleti e i Montecchi (sels), w. P. Argento (cnd), Milan RAI SO—Ancor di Fiori Sparsa Fonit Cetra ("Martini & Rossi" series) ▲ FCT CDMR 5006
Bellini, V.:Norma, w. M. Callas (sop), K. Baum (ten), N. Moscona (bass), G. Picco (cnd), Palacio Bellas Artes Orch, Palacio Bellas Artes Chorus *(rec live, Mexico City 5/23/50)* Melodram 2-▲ MEL 26018
Bellini, V.:Norma, w. M. Callas (sop), M. Del Monaco (ten), N. Zaccaria (bass), A. Votto (cnd), La Scala Orch, La Scala Chorus *(rec 12/7/55)* HRE 2-▲ 1007-2
Bellini, V.:Norma, w. Maria Callas (sop), Gabriella Carturan (mez), Mario del Monaco (ten), Giuseppe Zampieri (ten), Nicola Zaccaria (bass), A. Votto (cnd), La Scala Orch, La Scala Chorus Melodram 2-▲ CDM 26036
Berlioz, H.:La Damnation de Faust, w. Ettore Bastianini (bar), Plinio Clabassi (bass), Ruggero Bondino (sgr), P. Maag (cnd), *(orch unknown)* Great Opera Performances 2-▲ GOP 776
Berlioz, H.:Les Troyens (sels), w. N. Rankin (mez), M. del Monaco (ten), R. Kubelik (cnd), La Scala Orch [I] *(rec May 27, 1960)* VAI Audio ▲ VAIA 1026 [ADD]
Bizet, G.:Carmen, w. H. Gueden (sop), N. Gedda (ten), H. von Karajan (cnd), Vienna SO, Vienna Singverein *(rec live, Vienna Oct. 1954)* Melodram 2-▲ MEL 27012
Bizet, G.:Carmen (sels), w. G. di Stefano (ten), H. von Karajan (cnd), La Scala Orch, La Scala Chorus—14 arias [F] *(rec live, Milan, 1/18/55)* Arkadia 3-▲ 221 [ADD]
Cilea, F.:Adriana Lecouvreur, w. M. Olivero (sop), F. Corelli (ten), E. Bastianini (bar), M. Rossi (cnd), Naples Teatro San Carlo Orch, Naples Teatro San Carlo Chorus [I] *(rec live 11/28/59)* Melodram 2-▲ MEL 27009 (m) [AAD]
Cilea, F.:Adriana Lecouvreur, w. Magda Olivero (sop), Franco Corelli (ten), Ettore Bastianini (bar), M. Rossi (cnd), Naples Teatro San Carlo Orch, Naples Teatro San Carlo Chorus *(rec Naples, Nov 28, 1959)* Agorá Music ("Phoenix" series) 2-▲ 502
Cimarosa, D.:Il Matrimonio segreto, w. Alda Noni (sop), Riccardo Cassinelli (ten), Cesare Valletti (ten), Sesto Bruscantini (bar), Rovero (sgr), M. Wolf-Ferrari (cnd), Florence Maggio Musicale Orch *(rec 1950)* Cetra Classic 2-▲ CDO 32
Cimarosa, D.:Il Matrimonio segreto (sels), w. RAI SO, *(unknown RAI Chorus)*—arias:sels. unknown Cetra Classic ("Classics Collection" series) ▲ 111 [ADD]
Cimarosa, D.:Gli Orazii e i Curiazzi, w. A. Vercelli (mez), G. Del Signore (ten), T. Spataro (ten), C. M. Giulini (cnd), Milan RAI SO, Milan RAI Chorus [I] *(rec live 4/13/52)* Melodram 2-▲ CDM 29500 [AAD]
Donizetti, G.:Anna Bolena, w. L. Gencer (sop), A. Bertocci (ten), P. Clabassi (bass), G. Gavazzeni (cnd), Milan RAI SO, Milan RAI Chorus *(rec 1958)* Memories 2-▲ MEM 4517 [AAD]
Donizetti, G.:Anna Bolena, w. Maria Callas (sop), Gabriella Carturan (mez), Gianni Raimondi (ten), Plinio Clabassi (bass), Nicola Rossi Lemmeni (sgr), Luigi Rumo (sgr), G. Gavazzeni (cnd), La Scala Orch, La Scala Chorus Great Opera Performances 2-▲ GOP 768
Donizetti, G.:Anna Bolena, w. M. Callas (sop), G. Raimondi (ten), G. Gavazzeni (cnd), La Scala Orch, La Scala Chorus [I] *(rec live, 4/17/57)* Melodram 2-▲ MEL 26010
Donizetti, G.:Anna Bolena, w. Leyla Gencer (sop), Aldo Bertocci (ten), Plinio Clabassi (bass), G. Gavazzeni (cnd), Milan RAI SO, Milan RAI Chorus *(rec July 11, 1958)* Agorá Music ("Phoenix" series) 2-▲ 503
Donizetti, G.:Anna Bolena, w. M. Callas (sop—Anna Bolena), G. Simionato (mez—Giovanna Seymour), N. Rossi-Lemeni (bass—Enrico VIII), G. Gavazzeni (cnd), Milan RAI SO, Milan RAI Chorus *(rec May 14, 1957)* EMI Classics ▲ CDMB 64941
Donizetti, G.:Anna Bolena, w. M. Callas (sop—Anna Bolena), G. Simionato (mez—Giovanna), G. Raimondi (ten—Percy), N. Rossi-Lemeni (bass—King), G. Gavazzeni (cnd), La Scala Orch, La Scala Chorus [I] *(rec live, Milan 4/14/57)* Verona 2-▲ 27090/91
Donizetti, G.:La favorita, w. G. di Stefano (ten), E. Mascherini (bar), C. Siepi (bass-bar), Rodriguez (sgr), R. Cellini (cnd), Palacio Bellas Artes Orch, Palacio Bellas Artes Chorus [I] *(rec live, Mexico City, 7/12/49)* Standing Room Only 2-▲ SRO 816-2 [ADD]

Simionato, Giulietta (mez) (cont.)
Donizetti, G.:La favorita, w. S. Zanolli (sop), G. Raimondi (ten), M. Zanasi (bar), N. Zaccaria (bass), F. Previtali (cnd), Naples Teatro San Carlo Orch, Naples Teatro San Carlo Chorus [I] *(rec live, Naples 5/12/63)* Golden Age of Opera 2-▲ GAO 105/06 [ADD]
Falla, M. de:Atlántida, w. T. Stratas (sop), R. Browne (sgr), Halley (sgr), T. Schippers (cnd), La Scala Orch, La Scala Chorus *(rec live, Milan 6/18/62)* Memories 2-▲ HR 4464/65 [ADD]
Giordano, U.:Andrea Chénier, w. M. Caniglia (sop), B. Gigli (ten), G. Bechi (bar), G. Taddei (bar), I. Tajo (bass), O. de Fabritiis (cnd), La Scala Orch, La Scala Chorus [I] *(rec 1941, HMV DB 5423/35)* Angel ("Studio" series) 2-▲ CDHB 69996 (m) [ADD]
Giordano, U.:Andrea Chénier, w. Maria Caniglia (sop—Maddalena), Maria Huder (mez—Bersi), Vittoria Palombini (mez—Madelon), Giulietta Simionato (mez—Contessa), Beniamino Gigli (ten—Andrea), Adelio Zagonara (ten—Incroyable/Abbé), Gino Bechi (bar—Carlo), Leone Paci (bar—Mathieu), Giuseppe Taddei (b-bar—Pietro/Fouquier), Italo Tajo (b-bar—Roucher), Gino Conti (bass—Master/Schmidt), O. de Fabritiis (cnd), La Scala Orch, La Scala Chorus *(rec Nov 1941)* Arkadia ("The 78's" series) 2-▲ 78012 [ADD]
Giulietta Simionato *(rec live, 1956–1962)* Memories ("Great Voices" series) 2-▲ MEM 4386 (m)
Gluck, C.W.:Orfeo ed Euridice, w. S. Jurinac (sop), G. Sciutti (sop), H. von Karajan (cnd), Vienna PO, Vienna State Opera Chorus *(rec live 1959)* Memories 2-▲ HR 4382/83 (m)
Mascagni, P.:Arias, w. Renata Scotto (sop), Turin Lyric Orch—arias from Lodoletta & Cavalleria Rusticana Cetra Classic ("Classics Collection" series) ▲ 111 [ADD]
Mascagni, P.:Cavalleria rusticana, w. G. Simionato (sop—Santuzza), F. Cadoni (mez—Lola), L. Pellogrino (cta—Lucia), A. Braschi (ten—Turiddu), C. Tagliabue (bar—Alfio), A. Basile (cnd), Italian Lyric Orch, Turin Cetra Chorus *(rec Turin, 1950)* Cetra Classic 2-▲ CDO 27 [ADD]
Mascagni, P.:Cavalleria rusticana, w. L. Bruna Rasa (sop), B. Gigli (ten), G. Bechi (bar), P. Mascagni (cnd), La Scala Orch, La Scala Chorus [I] *(rec 1940)* EMI Classics ("Studio" series) 2-▲ CDHB 69987 (m) [ADD]
Mascagni, P.:Cavalleria rusticana, w. L.B. Rasa (sop), M. Marucucci (mez), B. Gigli (ten), G. Bechi (bar), P. Mascagni (cnd), La Scala Orch, La Scala Chorus *(rec 1940)* Nimbus 2-▲ NI 7843/44 [ADD]
Mascagni, P.:Cavalliera rusticana, w. Lina Bruna-Rasa (sop), Benia Gigli (ten), Giuseppe Nessi (ten), Gino Bechi (bar), Carlo Galeffi (bar), P. Mascagni (cnd), La Scala Orch, La Scala Chorus *(rec Milan, 1940)* Phonographe 2-▲ PHG CD 5066
Mascagni, P.:Cavalleria rusticana (sels), w. G. Di Stefano (ten), A. Votto (cnd), La Scala Orch, La Scala Chorus—Tu qui Santuzza [I] *(rec live, Milan, 5/10/55)* Standing Room Only 2-▲ SRO 816-2 [ADD]
Massenet, J.:Werther, w. D. Gatta (sop—Sofia), I. Ligabue (sop—Kaethlen), G. Simionato (mez—Charlotte), F. Tagliavini (ten—Werther), V. Pandano (ten—Schmidt), E. Campi (bass—Johann), S. Bruscantini (bass—Le Bailli), F. Capuana (cnd), La Scala Orch, La Scala Chorus *(rec Apr. 21, 1951)* Bongiovanni 2-▲ GB 1101/02 [ADD]
Massenet, J.:Werther (sels), w. P. Argento (cnd), Milan RAI SO—Oh Werther! Mio Werther! Fonit Cetra ("Martini & Rossi" series) ▲ FCT CDMR 5006
Meyerbeer, G.:Les Huguenots, w. J. Sutherland (sop), F. Cossotto (mez), F. Corelli (ten), V. Ganzarolli (bar), N. Ghiaurov (bass), G. Tozzi (bass), G. Gavezzeni (cnd), La Scala Orch, La Scala Chorus [I] *(rec live 5/28/62)* Melodram 3-▲ MEL 37026 (m) [AAD]
Rossini, G.:Arias, *(orch & chorus unknown)*—arias from Il Barbiere di Siviglia; La Cenerentola Cetra Classic ("Classics Collection" series) ▲ 111 [ADD]
Rossini, G.:Il barbiere di Siviglia, w. R. Broilo (sop—Berta), G. Simionato (mez—Rosina), L. Infantino (ten—Almaviva), G. Taddei (bar—Figaro), C. Badioli (bass—Bartolo), A. Cassinelli (bass—Basilio), F. Previtali (cnd), Milan RAI SO, Milan RAI Chorus *(rec 1950)* Cetra Classic 2-▲ CDO 6 [AAD]
Rossini, G.:La Cenerentola, w. Ornella Rovero (sop), Miti Truccato Pace (mez), Cesare Valletti (ten), Saturno Meletti (bar), Vito Susca (bass), Cristiano Dalamangas (sgr), M. Rossi (cnd), Turin RAI Orch, Bruno Erminero (cnd), Turin RAI Chorus Fonit Cetra ("Classic Collection" series) ▲ FCT CDON 34
Rossini, G.:Tancredi (sels), w. P. Argento (cnd), Milan RAI SO—Di Tanti Palpiti, Di Tante Pene Fonit Cetra ("Martini & Rossi" series) ▲ FCT CDMR 5006
Simionato & Di Stefano, w. Giuseppe Di Stefano (ten), Milan RAI Orch, Milan RAI Chorus [cnd:Nino Sanzogno] *(rec Nov. 26, 1956)* Incontri Memorabili ▲ CDMR 5015
Thomas, A.:Mignon (sels), w. P. Argento (cnd), Milan RAI SO—Io Consoco un Garzoncello di Boemia Che le Guance Ha Smunte e Sparute Fonit Cetra ("Martini & Rossi" series) ▲ FCT CDMR 5006
Thomas, A.:Mignon (sels), w. G. Di Stefano (ten), C. Siepi (b-bar), G. Picco (cnd), Palacio Bellas Artes Orch, Palacio Bellas Artes Chorus *(rec live, Mexico City, 6/28/49)* Golden Age of Opera 2-▲ GAO 128/29 [ADD]
Verdi, G.:Aida, w. Maria Callas (sop—Aida), Joan Sutherland (sop—Priestess), Giulietta Simionato (cta—Amneris), Kurt Baum (ten—Radames), Hector Thomas (ten—Messenger), Jess Walters (bar—Amonasro), Michael Langdon (bass—King), Giulio Neri (bass—Ramfis), J. Barbirolli (cnd), Royal Opera House Orch, Royal Opera House Chorus Covent Garden *(rec Covent Garden, London, June 10, 1953)* Legato Classics 2-▲ LCD 187-2
Verdi, G.:Aida, w. Antonietta Stella (sop—Aida), Mirella Parutto (sop—Priestess), Giulietta Simionato (mez—Amneris), Giuseppe DiStefano (ten—Radames), Giuseppe Zampiere (ten—Messenger), Giangiacomo Guelfi (bar—Amonasro), Silvio Maionica (bass—King of Egypt), Nicola Zaccaria (bass—Ramfis), A. Votto (cnd), La Scala Orch, La Scala Chorus *(rec Milan, Dec 7, 1956)* Legato Classics 2-▲ LCD 204-2 [ADD]
Verdi, G.:Aida, w. M. Callas (sop), K. Baum (ten), R. Weede (bar), G. Picco (cnd), Palacio Bellas Artes Orch, Palacio Bellas Artes Chorus *(rec live, Mexico City 5/30/50)* Melodram ▲ MLO 26009 [ADD]
Verdi, G.:Aida, w. R. Tebaldi (sop), C. Bergonzi (ten), C. MacNeil (bar), A. van Mill (bass), H. von Karajan (cnd), Vienna PO, Vienna State Opera Chorus [I] London 3-▲ 414087-2 [ADD]
Verdi, G.:Aida, w. R. Tebaldi (sop), C. Bergonzi (ten), C. MacNeil (bar), A. van Mill (bass), H. von Karajan (cnd), Vienna PO, Vienna State Opera Chorus [I] London ("Jubilee" series) ▲ 417763-2 [ADD]
Verdi, G.:Arias, w. Renata Scotto (sop), Turin Lyric Orch—arias from La Traviata & Aida Cetra Classic ("Classics Collection" series) ▲ 111 [ADD]
Verdi, G.:Un ballo in maschera, w. B. Nilsson (sop), C. Bergonzi (ten), C. MacNeil (bar), G. Solti (cnd), St. Cecilia Academy Orch Rome, St. Cecilia Academy Chorus Rome [I] London 2-▲ 425655-2 [ADD]
Verdi, G.:Un ballo in maschera, w. M. Callas (sop), E. Ratti (sop), G. di Stefano (ten), E. Bastianini (bar), G. Gavazzeni (cnd), La Scala Orch, La Scala Chorus [I] *(rec live 12/7/57)* Arkadia 2-▲ 519 (m) [AAD]
Verdi, G.:Un ballo in maschera, w. M. Callas (sop), E. Ratti (sop), G. di Stefano (ten), E. Bastianini (bar), G. Gavazzeni (cnd), La Scala Orch, La Scala Chorus *(rec 1957)* Melodram ▲ MLO 26039 [ADD]
Verdi, G.:Don Carlos, w. S. Jurinac (sop), E. Fernandi (ten), E. Bastianini (bar), C. Siepi (b-bar), H. von Karajan (cnd), Vienna PO, Vienna State Opera Chorus [I] *(rec live, Salzburg 7/26/58)* Arkadia 2-▲ 220 [ADD]
Verdi, G.:Falstaff, w. M. Freni (sop), I. Ligabue (sop), R. Elias (mez), R. Krause (ten), G. Evans (bar), R. Merrill (bar), G. Solti (cnd), RCA Italian Opera Orch, RCA Italiana Opera Chorus [I] London 2-▲ 417168-2 [ADD]
Verdi, G.:Falstaff, w. Anna Moffo (sop—Nannetta), Renata Tebaldi (sop—Alice Ford), Anna Maria Canali (mez—Meg Page), Giulietta Simionato (mez—Dame Quickly), Mariano Caruso (ten—Doctor Caius), Alvinio Misciano (ten—Fenton), Luigi Vellucci (ten—Bardolfo), Tito Gobi (bar—Falstaff), Carnell MacNeil (bar—Ford), Kenneth Smith (bass-Pistola), T. Serafin (cnd), *(orch unknown) (rec Chicago, 1958)* Legato Classics 2-▲ LCD 206-2 [ADD]
Verdi, G.:La forza del destino, w. R. Tebaldi (sop), M. del Monaco (ten), E. Bastianini (bar), C. Siepi (b-bar), F. Molinari-Pradelli (cnd), St. Cecilia Academy Orch Rome, St. Cecilia Academy Chorus Rome [I] London 3-▲ 421598-2 [ADD]
Verdi, G.:Otello, w. H. Gueden (sop), M. del Monaco (ten), A. Protti (bar), C. Siepi (b-bar), A. Erede (cnd), St. Cecilia Academy Orch Rome, St. Cecilia Academy Chorus Rome London 2-▲ 440242-2 [ADD]
Verdi, G.:Rigoletto, w. Hilde Gueden (sop—Gilda), Piero de Palma (ten—Borsa), Luisa Ribacchi (mez—Giovanna), Giulietta Simionato (mez—Maddalena), Mario del Monaco (ten—Duca de Mantova), Aldo Protti (bar—Rigoletto), Fernando Corena (bass—Conte Monterone), Cesare Siepi (bass—Sparafucile), A. Erede (cnd), St. Cecilia Academy Orch Rome, St. Cecilia Academy Chorus Rome Theorema ▲ TH 121179/180

Simionato, Giulietta (mez) (cont.)
Verdi, G.:Il trovatore, w. M. Callas (sop), K. Baum (ten), L. Warren (bar), G. Picco (cnd), Palacio Bellas Artes Orch, Palacio Bellas Artes Chorus *(rec live, Mexico City 6/20/50)* Melodram 2-▲ CDM 26017
Verdi, G.:Il trovatore, w. G. Tucci (sop), C. Bergonzi (ten), P. Cappuccilli (bar), G. Gavazzeni (cnd), La Scala Orch, La Scala Chorus *(rec live, Moscow 1965)* Melodram 2-▲ MEL 27008

Simionescu, Elena (sop)
Verdi, G.:La traviata, w. Elena Simionescu (sop—Annina), Virginia Zeani (sop—Violetta Valery), Elisabeta Neculce-Cartis (mez—Flora Bervoix), Ion Buzea (ten—Alfredo Germont), Vasile Moldoveanu (ten—Gastone/Viconte de Letorieres/Giuseppe), Teodor Panea (ten—Flora's Servant), Constantin Dumitru (bar—Commissioner/Baron Douphol), Nicolae Herlea (bar—Giorgio Germont), Valentin Loghin (bass—Marchese D'Obigny), Nicolae Rafael (bass—Doctor Grenvil), J. Bobescu (cnd), Romanian Opera Orch, Stelian Olariu (cnd), Romanian Opera Chorus *(rec 1968)* Vox Box 2-▲ CDX 5154

Simon, François (nar)
Stravinsky, I.:L'Histoire du soldat, w. J. V. Gilles (nar), W. Jacques (the Devil), E. Ansermet (cnd), Swiss Romande Orch members [F] *(rec 4/17/52)* Claves ▲ CD 8918 (m) [ADD]

Simone, A. R. de (sop)
Gluck, C.W.:L'Innocenza giustificata, w. B. Lucarini (sop—Flaminia), A. Ruffini (sop—Claudia), A. R. de Simone (sop—Flavio), U. Benelli (bar—Valerio), G. Catalucci (cnd), In Canto di Terni Youth Orch [I] *(rec live 9/90)* Bongiovanni 2-▲ GB 2111/12 [DDD]
Pergolesi, G.B.:Cants da camera, w. R. Gini (cnd), Concerto Ensemble *(rec Feb. 25–28, 1991)* Tactus ▲ TC 711601

Simone, Bruno de (bar)
Cimarosa, D.:Il Matrimonio segreto, w. D. Mazzuccato (sop), E. Dara (bar), A. Cavallaro (cnd), Marchigiana PO Nuova Era ▲ NUO 7014 [DDD]
Grétry, A.-E.-M.:Denys le tyran, w. S. Donzelli (sgr), R. Franceschetto (sgr), C. Di Segni (ten), F. Vizioli (cnd), Italian International Orch, Ars Pulcherrima Artium Chorus [F] *(rec live, Fermo, Palazzo Sassatelli, 1989)* Memories ▲ DR 3106 [DDD]
Rossini, G.:La cambiale di matrimonio, w. A. Rossi (sop), M. Comencini (ten), B. Praticò (bar), M. Viotti (cnd), English CO [I] Claves 8-▲ CD 9200 [DDD]
Rossini, G.:La cambiale di matrimonio, w. Alessandra Rossi (sop), Maurizio Comencini (ten), Bruno Praticò (bar), Valeria Baiano (bass), Francesco Facini (bass), M. Viotti (cnd), English CO Claves ▲ 50-9101

Simoneau, Léopold (ten)
Bach, J.S.:Mass in b, BWV 232, w. P. Alarie (sop), N. Merriman (cta), G. Neidlinger (bass), H. Scherchen (cnd), Vienna State Opera Orch, Vienna Academy Chorus [L] MCA Classics 2-▲ MCAD2-9821 [AAD]
Berlioz, H.:Requiem, "Grande Messe des Morts", w. C. Munch (cnd), Boston SO, New England Conservatory Chorus *(rec Apr 1959)* RCA Victor Gold Seal 8-▲ 0902-68444-2 [ADD]
Bizet, G.:Les Pêcheurs de perles, w. P. Alerie (sgr), X. Depraz (bass), J. Fournet (cnd), Lamoureux Orch *(rec 1953)* Philips 2-▲ 434782-2
Duparc, H.:Songs Voce della Luna ▲ VL 2013-1
Mozart, W.A.:Arias, w. I. Hollweg (sop), L. Marshall (sop), G. Unger (ten), G. Frick (bass), T. Beecham (cnd), Royal PO, Beecham Choral Society EMI Classics 2-▲ CDHB 63715
Mozart, W.A.:Così fan tutte, w. E. Schwarzkopf (sop), L. Otto (sop), N. Merriman (mez), R. Panerai (bar), S. Bruscantini (bar), H. von Karajan (cnd), Philharmonia Orch, Philharmonia Chorus [I] EMI Classics ("Studio" series) 3-▲ CDHC 69635 (m) [ADD]
Mozart, W.A.:Così fan tutte (sels), w. Lisa Otto (sop), Elizabeth Schwarzkopf (sop), Nan Merriman (mez), Rolando Panerai (bar), Sesto Bruscantini (bass), H. von Karajan (cnd), Philharmonia Orch Classics for Pleasure ("Eminence" series) ▲ CDEMX 2211 [DDD]
Mozart, W.A.:Don Giovanni, w. E. Grümmer (sop—D. Anna), R. Streich (sop—Zerlina), L. Della Casa (sop—D. Elvira), L. Simoneau (ten—Don Ottavio), C. Siepi (bass-baritone—Don Giovanni), W. Berry (bass—Masetto), G. Frick (bass—Il Commendatore), F. Corena (bass—Leporello), D. Mitropoulos (cnd), Vienna PO, Vienna State Opera Chorus *(rec Salzburg, July 24, 1956)* Sony Classical 3-▲ SM3K 64263 [ADD]
Mozart, W.A.:Don Giovanni, w. E. Grümmer (sop), L. Della Casa (sop), R. Streich (sop), C. Siepi (b-bar), G. Frick (bass), W. Berry (bass), F. Corena (bass), D. Mitropoulos (cnd), Vienna PO, Vienna State Opera Chorus [I] *(rec live, Salzburg, July 24, 1956)* Arkadia 3-▲ 552 (m) [ADD]
Mozart, W.A.:Entführung, w. I. Hollweg (sop), L. Marshall (sop), G. Unger (ten), G. Frick (bass), T. Beecham (cnd), Royal PO, Beecham Choral Society EMI Classics 2-▲ CDHB 63715
Mozart, W.A.:Requiem, w. I. Seefried (sop), J. Tourel (mez), W. Warfield (bar), B. Walter (cnd), New York PO *(rec 1956)* Historical Performers ▲ HPS 12 [ADD]
Mozart, W.A.:Zauberflöte, w. H. Gueden (sop), W. Lipp (sop), W. Berry (bass), K. Bohme (bass), K. Böhm (cnd), Vienna PO, Vienna State Opera Chorus London ("Grand Opera" series) 2-▲ 414362-2 [ADD]
Mozart, W.A.:Zauberflöte, w. L. Della Casa (sop), E. Köth (sop), G. Sciurri (sop), W. Berry (bass), K. Böhme (bass), G. Szell (cnd), Vienna PO, Vienna State Opera Chorus [G] *(rec live at the Salzburg Festival, July 27, 1959)* Melodram ("Connaisseur" series) 2-▲ MEL 27505 (m) [AAD]

Simonsen, Annette (mez)
Maegaard, J.:Elegy, w. Henrik Brendstrup (vc), Eva Feldbæk (org) *(rec Copenhagen, 1995–96)* Marco Polo/Dacapo ▲ 8.224050 [DDD]
Schnittke, A.:Penitential Psalms, w. Eva Bruun Hansen (sop), Elisabeth Rehling (sop), Maria Streijffert (alt), Karl-Gustav Andersson (ten), Poul Vejbo (ten), Stefan Parkman (cnd), Danish National Radio Choir Chandos ▲ CHAN 9480

Simpson, Glenda (mez)
Bach, J.S.:Mass in b, BWV 232, w. S. McNair (sop), D. Ziegler (mez), J. Aler (ten), W. Stone (bar), T. Paul (bass), R. Shaw (cnd), Atlanta SO, Atlanta Chamber Chorus [L] Telarc 2-▲ CD 80233 [DDD]
Now What Is Love?, w. Barry Mason (lt/baroque gtr/chit) Amon Ra ▲ CDSAR 50 [DDD]

Simpson, Marietta (mez)
Bach, J.S.:Magnificat, BWV 243, w. P. Jensen (sop), D. Upshaw (sop), D. Gordon (ten), W. Stone (bar), R. Shaw (cnd), Atlanta SO, Atlanta Chamber Chorus Telarc ▲ CD 80194 [DDD]
Beethoven, L. van:Mass, Op. 86, w. H. Schellenberg (mez), J. Humphrey (ten), M. Myers (ten), R. Shaw (cnd), Atlanta SO, Atlanta Sym Chorus [L] Telarc ▲ CD 80248 [DDD]
Gershwin, G.:Porgy & Bess, w. C. Haymon (sop—Bess), C. Clarey (sop—Serena), M. Simpson (sop—Maria), D. Evans (ten—Sporting Life), G. Baker (bar—Crown), W. White (bar—Porgy), S. Rattle (cnd), London PO, Glyndebourne Festival Chorus EMI Classics 3-▲ CDCC 49568
Janácek, L.:Slavonic Mass, w. C. Brewer (sop), K. Dent (ten), R. Roloff (bass), R. Shaw (cnd), Atlanta SO, Atlanta Sym Chorus [Sla] Telarc ▲ CD 80287 [DDD]
Mendelssohn, F.:Elijah, w. Barbara Bonney (sop), Henriette Schellenberg (sop), Florence Quivar (mez), Reid Bartelme (trb), Jerry Hadley (ten), Richard Clement (ten), Thomas Hampson (bar), Thomas Paul (bar), R. Shaw (cnd), Atlanta SO, Atlanta Sym Chorus [E] *(rec Symphony Hall, Woodruff Arts Center, Atlanta, GA, Nov. 5–7, 1994)* Telarc 2-▲ CD 80389 [DDD]
Schubert, Franz:Mass 6, w. B. Valente (sop), J. Humphrey (ten), G. Siebert (ten), M. Myers (ten), R. Shaw (cnd), Atlanta SO, Atlanta Sym Chorus [L] Telarc ▲ CD 80212 [DDD]
Szymanowski, K.:Stabat Mater, w. C. Goerke (sop), V. Ledbetter (bar), R. Shaw (cnd), Atlanta SO, Atlanta Sym Chorus *(rec Atlanta, Nov. 7–8, 1993)* Telarc ▲ CD 80362 [DDD]
Vivaldi, A.:Gloria, RV.589, w. D. Upshaw (sop), P. Jensen (sop), D. Gordon (ten), W. Stone (bar), R. Shaw (cnd), Atlanta SO, Atlanta Chamber Chorus Telarc ▲ CD 80194 [DDD]

Simson, Julie (mez)
Mahler, G.:Sym 8, w. Oksana Krovytska (sop—Magna Peccatrix), Sheila Smith (sop—Una poenitentium), Shauna Southwick (sop—Mater gloriosa), Kristine Jepson (mez—Maria Aegyptiaca), Julie Simson (mez—Mulier Samaritana), Kurt Hansen (ten—Doctor Marianus), Brian Steele (bar—Pater ecstaticus), Eugene Green (b-bar—Pater profundus), R. Olson (cnd), Colorado MahlerFest Orch, Colorado MahlerFest Chorale, Colorado Mormon Chorale, Colorado Children's Chorale *(rec MahlerFest VIII, Boulder, CO, Jan 14–15, 1995)* MahlerFest 2-▲ MF8-1
Parker, H.:Hora novissima, w. A. Soranno (sop), K. Hall (b-bar), D. Andersen (b-bar), J. Levick (cnd), Nebraska CO, Abendmusik Chorus, Nebraska Wesleyan Univ Choir Albany 2-▲ TROY 124/25

Sinatra, Frank (sgr)
Loesser, F.:Guys & Dolls, w. B. Crosby (sgr), D. Martin (sgr), J. Stafford (sgr), D. Shore (sgr), D. Reynolds (sgr), C. Dennis (sgr), A. Sherman (sgr), S. Davis Jr. (sgr), *(other artists unknown)* [studio cast] Reprise ▲ 45014-2 [AAD] ■ 45014-4
Porter, C.:High Society, w. B. Crosby (sgr), *(other artists unknown)* Capitol ▲ C21S 93787

Sinclair, Bernard (bar)
Lehár, F.:Das Land des Lächelns (sels), w. Ana-Maria Miranda (sop), Brigitte Krafft (sgr), J. Doussard (cnd), *(orch unknown)* [F] Forlane ▲ FOR 16715 [DDD]

Sinclair, Carolyn (sop)
Clarke, J.:Songs, w. Michael Jarvis (hpd), Margaret Gay (vc)—Celia is Soft; Long Has Pastora Rul'd the Plain; So Sweets the Charms of Love; Alas, Here Lies the Poor Alonzo Slain; Divine Astrea Hither Flew; Lord, What's Come to My Mother; I'se No More to Shady Coverts; Jockey Was a Dawdy Lad; The Bonny Grey Ey'd Morn; Jockey Was as Brisk & Blith a Lad *(rec St. Lawrence the Martyr Church, Hamilton, Ontario)* Hungaroton ▲ HCD 31602 [DDD]
Eccles, J.:Songs, w. Michael Jarvis (hpd), Margaret Gay (vc)—Stay, Ah Turn; Love is An Empty, Airy Name; If I Hear Orinda Swear; E'er Since You Came into My Sight; My Lover Has An Inconstant Mind; I'll Hurry Thee Hence; I Burn, My Brain Consumes to Ashes *(rec St. Lawrence the Martyr Church, Hamilton, Ontario)* Hungaroton ▲ HCD 31602 [DDD]
Purcell, H.:Songs, w. Margaret Gay (vc), Michael Jarvis (hpd)—Ah! How Sweet It is to Love; I Sigh'd & Owned My Love; Sweeter Than Roses; Whilst I with Grief Did on You Look; Oh! How You Protest; 'Twas Within a Furlong of Edinborough Town; Man is For the Woman Made; Ah Me! To Many Deaths Decreed; Oh! Lead Me to Some Peaceful Gloom; Lads & Lasses, Blith & Gay *(rec St. Lawrence the Martyr Church, Hamilton, Ontario)* Hungaroton ▲ HCD 31602 [DDD]

Sinclair, Jeanette (sop)
Rossini, G.:Le Comte Ory, w. M. Sinclair (cta), J. Oncina (ten), M. Roux (bar), V. Gui (cnd), Glyndebourne Festival Orch, Glyndebourne Festival Chorus *(rec 1956)* EMI Classics 2-▲ CDMB 64180

Sinclair, Monica (cta)
Donizetti, G.:La fille du régiment, w. J. Sutherland (sop), L. Pavarotti (ten), S. Maias (bass), R. Bonynge (cnd), Royal Opera House Orch [F] London 2-▲ 414520-2 [ADD]
Handel, G.F.:Messiah, w. Jennifer Vyvyan (sop), Jon Vickers (ten), Giorgio Tozzi (bass), T. Beecham (cnd), Royal PO *(rec 1959)* RCA Gold Seal 3-▲ 09026-61266-2
Handel, G.F.:Messiah (sels), w. Jennifer Vyvyan (sop), Jon Vickers (ten), Giorgio Tozzi (bass), T. Beecham (cnd), Royal PO, John McCarthy (cnd), Royal Choral Society—Ov; Comfort Ye My People; Every Valley Shall Be Exalted; And the Glory of the Lord; And He Shall Purify; O Thou That Tellest Good Tidings; For unto Us a Child is Born; Pastoral Symphony; There Were Shepherds Abiding; And the Angel Said unto Them; And Suddenly There Was; Glory to God in the Highest; He Shall Feed His Flock; Come unto Him; Behold the Lamb of God; He Was Despised; All We Like Sheep Have Gone Astray; Hallelujah!; I Know That My Redeemer Liveth; The Trumpet Shall Sound *(rec Walthamstow Town Hall, London, June–Aug 1959)* RCA Victor ▲ 09026-68159-2 [ADD]
Mozart, W.A.:Nozze di Figaro, w. S. Jurinac (sop), G. Sciutti (sop), R. Stevens (mez), D. McCoshan (ten), H. Cuenod (ten), G. Griffith (bar), S. Bruscantini (b-bar), F. Calabrese (bass), V. Gui (cnd), Glyndebourne Festival Orch, Glyndebourne Festival Chorus Classics for Pleasure ▲ CDCFP 4724 [ADD]
Mozart, W.A.:Requiem, w. Elsie Morison (sop), Alexander Young (ten), Marian Nowakowski (bass), T. Beecham (cnd), Royal PO, BBC Sym Chorus *(rec 1958)* Theorema ▲ TH 121151
Rossini, G.:Le Comte Ory, w. J. Sinclair (sop), J. Oncina (ten), M. Roux (bar), V. Gui (cnd), Glyndebourne Festival Orch, Glyndebourne Festival Chorus *(rec 1956)* EMI Classics 2-▲ CDMB 64180
Walton, W.:Troilus & Cressida (sels), w. E. Schwarzkopf (sop), P. Pears (ten), R. Lewis (ten), W. Walton (cnd), Philharmonia Orch—scenes EMI Classics ▲ ZDM 64199

Singer, Mark (bar)
Handel, G.F.:Faramondo, w. Julianne Baird (sop—Clotilde), Mary Ellen Callahan (sop—Adolfo), D'Anna Fortunado (mez—Faramondo), Jennifer Lane (mez—Rosimonda), Drew Minter (alt—Gernando), Peter Castaldi (bar—Gustavo), Mark Singer (bar—Tebaldo), Edward Brewer (hpd), R. Palmer (cnd), Brewer CO [period instrs] Vox Classics 3-▲ VOX3 7536 [DDD]
Rorem, N.:3 Sisters Who Are Not Sisters, w. Andrea Matthews (sop—Jenny), Carol Flamm (sgr—Helen), Madeline Tsingopoulos (sgr—Ellen), Frederick Urrey (ten—Samuel), Mark Singer (sgr—Sylvester), John Van Buskirk (pno) Newport Classic ▲ NPT 85594 [DDD]

Singher, Martial (bar)
Berlioz, H.:La Damnation de Faust, w. Suzanne Danco (sop), David Poleri (ten), Donald Gramm (bass), McHenry Boatwright (bass), Joseph de Pasquale (va), Louis Speyer (hn), C. Munch (cnd), Boston SO, Harvard Glee Club, Radcliffe Choral Society *(rec Feb 1954)* RCA Victor Gold Seal 8-▲ 0902-668444-2 [ADD]
Berlioz, H.:La Damnation de Faust, w. S. Danco (sop), D. Poleri (ten), D. Gramm (bass), C. Munch (cnd), Boston SO, Harvard Glee Club [F] RCA Gold Seal 2-▲ 7940-2-RG [ADD]
Brahms, J.:Liebeslieder Waltzes SATB, w. B. Valente (sop), M. Kleinman (cta), W. Conner (ten), R. Serkin (pno), L. Fleisher (pno) [G] Sony Classical ("Essential Classics" series) ▲ SBK 48176 ■ SBT 48176
Offenbach, J.:Les Contes d'Hoffmann, w. L. Amara (sop), R. Peters (sop), R. Stevens (mez), R. Tucker (ten), P. Monteux (cnd), Metropolitan Opera Orch, New York Metropolitan Opera Chorus Stradivarius 2-▲ DAT 12302
Stravinsky, I.:L'Histoire du soldat, w. M. Milhaud (nar), J.-P. Aumont (the Soldier), L. Stokowski (cnd), *(orch unknown)* [F] *(rec 1967)* Vanguard Classics ▲ OVC 8004 [ADD]

Singher, Martial (nar)
Honegger, A.:Le Roi David, w. Netania Davrath (sop), Jean Preston (mez), Marvin Sorenson (ten), M. Milhaud (nar), M. Abravanel (cnd), Utah SO [F] Vanguard Classics ▲ OVC 4038 [ADD]

Singstreu, H. (sop)
Gounod, C.:Faust, w. H. Singstreu (sop—Margarete), H. Rosvaenge (ten—Faust), M. Bohnen (bass—Mephistopheles), H. Steiner (cnd), Berlin RSO, Berlin Radio Chorus *(rec 1938)* Myto 2-▲ MCD 94196

Sinimberghi, Gino (ten)
Donizetti, G.:Requiem Mass, w. G. Tucci (sop), A. Lazzarini (mez), I. Sardi (bass), F. Maero (sgr), F. Molinari-Pradelli (cnd), Milan RAI SO, Milan RAI Chorus [L] *(rec live, Milan 3/21/61)* Memories ▲ HR 4131 [ADD]
Massenet, J.:Thérèse, w. Agnes Baltsa (mez—Thérèse), Francisco Araiza (ten—Armand), Gino Sinimberghi (ten—Officer), George Fortune (bass—André), Giancarlo Luccardi (bass—Morel), Eftimios Michalopoulos (sgr—Officer/Municipal Officer), G. Albrecht (cnd), Rome RAI SO, Giuseppe Piccillo (cnd), Rome RAI Chorus Orfeo ▲ 387961 [DDD]
Mercadante, S.:Il bravo, w. Miwako Matsumoto (sop—Violetta), Giovanna di Rocco (sop—Michelina), William Johns (ten—Il Bravo), Antonio Savastano (ten—Pisani), Gino Sinimberghi (ten—Cappello), Loris Gambelli (bass—Marco), Mario Machì (bass—Luigi), Paolo Washington (bass—Foscari), Maria Parazzini (sgr—Teodora), G. Ferro (cnd), Rome Opera Orch, Rome Opera Chorus *(rec Rome, Dec 30, 1976)* Italia 3-▲ CDC 94 [ADD]
Rossini, G.:La donna del lago, w. A. Balboni (sop), M. Caballé (sop), J. Hamari (mez), F. Bonisolli (ten), R. Bottazzo (ten), P. Washington (bass), P. Bellugi (cnd), Turin RAI Orch, Turin RAI Chorus *(rec live, Torino, 1970)* Foyer 2-▲ FOY 2028 [AAD]
Rossini, G.:L'occassione fa il ladro, w. C. Fusco (sop), M. T. Pace (mez), I. Tajo (bass), R. Gonzales (sgr), L. Colonna (cnd), Naples Alessandro Scarlatti RAI Orch [I] *(rec live, Naples, Sept. 29, 1963)* Arkadia ▲ 602 [ADD]
Rota, N.:Mysterium, w. A. Tuccari (sop), C. Vozza (mez), U. Trama (bass), A. Renzi (cnd), Pro Civitate Christiana di Assisi Orch, Pro Civitate Christiana di Assisi Chorus *(rec live 1962)* Claves ▲ CD 9323 [DDD]

Sinyavskaya, Tamara (mez)
Glinka, M.:Russlan & Ludmilla, w. Nina Fomina (sop—Gorislava), Bela Rudenko (sop—Ludmilla), Tamara Sinyavskaya (mez—Ratmir), Boris Morozov (bass—Farlaf), Evgeny Nesterenko (bass—Russlan), Valeri Yaroslavtsev (bass—Svetozar), Y. Simonov (cnd), Bolshoi Theater Orch, Bolshoi Theater Chorus *(rec Moscow, 1978–1979)* Melodiya ("The Russian Opera" series) 3-▲ 74321-29348-2 [ADD]
Tchaikovsky, P.:Eugene Onegin, w. Lidiya Chernikh (sop), Alexander Vedernikov (bass), Alexander Fedin (sgr), Yuri Mazurok (sgr), V. Fedoseyev (cnd), USSR SO, Moscow SO, Fernseh SO Audiophile Classics ("Legacy Collection" series) 2-▲ 101.751

Sioli (sgr)
Mercadante, S.:La Vestale, w. G. Dimitrova (sop), D. Vejzovic (sop), G. Cecchele (ten), Romanò (sgr), Cepreaga (sgr), Kliskic (sgr), Boldrini (sgr), V. Sutej (cnd), Spalato National Theater Orch, Spalato National Theater Chorus [I] *(rec 4/9/87)* Bongiovanni 2-▲ GB 2065/66 [DDD]

Sipes, Theodore (bar)
Hanson, H.:Pieces (4) Bar, w. Barbara Harbach (org), R. Shewan (cnd), Roberts Wesleyan College Chorale Albany ▲ TROY 129 [ADD]

Sirkiä, Raimo (ten)
Mahler, G.:Sym 8, w. Majken Bjerno (sop), Henriette Bonde-Hansen (sop), Inga Nielsen (sop), Kirsten Dolberg (alt), Anne Gjevang (alt), Jorma Hynninen (bar), Carsten Stabell (bass), L. Segerstam (cnd), Danish National RSO, Copenhagen Boys' Choir, Berlin Phil Choir, Danish National Radio Choir Chandos 2-▲ CHAN 9305/06 [DDD]
Merikanto, A.:Juha, w. Eeva-Liisa Saarinen (mez), Jorma Hynninen (bar), J.-P. Saraste (cnd), Finnish RSO Ondine 2-▲ ODE 872

Sirota, Gershon (cant)
Echoes of the Temple:Cantors in Prayer & Folksong, w. Pierre Pinchik (cant), Samuel Vigoda (cant), Joseph Rosenblatt (cant), Arthur Tracy (cant), et al. *(rec 1914–36)* Pearl ▲ PEA 9126 [ADD]

Sitwell, Edith (nar)
Walton, W.:Façade, w. Constant Lambert (nar), W. Walton (cnd), chamber orch Claremont ▲ CDGSE 785065

Siu, Leon (sgr)
Tanner, J.:Boy with Goldfish, w. M. Elliott (sgr), L. Holdridge (cnd), London SO, Nigel Brooks Chorale Albany ▲ TROY 053 [DDD]

Sivall, Olle (ten)
Verdi, G.:Rigoletto, w. M. Hallin (sop), B. Nordin (sop), K. Meyer (mez), B. Ericson (mez), Kjellgren (mez), N. Gedda (ten), H. Hasslo (bar), I. Wixell (bar), B. Alstergård (bar), A. Tyrén (bass), S. Ehrling (cnd), Stockholm Royal Opera House Orch, Stockholm Royal Opera Chorus *(rec live Jan. 18, 1959)* BIS ▲ CD 296 [AAD]
Verdi, G.:Il trovatore (sels), w. Hjördis Schymberg (sop), Kerstin Meyer (mez), Jussi Björling (ten), Hugo Hasslo (bar), H. Sandberg (cnd), Royal Opera Orch, Royal Opera House Chorus Covent Garden—Non son tuo figlio?; Mal reggendo all'aspro assalto; Quale d'armi fragor; Ah! sì, ben mio, coll'essere; L'onda de' suoni mistici; Di quella pira l'orrendo foco; Miserere d'un'alma già vicina; Madre?...non dormi?; Se m'ami ancor; Ciell...non m'inganna; Ti scosta... *(rec Royal Opera, Stockholm, Mar 6, 1960)* Myto ▲ MCD 953130

Siveri, Paolo (sgr)
Verdi, G.:Il trovatore, w. Maria Callas (sop), Cloe Elmo (cta), Giacomo Lauri-Volpi (ten), T. Serafin (cnd), Naples Teatro San Carlo Orch, Naples Teatro San Carlo Chorus *(rec Theatre of San Carlo, Naples, Jan. 27, 1951)* Pantheon 2-▲ PHE 6636 (m)

Sjöberg, Erik (ten)
Beethoven, L. van:Sym 9, "Choral Sym", w. Kerstin Lindberg-Torlind (sop), Else Jena (mez), Holger Byrding (bass), F. Busch (cnd), Danish National RSO, Danish National Radio Choir Arlecchino ARL

Sjöberg, Ingela Högerås (sop)
Schnittke, A.:Requiem, w. K. Salomonsson (sop), L. Lindholm (sop), A. F. Eker (cta), N. Högman (ten), S. Parkman (cnd), Stockholm Sinfonietta, Uppsala Academic Chamber Choir [L] BIS ▲ CD 497 [DDD]

Sjögren, Lars (ten)
Nilsson, T.:Music of, w. Ingmari Landin (alt), Lage Wedin (bass), Jerker Halldén (fl), Nils-Erik Sparf (vn), Hans-Ola Ericsson (org), Anders Loguin (perc), Torsten Nilsson (cnd), Gustaf Sjökvist (cnd), Swedish Radio Chorus—Ordinarium Missae; Balthasar/Daniel; Drei Gedichte Phono Suecia ▲ PHN 40 [AAD]
Nilsson, T.:Out of Earthly Night, w. Gudrun Bruna (sop), Marianne Mellnäs (sop), Kaysa Halldin (alt), Göran Swartz (bass), Sture Hedin (sgr), Ola Kyhlberg (sgr), Lars Ljungman (sgr), Nils Philipson (sgr), Ulrik Quale (sgr), Nils Spangenberg (sgr), Britta Therén (sgr), Karl-Erik Welin (org), Torsten Nilsson (cnd), Oscar's Motet Choir *(rec Oscar's Church, Stockholm, Sweden, Apr 26–27, 1978)* BIS ▲ CD 138 [AAD]

Sjöstedt, Margaret (sop)
Bach, J.S.:Magnificat, BWV 243, w. M. Coertse (sop), H. Rössl-Majdan (mez), A. Dermota (ten), F. Guthrie (bass), F. Prohaska (cnd), Vienna State Opera Orch, Vienna State Opera Chorus [L] *(rec June 1957)* Vanguard Classics ("The Bach Guild" series) ▲ OVC 2010 [ADD]
Giordano, U.:Andrea Chénier, w. H. Konetzni (sop—Madelon), M. Sjöstedt (sop—Bersi), R. Tebaldi (sop—Maddalena de Coigny), E. Höngen (cta—La Contessa de Coigny), F. Corelli (ten—Andrea Chénier), E. Bastianini (bar—C. Gérard), K. Paskalis (bar—Pietro Fléville), L. Welter (bar—Fouquier Tinville), A. Pernerstorfer (b-bar—Mathieu), L. von Matačić (cnd), Vienna State Opera Orch, Vienna State Opera Chorus *(rec Vienna, June 26, 1960)* Fortissimo 2-▲ CDE 3003 [ADD]

Sjöstedt, S. (sgr)
Hallén, A.:Harald der Wiking (act III, final scene), w. M. Meyerson (sgr—Berta), S. Lindström (sgr—Sigrun), A. Ljungholm (sgr—Harald), S. Sjöstedt (sgr—Sigleif), K. Jacobsson (sgr—Gudmund/Torgrim), S. Rybrant (cnd), Malmö SO, Malmö Radio Chorus [G] *(rec 6/6/74)* Musica Sveciae ▲ MSCD 621 [AAD]

Skinner, John York (alt)
Handel, G.F.:Partenope, w. Krisztina Laki (sop), Helga Müller-Molinari (mez), René Jacobs (alt), S. Kuijken (cnd), La Petite Bande Editio Classica 3-▲ 77109-2-RG [ADD]

Skladal (sgr)
Marschner, H.A.:Der Vampyr, w. L. Synek (sop), L. Heppe (ten), G. Oeggl (bar), Rathauscher (sgr), Sperlbauer (sgr), Weise (sgr), K. Tenner (cnd), Vienna RSO, Vienna Radio Chorus [G] *(rec live, Vienna, 4/9/51)* Memories 2-▲ HR 4466/67 [ADD]

Skoglund, Annika (mez)
Sandström, S.-D.:The High Mass, w. Lena Hoel (sop), Sara Olsson (sop), Siri Torjesen (sop), Marianne Eklöf (mez), Peter Bengtson (org), L. Segerstam (cnd), Swedish RSO, Eric Ericson Chamber Choir *(rec live, Berwald Hall, Stockholm, Nov. 25 & 26, 1994)* Caprice 2-▲ CAP 22036

Sköld, Clas (sgr)
Berwald, F.:Estrella de Soria (sels), w. L. Nordin (sop), K. Dalayman (sgr), S. Smith (sgr), A. Lorentzson (sgr), S. Westerberg (cnd), Helsingborg SO, Malmö Chamber Choir Musica Sveciae ▲ MSV 523 [DDD]

Skov, Susanne (sop)
Britten, H.:Flower Songs, w. J. Koch (pno), C. Bjørkøe (pno), Safri Duo, La Camerata Danica ▲ DCD 8154
Grainger, P.:Songs, w. J. Koch (pno), C. Bjørkøe (pno), M. Bojesen (cnd), Camerata, Safri Duo—No Nighean Dhu; O Mistress Mine; 6 Dukes Went a-Fishing; Mary Thompson; Old Irish Tune Danica ▲ DCD 8154
Holmboe, V.:Songs, w. J. Koch (pno), C. Bjørkøe (pno), Safri Duo—Americana Danica ▲ DCD 8154
Nørholm, I.:Songs, w. J. Koch (pno), C. Bjørkøe (pno), Camerata, Safri Duo—Song at Sunset Danica ▲ DCD 8154

Skovhus, Boje (bar)
Britten, H.:War Requiem, w. L. Orgonasova (sop), A. Rolfe-Johnson (ten), J. E. Gardiner (cnd), North German RSO, Monteverdi Choir London, North German Radio Chorus, Tölz Boys' Choir Deutsche Grammophon 2-▲ 437801-2
Lehár, F.:Die lustige Witwe, w. Cheryl Studer (sop), Barbara Bonney (sop), Bryn Terfel (b-bar), J.E. Gardiner (cnd), Vienna PO, Monteverdi Choir London Deutsche Grammophon ▲ 439911-2
Mozart, W.A.:Don Giovanni, w. Christine Brewer (sop—Donna Anna), Nuccia Focile (sop—Zerlina), Felicity Lott (sop—Donna Elvira), Jerry Hadley (ten—Don Ottavio), Bo Skovhus (bar—Don Giovanni), Umberto Chiummo (bass—Masetto/Il Commendatore), Alessandro Corbelli (bass—Leporello), C. Mackerras (cnd), Scottish CO, Scottish Chamber Chorus *(rec Usher Hall, Edinburgh, Scotland, July 31–Aug 11, 1995)* Telarc 3-▲ CD 80420 [DDD]
Mozart, W.A.:Nozze di Figaro, w. Cecilia Bartoli (sop—Cherubino), Sylvia McNair (sop—Susanna), Cheryl Studer (sop—Countess Almaviva), Lucio Gallo (bar—Figaro), Boje Skovhus (bar—Count Almaviva), C. Abbado (cnd), Vienna PO, Vienna State Opera Chorus Deutsche Grammophon 3-▲ 445903-2
Orff, C.:Carmina burana, w. S. Jo (sop), J. Kowalski (alt), Z. Mehta (cnd), London PO, London Phil Choir, Southend Boys' Choir Teldec ▲ 74886-2

Skovhus, Boje (bar) (cont.)
Schumann, C.:Songs, w. Helmut Deutsch (pno)—Liebeszauber; Der Mond kommt still gegangen; Die stille Lotosblume; Liebst du um Schönheit; Warum willst du and're fragen; Ich hab' in deinem Auge; Die gute Nacht; Ich stand in dunklen Träumen; Sie Liebten sich beide; Volkslied; Lorelei Sony Classical ▲ SK 62372
Schumann, R.:Dichterliebe, w. Helmut Deutsch (pno) Sony Classical ▲ SK 62372
Schumann, R.:Liederkreis, Op. 24, w. Helmut Deutsch (pno) Sony Classical ▲ SK 62372
Strauss, R.:Arabella (sels), w. P. Coburn (sop), R. Klepper (sop), M. Borst (mez), F. Hawlata (bass), M. Honeck (cnd), Munich RSO Capriccio ▲ 10481 [DDD]
Strauss, R.:Ariadne auf Naxos, w. P. Coburn (sop), R. Klepper (sop), M. Borst (mez), F. Hawlata (bass), M. Honeck (cnd), Munich RSO Capriccio ▲ 10481 [DDD]
Strauss, R.:Capriccio (sels), w. P. Coburn (sop), R. Klepper (sop), M. Borst (mez), F. Hawlata (bass), M. Honeck (cnd), Munich RSO Capriccio ▲ 10481 [DDD]
Strauss, R.:Der Rosenkavalier (sels), w. P. Coburn (sop), R. Klepper (sop), M. Borst (mez), F. Hawlata (bass), M. Honeck (cnd), Munich RSO Capriccio ▲ 10481 [DDD]
Thomas, A.:Hamlet, w. Alexandrina Pendachanska (sop), Viorica Cortez (mez), R. Giovanetti (cnd), ORF SO, Arnold Schoenberg Choir *(rec live, 1994)* Serenissima 3-▲ SER 360147
Zemlinsky, A. von:Lyric Sym, w. Luba Orgonasova (sop), C. P. Flor (cnd), North German RSO *(rec Musikhalle, Hamburg, Sept 8-10, 1994)* RCA Red Seal ▲ 09026-68111-2 [DDD]
Zemlinsky, A. von:Songs, w. Helmut Deutsch (pno)—Under Blooming Trees; In the Current; Last Request; In Spring; Welcome, Op. 7/2; Blissful Hour, Op. 10/2 *(rec Hannover, Dec 10-11, 1994)* RCA Red Seal ▲ 09026-68111-2 [DDD]

Skram, Knut (b-bar)
Bach, J.S.:Cant 82, w. Brynjar Hoff (ob), A. Ardal (cnd), Canticum Novum CO *(rec Greverud Church, Oslo, Norway, June 8 & 9 & Sept 23, 197)* BIS ▲ CD 101 [AAD]
Grieg, E.:The Mountain Thrall, w. T. Schuback (cnd), Gothenburg CO *(rec Gothenburg Concert Hall, Sweden, Mar 21-23, 1976)* BIS ▲ CD 43 [AAD]
Grieg, E.:Songs, w. M. Hirsti (sop), R. Jansen (pno)—7 Children's Songs, Op. 61; Haugtussa, Op. 67; Songs from Haugtussa not included in Op. 67; Clara's Song; I Love You, Dear; The Princess; Sighs; Morning Prayer at School Victoria ▲ VCD 19040
Grieg, E.:Songs, w. Eva Knardahl (pno)—Ragnhild; Ragna; Langs ei å; En Svane; Min tanke er et mægtigt fjeld *(rec Gothenburg Concert Hall, Sweden, Mar 21-23, 1976)* BIS ▲ CD 43 [AAD]
Grieg, E.:Songs, w. R. Jansen (pno)—four songs from Melodies of the Heart Op. 5; twelve songs from Op. 33—The youth; Last spring; The wounded heart; The berry; Beside the stream; A vision; The old mother; The first thing; At Rondane; A piece on friendship; Faith; The goal; Six elegiac songs, Op. 59; The mountain thrall, Op. 32 Victoria ▲ VCD 19039
Grieg, E.:Songs, w. M. Hirsti (sop), K. M. Sandve (ten), R. Jansen (pno)—Four Songs, Op. 15; 3 Songs from Peer Gynt; 5 Songs by Vilhelm Krag, Op. 60; 6 Songs by Holger Drachmann, Op. 49 [N] *(rec March & Dec. 1991)* Victoria ▲ VCD 19038 [DDD]
Grieg, E.:Songs, w. M. Hirsti (sop), K. M. Sandve (ten), R. Jansen (pno)—For L.M. Lindeman's Silver Wedding Anniversary; The Blueberry; Yuletide Cradle Song; Devoutest of Maidens; Little Lad; The Forgotten Maid; The White & Red, Red Roses Victoria ▲ VCD 19044
Grieg, E.:Songs, w. M. Hirsti (sop), K. M. Sandve (ten), R. Jansen (pno)—Songs & Ballads by Munch, Op. 9; 5 Poems by Paulsen, Op. 26; Romances, Op. 39; 5 Songs by Benzon, Op. 69; 5 Songs by Benzon, Op. 70 Victoria ▲ VCD 19043
Grieg, E.:Songs, w. M. Hirsti (sop), C. Pfeiler (mez), K. M. Sandve (ten), R. Jansen (pno)—4 Songs, Op. 2; 4 Songs by Christian Winther, Op. 10; 9 Songs, Op. 18; 6 Songs by Ibsen, Op. 25 Victoria ▲ VCD 19042
Grieg, E.:Songs, w. M. Hirsti (sop), C. Pfeiler (mez), K. M. Sandve (ten), R. Jansen (pno)—Op. 4, Nos. 1, 2, 3, 4, 5 & 6; Op. 21, Nos. 1, 2, 3 & 4; Op. 44, Nos. 1, 2, 3, 4, 5 & 6; Op. 48, Nos. 1, 2, 3, 4, 5 & 6; Op. 58, Nos. 1, 2, 3, 4 & 5 [N, G] Victoria ▲ VCD 19041
Strauss, E.:Songs, w. E. Knardahl (pno)—Krämerspiegel (12 songs), Op. 66 [G] *(rec March 21-23, 1976)* BIS ▲ CD 49 [AAD]

Skulski, Florian (bar)
Moniuszko, S.:Haunted Manor, w. Bozena Betley-Siradzka (sop—Hanna), Anna Witkowska (sop—Marta/Stara Niewiasta), Wiera Baniewicz (mez—Jadwiga), Aleksandra Imalska (mez—Czesnikowa), Kazimierz Dluha (Grzes), Zdzislaw Nikodem (ten—Damazy), Wieslaw Ochman (ten—Stefan), Andrzej Hiolski (bar—Miecznik), Florian Skulski (bar—Maciej), Leonard Mróz (bass—Zbigniew), Andrzej Saciuk (bass—Skoluba), J. Krenz (cnd), Cracow Polish Radio-TV Orch, Cracow Polish Radio-TV Chorus *(rec Cracovia, 1978)* Agora Music ("Phoenix" series) 3-▲ 509 [ADD]
Szymanowski, K.:King Roger, w. B. Zagórzanka (sop—Roger), S. Kowalski (ten—Shepherd), Z. Nikodem (ten—Edrisi), F. Skulski (bar—Roger II), R. Satanowski (cnd), Warsaw Teatr Wielki Orch, Warsaw Teatr Wielki Chorus [Polish] Koch Schwann 2-▲ CD 314 014 [DDD]

Škvárová, Yvona (cta)
Kozeluch, Joh. A.:Missa Pastoralis, w. S. Losová (sop), M. Švejda (ten), M. Podskalský (bass), B. Kulínský (cnd), Prague PO, Prague Radio Chorus Multisonic ▲ 31 0003-2 [ADD]

Slabbert, Wicus (sgr)
Zemlinsky, A. von:Kleider machen Leute, w. E. Mathis (sop), H. Winkler (ten), V. Vogel (ten), C. Otelli (bar), H. Franzen (bass), R. Scholze (bass), R. Weikert (cnd), Zurich Opera Orch, Zurich Opera House Chorus [G] *(rec live, Zurich Opera House, 6/29/90)* Koch Schwann 2-▲ CD 314 069 [DDD]

Sladdon, J. (sgr)
Taylor, B.J.:Wuthering Heights, w. Dave Willets (sgr), L. Garrett (sop), C. Carter (sgr), S. Campbell (sgr), Philharmonia Orch, Contorum Choir Silva America ▲ SSD 1008 ▮ SSC 1008

Slatinaru, Maria (sop)
Puccini, G.:Turandot, w. Teodora Lucaciu (sop—Liù), Maria Slatinaru (sop—Princess Turandot), Corneliu Finateanu (ten—Pong), George Mircea (ten—Emperor Altoum), Ludovic Speiss (ten—Prince Calaf), Valentin Teodorian (ten—Pang), Octav Enigarescu (bar—Ping), Dionisie Konya (bar—A Mandarin), Mircea Stefanescu (bar—The Prince of Persia), Nicolae Florei (bass—Timur), C. Litvin (cnd), Romanian Radio-TV Orch, Romanian Radio-TV Chorus *(rec Jan 1970)* Vox Box 2-▲ CDX 5160

Slavova, Mariana (sop)
Verdi, G.:Requiem Mass, w. Joke Kramer (mez), Alexander Stevenson (ten), Peter Lika (bass), P. Kuentz (cnd), Paul Kuentz Orch, Paul Kuentz Choir Pierre Verany 2-▲ PVY 730054 [DDD]

Šlepkovská, Denisa (mez)
Respighi, O.:La bella dormente nel bosco, w. Ivana Czaková (sop—Old Woman/Green Fairy), Adriana Kohútková (sop—Blue Fairy/Nightingale), Henrietta Lednárová (sop—Frog/Spindle), Jana Valásková (sop—Princess), Dagmar Pecková (mez—Cuckoo/Cat), Denisa Šlepkovská (mez—Queen/Duchess), Karol Bernáth (ten—Doctor), Guillermo Dominguez (ten—Prince April), Igor Pasek (ten—Jester), Ján Durčo (bar—Ambassador), Richard Haan (bar—King/Woodcutter), Stanislav Benacka (bass—Doctor), Anton Kúrnava (bass—Doctor), Marián Smolárik (bass—Doctor), M. Adriano (nar—Mr. Dollar Chèques), M. Adriano (cnd), Slovak RSO Bratislava, Ján Rozehnal (cnd), Slovak Phil Chorus *(rec Concert Hall of the Slovak Radio, Bratislava, June 8-20, 1994)* Marco Polo ("Opera Classics" series) ▲ 8.223742 [DDD]
Respighi, O.:Liriche su parole di poeti armeni, w. Vladimír Havran (fl), Michal Sintál (ob), Gabriel Koncer (cl), Ivan Viskup (b cl), Ivan Paulicka (bn), Frantisek Kovács (trbn), Katarína Vavreková (hp), M. Adriano (cnd) [arr. for chamber group by Adriano] *(rec Slovak Radio Concert Hall, Bratislava, Jan. 4-9, Feb. 19 & June)* Marco Polo ▲ 8.223595 [DDD]
Respighi, O.:Lucrezia, w. Adriana Kohútková (sop—Venilia), Michela Remor (sop—Lucrezia), Stefania Kaluza (mez—La Voce), Denisa Šlepkovská (mez—Servia), Ludovít Ludha (ten—Collatino), Igor Pasek (ten—Bruto), Ján Durčo (bar—Tito/Valerio), Richard Haan (bar—Tarquinio), Rado Hanák (bass—Arunte/Spurio Lucrezio) *(rec Concert Hall of the Slovak Radio, Bratislava, June 9-16, 1994)* Marco Polo ▲ 8.223717 [DDD]

Slezak, Leo (ten)
Lebendige Vergangenheit *(rec 1905 & 1907)* Preiser ▲ PRE CD 89136
Leo Slézak Sings *(rec 1928-29 for Grammophon)* Preiser ("Lebendige Vergangenheit" series) ▲ PRE 89203 (m) [AAD]
Mozart, W.A.:Entführung (sels), w. Maria Ivogün (sop), Richard Tauber (ten), K. Alwin (cnd), Vienna State Opera Orch—Hier soll ich dich; Konstanze!... wie ängstlich; Martern aller Arten *(rec 1905 - 1944)* Minerva ▲ MN A14 [ADD]

Slezak, Leo (ten) (cont.)
Opera Arias & Duets (rec. 1905-1908 from G & T 78 r) Preiser ("Lebendige Vergangenheit" series) ▲ PRE 89020 (m) [AAD]
Verdi, G.:Il trovatore (sels), w. J. Biel (ten), F. Tamagno (ten), L.-A. Escalaïs (ten), M. Gilion (ten), E. Caruso (ten), A. Paoli (ten), G. Zenatello (ten), J. Sembach (ten), F. Constantino (ten), G. Martinelli (ten), B. De Muro (ten), N. Fusati (ten), N. Piccaluga (ten), G. Lauri-Volpi (ten), A. Pertile (ten), E. Bergamaschi (ten), R. Tauber (ten), J. O'Sullivan (ten), H. Roswaenge (ten), G. Taccani (ten), V. Lois (ten), H. Lazaro (ten), A. Lindi (ten), A. Cortis (ten), F. Merli (ten), F. Völker (ten), J. Kiepura (ten), J. Schmidt (ten), J. Bjoerling (ten), B. Gigli (ten), A. Salvarezza (ten), J. Soler (ten), M. Filippeschi (ten)—34 performances of the Act III tenor aria "Di quella pira!," *(rec from 1903-1956)* Bongiovanni ▲ GB 1051 [AAD]

Sliwa, Bogdan (bar)
Elsner, J.:Passio Domini Nostri Jesu Christi, w. Bozena Harasimowicz (sop), Krzysztof Szmyt (ten), Czeslaw Galka (bar), Piotr Nowacki (bass), K. Kord (cnd), Warsaw PO, Henryk Wojnarowski (cnd), Ewa Marchwicka (cnd), Warsaw National Phil Chorus, E. Mlynarski State School of Music Children's Choir *(rec National Philharmonic, Warsaw, 1990)* Polskie Nagrania ▲ PNCD 078 [DDD]

Slobodskaya, Oda (sop)
Oda Slobodskaya & Vladimir Rosing in Russian Art Song, w. Slobodskaya, Oda (sop), Vladimir Rosing (ten) Pearl ▲ PEA 9021 [AAD]

Slonicka, Halina (sop)
Moniuszko, S.:Haunted Manor, w. Bozena Brun-Baranska (mez), Barbara Lawcewicz (mez), Krystyna Szczepanska (mez), Zdzislaw Nikodem (ten), Bogdan Paprocki (ten), Andrzej Hiolski (bar), Edmund Kossowski (bass), Bernard Ladysz (bass), W. Rowicki (cnd), Warsaw State Opera House Orch, Warsaw National Opera Chorus *(rec Warsaw, 1965)* Polskie Nagrania ▲ PNCD 093 [AAD]
Moniuszko, S.:Mass in E♭, w. A. Malewicz (mez), W. Pilewski (bass), E. Kajdasz (cnd), Warsaw CO, Polish Radio Chorus Olympia ▲ OLY 395 [ADD]
Moniuszko, S.:Sacred Music, w. A. Malewicz (mez), W. Pilewski (bass), E. Kajdasz (cnd), Warsaw CO, Polish Radio Chorus—Ne memineris; Vide humilitatem meam; Litanie Ostrobramskie, No. 1 Olympia ▲ OLY 395 [ADD]

Sloniowska, Halina (sop)
Moniuszko, S.:Halka, w. Barbara Nieman (sop), Jan Góralski (ten), Bogdan Paprocki (ten), Leslaw Pawluk (ten), Kazimierz Pustelak (ten), Andrzej Hiolski (bar), Edmund Kossowski (bass), Edward Pawlak (bass), Z. Gorzynski (cnd), Warsaw State Opera House Orch, Warsaw National Opera Chorus *(rec Warsaw, 1965)* Polskie Nagrania ▲ PNCD 092 [AAD]

Slowakiewicz, Alicia (sop)
Gluck, C.W.:La Corona, w. H. Gorzynska (sop), L. Juranek (sop), B. Nowicka (mez), T. Bugaj (cnd), Warsaw Sinfonia [I] Orfeo 2-▲ 135872 [DDD]

Slowioczek, Klement (bar)
Krása, H.:Chamber Music, w. I. Berix (cl), La Roche String Quartet—String Quartet (1923); Tanz for String Trio (1943); Theme & Variations for String Quartet; Three Songs for Baritone, Clarinet, Viola & Cello (1943) Channel Classics ▲ CCS 3792 [DDD]

Sluis, Mieke van der (sop)
Bach, J.S.:Cant 205, w. R. Jacobs (ct), C. Prégardien (ten), D. Thomas (bass), G. Leonhardt (cnd), Orch of the Age of Enlightenment [G] Philips ▲ 432161-2 [DDD]
Bach, J.S.:Cant 214, w. R. Jacobs (ct), C. Prégardien (ten), D. Thomas (bass), G. Leonhardt (cnd), Orch of the Age of Enlightenment [G] Philips ▲ 432161-2 [DDD]
Biber, H. von:Requiem à 15, w. Marta Almajano (sop), John Elwes (ten), Mark Padmore (ten), Frans Huijts (bar), Harry van der Kamp (bass), G. Leonhardt (cnd), Netherlands Bach Society Baroque Orch, Netherlands Bach Society Choir *(rec Utrecht, Germany, Oct 22-24, 1994)* Deutsche Harmonia Mundi ▲ 05472-77344-2 [DDD]
Couperin, F.:Leçons de ténèbres (for Good Friday), w. G. Laurens (mez), P. Monteilhet (lt), M. Muller (vl), L. Boulay (hpd/org)—[L] Erato (Musifrance) ▲ 2292-45012-2 [DDD]
Couperin, F.:Magnificat, w. G. Laurens (mez), P. Monteilhet (lt), M. Muller (vl), L. Boulay (hpd/org)—[L] Erato (Musifrance) ▲ 2292-45012-2 [DDD]
Desmarets, H.:Sacred Music, w. Barbara Schlick (sop), Harry Geraerts (ct), Fiori Musicali, New College Choir Oxford—Deux grands motets lorrains; Mystères de notre seigneur Jésus-Christ Erato ▲ ERA SEL 98529 [ADD]
Fux, J.J.:Dafne in Lauro, w. L. Akerlund (sop), S. Piccollo (sop), G. Lesne (alt), M. Klietmann (ten), R. Clemencic (cnd), Clemencic Consort, La Cappella Vocal Ensemble [I] Nuova Era ("Ancient Music" series) 2-▲ 6930/31 [DDD]
Handel, G.F.:Tamerlano, w. Isabelle Poulenard (sop—Irene), Mieke van der Sluis (sop—Asteria), René Jacobs (alt—Andronico), Henri Ledroit (ct—Tamerlano), John Elwes (ten—Bajazet), Gregory Reinhart (bass—Leone), J. Malgoire (cnd), La Grande Ecurie et la Chambre du Roy *(rec 1983)* Sony Classical 3-▲ SM3K 37893
Handel, G.F.:Te Deum, "Caroline", w. Graham Pushee (alt), Harry Van Berne (ten), Harry van der Kamp (bass), W. Helbich (cnd), Bremen Baroque Orch, Alfelder Vocal Ensemble CPO ▲ CPO 999244 [DDD]
Handel, G.F.:The Ways of Zion Do Mourn, w. Graham Pushee (alt), Harry van Berne (ten), Harry van der Kamp (bass), W. Helbich (cnd), Bremen Baroque Orch, Alfelder Vocal Ensemble CPO ▲ CPO 999244 [DDD]
Monteverdi, C.:Arias & Duets, w. A. Köhler (alt), Lautten Compagney—Sancta Maria; Ego flos campi; O bone Jesu; Laudate Dominum; Venite, venite; Fugge, fugge anima mea; Ballo delle Ingrate; Vorrei baciarti; Ed è pur dunque vero; Di far sempre gioire; Eri già tutta mia; O rosetta che rosetta/Non così tosto io miro; Quel sguardo sdegnosetto; Sinfonia; Adagiati, Poppea, Pur ti miro Capriccio ▲ 10 470 [DDD]
Steffani, A.:Stabat Mater, w. Marta Almajano (sop), John Elwes (ten), Mark Padmore (ten), Harry van der Kamp (bass), G. Leonhardt (cnd), Netherlands Bach Society Baroque Orch, Netherlands Bach Society Choir *(rec Utrecht, Germany, Oct 22-24, 1994)* Deutsche Harmonia Mundi ▲ 05472-77344-2 [DDD]
Telemann, G.P.:Hamburger Admiralitätsmusik, w. Mieke van der Sluis (sop—Hammonia), Graham Pushee (ten—Themis), Rufus Müller (ten—Mercurius), Klaus Mertens (bass—Neptunius), David Thomas (bass—Mars), Michael Schopper (bass—Albis), W. Helbich (cnd), Bremen Baroque Orch, Alsfeld Vocal Ensemble *(rec Nov 9, 1995)* CPO 2-▲ CPO 999373-2 [DDD]
Torrejón Y Velasco, T. de:La purpura de la rosa, w. P. Mildenhall (sop), J. Benet (ten), A. Martin (bar), R. Clemencic (cnd), Clemencic Consort, La Cappella Vocal Ensemble [Sp] Nuova Era ("Ancient Music" series) ▲ 6936 [DDD]
Valls, F.:Scala Arentina Mass, w. S. Paiu (sop), B. Lettinga (alt), D. Cordier (ct), J. Elwes (ten), H. van der Kamp (bass), G. Leonhardt (cnd), Netherlands Bach Society Baroque Orch, Netherlands Bach Society Choir Deutsche Harmonia Mundi ▲ 05472-77277-2
Vivaldi, A.:L'Olimpiade, w. L. Meeuwsen (sop), E. von Magnus (alt), G. Lesne (alt), A. Christofelis (alt), W. Oberholtzer (bar), A. Walker Schultze (bass), R. Clemencic (cnd), Clemencic Consort, La Cappella Vocal Ensemble [I] *(rec live, Paris, 2/8-10/90)* Nuova Era ("Ancient Music" series) 2-▲ 6932/33 [DDD]

Sluys, To van der (sop)
Beethoven, L. van:Sym 9, "Choral Sym", w. Suze Luger (cta), Louis van Tulder (ten), Willem Ravelli (bass), W. Mengelberg (cnd), Royal Concertgebouw Orch, Toonkunst Chorus *(rec 1938)* Music & Arts ▲ CD 918

Smart, M. (sop)
Smart, G.:Music of, w. B. Theurer (tpt), G. Smart (pno), Franciscan Quartet—Trumpeter Swan; Fanfare, Invocation & Alleluia Capstone ▲ CPS 8612 CD [DDD]

Smeets, Roger (sgr)
Loevendie, T.:Gassir, the Hero, w. Claron McFadden (sop—Partridge/Priestess), Timothy Wilson (alt—Shamsi), Christopher Gillett (ten—Safi), Robert Poulton (bar—Gassir), Lieuwe Visser (bass—Yemni), Roger Smeets (sgr—Rafi), D. Porcelijn (cnd), Asko Ensemble *(rec live, Amsterdam Studios, June 14-15, 1993)* Donemus ▲ CV 35

Smimic, Goran (sgr)
Schreker, F.:Irrelohe, w. Eva Randová (mez—Old Lola), Michael Pabst (ten—Count Heinrich), Monte Pederson (bar—Peter), Neven Belamaric (sgr—The Parson), Luana Devol (sgr—Eva), Sebastian Holecek (sgr—The Miller), Goran Smimic (sgr—The Forester) Sony Classical 2-▲ S2K 66850

Smirnov, Dmitri (ten)
Dmitri Smirnov *(rec 1912–24)* Pearl ▲ PEA 9106 [ADD]

Smit, Henk (bass)
Boito, A.:Mefistofele (sels), w. M. Olivero (sop—Margherita), M. Frusoni (ten—Faust), H. Smit (b-bar—Mefistofele), A. Kerjens (cnd), *(orch unknown)*—Act III *(rec live May 5, 1973)* VAI Audio 2-▲ VAIA 1062 [ADD]
Cilea, F.:Adriana Lecouvreur (sels), w. M. Olivero (sop—Adriana), M. Frusoni (ten—Maurizio), H. Smit (bass-bar—Michonnet), A. Kerjens (cnd), *(orch unknown)*—Act IV *(rec live May 5, 1973)* VAI Audio 2-▲ VAIA 1062 [ADD]

Smith (sgr)
Penderecki, K.:Polish Requiem, w. I. Haubold (sop), G. Winogrodska (mez), Z. Terzakis (ten), K. Penderecki (cnd), North German RSO, North German Radio Chorus [L] *(rec live, Lucerne, 1989)* Deutsche Grammophon 2-▲ 429720-2 [DDD]

Smith (spkr)
Plog, A.:Animal Ditties 2, w. A. Plog (tpt), Davis (pno) Crystal ▲ CD 663 [DDD]

Smith, Angus (ten)
Dunstable, J.:Sacred Music, w. Robert Harre Jones (ct), Charles Daniels (ten), D. Greig (cnd), Orlando Consort—Missa Rex Seculorum; Ave Maris Stella; Gloria in Canon; O Crux Gloriosa; Descendi in Ortum Meum; Speciosa Facta Es; Sub Tuam Portectionem; Veni Sancte Spiritus; Albanus Roseo Rutilat; Specialis Virgo; Preco Preheminencie; Salve Regina Metronome ▲ 1009
Lalande, M.-R. de:Confitebor tibi, Domine, w. G. Fisher (sop), O. Johnston (trb), C. Daniels (ct), S. Varcoe (bass), E. Higginbottom (cnd), King's Consort, Oxford New College Choir [L] Erato (Musifrance) ▲ 2292-45014-2 [DDD]
Lalande, M.-R. de:De profundis solo Voices, Orch & Chorus, w. G. Fisher (sop), O. Johnston (trb), C. Daniels (ct), S. Varcoe (bass), E. Higginbottom (cnd), King's Consort, New College Choir Oxford [L] Erato (Musifrance) ▲ 2292-45014-2 [DDD]
Lalande, M.-R. de:Miserere, w. G. Fisher (sop), O. Johnston (trb), C. Daniels (ct), S. Varcoe (bass), E. Higginbottom (cnd), King's Consort, Oxford New College Choir [L] Erato (Musifrance) ▲ 2292-45014-2 [DDD]

Smith, Carol (mez)
Beethoven, L. van:Missa Solemnis, w. E. Farrell (sop), R. Lewis (ten), K. Borg (bass), L. Bernstein (cnd), New York PO, Westminster Choir [L] Sony Classical 2-▲ SM2K 47522 [ADD]
Debussy, C.:La Damoiselle élue, w. V. de los Angeles (sop), C. Munch (cnd), Boston SO, Radcliffe Choral Society [F] RCA Gold Seal 2-▲ 7940-2-RG [ADD]
Mascagni, P.:Cavalleria rusticana, w. Z. Milanov (sop), J. Björling (ten), R. Merrill (bar), R. Cellini (cnd), RCA Victor SO, Robert Shaw Chorale [I] RCA Gold Seal ▲ 6510-2-RG [ADD]

Smith, D. (bar)
Bach, J.S.:St. John Passion, w. P. Curtin (sop), E. Thomann (sop), E. Alberts (cta), W. Kmentt, J. Van Kesteren (ten), R. Springer (bar), O. Wiener (bar), F. Guthrie (bass), F. Lukasowsky (bass), H. Scherchen (cnd), Vienna State Opera Orch, Vienna Academy Chorus [G] *(rec ca 1960)* MCA Classics 2-▲ MCAD2-9804
Dittersdorf, K.D. von:Arcifanfano, King of Fools, or It's Always Too Late to Learn, w. P. Brooks (sop), A. Russell (sop), E. Steber (sop), J. McCollum (ten), J. Sopher (ten), H. Rehfuss (bar), N. Jenkins (cnd), Clarion Music Society Orch, Clarion Music Society Chorus [E] *(rec live, New York 1965)* VAI Audio 2-▲ VAIA 1010-2 (m) [ADD]

Smith, Damien (bar)
Wallace, V.:Maritana, w. Majella Cullagh (sop), Lynda Lee (mez), Paul Charles Clarke (ten), Ian Caddy (bar), Quentin Hayes (bass), P. O. Duinn (cnd), RTE Concert Orch, RTE Phil Choir *(rec O'Reilly Hall, Dublin, Sept 1995)* Marco Polo 2-▲ 8.223406-7 [DDD]

Smith, David (bar)
Handel, G.F.:Judas Maccabaeus, w. Martina Arroyo (sop), Mary Davenport (mez), Lawrence Avery (ten), Jan Peerce (ten), T. Scherman (cnd), Vienna State Opera Orch, Vienna Academy Chorus Vox Box 2-▲ CDX 5125 [ADD]

Smith, Fran (sgr)
Davies, S.:What Is the Matter in Amy Glennon?, w. Gregory Whitehead (nar—The Idea), Sheila Davies (nar—Amy Glennon/Chorus), Piers McKenzie (nar—Auctioneer), Amy Newburg (sgr), Barney Jones (nar—The Fathers) ▲ WN 0013

Smith, Jaclyn (nar)
Saint-Saëns, C.:Carnival of the Animals, w. M. Golabek (nar), R. Golabek (nar), F. Savage (nar), C. Heston (nar), J. E. Jones (nar), B. White (nar), L. Redgrave (nar), W. Shatner (nar), J. Rivers (nar), T. Danson (nar), L. Tomlin (nar), D. Raffin (nar), A. Hepburn (nar), D. Moore (nar), W. Matthau (nar), L. Schifrin (cnd), Hollywood CO Dove Audio ▲ DOV 30700

Smith, Jason (bar)
Stuart, P.:Kill Bear Comes Home, w. Elana Gizzi (sop—Hasty Girl), Mi-Kyung Huh (sop—Cold Feet), Therese Murray (sop—Song Bird), Cherie Pfeil (sop—1st Sister), Renia Shukis (sop—2nd Sister), Riki Connaughton (mez—4th Sister), Lucy Fee (mez—3rd Sister), David Averbach (ten—Song Leader), Mark Schmidt (ten—Kill Bear), Jason Smith (bar—Cheif Wife Hunter), P. Stuart (cnd), Rochester Opera Theater Orch, Rochester Opera Theater Chorus VM ▲ DRK 154 [DDD]

Smith, Jennifer (sop)
Bach, J.S.:Cant 208, "Hunting Cant", w. E. Kirkby (sop), S. Davies (ten), M. George (b-bar), R. Goodman (cnd), Parley of Instruments [G] Hyperion ▲ CDA 66169
Bach, J.S.:Mass in b, BWV 232, w. M. Chance (ct), N. van der Meel (ten), H. van der Kamp (bass), F. Brüggen (cnd), Orch of the 18th Century, Netherlands Chamber Choir [L] *(rec live)* Philips ("Digital Classics" series) 2-▲ 426238-2 [DDD]
Berlioz, H.:Le Jeune pâtre breton, w. C. Mackerras (cnd), Philharmonia Orch IMP ("BBC Radio Classics" series) ▲ IMP 5691532
Berlioz, H.:Les Nuits d'été, w. C. Mackerras (cnd), Philharmonia Orch IMP ("BBC Radio Classics" series) ▲ IMP 5691532
Handel, G.F.:Amadigi di Gaula, w. E. Harrhy (sop—Melissa), J. Smith (sop—Oriana), P. Bertin (mez—Orgando), B. Fink (cta—Dardano), N. Stutzmann (cta—Amadigi), M. Minkowski (cnd), Louvre Musicians, Louvre Choir [I] Erato 2-▲ 2292-45490-2 [DDD]
Handel, G.F.:Messiah, w. Helen Kucharek (sop), Linda Finnie (mez), Niel Mackie (ten), Rodney Macann (b-bar), T. Dean (cnd), Pro Christe Orch, Pro Christe Choir *(rec St. Augustine's Church, Kilburn, London, 1986)* Guild 2-▲ GMDD 7112/3 [ADD]
Handel, G.F.:Ottone, Rè di Germania, w. Jennifer Smith (sop—Gismonda), Catherine Denley (mez—Matilda), James Bowman (ct—Ottone), Dominique Visse (ct—Adelberto), Michael George (bass—Emireno), R. King (cnd), King's Consort Hyperion 3-▲ CDA 66751/53
Handel, G.F.:Il Trionfo del Tempo e del Disinganno, w. Isabelle Poulenard (sop), Nathalie Stutzmann (cta), John Elwes (ten), M. Minkowski (cnd), Louvre Musicians Erato 2-▲ 2292-45351-2 ZA
Lully, J.-B.:Phaëton, w. V. Gens (sop), R. Yakar (sop), H. Crook (ten), J.-P. Fouchécourt (ten), M. Minkowski (cnd), Musiciens du Louvres Erato 2-▲ 91737
Monteverdi, C.:Orfeo, w. P. Kwella (sop), E. Kirkby (sop), N. Rogers (ten), S. Varcoe (bar), D. Thomas (bass), N. Rogers (cnd), London Cornett & Sackbutt Ensemble, C. Medlam (cnd), London Baroque Chiaroscuro EMI Classics ▲ CDMB 64947
Mozart, W.A.:Requiem, w. Helen Watts (cta), Ian Partridge (ten), Stafford Dean (bass), M. Atzmon (cnd), BBC Welsh National SO, BBC Choral Society IMP ("BBC Radio" series) ▲ IMP 5691452
Purcell, H.:Hail, Bright Cecilia, w. B. Gordon (alt), A. Stafford (alt), P. Elliot (ten), S. Varcoe (bar), D. Thomas (bass), J.E. Gardiner (cnd), English Baroque Soloists, Monteverdi Choir London Erato ("Gardiner Purcell Collection" series) ▲ 96554-2
Purcell, H.:King Arthur, w. Gillian Fisher (sop), E. Priday (sop), Gill Ross (sop), A. Stafford (alt), P. Elliot (ten), S. Varcoe (bar), J.E. Gardiner (cnd), English Baroque Soloists, Monteverdi Choir London Erato ("Gardiner Purcell Collection" series) 2-▲ 96552-2
Purcell, H.:King Arthur, w. G. Fisher (sop), E. Priday (sop), G. Ross (sop), A. Stafford (alt), P. Elliott (ten), S. Varcoe (bar), J.E. Gardiner (cnd), English Baroque Soloists, Monteverdi Choir London Erato 2-▲ 2292-45211-2 ZA
Purcell, H.:King Arthur (sels), w. G. Fisher (sop), E. Priday (sop), G. Ross (sop), J. E. Gardiner (cnd), English Baroque Soloists, Monteverdi Choir Erato ▲ 45919-2

Smith, Jennifer (sop) (cont.)
Purcell, H.:Odes & Welcome Songs (misc), w. E. Priday (sop), K. Amps (sop), M. Chance (ct), Wilson (sgr), J. M. Ainsley (ten), S. Richardson (bar), T. Pinnock (cnd), English Concert, *(chorus unknown)* —Come ye Sons of Art; Welcome to All the Pleasures; Of Old, When Heroes Thought it Base Archiv ▲ 427663-2 [DDD]
Rameau, J.P.:Platée, w. G. Ragon (ten), G. de Mey (ten), M. Minkowski (cnd), Louvre Musicians, Françoise Herr Vocal Ensemble [F] Erato ("Musifrance" series) 2-▲ 2292-45028-2 [DDD]
Stravinsky, I.:Pulcinella, w. J. Fryatt (ten), M. King (bass), S. Rattle (cnd), Northern Sinfonia of England EMI Classics ▲ CDM 64739

Smith, Kenneth (bass)
Verdi, G.:Falstaff, w. Anna Moffo (sop—Nannetta), Renata Tebaldi (sop—Alice Ford), Anna Maria Canali (mez—Meg Page), Giulietta Simionato (mez—Dame Quickly), Mariano Caruso (ten—Doctor Caius), Alvinio Misciano (ten—Fenton), Luigi Vellucci (ten—Bardolfo), Tito Gobi (bar—Falstaff), Carnell MacNeil (bar—Ford), Kenneth Smith (bass-Pistola), T. Serafin (cnd), *(orch unknown) (rec Chicago, 1958)* Legato Classics 2-▲ LCD 206-2 [ADD]

Smith, Kevin (ct)
Brassart, J.:Ave Maria, w. A. Teichert-Hailperin (sop), W. Jochesn (ten), M. Nitz (ten), Helga Weber Instrumental Circle Entrée ▲ 0041 [ADD]
Dufay, G.:Magnificat, w. A. Teichert-Hailperin (sop), W. Jochesn (ten), Helga Weber Instrumental Circle—Octavi toni for 3 voices Entrée ▲ 0041 [ADD]
Dunstable, J.:Sacred Music, w. A. Teichert-Hailperin (sop), W. Jochens (ten), M. Nitz (ten), H. Deutsch (bar), Helga Weber Instrumental Circle—Sancta Maria; Beata dei genetrix; Beata mater et innupta virgo; Speciosa facta es; Alma redemptoris mater Entrée ▲ 0041 [ADD]
Hildegard Of Bingen:Sacred Songs, w. A. Teichert-Hailperin (sop), W. Jochens (ten), M. Nitz (ten), H. Deutsch (bar), Helga Weber Instrumental Circle—Caritas abundat in omnia; O virtus sapientiae; O quam mirabilis; Hodie aperuit nobis clausa porta; Alleluia. O virga, mediatrix; O clarissima mater; O frodens virga Entrée ▲ 0041 [ADD]
Love Songs from the 14th & 15th Centuries, w. Almut Teichert-Hailperin (sop), Wilfried Jochens (ten), Martin Nitz (ten), Instrumentalkreis Helga Weber Entrée ▲ CHE 0042-2 [ADD]
Mozart, W.A.:Missa, K.317, w. Janet Price (sop), Anthony Rolfe-Johnson (ten), Graham Titus (bass), M. Davies (cnd), BBC Northern SO, Leeds Phil Chorus IMP ("BBC Radio Classics" series) ▲ IMP 5691552

Smith, M. (sgr)
Porter, C.:A Swell Party, w. A. Richards (sgr), N. Grace (sgr), A. Woods (sgr), D. Keman (sgr), *(other artists unknown)* [1992 London cast] Silva America ▲ SSD 1006 [DDD] ■ SSC 1006

Smith, Malcolm (bass)
Massenet, J.:Manon, w. Beverly Sills (sop—Manon), Plácido Domingo (ten—Des Grieux), Nico Castel (ten—Guillot), Richard Fredricks (bar—Lescaut), Robert Hale (bar—De Brétigny), Malcom Smith (bass—Count de Grieux), J. Rudel (cnd), New York City Opera Orch, New York City Opera Chorus *(rec live, New York, 1969)* Melodram 2-▲ IMC 205008 [ADD]
Still, W.G.:Tristan und Isolde, w. C. Ligendza (sop), S. Anderson (cta), C. Heater (ten), A. Svorc (bass), L. Toffolo (cnd), Trieste Teatro Comunale Giuseppe Verdi Orch, Trieste Teatro Comunale G. Verdi Chorus [G] *(rec live, Trieste, 12/13/69)* Melodram 3-▲ MEL 37072 (m) [AAD]

Smith, Marilyn Hill (sop)—see Hill Smith, Marilyn

Smith, Norwood (sgr)
Strauss (II), Joh.:Eine Nacht in Venedig, w. Nola Fairbanks (sgr—Ciboletta), Thomas Tibbett Hayward (sgr—Mario), Laurel Hurley (sgr—Nina), David Kurlan (sgr—Senator Bartoldi), Guen Omeron (sgr—Barbara), Jack Russell (sgr—Duke of Palobino), Kenneth Schon (sgr—Filippo Del Aqua), Norwood Smith (sgr—Caramello), Enzo Stuarti (sgr—Pappacoda) *(rec Belock Recording Studio, Bayside, NY)* Everest ▲ EVC 9036 [AAD]

Smith, S. (sgr)
Berwald, F.:Estrella de Soria (sels), w. L. Nordin (sop), K. Dalayman (sgr), A. Lorentzson (sgr), C. Sköld (sgr), S. Westerberg (cnd), Helsingborg SO, Malmö Chamber Choir Musica Sveciae ▲ MSV 523 [DDD]

Smith, Sheila (sop)
Mahler, G.:Sym 8, w. Oksana Krovytska (sop—Magna Peccatrix), Sheila Smith (sop—Una poenitentium), Shauna Southwick (sop—Mater gloriosa), Kristine Jepson (mez—Maria Aegyptiaca), Julie Simson (mez—Mulier Samaritana), Kurt Hansen (ten—Doctor Marianus), Brian Steele (bar—Pater ecstaticus), Eugene Green (b-bar—Pater profundus), R. Olson (cnd), Colorado MahlerFest Orch, Colorado MahlerFest Chorale, Colorado Mormon Chorale, Colorado Children's Chorale *(rec MahlerFest VIII, Boulder, CO, Jan 14–15, 1995)* MahlerFest 2-▲ MF8-1

Smith, Stephen (sgr)
Kraus, J.M.:Proserpin, w. Hillevi Martinpelto (sop), Susanne Rydén (sop), Anna Eklund-Tarantino (sgr), Peter Mattei (bar), Lars Arvidson (bass), M. Tatlow (cnd), Stockholm CO, Stockholm Chamber Choir Musica Sveciae 2-▲ MSCD 422/23 [DDD]

Smitt-Walter, K. (bar)
Lortzing, A.:Die beiden Schützen, w. K. Nentwig (sop), P. Kuen (ten), B. Kusche (bar), M. Pröbstl (bass), J. Koetsier (cnd), Bavarian RSO *(rec 1950)* Memories 2-▲ MEM 4546 [ADD]

Smolárik, Marián (bass)
Respighi, O.:La bella dormente nel bosco, w. Ivana Czaková (sop—Old Woman/Green Fairy), Adriana Kohútková (sop—Blue Fairy/Nightingale), Henrietta Lednárová (sop—Frog/Spindle), Jana Valásková (sop—Princess), Dagmar Pecková (mez—Cuckoo/Cat), Denisa Slepkovská (mez—Queen/Duchess), Karol Bernáth (ten—Doctor), Guillermo Dominguez (ten—Prince April), Igor Pasek (ten—Jester), Ján Durčo (bar—Ambassador), Richard Haan (bar—King/Woodcutter), Stanislav Benacka (bass—Doctor), Anton Kúrnava (bass—Doctor), Marián Smolárik (bass—Doctor), M. Adriano (nar—Mr. Dollar Chèques), M. Adriano (cnd), Slovak RSO Bratislava, Ján Rozehnal (cnd), Slovak Phil Chorus *(rec Concert Hall of the Slovak Radio, Bratislava, June 8–20, 1994)* Marco Polo ("Opera Classics" series) ▲ 8.223742 [DDD]

Smolenskaya, Elena (sop)
Tchaikovsky, P.:Queen of Spades, w. Evgenya Verbitskaya (mez), Georgi Nelepp (ten), Pavel Lisitsian (bar), A. Melik-Pashayev (cnd), Bolshoi Opera Orch, Bolshoi Theater Chorus Arlecchino 3- ARL

Smycková, Jarmila (sop)
Novák, V.:Storm, w. Jarmila Zilková (sop), Frantisek Livora (ten), Z. Košler (cnd), Czech PO, Czech Phil Chorus Supraphon ▲ SUP CD 3088

Smythe, Russel (bar)
Donizetti, G.:L'assedio di Calais, w. E. Harrhy (sop), D. Jones (mez), R. Serbo (ten), J. Treleaven (ten), D. Parry (cnd), Philharmonia Orch, Geoffrey Mitchell Choir Opera Rara 2-▲ OR 9 [DDD]
Rameau, J.P.:Hippolyte et Aricie, w. Véronique Gens (sop), Bernarda Fink (cta), Jean-Paul Fouchécourt (ten), Laurent Naouri (bar), M. Minkowski (cnd), Louvre Musicians, Sagittarius Vocal Ensemble Archiv 3-▲ 445853-2

Snarski, Andréa (bar)
Marschner, H.A.:Der Vampyr, w. Carole Farley (sop—Malwina), Nucci Condò (mez—Suse), Oslavio Di Credico (ten—George Dibdin), Josef Protschka (ten—Edgar Aubry), Romano Truffelli (ten—Richard Scrop), Martin Egel (bar—Sir Humphrey Davenaut), Andréa Snarski (bar—Toms Blunt), Siegmund Nimsgern (b-bar—Lord Ruthven), Armando Caforio (bass—Robert Green), Peter Boom (sgr—Il capo dei Vampiri), Carlo Di Giacomo (sgr—James Gadshill), Wolfgang Lenz (sgr—Sir Berkley), Galina Pisarenko (sgr—Janthe), Renzo Scorsoni (sgr—Un servitore di Berkley), Anastasia Tomaszewska Schepis (sgr—Emmy), G. Neuhold (cnd), Rome RAI SO, Rome RAI Chorus *(rec Rome, Jan 26, 1980)* Italia 2-▲ CDC 99 [ADD]

Snashall, Mark (trb)
Herrmann, B.:Wuthering Heights, w. M. Beaton (sop—Catherine), P. Bowden (mez—Isabella), E. Bainbridge (mez—Nelly), M. Snashall (trb—Hareton), D. Bell (bar—Heathcliff), J. Kitchiner (bar—Hindley), J. Ward (bar—Edgar), M. Rippon (bass—Joseph), D. Kelly (bass—Mr. Lockwood), B. Herrmann (cnd), Pro Arte Orch *(rec 1965–66)* Unicorn-Kanchana 3-▲ UKCD 2050/51/52 [ADD]

Snellincks, Dirk (bass)
Hasse, J.A.:Miserere in e, w. Greta de Reyghere (sop), Dina Grossberger (mez), Ian Honeyman (ten), Il Fondamento Opus 111 ▲ OPS 3080

▲ = CD ♦ = Enhanced CD Δ = MD ■ = Cassette Tape □ = DCC

Snellincks, Dirk (bass) (cont.)
Hasse, J.A.:Requiem, w. Greta de Reyghere (sop), Dina Grossberger (mez), Ian Honeyman (ten), Il Fondamento Ensemble Opus 111 ▲ OPS 3080

Snellings, Dirk (bass)
Haydn, M.:Missa Pro Defuncto Archiepiscopo Sigismundo, w. Lena Lootens (sop), Cornelia Salje (alt), Bernard Loonens (ten), Philippe Benoit (cnd), Vivente Voce Choir *(rec Steurbaut Sound Recording Centre)* René Gailly ▲ CD 87125 [DDD]
Haydn, M.:Motets, w. Lena Lootens (sop), Cornelia Salje (alt), Bernard Loonens (ten), Philippe Benoit (cnd), Vivente Voce Choir—Aria de Passione Domini *(rec Steurbaut Sound Recording Centre)* René Gailly ▲ CD 87125 [DDD]

Soanea, Ioan (bar)
Puccini, G.:Madama Butterfly, w. Eugenia Moldoveanu (sop—Madama Butterfly), Mihaela Agachi (mez—Suzuki), Corina Circa (mez—Kate Pinkerton), Emil Gherman (ten—B.F. Pinkerton), Stefan Popescu (ten—Goro), Ioan Soanea (bar—The Bonze/Yakuside), Eduard Tumageanian (bar—Sharpless), Alexandru Kopeczi (bass—Prince Yamadori), Mircea Moisa (bass—Commissioner), P. Popescu (cnd), Satu Mare PO, Cluj-Napoca Phil Chorus *(rec 1979)* Vox Box 2-▲ CDX 5155

Sobehartova, Jitka (sop)
Dvořák, A.:The Spectre's Bride, Op. 69, w. Jiri Kubik (ten), Jan Markvart (bar), Bratislava Philharmonic Chorus, P. Tiboris (cnd), Bohuslav Martinů PO [Cz] *(rec Nov. 26–30, 1993)* Elysium ▲ GRK 700 [DDD]

Söderström, Elisabeth (sop)
Beethoven, L. van:Missa Solemnis, w. M. Höffgen (cta), W. Kmentt (ten), M. Talvela (bass), O. Klemperer (cnd), New Philharmonia Orch, New Philharmonia Chorus [L] EMI Classics ("Studio" series) 2-▲ CDMB 69538 [ADD]
Blomdahl, K.-B.:...the voyage this night, w. Y. Ahronovitch (cnd), Stockholm PO Caprice ▲ CAP 21365 [AAD]
Britten, H.:Folksong Arrs, w. R. Tear (ten), N. Marriner (cnd), Northern Sinfonia of England—Bonny Earl O'Moray; Oliver Cromwell; O Waly, Waly; The Plough Boy EMI Classics ▲ CDM 69522
Britten, H.:Les Illuminations, w. G. Levine (cnd), English CO Arabesque ▲ Z 6603
Britten, H.:Our Hunting Fathers, w. N. Marriner, Northern Sinfonia of England EMI Classics ▲ CDM 69522
Britten, H.:War Requiem, w. R. Tear (ten), T. Allen (bar), S. Rattle (cnd), City of Birmingham SO, City of Birmingham Sym Chorus, Christ Church Boys' Chorus [E,L] EMI Classics 2-▲ CDC 47033
Debussy, C.:Pelléas et Mélisande, w. Y. Minton (mez), G. Shirley (ten), D. McIntyre (bass-bar), D. Ward (bass), P. Boulez (cnd), Royal Opera House Orch, Royal Opera House Chorus Covent Garden Sony Classical (Pierre Boulez Edition) 3-▲ SM3K 47265
Elisabeth Söderström & Kerstin Meyer, w. Kerstin Meyer (mez), Jan Eyron (pno) *(rec Nov. 1–3, 1974)* BIS ▲ CD 17 [AAD]
Gluck, C.W.:Orfeo ed Euridice, w. Ruth-Margret Pütz (sop), Dietrich Fischer-Dieskau (bar), F. Leitner (cnd), Cappella Coloniensis, Cologne Radio Chorus *(rec live, Cologne, Nov. 8, 1964)* Orfeo d'or 2-▲ 391952
Grieg, E.:Peer Gynt Suites, Opp. 46 & 55, w. A. Davis (cnd), New Philharmonia Orch *(rec Apr. 9–10, 1976)* Sony Classical ▲ SBK 53257; ■ SBT 53257
Humperdinck, E.:Hänsel und Gretel, w. I. Cotrubas (sop), F. von Stade (mez), C. Ludwig (mez), S. Nimsgern (b-bar), J. Pritchard (cnd), Gürzenich Orch [G] CBS 2-▲ M2K 35898 [ADD]
Janácek, L.:Jenůfa, w. L. Popp (sop), E. Randová (mez), M. Dvorsky (ten), W. Ochman (ten), C. Mackerras (cnd), Vienna PO [Cz] London 2-▲ 414483-2 [DDD]
Janácek, L.:Káťa Kabanová, w. N. Kniplová (mez), P. Dvorský (ten), V. Krejčík (ten), Z. Svehla (ten), D. Jedlička (bass), C. Mackerras (cnd), Vienna PO London 2-▲ 421852-2 [DDD]
Janácek, L.:The Makropulos Affair, w. V. Krejčík (ten), Z. Švehla (ten), V. Zítek (ten), D. Jedlička (bass), C. Mackerras (cnd), Vienna PO, Vienna Opera Chorus London 2-▲ 430372-2 [ADD]
Janácek, L.:Slavonic Mass, w. Drahomíra Drobkova (cta), František Livora (ten), Richard Novák (bass), C. Mackerras (cnd), Czech PO, Czech Phil Chorus Supraphon ▲ SUP 103575 [DDD]
Larsson, L.-E.:God in Disguise, w. E. Sandaen (bar), L. Ekborg (nar), S. Westerberg (cnd), Swedish SO Swedish Society ▲ SCD 1020
Lidholm, I.:Nausikaa Alone, w. S. Westerberg (cnd), Swedish RSO, Swedish Radio Chorus Caprice ▲ CAP 21366 [AAD]
Mahler, G.:Das Klagende Lied, w. E. Lear (sop), G. Hoffman (mez), S. Burrows (ten), E. Haefliger (ten), G. Nienstedt (bass), P. Boulez (cnd), London SO, London Sym Chorus Sony Classical ("Pierre Boulez Edition" series) ▲ SK 45841
Monteverdi, C.:Incoronazione, w. H. Donath (sop), C. Berberian (sop), P. Esswood (ct), N. Harnoncourt (cnd), Vienna Concentus Musicus [I] Teldec 4-▲ 2292-42547-2
Mozart, W.A.:Nozze di Figaro, w. R. Grist (sop), T. Berganza (mez), G. Evans (bar), O. Klemperer (cnd), New Philharmonia Orch, John Alldis Choir EMI Classics 3-▲ CDMC 63849
Nystroem, G.:Sym 3, w. S. Westerberg (cnd), Swedish RSO Swedish Society ▲ SCD 1015
Orff, C.:Carmina burana, w. G. Bäckelin (ten), S. Svanholm (ten), H. Schmidt-Isserstedt (cnd), Stockholm PO, Stockholm Phil Chorus *(rec live, 11/26/54)* BIS 8-▲ CD 421/24 (m/s) [AAD]
Örhängen, w. Hakan Sund (pno), Clas Pehrsson (rec) *(rec June 15–18, 1981)* BIS ▲ CD 187 [AAD]
Pergolesi, G.B.:Il maestro di musica, w. L. Gardelli (cnd), Drottningholm CO Swedish Society ▲ SCD 1029
Schubert, Franz:Songs (misc), w. P. Badura-Skoda (pno) [on 1824 Conrad Graf piano]—13 songs—D.118, 162, 216, 257, 328, 367, 544, 717, 720, 764, 877/2-4 [G] Astrée ▲ E 7783 [DDD]
Shostakovich, D.:From Jewish Folk Poetry, w. O. Wenkel (cta), R. Karczykowski (ten), B. Haitink (cnd), Royal Concertgebouw Orch London ▲ 417581-2 [DDD/ADD]
Stenhammar, W.:Serenade, w. N. Gedda (ten), R. Kubelik (cnd), Stockholm PO Swedish Society ▲ SCD 1016
Zemlinsky, A. von:Lyric Sym, w. D. Duesing (bar), B. Klee (cnd), Berlin RSO [G] Koch Schwann ▲ CD 311 053 [ADD]

Soffel, Doris (mez)
Bach, J.S.:Cant 26, w. A. Augér (sop), A. Kraus (ten), P. Huttenlocher (bar), H. Rilling (cnd), Stuttgart Bach Collegium, Gächinger Kantorei [G] *(rec 1979 & 1980)* Hänssler Classic ▲ 98.821 [AAD]
Bach, J.S.:Cant 121, w. A. Augér (sop), A. Kraus (ten), W. Schöne (bass), H. Rilling (cnd), Stuttgart Bach Collegium, Gächinger Kantorei [G] *(rec Feb & Apr 1980)* Hänssler Classic ▲ 98.824 [AAD]
Bach, J.S.:Cant 133, w. A. Augér (sop), A. Baldin (ten), P. Huttenlocher (bar), H. Rilling (cnd), Stuttgart Bach Collegium, Gächinger Kantorei [G] *(rec Feb–Mar 1980)* Hänssler Classic ▲ 98.826 [AAD]
Bach, J.S.:Cant 182, w. A. Baldin (ten), P. Huttenlocher (bar), H. Rilling (cnd), Stuttgart Bach Collegium, Gächinger Kantorei [G] *(rec 1975)* Hänssler Classic ▲ 98.880 [AAD]
Bach, J.S.:Cant 196, w. A. Baldin (ten), N. Tüller (b-bar), H. Rilling (cnd), Bach Ensemble *(rec Jan 1975)* Hänssler Classic ▲ 98.828 [AAD]
Beethoven, L. van:Sym 9, "Choral Sym", w. H. Donath (sop), S. Jerusalem (ten), P. Lika (bass), S. Celibidache (cnd), Munich PO, Munich Phil Chorus *(rec Mar. 19, 1989)* Exclusive ▲ EXL 15 [AAD]
Donizetti, G.:Anna Bolena, w. Katia Ricciarelli (sop), Pietro Ballo (ten), Nicolai Ghiuselev (bass), E. Pidò (cnd), Palermo Teatro Massimo Orch, Palermo Teatro Massimo Chorus *(rec live, 1991)* Serenissima 3-▲ SER 360111
Haydn, J.:Mass 3, "Cäcilienmesse", w. Lucia Popp (sop), Rudolf Laubenthal (ten), Kurt Moll (bass), R. Kubelik (cnd), Bavarian RSO, Bavarian Radio Chorus [L] Orfeo 2-▲ 032822 [DDD]
Mahler, G.:Kindertotenlieder, w. E. Inbal (cnd), Vienna SO *(rec Konzerthaus, Vienna, June 9–10, 1992)* Denon/PCM Digital ▲ DEN 75969 [DDD]
Mahler, G.:Lieder eines fahrenden Gesellen, w. E. Inbal (cnd), Vienna SO *(rec Konzerthaus, Vienna, July 4–5, 1992)* Denon/PCM Digital ▲ DEN 75969 [DDD]
Mahler, G.:Songs from Rückert, w. E. Inbal (cnd), Vienna SO *(rec Konzerthaus, Vienna, July 4–5, 1992)* Denon/PCM Digital ▲ DEN 75969 [DDD]
Mahler, G.:Sym 3, w. E. Inbal (cnd), Frankfurt RSO, Frankfurt Radio Chorus [G] Denon 2-▲ 7828/29 [DDD]
Wolf, H.:Der Corregidor, w. H. Donath (sop), W. Hollweg (ten), P. Maus (ten), K. Moll (bass), D. Fischer-Dieskau (bar), G. Albrecht (cnd), Berlin RSO [G] Koch Schwann 2-▲ CD 314 010
Zemlinsky, A. von:Eine florentinische Tragödie, w. K. Riegel (ten), G. Sarabia (bar), G. Albrecht (cnd), Berlin RSO [G] Koch Schwann ▲ CD 314012 [DDD]

Sojer, Hans (ten)
Weill, K.:The Seven Deadly Sins, w. B. Fassbaender (mez), K.-H. Brandt (ten), H. Komatsu (bass), I. Urbas (bass), C. Garben (cnd), North German Radio PO Harmonia Mundi France ▲ HMC 901420

Solari, Cristy (ten)
Cristy Solari Bongiovanni ▲ GB 1090 [ADD]

Soldh, Anita (sop)
Lundquist, I.T.:Sym 7, w. Olle Persson (bar), S. Ehrling (cnd), Swedish RSO, Mikaeli Chamber Choir Caprice ▲ CAP 21419 [DDD]

Solén, C. (ten)
Lindberg, O.:Requiem, w. I. Sörenson (sop), E. Thallang (alt), E. Saedén (bass), O. Johansson (org), H. Kyhle (cnd), Stockholm Univ College of Music Orch, Englebrekt Church Oratory Choir *(rec Nov. 2, 1980)* Sterling ▲ CDS 1013

Soler, José (ten)
Giordano, U.:Andrea Chénier, w. Renata Tebaldi (sop), Ugo Savarese (bar), A. Basile (cnd), Turin RAI SO Fonit Cetra ("Classic Collection" series) 2-▲ FCT CDO 24
Verdi, G.:Il trovatore (sels), w. J. Biel (ten), F. Tamagno (ten), L.-A. Escalaïs (ten), M. Gilion (ten), E. Caruso (ten), A. Paoli (ten), G. Zenatello (ten), J. Sembach (ten), L. Slezak (ten), F. Constantino (ten), G. Martinelli (ten), B. De Muro (ten), N. Fusati (ten), N. Piccaluga (ten), G. Lauri-Volpi (ten), A. Pertile (ten), E. Bergamaschi (ten), R. Tauber (ten), J. O'Sullivan (ten), H. Roswaenge (ten), G. Taccani (ten), V. Lois (ten), H. Lazaro (ten), A. Lindi (ten), A. Cortis (ten), F. Merli (ten), F. Völker (ten), J. Kiepura (ten), J. Schmidt (ten), J. Bjoerling (ten), B. Gigli (ten), A. Salvarezza (ten), M. Filippeschi (ten)—34 performances of the Act III tenor aria "Di quella pira!," *(rec from 1903–1956)* Bongiovanni ▲ GB 1051 [AAD]

Soles, Nanette (mez)
Britten, H.:Hymn to St. Cecilia, w. Christine Goerke (sop), Matthew Pittman (ten), Leonard Ratzlaff (bass), Robert Shaw (cnd), Robert Shaw Festival Singers *(rec Church of St. Pierre, Gramat, France, July 26–28, 1994)* Telarc ▲ CD 80408 [DDD]
Debussy, C.:Chansons (3) de Charles d'Orléans, w. Julie McCoy (sop), Pam Elrod (mez), Charles Bruffy (ten), Leonard Ratzlaff (bass), Robert Shaw (cnd), Robert Shaw Festival Singers *(rec Church of St. Pierre, Gramat, France, July 26–28, 1994)* Telarc ▲ CD 80408 [DDD]
Ravel, M.:Chansons, w. Mara Bonde (sop), Charles Bruffy (ten), Bruce Tammen (bass), Robert Shaw (cnd), Robert Shaw Festival Singers *(rec Church of St. Pierre, Gramat, France, July 26–28, 1994)* Telarc ▲ CD 80408 [DDD]

Solman, Miro (sgr)
Marinuzzi, G.:Jacquerie, w. Ilaria Galgani (sop), Antonio Salvadori (bar), Martine Surais (sgr), A. Licata (cnd), Catania Teatro Massimo Bellini Orch, Catania Teatro Massimo Bellini Chorus *(rec Catania, 1994)* Nuova Era 2-▲ NUO 7200 [DDD]

Sólyom-Nagy, Sándor (bar)
Beethoven, L. van:Syms (comp), w. Éva Andor (sop), Márta Szirmay (cta), György Korondi (ten), J. Ferencsik (cnd), Hungarian State Orch, Miklós Forrai (cnd), Budapest Chorus *(rec 1969, 1971, 1974–76)* Classical Diamonds 6-▲ 4013–18 [ADD]
Beethoven, L. van:Sym 9, "Choral Sym", w. E. Andor (sop), H. Szirmay (cta), G. Korondy (ten), J. Ferencsik (cnd), Hungarian PO, Budapest Phil Chorus Laserlight ▲ 15 905
Erkel, F.:Bánk Bán, w. K. Agay (sop), E. Komlóssy (cta), J. Réti (ten), J. Simándy (ten), J. Ferencsik (cnd), Budapest PO, Hungarian State Opera Chorus [Hun] *(rec 1969)* Hungaroton 2-▲ HCD 11376/77 [ADD]
Erkel, F.:Hunyadi László, w. M. Kalmár (sop), S. Sass (sop), D. Gulyás (ten), A. Molnar (ten), I. Gáti (bar), J. Kovács (cnd), Hungarian State Opera Orch, Hungarian State Opera Chorus [Hun] Hungaroton 3-▲ HCD 12581/83 [DDD]
Kodály, Z.:Háry János, w. Takács (sgr), J. Gregor (bass), J. Ferencsik (cnd), Hungarian State Opera Orch [Hun] Hungaroton 2-▲ HCD 12837/38
Liszt, F.:Christus, w. Veronika Kincses (sop), Tamara Takács (mez), Robert Nagy (ten), László Polgár (bass), A. Dorati (cnd), Hungarian State Orch, Hungarian Radio-TV Chorus [L] Hungaroton 3-▲ HCD 12831/33 [DDD]
Liszt, F.:Hungaria 1848, w. M. Temesi (sop), A. Molnár (ten), I. Zámbó (cnd), Hungarian State Orch, Hungarian People's Army Male Chorus—composed as a salute to the Hungarian revolution [G] Hungaroton ▲ HCD 12748 [DDD]
Respighi, O.:La Fiamma, w. I. Tokody (sop), T. Takács (mez), P. Kelen (ten), L. Gardelli (cnd), Hungarian State Orch, Hungarian State Chorus [I] Hungaroton 3-▲ HCD 12591/93 [DDD]
Strauss, R.:Guntram, w. I. Tokody (sop), R. Goldberg (ten), I. Gáti (bar), E. Queler (cnd), Hungarian State Orch, Hungarian People's Army Male Chorus [G] CBS 2-▲ M2K 39737 [DDD]

Somigli, Franca (sop)
Verdi, G.:Falstaff, w. Augusta Ottrabella (sop—Nannetta), Franca Somigli (sop—Alice), Angelica Cravcenko (mez—Mrs. Quickly), Mita Vasari (mez—Meg), Dino Borgioli (ten—Fenton), Giuseppe Nessi (ten—Bardolfo), Alfredo Tedeschi (ten—Dr. Cajus), Piero Biasini (bar—Ford), Mariano Stabile (bar—Falstaff), Virgilio Lazzari (bass—Pistola), A. Toscanini (cnd), Vienna PO, Vienna State Opera Chorus *(rec Salzburg, Aug 23, 1937)* Minerva 2-▲ MN A36/37 (m) [ADD]

Sommer, Ditha (sop)
Wagner, R.:Der Ring des Nibelungen, w. Liselotte Becker-Egner (sop—Woglinde/Ortlinde/Wellgunde), Angelika Berger (sop—Wellgunde/Waltraute), Siw Ericsdotter (sop—Norn 3), Heidemaria Ferch (sop—Freia/Gerhilde), Bella Jasper (sop—Helmwige/Waldvogel/Woglinde), Ditha Sommer (sop—Sieglinde/Gutrune), Ursula Boese (mez—Erda), Ruth Hesse (mez—Fricka), Nadezda Kniplová (mez—Brünnhilde), Margit Kobeck (mez—Schwertleite/Norn 2), Hilde Rosner (mez—Flosshilde/Siegrunde), Erica Schubert (mez—Grimgerde/Flosshilde), Ingrid Göritz (cta—Rossweisse/Norn 1), Herbert Doussant (ten—Froh), Herold Kraus (ten—Mime), Gerald McKee (ten—Siegmund/Siegfried), Fritz Uhl (ten—Loge), Rudolf Knoll (bar—Gunther/Donner), Rolf Polke (bass-bar—Wotan/Wanderer), Rolf Kühne (bass—Alberich), Takao Okamura (bass—Fafner), Otto von Rohr (bass—Hagen/Fasolt/Hunding), H. Swarowsky (cnd), Czech PO, Prague National Theater Orch *(rec June 3 & 5, July 26–31, A)* Weltbild Classics 14-▲ 703769 [ADD]

Sommerschuh, Gerda (sop)
Mozart, W.A.:Nozze di Figaro, w. Irma Beilke (sop), Helena Braun (sop), Josef Witt (ten), Hans Hotter (bar), Erich Kunz (bar), Gustav Neidlinger (b-bar), C. Krauss (cnd), Vienna PO, Vienna State Opera Chorus *(rec live, Salzburg Festival, Aug. 1942)* Preiser 3-▲ PRE 90203 [ADD]
Wagner, R.:Götterdämmerung, w. Birgit Nilsson (sop—Brünnhilde), Leonie Rysanek (sop—Gutrune), Gerda Sommerschuh (sop—Woglinde), Elisabeth Lindermeier (sop—Wellgunde), Ruth Michaelis (sop—Flohilde), Marianne Schech (sop—Dritte Norne), Ira Malaniuk (mez—Waltraute), Irmgarth Barth (mez—Erste Norne), Hertha Töpper (mez—Zweite Norne), Bernd Aldenhoff (ten—Siegfried), Hermann Uhde (bar—Gunther), Gottlob Frick (bass—Hagen), H. Knappertsbusch (cnd), Bavarian State Opera Orch, Bavarian State Opera Chorus *(rec live, Prinzregententheater, Sept. 1, 1955)* Orfeo 4-▲ 356944 (m)

Song, J. (voc/kayagum)
Song, J.:Improvs, w. M. Turner (vc & voc [left channel])—Reclusive Prayer; Love & Fear; Dancing Dead; Colours; Harbor My Distant Whisper; Genealogy; Frontier Guard; Precious Few; Han River Elegy; Squirm und Drag; Stories O.O. Discs ▲ OO 10 [DDD]

Sonnenberg, Melanie (mez)
Brahms, J.:Alto Rhap, w. T. Seelig (cnd), Fort Worth CO, Turtle Creek Chorale *(rec Meyerson Symphony Center, Dallas, June 15–16, 1995)* Reference ▲ RR 67 [DDD]
Schubert, Franz:Choral Part-Songs, w. T. Seelig (cnd), Fort Worth CO, Turtle Creek Chorale—Ständchen *(rec Meyerson Symphony Center, Dallas, June 15–16, 1995)* Reference ▲ RR 67 [DDD]

Sonnenschmidt, Rosina (sop)
Isabella Leonarda:Motets, w. Sephira Ensemble Stuttgart [period instrs]—Alta del ciel regina (from Op. 14) & Veni amor, veni Jesu (from Op. 15) [L] Bayer 2-▲ 100078/79 [DDD]
Strozzi, B.:Arias & Cants, w. Sephira Ensemble Stuttgart—nine soprano arias & cantatas, from Opp. 2,6,7 & 8 [period instrs] [I,L] Bayer 2-▲ 100078/79 CD [DDD]

Sonnerstedt, Bernhard (bar)
Brahms, J.:Ein Deutsches Requiem, w. K. Lindberg-Torlind (sop), W. Furtwängler (cnd), Stockholm PO *(rec 1948)* Music & Arts 2-▲ CD 289 (m) [AAD]

Sonntag, Ulrike (sop)
Bach, Joh. Christian:Amadis des Gaules, w. Hobarth, Verebies, Wagner, Schöne, H. Rilling (cnd), Bach Collegium, Gächinger Kantorei [G] Hänssler Classic 2-▲ 98.963 [DDD]
Hindemith, P.:Das Unaufhörliche, w. Robert Wörle (ten), Siegfried Lorenz (bar), Artur Korn (bass), L. Zagrosek (cnd), Berlin RSO, Berlin Radio Chorus Wergo 2-▲ WER 66032
Milhaud, D.:Cataloque de fleurs, w. Irmela Nolte (fl), Deborah Marshall (cl), Michael Weigel (bn), Renate Eggebrecht (vn), Stefan Berg (va), Friedemann Kupsa (vc), Arpat György (db) *(rec Ludwigsburg, Germany, Jan. 1995)* Troubadisc ▲ TROCD 01410 [DDD]
Milhaud, D.:Machines agricoles, w. Irmela Nolte (fl), Deborah Marshall (cl), Michael Weigel (bn), Renate Eggebrecht (vn), Stefan Berg (va), Friedemann Kupsa (vc), Arpat György (db) *(rec Ludwigsburg, Germany, Jan. 1995)* Troubadisc ▲ TROCD 01410 [DDD]
Milhaud, D.:Qt 3 Strs, w. Fanny Mendelssohn String Quartet *(rec Ludwigsburg, Germany, Jan. 1995)* Troubadisc ▲ TROCD 01410 [DDD]
Milhaud, D.:Songs, w. Rudolf Jansen (pno) *(rec Sept. 1994)* Troubadisc ▲ TROCD 01409 [DDD]
Stravinsky, I.:Les Noces, w. C. Kallisch (cta), M. Schäfer (ten), P. Lika (bass), C. Rausch (bass), et al., W. Schäfer (cnd), Frankfurt Kantorei [G] Koch Schwann ▲ 314 021 [DDD]

Soomer, Walter (sgr)
Wagner, R.:Arias & Scenes, w. Emmy Destinn (sop), Lilly Hafgren (sop), Frida Leider (sop), Emmi Leisner (cta), Ernst Kraus (ten), Lauritz Melchoir (ten), Leopold Demuth (bar), Friedrich Schorr (b-bar), Michael Bohynen (bass), Paul Knupfer (bass), Richard Mayr (bass), Heinrich Hensel (sgr) Iron Needle ▲ 1307 (m)

Soós, Emese (sop)
Górecki, H.-M.:Sym 2, "Copernican Sym", w. Tamás Altorjay (bar), T. Pál (cnd), Fricsay SO Stradivarius ▲ STV 33324 [DDD]

Sopher, Joseph (ten)
Dittersdorf, K.D. von:Arcifanfano, King of Fools, or It's Always Too Late to Learn, w. P. Brooks (sop), A. Russell (sop), E. Steber (sop), J. McCollum (ten), H. Rehfuss (bar), D. Smith (bar), N. Jenkins (cnd), Clarion Music Society Orch, Clarion Music Society Chorus [E] *(rec live, New York 1965)* VAI Audio 2-▲ VAIA 1010-2 (m) [ADD]

Soranno, Anna (sop)
Parker, H.:Hora novissima, w. J. Simson (mez), K. Hall (b-bar), D. Andersen (b-bar), J. Levick (cnd), Nebraska CO, Abendmusik Chorus, Nebraska Wesleyan Univ Choir Albany 2-▲ TROY 124/25

Sordello, Enzo (bar)
Cilea, F.:Adriana Lecouvreur, w. M. Olivero (sop), M. L. Nave (mez), P. Domingo (ten), A. Silipigni (cnd), *(orch unknown)* [I] *(rec 1973)* Legato Classics 2-▲ LCD 140-2 [ADD]
Cilea, F.:Adriana Lecouvreur, w. L. Gencer (sop—Adriana), A. Lazzarini (mez—Princess), F. Ricciardi (ten—Abbot), A. Zambon (ten—Maurizio), E. Sordello (bar—Michonnet), A. Zerbini (bass—Prince), O. de Fabritiis (cnd), Naples Teatro San Carlo Orch, Naples Teatro San Carlo Chorus *(rec Dec. 17, 1966)* Golden Age of Opera 2-▲ GAO 143/44 [ADD]
Puccini, G.:Madama Butterfly, w. R. Tebaldi (sop), F. Cossotto (mez), C. Bergonzi (ten), T. Serafin (cnd), St. Cecilia Academy Orch Rome, St. Cecilia Academy Chorus Rome [I] London 2-▲ 425531-2 [ADD]
Puccini, G.:Madama Butterfly (sels), w. R. Tebaldi (sop), C. Bergonzi (ten), T. Serafin (cnd), St. Cecilia Academy Orch Rome, St. Cecilia Academy Chorus Rome London ▲ 417733-2 [ADD]
Puccini, G.:Madama Butterfly (sels), w. R. Tebaldi (sop), F. Cossotto (mez), C. Bergonzi (ten), T. Serafin (cnd), St. Cecilia Academy Orch Rome, St. Cecilia Academy Chorus Rome [I] London ("Opera Gala" series) ▲ 421873-2 [ADD]
Spontini, G.:La vestale, w. M. Callas (sop), N. Rossi-Lemeni (bass), F. Corelli (ten), V. Tatozzi (bar), N. Zaccaria (bass), A. Votto (cnd), La Scala Orch, La Scala Chorus Great Opera Performances ▲ GOP 741
Spontini, G.:La vestale, w. M. Callas (sop), F. Corelli (ten), A. Votto (cnd), La Scala Orch, La Scala Chorus [I] *(rec live, Milan, 12/7/54)* Melodram 2-▲ MEL 26008
Spontini, G.:La vestale (sels), w. M. Callas (sop), A. Corelli (bar), A. Votto (cnd), La Scala Orch, La Scala Chorus [I]—3 scenes *(rec live, Milan, 12/7/54)* Verona 2-▲ 28003/04
Verdi, G.:Il trovatore, w. M. Caballé (sop), P. Domingo (ten), K. Andersson (cnd), New Orleans Opera Orch, New Orleans Opera Chorus [I] *(rec live 3/14/68)* Melodram 2-▲ MEL 27047 [AAD]

Sorell, Christiane (sop)
Bach, J.S.:St. Luke Passion, w. Maura Moreira (alt), Kurt Equiluz (ten), Franz Wimer (bass), Josef Nebois (org), G. Barati (cnd), Vienna State Opera Orch, Akademie Chamber Choir Soloists Sarx 2-▲ SRX 2026 [ADD]
Haydn, J.:Mass 14, "Harmoniemesse", w. Elisabeth Thoman (sop), Rose Bahl (cta), Maura Moreira (cta), Kurt Equiluz (ten), Gerhard Eder (bass), P. Wimburger (bass), G. Barati (cnd), Vienna State Opera Orch, Vienna Academy Chamber Choir *(rec 1964)* Tuxedo ▲ TUXCD 1055 [ADD]

Sorell, L. (mez)
Wagner, R.:Das Liebesverbot, w. H. Zadek (cta), A. Dermota (ten), K. Equiluz (ten), L. Welter (bar), Imdahl (sgr), R. Heger (cnd), Austrian RSO, Austrian Radio Chorus *(rec live, Vienna, 1962)* Melodram 2-▲ MEL 27052 [AAD]

Sorensen, Marvin (ten)
Handel, G.F.:Judas Maccabaeus, w. Martina Arroyo (sop), Grace Bumbry (mez), J. McCollum (ten), D. Watts (bass), M. Abravanel (cnd), Utah SO, Utah Sym Chorus [E] *(rec ca. 1959; originally rele)* MCA Classics 3-▲ MCAD3-10515 [ADD]

Sörenson, Iwa (sop)
Lindberg, O.:Requiem, w. E. Thallang (alt), C. Solén (ten), E. Saedén (bass), O. Johansson (org), H. Kyhle (cnd), Stockholm Univ College of Music Orch, Englebrekt Church Oratory Choir *(rec Nov. 2, 1980)* Sterling ▲ CDS 1013
Stenhammar, W.:Sången, w. Anne Sofie von Otter (mez), Stefan Dahlberg (ten), Per-Arne Wahlgren (bar), H. Blomstedt (cnd), Swedish RSO, Swedish Radio Chorus, Stockholm State Academy of Music Chamber Choir, Adolf Fredrik Music School Children's Choir Caprice ▲ CAP 21358

Sorenson, Marvin (ten)
Honegger, A.:Le Roi David, w. Netania Davrath (sop), Jean Preston (mez), M. Singher (nar), M. Milhaud (nar), M. Abravanel (cnd), Utah SO [F] Vanguard Classics ▲ OVC 4038 [ADD]

Sormova, Nada (sop)
Fibich, Z.:The Romance of Spring, w. Karel Prusa (bass), F. Vajnar (cnd), Prague RSO, Prague Radio Chorus Supraphon ▲ SUP 3197
Smetana, B.:The 2 Widows, w. M. Machotková (sop), J. Zahradnicek (ten), F. Jílek (cnd), Prague National Theater Orch, Prague National Theater Chorus [Cz] *(rec 1975)* Supraphon 2-▲ SUP 11 2122 [AAD]

Sorokina, Tamara (sgr)
Mussorgsky, M.:Boris Godunov, w. Irina Arkhipova (mez—Marina Mnishek), Evgenya Verbitskaya (mez—Nurse to Xenia), Valentina Klepatskaya (sgr—Fyodor), Tamara Sorokina (sgr—Xenia), Anton Grigoryev (ten—Simpleton), Vladimir Ivanovsky (ten—Grigory, the Pretender), Gyorgy Shulpin (bar—Prince Shuisky), Alexey Geleva (bass—Varlaam), Ivan Petrov (bass—Boris Godounov), Mark Reshetin (bass—Pimen), Alexi Ivanov (sgr—Andrei Shchelkalov), Evgeny Kibkalo (sgr—Rangoni), A. Melik-Pashayev (cnd), Bolshoi Theater Orch, Bolshoi Theater Chorus *(rec Moscow, 1962)* Melodiya ("The Russian Opera" series) 3-▲ 74321-29349-2 [ADD]

Sotin, Hans (bass)
Beethoven, L. van:Fidelio, w. G. Janowitz (sop), L. Popp (sop), R. Kollo (ten), D. Fischer-Dieskau (bar), L. Bernstein (cnd), Vienna PO, Vienna State Opera Chorus [G] Deutsche Grammophon 2-▲ 419436-2 [ADD]
Beethoven, L. van:Fidelio, w. H. Behrens (sop), S. Ghazarian (sop), P. Hofmann (ten), T. Adam (b-bar), G. Solti (cnd), Chicago SO, Chicago Sym Chorus [G] London 2-▲ 410227-2 [DDD]
Haydn, J.:Mass 10, "Kriegsmesse", "Paukenmesse", w. Judith Blegen (sop), Brigette Fassbaender (mez), Claes Hakan Ahnsjö (ten), L. Bernstein (cnd), Bavarian RSO, Bavarian Radio Chorus [L] Philips ▲ 412734-2 [DDD]
Lortzing, A.:Der Wildschütz, oder Die Stimme der Natur, w. Edith Mathis (sop), Peter Schreier (ten), Gottfried Hornik (bar), B. Klee (cnd), Berlin State Chorus *(rec Berlin, 1982)* Berlin Classics 2-▲ BER 1143 [ADD]

Sotin, Hans (bass) (cont.)
Mahler, G.:Sym 8, w. Hanneke van Bork (sop), Ileana Cotrubas (sop), Heather Harper (sop), Brigit Finnila (mez), Marianne Dieleman (cta), William Cochran (ten), Hermann Prey (bar), B. Haitink (cnd), Royal Concertgebouw Orch Philips ("Solo" series) ▲ 446195-2
Mahler, G.:Sym 8, w. S. Jo (sop), C. Studer (sop), W. Meier (mez), K. Lewis (ten), T. Allen (bar), G. Sinopoli (cnd), Philharmonia Orch, Philharmonia Chorus, Southend Boys' Choir [G] Deutsche Grammophon 2-▲ 435433-2
Mozart, W.A.:Così fan tutte, w. M. Price (sop), L. Popp (sop), Y. Minton (mez), L. Alva (ten), G. Evans (bar), O. Klemperer (cnd), New Philharmonia Orch, John Alldis Choir EMI Classics 3-▲ CDMC 63845
Mozart, W.A.:Missa, K.427, w. I. Cotrubas (sop), K. Te Kanawa (sop), W. Krenn (ten), R. Leppard (cnd), New Philharmonia Orch, John Alldis Choir [L] EMI Classics ▲ CDC 47385
Still, W.G.:Tristan und Isolde, w. C. Ligendza (sop), R. Baldani (mez), H. Hopf (ten), A. Dermota (ten), G. Neidlinger (bass), C. Kleiber (cnd), Vienna State Opera Orch, Vienna State Opera Chorus *(rec Oct. 7, 1973)* Exclusive 3-▲ EXL 18 [ADD]
Still, W.G.:Tristan und Isolde, w. Catarina Ligendza (sop), Ruša Baldani (mez), Hans Hopf (ten), C. Kleiber (cnd), Vienna PO, Vienna State Opera Chorus *(rec Vienna, Oct. 7, 1973)* Pantheon 3-▲ PHE 6601 (m)
Stravinsky, I.:Oedipus Rex, w. A. S. von Otter (mez/sop), V. Cole (ten), N. Gedda (ten), S. Estes (bass), P. Chéreau (nar), E.-P. Salonen (cnd), Swedish RSO, *(chorus unknown)* Sony Classical ▲ SK 48057
Wagner, R.:Lohengrin, w. J. Norman (sop), E. Randová (mez), P. Domingo (ten), D. Fischer-Dieskau (bar), S. Nimsgern (b-bar), G. Solti (cnd), Vienna PO, Vienna State Opera Chorus [G] London 4-▲ 421053-2 [DDD]
Wagner, R.:Lohengrin, w. J. Norman (sop), E. Randová (mez), P. Domingo (ten), D. Fischer-Dieskau (bar), S. Nimsgern (b-bar), G. Solti (cnd), Vienna PO, Vienna State Opera Chorus [G] London ▲ 425530-2 [DDD]
Wagner, R.:Die Meistersinger von Nürnberg, w. Hannelore Bode (sop), Jean Cox (ten), Klaus Hirte (bar), Karl Ridderbusch (bass), S. Varviso (cnd), Bayreuth Festival Orch, Bayreuth Festival Chorus [1974] [G] Philips 4-▲ 434611-2 [ADD]
Wagner, R.:Die Meistersinger von Nürnberg, w. Hannelore Bode (sop), Jean Cox (ten), Klaus Hirte (bar), Karl Ridderbusch (bass), S. Varviso (cnd), Bayreuth Festival Orch, Bayreuth Festival Chorus [1974] Philips 32-▲ 434420-2 [ADD/DDD]
Wagner, R.:Parsifal, w. W. Meier (mez), P. Hofmann (ten), F. Mazura (bar), S. Estes (bass), M. Salminen (bass), J. Levine (cnd), Bayreuth Festival Orch, Bayreuth Festival Chorus [1985] [G] Philips 4-▲ 434616-2 [DDD]
Wagner, R.:Tannhäuser, w. H. Dernesch (sop), C. Ludwig (mez), A. Kollo (ten), H. Braun (bar), G. Solti (cnd), Vienna PO [Paris version] [G] London 3-▲ 414581-2 [ADD]

Sotkilava, Zurab (ten)
Mussorgsky, M.:Boris Godunov (sels), *(cnd & orch unknown)* Sony Classical ▲ SMK 57653
Russian Vocal School Russian Compact Disc ("Talents of Russia" series) ▲ RCD 16013 [ADD]
Tchaikovsky, P.:Eugene Onegin (sels), *(cnd & orch unknown)* Sony Classical ▲ SMK 57653
Tchaikovsky, P.:Iolanta (sels), *(orch unknown)* Sony Classical ▲ SMK 57653
Tchaikovsky, P.:Queen of Spades (sels), w. *(orch unknown)* Sony Classical ▲ SMK 57653

Soto, Eduardo (bass)
Meyerbeer, G.:L'Africiane, w. Montserrat Caballe (sop—Selika), Christine Weidinger (sop—Inez), Miriam Ucelay (mez—Anna), Placido Domingo (ten—Vasco de Gama), Guillermo Sarabia (bar—Nelusko), Juan Thomas (b-bar—High Priest of Brahma), Dimiter Petkov (bass—Don Pedro), Juan Pons (bass—Don Diego), Eduardo Soto (bass—Grand Inquisitor), A. de Almeida (cnd), Barcelona Teatro Liceo Orch, Barcelona Gran Teatro de Liceo Chorus *(rec Barcelona, Nov 27, 1977)* Legato Classics 2-▲ LCD 208-2 [ADD]

Soucek, Jaroslav (bar)
Foerster, J.B.:Eva, w. Eva Depoltová (sop), Anna Barová (mez), Leo Marian Vodicka (ten), F. Vajnar (cnd), Prague RSO, Prague Radio Chorus *(rec 1982)* Supraphon 2-▲ SUP 3001

Souez, Ina (sop)
Mozart, W.A.:Così fan tutte, w. L. Helletsgrüber (sop), I. Eisinger (sop), H. Nash (ten), W. Domgraf-Fassbüander (bar), J. Brownlee (bar), F. Busch (cnd), Glyndebourne Festival Orch, Glyndebourne Festival Chorus [I] *(rec 1935)* Pearl 3-▲ PEAS 9406 (m) [AAD]
Mozart, W.A.:Così fan tutte, w. Irene Eisinger (sop—Despina), Luise Helletsgruber (sop—Dorabella), Ina Souez (sop—Fiordiligi), Heddle Nash (ten—Ferrando), John Brownlee (bass—Don Alfonso), Willi Domgraf-Fassbaender (bass—Guglielmo), F. Busch (cnd), Glyndebourne Festival Orch, Glyndebourne Festival Chorus *(rec June 25-28, 1935)* Arkadia ("The 78's" series) 2-▲ 78011 [ADD]
Mozart, W.A.:Don Giovanni, w. L. Helletsgrüber (sop), A. Mildmay (sop), K. von Pataky (ten), J. Brownlee (bar), R. Henderson (bar), T. Franklin (bar), S. Baccaloni (bass), F. Busch (cnd), Glyndebourne Festival Orch, Glyndebourne Festival Chorus [I] *(rec 1936, orig. issued by HMV)* Pearl 3-▲ PEAS 9369 (m) [AAD]
Mozart, W.A.:Songs, w. M. Callas (sop), E. Grümmer (sop), E. Schwarzkopf (sop), R. Scotto (sop), T. Lemnitz (sop), E. Berger (sop), S. Jurinac (sop), E. Schumann (sop), E. Rethberg (sop), L. Lehmann (sop), N. Gedda (ten), J. McCormack (ten), H. Roswenge (ten), H. Nash (ten), T. Gobbi (bar), G. Hüsch (bar), E. Kunz (bar), G. Frick (bass), E. Pinza (bass), A. Kipnis (bass) EMI Classics 4-▲ CDMD 63750

Soukupová, Věra (mez)
Beethoven, L. van:Sym 9, "Choral Sym", w. Gabriela Benackova-Cápova (sop), Vilem Pribyl (ten), Karel Prusa (bass), L. von Matačić (cnd), Czech PO Praga ▲ PR 250076
Dvořák, A.:Biblical Songs, Op. 99, w. Ivan Moravec (pno) Supraphon ▲ SUP 0206 [AAD]
Dvořák, A.:Rusalka, w. G. Beňačkova (sop), W. Ochman (ten), R. Novák (bass), V. Neumann (cnd), Czech PO, Prague Phil Chorus [Cz] Supraphon 3-▲ 10 3641 [DDD]
Dvořák, A.:Rusalka, w. G. Beňačkova (sop), W. Ochman (ten), R. Novák (bass), V. Neumann (cnd), Czech PO, Prague Phil Chorus [Cz] Supraphon Collection ▲ 11 0617-2 [DDD]
Dvořák, A.:Rusalka (sels), w. Gabriela Benačková (sop), Richard Novák (bass), V. Neumann (cnd), Czech PO, Czech Chorus Supraphon ▲ SUP 112252 [DDD]
Dvořák, A.:St Ludmilla, w. Eva Zikmundová (mez), Beno Blachut (ten), Richard Novák (bass), V. Smetáček (cnd), Prague SO, Czech Phil Chorus *(rec 1963)* Supraphon 2-▲ SUP 112141 [AAD]
Janácek, L.:Amarus, w. Vilém Přibyl (ten), F. Jílek (cnd), Czech PO, Josef Veselka (cnd), Prague Phil Chorus *(rec Czech Raio Broadcast, 1974)* Praga ▲ PR 250100
Janácek, L.:The Diary of One Who Disappeared, w. Stepanka Stepanova (mez), Beno Blachut (ten), Nicolai Gedda (ten), Josef Paleníček (pno), Prague Radio Women's Chorus, Czech Chamber Singers Female Chorus—contains 2 complete performances *(rec 1984 & 1956)* Supraphon ▲ SUP 0022 [DDD/ADD]
Janácek, L.:Slavonic Mass, w. Gabriela Benacková (sop), Frantisek Livora (ten), Karel Pruss (bass), V. Neumann (cnd), Czech PO, Czech Phil Chorus Panton ▲ PAN 811217
Kabeláč, M.:Cradlesongs Supraphon ▲ SUP 3020
Smetana, B.:The Brandenbergers in Bohemia, w. A. Vetava (ten), K. Kalas (bar), J.H. Tichý (cnd), Prague National Theater Orch, Prague National Theater Chorus [G] Supraphon 2-▲ SUP 111802 [AAD]
Smetana, B.:Libuše, w. G. Benackova (sop), V. Zitek (ten), Z. Košler (cnd), Prague National Theater Orch, Prague National Theater Chorus Supraphon 3-▲ SUP 111276 [DDD]
Smetana, B.:The Secret, w. Daniela Šounová-Brouková (sop), Leo Marian Vodička (ten), Z. Košler (cnd), Prague National Theater Orch Supraphon 2-▲ SUP 112177 [ADD]
Smetana, B.:Viola, w. Daniela Šounová-Brouková (sop), Leo Marian Vodička (ten), Z. Košler (cnd), Prague National Theater Orch Supraphon ▲ SUP 112177 [ADD]
Wagner, R.:Der Ring des Nibelungen, w. B. Nilsson (sop), L. Rysanek (sop), K. Dvořaková (sop), M. Mödl (sop), A. Burmeister (mez), V. Soukupova (mez), E. Wohlfahrt (ten), W. Windgassen (ten), T. Stewart (bar), T. Adam (b-bar), G. Neidlinger (b-bar), K. Böhme (bass), G. Nienstedt (bass), K. Böhm (cnd), Bayreuth Festival Orch, Bayreuth Festival Chorus [G] *(rec live, 1966-67)* Philips 14-▲ 420325-2 [ADD]

Souleimanov, Stanislav (bass)
Rimsky-Korsakov, N.:Christmas Eve, w. Ekaterina Koudriavtchenko (sop), Elena Zaremba (mez), Vladimir Bogtatchov (ten), Alexei Maslennikov (ten), Viatcheslav Voinarovski (ten), Viatcheslav Verestnikov (bar), Maxime Mikhailov (bass), M. Yurovski (cnd), Moscow Forum Theater Orch, Yurloff Academic Choir Russian Season 4-▲ CMX 388054

▲ = CD ♦ = Enhanced CD Δ = MD ■ = Cassette Tape □ = DCC

Souliotis, Elena (sop)
Boito, A.:Mefistofele, w. R. Tebaldi (sop—Margheritta), E. Souliotis (sop—Elena), M. Mackenzie (mez—Marta), M. Ruggiero (mez—Pantalis), A. Kraus (ten—Faust), H. Kraus (ten—Wagner), N. Ghiaurov (bass—Mefistofele), N. Sanzogno (cnd), *(orch unknown)* Ornamenti 2-▲ FE 101
Mussorgsky, M.:Khovanshchina, w. Mietta Sighele (sop—Emma), Elena Souliotis (sop—Susanna), Fiorenza Cossotto (mez—Marfa), Herbert Handt (ten—Scribe), Veriano Luchetti (ten—Prince Andrey Khovansky), Ludovic Spiess (ten—Prince Vasily Golitsin), Claudio Strudthoff (ten—Streshnev), Angelo Marchiandi (bar—Kuz'ka), Teodoro Rovetta (bar—1st Strel'tsi), Siegmund Nimsgern (b-bar—Shaklovity), Cesare Siepi (b-bar—Dosifey), Carlo del Bosco (bass—2nd Strel'tsi), Ubaldo Carosi (bass—Varsonofiev), Nicolai Ghiaurov (bass—Prince Ivan Khovnasky), Giovanni Sciarpeletti (bass—Pastor), B. Leskovich (cnd), Rome RAI SO, Rome RAI Chorus—also includes bonus Act V [w Boris Christoff] (Rome, 1958) *(rec Rome, 1973)* Bella Voce 3-▲ BLV 107.402 [AAD]

Souljois, Elena (sop)
Puccini, G.:Il trittico, w. M. Freni (sop), G. Giacomini (ten), R. Alagna (ten), J. Pons (bar), L. Nucci (bar), B. Bartoletti (cnd), Florence Maggio Musicale Orch, Florence Maggio Musicale Chorus London 3-▲ 436261-2 [DDD]

Soumagnas, Jean-Louis (sgr)
Gounod, C.:Le Médecin malgré lui, w. Lina Dachary (sop), Monique Stiot (mez), Michel Hamel (ten), Joseph Peyron (ten), Christophe Benoit (bar), Janine Capderou (sgr), J.-C. Hartemann (cnd), ORTF Lyric Orch Musidisc ▲ MUS 202322 [AAD]

Šounová-Brouková, Daniela (sop)
Dvořák, A.:The Jacobin, w. V. Přibyl (ten), K. Berman (bass), J. Pinkas (cnd), Brno State PO, Kühn Chorus Supraphon 2-▲ SUP 11 2190 [AAD]
Smetana, B.:The Secret, w. Vera Soukupová (mez), Leo Marian Vodička (ten), Z. Košler (cnd), Prague National Theater Orch Supraphon 2-▲ SUP 112177 [ADD]
Smetana, B.:Viola, w. Vera Soukupová (mez), Leo Marian Vodička (ten), Z. Košler (cnd), Prague National Theater Orch Supraphon ▲ SUP 112177 [ADD]

Southwick, Shauna (sop)
Mahler, G.:Sym 8, w. Oksana Krovytska (sop—Magna Peccatrix), Sheila Smith (sop—Una poenitentium), Shauna Southwick (sop—Mater gloriosa), Kristine Jepson (mez—Maria Aegyptiaca), Julie Simson (mez—Mulier Samaritana), Kurt Hansen (ten—Doctor Marianus), Brian Steele (bar—Pater ecstaticus), Eugene Green (b-bar—Pater profundus), R. Olson (cnd), Colorado MahlerFest Orch, Colorado MahlerFest Chorale, Colorado Mormon Chorale, Colorado Children's Chorale *(rec MahlerFest VIII, Boulder, CO, Jan 14-15, 1995)* MahlerFest 2-▲ MF8-1

Soutter, Winifred (sop)
Horder, M.:Songs (40), w. Peter Allanson (bar), Carl Murray (bar), Stephen Betteridge (pno), Gordon Kirkwood (pno) Symposium ▲ 1039

Souza, Noemi (cta)
Verdi, G.:Rigoletto, w. Renata Scotto (sop—Gilda), Stella Maris Silva (sop—Giovanna), Martha Carrizo (mez—Page), Carmen de la Mata (mez—Countess Ceprano), Noemi Souza (cta—Maddalena), Horacio Mastrango (ten—Borso), Richard Tucker (ten—Duke of Mantua), Cornell MacNeil (bar—Rigoletto), Riccardo Yost (bar—Marullo), Guerrino Boschetti (bass—Usher), Tulio Gagliardo (bass—Count Ceprano), Victor de Narké (bass—Monterone), William Wilderman (bass—Sparafucile), F. Previtali (cnd), Buenos Aires Teatro Colón Orch, Buenos Aires Teatro Colón Chorus *(rec Colon Theater, Buenos Aires, Aug. 22, 1967)* Legato Classics 2-▲ LCD 198-2

Souzay, Gérard (bar)
Berlioz, H.:L'Enfance du Christ, w. F. Kopleff (cta), C. Valletti (ten), G. Tozzi (bass), C. Munch (cnd), Boston SO, New England Conservatory Chorus RCA Gold Seal 2-▲ 09026-61234-2
Berlioz, H.:L'Enfance du Christ, w. Florence Kopleff (cta), Ceasare Valletti (ten), Lucien Oliver (bar), Giorgio Tozzi (bass), C. Munch (cnd), Boston SO, New England Conservatory Chorus *(rec Dec 1956)* RCA Victor Gold Seal 8-▲ 0902-668444-2 [ADD]
Boismortier, J.B. de:L'Automne, w. J.-F. Paillard (cnd), Jean-François Paillard CO Erato ▲ ERA 97416 [ADD]
Campra, A.:Cants françaises, w. J.-F. Paillard (cnd), Jean-François Paillard CO—Les femmes Erato ▲ ERA 97416 [ADD]
Courbois, P.:Dom Quichotte, w. J.-F. Paillard (cnd), Jean-François Paillard CO Erato ▲ ERA 97416 [ADD]
Duparc, H.:Songs, w. Dalton Baldwin (pno)—L'invitation au voyage; Extase; Phidylé; Le manoir de Rosemonde; Lamento; Soupir [F] Denon ▲ CO 2252 [DDD]
Fauré, G.:La bonne chanson, w. Dalton Baldwin (pno) [F] Denon ▲ CO 2252 [DDD]
Fauré, G.:Requiem, w. S. Danco (sop), E. Ansermet (cnd), Swiss Romande Orch, Tour de Peliz Union Chorus London ("Weekend Classics" series) ▲ 421026-2 [AAD]
Fauré, G.:Songs, w. Ameling (sop), D. Baldwin (pno) [complete edition of Fauré's songs] EMI Classics 4-▲ CDMD 64079
Massenet, J.:Manon, w. B. Sills (sop), N. Gedda (ten), G. Bacquier (bar), J. Rudel (cnd), New Philharmonia Orch, Ambrosian Opera Chorus [F] EMI Classics ("Studio" series) 3-▲ CDMC 69831 [ADD]
Poulenc, F.:Songs, w. E. Ameling (sop), D. Baldwin (pno)—complete EMI Classics 4-▲ CDMD 64087
Rameau, J.P.:Castor et Pollux, w. M. Schéle (sop), J. Scovotti (sop), R. Leanderson (bar), J. Villisech (bass), N. Harnoncourt (cnd), Vienna Concentus Musicus Teldec 4-▲ 42510-2
Rameau, J.P.:Thétis, w. J.-F. Paillard (cnd), Jean-François Paillard CO Erato ▲ ERA 97416 [ADD]
Ravel, M.:Don Quichotte à Dulcinée, w. Dalton Baldwin (pno) [F] Denon ▲ CO 2252 [DDD]

Soville, Floriana (mez)
Fioravanti, V.:Le cantatrici villane, w. G. Manci (sop—Agata), M. Mauro (sop—Nunziella), M. A. Peters (sop—Rosa), F. Sovilla (mez—Giannetta), E. Palacio (ten—Carlino), G. Gatti (bar—Don Bucefalo), D. Serraiocco (bass—Don Marco), R. Tigani (cnd), Frosinone Licinio Refice Conservatory SO *(rec Oct. 22, 23 & 25, 1992; [])* Bongiovanni 2-▲ GB 2135/36 [DDD]

Sovilla, Floriana (sop)
Donizetti, G.:Imelda de' Lambertazzi, w. D. D'Auria (sop), F. Tenzi (ten), A. Martin (bar), G. Sarti (bar), M. Andreae (cnd), Swiss-Italian Radio-TV Orch, Swiss-Italian Radio-TV Chorus [I] *(rec live)* Nuova Era 2-▲ 6778/79 [DDD]

Sowiak, Oksana (mez)
Lutoslawski, W.:Die Strohkette, w. Barbara Miller (sop), Robert Dohn (fl), Willy Schnell (ob), Martin Klose (cl), Hartmut Stute (cl), Karl Steinbrecher (bn), A. Grüber (cnd) Vox Box 2-▲ CDX 5133

Soxman, David (bass)
Moore, D.:Devil & Daniel Webster, w. Joyce Guyer (sop—Mary Stone), Benjamin Bongers (ten—Walter Butler), Michael Philip Davis (ten—Simon Girty), Matthew Foerschler (ten—Miser Stephens), Darren Keith Woods (ten—Mr. Scratch), Michael Lanman (bass—Blackbeard Teach), David Soxman (bass—Clerk), Brian Steele (bass—Daniel Webster), John Stephens (bass—Jabez Stone), Andrew Stuckey (bass—King Philip), Robert Gibby Brand (actor), Cary Miller (actor), R. Patterson (cnd), Kansas City SO, Kansas City Lyric Opera Chorus *(rec Sept 1995)* Newport Classic ▲ NPD 85585 [DDD]

Soyer, Roger (bass)
Berlioz, H.:La Damnation de Faust, w. M. Horne (mez—Marguerite), N. Gedda (ten—Faust), R. Soyer (bass—Mephistofeles), D. Petkov (bass—Brander), G. Prêtre (cnd), Rome RAI SO, Rome RAI Chorus *(rec live 1/11/69)* Arkadia 4-▲ 461 [ADD]
Berlioz, H.:L'Enfance du Christ, w. Victoria de los Angeles (sop), Nicolai Gedda (ten), Ernest Blanc (bar), A. Cluytens (cnd), Paris Conservatory Societé des Concerts Orch, René DuClos Chorus EMI Classics ("Doublefforte" series) 2-▲ CDFB 68586
Berlioz, H.:Les Troyens, w. B. Lindholm (sop), J. Veasey (mez), J. Vickers (ten), P. Glossop (bar), C. Davis (cnd), Royal Opera House Orch [F] Philips 4-▲ 416432-2 [ADD]
Bizet, G.:Les Pêcheurs de perles, w. I. Cotrubas (sop), A. Vanzo (ten), G. Sarabia (bar), G. Prêtre (cnd), Paris Opera Orch, Paris Opera Chorus Classics for Pleasure ▲ CDCFP 4721 [ADD]
Delibes, L.:Lakmé, w. M. Mesplé (sop), D. Millet (sop), C. Burles (ten), A. Lombard (cnd), Paris Opéra-Comique Orch, Paris Opéra-Comique Chorus EMI Classics 2-▲ CDCB 49430
Delibes, L.:Lakmé (sels), w. M. Mesplé (sop), D. Millet (sop), C. Burles (ten), A. Lombard (cnd), Paris Opéra-Comique Orch, Paris Opéra-Comique Chorus EMI Classics ▲ ZDM 63447

Soyer, Roger (bass) (cont.)
Donizetti, G.:Maria Stuarda, w. J. Sutherland (sop), H. Tourangeau (mez), L. Pavarotti (ten), J. Morris (bass), R. Bonynge (cnd), Bologna Teatro Comunale Orch, Bologna Teatro Comunale Chorus [I] London 2-▲ 425410-2 [ADD]
Rameau, J.P.:Dardanus, w. C. Eda-Pierre (sop), F. von Stade (mez), G. Gautier (ten), J. Van Dam (b-bar), R. Leppard (cnd), Paris Lyon Opera Orch, Paris Lyon Opera Chorus Erato 2-▲ 95312-2
Schubert, Ferdinand:Requiem, w. D. Degos (trb), K. Markus (ten), J. Galard (org), J.-P. Lore (cnd), French Oratorio Orch, J.-P. Lore Vocal Ensemble, Petits Chanteurs de Notre Dame de la Joie *(rec Nov. 9-11, 1980 & Jan. 25)* Esoldun ▲ MOS 1003 [ADD]
Schubert, Franz:Requiem, w. D. Degos (trb), K. Markus (ten), J. Galard (org), J.-P. Lore (cnd), French Oratorio Orch, J.-P. Lore Vocal Ensemble, Petits Chanteurs de Notre Dame de la Joie *(rec Nov. 9-11, 1980 & Jan. 25)* Esoldun ▲ MOS 1003 [ADD]

Spacagna, Maria (sop)
Cilea, F.:L'Arlesiana, w. E. Zilio (mez), P. Kelen (ten), B. Póka (bar), T. Clementis (bass), C. Rosekrans (cnd), Hungarian State Orch, Hungarian State Chorus Quintana 2-▲ QUI 903067/68
Delibes, L.:Lakmé, w. M. Spacagna (sop—Ellen), R. Welting (sop—Lakmé), A. Kraus (ten—Gérald), D. Holloway (bar—Frédéric), P. Plishka (bass—Nilakantha), N. Rescigno (cnd), Dallas Civic Opera Orch *(rec Nov. 1980)* Ornamenti 2-▲ FE 108 [ADD]
Mascagni, P.:Lodoletta, w. P. Kelen (ten), B. Szilágyi (bar), M. Kálmándi (bar), L. Polgár (bass), C. Rosekrans (cnd), Hungarian State Orch, Hungarian State Choruses [I] Hungaroton 2-▲ HCD 31307/08 [DDD]
Puccini, G.:Madama Butterfly, w. Sharon Grahm (mez), Vivica Genaux (mez), Richard di Renzi (ten), Richard Markley (ten), Erich Parce (bar), James Butler (bass), C. Rosenkrans (cnd), Hungarian State Opera Orch, Anikó Katona (cnd), Hungarian State Opera Chorus—3 versions *(rec Italian Institute, Budapest, Sept 5-21, 1995)* Vox Classics 4-▲ VOX4 7525 [DDD]

Špaček, Jozef (bar)
Puccini, G.:Tosca (sels), w. Nelly Miricioiu (sop—Tosca), Giorgio Lamberti (ten—Cavaradossi), Miroslav Dvorsky (ten—Spoletta), Silvano Carroli (bar—Baron Scarpia), Jozef Spaček (bar—Sacristan), Jan Durco (bass—Sciarrone), Stanislav Benačka (bass—Gaoler), A. Rahbari (cnd), Czech-Slovak RSO Bratislava, Slovak Phil Chorus *(rec Concert Hall of the Slovak Radio, Bratislava, Apr. 7-14, 1990)* Naxos ▲ 8.553153 [DDD]
Verdi, G.:Rigoletto, w. A. Ferrarini (sop), Y. Ramiro (ten), E. Tumagian (bar), A. Rahbari (cnd), Czech-Slovak RSO Bratislava, Slovak Phil Chorus [I] Naxos 2-▲ 8.660013/14 [DDD]

Špaček, Jozef (bass)
Verdi, G.:La traviata (sels), w. Monika Krause (sop), Ivica Neshybová (sop), Rannveig Braga (mez), Yordy Ramiro (ten), Gerog Tichy (bar), Ladislav Neshyba (bass), A. Rahbari (cnd), Czech-Slovak RSO Bratislava, Jan Rozehnal (cnd), Slovak Phil Chorus—Prelude act I; Libiam ne'lieti calici; Un dí, felice; È strano! Ah, fors'e lui; Follie!...sempre libera; Lunge da lei...de'miei bollenti spiriti; O Mio rimorosol; Pura si come un angelo...Dite alla giovine; Dammi tu forza; Di Provenza il mar; Noi siamo zingarelle; Prelude act III; Teneste la promessa...Addio del passato; Signora! Che t'accade?; Ah, Violetta! *(rec Bratislava Concert Hall, Dec 1990)* Naxos ▲ 8.553041 [DDD]

Spada, Enrico (sgr)
Verdi, G.:Otello, w. Maria Carbone (sgr), Nicola Fusati (ten), Piero Girardi (ten), Corrado Zambelli (ten), Apollo Granforte (bar), C. Sabajno (cnd), La Scala Orch, La Scala Chorus Grammofono 2000 2-▲ GRM 78651

Spägele, Mona (sop)
Luneburg 1647, w. Ensemble Lanterly, Werner Buchin (alt), Albrecht Pohl (bass) MD + G ▲ MDG CD 6050647
Schelle, J.:Actus Musicus auf Weyh-Nachten, w. Wilfried Jochens (ten), H. Arman (cnd), Schütz Academy *(rec Dec 15-18, 1992)* Capriccio ▲ 10508 [DDD]
Schütz, H.:Cantiones sacrae, w. Ralf Popken (alt), Rogers Covey-Crump (ten), John Potter (ten), Peter Kooj (bass), Thomas Ihlenfeldt (chit), Manfred Cordes (org)—complete 40 motets CPO 2-▲ 999405-2 [DDD]
Schütz, H.:Weihnachtshistorie, w. Wilfried Jochens (ten), H. Arman (cnd), Schütz Academy *(rec Dec 15-18, 1992)* Capriccio ▲ 10508 [DDD]

Spagnoli, Pietro (bar)
Carissimi, G.:Oratorio della Santissima Vergine, w. P. Borri (sop), A. M. Ferrante (sop), P. Pace (sop), A. Christofellis (alt), L. Petroni (ten), F. Sclaverano (ten), R. Abbondanza (bass), M. Mondelli (bass), F. Colusso (cnd), Seicentonovecento Ensemble [I] Bongiovanni ▲ GB 10011 [DDD]
Carissimi, G.:Oratorio di Daniele Profeta, w. P. Borri (sop), A. M. Ferrante (sop), P. Pace (sop), A. Christofellis (alt), L. Petroni (ten), F. Sclaverano (ten), R. Abbondanza (bass), M. Mondelli (bass), F. Colusso (cnd), Seicentonovecento Ensemble [I] Bongiovanni ▲ GB 10011 [DDD]
Donizetti, G.:L'elisir d'amore, w. M. Devia (sop), B. Pratico (bar), M. Viotti (cnd), English CO, Tallis Chamber Choir Erato 2-▲ 4509-91701-2
Mascagni, P.:Messa di gloria, w. I. Zennaro (ten), F. Colusso (cnd), Seicentonovecento Ensemble Musicaimmagine ▲ MR 10001 [DDD]
Rossini, G.:Messa di gloria, w. A. C. Antonacci (sop), B. Manca Di Nissa (cta), F. Araiza (ten), R. Gambill (ten), S. Accardo (cnd), St. Cecilia Academy Orch Rome, St. Cecilia Academy Chorus Rome *(rec Mar. 1-2, 1992)* Ricordi ▲ RFCD 2012 [DDD]
Rossini, G.:La pietra del paragone, w. Tiziana Carraro (sop—Fulvia), Elisabetta Gutierrez (mez—Baronessa Aspasia), Sara Mingardo (cta—Clarice), William Matteuzzi (ten—Giocondo), Marco Camastra (bar—Pacuvio), Pietro Spagnoli (bar—Conte Asdrubale), Gioacchino Zarrelli (bar—Fabrizio), Josè Fardilha (bass—Macrobio), B. Aprea (cnd), Graz SO, Sluk Chamber Chorus Bratislava *(rec 1993)* Bongiovanni 2-▲ GB 2179/80 [DDD]
Rossini, G.:Il Signor Bruschino, w. P. Orciani (sop), K. Lytting (mez), L. Canonici (ten), F. Massa (ten), B. Praticò (bar), N. de Carolis (b-bar), M. Viotti (cnd), Turin PO [I] Claves 8-▲ CD 9200 [DDD]
Rossini, G.:Il Signor Bruschino, w. Patrizia Orciani (sop), Katia Lytting (mez), Luca Canonici (ten), Fulvio Massa (ten), Bruno Praticò (bar), Natale de Carolis (b-bar), M. Viotti (cnd), Turin PO Claves 2-▲ 50-8904/5
Rossini, G.:Tancredi, w. Sumi Jo (sop—Amenaide), Lucretia Lendi (mez—Roggiero), Anna Maria di Micco (mez—Isaura), Ewa Podles (cta—Tancredi), Stanford Olsen (ten—Argirio), Pietro Spagnoli (bar—Orbazzano), Ewald Demeyere (hpd), Lieven Baert (vc), Franck Coryn (db), A. Zedda (cnd), Collegium Instrumentale Brugense, Capella Brugensis *(rec Poissy Theatre & Centre Musical-Lyrique-Phonographique, Ile de France, Jan. 26-31, 1994)* Naxos ("Opera Classics" series) 2-▲ 8.660037/38 [DDD]

Spangenberg, Nils (sgr)
Nilsson, T.:Out of Earthly Night, w. Gudrun Bruna (sop), Marianne Mellnäs (sop), Kaysa Hälldin (alt), Lars Sjögren (ten), Göran Swartz (bass), Sture Hedin (sgr), Ola Kyhlberg (sgr), Lars Ljungman (sgr), Nils Philipson (sgr), Ulrik Quale (sgr), Britta Therén (sgr), Karl-Erik Welin (org), Torsten Nilsson (cnd), Oscar's Motet Choir *(rec Oscar's Church, Stockholm, Sweden, Apr 26-27, 1978)* BIS ▲ CD 138 [AAD]

Spani, Hina (sop)
Hina Spani Pearl ▲ PEA 9196
Hina Spani, w. La Scala Orch [cnd:Carlo Sabajno], double quintet [cnd:Gino Nastrucci] *(rec 1927-1930 for HMV)* Preiser ("Lebendige Vergangenheit" series) ▲ PRE 89037 (m) [AAD]
Verdi, G.:Otello (sels), w. C. Muzio (sop), R. Ponselle (sop), E. Caruso (ten), N. Fusati (ten), L. Melchior (ten), F. Merli (ten), F. Tamagno (ten), B. Franci (bar), V. Maurel (bar), R. Stracciari (bar), T. Ruffo (bar) *(rec 1906-1933)* Music Memoria ▲ 30219

Spani, Paul (ten)
Strauss (II), Joh.:Der Zigeunerbaron, w. Emmy Loose (sop—Arsena), Gerda Scheyrer (sop—Saffi), Elisabeth Fez (cta—Mirabella), Hilde Rössl-Majdan (cta—Czipra), Waldemar Kmentt (ten—Barinkay), Paul Spani (ten—Ottokar), Erich Kunz (bar—Homonay), Kurt Preger (bar—Zsupan), Eberhard Wächter (bass—Carnero), A. Paulik (cnd), Vienna State Opera Orch, Vienna State Opera Chorus *(rec Brahmssaal, Vienna, Austria, June 1956)* Vanguard Classics 2-▲ OVC 8082/83 [ADD]

Sparbo, Njål (bar)
Habbestad, K.:Moster Suite, w. Kristin Kjølberg (sop), Odd Lund (goat's hn), T. Mikkelsen (cnd), Lithuanian National SO, Oslo Phil Women's Chamber Choir Norway Music ▲ 2912
Habbestad, K.:One Night on Earth, w. T. Mikkelsen (cnd), Lithuanian National SO Norway Music 2-▲ 2911

Sparbo, Njål (bar) (cont.)
Nordheim, A.:Music of, w. Siri Torjesen (sop), I. Bergby (cnd), Bit 20 Ensemble—Magic Island; Tractatus; Part for 6 Basses; Aftonland [Evening Land]; 3 Voci; Part for Va, Hpd & Perc; Qt for Strs; Response for Org, Perc & Tape — Norway Music 2-▲ CD 4990

Sparer, Rachel (sop)
Mascagni, P.:Silvano, w. Rachel Sparer (sop—Matilde), Lorraine DiSimone (mez—Rosa), Joseph Wolverton (ten—Silvano), Bojan Knezevic (bar—Renzo), P. Tiboris (cnd), Bohuslav Martinů PO *(rec SUNY Performing Arts Center Theatre, Purchase, NY, May 23–25, 1995)* — Elysium ▲ GRK 707 [DDD]

Spataro, Tomaso (ten)
Cimarosa, D.:Gli Orazii e i Curiazzi, w. G. Simionato (mez), A. Vercelli (mez), G. Del Signore (ten), C. M. Giulini (cnd), Milan RAI SO, Milan RAI Chorus [I] *(rec live 4/13/52)* — Melodram 2-▲ CDM 29500 [AAD]

Späth, Christoph (ten)
Mozart, W.A.:Nozze di Figaro, w. C. Margiono (sop), B. Bonney (sop), I. Rey (sop), A. Murray (mez, P.–L. Lang (mez), P. Langridge (ten), T. Hampson (bar), K. Moll (bass), A. Scharinger (bass), K. Langan (bass), N. Harnoncourt (cnd), Royal Concertgebouw Orch, Netherlands Opera Chorus *(rec Amsterdam, May 1993)* — Teldec 3-▲ 90861-2 [DDD]

Spatzek, H. (sop)
Mozart, W.A.:Songs, w. C. Knebel (pno) — ARS Produktion ▲ ARS 368321 [DDD]
Stavenhagen, B.:Songs, w. T. Pfeiffer (bar), H.–R. Förster (cnd), Vogtland PO Greiz/Reichenbach — ebs ▲ ebs 6079 [DDD]

Speca, Paolo (bar)
Albanese, G.:Songs, w. Luana Gentile (sop), Antonella Trovarelli (sop), Marina Gentile (mez), Stefano Consolini (ten), Andrea De Mele (vn), Sirio Benedetto (sax), Roberto Rupo (pno)—Aria di Natale; Duettino e coro muto (w. Carlo Moreno) [both w. Giorgina Dell'Immagine, Tito Petralia (cnd), EIAR Orch & Chorus]; Passione (M. Gentile); Serenata (Speca); Alzati, o bella... (Trovarelli); Mattinata (Speca); Il sogno d'una suora (Trovarelli); Ninna Nanna (M. Gentile); Barcarola (Rupo); Madrigale (L. Gentile); Ninna nanna...900 (L. Gentile); Variazioni (L. Gentile); Non so qual io mi voglia... (L. Gentile); Io sono un augellin... (L. Gentile); Bravo, bene, bis...(va bene) (Consolini & Di Benedetto); Che caviale (Consolini); Ma non sapete chi sono io? (Consolini & L. & M. Gentile); Grappoli di stelle (Consolini); Notte di Capri (Consolini & Di Mele); Una rosa di ferro battuto (Consolini, Speca & L. & M. Gentile) *(rec Ortona, Teatro Zambra, Feb 21, 22, 23 & Mar 1 &)* — Bongiovanni ▲ GB 5054-2 [DDD]
Tosti, P.F.:Canti populari e romanze abruzzesi, w. C. Di Censo (sop), M. Gentile (mez), W. Omaggio (ten), I. Crissante (pno) — Nuova Era ▲ NUO 7166 [DDD]

Speiser, Elisabeth (sop)
Bach, J.S.:Cant 204, w. Helmuth Steinkraus (fl), Willi Schnell (ob), Dietmar Keller (ob), Susanne Lautenbacher (vn), R. Ewerhart (cnd), Württemberg CO *(rec 1966)* — Vox Box 3-▲ CD3X 3039
Bach, J.S.:Cant 208, "Hunting Cant", w. Helen Donath (sop), Wilfrid Jochims (ten), Jakob Stämpfli (bass), H. Rilling (cnd), Stuttgart Bach Collegium, Stuttgart Memorial Church Figuralchor *(rec Southwest Sound Studio, Stuttgart-Bottnang, May 1965)* — Musicaphon ▲ 51351 [AAD]
Bach, J.S.:Cant 209, w. Helmuth Steinkraus (fl), Martin Galling (hpd), R. Ewerhart (cnd), Württemberg CO *(rec 1966)* — Vox Box 3-▲ CD3X 3039
Bach, J.S.:Cant 211, "Coffee Cant", w. Wilfrid Jochims (nar), Elisabeth Speiser (sop—Lieschen), Claus Ocker (bass—Schlendrian), R. Ewerhart (cnd), Württemberg CO *(rec 1966)* — Vox Box 3-▲ CD3X 3039
Berg, A.:Schliesse mir die Augen beide, w. I. Gage (pno)—both versions [G] — Jecklin ▲ JD 561-2 [ADD]
Berg, A.:Songs, Op. 2, w. Irwin Gage (pno) [G] — Jecklin ▲ JD 561-2 [ADD]
Carissimi, G.:Cants Sop Kbd, w. H.L. Hirsch (hpd)—Lamento della Maria Stuarda *(rec 1979)* — Jecklin-Disco ▲ JD 5004-2 [ADD]
Fröhlich, F.T.:Choral Music, w. P. Steiner (ten), J. Krattiger (bass), B. Billeter (pno), C. Spring (pno), Winterthur Vocal Ensemble [G] *(rec 1988)* — Jecklin-Disco ▲ JD 627-2 [ADD]
Gluck, C.W.:Orfeo ed Euridice, w. E. Gale (sop), J. Baker (mez), R. Leppard (cnd), London PO — Erato 2-▲ 2292-45864-2
Handel, G.F.:German Arias, H.202-210, w. Kathy Gohl (vn), Jap Schröder (vn), Johann Sonnleitner (hpd) [G] *(rec 1984)* — Jecklin-Disco ▲ JD 589-2 [ADD]
Haydn, J.:Arianna a Naxos, w. John Buttrick (pno) [I] *(rec 1987)* — Jecklin-Disco ▲ JD 621-2 [ADD]
Haydn, J.:Canzonettas, w. John Buttrick (pno)—Nos. 32, 34, 41, 42, 50 [E] *(rec 1987)* — Jecklin-Disco ▲ JD 621-2 [ADD]
Kreutzer, C.:Das Mühlrad, w. H.–R. Stalder (cl), R. Junghanns (kbd) [period instrs] *(rec 1984)* — Jecklin-Disco ▲ JD 587-2 [ADD]
Martin, F.:Requiem, w. R. Bollen (cta), E. Tappy (ten), P. Lagger (bass), A. Luy (org), F. Martin (cnd), Swiss-Italian Orch, Union Chorale, Choir of Our Lady of Lausanne, Ars Laeta Vocal Group *(rec live, May 4, 1973)* — Jecklin-Disco ▲ JD 631-2 [ADD]
Mozart, W.A.:Notturnos Sops, w. V. Gohl (cta), K. Widmer (bass), H.R. Stalder (cl), R. Kubli (bas hn), H. Leuthold (bas hn) [I] *(rec 1968)* — Jecklin-Disco ▲ JD 549-2 [ADD]
Mozart, W.A.:Più non si trovano, w. V. Gohl (cta), K. Widmer (bass), H.R. Stalder (cl), R. Kubli (bas hn), H. Leuthold (bas hn) [I] *(rec 1968)* — Jecklin-Disco ▲ JD 549-2 [ADD]
Schoenberg, A.:Songs, Op. 2, w. I. Gage (pno) [G] *(rec 1981)* — Jecklin-Disco ▲ JD 561-2 [ADD]
Schubert, Franz:Songs (misc), w. J. Buttrick (pno)—20 songs [G] *(rec 1988)* — Jecklin-Disco ▲ JD 630-2 [ADD]

Speiss, Ludovic (ten)
Puccini, G.:Turandot, w. Teodora Lucaciu (sop—Liù), Maria Slatinaru (sop—Princess Turandot), Corneliu Finateanu (ten—Pong), George Mircea (ten—Emperor Altoum), Ludovic Speiss (ten—Prince Calaf), Valentin Teodorian (ten—Pang), Octav Enigarescu (bar—Ping), Dionisie Konya (bar—A Mandarin), Mircea Stefanescu (bar—The Prince of Persia), Nicolae Florei (bass—Timur), C. Litvin (cnd), Romanian Radio-TV Orch, Romanian Radio-TV Chorus *(rec Jan 1970)* — Vox Box 2-▲ CDX 5160
Verdi, G.:La forza del destino, w. Maria Nistor-Slatinaru (sop—Donna Leonora), Mihaela Mariacineanu (mez—Curra), Zenaida Pally (mez—Preziosilla), Ludovic Speiss (ten—Don Alvaro), Ion Stoian (ten—Trabucco), Nicolae Herlea (bar—Don Carlo), Nicolae Florei (bass—Padre Guardiano) Constantin Gabor (bass—Fra Melitone), Dan Musetescu (bass—An Alcalde), Mihai Panghe (bass—Marquis of Calatrava), C. Litvin (cnd), Romanian Radio-TV Orch, Romanian Radio-TV Chorus *(rec Jan 1970)* — Vox Box 3-▲ CD3X 3038

Spence, Patricia (mez)
Arne, T.:Artaxerxes, w. Catherine Bott (sop), Philippa Hyde (sgr), Christopher Robson (alt), Richard Edgar-Wilson (ten), Ian Partridge (ten), R. Goodman (cnd), Parley of Instruments — Hyperion ("The English Orpheus" series) 2-▲ CDA 67051/2
Bernstein, L.:Songfest, w. Linda Hohenfeld (sop), Wendy White (mez), Walter Plante (ten), Vernon Hartman (bar), John Cheek (bass), L. Slatkin (cnd), St. Louis SO — RCA Red Seal ▲ 09026-61581-2
Duruflé, M.:Requiem, w. François le Roux (bar), D. Keene (cnd), Voices of Ascension Orch, Voices of Ascension Chorus *(rec Church of the Ascension, New York City, June 5–6, 1994)* — Delos ▲ DE 3169 [DDD]
Handel, G.F.:Judas Maccabaeus, w. Linda Saffer (sop), Brian Asawa (ct), Guy de Mey (ten), Leroy Kromm (b-bar), David Thomas (bass), N. McGegan (cnd), Philharmonia Baroque Orch, Univ of California at Berkeley Chamber Chorus [E] *(rec Nov. 15–18, 1992)* — Harmonia Mundi USA 2-▲ HMU 907077/78
Handel, G.F.:Messiah, w. Lorraine Hunt (sop), Janet Williams (sop), Drew Minter (alt), Jeffery Thomas (ten), William Parker (bar), N. McGegan (cnd), Philharmonia Baroque Orch, Univ of California at Berkeley Chamber Chorus—standard version of Messiah *occupies the first sections of each of the three CDs, one part per disc. Each part is followed, after a significant pause, by alternative versions of certain sections of the preceding material, 13 altogether. [E]* — Harmonia Mundi USA 3-▲ HMU 907050/52
Handel, G.F.:Messiah (sels), w. Lorraine Hunt (sop), Janet Williams (sop), Drew Minter (alt), Jeffery Thomas (ten), William Parker (bar), N. McGegan (cnd), Philharmonia Baroque Orch, Univ of California at Berkeley Chamber Chorus [E] — Harmonia Mundi USA ("Nightingale" series) ▲ HMN 907601
Handel, G.F.:Messiah (sels), w. Lorraine Hunt (sop), Janet Williams (sop), Drew Minter (alt), Jeffery Thomas (ten), William Parker (bar), N. McGegan (cnd), Philharmonia Baroque Orch, Univ of California at Berkeley Chamber Chorus — Harmonia Mundi USA ▲ HMU 907120

Spence, Patricia (mez) (cont.)
Handel, G.F.:Ottone, Rè di Germania, w. Julianna Gondek (sop), Lisa Saffer (sop), Drew Minter (alt), R. Popken (alt), Michael Dean (b-bar), N. McGegan (cnd), Freiburg Baroque Orch *(rec June 9–12, 1992)* — Harmonia Mundi USA 3-▲ HMU 907073/75
Handel, G.F.:La Rezurrezione, w. Linda Saffer (sop), Judith Nelson (mez), Jeffery Thomas (ten), Michael George (bass), N. McGegan (cnd), Philharmonia Baroque Orch [I] — Harmonia Mundi USA 2-▲ HMU 907027/28

Spencer, Keith (bar)
Brahms, J.:Ein Deutsches Requiem, w. Marvis Martin (sop), T.M. Sleeper (cnd), Univ of Miami SO, Univ of Miami Chorale — Cane ▲ CR 1003

Sperlbauer (sgr)
Marschner, H.A.:Der Vampyr, w. L. Synek (sop), L. Heppe (ten), G. Oeggl (bar), Rathauscher (sgr), Skladal (sgr), Weise (sgr), K. Tenner (cnd), Vienna RSO, Vienna Radio Chorus [G] *(rec live, Vienna, 4/9/51)* — Memories 2-▲ HR 4466/67 [ADD]

Sperry, Paul (ten)
Kraft, William:The Sublime & the Beautiful, w. W. Kraft (cnd), Pittsburgh New Music Ensemble [E] *(rec 1984)* — CRI ▲ CD 639 [ADD/DDD]
Luening, O.:No Jerusalem But This, w. K. Sullivan (sop), Jacqueline Pierce (sop), M. Moliterno (bar), P. Wilder (sgr), S. Rosser (sgr), A. Goodman (cnd), Music Project CO, Goodman Chamber Choir [E] *(rec 6/6/90)* — CRI ▲ CD 600 [DDD]
Paul Sperry Sings American Cycles & Sets, w. Irma Vallecillo (pno) — Albany ▲ TROY 058 [DDD]
Paul Sperry Sings an American Sampler:From Billings to Bolcom, w. Irma Vallecillo (pno) — Albany ▲ TROY 081 [DDD]
Paul Sperry Sings Romantic American Songs, w. Irma Vallecillo (pno) — Albany ▲ TROY 043-2 [ADD]
Paulus, S.:Artsongs, w. I. Vallecillo (pno) [E] — Albany ▲ TROY 036-2 [DDD]
Rands, B.:Canti del Sole, w. C. Plantamura (sop), B. Rands (cnd), SONOR Ensemble of Univ of California San Diego — CRI ▲ CD 591 [ADD]
Songs of an Innocent Age, w. Irma Vallecillo (pno) — Albany ▲ TROY 034-2 [ADD]
Welcher, D.:Evening Scenes, w. D. Welcher (cnd), Voices of Change — Crystal ▲ CD 740
Wilson, R.:The Ballad of Longwood Glen, w. N. Allen (hp) — CRI ▲ CD 602 [ADD]

Spierting, Gert (ten)
Schütz, H.:St. John Passion, w. Herta Flebbe (sop), Johannes Hoeflin (ten—Evangelist), Rolf Bössow (ten—Pilate), Jakob Stämpfli (bass—Jesus), Teinhard Tuge (bass—soliloquies), W. Ehmann (cnd), Westphalia Kantorei *(rec Münster zu Herfor, Sept. 1961)* — Cantate ▲ 57602 [ADD]

Spiess, Ludovic (ten)
Classics Go to the Movies, Vol. 5, w. Hannes Käster (org), Salzburg Mozarteum Orch, Bavarian RSO, Ludovic Spiess (ten), Virginia Zeani (sop), Rumanian Opera Orch, Rumanian Radio-TV Studio Orch, Sofia PO, Budapest SO, Philharmonia Orch — LaserLight ▲ 15 645
Mussorgsky, M.:Khovanshchina, w. Mietta Sighele (sop—Emma), Elena Souliotis (sop—Susanna), Fiorenza Cossotto (mez—Marfa), Herbert Handt (ten—Scribe), Veriano Luchetti (ten—Prince Andrey Khovansky), Ludovic Spiess (ten—Prince Vasily Golitsin), Claudio Strudthoff (ten—Streshnev), Angelo Marchiandi (bar—Kuz'ka), Teodoro Rovetta (bar—1st Strel'tsi), Siegmund Nimsgern (b-bar—Shaklovity), Cesare Siepi (b-bar—Dosifey), Carlo del Bosco (bass—2nd Strel'tsi), Ubaldo Carosi (bass—Varsonofiev), Nicolai Ghiaurov (bass—Prince Ivan Khovnasky), Giovanni Sciarpeletti (bass—Pastor), B. Leskovich (cnd), Rome RAI SO, Rome RAI Chorus—also includes bonus Act V [w Boris Christoff] (Rome, 1958) *(rec Rome, 1973)* — Bella Voce 3-▲ BLV 107.402 [AAD]
Puccini, G.:La Bohème, w. Elvira Cirje-Druica (sop—Musetta), Eugenia Moldoveanu (sop—Mimi), Andrei Borsos (ten—Parpignol), Constantin Gabor (ten—Alcindoro), Ludovic Spiess (ten—Rodolfo), Lucian Marinescu (bar—Schaunard), David Ohanesian (bar—Marcello), Pompei Harasteanu (bass—Benoit), Dan Zancu (bass—Colline), C. Petrovici (cnd), Romanian Opera Orch, Romanian Opera Chorus *(rec 1982)* — Vox Box 2-▲ CDX 5156
Smetana, B.:Dalibor, w. L. Rysanek (sop), E. Wächter (bar), J. Krips (cnd), Vienna State Opera Orch, Vienna State Opera Chorus *(rec live, Vienna, 10/19/69)* — Myto 2-▲ 2 MCD 92465 [ADD]

Spina, Steve La (bass)
Red Square Blue Russian Composers, w. Fred Hersch (pno), James Newton (fl), Toots Thielemans (hmc), Phil Woods (a sax), Erik Friedlander (vc), Jeff Hirshfield (drums) — Angel ▲ CDC 54743

Spingler, Renate (sop)
Dessau, P.:Haggada, w. Sabine Ritterbusch (sop), Yvi Jänicke (alt), Peter Galliard (ten—Rabbi Tarfon/Jude/ten solo), Gabriel Sadé (ten—Pharaoh), Jochen Schmeckenbechier (bar—Rabbi Jehoschua), Bernd Weikl (bar—Moses), Matthias Hölle (bass—Speaker/Rabbi Akiwa), Alfred Muff (bass—Father/Rabbi Eleasar), Johann Tilli (bass—Rabbi Elieser/bass solo), G. Albrecht (cnd), Hamburg State PO, Berlin Carl Maria Von Weber Men's Choir, Hamburg Alsterspatzen, North German Radio Chorus [G] *(rec Musikhalle, Hamburg, Sept 4 & 5, 1994)* — Capriccio 2-▲ 10590/91 [DDD]
Liebermann, R.:Medea, w. Françoise Pollet (sop—Medea), Yvi Jänicke (cta—Chalkiope), Zdena Furmančoková (sgr—Syrinx), Dagmar Hesse (sgr—Aiglaia), Hanne Krogen (sgr—Kore), Michaela Lucas (sgr—Oinone), Renate Spingler (sgr—Silene), Jochen Kowalski (ct—Kreon), Aage Haugland (bass—Jason), G. Albrecht (cnd), Hamburg State PO, Hamburg State Opera Chorus *(rec live, Hamburg, Germany, Sept 24, 1995)* — Musiques Suisses ▲ 6126 [DDD]

Spinrad, Norman (voc)
East/West, w. Richard Pinhas (syns/gtr), Dominique E. (voc), Patrick Gauthier (syn), G. Grunblatt (syn), François Auger (perc), Steve Shehan (perc), Didier Batard (bass gtr) — Cuneiform ▲ Rune 31

Spitzer (bass)
Schubert, Franz:Mass 3, w. R. Hansmann (sop), M. Lipovšek (mez), J. Reinprecht (ten), F. Wolf (cnd), St. Augustin Orch, St. Augustin Chorus — Preiser ▲ 93325

Spoorenberg, Erna (sop)
Beethoven, L. van:Christus am Ölberg, w. Erna Spoorenberg (sop—Seraph), Fritz Wünderlich (ten—Jesus), Hermann Schey (bass—Petrus), H. Spruit (cnd), Netherlands Radio PO, Groot Omroep Choir *(rec Mar 8, 1957)* — Bella Voce ▲ 7003 [AAD]
Bizet, G.:Les Pêcheurs de perles, w. A. Vanzo (ten), J. Joris (bar), G. Hoekman (bass), J. Fournet (cnd), Netherlands Radio PO [F] *(rec live, 1963)* — Verona 2-▲ 2707/08 (m) [AAD]
Bizet, G.:Les Pêcheurs de perles (sels), w. Alain Vanzo (ten), J. Fournet (cnd), Groot Radio PO, Groot Chorus *(rec Amsterdam, 1963)* — Bella Voce 2-▲ 107.208
Gounod, C.:Roméo et Juliette, w. Alain Vanzo (ten), J. Fournet (cnd), Groot Radio PO, Groot Chorus *(rec Amsterdam, Jan 1966)* — Bella Voce 2-▲ 107.208

Sporka, Richard (ten)
Dvořák, A.:Armida, w. Joanna Borowska (sop—Armida), Monika Brychtová (sgr—Siren), Wieslaw Ochman (ten—Rinald), Richard Sporka (ten—Dudo), Jan Markvart (bar—Sven), Pavel Daniluk (bass—King), George Fortune (bass—Ismen), Zdenek Harvánek (bass—Ubald), Miloslav Podskalský (bass—Peter), Milan Bürger (sgr—Gernand), Roman Janál (sgr—Muezzin/Hlasatel), Vratislav Kříz (sgr—Gottfried), Vladimír Nacházel (sgr—Roger), G. Albrecht (cnd), Czech PO, Prague Chamber Choir *(rec 1995)* — Orfeo 2-▲ 404962 [DDD]
Mozart, W.A.:Missa, K.317, w. Ludmila Vernerova (sop), Marta Benackova (mez), Ladislav Nezhyba (bass), G. Delogu (cnd), Prague Virtuosi, Prague Chamber Choir *(rec Domovina Studio, Prague, June 4–6, 1994)* — Discover International ▲ DI 920260 [DDD]
Mozart, W.A.:Vesperae solennes, w. Ludmila Vernerova (sop), Marta Benackova (mez), Ladislav Nezhyba (bass), G. Delogu (cnd), Prague Virtuosi, Prague Chamber Choir *(rec Domovina Studio, Prague, June 4–6, 1994)* — Discover International ▲ DI 920260 [DDD]
Zelenka, J.D.:Missa sanctissimae trinitatis, w. Anna Hlavenková (sop), Magdalena Kozená (alt), Lubomir Moravec (alt), Stanislav Predota (ten), Michal Pospí il (bass), M. Stryncl (cnd), Musica Florea — Studio Matou ▲ MAT 17 [DDD]

Spotorno, Mariangela (sop)
Donizetti, G.:L'elisir d'amore, w. Alessandra Ruffini (sop—Adina), Mariangela Spotorno (sop—Gianetta), Vincenzo La Scola (ten—Nemorino), Simone Alaimo (bar—Dulcamara), Roberto Frontali (bar—Belcore), P.G. Morandi (cnd), Hungarian State Opera Orch, Anikó Katona (cnd), Hungarian State Opera Chorus *(rec Budapest, July 1995)* — Naxos 2-▲ 8.60045-6 [DDD]

Sprawls, Charles (bass)
Britten, H.:Rejoice in the Lamb, w. Susan Ashe (sop), Cynthia Calabrese (alt), Victor Floyd (ten), Alfred Calabrese (cnd), Britten Singers — ACA Digital Recording ▲ CM 20039

Springer, Ingeborg (mez)
Humperdinck, E.:Hänsel und Gretel, w. G. Schöter (sop), P. Schrier (ten), T. Adam (bar), O. Suitner (cnd), Dresden Staatskapelle, Dresden Kreuz Choir
Berlin Classics ("Eterna" series) 2-▲ BER 2007 [ADD]

Springer, Renate (sop)
Mozart, W.A.:Zauberflöte, w. Birgit Been (sop), Nathalie Boissy (sop), Marianne Seibel (sop), Elizabeth Vidal (sop), Eleanor James (mez), Salvador Guzman (ten), Herbert Hechenberger (ten), Wolfgang Newmann (ten), Klaus Häger (bass), Philip Langshaw (bass), Hans-Georg Moser (bass), P. Kuentz (cnd), Paul Kuentz Orch, Francis Bardot (cnd), Maitrise des Hauts-de-Seine members, Paul Kuentz Choirs
Pierre Verany 2-▲ PVY 730055 [DDD]

Springer, Robert (bar)
Bach, J.S.:St. John Passion, w. P. Curtin (sop), E. Thomann (sop), E. Alberts (cta), W. Kmentt, J. Van Kesteren (ten), O. Wiener (bar), D. Smith (b-bar), F. Guthrie (bass), F. Lukasowsky (bass), H. Scherchen (cnd), Vienna State Opera Orch, Vienna Academy Chorus [G] *(rec ca 1960)*
MCA Classics 2-▲ MCAD2-9804

Sramek, Alfred (bar)
Dvořák, A.:Mass, w. G. Schmid (sop), J. Bernheimer (mez), J. Reinprecht (ten), F. Wolf (cnd), St. Augustin Orch, St. Augustin Chorus [L] *(rec 1987)* Preiser ▲ 93378 [ADD]
Mozart, W.A.:Don Giovanni, w. L. Price (sop), L. Popp (sop), S. Sass (sop), S. Burrows (ten), G. Bacquier (bar), B. Weikl (bar), K. Moll (bass), G. Solti (cnd), London PO, London Opera Chorus
London ("Grand Opera" series) 3-▲ 425169-2 [ADD]

Stabell, Carsten (bass)
Jensen, L.I.:The Return, w. A. Bolstad (sop), R. Sterne (alt), H. Bjørkey (ten), I. Gilhuus (ten), P. Vollestad (bar), O.K. Ruud (cnd), Trondheim SO, Trondheim Sym Chorus, Nidarso Cathedral Choir
Simax 2-▲ PSC 3109
Mahler, G.:Sym 8, w. Majken Bjerno (sop), Henriette Bonde-Hansen (sop), Inga Nielsen (sop), Kirsten Dolberg (alt), Anne Gjevang (alt), Raimo Sirkiä (ten), Jorma Hynninen (bar), L. Segerstam (cnd), Danish National RSO, Copenhagen Boys' Choir, Berlin Phil Choir, Danish National Radio Choir
Chandos 2-▲ CHAN 9305/06 [DDD]

Stabile, Mariano (bar)
The Italian Vocal Tradition, Vol. 1:The Voices of Toscanini, w. Toti dal Monte (sop), Claudio Muzio (sop), Rosetta Pampanini (sop), Biata Scacciati (sop), Giacomo Lauri-Volpi (ten), Francesco Merli (ten), Aureliano Pertile (ten), Carlo Galeffi (bar), Riccardo Stracciari (bar), Nazzareno de Angel *(rec 1921-35)*
Iron Needle ▲ 1304
Mozart, W.A.:Don Giovanni, w. G. Grob-Prandl (sop), H. Konetzni (sop), A. Pernerstorfer (b-bar), O. Czerwenka (bass), H. Swarowsky (cnd), Vienna SO, Vienna State Opera Chorus *(rec 1950)*
Preiser 2-▲ PRE 90166 [AAD]
Mozart, W.A.:Nozze di Figaro, w. Jarmila Novotna (sop), Aulikki Rautawaara (sop), Esther Réthy (sop), Agostino Lazzari (ten), Ezio Pinza (bass), B. Walter (cnd), Vienna PO, Vienna State Opera Chorus *(rec live, 1937)* Melodram ▲ CDI 205003
Mozart, W.A.:Nozze di Figaro (sels), w. Elisabeth Schumann (sop), Ninon Vallin (sop) *(rec 1905 - 1944)*
Minerva ▲ MN A14 [ADD]
Puccini, G.:Manon Lescaut (sels), w. M. Favero (sop), R. Tebaldi (sop), J. Gardino (mez), G. Malipiero (ten), G. Nessi (ten), T. Pasero (b-bar), C. Forti (bass), A. Toscanini (cnd), La Scala Orch, La Scala Chorus—Intermezzo; Act 3 *(rec live, Milan, May 18, 1946)*
Arkadia ("Historical Performances" series) 2-▲ 604 (m)
Verdi, G.:Falstaff, w. Augusta Ottrabella (sop—Nannetta), Franca Somigli (sop—Alice), Angelica Cravcenko (mez—Mrs. Quickly), Mita Vasari (mez—Meg), Dino Borgioli (ten—Fenton), Giuseppe Nessi (ten—Bardolfo), Alfredo Tedeschi (ten—Dr. Cajus), Piero Biasini (bar—Ford), Mariano Stabile (bar—Falstaff), Virgilio Lazzari (bass—Pistola), A. Toscanini (cnd), Vienna PO, Vienna State Opera Chorus *(rec Salzburg, Aug 23, 1937)* Minerva 2-▲ MN A36/37 (m) [ADD]
Verdi, G.:Falstaff, w. Dino Borgioli (ten), Ismildo Tedeschi (ten), A. Toscanini (cnd), Vienna PO, Vienna State Opera Chorus *(rec live, Salzburg Festival, 1936)* Arkadia 2-▲ 625

Stacewicz, R. (sop)
Gorczycki, G.G.:Sacred Choral Music, w. I. Tkaczyk (alt), A. Pagowska (alt), E. Sasiadek (ten), W. Brychcy (bass), Wroclaw Orch, S. Galonski (cnd), Edmund Kajdasz (cnd), Capella Bydgostiensis Pro Musica Antiqua, Madrigalists Choir, Polish Radio Chorus—Completorium; In virtute tua; Iudica me deus; Laetatus sum; Missa paschalis [L] *(rec 1966)* Olympia ▲ OCD 320 [AAD]

Stade, Frederica von (mez)
Basic 100, Vol. 63, w. Judith Blegen (sop), Philadelphia Orch [cnd:Eugene Ormandy]
RCA Victor ▲ 09026-68088-2 ■ 09026-68088-4
Berlioz, H.:La Damnation de Faust, w. K. Riegel (ten), J. Van Dam (b-bar), G. Solti (cnd), Chicago SO, Chicago Sym Chorus London 2-▲ 414680-2 [DDD]
Bernstein, L.:Arias & Barcarolles, w. Thomas Hampson (bar), M. Tilson Thomas (cnd), London SO *(rec Henry Wood Hall, London, Sept 1993)* Deutsche Grammophon ▲ 439926-2 [DDD]
Bernstein, L.:Music of, w. J. Norman (sop), K. Te Kanawa (sop), J. Anderson (sop), C. Ludwig (mez), T. Troyanos (mez), J. Carreras (ten), D. Garrison (ten), J. Hadley (ten), T. Hampson (bar), T. Daly (sgr), G. Kremer (vn), M. Rostropovich (vc), M.T. Thomas (va), L. Bernstein (cnd), *(orch unknown)*—various popular works Deutsche Grammophon ▲ 439251-2 ■ 439251-4
Brubeck, C.:Songs, w. Jenny Elkus (sgr), Bill Crofut (sgr/banjo), Chris Brubeck (sgr/trbn/pno/db), Mark Vinci (fl), Frank Brown (cl), Edward Arron (vc), Dan Brubeck (dr/perc)—The Distance between Us; La Paloma azul; Strange Meadowlark; Across Your Dreams; Summer Song; Polly; Blue Rondo-A Tribute to Dave; Autumn in Our Town; Thinking of You Thinking of Me; It's a Raggy Waltz; Heart of Winter; In the Grace of Your Room; Lonely on Both Ends of the Road *(rec Sandisfield, MA; Fantasy Studios, Berkeley, CA)* Telarc ▲ CD 80467 [DDD]
Canteloube, J.:Songs of Auvergne, w. A. de Almeida (cnd), Royal PO CBS ▲ MK 37299 [DDD]
Cavalli, P.F.:Music of, w. R. Leppard (cnd), Scottish CO—Lamento di Cassandra; Lamento di Clori; Numi Ciechi Piodi Me Erato ▲ 98504-2
Debussy, C.:Pelléas et Mélisande, w. N. Denize (mez), G. Raimondi (ten), R. Stilwell (bar), J. Van Dam (bass-bar), H. von Karajan (cnd), Berlin PO, German Opera Chorus [F]
EMI Classics 3-▲ CDCC 49350 [ADD]
Debussy, C.:Songs, w. D. Baldwin (pno)—complete edition of Debussy's songs
EMI Classics 3-▲ CDMC 64095
Divas in Song:Marylin Horne, a 60th Birthday Celebration, w. Montserrat Caballé (sop), H. Donath (sop), R. A. Swenson (sop), R. Fleming (mez), S. Ramey (bass), J. Levine (cnd), M. Katz (pno), W. Jones (pno), K. Donath (pno), Manuel Burgueras (pno) RCA Red Seal ▲ 09026-62547-2
Dvořák, A.:Music of, w. Itzhak Perlman (vn), Yo-Yo Ma (vc), Rudolf Firkusny (pno), S. Ozawa (cnd), Boston SO, Czech Phil Chorus—Carnival Ov., Op. 92; Romance in f for Vn & Orch, Op. 11; Klid [Silent Woods] for Vc & Orch, Op. 68/5; Humoresque in Gb, Op. 101/1 & 7; Mesicku na nebi hlubokém [from Rusalka, Op. 114]; Psalm 149 for Chorus & Orch, Op. 79; Gypsy Songs for Voice & Piano, Op. 55/4 & 5; Allegro [from Trio for Vn, Vc & Pno, Op. 90]; Slavonic Dances, Op. 72/2 & 7 *(rec Smetana Hall, Prague, Dec. 16, 1993)* Sony Classical ("Front Line" series) ▲ SK 46687 [DDD]; ■ ST 46687
Great American Songwriter's, w. Hubbard, Bruce (bar), Kiri Te Kanawa (sop), Thomas Hampson (bar)
Angel ▲ CDM 64670
Haydn, J.:Arias [I] Philips ▲ 420084-2 [ADD]
Haydn, J.:Mass 14, "Harmoniemesse", w. Judith Blegen (sop), Kenneth Riegel (ten), Simon Estes (bass), L. Bernstein (cnd), New York PO, Westminster Choir [L] *(rec 1966)*
Sony Classical 2-▲ SM2K 47560 [ADD]
Humperdinck, E.:Hänsel und Gretel, w. I. Cotrubas (sop), E. Söderström (sop), C. Ludwig (mez), S. Nimsgern (b-bar), J. Pritchard (cnd), Gürzenich Orch [G] CBS 2-▲ M2K 35898 [ADD]
James Levine's 25th Anniversary Metropolitan Opera Gala, w. J. Levine (cnd), Metropolitan Opera Orch, Ileana Cotrubas (sop), Renée Fleming (sop), Hei-Kyung Hong (sop), Karita Mattila (sop), Birgit Nilsson (sop), Ruth Ann Swenson (sop), Kiri Te Kanawa (sop), Deborah Voigt (sop), Grace Bumbry (mez), Heidi Grant Murphy (mez), Anne Sofie von Otter (mez) *(rec live, Metropolitan Opera House, New York, Apr 27, 1996)* Deutsche Grammophon ▲ 449177-2 [DDD]
Kern, J.:Show Boat, w. P. O'Hara (sop), T. Stratas (sop), K. Burns (mez), D. Garrison (ten), J. Hadley (ten), B. Hubbard (bar), J. McGlinn (cnd), London Sinfonietta, Ambrosian Opera Chorus
EMI Classics ▲ ZDC 49847

Stade, Frederica von (mez) (cont.)
Kern, J.:Show Boat, w. P. O'Hara (sop), T. Stratas (sop), K. Burns (mez), D. Garrison (ten), J. Hadley (ten), B. Hubbard (bar), J. McGlinn (cnd), London Sinfonietta, Ambrosian Opera Chorus, Ambrosian Singers EMI Classics 3-▲ A23 49108
Kern, J.:Show Boat, w. T. Stratas (sop), J. Hadley (ten), B. Hubbard (bar), P. O'Hara (sgr), K. Burns (mez), N. Kulp (sgr), J. McGlinn (cnd), London Sinfonietta, Ambrosian Chorus [original orchd Robert Russell Bennett]—also includes 45 minutes of music intended for the original performance but never included, plus music from revivals and films [1988 studio cast] Angel 3-▲ A23 49108 [DDD]
Mahler, G.:Lieder eines fahrenden Gesellen, w. A. Davis (cnd), London PO
Sony Classical ("Essential Classics" series) ▲ SBK 46535 [ADD] ■ SBT 46535
Mahler, G.:Songs from Rückert, w. A. Davis (cnd), London PO *(rec Dec. 8-16, 1978)*
Sony Classical ("Essential Classics" series) ▲ SBK 53518 [ADD] ■ SBT 53518
Massenet, J.:Cendrillon, w. R. Welting (sop), N. Gedda (ten), J. Bastin (bass), J. Rudel (cnd), Philharmonia Orch, Ambrosian Opera Chorus [F] CBS 2-▲ M2K 35194 [ADD]
Massenet, J.:Chérubin, w. D. Upshaw (sop), M. Anderson (cta), S. Ramey (bass), P. Steinberg (cnd), Munich RSO, Bavarian State Opera Chorus RCA Red Seal 2-▲ 09026-60593-2 [DDD]
Massenet, J.:Werther, w. J. Carreras (ten), T. Allen (bar), R. Lloyd (b-bar), C. Davis (cnd), Royal Opera House Orch Covent Garden, Royal Opera House Chorus Covent Garden [F]
Philips 2-▲ 416654-2 [ADD]
Mendelssohn, F.:A Midsummer Night's Dream (comp), w. J. Blegen (sop), E. Ormandy (cnd), Mendelssohn Club Chorus Philadelphia [G] RCA Red Seal ▲ RCD1-2084
Mendelssohn, F.:A Midsummer Night's Dream (comp), w. Kathleen Battle (sop), Judi Dench (nar), S. Ozawa (cnd), Boston SO, Tanglewood Festival Chorus Deutsche Grammophon ▲ 439897-2
Mendelssohn, F.:Songs, w. M. Horne (mez), M. Katz (pno)—4 Duets RCA Red Seal ▲ 09026-61681-2
Monteverdi, C.:Music of, w. R. Leppard (cnd), Scottish CO—Lamento di Ottavia; Aria di Ottavia; Et è pur dunque vero Erato ▲ 98504-2
Mozart, W.A.:Arias, *(cnd & orch unknown)* [I] Philips ▲ 420084-2 [ADD]
Mozart, W.A.:Complete Mozart Edition, w. L. Popp (sop), J. Baker (mez), Y. Minton (mez), S. Burrows (ten), R. Lloyd (b-bar), C. Davis (cnd), Royal Opera House Orch, Royal Opera House Chorus Covent Garden Philips 2-▲ 422544-2 [ADD]
Mozart, W.A.:Così fan tutte, w. T. Stratas (sop), K. Te Kanawa (sop), A. Lombard (cnd), Strasbourg PO, Rhine Opera Chorus Erato 3-▲ 98494-2
Mozart, W.A.:Così fan tutte (sels), w. R. Leppard (cnd), Scottish CO Erato ▲ 98504-2
Mozart, W.A.:Missa, K.427, w. A. Augér (sop), F. Lopardo (ten), C. Hauptmann (bass), L. Bernstein (cnd), Bavarian RSO, Bavarian Radio Chorus *(rec live April 1990)*
Deutsche Grammophon ▲ 431791-2 [DDD] □ 431791-5
Mozart, W.A.:Nozze di Figaro, w. K. Te Kanawa (sop), L. Popp (sop), T. Allen (bar), S. Ramey (bass), K. Moll (bass), G. Solti (cnd), London PO [I] London 3-▲ 410150-2 [DDD]
Mozart, W.A.:Nozze di Figaro, w. Mirella Freni (sop), Gundala Janowitz (sop), Jane Berbié (mez), Michel Sénéchal (ten), José Van Dam (b-bar), Kurt Moll (bass), G. Solti (cnd), Paris Opera Orch, Paris Opera Chorus *(rec live, Paris, Apr 7, 1973)* Agorá ("Phoenix" series) 3-▲ 515
Mozart, W.A.:Nozze di Figaro (sels), w. K. Te Kanawa (sop), L. Popp (sop), T. Allen (bar), S. Ramey (bass), K. Moll (bass), G. Solti (cnd), London PO [I] London ▲ 417395-2 [DDD] □ 417395-5
Offenbach, J.:Music of, w. A. de Almeida (cnd), Scottish CO—Ov; Lettre de la Périchole; Ah! que les homes sont bêtes!; Ariette de la griserie; Entr'acte [all from La Périchole]; Chanson de la fille du tambour-major [from La Fille du tambour-major]; Amours divins [from La Belle Hélène]; Ov; Couplets de pomme; J'en prendrai un, deux, trois [all from Pomme d'api]; Couplets de l'alphabet [from Madame l'Archiduc]; Ov [from La Romance de la rose]; Rondeau et valse [from La Vie parisienne]; Couplets du berger joli [from Orphée aux enfers]; Ov; Couplets de Boulette; Couplets de la rosière [all from Barbe Bleu]; Ov; Dites-lui; Ah! que j'aime les militaires! [all from La Grande-Duchesse de Gérolstein] *(rec City Hall, Glasgow, Scotland, Dec 16-18, 1994)* RCA Red Seal ▲ 09026-68116-2 [DDD]
Porter, C.:Anything Goes, w. J. McGlinn (sgr), K. Criswell (sop), C. Groenendaal (sgr), J. Gilford (sgr), London SO, Ambrosian Chorus [original 1934 Broadway version w. original orchestration by Robert Russell Bennett & Hans Spialek] Angel ▲ CDC 49848-2 [DDD]
Portrait of Frederica von Stade CBS ▲ MK 39315 ■ MT 39315
Rameau, J.P.:Dardanus, w. C. Eda-Pierre (sop), G. Gautier (ten), R. Soyer (bar), J. Van Dam (b-bar), R. Leppard (cnd), Paris Lyon Opera Orch, Paris Lyon Opera Chorus Erato 2-▲ 95312-2
Ravel, M.:Shéhérazade Mez, w. S. Ozawa (cnd), Boston SO [F] CBS ■ IMT 36665 (D)
Rodgers, R.:The Sound of Music, w. E. Farrell (sop), Håkan Hagegård (bar), B. Daniels (sgr), L. D. von Schlanbusch (sgr), et al., E. Kunzel (cnd), Cincinnati Pops Orch, May Festival Chorus [1987 studio cast]
Telarc ▲ CD 80162 [DDD] ■ CS 30162
Rossini, G.:Arias, *(orch unknown)* [I] Philips ▲ 420084-2 [ADD]
Rossini, G.:Music of, w. M. Fortuna (sop), M. Lerner (sop), D. Voigt (sop), M. Horne (mez), K. Kuhlmann (mez), R. Blake (ten), C. Estep (ten), C. Merritt (ten), T. Hampson (b-bar), H. Runey (b-bar), J. Opalach (bass), S. Ramey (bass), R. Norrington (cnd), Orch of St. Luke's, New York Concert Chorale
EMI Classics ▲ CDC 54643
Rossini, G.:Otello, w. J. Carreras (ten), S. Fisichella (ten), S. Ramey (bass), J. López-Cobos (cnd), Philharmonia Orch, Ambrosian Opera Chorus [I] Philips 2-▲ 432456-2 [ADD]
Schumann, R.:Frauenliebe und -leben, w. M. Horne (mez), M. Katz (pno) [sung as duet]
RCA Red Seal ▲ 09020-01081-2
Simple Gifts, w. Mormon Tabernacle Choir, Utah SO [cnd:Joseph Silverstein], John Longhurst (org)
London ▲ 436284-2 LH [DDD]
Songs of the Cat, w. Garrison Keillor (sgr/nar)
RCA Victor ▲ 09026-61161-2 [DDD] ■ 09026-61161-4 (CrO2)
Strauss, R.:Der Rosenkavalier (sels), w. K. Battle (sop), R. Fleming (sop), A. Schmidt (bar), C. Abbado (cnd), Berlin PO *(rec Dec. 31, 1992)* Sony Classical ▲ SK 52565
Verdi, G.:La traviata (sels), w. Loretta di Franco (sop), Joan Sutherland (sop), Leo Goeke (ten), Lou Marcella (ten), Luciano Pavarotti (ten), Gene Boucher (bar), Raymond Gibbs (bar), Sherrill Milnes (bar), Louis Sgarro (bar), John Trehy (bar) Budget ("The Greatest Voice in Opera" series) ▲ SYP 112
Voyage à Paris, w. Martin Katz (pno) RCA Red Seal ▲ 09026-62711-2

Stader, Maria (sop)
Bach, J.S.:Cant 57, w. Heinz Rehfuss (bass), J.-M. Auberson (cnd), Vienna Opera Orch
FNAC Music ("Via Classics" series) ▲ 642329
Bach, J.S.:Magnificat, BWV 243, w. H. Töpper (cta), E. Haefliger (ten), D. Fischer-Dieskau (bar), K. Richter (cnd), Munich Bach Orch, Munich Bach Choir [L]
Deutsche Grammophon ("Galleria" series) ▲ 419466-2 [ADD]
Bach, J.S.:Mass in b, BWV 232, w. Sieglinde Wagner (mez), Ernst Haefliger (ten), Theo Adam (b-bar), R. Mauersberger (cnd), Dresden State Orch, Dresden Kreuz Choir *(rec 1958)*
Berlin Classics ▲ BER 9171
Beethoven, L. van:Fidelio, w. S. Jurinac (sop), H. Peerce (ten), H. Knappertsbusch (cnd), Bavarian State Opera Orch, Bavarian State Opera Chorus [G] *(rec ca. 1961)*
MCA Classics 2-▲ MCAD2-9809 [AAD]
Beethoven, L. van:Missa Solemnis, w. E. Cavalti (mez), E. Haefliger (ten), H. Rehfuss (bass), C. Schuricht (cnd), Hamburg SO, St. Hedwig's Cathedral Choir *(rec Sept. 15, 1957)*
Archipon 2-▲ ARCH 2.1CD (m) [ADD]
Brahms, J.:Ein Deutsches Requiem, w. H. Prey (bar), C. Schuricht (cnd), Stuttgart RSO, Stuttgart Radio Chorus, Frankfurt Radio Chorus *(rec Nov. 7, 1959)* Archipon ▲ ARCH 2.2CD (m) [ADD]
Bruckner, A.:Mass 3, w. C. Hellmann (mez), E. Haefliger (ten), K. Borg (bass), E. Jochum (cnd), Bavarian RSO, Bavarian Radio Chorus Deutsche Grammophon ("The Originals" series) 2-▲ 447409-2
Bruckner, A.:Mass 3, w. A. Hellmann (alt), E. Haefliger (ten), K. Borg (bass), E. Jochum (cnd), Bavarian RSO, Bavarian Radio Chorus [L] Deutsche Grammophon 4-▲ 423127-2 [ADD]
Bruckner, A.:Psalm 150, w. E. Jochum (cnd), Berlin PO, Deutsche Opera Chorus [L]
Deutsche Grammophon 4-▲ 423127-2 [ADD]
Bruckner, A.:Te Deum, w. S. Wagner (mez), E. Haefliger (ten), P. Lagger (bass), E. Jochum (cnd), Berlin PO, German Opera Chorus [L] Deutsche Grammophon 4-▲ 423127-2 [ADD]
Dvořák, A.:Requiem Mass, w. Sieglinde Wagner (cta), Ernst Haefliger (ten), Kim Borg (b-bar), K. Ančerl (cnd), Czech PO, Czech Chorus Deutsche Grammophon ("Double" series) 2-▲ 437377-2
Haydn, J.:Mass 3, "Cäcilienmesse", w. Marga Höffgen (cta), Richard Holm (ten), Josef Greindl (bass), E. Jochum (cnd), Bavarian RSO, Bavarian Radio Chorus Deutsche Grammophon 2-▲ 437383-2 [ADD]

Stader, Maria (sop) (cont.)
Mozart, W.A.:Don Giovanni, w. I. Seefried (sop), S. Jurinac (sop), E. Haefliger (ten), D. Fischer-Dieskau (bar), K. C. Kohn (bass), F. Fricsay (cnd), Berlin RSO Deutsche Grammophon 3-▲ 437341-2
Mozart, W.A.:Exsultate, w. F. Fricsay (cnd), Berlin RIAS SO Deutsche Grammophon 2-▲ 437383-2 [ADD]
Mozart, W.A.:Litaniae Lauretanae, K.195, w. G. König (cnd), Berlin RIAS SO, Berlin RIAS Chamber Choir Deutsche Grammophon 2-▲ 437383-2
Mozart, W.A.:Missa, K.317, w. Sieglinde Wagner (mez), Helmut Krebs (ten), Josef Griendl (bass), I. Markevitch (cnd), Berlin PO, St. Hedwig's Cathedral Choir Deutsche Grammophon 2-▲ 437383-2
Mozart, W.A.:Missa, K.427, w. Annelohre Cahnbley (sop), George Maran (ten), Walter Raninger (bass), B. Paumgartner (cnd), Salzburg Mozarteum Orch, Salzburg Radio Chorus, Salzburg Mozarteum Chorus *(rec Aug 16, 1958)* Orfeo d'or ("Festspiel Dokumente" series) ▲ 397951 (m)
Mozart, W.A.:Missa, K.427, w. G. König (cnd), Berlin RIAS SO, Berlin RIAS Chamber Choir Deutsche Grammophon 2-▲ 437383-2
Mozart, W.A.:Nozze di Figaro, w. I. Seefried (sop), H. Töpper (mez), D. Fischer-Dieskau (bar), R. Capecchi (bar), I. Sardi (bass), F. Fricsay (cnd), Berlin RSO [G] *(rec 1960)* Deutsche Grammophon 3-▲ 437671-2
Mozart, W.A.:Vesperae de Dominica, w. G. König (cnd), Berlin RIAS SO, Berlin RIAS Chamber Choir Deutsche Grammophon 2-▲ 437383-2
Mozart, W.A.:Vesperae solennes, w. G. König (cnd), Berlin RIAS SO, Berlin RIAS Chamber Choir Deutsche Grammophon 2-▲ 437383-2
Schubert, Franz:Songs (misc), w. William Kapell (pno) *(rec 1940–53)* Pearl ▲ PEA 9194
Verdi, G.:Requiem Mass, w. M. Höffgen (cta), F. Wunderlich (ten), G. Frick (bass), H. Müller-Kray (cnd), South German RSO, South German Radio Sym Chorus *(rec live, Stuttgart, 11/2/60)* Myto 2-▲ 2 MCD 91648 [ADD]
Verdi, G.:Requiem Mass, w. Marjana Radev (mez), Helmut Krebs (ten), Kim Borg (bass), F. Fricsay (cnd), Berlin RIAS SO, Berlin RIAS Chamber Choir, St. Hedwig Cathedral Choir *(rec Jesus-Christus Church, Berlin, Sept 1953)* Deutsche Grammophon ("The Originals" series) ▲ 447442-2 [ADD]

Staehelin, F. (sgr)
Marx, K.:When Jesus Left His Mother, w. W. Pailer (bass), C. Näf (cnd), Amarillis Instrumental Ensemble, Feld Evangelistic Kantorei, Amarillis Vocal Ensemble [G] *(rec 6/89)* FSM ▲ FCD 97737 [DDD]

Staempfli, Jacob (bass)
Bach, J.S.:Cant 57, w. K. Ristenpart (cnd), Sarre CO, Sarre Choir Accord ▲ ACD 202652 [AAD]
Bach, J.S.:Cant 82, w. K. Ristenpart (cnd), Sarre CO, Sarre Choir Accord ▲ ACD 202652 [AAD]
Bach, J.S.:Cant 159, w. K. Ristenpart (cnd), Sarre CO, Sarre Choir Accord ▲ ACD 202652 [AAD]

Stafford, Ashley (ct)
Purcell, H.:Anthems & Services, w. Tom Seligman (trb), James Bowman (ct), John Mark Ainsley (ten), Andrew Gant (ten), Michael George (bass), Charles Pott (bass), R. King (cnd), King's Consort, King's Consort—O Sing unto the Lord; My beloved spake *(rec St Jude-on-the-Hill, London, Dec 20–21, 1968)* United ▲ CAL 88002 [DDD]
Purcell, H.:Hail. Bright Cecilia, w. J. Smith (sop), B. Gordon (alt), P. Elliot (ten), S. Varcoe (bar), D. Thomas (bass), J.E. Gardiner (cnd), English Baroque Soloists, Monteverdi Choir London Erato ("Gardiner Purcell Collection" series) ▲ 96554-2
Purcell, H.:King Arthur, w. J. Smith (sop), G. Fisher (sop), E. Priday (sop), G. Ross (sop), P. Elliott (ten), S. Varcoe (bar), J.E. Gardiner (cnd), English Baroque Soloists, Monteverdi Choir London Erato 2-▲ 2292-45211-2 ZA
Purcell, H.:King Arthur, w. Gillian Fisher (sop), E. Priday (sop), Gill Ross (sop), J. Smith (sop), P. Elliot (ten), S. Varcoe (bar), J.E. Gardiner (cnd), English Baroque Soloists, Monteverdi Choir London Erato ("Gardiner Purcell Collection" series) 2-▲ 96552-2

Stafford, J. (sgr)
Loesser, F.:Guys and Dolls, w. F. Sinatra (sgr), B. Crosby (sgr), D. Martin (sgr), D. Shore (sgr), D. Reynolds (sgr), C. Dennis (sgr), A. Sherman (sgr), S. Davis Jr. (sgr), *(other artists unknown)* [studio cast] Reprise ▲ 45014-2 [AAD] ■ 45014-4

Stahelová, Mária (sgr)
Puccini, G.:Madama Butterfly (sels), w. Miriam Gauci (sop—Madama Butterfly), Nelly Boschkowa (mez—Suzuki), Yordi Ramiro (ten—F.B. Pinkerton), Jozef Abel (ten—Goro), Georg Tichy (bass—Sharpless), Anna Tomkovicová (sgr), Elena Hanzelová (sgr) *(rec Concert Hall of the Czecho-Slovak Radio, Bratislava, May 2–10, 1991)* Naxos ▲ 8.553152 [DDD]

Stahl, H. (ten)
Gottlieb, J.:Sacred Music, w. M. Stone (sop), H. Reps (mez), D. Lefkowitz (ten), R. Abelson (bar), R. Botton (bar), P. Newman (reader), S. Sturk (cnd), Metropolitan Brass Ensemble, New York Motet Choir Premier ("Composer" series) ▲ PRCD 1018 [DDD]

Stahlman, Sylvia (sop)
Ward, R.:Songs for Pantheists, w. W. Strickland (cnd), Polish National RSO Katowice [F] CRI ■ C 206

Staley, J. (voc)
Lebaron, A.:Con for Active Frogs, w. G. Cartwright (voc), D. Shea (voc), W. Trigg (perc), A. LeBaron (cnd), New Music Consort [E] Mode ▲ 30

Stamm, Harald (bass)
Dittersdorf, K.D. von:Doctor und Apotheker, w. Hildegard Uhrmacher (sop—Leonore), Donna Woodward (sop—Rosalia), Waltraud Meier (mez—Claudia), Martin Finke (ten—Sichel), Frieder Lang (ten—Gotthold), Alois Perl (ten—Gallus), Gerhard Unger (ten—Sturmwald), Thomas Pfeiffer (bar—Police Commisioner), Wolfgang Schöne (bar—Krautmann), Harald Stamm (bass—Stössel), J. Lockhart (cnd), Rhine State PO Bayer 2-▲ BR 100 238/39 [DDD]
Haydn, J.:Die Schöpfung, w. Edith Mathis (sop), Christoph Prégardien (ten), M. Atzmon (cnd), World SO, Pécs Chamber Choir, Berlin Academy of Arts Chamber Choir, Shin-Yuh Kai Choir [G] *(rec Basilica San Francesco in Assisi, as part of the IPPNW "Hiroshima Concert 1990")* BIS 2-▲ CD 493/94 [DDD]
Hindemith, P.:Mathis der Maler, w. Josef Protschka (ten), Hermann Winkler (ten), Roland Hermann (bar), Victor von Halem (bass), G. Albrecht (cnd), Cologne RSO Wergo 3-▲ WER 6255-2
Schoeck, O.:Massimilla Doni, w. E. Mathis (sop), A. Küttenbaum (mez), H. Winkler (ten), G. Albrecht (cnd), Cologne RSO, Cologne Radio Chorus [G] Koch Schwann 2-▲ CD 314025 [DDD]
Schreker, F.:Der Schatzgräber, w. G. Schnaut (sop), J. Protschka (ten), H. Helm (bar), G. Albrecht (cnd), Hamburg State Opera Orch, Hamburg State Opera Chorus [G] *(rec live 5/89)* Capriccio 2-▲ 60010-2 [DDD]
Schumann, R.:Genoveva, w. J. Faulkner (sop—Genoveva), R. Behle (sop—Margaretha), K. Lewis (ten—Golo), A. Titus (bar—Siegfried), H. Stamm (bass—Hidulfus, Caspar), J. Tilli (bass—Balthasar), G. Albrecht (cnd), Hamburg State PO, Hamburg State Opera Chorus [G] *(rec 1992)* Orfeo 2-▲ 289932 [DDD]

Stämpfli, Jakob (bass)
Bach, J.S.:Cant 208, "Hunting Cant", w. Helen Donath (sop), Elisabeth Speiser (sop), Wilfrid Jochims (ten), H. Rilling (cnd), Stuttgart Bach Collegium, Stuttgart Memorial Church Figuralchor *(rec Southwest Sound Studio, Stuttgart-Bottnang, May 1965)* Musicaphon ▲ 51351 [AAD]
Bach, J.S.:Cant 213, w. Sheila Armstrong (sop), Hertha Töpper (alt), Theo Altmeyer (ten), H. Rilling (cnd), Stuttgart Bach Collegium *(rec 1967)* Musicaphon ▲ 51356 [AAD]
Bach, J.S.:Cant 249a, w. Edith Mathis (sop), Hetty Plümacher (alt), Theo Altmeyer (ten), H. Rilling (cnd), Stuttgart Bach Collegium, Stuttgart Memorial Church Figuralchor *(rec Gedächtniskirche Stuttgart, Mar 1967)* Musicaphon ▲ 51357 [AAD]
Schubert, Franz:Winterreise, w. Eke Mendez (pno) Accord ▲ ACD 221142 [DDD]
Schütz, H.:St. John Passion, w. Herta Flebbe (sop), Johannes Hoeflin (ten—Evangelist), Rolf Bössow (ten—Pilate), Gert Spierting (ten), Jakob Stämpfli (bass—Jesus), Teinhard Tuge (bass—soliloquies), W. Ehmann (cnd), Westphalia Kantorei *(rec Münster zu Herfor, Sept. 1961)* Cantate ▲ 57602 [ADD]

Stanley, G. (sgr)
Mozart, W.A.:Mitridate, w. M. Zara (sop), E. Gabry (sgr), L. Hager (cnd), Salzburg Mozarteum Orch [I] *(rec live in Salzburg, Jan. 31, 1970)* Memories 2-▲ HR 4156/57 (m) [ADD]

Stapp, Olivia (mez)
Griffes, C.T.:Impressions, w. D. Richardson (pno) [F] New World ▲ NW 273-2 [ADD]

Stark, Paulina (sop)
American-Jewish Art Songs, w. Nadine Shank (pno) Centaur ▲ CRC 2108

Stasio, Anna di (mez)
Alfano, F.:Risurrezione, w. M. Olivero (Katiusha), Gismondo (Prince Dmitri), A. Boyer (Simonson), E. Boncompagni (cnd), Turin RAI Orch [I] *(rec live, Oct 22, 1971)* Standing Room Only 2-▲ SRO 839-2 [ADD]
Bellini, V.:I Puritani, w. A. Maliponte (sop—Elvira), A. di Stasio (sop—Enrichetta di Francia), A. Kraus (ten—Lord Arturo Talbo), A. Pedroni (ten—Bruno Roberton), P. Cappuccilli (bar—Sir Riccardo Forth), R. Raimondi (bass—Sir Giorgio), G. Gavazzeni (cnd), Catania Teatro Massimo Bellini Orch, Catania Teatro Massimo Bellini Chorus *(rec Feb. 6, 1972)* Ornamenti 2-▲ FE 107 [ADD]
Donizetti, G.:La fille du régiment, w. M. Freni (sop), L. Pavarotti (ten), W. Ganzarolli (bar), W. Monachesi (bar), N. Sanzogno (cnd), La Scala Orch, La Scala Chorus [I] *(rec live, 2/11/69)* Verona 2-▲ 27046/47 (m) [AAD]
Donizetti, G.:La fille du régiment, w. M. Freni (sop), L. Pavarotti (ten), W. Ganzarolli (bar), W. Monachesi (bar), N. Sanzogno (cnd), La Scala Orch, La Scala Chorus [I] *(rec live, 2/11/69)* Melodram 2-▲ MEL 27045
Donizetti, G.:La fille du régiment (sels), w. Mirella Freni (sop), Angelo Mercuriali (ten), Luciano Pavarotti (ten), Wladimiro Ganzarolli (bar), Walter Monachesi (bar), Giuseppe Morresi (bass), V. Gullino (sgr), Luisa Rezzadore (sgr), N. Sanzogno (cnd), La Scala Orch, La Scala Chorus Budget ("The Greatest Voice in Opera" series) ▲ SYP 108
Donizetti, G.:Lucia di Lammermoor (sels), w. Renato Scotto (sop), Luciano Pavarotti (ten), F. Molinari-Pradelli (cnd), Turin RAI SO—Egli s'avanza; Sulla tomba che rinserra *(rec Torino, Oct 10, 1967)* Goldies ▲ GLD 63202 [ADD]
Giordano, U.:Andrea Chénier, w. Renata Tebaldi (sop—Maddalena), Anna di Stasio (mez—Bersi), Amalia Pini (mez—Madelon/Contessa), Mario Del Monaco (ten—Andrea Chenier), Antonio Pirino (ten—L'Incredibile/Abate), Aldo Protti (bar—Carlo Gerard), Arturo La Porta (bass/bar—Mathieu/Fleville), Silvano Pagliuca (bass/bar—Roucher/Fouquier-Tinville), Giorgio Onesti (bass—Dumas/Schmidt/Major-domo), F. Capuana (cnd), Italian Lyric Orch, Italian Lyric Chorus *(rec Tokyo, Oct 1, 1961)* Legato Classics 2-▲ LCD 214-2 [ADD]
Gounod, C.:Faust, w. Renata Scotto (sop—Margherita), Anna di Stasio (mez—Marta), Flaviano Labò (ten—Faust), Edoardo Gimenez (ten—Siebel), Piero Cappuccilli (bar—Valentino), Bruno Grella (bar—Wagner), Ruggero Raimondi (bass—Mefistofele), M. Gusella (cnd), Margherita Theater Orch, Margherita Theater Chorus *(rec Genova, 1970)* Golden Age of Opera 2-▲ GAO 170/71 [ADD]
Mascagni, P.:Cavalleria rusticana, w. E. Suliotis (sop), S. Malagu (mez), M. Del Monaco (ten), T. Gobbi (bar), S. Varviso (cnd), Rome Opera Orch, Rome Opera Chorus [I] IMP Collectors Series ▲ IMPX 9018 [AAD]
Ponchielli, A.:La Gioconda, w. Leyla Gencer (sop), Gianni Raimondi (ten), Ruggero Raimondi (bass), B. Bartoletti (cnd), Rome Opera Orch, Rome Opera Chorus Melodram 3-▲ CDM 37092
Puccini, G.:Madama Butterfly, w. R. Tebaldi (sop), G. Raimondi (ten), G. Valdengo (bar), A. Questa (cnd), *(orch & chorus unknown)* [I] *(rec live, Arena Flegrea, Naples 8/9/58)* Standing Room Only 2-▲ SRO 825-2 [ADD]
Puccini, G.:Madama Butterfly, w. R. Scotto (sop), C. Bergonzi (ten), R. Panerai (bar), J. Barbirolli (cnd), Rome Opera Orch, Rome Opera Chorus [I] EMI Classics ("Studio" series) ▲ CDM 63411 ■ EG 63411
Rossini, G.:Il barbiere di Siviglia (sels), w. R. Scotto (sop), A. Kraus (ten), A. Protti (bar), C. Badioli (bass), E. Campi (bass), V. Bellezza (cnd), Naples Teatro San Carlo Orch, Naples Teatro San Carlo Chorus *(rec July 26, 1958)* Golden Age of Opera 2-▲ GAO 137/38 [ADD]
Verdi, G.:Ernani, w. Margherita Roberti (sop), Athos Cesarini (ten), Mario del Monaco (ten), Ettore Bastianini (bar), Mario Rinaudo (bass), Nicola Rossi-Lemeni (bass), F. Previtali (cnd), Naples Teatro San Carlo Orch, Naples Teatro San Carlo Chorus Melodram 2-▲ CDM 270100
Verdi, G.:Otello, w. G. Jones (sop—Desdemona), A. di Stasio (mez—Emilia), J. McCracken (ten—Otello), P. de Palma (ten—Cassio), D. Fischer-Dieskau (bar—Iago), J. Barbirolli (cnd), New Philharmonia Orch, Ambrosian Opera Chorus EMI Classics ▲ CDMB 65296

Staskiewicz, Stanislas (sgr)
Adam, A.:Le Chalet, w. Denise Boursin (sop), Joseph Peyron (ten), A. Wolff (cnd), ORTF Lyric Orch Musidisc ▲ MUS 201942 [AAD]
Adam, A.:Le Farfadet, w. Denise Boursin (sop), Joseph Peyron (ten), A. Wolff (cnd), ORTF Lyric Orch Musidisc ▲ MUS 201942 [AAD]

Staufenbiel, Brian (ten)
Bowles, P.:Scènes d'Anabase, w. Roger Weismeyer (ob), Irene Herrmann (pno) Koch International Classics ▲ KIC 7343 [DDD]
Bowles, P.:Songs, w. Irene Herrmann (pno) Koch International Classics ▲ KIC 7343 [DDD]

Stavad, Hanne (cta)
Brahms, J.:Songs, w. Peter Westenholz (pno), Morten Zeuthen (vc)—Von ewiger Liebe, Op. 43/1; Die Mainacht, Op. 43/2 Danica ▲ DCD 8143
Brahms, J.:Songs, Op. 91, w. Peter Westenholz (pno), Morten Zeuthen (vc) Danica ▲ DCD 8143
Heise, P.:Songs, w. Peter Westenholz (pno), Morten Zeuthen (vc)—Gudrans Sorg [song cycle] Danica ▲ DCD 8143
Lutoslawski, W.:Songs, w. Peter Westenholz (pno), Morten Zeuthen (vc)—5 Songs after poems by Illakowicz Danica ▲ DCD 8143
Nielsen, C.:Songs, w. Peter Westenholz (pno), Morten Zeuthen (vc)—Det bodes der for Af Op. 6; I Seraillets Have Af Op. 4; Har Dagen sauket al sin sorg Af Op. 4 Danica ▲ DCD 8143
Nørgård, P.:Short Songs, w. Peter Westenholz (pno), Morten Zeuthen (vc) Danica ▲ DCD 8143
Schubert, Franz:Songs (misc), w. Peter Westenholz (pno), Morten Zeuthen (vc)—Der Tod und das Mädchen, D.531; Ganymed, D.544; Lachen und Weinen, D.777; Seligkeit, D.433; Wanderes nachlied II, D.768 Danica ▲ DCD 8143

Stavny, Andrey (bar)
Rimsky-Korsakov, N.:Songs, w. Anna Kovaleva (sop), Marianna Tarassova (mez), Konstantine Plužnikov (ten), Nikolai Okhotnikov (bass), Yury Serov (pno)—4 Romances, Op. 2; 4 Romances, Op. 3; 4 Romances, Op. 4; 4 Romances, Op. 7; 6 Romances, Op. 8; 2 Romances, Op. 25; 4 Romances, Op. 26; 4 Romances, Op. 27 *(rec St. Catherine's Lutheran Church, St. Petersburg, Sept–Dec 1993)* Russian Compact Disc ▲ RDCD 10051 [DDD]

Stavru, Cornel (ten)
Leoncavallo, R.:Pagliacci, w. Arta Florescu (sop—Nedda), Cornel Stavru (ten—Canio), Valentin Teodorian (ten—Beppe), Nicolae Herlea (bar—Tonio), Ladislau Konya (bar—Silvio), M. Popa (cnd), Bucharest Opera & Ballet Theater Orch, Bucharest Opera & Ballet Theater Chorus *(rec 1966)* Vox Box 2-▲ CDX 5161
Mascagni, P.:Cavalleria rusticana, w. Marina Krilovici (sop—Santuzza), Viorica Cortez (mez—Lola), Milka Nistor (mez—Lucia), Cornel Stavru (ten—Turiddu), David Ohanesian (bar—Alfio), M. Popa (cnd), Bucharest Opera & Ballet Theater Orch, Bucharest Opera & Ballet Theater Chorus *(rec 1966)* Vox Box 2-▲ CDX 5161
Verdi, G.:Il trovatore, w. Elena Dima (sop—Leonora), Victoria Draganescu (sop—Ines), Zenaida Pally (mez—Azucena), Ion Buzea (ten—Duke of Mantua), Constantin Iliescu (ten—Ruiz), Cornel Stavru (ten—Manrico), Octav Enigarescu (bar—Count di Luna), Constantin Dumitru (bass—Ferrando), E. Massini (cnd), Romanian Opera Orch, Romanian Opera Chorus *(rec 1960–61)* Vox Box 2-▲ CDX 5163

Stcherbakov, Vladimir (ten)
Dargomyzhsky, A.:Arias, w. Nina Terentieva (mez), A. Tchistiakov (cnd), *(orch unknown)*—Russalka; The Stone Guest Le Chant du Monde ▲ RUS 288 086
Mussorgsky, M.:Arias, w. Nina Terentieva (mez), A. Tchistiakov (cnd), *(orch unknown)*—Boris Godunov; Khovanshchina; Khovansky's duet; Marfa & Audrey; Marfa's song Le Chant du Monde ▲ RUS 288 086
Rimsky-Korsakov, N.:Arias, w. Nina Terentieva (mez), A. Tchistiakov (cnd), *(orch unknown)*—Lel's Song; Sadko; Snegurochka Le Chant du Monde ▲ RUS 288 086

Stearman, Steven (bass)
Scelsi, G.:Anahit, w. Paul Zukofsky (vn), Julie Bogorad (fl), Peggy Russell (fl), Courtney Westcott (fl), Lawrence McDonald (cl), Joan Waryha (cl), Jean Hansen (b cl), Bill Suite (e hn), Nita VanPelt (sax), Bob Zobal (tpt), John Carter (trbn), Martin Lydecker (trbn), Stan Cortman (hn), Robert Ward (hn), William Curry (va), Jody Rowitsch (va), Irene Wade (va), Anne Fagerburg (vc), John Gockel (vc), Sue Manz (bass) Itit□(rec Oberlin Conservatory of Music, Oct 8, 1973) CP² ▲ CP2 108 [AAD]

▲ = CD ♦ = Enhanced CD Δ = MD ■ = Cassette Tape □ = DCC

Stearns, Jason (bar)
Corigliano, J.:Of Rage & Remembrance, w. Michelle DeYoung (mez), Michael Accinno (boy sop), Robert Baker (ten), Michael Forest (ten), James Shaffran (bar), L. Slatkin (cnd), National SO Washington D.C., Washington Oratorio Society Men's Chorus *(rec J. F. K. Center for the Performing Arts, Washington, D. C., Nov 9–11, 1995 & Apr 19 &)* RCA Red Seal ▲ 09026-68450-2 [DDD]

Steber, Eleanor (sop)
Bach, J.S.:Cant 21, w. M. Rudolf (cnd), Columbia SO—Sighing, Weeping *(rec Columbia 30th St. Studios, New York, Sept 20, 1951)* Sony Classical ("Masterworks Heritage" series) ▲ MHK 62356 [ADD]
Bach, J.S.:Cant 68, w. M. Rudolf (cnd), Columbia SO—My Heart Ever Faithful *(rec Columbia 30th St. Studios, New York, Sept 20, 1951)* Sony Classical ("Masterworks Heritage" series) ▲ MHK 62356 [ADD]
Barber, S.:Vanessa, w. G. Resnik (sop), R. Elias (mez), N. Gedda (ten), G. Tozzi (bass), D. Mitropoulos (cnd), Metropolitan Opera Orch, Metropolitan Opera Chorus [E] RCA Gold Seal ▲ 7899-2-RG [ADD]
Beethoven, L. van:Ah, perfido!, w. J. Levine (cnd), *(orch unknown)* *(rec live, Cleveland 5/5/70)* VAI Audio ▲ VAIA 1012 (m/s) [ADD]
Berlioz, H.:La Captive, w. J.-P. Morel (cnd), Columbia SO *(rec Columbia 30th St. Studios, New York, May 19, 1954)* Sony Classical ("Masterworks Heritage" series) ▲ MHK 62356 [ADD]
Berlioz, H.:Le Jeune pâtre breton, w. J.-P. Morel (cnd), Columbia SO *(rec Columbia 30th St. Studios, New York, May 19, 1954)* Sony Classical ("Masterworks Heritage" series) ▲ MHK 62356 [ADD]
Berlioz, H.:Les Nuits d'été, w. D. Mitropoulos (cnd), Columbia SO *(rec Columbia 30th St. Studios, New York, May 19, 1954)* Sony Classical ("Masterworks Heritage" series) ▲ MHK 62356 [ADD]
Berlioz, H.:Les Troyens, w. R. Resnik (mez—Dido), E. Steber (sop—Cassandra), R. Cassily (ten—Aeneas), R. Lawrence (cnd), American Opera Society Orch, American Opera Society Chorus *(rec live, Carnegie Hall, 12/29/59 & 1/12/60)* VAI Audio 3-▲ VAIA 1006-3 [ADD]
Berlioz, H.:Zaïde, w. J.-P. Morel (cnd), Columbia SO *(rec Columbia 30th St. Studios, New York, May 19, 1954)* Sony Classical ("Masterworks Heritage" series) ▲ MHK 62356 [ADD]
Dittersdorf, K.D. von:Arcifanfano, King of Fools, or It's Always Too Late to Learn, w. P. Brooks (sop), A. Russell (sop), J. McCollum (ten), J. Sopher (ten), H. Rehfuss (bar), D. Smith (bar), N. Jenkins (cnd), Clarion Music Society Orch, Clarion Music Society Chorus [E] *(rec live, New York 1965)* VAI Audio 2-▲ VAIA 1010-2 (m) [ADD]
Eleanor Steber RCA Gold Seal ▲ 60521-2-RG [ADD]
The Eleanor Steber Collections, Vol. 1 *(rec 1938–1951)* VAI Audio ▲ VAIA 1072
Eleanor Steber in Concert 1956–1958 VAI Audio 2-▲ VAIA 1005-2 (m) [ADD]
Handel, G.F.:Messiah (sels), w. M. Rudolf (cnd), Columbia SO—I Know That My Redeemer Liveth *(rec Columbia 30th St. Studios, New York, Sept 18, 1951)* Sony Classical ("Masterworks Heritage" series) ▲ MHK 62356 [ADD]
Haydn, J.:Die Schöpfung (sels), w. M. Rudolf (cnd), Columbia SO—With Verdure Clad *(rec Columbia 30th St. Studios, New York, Sept 18, 1951)* Sony Classical ("Masterworks Heritage" series) ▲ MHK 62356 [ADD]
Her First Recordings, w. Armand Tokatyan (ten), Lucielle Browning (mez), Pino Bontempi (sgr), Annamary Dickey (sgr), George Cehanovsky (bar), Lorenzo Alvary ((bass), A. Kent (bar), Raoul Jobin (ten), Norman Cordon (bass) VAI Audio ▲ VAIA 1023 (m) [ADD]
In Memoriam Cantabile ("Biographies in Music") ▲ BIM 712-1
Love's Secrets & Other Songs By American Composers, w. illdred Miller (mez), John McCollum (ten), Donald Gramm (bass-bar), Edwin Biltcliffe (pno), Richard Cumming (pno) Vox Box ("The American Composers" series) 2-▲ CDX 5129
Mendelssohn, F.:Elijah (sels), w. M. Rudolf (cnd), Columbia SO—Hear Ye, Israel! *(rec Columbia 30th St. Studios, New York, Sept 18, 1951)* Sony Classical ("Masterworks Heritage" series) ▲ MHK 62356 [ADD]
Mozart, W.A.:Arias, *(cnd & orch unknown)*—Exsultate, jubilate; Tu virginum corona; Alleluia [all from Exsultate, jubilate]; L'amerò, sarò costante [from Il re pastore; w. Felix Eyle (violin)]; d'Oreste, d'Ajace [from Idomeneo]; Deh vieni, non tardar; Voi che sapete; Porgi amor; Dove sono i bei mementi [all from Le nozze di Figaro]; Resta, o cara; Or che il cielo; Nehmt meinen Dank, ihr holden Gönner [all concert arias] VAI Audio ▲ VAIA 1031 [ADD]
Mozart, W.A.:Arias, w. I. Cotrubas (sop), K. Te Kanawa (sop), R. Stevens (mez), P. Domingo (ten), S. Jerusalem (ten), G. London (bar), E. Pinza (bass)—arias & duets from Don Giovanni, Le nozze di Figaro, Die Zauberflöte, etc. *(rec 1941–1978)* CBS Masterworks ▲ MDK 46579 [AAD] ■ MGT 46579
Mozart, W.A.:Nozze di Figaro, w. Bidu Sayao (sop—Susanna), Eleanor Steber (sop—Countess Almaviva), Jarmila Novotna (sop—Cherubino), Ira Petina (sop—Marcellina), John Brownlee (bar—Count Almaviva), Salvatore Baccaloni (bass—Bartolo), Ezio Pinza (bass—Figaro), B. Walter (cnd), *(orch unknown)* The Fourties 2-▲ ENT FT 1509
Puccini, G.:La fanciulla del West, w. M. del Monaco (ten), G. Guelfi (bar), D. Mitropoulos (cnd), Venice Teatro La Fenice Orch, Venice Teatro La Fenice Chorus *(rec live, 6/15/54)* Arkadia 2-▲ 565 (m)
Strauss, R.:4 Last Songs, w. J. Levine (cnd), *(orch unknown)* *(rec live, Cleveland, 5/5/70)* VAI Audio ▲ VAIA 1012 (m/s) [ADD]
Strauss, R.:Die Frau ohne Schatten (sels), w. C. Goltz (sop), I. Steingruber (sop), S. Svanholm (ten), O. Wiener (bass), K. Böhm (cnd), *(orch unknown)*—selections from Act Two (Sieh, Amme, sieh...Würde ich lieber selber zu Stein!) & Act Three (Vater, bist du's?...) *(rec live, Munich, 6/4/53)* VAI Audio ▲ VAIA 1012 (m/s) [ADD]
Wagner, R.:Lohengrin, w. A. Varnay (sop), W. Windgassen (ten), H. Uhde (bar), J. Greindl (bass), J. Keilberth (cnd), Bayreuth Festival Orch, Bayreuth Festival Chorus *(rec live, Bayreuth Festival, 1953)* Teldec ("Historic" series) 4-▲ 93674

Stedman, Erin (sop)
Shewan, S.:Magnificat, w. Kimberly Higgins (alt), Robert Dingman (ten), Alexander Burgess (bar), Paul Shewan (tpt), Barbara Hull (tpt), Nanita Wilson (hn), Scott Emmons (trbn), Kirk Kettinger (tuba), Ann Musser Honeywell (org) Albany ▲ TROY 149 [DDD]
Shewan, S.:The Voice of the Lord in the Storm, w. Kimberly Higgins (alt), Robert Dingman (ten), Alexander Burgess (bar), Paul Shewan (tpt), Barbara Hull (tpt), Nanita Wilson (hn), Scott Emmons (trbn), Kirk Kettinger (tuba), Ann Musser Honeywell (org) Albany ▲ TROY 149 [DDD]

Steele, Brian (bar)
Mahler, G.:Sym 8, w. Oksana Krovytska (sop—Magna Peccatrix), Sheila Smith (sop—Una poenitentium), Shauna Southwick (sop—Mater gloriosa), Kristine Jepson (mez—Maria Aegyptiaca), Julie Simson (mez—Mulier Samaritana), Kurt Hansen (ten—Doctor Marianus), Brian Steele (bar—Pater ecstaticus), Eugene Green (b-bar—Pater profundus), R. Olson (cnd), Colorado MahlerFest Orch, Colorado MahlerFest Chorale, Colorado Mormon Chorale, Colorado Children's Chorale *(rec MahlerFest VIII, Boulder, CO, Jan 14–15, 1995)* MahlerFest 2-▲ MF8-1
Moore, D.:Ballad of Baby Doe, w. Jan Grissom (sop—Baby Doe), Dana Kreuger (mez—Augusta), Myrna Paris (cta—Mama), Brian Steele (bar—Horace), Mark Freiman (b-bar—W. J. Bryan), J. Moriarty (cnd), Central City Opera Orch, Central City Opera Chorus *(rec Central City, CO)* Newport Classic 2-▲ NPD 85593/2 [DDD]

Steele, Brian (bass)
Moore, D.:Devil & Daniel Webster, w. Joyce Guyer (sop—Mary Stone), Benjamin Bongers (ten—Walter Butler), Michael Philip Davis (ten—Simon Girty), Matthew Foerschler (ten—Miser Stephens), Darren Keith Woods (ten—Mr. Scratch), Michael Lanman (bass—Blackbeard Teach), David Soxman (bass—Clerk), Brian Steele (bass—Daniel Webster), John Stephens (bass—Jabez Stone), Andrew Stuckey (bass—King Philip), Robert Gibby Brand (actor), Cary Miller (actor), R. Patterson (cnd), Kansas City SO, Kansas City Lyric Opera Chorus *(rec Sept 1995)* Newport Classic ▲ NPD 85585 [DDD]

Steele, Lucy (sgr)
Hildegard Of Bingen:Sacred Songs, w. Jocelyn West (sgr), Vivien Ellis (sgr), Stevie Wishart (sgr/h-g), Hester Briant (sgr), Fiona Cunningham (sgr), Tara Franks (sgr), Emily Levy (sgr), Vickie Couperim (sgr), Julie Murphy (sgr), Oxford Girls' Choir—Honey & milk beneath her tongue; Ursula's virgins; The devil's virgins; Place of the ancient heart; Zeal of divinity; O fiery spirit; Red river falling; O orzchis ecclesia, Living-light angels; The clouds are grieving; The firstwoman; From their homeland; But the devil mocked; Song to Ecclesia *(rec Toddington, Gloucestershire, England, May 6–8, 1995)* Celestial Harmonies ▲ 13127-2

Steele, Tommy (sgr)
Loesser, F.:Hans Christian Andersen, w. Sally Ann Howes (sgr), et. al.—1977 revised stage version; London cast recording DRG ▲ 13116CD

Stefanescu, Adrian (bass)
Puccini, G.:Tosca, w. Virginia Zeani (sop—Floria Tosca), Emilia Oprea (mez—Shepherd), Nicolae Andreescu (ten—Spoletta), Corneliu Fanateanu (ten—Mario Cavaradossi), Nicolae Herlea (bar—Baron Scarpia), Gheorghe Crasnaru (bass—Cesare Angelotti), Constantin Gabor (bass—Sacristan), Pompei Harasteanu (bass—Jailer), Adrian Stefanescu (bass—Sciarrone), C. Trailescu (cnd), Romanian Opera Orch, Romanian Opera Chorus *(rec Sept 1977)* Vox Box 2-▲ CDX 5153

Stefanescu, Mircea (bar)
Puccini, G.:Turandot, w. Teodora Lucaciu (sop—Liù), Maria Slatinaru (sop—Princess Turandot), Corneliu Finateanu (ten—Pong), George Mircea (ten—Emperor Altoum), Ludovic Speiss (ten—Prince Calaf), Valentin Teodorian (ten—Pang), Octav Enigarescu (bar—Ping), Dionisie Konya (bar—A Mandarin), Mircea Stefanescu (bar—The Prince of Persia), Nicolae Florei (bass—Timur), C. Litvin (cnd), Romanian Radio-TV Orch, Romanian Radio-TV Chorus *(rec Jan 1970)* Vox Box 2-▲ CDX 5160

Stefano, Donato di (sgr)
Donizetti, G.:Linda di Chamounix, w. Mariella Devia (sop—Linda), Sonia Ganassi (mez—Pierotto), Francesca Provvisionato (mez—Maddalena), Luca Canonici (ten—Carlo), Alfonso Antoniozzi (bass—Il Marchese di Boisfleury), Petteri Salomaa (bass—Antonio), Boguslaw Fiksinski (sgr—L'intendente), Donato Di Stefano (sgr—Il Prefetto), G. Bellini (cnd), Eastern Netherlands Orch, Andrew Wise (cnd), National Reisopera Choir *(rec Muziekcentrum Enschede, Holland, June 24–July 2, 1992)* Arts Music 3-▲ 47151-2 [DDD]

Stefano, Giuseppe di (ten)
Arias, w. Birgit Nilsson (sop), Leontyne Price (sop) Legato Classics 2-▲ LCD 153-2 (m) [ADD]
Bellini, V.:I Puritani, w. M. Callas (sop), R. Panerai (bar), N. Rossi-Lemeni (bass), T. Serafin (cnd), La Scala Orch, La Scala Chorus [I] EMI Classics 2-▲ CDCB 47308 (m) [ADD]
Bellini, V.:I Puritani, w. M. Callas (sop), Campolonghi (sgr), R. Silva (bass), G. Picco (cnd), Palacio Bellas Artes Orch, Palacio Bellas Artes Chorus [I] *(rec live, Mexico City 5/29/52)* Melodram 2-▲ MEL 26027 (m) [AAD]
Bizet, G.:Carmen (sels), w. G. Simionato (mez), H. von Karajan (cnd), La Scala Orch, La Scala Chorus—14 arias [F] *(rec live, Milan, 1/18/55)* Arkadia 3-▲ 221 [ADD]
Chicago 1950, w. Bidu Sayao (sop), Renata Tebaldi (sop), Chicago Radio Orch [cnd:Gaetano Merola] Myto ▲ MCD 924.67 [ADD]
Donizetti, G.:La favorita, w. G. Simionato (mez), E. Mascherini (bar), C. Siepi (bass-bar), Rodriguez (sgr), R. Cellini (cnd), Palacio Bellas Artes Orch, Palacio Bellas Artes Chorus [I] *(rec live, Mexico City, 7/12/49)* Standing Room Only 2-▲ SRO 816-2 [ADD]
Donizetti, G.:Lucia di Lammermoor, w. M. Callas (sop), G. Zampieri (ten), R. Panerai (bar), G. Modesti (bass), H. von Karajan (cnd), La Scala Orch, La Scala Chorus *(rec 1954)* Melodram 2-▲ MLO 26040 [DDD]
Donizetti, G.:Lucia di Lammermoor, w. M. Callas (sop), R. Panerai (bar), H. von Karajan (cnd), La Scala Orch, La Scala Chorus [I] *(rec live, Milan 1/18/54)* Standing Room Only 2-▲ SRO 831-2 [ADD]
Donizetti, G.:Lucia di Lammermoor, w. M. Callas (sop), R. Panerai (bar), N. Zaccaria (bass), H. von Karajan (cnd), RIAS SO, La Scala Chorus [I] *(rec live, 1955)* EMI Classics (Studio) 2-▲ CDMB 63631 [ADD]
Donizetti, G.:Lucia di Lammermoor, w. M. Callas (sop), R. Panerai (bar), N. Zaccaria (bass), H. von Karajan (cnd), RIAS SO, La Scala Chorus [I] *(rec 9/29/55)* Verona 2-▲ 2709/10 (m) [AAD]
Donizetti, G.:Lucia di Lammermoor, w. M. Callas (sop), R. Panerai (bar), N. Zaccaria (bass), H. von Karajan (cnd), RIAS SO, La Scala Chorus [I] *(rec 9/29/55)* Melodram 2-▲ MEL 26004
Donizetti, G.:Lucia di Lammermoor, w. M. Callas (sop), Campolonghi (sgr), G. Picco (cnd), Palacio Bellas Artes Orch, Palacio Bellas Artes Chorus [I] *(rec live, Mexico City 6/10/52)* Myto 2-▲ 2 MCD 91340 [ADD]
Donizetti, G.:Lucia di Lammermoor, w. M. Callas (sop), T. Gobbi (bar), R. Arie (bass), T. Serafin (cnd), Florence Maggio Musicale Orch [I] EMI Classics (Studio) 2-▲ CDMB 69980 (m) [ADD]
Donizetti, G.:Lucia di Lammermoor, w. R. Scotto (sop), E. Bastianini (bar), N. Sanzogno (cnd), La Scala Orch, La Scala Chorus *(rec 1959)* Enterprise (Palladio) 2-▲ ENTPD 4117 [ADD]
Duets, w. Callas, Maria (sop), Guido Picco (cnd) *(rec live, Mexico City, 1952)* Melodram 2-▲ CDM 26028 (m) [AAD]
Famous Love Duets, Vol. 2, w. Gianna d'Angelo (sop), Montserrat Caballé (sop), Maria Callas (sop), Renata Scotto (sop), Beverly Sills (sop), Renata Tebaldi (sop), José Carreras (ten), Mario Del Monaco (ten), Plácido Domingo (ten), Luciano Pava Enterprise ("Documents" series) ▲ ENTLV 999
The Farewell Recitals, w. Maria Callas (sop), Ivor Newton (pno) *(rec Philadelphia & Miami & Cincinnati)* Ornamenti 2-▲ FE 124
Giordano, U.:Fedora, w. R. Tebaldi (sop), Mizzetti (sgr), M. Sereni (bar), A. Basile (cnd), Naples Teatro San Carlo Orch, Naples Teatro San Carlo Chorus [I] *(rec live, 1961)* Legato Classics 2-▲ LCD 158-2 (m) [ADD]
Giuseppe di Stefano:The Early Years Bongiovanni ▲ GB 1141 [ADD]
The Glory of Italy *(rec live, 1948–1956)* Cantabile ("Biographies in Music" series) 2-▲ BIM 704-2 (m)
Grandi Voci:Giuseppe di Stefano *(rec 1955–59)* London ▲ 440403-2 [ADD]
Italian Songs London ▲ 417794-2 LM
Lehàr, F.:Das Land des Lächelns, w. Dagmar Koller (sop), Valorie Goodall (sop), Heinz Holecek (bass), H. Lambrecht (cnd), Vienna Volksoper Orch [G] *(rec 1967)* Preiser ▲ 93144 [ADD]
Lehàr, F.:Der Zarewitsch (sels), w. D. Koller (sop), H. Holecek (bar), E.-G. Scherzer (cnd), Vienna Operetta Orch, Original Volga Cossacks Koch Schwann ▲ SCH 312732 [ADD]
Leoncavallo, R.:Pagliacci, w. M. Callas (sop), T. Gobbi (bar), R. Panerai (bar), T. Serafin (cnd), La Scala Orch [I] EMI Classics 3-▲ CDCC 47981 [ADD]
Liederabend, w. Rudolf Bibl (pno) *(rec Vienna, June 22, 1968)* Koch Schwann ▲ SCH 318332
The Martini & Rossi Concerts, Vol. 3, w. Margherita Carosio (sop), Turin RAI Orch [cnd:Oliviero de Fabritiis] Fonit Cetra ("Martini & Rossi" series) ▲ FCT CDMR 5003
Mascagni, P.:Cavalleria rusticana, w. M. Callas (sop), E. Ticozzi (mez), R. Panerai (bar), T. Serafin (cnd), La Scala Orch, La Scala Chorus [I] EMI Classics 3-▲ CDCC 47981 [ADD]
Mascagni, P.:Cavalleria rusticana (sels), w. G. Simionato (mez), A. Votto (cnd), La Scala Orch, La Scala Chorus—Tu qui Santuzza [I] *(rec live, Milan, 5/10/55)* Standing Room Only 2-▲ SRO 816-2 [ADD]
Massenet, J.:Manon (sels), w. M. Favero (sop), M. Borriello (bar), M. Mainardi (bar), A. Guarnieri (cnd), La Scala Orch, La Scala Chorus *(rec live, Milan, 3/15/47)* Myto ▲ 1 MCD 90526 [ADD]
Neapolitan Songs, w. . M. Guarino (cnd) EMI Classics ▲ CDC 47838
1944:His 1st Recordings Grammofono 2000 ▲ GRM 78635
Il Nostro Concerto Replay ▲ 8007
O sole mio Replay Music ▲ 4038
Opera Arias *(rec live, 1947–1963)* Memories 2-▲ MEM 4372 (m) [ADD]
Operatic Arias *(rec live, 1952–1963)* Suite ▲ STE 5008 [ADD]
Ponchielli, A.:La Gioconda, w. Zinka Milanov (sop—La Gioconda), Rosalind Elias (mez—Laura), Belan Amparan (cta—La Cieca), Giacomo Cottino (ten—Isepo), Giuseppe Di Stefano (ten—Enzo Grimaldo), Fernando Valentini (bar—Zuane/Un Nocchiero), Leonard Warren (bar—Barnaba), Virgilio Carbonari (bass—Un Cantore), Plinio Clabassi (bass—Alvise Badoero), F. Previtali (cnd), St. Cecilia Academy Orch Rome, St. Cecilia Academy Chorus Rome Theorema 3-▲ TH 121182/184
Puccini, G.:La Bohème, w. M. Callas (sop), A. Moffo (sop), R. Panerai (bar), A. Votto (cnd), La Scala Orch, La Scala Chorus [I] *(rec 1956)* EMI Classics 2-▲ CDCB 47475 (m) [ADD]
Puccini, G.:La Bohème, w. Licia Albanese (sop—Mimì), Audrey Schuh (sop—Musetta), Giuseppe di Stefano (ten—Rodolfo), Arthur Cosenza (bar—Schaunard), Giuseppe Valdengo (bar—Marcello), Norman Treigle (bass—Colline), Warren Gadpaille (bass—Benoît/Alcindoro), Thomas Carter (sgr—Parpignol), Harold Crane (sgr—Custom House Official), Steve Harun (sgr—Sergeant), R. Cellini (cnd), New Orleans Opera Orch, New Orleans Opera Chorus *(rec Nov 1959)* VAI Audio 2-▲ VAIA 1119-2 [ADD]
Puccini, G.:Manon Lescaut, w. M. Callas (sop), Fioravanti (sgr), T. Serafin (cnd), La Scala Orch, La Scala Chorus [I] EMI Classics 2-▲ CDCB 47392 (m)
Puccini, G.:Tosca, w. L. Price (sop), G. Taddei (bar), H. von Karajan (cnd), Vienna PO, Vienna State Opera Chorus [I] London 2-▲ 421670-2 [ADD]

VOCALISTS

Stefano, Giuseppe di (ten) (cont.)

Puccini, G.:Tosca, w. M. Callas (sop), Campolonghi (sgr), G. Picco (cnd), Palacio Bellas Artes Orch, Palacio Bellas Artes Chorus [I] *(rec live, Mexico City 1952)* Melodram 2-▲ 26028 (m) [AAD]

Puccini, G.:Tosca, w. M. Callas (sop), T. Gobbi (bar), V. de Sabata (cnd), La Scala Orch, La Scala Chorus [I] *(rec 1953)* EMI Classics 2-▲ CDCB 47174 (m) 2-■ 4AV 34047 (m)

Puccini, G.:Tosca, w. Renata Tebaldi (sop—Floria Tosca), Guiseppe di Stefano (ten—Mario Cavardossi), Rinaldo Pelizzoni (ten—Spoletta), Ettore Bastianini (bar—Baron Scarpia), Carlo Badioli (bass—Sacristan), Guiseppe Moresi (bass—Sciarrone), Franco Piva (bass—Jailer), Nicola Zaccaria (bass—Cesare Angelotti), G. Gavazzeni (cnd) *(rec Great Auditorium, Brussels World Fair, 1958)* Legato Classics 2-▲ LCD 2092 [ADD]

Puccini, G.:Tosca (sels), w. M. Callas (sop), G. Picco (cnd), Palacio Bellas Artes Orch, Palacio Bellas Artes Chorus—nine arias & duets [I] *(rec live, Mexico City, 7/1/52)* Standing Room Only 2-▲ SRO 820-2 [ADD]

Puccini, G.:Turandot, w. B. Nilsson (sop), L. Price (sop), T. Gobbi (bar), F. Molinari-Pradelli (cnd), Vienna State Opera Orch, Vienna State Opera Chorus [I] *(rec live, 6/22/61)* Legato Classics 2-▲ LCD 153-2 (m) [ADD]

Simionato & Di Stefano, w. Giulietta Simionato (mez), Milan RAI Orch, Milan RAI Chorus [cnd:Nino Sanzogno] *(rec Nov. 26, 1956)* Incontri Memorabili ▲ CDMR 5015

Strauss (II), Joh.:Die Fledermaus, w. H. Gueden (sop), R. Streich (sop), G. Stolze (ten), G. Zampieri (ten), E. Wächter (bar), W. Berry (bass), E. Kunz (bar), H. von Karajan (cnd), Vienna State Opera Orch, Vienna State Opera Chorus [G] Arkadia 3-▲ 215 (m) [ADD]

Thomas, A.:Mignon (sels), w. G. Simionato (mez), C. Siepi (b-bar), G. Picco (cnd), Palacio Bellas Artes Orch, Palacio Bellas Artes Chorus *(rec live, Mexico City, 6/28/49)* Golden Age of Opera 2-▲ GAO 128/29 [ADD]

Torna a Surriento:Italian Songs London ("Jubilee" series) ▲ 417794-2 LM [ADD]

Verdi, G.:Aida, w. Antonietta Stella (sop—Aida), Mirella Parutto (sop—Priestess), Giulietta Simionato (mez—Amneris), Giuseppe DiStefano (ten—Radames), Giuseppe Zampiere (ten—Messenger), Giangiacomo Guelfi (bar—Amonasro), Silvio Maionica (bass—King of Egypt), Nicola Zaccaria (bass-Ramfis), A. Votto (cnd), La Scala Orch, La Scala Chorus *(rec Milan, Dec 7, 1956)* Legato Classics 2-▲ LCD 204-2 [ADD]

Verdi, G.:Arias, w. M. Callas (sop), M. Gavazzeni (ten), C.M. Giulini (cnd), La Scala Orch—E strano...Sempre libera;—Ecco l'orrido campo...Ma dall' arido stelo Myto 2-▲ MCD 89003 (m) [ADD]

Verdi, G.:Un ballo in maschera, w. M. Callas (sop), E. Ratti (sop), G. Simionato (mez), E. Bastianini (bar), G. Gavazzeni (cnd), La Scala Orch, La Scala Chorus [I] *(rec live 12/7/57)* Arkadia 2-▲ 519 (m) [AAD]

Verdi, G.:Un ballo in maschera, w. M. Callas (sop), E. Ratti (sop), G. Simionato (mez), E. Bastianini (bar), G. Gavazzeni (cnd), La Scala Orch, La Scala Chorus *(rec 1957)* Melodram ▲ MLO 26039 [ADD]

Verdi, G.:Un ballo in maschera, w. M. Callas (sop), E. Ratti (sop), F. Barbieri (mez), T. Gobbi (bar), A. Votto (cnd), La Scala Orch, La Scala Chorus [I] *(rec 1956)* EMI Classics 2-▲ CDCB 47498 (m)

Verdi, G.:La forza del destino, w. Zinka Milanov (sop—Donna Leonora di Vargas), Rosalind Elias (mez—Preziosilla), Luisa Gioia (sgr—Curra), Angelo Mercuriali (ten—Trabuco), Giuseppe di Stefano (ten—Son Alvaro), Leonard Warren (bar—Don Carlos di Vargas), Giorgio Tozzi (b-bar—Padre guardiano), Dino Mantovani (bar—Fra Melitone), Paolo Washington (b-bar—Il marchese di Calatrava), Virgilio Carbonari (b-bar—un alcalde), Sergio Liviabella (sgr—un chirurgo), F. Previtali (cnd), St. Cecilia Academy Orch Rome, St. Cecilia Academy Chorus Rome [I] London ▲ 443678-2 [ADD]

Verdi, G.:La forza del destino, w. Leyla Gencer (sop—Leonora), Gabriella Carturan (mez—Preziosilla), Giuseppe di Stefano (ten—Don Alvaro), Aldo Protti (bar—Don Carlo), Cesare Siepi (b-bar), Franco Calabrese (bass—Marchese di Calatrava), Enrico Campi (bass—Fra Melitone), A. Votto (cnd), La Scala Orch, La Scala Chorus *(rec Bühnen der Stadt, Köln, July 5, 1957)* Agorá Music ("Phoenix" series) 3-▲ 510 [ADD]

Verdi, G.:La forza del destino, w. Leyla Gencer (sop), Aldo Protti (bar), Cesare Siepi (bass), A. Votto (cnd), La Scala Orch, La Scala Chorus *(rec La Scala Theatre, Milan, July 5, 1957)* Pantheon 3-▲ PHE 6627 (m)

Verdi, G.:La forza del destino, w. L. Gencer (sop), G. Carturan (mez), A. Priotti (bar), C. Siepi (b-bar), A. Votto (cnd), *(orch unknown)* *(rec live, Cologne 1957)* Melodram 3-▲ MEL 37010

Verdi, G.:La forza del destino, w. Zinka Milanov (sop), Rosalind Elias (mez), Leonard Warren (bar), Giorgio Tozzi (bass), Paolo Washington (bass), F. Previtali (cnd), St. Cecilia Academy Orch Rome, St. Cecilia Academy Chorus Rome *(rec 1959)* Theorema 3-▲ TH 121157/59

Verdi, G.:Requiem Mass, w. H. Nelli (sop), F. Barbieri (mez), C. Siepi (b-bar), A. Toscanini (cnd), NBC SO, Robert Shaw Chorale [L] RCA Gold Seal 2-▲ 60299-2-RG (m) [ADD] 2-■ 60299-4-RG (CrO2)

Verdi, G.:Requiem Mass, w. Elizabeth Schwarzkopf (sop), Oralia Dominguez (mez), Cesare Siepi (b-bar), V. de Sabata (cnd), La Scala Orch, La Scala Chorus Theorema 2-▲ TH 121123/24

Verdi, G.:Rigoletto, w. M. Callas (sop), Campolonghi (sgr), U. Mugnai (cnd), Palacio Bellas Artes Orch, Palacio Bellas Artes Chorus [I] *(rec live, Mexico City, 6/17/52)* Melodram 2-▲ CDM 26023

Verdi, G.:Rigoletto (sels), w. C. O'Connor (sop), O. Dominguez (mez), G. Valdengo (bar), I. Rufino (bass), R. Cellini (cnd), Palacio Bellas Artes Orch, Palacio Bellas Artes Chorus [abridged performance] *(rec live, Mexico City 6/22/48)* Golden Age of Opera 2-▲ GAO 128/29 [ADD]

Verdi, G.:La traviata, w. M. Callas (sop), Campolonghi (bar), U. Mugnai (cnd), Palacio Bellas Artes Orch, Palacio Bellas Artes Chorus [I] *(rec live, Mexico City, 6/3/52)* Melodram 2-▲ CDM 26021

Verdi, G.:La traviata, w. M. Callas (sop), E. Bastianini (bar), C. M. Giulini (cnd), La Scala Orch, La Scala Chorus [I] *(rec live 5/28/55)* Arkadia 2-▲ 501 (m) [AAD]

Verdi, G.:La traviata, w. M. Callas (sop), E. Bastianini (bar), C. M. Giulini (cnd), La Scala Orch, La Scala Chorus [I] *(rec 1955)* EMI Classics (Studio) 2-▲ CDMB 63628 (m) [ADD]

Verdi, G.:La traviata (sels), w. Elizabeth Schwarzkopf (sop), Oralia Dominguez (mez), Cesare Siepi (b-bar), V. de Sabata (cnd), La Scala Orch, La Scala Chorus—Preludes to Acts I & III Theorema 2-▲ TH 121123/24

Voce 'e notte Replay Music ▲ 4032

World Stars Sing Operetta, w. Anna Moffo (sop), Lucia Popp (sop), José Carreras (ten), Ants Kollo (ten), Thomas Moser (ten), Hermann Prey (bar), Karl Ridderbusch (bass), et al., various orchs *(rec 1968-1985)* Acanta ▲ 42941

Stefanoni, Marco (bass)

Verdi, G.:Un ballo in maschera, w. M. Curtis Verna (sop—Amelia), M. Erato (sop—Oscar), P. Tassinari (cta—Ulrica), F. Tagliavini (ten—Riccardo), G. Valdengo (bar—Renato), A. Albertini (bar—Silvano), M. Stefanoni (bass—Samuel), V. Susca (bass—Tom), A. Questa (cnd), Turin RAI SO, Turin RAI Chorus *(rec 1954)* Cetra Classic 2-▲ CDO 13 [AAD]

Stefanowicz, Artur (ct)

Mozart, W.A.:Arias, w. K. Teutsch (cnd), Sinfonia Varsovia—Mitridate, Rè di Ponto, K.87; Apollo et Hyacinthus, K.38; Ascanio in Alba, K.111; Ombra Felice, K.255 *(rec Polish Radio, Warsaw, Feb 1991)* Polskie Nagrania ▲ PNCD 110 [DDD]

Pergolesi, G.B.:Stabat mater, w. Brigitte Fournier (sop), A. Mysinski (cnd), Warsaw Soloists *(rec Warsaw Philharmonic Concert Hall, Warsaw, 1992)* Elysium ▲ GRK 705 [DDD]

Vivaldi, A.:Stabat Mater, w. Brigitte Fournier (sop), A. Mysinski (cnd), Warsaw Soloists *(rec Warsaw Philharmonic Concert Hall, Warsaw, 1992)* Elysium ▲ GRK 705 [DDD]

Steffan, Sophia (cta)

Glanville-Hicks, P.:Nausicaa, w. Teresa Stratas (sop—Nausicaa), Sophia Steffan (cta—Queen Arete), Michalis Heliotis (ten—Antinous/Priest), George Moutsios (ten—Eurymachus), Edward Ruhl (ten—Phemius), George Tsantikos (ten—Clytoneus), Vassilis Koundouris (bar—Messenger), John Modenos (bar—Aethon), Spiro Malas (bass—King Alcinous), C. Surinach (cnd), Athens SO, Athens Sym Chorus *(rec Athens Festival, 1961)* CRI ▲ CD 695 [ADD]

Steffan, Sophia (sop)

Glanville-Hicks, P.:Nausicaa (sels), w. Teresa Stratas (sop), Spiro Malas (bass), Michalis Helii (sgr), Michalis Heliots (sgr), George Moutsio (sgr), Edward Ruhl (sgr), George Tsantikos (sgr), C. Surinach (cnd), Athens SO, Athens Sym Chorus CRI ▲ CD 695 [ADD]

Steffek, Hanny (sop)

Gluck, C.W.:Orfeo ed Euridice, w. H. Steffek (sop—Amore), T. Stich-Randall (mez—Euridice), M. Forrester (cta—Orfeo), C. Mackerras (cnd), Vienna State Opera Orch, Vienna State Opera Chorus [Italian version w. additions composed for the French production] *(rec 6/66)* Vanguard Classics 2-▲ OVC 4039/40 [ADD]

Steffek, Hanny (sop) (cont.)

Lehár, F.:Die lustige Witwe, w. E. Schwarzkopf (sop), N. Gedda (ten), E. Wächter (bar), L. von Matačič (cnd), Philharmonia Orch, Philharmonia Chorus [G] EMI Classics 2-▲ CDCB 47177

Mozart, W.A.:Così fan tutte, w. E. Schwarzkopf (sop), C. Ludwig (mez), A. Kraus (ten), G. Taddei (bar), W. Berry (bass), K. Böhm (cnd), Philharmonia Orch, Philharmonia Chorus [I] EMI Classics ("Studio" series) 3-▲ CDMC 69330 [ADD]

Steffen, Jan Moritz (sgr)

Waits, T.:The Black Rider:The Casting of Magic Bullets, w. Angelika Thomas (sgr—Anne), Annette Paulmann (sgr—Kätchen), Sona Cervena (sgr—Bird/Messenger/Spoonwoman), Monika Tahal (sgr—Witness/Bird/Shrink/Wilhelm's Double/Skeleton), Susi Eisenkolb (sgr—Bridesmaid/Pegleg's Double), Heinz Vossbrink (sgr—Kuno), Dominique Horwitz (sgr—Pegleg), Gerd Kunath (sgr—Bertram), Stefan Kurt (sgr—Wilhelm), Klaus Schreiber (sgr—Robert/Man on Stag/Georg Schmid), Jörg Holm (Old Uncle/Duke), Jan Moritz Steffen (sgr—Young Kuno/Bird/Shrink/Skeleton), Tom Waits (vocals/coliope/organ/chamberlain/mar/emax/guitar/train whistle), Ralph Carney (saxophone/bass clarinet/baritone horn), Bill Douglas (bass instrument), Kenny Wollesen (perc) Island ▲ 314518559-2

Steiger, R. (sgr)

Rodgers, R.:Oklahoma!, w. Gordon MacRae (sgr), S. Jones (sgr), Gloria Grahame (sgr), Gene Nelson (sgr), C. Greenwood (sgr), J. Whitmore (sgr) *(rec 1955)* Broadway Angel ▲ ZDM 64691 ■ EG 64691

Stein, Barbara (alt)

Ernst, S.:Seven Miniatures on Japanese Haiku, w. Hertha Rosa-Herseni (vc), Susanne Geiger (pno) Vienna Modern Masters ▲ VMM 2018 [DDD]

Steiner, Elisabeth (mez)

Gluck, C.W.:Iphigénie en Aulide, w. Inge Borkh (sop—Klytämnestra), Christa Ludwig (mez—Iphigenie), Elisabeth Steiner (mez—Artemis), James King (ten—Achilles), Otto Edelmann (b-bar), Alois Pernerstorfer (b-bar), Walter Berry (bass), K. Böhm (cnd), Vienna PO, Salzburg Festival Chamber Choir, Vienna State Opera Chorus *(rec Salzburg, Aug 3, 1962)* Orfeo d'or ("Festspiel Dikumente" series) 2-▲ C 428962 (m) [ADD]

Schultze, N.:Das kalte Herz, w. Grit van Jüten (sop), Heinz Kruse (ten), Detelf Zywietz (sgr), N. Schutze (cnd), Cologne RSO, Händel Collegium Koch Schwann 2-▲ SCH 318002 [DDD]

Strauss (II), Joh.:Eine Nacht in Venedig (sels), w. J. Scovotti (sop), E. Schary (mez), C. Bini (ten), F. Stricker (ten), W. Brendel (bar), E. Märzendorfer (cnd), Hungarian State Orch, Hungarian State Chorus [G] Acanta ▲ CD 43809 [DDD]

Steiner, Paul (ten)

Fröhlich, F.T.:Choral Music, w. E. Speiser (sop), J. Krattiger (bass), B. Billeter (pno), C. Spring (pno), Winterthur Vocal Ensemble [G] *(rec 1988)* Jecklin-Disco ▲ JD 627-2 [ADD]

Steingruber, Ilona (sop)

Beethoven, L. van:Cant on the Death of the Emperor Joseph II, w. Alfred Poell (b-bar), C. Krauss (cnd), Vienna SO, Vienna Academy Chamber Choir *(rec live, 1953)* Originals ▲ ORISH 825 [ADD]

Beethoven, L. van:Missa Solemnis, w. Else Schuerhoff (alt), Ernst Majkut (ten), Otto Wiener (bass), O. Klemperer (cnd), Vienna SO, Akademie Chamber Choir *(rec Vienna, 1950)* Vox Legends 2-▲ CDX2 5527

Schubert, Franz:Die Verschworenen, w. Ilona Steingruber (sop—Countess), Elizabeth Roon (mez—Helene), Laurence Dutoit (trb—Isella), Walter Anton (ten—Udolin), Walter Berry (bar—Count), Rudolf Kreutzberger (sgr—Astolf), F. Grossmann (cnd), Vienna SO, Vienna Academy Chamber Choir Theorema ▲ TH 121178

Strauss, R.:Die Frau ohne Schatten (sels), w. E. Steber (sop), C. Goltz (sop), S. Svanholm (ten), O. Wiener (bass), K. Böhm (cnd), *(orch unknown)*—selections from Act Two (Sieh, Amme, sieh...Würde ich lieber selber zu Stein!) & Act Three (Vater, bist du's?...) *(rec live, Munich, 6/4/53)* VAI Audio ▲ VAIA 1012 (m/s) [ADD]

Steinsky, Ulrike (sop)

Mozart, W.A.:Zauberflöte, w. B. Hendricks (sop—Pamina), J. Anderson (sop—Queen of the Night), U. Steinsky (sop—Papagena), J. Hadley (ten—Tamino), T. Allen (bar—Papageno), R. Lloyd (bass—Sarastro), C. Mackerras (cnd), Scottish CO, Scottish Chamber Chorus [G] Telarc 2-▲ CD 80302 [DDD]

Stejskal, Margot (sop)

Strauss, R.:Der Rosenkavalier (sels), w. A. Pusar-Jeric (sop), A. Jahns (mez), U. Walther (cta), R. Haunstein (bar), T. Adam (b-bar), H. Vonk (cnd), Dresden Staatskapelle, Dresden State Chorus [G] *(rec live 2/85)* Denon ▲ CO 8010 [DDD]

Stella, Antonietta (sop)

Antonietta Stella Melodram 2-▲ CDM 27014 (m) [AAD]

Donizetti, G.:Linda di Chamounix, w. C. Valletti (ten), R. Capecchi (bar), G. Taddei (bar), T. Serafin (cnd), Naples Teatro San Carlo Orch, Naples Teatro San Carlo Chorus *(rec 1959)* Andromeda ▲ ANR 2509 [ADD]

Giordano, U.:Andrea Chénier, w. A. Stella (sop—Maddalena), F. Corelli (ten—Andrea Chénier), M. Sereni (bar—Carlo Gerard), G. Santini (cnd), Rome Opera Orch, Rome Opera Chorus EMI Classics ▲ CDMB 65287

Rosanna Carteri, Antonietta Stella & Beniamino Gigli, w. Rosanna Carteri (sop), Beniamino Gigli (ten), Rome RAI SO, Rome RAI Chorus [cnd:Nino Antonellini], Milan RAI SO [cnd:Nino Sanzogno] *(rec Milan & Sanremo, Feb. 9, 1953 & Dec. 21, 1)* Incontri memorabili ("Martini & Rossi Concert" series) ▲ CDMR 5005 [ADD]

Spontini, G.:Agnes von Hohensaufen, w. M. Caballé (sop), B. Prevedi (ten), G. Guelfi (bar), R. Muti (cnd), Rome Radio Orch, Rome RAI Chorus [I] *(rec live, 4/30/70)* Myto 2-▲ 2 MCD 90215 (m) [ADD]

Stella, Cossotto & Monaco, w. Fiorenza Cossotto (mez), Mario Del Monaco (ten), Ferruccio Scaglia (cnd), Milan RAI SO, Rome RAI SO *(rec Martini & Rossi Concert, 1959 & 1960)* Incontri Memorabili ▲ CDMR 5031

Verdi, G.:Aida, w. F. Barbieri (mez), F. Corelli (ten), A. Colzani (bar), M. Petri (bar), V. Gui (cnd), Naples Teatro San Carlo Orch, Naples Teatro San Carlo Chorus [I] *(rec live, Naples 11/2/55)* Golden Age of Opera 2-▲ GAO 116/17 [ADD]

Verdi, G.:Aida, w. Antonietta Stella (sop—Aida), Mirella Parutto (sop—Priestess), Giulietta Simionato (mez—Amneris), Giuseppe DiStefano (ten—Radames), Giuseppe Zampiere (ten—Messenger), Giangiacomo Guelfi (bar—Amonasro), Silvio Maionica (bass—King of Egypt), Nicola Zaccaria (bass-Ramfis), A. Votto (cnd), La Scala Orch, La Scala Chorus *(rec Milan, Dec 7, 1956)* Legato Classics 2-▲ LCD 204-2 [ADD]

Verdi, G.:Arias, w. F. Scaglia (cnd), Rome Italian Radio-TV Orch—arias from Ernani & Forza del destino [I] *(rec live 9/5/59)* Melodram 2-▲ MEL 27068 (m) [AAD]

Verdi, G.:Aroldo, w. G. Penno (ten), A. Protti (bar), F. Novelli (bar), T. Serafin (cnd), Florence Maggio Musicale Orch, Florence Maggio Musicale Chorus [I] *(rec live 6/3/53)* Melodram 2-▲ MEL 27014 (m) [AAD]

Verdi, G.:Attila, w. Gianfranco Cecchele (ten), Giangiacomo Guelfi (bar), Ruggiero Raimondi (bass), R. Muti (cnd), Rome RAI Orch, Rome RAI Chorus *(rec live 1970)* Memories 2-▲ HR 4178/79 (m)

Verdi, G.:Attila, w. Gianfranco Cecchele (ten), Giangiacomo Guelfi (bar), Ruggiero Raimondi (bass), R. Muti (cnd), Rome RAI SO, Rome RAI Chorus *(rec Rome, Nov. 21, 1970)* Pantheon 2-▲ PHE 6642 (m)

Verdi, G.:La battaglia di Legnano, w. F. Corelli (ten), E. Bastianini (bar), G. Gavazzeni (cnd), La Scala Orch, La Scala Chorus [I] *(rec live 12/7/61)* Myto 2-▲ 2 MCD 89010 (m) [ADD]

Verdi, G.:Simon Boccanegra, w. A. Stella (sop—Maria), C. Bergonzi (ten—Gabriele), G. Giorgetti (bar—Pietro), W. Monachesi (bar—Paolo), M. Petri (bar—Jacopo), P. Silveri (bar—Simon), F. Molinari-Pradelli (cnd), Rome Radio Orch, Rome RAI Chorus *(rec 1951)* Cetra Classic ▲ CDO 23 [ADD]

Verdi, G.:Il trovatore, w. M. Fiorentini (mez), F. Cossotto (mez), F. Corelli (ten), E. Bastianini (bar), I. Vinco (bass), G. Gavazzeni (cnd), La Scala Orch, La Scala Chorus [I] *(rec live, Milan, 12/7/62)* Claque 2-▲ CLQ 2013 (m)

Verdi, G.:Il trovatore, w. M. Fiorentini (mez), F. Cossotto (mez), F. Corelli (ten), E. Bastianini (bar), I. Vinco (bass), G. Gavazzeni (cnd), La Scala Orch, La Scala Chorus *(rec live, Milan, 12/7/62)* Melodram 2-▲ MEL 27068 (m) [AAD]

Stella, Antonietta (sop) (cont.)
Verdi, G.:I vespri siciliani, w. A. Stella (sop—Elena), M. Filippeschi (ten—Arrigo), G. Taddei (bar—Monforte), B. Ladysz (bass—Procida), T. Serafin (cnd), Palermo Teatro Massimo Orch, Palermo Teatro Massimo Chorus *(rec Jan. 18, 1957)* Golden Age of Opera 2-▲ GAO 145/46 [ADD]

Stemmler, T. (nar)
Henry VIII:Songs, Ballads & Instrumental Pieces, w. M. Valentin (cnd), Isaak Ensemble Heidelberg—The Isaak Ensemble plays 26 pieces, & Stemmler reads 9 of Henry's love letters to Anne Boleyn [E,F] Bayer ▲ 100132 [DDD]

Stene, Randi (cta)
Janácek, L.:Slavonic Mass, w. T. Kiberg (sop), P. Svensson (ten), U. Cold (bass), C. Mackerras (cnd), Danish National RSO, Danish National Radio Choir, Copenhagen Boys' Choir Chandos ▲ CHAN 9310 [DDD]

Stenhammar, S. (sop)
Guyonnet, J.:La Cantate interrompue, w. F. Rochaix (nar), S. Stenhammar (sop), S. Seban (pno), G. Calame (pno), E. Séjourne (perc), P. Geiss, E. Tarr (tpt), B. Nilsson (tpt), H. Ries (trbn), H. Rückert (trbn), J.-M. Collet, J. Guyonnet (cnd), Geneva Collegium Academicum [F] *(rec Nov. 15, 1986)* Grammont ▲ CTSP 30-2
Widmer, E.:Caititi-Lua Nova, w. E. Widmer (cnd), Collegium Academicum Soloists *(rec May 23, 1980)* Grammont ▲ CTSP 32-2 [ADD]

Stenkina, Valeria (alt)
Gounod, C.:Ave Maria, w. A. Titov (pno) Infinity Digital ▲ QK 57254 [DDD]
Gounod, C.:Ave Maria, w. Alexander Titov (pno) Infinity Digital ▲ QK 69255 [DDD]
Schubert, Franz:Ave Maria! Jungfrau mild!, w. Alexander Titov (pno) Infinity Digital ▲ QK 69255 [DDD]
Schubert, Franz:Ave Maria! Jungfrau mild!, w. A. Titov (pno) Infinity Digital ▲ QK 57254 [DDD]

Stensvold, Terje (bass)
Braein, E.F.:Anne Pedersdotter, w. K. Ekeberg (sop—Anne Pedersdotter), V. Hanssen (mez—Merete Beyer), R. Eriksen (alt—Herlofs-Marte), I. M. Brekke (alt—Bente), K. M. Sandve (ten—Martin Beyer), C. Ehrstedt (ten—Master Olaus), A. Helleland (ten—David), T. Gilje (ten—Jørund), S. A. Thorsen (bar—Master Johannes), S. Carlsen (bass—Absalon Pedersøn Beyer), T. Stensvold (bass—Master Laurentius), G. Oskarsson (bass—Jens Schelderup), P. Andersson (cnd), Norwegian National Opera Orch, Norwegian National Opera Chorus Simax 2-▲ PSC 3121

Štěpánová, Olga (alt)
Schnittke, A.:Requiem, w. Zdena Kloubová (sop), Vladimír Dolezal (ten), J. Belohlávek (cnd), Prague SO, Kühn Chorus *(rec live, Smetana Hall, Municipal House, Prague, Dec 19, 1990)* Panton ("60 Years of the Prague SO" series) ▲ PAN 811374 [ADD]

Stepanova, Stepanka (mez)
Janácek, L.:The Diary of One Who Disappeared, w. Věra Soukupová (mez), Beno Blachut (ten), Nicolai Gedda (ten), Josef Paleníček (pno), Prague Radio Women's Chorus, Czech Chamber Singers Female Chorus—contains 2 complete performances *(rec 1984 & 1956)* Supraphon ▲ SUP 0022 [DDD/ADD]

Stephens, John (bass)
Moore, D.:Devil & Daniel Webster, w. Joyce Guyer (sop—Mary Stone), Benjamin Bongers (ten—Walter Butler), Michael Philip Davis (ten—Simon Girty), Matthew Foerschler (ten—Miser Stephens), Darren Keith Woods (ten—Mr. Scratch), Michael Lanman (bass—Blackbeard Teach), David Soxman (bass—Clerk), Brian Steele (bass—Daniel Webster), John Stephens (bass—Jabez Stone), Andrew Stuckey (bass—King Philip), Robert Gibby Brand (actor), Cary Miller (actor), R. Patterson (cnd), Kansas City SO, Kansas City Lyric Opera Chorus *(rec Sept 1995)* Newport Classic ▲ NPD 85585 [DDD]

Stephens, Pamela Helen (mez)
Haydn, J.:Mass 12, "Theresienmesse", w. Janine Watson (sop), Mark Padmore (ten), Stephen Varcoe (bass), R. Hickox (cnd), Collegium Musicum 90 Chandos ▲ CHAN 0592
Purcell, H.:Dido & Aeneas, w. Rebecca Evans (sop—Belinda), Maria Ewing (sop—Dido), Mary Plazas (sop—1st witch), Patricia Rozario (sop—2nd woman), Sally Burgess (mez—Sorceress), Pamela Helen Stephens (mez—2nd witch), James Bowman (ct—Spirit), Jamie MacDougal (ten—Sailor), Karl Daymond (bar—Aeneas), R. Hickox (cnd), Collegium Musicum 90 Chandos ("Early Music" series) ▲ CHAN 0586 [DDD]
Sullivan, A.:The Yeomen of the Guard, w. Felicity Palmer (sop—Dame Carruthers), Pamela Helen Stephens (mez—Phoebe Meryll), Neill Archer (ten—Col Fairfax), Peter Hoare (ten—Leonard Meryll), Ralph Mason (ten—1st Yeoman), Donald Maxwell (bar—Wilfred Shadbolt), Peter Savidge (bar—Lieutenant Sir Richard Cholmondely), Donald Adams (bass—Sergeant Meryll), Richard Suart (bass—Jack Point), Peter Lloyd Evans (sgr—2nd Yeoman), Alwyn Mellor (sgr—Elsie Maynard), Clare O'Neill (sgr—Kate), C. Mackerras (cnd), Welsh National Opera Orch, Welsh National Opera Chorus *(rec Brangwyn Hall, Swasea, Wales, Apr 18-30 & May 1, 1995)* Telarc 2-▲ CD 80404 [DDD]

Stephenson, David (bass)
Handel, G.F.:Messiah (sels), w. Catherine Bott (sop), Clare Henry (cta), Gareth Roberts (ten), D. Jackson (cnd), London SO—Comfort Ye, My People, Saith Your God; Every Valley Shall Be Exalted; And the Glory of the Lord Shall Be Revealed; And He Shall Purify the Sons of Levi; For unto Us a Child Is Born; Pifa; Rejoice Greatly, O Daughter of Zion; Air:He Shall Feed His Flock Like a Shepherd; Behold the Lamb of God; He Was Despised and Rejected of Men; All We Like Sheep Have Gone Astray; The Trumpet Shall Sound; Chorus:Hallelujah! For the Lord God Omnipotent Reigneth Special Music Co. 2-▲ S2D 5110 [DDD]
Handel, G.F.:Messiah (sels), w. Catherine Bott (sop), Clare Henry (cta), Gareth Roberts (ten), D. Jackson (cnd), London SO—Comfort Ye, My People, Saith Your God; Every Valley Shall Be Exalted; And the Glory of the Lord Shall Be Revealed; And He Shall Purify the Sons of Levi; For unto Us a Child Is Born; Pifa; Rejoice Greatly, O Daughter of Zion; Air:He Shall Feed His Flock Like a Shepherd; Behold the Lamb of God; He Was Despised and Rejected of Men; All We Like Sheep Have Gone Astray; The Trumpet Shall Sound; Chorus:Hallelujah! For the Lord God Omnipotent Reigneth Special Music Co. ▲ SCD 5102 [DDD]

Stephenson, Donna (mez)
Johnson, H.:Emily Dickinson Songs, w. E. A. Holding (pno)—I. Exultation (1957), II. Mortal my friend (1956), III. If pain for peace prepares (1959) Albany ▲ TROY 061 [DDD]

Stepien, Jozef (ten)
Szymanowski, K.:Harnasie, w. R. Satanowski (cnd), Warsaw Opera Orch, Warsaw National Opera Chorus Koch Schwann ▲ CD 311064 [DDD]

Sterne, Randi (alt)
Jensen, L.I.:The Return, w. A. Bolstad (sop), H. Bjørkey (ten), I. Gilhuus (ten), P. Vollestad (bar), C. Stabell (bass), O.K. Ruud (cnd), Trondheim SO, Trondheim Sym Chorus, Nidarso Cathedral Choir Simax 2-▲ PSC 3109

Steur, Rene (bass)
Biber, H. von:Requiem à 15, w. E. Bongers (sop), A. Grimm (sop), K. Wessel (alt), P. de Groot (alt), M. Reyans (ten), S. Davies (ten), K.-J. de Koning (bass), T. Koopman (cnd), Amsterdam Baroque Orch, Amsterdam Baroque Choir Erato ▲ 91725
Biber, H. von:Vesperae longiores ac breviores una cum litaniis Laurentanis, w. E. Bongers (sop), A. Grimm (sop), K. Wessel (alt), P. de Groot (alt), M. Reyens (ten), S. Davies (ten), K.-J. de Koning (bass), T. Koopman (cnd), Amsterdam Baroque Orch, Amsterdam Baroque Choir Erato ▲ 91725

Stevens, Charles Robert (bar)
Talma, L.:Voices of Peace, w. Rosalind Rees (sop), Scott Whittaker (ten), G. Smith (cnd), Adirondack CO, Gregg Smith Singers Vox Box ("The American Composers" series) 3-▲ CDX 3037

Stevens, Dora (sop)
Walton, W.:Façade, w. H. Foss (pno)—(3 songs) Daphne; Through Gilded Trellises; Old Sir Faulk *(rec Mar. 20, 1940)* Dutton Laboratories ▲ CDAX 8003 [ADD]

Stevens, Risë (mez)
Bizet, G.:Carmen (sels), w. N. Conner (sop), R. Jobin (ten), R. Weede (bar), G. Sébastian (cnd), Metropolitan Opera Orch, New York Metropolitan Opera Chorus [F] Odyssey ■ YT 32102 (m)
Mozart, W.A.:Arias, w. E. Steber (sop), I. Cotrubas (sop), K. Te Kanawa (sop), P. Domingo (ten), S. Jerusalem (ten), G. London (bar), E. Pinza (bass)—arias & duets from Don Giovanni, Le nozze di Figaro, Die Zauberflöte, etc. *(rec 1941–1978)* CBS Masterworks ▲ MDK 46579 [AAD] ■ MGT 46579
Mozart, W.A.:Nozze di Figaro, w. S. Jurinac (sop), G. Sciutti (sop), M. Sinclair (cta), D. McCoshan (ten), H. Cuénod (ten), G. Griffith (bar), S. Bruscantini (b-bar), F. Calabrese (bass), V. Gui (cnd), Glyndebourne Festival Orch, Glyndebourne Festival Chorus Classics for Pleasure ▲ CDCFP 4724 [ADD]

Stevens, Risë (mez) (cont.)
Offenbach, J.:Les Contes d'Hoffmann, w. L. Amara (sop), R. Peters (sop), R. Tucker (ten), M. Singher (bar), P. Monteux (cnd), Metropolitan Opera Orch, New York Metropolitan Opera Chorus Stradivarius 2-▲ DAT 12302
Saint-Saëns, C.:Samson et Dalila, w. Risë Stevens (mez—Dalila), Ramón Vinay (ten—Samson), Thomas Carter (ten—1st Philistine), Tony Lopez (ten—Philistine Messenger), Joseph Mordino (bar—High Priest), Arthur Cosenza (bass—Abimélech), Joseph Knight (bass—2nd Philistine), Ara Berberian (bass—Old Hebrew), R. Cellini (cnd), New Orleans Opera Orch, New Orleans Opera Chorus *(rec live, Apr 2, 1960)* VAI Audio 2-▲ VAIA 1055-2 [ADD]

Stevenson, Adlai (nar)
Copland, A.:Lincoln Portrait, w. E. Ormandy (cnd), Philadelphia Orch Sony Classical ("Essential Classics" series) ▲ SBK 62401 ■ SBT 62401

Stevenson, Alexander (ten)
Bach, J.S.:St. John Passion, w. Barbara Schlick (sop), Ingeborg Most (alt), Edrian Brand (ten), Philip Langshaw (bass), Peter Lika (bass), P. Kuentz (cnd), Paul Kuentz Orch, Paul Kuentz Choir Pierre Verany 2-▲ PVY 730051 [DDD]
Handel, G.F.:Messiah (sels), w. Barbara Schlick (sop), Jean Nirouet (ct), Philip Langshaw (bass), P. Kuentz (cnd), Paul Kuentz Orch, Paul Kuentz Choir Pierre Verany ▲ PVY 730045
Mozart, W.A.:Missa, K.317, w. Mechtild Georg (sop), Barbara Schlick (sop), Philip Langshaw (bass), P. Kuentz (cnd), Paul Kuentz Orch, Paul Kuentz Choir Pierre Verany ▲ PVY 730041
Orff, C.:Carmina burana, w. Elisabeth Vidal (sop), André Cognet (bass), P. Kuentz (cnd), Paul Kuentz Orch, Paul Kuentz Choir, Mouez Armor Chorale, Lorient Conservatory Chorus, Notre Dame College Chorus Pierre Verany ▲ PVY 730044
Verdi, G.:Requiem Mass, w. Mariana Slavova (sop), Joke Kramer (mez), Peter Lika (bass), P. Kuentz (cnd), Paul Kuentz Orch, Paul Kuentz Choir Pierre Verany 2-▲ PVY 730054 [DDD]

Stewart, John (ten)
Argento, D.:To Be Sung Upon The Water, w. Charles Russo (cl/b cl), Donald Hassard (pno) Phoenix ▲ PHCD 129
Britten, H.:Canticle II, w. Ellen Shade (sop), Martin Katz (pno) Phoenix ▲ PHCD 129
Britten, H.:Sonnets of Michelangelo, w. Martin Katz (pno) Phoenix ▲ PHCD 129
Rorem, N.:Dialogues, w. Anita Darian (sop), Richard Cumming (pno), Ned Rorem (pno) Phoenix ▲ PHCD 116 [AAD]
Rorem, N.:King Midas, w. Sandra Walker (mez), Anne Schein (pno) Phoenix ▲ PHCD 126

Stewart, Patrick (nar)
Prokofiev, S.:Peter & the Wolf, w. K. Nagano (cnd), Lyon Opera Orch *(rec Lyon, Oct. 12-16, 1993)* Erato ▲ 97418-2 [DDD] ■ 97418-4

Stewart, Peter (bar)
Hoiby, L.:Songs, w. Lee Hoiby (pno)—I Was There [Beginning My Studies/I Was There/A Clear Midnight/O Captain! My Captain!/Joy, Shipmate, Joy!; poems by Whitman]; 2 Songs of Innocence [The Lamb/The Shepherd; poems by Blake]; An Immorality [by Pound]; O Florida [Floral Decorations for Bananas/Gubbinal/Continual Conversation With A Silent Man/Before My Door/O Florida, Venereal Soil; poems by Stevens]; Why Don't You? [by Beers]; Night [Anon]; What if... [by Coleridge]; Investiture at Cecconi's [by James Merrill]; Where the Music Comes From [by Lee Hoiby] *(rec Rutgers Church, NYC, Sept. 13–14, 1993)* CRI ▲ CD 685 [DDD]

Stewart, Ruth (mez)
Wagner, R.:Das Rheingold, w. L. Otto (sop), M. Muszely (sop), J. Blatter (mez), S. Wagner (mez), R. Schock (ten), H. Melchert (ten), F. Frantz (bass), B. Kusche (bass), J. Metternich (bass), R. Kempe (cnd), Berlin Staatskapelle *(rec Mar. 1959)* Berlin Classics ("Eterna" series) ▲ BER 2035 [ADD]

Stewart, Thomas (bar)
Krenek, E.:Jonny spielt auf, w. E. Lear (sop—Anita), L. Popp (sop—Yvonne), W. Blankenship (ten—Max), K. Equiluz (ten—Station Announcer), L. Heppe (ten—Manager), T. Stewart (bar—Daniello), G. Feldhof (bass—Jonny), H. Hollreiser (cnd), Vienna State Opera Orch [G] Vanguard Classics ▲ OVC 8048 [ADD]
Mahler, G.:Des Knaben Wunderhorn, w. E. Lear (sop), R. Kraus (cnd), Berlin PO *(rec 1962 & 1983)* VAI Audio ▲ VAIA 1061 (m) [ADD]
Orff, C.:Die Kluge, w. L. Popp (sop), J. Van Kesteren (ten), F. Crass (bass), G. Frick (bass), K. Eichhorn (cnd), Munich RSO Eurodisc 2-▲ 69069-2-RG [ADD]
Orff, C.:Der Mond—Ein kleines Welttheater, w. J. Van Kesteren (ten), F. Crass (bass), G. Frick (bass), K. Eichhorn (cnd), Munich RSO Eurodisc 2-▲ 69069-2-RG [ADD]
Strauss, R.:Arias, w. E. Lear (sop), *(orch unknown)*—2 duets from Arabella—Sie wollen mich heiraten; Das war sehr gut *(rec live ca. 1970/1972)* VAI Audio ▲ VAIA 1011 (m/s) [ADD]
Wagner, R.:Arias & Scenes, w. E. Lear (sop), *(orch unknown)*—soprano arias from Lohengrin, Tannhäuser; baritone arias from Fliegende Holländer, Tannhäuser, Walküre *(rec live ca. 1970/1972)* VAI Audio ▲ VAIA 1011 (m/s) [ADD]
Wagner, R.:Die Meistersinger von Nürnberg, w. Gundula Janowitz (sop), Brigitte Fassbaender (mez), Sándor Kónya (ten), Gerhard Unger (ten), Thomas Helmsey (bar), Franz Crass (bass), R. Kubelik (cnd), Bavarian RSO, Bavarian Radio Chorus *(rec 1967)* Calig 4-▲ 5097174 [ADD]
Wagner, R.:Die Meistersinger von Nürnberg, w. G. Janowitz (sop), B. Fassbaender (mez), S. Kónya (ten), G. Unger (ten), F. Crass (bass), T. Hemsley (bass), R. Kubelik (cnd), Bavarian RSO, Bavarian Radio Chorus [G] *(rec live, Munich, Oct. 1967)* Myto 4-▲ 4 MCD 92569 [ADD]
Wagner, R.:Parsifal, w. G. Jones (sop), J. King (ten), D. McIntyre (b-bar), K. Ridderbusch (bass), F. Crass (bass), P. Boulez (cnd), Bayreuth Festival Orch, Bayreuth Festival Chorus [G] *(rec 1970)* Deutsche Grammophon 3-▲ 435718-2 [ADD]
Wagner, R.:Der Ring des Nibelungen, w. B. Nilsson (sop), L. Rysanek (sop), K. Dvořaková (sop), M. Mödl (sop), A. Burmeister (mez), V. Soukupova (mez), E. Wohlfahrt (ten), W. Windgassen (ten), T. Stewart (bar), T. Adam (b-bar), G. Neidlinger (b-bar), K. Böhme (bass), G. Nienstedt (bass), K. Böhm (cnd), Bayreuth Festival Orch, Bayreuth Festival Chorus [G] *(rec live, 1966–67)* Philips 14-▲ 420325-2 [ADD]

Steyer, Arlette (sop)
Lalande, M.-R. de:Motets, w. V. Gens (sop), S. Piau (sop), J.-P. Fouchécourt (ten), F. Piolino (ten), J. Corréas (bass), W. Christie (cnd), Les Arts Florissants [L] Harmonia Mundi France ▲ HMC 901351
Lalande, M.-R. de:Te Deum, w. V. Gens (sop), S. Piau (sop), J.-P. Fouchécourt (ten), F. Piolino (ten), J. Corréas (bass), W. Christie (cnd), Les Arts Florissants [L] Harmonia Mundi France ▲ HMC 901351

Stich-Randall, Teresa (sop)
Bach, J.S.:Cant 51, w. K. Ristenpart (cnd), Sarre CO Accord ▲ ACD 200042
Bach, J.S.:Cant 78, w. D. Hermann (sop), A. Dermota (ten), H. Braun (bar), F. Prohaska (cnd), Bach Guild Orch, Bach Guild Chorus [G] *(rec May 1954)* Vanguard Classics ("The Bach Guild" series) ▲ OVC 2009 [ADD]
Bach, J.S.:Cant 106, "Actus tragicus", w. D. Hermann (sop), A. Dermota (ten), H. Braun (bar), F. Prohaska (cnd), Bach Guild Orch, Bach Guild Chorus [G] *(rec May 1954)* Vanguard Classics ("The Bach Guild" series) ▲ OVC 2009 [ADD]
Cherubini, L.:Ali Baba, ou Les Quarante voleurs, w. A. Kraus (ten), V. Ganzarolli (bar), N. Sanzogno (cnd), La Scala Orch, La Scala Chorus *(rec 1963)* Memories 2-▲ MEM 4513 [ADD]
Cimarosa, D.:Les Astuzie femminili (sels), w. Sesto Bruscantini (bass), M. Rossi (cnd), Turin RAI SO—Le figliole che so' de vent'anni *(rec Concerto Martini & Rossi, Torino, Nov 9, 1959)* Incontri Memorabili ▲ 5027 [ADD]
Gluck, C.W.:Orfeo ed Euridice, w. H. Steffek (sop—Amore), T. Stich-Randall (mez—Euridice), M. Forrester (cta—Orfeo), C. Mackerras (cnd), Vienna State Opera Orch, Vienna State Opera Chorus [Italian version w. additions composed for the French production] *(rec 6/66)* Vanguard Classics 2-▲ OVC 4039/40 [ADD]
Haydn, J.:Die Jahreszeiten, w. Helmut Kretschmar (ten), Erik Wenk (bass), W. Goehr (cnd), North German RSO, Hamburg Chorus *(rec 1966)* FNAC Music 2-▲ 642325
Haydn, J.:Die Schöpfung, w. Anny Felbermayer (sop—Eve), Teresa Stich-Randall (sop—Gabriel), Anton Dermota (ten—Uriel), Paul Schöffler (b-bar—Adam), Frederick Guthrie (bass—Raphael), Franz Holletschek (cembalo), M. Wöldike (cnd), Vienna State Opera Orch, Vienna State Opera Chorus *(rec Musikverein, Vienna, Austria, May 1955)* Vanguard Classics 2-▲ SVC 34/35 [AAD]

Stich-Randall, Teresa (sop) (cont.)

Lehár, F.:Die lustige Witwe, w. Teresa Stich-Randall (mez—Missia Palmieri), Monique Stiot (mez—Manon), Germaine Duclos (sgr—Praskovia), Linda Felder (sgr—Olga), Christiane Jacquin (sgr—Nadia), Jeannette Levasseur (sgr—Sylviane), Henri Legay (ten—Camille de Coutançon), Joseph Peyron (ten—Kromsky), Robert Destain (sgr—Baron Popoff), Michel Fauche (sgr—Pristich), Gérard Friedmann (sgr—Lerida), Jacques Gilet (sgr—Bogdanowitch), Jean Guy Henneveux (sgr—Prince Danilo), Serge Klin (sgr—Figg), Jacques Villa (sgr—D'Estillac), A. Sibert (cnd), Belgian Radio-TV Orch, Belgian Radio-TV Chorus *(rec Grand Auditorium, Belgium, Apr 30, 1970)* Studio SM 2-▲ 2160 [AAD]

Mozart, W.A.:Arias, w. Sesto Bruscantini (bass), M. Rossi (cnd), Turin RAI SO—Martern aller Arten [from Entführung aus dem Serail]; Tutto è disposto; E Susanna non vien! [both from Le nozze di Figaro]; Ei parte... Per pietá, ben mio perdona [from Cosi fan tutte]; Crudele ... Non mi dir, bell'idol mio [from Don Giovanni] *(rec Concerto Martini & Rossi, Torino, Nov 9, 1959)* Incontri Memorabili ▲ 5027 [ADD]

Mozart, W.A.:Cosi fan tutte, w. M. Adani (sop), T. Berganza (mez), L. Alva (ten), A. Cortis (ten), R. Panerai (bar), H. Rosbaud (cnd), Paris Conservatory Societé des Concerts Orch, Aix-en-Provence Festival Chorus [I] *(rec live, Aix-en-Provence, July 26, 1957)* Melodram 3-▲ MEL 37084 [AAD]

Mozart, W.A.:Don Giovanni, w. M. Caballé (sop), E. Wächter (bar), E. Kunz (bar), M. Gielen (cnd), Naples Teatro San Carlo Orch, Naples Teatro San Carlo Chorus [I] *(rec live, Lisbon, 1960)* Standing Room Only 2-▲ SRO 813-2 [ADD]

Mozart, W.A.:Don Giovanni, w. Leyla Gencer (sop—Donn'Elvra), Teresa Stich-Randall (mez—Donn'Anna), Sesto Bruscantini (bar—Leporello), Mario Petri (bar—Don Giovanni), F. Molinari-Pradelli (cnd), Milan RAI SO, Milan RAI Chorus Stradivarius 3-▲ STV DTM 12321 [ADD]

Mozart, W.A.:Entführung, w. Nicolai Gedda (ten), Michel Sénéchal (ten), Carmen Prieto (sgr), H. Rosbaud (cnd), Paris Conservatory Societé des Concerts Orch, Elisabeth Brasseur Chorale *(rec Aix-en-Provence Festival, France, 1954)* Agorá ("Phoenix" series) 2-▲ 512

Mozart, W.A.:Exsultate, w. K. Ristenpart (cnd), Sarre CO Accord ▲ ACD 200042

Mozart, W.A.:Missa, K.317, w. Bianca Maria Casoni (alt), Pietro Bottazzo (ten), K. Ristenpart (cnd), Sarre CO, Herbert Schmolzi (cnd), Sarrebrück Conservatory Choir Accord ▲ ACD 220252 [AAD]

Mozart, W.A.:Missa, K.427, w. K. Ristenpart (cnd), Sarre CO Accord ▲ ACD 200042

Mozart, W.A.:Nozze di Figaro (sels), w. R. Pütz (sop), T. Berganza (mez), A.-R. Johnson (ten), G. Bacquier (bar), F. Corena (bass), H. Wallberg (cnd), Swiss Romande Orch, Swiss Romande Chorus—Act IV Melodram 2-▲ CDM 27094 [ADD]

Mozart, W.A.:Songs, w. H. Rosbaud (pno)—(3) Abendempfindung (lied), K.523; Dans un bois solitaire (arietta), K.308; Oiseaux, si tous les ans (arietta), K.307 *(rec live, Aix-en-Provence July 31,1956)* Melodram 2-▲ CDM 26524 [ADD]

Mozart, W.A.:Songs, w. Jacqueline Bonneau (pno)—La violette; Sentiment du soir; L'image du rêve; Viens, chère cithare; Nostalgie du printemps; A chloé; Chant de séparation Accord ▲ ACD 201452 [AAD]

Mozart, W.A.:Thamos, w. A. Deloire (mez), J. Traxel (ten), T. Adam (b-bar), M. Rossi (cnd), Cologne RSO, Cologne Radio Chorus [G] *(rec live, Cologne May 20, 1956)* Melodram 3-▲ CDM 37084 [AAD]

Mozart, W.A.:Vesperae solennes, w. Bianca Maria Casoni (alt), Pietro Bottazzo (ten), K. Ristenpart (cnd), Sarre CO, Herbert Schmolzi (cnd), Sarrebrück Conservatory Choir Accord ▲ ACD 220252 [AAD]

Rossini, G.:Il barbiere di Siviglia (sels), w. Sesto Bruscantini (bass), M. Rossi (cnd), Turin RAI SO—Largo al factotum *(rec Concerto Martini & Rossi, Torino, Nov 9, 1959)* Incontri Memorabili ▲ 5027 [ADD]

Schubert, Franz:Songs (misc), w. Jacqueline Bonneau (pno)—A la musique; Petite rose des bruyères; Tu es le repos; Rire et pleurer; La truite; Foi printanière; Ave maria; Amour sans repos; Nuit et rêves Accord ▲ ACD 201452 [AAD]

Strauss, R.:Der Rosenkavalier, w. E. Schwarzkopf (sop), C. Ludwig (mez), O. Edelmann (bass), H. von Karajan (cnd), Philharmonia Orch [G] EMI Classics 3-▲ CDCX 49354 [ADD] 3-■ 3CDX 3970

Strauss, R.:Der Rosenkavalier, w. Elisabeth Schwarzkopf (sop), Christa Ludwig (mez), Otto Edelmann (b-bar), H. von Karajan (cnd), Philharmonia Orch, Philharmonia Chorus *(rec 1956)* EMI Classics ▲ CDCX 56113 (m)

Strauss, R.:Der Rosenkavalier (sels), w. E. Schwarzkopf (sop), C. Ludwig (mez), O. Edelmann (bass), H. von Karajan (cnd), Philharmonia Orch, Philharmonia Chorus EMI Classics ▲ ZDM 63452

Teresa Stich-Randall, w. Stich-Randall, Teresa (sop), Hans Rosbaud (pno) *(rec July 31, 1956)* Memoire Vive ▲ 262008 (m) [ADD]

Verdi, G.:Ernani (sels), w. Sesto Bruscantini (bass), M. Rossi (cnd), Turin RAI SO—Gran Dio!... Ohe de' verd'anni miei *(rec Concerto Martini & Rossi, Torino, Nov 9, 1959)* Incontri Memorabili ▲ 5027 [ADD]

Verdi, G.:Falstaff, w. Herva Nelli (sop), Cloë Elmo (cta), Frank Guarrera (bar), Giuseppe Valdengo (bar), A. Toscanini (cnd), *(orch unknown) (rec 1950)* Music & Arts 2-▲ CD 248 [ADD]

Stignani, Ebe (mez)

Bellini, V.:Norma, w. M. Callas (sop), J. Sutherland (sop), M. Picchi (ten), G. Vaghi (bass), V. Gui (cnd), Royal Opera House Orch, Royal Opera House Chorus Covent Garden [I] *(rec live, Covent Garden 11/52)* Legato Classics 2-▲ LCD 130-2 (m) [AAD]

Bellini, V.:Norma, w. M. Callas (sop), J. Sutherland (sop), M. Picchi (ten), G. Vaghi (bass), V. Gui (cnd), Royal Opera House Orch, Royal Opera House Chorus Covent Garden [I] *(rec live, Covent Garden 11/52)* Verona 3-▲ 27018/20 (m) [AAD]

Bellini, V.:Norma, w. Maria Callas (sop), Joan Sutherland (sop), Mirto Picchi (ten), Paul Asciak (sgr), V. Gui (cnd), Royal Opera House Orch, Royal Opera House Chorus Covent Garden *(rec live, London, 1952)* Enterprise ("Documents" series) 3-▲ ENTLV 968 [ADD]

Bellini, V.:Norma, w. Gina Signa (sop), Giovanni Breviario (ten), Tancredi Pasero (bass), V. Gui (cnd), Turin EIAR SO, Turin EIAR Chorus *(rec 1937)* Grammofono 2000 2-▲ GRM 78583

Bellini, V.:Norma, w. M. Callas (sop), M. Filippeschi (ten), N. Rossi-Lemeni (bass), T. Serafin (cnd), La Scala Orch, La Scala Chorus [I] EMI Classics 3-▲ CDC 47303 (m)

Bellini, V.:Norma, w. Gina Cigna (sop—Norma), Ebe Stignani (sop—Adalgisa), Adriana Perris (mez—Clotilde), Giovanni Breviario (ten—Pollione), Emilio Renzi (ten—Flavio), Tancredi Pasero (bass—Oroveso), V. Gui (cnd), EIAR Orch, Achille Consoli (cnd), EIAR Chorus *(rec Aug/Sept 1937)* Arkadia ("The 78's" series) 2-▲ 78010 [ADD]

Bellini, V.:Norma, w. J. Sutherland (sop), M. Callas (sop), M. Picchi (ten), G. Vaghi (bass), V. Gui (cnd), Royal Opera House Orch, Royal Opera House Chorus Covent Garden [I] *(rec live, Covent Garden 11/52)* Melodram 2-▲ MEL 26025

Bellini, V.:Norma, w. G. Cigna (sop), G. Breviario (ten), T. Pasero (bass), V. Gui (cnd), Turin EIAR SO, Turin EIAR Chorus *(rec 1937)* Memories 2-▲ MEM 4552 [ADD]

Bellini, V.:Norma, w. G. Cigna (sop), G. Breviario (ten), V. Gui (cnd), EIAR Orch, EIAR Chorus [I] *(rec 1936 for Cetra)* Pearl 2-▲ PEAS 9422 (m) [AAD]

Bizet, G.:Carmen (sels), w. R. Gigli (sop), B. Gigli (ten), *(orch unknown)* Melodram ▲ CD 15005 (m)

De Cavalieri, Fineschi, Olivero, Stignani, Tassinari, w. Anna de Cavalieri (sop), Ornella Fineschi (sop), Magda Olivero (sop), Pia Tassinari (mez), Rome RAI SO, Milan RAI SO *(rec 1953-58)* Incontri Memorabili ("Martini & Rossi Concerts" series) ▲ 5020

Ebe Stignani, Nicola Lemeni, w. Nicola Rossi Lemeni (bass), Milan RAI SO [cnd:Angelo Questa] *(rec Jan. 31, 1955)* Incontri Memorabili ("Martini & Rossi Concerts" series) ▲ 5013

Mozart, W.A.:Requiem, w. P. Tassinari (sop), F. Tagliavini (ten), I. Tajo (bass), V. de Sabata (cnd), RAI Orch, *(unknown RAI Chorus) (rec Apr. 1939)* Cetra Classic ▲ CDO 1 [AAD]

Opera Arias, w. Turin EIAR Sym *(rec 1937-1941)* Preiser ("Lebendige Vergangenheit" series) ▲ PRE 89014 (m) [AAD]

Verdi, G.:Aida, w. R. Tebaldi (sop), M. del Monaco (ten), A. Protti (bar), F. Corena (bass), A. Erede (cnd), St. Cecilia Academy Orch Rome, St. Cecilia Academy Chorus Rome London 2-▲ 440239-2 [ADD]

Verdi, G.:Aida, w. Maria Caniglia (sop—Aida), Ebe Stignani (mez—Amneris), Beniamino Gigli (ten—Radamés), Armando Borgioli (bar—Amonasro), T. Beecham (cnd), London SO, London Sym Chorus *(rec Royal Opera House, Covent Garden, May 24, 1939)* Enterprise ("The Radio Years" series) 2-▲ ENT RY 62

Verdi, G.:Aida, w. Renata Tebaldi (sop—Aida), Ebe Stignani (mez—Amneris), Mario Del Monaco (ten—Radamès), Piero de Palma (ten—Messenger), Aldo Protti (bar—Amonasro), Fernando Corena (bass—King), Dario Caselli (bass—Ramfis), A. Erede (cnd), St. Cecilia Academy Orch Rome, St. Cecilia Academy Chorus Rome *(rec 1952)* Theorema 2-▲ TH 121133/34

Stignani, Ebe (mez) (cont.)

Verdi, G.:Aida (sels), w. M. Callas (sop), M. Picchi (ten), R. De Falchi (bar), G. Neri (bass), V. Bellezza (cnd), Rome Opera Orch—five arias with Callas (solo, three duets & quintet) *(rec live 10/2/50)* Melodram 2-▲ CDM 26019 [AAD]

Verdi, G.:Aida (sels), w. O. Rovere (sop), M. Filippeschi (ten), C. Cava (bass), B. McFerrin (sgr), V. Bellezza (cnd), Naples Teatro San Carlo Orch, Naples Teatro San Carlo Chorus [I] [highlights] *(rec live, Arena Flegrea, Naples, 7/15/56)* Golden Age of Opera ▲ GAO 130 [ADD]

Verdi, G.:Un ballo in maschera, w. A. Cerquetti (sop), G. Poggi (ten), E. Bastianini (bar), E. Tieri (cnd), Florence Teatro Comunale Orch, Florence Teatro Comunale Chorus [I] *(rec live 1/6/57)* Standing Room Only 2-▲ SRO 804-2 (m) [ADD]

Verdi, G.:Don Carlos, w. M. Caniglia (sop—Elisabeth de Valois), G. Sciutti (sop—Page), E. Stignani (mez—Princess Eboli), M. Picchi (ten—Don Carlos), M. Ponz de L. (ten—Count of Lerma), P. Silveri (bar—Rodrigue), N. Rossi Lemeni (bass—Philip II), G. Neri (bass—Grand Inquisitor), A. Gaggi (bass—Old Monk), F. Previtali (cnd), Rome RAI SO, Rome RAI Chorus *(rec Rome, 1951)* Cetra Classic 3-▲ CDO 25 [ADD]

Verdi, G.:La forza del destino, w. Maria Caniglia (sop), Galliano Masini (ten), Carlo Tagliabue (bar), Tancredi Pasero (bass), G. Marinuzzi (cnd), EIAR Orch, EIAR Chorus *(rec 1941)* Grammofono 2000 ▲ GRM 78567 (m)

Verdi, G.:Requiem Mass, w. Maria Caniglia (sop), Benjamino Gigli (ten), Ezio Pinza (bass), T. Serafin (cnd), Rome Opera Orch, Rome Opera Chorus *(rec 1939)* Pearl ▲ PEA 9162 [ADD]

Verdi, G.:Requiem Mass, w. Maria Caniglia (sop), Beniamino Gigli (ten), Ezio Pinza (bass), T. Serafin (cnd), La Scala Orch, La Scala Chorus *(rec 1939)* Phonographie ▲ PHG 5012 [ADD]

Verdi, G.:Requiem Mass (sels), w. M. Caniglia (sop), B. Gigli (ten), T. Pasero (bass), V. de Sabata (cnd), Rome CO, Rome RAI Chorus, Turin RAI Chorus—Dies irae; Sanctus; Libera me *(rec Dec. 14, 1940)* Legato Classics 2-▲ LCD 178-2

Verdi, G.:Il trovatore, w. M. Callas (sop), G. Penno (ten), C. Tagliabue (bar), A. Votto (cnd), La Scala Orch, La Scala Chorus [I] *(rec live 2/23/53)* Myto 2-▲ 2 MCD 90213 (m) [ADD]

Stiles-Allen, Lilian (sop)

Vaughan Williams, R.:Serenade to Music, w. Isobel Baillie (sop), Elsie Suddaby (sop), Eva Turner (sop), Margaret Balfour (cta), Muriel Brunskill (cta), Astra Desmond (cta), Mary Jarred (cta), Parry Jones (ten), Heddle Nash (ten), Frank Titterton (ten), Walter Widdop (ten), Roy Henderson (bar), Harold Williams (bar), Norman Allin (bass), Robert Easton (bass), H. Wood (cnd), BBC SO *(rec Abbey Road, Oct 15, 1938)* Claremont ▲ CDGSE 785066

Stilwell, Richard (bar)

Brahms, J.:Ein Deutsches Requiem, w. A. Augér (sop), R. Shaw (cnd), Atlanta SO, Atlanta Sym Chorus [G] Telarc 2-▲ CD 80092 [DDD]

Debussy, C.:Pelléas et Mélisande, w. N. Denize (mez), F. von Stade (mez), G. Raimondi (ten), J. Van Dam (bass-bar), H. von Karajan (cnd), Berlin PO, German Opera Chorus [F] EMI Classics 3-▲ CDCC 49350 [ADD]

Handel, G.F.:Messiah, w. Kaaren Erickson (sop), Sylvia McNair (sop), Alfreda Hodgson (cta), Jon Humphrey (ten), R. Shaw (cnd), Atlanta SO, Atlanta Sym Chorus [E] Telarc ▲ CD 80103 [DDD]; ■ CS 30103 (D)

Handel, G.F.:Messiah, w. Kaaren Erickson (sop), Sylvia McNair (sop), Alfreda Hodgson (cta), Jon Humphrey (ten), R. Shaw (cnd), Atlanta SO, Atlanta Sym Chorus [E] Telarc 2-▲ CD 80093-2 [DDD]

Sting (nar)

Prokofiev, S.:Peter & the Wolf, w. C. Abbado (cnd), CO of Europe Deutsche Grammophon ▲ 429396-2 [DDD] □ 429396-5

Stiot, Monique (mez)

Gounod, C.:Le Médecin malgré lui, w. Lina Dachary (sop), Michel Hamel (ten), Joseph Peyron (ten), Christophe Benoit (bar), Janine Capderou (sgr), Jean-Louis Soumagnas (sgr), J.-C. Hartemann (cnd), ORTF Lyric Orch Musidisc ▲ MUS 202322 [AAD]

Hahn, R.:O mon del inconnul, w. Christiane Château (sop), Lina Dachary (sop), Michel Hamel (ten), Joseph Peyron (ten), Aimé Doniat (bar), Dominique Tirmont (bar), Philippe Gaudin (sgr), Jacques Provins (sgr), J. Brebion (cnd), ORTF Lyric Orch Musidisc ▲ MUS 202562 [AAD]

Lehár, F.:Die lustige Witwe, w. Teresa Stich-Randall (mez—Missia Palmieri), Monique Stiot (mez—Manon), Germaine Duclos (sgr—Praskovia), Linda Felder (sgr—Olga), Christiane Jacquin (sgr—Nadia), Jeannette Levasseur (sgr—Sylviane), Henri Legay (ten—Camille de Coutançon), Joseph Peyron (ten—Kromsky), Robert Destain (sgr—Baron Popoff), Michel Fauche (sgr—Pristich), Gérard Friedmann (sgr—Lerida), Jacques Gilet (sgr—Bogdanowitch), Jean Guy Henneveux (sgr—Prince Danilo), Serge Klin (sgr—Figg), Jacques Villa (sgr—D'Estillac), A. Sibert (cnd), Belgian Radio-TV Orch, Belgian Radio-TV Chorus *(rec Grand Auditorium, Belgium, Apr 30, 1970)* Studio SM 2-▲ 2160 [AAD]

Stocker, Eduard (bass)

Wolf, H.:Goethe-Lieder (sels), w. Magda Rusy (pno)—Grenzen der Menscheit; Genialisch treiben; Der Schäfer; Blumengruss; Gleich und gleich; Harfenspieler 1-11; Königlich gebet; Sankt Nepomuks vorabend; Der Rattenfänger; Frühling übers Jahr; Anakreons grab; Cophtisches Lied I & II; Phänomen Accord ▲ ACD 202792 [AAD]

Stoffel, David (b-bar)

Songs with a Touch of Bass, w. Milton Masciadri (db), Ivan Frazier (pno) *(rec Central Presbyterian Church, Athens, GA 1995)* ACA Digital Recording ▲ CM 20030

Stoian, Ion (ten)

Verdi, G.:La forza del destino, w. Maria Nistor-Slatinaru (sop—Donna Leonora), Mihaela Mariacineanu (mez—Curra), Zenaida Pally (mez—Preziosilla), Ludovic Speiss (ten—Don Alvaro), Ion Stoian (ten—Trabucco), Nicolae Herlea (bar—Don Carlo), Nicolae Florei (bass—Padre Guardiano) Constantin Gabor (bass—Fra Melitone), Dan Musetescu (bass—An Alcalde), Mihai Panghe (bass—Marquis of Calatrava), C. Litvin (cnd), Romanian Radio-TV Orch, Romanian Radio-TV Chorus *(rec Jan 1970)* Vox Box 3-▲ CD3X 3038

Stoilov, Nikolai (bass)

Rimsky-Korsakov, N.:Golden Cockerel, w. Yavora Stoilova (sop—Golden Cockerel), Elena Stoyanova (sop—Queen), Evgenia Babacheva (mez—Amelfa), Lyubomir Bodourov (ten—Prince), Lyubomir Dyakovski (ten—Astrologer), Emil Ugrinov (bar—Afron), Nikolai Stoilov (bass—Tsar), Kosta Videv (bass—Polkan), D. Manolov (cnd), Sofia National Opera Orch, Sofia National Opera Chorus *(rec Sofia, 1985)* Capriccio 2-▲ 10760/61 [DDD]

Stoilova, Yavora (sop)

Rimsky-Korsakov, N.:Golden Cockerel, w. Yavora Stoilova (sop—Golden Cockerel), Elena Stoyanova (sop—Queen), Evgenia Babacheva (mez—Amelfa), Lyubomir Bodourov (ten—Prince), Lyubomir Dyakovski (ten—Astrologer), Emil Ugrinov (bar—Afron), Nikolai Stoilov (bass—Tsar), Kosta Videv (bass—Polkan), D. Manolov (cnd), Sofia National Opera Orch, Sofia National Opera Chorus *(rec Sofia, 1985)* Capriccio 2-▲ 10760/61 [DDD]

Stokes, Nancy (sop)

Bizet, G.:Carmen, w. Laura Bustamante (sop—Frasquita), Ximena Riveros (sop—Mercedes), Nancy Stokes (sop—Micaela), Regina Resnik (mez—Carmen), Plácido Domingo (ten—Don José), Ismildo Tedeschi (ten—Remendado), Ramon Vinay (ten—Escamillo), Juan Charles (ten/bar—Dancaire), Agustin Letelier (bar—Morles), Jorge Algorta (bass—Zuniga), A. Guadagno (cnd), Santiago Teatro Municipale Orch, Santiago Teatro Municipale Chorus *(rec Santiago Municipal Theater, Sept. 4, 1967)* Legato Classics 2-▲ LCD 194-2 [ADD]

Stoklassa, Gertraut (sop)

Weber, C.M. von:Missa sancta 2, w. Emmy Lisken (cta), Manfred Raucamp (ten), Hans Kagel (bass), R. Bader (cnd), Stuttgart PO, Stuttgart Phil Chorus Koch Schwann ▲ SCH CD 316372

Stoleriu, Georgeta (sop)

5 Centuries of German Music in Transylvania, w. H. Andreescu (cnd), Bucharest Virtuosi, Adrian Petrescu (ob), René Cristian Popescu (vn), Gabriel Bala (va), Stefan Thomasz (db), Nicolae Licaret (hpd) Electrecord ▲ ELC EDC 168 [DDD]

Stolfova-Bandova, Hana (cta)

Dvořák, A.:Stabat Mater, w. Eva Jenisova (sop), Vladimir Dolezal (ten), Jiri Sulzenka (bass), L. Svárovský (cnd), Czech PO, Petr Fiala (cnd), Brno Czech Phil Chorus Supraphon 2-▲ SUP CD 3093

Stolte, Adele (sop)

Beethoven, L. van:Songs, w. P. Schreier (ten), W. Olbertz (pno)—Scherlieder; Ariettas (4) & duet, Op. 82; Ernste Lieder Berlin Classics ▲ BER 2084 [DDD]

▲ = CD ♦ = Enhanced CD Δ = MD ■ = Cassette Tape □ = DCC

Stolte, Adele (sop) (cont.)
Mozart, W.A.:Bastien und Bastienne, w. Peter Schreier (ten), Theo Adam (bass), H. Koch (cnd), Berlin CO — Berlin Classics ▲ BER 9129

Stolze, Gerhard (ten)
Berg, A.:Wozzeck, w. E. Lear (sop—Marie), F. Wunderlich (ten—Andres), G. Stoltze (ten—The Captain), D. Fischer-Dieskau (bar—Wozzeck), K. Böhm (cnd), German Opera Orch, German Opera Chorus [G] *(rec 1965)* — Deutsche Grammophon 3-▲ 435705-2 [ADD]
Orff, C.:Carmina burana, w. Gundula Janowitz (sop), Dietrich Fischer-Dieskau (bar), E. Jochum (cnd), Berlin German Opera Orch, Berlin German Opera Chorus *(rec Ufa-Studio, Berlin, Oct 1967)* — Deutsche Grammophon ▲ 447437-2 [ADD]
Orff, C.:Carmina burana, w. G. Janowitz (sop), D. Fischer-Dieskau (bar), G.L. Jochum (cnd), German Opera Orch, German Opera Chorus [G, L] — Deutsche Grammophon ("Galleria" series) ▲ 423886-2 [ADD]
Pfitzner, H.:Palestrina, w. S. Jurinac (sop), C. Ludwig (mez), F. Wunderlich (ten), O. Wiener (bar), G. Frick (bass), W. Berry (bass), R. Heger (cnd), Vienna State Opera Orch, Vienna State Opera Chorus *(rec live, Vienna 12/16/64)* — Myto 3-▲ 3 MCD 92259 [ADD]
Strauss (II), Joh.:Die Fledermaus, w. H. Gueden (sop), R. Streich (sop), G. Di Stefano (ten), G. Zampieri (ten), E. Wächter (bar), W. Berry (bass), E. Kunz (bar), H. von Karajan (cnd), Vienna State Opera Orch, Vienna State Opera Chorus [G] — Arkadia 3-▲ 215 (m) [ADD]
Strauss, R.:Elektra, w. B. Nilsson (sop), M. Collier (sop), R. Resnik (mez), T. Krause (bar), G. Solti (cnd), Vienna PO [G] — London 2-▲ 417345-2 [ADD]
Strauss, R.:Der Rosenkavalier, w. Erika Köth (sop—Sophie), Annelie Waas (sop—Marianne), Claire Watson (sop—Marschallin), Hertha Töpper (mez—Octavian), Brigitte Fassbaender (cta—Annina), Gerhard Stolze (ten—Valzacchi), Fritz Wunderlich (ten—Singer), Otto Wiener (bar—Faninal), Kurt Böhme (bass—Baron), J. Keilberth (cnd), Bavarian State Opera Orch, Bavarian State Opera Chorus *(rec Munich Opera Festival, National Theater, May 21, 1965)* — Orfeo d'or 3-▲ 425963
Strauss, R.:Salome, w. L. Rysanek (sop), A. Varnay (sop/mez), D. Fischer-Dieskau (bar), F. Leitner (cnd), Bavarian State Opera Orch *(rec live, Monaco, 1971)* — Melodram 2-▲ MEL 27098
Strauss, R.:Salome, w. B. Nilsson (sop), G. Hoffman (mez), W. Kmentt (ten), E. Wächter (bar), G. Solti (cnd), Vienna PO [G] — London 2-▲ 414414-2 [ADD]
Wagner, R.:Der Ring des Nibelungen, w. B. Nilsson (sop), K. Flagstad (sop), R. Crespin (sop), C. Watson (sop), C. Ludwig (mez), J. Madeira (mez), S. Svanholm (ten), J. King (ten), W. Windgassen (ten), G. London (bar), D. Fischer-Dieskau (bar), H. Hotter (b-bar), G. Neidlinger (b-bar), G. Frick (bass), G. Solti (cnd), Vienna PO [G] — London 15-▲ 414100-2 [ADD]
Wagner, R.:Siegfried, w. A. Varnay (sop), W. Windgassen (ten), A. Andersson (ten), H. Hotter (b-bar), J. Greindl (bass), H. Knappertsbusch (cnd), Bayreuth Festival Orch, Bayreuth Festival Chorus [G] *(rec live 1958)* — Arkadia 4-▲ 443 [AAD]
Wagner, R.:Siegfried, w. B. Nilsson (sop), W. Windgassen (ten), H. Hotter (b-bar), G. Neidlinger (b-bar), G. Solti (cnd), Vienna PO [G] — London 4-▲ 414110-2 [ADD]
Wagner, R.:Tannhäuser, w. V. de Los Angeles (sop), G. Bumbry (mez), W. Windgassen (ten), D. Fischer-Dieskau (bar), T. Adam (b-bar), J. Greindl (bass), F. Crass (bass), W. Sawallisch (cnd), Bayreuth Festival Orch, Bayreuth Festival Chorus [G] *(rec 1961)* — Myto 3-▲ MCD 93277

Stone, M. (sop)
Gottlieb, J.:Sacred Music, w. H. Reps (mez), D. Lefkowitz (ten), H. Stahl (ten), R. Abelson (bar), R. Botton (bar), P. Newman (reader), S. Sturk (cnd), Metropolitan Brass Ensemble, New York Motet Choir — Premier ("Composer" series) ▲ PRCD 1018 [DDD]

Stone, William (bar)
Bach, J.S.:Magnificat, BWV 243, w. P. Jensen (sop), D. Upshaw (sop), M. Simpson (mez), D. Gordon (ten), R. Shaw (cnd), Atlanta SO, Atlanta Chamber Chorus — Telarc ▲ CD 80194 [DDD]
Bach, J.S.:Mass in b, BWV 232, w. S. McNair (sop), G. Simpson (mez), D. Ziegler (mez), J. Aler (ten), T. Paul (bass), R. Shaw (cnd), Atlanta SO, Atlanta Chamber Chorus [L] — Telarc 2-▲ CD 80233 [DDD]
Hindemith, P.:When Lilacs Last In The Dooryard Bloom'd, w. Jan DeGaetani (mez), R. Shaw (cnd), Atlanta SO, Atlanta Sym Chorus [E] — Telarc ▲ CD 80132 [DDD]
Mozart, W.A.:Missa, K.427, w. Edith Wiens (sop), Delores Ziegler (mez), John Aler (ten), R. Shaw (cnd), Atlanta SO, Atlanta Sym Chorus [L] — Telarc 2-▲ CD 80150 [DDD]
Schubert, Franz:Mass 2, w. D. Upshaw (sop), D. Gordon (ten), R. Shaw (cnd), Atlanta SO, Atlanta Sym Chorus [L] — Telarc ▲ CD 80212 [DDD]
Telemann, G.P.:Der Tag des Gerichts, w. Patrice Michaels Bell (sop), Sandra Walker (mez), Karen Brunssen (mez), Bruce Fowler (ten), Kurt R. Hansen (ten), Douglas Anderson (bar), T. Wikman (cnd), Music of the Baroque Orch, Baroque Music Chorus *(rec live, St. Paul's United Church of Christ, Feb 23, 1992)* — Music of the Baroque 2-▲ MB 107
Vivaldi, A.:Gloria, RV.589, w. D. Upshaw (sop), P. Jensen (sop), M. Simpson (mez), D. Gordon (ten), R. Shaw (cnd), Atlanta SO, Atlanta Chamber Chorus — Telarc ▲ CD 80194 [DDD]
Walton, W.:Belshazzar's Feast, w. R. Shaw (cnd), Atlanta SO, Atlanta Sym Chorus [E] — Telarc ▲ CD 80181 [DDD]

Storojev, M. (sgr)
Glinka, M.:Songs, w. V. Bogachev (ten), Montreal Musici — Chandos ▲ CHAN 9149 [DDD]

Storojev, Nikita (bass)
Górecki, H.-M.:Beatus Vir, w. J. Nelson (cnd), Czech PO, Prague Phil Chorus — Argo ▲ 436835-2 [DDD]
Prokofiev, S.:Ivan the Terrible Cta, w. L. Finnie (mez), N. Järvi (cnd), Philharmonia Orch, Philharmonia Chorus — Chandos ▲ CHAN 8977 [DDD]
Schifrin, L.:Cantos Aztecas, w. P. Domingo (ten), C. Julian (sop), M. Felix (sgr), L. Schifrin (cnd), Mexican State SO, Mexico City Chorus [Sp] *(rec live 10/29/88)* — Pro Arte ▲ CDD 494 [DDD]
Shostakovich, D.:Song of the Forest, w. M. Kotliarov (ten), V. Ashkenazy (cnd), Royal PO, Brighton Festival Chorus, New London Children's Choir — London ▲ 436762-2 [DDD]
Shostakovich, D.:Sym 13, w. O. Kamu (cnd), City of Birmingham SO, City of Birmingham Sym Chorus [R] — Chandos ▲ CHAN 8540 [DDD]
Shostakovich, D.:Sym 14, w. E. Holleque (sop), Y. Turovsky (cnd), Montreal Musici — Chandos ▲ CHAN 8607 [DDD]

Stosch, A. von (sop)
Wagner, R.:Götterdämmerung (sels), w. F. Leider (sop), L. Melchior (ten), H. Janssen (bar), W. Schirp (bass), *(cnd & orch unknown)*—Act 2, Scenes 4 & 5 *(w. Furtwängler, Royal Opera House Orch. & Cho., 1938)*; Act 3, Schweigt eures Jammers *(Frida Leider & E. Marherr-Wagner, Blech, Berlin State Opera Orch., 1928)* — Pearl ▲ PEA 9331 (m) [AAD]

Stoska, Polyna (sgr)
Weill, K.:Street Scene, w. Anne Jeffreys (sgr), M. Abravanel (cnd), Brian Sullivan Orch *(rec 1949)* — CBS ▲ MK 44668 (m) [ADD]

Stoyanova, Elena (sop)
Orff, C.:Catulli Carmina, w. K. Kaludov (ten), M. Milkov (cnd), Bulgarian Radio-TV SO, Bulgarian Radio-TV Chorus [L] *(rec live in Sofia, 1988)* — Forlane ▲ FOR 16610 [DDD]
Rimsky-Korsakov, N.:Golden Cockerel, w. Yavora Stoilova (sop—Golden Cockerel), Elena Stoyanova (sop—Queen), Evgenia Babacheva (mez—Amelfa), Lyubomir Bodourov (ten—Prince), Lyubomir Dyakovski (ten—Astrologer), Emil Ugrinov (bar—Afron), Nikolai Stoilov (bass—Tsar), Kosta Videv (bass—Polkan), D. Manolov (cnd), Sofia National Opera Orch, Sofia National Opera Chorus *(rec Sofia, 1985)* — Capriccio 2-▲ 10760/61 [DDD]

Stracciari, Riccardo (bar)
The Italian Vocal Tradition, Vol. 1:The Voices of Toscanini, w. Toti dal Monte (sop), Claudio Muzio (sop), Rosetta Pampanini (sop), Biata Scacciati (sop), Giacomo Lauri-Volpi (ten), Francesco Merli (ten), Aureliano Pertile (ten), Carlo Galeffi (bar), Mariano Stabile (bar), Nazzareno de Angel *(rec 1921–35)* — Iron Needle ▲ 1304
Recital:5 Arias & 5 Songs — Music Memoria 2-▲ 30276/77
Riccardo Stracciari *(rec 1925)* — Preiser ("Lebendige Vergangenheit" series) ▲ PRE 89003 (m) [AAD]
Riccardo Stracciari *(rec 1917–28)* — Pearl ▲ PEA 9178 [ADD]
Rossini, G.:Il barbiere di Siviglia, w. M. Capsir (sop), D. Borgioli (ten), S. Baccaloni (bass), V. Bettoni (bass), L. Molajoli (cnd), La Scala Orch, La Scala Chorus *(rec 1929 for Columbia Records)* — Music Memoria 2-▲ 30276/77

Stracciari, Riccardo (bar) (cont.)
Rossini, G.:Il barbiere di Siviglia, w. Cesira Ferrari (mez—Berta), Mercedes Capsir (cta—Rosina), Dino Borgioli (ten—Count), Salvatore Baccaloni (bar—Bortolo), Aristide Baracchi (bar—Officer), Riccardo Stracciari (bar—Figaro), Vincenzo Bettoni (bass—Don Basilio), Attilo Bordonali (bass—Fiorello), L. Molajoli (cnd), La Scala Orch, La Scala Chorus *(rec 1930)* — Arkadia ("The 78's" series) 2-▲ 78008 [ADD]
Verdi, G.:Otello (sels), w. C. Muzio (sop), R. Ponselle (sop), H. Spani (sop), E. Caruso (ten), N. Fusati (ten), L. Melchior (ten), F. Merli (ten), F. Tamagno (ten), B. Franci (bar), V. Maurel (bar), T. Ruffo (bar) *(rec 1906–1933)* — Music Memoria ▲ 30219
Verdi, G.:Rigoletto, w. Mercedes Capsir (sop), Dino Borgioli (ten), Duilio Baronti (bass), Ernesto Dominici (bass), Anna Masetti Bassi (sgr) *(rec 1930)* — Grammofono 2000 2-▲ GRM 78632
Verdi, G.:Rigoletto, w. Mercedes Capsir (sop), Dino Borgioli (ten), Ernesto Dominici (bass), L. Molajoli (cnd), La Scala Orch, La Scala Chorus — Phonographe 2-▲ PHG 5036 [ADD]

Straka, Peter (ten)
Janácek, L.:Fate, w. Lívia Ághová (sop—Míla), Ludmila Nováková (sop—Frl. Stuhlá/Součková), Marta Benačková (cta—Mílas Mother), Stefan Margita (ten—Dr. Suda/Hrázda), Peter Straka (ten—Zivný), Ivan Kusnjer (bar—Konečny/Verva), Peter Mikuláš (bass—Lhotský), G. Albrecht (cnd), Czech PO, Prague Chamber Choir *(rec 1995)* — Orfeo ▲ 384 951 [DDD]
Mendelssohn, F.:Sym 2, w. C. Haymon (sop), A. Hagley (sop), W. Weller (cnd), Philharmonia Orch, Philharmonia Chorus [G] — Chandos ▲ CHAN 8995 [DDD]

Straley, Susan Faust (sop)
Constantinides, D.:Intimations, w. Susan Faust Straley (sop—Ellen), Cynthia Dewey (sgr—Celeste), D. Constantinides (cnd), Louisiana State Univ New Music Ensemble — Capstone ▲ CPS 8632
Constantinides, D.:Vocal Music, w. Cynthia Dewey (nar), Angela DeVerger (sop), Evelyn Petros (sop), Eugenia Epperson (fl), Richard Jernigan (cl), Kelly Smith Toney (vn), Hye-Yun Chung (hp), Stephen Brown (pno), John Raush (perc), D. Constantinides (cnd), Louisiana State Univ New Music Ensemble—Reflections IV for Sop, Fl, Hp & Pno; Intimations [1 Act Opera]; 4 Songs on Poems by Sappho; Mutability for Sop & Str Qt.; 4 Greek Songs — Vestige ▲ 04

Stramaglia, Isabella (sop)
Verdi, G.:Un ballo in maschera, w. Ghena Dimitrova (sop—Amelia), Isabella Stramaglia (sop—Oscar), Mirna Pecile (cta—Ulrica), Mario Carlin (ten—Un giudice), José Carreras (ten—Riccardo), Piero Cappuccilli (bar—Renato), Massimiliano Malaspina (bass—Samuel), Americo de Santis (bass—Silvano), Francesco Signor (bass—Tom), Ivan Del Manto (sgr—Un servo), G. Patanè (cnd), Parma Teatro Regio Orch *(rec Teatro Regio, Dec. 26, 1972)* — Golden Age of Opera 2-▲ GAO 183/84

Stratas, Teresa (sop)
Berg, A.:Lulu, w. Y. Minton (mez), V. Schwarz (sop), K. Riegel (ten), F. Mazura (bar), P. Boulez (cnd), Paris Opera Orch—Act 3 [G] — Deutsche Grammophon 3-▲ 415489-2 [ADD]
Falla, M. de:Atlántida, w. G. Simionato (mez), R. Browne (sgr), Halley (sgr), T. Schippers (cnd), La Scala Orch, La Scala Chorus *(rec live, Milan 6/18/62)* — Memories 2-▲ HR 4464/65 [ADD]
Glanville-Hicks, P.:Nausicaa, w. Teresa Stratas (sop—Nausicaa), Sophia Steffan (cta—Queen Arete), Michalis Heliotis (ten—Antinous/Priest), George Moutsios (ten—Eurymachus), Edward Ruhl (ten—Phemius), George Tsantikos (ten—Clytoneus), Vassilis Koundouris (bar—Messenger), John Modenos (bar—Aethon), Spiro Malas (bass—King Alcinous), C. Surinach (cnd), Athens SO, Athens Sym Chorus *(rec Athens Festival, 1961)* — CRI ▲ CD 695 [ADD]
Glanville-Hicks, P.:Nausicaa (sels), w. Spiro Malas (bass), Michalis Helii (sgr), Michalis Heliots (sgr), George Moutsio (sgr), Edward Ruhl (sgr), Sophia Steffan (sop), George Tsantikos (sgr), C. Surinach (cnd), Athens SO, Athens Sym Chorus — CRI ▲ CD 695 [ADD]
Kern, J.:Show Boat, w. F. von Stade (mez), J. Hadley (ten), B. Hubbard (bar), P. O'Hara (sgr), K. Burns (mez), N. Kulp (sgr), J. McGlinn (cnd), London Sinfonietta, Ambrosian Chorus [original orchd Robert Russell Bennett]—also includes 45 minutes of music intended for the original performance but never included, plus music from revivals and films [1988 studio cast] — Angel 3-▲ A23 49108 [DDD]
Kern, J.:Show Boat, w. P. O'Hara (sop), K. Burns (mez), F. von Stade (mez), D. Garrison (ten), J. Hadley (ten), B. Hubbard (bar), J. McGlinn (cnd), London Sinfonietta, Ambrosian Opera Chorus — EMI Classics ▲ ZDC 49847
Kern, J.:Show Boat, w. P. O'Hara (sop), K. Burns (mez), F. von Stade (mez), D. Garrison (ten), J. Hadley (ten), B. Hubbard (bar), J. McGlinn (cnd), London Sinfonietta, Ambrosian Opera Chorus, Ambrosian Singers — EMI Classics 3-▲ A23 49108
Lehár, F.:Die lustige Witwe, w. E. Harwood (sop), W. Hollweg (ten), R. Kollo (ten), Z. Kelemen (bar), H. von Karajan (cnd), Berlin PO, German Opera Chorus [G] *(rec 1972)* — Deutsche Grammophon 2-▲ 435712-2 [ADD]
Leoncavallo, R.:Pagliacci, w. Teresa Stratas (sop—Nedda), Placido Domingo (ten—Canio), Juan Pons (bar—Tonio), G. Prêtre (cnd), La Scala Orch, La Scala Chorus — Philips ("Duo" series) 2-▲ 454 265-2
Leoncavallo, R.:Pagliacci, w. P. Domingo (ten), J. Pons (bar), G. Prêtre (cnd), La Scala Orch, La Scala Chorus [I] — Philips 2-▲ 411484-2
Mozart, W.A.:Così fan tutte, w. K. Te Kanawa (sop), F. von Stade (mez), A. Lombard (cnd), Strasbourg PO, Rhine Opera Chorus — Erato 3-▲ 98494-2
Mozart, W.A.:Nozze di Figaro, w. S. Jurinac (sop), T. Berganza (mez), N. Condò (mez), A. Lazzari (ten), S. Bruscantini (bar), M. Petri (bass), G. Tadeo (bass), A. Mariotti (bass), Z. Mehta (cnd), *(orch unknown) (rec 1968)* — Great Opera Performances 3-▲ GOP 712
Smetana, B.:The Bartered Bride, w. R. Kollo (ten), W. Berry (b-bar), A. Malta (bass), J. Krombholc (cnd), Munich RSO — Eurodisc 2-▲ 7795-2-RG [ADD]
Verdi, G.:La traviata (sels), w. F. Wunderlich (ten), H. Prey (bar), G. Patanè (cnd), Bavarian State Opera Orch, Bavarian State Opera Chorus—substantial selections from Acts 1–3 *(rec live, Munich, 3/28/65)* — Myto 2-▲ 2 MCD 91648 [ADD]
Weill, K.:Songs [E,G,F] — Elektra/Nonesuch ▲ 79019-2 [DDD] ■ D1-79019 (D)
Weill, K.:Songs, w. G. Schwarz (cnd), chamber sym — Elektra/Nonesuch ▲ 79131-2 [ADD] ■ 79131-4

Strauss, I. (sgr)
Albert, E. d':Tiefland, w. Schock, Feldhoff, Sardi, H. Zanotelli (cnd), Berlin SO — Eurodisc 2-▲ 7797-2-RG [ADD]

Strebel, Reinhard (bass)
Wehrli, W.:Ein weltliches Requiem, w. R. Amsler (sop), D. Labusch (cta), B. Hunziker (ten), K. Girod (cnd), Aargauer CO, Aargauer Chamber Choir *(rec live Jan. 12, 1992)* — Jecklin ▲ JS 276-2 [DDD]

Streckmann, Ulrich (bass)
Schubert, Franz:Deutsche Messe, w. Alexander Seitz (trb), Robert Wörle (ten), R. Kammler (cnd), Munich Residenz CO, Augsburg Cathedral Boys' Choir — Calig ▲ CAL 50952 [DDD]
Schubert, Franz:Mass 2, w. Alexander Seitz (trb), Robert Wörle (ten), R. Kammler (cnd), Munich Residenz CO, Augsburg Cathedral Boys' Choir — Calig ▲ CAL 50952 [DDD]

Streep, Meryl (nar)
Poulenc, F.:Babar, w. Mona Golabek (pno), René Golabek (pno) [E] — Koch Schwann ▲ KIC CD 7368 ■ KIC MC 4368; 7371 (blister pack)
Ravel, M.:Ma mère l'oye suite, w. Mona Golabek (pno), René Golabek (pno), J. Falletta (cnd), New Zealand SO [E] — Koch Schwann ▲ KIC CD 7368 ■ KIC MC 4368; 7371 (Blister Pack)

Streetman, Curtis (bar)
Purcell, H.:Dido & Aeneas, w. Cassandra Hoffman (sop—Belinda), Arlene Travis (sop—2nd Witch), Desirée Halac (mez—Sorceress/Spirit), Jennifer Lane (mez—Dido), Elizabeth Norman (alt), Thomas Bogdan (ten—A Sailor), Michael Brown (bar—Aeneas), Curtis Streetman (bar), Caitriona O'Leary (sgr—2nd Woman), Sarah Pillow (sgr—1st Witch), B. Brookshire (cnd), San Cassiano Musici *(rec St. Ignatius of Antioch Episcopal Church, New York City, Spring 1995)* — Vox Classics ▲ VOX 7518

Streich, Rita (sop)
Humperdinck, E.:Hänsel und Gretel, w. Sena Jurinac (sop), Elisabeth Schwarzkopf (sop), Vittoria Palombini (mez), Rolando Panerai (bar), Bruna Ronshini (sgr), H. von Karajan (cnd), Milan Italian Radio-TV Orch, Milan RAI Chorus — Stradivarius 2-▲ STV 12314
Mozart, W.A.:Don Giovanni, w. E. Grümmer (sop), L. Della Casa (sop), L. Simoneau (ten), C. Siepi (b-bar), G. Frick (bass), W. Berry (bass), F. Corena (bass), D. Mitropoulos (cnd), Vienna PO, Vienna State Opera Chorus [I] *(rec live, Salzburg, July 24, 1956)* — Arkadia 3-▲ 552 (m) [ADD]

Streich, Rita (sop) (cont.)
Mozart, W.A.:Don Giovanni, w. E. Grümmer (sop—D. Anna), R. Streich (sop—Zerlina), L. Della Casa (sop—D. Elvira), L. Simoneau (ten—Don Ottavio), C. Siepi (bass-baritone—Don Giovanni), W. Berry (bass—Masetto), G. Frick (bass—Il Commendatore), F. Corena (bass—Leporello), D. Mitropoulos (cnd), Vienna PO, Vienna State Opera Chorus *(rec Salzburg, July 24, 1956)* Sony Classical 3-▲ SM3K 64263 [ADD]
Mozart, W.A.:Entführung, w. S. Barabas (sop), A. Dermota (ten), H. Krebs (ten), J. Greindl (bass), F. Fricsay (cnd), Berlin RSO, Berlin Radio Chorus [G] *(rec Jesus-Christuskirche, Berlin-Dahlem, Dec. 19-21, 1949)* Myto 2-▲ 2 MCD 92361 [ADD]
Mozart, W.A.:Zauberflöte, w. E. Schwarzkopf (sop), A. Noni (sop), N. Gedda (ten), G. Taddei (bar), M. Petri (bass), H. von Karajan (cnd), Rome Radio Orch, Rome RAI Chorus [I] *(rec live, Dec. 19, 1953)* Myto 2-▲ 2 MCD 89007 (m) [ADD]
Strauss (II), Joh.:Die Fledermaus, w. A. Schlemm (mez), P. Anders (ten), H. Krebs (ten), F. Fricsay (cnd), Berlin RSO, Berlin Radio Chorus [G] *(rec live, Berlin, 11/8/49)* Melodram 2-▲ MEL 29001 (m) [AAD]
Strauss (II), Joh.:Die Fledermaus, w. E. Schwarzkopf (sop), N. Gedda (ten), H. Krebs (ten), R. Christ (ten), E. Kunz (bar), K. Dönch (bar), H. von Karajan (cnd), Philharmonia Orch, Philharmonia Chorus [G] EMI Classics ("Studio" series) 2-▲ CDHB 69531 (m) [ADD]
Strauss (II), Joh.:Die Fledermaus, w. H. Gueden (sop), G. Di Stefano (ten), G. Stolze (ten), G. Zampieri (ten), E. Wächter (bar), W. Berry (bass), E. Kunz (bar), H. von Karajan (cnd), Vienna State Opera Orch, Vienna State Opera Chorus [G] Arkadia 3-▲ 215 (m) [ADD]
Strauss (II), Joh.:Eine Nacht in Venedig (sels), w. Christine Gorner (sop), Cesare Curzi (ten), Nicolai Gedda (ten), Christian Oppleberg (bar), F. Allers (cnd), Graunke SO, Graunke Chorus Emperor Operetta ▲ KO 86345
Strauss (II), Joh.:Der Zigeunerbaron (sels), w. Grace Bumbry (mez), Biserka Cvejic (mez), Gisela Litz (alt), Nicolai Gedda (ten), Hermann Prey (bar), Kurt Bohme (bass), F. Allers (cnd), Munich Bavarian State Opera Orch, Munich Bavarian State Opera Chorus Emperor Operetta ▲ KO 86346
Strauss, R.:Ariadne auf Naxos, w. E. Schwarzkopf (sop), I. Seefried (sop), L. Otto (sop), G. Hoffman (mez), R. Schock (ten), G. Unger (ten), H. Cuénod (ten), H. Prey (bar), F. Ollendorff (bass), H. von Karajan (cnd), Philharmonia Orch [G] *(rec 1954)* EMI Classics ("Studio" series) 2-▲ CDMB 69296 (m) [ADD]
Strauss, R.:Ariadne auf Naxos, w. Elisabeth Schwarzkopf (sop—Ariadne/Prima Donna), Irmgard Seefried (sop—Zerbinetta), Rita Streich (sop—The Composer), Rudolf Schock (ten—Bacchus), H. von Karajan (cnd), Philharmonia Orch EMI Classics 2-▲ CDCB 55176
Weber, C.M. von:Der Freischütz, w. Irmgard Seefried (sop), Richard Holm (ten), Eberhard Wächter (bar), Kurt Böhme (b-bar), E. Jochum (cnd), Bavarian RSO, Bavarian Radio Chorus Deutsche Grammophon 2-▲ 439717-2 [ADD]

Streiff, Danièle (sop)
Massenet, J.:Cléopâtre, w. B. Harries (sop), M. Olmeda (sop), J. Maurette (ten), D. Henry (bar), M. Hacquard (bar), P. Fournillier (cnd), St.-Etienne Nouvel Orch, Saint-Etienne Nouvel Chorus [F] *(rec live, Massenet Festival in Saint-Etienne 1990)* Koch Schwann 2-▲ 3-1032-2 [DDD]

Streijffert, Maria (alt)
Schnittke, A.:Penitential Psalms, w. Eva Bruun Hansen (sop), Elisabeth Rehling (sop), Annette Simonsen (alt), Karl-Gustav Andersson (ten), Poul Vejbo (ten), Stefan Parkman (cnd), Danish National Radio Choir Chandos ▲ CHAN 9480

Streinz, W. (bass)
Nicolai, O.:Lustigen Weiber, w. I. Bielke (sop), M. L. Schilp (mez), W. Ludwig (ten), G. Hann (bass), A. Rother (cnd), Berlin RSO, Berlin State Opera Chorus *(rec May 2, 1943)* Preiser 2-▲ PRE 90208 [ADD]

Streit, Kurt (ten)
Brahms, J.:Liebeslieder Waltzes SATB, w. Barbara Bonney (sop), Anne Sofie von Otter (mez), Olaf Bär (bar), Bengt Forsberg (pno), Helmut Deutsch (pno) EMI Classics ▲ CDC 55430
Brahms, J.:Neue Liebeslieder Waltzes, w. Barbara Bonney (sop), Anne Sofie von Otter (mez), Olaf Bär (bar), Bengt Forsberg (pno), Helmut Deutsch (pno) EMI Classics ▲ CDC 55430
Mozart, W.A.:Entführung, w. C. Studer (sop), E. Szmytka (sop), R. Gambill (ten), G. Missenhardt (bar), M. Heltau (nar), B. Weil (cnd), Vienna SO, Vienna State Opera Chorus Sony Classical 2-▲ S2K 48053
Mozart, W.A.:Entführung (sels), w. C. Studer (sop), E. Szmytka (sop), R. Gambill (ten), Gunter Missenhardt (bar), B. Weil (cnd), Vienna SO, Vienna State Opera Chorus *(rec Vienna, Apr. 2-10, 1991)* Sony Classical ("Opera Highlights" series) ▲ SMK 53500 [DDD]
Mozart, W.A.:Zauberflöte, w. B. Bonney (sop—Pamina), S. Jo (sop—Queen of the Night), K. Streit (ten—Tamino), G. Cachemaille (b-bar—Papageno), K. Sigmundsson (bass—Sarastro), A. Östman (cnd), Drottningholm Court Theater Orch, Drottingholm Court Thea Chorus L'Oiseau-Lyre 2-▲ 440085-2 [DDD]
Schoeck, O.:Der Sänger, w. Wolfram Rieger (pno) *(rec Pere Casulleras, Christine Rosse, CH-Waldenburg, Apr, 1995)* Jecklin ▲ JD 679-2 [DDD]
Schoeck, O.:Spielmannsweisen, w. Gudrun Haag (hp) *(rec Pere Casulleras, Christine Rosse, CH-Waldenburg, Apr, 1995)* Jecklin ▲ JD 679-2 [DDD]
Schumann, R.:Spanisches Liederspiel, w. Barbara Bonney (sop), Anne Sofie von Otter (mez), Olaf Bär (bar), Bengt Forsberg (pno), Helmut Deutsch (pno) EMI Classics ▲ CDC 55430

Stricker, Frieder (ten)
Strauss (II), Joh.:Eine Nacht in Venedig (sels), w. J. Scovotti (sop), E. Schary (mez), E. Steiner (mez), C. Bini (ten), W. Brendel (bar), E. Märzendorfer (cnd), Hungarian State Orch, Hungarian State Chorus [G] Acanta ▲ CD 43809 [DDD]

Strienz, Wilhelm (bass)
Lortzing, A.:Zar und Zimmermann, w. M. Gripekoven (sop—Marie), E. Mayer (cta—Widow Browe), H. Buchta (ten—Peter Ivonov), H. Schmid-Berikoven (ten—Marquis de Chateauneuf), G. Hann (b-bar—Tsar Peter I), W. Strienz (b-bar—Van Bett), B. Müller (bass) Myto 2-▲ MCD 943103
Mozart, W.A.:Entführung (sels), w. H. Zimmermann (cnd), Berlin RSO—6 arias [G] Melodram 2-▲ MEL 27056 (m) [AAD]
Mozart, W.A.:Zauberflöte, w. T. Lemnitz (sop), E. Berger (sop), I. Beilke (sop), H. Roswaenge (ten), H. Tessmer (ten), G. Hüsch (bar), T. Beecham (cnd), Berlin PO, Favre Chorus [without dialog; G] *(rec 1937-38 for HMV)* EMI Classics ("Great Recordings of the Century" series) 2-▲ CDHB 61034 (m) [ADD]
Mozart, W.A.:Zauberflöte, w. T. Lemnitz (sop), E. Berger (sop), I. Beilke (sop), H. Roswaenge (ten), H. Tessmer (ten), G. Hüsch (bar), T. Beecham (cnd), Berlin PO, Favre Chorus [without dialog; G] *(rec 1937-38 for HMV)* Pearl 2-▲ PEAS 9371 (m) [AAD]
Mozart, W.A.:Zauberflöte, w. T. Lemnitz (sop), E. Berger (sop), I. Beilke (sop), H. Roswaenge (ten), H. Tessmer (ten), G. Hüsch (bar), T. Beecham (cnd), Berlin PO, Favre Chorus [without dialog; G] *(rec 1937-38 for HMV)* Melodram 2-▲ MEL 27056 (m) [AAD]
Mozart, W.A.:Zauberflöte, w. E. Berger (sop), T. Lemnitz (sop), I. Beilke (sop), H. Roswaenge (ten), G. Hüsch (bar), T. Beecham (cnd), Berlin PO, Vereinigung Favres Soloists [G] *(rec Nov. 1937 & Feb.-Mar. 193)* Nimbus ("Prima Voce" series) 2-▲ NI 7827/8 (m) [ADD]
A Selection of the Great German Bass's Best Recordings *(rec 1926-40)* Pearl ▲ PEA 9155 [ADD]
Wilhelm Strienz *(rec 1935-40)* Preiser ("Lebendige Vergangenheit" series) ▲ PRE 89089 [AAD]

Stringer, Robert (trb)
Celestial Christmas 4, w. Worcester Cathedral Choir, Raymond Johnston (org) Celestial Harmonies ▲ 13077-2

Stritch, E. (sgr)
Rodgers, R.:Pal Joey, w. H. Gallagher (sgr), P. Northrop (sgr) [1952 revival cast] Broadway Angel ▲ ZDM 64696 ■ EG 64696

Striuli, Carlo (sgr)
Wolf-Ferrari, E.:Il campiello, w. D. Mazzucato (Gasparina), G. Devinu (Lucieta), M. Bolgan (Gnese), C. de Mola (Orsola), U. Benelli (Dona Cate Panciana), M. Rene Cosotti (Dona Pasqua Polegana), M. Comencini (Zorozeto), M. Biscotti (Astolfi), I. D'Arcangelo (Anzoleto), C. Striuli (Fabrizio del Ritorti), N. Bareza (cnd), Trieste Teatro Comunale Giuseppe Verdi Orch, Trieste Teatro Comunale G. Verdi Chorus *(rec Feb. 1992)* Ricordi 2-▲ RFCD 2014 [DDD]

Strow-Piccolo (sgr)
Mascagni, P.:Nerone, w. R. Didonè (sop), D. Di Domenico (ten), S. Cowan (bar), M. Dirks (bar), Harry Peeters (bass), Shapero (sgr), Tcholakov (sgr), K. Bakels (cnd), Hilversum RSO, Hilversum Chorus [I] Bongiovanni 2-▲ GB 2052/53 [DDD]

Struckmann, Falk (bar)
Beethoven, L. van:Sym 9, "Choral Sym", w. A. Marc (sop), I. Vermillion (mez), S. Jerusalem (ten), D. Barenboim (cnd), Berlin State Opera Orch, Berlin State Opera Chorus Erato ▲ 94353-2

Strudthoff, Claudio (ten)
Mussorgsky, M.:Khovanshchina, w. Mietta Sighele (sop—Emma), Elena Souliotis (sop—Susanna), Fiorenza Cossotto (mez—Marfa), Herbert Handt (ten—Scribe), Veriano Luchetti (ten—Prince Andrey Khovansky), Ludovic Spiess (ten—Prince Vasily Golitsin), Claudio Strudthoff (ten—Streshnev), Angelo Marchiandi (bar—Kuz'ka), Teodoro Rovetta (bar—1st Strel'tsi), Siegmund Nimsgern (b-bar—Shaklovity), Cesare Siepi (b-bar—Dosifey), Carlo del Bosco (bass—2nd Strel'tsi), Ubaldo Carosi (bass—Varsonofiev), Nicolai Ghiaurov (bass—Prince Ivan Khovnasky), Giovanni Sciarpeletti (bass—Pastor), B. Leskovich (cnd), Rome RAI SO, Rome RAI Chorus—also includes bonus Act V [w Boris Christoff] (Rome, 1958) *(rec Rome, 1973)* Bella Voce 3-▲ BLV 107.402 [AAD]

Struplová, Eva (sop)
Janácek, L.:Vocal Music, w. Stanislav Predota (ten), Hanus Barton (pno), Adam Skoumal (pno), L. Cerny (cnd), *(ensemble unknown)*, Milan Uherek (cnd), Severácek Children's Choir—Little Queens; Folk Poetry from Hukvaldy; Folk Nocturnes; Nursery Rhymes Studio Matous ▲ MAT 16 [DDD]

Stryczek, Karl-Heinz (bass)
Beethoven, L. van:Sym 9, "Choral Sym", w. E. Wiens (sop), U. Walther (cta), R. Goldberg (ten), H. Blomstedt (cnd), Dresden Staatskapelle, Dresden State Opera Chorus, Dresden Sym Chorus—final chorus Capriccio ▲ 10 914 [DDD]

Stuart, Richard (bar)
Sullivan, A.:The Mikado, w. M. McLaughlin (sop), A. Howells (mez), J. Watson (sop), F. Palmer (sop/mez), D. Adams (bass), A. Rolfe Johnson (ten), R. Van Allan (bass), N. Folwell (bar), C. Mackerras (cnd), Welsh National Opera Orch, Welsh National Opera Chorus—Ov & dialogue omitted [E] Telarc ▲ CD 80284 [DDD]; ■ CS 30284 (D)

Stuarti, Enzo (sgr)
Strauss (II), Joh.:Eine Nacht in Venedig, w. Nola Fairbanks (sgr—Ciboletta), Thomas Tibbett Hayward (sgr—Mario), Laurel Hurley (sgr—Nina), David Kurlan (sgr—Senator Bartoldi), Guen Omeron (sgr—Barbara), Jack Russell (sgr—Duke of Palobino), Kenneth Schon (sgr—Filippo Del Aqua), Norwood Smith (sgr—Caramello), Enzo Stuarti (sgr—Pappacoda) *(rec Belock Recording Studio, Bayside, NY)* Everest ▲ EVC 9036 [AAD]

Stuckey, Andrew (bass)
Moore, D.:Devil & Daniel Webster, w. Joyce Guyer (sop—Mary Stone), Benjamin Bongers (ten—Walter Butler), Michael Philip Davis (ten—Simon Girty), Matthew Foerschler (ten—Miser Stephens), Darren Keith Woods (ten—Mr. Scratch), Michael Lanman (bass—Blackbeard Teach), David Soxman (bass—Clerk), Brian Steele (bass—Daniel Webster), John Stephens (bass—Jabez Stone), Andrew Stuckey (bass—King Philip), Robert Gibby Brand (actor), Cary Miller (actor), R. Patterson (cnd), Kansas City SO, Kansas City Lyric Opera Chorus *(rec Sept 1995)* Newport Classic ▲ NPD 85585 [DDD]

Studer, Cheryl (sop)
Barber, S.:Songs, w. T. Hampson (b-bar), J. Browning (pno), Emerson String Quartet Deutsche Grammophon 2-▲ 435867-2 [DDD]
Beethoven, L. van:Ah, perfido!, w. C. Abbado (cnd), Berlin PO Deutsche Grammophon ▲ 435617-2 [DDD]
Beethoven, L. van:Missa Solemnis, w. J. Norman (sop), P. Domingo (ten), K. Moll (bass), J. Levine (cnd), Vienna PO, Leipzig Radio Chorus, Eric Ericson Chamber Chorus Deutsche Grammophon 2-▲ 435770-2 [DDD]
Cheryl Studer:A Portrait, w. Gabriele Ferro (cnd), Bernard Haitink (cnd), Riccardo Muti (cnd), Wolfgang Sawallisch (cnd), Jeffrey Tate (cnd) EMI Classics ▲ CDC 55350
Coloratura Arias, w. Munich Radio Orch [cnd:G. Ferro] EMI Classics ▲ CDC 49961
Donizetti, G.:Lucia di Lammermoor, w. P. Domingo (ten), J. Pons (bar), S. Ramey (bass), I. Marin (cnd), London SO Deutsche Grammophon 2-▲ 435309-2
Donizetti, G.:Lucia di Lammermoor (sels), w. Cheryl Studer (sop—Lucia), Plácido Domingo (ten—Edgardo), I. Marin (cnd), London SO—Io di te memoria viva... Ah, Verranno a te sull'aure [Act I] Deutsche Grammophon ▲ 447270-2 [DDD] ■ 447 270-4
Donizetti, G.:Requiem Mass, w. H. Müller-Molinari (mez), A. Baldin (ten), J. P. Bogart (bass), J.-H. Rootering (bass), M. A. G. Martínez (cnd), Bamberg SO, Bamberg Sym Chorus [L] Orfeo ▲ 172881 [DDD]
Floyd, C.:Susannah, w. C. Studer (sop—Sussanah Polk), J. Hadley (ten—Sam Polk), S. Ramey (bass—Rev. Olin Blitch), K. Nagano (cnd), Paris Lyon Opera Orch, Paris Lyon Opera Chorus Virgin Classics ▲ CDCB 45039
Gounod, C.:Faust, w. R. Leech (ten), T. Hampson (bar), J. Van Dam (b-bar), M. Plasson (cnd), Toulouse Capitole Orch, Toulouse Capitole Chorus, *(highlights from the above)* EMI Classics ▲ CDC 54358 [DDD]
Gounod, C.:Faust, w. R. Leech (ten), T. Hampson (bar), J. Van Dam (b-bar), M. Plasson (cnd), Toulouse Capitole Orch, Toulouse Capitole Chorus EMI Classics 3-▲ CDCC 54228 [DDD]
In Salzburg, w. Irwin Gage (pno) Deutsche Grammophon ▲ 437784-2
Lehár, F.:Die lustige Witwe, w. Barbara Bonney (sop), Boje Skovhus (bar), Bryn Terfel (b-bar), J.E. Gardiner (cnd), Vienna PO, Monteverdi Choir London Deutsche Grammophon ▲ 439911-2
Mad About Angels, w. Christa Ludwig (mez), Anne Sofie von Otter (mez), José Carreras (ten), New York PO [cnd:Leonard Bernstein], English Baroque Soloists [cnd:John Eliot Gardiner], Philharmonia Orch, Philharmonia Chorus [cnd:Carlo Maria Giulini], et. al. Deutsche Grammophon ▲ 449113-2 ■ 449113-4
Mad About Love, w. Kiri Te Kanawa (sop), José Carreras (ten), Jerry Hadley (ten), Philharmonia Orch [cnd:Giuseppe Sinopoli], Bastille Opera Orch [cnd:Myung-Whun Chung], Boston SO [cnd:Seiji Ozawa], Vienna PO [cnd:John Eliot Gardiner, James Levine] Deutsche Grammophon ▲ 449112-2 ■ 449112-4
Mahler, G.:Das Klagende Lied, w. W. Meier (mez), R. Goldberg (ten), T. Allen (bar), G. Sinopoli (cnd), Philharmonia Orch, Shin-Yuh Kai Chorus *(rec live, Japan 1990)* Deutsche Grammophon ▲ 435382-2 [DDD]
Mahler, G.:Sym 2, w. W. Meier (mez), C. Abbado (cnd), Vienna PO, Arnold Schoenberg Choir Deutsche Grammophon ▲ 439953-2
Mahler, G.:Sym 8, w. Sylvia McNair (sop), Andrea Rost (sop), Anne Sofie von Otter (mez), Rosemarie Lang (cta), Peter Seiffert (ten), Bryn Terfel (bar), Jan-Hendrik Rootering (bass), C. Abbado (cnd), Berlin PO, Berlin Radio Chorus, Prague Phil Chorus, Tölz Boys' Choir Deutsche Grammophon ("4D Audio" series) 2-▲ 445843-2
Mahler, G.:Sym 8, w. S. Jo (sop), W. Meier (mez), K. Lewis (ten), T. Allen (bar), H. Sotin (bass), G. Sinopoli (cnd), Philharmonia Orch, Philharmonia Chorus, Southend Boys' Choir [G] Deutsche Grammophon 2-▲ 435433-2
Massenet, J.:Hérodiade, w. Cheryl Studer (sop—Salomé), Nadine Denize (mez—Hérodiade), Ben Heppner (ten—Jean), José Van Dam (b-bar—Phanuel), Thomas Hampson (bass—Hérode), M. Plasson (cnd), Toulouse Capitole Orch, Toulouse Capitole Chorus EMI Classics 3-▲ CDCC 55378
Mozart, W.A.:Arias, w. N. Marriner (cnd), Academy of St. Martin in the Fields—arias from Die Zauberflöte, Le nozze di Figaro, Così fan tutte & Die Entführung aus dem Serail Philips ("Solo" series) ▲ 442410-2
Mozart, W.A.:Don Giovanni, w. C. Vaness (sop), W. Shimell (bar), S. Ramey (bass), R. Muti (cnd), Vienna PO EMI Classics 3-▲ CDCC 54255
Mozart, W.A.:Don Giovanni (sels), w. C. Vaness (sop), R. Muti (cnd), Vienna PO EMI Classics ▲ CDC 54323
Mozart, W.A.:Entführung, w. E. Szmytka (sop), K. Streit (ten), R. Gambill (ten), G. Missenhardt (bar), M. Heltau (nar), B. Weil (cnd), Vienna SO, Vienna State Opera Chorus Sony Classical 2-▲ S2K 48053
Mozart, W.A.:Entführung (sels), w. E. Szmytka (sop), K. Streit (ten), R. Gambill (ten), Gunter Missenhardt (bar), B. Weil (cnd), Vienna SO, Vienna State Opera Chorus *(rec Vienna, Apr. 2-10, 1991)* Sony Classical ("Opera Highlights" series) ▲ SMK 53500 [DDD]

Studer, Cheryl (sop) (cont.)
Mozart, W.A.:Nozze di Figaro, w. Cecilia Bartoli (sop—Cherubino), Sylvia McNair (sop—Susanna), Cheryl Studer (sop—Countess Almaviva), Lucio Gallo (bar—Figaro), Boje Skovhus (bar—Count Almaviva), C. Abbado (cnd), Vienna PO, Vienna State Opera Chorus Deutsche Grammophon 3-▲ 445903-2
Mozart, W.A.:Zauberflöte, w. K. Te Kanawa (sop), E. Lind (sop), F. Araiza (ten), O. Bär (bar), S. Ramey (bass), N. Marriner (cnd), Academy of St. Martin in the Fields, Ambrosian Opera Chorus [G] Philips 2-▲ 426276-2 [DDD]
Mozart, W.A.:Zauberflöte (sels), w. K. Te Kanawa (sop), E. Lind (sop), F. Araiza (ten), O. Bär (bar), S. Ramey (bass), N. Marriner (cnd), Academy of St. Martin in the Fields Philips ▲ 438495-2
Offenbach, J.:Les Contes d'Hoffmann, w. J. Norman (sop), E. Lind (sop), A. Sofie von Otter (mez), F. Araiza (ten), S. Ramey (bass), J. Tate (cnd), Dresden Staatskapelle Philips ▲ 438502-2
Offenbach, J.:Les Contes d'Hoffmann, w. J. Norman (sop), E. Lind (sop), A. S. von Otter (mez), F. Araiza (ten), S. Ramey (bass), J. Tate (cnd), Dresden Staatskapelle Philips 3-▲ 422374-2 [DDD]
Rossini, G.:Guillaume Tell, w. C. Merritt (ten), G. Zancanaro (bar), R. Muti (cnd), La Scala Orch, La Scala Chorus [I] *(rec live, 12/7/88)* Philips 4-▲ 422391-2 [DDD]
Rossini, G.:Semiramide, w. J. Larmore (mez), F. Lopardo (ten), S. Ramey (bass), I. Marin (cnd), London SO, Ambrosian Opera Chorus Deutsche Grammophon ▲ 437797-2
Schubert, Franz:Fierrabras, w. K. Mattila (sop), R. Gambill (ten), T. Hampson (bar), R. Holl (bass), L. Polgar (bass), C. Abbado (cnd), CO of Europe, Arnold Schoenberg Choir [G] *(rec live)* Deutsche Grammophon 2-▲ 427341-2 [DDD]
Schubert, Franz:Songs (misc), w. I. Gage (pno)—Die Forelle; Nacht und Träume; Im Frühling; Klage der Ceres; etc. [G] Deutsche Grammophon ▲ 431773-2 [DDD]
Strauss, R.:Elektra, w. E. Marton (sop), M. Lipovsek (mez), H. Winkler (ten), B. Weikl (bar), W. Sawallisch (cnd), Bavarian RSO, Bavarian Radio Chorus EMI Classics 2-▲ CDCB 54067
Strauss, R.:4 Last Songs, w. G. Sinopoli (cnd), Dresden Staatskapelle Deutsche Grammophon ▲ 439865-2
Strauss, R.:Die Frau ohne Schatten, w. U. Vinzing (sop), H. Schwarz (mez), R. Kollo (ten), A. Muff (bass), Schmidt (sgr), W. Sawallisch (cnd), Bavarian RSO, Bavarian Radio Chorus [uncut version] [G] EMI Classics 3-▲ CDCC 49074 [DDD]
Strauss, R.:Die Frau ohne Schatten, w. U. Vinzing (sop), H. Schwarz (mez), R. Kollo (ten), A. Muff (bass), Schmidt (sgr), W. Sawallisch (cnd), Bavarian RSO, Bavarian Radio Chorus [G] EMI Classics ▲ CDC 54494 [DDD]
Strauss, R.:Salome, w. L. Rysanek (sop), H. Hiestermann (ten), B. Terfel (b-bar), G. Sinopoli (cnd), Berlin German Opera Orch Deutsche Grammophon 2-▲ 431810-2 [DDD]
Verdi, G.:Attila, w. N. Shicoff (ten), G. Zancanaro (bar), S. Ramey (bass), R. Muti (cnd), La Scala Orch, La Scala Chorus [I] EMI Classics 2-▲ CDCB 49952 [DDD]
Verdi, G.:Requiem Mass, w. M. Lopivšek (cta), J. Carreras (ten), R. Riamondi (bass), C. Abbado (cnd), Vienna PO, Vienna State Opera Chorus Deutsche Grammophon 2-▲ 435884-2
Verdi, G.:quattro pezzi sacri, w. M. Lopivšek (cta), J. Carreras (ten), R. Riamondi (bass), C. Abbado (cnd), Vienna PO, Vienna State Opera Chorus Deutsche Grammophon 2-▲ 435884-2
Wagner, R.:Götterdämmerung, w. H. Behrens (sop), H. Schwarz (mez), R. Goldberg (ten), B. Weikl (bar), E. Wlaschiha (bar), M. Salminen (bass), J. Levine (cnd), Metropolitan Opera Orch, New York Metropolitan Opera Chorus Deutsche Grammophon 4-▲ 429385-2 [DDD]
Wagner, R.:Lohengrin, w. P. Frey (ten), M. Schenk (bass), P. Schneider (cnd), Bayreuth Festival Orch, Bayreuth Festival Chorus [G] Philips 4-▲ 434602-2 [DDD]
Wagner, R.:Lohengrin, w. Waltraud Meier (mez), Siegfried Jerusalem (ten), Andreas Schmidt (bar), Harmut Welker (bar), Kurt Moll (bass), C. Abbado (cnd), Vienna PO Deutsche Grammophon 3-▲ 437808-2
Wagner, R.:Lohengrin, w. P. Frey (ten), M. Schenk (bass), P. Schneider (cnd), Bayreuth Festival Orch, Bayreuth Festival Chorus Philips 32-▲ 434420-2 [ADD/DDD]
Wagner, R.:Lohengrin (sels), w. W. Meier (mez), S. Jerusalem (ten), B. Terfel (bar), C. Abbado (cnd), Berlin PO Deutsche Grammophon ▲ 439768-2
Wagner, R.:Lohengrin (sels), w. G. Schnaut (sop), P. Frey (ten), M. Schenk (bass), P. Schneider (cnd), Bayreuth Festival Orch, Bayreuth Festival Chorus Philips ▲ 438500-2
Wagner, R.:Die Meistersinger von Nürnberg, w. C. Studer (sop—Eva), B. Heppner (ten—Walther von Stolzing), B. Weikl (bar—Hans Sachs), S. Lorenz (b-bar—Sixtus Beckmesser), K. Moll (bass—Veit Pogner), W. Sawallisch (cnd), Bavarian State Opera Orch, Bavarian State Opera Chorus EMI Classics ▲ CDCD 55142
Wagner, R.:Die Meistersinger von Nürnberg (sels), w. W. Meier (mez), S. Jerusalem (ten), B. Terfel (bar), C. Abbado (cnd), Berlin PO Deutsche Grammophon ▲ 439768-2
Wagner, R.:Rienzi, der Letzte der Tribunen, w. Cheryl Studer (sop—Irene), René Kollo (ten—Rienzi), Friedrich Lenz (ten—Gesandte), Norbert Orth (ten—Baroncelli), Bodo Brinkmann (bar—Paolo Orsini), Keith Engen (bass—Cecco del Vecchio), Raimund Grumbach (bass—Gesandte), Jan-Hendrik Rootering (bass—Steffano Colonna), Carmen Anhorn (sgr—Ein Friedensbote), Karl Helm (sgr—Kardinal Orvieto), John Janssen (sgr—Adriano), Alfred Kuhn (sgr—Gesandte), Hans Wilbrink (sgr—Gesandte), W. Sawallisch (cnd), Bavarian State Opera Orch, Bavarian State Opera Chorus *(rec live, July 6, 1983)* Orfeo d'or 3-▲ 346953
Wagner, R.:Der Ring des Nibelungen (sels), w. E. Marton (sop), K. Te Kanawa (sop), M. Lipovšek (mez), S. Jerusalem (ten), R. Goldberg (ten), P. Haage (ten), J. Morris (bass), B. Haitink (cnd), Bayer RSO EMI Classics ▲ ZDC 54633
Wagner, R.:Tannhäuser, w. A. Baltsa (mez), P. Domingo (ten), A. Schmidt (bar), M. Salminen (bass), G. Sinopoli (cnd), Philharmonia Orch, Royal Opera House Chorus Covent Garden Deutsche Grammophon ▲ 435405-2 [DDD]
Wagner, R.:Tannhäuser, w. A. Baltsa (mez), P. Domingo (ten), A. Schmidt (bar), M. Salminen (bass), G. Sinopoli (cnd), Philharmonia Orch, Royal Opera House Chorus Covent Garden [G] Deutsche Grammophon 3-▲ 427625-2 [DDD]
Wagner, R.:Tannhäuser (sels), w. W. Meier (mez), S. Jerusalem (ten), B. Terfel (bar), C. Abbado (cnd), Berlin PO Deutsche Grammophon ▲ 439768-2
Wagner, R.:Tristan und Isolde (prelude & liebestod), w. G. Sinopoli (cnd), Dresden Staatskapelle Deutsche Grammophon ▲ 439865-2
Wagner, R.:Die Walküre (sels), w. W. Meier (mez), S. Jerusalem (ten), B. Terfel (bar), C. Abbado (cnd), Berlin PO Deutsche Grammophon ▲ 439768-2
Wagner, R.:Wesendonck Songs, w. G. Sinopoli (cnd), Dresden Staatskapelle Deutsche Grammophon ▲ 439865-2

Studer, Ulrich (bar)
Handel, G.F.:Serse, w. Barbara Hendricks (sop—Romilda), Anne-Marie Rodde (sop—Atalanta), Carolyn Watkinson (cta—Xerxes), Otrun Wenkel (cta—Amastre), Paul Esswood (ct—Arsamene), Ulrich Studer (bar—Elviro), Ulrik Cold (bass—Ariodate), J. Malgoire (cnd), La Grande Ecurie et la Chambre du Roy *(rec Paris, 1979)* Sony Classical 3-▲ SM3K 36941

Studholme, Marion (sop)
Sullivan, A.:The Mikado, w. J. Wakefield (ten), C. Revill (bar), D. Dowling (bar), J. Holmes (bass), A. Faris (cnd), Sadler's Wells Opera Orch, Sadler's Wells Opera Chorus Classics for Pleasure 2-▲ CDCFP 4730 [ADD]
Sullivan, A.:Music of, w. J. Allister (cta), E. Bohan (ten), I. Wallace (bar), M. Dods (cnd), London Concert Orch, English Chorale—sels. from Gondoliers; H.M.S. Pinafore; Mikado; Pirates of Penzance PWK Classics ▲ PWK 1157 [AAD]

Stumpf (sgr)
Bach, J.S.:Cant 110, w. W. Wiedl (trb), S. Frangoulis (trb), P. Esswood (ct), K. Equiluz (ten), M. van Egmond (b-bar), S. Lorenz (b-bar), N. Harnoncourt (cnd), Vienna Concentus Musicus, Tölz Boys' Choir [G] Teldec 2-▲ 2292-42603-2

Stumphius, Annegeer (sop)
Bach, J.S.:Mass in b, BWV 232, w. C. Kallisch (alto), R. Wörle (ten), A. Schmidt (bass), H.-M. Schneidt (cnd), Munich Bach Orch, Munich Bach Choir *(rec Mar 21, 1992)* Calig 2-▲ CAL 5029/30 [ADD]
Gluck, C.W.:La Recontre imprévue, w. J. Kaufmann (sop—Rezia), A. Stumphius (sop—Dardané), A.-M. Rodde (sop—Amine), I. Vermillion (mez—Balkis), R. Gambill (ten—Ali), C. H. Ahnsjö (ten—Osmin), J.-H. Rootering (bass—Un Calender), L. Hager (cnd), Munich RSO Orfeo 2-▲ 242912 [DDD]
Verhulst, J.:Songs, w. Nico Van der Meel (ten), Leo Van Doeselaar (pno)—25 sels NM Classics ▲ NM 92029

Stupárkova-Majtnerová, Jana (sop)
Báchorek, M.:Lidice, w. Karel Průša (bar), Osvald Albín (speaker), Jan Vlasák (speaker), O. Trhlík (cnd), Ostrava Janáček PO, Ostrava Janáček Mixed Chorus *(rec Smetana Hall of Prague's Municipal House, Feb 10 & 11, 1988)* Panton ▲ 811338-2 [AAD]
Báchorek, M.:Music of, w. Osvald Albin (nar), Otakar Brousek (nar), Jan Vlassak (nar), Brigita Šulcová (sop), Drahomira Drobková (cta), Karel Průša (bass), Pavel Kamas (sgr), Jan Kyzlink (sgr), Jana Stuperkova-Majtnerova (sgr), Bretislav Vojkuvka (sgr), O. Trhlík (cnd), Ostrava Janáček PO, Prague SO, Ostrava Janáček Chorus, Ostrava Women's Chamber Chorus, Permoník Children's Chorus—Lidice; Stereofonietta; Hukvald Poem Panton ▲ PAN 811338 [AAD/DDD]

Stutzmann, Nathalie (cta)
Bach, J.S.:Cant 54, w. Roy Goodman (vn), R. Goodman (cnd), Hanover Band *(rec Watford Town Hall, Hertfordshire, U.K, Jan 31–Feb 3, 1994)* RCA Red Seal ▲ 09026-62655-2 [DDD]
Bach, J.S.:Cant 82, w. Anthony Robson (ob), Roy Goodman (org), R. Goodman (cnd), Hanover Band *(rec Watford Town Hall, Hertfordshire, U.K, Jan 31–Feb 3, 1994)* RCA Red Seal ▲ 09026-62655-2 [DDD]
Bach, J.S.:Cant 170, w. Anthony Robson (ob), Roy Goodman (org), Alistair Ross (org), R. Goodman (cnd), Hanover Band *(rec Watford Town Hall, Hertfordshire, U.K, Jan 31–Feb 3, 1994)* RCA Red Seal ▲ 09026-62655-2 [DDD]
Brahms, J.:Alto Rhap, w. C. Davis (cnd), Bavarian RSO, Bavarian Radio Chorus RCA Red Seal ▲ 09026-61201-2
Debussy, C.:Ariettes oubliées, w. C. Collard (pno) [F] RCA Red Seal ▲ 09026-60899-2
Debussy, C.:Chansons de Bilitis, w. C. Collard (pno) [F] RCA Red Seal ▲ 09026-60899-2
Debussy, C.:Poèmes (5) de Baudelaire, w. C. Collard (pno) [F] RCA Red Seal ▲ 09026-60899-2
Fauré, G.:Songs, w. C. Collard (pno)—28 songs RCA Red Seal ▲ 09026-61439-2
Handel, G.F.:Amadigi di Gaula, w. E. Harrhy (sop—Melissa), J. Smith (sop—Oriana), P. Bertin (mez—Orgando), B. Fink (cta—Dardano), N. Stutzmann (cta—Amadigi), M. Minkowski (cnd), Louvre Musicians, Louvre Choir [I] Erato 2-▲ 2292-45490-2 [DDD]
Handel, G.F.:Arias, w. R. Goodman (cnd), Hanover Band—arias from Aci, Galatea e Polifemo, Floridante, Giulio Cesare in Egitto, Orlando, Partenope, Radamisto, Rinaldo [I] RCA Red Seal ▲ 09026-61205-2
Handel, G.F.:Il Trionfo del Tempo e del Disinganno, w. Isabelle Poulenard (sop), Jennifer Smith (sop), John Elwes (ten), M. Minkowski (cnd), Louvre Musicians Erato 2-▲ 2292-45351-2 ZA
Mozart, W.A.:Arias, w. V. Spivakov (cnd), Moscow Virtuosi—Ombra felice, K.255; Io ti lascio, oh cara, addio, K.Anh.245 *(rec Reitstadel, Neumarkt, Germany, July 27–30, 1994)* RCA Red Seal ▲ 09026-68187-2 [DDD]
Mozart, W.A.:Ascanio (sels), w. V. Spivakov (cnd), Moscow Virtuosi—Ahimè! Che veggio mai?; Al mio ben mi veggio avanti; Perchè tacer degg'io?; Cara, lontano ancora; Ah di sì nobil alma *(rec Reitstadel, Neumarkt, Germany, July 27–30, 1994)* RCA Red Seal ▲ 09026-68187-2 [DDD]
Mozart, W.A.:Betulia (sels), w. V. Spivakov (cnd), Moscow Virtuosi—Prigionier che fa ritorno; Parto inerme, e non pavento *(rec Reitstadel, Neumarkt, Germany, July 27–30, 1994)* RCA Red Seal ▲ 09026-68187-2 [DDD]
Mozart, W.A.:Mitridate (sels), w. V. Spivakov (cnd), Moscow Virtuosi—Venga pur, minacci e frema; Ah, giacchè son tradito; Son reo, l'error confesso; Vadasi...Oh ciel; Già dagli occhi il velo è tolto; Va, l'error mio palesa *(rec Reitstadel, Neumarkt, Germany, July 27–30, 1994)* RCA Red Seal ▲ 09026-68187-2 [DDD]
Pergolesi, w. Elizabeth Norberg-Schulz (sop), Hanover Band, Ray Goodman (org) RCA Red Seal ▲ 09026-61215-2
Ravel, M.:Histoires naturelles, w. C. Collard (pno) [F] RCA Red Seal ▲ 09026-60899-2
Ropartz, G.:Sym 3, w. F. Pollet (sop), T. Dran (ten), F. Vassar (b-bar), M. Plasson (cnd), Toulouse Capitole Orch, Orféon Donostiarra EMI Classics ▲ CDM 64689-2
Schubert, Franz:Mass 4, w. M. Pares-Reyna (sop), Fletcher (ten), P. Fourcade (bass), M. Piquemal (cnd), Harmonia Nova Orch Ensemble, Michel Piquemal Vocal Ensemble [L] Gallo ▲ CD 584 [DDD]
Schumann, R.:Dichterliebe, w. C. Collard (pno) [G] RCA Red Seal ▲ 09026-61187-2
Schumann, R.:Frauenliebe und -leben, w. C. Collard (pno) [G] RCA Red Seal ▲ 09026-61187-2
Schumann, R.:Gedichte, Op. 135, w. Michel Dalberto (pno) Erato ("Recital" series) ▲ 98505-2
Schumann, R.:Liederkreis, Op. 39, w. C. Collard (pno) RCA Red Seal ▲ 09026-61728-2
Schumann, R.:Myrthen, w. Michel Dalberto (pno) Erato ("Recital" series) ▲ 98505-2
Schumann, R.:Songs, w. C. Collard (pno)—6 songs from Dem Liederbuch eines Malers [G] RCA Red Seal ▲ 09026-61187-2
Schumann, R.:Songs, w. C. Collard (pno)—Opp. 27, 51, 77 & 96 RCA Red Seal ▲ 09026-61728-2
Vivaldi, A.:Stabat Mater Cta, w. V. Spivakov (cnd), Moscow Virtuosi [L] RCA Red Seal ▲ 60240-2-RC [DDD]
Wagner, R.:Songs, w. G. Oppitz (pno)—Mignonne; Waiting [from 3 Melodies]; All Things Are but Fleeting Images; 2 Grenadiers; In the Greenhouse [study for Tristan und Isolde] *(rec Villa Wahnfried, Wagner-Museum, Bayreuth, Mar 30–Apr 3, 1993)* BMG ▲ 61843-2

Suart, Richard (bass)
Sullivan, A.:HMS Pinafore, w. F. Palmer (sop—Little Buttercup), R. Evans (mez—Josephine), M. Schade (ten—Ralph Rackstraw), T. Allen (bar—Capt. Corcoran), R. Suart (bass—Rt. Hon. Sir Joseph Porter, K.C.B.), D. Adams (bass—Dick Deadeye), R. Van A. (bass—Bill Bobstay), C. Mackerras (cnd), Welsh National Opera Orch, Welsh National Opera Chorus *(rec Swansea, Wales, June 5–8, 1994)* Telarc ▲ CD 80374 [DDD]
Sullivan, A.:The Pirates of Penzance, w. R. Evans (sop—Mabel), G. Knight (mez—Ruth), J. Gossage (mez—Edith), J. M. Ainsley (ten—Frederic), R. Suart (bar—Maj.-Gen. Stanley), N. Folwell (bar—Samuel), D. Adams (b-bar—Pirate King), R. Van Allan (bass—Sergeant of Police), C. Mackerras (cnd), Welsh National Opera Orch, Welsh National Opera Chorus *(rec May 4–6, 1993)* Telarc ▲ CD 80353 [DDD]; ■ CS 30353
Sullivan, A.:Trial by Jury, w. Rebecca Evans (sop—Plaintiff), Barry Banks (ten—Defendant), Gareth Rhys-Davies (bar—Foreman of the Jury), Peter Savidge (bar—Counsel for the Plaintiff), Donald Adams (bass—Usher), Richard Suart (bass—The Learned Judge), C. Mackerras (cnd), Welsh National Opera Orch, Welsh National Opera Chorus *(rec Brangwyn Hall, Swasea, Wales, Apr 18–30 & May 1, 1995)* Telarc 2-▲ CD 80404 [DDD]
Sullivan, A.:The Yeomen of the Guard, w. Felicity Palmer (sop—Dame Carruthers), Pamela Helen Stephens (mez—Phoebe Meryll), Neill Archer (ten—Col Fairfax), Peter Hoare (ten—Leonard Meryll), Ralph Mason (ten—1st Yeoman), Donald Maxwell (bar—Wilfred Shadbolt), Peter Savidge (bar—Lieutenant Sir Richard Cholmondely), Donald Adams (bass—Sergeant Meryll), Richard Suart (bass—Jack Point), Peter Lloyd Evans (sgr—2nd Yeoman), Alwyn Mellor (sgr—Elsie Maynard), Clare O'Neill (sgr—Kate), C. Mackerras (cnd), Welsh National Opera Orch, Welsh National Opera Chorus *(rec Brangwyn Hall, Swasea, Wales, Apr 18–30 & May 1, 1995)* Telarc 2-▲ CD 80404 [DDD]

Suaste, Jesús (bar)
Revueltas, S.:Music of, w. Lourdes Ambriz (sop), E. Diemecke (cnd), Camerata de las Américas, Latin American String Quartet, Juan D. Tercero Vocal Octet—Troka; Cuauhnáhuac; The Owl; Frogs; Duet for Duck & Canary; Why Do You Believe?; Walking; Scenes from Childhood; 4 Little Pieces; The Knifesharpener; Market; Sensemayá *(rec Mexico City, Sept 1996)* Dorian ▲ 90244 [DDD]

Sublet, P. (sgr)
Stockhausen, K.:Tierkreis Pno, w. J.-J. Dünki (pno)—Scorpio & Pisces *(rec May 27 & Sept. 18, 1992)* Jecklin ▲ JS 289-2 [ADD]

Subrata, Faridah (mez)
Respighi, O.:Aretusa, w. M. Adriano (cnd), Czech-Slovak RSO Bratislava [I] Marco Polo ▲ 8.223347 [DDD]
Respighi, O.:Liriche dal Poema paradisiaco di Gabriele d'Annunzio, w. M. Adriano (cnd), Czech-Slovak RSO Bratislava [arr. by Adriano for voice, harp, keyboards & strings] [I] Marco Polo ▲ 8.223347 [DDD]
Respighi, O.:La Sensitiva, w. M. Adriano (cnd), Czech-Slovak RSO Bratislava [I] Marco Polo ▲ 8.223347 [DDD]
Respighi, O.:Il Tramonto, w. M. Adriano (cnd), Czech-Slovak RSO Bratislava [I] Marco Polo ▲ 8.223347 [DDD]

Šubrtová, Milada (sop)
Dvořák, A.:Rusalka, w. Ivo Zídek (ten), Eduard Haken (bass), Z. Chalabala (cnd), Prague National Theater Orch, Prague National Theater Chorus Supraphon 2-▲ SUP 0013 [AAD]
Skroup, F.:Columbus (sels), w. B. Blachut (ten), Z. Otava (bar), F. Dyk (cnd), Prague RSO, Prague Radio Chorus *(rec 1962)* Multisonic ("Prague Opera Collection" series) ▲ 31 0153
Smetana, B.:The Devil's Wall, w. Ivana Mixová (mez), Vaclav Bednář (bass), Z. Chalabala (cnd), Prague National Theater Orch, Prague National Theater Chorus *(rec Prague, 1960)* Supraphon 2-▲ SUP 112201 [AAD]

Suchánková, J. (sop)
Klein, G.:Madrigals, w. M. Čejková (sop), H. Pracnové (alt), K. Kozunik (ten), J. Belor (bar) *(rec Oct. 20 & 21, 1992)* Koch International Classics ▲ KIC 7230-2 [DDD]

Suddaby, Elsie (sop)
Vaughan Williams, R.:Serenade to Music, w. I. Baillie (sop), S. Allen (sop), E. Turner (sop), M. Balfour (cta), A. Desmond (cta), M. Brunskill (cta), M. Jarred (cta), H. Nash (ten), W. Widdop (ten), P. Jones (ten), F. Titterton (ten), R. Henderson (bass), R. Easton (bass), H. Williams (bass), N. Allin (bass), H. Wood (cnd), BBC SO [E] *(rec 10/15/38)* Pearl ▲ GEMMCD 9342 (m) [AAD]
Vaughan Williams, R.:Serenade to Music, w. Isobel Baillie (sop), Lilian Stiles-Allen (sop), Eva Turner (sop), Margaret Balfour (cta), Muriel Brunskill (cta), Astra Desmond (cta), Mary Jarred (cta), Parry Jones (ten), Heddle Nash (ten), Frank Titterton (ten), Walter Widdop (ten), Roy Henderson (bar), Harold Williams (bar), Norman Allin (bass), Robert Easton (bass), H. Wood (cnd), BBC SO *(rec Abbey Road, Oct 15, 1938)* Claremont ▲ CDGSE 785066
Vaughan Williams, R.:Serenade to Music, w. I. Baillie (sop), S. Allen (sop), E. Turner (sop), M. Balfour (cta), A. Desmond (cta), M. Brunskill (cta), M. Jarred (cta), H. Nash (ten), W. Widdop (ten), P. Jones (ten), F. Titterton (ten), R. Henderson (bass), R. Easton (bass), H. Williams (bass), N. Allin (bass), H. J. Wood (cnd), BBC SO Dutton Laboratories ▲ CDAX 8004 [ADD]
Vaughan Williams, R.:A Song of Thanksgiving, w. *(nar unknown)*, A. Boult (cnd), BBC SO, BBC Children's Chorus Intaglio ▲ ING 757 [ADD]
Wagner, R.:Der Ring des Nibelungen (sels), w. Florence Austral (sop), Frieda Leider (sop), Göta Ljunberg (sop), Walter Widdop (ten), Horst Laubenthal (ten), Lauritz Melchoir (ten), Friedrich Schorr (bar), Rudolf Bockelmann (b-bar), Ivar Andresen (bass), Emmanuel List (bass), Collingwood, Blech, Coates, Barbirolli, Heger, Alwin, Muck (cnd), London SO—scenes from Siegriend & Götterdämmerung; 90 Motives from Der Ring [w. Collingwood & LSO] Pearl 7-▲ PEA 9137 [ADD]

Suez, Ina (sop)
Mozart, W.A.:Così fan tutte (sels), w. Heddle Nash (ten), C. Raybould (cnd), *(orch unknown)*—Hier soll ich dich; Konstanzel... wie ängstlich; Martern aller Arten *(rec 1905 - 1944)* Minerva ▲ MN A14 [ADD]

Suhubiette, Joel (ten)
Palestrina, G.:Sacred Music, w. Catherine Greuillet (sop), Thierry Gregoire (alt), Pierre Sciema (alt), Bruno Boterf (ten), Jean-Luc Baudoin (ten), Jean-Claude Sarragosse (bass), Laurent Stewart (org), Françoise Lasserre (cnd), Champagne-Ardenne Akademia Regional Vocal Ensemble—Ave maria; Salve regina; Vergine bella; Vergine saggia; Virgine pura; Virgine santa; Vergine sola; Vergine chiara; Vergine, quante lagrime; Vergine, tale è terra; Ave mundi spes; Ave regina coelorum; Alma redemptoris mater; Regina coieli laetare; Salve regina; Magnificat; others *(rec Convent of the Annunciation Dominican Church, Paris, Jan., 1994)* Pierre Verany ▲ PVY 794041 [DDD]

Sukowa, Barbara (nar)
Schoenberg, A.:Pierrot lunaire, w. R. de Leeuw (cnd), Schoenberg Ensemble [G] Koch Schwann ▲ CD 310 117 [DDD]

Šulcová, Brigita (sop)
Báchorek, M.:Music of, w. Osvald Albin (nar), Otakar Brousek (nar), Jan Vlassak (nar), Drahomira Drobková (cta), Karel Průša (bass), Pavel Kamas (sgr), Jan Kyzlink (sgr), Jana Stuperkova-Majtnerova (sgr), Bretislav Vojkuvka (sgr), O. Trhlík (cnd), Ostrava Janáček PO, Prague SO, Ostrava Janáček Chorus, Ostrava Women's Chamber Chorus, Permoník Children's Chorus—Lidice; Stereofonietta; Hukvald Poem Panton ▲ PAN 811338 [AAD/DDD]
Báchorek, M.:Stereofonietta, w. Jan Kyzlink (bar), O. Trhlík (cnd), Ostrava Janáček PO *(rec Smetana Hall of Prague's Municipal House, Feb 10 & 11, 1988)* Panton ▲ 811338-2 [AAD]
Havelka, S.:Music of, w. Anna Barova (cta), Vladimir Dolezal (ten), Richard Novak (bass), V. Neumann (cnd), Czech PO, Prague Phil Chorus—Epistola de M. Hieronymi De Praga Supplicio Panton ▲ PAN 810966
Slavický, K.:Sinfonietta 4, w. Rudolf Pellar (nar), Václav Rabas (org), J. Belohlávek (cnd), Prague SO *(rec Dvořák Hall of Rudolfinum, Prague, Sept. 6 & 8, 1986)* Panton ("Protokol XX" series) ▲ PAN 811142 [DDD]

Suliotis, Elena (sop)
Catalani, A.:Loreley, w. G. Talarico (ten), P. Cappuccilli (bar), G. Gavazzeni (cnd), La Scala Orch, La Scala Chorus *(rec 1968)* Memories 2-▲ MEM 4511 [ADD]
Mascagni, P.:Cavalleria rusticana, w. S. Malagu (mez), A. Di Stasio (mez), M. Del Monaco (ten), T. Gobbi (bar), S. Varviso (cnd), Rome Opera Orch, Rome Opera Chorus [I] IMP Collectors Series ▲ IMPX 9018 [AAD]
Verdi, G.:Nabucco, w. B. Prevedi (ten), T. Gobbi (ten), C. Cava (bass), L. Gardelli (cnd), Vienna State Opera Orch, Vienna State Opera Chorus [I] London 2-▲ 417407-2 [ADD]

Sullé, Sylvie (mez)
Bruneau, A.:Lazare, w. Françoise Pollet (sop), Mary Saint-Palais (sop), Jean-Luc Viala (ten), Laurent Naouri (b-bar), J. Mercier (cnd), French National Orch, Maîtrise de Paris, Vittoria French Regional Choir Adès ▲ ADE 204512
Bruneau, A.:Requiem, w. Françoise Pollet (sop), Mary Saint-Palais (sop), Jean-Luc Viala (ten), Laurent Naouri (b-bar), J. Mercier (cnd), French National Orch, Maîtrise de Paris, Vittoria French Regional Choir Adès ▲ ADE 204512
Debussy, C.:La Damoiselle élue, w. M. Delünsch (sop), J.-C. Casadesus (cnd), Lille National Orch, Michel Piquemal Vocal Ensemble Harmonia Mundi France ▲ HMC 901490
Honegger, A.:Le Roi David, w. Alessandra Marc (sop), Laurence Dale (ten), D. Mesguich (nar), J.-C. Casadesus (cnd), Lille National Orch EMI Classics ▲ CDC 54793

Sullivan, K. (sop)
Luening, O.:No Jerusalem But This, w. Jacqueline Pierce (sop), Paul Sperry (ten), M. Moliterno (bar), P. Wilder (sgr), S. Rosser (sgr), A. Goodman (cnd), Music Project CO, Goodman Chamber Choir [E] *(rec 6/6/90)* CRI ▲ CD 600 [DDD]

Sullivan, L. (sgr)
Lerner, A.J.:Brigadoon, w. D. Brooks (sgr), M. Bell (sgr), P. Britton (sgr) [1947 Broadway original cast] RCA ▲ 1001-2 RG [ADD] ■ 1001-4 RG

Sulzenko, Jiří (bass)
Dvořák, A.:Stabat Mater, w. Eva Jenisova (sop), Hana Stolfova-Bandova (cta), Vladimir Dolezal (ten), L. Svárovský (cnd), Czech PO, Petr Fiala (cnd), Brno Czech Phil Chorus Supraphon 2-▲ SUP CD 3093
Puccini, G.:La Bohème (sels), w. Luba Orgonasova (sop—Mimì), Carmen Gonzales (sop—Musetta), Jonathan Welch (ten—Rudolfo), Fabio Previati (bar—Marcello), Boaz Senator (bar—Schaunard), Ivan Urbas (bass—Colline), Jiri Sulzenko (bass—Alcindoro), W. Humburg (cnd), Czech-Slovak RSO Bratislava, Bratislava Children's Choir, Slovak Phil Chorus *(rec Concert Hall, Czecho-Slovak Radio, Bratislava, Apr. 23-May 4, 1990)* Naxos ▲ 8.553151 [DDD]
Vanhal, J.B.:Missa Solemnis, w. Marta Filová (sop), Marta Benačková (mez), Jörg Dürmüller (ten), V. Neumann (cnd), Prague Virtuosi, Prague Chamber Choir—Kyrie eleison, Adagio— Allegro; Christe eleison, Andante; Kyrie eleison, Allegro; Gloria, Allegro moderato; Laudamus te, Andante; Gratias agimus tibi, Allegro moderato; Domine Deus, Rex caelestis, andante; Domine Deus, Agnus Dei, Adagio; Quoniam tu solus sanctus, Allegro moderato, Cum sancto spiritu, Allegro; Credo, Allegro moderato, Et incarnatus est. Adagio; Et resurrexit, Allegro moderato; Sanctus, Adagio—Osanna, Allegro; Benedictus, Andante—Osanna, Allegro; Agnus Dei, Adagio; Dona nobis pacem, Allegro *(rec Evangelische Kirche der böhmischen Brüder, Prag, Sept 25-28, 1994)* Orfeo ▲ C 353 951 A [DDD]

Sumegi, Daniel (bass)
Bellini, V.:Beatrice di Tenda, w. E. Gruberová (sop—Beatrice), V. Kasarova (mez—Agnese), D. Bernardini (ten—Orombello), B. Robinšak (ten—Anichino), I. Morosov (ten—Filippo Maria Visconti), D. Sumegi (bass—Rizzardo), P. Steinberg (cnd), Austrian RSO, Austrian Radio Chorus [I] *(rec live, Vienna Concert House 1/30 & 2/1/92)* Nightingale Classics 2-▲ NC 070560-2 [DDD]

Summers, Hilary (cta)
Handel, G.F.:Messiah, w. Lynne Dawson (sop), John Mark Ainsley (ten), Alastair Miles (bass), R. Goodman (cnd), Brandenburg Consort, Stephen Cleobury (cnd), King's College Choir Cambridge [1752 version] Argo 2-▲ 440672-2 [DDD]
Nyman, M.:Noises, w. Catherine Bott (sop), Ian Bostridge (ten), Andrew Findon (sax), David Roach (sax), D. Debart (cnd), Basse Normandie Instrumental Ensemble *(rec Caen, June 1991 & Abbey Road Studios, London, June 1993)* Argo ▲ 440842-2 [DDD]

Summers, Joan (sop)
Puccini, G.:Suor angelica, w. Elisabeth Carron (sop—Angelica), Joan Summers (sop—Genovieffa), Donna Owen (sop—Dolcina), Lou Ann Wyckoff (sop—Alms collector), Hanna Owen (sop—novice), Anthea De Forest (sop—novice), Charlotte Povia (mez—Abbess), Beverly Evans (mez—Monitress), Kay Creed (mez—Mistress), La Vergne Monette (sop/mez—lay sister), Joan August (sop/mez—lay sister), Pearle Goldsmith (sop/mez—other sister), Lila Herbert (sop/mez—other sister), Jodell Kenting (sop/mez—other sister), Ann Pretzat (sop/mez—other sister), Evelyn Sachs (cta—Princess), F. Patanè (cnd), *(orch unknown)* *(rec New York, Feb 23, 1967)* Legato Classics ▲ LCD 212-1 [ADD]

Summers, Jonathan (bar)
Balfe, M.W.:The Bohemian Girl, w. N. Thomas (sop), P. Power (ten), R. Bonynge (cnd), Irish National SO, Ireland National Sym Chorus Argo 2-▲ 433324-2 [DDD]
Britten, H.:Gloriana, w. J. Barstow (sop—Queen Elizabeth I), D. Jones (mez—Lady Essex), P. Langridge (ten—Earl of Essex), J. M. Ainsley (ten—Spirit of the Masque), J. Summers (bar—Lord Mountjoy), J. Shirley-Quirk (bar—Recorder of Norwich), B. Terfel (b-bar—Henry Cuffe), C. Mackerras (cnd), Welsh National Opera Orch, Welsh National Opera Chorus Argo 2-▲ 440213-2 [DDD]
Britten, H.:Peter Grimes, w. H. Harper (sop), J. Vickers (ten), C. Davis (cnd), Royal Opera House Orch, Royal Opera House Chorus Covent Garden [E] Philips 2-▲ 432578-2 [ADD]
Donizetti, G.:Lucrezia Borgia, w. J. Sutherland (sop—Lucrezia Borgia), A. Howells (mez—Maffio Orsini), A. Kraus (ten—Gennaro), R. Leggate (ten—Liverotto), J. Summers (bar—Apostolo Gazella), P. Hudson (bass-bar—Gubetta), S. Dean (bass—Don Alfonso), R. Bonynge (cnd), Royal Opera House Orch *(rec London, Apr. 9, 1980)* Ornamenti 2-▲ FE 111 [ADD]
Leoncavallo, R.:La Bohème, w. L. Mazzaria (sop), M. Senn (mez), B. Praticò (sgr), M. Malagnini (sgr), J. Latham-König (cnd), Venice Teatro La Fenice Orch, Venice Teatro La Fenice Chorus *(rec live, 1990)* Nuova Era 3-▲ 6917/19 [DDD]
Orff, C.:Carmina burana, w. A. Augér (sop), J. Van Kesteren (ten), R. Muti (cnd), Philharmonia Orch, Philharmonia Chorus [G, L] EMI Classics ▲ CDC 47100
Saint-Saëns, C.:Samson et Dalila, w. J. Carreras (ten), A. Baltsa (mez), Estes (bass), Burchuladze (bass), C. Davis (cnd), Bavarian RSO, Bavarian Radio Chorus Philips 2-▲ 426243-2 [DDD]
Saint-Saëns, C.:Samson et Dalila (sels), w. A. Baltsa (mez), J. Carreras (ten), D. George (ten), S. Estes (bass), P. Burchuladze (bass), C. Davis (cnd), Bavarian RSO Philips ▲ 438504-2
Vaughan Williams, R.:Sym 1, w. F. Lott (sop), B. Haitink (cnd), London SO, London Sym Chorus [E] EMI Classics ▲ CDC 49911 [DDD]

Summers, Lydia (mez)
Verdi, G.:Aida (sels), w. Rose Bampton (sop), Arthur Carron (ten), Leonard Warren (bar), W. Pelletier (cnd), Philadelphia studio musicians, New York studio musicians—Ritorna vincitor!; Rivedrai le foreste imbalsamate; Odimi, Aida; La fatal pietra...O terra, addio! *(rec Academy of Music, Philadelphia & Town Hall, New York, May 30 & June 17, 1940)* VAI Audio ▲ VAIA 1084
Wagner, R.:Tristan und Isolde (sels), w. Rose Bampton (sop), Arthur Carron (ten), W. Steinberg (cnd), Philadelphia studio musicians, New York studio musicians—Wohl kenn' ich Irlands Königin; O sink' hernieder; Wohin nun Tristan scheidet; Mild und leise *(rec Academy of Music, Philadelphia & Town Hall, New York, May 26 & 27, 1940)* VAI Audio ▲ VAIA 1084

Sundquist, Erik (bar)
Leoncavallo, R.:Pagliacci, w. R. Moberg [sop—Nedda], J. Bjoerling [ten—Canio], E. Sundquist [bar—Tonio], L. Gardelli (cnd), Milan RAI SO, Milan RAI Chorus [Sw] *(rec live, Stockholm, 12/8/54)* Legato Classics ▲ LCD 155-1 [ADD]

Sunnegardh, Thomas (ten)
Wagner, R.:Das Rheingold, w. Gabriele Fontana (sop—Woglinde), Nancy Gustafson (sop—Freia), Ildiko Komlosi (mez—Wellgunde), Hanna Schwarz (mez—Fricka), Elena Zaremba (mez—Erda), Margareta Hintermeier (cta—Flosshilde), Kim Begley (ten—Loge), Peter Schreier (ten—Mime), Thomas Sunnegardh (ten—Froh), Robert Hale (bass-bar—Wotan), Walter Fink (bass—Fafner), Franz-Josef Kapellmann (bass—Alberich), Jan-Hendrik Rootering (bass—Fasolt), Eike Wilm Schulte (bass—Donner), C. von Dohnányi (cnd), Cleveland Orch *(rec Severance Hall, Cleveland, Ohio, Dec 1993)* London 2-▲ 443690-2

Supervia, Conchita (mez)
Bizet, G.:Carmen (sels), w. Gaston Micheletti (ten), *(orch unknown)* Forlane ▲ FRL 16718 [ADD]
Bizet, G.:Carmen (sels), w. A. Vavon (sop), A. Bernadet (mez), J.-F. Delmas (b-bar), G. Micheletti (ten), A. Endreze (bar), G. Cloëz (cnd), Paris Opéra-Comique Orch, Paris Opéra-Comique Chorus—14 arias & scenes [F] *(rec Paris, 1930)* The Classical Collector ▲ FDC 2002 (m) [AAD]
Bizet, G.:Carmen (sels), w. A. Vavon (sop), A. Bernadet (mez), G. Micheletti (ten), A. Endreze (bar), G. Cloëz (cnd), Paris Opéra-Comique Orch, Paris Opéra-Comique Chorus—8 arias & scenes *(rec Paris 1930)* Nimbus ("Prima Voce" series) 2-▲ NI 7836/7 [ADD]
Conchita Supervia, w. Angelo Albergoni (cnd) *(rec 1927-1928)* Preiser (Lebendige Vergangenheit) ▲ 89023 (m) [ADD]
Conchita Supervia, Vol. 1 *(rec 1930-1932)* Pearl ▲ PEA 9975 [ADD]
Falla, M. de:Canciones populares españolas (7), w. F. Marshall (pno) *(rec , Paris 1930)* Nimbus (Prima Voce) 2-▲ NI 7836/7 [ADD]
Supervia in Opera & Song *(rec 1927-1932)* Nimbus ("Prima Voce" series) 2-▲ NI 7836/7 [ADD]
The Unknown Supervia *(rec 1929-1934)* Pearl ▲ PEA 9969 (m) [AAD]

Surais, Martine (sop)
Marinuzzi, G.:Jacquerie, w. Ilaria Galgani (sop), Antonio Salvadori (bar), Miro Solman (sgr), A. Licata (cnd), Catania Teatro Massimo Bellini Orch, Catania Teatro Massimo Bellini Chorus *(rec Catania, 1994)* Nuova Era 2-▲ NUO 7200 [DDD]

Surian, Giorgio (bass)
Donizetti, G.:La favorita, w. Gloria Scalchi (mez), Luca Canonici (ten), René Massis (bar), D. Renzetti (cnd), Milan RAI SO, Milan RAI Chorus Fonit Cetra ("Ricordi" series) 3-▲ FCT RFCD 2015
Gluck, C.W.:Iphigénie en Tauride, w. C. Vaness (sop—Iphigénie), S. Brunet (sop—Diane), G. Winbergh (ten—Pylade), T. Allen (bar—Oreste), G. Surian (bass—Thoas), R. Muti (cnd), La Scala Orch, La Scala Chorus *(rec Mar. 14-26, 1992)* Sony Classical 2-▲ S2K 52492 [DDD]
Paisiello, G.:Nina, o sia La pazza per amore, w. M. Bolgan (sop), F. Pediconi (sop), D. Bernardini (ten), F. Musinu (bass), R. Bonynge (cnd), Catania Teatro Massimo Bellini Orch, Catania Teatro Massimo Bellini Chorus [I] *(rec live 1989)* Nuova Era 2-▲ 6872/73 [DDD]
Rossini, G.:Bianca e Falliero, w. K. Ricciarelli (sop—Bianca), M. Horne (mez—Falliero), C. Merritt (ten—Contareno), D. Renzetti (cnd), *(orch & chorus unknown)* *(rec live, 1986)* Legato Classics 3-▲ LCD 138-3 [ADD]
Rossini, G.:Demetrio e Polibio, w. Christine Weidinger (sop—Lisinga), Sara Mingardo (cta—Siveno), Anna Laura Longo (sgr—Olmira), Dalmacio Gonzales (ten—Demetrio/Eumene), Giorgio Surjan (bass—Polibio), Martino Fullone (sgr—Onao), M. Carraro (cnd), Graz SO, Bratislava Chamber Chorus *(rec live, Martina Franca Opera Festival, Italy, July 27, 1992)* Dynamic 2-▲ CDS 171/1-2 [DDD]

Surikov, N. (bar)
Rachmaninoff, S.:Spring, w. A. Tchistiakov (cnd), Moscow Choral Academy Orch, Moscow Choral Academy Russian Season ("Russian Season" series) ▲ LDC 288069
Taneyev, S.:Choral Music, w. N. Terentieva (mez), A. Tchistiakov (cnd), Moscow Choral Academy Choir—St. John's of Damascus Russian Season ▲ LDC 288069
Tchaikovsky, P.:Moscow, w. N. Terntieva (mez), A. Tchistiakov (cnd), Moscow Choral Academy Choir Russian Season ▲ LDC 288069

Susca, Vito (bass)
Massenet, J.:Werther, w. L. Gencer (sop—Carlotta), G. Tavolaccini (sop—Sofia), F. Tagliavini (ten—Werther), M. Borriello (bar—Alberto), E. Mocchiutti (bar—Johann), V. Susca (bass—Il Podestà), R. Botteghelli (bass—Schmidt), C.F. Cillario (cnd), *(orch unknown)* Arkadia 2-▲ 599 [ADD]

▲ = CD ♦ = Enhanced CD Δ = MD ■ = Cassette Tape ▯ = DCC

Susca, Vito (bass) (cont.)

Rossini, G.:La Cenerentola, w. Ornella Rovero (sop), Miti Truccato Pace (mez), Giulietta Simionato (mez), Cesare Valletti (ten), Saturno Meletti (bar), Cristiano Dalamangas (sgr), M. Rossi (cnd), Turin RAI Orch, Bruno Erminero (cnd), Turin RAI Chorus — Fonit Cetra ("Classic Collection" series) ▲ FCT CDON 34

Verdi, G.:Un ballo in maschera, w. M. Curtis Verna (sop—Amelia), M. Erato (sop—Oscar), P. Tassinari (cta—Ulrica), F. Tagliavini (ten—Riccardo), G. Valdengo (bar—Renato), A. Albertini (bar—Silvano), M. Stefanoni (bass—Samuel), V. Susca (bass—Tom), A. Questa (cnd), Turin RAI SO, Turin RAI Chorus *(rec 1954)* — Cetra Classic 2-▲ CDO 13 [AAD]

Verdi, G.:Rigoletto, w. Gianna D'Angelo (sop), Aldo Protti (bar), Giorgio Tadeo (bass), F. Molinari-Pradelli (cnd), Trieste Teatro Comunale Giuseppe Verdi Orch, Trieste Teatro Comunale G. Verdi Chorus — Melodram 2-▲ CDM 27006

Verdi, G.:Simon Boccanegra, w. Leyla Gencer (sop), Glade Peterson (ten), Giuseppe Zampieri (ten), Tito Gobbi (bar), Rolando Panerai (bar), Giorgio Tozzi (bass), G. Gavazzeni (cnd), *(orch unknown)* — Great Opera Performances 2-▲ GOP 767

Wagner, R.:Die Meistersinger von Nürnberg, w. Bruna Rizzoli (sop), Fernanda Cadoni (mez), Luigi Infantino (ten), Vito Tatone (ten), Renato Capecchi (bar), Giuseppe Taddei (bar), Boris Christoff (bass), Giovanni Ciavola (bass), James Loomis (bass), Silvo Maionica (bass), Raimondo Botteghelli (sgr), Walter Brunelli (sgr), Carlo Franzini (sgr), Ezio de Giorgi (sgr), Renzo Gonzales (sgr), L. von Matačić (cnd), Turin RAI Radio-TV SO, Turin RAI Chorus — Stradivarius 4-▲ STV 12310

Suska, Katarzyna (cta)

Nicolai, O.:Te Deum, w. Bozena Betley (sop), Zofie Kilanowicz (sop), Henryk Grychnik (ten), Czeslaw Galka (bar), Jerzy Gruszczynski (bass), R. Bader (cnd), Cracow PO, Cracow Phil Chorus — Koch Schwann ▲ SCH CD 310872

Suppé, F. von:Requiem, w. Aleksandra Baranska (sop), Jerzy Knetig (ten), Andrjez Hiolski (bass), R. Bader (cnd), Cracow PO, Cracow Phil Chorus — Koch Schwann ▲ SCH CD 312482

Süss, Reiner (bar)

Dessau, P.:Einstein, w. Peter Schreier (ten), Theo Adam (bass), O. Suitner (cnd), Berlin Staatskapelle, Berlin State Opera Chorus — Berlin Classics 2-▲ BER CD 9109

Dessau, P.:Leonce & Lena, w. C. Nossek (sop), E. Büchner (bar), O. Suitner (cnd), Berlin Staatskapelle — Berlin Classics ▲ BER 1074 [ADD]

Dessau, P.:Puntila, w. Annelies Brumeister (mez—Lsins), Erich Witte (ten—Fredrick), Reiner Süss (bar—Johannes Puntila), P. Dessau (cnd), Berlin State Opera Orch, Berlin State Chorus *(rec Berlin, May 1988)* — Berlin Classics 2-▲ BER 2184 [ADD]

Prokofiev, S.:Betrothal in a Monastery (sels), w. A. Burmeister (mez), E. Büchner (bar), H. Kegel (cnd), Leipzig RSO [G] — Berlin Classics ▲ BER 2081 [ADD]

Telemann, G.P.:Cants, w. Leipzig St. Thomas Church Choir members—Der Schulmeister; Trauer-Musik eines kunsterfahrenen Canarienvogels; Sagt, ihr alleerschonsten Lippen; Die Hoffnung ist mein Leben — Berlin Classics ▲ BER 9135 [DDD]

Süssmann, Sofie-Christine (mez)

Brahms, J.:Gypsy Songs (8), w. D. Baldwin (pno) [G] — Arcobaleno ▲ SBCD 1506

Fauré, G.:La Chanson d'Eve, w. D. Baldwin (pno) [F] — Arcobaleno ▲ SBCD 1506 SBCD 1506

Schumann, R.:Frauenliebe und -leben, w. D. Baldwin (pno) [G] — Arcobaleno ▲ SBCD 1506

Sutcliffe, Tom (ct)

Bach, J.S.:St. Matthew Passion, w. J. Bowman (ct), P. Esswood (ct), K. Equiluz (ten), M. van Egmond (b-bar), N. Harnoncourt (cnd), Vienna Concentus Musicus [G] — Teldec 3-▲ 2292-42509-2 [AAD]

Suter, Heinz (bass)

Kraft, Walter:Christus, w. Anna Senn-Dähler (sop), Barbara Künzler (sop), Barbara Sutter (sop), Christine Guy (alt), Heidi Uhlmann (alt), Daniel Zellweger (alt), Matthias Senn (ten), Mikoto Usami (ten), Wolfgang Pailer (bass), Klaus Knall (cnd), Evangelische Singgemeinde Choirs *(rec Ostdorf bei Balingen, Oct. 8-11, 1986)* — Cantate 2-▲ 58004 [DDD]

Suthaus, Ludwig (ten)

Cherubini, L.:Médée (sels), w. I. Borkh (sop—Medea), L. Suthaus (ten—Giasone), V. Gui (cnd), Berlin State Opera Orch, Berlin State Opera Chorus—3 soprano arias & 3 duets *(rec live, Berlin 1958)* — Melodram 2-▲ CDM 27087 [ADD]

Wagner, R.:Lohengrin (sels)—Inbrunst im Herz — Myto 3-▲ MCD 93381

Wagner, R.:Die Meistersinger von Nürnberg, w. H. Scheppan (sop), E. Kunz (bar), P. Schöffler (b-bar), H. Abendroth (cnd), Bayreuth Festival Orch, Bayreuth Festival Chorus *(rec 1943)* — Preiser ▲ PRE 90174 [AAD]

Wagner, R.:Der Ring des Nibelungen, w. Gré Brouwenstein (sop—Freia/Sieglinde), Ilse Hollweg (sop—Waldvogel), Gerda Lammers (sop—Ortlinde), Paula Lenchner (sop—Wellgunde/Gerhilde), Hilde Scheppan (sop—Helmwige), Astrid Varnay (sop—Brünnilde/3rd Norn), Lore Wissmann (sop—Woglinde), Maria von Ilosvay (mez—Flosshilde/Schwertleite/2nd Norn), Louise Charlotte Kamps (mez—Siegrune), Jean Madeira (mez—Erda/Rossweisse/1st Norn), Georgine van Milinkovic (mez—Fricka/Grimgerde), Elisabeth Schärtel (mez—Waltraute), Paul Kuën (ten—Mime), Ludwig Suthaus (ten—Loge), Josef Traxel (ten—Froh), Wolfgang Windgassen (ten—Siegmund/Siegfried), Alfons Herwig (bar—Donner), Hermann Uhde (bar—Gunther), Hans Hotter (b-bar—Wotan), Gustav Neidlinger (b-bar—Alberich), Josef Griendl (bass—Fasolt/Hunding/Hagen), Arnold van Mill (bass—Fafner), H. Knappertsbusch (cnd), Bayreuth Festival Orch, Bayreuth Festival Chorus *(rec live, Bayreuth, Aug 13-17, 1956)* — Golden Melodram 14-▲ GM 1.001 [ADD]

Wagner, R.:Tannhäuser (sels)—In fernem Land — Myto 3-▲ MCD 93381

Wagner, R.:Tristan und Isolde (acts 2 & 3), w. E. Schlüter (sop), M. Klose (cta), J. Prohaska (ten), G. Frick (bass), W. Furtwängler (cnd), Berlin State Opera Orch, Berlin State Opera Chorus [G] *(rec live, Berlin, 10/3/47)* — Arkadia 2-▲ 358 [ADD]

Wagner, R.:Die Walküre (sels), w. B. Nilsson (sop), L. Rysanek (sop), H. von Karajan (cnd), La Scala Orch—nine selections from Acts 1 & 2 *(rec live in Milan, 4/21/58)* — Hunt Productions 12-▲ 12 CDKAR 223 (m) [ADD]

Sutherland, Joan (sop)

The Age of Bel Canto, w. London PO, London SO [cnd:Richard Bonynge] — London ("Opera Gala" series) ▲ 421881-2 LA [ADD]

The Age of Bel Canto, w. Marilyn Horne (mez), Richard Conrad (bar), London SO [cnd:Richard Bonynge], London Sym Chorus — London ("The Classic Sound" series) ▲ 448594-2

Arias *(rec 1962-63)* — Melodram 3-▲ CDM 37026 (m) [AAD]

The Art of the Prima Donna — London 2-▲ 425493-2 LM2 [ADD]

Bellini, V.:Ariette da camera (6)—5 arias from Norma, Puritani, Sonnambula — London ("Grand Opera" series) 3-▲ 433706-2 [ADD]

Bellini, V.:Beatrice di Tenda, w. L. Pavarotti (ten), R. Bonynge (cnd), London SO, Ambrosian Opera Chorus — London ("Grand Opera" series) 3-▲ 433706-2 [ADD]

Bellini, V.:Norma, w. F. Cossotto (mez), C. Craig (ten), I. Vinco (bass), R. Bonynge (cnd), Buenos Aires Teatro Colón Orch, Buenos Aires Teatro Colón Chorus *(rec live 7/2/69)* — Ediciones Teatro Colon 3-▲ ETC 101 [AAD]

Bellini, V.:Norma, w. M. Horne (mez), J. Alexander (ten), R. Cross (bass), R. Bonynge (cnd), London SO, London Sym Chorus [I] — London 3-▲ 425488-2 [ADD]

Bellini, V.:Norma, w. M. Caballé (sop), L. Pavarotti (sop), S. Ramey (bass), R. Bonynge (cnd), Welsh National Opera Orch, Welsh National Opera Chorus [I] — London 3-▲ 414476-2 [DDD]

Bellini, V.:Norma, w. M. Callas (sop), E. Stignani (mez), M. Picchi (ten), G. Vaghi (bass), V. Gui (cnd), Royal Opera House Orch, Royal Opera House Chorus Covent Garden [I] *(rec live, Covent Garden 11/52)* — Legato Classics 2-▲ LCD 130-2 (m) [AAD]

Bellini, V.:Norma, w. M. Callas (sop), E. Stignani (mez), M. Picchi (ten), G. Vaghi (bass), V. Gui (cnd), Royal Opera House Orch, Royal Opera House Chorus Covent Garden [I] *(rec live, Covent Garden 11/52)* — Verona 3-▲ 27018/20 (m) [AAD]

Bellini, V.:Norma, w. Maria Callas (sop), Ebe Stignani (cta), Mirto Picchi (ten), Paul Asciak (sgr), V. Gui (cnd), Royal Opera House Orch, Royal Opera House Chorus Covent Garden *(rec live, London, 1952)* — Enterprise ("Documents" series) 3-▲ ENTLV 968 [ADD]

Bellini, V.:Norma, w. M. Callas (sop), E. Stignani (mez), M. Picchi (ten), G. Vaghi (bass), V. Gui (cnd), Royal Opera House Orch, Royal Opera House Chorus Covent Garden [I] *(rec live, Covent Garden 11/52)* — Melodram 2-▲ MEL 26025

Bellini, V.:Norma (sels), w. M. Horne (mez), J. Alexander (ten), R. Cross (bass), R. Bonynge (cnd), London SO, London Sym Chorus [I] — London ("Opera Gala" series) ▲ 421886-2 [ADD]

Sutherland, Joan (sop) (cont.)

Bellini, V.:I Puritani, w. J. Sutherland (sop—Elvira), N. Gedda (ten—Arturo), E. Blanc (bar—Riccardo), J. Diaz (bass—Giorgio), R. Bonynge (cnd), *(orch unknown)* [I] *(rec live, Philadelphia 4/18/63)* — Standing Room Only 2-▲ SRO 838-2 [ADD]

Bellini, V.:I Puritani, w. L. Pavarotti (ten), P. Cappuccilli (bar), N. Ghiaurov (bass), R. Bonynge (cnd), London SO [I] — London 3-▲ 417588-2 [ADD]

Bellini, V.:I Puritani (sels), w. D. Cole (sop), A. Kraus (ten), R. Wolansky (bar), N. Ghiuselev (bass), R. Bonynge (cnd), San Francisco Opera Orch, San Francisco Opera Chorus *(rec live, San Francisco, 9/2/66)* — Golden Age of Opera ▲ GAO 133 [ADD]

Bellini, V.:I Puritani (sels), w. N. Filacuridi (sgr), E. Blanc (bar), G. Modesti (bass), *(orch unknown)* *(rec live, Edinburgh, Sept. 8, 1960)* — Standing Room Only 2-▲ SRO 841-2 [ADD]

Bellini, V.:La sonnambula, w. L. Pavarotti (ten), N. Ghiaurov (bass), R. Bonynge (cnd), National PO London [I] — London 2-▲ 417424-2 [DDD]

Bellini, V.:La sonnambula, w. R. Cioni (ten), E. Flagello (bass), *(cnd & orch unknown)* *(rec live Dec. 5, 1961")* — Standing Room Only 2-▲ SRO 841-2 [ADD]

Bellini, V.:La sonnambula (sels), w. T. Serafin (cnd), Royal Opera House Orch, Royal Opera House Chorus Covent Garden—seven arias & scenes [I] *(rec live, Covent Garden 1960)* — Myto 2-▲ 2 MCD 90529 [ADD]

Bizet, G.:Carmen, w. Regina Resnik (mez), Mario del Monaco (ten), T. Schippers (cnd), Swiss Romande Orch — London ("Double Decca" series) 2-▲ 443871-2

Bizet, G.:Carmen, w. R. Resnik (mez), M. Del Monaco (ten), T. Krause (bar), T. Schippers (cnd), Swiss Romande Orch — London 2-▲ 411630-2 [ADD]

Cilea, F.:Adriana Lecouvreur, w. C. Bergonzi (ten), L. Nucci (bar), R. Bonynge (cnd), Welsh National Opera Orch, Welsh National Opera Chorus — London 2-▲ 425815-2 [DDD]

Coloratura Spectacular — London ▲ 417814-2 LH [ADD]

Delibes, L.:Lakmé, w. A. Vanzo (ten), G. Bacquier (bar), R. Bonynge (cnd), Monte Carlo Opera Orch [F] — London 2-▲ 425485-2 [ADD]

Donizetti, G.:Anna Bolena, w. S. Mentzer (mez), B. Manca di Nissa (cta), J. Hadley (ten), S. Ramey (bass), R. Bonynge (cnd), Welsh National Opera Orch [I] — London 3-▲ 421096-2 [DDD]

Donizetti, G.:L'elisir d'amore, w. L. Pavarotti (ten), D. Cossa (bar), S. Malas (bass), R. Bonynge (cnd), English CO [I] — London 2-▲ 414461-2 [ADD]

Donizetti, G.:Emilia di Liverpool (sels), w. A. Cantelo (sop), W. McAlpine (ten), D. Dowling (bar), H. Alan (bass), J. Pritchard (cnd), Royal Liverpool PO, Liverpool Music Group Singers—13 arias from Act 1, & 4 from Act 2 [I] *(rec live, Liverpool Sept. 1957)* — Myto ▲ 1 MCD 91545 [ADD]

Donizetti, G.:La fille du régiment, w. M. Sinclair (cta), L. Pavarotti (ten), S. Maias (bass), R. Bonynge (cnd), Royal Opera House Orch [F] — London 2-▲ 414520-2 [ADD]

Donizetti, G.:La fille du régiment, w. R. Resnik (mez), A. Kraus (ten), S. Maias (bass), R. Bonynge (cnd), Chicago Lyric Opera Orch, Chicago Lyric Opera Chorus [F] *(rec Nov. 20, 1973)* — Myto 2-▲ MCD 93276

Donizetti, G.:Lucia di Lammermoor, w. J. McDonald (sop), M. Elkins (mez), J. Bowman (alt), J. Gibin (ten), J. Rouleau (bass), Shaw (sgr), T. Serafin (cnd), Royal Opera House Orch, Royal Opera House Chorus Covent Garden—3 duets from Act 1, & 3 soprano solo arias from Act 2 [I] — Myto ▲ 1 MCD 91545 [ADD]

Donizetti, G.:Lucia di Lammermoor, w. R. Cioni (ten), R. Merrill (bar), C. Siepi (bass-bar), J. Pritchard (cnd), St. Cecilia Academy Orch Rome, St. Cecilia Academy Chorus Rome [I] — London 2-▲ 411622-2 [ADD]

Donizetti, G.:Lucia di Lammermoor, w. L. Pavarotti (ten), S. Milnes (bar), N. Ghiaurov (bass), R. Bonynge (cnd), Royal Opera House Orch [I] — London 3-▲ 410193-2 [ADD]

Donizetti, G.:Lucia di Lammermoor (sels), w. L. Pavarotti (ten), S. Milnes (bar), N. Ghiaurov (bass), R. Bonynge (cnd), Royal Opera House Orch, Royal Opera House Chorus Covent Garden [I] — London ("Opera Gala" series) ▲ 421885-2 [ADD]

Donizetti, G.:Lucrezia Borgia, w. J. Sutherland (sop—Lucrezia Borgia), A. Howells (mez—Maffio Orsini), A. Kraus (ten—Gennaro), R. Leggate (ten—Liverotto), J. Summers (bar—Apostolo Gazella), P. Hudson (bass-bar—Gubetta), S. Dean (bass—Don Alfonso), R. Bonynge (cnd), Royal Opera House Orch *(rec London, Apr. 9, 1980)* — Ornamenti 2-▲ FE 111 [ADD]

Donizetti, G.:Lucrezia Borgia, w. M. Horne (mez), G. Aragall (ten), I. Wixell (bar), R. Bonynge (cnd), National PO London [I] — London 2-▲ 421497-2 [ADD]

Donizetti, G.:Maria Stuarda, w. H. Tourangeau (mez), L. Pavarotti (ten), R. Soyer (bar), J. Morris (bass), R. Bonynge (cnd), Bologna Teatro Comunale Orch, Bologna Teatro Comunale Chorus [I] — London 2-▲ 425410-2 [ADD]

An Evening To Remember, w. Australian Pops Orch — DRG ▲ 13103

Gounod, C.:Faust, w. F. Corelli (ten), N. Ghiaurov (bass), R. Bonynge (cnd), London SO, Ambrosian Opera Chorus [F] — London ("Grand Opera" series) 3-▲ 421240-2 [AAD]

Grandi Voci:Joan Sutherland *(rec 1959-1960)* — London ▲ 440404-2 [ADD]

Great Sopranos of Our Time, w. Maria Callas (sop), Renata Scotto (sop), Montserrat Caballé (sop), Elisabeth Schwarzkopf (sop), Victoria de los Angeles (sop), Mirella Freni (sop), Ileana Cotrubas (sop), Edita Gruberova (sop) — Classics for Pleasure ▲ CDEMX 9519 [ADD]

Greatest Hits — London ("Jubilee" series) ▲ 417780-2 LM [ADD]

Handel, G.F.:Alcina, w. N. Proctor (cta), van Dick (sgr), F. Leitner (cnd), Cappella Coloniensis, Cologne Radio Chorus [I] *(rec live, 1959)* — Verona 3-▲ 27011/13 (m) [AAD]

Handel, G.F.:Alcina, w. M. Freni (sop), T. Berganza (mez), R. Bonynge (cnd), London SO — London ("Grand Opera" series) 3-▲ 433723-2 [ADD]

Handel, G.F.:Alcina, w. N. Procter (cta), N. Monti (ten), F. Wunderlich (ten), T. Hemsley (bar), F. Leitner (cnd), Cappella Coloniensis, Cologne Radio Chorus — Melodram 3-▲ CDM 37002

Handel, G.F.:Alcina (sels), w. F. Leitner (cnd), Cappella Coloniensis—(2 arias) Di, cor mio, quanto l'amai; Ah! mio cor! scherrito sei [I] *(rec live May 15, 1959)* — Myto 2-▲ 2 MCD 90529 [ADD]

Handel, G.F.:Alcina (sels), *(orch unknown)* — Memories 2-▲ MEM 4585 [ADD]

Handel, G.F.:Giulio Cesare in Egitto (sels), w. Marilyn Horne (mez), R. Bonynge (cnd), London New SO — London ("Grand Opera" series) 3-▲ 433723-2 [ADD]

Handel, G.F.:Messiah, w. Huguette Tourangeau (mez), Werner Krenn (ten), Tom Krause (bar), R. Bonynge (cnd), English CO, Ambrosian Singers [E] — London ("Serenata" series) 2-▲ 433740-2 [ADD]

Handel, G.F.:Messiah, w. Grace Bumbry (mez), Kenneth McKeller (ten), Joseph Ward (bar), A. Boult (cnd), London PO — London 3-▲ 433003-2 [ADD]

Handel, G.F.:Messiah (sels), w. Grace Bumbry (mez), Kenneth McKellar (ten), Joseph Ward (bar), A. Boult (cnd), London SO, London Sym Chorus—arias & choruses — London ("Weekend Classics" series) ▲ 417879-2 [AAD] ■ 417879-4

Handel, G.F.:Rodelinda, Regina de' Longobardi, w. Joan Sutherland (sop—Rodelinda), Margaretha Elkins (mez—Bertarido's sister), Huguette Tourangeau (mez—Bertarido), Cora Canne-Meijer (alt—Unulfo), Eric Tappy (ten—Grimoaldo), Pieter van der Berg (bass—Garibaldo), R. Bonynge (cnd), Netherlands CO *(rec Amsterdam, June 30, 1973)* — Bella Voce 2-▲ BLV 107.206 [AAD]

Handel, G.F.:Rodelinda, Regina de' Longobardi, w. Janet Baker (mez), Raimund Herincx (bar), C. Farncombe (cnd), Philomusica Orch, Chandos Choir *(rec 1959)* — Memories 2-▲ MEM 4577 [ADD]

Handel, G.F.:Rodelinda, Regina de' Longobardi (sels) — Memories 2-▲ MEM 4585 [ADD]

Haydn, J.:L'Anima del filosofo, or Orfeo ed Euridice, w. Nicolai Gedda (ten), R. Bonynge (cnd), Scottish National Orch, Scottish National Chorus *(rec live)* — Verona 2-▲ VER 28018

Haydn, J.:L'Anima del filosofo, or Orfeo ed Euridice, w. Nicolai Gedda (ten), R. Bonynge (cnd), Scottish National Orch [I] *(rec live Edinburgh International Festival, 1967)* — Myto 2-▲ 2 MCD 90529 [ADD]

Home Sweet Home, w. Richard Bonynge (cnd), New Philharmonia Orch, Ambrosian Light Opera Chorus — London ▲ 425048-2 LC [ADD]

Lehár, F.:Die lustige Witwe (sels), w. R. Resnik (mez), W. Krenn (ten), R. Bonynge (cnd), National PO London, Ambrosian Singers—overture & highlights from Acts 1 & 2 — London ("Opera Gala" series) ▲ 421884-2 [ADD]

Live from Lincoln Center, w. Marilyn Horne (mez), Luciano Pavarotti (ten) — London 2-▲ 417587-2 LH [DDD]

Live Recordings, 1955-1964 — Melodram 2-▲ CDM 26515 (m) [AAD]

Massenet, J.:Le Roi de Lahore, w. L. Lima (ten), S. Milnes (bar), N. Ghiaurov (bass), R. Bonynge (cnd), National PO London, London Voices — London ("Grand Opera" series) 2-▲ 433851-2 [DDD]

Sutherland, Joan (sop) (cont.)
Meyerbeer, G.:Les Huguenots, w. F. Cossotto (mez), G. Simionato (mez), F. Corelli (ten), V. Ganzarolli (bar), N. Ghiaurov (bass), G. Tozzi (bass), G. Gavezzeni (cnd), La Scala Orch, La Scala Chorus [l] *(rec live 5/28/62)* Melodram 3-▲ MEL 37026 (m) [AAD]
Meyerbeer, G.:Les Huguenots, w. M. Arroyo (sop), H. Tourangeau (mez), A. Vrenios (ten), D. Cossa (bar), G. Bacquier (bar), N. Ghiuselev (bass), R. Bonynge (cnd), New Philharmonia Orch, Ambrosian Opera Chorus London ("Grand Opera" series) 4-▲ 430549-2 [AAD]
Mozart, W.A.:Don Giovanni (sels), w. Joan Sutherland (sop—Donna Anna), K. Böhm (cnd), *(orch unknown)* Memories 2-▲ MEM 4585 [ADD]
Mozart, W.A.:Don Giovanni (sels), w. E. Schwarzkopf (sop), G. Sciutti (sop), L. Alva (ten), E. Wächter (bar), C. M. Giulini (cnd), Philharmonia Orch EMI Classics ▲ ZDM 63078
Offenbach, J.:Les Contes d'Hoffmann, w. H. Tourangeau (mez), P. Domingo (ten), H. Cuénod (ten), G. Bacquier (bar), R. Bonynge (cnd), Swiss Romande Orch London 2-▲ 417363-2 [ADD]
Operatic Duets, w. Luciano Pavarotti (ten) London ▲ 400058-2 LH
Operatic Duets, w. Luciano Pavarotti (ten) London ("Opera Gala" series) ▲ 421894-2 LM [ADD]
Operetta Gala, w. Richard Bonynge (cnd), New Philharmonia Orch, Swiss Romande Orch, Ambrosian Light Opera Chorus London ("Opera Gala" series) ▲ 421880-2 LA [ADD]
Puccini, G.:Arias, w. M. Caballé (sop), M. Chiara (sop), M. Freni (sop), B. Nilsson (sop), R. Tebaldi (sop), F. Corelli (ten), L. Pavarotti (ten), S. Milnes (bar) London ▲ 421315-2 [ADD]
Puccini, G.:Turandot, w. M. Caballé (sop), L. Pavarotti (ten), N. Ghiaurov (bass), Z. Mehta (cnd), London PO, John Alldis Choir [l] London 2-▲ 414274-2 [ADD]
Puccini, G.:Turandot (sels), w. M. Caballé (sop), L. Pavarotti (ten), N. Ghiaurov (bass), Z. Mehta (cnd), London PO London ▲ 421320-2 [ADD] ▮ 421320-4
Romantic French Arias, w. Richard Bonynge (cnd), Swiss Romande Orch, Geneva Grand Theater Chorus London ("Opera Gala" series) ▲ 421879-2 LA [ADD]
Romantic Trios, w. Barry Tuckwell (hn), Richard Bonynge (cnd) London ▲ 421552-2 LH [ADD]
Rossini, G.:Semiramide, w. M. Horne (mez), J. Serge (ten), J. Rouleau (bass), S. Malas (bass), R. Bonynge (cnd), London SO, Ambrosian Singers [l] *(rec 1966)* London 3-▲ 425481-2 [ADD]
Rossini, G.:Semiramide, w. M. Horne (mez), Myers (sgr), Grant (sgr), R. Bonynge (cnd), New Philharmonia Orch, Ambrosian Opera Chorus [l] *(rec live at the Theatre Royal, Drury Lane, 2/9/69)* Arkadia 2-▲ 579 (m) [ADD]
Rossini, G.:Semiramide (sels), w. *(orch & cnd unknown)* Memories 2-▲ MEM 4585 [ADD]
Thomas, A.:Hamlet, w. S. Milnes (bar), R. Bonynge (cnd), Welsh National Opera Orch, Welsh National Opera Chorus London ("Grand Opera" series) 3-▲ 433857-2 [DDD]
Verdi, Bellini, & Donizetti Arias London ▲ 421305-2 LA [ADD]
Verdi, G.:Aida, w. Maria Callas (sop—Aida), Joan Sutherland (sop—Priestess), Giulietta Simionato (cta—Amneris), Kurt Baum (ten—Radames), Hector Thomas (ten—Messenger), Jess Walters (bar—Amonasro), Michael Langdon (bass—King), Giulio Neri (bass—Ramfis), J. Barbirolli (cnd), Royal Opera House Orch, Royal Opera House Chorus Covent Garden *(rec Covent Garden, London, June 10, 1953)* Legato Classics 2-▲ LCD 187-2
Verdi, G.:Arias, w. K. Battle (sop), J. Anderson (sop), M. Price (sop), L. Pavarotti (ten), L. Nucci (bar)—includes favorite arias from Aida, Ballo in maschera, Don Carlos, Nabucco, Rigoletto, Traviata, Trovatore London ("Ovation" series) ▲ 430748-2 [DDD]
Verdi, G.:I masnadieri, w. F. Bonisolli (ten), M. Manuguerra (bar), S. Ramey (bass), R. Bonynge (cnd), Welsh National Opera Orch, Welsh National Opera Chorus London ("Grand Opera" series) 2-▲ 433854-2 [DDD]
Verdi, G.:Requiem Mass, w. M. Horne (mez), L. Pavarotti (ten), M. Talvela (bass), G. Solti (cnd), Vienna PO, Vienna State Opera Chorus [L] London 2-▲ 411944-2 [ADD]
Verdi, G.:Rigoletto, w. H. Tourangeau (mez), L. Pavarotti (ten), S. Milnes (bar), M. Talvela (bass), R. Bonynge (cnd), London SO, London Sym Chorus [l] London 2-▲ 414269-2 [ADD]
Verdi, G.:Rigoletto, w. Joan Sutherland (sop—Gilda), Renato Cioni (ten—Duke), Cornell MacNeil (bar—Rigoletto), N. Sanzogno (cnd), St. Cecilia Academy Orch Rome, St. Cecilia Academy Chorus Rome London ("Double Decca" series) 2-▲ 443853-2
Verdi, G.:La traviata, w. L. Pavarotti (ten), M. Manuguerra (bar), R. Bonynge (cnd), National PO London, London Opera Chorus [l] London ▲ 400057-2 [DDD] ▮ 400057-4
Verdi, G.:La traviata, w. L. Pavarotti (ten), M. Manuguerra (bar), R. Bonynge (cnd), National PO London, London Opera Chorus [l] London 2-▲ 430491-2 [DDD]
Verdi, G.:La traviata, w. C. Bergonzi (ten), R. Merrill (bar), J. Pritchard (cnd), Florence Maggio Musicale Orch, Florence Maggio Musicale Chorus [l] London 2-▲ 411877-2 [ADD]
Verdi, G.:La traviata (sels), w. C. Bergonzi (ten), R. Merrill (bar), J. Pritchard (cnd), Florence Maggio Musicale Orch London ▲ 421325-2 [ADD]
Verdi, G.:La traviata (sels), w. Loretta di Franco (sop), Frederica von Stade (mez), Leo Goeke (ten), Lou Marcella (ten), Luciano Pavarotti (ten), Gene Boucher (bar), Raymond Gibbs (bar), Sherrill Milnes (bar), Louis Sgarro (bar), John Trehy (bar) Budget ("The Greatest Voice in Opera" series) ▲ SYP 112
Verdi, G.:Il trovatore, w. M. Horne (mez), L. Pavarotti (ten), I. Wixell (bar), N. Ghiaurov (bass), R. Bonynge (cnd), National PO London [l] London 2-▲ 417137-2 [ADD]
Verdi, G.:Il trovatore (sels), w. M. Horne (mez), L. Pavarotti (ten), R. Bonynge (cnd), National PO London London ▲ 421310-2 [ADD]

Sutliff (sgr)
Donizetti, G.:Don Pasquale, w. Ileana Cotrubas (sop), Alfredo Kraus (ten), Wladimiro Ganzarolli (bar), Vincente Sardinero (bar), B. Bartoletti (cnd), Chicago Lyric Opera Orch, Chicago Lyric Opera Chorus *(rec live, Chicago, Nov. 2, 1974)* Arkadia 2-▲ 490

Sutter, Barbara (sop)
Kraft, Walter:Christus, w. Anna Senn-Dähler (sop), Barbara Künzler (sop), Christine Guy (alt), Heidi Uhlmann (alt), Daniel Zellweger (alt), Matthias Senn (ten), Mikoto Usami (ten), Wolfgang Pailer (bass), Heinz Suter (bass), Klaus Knall (cnd), Evangelische Singgemeinde Choirs *(rec Ostdorf bei Balingen, Oct. 8–11, 1986)* Cantate 2-▲ 58004 [DDD]

Sutton, Vern (nar)
Argento, D.:A Waterbird Talk, w. R.A. Clark (cnd), Manhattan CO Newport Classic ▲ NPD 85602 [DDD]

Sutton, Vern (ten)
Argento, D.:Letters from Composers, w. Van (gtr) [E] CRI ▮ C 291
Argento, D.:Postcard from Morocco, w. S. Roche, B. Brandt, J. Hardy, Y. Marshall, V. Sutton, B. Busse, M. Foreman, P. Brunelle (cnd), Minnesota Opera Orch CRI 2-▲ CD 614 [ADD]

Suzuki, Atsuko (sgr)
Wagner, R.:Lohengrin, w. Sharon Sweet (sop—Elsa), Eva Marton (sop—Ortrud), Ben Heppner (ten—Lohengrin), Anton Rosner (ten—Nobleman), Heinrich Weber (ten—Nobleman), Jan-Hendrik Rootering (bar—Heinrich der Vögler), Sergei Leiferkus (bar—Friedrich von Telramund), Bryn Terfel (b-bar—King's Herald), Barbara Fleckenstein (sgr—Page), Atsuko Suzuki (sgr—Page), Gisela Ulmann (sgr—Page), Marion Rambausek (sgr—Page), Dankwart Siegele (sgr—Nobleman), Jürgen Weiss (sgr—Nobleman), C. Davis (cnd), Bavarian SO, Bavarian State Opera Chorus, Bavarian Radio Chorus *(rec Residenz Herkulesaal, Munich, May 14–28, 1994)* RCA Red Seal 3-▲ 09026-62646-2 [DDD]
Wagner, R.:Lohengrin (sels), w. Eva Marton (sop—Ortrud), Sharon Sweet (sop—Elsa von Brabant), Barbara Fleckenstein (sgr—Page), Marion Rambausek (sgr—Page), Atsuko Suzuki (sgr—Page), Gisela Ulmann (sgr—Page), Ben Heppner (ten—Lohengrin), Anton Rosner (ten—Nobleman), Heinrich Weber (ten—Nobleman), Sergei Leiferkus (bar—Friedrich von Telramund), Bryn Terfel (b-bar—King's Herald), Jan-Hendrik Rootering (bass—Henry the Fowler), Dankwart Siegele (sgr—Nobleman), Jürgen Weiss (sgr—Nobleman), C. Davis (cnd), Bavarian RSO, Michael Gläser (cnd), Udo Mehrpohl (cnd), Bavarian Radio Chorus, Bavarian State Opera Chorus—Seht! Seht! [from Act 1, Scene 2]; Nun sei bedankt, mein lieber Schwan!; Wenn ich im Kampfe für dich siege; Welch holde Wunder muss ich sehen?; Nun hört mich und achtet wohl; Durch Gottes Sieg ist jetzt dein Leben mein [all from Act 1, Scene 3]; Treulich geführt ziehet dahin [from Act 3, Scene 1]; Wie hehr erkenn' ich unsrer Liebe Wesen!; Höchstes Vertrau'n hast du mir schon zu danken; Weh' nun ist all' unser Glück dahin! [all from Act 3, Scene 2]; In fernem Land, unnahbar euren Schritten [from Act 3, Scene 3] *(rec Munich, Mar 14–28, 1994)* RCA Red Seal ▲ 09026-68239-2 [DDD]

Suzuki, Pat (sgr)
Rodgers, R.:Flower Drum Song, w. M. Umeki (sgr), J. Hall (sgr) [1958 cast] Columbia ▲ CK 02009 ▮ JST 02009

Svab, Alessandro (bar)
Rossini, G.:La pietra del paragone, w. M. C. Nocentini (sop), A. Trovarelli (mez), H. M. Molinari (cta), P. Barbacini (ten), V. Di Matteo (bar), R. Scaltriti (bar), P. Rumetz (bass), C. Desderi (cnd), Camerata Musicale Orch, Modeno Teatro Comunale Chorus [l] *(rec 1992)* Nuova Era 2-▲ 7132/33 [DDD]

Svanholm, Set (ten)
Gluck, C.W.:Iphigénie en Aulide (sels), w. Helena Braun (sop—Klytämnestra), Hilde Konetzni (sop—Iphigenie), Set Svanholm (ten—Achilles), Paul Schöffler (b-bar—Agamemnon), L. Ludwig (cnd), Vienna State Opera Orch *(rec Vienna, Oct. 29, 1942)* Koch Schwann ▲ SCH 314692 [ADD]
Orff, C.:Carmina burana, w. E. Söderström (sop), G. Bäckelin (ten), H. Schmidt-Isserstedt (cnd), Stockholm PO, Stockholm Phil Chorus *(rec live, 11/26/54)* BIS 8-▲ CD 421/24 (m/s) [AAD]
Rossini, G.:Il barbiere di Siviglia (sels), w. Birgit Nilsson (sop), Sigurd Björling (bar), Ehrling, Grevillius, Larsson, Mann, Sandberg (cnd), Royal Stockholm PO, Swedish RSO—Largo al factotum Bluebell ▲ BLU 058 [ADD]
Söderman, A.:King Heimer & Aslog, *(orch unknown)* Bluebell ▲ BLU 058 [ADD]
Strauss, R.:Ariadne auf Naxos (sels), w. Birgit Nilsson (sop), Sigurd Björling (bar), *(orch unknown)*—Circe, Circe kannst du mich hören? Bluebell ▲ BLU 058 [ADD]
Strauss, R.:Ariadne auf Naxos (sels), w. Adele Kern (sop—Zerbinetta), Anny Konetzni (sop—Ariadne), Set Svanholm (ten—Bacchus), Else Schulz (sgr—Composer), R. Moralt (cnd), Vienna State Opera Orch *(rec Vienna, Oct. 16, 1941)* Koch Schwann 2-▲ SCH 314625 [ADD]
Strauss, R.:Die Frau ohne Schatten (sels), w. E. Steber (sop), C. Goltz (sop), I. Steingruber (sop), O. Wiener (bass), K. Böhm (cnd), *(orch unknown)*—selections from Act Two (Sieh, Amme, sieh...Würde ich lieber selber zu Stein!) & Act Three (Vater, bist du's?...) *(rec live, Munich, 6/4/53)* VAI Audio ▲ VAIA 1012 (m/s) [ADD]
Verdi, G.:Otello (sels), w. Birgit Nilsson (sop), Sigurd Björling (bar), Ehrling, Grevillius, Larsson, Mann, Sandberg (cnd), Royal Stockholm PO, Swedish RSO—Desdemona real...Ora e per sempre adio...Si, pel ciel marmoreo giuro! Bluebell ▲ BLU 058 [ADD]
Wagner, R.:Arias & Scenes, w. Birgit Nilsson (sop), Sigurd Björling (bar), Ehrling, Grevillius, Larsson, Mann, Sandberg (cnd), Royal Stockholm PO, Swedish RSO—Morgenlich leuchtend [from Die Meistersinger von Nürnberg]; Ein Schwert verhiess mir der Vater [from Die Walküre]; Mime hiess ein mürrischer Zwerg...Brünnhilde, heilige Braut [from Götterdämmerung] Bluebell ▲ BLU 058 [ADD]
Wagner, R.:Arias & Scenes, w. F. Weissmann (cnd), *(orch unknown)*—selections from Lohengrin, Tannhäuser, Meistersinger, Walküre, Siegfried (w. Eileen Farrell (sop)) [G] *(rec 1947–50)* Myto ▲ 1 MCD 93174
Wagner, R.:Der fliegende Holländer (sels), w. Maria Nemeth (sop—Senta), Set Svanholm (ten—Erik), Joel Berglund (bar—Holländer), L. Reichwein (cnd), Vienna State Opera Orch *(rec Vienna, Sept. 28, 1942)* Koch Schwann ▲ SCH 314692 [ADD]
Wagner, R.:Götterdämmerung, w. M. Fuchs (sop), H. Scheppan (sop), R. Burg (bar), F. Dalberg (bass), K. Elmendorff (cnd), Bayreuth Festival Orch, Bayreuth Festival Chorus *(rec July 21, 1942)* Preiser 4-▲ PRE 90164 [AAD]
Wagner, R.:Götterdämmerung (sels), w. Set Svanholm (ten—Siegfried), Paul Schöffler (b-bar—Gunther), Herbert Alsen (bass—Hagen), H. Knappertsbusch (cnd), Vienna State Opera Orch *(rec Vienna, June 27, 1941)* Koch Schwann ▲ SCH 314692 [ADD]
Wagner, R.:Die Meistersinger von Nürnberg (sels), w. Maria Reining (sop—Eva), Set Svanholm (ten—Walther), Paul Schöffler (b-bar—Hans Sachs), K. Böhm (cnd), Vienna State Opera Orch *(rec Vienna, Jan. 31, 1943)* Koch Schwann ▲ SCH 314692 [ADD]
Wagner, R.:Das Rheingold, w. K. Flagstad (sop), J. Madeira (mez), G. London (bar), G. Neidlinger (b-bar), K. Böhme (bass), G. Solti (cnd), Vienna PO [G] London 3-▲ 414101-2 [ADD]
Wagner, R.:Rienzi, der Letzte der Tribunen, w. C. Ludwig (mez), P. Schoeffler (b-bar), J. Krips (cnd), *(orch unknown)* [G] *(rec live, Vienna, 1960)* Melodram 2-▲ MEL 27023
Wagner, R.:Der Ring des Nibelungen, w. K. Flagstad (sop), H. Konetzni (sop), E. Höngen (cta), G. Treptow (ten), M. Lorenz (ten), F. Frantz (b-bar), L. Weber (bass), B. Herrmann (bass), W. Furtwängler (cnd), La Scala Orch, La Scala Chorus *(rec live 1950)* Arkadia 12-▲ 351 [ADD]
Wagner, R.:Der Ring des Nibelungen, w. Kirsten Flagstad (sop), Hilde Konetzni (sop), Elisabeth Höngen (cta), Max Lorenz (ten), Günther Treptow (ten), Josef Hermann (bar), Ludwig Weber (bass), Ferdinand Franz (sgr), W. Furtwängler (cnd), La Scala Orch, La Scala Chorus *(rec Milan, 1950)* Music & Arts 12-▲ CD 914
Wagner, R.:Der Ring des Nibelungen, w. B. Nilsson (sop), K. Flagstad (sop), R. Crespin (sop), C. Watson (sop), C. Ludwig (mez), J. Madeira (mez), J. King (ten), G. Stolze (ten), W. Windgassen (ten), G. London (bar), D. Fischer-Dieskau (bar), H. Hotter (b-bar), G. Neidlinger (b-bar), G. Frick (bass), G. Solti (cnd), Vienna PO [G] London 15-▲ 414100-2 [ADD]
Wagner, R.:Der Ring des Nibelungen (sels), w. Adele Kern (sop), Anny Konetzni (sop), Hilde Konetzni (sop), Elisabeth Schumann (sop), Enid Szantho (cta), Josef Kalenberg (ten), Max Lorenz (ten), Erich Zimmermann (ten), Hans Hotter (bar), Jaro Prohaska (bar), Emil Schipper (bar), Paul Schöffler (b-bar), Ludwig Hoffmann (bass), H. Knappertsbusch (cnd), Vienna State Opera Orch *(rec Vienna, 1937–1943)* Koch Schwann 2-▲ SCH 314742 [ADD]
Wagner, R.:Tannhäuser (sels), w. Set Svanholm (ten—Tannhäuser), Alfred Poell (bar—Wolfram), L. Reichwein (cnd), Vienna State Opera Orch *(rec Vienna, Oct. 11, 1942)* Koch Schwann ▲ SCH 314692 [ADD]
Wagner, R.:Tristan und Isolde (sels), w. K. Flagstad (sop), V. Ursuleac (sop), H. Hotter (b-bar), E. Kleiber (cnd), Buenos Aires Teatro Colón Orch, Buenos Aires Teatro Colón Chorus—highlights from Acts 1–3 [G] *(rec live, 1948)* Melodram 2-▲ MEL 25007 (m) [AAD]
Wagner, R.:Die Walküre (sels), w. Hilde Konetzni (sop—Sieglinde), Max Lorenz (ten—Siegmund), Julius Pölzer (ten—Siegmund), Set Svanholm (ten—Siegmund), Knappertsbusch, Martin (cnd), Vienna State Opera Orch Koch Schwann ▲ SCH 314692 [ADD]
Wagner, R.:Die Walküre (act 1/scene 3), w. Rose Bampton (sop), A. Toscanini (cnd), NBC SO, NBC Sym Chorus [G] *(rec rehearsals & performance, New York, 4/4–6/47)* Myto 2-▲ 2 MCD 90316 (m) [ADD]
Weber, C.M. von:Der Freischütz (sels), w. Birgit Nilsson (sop), Sigurd Björling (bar), Ehrling, Grevillius, Larsson, Mann, Sandberg (cnd), Royal Stockholm PO, Swedish RSO—Durch die Wälder, durch die Auen Bluebell ▲ BLU 058 [ADD]
Weber, C.M. von:Der Freischütz (sels), w. Set Svanholm (bar—Max), Franz Norman (bass—Kuno), Marjan Rus (bass—Kaspar), H. Knappertsbusch (cnd), Vienna State Opera Orch *(rec Vienna, June 18, 1941)* Koch Schwann ▲ SCH 314692 [ADD]

Sved, Alexander (bar)
Il Mito Dell'Opera Bongiovanni ▲ GB 1081
Verdi, G.:Aida (sels), w. Paula Takács (sop), F. Molinari-Pradelli (cnd), Hungarian State Opera Orch—Ciel! Mio padre *(rec Mar 24, 1956)* Hungaroton ("Great Hungarian Voices" series) ▲ HCD 31614 [ADD]
Verdi, G.:Un ballo in maschera, w. Stella Andreva (sop—Oscar), Zinka Milanov (sop—Amelia), Bruna Castagna (cta—Ulrica), Jussi Björling (ten—Riccardo), Lodovico Oliviero (ten—Un Servo D'Amelia), John Cartet (bar—Un Giudice), Alexander Sved (bar—Renato), Normann Cordon (bass—Samuel), Arthur Kent (bass—Silvano), Nicola Moscona (bass—Tom), E. Panizza (cnd), *(orch unknown)* *(rec live, New York, Dec. 14, 1940)* The Fourties 2-▲ ENT FT 1515
Verdi, G.:Un ballo in maschera (sels), w. V. Komor (cnd), Hungarian State Opera Orch—Alla vita che t'arride; Alzati!...ERi tu, che macchiavi *(rec June 7, 1954)* Hungaroton ("Great Hungarian Voices" series) ▲ HCD 31614 [ADD]
Verdi, G.:Falstaff (sels), w. F. Molinari-Pradelli (cnd), Hungarian State Opera Orch—L'onore! Ládri *(rec Apr 29, 1955)* Hungaroton ("Great Hungarian Voices" series) ▲ HCD 31614 [ADD]
Verdi, G.:La forza del destino (sels), w. Róbert Ilosfalvy (ten), Rubányi, Molinari-Pradelli (cnd), Hungarian State Opera Orch—Solenne in quest'ora; Urna fatale *(rec 1955)* Hungaroton ("Great Hungarian Voices" series) ▲ HCD 31614 [ADD]
Verdi, G.:Macbeth (sels), w. V. Vaszy (cnd), Hungarian State Opera Orch—Perfidi! All'anglo...Pietà, rispetto, amore *(rec Oct 21, 1954)* Hungaroton ("Great Hungarian Voices" series) ▲ HCD 31614 [ADD]

▲ = CD ♦ = Enhanced CD Δ = MD ▮ = Cassette Tape □ = DCC

Sved, Alexander (bar) (cont.)
Verdi, G.:Rigoletto (sels), w. Mária Gyurkovics (sop), Olga Szönyi (mez), Ernö Kenéz (ten), János Fodor (bar), József Bódy (bass), Kórodi, Molinari-Pradelli (cnd), Hungarian State Opera Orch—Pari siamo!; Figlia! Mio padre! A te dappresso; Cortigiani! Vil' razza dannata; Tutte le feste al tempio...Ah! solo per me!; Chi è mai... *(rec 1955-56)* Hungaroton ("Great Hungarian Voices" series) ▲ HCD 31614 [ADD]

Svedenbrandt, Georg (bass)
Mascagni, P.:Cavalleria rusticana, w. A. Nordmo-Lövberg (sop), A. Bjoerling (sop), M. Sehlmark (cta), J. Bjoerling (ten), K. Bendix (cnd), Stockholm Royal Opera House Orch, Stockholm Royal Opera Chorus [I, Sw] *(rec live, Stockholm, 12/8/54)* Legato Classics ▲ LCD 164-1 [ADD]

Svehla, Zdenek (ten)
Janácek, L.:Kát'a Kabanová, w. E. Söderström (sop), N. Kniplová (mez), P. Dvorský (ten), V. Krejčík (ten), D. Jedlička (bass), C. Mackerras (cnd), Vienna PO London 2-▲ 421852-2 [ADD]
Janácek, L.:The Makropulos Affair, w. E. Söderström (sop), V. Krejčík (ten), V. Zítek (ten), D. Jedlička (bass), C. Mackerras (cnd), Vienna PO, Vienna Opera Chorus London 2-▲ 430372-2 [ADD]
Roussel, A.:Evocations, w. Marie Mrázová (cta), Jindřich Jindrák (bar), Z. Košler (cnd), Czech PO, Czech Phil Chorus Supraphon ▲ SUP 111823 [AAD]

Švejda, Miroslav (ten)
Kozeluch, Joh. A.:Missa Pastoralis, w. S. Losová (sop), Y. Škvárová (cta), M. Podskalský (bass), B. Kulínský (cnd), Prague PO, Prague Radio Chorus Multisonic ▲ 31 0003-2 [ADD]
Smetana, B.:Choral Music, w. Vratislav Jahna (bar), Jaroslav Horáček (bass), Z. Košler (cnd), Prague SO, Prague Radio Chorus, Czech Phil Chorus Supraphon ▲ SUP CD 3040

Svendén, Brigitta (mez)
Elgar, E.:Songs, w. J. Carewe (cnd), Nice PO [E] *(rec 7 & 11/90)* Forlane ▲ FOR 16642 [DDD]
Mahler, G.:Kindertotenlieder, w. J. Carewe (cnd), Nice PO [G] *(rec 7 & 11/90; no texts)* Forlane ▲ FOR 16642 [DDD]
Rangström, T.:Songs, w. H. Hagegård (bar), T. Schuback (pno) Musica Sveciae ▲ MSV 629 [DDD]
Wagner, R.:Götterdämmerung, w. A. Evans (sop—Brünnhilde), E.-M. Bundschuh (sop—Gutrune), H. Leidland (sop—Woglinde), A. Küttenbaum (sop—Wellgunde), W. Meier (mez—Waltraute), B. Svendén (mez—1st Norn), J. Turner (mez), *(cnd & orch unknown)* Teldec 4-▲ 4509-94194-2 [DDD]
Wagner, R.:Das Rheingold, w. C. Ludwig (mez), S. Jerusalem (ten), H. Zednik (ten), E. Wlaschiha (bar), J. Morris (bass), J. Levine (cnd), Metropolitan Opera Orch [G] Deutsche Grammophon 3-▲ 427607-2 [DDD]
Wagner, R.:Siegfried, w. H. Behrens (sop), R. Goldberg (ten), J. Morris (bass), J. Levine (cnd), Metropolitan Opera Orch, New York Metropolitan Opera Chorus [G] Deutsche Grammophon 4-▲ 429407-2 [DDD]
Wagner, R.:Siegfried, w. A. Evans (sop—Brünhilde), H. Leidland (sop—Waldvogel), B. Svendén (mez—Erda), S. Jerusalem (ten—Siegfried), G. Clark (ten—Mime), J. Tomlinson (bass—Der Wanderer), G. von Kannen (bass—Alberich), P. Kang (bass), *(cnd & orch unknown)* Teldec 4-▲ 4509-94193-2 [DDD]
Zemlinsky, A. von:Songs to Poems by Maurice Maeterlinck, w. J. Carewe (cnd), Nice PO [G] Forlane ▲ FOR 16642 [DDD]

Svensson, Peter (ten)
Janácek, L.:Slavonic Mass, w. T. Kiberg (sop), R. Stene (cta), U. Cold (bass), C. Mackerras (cnd), Danish National RSO, Danish National Radio Choir, Copenhagen Boys' Choir Chandos ▲ CHAN 9310 [DDD]
Kodály, Z.:Psalmus hungaricus, w. C. Mackerras (cnd), Danish National RSO, Danish National Radio Choir, Copenhagen Boys' Choir Chandos ▲ CHAN 9310 [DDD]
Tobias, R.:Des Jonah Sendung, w. Pille Lill (sop), Urve Tauts (mez), Raimo Laukka (bar), Mati Palm (bass), Ines Maidre (org), N. Järvi (cnd), Estonian State SO, Oratorio Choir, Estonian Phil Chamber Choir, Tallinn Boys' Choir *(rec Estonia Concert Hall, Tallinn, Estonia, June 23-29, 1995)* BIS 2-▲ CD 731/732 [DDD]

Sverdlik, Daniel (sgr)
Monk, M.:Key, w. Meredith Monk (sgr/elec org/jews hp), Dick Higgins (sgr), Collin Walcott (sgr/mrdingam), Mark Berger (nar), Lanny Harrison (nar) *(rec live, Gary Weis' loft, Santa Monica, CA, Ace Gallery, Los Angeles, CA, The House, New York City, The Farm, Los Angeles, CA, July 1970-Jan 1971)* Lovely Music ▲ LCD 1051 [ADD]

Svetlev, Mikhail (ten)
Mussorgsky, M.:Boris Godunov, w. S. Mineva (mez—Marina), M. Svetlev (ten—Gregory), N. Ghiaurov (bass—Boris), N. Ghiuselev (bass—Pimen), E. Tchakarov (cnd), Sofia Festival Orch, Sofia National Opera Chorus [R] Sony Classical ("Russian Opera" series) 3-▲ S3K 45763

Švorc, Antonín (bar)
Schoenberg, A.:Die glückliche Hand, w. Z. Košler (cnd), Czech PO *(rec 1981)* Praga ▲ PR 250082

Švorc, Antonín (bass)
Still, W.G.:Tristan und Isolde, w. C. Ligendza (sop), S. Anderson (cta), C. Heater (ten), M. Smith (bass), L. Toffolo (cnd), Trieste Teatro Comunale Giuseppe Verdi Orch, Trieste Teatro Comunale G. Verdi Chorus [G] *(rec live, Trieste, 12/13/69)* Molodram 3-▲ MEL 37072 (m) [AAD]

Swanson, Catherine (sop)
Mendelssohn, F.:Die Hochzeit des Camacho, w. R. Schudel (sop—Quiteria), C. Swanson (sop—Lucinda), C. Bieber (ten—Basilio), W. Mok (ten—Vivaldo), V. Horn (ten—Camacho), R. Lukas (bar—Carrasco), J. Becker (bass—Sancho Panza), W. Murray (bass—Don Quixote), B. Klee (cnd), Berlin RSO, Berlin Radio Chorus [G] Koch Schwann 2-▲ 314042 [DDD]

Swarthout, Gladys (mez)
Chausson, E.:Poème de l'amour et de la mer, w. P. Monteux (cnd), San Francisco SO RCA Gold Seal ("Pierre Monteux Edition" series) ▲ 09026-61899-2
Opera Stars Sing on Radio, Vol. 1:Unpublished Broadcasts from the Fourties, w. Dusolina Giannini (sop), Helen Traubel (sop), Richard Crooks (ten), Lauritz Melchior (ten), Robert Merrill (bar), Lawrence Tibbett (bar), Ezio Pinza (bass) Enterprise ("The Radio Years" series) ▲ ENTRY 11

Swartz, Göran (bass)
Nilsson, T.:Out of Earthly Night, w. Gudrun Bruna (sop), Marianne Mellnäs (sop), Kaysa Hälldin (alt), Lars Sjögren (ten), Sture Hedin (sgr), Ola Kyhlberg (sgr), Lars Ljungman (sgr), Nils Philipson (sgr), Ulrik Quale (sgr), Nils Spangenberg (sgr), Britta Therén (sgr), Karl-Erik Welin (org), Torsten Nilsson (cnd), Oscar's Motet Choir *(rec Oscar's Church, Stockholm, Sweden, Apr 26-27, 1978)* BIS ▲ CD 138 [AAD]

Sweeney, Donald (bass)
Finzi, G.:In terra pax, w. Libby Crabtree (sop), D. Hill (cnd), Bournemouth SO, Winchester Cathedral Choir, Waynflete Singers *(rec Winchester Cathedral, Jan 10-13, 1994)* London ▲ 444130-2 [DDD]
Vaughan Williams, R.:Fant on Christmas Carols, w. David Dunnett (org), D. Hill (cnd), Bournemouth SO, Winchester Cathedral Choir, Waynflete Singers *(rec Winchester Cathedral, Jan 10-13, 1994)* London ▲ 444130-2 [DDD]

Sweet, Sharon (sop)
Mozart, W.A.:Don Giovanni, w. K. Mattila (sop), M. McLaughlin (sop), F. Araiza (ten), T. Allen (bar), S. Alaimo (b-bar), R. Lloyd (bass), N. Marriner (cnd), Academy of St. Martin in the Fields, Ambrosian Opera Chorus Philips 3-▲ 432129-2 [DDD]
Verdi, G.:Falstaff, w. M. Horne (mez), F. Lopardo (ten), R. Panerai (bar), A. Titus (bar), C. Davis (cnd), Bavarian RSO, Bavarian Radio Chorus RCA Red Seal 2-▲ 09026-60705-2 [DDD]
Verdi, G.:Pezzi sacri, w. C. M. Giulini (cnd), Berlin PO, Ernst Senff Chorus Sony Classical ▲ SK 46491
Wagner, R.:Lohengrin, w. Sharon Sweet (sop—Elsa), Eva Marton (sop—Ortrud), Ben Heppner (ten—Lohengrin), Anton Rosner (ten—Nobleman), Heinrich Weber (ten—Nobleman), Jan-Hendrik Rootering (bar—Heinrich der Vögler), Sergei Leiferkus (bar—Friedrich von Telramund), Bryn Terfel (b-bar—King's Herald), Barbara Fleckenstein (sgr—Page), Atsuko Suzuki (sgr—Page), Gisela Ulmann (sgr—Page), Marion Rambausek (sgr—Page), Dankwart Siegele (sgr—Nobleman), Jürgen Weiss (sgr—Nobleman), C. Davis (cnd), Bavarian SO, Bavarian State Opera Chorus, Bavarian Radio Chorus *(rec Residenz Herkulesaal, Munich, May 14-28, 1994)* RCA Red Seal 3-▲ 09026-62646-2 [DDD]

Sweet, Sharon (sop) (cont.)
Wagner, R.:Lohengrin (sels), w. Eva Marton (sop—Ortrud), Sharon Sweet (sop—Elsa von Brabant), Barbara Fleckenstein (sgr—Page), Marion Rambausek (sgr—Page), Atsuko Suzuki (sgr—Page), Gisela Ulmann (sgr—Page), Ben Heppner (ten—Lohengrin), Anton Rosner (ten—Nobleman), Heinrich Weber (ten—Nobleman), Sergei Leiferkus (bar—Friedrich von Telramund), Bryn Terfel (b-bar—King's Herald), Jan-Hendrik Rootering (bass—Henry the Fowler), Dankwart Siegele (sgr—Nobleman), Jürgen Weiss (sgr—Nobleman), C. Davis (cnd), Bavarian RSO, Michael Gläser (cnd), Udo Mehrpohl (cnd), Bavarian Radio Chorus, Bavarian State Opera Chorus—Seht! Seht! [from Act 1, Scene 2]; Nun sei bedankt, mein lieber Schwan!; Wenn ich im Kampfe für dich siege; Welch holde Wunder muss ich sehen?; Nun höret mich und achtet wohl; Durch Gottes Sieg ist jetzt dein Leben mein [all from Act 1, Scene 3]; Treulich geführt ziehet dahin [from Act 3, Scene 1]; Wie hehr erkenn' ich unsrer Liebe Wesen!; Höchstes Vertrau'n hast du mir schon zu danken; Weh' nun ist all' unser Glück dahin! [all from Act 3, Scene 2]; In fernem Land, unnahbar euren Schritten [from Act 3, Scene 3] *(rec Munich, Mar 14-28, 1994)* RCA Red Seal ▲ 09026-68239-2 [DDD]
Weber, C.M. von:Der Freischütz, w. R. Ziesack (sop), A. Schmidt (bar), M. Hölle (bass), M. Janowski (cnd), German SO, Berlin Radio Chorus RCA Red Seal 2-▲ 09026-62538-2

Swensen, Robert (ten)
Adam, A.:Le Postillon de Lunjumeau, w. P. Coburn (sop), J. Linn (bar), P. Lika (bass), K. Arp (cnd), Kaiserslautern Radio Orch, Stuttgart Chamber Choir [G] Capriccio 2-▲ 60040-2 [DDD]
Gazzaniga, G.:Don Giovanni, w. P. Coburn (sop), J. Kaufmann (sop), J. Aler (ten), J.-L. Chaignaud (bar), G. von Kannen (bass), A. Scharinger (bass), S. Soltesz (cnd), Munich RSO, Munich Radio Chorus [I] Orfeo 2-▲ 214902 [DDD]

Swenson, Kari (sop)
Walth, G.:Spring Songs, w. Julie Schwarz (pno)—Spring Meyer ▲ MC 0108

Swenson, Lois (sop)
Meisner, D.:He Who Dwells, w. Deirdre Fay (ob), Julie Schwartz (pno) Meyer ▲ MC 0108

Swenson, Ruth Ann (sop)
Bellini, V.:I Puritani (sels), w. N. Rescigno (cnd), London PO—O rendetemi la speme *(rec Nov. 11-19, 1993)* EMI Classics ▲ CDC 54827 [DDD]
Bellini, V.:La sonnambula (sels), w. N. Rescigno (cnd), London PO—A te dilette...Come per me sereno *(rec Nov. 11-19, 1993)* EMI Classics ▲ CDC 54827 [DDD]
I Carry Your Heart, w. Warren Jones (pno), Charles Neidich (cl) EMI Classics ▲ CDC 56158
Divas in Song:Marylin Horne, a 60th Birthday Celebration, w. Montserrat Caballé (sop), H. Donath (sop), F. von Stade (mez), R. Fleming (mez), S. Ramey (bass), J. Levine (cnd), M. Katz (pno), W. Jones (pno), K. Donath (pno), Manuel Burgueras (pno) RCA Red Seal ▲ 09026-62547-2
Donizetti, G.:Linda di Chamounix (sels), w. N. Rescigno (cnd), London PO—Ah! tardai tropp...O luce di quest'anima *(rec Nov. 11-19, 1993)* EMI Classics ▲ CDC 54827 [DDD]
Donizetti, G.:Lucia di Lammermoor (sels), w. N. Rescigno (cnd), London PO—Regnava nel silenzio...Quando, rapito in estasi *(rec Nov. 11-19, 1993)* EMI Classics ▲ CDC 54827 [DDD]
Gounod, C.:Roméo et Juliette, w. Susan Graham (sop—Stephano), Ruth Ann Swenson (sop—Juliette), Sarah Walker (mez—Gertrude), Paul Charles Clarke (ten—Tybalt), Placido Domingo (ten—Roméo), Kurt Ollmann (bar—Mercutio), Alastair Miles (bass—Frère Laurent), David Pittman-Jennings (bass—Le Duc), Alain Vernhes (bass—Capulet), L. Slatkin (cnd), Munich RSO, Munich Radio Chorus *(rec Studio 1, Bavarian Radio, Munich, Nov 29 - Dec 10, 1995)* RCA Red Seal 2-▲ 09026-68440-2 [DDD]
Gounod, C.:Roméo et Juliette (sels), w. N. Rescigno (cnd), London PO—Ah! Je veux vivre *(rec Nov. 11-19, 1993)* EMI Classics ▲ CDC 54827 [DDD]
James Levine's 25th Anniversary Metropolitan Opera Gala, w. J. Levine (cnd), Metropolitan Opera Orch, Ileana Cotrubas (sop), Renée Fleming (sop), Hei-Kyung Hong (sop), Karita Mattila (sop), Birgit Nilsson (sop), Kiri Te Kanawa (sop), Deborah Voigt (sop), Grace Bumbry (mez), Heidi Grant Murphy (mez), Anne Sofie von Otter (mez) *(rec live, Metropolitan Opera House, New York, Apr 27, 1996)* Deutsche Grammophon ▲ 449177-2 [DDD]
Meyerbeer, G.:L'Africaine (sels), w. N. Rescigno (cnd), London PO—Adieu, mon doux rivage *(rec Nov. 11-19, 1993)* EMI Classics ▲ CDC 54827 [DDD]
Meyerbeer, G.:Dinorah (sels), w. N. Rescigno (cnd), London PO—Ombre légère, qui suis mes pas *(rec Nov. 11-19, 1993)* EMI Classics ▲ CDC 54827 [DDD]
Meyerbeer, G.:Les Huguenots (sels), w. N. Rescigno (cnd), London PO—Obeau pays de la Touraine! *(rec Nov. 11-19, 1993)* EMI Classics ▲ CDC 54827 [DDD]
Puccini, G.:La Bohème, w. Leontina Vaduva (sop—Mimi), Ruth Ann Swenson (sop—Musetta), Roberto Alagna (ten—Rodolfo), Simon Keenlyside (bar—Schaunard), Thomas Hampson (bar—Marcello), Samuel Ramey (bass—Colline), Enrico Fissore (bass—Benoit), A. Pappano (cnd), Philharmonia Orch EMI Classics 2-◆ CDCB 56120

Swistro, C. (sop)
Pinkham, D.:Wedding Cant, w. T. W. Bridge (ten), B. Bruns (pno), Boston Cecilia *(rec Dec. 1992)* Koch International Classics ▲ KIC 7180 [DDD]

Sylvan, Sanford (bar)
Adams, J.:The Death of Klinghoffer, w. S. Friedman (mez), J. Maddalena (bar), T. Hammons (bar), K. Nagano (cnd), Lyon Opera Orch, English Opera Group Chorus Elektra/Nonesuch 2-▲ 79281-2 2-■ 79281-4
Adams, J.:Nixon in China, w. *(other soloists unknown)*, E. de Waart (cnd), Orch of St. Luke [E] Elektra/Nonesuch 3-▲ 79177-2 2-■ 79177-4
Adams, J.:Nixon in China (sels), w. *(other soloists unknown)*, E. de Waart (cnd), Orch of St. Luke [E] Elektra/Nonesuch ▲ 79193-2 ■ 79193-4
Adams, J.:Wound Dresser, w. J. Adams (cnd), Orch of St. Luke Elektra/Nonesuch ▲ 79218-2 [DDD] ■ 79218-4 (D)
Bach, J.S.:Cant 140, w. H. Schellenberg (sop), J. Humphrey (ten), B. H. Moyse (cnd), Orch of St. Luke MusicMasters ▲ 7059-2-C [DDD]
Bach, J.S.:Magnificat, BWV 243, w. M. A. Kruger (sop), H. Schellenberg (sop), M. Westbrook-Geha (mez), I. Humphrey (ten), B. H. Moyse (cnd), Orch of St. Luke MusicMasters ▲ 7059-2-C [DDD]
Barber, S.:Hermit Songs, w. D. Breitman (pno) Elektra/Nonesuch ▲ 79259-2
Chanler, T.:Epitaphs (8), w. D. Breitman (pno) Elektra/Nonesuch ▲ 79259-2
Copland, A.:Poems (8) of Emily Dickinson, w. D. Breitman (pno) Elektra/Nonesuch ▲ 79259-2
Crumb, G.:Songs, Drones & Refrains of Death, w. Speculum Musicae—[Sp] *(rec 6/17/90)* Bridge ▲ BCD 9028 [DDD]
Geller, T.:Where Silence Reigns, w. G. Schuller (cnd), Collage New Music Ensemble GM ▲ GM2032CD
Harbison, J.:The Flight into Egypt, w. Roberta Anderson (sop), D. Hoose (cnd), Cantata Ensemble, Cantata Singers [E] New World ▲ 80395-2 [DDD]
Harbison, J.:Words From Paterson, w. Boston Sym Chamber Players Elektra/Nonesuch ▲ 79189-2 ■ 79189-4
Schubert, Franz:Die Schöne Müllerin, w. D. Breitman (pno) Elektra/Nonesuch ▲ 79293-2
Tippett, M.:The Ice Break, w. H. Harper (sop), D. Wilson-Johnson (bar), D. Atherton (cnd), London Sinfonietta, London Sym Chorus [E] Virgin Classics ▲ 59048 [DDD]
York, W.:Native Songs, w. N. Armstrong (sop), S. Downey (sgr), R. Woodhouse (sgr), P. Friedland (fl), J. Fischer (pno), J. Russell Smith (perc) *(rec May 1987)* New World ▲ 80439-2

Sylvester, Michael (ten)
Verdi, G.:Don Carlos (sels), w. J. Bunnell (sop), A. Millo (sop), D. Zajick (mez), V. Chernov (bar), F. Furlanetto (bass), P. Plishka (bass), J. Levine (cnd), Metropolitan Opera Orch, New York Metropolitan Opera Chorus *(rec New York, Apr. 20-May 14, 1992)* Sony Classical ("Opera Highlights" series) ▲ SMK 53507 [DDD]

Synek, Liane (sop)
Marschner, H.A.:Der Vampyr, w. L. Heppe (ten), G. Oeggl (bar), Rathauscher (sgr), Skladal (sgr), Sperlbauer (sgr), Weise (sgr), K. Tenner (cnd), Vienna RSO, Vienna Radio Chorus [G] *(rec live, Vienna, 4/9/51)* Memories 2-▲ HR 4466/67 [ADD]

Syule, Tamash (bass)
Mahler, G.:Sym 8, w. Lyudmila Hadzhieva (sop), Maria Temeshi (sop), Darina Takova (sop), Tamara Takac (alt), Boryana Tabakova (alt), Janos Bandi (ten), Pal Kovacs (bar), E. Tabakov (cnd), Sofia PO, Bulgarian National Chorus, Bulgarian National Radio Chorus, Bulgarian National Radio Children's Choir *(rec National Palace of Culture, Sofia, June 1991)* Capriccio 15-▲ 49043 [DDD]

Szabó, Bálint (bass)
Bretan, N.:The Evening Star, w. Adriana Croitoru (sop—King's Daughter), Elena Casian (mez—Lady-in-Waiting), Marius Budoiu (ten—Mariner), Ioan Pojar (ten—Page), Ionel Voineag (ten—Evening Star), Bálint Szabó (bass—Michael the Archangel), B. Hary (cnd), Transylvania PO Cluj *(rec Cluj, Sept 1994)* Nimbus ▲ NI 5463 [DDD]

Szabó, Ida (sop)
Rachmaninoff, S.:Liturgy of St John Chrysostom, w. Tamás Bubnó (ten), Ákos Ambrus (bar), Zoltán Kocsis (cnd), Tomkins Vocal Ensemble *(rec 1995)* Hungaroton 2-▲ HCD 31610/11 [DDD]

Szameit, Sabine (sop)
Steffani, A.:Enrico Leone, w. R. Popken (alt), M. Frimmer (sop), N. Yoko (cta), C. Guber (cta), D. Diwiak (ten), G. Faulstich (bar), L. Rovatkay (cnd), Cappela Agostino Steffani [period instrs] [I] Calig ▲ CAL 50855 [DDD]

Szantho, Enid (cta)
Wagner, R.:Der Ring des Nibelungen (sels), w. Adele Kern (sop), Anny Konetzni (sop), Hilde Konetzni (sop), Elisabeth Schumann (sop), Josef Kalenberg (ten), Max Lorenz (ten), Set Svanholm (ten), Erich Zimmermann (ten), Hans Hotter (bar), Jaro Prohaska (bar), Emil Schipper (bar), Paul Schöffler (b-bar), Ludwig Hoffmann (bass), H. Knappertsbusch (cnd), Vienna State Opera Orch *(rec Vienna, 1937–1943)* Koch Schwann 2-▲ SCH 314742 [ADD]
Wagner, R.:Siegfried (sels), w. E. Szantho (cta—Erda), M. Lorenz (ten—Siegfried), W. Wernigk (ten—Mime), L. Hoffmann (bass—Wanderer), H. Knappertsbusch (cnd), Vienna State Opera Orch, Vienna State Opera Chorus *(rec June 16, 1937)* Koch Schwann 2-▲ SCH 314602

Szczepanska, Krystyna (mez)
Bizet, G.:Carmen (sels), w. Krystyna Szczepanska (alt—Carmen), Bogdan Paprocki (ten—Don José), Andrzej Hiolski (bar—Escamillo), Alina Bolechowska (sgr—Micaela), J. Semkow (cnd), Warsaw PO, Warsaw National Phil Chorus Polskie Nagrania ▲ PNCD 213 [AAD]
Moniuszko, S.:Haunted Manor, w. Halina Slonicka (sop), Bozena Brun-Baranska (mez), Barbara Lawcewicz (mez), Zdzislaw Nikodem (ten), Bogdan Paprocki (ten), Andrzej Hiolski (bar), Edmund Kossowski (bass), Bernard Ladysz (bass), W. Rowicki (cnd), Warsaw State Opera House Orch, Warsaw National Opera Chorus *(rec Warsaw, 1965)* Polskie Nagrania ▲ PNCD 093 [AAD]
Penderecki, K.:Utrenia, w. Delfina Ambroziak (sop), Stefania Woytowicz (sop), Kazimierz Pustelak (ten), Boris Carmeli (bass), Wlodzimierz Denysenko (bass), A. Markowski (cnd), Warsaw PO, Józef Bok (cnd), Stanislaw Skoraczewski (cnd), Warsaw National Phil Chorus, Pioneer Choir *(rec Warsaw, 1973)* Polskie Nagrania ▲ PNCD 018
Szymanowski, K.:Stabat Mater, w. Stefania Woytowicz (sop), Andrzej Hiolski (bar), W. Rowicki (cnd), Warsaw PO, Warsaw National Phil Chorus *(rec Concert Hall at the National PO, Warsaw, 1961)* Polskie Nagrania ▲ PLN 063 [ADD]

Sze, Yi-Kwei (bass)
Berlioz, H.:Les Nuits d'été, w. V. de los Angeles (sop), M. Roggero (mez), L. Chabay (ten), C. Munch (cnd), Boston SO RCA Gold Seal 2-▲ 09026-60681-2
Berlioz, H.:Roméo et Juliette, w. Margaret Roggero (mez), Leslie Chabay (ten), C. Munch (cnd), Boston SO, Harvard Glee Club, Radcliffe Choral Society *(rec Feb 1953)* RCA Victor Gold Seal 8-▲ 0902-668444-2 [ADD]
Berlioz, H.:Roméo et Juliette, w. M. Roggero (mez), L. Chabay (ten), C. Munch (cnd), Boston SO, Harvard Glee Club, Radcliffe Choral Society RCA Gold Seal 2-▲ 09026-60681-2

Szechowska, Maria (sop)
Liszt, F.:Legend of Saint Elizabeth, w. Doreen Millmann (mez), Klaus Lapins (bar), István Bercewy (bass), S. Heinrich (cnd), Warsaw RSO, Warsaw Radio Chorus [G] *(rec 1983)* Koch Schwann 2-▲ 3-1291-2 [ADD]

Székely, Mihály (bass)
Bartók, B.:Bluebeard's Castle, w. O. Szönyi (sop), A. Dorati (cnd), London SO Mercury Living Presence ▲ 434325-2 [ADD]
Bartók, B.:Bluebeard's Castle, w. *(other soloists unknown)*, G. Sébastian (cnd), Budapest RSO *(rec 1951)* Arlecchino ▲ ARL109
Bartók, B.:Bluebeard's Castle, w. K. Palánkay (sop), J. Ferencsik (cnd), Budapest PO [Hun] *(rec 1956)* Hungaroton ▲ HCD 11001 (m) [ADD]

Székelyhidy, Ferenc (ten)
Bartók, B.:Pno Music, w. B. Bartók (pno), V. Medgyaszay (sop), M. Basilides (cta), J. Szigeti (vn), B. Goodman (cl), D. Bartók Pásztory (pno), H. J. Baker, E. J. Rubsam (perc)—studio, broadcast & piano roll recordings of music by Bartók, Kodály, Beethoven, Debussy, Liszt & Scarlatti, chronologically arranged from ca. 1920 through 1945—Sonatina; 6 Romanian Folk Dances; Evening in Transylvania; 8 sels. from 15 Hungarian Peasant Songs; Suite, Op. 14 (both the issued & test recordings); Allegro barbaro; 5 sels. from 2 Romanian Dances, 3 Burlesques, 10 Easy Pieces & 14 Bagatelles; & 4 Sons. by D. Scarlatti (test recordings); 8 sels. from 15 Hungarian Peasant Songs; 4 sels. from 9 Little Piano Pieces, Petite Suite & 3 Rondos on Folk Melodies; & "Sursum corda" from Liszt's Années de pèlerinage; 20 Hungarian Folk Songs; 5 Hungarian Folk Tunes; 8 Hungarian Folksongs; Hungarian Folk Tunes; 6 Romanian Folk Dances; Rhap. 1 Violin & Piano; Contrasts for Clarinet, Violin & Piano; 2 sels. from Mikrokosmos; 32 sels. from Mikrokosmos; Rhap. 1; Son. No. 2; Beethoven's "Kreutzer" Son.; Debussy's Son. 3; Son. 2 Pianos & Percussion; Petite Suite; 3 Hungarian Folk Tunes; 11 sels. from Improvs. on Hungarian Peasant Songs; Mikrokosmos; 3 Rondos on Folk Melodies; 9 Little Piano Pieces; 14 Bagatelles; 15 sels. from For Children & 2 sels. from 10 Easy Pieces Hungaroton 6-▲ HCD 12326/31 (m) [ADD]
Kodály, Z.:Hungarian Folk Music, w. V. Medgyaszay (sop), M. Basilides (mez), B. Bartók (pno) [arr. by Kodály for solo voice & piano]—20 Hungarian folk songs *(rec Budapest, 1928)* Hungaroton 6-▲ HCD 12326/31 (m) [ADD]

Szemere, László (ten)
Einem, G. von:Der Prozess, w. Lisa Della Casa (sop—Frl. Bürstner/Die Frau des Gerichtsdieners/Leni), Peter Klein (ten—Der Direktorstellvertreter/Der Student), Max Lorenz (ten—Josef K.), Erich Majkut (ten—Ein Bursche), László Szemere (ten—Titorelli), Alois Pernerstorfer (b-bar—Willem/Der Gerichtsdiener), Alfred Poell (b-bar—Der Advokat), Walter Berry (bass—Franz/Kanzleidirektor), Oskar Czerwenka (bass—Der Untersuchungsrichter/Der Prügler), Ludwig Hofmann (bass—Der Aufseher/Ein Passant/Der Geistliche/Der Fabrikant), Polly Batic (sgr—Frau Grubach), Endreh Koreh (sgr—Albert K.), Luise Leitner (sgr—Ein buckliges Mädchen), K. Böhm (cnd), Vienna PO, Vienna State Opera Chorus *(rec Aug 17, 1953)* Orfeo d'or ("Festspiel Dokumente" series) 2-▲ 392952 (m)
Strauss, R.:Die Liebe der Danae, w. A. Kupper (sop), J. Traxel (ten), P. Schöffler (b-bar), C. Krauss (cnd), Vienna PO, Vienna State Opera Chorus [G] *(rec live, Salzburg, 8/14/52)* Melodram 3-▲ MEL 37061 (m) [AAD]

Szendrényi, Katalin (sop)
Mahler, G.:Das Klagende Lied, w. Klára Takács (cta), Dénes Gulyás (ten), A. Ligeti (cnd), Budapest SO, Péter Erdei (cnd), Hungarian Radio-TV Chorus Classical Diamonds ▲ CLD 4010 [DDD]

Szerda, A. (voc)
Stravinsky, I.:L'Histoire du soldat, w. H. Schimmelpfennig (nar), M. Hoffmann (the Soldier), P. Leiner (cnd), Contemporano Ensemble Bayer ▲ 100207 [DDD]

Sziklay, Erika (nar)
Schoenberg, A.:Pierrot lunaire, w. A. Mihály (cnd), Budapest CO [G] Hungaroton ▲ HCD 11385 [ADD]

Sziklay, Erika (sop)
Boulez, P.:Improvisations sur Mallarmé I & II, w. A. Mihály (cnd), Budapest CO [F] Hungaroton ▲ HCD 11385 [ADD]
Webern, A.:Canons on Latin Texts, w. A. Mihály (cnd), Budapest CO [L] Hungaroton ▲ HCD 11385 [ADD]
Webern, A.:Songs, Op. 8, w. A. Mihály (cnd), Budapest CO [G] Hungaroton ▲ HCD 11385 [ADD]

Szilágyi, Béla (bar)
Caldara, A.:Stabat Mater, w. I. Verebics (sop), É. Lax (mez), G. Kállay (ten), E. Kollár (cnd), Concerto Armonico Budapest, Monteverdi Chamber Choir [L] Hungaroton ▲ HCD 31273 [DDD]
Handel, G.F.:Agrippina, w. S. Bradshaw (sop), W. Hill (sop), L. Saffer (sop), G. Banditelli (cta), D. Minter (alt), R. Popken (alt), M. Dean (b-bar), N. Isherwood (bass), N. McGegan (cnd), Capella Savaria [period instrs] [I] Harmonia Mundi USA 3-▲ HMU 907063/65 ■ HMU 407063/65

Szilágyi, Béla (bar) (cont.)
Mascagni, P.:Lodoletta, w. M. Spacagna (sop), P. Kelen (ten), M. Kálmándi (bar), L. Polgár (bass), C. Rosekrans (cnd), Hungarian State Orch, Hungarian State Choruses [I] Hungaroton 2-▲ HCD 31307/08 [DDD]

Szimándy (sgr)
Lehár, F.:Das Land des Lächelns (sels), w. Házy (sop), Magda Kalmár (sop), Bende (sgr), G. Oberfrank (cnd), Budapest SO, Hungarian Radio-TV Chorus [Hun] Hungaroton ▲ HCD 16809 [ADD]

Szirmay, Márta (cta)
Beethoven, L. van:Syms (comp), w. Éva Andor (sop), György Korondi (ten), Sándor Sólyom-Nagy (bar), J. Ferencsik (cnd), Hungarian State Orch, Miklós Forrai (cnd), Budapest Chorus *(rec 1969, 1971, 1974–76)* Classical Diamonds 6-▲ 4013-18 [ADD]
Beethoven, L. van:Sym 9, "Choral Sym", w. E. Andor (sop), G. Korondy (ten), S. Solyom-Nagy (bar), J. Ferencsik (cnd), Hungarian PO, Budapest Phil Chorus Laserlight ▲ 15 905

Szita, Bori (sgr)
Make Wonder:Songs from Operettas, w. Magda Kalmár (sop), Éva Köteles (sgr), Judit Takács (sgr), Budapest SO [cnd:Tamás Bródy], Hungarian State Orch [cnd:András Sebestyén] Hungaroton ▲ HCD 16613 [AAD]

Szklarecka, Grazyna (sop)
Zimmermann, U.:Die weisse Rose (sels), w. F. Schiller (bar), U. Zimmermann (cnd), Musica Viva Ensemble [scenes for 2 solo voices & instrumental ensemble] Berlin Classics ("Eterna" series) ▲ BER 2060 [DDD]

Szmyt, Krysztof (ten)
Elsner, J.:Passio Domini Nostri Jesu Christi, w. Bozena Harasimowicz (sop), Czeslaw Galka (bar), Bogdan Sliwa (bar), Piotr Nowacki (bass), K. Kord (cnd), Warsaw PO, Henryk Wojnarowski (cnd), Ewa Marchwicka (cnd), Warsaw National Phil Chorus, E. Mlynarski State School of Music Children's Choir *(rec National Philharmonic, Warsaw, 1990)* Polskie Nagrania ▲ PNCD 078 [DDD]
Elsner, J.:Passio Domini Nostri Jesu Christi, w. B. Harasimowicz (sop), C. Galka (bar), P. Nowacki (bass), K. Kord (cnd), Warsaw National Philharmonic SO, Warsaw National Philharmonic Sym Chorus *(rec 1990)* Muza ▲ PNCD 078 [DDD]

Szmytka, Elzbieta (sop)
Gazzaniga, G.:Don Giovanni, w. L. Serra (sop), E. Schmid-Lienbacher (sop), D. Johnson (sgr), F. Furlanetto (bass), B. Weil (cnd), Tafelmusik Sony Classical ("Vivarte" series) ▲ SK 46693
Górecki, H.-M.:Good Night, w. Paul Edmund-Davies (a fl), Huub Righarts (perc), Mireille Gleizes (pno) *(rec Abbey Bonne Espérance, Vellereille-les-Brayeux, Belgium; July 17–19, 1995)* Telarc ▲ CD-80417 [DDD]
Lehár, F.:Die lustige Witwe, w. F. Lott (sop), J. Aler (ten), T. Hampson (b-bar), D. Bogarde (nar), F. Welser-Möst (cnd), London PO, Glyndebourne Festival Chorus EMI Classics ▲ CDCB 55152
Mozart, W.A.:Così fan tutte, w. K. Mattila (sop), A. S. von Otter (mez), F. Araiza (ten), T. Allen (bar), J. van Dam (b-bar), N. Marriner (cnd), Academy of St. Martin in the Fields, Ambrosian Opera Chorus [I] Philips 3-▲ 422381-2 [DDD]
Mozart, W.A.:Entführung, w. C. Studer (sop), K. Streit (ten), R. Gambill (ten), G. Missenhardt (bar), M. Heltau (nar), B. Weil (cnd), Vienna SO, Vienna State Opera Chorus Sony Classical 2-▲ S2K 48053
Mozart, W.A.:Entführung (sels), w. C. Studer (sop), K. Streit (ten), R. Gambill (ten), Gunter Missenhardt (bar), B. Weil (cnd), Vienna SO, Vienna State Opera Chorus *(rec Vienna, Apr. 2–10, 1991)* Sony Classical ("Opera Highlights" series) ▲ SMK 53500 [DDD]
Szymanowski, K.:Litany to the Virgin Mary, w. F. Quivar (cta), J. Garrison (ten), J. Connell (bass), S. Rattle (cnd), City of Birmingham SO, City of Birmingham Sym Chorus EMI Classics ▲ CDC 55121
Szymanowski, K.:Stabat Mater, w. F. Quivar (mez), J. Connell (bass), S. Rattle (cnd), City of Birmingham SO, City of Birmingham Sym Chorus EMI Classics ▲ CDC 55121

Szobek, Márta (sgr)
Csenki, I.:Gypsy Dances of Hungary, w. R. Lantos (cnd), Hungarian State Folk Ensemble Orch, Hungarian State Folk Ensemble Chorus *(rec 1969)* Hungaroton ▲ HCD 18008 [AAD]

Szőkefalvi-Nagy (sgr)
Vivaldi, A.:Magnificat, RV.611, w. T. Takács (mez), J. Németh (mez), Bátori (sgr), Kovács (sgr), F. Szekeres (cnd), Budapest Strings, Budapest Madrigal Choir [L] Hungaroton ▲ HCD 31259 [DDD]

Szőnyi, Olga (sop)
Bartók, B.:Bluebeard's Castle, w. M. Székely (bass), A. Dorati (cnd), London SO Mercury Living Presence ▲ 434325-2 [ADD]
Szokolay, S.:Blood Wedding, w. E. Házy (sop), E. Komlóssy (cta), Faragó (sgr), A. Kórodi (cnd), Hungarian State Opera Orch, Hungarian State Opera Chorus [Hun] Hungaroton 2-▲ HCD 11262/63 [ADD]
Verdi, G.:Rigoletto (sels), w. Mária Gyurkovics (sop), Ernő Kenéz (ten), János Fodor (bar), Alexander Svéd (bar), József Bódy (bass), Kórodi, Molinari-Pradelli (cnd), Hungarian State Opera Orch—Pari siamo!; Figlia! Mio padre! A te dappresso; Cortigiani! Vil' razza dannata; Tutte le feste al tempio...Ah! solo per me!; Chi è mai... *(rec 1955–56)* Hungaroton ("Great Hungarian Voices" series) ▲ HCD 31614 [ADD]

Szostek-Radkowa, Krystyna (mez)
Baird, T.:Tomorrow, w. J. Artysz (bar), E. Pawlak (bass), J. Ostrowski (nar), R. Czajkowski (cnd), Poznan Philharmonic SO [Pol] Olympia ▲ OCD 326 [AAD]
Bizet, G.:Carmen (sels), w. Ryszard Karczykowski (ten), Monika Chabros (sgr) *(other artists unknown)* —Habanera z I aktu; Aris Don Jose z II aktu; Aria Micaeli z III aktu Polskie Nagrania ▲ PNCD 080 [AAD]
Mozart, W.A.:Requiem, w. Barbara Nieman (sop), Wieslaw Ochman (ten), Leonard Mróz (bass), K. Kord (cnd), Warsaw PO, Henryk Wojnarowski (cnd), Warsaw National Phil Chorus *(rec Warsaw, 1979)* Polskie Nagrania ▲ PNCD 135 [ADD]
Szymanowski, K.:Demeter, w. Polish National RSO Katowice, Polish Radio Women's Choir *(rec Concert Hall at the National PO, Warsaw, 1982)* Polskie Nagrania ▲ PLN 063 [ADD]
Szymanowski, K.:Stabat Mater, w. J. Gadulanka (sop), A. Hlolski (bar), K. Stryja (cnd), Polish State PO, Polish State Phil Chorus Marco Polo ▲ 8.223293 [DDD]

Szramek, A. (sgr)
Berg, A.:Lulu, w. A. Silja (sop), B. Fassbaender (mez), W. Berry (b-bar), K. Moll (bass), H. Hotter (b-bar), C. von Dohnányi (cnd), Vienna PO London 2-▲ 430415-2 [ADD]

Szücs, Márta (sop)
Caldara, A.:Magnificat, w. K. Takács (cta), D. Gulyás (ten), T. Bátor (bass), F. Szekeres (cnd), Budapest Strings, Budapest Madrigal Choir [L] Hungaroton ▲ HCD 31259 [DDD]
Sammartini, G.B.:Magnificat in B♭, w. Takács (alt), Gulyás (ten), Bátor (bass), F. Szekeres (cnd), Budapest Strings, Budapest Madrigal Choir [L] Hungaroton ▲ HCD 31259 [DDD]

Szücs, Robert (bass)
Vivaldi, A.:Magnificat, RV.610, w. T. Takács (mez), D. Gulyás (ten), T. Bátor (bass), F. Szekeres (cnd), Budapest Strings, Budapest Madrigal Choir [L] Hungaroton ▲ HCD 31259 [DDD]

Szwajgier, Olga (sop)
Penderecki, K.:Dies Irae, w. Z. Jankovski (ten), L. Mróz (bass), S. Kawalla (cnd), Polish Radio-TV SO, Polish Radio-TV Chorus [L] Vienna Modern Masters ▲ VMM 3015 [DDD]
Stachowski, M.:Madrigali dell'estate, w. Silesian String Quartet members *(rec Apr. 1–6, 1987)* Polskie Nagrania ▲ PLN 076 [ADD]

Tabachuk, Tatjana (mez)
Tchaikovsky, P.:Iolanta, w. Michaela Gurevich (sop—Iolanta), Jaqueline Miura (sop—Brigitta), Tatjana Tabachuk (mez—Martha), Annette Kuhn (mez—Laura), Ian Denolfo (ten—Godefroy), Keith Alexander Bolves (ten—Alméric), Alexander Ben (bar—Robert), Georg Lehner (bar—Ibn-Hakia), Arutiun Kotchinian (bass—René), Kurt Geysen (bass—Bertrand), H. Rotman (cnd), Warsaw PO, ECOV Ensemble Members *(rec Vooruit Center of the Arts, Ghent, Belgium, Aug 28–29, 1993)* CPO 2-▲ CPO 999456-2 [DDD]

Tabakova, Boryana (alt)
Mahler, G.:Sym 8, w. Lyudmila Hadzhieva (sop), Maria Temeshi (sop), Darina Takova (sop), Tamara Takac (alt), Janos Bandi (ten), Pal Kovacs (bar), Tamash Syule (bass), E. Tabakov (cnd), Sofia PO, Bulgarian National Chorus, Bulgarian National Radio Chorus, Bulgarian National Radio Children's Choir *(rec National Palace of Culture, Sofia, June 1991)* Capriccio 15-▲ 49043 [DDD]

Tabery, Vandaa (mez)
Handel, G.F.:Scipione, w. Doris Lamprecht (sop), Sandrine Piau (sop), Guy Flechter (ten), Olivier Lalouette (bass), C. Rousset (cnd), Les Talens Lyriques [I] FNAC Music 3-▲ 592245 [DDD]

Tabiadon, Adelisa (mez)
Mercadante, S.:Il bravo, w. J. Perry (sop), D. Di Domenico (ten), S. Bertocchi (ten), S. Antonucci (bar), B. Aprea (cnd), Italian International Orch, Slovak Phil Chorus [I] *(rec live 7/28–31/90)* Nuova Era 3-▲ 6971/73 [DDD]

Taborsky, Maria (sop)
Weber, C.M. von:Missa sancta 1, w. Gerda Kink (cta), Hermann Pöllmann (ten), Hans Huber (bass), Gisela Schindler (org), E. Ehret (cnd), St. Michael Orch Munich, St. Michael Chorus Munich Koch Schwann ▲ SCH CD 316372
Weber, C.M. von:Missa sancta 2, w. Gerda Kink (alt), Hermann Pöllmann (ten), Hans Huber (bass), Gisela Schindler (org), E. Ehret (cnd), Munich St. Michael's Orch, Munich St. Michael Choir Studio SM ▲ D 2454 [ADD]

Taccani, G. (ten)
Verdi, G.:Il trovatore (sels), w. J. Biel (ten), F. Tamagno (ten), L.-A. Escalaïs (ten), M. Gilion (ten), E. Caruso (ten), A. Paoli (ten), G. Zenatello (ten), J. Sembach (ten), L. Slezak (ten), F. Constantino (ten), G. Martinelli (ten), B. De Muro (ten), N. Fusati (ten), N. Piccaluga (ten), G. Lauri-Volpi (ten), A. Pertile (ten), E. Bergamaschi (ten), R. Tauber (ten), J. O'Sullivan (ten), H. Roswaenge (ten), V. Lois (ten), H. Lazaro (ten), A. Lindi (ten), A. Cortis (ten), F. Merli (ten), F. Völker (ten), J. Kiepura (ten), J. Schmidt (ten), J. Bjoerling (ten), B. Gigli (ten), A. Salvarezza (ten), J. Soler (ten), M. Filippeschi (ten)—34 performances of the Act III tenor aria "Di quella pira!," *(rec from 1903–1956)* Bongiovanni ▲ GB 1051 [AAD]

Tachikawa, Akira (ct)
Bach, J.S.:Cant 4, w. Yumiko Kurisu (sop), Koki Katano (ten), Peter Kooy (bass), M. Suzuki (cnd), Japan Bach Collegium *(rec Kobe Shoin Women's University, Japan, June - July 1995)* BIS ▲ CD 751 [DDD]
Bach, J.S.:Cant 150, w. Yumiko Kurisu (sop), Koki Katano (ten), Peter Kooy (bass), M. Suzuki (cnd), Japan Bach Collegium *(rec Kobe Shoin Women's University, Japan, June - July 1995)* BIS ▲ CD 751 [DDD]
Bach, J.S.:Cant 196, w. Yumiko Kurisu (sop), Koki Katano (ten), Peter Kooy (bass), M. Suzuki (cnd), Japan Bach Collegium *(rec Kobe Shoin Women's University, Japan, June - July 1995)* BIS ▲ CD 751 [DDD]

Taddei, Giuseppe (bar)
Arias & Duets (1974–1986), w. P. Domingo (ten), L. Pavarotti (ten), et al., Vienna State Opera Orch [var. cnd] Acanta ▲ 49402
Cilea, F.:Adriana Lecouvreur (sels), w. Renata Tebaldi (sop—Adriana), Piero de Palma (ten—Abate), Gianni Poggi (ten—Maurizio), Giuseppe Taddei (bar—Michonnet), Augusto Romani (bass—Prince), G. Santini (cnd), Naples Teatro San Carlo Orch, Naples Teatro San Carlo Chorus—Del sultano Amurate...Io son l'umile ancella; Giusto Cielo! che feci in tal giorno; Salvatemi! salvatemi!...Scostatevi, profani! *(rec San Carlo Theater, Naples, Dec. 26, 1952)* Legato Classics 2-▲ LCD 193-2 [ADD]
Cilea, F.:Adriana Lecouvreur (sels), w. Gabriella Tucci (sop), A. Basile (cnd), Turin Radio-TV SO—Ecco il monologo... *(rec Concerto Martini & Rossi, Turin, Feb 15, 1960)* Incontri Memorabili ▲ 5029 [ADD]
Donizetti, G.:Arias, w. Gabriella Tucci (sop), A. Basile (cnd), Turin Radio-TV SO—Vien Leonora [from La Favorita]; Ah! tardi, troppo [from Linda di Chamounix] *(rec Concerto Martini & Rossi, Turin, Feb 15, 1960)* Incontri Memorabili ▲ 5029 [ADD]
Donizetti, G.:Belisario, w. L. Gencer (sop), M. Pecile (cta), U. Grilli (ten), N. Zaccaria (bass), G. Gavazzeni (cnd), Venice Teatro La Fenice Orch, Venice Teatro La Fenice Chorus [I] *(rec live, Venice 5/14/69)* Melodram 2-▲ MEL 27051 [AAD]
Donizetti, G.:Belisario, w. L. Gencer (sop), M. Pecile (cta), U. Grilli (ten), N. Zaccaria (bass), G. Gavazzeni (cnd), Venice Teatro La Fenice Orch, Venice Teatro La Fenice Chorus [I] *(rec live in Venice, 5/14/69)* Verona 2-▲ 27048/49 (m) [AAD]
Donizetti, G.:L'elisir d'amore, w. Rosanna Carteri (sop—Adina), Luigi Angela Vercelli (mez—Gianetta), Luigi Alva (ten—Nemorino), Rolando Panerai (bar—Belcore), Giuseppe Taddei (bar—Dulcamara), T. Serafin (cnd), La Scala Orch, La Scala Chorus EMI Classics 2-▲ CDMB 65658
Donizetti, G.:L'elisir d'amore, w. R. Scotto (sop), C. Bergonzi (ten), P. Cava (ten), G. Gavazzeni (cnd), Florence Maggio Musicale Orch, Florence Maggio Musicale Chorus *(rec live 1967)* Memories 2-▲ HR 4129/30 (s)
Donizetti, G.:L'elisir d'amore, w. Renata Scotto (sop), Carlo Bergonzi (ten), Carlo Cava (bass), G. Gavazzeni (cnd), Florence Teatro Comunale Orch, Florence Teatro Comunale Chorus *(rec June 1967)* Pantheon 2-▲ PHE 6612 (m)
Donizetti, G.:Linda di Chamounix, w. A. Stella (sop), C. Valletti (ten), R. Capecchi (bar), T. Serafin (cnd), Naples Teatro San Carlo Orch, Naples Teatro San Carlo Chorus *(rec 1959)* Andromeda ▲ ANR 2509 [ADD]
Giordano, U.:Andrea Chénier, w. Maria Caniglia (sop—Maddalena), Maria Huder (mez—Bersi), Vittoria Palombini (mez—Madelon), Giulietta Simionato (mez—Contessa), Beniamino Gigli (ten—Andrea), Adelio Zagonara (ten—Incroyable/Abbé), Gino Bechi (bar—Carlo), Leone Paci (bar—Mathieu), Giuseppe Taddei (b-bar—Pietro/Fouquier), Italo Tajo (b-bar—Roucher), Gino Conti (bass—Master/Schmidt), O. de Fabritiis (cnd), La Scala Orch, La Scala Chorus *(rec Nov 1941)* Arkadia ("The 78's" series) 2-▲ 78012 [ADD]
Giordano, U.:Andrea Chénier, w. M. Caniglia (sop), G. Simionato (mez), B. Gigli (ten), G. Bechi (bar), I. Tajo (bass), O. de Fabritiis (cnd), La Scala Orch, La Scala Chorus [I] *(rec 1941, HMV DB 5423/35)* Angel ("Studio" series) 2-▲ CDHB 69996 (m) [ADD]
Giuseppe Taddei, w. Arturo Basile (cnd), Fernando Previtali (cnd), Angelo Questa (cnd), RAI SO *(rec 1955)* Cetra Classics ▲ CDON 109
Leoncavallo, R.:Pagliacci, w. Joan Carlyle (sop—Nedda/Colombina), Carlo Bergonzi (ten—Canio/Pagliaccio), Franco Ricciardi (ten—Villager), Ugo Benelli (bar—Peppe/Arlecchino), Rolando Panerai (bar—Silvio), Giuseppe Taddei (bar—Tonio/Taddeo), Giuseppe Morresi (bass—Villager), H. von Karajan (cnd), La Scala Orch, La Scala Chorus *(rec La Scala, Milan, Oct 1965)* Deutsche Grammophon ("The Originals" series) ▲ 449727-2 [ADD]
Leoncavallo, R.:Pagliacci, w. J. Carlyle (sop), C. Bergonzi (ten), U. Benelli (bar), R. Panerai (bar), H. von Karajan (cnd), La Scala Orch [I] Deutsche Grammophon 3-▲ 419257-2 [ADD]
Massenet, J.:Hérodiade (sels), w. Gabriella Tucci (sop), A. Basile (cnd), Turin Radio-TV SO—Divine volupté *(rec Concerto Martini & Rossi, Turin, Feb 15, 1960)* Incontri Memorabili ▲ 5029 [ADD]
Meyerbeer, G.:Les Huguenots, w. A. Pastori (sop), A. de Cavalieri (mez), G. Lauri-Volpi (ten), G. Tozzi (bass), N. Zaccaria (bass), T. Serafin (cnd), Milan RAI SO, Milan RAI Chorus *(rec 1956)* Memories 3-▲ MEM 4566 [ADD]
Mozart, W.A.:Così fan tutte, w. E. Schwarzkopf (sop), H. Steffek (sop), C. Ludwig (mez), A. Kraus (ten), W. Berry (bass), K. Böhm (cnd), Philharmonia Orch, Philharmonia Chorus [I] EMI Classics ("Studio" series) 3-▲ CDMC 69330 [ADD]
Mozart, W.A.:Don Giovanni (sels), w. Gabriella Tucci (sop), A. Basile (cnd), Turin Radio-TV SO—Madamina il catalogo è questo *(rec Concerto Martini & Rossi, Turin, Feb 15, 1960)* Incontri Memorabili ▲ 5029 [ADD]
Mozart, W.A.:Nozze di Figaro, w. E. Schwarzkopf (sop), G. Sciurri (sop), H. Prey (bar), C. M. Giulini (cnd), Residentie Orch The Hague, Netherlands Chamber Choir [I] *(rec live, Holland Festival, 1961)* Verona 3-▲ 27092/94
Mozart, W.A.:Nozze di Figaro, w. A. Moffo (sop), E. Schwarzkopf (sop), F. Cossotto (mez), E. Wächter (bar), C. M. Giulini (cnd), Philharmonia Orch, Philharmonia Chorus [I] EMI Classics ("Studio" series) 2-▲ CDMB 63266 [ADD]
Mozart, W.A.:Nozze di Figaro (sels), w. A. Moffo (sop), E. Schwarzkopf (sop), F. Cossotto (mez), E. Wächter (bar), C. M. Giulini (cnd), Philharmonia Orch, Philharmonia Chorus—sels. EMI Classics ("Studio" series) ▲ CDM 63409
Mozart, W.A.:Zauberflöte, w. E. Schwarzkopf (sop), R. Streich (sop), A. Noni (sop), N. Gedda (ten), M. Petri (bass), H. von Karajan (cnd), Rome Radio Orch, Rome RAI Chorus [I] *(rec live, Dec. 19, 1953)* Myto 2-▲ 2 MCD 89007 (m) [ADD]

Taddei, Giuseppe (bar) (cont.)
Puccini, G.:La Bohème, w. M. Freni (sop), H. Gueden (sop), G. Raimondi (ten), H. von Karajan (cnd), Vienna State Opera Orch, Vienna State Opera Chorus [I] *(rec live 11/30/63)* Melodram 2-▲ MELCD 27007
Puccini, G.:Gianni Schicchi, w. G. Rapisardi (sop), A. Dubbini (mez), G. Savio (ten), A. Simonetto (cnd), Turin RAI SO [I] *(rec 10/5/49)* Preiser ▲ 90074 (m) [AAD]
Puccini, G.:Gianni Schicchi, w. Grete Rapisardi (sop), Giuseppe Savio (ten), A. Simonetto (cnd), *(orch & chorus unknown)* Cetra Classic ▲ 363
Puccini, G.:Madama Butterfly, w. C. Petrella (sop—Madama Butterfly), M. Masini (mez—Suzuki), M. C. Foscale (sgr—Kate Pinkerton), F. Tagliavini (ten—Pinkerton), M. Caruso (ten—Goro), G. Taddei (bar—Sharpless), A. Albertini (bar—Yamadori), A. Biancardo (bass—Bonze), A. Questa (cnd), Turin RAI Orch, Cetra Chorus *(rec 1953)* Cetra Classic 2-▲ CDO 10 [AAD]
Puccini, G.:Manon Lescaut, w. M. Freni (sop—Manon), C. Bartoli (mez—Musici I), L. Pavarotti (ten—Des Grieux), R. Vargas (ten—Edmondo), D. Croft (ten—Lescaut), G. Taddei (bar—Geronte), J. Levine (cnd), Metropolitan Opera Orch, New York Metropolitan Opera Chorus [I] *(rec 1992)* London ▲ 440200-2 [DDD]
Puccini, G.:Suor angelica (sels), w. Gabriella Tucci (sop), A. Basile (cnd), Turin Radio-TV SO—Senza mamma *(rec Concerto Martini & Rossi, Turin, Feb 15, 1960)* Incontri Memorabili ▲ 5029 [ADD]
Puccini, G.:Tosca, w. L. Price (sop), G. di Stefano (ten), H. von Karajan (cnd), Vienna PO, Vienna State Opera Chorus [I] London 2-▲ 421670-2 [ADD]
Puccini, G.:Tosca, w. Leyla Gencer (sop), Melchiorre Luise (bass), Vittorio de Santis (sgr), V. Bellezza (cnd), *(orch & chorus unknown)* *(rec live, Naples, Mar. 21, 1955)* Great Opera Performances 2-▲ GOP 751
Recital Melodram ▲ CDM 16509
Rossini, G.:Il barbiere di Siviglia, w. R. Broilo (sop—Berta), G. Simionato (mez—Rosina), L. Infantino (ten—Almaviva), G. Taddei (bar—Figaro), C. Badioli (bass—Bartolo), A. Cassinelli (bass—Basilio), F. Previtali (cnd), Milan RAI SO, Milan RAI Chorus *(rec 1950)* Cetra Classic 2-▲ CDO 6 [AAD]
Sings Arias & Neapolitan Songs, w. various orchs Preiser ▲ PRE 90020 (m) [AAD]
Teresa Berganza, Giuseppe Taddei, w. Teresa Berganza (mez), Milan RAI SO [cnd:Frieder Weissmann] *(rec Dec. 16, 1957)* Incontri Memorabili ("Martini & Rossi Concerts" series) ▲ 5025
Verdi, G.:Aida, w. M. Callas (sop), O. Dominguez (mez), M. Del Monaco (ten), O. de Fabritiis (cnd), Palacio Bellas Artes Orch, Palacio Bellas Artes Chorus *(rec live, Mexico City 7/3/51)* Melodram 2-▲ CDM 26015
Verdi, G.:Arias, w. Gabriella Tucci (sop), A. Basile (cnd), Turin Radio-TV SO—Tacea la notte placida [from Il Trovatore]; Ave Maria! [from Otello] *(rec Concerto Martini & Rossi, Turin, Feb 15, 1960)* Incontri Memorabili ▲ 5029 [ADD]
Verdi, G.:Ernani, w. Caterina Mancini (sop), Vittorio Pandano (ten), Gino Penno (ten), Giacomo Vaghi (bar), Ezio Achilli (sgr), Licia Rossini (sgr), F. Previtali (cnd), Rome RAI SO, Rome RAI Chorus Cetra Classic 2-▲ CDON 39 [ADD]
Verdi, G.:Macbeth, w. Leyla Gencer (sop), Mirto Picchi (ten), Ferruccio Mazzoli (bass), V. Gui (cnd), Palermo Teatro Massimo Orch, Palermo Teatro Massimo Chorus *(rec Palermo, Jan. 14, 1960)* Pantheon 2-▲ PHE 6604 (m)
Verdi, G.:Macbeth, w. B. Nilsson (sop), B. Prevedi (ten), T. Schippers (cnd), St. Cecilia Academy Orch Rome, St. Cecilia Academy Chorus Rome London ("Grand Opera" series) 2-▲ 433039-2 [ADD]
Verdi, G.:Rigoletto, w. L. Pagliughi (sop—Gilda), I. Colasanti (mez—Maddalena), F. Tagliavini (ten—Duca), A. Albertini (bar—Il Cavaliere Marullo), G. Taddei (bar—Rigoletto), G. Neri (bass—Sparafucile), A. Zerbini (bass—Conte di Monterone), A. Questa (cnd), Turin RSO, Turin Radio Chorus *(rec 1953)* Cetra Classics 2-▲ CDO 11 [AAD]
Verdi, G.:La traviata, w. M. Callas (sop), Giron (sgr), C. Valletti (ten), O. de Fabritiis (cnd), Palacio Bellas Artes Orch, Palacio Bellas Artes Chorus [I] *(rec live, Mexico City, 7/17/51)* Melodram 2-▲ CDM 26019 [AAD]
Verdi, G.:La traviata (sels), w. Anna de Santis (sop—Annina), Renata Tebaldi (sop—Violetta), Giuseppe Campora (ten—Alfredo), Gerardo Gaudioso (bar—Doupho), Giuseppe Taddei (bar—Germont), Antonio Picillo (bass—Grenvil), G. Santini (cnd), Naples Teatro San Carlo Orch, Naples Teatro San Carlo Chorus—E strano...Ah, fors'e lui; Follie!...Sempre libera; Pero l'attendo...Amami, Alfredo; Invitato a qui seguirmi; Alfredo, Alfredo, di questo core; Teneste la promessa...Addio del passato; Ma se tornando...Ah! Gran Dio! Morir si giovine; Se una pudica vergine *(rec San Carlo Theater, Naples, Jan. 17, 1952)* Legato Classics 2-▲ LCD 193-2 [ADD]
Verdi, G.:I vespri siciliani, w. A. Stella (sop—Elena), M. Filippeschi (ten—Arrigo), G. Taddei (bar—Monforte), B. Ladysz (bass—Procida), T. Serafin (cnd), Palermo Teatro Massimo Orch, Palermo Teatro Massimo Chorus *(rec Jan. 18, 1957)* Golden Age of Opera 2-▲ GAO 145/46 [ADD]
Wagner, R.:Die Meistersinger von Nürnberg, w. Bruna Rizzoli (sop), Fernanda Cadoni (mez), Luigi Infantino (ten), Vito Tatone (ten), Renato Capecchi (bar), Boris Christoff (bass), Giovanni Ciavola (bass), James Loomis (bass), Silvo Maionica (bass), Vito Susca (bass), Raimondo Botteghelli (sgr), Walter Brunelli (sgr), Carlo Franzini (sgr), Ezio de Giorgi (sgr), Renzo Gonzales (sgr), L. von Matačić (cnd), Turin RAI Radio-TV SO, Turin RAI Chorus Stradivarius 4-▲ STV 12310

Tadeo, Giorgio (bass)
Mozart, W.A.:Nozze di Figaro, w. S. Jurinac (sop), T. Stratas (sop), T. Berganza (mez), N. Condò (mez), A. Lazzari (ten), S. Bruscantini (bar), M. Petri (bass), A. Mariotti (bass), Z. Mehta (cnd), *(orch unknown)* *(rec 1968)* Great Opera Performances 3-▲ GOP 712
Mozart, W.A.:Nozze di Figaro, w. L. Cherici (sop), K. Mattila (sop), M. McLaughlin (sop), M. Bacelli (mez), N. Curiel (mez), U. Benelli (ten), L. Gallo (bar), A. Nosotti (bass), M. Pertusi (bass), G. Tadeo (bass), Z. Mehta (cnd), Florence Maggio Musicale Orch, Florence Maggio Musicale Chorus Sony Classical ▲ SK 53286
Puccini, G.:Manon Lescaut (sels), w. Carlo Gaifa (ten), Giuseppe Giacomini (ten), Guido Mazzini (bass), Angeles Gulin (sgr), M. Arena (cnd), *(orch unknown)*—Tra voi belle; Cortese damigella; Donna non vidi mai; Vedete, io son fedele; Tu, tu, amore; Ah! Manon, mi tradisce; Lescaut!; Ansia eterna crudel; No, pazzo son; Tutta su me ti posa; Manon...senti amor mio *(rec Treviso, Oct. 16, 1974)* Golden Age of Opera 2-▲ GAO 189/90 [ADD]
Rossini, G.:Il barbiere di Siviglia (sels), w. G. d' Angelo (sop), G. Carturan (mez), N. Monti (ten), R. Capecchi (bar), G. Giorgetti (bar), C. Cava (bass), B. Bartoletti (cnd), Bavarian RSO IMP Collectors Series ▲ IMPX 9022 [AAD]
Verdi, G.:Rigoletto, w. Gianna D'Angelo (sop), Aldo Protti (bar), Vito Susca (bass), F. Molinari-Pradelli (cnd), Trieste Teatro Comunale Giuseppe Verdi Orch, Trieste Teatro Comunale G. Verdi Chorus Melodram 2-▲ CDM 27006

Tagger, Nicola (sgr)
Rossini, G.:Zelmira, w. Virginia Zeani (sop), Anna Maria Rota (cta), Enrico Campi (bass), Guido Mazzini (bass), Paolo Washington (bass), Gastone Limarilli (sgr), Giuseppe Moretti (sgr), C. Franci (cnd), *(orch unknown)* Great Opera Performances 2-▲ GOP 780

Tagliabue, Carlo (bar)
Carlo Tagliabue, w. Margherita Carosio (sop), Ettore Bergamaschi (ten), Zinka Milanov (sop), Bruna Castagna (cta), Frederick Jagel (ten), Norman Cordon (bass), Renata Tebaldi (sop), Alfredo Colella (bass) *(rec in studio and live, 1928–1951)* Bongiovanni ▲ GB 1070-2 [ADD]
Carlo Tagliabue:Opera Arias Preiser ("Lebendige Vergangenheit" series) ▲ PRE 89015 (m) [AAD]
Flotow, F. von:Martha, w. E. Rizzieri (sop—Lady Enrichetta), P. Tassinari (sop—Nancy), F. Tagliavini (ten—Lionello), C. Tagliabue (bar—Plumkett), B. Carmassi (bass—Sir Tristano), F. Molinari-Pradelli (cnd), Turin RAI Orch, Turin RAI Chorus *(rec 1953; Italian libretto)* Cetra Classic 2-▲ CDO 7 [AAD]
Giordano, U.:Madame Sans-Gêne, w. Magda László (sop—Caterina), Carlo Tagliabue (bar—Napoleone), Renato Berti (sgr—Despréaux), Irene Callaway (sgr—Toniotta/Carolina), Danilo Cestari (sgr—Neipperg/Vinaigre), Maria Luisa Malacchi (sgr—Giulia/Principessa Elisa), Carlo Perucci (sgr—Fouché), Danilo Vega (sgr—Lefebvre), Enzo Viaro (sgr—De Brigode/Gelsomino), A. Basile (cnd), Milan RAI SO, Milan RAI Chorus *(rec Milan, Aug 10, 1957)* Bongiovanni 2-▲ GB 1129/30
Leoncavallo, R.:Pagliacci, w. C. Gavazzi (sop—Nedda), C. Bergonzi (ten—Canio), S. Di Tommaso (ten—Beppe), C. Tagliabue (bar—Tonio), M. Rossi (bar—Silvio), A. Simonetto (cnd), Turin RAI SO, Turin RAI Chorus *(rec Turin, 1951)* Cetra Classic 2-▲ CDO 27 [ADD]
Mascagni, P.:L'amico Fritz, w. R. Carteri (sop—Suzel), R. Corsi (mez—Beppe), C. Valletti (ten—Fritz), C. Tagliabue (bar—David), V. Gui (cnd), Milan RAI SO, Milan RAI Chorus *(rec live, Apr. 25, 1953)* Bongiovanni 2-▲ GB 1098/99 [ADD]

Tagliabue, Carlo (bar) (cont.)
Mascagni, P.:Cavalleria rusticana, w. G. Simionato (sop—Santuzza), F. Cadoni (mez—Lola), L. Pellegrino (cta—Lucia), A. Braschi (ten—Turiddu), C. Tagliabue (bar—Alfio), A. Basile (cnd), Italian Lyric Orch, Turin Cetra Chorus *(rec Turin, 1950)* Cetra Classic 2-▲ CDO 27 [ADD]
Verdi, G.:La forza del destino, w. Maria Caniglia (sop), Ebe Stignani (mez), Galliano Masini (ten), Tancredi Pasero (bass), G. Marinuzzi (cnd), EIAR Orch, EIAR Chorus *(rec 1941)* Grammofono 2000 ▲ GRM 78567 (m)
Verdi, G.:Rigoletto (sels), w. A. Pastori (sop), Antonioli (ten), U. Rapalo (cnd), Naples Teatro San Carlo Orch, Naples Teatro San Carlo Chorus [l] *(rec live, Naples, 1/20/56)* The Golden Age of Opera ▲ GAO 115 [ADD]
Verdi, G.:La traviata, w. Renata Tebaldi (sop—Violetta), Giacinto Prandelli (ten—Alfredo), Carlo Tagliabue (bar—Germont), T. Serafin (cnd), Naples Teatro San Carlo Orch, Naples Teatro San Carlo Chorus *(rec Arena Flegrea, Naples, July 3, 1954)* Golden Age of Opera 2-▲ GAO 191/192 [ADD]
Verdi, G.:Il trovatore, w. M. Callas (sop), E. Stignani (mez), G. Penno (ten), A. Votto (cnd), La Scala Orch, La Scala Chorus [l] *(rec live 2/23/53)* Myto 2-▲ 2 MCD 90213 (m) [ADD]
Verdi, G.:I vespri siciliani, w. A. Cerquetti (sop), Ortica (sgr), B. Christoff (bass), M. Rossi (cnd), Turin Radio Orch, Turin Radio Chorus [l] *(rec live, Turin, 11/16/55)* Claque 2-▲ CLQ 2017 (m)
Wagner, R.:Tannhäuser (sels), w. R. Tebaldi (sop), H. Beirer (ten), B. Christoff (bass), K. Böhm (cnd), Naples Teatro San Carlo Orch, Naples Teatro San Carlo Chorus—10 soprano solo, duet & ensemble arias Acts 2 & 3 [l; Hans Beirer (Tannhäuser) sings in German] *(rec live, Naples, 3/12/50)* Standing Room Only ▲ SRO 834-1 [ADD]
Zandonai, R.:Francesca da Rimini, w. M. Caniglia (sop—Francesca), A. M. Canali (mez—Altichiara), A. Bertocci (ten—Ser Toldo Berardengo), M. Carlin (ten—Malatestino), G. Prandelli (ten—Paolo), C. Tagliabue (bar—Giovanni), E. Campi (bass—Il Giuliare/Il Torrigiano), A. Guarnieri (cnd), Rome RAI SO, Rome RAI Chorus *(rec 1952)* Cetra Classic ▲ CDO 22 [ADD]

Tagliasacchi, M. (sop)
Donizetti, G.:La fille du régiment, w. L. Serra (sop), W. Matteuzzi (ten), E. Dara (bar), B. Campanella (cnd), Bologna Teatro Comunale Orch, Bologna Teatro Comunale Chorus [l] *(rec live, 2/16–26/89)* Nuova Era 2-▲ 6791/92 [DDD]

Tagliavini, Ferruccio (ten)
Bellini, V.:La sonnambula, w. L. Pagliughi (sop—Amina), W. Ruggeri (sop—Lisa), A. M. Anelli (mez—Teresa), F. Tagliavini (ten—Elvino), P. L. Latinucci (bass—Alessio), C. Siepi (bass—Conte Rodolfo), F. Capuana (cnd), Turin RSO, Turin Radio Chorus *(rec 1952)* Fonit Cetra ("Classic Collection" series) 2-▲ FCT CDO 16 [AAD]
Bellini, V.:La sonnambula (sels), w. P. Argento (cnd), Milan RAI SO—L'anel ti dono Fonit Cetra ("Martini & Rossi" series) ▲ FCT CDMR 5006
Bizet, G.:Carmen (sels), w. P. Argento (cnd), Milan RAI SO—Il Fior Che Avevi a Me Tu Dato Nella Prigion Io l'Ho Serbato Fonit Cetra ("Martini & Rossi" series) ▲ FCT CDMR 5006
Bizet, G.:Les Pêcheurs de perles, w. M. Pobbe (sop), U. Savarese (bar), C. Cava (bass), O. de Fabritiis (cnd), Naples Teatro San Carlo Orch, Naples Teatro San Carlo Chorus [l] *(rec live 1/4/59)* Melodram 2-▲ MEL 27069 (m) [AAD]
Boito, A.:Mefistofele, w. M. Pobbe (sop—Margherita), D. De Cecco (sop—Elena), E. Ticozzi (mez—Marta), F. Tagliavini (ten—Faust), G. Neri (bass—Mefistofele), A. Questa (cnd), Turin RSO, Turin Teatro Regio Chorus *(rec 1954)* Cetra Classic ▲ CDO 19
The Cetra Recordings, 1940–43 Enterprise ("Vocal Archives" series) ▲ ENT VA 1131
Cilea, F.:L'Arlesiana, w. L. di Lelio (sop), P. Tassinari (sop), G. Galli (bar), P. Silveri (bar), B. Carmassi (bass), A. Zerbini (bass), A. Basile (cnd), Turin RAI Orch, Turin RAI Chorus *(rec 1951)* Cetra Classics ▲ CDO 21 [AAD]
Donizetti, G.:L'elisir d'amore (sels), w. P. Argento (cnd), Milan RAI SO—Una Furtiva Lacrima Fonit Cetra ("Martini & Rossi" series) ▲ FCT CDMR 5006
Donizetti, G.:Lucia di Lammermoor, w. M. Callas (sop), P. Cappuccilli (bar), B. Ladysz (bass), T. Serafin (cnd), Philharmonia Orch [l] EMI Classics 2-▲ CDCB 47440
Donizetti, G.:Maria Stuarda, w. L. Gencer (sop), S. Verrett (mez), F. Molinari-Pradelli (cnd), Florence Maggio Musicale Orch, Florence Maggio Musicale Chorus *(rec 1967)* Memories 2-▲ MEM 4504 [AAD]
Donizetti, G.:Maria Stuarda (sels), w. L. Gencer (sop), S. Verrett (mez), F. Molinari-Pradelli (cnd), Florence Maggio Musicale Orch, Florence Maggio Musicale Chorus, 11 arias from Acts 2 & 3 [l] *(rec 5/2/67)* Myto 2-▲ 2 MCD 91137 [ADD]
The Early Operatic Recordings 1940–43, w. EIAR Orch [cnd:Ugo Tansini] Centaur ▲ CRC 2164
Flotow, F. von:Martha, w. E. Rizzieri (sop—Lady Enrichetta), P. Tassinari (sop—Nancy), F. Tagliavini (ten—Lionello), C. Tagliabue (bar—Plumkett), B. Carmassi (bass—Sir Tristano), F. Molinari-Pradelli (cnd), Turin RAI Orch, Turin RAI Chorus *(rec 1953; Italian libretto)* Cetra Classic 2-▲ CDO 7 [AAD]
Gertrud Grob-Prandl, Ferruccio Tagliavini, w. Gertrud Grob-Prandl (sop), Milan RAI SO [cnd:Oliviero de Fabritiis] *(rec Dec. 24, 1953)* Incontri Memorabili ("Martini & Rossi Concerts" series) ▲ 5004
Giordano, U.:Fedora, w. Pia Tassinari (sop), Meletti (sgr), Micheluzzi (sgr), Mascolo (sgr), Jolanda Torriani (sgr), O. Fabritiis (cnd), Milan RAI SO, Milan RAI Chorus *(rec live, July 10, 1954)* Arkadia 2-▲ 493
Live Recordings 1952–1959 Memories ("Great Voices" series) 2-▲ MEM 4444 [ADD]
Mascagni, P.:L'amico Fritz, w. P. Tassinari (sop—Suzel), A. Pini (mez—Beppe), F. Tagliavini (ten—Fritz), A. Giannotti (ten—Frederico), S. Meletti (bar—David), P. L. Latinucci (bass—Hanezò), P. Mascagni (cnd), Turin RSO, Turin Radio Chorus *(rec 1941)* Cetra Classic 2-▲ CDO 18
Massenet, J.:Manon, w. V. De los Angeles (sop), A. Poli (bar), N. Annovazzi (cnd), Rome Opera Orch, Rome Opera Chorus *(rec live 1957)* Melodram 2-▲ MEL 27082
Massenet, J.:Manon (sels), w. P. Argento (cnd), Milan RAI SO—En fermant les yeux, je vois Fonit Cetra ("Martini & Rossi" series) ▲ FCT CDMR 5006
Recital, 1941–1950 Myto ▲ MCD 933.82
Massenet, J.:Werther, w. L. Gencer (sop—Carlotta), G. Tavolaccini (sop—Sofia), F. Tagliavini (ten—Werther), M. Borriello (bar—Alberto), E. Mocchiutti (bar—Johann), V. Susca (bass—Il Podestà), R. Botteghelli (bass—Schmidt), C.F. Cillario (cnd), *(orch unknown)* Arkadia 2-▲ 599 [ADD]
Massenet, J.:Werther, w. D. Gatta (sop—Sofia), I. Ligabue (sop—Kaethlen), G. Simionato (mez—Charlotte), F. Tagliavini (ten—Werther), V. Pandano (ten—Schmidt), E. Campi (bass—Johann), S. Bruscantini (bass—Le Bailli), F. Capuana (cnd), La Scala Orch, La Scala Chorus *(rec Apr. 21, 1951)* Bongiovanni 2-▲ GB 1101/02 [ADD]
Massenet, J.:Werther, w. L. Gencer (sop), F. Tagliavini (ten)., C.F. Cillario (cnd), Trieste Teatro Comunale Giuseppe Verdi Orch *(rec 1959)* Memories 2-▲ MEM 4554 [ADD]
Massenet, J.:Werther, w. M. Cortis (bar), P.L. Latinucci (bass), F. Molinari-Pradelli (cnd), Turin RAI SO *(rec 1953)* Cetra Classic 2-▲ CDO 15 [AAD]
Mozart, W.A.:Requiem, w. P. Tassinari (sop), E. Stignani (mez), I. Tajo (bass), V. de Sabata (cnd), RAI Orch, *(unknown RAI Chorus)* *(rec Apr. 1939)* Cetra Classic ▲ CDO 1 [AAD]
Puccini, G.:Madama Butterfly, w. C. Petrella (sop—Madama Butterfly), M. Masini (mez—Suzuki), M. C. Foscale (sgr—Kate Pinkerton), F. Tagliavini (ten—Pinkerton), M. Caruso (ten—Goro), G. Taddei (bar—Sharpless), A. Albertini (bar—Yamadori), A. Biancardo (bass—Bonze), A. Questa (cnd), Turin RAI Orch, Cetra Chorus *(rec 1953)* Cetra Classic 2-▲ CDO 10 [AAD]
Puccini, G.:Tosca, w. B. Nilsson (sop), R. Vinay (ten), C. Maresco (cnd), Philadelphia Opera Orch, Philadelphia Opera Chorus *(rec Apr. 10, 1963)* Melodram 2-▲ MLO 270112 [ADD]
Puccini, G.:Tosca, w. R. Tebaldi (sop), T. Gobbi (bar), F. Molinari-Pradelli (cnd), Royal Opera House Orch, Royal Opera House Chorus Covent Garden [l] *(rec live at Covent Garden, 6/30/55)* Legato Classics 2-▲ LCD 157-2 (m) [ADD]
Spontini, G.:Olympia, w. J. Varady (sop), S. Toczyska (mez), D. Fischer-Dieskau (bar), G. Fortune (bass), J. Becker (bass), G. Albrecht (cnd), Berlin RSO, Berlin Radio Chorus [Paris version] Orfeo 2-▲ 137862 [DDD]
Spontini, G.:La vestale, w. R. Scotto (sop), O. Dominguez (mez), M. Picchi (ten), V. Gui (cnd), Florence Maggio Musicale Orch, Florence Maggio Musicale Chorus [l] *(rec live 5/5/70)* Melodram ("Connaisseur" series) 2-▲ CDM 27512 [ADD]
Verdi, G.:Un ballo in maschera, w. M. Curtis Verna (sop—Amelia), M. Erato (sop—Oscar), P. Tassinari (cta—Ulrica), F. Tagliavini (ten—Riccardo), G. Valdengo (bar—Renato), A. Albertini (bar—Silvano), M. Stefanoni (bass—Samuel), V. Susca (bass—Tom), A. Questa (cnd), Turin RAI SO, Turin RAI Chorus *(rec 1954)* Cetra Classic 2-▲ CDO 13 [AAD]

Tagliavini, Ferruccio (ten) (cont.)
Verdi, G.:Rigoletto, w. L. Pagluighi (sop—Gilda), I. Colasanti (mez—Maddalena), F. Tagliavini (ten—Duca), A. Albertini (bar—Il Cavaliere Marullo), G. Taddei (bar—Rigoletto), G. Neri (bass—Sparafucile), A. Zerbini (bass—Conte di Monterone), A. Questa (cnd), Turin RSO, Turin Radio Chorus *(rec 1953)* Cetra Classics 2-▲ CDO 11 [AAD]

Tagliavini, Franco (ten)
Berlioz, H.:Te Deum, w. C. Davis (cnd), London SO, London Sym Chorus, Wandsworth School Boys' Chorus [L] Philips ▲ 416660-2 [ADD]
Franco Tagliavini:Recital Myto ▲ 952126

Taha, Claudia (sop)
Kinkel, J.:Songs, w. Heidi Kommerell (pno)—Wunsch, Op. 7/2; An den Mond, Op. 7/5; Die Zigeuner, Op. 7/6; Verlornes Glück, Op. 6/3; Vorüberfahrt, Op. 7/3; Nachtlied, Op. 7/6 Bayer ▲ 100248 [DDD]
Lang, J.:Songs, w. Heidi Kommerell (pno)—14 sels including Erinnerung; Den Abschied schnell genommen, Op. 15/1; An de See, Op. 14/4; Am Flusse, Op. 14/2; Frühzeitiger Frühling, Op. 6/3; In weite Ferne, Op. 15/3; Auf dem See in tausend Sterne, Op. 14/6 Bayer ▲ 100248 [DDD]
Spohr, L.:Faust, w. M. Vier (b-bar), E. von Jordis (bass), G. Moull (cnd), Bielefeld PO, Bielefeld Opera Chorus [1852 version] *(rec live, June 1993)* CPO 2-▲ CPO 999247 [DDD]

Tahal, Monika (sgr)
Waits, T.:The Black Rider:The Casting of Magic Bullets, w. Angelika Thomas (sgr—Anne), Annette Paulmann (sgr—Kätchen), Sona Cervena (sgr—Bird/Messenger/Spoonwoman), Monika Tahal (sgr—Witness/Bird/Shrink/Wilhelm's Double/Skeleton), Susi Eisenkolb (sgr—Bridesmaid/Pegleg's Double), Heinz Vossbrink (sgr—Kuno), Dominique Horwitz (sgr—Pegleg), Gerd Kunath (sgr—Bertram), Stefan Kurt (sgr—Wilhelm), Klaus Schreiber (sgr—Robert/Man on Stag/Georg Schmid), Jörg Holm (Old Uncle/Duke), Jan Moritz Steffen (sgr—Young Kuno/Bird/Shrink/Skeleton), Tom Waits (vocals/coliope/organ/chamberlain/mar/emax/guitar/train whistle), Ralph Carney (saxophone/bass clarinet/baritone horn), Bill Douglas (bass instrument), Kenny Wollesen (perc) Island ▲ 314518559-2

Taillon, Jocelyne (mez)
Auber, D.-F.:Le Domino noir, w. Sumi Jo (sop), Doris Lamprecht (sop), Martine Olmeda (sop), Isabelle Vernet (sop), Bruce Ford (ten), Patrick Power (ten), Gilles Cachemaille (bar), Jules Bastin (bass), R. Bonynge (cnd), English CO, London Voices London 2-▲ 440646-2
Enescu, G.:Oedipe, w. B. Hendricks (sop), B. Fassbaender (mez), M. Lipovšek (mez), N. Gedda (ten), J. Aler (ten), G. Bacquier (bar), Quilico (bar), J. Van Dam (bass-bar), L. Foster (cnd), Monte Carlo PO, Orféon Donostiarra, Petits Chanteurs de Monaco [F] EMI Classics 2-▲ CDCB 54011 [DDD]
Offenbach, J.:Les Contes d'Hoffmann, w. L. Serra (sop), R. Plowright (sop), J. Norman (sop), A. Murray (mez), J. Taillon (mez), N. Shicoff (ten), A. Oliver (ten), R. Tear (ten), J. Van Dam (b-bar), D. Duesing (bar), K. Rydl (bass), S. Cambreling (cnd), Brussels Théâtre de la Monnaie Orch [F] EMI Classics 3-▲ CDCC 49641 [DDD]
Ravel, M.:L'Enfant et les sortilèges, w. Arleen Augér (sop), Marilyn Richardson (sop), Jane Berbié (mez), Linda Finnie (mez), Davenny Wyner (mez), Philip Langridge (ten), Philippe Huttenlocher (bar), Jules Bastin (bass), A. Previn (cnd), London SO, Ambrosian Opera Chorus Classics for Pleasure ("Eminence" series) ▲ CFP 2241

Taino, Franco (bass)
Strauss, R.:Der Rosenkavalier, w. Jarmila Barton (sop—Marianne), Lisa Della Casa (sop—Sophie), Sena Jurinac (sop—Octavian), Ilva Ligabue (sop—Orphan), Elisabeth Schwarzkopf (sop—Marschallin), Else Schürhoff (mez—Annina), Luisa Villa (mez—Milliner), Hugues Cuénod (ten—Marschallin's majordomo), Erich Majkut (ten—Valzacchi), Giuseppe Nessi (ten—Animal seller), Luciano Della Pergola (ten—Lackey/Faninal's majordomo), Antonio Pirino (ten—An Italian Singer), Gino Del Signore (ten—Lackey/Waiter), Erich Kunz (bar—Herr von Faninal), Paolo Pedani (bar—Lackey), Attilo Barbesi (bass—Lackey/Waiter), Enrico Campi (bass—Waiter), Otto Edelmann (bass—Baron Ochs), Bruno Fichtinger (bass—Notary), Franco Taino (bass—Waiter), Maria Amadini (sgr—Orphan), Pina Carrillo (sgr—Orphan), Joszi Trojan Regar (sgr—Innkeeper), H. von Karajan (cnd), La Scala Orch, La Scala Chorus *(rec La Scala Theater, Milan, Jan. 26, 1952)* Legato Classics 3-▲ LCD 197-3

Tajo, Italo (bass)
Giordano, U.:Andrea Chénier, w. Maria Caniglia (sop—Maddalena), Maria Huder (mez—Bersi), Vittoria Palombini (mez—Madelon), Giulietta Simionato (mez—Contessa), Beniamino Gigli (ten—Andrea), Adelio Zagonara (ten—Incroyable/Abbé), Gino Bechi (bar—Carlo), Leone Paci (bar—Mathieu), Giuseppe Taddei (b-bar—Pietro/Fouquier), Italo Tajo (b-bar—Roucher), Gino Conti (bass—Master/Schmidt), O. de Fabritiis (cnd), La Scala Orch, La Scala Chorus *(rec Nov 1941)* Arkadia ("The 78's" series) 2-▲ 78012 [ADD]
Giordano, U.:Andrea Chénier, w. M. Caniglia (sop), G. Simionato (mez), B. Gigli (ten), G. Bechi (bar), G. Taddei (bar), O. de Fabritiis (cnd), La Scala Orch, La Scala Chorus [l] *(rec 1941, HMV DB 5423/35)* Angel ("Studio" series) 2-▲ CDHB 69996 (m) [ADD]
Gounod, C.:Faust (sels), w. R. Tebaldi (sop), F. Cadoni (mez), M. Filippeschi (ten), R. Panerai (bar), F. Patanè (cnd), Naples Teatro San Carlo Orch, Naples Teatro San Carlo Chorus—Act IV, Scenes 1 & 2 & Act V, Scene 2 *(rec live, 4/26/51)* Standing Room Only 2-▲ SRO 810-2 [ADD]
Mozart, W.A.:Nozze di Figaro, w. G. Gatti (sop), A. Noni (sop), G. Sciurri (sop), J. Gardino (mez), M.T. Pace (mez), A. Mercuriali (ten), S. Bruscantini (bar), F. Corena (bass), F. Previtali (cnd), Rome RAI Orch [l] *(rec 1951)* Cetra Classic 2-▲ CDO 12
Mozart, W.A.:Requiem, w. P. Tassinari (sop), E. Stignani (mez), F. Tagliavini (ten), V. de Sabata (cnd), RAI Orch, *(unknown RAI Chorus)* *(rec Apr. 1939)* Cetra Classic ▲ CDO 1 [AAD]
Puccini, G.:Manon Lescaut, w. K. Te Kanawa (sop), J. Carreras (ten), P. Coni (bar), R. Chailly (cnd), Bologna Teatro Comunale Orch [l] London 2-▲ 421426-2 [DDD]
Rossini, G.:L'occassione fa il ladro, w. C. Fusco (sop), M. T. Pace (mez), G. Sinimberghi (ten), R. Gonzales (sgr), L. Colonna (cnd), Naples Alessandro Scarlatti RAI Orch [l] *(rec live, Naples, Sept. 29, 1963)* Arkadia ▲ 602 [ADD]
Verdi, G.:Macbeth, w. M. Callas (sop), G. Penno (ten), E. Mascherini (bar), V. de Sabata (cnd), *(orch unknown)* *(rec Milan, 1952)* Great Opera Performances 2-▲ GOP 750

Takács (alt)
Sammartini, G.B.:Magnificat in B♭, w. Szűcs (sop), Gulyás (ten), Bátor (bass), F. Szekeres (cnd), Budapest Strings, Budapest Madrigal Choir [L] Hungaroton ▲ HCD 31259 [DDD]

Takács (sgr)
Kodály, Z.:Háry János, w. S. Sólyom-Nagy (bar), J. Gregor (bass), J. Ferencsik (cnd), Hungarian State Opera Orch [Hun] Hungaroton 2-▲ HCD 12837/38

Takács, Judit (sgr)
Make Wonder:Songs from Operettas, w. Magda Kalmár (sop), Éva Köteles (sgr), Bori Szita (sgr), Budapest SO [cnd:Tamás Bródy], Hungarian State Orch [cnd:András Sebestyén] Hungaroton ▲ HCD 16613 [AAD]

Takács, Klára (cta)
Caldara, A.:Magnificat, w. M. Szűcs (sop), D. Gulyás (ten), T. Bátor (bass), F. Szekeres (cnd), Budapest Strings, Budapest Madrigal Choir [L] Hungaroton ▲ HCD 31259 [DDD]
Mahler, G.:Das Klagende Lied, w. Katalin Szendrényi (sop), Dénes Gulyás (ten), A. Ligeti (cnd), Budapest SO, Péter Erdei (cnd), Hungarian Radio-TV Chorus Classical Diamonds ▲ CLD 4010 [DDD]

Takács, Paula (sop)
Verdi, G.:Aida (sels), w. Alexander Svéd (bar), F. Molinari-Pradelli (cnd), Hungarian State Opera Orch—Ciel! Mio padre *(rec Mar 24, 1956)* Hungaroton ("Great Hungarian Voices" series) ▲ HCD 31614 [ADD]

Takács, Tamara (mez)
Brahms, J.:Ernste Gesänge, w. J. Jandó (pno) [G] *(rec 1989)* Naxos ▲ 8.550400 [DDD]
Cherubini, L.:Médée, w. M. Kalmar (sop), S. Sass (sop), V. Luchetti (ten), K. Kovats (bass), L. Gardelli (cnd), Budapest SO, Hungarian Radio Chorus [l] Hungaroton 2-▲ HCD 11904/05
Liszt, F.:Christus, w. Veronika Kincses (sop), Robert Nagy (ten), Sándor Sólyom-Nagy (bar), László Polgár (bass), A. Dorati (cnd), Hungarian State Orch, Hungarian Radio-TV Chorus [L] Hungaroton 3-▲ HCD 12831/33 [DDD]
Liszt, F.:Hungarian Coronation Mass, w. V. Kincses (sop), D. Gulyas (ten), L. Polgar (bass), G. Lehel (cnd), Budapest SO, Hungarian Radio Chorus [L] Hungaroton ▲ HCD 12148
Liszt, F.:Missa solemnis, w. V. Kincses (mez), G. Korondy (ten), J. Gregor (bass), A. Ferencsik (cnd), Budapest SO, Budapest Sym Chorus [L] Hungaroton ▲ HCD 11861

▲ = CD ♦ = Enhanced CD Δ = MD ■ = Cassette Tape □ = DCC

Takács, Tamara (mez) (cont.)

Liszt, F.:Septam sacramenta, w. J. Bándi (ten), G. Kallay (ten), K. Kaváts (bar), Zsuzsa Elekes (org), I. Zámbó (cnd), Hungarian State Orch, Hungarian People's Army Male Chorus, Jeunesses Musicales Women's Chorus [L] Hungaroton ▲ HCD 12748 [DDD]

Mahler, G.:Sym 8, w. Lyudmila Hadzhieva (sop), Maria Temeshi (sop), Darina Takova (sop), Boryana Tabakova (alt), Janos Bandi (ten), Pal Kovacs (bar), Tamash Syule (bass), E. Tabakov (cnd), Sofia PO, Bulgarian National Chorus, Bulgarian National Radio Chorus, Bulgarian National Radio Children's Choir *(rec National Palace of Culture, Sofia, June 1991)* Capriccio 15–▲ 49043 [DDD]

Puccini, G.:Madama Butterfly, w. V. Kincses (sop), P. Dvorsky (ten), L. Miller (bar), G. Patanè (cnd), Hungarian State Opera Orch, Hungarian State Opera Chorus [I] Hungaroton 2–▲ HCD 12256/57

Respighi, O.:Belfagor, w. S. Sass (sop), G. Lamberti (ten), L. Miller (bar), L. Polgár (bass), L. Gardelli (cnd), Hungarian State Orch, Hungarian State Chorus [I] Hungaroton 2–▲ HCD 12850/51 [DDD]

Respighi, O.:La Fiamma, w. I. Tokody (sop), P. Kelen (ten), S. Sólyom-Nagy (bar), L. Gardelli (cnd), Hungarian State Orch, Hungarian State Chorus [I] Hungaroton 3–▲ HCD 12591/93 [DDD]

Schubert, Franz:Songs (misc), w. J. Jandó (gtr)—An die Musik; Heidenröslein; Die Forelle; Auf dem Wasser zu singen; Du bist die Ruh; Im Frühling; Wandrers; Nach und Träume; Der Zwerg; Gretchen am Spinnrade; Die junge Nonne; Lied der Mignon I; Lied der Mignon II; Lied der Mignon III; Suleikas Gesang I; Suleikas Gesang II; Der tod und das Mädchen; Erikönig [G] *(rec Oct. 8–11, 1991)* Naxos ▲ 8.550476 [DDD]

Schumann, R.:Frauenliebe und -leben, w. J. Jandó (pno) [G] *(rec 1989)* Naxos ▲ 8.550400 [DDD]

Vivaldi, A.:Cants, w. F. Szekeres (cnd), Hungarian State Orch—RV. 684, "Cessate omai cessate" [I] Hungaroton ▲ HCD 12087

Vivaldi, A.:Magnificat, RV.610, w. D. Gulyás (ten), T. Bátor (bass), R. Szücs (bass), F. Szekeres (cnd), Budapest Strings, Budapest Madrigal Choir [L] Hungaroton ▲ HCD 31259 [DDD]

Vivaldi, A.:Magnificat, RV.611, w. J. Németh (mez), Bátori (sgr), Kovács (sgr), Szőkefalvi-Nagy (sgr), F. Szekeres (cnd), Budapest Strings, Budapest Madrigal Choir [L] Hungaroton ▲ HCD 31259 [DDD]

Vivaldi, A.:L'Olimpiade (sels), w. M. Zempléni (sop), Horváth (sgr), Káplán (sgr), L. Miller (bar), I. Gáti (bar), K. Kováts (bass), F. Szekeres (cnd), Hungarian State Orch, Budapest Madrigal Choir [I] White Label ▲ HRC 073 [ADD]

Wagner, R.:Wesendonck Songs, w. J. Jandó (pno) [G] *(rec 1989)* Naxos ▲ 8.550400 [DDD]

Takemoto, Setsuko (mez)

Mahler, G.:Sym 2, w. Junko Ioka (sop), T. Asahina (cnd), Osaka PO, Hakaru Matsuoka (cnd), Yutaka Tomizawa (cnd), Musashino Chorus *(rec Suntory Hall, Tokyo, July 23, 1995)* Canyon Classics 2–▲ 335

Takova, Darina (sop)

Mahler, G.:Sym 8, w. Lyudmila Hadzhieva (sop), Maria Temeshi (sop), Tamara Takac (alt), Boryana Tabakova (alt), Janos Bandi (ten), Pal Kovacs (bar), Tamash Syule (bass), E. Tabakov (cnd), Sofia PO, Bulgarian National Chorus, Bulgarian National Radio Chorus, Bulgarian National Radio Children's Choir *(rec National Palace of Culture, Sofia, June 1991)* Capriccio 15–▲ 49043 [DDD]

Talarico, Gianfranco (ten)

Catalani, A.:Loreley, w. E. Suliotis (sop), P. Cappuccilli (bar), G. Gavazzeni (cnd), La Scala Orch, La Scala Chorus *(rec 1968)* Memories 2–▲ MEM 4511 [ADD]

Talvela, Martti (bass)

Beethoven, L. van:Missa Solemnis, w. E. Söderström (sop), M. Höffgen (cta), W. Kmentt (ten), O. Klemperer (cnd), New Philharmonia Orch, New Philharmonia Chorus [L] EMI Classics ("Studio" series) 2–▲ CDMB 69538 [ADD]

Beethoven, L. van:Missa Solemnis, w. Margaret Price (sop), Christa Ludwig (mez), Wieslaw Ochman (ten), K. Böhm (cnd), Vienna PO, Vienna State Opera Chorus *(rec 1957)* Deutsche Grammophon ("Double" series) 2–▲ 437386–2 [ADD]

Kilpinen, Y.:Songs, w. I. Gage (pno)—kirkkorannassa, Op. 54/2; Kesäyö, Op. 23/3; Laululle, Op. 52/3; Tunturille, Op. 52/4; Vanha Kirkko, Op. 54/1; Suvilaulu, Op. 54/3; Jänkä, Op. 52/1; Rannalta, Op. 23/1 Finlandia ▲ 4509–95846–2 [ADD]

Kokkonen, J.:The Last Temptations, w. Ritva Auvinen (sop), U. Söderblom (cnd), Savonlinna Opera Festival Orch, Savonlinna Opera Festival Chorus Finlandia 2–▲ FIN 104 [AAD]

Mahler, G.:Sym 8, w. A. Augér (sop), H. Harper (sop), L. Popp (sop), Y. Minton (mez), H. Watts (cta), A. Kollo (ten), J. Shirley-Quirk (bar), G. Solti (cnd), Chicago SO, Vienna State Opera Chorus, Vienna Boys' Choir, Vienna Singverein [G,L] London 2–▲ 414493–2 [ADD]

Mozart, W.A.:Arias, w. I. Cotrubas (sop), E. Gruberova (sop), L. Price (sop), J. Varady (sop), L. Popp (mez), F. Araiza (ten), P. Domingo (ten), P. de Palma (ten), P. Schreier (ten), F. Wunderlich (ten), S. Milnes (bar), A. Titus (bar)—sels. from Entführung aus dem Serail, Così fan tutte, Don Giovanni, Idomeneo, Die Zauberflöte, Le nozze di Figaro Eurodisc ▲ 69256–2–RG [ADD]

Mozart, W.A.:Don Giovanni (sels), w. R. Grist (sop), B. Nilsson (sop), M. Arroyo (sop), P. Schreier (ten), D. Fischer-Dieskau (bar), K. Böhm (cnd), Prague National Theater Orch IMP Collectors Series ▲ IMPX 9023 [AAD]

Mozart, W.A.:Entführung, w. E. Gruberova (sop), K. Battle (sop), G. Winbergh (ten), H. Zednik (ten), Will Quadflieg (nar), G. Solti (cnd), Vienna PO [G] London 2–▲ 417402–2 [DDD]

Mozart, W.A.:Zauberflöte, w. P. Lorengar (sop), C. Deutekom (sop), S. Burrows (ten), H. Prey (bar), D. Fischer-Dieskau (bar), G. Solti (cnd), Vienna PO [G] London 3–▲ 414568–2

Mozart, W.A.:Zauberflöte (sels), w. Pilar Lorengar (sop), Cristina Deutekom (sop), Stuart Burrows (ten), Hermann Prey (bar), G. Solti (cnd), Vienna PO London ▲ 421302–2 [ADD]

Mussorgsky, M.:Boris Godunov, w. N. Gedda (ten—Dmitri), M. Talvela (bass—Boris), J. Semkow (cnd), Cracow RSO, Cracow Radio Chorus EMI Classics ▲ CDCC 54377

Mussorgsky, M.:Songs & Dances, w. R. Gothóni (pno) Finlandia ▲ 4509–95846–2 [ADD]

Mussorgsky, M.:Songs & Dances, w. N. Järvi (cnd), Finnish RSO [orch. arr. by Aho] BIS ▲ CD 325

Rachmaninoff, S.:Songs, w. R. Gothóni (pno)—A Dream, Op. 8/5; The harvest of Sorrow, Op. 4/5; Night Is Mournful, Op. 26/12; Oh, Never Sing to Me Again, Op. 4/4; Christ Is Risen, Op. 26/6 Finlandia ▲ 4509–95846–2 [ADD]

Schubert, Franz:Winterreise, w. R. Gothóni (pno) [G] BIS ▲ CD 253 [DDD]

Verdi, G.:Don Carlos, w. Gundula Janowitz (sop), Shirley Verrett (mez), Franco Corelli (ten), Eberhard Waechter (bar), Nicolai Ghiaurov (bass), H. Stein (cnd), Vienna PO, Vienna State Opera Chorus *(rec Vienna, Oct. 25, 1970)* Pantheon 2–▲ PHE 6614

Verdi, G.:Requiem Mass, w. J. Sutherland (sop), M. Horne (mez), L. Pavarotti (ten), G. Solti (cnd), Vienna PO, Vienna State Opera Chorus [L] London 2–▲ 411944–2 [ADD]

Verdi, G.:Rigoletto, w. J. Sutherland (sop), H. Tourangeau (mez), L. Pavarotti (ten), S. Milnes (bar), R. Bonynge (cnd), London SO, London Sym Chorus [I] London 2–▲ 414269–2 [ADD]

Wagner, R.:Der fliegende Holländer, w. A. Silja (sop), E. Kozub (ten), T. Adam (b-bar), O. Klemperer (cnd), New Philharmonia Orch, BBC Sym Chorus [G] EMI Classics ("Studio" series) 3–▲ CDMC 63344 [ADD]

Wagner, R.:Der fliegende Holländer, w. Anja Silja (sop—Senta), Anneliese Burmeister (mez—Mary), Ernst Kozub (ten—Erik), Gerhard Unger (ten—Steersman), Theo Adam (bass—Dutchman), Martti Talvela (bass—Daland), O. Klemperer (cnd), New Philharmonia Orch, BBC Sym Chorus EMI Classics 3–▲ CDCC 55179

Wagner, R.:Der fliegende Holländer, w. Martin (sop), A. Kollo (ten), N. Bailey (bar), G. Solti (cnd), Chicago SO, Chicago Sym Chorus [G] London 2–▲ 414551–2 [ADD]

Wagner, R.:Tannhäuser, w. S. Jurinac (sop), B. Martin (sop), H. Beirer (ten), H. Braun (bar), W. Sawallisch (cnd), La Scala Orch, La Scala Chorus [G] *(rec live, Milan 4/13/67)* Melodram 3–▲ CDM 37091 [ADD]

Wagner, R.:Tristan und Isolde, w. B. Nilsson (sop), C. Ludwig (mez), W. Windgassen (ten), E. Wächter (bar), K. Böhm (cnd), Bayreuth Festival Orch, Bayreuth Festival Chorus [G] *(rec Bayreuth Festival, 1966)* Deutsche Grammophon 3–▲ 419889–2 [ADD]

Wagner, R.:Tristan und Isolde, w. B. Nilsson (sop), C. Ludwig (mez), W. Windgassen (ten), E. Wächter (bar), K. Böhm (cnd), Bayreuth Festival Orch, Bayreuth Festival Chorus [G] Philips 3–▲ 434425–2 [ADD]

Wagner, R.:Die Walküre (act 1), w. E. Martón (sop), L. Hofmann (bass), Z. Mehta (cnd), New York PO [G] CBS ▲ MK 39745 [DDD]

Tamagno, Francesco (ten)

The Complete Recordings (1903–04), w. pno accompaniment Opal ▲ CD 9846 (m) [AAD]

Francesco Tamagno, w. *(rec 1903–04)* Symposium 2–▲ SYM 1186/87

Tamagno, Francesco (ten) (cont.)

Verdi, G.:Otello (sels), w. C. Muzio (sop), R. Ponselle (sop), H. Spani (sop), E. Caruso (ten), N. Fusati (ten), L. Melchior (ten), F. Merli (ten), B. Franci (bar), V. Maurel (bar), R. Stracciari (bar), T. Ruffo (bar) *(rec 1906–1933)* Music Memoria ▲ 30219

Verdi, G.:Il trovatore (sels), w. J. Biel (ten), L.-A. Escalaïs (ten), M. Gilion (ten), E. Caruso (ten), A. Paoli (ten), G. Zenatello (ten), J. Sembach (ten), L. Slezak (ten), F. Constantino (ten), G. Martinelli (ten), B. De Muro (ten), N. Fusati (ten), N. Piccaluga (ten), G. Lauri-Volpi (ten), A. Pertile (ten), E. Bergamaschi (ten), R. Tauber (ten), J. O'Sullivan (ten), H. Roswaenge (ten), G. Taccani (ten), V. Lois (ten), H. Lazaro (ten), A. Lindi (ten), A. Cortis (ten), F. Merli (ten), F. Völker (ten), J. Kiepura (ten), J. Schmidt (ten), J. Bjoerling (ten), B. Gigli (ten), A. Salvarezza (ten), J. Soler (ten), M. Filippeschi (ten)—34 performances of the Act III tenor aria "Di quella pira!," *(rec from 1903–1956)* Bongiovanni ▲ GB 1051 [AAD]

The World of Singing, Vol. 3:The Italian School, Part 1:The Italian Tenors Before World War I (1902–13), w. Antonio Aramburo (ten), Alessandro Bonci (ten), Giuseppe Borgatti (ten), Enrico Caruso (ten), Edoardo Garbin (ten), Fiorello Giraud (ten), Fernando de Lucia (ten), Francesco Marconi (ten), Giovanni Battista de Negri (ten), Antonio Paoli (ten), et. al. Enterprise ("Vocal Archives" series) 3–▲ ENT VA 2104

Tamar, Jano (sop)

Cherubini, L.:Médée, w. Patrizia Ciofi (sgr), Luca Lombardo (sgr), Magali Damonte (sgr), Jean-Philippe Courtis (bass), P. Fournillier (cnd), Italian International Opera Orch, Sluk Chamber Chorus Bratislava *(rec Martina Franca Festival, 1995)* Nuova Era 2–▲ NUO 7253

Tammen, Bruce (bass)

Ravel, M.:Chansons, w. Mara Bonde (sop), Nannette Soles (mez), Charles Bruffy (ten), Robert Shaw (cnd), Robert Shaw Festival Singers *(rec Church of St. Pierre, Gramat, France, July 26–28, 1994)* Telarc ▲ CD 80408 [DDD]

Tanaka, Shoko (nar)

Lieber, E.:Tomb of Hasegawa, w. Edvard Lieber (pno) Concord Concerto ▲ CCD 42027 [ADD]

Tandura, Elisabetta (mez)

Donizetti, G.:Il furioso all'isola di Santo Domingo, w. P. Antonucci (sop), L. Serra (sop), L. Canonici (ten), R. Coviello (bar), Picconi (sgr), C. Rizzi (cnd), Piacenza SO, Piacenza Chorus [I] *(rec live, 11/10/87)* Bongiovanni 3–▲ GB 2056/58 [DDD]

Tappy, Eric (ten)

Handel, G.F.:Rodelinda, Regina de' Longobardi, w. Joan Sutherland (sop—Rodelinda), Margaretha Elkins (mez—Bertarido's sister), Huguette Tourangeau (mez—Bertarido), Cora Canne-Meijer (alt—Unulfo), Eric Tappy (ten—Grimoaldo), Pieter van der Berg (bass—Garibaldo), R. Bonynge (cnd), Netherlands CO *(rec Amsterdam, June 30, 1973)* Bella Voce 2–▲ BLV 107.206 [AAD]

Martin, F.:Le Mystère de la Nativité, w. Elly Ameling (sop), Aafje Heynis (cta), Hugues Cuénod (ten), Louis Devos (ten), Pierre Bollet (bar), Derrik Olsen (bar), Charles Clavensy (b-bar), André Vessières (bass), E. Ansermet (cnd), Swiss Romande Orch, Jeunes de l'Eglise Chorus, Ceneva Motet Chorus Cascavelle 2–▲ CVL 2006 [ADD]

Martin, F.:Pilate, w. Ariette Chedel (cta), Eugenia Zareska (mez), Derrik Olsen (bar), Jean-Christoph Benoit (bar), E. Ansermet (cnd), Swiss Romande Orch, Lausanne Pro Arte Choir Cascavelle 2–▲ CVL 2006 [ADD]

Martin, F.:Requiem, w. E. Speiser (sop), R. Bollen (cta), P. Lagger (bass), A. Luy (org), F. Martin (cnd), Swiss-Italian Orch, Union Chorale, Choir of Our Lady of Lausanne, Ars Laeta Vocal Group *(rec live, May 4, 1973)* Jecklin-Disco ▲ JD 631–2 [ADD]

Monteverdi, C.:Madrigals, w. Basia Retchitzka (sop), Rodolfo Malacarne (ten), Laerte Malaguti (bar), James Loomis (bass), E. Loehrer (cnd), Lugano Chamber Society Orch, Lugano Chamber Society Chorus—8 Madrigali Guerrieri e Amorosi Accord ▲ ACD 220872

Regamey, C.:Alpha, w. A. Jordan (cnd), Swiss-Italian Orch [F] Grammont ▲ CTSP 5–2 [ADD]

Taraschenko, Vitaly (ten)

Rachmaninoff, S.:Francesca da Rimini, w. N. Vasiliev (bar), V. Matorin (bass), A. Tchistiakov (cnd), Bolshoi Theater SO Soloists Russian Season ("Russian Season" series) ▲ LDC 288081

Tarassova, Marianna (mez)

Rimsky-Korsakov, N.:Songs, w. Anna Kovaleva (sop), Konstantine Pluzhnikov (ten), Andrey Stavny (bar), Nikolai Okhotnikov (bass), Yury Serov (pno)—4 Romances, Op. 2; 4 Romances, Op. 3; 4 Romances, Op. 4; 4 Romances, Op. 7; 6 Romances, Op. 8; 2 Romances, Op. 25; 4 Romances, Op. 26; 4 Romances, Op. 27 *(rec St. Catherine's Lutheran Church, St. Petersburg, Sept–Dec 1993)* Russian Compact Disc ▲ RDCD 10051 [DDD]

Tarastchenko, Vitaly (ten)

Rachmaninoff, S.:Aleko, w. Natalia Erassova (sop), Galina Borissova (cta), Vladimir Matorin (bass), Viatcheslav Potchapski (bass), A. Tchistiakov (cnd), Bolshoi Theater Orch, Russian State Choir Russian Season 3–▲ CMX 388053

Rachmaninoff, S.:Francesca da Rimini, w. Maria Lapina (sop), Nikolaï Vassiliev (ten), Nikolaï Mechetniak (bar), Vladimir Matorin (bass), A. Tchistiakov (cnd), Bolshoi Theater Orch, Russian State Choir Russian Season 3–▲ CMX 388053

Rimsky-Korsakov, N.:A May Night, w. Maria Lapina (sop), Natalia Erassova (mez), Elena Okolycheva (cta), Alexander Arkhipov (ten), Piotr Glouboky (bass), Viatcheslav Potchapski (bass), A. Tchistiakov (cnd), Bolshoi Theater Orch, Russian State Choir Russian Season 4–▲ CMX 388054

Tarrès, Enriqueta (sop)

Meyerbeer, G.:Les Huguenots, w. Jeanette Scovotti (sop—Urbain), Rita Shane (sop—Marguerite de Valois), Enriqueta Tarrès (sop—Valentine), Nicolai Gedda (ten—Raoul de Nangis), Justino Diaz (bass—Marcel), Dimiter Petkov (bass—Le Comte de Saint-Bris), E. Märzendorfer (cnd), Austrian RSO, Austrian Radio Chorus *(rec Vienna, Feb 17, 1971)* Myto 2–▲ MCD 961141

Mozart, W.A.:Idomeneo, w. Gundula Janowitz (sop), Richard Lewis (ten), Luciano Pavarotti (ten), J. Pritchard (cnd), London PO, Glyndebourne Festival Chorus [I] *(rec live at Royal Albert Hall, Aug. 17, 1964)* Verona 2–▲ 27038/39 (m) [AAD]

Mozart, W.A.:Idomeneo, w. Gundula Janowitz (sop), Richard Lewis (ten), Luciano Pavarotti (ten), J. Pritchard (cnd), London PO, Glyndebourne Festival Chorus [I] *(rec live, Royal Albert Hall, London Aug. 17, 1964)* Melodram 2–▲ MEL 27003 (m)

Mozart, W.A.:Idomeneo (sels), w. Gundula Janowitz (sop), David Hughes (ten), Richard Lewis (ten), Luciano Pavarotti (ten), Neilson Taylor (bar), Dennis Wicks (bass), J. Pritchard (cnd), London PO, Glyndebourne Festival Chorus Budget ("The Greatest Voice in Opera" series) ▲ SYP 107

Tassel, Charles van (bar)

Andriessen, L.:Mausoleum, w. David Barick (bar), R. de Leeuw (cnd), Asko Ensemble, Schoenberg Ensemble Donemus ▲ CV 20

Massenet, J.:Thérèse, w. J. Piland (sop), H. Haskin (ten), L. Vis (cnd), Netherlands PO, Netherlands Theater Chorus [F] Canal Grande ▲ CG 9220 [DDD]

Tassinari, Pia (sop)

Bizet, G.:Carmen (sels), w. Margherita Benetti (sop—Micaela), Pia Tassinari (sop—Carmen), Franco Corelli (ten—Don José), Giangiacomo Guelfi (bar—Escamillo), A. Basile (cnd), Turin RAI Orch—[Act. 1] È l'amore uno strano augello; Josè!...Micaela!...Ah! mi parla di lei; Mia madre io vedo ancor, sì, sì; Presso il bastion di Siviglia; Tacer, dì, non vuoi tu?; [Act 2] Con voi ber; Alto là! Chi va là ; Il fior che avevi a me tu dato; [Act 3] Andiam, nostra sorte sappiam!; [Act 4] Largo! Largo! L'Alcade; Sei tu?...Son io; Più non m'ama il tuo cor? *(rec Torino Dec. 15, 1961)* Myto ▲ MCD 953132

Cilea, F.:L'Arlesiana, w. L. di Lelio (sop), F. Tagliavini (ten), G. Galli (bar), P. Silveri (bar), B. Carmassi (bass), A. Zerbini (bass), A. Basile (cnd), Turin RAI Orch, Turin RAI Chorus *(rec 1951)* Cetra Classics ▲ CDO 21 [AAD]

De Cavalieri, Fineschi, Olivero, Stignani, Tassinari, w. Cavalieri, Anna de (sop), Ornella Fineschi (sop), Magda Olivero (sop), Ebe Stignani (mez), Rome RAI SO, Milan RAI SO *(rec 1953–58)* Incontri Memorabili ("Martini & Rossi Concerts" series) ▲ 5020

Flotow, F. von:Martha, w. E. Rizzieri (sop—Lady Enrichetta), P. Tassinari (sop—Nancy), F. Tagliavini (ten—Lionello), C. Tagliabue (bar—Plumkett), B. Carmassi (bass—Sir Tristano), F. Molinari-Pradelli (cnd), Turin RAI Orch, Turin RAI Chorus *(rec 1953; Italian libretto)* Cetra Classic 2–▲ CDO 7 [AAD]

Giordano, U.:Fedora, w. Ferruccio Tagliavini (ten), Meletti (sgr), Micheluzzi (sgr), Mascolo (sgr), Jolanda Torriani (sgr), O.. Fabritiis (cnd), Milan RAI SO, Milan RAI Chorus *(rec live, July 10, 1954)* Arkadia 2–▲ 493

Mascagni, P.:L'amico Fritz, w. P. Tassinari (sop—Suzel), A. Pini (mez—Beppe), F. Tagliavini (ten—Fritz), A. Giannotti (ten—Frederico), S. Meletti (bar—David), P. L. Latinucci (bass—Hanezò), P. Mascagni (cnd), Turin RSO, Turin Radio Chorus *(rec 1941)* Cetra Classic 2–▲ CDO 18

VOCALISTS

Tassinari, Pia (sop) (cont.)
Mozart, W.A.:Requiem, w. E. Stignani (mez), F. Tagliavini (ten), I. Tajo (bass), V. de Sabata (cnd), RAI Orch, *(unknown RAI Chorus) (rec Apr. 1939)* Cetra Classic ▲ CDO 1 [AAD]
Verdi, G.:Un ballo in maschera, w. M. Curtis Verna (sop—Amelia), M. Erato (sop—Oscar), P. Tassinari (cta—Ulrica), F. Tagliavini (ten—Riccardo), G. Valdengo (bar—Renato), A. Albertini (bar—Silvano), M. Stefanoni (bass—Samuel), V. Susca (bass—Tom), A. Questa (cnd), Turin RAI SO, Turin RAI Chorus *(rec 1954)* Cetra Classic 2-▲ CDO 13 [AAD]
Verdi, G.:Falstaff, w. Pia Tassinari (sop—Alice Ford), Ines Alfani Tellini (sop—Nannetta), Aurora Buades (mez—Quickly), Rita Monticone (mez—Meg Page), Roberto D'Alessio (ten—Fenton), Giuseppe Nessi (ten—Bardolfo), Emilio Venturini (ten—Dr. Caius), Emilio Ghirardini (bar—Ford), Giacomo Rimini (bar—Sir John Falstaff), Salvatore Baccaloni (bass—Pistola), L. Molajoli (cnd), Milan SO, La Scala Chorus *(rec La Scala Theatre, Milan, Apr. 1932)* VAI Audio 2-▲ VAIA 1098-2

Tatone, Vito (ten)
Wagner, R.:Die Meistersinger von Nürnberg, w. Bruna Rizzoli (sop), Fernanda Cadoni (mez), Luigi Infantino (ten), Renato Capecchi (bar), Giuseppe Taddei (bar), Boris Christoff (bass), Giovanni Ciavola (bass), James Loomis (bass), Silvo Maionica (bass), Vito Susca (bass), Raimondo Botteghelli (sgr), Walter Brunelli (sgr), Carlo Franzini (sgr), Ezio de Giorgi (sgr), Renzo Gonzales (sgr), L. von Matačić (cnd), Turin RAI Radio-TV SO, Turin RAI Chorus Stradivarius 4-▲ STV 12310

Tatozzi, Vittorio (bar)
Bellini, V.:I Capuleti e i Montecchi (sels), w. F. Cossotto (mez), R. Gavarini (ten), L. Maazel (cnd), Rome RAI Orch, Rome RAI Chorus—2 solo tenor arias & 1 mezzo-bass duet [I] *(rec live 10/23/58)* Melodram ("Connaisseur" series) 2-▲ CDM 27509 [ADD]
Spontini, G.:La vestale, w. M. Callas (sop), N. Rossi-Lemeni (bass), F. Corelli (ten), E. Sordello (bar), N. Zaccaria (bass), A. Votto (cnd), La Scala Orch, La Scala Chorus Great Opera Performances ▲ GOP 741

Tattermuschová, Helena (sop)
Janácek, L.:The Cunning Little Vixen, w. Helena Tattermuschova (sop—Cunning Little Vixen), Eva Zikmundová (sop—The Fox), B. Gregor (cnd), Prague National Theater Orch, Prague National Theater Chorus *(rec 1970)* Supraphon 2-▲ SUP 3071
Janácek, L.:The Makropulos Affair, w. Libuse Prylova (sop), Rudolf Vanasek (ten), Ivo Zidek (ten), B. Gregor (cnd), Prague National Orch, Prague National Theater Chorus *(rec mid 1960's)* Supraphon 2-▲ SUP 108351 [AAD]

Tatum, N. (sop)
Flagello, N.:Contemplations, w. N. Flagello (cnd), Rome SO Phoenix ▲ PHCD 125 [ADD]

Tauber, Richard (ten)
The Acoustic Lieder Recordings (1919-1926) Pearl ▲ PEA 9901 (m) [AAD]
Arias & Duets, w. Lotte Lehmann (sop), Elisabeth Rethberg (sop), et al. *(rec 1919–26)* Preiser 2-▲ PRE 89219
Bizet, G.:Carmen (sels)—Air de fleur Minerva ▲ 5 (m) [ADD]
Flotow, F. von:Martha (sels)—Ach so fromm Minerva ▲ 5 (m) [ADD]
Great Love Duets, w. Erna Berger (sop), Miliza Korjus (sop), Lotte Lehmann (sop), Frida Leider (sop), Charles Kullman (ten), Lauritz Melchior (ten), Helge Roswaenge (ten), Tito Schipa (ten), et al. Pearl ▲ PEA 9217
Lehár, F.:Music of, w. E. Réthy (sop), M. Reining (sop), J. Novotna (sop), F. Lehár (cnd), Vienna SO, Vienna PO—6 orchestral sels. *(Musikalische Memorien I–IV; Die lustige Witwe—Overture; Eva—Prelude)*; 4 Arias from Giuditta *(Du bist meine Sonne—Tauber; Freunde, das Leben ist lebenswert—Tauber; Schön wie die blaue Sommernacht—Novotna & Tauber; Schönste der Frauen—Tauber)*; 1 Song & 5 Arias sung by Esther Rethy *(Wien, du bist das Herz der Welt; Giuditta—Meine Lippen, sie küssenso heiss; Paganini—Liebe, du Himmel auf Erden; Schön ist die Welt—Ich bin verliebt; Der Zarewitsch—Einer wird kommen; Zigeunerliebe—Hör ich Cymbalklänge)*; 2 Arias sung by Maria Reining *(Eva—Im heimlichen Dämmer der silbernen Ampel; Friederike—Warum hast du mich wachgeküsst?) (rec 1934–1942 Odeon & HMV rec)* Preiser ▲ 90150 (m) [AAD]
Lehár, F.:Music of, w. F. Lehár (cnd), Zurich RSO—Music from Das Land des Lächelns; Giuditta; Der Graf von Luxemburg; Das Füstenkind; others *(rec June 5, 1946)* Koch Schwann ▲ SCH 310982 [AAD]
Leoncavallo, R.:Pagliacci (sels)—Prologue Minerva ▲ 5 (m) [ADD]
Lotte Lehmann, w. Lotte Lehmann (sop), Jan Kiepura (ten) Pearl ▲ PEA 9409 (m) [ADD]
Lotte Schöne & Richard Tauber in Operetta Nimbus ("Prima Voce" series) ▲ NI 7833 [ADD]
Mozart, W.A.:Arias—Dalla sua pace; Il mio tesoro [both from Don Giovanni]; Konstanze, Konstanze [from Die Entführung aus dem Serail]; Dies Bildnis [from Die Zauberflöte] Minerva ▲ 5 (m) [ADD]
Mozart, W.A.:Entführung (sels), w. Maria Ivogün (sop), Leo Slezak (ten), K. Alwin (cnd), Vienna State Opera Orch—Hier soll ich dich; Konstanze!... wie ängstlich; Martern aller Arten *(rec 1905 - 1944)* Minerva ▲ MN A14 [ADD]
My Heart's Delight:Operetta Gems & Songs of Romance *(rec 1928–43)* ASV ("Living Era" series) ▲ ASL 5146 [ADD]
My Love for You Memoir Classics ▲ CDMOIR 433
Offenbach, J.:Les Contes d'Hoffmann (sels)—Legend von Kleinsach; Ha, wie in meiner Seele Minerva ▲ 5 (m) [ADD]
Only a Rose Memoir Classics ▲ CDMOIR 421 [ADD]
Puccini, G.:Arias—Recondita armonia; E lucevan le stelle [both from Tosca]; Addio fiorito asil [from Madama Butterfly]; Non piangere Liù; Nessun dorma [both from Turandot] Minerva ▲ 5 (m) [ADD]
Richard Tauber In Concert 1937-1947 Eklipse 2-▲ EKR CD5
Richard Tauber In Concert *(rec 7/18/39)* Standing Room Only 2-▲ SRO 830-2 [ADD]
Richard Tauber:Operatic Arias *(rec 1923–39)* Pearl ▲ PEA 9145 [ADD]
Richard Tauber Sings Lieder:12 German Folk Songs, w. Mischa Spoliansky (pno) *(rec 1926)* Pearl ▲ PEA 9370 (m) [AAD]
Schubert, Franz:Winterreise, w. M. Spoliansky (pno)—12 selections—Nos. 1, 5, 6, 8, 11, 13, 15, 18, 20, 21, 22, 24 [G] *(rec 6/20/27 for Parlophone–Od)* Pearl ▲ PEA 9370 (m) [AAD]
Schumann, R.:Songs, w. Percy Kahn (pno)—4 songs—Widmung, Op. 25/1; Der Nussbaum, Op. 25/3; Aus den Östlichen Rosen, Op. 25/25; Mondnacht, Op. 39/5 [G] *(rec 1935/36 for Parlophone)* Pearl ▲ PEA 9370 (m) [AAD]
The Singing Dream *(rec 1927–34 from Parlophone/O)* Pearl ▲ PEA 9444 (m) [AAD]
Sings German Folk Songs *(rec 1926–35)* Bel Age ▲ 103.002 [ADD]
Sings Lieder, w. orch Pearl ▲ PEA 9381 (m) [ADD]
Sings Light Music of the '20s & '30s, w. orch *(rec. 1920–1935)* Pearl ▲ PEA 9416 (m) [ADD]
Smetana, B.:The Bartered Bride, w. H. Konetzni (sop), F. Krenn (bass), T. Beecham (cnd), Royal Opera House Orch, Royal Opera House Chorus Covent Garden [G] *(rec live, Covent Garden, 5/1/39)* Standing Room Only 2-▲ SRO 830-2 [ADD]
Tauber in Opera *(rec 1920–28 for Odeon)* Nimbus ("Prima Voce" series) ▲ NI 7830 [ADD]
Verdi, G.:Arias—Questa o quella; La donna è mobile [both from Rigoletto]; Ah, sì, ben mio; Di quella pira [both from Il Trovatore]; De' miei bollenti spiriti [from La traviata] Minerva ▲ 5 (m) [ADD]
Verdi, G.:Il trovatore (sels), w. J. Biel (ten), F. Tamagno (ten), L.-A. Escalaïs (ten), M. Gilion (ten), E. Caruso (ten), A. Paoli (ten), G. Zenatello (ten), J. Sembach (ten), L. Slezak (ten), F. Constantino (ten), G. Martinelli (ten), B. De Muro (ten), N. Fusati (ten), N. Piccaluga (ten), G. Lauri-Volpi (ten), A. Pertile (ten), E. Bergamaschi (ten), J. O'Sullivan (ten), H. Roswaenge (ten), G. Taccani (ten), V. Lois (ten), H. Lazaro (ten), A. Lindi (ten), A. Cortis (ten), F. Merli (ten), F. Völker (ten), J. Kiepura (ten), J. Schmidt (ten), J. Bjoerling (ten), B. Gigli (ten), A. Salvarezza (ten), J. Soler (ten), M. Filippeschi (ten)—34 performances of the Act III tenor aria "Di quella pira!," *(rec from 1903–1956)* Bongiovanni ▲ GB 1051 [AAD]
You Are My Heart's Delight *(rec 1927–42)* Pearl ▲ PEA 7042 [AAD]

Tauberová, Maria (sop)
Martinů, B.:Julietta, w. I. Zidek (ten), J. Krombholc (cnd), Prague National Theater Orch, Prague National Theater Chorus [Cz] *(rec 1964)* Supraphon 3-▲ 10 8176-2 [AAD]
Novák, V.:Storm, w. Drahomira Tikalová (sop), Beno Blachut (ten), Ladislav Mráz (bar), J. Krombholc (cnd), Czech PO, Czech Phil Chorus *(rec 1956)* Supraphon 2-▲ SUP 111982 (m) [DDD]

Taubmann, Horst (ten)
Strauss, R.:Arabella, w. M. Reining (sop), L. Della Casa (sop), H. Hotter (b-bar), K. Böhm (cnd), Vienna PO *(rec Salzburg Festival, 1947)* Deutsche Grammophon 3-▲ 445342-2 (m) [ADD]

Tauts, Urre (mez)
Tobias, R.:Des Jonah Sendung, w. Pille Lill (sop), Peter Svensson (ten), Raimo Laukka (bar), Mati Palm (bass), Ines Maidre (org), N. Järvi (cnd), Estonian State SO, Oratorio Choir, Estonian Phil Chamber Choir, Tallinn Boys' Choir *(rec Estonia Concert Hall, Tallinn, Estonia, June 23–29, 1995)* BIS 2-▲ CD 731/732 [DDD]
Tubin, E.:Requiem for Fallen Soldiers, w. E. Klas (cnd), Estonian National Male Choir Ondine 2-▲ ODE 783-2D [DDD]

Tavolaccini, Giuliana (sop)
Massenet, J.:Werther, w. L. Gencer (sop—Carlotta), G. Tavolaccini (sop—Sofia), F. Tagliavini (ten—Werther), M. Borriello (bar—Alberto), E. Mocchiutti (bar—Johann), V. Susca (bass—Il Podestà), R. Botteghelli (bass—Schmidt), C.F. Cillario (cnd), *(orch unknown)* Arkadia 2-▲ 599 [ADD]
Verdi, G.:La traviata, w. Renata Scotto (sop—Violetta Valery), Giuliana Tavolaccini (sop—Flora Bervoix), Gianni Raimondi (ten—Alfredo Germont), Ettore Bastianini (bar—Giorgio Germont), A. Votto (cnd), La Scala Orch, La Scala Chorus *(rec La Scala Theatre, Milan, 1963)* Deutsche Grammophon 2-▲ 439720-2 [ADD]
Verdi, G.:La traviata (sels), w. R. Scotto (sop), A. Bonato (sop), G. Raimondi (ten), E. Bastianini (bar), A. Votto (cnd), La Scala Orch, La Scala Chorus IMP Collectors Series ▲ IMPX 9025 [AAD]

Taylor (sgr)
Verdi, G.:I vespri siciliani, w. J. Brumaire (sop), P. Bowden (mez), Bonhomme (sgr), Baran (sgr), M. Rossi (cnd), BBC Concert Orch, BBC Concert Chorus [original French version] *(rec live, London, 5/10/69)* Arkadia 3-▲ 456 [ADD]

Taylor, Daniel (ct)
Jommelli, N.:Didone abbandonata, w. Dorothea Röschmann (sop), Mechthild Bach (mez), Martina Borst (mez), William Kendall (ct), Arno Raunig (ct), F. Bernius (cnd), Stuttgart CO—Didone; Enea; Iarba; Selene; Araspe; Osmida Orfeo 3-▲ CD 381953 [DDD]

Taylor, James (ten)
Bach, J.S.:Cant 66, w. Barbara Schlick (sop), Kai Wessel (alt), Peter Kooy (bass), Philippe Herreweghe (cnd), Collegium Vocale Harmonia Mundi France ▲ HMC 901513
Bach, J.S.:Cant 201, w. Maria Cristina Kiehr (sop), Andreas Scholl (ct), Kurt Azeberger (ten), Roman Trekel (bar), Peter Lika (bass), R. Jacobs (cnd), Berlin Academy for Early Music, Berlin Chamber Chorus Harmonia Mundi France 2-▲ HMC 901544.45
Bach, J.S.:Cant 213, w. Efrat Ben-Nun (sop), Andreas Scholl (ct), Klaus Häger (bass), R. Jacobs (cnd), Berlin Academy for Early Music, Berlin Chamber Chorus Harmonia Mundi France 2-▲ HMC 901544.45
Bach, J.S.:Easter Oratorio, w. Barbara Schlick (sop), Kai Wessel (alt), Peter Kooy (bass), Philippe Herreweghe (cnd), Collegium Vocale Harmonia Mundi France ▲ HMC 901513
Beethoven, L. van:Missa Solemnis, w. Rosa Mannion (sop), Birgit Remmert (alt), Cornelius Hauptmann (bass), P. Herreweghe (cnd), Champs Elysées Theater Orch, Chapelle Royale Choir, Collegium Vocale *(rec Auditorium Stravinski de Montreux, Feb. 20–21, 1995)* Harmonia Mundi France ▲ HMC 901557
Dvořák, A.:Stabat Mater, w. Marina Shaguch (sop), Ingeborg Danz (alt), Thomas Quasthoff (bass), H. Rilling (cnd), Oregon Bach Festival Orch, Oregon Bach Festival Choir *(rec Silva Concert Hall, Hult Center for the Performing Arts, Eugene, Oregon, July 8–11, 1995)* Hänssler Classic ("Exclusive" series) 2-▲ CD 98.935 [DDD]
Mendelssohn, F.:St. Paul, w. Melanie Diener (sop), Annette Markert (mez), Matthias Görne (bass), P. Herreweghe (cnd), Champs Elysées Theater Orch, Chapelle Royale Choir, Collegium Vocale *(rec Stravinsky Auditorium, Montreaux)* Harmonia Mundi France 2-▲ HMC 901584.85

Taylor, Janice (mez)
Bach, J.S.:Cant 63, w. S. McNair (sop), D. Gordon (ten), D. Lichti (b-bar), G. Funfgeld (cnd), Bach Festival Orch, Bethlehem Bach Choir—plus Sanctus from Mass in b, BWV 232 [G] Dorian ▲ DOR 90113 [DDD]
Beethoven, L. van:Missa Solemnis, w. S. McNair (sop), J. Aler (ten), T. Krause (bar), R. Shaw (cnd), Atlanta SO, Atlanta Sym Chorus [L] Telarc 2-▲ CD 80150 [DDD]
Handel, G.F.:Messiah, w. Leslie Fagan (sop), Mark Dubois (ten), Gary Relyea (b-bar), G. Fagan (cnd), Concert Players Orch, Gerald Fagan Singers, London Fanshawe Symphonic Chorus Doremi 2-▲ 9306 [DDD]
Prokofiev, S.:Alexander Nevsky, w. Z. Macal (cnd), Milwaukee SO, Milwaukee Sym Chorus *(rec Oct. 29, 1990)* Koss Classics ▲ KC 1016 [DDD]

Taylor, Neilson (bar)
Massenet, J.:Sapho, w. Jenny Hill (sop), Laura Sarti (mez), Bernard Dickerson (ten), Alexander Oliver (ten), George Macpherson (bass), Milla Andrew (sgr), B. Keefe (cnd), BBC SO, BBC Sym Chorus *(rec live, 1973)* Memories 2-▲ MEM 4601 [AAD]
Mozart, W.A.:Idomeneo (sels), w. Gundula Janowitz (sop), Enriqueta Tarres (sop), David Hughes (ten), Richard Lewis (ten), Luciano Pavarotti (ten), Dennis Wicks (bass), J. Pritchard (cnd), London PO, Glyndebourne Festival Chorus Budget ("The Greatest Voice in Opera" series) ▲ SYP 107

Taylor, Paul (ten)
Scarlatti, D.:Stabat mater, w. J. Kennard (sop), J. Poole (cnd), BBC Singers *(rec 1976)* Sony Classical ("Essential Classics" series) ▲ SBK 48282 [AAD] ■ SBT 48282

Taylor, Rose (mez)
Ligeti, G.:The Ligeti Edition, w. Phyllis Bryn-Julson (sop), Rosemary Hardy (sop), Christiane Oelze (sop), Sibylle Ehlert (sgr), Omar Ebrahim (bar), Pierre-Laurent Aimard (pno), E.-P. Salonen (cnd), Philharmonia Orch, King's Singers—Vocal Works; Madrigals; Mysteries; Adventures; Songs; Nonsense Madrigals Sony Classical ▲ SK 62311

Taylor, S. (ct)
Dvořák, A.:Mass, w. Coupe (trb), P. Cave (ten), S. Foulkes (bass), A. Pinel (org), M. Archer (cnd), Bristol Cathedral Choir [L] Meridian ▲ CDE 84188

Tcholakov (sgr)
Mascagni, P.:Nerone, w. R. Didonè (sop), D. Di Domenico (ten), S. Cowan (bar), M. Dirks (bar), Harry Peeters (bass), Shapero (sgr), Strow-Piccolo (sgr), K. Bakels (cnd), Hilversum RSO, Hilversum Chorus [I] Bongiovanni 2-▲ GB 2052/53 [DDD]

Teal, Julie (sgr)
Handel, G.F.:Serse, w. L. Atkinson (trb), D. Cole (sop), A. Terzian (mez), A. Andersson (ten), T. Allen (bar), Schumann-Halley (sgr), A. Duczmal (cnd), Amadeus CO [I] *(rec live recording produced by "Studios Classique Berlin")* Koch Schwann 3-▲ CD SC 100 300 [DDD]

Tear, Robert (ten)
Bach, C.P.E.:Magnificat, w. F. Palmer (sop), H. Watts (cta), S. Roberts (b-bar), P. Ledger (cnd), Academy of St. Martin in the Fields, King's College Choir Cambridge London ("Jubilee" series) ▲ 421148-2 [ADD]
Bach, J.S.:Cant 82, w. J. Baker (sop), J. Shirley-Quirk (bar), N. Marriner (cnd), Academy of St. Martin in the Fields London ("Jubilee" series) ▲ 430260-2 [ADD]
Bach, J.S.:Cant 159, w. J. Baker (sop), J. Shirley-Quirk (bar), N. Marriner (cnd), Academy of St. Martin in the Fields London ("Jubilee" series) ▲ 430260-2 [ADD]
Bach, J.S.:Cant 170, w. J. Baker (sop), J. Shirley-Quirk (bar), N. Marriner (cnd), Academy of St. Martin in the Fields London ("Jubilee" series) ▲ 430260-2 [ADD]
Bach, J.S.:Christmas Oratorio, w. Elly Ameling (sop), Janet Baker (mez), Dietrich Fischer-Dieskau (bar), P. Ledger (cnd), Academy of St. Martin in the Fields, King's College Choir Cambridge *(rec 1976)* EMI Classics ("Doublefforte" series) 2-▲ CDFB 69503
Bach, J.S.:Magnificat, BWV 243, w. L. Popp (sop), A. Pashley (sop), J. Baker (mez), D. Barenboim (cnd), New Philharmonia Orch, New Philharmonia Chorus EMI Classics ▲ CDM 64634-2
Bach, J.S.:Magnificat, BWV 243, w. Anne Pashley (sop), Lucia Popp (sop), Janet Baker (mez), Thomas Hemsley (bar), D. Barenboim (cnd), New Philharmonia Orch, New Philharmonia Chorus *(rec All Saints, Tooting, London, May 1968)* EMI Classics ▲ CDK 65334 [ADD]
Bach, J.S.:Magnificat, BWV 243, w. F. Palmer (sop), H. Watts (cta), S. Roberts (b-bar), P. Ledger (cnd), Academy of St. Martin in the Fields, King's College Choir Cambridge London ("Jubilee" series) ▲ 421148-2 [ADD]
Bach, J.S.:Mass in b, BWV 232, w. M. Marshall (sop), J. Baker (mez), S. Ramey (bass), N. Marriner (cnd), Academy of St. Martin in the Fields, *(chorus unknown)* [L] Philips 2-▲ 416415-2 [ADD]

Tear, Robert (ten) (cont.)

Bach, J.S.:St. Matthew Passion, w. F. Lott (sop), A. Hodgson (cta), J. Shirley–Quirk (bar), S. Roberts (bar), D. Willcocks (cnd), Thames CO, Bach Choir [E] ASV Quicksilva 3–▲ ASQ 324 [ADD]

Beethoven, L. van:Mass, Op. 86, w. A. Tomwa–Sintow (sop), P. Payne (mez), R. Lloyd (bass), C. Davis (cnd), London SO, London Sym Chorus [G] Philips 2–▲ 438362–2

Beethoven, L. van:Missa Solemnis, w. A. Tomwa–Sintow (sop), P. Payne (mez), R. Lloyd (bass), C. Davis (cnd), London SO, London Sym Chorus [G] Philips 2–▲ 438362–2

Beethoven, L. van:Missa Solemnis, w. Ileana Cotrubas (sop), Kathleen Kuhlmann (mez), Gwynne Howell (bass), J. Pritchard (cnd), BBC SO, BBC Singers IMP ("BBC Radio Classics" series) ▲ IMP 5691552

Beethoven, L. van:Sym 9, "Choral Sym", w. H. Harper (sop), A. Hodgson (cta), G. Howell (bass), R. Hickox (cnd), Northern Sinfonia of England, London Sym Chorus members ASV Quicksilva ▲ ASQ 6069 [DDD]

Britten, H.:Ballad of Heroes, w. S. Rattle (cnd), City of Birmingham SO, City of Birmingham Sym Chorus [E] *(rec 7/90)* EMI Classics 2–▲ CDCB 54270 [DDD]

Britten, H.:Folksong Arrs, w. E. Söderström (sop), N. Marriner (cnd), Northern Sinfonia of England—Bonny Earl O'Moray; Oliver Cromwell; O Waly, Waly; The Plough Boy EMI Classics ▲ CDM 69522

Britten, H.:Praise We Great Men, w. A. Hargan (sop), M. King (alt), W. White (bass), S. Rattle (cnd), City of Birmingham SO, City of Birmingham Sym Chorus [E] *(rec July, 1990)* EMI Classics 2–▲ ZDCB 54270 [DDD]

Britten, H.:Serenade, Op. 31, w. A. Civil (hn), R. Armstrong (cnd), Welsh National Opera Orch EMI Classics ▲ CDM 69522

Britten, H.:Spring Sym, w. Eiddwen Harrhy (sop), Linda Finnie (cta), G. Rozhdestvensky (cnd), BBC SO, BBC Sym Chorus, London Voices, Southend Boys' Choir IMP ("BBC Radio Classics" series) ▲ IMP 5691752

Britten, H.:Spring Sym, w. S. Armstrong (sop), J. Baker (mez), A. Previn (cnd), London SO, London Sym Chorus EMI Classics ▲ CDM 64736

Britten, H.:War Requiem, w. E. Söderström (sop), T. Allen (bar), S. Rattle (cnd), City of Birmingham SO, City of Birmingham Sym Chorus, Christ Church Boys' Chorus [E,L] EMI Classics 2–▲ CDC 47033

Butterworth, G.:Songs (3) Voc & Strs, w. T. Allen (bar), Rattle, Handley (cnd), City of Birmingham SO EMI Classics ▲ CDM 64731

Delius, F.:Music of, w. J. Barbirolli (cnd), Hallé Orch, London SO, Ambrosian Singers—Brigg Fair; In a Summer Garden; On Hearing the First Cuckoo in Spring; Summer Night on the River; A Song before Sunrise; Intermezzo & Serenade [from Hassan]; La Calinda; Late Swallows; Intermezzo [from Fennimore & Gerda]; The Walk to Paradise Garden; Prelude [from Irmelin]; A Song of Summer; Appalachia; rehearsal of Appalachia EMI Classics ▲ ZDMB 65119

Elgar, E.:The Apostles, w. S. Armstrong (sop), H. Watts (cta), J. C. Case (bar), B. Luxon (bar), C. Grant (bass), A. Boult (cnd), London PO, London Phil Chorus, Downe House School Choir [E] EMI Classics ▲ CDMB 64206

Elgar, E.:The Dream of Gerontius, w. Alfreda Hodgson (cta), Benjamin Luxon (bar), A. Gibson (cnd), Scottish National Orch, Scottish National Chorus CRD 2–▲ 33267

Elgar, E.:Songs, w. T. Allen (bar), Rattle, Handley (cnd), City of Birmingham SO EMI Classics ▲ CDM 64731

Handel, G.F.:Dixit Dominus (sels), w. Teresa Zylis–Gara (sop), Janet Baker (mez), D. Willcocks (cnd), King's College Choir Cambridge—Dixit Dominus [chorus w. solos]; Gloria [chorus] *(rec King's College Chapel, Cambridge, Aug. 1965)* EMI Classics ▲ CDK 65336 [ADD]

Handel, G.F.:Messiah, w. Elisabeth Harwood (sop), Janet Baker (mez), Paul Esswood (ct), Raimund Herincx (bass), C. Mackerras (cnd), English CO, Ambrosian Singers [E] Angel ("Studio" series) 2–▲ CDMB 62748 [ADD]

Handel, G.F.:Messiah, w. Elisabeth Harwood (sop), Janet Baker (mez), Paul Esswood (ct), Raimund Herincx (bass), C. Mackerras (cnd), English CO, Ambrosian Singers [E] Angel ("Studio" series) ▲ CDM 69040

Handel, G.F.:Ode for St. Cecilia's Day, w. Jill Gomez (sop), P. Ledger (cnd), English CO, King's College Choir Cambridge [E] ASV ▲ ASV 512 [DDD]

Handel, G.F.:Salve Regina, w. Janet Baker (mez), Helen Watts (cta), Benjamin Luxon (bar), John Shirley–Quirk (bar), R. Leppard (cnd), English CO, London Voices Erato 3–▲ 2292–45994–2

Haydn, J.:Mass 12, "Theresienmesse", w. Lucia Popp (sop), Rosalind Elias (mez), Paul Hudson (bass), L. Bernstein (cnd), London SO, London Sym Chorus [L] Sony Classical 2–▲ SM2K 47522 [ADD]

Janácek, L.:The Cunning Little Vixen, w. L. Watson (sop), E. Bainbridge (mez), G. Knight (mez), D. Montague (mez), J. Dobson (ten), T. Allen (bar), G. Howell (bass), S. Rattle (cnd), Royal Opera House Orch [E] EMI Classics 2–▲ CDCB 54212

Mahler, G.:Das Klagende Lied, w. Teresa Cahill (sop), Janet Baker (mez), Gwynne Howell (bass), G. Rozhdestvensky (cnd), BBC SO, BBC Sym Chorus IMP ("BBC Radio" series) ▲ IMP 5691412

Mahler, G.:Das Klagende Lied, w. H. Döse (sop), A. Hodgson (cta), S. Rae, S. Rattle (cnd), City of Birmingham SO, City of Birmingham Sym Chorus EMI ▲ CDC 47089

Mahler, G.:Das Lied von der Erde, w. Jean Rigby (mez), M. Wiggelsworth (cnd), Premiere Ensemble [arr. Schoenberg] RCA Red Seal ▲ 09026–68043–2

Mendelssohn, F.:Sym 2, w. E. Wiens (sop), J. Howarth (sop), F. d' Avalos (cnd), Philharmonia Orch, Bach Choir IMP Masters ▲ IMP MCD 83 [DDD]

Monteverdi, C.:Vespro della Beata Vergine, w. Elly Ameling (sop), Norma Burrowes (sop), Charles Brett (ct), Anthony Rolfe Johnson (ten), Martyn Hill (ten), Peter Knapp (bass), John Noble (bass), Munrow, Ledger (cnd), London Early Music Consort EMI Classics ("Doublefforte" series) 2–▲ CDFB 68631

Monteverdi, C.:Vespro della Beata Vergine, w. Elly Ameling (sop), Norma Burrowes (sop), Charles Brett (ct), Martyn Hill (ten), Anthony Rolfe–Johnson (ten), Peter Knapp (bass), John Noble (bass), Francis Grier (org/hpd), James Lancelot (org/hpd), Andrew Leach (org/hpd), P. Ledger (cnd), London Early Music Consort, King's College Choir Cambridge—Nigra sum [con.]; Laudate pueri [psalm]; Sancta Maria [son. sopra]; Magnificat *(rec Chapel of King's College, Cambridge, July & Aug. 1975)* EMI Classics ▲ CDK 65339 [ADD]

Mozart, W.A.:Complete Mozart Edition, w. C. Eda–Pierre (sop), N. Burrowes (sop), S. Burrows (ten), C. Davis (cnd), Academy of St. Martin in the Fields, John Alldis Choir Philips 2–▲ 422538–2 [ADD]

Mozart, W.A.:Complete Mozart Edition, w. M. Price (sop), L. Serra (sop), P. Schreier (ten), T. Adam (b–bar), K. Moll (bass), C. Davis (cnd), Dresden Staatskapelle, Dresden State Chorus Philips 3–▲ 422543–2 [ADD]

Mozart, W.A.:Requiem, w. I. Cotrubas (sop), H. Watts (cta), J. Shirley–Quirk (bar), N. Marriner (cnd), Academy of St. Martin in the Fields, Academy of St. Martin in the Fields Chorus [L] London ▲ 417746–2 [ADD]

Mozart, W.A.:Zauberflöte, w. M. Price (sop—Pamina), L. Serra (sop—Queen of the Night), M. Venuti (sop—Papagena), M. McLaughlin (sop—1st Lady), A. Murray (mez—2nd Lady), H. Schwarz (cta—3rd Lady), F. Höher (trb—1st Boy), M. Diedrich (trb—2nd Boy), F. Klos (trb—3rd Boy), P. Schreier (ten—Tamino), R. Tear (ten—Monostatos), R. Goldberg (ten—1st Armoured Man), K. Moll (bass—Sarastro), H. Rech (bass—2nd Armoured Man), C. Davis (cnd), Dresden Staatskapelle, Leipzig Radio Chorus Philips ("Duo" series) 2–▲ 442568–2

Offenbach, J.:Les Contes d'Hoffmann, w. L. Serra (sop), R. Plowright (sop), J. Norman (sop), A. Murray (mez), J. Taillon (mez), N. Shicoff (ten), A. Oliver (ten), R. Tear (ten), J. Van Dam (b–bar), D. Duesing (bar), K. Rydl (bass), S. Cambreling (cnd), Brussels Théâtre de la Monnaie Orch [F] EMI Classics 3–▲ CDCC 49641 [DDD]

Puccini, G.:Manon Lescaut, w. M. Caballé (sop—Manon Lescaut), P. Domingo (ten—Des Grieux), R. Tear (ten—Edmondo), V. Sardinero (bar—Lescaut), N. Mangin (bass—Geronte), B. Bartoletti (cnd), New Philharmonia Orch, Ambrosian Opera Chorus EMI Classics ▲ CDMB 64852

Schubert, Franz:Winterreise, w. P. Ledger (pno) ASV Quicksilva ▲ QS 6085 [ADD]

Sullivan, A.:Music of, w. V. Masterson (sop), S. Armstrong (sop), B. Luxon (bar), Alwyn, Hickox (cnd), Bournemouth Sinfonietta, Northern Sinfonietta of England—sels. from all operettas of Gilbert & Sullivan EMI Classics ▲ CDM 64393

Tippett, M.:King Priam, w. Heather Harper (sop—Hecuba), Linda Hirst (sop—Serving Woman), Felicity Palmer (sop—Andromache), Julian Saipe (sop—Paris), Yvonne Minton (mez—Helen), Ann Murray (mez—Nurse), Kenneth Bowen (ten—Hermes), Peter Hall (ten—Young Guard), Philip Langridge (ten—Paris), Robert Tear (ten—Achilles), Thomas Allen (bar—Hector), Norman Bailey (bar—Priam), Stephen Roberts (bar—Patroclus), David Wilson–Johnson (bar—Old Man), D. Atherton (cnd), London Sinfonietta, London Sinfonietta Chorus Chandos ▲ CHAN 9406/7 [DDD]

Tippett, M.:The Mask of Time, w. F. Robinson (sop), S. Walker (mez), J. Cheek (bass), A. Davis (cnd), BBC SO, BBC Sym Chorus EMI Classics ▲ ZDMB 64111

Vaughan Williams, R.:On Wenlock Edge, w. V. Handley (cnd), City of Birmingham SO [orch. version] EMI Classics ▲ CDM 64731

Weill, K.:The Seven Deadly Sins, w. J. Migenes (sop), S. Kale (ten), A. Opie (bar), R. Kennedy (bass), M. Tilson Thomas (cnd), London SO CBS ▲ MK 44529 [DDD]

Tebaldi, Renata (sop)

Boito, A.:Mefistofele, w. M. del Monaco (ten), C. Siepi (bass), T. Serafin (cnd), St. Cecilia Academy Orch Rome, St. Cecilia Academy Chorus Rome *(rec 1958)* London ▲ 440054–2

Boito, A.:Mefistofele, w. C. Bergonzi (ten), N. Ghiaurov (bass), L. Gardelli (cnd), *(orch unknown)* *(rec live, New York 1/25/66)* Standing Room Only 2–▲ SRO 824–2 [ADD]

Boito, A.:Mefistofele, w. R. Tebaldi (sop—Margheritta), E. Souliotis (sop—Elena), M. Mackenzie (mez—Marta), M. Ruggiero (mez—Pantalis), A. Kraus (ten—Faust), H. Kraus (ten—Wagner), N. Ghiaurov (bass—Mefistofele), N. Sanzogno (cnd), *(orch unknown)* Ornamenti 2–▲ FE 101

Callas & Tebaldi:The Early Recordings, w. Maria Callas (sop) Andromeda 2–▲ ANR 2518/19

Carlo Tagliabue, w. Carlo Tagliabue (bar), Margherita Carosio (sop), Ettore Bergamaschi (ten), Zinka Milanov (sop), Bruna Castagna (cta), Frederick Jagel (ten), Norman Cordon (bass), Alfredo Colella (bass) *(rec in studio and live, 1928–1951)* Bongiovanni ▲ GB 1070–2 [ADD]

Catalani, A.:La Wally, w. C. Bergonzi (ten), P. Glossop (bar), F. Corena (bass), F. Cleva (cnd), American Opera Society Orch, American Opera Society Chorus *(rec Mar. 13, 1968)* Intaglio 2–▲ ING 764 [ADD]

Catalani, A.:La Wally, w. G. Prandelli (ten), S. Majonica (bass), G. Santini (cnd), Rome RAI SO, Rome RAI Chorus *(rec 1960)* Enterprise (Palladio) 2–▲ ENTPD 4165 [ADD]

Catalani, A.:La Wally, w. L. Marimpietri (sop), M. del Monaco (ten), P. Cappuccilli (bar), Justino Diaz (bass), F. Cleva (cnd), Monte Carlo Opera Orch, Turin Lyric Chorus [I] London 2–▲ 425417–2 [ADD]

Catalani, A.:La Wally, w. R. Scotto (sop), M. del Monaco (ten), G. Guelfi (bar), C.M. Giulini (cnd), *(orch unknown)* *(rec Milan, 1953)* Great Opera Performances 2–▲ GOP 734

Catalani, A.:La Wally, w. R. Scotto (sop—Walter), R. Tebaldi (sop—Wally), J. Gardino (mez—Afra), M. Del Monaco (ten—Giuseppe Hagenbach), G.G. Guelfi (bar—Vincenzo Gellner), G. Tozzi (bass—Stromminger), C. M. Giulini (cnd), La Scala Orch, La Scala Chorus *(rec Dec. 7, 1953)* Legato Classics 2–▲ LCD 177–2 [ADD]

Catalani, A.:La Wally (sels), w. C. Bergonzi (ten), *(sels unknown)* *(rec Carnegie Hall, 1968)* Great Opera Performances 2–▲ GOP 734

Chicago 1950, w. Giuseppe Di Stefano (ten), Bidu Sayao (sop), Chicago Radio Orch [cnd:Gaetano Merola] Myto ▲ MCD 924.67 [ADD]

Cilea, F.:Adriana Lecouvreur, w. M. del Monaco (ten), F. Capuana (cnd), St. Cecilia Academy Orch Rome, St. Cecilia Academy Chorus Rome London 2–▲ 430256–2 [ADD]

Cilea, F.:Adriana Lecouvreur (sels), w. Renata Tebaldi (sop—Adriana), Piero de Palma (ten—Abate), Gianni Poggi (ten—Mauriczio), Giuseppe Taddei (bar—Michonnet), Augusto Romani (bass—Prince), G. Santini (cnd), Naples Teatro San Carlo Orch, Naples Teatro San Carlo Chorus—Del sultano Amurate...Io son l'umile ancella; Giusto Cielo! che feci in tal giorno; Salvatemi! salvatemi!...Scostatevi, profani! *(rec San Carlo Theater, Naples, Dec. 26, 1952)* Legato Classics 2–▲ LCD 193–2 [ADD]

The Early Recordings (1949–1952), w. Alberto Erede (cnd), St. Cecilia Academy Orch, Swiss Romande Orch London ("Historic" series) ▲ 425989–2 LM [ADD]

Famous Love Duets, Vol. 2, w. Gianna d'Angelo (sop), Montserrat Caballé (sop), Maria Callas (sop), Renata Scotto (sop), Beverly Sills (sop), Renata Tebaldi (sop), José Carreras (ten), Mario Del Monaco (ten), Giuseppe Di Stefano (ten), Plácido Domingo (ten), et. al. Enterprise ("Documents" series) ▲ ENTLV 999

Giordano, U.:Andrea Chénier, w. U. Savarese (bar), A. Basile (cnd), Turin RAI SO Cetra Classic 2–▲ CDO 24

Giordano, U.:Andrea Chénier, w. H. Konetzni (sop—Madelon), M. Sjöstedt (sop—Bersi), R. Tebaldi (sop—Maddalena de Coigny), E. Höngen (cta—La Contessa de Coigny), F. Corelli (ten—Andrea Chénier), E. Bastianini (bar—C. Gérard), K. Paskalis (bar—Pietro Fléville), L. Welter (bar—Fouquier Tinville), A. Pernerstorfer (b–bar—Mathieu), L. von Matačić (cnd), Vienna State Opera Orch, Vienna State Opera Chorus *(rec Vienna, June 26, 1960)* Fortissimo 2–▲ CDE 3003 [ADD]

Giordano, U.:Andrea Chénier, w. Renata Tebaldi (sop—Maddalena), Anna di Stasio (mez—Bersi), Amalia Pini (mez—Madelon/Contessa), Mario Del Monaco (ten—Andrea Chenier), Antonio Pirino (ten—L'Incredibile/Abate), Aldo Protti (bar—Carlo Gerard), Arturo La Porta (bass/bar—Mathieu/Fleville), Silvano Pagliuca (bass/bar—Roucher/Fouquier–Tinville), Giorgio Onesti (bass—Dumas/Schmidt/Major–domo), F. Capuana (cnd), Italian Lyric Orch, Italian Lyric Chorus *(rec Tokyo, Oct 1, 1961)* Legato Classics 2–▲ LCD 214–2 [ADD]

Giordano, U.:Andrea Chénier, w. José Soler (ten), Ugo Savarese (bar), A. Basile (cnd), Turin RAI SO Fonit Cetra ("Classic Collection" series) 2–▲ FCT CDO 24

Giordano, U.:Andrea Chénier, w. F. Corelli (ten), E. Bastianini (bar), L. von Matačić (cnd), *(orch unknown)*—eleven arias [I] *(rec live, Vienna, 6/26/60)* Standing Room Only 2–▲ SRO 821–2 [ADD]

Giordano, U.:Andrea Chénier (sels), w. F. Barbieri (mez), M. del Monaco (ten), P. Silveri (bar), V. de Sabata (cnd), La Scala Orch, La Scala Chorus—14 arias from Acts 1–3 [I] *(rec live, Milan, 3/6/49)* Myto ▲ 1 MCD 90634 [ADD]

Giordano, U.:Andrea Chénier (sels), w. R. Tucker (ten), *(orch unknown)*—Ecco l'altare...Ora soave; Come un bel di di maggio; Vicino a te s'acqueta *(rec 1956–63)* Standing Room Only ▲ SRO 8441 [ADD]

Giordano, U.:Fedora, w. Mizzetti (sgr), G. di Stefano (ten), M. Sereni (bar), A. Basile (cnd), Naples Teatro San Carlo Orch, Naples Teatro San Carlo Chorus [I] *(rec live, 1961)* Legato Classics 2–▲ LCD 158–2 (m) [ADD]

Gounod, C.:Faust (sels), w. F. Cadoni (mez), M. Filippeschi (ten), R. Panerai (bar), I. Tajo (bass), F. Patanè (cnd), Naples Teatro San Carlo Orch, Naples Teatro San Carlo Chorus—Act IV, Scenes 1 & 2 & Act V, Scene 2 *(rec live, 4/26/51)* Standing Room Only 2–▲ SRO 810–2 [ADD]

Grandi Voci:Renata Tebaldi *(rec 1954–55, 1957–59, 1962 &)* London ▲ 440408–2 [ADD]

Her Early Recordings in Europe Originals ▲ ORI SH 963

Homage to Renata Tebaldi Great Opera Performances 2–▲ GOP 721

La Leggendaria Tebaldi:A 40th Anniversary Tribute Legato Classics ▲ LCD 138–1 [ADD]

Lincke, P.:Frau Luna (sels), w. Ingeborg Hallstein (sop), Willi Brokmeier (ten), W. Schmidt–Boelcke (cnd), Bavarian RSO, Bavarian Radio Chorus [G] Acanta ▲ CD 42484 [DDD]

Mascagni, P.:Cavalleria rusticana, w. J. Bjoerling (ten), A. Erede (cnd), Florence Maggio Musicale Orch, Florence Maggio Musicale Chorus *(rec Sept. 1957)* London ("Historic" series) ▲ 425985–2 [ADD]

Operatic Duets, w. Jussi Björling (ten), Licia Albanese (sop), Zinka Milanov (sop), Robert Merrill (bar) RCA Gold Seal ▲ 7799–2–RG (m) [ADD] ■ 7799–4–RG (CrO2)

Ponchielli, A.:La Gioconda, w. C. Bergonzi (ten), *(other soloists unknown),* L. Gardelli (cnd), St. Cecilia Academy Orch Rome, St. Cecilia Academy Chorus Rome London 3–▲ 430042–2 [ADD]

A Portrait of the Artist, 1949–1958 Legato Classics ▲ LCD 115–1 (m) [AAD]

Public Performances 1951–1961 Memories ("Great Voices" series) 2–▲ MEM 4235 (m) [ADD]

Puccini, G.:Arias, w. Maria Callas (sop), *(orch unknown)*—sels from La Bohème, Tosca & Madama Butterfly *(rec 1953–64)* Andromeda ▲ ANR 2546 [ADD]

Puccini, G.:Arias, w. M. Caballé (sop), M. Chiara (sop), M. Freni (sop), B. Nilsson (sop), J. Sutherland (sop), F. Corelli (ten), L. Pavarotti (ten), S. Milnes (bar) London ▲ 421315–2 [ADD]

Puccini, G.:La Bohème, w. H. Gueden (sop), G. Prandelli (ten), G. Inghilleri (bar), F. Corena (bass), Raphäel Arié (bass), A. Erede (cnd), St. Cecilia Academy Orch Rome, St. Cecilia Academy Chorus Rome London 2–▲ 440233–2 [ADD]

Puccini, G.:La Bohème, w. G. d'Angelo (sop), C. Bergonzi (ten), E. Bastianini (bar), C. Siepi (b–bar), T. Serafin (cnd), St. Cecilia Academy Orch Rome, St. Cecilia Academy Chorus Rome [I] London 2–▲ 425534–2 [ADD]

Puccini, G.:La Bohème, w. C. Bergonzi (ten), E. Bastianini (bar), C. Siepi (b–bar), T. Serafin (cnd), St. Cecilia Academy Orch Rome, St. Cecilia Academy Chorus Rome Enterprise ("Flowers" series) 2–▲ ENTBL 15 [ADD]

Puccini, G.:La Bohème, w. Candida (sgr), F. Corelli (ten), F. Guarrera (bar), J. Hines (bass), A. Guadagno (cnd), *(orch & chorus unknown)* [I] *(rec live, Philadelphia 12/2/69)* Standing Room Only 2–▲ SRO 821–2 [ADD]

Tebaldi, Renata (sop) (cont.)

Puccini, G.:La Bohème, w. E. Ribetti (mez), E. Avolanti (ten), G. Lauri Volpi (ten), T. Gobbi (bar), S. Meletti (bar), C. Badioli (bass), G. Neri (bass), G. Santini (cnd), *(orch unknown) (rec 1951)* Great Opera Performances ▲ GOP 743
Puccini, G.:La Bohème (sels), w. C. Bergonzi (ten), E. Bastianini (bar), C. Siepi (b-bar), T. Serafin (cnd), St. Cecilia Academy Orch Rome, St. Cecilia Academy Chorus Rome—scenes & arias London ▲ 421301-2 [ADD]
Puccini, G.:La fanciulla del West, w. M. del Monaco (ten), C. MacNeil (bar), G. Tozzi (bass), F. Capuana (cnd), St. Cecilia Academy Orch Rome, St. Cecilia Academy Chorus Rome [I] London 2-▲ 421595-2 [ADD]
Puccini, G.:Madama Butterfly, w. A. di Stasio (mez), G. Raimondi (ten), G. Valdengo (bar), A. Questa (cnd), *(orch & chorus unknown)* [I] *(rec live, Arena Flegrea, Naples 8/9/58)* Standing Room Only 2-▲ SRO 825-2 [ADD]
Puccini, G.:Madama Butterfly, w. F. Cossotto (mez), C. Bergonzi (ten), E. Sordello (bar), T. Serafin (cnd), St. Cecilia Academy Orch Rome, St. Cecilia Academy Chorus Rome [I] London 2-▲ 425531-2 [ADD]
Puccini, G.:Madama Butterfly (sels), w. C. Bergonzi (ten), E. Sordello (bar), T. Serafin (cnd), St. Cecilia Academy Orch Rome, St. Cecilia Academy Chorus Rome London ▲ 417733-2 [ADD]
Puccini, G.:Madama Butterfly (sels), w. F. Cossotto (mez), C. Bergonzi (ten), E. Sordello (bar), T. Serafin (cnd), St. Cecilia Academy Orch Rome, St. Cecilia Academy Chorus Rome [I] London ("Opera Gala" series) ▲ 421873-2 [ADD]
Puccini, G.:Manon Lescaut, w. M. del Monaco (ten), F. Molinari-Pradelli (cnd), St. Cecilia Academy Orch Rome, St. Cecilia Academy Chorus Rome London 2-▲ 430253-2 [ADD]
Puccini, G.:Manon Lescaut (sels), w. M. Favero (sop), J. Gardino (mez), G. Malipiero (ten), G. Nessi (ten), M. Stabile (bar), T. Pasero (b-bar), C. Forti (bass), A. Toscanini (cnd), La Scala Orch, La Scala Chorus—Intermezzo; Act 3 *(rec live, Milan, May 18, 1946)* Arkadia ("Historical Performances" series) 2-▲ 604 (m)
Puccini, G.:Manon Lescaut (sels), w. R. Tucker (ten), *(orch unknown)*—Donna non vidi mai; Vedete? lo son fedele; E ver!...In quelle trine morbide; L'ora, o Tirsi!; Oh, saro la piu bella!; Tu soffri?..Vedi, vedi, son io che piango; Sola, perduta, abbandonata; Fra le tue braccia amore *(rec between 1956-63)* Standing Room Only ▲ SRO 8441 [ADD]
Puccini, G.:Tosca, w. Renata Tebaldi (sop—Floria Tosca), Guiseppe di Stefano (ten—Mario Cavardossi), Rinaldo Pelizzoni (ten—Spoletta), Ettore Bastianini (bar—Baron Scarpia), Carlo Badioli (bass—Sacristan), Guiseppe Moresi (bass—Sciarrone), Franco Piva (bass—Jailer), Nicola Zaccaria (bass—Cesare Angelotti), G. Gavazzeni (cnd) *(rec Great Auditorium, Brussels World Fair, 1958)* Legato Classics 2-▲ LCD 2092 [ADD]
Puccini, G.:Tosca, w. R. Tebaldi (sop—Tosca), F. Corelli (ten—Cavaradossi), A. Colzani (bar—Scarpia), P. L. Latinucci (b-bar—Sacristan), G. Beloni (bass—Angelotti), M. Parenti (cnd), Livorno Teatro La Gran Guardia Orch, Livorno Teatro La Gran Guardia Chorus *(rec live Sept. 21, 1959)* Legato Classics 2-▲ LCD 171-2 [ADD]
Puccini, G.:Tosca, w. M. del Monaco (ten), F. Molinari-Pradelli (cnd), St. Cecilia Academy Orch Rome, St. Cecilia Academy Chorus Rome London 2-▲ 411871-2 [ADD]
Puccini, G.:Tosca, w. G. Campora (ten), Enzo Mascherini (bar), F. Corena (bass), A. Erede (cnd), St. Cecilia Academy Orch Rome, St. Cecilia Academy Chorus Rome Enterprise 2-▲ ENTPD 4106 [ADD]
Puccini, G.:Tosca, w. Gian Franco Volante (trb), Piero de Palma (ten), Giuseppe Campora (ten), Enzo Mascherini (bar), Fernando Corena (bass), Dario Caselli (bass), Antonio Sacchetti (bass), A. Erede (cnd), St. Cecilia Academy Orch Rome, St. Cecilia Academy Chorus Rome *(rec 1952)* Andromeda 2-▲ ANR 2539 [ADD]
Puccini, G.:Tosca, w. G. Campora (ten), Enzo Mascherini (bar), F. Corena (bass), A. Erede (cnd), St. Cecilia Academy Orch Rome, St. Cecilia Academy Chorus Rome London 2-▲ 440236-2 [ADD]
Puccini, G.:Tosca, w. F. Tagliavini (ten), T. Gobbi (bar), F. Molinari-Pradelli (cnd), Royal Opera House Orch, Royal Opera House Chorus Covent Garden [I] *(rec live at Covent Garden, 6/30/55)* Legato Classics 2-▲ LCD 157-2 (m) [ADD]
Puccini, G.:Turandot, w. B. Nilsson (sop), J. Bjoerling (ten), G. Tozzi (bass), E. Leinsdorf (cnd), Rome Opera Orch, Rome Opera Chorus [I] RCA Red Seal 2-▲ 5932-2-RC 3-■ AGK3-3970
Puccini, G.:Turandot, w. Birgit Nilsson (sop—Turandot), Renata Tebaldi (sop—Liù), Jussi Björling (ten—Calaf), Alessio De Paolis (ten—Emperor Altoum), Piero de Palma (ten—Pang), Mario Sereni (bar—Ping), Adelio Zagonara (bar—Prince of Persia), Giorgio Tozzi (bass—Timur), Tommaso Frascati (bass—Pong), Leonardo Monreale (bass—Mandarin), E. Leinsdorf (cnd), Rome Opera Orch, Rome Opera Chorus *(rec Rome Opera House, July 3-11, 1959)* RCA Living Stereo 2-▲ 09026-62687-2 [ADD]
Puccini, G.:Turandot, w. I. Borkh (sop), M. del Monaco (ten), A. Erede (cnd), St. Cecilia Academy Orch Rome, St. Cecilia Academy Chorus Rome London 2-▲ 433761-2 [ADD]
Renata Tebaldi London ▲ 421312-2 LA [ADD]
Renata Tebaldi alla Scala, w. Martin Katz (pno) *(rec May 20, 1974)* Myto ▲ MCD 943105
Renata Tebaldi in Concert, w. Milan RAI Orch [cnd:Nino Sanzogno] *(rec Nov 30, 1953)* Standing Room Only 2-▲ SRO 824-2 [ADD]
La Tebaldi London 2-▲ 430481-2 [ADD]
Tebaldi, Barbieri & Valletti, w. Fedora Barbieri (mez), Cesare Valletti (ten), Fighera, Nino Sanzogno (cnd), Turin RAI SO, Milan RAI SO *(rec Martini & Rossi Concert, 1951 & 1953)* Incontri Memorabili ▲ CDMR 5012
Verdi, G.:Aida, w. E. Stignani (mez), M. del Monaco (ten), A. Protti (bar), F. Corena (bass), A. Erede (cnd), St. Cecilia Academy Orch Rome, St. Cecilia Academy Chorus Rome London 2-▲ 440239-2 [ADD]
Verdi, G.:Aida, w. G. Simionato (mez), C. Bergonzi (ten), C. MacNeil (bar), A. van Mill (bass), H. von Karajan (cnd), Vienna PO, Vienna State Opera Chorus [I] London ("Jubilee" series) ▲ 417763-2 [ADD]
Verdi, G.:Aida, w. G. Simionato (mez), C. Bergonzi (ten), C. MacNeil (bar), A. van Mill (bass), H. von Karajan (cnd), Vienna PO, Vienna State Opera Chorus [I] London 3-▲ 414087-2 [ADD]
Verdi, G.:Aida, w. Renata Tebaldi (sop—Aida), Ebe Stignani (mez—Amneris), Mario Del Monaco (ten—Radamès), Piero de Palma (ten—Messenger), Aldo Protti (bar—Amonasro), Fernando Corena (bass—King), Dario Caselli (bass—Ramfis), A. Erede (cnd), St. Cecilia Academy Orch Rome, St. Cecilia Academy Chorus Rome *(rec 1952)* Theorema 2-▲ TH 121133/34
Verdi, G.:Arias, w. Maria Callas (sop), *(orchs & choruses unknown)*—sels from La traviata, Il Trovatore & Un ballo in maschera *(rec 1953-64)* Andromeda ▲ ANR 2546 [ADD]
Verdi, G.:Un ballo in maschera, w. L. Pavarotti (ten), S. Milnes (bar), B. Bartoletti (cnd), St. Cecilia Academy Orch Rome, St. Cecilia Academy Chorus Rome London ▲ 440042-2
Verdi, G.:Don Carlos, w. G. Bumbry (mez), C. Bergonzi (ten), D. Fischer-Dieskau (bar), N. Ghiaurov (bass), G. Solti (cnd), Royal Opera House Orch Covent Garden, Royal Opera House Chorus Covent Garden [1886 5-act Italian version] [I] London 3-▲ 421114-2 [ADD]
Verdi, G.:Falstaff, w. Anna Moffo (sop—Nannetta), Renata Tebaldi (sop—Alice Ford), Anna Maria Canali (mez—Meg Page), Giulietta Simionato (mez—Dame Quickly), Mariano Caruso (ten—Doctor Caius), Alvinio Misciano (ten—Fenton), Luigi Vellucci (ten—Bardolfo), Tito Gobi (bar—Falstaff), Cornell MacNeil (bar—Ford), Kenneth Smith (bass-Pistola), T. Serafin (cnd), *(orch unknown) (rec Chicago, 1958)* Legato Classics 2-▲ LCD 206-2 [ADD]
Verdi, G.:La forza del destino, w. G. Simionato (mez), M. del Monaco (ten), E. Bastianini (bar), C. Siepi (b-bar), F. Molinari-Pradelli (cnd), St. Cecilia Academy Orch Rome, St. Cecilia Academy Chorus Rome [I] London 3-▲ 421598-2 [ADD]
Verdi, G.:La forza del destino, w. O. Dominguez (mez), F. Corelli (ten), R. Capecchi (bar), E. Bastianini (bar), B. Christoff (bass), F. Molinari-Pradelli (cnd), Naples Teatro San Carlo Orch, Naples Teatro San Carlo Chorus *(rec Oct. 1 1958)* Melodram 3-▲ MLO 370102 [AAD]
Verdi, G.:La forza del destino (sels), w. F. Corelli (ten), F. Molinari-Pradelli (cnd), Naples Teatro San Carlo Orch, Naples Teatro San Carlo Chorus *(rec live Mar. 15, 1958)* Legato Classics 2-▲ LCD 171-2 [ADD]
Verdi, G.:Giovanna d'Arco, w. Renata Tebaldi (sop—Giovanna), Gino Penno (ten—Carlo VII), Luciano Della Pergola (ten—Delil), Ugo Savarese (bar—Giacomo), Ignio Ricco (bass—Talbot), G. Santini (cnd), Naples Teatro San Carlo Orch, Naples Teatro San Carlo Chorus *(rec San Carlo Theater, Naples, Mar. 15, 1951)* Legato Classics 2-▲ LCD 193-2 [ADD]

Tebaldi, Renata (sop) (cont.)

Verdi, G.:Giovanna d'Arco, w. C. Bergonzi (ten), R. Panerai (bar), A. Simonetto (cnd), Milan RAI Orch, Milan RAI Chorus [I] *(rec live)* Melodram 2-▲ 27021
Verdi, G.:Giovanna d'Arco, w. Carlo Bergonzi (ten), Rolando Panerai (bar), A. Simonetto (cnd), Milan RAI SO, Milan RAI Chorus *(rec Milan, May 26, 1951)* Pantheon 2-▲ PHE 6610 (m)
Verdi, G.:Otello, w. M. del Monaco (ten), L. Warren (bar), A. Votto (cnd), La Scala Orch, La Scala Chorus *(rec July 1, 1954)* Melodram 2-▲ MLO 270101 [AAD]
Verdi, G.:Otello, w. M. Del Monaco (ten), A. Protti (bar), H. von Karajan (cnd), Vienna PO [I] London 2-▲ 411618-2 [ADD]
Verdi, G.:Otello, w. Renata Tebaldi (sop—Desdemona), Luisa Ribacchi (mez—Emilia), Angelo Mercuriali (ten—Roderigo), Mario del Monaco (ten—Otello), Piero de Palma (ten—Cassio), Aldo Protti (bar—Iago), Dario Caselli (bass—A Herald), Fernando Corena (bass—Lodovico), Pierluigi Martinucci (bass—Montano), A. Erede (cnd), St. Cecilia Academy Orch Rome, St. Cecilia Academy Chorus Rome Theorema ▲ TH 121141/142
Verdi, G.:Otello (sels), w. K. Adler (cnd), *(orch unknown)*—Piangea cantanda...Salce, salce; Ave Maria [I] *(rec live, Los Angeles 8/30/56)* Standing Room Only 2-▲ SRO 825-2 [ADD]
Verdi, G.:Rigoletto, w. M. del Monaco (ten), A. Protti (bar), P. de Palma (bass), F. Corena (bass), A. Erede (cnd), St. Cecilia Academy Orch Rome, St. Cecilia Academy Chorus Rome London 2-▲ 440245-2 [ADD]
Verdi, G.:Simon Boccanegra, w. Renata Tebaldi (sop—Maria Boccanegra), Penelope Jensen (mez—Maria's Maidservant), Richard Tucker (ten—Gabriele Adorno), Rod MacWerter (ten—Paolo), Cornell MacNeil (bar—Simon Boccanegra), Ara Berberian (bar—Pietro), Ezio Flagello (bass—Jacopo Fiesco), Franco Iglesias (bass—Paolo), J. Levine (cnd), *(orch unknown) (rec live, Miami, 1970)* Legato Classics 2-▲ LCD 189-2 [ADD]
Verdi, G.:Simon Boccanegra (sels), w. R. Tucker (ten)—Cielo di stelle orbato; Il Doge qui; Tu qui?...Amelia! *(rec between 1956-63)* Standing Room Only ▲ SRO 8441 [ADD]
Verdi, G.:La traviata, w. Renata Tebaldi (sop—Violetta), Giacinto Prandelli (ten—Alfredo), Carlo Tagliabue (bar—Germont), T. Serafin (cnd), Naples Teatro San Carlo Orch, Naples Teatro San Carlo Chorus *(rec Arena Flegrea, Naples, July 3, 1954)* Golden Age of Opera 2-▲ GAO 191/192 [ADD]
Verdi, G.:La traviata, w. G. Prandelli (ten), G. Orlandini (bar), C. M. Giulini (cnd), Milan RAI Orch, Milan RAI Chorus *(rec live 5/28/52)* Standing Room Only 2-▲ SRO 810-2 [ADD]
Verdi, G.:La traviata, w. et al., F. Molinari-Pradelli (cnd), St. Cecilia Academy Orch Rome, St. Cecilia Academy Chorus Rome London 2-▲ 430250-2 [ADD]
Verdi, G.:La traviata (sels), w. N. Filacuridi (ten), U. Savarese (bar), T. Serafin (cnd), Florence Maggio Musicale Orch, Florence Maggio Musicale Chorus *(rec live, Florence 1956)* Melodram ▲ MEL 15006
Verdi, G.:La traviata (sels), w. Anna de Santis (sop—Annina), Renata Tebaldi (sop—Violetta), Giuseppe Campora (ten—Alfredo), Gerardo Gaudioso (bar—Douphol), Giuseppe Taddei (bar—Germont), Antonio Picillo (bass—Grenvil), G. Santini (cnd), Naples Teatro San Carlo Orch, Naples Teatro San Carlo Chorus—E strano...Ah, fors'e lui; Follie!...Sempre libera; Pero l'attendo...Amami, Alfredo; Invitato a qui seguirmi; Alfredo, Alfredo, di questo core; Teneste la promessa...Addio del passato; Ma se tornando...Ah! Gran Dio! Morir si giovine; Se una pudica vergine *(rec San Carlo Theater, Naples, Jan. 17, 1952)* Legato Classics 2-▲ LCD 193-2 [ADD]
Wagner, R.:Lohengrin (sels), w. R. Tebaldi (sop—Elsa), E. Nicolai (mez—Ortrud), G. Penno (ten—Lohengrin), G. Guelfi (bar—Telramund), G. Neri (bass—Heinrich), G. Santini (cnd), Naples Teatro San Carlo Orch, Naples Teatro San Carlo Chorus—8 soprano duets/trio from Acts 1-3 [I] *(rec live, Naples, 12/26/54)* Standing Room Only ▲ SRO 834-1 [ADD]
Wagner, R.:Tannhäuser (sels), w. H. Beirer (ten), C. Tagliabue (bar), B. Christoff (bass), K. Böhm (cnd), Naples Teatro San Carlo Orch, Naples Teatro San Carlo Chorus—10 soprano solo, duet & ensemble arias Acts 2 & 3 [I; Hans Beirer (Tannhäuser) sings in German] *(rec live, Naples, 3/12/50)* Standing Room Only ▲ SRO 834-1 [ADD]

Tedeschi, Alfredo (ten)

Verdi, G.:Falstaff, w. Augusta Ottrabella (sop—Nannetta), Franca Somigli (sop—Alice), Angelica Cravcenko (mez—Mrs. Quickly), Mita Vasari (mez—Meg), Dino Borgioli (ten—Fenton), Giuseppe Nessi (ten—Bardolfo), Alfredo Tedeschi (ten—Dr. Cajus), Piero Biasini (bar—Ford), Mariano Stabile (bar—Falstaff), Virgilio Lazzari (bass—Pistola), A. Toscanini (cnd), Vienna PO, Vienna State Opera Chorus *(rec Salzburg, Aug 23, 1937)* Minerva 2-▲ MN A36/37 (m) [ADD]

Tedeschi, Ismildo (ten)

Bizet, G.:Carmen, w. Laura Bustamante (sop—Frasquita), Ximena Riveros (sop—Mercedes), Nancy Stokes (sop—Micaela), Regina Resnik (mez—Carmen), Plácido Domingo (ten—Don José), Ismildo Tedeschi (ten—Remendado), Ramon Vinay (ten—Escamillo), Juan Charles (ten/bar—Dancaire), Agustin Letelier (bar—Morles), Jorge Algorta (bass—Zuniga), A. Guadagno (cnd), Santiago Teatro Municipale Orch, Santiago Teatro Municipale Chorus *(rec Santiago Municipal Theater, Sept. 4, 1967)* Legato Classics 2-▲ LCD 194-2 [ADD]
Verdi, G.:Falstaff, w. Dino Borgioli (ten), Mariano Stabile (bar), A. Toscanini (cnd), Vienna PO, Vienna State Opera Chorus *(rec live, Salzburg Festival, 1936)* Arkadia 2-▲ 625

Tedesco, Alfio (ten)

Verdi, G.:Ernani (sels), w. Grace Anthony (sop), Giuseppe De Luca (bar)—O sommo Carlo *(rec 1928)* Minerva ▲ MN-A23 [ADD]

Tedesco, Sergio (ten)

Donizetti, G.:Le Convenienze Teatrali, w. M.A. Peters (sop), A. Cicogna (mez), R. Scaltriti (bar), B. Rigacci (cnd), Emilia Romagna Arturo Toscanini SO, Lugo Teatro Comunale Rossini Chorus [I] *(rec live, 6/90)* Bongiovanni 2-▲ GB 2091/92 [DDD]
Lattuada, F.:Le Preziose ridicole, w. S. Valayre (sop—Madelon), A. Catarci (sop—Marotte), A. Cicogna (mez—Cathos), S. Tedesco (ten—La Grange), E. Di Cesare (ten—Mascarille), A. Veccia (bar—Croissy), R. Servile (bar—Jodelet), E. Fissore (bass—Gorgibus), E. Romagna (cnd), Toscanini SO, G. Masini (cnd), Rossini Teatro Comunale Chorus [I] *(rec live, 1991)* Ermitage ▲ ERM 404 [DDD]

Tegzes, Maria (sop)

Eisler, H.:Songs, w. G. Burleson (pno)—Die Maske des Bösens; Lied eines Freudenmädchens; Hollywood Elegy; Wie der Wind weht; Lied der Kupplerin; Andere die Welt, sie braucht es Neuma ▲ 45083 [DDD]
Electro Accoustic Music III, w. Camilla Hoitenga (fl), William Buonocore (gtr), Jacques Linder (pno), Robert McCormick (perc) Neuma ▲ 450-87 [DDD]
Harsh, E.:Songs, w. Geoffery Burleson (pno)—be not the slave of words/i fear loquacios odes Neuma ▲ 45083 [DDD]
Korde, S.:Rasa, w. *(other parts unknown)* Neuma ▲ 450-85 [DDD]
Risset, J.-C.:Autre face Neuma ▲ 450-73 [DDD]
Schoenberg, A.:The Cabaret Songs, w. G. Burleson (pno) Neuma ▲ 45083 [DDD]
Westergaard, P.:Ariel Music, w. M. Pratt (cnd), Group for Contemporary Music CRI ▲ CD 696 [DDD]

Tei, Enzo (sgr)

Donizetti, G.:Il Duca d'Alba, w. Wladimiro Ganzarolli (bar), Louis Quilico (bar), Ivana Tosini (sgr), T. Schippers (cnd), Trieste PO *(rec live at the Spoleto Festival, June 11, 1959)* Memories 2-▲ MEM 4579 [ADD]

Teichert-Hailperin, Almut (sop)

Brassart, J.:Ave Maria, w. K. Smith (ct), W. Jochesn (ten), M. Nitz (ten), Helga Weber Instrumental Circle Entrée ▲ 0041 [ADD]
Dufay, G.:Magnificat, w. K. Smith (ct), W. Jochesn (ten), Helga Weber Instrumental Circle—Octavi toni for 3 voices Entrée ▲ 0041 [ADD]
Dunstable, J.:Sacred Music, w. K. Smith (ct), W. Jochens (ten), M. Nitz (ten), H. Deutsch (bar), Helga Weber Instrumental Circle—Sancta Maria; Beata dei genetrix; Beata mater et innupta virgo; Speciosa facta es; Alma redemptoris mater Entrée ▲ 0041 [ADD]
Hildegard Of Bingen:Sacred Songs, w. K. Smith (ct), W. Jochens (ten), M. Nitz (ten), H. Deutsch (bar), Helga Weber Instrumental Circle—Caritas abundat in omnia; O virtus sapientiae; O quam mirabilis; Hodie aperuit nobis clausa porta; Alleluia. O virga, mediatrix; O clarissima mater; O frodens virga Entrée ▲ 0041 [ADD]
Love Songs from the 14th & 15th Centuries, w. Kevin Smith (ct), Wilfried Jochens (ten), Martin Nitz (ten), Instrumentalkreis Helga Weber Entrée ▲ CHE 0042-2 [ADD]

Te Kanawa, Kiri (sop)

Ave Maria Philips ▲ 412629-2 PH [DDD] ■ 412629-4 PH (D) □ 412629-5

▲ = CD ♦ = Enhanced CD Δ = MD ■ = Cassette Tape □ = DCC

Te Kanawa, Kiri (sop) (cont.)

Bach, J.S.:St. Matthew Passion, w. A. S. von Otter (mez), H. P. Blochwitz (ten), A. Rolfe Johnson (ten), O. Bär (bar), T. Krause (bass), G. Solti (cnd), Chicago SO, Chicago Sym Chorus, Glen Ellyn Children's Chorus [G] London 3-▲ 421177-2 [DDD]
Bach, J.S.:St. Matthew Passion (sels), w. A. S. von Otter (mez), H. P. Blochwitz (ten), A. Rolfe Johnson (ten), O. Bär (bar), T. Krause (bass), G. Solti (cnd), Chicago SO, Chicago Sym Chorus, Glen Ellyn Children's Chorus [G] London ▲ 425691-2 [DDD]
Beethoven, L. van:Cant on the Death of the Emperor Joseph II, w. Y. Newman (mez), D. Barrett (bar), M. Langdon (bass), C. Davis (cnd), BBC SO, BBC Chorus, BBC Choral Society [G] *(rec live Oct. 7, 1970)* Intaglio ▲ INCD 7361 [ADD]
Beethoven, L. van:Sym 9, "Choral Sym", w. E. Jochum (cnd), London SO, London Sym Chorus EMI Classics ▲ CDM 64633
Bernstein, L.:Music of, w. J. Norman (sop), J. Anderson (sop), F. von Stade (mez), C. Ludwig (mez), T. Troyanos (mez), J. Carreras (ten), D. Garrison (ten), J. Hadley (ten), T. Hampson (bar), T. Daly (sgr), G. Kremer (vn), M. Rostropovich (vc), M.T. Thomas (va), L. Bernstein (cnd), *(orch unknown)*—various popular works Deutsche Grammophon ▲ 439251-2 ■ 439251-4
Bernstein, L.:West Side Story, w. T. Troyanos (mez), J. Carreras (ten), K. Ollmann (bass), L. Bernstein (cnd), *(orch unknown)* [E] Deutsche Grammophon ▲ 415963-2 [DDD] ■ 415963-4 □ 415963-5
Bernstein, L.:West Side Story (sels) London ▲ 440280-2 ■ 440280-4
Bizet, G.:Carmen, w. T. Troyanos (mez), P. Domingo (ten), J. Van Dam (b-bar), G. Solti (cnd), London PO [F] London ▲ 421300-2 [ADD]
Bizet, G.:Carmen, w. T. Troyanos (mez), P. Domingo (ten), J. Van Dam (b-bar), G. Solti (cnd), London PO [F] London 3-▲ 414489-2 [ADD]
Bizet, G.:Carmen, w. Shirley Verrett (mez), Placido Domingo (ten), José Van Dam (b-bar), G. Solti (cnd), Royal Opera House Orch, Royal Opera House Chorus Covent Garden *(rec live, London, 1973)* Arkadia 3-▲ 498
Blue Skies, w. Nelson Riddle Orch London ▲ 414666-2 LH [DDD]
Brahms, J.:Ein Deutsches Requiem, w. B. Weikl (bar), G. Solti (cnd), Chicago SO, Chicago Sym Chorus [G] London 2-▲ 414627-2 [ADD]
Canteloube, J.:Songs of Auvergne, w. J. Tate (cnd), English CO—series 1-5 *(rec Kingsway Hall, London, Aug 16-19, 1982 & Sept 26)* London ("Double Decker" series) 2-▲ 444995-2 [DDD]
Canteloube, J.:Songs of Auvergne, w. J. Tate (cnd), English CO London ▲ 411730-2
Christmas with Kiri, w. Carl Davis, Philharmonia Orch, London Voices London ▲ 414632-2 LH [DDD]
Come to the Fair (Danny Boy & Other British Folksongs) EMI Classics ▲ CDC 47080 [DDD] ■ 4DS 38097 (D)
Delius, F.:A Mass of Life, w. P. Bowden (mez), R. Dowd (ten), J. Shirley-Quirk (bar), N. del Mar (cnd), BBC SO, BBC Sym Chorus *(rec live, London 5/3/71)* Intaglio 2-▲ INCD 702-2 [ADD]
Fauré, G.:Requiem, w. S. Milnes (bar), C. Dutoit (cnd), Montreal SO, Montreal Sym Chorus [L] London ▲ 421440-2 [DDD] □ 421440-5
French Opera Arias, w. Royal Opera Orch [cnd:Jeffrey Tate] Angel ▲ CDC 49863 [DDD]
Gershwin, G.:Music of Angel ▲ CDC 47454 ■ 4DS 47454
Gershwin, G.:Songs, w. J. McGlinn (cnd), New Princess Theater Orch EMI Classics ▲ CDC 47454 [DDD]
Gounod, C.:Faust, w. F. Araiza (ten), E. Nesterenko (bass), C. Davis (cnd), Bavarian RSO, Bavarian Radio Chorus [F] Philips 3-▲ 420164-2 [DDD]
Great American Songwriter's, w. Bruce Hubbard (bar), Frederica von Stade (mez), Thomas Hampson (bar) Angel ▲ CDM 64670
Great Love Scenes, w. Plácido Domingo (ten), R. Scotto (sop), I. Cotrubas (sop) CBS ▲ MK 39030 ■ MT 39030
Handel, G.F.:Arias—features arias from Rinaldo, Alcina, Giulio Cesare, Agrippina, Amadigi, Ariodante & Giustino Philips ▲ 434992-2
Handel, G.F.:Messiah, w. Anne Gjevang (mez), Richard Lewis (ten), Gwynne Howell (bass), G. Solti (cnd), Chicago SO, Chicago Sym Chorus [E] London 2-▲ 414396-2 [DDD]
Handel, G.F.:Messiah (sels), w. Anne Gjevang (mez), Richard Lewis (ten), Gwynne Howell (bass), G. Solti (cnd), Chicago SO, Chicago Sym Chorus—arias & choruses London ▲ 430098-2 [DDD] ■ 430098-4
Heart to Heart Angel ▲ CDQ 54299 ■ 4DQ 54299
Herrmann, B.:Film Music, w. C. Gerhardt (cnd), National PO London—On Dangerous Ground; Citizen Kane; Beneath the 12-Mile Reef; Hanover Square; White Witch Doctor RCA ▲ 0707-2-RG [ADD] ■ 0707-4-RG
Italian Opera Arias, w. London SO [cnd:M. W. Chung] EMI Classics ▲ CDC 54062
James Levine's 25th Anniversary Metropolitan Opera Gala, w. J. Levine (cnd), Metropolitan Opera Orch, Ileana Cotrubas (sop), Renée Fleming (sop), Hei-Kyung Hong (sop), Karita Mattila (sop), Birgit Nilsson (sop), Ruth Ann Swenson (sop), Deborah Voigt (sop), Grace Bumbry (mez), Heidi Grant Murphy (mez), Anne Sofie von Otter (mez) *(rec live, Metropolitan Opera House, New York, Apr 27, 1996)* Deutsche Grammophon ▲ 449177-2 [DDD]
Kern, J.:Music of, w. J. McGlinn (cnd), London Sinfonietta Angel ▲ CDQ 54527 ■ 4DQ 54527
Kiri:Her Greatest Hits London ▲ 443600-2 [DDD] ■ 443600-4
Kiri in Recital, w. Roger Vignoles (pno) London ▲ 425820-2 LH [DDD]
Kiri on Broadway London ▲ 440280-2 ■ 440280-4
The Kiri Selection Angel ▲ CDQ 54530
Kiri Sidetracks, w. André Previn (pno), Mundell Lowe (gtr), Ray Brown (db) Philips ▲ 434092-2 PH [DDD] ■ 434092-4 PH (D)
Kiri Sings Kern, w. London Sinfonietta [cnd:John McGlinn] Angel ▲ CDQ 54527 ■ 4DQ 54527
Kiri Te Kanawa EMI Classics ("Diva" series) ▲ CDM 65578
Lerner, A.J.:My Fair Lady (sels) London ▲ 440280-2 ■ 440280-4
A Little Christmas Music, w. King's Singers, City of London Brass Quintet, City of London Sinfonia [cnd:R. Hickox] EMI Classics ▲ CDC 49909
McCartney, P.:Liverpool Oratorio, w. S. Burgess (mez), J. Hadley (ten), W. White (bass), C. Davis (cnd), Royal Liverpool PO, Royal Liverpool Phil Choir EMI Classics 2-▲ CDQB 54371 2-■ 4D2Q 54371
Mad About Love, w. Cheryl Studer (sop), José Carreras (ten), Jerry Hadley (ten), Philharmonia Orch [cnd:Giuseppe Sinopoli], Bastille Opera Orch [cnd:Myung-Whun Chung], Boston SO [cnd:Seiji Ozawa], Vienna PO [cnd:John Eliot Gardiner, James Levine] Deutsche Grammophon ▲ 449112-2 ■ 449112-4
Mahler, G.:Sym 2, w. M. Horne (mez), S. Ozawa (cnd), Boston SO, Tanglewood Festival Chorus [G] Philips 2-▲ 420824-2 [DDD]
Mahler, G.:Sym 4, w. G. Solti (cnd), Chicago SO [G] London ▲ 410188-2 [DDD]
Mozart, W.A.:Arias, w. A. Davis (cnd), London SO—from Die Zauberflöte, Così fan tutte, Idomeneo, Zaide, Lucio Silla; others [G,I] Philips ▲ 411148-2 [DDD]
Mozart, W.A.:Arias, w. E. Steber (sop), I. Cotrubas (sop), R. Stevens (mez), P. Domingo (ten), S. Jerusalem (ten), G. London (bar), E. Pinza (bass)—arias & duets from Don Giovanni, Le nozze di Figaro, Die Zauberflöte, etc. *(rec 1941-1978)* CBS Masterworks ▲ MDK 46579 [AAD] ■ MGT 46579
Mozart, W.A.:Arias, w. G. Fischer (cnd), Vienna CO—(7 concert arias) K.272, K.583, K.73d (79), K.582, K.490, K.528, K.383 [G,I] London ▲ 417756-2 [ADD]
Mozart, W.A.:Arias, w. J. Tate (cnd), English CO—from Die Entführung aus dem Serail; Mitridate, Re di Ponto; Don Giovanni; concert arias, K.369 & K.505 [G,I] Philips ▲ 420950-2 [DDD]
Mozart, W.A.:Arias—Le Nozze de Figaro *(Porgo amor; E Susanno non vienl...Dove sono)*, Der Shauspieldirektor *(Bester Jungling)* & seven concert arias *(K.272; K.583/1 & 2; K.528; K.490; K.73d; K. 79)* *(rec 1980; 1981 & 1990)* London ▲ 440401-2 [ADD/DDD]
Mozart, W.A.:Ave verum corpus, w. A. Sofie von Otter (mez), A. R. Johnson (ten), R. Lloyd (bass), N. Marriner (cnd), Academy of St. Martin in the Fields, Academy Chorus *(rec London, Mar. 10-12, 1993)* Philips ▲ 438999-2
Mozart, W.A.:Complete Mozart Edition, w. M. Arroyo (sop), M. Freni (sop), S. Burrows (ten), I. Wixell (bar), C. Davis (cnd), Royal Opera House Orch, Royal Opera House Chorus Covent Garden Philips 3-▲ 422541-2 [ADD]
Mozart, W.A.:Così fan tutte, w. Marie McLaughlin (sop), Ann Murray (mez), Hans-Peter Blochwitz (ten), Thomas Hampson (bar), G. Furlanetto (bar), J. Levine (cnd), Vienna PO, Vienna State Opera Chorus [I] Deutsche Grammophon 3-▲ 423897-2 [DDD]

Te Kanawa, Kiri (sop) (cont.)

Mozart, W.A.:Così fan tutte, w. T. Stratas (sop), F. von Stade (mez), A. Lombard (cnd), Strasbourg PO, Rhine Opera Chorus Erato 3-▲ 98494-2
Mozart, W.A.:Don Giovanni, w. E. Moser (sop), T. Berganza (mez), K. Riegel (ten), G. Raimondi (ten), J. Van Dam (b-bar), J. Macurdy (bass), L. Maazel (cnd), Paris Opera Orch, Paris Opera Chorus [I] CBS 3-▲ M3K 35192
Mozart, W.A.:Don Giovanni (sels), w. E. Moser (sop), T. Berganza (mez), K. Riegel (ten), G. Raimondi (ten), J. Van Dam (b-bar), J. Macurdy (bass), L. Maazel (cnd), Paris Opera Orch CBS ■ MT 35859
Mozart, W.A.:Don Giovanni (sels), w. Teresa Berganza (mez), José Van Dam (bass-bar), Ruggero Raimondi (bass), L. Maazel (cnd), Paris Opera Orch, Paris Opera Chorus Sony Classical ("Essential Classics" series) ▲ SBK 62663 ■ SBT 62663
Mozart, W.A.:Exsultate, w. C. Davis (cnd), London SO [L] Philips ▲ 412873-2 [ADD]
Mozart, W.A.:Kyrie, K.341, w. E. Bainbridge (mez), A. Davies (ten), G. Howell (bass), C. Davis (cnd), London SO, London Sym Chorus [L] Philips ▲ 412873-2
Mozart, W.A.:Missa, K.427, w. I. Cotrubas (sop), W. Krenn (ten), H. Sotin (bass), R. Leppard (cnd), New Philharmonia Orch, John Alldis Choir [L] EMI Classics ▲ CDC 47385
Mozart, W.A.:Missa, K.427, w. A. Sofie von Otter (mez), A. R. Johnson (ten), R. Lloyd (bass), N. Marriner (cnd), Academy of St. Martin in the Fields, Academy of St. Martin in the Fields Chorus *(rec London, Mar. 10-12, 1993)* Philips ▲ 438999-2
Mozart, W.A.:Nozze di Figaro, w. L. Popp (sop), F. von Stade (mez), T. Allen (bar), S. Ramey (bass), K. Moll (bass), G. Solti (cnd), London PO [I] London 3-▲ 410150-2 [DDD]
Mozart, W.A.:Nozze di Figaro (sels), w. L. Popp (sop), F. von Stade (mez), T. Allen (bar), S. Ramey (bass), K. Moll (bass), G. Solti (cnd), London PO [I] London ▲ 417395-2 [DDD] □ 417395-5
Mozart, W.A.:Vesperae solennes, w. E. Bainbridge (mez), A. Davies (ten), G. Howell (bass), C. Davis (cnd), London SO, London Sym Chorus [L] Philips ▲ 412873-2 [ADD]
Mozart, W.A.:Zauberflöte, w. C. Studer (sop), E. Lind (sop), F. Araiza (ten), O. Bär (bar), S. Ramey (bass), N. Marriner (cnd), Academy of St. Martin in the Fields, Ambrosian Opera Chorus [G] Philips 2-▲ 426276-2 [DDD]
Mozart, W.A.:Zauberflöte (sels), w. C. Studer (sop), E. Lind (sop), F. Araiza (ten), O. Bär (bar), S. Ramey (bass), N. Marriner (cnd), Academy of St. Martin in the Fields Philips ▲ 438495-2
Our Christmas Songs for You, w. Roberto Alagna (ten), Thomas Hampson (bar), Jonathan Tunick (cnd), *(orch unknown)* EMI Classics ▲ CDC 56176
Porter, C.:Kiss Me, Kate (sels) London ▲ 440280-2 ■ 440280-4
Porter, C.:Music of, w. P. Matz (cnd), New World SO Angel ▲ CDQ 55050 ■ 4DQ 55050
A Portrait of Kiri Te Kanawa London ▲ 417645-2 LH ■ 417645-4
A Portrait of Kiri Te Kanawa CBS ▲ MK 39208 ■ MT 39208
Puccini, G.:Arias, w. J. Pritchard (cnd), London PO [I] CBS ▲ MK 37298 [DDD] ■ IMT 37298 (D)
Puccini, G.:Manon Lescaut, w. J. Carreras (ten), P. Coni (bar), I. Tajo (bass), R. Chailly (cnd), Bologna Teatro Comunale Orch [I] London 2-▲ 421426-2 [DDD]
Puccini, G.:Music of, w. Eva Marton (sop), José Carreras (ten), Luciano Pavarotti (ten), Richard Tucker (ten), *(other artists unknown)*—19 arias & duets from La bohème, Gianni Schicchi, Madama Butterfly, La Rondine, Tosca & Turandot *(six mono & 13 stereo recordings)* CBS ▲ MLK 45809 [AAD/ADD/D ■ MLT 45809
Puccini, G.:La Rondine, w. M. Nicolesco (sop), P. Domingo (ten), D. Rendall (ten), L. Nucci (bar), L. Maazel (cnd), London SO, Ambrosian Opera Chorus [I] CBS 2-▲ M2K 37852 [DDD]
Puccini, G.:Tosca (sels), w. J. Aragall (ten), L. Nucci (bar), G. Solti (cnd), National PO London, Welsh National Opera Chorus London ▲ 421611-2 [DDD]
Robbins, R.:Film Music, w. *(other artists unknown)*—A Room with a View; Howard's End; Maurice Angel ▲ ZDMC 28956
Rodgers, R.:Music of—sels from Carousel & The Sound of Music London ▲ 440280-2 ■ 440280-4
Schubert, Franz:Songs (misc), w. Elly Ameling (sop), Judith Blegen (sop), Judith Raskin (sop)—Rastlose Liebe; Gretchen am Spinnrade; Trockne Blumen; Nur wer die Sehnsucht kennt Sony Classical ("Essential Classics" series) ▲ SBK 62422 ■ SBT 62422
Songs of Inspiration, w. Julius Rudel, Utah SO, Mormon Tabernacle Choir London ▲ 425431-2 LH [DDD]
Strauss (II), Joh.:Die Fledermaus, w. E. Gruberová (sop), B. Fassbaender (mez), W. Brendel (bar), R. Leech (ten), O. Bär (bar), T. Krause (bar), A. Previn (cnd), Vienna PO, Vienna State Opera Chorus [G] Philips 2-▲ 432157-2 [DDD]
Strauss (II), Joh.:Die Fledermaus (sels), w. E. Gruberova (sop), B. Fassbaender (mez), R. Leech (ten), W. Brendel (bar), O. Bär (bar), A. Previn (cnd), Vienna PO Philips ▲ 438503-2
Strauss, R.:Arabella, w. Fontana (sgr), H. Dernesch (sop/mez), F. Grundheber (bar), J. Tate (cnd), Royal Opera House Orch [G] London 3-▲ 417623-2 [DDD]
Strauss, R.:Capriccio, w. Kiri Te Kanawa (sop—Gräfin), Brigitte Fassbaender (mez—Clairon), Uwe Heilmann (ten—Flamand), Werner Hollweg (ten—Taupe), Olaf Bär (bar—Olivier), Håkan Hagegård (bar—Graf), Victor von Halem (b-bar—La Roche), U. Schirmer (cnd), Vienna PO [G] *(rec Vienna, Dec 1993)* London 2-▲ 444405-2 [DDD]
Strauss, R.:4 Last Songs, w. A. Davis (cnd), London SO [G] CBS ▲ MK 35140 ■ MT 35140
Strauss, R.:4 Last Songs, w. G. Solti (cnd), Vienna PO [G] London ▲ 430511-2 [DDD]
Strauss, R.:Der Rosenkavalier, w. B. Hendricks (sop), A. S. von Otter (mez), B. Haitink (cnd), Dresden Staatskapelle EMI Classics 3-▲ CDCC 54259
Strauss, R.:Der Rosenkavalier (sels), w. B. Hendricks (sop), A. S. von Otter (mez), R. Leech (ten), K. Rydl (bass), B. Haitink (cnd), Dresden Staatskapelle, Dresden State Opera Chorus EMI Classics ▲ ZDC 54493
Strauss, R.:Songs, w. G. Solti (pno)—Malven; Hat gesagt; Muttertandelei; Madrigal; Ständchen; Schlechtes Wetter; Allerseelen; Die Nacht; Cäcilie; All mein Gedanken; Begegnung; Morgen; Zueignung [G] London ▲ 430511-2 [DDD]
Strauss, R.:Songs, w. A. Davis (cnd), London SO—6 songs CBS ▲ MK 35140 ■ MT 35140
Tchaikovsky, P.:Eugene Onegin, w. K. Te Kanawa (sop—Tatiana), P. Bardon (mez—Olga), N. Rosenshein (ten—Lensky), T. Hampson (b-bar—Eugene Onegin), J. Connell (bass—Prince Gremin), C. Mackerras (cnd), Welsh National Opera Orch, Welsh National Opera Chorus [E] EMI Classics ▲ CDCB 55004
Verdi, G.:Arias [I] CBS ▲ MK 37298 [DDD] ■ IMT 37298 (D)
Verdi, G.:Otello, w. L. Pavarotti (ten), L. Nucci (bar), G. Solti (cnd), Chicago SO, Chicago Sym Chorus [I] London 2-▲ 433669-2 [DDD]
Verdi, G.:Simon Boccanegra, w. J. Aragall (ten), L. Nucci (bar), P. Burchuladze (bass), G. Solti (cnd), La Scala Orch, La Scala Chorus [I] London 2-▲ 425628-2 [DDD]
Verdi, G.:La traviata, w. A. Kraus (ten), D. Hvorostovsky (bar), Z. Mehta (cnd), Florence Maggio Musicale Orch, Florence Maggio Musicale Chorus [I] Philips 2-▲ 438238-2
Villa-Lobos, H.:Bachiana brasileira 5, w. R.E. Harrell (cnd), Ensemble London ▲ 411730-2 [DDD]
Villa-Lobos, H.:Bachiana brasileira 5, w. Lynn Harrell (vc) *(other cellists unknown)* *(rec Walthamstow Town Hall, June 24, 1984)* London ("Double Decker" series) 2-▲ 444995-2 [DDD]
Wagner, R.:Der Ring des Nibelungen (sels), w. E. Marton (sop), C. Studer (sop), M. Lipovšek (mez), S. Jerusalem (ten), R. Goldberg (ten), P. Haage (ten), J. Morris (bass), B. Haitink (cnd), Bayer RSO EMI Classics ▲ ZDC 54633
Wagner, R.:Siegfried, w. E. Marton (sop), S. Jerusalem (ten), P. Haage (ten), J. Morris (bass), B. Haitink (cnd), Bavarian RSO [G] EMI Classics 4-▲ CDCD 54290
Wagner, R.:Tannhäuser (sels), w. R. Kollo (ten), Håkan Hagegård (bar), W. Meier (mez), M. Holle (bass), M. Janowski (cnd), Philharmonia Orch, Ambrosian Singers; music from film soundtrack for Meeting Venus Teldec ▲ 2292 46336-2 [DDD] ■ 2292 46336-4 □ 2292 46336-5
Wagner, R.:Tannhäuser (sels), w. W. Meier (mez), R. Kollo (ten), H. Hagegard (bar), M. Janowski (cnd), Philharmonia Orch, Ambrosian Singers Teldec ▲ 46336-2 ■ 46336-4
Weill, K.:One Touch of Venus (sels) London ▲ 440280-2 ■ 440280-4
The Young Kiri (Early Recordings, 1964-70), w. various orchs London 2-▲ 430325-2 LH2 [ADD]

Telese, Maryanne (sop)

Let My Song Fill Your Heart:A Remembrance of the American Concert Song, w. Arthur Woodley (bass), Peter Howard (pno), Joseph Smith (pno) Premier ▲ PR 1002

Tellini, Ines Alfani (sop)

Bizet, G.:Carmen, w. Aurora d'Alessio Buades (cta), Aureliano Pertile (ten), Benvenuto Franci (bar), L. Molajoli (cnd), La Scala Orch, La Scala Chorus *(rec Milan, 1933)* Phonographie 2-▲ PHG 5013 [ADD]

Tellini, Ines Alfani (sop) (cont.)
Verdi, G.:Falstaff, w. Pia Tassinari (sop—Alice Ford), Ines Alfani Tellini (sop—Nannetta), Aurora Buades (mez—Quickly), Rita Monticone (mez—Meg Page), Roberto D'Alessio (ten—Fenton), Giuseppe Nessi (ten—Bardolfo), Emilio Venturini (ten—Dr. Caius), Emilio Ghirardini (bar—Ford), Giacomo Rimini (bar—Sir John Falstaff), Salvatore Baccaloni (bass—Pistola), L. Molajoli (cnd), Milan SO, La Scala Chorus *(rec La Scala Theatre, Milan, Apr. 1932)* VAI Audio 2-▲ VAIA 1098-2

Telva, Marion (mez)
Beethoven, L. van:Missa Solemnis, w. E. Rethberg (sop), G. Martinelli (ten), E. Pinza (bass), A. Toscanini (cnd), New York PO, Westminster Choir [L] *(rec live, New York 4/28/35)* Melodram 2-▲ CDM 28036 [ADD]

Temesi, Maria (sop)
Liszt, F.:Hungaria 1848, w. A. Molnár (ten), S. Sólyom-Nagy (bar), I. Zámbó (cnd), Hungarian State Orch, Hungarian People's Army Male Chorus—composed as a salute to the Hungarian revolution [G] Hungaroton ▲ HCD 12748 [DDD]
Mahler, G.:Sym 8, w. Lyudmila Hadzhieva (sop), Darina Takova (sop), Tamara Takac (alt), Boryana Tabakova (alt), Janos Bandi (ten), Pal Kovacs (bar), Tamash Syule (bass), E. Tabakov (cnd), Sofia PO, Bulgarian National Chorus, Bulgarian National Radio Chorus, Bulgarian National Radio Children's Choir *(rec National Palace of Culture, Sofia, June 1991)* Capriccio 15-▲ 49043 [DDD]

Temperley, Jean (mez)
Ketèlbey, A.W.:Music of, w. V. Mdegley (ten), L. Pearson (pno), J. Lanchbery (cnd), Philharmonia Orch, Ambrosian Singers—In a Persian Market; In a Monastery Garden; Chal Romano; In the Mystic Land of Egypt; The Clock and the Dresden Figures; Bells across the Meadows; In a Chinese Temple; In the Moonlight; Sanctuary of the Heart Classics for Pleasure ▲ CDCFP 4637 [ADD]

Temple, Richard (bar)
Sullivan, A.:The Pirates of Penzance (sels)—I am a pirate king; Poor wand'ring one Symposium ▲ 1123

Temple, Wilfred (sgr)
Dibdin, C.:Lionel & Clarissa (sels), w. O. Groves (sgr), A. Reynolds (cnd), Hammersmith Lyric Theater Orch *(rec 1925 for HMV)* Pearl ▲ PEA 9917 (m) [AAD]

Tenko (sgr)
Sato, M.:Improvs, w. Michihiro Sato (tsugaru shamisen), Bill Frisell (elec gtr), Fred Frith (elec gtr), Mark Miller (elec bass), Nicolas Collins (elec), Christian Marclay (turntables), Steve Colemann (sax), Tom Cora (vc), Joey Baron (perc), Mark Dresser (elec bass), Gerry Hemingway (perc), Toh Ban Djan [Ikue Mori (perc), Luli Shioi (elec bass/sgr)], Semantics [Elliott Sharp (electric gtr/bass), Samm Bennett (perc), Ned Rothenberg (sax)]—23 improvisations with various accompaniment combinations *(rec Baby Monster Studio, NY, Apr. 11-16, 1988)* Hat Hut ▲ hat ART CD 6015 [ADD]

Tenzi, Fausto (ten)
Donizetti, G.:Imelda de' Lambertazzi, w. D. D'Auria (sop), F. Sovilla (sop), A. Martin (bar), G. Sarti (bar), M. Andreae (cnd), Swiss-Italian Radio-TV Orch, Swiss-Italian Radio-TV Chorus [I] *(rec live)* Nuova Era 2-▲ 6778/79 [DDD]
Leoncavallo, R.:Arias, w. R. Negri (piano)—19 unpublished arias Nuova Era ▲ NUO 7178 [DDD]

Teodorian, Valentin (ten)
Constantinescu, P.:The Nativity, w. E. Petrescu (sop), M. Kessler (mez), H. Bömches (bass), M. Basarab (cnd), Bucharest George Enescu PO, Bucharest George Enescu Phil Chorus *(rec 1977)* Olympia ▲ OCD 402 [AAD]
Leoncavallo, R.:Pagliacci, w. Arta Florescu (sop—Nedda), Cornel Stavru (ten—Canio), Valentin Teodorian (ten—Beppe), Nicolae Herlea (bar—Tonio), Ladislau Konya (bar—Silvio), M. Popa (cnd), Bucharest Opera & Ballet Theater Orch, Bucharest Opera & Ballet Theater Chorus *(rec 1966)* Vox Box 2-▲ CDX 5161
Puccini, G.:Turandot, w. Teodora Lucaciu (sop—Liù), Maria Slatinaru (sop—Princess Turandot), Corneliu Finateanu (ten—Pong), George Mircea (ten—Emperor Altoum), Ludovic Speiss (ten—Prince Calaf), Valentin Teodorian (ten—Pang), Octav Enigarescu (bar—Ping), Dionisie Konya (bar—A Mandarin), Mircea Stefanescu (bar—The Prince of Persia), Nicolae Florei (bass—Timur), C. Litvin (cnd), Romanian Radio-TV Orch, Romanian Radio-TV Chorus *(rec Jan 1970)* Vox Box 2-▲ CDX 5160
Rossini, G.:Il barbiere di Siviglia, w. Magda Ianculescu (sop—Rosina), Maria Sandulescu (mez—Berta), Valentin Teodorian (ten—Count Almaviva), Nicolae Herlea (bar—Figaro), Stefan Petrescu (bar—Fiorello), Constantin Gabor (bass—Don Bartolo), Valentin Loghin (bass—Don Basilio), M. Brediceanu (cnd), Romanian Opera Orch, Romanian Opera Chorus *(rec 1960-61)* Vox Box 2-▲ CDX 5159

Terentieva, Nina (mez)
Dargomyzhsky, A.:Arias, w. Vladimir Stcherbakov (ten), A. Tchistiakov (cnd), *(orch unknown)*—Russalka; The Stone Guest Le Chant du Monde ▲ RUS 288 086
Mussorgsky, M.:Arias, w. Vladimir Stcherbakov (ten), A. Tchistiakov (cnd), *(orch unknown)*—Boris Godunov; Khovanshchina; Khovansky's duet; Marfa & Audrey; Marfa's song Le Chant du Monde ▲ RUS 288 086
Rimsky-Korsakov, N.:Arias, w. Vladimir Stcherbakov (ten), A. Tchistiakov (cnd), *(orch unknown)*—Lel's Song; Sadko; Snegurochka Le Chant du Monde ▲ RUS 288 086
Rimsky-Korsakov, N.:Kaschei the Immortal, w. I. Jourina (sop), A. Arkhipov (ten), V. Verestnikov (bar), V. Matorin (bass), A. Tchistiakov (cnd), Bolshoi Theater Orch, Yurloff Russian Choir [Russian] Russian Season ("Russian Season" series) ▲ LDC 288046 [DDD]
Taneyev, S.:Choral Music, w. N. Surikov (bar), A. Tchistiakov (cnd), Moscow Choral Academy Choir—St. John's of Damascus Russian Season ▲ LDC 288069

Terfel, Bryn (b-bar)
Beethoven, L. van:Sym 9, "Choral Sym", w. Jane Eaglen (sop), Waltraud Meier (cta), Ben Heppner (ten), C. Abbado (cnd), Berlin PO, Swedish Radio Chorus, Eric Ericson Chamber Choir *(rec Salzburg Easter Festival, 1996)* Sony Classical ▲ SK 62634 Δ SM 62634
Beethoven, L. van:Sym 9, "Choral Sym", w. Joan Rodgers (sop), Della Jones (alt), Peter Bronder (ten), C. Mackerras (cnd), Royal Liverpool PO, Royal Liverpool Phil Choir Classics for Pleasure ("Eminence" series) ▲ CFP 2186 [DDD]
Beethoven, L. van:Die Weihe des Hauses (incidental music), w. Sylvia McNari (sop), Bruno Ganz (narr), C. Abbado (cnd), Berlin PO, Berlin Radio Chorus *(rec Great Hall, Philharmonie, Berlin)* Deutsche Grammophon ▲ 447748-2 [DDD]
Brahms, J.:Ein Deutsches Requiem, w. A. M. Blasi (sop), E. Schloter (org), C. Davis (cnd), Bavarian RSO, Bavarian Radio Chorus [G] RCA Red Seal ▲ 09026-60868-2
Britten, H.:Gloriana, w. J. Barstow (sop—Queen Elizabeth I), D. Jones (mez—Lady Essex), P. Langridge (ten—Earl of Essex), J. M. Ainsley (ten—Spirit of the Masque), J. Summers (bar—Lord Mountjoy), J. Shirley-Quirk (bar—Recorder of Norwich), B. Terfel (b-bar—Henry Cuffe), C. Mackerras (cnd), Welsh National Opera Orch, Welsh National Opera Chorus Argo 2-▲ 440213-2 [DDD]
Delius, F.:Sea Drift, w. R. Hickox (cnd), Bournemouth SO, Bournemouth Chorus Chandos ▲ CHAN 9214 [DDD]
Delius, F.:Songs of Farewell, w. R. Hickox (cnd), Bournemouth SO, Bournemouth Chorus Chandos ▲ CHAN 9214 [DDD]
Delius, F.:Songs of Sunset, w. S. Burgess (mez), R. Hickox (cnd), Bournemouth SO, Bournemouth Chorus Chandos ▲ CHAN 9214 [DDD]
Elgar, E.:The Apostles, w. A. Hargan (sop), A. Hodgson (cta), D. Rendall (ten), S. Roberts (bar), R. Lloyd (bass), R. Hickox (cnd), London SO, London Sym Chorus [E] Chandos 2-▲ CHAN 8875/76 [DDD]
Handel, G.F.:Messiah, w. Joan Rodgers (sop), Della Jones (mez), Christopher Robson (ct), Philip Langridge (ten), R. Hickox (cnd), Collegium Musicum 90 [period instrs] [E] Chandos ("Chaconne" series) 2-▲ CHAN 0522/23 [DDD]
Handel, G.F.:Messiah (sels), w. Patrizia Kwella (sop), Catherine Denley (mez), John Mark Ainsley (ten), M. Stephenson (cnd), London Musici, London Chamber Choir Conifer Classics ▲ 74321-15354-2
Ireland, J.:Greater Love Hath No Man, w. P. Bott (sop), R. Hickox (cnd), London SO, London Sym Chorus [E] Chandos ▲ CHAN 8879 [DDD]
Ireland, J.:These Things shall Be, w. R. Hickox (cnd), London SO, London Sym Chorus [E] Chandos ▲ CHAN 8879 [DDD]
Ireland, J.:Vexilla Regis, w. P. Bott (sop), T. Shaw (mez), J. Oxley (ten), R. Hickox (cnd), London SO, London Sym Chorus [L] Chandos ▲ CHAN 8879 [DDD]

Terfel, Bryn (b-bar) (cont.)
James Levine's 25th Anniversary Metropolitan Opera Gala, w. J. Levine (cnd), Metropolitan Opera Orch, Ileana Cotrubas (sop), Renée Fleming (sop), Hei-Kyung Hong (sop), Karita Mattila (sop), Birgit Nilsson (sop), Ruth Ann Swenson (sop), Kiri Te Kanawa (sop), Deborah Voigt (sop), Grace Bumbry (mez), Heidi Grant Murphy (mez), Anne Sofie von Otter (mez) *(rec live, Metropolitan Opera House, New York, Apr 27, 1996)* Deutsche Grammophon ▲ 449177-2 [DDD]
Last Night of the Proms, w. Evelyn Glennie (mar), Andrew Davis (cnd), BBC SO, BBC Sym Chorus, BBC Singers *(rec Royal Albert Hall, Sep. 10, 1994)* Teldec ▲ 97868-2 [DDD]
Lehár, F.:Die lustige Witwe, w. Cheryl Studer (sop), Barbara Bonney (sop), Boje Skovhus (bar), J.E. Gardiner (cnd), Vienna PO, Monteverdi Choir London Deutsche Grammophon ▲ 439911-2
Mahler, G.:Kindertotenlieder, w. G. Sinopoli (cnd), *(orch unknown)* Deutsche Grammophon ("4D Audio" series) ▲ 447578-2
Mahler, G.:Sym 8, w. Sylvia McNair (sop), Andrea Rost (sop), Cheryl Studer (sop), Anne Sofie von Otter (mez), Rosemarie Lang (cta), Peter Seiffert (ten), Jan-Hendrik Rootering (bass), C. Abbado (cnd), Berlin PO, Berlin Radio Chorus, Prague Phil Chorus, Tölz Boys' Choir Deutsche Grammophon ("4D Audio" series) 2-▲ 445843-2
Monteverdi, C.:Vespro della Beata Vergine, w. A. Monoyios (sop), M. Pennicchi (sop), M. Chance (ct), G. Tucker (ten), N. Robson (ten), S. Naglia (ten), A. Miles (bass), J. E. Gardiner (cnd), English Baroque Soloists, His Majesties Sagbutts & Cornetts, London Monteverdi Choir Archiv 2-▲ 429565-2 [DDD]
Mozart, W.A.:Idomeneo, w. Heidi Grant-Murphy (sop—Ilia), Carol Vaness (sop—Elettra), Cecilia Bartoli (mez—Idamante), Plácido Domingo (ten—Idomeneo), Frank Lopardo (ten—High Priest), Thomas Hampson (bar—Arbace), Bryn Terfel (b-bar—The Voice), J. Levine (cnd), Metropolitan Opera Orch, Raymond Hughes (cnd), New York Metropolitan Opera Chorus *(rec Manhattan Center Studios, New York, Mar & Apr 1994)* Deutsche Grammophon 3-▲ 447 737-2 [DDD]
Mozart, W.A.:Nozze di Figaro, w. A. Hagley (sop), H. Martinpelto (sop), R. Gilfrey (bar), J. E. Gardiner (cnd), English Baroque Soloists, Monteverdi Choir London [G] Archiv 3-▲ 439871-2 [DDD]
Mozart, W.A.:Nozze di Figaro (sels), w. J. E. Gardiner (cnd), *(orch unknown)* Deutsche Grammophon ("4D Audio" series) ▲ 447578-2
Opera Arias, w. Metropolitan Opera Orch [cnd:James Levine] Deutsche Grammophon ▲ 4458862 GH [DDD]
Rodgers, R.:Music of, w. P. Daniel (cnd), English Northern Philharmonia—Oh, What a Beautiful Mornin'; The Surrey with the Fringe on Top [both from Oklahoma!]; It Might as Well Be Spring [from State Fair]; Some Enchanted Evening; Bali Ha'i; Younger than Springtime; This Nearly Was Mine [all from South Pacific]; There Is Nothin' Like a Dame [from South Pacific; w. Stephen Briggs (ten), Keith Mills (ten), Maurice Bowen (bass), Stephen Dowson (bass), Chorus of Opera North]; If I Loved You; Soliloquy [both from Carousel]; June Is Bustin' Out All Over; You'll Never Walk Alone [both from Carousel; w. Chorus of Opera North]; Something Wonderful; I Have Dreamed [both from The King & I]; So Far; A Fellow Needs a Girl; Come Home [all from Allegro]; What a Lovely Day for a Wedding [from Allegro; w. Keith Mills (ten), Chorus of Opera North]; No Other Love [from Me & Juliet], Edelweiss [from The Sound of Music] *(rec Main Hall, Albert Halls, Bolton, Oct 1995)* Deutsche Grammophon ▲ 449163-2 [DDD]
Strauss, R.:Salome, w. Catherine Malfitano (sop), Hanna Schwarz (mez), Kenneth Riegel (ten), C. von Dohnányi (cnd), Vienna PO London 2-▲ 444178-2
Strauss, R.:Salome, w. C. Studer (sop), L. Rysanek (sop), H. Hiestermann (ten), G. Sinopoli (cnd), Berlin German Opera Orch Deutsche Grammophon 2-▲ 431810-2 [DDD]
Stravinsky, I.:Oedipus Rex, w. J. Norman (sop), P. Langridge (ten), P. Schreier (ten), S. Ozawa (cnd), Saito Kinen Orch Philips ▲ 438865-2
Vaughan Williams, R.:Dona nobis pacem, w. Y. Kenny (sop), R. Hickox (cnd), London SO, London Sym Chorus, St. Paul's Cathedral Choristers EMI Classics ▲ CDC 54788
Vaughan Williams, R.:Sancta civitas, w. P. Langridge (ten), R. Hickox (cnd), London SO, London Sym Chorus, St. Paul's Cathedral Choirsters EMI Classics ▲ CDC 54788
Vaughan Williams, R.:The Shepherds of the Delectable Mountains, w. L. Kitchen (sop), J.-M. Ainsley (ten), A. Thompson (ten), A. Opie (bar), J. Best (bass), M. Best (cnd), City of London Sinfonia [E] Hyperion ▲ CDA 66569 [DDD]
Wagner, R.:Lohengrin, w. Sharon Sweet (sop—Elsa), Eva Marton (sop—Ortrud), Ben Heppner (ten—Lohengrin), Anton Rosner (ten—Nobleman), Heinrich Weber (ten—Nobleman), Jan-Hendrik Rootering (bar—Heinrich der Vögler), Sergei Leiferkus (bar—Friedrich von Telramund), Bryn Terfel (b-bar—King's Herald), Barbara Fleckenstein (sgr—Page), Atsuko Suzuki (sgr—Page), Gisela Ulmann (sgr—Page), Marion Rambausek (sgr—Page), Dankwart Siegele (sgr—Nobleman), Jürgen Weiss (sgr—Nobleman), C. Davis (cnd), Bavarian SO, Bavarian State Opera Chorus, Bavarian Radio Chorus *(rec Residenz Herkulesaal, Munich, May 14-28, 1994)* RCA Red Seal 3-▲ 09026-62646-2 [DDD]
Wagner, R.:Lohengrin (sels), w. C. Studer (sop), W. Meier (mez), S. Jerusalem (ten), C. Abbado (cnd), Berlin PO Deutsche Grammophon ▲ 439768-2
Wagner, R.:Lohengrin (sels), w. Eva Marton (sop—Ortrud), Sharon Sweet (sop—Elsa von Brabant), Barbara Fleckenstein (sgr—Page), Marion Rambausek (sgr—Page), Atsuko Suzuki (sgr—Page), Gisela Ulmann (sgr—Page), Ben Heppner (ten—Lohengrin), Anton Rosner (ten—Nobleman), Heinrich Weber (ten—Nobleman), Sergei Leiferkus (bar—Friedrich von Telramund), Bryn Terfel (b-bar—King's Herald), Jan-Hendrik Rootering (bass—Henry the Fowler), Dankwart Siegele (sgr—Nobleman), Jürgen Weiss (sgr—Nobleman), C. Davis (cnd), Bavarian RSO, Michael Gläser (cnd), Udo Mehrpohl (cnd), Bavarian Radio Chorus, Bavarian State Opera Chorus—Seht! Seht! [from Act 1, Scene 2]; Nun sei bedankt, mein lieber Schwan!; Wenn ich im Kampfe für dich siege; Welch holde Wunder muss ich sehen?; Nun höret mich und achtet wohl; Durch Gottes Sieg ist jetzt dein Leben mein [all from Act 1, Scene 3]; Treulich geführt ziehet dahin [from Act 3, Scene 1]; Wie hehr erkenn' ich unsrer Liebe Wesen!; Höchstes Vertrau'n hast du mir schon zu danken; Weh' nun ist all' unser Glück dahin! [all from Act 3, Scene 2]; In fernem Land, unnahbar euren Schritten [from Act 3, Scene 3] *(rec Munich, Mar 14-28, 1994)* RCA Red Seal ▲ 09026-68239-2 [DDD]
Wagner, R.:Die Meistersinger von Nürnberg (sels), w. C. Studer (sop), W. Meier (mez), S. Jerusalem (ten), C. Abbado (cnd), Berlin PO Deutsche Grammophon ▲ 439768-2
Wagner, R.:Die Meistersinger von Nürnberg (sels), w. J. E. Gardiner (cnd), *(orch unknown)* Deutsche Grammophon ("4D Audio" series) ▲ 447578-2
Wagner, R.:Tannhäuser (sels), w. C. Studer (sop), W. Meier (mez), S. Jerusalem (ten), C. Abbado (cnd), Berlin PO Deutsche Grammophon ▲ 439768-2
Wagner, R.:Tannhäuser (sels), w. J. E. Gardiner (cnd), *(orch unknown)* Deutsche Grammophon ("4D Audio" series) ▲ 447578-2
Wagner, R.:Die Walküre (sels), w. C. Studer (sop), W. Meier (mez), S. Jerusalem (ten), C. Abbado (cnd), Berlin PO Deutsche Grammophon ▲ 439768-2
Walton, W.:Belshazzar's Feast, w. A. Litton (cnd), Bournemouth SO, Bournemouth Sym Chorus, L'Inviti, Waynflete Singers *(rec Winchester Cathedral, Feb 1995)* London ▲ 448134-2 [DDD]

Terkal, Karl (ten)
Benatzky, R.:Im weissen Rössl (sels), w. F. Loor (sop), H. Brauner (cta), K. Equiluz (ten), F. Bauer-Theussl (cnd), Vienna Volksoper Orch, Vienna Volksoper Chorus [G] Koch Präsent ▲ CD 399225 [AAD]

Terner, Helga (sop)
Auber, D.-F.:Fra Diavolo, w. G. Neumann (ten), E. Büchner (bar), W.-D. Hauschild (cnd), Berlin RSO Berlin Classics ▲ BER 2140 [ADD]
Bach, J.S.:Cant 4, w. Ortrun Wenkel (cta), Peter Schreier (ten), Eberhard Büchner (ten), H.-J. Rotzsch (cnd), Leipzig Gewandhaus Orch, Leipzig St. Thomas Church Choir, Leipzig New Bach Collegium Musicum Berlin Classics ▲ BER 2067 [ADD]
Bach, J.S.:Cant 31, w. Ortrun Wenkel (cta), Peter Schreier (ten), Eberhard Büchner (ten), H.-J. Rotzsch (cnd), Leipzig Gewandhaus Orch, Leipzig St. Thomas Church Choir, Leipzig New Bach Collegium Musicum Berlin Classics ▲ BER 2067 [ADD]
Bach, J.S.:Cant 31, w. Eberhard Büchner (ten), Siegfried Lorenz (bar), Hermann Christian Polster (bass), Lang (sgr), Weimann (sgr), H.-J. Rotzsch (cnd), Leipzig Gewandhaus Orch, St. Thomas Choir Berlin Classics ▲ BER 9025 [ADD]
Bach, J.S.:Cant 66, w. Eberhard Büchner (ten), Siegfried Lorenz (bar), Hermann Christian Polster (bass), Lang (sgr), Weimann (sgr), H.-J. Rotzsch (cnd), Leipzig Gewandhaus Orch, St. Thomas Choir Berlin Classics ▲ BER 9025 [ADD]

Terner, Helga (sop) (cont.)
Bach, J.S.:Cant 106, "Actus tragicus", w. Eberhard Büchner (ten), Siegfried Lorenz (bar), Hermann Christian Polster (bass), Lang (sgr), Weimann (sgr), H.-J. Rotzsch (cnd), Leipzig Gewandhaus Orch, St. Thomas Choir — Berlin Classics ▲ BER 9025 [ADD]
Bach, J.S.:Cant 134, w. Ortrun Wenkel (cta), Peter Schreier (ten), Eberhard Büchner (ten), H.-J. Rotzsch (cnd), Leipzig Gewandhaus Orch, Leipzig New Bach Collegium Musicum, Leipzig St. Thomas Church Choir — Berlin Classics ▲ BER 2067 [ADD]

Terntieva, N. (mez)
Tchaikovsky, P.:Moscow, w. N. Surikov (bar), A. Tchistiakov (cnd), Moscow Choral Academy Choir — Russian Season ▲ LDC 288069

Terrani, Lucia Valentini (mez)
Handel, G.F.:Messiah, w. Patricia Schuman (sop), Bruce Ford (ten), Gwynne Howell (bass), Bernard Soustrot (tpt), C. Scimone (cnd), Venice Solisti, John McCarthy (cnd), Ambrosian Singers *(rec S. Francisco Church, Schio, Italy, June 23–30, 1989)* — Arts 2-▲ 471052 [DDD]
Haydn, J.:Arianna a Naxos, w. Maurizio Carnelli (pno) — Kicco Classic ▲ KC 196 [DDD]
Pergolesi, G.B.:Stabat mater (sels), w. A. Zedda (cnd), Turin RAI SO — Kicco Classic ▲ 195
Rossini, G.:Arias, w. A. Zedda (cnd), Turin RAI SO—from Otello; Cenerentola; Barbiere di Siviglia; Maometto II; Italiana in Algeri; Donna del Lago — Kicco Classic ▲ 195
Rossini, G.:La Cenerentola, w. E. Ravaglia (sop), F. Araiza (ten), E. Dara (bar), G. Ferro (cnd), Cappella Coloniensis, Cologne Radio Chorus [I] — Sony Classical 2-▲ S2K 46433 [ADD]
Rossini, G.:La donna del lago, w. K. Ricciarelli (sop), D. Raffanti (ten), S. Ramey (bass), M. Pollini (cnd), CO of Europe, Prague Phil Chorus [I] — CBS 2-▲ M2K 39311 [DDD]
Rossini, G.:Giovanna d'Arco, w. Maurizio Carnelli (pno) — Kicco Classic ▲ KC 196 [DDD]
Rossini, G.:L'italiana in Algeri, w. U. Benelli (ten), S. Bruscantini (bar), A. Mariotti (bass), G. Bertini (cnd), Dresden State Orch [I] — Acanta 2-▲ CD 42308 [DDD]
Rossini, G.:L'italiana in Algeri, w. L. Rizzi (cta), W. Ganzarolli (bar), E. Dara (bar), G. Ferro (cnd), Capella Coloniensis, Cologne Radio Chorus [period instrs] [I] — CBS 2-▲ M2K 39048 [ADD]
Rossini, G.:Songs, w. Maurizio Carnelli (pno)—Addio di Rossini; Canzonetta spagnola; Ave Maria; La danza — Kicco Classic ▲ KC 196 [DDD]
Rossini, G.:Stabat Mater, w. Beatrice Haldas (sop), Antonio Savastano (ten), Raffaele Arié (bass), E. Loehrer (cnd), Swiss-Italian Radio-TV Orch, Swiss-Italian Radio-TV Chorus — Accord ▲ ACD 201752 [AAD]
Verdi, G.:Nabucco, w. G. Dimitrova (sop), P. Domingo (ten), P. Cappuccilli (bar), E. Nesterenko (bass), G. Sinopoli (cnd), German Opera Orch, German Opera Chorus [I] — Deutsche Grammophon 2-▲ 410512-2 [DDD]

Terrasson, Rene (sgr)
Offenbach, J.:Barbe-bleue, w. Henri Legay (ten), René Lenoty (ten), Aimé Doniat (bar), J. Doussard (cnd), ORTF Lyric Orch, ORTF Lyric Chorale *(rec 1967)* — Memories 2-▲ MEM 4591 [ADD]

Terzakis, Zahos (ten)
Lehár, F.:Music of, w. H. Martinpelto (sop), E. Smola (cnd), BRTN PO—Die lustige Witwe *(Ov.)*, Paganini *(Gern hab' ich die Frau'n geküsst; Niemand liebt dich so wie ich)*, Der Graf von Luxemburg *(Es duftet nach Trèfle incarnat; Faschungsmarsch)*, Friederike *(O Mädchen, mein Mädchen)*, Zigeunerliebe *(Hör' ich Cymbalklänge; Zorika, Zorika)*, Schön ist die Welt *(Schön ist die Welt)*, Das Land des Lächelns *(Chinesischer Tanz; Dein ist mein ganzes Herz)*, Eva *(Fräulein Frau das klingt doch nicht gewöhnlich; Nur das eine Wort sprich es aus)*, Giuditta *(Intermezzo; Du bist meine Sonne; Herr Käpitan, der Weg ist weit; Schönste der Frau'n; Freunde, das Leben ist lebenswert)* — Eufoda ▲ EUF 1188 [DDD]
Penderecki, K.:Als Jakob erwachte, w. Jadwiga Gadulanka (sop), Piotr Nowacki (bass), K. Penderecki (cnd), Royal Stockholm PO, Stockholm Royal Theater Opera Chorus — Chandos 2-▲ CHAN 9459
Penderecki, K.:Polish Requiem, w. Jadwiga Gadulanka (sop), Piotr Nowacki (bass), K. Penderecki (cnd), Royal Stockholm PO, Stockholm Royal Theater Opera Chorus — Chandos 2-▲ CHAN 9459
Penderecki, K.:Polish Requiem, w. I. Haubold (sop), G. Winogrodska (mez), Smith (sgr), K. Penderecki (cnd), North German RSO, North German Radio Chorus [L] *(rec live, Lucerne, 1989)* — Deutsche Grammophon 2-▲ 429720-2 [DDD]

Terzian, Anita (mez)
Handel, G.F.:Alessandro, w. L. Atkinson (trb), Watson (sop), B. J. Rieders (cta), T. Poole (ten), D. Price (ten), Andersson (sgr), M. Nowakowski (cnd), Sinfonia Varsovia [I] *(rec live)* — Koch Schwann 3-▲ CD SC 100 303 [DDD]
Handel, G.F.:Serse, w. L. Atkinson (trb), D. Cole (sop), A. Andersson (ten), T. Allen (bar), Schumann-Halley (sgr), J. Teal (sgr), A. Duczmal (cnd), Amadeus CO [I] *(rec live recording produced by "Studios Classique Berlin")* — Koch Schwann 3-▲ CD SC 100 300 [DDD]

Teschemacher, Margharete (sop)
Margarete Teschemacher (1903–1959), w. various Berlin orchs, Karl Böhm (cnd), Hanns Udo Müller (cnd), Bruno Seidler-Winkler (cnd), Fritz Zann (cnd) *(rec 1933–1939 HMV recordings)* — Preiser ("Lebendige Vergangenheit" series) ▲ PRE 89049 (m) [AAD]
Mozart, W.A.:Don Giovanni, w. M. Schech (sop), H. Hopf (ten), M. Ahlersmeyer (bar), K. Böhme (bass), G. Frick (bass), K. Elmendorff (cnd), Saxon State Orch, Dresden State Opera Chorus [G] *(rec 1943)* — Berlin Classics ("Dokumente" series) 3-▲ BER 2048 [ADD]
Wagner, R.:Arias & Scenes, w. Kathe Heidersbach (sop), Maria Reining (sop), Hilde Scheppan (sop), Margarete Klose (mez), Max Lorenz (ten), Jaro Prohaska (bar), Karl Schmitt-Walter (bar), Kurt Böhme (bass), *(orch unknown)*—selections from Rienzi; Der Fliegende Holländer; Tannhäuser; Lohengrin; Tristan und Isolde; Die Meistersinger von Nürnberg; Die Walküre & Götterdämmerung *(rec 1927–1944)* — Phonographe 2-▲ PHG 5016 [AAD]
Wagner, R.:Die Meistersinger von Nürnberg (sels), w. H. Jung (mez), M. Kremer (ten), T. RA. (ten), E. Fuchs (bar), H.-H. Nissen (bar), S. Nilsson (bass), K. Böhm (cnd), Saxon State Orch—Act. 3 *(rec 1939)* — Pearl 2-▲ PEA 9121 [ADD]
Wagner, R.:Die Walküre (act 1), w. M. Lorenz (ten), K. Böhme (bass), K. Elmendorff (cnd), Saxon State Orch [G] *(rec 9/21/44)* — Preiser ▲ 90015 (m) [AAD]
Wolf, H.:Der Corregidor, w. M. Fuchs (sop), K. Erb (ten), J. Herrmann (bar), K. Böhme (b-bar), G. Hann (bass), G. Frick (bass), K. Elmendorff (cnd), Saxon State Orch, Saxon State Chorus *(rec 1944)* — Preiser 2-▲ PRE 90182 [AAD]

Tessmer, Heinrich (ten)
Mozart, W.A.:Zauberflöte, w. T. Lemnitz (sop), E. Berger (sop), I. Beilke (sop), H. Roswaenge (ten), G. Hüsch (bar), W. Strienz (bass), T. Beecham (cnd), Berlin PO, Favre Chorus [without dialog; G] *(rec 1937–38 for HMV)* — Pearl 2-▲ PEAS 9371 (m) [AAD]
Mozart, W.A.:Zauberflöte, w. T. Lemnitz (sop), E. Berger (sop), I. Beilke (sop), H. Roswaenge (ten), G. Hüsch (bar), W. Strienz (bass), T. Beecham (cnd), Berlin PO, Favre Chorus [without dialog; G] *(rec 1937–38 for HMV)* — EMI Classics ("Great Recordings of the Century" series) 2-▲ CDHB 61034 (m) [ADD]
Mozart, W.A.:Zauberflöte, w. T. Lemnitz (sop), E. Berger (sop), I. Beilke (sop), H. Roswaenge (ten), G. Hüsch (bar), W. Strienz (bass), T. Beecham (cnd), Berlin PO, Favre Chorus [without dialog; G] *(rec 1937–38 for HMV)* — Melodram 2-▲ MEL 27056 (m) [AAD]

Testi, Lorenzo (bar)
Cilea, F.:Gloria, w. M. Roberti (sop), A. M. Rota (cta), F. Labò (ten), A. Albertini (bar), E. Campi (bass), F. Mazzoli (bass), F. Previtali (cnd), Turin RAI Orch, Turin RAI Chorus [I] *(rec live, Turin July 8, 1969)* — Memories ▲ HR 4472 [ADD]

Tetrazzini, Luisa (sop)
Bellini, V.:Arias, *(orchs unknown)*—Ah, non credea mirarti; Come per me sereno [both from La Sonnambula]; Vien' diletto [from I Puritani] — Minerva ▲ MN A13 [ADD]
Bellini, V.:I Puritani (sels), w. *(other artists unknown)*—Vien Diletto — Enterprise ("Vocal Archives" series) ▲ ENT VA 1122
Bellini, V.:La sonnambula (sels), w. *(other artists unknown)*—Ah, Non Credea Mirarti; Come per Me Sereno...Sovra il Sen — Enterprise ("Vocal Archives" series) ▲ ENT VA 1122
The Complete Known Recordings [1903–1922] — Pearl 5-▲ PEA 9220 (m) [AAD]
Donizetti, G.:Linda di Chamounix (sels), w. *(other artists unknown)*—O, Luce di Quest'anima — Enterprise ("Vocal Archives" series) ▲ ENT VA 1122
Donizetti, G.:Lucia di Lammermoor (sels), w. *(other artists unknown)*—Splendon le sacre faci; Regnava nel Silenzio...Quando Rapito in Estasi — Enterprise ("Vocal Archives" series) ▲ ENT VA 1122
The London Recordings — EMI Classics 3-▲ CDHC 63802

Tetrazzini, Luisa (sop) (cont.)
Rossini, G.:Arias, *(orch unknown)*—Una voce poco fa [from Il barbiere di Siviglia]; Bel Raggio lusinghier [from Semiramide] — Minerva ▲ MN A13 [ADD]
Rossini, G.:Il barbiere di Siviglia (sels), w. *(other artists unknown)*—Una Voce Poco Fa — Enterprise ("Vocal Archives" series) ▲ ENT VA 1122
Rossini, G.:Semiramide (sels), w. *(other artists unknown)*—Bel Raggio Lusinghier — Enterprise ("Vocal Archives" series) ▲ ENT VA 1122
Tetrazzini (rec. 1908–1914) — Nimbus ("Prima Voce" series) ▲ NI 7808-2 (m) [ADD]
Verdi, G.:Arias, w. *(other artists unknown)*—Caro Nome [from Rigoletto]; È Stranol...Ah, Fors'è Lui Folliel...Sempre Libera; Addio del Passato [both from La traviata]; Saper Vorreste [from Un ballo in maschera]; Mercè, Dilette Amiche [from I vespri siciliani]; L'insana parola...I Sacri Nomi [from Aida]; Cruda sventura [from La forza del destino] — Enterprise ("Vocal Archives" series) ▲ ENT VA 1122
Verdi, G.:Arias, *(orchs unknown)*—Caro nome [from Rigoletto]; E' stranol...Ah, fors'è lui; Folliel...Sempre libera; Addio, del passato [all from La traviata]; Saper vorreste [from Un ballo in maschera]; Mercè, dilette amiche [from I vespri siciliani]; L'insana parola...I sacri nomi [from Aida]; Cruda sventura [from La forza del destino] — Minerva ▲ MN A13 [ADD]

Tevdorashvili, Vasiko (sgr)
Kancheli, G.:Morning Prayers, w. Natalia Pschenitschnikova (alto flute), D. R. Davies (cnd), Stuttgart CO *(rec Apr. 1994)* — ECM New Series ▲ 78118-21510-2 [DDD]

Teyte, Margaret (sop)
Maggie Teyte:In Concert *(rec 1935 & 1948)* — VAI Audio ▲ VAIA/IPA 1066-2 [ADD](m)
Maggie Teyte Live (1934–1948) (rec. mostly from USA radio broadcasts, 1945–1948) — Pearl ▲ PEA 9326 (m) [AAD]

Thallaug, Edith (mez)
Brahms, J.:Duets, Op. 28, w. E. Hagegůrd (ten), L. Negro (pno) *(rec Nacka Aula, Nacka Sweden, Dec. 20–22, 1976)* — BIS ▲ CD 70 [AAD]
Brahms, J.:Duets, Op. 28, w. Erland Hagegard (bar), Lucia Negro (pno) *(rec Nacka Aula, Nacka, Sweden, 1976)* — BIS ▲ CD 77 [AAD]
Lindberg, O.:Requiem, w. I. Sörenson (sop), C. Solén (ten), E. Saedén (bass), O. Johansson (org), H. Kyhle (cnd), Stockholm Univ College of Music Orch, Englebrekt Church Oratory Choir *(rec Nov. 2, 1980)* — Sterling ▲ CDS 1013
Schumann, R.:Spanisches Liederspiel, w. Märta Schéle (sop), Gösta Winbergh (ten), Erland Hagegard (bar), Lucia Negro (pno) *(rec Nacka Aula, Nacka, Sweden, 1976)* — BIS ▲ CD 77 [AAD]

Thames, Jeanine (sop)
Mozart, W.A.:Entführung, w. S. Greenberg (sop), J. Van Der Schaaf (ten), W. Gahmlich (ten), K. Rydl (bass), M. Viotti (cnd), Frankfurt RSO, Bamberg Sym Chorus — LaserLight ▲ 14117 [DDD]
Mozart, W.A.:Entführung, w. S. Greenburg (sop), J. van der Schaaf (ten), W. Gahmlich (ten), K. Rydl (bass), Trissenaar (sgr), M. Viotti (cnd), Frankfurt RSO, Bamberg Sym Chorus — Capriccio 2-▲ 10 403/04

Thatcher, Margaret (nar)
Copland, A.:Lincoln Portrait, w. W. Morris (cnd), London SO — EMI Classics ▲ CDC 54539-2 [DDD]

Thau, Pierre (bass)
Debussy, C.:Pelléas et Mélisande, w. C. Alliot-Lugaz (sop), F. Golfier (sop), C. Carlson (mez), D. Henry (ten), G. Cachemaille (bar), C. Dutoit (cnd), Montreal SO, Montreal Sym Chorus [F] — London 2-▲ 430502-2 [DDD]

Thaw, David (ten)
Strauss, R.:Der Rosenkavalier, w. Claire Watson (sop—Feldmarschallin), Lucia Popp (sop—Sophie), Annelie Waas (sop—Marianne), Brigitte Fassbaender (mez—Octavian), Margarethe Bence (ct—Annina), David Thaw (ten—Valzacchi), Karl Ridderbusch (bass—Baron Ochs), Benno Kusche (bass—Herr von Faninal), Albrecht Peter (bass—Police Inspector), C. Kleiber (cnd), Bavarian State Orch, Bavarian State Chorus *(rec live, Münchner Festspiele, July 20, 1974)* — Arkadia 3-▲ 486 [ADD]

Thaysen, Eva Hess (sop)
Nielsen, C.:Songs, w. Mette Ejsing (alt), John Laursen (ten), Lars Thodberg Bertelsen (bar), Frode Stengaard (org), Tove Lønskov (pno)—Little Helle; Sir Oluf's Song; Dance-Song; Dawn [all from the play Sir Oluf He Rides]; The Storm Wages over the Dark Waters; My Girl Is as Fair as Amber; The Day the Eagle was Ready to Fly; A Mother was Told at the Feast; The Thistle Crop Looks Promising; Once When Death was Awaited; So Bitter was My Heart; Like a Venturous Fleet at Anchor [all from the play The Mother]; The Sign & the Word of the Cross; Of All the Flowers that Grow on Earth; As the Golden Sun Breaks Through; There is a Path; It Is No Great Struggle; Daffodil, Why Are You Here? [all from Hymns & Sacred Songs]; The Sun Springs Out Like a Rose [from the play Cosmus]; The Great Master Comes; See My Fragile Web; Our Eyes May Rejoice; When Summer's Song is Sung; Earth in Whose Embrace [all from 20 Popular Melodies]; Of What are You Singing? [The Lark]; Teach Me, O Stars of Night [both from 4 Popular Melodies]; Italian Shepherd's Song; We Love You, Our Lofty North!; Vocalise; The Power that Gave Me My Little Song [all from Amor & the Poet]; May Song [Merrily, with Joyful Song!] — Rondo Grammofon ▲ RCD 8329
Nielsen, C.:Sym 3, w. Lars Thodberg Bertelsen (bar), E. Serov (cnd), Odense SO — Kontrapunkt ▲ KPT 32203

Thebom, Blanche (mez)
Mozart, W.A.:Così fan tutte (sels), w. S. Jurinac (sop), A. Noni (sop), R. Lewis (ten), E. Kunz (bar), M. Borriello (bar), F. Busch (cnd), Glyndebourne Festival Orch *(rec Glyndebourne Festival, 1950)* — Testament ▲ TES SBT 1040 [ADD]

Therén, Britta (sgr)
Nilsson, T.:Out of Earthly Night, w. Gudrun Bruna (sop), Marianne Mellnäs (sop), Kaysa Hälldin (alt), Lars Sjögren (ten), Göran Swartz (bass), Sture Hedin (sgr), Ola Kyhlberg (sgr), Lars Ljungman (sgr), Nils Philipson (sgr), Ulrik Quale (sgr), Nils Spangenberg (sgr), Karl-Erik Welin (org), Torsten Nilsson (cnd), Oscar's Motet Choir *(rec Oscar's Church, Stockholm, Sweden, Apr 26–27, 1978)* — BIS ▲ CD 138 [AAD]

Theyard, Harry (ten)
Refice, L.:Cecilia, w. R. Scotto (sop), G. Fourié (sgr), A. Campori (cnd), *(orch unknown)*—abriged version *(rec live 1976)* — Vai Audio ▲ VAIA 1042 [ADD]

Thiegem, D. van (voc)
Ashley, R.:Perfect Lives [Private Parts], w. R. Ashley (nar), "Blue" G. Tyranny (kbds), J. Kroesen (voc), P. Gordon (pre-recorded orchestral beds) — Lovely Music 3-▲ LCD 4917.3 [ADD] 2-■ LMC 4913/4947

Thiem, Klaus (bar)
Wolf, H.:Christnacht, w. S. Inou-Heller (sop), M.-L. Wilke (mez), U. Gronostay (cnd), Berlin RSO, Berlin Radio Chorus [G] — Koch Schwann ▲ CD 313013 [DDD]

Thill, Georges (ten)
Charpentier, G.:Louise, w. N. Vallin (sop—Louise), C. Gaudel (sop—Irma), A. Lecouvreur (mez—Mother), G. Thill (ten—Julien), A. Pernet (bass—Father), E. Bigot (cnd), Raugel Orch, Raugel Chorus *(rec 1936)* — Nimbus (Prima Voce) ▲ NI 7829 (m) [ADD]
Charpentier, G.:Louise (abridged ed), w. N. Vallin (sop—Louise), C. Gaudel (mez—Irma), A. Lecouvreur (cta—La Mère), G. Thill (ten—Julien), A. Pernet (bass—La Père), E. Bigot (cnd), *(orch & chorus unknown)* [F] *(rec 1935 for Columbia Records)* — Music Memoria 3-▲ 30223
Georges Thill *(rec 1925–1936 for Columbia)* — Pearl ▲ PEA 9947 (m) [AAD]
King of the French Tenors — Music Memoria ▲ 30190
Leoncavallo, R.:Pagliacci (sels), w. Enrico Caruso (ten), Antonio Paoli (ten), Giovanni Zenatello (ten), Amedeo Bassi (ten), Hermann Jadlowker (ten), Fernand Ansseau (ten), Hipolito Lazaro (ten), Nino (Filippo) Piccaluga (ten), Mario Chamlee (ten), Giacomo Lauri-Volpi (ten), Miguel Fleta (ten), Giovanni Martinelli (ten), Aureliano Pertile (ten), Alessandro Valente (ten), Francesco Merli (ten), Lauritz Melchior (ten), Marcel Wittrisch (ten), Joseph Schmidt (ten), Beniamino Gigli (ten), Giuseppe Lugo (ten), Helge Roswaenge (ten), Jussi Bjoerling (ten)—23 versions of the tenor aria "Vesti la giubba" *(rec 1907–1944)* — Bongiovanni ▲ GB 1071 [ADD]
Wagner, R.:Arias & Scenes, w. K. Flagstad (sop), E. Rethberg (sop), B. Nilsson (sop), E. Schumann (sop), F. Leider (sop), L. Melchior (ten), G. Thill (ten), A. Pertile (ten), G. Hüsch (bar), F. Schorr (b-bar), H. Hotter (b-bar), A. Kipnis (bass), *(orch unknown)* — EMI Classics ("Studio" series) 4-▲ CDMC 64008

Thingboe, Eva Lillian (mez)
Corghi, A.:Divara—Wasser und Blut, w. Susanna von der Burg (sop—Divara), Suzanne McLeod (mez—Else Windscherer), Eva Lillian Thingboe (mez—Hille Feiken), Robert Schwarts (ten—Lame Man), Heinz Fitz (spkr—Bernd Knipperdollinck), Hanslutz Hildmann (spkr—Jan Matthys), Michael Holm (spkr—Bernhard Rothmann), Christopher Krieg (spkr—Jan van Leiden), W. Humburg (cnd), Münster SO, Münster City Theater Chorus [G] *(rec Grosses Haus, Münster State Theater, Nov. 27–29, 1993)* Marco Polo 2-▲ 8.223706/07 [DDD]

Thomann, Elisabeth (sop)
Bach, J.S.:St. John Passion, w. P. Curtin (sop), E. Alberts (cta), W. Kmentt, J. Van Kesteren (ten), R. Springer (bar), O. Wiener (bar), D. Smith (b-bar), F. Guthrie (bass), F. Lukasowsky (bass), H. Scherchen (cnd), Vienna State Opera Orch, Vienna Academy Chorus [G] *(rec ca 1960)* MCA Classics 2-▲ MCAD2-9804
Haydn, J.:Mass 6, "Nikolai-messe", "6/4-Takt-Messe", w. Rose Bahl (cta), Kurt Equiluz (ten), G. Barati (cnd), Vienna State Opera Orch, Vienna Academy Chamber Choir *(rec 1964)* Tuxedo ▲ TUXCD 1055 [ADD]
Haydn, J.:Mass 10, "Kriegsmesse", "Paukenmesse", w. Elfriede Jahn (alt), Stafford Wing (ten), Eishi Kawamura (bass), H. Gillesberger (cnd), Vienna State Opera Orch, Vienna Chamber Choir *(rec 1965)* Tuxedo ▲ TUXCD 1025
Haydn, J.:Mass 14, "Harmoniemesse", w. Christiane Sorell (sop), Rose Bahl (cta), Maura Moreira (cta), Kurt Equiluz (ten), Gerhard Eder (bass), P. Wimburger (bass), G. Barati (cnd), Vienna State Opera Orch, Vienna Academy Chamber Choir *(rec 1964)* Tuxedo ▲ TUXCD 1055 [ADD]
Schubert, Franz:Deutsche Messe, w. Gertrude Jahn (alt), Stafford Wing (ten), Kunikazu Ohashi (bass), H. Gillesberger (cnd), Vienna SO, Vienna Chamber Choir Tuxedo ▲ TUXCD 1074 [ADD]
Schubert, Franz:Mass 3, w. Gertrude Jahn (alt), Stafford Wing (ten), Kunikazu Ohashi (bass), H. Gillesberger (cnd), Vienna SO, Vienna Chamber Choir Tuxedo ▲ TUXCD 1074 [ADD]

Thomas (sgr)
Handel, G.F.:Israel in Egypt, w. Nancy Argenta (sop), Emily Van Evera (sop), Jan Wilson (mez), Anthony Rolfe Johnson (ten), White (sgr), A. Parrott (cnd), Taverner Players, Taverner Choir [E] EMI Classics 2-▲ CDCB 54018 [DDD]
Strauss, R.:Die Frau ohne Schatten, w. L. Rysanek (sop), Hoffman (sgr), H. von Karajan (cnd), Vienna State Opera Orch, Vienna State Opera Chorus [G] *(rec live, Vienna, 6/11/64)* Arkadia 3-▲ 207 (m) [ADD]

Thomas, Angelika (sgr)
Waits, T.:The Black Rider:The Casting of Magic Bullets, w. Angelika Thomas (sgr—Anne), Annette Paulmann (sgr—Kätchen), Sona Cervena (sgr—Bird/Messenger/Spoonwoman), Monika Tahal (sgr—Witness/Bird/Shrink/Wilhelm's Double/Skeleton), Susi Eisenkolb (sgr—Bridesmaid/Pegleg's Double), Heinz Vossbrink (sgr—Kuno), Dominique Horwitz (sgr—Pegleg), Gerd Kunath (sgr—Bertram), Stefan Kurt (sgr—Wilhelm), Klaus Schreiber (sgr—Robert/Man on Stag/Georg Schmid), Jörg Holm (Old Uncle/Duke), Jan Moritz Steffen (sgr—Young Kuno/Bird/Shrink/Skeleton), Tom Waits (vocals/coliope/organ/chamberlain/mar/emax/guitar/train whistle), Ralph Carney (saxophone/bass clarinet/baritone horn), Bill Douglas (bass instrument), Kenny Wollesen (perc) Island ▲ 314518559-2

Thomas, David (bass)
Bach, J.S.:Cant 205, w. M. van der Sluis (sop), R. Jacobs (ct), C. Prégardien (ten), G. Leonhardt (cnd), Orch of the Age of Enlightenment [G] Philips ▲ 432161-2 [DDD]
Bach, J.S.:Cant 214, w. M. van der Sluis (sop), R. Jacobs (ct), C. Prégardien (ten), G. Leonhardt (cnd), Orch of the Age of Enlightenment [G] Philips ▲ 432161-2 [DDD]
Bach, J.S.:Magnificat, BWV 243, w. E. Kirkby (sop), J. Nelson (sop), C. Watkinson (cta), P. Elliott (ten), S. Preston (cnd), Academy of Ancient Music, Christ Church Cathedral Choir Oxford [E♭ version; L] L'Oiseau-Lyre ▲ 414678-2 [ADD]
Bach, J.S.:Mass in b, BWV 232, w. E. Kirkby (sop), E. Van Evera (sop), R. Covey-Crump (ct), A. Parrott (cnd), Taverner Consort, Taverner Players, Tölz Boys' Choir [L] EMI Classics 2-▲ ZDCB 47292-2 [DDD]
Burgon, G.:The Fall of Lucifer, w. J. Bowman (ct), R. Covey-Crump (ten), G. Burgon (cnd), Endymion Ensemble, M. Greenall (cnd), Elysian Singers London Silva Classics ▲ SIL 6002 [DDD]
Caccini, G.:Arias, w. Anthony Rooley (chit) Musica Oscura ("The Orpheus Circle" series) ▲ MOS 70974
Handel, G.F.:Apollo e Dafne, w. Judith Nelson (sop), N. McGegan (cnd), Philharmonia Baroque Orch Harmonia Mundi France ("Musique d'abord" series) ▲ HMA 1905157
Handel, G.F.:Arias, w. N. McGegan (cnd), Philharmonia Baroque Orch—17 arias from Acis & Galatea, Athaliah, Deborah, Esther, Ezio, Orlando, Sosarme, Tolomeo [composed for Italian bass Antonio Montagnana] [E,I] Harmonia Mundi USA ▲ HMU 907016
Handel, G.F.:Arias, w. Lisa Saffer (sop—Cuzzoni), Lorraine Hunt (mez—Durastanti), Drew Minter (ct—Senesino), David Thomas (bass—Montagnana), N. McGegan (cnd), Philharmonia Baroque Orch Harmonia Mundi 4-▲ HMX 2907171.74
Handel, G.F.:Judas Maccabaeus, w. Linda Saffer (sop), Patricia Spence (mez), Brian Asawa (ct), Guy de Mey (ten), Leroy Kromm (b-bar), N. McGegan (cnd), Philharmonia Baroque Orch, Univ of California at Berkeley Chamber Chorus [E] *(rec Nov. 15–18, 1992)* Harmonia Mundi USA 2-▲ HMU 907077/78
Handel, G.F.:Messiah, w. Emma Kirkby (sop), Emily Van Evera (sop), Margaret Cable (mez), James Bowman (ct), Joseph Cornwell (ten), A. Parrott (cnd), Taverner Consort, Taverner Choir [E] EMI Classics 2-▲ CDCB 49801 [DDD]
Handel, G.F.:Messiah, w. Emma Kirkby (sop), Judith Nelson (mez), Carolyn Watkinson (cta), Paul Elliott (ten), C. Hogwood (cnd), Academy of Ancient Music London 2-▲ 430488-2 [DDD]
Handel, G.F.:Orlando, w. Arleen Augér (sop), Emma Kirkby (sop), Catherine Robbin (mez), James Bowman (ct), C. Hogwood (cnd), Academy of Ancient Music L'Oiseau-Lyre 3-▲ 430845-2 [DDD]
Handel, G.F.:Semele, w. Norma Burrowes (sop), Patrizia Kwella (sop), Elizabeth Priday (sop), Catherine Denley (mez), Della Jones (mez), Timothy Penrose (alt), Anthony Rolfe-Johnson (ct), Maldwyn Davies (ten), Robert Lloyd (b-bar), J. E. Gardiner (cnd), English Baroque Soloists, Monteverdi Choir London Erato 2-▲ 2292-45982-2
Handel, G.F.:Susanna, w. Jill Feldman (sop), Lorraine Hunt (sop), Drew Minter (alt), Jeffery Thomas (ten), William Parker (bar), N. McGegan (cnd), Philharmonia Baroque Orch, Univ of California at Berkeley Chamber Chorus [E] Harmonia Mundi USA 3-▲ HMU 907030/32
Handel, G.F.:Susanna (sels), w. Jill Feldman (sop), Lorraine Hunt (sop), Drew Minter (alt), Jeffrey Thomas (ten), William Parker (bar), N. McGegan (cnd), Philharmonia Baroque Orch Harmonia Mundi France ▲ HMU 907168
Handel, G.F.:Susanna (sels), w. Jill Feldman (sop), Lorraine Hunt (sop), Drew Minter (alt), Jeffery Thomas (ten), William Parker (bar), N. McGegan (cnd), Philharmonia Baroque Orch, Univ of California at Berkeley Chamber Chorus [E] Harmonia Mundi USA ("Nightingale" series) ▲ HMN 907601
Handel, G.F.:Theodora, w. Lorraine Hunt (sop—Theodora), Jennifer Lane (mez—Irene), Drew Minter (alt—Didymus), Jeffery Thomas (ten—Septimius), David Thomas (bass—Valens), N. McGegan (cnd), Philharmonia Baroque Orch, Univ of California at Berkeley Chamber Chorus [period instrs] [E] *(rec 9/91)* Harmonia Mundi USA 3-▲ HMU 907060/62 [DDD]
Handel, G.F.:Theodora (sels), w. Lorraine Hunt (sop), Jennifer Lane (mez), Drew Minter (ct), Jeffrey Thomas (ten), N. McGegan (cnd), Philharmonia Baroque Orch, Univ of California at Berkeley Chamber Chorus Harmonia Mundi France ▲ HMU 907188
Haydn, J.:Die Schöpfung, w. Arleen Augér (sop), Philip Langridge (ten), S. Rattle (cnd), City of Birmingham SO, City of Birmingham Sym Chorus [E] EMI Classics 2-▲ CDCB 54159 [DDD]
Johnson, Robert:Music for Shakespeare's Plays, w. E. Kirkby (sop), A. Rooley (lt) Virgin Classics ▲ CDC 59321
Monteverdi, C.:Orfeo, w. P. Kwella (sop), E. Kirkby (sop), J. Smith (sop), N. Rogers (ten), S. Varcoe (bar), N. Rogers (cnd), London Cornett & Sackbutt Ensemble, C. Medlam (cnd), London Baroque Chiaroscuro EMI Classics 2-▲ CDMB 64947
Monteverdi, C.:Ritorno d'Ulisse, w. L. Hunt (sop), C. Högman (sop), B. Fink (cta), D. Vissé (ct), C. Prégardien (ten), G. Tucker (ten), R. Jacobs (ct), Concerto Vocale [I] Harmonia Mundi France 3-▲ HMC 901427/29
Monteverdi, C.:Selva morale e spirituale (sels), w. E. Kirkby (sop), I. Partridge (ten), Parley of Instruments [L] Hyperion ▲ CDA 66021 [DDD]

Thomas, David (bass) (cont.)
Monteverdi, C.:Vespro della Beata Vergine, w. A. Mellon (sop), G. Laurens (mez), H. Crook (ten), P. Herreweghe (cnd), Toulouse Saqueboutiers, Chapelle Royale Choir, Collegium Vocale [L] Harmonia Mundi France 2-▲ HMC 901247/48 [DDD]
Mozart, W.A.:Music of, w. Gundula Janowitz (sop), Julia Bernheimer (mez), Martyn Hill (ten), Anthony Halstead (hn), Colin Lawson (b cl), Christopher Kite (pno), R. Goodman (cnd), Hanover Band—Cons for Hn, K.412, 417, 447, 494a & 495; Sym No. 40; Con for Cl; Eine kleine Nachtmusik; Requiem; Sym No. 41; Con No. 20 for Pno; Serenata Notturna Nimbus 4-▲ NI 1791 [DDD]
Mozart, W.A.:Requiem, w. G. Janowitz (sop), J. Bernheimer (mez), M. Hill (ten), R. Goodman (cnd), Hanover Band, Hanover Chorus [period instruments; H.C. Robbins Landon edition] Nimbus 4-▲ NI 1791 [DDD]
Mozart, W.A.:Requiem, w. G. Janowitz (sop), J. Bernheimer (mez), M. Hill (ten), R. Goodman (cnd), Hanover Band, Hanover Chorus [period instruments; H.C. Robbins Landon's edition; L] Nimbus ▲ NI 5241-2 [DDD]
Puliaschi, G.D.:Arias, w. Anthony Rooley (chit) Musica Oscura ("The Orpheus Circle" series) ▲ MOS 70974
Purcell, H.:Dido & Aeneas, w. E. Kirkby (sop), J. Nelson (sop), A. Parrott (cnd), Taverner Players, Taverner Choir [E] Chandos ("Chaconne" series) ▲ CHAN 0521 [DDD]
Purcell, H.:Dido & Aeneas, w. Catherine Bott (sop—Dido), Emma Kirkby (sop—Belinda), Michael Chance (alt—Spirit), John Mark Ainsley (bar—Aeneas), David Thomas (bar—Sorceress), C. Hogwood (cnd), Academy of Ancient Music L'Oiseau-Lyre ▲ 436992-2 [DDD]
Purcell, H.:Hail, Bright Cecilia, w. J. Smith (sop), B. Gordon (alt), A. Stafford (alt), P. Elliot (ten), S. Varcoe (bar), J.E. Gardiner (cnd), English Baroque Soloists, Monteverdi Choir London Erato ("Gardiner Purcell Collection" series) ▲ 96554-2
Purcell, H.:The Indian Queen, w. Catherine Bott (sop—Orazia/Married Woman), Emma Kirkby (sop—Indian Girl/Zempoalla/Cupid), John Mark Ainsley (ten—Indian Boy/Fame/Follower of Cupid/Aerial Spirits), Julian Podger (ten—Follower of Envy/Aerial Spirit), Gerald Finley (bar—Conjurer/Hymen/Follower of Cupid), Helen Parker (sgr—Aerial Spirits), David Thomas (bass—Envy/High Priest/Married Man/Follower of Cupid), Simon Berridge (sgr—Follower of Envy), Libby Crabtree (sgr—Follower of Hymen/Aerial Spirit), Tommy Williams (sgr—God of Dreams), C. Hogwood (cnd), Academy of Ancient Music *(rec Walthamstow Assembly Hall, London, July 1994)* L'Oiseau-Lyre ▲ 444339-2 [DDD]
Purcell, H.:Music for the Theater, w. E. Kirkby (sop), J. Nelson (sop), J. Bowman (ct), M. Hill (ten), R. Covey-Crump (ten), C. Keyte (bass), C. Hogwood (cnd), Academy of Ancient Music L'Oiseau-Lyre 6-▲ 425893-2 [ADD]
Purcell, H.:Songs, w. E. Kirkby (sop), A. Rooley (lt) Hyperion ▲ CDA 66056 [DDD]
Purcell, H.:Songs, w. Jean Nibbs (sop), Geoffrey Mitchell (ct), Peter Hall (ten), Margaret Phillips (org), Michael Howard (cnd), Cantores in Ecclesia—Hear My Prayer, O Lord; Song of the 3 Children; Remember Not, Lord, Our Offences; Voluntary for Single Organ; Magnificat & Nunc Dimittis in g; Thy Work is a Lantern; Burial Sentences for Queen Mary [Man That is Born of a Woman; In the Midst of Life We Are in Death; Thou Knowest, Lord, the Secrets of Our Hearts]; O God, Thou Art My God; Magnificat & Nunc Dimittis in B♭; Voluntary on the 100th Psalm Tune; Turn Thou Us, O Good Lord; O Give Thanks Unto the Lord [Psalm 106] IMP ("BBC Radio Classics" series) ▲ IMP 9126
Stradella, A.:L'anime del purgatorio, w. Emma Kirkby (sop), Evelyn Tubb (sop), Richard Wistreich (b-bar), Consort of Musicke Musica Oscura ▲ OSC 70984 [DDD]
Stradella, A.:L'anime del purgatorio, w. Emma Kirkby (sop), Evelyn Tubb (sop), Richard Wistreich (bass), A. Rooley (cnd), Consort of Musicke Musica Oscura ("Favola in Musica" series) ▲ MOS 70984
Stravinsky, I.:Pulcinella, w. A. Murray (mez), M. Hill (ten), R. Hickox (cnd), City of London Sinfonia Virgo ▲ CDZ 61107
Telemann, G.P.:Hamburger Admiralitätsmusik, w. Mieke van der Sluis (sop—Hammonia), Graham Pushee (ten—Themis), Rufus Müller (ten—Mercurius), Klaus Mertens (bass—Neptunius), David Thomas (bass—Mars), Michael Schopper (bass—Albis), W. Helbich (cnd), Bremen Baroque Orch, Alsfeld Vocal Ensemble *(rec Nov 9, 1995)* CPO 2-▲ CPO 999373-2 [DDD]
Vivaldi, A.:Gloria, RV.589, w. J. Nelson (sop), E. Kirkby (sop), C. Watkinson (cta), P. Elliott (ten), S. Preston (cnd), Academy of Ancient Music, Christ Church Cathedral Choir Oxford [L] L'Oiseau-Lyre ▲ 414678-2 [ADD]
Wagner, R.:Der Ring des Nibelungen, w. R. Crespin (sop), G. Janowitz (sop), C. Ludwig (mez), H. Dernesch (mez), J. Vickers (ten), D. Fischer-Dieskau (bar), H. von Karajan (cnd), Berlin PO *(rec live at Salzburg Easter Festivals, 1967–1970)* Arkadia 12-▲ 223 (m) [ADD]
Wagner, R.:Der Ring des Nibelungen, w. R. Crespin (sop), G. Janowitz (sop), C. Ludwig (mez), H. Dernesch (mez), J. Vickers (ten), D. Fischer-Dieskau (bar), H. von Karajan (cnd), Berlin PO *(rec late 1960s)* Deutsche Grammophon 15-▲ 435211-2 [ADD]

Thomas, Glynne (sgr)
Verdi, G.:Macbeth, w. Amy Shuard (sop—Lady Macbeth), Noreen Berry (mez—Lady-in-waiting), John Dobson (ten—Malcolm), André Turp (ten—Macduff), Tito Gobbi (bar—Macbeth), Edgar Boniface (bass—Servant), Rydderch Davies (bass—Doctor), Forbes Robinson (bass—Banco), Jean Holmes (sgr—Apparition), Celia Penny (sgr—Apparition), Glynne Thomas (sgr—Apparition), Brian Wrigt (sgr—Araldo), F. Molinari-Pradelli (cnd), Royal Opera House Orch, Royal Opera House Chorus Covent Garden *(rec London, Apr 8, 1960)* Bella Voce 2-▲ 7203 [AAD]

Thomas, Hector (ten)
Verdi, G.:Aida, w. Maria Callas (sop—Aida), Joan Sutherland (sop—Priestess), Giulietta Simionato (cta—Amneris), Kurt Baum (ten—Radames), Hector Thomas (ten—Messenger), Jess Walters (bar—Amonasro), Michael Langdon (bass—King), Giulio Neri (bass—Ramfis), J. Barbirolli (cnd), Royal Opera House Orch, Royal Opera House Chorus Covent Garden *(rec Covent Garden, London, June 10, 1953)* Legato Classics 2-▲ LCD 187-2

Thomas, Jeffrey (ten)
Bach, J.S.:Cant 8, w. J. Baird (sop), S. Rickards (alt), J. Weaver (bass), J. Thomas (cnd), American Bach Soloists [G] Koch International Classics ▲ KIC 7163-2 [DDD]
Bach, J.S.:Cant 55, w. J. Thomas (cnd), American Bach Soloists [G] *(rec Apr & Oct 1990)* Koch International Classics ▲ KIC 7138-2 [DDD]
Bach, J.S.:Cant 156, w. S. Rickards (alt), J. Weaver (bass), J. Thomas (cnd), American Bach Soloists [G] Koch International Classics ▲ KIC 7163-2 [DDD]
Bach, J.S.:Cant 198, w. J. Nelson (sop), J. Malafronte (mez), W. Sharp (bar), J. Thomas (cnd), American Bach Soloists [G] Koch International Classics ▲ KIC 7163-2 [DDD]
Bach, J.S.:St. John Passion, w. J. Baird (sop), J. Bryden (sop), D. Ripley (bar), J. Weaver (bass), K. Slowik (cnd), Smithsonian Chamber Players, Smithsonian Chamber Chorus [period instrs] [G] *(Slowik performs the original 1724 version, & includes the two choruses & three arias added to Bach's 1725 revision as appended tracks at the end of the discs, allowing the listener to either ignore the end tracks & hear the standard version or program the discs to play the 1725 sequence)* Smithsonian Collection 5-▲ ND 0380 [DDD]
Beethoven, L. van:Sym 9, "Choral Sym", w. Gwyneth Jones (sop), Tatiana Troyanos (mez), Karl Ridderbusch (bass), K. Böhm (cnd), Vienna PO, Vienna State Opera Chorus Deutsche Grammophon ("Double" series) 2-▲ 437368-2
Handel, G.F.:Messiah, w. Lorraine Hunt (sop), Janet Williams (sop), Patricia Spence (mez), Drew Minter (alt), William Parker (bar), N. McGegan (cnd), Philharmonia Baroque Orch, Univ of California at Berkeley Chamber Chorus—standard version of Messiah *occupies the first sections of each of the three CDs, one part per disc. Each part is followed, after a significant pause, by alternative versions of certain sections of the preceding material, 13 altogether. [E]* Harmonia Mundi USA 3-▲ HMU 907050/52
Handel, G.F.:Messiah (sels), w. Lorraine Hunt (sop), Janet Williams (sop), Patricia Spence (mez), Drew Minter (alt), William Parker (bar), N. McGegan (cnd), Philharmonia Baroque Orch, Univ of California at Berkeley Chamber Chorus Harmonia Mundi USA ▲ HMU 907120
Handel, G.F.:Messiah (sels), w. Lorraine Hunt (sop), Janet Williams (sop), Patricia Spence (mez), Drew Minter (alt), William Parker (bar), N. McGegan (cnd), Philharmonia Baroque Orch, Univ of California at Berkeley Chamber Chorus [E] Harmonia Mundi USA ("Nightingale" series) ▲ HMN 907601
Handel, G.F.:La Rezurrezione, w. Linda Saffer (sop), Judith Nelson (mez), Patricia Spence (mez), Michael George (bass), N. McGegan (cnd), Philharmonia Baroque Orch [I] Harmonia Mundi USA 2-▲ HMU 907027/28

Thomas, Jeffrey (ten) (cont.)
Handel, G.F.:Susanna, w. Jill Feldman (sop), Lorraine Hunt (sop), Drew Minter (alt), William Parker (bar), David Thomas (bass), N. McGegan (cnd), Philharmonia Baroque Orch, Univ of California at Berkeley Chamber Chorus [E] Harmonia Mundi USA 3-▲ HMU 907030/32
Handel, G.F.:Susanna (sels), w. Jill Feldman (sop), Lorraine Hunt (sop), Drew Minter (alt), William Parker (bar), David Thomas (bass), N. McGegan (cnd), Philharmonia Baroque Orch Harmonia Mundi France ▲ HMU 907168
Handel, G.F.:Susanna (sels), w. Jill Feldman (sop), Lorraine Hunt (sop), Drew Minter (alt), William Parker (bar), David Thomas (bass), N. McGegan (cnd), Philharmonia Baroque Orch, Univ of California at Berkeley Chamber Chorus [E] Harmonia Mundi USA ("Nightingale" series) ▲ HMN 907601
Handel, G.F.:Theodora, w. Lorraine Hunt (sop—Theodora), Jennifer Lane (mez—Irene), Drew Minter (alt—Didymus), Jeffery Thomas (ten—Septimius), David Thomas (bass—Valens), N. McGegan (cnd), Philharmonia Baroque Orch, Univ of California at Berkeley Chamber Chorus [period instrs] [E] *(rec 9/91)* Harmonia Mundi USA 3-▲ HMU 907060/62 [DDD]
Handel, G.F.:Theodora (sels), w. Lorraine Hunt (sop), Jennifer Lane (mez), Drew Minter (ct), David Thomas (bass), N. McGegan (cnd), Philharmonia Baroque Orch, Univ of California at Berkeley Chamber Chorus Harmonia Mundi France ▲ HMU 907188
Haydn, J.:Mass 11, "Nelsonmesse", "Imperial Mass", "Coronation Mass", w. Janet Baker (sop), Pamela Dellal (mez), James Maddalena (bar), M. Pearlman (cnd), Banchetto Musicale [L] Arabesque ▲ Z 6560 [DDD]
Monteverdi, C.:Orfeo, w. Jennifer Lane (mez), Michael Brown (sgr), Dana Hanchard (sgr), Timothy Leigh Evans (sgr), Paul Shipper (sgr), G. Toth (cnd), ARTEK Lyrichord 2-▲ LYR 9002 [DDD]
Mozart, W.A.:Missa, K.427, w. Nancy Armstrong (sop), Dominique Labelle (sop), Richard Morrison (bass), A. Parrott (cnd), Boston Early Music Festival Orch, Handel & Haydn Society Chorus [L] Denon ▲ CO 79573 [DDD]
Purcell, H.:The Fairy Queen, w. C. Bott (sop), M. Schopper (bass), T. Koopman (cnd), Amsterdam Baroque Orch, Amsterdam Baroque Choir Erato 2-▲ 98507-2
Schoenberg, A.:Gurrelieder, w. M. Napier (sop), Y. Minton (mez), K. Bowman (sgr), G. Reich (nar), S. Nimsgern (b-bar), P. Boulez (cnd), BBC SO *(rec Oct. 26–Dec. 06, 1974)* Sony Classical 2-▲ SM2K 48459 [ADD]
Wagner, R.:Lohengrin, w. A. Varnay (sop), I. Bjoner (sop), G. Neidlinger (b-bar), W. Sawallisch (cnd), La Scala Orch, Prague Phil Chorus [G] *(rec live, Milan 1965)* Melodram 3-▲ MEL 37067 [AAD]
Wagner, R.:Lohengrin, w. E. Grümmer (sop), C. Ludwig (mez), D. Fischer-Dieskau (bar), G. Frick (bass), R. Kempe (cnd), Vienna PO, Vienna State Opera Chorus [G] EMI Classics 3-▲ CDCC 49017 [ADD]
Wagner, R.:Parsifal, w. I. Dalis (mez), G. London (bar), H. Hotter (b-bar), G. Neidlinger (b-bar), H. Knappertsbusch (cnd), Bayreuth Festival Orch, Bayreuth Festival Chorus [1962] [G] Philips 4-▲ 416390-2 [ADD]

Thomas, John Charles (bar)
An American Classic Nimbus ("Prima Voce" series) ▲ NI 7838 (m) [AAD]
Home on the Range *(rec 1923–1941 for HMV, Victor)* Pearl ▲ PEA 9977 [AAD]

Thomas, John Patrick (voc)
Cage, J.:Ryoanji, w. Gudrun Reschke (ob), Eberhard Blum (fl), Iven Hausmann (trbn), Robert Black (db), Jan Williams (perc) *(rec Akademie der Künste, Berlin, June 22, 1995)* Hat Hut ("Now" series) ▲ hat ART CD 6183 [DDD]

Thomas, Juan (bass)
Meyerbeer, G.:L'Africiane, w. Montserrat Caballe (sop—Selika), Christine Weidinger (sop—Inez), Miriam Ucelay (mez—Anna), Placido Domingo (ten—Vasco de Gama), Guillermo Sarabia (bar—Nelusko), Juan Thomas (b-bar—High Priest of Brahma), Dimiter Petkov (bass—Don Pedro), Juan Pons (bass—Don Diego), Eduardo Soto (bass—Grand Inquisitor), A. de Almeida (cnd), Barcelona Teatro Liceo Orch, Barcelona Gran Teatro de Liceo Chorus *(rec Barcelona, Nov 27, 1977)* Legato Classics 2-▲ LCD 208-2 [ADD]

Thomas, Marjorie (cta)
Davies, P.M.:Miss Donnithorne's Maggot, w. P. M. Davies (cnd), Fires of London *(rec digital rec'g)* Unicorn-Kanchana ▲ DKP CD 9052 [ADD/DDD]
Elgar, E.:The Music Makers, w. M. Sargent (cnd), Leeds Philharmonic Society, London SO, Huddersfield Choral Society, Royal Choral Society *(rec live, Royal Albert Hall April 29, 1965)* Intaglio ▲ INCD 7351 [ADD]
Handel, G.F.:Messiah, w. Elsie Morison (sop), Richard Lewis (ten), James Milligan (bass), M. Sargent (cnd), Royal Liverpool PO, Huddersfield Choral Society Classics for Pleasure 2-▲ CDCFP 4718 [ADD]
Handel, G.F.:Messiah (sels), w. Elsie Morison (sop), Richard Lewis (ten), James Milligan (bass), Eric Chadwick (org), M. Sargent (cnd), Royal Liverpool PO, Huddersfield Choral Society Classics for Pleasure ▲ CDCFP 9007 [ADD]

Thomas, Nova (sop)
Balfe, M.W.:The Bohemian Girl, w. P. Power (ten), J. Summers (bar), R. Bonynge (cnd), Irish National SO, Ireland National Sym Chorus Argo 2-▲ 433324-2 [DDD]

Thomas, Tracy (sop)
Schubert, Franz:Der Graf von Gleichen, w. Gwendolyn Coleman (sop), Karen Driscoll (sop), Brad Diamond (ten), John M. Koch (bar), G. Samuel (cnd), Cincinnati PO, CCM Chamber Choir *(rec Corbett Auditorium, Univ of Cincinnati, Mar 12–13, 1994)* Centaur 2-▲ 2281/2282 [DDD]

Thomaschke, Thomas (bass)
Mendelssohn, Fanny:Oratorio, w. I. Lippitz (sop), Annemarie Fischer-Kunz (cta), H. Hatano (ten), E.M. Blankenburg (cnd), Cologne Youth Orch, Cologne Youth Chorus CPO ▲ CPO 999009-2 [DDD]

Thompson, Adrian (ten)
Bush, G.:A Summer Serenade, w. R. Hickox (cnd), City of London Sinfonia, Westminster Singers [E] Chandos ▲ CHAN 8864 [DDD]
Gay, J.:The Beggar's Opera, w. S. Walker (mez), B. Hoskins (sgr), C. Daniels (ten), I. Caddy (b-bar), J. Barlow (cnd), Broadside Band [E] Hyperion 2-▲ CDA 66591/92
Mendelssohn, Fanny:Songs, w. Michaela Krämer (sop), Gerhild Romberger (alt), Gerrit Miehlke (bass), Richard Braun (pno), Willi Gundlach (cnd), Dortmund Univ Chamber Choir—Morgendämmerung; Im Herbste; Unter des Laubdachs Hut; Ich stand gelehnet an den Mast; Mitternacht; Abschied; Lockung; Abend; Aus meinen Tränen; Wenn ich in deine Augen seh'; Im wunderschönen Monat Mai; Schöne Fremde; Schweigend sinkt die Nacht hernieder; Nacht liegt auf den fremden Wegen; Hochzeitsbitter; Wandl' ich in dem Wald; Frühzeitiger Frühling; Blumengruss; O Herbst; Schilflied; Feldlied; März; Lichter Mai; Waldruhe; Nachtreigen *(rec Musikhochschule Detmold, Dortmund, Oct 1995)* Thorofon ▲ CTH 2299 [DDD]
Schubert, Franz:Songs (comp), w. G. Johnson (pno)—early songs, between D.10 & D.134 [G] Hyperion ▲ CDJ 33012 [DDD]
Vaughan Williams, R.:The Shepherds of the Delectable Mountains, w. L. Kitchen (sop), J.-M. Ainsley (ten), A. Opie (bar), B. Terfel (b-bar), J. Best (bass), M. Best (cnd), City of London Sinfonia [E] Hyperion ▲ CDA 66569 [DDD]

Thompson, Jeanette (sop)
Negro Spirituals, w. Ieper Chamber Choir, David Miller (pno) Pavane ▲ ADW 7267 [DDD]

Thompson, Martin (ten)
Bellini, V.:Beatrice di Tenda, w. L. Aliberti (sop), C. Capasso (treble), P. Gavanelli (bass), F. Luisi (cnd), Berlin German Opera Orch, Berlin German Opera Chorus Berlin Classics 2-▲ BER 1042 [DDD]

Thorborg, Kerstin (mez)
Beethoven, L. van:Sym 9, "Choral Sym", w. Jarmila Novotna (sop), Jan Pierce (ten), Nicola Moscona (bass), A. Toscanini (cnd), NBC SO, Westminster Choir *(rec 1939)* LYS ▲ LYS 128
Beethoven, L. van:Sym 9, "Choral Sym", w. Jarmila Novotná (sop), Jan Peerce (ten), Nicola Moscona (bass), A. Toscanini (cnd), NBC SO, Westminster Choir *(rec New York City, 1939)* Grammofono 2000 ▲ GRM 78524 (m)
Kerstin Thorborg *(rec 1933–40)* Preiser ("Lebendige Vergangenheit" series) ▲ PRE 89084 [AAD]
Mahler, G.:Das Lied von der Erde, w. C. Martin Öhmann (ten), C. Schuricht (cnd), Royal Concertgebouw Orch *(rec live, Amsterdam, Oct. 5, 1939)* Archipon ▲ ARCH 3.1 (m) [ADD]
Mahler, G.:Das Lied von der Erde, w. Carl Martin Öhman (ten), C. Schuricht (cnd), Royal Concertgebouw Orch *(rec live, Amsterdam, Oct 5, 1939)* Minerva ▲ MN A30 (m) [ADD]
Mahler, G.:Das Lied von der Erde, w. V. Talich (cnd), Stockholm PO—sels. *(rec live, 11/7/34)* BIS 8-▲ CD 421/24 (m/s) [AAD]

Thorborg, Kerstin (mez) (cont.)
Mahler, G.:Das Lied von der Erde, w. Charles Kullmann (ten), B. Walter (cnd), Vienna PO *(rec Vienna, May 1936)* Grammofono 2000 ▲ GRM 78553
Mahler, G.:Das Lied von der Erde, w. C. Kullman (ten), B. Walter (cnd), Vienna PO Enterprise ("Palladio" series) ▲ ENTPD 4172 [ADD]
Mahler, G.:Songs, w. B. Walter (cnd), Vienna PO—Ich bin der Welt abhanden gekommen [G] *(rec live, Vienna, 5/24/36)* Music & Arts ▲ CD 749-1 (m) [AAD]
Mahler, G.:Songs from Rückert, w. B. Walter (cnd), Vienna PO—Ich bin der Welt abhanden gekommen [G] *(rec live in the Musikvereinsaal, Vienna, 5/24/36)* Pearl ▲ PEA 9413 (m) [AAD]
Mozart, W.A.:Requiem, w. E. Schumann (sop), A. Dermota (ten), A. Kipnis (bass), B. Walter (cnd), Vienna PO, Vienna State Opera Chorus EMI Classics ("Great Recordings of the Century" series) 3-▲ CDHC 63912
Mussorgsky, M.:Boris Godunov, w. René Maison (ten), Alexander Kipnis (bass), G. Szell (cnd), New York Metropolitan Opera Orch, New York Metropolitan Opera Chorus *(rec live, Feb 13, 1943)* The Fourties 2-▲ ENT 1505
Still, W.G.:Tristan und Isolde, w. Kirsten Flagstad (sop), Lauritz Melchoir (ten), Ludwig Hofmann (bass), Julius Huehn (sgr), A. Bodanzky (cnd), *(orch unknown)* *(rec Jan 2, 1937)* Enterprise ("The Fourties" series) 3-▲ ENT 304
Wagner, R.:Götterdämmerung (sels), w. Frida Leider (sop), Lauritz Melchior (ten), Herbert Janssen (bar), Emanuel List (bass), Maria Nezadál (sgr), T. Beecham (cnd), London PO, Royal Opera House Chorus Covent Garden *(rec Covent Garden, London, 1936)* Preiser ▲ PRE 90266
Wagner, R.:Götterdämmerung (sels), w. F. Leider (sop), Nezadál (sop), L. Melchior (ten), H. Janssen (bar), L. Weber (bass), T. Beecham (cnd), London PO, Royal Opera House Chorus Covent Garden [G] *(rec from 1925 Polydor & 1929)* Legato Classics 2-▲ LCD 146-2 (m) [ADD]
Wagner, R.:Die Walküre, w. Helen Traubel (sop), Astrid Varnay (sop), Lauritz Melchoir (ten), Friedrich Schorr (b-bar), E. Leinsdorf (cnd), *(orch unknown)* *(rec Dec 6, 1941)* Enterprise ("The Forties" series) 2-▲ ENT 318

Thorngren, Jane (sop)
Satoh, S.:Stabat mater, w. Bart Folse (cnd), Pro Arte Chorale New Albion ▲ NA 016 [DAD]

Thornton, James (bar)
Walton, W.:Troilus & Cressida, w. Judith Howarth (sop—Cressida), Arthur Davies (ten—Troilus), Nigel Robson (ten—Pandarus), Brian Cookson (ten—3rd Watchman), Peter Bodenham (ten—Priest), Keith Mills (ten—Soldier), Alan Opie (bar—Diomede), James Thornton (bar—Antenor), Clive Bayley (bass—Calkas), David Owen-Lewis (bass—Horaste), R. Hickox (cnd), English Northern Philharmonia, Opera North Chorus Chandos 2-▲ CHAN 9370/71 [DDD]

Thornton-Holmes, Christopher (bar)
Donizetti, G.:Emilia di Liverpool, w. Y. Kenny (sop), A. Mason (sop), B. Mills (sop), C. Merritt (ten), S. Bruscantini (bar), G. Dolton (bar), D. Parry (cnd), Philharmonia Orch, Geoffrey Mitchell Choir—complete opera, without dialogue Opera Rara 3-▲ OR 8
Donizetti, G.:L'Eremitaggio di Liverpool, w. Y. Kenny (sop), A. Mason (sop), B. Mills (sop), C. Merritt (ten), S. Bruscantini (bar), G. Dolton (bar), D. Parry (cnd), Philharmonia Orch, Geoffrey Mitchell Choir—complete opera, without dialogue Opera Rara 3-▲ OR 8

Thors, Andréas (boy sop)
Nielsen, C.:Choral Music, w. Å. Bäverstam (sop), L. Ekdahl (girl sop), K. M. Sandve (ten), P. Hoyer (bar), E.-P. Salonen (cnd), Swedish RSO, Stockholm Boys' Choir, Swedish Radio Chorus—Springtime in Funen; The Blind Musician; The Old People; Dance Ballad *(rec Sept. 16–18, 1991)* Sony Classical ▲ SK 53276 [DDD]

Thorsen, Stein Arild (bar)
Braein, E.F.:Anne Pedersdotter, w. K. Ekeberg (sop—Anne Pedersdotter), V. Hanssen (mez—Merete Beyer), R. Eriksen (alt—Herlofs-Marte), I. M. Brekke (alt—Bente), K. M. Sandve (ten—Martin Beyer), C. Ehrstedt (ten—Master Olaus), A. Helleland (ten—David), T. Gilje (ten—Jørund), S. A. Thorsen (bar—Master Johannes), S. Carlsen (bass—Absalon Pedersøn Beyer), T. Stensvold (bass—Master Laurentius), G. Oskarsson (bass—Jens Schelderup), P. Andersson (cnd), Norwegian National Opera Orch, Norwegian National Opera Chorus Simax 2-▲ PSC 3121

Thresh, J. (sgr)
Puccini, G.:Madama Butterfly, w. V. de los Angeles (sop), R. Nadell (mez), B. Faulkner (sgr), W. Fredericks (sgr), D. Bernard (sgr), R. Torigi (sgr), A. Cosenza (bar), W. Herbert (cnd), New Orleans Opera Orch, New Orleans Opera Chorus *(rec live March 18, 1954)* Legato Classics 2-▲ LCD 168-2 [ADD]

Thurn, P. im (bar)
Prokofiev, S.:Eugene Onegin, w. T. West (nar), K. Fuge (sop), J. Walker (bass), E. Downes (cnd), Sinfonia 21, New Company Chandos 2-▲ CHAN 9318/19 [DDD]

Tibbels, Nicole (sop)
Britten, H.:A Boy Was Born, w. S. Leonard (sop), S. Bickley (mez), P. Hall (ten), G. Jess (bass), T. Edwards (cnd), London Sinfonietta Chorus, St. Paul's Cathedral Choristers Virgin Classics ▲ CDC 59136
Britten, H.:Hymn to St. Cecilia, w. S. Leonard (sop), S. Bickley (mez), P. Hall (ten), G. Jess (bass), T. Edwards (cnd), London Sinfonietta Chorus, St. Paul's Cathedral Choir Virgin Classics ▲ CDC 59136
Britten, H.:Sonnets of Michelangelo, w. S. Leonard (sop), S. Bickley (mez), P. Hall (ten), G. Jess (bass), T. Edwards (cnd), London Sinfonietta Chorus, Choristers of St. Paul's Cathedral Virgin Classics ▲ CDC 59136

Tibbett, Lawrence (bar)
At His Magnificent Best Cantabile ("Biographies in Music" series) ▲ BIM 706-1 (m)
The Best of Lawrence Tibbett (rec. 1927–1935) Pearl ▲ PEA 9307 (m) [AAD]
The Emperor Tibbett *(rec from 78 rpm & live broadcasts, 1926–1941)* Pearl 2-▲ PEA 9452 (m) [AAD]
From Broadway to Hollywood *(rec 1927–1936)* Hermes ▲ HRM 6005 [ADD]
Lawrence Tibbett RCA Gold Seal ▲ 7808-2-RG (m) [ADD]
Lawrence Tibbett:His Rarities & Famous Performances on Radio, Films & Records (1930–43) Enterprise ("The Radio Years" series) ▲ ENT RY 29 (m)
Opera Stars Sing on Radio, Vol. 1:Unpublished Broadcasts from the Fourties, w. Dusolina Giannini (sop), Helen Traubel (sop), Gladys Swarthout (cta), Richard Crooks (ten), Lauritz Melchoir (ten), Robert Merrill (bar), Ezio Pinza (bass) Enterprise ("The Radio Years" series) ▲ ENTRY 11
Tibbett in Opera *(rec 1926–1939 for Victor)* Nimbus ("Prima Voce" series) ▲ NI 7825 [ADD]
Verdi, G.:Un ballo in maschera (sels), w. Maria Caniglia (sop), Gina Cigna (sop), Fedora Barbieri (mez), Enrico Carusa (ten), Beniamino Gigli (ten), Giovanni Zenatello (ten), Carlo Galeffi (bar), *(various orchs & cnds)* *(rec 1911–43)* Grammofono 2000 ▲ GRM 78527 (m)
Verdi, G.:La forza del destino, w. Stella Roman (sop), Frederick Jagel (ten), Salvatore Baccaloni (bass), Ezio Pinza (bass), B. Walter (cnd), New York Metropolitan Opera Orch *(rec live, Jan 23, 1943)* The Fourties 2-▲ ENT 1503
Verdi, G.:Otello, w. Elisabeth Rethberg (sop), Giovanni Martinelli (ten), E. Panizza (cnd), *(orch unknown)* *(rec Feb 12, 1938)* Enterprise ("The Fourties" series) 2-▲ ENT 309
Verdi, G.:Otello (sels), w. H. Jepson (sop), G. Martinelli (ten), N. Massue (ten), W. Pelletier (cnd), Metropolitan Opera Orch, New York Metropolitan Opera Chorus—eleven arias & scenes *(rec 1939)* Pearl ▲ GEMMCD 9914 (m) [AAD]
Verdi, G.:La traviata, w. Rosa Ponselle (sop—Violetta), Henriette Wakefield (sop—Annina), Frederick Jagel (ten—Alfredo), Alfredo Gandolfi (bar—Baron), Lawrence Tibbett (bar—Giorgio), E. Panizza (cnd), *(orch unknown)* *(rec live, New York, Jan. 5, 1935)* The Fourties 2-▲ ENT FT 1513
Wagner, R.:Der Ring des Nibelungen, w. A. Davis (sop), F. Jagel (ten), L. Stokowski (cnd), Philadelphia Orch *(rec 1933–1939)* Pearl 2-▲ CD 9076 [ADD]

Ticciati, Hugo (trb)
Britten, H.:Curlew River, w. Mark Milhofer (ten), Mark Evans (bar), Gwynn Hughes Jones (bar), Matthew Hargreaves (bass), D. Angus (cnd), Guildhall Chamber Ensemble Koch Schwann ▲ SCH 313972

Tichy, Georg (bass)
Haydn, J.:Applausus:Jubilaeum virtutis Palatium, w. Florian Erdl (sgr), Gert Füssi (sgr), Christian Graf (sgr), Helmut Wildhaber (ten), P. Angerer (cnd), Vienna Concilium Musicum [period instrs] Koch Schwann ▲ SCH 314092

Tichy, Georg (bass) (cont.)
Puccini, G.:Madama Butterfly (sels), w. Miriam Gauci (sop—Madama Butterfly), Nelly Boschkowa (mez—Suzuki), Yordi Ramiro (ten—F.B. Pinkerton), Jozef Abel (ten—Goro), Georg Tichy (bass—Sharpless), Anna Tomkovicová (sgr), Mária Stahelová (sgr), Elena Hanzelová (sgr) *(rec Concert Hall of the Czecho-Slovak Radio, Bratislava, May 2-10, 1991)* Naxos ▲ 8.553152 [DDD]

Tichy, Gerog (bass)
Verdi, G.:La traviata (sels), w. Monika Krause (sop), Ivica Neshybová (sop), Rannveig Braga (mez), Yordy Ramiro (ten), Ladislav Neshyba (bass), Jozef Špaček (bass), A. Rahbari (cnd), Czech-Slovak RSO Bratislava, Jan Rozehnal (cnd), Slovak Phil Chorus—Prelude act I; Libiam ne'lieti calici; Un dí, felice; È strano! Ah, fors'e lui; Follie!...sempre libera; Lunge da lei...de'miei bollenti spiriti; O Mio rimorosol; Pura si come un angelo...Dite alla giovine; Dammi tu forza; Di Provenza il mar; Noi siamo zingarelle; Prelude act III; Teneste la promessa...Addio del passato; Signora! Che t'accade?; Ah, Violetta! *(rec Bratislava Concert Hall, Dec 1990)* Naxos ▲ 8.553041 [DDD]

Ticinelli-Fattori, Luciana (sop)
Palestrina, G.:Sacred Music, w. Maria Minetto (mez), Laerte Malaguti (bar), James Loomis (bass), E. Loehrer (cnd), Lugano Chamber Society Instrumental Ensemble, Lugano Chamber Society Chorus—Vexilla Regis Prodeunt; Adoramus Te; Laudario Di Cortona Accord ▲ ACD 201562 [AAD]

Ticozzi, Ebe (mez)
Boito, A.:Mefistofele, w. M. Pobbe (sop—Margherita), D. De Cecco (sop—Elena), E. Ticozzi (mez—Marta), F. Tagliavini (ten—Faust), G. Neri (bass—Mefistofele), A. Questa (cnd), Turin RSO, Turin Teatro Regio Chorus *(rec 1954)* Fonit Cetra ("Classic Collection" series) 2-▲ FCT CDO 19
Mascagni, P.:Cavalleria rusticana, w. M. Callas (sop), G. di Stefano (ten), R. Panerai (bar), T. Serafin (cnd), La Scala Orch, La Scala Chorus [I] EMI Classics 3-▲ CDCC 47981 [ADD]

Tiilikainen, Sauli (bar)
Bergman, E.:The Singing Tree, w. K. Hannula (sop), C. Hellekant (cta), P. Lindroos (ten), P. Salomaa (bass), M. Wallén (bass), U. Söderblom (cnd), Finnish National Opera Orch, Dominante Chamber Choir, Tapiola Chamber Choir Ondine 2-▲ ODE 794-2D [DDD]
Kortekangas, O.:Grand Hotel, w. E.-L. Saarinen (mez), K. Laurikainen (speaker), Pohjola, Söderström (cnd), Avanti! CO, Finnish Chamber Chorus, Tapiola Chorus [Fin] Ondine ▲ ODE 749-2 [ADD]
Merikanto, O.:Music of, w. Eeva-Liisa Saarinen (mez), Jorma Hynninen (bar), Kaija Saarikettu (vn), Erkki Rautio (vc), Pertti Eerola (pno), Ralf Gothoni (pno), Raija Kerppo (pno), Izumi Tateno (pno), Tauno Satomaa (cnd), Candomino Choir—Summer Evening (waltz); Valse lente; Romance; On the Highest Tree-Top; Annina; Bye, Bye Lullabye; The Weeping Flute; At Sea; Hey My Heart; Where Rustling Birches Bend; Play Softly, the Tune of Mourning; Fairy Tale by the Fireside; Idyll; Scherzo, Op. 6/4; O Dost Thou Remember That Hymn; Lade Ladoga; Why Do I Sing; The Thunderbird; The Happy Ones; Summer Evening's Idyll Finlandia ▲ FIN 500432 [AAD/DDD]
Sibelius, J.:Everyman, w. Lilli Paasikivi (mez), Petri Lehto (ten), Leena Saarenpää (pno), Pauli Pietiläinen (org), O. Vänskä (cnd), Lahti SO, Lahti Chamber Choir *(rec Church of the Cross, Lahti, Finland, Jan 11-13, 1995)* BIS ▲ CD-735 [DDD]
Sibelius, J.:The Tempest, w. R. Viljakainen (sop), M. Groop (mez), J. Silvasti (ten), J. Hynninen (bar), J.-P. Saraste (cnd), Finnish RSO, Finnish Opera Festival Chorus Ondine ▲ ODE 813 [DDD]

Tikalová, Drahomira (sop)
Dvořák, A.:Stabat Mater, w. Marta Krasova (cta), Beno Blachut (ten), Karel Kalas (bass), V. Talich (cnd), Czech PO, Czech Phil Chorus *(rec 1952)* Supraphon 2-▲ SUP 111902 [ADD]
Dvořák, A.:Vanda, w. Stefa Petrova (mez), Beno Blachut (ten), Karel Kalas (bass), F. Dyk (cnd), Prague RSO, Jiri Pinkas (cnd), Prague Radio Chorus *(rec 1951)* Supraphon ("Hidden Treasures from Prague" series) 2-▲ SUP CD 3007 (m)
Janácek, L.:Kát'a Kabanová, w. B. Blachut (ten), J. Krombholc (cnd), Prague National Theater Orch, Prague National Theater Chorus Supraphon 2-▲ SUP 108016 [ADD]
Novák, V.:Storm, w. Maria Tauberová (sop), Beno Blachut (ten), Ladislav Mráz (bar), J. Krombholc (cnd), Czech PO, Czech Phil Chorus *(rec 1956)* Supraphon 2-▲ SUP 111982 (m) [ADD]
Smetana, B.:The Bartered Bride, w. Ivo Zidek (ten), Eduard Haken (bass), Z. Chalabala (cnd), Prague National Theater Orch, Prague National Theater Chorus Supraphon 2-▲ SUP 0040 [AAD]

Tilli, Johann (bass)
Dessau, P.:Haggada, w. Sabine Ritterbusch (sop), Renate Spingler (sop), Yvi Jänicke (alt), Peter Galliard (ten—Rabbi Tarfon/Jude/ten solo), Gabriel Sadé (ten—Pharaoh), Jochen Schmeckenbecher (bar—Rabbi Jehoschua), Bernd Weikl (bar—Moses), Matthias Hölle (bass—Speaker/Rabbi Akiwa), Alfred Muff (bass—Father/Rabbi Eleasar), Johann Tilli (bass—Rabbi Elieser/bass solo), G. Albrecht (cnd), Hamburg State PO, Berlin Carl Maria Von Weber Men's Choir, Hamburg Alsterspatzen, North German Radio Chorus [G] *(rec Musikhalle, Hamburg, Sept 4 & 5, 1994)* Capriccio 2-▲ 10590/91 [DDD]
Schumann, R.:Genoveva, w. J. Faulkner (sop—Genoveva), R. Behle (sop—Margaretha), K. Lewis (ten—Golo), A. Titus (bar—Siegfried), H. Stamm (bass—Hidulfus, Caspar), J. Tilli (bass—Balthasar), G. Albrecht (cnd), Hamburg State PO, Hamburg State Opera Chorus [G] *(rec 1992)* Orfeo 2-▲ 289932 [DDD]

Timberlake, S. (bass)
Prokofiev, S.:Ivan the Terrible, w. C. Carlson (mez), L. Slatkin (cnd), St. Louis SO, St. Louis Sym Chorus [R] Vox Box 2-▲ CDX 5021 [ADD]

Tindall, Paul (sgr)
Handel, G.F.:Israel in Egypt, w. Ruth Holton (sop), Elisabeth Friday (sgr), Michael Chance (alt), Philip Salmon (ten), J. E. Gardiner (cnd), English Baroque Soloists, Monteverdi Choir London Philips ▲ 432110-2

Tindall, Paul (ten)
Purcell, H.:Dido & Aeneas, w. Ruth Holton (sop—Belinda), Elisabeth Priday (sop—2nd Woman), Donna Deam (sop—1st Witch), Shauna Beesley (sop—2nd Witch), Teresa Shaw (mez—Sorceress), Carolyn Watkinson (cta—Dido), Jonathan Peter Kenny (alt—Spirit), Paul Tindall (ten—Sailor), George Mosley (bass—Aeneas), J.E. Gardiner (cnd), English Baroque Soloists, Monteverdi Choir London *(rec Saint George's, Bristol, UK, July 12-14, 1990)* Philips ▲ 432114-2
Purcell, H.:Welcome to All the Pleasures, w. Ruth Holton (sop), Nicola Jenkin (sop), Michael Chance (alt), George Mosly (bass), J.E. Gardiner (cnd), English Baroque Soloists, Monteverdi Choir London *(rec Saint George's, Bristol, UK, July 12-14, 1990)* Philips ▲ 432114-2

Tinsley, Pauline (sop)
Handel, G.F.:Music of, w. James Bowman (ct), Anthony Rolfe-Johnson (ten), David Wilson-Johnson (ten), Simon Preston (org), R. Leppard (cnd), English CO, London Phil Chorus—Zadok the Priest; Eternal Source of Light Divine; Tamerlano Ov; Dead March [from Saul]; When the Ear Heard Her; She Delivered the Poor That Cried; Their Bodies Are Buried in Peace; Glory Be to the Father; As It Was in the Beginning; Con a Due Cori in B♭; Waft Her Angels to the Skies; Con in g for Org, Op. 7/5; Hallelujah Chorus [from The Messiah] IMP ("BBC Radio Classics" series) ▲ IMP 5691522

Tippe, Corinna (sop)
Hoffmann, E.T.A.:Undine, w. Barbara Baier (sop—Berthalda), Heidrun Plesch (sop—Undine), Corinna Tippe (sop—Die Herzogin), Maria Hiefinger (mez—Fisherman's Wife), Achim Schamberger (ten—Der Herzog), Johannes Beck (bar—Ritter Huldbrand von Ringstetten), Michael Albert (bass—Fisherman), Ulrich Bosch (bass—Heilmann), Bernd Hofmann (bass—Kühleborn), H. Dechant (cnd), Bamberg Youth Orch Bayer 3-▲ 100256/58 [DDD]

Tirmont, Dominique (bar)
Hahn, R.:O mon bel inconnu!, w. Christiane Château (sop), Lina Dachary (sop), Monique Stiot (mez), Michel Hamel (ten), Joseph Peyron (ten), Aimé Doniat (bar), Philippe Gaudin (sgr), Jacques Provins (sgr), J. Brebion (cnd), ORTF Lyric Orch Musidisc 2-▲ MUS 202562 [AAD]

Tirmont, Edmond (ten)
Gounod, C.:Roméo et Juliette, w. Yvonne Gall (sop—Juliette), Champell (sop—Stéphano), Jeanne Goulancourt (mez—Gertrude), Agustarello Affre (ten—Roméo), Edmond Tirmont (ten—Tybalt), Alexis Boyer (bar—Mercutio), Pierre Dupré (bar—Paris), Hypolite Belhomme (bar—Grégorio), Marcel Journet (bass—Frère Laurent), Henri Albers (bass—Capulet), Valermont (bass—The Duke), F. Rühlmann (cnd), Paris Opéra-Comique Orch, Paris Opéra-Comique Chorus *(rec 1912)* VAI Audio ▲ VAIA 1064-3 F

Tisi, Ezio Maria (sgr)
Rossini, G.:La gazetta, w. Teresa Verdera (sop), Gianpiero Ruggeri (sgr), Kasimierz Sergiel (sgr), W. Keitel (cnd), Minsk Orch, Motet & Madrigal Posen Chamber Chorus Deutsche Schallplatten ▲ DS 1053

Tisi, Ezio Maria (voc)
Cicognini, A.:The Bicycle Thief (sels), w. N. Samale (cnd), Sinfonia Orch delle Marche, St. Cecilia di Fabriano Legend ▲ CD 23 [DDD]
Cicognini, A.:Gold of Naples (sels), w. N. Samale (cnd), Sinfonia Orch delle Marche, St. Cecilia di Fabriano Legend ▲ CD 23 [DDD]
Cicognini, A.:The Last Judgement (sels), w. N. Samale (cnd), Sinfonia Orch delle Marche, St. Cecilia di Fabriano Legend ▲ CD 23 [DDD]
Cicognini, A.:Miracle in Milan (sels), w. N. Samale (cnd), Sinfonia Orch delle Marche, St. Cecilia di Fabriano Legend ▲ CD 23 [DDD]
Cicognini, A.:TheRoof (sels), w. N. Samale (cnd), Sinfonia Orch delle Marche, St. Cecilia di Fabriano Legend ▲ CD 23 [DDD]
Cicognini, A.:Shoeshine (sels), w. N. Samale (cnd), Sinfonia Orch delle Marche, St. Cecilia di Fabriano Legend ▲ CD 23 [DDD]
Cicognini, A.:Umberto D (sels), w. N. Samale (cnd), Sinfonia Orch delle Marche, St. Cecilia di Fabriano Legend ▲ CD 23 [DDD]

Titta, Enzo (bass)
Puccini, G.:La fanciulla del West (sels), w. Magda Olivero (sop—Minnie), Corinna Vozza (mez—Wowkle), Paolo Caroli (ten—Harry), Giacomo Lauri-Volpi (ten—Dick Johnson), Marco Rogani (ten—Pony Express Rider), Salvatore di Tommaso (ten—Trin), Adelio Zagonara (ten—Nick), Virgilio Ascorro (bar—Sid), Alfredo Colella (bar—Jake Wallace), Giuseppe Forgione (bar—Bello), Giancarlo Guelfi (bar—Jack Rance), Arturo la Porta (bar—Sonora), Gino Conti (bass—José Castro), Piere Passarotti (bass—Bill), Enzo Titta (bass—Larkens), Giulio Tomei (bass—Ashby), V. Bellezza (cnd), Rome Opera Orch, Rome Opera Chorus—Minnie, dalla mia casa son partito; Laggiù nel Soledad; Chi c'è per farmi i ricci; Oh! Mister Johnson, siete rimasto; Non so ben neppur io; Io non son che una povera fanciulla; No, Minnie, non piangete; Vorrei mettermi queste; Hallo!; Oh, se sapeste; Credo che abbiate torto; Ma ti giuro ch'io non ti lascio più; Vieni fuori!; Una parola sola!...Or son sei mesi; Che c'è di nuovo Jack?; È là; Siete pronto; Ch'ella mi creda; È Minnie!...È Minnie! *(rec Rome, Mar. 30, 1957)* Golden Age of Opera ▲ GAO 180 [ADD]

Titterton, Frank (ten)
Vaughan Williams, R.:Serenade to Music, w. I. Baillie (sop), E. Suddaby (sop), S. Allen (sop), E. Turner (sop), M. Balfour (cta), A. Desmond (cta), M. Brunskill (cta), M. Jarred (cta), H. Nash (ten), W. Widdop (ten), P. Jones (ten), R. Henderson (bass), R. Easton (bass), H. Williams (bass), N. Allin (bass), H. J. Wood (cnd), BBC SO Dutton Laboratories ▲ CDAX 8004 [ADD]
Vaughan Williams, R.:Serenade to Music, w. I. Baillie (sop), E. Suddaby (sop), S. Allen (sop), E. Turner (sop), M. Balfour (cta), A. Desmond (cta), M. Brunskill (cta), M. Jarred (cta), H. Nash (ten), W. Widdop (ten), P. Jones (ten), R. Henderson (bass), R. Easton (bass), H. Williams (bass), N. Allin (bass), H. Wood (cnd), BBC SO [E] *(rec 10/15/38)* Pearl ▲ GEMMCD 9342 (m) [AAD]
Vaughan Williams, R.:Serenade to Music, w. Isobel Baillie (sop), Lilian Stiles-Allen (sop), Elsie Suddaby (sop), Eva Turner (sop), Margaret Balfour (cta), Muriel Brunskill (cta), Astra Desmond (cta), Mary Jarred (cta), Parry Jones (ten), Heddle Nash (ten), Walter Widdop (ten), Roy Henderson (bar), Harold Williams (bar), Norman Allin (bass), Robert Easton (bass), H. Wood (cnd), BBC SO *(rec Abbey Road, Oct 15, 1938)* Claremont ▲ CDGSE 785066

Titus, Alan (bar)
Beethoven, L. van:Cant on the Death of the Emperor Joseph II, w. Markus Schäfer (ten), Bodil Arnesen (sgr), K.A. Rickenbacher (cnd), Berlin RSO, Berlin Radio Chorus Koch Schwann ▲ SCH 314352 [DDD]
Bizet, G.:Carmen, w. D. Palade (sop), G. Alperyn (mez), G. Lamberti (ten), et al., A. Rahbari (cnd), Czech-Slovak RSO Bratislava, Slovak Phil Chorus, Bratislava Children's Choir [F] Naxos 3-▲ 8.660005/07 [DDD]
Bizet, G.:Carmen (sels), w. D. Palade (sop—Micaëla), A. Liebeck (sop—Frasquita), G. Alperyn (mez—Carmen), D. Schaechter (mez—Mercédès), G. Lamberti (ten—Don José), M. Dvorsky (ten—Remandado), J. Durco (ten—Cancairo), A. Titus (bar—Escamillo), V. Chmelo (bar—Morales), D. Rigosa (bass—Zuniga), A. Rahbari (cnd), Czech-Slovak RSO Bratislava, Slovak Phil Chorus, Bratislava Children's Choir *(rec July 1990)* Naxos ▲ 8.550727 [DDD]
Catalani, A.:La Wally, w. E. Marton (sop), F. Araiza (ten), F. Ellero d'Artegna (bass), P. Steinberg (cnd), Munich RSO, Bavarian Radio Chorus [I] Eurodisc 2-▲ 69073-2-RC [DDD] ■ 69073-4-RC (CrO2)
Donizetti, G.:Don Pasquale, w. Beverly Sills (sop), Alfredo Kraus (ten), Donald Gramm (b-bar), S. Caldwell (cnd), London SO, Ambrosian Opera Chorus EMI Classics 2-▲ CDMB 66030
Haydn, J.:Mass 10, "Kriegsmesse", "Paukenmesse", w. Patricia Wells (sop), Gwendoline Killebrew (mez), Michael Devlin (b-bar), L. Bernstein (cnd), *(orch unknown)*, Norman Scribner Choir [L] *(rec 1973)* Sony Classical ("Bernstein:The Royal Edition" series) 2-▲ SM2K 47563 [ADD]
Killmayer, W.:Yolimba, w. M. Venuti (sop—Yolimba), A. Titus (bar—Möhringer), P. Schneider (cnd), Munich RSO, Bavarian Radio Chorus [G] Orfeo ▲ 257921 [DDD]
Mozart, W.A.:Arias, w. I. Cotrubas (sop), E. Gruberova (sop), L. Price (sop), J. Varady (sop), L. Popp (mez), F. Araiza (ten), P. Domingo (ten), P. de Palma (ten), P. Schreier (ten), F. Wunderlich (ten), S. Milnes (bar), M. Talvela (bass)—sels. from Entführung aus dem Serail, Così fan tutte, Don Giovanni, Idomeneo, Die Zauberflöte, Le nozze di Figaro Eurodisc ▲ 69256-2-RG [ADD]
Mozart, W.A.:Don Giovanni, w. J. Varady (sop), A. Augér (sop), E. Mathis (sop), T. Moser (ten), R. Panerai (bar), R. Scholze (bass), J.-H. Rootering (bass), R. Kubelik (cnd), Bavarian RSO, Bavarian Radio Chorus [I] Eurodisc 3-▲ 7798-2 [DDD]
Schumann, R.:Genoveva, w. J. Faulkner (sop—Genoveva), R. Behle (sop—Margaretha), K. Lewis (ten—Golo), A. Titus (bar—Siegfried), H. Stamm (bass—Hidulfus, Caspar), J. Tilli (bass—Balthasar), G. Albrecht (cnd), Hamburg State PO, Hamburg State Opera Chorus [G] *(rec 1992)* Orfeo 2-▲ 289932 [DDD]
Verdi, G.:Falstaff, w. S. Sweet (sop), M. Horne (mez), F. Lopardo (ten), R. Panerai (bar), C. Davis (cnd), Bavarian RSO, Bavarian Radio Chorus RCA Red Seal 2-▲ 09026-60705-2 [DDD]

Titus, Graham (bass)
Mozart, W.A.:Missa, K.317, w. Janet Price (sop), Kevin Smith (ct), Anthony Rolfe-Johnson (ten), M. Davies (cnd), BBC Northern SO, Leeds Phil Chorus IMP ("BBC Radio Classics" series) ▲ IMP 5691552
Tavener, J.:Innocence, w. Patricia Rozario (sop), Leigh Nixon (ten), Alice Neary (vc), Charles Fullbrook (bells), Martin Baker (org), Martin Neary (cnd), Westminster Abbey Choir *(rec Westminster Abbey, May 1-5, 1995)* Sony Classical ▲ SK 66613 [DDD]

Titze, Robert (bass)
Schumann, R.:Requiem Mignon, w. Christa Lehnert (sop), Edith Mathis (sop), Maura Moreira (cta), Margarete Witte-Waldbauer (alt), R. Wagner (cnd), Innsbruck SO, Innsbruck Chorus *(rec Innsbruck, 1963)* Allegretto ▲ ACD 8190

Tkaczyk, I. (alt)
Gorczycki, G.G.:Sacred Choral Music, w. R. Stacewicz (sop), A. Pagowska (alt), E. Sasiadek (ten), W. Brychcy (bass), Wroclaw Orch, S. Galonski (cnd), Edmund Kajdasz (cnd), Capella Bydgostiensis Pro Musica Antiqua, Madrigalists Choir, Polish Radio Chorus—Completorium; In virtute tua; Iudica me deus; Laetatus sum; Missa paschalis [L] *(rec 1966)* Olympia ▲ OCD 320 [AAD]

Tobiasson, Ingrid (cta)
The Most Beloved Opera Choruses, w. [cnd:Sixten Ehrling], Royal Swedish Opera Chorus, Carina Morling (mez), Magnus Kyhle (ten), Anders Lorentzon (bass) Caprice ▲ CAP 21520

Toborsky, M. (sop)
Weber, C.M. von:Gloria et honore, w. E. Ehret, St. Michael Orch Munich, St. Michael Chorus Munich Koch Schwann ▲ CD 313 055 [ADD]
Weber, C.M. von:In die solemnitatis, w. E. Ehret (cnd), St. Michael's Orch, St. Michael's Chorus Koch Schwann ▲ CD 313 055 [ADD]

Toczyska, Stefania (mez)
Chopin, F.:Songs Sop (comp), w. Janusz Olejniczak (pno)—Op. 74/6, 9, 16 & 17 *(rec Rzeszow, May 15-17, 1995)* Selene ▲ CD 9503.26 [DDD]
Glinka, M.:A Life for the Tsar, w. A. Pendachanska (sop), C. Merritt (ten), B. Martinovich (bass), E. Tchakarov (cnd), Sofia Festival Orch, Sofia National Opera Chorus [R] Sony Classical 3-▲ S3K 46487 [DDD]

Toczyska, Stefania (mez) (cont.)
Karlowicz, M.:Songs, w. Janusz Olejniczak (pno)—Op. 1/1-3, 5 & 6; Op. 3/1-5 & 7; Pod jaworem; Po szerokim; O, nie wiesz!; Z nowa wiosna *(rec Rzeszow, May 15-17, 1995)* Selene ▲ CD 9503.26 [DDD]
Moniuszko, S.:Songs, w. Janusz Olejniczak (pno)—Piesn wieczorna; Zlota rybka; Kozak; Ojcze z niebios *(rec Rzeszow, May 15-17, 1995)* Selene ▲ CD 9503.26 [DDD]
Scriabin, A.:Sym 1, w. M. Myers (ten), R. Muti (cnd), Philadelphia Orch, Philadelphia Choral Arts Society EMI Classics 3-▲ CDC 54251
Spontini, G.:Olympia, w. J. Varady (sop), F. Tagliavini (ten), D. Fischer-Dieskau (bar), G. Fortune (bass), J. Becker (bass), G. Albrecht (cnd), Berlin RSO, Berlin Radio Chorus [Paris version] Orfeo 2-▲ 137862 [DDD]
Verdi, G.:Il trovatore, w. Katia Ricciarelli (sop), José Carreras (ten), Yuri Mazurok (bar), C. Davis (cnd), Royal Opera House Orch, Royal Opera House Chorus Covent Garden Philips ("Two-Fers" series) 2-▲ 446151-2

Todd, Phillip (ten)
Couperin, F.:Leçons de ténèbres (for Good Friday), w. A. Deller (ct), R. Perulli (va da gamba), M. Chapuis (org) [L] Musique d'Abord ▲ HMA 190210
Purcell, H.:The Prophetess, or The History of Dioclesian, w. H. Sheppard (sop), S. Le Sage (sop), A. Deller (ct), M. Worthley (ten), M. Bevan (bar), A. Deller (cnd), Vienna Concentus Musicus—also includes incidental music from the play *(rec June 1965)* Vanguard Classics ("The Bach Guild" series) ▲ OVC 2517 [ADD]

Todorovic, Zoran (sgr)
Künneke, E.:The Alluring Flame, w. Birgit Fandrey (sgr—Dolores), Christianne Hossfeld (sgr—Lisbeth), Maria Mallé (sgr), Jürgen Sacher (ten—Master), Ralf Lukas (bar—Hoffman), Gerd Grochowski (sgr—1st Neighbor), Gerhard Peters (sgr—Friedrich), Zoran Todorovic (sgr—Jacinto), Theodor Weimer (sgr—2nd Neighbor), P. Falk (cnd), Cologne RSO, Cologne Radio Chorus *(rec Cologne, Nov 7-26, 1994)* Capriccio ▲ 10753 [DDD]

Tokatyan, Armand (ten)
Her First Recordings, w. Steber, Eleanor (sop), Lucielle Browning (mez), Pino Bontempi (sgr), Annamary Dickey (sgr), George Cehanovsky (bar), Lorenzo Alvary ((bass), A. Kent (bar), Raoul Jobin (ten), Norman Cordon (bass) VAI Audio ▲ VAIA 1023 (m) [ADD]

Tokody, Ilona (sop)
Live in Tokyo, w. Masahiro Saitoh (pno) *(rec Apr. 20, 1991)* Live Notes ▲ WWCC 7220
Mascagni, P.:Iris, w. P. Domingo (ten), J. Pons (bar), G. Patanè (cnd), Munich RSO, Bavarian Radio Chorus CBS 2-▲ M2K 45526
Portrait of the Artist *(rec live, 1991-92)* VAI Audio ▲ VAIA 1009 [ADD/DDD]
A Portrait of the Artist Standing Room Only ▲ SRO 823-1 [ADD]
Puccini, G.:Arias, w. Juan Pons (bar), E. Lukács (cnd), Hungarian State Opera Orch—O mio babbino caro [from Gianni Schicchi] *(rec live, Franz Liszt Music Academy, Budapest, Hungary, June 4, 1994)* VAI Audio ▲ VAIA 1089
Puccini, G.:Suor angelica, w. Barlay (sgr), B. Póka (bar), L. Gardelli (cnd), Hungarian State Opera Orch, Hungarian State Opera Chorus [I] Hungaroton ▲ HCD 12490
Puccini, G.:Il tabarro, w. G. Lamberti (ten), S. Nimsgern (bar), G. Patanè (cnd), Munich RSO [I] Eurodisc ▲ 7775-2-RC [DDD]
Respighi, O.:La Fiamma, w. T. Takács (mez), P. Kelen (ten), S. Sólyom-Nagy (bar), L. Gardelli (cnd), Hungarian State Orch, Hungarian State Chorus [I] Hungaroton 3-▲ HCD 12591/93 [DDD]
Strauss, R.:Guntram, w. R. Goldberg (ten), S. Sólyom-Nágy (bar), I. Gáti (bar), E. Queler (cnd), Hungarian State Orch, Hungarian People's Army Male Chorus [G] CBS 2-▲ M2K 39737 [DDD]
Tosti, P.F.:songs, w. Juan Pons (bar), E. Lukács (cnd), Hungarian State Opera Orch—'A Vucchella *(rec live, Franz Liszt Music Academy, Budapest, Hungary, June 4, 1994)* VAI Audio ▲ VAIA 1089
Verdi, G.:arias, w. Juan Pons (bar), E. Lukács (cnd), Hungarian State Opera Orch—Favella il Doge ad Amelia Grimaldi? [duet from Simon Boccanegra]; Di Provenza il mar; Un dì, quando le veneri...Dite alla giovine [both from La Traviata]; Pace, pace, mio Dio! [from La Forza del Destino]; Udiste? Come albeggi, la scure al figlio [duet from Il Trovatore]; Cortigiani, vil razza dannata; Mio padre! Dio! mia Gilda...Tutte le feste [both from Rigoletto]; Cielǃ Mio padre! [from Aida] *(rec live, Franz Liszt Music Academy, Budapest, Hungary, June 4, 1994)* VAI Audio ▲ VAIA 1089

Tomanelli, Carlo (bass)
Rossini, G.:Il barbiere di Siviglia, w. Roberta Peters (sop—Rosina), Margaret Roggero (mez—Berta), Cesare Valletti (ten—Count Almaviva), Calvin Marsh (bar—Fiorello/Sergeant), Robert Merrill (bar—Figaro), Fernando Corena (bass—Dr. Bartolo), Carlo Tomanelli (bass—Ambrogio), Giorgio Tozzi (bass—Don Basilio), E. Leinsdorf (cnd), Metropolitan Opera Orch, New York Metropolitan Opera Chorus *(rec Manhattan Center, New York, Sept 1-11, 1958)* RCA Living Stereo 3-▲ 09026-68552-2 [ADD]

Tomaszewska Schepis, Anastasia (sgr)
Marschner, H.A.:Der Vampyr, w. Carole Farley (sop—Malwina), Nucci Condò (mez—Suse), Oslavio Di Credico (ten—George Dibdin), Josef Protschka (ten—Edgar Aubry), Romano Truffelli (ten—Richard Scrop), Martin Egel (bar—Sir Humphrey Davenaut), Andréa Snarski (bar—Toms Blunt), Siegmund Nimsgern (b-bar—Lord Ruthven), Armando Caforio (bass—Robert Green), Peter Boom (sgr—Il capo dei Vampiri), Carlo Di Giacomo (sgr—James Gadshill), Wolfgang Lenz (sgr—Sir Berkley), Galina Pisarenko (sgr—Janthe), Renzo Scorsoni (sgr—Un servitore di Berkley), Anastasia Tomaszewska Schepis (sgr—Emmy), G. Neuhold (cnd), Rome RAI SO, Rome RAI Chorus *(rec Rome, Jan 26, 1980)* Italia 2-▲ CDC 99 [ADD]

Tomei, Giulio (bass)
Arias & Duets, w. Beniamino Gigli (ten), Iva Pacetti (sop) EMI Classics ▲ CDH 61052
Puccini, G.:La fanciulla del West (sels), w. Magda Olivero (sop—Minnie), Corinna Vozza (mez—Wowkle), Paolo Caroli (ten—Harry), Giacomo Lauri-Volpi (ten—Dick Johnson), Marco Rogani (ten—Pony Express Rider), Salvatore di Tommaso (ten—Trin), Adelio Zagonara (ten—Nick), Virgilio Ascorro (bar—Sid), Alfredo Colella (bar—Jake Wallace), Giuseppe Forgione (bar—Bello), Giancarlo Guelfi (bar—Jack Rance), Arturo la Porta (bar—Sonora), Gino Conti (bass—José Castro), Piere Passarotti (bass—Bill), Enzo Titta (bass—Larkens), Giulio Tomei (bass—Ashby), V. Bellezza (cnd), Rome Opera Orch, Rome Opera Chorus—Minnie, dalla mia casa son partito; Laggiù nel Soledad; Chi c'è per farmi i ricci; Oh! Mister Johnson, siete rimasto; Non so ben neppur io; Io non son che una povera fanciulla; No, Minnie, non piangete; Vorrei mettermi queste; Hallo!; Oh, se sapeste; Credo che abbiate torto; Ma ti giuro ch'io non ti lascio più; Vieni fuori!; Una parola sola!...Or son sei mesi; Che c'è di nuovo Jack?; È là; Siete pronto; Ch'ella mi creda; È Minnie!...È Minnie! *(rec Rome, Mar. 30, 1957)* Golden Age of Opera ▲ GAO 180 [ADD]

Tomicich, Aurio (bass)
Bellini, V.:Bianca e Fernando, w. Y. O. Shin (sop), G. Kunde (ten), W. Coppola (ten), A. Licata (cnd), Catania Teatro Massimo Bellini Orch, Catania Teatro Massimo Bellini Chorus Nuova Era 2-▲ NUO 7076 [DDD]
Morlacchi, F.:Nuovo barbiere, w. A. Ruffini (sop), G. Gatti (sop), M. Comencini (ten), R. Franceschetto (sgr), G. Catalucci (cnd), Orch Giovanile In Canto [I] *(rec live 9/9/89)* Bongiovanni 2-▲ GB 2085/86 [DDD]
Smareglia, A.:La falena, w. Leyla Gencer (sop—La Falena), Rita Lantieri (sop—Albina, sua figlia), Ruggero Bondino (ten—Re Stellio), Dario Zerial (ten—Il ladro), Mario D'Anna (bar—Il vecchio Uberto), Aurio Tomicich (bass—Morio), Giuseppe Botta (sgr—Un marinaio), G. Gavazzeni (cnd), Trieste Teatro Comunale Giuseppe Verdi Orch, Trieste Teatro Comunale G. Verdi Chorus *(rec Trieste, Mar 18, 1876)* Bongiovanni 2-▲ GB 1131/32

Tomkovicová, Anna (sgr)
Puccini, G.:Madama Butterfly (sels), w. Miriam Gauci (sop—Madama Butterfly), Nelly Boschkowa (mez—Suzuki), Yordi Ramiro (ten—F.B. Pinkerton), Jozef Abel (ten—Goro), Georg Tichy (bass—Sharpless), Mária Stahelová (sgr), Elena Hanzelová (sgr) *(rec Concert Hall of the Czecho-Slovak Radio, Bratislava, May 2-10, 1991)* Naxos ▲ 8.553152 [DDD]

Tomlin, Lily (nar)
Saint-Saëns, C.:Carnival of the Animals, w. M. Golabek (nar), R. Golabek (nar), F. Savage (nar), C. Heston (nar), J. E. Jones (nar), B. White (nar), L. Redgrave (nar), W. Shatner (nar), J. Rivers (nar), T. Danson (nar), D. Raffin (nar), A. Hepburn (nar), D. Moore (nar), W. Matthau (nar), J. Smith (nar), L. Schifrin (cnd), Hollywood CO Dove Audio ▲ DOV 30700

Tomlinson, John (bass)
Bartók, B.:Bluebeard's Castle, w. Anne Sofie von Otter (mez—Judith), John Tomlinson (bass—Duke Bluebeard), Sandor Eles (nar), B. Haitink (cnd), Berlin PO *(rec Berlin)* EMI Classics ▲ CDC 56162
Bartók, B.:Cant Profana, "The Giant Stags", w. J. Aler (ten), P. Boulez (cnd), Chicago SO, Chicago Sym Chorus Deutsche Grammophon ▲ 435863-2 [DDD]
Handel, G.F.:Acis & Galatea [arr Mozart], w. B. Bonney (sop), J. MacDougall (ten), M. Schäfer (ten), T. Pinnock (cnd), English Concert, English Concert Choir London 2-▲ 425792-2
Handel, G.F.:Messiah, w. Arleen Augér (sop), Anne Sofie von Otter (mez), Michael Chance (ct), Howard Crook (ten), T. Pinnock (cnd), English CO, English Concert Choir [E] Archiv 2-▲ 423630-2 [DDD]
Handel, G.F.:Messiah (sels), w. Arleen Augér (sop), Anne Sofia von Otter (mez), Michael Chance (ct), Paul Crook (ten), T. Pinnock (cnd), English CO, English Concert Choir [E] Archiv ▲ 427664-2 [DDD] ■ 427664-4
Martinů, B.:The Greek Passion, w. Helen Field (sop), John Mitchinson (ten), Phillip Joll (b-bar), C. Mackerras (cnd), Brno State PO, Czech Phil Chorus [E] *(rec 1981)* Supraphon 2-▲ 10 3611-2 [DDD]
Mozart, W.A.:Così fan tutte (sels), w. L. Cuberli (sop), J. Rodgers (sop), C. Bartoli (mez), D. Barenboim (cnd), Berlin PO, Berlin RIAS Chamber Choir Erato ▲ 94821
Mozart, W.A.:Don Giovanni (sels), w. L. Cuberli (sop), J. Rodgers (sop), F. Furlanetto (bass), D. Barenboim (cnd), Berlin PO, Berlin RIAS Chamber Choir Erato ▲ 94823
Stravinsky, I.:Oedipus Rex, w. M. Lipovsek (mez), A. Rolfe-Johnson (ten), F. Welser-Möst (cnd), London PO, London Phil Chorus EMI Classics ▲ CDC 54445
Stravinsky, I.:Pulcinella, w. Y. Kenny (sop), J. Aler (ten), E.-P. Salonen (cnd), London Sinfonietta Sony Classical ▲ SK 45965
Stravinsky, I.:Renard, w. J. Aler (ten), N. Robson (ten), D. Wilson-Johnson (bar), E.-P. Salonen (cnd), London Sinfonietta Sony Classical ▲ SK 45965
Wagner, R.:Götterdämmerung, w. E. Marton (sop), S. Jerusalem (ten), T. Hampson (bar), B. Haitink (cnd), Bavarian RSO [G] EMI Classics 4-▲ CDCD 54485
Wagner, R.:Das Rheingold, w. L. Finnie (mez—Fricka), G. Clark (ten—Loge), J. Tomlinson (bar—Wotan), B. Brinkmann (bar—Donner), D. Barenboim (cnd), Bayreuth Festival Orch, Bayreuth Festival Chorus [G] Teldec 2-▲ 4509-91185-2
Wagner, R.:Siegfried, w. A. Evans (sop—Brünhilde), H. Leidland (sop—Waldvogel), B. Svendén (mez—Erda), S. Jerusalem (ten—Siegfried), G. Clark (ten—Mime), J. Tomlinson (bass—Der Wanderer), G. von Kannen (bass—Alberich), P. Kang (bass), *(cnd & orch unknown)* Teldec 4-▲ 4509-94193-2 [DDD]
Wagner, R.:Die Walküre (sels), w. F. d' Avalos (cnd), Philharmonia Orch—Wotan's Farewell & Magic Fire Music [G] ASV ▲ ASV 666 [DDD]
Weill, K.:The Seven Deadly Sins, w. E. Ross (sop), A. R. Johnson (ten), I. Caley (ten), M. Rippon (bass), S. Rattle (cnd), City of Birmingham SO EMI Classics ▲ CDM 64739

Tommaso, A. di (bass)
Rossini, G.:Il barbiere di Siviglia (sels), w. M. Resemba (sop), N. Sabatano (sop), F. de Lucia (ten), F. Novelli (bar), G. Schottler (bass), S. Valentino (bass), S. Sassano (cnd), Naples Teatro San Carlo Orch, Naples Teatro San Carlo Chorus [I] *(rec 1918 for Phonotype)* Standing Room Only ▲ SRO 819-1 [ADD]

Tommaso, Salvatore di (ten)
Leoncavallo, R.:Pagliacci, w. C. Gavazzi (sop—Nedda), C. Bergonzi (ten—Canio), S. Di Tommaso (ten—Beppe), C. Tagliabue (bar—Tonio), M. Rossi (bar—Silvio), A. Simonetto (cnd), Turin RAI SO, Turin RAI Chorus *(rec Turin, 1951)* Cetra Classic 2-▲ CDO 27 [ADD]
Puccini, G.:La fanciulla del West (sels), w. Magda Olivero (sop—Minnie), Corinna Vozza (mez—Wowkle), Paolo Caroli (ten—Harry), Giacomo Lauri-Volpi (ten—Dick Johnson), Marco Rogani (ten—Pony Express Rider), Salvatore di Tommaso (ten—Trin), Adelio Zagonara (ten—Nick), Virgilio Ascorro (bar—Sid), Alfredo Colella (bar—Jake Wallace), Giuseppe Forgione (bar—Bello), Giancarlo Guelfi (bar—Jack Rance), Arturo la Porta (bar—Sonora), Gino Conti (bass—José Castro), Piere Passarotti (bass—Bill), Enzo Titta (bass—Larkens), Giulio Tomei (bass—Ashby), V. Bellezza (cnd), Rome Opera Orch, Rome Opera Chorus—Minnie, dalla mia casa son partito; Laggiù nel Soledad; Chi c'è per farmi i ricci; Oh! Mister Johnson, siete rimasto; Non so ben neppur io; Io non son che una povera fanciulla; No, Minnie, non piangete; Vorrei mettermi queste; Hallo!; Oh, se sapeste; Credo che abbiate torto; Ma ti giuro ch'io non ti lascio più; Vieni fuori!; Una parola sola!...Or son sei mesi; Che c'è di nuovo Jack?; È là; Siete pronto; Ch'ella mi creda; È Minnie!...È Minnie! *(rec Rome, Mar. 30, 1957)* Golden Age of Opera ▲ GAO 180 [ADD]

Tomowa-Sintow, Anna (sop)
Beethoven, L. van:Mass, Op. 86, w. P. Payne (mez), R. Tear (ten), R. Lloyd (bass), C. Davis (cnd), London SO, London Sym Chorus [G] Philips 2-▲ 438362-2
Beethoven, L. van:Missa Solemnis, w. P. Payne (mez), R. Tear (ten), R. Lloyd (bass), C. Davis (cnd), London SO, London Sym Chorus [G] Philips 2-▲ 438362-2
Beethoven, L. van:Missa Solemnis, w. Annelies Burmeister (alt), Peter Schreier (ten), Hermann Christian Polster (bass), Gerhard Bosse (vn), Hannes Kastner (org), K. Masur (cnd), Leipzig Gewandhaus Orch, Leipzig Radio Chorus Berlin Classics ("Masur Edition" series) ▲ BER 9160
Brahms, J.:Ein Deutsches Requiem, w. J. van Dam (b-bar), H. von Karajan (cnd), Berlin PO, Vienna Singverein [G] *(rec 1976)* EMI Classics ▲ CDM 69229 [ADD]
Famous Opera Arias, w. Munich Radio Orch [cnd:Peter Sommer] Orfeo ▲ S 106841A [DDD]
Korngold, E.W.:Das Wunder der Heliane, w. R. Runkel (cta), N. Gedda (ten), J. D. de Haan (ten), H. Welker (bar), R. Pape (bass), J. Mauceri (cnd), Berlin RSO [G] London 3-▲ 436636-2 [DDD]
Mozart, W.A.:Così fan tutte (sels), w. I. Stefanov (cnd), Bulgarian RSO—Come scoglio; Un'aura amorosa LaserLight ▲ 15 890 [DDD]
Mozart, W.A.:Don Giovanni, w. K. Battle (sop), A. Baltsa (mez), G. Winbergh (ten), S. Ramey (bass), F. Furlanetto (bass), P. Burchuladze (bass), H. von Karajan (cnd), Berlin PO, German Opera Chorus [I] Deutsche Grammophon 3-▲ 419179-2 [DDD]
Mozart, W.A.:Don Giovanni (sels), w. T. Zylis-Gara (sop), E. Mathis (sop), S. Milnes (bar), W. Berry (bass), K. Böhm (cnd), Vienna PO, Vienna State Opera Chorus—Scenes & Arias Deutsche Grammophon ▲ 429823-2 [ADD]
Mozart, W.A.:Don Giovanni (sels), w. K. Battle (sop), A. Baltsa (mez), G. Winbergh (ten), S. Ramey (bass), F. Furlanetto (bass), P. Burchuladze (bass), H. von Karajan (cnd), Berlin PO, German Opera Chorus [I] Deutsche Grammophon ▲ 419635-2 [DDD]
Mozart, W.A.:Missa, K.317, w. A. Baltsa (mez), W. Krenn (ten), J. van Dam (b-bar), H. von Karajan (cnd), Berlin PO, Vienna Singverein Deutsche Grammophon ▲ 429820-2 [ADD]
Mozart, W.A.:Missa, K.317, w. A. Baltsa (mez), W. Krenn (ten), J. van Dam (b-bar), H. von Karajan (cnd), Berlin PO, Vienna Singverein [L] Deutsche Grammophon ("Galleria" series) 2-▲ 423913-2 [ADD]
Mozart, W.A.:Nozze di Figaro (sels), w. José van Dam (b-bar), Controbas (sgr), H. von Karajan (cnd), Vienna PO London ▲ 421317-2 [ADD]
Mozart, W.A.:Requiem, w. A. Baltsa (mez), W. Krenn (ten), J. van Dam (b-bar), H. von Karajan (cnd), Berlin PO, Vienna Singverein Deutsche Grammophon ▲ 429821-2 [ADD] ■ 429821-4
Mozart, W.A.:Requiem, w. A. Baltsa (mez), W. Krenn (ten), J. van Dam (b-bar), H. von Karajan (cnd), Berlin PO, Vienna Singverein [L] Deutsche Grammophon ("Galleria" series) ▲ 419867-2 [ADD] ■ 419867-4
Mozart, W.A.:Requiem, w. H. Müller Molinari (cta), V. Cole (ten), P. Burchuladze (bass), H. von Karajan (cnd), Vienna PO, Vienna Singverein [L] Deutsche Grammophon ("Karajan Gold" series) ▲ 439023-2 [DDD]
Mozart, W.A.:Zauberflöte, w. Edith Mathis (sop), Karin Ott (sop), Janet Perry (sop), Agnes Baltsa (mez), Hannah Schwarz (mez), Francisco Araiza (ten), Gottfried Hornik (bar), José Van Dam (b-bar), H. von Karajan (cnd), Berlin PO, German Opera Chorus [G] Deutsche Grammophon 3-▲ 410967-2 [DDD]
Mozart, W.A.:Zauberflöte (sels), w. Edith Mathis (sop), Karin Ott (sop), Janet Perry (sop), Agnes Baltsa (mez), Hannah Schwarz (mez), Francisco Araiza (ten), Gottfried Hornik (bar), José Van Dam (b-bar), H. von Karajan (cnd), Berlin PO, German Opera Chorus [G] Deutsche Grammophon ▲ 415287-2 [DDD]
Strauss, R.:Ariadne auf Naxos, w. K. Battle (sop), A. Baltsa (mez), G. Lakes (ten), H. Prey (bar), J. Levine (cnd), Vienna PO Deutsche Grammophon 2-▲ 419225-2 [DDD]

Tomowa-Sintow, Anna (sop) (cont.)
Strauss, R.:Der Rosenkavalier, w. J. Perry (sop), A. Baltsa (mez), K. Moll (bass), H. von Karajan (cnd), Vienna PO, Vienna State Opera Chorus [G] Deutsche Grammophon 3-▲ 423850-2 [DDD]
Tchaikovsky, P.:Eugene Onegin, w. R. Troeva-Mircheva (cta), N. Gedda (ten), Y. Mazurok (bar), N. Ghiuselev (bass), E. Tchakarov (cnd), Sofia Festival Orch, Sofia National Opera Chorus [R] Sony Classical 2-▲ S2K 45539 [DDD]
Verdi, G.:Arias, w. R. Raichev (cnd), Sofia PO—Air de Leonore [from Act 4 of La forza del destino]; Airs d'Aida [from Scenes 1 & 5 for Aida]; Willow Song; Ave Maria [both from Othello]; Air de Abigail [from Nabucco]; Récitatif et cavatine d'Elvire [from Hernani]; Scène et air de Violetta; Air de Violetta [both from La traviata] Forlane ▲ FRL 10506 [AAD]
Verdi, G.:Requiem Mass, w. Agnes Baltsa (mez), José Carreras (ten), José Van Dam (bass-bar), H. von Karajan (cnd), Vienna PO, Vienna State Opera Chorus, Sofia National Opera Chorus *(rec Great Hall, Musikverein, Vienna, June 1984)* Deutsche Grammophon 2-▲ 439033-2 [DDD]
Wagner, R.:Lohengrin, w. D. Vejzovic (sop), A. Kollo (ten), S. Nimsgern (b-bar), K. Ridderbusch (bass), H. von Karajan (cnd), Berlin PO, German Opera Chorus [G] EMI Classics ("Studio" series) 4-▲ CDMD 69314 [ADD]

Tong, John (nar)
Lumsdaine, D.:Aria for Edward John Eyre, w. M. Qualfe (sop), P. Gwynne (nar), D. Stanhope (cnd), Seymour Group Vox Australis ▲ VAST 011

Tonini, Daniele (bass)
Scarlatti, A.:Concerti sacri, motetti, w. Ilaria Galgani (sop), Susanna Anselmi (cta), Luca Casalin (ten), Il Ruggiero—Nos. 6-10 Tactus ▲ TC 661904 [DDD]
Scarlatti, A.:Concerti sacri, motetti, w. Ilaria Galgani (sop), Susanna Anselmi (cta), Luca Casalin (ten), Il Ruggiero—Nos. 1-5 Tactus ▲ TC 661903 [DDD]

Tonkha, Vladimir (nar)
Takahashi, Y.:Music of, w. Kazuko Takada (shamisen/sgr), Yumiko Tanaka (b shamisen), Ko Ishikawa (mouth org), Kishiko Suzumi (va), Ayumi Shimonoto (shamisen/sgr), Yuji Takahashi (pno)—Sugagaki Kuzushi; Mimi No Ho; Kagehime No Michiyuki; Yubi-Tomyo [Finger Light] Tzadik ▲ TZA 7010 [DDD]

Topol (sgr)
Broadway, w. Ethel Merman (sgr), Judy Holliday (sgr), Dick van Dyke (sgr), Doris Day (sgr), Mary Martin (sgr), Jill Haworth (sgr), William Warfield (sgr), et al.
Sony Classical ("Greatest Hits" series) ▲ MLK 62365 ■ MLT 62365

Töpper, Hertha (mez)
Bach, J.S.:Cant 213, w. Sheila Armstrong (sop), Theo Altmeyer (ten), Jakob Stämpfli (bass), H. Rilling (cnd), Stuttgart Bach Collegium *(rec 1967)* Musicaphon ▲ 51356 [AAD]
Bach, J.S.:Magnificat, BWV 243, w. M. Stader (sop), E. Haefliger (ten), D. Fischer-Dieskau (bar), K. Richter (cnd), Munich Bach Orch, Munich Bach Choir [L]
Deutsche Grammophon ("Galleria" series) ▲ 419466-2 [ADD]
Bach, J.S.:Mass in b, BWV 232, w. L. Marshall (sop), P. Pears (ten), K. Borg (bass), E. Jochum (cnd), Bavarian RSO, Bavarian Radio Chorus Philips 2-▲ 438739-2
Bach, J.S.:St. John Passion, w. Evelyn Lear (sop), Ernst Haefliger (ten), Hermann Prey (bar), Kieth Engen (bass), K. Richter (cnd), Munich Bach Orch, Munich Bach Choir
Deutsche Grammophon ("2CD" series) 2-▲ 453 007-2
Bach, J.S.:St. Matthew Passion, w. I. Seefried (sop), A. Fahberg (sop), E. Haefliger (ten), D. Fischer-Dieskau (bar), K. Engen (bass), M. Proebstl (bass), K. Richter (cnd), Munich Bach Orch, Munich Bach Choir Archiv ▲ 439338-2 [ADD]
Handel, G.F.:Judas Maccabaeus, w. Gundula Janowitz (sop), Peter Schreier (ten), Ernest Haefliger (ten), Theo Adam (bass), Siegfried Vogel (bass), H. Koch (cnd), Berlin RSO, Berlin Radio Chorus
Berlin Classics 2-▲ BER 9112
Mozart, W.A.:Nozze di Figaro, w. M. Stader (sop), I. Seefried (sop), D. Fischer-Dieskau (bar), R. Capecchi (bar), I. Sardi (bass), F. Fricsay (cnd), Berlin RSO [G] *(rec 1960)*
Deutsche Grammophon 3-▲ 437671-2
Mussorgsky, M.:Boris Godunov, w. Martha Mödl (sop—Marina Mniszek), Lotte Schädle (sop—Xenia), Dorothea Siebert (mez—Fyodor), Hertha Töpper (mez—Xenia's wet-nurs), Karl Hermann Bennert (Boyer Khrushchyov), Lorenz Fehenberger (ten—Prince Shuysky), Hans Hopf (ten—Grigory), Karl Ostertag (ten—Missail), Hans Hotter (b-bar—Boris Godunov), Hermann Uhde (bar—Andrey Shchelkalov), Kurt Böhme (bass—Varlaam), Kim Borg (bass—Pimen), Kieth Engen (bass—Lewicki), Adolf Keil (bass—Nikitich), Benno Kusche (bar—Rangoni), Heinz Maria Linz (bass—Czernikowski), E. Jochum (cnd), Bavarian RSO, Bavarian Radio Chorus *(rec Munich, May 1957)* Myto 3-▲ MCD 953131
Nicolai, O.:Lustigen Weiber, w. Erika Köth (sop), Maria Rogner (sgr), Hans Günter Nöcker (b-bar), Kim Borg (bass), Naan Pödl (sgr), F. Rieger (cnd), Bavarian RSO, Bavarian Chorus *(rec 1960's)*
Pantheon 2-▲ PHE 6660 (m)
Schmidt, F.:Das Buch mit sieben Siegeln, w. Anton Dermota (ten), Thomas Moser (ten), Robert Holl (bass), A.J. Hochstrasser (cnd), Lower Austria Tonkünst Orch, Graezer Concert Choir *(rec 1975)*
Preiser 2-▲ PRE 93263 [ADD]
Schoenberg, A.:Gurrelieder, w. I. Borkh (sop), H. Schachtschneider (ten), L. Fehenberger (ten), K. Engen (bass), R. Kubelik (cnd), Bavarian RSO—also includes songs by Berg, Schoenberg & Webern
Deutsche Grammophon ("20th Century Classics" series) ▲ 431744-2 [ADD]
Strauss, R.:Der Rosenkavalier, w. Erika Köth (sop—Sophie), Annelie Waas (sop—Marianne), Claire Watson (sop—Marschallin), Hertha Töpper (mez—Octavian), Brigitte Fassbaender (cta—Annina), Gerhard Stolze (ten—Valzacchi), Fritz Wunderlich (ten—Singer), Otto Wiener (bar—Faninal), Kurt Böhme (bass—Baron), J. Keilberth (cnd), Bavarian State Opera Orch, Bavarian State Opera Chorus *(rec Munich Opera Festival, National Theater, May 21, 1965)* Orfeo d'or 3-▲ 425963
Strauss, R.:Salome, w. Astrid Varnay (sop—Salome), Hertha Töpper (mez—Der Page der Herodias), Margarete Klose (cta—Herodias), Hans Hopf (ten—Narraboth), Karl Hoppe (ten—1st Nazarene), Karl Ostertag (ten—1st Jew), Julius Patzak (ten—Herodes), Hans Braun (bar—Jochanaan), Benno Kusche (bar—2nd Soldier), Adolf Keil (bass—1st Soldier), Hans Hermann Nissen (bass—Ein Kappadozier), Max Proebstl (bass—2nd Nazarene), Walter Carnotch (sgr—4th Jew), Emil Graf (sgr—3rd Jew), Paul Kaussen (sgr—2nd Jew), Hildegard Limmer (sgr—A slave), Georg Witter (sgr—5th Jew), H. Weigert (cnd), Bavarian RSO *(rec June 21-25, 1953)* Bella Voce 2-▲ BLV 7210 [AAD]
Wagner, R.:Götterdämmerung, w. Birgit Nilsson (sop—Brünnhilde), Leonie Rysanek (sop—Gutrune), Gerda Sommerschuh (sop—Woglinde), Elisabeth Lindermeier (sop—Wellgunde), Ruth Michaelis (sop—Flohilde), Marianne Schech (sop—Dritte Norne), Ira Malaniuk (mez—Waltraute), Irmgarth Barth (mez—Erste Norne), Hertha Töpper (mez—Zweite Norne), Bernd Aldenhoff (ten—Siegfried), Hermann Uhde (bar—Gunther), Gottlob Frick (bass—Hagen), H. Knappertsbusch (cnd), Bavarian State Opera Orch, Bavarian State Opera Chorus *(rec live, Prinzregententheater, Sept. 1, 1955)*
Orfeo 4-▲ 356944 (m)

Toppin, Louise (sgr)
Banfield, W.:Prophetess II, w. Howard Watkins (pno) Innova ▲ 510 [DDD]

Torbus-Mierzwiakow, Irena (sop)
Kabeláč, M.:Euphemias Mysterion [Gk] Supraphon ▲ SUP 3020

Torday, Robert (b-bar)
Handel, G.F.:Messiah, w. Max Emanuel Cencic (sop), Charles Humphries (ct), Ivan Sharpe (ten), P. Marschik (cnd), Academy of London Orch, Martin Schebesta (cnd), Vienna Boys' Choir *(rec Symphony Hall, Birmingham & Barbican Center, London, Nov 17 & 19, 1994)*
Capriccio 2-▲ 60068-2 [DDD]

Torigi, Richard (bar)
Puccini, G.:Madama Butterfly, w. V. de los Angeles (sop), R. Nadell (mez), B. Faulkner (sgr), W. Fredericks (sgr), J. Thresh (sgr), D. Bernard (sgr), A. Cosenza (bar), W. Herbert (cnd), New Orleans Opera Orch, New Orleans Opera Chorus *(rec live March 18, 1954)*
Legato Classics 2-▲ LCD 168-2 [ADD]
Puccini, G.:Madama Butterfly, w. Dorothy Kirsten (sop—Madama Butterfly), Rosalind Nadell (mez—Suzuki), Eileen Ireland (mez—Kate), Daniele Barioni (ten—Pinkerton), Thomas Carter (ten—Goro), Arthur Cosenza (ten—Yamadori), Richard Torigi (bar—Sharpless), Rodney Hall (bass—The Bronze), Harold Crane (bass—Commissioner), R. Cellini (cnd), New Orleans Opera Orch, New Orleans Opera Chorus *(rec live, Mar 1960)* VAI Audio 2-▲ VAIA 1054-2

Torigi, Richard (bar) (cont.)
Verdi, G.:Falstaff, w. Vivian Della Chiesa (sop—Alice), Audrey Schuh (sop—Nannetta), Lizabeth Pritchett (mez—Quickly), Evelyn Sachs (mez—Meg), André Turp (ten—Fenton), Virginio Assandri (ten—Caius), Luigi Vellucci (ten—Bardolfo), Leonard Warren (bar—Falstaff), Richard Torigi (bar—Ford), R. Cellini (cnd), New Orleans Opera Orch, New Orleans Opera Chorus *(rec live, May 5, 1956)*
VAI Audio 2-▲ VAIA 1056-2

Torjesen, Siri (sop)
Nordheim, A.:Music of, w. Njål Sparbo (bar), I. Bergby (cnd), Bit 20 Ensemble—Magic Island; Tractatus; Part for 6 Basses; Aftonland [Evening Land]; 3 Voci; Part for Va, Hpd & Perc; Qt for Strs; Response for Org, Perc & Tape Norway Music 2-▲ CD 4990
Sandström, S.-D.:The High Mass, w. Lena Hoel (sop), Sara Olsson (sop), Marianne Eklöf (mez), Annika Skoglund (mez), Peter Bengtson (org), L. Segerstam (cnd), Swedish RSO, Eric Ericson Chamber Choir *(rec live, Berwald Hall, Stockholm, Nov. 25 & 26, 1994)* Caprice 2-▲ CAP 22036

Tornasaetti, Bruno (bar)
Leoncavallo, R.:Pagliacci, w. Joan Carlyle (sop—Nedda), Jon Vickers (ten—Canio), José Noit (ten—Beppe), Cornell MacNeil (bar—Tonio), Bruno Tornasaetti (bar—Silvio), B. Bartoletti (cnd), *(orch unknown) (rec live, Buenos Aires, 1968)* VAI Audio ▲ VAIA 1014 [ADD]

Torntoft, Preben (trb)
Danish Songs, w. pno accompaniment (Rec. 1951-1953) Danacord ▲ DACOCD 347 (m) [ADD]

Toro, Puli (mez)
Puccini, G.:Tosca, w. Birgit Nilsson (sop—Floria Tosca), Puli Toro (mez—Shepherd), Jose Carreras (ten—Mario Cavaradossi), Joaquin Romaguera (ten—Spoleta), James Billings (bar—Sacristan), Richard Fredricks (bar—Baron Scarpa), Samuel Ramey (bass—Cesare Angelotti), William Ledbetter (sgr—Sciarrone), Richard Park (sgr—Cardinal), Don Yule (sgr—Jailer), J. Rudel (cnd), *(orch & chorus unknown) (rec Nov 13, 1974)* Legato Classics 2-▲ LCD-200-2

Torre, Philip (sgr)
Rorem, N.:Miss Julie, w. Theodora Fried (sgr—Miss Julie), Heather Sarris (sgr—Christine, the cook), Laurelyn Watson (sgr—Young Girl), David Blackburn (sgr—Mr. Niels), Mark Mulligan (sgr—Young Boy), Philip Torre (sgr—John, the valet), Judd Ernster (bass), D. Gilbert (cnd), Manhattan School of Music Opera Orch, Manhattan School of Music Opera Chorus Newport Classic 2-▲ NPT 85605 [DDD]

Torres, Victor (bar)
Monteverdi, C.:Vespro della Beata Vergine, w. Barbara Borden (sop), Maria Cristina Kiehr (sop), Andreas Scholl (alt), John Bowen (ten), Andrew Murgatroyd (ten), Antonio Abete (bass), Jelle Draijer (bass), René Jacobs (cnd), Concerto Vocale, Netherlands Chamber Choir Harmonia Mundi 2-▲ 901566.67

Torri, Rosina (sop)
Puccini, G.:La Bohème, w. T. Vitulli (sop), A. Giorgini (ten), E. Badini (bar), L. Manfrini (bass), C. Sabajno (cnd), La Scala Orch [I] *(rec 1927)* InSync 2-■ C 4131/2 (m)
Puccini, G.:La Bohème, w. Rosina Torri (sop—Mimi), Thea Vitulli (sop—Musetta), Aristodemo Giorgini (ten—Rodolfo), Giuseppe Nessi (ten—Parpignol), Ernesto Badini (bar—Marcello), Aristide Baracchi (bar—Schaunard), Luigi Manfrini (bass—Colline), Salvatore Baccaloni (bass—Benoit/Alcindoro), C. Sabajno (cnd), La Scala Orch, La Scala Chorus *(rec 1928)* VAI Audio 2-▲ VAIA 1078-2

Torriani, Jolanda (sgr)
Giordano, U.:Fedora, w. Pia Tassinari (sop), Ferruccio Tagliavini (ten), Meletti (sgr), Micheluzzi (sgr), Mascolo (sgr), O.. Fabritiis (cnd), Milan RAI SO, Milan RAI Chorus *(rec live, July 10, 1954)*
Arkadia 2-▲ 493

Torzewski, Marek (ten)
Nono, L.:Canto sospeso, w. B. Bonney (sop), S. Otto (alt), S. Lothar (nar), B. Ganz (nar), Berlin Radio Chorus *(rec Dec. 9-11, 1992)* Sony Classical ▲ SK 53360 [DDD]

Toscani, Rina Gallo (mez)
Mascagni, P.:Cavalleria rusticana, w. L. Bruna Rasa (sop), M. Meloni (mez), A. Melandri (ten), A. Poli (bar), P. Mascagni (cnd), Holland Italian Opera Orch, Italian d'Olanda Opera Chorus [I] *(rec live at the Royal Theatre in the Hague, 11/7/38)* Bongiovanni ▲ GB 1050 (m) [AAD]

Tosi, Giancarlo (bass)
Martin Y Soler, V.:Il Tutore Burlato, w. Liliana Marzano (sop—Menica), Maria Angeles Peters (sop—Violante), Juan Diego Florez (ten—Anselmo), Ernesto Palacio (ten—Il Cavaliere), Marcello Lippi (bar—Pippo), Giancarlo Tosi (bass—Don Fabrizio), Michela Forgione (hpd), M. Harth-Bedoya (cnd), Dianopolis Bulgarian CO *(rec VI Festival Internazionale di Gerace nella Chiesa di San Francesco, Aug 16, 1994)* Bongiovanni 2-▲ GB 2175/76-2 [DDD]

Tosini, Ivana (sgr)
Donizetti, G.:Il Duca d'Alba, w. Wladimiro Ganzarolli (bar), Louis Quilico (bar), Enzo Tei (sgr), T. Schippers (cnd), Trieste PO *(rec live at the Spoleto Festival, June 11, 1959)*
Memories 2-▲ MEM 4579 [ADD]

Toso, Maria Teresa (alt)
Salieri, A.:La passione di Gesù Cristo, w. Daniela Citino (sop), Nikola Yovanovitch (ten), Mario Scardoni (bass), Giovanna Scardoni (voc), A. Turco (cnd), Verona Cathedral Cappella Musicale *(rec Verona Cathedral, Italy, Mar 30, 1995)* Bongiovanni ▲ GB 2190 [DDD]

Tószeghi, A. von (alt)
Haller, H.:Nocturnes (3), w. H. Salquin (pno) Grammont ▲ CTSP 10-2 [ADD]

Toth (sgr)
Crumb, G.:Night Music I, w. G. Crumb (cnd), *(orch unknown)* CRI ■ ACS 6008

Tourangeau, Huguette (mez)
Donizetti, G.:Maria Stuarda, w. J. Sutherland (sop), L. Pavarotti (ten), R. Soyer (bar), J. Morris (bass), R. Bonynge (cnd), Bologna Teatro Comunale Orch, Bologna Teatro Comunale Chorus [I]
London 2-▲ 425410-2 [ADD]
Falla, M. de:El amor brujo, w. C. Dutoit (cnd), Montreal SO London ▲ 430703-2 [DDD]
Handel, G.F.:Messiah, w. Joan Sutherland (sop), Werner Krenn (ten), Tom Krause (bar), R. Bonynge (cnd), English CO, Ambrosian Singers [E] London ("Serenata" series) 2-▲ 433740-2 [ADD]
Handel, G.F.:Rodelinda, Regina de' Longobardi, w. Joan Sutherland (sop—Rodelinda), Margaretha Elkins (mez—Bertarido's sister), Huguette Tourangeau (mez—Bertarido), Cora Canne-Meijer (alt—Unulfo), Eric Tappy (ten—Grimoaldo), Pieter van der Berg (bass—Garibaldo), R. Bonynge (cnd), Netherlands CO *(rec Amsterdam, June 30, 1973)* Bella Voce 2-▲ BLV 107.206 [AAD]
Meyerbeer, G.:Les Huguenots, w. J. Sutherland (sop), M. Arroyo (sop), A. Vrenios (ten), D. Cossa (bar), G. Bacquier (bar), N. Ghiuselev (bass), R. Bonynge (cnd), New Philharmonia Orch, Ambrosian Opera Chorus London ("Grand Opera" series) 4-▲ 430549-2 [AAD]
Offenbach, J.:Les Contes d'Hoffmann, w. J. Sutherland (sop), P. Domingo (ten), H. Cuénod (ten), G. Bacquier (bar), R. Bonynge (cnd), Swiss Romande Orch London 2-▲ 417363-2 [ADD]
Verdi, G.:Rigoletto, w. J. Sutherland (sop), L. Pavarotti (ten), S. Milnes (bar), M. Talvela (bass), R. Bonynge (cnd), London SO, London Sym Chorus [I] London 2-▲ 414269-2 [ADD]

Tourel, Jennie (mez)
Berlioz, H.:La Mort de Cléopâtre, w. L. Bernstein (cnd), New York PO
Sony Classical 2-▲ SM2K 47526 [ADD]
Foss, L.:Song of Songs, w. L. Bernstein (cnd), New York PO [E] Sony Classical ▲ SMK 47533 [ADD]
Mahler, G.:Kindertotenlieder, w. L. Bernstein (cnd), New York PO *(rec 1960)*
Sony Classical ("Bernstein:The Royal Edition" series) 2-▲ SM2K 47576 [ADD]
Mahler, G.:Songs, w. L. Bernstein (cnd), New York PO—3 Rückert Songs:Ich atmet' einen linden Duft; Ich bin der Welt abhanden gekommen; Um Mitternacht; plus Das Irdische Leben from Knaben Wunderhorn *(rec 1960)*
Sony Classical ("Bernstein:The Royal Edition" series) 2-▲ SM2K 47576 [ADD]
Mozart, W.A.:Ch'io mi scordi di te, w. M. Horszowski (pno), P. Casals (cnd), Perpignan Festival Orch *(rec Perpignan, France, July 15-16, 1951)*
Sony Classical ("The Casals Edition" series) ▲ SMK 58984 [ADD]
Mozart, W.A.:Requiem, w. I. Seefried (sop), L. Simoneau (ten), W. Warfield (bar), B. Walter (cnd), New York PO *(rec 1956)* Historical Performers ▲ HPS 12 [ADD]
The Tsar, w. Philadelphia Orch [cnd:Eugene Ormandy], André Kostelanetz (cnd), Claudio Abbado (cnd), Chicago SO, et al. Sony Classical ("Greatest Hits" series) ▲ MLK 62683 ■ MLT 62683

Tourne, Teresa (sop)
Falla, M. de:El retablo de maese Pedro, w. P. Lavigren (ten), R. Cesari (bar), P. de Freitas Branco (cnd), Madrid Concert Orch EMI Classics 2-▲ ZDMB 64555

Towers, C. (sgr)
Rodgers, R.:The King & I, w. Y. Brynner (sgr), *(other artists unknown)* [1977 Broadway revival cast] RCA ▲ RCD 12610 ■ ABK 12610

Toyoda, Kiyomi (sop)
Kawanami, T.:Ondine, w. T. Otaka (cnd), Tokyo PO Camerata ▲ 32CM 295

Tozzi, Giorgio (bass)
Barber, S.:Vanessa, w. E. Steber (sop), G. Resnik (sop), R. Elias (mez), N. Gedda (ten), D. Mitropoulos (cnd), Metropolitan Opera Orch, Metropolitan Opera Chorus [E] RCA Gold Seal ▲ 7899-2-RG [ADD]
Beethoven, L. van:Fidelio, w. Judith Blegen (sop), Leonie Rysanek (sop), Jon Vickers (ten), Walter Berry (bass), John Macurdy (bass), K. Böhm (cnd), San Francisco Opera Orch, San Francisco Opera Chorus Melodram 2-▲ CDM 27086
Berlioz, H.:L'Enfance du Christ, w. Florence Kopleff (cta), Ceasare Valletti (ten), Gérard Souzay (bar), Lucien Oliver (bar), C. Munch (cnd), Boston SO, New England Conservatory Chorus *(rec Dec 1956)* RCA Victor Gold Seal 8-▲ 0902-668444-2 [ADD]
Berlioz, H.:L'Enfance du Christ, w. F. Kopleff (cta), C. Valletti (ten), G. Souzay (bar), C. Munch (cnd), Boston SO, New England Conservatory Chorus RCA Gold Seal 2-▲ 09026-61234-2
Catalani, A.:La Wally, w. R. Scotto (sop—Walter), R. Tebaldi (sop—Wally), J. Gardino (mez—Afra), M. Del Monaco (ten—Giuseppe Hagenbach), G.G. Guelfi (bar—Vincenzo Gellner), G. Tozzi (bass—Stromminger), C. M. Giulini (cnd), La Scala Orch, La Scala Chorus *(rec Dec. 7, 1953)* Legato Classics 2-▲ LCD 177-2 [ADD]
Christmas Treasures, w. Leontyne Price (sop), Marian Anderson (cta), Rosalind Elias (mez), Mario Lanza (ten), Arthur Fiedler (cnd), Leopold Stokowski (cnd), Robert Shaw Chorale RCA Living Stereo ▲ 09026-61867-2 ■ 09026-61867-4
Donizetti, G.:Lucia di Lammermoor, w. Roberta Peters (sop—Lucia), Mitì Truccato Pace (mez—Alisa), Jan Peerce (ten—Edgardo), Piero de Palma (ten—Lord Arturo Bucklaw), Mario Carlin (ten—Normanno), Philip Maero (bar—Lord Enrico Ashton), Giorgio Tozzi (bass—Raimondo), E. Leinsdorf (cnd), Rome Opera Orch, Rome Opera Chorus *(rec Rome Opera House, Aug 5-14, 1957)* RCA Living Stereo 2-▲ 09026-68537-2 [ADD]
Handel, G.F.:Messiah, w. Jennifer Vyvyan (sop), Monica Sinclair (cta), Jon Vickers (ten), T. Beecham (cnd), Royal PO *(rec 1959)* RCA Gold Seal 3-▲ 09026-61266-2
Handel, G.F.:Messiah (sels), w. Jennifer Vyvyan (sop), Monica Sinclair (mez), Jon Vickers (ten), T. Beecham (cnd), Royal PO, John McCarthy (cnd), Royal Choral Society—Ov; Comfort Ye My People; Every Valley Shall Be Exalted; And the Glory of the Lord; And He Shall Purify; O Thou That Tellest Good Tidings; For unto Us a Child is Born; Pastoral Symphony; There Were Shepherds Abiding; And the Angel Said unto Them; And Suddenly There Was; Glory to God in the Highest; He Shall Feed His Flock; Come unto Him; Behold the Lamb of God; He Was Despised; All We Like Sheep Have Gone Astray; Hallelujah!; I Know That My Redeemer Liveth; The Trumpet Shall Sound *(rec Walthamstow Town Hall, London, June-Aug 1959)* RCA Victor ▲ 09026-68159-2 [ADD]
Meyerbeer, G.:Les Huguenots, w. J. Sutherland (sop), F. Cossotto (mez), G. Simionato (mez), F. Corelli (ten), V. Ganzarolli (bar), N. Ghiaurov (bass), G. Gavezzeni (cnd), La Scala Orch, La Scala Chorus [I] *(rec live 5/28/62)* Melodram 3-▲ MEL 37026 (m) [AAD]
Meyerbeer, G.:Les Huguenots, w. A. Pastori (sop), A. de Cavalieri (mez), G. Lauri-Volpi (ten), G. Taddei (bar), N. Zaccaria (bass), T. Serafin (cnd), Milan RAI SO, Milan RAI Chorus *(rec 1956)* Memories 3-▲ MEM 4566 [ADD]
Puccini, G.:La Bohème, w. A. Moffo (sop), F. Costa (mez), G. Tucker (ten), R. Merrill (bar), E. Leinsdorf (cnd), Rome Opera Orch, Rome Opera Chorus [I] RCA Gold Seal 2-▲ 3969-2-RG [ADD] 2-■ 3969-4-RG (CrO2)
Puccini, G.:La Bohème (sels), w. A. Moffo (sop), F. Costa (mez), G. Tucker (ten), R. Merrill (bar), E. Leinsdorf (cnd), Rome Opera Orch, Rome Opera Chorus RCA Gold Seal ▲ 60189-2-RG [ADD] ■ 60189-4-RG (CrO2)
Puccini, G.:La fanciulla del West, w. R. Tebaldi (sop), M. del Monaco (ten), C. MacNeil (bar), F. Capuana (cnd), St. Cecilia Academy Orch Rome, St. Cecilia Academy Chorus Rome [I] London 2-▲ 421595-2 [ADD]
Puccini, G.:Turandot, w. B. Nilsson (sop), R. Tebaldi (sop), J. Bjoerling (ten), E. Leinsdorf (cnd), Rome Opera Orch, Rome Opera Chorus [I] RCA Red Seal 2-▲ 5932-2-RC 3-■ AGK3-3970
Puccini, G.:Turandot, w. Birgit Nilsson (sop—Turandot), Renata Tebaldi (sop—Liù), Jussi Björling (ten—Calaf), Alessio De Paolis (ten—Emperor Altoum), Piero de Palma (ten—Pang), Mario Sereni (bar—Ping), Adelio Zagonara (bar—Prince of Persia), Giorgio Tozzi (bass—Timur), Tommaso Frascati (bass—Pong), Leonardo Monreale (bass—Mandarin), E. Leinsdorf (cnd), Rome Opera Orch, Rome Opera Chorus *(rec Rome Opera House, July 3-11, 1959)* RCA Living Stereo 2-▲ 09026-62687-2 [ADD]
Puccini, G.:Turandot, w. Montserrat Caballé (sop—Turandot), Leona Mitchell (sop—Liu), Remy Corazza (ten—Pang), Joseph Franck (ten—Pong), Robert Johnson (ten—Prince of Persia), Raymond Manton (ten—Altoum), Luciano Pavarotti (ten—Calaf), Aldo Bramante (bar—a mandarin), Dale Duesing (bar—Ping), Giorgio Tozzi (bass—Timur), R. Chailly (cnd), *(orch unknown)* *(rec San Francisco, Nov. 4, 1977)* Legato Classics 2-▲ LCD 188-2
Rossini, G.:Il barbiere di Siviglia, w. T. Berganza (mez), R. Casellato (ten), S. Bruscantini (bar), B. Bartoletti (cnd), Buenos Aires Teatro Colón Orch, Buenos Aires Teatro Colón Chorus [I] *(rec 1969)* Golden Age of Opera 2-▲ GAO 149/50
Rossini, G.:Il barbiere di Siviglia, w. R. Peters (sop), C. Valletti (ten), R. Merrill (bar), F. Corena (bass), E. Leinsdorf (cnd), Metropolitan Opera Orch, New York Metropolitan Opera Chorus [I] RCA Gold Seal 3-▲ 6505-2-RG [ADD] 2-■ 6505-4-RG (CrO2)
Rossini, G.:Il barbiere di Siviglia, w. Roberta Peters (sop—Rosina), Margaret Roggero (mez—Berta), Cesare Valletti (ten—Count Almaviva), Calvin Marsh (bar—Fiorello/Sergeant), Robert Merrill (bar—Figaro), Fernando Corena (bass—Dr. Bartolo), Carlo Tomanelli (bass—Ambrogio), Giorgio Tozzi (bass—Don Basilio), E. Leinsdorf (cnd), Metropolitan Opera Orch, New York Metropolitan Opera Chorus *(rec Manhattan Center, New York, Sept 1-11, 1958)* RCA Living Stereo 3-▲ 09026-68552-2 [ADD]
Rossini, G.:Il barbiere di Siviglia (sels), w. R. Peters (sop), C. Valletti (ten), R. Merrill (bar), F. Corena (bass), E. Leinsdorf (cnd), Metropolitan Opera Orch, New York Metropolitan Opera Chorus RCA Gold Seal ▲ 60188-2-RG [ADD] ■ 60188-4-RG (CrO2)
Verdi, G.:Aida, w. L. Price (sop), R. Gorr (mez), J. Vickers (ten), R. Merrill (bar), G. Solti (cnd), Rome Opera Orch, Rome Opera Chorus [I] London ▲ 421860-2 [ADD]
Verdi, G.:Aida, w. L. Price (sop), R. Gorr (mez), J. Vickers (ten), R. Merrill (bar), G. Solti (cnd), Rome Opera Orch, Rome Opera Chorus [I] London 3-▲ 417416-2 [ADD]
Verdi, G.:La forza del destino, w. Zinka Milanov (sop), Rosalind Elias (mez), Giuseppe Di Stefano (ten), Leonard Warren (bar), Paolo Washington (bass), F. Previtali (cnd), St. Cecilia Academy Orch Rome, St. Cecilia Academy Chorus Rome *(rec 1959)* Theorema 3-▲ TH 121157/59
Verdi, G.:La forza del destino, w. Zinka Milanov (sop—Donna Leonora di Vargas), Rosalind Elias (mez—Preziosilla), Luisa Gioia (sgr—Curra), Angelo Mercuriali (ten—Trabuco), Giuseppe di Stefano (ten—Son Alvaro), Leonard Warren (bar—Don Carlos di Vargas), Giorgio Tozzi (b-bar—Padre guardiano), Dino Mantovani (bar—Fra Melitone), Paolo Washington (b-bar—Il marchese di Calatrava), Virgilio Carbonari (b-bar—un alcalde), Sergio Liviabella (sgr—un chirurgo), F. Previtali (cnd), St. Cecilia Academy Orch Rome, St. Cecilia Academy Chorus Rome [I] London ▲ 443678-2 [ADD]
Verdi, G.:Luisa Miller, w. A. Moffo (sop), S. Verrett (mez), C. Bergonzi (ten), C. MacNeil (bar), F. Cleva (cnd), RCA Italian Opera Orch [I] RCA Gold Seal 2-▲ 6646-2-RG [ADD]
Verdi, G.:Requiem Mass, w. L. Price (sop), R. Elias (mez), J. Björling (ten), F. Reiner (cnd), Vienna PO, Vienna Singverein [L] London 2-▲ 421608-2 [ADD]
Verdi, G.:Requiem Mass, w. Leontyne Price (sop), Rosalind Elias (mez), Jussi Björling (ten), F. Reiner (cnd), Vienna PO, French Musical Society Vocal Group *(rec 1959)* London ("Double Decker" series) 2-▲ 444833-2 [ADD]
Verdi, G.:Requiem Mass, w. L. Price (sop), N. Merriman (mez), R. Tucker (ten), E. Ormandy (cnd), Philadelphia Orch *(rec live Apr. 6, 1957)* Standing Room Only ▲ SRO 842-1 [ADD]
Verdi, G.:Rigoletto, w. R. Peters (sop), J. Björling (ten), R. Merrill (bar), J. Perlea (cnd), Rome Opera Orch, Rome Opera Chorus [I] RCA Gold Seal 2-▲ 60172-2-RG [ADD] 2-■ 60172-4-RG (CrO2)

Tozzi, Giorgio (bass) (cont.)
Verdi, G.:Simon Boccanegra, w. Leyla Gencer (sop), Glade Peterson (ten), Giuseppe Zampieri (ten), Tito Gobbi (bar), Rolando Panerai (bar), Vito Susca (bass), G. Gavazzeni (cnd), *(orch unknown)* Great Opera Performances 2-▲ GOP 767
Verdi, G.:Il trovatore, w. L. Price (sop), R. Elias (mez), G. Tucker (ten), L. Warren (bar), A. Basile (cnd), Rome Opera Orch RCA Gold Seal 2-▲ 60560-2-RG [ADD] 2-■ 60560-4-RG (CrO2)
Wagner, R.:Der fliegende Holländer, w. L. Rysanek (sop), K. Liebl (ten), G. London (bar), A. Dorati (cnd), Royal Opera House Orch, Royal Opera House Chorus Covent Garden [G] London 2-▲ 417319-2 [ADD]

Tracy, Arthur (cant)
Echoes of the Temple:Cantors in Prayer & Folksong, w. Gershon Sirota (cant), Pierre Pinchik (cant), Samuel Vigoda (cant), Joseph Rosenblatt (cant), et al. *(rec 1914-36)* Pearl ▲ PEA 9126 [ADD]

Traesdal, Tove (mez)
Brahms, J.:Songs, w. Einar Henning Smebye (pno)—8 songs, Op. 57 Victoria ▲ VCD 19106
Grieg, E.:Songs, w. Einar Henning Smebye (pno)—6 German Songs, Op. 48 Victoria ▲ VCD 19106
Heise, P.:Songs, w. Einar Henning Smebye (pno)—Gudrun's Grief [Dengang var Gudrn beredt til døden; Hos sad jarlers aedle hustruer; Da sagde Herborg; Da sagde Gullrönd; Engang Gudrun end ham skuede; Saa var min Sigurd] Victoria ▲ VCD 19106
Ravel, M.:Histoires naturelles, w. Einar Henning Smebye (pno) Victoria ▲ VCD 19106

Trakas, Christopher (bar)
Respighi, O.:Il Tramonto, w. Venice String Quartet [I] Koch International Classics ▲ KIC 7215 [DDD]

Trama, Ugo (bass)
Bellini, V.:Il pirata, w. M. Caballè (sop), F. Raffanelli (sop), G. Baratti (ten), F. Labò (ten), P. Cappuccilli (bar), E. Ghiglia (cnd), *(orch unknown)* *(rec Florence, 1967)* Great Opera Performances ▲ GOP 729
Concerti, w. Magda Olivero (sop), D. Antoioli (sgr), A. Protti (bar), K. Ostar (sgr), Fulvio Vernizzi (cnd) Great Opera Performances 2-▲ GOP 709
Mercadante, S.:Elisa e Claudio, w. Virginia Zeani (sop), Agostino Lazzari (ten), Domenico Trimarchi (bar), Fiorini (sgr), U. Rapalo (cnd), Naples Teatro San Carlo Orch, Naples Teatro San Carlo Chorus *(rec live, Naples, 1/31/71)* Melodram 2-▲ MEL 27099 [ADD]
Rossini, G.:La Cenerentola, w. T. Berganza (mez), L. Alva (ten), R. Capecchi (bar), C. Abbado (cnd), London SO, London Sym Chorus [I] Deutsche Grammophon 2-▲ 423861-2 [ADD]
Rota, N.:Mysterium, w. A. Tuccari (sop), C. Vozza (mez), G. Sinimberghi (ten), A. Renzi (cnd), Pro Civitate Christiana di Assisi Orch, Pro Civitate Christiana di Assisi Chorus *(rec live 1962)* Claves ▲ CD 9323 [DDD]

Traube, Claude (ten)
Mendelssohn, F.:Psalm 42, w. Y. Perrin (sop), M. Schwartz (mez), O. Dufour (ten), P. Huttenlocher (bar), C. Ossola (bass), M. Hutin (bass), C. Liang-Sheng (cnd), Geneva SO, Geneva Univ Chorus Gallo ▲ CD 635 [AAD]
Mendelssohn, F.:Psalm 95, w. Y. Perrin (sop), M. Schwartz (mez), O. Dufour (ten), P. Huttenlocher (bar), C. Ossola (bass), M. Hutin (bass), C. Liang-Sheng (cnd), Geneva SO, Geneva Univ Chorus Gallo ▲ CD 635 [AAD]
Mendelssohn, F.:Psalm 115, w. Y. Perrin (sop), M. Schwartz (mez), O. Dufour (ten), P. Huttenlocher (bar), C. Ossola (bass), M. Hutin (bass), C. Liang-Sheng (cnd), Geneva SO, Geneva Univ Chorus Gallo ▲ CD 635 [AAD]

Traubel, Helen (sop)
Helen Traubel Rarities on Radio *(rec 1937-44)* Enterprise ("The Radio Years" series) ▲ ENTRY 10 (m)
Opera Stars Sing on Radio, Vol. 1:Unpublished Broadcasts from the Fourties, w. Dusolina Giannini (sop), Gladys Swarthout (cta), Richard Crooks (ten), Lauritz Melchoir (ten), Robert Merrill (bar), Lawrence Tibbett (bar), Ezio Pinza (bass) Enterprise ("The Radio Years" series) ▲ ENTRY 11
Rodgers, R.:Pipe Dream, w. W. Johnson (sgr), J. Tyler (sgr) [1955 Broadway cast] RCA ▲ 09026-61481-2 ■ 09026-61481-4
Romberg, S.:Deep in My Heart, w. J. Ferrer (sgr), R. Clooney (sgr), Gene Kelly (sgr), F. Kelly (sgr), V. Damone (sgr), J. Powell (sgr), A. Miller (sgr), W. Olvis (sgr), C. Richards (sgr), H. Keel (sgr), T. Martin (sgr), J. Weldon (sgr) Sony Music Special Products ▲ AK 47703
Wagner, R.:Arias & Scenes—Arias from Tannhauser; Tristan & Isolde; Lohengrin; Die Walkure *(rec 1940 & 1945)* Preiser ▲ PRE CD 89120
Wagner, R.:Götterdämmerung (sels), w. L. Melchior (ten), A. Toscanini (cnd), NBC SO—Dawn, Rhine Journey, Death & Funeral Music; Immolation Scene RCA Gold Seal ▲ 09026-60304-2 ■ 09026-60304-4
Wagner, R.:Götterdämmerung (siegfried's funeral), w. Herbert Janssen (bar), Doris Doré (sgr), A. Rodzinski (cnd), New York PO *(rec Carnegie Hall, New York City, Nov 25, 1945)* Enterprise ("The Radio Years" series) ▲ ENT RY 55
Wagner, R.:Lohengrin, w. H. Traubel (sop—Elsa), A. Varnay (sop—Ortrud), L. Melchior (ten—Lohengrin), F. Guerrera (bar—Herald), H. Janssen (bar—Telramund), D. Ernster (bass—King Heinrich), F. Stiedry (cnd), Metropolitan Opera Orch, New York Metropolitan Opera Chorus *(rec live Jan. 6, 1950)* Danacord 3-▲ DACOCD 322/24 [AAD]
Wagner, R.:Das Rheingold (sels), w. Herbert Janssen (bar), Doris Doré (sgr), A. Rodzinski (cnd), New York PO—Entry of the Gods into Valhalla *(rec Carnegie Hall, New York City, Nov 25, 1945)* Enterprise ("The Radio Years" series) ▲ ENT RY 55
Wagner, R.:Der Ring des Nibelungen (sels), w. Lauritz Melchoir (ten), A. Toscanini (cnd), NBC SO—Complete Scene III [from Act 1 of Die Walküre]; Dawn & Bruennhilde; Siegfried's Funeral Music; Brunnhilde Immolation [all from Götterdämmerung] *(rec 1941)* Grammofono 2000 ▲ GRM 78564
Wagner, R.:Siegfried (waldweben), w. Herbert Janssen (bar), Doris Doré (sgr), A. Rodzinski (cnd), New York PO *(rec Carnegie Hall, New York City, Nov 25, 1945)* Enterprise ("The Radio Years" series) ▲ ENT RY 55
Wagner, R.:Tannhäuser, w. Lauritz Melchior (ten/bar), Herbert Janssen (bar), Alexander Kipnis (bass), G. Szell (cnd), *(orch unknown)* Enterprise ("The Radio Years" series) 3-▲ ENT RY 26 (m)
Wagner, R.:Die Walküre, w. Astrid Varnay (sop), Kerstin Throborg (cta), Lauritz Melchoir (ten), Friedrich Schorr (b-bar), E. Leinsdorf (cnd), *(orch unknown)* *(rec Dec 6, 1941)* Enterprise ("The Forties" series) 2-▲ ENT 318
Wagner, R.:Die Walküre (sels), w. L. Melchior (ten), A. Toscanini (cnd), NBC SO—Act 1, Scene 3 [G] RCA Gold Seal ▲ 60264-2-RG [ADD] ■ 60264-4-RG (CrO2)
Wagner, R.:Die Walküre (act 3), w. Herbert Janssen (bar), Doris Doré (sgr), A. Rodzinski (cnd), New York PO *(rec Carnegie Hall, New York City, Nov 25, 1945)* Enterprise ("The Radio Years" series) ▲ ENT RY 55
Wagner, R.:Wesendonck Songs, w. L. Stokowski (cnd), Philadelphia Orch—3 songs only—Im Treibhaus, Schmerzen & Träume *(rec 1940 for Victor)* Pearl ▲ PEA 9486 (m) [AAD]

Travis, Arlene (sop)
Purcell, H.:Dido & Aeneas, w. Cassandra Hoffman (sop—Belinda), Arlene Travis (sop—2nd Witch), Desirée Halac (mez—Sorceress/Spirit), Jennifer Lane (mez—Dido), Elizabeth Norman (alt), Thomas Bogdan (ten—A Sailor), Michael Brown (bar—Aeneas), Curtis Streetman (bar), Caitriona O'Leary (sgr—2nd Woman), Sarah Pillow (sgr—1st Witch), B. Brookshire (cnd), San Cassiano Musici *(rec St. Ignatius of Antioch Episcopal Church, New York City, Spring 1995)* Vox Classics ▲ VOX 7518

Trawinska-Moroz, Urszula (sop)
Bel Canto, w. Polish Radio-TV Orch [cnd:Jan Pruszak, Wlodzimierz Kamirski] Polskie Nagrania Edition ▲ ECD 063

Traxel, Josef (ten)
Mozart, W.A.:Thamos, w. T. Stich-Randall (mez), A. Deloire (mez), T. Adam (b-bar), M. Rossi (cnd), Cologne RSO, Cologne Radio Chorus [G] *(rec live, Cologne May 20, 1956)* Melodram 3-▲ CDM 37084 [AAD]
Strauss, R.:Die Liebe der Danae, w. A. Kupper (sop), L. Szemere (ten), P. Schöffler (b-bar), C. Krauss (cnd), Vienna PO, Vienna State Opera Chorus [G] *(rec live, Salzburg, 8/14/52)* Melodram 3-▲ MEL 37061 (m) [AAD]
Wagner, R.:Der fliegende Holländer, w. A. Varnay (sop), G. London (bar), A. van Mill (bass), J. Keilberth (cnd), Bayreuth Festival Orch, Bayreuth Festival Chorus [G] *(rec live, Bayreuth, 7/25/56)* Myto 2-▲ 2 MCD 93175

Traxel, Josef (ten) (cont.)
Wagner, R.:Der Ring des Nibelungen, w. Gré Brouwenstein (sop—Freia/Sieglinde), Ilse Hollweg (sop—Waldvogel), Gerda Lammers (sop—Ortlinde), Paula Lenchner (sop—Wellgunde/Gerhilde), Hilde Scheppan (sop—Helmwige), Astrid Varnay (sop—Brünnilde/3rd Norn), Lore Wissmann (sop—Woglinde), Maria von Ilosvay (mez—Flosshilde/Schwertleite/2nd Norn), Louise Charlotte Kamps (mez—Siegrune), Jean Madeira (mez—Erda/Rossweisse/1st Norn), Georgine van Milinkovic (mez—Fricka/Grimgerde), Elisabeth Schärtel (mez—Waltraute), Paul Kuën (ten—Mime), Ludwig Suthaus (ten—Loge), Josef Traxel (ten—Froh), Wolfgang Windgassen (ten—Siegmund/Siegfried), Alfons Herwig (bar—Donner), Hermann Uhde (bar—Gunther), Hans Hotter (b-bar—Wotan), Gustav Neidlinger (b-bar—Alberich), Josef Griendl (bass—Fasolt/Hunding/Hagen), Arnold van Mill (bass—Fafner), H. Knappertsbusch (cnd), Bayreuth Festival Orch, Bayreuth Festival Chorus *(rec live, Bayreuth, Aug 13–17, 1956)* Golden Melodram 14-▲ GM 1.001 [ADD]

Tree, David (ten)
Puccini, G.:Madama Butterfly, w. V. de los Angeles (sop—Madama Butterfly), B. Howitt (mez—Suzuki), J. Livingston (mez—Kate), J. Lanigan (ten—Pinkerton), D. Tree (ten—Goro), D. A. (ten—Yamadori), G. Evans (bar—Sharpless), M. Langdon (bass—Bonzo), R. Kempe (cnd), Royal Opera House Orch, Royal Opera House Chorus Covent Garden *(rec London, May 1957)* Ornamenti 2-▲ FE 112 [ADD]

Tréguier, Christian (bar)
Dao, N.-T.:Les Enfants d'Izieu, w. Sophie Boulin (sop), Eric Trémolières (ten), S. Gualda (cnd), Radio France PO Musique Francaise d'Aujourd'hui ("Collection MFA–Radio France" series) ▲ MFA 216003
Massenet, J.:Esclarmonde, w. Denia Mazzola (sop), José Sempere (ten), Hélène Parraguin (sgr), P. Fournillier (cnd), Franz Liszt SO, Massenet Festival Choir *(rec live, Massenet Festival, Saint-Étienne)* Koch Schwann 3-▲ SCH 312692 [DDD]
Massenet, J.:Grisélidis, w. Michèle Command (sop), Brigitte Desnoues (sop), Jean-Luc Viala (ten), Didier Henry (bar), Maurice Sieyes (bar), Jean-Philippe Courtis (bass), Claire Larcher (sgr), P. Fournillier (cnd), Franz Liszt SO, Budapest Lyon Chorus Koch Schwann 2-▲ SCH 312702 [DDD]

Trehy, John (bar)
Verdi, G.:La traviata (sels), w. Loretta di Franco (sop), Joan Sutherland (sop), Frederica von Stade (mez), Leo Goeke (ten), Lou Marcella (ten), Luciano Pavarotti (ten), Gene Boucher (bar), Raymond Gibbs (bar), Sherrill Milnes (bar), Louis Sgarro (bar), John Trehy (bar) Budget ("The Greatest Voice in Opera" series) ▲ SYP 112

Treigle, Norman (bass)
Boito, A.:Mefistofele, w. M. Caballé (sop), P. Domingo (ten), J. Rudel (cnd), London SO, Ambrosian Opera Chorus [I] EMI Classics 2-▲ CDCB 49522 [ADD]
Floyd, C.:Markheim, w. Norman Treigle (bass—Markheim), Audrey Schuh (sgr—Tess), Alan Crofoot (sgr—Josiah Creach), William Diard (sgr—Stranger), K. Andersson (cnd), New Orleans Opera Orch, New Orleans Opera Chorus *(rec New Orleans, LA, Mar. 31 & Apr. 2, 1966)* VAI Audio ▲ VAIA 1107
Floyd, C.:Susannah, w. Phyllis Curtin (sop—Susannah Polk), Richard Cassilly (ten—Sam Polk), Norman Treigle (bass—Olin Blitch), Marietta Muhs Cosenza (sgr—Mrs. McLean), Marilyn Davidson (sgr—Mrs. Gleaton), Kay Long (sgr—Mrs. Hayes), Jean Young (sgr—Mrs. Ott), Alton Brim (sgr—Elder Hayes), Thomas Carter (sgr—Elder Gleaton), Jack Davis (sgr—Elder McLean), Keith Kaldenberg (sgr—Little Bat McLean), Burton Parker (sgr—Elder Ott), K. Andersson (cnd), New Orleans Opera Orch, New Orleans Opera Chorus *(rec Mar 31, 1962)* VAI Audio 2-▲ VAIA 1115-2 [ADD]
Handel, G.F.:Giulio Cesare in Egitto, w. Beverly Sills (sop), Maureen Forrester (cta), Fritz Wolff (ten), Spiro Malas (bass), J. Redel (cnd), New York City Opera Orch, New York City Opera Chorus RCA Gold Seal 2-▲ 6182-2-RG [ADD]
Offenbach, J.:Les Contes d'Hoffmann, w. Beverly Sills (sop—Olympia/Giulietta/Antonia/Stella), Edith Evans (mez—Nicklausse/Mother's Voice), Michael Devlin (ten—Spalanzani), André Turp (ten—Hoffmann), Luigi Vellucci (ten—Andrès/Cochenille/Pitichinaccio/Frantz), Donald Bernard (bar—Luther/Schlemil), Norman Treigle (bass—Lindorf/Coppélius/Dapertutto/Dr. Miracle), John West (bass—Crespel), Alton Brim (sgr—Nathanaël), Rodney Hall (sgr—Hermann), K. Andersson (cnd), New Orleans Opera Orch, New Orleans Opera Chorus *(rec Feb 27, 1964)* VAI Audio 2-▲ VAIA 1121-2 [ADD]
Puccini, G.:La Bohème, w. Licia Albanese (sop—Mimì), Audrey Schuh (sop—Musetta), Giuseppe di Stefano (ten—Rodolfo), Arthur Cosenza (bar—Schaunard), Giuseppe Valdengo (bar—Marcello), Norman Treigle (bass—Colline), Warren Gadpaille (bass—Benoît/Alcindoro), Thomas Carter (sgr—Parpignol), Harold Crane (sgr—Custom House Official), Steve Harun (sgr—Sergeant), R. Cellini (cnd), New Orleans Opera Orch, New Orleans Opera Chorus *(rec Nov 1959)* VAI Audio 2-▲ VAIA 1119-2 [ADD]
Verdi, G.:Un ballo in maschera (sels), w. A. Schuh (sgr), Larrimore (sgr), J. Bjørling (ten), M. Rothmüller (bar), J. Morris (bass), Feux (sgr), W. Herbert (cnd), *(orch unknown)* [I] *(rec live, New Orleans, 4/22/50)* Legato Classics ▲ LCD 154-1 (m) [ADD]

Trekel, Roman (bar)
Bach, J.S.:Cant 201, w. Maria Cristina Kiehr (sop), Andreas Scholl (ct), James Taylor (ten), Kurt Azeberger (ten), Peter Lika (bass), R. Jacobs (cnd), Berlin Academy for Early Music, Berlin Chamber Chorus Harmonia Mundi France 2-▲ HMC 901544.45
Schoeck, O.:Unter Sternen, w. Christoph Keller (pno) *(rec Pere Casulleras, Christine Rossi, CH-Waldenburg Jun 1995)* Jecklin ▲ JD 678-2 [DDD]

Treleaven, John (ten)
Donizetti, G.:L'assedio di Calais, w. E. Harrhy (sop), D. Jones (mez), R. Serbo (ten), R. Smythe (bar), D. Parry (cnd), Philharmonia Orch, Geoffrey Mitchell Choir Opera Rara 2-▲ OR 9 [DDD]

Trémolières, Eric (ten)
Dao, N.-T.:Les Enfants d'Izieu, w. Sophie Boulin (sop), Christian Tréguier (bass), S. Gualda (cnd), Radio France PO Musique Francaise d'Aujourd'hui ("Collection MFA–Radio France" series) ▲ MFA 216003

Tremper, Susanne (sgr)
Weill, K.:Mahagonny, w. U. Lemper (sop), H. Jungwirth (sop), H. Wildhaber (ten), P. Haage (ten), T. Mohr (bar), Jeffrey Cohen (pno), J. Mauceri (cnd), Berlin RIAS Chamber Ensemble [G] London ▲ 430168-2 [DDD]
Weill, K.:The Seven Deadly Sins, w. U. Lemper (sop), H. Jungwirth (sop), H. Wildhaber (ten), P. Haage (ten), T. Mohr (bar), J. Mauceri (cnd), Berlin RIAS Chamber Ensemble [G] London ▲ 430168-2 [DDD]
Weill, K.:The Threepenny Opera, w. U. Lemper (sop), Milva (sgr), H. Dernesch (mez), R. Kollo (ten), M. Adorf (sgr), W. Reichmann (sgr), J. Mauceri (cnd), Berlin RIAS Sinfonietta, Berlin RIAS Chamber Choir [G] London ▲ 430075-2 [DDD]

Treptow, Günther (ten)
Wagner, R.:Parsifal, w. Anny Konetzni (sop—Kundry), Günther Treptow (ten—Parsifal), Paul Schöffler (bar—Amfortas), Hans Braun (bass—Titurel), Adolf Vogel (bass—Klingsor), Ludwig Weber (bass—Gurnemanz), R. Moralt (cnd), Vienna SO, Vienna State Opera Chorus *(rec Vienna)* Myto 4-▲ 4 MCD 954.136
Wagner, R.:Der Ring des Nibelungen, w. K. Flagstad (sop), H. Konetzni (sop), E. Höngen (cta), S. Svanholm (ten), M. Lorenz (ten), F. Frantz (b-bar), L. Weber (bass), B. Herrmann (bass), W. Furtwängler (cnd), La Scala Orch, La Scala Chorus *(rec live 1950)* Arkadia 12-▲ 351 [ADD]
Wagner, R.:Der Ring des Nibelungen, w. Kirsten Flagstad (sop), Hilde Konetzni (sop), Elisabeth Höngen (cta), Max Lorenz (ten), Set Svanholm (ten), Josef Hermann (bar), Ludwig Weber (bass), Ferdinand Franz (sgr), W. Furtwängler (cnd), La Scala Orch, La Scala Chorus *(rec Milan, 1950)* Music & Arts 12-▲ CD 914
Wagner, R.:Tristan und Isolde, w. Helena Braun (sop—Isolde), Margarete Klose (mez—Brangäne), Günther Treptow (ten—Tristan), Paul Kuen (ten—Ein Hirte), Albrecht Peter (bar—Melot), Fritz Richard Bender (bar—Ein Steuermann), Ferdinand Frantz (b-bar—König Marke), Paul Schöffler (b-bar—Kurwenal), H. Knappertsbusch (cnd), Bavarian State Opera Orch, Bavarian State Opera Chorus *(rec live, Prinzregententheater, July 23, 1950)* Orfeo 3-▲ 355
Wagner, R.:Die Walküre (sels), w. Hilde Konetzni (sop—Sieglinde), Günther Treptow (ten—Siegmund), Herbert Alsen (bass—Hunding), R. Moralt (cnd), Vienna SO—Act 1 Myto 4-▲ 4 MCD 954.136

Tretom, M. (sop)
Wikström, I.:Den Brottsliga Modern, w. E. Saeden (bar), A. Häggstam (bass), Nordisk CO Proprius ▲ 9069

Trévi, J. de (ten)
Berlioz, H.:La Damnation de Faust, w. M. Berthon (sop), C. Panzéra (bar), P. Coppola (cnd), Pasdeloup Concerts Association Orch, St. Gervais Chorus *(rec 1930)* Pearl ▲ PEA 9080 [ADD]

Trévi, J. de (ten) (cont.)
Berlioz, H.:La Damnation de Faust (sels), w. M. Berthon (sop), C. Panzéra (bar), L. Morturier (sgr), P. Coppola (cnd), Pasdeloup Orch, St. Gervais Chorus [abridged vers] [F] *(rec 1931)* The Classical Collector 2-▲ FDC2 2006 [AAD]

Trevisan, Antonella (mez)
Verdi, G.:La traviata, w. T. Fabbricini (sop—Violetta), A. Trevisan (mez—Annina), N. Curiel (mez—Flora), R. Alagna (ten—Alfredo), E. Cossutta (ten—Gastone), E. Gavazzi (ten—Giuseppe), O. Mori (bar—Douphol), E. Capuano (bass—d'Obigny), F. Musinu (bass—Grenvil), R. Muti (cnd), La Scala Orch, La Scala Chorus Sony Classical 2-▲ S2K 52486 [DDD]

Trevor, Caroline (alt)
Bach, J.S.:Magnificat, BWV 243, w. Anna Crookes (sop), Jayne Whitaker (sop), Timothy Robinson (ten), Nicholas Gedge (b-bar), N. Ward (cnd), Northern CO, Oxford Schola Cantorum *(rec St. Peter's Church, Hale, Cheshire, Dec. 2, 1993)* Naxos ▲ 8.550763 [DDD]
Britten, H.:Hymn to St. Cecilia, w. N. Jenkin (sop), R. Dean (sop), P. Daggett (ten), S. Birchall (bass), H. Christophers (cnd), The Sixteen *(rec 1 & 4/91)* Collins Classics ▲ 12862 [DDD]
Dowland, J.:Lachrimae, or Seaven Teares, w. J. Heringman (Renaissance lt), Rose Consort of Viols Amon Ra ▲ CD-SAR 55 [DDD]
Vivaldi, A.:Gloria, RV.589, w. Anna Crookes (sop), Jayne Whitaker (sop), Christine Swain (ob), Robert Glenton (vc), Christopher Stokes (org), N. Ward (cnd), Northern CO, Oxford Schola Cantorum *(rec St. Peter's Church, Hale, Cheshire, Dec. 3, 1993)* Naxos ▲ 8.550767 [DDD]

Trew, Graham (bar)
Butterworth, G.:Songs (6) from *A Shropshire Lad*, w. R. Vignoles (pno) [E] *(rec 8/79)* Meridian ▲ CDE84185
Gurney, I.:The Western Playland, w. R. Vignoles (pno), Coull String Quartet [E] Meridian ▲ CDE84185
Peel, G.:In Summertime on Bredon, w. R. Vignoles (pno) [E]—When the Lad for Longing Sighs; Reveille; In Summertime on Bredon *(rec 8/79)* Meridian ▲ CDE84185
Somervell, A.:The Shropshire Lad, w. R. Vignoles (pno) [E] *(rec 8/79)* Meridian ▲ CDE84185

Trexler, Roswitha (mez)
Henze, H.-W.:Voices, w. Joachim Vogt (ten), H. Neumann (cnd), Leipzig RSO members Berlin Classics 2-▲ BER 2180 [DDD]

Trexler, Roswitha (sop)
Berg, A.:Early Songs, w. John Tilbury (pno) Berlin Classics ▲ BER 9049 [DDD]
Eisler, H.:Songs, w. Jutta Czapski (pno) Berlin Classics ("Hanns Eisler Edition" series) 2-▲ BER 9229
Webern, A.:Songs, w. Rolf-Dieter Arens (pno), C.P. Flor (cnd), Berlin SO Berlin Classics ▲ BER 9049 [DDD]

Trimarchi, Domenico (bar)
Bellini, V.:La straniera, w. R. Scotto (sop), E. Zilio (mez), R. Cioni (ten), E. Campi (bass), N. Sanzogno (cnd), Palermo Teatro Massimo Orch, Palermo Teatro Massimo Chorus [I] *(rec live, Palermo, 1968)* Melodram 2-▲ 27039
Bellini, V.:La straniera, w. R. Scotto (sop), E. Zilio (mez), R. Cioni (ten), E. Campi (bass), N. Sanzogno (cnd), Palermo Teatro Massimo Orch, Palermo Teatro Massimo Chorus [I] *(rec live, Palermo, 1968)* Verona 2-▲ 27097/98
Donizetti, G.:Lucia di Lammermoor (sels), w. Christina Deutekom (sop—Lucia), Luciano Pavarotti (ten—Edgardo), Domenico Trimarchi (bar—Enrico Ashton), Silviano Pagliuca (bass—Raimondo Bidebent), C.M. Guilini (cnd), Naples Teatro San Carlo Orch, Naples Teatro San Carlo Chorus Budget ("The Greatest Voice in Opera" series) ▲ SYP 103
Massenet, J.:Werther, w. E. Ravaglia (sop), B. Casoni (mez), C. Bergonzi (ten), O. de Fabritiis (cnd), Naples Teatro San Carlo Orch, Naples Teatro San Carlo Chorus [I] *(rec live, Naples, 2/13/69)* Melodram 2-▲ 27058 [AAD]
Massenet, J.:Werther, w. V. Zeani (sop), A. Kraus (ten), M. Basiola (bar), A. Votto (cnd), *(orch unknown) (rec Palermo, 1971)* Great Opera Performances 2-▲ GOP 749
Mercadante, S.:Elisa e Claudio, w. Virginia Zeani (sop), Agostino Lazzari (ten), Ugo Trama (bass), Fiorini (sgr), U. Rapalo (cnd), Naples Teatro San Carlo Orch, Naples Teatro San Carlo Chorus *(rec live, Naples, 1/31/71)* Melodram 2-▲ MEL 27099 [ADD]
Rossini, G.:Il barbiere di Siviglia (sels), w. A. Baltsa (mez), S. Burgess (mez), F. Araiza (ten), T. Allen (bar), R. Lloyd (bass), N. Marriner (cnd), Academy of St. Martin in the Fields Philips ▲ 438498-2

Trissenaar (sgr)
Mozart, W.A.:Entführung, w. S. Greenburg (sop), J. Thames (sop), J. van der Schaaf (ten), W. Gahmlich (ten), K. Rydl (bass), M. Viotti (cnd), Frankfurt RSO, Bamberg Sym Chorus Capriccio 2-▲ 10 403/04

Tro, Silva (sgr)
Bretón, T.:La Verbena de la paloma, w. Maria Bayo (sop), Raquel Pierotti (sop), Plácido Domingo (ten), Enrique Baquerizo (sgr), Rafael Castejon (sgr), Milagros Martin (sgr), A. Ros-Marbá (cnd), Madrid SO Valois ("Zarauela" series) ▲ V 4725

Troetschel, Elfriede (sop)
Mahler, G.:Sym 4, w. O. Klemperer (cnd), Berlin RSO *(rec live, 1956)* Originals ▲ ORISH 823 [ADD]

Troeva-Mircheva, Rossitza (cta)
Puccini, G.:Madama Butterfly, w. Raina Kabaivanska (sop—Madama Butterfly), Alexandrina Milcheva (mez—Suzuki), Rossitza Troeva-Mircheva (cta—Kate Pinkerton), Nazzareno Antinori (ten—F.B. Pinkerton), Roumen Doikov (ten—Goro), Werther Vrachovski (ten—Il Principe Yamadori), Nelson Portella (bar—Sharpless), Kosta Dinkov (bass—Lo zio Bonzo), G. Bellini (cnd), Sofia PO, Svetoslav Obrenetov Bulgarian National Chorus *(rec Sophia, Bulgaria, Dec 1–13, 1982)* Arts Music 2-▲ 447161-2 [DDD]
Tchaikovsky, P.:Eugene Onegin, w. A. Tomowa-Sintow (sop), N. Gedda (ten), Y. Mazurok (bar), N. Ghiuselev (bass), E. Tchakarov (cnd), Sofia Festival Orch, Sofia National Opera Chorus [R] Sony Classical 2-▲ S2K 45539 [DDD]

Trogu (sgr)
Vivaldi, A.:Beatus vir, R.795, w. Caterina Calvi (sop), Susanna Moncayo Von Hase (cta), Vincenzo Manno (ten), Bonitatibus (sgr) Agora Music ▲ 001
Vivaldi, A.:Gloria (& Intro), RV.588, w. Caterina Calvi (sop), Susanna Moncayo Von Hase (cta), Vincenzo Manno (ten), Bonitatibus (sgr) Agora Music ▲ 001

Troitskaya, Natalia (sop)
Janácek, L.:Slavonic Mass, w. E. Randova (cta), K. Kaludov (ten), S. Leiferkas (bass), T. Trotter (org), C. Dutoit (cnd), Montreal SO, Montreal Sym Chorus London ▲ 436211-2

Troselj, Ivana (sgr)
McLean, B.:Rainforest Images, w. Panaiotis (sgr), K. Ryan (sgr), P. McLean (sgr/rcr/vn), B. McLean (rcr/clariflute), B. Dickie (didgeridoo) Capstone ▲ CPS 8617n

Trost, Rainer (sgr)
Mendelssohn, F.:St. Paul, w. Soile Isokoski (sop), Peter Lika (bass), C. Spering (cnd), Das Neue Orch Opus 111 2-▲ OPS 30-135/136

Trotta, Bernardino (sgr)
Rossini, G.:Armida, w. C. Deutekom (sop), P. Bottazzo (ten), O. Garaventa (ten), E. Gimenez (ten), A. Maddalena (bass), G. Antonini (bass), C. Franci (cnd), Venice Teatro La Fenice Orch, Venice Teatro La Fenice Chorus *(rec live, Venice, 1970)* Foyer 2-▲ FOY 2030 [AAD]
Verdi, G.:Un giorno di regno, w. Maria Casula (sop), Angelo Romero (bar), Enrico Fissore (bass), Franca Fabbri (sgr), Michele Guento (sgr), Islen Moubayed (sgr), Ruggero Rado (sgr), A. Zedda (cnd), *(orch unknown)* Great Opera Performances 2-▲ GOP 782

Troupova-Wilke, Irena (sop)
Monteverdi, C.:Vespers, w. Susanne Ryden (sop), Detlef Bratschke (alt), Erich Mentzel (ten), Hermann Oswald (ten), Manuel Warwitz (ten), Thomas Herberich (bass), Günther Schmidt (bass), H. Arman (cnd), Schütz Academy Capriccio ▲ CD 10521 [DDD]

Trovarelli, Antonella (mez)
Albanese, G.:Songs, w. Luana Gentile (sop), Marina Gentile (mez), Stefano Consolini (ten), Paolo Speca (bar), Andrea De Mele (vn), Sirio Benedetto (sax), Roberto Rupo (pno)—Aria di Natale; Duettino e coro muto (w. Carlo Moreno) [both w. Giorgina Dell'Immagine, Tito Petralia (cnd), EIAR Orch & Chorus]; Passione (M. Gentile); Serenata (Speca); Alzati, o bella... (Trovarelli); Mattinata (Speca); Il sogno d'una suora (Trovarelli); Ninna Nanna (M. Gentile); Barcarola (Rupo); Madrigale (L. Gentile); Ninna nanna...900 (L. Gentile); Variazioni (L. Gentile); Non so qual io mi voglia... (L. Gentile); Io sono un augellin... (L. Gentile); Bravo, bene, bis...(va bene) (Consolini & Di Benedetto); Che caviale (Consolini); Ma non sapete chi sono io? (Consolini & L. & M. Gentile); Grappoli di stelle (Consolini); Notte di Capri (Consolini & Di Mele); Una rosa di ferro battuto (Consolini, Speca & L. & M. Gentile) *(rec Ortona, Teatro Zambra, Feb 21, 22, 23 & Mar 1 &)* Bongiovanni ▲ GB 5054-2 [DDD]
Rossini, G.:La pietra del paragone, w. M. C. Nocentini (sop), H. M. Molinari (cta), P. Barbacini (ten), V. Di Matteo (bar), R. Scaltriti (bar), A. Svab (bar), P. Rumetz (bass), C. Desderi (cnd), Camerata Musicale Orch, Modeno Teatro Comunale Chorus [l] *(rec 1992)* Nuova Era 2-▲ 7132/33 [DDD]

Troxell, Richard (ten)
Puccini, G.:Madama Butterfly, w. Ying Huang (sop), J. Conlon (cnd), Orch de Paris—Original Motion Picture Soundtrack based on the opera by Puccini Sony Classical ▲ S2K 69258
Puccini, G.:Madama Butterfly (sels), w. Ying Huang (sop—Cio-Cio-San), Constance Hauman (mez—Kate Pinkerton), Ning Liang (mez—Suzuki), Richard Troxell (ten—B. F. Pinkerton), Richard Cowan (sgr—Sharpless), Jing Ma Fan (sgr—Goro), Christopheren Nomura (sgr—Prince Yamadori), J. Conlon (cnd), Orch de Paris—Dovunque al Mondo; B. F. Pinkerton Giù; Bimba, Bimba, Non Piangere; Ah! Vien! Sei Mia!; Un Bel Dì; Ora a Noi; Petali d'Ogni Fior; Coro a Bocca Chiusa; Prelude; Io So Che Alle Sue Pene; Ah! Son Vil!; E Sia! A Lui Devo Obbedir; Butterfly! *(rec Olivier Messiaen Auditorium, Paris, 1996)* Sony Classical ▲ SK 61972 [DDD]

Troyanos, Tatiana (mez)
Beethoven, L. van:Sym 9, "Choral Sym", w. Gwyneth Jones (sop), Jess Thomas (ten), Karl Ridderbusch (bass), K. Böhm (cnd), Vienna PO, Vienna State Opera Chorus Deutsche Grammophon ("Double" series) 2-▲ 437368-2
Bernstein, L.:Music of, w. J. Norman (sop), K. Te Kanawa (sop), J. Anderson (sop), F. von Stade (mez), C. Ludwig (mez), J. Carreras (ten), D. Garrison (ten), J. Hadley (ten), T. Hampson (bar), T. Daly (sgr), G. Kremer (vn), M. Rostropovich (vc), M.T. Thomas (va), L. Bernstein (cnd), *(orch unknown)*—various popular works Deutsche Grammophon ▲ 439251-2 ■ 439251-4
Bernstein, L.:West Side Story, w. K. Te Kanawa (sop), J. Carreras (ten), K. Ollmann (bass), L. Bernstein (cnd), *(orch unknown)* [E] Deutsche Grammophon ▲ 415963-2 [DDD] ■ 415963-4 □ 415963-5
Bizet, G.:Carmen, w. K. Te Kanawa (sop), P. Domingo (ten), J. Van Dam (b-bar), G. Solti (cnd), London PO [F] London ▲ 421300-2 [ADD]
Bizet, G.:Carmen, w. K. Te Kanawa (sop), P. Domingo (ten), J. Van Dam (b-bar), G. Solti (cnd), London PO [F] London 3-▲ 414489-2 [ADD]
Donizetti, G.:Lucrezia Borgia, w. L. Gencer (sop), J. Carrreras (ten), N. Rescigno (cnd), Dallas Civic Opera Orch, Dallas Civic Opera Chorus *(rec 1973)* Melodram 2-▲ MLO 270109 [ADD]
Mahler, G.:Sym 2, w. Felicity Palmer (sop/mez), P. Boulez (cnd), BBC SO, Paris Conservatory Société des Concerts Orch, BBC Sym Chorus Originals 2-▲ ORISH 855
Mahler, G.:Sym 2, w. F. Palmer (sop), P. Boulez (cnd), BBC SO, BBC Choral Society, London Phil Choir Enterprise 2-▲ LV 915/916
Mozart, W.A.:Complete Mozart Edition, w. Jessye Norman (sop), I. Cotrubas (sop), H. Donath (sop), W. Hollweg (ten), H. Prey (bar), H. Schmidt-Isserstedt (cnd), North German RSO Philips 3-▲ 422534-2 [ADD]
Mozart, W.A.:Così fan tutte, w. L. Price (sop), J. Raskin (sop), G. Shirley (ten), S. Milnes (bar), E. Leinsdorf (cnd), New Philharmonia Orch, New Philharmonia Chorus [I] RCA Gold Seal 3-▲ 6677-2 [ADD]
Mozart, W.A.:Missa brevis, K.220, w. E. Mathis (spo), H. Laubenthal (ten), K. Engen (bass) Deutsche Grammophon ▲ 429820-2 [ADD]
Mozart, W.A.:Nozze di Figaro (sels), w. G. Janowitz (sop), E. Mathis (sop), D. Fischer-Dieskau (bar), H. Prey (bar), K. Böhm (cnd), Berlin German Opera Orch—Scenes & Arias Deutsche Grammophon ▲ 429822-2 [ADD]
Schoenberg, A.:Gurrelieder, w. J. Norman (sop), J. McCracken (ten), D. Arnold (bar), S. Ozawa (cnd), Boston SO, Tanglewood Festival Chorus Philips 2-▲ 412511-2
Strauss, R.:Ariadne auf Naxos, w. L. Rysanek (sop), J. Scovotti (sop), J. King (ten), P. Schöffler (b-bar), K. Böhm (cnd), Vienna State Opera Orch, Vienna State Opera Chorus *(rec 1967)* Melodram 2-▲ MLO 270105 [ADD]
Strauss, R.:Der Rosenkavalier, w. E. Mathis (sop), C. Ludwig (mez), O. Wiener (bar), T. Adam (b-bar), K. Böhm (cnd), Vienna PO *(rec Salzburg Festival, 1969)* Deutsche Grammophon 3-▲ 445338-2 [ADD]

Truffelli, Romano (ten)
Marschner, H.A.:Der Vampyr, w. Carole Farley (sop—Malwina), Nucci Condò (mez—Suse), Oslavio Di Credico (ten—George Dibdin), Josef Protschka (ten—Edgar Aubry), Romano Truffelli (ten—Richard Scrop), Martin Egel (bar—Sir Humphrey Davenaut), Andréa Snarski (bar—Toms Blunt), Siegmund Nimsgern (b-bar—Lord Ruthven), Armando Caforio (bass—Robert Green), Peter Boom (sgr—Il capo dei Vampiri), Carlo Di Giacomo (sgr—James Gadshill), Wolfgang Lenz (sgr—Sir Berkley), Galina Pisarenko (sgr—Janthe), Renzo Scorsoni (sgr—Un servitore di Berkley), Anastasia Tomaszewska Schepis (sgr—Emmy), G. Neuhold (cnd), Rome RAI SO, Rome RAI Chorus *(rec Rome, Jan 26, 1980)* Italia 2-▲ CDC 99 [ADD]

Trundt, Henny (sop)
Wagner, R.:Götterdämmerung (sels), w. Henny Trundt (sop—Brünnhilde), Josef Kalenberg (ten—Siegfried), Emil Schipper (bar—Gunther), Josef von Manowarda (bass—Hagen), C. Krauss (cnd), Vienna State Opera Orch *(rec Mar. 7, 1933)* Koch Schwann 2-▲ SCH 314642 [ADD]

Truplová, Eva (sop)
Janácek, L.:Moravian Folk Poetry, w. Stanislav Predota (ten), Adam Skoumal (pno) Studio Matou ▲ MAT 15 [DDD]

Tsantikos, George (ten)
Glanville-Hicks, P.:Nausicaa, w. Teresa Stratas (sop—Nausicaa), Sophia Steffan (cta—Queen Arete), Michalis Heliotis (ten—Antinous/Priest), George Moutsios (ten—Eurymachus), Edward Ruhl (ten—Phemius), George Tsantikos (ten—Clytoneus), Vassilis Koundouris (bar—Messenger), John Modenos (bar—Aethon), Spiro Malas (bass—King Alcinous), C. Surinach (cnd), Athens SO, Athens Sym Chorus *(rec Athens Festival, 1961)* CRI ▲ CD 695 [ADD]
Glanville-Hicks, P.:Nausicaa (sels), w. Teresa Stratas (sop), Spiro Malas (bass), Michalis Helii (sgr), Michalis Heliots (sgr), George Moutsio (sgr), Edward Ruhl (sgr), Sophia Steffan (sop), C. Surinach (cnd), Athens SO, Athens Sym Chorus CRI ▲ CD 695 [ADD]

Tschammer, Hans (bass)
Beethoven, L. van:Fidelio (sels), w. Evelyn Herlitzius (sop—Leonore), Ruth Ziesak (sop—Marzelline), Stig Andersen (ten—Florestan), Herbert Lippert (ten—Jaquino), Albert Dohmen (bar—Don Pizarro), Andreas Kohn (bass—Don Fernando), Hans Tschammer (bass—Rocco), G. Solti (cnd), World Orch for Peace, London Voices—Finale Act II *(rec Victoria Hall, Geneva, July 5, 1995)* London ▲ 448901-2 [DDD]
Beethoven, L. van:Missa Solemnis, w. C. Vaness (sop), W. Meier (mez), H.-P. Blochwitz (ten), J. Tate (cnd), English CO, Tallis Chamber Choir [L] EMI Classics ▲ CDC 49950 [DDD]
Wagner, R.:Das Rheingold, w. M. Lipovšek (mez), J. Rappé (ten), H. Zednik (ten), P. Haage (ten), A. Schmidt (bar), T. Adam (b-bar), K. Rydl (bass), J. Morris (bass), B. Haitink (cnd), Bavarian RSO [G] EMI Classics 2-▲ CDCB 49853 [DDD]

Tsimitselis, L. (sop)
Haydn, M.:Vesperae pro festo Sanctorum Innocentium, w. A. Schram (sop), O. Messerli (alt), A. von Aarburg (cnd), Capella Concertante, Zurich Boys' Choir [L] *(rec 12/89)* Tudor ▲ 754 [DDD]

Tsingopoulos, Madeline (sgr)
Rorem, N.:A Childhood Miracle, w. Michele Couture (sop—Peony), Darcy Dunn (sgr—Violet), Madeline Tsingopoulos (sgr—Mother), Mary Cidoni (sgr—Emma), Patrick Greene (sgr—Snowman), Peter Castaldi (sgr—Father), R. E. Harrell (cnd), Magic Circle CO Newport Classic ▲ NPT 85594 [DDD]

Tsingopoulos, Madeline (sgr) (cont.)
Rorem, N.:3 Sisters Who Are Not Sisters, w. Andrea Matthews (sop—Jenny), Carol Flamm (sgr—Helen), Madeline Tsingopoulos (sgr—Ellen), Frederick Urrey (ten—Samuel), Mark Singer (sgr—Sylvester), John Van Buskirk (pno) Newport Classic ▲ NPT 85594 [DDD]

Tuand, Carlo (ten)
Bellini, V.:I Puritani, w. Edita Gruberova (sop), Katia Lytting (mez), Justin Lavender (ten), Ettore Kim (bar), Francesco Ellero d'Artegna (bass), Dankwart Siegele (bass), F. Luisi (cnd), Munich RSO, Bavarian Radio Chorus Nightingale Classics 3-▲ NIG 70562

Tubb, Evelyn (sop)
Bringing Light to the Unknown, w. Consort of Musicke, Emma Kirkby (sop), et al. Musica Oscura ▲ OSC 280826 [DDD]
The Dark Is My Delight, w. Michael Fields (lt) Musica Oscura ("Women in Song" series) ▲ MOS 70980
The Mad Lover, w. Frances Kelly (triple hp) Musica Oscura ("The Orpheus Circle" series) ▲ MOS 70987
Monteverdi, C.:Ballo delle ingrate, w. Emma Kirkby (sop), Barbara Nichols (sop), Maria Ewing (sop), A. Rooley (cnd), Consort of Musicke [I] Virgin Classics ▲ 59606 [DDD]
Stradella, A.:L'anime del purgatorio, w. Emma Kirkby (sop), David Thomas (bass), Richard Wistreich (bass), A. Rooley (cnd), Consort of Musicke Musica Oscura ("Favola in Musica" series) ▲ MOS 70984

Tuccari, Angelic (sop)
Paisiello, G.:Fedra, w. O. Beggiato (sop), R. Mattioli (sop), L. Udovick (sop), A. Lazzari (ten), A. Questa (cnd), Milan RAI SO, Milan RAI Chorus *(rec 1958)* Memories 2-▲ MEM 4502 [AAD]
Pergolesi, G.B.:La serva padrona, w. Sesto Bruscantini (bar), Milan RAI Lyric Orch Cetra Classic ▲ CDO 33
Rota, N.:Mysterium, w. C. Vozza (mez), G. Sinimberghi (ten), U. Trama (bass), A. Renzi (cnd), Pro Civitate Christiana di Assisi Orch, Pro Civitate Christiana di Assisi Chorus *(rec live 1962)* Claves ▲ CD 9323 [DDD]

Tucci, Gabriella (sop)
Bellini, V.:I Puritani (sels), w. Gabriella Tucci (sop—Elvira), Vittorina Magnaghi (mez—Enrichetta di Francia), Luciano Pavarotti (ten—Lord Arturo Talbo), Aldo Protti (bar—Sir Riccardo Forth), Ruggero Raimondi (bass—Sir Giorgio), A. Quadri (cnd), Vincenzo Bellini Theater Orch, Catania Teatro Massimo Bellini Chorus Budget ("The Greatest Voice in Opera" series) ▲ SYP 106
Bellini, V.:I Puritani (sels), w. L. Pavarotti (ten), A. Protti (bar), R. Raimondi (bass), A. Quadri (cnd), Catania Teatro Massimo Bellini Orch, Catania Teatro Massimo Bellini Chorus [I] *(rec live, Catania 3/22/68)* Verona 3-▲ 27029/31
Bellini, V.:I Puritani (sels), w. L. Pavarotti (ten), A. Protti (bar), R. Raimondi (bass), A. Quadri (cnd), Catania Teatro Massimo Bellini Orch, Catania Teatro Massimo Bellini Chorus [I] *(rec live, Catania 3/22/68)* Melodram ▲ MEL 15001
Cilea, F.:Adriana Lecouvreur (sels), w. Guiseppe Taddei (bar), A. Basile (cnd), Turin Radio-TV SO—Ecco il monologo... *(rec Concerto Martini & Rossi, Turin, Feb 15, 1960)* Incontri Memorabili ▲ 5029 [ADD]
Donizetti, G.:Arias, w. Guiseppe Taddei (bar), A. Basile (cnd), Turin Radio-TV SO—Vien Leonora [from La Favorita]; Ah! tardi, troppo [from Linda di Chamounix] *(rec Concerto Martini & Rossi, Turin, Feb 15, 1960)* Incontri Memorabili ▲ 5029 [ADD]
Donizetti, G.:Requiem Mass, w. A. Lazzarini (mez), G. Sinimberghi (ten), I. Sardi (bass), F. Maero (sgr), F. Molinari-Pradelli (cnd), Milan RAI SO, Milan RAI Chorus [L] *(rec live, Milan 3/21/61)* Memories ▲ HR 4131 [ADD]
Massenet, J.:Hérodiade (sels), w. Guiseppe Taddei (bar), A. Basile (cnd), Turin Radio-TV SO—Divine volupté *(rec Concerto Martini & Rossi, Turin, Feb 15, 1960)* Incontri Memorabili ▲ 5029 [ADD]
Mozart, W.A.:Don Giovanni (sels), w. Guiseppe Taddei (bar), A. Basile (cnd), Turin Radio-TV SO—Madamina il catalogo è questo *(rec Concerto Martini & Rossi, Turin, Feb 15, 1960)* Incontri Memorabili ▲ 5029 [ADD]
Piccinni, N.:Didon, w. O. Mori (bass), M. Petri (bass), M. Rossi (cnd), Naples RAI Orch, Naples RAI Chorus *(rec live 4/16/70)* Arkadia 2-▲ 596 [ADD]
Puccini, G.:Suor angelica (sels), w. Guiseppe Taddei (bar), A. Basile (cnd), Turin Radio-TV SO—Senza mamma *(rec Concerto Martini & Rossi, Turin, Feb 15, 1960)* Incontri Memorabili ▲ 5029 [ADD]
Verdi, G.:Arias, w. Guiseppe Taddei (bar), A. Basile (cnd), Turin Radio-TV SO—Tacea la notte placida [from Il Trovatore]; Ave Maria! [from Otello] *(rec Concerto Martini & Rossi, Turin, Feb 15, 1960)* Incontri Memorabili ▲ 5029 [ADD]
Verdi, G.:Il trovatore, w. G. Simionato (mez), C. Bergonzi (ten), P. Cappuccilli (bar), G. Gavazzeni (cnd), La Scala Orch, La Scala Chorus *(rec live, Moscow 1965)* Melodram 2-▲ MEL 27008

Tuček, René (bar)
Dvořák, A.:King & Charcoal Burner, w. Drahonira Drobkova (cta), Viktor Koci (ten), Dalibor Jedlicka (bass), J. Chaloupka (cnd), Prague National Theater Orch, Milan Maly (cnd), Prague National Theater Chorus [final version] *(rec 1989)* Supraphon ("Hidden Treasures from Prague" series) ▲ SUP CD 3078
Martinů, B.:Alexandre bis, w. J. Krátká (sop), A. Barová (mez), R. Novák (ten), F. Jílek (cnd), Brno Janáček Opera Orch Supraphon ▲ SUP 11 2140 [AAD]
Martinů, B.:Comedy on the Bridge, w. J. Krátká (sop), A. Barová (mez), R. Novák (ten), F. Jílek (cnd), Brno Janáček Opera Orch Supraphon ▲ SUP 11 2140 [AAD]

Tucker, Gene (ten)
Berlioz, H.:Messe solennelle Bar, w. Terry Cook (bass), Rosa Lamoreaux (sgr), J. Reilly Lewis (cnd), Washington National Cathedral Choral Society Koch International Classics ▲ KIC 7204 [DDD]
Halévy, F.:La Juive, w. M. Le Bris (sop), Y. Hayashi (sop), Sabate (sgr), A. Guadagno (cnd), *(orch & chorus unknown)* [F] *(rec live, London, 1973)* Legato Classics 2-▲ LCD 120-2 [AAD]
Monteverdi, C.:Ritorno d'Ulisse, w. L. Hunt (sop), C. Högman (sop), B. Fink (cta), D. Vissé (ct), C. Prégardien (ten), D. Thomas (bass), R. Jacobs (cnd), Concerto Vocale [I] Harmonia Mundi France 3-▲ HMC 901427/29
Monteverdi, C.:Vespro della Beata Vergine, w. A. Monoyios (sop), M. Pennicchi (sop), M. Chance (ct), N. Robson (ten), S. Naglia (ten), B. Terfel (b-bar), A. Miles (bass), J. E. Gardiner (cnd), English Baroque Soloists, His Majesties Sagbutts & Cornetts, London Monteverdi Choir Archiv 2-▲ 429565-2 [DDD]
Mozart, W.A.:Missa brevis, K.194, w. M. Busching (mez), P. Fay (bar), C. Dill Smith (sgr), H. Mardirosian (cnd), St. Thomas Moore Cathedral Orch, St. Thomas Moore Cathedral Chorus [L] Centaur ▲ CRC 2074 [DDD]
Mozart, W.A.:Tantum ergo, w. Carolyn Dill Smith (sop), Marianna Busching (mez), Peter Fay (bar), H. Mardirosian (cnd), St. Thomas Moore Cathedral Orch, St. Thomas Moore Cathedral Chorus [L] Centaur ▲ CRC 2074 [DDD]
Mozart, W.A.:Vesperae de Dominica, w. C. Dill Smith (sop), M. Busching (mez), P. Fay (bar), H. Mardirosian (cnd), St. Thomas Moore Cathedral Orch, St. Thomas Moore Cathedral Chorus [L] Centaur ▲ CRC 2074 [DDD]
Puccini, G.:La Bohème, w. A. Moffo (sop), F. Costa (mez), R. Merrill (bar), G. Tozzi (bass), E. Leinsdorf (cnd), Rome Opera Orch, Rome Opera Chorus [I] RCA Gold Seal 2-▲ 3969-2-RG [ADD] 2-■ 3969-4-RG (CrO2)
Puccini, G.:La Bohème (sels), w. A. Moffo (sop), F. Costa (mez), R. Merrill (bar), G. Tozzi (bass), E. Leinsdorf (cnd), Rome Opera Orch, Rome Opera Chorus RCA Gold Seal ▲ 60189-2-RG [ADD] ■ 60189-4-RG (CrO2)
Puccini, G.:Madama Butterfly, w. L. Price (sop), R. Elias (mez), P. Maero (bar), E. Leinsdorf (cnd), RCA Italian Opera Orch [I] RCA Red Seal 2-▲ 6160-2-RC [ADD]
Puccini, G.:Madama Butterfly (sels), w. L. Price (sop), R. Elias (mez), P. Maero (bar), E. Leinsdorf (cnd), RCA Italian Opera Orch [I] RCA ■ RK 1048
Verdi, G.:Aida, w. M. Callas (sop), F. Barbieri (mez), T. Gobbi (ten), N. Zaccaria (bass), T. Serafin (cnd), La Scala Orch, La Scala Chorus [I] EMI Classics 3-▲ CDCC 49030 [ADD]
Verdi, G.:Aida, w. H. Nelli (sop), E. Gustavson (mez), G. Valdengo (bar), A. Toscanini (cnd), NBC SO, Robert Shaw Chorale [I] RCA Gold Seal 3-▲ 60251-2-RG (m) [ADD] 2-■ 60251-4-RG (CrO2)
Verdi, G.:Aida, w. H. Nelli (sop), E. Gustavson (mez), G. Valdengo (bar), A. Toscanini (cnd), NBC SO, Robert Shaw Chorale [I] RCA Gold Seal 7-▲ 60326-2-RG (m) [ADD] 6-■ 60326-4-RG (CrO2)
Verdi, G.:Arias, w. E. Farrell (sop) [duets] Odyssey ■ YT 35935
Verdi, G.:Un ballo in maschera, w. C. Deutekom (sop), R. Bruson (bar), R. Muti (cnd), Florence Teatro Comunale Orch, Florence Teatro Comunale Chorus *(rec live, Florence 1972)* Foyer 2-▲ FOY 2047 [AAD]

Tucker, Gene (ten) (cont.)
Verdi, G.:La traviata, w. A. Moffo (sop), R. Merrill (bar), F. Previtali (cnd), Rome Opera Orch [I] RCA Gold Seal ▲ 60204-2-RG [ADD] ■ 60204-4-RG
Verdi, G.:La traviata, w. A. Moffo (sop), R. Merrill (bar), F. Previtali (cnd), Rome Opera Orch [I] RCA Gold Seal 2-▲ 4144-2-RG [ADD] 2-■ 4144-4-RG
Verdi, G.:Il trovatore, w. L. Price (sop), R. Elias (mez), L. Warren (bar), G. Tozzi (bass), A. Basile (cnd), Rome Opera Orch RCA Gold Seal 2-▲ 60560-2-RG [ADD] 2-■ 60560-4-RG (CrO2)
Verdi, G.:Il trovatore, w. M. Caballé (sop), M. Zanasi (bar), T. Schippers (cnd), Florence Maggio Musicale Orch, Florence Maggio Musicale Chorus [I] *(rec live 1968)* Melodram 2-▲ MEL 27035
Verdi, G.:Il trovatore, w. M. Caballé (sop), M. Zanasi (bar), T. Schippers (cnd), Florence Maggio Musicale Orch, Florence Maggio Musicale Chorus *(rec 1968)* Memories ▲ MEM 4521 [ADD]

Tucker, Laura (mez)
Purcell, H.:Dido & Aeneas, w. Nancy Maultsby (sop—Dido), Susannah Waters (sop—Belinda), Margaret O'Keefe (sop—1st Witch), Sharon Baker (sop—2nd Woman), Laura Tucker (mez—Sorceress), Donna Ames (alt—Spirit), Richard Clement (ten—Sailor), Russell Braun (bar—Aeneas), M. Pearlman (cnd), Boston Baroque Orch Telarc ▲ CD 80424 [DDD]

Tucker, Mark (ten)
Bach, J.S.:Mass in b, BWV 232, w. N. Argenta (sop), C. Denley (mez), S. Varcoe (b-bar), R. Hickox (cnd), Collegium Musicum 90 Chandos ("Chaconne" series) 2-▲ CHAN 0533/34 [DDD]
Monteverdi, C.:Incoronazione, w. Constanze Backes (sop—Valletto), Catherine Bott (sop—Drusilla/Pallade/La Virtù), Dana Hanchard (sop—Nerone), Sylvia McNair (sop—Poppea), Marinella Pennicchi (sop—Amore/Damigella), Annie Sofie von Otter (mez—Ottavia/Venere/La Fortuna), Julian Clarkson (alt—Littore/Mercurio), Bernarda Fink (cta—Arnalta), Roberto Balconi (ct—Nutrice), Michael Chance (ct—Ottone), Nigel Robson (ten—Liberto/Soldato Secondo), Mark Tucker (ten—Lucano/Soldato Primo), Francesco Ellero d'Artegna (bass—Seneca), J. E. Gardiner (cnd), English Baroque Soloists *(rec Queen Elizabeth Hall, South Bank Ctr, London, Dec 1993)* Archiv 3-▲ 447088-2
Purcell, H.:King Arthur, w. N. Argenta (sop), J. Gooding (sop), L. Perillo (sop), J. MacDougall (ten), G. Finley (bar), B. Bannatyne-Scott (bass), T. Pinnock (cnd), English Concert, *(chorus unknown)* Archiv 2-▲ 435490-2 [DDD]

Tucker, Richard (ten)
Donizetti, G.:Lucia di Lammermoor (sels), w. Renata Scotto (sop—Lucia), Ruth Carron (mez—Alisa), Richard Tucker (ten—Edgardo), Matteo Manuguerra (bar—Enrico), Robert Hale (bass-bar—Raimondo), A. Guadagno (cnd), *(orch & chorus unknown)*—Lucia, perdona...Verranno a te; Sconsigliato! In queste porte; Il dolce suono; Non mi guardar si fiero...Spargi d'amaro pianto; Tombe degli avi miei...Fra poco a me ricovero; Tu che a Dio spiegasti l'ali *(rec Philadelphia, 1973)* Legato Classics 2-▲ LCD 198-2
The Essence of Verismo:A 50th Anniversary Tribute Legato Classics ▲ LCD 184-1 [ADD]
Giordano, U.:Andrea Chénier (sels), w. R. Tebaldi (sop), *(orch unknown)*—Ecco l'altare...Ora soave; Come un bel di di maggio; Vicino a te s'acqueta *(rec 1956-63)* Standing Room Only ▲ SRO 8441 [ADD]
Gounod, C.:Faust, w. V. de los Angeles (sop), C. Ward (sgr), M. Mayhoff (sgr), H. Noel (sgr), N. Moscona (bass), D. Bernard (sgr), W. Herbert (cnd), New Orleans Opera Orch [F] *(rec Feb. 26, 1953)* Legato Classics 2-▲ LCD 167-2 [AAD]
In Memoriam Odyssey ■ YT 35498
Leoncavallo, R.:Pagliacci, w. Mietta Sighele (sop), Kari Murmela (bar), Walter Alberti (bar), R. Muti (cnd), Florence Maggio Musicale Orch, Florence Maggio Musicale Chorus *(rec Florence, 1971)* Memories ▲ MEM 4576 [ADD]
Leoncavallo, R.:Pagliacci, w. M. Sighele (sop), E. Lorenzi (ten), K. Nurmela (bar), R. Muti (cnd), Florence Teatro Comunale Orch, Florence Teatro Comunale Chorus *(rec live, Florence, 1971)* Foyer ▲ FOY 2050 [AAD]
Live from Carnegie Hall, Jan. 7, 1973, w. R. Merrill (bar) *(rec Carnegie Hall, NYC Jan. 7, 1973)* Teldec 2-▲ 93706-2
Offenbach, J.:Les Contes d'Hoffmann, w. L. Amara (sop), R. Peters (sop), R. Stevens (mez), M. Singher (bar), P. Monteux (cnd), Metropolitan Opera Orch, New York Metropolitan Opera Chorus Stradivarius 2-▲ DAT 12302
A Passover Seder Festival Sony Masterworks ▲ MDK 48304 ■ MGT 48304
A Portrait of the Artist *(rec live rec'gs, 1950-1972)* Legato Classics ▲ LCD 104-1 (m) [ADD]
Puccini, G.:Madama Butterfly (sels), w. Leontyne Price (sop), Rosalind Elias (mez), Piero De Palma (ten), Phillip Maero (bar), E. Leinsdorf (cnd), RCA Italian Opera Orch, RCA Italiana Opera Chorus RCA Victor ▲ 09026-68089-2; ■ 09026-68089-4
Puccini, G.:Manon Lescaut (sels), w. R. Tebaldi (sop), *(orch unknown)*—Donna non vidi mai; Vedete? Io son fedele; E ver!...In quelle trine morbide; L'ora, o Tirsi!; Oh, saro la piu bella!; Tu soffri?..Vedi, vedi, son io che piango; Sola, perduta, abbandonata; Fra le tue braccia amore *(rec between 1956-63)* Standing Room Only ▲ SRO 8441 [ADD]
Puccini, G.:Music of, w. Kiri Te Kanawa (sop), Eva Marton (sop), José Carreras (ten), Luciano Pavarotti (ten), *(other artists unknown)*—19 arias & duets from La bohème, Gianni Schicchi, Madama Butterfly, La Rondine, Tosca & Turandot *(six mono & 13 stereo recordings)* CBS ▲ MLK 45809 [AAD/ADD/D ■ MLT 45809
Richard Tucker *(rec live 1949-1968)* Memories ("Great Voices" series) 2-▲ MEM 4134 (m)
Richard Tucker In Recital, w. pno accompaniment *(rec New York recitals, 1972 & 1974)* HRE ▲ 1003-1 [ADD]
Verdi, G.:Music of, w. Eileen Farrell (sop) [w. Vienna State Opera Orch [cnd:Nello Santi], Columbia SO [cnd:Fausto Cleva], New Philharmonia Orch [cnd:Franz Allers]]—arias & duets from Aida; Un ballo in maschera; I Lombardi; I due Foscari; Simon Boccanegra; Il trovatore; Luisa Miller; Rigoletto; I vespri siciliani; La forza del destino; Otello Sony Classical ("Masterworks Heritage" series) ▲ MHK 62357
Verdi, G.:Requiem Mass, w. L. Amara (sop), M. Forrester (cta), G. London (bar), E. Ormandy (cnd), Philadelphia Orch, Westminster Choir Sony Classical ▲ SB2K 53252
Verdi, G.:Requiem Mass, w. L. Price (sop), N. Merriman (mez), G. Tozzi (bass), E. Ormandy (cnd), Philadelphia Orch *(rec live Apr. 6, 1957)* Standing Room Only ▲ SRO 842-1 [ADD]
Verdi, G.:Requiem Mass, w. L. Amara (sop), M. Forrester (cta), G. London (bar), E. Ormandy (cnd), Philadelphia Orch, Westminster Choir [L] Odyssey ■ YT 35230
Verdi, G.:Rigoletto, w. Renata Scotto (sop—Gilda), Stella Maris Silva (sop—Giovanna), Martha Carrizo (mez—Page), Carmen de la Mata (mez—Countess Ceprano), Noemi Souza (cta—Maddalena), Horacio Mastrango (ten—Borso), Richard Tucker (ten—Duke of Mantua), Cornell MacNeil (bar—Rigoletto), Riccardo Yost (bar—Marullo), Guerrino Boschetti (bass—Usher), Tulio Gagliardo (bass—Count Ceprano), Victor de Narké (bass—Monterone), William Wilderman (bass—Sparafucile), F. Previtali (cnd), Buenos Aires Teatro Colón Orch, Buenos Aires Teatro Colón Chorus *(rec Colon Theater, Buenos Aires, Aug. 22, 1967)* Legato Classics 2-▲ LCD 198-2
Verdi, G.:Simon Boccanegra, w. Renata Tebaldi (sop—Maria Boccanegra), Penelope Jensen (mez—Maria's Maidservant), Richard Tucker (ten—Gabriele Adorno), Rod MacWerter (ten—Paolo), Cornell MacNeil (bar—Simon Boccanegra), Ara Berberian (bar—Pietro), Ezio Flagello (bass—Jacopo Fiesco), Franco Iglesias (bass—Paolo), J. Levine (cnd), *(orch unknown)* *(rec live, Miami, 1970)* Legato Classics 2-▲ LCD 189-2 [ADD]
Verdi, G.:Simon Boccanegra (sels), w. R. Tebaldi (sop)—Cielo di stelle orbato; Il Doge qui; Tu qui?...Amelia! *(rec between 1956-63)* Standing Room Only ▲ SRO 8441 [ADD]
Verdi, G.:Il trovatore, w. Katia Ricciarelli (sop), Renato Bruson (bar), Zanibelli (sgr), A. Erede (cnd), Parma Teatro Regio Orch *(rec Parma, 1971)* Golden Age of Opera 2-▲ GAO 193/194

Tucker, Sophie (sgr)
Monteverdi, C.:Ritorno d'Ulisse, w. Gloria Banditelli (cta), Villanueva (sgr), A. Curtis (cnd), Sonatori de la Gioiosa Marca [I] Nuova Era ("Ancient Music" series) 3-▲ 7103/05 [DDD]

Tugarinova, Tatiana (mez)
Borodin, A.:Prince Igor, w. Elana Obraztsova (mez—Konchakovna), Tatiana Tugarinova (mez—Yaroslavna), Vladimir Atlantov (ten—Vladimir Igoryevich), Artur Eisen (bass—Vladimir Galitsky), Ivan Petrov (bass—Igor Svyatoslavich), Alexander Vedernikov (bass—Konchak), M. Ermler (cnd), Bolshoi Theater Orch, Bolshoi Theater Chorus *(rec Moscow, 1969)* Melodiya ("The Russian Opera" series) 3-▲ 74321-29346-2 [ADD]

Tuge, Teinhard (bass)
Schütz, H.:St. John Passion, w. Herta Flebbe (sop), Johannes Hoeflin (ten—Evangelist), Rolf Bössow (ten—Pilate), Gert Spierting (ten), Jakob Stämpfli (bass—Jesus), Teinhard Tuge (bass—soliloquies), W. Ehmann (cnd), Westphalia Kantorei *(rec Münster zu Herfor, Sept. 1961)* Cantate ▲ 57602 [ADD]

Tukur, U. (sgr)
Beethoven, L. van:Egmont (incidental music), w. R. Ziesak (sop), G. Albrecht (cnd), Hamburg State PO [G] Orfeo ▲ 288921 [DDD]

Tüller, Niklaus (bass)
Bach, J.S.:Cant 59, w. A. Augér (sop), H. Rilling (cnd), Stuttgart Bach Collegium, Gächinger Kantorei [G] *(rec 1976-77)* Hänssler Classic ▲ 98.886 [AAD]
Bach, J.S.:Cant 113, w. A. Augér (sop), G. Schreckenbach (cta), A. Kraus (ten), H. Rilling (cnd), Stuttgart Bach Collegium, Gächinger Kantorei Hänssler Classic ▲ 98.810 [ADD]
Bach, J.S.:Cant 122, w. A. Augér (sop), G. Schreckenbach (cta), A. Kraus (ten), H. Rilling (cnd), Stuttgart Bach Collegium, Frankfurt Kantorei [G] *(rec Feb 1972)* Hänssler Classic ▲ 98.826 [AAD]
Bach, J.S.:Cant 136, w. H. Watts (cta), K. Equiluz (ten), H. Rilling (cnd), Stuttgart Bach Collegium, Gächinger Kantorei Hänssler Classic ▲ 98.806 [AAD]
Bach, J.S.:Cant 163, w. A. Augér (sop), H. Watts (cta), A. Kraus (ten), H. Rilling (cnd), Stuttgart Bach Collegium, Gächinger Kantorei [G] *(rec 1976 & 1977)* Hänssler Classic ▲ 98.820 [AAD]
Bach, J.S.:Cant 167, w. K. Graf (sop), H. Gardow (sop), A. Kraus (ten), H. Rilling (cnd), Stuttgart Bach Collegium, Remembrance Florid Church Chorus Hänssler Classic ▲ 98.803 [AAD]
Bach, J.S.:Cant 190, w. H. Watts (cta), K. Equiluz (ten), H. Rilling (cnd), Stuttgart Bach Collegium, Gächinger Kantorei [G] Hänssler Classic ▲ 98.870 [AAD]
Bach, J.S.:Cant 196, w. D. Soffel (cta), A. Baldin (ten), H. Rilling (cnd), Bach Ensemble *(rec Jan 1975)* Hänssler Classic ▲ 98.828 [AAD]
Moeschinger, A.:Cant, w. F. Lang (ten), Bern Ad Hoc Ensemble—Prelude & Dialogue [F] Grammont ▲ CTSP 1-2 [ADD]
Moser, R.:Wortabend, w. K. Graf (sop), M. Venzago (cnd), Basel RSO Soloists [G] Grammont ▲ CTSP 12-2 [ADD]
Schoeck, O.:Notturno, w. Bern String Quartet Accord ▲ ACD 220772 [AAD]
Schoeck, O.:Songs (comp), w. C. Keller (pno)—16 songs *(rec March 1992)* Jecklin-Disco ▲ JD 673-2 [DDD]
Schoeck, O.:Songs (misc), w. Christoph Keller (pno)—Eichendorff Songs, Op. 20/1-14 Accord ▲ ACD 220772 [AAD]

Tullio, Eileen di (sop)
The Art of Eileen di Tullio Legato Classics ▲ LCD 196-1

Tumagian, Eduard (bar)
Brahms, J.:Ein Deutsches Requiem, w. M. Gauci (sop), A. Rahbari (cnd), Czech-Slovak RSO Bratislava, Slovak Phil Chorus *(rec June 1992)* Naxos ▲ 8.550213 [DDD]
Duets & Arias from Italian Operas, w. G. Aragall (ten), A. Rahbari (cnd), Czech-Slovak RSO Bratislava Naxos ▲ 8.550684 [DDD]
Puccini, G.:Madama Butterfly, w. Eugenia Moldoveanu (sop—Madama Butterfly), Mihaela Agachi (mez—Suzuki), Corina Circa (mez—Kate Pinkerton), Emil Gherman (ten—B.F. Pinkerton), Stefan Popescu (ten—Goro), Ioan Soanea (bar—The Bonze/Yakuside), Eduard Tumageanian (bar—Sharpless), Alexandru Kopeczi (bass—Prince Yamadori), Mircea Moisa (bass—Commissioner), P. Popescu (cnd), Satu Mare PO, Cluj-Napoca Phil Chorus *(rec 1979)* Vox Box 2-▲ CDX 5155
Verdi, G.:Rigoletto, w. A. Ferrarini (sop), Y. Ramiro (ten), J. Spaček (bar), A. Rahbari (cnd), Czech-Slovak RSO Bratislava, Slovak Phil Chorus [I] Naxos 2-▲ 8.660013/14 [DDD]

Tunell, Lisa (cta)
Beethoven, L. van:Sym 9, "Choral Sym", w. H. Schymberg (sop), G. Bäckelin (ten), S. Björling (bar), W. Furtwängler (cnd), Stockholm Concert Society Orch *(rec Dec. 1, 1943)* Music & Arts ▲ CD 774 [AAD]
Beethoven, L. van:Sym 9, "Choral Sym", w. G. Bckelin (ten), S. Björling (bass), W. Furtwängler (cnd), Stockholm PO *(rec Dec. 1, 1943)* Music & Arts ▲ CD 2002 [AAD]

Tung, Y. S. (sgr)
Rodgers, R.:Flower Drum Song, w. K. Scott (sgr), I. Shepley (sgr), Y. Saki (sgr), T. Hebert (sgr) [1960 London cast] Angel ▲ ZDM 89953

Turati, Giancarlo (ten)
Bellini, V.:Norma, w. Margherita Rinaldi (sop—Adalgisa), Renata Scotto (sop—Norma), Giuseppina Arista (mez—Clotilde), Ermanno Mauro (ten—Pollione), Giancarlo Turati (ten—Flavio), Agostino Ferrin (bass—Oroveso), R. Muti (cnd), Florence Teatro Comunale Orch, Florence Teatro Comunale Chorus *(rec Florence, Dec 19, 1978)* Legato Classics 2-▲ LCD 203-2

Türk, Gerd (ten)
Bach, J.S.:St. John Passion, w. B. Schlick (sop), K. Wessel (alto), G. de Mey (ten), K. Mertens (b-bar), P. Kooy (bass), T. Koopman (cnd), Amsterdam Baroque Orch, Netherlands Bach Society Choir Erato 2-▲ 94675-2
Barbarino, B.:Sacred Music, w. R. Wilson (cnd), Musica Fiata—O sacrum convivium *(rec St. Osdag Church, Mandelsloh, Germany, June 11-15, 1994)* Sony Classical ("Vivarte" series) 2-▲ S2K 66254 [DDD]
Biber, H. von:Chi la dura la vince, w. Barbara Schlick (sop), Gotthold Schwarz (bass), Xenia Meijer (sgr), W. Brunner (cnd), Salzburg Hofmusik CPO 3-▲ CPO 999258 [DDD]
Caldara, A.:Maddalena ai Piedi di Cristo, w. Maria Cristina Kiehr (sop), Rosa Dominguez (sop), Bernarda Fink (cta), Andreas Scholl (ct), Ulrich Messthaler (bass), R. Jacobs (cnd), Schola Cantorum Basiliensis Instrumental Ensemble Harmonia Mundi France 2-▲ HMC 905221.22
Caldara, A.:Stabat Mater, w. Monika Frimmer (sop), Gloria Banditelli (mez), Peter Frank (bass), L. Rovatkay (cnd), Capella Agostino Steffani, Westphalia Kantorei EMI Classics ▲ CDC 54845
Cavalli, P.F.:Vespero della beata Vergine Maria, w. Barbara Borden (sop), Emily van Evera (sop), Markus Brutscher (ten), Mark Padmore (ten), Rodrigo del Pozo (ten), Harry van der Kamp (bass), Peter Zimpel (sgr), Bruce Dickey (sackbut), Charles Toet (sackbut), Concerto Palatino, Schola Cantorum Basiliensis Harmonia Mundi France ("Documenta" series) 2-▲ HMC 905219/20
Gabrieli, G.:Music of, w. David Cordier (alt), Wilfried Jochens (ten), Rufus Müller (ten), Harry van der Kamp (bass), R. Wilson (cnd), Musica Fiata, La Capella Ducale—Toccata [arr Wilson]; Buccinate in neomenia tuba à 19; Canzon XVII à 12; Dulcis Jesu patris imago [Son con voce à 20]; Timor et remor à 6; Son con 3 Vns; Son XIX à 15; In ecclesiis à 14; Canzon V à 7; Jubilate Deo à 10; Son XVIII à 14; Cantate Domino à 8; Canzon primi toni à 10; Misericordia tua Domine à 12; Canzon X à 8; Toccata primi toni; Magnificat à 33 [reconstructed by Wilson]; Benedictus es Dominus à 8 *(rec St. Osdag Church, Mandelsloh, Germany, June 11-15, 1994)* Sony Classical ("Vivarte" series) 2-▲ S2K 66254 [DDD]
Grandi, A.:Sacred Music, w. David Cordier (alt), Wilfried Jochens (ten), Rufus Müller (ten), Harry van der Kamp (bass), R. Wilson (cnd), Musica Fiata, La Capella Ducale—Heu mihi [Dialogo à 4]; O quam tu pulchra es; Cantemus Domino; Salvum me fac, Deus [Basso solo] *(rec St. Osdag Church, Mandelsloh, Germany, June 11-15, 1994)* Sony Classical ("Vivarte" series) 2-▲ S2K 66254 [DDD]
Mangold, C.A.:Abraham, w. Monika Frimmer (sop), Georg Mechthild (mez), B Gärtner (ten), Giles Cachemaille (bar), Philadelphia Orch, Darmstadt Concert Choir Christophorus 2-▲ 77172
Mozart, W.A.:Requiem, w. M. Figueras (sop), C. Schubert (alt), J. Schreckenberger (bass), J. Savall (cnd), La Capella Reial de Catalunya, Le Concert des Nations Astrée ▲ E 8759
Pergolesi, G.B.:Stabat mater, w. Monika Frimmer (sop), Gloria Banditelli (mez), Peter Frank (bass), L. Rovatkay (cnd), Capella Agostino Steffani, Westphalia Kantorei EMI Classics ▲ CDC 54845
Vivaldi, A.:Son al St. Sepolcro, w. Monika Frimmer (sop), Gloria Banditelli (mez), Peter Frank (bass), L. Rovatkay (cnd), Capella Agostino Steffani, Westphalia Kantorei EMI Classics ▲ CDC 54845

Turner, Claramae (mez)
Berlin, I.:Annie Get Your Gun, w. E. Merman (sgr), R. Middleton (sgr), L. Bibb (sgr), K. Carnes (sgr), J. Garth (sgr), R. Lenn (sgr), J. Blackton (cnd) [1946 cast] MCA Classics ▲ MCAD 10047 [AAD] ■ MCAC 10047
Ponchielli, A.:La Gioconda (sels), w. Z. Milanov (sop), R. Turrini (sgr), C. Bardelli (bar), W. Herbert (cnd), *(orch & chorus unknown)*—abridged:the part of Goiconda [Milanov] is presented complete [I] *(rec live, New Orleans, 11/5/53)* Standing Room Only ▲ SRO 814-1 [ADD]
Rodgers, R.:Carousel, w. Gordon MacRae (sgr), S. Jones (sgr), C. Mitchell (sgr), B. Ruick (sgr), R. Rounseville (sgr) *(rec 1956)* Broadway Angel ▲ ZDM 64692 ■ EG 64692

Turner, Eva (sop)
Hardelot, G. d':Songs—Because; Sometimes in My Dreams Claremont ▲ CDGSE 785066
Ponchielli, A.:La Gioconda (sels), w. L. Molajoli (cnd), *(orch unknown)*—Suicidio!; Già ti veggo [w. Erminia Rubadi (mez), Fernandino Ciniselli (ten), Leone Paci (bar), Bruno Carmazzi (bass), La Scala Chorus] Claremont ▲ CDGSE 785066

Turner, Eva (sop) (cont.)
Puccini, G.:Arias—In questa reggia [from Turandot]; Vissi d'arte [from Tosca] [both w. Lorenzo Molajoli (cnd)]; Entrance of Butterfly [from Madama Butterfly; w. George Hancock (bar)]; In questa reggia [from Turandot; w. Dino Borgioli (ten)] Claremont ▲ CDGSE 785066
Vaughan Williams, R.:Serenade to Music, w. I. Baillie (sop), E. Suddaby (sop), S. Allen (sop), M. Balfour (cta), A. Desmond (cta), M. Brunskill (cta), M. Jarred (cta), H. Nash (ten), W. Widdop (ten), P. Jones (ten), F. Titterton (ten), R. Henderson (bass), R. Easton (bass), H. Williams (bass), N. Allin (bass), H. J. Wood (cnd), BBC SO Dutton Laboratories ▲ CDAX 8004 [ADD]
Vaughan Williams, R.:Serenade to Music, w. I. Baillie (sop), E. Suddaby (sop), S. Allen (sop), M. Balfour (cta), A. Desmond (cta), M. Brunskill (cta), M. Jarred (cta), H. Nash (ten), W. Widdop (ten), P. Jones (ten), F. Titterton (ten), R. Henderson (bass), R. Easton (bass), H. Williams (bass), N. Allin (bass), H. Wood (cnd), BBC SO [E] *(rec 10/15/38)* Pearl ▲ GEMMCD 9342 (m) [AAD]
Vaughan Williams, R.:Serenade to Music, w. Isobel Baillie (sop), Lilian Stiles-Allen (sop), Elsie Suddaby (sop), Margaret Balfour (cta), Muriel Brunskill (cta), Astra Desmond (cta), Mary Jarred (cta), Parry Jones (ten), Heddle Nash (ten), Frank Titterton (ten), Walter Widdop (ten), Roy Henderson (bar), Harold Williams (bar), Norman Allin (bass), Robert Easton (bass), H. Wood (cnd), BBC SO *(rec Abbey Road, Oct 15, 1938)* Claremont ▲ CDGSE 785066
Verdi, G.:Aida (sels), w. L. Molajoli (cnd), *(orch unknown)*—Ritorna vincitor [2 versions]; Qui Radames verrà...O patria mia; Gloria all' Egitto [w. Erminia Rubadi (mez), Fernandino Ciniselli (ten), Leone Paci (bar), Bruno Carmazzi (bass), La Scala Chorus] Claremont ▲ CDGSE 785066

Turner, Jane (mez)
Wagner, R.:Götterdämmerung, w. A. Evans (sop—Brünnhilde), E.-M. Bundschuh (sop—Gutrune), H. Leidland (sop—Woglinde), A. Küttenbaum (sop—Wellgunde), W. Meier (mez—Waltraute), B. Svendén (mez—1st Norn), *(cnd & orch unknown)* Teldec 4-▲ 4509-94194-2 [DDD]

Turner, Paul (bass)
Haydn, J.:Stabat Mater, w. R. Lampo (sop), S. Zaramella (alt), V. Martino (ten), D. Ferrari (cnd), Milan Sinfonietta, Concentus Musicae Antiquae Vocal Group Nuova Era ▲ NUO 7170 [DDD]

Turner, Richard (ten)
Voices That Are Gone:Songs from Victorian America, w. Anne Beetem (pno) Corvus ▲ RT 1196

Turner-Butler (alt)
Pergolesi, G.B.:Stabat mater, w. Tynes (sop), M. Bruni (cnd), Prague CO, Czech Phil Chorus [L] *(rec 1968)* Supraphon Collection ▲ 11 0620-2 [ADD]

Turp, André (ten)
Berlioz, H.:La Damnation de Faust, w. Regine Crespin (sop), Michelle Roux (bar), P. Monteux (cnd), London SO *(rec live, Mar 1962)* Music & Arts 2-▲ CD 928
Berlioz, H.:Roméo et Juliette, w. R. Resnik (mez), J. Ward (bar), P. Monteux (cnd), London SO, London Sym Chorus [F] MCA Classics 2-▲ MCAD2-9805
Offenbach, J.:Les Contes d'Hoffmann, w. Beverly Sills (sop—Olympia/Giulietta/Antonia/Stella), Edith Evans (mez—Nicklausse/Mother's Voice), Michael Devlin (ten—Spalanzani), André Turp (ten—Hoffmann), Luigi Vellucci (ten—Andrès/Cochenille/Pitichinaccio/Frantz), Donald Bernard (bar—Luther/Schlemil), Norman Treigle (bass—Lindorf/Coppélius/Dapertutto/Dr. Miracle), John West (bass—Crespel), Alton Brim (sgr—Nathanaël), Rodney Hall (sgr—Hermann), K. Andersson (cnd), New Orleans Opera Orch, New Orleans Opera Chorus *(rec Feb 27, 1964)* VAI Audio 2-▲ VAIA 1121-2 [ADD]
Verdi, G.:Falstaff, w. Vivian Della Chiesa (sop—Alice), Audrey Schuh (sop—Nannetta), Lizabeth Pritchett (mez—Quickly), Evelyn Sachs (mez—Meg), André Turp (ten—Fenton), Virginio Assandri (ten—Caius), Luigi Vellucci (ten—Bardolfo), Leonard Warren (bar—Falstaff), Richard Torigi (bar—Ford), R. Cellini (cnd), New Orleans Opera Orch, New Orleans Opera Chorus *(rec live, May 5, 1956)* VAI Audio 2-▲ VAIA 1056-2
Verdi, G.:Macbeth, w. Amy Shuard (sop—Lady Macbeth), Noreen Berry (mez—Lady-in-waiting), John Dobson (ten—Malcolm), André Turp (ten—Macduff), Tito Gobbi (bar—Macbeth), Edgar Boniface (bass—Servant), Rydderch Davies (bass—Doctor), Forbes Robinson (bass—Banco), Jean Holmes (sgr—Apparition), Celia Penny (sgr—Apparition), Glynne Thomas (sgr—Apparition), Brian Wrigt (sgr—Araldo), F. Molinari-Pradelli (cnd), Royal Opera House Orch, Royal Opera House Chorus Covent Garden *(rec London, Apr 8, 1960)* Bella Voce 2-▲ 7203 [AAD]

Turrini, R. (sgr)
Ponchielli, A.:La Gioconda (sels), w. Z. Milanov (sop), C. Turner (mez), C. Bardelli (bar), W. Herbert (cnd), *(orch & chorus unknown)*—abridged:the part of Goiconda [Milanov] is presented complete [I] *(rec live, New Orleans, 11/5/53)* Standing Room Only ▲ SRO 814-1 [ADD]

Tütler, N. (bass)
Bach, J.S.:Cant 23, w. A. Augér (sop), H. Watts (cta), A. Baldin (ten), H. Rilling (cnd), Stuttgart Bach Collegium, Gächinger Kantorei [G] *(rec 1977)* Hänssler Classic ▲ 98.879 [AAD]
Bach, J.S.:Cant 181, w. A. Augér (sop), G. Schnaut (mez), G. Schreckenbach (cta), K. Equiluz (ten), H. Rilling (cnd), Stuttgart Bach Collegium, Gächinger Kantorei [G] *(rec 1981)* Hänssler Classic ▲ 98.878 [AAD]

Tweed, Pauline (sgr)
Waydith, G. von:Jesus before Herod, w. Michael Best (ten—Jappeticus), Christopher Lindbloom (sgr—Philippo/Herod), Eileen Moss (sgr—Pabula), Vincent Russo (sgr—Pabo), Stephen A. Scot-Shepherd (sgr—Luke the Evangelist), Pauline Tweed (sgr—1st & 2nd girls), P. Erös (cnd), San Diego SO, San Diego Master Chorale *(rec 1979)* VAI Audio 2-▲ VAIA 1095-2 [ADD]

Tyeska, James (bar)
Flowering of Vocal Music in America, 1767-1823, w. Susan Belling (sop), Cynthia Clarey (sop), Barbara Wallace (sop), Debra Vanderlinde (sop), D'Anna Fortunato (mez), Evelyn Petros (mez), Charles Bressler (ten), Richard Anderson (bar), Joseph McKee (bass), Cynthia Otis (hp), Leonard Rav New World ▲ 80467-2

Tyler, J. (sgr)
Rodgers, R.:Pipe Dream, w. H. Traubel (sop), W. Johnson (sgr) [1955 Broadway cast] RCA ▲ 09026-61481-2 ■ 09026-61481-4

Tynes (sop)
Pergolesi, G.B.:Stabat mater, w. Turner-Butler (alt), M. Bruni (cnd), Prague CO, Czech Phil Chorus [L] *(rec 1968)* Supraphon Collection ▲ 11 0620-2 [ADD]

Tyrén, Arne (bass)
Verdi, G.:Rigoletto, w. M. Hallin (sop), B. Nordin (sop), K. Meyer (mez), B. Ericson (mez), Kjellgren (mez), N. Gedda (ten), O. Sivall (ten), H. Hasslo (bar), I. Wixell (bar), B. Alstergård (bar), S. Ehrling (cnd), Stockholm Royal Opera House Orch, Stockholm Royal Opera Chorus *(rec live Jan. 18, 1959)* BIS ▲ CD 296 [AAD]

Tzatcheva, Roumiana (alt)
Bach, J.S.:Christmas Oratorio, w. Ludmila Hadjieva (sop), Lubomir Diacovski (ten), Plamen Hidjov (bass), Tabakov, Kralev (cnd), Madrigal Chamber Ensemble, Sofia CO Soloists Pentagon 3-▲ 302 [DDD]

Ucelay, Miriam (mez)
Meyerbeer, G.:L'Africiane, w. Montserrat Caballe (sop—Selika), Christine Weidinger (sop—Inez), Miriam Ucelay (mez—Anna), Placido Domingo (ten—Vasco de Gama), Guillermo Sarabia (bar—Nelusko), Juan Thomas (b-bar—High Priest of Brahma), Dimiter Petkov (bass—Don Pedro), Juan Pons (bass—Don Diego), Eduardo Soto (bass—Grand Inquisitor), A. de Almeida (cnd), Barcelona Teatro Liceo Orch, Barcelona Gran Teatro de Liceo Chorus *(rec Barcelona, Nov 27, 1977)* Legato Classics 2-▲ LCD 208-2 [ADD]

Ude, Armin (ten)
Brahms, J.:Liebeslieder Waltzes SATB, w. Barbara Hoene (sop), Gisela Pohl (alt), Siegfried Lorenz (bar), Klaus Bässler (pno), Dieter Zechlin (pno), W.-D. Hauschild (cnd), Berlin RSO Berlin Classics ▲ BER 9269
Brahms, J.:Neue Liebeslieder Waltzes, w. Barbara Hoene (sop), Gisela Pohl (alt), Siegfried Lorenz (bar), Klaus Bässler (pno), Dieter Zechlin (pno), W.-D. Hauschild (cnd), Berlin RSO Berlin Classics ▲ BER 9269
Saint-Saëns, C.:Oratorio de Noël, w. Ute Selbig (sop), Elisabeth Wilke (mez), Annette Markert (cta), Egbert Junghans (bar), Jutta Zoff (hp), Michael-Christfield Winkler (org), M. Flämig (cnd), Dresden PO, Dresden Kreuz Choir *(rec Dresden, Mar & Apr 1987)* Capriccio ▲ 10216 [DDD]

Udovich, Lucille (sop)
Paisiello, G.:Fedra, w. O. Beggiato (sop), R. Mattioli (sop), A. Tuccari (sop), A. Lazzari (ten), A. Questa (cnd), Milan RAI SO, Milan RAI Chorus *(rec 1958)* Memories 2-▲ MEM 4502 [AAD]

Udovich, Lucille (sop) (cont.)
Puccini, G.:Turandot (sels), w. L. Gencer (sop), F. Corelli (ten), O. de Fabritiis (cnd), Naples Teatro San Carlo Orch, Naples Teatro San Carlo Chorus—Signore ascolta; Il nome che cercate..tu che di gel sei cinta *(rec Jan. 13, 1962)* Golden Age of Opera 2-▲ GAO 143/44 [ADD]
Spontini, G.:Agnes von Hohensaufen, w. D. Dow (sop), F. Corelli (ten), A. Colzani (bar), G. Guelfi (bar), V. Gui (cnd), Florence Maggio Musicale Orch, Florence Maggio Musicale Chorus [I] *(rec live 5/9/54)* Melodram 2-▲ MEL 27055 (m) [AAD]

Uecker, Korliss (sop)
Schumann, C.:Songs, w. J. Polk (pno)—19 lieder—Am Strand; Volkslied; Er ist gekommen in Sturm und Regen; Liebst du um Schönheit; Warum willst du and're fragen; Ich stand in dunklen Träumen; Sie liebten sich beide; Liebeszauber; Der Mond kommt still gegangen; Ich hab' in deinem Auge; Die stille Lotosblume; Loreley; O weh des Scheidens; Beim Abscheid; Was weinst du, Blümlein; An einem lichten Morgen; Geheimes Flüstern hier und dort; Das ist ein Tag, der klingen mag; Das Veilchen [G] Arabesque ▲ Z 6624 [DDD]

Ugrinov, Emil (bar)
Rimsky-Korsakov, N.:Golden Cockerel, w. Yavora Stoilova (sop—Golden Cockerel), Elena Stoyanova (sop—Queen), Evgenia Babacheva (mez—Amelfa), Lyubomir Bodourov (ten—Prince), Lyubomir Dyakovski (ten—Astrologer), Emil Ugrinov (bar—Afron), Nikolai Stoilov (bass—Tsar), Kosta Videv (bass—Polkan), D. Manolov (cnd), Sofia National Opera Orch, Sofia National Opera Chorus *(rec Sofia, 1985)* Capriccio 2-▲ 10760/61 [DDD]

Uhde, Hermann (bar)
Mussorgsky, M.:Boris Godunov, w. Martha Mödl (sop—Marina Mniszek), Lotte Schädle (sop—Xenia), Dorothea Siebert (mez—Fyodor), Hertha Töpper (mez—Xenia's wet-nurs), Karl Hermann Bennert (Boyer Khrushchyov), Lorenz Fehenberger (ten—Prince Shuysky), Hans Hopf (ten—Grigory), Karl Ostertag (ten—Missail), Hans Hotter (b-bar—Boris Godunov), Hermann Uhde (bar—Andrey Shchelkalov), Kurt Böhme (bass—Varlaam), Kim Borg (bass—Pimen), Kieth Engen (bass—Lewicki), Adolf Keil (bass—Nikitich), Benno Kusche (bar—Rangoni), Heinz Maria Linz (bass—Czernikowski), E. Jochum (cnd), Bavarian RSO, Bavarian Radio Chorus *(rec Munich, May 1957)* Myto 3-▲ MCD 953131
Orff, C.:Antigonae, w. Christel Goltz (sop), Paul Kuen (ten), Karl Ostertag (ten), Benno Kusche (bar), N. Barth (bar), G. Solti (cnd), Bavarian State Opera Orch, Bavarian State Opera Chorus *(rec Prinzregententheater, Jan. 12, 1951)* Orfeo d'or 2-▲ 407952
Strauss, R.:Die ägyptische Helena, w. Annelies Kupper (sop—Aithra), Leonie Rysanek (sop—Helena), Ira Malaniuk (cta—Omniscient Seashell), Bernd Aldenhoff (ten—Menelas), Richard Holm (ten—Da-ud), Hermann Uhde (bar—Altair), J. Keilberth (cnd), Bavarian State Opera Orch, Bavarian State Opera Chorus *(rec Munich Opera Festival, Prince Regent Theater, Aug 10, 1956)* Orfeo d'or 2-▲ 424962
Strauss, R.:Die ägyptische Helena, w. L. Rysanek (sop), A. Kupper (sop), B. Aldenhoff (ten), J. Keilberth (cnd), Bavarian State Opera Orch, Bavarian State Opera Chorus [G] *(rec live, Munich, 8/27/56)* Melodram 2-▲ MEL 27066 (m) [AAD]
Wagner, R.:Der fliegende Holländer, w. A. Varnay (sop), W. Windgassen (ten), L. Weber (bass), H. Knappertsbusch (cnd), Bayreuth Festival Orch, Bayreuth Festival Chorus [G] *(rec live)* Arkadia 2-▲ 421 [ADD]
Wagner, R.:Götterdämmerung, w. Birgit Nilsson (sop—Brünnhilde), Leonie Rysanek (sop—Gutrune), Gerda Sommerschuh (sop—Woglinde), Elisabeth Lindermeier (sop—Wellgunde), Ruth Michaelis (sop—Flohilde), Marianne Schech (sop—Dritte Norne), Ira Malaniuk (mez—Waltraute), Irmgarth Barth (mez—Erste Norne), Hertha Töpper (mez—Zweite Norne), Bernd Aldenhoff (ten—Siegfried), Hermann Uhde (bar—Gunther), Gottlob Frick (bass—Hagen), H. Knappertsbusch (cnd), Bavarian State Opera Orch, Bavarian State Opera Chorus *(rec live, Prinzregententheater, Sept. 1, 1955)* Orfeo 4-▲ 356944 (m)
Wagner, R.:Götterdämmerung (sels), w. A. Varnay (sop), E. Grümmer (sop), B. Aldenhoff (ten), G. Frick (bass), J. Greindl (bass), H. Knappertsbusch (cnd), Bavarian State Opera Orch, Bayreuth Festival Orch, Bavarian State Opera Chorus, Bayreuth Festival Chorus [G] *(rec live 1955 & 1957)* Melodram 4-▲ MEL 46106 (m) [AAD]
Wagner, R.:Lohengrin, w. E. Steber (sop), A. Varnay (sop), W. Windgassen (ten), J. Greindl (bass), J. Keilberth (cnd), Bayreuth Festival Orch, Bayreuth Festival Chorus *(rec live, Bayreuth Festival, 1953)* Teldec ("Historic" series) 4-▲ 93674
Wagner, R.:Lohengrin, w. B. Nilsson (sop), A. Varnay (sop), W. Windgassen (ten), E. Jochum (cnd), Bayreuth Festival Orch, Bayreuth Festival Chorus *(rec live, Bayreuth 1954)* Melodram 3-▲ MEL 36104
Wagner, R.:Der Ring des Nibelungen, w. Gré Brouwenstein (sop—Freia/Sieglinde), Ilse Hollweg (sop—Waldvogel), Gerda Lammers (sop—Ortlinde), Paula Lenchner (sop—Wellgunde/Gerhilde), Hilde Scheppan (sop—Helmwige), Astrid Varnay (sop—Brünnilde/3rd Norn), Lore Wissmann (sop—Woglinde), Maria von Ilosvay (mez—Flosshilde/Schwertleite/2nd Norn), Louise Charlotte Kamps (mez—Siegrune), Jean Madeira (mez—Erda/Rossweisse/1st Norn), Georgine van Milinkovic (mez—Fricka/Grimgerde), Elisabeth Schärtel (mez—Waltraute), Paul Kuën (ten—Mime), Ludwig Suthaus (ten—Loge), Josef Traxel (ten—Froh), Wolfgang Windgassen (ten—Siegmund/Siegfried), Alfons Herwig (bar—Donner), Hermann Uhde (bar—Gunther), Hans Hotter (b-bar—Wotan), Gustav Neidlinger (b-bar—Alberich), Josef Greindl (bass—Fasolt/Hunding/Hagen), Arnold van Mill (bass—Fafner), H. Knappertsbusch (cnd), Bayreuth Festival Orch, Bayreuth Festival Chorus *(rec live, Bayreuth, Aug 13-17, 1956)* Golden Melodram 14-▲ GM 1.001 [ADD]

Uherek, Jiří (sgr)
Bruckner, A.:Mass 3, w. Dagmar Masková (sgr), Vladimír Nacházel (sgr), Jiří Novotný (sgr), Jiří Seiler (sgr), Eva Zbytovská (sgr), Jan Votava (trbn), Josef Kšica (org), Josef Pancík (cnd), Prague Chamber Choir Orfeo ▲ 327 951 [DDD]
Bruckner, A.:Motets, w. Dagmar Masková (sgr), Vladimír Nacházel (sgr), Jiří Novotný (sgr), Jiří Seiler (sgr), Eva Zbytovská (sgr), Jan Votava (trbn), Josef Kšica (org), Josef Pancík (cnd), Prague Chamber Choir—Locus iste; Afferentur regi; Ave Maria (2); Pange lingua; Pange lingua (phrygisch); Tantum ergo (2); Libera me; Os iusti; Virga jesse; Vexilla regis; Christus factus est; Tota pulchra es Maria; Ecce sacerdos magnus Orfeo ▲ 327 951 [DDD]

Uhl, Fritz (ten)
Wagner, R.:Der Ring des Nibelungen, w. Liselotte Becker-Egner (sop—Woglinde/Ortlinde/Wellgunde), Angelika Berger (sop—Wellgunde/Waltraute), Siw Ericsdotter (sop—Norn 3), Heidemaria Ferch (sop—Freia/Gerhilde), Bella Jasper (sop—Helmwige/Waldvogel/Woglinde), Ditha Sommer (sop—Sieglinde/Gutrune), Ursula Boese (mez—Erda), Ruth Hesse (mez—Fricka), Nadezda Kniplová (mez—Brünnhilde), Margit Kobeck (mez—Schwertleite/Norn 2), Hilde Rosner (mez—Flosshilde/Siegrunde), Erica Schubert (mez—Grimgerde/Flosshilde), Ingrid Göritz (cta—Rossweisse/Norn 1), Herbert Doussant (ten—Froh), Herold Kraus (ten—Mime), Gerald McKee (ten—Siegmund/Siegfried), Fritz Uhl (ten—Loge), Rudolf Knoll (bar—Gunther/Donner), Rolf Polke (bass-bar—Wotan/Wanderer), Rolf Kühne (bass—Alberich), Takao Okamura (bass—Fafner), Otto von Rohr (bass—Hagen/Fasolt/Hunding), H. Swarowsky (cnd), Czech PO, Prague National Theater Orch *(rec June 3 & 5, July 26-31, A)* Weltbild Classics 14-▲ 703769 [ADD]

Uhle, H.-M. (ten)
Mauersberger, R.:St. Luke, w. A. Bassenge (alt), Thüringian Academic Sing Circle *(rec May 24-26, 1991)* Thorofon ▲ CTH 2127 [DDD]
Wagner, R.:Parsifal, w. C. Ludwig (mez), E. Höngen (cta), H. Hotter (b-bar), T. Franc (bass), W. Berry (bass), H. von Karajan (cnd), Vienna State Opera Orch, Vienna State Opera Chorus [G] *(rec live 4/1/61)* Arkadia 3-▲ 219 (m) [ADD]
Wagner, R.:Tristan und Isolde, w. B. Nilsson (sop), R. Resnik (mez), R. Krause (ten), A. van Mill (bass), G. Solti (cnd), Vienna PO [G] London ("Grand Opera" series) 4-▲ 430234-2 [ADD]

Uhlmann, Heidi (alt)
Kraft, Walter:Christus, w. Anna Senn-Dähler (sop), Barbara Künzler (sop), Barbara Sutter (sop), Christine Guy (alt), Daniel Zellweger (alt), Matthias Senn (ten), Mikoto Usami (ten), Wolfgang Pailer (bass), Heinz Suter (bass), Klaus Knall (cnd), Evangelische Singgemeinde Choirs *(rec Ostdorf bei Balingen, Oct. 8-11, 1986)* Cantate 2-▲ 58004 [DDD]

Uhrmacher, Hildegard (sop)
Dittersdorf, K.D. von:Doctor und Apotheker, w. Hildegard Uhrmacher (sop—Leonore), Donna Woodward (sop—Rosalia), Waltraud Meier (mez—Claudia), Martin Finke (ten—Sichel), Frieder Lang (ten—Gotthold), Alois Perl (ten—Gallus), Gerhard Unger (ten—Sturmwald), Thomas Pfeiffer (bar—Police Commisioner), Wolfgang Schöne (bar—Krautmann), Harald Stamm (bass—Stössel), J. Lockhart (cnd), Rhine State PO Bayer 2-▲ BR 100 238/39 [DDD]

Ulbrich, Andrea (mez)
Mendelssohn, F.:Die Hochzeit des Camacho, w. R. Hofman (sop—Quiteria), A. Ulbrich (mez—Lucinda), S. Weir (ten—Basilio), H. Rhys-Evans (ten—Vivaldo), N. van der Meel (ten—Camacho), W. Wild (bar—Carrasco), U. Malmberg (bass—Sancho Panza), U. Cold (bass—Don Quixote), J. van Immerseel (cnd), Anima Eterna Orch, Aachen Boys Choir, Chor Modus Novus [G] *(rec Sept. 19–22, 1992)* Channel Classics 2-▲ CCS 5593 [DDD]

Ulfung, Ragnar (ten)
Verdi, G.:Un ballo in maschera (sels), w. Erik Saeden (bar), Lovberg (sgr), C. Savina (cnd), Stockholm Royal Opera House Orch—Act III excerpts *(rec 1966)* Arkadia 2-▲ 488

Ulmann, Gisela (sgr)
Wagner, R.:Lohengrin, w. Sharon Sweet (sop—Elsa), Eva Marton (sop—Ortrud), Ben Heppner (ten—Lohengrin), Anton Rosner (ten—Nobleman), Heinrich Weber (ten—Nobleman), Jan-Hendrik Rootering (bar—Heinrich der Vögler), Sergei Leiferkus (bar—Friedrich von Telramund), Bryn Terfel (b-bar—King's Herald), Barbara Fleckenstein (sgr—Page), Atsuko Suzuki (sgr—Page), Gisela Ulmann (sgr—Page), Marion Rambausek (sgr—Page), Dankwart Siegele (sgr—Nobleman), Jürgen Weiss (sgr—Nobleman), C. Davis (cnd), Bavarian SO, Bavarian State Opera Chorus, Bavarian Radio Chorus *(rec Residenz Herkulessaal, Munich, May 14–28, 1994)* RCA Red Seal 3-▲ 09026-62646-2 [DDD]
Wagner, R.:Lohengrin (sels), w. Eva Marton (sop—Ortrud), Sharon Sweet (sop—Elsa von Brabant), Barbara Fleckenstein (sgr—Page), Marion Rambausek (sgr—Page), Atsuko Suzuki (sgr—Page), Gisela Ulmann (sgr—Page), Ben Heppner (ten—Lohengrin), Anton Rosner (ten—Nobleman), Heinrich Weber (ten—Nobleman), Sergei Leiferkus (bar—Friedrich von Telramund), Bryn Terfel (b-bar—King's Herald), Jan-Hendrik Rootering (bass—Henry the Fowler), Dankwart Siegele (sgr—Nobleman), Jürgen Weiss (sgr—Nobleman), C. Davis (cnd), Bavarian RSO, Michael Gläser (cnd), Udo Mehrpohl (cnd), Bavarian Radio Chorus, Bavarian State Opera Chorus—Seht! Seht! [from Act 1, Scene 2]; Nun sei bedankt, mein lieber Schwan!; Wenn ich im Kampfe für dich siege; Welch holde Wunder muss ich sehen?; Nun höret mich und achtet wohl; Durch Gottes Sieg ist jetzt dein Leben mein [all from Act 1, Scene 3]; Treulich geführt ziehet dahin [from Act 3, Scene 1]; Wie hehr erkenn' ich unsrer Liebe Wesen!; Höchstes Vertrau'n hast du mir schon zu danken; Weh' nun ist all' unser Glück dahin! [all from Act 3, Scene 2]; In fernem Land, unnahbar euren Schritten [from Act 3, Scene 3] *(rec Munich, Mar 14–28, 1994)* RCA Red Seal ▲ 09026-68239-2 [DDD]

Ulrich, Emilie (sop)
Vilhelm Herold, w. Vilhelm Herold (ten), Johanne Brun (sop), Helge Nissen (b-bar) Nimbus ("Prima Voce" series) ▲ NI 7880 [ADD]

Umeki, M. (sgr)
Rodgers, R.:Flower Drum Song, w. P. Suzuki (sgr), J. Hall (sgr) [1958 cast] Columbia ▲ CK 02009 ■ JST 02009

Unander-Scharin, Carl (ten)
The Royal Court of the Vasa Kings, 1523–1611, w. Mikael Bellini (ct), Lennart Löwgren (ct), Lars Arvidson (bass), Sven-Anders Benktsson (bass), Sven Aberg (six-course Renaissance lt), Hortus Musicus, Tallinn [cnd:Andres Mustonen] Musica Sveciae ▲ MSV 202 [DDD]

Unger, Gerhard (ten)
Beethoven, L. van:Fidelio, w. I. Hallstein (sop), C. Ludwig (mez), J. Vickers (ten), W. Berry (bass), G. Frick (bass), O. Klemperer (cnd), Philharmonia Orch, Philharmonia Chorus [G]; w. minimal dialog EMI Classics ("Studio" series) 2-▲ CDMB 69324 [ADD]
Beethoven, L. van:Fidelio, w. Ingeborg Hallstein (sop—Marzelline), Christa Ludwig (mez—Leonore/Fidelio), Gerhard Unger (ten—Jaquino), Jon Vickers (ten—Florestan), Walter Berry (bass—Pizarro), Franz Crass (bass—Don Fernando), Gottlob Frick (bass—Rocco), O. Klemperer (cnd), Philharmonia Orch, Philharmonia Chorus EMI Classics 2-▲ CDCB 55170
Cornelius, P.:Der Barbier von Bagdad, w. E. Schwarzkopf (sop), G. Hoffman (cta), N. Gedda (ten), O. Czerwenka (bass), E. Leinsdorf (cnd), Philharmonia Orch, Philharmonia Chorus EMI Classics ▲ CDMB 65284
Dittersdorf, K.D. von:Doctor und Apotheker, w. Hildegard Uhrmacher (sop—Leonore), Donna Woodward (sop—Rosalia), Waltraud Meier (mez—Claudia), Martin Finke (ten—Sichel), Frieder Lang (ten—Gotthold), Alois Perl (ten—Gallus), Gerhard Unger (ten—Sturmwald), Thomas Pfeiffer (bar—Police Commisioner), Wolfgang Schöne (bar—Krautmann), Harald Stamm (bass—Stössel), J. Lockhart (cnd), Rhine State PO Bayer 2-▲ BR 100 238/39 [DDD]
Mozart, W.A.:Arias, w. I. Hollweg (sop), L. Marshall (sop), L. Simoneau (ten), G. Frick (bass), T. Beecham (cnd), Royal PO, Beecham Choral Society EMI Classics 2-▲ CDHB 63715
Mozart, W.A.:Entführung, w. I. Hollweg (sop), L. Marshall (sop), L. Simoneau (ten), G. Frick (bass), T. Beecham (cnd), Royal PO, Beecham Choral Society EMI Classics 2-▲ CDHB 63715
Mozart, W.A.:Entführung, w. Reri Grist (sop—Blondchen), Anneliese Rothenberger (sop—Konstanze), Gerhard Unger (ten—Pedrillo), Fritz Wunderlich (ten—Belmonte), Fernando Corena (bass—Osmin), Michael Heltau (nar—Selim), Z. Mehta (cnd), Vienna PO, Vienna State Opera Chorus *(rec July 28, 1965)* Orfeo d'or ("Festspiel Dokumente" series) 2-▲ 392952 (m)
Mozart, W.A.:Zauberflöte, w. Reri Grist (sop), Edita Gruberová (sop), Edith Mathis (sop), Rene Kollo (ten), Hermann Prey (bar), José Van Dam (b-bar), Peter Meven (bass), H. von Karajan (cnd), Vienna PO, Vienna State Opera Chorus *(rec live, Salzburg, July 26, 1974)* Arkadia 2-▲ 233
Orff, C.:Carmina burana, w. L. Popp (sop), R. Wolansky (bar), J. Noble (bar), R. Frühbeck de Burgos (cnd), New Philharmonia Orch, New Philharmonia Chorus EMI Classics ▲ CDM 64328
Strauss, R.:Ariadne auf Naxos, w. E. Schwarzkopf (sop), I. Seefried (sop), R. Streich (sop), L. Otto (sop), G. Hoffman (mez), R. Schock (ten), H. Cuénod (ten), H. Prey (bar), F. Ollendorff (bass), H. von Karajan (cnd), Philharmonia Orch [G] *(rec 1954)* EMI Classics ("Studio" series) 2-▲ CDMB 69296 (m) [ADD]
Wagner, R.:Der fliegende Holländer, w. Anja Silja (sop—Senta), Anneliese Burmeister (mez—Mary), Ernst Kozub (ten—Erik), Gerhard Unger (ten—Steersman), Theo Adam (bass—Dutchman), Martti Talvela (bass—Daland), O. Klemperer (cnd), New Philharmonia Orch, BBC Sym Chorus EMI Classics 3-▲ CDCC 55179
Wagner, R.:Die Meistersinger von Nürnberg, w. E. Schwarzkopf (sop), I. Malaniuk (cta), H. Hopf (ten), E. Kunz (bar), O. Edelmann (b-bar), F. Dalberg (bass), H. von Karajan (cnd), Bayreuth Festival Orch, Bayreuth Festival Chorus [G] *(rec 1951)* EMI Classics ("Great Recordings of the Century" series) 4-▲ CDHD 63500 (m) [ADD]
Wagner, R.:Die Meistersinger von Nürnberg, w. E. Grümmer (sop), M. Höffgen (cta), R. Schock (ten), H. Prey (bar), B. Kusche (bar), F. Frantz (b-bar), G. Frick (bass), R. Kempe (cnd), Berlin PO *(rec 1956)* EMI Classics 4-▲ CDMD 64154
Wagner, R.:Die Meistersinger von Nürnberg, w. G. Janowitz (sop), B. Fassbaender (mez), S. Kónya (ten), T. Stewart (bar), F. Crass (bass), T. Hemsley (bass), R. Kubelik (cnd), Bavarian RSO, Bavarian Radio Chorus [G] *(rec live, Munich, Oct. 1967)* Myto 4-▲ 4 MCD 92569 [ADD]
Wagner, R.:Die Meistersinger von Nürnberg, w. Tiana Lemnitz (sop—Eva), Bernd Aldenhoff (ten—Walther von Stolzing), Gerhard Unger (ten—David), Ferdinand Frantz (b-bar—Hans Sachs), Kurt Boehme (bass—Veit Pogner), Heinrich Pflanzl (bass—Sixtus Beckmesser), R. Kempe (cnd), Saxon State Orch *(rec Dresden, 1951)* Myto 4-▲ MCD 961138
Wagner, R.:Die Meistersinger von Nürnberg, w. Gundula Janowitz (sop), Brigitte Fassbaender (mez), Sándor Kónya (ten), Thomas Helmsey (bar), Thomas Stewart (bar), Franz Crass (bass), R. Kubelik (cnd), Bavarian RSO, Bavarian Radio Chorus *(rec 1967)* Calig 4-▲ 5097174 [ADD]

Uppman, Theodor (bar)
Britten, H.:Billy Budd, w. P. Pears (ten), H. Alan (bar), G. Evans (b-bar), F. Dalberg (bass), B. Britten (cnd), Royal Opera House Orch, Royal Opera House Chorus Covent Garden *(rec Dec. 1, 1951)* VAI Audio 3-▲ VAIA 1034-3 [ADD]

Upshaw, Dawn (sop)
Bach, J.S.:Magnificat, BWV 243, w. P. Jensen (sop), M. Simpson (mez), D. Gordon (ten), W. Stone (bar), R. Shaw (cnd), Atlanta SO, Atlanta Chamber Chorus Telarc ▲ CD 80194 [DDD]

Upshaw, Dawn (sop) (cont.)
Barber, S.:Knoxville:Summer of 1915, w. D. Zinman (cnd), Orch of St. Luke Elektra/Nonesuch ▲ 79187-2 ■ 79187-4
Canteloube, J.:Songs of Auvergne, w. K. Nagano (cnd), Lyon Opera Orch *(rec Lyon, Apr. 1–4, 1994)* Erato ▲ 96559-2 [DDD]
Charpentier, M.-A.:Magnificat, w. A. Murray (mez), E. Robinson (mez), J. Aler (ten), K. Moll (bass), N. Marriner (cnd), Academy of St. Martin in the Fields, Academy of St. Martin in the Fields Chorus EMI Classics ▲ CDC 54284
Charpentier, M.-A.:Te Deum in C, w. A. Murray (mez), E. Robinson (mez), J. Aler (ten), K. Moll (bass), N. Marriner (cnd), Academy of St. Martin in the Fields, Academy of St. Martin in the Fields Chorus EMI Classics ▲ CDC 54284
Copland, A.:Old American Songs, w. T. Hampson (bar), H. Wolff (cnd), St. Paul CO Teldec ▲ 77310
Copland, A.:Poems (8) of Emily Dickinson, w. H. Wolff (cnd), St. Paul CO Teldec ▲ 77310
Debussy, C.:La Damoiselle élue, w. P. Rasmussen (mez), E.-P. Salonen (cnd), Los Angeles PO, Los Angeles Master Chorale Women's Voices *(rec Feb. 22, 1993)* Sony Classical ▲ SK 58952 [DDD]
Donizetti, G.:L'elisir d'amore, w. K. Battle (sop), L. Pavarotti (ten), E. Dara (bar), L. Nucci (bar), J. Levine (cnd), Metropolitan Orch, New York Metropolitan Opera Chorus Deutsche Grammophon 2-▲ 429744-2 [DDD]
Gershwin, G.:Oh, Kay!, w. Dawn Upshaw (sop—Kay), Kurt Ollmann (bar—Jimmy Winter), Adam Arkin (sgr—Shory McGee), E. Stern (cnd), *(orch unknown)* Elektra/Nonesuch ▲ 79361-2 ■ 79361-4
The Girl with Orange Lips, w. Upshaw, Dawn (sop) Elektra/Nonesuch ▲ 79262-2 ZK ■ 79262-4 AW
Górecki, H.-M.:Sym 3, "Sym of Sorrowful Songs", w. D. Zinman (cnd), London Sinfonietta Elektra/Nonesuch ▲ 79282-2 ■ 79282-4
Harbison, J.:Mirabai Songs, w. D. Zinman (cnd), Orch of St. Luke's Elektra/Nonesuch ▲ 79187-2 ■ 79187-4
Harbison, J.:Simple Daylight, w. Boston Sym Chamber Players Elektra/Nonesuch ▲ 79189-2 ■ 79189-4
Haydn, J.:Die Schöpfung, w. Jon Humphrey (ten); John Cheek (bass), R. Shaw (cnd), Atlanta SO, Atlanta Chamber Chorus [E] Telarc 2-▲ CD 80298 [DDD]
Lutoslawski, W.:Chantefleurs et Chantefables, w. E.-P. Salonen (cnd), Los Angeles PO *(rec Los Angeles, Nov 14, 17 & 18, 1994)* Sony Classical ▲ SK 67189 [DDD]
Mahler, G.:Sym 4, w. C. von Dohnányi (cnd), Cleveland Orch *(rec May 1992)* London ▲ 440315-2 [DDD]
Massenet, J.:Chérubin, w. F. von Stade (mez), M. Anderson (cta), S. Ramey (bass), P. Steinberg (cnd), Munich RSO, Bavarian State Opera Chorus RCA Red Seal 2-▲ 09026-60593-2 [DDD]
Menotti, G.C.:The Old Maid & the Thief, w. D. Zinman (cnd), Orch of St. Luke—Act 1, Scene 6, "What a curse for a woman is a timid man" Elektra/Nonesuch ▲ 79187-2 ■ 79187-4
Mozart, W.A.:Finta giardiniera, w. E. Gruberova (sop), C. Margiono (sop), M. Bacelli (sop), U. Heilmann (ten), A. Scharinger (bass), N. Harnoncourt (cnd), Vienna Concentus Musicus Teldec 3-▲ 72309-2
Mozart, W.A.:Zauberflöte, w. B. Hoch (sop), A. Rolfe Johnson (ten), A. Schmidt (bar), R. Norrington (cnd), London Classical Players [period instrs] EMI Classics 2-▲ CDCB 54287
Mozart, W.A.:Zauberflöte (sels), w. B. Hoch (sop), A. Rolfe Johnson (ten), A. Schmidt (bar), R. Norrington (cnd), London Classical Players [period instrs] EMI Classics ▲ CDC 54492
Schoenberg, A.:Qt 2 Strs, w. Arditti String Quartet Montaigne 2-▲ MO 782024
Schubert, Franz:Mass 2, w. D. Gordon (ten), W. Stone (bass), R. Shaw (cnd), Atlanta SO, Atlanta Sym Chorus [L] Telarc ▲ CD 80212 [DDD]
Stravinsky, I.:The Rake's Progress, w. D. Zinman (cnd), Orch of St. Luke—Act 1, Scene 3, "No word from Tom" Elektra/Nonesuch ▲ 79187-2 ■ 79187-4
Vivaldi, A.:Gloria, RV.589, w. P. Jensen (sop), M. Simpson (mez), D. Gordon (ten), W. Stone (bar), R. Shaw (cnd), Atlanta SO, Atlanta Chamber Chorus Telarc ▲ CD 80194 [DDD]
Wolf, H.:Italienische Liederbücher (comp), w. Olaf Bär (bar), Helmut Deutsch (pno) EMI Classics ▲ CDC 55618

Uray, Peter (nar)
Benda, G.A.:Medea, w. Hertha Schell (nar), Brigitte Quadlbauer (nar), C. Benda (cnd), Prague CO *(rec Prague, Nov 1994)* Naxos ▲ 8.553346 [DDD]

Urb, Kaia (sop)
Tüür, E.-S.:Requiem in memoriam Peeter Lilje, w. Tiit Kogermann (ten), T. Kaljuste (cnd), Tallinn CO, Estonian Phil Chamber Choir *(rec Estonia Concert Hall, Tallinn, 1994–95)* ECM ("ECM New" series) ▲ ECM 1590 [DDD]

Urban, Friederike (sop)
Mauersberger, R.:Geh aus, mein Herz, und suche Freude, w. Sabine Dicke (sop), Dorothea Schmidt (sop), Annette Bassenge (alt), Christiane Fischer (alt), Sabine Hering (alt), Johannes Unger (org), Wolfgang Unger (dir), Thüringian Academic Sing Circle Thorofon ▲ CTH 2245 [DDD]

Urbanová, Eva (sgr)
Opera Arias, w. Prague SO [cnd:Jiří Bělohlávek] Supraphon ▲ SUP 111851 [DDD]
Smetana, B.:Dalibor, w. Leo Maria Vodička (ten), Iván Kusnjer (bar), Z. Košler (cnd), Prague National Theater Orch, Prague National Theater Chorus Supraphon 2-▲ SUP 0077 [DDD]

Urbanová, Eva (sop)
Dvořák, A.:The Spectre's Bride, Op. 110, w. Ludovit Ludha (ten), Ivan Kusnjer (b-bar), J. Belohlávek (cnd), Prague SO, Pavel Kühn (cnd), Prague Phil Chorus *(rec live, 1995)* Supraphon ▲ SUP 3091
Smetana, B.:Libuše, w. Leo Marian Vodička (ten), O. Dohnányi (cnd), Prague National Theater Orch, Prague National Theater Chorus Supraphon 2-▲ SUP 3200

Urbas, Ivan (bass)
Puccini, G.:La Bohème (sels), w. Luba Orgonasova (sop—Mimì), Carmen Gonzales (sop—Musetta), Jonathan Welch (ten—Rudolfo), Fabio Previati (bar—Marcello), Boaz Senator (bar—Schaunard), Ivan Urbas (bass—Colline), Jiri Sulzenko (bass—Alcindoro), W. Humburg (cnd), Czech-Slovak RSO Bratislava, Bratislava Children's Choir, Slovak Phil Chorus *(rec Concert Hall, Czecho-Slovak Radio, Bratislava, Apr. 23–May 4, 1990)* Naxos ▲ 8.553151 [DDD]
Weill, K.:The Seven Deadly Sins, w. B. Fassbaender (mez), K.-H. Brandt (ten), H. Sojer (ten), H. Komatsu (bass), C. Garben (cnd), North German Radio PO Harmonia Mundi France ▲ HMC 901420

Uria-Monzon, Béatrice (mez)
Berlioz, H.:La Mort de Cléopâtre, w. J.-C. Casadesus (cnd), Lille National Orch Harmonia Mundi France ▲ HMC 901542
Bizet, G.:Carmen (sels), w. Léontina Vaduva (sop), Christian Papis (ten), Vincent Le Texier (bar), A. Lombard (cnd), Bordeaux-Aquitaine National Orch—Toréador & other great arias Valois ▲ V 4769
Fauré, G.:Songs, w. Natalie Dessay (sop), Jean-Paul Fouchécourt (ten), François Le Roux (bar), Jeff Cohen (pno)—complete songs grouped by poets [Leconte de Lisle; Charles Baudelaire; Paul Verlaine; Jean de la Ville de Mirmont; Armand Silvestre; Victor Hugo; Théophile Gautier; 5 Melodies of Venice; Sully Prudhomme; Albert Samain; Louis Pommey; Paul de Chodens; Marc Monnier; Romain Bussine; Victor Wilder; Georgette Deblads; Villiers de l'Isle Adam; Charles Grandmougin; Henri de Régnier; Stéphan Bordèse; Charles Van Lerberghe; Baronne de Brimont; Maurice Maeterlinck; Edmond Haraucourt; Molière REM 4-▲ REM 311179 [DDD]

Uribe, Luz Angélica (sop)
Delgado, F.:Choral Music, w. Martha Molinar (sop), Ana Paula Abitia (mez), Alfredo Mendoza (ten), Noé Colín (bass), B. J. Echenique (cnd), Mexico City CO, Alfredo Mendoza (cnd), Schola Cantorum—Te Deum al Sr. Felipe de Jesús Urtext ▲ URT 2001 [DDD]
Jerusalem, I.:Choral Music, w. Martha Molinar (sop), Ana Paula Abitia (mez), Alfredo Mendoza (ten), Noé Colín (bass), B. J. Echenique (cnd), Mexico City CO, Alfredo Mendoza (cnd), Schola Cantorum—Magnificat a Dos Voces; Misa en Sol Mayor a 8 Voces Urtext ▲ URT 2001 [DDD]

Urrey, Frederick (ten)
Argento, D.:Elizabethan Songs (6), w. R.A. Clark (cnd), Manhattan CO Newport Classic ▲ NPD 85602 [DDD]
Foster, S.C.:Songs, w. J. Baird (sop), L. Russell (alt/mountain dulcimer), J. Van Buskirk (pno), R. Enslow (fid)—The Glendy Burke; Nelly Was a Lady; Melinda May; The Soirée Polka; The Moustache Song; O Willie, Is It You, Dear?; Mr. & Mr Albany ▲ TROY 119
Handel, G.F.:Ezio, w. Julianne Baird (sop—Fulvia), Jennifer Lane (mez—Onoria), D'Anna Fortunato (cta—Ezio), Raymond Pellerin (alt—Emperor), Frederick Urrey (ten—Massimo), Nathaniel Watson (bar—Varo), Johannes Somary (org), R.A. Clark (cnd), Manhattan CO *(rec St. Jean Baptiste Church, New York, Mar. 1994)* Vox Classics 2-▲ VOX 27503 [DDD]

Urrey, Frederick (ten) (cont.)
Handel, G.F.:Muzio Scevola, w. Julianne Baird (sop—Clelia), Andrea Matthews (sop—Fidalma), Erie Mills (sop—Orazio), D'Anna Fortunato (mez—Muzio), Jennifer Lane (mez—Irene), Frederick Urrey (ten—Tarquino), John Ostendorf (b-bar—Porsenna), R. Palmer (cnd), Brewer Baroque CO [period instrs] [I] *(rec 10/91)* Newport Classic 2-▲ NPD 85540/2 [DDD]
Handel, G.F.:Siroe, Rè di Persia, w. Andrea Matthews (sop), Julianne Baird (mez), D'Anna Fortunato (mez), Steven Rickards (ct), John Ostendorf (b-bar), R. Palmer (cnd), Brewer Baroque CO [period instrs] [I] Newport Classic 3-▲ NCD 60125 [DDD]
O Mistress Mine:A Collection of English Lute Songs, w. Ronn McFarlane (lt) Dorian ▲ DOR 90136 [DDD]
Rorem, N.:3 Sisters Who Are Not Sisters, w. Andrea Matthews (sop—Jenny), Carol Flamm (sgr—Helen), Madeline Tsingopoulos (sgr—Ellen), Frederick Urrey (ten—Samuel), Mark Singer (sgr—Sylvester), John Van Buskirk (pno) Newport Classic ▲ NPT 85594 [DDD]
Wallach, J.:Mourning Madrigals, w. K. Birnbaum (sop), C. Abraham (fl), A. Tarantiles (hp) [E] Capstone ▲ CPS 8613

Ursuleac, Viorica (sop)
Strauss, R.:Die ägyptische Helena (sels), w. V. Ursuleac (sop—Helena), F. Völker (ten—Menelas), H. Roswaenge (ten—Da-Ud), E. Kunz (bar—Arbace), C. Krauss (cnd), Vienna State Opera Orch, Vienna State Opera Chorus *(rec Sept. 20, 1933)* Koch Schwann 2-▲ SCH 314552 [ADD]
Strauss, R.:Arabella (sels), w. Margit Bokor (sop—Zdenka), Viorica Ursuleac (sop—Arabella), Alfred Jerger (bar—Mandryka), Richard Mayr (bass—Waldner), C. Krauss (cnd), Vienna State Opera Orch *(rec Vienna, Oct. 29, 1933)* Koch Schwann 2-▲ SCH 314625 [ADD]
Strauss, R.:Ariadne auf Naxos, w. Erna Berger (sop), Miliza Korjus (sop), Helge Rosvaenge (ten), *(other soloists unknown)*, C. Krauss (cnd), Vienna State Opera Orch, Vienna State Opera Chorus *(rec 1935)* Arlecchino 3- ARL
Strauss, R.:Ariadne auf Naxos, w. Erna Berger (sop), Helge Roswaenge (ten), Karl Hammes (bar), C. Krauss (cnd), Berlin Reich RSO *(rec Berlin, 1935)* Preiser ▲ PRE 90259
Strauss, R.:Capriccio (sels), w. V. Ursuleac (sop—Die Gräfin), F. Klarwein (ten—Flamand), H. Hotter (b-bar—Olivier), G. Hann (b-bar—La Roche), G. Wieter (bass—Der Haushofmeister), C. Krauss (cnd), Bavarian State Opera Orch *(rec 1942)* Myto ▲ MCD 943104
Strauss, R.:Die Frau ohne Schatten (sels), w. Viorica Ursuleac (sop—Die Kaiserin), Gertrude Rünger (cta/sop—Elisabetta), Franz Völker (ten—Der Kaiser), C. Krauss (cnd), Vienna State Opera Orch *(rec Vienna, June 1, 1933)* Koch Schwann 2-▲ SCH 314662 [ADD]
Strauss, R.:Friedenstag, w. Viorica Ursuleac (sop—Maria), Anton Dermota (ten—Ein Piemonteser), Hans Hotter (b-bar—Kommandant), Herbert Alsen (bass—Wachtmeister), C. Krauss (cnd), Vienna State Opera Orch *(rec Vienna, Oct. 16, 1941)* Koch Schwann 2-▲ SCH 314625 [ADD]
Strauss, R.:Der Rosenkavalier, w. Adele Kern (sop), Georgine von Milinkovic (mez), Georg Hann (bass), Ludwig Weber (bass), C. Krauss (cnd), Bavarian State Opera Orch, Bavarian State Opera Chorus *(rec Munich, June 1942)* Preiser 3-▲ PRE 90218
Strauss, R.:Songs, w. C. Krauss (pno)—Madrigal, Op. 15/1; Dem Herzenähnlich, Op. 15/4; Lob des Leidens, Op. 15/3; Seitdem dein Aug' in meines schaute, Op. 17/1; Muttertändelei, Op. 43/2; Blindenklage, Op. 56/2; Für fünfzehn Myto ▲ MCD 943104
Verdi, G.:Don Carlos (sels), w. Viorica Ursuleac (sop—Elisabetta), Franz Völker (ten—Don Carlo), Josef von Manowarda (bass—Filippo), C. Krauss (cnd), Vienna State Opera Orch *(rec Vienna, Feb. 25, 1933)* Koch Schwann 2-▲ SCH 314662 [ADD]
Verdi, G.:Otello (sels), w. Viorica Ursuleac (sop—Desemona), Franz Völker (ten—Otello), Josef von Manowarda (bass—Iago), C. Krauss (cnd), Vienna State Opera Orch *(rec Vienna, Dec. 15, 1933)* Koch Schwann 2-▲ SCH 314662 [ADD]
Wagner, R.:Der fliegende Holländer, w. Luise Willer (mez), Karl Ostertag (ten), Hans Hotter (b-bar), Georg Hann (bass), C. Krauss (cnd), Bavarian State Opera Orch, Bavarian State Opera Chorus *(rec Mar 13-16, 1944)* Preiser 2-▲ PRE 90250 [ADD]
Wagner, R.:Die Meistersinger von Nürnberg (sels), w. V. Ursuleac (sop—Eva), F. Völker (ten—Walther), A. Jerger (b-bar—Hans Sachs), C. Krauss (cnd), Vienna State Opera Orch, Vienna State Opera Chorus *(rec Apr. 13, 1934)* Koch Schwann 2-▲ SCH 314602
Wagner, R.:Die Meistersinger von Nürnberg (sels), w. V. Ursuleac (sop—Eva), M. Lorenz (ten—Walther), E. Zimmermann (ten—David), A. Jerger (b-bar—Hans Sachs), C. Krauss (cnd), Vienna State Opera Orch, Vienna State Opera Chorus *(rec Feb. 26, 1933)* Koch Schwann 2-▲ SCH 314562 [ADD]
Wagner, R.:Die Meistersinger von Nürnberg (sels), w. Viorica Ursuleac (sop—Eva), Rudolf Bockelmann (ten—Hans Sachs), Josef Kalenberg (ten—Walther), Hermann Wiedemann (bar—Beckmesser), C. Krauss (cnd), Vienna State Opera Orch, Vienna State Opera Chorus *(rec Jan. 20, 1933)* Koch Schwann 2-▲ SCH 314642 [ADD]
Wagner, R.:Tristan und Isolde (sels), w. K. Flagstad (sop), S. Svanholm (ten), H. Hotter (b-bar), E. Kleiber (cnd), Buenos Aires Teatro Colón Orch, Buenos Aires Teatro Colón Chorus—highlights from Acts 1-3 [G] *(rec live, 1948)* Melodram 2-▲ MEL 25007 (m) [AAD]
Wagner, R.:Die Walküre (sels), w. Viorica Ursuleac (sop—Sieglinde), Hilde Konetzni (sop—Sieglinde), Gertrude Rünger (sop—Brünnhilde), Franz Völker (ten—Siegmund), Richard Mayr (bass—Hunding), Krauss, Knappertsbusch (cnd), Vienna State Opera Orch Koch Schwann 2-▲ SCH 314662 [ADD]

Usami, Mikoto (ten)
Kraft, Walter:Christus, w. Anna Senn-Dähler (sop), Barbara Künzler (sop), Barbara Suttor (sop), Christine Guy (alt), Heidi Uhlmann (alt), Daniel Zellweger (alt), Matthias Senn (ten), Wolfgang Pailer (bass), Heinz Suter (bass), Klaus Knall (cnd), Evangelische Singgemeinde Choirs *(rec Ostdorf bei Balingen, Oct. 8-11, 1986)* Cantate 2-▲ 58004 [DDD]

Ustinova, Elena (sop)
Rachmaninoff, S.:The Bells, w. K. Westi (ten), J. Hynninen (bar), D. Kitayenko (cnd), Danish National RSO, Danish National Radio Choir Chandos ▲ CHAN 8966 [DDD]

Ustuk, Ayhan (sgr)
Mercadante, S.:Caritea, regina di Spagna, w. Nana Gordaze (sgr), Sonia Lee (sgr), Jacek Laszczkowski (sgr), Nicolas Rivenq (bar), Gregory Bonfatti (sgr), G. Carella (cnd), Italian International Opera Orch, Bratislava Camera Chorus *(rec Italy, 1995)* Nuova Era 3-▲ NUO 7258

Usunow, Dimiter (ten)
Mussorgsky, M.:Boris Godunov, w. N. Dobrianova (sop), S. Jurinac (sop), N. Ghiaurov (bass), N. Ghiuselev (bass), A. Diakov (bass), H. von Karajan (cnd), Vienna PO, Vienna State Opera Chorus [R] *(rec live in Salzburg, 7/26/64)* Arkadia 2-▲ 210 (m) [ADD]

Ütő, Endre (bass)
Durkó, Z.:Burial Prayer, w. Attila Fülöp (ten), G. Lehel (cnd), Budapest SO, Ferenc Sapszon (cnd), Hungarian Radio-TV Chorus *(rec 1975)* Hungaroton ▲ HCD 31654 [AAD]

Vaccari, Patrizia (sop)
Perti, G.A.:Liturgy for Good Friday, w. Maura Pederzoli (sop), Cristina Calzolari (sop), Alida Oliva (sop), Claudia Bugli (sop), Lucia Bagnoli (alt), Cinzia Meneghel (alt), Renzo Bez (alt), Alessandro Carmignani (alt), Michel van Goethem (alt), Mauro Collina (ten), Vincenzo Di Donato (ten), Paolo Fanciullacci (ten), Giovanni Caccamo (ten), Paolo Da Col (ten), Sergio Foresti (bass), Marco Scavazza (bass), Luca Ferracin (bass), Paride Montanari (bass), Liuwe Tamminga (org), Sergio Vartolo (org), S. Vartolo (cnd), Bologna San Petronio Capella Musicale Orch—Omnes amici mei; De lamentatione Jeremiae Prophetae:Heth. Cogitavit; Velum templi; Vinea mea; De lamentatione Jeremiae Prophetae:Lamed. Matribus suis; Tamquam ad latronem; Tenebrae factae sunt; Animam meam; Tradiderunt me; Jesum tradidit; De lamentatione Jeremiae Prophetae:Aleph. Ego vir; Caligaverunt *(rec St. Petronio Basilica, Bologna, Mar 28-31, 1995)* Naxos ▲ 8.553321 [DDD]
Vivaldi, A.:Gloria, RV.589, w. R. Invernizzi (sop), R. Balconi (ct), L. Gariboldi (ten), C. Gubert (cnd), Padua Bach Academy CO, Padua Bach Academy Chamber Chorus Rivoalto ▲ RIV 9301 [DDD]
Vivaldi, A.:Magnificat, RV.610, w. R. Invernizzi (sop), R. Balconi (ct), L. Gariboldi (ten), C. Gubert (cnd), Padua Bach Academy CO, Padua Bach Academy Chamber Chorus Rivoalto ▲ RIV 9301 [DDD]

Vaduva, Leontina (sop)
Bizet, G.:Carmen (sels), w. Béatrice Uria-Monzon (mez), Christian Papis (ten), Vincent Le Texier (bar), A. Lombard (cnd), Bordeaux-Aquitaine National Orch—Toréador & other great arias Valois ▲ V 4769
Puccini, G.:La Bohème, w. Leontina Vaduva (sop—Mimi), Ruth Ann Swenson (sop—Musetta), Roberto Alagna (ten—Rodolfo), Simon Keenlyside (bar—Schaunard), Thomas Hampson (bar—Marcello), Samuel Ramey (bass—Colline), Enrico Fissore (bass—Benoit), A. Pappano (cnd), Philharmonia Orch EMI Classics 2-♦ CDCB 56120

Vaduva, Leontina (sop) (cont.)
Verdi, G.:Rigoletto, w. J. Larmore (mez), R. Leech (ten), A. Agache (bar), S. Ramey (bass), C. Rizzi (cnd), Welsh National Opera Orch Teldec ▲ 90851-2

Vaghi, Giacomo (bass)
Bellini, V.:Norma, w. M. Callas (sop), J. Sutherland (sop), E. Stignani (mez), M. Picchi (ten), V. Gui (cnd), Royal Opera House Orch, Royal Opera House Chorus Covent Garden [I] *(rec live, Covent Garden 11/52)* Legato Classics 2-▲ LCD 130-2 (m) [AAD]
Bellini, V.:Norma, w. M. Callas (sop), J. Sutherland (sop), E. Stignani (mez), M. Picchi (ten), V. Gui (cnd), Royal Opera House Orch, Royal Opera House Chorus Covent Garden [I] *(rec live, Covent Garden 11/52)* Verona 3-▲ 27018/20 (m) [AAD]
Bellini, V.:Norma, w. J. Sutherland (sop), M. Callas (sop), E. Stignani (mez), M. Picchi (ten), V. Gui (cnd), Royal Opera House Orch, Royal Opera House Chorus Covent Garden [I] *(rec live, Covent Garden 11/52)* Melodram 2-▲ MEL 26025
Verdi, G.:Ernani, w. Caterina Mancini (sop), Vittorio Pandano (ten), Gino Penno (ten), Giuseppe Taddei (bar), Ezio Achilli (sgr), Licia Rossini (sgr), F. Previtali (cnd), Rome RAI SO, Rome RAI Chorus Cetra Classic 2-▲ CDON 39 [ADD]
Verdi, G.:La forza del destino (sels), w. G. Cigna (sop—Leonora), E. Ghirardini (bar—Melitone), G. Vaghi (bar—Guardiano), O. de Fabritiis (cnd), Rome RAI Orch, Rome RAI Chorus *(rec Oct. 10, 1938)* Legato Classics 2-▲ LCD 173-2 [ADD]
Verdi, G.:Luisa Miller, w. L. Kelston (sop—Luisa), M.T. Pace (mez—Federica), G. Larui-Volpi (ten—Rodolfo), S. Colombo (bar—Miller), G. Vaghi (bar—Count Walter), D. Baronti (bass—Wurm), M. Rossi (cnd), Rome RAI Orch, Rome RAI Chorus *(rec 1951)* Cetra Classic 2-▲ CDO 17 [AAD]

Vaillancourt, Pauline (sop)
Provost, S.:L'Adorable verrotière, w. Michel Forgues (nar), L. Vaillancourt (cnd), Nouvel Ensemble Moderne *(rec Studio 12, Maison de Radio-Canada, Montreal, May 12, 1993)* Ummus ▲ UMM 109
Vivier, C.:Kopernikus, "A Ritual Opera of Death", w. Y. Parent (sop), P. Vaillancourt (sop), M.-D. Parent (sop), J. Fleury (cta), D. Doane (ten), M. Ducharme (bar), Y. Saint-Amant (bass), F. Martel (cl), M. Bélanger (vn), L. Bouchard (tpt), L. Vaillancourt (cnd), *(orch unknown)* *(rec Feb. 1991)* CBC ("Musica Viva" series) ▲ MVCD 1047 [DDD]

Valásková, Jana (sop)
Respighi, O.:La bella dormente nel bosco, w. Ivana Czaková (sop—Old Woman/Green Fairy), Adriana Kohútková (sop—Blue Fairy/Nightingale), Henrietta Lednárová (sop—Frog/Spindle), Jana Valásková (sop—Princess), Dagmar Pecková (mez—Cuckoo/Cat), Denisa Slepkovská (mez—Queen/Duchess), Karol Bernáth (ten—Doctor), Guillermo Dominguez (ten—Prince April), Igor Pasek (ten—Jester), Ján Durco (bar—Ambassador), Richard Haan (bar—King/Woodcutter), Stanislav Benacka (bass—Doctor), Anton Kúrnava (bass—Doctor), Marián Smolárik (bass—Doctor), M. Adriano (nar—Mr. Dollar Chèques), M. Adriano (cnd), Slovak RSO Bratislava, Ján Rozehnal (cnd), Slovak Phil Chorus *(rec Concert Hall of the Slovak Radio, Bratislava, June 8-20, 1994)* Marco Polo ("Opera Classics" series) ▲ 8.223742 [DDD]
Respighi, O.:La Primavera, w. Henrietta Lednárová (sop—Prima fanciulla), Jana Valásková (sop—Sirvard), Beata Geriová (mez—Seconda fanciulla), Miroslav Dvorský (ten—Il giovine), Richard Haan (bar—L'orante), Vladimír Kubovčík (bass—Il vecchio), Vera Rasková (fl), M. Adriano (cnd), Slovak RSO Bratislava, Slovak Phil Chorus *(rec Slovak Radio Concert Hall, Bratislava, Jan. 4-9, Feb. 19 & June)* Marco Polo ▲ 8.223595 [DDD]

Valayre, Sylvie (sop)
Lattuada, F.:Le Preziose ridicole, w. S. Valayre (sop—Madelon), A. Catarci (sop—Marotte), A. Cicogna (mez—Cathos), S. Tedesco (ten—La Grange), E. Di Cesare (ten—Mascarille), A. Veccia (bar—Croissy), R. Servile (bar—Jodelet), E. Fissore (bass—Gorgibus), E. Romagna (cnd), Toscanini SO, G. Masini (cnd), Rossini Teatro Comunale Chorus [I] *(rec live, 1991)* Ermitage ▲ ERM 404 [DDD]

Valdengo, Giuseppe (bar)
Puccini, G.:La Bohème, w. Licia Albanese (sop—Mimi), Audrey Schuh (sop—Musetta), Giuseppe di Stefano (ten—Rodolfo), Arthur Cosenza (bar—Schaunard), Giuseppe Valdengo (bar—Marcello), Norman Treigle (bass—Colline), Warren Gadpaille (bass—Benoît/Alcindoro), Thomas Carter (sgr—Parpignol), Harold Crane (sgr—Custom House Official), Steve Harun (sgr—Sergeant), R. Cellini (cnd), New Orleans Opera Orch, New Orleans Opera Chorus *(rec Nov 1959)* VAI Audio 2-▲ VAIA 1119-2 [ADD]
Puccini, G.:Madama Butterfly, w. R. Tebaldi (sop), A. di Stasio (mez), G. Raimondi (ten), A. Questa (cnd), *(orch & chorus unknown)* [I] *(rec live, Arena Flegrea, Naples 8/9/58)* Standing Room Only 2-▲ SRO 825-2 [ADD]
Verdi, G.:Aida, w. H. Nelli (sop), E. Gustavson (mez), G. Tucker (ten), A. Toscanini (cnd), NBC SO, Robert Shaw Chorale [I] RCA Gold Seal 3-▲ 60251-2-RG (m) [ADD] 2-■ 60251-4-RG (CrO2)
Verdi, G.:Aida, w. H. Nelli (sop), E. Gustavson (mez), G. Tucker (ten), A. Toscanini (cnd), NBC SO, Robert Shaw Chorale [I] RCA Gold Seal 7-▲ 60326-2-RG (m) [ADD] 6-■ 60326-4-RG (CrO2)
Verdi, G.:Un ballo in maschera, w. M. Curtis Verna (sop—Amelia), M. Erato (sop—Oscar), P. Tassinari (cta—Ulrica), F. Tagliavini (ten—Riccardo), G. Valdengo (bar—Renato), A. Albertini (bar—Silvano), M. Stefanoni (bass—Samuel), V. Susca (bass—Tom), A. Questa (cnd), Turin RAI SO, Turin RAI Chorus *(rec 1954)* Cetra Classic 2-▲ CDO 13 [AAD]
Verdi, G.:Falstaff, w. Herva Nelli (sop), Teresa Stich-Randall (sop), Cloë Elmo (cta), Frank Guarrera (bar), A. Toscanini (cnd), *(orch unknown)* *(rec 1950)* Music & Arts 2-▲ CD 248 [ADD]
Verdi, G.:Otello, w. H. Nelli (sop), R. Vinay (ten), A. Toscanini (cnd), NBC SO [I] RCA Gold Seal 2-▲ 60302-2-RG [ADD] 2-■ 60302-4-RG (CrO2)
Verdi, G.:Rigoletto (sels), w. C. O'Connor (sop), O. Dominguez (mez), G. Di Stefano (ten), I. Rufino (bass), R. Cellini (cnd), Palacio Bellas Artes Orch, Palacio Bellas Artes Chorus [abridged performance] *(rec live, Mexico City 6/22/48)* Golden Age of Opera 2-▲ GAO 128/29 [ADD]

Valente (sop)
Respighi, O.:Lauda per la Natività del Signore, w. M. Forrester (cta), Gordon (ten), M. Korn (cnd), Concerto Soloists Instrumental Ensemble, Philadelphia Singers RCA Red Seal ▲ 7787-2-RC [DDD] ■ 7787-4-RC (CrO2)

Valente, Alessandro (ten)
Alessandro Valente *(rec 1927-30)* Preiser ("Lebendige Vergangenheit" series) ▲ PRE 89126
del Tredici, D.:Night Conjure-Verse, w. M. Burgess (sop), D. del Tredici (cnd), Marlboro Festival Ensemble [E] CRI ■ ACS 6004
Leoncavallo, R.:Pagliacci, w. Adelaide Saraceni (sop—Nedda), Alessandro Valente (ten—Canio), Nello Palai (ten—Beppe), Apollo Granforte (bar—Tonio), Leonildo Basi (bass—Silvio), C. Sabajno (cnd), La Scala Orch, La Scala Chorus *(rec Apr, Sept 1929 & Jan 1930)* VAI Audio 2-▲ VAIA 1082-2
Leoncavallo, R.:Pagliacci (sels), w. Enrico Caruso (ten), Antonio Paoli (ten), Giovanni Zenatello (ten), Amedeo Bassi (ten), Hermann Jadlowker (ten), Fernand Ansseau (ten), Hipolito Lazaro (ten), Nino (Filippo) Piccaluga (ten), Mario Chamlee (ten), Giacomo Lauri-Volpi (ten), Miguel Fleta (ten), Giovanni Martinelli (ten), Aureliano Pertile (ten), Georges Thill (ten), Francesco Merli (ten), Lauritz Melchior (ten), Marcel Wittrisch (ten), Joseph Schmidt (ten), Beniamino Gigli (ten), Giuseppe Lugo (ten), Helge Roswaenge (ten), Jussi Bjoerling (ten)—23 versions of the tenor aria "Vesti la giubba" *(rec 1907-1944)* Bongiovanni ▲ GB 1071 [ADD]

Valente, Benita (sop)
Bach, J.S.:Psalms (4), w. Judith Malafronte (alt), J. Thomas (cnd), American Bach Soloists—Psalm 51:Tilge, Höchter, meine Sünden Koch International Classics ▲ KIC 7237 [DDD]
Beethoven, L. van:Sym 9, "Choral Sym", w. F. Kopleff (cta), J. Hadley (ten), J. Cheek (bass), R. Shaw (cnd), Atlanta SO, Atlanta Sym Chorus Pro Arte ▲ CDD 245 [DDD]
Brahms, J.:Liebeslieder Waltzes SATB, w. M. Kleinman (cta), W. Conner (ten), M. Singher (bar), R. Serkin (pno), L. Fleisher (pno) [G] Sony Classical ("Essential Classics" series) ▲ SBK 48176 ■ SBT 48176
Brahms, J.:Songs, w. R. Goode (pno) [G] InSync ■ C 4150
Dallapiccola, L.:Parole di San Paolo, w. J. Thome (cnd), Orch of Our Time Vox Box 2-▲ CDX 5144
Debussy, C.:Ariettes oubliées, w. Lydia Artymiw (pno) *(rec Rutgers Church, New York City, Jan 23-26, 1989)* Centaur ▲ CRC 2220 [DDD]
Debussy, C.:Chansons de jeunesse (4), w. Lydia Artymiw (pno) *(rec Rutgers Church, New York City, Jan 23-26, 1989)* Centaur ▲ CRC 2220 [DDD]
Debussy, C.:Fêtes galantes 1, w. Lydia Artymiw (pno) *(rec Rutgers Church, New York City, Jan 23-26, 1989)* Centaur ▲ CRC 2220 [DDD]
del Tredici, D.:Night Conjure-Verse, w. Mary Burgess (mez), D. del Tredici (cnd), Marlboro Festival Players CRI ("American Masters" series) ▲ CD 689 [DDD]

Valente, Benita (sop) (cont.)
Fauré, G.:Mélodies 'de Venise', Op. 58, w. Lydia Artymiw (pno)—Mandoline; En Sourdine; Green; A Clymene; C'est l'extase; Au bord de l'eau; Fleur jetée [all texts Verlaine] *(rec Rutgers Church, New York City, Jan 23–26, 1989)* Centaur ▲ CRC 2220 [DDD]
Haydn, J.:The Seven Last Words of Christ on the Cross, w. Jan DeGaetani (mez), Jon Humphrey (ten), Thomas Paul (bar), Juilliard String Quartet Sony Classical ▲ SK 44914 [DDD]
Love Songs & Lullabies, w. Sharon Isbin (gtr), Thomas Allen (bar), Guadencio Thiago de Mello (perc), Julia Bogorad (fl) Virgin Classics ▲ 59226
Mahler, G.:Sym 2, w. M. Forrester (cta), G. Kaplan (cnd), London SO, London Sym Chorus MCA Classics 2–▲ MCAD 11011 [DDD]; 2–■ MCAC 11011 (D)
Mahler, G.:Sym 2, w. Maureen Forrester (cta), G. Kaplan (cnd), London SO, Ardwyn Singers, BBC Welsh Chorus, Cardiff Polyphonic Choir, Dyfed Choir Conifer Classics 2–▲ 75605–51277–2 [DDD]
Mozart, W.A.:Songs, w. R. Goode (pno) [G,I] InSync ■ C 4150
Schubert, Franz:Der Hirt auf dem Felsen, w. H. Wright (cl), R. Serkin (pno) [G] *(rec 1960)* Sony Classical ▲ SMK 45901 [ADD/DDD] ■ SMT 45901
Schubert, Franz:Der Hirt auf dem Felsen, w. H. Wright (cl), R. Serkin (pno) [G] Sony Classical ("Essential Classics" series) ▲ SBK 48176 ■ SBT 48176
Schubert, Franz:Mass 6, w. M. Simpson (mez), J. Humphrey (ten), G. Siebert (ten), M. Myers (ten), R. Shaw (cnd), Atlanta SO, Atlanta Sym Chorus [L] Telarc ▲ CD 80212 [DDD]
Schubert, Franz:Songs (misc), w. R. Goode (pno) [G] InSync ■ C 4150
Shostakovich, D.:From Jewish Folk Poetry, w. Jan de Gaetani (mez), Jon Humphrey (ten), Samuel Lipman (pno) *(rec live, Aspen Music Festival, 1980)* Bridge ▲ BCD 9048 [ADD]
Vaughan Williams, R.:Sym 1, w. T. Allen (bar), L. Slatkin (cnd), Philharmonia Orch, Philharmonia Chorus RCA Red Seal ▲ 09026–61197–2
Wolf, H.:Italienische Liederbücher (sels), w. R. Goode (pno) [G] InSync ■ C 4150

Valente, Valentina (sop)
Mussorgsky, M.:Boris Godunov, w. V. Valente (sop—Xenia), E. Gorochovskaya (mez—Nurse), L. Nichiteanu (mez—Fyodor), E. Zarmeba (mez—Hostess), M. Lipovšek (cta—Marina), P. Langridge (ten—Prince Shuisky), H. Wildhaber (ten—Misail), A. Fedin (ten—Simpleton), S. Leiferkus (bar—Rangoni), A. Kotcherga (bass—B: Godounov), A. Shagidullin (bass—Shchelkalov), S. Ramey (bass—Pimen), S. Larin (bass—Girgory), G. Nikolsky (bass—Varlaam), C. Abbado (cnd), Berlin PO, Tölz Boys' Choir, Berlin Radio Chorus, Slovak Phil Chorus *(rec Nov. 7–30, 1993)* Sony Classical 3–▲ S3K 58977 [DDD]

Valenti, Monica (sop)
Salieri, A.:Axur, Re d'Ormus, w. A. Martin (bar), E. Mei (sop), C. Rayam (ten), E. Nova (bass), A. Vespasiani (mez), R. Clemencic (cnd), Guido d'Arezzo Orch, Guido d'Arezzo Chorus [I] *(rec live 1989)* Nuova Era 3–▲ 6852/54 [DDD]

Valentini, Fernando (bar)
Ponchielli, A.:La Gioconda, w. Zinka Milanov (sop—La Gioconda), Rosalind Elias (mez—Laura), Belan Amparan (cta—La Cieca), Giacomo Cottino (ten—Isepo), Giuseppe Di Stefano (ten—Enzo Grimaldo), Fernando Valentini (bar—Zuane/Un Nocchiero), Leonard Warren (bar—Barnaba), Virgilio Carbonari (bass—Un Cantore), Plinio Clabassi (bass—Alvise Badoero), F. Previtali (cnd), St. Cecilia Academy Orch Rome, St. Cecilia Academy Chorus Rome Theorema 3–▲ TH 121182/184

Valentini-Terrani, L. (mez)
Pergolesi, G.B.:Stabat mater, w. M. Marshall (sop), C. Abbado (cnd), London SO [L] Deutsche Grammophon ▲ 415103–2 [DDD]
Rossini, G.:Arias, w. A. Zedda (cnd), Turin RAI SO, Turin RAI Chorus—Tancredi:Oh patria!...Di tanti palpiti; Otello:Assisa a' piè d'un salice; Semiramide:Eccomi alfine in Babilonia; Maometto II:Non temer:d'un basso affetto; Il barbiere di Siviglia:Una voce poco fa; La Cenerentola:Della fortuna instabile *(rec between Sept. 1980 & Oct.)* Italia ▲ CDC 66 [AAD]
Vivaldi, A.:Gloria, RV.589, w. T. Berganza (mez), R. Muti (cnd), New Philharmonia Orch, New Philharmonia Chorus [L] EMI Classics ▲ CDC 47990 [ADD]
Vivaldi, A.:Magnificat, RV.611, w. T. Berganza (mez), R. Muti (cnd), New Philharmonia Orch, New Philharmonia Chorus [L] EMI Classics ▲ CDC 47990 [ADD]
Vivaldi, A.:Orlando Furioso, w. V. de los Angeles (sop), M. Horne (mez), C. Gonzales (mez), Kosma (sgr), S. Bruscantini (bar), N. Zaccaria (bass), C. Scimone (cnd), Venice Solisti Erato 3–▲ 2292–45147–2 ZB

Valentino, Francesco (sgr)
Verdi, G.:Il trovatore, w. Norina Greco (sop), Bruna Castagna (mez), Jussi Björling (ten), Nicola Moscona (bass), F. Calusio (cnd), *(orch & chorus unknown)* Enterprise ("The Radio Years" series) 2–▲ ENT 44 (m)

Valentino, Frank (bar)
Puccini, G.:La Bohème, w. L. Albanese (sop), A. McKnight (sop), J. Peerce (ten), A. Toscanini (cnd), NBC SO, NBC Sym Chorus [I] RCA Gold Seal 2–▲ 60288–2–RG [ADD] 2–■ 60288–4–RG (CrO2)
Verdi, G.:Rigoletto (sels), w. Nan Merriman (mez), Jan Peerce (ten), Nicola Moscona (bass), G. Ribla (sgr), A. Toscanini (cnd), NBC SO—Act III (complete) Enterprise ("The Radio Years" series) ▲ ENT 48
Verdi, G.:Rigoletto (act 3), w. Nan Merriman (mez), Jan Peerce (ten), Nicola Moscona (bass), G. Ribla (sgr), A. Toscanini (cnd), NBC SO [I] *(rec New York, 7/25/43)* Melodram 2–▲ MEL 28022 (m) [AAD]
Verdi, G.:Il trovatore, w. Norina Greco (sop—Leonora), Bruna Castagna (cta—Azucena), Jussi Björling (ten—Manrico), Francesco Valentino (bar—Count di Luna), Nicola Moscona (bass—Ferrando), F. Calusio (cnd), *(orch unknown) (rec live, New York, Jan. 11, 1941)* The Fourties 2–▲ ENT FT 1507

Valentino, Stefano (bass)
Rossini, G.:Il barbiere di Siviglia (sels), w. M. Resemba (sop), N. Sabatano (sop), F. de Lucia (ten), F. Novelli (bar), G. Schottler (bass), A. di Tommaso (bass), S. Sassano (cnd), Naples Teatro San Carlo Orch, Naples Teatro San Carlo Chorus [I] *(rec 1918 for Phonotype)* Standing Room Only ▲ SRO 819–1 [ADD]

Valermont (bass)
Gounod, C.:Roméo et Juliette, w. Yvonne Gall (sop—Juliette), Champell (sop—Stéphano), Jeanne Goulancourt (mez—Gertrude), Agustarello Affre (ten—Roméo), Edmond Tirmont (ten—Tybalt), Alexis Boyer (bar—Mercutio), Pierre Dupré (bar—Paris), Hypolite Belhomme (bar—Grégorio), Marcel Journet (bass—Frère Laurent), Henri Albers (bass—Capulet), Valermont (bass—The Duke), F. Rühlmann (cnd), Paris Opéra-Comique Orch, Paris Opéra-Comique Chorus *(rec 1912)* VAI Audio ▲ VAIA 1064–3 F

Valero, Fernando (ten)
The World of Singing, Vol. 3:The Italian School, Part 1:The Italian Tenors Before World War I (1902–13), w. Antonio Aramburo (ten), Alessandro Bonci (ten), Giuseppe Borgatti (ten), Enrico Caruso (ten), Edoardo Garbin (ten), Fiorello Giraud (ten), Fernando de Lucia (ten), Francesco Marconi (ten), Giovanni Battista de Negri (ten), Antonio Paoli (ten), et. al Enterprise ("Vocal Archives" series) 3–▲ ENT VA 2104

Valjakka, Taru (sop)
Segerstam, L.:Songs of Experience, w. L. Segerstam (cnd), Austrian RSO *(rec Grosses Konzerthaussaal, Vienna, Apr. 14, 1976)* BIS ▲ CD 39 [AAD]

Válka, Josef (ten)
Janáček, L.:Šárka, w. A. Nováková (sop), A. Jurecka (ten), K. Kunc (bass), B. Bakala (cnd), Brno RSO, Brno Radio Chorus *(rec live, 1953)* Multisonic ("Prague Spring Collection" series) ▲ 31 0154 [ADD]

Vallee, Rudy (sgr)
Loesser, F.:How to Succeed in Business without Really Trying, w. R. Morse (sgr), *(other artists unknown)* [1961 Broadway cast] RCA ▲ 60352–2 RG [ADD] ■ 60352–4 RG
Rodgers, R.:Music of, w. B. Crosby (sgr), J. Macdonald (sgr), A. Jolson (sgr), et al., Whiteman, Sinatra (cnd), Whiteman Orch, Sinatra Orch, Paramount Studio Orch—On Your Toes; Jumbo; Present Arms; One Dam Thing After Another; The Boys from Syracuse; Heads Up; Lido Lady; Peggy Ann; Love Me Tonight; Higher & Higher; Spring is Here; The Girl Friend; Simple Simon; Hallelujah; I'm a Bum Pearl ("Flapper" series) ▲ PAST CD 9794 [AAD]

Vallejo, Daniel Galvez (ten)
Berlioz, H.:La Mort de Sardanapale, w. J.-C. Casadesus (cnd), Lille National Orch Harmonia Mundi France ▲ HMC 901542
Berlioz, H.:La Mort d'Orphée, w. J.-C. Casadesus (cnd), Lille National Orch Harmonia Mundi France ▲ HMC 901542

Valletti, Cesare (ten)
Bellini, V.:La sonnambula, w. M. Callas (sop), G. Carturan (mez), G. Modesti (bass), L. Bernstein (cnd), La Scala Orch, La Scala Chorus [I] *(rec live, 3/5/55)* Myto 2–▲ 2 MCD 89006 (m) [ADD]
Berlioz, H.:L'Enfance du Christ, w. Florence Kopleff (cta), Gérard Souzay (bar), Lucien Oliver (bar), Giorgio Tozzi (bass), C. Munch (cnd), Boston SO, New England Conservatory Chorus *(rec Dec 1956)* RCA Victor Gold Seal 8–▲ 0902–668444–2 [ADD]
Berlioz, H.:L'Enfance du Christ, w. F. Kopleff (cta), G. Souzay (bar), G. Tozzi (bass), C. Munch (cnd), Boston SO, New England Conservatory Chorus RCA Gold Seal 2–▲ 09026–61234–2
Cesare Valletti *(rec live, 1954–60)* Memories ("Great Voices" series) 2–▲ MEM 4191 (m)
Cimarosa, D.:Il Matrimonio segreto, w. Alda Noni (sop), Giulietta Simionato (mez), Riccardo Cassinelli (ten), Sesto Bruscantini (bar), Rovero (sgr), M. Wolf-Ferrari (cnd), Florence Maggio Musicale Orch *(rec 1950)* Cetra Classic 2–▲ CDO 32
Donizetti, G.:Don Pasquale, w. A. Noni (sop—Norina), C. Valletti (ten—Ernesto), M. Borriello (bar—Dr. Malatesta), S. Bruscantini (bass-bar—Pasquale), M. Rossi (cnd), Turin RAI SO, Turin RAI Chorus *(rec 1952)* Cetra Classic 2–▲ CDO 14 [AAD]
Donizetti, G.:L'elisir d'amore, w. Alda Noni (sop), Sesto Bruscantini (bar), G. Gavazzeni (cnd), Rome RAI SO, Rome RAI Chorus *(rec 1952)* Fonit Cetra ("Classic Collection" series) 2–▲ FCT CDO 5 [AAD]
Donizetti, G.:La fille du régiment, w. Lina Pagliughi (sop), Rina Corsi (mez), Sesto Bruscantini (bar), Eraldo Coda (bar), M. Rossi (cnd), Milan RAI Lyric Orch, Milan RAI Chorus *(rec 1950)* Cetra Classic 2–▲ CDON 38 [ADD]
Donizetti, G.:Linda di Chamounix, w. A. Stella (sop), R. Capecchi (bar), G. Taddei (bar), T. Serafin (cnd), Naples Teatro San Carlo Orch, Naples Teatro San Carlo Chorus *(rec 1959)* Andromeda ▲ ANR 2509 [ADD]
Maria Coleva, Cesare Valletti, w. Maria Coleva (sop), Rome RAI SO [cnd:Rigacci] *(rec Dec. 4, 1961)* Incontri Memorabili ("Martini & Rossi Concerts" series) ▲ 5030
Mascagni, P.:L'amico Fritz, w. R. Carteri (sop—Suzel), R. Corsi (mez—Beppe), C. Valletti (ten—Fritz), C. Tagliabue (bar—David), V. Gui (cnd), Milan RAI SO, Milan RAI Chorus *(rec live, Apr. 25, 1953)* Bongiovanni 2–▲ GB 1098/99 [ADD]
Massenet, J.:Werther, w. J. Guido (sop—Sophie), N. Rankin (sop—Charlotte), C. Valletti (ten—Werther), A. Cosenza (bar—Albert), R. Cellini (cnd), New Orleans Opera Orch *(rec 1956)* Golden Age of Opera 2–▲ GAO 141/42 [ADD]
Mozart, W.A.:Don Giovanni, w. Birgit Nilsson (sop—Donna Anna), Leontyne Price (sop—Donna Elvira), Eugenia Ratti (sop—Zerlina), Cesare Valletti (ten—Don Ottavio), Heinz Blankenburg (bar—Masetto), Fernando Corena (b-bar—Leporello), Arnold van Mill (b-bar—Il Commendatore), Cesare Siepi (b-bar—Don Giovanni), E. Leinsdorf (cnd), Vienna PO, Vienna State Opera Chorus [I] London 3–▲ 444594–2 [ADD]
Puccini, G.:Madama Butterfly, w. A. Moffo (sop), R. Elias (mez), R. Cesari (bar), E. Leinsdorf (cnd), Rome Opera Orch, Rome Opera Chorus [I] RCA Gold Seal 2–▲ 4145–2–RG [ADD]
Puccini, G.:Madama Butterfly, w. A. Moffo (sop), R. Elias (mez), R. Cesari (bar), E. Leinsdorf (cnd), Rome Opera Orch, Rome Opera Chorus [I] RCA Gold Seal ▲ 60202–2–RG [ADD] ■ 60202–4–RG
Rossini, G.:Il barbiere di Siviglia, w. R. Peters (sop), R. Merrill (bar), G. Tozzi (bass), F. Corena (bass), E. Leinsdorf (cnd), Metropolitan Opera Orch, New York Metropolitan Opera Chorus [I] RCA Gold Seal 3–▲ 6505–2–RG [ADD] 2–■ 6505–4–RG (CrO2)
Rossini, G.:Il barbiere di Siviglia, w. D. Gatta (sop), G. Bechi (bar), N. Rossi-Lemeni (bass), V. de Sabata (cnd), La Scala Orch, La Scala Chorus *(rec 1952)* Memories 2–▲ MEM 4525 [AAD]
Rossini, G.:Il barbiere di Siviglia, w. Roberta Peters (sop—Rosina), Margaret Roggero (mez—Berta), Cesare Valletti (ten—Count Almaviva), Calvin Marsh (bar—Fiorello/Sergeant), Robert Merrill (bar—Figaro), Fernando Corena (bass—Dr. Bartolo), Carlo Tomanelli (bass—Ambrogio), Giorgio Tozzi (bass—Don Basilio), E. Leinsdorf (cnd), Metropolitan Opera Orch, New York Metropolitan Opera Chorus *(rec Manhattan Center, New York, Sept 1–11, 1958)* RCA Living Stereo 3–▲ 09026–68552–2 [ADD]
Rossini, G.:Il barbiere di Siviglia (sels), w. R. Peters (sop), R. Merrill (bar), G. Tozzi (bass), F. Corena (bass), E. Leinsdorf (cnd), Metropolitan Opera Orch, New York Metropolitan Opera Chorus RCA Gold Seal ▲ 60188–2–RG [ADD] ■ 60188–4–RG (CrO2)
Rossini, G.:La Cenerentola, w. Ornella Rovero (sop), Miti Truccato Pace (mez), Giulietta Simionato (mez), Saturno Meletti (bar), Vito Susca (bass), Cristiano Dalamangas (sgr), M. Rossi (cnd), Turin RAI Orch, Bruno Erminero (cnd), Turin RAI Chorus Fonit Cetra ("Classic Collection" series) 2–▲ FCT CDON 34
Tebaldi, Barbieri & Valletti, w. Renata Tebaldi (sop), Fedora Barbieri (mez), Fighera, Nino Sanzogno (cnd), Turin RAI SO, Milan RAI SO *(rec Martini & Rossi Concert, 1951 & 1953)* Incontri Memorabili ▲ CDMR 5012
Verdi, G.:La traviata, w. M. Callas (sop), Giron (sgr), G. Taddei (bar), O. de Fabritiis (cnd), Palacio Bellas Artes Orch, Palacio Bellas Artes Chorus [I] *(rec live, Mexico City, 7/17/51)* Melodram 2–▲ CDM 26019 [AAD]
Verdi, G.:La traviata, w. M. Callas (sop), A. Zanasi (bass), N. Rescigno (cnd), Royal Opera House Orch, Royal Opera House Chorus Covent Garden [I] *(rec live 6/20/58)* Melodram 2–▲ MEL 26007 (m)
Verdi, G.:La traviata, w. M. Callas (sop), A. Zanasi (bass), N. Rescigno (cnd), Royal Opera House Orch, Royal Opera House Chorus Covent Garden [I] *(rec live 6/20/58)* Verona 2–▲ 27054/55 (m) [AAD]
The Voices of Living Stereo, Vol. 2, w. Eileen Farrell (sop), Birgit Nilsson (sop), Roberta Peters (sop), Leontyne Price (sop), Galina Vishnevskaya (sop), Rosalind Elias (mez), Shirley Verrett (mez), Marian Anderson (cta), Maureen Forrester (cta), Sergio Franchi (ten), Mario Lanza (ten), Richard Lewis (ten), Jan Pee, Alexander Dedyukhin (pno), Franz Rupp (pno), Leo Taubman (pno), George Trovillo (pno), Charles Wadsworth (pno), Boston Pops Orch [cnd:Arthur Fiedler], Boston SO [cnd:Charles Munch], Chicago SO [cnd:Fritz Reiner], RCA Victor Orch, RCA Victor Chorus [cnd:Wa *(rec Boston & Chicago & New York & Rome, 1957–1964)* RCA Living Stereo ▲ 09026–68167–2 [ADD]

Vallin, Marie-Claude (sop)
Airs de Cour:French Court Music from the 17th Century, w. Max van Egmond (bass), Lutz Kirchhof (renaissance lt) Sony Classical ("Vivarte" series) ▲ SK 48250 [DDD]
Haydn, J.:Ave regina, w. Bob Van Asperen (org), B. Weil (cnd), L'Archibudelli, Tölz Boys' Choir *(rec Bad Tölz, Germany, Jan. 2–4, 1993)* Sony Classical ("Vivarte" series) ▲ SK 53368 [DDD]
Love Songs & Dances:Consort Music for Lute & Voices from "Pratum Musicum", w. Kirchhof, Lutz (lt), Claudio Cavina (altus), Max van Egmond (bar), Sabine Dreier (trns fl), Petra Manz (vl) *(rec Evangelische Kirche, St Osdag, Mandelsloh, Germany, Nov 21–24, 1994)* Sony Classical ("Vivarte" series) ▲ SK 66263 [DDD]
Puccini, G.:Tosca (sels), w. E. di Mazzei (ten), P. Payen (bar), A. Endrèze (bar), G. Cloëz (cnd), Paris Opéra-Comique Orch, Paris Opéra-Comique Chorus [abridged version] [F] *(rec 1932)* Music Memoria ▲ 30376

Vallin, Ninon (sop)
Charpentier, G.:Louise, w. N. Vallin (sop—Louise), C. Gaudel (sop—Irma), A. Lecouvreur (mez—Mother), G. Thill (ten—Julien), A. Pernet (bass—Father), E. Bigot (cnd), Raugel Orch, Raugel Chorus *(rec 1936)* Nimbus (Prima Voce) ▲ NI 7829 (m) [ADD]
Charpentier, G.:Louise (abridged ed), w. N. Vallin (sop—Louise), C. Gaudel (mez—Irma), A. Lecouvreur (cta—La Mère), G. Thill (ten—Julien), A. Pernet (bass—La Père), E. Bigot (cnd), *(orch & chorus unknown)* [F] *(rec 1935 for Columbia Records)* Music Memoria 3–▲ 30223
Falla, M. de:El amor brujo (sels), w. G. Cloëz (cnd)—En la Cueva:Canción del amor dolido; Escena:Canción del Fuego fatuo; Danza de Juego de Amor *(rec 1930)* VAI Audio ▲ VAIA 1127 [ADD]
Falla, M. de:Canciones populares españolas (7), w. Godfroy Andolfi (pno)—Seguidilla murciana; Nana; Jota *(rec 1930)* VAI Audio ▲ VAIA 1127 [ADD]
Mozart, W.A.:Nozze di Figaro (sels), w. Mariano Stabile (bar), Elisabeth Schumann (sop) *(rec 1905 – 1944)* Minerva ▲ MN A14 [ADD]
Nin, J.:Songs, w. Joaquín Nin (pno)—Tonada de la niña perdida; Canto andaluz; Granadina; Montañesa; El jilguerillo con pico de oro; Malagueña; Polo *(rec 1931)* VAI Audio ▲ VAIA 1127 [ADD]
Opera & Mélodie, w. Vallin, Ninon (sop), various orchs & pno accompaniment, rec. ca. 1927–1938 from Odws□Pearl ▲ PEA 9948 (m) [ADD]
Schumann, R.:Frauenliebe und -leben, w. Godfroy Andolfi (pno) [Fr. trans. Jules Barbier] *(rec 1920)* VAI Audio ▲ VAIA 1127 [ADD]

Vallin, Ninon (sop) (cont.)

Schumann, R.:Liederkreis, Op. 39, w. Godfroy Andolfi (pno)—Au loin *(rec 1931)* VAI Audio ▲ VAIA 1127 [ADD]

Strauss, R.:Songs, w. Godfroy Andolfi (pno)—Sérénade; Rêve crépusculaire *(rec 1931)* VAI Audio ▲ VAIA 1127 [ADD]

Valori, Nino (ten)

Verdi, G.:Ernani, w. Licia Galvano (sop—Giovanna), Leyla Gencer (sop—Elvira), Carlo Bergonzi (ten—Ernani), Nino Valori (ten—Don Riccardo), Piero Cappuccilli (bar—Don Carlo), Alessandro Cassis (bar—Jago), Ruggero Raimondi (bass—Don Ruy Gomez de Silva), G. Gavazzeni (cnd), Catania Teatro Massimo Bellini Orch, Catania Teatro Massimo Bellini Chorus *(rec live, Catania, Jan 15, 1972)* Arkadia 2–▲ 621 [ADD]

Vanasek, Rudolf (ten)

Janácek, L.:The Makropulos Affair, w. Libuse Prylova (sop), Helena Tattermuschová (sop), Ivo Zídek (ten), B. Gregor (cnd), Prague National Orch, Prague National Theater Chorus *(rec mid 1960's)* Supraphon 2–▲ SUP 108351 [AAD]

Vanaud, Marcel (bar)

Verdi, G.:Arias, w. R. Rossel (cnd), Wallonie Opera Royal Orch—Nabucco; Stiffelio; Rigoletto; Il Trovatore; La Traviata; Un Ballo in Maschera; La Forza del destino; Don Carlo Ligia Digital ▲ 0203035

Van Berne, Harry (ten)

Charpentier, M.–A.:Motets for Double Choir, w. B. Schlick (sop), N. Zijlstra (sop), K. Wessel (alt), D. Visse (ct), C. Prégardien (ten), P. Kooy (bass), K. Martens (bass), T. Koopman (cnd), Amsterdam Baroque Orch—Canticum pro pace; Josué; Mors Saulis et Jonathae; Praelium Michaelis; Quam dilecta; 3 Leçons de Ténèbres Erato (Musifrance) ▲ 2292–45822–2 ZA

Handel, G.F.:Te Deum, "Caroline", w. Mieke van der Sluis (sop), Graham Pushee (alt), Harry van der Kamp (bass), W. Helbich (cnd), Bremen Baroque Orch, Alfelder Vocal Ensemble CPO ▲ CPO 999244 [DDD]

Handel, G.F.:The Ways of Zion Do Mourn, w. Mieke van der Sluis (sop), Graham Pushee (alt), Harry van der Kamp (bass), W. Helbich (cnd), Bremen Baroque Orch, Alfelder Vocal Ensemble CPO ▲ CPO 999244 [DDD]

Van Dam, José (b–bar)

Berlioz, H.:La Damnation de Faust, w. F. von Stade (mez), K. Riegel (ten), G. Solti (cnd), Chicago SO, Chicago Sym Chorus London 2–▲ 414680–2 [DDD]

Berlioz, H.:L'Enfance du Christ, w. A. S. von Otter (mez), Johnson (sgr), G. Cachemaille (bar), J. Bastin (bass), J.E. Gardiner (cnd), Lyon Opera Orch, Monteverdi Choir London [F] Erato 2–▲ 2292–45275–2 [DDD]

Bizet, G.:Carmen, w. T. Troyanos (mez), K. Te Kanawa (sop), P. Domingo (ten), G. Solti (cnd), London PO [F] London 3–▲ 414489–2 [ADD]

Bizet, G.:Carmen, w. T. Troyanos (mez), K. Te Kanawa (sop), P. Domingo (ten), G. Solti (cnd), London PO [F] London ▲ 421300–2 [ADD]

Bizet, G.:Carmen, w. Kiri Te Kanawa (sop), Shirley Verrett (mez), Placido Domingo (ten), G. Solti (cnd), Royal Opera House Orch, Royal Opera House Chorus Covent Garden *(rec live, London, 1973)* Arkadia 3–▲ 498

Bizet, G.:Carmen (sels), w. K. Ricciarelli (sop), A. Baltsa (mez), J. Carreras (ten), H. von Karajan (cnd), Berlin PO, Paris Opera Chorus [F] Deutsche Grammophon ▲ 413322–2 [DDD]

Brahms, J.:Ein Deutsches Requiem, w. A. Tomowa–Sintow (sop), H. von Karajan (cnd), Berlin PO, Vienna Singverein [G] *(rec 1976)* EMI Classics ▲ CDM 69229 [ADD]

Brahms, J.:Ein Deutsches Requiem, w. B. Hendricks (sop), H. von Karajan (cnd), Vienna PO, Vienna Singverein [G] *(rec 1986)* Deutsche Grammophon ▲ 431651–2 [DDD]

Charpentier, G.:Louise, w. B. Sills (sop—Louise), M. Dunn (mez—Louise's Mother), N. Gedda (ten—Julien), J. Van Dam (bass–bar—Louise's Father), J. Rudel (cnd), Paris Opera Orch, Paris Opera Chorus EMI Classics ▲ CDMC 65299

Debussy, C.:Pelléas et Mélisande, w. M. Ewing (sop), C. Ludwig (mez), F. Le Roux (bar), J.–P. Courtis (bass), C. Abbado (cnd), Vienna PO, Vienna State Opera Chorus Deutsche Grammophon 2–▲ 435344–2 [DDD]

Debussy, C.:Pelléas et Mélisande, w. N. Denize (mez), F. von Stade (mez), G. Raimondi (ten), R. Stilwell (bar), H. von Karajan (cnd), Berlin PO, German Opera Chorus [F] EMI Classics 3–▲ CDCC 49350 [ADD]

Enescu, G.:Oedipe, w. B. Hendricks (sop), B. Fassbaender (mez), M. Lipovšek (mez), J. Taillon (mez), N. Gedda (ten), J. Aler (ten), G. Bacquier (bar), Quilico (bar), L. Foster (cnd), Monte Carlo PO, Orféon Donostiarra, Petits Chanteurs de Monaco [F] EMI Classics 2–▲ CDCB 54011 [DDD]

Gluck, C.W.:Iphigénie en Aulide, w. L. Dawson (sop), A. S. von Otter (mez), J. Aler (ten), Lyon Opera Orch, J. E. Gardiner (cnd), Monteverdi Choir London Erato ("Musifrance" series) 2–▲ 2292–45003–2–ZA [DDD]

Gounod, C.:Faust, w. C. Studer (sop), R. Leech (ten), T. Hampson (bar), M. Plasson (cnd), Toulouse Capitole Orch, Toulouse Capitole Chorus, *(highlights from the above)* EMI Classics ▲ CDC 54358 [DDD]

Gounod, C.:Faust, w. C. Studer (sop), R. Leech (ten), T. Hampson (bar), M. Plasson (cnd), Toulouse Capitole Orch, Toulouse Capitole Chorus EMI Classics 3–▲ CDCC 54228 [DDD]

Gounod, C.:Mors et vita, w. B. Hendricks (sop), N. Denize (mez), J. Aler (ten), M. Plasson (cnd), Toulouse Capitole Orch, Orféon Donostiarra [F] *(rec 1/92)* EMI Classics 2–▲ CDCB 54459

Gounod, C.:Roméo et Juliette, w. C. Malfitano (sop), A. Kraus (ten), L. Quilico (bar), G. Bacquier (bar), M. Plasson (cnd), Toulouse Capitole Orch, Toulouse Capitole Chorus [F] EMI Classics 3–▲ CDCC 47365

Gounod, C.:Songs, w. J.–P. Collard (pno)—Medjé; Envoi de fleurs; Si la mort est le but; Crépuscule; Hymne à la nuit EMI Classics ▲ CDC 54818

Les grands airs italiens, w. Loire PO [cnd:Marc Soustrot] Forlane ▲ FOR 16681 [DDD]

Ibert, J.:Chansons de Don Quichotte, w. K. Nagano (cnd), Lyon Opera Orch Virgin Classics ▲ CDC 59236

Mahler, G.:Kindertotenlieder, w. J.–C. Casadesus (cnd), Lille National Orch [G] Forlane ▲ FOR 16553 [DDD]

Mahler, G.:Des Knaben Wunderhorn—Le cor merveilleux de l'enfant Forlane ▲ FRL 302270 [ADD]

Mahler, G.:Des Knaben Wunderhorn, w. J.–C. Casadesus (cnd), Lille National Orch—2 sels. Forlane ▲ FOR 16553 [DDD]

Mahler, G.:Songs from Rückert, w. J.–C. Casadesus (cnd), Lille National Orch [G] Forlane ▲ FOR 16553 [DDD]

Mahler, G.:Songs from Rückert Forlane ▲ FRL 302270 [ADD]

Mahler, G.:Syms, w. J. Blegen (sop), B. Hendricks (sop), M. Price (sop), G. Zeumer (sop), H. Wittek (trb), A. Baltsa (mez), C. Ludwig (mez), K. Riegel (ten), H. Prey (bar), A. Schmidt (bar), L. Bernstein (cnd), New York PO, Royal Concertgebouw Orch, Vienna PO, Westminster Choir, New York Choral Artists, Brooklyn Boys' Choir, Vienna Boys' Choir, Vienna State Opera Chorus, Vienna Singverein Deutsche Grammophon 13–▲ 435162–2 [DDD]

Mahler, G.:Sym 8, w. J. Blegen (sop), M. Price (sop), G. Zeumer (sop), A. Baltsa (mez), K. Riegel (ten), H. Prey (bar), A. Schmidt (bar), L. Bernstein (cnd), Vienna PO, Vienna State Opera Chorus, Vienna Boys' Choir *(rec Salzburg Festival, 1975)* Deutsche Grammophon 2–▲ 435102–2 [ADD]

Martin, F.:Monologe (6) aus "Jedermann", w. K. Nagano (cnd), Lyon Opera Orch Virgin Classics ▲ CDC 59236

Massenet, J.:Don Quichotte, w. T. Berganza (mez—La Belle Dulcinée), A. Fondary (bar—Sancho Pana), J. Van Dam (b–bar—Don Quichotte), M. Plasson (cnd), Toulouse Capitole Orch, Toulouse Capitole Chorus EMI Classics ▲ CDCB 54767

Massenet, J.:Hérodiade, w. Cheryl Studer (sop—Salomé), Nadine Denize (mez—Hérodiade), Ben Heppner (ten—Jean), José Van Dam (b–bar—Phanuel), Thomas Hampson (bass—Hérode), M. Plasson (cnd), Toulouse Capitole Orch, Toulouse Capitole Chorus EMI Classics 3–▲ CDCC 55378

Massenet, J.:Songs, w. J.–P. Collard (pno)—Les mains; Berceuse; La mort de la cigale; Elégie [w. G. Rouge (cello)] EMI Classics ▲ CDC 54818

Mozart, W.A.:Arias, w. J.–P. Wallez (cnd), Paris Orchestral Ensemble—from Così fan tutte, Don Giovanni, Le nozze di Figaro, Die Zauberflöte; (2 concert arias) K. 513 & K.541 [G,I] *(rec live Nov. 22, 1986)* Forlane ▲ FOR 16562 [DDD]

Van Dam, José (b–bar) (cont.)

Mozart, W.A.:Così fan tutte, w. K. Mattila (sop), E. Szmytka (sop), A. S. von Otter (mez), F. Araiza (ten), T. Allen (bar), N. Marriner (cnd), Academy of St. Martin in the Fields, Ambrosian Opera Chorus [I] Philips 3–▲ 422381–2 [DDD]

Mozart, W.A.:Don Giovanni, w. E. Moser (sop), K. Te Kanawa (sop), T. Berganza (mez), K. Riegel (ten), G. Raimondi (ten), J. Macurdy (bass), L. Maazel (cnd), Paris Opera Orch, Paris Opera Chorus [I] CBS 3–▲ M3K 35192

Mozart, W.A.:Don Giovanni (sels)—Air de Leparella; Air de Don Giovanni; Air du Champagne; Air de Don Giovanni [Canzonetta] Forlane ▲ FRL 302270 [ADD]

Mozart, W.A.:Don Giovanni (sels), w. Kiri Te Kanawa (sop), Teresa Berganza (mez), Ruggero Raimondi (bass), L. Maazel (cnd), Paris Opera Orch, Paris Opera Chorus Sony Classical ("Essential Classics" series) ▲ SBK 62663 ■ SBT 62663

Mozart, W.A.:Don Giovanni (sels), w. E. Moser (sop), K. Te Kanawa (sop), T. Berganza (mez), K. Riegel (ten), G. Raimondi (ten), J. Macurdy (bass), L. Maazel (cnd), Paris Opera Orch CBS ■ MT 35859

Mozart, W.A.:Missa, K.317, w. A. Tomowa–Sintow (sop), A. Baltsa (mez), W. Krenn (ten), H. von Karajan (cnd), Berlin PO, Vienna Singverein Deutsche Grammophon ▲ 429820–2 [ADD]

Mozart, W.A.:Missa, K.317, w. A. Tomowa–Sintow (sop), A. Baltsa (mez), W. Krenn (ten), H. von Karajan (cnd), Berlin PO, Vienna Singverein [L] Deutsche Grammophon ("Galleria" series) 2–▲ 423913–2 [ADD]

Mozart, W.A.:Nozze di Figaro, w. Mirella Freni (sop), Gundala Janowitz (sop), Jane Berbié (mez), Frederica von Stade (mez), Michel Sénéchal (ten), Kurt Moll (bass), G. Solti (cnd), Paris Opera Orch, Paris Opera Chorus *(rec live, Paris, Apr 7, 1973)* Agorá ("Phoenix" series) 3–▲ 515

Mozart, W.A.:Nozze di Figaro, w. Mirella Freni (sop), Daniela Mazzucato (sop), Teresa Berganza (mez), Mirto Picchi (ten), Hermann Prey (bar), Paolo Montarsolo (bass), C. Abbado (cnd), La Scala Orch, La Scala Chorus *(rec live, Apr 22, 1974)* Arkadia 3–▲ 614

Mozart, W.A.:Nozze di Figaro, w. L. Popp (sop), B. Hendricks (sop), A. Baltsa (mez), G. Raimondi (ten), N. Marriner (cnd), Academy of St. Martin in the Fields, Ambrosian Opera Chorus [I] Philips 3–▲ 416370–2 [DDD]

Mozart, W.A.:Nozze di Figaro (sels), w. Anna Tomowa–Sintow (sop), Controbas (sgr), H. von Karajan (cnd), Vienna PO London ▲ 421317–2 [ADD]

Mozart, W.A.:Nozze di Figaro (sels)—Récitatif, auf du comte almaviva Forlane ▲ FRL 302270 [ADD]

Mozart, W.A.:Nozze di Figaro (sels), w. L. Popp (sop), B. Hendricks (sop), A. Baltsa (mez), G. Raimondi (ten), N. Marriner (cnd), Academy of St. Martin in the Fields, Ambrosian Opera Chorus [I] Philips ▲ 416870–2 [DDD]

Mozart, W.A.:Requiem, w. A. Tomowa–Sintow (sop), A. Baltsa (mez), W. Krenn (ten), H. von Karajan (cnd), Berlin PO, Vienna Singverein Deutsche Grammophon ▲ 429821–2 [ADD] ■ 429821–4

Mozart, W.A.:Requiem, w. A. Tomowa–Sintow (sop), A. Baltsa (mez), W. Krenn (ten), H. von Karajan (cnd), Berlin PO, Vienna Singverein [L] Deutsche Grammophon ("Galleria" series) ▲ 419867–2 [ADD] ■ 419867–4

Mozart, W.A.:Zauberflöte, w. Edith Mathis (sop), Karin Ott (sop), Janet Perry (sop), Anna Tomowa–Sintow (sop), Agnes Baltsa (mez), Hannah Schwarz (mez), Francisco Araiza (ten), Gottfried Hornik (bar), H. von Karajan (cnd), Berlin PO, German Opera Chorus [G] Deutsche Grammophon 3–▲ 410967–2 [DDD]

Mozart, W.A.:Zauberflöte, w. Reri Grist (sop), Edita Gruberová (sop), Edith Mathis (sop), Rene Kollo (ten), Gerhard Unger (ten), Hermann Prey (bar), Peter Meven (bass), H. von Karajan (cnd), Vienna PO, Vienna State Opera Chorus *(rec live, Salzburg, July 26, 1974)* Arkadia 2–▲ 233

Mozart, W.A.:Zauberflöte (sels), w. Edith Mathis (sop), Karin Ott (sop), Janet Perry (sop), Anna Tomowa–Sintow (sop), Agnes Baltsa (mez), Hannah Schwarz (mez), Francisco Araiza (ten), Gottfried Hornik (bar), H. von Karajan (cnd), Berlin PO, German Opera Chorus [G] Deutsche Grammophon ▲ 415287–2 [DDD]

Mozart, W.A.:Zauberflöte (sels)—Air de Papageno Forlane ▲ FRL 302270 [ADD]

Offenbach, J.:Les Contes d'Hoffmann, w. L. Serra (sop), R. Plowright (sop), J. Norman (sop), A. Murray (mez), J. Taillon (mez), N. Shicoff (ten), A. Oliver (ten), R. Tear (ten), D. Duesing (bar), K. Rydl (bass), S. Cambreling (cnd), Brussels Théâtre de la Monnaie Orch [F] EMI Classics 3–▲ CDCC 49641 [DDD]

Poulenc, F.:Le Bal masqué, w. K. Nagano (cnd), Lyon Opera Orch Virgin Classics ▲ CDC 59236

Poulenc, F.:Dialogues des Carmélites, w. C. Dubosc (sop), R. Yakar (sop), R. Gorr (mez), M. Dupuy (mez), K. Nagano (cnd), Lyon Opera Orch Virgin Classics ▲ CDCB 59227

Puccini, G.:La Bohème (sels)—Air de Colline Forlane ▲ FRL 302270 [ADD]

Rameau, J.P.:Dardanus, w. C. Eda–Pierre (sop), F. von Stade (mez), G. Gautier (ten), R. Soyer (bar), R. Leppard (cnd), Paris Lyon Opera Orch, Paris Lyon Opera Chorus Erato 2–▲ 95312–2

Ravel, M.:Don Quichotte à Dulcinée, w. P. Boulez (cnd), Ensemble InterContemporain [F] CBS ▲ MK 39023

Ravel, M.:Don Quichotte à Dulcinée, w. K. Nagano (cnd), Lyon Opera Orch Virgin Classics ▲ CDC 59236

Ravel, M.:Mélodies populaires grecques, w. P. Boulez (cnd), Ensemble InterContemporain [F] CBS ▲ MK 39023

Rossini, G.:Il barbiere di Siviglia (sels), *(orch unknown)* Forlane ▲ FRL 302270 [ADD]

Saint–Saëns, C.:Songs, w. J.–P. Collard (pno)—Rêverie; Clair de lune; Sonnet; Si vous n'avez rien à me dire; Le lever de la lune; Extase; Les cloches de la mer; Danse macabre; Le pas d'armes du roi Jean EMI Classics ▲ CDC 54818

Schubert, Franz:Schwanengesang, w. V. Afanassiev (pno) [G] Forlane ▲ FOR 16647 [DDD]

Schubert, Franz:Winterreise, w. D. Baldwin (pno) [G] Forlane ▲ FOR 16622 [DDD]

Schumann, R.:Dichterliebe, w. D. Baldwin (pno) [G] Forlane ▲ FOR 16595 [DDD]

Schumann, R.:Songs, w. D. Baldwin (pno)—12 Kerner–Lieder, Op. 35; Die beiden Grenadiere, Op. 49 [G] Forlane ▲ FOR 16595 [DDD]

Strauss, R.:Die Frau ohne Schatten, w. J. Varady (sop), H. Behrens (sop), P. Domingo (ten), G. Solti (cnd), Vienna PO, Vienna State Opera Chorus [G] London 3–▲ 436243–2

Strauss, R.:Salome, w. H. Behrens (sop), A. Baltsa (mez), H. Angervo (alt), K.W. Böhm (ten), W. Ochman (ten), H. von Karajan (cnd), Vienna PO EMI Classics 2–▲ CDCB 49358

Strauss, R.:Salome, w. K. Huffstodt (sop), H. Jossoud (mez), J. Dupouy (ten), J.L. Viala (ten), K. Nagano (cnd), Paris Lyon Opera Orch, Paris Lyon Opera Chorus Virgin Classics 2–▲ CDCB 59054

Verdi, G.:Aida, w. L. Freni (sop), K. Ricciarelli (sop), A. Baltsa (mez), J. Carreras (ten), P. Cappuccilli (bar), G. Raimondi (ten), H. von Karajan (cnd), Vienna PO, Vienna State Opera Chorus [I] EMI Classics (Studio) 3–▲ CDMC 69300 [ADD]

Verdi, G.:Don Carlos (sels)—Monologue de Philippe II Forlane ▲ FRL 302270 [ADD]

Verdi, G.:Falstaff, w. E. Norberg–Schulz (sop—Nannetta), L. Serra (sop—Alice), S. Graham (mez—Meg Page), M. Lipovsek (cta—Miss Quickly), K. Begley (ten—Dr. Caius), P. Conti (ten—Ford), M. Luperi (ten—Pistol), J. Van Dam (b–bar—Falstaff), P. LeFebvre (bass—Bardolph), G. Solti (cnd), Berlin PO, Berlin Radio Chorus London ▲ 440650–2 [DDD]

Verdi, G.:Requiem Mass, w. Anna Tomowa–Sintow (sop), Agnes Baltsa (mez), José Carreras (ten), H. von Karajan (cnd), Vienna PO, Vienna State Opera Chorus, Sofia National Opera Chorus *(rec Great Hall, Musikverein, Vienna, June 1984)* Deutsche Grammophon 2–▲ 439033–2 [DDD]

Verdi, G.:Rigoletto (sels)—Air de Rigoletto Forlane ▲ FRL 302270 [ADD]

Verdi, G.:Simon Boccanegra, w. Alberto Cupido (ten), Ned Barth (bar), Manfred Schenk (bass), Daniela Longhi (sgr), Dino Musio (sgr), M. Veltri (cnd), Marseille Opera Orch, Marseille Opera Chorus Lyrinx 3–▲ LYX 127 [DDD]

Wagner, R.:Arias & Scenes, w. J.–C. Casadesus (cnd), Lille National Orch—Der fliegende Holländer:Die Frist ist um; Tannhäuser:Blick ich umher; O du mein holder Abendstern; Die Meistersinger von Nürnberg:Was duftet doch der Flieder; Wahn! Wahn! überall Wahn; Die Walküre:Leb wohl! du kühnes, herrliches Kind [G] Forlane ▲ FOR 16633 [DDD]

Wagner, R.:Der fliegende Holländer, w. D. Vejzovic (sop), P. Hofmann (ten), Kurt Moll (bass), H. von Karajan (cnd), Berlin PO [G] EMI Classics 2–▲ CDMB 64650

Wagner, R.:Parsifal, w. D. Vejzovic (sop), P. Hofmann (ten), S. Nimsgern (b–bar), K. Moll (bass), H. von Karajan (cnd), Berlin PO, German Opera Chorus [G] Deutsche Grammophon 4–▲ 413347–2 [DDD]

Wagner, R.:Tannhäuser (sels)—Romance de l'étoile [Cavatine de Wolfram] Forlane ▲ FRL 302270 [ADD]

Wagner, R.:Die Walküre (sels)—Les adieux de Wotan Forlane ▲ FRL 302270 [ADD]

Vanderlinde, Debra (sop)

Flowering of Vocal Music in America, 1767–1823, w. Susan Belling (sop), Cynthia Clarey (sop), Barbara Wallace (sop), Debra Vanderlinde (sop), D'Anna Fortunato (mez), Evelyn Petros (mez), Charles Bressler (ten), Richard Anderson (bar), James Tyeska (bar), Joseph McKee (bass), Cynthia Otis (hp), et. al. New World ▲ 80467–2

Vandersteene, Zeger (ten)

Uy, P.:Choral pour la Paix, w. Dinah Bryant (sop), Philippe Huttenlocher (bar), Alain Carré (nar), Dominique Cornil (pno), G. Octors (cnd), Wallonie Royal CO, Denis Menier (cnd), Namur Chamber Choir *(rec Aulne, Belgium, 1995)* Cypres ▲ 2611 [DDD]

Zuidam, R.:Freeze, w. Susan Narucki (sop—Patty Hearst), Gerrie de Vries (mez), Martin Hargrove (bass), Jaco Huijpen (bass), S. Asbury (cnd), Asko Ensemble NM Classics 2–▲ NM 92047

Vanderwal, David (ten)

Bach, J.S.:St. John Passion, w. Tamara Matthews (sop), Jennifer Lane (alt), Mark Bleeke (ten—Evangelist), Kevin Walsh (bar—Pilate), Nathaniel Watson (bass—Jesus), E. Milnes (cnd), Trinity Baroque Orch, Trinity Cathedral Choir *(rec Trinity Cathedral, Portland, OR, Mar 31, 1996)* PGM 2–▲ PGM 111

Van Dyke, Dick (sgr)

Broadway, w. Ethel Merman (sgr), Judy Holliday (sgr), Doris Day (sgr), Topol (sgr), Mary Martin (sgr), Jill Haworth (sgr), William Warfield (sgr), et al. Sony Classical ("Greatest Hits" series) ▲ MLK 62365 ■ MLT 62365

Vane, Doris (sop)

Friml, R.:Film Music, w. H. Williams (bar), D. Oldham (ten), London Palladium Orch—The Vagabond King; The Blue Kitten; Rose Marie; The 3 Musketeers; The Firefly Pearl ("Flapper" series) ▲ PAST CD 9764 [AAD]

Gounod, C.:Faust, w. M. Licette (sop—Margarita), D. Vane (sop—Siebel), M. Brunskill (cta—Martha), H. Nash (ten—Faust), H. Williams (b-bar—Valentine), R. Easton (bass—Mephistopheles), R. Carr (bass—Wagner), T. Beecham (cnd), BBC SO, BBC Sym Chorus Dutton Laboratories 2–▲ CDAX 2001 [ADD]

Vane, Kyra (sop)

Kyra Vayne Preiser ("Lebendige Vergangenheit" series) ▲ PRE 89996 [AAD]

van Egmond, Max (bass)—see Egmond, Max van

Vanelli, Gino (bar)

Leoncavallo, R.:Pagliacci, w. Rosetta Pampanini (sop), Francesco Merli (ten), Giuseppe Nessi (ten), Carlo Galeffi (bar), *(orch unknown)* *(rec Milan, 1930)* Melodram ▲ IMC 102003

Puccini, G.:La Bohème, w. Luba Mirella (sop—Musetta), Rosetta Pampanini (sop—Mimì), Luigi Marini (ten—Rodolfo), Giuseppe Nessi (ten—Alcindoro), Aristide Baracchi (bar—Schaunard), Gino Vanelli (bar—Marcello), Salvatore Baccaloni (bass—Benoit), Tancredi Pasero (bass—Colline), L. Molajoli (cnd), La Scala Orch, La Scala Chorus Bongiovanni 2–▲ 1125/26 [ADD]

Puccini, G.:Madama Butterfly, w. R. Pampanini (sop), A. Granda (ten), G. Nessi (ten), S. Baccaloni (bass), L. Malajoli (cnd), La Scala Orch, La Scala Chorus *(rec 1928)* Centaur 2–▲ CRC 2196/97

Puccini, G.:Madama Butterfly, w. Rosetta Pampanini (sop—Madama Butterfly), Conchita Velasquez (mez—Suzuki), Cesira Ferrari (mez—Kate Pinkerton), Alessandro Granda (ten—F. B. Pinkerton), Giuseppe Nessi (ten—Goro), Aristide Baracchi (bar—Il Principe Yamadori), Gino Vanelli (bar—Sharpless), Lino Bonardi (bass—Il Commissario Imperiale), Salvatore Baccaloni (bass—Lo zio Bonzo), L. Molajoli (cnd), La Scala Orch, La Scala Chorus Bongiovanni 2–▲ 1123/24 [ADD]

Vaness, Carol (sop)

Beethoven, L. van:Missa Solemnis, w. W. Meier (mez), H.-P. Blochwitz (ten), H. Tschammer (bass), J. Tate (cnd), English CO, Tallis Chamber Choir [L] EMI Classics ▲ CDC 49950 [DDD]

Donizetti, G.:Anna Bolena (sels), w. Melinda Paulsen (cta), Dennis O'Neill (ten), Anton Rosner (ten), Ambrogio Riva (bass), R. Abbado (cnd), Munich RSO, Bavarian Radio Chorus—Final Scene & Aria [from Act II] *(rec Studio 1, Bavaria, Apr 13–17, 1993)* RCA Red Seal ▲ 09026–61828–2 [DDD]

Gluck, C.W.:Iphigénie en Tauride, w. C. Vaness (sop—Iphigénie), S. Brunet (sop—Diane), G. Winbergh (ten—Pylade), T. Allen (bar—Oreste), G. Surian (bass—Thoas), R. Muti (cnd), La Scala Orch, La Scala Chorus *(rec Mar. 14–26, 1992)* Sony Classical 2–▲ S2K 52492 [DDD]

Mozart, W.A.:Arias, w. P. Domingo (ten), E. Cohn (cnd), Munich RSO—arias from Clemenza di Tito, Così fan tutte, Don Giovanni, Entführung aus dem Serail, La finta giardineira, Idomeneo, Le nozze di Figaro, Die Zauberflöte EMI Classics ▲ CDC 54329

Mozart, W.A.:Arias, w. L. Hager (cnd), Munich RSO—(11) from Clemenza di Tito, Così fan tutte, Don Giovanni, Idomeneo, Le nozze di Figaro [I] RCA Red Seal ▲ 60562–2–RC [DDD]

Mozart, W.A.:Clemenza, w. Christine Barbaux (sop—Servilia), Carol Vaness (sop—Viellia), Martha Senn (mez—Annio), Delores Ziegler (mez—Sesto), Gösta Winbergh (ten—Tito), László Polgár (bass—Publio), R. Muti (cnd), Vienna PO, Vienna State Opera Chorus *(rec live, Salzburg Festival, 1988)* EMI Classics 2–▲ CDCB 55489

Mozart, W.A.:Così fan tutte, w. Delores Ziegler (mez), C. Watson (cta), J. Aler (ten), D. Duesing (bar), C. Desderi (bar), B. Haitink (cnd), London PO, Glyndebourne Festival Chorus EMI Classics 3–▲ CDCC 47727

Mozart, W.A.:Don Giovanni, w. M. Ewing (sop), E. Gale (sop), K. Lewis (ten), T. Allen (bar), R. Van Allan (bass), B. Haitink (cnd), London PO, Glyndebourne Festival Chorus [I] EMI Classics 3–▲ CDCC 47036 [DDD]

Mozart, W.A.:Don Giovanni, w. S. Studer (sop), W. Shimell (bar), S. Ramey (bass), R. Muti (cnd), Vienna PO EMI Classics 3–▲ CDCC 54255

Mozart, W.A.:Don Giovanni (sels), w. C. Studer (sop), R. Muti (cnd), Vienna PO EMI Classics ▲ CDC 54323

Mozart, W.A.:Idomeneo, w. Heidi Grant-Murphy (sop—Ilia), Carol Vaness (sop—Elettra), Cecilia Bartoli (mez—Idamante), Plácido Domingo (ten—Idomeneo), Frank Lopardo (ten—High Priest), Thomas Hampson (bar—Arbace), Bryn Terfel (b-bar—The Voice), J. Levine (cnd), Metropolitan Opera Orch, Raymond Hughes (cnd), New York Metropolitan Opera Chorus *(rec Manhattan Center Studios, New York, Mar & Apr 1994)* Deutsche Grammophon 3–▲ 447 737–2 [DDD]

Mozart, W.A.:Nozze di Figaro, w. Rebecca Evans (sop—Barbarina), Nuccia Focile (sop—Susanna), Suzanne Murphy (sop—Marcellina), Carol Vaness (sop—Countess Almaviva), Susanne Mentzer (mez—Cherubino), Ryland Davies (ten—Don Basilio/Don Curzio), Alessandro Corbelli (bar—Count Almaviva), Alfonso Antoniozzi (bass—Doctor Bartolo/Antonio), Alastair Miles (bass—Figaro), C. Mackerras (cnd), Scottish CO, Scottish Chamber Chorus *(rec Usher Hall, Edingurgh, Scotland, July 31–Aug. 12, 1994)* Telarc 3–▲ CD 80388 [DDD]

Verdi, G.:Macbeth (sels), w. Marisca Mulder (sop), Ambrogio Riva (bass), R. Abbado (cnd), Munich RSO, Bavarian Radio Chorus—Grand Sleepwalking Scene [from Act IV] *(rec Studio 1, Bavaria, Apr 13–17, 1993)* RCA Red Seal ▲ 09026–61828–2 [DDD]

Verdi, G.:Otello (sels), w. Melinda Paulsen (cta), R. Abbado (cnd), Munich RSO, Bavarian Radio Chorus—Canzone del salice; Ave Maria [both from Act IV] *(rec Studio 1, Bavaria, Apr 13–17, 1993)* RCA Red Seal ▲ 09026–61828–2 [DDD]

Verdi, G.:Requiem Mass, w. F. Quivar (mez), D. O'Neill (ten), C. Colombara (bass), C. Davis (cnd), Bavarian RSO, Bavarian Radio Chorus RCA Red Seal 2–▲ 09026–60902–2

Verdi, G.:La traviata (sels), w. Dennis O'Neill (ten), R. Abbado (cnd), Munich RSO, Bavarian Radio Chorus—Final Scene & Aria [from Act I] *(rec Studio 1, Bavaria, Apr 13–17, 1993)* RCA Red Seal ▲ 09026–61828–2 [DDD]

Verdi, G.:Il trovatore (sels), w. Dennis O'Neill (ten), Anton Rosner (ten), R. Abbado (cnd), Munich RSO, Bavarian Radio Chorus—Scene, Aria & Miserere [from Act IV] *(rec Studio 1, Munich, Apr 13–17, 1993)* RCA Red Seal ▲ 09026–61828–2 [DDD]

Van Evera, Emily (sop)

Bach, J.S.:Mass in b, BWV 232, w. E. Kirkby (sop), R. Covey-Crump (ct), D. Thomas (bass), A. Parrott (cnd), Taverner Consort, Taverner Players, Tölz Boys' Choir [L] EMI Classics 2–▲ ZDCB 47292–2 [DDD]

Cavalli, P.F.:Vespero della beata Vergine Maria, w. Barbara Borden (sop), Markus Brutscher (ten), Mark Padmore (ten), Rodrigo del Pozo (ten), Gerd Türk (ten), Harry van der Kamp (bass), Peter Zimpel (sgr), Bruce Dickey (sackbut), Charles Toet (sackbut), Concerto Palatino, Schola Cantorum Basiliensis Harmonia Mundi France ("Documenta" series) 2–▲ HMC 905219/20

Van Evera, Emily (sop) (cont.)

Handel, G.F.:Israel in Egypt, w. Nancy Argenta (sop), Jan Wilson (mez), Anthony Rolfe Johnson (ten), Thomas (sgr), White (sgr), A. Parrott (cnd), Taverner Players, Taverner Choir [E] EMI Classics 2–▲ CDCB 54018 [DDD]

Handel, G.F.:Messiah, w. Emma Kirkby (sop), Margaret Cable (alt), James Bowman (ct), A. Parrott (cnd), Taverner Players, Taverner Choir Virgin Classics 2–▲ ZDMB 61330

Handel, G.F.:Messiah, w. Emma Kirkby (sop), Margaret Cable (mez), James Bowman (ct), Joseph Cornwell (ten), David Thomas (bass), A. Parrott (cnd), Taverner Consort, Taverner Choir [E] EMI Classics 2–▲ CDCB 49801 [DDD]

Van Lunen, C. (sop)

Purcell, H.:Dido & Aeneas, w. R. A. Morgan (mez), D. Barick (bar), R. Shaw (cnd), Academy of the Begynhof Amsterdam [E] Globe ▲ GLO 5020 [DDD]

Van Mill, Arnold (bass)

Mozart, W.A.:Don Giovanni, w. Birgit Nilsson (sop—Donna Anna), Leontyne Price (sop—Donna Elvira), Eugenia Ratti (sop—Zerlina), Cesare Valletti (ten—Don Ottavio), Heinz Blankenburg (bar—Masetto), Fernando Corena (b-bar—Leporello), Arnold van Mill (b-bar—Il Commendatore), Cesare Siepi (b-bar—Don Giovanni), E. Leinsdorf (cnd), Vienna PO, Vienna State Opera Chorus [I] London 3–▲ 444594–2 [ADD]

Mozart, W.A.:Entführung, w. Rosemarie Ronisch (sop), Jutta Vulpius (sop), Rolf Apreck (ten), Jurgen Forster (ten), O. Suitner (cnd), Dresden State Opera Orch, Dresden State Opera Chorus Berlin Classics 2–▲ BER 9116

Verdi, G.:Aida, w. R. Tebaldi (sop) G. Simionato (mez), C. Bergonzi (ten), C. MacNeil (bar), H. von Karajan (cnd), Vienna PO, Vienna State Opera Chorus [I] London 3–▲ 414087–2 [ADD]

Verdi, G.:Aida, w. R. Tebaldi (sop) G. Simionato (mez), C. Bergonzi (ten), C. MacNeil (bar), H. von Karajan (cnd), Vienna PO, Vienna State Opera Chorus [I] London ("Jubilee" series) ▲ 417763–2 [ADD]

Wagner, R.:Der fliegende Holländer, w. A. Varnay (sop), J. Traxel (ten), G. London (bar), J. Keilberth (cnd), Bayreuth Festival Orch, Bayreuth Festival Chorus [G] *(rec live, Bayreuth, 7/25/56)* Myto 2–▲ 2 MCD 93175

Wagner, R.:Der fliegende Holländer (sels), w. S. Jurinac (sop), N. Bailey (bar), F. Adam (cnd), Strasbourg Opera Orch, Strasbourg Opera Chorus—Senta's ballad (Jo-ho-hoe!...Traft ihr das Schiff) & Willst Du des Vaters Wahl [G] *(rec live, Strasbourg, 11/25/69)* Melodram 3–▲ CDM 37091 [ADD]

Wagner, R.:Der Ring des Nibelungen, w. Gré Brouwenstein (sop—Freia/Sieglinde), Ilse Hollweg (sop—Waldvogel), Gerda Lammers (sop—Ortlinde), Paula Lenchner (sop—Wellgunde/Gerhilde), Hilde Scheppan (sop—Helmwige), Astrid Varnay (sop—Brünnilde/3rd Norn), Lore Wissmann (sop—Woglinde), Maria von Ilosvay (mez—Flosshilde/Schwertleite/2nd Norn), Louise Charlotte Kamps (mez—Siegrune), Jean Madeira (mez—Erda/Rossweisse/1st Norn), Georgine van Milinkovic (mez—Fricka/Grimgerde), Elisabeth Schärtel (mez—Waltraute), Paul Kuën (ten—Mime), Ludwig Suthaus (ten—Loge), Josef Traxel (ten—Froh), Wolfgang Windgassen (ten—Siegmund/Siegfried), Alfons Herwig (bar—Donner), Hermann Uhde (bar—Gunther), Hans Hotter (b-bar—Wotan), Gustav Neidlinger (b-bar—Alberich), Josef Griendl (bass—Fasolt/Hunding/Hagen), Arnold van Mill (bass—Fafner), H. Knappertsbusch (cnd), Bayreuth Festival Orch, Bayreuth Festival Chorus *(rec live, Bayreuth, Aug 13–17, 1956)* Golden Melodram 14–▲ GM 1.001 [ADD]

Wagner, R.:Tristan und Isolde, w. B. Nilsson (sop), R. Resnik (mez), H.-M. Uhle (ten), R. Krause (ten), G. Solti (cnd), Vienna PO [G] London ("Grand Opera" series) 4–▲ 430234–2 [ADD]

Vanni, Helen (mez)

Rorem, N.:Gloria, w. Phyllis Curtin (sop), Ned Rorem (pno) Phoenix ▲ PHCD 126

Schoenberg, A.:Songs, w. Ellen Faull (sop), Donald Gramm (b-bar), Glenn Gould (pno)—Zwei Gesange, Op. 1; Vier Lieder, Op. 2; Das Buch der hängenden Gärten; Sechs Lieder, Op. 3; Zwei Balladen, Op. 12; Drei Lieder, Op. 48; Zwei Lieder, Op. 14; Zwei Lieder, Op. Posth.; Acht Lieder, Op. 6 Sony Classical ("Glen Gould Edition" series) 2–▲ SM2K 52667

Van Tulder, Louis (ten)

Beethoven, L. van:Sym 9, "Choral Sym", w. To de Sluys (sop), Suze Luger (cta), Willem Ravelli (bass), W. Mengelberg (cnd), Royal Concertgebouw Orch, Toonkunst Chorus *(rec 1938)* Music & Arts ▲ CD 918

Verdi, G.:Requiem Mass, w. I. Auez (sop), L. Fischer (cta), H. Schey (bar), C. Schuricht (cnd), Royal Concertgebouw Orch, Amsterdam Toonkunst Choir *(rec live, Amsterdam, Nov. 2, 1939)* Archipon 2–▲ ARC 3.2/3 (m) [ADD]

Vanzo, Alain (ten)

Bizet, G.:Les Pêcheurs de perles, w. E. Spoorenberg (sop), J. Joris (bar), G. Hoekman (bass), J. Fournet (cnd), Netherlands Radio PO [F] *(rec live, 1963)* Verona 2–▲ 2707/08 (m) [AAD]

Bizet, G.:Les Pêcheurs de perles, w. I. Cotrubas (sop), G. Sarabia (bar), R. Soyer (bass), G. Prêtre (cnd), Paris Opera Orch, Paris Opera Chorus Classics for Pleasure ▲ CDCFP 4721 [ADD]

Bizet, G.:Les Pêcheurs de perles (sels), w. Erna Spoorenberg (sop), J. Fournet (cnd), Groot Radio PO, Groot Chorus *(rec Amsterdam, 1963)* Bella Voce 2–▲ 107.208

Delibes, L.:Lakmé, w. J. Sutherland (sop), G. Bacquier (bar), R. Bonynge (cnd), Monte Carlo Opera Orch [F] London 2–▲ 425485–2 [ADD]

Donizetti, G.:Lucrezia Borgia, w. Montserrat Caballé (sop), Jane Berbié (mez), Kostas Paskalis (bar), Arnold Voketaitis (bass-bar), L. D. Clements (sgr), Adib Fazah (sgr), Mauro Lampi (sgr), Vern Shinall (sgr), Jerold Siena (sgr), William Wiederanders (sgr), J. Perlea (cnd), New York City Opera Orch, New York City Chorus Great Opera Performances 2–▲ GOP 769

Donizetti, G.:Lucrezia Borgia, w. M. Caballé (sop), J. Berbié (mez), K. Paskalis (bar), J. Perlea (cnd), *(orch & chorus unknown)* [I] *(rec live in New York, 4/20/65)* Standing Room Only 2–▲ SRO 801–2 (m) [ADD]

Gounod, C.:Roméo et Juliette, w. Erna Spoorenberg (sop), J. Fournet (cnd), Groot Radio PO, Groot Chorus *(rec Amsterdam, Jan 1966)* Bella Voce 2–▲ 107.208

Vaquelin, Jean-Paul (sgr)

Boieldieu, F.-A.:Le Calife de Bagdad, w. Christiane Eda-Pierre (sop), Jane Berbié (mez), Jeannine Collard (mez), Jean Giraudeau (ten), L. Fourestier (cnd), ORTF Lyric Orch, ORTF Lyric Chorale Musidisc ▲ MUS 201852 [AAD]

Varady, Julia (sop)

Beethoven, L. van:Missa Solemnis, w. Iris Vermillion (mez), Vinson Cole (ten), Rene Pape (bass), Kolja Blacher (vn), G. Solti (cnd), Berlin PO, Berlin Radio Chorus London ▲ 444337–2 [DDD]

Leoncavallo, R.:Pagliacci (sels), w. M. Freni (sop), L. Pavoratti (ten), P. Cappuccilli (bar), I. Wixell (bar), G. Gavazzeni (cnd), National PO London London ▲ 421870–2 [ADD]

Mascagni, P.:Cavalleria rusticana, w. L. Pavarotti (ten), P. Cappuccilli (bar), G. Gacazzeni (cnd), National PO London, National Phil London Chorus [I] London 2–▲ 414590–2 [ADD]

Mascagni, P.:Cavalleria rusticana (sels), w. Mirella Freni (sop), Luciano Pavoratti (ten), Piero Cappuccilli (bar), Ingvar Wixel (bar), G. Gavazzeni (cnd), National PO London London ▲ 421870–2 [ADD]

Meyerbeer, G.:Gli amori di Teolinda, w. J. Fadle (cl), G. Albrecht (cnd), Berlin RSO, Berlin RIAS Chamber Choir [I] Orfeo ▲ 054831 [DDD]

Mozart, W.A.:Arias, w. Arleen Augér (sop), Kathleen Battle (sop), Irma Beilke (sop), Helena Braun (sop), Lisa Della Casa (sop), Maria Cebotari (sop), Ileana Cotrubas (sop), Helen Donath (sop), Mirella Freni (sop), Reri Grist (sop), Edita Gruberova (sop), Elisabeth Grümmer (sop), Hilde Güden (sop), Ingeborg Hallstein (sop), Luise Helletsgruber (sop), Gundula Janowitz (sop), Sena Jurinac (sop), Erika Köth (sop), Evelyn Lear (sop), Wilma Lipp (sop), Margaret Marshall (sop), Edith Mathis (sop), Jarmila Novotna (sop), Margherita Perras (sop), Lucia Popp (sop), Elisabeth Rethberg (sop), Anneliese Rothenberger (sop), Elisabeth Schumann (sop), Elisabeth Schwarzkopf (sop), Graziella Sciutti (sop), Irmgard Seefried (sop), Graziella Sciutti (sop), Agnes Baltsa (mez), Margit Bokor (mez), Brigitte Fassbaender (mez), Christa Ludwig (mez), Ann Murray (mez), Francisco Araiza (ten), Anton Dermota (ten), Helge Rosvaenge (ten), Rudolf Schock (ten), Peter Schreier (ten), Leopold Simoneau (ten), Eric Tappy (ten), Richard Tauber (ten), Gösta Winbergh (ten), Josef Witt (ten), Fritz Wunderlich (ten), Christian Boesch (bar), Willy Domgraf-Fassbaender (bar), Karl Dönch (bar), Dietrich Fischer-Dieskau (bar), Erich Kunz (bar), Eberhard Wächter (bar), Hans Hotter (b-bar), Paul Schöffler (b-bar), Cesare Siepi (b-bar), José Van Dam (b-bar), Walter Berry (bass), Geraint Evans (bass), Nicolai Ghiaurov (bass), Alexander Kipnis (bass), Richard Mayr (bass), Kurt Moll (bass), James Morris (bass), Ezio Pinza (bass), Martti Talvela (bass), Giorgio Tozzi (bass), Hans Duhan (sgr), Res Fischer (sgr), Marie Gerhart (sgr), *(various orchs & cnds)*—sels from Idomeneo, Die Entführung aus der Serail, Le nozze di Figaro, Don Giovanni, Così fan tutte, Die Zauberflöte & various arias Orfeo d'or ("Festspiel Dokumente" series) 5–▲ 408955

1458 ▲ = CD ♦ = Enhanced CD Δ = MD ■ = Cassette Tape □ = DCC

Varady, Julia (sop) (cont.)
Mozart, W.A.:Arias, w. I. Cotrubas (sop), E. Gruberova (sop), L. Price (sop), L. Popp (mez), F. Araiza (ten), P. Domingo (ten), P. de Palma (ten), P. Schreier (ten), F. Wunderlich (ten), S. Milnes (bar), A. Titus (bar), M. Talvela (bass)—sels. from Entführung aus dem Serail, Così fan tutte, Don Giovanni, Idomeneo, Die Zauberflöte, Le nozze di Figaro Eurodisc ▲ 69256-2-RG [ADD]
Mozart, W.A.:Complete Mozart Edition, w. B. Hendricks (sop), S. Mentzer (mez), F. Araiza (ten), T. Allen (bar), C. Davis (cnd), Bavarian RSO Philips 3-▲ 422537-2 [ADD]
Mozart, W.A.:Complete Mozart Edition, w. A. Augér (sop), E. Mathis (sop), H. Donath (sop), P. Schreier (ten), L. Hager (cnd), Salzburg Mozarteum Orch Philips 3-▲ 422532-2 [ADD]
Mozart, W.A.:Don Giovanni, w. A. Augér (sop), E. Mathis (sop), T. Moser (ten), A. Titus (bar), R. Panerai (bar), R. Scholze (bass), J.-H. Rootering (bass), R. Kubelik (cnd), Bavarian RSO, Bavarian Radio Chorus [I] Eurodisc 3-▲ 7798-2 [DDD]
Mozart, W.A.:Songs, w. E. Bashkirowa (pno)—(10 songs) Ridente la calma, K.152; Oiseaux, si tous les ans, K.307; Dans un bois solitaire, K.308; An die Einsamkeit, K.391; Der Zauberer, K.472; Das Veilchen, K.476; Die Alte, K.517; Als Luise die Briefe..., K.520; Abendempfindung, K.523; Un moto di gioia, K.579 [F,G,I] Orfeo ▲ 248921 [DDD]
Shostakovich, D.:Poems of Marina Tsvetayeva, Op. 143a, w. B. Haitink (cnd), Royal Concertgebouw Orch London ▲ 417514-2 [DDD]
Shostakovich, D.:Sym 14, w. D. Fischer-Dieskau (bar), O. Wenkel (cta), B. Haitink (cnd), Royal Concertgebouw Orch London ▲ 417514-2 [DDD]
Spohr, L.:German Songs , Op. 103, w. H. Schöneberger (cl), H. Höll (pno) [G] Orfeo ▲ 103841 [DDD] ■ M 103841A
Spohr, L.:Jessonda, w. R. Behle (sop), T. Moser (ten), D. Fischer-Dieskau (bar), K. Moll (bass), G. Albrecht (cnd), Hamburg State PO, Hamburg State Opera Chorus [G] Orfeo 2-▲ 240912 [DDD]
Spontini, G.:Olympia, w. S. Toczyska (mez), F. Tagliavini (ten), D. Fischer-Dieskau (bar), G. Fortune (bass), J. Becker (bass), G. Albrecht (cnd), Berlin RSO, Berlin Radio Chorus [Paris version] Orfeo 2-▲ 137862 [DDD]
Strauss (II), Joh.:Die Fledermaus, w. L. Popp (sop), A. Kollo (ten), H. Prey (bar), I. Rebroff (bass), E. Kleiber (cnd), Bavarian State Opera Orch [G] Deutsche Grammophon 2-▲ 415646-2 [ADD]
Strauss, R.:Arabella, w. H. Donath (sop), D. Fischer-Dieskau (bar), A. Schmidt (bar), W. Berry (bass), W. Sawallisch (cnd), Bavarian State Orch Orfeo 2-▲ 169882 [DDD]
Strauss, R.:Ariadne auf Naxos, w. J. Norman (sop), E. Gruberova (sop), P. Frey (ten), O. Bär (bar), D. Fischer-Dieskau (bar), K. Masur (cnd), Leipzig Gewandhaus Orch [G] Philips 2-▲ 422084-2 [DDD]
Strauss, R.:Feuersnot, w. B. Weikl (bar), H. Berger-Tuna (bass), H. Fricke (cnd), Munich RSO, Bavarian Radio Chorus [G] Acanta 2-▲ 43530-1-2 [DDD]
Strauss, R.:Die Frau ohne Schatten, w. H. Behrens (sop), P. Domingo (ten), J. Van Dam (b-bar), G. Solti (cnd), Vienna PO, Vienna State Opera Chorus [G] London 3-▲ 436243-2
Strauss, R.:Songs, w. E. Bashkirowa (pno)—Schlagende Herzen, Op. 29/2; Meinem Kinde, Op. 37/3; Befreit, Op. 39/4; Waldseligkeit, Op. 49/1; Frühlingsfeier, Op. 56/5; Ich wollt' ein Sträusslein binden, Op. 68/2; Säusle, liebe Myrte, Op. 68/3; Schlechtes Wetter, Op. 69/5 [G] Orfeo ▲ 248921 [DDD]
Tchaikovsky, P.:Songs, w. A. Riemann (pno)—Songs, Opp. 65 & 73 Orfeo ▲ 053851
Verdi, G.:Arias, w. D. Fischer-Dieskau (cnd), Bavarian State Orch—Ben io t'invenni [from Nabucco]; Tacea la notte; Timor di me [both from Il Trovatore]; È strano [w. Lothar Odinius (ten)]; Teneste la promessa–Attendo,attendo [both from La traviata]; Ecco l'orrido campo–Ma dall'arido stelo divulsa; Morrò, ma prima in grazia [both from Un ballo in maschera]; Pace, pace, mio dio [from La forza del destino] *(rec Studio 1, Bavarian Radio, Jan 23, 25, 26 & 28, 1995)* Orfeo ▲ 186951 [DDD]
Wagner, R.:Arias & Scenes, w. Peter Seiffert (ten), D. Fischer-Dieskau (cnd), Bavarian State Orch, Bavarian State Chorus—Lohengrin:Ov; 'Wedding March & Chorus'; Tannhäuser:'Dich, teure Halle'; Ov Act 2; 'Gepriesen sei die Stunde'; Walküre:'Ein Schwert verhiess mir der Vater' EMI Classics ▲ CDC 56138

Varcoe, Stephen (bar)
Bach, J.S.:Cant 106, "Actus tragicus", w. N. Argenta (sop), M. Chance (ct), A. Rolfe Johnson (ten), J. E. Gardiner (cnd), English Baroque Soloists, Monteverdi Choir London [G] Archiv ▲ 429782-2 [DDD]
Bach, J.S.:Cant 131, w. W. Kendall (ten), J. E. Gardiner (cnd), English Baroque Soloists, Monteverdi Choir London Erato ▲ 2292-45988-2
Bach, J.S.:Cant 140, w. R. Holton (sop), A. Rolfe Johnson (ten), J. E. Gardiner (cnd), English Baroque Soloists, Monteverdi Choir London [G] Archiv ▲ 431809-2 [DDD]
Bach, J.S.:Cant 147, w. R. Holton (sop), M. Chance (ct), A. Rolfe Johnson (ten), J. E. Gardiner (cnd), English Baroque Soloists, Monteverdi Choir London [G] Archiv ▲ 431809-2 [DDD]
Bach, J.S.:Cant 198, w. N. Argenta (sop), M. Chance (ct), A. Rolfe Johnson (ten), J. E. Gardiner (cnd), English Baroque Soloists, Monteverdi Choir London [G] Archiv ▲ 429782-2 [DDD]
Bach, J.S.:Magnificat, BWV 243, w. T. Bonner (sop), E. Kirkby (sop), M. Chance (ct), J. M. Ainsley (ten), R. Hickox (cnd), Collegium Musicum 90 Chandos ("Chaconne" series) ▲ CHAN 0518 [DDD]
Bach, J.S.:Mass in b, BWV 232, w. N. Argenta (sop), C. Denley (mez), M. Tucker (ten), R. Hickox (cnd), Collegium Musicum 90 Chandos ("Chaconne" series) 2-▲ CHAN 0533/34 [DDD]
Bach, J.S.:St. Matthew Passion, w. N. Argenta (sop), L. Lee (mez), J. Kenny (alt), J. MacDougall (ten), R. Müller (ten), R. Jackson (bar), P. Goodwin (cnd), *(orch & chorus unknown)* United 2-▲ UNI 89301 [DDD]
Bach, J.S.:St. Matthew Passion (sels), w. N. Argenta (sop), L. Lee (mez), J. Kenny (alt), J. MacDougall (ten), R. Müller (ten), R. Jackson (bar), P. Goodwin (cnd), *(orch & chorus unknown) (rec St. George's Theater, London, Feb 24-27, 1994)* United ▲ UNI 88030 [DDD]
Blow, J.:Anthems, w. Joseph Cornwell (ten), Robin Blaze (sgr), D. Hill (cnd), Parley of Instruments, Winchester Cathedral Choir Hyperion 2-▲ CDA 67031/32
Britten, B.:Cant misericordium, w. J. M. Ainsley (ten), R. Hickox (cnd), City of London Sinfonia, Britten Singers [L] Chandos ▲ CHAN 8997 [DDD]
Bush, G.:Farewell, Earth's Bliss, w. R. Hickox (cnd), City of London Sinfonia [E] Chandos ▲ CHAN 8864 [DDD]
Bush, G.:Songs (4) from The Hesperides, w. R. Hickox (cnd), City of London Sinfonia [E] Chandos ▲ CHAN 8864 [DDD]
Butterworth, G.:Songs (3) Voc & Strs, w. R. Hickox (cnd), City of London Sinfonia [E] Chandos ▲ CHAN 8743 [DDD]
Butterworth, G.:Songs (6) from *A Shropshire Lad*, w. R. Hickox (cnd), City of London Sinfonia [E] Chandos ▲ CHAN 8743 [DDD]
Campra, A.:Messe de Requiem, w. E. Baudry (sop), M. Zanetti (sop), J. Benet (ten), J. Elwes (ten), P. Herreweghe (cnd), La Chapelle Royale Orch [L] Harmonia Mundi France ▲ HMC 901251
Christmas Day in the Morning, w. Cambridge Singers, City of London Sinfonia [cnd:John Rutter] Collegium ▲ COLCD 121 ■ COLCS 121
Elgar, E.:Songs, w. R. Hickox (cnd), City of London Sinfonia—Pleading, Op. 48/1; Twilight, Op. 59/6 [E] Chandos ▲ CHAN 8743 [DDD]
Fauré, G.:Requiem, w. C. Ashton (sop), J. Rutter (cnd), City of London Sinfonia members, Cambridge Singers [1893 ver.] [L] Collegium ▲ COLCD 109 [DDD] ■ COLC 109 (D)
Finzi, G.:Let us garlands bring, w. R. Hickox (cnd), City of London Sinfonia [E] Chandos ▲ CHAN 8743 [DDD]
Finzi, G.:Requiem da Camera, w. R. Hickox (cnd), City of London Sinfonia, Britten Singers [E] Chandos ▲ CHAN 8997 [DDD]
Finzi, G.:Song Cycles Bar, w. C. Benson (pno)—Earth & Air & Rain, Op. 15; Before & After Summer, Op. 16; I Said to Love, Op. 19b [E] Hyperion 2-▲ CDA 66161/62
Grainger, P.:Songs, w. Penelope Thwaites (pno)—The Lost Lady Found; Creeping Jane; Bold William Taylor; 6 Dukes Went a-Fishin'; The British Waterside; The Pretty Maid Milking Her Cow; Hard Hearted Barb'ra; Willow, Willow; Shallow Brown; Bonnie George Campbell; Drowned; Leezie Lindsay; Willie's Gone to Melville Castle; Lukannon; Northern Ballad; Ride with an Idle Whip; The Men of the Sea; Merciful Town; Soldier, Soldier; Sailor's Chanty; The Secret of the Sea Chandos ("The Grainger Edition" series) ▲ CHAN 9503

Varcoe, Stephen (bar) (cont.)
Hahn, R.:Songs, w. Felicity Lott (sop), Susan Bickley (mez), Ian Bostridge (ten), Graham Johnson (pno), Stephen Layton (cnd), London Choral Society—[CD 1] Si mes vers avaient des ailes; Paysage; Rêverie; Offrande; Mai; Infidelité; Seule; Les Cygnes; Nocturne; 3 jours de vendange; D'une prison; Séraphine; L'Heure exquise; Fêtes galantes; 12 Rondels; [CD 2] Quand la nuit n'est pas étoilée; Le Plus beau présent; Sur l'eau; Le Rossignol des lilas; A Chloris; Ma jeunesse; Puisque j'ai mis ma lèvre; Etudes Latines; La Nymphe de la Source; Au Rossignol; Je me souviens; Air de la lettre; C'est très vilain d'être infidèle; C'est sa banlieue; Nous avons fait un beau voyage; La Dernière Valse Hyperion ("The Hyperion French Song Edition" series) 2-▲ CDA 67141/42
Handel, G.F.:The Triumph of Time & Truth, w. James Goodman (trb), Fisher (sop), Emma Kirkby (sop), Charles Brett (ct), Ian Partridge (ten), D. Darlow (cnd), London Handel Orch, London Handel Chorus [E] Hyperion 2-▲ CDA 66071/72
Haydn, J.:Mass 12, "Theresienmesse", w. Janine Watson (sop), Pamela Helen Stephen (mez), Mark Padmore (ten), R. Hickox (cnd), Collegium Musicum 90 Chandos ▲ CHAN 0592
Holst, G.:Savitri, w. F. Palmer (sop), P. Langridge (ten), R. Hickox (cnd), City of London Sinfonia, Hickox Singers Hyperion ▲ CDA 66099 [DDD]
If There Were Dreams to Sell:English Orchestral Songs, w. City of London Sinfonia [cnd:Richard Hickox] Chandos ▲ CHAN 8743 [DDD]
Lalande, M.-R. de:Confitebor tibi, Domine, w. G. Fisher (sop), O. Johnston (trb), C. Daniels (ct), A. Smith (ten), E. Higginbottom (cnd), King's Consort, Oxford New College Choir [L] Erato (Musifrance) ▲ 2292-45014-2 [DDD]
Lalande, M.-R. de:De profundis solo Voices, Orch & Chorus, w. G. Fisher (sop), O. Johnston (trb), C. Daniels (ct), A. Smith (ten), E. Higginbottom (cnd), King's Consort, New College Choir Oxford [L] Erato (Musifrance) ▲ 2292-45014-2 [DDD]
Lalande, M.-R. de:Miserere, w. G. Fisher (sop), O. Johnston (trb), C. Daniels (ct), A. Smith (ten), E. Higginbottom (cnd), King's Consort, Oxford New College Choir [L] Erato (Musifrance) ▲ 2292-45014-2 [DDD]
Monteverdi, C.:Orfeo, w. P. Kwella (sop), E. Kirkby (sop), J. Smith (sop), N. Rogers (ten), D. Thomas (bass), N. Rogers (cnd), London Cornett & Sackbutt Ensemble, C. Medlam (cnd), London Baroque Chiaroscuro EMI Classics ▲ CDMB 64947
La Procession:80 Years of French Song (1839-1919), w. Graham Johnson (pno) Hyperion ▲ CDA 66248 [DDD]
Purcell, H.:Anthems & Services, w. J. Bowman (ct), R. Covey-Crump (ten), C. Daniels (ten), M. George (bass), R. King (cnd), King's Consort, New College Choir Oxford—My heart is inditing; The way of God is an undefiled way; Sing unto God; Behold, I bring you glad tidings; Since God so tender a regard; Early, O Lord, my fainting soul; Sleep, Adam, sleep and take thy rest; Awake, ye dead; The earth trembled; Lord not to us but to thy name; O all ye people, clap your hands Hyperion ▲ CDA 66644
Purcell, H.:Dido & Aeneas, w. L. Dawson (sop), A. S. von Otter (mez), N. Rogers (ten), T. Pinnock (cnd), English Concert, *(chorus unknown)* [E] Archiv ▲ 427624-2 [DDD]
Purcell, H.:Hail. Bright Cecilia, w. J. Smith (sop), B. Gordon (alt), A. Stafford (alt), P. Elliot (ten), D. Thomas (bass), J.E. Gardiner (cnd), English Baroque Soloists, Monteverdi Choir London Erato ("Gardiner Purcell Collection" series) ▲ 96554-2
Purcell, H.:King Arthur, w. J. Smith (sop), G. Fisher (sop), E. Priday (sop), G. Ross (sop), A. Stafford (alt), P. Elliott (ten), J.E. Gardiner (cnd), English Baroque Soloists, Monteverdi Choir London Erato 2-▲ 2292-45211-2 ZA
Purcell, H.:King Arthur, w. Gillian Fisher (sop), E. Priday (sop), Gill Ross (sop), J. Smith (sop), A. Stafford (alt), P. Elliot (ten), J.E. Gardiner (cnd), English Baroque Soloists, Monteverdi Choir London Erato ("Gardiner Purcell Collection" series) 2-▲ 96552-2
Purcell, H.:The Prophetess, or The History of Dioclesian, w. L. Dawson (sop), Gillian Fisher (sop), R. Covey-Crump (ten), P. Elliot (ten), M. George (bass), J.E. Gardiner (cnd), Monteverdi Orch, Monteverdi Choir London Erato ("Gardiner Purcell Collection" series) 2-▲ 96556-2
Purcell, H.:Timon of Athens, w. L. Dawson (sop), Gillian Fisher (sop), R. Covey-Crump (ten), P. Elliot (ten), M. George (bass), J.E. Gardiner (cnd), Monteverdi Orch, Monteverdi Choir London Erato ("Gardiner Purcell Collection" series) 2-▲ 96556-2
Quilter, R.:Shakespeare Songs, Op. 6, w. R. Hickox (cnd), City of London Sinfonia [E] Chandos ▲ CHAN 8743 [DDD]
Schoenberg, A.:Serenade Cl, w. 20th Century Classics Ensemble Koch International Classics ▲ KIC 7263-2 [DDD]
Schubert, Franz:Songs (comp), w. G. Johnson (pno)—13 songs—D.111, 351, 361, 525, 526, 536, 553, 562, 565, 639, 743, 766, 881 [G] Hyperion ▲ CDJ 33002 [DDD]
Stravinsky, I.:Abraham & Isaac, w. R. Craft (cnd), Orch of St. Luke MusicMasters ▲ 01612-67158-2
Vaughan Williams, R.:Songs, w. R. Hickox (cnd), City of London Sinfonia—3 songs from *The House of Life*—Love-Sight; Silent Noon; Heart's Haven [E] Chandos ▲ CHAN 8743 [DDD]

Vardaman, L. (sop)
Dvorak, C.:Amanda Mandelal, w. R. Rosales (sop), M. Lifchitz (cnd), North/South Consonance Ensemble North/South Recordings ▲ NS 1004 [DDD]
Greenberg, L.:This Man Was Your Brother, w. R. Rosales (sop), M. Lifchitz (cnd), North/South Consonance Ensemble North/South Recordings ▲ NS 1004 [DDD]
Greenberg, L.:La Vida Es Sueño, w. R. Rosales (sop), M. Lifchitz (cnd), North/South Consonance Ensemble North/South Recordings ▲ NS 1004 [DDD]
Lifchitz, M.:Canto de paz, w. L. Weiss (fl), G. Kitzis (vn), N. Ives (vc), M. Lifchitz (pno) Opus One ▲ 149
Lifchitz, M.:Of Bondage & Freedom, w. R. Rosales (sop), M. Lifchitz (cnd), North/South Consonance Ensemble North/South Recordings ▲ NS 1004 [DDD]
Pleskow, R.:Arabesques, w. R. Rosales (sop), M. Lifchitz (cnd), North/South Consonance Ensemble North/South Recordings ▲ NS 1004 [DDD]

Varga, Erzsébet (sgr)
Gulyás, L.:Triple Jumping Dance, w. R. Lantos (cnd), Hungarian State Folk Ensemble Orch, Hungarian State Folk Ensemble Chorus *(rec 1969)* Hungaroton ▲ HCD 18008 [AAD]

Vargas, Milagro (sop)
Glass, Philip:Songs from the Trilogy, w. L. Childs (spkr), P. Esswood, D. Perry (ten), Philip Glass Ensemble CBS ▲ MK 45580 ■ FMT 45580

Vargas, Ramon (ten)
Bellini, V.:Zaira, w. K. Ricciarelli (sop), A. Papadjakou (cta), S. Alaimo (ten), P. Olmi (cnd), Catania Teatro Massimo Bellini Orch, Catania Teatro Massimo Bellini Chorus [I] *(rec live 1990)* Nuova Era 2-▲ 6982/83 [DDD]
Bellini, V.:Zaira (sels), w. K. Ricciarelli (sop), P. Olmi (cnd), Catania Teatro Massimo Bellini Orch, Catania Teatro Massimo Bellini Chorus Nuova Era ▲ NUO 7187 [DDD]
Christmas with Ramón Vargas, w. Vienna Concilium Musicum [cnd:Paul Angerer], Lucerne Boy's Choir *(rec live, Jesuitenkirche in Lucerne, Dec 21, 1995)* Claves ▲ CD 509612 [DDD]
Donizetti, G.:Arias, w. M. Viotti (cnd), English CO—includes arias from Anna Bolena; Don Pasquale; Lucia di Lammermoor; Linda di Chamounix; L'Elisir d'amore; Le duc d'Alba Claves ▲ 50-9202
Puccini, G.:Manon Lescaut, w. M. Freni (sop—Manon), C. Bartoli (mez—Musici I), L. Pavarotti (ten—Des Grieux), R. Vargas (ten—Edmondo), D. Croft (ten—Lescaut), G. Taddei (bar—Geronte), J. Levine (cnd), Metropolitan Opera Orch, New York Metropolitan Opera Chorus [I] *(rec 1992)* London ▲ 440200-2 [DDD]
Rossini, G.:Arias, w. M. Viotti (cnd), English CO—arias from Barbiere di Siviglia, Donna del Lago, Italiana in Algeri, Occasione fa il Ladro [I] Claves ▲ CD 9202 [DDD]
Rossini, G.:Il barbiere di Siviglia, w. I. Kertesi (sop—Berta), S. Ganassi (mez—Rosina), R. Vargas (ten—Almaviva), A. Romero (bar—Dr. Bartolo), R. Servile (bar—Figaro), F. de Grandis (bass—Basilio), K. Sárkány (bass—Fiorello), A. Déri (pno), B. Sztankovits (gtr), W. Humburg (cnd), Failoni CO, Hungarian Radio Chorus *(rec Nov. 16-28, 1992)* Naxos 3-▲ 8.660027/29 [DDD]
Rossini, G.:La scala di seta, w. Teresa Ringholz (sop), Francesca Provvisionata (mez), Fulvio Massa (ten), Alessandro Corbelli (bar), Natale de Carolis (b-bar), M. Viotti (cnd), English CO Claves 2-▲ 9219/20
Rossini, G.:Tancredi, w. Veronica Cangemi (sop—Roggiero), Eva Mei (sop—Amenaide), Vasselina Kasarova (mez—Tancredi), Melinda Paulsen (cta—Isaura), Ramón Vargas (ten—Argirio), Harry Peeters (bass—Orbazzano), Janos Maté (vn), Gottfried Greiner (vc), Ingo Nawra (db), David Syrus (hpd), R. Abbado (cnd), Munich RSO, Bavarian Radio Chorus *(rec Studio 1, Munich, July 17-30, 1995)* RCA Red Seal 3-▲ 09026-68349-2 [DDD]

Vargas, Ramon (ten) (cont.)
Verdi, G.:Falstaff, w. Maureen O'Flynn (sop), Daniela Dessi (sop), Bernadette Manca di Nissa (mez), Delores Ziegler (mez), Ernesto Gavazzi (ten), Paolo Barbacini (ten), Juan Pons (bar), Roberto Frontali (bar), Luigi Roni (bass), R. Muti (cnd), La Scala Orch, La Scala Chorus *(rec Milan La Scala Theater, Italy, Mar. 29 & 31)* Sony Classical ▲ S2K 58961 [DDD]

Varjabed, David (bar)
Operatic Arias & Neapolitan Songs, w. Yerevan RSO [cnd:Rafael Mangasarian], Yerevan String Orch [cnd:Kevork Adjemian] Doremi ▲ DHR 71121 [AAD]

Varnay, Astrid (sop)
Great Voices:Astrid Varnay *(rec 1951–54)* Memories 2–▲ MEM 4560 [ADD]
Janácek, L.:Jenůfa, w. H. Hillebrecht (sop), W. Cochran (ten), Cox (sgr), R. Kubelik (cnd), Bavarian State Opera Orch, Bavarian State Opera Chorus [G] *(rec live in Munich, Mar. 17, 1970)* Myto 2–▲ 2 MCD 90422 [ADD]
Janácek, L.:Jenůfa (sels), w. M. Collier (sop), R. Cassilly (ten), J. Lanigan (ten), R. Kubelik (cnd), Royal Opera House Orch, Royal Opera House Chorus Covent Garden—eight solo, duet & trio arias featuring Astrid Varnay [G] *(rec live at Covent Garden, Feb. 24, 1968)* Myto 2–▲ 2 MCD 90422 [ADD]
Leoncavallo, R.:Pagliacci, w. M. Caballé (sop), R. Scotto (sop), J. Hamari (mez), J. Carreras (ten), M. Manuguerra (bar), T. Allen (bar), K. Nurmela (bar), U. Benelli (bar), R. Muti (cnd), Philharmonia Orch, Ambrosian Opera Chorus EMI Classics 2–▲ CDMB 63650
Mascagni, P.:Cavalleria rusticana, w. Ruth Falcon (sop—Lola), Leonie Rysanek (sop—Santuzza), Astrid Varnay (sop—Mamma Lucia), Plácido Domingo (ten—Turiddu), Benito di Bella (bar—Alfio), N. Santi (cnd), Munich National Theater Orch, Munich National Theater Chorus *(rec Munich, Dec 25, 1978)* Legato Classics ▲ LCD 202–1
Opera Arias, w. Varnay, Astrid (sop), Austrian Tonkünstler Orch [cnd:Herman Weigert] *(rec live, 6/19–20/51)* Melodram ▲ CDM 16504 (m)
Strauss, R.:Elektra, w. M. Mödl (sop/mez), H. Hillebrecht (sop), J. King (ten), E. Wächter (bar), H. von Karajan (cnd), Vienna PO, Vienna State Opera Chorus [G] *(rec 1964)* Melodram 2–▲ MEL 27044 [AAD]
Strauss, R.:Elektra (sels), w. H. Hillebrecht (sop), J. King (ten), H. von Karajan (cnd), Vienna PO, Vienna State Opera Chorus [G] *(rec live in Salzburg, 8/11/64)* Arkadia 3–▲ 213 (m) [ADD]
Strauss, R.:Salome, w. Astrid Varnay (sop—Salome), Hertha Töpper (mez—Der Page der Herodias), Margarete Klose (cta—Herodias), Hans Hopf (ten—Narraboth), Karl Hoppe (ten—1st Nazarene), Karl Ostertag (ten—1st Jew), Julius Patzak (ten—Herodes), Hans Braun (bar—Jochanaan), Benno Kusche (bar—2nd Soldier), Adolf Keil (bass—1st Soldier), Hans Hermann Nissen (bass—Ein Kappadozier), Max Proebstl (bass—2nd Nazarene), Walter Carnotch (sgr—4th Jew), Emil Graf (sgr—3rd Jew), Paul Kaussen (sgr—2nd Jew), Hildegard Limmer (sgr—A slave), Georg Witter (sgr—5th Jew), H. Weigert (cnd), Bavarian RSO *(rec June 21–25, 1953)* Bella Voce 2–▲ BLV 7210 [AAD]
Strauss, R.:Salome, w. L. Rysanek (sop), G. Stolze (ten), D. Fischer-Dieskau (bar), F. Leitner (cnd), Bavarian State Opera Orch *(rec live, Monaco, 1971)* Melodram 2–▲ MEL 27098
Verdi, G.:Macbeth, w. Astrid Varnay (sop—Lady Macbeth), Trude Roesler (mez—Lady-in-waiting), Hasso Eschert (ten—Malcolm), Walter Geisler (ten—Macduff), Joseph Metternich (bar—Macbeth), Ludwig Weber (bass—Banquo), R. Kraus (cnd), West German Orch, West German Chorus *(rec Cologne, 1954)* Myto 2–▲ 952128
Wagner, R.:Der fliegende Holländer, w. J. Traxel (ten), G. London (bar), A. van Mill (bass), J. Keilberth (cnd), Bayreuth Festival Orch, Bayreuth Festival Chorus [G] *(rec live, Bayreuth, 7/25/56)* Myto 2–▲ 2 MCD 93175
Wagner, R.:Der fliegende Holländer, w. W. Windgassen (ten), H. Uhde (bar), L. Weber (bass), H. Knappertsbusch (cnd), Bayreuth Festival Orch, Bayreuth Festival Chorus [G] *(rec live)* Arkadia 2–▲ 421 [ADD]
Wagner, R.:Götterdämmerung (sels), w. E. Grümmer (sop), B. Aldenhoff (ten), H. Uhde (bar), G. Frick (bass), J. Greindl (bass), H. Knappertsbusch (cnd), Bavarian State Opera Orch, Bayreuth Festival Orch, Bavarian State Opera Chorus, Bayreuth Festival Chorus [G] *(rec live 1955 & 1957)* Melodram 4–▲ MEL 46106 (m) [AAD]
Wagner, R.:Lohengrin, w. L. Rysanek (sop), S. Kónya (ten), E. Blanc (bar), A. Cluytens (cnd), Bayreuth Festival Orch, Bayreuth Festival Chorus [G] *(rec live, 7/23/58)* Myto 3–▲ MCD 89002 (m) [ADD]
Wagner, R.:Lohengrin, w. B. Nilsson (sop), W. Windgassen (ten), H. Uhde (bar), E. Jochum (cnd), Bayreuth Festival Orch, Bayreuth Festival Chorus *(rec live, Bayreuth 1954)* Melodram 3–▲ MEL 36104
Wagner, R.:Lohengrin, w. E. Steber (sop), W. Windgassen (ten), H. Uhde (bar), J. Greindl (bass), J. Keilberth (cnd), Bayreuth Festival Orch, Bayreuth Festival Chorus *(rec live, Bayreuth Festival, 1953)* Teldec ("Historic" series) 4–▲ 93674
Wagner, R.:Lohengrin, w. I. Bjoner (sop), J. Thomas (ten), G. Neidlinger (b-bar), W. Sawallisch (cnd), La Scala Orch, Prague Phil Chorus [G] *(rec live, Milan 1965)* Melodram 3–▲ MEL 37067 [AAD]
Wagner, R.:Lohengrin, w. H. Traubel (sop—Elsa), A. Varnay (sop—Ortrud), L. Melchior (ten—Lohengrin), F. Guerrera (bar—Herald), H. Janssen (bar—Telramund), D. Ernster (bass—King Heinrich), F. Stiedry (cnd), Metropolitan Opera Orch, New York Metropolitan Opera Chorus *(rec live Jan. 6, 1950)* Danacord 3–▲ DACOCD 322/24 [AAD]
Wagner, R.:Der Ring des Nibelungen, w. Gré Brouwenstein (sop—Freia/Sieglinde), Ilse Hollweg (sop—Waldvogel), Gerda Lammers (sop—Ortlinde), Paula Lenchner (sop—Wellgunde/Gerhilde), Hilde Scheppan (sop—Helmwige), Astrid Varnay (sop—Brünnilde/3rd Norn), Lore Wissmann (sop—Woglinde), Maria von Ilosvay (mez—Flosshilde/Schwertleite/2nd Norn), Louise Charlotte Kamps (mez—Siegrune), Jean Madeira (mez—Erda/Rossweisse/1st Norn), Georgine van Milinkovic (mez—Fricka/Grimgerde), Elisabeth Schärtel (mez—Waltraute), Paul Kuën (ten—Mime), Ludwig Suthaus (ten—Loge), Josef Traxel (ten—Froh), Wolfgang Windgassen (ten—Siegmund/Siegfried), Alfons Herwig (bar—Donner), Hermann Uhde (bar—Gunther), Hans Hotter (b-bar—Wotan), Gustav Neidlinger (b-bar—Alberich), Josef Griendl (bass—Fasolt/Hunding/Hagen), Arnold van Mill (bass—Fafner), H. Knappertsbusch (cnd), Bayreuth Festival Orch, Bayreuth Festival Chorus *(rec live, Bayreuth, Aug 13–17, 1956)* Golden Melodram 14–▲ GM 1.001 [ADD]
Wagner, R.:Siegfried, w. R. Siewert (cta), B. Aldenhoff (ten), P. Kuen (ten), S. Björling (bar), H. Pflanzl (bass), F. Dalberg (bass), H. von Karajan (cnd), Bayreuth Festival Orch, Bayreuth Festival Chorus [G] *(rec live 1951)* Melodram 4–▲ MEL 46106 (m) [AAD]
Wagner, R.:Siegfried, w. W. Windgassen (ten), A. Andersson (ten), G. Stoltze (ten), H. Hotter (b-bar), J. Greindl (bass), H. Knappertsbusch (cnd), Bayreuth Festival Orch, Bayreuth Festival Chorus [G] *(rec live 1958)* Arkadia 4–▲ 443 [AAD]
Wagner, R.:Siegfried (sels), w. B. Aldenhoff (ten), H. Knappertsbusch (cnd), Bayreuth Festival Orch, Bayreuth Festival Chorus—Act 3 Scene 3 [G] *(rec live 1957)* Arkadia 4–▲ 443 [AAD]
Wagner, R.:Die Walküre, w. Helen Traubel (sop), Kerstin Throborg (cta), Lauritz Melchoir (ten), Friedrich Schorr (b-bar), E. Leinsdorf (cnd), *(orch unknown)* *(rec Dec 6, 1941)* Enterprise ("The Forties" series) 2–▲ ENT 318
Wagner, R.:Die Walküre (act 3), w. A. Varnay (sop—Brünnhilde), L. Rysanek (sop—Sieglinde), S. Björling (bar—Wotan), H. von Karajan (cnd), Bayreuth Festival Orch *(rec Aug. 12, 1951)* EMI Classics ▲ ZDH 64704

Vasari, Mita (mez)
Verdi, G.:Falstaff, w. Augusta Ottrabella (sop—Nannetta), Franca Somigli (sop—Alice), Angelica Cravcenko (mez—Mrs. Quickly), Mita Vasari (mez—Meg), Dino Borgioli (ten—Fenton), Giuseppe Nessi (ten—Bardolfo), Alfredo Tedeschi (ten—Dr. Cajus), Piero Biasini (bar—Ford), Mariano Stabile (bar—Falstaff), Virgilio Lazzari (bass—Pistola), A. Toscanini (cnd), Vienna PO, Vienna State Opera Chorus *(rec Salzburg, Aug 23, 1937)* Minerva 2–▲ MN A36/37 (m) [ADD]

Vasconcelos, Nana (sgr)
Gohl, M.:The West, w. Seamus Eagan (sgr), Jay Ungar (vn), Molly Mason (gtr), *(other artists unknown)*, M. Gohl (cnd), Black Elk Voices Sony Classical ▲ SK 62727 ■ ST 62727
Hassell, J.:Vernal Equinox, w. Jon Hassell (tpt), Nana Vasconcelos, et al. (perc) Lovely Music ▲ LCD 1021 [ADD]

Vasiliev, Nikolai (bar)
Rachmaninoff, S.:Francesca da Rimini, w. V. Taraschenko (ten), V. Matorin (bass), A. Tchistiakov (cnd), Bolshoi Theater SO Soloists Russian Season ("Russian Season" series) ▲ LDC 288081

Vásquez, Hector (bar)
Massenet, J.:Hérodiade (sels), w. Renée Fleming (sop—Salomé), Dolora Zajick (mez—Hérodiade), Plácido Domingo (ten—Jean), Juan Pons (bar—Hérode), Hector Vásquez (bar—Vitellius), Kenneth Cox (bass—Phanuel), V. Gergiev (cnd), San Francisco Opera Orch, San Francisco Opera Chorus—highlights *(rec San Francisco Opera, Nov 1994)* Sony Classical ▲ SK 61965

Vassar, Frédéric (b-bar)
Cornelius, P.:Stabat Mater, w. D. Borst (sop), J. Mayeur (cta), J.-L. Viala (ten), M. Piquemal (cnd), Cannes-Provençe Alpes-Côte d'Azur Regional Orch, Cannes Regional Chorus Musique d'Abord ▲ HMA 1905206
Mascagni, P.:Il piccolo Marat, w. S. Neves (sop—Mariella), C. Pfeiler (mez—Principessa di Fleury), D. Galvez-Vallejo (ten—Marat), S. Cowan (bar—Soldier), M. Dirks (bar—Il Ladro), F. Vassar (bass—L'Orco), H. Claessens (bass—Spy), K. Bakels (cnd), Netherlands RSO, Netherlands Radio Chorus *(rec Feb. 9, 1992)* Bongiovanni 2–▲ GB 2168/69 [DDD]
Ropartz, G.:Sym 3, w. F. Pollet (sop), N. Stutzmann (cta), T. Dran (ten), M. Plasson (cnd), Toulouse Capitole Orch, Orféon Donostiarra EMI Classics ▲ CDM 64689-2

Vassilev, Assen (bass)
Shostakovich, D.:The Execution of Stepan Razin, w. A. Andreev (cnd), Varna PO, Varna Phil Chorus [R] Koch International Classics ▲ KIC 7017-2 [DDD] ■ 3-7017-4 (D)
Stoyanov, L.:Liturgia Solemnis, w. M. Mtakiev (cnd), Varna PO, Slavonic Voices Male Chamber Choir [Slavonic] Koch International Classics ▲ KIC 7033-2 [DDD] ■ 3-7033-4 (D)
Sviridov, G.:Oratorio pathétique, w. A. Andreev (cnd), Varna PO, Varna Phil Chorus [R] Koch International Classics ▲ KIC 7017-2 [DDD] ■ 3-7017-4 (D)

Vassilev, Valentin (ten)
Gesualdo, D.C.:Madrigals, w. V. Kissyova (sop), N. Pankova (sop), A. Bovarian (alt), K. Mirinski (bass), S. Kralev (cnd), Sofia Madrigal—Io tacerò; Invan dunque o crudele; Moro lasso al mio duolo; Dolcissima mia vita Gega ▲ GD 174 [DDD]
Monteverdi, C.:Madrigals, w. V. Kissyova (sop), N. Pankova (sop), A. Bovarian (alt), K. Mirinski (bass), S. Kralev (cnd), Sofia Madrigal Ensemble—Psalmus 121, "Laetatus sum"; Batto qui pianse; Chiome d'oro; Amor che deggio far?; O come sei gentile; Psalmus 147, "Lauda Jerusalem" Gega ▲ GD 174 [DDD]
Schütz, H.:Motets (misc), w. V. Kissyova (sop), A. Ivanova (sop), N. Pankova (sop), A. Bovarian (alt), K. Mirinski (bass), S. Kralev (cnd), Sofia Madrigal—Christe Deus adjuva; Verbum caro factum est; Te Christe supplex invoco; Veni redemtor gentium; Veni sancte Spiritus Gega ▲ GD 174 [DDD]

Vassiliev, Nikolai (ten)
Rachmaninoff, S.:Francesca da Rimini, w. Maria Lapina (sop), Vitaly Tarastchenko (ten), Nikolaï Mechetniak (bar), Vladimir Matorin (bass), A. Tchistiakov (cnd), Bolshoi Theater Orch, Russian State Choir Russian Season 3–▲ CMX 388053

Vassilieva, Elena (sop)
Raskatov, A.:Pas de deux, w. Claude Delangle (s sax/t sax) *(rec Paris, July 1995)* BIS ▲ CD 765 [DDD]

Vaughan, Elizabeth (sop)
Haydn, J.:Mass 11, "Nelsonmesse", "Imperial Mass", "Coronation Mass", w. Janet Baker (mez), N. Marriner (cnd), Academy of St. Martin in the Fields, King's College Choir Cambridge London ("Jubilee" series) ▲ 421146-2 [ADD]
Pergolesi, G.B.:Magnificat in C, w. Janet Baker (cta), Ian Partridge (ten), Christopher Keyte (bass), D. Willcocks (cnd), Academy of St. Martin in the Fields, King's College Choir Cambridge *(rec 1966)* London 2–▲ 443868-2 [ADD]
Vivaldi, A.:Gloria, RV.589, w. J. Baker (mez), N. Marriner (cnd), Academy of St. Martin in the Fields, King's College Choir Cambridge London ("Jubilee" series) ▲ 421146-2 [ADD]

Vaughan, S. (sgr)
Gershwin, G.:Porgy & Bess (sels), w. M. Tilson Thomas (cnd), Los Angeles PO, Jazz Trio [overture & song medley arr. Marty Paitch] CBS ▲ MK 42516 [ADD/DDD] ■ FMT 42516

Vauquet, A. (alt)
Vuataz, R.:Ballade, w. U. Rüttimann (pno) *(rec Feb. 20, 1980)* Grammont ▲ CTSP 7-2 [ADD]

Vavon, Andrée (sop)
Bizet, G.:Carmen (sels), w. C. Supervia (mez), A. Bernadet (mez), J.-F. Delmas (b-bar), G. Micheletti (ten), A. Endreze (bar), G. Cloëz (cnd), Paris Opéra-Comique Orch, Paris Opéra-Comique Chorus—14 arias & scenes [F] *(rec Paris, 1930)* The Classical Collector ▲ FDC 2002 (m) [AAD]
Bizet, G.:Carmen (sels), w. C. Supervia (mez), A. Bernadet (mez), G. Micheletti (ten), A. Endreze (bar), G. Cloëz (cnd), Paris Opéra-Comique Orch, Paris Opéra-Comique Chorus—8 arias & scenes *(rec Paris 1930)* Nimbus ("Prima Voce" series) 2–▲ NI 7836/7 [ADD]

Vayne, Kyra (sop)
Kyra Vayne, Vol. 2 *(rec 1945–64)* Preiser ("Lebendige Vergangenheit" series) ▲ PRE 89993

Veasey, Josephine (mez)
Berlioz, H.:Benvenuto Cellini, w. J. Carlyle (sop), K. Lewis (ten), Kentish, Cameron, Bushby, Garrard, Ward, A. Dorati (cnd), BBC SO, BBC Sym Chorus [E] *(rec live, Royal Festival Hall, 1964)* Music & Arts 2–▲ CD 618 (m) [AAD]
Berlioz, H.:La Damnation de Faust, w. N. Gedda (ten), G. Bastin (bar), C. Davis (cnd), London SO, London Sym Chorus, Ambrosian Singers [F] Philips 2–▲ 416395-2 [ADD]
Berlioz, H.:Les Troyens, w. B. Lindholm (sop), J. Vickers (ten), P. Glossop (bar), R. Soyer (bass), C. Davis (cnd), Royal Opera House Orch [F] Philips 4–▲ 416432-2 [ADD]
Britten, H.:A Midsummer Night's Dream, w. E. Harwood (sop), H. Watts (cta), A. Deller (ct), P. Pears (ten), J. Shirley-Quirk (bar), B. Britten (cnd), London SO, London Sym Chorus [E] London 2–▲ 425663-2 [ADD]
Verdi, G.:Otello, w. Raina Kabaivanska (sop), John Lanigan (ten), Mario del Monaco (ten), Tito Gobbi (bar), G. Solti (cnd), Royal Opera House Orch, Royal Opera House Covent Garden Chorus *(rec June 30, 1962)* Memories ▲ MEM 4583 [AAD]

Veccia, Angelo (bar)
Lattuada, F.:Le Preziose ridicole, w. S. Valayre (sop—Madelon), A. Catarci (sop—Marotte), A. Cicogna (mez—Cathos), S. Tedesco (ten—La Grange), E. Di Cesare (ten—Mascarille), A. Veccia (bar—Croissy), R. Servile (bar—Jodelet), E. Fissore (bass—Gorgibus), E. Romagna (cnd), Toscanini SO, G. Masini (cnd), Rossini Teatro Comunale Chorus [I] *(rec live, 1991)* Ermitage ▲ ERM 404 [DDD]

Vedernikov, Alexander (bass)
Borodin, A.:Prince Igor, w. Elena Obraztsova (mez—Konchakovna), Tatiana Tugarinova (mez—Yaroslavna), Vladimir Atlantov (ten—Vladimir Igoryevich), Artur Eisen (bass—Vladimir Galitsky), Ivan Petrov (bass—Igor Svyatoslavich), Alexander Vedernikov (bass—Konchak), M. Ermler (cnd), Bolshoi Theater Orch, Bolshoi Theater Chorus *(rec Moscow, 1969)* Melodiya ("The Russian Opera" series) 3–▲ 74321-29346-2 [ADD]
Tchaikovsky, P.:Eugene Onegin, w. Lidiya Chernikh (sop), Tamara Sinyavskaya (mez), Alexander Fedin (sgr), Yuri Mazurok (sgr), V. Fedoseyev (cnd), USSR SO, Moscow SO, Fernseh SO Audiophile Classics ("Legacy Collection" series) 2–▲ 101.751

Vega, Danilo (sgr)
Giordano, U.:Madame Sans-Gêne, w. Magda László (sop—Caterina), Carlo Tagliabue (bar—Napoleone), Renato Berti (sgr—Despréaux), Irene Callaway (sgr—Toniotta/Carolina), Danilo Cestari (sgr—Neipperg/Vinaigre), Maria Luisa Malacchi (sgr—Giulia/Principessa Elisa), Carlo Perucci (sgr—Fouché), Danilo Vega (sgr—Lefebvre), Enzo Viaro (sgr—De Brigode/Gelsomino), A. Basile (cnd), Milan RAI SO, Milan RAI Chorus *(rec Milan, Aug 10, 1957)* Bongiovanni 2–▲ GB 1129/30

Vejbo, Poul (ten)
Schnittke, A.:Penitential Psalms, w. Eva Bruun Hansen (sop), Elisabeth Rehling (sop), Annette Simonsen (alt), Maria Streijffert (alt), Karl-Gustav Andersson (ten), Stefan Parkman (cnd), Danish National Radio Choir Chandos ▲ CHAN 9480

Vejzovic, Dunja (mez)
Berg, A.:Wozzeck (sels), w. C. Kleiber (cnd), Vienna PO, Vienna Boys' Choir *(rec Feb. 28, 1982)* Exclusive ▲ EXL 47 [ADD]
Brahms, J.:Alto Rhap, w. C. Eschenbach (cnd), Houston SO EMI Classics ▲ CDC 45006
Brahms, J.:Alto Rhap, w. C. Eschenbach (cnd), Houston SO, Houston Sym Male Chorus Virgin Classics 2–▲ CUVB 61226

Vejzovic, Dunja (mez) (cont.)
Massenet, J.:Hérodiade, w. M. Caballé (sop—Salomé), D. Vejzovic (mez—Hérodiade), J. Carreras (ten—Jean), J. Pons (bar—Hérode), E. Serra (bar—Vitellius), V. Esteve (bar—High Priest), R. Kennedy (bass—Phanuel), J. Delacôte (cnd), Barcelona Teatro Liceo Orch, Barcelona Gran Teatro de Liceo Chorus *(rec Jan. 6, 1984)* Legato Classics 2-▲ LCD 182 [ADD]
Mercadante, S.:La Vestale, w. G. Dimitrova (sop), G. Cecchele (ten), Romanò (sgr), Cepreaga (sgr), Kliskic (sgr), Sioli (sgr), Boldrini (sgr), V. Sutej (cnd), Spalato National Theater Orch, Spalato National Theater Chorus [I] *(rec 4/9/87)* Bongiovanni 2-▲ GB 2065/66 [DDD]
Wagner, R.:Der fliegende Holländer, w. P. Hofmann (ten), J. Van Dam (b-bar), Kurt Moll (bass), H. von Karajan (cnd), Berlin PO [G] EMI Classics 2-▲ CDMB 64650
Wagner, R.:Lohengrin, w. A. Tomowa-Sintow (sop), A. Kollo (ten), S. Nimsgern (b-bar), K. Ridderbusch (bass), H. von Karajan (cnd), Berlin PO, German Opera Chorus [G] EMI Classics ("Studio" series) 4-▲ CDMD 69314 [ADD]
Wagner, R.:Parsifal, w. P. Hofmann (ten), J. Van Dam (b-bar), S. Nimsgern (b-bar), K. Moll (bass), H. von Karajan (cnd), Berlin PO, German Opera Chorus [G] Deutsche Grammophon 4-▲ 413347-2 [DDD]

Velasquez, Conchita (mez)
Puccini, G.:Madama Butterfly, w. Rosetta Pampanini (sop—Madama Butterfly), Conchita Velasquez (mez—Suzuki), Cesira Ferrari (mez—Kate Pinkerton), Alessandro Granda (ten—F. B. Pinkerton), Giuseppe Nessi (ten—Goro), Aristide Baracchi (bar—Il Principe Yamadori), Gino Vanelli (bar—Sharpless), Lino Bonardi (bass—Il Commissario Imperiale), Salvatore Baccaloni (bass—Lo zio Bonzo), L. Molajoli (cnd), La Scala Orch, La Scala Chorus Bongiovanni 2-▲ 1123/24 [ADD]

Vele, Luděk (bass)
Dvořák, A.:Stabat Mater, w. L. Aghová (sop), M. Schiml (sop), A. Baldin (ten), J. Belohlávek (cnd), Czech PO, Prague Phil Chorus [L] Chandos 2-▲ CHAN 8985/86 [DDD]
Reicha, A.:Requiem, w. V. Hrubá-Freiberger (sop), A. Barová (mez), V. Dolezal (ten), L. Mátl (cnd), Dvořák CO, Czech Phil Chorus [L] Supraphon ▲ 11 0332-2 [DDD]
Slavicky, K.:Psalmi, w. Salome Losová (sop), Dagmar Pecková (cta), Vladimír Dolezal (ten), Jan Hora (org), P. Kühn (cnd), Kühn Chorus *(rec Dvořák Hall of Rudolfinum, Prague, Mar. 14-16, 1989)* Panton ("Protokol XX" series) ▲ PAN 811142 [DDD]

Velis, Andrea (ten)
Puccini, G.:Tosca, w. Leonie Rysanek (sop), Russell Christopher (ten), Clifford Harvuot (bar), Cornell MacNeil (bar), Fernando Corena (bass), Paul Plishka (bass), F. Molinari-Pradelli (cnd), San Francisco Opera Orch, San Francisco Opera Chorus Melodram 2-▲ CDM 27508

Veljanov, A. (nar)
Popp, M.:Ludus Danielis, w. T. Schlierf (spkr), P. Pöppel (sgr), S. Hausen (sgr), M. Popp (cnd), Estampie *(rec Jan. 1-10, 1993)* Christophorus ▲ 77144 [DDD]

Vellard, Dominique (sgr)
Nova Cantica:Latin Songs of the High Middle Ages, w. Emmanuel Bonnardot, Schola Cantorum Basiliensis Deutsche Harmonia Mundi ▲ 77196-2-RC [DDD]

Vellucci, Luigi (ten)
Offenbach, J.:Les Contes d'Hoffmann, w. Beverly Sills (sop—Olympia/Giulietta/Antonia/Stella), Edith Evans (mez—Nicklausse/Mother's Voice), Michael Devlin (ten—Spalanzani), André Turp (ten—Hoffmann), Luigi Vellucci (ten—Andrès/Cochenille/Pitichinaccio/Frantz), Donald Bernard (bar—Luther/Schlemil), Norman Treigle (bass—Lindorf/Coppélius/Dapertutto/Dr. Miracle), John West (bass—Crespel), Alton Brim (sgr—Nathanaël), Rodney Hall (sgr—Hermann), K. Andersson (cnd), New Orleans Opera Orch, New Orleans Opera Chorus *(rec Feb 27, 1964)* VAI Audio 2-▲ VAIA 1121-2 [ADD]
Verdi, G.:Falstaff, w. Vivian Della Chiesa (sop—Alice), Audrey Schuh (sop—Nannetta), Lizabeth Pritchett (mez—Quickly), Evelyn Sachs (mez—Meg), André Turp (ten—Fenton), Virginio Assandri (ten—Caius), Luigi Vellucci (ten—Bardolfo), Leonard Warren (bar—Falstaff), Richard Torigi (bar—Ford), R. Cellini (cnd), New Orleans Opera Orch, New Orleans Opera Chorus *(rec live, May 5, 1956)* VAI Audio 2-▲ VAIA 1056-2
Verdi, G.:Falstaff, w. Anna Moffo (sop—Nannetta), Renata Tebaldi (sop—Alice Ford), Anna Maria Canali (mez—Meg Page), Giulietta Simionato (mez—Dame Quickly), Mariano Caruso (ten—Doctor Caius), Alvinio Misciano (ten—Fenton), Luigi Vellucci (ten—Bardolfo), Tito Gobi (bar—Falstaff), Carnell MacNeil (bar—Ford), Kenneth Smith (bass-Pistola), T. Serafin (cnd), *(orch unknown) (rec Chicago, 1958)* Legato Classics 2-▲ LCD 206-2 [ADD]

Venditelli, Giuseppe (ten)
Puccini, G.:Manon Lescaut (sels), w. Magda Olivero (sop—Manon), Giuseppe Venditelli (ten—Chevalier), P. Argento (cnd), Turin RAI SO—Oh, sarò la più bella! [Act 2] *(rec Turin, July 2, 1975)* Bella Voce 2-▲ BLV 107.221 [AAD]

Ventre, Carlo (ten)
Pacini, G.:Saffo, w. Francesca Pedaci (sop—Saffo), Gemma Bertagnolli (sop—Dirce), Mariana Pentcheva (mez—Climene), Carlo Ventre (ten—Faone), Aled Hall (ten—Ippia), Roberto de Candia (bar—Alcandro), Davide Baronchelli (bass—Lisimaco), M. Benini (cnd), Irish National SO, Lubomír Mátl (cnd), Wexford Festival Opera Chorus *(rec Wexford, Oct & Nov 1995)* Marco Polo 2-▲ 8.223883-4 [DDD]

Ventriglia, Franco (bass)
Donizetti, G.:Il Duca d'Alba, w. Renato Cioni (ten), Wladimiro Ganzarolli (bar), T. Schippers (cnd), Trieste PO Melodram ▲ CDM 27036

Ventris, Christopher (sgr)
Weir, J.:Blond Eckbert, w. Anne-Marie Owens (mez), Nicholas Folwell (bar), Nerys Jones (sgr), S. Edwards (cnd), English National Opera Orch Collins Classics ▲ COL 1461

Ventura, Elvino (ten)
The World of Singing, Vol 4:The Italian School Part 1:Tenors before World War I, Book 2, w. Edoardo Garbin (ten), Fiorello Giraud (ten), Florencio Costantino (ten), Antonio Paoli (ten), Giuseppe Borgatti (ten), Carlo Albani (ten), Enrico Caruso (ten), Amedeo Bassi (ten), Piero Schivazzi (ten), Giovanni Zenatello (ten) Enterprise ("Vocal Archives" series) 3-▲ ENT VA 2107

Venturi, Paride (ten)
Verdi, G.:Macbeth, w. Grace Bumbry (mez—Lady Macbeth), Luciano Saldari (ten—Macduff), Paride Venturi (ten—Malcolm), Renato Bruson (bar—Macbeth), Agostino Ferrin (bass—Banquo), A. Gatto (cnd), Bologna Teatro Comunale Orch, Bologna Teatro Comunale Chorus *(rec Bologna, Mar. 18, 1975)* Golden Age of Opera 2-▲ GAO 185/86 [ADD]

Venturini, Emilio (ten)
Bellini, V.:I Puritani, w. Mirella Freni (sop), Mirelle Fiorentini (mez), Luciano Pavarotti (ten), Sesto Bruscantini (bar), Giovanni Antonini (bass), Bonaldo Giaiotti (bass), R. Muti (cnd), Rome RAI SO, Rome RAI Chorus Melodram 2-▲ CDM 27062
Donizetti, G.:Lucia di Lammermoor, w. M. Capsir (sop—Lucia), E. de Muro Lomanto (ten—Sir Ravenswood), E. Venturini (ten—Lord Bucklaw), E. Molinari (bar—Lord Ashton), S. Baccaloni (bass—Bidebent), L. Molajoli (cnd), La Scala Orch, La Scala Chorus *(rec 1933)* Myto 2-▲ 2MCD 94299
Verdi, G.:Falstaff, w. Pia Tassinari (sop—Alice Ford), Ines Alfani Tellini (sop—Nannetta), Aurora Buades (mez—Quickly), Rita Monticone (mez—Meg Page), Roberto D'Alessio (ten—Fenton), Giuseppe Nessi (ten—Bardolfo), Emilio Venturini (ten—Dr. Caius), Emilio Ghirardini (bar—Ford), Giacomo Rimini (bar—Sir John Falstaff), Salvatore Baccaloni (bass—Pistola), L. Molajoli (cnd), Milan SO, La Scala Chorus *(rec La Scala Theatre, Milan, Apr. 1932)* VAI Audio 2-▲ VAIA 1098-2

Venuti, Maria (sop)
Bach, J.S.:Mass in b, BWV 232, w. C. Kallisch (cta), C. Prégardien (ten), A. Scharinger (bass), E. Ortner (cnd), Salzburg Baroque Ensemble, Arnold Schoenberg Choir Koch Schwann 2-▲ SCH 312512 [DDD]
Handel, G.F.:Samson, w. Roberta Alexander (sop), Jochen Kowalski (ct), Anthony Rolfe Johnson (ten), Aalstair Miles (bass), Anton Scharinger (bass), N. Harnoncourt (cnd), Vienna Concentus Musicus, Arnold Schoenberg Choir Teldec ▲ 74871-2
Killmayer, W.:Yolimba, w. M. Venuti (sop—Yolimba), A. Titus (bar—Möhringer), P. Schneider (cnd), Munich RSO, Bavarian Radio Chorus [G] Orfeo ▲ 257921 [DDD]

Venuti, Maria (sop) (cont.)
Mozart, W.A.:Zauberflöte, w. M. Price (sop—Pamina), L. Serra (sop—Queen of the Night), M. Venuti (sop—Papagena), M. McLaughlin (sop—1st Lady), A. Murray (mez—2nd Lady), H. Schwarz (cta—3rd Lady), F. Höher (trb—1st Boy), M. Diedrich (trb—2nd Boy), F. Klos (trb—3rd Boy), P. Schreier (ten—Tamino), R. Tear (ten—Monostatos), R. Goldberg (ten—1st Armoured Man), K. Moll (bass—Sarastro), H. Rech (bass—2nd Armoured Man), C. Davis (cnd), Dresden Staatskapelle, Leipzig Radio Chorus Philips ("Duo" series) 2-▲ 442568-2
Warren, E.R.:The Sleeping Beauty, w. Maria Venuti (mez—Princess), Thomas Hampson (bar—Prince), Gerd Nienstedt (b-bar—King), David Lutz (pno), B. Ferden (cnd), Cracow RSO, Cracow Radio Chorus *(rec Church of the Bernardines, Cracow, Poland, June 21-24, 1993)* Cambria ▲ CD 1095 [DDD]

Verbitskaya, Evgenya (mez)
Mussorgsky, M.:Boris Godunov, w. Irina Arkhipova (mez—Marina Mnishek), Evgenya Verbitskaya (mez—Nurse to Xenia), Valentina Klepatskaya (sgr—Fyodor), Tamara Sorokina (sgr—Xenia), Anton Grigoryev (ten—Simpleton), Vladimir Ivanovsky (ten—Grigory, the Pretender), Gyorgy Shulpin (bar—Prince Shuisky), Alexey Geleva (bass—Varlaam), Ivan Petrov (bass—Boris Godounov), Mark Reshetin (bass—Pimen), Alexi Ivanov (sgr—Andrei Shchelkalov), Evgeny Kibkalo (sgr—Rangoni), A. Melik-Pashayev (cnd), Bolshoi Theater Orch, Bolshoi Theater Chorus *(rec Moscow, 1962)* Melodiya ("The Russian Opera" series) 3-▲ 74321-29349-2 [ADD]
Prokofiev, S.:War & Peace, w. Galina Vishnevskaya (sop—Natasha Rostovoa), Irina Arkhipova (mez—Hélène Bezukhova), Evgenya Verbitskaya (mez—Marya Akhrosimova), Alexi Maslennikov (ten—Anatole Kuragin), Vladimir Petrov (ten—Pierre Bezukhov), Pavel Lisitsian (bar—Napoleon), Alexi Krivchenya (bass—Field-Marshall Kutuzov), Evgeny Kibkalo (sgr—Prince Andrei Bolkonsky), A. Melik-Pashayev (cnd), Bolshoi Theater Orch, Bolshoi Theater Chorus *(rec Moscow, 1961)* Melodiya ("The Russian Opera" series) 3-▲ 74321-29350-2 [ADD]
Tchaikovsky, P.:Queen of Spades, w. Elena Smolenskaya (sop), Georgi Nelepp (ten), Pavel Lisitsian (bar), A. Melik-Pashayev (cnd), Bolshoi Opera Orch, Bolshoi Theater Chorus Arlecchino 3- ARL

Vercelli, Angela (mez)
Cimarosa, D.:Gli Orazii e i Curiazzi, w. G. Simionato (mez), G. Del Signore (ten), T. Spataro (ten), C. M. Giulini (cnd), Milan RAI SO, Milan RAI Chorus [I] *(rec live 4/13/52)* Melodram 2-▲ CDM 29500 [AAD]
Donizetti, G.:L'elisir d'amore, w. Rosanna Carteri (sop—Adina), Luigi Angela Vercelli (mez—Gianetta), Luigi Alva (ten—Nemorino), Rolando Panerai (bar—Belcore), Giuseppe Taddei (bar—Dulcamara), T. Serafin (cnd), La Scala Orch, La Scala Chorus EMI Classics 2-▲ CDMB 65658

Verdera, Teresa (sop)
Rossini, G.:La gazetta, w. Gianpiero Ruggeri (sgr), Kasimierz Sergiel (sgr), Ezio Maria Tisi (sgr), W. Keitel (cnd), Minsk Orch, Motet & Madrigal Posen Chamber Chorus Deutsche Schallplatten ▲ DS 1053

Verducci, Alessandro (bass)
Bellini, V.:La sonnambula, w. M. Devia (sop), L. Canonici (ten), M. Viotti (cnd), Piacenza SO, Piacenza Chorus [I] *(rec live 11/88)* Nuova Era 2-▲ 6764/65 [DDD]

Verebics, Ibolya (sop)
Bach, Joh. Christian:Amadis des Gaules, w. Sonntag, Hobarth, Wagner, Schöne, H. Rilling (cnd), Bach Collegium, Gächinger Kantorei [G] Hänssler Classic 2-▲ 98.963 [DDD]
Bach, J.S.:St. Matthew Passion, w. R. Kiss (sop), Á. Csenki (mez), J. Németh (mez), P. Cser (ten), J. Mukk (ten), I. Gati (bar), F. Korpás (bar), P. Köves (bass), G. Oberfrank (cnd), Hungarian State SO, Hungarian Festival Choir, Hungarian Radio Children's Choir [G] *(rec Feb 1993)* Naxos 3-▲ 8.550832/34 [DDD]
Brixi, F.X.:Missa Interga, w. C. Borchers (cta), S. Weir (ten), Genhardt (bass), H. Rilling (cnd), Prague CO, Kühn Chorus Supraphon ▲ 11 0092-2 [DDD]
Brixi, F.X.:Opus Patheticum de Septem Doloribus Beatae Mariae Virginis, w. C. Borchers (cta), S. Weir (ten), Genhardt (bass), H. Rilling (cnd), Prague CO, Kühn Chorus Supraphon ▲ 11 0092-2 [DDD]
Caldara, A.:Stabat Mater, w. E. Lax (mez), G. Kállay (ten), B. Szilágyi (bar), E. Kollár (cnd), Concerto Armonico Budapest, Monteverdi Chamber Choir [L] Hungaroton ▲ HCD 31273 [DDD]
Haydn, M.:Missa Pro Defuncto Archiepiscopo Sigismundo, w. Judit Németh (mez), Martin Klietmann (ten), József Moldvay (bass), H. Rilling (cnd), Franz Liszt CO, Hungarian Radio-TV Chorus [L] Hungaroton ▲ HCD 31022 [DDD]
Haydn, M.:Missa Sancti Francisci, w. Judit Németh (mez), Martin Klietmann (ten), József Moldvay (bass), H. Rilling (cnd), Franz Liszt CO, Hungarian Radio-TV Chorus [L] Hungaroton ▲ HCD 31022 [DDD]
Mozart, W.A.:Alma Dei creatoris, w. Judit Németh (cta), József Mukk (ten), József Moldvay (bar), Gábor Oláh (bar), István Ella (org), János Reményi (cnd), Hungarian Radio-TV Children's Chorus Girls' Voices, Hungarian Radio-TV Male Chamber Choir *(rec Hungaroton Studio, June 14-16, 1991)* Hungaroton ▲ HCD 4003 [DDD]
Mozart, W.A.:Ave verum corpus, w. Judit Németh (cta), József Mukk (ten), József Moldvay (bar), Gábor Oláh (bar), István Ella (org), János Reményi (cnd), Hungarian Radio-TV Children's Chorus Girls' Voices, Hungarian Radio-TV Male Chamber Choir *(rec Hungaroton Studio, June 14-16, 1991)* Hungaroton ▲ HCD 4003 [DDD]
Mozart, W.A.:Miserere, w. Judit Németh (cta), József Mukk (ten), József Moldvay (bass), Gábor Oláh (bar/Gregorian intonations), István Ella (org), János Reményi (cnd), Hungarian Radio-TV Children's Chorus Girls' Voices, Hungarian Radio-TV Male Chamber Choir *(rec Hungaroton Studio, June 14-16, 1991)* Hungaroton ▲ HCD 4003 [DDD]
Mozart, W.A.:Misericordias Domini, w. Judit Németh (cta), József Mukk (ten), József Moldvay (bass), Gábor Oláh (bar/Gregorian intonations), István Ella (org), János Reményi (cnd), Hungarian Radio-TV Children's Chorus Girls' Voices, Hungarian Radio-TV Male Chamber Choir *(rec Hungaroton Studio, June 14-16, 1991)* Hungaroton ▲ HCD 4003 [DDD]
Mozart, W.A.:Missa, K.427, w. C. Oelze (sop), S. Weir (ten), O. Widmer (bass), H. Rilling (cnd), Stuttgart Bach Collegium, Gächinger Kantorei [L] Hänssler Classic 2-▲ 98.979 [DDD]
Mozart, W.A.:Missa brevis, K.65, w. Judit Németh (cta), József Mukk (ten), József Moldvay (bass), Gábor Oláh (bar/Gregorian intonations), István Ella (org), János Reményi (cnd), Hungarian Radio-TV Children's Chorus Girls' Voices, Hungarian Radio-TV Male Chamber Choir *(rec Hungaroton Studio, June 14-16, 1991)* Hungaroton ▲ HCD 4003 [DDD]
Mozart, W.A.:Missa brevis, K.194, w. Judit Németh (cta), József Mukk (ten), József Moldvay (b), Gábor Oláh (bar/Gregorian intonations), István Ella (org), János Reményi (cnd), Hungarian Radio-TV Children's Chorus Girls' Voices, Hungarian Radio-TV Male Chamber Choir *(rec Hungaroton Studio, June 14-16, 1991)* Hungaroton ▲ HCD 4003 [DDD]
Mozart, W.A.:Sancta Maria, w. Judit Németh (cta), József Mukk (ten), József Moldvay (bass), Gábor Oláh (bar/Gregorian intonations), István Ella (org), János Reményi (cnd), Hungarian Radio-TV Children's Chorus Girls' Voices, Hungarian Radio-TV Male Chamber Choir *(rec Hungaroton Studio, June 14-16, 1991)* Hungaroton ▲ HCD 4003 [DDD]

Verestnikov, Vladislav (bar)
Rachmaninoff, S.:The Miserly Knight, w. Mikhail Krutikov (sgr), Vladimir Kudriashov (sgr), Alexander Arkhipov (sgr), Piotr Gluboky (sgr), A. Tchistiakov (cnd), Bolshoi Theater Orch, Russian State Choir Russian Season 3-▲ CMX 388053
Rimsky-Korsakov, N.:Christmas Eve, w. Ekaterina Koudriavtchenko (sop), Elena Zaremba (mez), Vladimir Bogtatchov (ten), Alexei Maslennikov (ten), Viatcheslav Voinarovski (ten), Maxime Mikhailov (bass), Stanislav Souleimanov (bass), M. Yurovski (cnd), Moscow Forum Theater Orch, Yurloff Academic Choir Russian Season 4-▲ CMX 388054
Rimsky-Korsakov, N.:Kaschei the Immortal, w. I. Jourina (sop), N. Terentieva (mez), A. Arkhipov (ten), V. Matorin (bass), A. Tchistiakov (cnd), Bolshoi Theater Orch, Yurloff Russian Choir [Russian] Russian Season ("Russian Season" series) ▲ LDC 288046 [DDD]

Verhaeghe, Claudie (sop)
Chopin, F.:Songs Sop (comp), w. J. Micault (pno) [Pol] Arcobaleno ▲ SBCD 8100
Mendelssohn, Fanny:Songs, w. Jean Micault (pno)—Opp. 1 & 7 Arcobaleno ▲ AAOC 9329
Schumann, C.:Songs, w. Jean Micault (pno)—Opp. 12 & 13 Arcobaleno ▲ AAOC 9329
Werfel, A.M.:Songs, w. Jean Micault (pno)—7 sels Arcobaleno ▲ AAOC 9329

Verkinderen (sgr)
Charpentier, M.-A.:Leçons de ténèbres, H. 96-110, w. J. Nelson (mez), R. Jacobs (cnd), Concerto Vocale—H.105, 106, 110 [L] Harmonia Mundi France ▲ HMC 901007

Vermillion, Iris (mez)
Beethoven, L. van:Missa Solemnis, w. Julia Varady (sop), Vinson Cole (ten), Rene Pape (bass), Kolja Blacher (vn), G. Solti (cnd), Berlin PO, Berlin Radio Chorus London ▲ 444337-2 [DDD]
Beethoven, L. van:Sym 9, "Choral Sym", w. A. Marc (sop), S. Jerusalem (ten), F. Struckmann (bar), D. Barenboim (cnd), Berlin State Opera Orch, Berlin State Opera Chorus Erato ▲ 94353-2
Gluck, C.W.:La Recontre imprévue, w. J. Kaufmann (sop—Rezia), A. Stumphius (sop—Dardané), A.-M. Rodde (sop—Amine), I. Vermillion (mez—Balkis), R. Gambill (ten—Ali), C. H. Ahnsjö (ten—Osmin), J.-H. Rootering (bass—Un Calender), L. Hager (cnd), Munich RSO Orfeo 2-▲ 242912 [DDD]
Graun, K.H.:Cesare e Cleopatra, w. Janet Williams (sop), Lynne Dawson (sop), Robert Gambill (ten), R. Jacobs (cnd), Concerto Cologne Harmonia Mundi France 3-▲ HMC 901561.63
Mozart, W.A.:Complete Mozart Edition, w. A. M. Blasi (sop), S. McNair (sop), J. Hadley (ten), C. H. Ahnsjö (ten), N. Marriner (cnd), Academy of St. Martin in the Fields Philips 2-▲ 422535-2 [ADD]
Reger, M.:Songs, w. Peter Stamm (pno)—Es schläft ein stiller Garten, Op. 98/4; Winterahnung, Op. 4/3; Im April, Op. 4/4; Ein Paar, Op. 55/9; Nelken, Op.15/3; Hat gesagt–Bleibt's nicht dabei, Op.75/12; Die blunten Kühe, Op. 70/4; Schlummerlied; Flötenspierlerin, Op. 88/3; Totensprache, Op. 62/12; Leise, leise weht irh Lüfte, Op. 97/2; Der bescheidene Schäfer, Op. 97/4; Mittag, Op. 76/35; Vor der Liebe, Op. 76/32; Waldeinsamkeit, Op. 76/3; Der verliebte Jäger, Op. 76/13; Traum durch dir Dämmerung. Op. 35/3; Aeolscharfe, Op. 75/11; Ein Drängen, Op. 97/3; Einsamkeit, Op. 75/18; An die Hoffnung, Op. 124 *(rec Jan & Nov 1995)* CPO ▲ 999317-2 [DDD]
Schulhoff, E.:The Flames, w. Jane Eaglen (sop—Donna Anna, Nun, Woman, Marguerite), Carola Höhn (sop—Shadow), Celina Lindsley (sop—Shadow), Regina Schudel (sop—Shadow), Iris Vermillion (mez—La Morte), Christiane Berggold (alt—Shadow), Kaja Borris (alt—Shadow), Elvira Dressen (alt—Shadow), Kurt Westi (ten—Don Juan), Johann-Werner Prein (bass—Commendatore), Gerd Wolf (bass—Harlequin), J. Mauceri (cnd), Berlin German SO, Berlin RIAS Chamber Choir *(rec Jesus-Christus Church, Berlin Dahlem, Oct 1993/Apr 1994)* London 2-▲ 444630-2 [DDD]
Ullmann, V.:Kaiser von Atlantis, w. C. Oelze (sop—Bubikopf), I. Vermillion (mez—The Drummer), M. Petzold (ten—A Soldier), M. Kraus (ten—Kaiser Overall), H. Lippert (ten—Harlekin), F. Mazura (bar—The Loudspeaker), W. Berry (bass—Death), L. Zagrosek (cnd), Leipzig Gewandhaus Orch London ▲ 440854-2 [DDD]
Wagner, R.:Der fliegende Holländer, w. H. Beherns (sop—Senta), I. Vermillion (mez—Mary), U. Heilmann (ten—Helmsman), J. Protschka (ten—Erik), R. Hale (bar—The Dutchman), K. Rydl (bass—Daland), C. von Dohnányi (cnd), Vienna PO, Vienna State Opera Chorus London 2-▲ 436418-2 [DDD]
Zemlinsky, A. von:Songs (misc), w. Ruth Ziesak (sop), Hans Peter Blochwitz (ten), Andreas Schmidt (bar), Cord Garben (pno)—Die schlanke Wasserlilie; Gute Nacht; Liebe und Frühling; Ich sah mein eigen Angesicht; In der Ferne; Waldgespräch; Der Rosenband; Abendstern; Des Mädchens Klage; Der Morgenstern; Wandl' ich im Wald des Abends; Orientalisches Sonett; Süsse, süsse Sommernacht; Herbsten; Nun schwillt der See so bang; In der Sonnengasse; Herr Bombardil; Es war ein alter König; Über eine Wiege; Mädel, kommst du mit zum Tanz?; Jane Grey; Der verlorene Haufen; Vorspiel; Ansturm; Auf See; Noch spür ich ihren Atem; Hörtest du denn nicht hinein; Die Beiden; Harmonie des Abends; Und einmal gehst du *(rec Stuttgart & Berlin, Germany, Mar. 30–June 8, 1993)* Sony Classical ▲ SK 57960

Verna, M. Curtis (sop)
Verdi, G.:Aida, w. M. Pirazzini (cta), F. Corelli (ten), G. Guelfi (bar), G. Neri (bass), A. Questa (cnd), Turin RAI SO, Turin RAI Chorus *(rec 1956)* Enterprise ("Palladio") 2-▲ ENT PD 4184 [ADD]
Verdi, G.:Un ballo in maschera, w. M. Curtis Verna (sop—Amelia), M. Erato (sop—Oscar), P. Tassinari (cta—Ulrica), F. Tagliavini (ten—Riccardo), G. Valdengo (bar—Renato), A. Albertini (bar—Silvano), M. Stefanoni (bass—Samuel), V. Susca (bass—Tom), A. Questa (cnd), Turin RAI SO, Turin RAI Chorus *(rec 1954)* Cetra Classic 2-▲ CDO 13 [AAD]

Vernerova, Ludmila (sop)
Mozart, W.A.:Missa, K.317, w. Marta Benackova (mez), Richard Sporka (ten), Ladislav Nezhyba (bass), G. Delogu (cnd), Prague Virtuosi, Prague Chamber Choir *(rec Domovina Studio, Prague, June 4–6, 1994)* Discover International ▲ DI 920260 [DDD]
Mozart, W.A.:Vesperae solennes, w. Marta Benackova (mez), Richard Sporka (ten), Ladislav Nezhyba (bass), G. Delogu (cnd), Prague Virtuosi, Prague Chamber Choir *(rec Domovina Studio, Prague, June 4–6, 1994)* Discover International ▲ DI 920260 [DDD]

Vernet, Isabelle (sop)
Auber, D.-F.:Le Domino noir, w. Sumi Jo (sop), Doris Lamprecht (sop), Martine Olmeda (sop), Jocelyne Taillon (mez), Bruce Ford (ten), Patrick Power (ten), Gilles Cachemaille (bar), Jules Bastin (bass), R. Bonynge (cnd), English CO, London Voices London 2-▲ 440646-2
Berlioz, H.:Les Nuits d'été, w. Laurent Martin (pno) Ligia Digital ▲ 0201032
Berlioz, H.:Songs, w. Laurent Martin (pno)—La Belle Isabeau; Le Chasseur danois; Le Dépit de la bergère; Le Jeune patre Bréton; La Mort d'Ophélie; Petit oiseau; Zaide Ligia Digital ▲ 0201032
Gounod, C.:Songs, w. L. Martin (pno)—Venise; Le lever; Le chant de Eurydice; Départ; Déesse ou femme; Chanson de printemps; Aubade; Repentir; O ma belle rebelle; Medjé; Marguerite; A toi mon coeur; L'absent; Tombez mes ailes; Le calme; Si la mort est le but; Noël; Ave Maria Ligia Digital ▲ 0201010 [DDD]

Vernhes, Alain (bass)
Gounod, C.:Roméo et Juliette, w. Susan Graham (sop—Stephano), Ruth Ann Swenson (sop—Juliette), Sarah Walker (mez—Gertrude), Paul Charles Clarke (ten—Tybalt), Placido Domingo (ten—Roméo), Kurt Ollmann (bar—Mercutio), Alastair Miles (bass—Frère Laurent), David Pittman-Jennings (bass—Le Duc), Alain Vernhes (bass—Capulet), L. Slatkin (cnd), Munich RSO, Munich Radio Chorus *(rec Studio 1, Bavarian Radio, Munich, Nov 29 - Dec 10, 1995)* RCA Red Seal 2-▲ 09026-68440-2 [DDD]

Verreau, Richard (sgr)
Berlioz, H.:La Damnation de Faust, w. Pierre Mollet (bar—Brandler), Michel Roux (bar—Méphistophélès), Consuelo Rubio (sgr—Marguerite), Richard Verreau (sgr—Faust) Theorema 2-▲ TH 121170/171

Verrett, Shirley (mez)
Berlioz, H.:Les Troyens, w. M. Horne (mez), N. Gedda (ten), V. Luchetti (ten), R. Massard (bar), G. Prêtre (cnd), Rome RAI SO, Rome RAI Chorus [F] *(rec live 5/30/69)* Melodram 3-▲ MEL 37060 [AAD]
Berlioz, H.:Les Troyens, w. M. Horne (mez), N. Gedda (ten), V. Luchetti (ten), R. Massard (bar), G. Prêtre (cnd), Rome RAI SO, Rome RAI Chorus *(rec live 5/30/69)* Arkadia 4-▲ 461 [ADD]
Berlioz, H.:Les Troyens (sels), *(orch unknown)* *(rec 1969)* Arkadia ("Historical Performances" series) 2-▲ 495
Bizet, G.:Carmen, w. Kiri Te Kanawa (sop), Placido Domingo (ten), José Van Dam (b-bar), G. Solti (cnd), Royal Opera House Orch, Royal Opera House Chorus Covent Garden *(rec live, London, 1973)* Arkadia 3-▲ 498
Chausson, E.:Poème de l'amour et de la mer, w. G. Ferro (cnd), Turin RAI Orch Fonit Cetra ("Italia" series) ▲ FCT CDC 90
Donizetti, G.:Maria Stuarda, w. L. Gencer (sop), F. Tagliavini (ten), F. Molinari-Pradelli (cnd), Florence Maggio Musicale Orch, Florence Maggio Musicale Chorus *(rec 1967)* Memories 2-▲ MEM 4504 [AAD]
Donizetti, G.:Maria Stuarda, w. M. Caballé (sop), O. Garaventa (ten), C.F. Cillario (cnd), La Scala Orch, La Scala Chorus [I] *(rec live, Milan 4/20/71)* Myto 2-▲ 2 MCD 91137 [ADD]
Donizetti, G.:Maria Stuarda (sels), w. L. Gencer (sop), F. Tagliavini (ten), F. Molinari-Pradelli (cnd), Florence Maggio Musicale Orch, Florence Maggio Musicale Chorus, 11 arias from Acts 2 & 3 [I] *(rec 5/2/67)* Myto 2-▲ 2 MCD 91137 [ADD]
Gluck, C.W.:Orfeo ed Euridice, w. A. Moffo (sop), J. Raskin (sop), R. Fasano (cnd), Collegium Musicum Italicum Instrumental Ensemble, Rome Virtuosi RCA Gold Seal 2-▲ 7896-2-RG [ADD]
Great Operatic Duets, w. Montserrat Caballé (sop), Anton Guadagno (cnd), New Philharmonia Orch, Ambrosian Opera Chorus RCA Gold Seal ▲ 60818-2-RG [ADD]
Massenet, J.:Hérodiade (sels), w. G. Ferro (cnd), Turin RAI Orch—Je Ne l'Ai Pas Trouvée...Il Est Doux, Il Est Bon Fonit Cetra ("Italia" series) ▲ FCT CDC 90
Massenet, J.:Manon (sels), w. G. Ferro (cnd), Turin RAI Orch—Allons! Il le Faut!...Adieu Notre Petite Table; Je Marche sur Tous les Chemins...Obéissons Quand Leur Voix Appelle Fonit Cetra ("Italia" series) ▲ FCT CDC 90
Massenet, J.:Werther (sels), w. G. Ferro (cnd), Turin RAI Orch—Werther! Werther!...Je Vous Écris de Ma Petite Chambre Fonit Cetra ("Italia" series) ▲ FCT CDC 90

Verrett, Shirley (mez) (cont.)
Rodgers, R.:Carousel, w. M. Hayden (sgr), *(other artists unknown)* [1994 Broadway cast] Angel ▲ CDQ 55199 ■ 4DQ 55199
Rossini, G.:Mosè in Egitto, w. Teresa Zylis-Gara (sop), Ottavio Garaventa (ten), Giampaolo Corradi (bass), Nicolai Ghiaurov (bass), Mario Petri (bass), W. Sawallisch (cnd), Rome RAI Orch, Rome RAI Chorus *(rec live, Rome, 1968)* Italian Opera Rarities 2-▲ IOR 7724 [ADD]
Rossini, G.:The Siege of Corinth, w. B. Sills (sop), J. Diaz (bass), T. Schippers (cnd), London SO, Ambrosian Opera Chorus [I] *(rec London, 1974)* EMI Classics 3-▲ CDMC 64335
Rossini, G.:Stabat Mater, w. T. Zylis-Gara (sop), L. Pavarotti (ten), N. Zaccaria (bass), C. M. Giulini (cnd), Rome RAI Orch, Rome RAI Chorus [L] *(rec live 12/22/67)* Melodram 2-▲ MEL 28012
Rossini, G.:Stabat Mater, w. T. Zylis-Gara (sop), L. Pavarotti (ten), N. Zaccaria (bass), C.M. Giulini (cnd), Rome Radio Orch, Rome RAI Chorus [L] *(rec live 12/22/67)* Verona 2-▲ 27060/61 (m) [AAD]
Rossini, G.:Stabat Mater, w. Teresa Zylis-Gara (sop), Luciano Pavarotti (ten), Nicola Zaccaria (bass), C. M. Giulini (cnd), Rome RAI Orch, Rome RAI Chorus *(rec Rome, Dec. 1967)* Emozioni ▲ ARCD 2041
Saint-Saëns, C.:Samson et Dalila, w. Richard Cassilly (ten), Robert Massard (bar), G. Prêtre (cnd), La Scala Orch *(rec La Scala Theatre, May 30, 1969)* Arkadia ("Historical Performances" series) 2-▲ 495
Shirley Verrett in Opera RCA Gold Seal ▲ 09026-61457-2
Verdi, G.:Don Carlos, w. Gundula Janowitz (sop), Franco Corelli (ten), Eberhard Waechter (bar), Nicolai Ghiaurov (bass), Martti Talvela (bass), H. Stein (cnd), Vienna PO, Vienna State Opera Chorus *(rec Vienna, Oct. 25, 1970)* Pantheon 2-▲ PHE 6614
Verdi, G.:Luisa Miller, w. A. Moffo (sop), C. Bergonzi (ten), C. MacNeil (bar), G. Tozzi (bass), F. Cleva (cnd), RCA Italian Opera Orch [I] RCA Gold Seal 2-▲ 6646-2-RG [ADD]
Verdi, G.:Macbeth, w. Shirley Verrett (mez—Lady Macbeth), Plácido Domingo (ten—Macduff), Piero Cappuccilli (bar—Macbeth), Nicolai Ghiaurov (bass—Banco), C. Abbado (cnd), La Scala Orch, La Scala Chorus Deutsche Grammophon ("The Originals" series) ▲ 449 732-2
Verdi, G.:Rigoletto (sels), w. J. Anderson (sop), L. Pavarotti (ten), L. Nucci (bar), N. Ghiaurov (bass), R. Chailly (cnd), Bologna Teatro Comunale Orch, Bologna Teatro Comunale Chorus London ▲ 436097-2 [DDD]
Verdi, G.:Il trovatore, w. Antonella Banaudi (sop—Leonora), Barbara Frittoli (sop—Ines), Shirley Verrett (mez—Azucena), Enrico Facini (ten—Un messo), Piero de Palma (ten—Ruiz), Luciano Pavarotti (ten—Marico), Leo Nucci (bar—Il Conte di Luna), Roberto Scaltriti (bar—Un vecchio zingaro), Francesco Ellero d'Artegna (bass—Ferrando), Z. Mehta (cnd), Florence Maggio Musicale Orch, Florence Maggio Musicale Chorus *(rec Maggio Musicale Fiorentino Community Theater, June 18-July 2, 1990)* London 2-▲ 430694-2
The Voices of Living Stereo, Vol. 2, w. Eileen Farrell (sop), Birgit Nilsson (sop), Roberta Peters (sop), Leontyne Price (sop), Galina Vishnevskaya (sop), Rosalind Elias (mez), Marian Anderson (cta), Maureen Forrester (cta), Sergio Franchi (ten), Mario Lanza (ten), Richard Lewis (ten), Jan Pee, Alexander Dedyukhin (pno), Franz Rupp (pno), Leo Taubman (pno), George Trovillo (pno), Charles Wadsworth (pno), Boston Pops Orch [cnd:Arthur Fiedler], Boston SO [cnd:Charles Munch], Chicago SO [cnd:Fritz Reiner], RCA Victor Orch, RCA Victor Chorus [cnd:Wa *(rec Boston & Chicago & New York & Rome, 1957–1964)* RCA Living Stereo ▲ 09026-68167-2 [ADD]

Verrett, Shirley (sop)
Berlioz, H.:Les Troyens (sels), w. Shirley Verrett (sop—Didon), G. Prêtre (cnd), Rome RAI SO, Rome RAI Chorus *(rec live, Rome, May 30, 1969)* Arkadia ▲ 619 [ADD]
Purcell, H.:Dido & Aeneas, w. Helen Donath (sop—Belinda), Shirley Verrett (sop—Dido), Oralia Dominguez (mez—Sorceress), Carmen Lavani (alt—A Spirit), Margaret Lensky (cta—2nd Witch), Carlo Gaifa (ten—A Sailor), Dan Jordacescu (bar—Aeneas), Rosina Cavicchioli (sgr—A Woman), Lilia Teresita Reyes (sgr—1st Witch), R. Leppard (cnd), Turin RAI SO, Ambrosian Chorus *(rec Torino, May 20, 1971)* Arkadia ▲ 619 [ADD]

Verschaeve, Michel (bar)
Charpentier, M.-A.:Leçons de ténèbres, H. 96–110, w. Jan Caals (ten), Harry Ruyl (ten), Howard Crook (ct), Luc de Meulenaere (ct), Kurt Widmer (bass), L. Devos (cnd), Musica Polyphonica Erato 2-▲ ERA 96376 [DDD]

Verschaeve, Michel (bass)
Jacquet De La Guerre, E.:Le Raccomondement comique de Pierrot et de Nicole, w. I. Poulenard (sop), G. Guillard (hpd), *(ensemble unknown)* [F] Arion 2-▲ ARN 268012 [AAD]

Vespasiani, Ambra (mez)
Salieri, A.:Axur, Re d'Ormus, w. A. Martin (bar), E. Mei (sop), C. Rayam (ten), E. Nova (bass), M. Valenti (sop), R. Clemencic (cnd), Guido d'Arezzo Orch, Guido d'Arezzo Chorus [I] *(rec live 1989)* Nuova Era 3-▲ 6852/54 [DDD]

Vessières, André (bass)
Martin, F.:Le Mystère de la Nativité, w. Elly Ameling (sop), Aafje Heynis (cta), Hugues Cuénod (ten), Louis Devos (ten), Eric Tappy (ten), Pierre Bollet (bar), Derrik Olsen (bar), Charles Clavensy (b-bar), E. Ansermet (cnd), Swiss Romande Orch, Jeunes de l'Eglise Chorus, Ceneva Motet Chorus Cascavelle 2-▲ CVL 2006 [ADD]
Ravel, M.:L'Heure espagnole, w. S. Danco (mez—Concepcion), J. Giraudeau (ten—Gonzalve), M. Hamel (ten—Torquemada), J. Cameron (bar—Ramiro), A. Vessières (bass—Gomez), B. Maderna (cnd), BBC SO *(rec Nov. 1960)* Stradivarius ▲ STR 10062 [ADD]

Vetava, A. (ten)
Smetana, B.:The Brandenbergers in Bohemia, w. V. Soukupova (sop), K. Kalas (bar), J.H. Tichý (cnd), Prague National Theater Orch, Prague National Theater Chorus [G] Supraphon 2-▲ SUP 111802 [AAD]

Vezzani, César (ten)
Gounod, C.:Faust, w. M. Berthon (sop—Marguerite), C. Vezzani (ten—Faust), L. Musy (b-bar—Valentin), M. Journet (bass—Mephistofeles), H. Busser (cnd), Paris Opera Orch, Paris Opera Chorus [F] *(rec 1930)* Music Memoria 2-▲ 30187
Gounod, C.:Faust, w. M. Berthon (sop), M. Coiffier (sop), J. Montfort (mez), L. Musy (b-bar), M. Cozette (bar), M. Journet (bass), H. Busser (cnd), Paris Opera Orch, Paris Opera Chorus [F] *(rec 1930)* Pearl 2-▲ PEA 9987 [ADD]

Viala, Jean-Luc (ten)
Berlioz, H.:Messe solennelle Sop, w. Donna Brown (sop), Gilles Cachemaille (bar), J. E. Gardiner (cnd), Orch Révolutionnaire et Romantique, Monteverdi Choir London Philips ▲ 442137-2 ■ 442137-4 □ 442137-5
Berlioz, H.:Requiem, "Grande Messe des Morts", w. A. Lombard (cnd), Bordeaux-Aquitaine National Orch, Lubomír Mátl (cnd), Prague Phil Chorus, Slovak Phil Choir Forlane ▲ FRL 16639 [DDD]
Bruneau, A.:Lazare, w. Françoise Pollet (sop), Mary Saint-Palais (sop), Sylvie Sullé (mez), Laurent Naouri (b-bar), J. Mercier (cnd), French National Orch, Maîtrise de Paris, Vittoria French Regional Choir Adès ▲ ADE 204512
Bruneau, A.:Requiem, w. Françoise Pollet (sop), Mary Saint-Palais (sop), Sylvie Sullé (mez), Laurent Naouri (b-bar), J. Mercier (cnd), French National Orch, Maîtrise de Paris, Vittoria French Regional Choir Adès ▲ ADE 204512
Cornelius, P.:Stabat Mater, w. D. Borst (sop), J. Mayeur (cta), F. Vassar (bass-bar), M. Piquemal (cnd), Cannes-Provençe Alpes-Côte d'Azur Regional Orch, Cannes Regional Chorus Musique d'Abord ▲ HMA 1905206
Donizetti, G.:Messa di Gloria e Credo, w. Danielle Borst (sop), Hélène Jossoud (mez), Vincent Le Texier (bass-bar), M. Piquemal (cnd), Avignon-Provence Regional Lyric Orch, Provence-Alpes-Côte d'Azur Regional Choir Accord ▲ ACD 212142 [DDD]
Gluck, C.W.:La Recontre imprévue, w. C. Le Coz (sop), L. Dawson (sop), C. Dubosc (sop), S. Marin-Degor (sop), G. Fletcher (sgr), F. Dudziak (ten), G. de Mey (ten), J.-L. Viala (ten), G. Cachémaille (bar), J.-P. Lafont (bass), J. E. Gardiner (cnd), Paris Lyon Opera Orch, Paris Lyon Opera Chorus [F] Erato 2-▲ 2292-45516-2 [DDD]
Massenet, J.:Grisélidis, w. Michèle Command (sop), Brigitte Desnoues (sop), Didier Henry (bar), Maurice Sieyes (bar), Christian Treguier (bar), Jean-Philippe Courtis (bass), Claire Larcher (sgr), P. Fournillier (cnd), Franz Liszt SO, Budapest Lyon Chorus Koch Schwann 2-▲ SCH 312702 [DDD]
Prokofiev, S.:The Love for 3 Oranges (suite), w. C. Dubosc (sop), G. Gautier (ten), G. Bacquier (bar), J. Bastin (bass), K. Nagano (cnd), Paris Lyon Opera Orch, Paris Lyon Opera Chorus [F] Virgin Classics ▲ 59566 [DDD]

 ▲ = CD ♦ = Enhanced CD Δ = MD ■ = Cassette Tape □ = DCC

Viala, Jean-Luc (ten) (cont.)
Rossini, G.:Petite messe solennelle, w. Françoise Pollet (sop), Jacqueline Mayeur (mez), Michel Piquemal (bar), Raymond Alessandrini (pno), Emmanuel Mandrin (harm), Michel Piquemal (cnd), Michel Piquemal Vocal Ensemble Accord 2-▲ ACD 203562 [DDD]
Strauss, R.:Salome, w. K. Huffstodt (sop), H. Jossoud (mez), J. Dupouy (ten), J. van Dam (bar), K. Nagano (cnd), Paris Lyon Opera Orch, Paris Lyon Opera Chorus Virgin Classics 2-▲ CDCB 59054

Vialtzeva, Anastasia (sgr)
The World of Singing, Vol. 2:Singers of Imperial Russia, w. Nina Koshetz (sop), Evgenia Zbrueva (cta), Nicolai Figner (ten), Feodor Chaliapin (bass), Nina Friede (sgr), Maria Kouznetsova (sgr) Enterprise ("Vocal Archives" series) 2-▲ ENT VA 2102

Viard, Martine (voc)
Cage, J.:She Is Asleep, w. I. Berteletti (prepared pno), Hêlios Percussion Quartet Wergo ▲ WER 6203-2 [DDD]

Viaro, Enzo (sgr)
Giordano, U.:Madame Sans-Gêne, w. Magda László (sop—Caterina), Carlo Tagliabue (bar—Napoleone), Renato Berti (sgr—Despréaux), Irene Callaway (sgr—Toniotta/Carolina), Danilo Cestari (sgr—Neipperg/Vinaigre), Maria Luisa Malacchi (sgr—Giulia/Principessa Elisa), Carlo Perucci (sgr—Fouché), Danilo Vega (sgr—Lefebvre), Enzo Viaro (sgr—De Brigode/Gelsomino), A. Basile (cnd), Milan RAI SO, Milan RAI Chorus *(rec Milan, Aug 10, 1957)* Bongiovanni 2-▲ GB 1129/30

Vickers, Jon (ten)
Beethoven, L. van:Fidelio, w. Ingeborg Hallstein (sop—Marzelline), Christa Ludwig (mez—Leonore/Fidelio), Gerhard Unger (ten—Jaquino), Jon Vickers (ten—Florestan), Walter Berry (bass—Pizarro), Franz Crass (bass—Don Fernando), Gottlob Frick (bass—Rocco), O. Klemperer (cnd), Philharmonia Orch, Philharmonia Chorus EMI Classics 2-▲ CDCB 55170
Beethoven, L. van:Fidelio, w. Judith Blegen (sop), Leonie Rysanek (sop), Walter Berry (bass), John Macurdy (bass), Giorgio Tozzi (bass), K. Böhm (cnd), San Francisco Opera Orch, San Francisco Opera Chorus Melodram 2-▲ CDM 27086
Beethoven, L. van:Fidelio, w. S. Jurinac (sop), H. Hotter (b-bar), G. Frick (bass), O. Klemperer (cnd), Royal Opera House Orch, Royal Opera House Chorus Covent Garden [G] *(rec live, Covent Garden, 3/7/61)* Melodram 2-▲ MEL 27076 (m) [AAD]
Beethoven, L. van:Fidelio, w. I. Hallstein (sop), C. Ludwig (mez), G. Unger (ten), W. Berry (bass), G. Frick (bass), O. Klemperer (cnd), Philharmonia Orch, Philharmonia Chorus [G]; w. minimal dialog EMI Classics ("Studio" series) 2-▲ CDMB 69324 [ADD]
Berlioz, H.:Les Troyens, w. B. Lindholm (sop), J. Veasey (mez), P. Glossop (bar), R. Soyer (bass), C. Davis (cnd), Royal Opera House Orch [F] Philips 4-▲ 416432-2 [ADD]
Bizet, G.:Carmen, w. M. Freni (sop), G. Bumbry (mez), K. Paskalis (bar), R. Frühbeck de Burgos (cnd), Paris Opera Orch, Paris Opera Chorus [opéra comique version] [F] EMI Classics ("Studio" series) 2-▲ CDMB 63643 [ADD]
Bizet, G.:Carmen, w. G. Bumbry (sop), M. Freni (sop), J. Diaz (bass), H. von Karajan (cnd), Vienna PO, Vienna State Opera Chorus [F] *(rec live, Salzburg 1967)* Arkadia 3-▲ 221 [ADD]
Bizet, G.:Carmen (sels), w. Mirella Freni (sop), Grace Bumbry (mez), H. von Karajan (cnd), Vienna PO *(rec Salzburg, 1967)* Arkadia 3-▲ 498
Britten, H.:Peter Grimes, w. H. Harper (sop), J. Summers (bar), C. Davis (cnd), Royal Opera House Orch, Royal Opera House Chorus Covent Garden [E] Philips 2-▲ 432578-2 [ADD]
Cherubini, L.:Médée, w. M. Callas (sop), T. Berganza (mez), N. Zaccaria (bass), N. Rescigno (cnd), Dallas SO *(rec live, Dallas Civic Opera, State Fair Music Hall 11/6/58)* Melodram 2-▲ MEL 26016
Cherubini, L.:Médée, w. M. Callas (sop), F. Cossotto (mez), N. Zaccaria (bass), N. Rescigno (cnd), Royal Opera House Orch, Royal Opera House Chorus Covent Garden [I] *(rec live, Covent Garden, 6/30/59)* Melodram 2-▲ MEL 26005
Dvořák, A.:Zigeunermelodien, Op. 55, w. Richard Woitach (pno)—My Song Resounds, My Song of Love; Yon Lies the Moon, So Far, So Still; Dark in Flowing Linen; Soaring Ever Upward *(rec live, New York, Apr. 30, 1967)* VAI Audio ▲ VAIA 1032 [ADD]
Elgar, E.:The Dream of Gerontius, w. C. Shacklock (mez), M. Nowkovski (bass), J. Barbirolli (cnd), Rome Radio Orch, Rome RAI Chorus [E] *(rec live, Rome 11/20/57)* Arkadia 2-▲ 584 [ADD]
Handel, G.F.:Messiah, w. Jennifer Vyvyan (sop), Monica Sinclair (cta), Giorgio Tozzi (bass), T. Beecham (cnd), Royal PO *(rec 1959)* RCA Gold Seal 3-▲ 09026-61266-2
Handel, G.F.:Messiah (sels), w. Jennifer Vyvyan (sop), Monica Sinclair (mez), Giorgio Tozzi (bass), T. Beecham (cnd), Royal PO, John McCarthy (cnd), Royal Choral Society—Ov; Comfort Ye My People; Every Valley Shall Be Exalted; And the Glory of the Lord; And He Shall Purify; O Thou That Tellest Good Tidings; For unto Us a Child is Born; Pastoral Symphony; There Were Shepherds Abiding; And the Angel Said unto Them; And Suddenly There Was; Glory to God in the Highest; He Shall Feed His Flock; Come unto Him; Behold the Lamb of God; He Was Despised; All We Like Sheep Have Gone Astray; Hallelujah!; I Know That My Redeemer Liveth; The Trumpet Shall Sound *(rec Walthamstow Town Hall, London, June-Aug 1959)* RCA Victor ▲ 09026-68159-2 [ADD]
Handel, G.F.:Messiah (sels), w. Richard Woitach (pno)—Behold & See If There Be; But Thou Didst Not Leave His Soul in Hell *(rec live, New York, Apr. 30, 1967)* VAI Audio ▲ VAIA 1032 [ADD]
Italian Opera Arias, w. Rome Opera House Orch [cnd.:Tullio Serafin] *(rec Rome, July 1961)* VAI Audio ▲ VAIA 1016 [AAD]
Leoncavallo, R.:Pagliacci, w. Joan Carlyle (sop—Nedda), Jon Vickers (ten—Canio), José Noit (ten—Beppe), Cornell MacNeil (bar—Tonio), Bruno Tomasaetti (bar—Silvio), B. Bartoletti (cnd), *(orch unknown) (rec live, Buenos Aires, 1968)* VAI Audio ▲ VAIA 1014 [ADD]
Live Performances 1961-1970, w. Vickers, Jon (ten) Memories 2-▲ MEM 4394 (m) [ADD]
Mahler, G.:Das Lied von der Erde, w. J. Norman (sop), C. Davis (cnd), London SO [G] Philips ▲ 411474-2 [DDD]
Purcell, H.:Songs, w. Richard Woitach (pno)—Sweeter than Roses; There's Not a Swain of the Plain; Not All of My Torments; Man Is for the Woman Made *(rec live, New York, Apr. 30, 1967)* VAI Audio ▲ VAIA 1032 [ADD]
Saint-Saëns, C.:Samson et Dalila, w. R. Gorr (mez), E. Blanc (bar), G. Prêtre (cnd), Paris Opera Orch, René DuClos Chorus [F] EMI Classics 2-▲ CDCB 47895
Saint-Saëns, C.:Samson et Dalila (sels), w. R. Gorr (mez), E. Blanc (bar), G. Prêtre (cnd), Paris Opera Orch EMI Classics ▲ ZDM 63935
Scarlatti, A.:Cants, w. Richard Woitach (pno)—Cara e dolce; Difesa non ha; O dolcissima speranza; La speranza; Toglietemi la vita ancor *(rec live, New York, Apr. 30, 1967)* VAI Audio ▲ VAIA 1032 [ADD]
Schubert, Franz:Winterreise, w. P. Schaaf (pno) [G] *(rec live 10/2/83)* VAI Audio 2-▲ VAIA 1007-2 [ADD]
Schumann, R.:Dichterliebe, w. Richard Woitach (pno) *(rec live, New York, Apr. 30, 1967)* VAI Audio ▲ VAIA 1032 [ADD]
Verdi, G.:Aida, w. L. Price (sop), R. Gorr (mez), R. Merrill (bar), G. Tozzi (bass), G. Solti (cnd), Rome Opera Orch, Rome Opera Chorus [I] London 3-▲ 417416-2 [ADD]
Verdi, G.:Aida, w. L. Price (sop), R. Gorr (mez), R. Merrill (bar), G. Tozzi (bass), G. Solti (cnd), Rome Opera Orch, Rome Opera Chorus [I] London ▲ 421860-2 [ADD]
Verdi, G.:Aida, w. G. Jones (sop), Dourian (sgr), Shaw (sgr), E. Downes (cnd), Royal Opera House Orch, Royal Opera House Chorus Covent Garden [I] *(rec live, Covent Garden, 1/27/68)* Melodram 2-▲ MEL 27019
Verdi, G.:Don Carlos, w. G. Brouwenstein (sop—Elisabetta di Valois), F. Barbieri (mez—Princess Eboli), J. Vickers (ten—Don Carlo), T. Gobbi (bar—Rodrigo), B. Christoff (bass—Fillipo), C. M. Giulini (cnd), Royal Opera House Orch, Royal Opera House Chorus Covent Garden *(rec 1958)* Myto 3-▲ MCD 94197
Verdi, G.:Otello, w. M. Freni (sop), P. Glossop (bar), H. von Karajan (cnd), Vienna PO *(rec 1971)* Memories 2-▲ MEM 4533 [ADD]
Wagner, R.:Der Ring des Nibelungen, w. R. Crespin (sop), G. Janowitz (sop), C. Ludwig (mez), H. Dernesch (mez), D. Fischer-Dieskau (bar), D. Thomas (bass), H. von Karajan (cnd), Berlin PO *(rec live at Salzburg Easter Festivals, 1967-1970)* Arkadia 12-▲ 223 (m) [ADD]
Wagner, R.:Der Ring des Nibelungen, w. R. Crespin (sop), G. Janowitz (sop), C. Ludwig (mez), H. Dernesch (mez), D. Fischer-Dieskau (bar), D. Thomas (bass), H. von Karajan (cnd), Berlin PO *(rec late 1960s)* Deutsche Grammophon 15-▲ 435211-2 [ADD]
Wagner, R.:Tristan und Isolde, w. H. Dernesch (sop), C. Ludwig (mez), P. Schreier (ten), B. Weikl (bar), W. Berry (bass), K. Ridderbusch (bass), H. von Karajan (cnd), Berlin PO, German Opera Chorus [G] EMI Classics ("Studio" series) 4-▲ CDMD 69319 [ADD]

Vidal, Elisabeth (sop)
Mozart, W.A.:Zauberflöte, w. Birgit Been (sop), Nathalie Boissy (sop), Marianne Seibel (sop), Renate Springer (sop), Eleanor James (mez), Salvador Guzman (ten), Herbert Hechenberger (ten), Wolfgang Newmann (ten), Klaus Häger (bass), Philip Langshaw (bass), Hans-Georg Moser (bass), P. Kuentz (cnd), Paul Kuentz Orch, Francis Bardot (cnd), Maitrise des Hauts-de-Seine members, Paul Kuentz Choirs Pierre Verany 2-▲ PVY 730055 [DDD]
Orff, C.:Carmina burana, w. Alexander Stevensen (ten), André Cognet (bass), P. Kuentz (cnd), Paul Kuentz Orch, Paul Kuentz Choir, Mouez Armor Chorale, Lorient Conservatory Chorus, Notre Dame College Chorus Pierre Verany ▲ PVY 730044
Ravel, M.:L'Enfant et les sortilèges, w. M. Lagrange (sop), M. Damonte (mez), M. Mahé (mez), A. Chedel (cta), L. Pezzino (ten), M. Barrard (bar), V. le Texier (b-bar), A. Lombard (cnd), Bordeaux-Aquitaine National Orch, Bordeaux Grand Théâtre Municipal Chorus [F] Valois ▲ V 4670

Videnov, Lyubomir (bar)
Rimsky-Korsakov, N.:Snow Maiden, w. Stefka Evstatieva (sop—Kupava), Elena Zemenkova (sop—Snow Maiden), Alexandrina Milcheva (mez—Spring Fairy), Vessela Zorova (mez—wife), Stefka Mineva (alt—Lehl), Avram Andreev (ten—Tsar), Lyubomir Dyakovski (ten—Cottager, Sprite), Lyubomir Videnov (bar—Misgir), Nicola Ghiuselev (bass—King), S. Angelov (cnd), Bulgarian RSO, Bulgarian National Chorus *(rec Sofia, 1985)* Capriccio 3-▲ 10749-51 [DDD]

Videv, Kosta (bass)
Rimsky-Korsakov, N.:Golden Cockerel, w. Yavora Stoilova (sop—Golden Cockerel), Elena Stoyanova (sop—Queen), Evgenia Babacheva (mez—Amelfa), Lyubomir Bodourov (ten—Prince), Lyubomir Dyakovski (ten—Astrologer), Emil Ugrinov (bar—Afron), Nikolai Stoilov (bass—Tsar), Kosta Videv (bass—Polkan), D. Manolov (cnd), Sofia National Opera Orch, Sofia National Opera Chorus *(rec Sofia, 1985)* Capriccio 2-▲ 10760/61 [DDD]

Vier, Michael (bar)
Spohr, L.:Faust, w. C. Taha (sop), E. von Jordis (bass), G. Moull (cnd), Bielefeld PO, Bielefeld Opera Chorus [1852 version] *(rec live, June 1993)* CPO 2-▲ CPO 999247 [DDD]

Vighi, Giovanna (mez)
Donizetti, G.:Messa di Gloria e Credo, w. H. Mané (sop), P. Maus (ten), M. Machi (bass), R. Bader (cnd), Berlin RSO, St. Hedwig's Cathedral Choir [L] Koch Schwann ▲ CD 313031 [ADD]

Vignoli, Paolo (ten)
Burkhard, W.:Sacred Music, w. Fritz Näf (cnd), Basel Madrigalists—Die Sintflut; Christi Leidensverkundigung; Das Ezzolied Ars Musici ▲ 1146

Vigoda, Samuel (cant)
Echoes of the Temple:Cantors in Prayer & Folksong, w. Gershon Sirota (cant), Pierre Pinchik (cant), Joseph Rosenblatt (cant), Arthur Tracy (cant), et al. *(rec 1914-36)* Pearl ▲ PEA 9126 [ADD]

Vihavainen, Satu (sop)
Kokkonen, J.:Erekhtheion, w. W. Grönroos (bar), O. Vänskä (cnd), Lahti SO, Academic Choral Society [Fin] BIS ▲ CD 498 [DDD]
Kokkonen, J.:Requiem (in memoriam Maija Kokkonen), w. Jorma Hynninen (bar), U. Söderblom (cnd), Helsinki PO, Academic Choral Society Finlandia ▲ FIN 53353 [DDD]

Viljakainen, Raili (sop)
Sibelius, J.:The Tempest, w. M. Groop (mez), J. Silvasti (ten), J. Hynninen (bar), S. Tiilikainen (bar), J.-P. Saraste (cnd), Finnish RSO, Finnish Opera Festival Chorus Ondine ▲ ODE 813 [DDD]

Villa, Jacques (sgr)
Lehár, F.:Die lustige Witwe, w. Teresa Stich-Randall (mez—Missia Palmieri), Monique Stiot (mez—Manon), Germaine Duclos (sgr—Praskovia), Linda Felder (sgr—Olga), Christiane Jacquin (sgr—Nadia), Jeannette Levasseur (sgr—Sylviane), Henri Legay (ten—Camille de Coutançon), Joseph Peyron (ten—Kromsky), Robert Destain (sgr—Baron Popoff), Michel Fauche (sgr—Pristich), Gérard Friedmann (sgr—Lerida), Jacques Gilet (sgr—Bogdanowitch), Jean Guy Henneveux (sgr—Prince Danilo), Serge Klin (sgr—Figg), Jacques Villa (sgr—D'Estillac), A. Sibert (cnd), Belgian Radio-TV Orch, Belgian Radio-TV Chorus *(rec Grand Auditorium, Belgium, Apr 30, 1970)* Studio SM 2-▲ 2160 [AAD]

Villa, L. (sop)
Mozart, W.A.:Nozze di Figaro, w. E. Schwarzkopf (sop), I. Seefried (sop), S. Jurinac (sop), R. Panerai (bar), H. von Karajan (cnd), La Scala Orch, La Scala Chorus [I] *(rec live Feb. 4, 1954)* Melodram 3-▲ MEL 37075 [AAD]

Villa, Luisa (mez)
Strauss, R.:Der Rosenkavalier, w. Jarmila Barton (sop—Marianne), Lisa Della Casa (sop—Sophie), Sena Jurinac (sop—Octavian), Ilva Ligabue (sop—Orphan), Elisabeth Schwarzkopf (sop—Marschallin), Else Schürhoff (mez—Annina), Luisa Villa (mez—Milliner), Hugues Cuénod (ten—Marschallin's majordomo), Erich Majkut (ten—Valzacchi), Giuseppe Nessi (ten—Animal seller), Luciano Della Pergola (ten—Lackey/Faninal's majordomo), Antonio Pirino (ten—An Italian Singer), Gino Del Signore (ten—Lackey/Waiter), Erich Kunz (bar—Herr von Faninal), Paolo Pedani (bar—Lackey), Attilio Barbesi (bass—Lackey/Waiter), Enrico Campi (bass—Waiter), Otto Edelmann (bass—Baron Ochs), Bruno Fichtinger (bass—Notary), Franco Taino (bass—Waiter), Maria Amadini (sgr—Orphan), Pina Carrillo (sgr—Orphan), Joszi Trojan Regar (sgr—Innkeeper), H. von Karajan (cnd), La Scala Orch, La Scala Chorus *(rec La Scala Theater, Milan, Jan. 26, 1952)* Legato Classics 3-▲ LCD 197-3

Villa, Natale (bass)
Puccini, G.:Manon Lescaut, w. Maria Zamboni (sop—Manon), Anna Masetti-Bassi (mez—Singer), Francesco Merli (ten—Chevalier), Giuseppe Nessi (ten—Edmondo/Dancing Master/ Lamplighter), Lorenzo Conati (bar—Lescaut), Aristide Baracchi (bass—Innkeeper/Sergeant), Attilio Bordonali (bass—Geronte), Natale Villa (bass—Naval Captain), L. Molajoli (cnd), La Scala Orch, Vittore Veneziani (cnd), La Scala Chorus *(rec 1930)* Arkadia ("The 78's" series) 2-▲ 78014 [ADD]

Villanueva (sgr)
Monteverdi, C.:Ritorno d'Ulisse, w. Gloria Banditelli (cta), Tucker (sgr), A. Curtis (cnd), Sonatori de la Gioiosa Marca [I] Nuova Era ("Ancient Music" series) 3-▲ 7103/05 [DDD]

Villarroel, Veronica (sop)
Moreno Torroba, F.:Luisa Fernanda, w. Ana Rodrigo (mez), Plácido Domingo (ten), Juan Pons (bar), A. Ros-Marbá (cnd), Madrid SO Valois 2-▲ V 4759
Penella, M.:El gato montés, w. T. Berganza (mez), P. Domingo (ten), J. Pons (bar), M. Roa (cnd), Madrid SO [Sp] Deutsche Grammophon 2-▲ 435776-2 [DDD]

Villisech, Jacques (bass)
Bach, J.S.:St. John Passion, w. K. Equiluz (ten), M. Van Egmond (b-bar), N. Harnoncourt (cnd), Vienna Concentus Musicus, Vienna Boys' Choir soloists Teldec ▲ 2292-42492-2
Rameau, J.P.:Castor et Pollux, w. M. Schéle (sop), J. Scovotti (sop), R. Leanderson (bar), G. Souzay (bar), N. Harnoncourt (cnd), Vienna Concentus Musicus Teldec ▲ 42510-2

Vinay, Ramon (ten)
Bizet, G.:Carmen, w. Laura Bustamante (sop—Frasquita), Ximena Riveros (sop—Mercedes), Nancy Stokes (sop—Micaela), Regina Resnik (mez—Carmen), Plácido Domingo (ten—Don José), Ismildo Tedeschi (ten—Remendado), Ramon Vinay (ten—Escamillo), Juan Charles (ten/bar—Dancaire), Agustin Letelier (bar—Morles), Jorge Algorta (bass—Zuniga), A. Guadagno (cnd), Santiago Teatro Municipale Orch, Santiago Teatro Municipale Chorus *(rec Santiago Municipal Theater, Sept. 4, 1967)* Legato Classics 2-▲ LCD 194-2 [ADD]
Puccini, G.:Tosca, w. B. Nilsson (sop), F. Tagliavini (ten), C. Maresco (cnd), Philadelphia Opera Orch, Philadelphia Opera Chorus *(rec Apr. 10, 1963)* Melodram 2-▲ MLO 270112 [ADD]
Recital (rec. live, New York & London, 1948-1970) Melodram 2-▲ CDM 26519 [AAD]
Saint-Saëns, C.:Samson et Dalila, w. Risë Stevens (mez—Dalila), Ramón Vinay (ten—Samson), Thomas Carter (ten—1st Philistine), Tony Lopez (ten—Philistine Messenger), Joseph Mordino (bar—High Priest), Arthur Cosenza (bass—Abimélech), Joseph Knight (bass—2nd Philistine), Ara Berberian (bass—Old Hebrew), R. Cellini (cnd), New Orleans Opera Orch, New Orleans Opera Chorus *(rec live, Apr 2, 1960)* VAI Audio 2-▲ VAIA 1055-2 [ADD]
Verdi, G.:Otello, w. H. Nelli (sop), G. Valdengo (bar), A. Toscanini (cnd), NBC SO [I] RCA Gold Seal 2-▲ 60302-2-RG [ADD] 2-■ 60302-4-RG (CrO2)
Verdi, G.:Otello, w. Carla Martinis (sop—Desdemona), Sieglinde Wagner (mez—Emilia), Anton Dermota (ten—Cassio), Paul Schöffler (ten—Iago), Ramon Vinay (ten—Otello), Josef Greindl (bass—Lodovico), W. Furtwängler (cnd), Vienna PO, Vienna State Opera Chorus *(rec live, Salzburg Festival, Aug 7, 1951)* EMI Classics ▲ CDMB 65751

VOCALISTS

Vinay, Ramon (ten) (cont.)
Wagner, R.:Tannhäuser, w. G. Brouwenstijn (sop), D. Fischer-Dieskau (bar), J. Greindl (bass), J. Keilberth (cnd), Bayreuth Festival Orch, Bayreuth Festival Chorus *(rec live, Bayreuth, 1954)* Melodram 3-▲ MEL 36105
Wagner, R.:Tristan und Isolde, w. M. Mödl (sop), H. Hotter (b-bar), H. von Karajan (cnd), Bayreuth Festival Orch, Bayreuth Festival Chorus *(rec 1955)* Arkadia 4-▲ 528 (m) [AAD]

Vincent, Jo (sop)
Mahler, G.:Sym 2, w. K. Ferrier (cta), O. Klemperer (cnd), Royal Concertgebouw Orch [G] *(rec 7/12/51)* Verona 2-▲ 27062/63 (m) [AAD]
Mahler, G.:Sym 2, w. K. Ferrier (cta), O. Klemperer (cnd), Royal Concertgebouw Orch—abridged version of the 4th movt., "Urlicht," from the above rec'g Verona ▲ 27076 (m) [AAD]

Vincent, Lawrence (ten)
Warren, E.R.:The Legend of King Arthur:A Choral Sym, w. T. Hampson (bar), S. Kawalla (cnd), Cracow Polish Radio-TV SO [E] Cambria ▲ CD 1043 [DDD]

Vincenzi, Edda (sop)
Zandonai, R.:Francesca da Rimini, w. Lydia Marimpietri (sop—Biancofiore), Magda Olivero (sop—Francesca), Pinuccia Perotti (sop—Samaritana), Edda Vincenzi (sop—Garsenda), Gabriella Carturan (mez—Smaragdi), Biancamaria Casoni (mez—Altichiara), Anna Maria Rota (cta—Donella), Athos Cesarini (ten—Archer), Angelo Mercuriali (ten—Ser Toldo Berardengo), Mario del Monaco (ten—Paolo), Piero de Palma (ten—Malatestino), Rinaldo Pelizzoni (ten—Prisoner), Gianpiero Malaspina (bar—Gianciotto), Dino Mantovani (bar—Jester), Enrico Campi (bass—Ostasio), Giuseppe Morresi (bass—Tower warden), G. Gavazzeni (cnd), La Scala Orch, La Scala Chorus *(rec La Scala Theatre, Milan, June 4, 1959)* Legato Classics 2-▲ LCD 186-2

Vinciguerra, Maria (mez)
Donizetti, G.:Lucia di Lammermoor, w. Lina Pagliughi (sop—Lucia), Maria Vinciguerra (mez—Alisa), Armando Giannotti (ten—Normanno), Muzio Giovagnoli (ten—Arturo), Giovanni Malipiero (ten—Edgardo), Giuseppe Manacchini (bar—Enrico), Luciano Neroni (bass—Raimondo), U. Tansini (cnd), EIAR Orch, EIAR Chorus *(rec 1938)* Bongiovanni ("Il mito dell'opera" series) 2-▲ GB 1122-2 [ADD]
Donizetti, G.:Lucia di Lammermoor, w. Lina Pagliughi (sop—Lucia), Maria Vinciguerra (mez—Alisa), Armando Giannotti (ten—Normanno), Muzio Giovannoli (ten—Lord Arturo), Giovanni Malipiero (ten—Edgardo), Giuseppe Manacchini (bar—Lord Enrico), Luciano Neroni (bass—Raimondo), U. Tansini (cnd), EIAR Orch, EIAR Chorus *(rec Turin, 1942)* Melodram 2-▲ IMC 202004 [ADD]

Vinco, Ivo (bass)
Bellini, V.:Norma, w. J. Sutherland (sop), F. Cossotto (mez), C. Craig (ten), R. Bonynge (cnd), Buenos Aires Teatro Colón Orch, Buenos Aires Teatro Colón Chorus *(rec live 7/2/69)* Ediciones Teatro Colon 3-▲ ETC 101 [AAD]
Bellini, V.:Norma, w. Caballé (soprano—Norma), F. Cossotto (mez), B. Prevedi (ten), J. Carreras (ten), C. F. Cillario (cnd), Barcelona Teatro Liceo Orch, Barcelona Gran Teatro de Liceo Chorus [I] *(rec live, Barcelona 1/11/70)* Melodram 2-▲ CDM 27089 [ADD]
Bellini, V.:Norma (sels), w. M. Callas (sop), F. Cossotto (mez), G. Cecchele (ten), G. Prêtre (cnd), Paris Opera Orch, Paris Opera Chorus—sels. *(rec 1965)* Melodram ▲ MLO 16038 [ADD]
Bellini, V.:La sonnambula, w. R. Scotto (sop), A. Kraus (ten), N. Santi (cnd), Venice Teatro La Fenice Orch, Venice Teatro La Fenice Chorus [I] *(rec live, Venice 5/26/61)* Golden Age of Opera 2-▲ GAO 111/12 [ADD]
Ponchielli, A.:La Gioconda, w. M. Callas (sop), F. Cossotto (mez), I. Companeez (cta), P. M. Ferraro (ten), P. Cappuccilli (bar), A. Votto (cnd), La Scala Orch, La Scala Chorus EMI Classics ▲ CDCC 49518
Verdi, G.:Don Carlos, w. S. Jurinac (sop—Elisabetta), L. Rysanek (sop—Celestial Voice), F. Cossotto (mez—Princess Eboli), L. Dutoit (boy sop—Tebaldo), P. Domingo (ten—Don Carlo), E. Majkut (ten—Count of Lerma), M. Sereni (bar—Rodrigo), C. Siepi (bass—Philip II), I. Vinco (bass—Grand Inquisitor), T. Franc (bass—Friar), S. Varviso (cnd), Vienna State Opera Orch, Vienna State Opera Chorus Standing Room Only 2-▲ SRO 850 [ADD]
Verdi, G.:Nabucco, w. Mirella Parutto (sgr), Ettore Bastianini (bar), B. Bartoletti (cnd), *(orch unknown), (orch & chorus unknown) (rec live, Florence, Aug. 26, 1961)* Great Opera Performances 2-▲ GOP 751
Verdi, G.:Il trovatore, w. A. Stella (sop), M. Fiorentini (mez), F. Cossotto (mez), F. Corelli (ten), E. Bastianini (bar), G. Gavazzeni (cnd), La Scala Orch, La Scala Chorus *(rec live, Milan, 12/7/62)* Melodram 2-▲ MEL 27068 (m) [AAD]
Verdi, G.:Il trovatore, w. A. Stella (sop), M. Fiorentini (mez), F. Cossotto (mez), F. Corelli (ten), E. Bastianini (bar), G. Gavazzeni (cnd), La Scala Orch, La Scala Chorus [I] *(rec live, Milan, 12/7/62)* Claque 2-▲ CLQ 2013 (m)

Vink, Elena (sop)
de Leeuw, T.:Haiku II, w. E. Spanjaard (cnd), The Hague PO Donemus ▲ CV 23

Vinogradov, Georgi (ten)
Schumann, R.:Dichterliebe Preiser ▲ PRE 89118
Schumann, R.:Songs Preiser ▲ PRE 89118

Vinson, Brigitte (mez)
Chausson, E.:Duos, "La nuit" & "Le réveil", w. D. Collot (sop), J. Bouillat (ten), G. Wieclaw (bass), E. Strosser (pno), C. Desert (pno), J. Sourisse (cnd), Jean Sourisse Ensemble, Audite Nova Vocal Ensemble FNAC Music ▲ 592224 [DDD]
Debussy, C.:Songs, w. D. Collot (sop), J. Bouillat (ten), G. Wieclaw (bass), C. Desert (pno), E. Strosser (pno), J. Sourisse (cnd), Jean Sourisse Ensemble, Audite Nova Vocal Ensemble—3 chansons de Chateau D'Orleans FNAC Music ▲ 592224 [DDD]
Fauré, G.:Madrigal, w. D. Collot (sop), J. Bouillat (ten), G. Wieclaw (bass), C. Desert (pno), E. Strosser (pno) FNAC Music ▲ 592224 [DDD]
Fauré, G.:Pavane Orch, w. D. Collot (sop), J. Bouillat (ten), G. Wieclaw (bass), C. Desert (pno), E. Strosser (pno), J. Sourisse (cnd), Jean Sourisse Ensemble, Audite Nova Vocal Ensemble FNAC Music ▲ 592224 [DDD]
Fauré, G.:Songs, w. D. Collot (sop), J. Bouillat (ten), G. Wieclaw (bass), C. Desert (pno), E. Strosser (pno), J. Sourisse (cnd), Jean Sourisse Ensemble, Audite Nova Vocal Ensemble—Le Ruisseau, Op. 22; Puisqu'ici bas, Op. 10/1, Les Djinns, Op. 12 FNAC Music ▲ 592224 [DDD]
Ravel, M.:Songs, w. D. Collot (sop), J. Bouillat (ten), G. Wieclaw (bass), E. Strosser (pno), C. Desert (pno), J. Sourisse (cnd), Jean Sourisse Ensemble, Audite Nova Vocal Ensemble—3 a capella songs FNAC Music ▲ 592224 [DDD]
Saint-Saëns, C.:Choral Music, w. D. Collot (sop), J. Bouillat (ten), G. Wieclaw (bass), E. Strosser (pno), C. Desert (pno), J. Sourisse (cnd), Jean Sourisse Ensemble , Vocal Audite Nova Ensemble—Calme des nuits, Op. 68/1; Les fleurs et les arbres, Op. 68/2; Salterelle, Op. 74 FNAC Music ▲ 592224 [DDD]

Vinson, Brigitte (sop)
Bach, J.S.:Magnificat, BWV 243, w. Hélène Obadia (sop), Madeleine Jalabert (alt), Hervé Lamy (ten), Philip Langshaw (bass), P. Kuentz (cnd), Paul Kuentz Orch, Paul Kuentz Choir Pierre Verany ▲ PVY 730048

Vinzing, Ute (sop)
Strauss, R.:Die Frau ohne Schatten, w. C. Studer (sop), H. Schwarz (mez), R. Kollo (ten), A. Muff (bass), Schmidt (sgr), W. Sawallisch (cnd), Bavarian RSO, Bavarian Radio Chorus [uncut version] [G] EMI Classics 3-▲ CDCC 49074 [DDD]
Strauss, R.:Die Frau ohne Schatten, w. C. Studer (sop), H. Schwarz (mez), R. Kollo (ten), A. Muff (bass), Schmidt (sgr), W. Sawallisch (cnd), Bavarian RSO, Bavarian Radio Chorus [G] EMI Classics ▲ CDC 54494 [DDD]

Virgilio, Nicolas di (ten)
Beethoven, L. van:Sym 9, "Choral Sym", w. M. Arroy (sop), R. Sarfaty (mez), N. Scott (bass), L. Bernstein (cnd), New York PO, Juilliard Chorus *(rec New York, May 18, 1964)* Sony Classical ("Bernstein:The Royal Edition" series) Δ SM 47513 [ADD]

Visconti, Piero (ten)
Catalani, A.:Loreley, w. M. Colalillo (sop), M. L. Garbato (sop), A. Cassis (bar), N. Annovazzi (cnd), Lucca Teatro Comunale del Giglio Orch, Lucca Teatro Comunale del Giglio Chorus *(rec live 9/19/82)* Bongiovanni 2-▲ GB 2015/16 [ADD]

Vishnevskaya, Galina (sop)
Britten, H.:Poet's Echo, w. M. Rostropovich (vc) London 2-▲ 433200-2

Vishnevskaya, Galina (sop) (cont.)
Britten, H.:War Requiem, w. P. Pears (ten), D. Fischer-Dieskau (bar), B. Britten (cnd), London SO, London Sym Chorus [E,L] London 2-▲ 414383-2 [ADD]
Mahler, G.:Sym 2, w. Hilde Rössl-Majdan (alt), O. Klemperer (cnd), Vienna PO, Vienna Phil Chorus Music & Arts ▲ CD 881 [ADD]
Mussorgsky, M.:Boris Godunov, w. N. Gedda (ten), G. Raimondi (ten), M. Rostropovich (cnd), National SO Washington D.C., Washington Oratorio Society, Choral Arts Society [R] Erato 3-▲ 2292-45418-2 ZB [DDD]
Mussorgsky, M.:Sunless, w. M. Rostropovich (pno/vc), O. Kagan (vn), L. Mogilevskaya (pno) *(rec Jan. 17, 1973)* Russian Disc ▲ RUS 11003 [AAD]
Prokofiev, S.:War & Peace, w. Galina Vishnevskaya (sop—Natasha Rostovoa), Irina Arkhipova (mez—Hélène Bezukhova), Evgenya Verbitskaya (mez—Marya Akhrosimova), Alexi Maslennikov (ten—Anatole Kuragin), Vladimir Petrov (ten—Pierre Bezukhov), Pavel Lisitsian (bar—Napoleon), Alexi Krivchenya (bass—Field-Marshall Kutuzov), Evgeny Kibkalo (sgr—Prince Andrei Bolkonsky), A. Melik-Pashayev (cnd), Bolshoi Theater Orch, Bolshoi Theater Chorus *(rec Moscow, 1961)* Melodiya ("The Russian Opera" series) 3-▲ 74321-29350-2 [ADD]
Shostakovich, D.:Lady Macbeth of Mtsensk, w. B. Finnilä (mez), N. Gedda (ten), A. Haugland (bass), M. Rostropovich (cnd), London PO, Ambrosian Opera Chorus [R] EMI Classics 2-▲ CDCB 49955 [ADD]
Shostakovich, D.:Songs Sop, Op. 127, w. M. Rostropovich (pno/vc), O. Kagan (vn), L. Mogilevskaya (pno) *(rec Jan. 17, 1973)* Russian Disc ▲ RUS 11003 [AAD]
Shostakovich, D.:Sym 14, w. M. Reshetin (bass), R. Barshaï (cnd), Moscow CO *(rec Sept. 29, 1969)* Russian Disc ▲ RUS 11192 [ADD]
Stravinsky, I.:Songs, w. M. Rostropovich (pno/vc), O. Kagan (vn), L. Mogilevskaya (pno)—2 songs *(rec Jan. 17, 1973)* Russian Disc ▲ RUS 11003 [AAD]
Tchaikovsky, P.:Eugene Onegin, w. L. Avdeyeva (mez), S. Lemeshev (ten), Belov (sgr), Petrov (sgr), B. Khaikin (cnd), Bolshoi Theater Orch, Bolshoi Theater Chorus [R] *(rec ca. early '60s for Melodi)* Legato Classics 2-▲ LCD 163-2 (m) [ADD]
Tchaikovsky, P.:Iolanta, w. N. Gedda (ten), W. Groenroos (bar), M. Rostropovich (cnd), Orch de Paris Erato 2-▲ 45793-2
The Voices of Living Stereo, Vol. 2, w. Eileen Farrell (sop), Birgit Nilsson (sop), Roberta Peters (sop), Leontyne Price (sop), Rosalind Elias (mez), Shirley Verrett (mez), Marian Anderson (cta), Maureen Forrester (cta), Sergio Franchi (ten), Mario Lanza (ten), Richard Lewis (ten), Jan Pee, Alexander Dedyukhin (pno), Franz Rupp (pno), Leo Taubman (pno), George Trovillo (pno), Charles Wadsworth (pno), Boston Pops Orch [cnd:Arthur Fiedler], Boston SO [cnd:Charles Munch], Chicago SO [cnd:Fritz Reiner], RCA Victor Orch, RCA Victor Chorus [cnd:Wa *(rec Boston & Chicago & New York & Rome, 1957-1964)* RCA Living Stereo ▲ 09026-68167-2 [ADD]

Visse, Dominique (alt)
Handel, G.F.:Giulio Cesare in Egitto, w. Lynne Dawson (sop), Eirian James (mez), Guillemette Laurens (mez), James Bowman (alt), Nicolas Rivenq (bar); J. Malgoire (cnd), La Grande Écurie et la Chambre du Roy Astrée 3-▲ E 8558

Visse, Dominique (ct)
Campra, A.:Messe de Requiem, w. G. Ragon (ten), P. Harvey (bar), J. Malgoire (cnd), La Grande Écurie et la Chambre du Roy, Les Pages de la Chapelle *(rec Nov. 4-6, 1992)* FNAC Music ▲ 592223 [DDD]
Campra, A.:Misere, w. G. Ragon (ten), P. Harvey (bar), J. Malgoire (cnd), La Grande Écurie et la Chambre du Roy, Les Pages de la Chapelle *(rec Nov. 4-6, 1992)* FNAC Music ▲ 592223 [DDD]
Charpentier, M.-A.:Les Arts florissants, w. C. Dussaut (sop), J. Feldman (sop), A. Mellon (sop), G. Laurens (mez), P. Cantor (ten), G. Reinhart (bar), W. Christie (cnd), Les Arts Florissants [F] Musique d'Abord ▲ HMA 1901083
Charpentier, M.-A.:Le Malade imaginaire, w. C. Brua (sop), N. Rime (sop), M. Zanetti (sop), H. Crook (ten), J.-F. Gardeil (bar), W. Christie (cnd), Les Arts Florissants [F] Harmonia Mundi France ▲ HMC 901336
Charpentier, M.-A.:Motets for Double Choir, w. B. Schlick (sop), N. Zijlstra (sop), K. Wessel (alt), H. van Berne (ten), C. Prégardien (ten), P. Kooy (bass), K. Martens (bass), T. Koopman (cnd), Amsterdam Baroque Orch—Canticum pro pace; Josué; Mors Saulis et Jonathae; Praelium Michaelis; Quam dilecta; 3 Leçons de Ténèbres Erato (Musifrance) ▲ 2292-45822-2 ZA
Handel, G.F.:Giulio Cesare in Egitto, w. Barbara Schlick (sop), Jennifer Larmore (mez), Marianne Rørholm (mez), Bernarda Fink (cta), Derek Lee Ragin (ct), Oliver Lallouette (bass), Furio Zanasi (bass), R. Jacobs (cnd), Concerto Cologne [period instrs] Harmonia Mundi France 3-▲ HMC 901385/87
Handel, G.F.:Ottone, Rè di Germania, w. Jennifer Smith (sop—Gismonda), Catherine Denley (mez—Matilda), James Bowman (ct—Ottone), Dominique Visse (ct—Adelberto), Michael George (bass—Emireno), R. King (cnd), King's Consort Hyperion 3-▲ CDA 66751/53
Hasse, J.A.:Cleofide, w. Emma Kirkby (sop), Agnès Mellon (sop), Randall Wong (ct), Derek Lee Ragin (ct), David Cordier (alt), W. Christie (cnd), Cappella Coloniensis [I] Capriccio 4-▲ 10193/96 [DDD]
Monteverdi, C.:Ritorno d'Ulisse, w. L. Hunt (sop), C. Högman (sop), B. Fink (cta), C. Prégardien (ten), G. Tucker (ten), D. Thomas (bass), R. Jacobs (cnd), Concerto Vocale [I] Harmonia Mundi France 3-▲ HMC 901427/29
Mozart, W.A.:Requiem, w. Colette Alliot-Lugaz (sop), Martyn Hill (ten), G. Reinhart (bar), J. Malgoire (cnd), La Grande Écurie et la Chambre du Roy, Nord-Pas-de-Calais Choir [L] CBS ▲ MDK 44904 [DDD]
Vivaldi, A.:Montezuma (sels), w. J.-C. Malgoire (cnd), La Grande Écurie et la Chambre du Roy—Gl'oltraggidella sorte Astrée ▲ E 8552 [DDD]

Visser, Lieuwe (bass)
Bach, J.S.:Cant 70, w. W. Wiedl (trb), P. Esswood (ct), K. Equiluz (ten), N. Harnoncourt (cnd), Vienna Concentus Musicus, Tölz Boys' Choir [G] Teldec 2-▲ 2292-42572-2 [ADD]
Berlioz, H.:Choral Music, w. G. Garino (tenor), R. van der Meer (bass), J. Fournet (cnd), Dutch RSO, Dutch Radio Chorus—Le cinq mai, Op. 6; L'impériale, Op. 26; La mort d'Orphée; La révolution grecque, scène héroïque Denon ▲ CO 72886 [DDD]
Janssen, G.:Noach, w. Claron McFadden (sop—Noach's Wife), Lieuwe Visser (bass—Noach), Huib Rooymans (nar), L. Vis (cnd), New Artis Orch, Mondriaan Quartet, Ay-Kherel Ensemble *(rec Amsterdam, June 20-21, 1994)* Donemus 2-▲ CV 42/43
Loevendie, T.:Gassir, the Hero, w. Claron McFadden (sop—Partridge/Priestess), Timothy Wilson (alt—Shamsi), Christopher Gillett (ten—Safi), Robert Poulton (bar—Gassir), Lieuwe Visser (bass—Yemni), Roger Smeets (sgr—Rafi), D. Porcelijn (cnd), Asko Ensemble *(rec live, Amsterdam Studios, June 14-15, 1993)* Donemus ▲ CV 35

Vitale, Maria (sop)
Mercadante, S.:Il giuramento (sels), w. M. Pirazzini (mez), R. Panerai (bar), A. Berdini (bar), A. Simonetto (cnd), Milan RAI Orch, Milan RAI Chorus [I]—14 scenes & arias *(rec live, Milan, 4/5/51)* Myto 2-▲ 2 MCD 90632 [ADD]
Rossini, G.:Elisabetta, regina d'Inghilterra (sels), w. L. Pagliughi (sop), G. Campora (ten), Pinno (sgr), A. Simonetto (cnd), Milan RAI SO, Milan RAI Chorus—six arias [I] *(rec live, 4/27/53)* Myto 2-▲ 2 MCD 90530 [ADD]
Verdi, G.:I lombardi alla prima crociata, w. Renata Broilo (sop), Miriam Pirazzini (mez), Aldo Bertocci (ten), Mario Frosini (sgr), Mario Petri (bass), Bruno Franchi (sgr), Gustavo Gallo (sgr), Renato Pasquali (sgr), M. Wolf-Ferrari (cnd), Milan RAI Lyric Orch, Milan RAI Chorus *(rec 1954)* Cetra Classic 2-▲ CDON 41 [ADD]
Verdi, G.:Oberto, Conte di San Bonifacio, w. Elena Nicolai (mez), Giuseppe Modesti (bass), Gino Bonelli (sgr), Lydia Roan (sgr), A. Simonetto (cnd), Turin RAI Orch, Turin RAI Chorus Great Opera Performances 2-▲ GOP 774

Vitali, Marisa (sop)
Beethoven, L. van:Arias & Duets, w. Ernesto Palacio (ten), M. de Bernart (cnd), I Pomeriggi Musicali Orch—Soll ein Schuh nicht drücken; O welch' ein Leben! ein ganzes Meer! [both from Die schöne Schusterin]; Primo amore piacer del ciel; Ne' giorni tuoi felici [from Olimpiade] *(rec Milano, Apr 1994)* Arcadia ▲ 153 [DDD]
Beethoven, L. van:Egmont (incidental music), w. M. de Bernart (cnd), I Pomeriggi Musicali Orch *(rec Milano, Apr 1994)* Arcadia ▲ 153 [DDD]

1464 ▲ = CD ♦ = Enhanced CD Δ = MD ■ = Cassette Tape ▯ = DCC

Vitas, M. (sop)
Tchaikovsky, P.:Songs, w. K. Bogino (pno)—Do Not Believe My Friend; Not a Word, My Friend [both from 6 Songs, Op. 6]; Lullaby [from 6 Songs, Op. 16]; Say, What Does the Nightingale Sing [from 6 Songs, Op. 57]; 'Mid a Turbulent Ball [from 6 Songs, Op. 38]; Had I Known; In the Field [both from 7 Songs, Op. 47]; Lullaby in the Storm [from 16 Children's Songs, Op. 54]; O Senseless Night; I Shall Not Tell You Anything; O Nightingale [all from 12 Songs, Op. 60]; Zemphir's Song [I] Musicaimmagine ▲ MR 10011 [DDD]

Vitulli, Thea (sop)
Puccini, G.:La Bohème, w. R. Torri (sop), A. Giorgini (ten), E. Badini (bar), L. Manfrini (bass), C. Sabajno (cnd), La Scala Orch [I] *(rec 1927)* InSync 2-■ C 4131/2 (m)
Puccini, G.:La Bohème, w. Rosina Torri (sop—Mimi), Thea Vitulli (sop—Musetta), Aristodemo Giorgini (ten—Rodolfo), Giuseppe Nessi (ten—Parpignol), Ernesto Badini (bar—Marcello), Aristide Baracchi (bar—Schaunard), Luigi Manfrini (bass—Colline), Salvatore Baccaloni (bass—Benoit/Alcindoro), C. Sabajno (cnd), La Scala Orch, La Scala Chorus *(rec 1928)* VAI Audio 2-▲ VAIA 1078-2

Vivian (sop)
Mascagni, P.:Sì, w. A. Felle (sop), Maria Gentile (sop), M.G. Liguori (sop), Nicoletti (sgr), Comas (sgr), S. Sanna (cnd), Montepulciano Arts Center Orch, Montepulciano Arts Center Chorus [I] *(rec live, 7/24/87)* Bongiovanni 2-▲ GB 2050/51 [DDD]

Vivo, Graziano del (bass)
Bellini, V.:I Puritani, w. C. Deutekom (sop), F. Raffanelli (sop), N. Gedda (ten), S. Bruscantini (b-bar), A. Ferrin (bass), R. Muti (cnd), *(orch unknown) (rec 1970)* Great Opera Performances ▲ GOP 735
Catalani, A.:Edmea, w. M. Sokolinska Noto (sop), M. Frusoni (ten), M. Chingari (bar), P. Lefebvre (bass), A. Nosotti (bass), G. Pasella (bass), M. de Bernart (cnd), Lucca Teatro Comunale Giglio Orch, Lucca Teatro Comunale del Giglio Chorus [I] *(rec live 9/89)* Bongiovanni 2-▲ GB 2093/94 [DDD]

Vlachopoulos, Zoë (sop)
Gluck, C.W.:Orfeo ed Euridice (sels), w. A. Ayars (sop), K. Ferrier (cta), F. Stiedry (cnd), Southern PO, Glyndebourne Festival Chorus *(rec 1947)* Enterprise ("Palladio" series) ▲ ENTPD 4171 [ADD]

Vlasák, Jan (nar)
Báchorek, M.:Lidice, w. Jana Stupárkova–Majtnerová (sop), Karel Průša (bar), Osvald Albín (speaker), O. Trhlík (cnd), Ostrava Janáček PO, Ostrava Janáček Mixed Chorus *(rec Smetana Hall of Prague's Municipal House, Feb 10 & 11, 1988)* Panton ▲ 811338-2 [AAD]

Vlasov, Vitali (ten)
Shchedrin, R.:Dead Souls, w. Larisa Avdeyeva (mez—Korobochka), Galina Borisova (mez—Plyushkin), Alexi Maslennikov (ten—Selifan), Vladislav Piavko (ten—Nozdryov), Vitali Vlasov (ten—Manilov), Boris Morozov (bass—Sobakevich), Alexander Voroshilo (sgr—Chichikov), Y. Temirkanov (cnd), Bolshoi Theater Orch, Bolshoi Theater Chorus, Moscow Chamber Choir *(rec Moscow, 1982)* Melodiya ("The Russian Opera" series) 2-▲ 74321-29347-2 [ADD]

Vlassak, Jan (nar)
Báchorek, M.:Music of, w. Osvald Albín (nar), Otakar Brousek (nar), Brigita Šulcová (sop), Drahomira Drobková (cta), Karel Průša (bass), Pavel Kamas (sgr), Jan Kyzlink (sgr), Jana Stuperkova–Majtnerova (sgr), Bretislav Vojkuvka (sgr), O. Trhlík (cnd), Ostrava Janáček PO, Prague SO, Ostrava Janáček Chorus, Ostrava Women's Chamber Chorus, Permoník Children's Chorus—Lidice; Stereofonietta; Hukvald Poem Panton ▲ PAN 811338 [AAD/DDD]

Vlazinskaya (nar)
Schmidt, W.:The Sparrow and The Amazing Mr. Avaunt, w. P. Christ (ob) [E] Crystal ▲ CD 321

Vodička, Leo Marian (ten)
Foerster, J.B.:Eva, w. Eva Depoltová (sop), Anna Barová (mez), Jaroslav Soucek (bar), F. Vajnar (cnd), Prague RSO, Prague Radio Chorus *(rec 1982)* Supraphon 2-▲ SUP 3001
Janácek, L.:Amarus, w. Kvetoslava Nemeckova (sop), Vaclav Zitek (bar), Jan Hora (org), C. Mackerras (cnd), Czech PO, Lubomír Mátl (cnd), Czech Phil Chorus *(rec 1984)* Supraphon ▲ SUP CD 3045
Janácek, L.:Moravian Folk Poetry, w. Zdena Kloubová (sop), Radoslav Kvapil (pno) Unicorn–Kanchana ▲ DKP CD 9154
Smetana, B.:Dalibor, w. Eva Urbanová (sgr), Iván Kusnjer (bar), Z. Košler (cnd), Prague National Theater Orch, Prague National Theater Chorus Supraphon 2-▲ SUP 0077 [DDD]
Smetana, B.:The Kiss, w. Eva Deplotová (sop), Libuše Márová (mez), F. Vajnar (cnd), Brno Janáček Opera Orch, Brno Janáček Opera Chorus Supraphon 2-▲ SUP 112180 [AAD]
Smetana, B.:Libuše, w. Eva Urbanová (sop), O. Dohnányi (cnd), Prague National Theater Orch, Prague National Theater Chorus Supraphon 2-▲ SUP 3200
Smetana, B.:The Secret, w. Daniela Šounová-Brouková (sop), Vera Soukupová (mez), Z. Košler (cnd), Prague National Theater Orch Supraphon 2-▲ SUP 112177 [ADD]
Smetana, B.:Viola, w. Daniela Šounová-Brouková (sop), Vera Soukupová (mez), Z. Košler (cnd), Prague National Theater Orch Supraphon ▲ SUP 112177 [ADD]

Vogel, Adelheid (sop)
Draeseke, F.:Mysterium:Christus, w. C. Bischoff (sop), E. Dersen (alt), K. Markus (ten), H.J. Ritzerfeld (ten), P. Langshaw (bar), B. Kämpff (bass), J. Sonnenschmidt (org), U.-R. Follert (cnd), Breslau State PO, Evangelical Boys' Choir Palatine, Heilbronn Vocal Ensemble, Palatine Kurrende Bayer 5-▲ 100175/79

Vogel, Adolf (bass)
Wagner, R.:Parsifal, w. Anny Konetzni (sop—Kundry), Günther Treptow (ten—Parsifal), Paul Schöffler (bar—Amfortas), Hans Braun (bass—Titurel), Adolf Vogel (bass—Klingsor), Ludwig Weber (bass—Gurnemanz), R. Moralt (cnd), Vienna SO, Vienna State Opera Chorus *(rec Vienna)* Myto 4-▲ 4 MCD 954.136

Vogel, Siegfried (bass)
Handel, G.F.:Imeneo, w. Sylvia Geszty (sop), Renate Krahmer (sop), Hans-Joachim Rotzsch (ten), Günther Leib (bass), H.-T. Margraf (cnd), Halle Handel Festival Orch, Leipzig Radio Chorus *(rec 1966)* Berlin Classics ▲ BER 9110
Handel, G.F.:Judas Maccabaeus, w. Gundula Janowitz (sop), Hertha Töpper (alt), Peter Schreier (ten), Ernest Haefliger (ten), Theo Adam (bass), H. Koch (cnd), Berlin RSO, Berlin Radio Chorus Berlin Classics 2-▲ BER 9112
Nicolai, O.:Lustigen Weiber, w. H. Donath (sop), E. Mathis (sop), H. Schwarz (mez), K. Ludwig (ten), K.-E. Mercker (ten), P. Schreier (ten), C. Dormoy (bar), B. Weikl (bar), K. Moll (bass), B. Klee (cnd), Berlin Staatskapelle, Berlin State Opera Chorus *(rec July 3, 1976)* Berlin Classics ("Eterna" series) ▲ BER 2046-2 [ADD]
Verdi, G.:La forza del destino, w. G. Bumbry (sop—Leonora), H. Dernesch (sop—Preziosilla), N. Gedda (ten—Alvaro), H. Prey (bar—Don Carlos), G. Frick (bass—Pater Guardian), S. Vogel (bass—Marchese), G. Patanè (cnd), Dresden State Orch, Dresden State Opera Chorus *(rec Aug. 1965)* Berlin Classics ("Eterna" series) ▲ BER 2025-2 [ADD]
Wagner, R.:Lohengrin, w. E. Connell (sop), N. Armstrong (sop), P. Hofmann (ten), L. Roar (bass), B. Weikl (bass), W. Nelsson (cnd), Bayreuth Festival Orch, Bayreuth Festival Chorus CBS 3-▲ M3K 38594

Vogel, Volker (ten)
Zemlinsky, A. von:Kleider machen Leute, w. E. Mathis (sop), H. Winkler (ten), C. Otelli (bar), H. Franzen (bass), R. Scholze (bass), W. Slabbert (sgr), R. Weikert (cnd), Zurich Opera Orch, Zurich Opera House Chorus [G] *(rec live, Zurich Opera House, 6/29/90)* Koch Schwann 2-▲ CD 314 069 [DDD]

Vogt, Joachim (ten)
Henze, H.-W.:Voices, w. Roswitha Trexler (mez), H. Neumann (cnd), Leipzig RSO members Berlin Classics 2-▲ BER 2180 [DDD]

Voigt, Deborah (sop)
Beethoven, L. van:Fidelio, w. Elizabeth Norberg-Schulz (sop—Marzelline), Deborah Voigt (sop—Lenore), Ben Heppner (ten—Florestan), Michael Schade (ten—Jaquino), Günter von Kannaten (b-bar—Don Pizarro), Matthias Hölle (bass—Rocco), Thomas Quasthoff (bass—Don Fernando), C. Davis (cnd), Bavarian RSO, Bavarian Radio Chorus, Bavarian State Opera Men's Chorus *(rec Herkulessaal der Residenz, Munich, May 15-25, 1995)* RCA Victor 2-▲ 09026-68344-2 [DDD]
Berlioz, H.:Les Troyens, w. F. Pollet (sop—Dido), D. Voigt (sop—Cassandre), C. Dubosc (sop—Ascagne), H. Perraguin (cta—Anna), G. Lakes (ten—Aeneas), J.-L. Maurette (ten—Iopas), J. M. Ainsley (ten—Hylas), M. P. (ten—Panthee), G. Cross (ten—Sinon), G. Quilico (bar—Chorebe), J.-P. Courtis (b-bar—Narbal), M. Belleau (bass—Ghost of Hector), R. Schirrer (bass—Priam), C. Dutoit (cnd), Montreal SO, Montreal Sym Chorus London 4-▲ 443693-2 [DDD]

Voigt, Deborah (sop) (cont.)
James Levine's 25th Anniversary Metropolitan Opera Gala, w. J. Levine (cnd), Metropolitan Opera Orch, Ileana Cotrubas (sop), Renée Fleming (sop), Hei-Kyung Hong (sop), Karita Mattila (sop), Birgit Nilsson (sop), Ruth Ann Swenson (sop), Kiri Te Kanawa (sop), Grace Bumbry (mez), Heidi Grant Murphy (mez), Anne Sofie von Otter (mez) *(rec live, Metropolitan Opera House, New York, Apr 27, 1996)* Deutsche Grammophon ▲ 449177-2 [DDD]
Rossini, G.:Music of, w. M. Fortuna (sop), M. Lerner (sop), M. Horne (mez), K. Kuhlmann (mez), F. von Stade (mez), R. Blake (ten), C. Estep (ten), C. Merritt (ten), T. Hampson (b-bar), H. Runey (b-bar), J. Opalach (bass), S. Ramey (bass), R. Norrington (cnd), Orch of St. Luke's, New York Concert Chorale EMI Classics ▲ CDC 54643
Weber, C.M. von:Oberon, w. D. Ziegler (mez), G. Lakes (ten), B. Heppner (ten), J. Conlon (cnd), Cologne PO, Cologne Opera Chorus EMI Classics 2-▲ CDCB 54739

Voinarovski, Viatcheslav (ten)
Rimsky-Korsakov, N.:Christmas Eve, w. Ekaterina Koudriavtchenko (sop), Elena Zaremba (mez), Vladimir Bogtatchov (ten), Alexei Maslennikov (ten), Viatcheslav Verestnikov (bar), Maxime Mikhailov (bass), Stanislav Souleimanov (bass), M. Yurovski (cnd), Moscow Forum Theater Orch, Yurloff Academic Choir Russian Season 4-▲ CMX 388054

Voinea, Silvia (sop)
Donizetti, G.:Lucia di Lammermoor, w. Silvia Voinea (sop—Lucia), Lucia Cicoara (mez—Alisa), Florin Georgescu (ten—Edgardo), Gabriel Nastase (ten—Arturo), Nicolae Herlea (bar—Lord Enrico), Pompei Harasteanu (bass—Raimondo), C. Petrovici (cnd), Romanian Opera Orch, Romanian Opera Chorus *(rec 1984)* Vox Box 2-▲ CDX 5164

Voineag, Ionel (ten)
Bretan, N.:The Evening Star, w. Adriana Croitoru (sop—King's Daughter), Elena Casian (mez—Lady-in-Waiting), Marius Budoiu (ten—Mariner), Ioan Pojar (ten—Page), Ionel Voineag (ten—Evening Star), Bálint Szabó (bass—Michael the Archangel), B. Hary (cnd), Transylvania PO Cluj *(rec Cluj, Sept 1994)* Nimbus ▲ NI 5463 [DDD]

Vojkůvka, Bretislav (ten)
Báchorek, M.:Hukvald Poem, w. Drahomíra Drobková (sop), Pavel Kamas (bar), Otakar Brousek (reciter), O. Trhlík (cnd), Prague SO, Ostrava Female Chamber Chorus, Permoník Children's Chorus *(rec Smetana Hall of Prague's Municipal House, Feb 10 & 11, 1988)* Panton ▲ 811338-2 [DDD]
Báchorek, M.:Music of, w. Osvald Albín (nar), Otakar Brousek (nar), Jan Vlassak (nar), Brigita Šulcová (sop), Drahomira Drobková (cta), Karel Průša (bass), Pavel Kamas (sgr), Jan Kyzlink (sgr), Jana Stuperkova–Majtnerova (sgr), O. Trhlík (cnd), Ostrava Janáček PO, Prague SO, Ostrava Janáček Chorus, Ostrava Women's Chamber Chorus, Permoník Children's Chorus—Lidice; Stereofonietta; Hukvald Poem Panton ▲ PAN 811338 [AAD/DDD]

Voketaitis, Arnold (b-bar)
Donizetti, G.:Lucrezia Borgia, w. Montserrat Caballé (sop), Jane Berbié (mez), Alain Vanzo (ten), Kostas Paskalis (bar), L. D. Clements (sgr), Adib Fazah (sgr), Mauro Lampi (sgr), Vern Shinall (sgr), Jerold Siena (sgr), William Wiederanders (sgr), J. Perlea (cnd), New York City Opera Orch, New York City Chorus Great Opera Performances 2-▲ GOP 769
Rachmaninoff, S.:The Bells, w. Christos (sop), Walter Planté (ten), L. Slatkin (cnd), St. Louis SO, St. Louis Sym Chorus *(rec 1980)* Vox Box 3-▲ CD3X 3002 [ADD]
Rachmaninoff, S.:Spring, w. L. Slatkin (cnd), St. Louis SO, St. Louis Sym Chorus *(rec 1980)* Vox Box 3-▲ CD3X 3002 [ADD]

Volante, Gian Franco (trb)
Puccini, G.:Tosca, w. Ranata Tebaldi (sop), Piero de Palma (ten), Giuseppe Campora (ten), Enzo Mascherini (bar), Fernando Corena (bass), Dario Caselli (bass), Antonio Sacchetti (bass), A. Erede (cnd), St. Cecilia Academy Orch Rome, St. Cecilia Academy Chorus Rome *(rec 1952)* Andromeda 2-▲ ANR 2539 [ADD]

Voldby, Leni (mez)
This Is Denmark, w. I. Kessler (pno) (rec. Dec. 1990) Danacord ▲ DACOCD 377 [DDD]

Völker, Franz (ten)
Franz Völker Sings Lieder *(rec 1927-41)* Preiser ▲ PRE 89997 [ADD]
Franz Völker, Vol. 2 *(rec between 1933-41)* Preiser ▲ PRE 89070 [ADD]
In the Kingdom of Operettas *(rec 1927-38)* Preiser 2-▲ PRE 89221
The Legendary Singers at Lindenoper Berlin (1927-1945), w. Gitta Alpar (sop), Erna Berger (sop), Tiana Lemnitz (sop), Maria Müller (sop), Margarete Klose (cta), Peter Anders (ten), Max Lorenz (ten), Walter Ludwig (ten), Lauritz Melchior (ten), Rudolf Schock (ten), Willi Domgraf-Fassb *(rec 1927; 1937; 1941-45)* Minerva ▲ MN A21 [ADD]
Opera Arias, w. Berlin State Opera Orch [var. cnds] Preiser ("Lebendige Vergangenheit" series) ▲ PRE 89005 (m) [AAD]
Strauss, R.:Die ägyptische Helena (sels), w. V. Ursuleac (sop—Helena), F. Völker (ten—Menelas), H. Roswaenge (ten—Da-Ud), E. Kunz (bar—Arbace), C. Krauss (cnd), Vienna State Opera Orch, Vienna State Opera Chorus *(rec Sept. 20, 1933)* Koch Schwann 2-▲ SCH 314552 [ADD]
Strauss, R.:Die Frau ohne Schatten (sels), w. Viorica Ursuleac (sop—Die Kaiserin), Gertrude Rünger (cta/sop—Elisabetta), Franz Völker (ten—Der Kaiser), C. Krauss (cnd), Vienna State Opera Orch *(rec Vienna, June 1, 1933)* Koch Schwann 2-▲ SCH 314662 [ADD]
Verdi, G.:Don Carlos (sels), w. H. Konetzni (sop—Elisabetta), F. Völker (ten—Don Carlos), A. Kipnis (bass—Filippo), B. Walter (cnd), Vienna State Opera Orch, Vienna State Opera Chorus *(rec Dec. 16, 1936)* Koch Schwann 2-▲ SCH 314602
Verdi, G.:Don Carlos (sels), w. Viorica Ursuleac (sop—Elisabetta), Franz Völker (ten—Don Carlo), Josef von Manowarda (bass—Filippo), C. Krauss (cnd), Vienna State Opera Orch *(rec Vienna, Feb. 25, 1933)* Koch Schwann 2-▲ SCH 314662 [ADD]
Verdi, G.:Otello (sels), w. Viorica Ursuleac (sop—Desemona), Franz Völker (ten—Otello), Josef von Manowarda (bass—Iago), C. Krauss (cnd), Vienna State Opera Orch *(rec Vienna, Dec. 15, 1933)* Koch Schwann 2-▲ SCH 314662 [ADD]
Verdi, G.:Il trovatore (sels), w. J. Biel (ten), F. Tamagno (ten), L.-A. Escalaïs (ten), M. Gilion (ten), E. Caruso (ten), A. Paoli (ten), G. Zenatello (ten), J. Sembach (ten), L. Slezak (ten), F. Constantino (ten), G. Martinelli (ten), B. De Muro (ten), N. Fusati (ten), N. Piccaluga (ten), G. Lauri-Volpi (ten), A. Pertile (ten), E. Bergamaschi (ten), R. Tauber (ten), J. O'Sullivan (ten), H. Roswaenge (ten), G. Taccani (ten), V. Lois (ten), H. Lazaro (ten), A. Lindi (ten), A. Cortis (ten), F. Merli (ten), J. Kiepura (ten), J. Schmidt (ten), J. Bjoerling (ten), B. Gigli (ten), A. Salvarezza (ten), J. Soler (ten), M. Filippeschi (ten)—34 performances of the Act III tenor aria "Di quella pira!," *(rec from 1903-1956)* Bongiovanni ▲ GB 1051 [ADD]
Wagner, R.:Der fliegende Holländer, w. Maria Müller (sop), Joel Berglund (ten), Ludwig Hoffmann (bass), R. Kraus (cnd), Bayreuth Festival Orch, Bayreuth Festival Chorus *(rec live, Bayreuth, July 18, 1942)* Preiser 2-▲ PRE 90232 [ADD]
Wagner, R.:Lohengrin, w. M. Müller (sop), J. Prohaska (bar), A. Rother (cnd), Berlin Staatskapelle [G] *(rec 1942)* Preiser 3-▲ 90043 (m) [ADD]
Wagner, R.:Lohengrin (sels), w. Maria Müller (sop), Margarete Klose (mez), Joseph von Manowarda (bass), W. Furtwängler (cnd), Bayreuth Festival Orch, Bayreuth Festival Chorus—Prelude to Act III; Operatic sels. *(rec 1931)* Grammofono 2000 ▲ GRM 78515 [ADD]
Wagner, R.:Lohengrin (sels), w. Franz Völker (ten—Lohengrin), Josef von Manowarda (bass—King Henry), Zdenka Zika (sgr—Titurel), F. Rühlmann (cnd), Vienna State Opera Orch *(rec Vienna, June 3, 1933)* Koch Schwann 2-▲ SCH 314662 [ADD]
Wagner, R.:Lohengrin (sels), w. Maria Müller (sop—Elsa), Margarete Klose (mez—Ortrud), Franz Völker (ten—Lohengrin), Jaro Prohaska (bar—Telramund), Josef von Manowarda (bass—King Heinrich), H. Tietjen (cnd), Vienna State Opera Orch *(rec Vienna, 1938)* Koch Schwann 2-▲ SCH 314682 [ADD]
Wagner, R.:Die Meistersinger von Nürnberg (sels), w. V. Ursuleac (sop—Eva), F. Völker (ten—Walther), A. Jerger (b-bar—Hans Sachs), C. Krauss (cnd), Vienna State Opera Orch, Vienna State Opera Chorus *(rec Apr. 13, 1934)* Koch Schwann 2-▲ SCH 314602
Wagner, R.:Rienzi, der Letzte der Tribunen (sels), w. Rosette Andsy (cta—Adriano), Hermann Gallos (ten—Baroncelli), Karl Ettl (bass—Cecco), J. Krips (cnd), Vienna State Opera Orch *(rec Vienna, May 15, 1933)* Koch Schwann 2-▲ SCH 314662 [ADD]
Wagner, R.:Die Walküre (sels), w. Viorica Ursuleac (sop—Sieglinde), Hilde Konetzni (sop—Sieglinde), Gertrude Rünger (sop—Brünnhilde), Franz Völker (ten—Siegmund), Richard Mayr (bass—Hunding), Krauss, Knappertsbusch (cnd), Vienna State Opera Orch Koch Schwann 2-▲ SCH 314662 [ADD]

Völker, Franz (ten) (cont.)
Wagner, R.:Die Walküre (sels), w. Lotte Lehmann (sop—Sieglinde), Maria Jeritza (sop—Brünnhilde), Franz Völker (ten—Siegmund), Friedrich Schorr (bass—Wotan), C. Krauss (cnd), Vienna State Opera Orch *(rec Vienna, Sept. 14, 1933)* Koch Schwann ▲ SCH 314622 [ADD]
Wagner, R.:Die Walküre (sels), w. H. Konetzni (sop—Sieglinde), R. Merker (sop—Brünhilde), F. Völker (ten—Sigmund), L. Hofmann (bass—Wotan), B. Walter (cnd), Vienna State Opera Orch, Vienna State Opera Chorus *(rec Oct. 19, 1936)* Koch Schwann 2-▲ SCH 314592
Wagner, R.:Die Walküre (sels), w. Maria Jeritza (sop—Brünnhilde), Felice Hüni-Mišek (sop—Sieglinde), Franz Völker (ten—Siegmund), Friedrich Schorr (b-bar—Wotan), C. Krauss (cnd), Vienna State Opera Orch *(rec June 11, 1933)* Koch Schwann 2-▲ SCH 314642 [ADD]
Wagner, R.:Die Walküre (sels), w. Anny Konetzni (sop—Brunnhilde), Maria Müller (sop—Sieglinde), Franz Völker (ten—Siegmund), Walter Grossmann (bass—Wotan), W. Furtwängler (cnd), Vienna State Opera Orch *(rec Vienna, Feb. 13-17, 1936)* Koch Schwann 2-▲ SCH 314702 [ADD]

Volkert, Gudrun (sop)
Straus, O.:The Merry Nibelungs, w. Lisa Griffith (sop—Kriemhild), Gudrun Volkert (sop—Brunhilde), Daphne Evangelatos (cta—Ute), Gabriele Henkel (sgr—Giselher), Christine Mann (sgr—Vogel), Hein Heidbüchel (ten—Volker), Martin Gantner (sgr—Gunther), Gerd Grochowski (sgr—Dankwart), Michael Nowak (sgr—Siegfried), Josef Otten (sgr—Hagen), S. Köhler (cnd), Cologne RSO, Cologne Radio Chorus *(rec Cologne, Jan 31–Feb 17, 1995)* Capriccio ▲ 10752 [DDD]

Vollestad, Per (bar)
Grieg, E.:Songs, w. T. Mikkelsen (cnd), Lithuanian National SO—The Mountain Thrall, Op. 32; A Swan, Op. 25/2; 12 Songs to Poems by A.O. Vinje, Op. 35; I Walked One Balmy Summer Eve, Op. 26/2; Henrik Wergeland, Op. 58/3; From Monte Pincio, Op Simax ▲ PSC 1076
Grieg, E.:Songs, w. S. Hjelset (pno)—Op. 5, Nos. 1, 2, 3 & 4; Op. 15, No. 2; Op. 18, Nos. 1, 2, 3 & 7; Op. 21, Nos. 1 & 3; Op. 25, Nos. 1, 2, 3, 4, 5 & 6; Op. 26, Nos. 3, 4 & 5; Op. 39, No. 2; Op. 44, Nos. 3 & 5; Op. 48, Nos. 1, 2, 3, 5 & 6; Op. 49, Nos. 4 & 6; Op. 58, No. 2; Op. 59, Nos. 3 & 4; Op. 70, No. 3 [N, G] Simax ▲ PSC 1089 [DDD]
Jensen, L.I.:The Return, w. A. Bolstad (sop), R. Sterne (alt), H. Bjørkey (ten), I. Gilhuus (ten), C. Stabell (bass), O.K. Ruud (cnd), Trondheim SO, Trondheim Sym Chorus, Nidarso Cathedral Choir Simax 2-▲ PSC 3109
Mozart, W.A.:Così fan tutte, w. S. Isokoski (sop—Fiordiligi), N. Argenta (sop—Despina), M. Groop (mez—Dorabella), M. Schäfer (ten—Ferrando), P. Vollestad (bar—Guglielmo), H. Claessens (b-bar—Don Alfonso)., S. Kuijken (cnd), La Petite Bande, La Petite Bande Chorus Accent 3-▲ ACC 9296/98

Volpi, Guido (ten)
Guido Volpi Bongiovanni ▲ GB 1054-2 [ADD]

Vonk (ten)
Schubert, Franz:Mass 5, w. S. Chilcott (sop), R. Cyrille (alt), G. Schwarz (bass), R. Delcroix (cnd), Basque Bayonne-Côte Orch, Ametsa D'Irun Choir [L] Forlane ▲ FOR 16649 [DDD]

Vorapajev (ten)
Mozart, W.A.:Requiem, w. Jitka Pavlová (sop), Polovecova (mez), Gennadi Bezzubenkov (bass), M. Glinka (cnd), Ljubljana SO, Leningrad Chorus [L] Stradivari Classics ▲ SCD 6003 [DDD] ▮ SMC 6003 (D)

Voroshilo, Alexander (sgr)
Shchedrin, R.:Dead Souls, w. Larisa Avdeyeva (mez—Korobochka), Galina Borisova (mez—Plyushkin), Alexi Maslennikov (ten—Selifan), Vladislav Piavko (ten—Nozdryov), Vitali Vlasov (ten—Manilov), Boris Morozov (bass—Sobakevich), Alexander Voroshilo (sgr—Chichikov), Y. Temirkanov (cnd), Bolshoi Theater Orch, Bolshoi Theater Chorus, Moscow Chamber Choir *(rec Moscow, 1982)* Melodiya ("The Russian Opera" series) 2-▲ 74321-29347-2 [ADD]

Vorrasi, John (ten)
Songs, Dances & Fantasy, w. Jerry Fuller (db), Frederick Ockwell (pno), Kenneth Dorsch (hpd), William Ferris (pno), Steve Hartman (hp), Thomas Potter (bar), Anne Waller (gtr) Musical Arts Society ▲ CD 41589 [AAD] ▮ CS 41589
Sowerby, L.:Forsaken of Man, w. Alicia Clark (sop), Judith Compton (alt), Thomas Potter (bass), Paul Grizzell (bass), Matthew Greenberg (bass), Bruce Hall (sgr), Thomas Weisflog (org), William Ferris (cnd), William Ferris Chorale *(rec St. Thomas the Apostle Church, Chicago, June 1990)* New World ▲ 803942 [AAD]

Vortoluzzi, Bianca (cta)
Verdi, G.:Rigoletto (sels), w. Renata Scotto (sop—Gilda), Corinna Vozza (mez—Giovanna), Bianca Vortoluzzi (cta—Maddalena), Luciano Pavarotti (ten—Duke of Mantua), Kostas Paskalis (bar—Rigoletto), Paolo Washington (bass—Sparafucile), C. M. Guilini (cnd), Rome Opera Orch, Rome Opera Chorus Budget ("The Greatest Voice in Opera" series) ▲ SYP 104

Vossbrink, Heinz (sgr)
Waits, T.:The Black Rider:The Casting of Magic Bullets, w. Angelika Thomas (sgr—Anne), Annette Paulmann (sgr—Kätchen), Sona Cervena (sgr—Bird/Messenger/Spoonwoman), Monika Tahal (sgr—Witness/Bird/Shrink/Wilhelm's Double/Skeleton), Susi Eisenkolb (sgr—Bridesmaid/Pegleg's Double), Heinz Vossbrink (sgr—Kuno), Dominique Horwitz (sgr—Pegleg), Gerd Kunath (sgr—Bertram), Stefan Kurt (sgr—Wilhelm), Klaus Schreiber (sgr—Robert/Man on Stag/Georg Schmid), Jörg Holm (Old Uncle/Duke), Jan Moritz Steffen (sgr—Young Kuno/Bird/Shrink/Skeleton), Tom Waits (vocals/coliope/organ/chamberlain/mar/emax/guitar/train whistle), Ralph Carney (saxophone/bass clarinet/baritone horn), Bill Douglas (bass instrument), Kenny Wollesen (perc) Island ▲ 314518559-2

Votipka, Thelma (mez)
Bellini, V.:Norma, w. Gina Cigna (sop—Norma), Thelma Votipka (mez—Clotilde), Bruna Castagna (cta—Adalgisa), Giovanni Martinelli (ten—Pollione), Giodano Paltrinieri (ten—Flavio), Ezio Pinza (bass—Oroveso), E. Panizza (cnd), *(orch unknown)* *(rec live, New York, Feb. 20, 1937)* The Fourties 2-▲ ENT FT 1517
Donizetti, G.:Lucia di Lammermoor, w. Lily Pons (sop—Lucia), Thelma Votipka (mez—Alisa), Frederick Jagel (ten—Edgardo), John Brownlee (bar—Enrico), Ezio Pinza (bass—Raimondo), G. Papi (cnd), *(orch unknown)* The Fourties 2-▲ ENT FT 1511

Vozza, Corinna (mez)
Puccini, G.:La fanciulla del West (sels), w. Magda Olivero (sop—Minnie), Corinna Vozza (mez—Wowkle), Paolo Caroli (ten—Harry), Giacomo Lauri-Volpi (ten—Dick Johnson), Marco Rogani (ten—Pony Express Rider), Salvatore di Tommaso (ten—Trin), Adelio Zagonara (ten—Nick), Virgilio Ascorro (bar—Sid), Alfredo Colella (bar—Jake Wallace), Giuseppe Forgione (bar—Bello), Giancarlo Guelfi (bar—Jack Rance), Arturo la Porta (bar—Sonora), Gino Conti (bass—José Castro), Piere Passarotti (bass—Bill), Enzo Titta (bass—Larkens), Giulio Tomei (bass—Ashby), V. Bellezza (cnd), Rome Opera Orch, Rome Opera Chorus—Minnie, dalla mia casa son partito; Laggiù nel Soledad; Chi c'è per farmi i ricci; Oh! Mister Johnson, siete rimasto; Non so ben neppur io; Io non son che una povera fanciulla; No, Minnie, non piangete; Vorrei mettermi queste; Hallo!; Oh, se sapeste; Credo che abbiate torto; Ma ti giuro ch'io non ti lascio più; Vieni fuori!; Una parola sola!...Or son sei mesi; Che c'è di nuovo Jack?; È là; Siete pronto; Ch'ella mi creda; È Minnie!...È Minnie! *(rec Rome, Mar. 30, 1957)* Golden Age of Opera ▲ GAO 180 [ADD]
Rota, N.:Mysterium, w. A. Tuccari (sop), G. Sinimberghi (ten), U. Trama (bass), A. Renzi (cnd), Pro Civitate Christiana di Assisi Orch, Pro Civitate Christiana di Assisi Chorus *(rec live 1962)* Claves ▲ CD 9323 [DDD]
Verdi, G.:Rigoletto (sels), w. Renata Scotto (sop—Gilda), Corinna Vozza (mez—Giovanna), Bianca Vortoluzzi (cta—Maddalena), Luciano Pavarotti (ten—Duke of Mantua), Kostas Paskalis (bar—Rigoletto), Paolo Washington (bass—Sparafucile), C. M. Guilini (cnd), Rome Opera Orch, Rome Opera Chorus Budget ("The Greatest Voice in Opera" series) ▲ SYP 104

Vrachovski, Werther (ten)
Puccini, G.:Madama Butterfly, w. Raina Kabaivanska (sop—Madama Butterfly), Alexandrina Milcheva (mez—Suzuki), Rossitza Troeva-Mircheva (cta—Kate Pinkerton), Nazzareno Antinori (ten—F.B. Pinkerton), Roumen Doikov (ten—Goro), Werther Vrachovski (ten—Il Principe Yamadori), Nelson Portella (bar—Sharpless), Kosta Dinkov (bass—Lo zio Bonzo), G. Bellini (cnd), Sofia PO, Svetoslav Obrenetov Bulgarian National Chorus *(rec Sophia, Bulgaria, Dec 1-13, 1982)* Arts Music 2-▲ 447161-2 [DDD]

Vraspir, Lubomír (ten)
Carolling, w. Gabriela Beňačková (sop), Bambini di Praga [cnd:Jaroslav Krček], Tuma (org), Prague Brass Quintet Supraphon ▲ SUP 111417 [DDD]

Vraspir, Lubomír (ten) (cont.)
Krček, J.:Songs of Love, w. J. Fišer (vn), J. Krček (cnd), Musica Bohemica Panton ▲ 81 1030-2
Krček, J.:Sym 2, w. J. Krček (cnd), Musica Bohemica, *(chorus unknown)* Panton ▲ 81 1030-2
Krček, J.:Testamenti, w. J. Mihálíková (sop), J. Krček (cnd), Musica Bohemica, *(chorus unknown)* Panton ▲ 81 1030-2

Vredeveldt, John (ten)
Meijering, Chiel:St. Louis Blues, w. Andrea van Beek (sop), Francine van der Heijden (sop), Jeanette Huizinga (mez), Rein Kolpa (ten), Willem-Jan van Deuveren (ten), Gérard Bernts (bar), W. Megens (cnd), De Ereprijs Orch [I] *(rec Schouwburg Arnhem, Mar 10, 1995)* Donemus 2-▲ neos 01-02

Vrenios, Anastasios (ten)
Meyerbeer, G.:Les Huguenots, w. J. Sutherland (sop), M. Arroyo (sop), H. Tourangeau (mez), D. Cossa (bar), G. Bacquier (bar), N. Ghiuselev (bass), R. Bonynge (cnd), New Philharmonia Orch, Ambrosian Opera Chorus London ("Grand Opera" series) 4-▲ 430549-2 [AAD]

Vries, Gerrie de (mez)
Zuidam, R.:Freeze, w. Susan Narucki (sop—Patty Hearst), Zeger Vandersteene (ten), Martin Hargrove (bass), Jaco Huijpen (bass), S. Asbury (cnd), Asko Ensemble NM Classics 2-▲ NM 92047

Vries, Gerrie de (sop)
Vries, K. de:Diafonia, w. R. Boelens (sop), D. Porcelijn (cnd), Asko Ensemble Donemus ▲ CV 34

Vries, Müller de (sgr)
Mozart, W.A.:Bastien und Bastienne, w. Kirchner (sgr), Choy (sgr), R. Clemencic (cnd), Alpe Adria Ensemble [G] Nuova Era 2-▲ 7106/07 [DDD]
Rousseau, J.-J.:Le Devin du village, w. Kirchner (sgr), Choy (sgr), R. Clemencic (cnd), Alpe Adria Ensemble, Alpe Adria Chorus [F] Nuova Era 2-▲ 7106/07 [DDD]

Vulpius, Jutta (sop)
Mozart, W.A.:Entführung, w. Rosemarie Ronisch (sop), Rolf Apreck (ten), Jurgen Forster (ten), Arnold van Mill (bass), O. Suitner (cnd), Dresden State Opera Orch, Dresden State Opera Chorus Berlin Classics 2-▲ BER 9116

Vye, M. (sgr)
Rodgers, R.:Carousel, w. J. Raitt (sgr), J. Clayton (sgr), J. Darling (sgr), C. Johnson (sgr), E. Mattson (sgr), C. Baxter (sgr), J. Littau (cnd) [1945 cast] MCA Classics ▲ MCAD 10048 [AAD] ▮ MCAC 10048

Vyvyan, Jennifer (sop)
Bach, C.P.E.:Magnificat, w. Helen Watts (cta), Wilfred Brown (ten), Thomas Hemsley (bass), G. Jones (cnd), Geraint Jones Orch, Geraint Jones Singers EMI Classics ("Baroque" series) ▲ CDK 65737
Britten, H.:Owen Wingrave, w. S. Fisher (Miss Wingrave), H. Harper (Mrs. Coyle), J. Baker (Kate), P. Pears (Sir P. Wingrave; Narrator), B. Luxon (Owen Wingrave), J. Shirley-Quirk (Coyle), B. Britten, Wandworth School Boys' Choir, English CO London 2-▲ 433200-2
Britten, H.:The Turn of the Screw, w. O. Dyer (sop), A. Mandikian (mez), D. Hemmings (trb), G. Cross (ten), P. Pears (ten), B. Britten (cnd), English Opera Group Orch [E] London ▲ 425672-2 (m) [ADD]
Handel, G.F.:Messiah, w. Monica Sinclair (cta), Jon Vickers (ten), Giorgio Tozzi (bass), T. Beecham (cnd), Royal PO *(rec 1959)* RCA Gold Seal 3-▲ 09026-61266-2
Handel, G.F.:Messiah (sels), w. Monica Sinclair (mez), Jon Vickers (ten), Giorgio Tozzi (bass), T. Beecham (cnd), Royal PO, John McCarthy (cnd), Royal Choral Society—Ov; Comfort Ye My People; Every Valley Shall Be Exalted; And the Glory of the Lord; And He Shall Purify; O Thou That Tellest Good Tidings; For unto Us a Child is Born; Pastoral Symphony; There Were Shepherds Abiding; And the Angel Said unto Them; And Suddenly There Was; Glory to God in the Highest; He Shall Feed His Flock; Come unto Him; Behold the Lamb of God; He Was Despised; All We Like Sheep Have Gone Astray; Hallelujah!; I Know That My Redeemer Liveth; The Trumpet Shall Sound *(rec Walthamstow Town Hall, London, June–Aug 1959)* RCA Victor ▲ 09026-68159-2 [ADD]
Mendelssohn, F.:A Midsummer Night's Dream (sels), w. Marion Lowe (sop), P. Maag (cnd), London SO, Royal Opera House Women's Chorus Covent Garden—Op. 21; Op. 61, Nos 1, 3, 5, 7, 9, 11, 12 Classic Records ▲ CSCD 6001

Waag, Bjorn (sgr)
Schoenberg, A.:Die Jakobsleiter, w. Barbara Kilduff (sop—Seele 1), Jadwiga Rappé (cta—Sterbende), Wilfried Gahmlich (ten—Aufrührerischer), Cornelius Hauptmann (ten—Gabriel), Keith Lewis (ten—Berfener), Kurt Azesberger (bar—Mönch), Barbara Fuchs (sgr—Seele 2), Matteo de Monti (sgr—Ringender), Bjorn Waag (sgr—Auserwählter), E. Inbal (cnd), Frankfurt RSO, Robin Gritton (cnd), Berlin Radio Chorus *(rec Alte Oper, Frankfurt, Sept 6-9, 1994)* Denon ▲ CO 78977 [DDD]

Waara, S. (sgr)
Porter, C.:Fifty Million Frenchmen, w. H. McGillin (sgr), K. Criswell (sop), K. McClelland (sgr), S. Powell (sgr), K. Ziemba (sgr), J. Graae (sgr), J. Harder (sgr), P. Cass (sgr), J. LeClerc (sgr) [1991 studio cast] New World ▲ 80417-2 [DDD]

Waas, Annelie (sop)
Strauss, R.:Der Rosenkavalier, w. Erika Köth (sop—Sophie), Annelie Waas (sop—Marianne), Claire Watson (sop—Marschallin), Hertha Töpper (mez—Octavian), Brigitte Fassbaender (cta—Annina), Gerhard Stolze (ten—Valzacchi), Fritz Wunderlich (ten—Singer), Otto Wiener (bar—Faninal), Kurt Böhme (bass—Baron), J. Keilberth (cnd), Bavarian State Opera Orch, Bavarian State Opera Chorus *(rec Munich Opera Festival, National Theater, May 21, 1965)* Orfeo d'or 3-▲ 425963
Strauss, R.:Der Rosenkavalier, w. Claire Watson (sop—Feldmarschallin), Lucia Popp (sop—Sophie), Annelie Waas (sop—Marianne), Brigitte Fassbaender (mez—Octavian), Margaretthe Bence (ct—Annina), David Thaw (ten—Valzacchi), Karl Ridderbusch (bass—Baron Ochs), Benno Kusche (bass—Herr von Faninal), Albrecht Peter (bass—Police Inspector), C. Kleiber (cnd), Bavarian State Orch, Bavarian State Chorus *(rec live, Münchner Festspiele, July 20, 1974)* Arkadia 3-▲ 486 [ADD]

Wächter, Eberhard (bar)
Berg, A.:Wozzeck, w. A. Silja (sop), G. Jahn (mez), H. Laubenthal (ten), H. Zednik (ten), C. von Dohnányi (cnd), Vienna PO London 2-▲ 417348-2 [DDD]
Brahms, J.:Ein Deutsches Requiem, w. G. Janowitz (sop), H. von Karajan (cnd), Berlin PO, Vienna Singverein [G] Deutsche Grammophon ("Galleria" series) ▲ 427252-2 [ADD]
Lehár, F.:Die lustige Witwe, w. E. Schwarzkopf (sop), H. Steffek (sop), N. Gedda (ten), L. von Matačić (cnd), Philharmonia Orch, Philharmonia Chorus [G] EMI Classics 2-▲ CDCB 47177
Max Lorenz:Recital, 1933-1957, w. Max Lorenz (ten), Maria Reining (sop), Berlin RSO [cnd:Artur Rother], Bayreuth Festival Orch [cnd:Heinz Tietjen, Richard Strauss], German Large RSO [cnd:Rudolf Moralt, Max Schönherr, Anton Paulik], Hessen RSO [cnd:Kurt Schröder], Brenda Lewis (sop), Wolfgang Zimmer (bar) *(rec 1933–57)* Myto ▲ MCD 934.88
Millöcker, C.:Bettelstudent, w. Wilma Lipp (sop—Laura), Esther Rethy (sop—Bronislava), Rosette Anday (cta—Palmatica), Rudolf Christ (ten—Symon), Kurt Preger (ten—Ollendorf), Eberhard Wächter (bar—Jan), A. Paulik (cnd), Vienna Volksoper Orch, Vienna Volksoper Chorus *(rec Brahmssaal, Vienna, June 1995)* Omega 2-▲ OCD 1018/19 [ADD]
Mozart, W.A.:Don Giovanni, w. M. Caballé (sop), T. Stich-Randall (mez), E. Kunz (bar), M. Gielen (cnd), Naples Teatro San Carlo Orch, Naples Teatro San Carlo Chorus [I] *(rec live, Lisbon, 1960)* Standing Room Only 2-▲ SRO 813-2 [ADD]
Mozart, W.A.:Don Giovanni, w. L. Price (sop), H. Gueden (sop), G. Sciurri (sop), F. Wunderlich (ten), W. Berry (bass), H. von Karajan (cnd), Vienna PO, Vienna State Opera Chorus [I] *(rec live, 1963)* Verona 3-▲ 27065/67 (m) [AAD]
Mozart, W.A.:Don Giovanni (sels), w. E. Schwarzkopf (sop), G. Sciutti (sop), J. Sutherland (sop), L. Alva (ten), C. M. Giulini (cnd), Philharmonia Orch EMI Classics ▲ ZDM 63078
Mozart, W.A.:Nozze di Figaro, w. A. Moffo (sop), E. Schwarzkopf (sop), F. Cossotto (mez), G. Taddei (bar), C. M. Giulini (cnd), Philharmonia Orch, Philharmonia Chorus [I] EMI Classics ("Studio" series) 2-▲ CDMB 63266 [ADD]
Mozart, W.A.:Nozze di Figaro (sels), w. A. Moffo (sop), E. Schwarzkopf (sop), F. Cossotto (mez), G. Taddei (bar), C. M. Giulini (cnd), Philharmonia Orch, Philharmonia Chorus—sels. EMI Classics ("Studio" series) ▲ CDM 63409
Rossini, G.:Il barbiere di Siviglia, w. R. Grist (sop), F. Wunderlich (ten), O. Czerwenka (bass), Kunz (sgr), K. Böhm (cnd), Vienna State Opera Orch, Vienna State Opera Chorus *(rec live, Vienna 4/28/66)* Myto 2-▲ 2 MCD 91752 [ADD]
Smetana, B.:Dalibor, w. L. Rysanek (sop), L. Spiess (ten), J. Krips (cnd), Vienna State Opera Orch, Vienna State Opera Chorus *(rec live, Vienna, 10/19/69)* Myto 2-▲ 2 MCD 92465 [ADD]

Wächter, Eberhard (bar) (cont.)

Strauss (II), Joh.:Die Fledermaus, w. H. Gueden (sop), R. Streich (sop), G. Di Stefano (ten), G. Stolze (ten), G. Zampieri (ten), W. Berry (bass), E. Kunz (bar), H. von Karajan (cnd), Vienna State Opera Orch, Vienna State Opera Chorus [G] Arkadia 3–▲ 215 (m) [ADD]

Strauss (II), Joh.:Die Fledermaus, w. H. Gueden (sop), E. Köth (sop), R. Resnik (mez), W. Kmentt (ten), G. Zampieri (ten), W. Berry (bass), E. Kunz (bar), H. von Karajan (cnd), Vienna PO, Vienna State Opera Chorus, with Gala Sequence [G] London 2–▲ 421046–2 [ADD]

Strauss (II), Joh.:Die Fledermaus (sels), w. Wilma Lipp (sop), Gerda Scheyer (sop), Christa Ludwig (mez), Anton Dermota (ten), Walter Berry (bar), Erich Kunz (bar), O. Ackermann (cnd), Philharmonia Orch, London Phil Chorus Emperor Operetta ▲ KO 86340

Strauss (II), Joh.:Der Zigeunerbaron, w. Emmy Loose (sop—Arsena), Gerda Scheyrer (sop—Saffi), Elisabeth Fez (cta—Mirabella), Hilde Rössl-Majdan (cta—Czipra), Waldemar Kmentt (ten—Barinkay), Paul Spani (ten—Ottokar), Erich Kunz (bar—Homonay), Kurt Preger (bar—Zsupan), Eberhard Wächter (bass—Carnero), A. Paulik (cnd), Vienna State Opera Orch, Vienna State Opera Chorus *(rec Brahmssaal, Vienna, Austria, June 1956)* Vanguard Classics 2–▲ OVC 8082/83 [ADD]

Strauss, R.:Capriccio, w. E. Schwarzkopf (sop), A. Moffo (sop), C. Ludwig (mez), N. Gedda (ten), D. Fischer-Dieskau (bar), H. Hotter (b-bar), W. Sawallisch (cnd), Philharmonia Orch [G] EMI Classics 2–▲ CDCB 49014 (m) [ADD]

Strauss, R.:Elektra, w. B. Nilsson (sop), L. Rysanek (sop), R. Resnik (mez), W. Windgassen (ten), K. Böhm (cnd), *(orch unknown)* [G] *(rec live, Vienna 12/16/65)* Standing Room Only 2–▲ SRO 833–2 [ADD]

Strauss, R.:Elektra, w. A. Varnay (sop/mez), M. Mödl (sop/mez), H. Hillebrecht (sop), J. King (ten), H. von Karajan (cnd), Vienna PO, Vienna State Opera Chorus [G] *(rec 1964)* Melodram 2–▲ MEL 27044 [AAD]

Strauss, R.:Salome, w. B. Nilsson (sop), G. Hoffman (mez), G. Stolze (ten), W. Kmentt (ten), G. Solti (cnd), Vienna PO [G] London 2–▲ 414414–2 [ADD]

Verdi, G.:Don Carlos, w. Gundula Janowitz (sop), Shirley Verrett (mez), Franco Corelli (ten), Nicolai Ghiaurov (bass), Martti Talvela (bass), H. Stein (cnd), Vienna PO, Vienna State Opera Chorus *(rec Vienna, Oct. 25, 1970)* Pantheon 2–▲ PHE 6614

Verdi, G.:Falstaff, w. Ilva Ligabue (sop), Oralia Dominguez (mez), Luigi Alva (ten), Geraint Evans (bar), F. Previtali (cnd), *(orch unknown)* *(rec Teatro Colon, Buenos Aires, Aug. 30, 1963)* Ornamenti ("Gala Evenings, Teatro Colon") 2–▲ 119

Wagner, R.:Tannhäuser, w. Gré Brouwestijn (sop), Murray Dickie (ten), Karl Liebl (ten), Alois Pernerstorfer (b-bar), Deszö Ernster (bass), Walter Brunelli (sgr), Peter Harrower (sgr), Rosl Schweiger (sgr), Herta Wilfert (sgr), A. Rodzinski (cnd), Rome RAI Radio-TV SO, Rome RAI Chorus Stradivarius 3–▲ STV 12318

Wagner, R.:Tannhäuser, w. A. Silja (sop), G. Bumbry (mez), W. Windgassen (ten), J. Greindl (bass), W. Sawallisch (cnd), Bayreuth Festival Orch, Bayreuth Festival Chorus [Dresden version with Paris Venusberg music] [G] Philips 3–▲ 434607–2 [ADD]

Wagner, R.:Tannhäuser (sels), w. G. Brouwenstijn (sop), H. Wilfert (sgr), K. Liebl (ten), A. Rodzinski (cnd), Rome RAI Orch, Rome RAI Chorus *(rec Nov. 21 1957)* Myto 3–▲ MCD 93277

Wagner, R.:Tristan und Isolde, w. B. Nilsson (sop), C. Ludwig (mez), W. Windgassen (ten), M. Talvela (bass), K. Böhm (cnd), Bayreuth Festival Orch, Bayreuth Festival Chorus [G] *(rec Bayreuth Festival, 1966)* Deutsche Grammophon 3–▲ 419889–2 [ADD]

Wagner, R.:Tristan und Isolde, w. B. Nilsson (sop), C. Ludwig (mez), W. Windgassen (ten), M. Talvela (bass), K. Böhm (cnd), Bayreuth Festival Orch, Bayreuth Festival Chorus [G] Philips 3–▲ 434425–2 [ADD]

Weber, C.M. von:Der Freischütz, w. Irmgard Seefried (sop), Rita Streich (sop), Richard Holm (ten), Kurt Böhme (b-bar), E. Jochum (cnd), Bavarian RSO, Bavarian Radio Chorus Deutsche Grammophon 2–▲ 439717–2 [ADD]

Wadsworth, Michael (bar)

Weisgall, H.:Six Characters in Search of an Author, w. E. Byrne (sop—Stepdaughter), S. Foster (sop—Prompter), E. Furtal (sop—Coloratura), J. King (mez—Mezzo), N. Maultsby (mez—Mother), P. LoVerne (cta—Madame Pace), D. Pritchett (alt—Wardrobe Mistress), B. Fowler (ten—Tenore Boffo), K. Anderson (ten—Director), A. Schroeder (bar—Accompanist), P. Zawisza (bar—Stage Manager), R. Orth (bar—Father), G. Lehman (bar—Son), M. Wadsworth (b-bar—Basso Cantante), L. Schaenen (cnd), Chicago Lyric Opera Orch, Lyric Opera Center Chorus *(rec Chicago, June 14 & 16, 1990)* New World 2–▲ 80454–2

Wagemann, Rose (mez)

Hindemith, P.:Mathis der Maler, w. Urszula Koszut (sop), Trudeliese Schmidt (mez), Rose Wagemann (mez), William Cochran (ten), Donald Grobe (ten), James King (ten), Manfred Schmidt (ten), Dietrich Fischer-Dieskau (bar), Gerd Feldhoff (bass), Alexander Malta (bass), Peter Meven (bass), Karl Kreile (sgr), R. Kubelik (cnd), Bavarian RSO, Bavarian Radio Chorus EMI Classics 2–▲ CDCC 55237

Wager, Michael (nar)

Bernstein, L.:Sym 3, "Kaddish", w. M. Caballé (sop), L. Bernstein (cnd), Israel PO, *(chorus unknown)* Deutsche Grammophon 2–▲ 445245–2 [ADD]

Wagner, Friederike (sop)

Bach, J.S.:Cant 199, w. C. Brembeck (cnd), Capella Istropolitana [G] *(rec May 1991)* Naxos ▲ 8.550431 [DDD]

Bach, J.S.:Cant 202, "Wedding Cant", w. C. Brembeck (cnd), Capella Istropolitana [G] *(rec May 1991)* Naxos ▲ 8.550431 [DDD]

Bach, J.S.:Cant 209, w. C. Brembeck (cnd), Capella Istropolitana [G] *(rec May 1991)* Naxos ▲ 8.550431 [DDD]

Brixi, F.X.:Missa di Gloria, w. R. Schneider-Waterberg (alt), B. Hirtreiter (ten), M. Mantaj (bass), C. Hammer (org), W. Kelber (cnd), Munich Monteverdi Orch, Munich Concerto Vocale *(rec 1993)* Calig ▲ CAL 50927 [ADD]

Wagner, James (ten)

Verdi, G.:Messa per Rossini, w. G. Benačková-Cápova (sop), F. Quivar (mez), A. Agache (bar), A. Haugland (bass), H. Rilling (cnd), Stuttgart RSO, Gächinger Kantorei, Prague Phil Chorus [L] Hänssler Classic 2–▲ CD 98.949 [DDD] 2–■ MC 96.949 (D)

Weill, K.:Berlin Requiem, w. W. Holzmair (bar), H. Schmidt (cnd), Düsseldorf SO, Düsseldorf Sym Chorus [G] Koch Schwann ▲ CD 314 050 [DDD]

Weill, K.:Kiddush, w. M.-A. Schlingensiepen (cnd), Düsseldorf Choir Koch Schwann ▲ CD 314 050 [DDD]

Wagner, Lauren (sop)

American Song Recital, w. Fred Weldy (pno) Channel Classics ▲ CCS 5293 [DDD]

Wagner, Sieglinde (mez)

Bach, J.S.:Mass in b, BWV 232, w. Maria Stader (sop), Ernst Haefliger (ten), Theo Adam (b-bar), R. Mauersberger (cnd), Dresden State Orch, Dresden Kreuz Choir *(rec 1958)* Berlin Classics ▲ BER 9171

Bruckner, A.:Te Deum, w. M. Stader (sop), E. Haefliger (ten), P. Lagger (bass), E. Jochum (cnd), Berlin PO, German Opera Chorus [L] Deutsche Grammophon 4–▲ 423127–2 [ADD]

Dvořák, A.:Requiem Mass, w. Maria Stader (sop), Ernst Haefliger (ten), Kim Borg (b-bar), K. Ančerl (cnd), Czech PO, Czech Chorus Deutsche Grammophon ("Double" series) 2–▲ 437377–2

Furtwängler, W.:Te Deum, w. E. Mathis (sop), J. Dooley (alt), G. Jelden (ten), H. Chemin-Petit (cnd), Berlin PO *(rec live, 1967)* As Disc ▲ ASD 2506

Mozart, W.A.:Missa, K.317, w. Maria Stader (sop), Helmut Krebs (ten), Josef Griendl (bass), I. Markevitch (cnd), Berlin PO, St. Hedwig's Cathedral Choir Deutsche Grammophon 2–▲ 437383–2

Strauss (II), Joh.:Die Fledermaus, w. H. Gueden (sop), J. Patzak (ten), A. Dermota (ten), A. Jaresch (ten), A. Poell (b-bar), W. Lipp (sop), K. Preger (ten), C. Krauss (cnd), Vienna PO *(rec early 1950s)* London ("Historic" series) 2–▲ 425990–2 [AAD]

Verdi, G.:Otello, w. Carla Martinis (sop—Desdemona), Sieglinde Wagner (mez—Emilia), Anton Dermota (ten—Cassio), Paul Schöffler (ten—Iago), Ramon Vinay (ten—Otello), Josef Greindl (bass—Lodovico), W. Furtwängler (cnd), Vienna PO, Vienna State Opera Chorus *(rec live, Salzburg Festival, Aug 7, 1951)* EMI Classics ▲ CDMB 65751

Wagner, R.:Der fliegende Holländer, w. M. Schech (sop), G. Frick (ten), F. Wunderlich (ten), R. Schock (ten), D. Fischer-Dieskau (bar), F. Konwitschny (cnd), Berlin Staatskapelle Berlin Classics ("Eterna" series) 2–▲ BER 2097 [ADD]

Wagner, Sieglinde (mez) (cont.)

Wagner, R.:Der fliegende Holländer, w. Annelies Kupper (sop—Senta), Sieglinde Wagner (mez—Mary), Ernst Haefliger (ten—Steersman), Wolfgang Windgassen (ten—Erik), Josef Metternich (ten—Dutchman), Josef Greindl (bass—Daland), F. Fricsay (cnd), Berlin RIAS SO, Berlin RIAS Chamber Choir *(rec 1953)* Deutsche Grammophon 2–▲ 439714–2 (m) [ADD]

Wagner, R.:Das Rheingold, w. L. Otto (sop), M. Muszely (sop), J. Blatter (mez), R. Stewart (mez), S. Wagner (mez), R. Schock (ten), H. Melchert (ten), F. Frantz (bass), B. Kusche (bass), J. Metternich (bass), R. Kempe (cnd), Berlin Staatskapelle *(rec Mar. 1959)* Berlin Classics ("Eterna" series) ▲ BER 2035 [ADD]

Wagstaff, Lyndsay (sop)

Adams, J.:Grand Pianola Music, w. Kym Amps (sop), Ruth Holton (sop), Ellen Corver (pno), Sepp Grotenhuis (pno), S. Mosko (cnd), Netherlands Wind Ensemble Chandos ▲ CHAN 9363 [DDD]

Wahlgren, Per-Arne (bar)

Geijer, E.G.:Songs, w. Catharina Olsson (mez), Thomas Schuback (pno) Musica Sveciae ▲ MSV 519 [ADD]

Haeffner, J.C.F.:Electra (sels), w. H. Martinpelto (sop), G. Hoffstedt (sop), S. Dahlberg (ten), T. Schuback (cnd), Drottningholm Baroque Ensemble—3 recitatives & arias [Sw] *(rec 1989–90)* Musica Sveciae ▲ MSCD 426 [DDD]

Naumann, J.G.:Arias, w. G. Hoffstedt (sop), H. Martinpelto (sop), S. Dahlberg (ten), T. Schuback (cnd), Drottningholm Baroque Ensemble—sels. from Amphion & Cora och Alonzo [Sw] Musica Sveciae ▲ MSCD 426 [DDD]

Stenhammar, W.:Sången, w. Iwa Sörenson (sop), Anne Sofie von Otter (mez), Stefan Dahlberg (ten), H. Blomstedt (cnd), Swedish RSO, Swedish Radio Chorus, Stockholm State Academy of Music Chamber Choir, Adolf Fredrik Music School Children's Choir Caprice ▲ CAP 21358

Uttini, F.A.B.:Thetis och Pelée (sels), w. H. Martinpelto (sop), G. Hoffstedt (sop), S. Dahlberg (ten), T. Schuback (cnd), Drottningholm Baroque Ensemble [Sw] Musica Sveciae ▲ MSCD 426 [DDD]

Waite, Shelley (sop)

Brubeck, D.:To Hope!:A Celebration, w. Mark Bleeke (ten), Kevin Deas (b-bar), R. Gloyd (cnd), Cathedral Choral Society Orch, Dave Brubeck Quartet, Cathedral Choral Society Chorus *(rec Washington National Cathedral, Washington, D.C., June 12, 1995)* Telarc ▲ CD 80430 [DDD]

Waits, Tom (sgr)

Bryars, G.:Jesus' Blood Never Failed Me Yet, w. M. Riesman (cnd), Gavin Bryars Ensemble Philips ▲ 438823–2

Waits, T.:The Black Rider:The Casting of Magic Bullets, w. Angelika Thomas (sgr—Anne), Annette Paulmann (sgr—Kätchen), Sona Cervena (sgr—Bird/Messenger/Spoonwoman), Monika Tahal (sgr—Witness/Bird/Shrink/Wilhelm's Double/Skeleton), Susi Eisenkolb (sgr—Bridesmaid/Pegleg's Double), Heinz Vossbrink (sgr—Kuno), Dominique Horwitz (sgr—Pegleg), Gerd Kunath (sgr—Bertram), Stefan Kurt (sgr—Wilhelm), Klaus Schreiber (sgr—Robert/Man on Stag/Georg Schmid), Jörg Holm (Old Uncle/Duke), Jan Moritz Steffen (sgr—Young Kuno/Bird/Shrink/Skeleton), Tom Waits (vocals/coliope/organ/chamberlain/mar/emax/guitar/train whistle), Ralph Carney (saxophone/bass clarinet/baritone horn), Bill Douglas (bass instrument), Kenny Wollesen (perc) Island ▲ 314518559–2

Wakefield, Henriette (sop)

Verdi, G.:La traviata, w. Rosa Ponselle (sop—Violetta), Henriette Wakefield (sop—Annina), Frederick Jagel (ten—Alfredo), Alfredo Gandolfi (bar—Baron), Lawrence Tibbett (bar—Giorgio), E. Panizza (cnd), *(orch unknown)* *(rec live, New York, Jan. 5, 1935)* The Fourties 2–▲ ENT FT 1513

Wakefield, John (ten)

Handel, G.F.:Messiah, w. Heather Harper (sop), Helen Watts (cta), John Shirley-Quirk (bar), C. Davis (cnd), London SO, London Sym Chorus Philips 2–▲ 438356–2

Sullivan, A.:The Mikado, w. M. Studholme (sop), C. Revill (bar), D. Dowling (bar), J. Holmes (bass), A. Faris (cnd), Sadler's Wells Opera Orch, Sadler's Wells Opera Chorus Classics for Pleasure 2–▲ CDCFP 4730 [ADD]

Walcott, Collin (sgr/mrdingam)

Monk, M.:Key, w. Meredith Monk (sgr/elec org/jews hp), Daniel Sverdlik (sgr), Dick Higgins (sgr), Mark Berger (nar), Lanny Harrison (nar) *(rec live, Gary Weis' loft, Santa Monica, CA, Ace Gallery, Los Angeles, CA, The House, New York City, The Farm, Los Angeles, CA, July 1970–Jan 1971)* Lovely Music ▲ LCD 1051 [ADD]

Walker, Adalbert (bass)

Wagner, S.:Banadietrich, w. Beth Johanning (sop), Vivian Hanner (sgr), Volker Horn (ten), André Wenhold (bar), Andreas Schmidt (bar), V. Gailis (cnd), Thuringian SO, Rudolstadt Festival Chorus *(rec Rudolstädt, June 1995)* Marco Polo 2–▲ 8.223895–6 [DDD]

Walker, Ian (nar)

Walker, G.:Poem, w. A. Frascarelli (cnd), Capitol Chamber Artists Albany ▲ TROY 154 [DDD]

Walker, J. (bass)

Prokofiev, S.:Eugene Onegin, w. T. West (nar), K. Fuge (sop), P. im Thurn (bar), E. Downes (cnd), Sinfonia 21, New Company Chandos 2–▲ CHAN 9318/19 [DDD]

Walker, Malcolm (bar)

Debussy, C.:Pelléas et Mélisande, w. E. Manchet (sop—Mélisande), M. Walker (bar—Pelléas), J. Carewe (cnd), Nice PO, Nice Opera Chorus—no texts [F] *(rec 6/88)* Pierre Verany 2–▲ PV.788093/4 [DDD]

Walker, N. (sgr)

Bernstein, L.:On the Town, w. M. Martin (sgr), B. Comden (sgr), A. Green (sgr), Tutti Camarata Orch, Leonard Joy Orch, Lynn Murray Orch, Lynn Murray Chorus MCA Classics ▲ MCAD 10280 (m) [AAD]

Rodgers, R.:Music of, w. S. Bass (sgr), J. Andrews (sgr), P. Como (sgr), D. Reese (sgr), J. Jones (sgr), N. Luboff (sgr), M. Gold (sgr), H. Bowen (sgr), V. Damone (sgr), P. Nero (pno), J. P. Morgan (sgr), E. Fisher (sgr), B. Goodman (cl), Ann-Margaret (sgr), Shorty Rogers (sgr), D. Shore (sgr), T. Martin (sgr), M. King (sgr), A. Newley (sgr) RCA ▲ 8590–2 R ■ 8590–4 R

Walker, Norman (bass)

Elgar, E.:The Dream of Gerontius, w. G. Ripley (cta), H. Nash (ten), D. Noble (bar), M. Sargent (cnd), Liverpool PO, Huddersfield Choral Society Testament ▲ TES SBT 2025 [ADD]

Verdi, G.:La traviata, w. Maria Caniglia (sop—Violetta), Maria Huder (mez—Flora), Gladys Palmer (cta—Annina), Octave Dua (ten—Giuseppe), Beniamino Gigli (ten—Alfredo), Booth Hitchen (ten—D'Obigny), Adelio Zagonara (bar—Gastone), Aristide Baracchi (bar—Douphol), Mario Basiola (bar—Germont), Norman Walker (bass—Dr. Grenville), V. Gui (cnd), London PO, London Phil Chorus *(rec Royal Opera House, Covent Garden, May 22, 1939)* Minerva 2–▲ MN A28/29 (m) [ADD]

Walker, P. (sop)

Pacini, G.:Maria Tudor, w. M. Hill Smith (sop), K. Lewis (ten), C. Blades (bar), D. Parry (cnd), English SO *(rec 1983)* Italian Opera Rarities ▲ IOR 7714 [ADD]

Vaughan Williams, R.:5 Tudor Portraits, w. F. Harrison (alto), A. Boult (cnd), BBC SO, BBC Northern Singers Intaglio ▲ ING 757 [ADD]

Walker, Sarah (mez)

Brahms, J.:Songs, w. Roger Vignoles (pno)—Gypsy Songs, Op. 103; 6 Mädchenlieder; 2 Gesänge Meridian ▲ MER 84232 [DDD]

Brahms, J.:Songs, Op. 91, w. P. Silverthorne (va), J. Jacobson (pno) [G] Meridian ▲ CDE 84190

Britten, H.:Purcell Realizations, w. Susan Gritton (sop), Felicity Lott (sop), James Bowman (alto), John Mark Ainsley (ten), Anthony Rolfe Johnson (ten), Richard Jackson (bass), Simon Keenlyside (bass), Ian Bostridge (sgr), Graham Johnson (pno) Hyperion 2–▲ CDA 67061/62

British Music on Hyperion, w. Parley of Instruments, Roy Goodman (cnd), John Mark Ainsley (ten), Graham Johnson (pno), Salomon Quartet, BBC Scottish SO, Anthony Rolfe Johnson (ten), Royal PO, St. Paul's Cathedral Choir, Nash Ensemble, Martyn Hill (ten), Suasan Gritton (sop), Sarah Wal Hyperion ▲ HYP 15

Cabaret Songs, w. Roger Vignoles (pno) *(rec live 1982 & 1988)* Meridian ▲ 84167

Debussy, C.:Chansons de Bilitis, w. Roger Vignoles (pno) Unicorn-Kanchana ▲ UKCD 2078

Debussy, C.:Chansons de France (3), w. Roger Vignoles (pno) Unicorn-Kanchana ▲ UKCD 2078

Debussy, C.:Fêtes galantes 2, w. Roger Vignoles (pno) Unicorn-Kanchana ▲ UKCD 2078

Delius, F.:Songs, w. Felicity Lott (sop), Anthony Rolfe Johnson (ten), E. Fenby (cnd), Royal PO—Orchestral Songs; Songs w. Pno [Scandinavian, French & English] Unicorn-Kanchana ("Souvenir" series) ▲ UK 2075

Dreams and Fancies (Favorite Songs in English) CRD ▲ 3473 [DDD]

Walker, Sarah (mez) (cont.)
Dvořák, A.:Zigeunermelodien, Op. 55, w. Roger Vignoles (pno) Meridian ▲ MER 84232 [DDD]
Elgar, E.:The Music Makers, w. N. del Mar (cnd), BBC SO, BBC Singers, BBC Sym Chorus IMP ("BBC Radio Classics" series) ▲ IMP 5691672
Enescu, G.:Chansons (7) de Clément Marot, w. Roger Vignoles (pno) Unicorn–Kanchana ▲ UKCD 2078
Falla, M. de:El amor brujo, w. G. Simon (cnd), London SO [Sp] Chandos ▲ CHAN 8457 [DDD]
Fauré, G.:La bonne chanson, w. Nash Ensemble [F] CRD ▲ 3389 [ADD]
Fauré, G.:Songs, w. M. Martineau (pno)—Le Papillon et la fleur, Op. 1/1; Ici–bas!, Op. 8/3; Sérénade Toscane, Op. 3/2; Nocturne, Op. 43/2; Au bord de l'eau, Op. 8/1; Seule!, Op. 3/1; Larmes, Op. 51/1; Aurore, Op. 39/1; Fleur jetée, Op. 39/2; Le Pays des rêves, Op. 39/3; Les Roses d'Ispahan, Op. 39/4; Chanson, Op. 94; C'est la paix, Op. 114; La fée aux chansons, Op. 27/2; L'absent, Op. 5/3; Arpège, Op. 76/2; Le plus doux chemin, Op. 87/1; Accompagnement, Op. 85/3; Au Cimitière, Op. 51/2; Le Don silencieux, Op. 92; Chanson de Mélisande (1898); Clair de lune, Op. 46/2; Vocalise (1907); Puisqu'ici bas toute âme, Op. 10/1; Tarantelle, Op. 10/2 [F] *(rec 1991)* CRD ▲ 3477 [DDD]
Fauré, G.:Songs, w. M. Martineau (pno)—Le Jardin clos (cycle of 8 songs), Op. 106 (1914); plus 20 individual songs composed ca. 1861–1904—Mai, Op. 1/2; Chant d'automne, Op. 5/1; Rêve d'amour, Op. 5/2; Dans les ruines d'un abbaye (1867); L'aurore (ca. 1871); Après un rêve (ca. 1878); Tristesse, Op. 6/2; Nell, Op. 18/1; Automne, Op. 18/3; Les Berceaux, Op. 23/1; Notre amour, Op. 23/2; Le Secret, Op. 23/3; Noël, Op. 43/1; Les Présents, Op. 46/1; La Rose, Op. 51/4; En Prière (1890); La parfum impérissable, Op. 76/1; Soir, Op. 83/2; Dans la forêt de septembre, Op. 85/1; Le Ramier, Op. 87/2 CRD ▲ 3476 [DDD]
Gay, J.:The Beggar's Opera, w. B. Hoskins (sgr), A. Thompson (ten), C. Daniels (ten), I. Caddy (b–bar), J. Barlow (cnd), Broadside Band [E] Hyperion 2–▲ CDA 66591/92
Gounod, C.:Roméo et Juliette, w. Susan Graham (sop—Stephano), Ruth Ann Swenson (sop—Juliette), Sarah Walker (mez—Gertrude), Paul Charles Clarke (ten—Tybalt), Placido Domingo (ten—Roméo), Kurt Ollmann (bar—Mercutio), Alastair Miles (bass—Frère Laurent), David Pittman–Jennings (bass—Le Duc), Alain Vernhes (bass—Capulet), L. Slatkin (cnd), Munich RSO, Munich Radio Chorus *(rec Studio 1, Bavarian Radio, Munich, Nov 29 - Dec 10, 1995)* RCA Red Seal 2–▲ 09026–68440–2 [DDD]
Mozart, W.A.:Requiem, w. Y. Kenny (sop), W. Kendall (ten), D. Wilson–Johnson (bar), G. Guest (cnd), English CO, St. John's College Choir Cambridge [L] Chandos ▲ CHAN 8574 [DDD]
Ravel, M.:Chansons madécasses, w. Nash Ensemble Virgin Classics ▲ CDC 45016
Rorem, N.:King Midas, w. John Stewart (ten), Anne Schein (pno) Phoenix ▲ PHCD 126
Roussel, A.:Light, w. Roger Vignoles (pno) Unicorn–Kanchana ▲ UKCD 2078
Roussel, A.:Mélodies, w. Roger Vignoles (pno) Unicorn–Kanchana ▲ UKCD 2078
Roussel, A.:Poèmes chinois, w. Roger Vignoles (pno) Unicorn–Kanchana ▲ UKCD 2078
Schubert, Franz:Songs (comp), w. G. Johnson (pno)—18 songs—D.114, 208, 238, 259, 289, 290, 328, 418, 462, 463, 464, 465, 466, 495, 498, 614, 653, 920 [G] Hyperion ▲ CDJ 33008 [DDD]
The Sea, w. Thomas Allen (sgr), R. Vignoles (pno) Hyperion ▲ CDA 66165
Shakespeare's Kingdom Hyperion ▲ CDA 66136
Tchaikovsky, P.:Eugene Onegin, w. N. Focile (sop), I. Arkhipova (mez), F. Egerton (ten), D. Hvorostovsky (bar)., S. Bychkov (cnd), Orch de Paris Philips 2–▲ 438235–2
Telemann, G.P.:Der Tag des Gerichts, w. Patrice Michaels Bell (sop), Karen Brunssen (mez), Bruce Fowler (ten), Kurt R. Hansen (ten), William Stone (bar), Douglas Anderson (bar), T. Wikman (cnd), Music of the Baroque Orch, Baroque Music Chorus *(rec live, St. Paul's United Church of Christ, Feb 23, 1992)* Music of the Baroque 2–▲ MB 107
Tippett, M.:The Mask of Time, w. F. Robinson (sop), R. Tear (ten), J. Cheek (bass), A. Davis (cnd), BBC SO, BBC Sym Chorus EMI Classics ▲ ZDMB 64111
Vaughan Williams, R.:Hugh the Dover, w. R. Evans (sop), B. Bottone (ter), N. Jenkins (ten), A. Opie (bar), R. Van Allan (bass), M. Best (cnd), Corydon Orch, Corydon Singers, New London Children's Choir Hyperion 2–▲ CDA 66901/02

Wallace, Barbara (sop)
Flowering of Vocal Music in America, 1767–1823, w. Susan Belling (sop), Cynthia Clarey (sop), Debra Vanderlinde (sop), D'Anna Fortunato (mez), Evelyn Petros (mez), Charles Bressler (ten), Richard Anderson (bar), James Tyeska (bar), Joseph McKee (bass), Cynthia Otis (hp), Leonard Rav New World ▲ 80467–2

Wallace, Ian (bass)
Busoni, F.:Arlecchino or Die Fenster, w. E. Malbin (sop), M. Dickie (ten), G. Evans (bar), F. Ollendorf (bass), Glyndebourne Festival Chorus, J. Pritchard (cnd), Glyndebourne Festival Orch EMI Classics ▲ CDMB 65284
Handel, G.F.:Sosarme, Rè di Media, w. Margaret Ritchie (sop—Elmira), Alfred Deller (mez—Sosarme), Nancy Evans (mez—Erenice), Helen Watts (cta—Melo), John Kentish (ct—Argone), William Herbert (ten—King Haliate), Ian Wallace (bass—Altomaro), A. Lewis (cnd), St. Cecilia Academy Orch Rome, St. Anthony Singers Theorema 2–▲ TH 121194/195
Rossini, G.:Il barbiere di Siviglia, w. V. de los Angeles (sop), L. Alva (ten), C. Cava (bass), V. Gui (cnd), Royal PO, Glyndebourne Festival Chorus *(rec 1962)* EMI Classics 2–▲ CDMB 64162
Sullivan, A.:The Mikado, w. O. Brannigan (bass), R. Lewis (ten), G. Evans (bar), M. Sargent (cnd), Pro Arte Orch, Glyndebourne Festival Chorus EMI Classics 2–▲ CDMB 64403
Sullivan, A.:Music of, w. M. Studholme (sop), J. Allister (cta), E. Bohan (ten), M. Dods (cnd), London Concert Orch, English Chorale—sels. from Gondoliers; H.M.S. Pinafore; Mikado; Pirates of Penzance PWK Classics ▲ PWK 1157 [AAD]

Wallén, Martti (bass)
Bergman, E.:The Singing Tree, w. K. Hannula (sop), C. Hellekant (cta), P. Lindroos (ten), P. Salomaa (bass), S. Tiilikainen (bar), U. Söderblom (cnd), Finnish National Opera Orch, Dominante Chamber Choir, Tapiola Chamber Choir Ondine 2–▲ ODE 794–2D [DDD]

Waller, A. (bass)
Wagner, S.:Der Bärenhäuter, w. B. Johanning (sop—Luise), K. Likic (sop—Lene), T. Koon (sop—Gunda), V. Horn (ten—Hans Kraft), A. Feilhaber (ten—Nikolaus Spitz), R. Hartmann (bar—Kaspar Wild), A. Wenhold (bar—Stranger), A. Waller (bass—Devil), H. Kiichli (bass—Melchior Fröhlich), K. Bach (cnd), Thüringian SO, Thüringian State Theater Chorus *(rec Rudolstadt, July 25-31, 1993)* Marco Polo ("Opera Classics" series) 2–▲ 8.223713/4 [DDD]

Walley, Matthew (ten)
Balada, L.:Escenas borrascosas, w. Katy Shackelton–Williams (sop—Isabel), Nancy Maria Balach (mez—Beatriz), Matthew Walley (ten—Colón), J.P. Izquierdo (cnd), Carnegie Mellon PO, Robert Page (cnd), Carnegie Mellon Concert Choir, Carnegie Mellon Repertory Chorus New World ▲ 804982
Balada, L.:Escenas borrascosas, w. Kay Shackleton–Williams (sop—Isabel), Nancy Maria Balach (mez—Beatriz), Matthew Walley (ten—Colón), J.P. Izquierdo (cnd), Carnegie Mellon PO, Robert Page (cnd), Carnegie Mellon Concert Choir, Carnegie Mellon Repertory Chorus *(rec Carnegie Music Hall, Pittsburgh, PA, Apr 7-8, 1994)* New World ▲ 80498–2

Wallis, Delia (mez)
Mendelssohn, F.:A Midsummer Night's Dream (comp), w. Janice Watson (sop), A. Previn (cnd), London SO, London Sym Chorus [E] EMI Classics ▲ CDC 47163
Verdi, G.:Ernani (sels), w. Felicia Weathers (sop—Elvira), Delia Wallis (mez—Giovanna), Placido Domingo (ten—Ernani), Wynford Evans (ten—Don Riccardo), Piero Francia (bar—Don Carlo), Agostino Ferrin (bass—Don Ruy Gomex de Silva), Robert Holl (bass—Iago), E. Downes (cnd), Omroep Orch, Omroep Chorus *(rec Amsterdam, Jan 15, 1972)* Bella Voce ▲ BLV 107.004 [AAD]

Wallprecht, Klaus (sgr)
Delius, F.:A Village Romeo & Juliet, w. Eva–Christine Reimer (sgr), Karsten Russ (sgr), K. Seibel (cnd), Kiel PO CPO 2–▲ CPO 999328 [DDD]
Schillings, M. von:Mona Lisa, w. Beate Bilandzija (sgr), Albert Bonnema (sgr), K. Seibel (cnd), Kiel PO CPO 2–▲ CPO 999303 [DDD]

Wallström, Tord (bar)
Donizetti, G.:Maria Stuarda (sels), w. Lena Nordin (sop), Carina Morling (mez), Ingus Peterssons (ten), Anders Bergström (bar), Maria Wieslander (org), Sven Åberg (chit), Chrichan Larsson (vc), Nanette Nowels–Stenholm (pno), M. Guidarini (cnd), *(orch unknown)* Swedish Society ▲ SCD 1076
Kraus, J.M.:Soliman II, w. L. Hoel (sop), B. Ortendahl–Corin (sop), B.–O. Morgny (ten), P. Brunelle (cnd), Royal Swedish Opera Orch, Sweden Royal Opera Chorus Virgin Classics ▲ 59068 [DDD]

Walmsley-Clark, Penelope (sop)
The Best of Richard Hickox, w. R. Hickox (cnd), London SO, London Sym Chorus, John Graham–Hall (ten), D. Maxwell (bar), Southend Boys' Choir, London Voices IMP Classics 3–▲ TCD 1073 [DDD]
Harvey, J.:Song Offerings, w. G. Benjamin (cnd), London Sinfonietta Nimbus ▲ NI 5167 [DDD]
Holloway, R.:Sea Surface Full of Clouds, w. M. Cable (mez), C. Brett (alt), M. Hill (ten), R. Hickox (cnd), City of London Sinfonia Chandos ▲ CHAN 9228 [DDD]
Maderna, B.:Hyperion, w. B. Ganz (nar), J. Zoon (fl), P. Eötvös (cnd), Asko Ensemble, Les Jeunes Solistes Vocal Ensemble Montaigne 2–▲ MO 782014 [DDD]
Orff, C.:Carmina burana, w. J. Graham–Hall (ten), D. Maxwell (bar), R. Hickox (cnd), London SO, London Sym Chorus [G, L] IMP Classics ▲ PCD 855
Stockhausen, K.:Stimmung, w. K. Flowers (sop), Long (sgr), R. Covey–Crump (ten), P. Rose (bass), Hillier (sgr) Hyperion ▲ CDA 66115

Walsh, Kevin (bar)
Bach, J.S.:St. John Passion, w. Tamara Matthews (sop), Jennifer Lane (alt), Mark Bleeke (ten—Evangelist), David Vanderwal (ten), Kevin Walsh (bar—Pilate), Nathaniel Watson (bass—Jesus), E. Milnes (cnd), Trinity Baroque Orch, Trinity Cathedral Choir *(rec Trinity Cathedral, Portland, OR, Mar 31, 1996)* PGM 2–▲ PGM 111

Walston, R. (sgr)
Rodgers, R.:Me & Juliet, w. I. Bigley (sgr), B. Hayes (sgr), J. McCracken (sgr) [1953 Broadway cast] RCA ▲ 09026–61480–2 ■ 09026–61480–4

Walt, Deon van der (ten)
Donizetti, G.:La fille du régiment, w. Edita Gruberová (sop), Rosa Laghezza (mez), Philippe Fourcade (bass), François Castel (sgr), M. Panni (cnd), Munich RSO, Bavarian Radio Chorus Nightingale Classics 2–▲ NIG 70566
Mendelssohn, F.:Sym 2, w. Pamela Coburn (sop), Lioba Braun (alt), K.–F. Beringer (cnd), Austro–Hungarian PO *(rec Ansbach, July 1996)* Hänssler Classic 2–▲ CD 98.134 [DDD]

Walt, van der (sop)
Mozart, W.A.:Così fan tutte (sels), w. C. Margiono (sop), D. Ziegler (mez), G. Cachemaille (bar), N. Harnoncourt (cnd), Royal Concertgebouw Orch—sels. Teldec ▲ 9031–76455–2

Walter, Silja (nar)
Rütti, C.:Verena, die Quelle, w. I. Moore (cnd), Cambridge Instrumental Ensemble, Cambridge Voices Herald 2–▲ HAVPCD 186 [DDD]

Walters, Jess (bar)
Verdi, G.:Aida, w. Maria Callas (sop—Aida), Joan Sutherland (sop—Priestess), Giulietta Simionato (cta—Amneris), Kurt Baum (ten—Radames), Hector Thomas (ten—Messenger), Jess Walters (bar—Amonasro), Michael Langdon (bass—King), Giulio Neri (bass—Ramfis), J. Barbirolli (cnd), Royal Opera House Orch, Royal Opera House Chorus Covent Garden *(rec Covent Garden, London, June 10, 1953)* Legato Classics 2–▲ LCD 187–2

Walther, Ute (cta)
Beethoven, L. van:Sym 9, "Choral Sym", w. E. Wiens (sop), R. Goldberg (ten), K.–H. Stryczek (bass), H. Blomstedt (cnd), Dresden Staatskapelle, Dresden State Opera Chorus, Dresden Sym Chorus—final chorus Capriccio ▲ 10 914 [DDD]
Beethoven, L. van:Sym 9, "Choral Sym", w. A. Hargan (sop), E. Büchner (ten), K. Kováts (bass), H. Kegel (cnd), Dresden PO Capriccio ▲ 10 453 [DDD]
Strauss, R.:Der Rosenkavalier (sels), w. A. Pusar–Jeric (sop), M. Stejskal (sop), A. Jahns (mez), R. Haunstein (bar), T. Adam (b–bar), H. Vonk (cnd), Dresden Staatskapelle, Dresden State Chorus [G] *(rec live 2/85)* Denon ▲ CO 8010 [DDD]

Walton, Susana (nar)
Walton, W.:Façade, w. Richard Baker (nar), R. Hickox (cnd), City of London Sinfonia members [E] Chandos ▲ CHAN 8869 [DDD]

Wang, J. (sgr)
Barber, S.:Songs, w. C. Rosenberger (pno) [trans. cello & piano Bejun Mehta]—With Rue My Heart is Laden, Op. 2/2 & Sure on this Shining Night, Op. 13/3 Delos ▲ DE 3097 [DDD]

Wangemann, Hendrikje (sop)
Eisler, H.:Deutsche Sinfonie, w. Annette Markert (alt), Matthias Görne (bar), Peter Lika (bass), Gert Gütschow (speaker), Volker Schwarz (speaker), L. Zagrosek (cnd), Leipzig Gewandhaus Orch, Ernst Senff Chorus *(rec Gewandhaus, Leipzig, May 1995)* London ("Entartet Musik" series) ▲ 448389–2 [DDD]

Ward (sgr)
Berlioz, H.:Benvenuto Cellini, w. J. Carlyle (sop), J. Veasey (mez), K. Lewis (ten), Kentish, Cameron, Bushby, Garrard, A. Dorati (cnd), BBC SO, BBC Sym Chorus [E] *(rec live, Royal Festival Hall, 1964)* Music & Arts 2–▲ CD 618 (m) [AAD]

Ward, B. J. (sop)
Queen of the Night Dorchester Classics ▲ DRC 1001

Ward, C. (sgr)
Gounod, C.:Faust, w. V. de los Angeles (sop), M. Mayhoff (sgr), R. Tucker (ten), H. Noel (sgr), N. Moscona (bass), D. Bernard (sgr), W. Herbert (cnd), New Orleans Opera Orch [F] *(rec Feb. 26, 1953)* Legato Classics 2–▲ LCD 167–2 [AAD]

Ward, David (bass)
Debussy, C.:Pelléas et Mélisande, w. E. Söderström (sop), Y. Minton (mez), G. Shirley (ten), D. McIntyre (bass–bar), P. Boulez (cnd), Royal Opera House Orch, Royal Opera House Chorus Covent Garden Sony Classical (Pierre Boulez Edition) 3–▲ SM3K 47265
Monteverdi, C.:Ballo delle ingrate, w. April Cantelo (sop—Una dell' Ingrate), Eileen McLoughlin (sop—Amore), Alfred Deller (alt—Venere), David Ward (bass—Plutone), Julian Bream (lt), Desmond Dupre (vl), A. Deller (cnd), London Chamber Players *(rec Walthamstow Hall, London)* Vanguard Classics ▲ OVC 8100 [ADD]

Ward, Joseph (bar)
Berlioz, H.:Roméo et Juliette, w. R. Resnik (mez), A. Turp (ten), P. Monteux (cnd), London SO, London Sym Chorus [F] MCA Classics 2–▲ MCAD2–9805
Handel, G.F.:Messiah, w. Joan Sutherland (sop), Grace Bumbry (mez), Kenneth McKeller (ten), A. Boult (cnd), London PO London 3–▲ 433003–2 [ADD]
Handel, G.F.:Messiah (sels), w. Joan Sutherland (sop), Grace Bumbry (mez), Kenneth McKellar (ten), A. Boult (cnd), London SO, London Sym Chorus—arias & choruses London ("Weekend Classics" series) ▲ 417879–2 [AAD] ■ 417879–4
Herrmann, B.:Wuthering Heights, w. M. Beaton (sop—Catherine), P. Bowden (mez—Isabella), E. Bainbridge (mez—Nelly), M. Snashall (trb—Hareton), D. Bell (bar—Heathcliff), J. Kitchiner (bar—Hindley), J. Ward (bar—Edgar), M. Rippon (bass—Joseph), D. Kelly (bass—Mr. Lockwood), B. Herrmann (cnd), Pro Arte Orch *(rec 1965–66)* Unicorn–Kanchana 3–▲ UKCD 2050/51/52 [ADD]

Ward, K. (sgr)
Gershwin, G.:Crazy for You, w. R. Henshaw (sgr) [1992 London cast] RCA ▲ 09026–61933–2 ■ 09026–61933–4

Warfield, William (bar)
Broadway, w. Ethel Merman (sgr), Judy Holliday (sgr), Dick van Dyke (sgr), Doris Day (sgr), Topol (sgr), Mary Martin (sgr), Jill Haworth (sgr), et al. Sony Classical ("Greatest Hits" series) ▲ MLK 62365 ■ MLT 62365
Copland, A.:Old American Songs, w. A. Copland (cnd), Columbia SO [E] CBS ▲ MK 42430 [ADD]
Gershwin, G.:Porgy & Bess (sels), w. H. Boatwright (sop), L. Price (sop), S. Henderson (cnd), RCA Victor SO, RCA Victor Chorus [E] RCA Gold Seal ▲ 5234–2–RG [ADD]
Handel, G.F.:Messiah, w. Eileen Farrell (sop), Martha Lipton (cta), T. Cunningham (ten), E. Ormandy (cnd), Philadelphia Orch, Mormon Tabernacle Choir [E] CBS 2–▲ M2K 00607 ■ M2T 00607
Handel, G.F.:Messiah (sels), w. Adele Addison (sop), Russell Oberlin (ct), Edward Lloyd (ten), L. Bernstein (cnd), New York PO, Westminster Choir [E] CBS ▲ MYK 38481 ■ MYT 38481
Kern, J.:Show Boat, w. B. Cook (sop) [1966 revival cast] RCA ▲ 09026–61182–2 [ADD] ■ 09026–61182–4
Mozart, W.A.:Requiem, w. I. Seefried (sop), J. Tourel (mez), L. Simoneau (ten), B. Walter (cnd), New York PO *(rec 1956)* Historical Performers ▲ HPS 12 [ADD]
Stravinsky, I.:L'Histoire du soldat (sels), w. I. Hobson (cnd), Sinfonia da Camera [E] *(rec Feb. 1992)* Arabesque ▲ Z 6644

1468 ▲ = CD ♦ = Enhanced CD Δ = MD ■ = Cassette Tape ☐ = DCC

Warfield, William (nar)
Still, W.G.:Music of, w. Yolanda Williams (sop), Hilda Harris (alt), P. Brunelle (cnd), Plymouth Music Series Orch, Plymouth Music Series Chorus, Leigh Morris Chorale—Wailing Woman; Swanee River; And They Lynched Him on a Tree; Miss Sally's Party Collins Classics ▲ COL 1454
Walton, W.:Façade, w. I. Hobson (cnd), Sinfonia da Camera [E] *(rec Feb. 1992)* Arabesque ▲ Z 6644

Warren, L. Ann (sgr)
Mancini, H.:Victor/Victoria, w. J. Andrews (sgr), R. Preston (sgr) GNP Crescendo ▲ GNPD 8038

Warren, Leonard (bar)
His First Recordings (1940), w. Wilfrid Pelletier (cnd) *(rec Town Hall, New York City and Academy of Music, Philadelphia, May-June 1940)* VAI Audio ▲ VAIA 1017 (m) [ADD]
Leoncavallo, R.:Pagliacci, w. V. de los Angeles (sop), J. Björling (ten), R. Merrill (bar), R. Cellini (cnd), Columbus Orch, Robert Shaw Chorale EMI Classics ▲ ZDC 49503
Live Performances 1945-1959, w. Firestone Orch [cnd:Howard Barlow, unless otherwise stated] Memories 2-▲ MEM 4460 (m) [ADD]
Live Radio Broadcasts (1940-1958) Legato Classics ("Biographies in Music" series) ▲ BIM 707-1 (m)
On Tour in Russia, w. William Sektberg (pno) RCA Gold Seal ▲ 7807-2-RG (m) [ADD]
Ponchielli, A.:La Gioconda, w. Zinka Milanov (sop—La Gioconda), Rosalind Elias (mez—Laura), Belen Amparan (cta—La Cieca), Giacomo Cottino (ten—Isepo), Giuseppe Di Stefano (ten—Enzo Grimaldo), Fernando Valentini (bar—Zuane/Un Nocchiero), Leonard Warren (bar—Barnaba), Virgilio Carbonari (bass—Un Cantore), Plinio Clabassi (bass—Alvise Badoero), F. Previtali (cnd), St. Cecilia Academy Orch Rome, St. Cecilia Academy Chorus Rome Theorema 3-▲ TH 121182/184
Puccini, G.:Tosca, w. Z. Milanov (sop), J. Björling (ten), E. Leinsdorf (cnd), Rome Opera Orch, Rome Opera Chorus [I] RCA Gold Seal 2-▲ 4514-2-RG [ADD] 2-■ 4514-2-RG
Puccini, G.:Tosca (sels), w. Z. Milanov (sop), J. Björling (ten), E. Leinsdorf (cnd), Rome Opera Orch, Rome Opera Chorus RCA Gold Seal ▲ 60192-2-RG [ADD] ■ 60192-4-RG (CrO2)
Recital, 1941-1947 Myto ▲ MCD 935.93
Verdi, G.:Aida, w. Z. Milanov (sop), F. Barbieri (mez), J. Björling (ten), B. Christoff (bass), J. Perlea (cnd), Rome Opera Orch, Rome Opera Chorus [I] RCA Gold Seal ▲ 60201-2-RG (m) [ADD] ■ 60201-4-RG (m)
Verdi, G.:Aida, w. Z. Milanov (sop), F. Barbieri (mez), J. Björling (ten), B. Christoff (bass), J. Perlea (cnd), Rome Opera Orch, Rome Opera Chorus [I] RCA Gold Seal 3-▲ 6652-2-RG (m) [ADD] 3-■ ALK3-5380 (m)
Verdi, G.:Aida (sels), w. Rose Bampton (sop), Lydia Summers (mez), Arthur Carron (ten), W. Pelletier (cnd), Philadelphia studio musicians, New York studio musicians—Ritorna vincitor!; Rivedrai le foreste imbalsamate; Odimi, Aida; La fatal pietra...O terra, addio! *(rec Academy of Music, Philadelphia & Town Hall, New York, May 30 & June 17, 1940)* VAI Audio ▲ VAIA 1084
Verdi, G.:Arias—8 arias *(rec 1940)* VAI Audio ▲ VAIA 1017 (m) [ADD]
Verdi, G.:Un ballo in maschera, w. Zinka Milanov (sop), Jan Peerce (ten), B. Walter (cnd), *(orch unknown) (rec Jan 15, 1944)* Enterprise ("The Fourties" series) 2-▲ ENT 311
Verdi, G.:Falstaff, w. Vivian Della Chiesa (sop—Alice), Audrey Schuh (sop—Nannetta), Lizabeth Pritchett (mez—Quickly), Evelyn Sachs (mez—Meg), André Turp (ten—Fenton), Virginio Assandri (ten—Caius), Luigi Vellucci (ten—Bardolfo), Leonard Warren (bar—Falstaff), Richard Torigi (bar—Ford), R. Cellini (cnd), New Orleans Opera Orch, New Orleans Opera Chorus *(rec live, May 5, 1956)* VAI Audio 2-▲ VAIA 1056-2
Verdi, G.:La forza del destino, w. Zinka Milanov (sop), Rosalind Elias (mez), Giuseppe Di Stefano (ten), Giorgio Tozzi (bass), Paolo Washington (bass), F. Previtali (cnd), St. Cecilia Academy Orch Rome, St. Cecilia Academy Chorus Rome *(rec 1959)* Theorema 3-▲ TH 121157/59
Verdi, G.:La forza del destino, w. Z. Milanov (sop), M. Del Monaco (ten), G. Pechner (bar), W. Wildermann (bass), W. Herbert (cnd), *(orch unknown) (rec live 1953)* Legato Classics 2-▲ LCD 118-2 (m) [AAD]
Verdi, G.:La forza del destino, w. Zinka Milanov (sop—Donna Leonora di Vargas), Rosalind Elias (mez—Preziosilla), Luisa Gioia (sgr—Curra), Angelo Mercuriali (ten—Trabuco), Giuseppe di Stefano (ten—Son Alvaro), Leonard Warren (bar—Don Carlos di Vargas), Giorgio Tozzi (b-bar—Padre guardiano), Dino Mantovani (bar—Fra Melitone), Paolo Washington (b-bar—Il marchese di Calatrava), Virgilio Carbonari (b-bar—un alcalde), Sergio Liviabella (sgr—un chirurgo), F. Previtali (cnd), St. Cecilia Academy Orch Rome, St. Cecilia Academy Chorus Rome [I] London ▲ 443678-2 [ADD]
Verdi, G.:Macbeth, w. L. Rysanek (sop), C. Bergonzi (ten), J. Hines (bass), E. Leinsdorf (cnd), Metropolitan Opera Orch, New York Metropolitan Opera Chorus [I] RCA Gold Seal 2-▲ 4516-2-RG [ADD]
Verdi, G.:Otello, w. R. Tebaldi (sop), M. del Monaco (ten), A. Votto (cnd), La Scala Orch, La Scala Chorus *(rec July 1, 1954)* Melodram 2-▲ MLO 270101 [AAD]
Verdi, G.:Rigoletto (act 4), w. Z. Milanov (sop), N. Merriman (mez), J. Peerce (ten), A. Toscanini (cnd), NBC SO RCA Gold Seal ▲ 60276-2-RG [ADD] ■ 60276-4-RG (CrO2)
Verdi, G.:Simon Boccanegra (sels), w. Celia Garcia (sop—Maria Boccanegra), Mario Filippeschi (ten—Gabriele Adorno), Ignacio Ruffino (ten—Pietro), Leonard Warren (bar—Simon Boccanegra), Roberto Silva (bass—Jacopo Fiesco), Carlo Morelli (bass—Paolo), R. Cellini (cnd), Mexican National Opera Orch, Mexican National Opera Chorus *(rec Palacio de las Bellas Artes, Mexico City, July 4, 1950)* Legato Classics ▲ LCD 185-1 [ADD]
Verdi, G.:Il trovatore, w. M. Callas (sop), G. Simionato (mez), K. Baum (ten), G. Picco (cnd), Palacio Bellas Artes Orch, Palacio Bellas Artes Chorus *(rec live, Mexico City 6/20/50)* Melodram 2-▲ CDM 26017
Verdi, G.:Il trovatore, w. Z. Milanov (sop), F. Barbieri (mez), J. Björling (ten), R. Cellini (cnd), RCA Victor SO, Robert Shaw Chorale [I] RCA Gold Seal 2-▲ 6643-2-RG (m) [ADD] 2-■ CLK2-5377 (m)
Verdi, G.:Il trovatore, w. Z. Milanov (sop), F. Barbieri (mez), J. Björling (ten), R. Cellini (cnd), RCA Victor SO, Robert Shaw Chorale [I] RCA Gold Seal ▲ 60191-2-RG [ADD] ■ 60191-4-RG (CrO2)
Verdi, G.:Il trovatore, w. L. Price (sop), R. Elias (mez), G. Tucker (ten), G. Tozzi (bass), A. Basile (cnd), Rome Opera Orch RCA Gold Seal 2-▲ 60560-2-RG [ADD] 2-■ 60560-4-RG (CrO2)
Verdi, G.:Il trovatore (sels), w. M. Callas (sop), Feuss (sgr), C. Sagarminaga (ten), K. Baum (ten), G. Picco (cnd), Palacio Bellas Artes Orch, Palacio Bellas Artes Chorus—ten selections from Acts 1 & 4 [I] *(rec live, Mexico City 6/20/50)* Myto 2-▲ 2 MCD 90213 (m) [ADD]

Warwick, Dionne (sgr)
Plácido Domingo:The Best of Christmas in Vienna, w. Plácido Domingo (ten), José Carreras (ten), Charles Aznavour, Sissel Kyrkjebø, Vienna SO [cnd:Vjekoslav Sutej] *(rec Vienna)* Sony Classical ▲ SK 62696 ■ ST 62696

Warwitz, Manuel (ten)
Monteverdi, C.:Vespers, w. Susanne Ryden (sop), Irena Troupova-Wilke (sop), Detlef Bratschke (alt), Erich Mentzel (ten), Hermann Oswald (ten), Thomas Herberich (bass), Günther Schmidt (bass), H. Arman (cnd), Schütz Academy Capriccio ▲ CD 10521 [DDD]

Washington, Paolo (bass)
Donizetti, G.:Lucia di Lammermoor, w. R. Scotto (sop), A. Kraus (ten), Sesto Bruscantini (bass-bar), B. Rigacci (cnd), *(orch unknown) (rec 1963)* Great Opera Performances 2-▲ GOP 747
Donizetti, G.:Requiem Mass, w. L. Pavarotti (ten), M. Cortez (ten), R. Bruson (bar), G. Fackler (cnd), Arena di Verona Orch, Arena di Verona Chorus London ("Ovation" series) ▲ 425043-2 [ADD]
Mercadante, S.:Il bravo, w. Miwako Matsumoto (sop—Violetta), Giovanna di Rocco (sop—Michelina), William Johns (ten—Il Bravo), Antonio Savastano (ten—Pisani), Gino Sinimberghi (ten—Cappello), Loris Gambelli (bass—Marco), Mario Machì (bass—Luigi), Paolo Washington (bass—Foscari), Maria Parazzini (sgr—Teodora), G. Ferro (cnd), Rome Opera Orch, Rome Opera Chorus *(rec Rome, Dec 30, 1976)* Italia 3-▲ CDC 94 [ADD]
Puccini, G.:La Bohème, w. Ileana Cotrubas (sop—Mimì), Margherita Guglielmi (sop—Musetta), José Carreras (ten—Rodolfo), Saverio Porzano (ten—Parpignol), Regolo Romani (ten—Vendor), Claudio Giombi (bar—Benoit), Gianni Maffeo (bar—Schaunard), Angelo Romero (bar—Marcello), Alfredo Giacomotti (bass—Alcindoro), Carlo Meliciani (bass—Customs Officer), Giuseppe Morresi (bass—Sergeant), Paolo Washington (bass—Colline), G. Prêtre (cnd), La Scala Orch, La Scala Chorus *(rec Washington D.C., Sept 8, 1976)* Legato Classics 2-▲ LCD 201-2
Rossini, G.:La donna del lago, w. A. Balboni (sop), M. Caballé (sop), J. Hamari (mez), F. Bonisolli (ten), R. Bottazzo (ten), G. Sinimberghi (ten), P. Bellugi (cnd), Turin RAI Orch, Turin RAI Chorus *(rec live, Torino, 1970)* Foyer 2-▲ FOY 2028 [AAD]

Washington, Paolo (bass) (cont.)
Rossini, G.:Zelmira, w. Virginia Zeani (sop), Anna Maria Rota (cta), Enrico Campi (bass), Guido Mazzini (bass), Gastone Limarilli (sgr), Giuseppe Moretti (sgr), Nicola Tagger (sgr), C. Franci (cnd), *(orch unknown)* Great Opera Performances 2-▲ GOP 780
Verdi, G.:La forza del destino, w. Zinka Milanov (sop—Donna Leonora di Vargas), Rosalind Elias (mez—Preziosilla), Luisa Gioia (sgr—Curra), Angelo Mercuriali (ten—Trabuco), Giuseppe di Stefano (ten—Son Alvaro), Leonard Warren (bar—Don Carlos di Vargas), Giorgio Tozzi (b-bar—Padre guardiano), Dino Mantovani (bar—Fra Melitone), Paolo Washington (b-bar—Il marchese di Calatrava), Virgilio Carbonari (b-bar—un alcalde), Sergio Liviabella (sgr—un chirurgo), F. Previtali (cnd), St. Cecilia Academy Orch Rome, St. Cecilia Academy Chorus Rome [I] London ▲ 443678-2 [ADD]
Verdi, G.:La forza del destino, w. Zinka Milanov (sop), Rosalind Elias (mez), Giuseppe Di Stefano (ten), Leonard Warren (bar), Giorgio Tozzi (bass), F. Previtali (cnd), St. Cecilia Academy Orch Rome, St. Cecilia Academy Chorus Rome *(rec 1959)* Theorema 3-▲ TH 121157/59
Verdi, G.:Rigoletto (sels), w. Renata Scotto (sop—Gilda), Corinna Vozza (mez—Giovanna), Bianca Vortoluzzi (cta—Maddalena), Luciano Pavarotti (ten—Duke of Mantua), Kostas Paskalis (bar—Rigoletto), Paolo Washington (bass—Sparafucile), C. M. Guilini (cnd), Rome Opera Orch, Rome Opera Chorus Budget ("The Greatest Voice in Opera" series) ▲ SYP 104

Waters, Susannah (sop)
Purcell, H.:Dido & Aeneas, w. Nancy Maultsby (sop—Dido), Susannah Waters (sop—Belinda), Margaret O'Keefe (sop—1st Witch), Sharon Baker (sop—2nd Woman), Laura Tucker (mez—Sorceress), Donna Ames (alt—Spirit), Richard Clement (ten—Sailor), Russell Braun (bar—Aeneas), M. Pearlman (cnd), Boston Baroque Orch Telarc ▲ CD 80424 [DDD]

Watkinson, Carolyn (cta)
Bach, J.S.:Cants (misc), w. Edith Mathis (sop), Eberhard Büchner (ten), Peter Schreier (ten), Siegfried Lorenz (bar), Theo Adam (b-bar), P. Schreier (cnd), Berlin CO, Berlin Soloists Berlin Classics ▲ BER 9221
Bach, J.S.:Cant 5, w. A. Augér (sop), A. Baldin (ten), W. Schöne (bass), H. Rilling (cnd), Stuttgart Bach Collegium, Gächinger Kantorei [G] *(rec Feb & Oct 1979)* Hänssler Classic ▲ 98.816 [AAD]
Bach, J.S.:Cant 37, w. A. Augér (sop), A. Kraus (ten), P. Huttenlocher (bar), H. Rilling (cnd), Stuttgart Bach Collegium, Gächinger Kantorei [G] *(rec 1979)* Hänssler Classic ▲ 98.886 [AAD]
Bach, J.S.:Cant 146, w. P. Schreier (ten), P. Huttenlocher (bass), H. Rilling (cnd), Stuttgart Bach Collegium, Gächinger Kantorei [G] *(rec 1973)* Hänssler Classic ▲ 98.884 [AAD]
Bach, J.S.:Cant 169, w. H. Rilling (cnd), Württemberg CO, Gächinger Kantorei [G] *(rec 1983)* Hänssler Classic ▲ 98.815 [AAD]
Bach, J.S.:Cant 176, w. I. Nielsen (sop), W. Hedwein (bass), H. Rilling (cnd), Stuttgart Bach Collegium, Gächinger Kantorei Hänssler Classic ▲ 98.801 [AAD]
Bach, J.S.:Cant 180, w. A. Augér (sop), A. Kraus (ten), W. Heldwein (sop), H. Rilling (cnd), Stuttgart Bach Collegium, Gächinger Kantorei [G] *(rec Feb & Oct 1979)* Hänssler Classic ▲ 98.816 [AAD]
Bach, J.S.:Cant 205, w. Edith Mathis (sop), Julia Hamari (alt), Peter Schreier (ten), Siegfried Lorenz (bass), P. Schreier (cnd), Berlin CO, Berlin Soloists Berlin Classics ▲ BER 9224
Bach, J.S.:Cant 206, w. Edith Mathis (sop), Peter Schreier (ten), Siegfried Lorenz (bass), P. Schreier (cnd), Berlin CO, Berlin Soloists Berlin Classics ▲ BER CD 9225
Bach, J.S.:Cant 207, w. Edith Mathis (sop), Julia Hamari (alt), Peter Schreier (ten), Siegfried Lorenz (bass), P. Schreier (cnd), Berlin CO, Berlin Soloists Berlin Classics ▲ BER 9224
Bach, J.S.:Cant 215, w. Edith Mathis (sop), Peter Schreier (ten), Siegfried Lorenz (bass), P. Schreier (cnd), Berlin CO, Berlin Soloists Berlin Classics ▲ BER CD 9225
Bach, J.S.:Christmas Oratorio, w. B. Schlick (sop), K. Equiluz (ten), M. Brodard (bar), M. Corboz (cnd), Lausanne CO Erato ▲ 2292-45865-2
Bach, J.S.:Magnificat, BWV 243, w. E. Kirkby (sop), J. Nelson (sop), P. Elliott (ten), D. Thomas (bass), S. Preston (cnd), Academy of Ancient Music, Christ Church Cathedral Choir Oxford [E♭ version; L] L'Oiseau-Lyre ▲ 414678-2 [ADD]
Bach, J.S.:St. Matthew Passion, w. M. Marshall (sop), K. Equiluz (ten), G. Faulstisch (bar), P. Huttenlocher (bar), R. Johnson (bar), M. Corboz (cnd), Lausanne CO, Lausanne Vocal Ensemble Erato 3-▲ 2292-45375-2 GX
Beethoven, L. van:Missa Solemnis, w. M. Hirsti (sop), A. Murgatroyd (ten), M. George (bass), T. Kvam (cnd), Hanover Band, Oslo Cathedral Choir [period instrs] [L] Nimbus ▲ NI 5109 [DDD]
Beethoven, L. van:Syms (comp), w. B. , P. Schreier (tenor)(te, B. Haitink (cnd), Royal Concertgebouw Orch—[R. Holl (bass) in No. 9] Philips 5-▲ 442073-2
Handel, G.F.:Messiah, w. Emma Kirkby (sop), Judith Nelson (mez), Paul Elliott (ten), David Thomas (bass), C. Hogwood (cnd), Academy of Ancient Music London 2-▲ 430488-2 [DDD]
Handel, G.F.:Rinaldo, w. Sophie Boulin (sop—Donna), Ileana Cotrubas (sop—Almirena), Marie-Françoise Jacquelin (sop—Sirene), Nicole Leport (sop—Sirene), Jeanette Scovotti (sop—Armida), Carolyn Watkinson (cta—Rinaldo), Charles Brett (ct—Eustazio), Paul Esswood (ct—Goffredo), Armand Arapian (ten—Mago Christiano/Araldo), Ulrik Cold (bass—Argante), J. Malgoire (cnd), La Grande Écurie et la Chambre du Roy *(rec Paris, 1977)* Sony Classical 3-▲ SM3K 34592
Handel, G.F.:Serse, w. Barbara Hendricks (sop—Romilda), Anne-Marie Rodde (sop—Atalanta), Carolyn Watkinson (cta—Xerxes), Otrun Wenkel (cta—Amastre), Paul Esswood (ct—Arsamene), Ulrich Studer (bar—Elviro), Ulrik Cold (bass—Ariodate), J. Malgoire (cnd), La Grande Écurie et la Chambre du Roy *(rec Paris, 1979)* Sony Classical 3-▲ SM3K 36941
Handel, G.F.:Solomon, w. Nancy Argenta (sop), Barbara Hendricks (sop), Anthony Rolfe Johnson (ct), J. E. Gardiner (cnd), English Baroque Soloists, Monteverdi Choir London [E] Philips 2-▲ 412612-2 [DDD]
Haydn, J.:Arianna a Naxos, w. Glen Wilson (hpd) [I] *(rec 6/90)* Virgin Classics ▲ 59033 [DDD]
Haydn, J.:Canzonettas, w. Glen Wilson (hpd)—Nos. 25, 27-32, 36, 41, 42 [E] *(rec June 1990)* Virgin Classics ▲ 59033 [DDD]
Haydn, J.:Mass 11, "Nelsonmesse", "Imperial Mass", "Coronation Mass", w. Felicity Lott (sop), Maldwyn Davies (ten), David Wilson-Johnson (bar), T. Pinnock (cnd), English CO [L] Archiv ▲ 423097-2 [DDD]
Mendelssohn, F.:Athalie, w. Danielle Borst (sop), Brigitte Desnoues (sop), Jean-Marc Avocat (sgr), Souad Natech (sgr), B. Tetu (cnd), Lorraine PO, Lyon National Chorus Koch Schwann ▲ SCH 314282 [DDD]
Mozart, W.A.:Requiem, w. B. Schlick (sop), C. Prégardien (ten), H. van der Kamp (bass), T. Koopman (cnd), Amsterdam Baroque Orch, Netherlands Bach Society Choir [L] Erato ▲ 2292-45472-2 [DDD] ■ 2292-45472-4
Mozart, W.A.:Requiem, w. S. McNair (sop), F. Araiza (ten), R. Lloyd (b-bar), N. Marriner (cnd), Academy of St. Martin in the Fields, Academy Chorus [L] Philips ▲ 432087-2 [DDD]
Mozart, W.A.:Requiem, w. A. Augér (sop), S. Jerusalem (ten), S. Nimsgern (b-bar), H. Rilling (cnd), Stuttgart Bach Ensemble, Gächinger Kantorei [L] Odyssey ▲ MBK 42614 ■ YT 42614
Purcell, H.:Dido & Aeneas, w. Ruth Holton (sop—Belinda), Elisabeth Priday (sop—2nd Woman), Donna Deam (sop—1st Witch), Shauna Beesley (sop—2nd Witch), Teresa Shaw (mez—Sorceress), Carolyn Watkinson (cta—Dido), Jonathan Peter Kenny (alt—Spirit), Paul Tindall (ten—Sailor), George Mosley (bass—Aeneas), J.E. Gardiner (cnd), English Baroque Soloists, Monteverdi Choir London *(rec Saint George's, Bristol, UK, July 12-14, 1990)* Philips ▲ 432114-2
Schmidt, F.:Das Buch mit sieben Siegeln, w. Sylvia Greenberg (sop), Peter Schreier (ten), Thomas Moser (ten), Robert Holl (bass), Kurt Rydl (bass), L. Zagrosek (cnd), Austrian RSO, Vienna State Opera Chorus [G] Orfeo 2-▲ 143862 [DDD]
Vivaldi, A.:Beatus vir (Psalm 111), w. M. Burgess (sop), J. Chamonin (sop), J.-C. Malgoire (cnd), La Grande Écurie et la Chambre du Roy, Raphaël Passaquet Vocal Ensemble *(rec 1976)* Sony Classical ("Essential Classics" series) ▲ SBK 48280 [ADD] ■ SBT 48280
Vivaldi, A.:Gloria, RV.589, w. J. Nelson (sop), E. Kirkby (sop), P. Elliott (ten), D. Thomas (bass), S. Preston (cnd), Academy of Ancient Music, Christ Church Cathedral Choir Oxford [L] L'Oiseau-Lyre ▲ 414678-2 [ADD]
Vivaldi, A.:Gloria, RV.589, w. M. Burgess (sop), Jocelyne Chamonine (sop), J.-C. Malgoire (cnd), La Grande Écurie et la Chambre du Roy, Raphaël Passaquet Vocal Ensemble *(rec 1976)* Sony Classical ("Essential Classics" series) ▲ SBK 48280 [ADD] ■ SBT 48280

Watson (sgr)
Handel, G.F.:Israel in Egypt, w. Elizabeth Gale (sop), James Bowman (alt), Ian Partridge (ten), Tom McDonnell (bar), Alan Watt (bass), S. Preston (cnd), English CO, Christ Church Cathedral Choir Oxford London ("Jubilee" series) 2-▲ 421602-2 [ADD]

Watson (sgr) (cont.)

Saint-Saëns, C.:Requiem, w. Hewes (sgr), Weld (sgr), MacMaster (sgr), J. Somary (cnd), Amor Artis Orch, Amor Artis Chorale *(rec live)* Premier ▲ PRCD 1025 [DDD]

Watson (sop)

Handel, G.F.:Alessandro, w. L. Atkinson (trb), A. Terzian (mez), B. J. Rieders (cta), T. Poole (ten), D. Price (ten), Andersson (sgr), M. Nowakowski (cnd), Sinfonia Varsovia [I] *(rec live)* Koch Schwann 3-▲ CD SC 100 303 [DDD]

Watson, Carolyn (cta)

Mozart, W.A.:Così fan tutte, w. Carol Vaness (sop), Delores Ziegler (mez), J. Aler (ten), D. Duesing (bar), C. Desderi (bar), B. Haitink (cnd), London PO, Glyndebourne Festival Chorus EMI Classics 3-▲ CDCC 47727

Mozart, W.A.:Entführung, w. Yvonne Kenny (sop), Peter Schreier (ten), Wilfried Gamlich (ten), Matti Salminen (bass), Wolfgang Reichmann (nar), N. Harnoncourt (cnd), Zurich Mozart Opera Orch, Zurich Mozart Opera Chorus [G] Teldec 2-▲ 2292-42643-2

Watson, Claire (sop)

Britten, H.:Peter Grimes, w. P. Pears (ten), G. Evans (bar), B. Britten (cnd), Royal Opera House Orch, Royal Opera House Chorus Covent Garden [E] London 3-▲ 414577-2 [ADD]

Mozart, W.A.:Don Giovanni, w. C. Ludwig (mez), N. Gedda (ten), N. Ghiaurov (bass), O. Klemperer (cnd), New Philharmonia Orch, New Philharmonia Chorus EMI Classics 3-▲ CDMC 63841

Strauss, R.:Der Rosenkavalier, w. Erika Köth (sop—Sophie), Annelie Waas (sop—Marianne), Claire Watson (sop—Marschallin), Hertha Töpper (mez—Octavian), Brigitte Fassbaender (cta—Annina), Gerhard Stolze (ten—Valzacchi), Fritz Wunderlich (ten—Singer), Otto Wiener (bar—Faninal), Kurt Böhme (bass—Baron), J. Keilberth (cnd), Bavarian State Opera Orch, Bavarian State Opera Chorus *(rec Munich Opera Festival, National Theater, May 21, 1965)* Orfeo d'or 3-▲ 425963

Strauss, R.:Der Rosenkavalier, w. B. Fassbaender (mez), K. Ridderbusch (bass), C. Kleiber (cnd), Bavarian State Opera Orch *(rec 1977)* Exclusive 3-▲ EXL 49 [ADD]

Strauss, R.:Der Rosenkavalier, w. Claire Watson (sop—Feldmarschallin), Lucia Popp (sop—Sophie), Annelie Waas (sop—Marianne), Brigitte Fassbaender (mez—Octavian), Margaretthe Bence (ct—Annina), David Thaw (ten—Valzacchi), Karl Ridderbusch (bass—Baron Ochs), Benno Kusche (bass—Herr von Faninal), Albrecht Peter (bass—Police Inspector), C. Kleiber (cnd), Bavarian State Orch, Bavarian State Chorus *(rec live, Münchner Festspiele, July 20, 1974)* Arkadia 3-▲ 486 [ADD]

Wagner, R.:Der Ring des Nibelungen, w. B. Nilsson (sop), K. Flagstad (sop), R. Crespin (sop), C. Ludwig (mez), J. Madeira (mez), S. Svanholm (ten), J. King (ten), G. Stolze (ten), W. Windgassen (ten), G. London (bar), D. Fischer-Dieskau (bar), H. Hotter (b-bar), G. Neidlinger (b-bar), G. Frick (bass), G. Solti (cnd), Vienna PO [G] London 15-▲ 414100-2 [ADD]

Watson, Janice (sop)

Beethoven, L. van:Ah, perfido!, w. M. Best (cnd), Corydon Orch—aria only Hyperion ▲ CDA 66830

Beethoven, L. van:Mass, Op. 86, w. Jean Rigby (mez), John Mark Ainsley (ten), Gwynne Howell (bass), M. Best (cnd), Corydon Orch, Corydon Singers Hyperion ▲ CDA 66830

Beethoven, L. van:Ne' giorni tuoi felici, w. John Mark Ainsley (ten), M. Best (cnd), Corydon Orch Hyperion ▲ CDA 66830

Beethoven, L. van:Tremate, empi, tremate, w. Gwynne Howell (bass), M. Best (cnd), Corydon Orch Hyperion ▲ CDA 66830

Haydn, J.:Mass 12, "Theresienmesse", w. Pamela Helen Stephen (mez), Mark Padmore (ten), Stephen Varcoe (bass), R. Hickox (cnd), Collegium Musicum 90 Chandos ▲ CHAN 0592

Howells, H.:Missa sabrinensis, w. Della Jones (cta), Martyn Hill (ten), Donald Maxwell (bar), G. Rozhdestvensky (cnd), London SO, London Sym Chorus Chandos ▲ CHAN 9348 [DDD]

Lloyd, G.:John Socman (sels), w. D. Montague (mez), T. Booth (ten), D. Wilson-Johnson (bar), M. Rivers (bar), M. George (bass), G. Lloyd (cnd), Philharmonia Orch, London Voices Albany ▲ TROY 131 [DDD]

Lloyd, G.:A Litany, w. Jeremy White (bar), G. Lloyd (cnd), Philharmonia Orch, Guildford Choral Society *(rec Watford Town Hall, Mar 24–25, 1996)* Albany ▲ TROY 200 [DDD]

Maccunn, H.:The Dowie Dens o'Yarrow, w. Lisa Milne (sop), Jamie MacDougall (ten), Peter Sidhom (bar), Stephen Gadd (bass), M. Brabbins (cnd), BBC Scottish SO, Scottish Opera Chorus Hyperion ▲ CDA 66815

Maccunn, H.:Jeanie Deans (sels), w. Lisa Milne (sop), Jamie MacDougall (ten), Peter Sidhom (bar), Stephen Gadd (bass), M. Brabbins (cnd), BBC Scottish SO, Scottish Opera Chorus Hyperion ▲ CDA 66815

Maccunn, H.:Lay of Last Minstrel, w. Lisa Milne (sop), Jamie MacDougall (ten), Peter Sidhom (bar), Stephen Gadd (bass), M. Brabbins (cnd), BBC Scottish SO, Scottish Opera Chorus Hyperion ▲ CDA 66815

Maccunn, H.:Ship o' the Fiend, w. Lisa Milne (sop), Jamie MacDougall (ten), Peter Sidhom (bar), Stephen Gadd (bass), M. Brabbins (cnd), BBC Scottish SO, Scottish Opera Chorus Hyperion ▲ CDA 66815

Mendelssohn, F.:A Midsummer Night's Dream (comp), w. Delia Wallis (mez), A. Previn (cnd), London SO, London Sym Chorus [E] EMI Classics ▲ CDC 47163

Poulenc, F.:Gloria Sop, w. Y. P. Tortelier (cnd), BBC PO, BBC Singers Chandos ▲ CHAN 9341 [DDD]

Poulenc, F.:Stabat mater, w. Y. P. Tortelier (cnd), BBC PO, BBC Singers Chandos ▲ CHAN 9341 [DDD]

Sullivan, A.:The Mikado, w. M. McLaughlin (sop), A. Howells (mez), F. Palmer (sop/mez), D. Adams (bass), A. Rolfe Johnson (ten), R. Stuart (bar), R. Van Allan (bass), N. Folwell (bar), C. Mackerras (cnd), Welsh National Opera Orch, Welsh National Opera Chorus—Ov & dialogue omitted [E] Telarc ▲ CD 80284 [DDD]; ■ CS 30284 (D)

Wagner, R.:Götterdämmerung, w. B. Nilsson (sop), C. Ludwig (mez), W. Windgassen (ten), D. Fischer-Dieskau (bar), G. Frick (bass), G. Solti (cnd), Vienna PO [G] London 4-▲ 414115-2 [ADD]

Watson, Jean (cta)

Bach, J.S.:St. Matthew Passion, w. Nadine Conner (sop), William Hain (ten), Mack Harrell (bar), Herbert Janssen (bar), Lorenzo Alvary (bass), B. Walter (cnd), New York PO, New York Phil Chorus—Part I Minerva ▲ 20

Watson, Laurelyn (sgr)

Rorem, N.:Miss Julie, w. Theodora Fried (sgr—Miss Julie), Heather Sarris (sgr—Christine, the cook), Laurelyn Watson (sgr—Young Girl), David Blackburn (sgr—Mr. Niels), Mark Mulligan (sgr—Young Boy), Philip Torre (sgr—John, the valet), Judd Ernster (bass), D. Gilbert (cnd), Manhattan School of Music Opera Orch, Manhattan School of Music Opera Chorus Newport Classic 2-▲ NPT 85605 [DDD]

Watson, Lilian (sop)

Donizetti, G.:L'elisir d'amore, w. I. Cotrubas (sop), P. Domingo (ten), G. Evans (bar), I. Wixell (bar), J. Pritchard (cnd), Royal Opera House Orch, Royal Opera House Chorus Covent Garden *(rec 1977)* CBS 2-▲ M2K 34585 [ADD]

Handel, G.F.:Israel in Egypt, w. Elizabeth Gale (sop), James Bowman (alt), Ian Partridge (ten), Tom McDonnell (bass), Alan Watt (bass), S. Preston (cnd), English CO, Christ Church Cathedral Choir Oxford *(rec Chapel of Merton College, Oxford, 1975)* London 2-▲ 443470-2 [ADD]

Janácek, L.:The Cunning Little Vixen, w. E. Bainbridge (mez), G. Knight (mez), D. Montague (mez), J. Dobson (ten), R. Tear (ten), T. Allen (bar), G. Howell (bass), S. Rattle (cnd), Royal Opera House Orch [E] EMI Classics 2-▲ CDCB 54212

Watson, Nathaniel (bass)

Bach, J.S.:St. John Passion, w. Tamara Matthews (sop), Jennifer Lane (alt), Mark Bleeke (ten—Evangelist), David Vanderwal (ten), Kevin Walsh (bar—Pilate), Nathaniel Watson (bass—Jesus), E. Milnes (cnd), Trinity Baroque Orch, Trinity Cathedral Choir *(rec Trinity Cathedral, Portland, OR, Mar 31, 1996)* PGM 2-▲ PGM 111

Handel, G.F.:Sosarme, Rè di Media, w. Julinne Baird (sop—Elmira), D'Anna Fortunato (mez—Sosarme), Jennifer Lane (mez—Erenice), Drew Minter (ct—Melo), Rarmond Pellerin (ct—Argone), John Aler (ten—King Haliate), Nathaniel Watson (bass—Varo), Edward Brewer (hpd) Newport Classic 2-▲ NPT 85575 [DDD]

Watson, Nicholas (bar)

Barber, S.:Dover Beach, w. Alexander String Quartet *(rec July 1992)* Analekta ▲ CLCD 2009

Gershwin, G.:Lullaby, w. Alexander String Quartet *(rec July 1992)* Analekta ▲ CLCD 2009

Handel, G.F.:Ezio, w. Julianne Baird (sop—Fulvia), Jennifer Lane (mez—Onoria), D'Anna Fortunato (cta—Ezio), Raymond Pellerin (alt—Emperor), Frederick Urrey (ten—Massimo), Nathaniel Watson (bar—Varo), Johannes Somary (org), R.A. Clark (cnd), Manhattan CO *(rec St. Jean Baptiste Church, New York, Mar. 1994)* Vox Classics 2-▲ VOX 27503 [DDD]

Watson, Nicholas (bar) (cont.)

Imbrie, A.W.:Campion Songs, w. Joan Peterson (sop), Nancy Wertsch (alt), Mark Bleeke (ten), A. Korf (cnd), Parnassus *(rec Sept. 29, 1993)* New World ▲ 80441-2

Watt, Alan (bass)

Handel, G.F.:Israel in Egypt, w. Elizabeth Gale (sop), James Bowman (alt), Ian Partridge (ten), Tom McDonnell (bar), Watson (sgr), S. Preston (cnd), English CO, Christ Church Cathedral Choir Oxford London ("Jubilee" series) 2-▲ 421602-2 [ADD]

Handel, G.F.:Israel in Egypt, w. Elizabeth Gale (sop), Lillian Watson (sop), James Bowman (alt), Ian Partridge (ten), Tom McDonnell (bass), S. Preston (cnd), English CO, Christ Church Cathedral Choir Oxford *(rec Chapel of Merton College, Oxford, 1975)* London 2-▲ 443470-2 [ADD]

Watts, D. (bass)

Handel, G.F.:Judas Maccabaeus, w. Martina Arroyo (sop), Grace Bumbry (mez), J. McCollum (ten), Marvin Sorensen (ten), M. Abravanel (cnd), Utah SO, Utah Sym Chorus [E] *(rec ca. 1959; originally rele)* MCA Classics 3-▲ MCAD3-10515 [ADD]

Watts, Helen (cta)

Bach, C.P.E.:Magnificat, w. Jennifer Vyvyan (sop), Wilfred Brown (ten), Thomas Hemsley (bass), G. Jones (cnd), Geraint Jones Orch, Geraint Jones Singers EMI Classics ("Baroque" series) ▲ CDK 65737

Bach, C.P.E.:Magnificat, w. F. Palmer (sop), R. Tear (ten), S. Roberts (b-bar), P. Ledger (cnd), Academy of St. Martin in the Fields, King's College Choir Cambridge London ("Jubilee" series) ▲ 421148-2 [ADD]

Bach, J.S.:Cant 2, w. A. Baldin (ten), W. Heldwein (bass), H. Rilling (cnd), Stuttgart Bach Collegium, Gächinger Kantorei Hänssler Classic ▲ 98.801 [AAD]

Bach, J.S.:Cant 7, w. A. Kraus (ten), W. Schöne (bass), H. Rilling (cnd), Stuttgart Bach Collegium, Gächinger Kantorei Hänssler Classic ▲ 98.802 [AAD]

Bach, J.S.:Cant 8, w. A. Augér (sop), A. Kraus (ten), P. Huttenlocher (bar), H. Rilling (cnd), Stuttgart Bach Collegium, Gächinger Kantorei [G] *(rec 1979)* Hänssler Classic ▲ 98.813 [AAD]

Bach, J.S.:Cant 23, w. A. Augér (sop), A. Baldin (ten), N. Tütler (bass), H. Rilling (cnd), Stuttgart Bach Collegium, Gächinger Kantorei [G] *(rec 1977)* Hänssler Classic ▲ 98.879 [AAD]

Bach, J.S.:Cant 24, w. A. Augér (sop), K. Pugh (cta), A. Kraus (ten), W. Heldwein (bass), W. Schöne (bass), H. Rilling (cnd), Stuttgart Bach Collegium, Gächinger Kantorei Hänssler Classic ▲ 98.803 [AAD]

Bach, J.S.:Cant 27, w. R. Hansmann (sop), K. Equiluz (ten), M. Van Egmond (b-bar), J. Jürgens (cnd), Concerto Amsterdam, Monteverdi Choir London Teldec (Das alte Werke) ▲ 93687

Bach, J.S.:Cant 33, w. F. Lang (ten), P. Huttenlocher (bar), H. Rilling (cnd), Stuttgart Bach Collegium, Gächinger Kantorei Hänssler Classic ▲ 98.811 [AAD]

Bach, J.S.:Cant 34, w. A. Kraus (ten), W. Schöne (bass), Stuttgart Bach Collegium, Gächinger Kantorei Hänssler Classic ▲ 98.887 [AAD]

Bach, J.S.:Cant 38, w. A. Augér (sop), L.-M. Harder (ten), P. Huttenlocher (bar), H. Rilling (cnd), Stuttgart Bach Collegium, Gächinger Kantorei [G] *(rec Feb & Apr 1980)* Hänssler Classic ▲ 98.818 [AAD]

Bach, J.S.:Cant 44, w. A. Augér (sop), A. Baldin (ten), W. Schöne (bass), H. Rilling (cnd), Stuttgart Bach Collegium, Gächinger Kantorei [G] *(rec 1979)* Hänssler Classic ▲ 98.886 [AAD]

Bach, J.S.:Cant 46, w. A. Kraus (ten), W. Schöne (bass), H. Rilling (cnd), Stuttgart Bach Collegium, Gächinger Kantorei Hänssler Classic ▲ 98.808 [AAD]

Bach, J.S.:Cant 60, w. A. Kraus (ten), P. Huttenlocher (bar), H. Rilling (cnd), Stuttgart Bach Collegium, Gächinger Kantorei [G] *(rec 1977 & 1978)* Hänssler Classic ▲ 98.821 [AAD]

Bach, J.S.:Cant 62, w. I. Nielsen (sop), A. Baldin (ten), P. Huttenlocher (bar), H. Rilling (cnd), Stuttgart Bach Collegium, Gächinger Kantorei [G] *(rec Feb & Apr 1980)* Hänssler Classic ▲ 98.822 [AAD]

Bach, J.S.:Cant 67, w. W. Krenn (ten), T. Krause, E. Ansermet (cnd), Swiss Romande Orch, Lausanne Pro Arte Choir London ("Serenata" series) ▲ 433175-2 [ADD]

Bach, J.S.:Cant 83, w. A. Kraus (ten), W. Heldwein (bass), H. Rilling (cnd), Bach Ensemble [G] *(rec 1979)* Hänssler Classic ▲ 98.875 [AAD]

Bach, J.S.:Cant 86, w. A. Augér (mez), A. Kraus (ten), W. Heldwein (bass), H. Rilling (cnd), Stuttgart Bach Collegium, Gächinger Kantorei [G] *(rec 1979)* Hänssler Classic ▲ 98.885 [AAD]

Bach, J.S.:Cant 89, w. A. Augér (sop), P. Huttenlocher (bar), H. Rilling (cnd), Stuttgart Bach Collegium, Gächinger Kantorei [G] *(rec Sept & Dec 1977)* Hänssler Classic ▲ 98.818 [AAD]

Bach, J.S.:Cant 90, w. A. Kraus (ten), H. Rilling (cnd), Stuttgart Bach Collegium, Gächinger Kantorei [G] *(rec 1977 & 1978)* Hänssler Classic ▲ 98.821 [AAD]

Bach, J.S.:Cant 91, w. H. Donath (sop), A. Kraus (ten), W. Schöne (bass), H. Rilling (cnd), Stuttgart Bach Collegium, Württemberg CO, Gächinger Kantorei, Frankfurt Choir [G] *(rec Feb 1972)* Hänssler Classic ▲ 98.822 [AAD]

Bach, J.S.:Cant 92, w. A. Augér (sop), G. Schreckenbach (cta), A. Baldin (ten), P. Huttenlocher (bar), H. Rilling (cnd), Bach Ensemble [G] *(rec 1980)* Hänssler Classic ▲ 98.877 [AAD]

Bach, J.S.:Cant 99, w. A. Augér (sop), L.-M. Harder (ten), J. Bröcheler (bar), H. Rilling (cnd), Stuttgart Bach Collegium, Gächinger Kantorei [G] *(rec 1979)* Hänssler Classic ▲ 98.813 [AAD]

Bach, J.S.:Cant 101, w. A. Augér (sop), A. Baldin (ten), J. Bröcheler (bar), H. Rilling (cnd), Stuttgart Bach Collegium, Gächinger Kantorei Hänssler Classic ▲ 98.809 [AAD]

Bach, J.S.:Cant 115, w. A. Augér (sop), L.-M. Harder (ten), W. Schöne (bass), H. Rilling (cnd), Stuttgart Bach Collegium, Gächinger Kantorei [G] *(rec 1980)* Hänssler Classic ▲ 98.819 [AAD]

Bach, J.S.:Cant 116, w. A. Augér (sop), L.-M. Harder (ten), P. Huttenlocher (bar), H. Rilling (cnd), Stuttgart Bach Collegium, Gächinger Kantorei [G] *(rec 1980)* Hänssler Classic ▲ 98.820 [AAD]

Bach, J.S.:Cant 126, w. A. Kraus (ten), W. Schöne (bass), H. Rilling (cnd), Stuttgart Bach Collegium, Gächinger Kantorei [G] *(rec 1980)* Hänssler Classic ▲ 98.878 [AAD]

Bach, J.S.:Cant 130, w. E. Ameling (sop), W. Krenn (ten), T. Krause (bass), E. Ansermet (cnd), Swiss Romande Orch, Lausanne Pro Arte Choir London ("Serenata" series) ▲ 433175-2 [ADD]

Bach, J.S.:Cant 132, w. A. Augér (sop), K. Equiluz (ten), W. Schöne (bass), H. Rilling (cnd), Stuttgart Bach Collegium, Gächinger Kantorei [G] *(rec Sept 1976 & Jan & Apr 197)* Hänssler Classic ▲ 98.822 [AAD]

Bach, J.S.:Cant 135, w. A. Kraus (ten), P. Huttenlocher (bar), Stuttgart Bach Collegium, Gächinger Kantorei Hänssler Classic ▲ 98.802 [AAD]

Bach, J.S.:Cant 136, w. K. Equiluz (ten), N. Tüller (bass), H. Rilling (cnd), Stuttgart Bach Collegium, Gächinger Kantorei Hänssler Classic ▲ 98.806 [AAD]

Bach, J.S.:Cant 139, w. I. Nelson (sop), A. Kraus (ten), P. Huttenlocher (bar), H. Rilling (cnd), Stuttgart Bach Collegium, Gächinger Kantorei [G] *(rec 1979 & 1980)* Hänssler Classic ▲ 98.820 [AAD]

Bach, J.S.:Cant 144, w. A. Augér (sop), A. Kraus (ten), H. Rilling (cnd), Bach Ensemble [G] *(rec 1978)* Hänssler Classic ▲ 98.876 [AAD]

Bach, J.S.:Cant 148, w. K. Equiluz (ten), H. Rilling (cnd), Stuttgart Bach Collegium, Gächinger Kantorei [G] *(rec 1977)* Hänssler Classic ▲ 98.814 [AAD]

Bach, J.S.:Cant 158, w. R. Hansmann (sop), K. Equiluz (ten), M. Van Egmond (b-bar), J. Jürgens (cnd), Concerto Amsterdam, Monteverdi Choir London Teldec ("Das alte Werke" series) ▲ 93687

Bach, J.S.:Cant 163, w. A. Augér (sop), A. Kraus (ten), N. Tüller (bass), H. Rilling (cnd), Stuttgart Bach Collegium, Gächinger Kantorei [G] *(rec 1976 & 1977)* Hänssler Classic ▲ 98.820 [AAD]

Bach, J.S.:Cant 186, w. A. Augér (sop), K. Equiluz (ten), H. Rilling (cnd), Stuttgart Bach Collegium, Gächinger Kantorei Hänssler Classic ▲ 98.805 [AAD]

Bach, J.S.:Cant 190, w. K. Equiluz (ten), N. Tüller (b-bar), H. Rilling (cnd), Stuttgart Bach Collegium, Gächinger Kantorei [G] Hänssler Classic ▲ 98.870 [AAD]

Bach, J.S.:Cant 198, w. R. Hansmann (sop), K. Equiluz (ten), M. Van Egmond (b-bar), J. Jürgens (cnd), Concerto Amsterdam, Monteverdi Choir London Teldec (Das alte Werke) ▲ 93687

Bach, J.S.:Magnificat, BWV 243, w. E. Ameling (sop), H. van Bork (sop), W. Krenn (ten), T. Krause (bass), K. Münchinger (cnd), Stuttgart CO, Vienna Academy Chorus London ("Serenata" series) ▲ 433175-2 [ADD]

Bach, J.S.:Magnificat, BWV 243, w. F. Palmer (sop), R. Tear (ten), S. Roberts (b-bar), P. Ledger (cnd), Academy of St. Martin in the Fields, King's College Choir Cambridge London ("Jubilee" series) ▲ 421148-2 [ADD]

Bach, J.S.:Magnificat, BWV 243, w. A. Augér (sop), A. Murray (mez), A. Kraus (ten), P. Huttenlocher (bar), W. Schöne (bass), H. Rilling (cnd), Stuttgart Bach Collegium, Gächinger Kantorei *(rec 1979)* Sony Classical ("Essential Classics" series) ▲ SBK 48280 [ADD] ■ SBT 48280

Watts, Helen (cta) (cont.)

Beethoven, L. van:Sym 9, "Choral Sym", w. Heather Harper (sop), Alexander Young (ten), Donald McIntyre (bass), L. Stokowski (cnd), London SO, London Sym Chorus *(rec London, Sept 23, 1967)* Music & Arts ▲ MUA CD 943

Britten, H.:A Midsummer Night's Dream, w. E. Harwood (sop), J. Veasey (mez), A. Deller (ct), P. Pears (ten), J. Shirley-Quirk (bar), B. Britten (cnd), London SO, London Sym Chorus [E] London 2-▲ 425663-2 [ADD]

Elgar, E.:The Apostles, w. S. Armstrong (sop), R. Tear (ten), J. C. Case (bar), B. Luxon (bar), C. Grant (bass), A. Boult (cnd), London PO, London Phil Chorus, Downe House School Choir [E] EMI Classics ▲ CDMB 64206

Elgar, E.:The Light of Life, w. M. Marshall (sop), J. Shirley-Quirk (bar), C. Groves (cnd), Royal Liverpool PO, Royal Liverpool Phil Choir EMI Classics ▲ CDM 64732

Elgar, E.:The Light of Life (sels), w. M. Marshall (sop), J. Shirley-Quirk (bass), C. Groves (cnd), Royal Liverpool PO—Meditation EMI Classics ▲ CDM 64732

Handel, G.F.:Judas Maccabaeus, w. Heather Harper (sop), Alexander Young (ten), John Shirley-Quirk (bass), J. Somary (cnd), English CO, Amor Artis Chorale [E] *(rec 1979)* Vanguard Classics 2-▲ OVC 4071/72 [ADD]

Handel, G.F.:Judas Maccabaeus (sels), w. Heather Harper (sop), Alexander Young (ten), John Shirley-Quirk (bar), J. Somary (cnd), English CO, Amor Artis Chorale Vanguard Classics ▲ OVC 4073 [ADD]

Handel, G.F.:Messiah, w. Heather Harper (sop), John Wakefield (ten), John Shirley-Quirk (bar), C. Davis (cnd), London SO, London Sym Chorus Philips 2-▲ 438356-2

Handel, G.F.:Salve Regina, w. Janet Baker (mez), Robert Tear (ten), Benjamin Luxon (bar), John Shirley-Quirk (bar), R. Leppard (cnd), English CO, London Voices Erato 3-▲ 2292-45994-2

Handel, G.F.:Sosarme, Rè di Media, w. Margaret Ritchie (sop—Elmira), Alfred Deller (mez—Sosarme), Nancy Evans (mez—Erenice), Helen Watts (cta—Melo), John Kentish (ct—Argone), William Herbert (ten—King Haliate), Ian Wallace (bass—Altomaro), A. Lewis (cnd), St. Cecilia Academy Orch Rome, St. Anthony Singers Theorema 2-▲ TH 121194/195

Mahler, G.:Sym 2, w. H. Harper (sop), G. Solti (cnd), London SO, London Sym Chorus [G] London 2-▲ 425005-2 [ADD]

Mahler, G.:Sym 3, w. G. Solti (cnd), London SO, Ambrosian Chorus, Wandsworth School Boys' Choir [G] London 2-▲ 414254-2 [ADD]

Mahler, G.:Sym 8, w. A. Augér (sop), H. Harper (sop), L. Popp (sop), Y. Minton (mez), A. Kollo (ten), J. Shirley-Quirk (bar), M. Talvela (bass), G. Solti (cnd), Chicago SO, Vienna State Opera Chorus, Vienna Boys' Choir, Vienna Singverein [G,L] London 2-▲ 414493-2 [ADD]

Mozart, W.A.:Requiem, w. Jennifer Smith (sop), Ian Partridge (ten), Stafford Dean (bass), M. Atzmon (cnd), BBC Welsh National SO, BBC Choral Society IMP ("BBC Radio" series) ▲ IMP 5691452

Mozart, W.A.:Requiem, w. I. Cotrubas (sop), R. Tear (ten), J. Shirley-Quirk (bar), N. Marriner (cnd), Academy of St. Martin in the Fields, Academy of St. Martin in the Fields Chorus [L] London ▲ 417746-2 [ADD]

Tippett, M.:A Child Of Our Time, w. Jill Gomez (sop), Kenneth Wooliam (ten), John Shirley-Quirk (bar), G. Rozhdestvensky (cnd), BBC SO, BBC Sym Chorus IMP ("BBC Radio Classics" series) ▲ IMP 9130

Tippett, M.:The Midsummer Marriage, w. Joan Carlyle (sop—Joan), Elizabeth Harwood (sop—Beth), Elizabeth Bainbridge (mez), Helen Watts (cta—Sosostris), Stuart Burrows (ten—Jack), Alberto Remedios (ten—Mark), Stafford Dean (bass), Raimund Herincx (bass—King Fisher), C. Davis (cnd), Royal Opera House Orch, Royal Opera House Chorus Covent Garden Lyrita 2-▲ SRCD 2217

Vivaldi, A.:Stabat Mater Cta, w. J.-C. Malgoire (cnd), English Bach Festival Orch [L] *(rec 1977)* Sony Classical ("Essential Classics" series) ▲ SBK 48282 [AAD] ■ SBT 48282

Wagner, R.:Die Meistersinger von Nürnberg (sels), w. Heather Harper (sop), Alexander Young (ten), Donald McIntyre (bass), L. Stokowski (cnd), London SO, London Sym Chorus—Suite:Prelude Act III, Dance of the Apprentices, Entrance of the Mastersingers *(rec London, Sept 23, 1967)* Music & Arts ▲ MUA CD 943

Watzke, Rudolf (bass)

Beethoven, L. van:Sym 9, "Choral Sym", w. Erna Berger (sop), Gertrude Pitzinger (cta), Walther Ludwig (ten), W. Furtwängler (cnd), Berlin PO, Bruno Kittel Choir *(rec Queens Hall, London, May 1, 1937)* Music & Arts ▲ CD 818 [ADD]

Beethoven, L. van:Sym 9, "Choral Sym", w. Tilla Briem (sop), Elisabeth Höngen (cta), Peter Anders (ten), W. Furtwängler (cnd), Berlin PO, Bruno Kittel Choir *(rec 1942)* Grammofono 2000 ▲ GRM 78581

Beethoven, L. van:Sym 9, "Choral Sym", w. Tilla Briem (sop), Elisabeth Höngen (cta), Peter Anders (ten), W. Furtwängler (cnd), Berlin PO, Bruno Kittel Choir *(rec Mar 22, 1942)* Iron Needle 3-▲ IN 1348/50 [ADD]

Wayne, C. (sgr)

Schönberg, C.-M.:Miss Saigon, w. K. Criswell (sop), M. Freeman (cnd), West End Orch Pickwick ▲ PIC PWKS 4229

Weathers, Felicia (sop)

Smetana, B.:Dalibor (sels), w. S. Konya (ten), G. Nienstedt (bass), R. Kubelik (cnd), Bavarian RSO, Bavarian Radio Chorus—nine solo, duet & trio arias featuring tenor Sandor Konya as Dalibor, from Acts 1-3 *(rec live, Munich, 1968)* Myto 2-▲ 2 MCD 92465 [ADD]

Verdi, G.:Ernani (sels), w. Felicia Weathers (sop—Elvira), Delia Wallis (mez—Giovanna), Placido Domingo (ten—Ernani), Wynford Evans (ten—Don Riccardo), Piero Francia (bar—Don Carlo), Agostino Ferrin (bass—Don Ruy Gomex de Silva), Robert Holl (bass—Iago), E. Downes (cnd), Omroep Orch, Omroep Chorus *(rec Amsterdam, Jan 15, 1972)* Bella Voce ▲ BLV 107.004 [AAD]

Weaver, John (bass)

Bach, J.S.:Cant 8, w. J. Baird (sop), S. Rickards (alt), J. Thomas (ten), J. Thomas (cnd), American Bach Soloists [G] Koch International Classics ▲ KIC 7163-2 [DDD]

Bach, J.S.:Cant 156, w. S. Rickards (alt), J. Thomas (ten), J. Thomas (cnd), American Bach Soloists [G] Koch International Classics ▲ KIC 7163-2 [DDD]

Bach, J.S.:Mass in b, BWV 232, w. J. Baird (sop), J. Nelson (sop), N. Zylstra, J. Lane, Z. Muñoz, S. Rickards, P. Romano, W. Sharp, J. Thomas (cnd), American Bach Soloists Koch International Classics 2-▲ KIC 7194-2 [DDD]

Bach, J.S.:St. John Passion, w. J. Baird (sop), J. Bryden (sop), J. Thomas (ten), D. Ripley (bar), K. Slowik (cnd), Smithsonian Chamber Players, Smithsonian Chamber Chorus [period instrs] [G] *(Slowik performs the original 1724 version, & includes the two choruses & three arias added to Bach's 1725 revision as appended tracks at the end of the discs, allowing the listener to either ignore the end tracks & hear the standard version or program the discs to play the 1725 sequence)* Smithsonian Collection 5-▲ ND 0380 [DDD]

Weaver, Martha Jane (mez)

Paulus, S.:Voices, w. Frank Kelley (ten), J. Alexander (cnd), Pacific SO, Pacific Chorale Albany ▲ TROY 182

Webber, Aaron (trb)

Duruflé, M.:Mass, "Cum jubilo", w. Simon Keenlyside (bar), Natalie Clein (vc), Iain Simcock (org), James O'Donnell (cnd), Westminster Cathedral Choir Hyperion ▲ CDA 66757

Duruflé, M.:Motets on Gregorian Chants, Op. 10, w. Simon Keenlyside (bar), Natalie Clein (vc), Iain Simcock (org), J. O'Donnell (cnd), Westminster Cathedral Choir Hyperion ▲ CDA 66757

Duruflé, M.:Notre Père, w. Simon Keenlyside (bar), Natalie Clein (vc), Iain Simcock (org), J. O'Donnell (cnd), Westminster Cathedral Choir Hyperion ▲ CDA 66757

Duruflé, M.:Requiem, w. Simon Keenlyside (bar), Natalie Clein (vc), Iain Simcock (org), J. O'Donnell (cnd), Westminster Cathedral Choir Hyperion ▲ CDA 66757

Webber, Carol (sgr)

Donizetti, G.:Don Pasquale, w. Edoardo Gimenez (ten), Geraint Evans (bar), Mario D'Anna (sgr), H. Holt (cnd), *(orch unknown)* *(rec Seattle, 1981)* Ornamenti ("Gala Evenings, Teatro Colon" series) 2-▲ 121

Webber, Lynne (sop)

Babbitt, M.:Phonemena Sop & Pno, w. Jerry Kuderna (pno) *(rec Colombia Studios, NYC)* New World ▲ 80466-2

Weber, Heinrich (ten)

Humperdinck, E.:Königskinder, w. Dagmar Schellenberger (sop—Goose girl), Marilyn Schmiege (cta—Witch), Thomas Moser (ten—King's Son), Heinrich Weber (ten—Broommaker), Dietrich Henschel (bar—Fiddler), Andreas Kohn (bass—Woodcutter), F. Luisi (cnd), Munich RSO, Michael Gläser (cnd), Bavarian Radio Chorus *(rec live, Munich Herkulessaal, Mar 22-24, 1996)* Calig 3-CAL 5096870 [DDD]

Wagner, R.:Lohengrin, w. Sharon Sweet (sop—Elsa), Eva Marton (sop—Ortrud), Ben Heppner (ten—Lohengrin), Anton Rosner (ten—Nobleman), Heinrich Weber (ten—Nobleman), Jan-Hendrik Rootering (bar—Heinrich der Vögler), Sergei Leiferkus (bar—Friedrich von Telramund), Bryn Terfel (b-bar—King's Herald), Barbara Fleckenstein (sgr—Page), Atsuko Suzuki (sgr—Page), Gisela Ulmann (sgr—Page), Marion Rambausek (sgr—Page), Dankwart Siegele (sgr—Nobleman), Jürgen Weiss (sgr—Nobleman), C. Davis (cnd), Bavarian SO, Bavarian State Opera Chorus, Bavarian Radio Chorus *(rec Residenz Herkulesaal, Munich, May 14-28, 1994)* RCA Red Seal 3-▲ 09026-62646-2 [DDD]

Wagner, R.:Lohengrin (sels), w. Eva Marton (sop—Ortrud), Sharon Sweet (sop—Elsa von Brabant), Barbara Fleckenstein (sgr—Page), Marion Rambausek (sgr—Page), Atsuko Suzuki (sgr—Page), Gisela Ulmann (sgr—Page), Ben Heppner (ten—Lohengrin), Anton Rosner (ten—Nobleman), Heinrich Weber (ten—Nobleman), Sergei Leiferkus (bar—Friedrich von Telramund), Bryn Terfel (b-bar—King's Herald), Jan-Hendrik Rootering (bass—Henry the Fowler), Dankwart Siegele (sgr—Nobleman), Jürgen Weiss (sgr—Nobleman), C. Davis (cnd), Bavarian RSO, Michael Gläser (cnd), Udo Mehrpohl (cnd), Bavarian Radio Chorus, Bavarian State Opera Chorus—Seht! Seht! [from Act 1, Scene 2]; Nun sei bedankt, mein lieber Schwan!; Wenn ich im Kampfe für dich siege; Welch holde Wunder muss ich sehen?; Nun höret mich und achtet wohl; Durch Gottes Sieg ist jetzt dein Leben mein [all from Act 1, Scene 3]; Treulich geführt ziehet dahin [from Act 3, Scene 1]; Wie hehr erkenn' ich unsrer Liebe Wesen!; Höchstes Vertrau'n hast du mir schon zu danken; Weh' nun ist all' unser Glück dahin! [all from Act 3, Scene 2]; In fernem Land, unnahbar euren Schritten [from Act 3, Scene 3] *(rec Munich, Mar 14-28, 1994)* RCA Red Seal ▲ 09026-68239-2 [DDD]

Weber, Ludwig (bass)

Beethoven, L. van:Sym 9, "Choral Sym", w. I. Borkh (sop), R. Siewert (cta), R. Lewis (ten), R. Leibowitz (cnd), Royal PO, Beecham Choral Society [G] *(rec 6/61)* Chesky ▲ CD66 [ADD]

Einem, G. von:Dantons Tod, w. M. Cebotari (sop—Lucille Desmoulins), R. Anday (cta—Frau des Simon), P. Klein (ten—de Séchelles), J. Patzak (ten—Camille Desmoulins), J. Witt (ten—Robspierre), P. Schöffler (bar—Danton), L. Weber (bass—Saint Just), F. Fricsay (cnd), Vienna PO, Vienna State Opera Chorus *(rec Aug. 6, 1947)* Stradivarius 2-▲ STR 10067 [ADD]

Mozart, W.A.:Don Giovanni, w. Hedwig Jungkurth (sop—Elvira), Maria Reining (sop—Anna), Julius Patzak (ten—Ottavio), Karl Hammes (bar—Don Giovanni), Georg Hann (bass), Ludwig Weber (bass—Commandant), J. Keilberth (cnd), Stuttgart Reich RSO, Stuttgart Radio Chorus *(rec Mar, 1936)* Preiser 2-▲ PRE 90263

Pfitzner, H.:Von deutscher Seele, w. Trude Eipperle (sop), Luise Willer (mez), Julius Patzak (ten), C. Krauss (cnd), Vienna PO, Vienna State Opera Chorus *(rec Jan 1945)* Preiser 2-▲ PRE 90255 [ADD]

Strauss, R.:Der Rosenkavalier, w. M. Reining (sop), H. Gueden (sop), S. Jurinac (sop), E. Kleiber (cnd), Vienna PO, Vienna State Opera Chorus [G] London ("Historic" series) ▲ 425950-2 (m) [ADD]

Strauss, R.:Der Rosenkavalier, w. Adele Kern (sop), Viorica Ursuleac (sop), Georgine von Milinkovic (mez), Georg Hann (bass), C. Krauss (cnd), Bavarian State Opera Orch, Bavarian State Opera Chorus *(rec Munich, June 1942)* Preiser 3-▲ PRE 90218

Verdi, G.:Macbeth, w. Astrid Varnay (sop—Lady Macbeth), Trude Roesler (mez—Lady-in-waiting), Hasso Eschert (ten—Malcolm), Walter Geisler (ten—Macduff), Joseph Metternich (bar—Macbeth), Ludwig Weber (bass—Banquo), R. Kraus (cnd), West German Orch, West German Chorus *(rec Cologne, 1954)* Myto 2-▲ 952128

Wagner, R.:Der fliegende Holländer, w. A. Varnay (sop), W. Windgassen (ten), H. Uhde (bar), H. Knappertsbusch (cnd), Bayreuth Festival Orch, Bayreuth Festival Chorus [G] *(rec live)* Arkadia 2-▲ 421 [ADD]

Wagner, R.:Der fliegende Holländer (sels), w. Kirsten Flagstad (sop), Tiana Lemnitz (sop), Torsten Ralf (ten), Rudolf Bockelmann (b-bar), T. Beecham (cnd), Royal Opera House Orch, Royal Opera House Chorus Covent Garden Memories ("Golden" series) ▲ MEM 3003

Wagner, R.:Der fliegende Holländer (sels), w. K. Flagstad (sop), M. Lorenz (ten), H. Janssen (bar), F. Reiner (cnd), Royal Opera House Orch, Royal Opera House Chorus Covent Garden [G] *(rec live, Covent Garden, 6/11/37)* Standing Room Only ▲ SRO 808-1 (m) [ADD]

Wagner, R.:Götterdämmerung (sels), w. Kirsten Flagstad (sop), Tiana Lemnitz (sop), Torsten Ralf (ten), Rudolf Bockelmann (b-bar), T. Beecham (cnd), Royal Opera House Orch, Royal Opera House Chorus Covent Garden Memories ("Golden" series) ▲ MEM 3003

Wagner, R.:Götterdämmerung (sels), w. F. Leider (sop), Nezadál (sop), K. Thorborg (mez), L. Melchior (ten), H. Janssen (bar), T. Beecham (cnd), London PO, Royal Opera House Chorus Covent Garden [G] *(rec from 1925 Polydor & 1929)* Legato Classics 2-▲ LCD 146-2 (m) [ADD]

Wagner, R.:Lohengrin (sels), w. Kirsten Flagstad (sop), Tiana Lemnitz (sop), Torsten Ralf (ten), Rudolf Bockelmann (b-bar), T. Beecham (cnd), Royal Opera House Orch, Royal Opera House Chorus Covent Garden Memories ("Golden" series) ▲ MEM 3003

Wagner, R.:Die Meistersinger von Nürnberg (sels), w. Kirsten Flagstad (sop), Tiana Lemnitz (sop), Torsten Ralf (ten), Rudolf Bockelmann (b-bar), T. Beecham (cnd), Royal Opera House Orch, Royal Opera House Chorus Covent Garden Memories ("Golden" series) ▲ MEM 3003

Wagner, R.:Parsifal, w. Anny Konetzni (sop—Kundry), Günther Treptow (ten—Parsifal), Paul Schöffler (bar—Amfortas), Hans Braun (bass—Titurel), Adolf Vogel (bass—Klingsor), Ludwig Weber (bass—Gurnemanz), R. Moralt (cnd), Vienna SO, Vienna State Opera Chorus *(rec Vienna)* Myto 4-▲ 4 MCD 954.136

Wagner, R.:Parsifal (sels), w. E. Larcen (sop), H. Reimar (ten), C. Hartmann (bar), H. Knappertsbusch (cnd), Berlin German Opera Orch, Berlin German Opera Chorus—Act 3 *(rec 1943)* Enterprise ("Document" series) ▲ ENTLV 943 [ADD]

Wagner, R.:Parsifal (sels), w. Carl Hartmann (ten), Hans Reinmar (bar), Elsa Laren (sgr), H. Knappertsbusch (cnd), Berlin German Opera Orch, Berlin German Opera Chorus—complete Act 3 *(rec Berlin, March 31, 1942)* Grammofono 2000 ▲ GRM 78555

Wagner, R.:Das Rheingold, w. P. Brivkalne (sop), I. Malaniuk (cta), R. Siewert (cta), Fritz (sgr), Pflanzl (ten), S. Björling (bar), W. Faulhaber (bass), F. Dalberg (bass), H. von Karajan (cnd), Bayreuth Festival Orch, Bayreuth Festival Chorus [G] *(rec live 8/1/51)* Melodram 2-▲ MEL 26107 (m) [AAD]

Wagner, R.:Der Ring des Nibelungen, w. Kirsten Flagstad (sop), Hilde Konetzni (sop), Elisabeth Höngen (cta), Max Lorenz (ten), Set Svanholm (ten), Günther Treptow (ten), Josef Hermann (bar), Ferdinand Franz (sgr), W. Furtwängler (cnd), La Scala Orch, La Scala Chorus *(rec Milan, 1950)* Music & Arts 12-▲ CD 914

Wagner, R.:Der Ring des Nibelungen, w. K. Flagstad (sop), H. Konetzni (sop), E. Höngen (cta), G. Treptow (ten), S. Svanholm (ten), M. Lorenz (ten), F. Frantz (b-bar), B. Herrmann (bass), W. Furtwängler (cnd), La Scala Orch, La Scala Chorus *(rec live 1950)* Arkadia 12-▲ 351 [ADD]

Wagner, R.:Tristan und Isolde (sels), w. Kirsten Flagstad (sop), Tiana Lemnitz (sop), Torsten Ralf (ten), Rudolf Bockelmann (b-bar), T. Beecham (cnd), Royal Opera House Orch, Royal Opera House Chorus Covent Garden Memories ("Golden" series) ▲ MEM 3003

Webster, Douglas (bar)

Schoenfield, P.:Klezmer Rondos, w. C. Wincenc (fl), A. Neale (cnd), New York CO Solisti New World ▲ 80403-2 [DDD]

Webster, Gillian (sop)

Beethoven, L. van:Sym 9, "Choral Sym", w. Catherine Wyn-Rogers (cta), Martyn Hill (ten), Robert Hayward (bar), R. Leppard (cnd), Royal PO, Ambrosian Singers Tring ("Royal Philharmonic Collection" series) ▲ TRP 51 [DDD]

Wedin, Lage (bar)

Dallapiccola, L.:Il Prigioniero, w. Phyllis Bryn-Julson (sop), Sven-Erik Alexandersson (ten), Howard Haskin (ten), Jorma Hynninen (bar), E.-P. Salonen (cnd), Swedish RSO, Eric Ericson Chamber Choir Sony Classical ▲ SK 68323

Nilsson, T.:Music of, w. Ingmari Landin (alt), Lars Sjögren (ten), Jerker Halldén (fl), Nils-Erik Sparf (vn), Hans-Ola Ericsson (org), Anders Loguin (perc), Torsten Nilsson (cnd), Gustaf Sjökvist (cnd), Swedish Radio Chorus—Ordinarium Missae; Balthasar/Daniel; Drei Gedichte Phono Suecia ▲ PHN 40 [AAD]

Wedin, Lage (bar) (cont.)
Olsson, O.:Requiem, w. M. A. Häggander (sop), E. Paaske (cta), A. Andersson (ten), A. Öhrwall (cnd), Stockholm PO, Stockholm Phil Chorus Caprice ▲ CAP 21368 [DDD]

Weede, Robert (bar)
Bizet, G.:Carmen (sels), w. Risë Stevens (sop), N. Conner (sop), R. Jobin (ten), G. Sébastian (cnd), Metropolitan Opera Orch, New York Metropolitan Opera Chorus [F] Odyssey ■ YT 32102 (m)
Charpentier, M.-A.:Louise (sels), w. Grace Moore (sop), Josef Schmidt (ten), E. Rapée (cnd), Radio City Music Hall Orch, Radio City Music Hall Chorus—Depuis le jour Enterprise ("The Radio Years" series) ▲ ENT RY 58
Leoncavallo, R.:Pagliacci (sels), w. Grace Moore (sop), Josef Schmidt (ten), E. Rapée (cnd), Radio City Music Hall Orch, Radio City Music Hall Chorus—Stridono lassù Enterprise ("The Radio Years" series) ▲ ENT RY 58
Massenet, J.:Manon (sels), w. Grace Moore (sop), Josef Schmidt (ten), E. Rapée (cnd), Radio City Music Hall Orch, Radio City Music Hall Chorus—Obéissons quand leur voix appelle [Gavotte] Enterprise ("The Radio Years" series) ▲ ENT RY 58
Puccini, G.:La Bohème (sels), w. Grace Moore (sop), Josef Schmidt (ten), E. Rapée (cnd), Radio City Music Hall Orch, Radio City Music Hall Chorus—Che Gelida Manina; Sì, Mi Chiamano Mimì; O Soave Fanciulla Enterprise ("The Radio Years" series) ▲ ENT RY 58
Puccini, G.:Madama Butterfly (sels), w. Grace Moore (sop), Josef Schmidt (ten), E. Rapée (cnd), Radio City Music Hall Orch, Radio City Music Hall Chorus—Vogliatemi Bene Enterprise ("The Radio Years" series) ▲ ENT RY 58
Puccini, G.:Tosca, w. M. Callas (sop), M. Filippeschi (ten), U. Mugnai (cnd), Palacio Bellas Artes Orch, Palacio Bellas Artes Chorus [I] *(rec live, Mexico City, 6/8/50)* Standing Room Only 2-▲ SRO 820-2 [ADD]
Puccini, G.:Tosca, w. Maria Callas (sop), Mario Filippeschi (ten), Carlos Sagarminaga (ten), Ramon Alonso (bass), U. Mugnai (cnd), Palacio Bellas Artes Orch, Palacio Bellas Artes Chorus Melodram 3-▲ CDM 36032
Puccini, G.:Tosca (sels), w. Grace Moore (sop), Josef Schmidt (ten), E. Rapée (cnd), Radio City Music Hall Orch, Radio City Music Hall Chorus—Recondita Armonia; Vissi d'Arte; E Lucevan le Stelle; Te Deum Enterprise ("The Radio Years" series) ▲ ENT RY 58
Verdi, G.:Aida, w. M. Callas (sop), G. Simionato (mez), K. Baum (ten), G. Picco (cnd), Palacio Bellas Artes Orch, Palacio Bellas Artes Chorus *(rec live, Mexico City 5/30/50)* Melodram ▲ MLO 26009 [ADD]

Wegmann, Christoph (trb)
Bach, J.S.:Cant 152, w. T. Hampson (b-bar), N. Harnoncourt (cnd), Vienna Concentus Musicus [G] Teldec 2-▲ 2292-42632-2 [DDD]

Wegner, Walburga (sop)
Verdi, G.:Un ballo in maschera, w. Martha Mödl (sop—Ulrica), Walburga Wegner (sop—Amelia), Anny Schlemm (mez—Oscar), Lorenz Fehenberger (ten—Ricardo), Dietrich Fischer-Dieskau (bar—Renato), Wilhelm Schirp (bass—Samuel), Willy Schoneweib (bass—Tom), Gunther Wilhelms (bass—Silvan), Fritz Augustin (sgr—Ein Richter), Friedrich Himmelmann (sgr—Ein Diener Amelia), F. Busch (cnd), Cologne RSO, Bernhard Alois Zimmermann (cnd), Cologne Radio Chorus Calig 2-▲ 50946/47 (m) [ADD]

Weichert, Matthias (bass)
Berlinski, H.:Das Gebet Bonhoeffers, w. Nancy Gibson (sop), Olaf Georgi (fl), Bernhard Hentrich (vc), Herman Berlinski (org), Holger Miersch (cel), Martin Homann (perc), Hans-Christoph Rademann (cnd), Dresden Chamber Choir Vienna Modern Masters ▲ VMM 3027 [DDD]
Helmschrott, R.:Cross & Freedom, w. Helmut Schatz, Nancy Gibson (sop), Frieder Aurich (ten), Manfred Ball (nar), Anett Baumann (vn), Frank Phillipstch, Linda Robbins, Gerhard Wolf, Martin Homann (perc), Robert M. Helmschrott (org), H.-C. Rademann (cnd), Munich Trombone Quartet, Dresden Chamber Choir Vienna Modern Masters ▲ VMM 3027 [DDD]

Weidemann, Hermann (bar)
Wagner, R.:Parsifal (sels), w. A. Konetzni (sop), H. Grahl (ten), H. Alsen (bass), H. Knappertsbusch (cnd), Vienna State Opera Orch, Vienna State Opera Chorus *(rec Apr. 6, 1939)* Koch Schwann 2-▲ SCH 314522 [ADD]

Weidinger, Christine (sop)
Handel, G.F.:Rinaldo, w. Cecelia Gasdia (sop), Marylin Horne (mez), Ernesto Palacio (ten), J. Fisher (cnd), Venice Teatro La Fenice Orch *(rec live 1989)* Nuova Era 2-▲ 6813/14 [DDD]
Meyerbeer, G.:L'Africiane, w. Montserrat Caballe (sop—Selika), Christine Weidinger (sop—Inez), Miriam Ucelay (mez—Anna), Placido Domingo (ten—Vasco de Gama), Guillermo Sarabia (bar—Nelusko), Juan Thomas (b-bar—High Priest of Brahma), Dimiter Petkov (bass—Don Pedro), Juan Pons (bass—Don Diego), Eduardo Soto (bass—Grand Inquisitor), A. de Almeida (cnd), Barcelona Teatro Liceo Orch, Barcelona Gran Teatro de Liceo Chorus *(rec Barcelona, Nov 27, 1977)* Legato Classics 2-▲ LCD 208-2 [ADD]
Rossini, G.:Demetrio e Polibio, w. Christine Weidinger (sop—Lisinga), Sara Mingardo (cta—Siveno), Anna Laura Longo (sgr—Olmira), Dalmacio Gonzales (ten—Demetrio/Eumene), Giorgio Surjan (bass—Polibio), Martino Fullone (sgr—Onao), M. Carraro (cnd), Graz SO, Bratislava Chamber Chorus *(rec live, Martina Franca Opera Festival, Italy, July 27, 1992)* Dynamic 2-▲ CDS 171/1-2 [DDD]
Verdi, G.:Arias, w. R. A. Clark (cnd), Manhattan CO—Madre pietosa; Pace, pace, mio dio [both from La forza del destino]; Ernani, involami [from Ernani]; O patria mia [from Aida]; Act 1 Prelude; Una macchia [both from Macbeth; w. Darcy Dunn (sop), Peter Castaldi (bar)]; Act 1 Prelude; Addio del passato [both from La traviata]; Tacea la notte [from Il Trovatore; w. Mary Polis (mez)]; Morrò, ma prima in grazia [from Un ballo in maschera] Newport Classic ▲ NPD 85581 [DDD]

Weidlich, E. (sop)
Bizet, G.:Carmen, w. E. Höngen (cta), T. Ralf (ten), J. Herrmann (bar), K. Böhme (bass), K. Böhm (cnd), Dresden State Opera Orch, Dresden State Opera Chorus *(rec Dec. 4 & 5, 1942)* Preiser 2-▲ 90152 (m)

Weigelt (sgr)
Künneke, E.:Die grosse Sünderin (sels), w. M. Cunitz (sop), R. Schock (ten), Bajew (sgr), Gehly (sgr), Rau (sgr), Schröder (sgr), Marszalek (cnd), Cologne RSO, Cologne Radio Chorus [G] Acanta ▲ CD 42483 [DDD]

Weikl, Bernd (bar)
Beethoven, L. van:Sym 9, "Choral Sym", w. S. McNair (sop), U. Heilmann (ten), J. Van Nes (bar), K. Masur (cnd), Leipzig Gewandhaus Orch, London Radio Choir Philips ▲ 432995-2
Brahms, J.:Ein Deutsches Requiem, w. K. Te Kanawa (sop), G. Solti (cnd), Chicago SO, Chicago Sym Chorus [G] London 2-▲ 414627-2 [ADD]
Dessau, P.:Haggada, w. Sabine Ritterbusch (sop), Renate Spingler (sop), Yvi Jänicke (alt), Peter Galliard (ten—Rabbi Tarfon/Jude/ten solo), Gabriel Sadé (ten—Pharaoh), Jochen Schmeckenbecher (bar—Rabbi Jehoschua), Bernd Weikl (bar—Moses), Matthias Hölle (bass—Speaker/Rabbi Akiwa), Alfred Muff (bass—Father/Rabbi Eleasar), Johann Tilli (bass—Rabbi Elieser/bass solo), G. Albrecht (cnd), Hamburg State PO, Berlin Carl Maria Von Weber Men's Choir, Hamburg Alsterspatzen, North German Radio Chorus [G] *(rec Musikhalle, Hamburg, Sept 4 & 5, 1994)* Capriccio 2-▲ 10590/91 [DDD]
Gluck, C.W.:Alceste, w. J. Norman (sop), N. Gedda (ten), T. Krause (bar), S. Nimsgern (b-bar), S. Baudo (cnd), Bavarian RSO, Bavarian Radio Chorus, *(highlights of above)* Orfeo ▲ 027901 [DDD]
Gluck, C.W.:Alceste, w. J. Norman (sop), N. Gedda (ten), T. Krause (bar), S. Nimsgern (b-bar), S. Baudo (cnd), Bavarian RSO, Bavarian Radio Chorus [French version] Orfeo 3-▲ 027823 [DDD]
Haydn, J.:Die Schöpfung, w. Margaret Marshall (sop), Lucia Popp (sop), Vinson Cole (ten), Gwynne Howell (bass), R. Kubelik (cnd), Bavarian RSO, Bavarian Radio Chorus Orfeo 2-▲ 150852 [DDD] 2-■ 150852 (D)
Humperdinck, E.:Hänsel und Gretel, w. H. Behrens (sop—Gertrud, the Stepmother), R. Ziesak (sop—Gretel), R. Joshua (sop—Sandman), C. Schäfer (sop—Dew Fairy), J. Larmore (mez—Hänsel), H. Schwarz (cta—Nibblewitch), B. Weikl (bar—Peter, the Father), D. Runnicles (cnd), Bavarian RSO, Tölz Boys' Choir *(rec Munich, Feb. 1994)* Teldec 2-▲ 94549-2 [DDD]
Leoncavallo, R.:La Bohème, w. Lucia Popp (sop), Alexandrina Milcheva (mez), Franco Bonisolli (ten), H. Wallberg (cnd), Munich RSO, Bavarian Radio Chorus [I] Orfeo 2-▲ 023822 [DDD]
Mahler, G.:Des Knaben Wunderhorn, w. L. Popp (sop), J. Baker (mez), M. Dickie (ten), D. Fischer-Dieskau (bar), K. Tennstedt (cnd), London PO EMI Classics ▲ CDZB 62707
Mahler, G.:Das Lied von der Erde, w. L. Popp (sop), J. Baker (mez), M. Dickie (ten), D. Fischer-Dieskau (bar), P. Kletzki (cnd), Philharmonia Orch EMI Classics ▲ CDZB 62707

Weikl, Bernd (bar) (cont.)
Mozart, W.A.:Don Giovanni, w. L. Price (sop), L. Popp (sop), S. Sass (sop), S. Burrows (ten), G. Bacquier (bar), A. Sramek (bar), K. Moll (bass), G. Solti (cnd), London PO, London Opera Chorus London ("Grand Opera" series) 3-▲ 425169-2 [ADD]
Nicolai, O.:Lustigen Weiber, w. H. Donath (sop), E. Mathis (sop), H. Schwarz (mez), K. Ludwig (ten), K.-E. Mercker (ten), P. Schreier (ten), C. Dormoy (bar), K. Moll (bass), S. Vogel (bass), B. Klee (cnd), Berlin Staatskapelle, Berlin State Opera Chorus *(rec July 3, 1976)* Berlin Classics ("Eterna" series) ▲ BER 2046-2 [ADD]
Opera & Operetta Arias Acanta ▲ 43266
Operetta Recital, w. Austrian Radio Orch, Austrian Radio Chorus [cnd:Kurt Eichorn] Orfeo ▲ 077831
Orff, C.:Carmina burana, w. J. Anderson (sop), P. Creech (ten), J. Levine (cnd), Chicago SO, Chicago Sym Chorus [G,L] Deutsche Grammophon ▲ 415136-2 [DDD] ■ 415136-4
Schubert, Franz:Winterreise, w. Helmut Deutsch (pno) Nightingale Classics ▲ NIG CD 70960
Strauss, R.:Elektra, w. C. Studer (sop), E. Marton (sop), M. Lipovsek (mez), H. Winkler (ten), W. Sawallisch (cnd), Bavarian RSO, Bavarian Radio Chorus EMI Classics 2-▲ CDCB 54067
Strauss, R.:Feuersnot, w. J. Varady (sop), H. Berger-Tuna (bass), H. Fricke (cnd), Munich RSO, Bavarian Radio Chorus [G] Acanta 2-▲ 43530-1-2 [DDD]
Strauss, R.:Salome, w. E. Martón (sop), B. Fassbaender (mez/sop), H. Zednik (ten), R. Lewis (ten), Z. Mehta (cnd), Berlin PO *(rec live)* Sony Classical 2-▲ S2K 46717
Verdi, G.:Arias, w. H. Wallberg (cnd), Munich RSO—9 arias from Ballo in maschera, Don Carlos, Forza del destino, Macbeth, Otello, Rigoletto, Traviata, Trovatore [I] Acanta ▲ 43327
Wagner, R.:Götterdämmerung, w. H. Behrens (sop), C. Studer (sop), H. Schwarz (mez), R. Goldberg (ten), E. Wlaschiha (bar), M. Salminen (bass), J. Levine (cnd), Metropolitan Opera Orch, New York Metropolitan Opera Chorus Deutsche Grammophon 4-▲ 429385-2 [DDD]
Wagner, R.:Lohengrin, w. E. Connell (sop), N. Armstrong (sop), P. Hofmann (ten), L. Roar (bass), S. Vogel (bass), W. Nelsson (cnd), Bayreuth Festival Orch, Bayreuth Festival Chorus CBS 3-▲ M3K 38594
Wagner, R.:Die Meistersinger von Nürnberg, w. H. Bode (sop), J. Hamari (mez), A. Kollo (ten), N. Bailey (bar), K. Moll (bass), G. Solti (cnd), Vienna PO, Vienna State Opera Chorus [G] London 4-▲ 417497-2 [ADD]
Wagner, R.:Die Meistersinger von Nürnberg, w. C. Studer (sop—Eva), B. Heppner (ten—Walther von Stolzing), B. Weikl (bar—Hans Sachs), S. Lorenz (b-bar—Sixtus Beckmesser), K. Moll (bass—Veit Pogner), W. Sawallisch (cnd), Bavarian State Opera Orch, Bavarian State Opera Chorus EMI Classics ▲ CDCD 55142
Wagner, R.:Tannhäuser, w. Nadine Secunde (sop), Waltraude Meier (mez), Rene Kollo (ten), Z. Mehta (cnd), Bavarian State Opera Orch, Bavarian State Opera Chorus *(rec live, Munich, 1994)* Serenissima 3-▲ SER 360166
Wagner, R.:Tristan und Isolde, w. H. Dernesch (sop), C. Ludwig (mez), J. Vickers (ten), P. Schreier (ten), W. Berry (bass), K. Ridderbusch (bass), H. von Karajan (cnd), Berlin PO, German Opera Chorus [G] EMI Classics ("Studio" series) 4-▲ CDMD 69319 [ADD]
Wagner, R.:Tristan und Isolde (sels), w. H. Behrens (sop), Y. Minton (mez), P. Hofmann (ten), L. Bernstein (cnd), Bavarian RSO, Bavarian Radio Chorus Philips ▲ 438501-2

Weimann (sgr)
Bach, J.S.:Cant 31, w. Eberhard Büchner (ten), Siegfried Lorenz (bar), Hermann Christian Polster (bass), Lang (sgr), Termer (sgr), H.-J. Rotzsch (cnd), Leipzig Gewandhaus Orch, St. Thomas Choir Berlin Classics ▲ BER 9025 [ADD]
Bach, J.S.:Cant 66, w. Eberhard Büchner (ten), Siegfried Lorenz (bar), Hermann Christian Polster (bass), Lang (sgr), Termer (sgr), H.-J. Rotzsch (cnd), Leipzig Gewandhaus Orch, St. Thomas Choir Berlin Classics ▲ BER 9025 [ADD]
Bach, J.S.:Cant 106, "Actus tragicus", w. Eberhard Büchner (ten), Siegfried Lorenz (bar), Hermann Christian Polster (bass), Lang (sgr), Termer (sgr), H.-J. Rotzsch (cnd), Leipzig Gewandhaus Orch, St. Thomas Choir Berlin Classics ▲ BER 9025 [ADD]

Weimer, Theodor (sgr)
Künneke, E.:The Alluring Flame, w. Birgit Fandrey (sgr—Dolores), Christianne Hossfeld (sgr—Lisbeth), Maria Mallé (sgr), Jürgen Sacher (ten—Master), Ralf Lukas (bar—Hoffman), Gerd Grochowski (sgr—1st Neighbor), Gerhard Peters (sgr—Friedrich), Zoran Todorovic (sgr—Jacinto), Theodor Weimer (sgr—2nd Neighbor), P. Falk (cnd), Cologne RSO, Cologne Radio Chorus *(rec Cologne, Nov 7-26, 1994)* Capriccio ▲ 10753 [DDD]

Weinberger, H. (sgr)
York, W.:Songs on a Poem of Su Tung P'O, w. D. Ripley (bass), B. Lancaster (sgr) *(rec May 1987)* New World ▲ 80439-2

Weindl, M. (sop)
Lortzing, A.:Hans Sachs, w. K. Schmitt-Walter (bar), M. Loy (cnd), Frankenland State SO *(rec 1950)* Memories 2-▲ MEM 4550 [ADD]

Weiner, O. (ten)
Bach, J.S.:St. John Passion, w. P. Curtin (sop), E. Alberts (cta), W. Kmentt (ten), H. Scherchen (cnd), Vienna State Opera Orch, Vienna Academy Chorus *(rec 1962)* Enterprise ("Documents" series) ▲ ENT LV 925

Weinorowski, Wjacheslav (sgr)
Rubinstein, A.:The Demon, w. Ludmilla Andrew (sop—Nanny), Marina Mescheriakova (sop—Tamara), Alison Browner (mez—Angel), Anatoly Lochak (sgr—Demon), Richard Robson (sgr—Old Servant), Valery Serkin (sgr—Prince Sinodal), Wjacheslav Weinorowski (sgr—Messenger), Leonid Zimnenko (sgr—Prince Gudal), A. Anissimov (cnd), Irish National SO, Gregory Rose (cnd), Wexford Festival Opera Chorus *(rec Wexford, Oct & Nov, 1994)* Marco Polo 2-▲ 8.223781-2 [DDD]

Weins, Edith (sop)
Strauss, R.:Songs, w. Rudolf Jansen (pno)—Die Nacht, Op. 10/3; Auf ein Kind, Op. 47/1; Wiegenlied, O. Op. AV 41; Meinem Kinde, Op. 37/3; Wiegenlied, Op. 41/1; Muttertändelei, Op. 43/2; Gefunden, Op. 56/1; Blauer Sommer, Op. 31/1; Malven, O. Op.; Ein Röslein zog ich mir im Garten, O. Op. AV 49; Allerseelen, Op. 10/8; Ach Lieb, ich muss nun scheiden, Op. 21/3; Mein Herz ist stumm, Op. 19/6; Morgen, Op. 27/4; Ständchen, Op. 17/2; Freundliche Vision, Op. 48/1; Ruhe, meine Seele, Op. 27/1; Waldseligkeit, Op. 49/1; Einerlei, Op. 69/3; Schlechtes Wetter, Op. 69/5; Wir beide wollen springen, O. Op. AV 90; Zueignung, Op. 10/1 *(rec Glenn Gould Studio, CBC Toronto, Oct 31-Nov 3, 1994)* CBC ("Musica Viva" series) ▲ MVCD 1090 [DDD]

Weir, Scot (ten)
Brixi, F.X.:Missa Interga, w. I. Verebics (sop), C. Borchers (cta), Genhardt (bass), H. Rilling (cnd), Prague CO, Kühn Chorus Supraphon ▲ 11 0092-2 [DDD]
Brixi, F.X.:Opus Patheticum de Septem Doloribus Beatae Mariae Virginis, w. I. Verebics (sop), C. Borchers (cta), Genhardt (bass), H. Rilling (cnd), Prague CO, Kühn Chorus Supraphon ▲ 11 0092-2 [DDD]
Mendelssohn, F.:Die Hochzeit des Camacho, w. R. Hofman (sop—Quiteria), A. Ulbrich (mez—Lucinda), S. Weir (ten—Basilio), H. Rhys-Evans (ten—Vivaldo), N. van der Meel (ten—Camacho), W. Wild (bar—Carrasco), U. Malmberg (bass—Sancho Panza), U. Cold (bass—Don Quixote), J. van Immerseel (cnd), Anima Eterna Orch, Aachen Boys Choir, Chor Modus Novus [G] *(rec Sept. 19-22, 1992)* Channel Classics 2-▲ CCS 5593 [DDD]
Mozart, W.A.:Missa, K.427, w. C. Oelze (sop), J. Larmore (mez), P. Kooy (bass), P. Herreweghe (cnd), Champs Elysées Theater Orch, Chapelle Royale Choir, Collegium Vocale Harmonia Mundi France ▲ HMC 901393
Mozart, W.A.:Missa, K.427, w. C. Oelze (sop), I. Verebics (sop), O. Widmer (bass), H. Rilling (cnd), Stuttgart Bach Collegium, Gächinger Kantorei [L] Hänssler Classic 2-▲ 98.979 [DDD]
Mozart, W.A.:Requiem, w. C. Oelze (sop), I. Danz (mez), A. Schmidt (bar), H. Rilling (cnd), Stuttgart Bach Collegium, Gächinger Kantorei [L] Hänssler Classic 2-▲ 98.979 [DDD]

Weise (sgr)
Marschner, H.A.:Der Vampyr, w. L. Synek (sop), L. Heppe (ten), G. Oeggl (bar), Rathauscher (sgr), Skladal (sgr), Sperlbauer (sgr), K. Tenner (cnd), Vienna RSO, Vienna Radio Chorus [G] *(rec live, Vienna, 4/9/51)* Memories 2-▲ HR 4466/67 [ADD]

▲ = CD ♦ = Enhanced CD Δ = MD ■ = Cassette Tape □ = DCC

Weiss, Jürgen (sgr)

Wagner, R.:Lohengrin, w. Sharon Sweet (sop—Elsa), Eva Marton (sop—Ortrud), Ben Heppner (ten—Lohengrin), Anton Rosner (ten—Nobleman), Heinrich Weber (ten—Nobleman), Jan-Hendrik Rootering (bar—Heinrich der Vögler), Sergei Leiferkus (bar—Friedrich von Telramund), Bryn Terfel (b-bar—King's Herald), Barbara Fleckenstein (sgr—Page), Atsuko Suzuki (sgr—Page), Gisela Ulmann (sgr—Page), Marion Rambausek (sgr—Page), Dankwart Siegele (sgr—Nobleman), Jürgen Weiss (sgr—Nobleman), C. Davis (cnd), Bavarian SO, Bavarian State Opera Chorus, Bavarian Radio Chorus *(rec Residenz Herkulesaal, Munich, May 14-28, 1994)* RCA Red Seal 3-▲ 09026-62646-2 [DDD]

Wagner, R.:Lohengrin (sels), w. Eva Marton (sop—Ortrud), Sharon Sweet (sop—Elsa von Brabant), Barbara Fleckenstein (sgr—Page), Marion Rambausek (sgr—Page), Atsuko Suzuki (sgr—Page), Gisela Ulmann (sgr—Page), Ben Heppner (ten—Lohengrin), Anton Rosner (ten—Nobleman), Heinrich Weber (ten—Nobleman), Sergei Leiferkus (bar—Friedrich von Telramund), Bryn Terfel (b-bar—King's Herald), Jan-Hendrik Rootering (bass—Henry the Fowler), Dankwart Siegele (sgr—Nobleman), Jürgen Weiss (sgr—Nobleman), C. Davis (cnd), Bavarian RSO, Michael Gläser (cnd), Udo Mehrpohl (cnd), Bavarian Radio Chorus, Bavarian State Opera Chorus—Seht! Seht! [from Act 1, Scene 2]; Nun sei bedankt, mein lieber Schwan!; Wenn ich im Kampfe für dich siege; Welch holde Wunder muss ich sehen?; Nun höret mich und achtet wohl; Durch Gottes Sieg ist jetzt dein Leben mein [all from Act 1, Scene 3]; Treulich geführt ziehet dahin [from Act 3, Scene 1]; Wie hehr erkenn' ich unsrer Liebe Wesen!; Höchstes Vertrau'n hast du mir schon zu danken; Weh' nun ist all' unser Glück dahin! [all from Act 3, Scene 2]; In fernem Land, unnahbar euren Schritten [from Act 3, Scene 3] *(rec Munich, Mar 14-28, 1994)* RCA Red Seal ▲ 09026-68239-2 [DDD]

Weiss, Silvia (sgr)

Henze, H.-W.:Elegy for Young Lovers, w. Regina Schudel (sop), Richard Lloyd Morgan (bass), Lawrence Richard (bass), Helmut Bernhofen (sgr), Bruno Fath (sgr), Aurelia Hajek (sgr), B. Jones (cnd), Berlin Chamber Opera Orch *(rec Berlin)* Deutsche Schallplatten 2-▲ DS 1050

Welbat, Douglas (nar)

Mozart, W.A.:Zauberflöte, w. Constanze Backes (sop—Papagena), Christiane Oelze (sop—Pamina), Susan Roberts (sop—First Lady), Cyndia Sieden (sop—Queen of the Night), Carola Guber (cta—Second Lady), Maria Jonas (cta—Third Lady), Andreas Dieterich (trb—First Boy), Jan Andreas Mendel (trb—Second Boy), Florian Wöller (trb—Third Boy), Uwe Peper (ten—Monostatos), Nicolas Robertson (ten—First Man in Armor), Michael Schade (ten—Tamino), Gerald Finley (bar—Papageno), Noel Mann (bass—Second Man in Armour), Harry Peeters (bass—Sarastro), Detlef Roth (bass—Speaker/First Priest), Robert Burt (speaker—Third Priest), Robert Johnston (speaker—Second Priest), Wolfgang Knauer (speaker—Fourth Priest), Douglas Welbat (speaker—Second Priest), J. E. Gardiner (cnd), English Baroque Soloists, Monteverdi Choir London *(rec Forum am Schlosspark, Ludwigsburg, July 1995)* Archiv 2-▲ 449166-2

Welch, Jonathan (ten)

Puccini, G.:La Bohème, w. L. Orgonasova (sop), C. Gonzales (mez), F. Previati (bar), W. Humburg (cnd), *(orch unknown)*, Bratislava Children's Choir [I] Naxos 2-▲ 8.660003/04 [DDD]

Puccini, G.:La Bohème (sels), w. Luba Orgonasova (sop—Mimì), Carmen Gonzales (sop—Musetta), Jonathan Welch (ten—Rudolfo), Fabio Previati (bar—Marcello), Boaz Senator (bar—Schaunard), Ivan Urbas (bass—Colline), Jiri Sulzenko (bass—Alcindoro), W. Humburg (cnd), Czech-Slovak RSO Bratislava, Bratislava Children's Choir, Slovak Phil Chorus *(rec Concert Hall, Czecho-Slovak Radio, Bratislava, Apr. 23-May 4, 1990)* Naxos ▲ 8.553151 [DDD]

Weld (sgr)

Saint-Saëns, C.:Requiem, w. Hewes (sgr), MacMaster (sgr), Watson (sgr), J. Somary (cnd), Amor Artis Orch, Amor Artis Chorale *(rec live)* Premier ▲ PRCD 1025 [DDD]

Weldon, J. (sgr)

Romberg, S.:Deep in My Heart, w. H. Traubel (sgr), J. Ferrer (sgr), R. Clooney (sgr), Gene Kelly (sgr), F. Kelly (sgr), V. Damone (sgr), J. Powell (sgr), A. Miller (sgr), W. Olvis (sgr), C. Richards (sgr), H. Keel (sgr), T. Martin (sgr) Sony Music Special Products ▲ AK 47703

Welfing, H. M. (ten)

Bach, J.S.:Cant 70, w. A. Felbermayer (sop), E. Wiens (sop), N. Foster (bass), F. Prohaska (cnd), Vienna State Opera Orch, Vienna State Opera Chorus [G] *(rec June 1957)* Vanguard Classics ("The Bach Guild" series) ▲ OVC 2010 [ADD]

Welitsch, Ljuba (sop)

Mozart, W.A.:Don Giovanni, w. I. Seefried (sop), E. Schwarzkopf (sop), A. Dermota (ten), E. Kunz (bar), T. Gobbi (bar), A. Poell (b-bar), J. Greindl (bass), W. Furtwängler (cnd), Vienna PO, Vienna State Opera Chorus *(rec 1950)* Laudis 3-▲ LDS 4001 [AAD]

Recital Melodram 2-▲ CDM 26511 (m) [AAD]

Unforgettable Recitals:Ljuba Welitsch melodram 2-▲ CDI 204004 [ADD]

Welker, Hartmut (bar)

Korngold, E.W.:Das Wunder der Heliane, w. A. Tomowa-Sintow (sop), R. Runkel (cta), N. Gedda (ten), J. D. de Haan (ten), R. Pape (bass), J. Mauceri (cnd), Berlin RSO [G] London 3-▲ 436636-2 [DDD]

Wagner, R.:Lohengrin, w. Cheryl Studer (sop), Waltraud Meier (mez), Siegfried Jerusalem (ten), Andreas Schmidt (bar), Kurt Moll (bass), C. Abbado (cnd), Vienna PO Deutsche Grammophon 3-▲ 437808-2

Zomlinsky, A. von:Der Traumgörge, w. P. Coburn (sop), J. Martin (sop), G. M. Ronge (sop), B. Calm (mez), P. Haage (ten), H. Kruse (ten), J. Protschka (ten), M. Blasius (bass), V. von Halem (bass), G. Albrecht (cnd), Frankfurt RSO [G] Capriccio 2-▲ CD 10241/2 [DDD]

Weller, Dieter (bass)

Zemlinsky, A. von:Der Geburtstag der Infantin, w. B. Haldas (sop), I. Nielsen (sop), K. Riegel (ten), G. Albrecht (cnd), Berlin RSO, Berlin RIAS Women's Chamber Choir [G] Koch Schwann ▲ CD 314 013 [DDD]

Wells, Alison (sop)

Hopkins, B.:Music of, w. A. Balanescu (vn), R. Bernas (cnd), Music Projects London—En attendant for Flute, Oboe, Cello & Harpsichord; 2 Pomes for Soprano, Bass Cittern; Trumpet, Harp & Viola; Penandt for Violin; Sensation for Soprano, Saxophone, Trumpet, Harp & Viola NM Classics ▲ NMCD 014 [DDD]

Wells, Jeffrey (bass)

Barber, S.:Antony & Cleopatra, w. E. Hinds (sop), C. Badea (cnd), Spoleto Festival Orch, Westminster Choir [E] *(rec live at the Spoleto Festival in Spoleto, Italy, June 1983)* New World 2-▲ 322/24-2 [AAD]

Wells, Patricia (sop)

Cherubini, L.:Mass in d, w. Maureen Forrester (cta), George Shirley (ten), Justino Diaz (bass), N. Jenkins (cnd), Clarion Concerts Orch, Clarion Concerts Chorus *(rec Vanguard's 23rd Street Recording Studio)* Vanguard Classics ▲ SVC-44 [AAD]

Haydn, J.:Mass 10, "Kriegsmesse", "Paukenmesse", w. Gwendoline Killebrew (mez), Michael Devlin (b-bar), Alan Titus (bar), L. Bernstein (cnd), *(orch unknown)*, Norman Scribner Choir [L] *(rec 1973)* Sony Classical ("Bernstein:The Royal Edition" series) 2-▲ SM2K 47563 [ADD]

Mercadante, S.:Il giuramento, w. B. Wolff (mez), G. Colmagro (bar), M. Molese (sgr), T. Schippers (cnd), Juilliard Orch, Juilliard Chorus [I] *(rec live, Spoleto, 6/29/70)* Memories 2-▲ HR 4174/75 (m)

Mercadante, S.:Il giuramento, w. B. Wolff (mez), G. Colmagro (bar), M. Molese (sgr), T. Schippers (cnd), Juilliard Orch, Juilliard Chorus [I] *(rec live, Spoleto, 6/29/70)* Myto 2-▲ 2 MCD 90632 [ADD]

Welter, L. (bar)

Giordano, U.:Andrea Chénier, w. H. Konetzni (sop—Madelon), M. Sjöstedt (sop—Bersi), R. Tebaldi (sop—Maddalena de Coigny), E. Höngen (cta—La Contessa de Coigny), F. Corelli (ten—Andrea Chénier), E. Bastianini (bar—C. Gérard), K. Paskalis (bar—Pietro Fléville), L. Welter (bar—Fouquier Tinville), A. Pernerstorfer (b-bar—Mathieu), L. von Matačić (cnd), Vienna State Opera Orch, Vienna State Opera Chorus *(rec Vienna, June 26, 1960)* Fortissimo 2-▲ CDE 3003 [ADD]

Handel, G.F.:Judas Maccabaeus, w. Agnes Giebel (sop), Julianna Falk (cta), Fritz Wunderlich (ten), Pöld (sgr), R. Kubelik (cnd), Bavarian RSO, Bavarian Chorus [G] *(rec live 10/25/63)* Melodram 2-▲ MEL 28026 [AAD]

Wagner, R.:Das Liebesverbot, w. H. Zadek (cta), L. Sorell (mez), A. Dermota (ten), K. Equiluz (ten), Imdahl (sgr), R. Heger (cnd), Austrian RSO, Austrian Radio Chorus *(rec live, Vienna, 1962)* Melodram 2-▲ MEL 27052 [AAD]

Welting, Ruth (sop)

Delibes, L.:Lakmé, w. M. Spacagna (sop—Ellen), R. Welting (sop—Lakmé), A. Kraus (ten—Gérald), D. Holloway (bar—Frédéric), P. Plishka (bass—Nilakantha), N. Rescigno (cnd), Dallas Civic Opera Orch *(rec Nov. 1980)* Ornamenti 2-▲ FE 108 [ADD]

Massenet, J.:Cendrillon, w. F. von Stade (mez), N. Gedda (ten), J. Bastin (bass), J. Rudel (cnd), Philharmonia Orch, Ambrosian Opera Chorus [F] CBS 2-▲ M2K 35194 [ADD]

Wen, Cui (nar)

Bond, V.:Thinking Like a Mountain, w. V. Bond (cnd), Shanghai SO *(rec Shanghai Music Hall)* Protone ▲ NRPR 2205 [DDD]

Wenberg, Vittorio (sgr)

Puccini, G.:Madama Butterfly (sels), w. Margaret Sheridan (sop), Ida Mannarini (mez), Lionello Cecil (ten), Carlo Sabajno (pno) *(rec La Scala, 1929-30)* Romophone ("Opera Magna" series) 2-▲ 89001-2

Wendel, Christoph Johannes (sgr)

Schnittke, A.:Historia von D. Johann Fausten, w. Hanna Schwarz (mez—Fair Helen), Arno Raunig (alt—Mephostophiles), Eberhard Büchner (ten—Old Man), Jürgen Freier (bar—Dr. Johann Faustus), Jonathan Barreto-Ramos (sgr—Student), Jürgen Fersch (sgr—Student), Eberhard Lorenz (sgr—Erzähler), Christoph Johannes Wendel (sgr—Student), G. Albrecht (cnd), Hamburg State PO, Hamburg State Opera Chorus *(rec live, Hamburg, Germany)* RCA Red Seal 2-▲ 09026-68413-2

Wendlandt, William (bar)

Partch, H.:Barstow, w. Harry Partch (adapted gtr/voc), Christine Charnstrom (chromelodeon), Lee Hoiby (kitara) *(rec 1945)* Innova 4-▲ 401

Partch, H.:By the Rivers of Babylon, w. Christine Charnstrom (chromelodeon), Lee Hoiby (kithara), Harry Partch (adapted va) *(rec 1945)* Innova 4-▲ 401

Partch, H.:Dark Brother, w. Christine Charnstrom (chromelodeon), Lee Hoiby (kithara), Harry Partch (adapted va), Fralia Hancock (Indian dr) *(rec 1945)* Innova 4-▲ 401

Partch, H.:US Highball, w. Harry Partch (adapted gtr/voc), Christine Charnstrom (chromelodeon), Lee Hoiby (kitara), Fralia Hancock (db canon) *(rec 1946)* Innova 4-▲ 401

Wendlant, William (spkr)

Partch, H.:17 Lyrics by Li Po, w. Harry Partch (adapted va)—10 Lyrics [A Dream; An Encounter in the Field; On Hearing the Flute; The Intruder; I am a Peach Tree; With a Man of Leisure; A Midnight Farewell; Before the Cask of Wine; On the Ship of Spicewood; By the Great Wall] *(rec 1947)* Innova 4-▲ 401

Wendler, Attila (ten)

Franck, C.:Choral Music, w. Mariann Bódi (sop), Istvan Rácz (bass), Salomon Kamp (cnd), Debrecen Kodaly Choir—Quae est ista; Dextera Domini Hungaroton ▲ HCD 31579 [DDD]

Franck, C.:Messe solennelle, w. Dezsö Karasszon (org), Andrea Kocsis (hp), Zsolt Moinár (vc), Ferenc Nagy (db), Salomon Kamp (cnd), Debrecen Kodaly Choir Hungaroton ▲ HCD 31579 [DDD]

Wenglor, Ingeborg (sop)

Beethoven, L. van:Syms (comp), w. U. Zollenkopf (cta), Hans Joachim Rotzsch (ten), T. Adam (bass-bar), F. Konwitschny (cnd), Leipzig Gewandhaus Orch, Leipzig Radio Chorus *(rec 1959-1961)* Berlin Classics ("Eterna" series) 6-▲ BER 2005 [ADD]

Beethoven, L. van:Sym 9, "Choral Sym", w. Ursula Zollenkopf (alt), Hans Jochim Rotzsch (ten), Theo Adam (bass), F. Konwitschny (cnd), Leipzig Gewandhaus Orch, Leipzig Radio Chorus Polskie Nagrania Edition ▲ ECD 028

Wenhold, André (bar)

Wagner, S.:Banadietrich, w. Beth Johanning (sop), Vivian Hanner (sgr), Volker Horn (ten), Andreas Schmidt (bar), Adalbert Walker (bass), V. Gailis (cnd), Thuringian SO, Rudolstadt Festival Chorus *(rec Rudolstädt, June 1995)* Marco Polo 2-▲ 8.223895-6 [DDD]

Wagner, S.:Der Bärenhäuter, w. B. Johanning (sop—Luise), K. Likic (sop—Lene), T. Koon (sop—Gunda), V. Horn (ten—Hans Kraft), A. Feilhaber (ten—Nikolaus Spitz), R. Hartmann (bar—Kaspar Wild), A. Wenhold (bar—Stranger), A. Waller (bass—Devil), H. Kiichli (bass—Melchior Fröhlich), K. Bach (cnd), Thüringian SO, Thüringian State Theater Chorus *(rec Rudolstadt, July 25-31, 1993)* Marco Polo ("Opera Classics" series) 2-▲ 8.223713/4 [DDD]

Wagner, S.:Schwarzschwanenreich, w. Beth Johanning (sop—Linda), Kerstin Quandt (cta—Ursula), Walter Raffeiner (ten—Ludwig), Lucian Chioreanu (ten—A Boy), André Wenhold (bar—Oswald), Roland Hartmann (sgr—Tempter/Priest), Jutta Maria Schmitz (sgr—Ash-Woman), Ksenija Lukie (sgr—A Girl), K. Bach (cnd), Thüringian Saalfeld-Rudolstadt SO, Thüringian Landestheater Rudolstadt Chorus *(rec Thüringer Landestheater, Rudolstadt, June 1994)* Marco Polo 2-▲ 8.223777-8 [DDD]

Wenk, Erich (bass)

Brahms, J.:Liebeslieder Waltzes SATB, w. E. Berger (sop), G. Pfitzinger (alt), W. Ludwig (ten), E.-G. Scherzer (pno), G. Falbe (pno) *(rec 1959)* FNAC Music ▲ 642313

Brahms, J.:Neue Liebeslieder Waltzes, w. E. Berger (sop), G. Pfitzinger (alt), W. Ludwig (ten), E.-G. Scherzer (pno), G. Falbe (pno) *(rec 1959)* FNAC Music ▲ 642313

Haydn, J.:Die Jahreszeiten, w. Teresa Stich-Randall (mez), Helmut Kretschmar (ten), W. Goehr (cnd), North German RSO, Hamburg Chorus *(rec 1966)* FNAC Music 2-▲ 642325

Wenkel, Ortrun (cta)

Bach, J.S.:Cant 4, w. Helga Terner (sop), Peter Schreier (ten), Eberhard Büchner (ten), H.-J. Rotzsch (cnd), Leipzig Gewandhaus Orch, Leipzig St. Thomas Church Choir, Leipzig New Bach Collegium Musicum Berlin Classics ▲ BER 2067 [ADD]

Bach, J.S.:Cant 21, w. Arleen Augér (sop), Siegfried Jerusalem (ten), Peter Schreier (ten), Theo Adam (b-bar), H.-J. Rotzsch (cnd), New Bach Collegium Musicum, Leipzig St. Thomas Church Choir Berlin Classics ▲ BER 2175 [ADD]

Bach, J.S.:Cant 31, w. Helga Terner (sop), Peter Schreier (ten), Eberhard Büchner (ten), H.-J. Rotzsch (cnd), Leipzig Gewandhaus Orch, Leipzig St. Thomas Church Choir, Leipzig New Bach Collegium Musicum Berlin Classics ▲ BER 2067 [ADD]

Bach, J.S.:Cant 50, w. Arleen Auger (sop), Peter Schreier (ten), Theo Adam (b-bar), H.-J. Rotzsch (cnd), New Bach Collegium Musicum, Leipzig St. Thomas Church Choir Berlin Classics ▲ BER 2176 [ADD]

Bach, J.S.:Cant 79, w. Arleen Augér (sop), Peter Schreier (ten), Theo Adam (b-bar), H.-J. Rotzsch (cnd), New Bach Collegium Musicum, Leipzig St. Thomas Church Choir Berlin Classics ▲ BER 2176 [ADD]

Bach, J.S.:Cant 80, w. Arleen Augér (sop), Peter Schreier (ten), Theo Adam (b-bar), H.-J. Rotzsch (cnd), New Bach Collegium Musicum, Leipzig St. Thomas Church Choir Berlin Classics ▲ BER 2176 [ADD]

Bach, J.S.:Cant 134, w. Helga Terner (sop), Peter Schreier (ten), Eberhard Büchner (ten), H.-J. Rotzsch (cnd), Leipzig Gewandhaus Orch, Leipzig New Bach Collegium Musicum, Leipzig St. Thomas Church Choir Berlin Classics ▲ BER 2067 [ADD]

Bach, J.S.:Cant 137, w. Arleen Augér (sop), Peter Schreier (ten), Siegfried Jerusalem (ten), Theo Adam (b-bar), H.-J. Rotzsch (cnd), New Bach Collegium Musicum, Leipzig St. Thomas Church Choir Berlin Classics ▲ BER 2175 [ADD]

Bach, J.S.:Cant 192, w. Arleen Auger (sop), Peter Schreier (ten), Theo Adam (b-bar), H.-J. Rotzsch (cnd), New Bach Collegium Musicum, Leipzig St. Thomas Church Choir Berlin Classics ▲ BER 2176 [ADD]

Dvořák, A.:Stabat Mater, w. G. Benačková (sop), P. Dvorský (ten), J.-H. Rootering (bass), W. Sawallisch (cnd), Czech PO, Czech Phil Chorus [L] Supraphon 2-▲ 10 3561-2 [DDD]

Handel, G.F.:Serse, w. Barbara Hendricks (sop—Romilda), Anne-Marie Rodde (sop—Atalanta), Carolyn Watkinson (cta—Xerxes), Otrun Wenkel (cta—Amastre), Paul Esswood (ct—Arsamene), Ulrich Studer (bar—Elviro), Ulrik Cold (bass—Ariodate), J. Malgoire (cnd), La Grande Écurie et la Chambre du Roy *(rec Paris, 1979)* Sony Classical 3-▲ SM3K 36941

Mozart, W.A.:Requiem, w. Rachel Yakar (sop), Kurt Equiluz (ten), Robert Holl (bass), N. Harnoncourt (cnd), Vienna Concentus Musicus, Vienna State Opera Chorus [L] Teldec ▲ 2292-42911-2

Shostakovich, D.:From Jewish Folk Poetry, w. E. Söderström (sop), R. Karczykowski (ten), B. Haitink (cnd), Royal Concertgebouw Orch London ▲ 417581-2 [DDD/ADD]

Shostakovich, D.:Sym 14, w. J. Varady (sop), D. Fischer-Dieskau (bar), B. Haitink (cnd), Royal Concertgebouw Orch London ▲ 417514-2 [DDD]

Wennberg, Siv (sop)

Wagner, R.:Rienzi, der Letzte der Tribunen, w. Martin (sop), A. Kollo (ten), P. Schreier (ten), T. Adam (b-bar), H. Hollreiser (cnd), Dresden State Opera Orch, Dresden State Opera Chorus [G] EMI Classics ("Studio" series) 3-▲ CDMB 63980

Wentzel (sgr)
Menotti, G.C.:Goya, w. Josie de Guzman (sgr), Daner (sgr), Hernandez (sgr), S. Mercurio (cnd), Spoleto Festival Orch, Westminster Choir [I] *(rec live 1991)* Nuova Era 2-▲ 7060/61 [DDD]

Wenzel, Silke (sop)
Bach, J.S.:Cant 36, w. Reiner Schneider-Waterburg (alt), Kobie van Rensburg (ten), Christian Hilz (bass), W. Kelber (cnd), Munich Monteverdi Orch *(rec live, Dec 1995)* Calig ▲ 50963 [DDD]
Bach, J.S.:Cant 40, w. Reiner Schneider-Waterburg (alt), Kobie van Rensburg (ten), Christian Hilz (bass), W. Kelber (cnd), Munich Monteverdi Orch *(rec live, Dec 1995)* Calig ▲ 50963 [DDD]
Bach, J.S.:Cant 91, w. Reiner Schneider-Waterburg (alt), Kobie van Rensburg (ten), Christian Hilz (bass), W. Kelber (cnd), Munich Monteverdi Orch *(rec live, Dec 1995)* Calig ▲ 50963 [DDD]

Werner, Alfred (bar)
Strauss (II), Joh.:Die Fledermaus (sels), w. Ariane Calix (sop—Ida), Gabriele Fontana (sop—Rosalinde), Brigitte Karwautz (sop—Adele), Rohangiz Yachmi-Caucig (cta—Orlofsky), John Dickie (ten—Eisenstein), Josef Hopferwieser (ten—Alfred), Erich Wessner (ten—Dr. Blind), Andrea Martin (bar—Falke), Alfred Werner (bar—Frank), J. Wildner (cnd), Czech-Slovak RSO Bratislava, Bratislava City Chorus—Ov.; [Act I] Täubchen, das entflattert ist...; Ach, ich darf nicht hin zu dir; Nein, mit solchen Advokaten; Komm mit mir zum Souper; So muss allein ich bleiben; Trinke, Liebchen, trinke schnell; [Act II] Ein Souper heut' uns winkt; Ich lade gern mir Gäste ein; Mein Herr Marquis, ein Mann wie Sie; Dieser Anstand, so manierlich; Klänge der Heimat; Im Feuerstrom der Reben; Marianka komm und tanz me hier; [Act III] Entr'acte; Spiel' ich die Unschuld vom Lande; O Fledermaus, o Fledermaus *(rec Slovak Radio Concert Hall, Bratislava)* Naxos ▲ 8.553171 [DDD]

Werner, Regina (sop)
Bach, J.S.:Cant 29, w. Heidi Riess (alt), Hans-Joachim Rotzsch (ten), Hermann Christian Polster (bass), H.-J. Rotzsch (cnd), Leipzig Gewandhaus Orch, Leipzig St. Thomas Church Choir Berlin Classics ▲ BER CD 9055
Bach, J.S.:Cant 119, w. Heidi Riess (alt), Hans-Joachim Rotzsch (ten), Hermann Christian Polster (bass), H.-J. Rotzsch (cnd), Leipzig Gewandhaus Orch, Leipzig St. Thomas Church Choir Berlin Classics ▲ BER CD 9055
Haydn, J.:Die Schöpfung, w. Peter Schreier (ten), Theo Adam (bass), H. Koch (cnd), Berlin RSO, Berlin Radio Chorus Berlin Classics 2-▲ BER CD 9115

Wernigk, William (ten)
Wagner, R.:Siegfried (sels), w. E. Szantho (cta—Erda), M. Lorenz (ten—Siegfried), W. Wernigk (ten—Mime), L. Hoffmann (bass—Wanderer), H. Knappertsbusch (cnd), Vienna State Opera Orch, Vienna State Opera Chorus *(rec June 16, 1937)* Koch Schwann 2-▲ SCH 314602

Werres, Elisabeth (sop)
Hindemith, P.:Neues vom Tage, w. R. Ries (sgr), Claudio Nicolai (bar), J. Latham-König (cnd), Cologne RSO [G] Wergo 2-▲ WER 6192/93-2

Wertsch, Nancy (alt)
Imbrie, A.W.:Campion Songs, w. Joan Peterson (sop), Mark Bleeke (ten), Nathaniel Watson (bar), A. Korf (cnd), Parnassus *(rec Sept. 29, 1993)* New World ▲ 80441-2

Wesley-Smith, Olivia (sgr)
Wesley-Smith, M.:Snark-Hunting 2, w. Martin Wesley-Smith (elec) [excerpts from Boojum! (1986)] *(rec Electronic Music Studio, Sydney Conservatorium of Music)* Tall Poppies ▲ TP 072 [DDD]

Wessel, Kai (alt)
Bach, J.S.:Cant 66, w. Barbara Schlick (sop), James Taylor (ten), Peter Kooy (bass), Phillippe Herreweghe (cnd), Collegium Vocale Harmonia Mundi France ▲ HMC 901513
Bach, J.S.:Easter Oratorio, w. Barbara Schlick (sop), James Taylor (ten), Peter Kooy (bass), Phillippe Herreweghe (cnd), Collegium Vocale Harmonia Mundi France ▲ HMC 901513
Bach, J.S.:St. John Passion, w. B. Schlick (sop), G. de Mey (ten), G. Turk (ten), K. Mertens (b-bar), P. Kooy (bass), T. Koopman (cnd), Amsterdam Baroque Orch, Netherlands Bach Society Choir Erato 2-▲ 94675-2
Bach, J.S.:St. Matthew Passion, w. B. Schlick (sop), G. de Mey (ten), C. Pregardien (ten), P. Kooy (bass), T. Koopman (cnd), Amsterdam Baroque Orch, W. Cantryn (cnd), J. van Veldhoven (cnd), Breda Sacred Choir, Netherlands Bach Society Boys' Choir Erato ▲ 2292-45814-2
Bach, J.S.:St. Matthew Passion, w. B. Schlick (sop), G. de Mey (ten), P. Kooy (bass), T. Koopman (cnd), Amsterdam Baroque Orch Erato 2-▲ 94676-2
Biber, H. von:Requiem à 15, w. E. Bongers (sop), A. Grimm (sop), P. de Groot (alt), M. Reyans (ten), S. Davies (ten), R. Steur (bass), K.-J. de Koning (bass), T. Koopman (cnd), Amsterdam Baroque Orch, Amsterdam Baroque Choir Erato ▲ 91725
Biber, H. von:Vesperae longiores ac breviores una cum litaniis Laurentanis, w. E. Bongers (sop), A. Grimm (sop), P. de Groot (alt), M. Reyans (ten), S. Davies (ten), R. Steur (bass), K.-J. de Koning (bass), T. Koopman (cnd), Amsterdam Baroque Orch, Amsterdam Baroque Choir Erato ▲ 91725
Capricornus, S.F.:Theatrum musicum quod per duodecim scenas seu sacras cantiones aperuit, w. D. Collot (sop), L. S. Norin (mez), I. Honeyman (ten), S. Schreckenberger (bass), M. Gester (cnd), Parlement de Musique Opus 111 ▲ OPS 30-99
Charpentier, M.-A.:Motets for Double Choir, w. B. Schlick (sop), N. Zijlstra (sop), D. Visse (ct), H. van Berne (ten), C. Prégardien (ten), P. Kooy (bass), K. Martens (bass), T. Koopman (cnd), Amsterdam Baroque Orch—Canticum pro pace; Josué; Mors Saulis et Jonathae; Praelium Michaelis; Quam dilecta; 3 Leçons de Ténèbres Erato (Musifrance) ▲ 2292-45822-2 ZA
Scarlatti, A.:Passion Oratorio, w. M. Bach (sop), P. Geitner (sop), M. Schneider (cnd), La Stagione, Frankfurt Vocal Ensemble Capriccio 2-▲ CD 10 411/12
Wagner, R.:Die Meistersinger von Nürnberg (sels), w. E. Kunz (bar), G. Hann (bass), A. Rother (cnd), Berlin RSO, Berlin Radio Chorus—Act 2 Preiser ▲ PRE 90168 [AAD]

Wessner, Erich (ten)
Strauss (II), Joh.:Die Fledermaus (sels), w. Ariane Calix (sop—Ida), Gabriele Fontana (sop—Rosalinde), Brigitte Karwautz (sop—Adele), Rohangiz Yachmi-Caucig (cta—Orlofsky), John Dickie (ten—Eisenstein), Josef Hopferwieser (ten—Alfred), Erich Wessner (ten—Dr. Blind), Andrea Martin (bar—Falke), Alfred Werner (bar—Frank), J. Wildner (cnd), Czech-Slovak RSO Bratislava, Bratislava City Chorus—Ov.; [Act I] Täubchen, das entflattert ist...; Ach, ich darf nicht hin zu dir; Nein, mit solchen Advokaten; Komm mit mir zum Souper; So muss allein ich bleiben; Trinke, Liebchen, trinke schnell; [Act II] Ein Souper heut' uns winkt; Ich lade gern mir Gäste ein; Mein Herr Marquis, ein Mann wie Sie; Dieser Anstand, so manierlich; Klänge der Heimat; Im Feuerstrom der Reben; Marianka komm und tanz me hier; [Act III] Entr'acte; Spiel' ich die Unschuld vom Lande; O Fledermaus, o Fledermaus *(rec Slovak Radio Concert Hall, Bratislava)* Naxos ▲ 8.553171 [DDD]

West, Jayne (sop)
Koechlin, C.:Premier album de Lilian, w. F. Smith (fl), M. Amlin (pno) [F] Hyperion ▲ CDA 66414 [DDD]
Stravinsky, I.:The Rake's Progress, w. J. West (sop—Anne Trulove), S. Love (mez—Mother Goose), W. White (mez—Baba the Turk), J. Garrison (ten—Tome Rakewell), M. Lowrey (ten—Sellem), A. Woodley (bar—Father Truelove), J. Cheek (b-bar), *(orch unknown)* MusicMasters 2-▲ 01612-67131-2 [DDD]

West, Jocelyn (sgr)
Hildegard Of Bingen:Sacred Songs, w. Jocelyn West (sgr), Vivien Ellis (sgr), Stevie Wishart (sgr/h-g), Hester Briant (sgr), Fiona Cunningham (sgr), Tara Franks (sgr), Emily Levy (sgr), Lucy Steele (sgr), Vickie Couperin (sgr), Julie Murphy (sgr), Oxford Girls' Choir—Honey & milk beneath her tongue; Ursula's virgins; The devil's virgins; Place of the ancient heart; Zeal of divinity; O fiery spirit; Red river falling; O orzchis ecclesia, Living-light angels; The clouds are grieving; The firstwoman; From their homeland; But the devil mocked; Song to Ecclesia *(rec Toddington, Gloucestershire, England, May 6-8, 1995)* Celestial Harmonies ▲ 13127-2

West, John (bass)
Offenbach, J.:Les Contes d'Hoffmann, w. Beverly Sills (sop—Olympia/Giulietta/Antonia/Stella), Edith Evans (mez—Nicklausse/Mother's Voice), Michael Devlin (ten—Spalanzani), André Turp (ten—Hoffmann), Luigi Vellucci (ten—Andrès/Cochenille/Pitichinaccio/Frantz), Donald Bernard (bar—Luther/Schlemil), Norman Treigle (bass—Lindorf/Coppélius/Dapertutto/Dr. Miracle), John West (bass—Crespel), Alton Brim (sgr—Nathanaël), Rodney Hall (sgr—Hermann), K. Andersson (cnd), New Orleans Opera Orch, New Orleans Opera Chorus *(rec Feb 27, 1964)* VAI Audio 2-▲ VAIA 1121-2 [ADD]

West, Jon Frederic (ten)
Alfano, F.:Turandot, w. L. Kelm (Turandot), C. Keene (cnd), *(orch unknown), (chorus unknown)*—6 arias & duets [I] *(rec live, New York 1985)* Standing Room Only 2-▲ SRO 839-2 [ADD]

West, Lucretia (alt)
Mahler, G.:Kindertotenlieder, w. H. Knappertsbusch (cnd), Berlin PO [G] *(rec live, Berlin, 4/9/56)* Arkadia ▲ 710 (m) [ADD]
Mahler, G.:Lieder eines fahrenden Gesellen, w. H. Scherchen (cnd), Vienna State Opera Orch, Vienna Academy Chorus Theorema ▲ TH 121203/04
Mahler, G.:Sym 2, w. Mimi Coertse (sop), H. Scherchen (cnd), Vienna State Opera Orch Theorema 2-▲ TH 121203/04
Mahler, G.:Sym 2, w. M. Coertse (sop), H. Scherchen (cnd), Vienna State Opera Orch, Vienna State Opera Chorus *(rec 1958)* Enterprise ("Palladio" series) ▲ ENTPD 4180 [ADD]
Mahler, G.:Sym 2, w. M. Coertse (sop), H. Scherchen (cnd), London Phil SO, Vienna Academy Chorus MCA Classics ("Double Decker" series) 2-▲ MCAD2-99833 [AAD]
Mahler, G.:Sym 3, w. J. Barbirolli (cnd), Berlin PO, St. Hedwig's Cathedral Choir [G] *(rec live, 3/8/69)* Arkadia 3-▲ 719 [ADD]
Mozart, W.A.:Requiem, w. S. Jurinac (sop), H. Loeffler (ten), F. Gutherie (bass), R. Leibowitz (cnd), Vienna State Opera Orch, Vienna State Opera Chorus [L] *(rec 1958)* MCA Classics 2-▲ MCAD2 9816 [AAD]
Mozart, W.A.:Requiem, w. S. Jurinac (sop), H. Loeffler (ten), F. Gutherie (bass), H. Scherchen (cnd), Vienna State Opera Orch, Vienna State Opera Chorus *(rec 1958)* Andromeda ▲ ANR 2525 [ADD]

West, Timothy (nar)
Prokofiev, S.:Eugene Onegin, w. K. Fuge (sop), P. im Thurn (bar), J. Walker (bass), E. Downes (cnd), Sinfonia 21, New Company Chandos 2-▲ CHAN 9318/19 [DDD]
Walton, W.:Façade, w. Prunella Scales (nar), J. Glover (cnd), London Mozart Players [1951 version] [E] ASV ▲ ASV 679 [DDD/ADD]

Westbrook-Geha, Mary (mez)
Bach, J.S.:Magnificat, BWV 243, w. M. A. Kruger (sop), H. Schellenberg (sop), I. Humphrey (ten), S. Sylvan (bar), B. H. Moyse (cnd), Orch of St. Luke MusicMasters ▲ 7059-2-C [DDD]
Mozart, W.A.:Requiem, w. J. Bryden (sop), W. Hite (ten), S. Richardson (bar), A. Parrott (cnd), Boston Early Music Festival Orch, Boston Early Music Festival Chorus [L] Denon ▲ CO 77152 [DDD]

Westi, Kurt (ten)
Gade, N.W.:Korsfarerne, w. Rorholm (mez), Cold (bass), F. Rasmussen (cnd), Aarhus SO, Aarhus Sym Chorus [Da] BIS ▲ CD 465 [DDD]
Koppel, H.D.:Moses, w. Elisabeth Meyer-Topsøe (sop), Kirsten Dolberg (mez), Michael Kristensen (ten), Per Høyer (bar), Christian Christiansen (bass), O.A. Hughes (cnd), Danish National RSO, Jesper Grovw Jørgensen (cnd), Danish National Radio Choir *(rec Danish Radio Concert Hall, Mar 1996)* Marco Polo/Dacapo ▲ 8.224046 [DDD]
Nielsen, C.:Saul & David, w. T. Kiberg (sop), A. Gjevang (mez), P. Lindroos (ten), C. Christiansen (bass), A. Haugland (bass), J. Klint (bass), N. Järvi (cnd), Danish National RSO, Danish National Radio Choir [Da] Chandos 2-▲ CHAN 8911/12 [DDD]
Nielsen, C.:Songs, w. H. Metz (pno)—Den Danske sang er en ung blond pige; Der dukker af disen min faedrende jord; Farvel min velsignede fødeby; Grøn er varens haek; Hvem sidder der bag skaermen; Hvor sødt i sommeraftenstunden; I skyggen vi vanke; Jeg baerer med smil min byrde; Jeg laegger mig sa trygt til ro; Jeg ved en laerkerede; Min pige er lys som rav; Nu er dagen fuld af sang; Nu er da varen kommen; De refsnaes drenge, de samsø piger; Saenk kun dit hoved, du blomst; Se dig ud en sommerdag; Skal blomsterne da visne?; Solen er sa rød, mor; Den spillemand spiller pa strenge; Ud gar du nu pa livets vej; Underlige aftenlufte; Vender sig lykken fra dig [Da] Kontrapunkt ▲ 32047 [DDD]
Rachmaninoff, S.:The Bells, w. E. Ustinova (sop), J. Hynninen (bar), D. Kitayenko (cnd), Danish National RSO, Danish National Radio Choir Chandos ▲ CHAN 8966 [DDD]
Schulhoff, E.:The Flames, w. Jane Eaglen (sop—Donna Anna, Nun, Woman, Marguerite), Carola Höhn (sop—Shadow), Celina Lindsley (sop—Shadow), Regina Schudel (sop—Shadow), Iris Vermillion (mez—La Morte), Christiane Berggold (alt—Shadow), Kaja Borris (alt—Shadow), Elvira Dressen (alt—Shadow), Kurt Westi (ten—Don Juan), Johann-Werner Prein (bass—Commendatore), Gerd Wolf (bass—Harlequin), J. Mauceri (cnd), Berlin German SO, Berlin RIAS Chamber Choir *(rec Jesus-Christus Church, Berlin Dahlem, Oct 1993/Apr 1994)* London 2-▲ 444630-2 [DDD]

Westphal, Gert (voc)
Liszt, F.:Songs, w. M. Studer (pno)—Lenore; Der blinde Sänger; Der traurige Mönch; Des toten Dichters Liebe [G] *(rec 1982)* Jecklin-Disco ▲ JD 570-2 [ADD]
Nietzsche, F.:Pno Music, w. M. Studer (pno)—Das zerbrochene Ringlein [G] *(rec 1982)* Jecklin-Disco ▲ JD 570-2 [ADD]
Strauss, R.:Enoch Arden, w. J. Buttrick (pno) *(rec 1984)* Jecklin-Disco ▲ JD 592-2 [ADD]
Strauss, R.:Songs, w. M. Studer (pno)—Das Schloss am Meere [G] *(rec 1982)* Jecklin-Disco ▲ JD 570-2 [ADD]
Ullmann, V.:Die Weise von Liebe und Tod, w. Michael Allan (pno) *(rec Siemensvilla, Berlin-Lankwitz, Aug. 1994)* EDA ▲ EDA 008-2 [DDD]

Wettergren, Gertrud (mez)
Verdi, G.:Il trovatore, w. G. Cigna (sop—Leonora), G. Wettergren (mez—Azucena), M. Huder (mez—Ines), J. Björling (ten—Manrico), O. Dua (ten—Ruiz), C. Zambelli (ten—Ferrando), M. Basiola (bar—Count di Luna), L. Horsman (bar—Old Gypsy), V. Gui (cnd), Royal Opera Orch, Royal Opera House Chorus Covent Garden *(rec May 12, 1939)* Legato Classics 2-▲ LCD 173-2 [ADD]

Wheatley, C. (sgr)
Nielsen, C.:Sym 3, w. A. Browning (sop), J. Horenstein (cnd), BBC Northern SO Intaglio ▲ ING 738 [ADD]

Wheeler, K. (mez)
Rorem, N.:Hearing, w. R. Rees (sop), M. Galloway (ten), R. Hilley (bar), R. Wagner (cl), J. Hamlin (tpt), D. Starobin (mand), D. Davidson (vn), K. Askew (va), J. Babich (db), P. Suits (pno), D. Druckman (perc), G. Smith (cnd) Premier ▲ PRCD 1035 [ADD]

Whitaker, Jayne (sop)
Bach, J.S.:Magnificat, BWV 243, w. Anna Crookes (sop), Caroline Trevor (alt), Timothy Robinson (ten), Nicholas Gedge (b-bar), N. Ward (cnd), Northern CO, Oxford Schola Cantorum *(rec St. Peter's Church, Hale, Cheshire, Dec. 2, 1993)* Naxos ▲ 8.550763 [DDD]
Vivaldi, A.:Beatus vir, R.597, w. Carys-Anne Lane (sop), Christine Swain (ob), Robert Glenton (vc), Christopher Stokes (org), N. Ward (cnd), Northern CO, Oxford Schola Cantorum *(rec St. Peter's Church, Hale, Cheshire, Mar. 14, 1994)* Naxos ▲ 8.550767 [DDD]
Vivaldi, A.:Gloria, RV.589, w. Anna Crookes (sop), Caroline Trevor (alt), Christine Swain (ob), Robert Glenton (vc), Christopher Stokes (org), N. Ward (cnd), Northern CO, Oxford Schola Cantorum *(rec St. Peter's Church, Hale, Cheshire, Dec. 3, 1993)* Naxos ▲ 8.550767 [DDD]

White (sgr)
Handel, G.F.:Israel in Egypt, w. Nancy Argenta (sop), Emily Van Evera (sop), Jan Wilson (mez), Anthony Rolfe Johnson (ten), Thomas (sgr), A. Parrott (cnd), Taverner Players, Taverner Choir [E] EMI Classics 2-▲ CDCB 54018 [DDD]

White, Betty (nar)
Saint-Saëns, C.:Carnival of the Animals, w. M. Golabek (nar), R. Golabek (nar), F. Savage (nar), C. Heston (nar), J. E. Jones (nar), L. Redgrave (nar), W. Shatner (nar), J. Rivers (nar), T. Danson (nar), L. Tomlin (nar), D. Raffin (nar), A. Hepburn (nar), D. Moore (nar), W. Matthau (nar), J. Smith (nar), L. Schifrin (cnd), Hollywood CO Dove Audio ▲ DOV 30700

White, Jason (ten)
Soldier, D.:War Prayer, w. Dionne Freeney (alt), Wilbur Pauley (bass), R.A. Clark (cnd), Manhattan CO, Gospel Singers Newport Classic ▲ NPD 85589 [DDD]

White, Jeremy (bar)
Lloyd, G.:A Litany, w. Janice Watson (sop), G. Lloyd (cnd), Philharmonia Orch, Guildford Choral Society *(rec Watford Town Hall, Mar 24-25, 1996)* Albany ▲ TROY 200 [DDD]

White, Jeremy (bass)
Mendelssohn, F.:Elijah, w. R. Plowright (sop), L. Finnie (mez), J. Budd (trb), A. Davies (ten), R. Hickox (cnd), London SO, London Sym Chorus [E] Chandos 2-▲ CHAN 8774/75 [DDD]

White, Robert (ten)
Cage, J.:Four Walls, w. Joshua Pierce (pno) Albany ▲ TROY 197 [DDD]
Corigliano, J.:Irish Folk Songs (3), w. R. Wilson (fl) RCA Gold Seal ▲ 60395-2-RG [ADD]
Corigliano, J.:Poem in October, w. T. Nyfenger (fl), B. Lucarelli (ob), J. Rabbai (cl), Maurice Press (hpd), M. Press (cnd), American String Quartet RCA Gold Seal ▲ 60395-2-RG [ADD]
Handel, G.F.:Arias, w. I. Bolton (cnd), City of London Baroque Sinfonia Virgin Classics ▲ CDZ 59644
Mozart, W.A.:Missa, K.317, w. C. Bogard (sop), J. de Gaetani (mez), T. Paul (bass), D. Zinman (cnd), Rochester PO, Roberts Wesleyan College Chorale *(rec 1978)* Allegretto ▲ ACD 8164 [ADD] ■ ACS 8164
Palmer, G.M.:Chamber Music, w. Samuel Sanders (pno) Indiana Univ School of Music ▲ 0-253-35061-1
Schubert, Franz:Songs (misc), w. G. Johnson (pno) Virgin Classics ▲ CDZ 59650

White, W. (bar)
Gershwin, G.:Porgy & Bess, w. C. Haymon (sop—Bess), C. Clarey (sop—Serena), M. Simpson (sop—Maria), D. Evans (ten—Sporting Life), G. Baker (bar—Crown), W. White (bar—Porgy), S. Rattle (cnd), London PO, Glyndebourne Festival Chorus EMI Classics 3-▲ CDCC 49568
Mozart, W.A.:Requiem, w. F. Lott (sop), D. Jones (mez), K. Lewis (ten), F. Welser-Möst (cnd), London PO, London Phil Chorus EMI Classics ▲ CDM 63260

White, Wendy (mez)
Bernstein, L.:Songfest, w. Linda Hohenfeld (sop), Patricia Spence (mez), Walter Plante (ten), Vernon Hartman (bar), John Cheek (bass), L. Slatkin (cnd), St. Louis SO RCA Red Seal ▲ 09026-61581-2
Stravinsky, I.:The Rake's Progress, w. J. West (sop—Anne Trulove), S. Love (mez—Mother Goose), W. White (mez—Baba the Turk), J. Garrison (ten—Tome Rakewell), M. Lowrey (ten—Sellem), A. Woodley (bar—Father Truelove), J. Cheek (b-bar), *(orch unknown)* MusicMasters 2-▲ 01612-67131-2 [DDD]
Verdi, G.:Luisa Miller (sels), w. A. Millo (sop), F. Quivar (cta), P. Domingo (ten), V. Chernov (bar), J.-H. Rootering (bass), P. Plishka (bass), J. Levine (cnd), Metropolitan Opera Orch, New York Metropolitan Opera Chorus *(rec New York, May 2-18, 1991)* Sony Classical ("Opera Highlights" series) ▲ SMK 53508 [DDD]

White, Willard (bass)
Britten, H.:Praise We Great Men, w. A. Hargan (sop), M. King (alt), R. Tear (ten), S. Rattle (cnd), City of Birmingham SO, City of Birmingham Sym Chorus [E] *(rec July, 1990)* EMI Classics 2-▲ ZDCB 54270 [DDD]
Copland, A.:Old American Songs, w. G. McNaught (pno) [E] Chandos ▲ CHAN 8960 [DDD]
Handel, G.F.:Acis & Galatea, w. N. Burrowes (sop), M. Hill (ten), A. R. Johnson (ten), J. E. Gardiner (cnd), English Baroque Soloists [E] Archiv ▲ 423406-2 [ADD]
Handel, G.F.:Messiah, w. Yvonne Kenny (sop), Jean Rigby (cta), Thomas Randle (ten), O. A. Hughes (cnd), Royal PO, Royal Choral Society IMP Classics 2-▲ IMPDPCD 1106 [DDD]
McCartney, P.:Liverpool Oratorio, w. K. Te Kanawa (sop), S. Burgess (mez), J. Hadley (ten), C. Davis (cnd), Royal Liverpool PO, Royal Liverpool Phil Choir EMI Classics 2-▲ CDQB 54371 2-■ 4D2Q 54371
Mozart, W.A.:Requiem, w. Felicity Lott (sop), Cella Jones (mez), Keith Lewis (ten), David Bell (org), F. Welser-Möst (cnd), London PO, London Phil Choir Classics for Pleasure ("Eminence" series) ▲ CDEMX 2150 [DDD]
Mozart, W.A.:Requiem, w. Barbara Bonney (sop), Anne Sophie von Otter (mez), Hans-Peter Blochwitz (ten), J. E. Gardiner (cnd), English Baroque Soloists, Monteverdi Choir London [L] Philips ▲ 420197-2 [DDD]
Mozart, W.A.:Zauberflöte, w. Natalie Dessay (sop—Queen of the Night), Linda Kitchen (sop—Papagena), Rosa Mannion (sop—Pamina), Anna-Maria Panzarella (sop—First Lady), Doris Lamprecht (mez—Second Lady), Delphine Haidan (cta—Third Lady), Hans Peter Blochwitz (ten—Tamino), Steven Cole (ten—Monostatos), Chrisopher Josey (ten—First Priest/First Armed Man), Anton Scharinger (bar—Papageno), Reinhard Hagen (bass—Sarastro), Laurent Naouri (bass—Second Priest/Second Armed Man), Willard White (bass—Speaker), W. Christie (cnd), Les Arts Florissants *(rec Paris Oct 2-9 1995)* Erato 2-▲ 12705-2 [DDD]
Strauss, R.:Die ägyptische Helena, w. G. Jones (sop), M. Kastu (ten), B. Hendricks (sop), C. Rayam (ten), B. Finnilä (mez), A. Dorati (cnd), Detroit SO London ("Grand Opera" series) 2-▲ 430381-2 [AAD]
10 American Spirituals, w. Graeme McNaught (pno) Chandos ▲ CHAN 8960 [DDD]
Zemlinsky, A. von:Symphonische Gesänge, w. R. Chailly (cnd), Royal Concertgebouw Orch London ("Entartete Musik" series) ▲ 443569-2 [DDD]

Whitehead, A. H. (alt)
Lambert, C.:The Rio Grande, w. Hamilton Harty (pno), C. Lambert (cnd), Hallé Orch, St. Michaels' Singers Claremont ▲ CDGSE 785065

Whitehead, Gregory (nar)
Davies, S.:What Is the Matter in Amy Glennon?, w. Gregory Whitehead (nar—The Idea), Sheila Davies (nar—Amy Glennon/Chorus), Piers McKenzie (nar—Auctioneer), Fran Smith (sgr), Amy Newburg (sgr), Barney Jones (nar—The Fathers) ▲ WN 0013

Whitmore, J. (sgr)
Rodgers, R.:Oklahoma!, w. Gordon MacRae (sgr), S. Jones (sgr), R. Steiger (sgr), Gloria Grahame (sgr), Gene Nelson (sgr), C. Greenwood (sgr) *(rec 1955)* Broadway Angel ▲ ZDM 64691 ■ EG 64691

Whittaker, Scott (ten)
Talma, L.:Voices of Peace, w. Rosalind Rees (sop), Charles Robert Stevens (bar), G. Smith (cnd), Adirondack CO, Gregg Smith Singers Vox Box ("The American Composers" series) 3-▲ CDX 3037

Whittlesey, Christine (sop)
Birtwistle, H.:Settings (3) of Celan, w. P. Boulez (cnd), Ensemble InterContemporain Deutsche Grammophon ▲ 439910-2
Gubaidulina, S.:Hommage à T. S. Eliot, w. G. Kremer (vn), *(other instrs unknown)* *(rec 1987 tour of "Music from)* Deutsche Grammophon ▲ 427336-2 [DDD]
Kurtág, G.:Scenes from a Novel, w. M. Tacke (vn), T. Fichter (db), M. Fábián (cimbalom) *(rec Jan. 7-9, 1992)* Sony Classical ▲ SK 53290 [DDD]
Mason, B.:Realistic Virelais, w. I. Metzmacher (cnd), Ensemble Modern Bridge ▲ BCD 9045 [DDD]
Mason, B.:Self-Reverential Songs, w. I. Metzmacher (cnd), Ensemble Modern Bridge ▲ BCD 9045 [DDD]
Schoenberg, A.:Qt 2 Strs, w. Prazak String Quartet Praga ▲ PR 250056

Wick, Ursula (mez)
Kosma, J.:Le Ménagerie de Tristan, w. Gérard Wyss (pno) Gallo ▲ CD 831
Poulenc, F.:Songs, w. Gérard Wyss (pno)—Les chemins de l'amour; Le bestaire Gallo ▲ CD 831
Satie, E.:Songs, w. Gérard Wyss (pno)—Air du rat; Spleen; La grenouille américane; Air du poète; Chanson du chat; La diva de l'empire; Je te veux; Allons-y chochotte Gallo ▲ CD 831
Wiener, J.:Songs, w. Gérard Wyss (pno)—Septpetites histoires; Polka; 29-40 chantefleurs Gallo ▲ CD 831

Wickham, Henry (bar)
Parry, H.:A Garland of (6) Old-Fashioned Songs, w. Susie Allan (pno) Meridian ▲ MER 84279 [DDD]
Somervell, A.:Maud, w. Susie Allan (pno) Meridian ▲ MER 84279 [DDD]
Woodforde-Finden, A.:Indian Love Lyrics, w. Susie Allan (pno) Meridian ▲ MER 84279 [DDD]

Wicks, Dennis (bass)
Mozart, W.A.:Idomeneo (sels), w. Gundula Janowitz (sop), Enriqueta Tarres (sop), David Hughes (ten), Richard Lewis (ten), Luciano Pavarotti (ten), Neilson Taylor (bar), J. Pritchard (cnd), London PO, Glyndebourne Festival Chorus Budget ("The Greatest Voice in Opera" series) ▲ SYP 107
Puccini, G.:Tosca, w. Maria Callas (sop—Floria Tosca), Robert Bowman (ten—Spoletta), Renato Cioni (ten—Mario Cavaradossi), Eric Garrett (bar—Il Sagrestano), Tito Gobbi (bar—Scarpia), Victor Godfrey (bass—Casare Angelotti), Dennis Wicks (bass—Sciarrone), C. F. Cillario (cnd), Royal Opera House Orch, Royal Opera House Chorus Covent Garden *(rec London, 1964)* Melodram 2-▲ CDI 203003 [ADD]

Widdop, Walter (ten)
Bach, J.S.:Mass in b, BWV 232, w. E. Schumann (sop), M. Balfour (cta), F. Schorr (bar), A. Coates (cnd), London SO, London Phil Chorus [L] *(rec Kingsway Hall, London Mar-Apr 1929)* Pearl 2-▲ PEAS 9900 (m) [AAD]

Widdop, Walter (ten) (cont.)
Mussorgsky, M.:Boris Godunov (sels), w. Edward Halland (bass), Robert Gwynne (sgr), Franklin Kelsey (sgr), A. Coates (cnd), *(orch unknown)*—Revolutionary Scene, Act. IV *(rec Hayes, Studio B, Nov. 3, 1925)* Claremont ▲ GSE 785061
20 Great Basses Sing Great Arias *(rec 1905-42)* Pearl ▲ PEA 9122 [ADD]
Vaughan Williams, R.:Serenade to Music, w. I. Baillie (sop), E. Suddaby (sop), S. Allen (sop), E. Turner (sop), M. Balfour (cta), A. Desmond (cta), M. Brunskill (cta), M. Jarred (cta), H. Nash (ten), P. Jones (ten), F. Titterton (ten), R. Henderson (bass), R. Easton (bass), H. Williams (bass), N. Allin (bass), H. J. Wood (cnd), BBC SO Dutton Laboratories ▲ CDAX 8004 [ADD]
Vaughan Williams, R.:Serenade to Music, w. I. Baillie (sop), E. Suddaby (sop), S. Allen (sop), E. Turner (sop), M. Balfour (cta), A. Desmond (cta), M. Brunskill (cta), M. Jarred (cta), H. Nash (ten), P. Jones (ten), F. Titterton (ten), R. Henderson (bass), R. Easton (bass), H. Williams (bass), N. Allin (bass), H. Wood (cnd), BBC SO [E] *(rec 10/15/38)* Pearl ▲ GEMMCD 9342 (m) [AAD]
Vaughan Williams, R.:Serenade to Music, w. Isobel Baillie (sop), Lilian Stiles-Allen (sop), Elsie Suddaby (sop), Eva Turner (sop), Margaret Balfour (cta), Muriel Brunskill (cta), Astra Desmond (cta), Mary Jarred (cta), Parry Jones (ten), Heddle Nash (ten), Frank Titterton (ten), Roy Henderson (bar), Harold Williams (bar), Norman Allin (bass), Robert Easton (bass), H. Wood (cnd), BBC SO *(rec Abbey Road, Oct 15, 1938)* Claremont ▲ CDGSE 785066
Wagner, R.:Der Ring des Nibelungen (sels), w. Florence Austral (sop), Frieda Leider (sop), Elsie Suddaby (sop), Göta Ljunberg (sop), Horst Laubenthal (ten), Lauritz Melchior (ten), Friedrich Schorr (bar), Rudolf Bockelmann (b-bar), Ivar Andresen (bass), Emmanuel List (bass), Collingwood, Blech, Coates, Barbirolli, Heger, Alwin, Muck (cnd), London SO—scenes from Siegriend & Götterdämmerung; 90 Motives from Der Ring [w. Collingwood & LSO] Pearl 7-▲ PEA 9137 [ADD]
Wagner, R.:Tannhäuser (sels), w. Lauritz Melchior (ten), Friedrich Schorr (b-bar), Edward Halland (bass), A. Coates (cnd), London SO, New SO—Ov; Venusberg Bacchanale; 1st Pilgrims' Chorus; Wolfram's Cavatina; Prelude; Pilgrims' Return; Rome Narration *(rec 1925-30)* Claremont ▲ GSE 78 50 54
Walter Widdop *(rec between 1926 & 1930)* Pearl ▲ PEA 9122 [AAD]

Widmer, Kurt (bass)
Charpentier, M.-A.:Leçons de ténèbres, H. 96-110, w. Jan Caals (ten), Harry Ruyl (ten), Howard Crook (ct), Luc de Meulenaere (ct), Michel Verschaeve (bar), L. Devos (cnd), Musica Polyphonica Erato 2-▲ ERA 96376 [DDD]
Fauré, G.:Requiem, w. E. Mathis (sop), J. Fournet (cnd), Swiss Festival Orch, Lucerne Festival Chorus *(rec 1984)* Koch Treasure ▲ 31619-2 [DDD]
Haydn, J.:Die Jahreszeiten, w. Helen Donath (sop), A. Kraus (ten), W. Gönnenwein (cnd), Ludwigsburg Festival Orch, South German Madrigal Choir [G] Vox Box 2-▲ CDX 5045 [ADD]
Haydn, J.:Mass 14, "Harmoniemesse", w. Barbara Martig-Tüller (sop), Ria Bollen (alt), Adalbert Kraus (ten), Melitta Veits (org), D. Hellmann (cnd), Southwest German RSO Baden-Baden Calig ▲ CAL 50490
Haydn, J.:Die Schöpfung, w. Helen Donath (sop), Scherr (alt), Adalbert Kraus (ten), W. Gönnenwein (cnd), Ludwigsburg Festival Orch, South German Madrigal Choir [G] Vox Box 2-▲ CDX 5025 [ADD]
Keller, A.:Songs Bar & Pno, w. J. Wyttenbach (pno) [G] Grammont ▲ CTSP 19-2 [ADD]
Mozart, W.A.:Notturnos Sops, w. E. Speiser (sop), V. Gohl (cta), H.R. Stalder (cl), R. Kubli (bas hn), H. Leuthold (bas hn) [I] *(rec 1968)* Jecklin-Disco ▲ JD 549-2 [ADD]
Mozart, W.A.:Più non si trovano, w. E. Speiser (sop), V. Gohl (cta), H.R. Stalder (cl), R. Kubli (bas hn), H. Leuthold (bas hn) [I] *(rec 1968)* Jecklin-Disco ▲ JD 549-2 [ADD]
Saint-Saëns, C.:Oratorio de Noël, w. V. Schweizer (sop), E. Wiens (sop), H. Jung (mez), F. Melzer (ten), D. Hellmann (cnd), Mainz Bach Orch, Mainz Bach Choir *(rec 1976)* Calig ▲ CAL 50512 [AAD]
Schmid, E.:Gesänge der Zeit, w. J. Wyttenbach (pno) [G] *(rec. Oct. 31, 1975)* Grammont ▲ CTSP 33-2 [ADD]
Schmid, E.:Songs from Sonnets by Michelangelo-Rilke, w. J. Wyttenbach (pno) [G] *(rec. Oct. 31, 1975)* Grammont ▲ CTSP 33-2 [ADD]
Vogel, W.:Sprechlieder, w. W. Bärtschi (pno) [G] Grammont ▲ CTSP 14-2 [ADD]
Zelenka, J.D.:Lamentationes Jeremiae Prophetae, w. R. Jacobs (alt), G. de Mey (ten), R. Jacobs (cnd), Schola Cantorum Basiliensis Instrumental Ensemble Editio Classica ▲ 77112-2-RG [ADD]
Zemlinsky, A. von:Songs (misc), w. J.-J. Dünki (pno)—6 songs *(rec 1985)* Jecklin-Disco ▲ JD 594-2 [ADD]

Widmer, Oliver (bass)
Mozart, W.A.:Missa, K.427, w. C. Oelze (sop), I. Verebics (sop), S. Weir (ten), H. Rilling (cnd), Stuttgart Bach Collegium, Gächinger Kantorei [L] Hänssler Classic 2-▲ 98.979 [DDD]

Wiebe, Monika (sop)
Cherubini, L.:Masses, w. Helena Jungwirth (alt), Rodrigo Orrego (ten), Wolf Matthias Friedrich (bass), H.R. Zöbeley (cnd), Munich SO, Munich Motet Choir—Missa Solemnis Calig ▲ CAL 50914

Wiebel, Rudolf (bar)
Kol Nidre:Sacred Music of the Synagogue, w. Gloria Seipelt (alt), Leo Roth (ten), Werner Buschnakowski (org), Harry Foss (org), Leipzig RSO members, Jewish Congregation Choir Berlin, Leipzig Synagogue Choir EMI Classics ▲ CDM 65457

Wieclaw, G. (bass)
Chausson, E.:Duos, "La nuit" & "Le réveil", w. D. Collot (sop), B. Vinson (mez), J. Bouillat (ten), E. Strosser (pno), C. Docort (pno), J. Sourisse (cnd), Jean Sourisse Ensemble, Audite Nova Vocal Ensemble FNAC Music ▲ 592224 [DDD]
Debussy, C.:Songs, w. D. Collot (sop), B. Vinson (mez), J. Bouillat (ten), C. Desert (pno), E. Strosser (pno), J. Sourisse (cnd), Jean Sourisse Ensemble, Audite Nova Vocal Ensemble—3 chansons de Chateau D'Orleans FNAC Music ▲ 592224 [DDD]
Fauré, G.:Madrigal, w. D. Collot (sop), B. Vinson (mez), J. Bouillat (ten), C. Desert (pno), E. Strosser (pno) FNAC Music ▲ 592224 [DDD]
Fauré, G.:Pavane Orch, w. D. Collot (sop), B. Vinson (mez), J. Bouillat (ten), C. Desert (pno), E. Strosser (pno), J. Sourisse (cnd), Jean Sourisse Ensemble, Audite Nova Vocal Ensemble FNAC Music ▲ 592224 [DDD]
Fauré, G.:Songs, w. D. Collot (sop), B. Vinson (mez), J. Bouillat (ten), C. Desert (pno), E. Strosser (pno), J. Sourisse (cnd), Jean Sourisse Ensemble, Audite Nova Vocal Ensemble—Le Ruisseau, Op. 22; Puisqu'ici bas, Op. 10/1, Les Djinns, Op. 12 FNAC Music ▲ 592224 [DDD]
Ravel, M.:Songs, w. D. Collot (sop), B. Vinson (mez), J. Bouillat (ten), E. Strosser (pno), C. Desert (pno), J. Sourisse (cnd), Jean Sourisse Ensemble, Audite Nova Vocal Ensemble—3 a capella songs FNAC Music ▲ 592224 [DDD]
Saint-Saëns, C.:Choral Music, w. D. Collot (sop), B. Vinson (mez), J. Bouillat (ten), E. Strosser (pno), C. Desert (pno), J. Sourisse (cnd), Jean Sourisse Ensemble , Vocal Audite Nova Ensemble—Calme des nuits, Op. 68/1; Les fleurs et les arbres, Op. 68/2; Salterelle, Op. 74 FNAC Music ▲ 592224 [DDD]

Wiedemann, Hermann (bar)
Wagner, R.:Die Meistersinger von Nürnberg (sels), w. Viorica Ursuleac (sop—Eva), Rudolf Bockelmann (ten—Hans Sachs), Josef Kalenberg (ten—Walther), Hermann Wiedemann (bar—Beckmesser), C. Krauss (cnd), Vienna State Opera Orch, Vienna State Opera Chorus *(rec Jan. 20, 1933)* Koch Schwann 2-▲ SCH 314642 [ADD]
Wagner, R.:Das Rheingold (sels), w. Erich Zimmermann (ten—Mime), Herrmann Wiedemann (bar—Alberich), Josef von Manowarda (bass—Wotan), C. Krauss (cnd), Vienna State Opera Orch *(rec Feb. 28, 1933)* Koch Schwann 2-▲ SCH 314642 [ADD]

Wiedenmann, Reinhold (voc)
Eschenbach, W. von:Titurel, w. Osvaldo Parisi (lt)—2 fragments Koch Schwann ▲ SCH 318322 [DDD]

Wiederanders, William (sgr)
Donizetti, G.:Lucrezia Borgia, w. Montserrat Caballé (sop), Jane Berbié (mez), Alain Vanzo (ten), Kostas Paskalis (bar), Arnold Voketaitis (bass-bar), L. D. Clements (sgr), Adib Fazah (sgr), Mauro Lampi (sgr), Vern Shinall (sgr), Jerold Siena (sgr), J. Perlea (cnd), New York City Opera Orch, New York City Chorus Great Opera Performances 2-▲ GOP 769

Wiedl, Wilhelm (trb)
Bach, J.S.:Cant 69, w. P. Esswood (ct), K. Equiluz (ten), R. van der Meer (bass), N. Harnoncourt (cnd), Vienna Concentus Musicus, Concentus Musicus [G] Teldec 2-▲ 2292-42572-2 [ADD]
Bach, J.S.:Cant 70, w. P. Esswood (ct), K. Equiluz (ten), L. Visser (bass), N. Harnoncourt (cnd), Vienna Concentus Musicus, Tölz Boys' Choir [G] Teldec 2-▲ 2292-42572-2 [ADD]

Wiedl, Wilhelm (trb) (cont.)
Bach, J.S.:Cant 71, w. P. Esswood (ct), K. Equiluz (ten), R. van der Meer (bass), N. Harnoncourt (cnd), Vienna Concentus Musicus, Vienna Concentus Musicus Chorus [G]
Teldec 2-▲ 2292-42572-2 [ADD]
Bach, J.S.:Cant 72, w. P. Esswood (ct), R. van der Meer (bass), N. Harnoncourt (cnd), Vienna Concentus Musicus, Tölz Boys' Choir [G] Teldec 2-▲ 2292-42572-2 [ADD]
Bach, J.S.:Cant 80, w. P. Esswood (ct), K. Equiluz (ten), R. van der Meer (bass), N. Harnoncourt (cnd), Vienna Concentus Musicus [G] Teldec 2-▲ 2292-42577-2 [ADD]
Bach, J.S.:Cant 84, w. N. Harnoncourt (cnd), Vienna Concentus Musicus, Tölz Boys' Choir [G]
Teldec 2-▲ 2292-42578-2 [ADD]
Bach, J.S.:Cant 85, w. P. Esswood (ct), K. Equiluz (ten), N. Harnoncourt (cnd), Vienna Concentus Musicus, Vienna Concentus Musicus Chorus [G] Teldec 2-▲ 2292-42578-2 [ADD]
Bach, J.S.:Cant 86, w. P. Esswood (ct), K. Equiluz (ten), N. Harnoncourt (cnd), Vienna Concentus Musicus, Vienna Concentus Musicus Chorus [G] Teldec 2-▲ 2292-42578-2 [ADD]
Bach, J.S.:Cant 95, w. K. Equiluz (ten), P. Huttenlocher (bar), N. Harnoncourt (cnd), Vienna Concentus Musicus [G] Teldec 2-▲ 2292-42583-2 [ADD]
Bach, J.S.:Cant 96, w. P. Esswood (ct), K. Equiluz (ten), P. Huttenlocher (bar), N. Harnoncourt (cnd), Vienna Concentus Musicus [G] Teldec ▲ 2292-42583-2 [ADD]
Bach, J.S.:Cant 97, w. P. Esswood (ct), K. Equiluz (ten), P. Huttenlocher (bar), N. Harnoncourt (cnd), Vienna Concentus Musicus [G] Teldec ▲ 2292-42583-2 [ADD]
Bach, J.S.:Cant 99, w. P. Esswood (ct), K. Equiluz (ten), P. Huttenlocher (bar), N. Harnoncourt (cnd), Vienna Concentus Musicus [G] Teldec ▲ 2292-42584-2
Bach, J.S.:Cant 101, w. P. Esswood (ct), K. Equiluz (ten), P. Huttenlocher (bar), N. Harnoncourt (cnd), Vienna Concentus Musicus [G] Teldec ▲ 2292-42584-2
Bach, J.S.:Cant 102, w. P. Esswood (ct), K. Equiluz (ten), P. Huttenlocher (bar), N. Harnoncourt (cnd), Vienna Concentus Musicus [G] Teldec ▲ 2292-42584-2
Bach, J.S.:Cant 105, w. P. Esswood (ct), K. Equiluz (ten), M. van Egmond (b-bar), N. Harnoncourt (cnd), Vienna Concentus Musicus, Tölz Boys' Choir [G] Teldec ▲ 2292-42602-2
Bach, J.S.:Cant 110, w. S. Frangoulis (trb), P. Esswood (ct), Stumpf (sgr), K. Equiluz (ten), M. van Egmond (b-bar), S. Lorenz (b-bar), N. Harnoncourt (cnd), Vienna Concentus Musicus, Tölz Boys' Choir [G] Teldec 2-▲ 2292-42603-2

Wiedstruck, Yvonne (voc)
Pfitzner, H.:Der blumen Rache, w. Yvi Jänicke (cta), Yaron Windmüller (voc), R. Reuter (cnd), Berlin RSO, Berlin Radio Chorus CPO ▲ CPO 999158 [DDD]
Pfitzner, H.:Das dunkle Reich, w. Yvi Jänicke (cta), Yaron Windmüller (voc), R. Reuter (cnd), Berlin RSO, Berlin Radio Chorus CPO ▲ CPO 999158 [DDD]
Pfitzner, H.:Fons salutifer, w. Yvi Jänicke (cta), Yaron Windmüller (voc), R. Reuter (cnd), Berlin RSO, Berlin Radio Chorus CPO ▲ CPO 999158 [DDD]

Wiegold, Mary (sop)
Lumsdaine, D.:What Shall I Sing?, w. E. Pillinger (cl), I. Mitchell (cl) NM Classics ▲ NMCD 007 [DDD]
Mary Wiegold's Songbook, w. Composer's Ensemble NMC ▲ NMCD 003 [DDD]

Wiener, Otto (bar)
Bach, J.S.:St. John Passion, w. P. Curtin (sop), E. Thomann (sop), E. Alberts (cta), W. Kmentt, J. Van Kesteren (ten), R. Springer (bar), D. Smith (b-bar), F. Guthrie (bass), F. Lukasowsky (bass), H. Scherchen (cnd), Vienna State Opera Orch, Vienna Academy Chorus [G] *(rec ca 1960)*
MCA Classics 2-▲ MCAD2-9804
Beethoven, L. van:Missa Solemnis, w. Ilona Steingruber (sop), Else Schuerhoff (alt), Ernst Majkut (ten), O. Klemperer (cnd), Vienna SO, Akademie Chamber Choir *(rec Vienna, 1950)*
Vox Legends 2-▲ CDX2 5527
Haydn, J.:The Seven Last Words of Christ on the Cross, w. Albert (sop), John Van Kesteren (ten), Anatoli Babikian (bass), H. Scherchen (cnd), Vienna State Opera Orch, Vienna State Opera Chorus [oratorio version] [G] *(rec 1962)* MCA Classics 2-▲ MCAD2-9816 [AAD]
Mozart, W.A.:Grabmusik, w. Maria Seebach (sop), J. Messner (cnd), Salzburg Mozarteum Orch, Salzburg Cathedral Choir *(rec Aug 24, 1952)* Orfeo d'or ("Festspiel Dokumente" series) ▲ 396951
Pfitzner, H.:Palestrina, w. S. Jurinac (sop), C. Ludwig (mez), F. Wunderlich (ten), G. Stolze (ten), G. Frick (bass), W. Berry (bass), R. Heger (cnd), Vienna State Opera Orch, Vienna State Opera Chorus *(rec live, Vienna 12/16/64)* Myto 3-▲ 3 MCD 92259 [ADD]
Strauss, R.:Die Frau ohne Schatten (sels), w. E. Steber (sop), C. Goltz (sop), I. Steingruber (sop), S. Svanholm (ten), K. Böhm (cnd), *(orch unknown)*—selections from Act Two (Sieh, Amme, sieh...Würde ich lieber selber zu Stein!) & Act Three (Vater, bist du's?...) *(rec live, Munich, 6/4/53)*
VAI Audio ▲ VAIA 1012 (m/s) [ADD]
Strauss, R.:Der Rosenkavalier, w. Erika Köth (sop—Sophie), Annelie Waas (sop—Marianne), Claire Watson (sop—Marschallin), Hertha Töpper (mez—Octavian), Brigitte Fassbaender (cta—Annina), Gerhard Stolze (ten—Valzacchi), Fritz Wunderlich (ten—Singer), Otto Wiener (bar—Faninal), Kurt Böhme (bass—Baron), J. Keilberth (cnd), Bavarian State Opera Orch, Bavarian State Opera Chorus *(rec Munich Opera Festival, National Theater, May 21, 1965)* Orfeo d'or 3-▲ 425963
Strauss, R.:Der Rosenkavalier, w. E. Mathis (sop), C. Ludwig (mez), T. Troyanos (mez), T. Adam (b-bar), K. Böhm (cnd), Vienna PO *(rec Salzburg Festival, 1969)*
Deutsche Grammophon 3-▲ 445338-2 [ADD]

Wiener-Chenisheva (sop)
Verdi, G.:Requiem Mass, w. A. Milcheva-Nonova (mez), L. Bodourov (ten), N. Ghiuselev (bass), I. Marinov (cnd), Sofia State PO, Sofia State Chorus [L] Vivace 3-▲ E 326 [ADD]

Wiens, Edith (sop)
Bach, J.S.:Cant 70, w. A. Felbermayer (sop), H. M. Welfing (ten), N. Foster (bass), F. Prohaska (cnd), Vienna State Opera Orch, Vienna State Opera Chorus [G] *(rec June 1957)*
Vanguard Classics ("The Bach Guild" series) ▲ OVC 2010 [ADD]
Bach, J.S.:Cant 164, w. J. Hamari (cta), L.-M. Harder (ten), W. Heldwein (bass), H. Rilling (cnd), Stuttgart Bach Collegium, Gächinger Kantorei Hänssler Classic ▲ 98.811 [AAD]
Beethoven, L. van:Sym 9, "Choral Sym", w. U. Walther (cta), R. Goldberg (ten), K.-H. Stryczek (bass), H. Blomstedt (cnd), Dresden Staatskapelle, Dresden State Opera Chorus, Dresden Sym Chorus—final chorus Capriccio ▲ 10 914 [DDD]
Haydn, J.:Die Schöpfung, w. Barbara Bonney (mez), Hans-Peter Blochwitz (ten), Olaf Bär (bar), Jan-Herdrik Rootering (bass), N. Marriner (cnd), Stuttgart Radio Orch, Stuttgart Radio Chorus [G]
EMI Classics 2-▲ CDCB 54038 [DDD]
Mendelssohn, F.:Sym 2, w. J. Howarth (sop), R. Tear (ten), F. d' Avalos (cnd), Philharmonia Orch, Bach Choir IMP Masters ▲ IMP MCD 83 [DDD]
Mendelssohn, F.:Sym 2, w. B. Bonney (sop), P. Schreier (ten), K. Masur (cnd), Leipzig Gewandhaus Orch, Leipzig Gewandhaus Chorus [G] Teldec ▲ 2292-44178-2 ZK [DDD]
Mozart, W.A.:Missa, K.427, w. Delores Ziegler (mez), John Aler (ten), William Stone (bar), R. Shaw (cnd), Atlanta SO, Atlanta Sym Chorus [L] Telarc 2-▲ CD 80150 [DDD]
Mozart, W.A.:Requiem, w. Gabriele Schreckenbach (mez), Aldo Baldin (ten), Gerhard Faulstich (bar), U. Gronostay (cnd), Berlin RSO, Berlin RIAS Chamber Choir [L] LaserLight ▲ 15 882 [DDD]
Saint-Saëns, C.:Oratorio de Noël, w. V. Schweizer (sop), H. Jung (mez), F. Melzer (ten), K. Widmer (bass), D. Hellmann (cnd), Mainz Bach Orch, Mainz Bach Choir *(rec 1976)*
Calig ▲ CAL 50512 [AAD]
Schubert, Franz:Der Hirt auf dem Felsen, w. J. Valdepeñas (cl), R. Jansen (pno)
CBC ("Musica Viva" series) ▲ MVCD 1053 [DDD]
Schubert, Franz:Songs (misc), w. R. Jansen (pno)—An die Musik; An Silvia; Ariette der Claudine; Auf dem Wasser zu singen; Der Einsame; Fischerweise; Frühlingsglaube; Heidenröslein; Die junge Nonne; Der Jüngling an der Quelle; Lachen und Weinen; Liebhaber in allen Gestalten; Das Lied im Grünen; Die Mutter Erde; Nacht und Träume; Seligkeit; also, Romanze, D.787, No. 2 & Der Hirt auf dem Felsen, w. Joaquin Valdepeñas (clarinet) [G] CBC ("Musica Viva" series) ▲ MVCD 1053 [DDD]
Schumann, R.:Songs, w. Rudolf Jansen (pno)—Widmung, Op. 25/1; Schneeglöckchen, Op. 79/26; Volksliedchen, Op. 51/2; Jasminenstrauch, Op. 27/4; Lied der Braut, Op. 25/12; O ihr Herren, Op. 37/3; Aus den östlichen Rosen, Op. 25/25; Der Himmel hat eine Träne geweint, Op. 37/1; Mein schöner Stern, Op. 101/4; Zum Schluss, Op. 25/26; Aus den hebräischen Gesängen, Op. 25/15; An den Mond, Op. 95/2; Du bist wie eine Blume, Op. 25/24; Dein Angesicht, Op. 127/2
Cascavelle ▲ CVL 1029 [DDD]

Wiens, Edith (sop) (cont.)
Vaughan Williams, R.:Dona nobis pacem, w. B. Rayner Cook (bar), B. Thomson (cnd), London PO, London Phil Chorus [L] Chandos ▲ CHAN 8590 [DDD]

Wieter, Georg (bass)
Orff, C.:Die Kluge, w. E. Schwarzkopf (sop), R. Christ (ten), P. Kuén (ten), M. Cordes (bar), B. Kusche (bar), H. Prey (bar), G. Frick (bass), W. Sawallisch (cnd), Philharmonia Orch [G]
EMI Classics ("Studio" series) 2-▲ CDMB 63712 [ADD]
Orff, C.:Der Mond—Ein kleines Welttheater, w. Karl Erb (nar), Paul Kuen (ten—Lad 3), Josef Knapp (bar—Lad 2), Benno Kusche (bar—Lad 1), Georg Hann (bass—St. Peter), Georg Wieter (bass—Lad 4), Rudolf Wünzer (bass—The Farmer), Karl Hanft (sgr—Innkeeper), Willy Rösner (sgr—The Major), R. Alberth (cnd), Bavarian RSO, Bavarian Radio Chorus *(rec Studio 1, Bavarian Radio, Jan. 19-20, 1950)*
Calig ▲ CAL 50948 (m) [ADD]
Puccini, G.:La Bohème, w. Trude Eipperle (sop), Hildegarde Ranczak (sop), Alfons Fügel (ten), Carl Kronenberg (bar), Georg Hann (bass), Emil Graf (sgr), Otto Hillerbrandt (sgr), Karl Schmidt (sgr), C. Krauss (cnd), Bavarian State Opera Orch, Bavarian State Opera Chorus *(rec 1940)*
Preiser 2-▲ PRE 90275
Strauss, R.:Capriccio (sels), w. V. Ursuleac (sop—Die Gräfin), F. Klarwein (ten—Flamand), H. Hotter (b-bar—Olivier), G. Hann (b-bar—La Roche), G. Wieter (bass—Der Haushofmeister), C. Krauss (cnd), Bavarian State Opera Orch *(rec 1942)* Myto ▲ MCD 943104
Strauss, R.:Feuersnot, w. Maud Cunitz (sop—Diemut), Antonia Fahberg (sop—Elsbeth), Irmgard Barth (mez—Wigelis), Liselotte Nölser (sgr—Margret), Karl Ostertag (ten—Schweiker), Marcel Cordes (bar—Kunrad), Kieth Engen (bass—Kofel), Karl Hoppe (bass—Hämerlein), Max Proebstl (bass—Ortolf), Georg Wieter (bass—Jörg), R. Kempe (cnd), Bavarian State Opera Orch, Bavarian State Opera Chorus *(rec Munich Opera Festival, Prince Regent Theater, Aug 14, 1958)* Orfeo d'or 2-▲ 423962

Wijk, A. van (mez)
Schlegel, L.:Songs Mez, w. F. van Ruth (pno) [G] Attacca ▲ 8951-4 [DDD]

Wilbrink, Hans (sgr)
Wagner, R.:Rienzi, der Letzte der Tribunen, w. Cheryl Studer (sop—Irene), René Kollo (ten—Rienzi), Friedrich Lenz (ten—Gesandte), Norbert Orth (ten—Baroncelli), Bodo Brinkmann (bar—Paolo Orsini), Keith Engen (bass—Cecco del Vecchio), Raimund Grumbach (bass—Gesandte), Jan-Hendrik Rootering (bass—Steffano Colonna), Carmen Anhorn (sgr—Ein Friedensbote), Karl Helm (sgr—Kardinal Orvieto), John Janssen (sgr—Adriano), Alfred Kuhn (sgr—Gesandte), Hans Wilbrink (sgr—Gesandte), W. Sawallisch (cnd), Bavarian State Opera Orch, Bavarian State Opera Chorus *(rec live, July 6, 1983)*
Orfeo d'or 3-▲ 346953

Wild, Waldemar (bar)
Mendelssohn, F.:Die Hochzeit des Camacho, w. R. Hofman (sop—Quiteria), A. Ulbrich (mez—Lucinda), S. Weir (ten—Basilio), H. Rhys-Evans (ten—Vivaldo), N. van der Meel (ten—Camacho), W. Wild (bar—Carrasco), U. Malmberg (bass—Sancho Panza), U. Cold (bass—Don Quixote), J. van Immerseel (cnd), Anima Eterna Orch, Aachen Boys Choir, Chor Modus Novus [G] *(rec Sept. 19-22, 1992)*
Channel Classics 2-▲ CCS 5593 [DDD]

Wildbrunn, Helene (sop)
Helene Wildbrunn *(rec 1919-24)* Preiser ("Lebendige Vergangenheit" series) ▲ PRE 89097 [AAD]

Wilder, P. (sgr)
Luening, O.:No Jerusalem But This, w. K. Sullivan (sop), Jacqueline Pierce (sop), Paul Sperry (ten), M. Moliterno (bar), S. Rosser (sgr), A. Goodman (cnd), Music Project CO, Goodman Chamber Choir [E] *(rec 6/6/90)* CRI ▲ CD 600 [DDD]

Wilderman, William (bass)
Beethoven, L. van:Sym 9, "Choral Sym", w. Emilia Cundari (sop), Nell Rankin (mez), Albert Da Costa (ten), B. Walter (cnd), Columbia SO, Westminster Sym Choir *(rec American Legion Hall, Los Angeles, CA, Apr. 6, 1954)* Sony Classical ("Bruno Walter Edition, Vol. 2" series) ▲ SMK 64464 [ADD]
Verdi, G.:La forza del destino, w. Z. Milanov (sop), M. Del Monaco (ten), L. Warren (bar), G. Pechner (bar), W. Herbert (cnd), *(orch unknown)* *(rec live 1953)*
Legato Classics 2-▲ LCD 118-2 (m) [AAD]
Verdi, G.:Rigoletto, w. Renata Scotto (sop—Gilda), Stella Maris Silva (sop—Giovanna), Martha Carrizo (mez—Page), Carmen de la Mata (mez—Countess Ceprano), Noemi Souza (cta—Maddalena), Horacio Mastrango (ten—Borso), Richard Tucker (ten—Duke of Mantua), Cornell MacNeil (bar—Rigoletto), Riccardo Yost (bar—Marullo), Guerrino Boschetti (bass—Usher), Tulio Gagliardo (bass—Count Ceprano), Victor de Narké (bass—Monterone), William Wilderman (bass—Sparafucile), F. Previtali (cnd), Buenos Aires Teatro Colón Orch, Buenos Aires Teatro Colón Chorus *(rec Colon Theater, Buenos Aires, Aug. 22, 1967)* Legato Classics 2-▲ LCD 198-2

Wildhaber, Helmut (ten)
Haydn, J.:Applausus:Jubilaeum virtutis Palatium, w. Florian Erdl (sgr), Gert Füssi (sgr), Christian Graf (sgr), Georg Tichy (bass), P. Angerer (cnd), Vienna Concilium Musicum [period instrs]
Koch Schwann ▲ SCH 314092
Haydn, J.:Die Jahreszeiten, w. Krisztina Láki (sop), Peter Lika (bass), S. Kuijken (cnd), La Petite Bande, Flanders Opera Choir Virgin Classics 2-▲ ZDCB 59268
Haydn, J.:Mass 5, "Missa Sancti Josephi", "Grosse Orgelmesse", w. Dorthea Röschmann (sop), Bernarda Fink (cta), Klaus Mertens (bar), M. Haselböck (cnd), Vienna Academy, Hugo Distler Choir
Novalis ▲ 150095 [DDD]
Haydn, J.:Mass 7, "Kleine Orgelmesse", w. Dorthea Röschmann (sop), Bernarda Fink (cta), Klaus Mertens (bar), M. Haselböck (cnd), Vienna Academy, Hugo Distler Choir Novalis ▲ 150095 [DDD]
Haydn, J.:Salve regina, H.XXIIIb/2, w. Dorthea Röschmann (sop), Bernarda Fink (cta), Klaus Mertens (bar), M. Haselböck (cnd), Vienna Academy, Hugo Distler Choir Novalis ▲ 150095 [DDD]
Hummel, J.N.:Alma virgo, w. Amanda Halgrimson (sop), Susan McAdoo (mez), Petr Mikuláš (bass), Jan Engel (bass), M. Haselböck (cnd), Vienna Academy, Brünn Czech Phil Chorus
Koch Schwann ▲ SCH CD 317792
Hummel, J.N.:Mass in E♭, Op. 80, w. Amanda Halgrimson (sop), Susan McAdoo (mez), Petr Mikuláš (bass), Jan Engel (bass), M. Haselböck (cnd), Vienna Academy, Brünn Czech Phil Chorus
Koch Schwann ▲ SCH CD 317792
Hummel, J.N.:Quod quod in orbe, w. Amanda Halgrimson (sop), Susan McAdoo (mez), Petr Mikuláš (bass), Jan Engel (bass), M. Haselböck (cnd), Vienna Academy, Brünn Czech Phil Chorus
Koch Schwann ▲ SCH CD 317792
Mozart:Missa Solemnis & Salieri:Te Deum (The Coronation Mass for Leopold II in Prague, September 1791), w. Vienna Academy, Ruth Ziesak (sop), E. von Magnus (mez), G. Hornik (bass), Hugo Distler Chorus, Vienna Hofburg Chapel Choir Novalis ▲ 150087 [DDD]
Mozart, W.A.:Masonic Music, w. C. Prégardien (ten), G. Hornik (bass), P. Schneyder (bass), M. Haselböck (cnd), Vienna Academy, Chorus Viennensis—Masonic Cants., K.429, 471, 619, 623 & Songs, K.148, 468, 483, 484 [G] Novalis ▲ 150081 [DDD]
Mozart, W.A.:Missa solemnis, K.337, w. R. Ziesak (sop), E. von Magnus (alt), G. Hornik (bar), H. Hüttler (cant), M. Jankowitsch (cant), P. Jelosits (cant), I. Rainer (org), M. Haselböck (cnd), Vienna Academy, Vienna Hofburg Chapel Choir [L] *(rec Apr. 1992)* Novalis ▲ 150087 [DDD]
Mussorgsky, M.:Boris Godunov, w. V. Valente (sop—Xenia), E. Gorochovskaya (mez—Nurse), L. Nichiteanu (mez—Fyodor), E. Zarmeba (mez—Hostess), M. Lipovšek (cta—Marina), P. Langridge (ten—Prince Shuisky), H. Wildhaber (ten—Misail), A. Fedin (ten—Simpleton), S. Leiferkus (bar—Rangoni), A. Kotcherga (bass—B. Godounov), A. Shagidullin (bass—Shchelkalov), S. Ramey (bass—Pimen), S. Larin (bass—Girgory), G. Nikolsky (bass—Varlaam), C. Abbado (cnd), Berlin PO, Tölz Boys' Choir, Berlin Radio Chorus, Slovak Phil Chorus *(rec Nov. 7-30, 1993)*
Sony Classical 3-▲ S3K 58977 [DDD]
Weill, K.:Mahagonny, w. U. Lemper (sop), H. Jungwirth (sop), P. Haage (ten), T. Mohr (bar), S. Tremper (sgr), Jeffrey Cohen (pno), J. Mauceri (cnd), Berlin RIAS Chamber Ensemble [G]
London ▲ 430168-2 [DDD]
Weill, K.:The Seven Deadly Sins, w. U. Lemper (sop), H. Jungwirth (sop), P. Haage (ten), T. Mohr (bar), S. Tremper (sgr), J. Mauceri (cnd), Berlin RIAS Chamber Ensemble [G] London ▲ 430168-2 [DDD]

Wilfert, Herta (sgr)
Wagner, R.:Tannhäuser, w. Gré Brouwestijn (sop), Murray Dickie (ten), Karl Liebl (ten), Eberhard Waechter (bar), Alois Pernerstorfer (b-bar), Deszö Ernster (bass), Walter Brunelli (sgr), Peter Harrower (sgr), Rosl Schweiger (sgr), A. Rodzinski (cnd), Rome RAI Radio-TV SO, Rome RAI Chorus
Stradivarius 3-▲ STV 12318

Wilfert, Herta (sgr) (cont.)
Wagner, R.:Tannhäuser (sels), w. G. Brouwenstijn (sop), K. Liebl (ten), E. Wächter (bar), A. Rodzinski (cnd), Rome RAI Orch, Rome RAI Chorus *(rec Nov. 21 1957)* Myto 3–▲ MCD 93277

Wilhelms, Gunther (bass)
Verdi, G.:Un ballo in maschera, w. Martha Mödl (sop—Ulrica), Walburga Wegner (sop—Amelia), Anny Schlemm (mez—Oscar), Lorenz Fehenberger (ten—Ricardo), Dietrich Fischer-Dieskau (bar—Renato), Wilhelm Schirp (bass—Samuel), Willy Schoneweib (bass—Tom), Gunther Wilhelms (bass—Silvan), Fritz Augustin (sgr—Ein Richter), Friedrich Himmelmann (sgr—Ein Diener Amelia), F. Busch (cnd), Cologne RSO, Bernhard Alois Zimmermann (cnd), Cologne Radio Chorus Calig 2–▲ 50946/47 (m) [ADD]

Wilke, Elisabeth (mez)
Saint-Saëns, C.:Oratorio de Noël, w. Ute Selbig (sop), Annette Markert (cta), Armin Ude (ten), Egbert Junghans (bar), Jutta Zoff (hp), Michael-Christfield Winkler (org), M. Flämig (cnd), Dresden PO, Dresden Kreuz Choir *(rec Dresden, Mar & Apr 1987)* Capriccio ▲ 10216 [DDD]

Wilke, Marie-Luise (mez)
Wolf, H.:Christnacht, w. S. Inou-Heller (sop), K. Thiem (bar), U. Gronostay (cnd), Berlin RSO, Berlin Radio Chorus [G] Koch Schwann ▲ CD 313013 [DDD]

Will, Jacob (bass)
Suter, H.:Le Laudi di San Francesco d'Assisi, w. A. Michael (sop), J. Winklet (alt), A. Baldin (ten), P. Laubschet (org), Bern SO, T. Loosli (cnd), Bern Bach Choir, Sekundar School Children's Choir Ars Musici ▲ AM 1015–2 [DDD]

Willer, Luise (mez)
Pfitzner, H.:Von deutscher Seele, w. Trude Eipperle (sop), Julius Patzak (ten), Ludwig Weber (bass), C. Krauss (cnd), Vienna PO, Vienna State Opera Chorus *(rec Jan 1945)* Preiser 2–▲ PRE 90255 [ADD]
Wagner, R.:Der fliegende Holländer, w. Viorica Ursuleac (sop), Karl Ostertag (ten), Hans Hotter (b-bar), Georg Hann (bass), C. Krauss (cnd), Bavarian State Opera Orch, Bavarian State Opera Chorus *(rec Mar 13-16, 1944)* Preiser 2–▲ PRE 90250 [ADD]

Willetts, Dave (sgr)
Lloyd Webber, A.:Music of, w. L. Garrett (sgr), C. Corcoran (sgr), Gerard Casey (sgr), S. Campbell (sgr), Royal PO, Royal PO Pops Orch, Royal PO Concert Orch—sels from The Phantom of the Opera; Evita; Cats; Joseph & the Amazing Technicolor Dreamcoat; Jesus Christ Superstar; Tell Me on a Sunday; Song & Dance; Starlight Express; Sunset Boulevard Silva America 2–▲ SILCD 1044 [DDD] ■ SILMC 1044
Lloyd Webber, A.:Music of, w. L. Garrett (sgr), C. Corcoran (sgr), S. Campbell (sgr), *(other artists unknown)* —The Phantom of the Opera; Aspects of Love; Cats; Evita; Jesus Christ Superstar; Starlight Express Silva America ▲ SILCD 1022 [DDD] ■ SILMC 1022
Taylor, B.J.:Wuthering Heights, w. L. Garrett (sop), C. Carter (sgr), J. Sladdon (sgr), S. Campbell (sgr), Philharmonia Orch, Contorum Choir Silva America ▲ SSD 1008 ■ SSC 1008

Williams (sgr)
Gershwin, G.:Porgy & Bess (sels), w. Matthews, Long, Winters, Engel, *(orch unknown)* [E] Odyssey ■ YT 35501 (m)

Williams, A. (sgr)
Mancini, H.:Film Music, w. J. Mathis (sgr), L. Albright (sgr), B. Hackett (sgr), B. Greco (sgr), C. Byrd (sgr), P. Page (sgr), Mancini (cnd), Costa Orch, Conniff Orch, Mancini Orch—sels from Breakfast at Tiffany's; Peter Gunn; Mr. Lucky & others Columbia/Legacy ▲ CK 66505

Williams, C. (bar)
Siegmeister, E.:Langston Hughes Songs, w. Lazar (cnd), Washington Music Ensemble [E] CRI ■ C 532

Williams, Ellen (mez)
Hoekman, T.:Margarets, w. Terry Rhodes (sop), Timothy Hoekman (pno) Albany ▲ TROY 172 [DDD]
Hoiby, L.:Bermudas, w. Terry Rhodes (sop), Hsiao-mei Ku (vn), Jonathan Bagg (va), Fred Raimi (vc), Thomas Warburton (pno) Albany ▲ TROY 172 [DDD]
Jaffe, S.:Fort Juniper Songs, w. Terry Rhodes (sop), Stephen Jaffe (pno) Albany ▲ TROY 172 [DDD]
Kouneva, P.:Aeon, w. Terry Rhodes (sop), Penka Kouneva (pno), Lynn Glasscock (perc), Robbie Link (gtr) Albany ▲ TROY 172 [DDD]
Ward, R.:Lady Kate (sels), w. Terry Rhodes (sop), S. Tiley (cnd), *(orch unknown)*—Eve, I Can't Lie to an Old Friend Albany ▲ TROY 172 [DDD]
Ward, R.:Roman Fever (sels), w. Terry Rhodes (sop), S. Tiley (cnd), *(orch unknown)*—It's Still the Most Beautiful View in the World Albany ▲ TROY 172 [DDD]

Williams, Harold (bar)
Blitzstein, M.:Songs, w. R. Edwards (ten), L. Lehrman (pno)—songs & scenes from Reuben, Reuben [1955], Jane Pickens Show (title theme) [1949], Goloopchik [1946], Idiots First [1962], Juno [1957], New York Opera [1941], No For An Answer [1941], Parade [1935], Sacco & Vanzetti [1959] Premier ▲ PRCD 1005 [DDD]
Friml, R.:Film Music, w. D. Vane (sop), D. Oldham (ten), London Palladium Orch—The Vagabond King; The Blue Kitten; Rose Marie; The 3 Musketeers; The Firefly Pearl ("Flapper" series) ▲ PAST CD 9764 [AAD]
Gounod, C.:Faust, w. M. Licette (sop—Margarita), D. Vane (sop—Siebel), M. Brunskill (cta—Martha), H. Nash (ten—Faust), H. Williams (b-bar—Valentine), R. Easton (bass—Mephistopheles), R. Carr (bass—Wagner), T. Beecham (cnd), BBC SO, BBC Sym Chorus Dutton Laboratories 2–▲ CDAX 2001 [ADD]
Handel, G.F.:Messiah, w. Dora Labbette (sop), Muriel Brunskill (cta), Hubert Eisdell (ten), T. Beecham (cnd), BBC SO, BBC Choir *(rec 1927)* Pearl 2–▲ PEA 9456 [DDD]
Mendelssohn, F.:Elijah, w. Isobel Baillie (sop), Gladys Ripley (cta), James Johnston (ten), M. Sargent (cnd), Liverpool PO, Huddersfield Choral Society Dutton Laboratories 2–▲ DUT 2004 [ADD]
Sullivan, A.:The Mikado—The Mikado's song Symposium ▲ 1123
Vaughan Williams, R.:Serenade to Music, w. I. Baillie (sop), E. Suddaby (sop), S. Allen (sop), E. Turner (sop), M. Balfour (cta), A. Desmond (cta), M. Brunskill (cta), M. Jarred (cta), H. Nash (ten), W. Widdop (ten), P. Jones (ten), F. Titterton (ten), R. Henderson (bass), R. Easton (bass), N. Allin (bass), H. J. Wood (cnd), BBC SO Dutton Laboratories ▲ CDAX 8004 [ADD]
Vaughan Williams, R.:Serenade to Music, w. Isobel Baillie (sop), Lilian Stiles-Allen (sop), Elsie Suddaby (sop), Eva Turner (sop), Margaret Balfour (cta), Muriel Brunskill (cta), Astra Desmond (cta), Mary Jarred (cta), Parry Jones (ten), Heddle Nash (ten), Frank Titterton (ten), Walter Widdop (ten), Roy Henderson (bar), Norman Allin (bass), Robert Easton (bass), H. Wood (cnd), BBC SO *(rec Abbey Road, Oct 15, 1938)* Claremont ▲ CDGSE 785066
Vaughan Williams, R.:Serenade to Music, w. I. Baillie (sop), E. Suddaby (sop), S. Allen (sop), E. Turner (sop), M. Balfour (cta), A. Desmond (cta), M. Brunskill (cta), M. Jarred (cta), H. Nash (ten), W. Widdop (ten), P. Jones (ten), F. Titterton (ten), R. Henderson (bass), R. Easton (bass), N. Allin (bass), H. Wood (cnd), BBC SO [E] *(rec 10/15/38)* Pearl ▲ GEMMCD 9342 (m) [AAD]

Williams, Janet (sop)
Brahms, J.:Ein Deutsches Requiem, w. T. Hampson (bass), D. Barenboim (cnd), Chicago SO, Chicago Sym Chorus [G] Erato ▲ 92856–2
Cimarosa, D.:Il Matrimonio segreto, w. Susan Patterson (sop—Carolina), Janet Williams (mez—Elisseta), Gloria Banditelli (cta—Fidalma), William Matteuzzi (ten—Paolino), Alfonso Antoniozzi (bass—Geronimo), Petteri Salomaa (bass—Count Robinson), Hans Ludwig Hirsch (pno), G. Bellini (cnd), Eastern Netherlands Orch *(rec Muziekcentrum Enschede, Holland, Aug 26–Sept 8, 1991)* Arts 3–▲ 471172 [DDD]
Graun, K.H.:Cesare e Cleopatra, w. Lynne Dawson (sop), Iris Vermillion (mez), Robert Gambill (ten), R. Jacobs (cnd), Concerto Cologne Harmonia Mundi France 3–▲ HMC 901561.63
Graun, K.H.:Cesare e Cleopatra, w. Debora Beronesi (sop), Lynne Dawson (sop), Curtis Rayam (ten), R. Jacobs (cnd), Concerto Cologne, Berlin State Opera Chorus members Serenissima 3–▲ SER 360171 [DDD]
Handel, G.F.:Messiah, w. Lorraine Hunt (sop), Patricia Spence (mez), Drew Minter (alt), Jeffery Thomas (ten), William Parker (bar), N. McGegan (cnd), Philharmonia Baroque Orch, Univ of California at Berkeley Chamber Chorus—standard version of Messiah *occupies the first sections of each of the three CDs, one part per disc. Each part is followed, after a significant pause, by alternative versions of certain sections of the preceding material, 13 altogether. [E]* Harmonia Mundi USA 3–▲ HMU 907050/52
Handel, G.F.:Messiah (sels), w. Lorraine Hunt (sop), Patricia Spence (mez), Drew Minter (alt), Jeffery Thomas (ten), William Parker (bar), N. McGegan (cnd), Philharmonia Baroque Orch, Univ of California at Berkeley Chamber Chorus Harmonia Mundi USA ▲ HMU 907120

Williams, Janet (sop) (cont.)
Handel, G.F.:Messiah (sels), w. Lorraine Hunt (sop), Patricia Spence (mez), Drew Minter (alt), Jeffery Thomas (ten), William Parker (bar), N. McGegan (cnd), Philharmonia Baroque Orch, Univ of California at Berkeley Chamber Chorus [E] Harmonia Mundi USA ("Nightingale" series) ▲ HMN 907601

Williams, Karen (sop)
Fennimore, J.:Eventide, w. H. Johnsson (mez), P. Creech (ten), T. Rolek (cnd), Chelsea Chamber Ensemble [E] Albany ▲ TROY 023–2 [ADD]
Fennimore, J.:Songs (6), w. J. Fennimore (pno)—Winter love; Mary weeps for her child; The snow grew out of the sky last night; Infant joy; Now death has shut your eyes; My heart [E] Albany ▲ TROY 023–2 [ADD]

Williams, Malcolm (sgr)
Donizetti, G.:Il giovedì grasso, w. J. Gomez (sop), J. Hughes (mez), J. Peters (mez), U. Benelli (bar), B. Donlan (bar), F. Davià (bass), E. Esparza (sgr), D. Atherton (cnd), Eireann Radio-TV SO [I] *(rec live, 1970)* Memories ▲ HR 4482 [ADD]

Williams, Nancy (mez)
Bernstein, L.:Songfest, w. C. Dale (sop), R. Elias (mez), N. Rosenshein (ten), J. Reardon (bar), D. Gramm (b-bar), L. Bernstein (cnd), National SO Washington D.C. [E] Deutsche Grammophon ▲ 415965–2 [ADD]

Williams, O. (sgr)
Partch, H.:Revelation in the Courthouse Park, w. S. Costallos (sgr—Mom & Agave), C. Durham (ten—Sonny & Pentheus), M. Kimbrough (bar—Vendor & Herdsman), E. Earle (b-bar—Hobo & Tiresias), O. Babatunde (sgr—Dion & Dionysus), C. Roos (sgr—Mayor & Cadmus), O. Williams (sgr—Korypheus), R. Young (sgr—Cop & Guard), D. Mitchell (cnd), Partch Instrumentalists, marching band, *(chorus unknown)* [E] *(rec 10/87)* Tomato 2–▲ R2 70390 [DDD]

Williams, Roderick (bar)
Martin, F.:In terra pax, w. Judith Howarth (sop), Della Jones (cta), Martyn Hill (ten), Stephen Roberts (bass), M. Bamert (cnd), London PO, Laszlo Heltay (cnd), Brighton Festival Chorus Chandos ▲ CHAN 9465

Williams, Tommy (sgr)
Purcell, H.:The Indian Queen, w. Catherine Bott (sop—Orazia/Married Woman), Emma Kirkby (sop—Indian Girl/Zempoalla/Cupid), John Mark Ainsley (ten—Indian Boy/Fame/Follower of Cupid/Aerial Spirits), Julian Podger (ten—Follower of Envy/Aerial Spirit), Gerald Finley (bar—Conjurer/Hymen/Follower of Cupid), Helen Parker (sgr—Aerial Spirits), David Thomas (bass—Envy/High Priest/Married Man/Follower of Cupid), Simon Berridge (sgr—Follower of Envy), Libby Crabtree (sgr—Follower of Hymen/Aerial Spirit), Tommy Williams (sgr—God of Dreams), C. Hogwood (cnd), Academy of Ancient Music *(rec Walthamstow Assembly Hall, London, July 1994)* L'Oiseau-Lyre ▲ 444339–2 [DDD]

Williams, Yolanda (sop)
Still, W.G.:Music of, w. William Warfield (nar), Hilda Harris (alt), P. Brunelle (cnd), Plymouth Music Series Orch, Plymouth Music Series Chorus, Leigh Morris Chorale—Wailing Woman; Swanee River; And They Lynched Him on a Tree; Miss Sally's Party Collins Classics ▲ COL 1454

Williams-King, Anne (sop)
Bax, A.:Enchanted Summer, w. L. McWhirter (sop), V. Handley (cnd), Royal PO, Brighton Festival Chorus [E] Chandos ▲ CHAN 8625 [DDD]

Williamson, Vanessa (mez)
Handel, G.F.:Messiah, w. Ruth Holton (sop), James Griffett (ten), Lawrence Albert (bass), U. Walser (tpt), M. Brown (cnd), Gioia della Musica, Bmensky Akademicky Sbor Allegro 2–▲ ALGDPCD 1068 [DDD]
Handel, G.F.:Messiah (sels), w. Ruth Holton (sop), James Griffett (ten), L. Albert (bass), M. Brown (cnd), Gioia della Musica, Bmensky Akademicky Sbor Allegro ▲ ALG PCD 1078 [DDD]

Willis, Constance (mez)
Mozart, W.A.:Nozze di Figaro, w. Aulikki Rautawaara (sop), Audrey Mildmay (sop), John Heddle Nash (ten), Roy Henderson (bar), Willi Domgraf-Fassbaender (bar), F. Busch (cnd), Glyndebourne Festival Orch *(rec 1934)* Legend 2–▲ LGD 132 [ADD]
Mozart, W.A.:Nozze di Figaro, w. Aulikki Rautawaara (sop), Audrey Mildmay (sop), John Heddle Nash (ten), Roy Henderson (bar), Willi Domgraf-Fassbaender (bar), F. Busch (cnd), Glyndebourne Festival Orch, Glyndebourne Festival Chorus [I] *(rec 1934–35)* Pearl 2–▲ PEAS 9375 (m) [AAD]
Mozart, W.A.:Nozze di Figaro (sels), w. Luise Helletsgrüber (sop), Audrey Mildmay (sop), Aulikki Rautawaara (sop), John Heddle Nash (ten), Willi Domgraf-Fassbaender (bar), Roy Henderson (bar), Norman Allin (bass), F. Busch (cnd), Glyndebourne Festival Orch Pearl ▲ PEA CD 9230

Wilson, Tim (ten)
Verdi, G.:Il trovatore, w. A. Millo (sop), D. Zajick (mez), S. Kelly (cta), P. Domingo (ten), A. Laciura (ten), J. Morris (bass), G. Bater (bass), J. Levine (cnd), Metropolitan Opera Orch, New York Metropolitan Opera Chorus *(rec June 18, 1991)* Sony Classical 2–▲ S2K 48070 [DDD]

Willumsen, Marianne (sop)
Thommessen, O.A.:Gratia agimus, w. Geir Henning (pno) Caprice ▲ CAP 21403

Wilson (sgr)
Purcell, H.:Odes & Welcome Songs (misc), w. J. Smith (sop), E. Priday (sop), K. Amps (sop), M. Chance (ct), J. M. Ainsley (ten), S. Richardson (bar), T. Pinnock (cnd), English Concert, *(chorus unknown)* —Come ye Sons of Art; Welcome to All the Pleasures; Of Old, When Heroes Thought it Base Archiv ▲ 427663–2 [DDD]

Wilson, G. (ten)
Stravinsky, I.:Pulcinella, w. J. Graham-Hall (ten), J. Opalach (bass), G. Schwarz (cnd), Seattle SO Delos ▲ DE 3100 [DDD]

Wilson, Jan (mez)
Handel, G.F.:Israel in Egypt, w. Nancy Argenta (sop), Emily Van Evera (sop), Anthony Rolfe Johnson (ten), Thomas (sgr), White (sgr), A. Parrott (cnd), Taverner Players, Taverner Choir [E] EMI Classics 2–▲ CDCB 54018 [DDD]
Schafer, R.M.:Minnelieder, w. Pennsylvania Wind Quintet *(rec Unitarian Universalist Fellowship, State College, PA, May 1992–July 1993)* Centaur ▲ CRC 2225 [DDD]

Wilson, Lambert (nar)
Prokofiev, S.:Peter & the Wolf, w. M. Plasson (cnd), Toulouse Capitole Orch EMI Classics 2–▲ CDC 54465

Wilson, M. (sgr)
Sousa, J.P.:Songs, w. J. Guyer (sop), D. Buck (sgr)—(6 soprano solos, 7 baritone solos, & 5 duets) I've made my plans for the summer (1907); The love that lives forever (1917); Valse song [The Crystal lute - from *The American Maid*, 1909]; Oh, ye lilies white (1887); Girls who have loved [or The Mystery of History - from *The Free Lance*, 1905]; There's a mery brown thrush (1926); The fighting race (1919); A Serenade in Seville (1924); My own, my Geraldine (1887); Sweet Miss Industry (1887); I wonder (1888); You cannot tell how old they are by looking at their skirts (1923); Forever and a day (1927); Sweetheart, I'm waiting (1895); Blue Ridge, I'm coming back to you (1917); Love's radiant hour (1928); A rare old fellow (1881); The Stars and Stripes forever (1898) [E] Premier ▲ PRCD 1011 [DDD]

Wilson, Nat (b-bar)
Rameau, J.P.:Le Berger fidèle, w. Christine Brandes (sop), Ann Monoyios (sop), Howard Crook (ten), Concert Royal Newport Classic ▲ NPT 85555

Wilson, Steuart (ten)
Elgar, E.:The Dream of Gerontius (sels), w. M. Balfour (cta), H. Heyner (bar), E. Elgar (cnd), Royal Albert Hall Orch, Royal Choral Society [E] *(rec 1927)* Opal ▲ CD 9810 (m) [AAD]

Wilson, Timothy (alt)
Loevendie, T.:Gassir, the Hero, w. Claron McFadden (sop—Partridge/Priestess), Timothy Wilson (alt—Shamsi), Christopher Gillett (ten—Safi), Robert Poulton (bar—Gassir), Lieuwe Visser (bass—Yemni), Roger Smeets (sgr—Rafi), D. Porcelijn (cnd), Asko Ensemble *(rec live, Amsterdam Studios, June 14–15, 1993)* Donemus ▲ CV 35

Wilson, Timothy (ten)
Tavener, J.:Akathist of Thanksgiving, w. J. Bowman (ct), M. Baker (org), M. Neary (cnd), BBC SO, Westminster Abbey Choir, BBC Singers *(rec Jan. 21, 1994)* Sony Classical ▲ SK 64446 [DDD]

Wilson–Johnson, David (bar)
Bach, J.S.:St. John Passion, w. P. Kwella (sop), D. James (ct), W. Kendall (ten), I. Partridge (ten), M. George (bar), H. Christophers (cnd), The Sixteen Orch, The Sixteen [G] Chandos ("Chaconne" series) 2-▲ CHAN 0507/08 [DDD]
Berlioz, H.:La Damnation de Faust, w. J. Larmor (mez—Marguerite), K. Olsen (ten—Faust), D. Wilson-Johnson (bar—Méphistophélès), H. Claessens (bar—Brander), G. Neuhold (cnd), Flanders Royal PO, Düsseldorf Municipal Choral Society Bayer 2-▲ 500017/18 [DDD]
Boughton, R.:The Immortal Hour, w. A. Dawson (sop), R. Kennedy (bass), A. Melville (cnd), English CO, Geoffrey Mitchell Choir [E] Hyperion 2-▲ CDA 66101/02 [DDD]
Brahms, J.:Ein Deutsches Requiem, w. F. Lott (sop), R. Hickox (cnd), London SO, London Sym Chorus [G] Chandos ▲ CHAN 8942 [DDD]
Elgar, E.:Caractacus, w. J. Howarth (sop), A. Davies (ten), S. Roberts (bar), A.R. Miles (bass), R. Hickox (cnd), London SO, London Sym Chorus [E] *(rec 1992)* Chandos 2-▲ CHAN 9156/57 [DDD]
Elgar, E.:The Kingdom, w. M. Marshall (sop), F. Palmer (sop), Davies (ten), R. Hickox (cnd), London SO, London Sym Chorus [E] Chandos 2-▲ CHAN 8788/89 [DDD]
Fauré, G.:Requiem, w. Harry Escott (trb), D. Hill (cnd), City of London Sinfonia, Westminster Cathedral Choir IMP ▲ PCD 2015
Goss, J.:O Saviour of the World, w. Maldwyn Davies (ten), Andrew Lucas (org), John Scott (cnd), St. Paul's Cathedral Choir, St. Paul's Cathedral Special Choir Conifer Classics ▲ 75605–51193–2 [DDD]
Grainger, P.:Jungle Book (comp), w. John Mark Ainsley (ten), S. Layton (cnd), Polyphony Hyperion ▲ CDA 66863
Haydn, J.:Mass 11, "Nelsonmesse", "Imperial Mass", "Coronation Mass", w. Felicity Lott (sop), Carolyn Watkinson (cta), Maldwyn Davies (ten), T. Pinnock (cnd), English CO [L] Archiv ▲ 423097–2 [DDD]
Hughes, O.A.:Dewi Saint, w. Yvonne Kenny (sop), Martyn Hill (ten), O. A. Hughes (cnd), BBC Welsh National SO, BBC Welsh National Chorus [E] Chandos ▲ CHAN 8890 [DDD]
Lloyd, G.:John Socman (sels), w. J. Watson (sop), D. Montague (mez), T. Booth (ten), M. Rivers (bar), M. George (bass), G. Lloyd (cnd), Philharmonia Orch, London Voices Albany ▲ TROY 131 [DDD]
Martin, F.:Monologe (6) aus "Jedermann", w. M. Bamert (cnd), London PO Chandos ▲ CHAN 9411 [DDD]
Matthews, C.:Great Journey, w. L. Friend (cnd), Nash Ensemble Virgin Classics ▲ CDC 59061
Mozart, W.A.:Missa, K.317, w. L. Marshall (sop), A. Murray (mez), R. Covey-Crump (ten), S. Cleobury (cnd), English CO, King's College Choir Cambridge [L] Argo ▲ 411904–2 [DDD]
Mozart, W.A.:Missa, K.317, w. Y. Kenny (sop), K. Kuhlmann (mez), K. Lewis (ten), C. P. Flor (cnd), Philharmonia Orch, London Voices RCA Red Seal ▲ 09026–60812–2
Mozart, W.A.:Missa solemnis, K.337, w. L. Marshall (sop), A. Murray (mez), R. Covey-Crump (ten), S. Cleobury (cnd), English CO [L] Argo ▲ 411904–2 [DDD]
Mozart, W.A.:Requiem, w. Y. Kenny (sop), S. Walker (mez), W. Kendall (ten), G. Guest (cnd), English CO, St. John's College Choir Cambridge [L] Chandos ▲ CHAN 8574 [DDD]
Parry, H.:The Soul's Ransom, w. D. Jones (mez), M. Bamert (cnd), London PO, London Phil Chorus [E] Chandos ▲ CHAN 8990 [DDD]
Purcell, H.:The Fairy Queen, w. Lorraine Hunt (sop), Susan Bickley (mez), Catherine Pierard (mez), Howard Crook (ten), Mark Padmore (ten), Richard Wistreich (bass), R. Norrington (cnd), London Classical Players, Schütz Choir London EMI Classics ▲ CDCB 55234
Purcell, H.:Odes & Welcome Songs (misc), w. H. Cook (ten), J. Bowman (ct), C. Robson (ct), G. Leonhardt (hpd), G. Leonhardt (cnd), Orch of the Age of Enlightenment Virgin Classics ▲ CDC 59243
Rachmaninoff, S.:The Bells, w. S. Murphy (sop), K. Lewis (ten), N. Järvi (cnd), Scottish National Orch, Scottish National Chorus [R] Chandos ▲ CHAN 8476 [DDD]
Shostakovich, D.:Hamlet (incidental), w. M. Elder (cnd), City of Birmingham SO United ▲ UNI 88050
Shostakovich, D.:King Lear (incidental), w. M. Elder (cnd), City of Birmingham SO United ▲ UNI 88050
Smyth, E.:The Wreckers, w. Judith Howarth (sop), Anne-Marie Owens (mez), Annemarie Sand (mez), Justin Lavender (ten), Anthony Roden (ten), Peter Sidhom (bar), Brian Bannatyne-Scott (bass), O. de la Martinez (cnd), BBC PO, Huddersfield Choral Society *(rec live, Royal Albert Hall, London, July 31, 1994)* Conifer Classics 2-▲ 75605–51250–2
Stainer, J.:The Crucifixion, w. Maldwyn Davies (ten), Andrew Lucas (org), John Scott (cnd), St. Paul's Cathedral Choir, St. Paul's Cathedral Special Choir Conifer Classics ▲ 75605–51193–2 [DDD]
Stravinsky, I.:Renard, w. J. Aler (ten), N. Robson (ten), J. Tomlinson (bass), E.-P. Salonen (cnd), London Sinfonietta Sony Classical ▲ SK 45965
Tippett, M.:The Ice Break, w. H. Harper (sop), S. Sylvan (bar), D. Atherton (cnd), London Sinfonietta, London Sym Chorus [E] Virgin Classics ▲ 59048 [DDD]
Tippett, M.:King Priam, w. Heather Harper (sop—Hecuba), Linda Hirst (sop—Serving Woman), Felicity Palmer (sop—Andromache), Julian Saipe (sop—Paris), Yvonne Minton (mez—Helen), Ann Murray (mez—Nurse), Kenneth Bowen (ten—Hermes), Peter Hall (ten—Young Guard), Philip Langridge (ten—Paris), Robert Tear (ten—Achilles), Thomas Allen (bar—Hector), Norman Bailey (bar—Priam), Stephen Roberts (bar—Patroclus), David Wilson-Johnson (bar—Old Man), D. Atherton (cnd), London Sinfonietta, London Sinfonietta Chorus Chandos ▲ CHAN 9406/7 [DDD]
Vivaldi, A.:Sacred Choral Music, w. Susan Gritton (sop), Catherine Denley (mez), Lynton Atkinson (trb), Lisa Milne (sgr), R. King (cnd), King's Consort—Magnificat; Lauda, Jerusalem; Kyrie eleison; Credo in unum Deum; Dixit Dominus Hyperion ▲ CDA 66769
Walton, W.:Belshazzar's Feast, w. R. Hickox (cnd), London SO, London Sym Chorus Classics for Pleasure ("Eminence" series) ▲ CDEMX 2225 [DDD]

Wilson–Johnson, David (nar)
Schoenberg, A.:Ode to Napoleon, w. P. Boulez (cnd), BBC SO, Ensemble InterContemporain *(rec Mar. 31, 1980)* Sony Classical ▲ SMK 48463 [ADD]

Wilson–Johnson, David (ten)
Handel, G.F.:Music of, w. Pauline Tinsley (sop), James Bowman (ct), Anthony Rolfe-Johnson (ten), Simon Preston (org), R. Leppard (cnd), English CO, London Phil Chorus—Zadok the Priest; Eternal Source of Light Divine; Tamerlano Ov; Dead March [from Saul]; When the Ear Heard Her; She Delivered the Poor That Cried; Their Bodies Are Buried in Peace; Glory Be to the Father; As It Was in the Beginning; Con a Due Cori in B♭; Waft Her Angels to the Skies; Con in g for Org, Op. 7/5; Hallelujah Chorus [from The Messiah] IMP ("BBC Radio Classics" series) ▲ IMP 5691522

Wilton, Ebba (sop)
The Danish Nightingale Point ▲ PCD 5111

Wimberger, Peter (b-bar)
Haydn, J.:Mass 14, "Harmoniemesse", w. Christiane Sorell (sop), Elisabeth Thoman (sop), Rose Bahl (cta), Maura Moreira (cta), Kurt Equiluz (ten), Gerhard Eder (bass), G. Barati (cnd), Vienna State Opera Orch, Vienna Academy Chamber Choir *(rec 1964)* Tuxedo ▲ TUXCD 1055 [ADD]
Wagner, R.:Der Ring des Nibelungen (sels), w. M. Caballé (sop), Z. Mehta (cnd), New York PO—Rheingold *(Entry of the Gods)*, Walküre *(Ride of the Valkyries; Magic Fire Music)* Siegfried *(Waldweben)*, Götterdämmerung *(Rhine Journey & Funeral Music; Immolation Scene)* CBS ▲ MDK 44657 [DDD] ■ MDT 44657 (D)

Wimer, Franz (bass)
Bach, J.S.:St. Luke Passion, w. Christiane Sorell (sop), Maura Moreira (alt), Kurt Equiluz (ten), Josef Nebois (org), G. Barati (cnd), Vienna State Opera Orch, Akademie Chamber Choir Soloists Sarx 2-▲ SRX 2026 [ADD]

Wimmer, Hans-Georg (bass)
Bach, J.S.:St. Matthew Passion, w. Monika Frimmer (sop), Veronika Winter (sop), Lena Susanne Norin (alt), Wilfried Jochens (ten), Christoph Prégardien (ten), Klaus Mertens (bass), H. Max (cnd), Das Kliene Konzert, Rheinland Kantorei Capriccio 2-▲ 60 046 [DDD]
Homilius, G.A.:St. Matthew Passion, w. A. Monoyios (sop), U. Groenwald (cta), G. Türk, C. Prégardien (ten), K. Mertens (b-bar), Berlin Academy for Early Music, Leverkusen Cappella Vocale Berlin Classics 2-▲ BER 1046 [DDD]

Winbergh, Gösta (ten)
Donizetti, G.:Don Pasquale, w. M. Freni (sop), S. Bruscantini (bar), L. Nucci (bar), R. Muti (cnd), Philharmonia Orch, Ambrosian Opera Chorus EMI Classics 2-▲ CDCB 47068
Donizetti, G.:Don Pasquale (sels), w. M. Freni (sop), S. Bruscantini (bar), L. Nucci (bar), R. Muti (cnd), Philharmonia Orch, Ambrosian Opera Chorus EMI Classics ▲ CDC 54490

Winbergh, Gösta (ten) (cont.)
Gluck, C.W.:Iphigénie en Tauride, w. C. Vaness (sop—Iphigénie), S. Bruson (bar—Diane), G. Winbergh (ten—Pylade), T. Allen (bar—Oreste), G. Surian (bass—Thoas), R. Muti (cnd), La Scala Orch, La Scala Chorus *(rec Mar. 14–26, 1992)* Sony Classical 2-▲ S2K 52492 [DDD]
Haydn, J.:Die Schöpfung, w. Kathleen Battle (sop), Kurt Moll (bass), J. Levine (cnd), Berlin PO, Stockholm Radio Chorus, Stockholm Chamber Choir Deutsche Grammophon 2-▲ 427629–2 [DDD]
Mozart, W.A.:Clemenza, w. Christine Barbaux (sop—Servilia), Carol Vaness (sop—Viellia), Martha Senn (mez—Annio), Delores Ziegler (mez—Sesto), Gösta Winbergh (ten—Tito), László Polgár (bass—Publio), R. Muti (cnd), Vienna PO, Vienna State Opera Chorus *(rec live, Salzburg Festival, 1988)* EMI Classics 2-▲ CDCB 55489
Mozart, W.A.:Don Giovanni, w. A. Tomowa-Sintow (sop), K. Battle (sop), A. Baltsa (mez), S. Ramey (bass), F. Furlanetto (bass), P. Burchuladze (bass), H. von Karajan (cnd), Berlin PO, German Opera Chorus [I] Deutsche Grammophon 3-▲ 419179–2 [DDD]
Mozart, W.A.:Don Giovanni (sels), w. A. Tomowa-Sintow (sop), K. Battle (sop), A. Baltsa (mez), S. Ramey (bass), F. Furlanetto (bass), P. Burchuladze (bass), H. von Karajan (cnd), Berlin PO, German Opera Chorus [I] Deutsche Grammophon ▲ 419635–2 [DDD]
Mozart, W.A.:Entführung, w. E. Gruberova (sop), K. Battle (sop), H. Zednik (ten), M. Talvela (bass), Will Quadflieg (nar), G. Solti (cnd), Vienna PO [G] London 2-▲ 417402–2 [DDD]
Mozart, W.A.:Zauberflöte, w. S. Jo (sop), L. Orgonasova (sop), Martina Bovet (sop), H. Hagegard (bar), A. Jordan (cnd), Paris Orchestral Ensemble, Romande Chamber Choir, Pro Arte Lausanne Erato 2-▲ 2292–45469–2 [DDD]
Schumann, R.:Spanisches Liederspiel, w. Märta Schéle (sop), Edith Thallaug (alt), Erland Hagegard (bar), Lucia Negro (pno) *(rec Nacka Aula, Nacka, Sweden, 1976)* BIS ▲ CD 77 [AAD]
Strauss (II), Joh.:Songs, w. Friedrich Haider (pno) Nightingale Classics ▲ NIG 948

Windgassen, Wolfgang (ten)
Beethoven, L. van:Fidelio, w. S. Jurinac (sop), M. Mödl (sop), A. Poell (bar), O. Edelmann (bass), G. Frick (bass), W. Furtwängler (cnd), Vienna PO *(rec Oct. 1953)* EMI Classics 2-▲ CDHB 64496
Beethoven, L. van:Fidelio (sels), w. W. Furtwängler (cnd), Vienna PO—3 selections from Act 2—aria "Gott, welch' Dunkel hier...In des lebens Frühlingstagen," trio "Euch werde Lohn!" [w. Martha Mödl & Gottlob Frick] & duet "O namenlose Freude" [w. Martha Mödl] [G] *(rec 1953)* Memories 2-▲ HR 4424/25 [ADD]
Strauss, R.:Elektra, w. B. Nilsson (sop), L. Rysanek (sop), R. Resnik (mez), E. Wächter (bar), K. Böhm (cnd), *(orch unknown)* [G] *(rec live, Vienna 12/16/65)* Standing Room Only 2-▲ SRO 833–2 [ADD]
Wagner, R.:Arias & Scenes, *(orch unknown)*—selections from Götterdämmerung *(In Leid zu dem Wipfel...Brünnhilde heilige Braut—w. Neidlinger, Greindl, C. Krauss, Bayreuth 1953)*, Lohengrin *(Mein lieber Schwan, Das süsse Lied verhallt & In fernem Land—w. Nilsson, Varnay, Adam, Jochum, Bayreuth 1954)*, Siegfried *(Ist's eine Kunst...Her mit den Stücken...Notung! Notung!...Hoho! Hoho! Hoheil & Selige Öde...Das ist kein Mann—w. Krauss, Bayreuth 1953)*, Tristan *(Love Duet, etc.—w. Nilsson, Ludwig, Wächter, Böhm, Bayreuth 1966)* [G] Memories 2-▲ HR 4424/25 [ADD]
Wagner, R.:Der fliegende Holländer, w. Annelies Kupper (sop—Senta), Sieglinde Wagner (mez—Mary), Ernst Haefliger (ten—Steersman), Wolfgang Windgassen (ten—Erik), Josef Metternich (ten—Dutchman), Josef Greindl (bass—Daland), F. Fricsay (cnd), Berlin RIAS SO, Berlin RIAS Chamber Choir *(rec 1953)* Deutsche Grammophon 2-▲ 439714–2 (m) [ADD]
Wagner, R.:Der fliegende Holländer, w. A. Varnay (sop), H. Uhde (bar), L. Weber (bass), H. Knappertsbusch (cnd), Bayreuth Festival Orch, Bayreuth Festival Chorus [G] *(rec live)* Arkadia 2-▲ 421 [ADD]
Wagner, R.:Götterdämmerung, w. B. Nilsson (sop), J. Watson (sop), C. Ludwig (mez), D. Fischer-Dieskau (bar), G. Frick (bass), G. Solti (cnd), Vienna PO [G] London 4-▲ 414115–2 [ADD]
Wagner, R.:Lohengrin, w. E. Steber (sop), A. Varnay (sop), H. Uhde (bar), J. Greindl (bass), J. Keilberth (cnd), Bayreuth Festival Orch, Bayreuth Festival Chorus *(rec live, Bayreuth Festival, 1953)* Teldec ("Historic" series) 4-▲ 93674
Wagner, R.:Lohengrin, w. B. Nilsson (sop), A. Varnay (sop), H. Uhde (bar), E. Jochum (cnd), Bayreuth Festival Orch, Bayreuth Festival Chorus *(rec live, Bayreuth 1954)* Melodram 3-▲ MEL 36104
Wagner, R.:Die Meistersinger von Nürnberg, w. E. Grümmer (sop), T. Adam (b-bar), J. Greindl (bass), H. Knappertsbusch (cnd), Bayreuth Festival Orch, Bayreuth Festival Chorus [G] *(rec live, Bayreuth, 1960)* Melodram 4-▲ MEL 46103
Wagner, R.:Die Meistersinger von Nürnberg (sels), w. H. Hotter (b-bar), A. Cluytens (cnd), Bayreuth Festival Orch, Bayreuth Festival Chorus—Monologue & Duet from Act 3 [G] *(rec live, 1957)* Arkadia 4-▲ 440 (m) [AAD]
Wagner, R.:Das Rheingold, w. E. Schwarzkopf (sop), I. Malaniuk (cta), S. Björling (bar), Pflanzl (sgr), H. von Karajan (cnd), Bayreuth Festival Orch, Bayreuth Festival Chorus [G] *(rec live, 1951)* Arkadia 2-▲ 216 (m) [ADD]
Wagner, R.:Der Ring des Nibelungen, w. B. Nilsson (sop), K. Flagstad (sop), R. Crespin (sop), C. Watson (sop), C. Ludwig (mez), J. Madeira (mez), S. Svanholm (ten), J. King (ten), G. Stolze (ten), G. London (bar), D. Fischer-Dieskau (bar), H. Hotter (b-bar), G. Neidlinger (b-bar), G. Frick (bass), G. Solti (cnd), Vienna PO [G] London 15-▲ 414100–2 [ADD]
Wagner, R.:Der Ring des Nibelungen, w. B. Nilsson (sop), L. Rysanek (sop), K. Dvořaková (sop), M. Mödl (sop), A. Burmeister (mez), V. Soukupova (mez), E. Wohlfahrt (ten), T. Stewart (bar), T. Adam (b-bar), G. Neidlinger (b-bar), K. Böhme (bass), G. Nienstedt (bass), K. Böhm (cnd), Bayreuth Festival Orch, Bayreuth Festival Chorus [G] *(rec live, 1966–67)* Philips 14-▲ 420325–2 [ADD]
Wagner, R.:Der Ring des Nibelungen, w. Gré Brouwenstein (sop—Freia/Sieglinde), Ilse Hollweg (sop—Waldvogel), Gerda Lammers (sop—Ortlinde), Paula Lenchner (sop—Wellgunde/Gerhilde), Hilde Scheppan (sop—Helmwige), Astrid Varnay (sop—Brünnilde/3rd Norn), Lore Wissmann (sop—Woglinde), Maria von Ilosvay (mez—Flosshilde/Schwertleite/2nd Norn), Louise Charlotte Kamps (mez—Siegrune), Jean Madeira (mez—Erda/Rossweisse/1st Norn), Georgine van Milinkovic (mez—Fricka/Grimgerde), Elisabeth Schärtel (mez—Waltraute), Paul Kuën (ten—Mime), Ludwig Suthaus (ten—Loge), Josef Traxel (ten—Froh), Wolfgang Windgassen (ten—Siegmund/Siegfried), Alfons Herwig (bar—Donner), Hermann Uhde (bar—Gunther), Hans Hotter (b-bar—Wotan), Gustav Neidlinger (b-bar—Alberich), Josef Griendl (bass—Fasolt/Hunding/Hagen), Arnold van Mill (bass—Fafner), H. Knappertsbusch (cnd), Bayreuth Festival Orch, Bayreuth Festival Chorus *(rec live, Bayreuth, Aug 13–17, 1956)* Golden Melodram 14-▲ GM 1.001 [ADD]
Wagner, R.:Der Ring des Nibelungen (sels), w. Birgit Nilsson (sop—Brünnhilde), Leonie Rysanek (sop—Sieglinde), James King (ten—Siegmund), Theo Adam (b-bar—Wotan), Gustav Neidlinger (b-bar), Josef Greindl (bass), K. Böhm (cnd), Bayreuth Festival Orch *(rec Bayreuth, 1967)* Philips 2-▲ 454020–2
Wagner, R.:Der Ring des Nibelungen (sels), w. B. Nilsson (sop), H. Hotter (b-bar), G. Solti (cnd), Vienna PO London ▲ 421313–2 [ADD]
Wagner, R.:Siegfried, w. B. Nilsson (sop), E. Wohlfahrt (ten), T. Adam (b-bar), G. Neidlinger (b-bar), K. Böhm (cnd), Bayreuth Festival Orch, Bayreuth Festival Chorus [G] Philips 4-▲ 412483–2 [ADD]
Wagner, R.:Siegfried, w. A. Varnay (sop), A. Andersson (ten), G. Stoltze (ten), H. Hotter (b-bar), J. Greindl (bass), H. Knappertsbusch (cnd), Bayreuth Festival Orch, Bayreuth Festival Chorus [G] *(rec live 1958)* Arkadia 4-▲ 443 [AAD]
Wagner, R.:Siegfried, w. B. Nilsson (sop), G. Stolze (ten), H. Hotter (b-bar), G. Neidlinger (b-bar), G. Solti (cnd), Vienna PO [G] London 4-▲ 414110–2 [ADD]
Wagner, R.:Tannhäuser, w. A. Silja (sop), G. Bumbry (mez), E. Wächter (bar), J. Greindl (bass), W. Sawallisch (cnd), Bayreuth Festival Orch, Bayreuth Festival Chorus [Dresden version with Paris Venusberg music] [G] Philips 3-▲ 434607–2 [ADD]
Wagner, R.:Tannhäuser, w. V. de Los Angeles (sop), G. Bumbry (mez), G. Stolze (ten), D. Fischer-Dieskau (bar), T. Adam (b-bar), J. Greindl (bass), F. Crass (bass), W. Sawallisch (cnd), Bayreuth Festival Orch, Bayreuth Festival Chorus [G] *(rec 1961)* Myto 3-▲ MCD 93277
Wagner, R.:Tristan und Isolde, w. B. Nilsson (sop), C. Ludwig (mez), E. Wächter (bar), M. Talvela (bass), K. Böhm (cnd), Bayreuth Festival Orch, Bayreuth Festival Chorus [G] *(rec Bayreuth Festival, 1966)* Deutsche Grammophon 3-▲ 419889–2 [ADD]
Wagner, R.:Tristan und Isolde, w. B. Nilsson (sop), C. Ludwig (mez), E. Wächter (bar), M. Talvela (bass), K. Böhm (cnd), Bayreuth Festival Orch, Bayreuth Festival Chorus [G] Philips 3-▲ 434425–2 [ADD]
Wagner, R.:Tristan und Isolde (sels), w. B. Nilsson (sop), H. von Karajan (cnd), *(orch unknown)*—Love Duet *(rec 1959)* Arkadia 4-▲ 224

Windgassen, Wolfgang (ten) (cont.)
Wagner, R.:Tristan und Isolde (sels), w. Martha Mödl (sop—Isolde), Johanna Blatter (mez—Brangäne), Wolfgang Windgassen (ten—Tristan), A. Rother (cnd), Berlin City Opera Orch—Weh, ach wehe! dies zu dulden [rec. Nov 24., 1954]; Isolde!— Tristan! Geliebter! [rec. Oct. 24, 1954]; Lausch', Geliebter!— Lass mich sterben! [rec. Oct 24., 1954]; Mild und leise wie er lächelt [rec. Oct 22., 1952] Teldec ("Historic" series) ▲ 95516-2 [ADD]

Windmüller, Yaron (bar)
Ullmann, V.:Songs, w. Christine Schäfer (sop), Liat Himmelheber (mez), Axel Bauni (pno)—5 Liebeslieder, Op. 18; 6 Lieder, Op. 17; 3 Sonette, Op. 29; 6 Sonnets, Op. 34; Geistliche Lieder, Op. 20; Liederbuch das Hafis, op. 30; Der Mensch und sein Tag, Op. 47; Immer inmitten; Chinesische Lieder; 3 Lieder Orfeo 2-▲ 380952 [DDD]

Windmüller, Yaron (voc)
Pfitzner, H.:Der blumen Rache, w. Yvi Jänicke (cta), Yvonne Wiedstruck (sgr), R. Reuter (cnd), Berlin RSO, Berlin Radio Chorus CPO ▲ CPO 999158 [DDD]
Pfitzner, H.:Das dunkle Reich, w. Yvi Jänicke (cta), Yvonne Wiedstruck (voc), R. Reuter (cnd), Berlin RSO, Berlin Radio Chorus CPO ▲ CPO 999158 [DDD]
Pfitzner, H.:Fons salutifer, w. Yvi Jänicke (cta), Yvonne Wiedstruck (voc), R. Reuter (cnd), Berlin RSO, Berlin Radio Chorus CPO ▲ CPO 999158 [DDD]

Wing, Stafford (ten)
Haydn, J.:Mass 10, "Kriegsmesse", "Paukenmesse", w. Elisabeth Thomann (sop), Elfriede Jahn (alt), Eishi Kawamura (bass), H. Gillesberger (cnd), Vienna State Opera Orch, Vienna Chamber Choir *(rec 1965)* Tuxedo ▲ TUXCD 1025
Schubert, Franz:Deutsche Messe, w. Elisabeth Thomann (sop), Gertrude Jahn (alt), Kunikazu Ohashi (bass), H. Gillesberger (cnd), Vienna SO, Vienna Chamber Choir Tuxedo ▲ TUXCD 1074 [ADD]
Schubert, Franz:Mass 3, w. Elisabeth Thomann (sop), Gertrude Jahn (alt), Kunikazu Ohashi (bass), H. Gillesberger (cnd), Vienna SO, Vienna Chamber Choir Tuxedo ▲ TUXCD 1074 [ADD]

Winkler, Hermann (ten)
Hindemith, P.:Mathis der Maler, w. Josef Protschka (ten), Roland Hermann (bar), Victor von Halem (bass), Harald Stamm (bass), G. Albrecht (cnd), Cologne RSO Wergo 3-▲ WER 6255-2
Schoeck, O.:Massimilla Doni, w. E. Mathis (sop), A. Küttenbaum (mez), H. Stamm (bass), G. Albrecht (cnd), Cologne RSO, Cologne Radio Chorus [G] Koch Schwann 2-▲ CD 314025 [DDD]
Strauss, R.:Elektra, w. C. Studer (sop), E. Marton (sop), M. Lipovsek (mez), B. Weikl (bar), W. Sawallisch (cnd), Bavarian RSO, Bavarian Radio Chorus EMI Classics 2-▲ CDCB 54067
Zemlinsky, A. von:Kleider machen Leute, w. E. Mathis (sop), V. Vogel (ten), C. Otelli (bar), H. Franzen (bass), R. Scholze (bass), W. Slabbert (sgr), R. Weikert (cnd), Zurich Opera Orch, Zurich Opera House Chorus [G] *(rec live, Zurich Opera House, 6/29/90)* Koch Schwann 2-▲ CD 314 069 [DDD]

Winkler Prins, Djoke (sop)
Straesser, J.:Ramasasiri, w. A. van Beek (cnd), *(ensemble unknown) (rec June 26, 1981)* Donemus ▲ CV 44

Winklet, Jutta (alt)
Suter, H.:Le Laudi di San Francesco d'Assisi, w. A. Michael (sop), A. Baldin (ten), J. Will (bass), P. Laubschet (org), Bern SO, T. Loosli (cnd), Bern Bach Choir, Sekundar School Children's Choir Ars Musici ▲ AM 1015-2 [DDD]

Winogrodska, Grazyna (mez)
Penderecki, K.:Polish Requiem, w. I. Haubold (sop), Z. Terzakis (ten), Smith (sgr), K. Penderecki (cnd), North German RSO, North German Radio Chorus [L] *(rec live, Lucerne, 1989)* Deutsche Grammophon 2-▲ 429720-2 [DDD]
Stachowski, M.:Sapphic Odes, w. K. Penderecki (cnd), Polish National RSO Katowice *(rec Apr. 1-6, 1987)* Polskie Nagrania ▲ PLN 076 [ADD]

Winska, Aga (sop)
Chopin, F.:Mazurkas, w. Jerzy Sterczynski (pno)—Op. 6/1 & 4, Op. 7/1 & 3, Op. 24/1 & 2, Op. 33/2 & 3, Op. 50/1 & 2, Op. 67/1 & Op. 68/2 [all arr Viardot]; Op. 17/1 & 4 [arr Bordese] *(rec Rzeszow, June 28-30, 1995)* Selene ▲ CD 9504.27 [DDD]

Winslade, Glenn (ten)
Handel, G.F.:Messiah (sels), w. Felicity Lott (sop), Linda Finnie (mez), Henry Herford (bar), G. Malcolm (cnd), Scottish CO, Scottish Phil Singers IMP ("Classic" series) ▲ IMP 2031

Winter, Horst (ten)
Golden Operetta, Vol. 2:Operetta Melodies, w. F. Bauer-Theussl (cnd), Vienna Volksoper Orch, Vienna Volksoper Chorus, Renate Holm (sop), Lotte Rysanek (sop), Dagmar Hermann (mez), Kurt Equiluz (ten), et al. Koch Präsent ▲ 399 224 [AAD]

Winter, Kate (sop)
Stravinsky, I.:Les Noces, w. L. Seymour (cta), P. Jones (ten), R. Henderson (bar), I. Stravinsky (cnd), *(orch & chorus unknown)* EMI Classics 2-▲ ZDCB 54607

Winter, Veronika (sgr)
Austin, E.:An Die Nachgeborenen, w. Alex Bassermann (sgr), Kirsten Grünenpült (sgr), Sibylle Dotzauer (pno), Gerald Kegelmann (cnd), Heidelberg-Mannheim State Univ Chamber Choir Capstone ▲ CPS 8625

Winter, Veronika (sop)
Bach, J.S.:St. Matthew Passion, w. Monika Frimmer (sop), Lena Susanne Norin (alt), Wilfried Jochens (ten), Christoph Prégardien (ten), Klaus Mertens (bass), Hans-Georg Wimmer (bass), H. Max (cnd), Das Kliene Konzert, Rhineland Kantorei Capriccio 2-▲ 60 046 [DDD]
Telemann, G.P.:Auferstehung und Himmelfahrt Jesu, w. Monika Frimmer (sop), Matthias Koch (alt), Nico Van der Meel (ten), Klaus Mertens (bass), H. Max (cnd), Das Kliene Konzert, Rhineland Kantorei Capriccio ▲ CD 10596 [DDD]

Winters (sgr)
Gershwin, G.:Porgy & Bess (sels), w. Williams, Matthews, Long, Winters, Engel, *(orch unknown)* [E] Odyssey ■ YT 35501 (m)

Wintersteller, L. (sgr)
Rodgers, R.:Music of, w. V. Clark (sgr), Gregg Edelman (sgr), J. Graae (sgr), A. Reed (sgr)—Oklahoma; Carousel; The Sound of Music; South Pacific; Flower Drum Song; Cinderella & others Varèse Sarabande ▲ VSD 5516 ■ VSC 5516

Wirz, Clara (mez)
Janácek, L.:The Diary of One Who Disappeared, w. Peter Keller (ten), Mario Venzago (pno), Mario Venzago (cnd), Lucerne Singers Accord ▲ ACD 220312 [DDD]
Mozart, W.A.:Songs, w. A. M. Miranda (soprano), M. Quillevéré (ten), U. Reinemann (bar), C. Ivaldi (pno)—K.152, 307, 308, 346, 351, 436-439, 441, 441b, 472, 473, 506, 510, 520, 523, 524, 532, 549, 561, 625, & K.Anh 5 *(rec 1979)* Arion ▲ ARN 68161 [ADD]
Schumann, R.:Frauenliebe und -leben, w. Annibale Rebaudengo (pno) Accord ▲ ACD 201572 [AAD]

Wise, Patricia (sop)
Berg, A.:Lulu, w. P. Wise (sop—Lulu), B. Fassbaender (mez—Countess Geschwitz), H. Hotter (b-bar—Schigolch), J. Tate (cnd), French National Orch—Act 3 [G] *(rec live 9 & 10/91)* EMI Classics 3-▲ CDCC 54622 [DDD]
Mozart, W.A.:Missa, K.66, w. M. Aoyama (cta), P. Baillie (ten), H. Müller (bass), E. Hinreiner (cnd), Salzburg Camerata Academica, Salzburg RSO, Mozart Choir [L] *(rec May 1974)* Koch Treasure ▲ 316182 [ADD]
Verdi, G.:Rigoletto, w. P. Wise (sop—Gilda), B. Evans (sop—Giovanna), M. Yauger (mez—Maddalena), J. Carreras (ten—Duke), L. Quilico (bar—Rigoletto), J. Rudel (cnd), *(orch unknown) (rec Apr. 22, 1973)* Standing Room Only 2-▲ SRO 843 [ADD]

Wishart, Stevie (sgr/h-g)
Hildegard Of Bingen:Sacred Songs, w. Jocelyn West (sgr), Vivien Ellis (sgr), Hester Briant (sgr), Fiona Cunningham (sgr), Tara Franks (sgr), Emily Levy (sgr), Lucy Steele (sgr), Vickie Couperim (sgr), Julie Murphy (sgr), Oxford Girls' Choir—Honey & milk beneath her tongue; Ursula's virgins; The devil's virgins; Place of the ancient heart; Zeal of divinity; O fiery spirit; Red river falling; O orzchis ecclesia, Living-light angels; The clouds are grieving; The firstwoman; From their homeland; But the devil mocked; Song to Ecclesia *(rec Toddington, Gloucestershire, England, May 6-8, 1995)* Celestial Harmonies ▲ 13127-2

Wissmann, Lore (sop)
Wagner, R.:Der Ring des Nibelungen, w. Gré Brouwenstein (sop—Freia/Sieglinde), Ilse Hollweg (sop—Waldvogel), Gerda Lammers (sop—Ortlinde), Paula Lenchner (sop—Wellgunde/Gerhilde), Hilde Scheppan (sop—Helmwige), Astrid Varnay (sop—Brünnilde/3rd Norn), Lore Wissmann (sop—Woglinde), Maria von Ilosvay (mez—Flosshilde/Schwertleite/2nd Norn), Louise Charlotte Kamps (mez—Siegrune), Jean Madeira (mez—Erda/Rossweisse/1st Norn), Georgine van Milinkovic (mez—Fricka/Grimgerde), Elisabeth Schärtel (mez—Waltraute), Paul Kuën (ten—Mime), Ludwig Suthaus (ten—Loge), Josef Traxel (ten—Froh), Wolfgang Windgassen (ten—Siegmund/Siegfried), Alfons Herwig (bar—Donner), Hermann Uhde (bar—Gunther), Hans Hotter (b-bar—Wotan), Gustav Neidlinger (b-bar—Alberich), Josef Griendl (bass—Fasolt/Hunding/Hagen), Arnold van Mill (bass—Fafner), H. Knappertsbusch (cnd), Bayreuth Festival Orch, Bayreuth Festival Chorus *(rec live, Bayreuth, Aug 13-17, 1956)* Golden Melodram 14-▲ GM 1.001 [ADD]

Wistreich, Richard (bass)
Blow, J.:The Glorious Day Is Come, w. Suzie le Blanc (sop), Michael Chance (ct), Joseph Cornwell (ten), P. Holman (cnd), Parley of Instruments, Playford Consort Hyperion ▲ CDA 66770
Music from 17th Century Germany, w. His Majesties Sagbutts & Cornetts, Alistair Ross (org) Meridian ▲ 84096
The Musical Life of Samuel Pepys, w. Robin Jeffrey (thb/baroque gtr), chamber org & strs Saydisc ▲ CDSDL 385 [DDD]
Purcell, H.:The Fairy Queen, w. Lorraine Hunt (sop), Susan Bickley (mez), Catherine Pierard (mez), Howard Crook (ten), Mark Padmore (ten), David Wilson-Johnson (bar), R. Norrington (cnd), London Classical Players, Schütz Choir London EMI Classics ▲ CDCB 55234
Stradella, A.:L'anime del purgatorio, w. Emma Kirkby (sop), Evelyn Tubb (sop), David Thomas (bass), A. Rooley (cnd), Consort of Musicke Musica Oscura ("Favola in Musica" series) ▲ MOS 70984 [DDD]

Witkowska, Anna (sop)
Moniuszko, S.:Haunted Manor, w. Bozena Betley-Siradzka (sop—Hanna), Anna Witkowska (sop—Marta/Stara Niewiasta), Wiera Baniewicz (mez—Jadwiga), Aleksandra Imalska (mez—Czesnikowa), Kazimierz Dluha (Grzes), Zdzislaw Nikodem (ten—Damazy), Wieslaw Ochman (ten—Stefan), Andrzej Hiolski (bar—Miecznik), Florian Skulski (bar—Maciej), Leonard Mróz (bass—Zbigniew), Andrzej Saciuk (bass—Skoluba), J. Krenz (cnd), Cracow Polish Radio-TV Orch, Cracow Polish Radio-TV Chorus *(rec Cracovia, 1978)* Agora Music ("Phoenix" series) 3-▲ 509 [ADD]

Witt, Josef (ten)
Einem, G. von:Dantons Tod, w. M. Cebotari (sop—Lucille Desmoulins), R. Anday (cta—Frau des Simon), P. Klein (ten—de Séchelles), J. Patzak (ten—Camille Desmoulins), J. Witt (ten—Robspierre), P. Schöffler (bar—Danton), L. Weber (bass—Saint Just), F. Fricsay (cnd), Vienna PO, Vienna State Opera Chorus *(rec Aug. 6, 1947)* Stradivarius 2-▲ STR 10067 [ADD]
Mozart, W.A.:Nozze di Figaro, w. Irma Beilke (sop), Helena Braun (sop), Gerda Sommerschuh (sop), Hans Hotter (bar), Erich Kunz (bar), Gustav Neidlinger (b-bar), C. Krauss (cnd), Vienna PO, Vienna State Opera Chorus *(rec live, Salzburg Festival, Aug. 1942)* Preiser 3-▲ PRE 90203 [ADD]
Strauss, R.:Ariadne auf Naxos, w. M. Reining (sop), I. Seefried (sop), A. Noni (sop), M. Lorenz (ten), E. Kunz (bar), P. Schöffler (bass), K. Böhm (cnd), Vienna State Opera Orch *(rec Strauss' 80th Birthday Festival, June 11, 1944)* Preiser 2-▲ PRE 90217 [ADD]
Strauss, R.:Salome (sels), w. E. Schulz (sop—Salome), A. Dermota (ten—Narraboth), J. Witt (ten—Herodes), H. Hotter (bar—Jochanaan), P. Schöffler (b-bar—Jochanaan), R. Strauss (cnd), Vienna State Opera Orch, Vienna State Opera Chorus *(rec Feb. 15 & May 6, 1942)* Koch Schwann 2-▲ SCH 314532 [ADD]
Verdi, G.:Macbeth, w. E. Höngen (cta), M. Ahlersmeyer (bar), H. Alsen (bass), K. Böhm (cnd), Vienna State Opera Orch, Vienna State Opera Chorus *(rec 1943)* Preiser 2-▲ PRE 90175 [AAD]

Witt, Kerstin (mez)
Strauss, R.:Salome, w. J. Norman (sop), A. Markert (cta), W. Raffeiner (ten), R. Leech (ten), J. Morris (bass), S. Ozawa (cnd), Dresden Staatskapelle Philips 2-▲ 432153-2

Witte, Erich (ten)
Dessau, P.:Puntila, w. Annelies Brumeister (mez—Lsins), Erich Witte (ten—Fredrick), Reiner Süss (bar—Johannes Puntila), P. Dessau (cnd), Berlin State Opera Orch, Berlin State Chorus *(rec Berlin, May 1988)* Berlin Classics 2-▲ BER 2184 [ADD]
Weber, C.M. von:Abu Hassan, w. E. Schwarzkopf (sop), M. Bohnen (bass), L. Ludwig (cnd), Berlin RSO, Berlin Radio Chorus [G] *(rec Germany 1941)* Forlane ▲ FOR 16572 (m) [AAD]
Weber, C.M. von:Abu Hassan, w. Elisabeth Schwarzkopf (sop), Michael Bohnen (bass), L. Ludwig (cnd), Berlin RSO, Berlin Radio Chorus Grammofono 2000 ▲ GRM 78650

Wittek, Helmut (trb)
Bach, J.S.:Cant 185, w. P. Esswood (ct), K. Equiluz (ten), T. Hampson (b-bar), N. Harnoncourt (cnd), Vienna Concentus Musicus, Tölz Boys' Choir [G] Teldec 2-▲ 2292-44179-2 [DDD]
Mahler, G.:Syms, w. J. Blegen (sop), B. Hendricks (sop), M. Price (sop), G. Zeumer (sop), A. Baltsa (mez), C. Ludwig (mez), K. Riegel (ten), H. Prey (bar), A. Schmidt (bar), J. Van Dam (b-bar), L. Bernstein (cnd), New York PO, Royal Concertgebouw Orch, Vienna PO, Westminster Choir, New York Choral Artists, Brooklyn Boys' Choir, Vienna Boys' Choir, Vienna State Opera Chorus, Vienna Singverein Deutsche Grammophon 13-▲ 435162-2 [DDD]
Mahler, G.:Sym 4, w. L. Bernstein (cnd), Royal Concertgebouw Orch [G] Deutsche Grammophon ▲ 423007-2 [DDD]

Witter, Georg (sgr)
Strauss, R.:Salome, w. Astrid Varnay (sop—Salome), Hertha Töpper (mez—Der Page der Herodias), Margarete Klose (cta—Herodias), Hans Hopf (ten—Narraboth), Karl Hoppe (ten—1st Nazarene), Karl Ostertag (ten—1st Jew), Julius Patzak (ten—Herodes), Hans Braun (bar—Jochanaan), Benno Kusche (bar—2nd Soldier), Adolf Keil (bass—1st Soldier), Hans Hermann Nissen (bass—Ein Kappadozier), Max Proebstl (bass—2nd Nazarene), Walter Carnotch (sgr—4th Jew), Emil Graf (sgr—3rd Jew), Paul Kaussen (sgr—2nd Jew), Hildegard Limmer (sgr—A slave), Georg Witter (sgr—5th Jew), H. Weigert (cnd), Bavarian RSO *(rec June 21-25, 1953)* Bella Voce 2-▲ BLV 7210 [AAD]

Witte-Waldbauer, Margarete (alt)
Schumann, R.:Requiem Mignon, w. Christa Lehnert (sop), Edith Mathis (sop), Maura Moreira (cta), Robert Titze (bass), R. Wagner (cnd), Innsbruck SO, Innsbruck Chorus *(rec Innsbruck, 1963)* Allegretto ▲ ACD 8190

Wittrisch, Marcel (ten)
Leoncavallo, R.:Pagliacci (sels), w. Enrico Caruso (ten), Antonio Paoli (ten), Giovanni Zenatello (ten), Amedeo Bassi (ten), Hermann Jadlowker (ten), Fernand Ansseau (ten), Hipolito Lazaro (ten), Nino (Filippo) Piccaluga (ten), Mario Chamlee (ten), Giacomo Lauri-Volpi (ten), Miguel Fleta (ten), Giovanni Martinelli (ten), Aureliano Pertile (ten), Georges Thill (ten), Alessandro Valente (ten), Francesco Merli (ten), Lauritz Melchior (ten), Joseph Schmidt (ten), Beniamino Gigli (ten), Giuseppe Lugo (ten), Helge Roswaenge (ten), Jussi Bjoerling (ten)—23 versions of the tenor aria "Vesti la giubba" *(rec 1907-1944)* Bongiovanni ▲ GB 1071 [ADD]
Marcel Wittrisch:Opera Arias *(rec 1931-36)* Preiser ("Lebendige Vergangenheit" series) ▲ PRE 89024 (m) [AAD]
Mozart, W.A.:Zauberflöte (sels), w. Alexander Kipnis (b), Maria Galvany (sop), Eide Norena (sop), C. Schmalstich (cnd), Berlin State Opera Orch—Dies Bildnis (Act 1); O Isis und Osiris; Der Hölle Rache; Ach, ich fühl's *(rec 1905 - 1944)* Minerva ▲ MN A14 [ADD]

Wixell, Ingvar (bar)
Basic 100, Vol. 78, w. Raina Kabaivanska (sop), Luciano Pavarotti (ten), Rome Opera House Orch [cnd:Daniel Oren] RCA Victor ▲ 09026-68455-2 ■ 09026-68455-4
Donizetti, G.:L'elisir d'amore, w. I. Cotrubas (sop), L. Watson (sop), P. Domingo (ten), G. Evans (bar), J. Pritchard (cnd), Royal Opera House Orch, Royal Opera House Chorus Covent Garden *(rec 1977)* CBS 2-▲ M2K 34585 [ADD]
Donizetti, G.:L'elisir d'amore (sels), w. Reri Grist (sop), Luciano Pavarotti (ten), Sesto Bruscantini (bar), Maria Ambrosio (sgr), G. Patanè (cnd), San Francisco War Memorial Opera House Orch, San Francisco War Memorial Opera House Chorus *(rec live, San Francisco, 1969)* Budget ("The Greatest Voice in Opera" series) ▲ SYP 109
Donizetti, G.:Lucrezia Borgia, w. J. Sutherland (sop), M. Horne (mez), G. Aragall (ten), R. Bonynge (cnd), National PO London [I] London 2-▲ 421497-2 [ADD]
Leoncavallo, R.:Pagliacci, w. M. Freni (sop), L. Pavarotti (ten), G. Patanè (cnd), National PO London, National Phil London Chorus [I] London 2-▲ 414590-2 [ADD]

VOCALISTS

Wixell, Ingvar (bar) (cont.)

Leoncavallo, R.:Pagliacci (sels), w. J. Varady (sop), M. Freni (sop), L. Pavoratti (ten), P. Cappuccilli (bar), G. Gavazzeni (cnd), National PO London London ▲ 421870-2 [ADD]

Mascagni, P.:Cavalleria rusticana (sels), w. Julia Varady (sop), Mirella Freni (sop), Luciano Pavoratti (ten), Piero Cappuccilli (bar), G. Gavazzeni (cnd), National PO London London ▲ 421870-2 [ADD]

Mozart, W.A.:Complete Mozart Edition, w. K. Te Kanawa (sop), M. Arroyo (sop), M. Freni (sop), S. Burrows (ten), C. Davis (cnd), Royal Opera House Orch, Royal Opera House Chorus Covent Garden Philips 3-▲ 422541-2 [ADD]

Mozart, W.A.:Complete Mozart Edition, w. J. Norman (sop), M. Freni (sop), Y. Minton (mez), C. Davis (cnd), BBC SO, BBC Sym Chorus Philips 3-▲ 422540-2 [ADD]

Mozart, W.A.:Complete Mozart Edition, w. E. Mathis (sop), P. Schreier (ten), W. Hollweg (bar), B. Klee (cnd), Berlin Staatskapelle Philips 2-▲ 422536-2 [ADD]

Peterson-Berger, W.:Songs, w. J. Arnell (cnd), Stockholm PO—Arnljots hälsningssang till Jämtland; Bland skogens höga furustammar; Böljeby-vals; När jag för mig själv i mörka skogen gar [Sw] Musica Sveciae ▲ MSCD 617 [DDD]

Puccini, G.:La Bohème, w. K. Ricciarelli (sop), A. Putnam (sop), J. Carreras (ten), C. Davis (cnd), Royal Opera House Orch [I] Philips 2-▲ 416492-2 [ADD]

Puccini, G.:Madama Butterfly, w. R. Scotto (sop), P. Domingo (ten), L. Maazel (cnd), Philharmonia Orch, Ambrosian Singers [I] CBS 2-▲ M2K 35181 [AAD]

Puccini, G.:Tosca, w. M. Caballé (sop), J. Carreras (ten), C. Davis (cnd), Royal Opera House Orch Covent Garden [I] Philips 2-▲ 412885-2 [ADD]

Puccini, G.:Tosca, w. R. Kaibaivanska (sop—Floria), L. Pavarotti (ten—Mario), I. Wixell (bar—Scarpia), F. Federici (bass—Angelotti), D. Oren (cnd), Rome Opera Orch, Rome Opera Chorus RCA Red Seal ▲ 09026-61807-2; ■ 09026-61807-4

Puccini, G.:Tosca, w. R. Kaibaivanska (sop—Floria), L. Pavarotti (ten—Mario), I. Wixell (bar—Scarpia), F. Federici (bass—Angelotti), D. Oren (cnd), Rome Opera Orch, Rome Opera Chorus RCA Red Seal 2-▲ 09026-61806-2

Puccini, G.:Tosca (sels), w. Raina Kabaivanska (sop), Luciano Pavarotti (ten), D. Oren (cnd), Rome Opera Orch RCA ("Basic 100" series) ▲ 09026-68455-2 ■ 09026-68455-4

Puccini, G.:Il trittico, w. R. Scotto (sop), I. Cotrubas (sop), M. Horne (mez), P. Domingo (ten), T. Gobbi (bar), L. Maazel (cnd), London SO, Philharmonia Orch [I] CBS 3-▲ M3K 35912 [ADD]

Rangström, T.:Songs, w. J. Arnell (cnd), Stockholm PO—En visa om mig och narren Herkules; En visa om när jag var lustig; En visa till Karin när hon hade dansat; En visa till Karin ur fängelset; Kung Eriks sista visa [Sw] Musica Sveciae ▲ MSCD 617 [DDD]

Söderman, A.:King Heimer & Aslog, w. J. Arnell (cnd), Stockholm PO [Sw] Musica Sveciae ▲ MSCD 617 [DDD]

Stenhammar, W.:Florez och Blanzefor, w. S. Westerberg (cnd), Swedish RSO EMI Classics ▲ CDM 65081

Stenhammar, W.:Songs, w. J. Arnell (cnd), Stockholm PO—En positivvisa; Florez och Blanzeflor; I en skogskbacke; Kväll i Klara; Mellan broarna [Sw] *(rec 6/90)* Musica Sveciae ▲ MSCD 617 [DDD]

Verdi, G.:Un giorno di regno, w. J. Norman (sop), F. Cossotto (mez), J. Carreras (ten), V. Sardinero (bar), W. Ganzarolli (bar), P. Elvin (bass), A. Cassinelli (bass), L. Gardelli (cnd), Royal PO, Ambrosian Singers Philips 2-▲ 422429-2 [ADD]

Verdi, G.:Rigoletto, w. M. Hallin (sop), B. Nordin (sop), K. Meyer (mez), B. Ericson (mez), Kjellgren (mez), N. Gedda (ten), O. Sivall (ten), H. Hasslo (bar), B. Alstergård (bar), A. Tyrén (bass), S. Ehrling (cnd), Stockholm Royal Opera House Orch, Stockholm Royal Opera Chorus *(rec live Jan. 18, 1959)* BIS ▲ CD 296 [AAD]

Verdi, G.:Il trovatore, w. J. Sutherland (sop), M. Horne (mez), L. Pavarotti (ten), N. Ghiaurov (bass), R. Bonynge (cnd), National PO London [I] London 2-▲ 417137-2 [ADD]

Wlaschiha, Ekkehard (bass)

Beethoven, L. van:Fidelio, w. J. Norman (sop), P. Coburn (sop), R. Goldberg (ten), H.-P. Blochwitz (ten), A. Schmidt (bar), K. Moll (bass), B. Haitink (cnd), Dresden Staatskapelle, Dresden State Chorus [G] Philips 2-▲ 426308-2 [DDD]

Pfitzner, H.:Palestrina, w. C. Nossek (sop), R. Long (mez), P. Schreier (ten), S. Lorenz (bar), O. Suitner (cnd), Berlin Staatskapelle, Berlin State Opera Chorus Berlin Classics ▲ BER 1001

Wagner, R.:Götterdämmerung, w. H. Behrens (sop), C. Studer (sop), H. Schwarz (mez), R. Goldberg (ten), B. Weikl (bar), M. Salminen (bass), J. Levine (cnd), Metropolitan Opera Orch, New York Metropolitan Opera Chorus Deutsche Grammophon 4-▲ 429385-2 [DDD]

Wagner, R.:Parsifal, w. J. Norman (sop), P. Domingo (ten), K. Moll (bass), J. Morris (bass), J.-H. Rootering (bass), J. Levine (cnd), Metropolitan Opera Orch, New York Metropolitan Opera Chorus Deutsche Grammophon 4-▲ 437501-2

Wagner, R.:Das Rheingold, w. B. Svendén (sop), C. Ludwig (mez), S. Jerusalem (ten), H. Zednik (ten), J. Morris (bass), J. Levine (cnd), Metropolitan Opera Orch [G] Deutsche Grammophon 3-▲ 427607-2 [DDD]

Wagner, R.:Der Ring des Nibelungen (sels), w. J. Norman (sop), H. Behrens (sop), K. Battle (sop), J. Morris (mez), C. Ludwig (mez), R. Goldberg (ten), S. Jerusalem (ten), M. Salminen (bass), J. Levine (cnd), Metropolitan Opera Orch—The Compact Ring—Ride of the Valkyries Wotan's Farewell & Magic Fire Music, Forest Murmurs, Brünnhilde's Awakening, Siegfried's Funeral Music, Brünnhilde's Immolation, & others Deutsche Grammophon ▲ 437825-2

Wohlers, Rüdiger (ten)

Haydn, J.:Die Schöpfung, w. Norma Burrowes (sop), James Morris (bass), G. Solti (cnd), Chicago SO, Chicago Sym Chorus—sels. London ("Jubilee" series) ▲ 430739-2 [DDD]

Righini, V.:Te Deum, w. G. Resick (sop), M. Schiml (sop), V. von Halem (bass), G. Albrecht (cnd), Berlin RSO, Berlin Radio Chorus [L] Koch Schwann ▲ CD 313052 [ADD]

Wohlfahrt, Erwin (ten)

Wagner, R.:Der Ring des Nibelungen, w. B. Nilsson (sop), L. Rysanek (sop), K. Dvořaková (sop), M. Mödl (sop), A. Burmeister (mez), V. Soukupova (mez), W. Windgassen (ten), T. Stewart (bar), T. Adam (b-bar), G. Neidlinger (b-bar), K. Böhme (bass), G. Nienstedt (bass), K. Böhm (cnd), Bayreuth Festival Orch, Bayreuth Festival Chorus [G] *(rec live, 1966-67)* Philips 14-▲ 420325-2 [ADD]

Wagner, R.:Siegfried, w. B. Nilsson (sop), W. Windgassen (ten), T. Adam (b-bar), G. Neidlinger (b-bar), K. Böhm (cnd), Bayreuth Festival Orch, Bayreuth Festival Chorus [G] Philips 4-▲ 412483-2 [ADD]

Wolanski, Jan (bass)

Orff, C.:Carmina burana, w. A. M. Dahl (sop), B. Grek (ten), I. Stupel (cnd), Artur Rubinstein PO, Artur Rubinstein Phil Chorus *(rec Apr. 1991)* Danacord ▲ DACOCD 400 [DDD]

Wolansky, Raymond (bar)

Bellini, V.:I Puritani (sels), w. J. Sutherland (sop), D. Cole (sop), A. Kraus (ten), N. Ghiuselev (bass), R. Bonynge (cnd), San Francisco Opera Orch, San Francisco Opera Chorus *(rec live, San Francisco, 9/2/66)* Golden Age of Opera ▲ GAO 133 [ADD]

Orff, C.:Carmina burana, w. L. Popp (sop), G. Unger (ten), J. Noble (bar), R. Frühbeck de Burgos (cnd), New Philharmonia Orch, New Philharmonia Chorus EMI Classics ▲ CDM 64328

Schubert, Franz:Fierrabras, w. H. Plümacher (cta), F. Wunderlich (ten), O. von Rohr (bass), H. Müller-Kray (cnd), Bern State Orch, Berlin RIAS Chamber Choir, South Swiss Radio Chorus—abridged performance *(rec l959)* Myto ▲ MCD 89001 [ADD]

Wolf, Gerd (bass)

Matthus, S.:Mirabeau, w. Carola Höhn (sop—Marie Antoinette), Carola Fischer (cta—Eveline Le Jay), Peter-Jürgend Schmidt (ten—Ludwig XVI), Jürgen Freier (bar—Honoré-Gabriel de Riqueti), Gerd Wolf (bass—Victor Riqueti), H. Fricke (cnd), Berlin State Opera Orch, Berlin State Opera Chorus *(rec Berlin, 1989)* Berlin Classics 2-▲ BER 1075 [DDD]

Schulhoff, E.:The Flames, w. Jane Eaglen (sop—Donna Anna, Nun, Woman, Marguerite), Carola Höhn (sop—Shadow), Celina Lindsley (sop—Shadow), Regina Schudel (sop—Shadow), Iris Vermillion (mez—La Morte), Christiane Berggold (alt—Shadow), Kaja Borris (alt—Shadow), Elvira Dressen (alt—Shadow), Kurt Westi (ten—Don Juan), Johann-Werner Prein (bass—Commendatore), Gerd Wolf (bass—Harlequin), J. Mauceri (cnd), Berlin German SO, Berlin RIAS Chamber Choir *(rec Jesus-Christus Church, Berlin Dahlem, Oct 1993/Apr 1994)* London 2-▲ 444630-2 [DDD]

Wolff (sgr)

Bernstein, L.:Trouble in Tahiti, w. Atkinson (sgr), A. Winograd (cnd), MGM Studio SO [E] Polydor ▲ 827845-2 (m) ■ 827845-4 (m)

Künneke, E.:Der Vetter aus Dingsda (sels), w. G. Van Jüten (sop), Kollo (ten), B. Kusche (bar), Breck (sgr), Geese, Künneke (cnd), Cologne RSO, Cologne Radio Chorus [G] Acanta ▲ CD 43460 [DDD]

Wolff, Beverly (mez)

Donizetti, G.:Roberto Devereux, w. Montserrat Caballé (sop), Guido Fabbris (ten), Gianni Raimondi (ten), Walter Alberti (bar), Paolo Badoer (sgr), Carlo Micalucci (sgr), Carlo Padoan (sgr), B. Bartoletti (cnd), Venice Teatro La Fenice Orch, Venice Teatro La Fenice Chorus Great Opera Performances 2-▲ GOP 764

Mercadante, S.:Il giuramento, w. P. Wells (sop), G. Colmagro (bar), M. Molese (sgr), T. Schippers (cnd), Juilliard Orch, Juilliard Chorus [I] *(rec live, Spoleto, 6/29/70)* Myto 2-▲ 2 MCD 90632 [ADD]

Mercadante, S.:Il giuramento, w. P. Wells (sop), G. Colmagro (bar), M. Molese (sgr), T. Schippers (cnd), Juilliard Orch, Juilliard Chorus [I] *(rec live, Spoleto, 6/29/70)* Memories 2-▲ HR 4174/75 (m)

Rorem, N.:Poems of Love & the Rain, w. Ned Rorem (pno) Phoenix ▲ PHCD 108 [AAD]

Rorem, N.:Some Trees, w. P. Curtin (sop), D. Gramm (b-bar), N. Rorem (pno) [E] CRI ■ C 238

Rorem, N.:Some Trees, w. P. Curtin (sop), D. Gramm (bar), N. Rorem (pno) CRI ▲ CD 657 [ADD]

Rorem, N.:Songs, w. P. Curtin (sop), D. Gramm (bar) [E] CRI ■ C 238

Rossini, G.:La pietra del paragone, w. A. Elgar (sop), E. Bonazzi (mez), J. Carreras (ten), J. Reardon (bar), R. Murcell (bar), A. Foldi (b-bar), J. Diaz (bass), N. Jenkins (cnd), Clarion Concerts Orch, Clarion Concerts Chorus [I] *(rec. ca. 1972)* Vanguard Classics 3-▲ OVC 8043/45 [ADD]

Rossini, G.:Stabat Mater, w. M. Arroyo (sop), T. del Bianco (ten), J. Diaz (bass), T. Schippers (cnd), New York PO, Camerata Singers Sony Classical ▲ SB2K 53252

Wolff, Fritz (ten)

Handel, G.F.:Giulio Cesare in Egitto, w. Beverly Sills (sop), Maureen Forrester (cta), Spiro Malas (bass), Norman Treigle (bass), J. Redel (cnd), New York City Opera Orch, New York City Opera Chorus RCA Gold Seal 2-▲ 6182-2-RG [ADD]

Wagner, R.:Parsifal (sels), w. Alexander Kipnis (bass), Muck, Wagner (cnd), Bayreuth Festival Orch, Bayreuth Festival Chorus [1927]—Transformation Scene, Grail Scene, Flower Maidens Scene, Prelude to Act 3, Good Friday Music InSync ■ C 4137 (m)

Wolf-Michaux, Frédérique (cta)

Aperghis, G.:L'origine des espèces, w. Françoise Degeorges (sop), Donatienne Michel-Dansac (sop), Emmanuelle Zoll (sop), Valérie Joly (mez), Elena Andreyev (vc) Musique Française d'Aujourd'hui ▲ MFA 216004

Wöller, Florian (trb)

Mozart, W.A.:Zauberflöte, w. Constanze Backes (sop—Papagena), Christiane Oelze (sop—Pamina), Susan Roberts (sop—First Lady), Cyndia Sieden (sop—Queen of the Night), Carola Guber (cta—Second Lady), Maria Jonas (cta—Third Lady), Andreas Dieterich (trb—First Boy), Jan Andreas Mendel (trb—Second Boy), Florian Wöller (trb—Third Boy), Uwe Peper (ten—Monostatos), Nicolas Robertson (ten—First Man in Armor), Michael Schade (ten—Tamino), Gerald Finley (bar—Papageno), Noel Mann (bass—Second Man in Armour), Harry Peeters (bass—Sarastro), Detlef Roth (bass—Speaker/First Priest), Robert Burt (speaker—Third Priest), Robert Johnston (speaker—Second Priest), Wolfgang Knauer (speaker—Fourth Priest), Douglas Welbat (speaker—Second Priest), J. E. Gardiner (cnd), English Baroque Soloists, Monteverdi Choir London *(rec Forum am Schlosspark, Ludwigsburg, July 1995)* Archiv 2-▲ 449166-2

Wollitz, Eduard (bass)

Mozart, W.A.:Requiem, w. U. Buckel (sop), M. Bence (cta), H.-U. Mielsch (ten), R. Bader (cnd), Stuttgart PO, Böblingen Bach Choir Allegretto ▲ ACD 8060 [ADD] ■ ACS 8060

Wolverton, Joseph (ten)

Mascagni, P.:Silvano, w. Rachel Sparer (sop—Matilde), Lorraine DiSimone (mez—Rosa), Joseph Wolverton (ten—Silvano), Bojan Knezevic (bar—Renzo), P. Tiboris (cnd), Bohuslav Martinů PO *(rec SUNY Performing Arts Center Theatre, Purchase, NY, May 23-25, 1995)* Elysium ▲ GRK 707 [DDD]

Wong, Randall (ct)

Hasse, J.A.:Cleofide, w. Emma Kirkby (sop), Agnès Mellon (sop), Dominique Visse (ct), Derek Lee Ragin (ct), David Cordier (alt), W. Christie (cnd), Cappella Coloniensis [I] Capriccio 4-▲ 10193/96 [DDD]

Woodhouse, R. (sgr)

York, W.:Native Songs, w. N. Armstrong (sop), S. Sylvan (bar), S. Downey (sgr), P. Friedland (fl), J. Fischer (pno), J. Russell Smith (perc) *(rec May 1987)* New World ▲ 80439-2

Woodland, Rae (sop)

Bliss, A.:The Olympians, w. S. Minty (mez), T. Hemsley (bar), R. Herincx (bass), B. Fairfax (cnd), Polyphonia Orch, Ambrosian Singers *(rec 1972)* Intaglio 2-▲ ING 755 [ADD]

Bliss, A.:Rout, w. A. Bliss (cnd), London SO Lyrita ▲ SRCD 225 [ADD]

Handel, G.F.:Messiah, w. Oliver Johnston (trb), Norma Proctor (cta), Paul Esswood (ct), Stephen Roberts (bar), J. Tobin (cnd), English SO, London Choral Society [Handel's original orchestration] [E] *(rec 1976)* Protone ■ CSPR 166/67

Mahler, G.:Sym 2, w. Janet Baker (mez), L. Stokowski (cnd), London SO, BBC Chorus, BBC Choral Society, Goldsmith's Choral Union, Harrow Choral Society *(rec 1963)* Music & Arts ▲ CD 885 [AAD]

Woodley, Arthur (b-bar)

Burleigh, H.T.:Songs, w. Hilda Harris (mez), Philip Creech (ten), Steven Cole (ten), Joseph Smith (pno)—Now Sleeps the Crimson Petal; Promis' Lan'; Ethiopia Saluting the Colors; Lovely Dark & Lonely One; Love Watches; Almona; O, Night of Dream & Wonder; His Helmet's Blaze; I Hear His Footsteps, Music Sweet; Thou Art Weary; This is Nirvana; Ahmed's Song of Farewell; Through Moanin' Pines; The Frolic; In de Col' Moonlight; A Jubilee; On Bended Knees; A New Hiding-Place; Worth While; The Jungle Flower; Kashmiri Song; Among the Fuchsias; Till I Wake; By an' By; Ev'ry Time I Feel de Spirit; Deep River; Oh, Didn't it Rain; Swing Low, Sweet Chariot; Wade in de Water; Heav'n, Heav'n Premier ▲ PRCD 1041 [DDD]

Foster, S.C.:Old Folks at Home, w. S. Richman (cnd), Harmonie Ensemble/New York, Collegiate Chorale [arr Dvořák 1894] Music & Arts ▲ MUA CD 926

Gershwin, G.:Blue Monday Blues, w. A. Burton (sop), G. Hopkins (ten), W. Sharp (bar), J. J. Offenbach (b-bar), M. Alsop (cnd), Concordia Orch EMI Classics ▲ CDC 54851

Gershwin, G.:Porgy & Bess (sels), w. D. Newman (sop), H. de la Fuente (cnd), Mineria SO, New Philharmonia Orch, Oklahoma City Ambassors Choir IMP Classics ▲ IMPPCD 1057 [DDD]

Let My Song Fill Your Heart:A Remembrance of the American Concert Song, w. Maryanne Telese (sop), Peter Howard (pno), Joseph Smith (pno) Premier ▲ PR 1002

Stravinsky, I.:The Rake's Progress, w. J. West (sop—Anne Trulove), S. Love (mez—Mother Goose), W. White (mez—Baba the Turk), J. Garrison (ten—Tome Rakewell), M. Lowrey (ten—Sellem), A. Woodley (bar—Father Truelove), J. Cheek (b-bar), *(orch unknown)* MusicMasters 2-▲ 01612-67131-2 [DDD]

Woodman, Thomas (bar)

Vaughan Williams, R.:Songs, w. R. Golden (sop), N. Bean (vn), L. Rothfuss (pno)—From the House of Life; 4 Last Songs; Linden Lea; The Sky Above the Roof; Dreamland; Claribel; If I Were a Queen; 4 Poems by Fredegond Shove; Adieu; Think of Me; Along the Field *(rec Apr. 1992)* Koch International Classics ▲ KIC 7168 [DDD]

Woods, A. (sgr)

Porter, C.:A Swell Party, w. A. Richards (sgr), N. Grace (sgr), D. Keman (sgr), M. Smith (sgr), *(other artists unknown)* [1992 London cast] Silva America ▲ SSD 1006 [DDD] ■ SSC 1006

Woods, Darren Keith (ten)

Moore, D.:Devil & Daniel Webster, w. Joyce Guyer (sop—Mary Stone), Benjamin Bongers (ten—Walter Butler), Michael Philip Davis (ten—Simon Girty), Matthew Foerschler (ten—Miser Stephens), Darren Keith Woods (ten—Mr. Scratch), Michael Lanman (bass—Blackbeard Teach), David Soxman (bass—Clerk), Brian Steele (bass—Daniel Webster), John Stephens (bass—Jabez Stone), Andrew Stuckey (bass—King Philip), Robert Gibby Brand (actor), Cary Miller (actor), R. Patterson (cnd), Kansas City SO, Kansas City Lyric Opera Chorus *(rec Sept 1995)* Newport Classic ▲ NPD 85585 [DDD]

Woods, Sheryl (sop)

Handel, D.:The Poems of Our Climate, w. Pamela Watson (fl), Brian Delay (gtr), Val Griffen (vc), Anton Nel (pno), Jack Brennan (perc), James Culley (perc), Allen Otte (perc), G. Samuel (cnd) Vienna Modern Masters ▲ VMM 2019 [DDD]

Woodward, Donna (sop)

Dittersdorf, K.D. von:Doctor und Apotheker, w. Hildegard Uhrmacher (sop—Leonore), Donna Woodward (sop—Rosalia), Waltraud Meier (mez—Claudia), Martin Finke (ten—Sichel), Frieder Lang (ten—Gotthold), Alois Perl (ten—Gallus), Gerhard Unger (ten—Sturmwald), Thomas Pfeiffer (bar—Police Commisioner), Wolfgang Schöne (bar—Krautmann), Harald Stamm (bass—Stössel), J. Lockhart (cnd), Rhine State PO Bayer 2-▲ BR 100 238/39 [DDD]

Woody, T. (bar)

Howells, H.:Requiem, w. J. Barton (trb), P. Flight (ct), D. Honoré (ten), F. Burgomeister (cnd), Indianapolis Festival Orch, Christ Church Cathedral Men & Boys Choir Oxford Gothic ▲ G 49062 [DDD]

Woolf, Simon (trb)

Mendelssohn, F.:Elijah, w. Gwyneth Jones (sop), Janet Baker (mez), Nicolai Gedda (ten), Dietrich Fischer-Dieskau (bar), R. Frühbeck de Burgos (cnd), New Philharmonia Orch, New Philharmonia Chorus, Wandsworth School Boys' Choir *(rec 1968)* EMI Classics ("Doublefforte" series) 2-▲ CDFB 68601

Wooliam, Kenneth (ten)

Tippett, M.:A Child Of Our Time, w. Jill Gomez (sop), Helen Watts (cta), John Shirley-Quirk (bar), G. Rozhdestvensky (cnd), BBC SO, BBC Sym Chorus IMP ("BBC Radio Classics" series) ▲ IMP 9130

Wörle, Robert (ten)

Bach, J.S.:Mass in b, BWV 232, w. A. Stumphius (sop), C. Kallisch (alto), A. Schmidt (bass), H.-M. Schneidt (cnd), Munich Bach Orch, Munich Bach Choir *(rec Mar 21, 1992)* Calig 2-▲ CAL 5029/30 [ADD]

Busoni, F.:Turandot, w. C. Lindsley (sop), J. Protschka (ten), R. Pape (bass), G. Albrecht (cnd), Berlin RSO, Berlin RIAS Chamber Choir Capriccio ▲ 60039 [DDD]

Goldschmidt, B.:Der gewaltige Hahnrei, w. R. Alexander (sop), M. Posselt (sop), H. Lawrence (sop), M. Kraus (ten), M. Petzold (ten), C. Otelli (bar), L. Zagrosek (cnd), German SO, Berlin Radio Chorus London ▲ 440850-2 [DDD]

Goldschmidt, B.:Mediterranean Songs, w. R. Alexander (sop), M. Posselt (sop), H. Lawrence (sop), M. Kraus (ten), M. Petzold (ten), C. Otelli (bar), L. Zagrosek (cnd), German SO, Berlin Radio Chorus London ▲ 440850-2 [DDD]

Handel, G.F.:Judas Maccabaeus, w. M. Meier-Schmid (sop), Elisabeth von Magnus (alt), Jörg Dürmüller (ten), Franz-Josef Selig (bass), T. Fey (cnd), Schlierbach CO, Munich Motet Choir [E] Christophorus 2-▲ 77128 [DDD]

Hindemith, P.:Das Unaufhörliche, w. Ulrike Sonntag (sop), Siegfried Lorenz (bar), Artur Korn (bass), L. Zagrosek (cnd), Berlin RSO, Berlin Radio Chorus Wergo 2-▲ WER 66032

Holzbauer, I.:Günther von Schwarzburg, w. Clara McFadden (sop), Christoph Prégardien (ten), Michael Schopper (bass), M. Schneider (cnd), La Stagione CPO 3-▲ CPO 999265

Schubert, Franz:Deutsche Messe, w. Alexander Seitz (trb), Ulrich Streckmann (bass), R. Kammler (cnd), Munich Residenz CO, Augsburg Cathedral Boys' Choir Calig ▲ CAL 50952 [DDD]

Schubert, Franz:Mass 2, w. Alexander Seitz (trb), Ulrich Streckmann (bass), R. Kammler (cnd), Munich Residenz CO, Augsburg Cathedral Boys' Choir Calig ▲ CAL 50952 [DDD]

Worthley, Max (ten)

Purcell, H.:The Prophetess, or The History of Dioclesian, w. H. Sheppard (sop), S. Le Sage (sop), A. Deller (ct), P. Todd (ten), M. Bevan (bar), A. Deller (cnd), Vienna Concentus Musicus—also includes incidental music from the play *(rec June 1965)* Vanguard Classics ("The Bach Guild" series) ▲ OVC 2517 [ADD]

Woska, Elisabeth (nar)

Hiller, W.:Schulamit, w. Regina Klepper (sop), Edeltraud Knabel (alt), Michael Schopper (bass), Waltraut Mastrogiovanni-Kraxner (shofar), H.R. Zöbeley (cnd), Munich Residenz Orch, Munich Percussion Ensemble, Calw Aurelius Boys' Choir Soloists, Munich Motet Choir Wergo ▲ WER 6280-2

Strauss, R.:Enoch Arden, w. Begonia-Uriarte Mrongovius (pno) *(rec Kleiner Konzertsaal, Gasteig, Munich, June 18, 1986)* Arts Music ▲ 447260-2 [DDD]

Strauss, R.:Das Schloss am Meere, w. Karl-Hermann Mrongovius (pno) *(rec Kleiner Konzertsaal, Gasteig, Munich, June 18, 1986)* Arts Music ▲ 447260-2 [DDD]

Wosnitza, Cornella (sop)

Blacher, B.:Songs, w. Katharina Richter (sop), Markus Köhler (bar), Horst Göbel (pno), Chatschatur Kanajan (vn), Piotr Prysiasnik (vn), Fred Günther (va), Ithay Khen (vc), Christian Peters (sax), Markus Weidmann (bn)—3 Chansons; Ungereimtes; 4 Lieder; Nebel; 13 Ways of Looking at a Blackbird; 5 Sinnsprüche Omars des Zeitmachers; 3 Psalmen; Aprèslude; Francesca da Rimini; Jazz-Koloraturen Signum ▲ SIG X73-00 [DDD]

Wottrich, Endrik (sgr)

Braunfels, W.:Die Vögel, w. Helen Kwon (sop—Nightingale), Wolfgang Holzmair (bar—Hoopoe), Matthias Gorne (b-bar—Prometheus), Michael Krause (sgr—Loyal Friend), Endrik Wottrich (sgr—Good Hope), L. Zagrosek (cnd), Berlin German SO, Berlin Radio Chorus London ("Entartete Musik" series) ▲ 448 679-2

Cornelius, P.:Der Cid, w. Gertrud Ottenthal (sop), Ronnie Johansen (sgr), Robert Schunk (ten), Albert Dohmen (bar), Michael Schopper (bass), G. Kuhn (cnd), Berlin RSO, Berlin Radio Chorus Koch Schwann 2-▲ SCH 315222

Wottrich, Endrik (ten)

Korngold, E.W.:Der Ring des Polykrates, w. Beate Bilandzija (sop—Laura), Kirsten Blanck (sop—Lieschen), Endrik Wottrich (ten—Wilhelm), Jürgen Sacher (ten—Florian), Dietrich Henschel (bar—Peter), K. Seibel (cnd), German SO *(rec Jesus Christ Church, Dahlem, Sept 19-25, 1995)* CPO ▲ CPO 999402-2 [DDD]

Woytowicz, Stefania (sop)

Chopin, F.:Songs Sop (comp), w. Andrzej Bachleda (ten), Wanda Klimowicz (pno) *(rec Warsaw, 1960)* Polskie Nagrania ▲ PNCD 315

Górecki, H.-M.:Sym 3, "Sym of Sorrowful Songs", w. J. Katlewicz (cnd), Polish National RSO Katowice [Pol] *(rec 1977)* Olympia ▲ OCD 313 [AAD]

Górecki, H.-M.:Sym 3, "Sym of Sorrowful Songs", w. J. Katlewicz (cnd), Polish National SO *(rec May 1978)* Polskie Nagrania ▲ PNCD 215

Penderecki, K.:The Passion & Death of Our Lord Jesus Christ According to St. Luke, w. Leszek Herdegen (nar), Andrzej Hiolski (bar), Bernard Ladysz (bass), H. Czyz (cnd), Cracow PO, Cracow Phil Boys' Chorus, Cracow Phil Mixed Choir Polskie Nagrania 2-▲ PNCD 017 A/B

Penderecki, K.:Utrenia, w. Delfina Ambroziak (sop), Krystyna Szczepanska (mez), Kazimierz Pustelak (ten), Boris Carmeli (bass), Wlodzimierz Denysenko (bass), A. Markowski (cnd), Warsaw PO, Józef Bok (cnd), Stanislaw Skoraczewski (cnd), Warsaw National Phil Chorus, Pioneer Choir *(rec Warsaw, 1973)* Polskie Nagrania ▲ PNCD 018

Szymanowski, K.:Litany to the Virgin Mary, w. W. Rowicki (cnd), Warsaw PO, Warsaw National Phil Chorus—12-note Zither; Like a Dwarf Bush *(rec Concert Hall at the National PO, Warsaw, 1961)* Polskie Nagrania ▲ PLN 063 [ADD]

Szymanowski, K.:Stabat Mater, w. Krystyna Szczepanska (alt), Andrzej Hiolski (bar), W. Rowicki (cnd), Warsaw PO, Warsaw National Phil Chorus *(rec Concert Hall at the National PO, Warsaw, 1961)* Polskie Nagrania ▲ PLN 063 [ADD]

Szymanowski, K.:Sym 3, w. W. Rowicki (cnd), Warsaw PO, Warsaw National Phil Chorus *(rec Concert Hall at the National PO, Warsaw, 1961)* Polskie Nagrania ▲ PLN 063 [ADD]

Wrana, Hans (bass)

Schoeck, O.:Das Schloss Dürande (sels), w. Maria Cebotari (sop—Gabriele), Marta Fuchs (sop—Gräfin Morvaille), Brigitte Fassbaender (mez—Renald Willi Domgraf), Rut Berglund (cta—Priorin), Peter Anders (ten—Armand), Benno Arnold (ten—Jäger), Josef Greindl (bass—Nicole), Hans Wrana (bass—Jäger), Vasso Argyris (sgr—Volksredner), Otto Hüsch (sgr—Wildhüter), Leo Laschet (sgr—Jäger), Fritz Marcks (sgr—Jäger), Felix Schneider (sgr—Jäger), R. Heger (cnd)—Text; Ich kann es nicht glauben [from Act 1]; Text; Heil dir, du Feuerquelle [from Act 2]; Text; Gesucht und nicht gefunden [from Act 3]; Text; Der Jäger ist frei! [Act 3 Finale]; Text; Sie kommen mit Flinten und Stangen [Act 4]; Text; Du Narr des vermeintlichen Rechts [Act 4 finale]; Text *(rec live, Apr 1943)* Jecklin ▲ JD 692

Wright, Patricia (sop)

Jane Austen Songs, w. Jon Gillaspie (pno) Pearl ▲ PEA 9613 [DDD]

Wrigt, Brian (sgr)

Verdi, G.:Macbeth, w. Amy Shuard (sop—Lady Macbeth), Noreen Berry (mez—Lady-in-waiting), John Dobson (ten—Malcolm), André Turp (ten—Macduff), Tito Gobbi (bar—Macbeth), Edgar Boniface (bass—Servant), Rydderch Davies (bass—Doctor), Forbes Robinson (bass—Banco), Jean Holmes (sgr—Apparition), Celia Penny (sgr—Apparition), Glynne Thomas (sgr—Apparition), Brian Wrigt (sgr—Araldo), F. Molinari-Pradelli (cnd), Royal Opera House Orch, Royal Opera House Chorus Covent Garden *(rec London, Apr 8, 1960)* Bella Voce 2-▲ 7203 [AAD]

Wróblewski, Ryszard (ten)

Gloria Tibi Trinitas:Sacred Music of Slav Composers 18th-20th Centuries, w. [cnd:Andrzej Filaber], Warsaw Cathedral Choir, Jolanta Kaufman (sop), Anna Lubanska (alt), Czeslaw Galka (bass), Maciej Piwowarski (org) Polskie Nagrania Edition ▲ ECD 057 [DDD]

Wulkopf, Cornelia (mez)

Bach, J.S.:Mass in b, BWV 232, w. B. Bonney (sop), P. Schrier (ten), A. Scharinger (bass), S. Celibidache (cnd), Munich PO, Munich Bach Choir Exclusive ▲ EXL 33 [ADD]

Brahms, J.:Songs, w. K. Schilde (pno)—4 Ernste Gesänge, Op. 121 [G] Ars Produktion ▲ FCD 368305

Brahms, J.:Songs, Op. 91, w. R. Metzger (va), K. Schilde (pno) [G] Ars Produktion ▲ FCD 368305

Dvořák, A.:Biblical Songs, Op. 99, w. K. Schilde (pno) [G] Ars Produktion ▲ FCD 368305

Egk, W.:Peer Gynt, w. J. Perry (sop), N. Sharp (sop), H. Hopf (ten), R. Hermann (bar), H. Wallberg (cnd), Munich RSO, Bavarian Radio Chorus [G] Orfeo 2-▲ 005822 [DDD]

Forgotten Romantic Songs, Vol. 1, w. Klaus Schilde (pno), Manfred Neukirchner (hn) Ars Produktion ▲ FCD 368315 [DDD]

Sacred Horn Music, w. Allgäuer Horn Ensemble, U. Köbl (hn), M. Neukirchner (hn), J. Skudlik (org) Ars Produktion ▲ FCD 368304

Schubert, Franz:Lazarus, or Die Feier der Auferstehung, w. E. Mathis (sop), H. Schwarz (mez), W. Hollweg (ten), H. Laubenthal (ten), H. Prey (bar), G. Chmura (cnd), Stuttgart RSO, Stuttgart Radio Chorus [G] Orfeo ▲ 011101 [DDD]

Wunderlich, Fritz (ten)

Arias, Lieder & Popular Songs Deutsche Grammophon 5-▲ 435145-2 GX5

Beethoven, L. van:Christus am Ölberg, w. Erna Spoorenberg (sop—Seraph), Fritz Wünderlich (ten—Jesus), Hermann Schey (bass—Petrus), H. Spruit (cnd), Netherlands Radio PO, Groot Omroep Choir *(rec Mar 8, 1957)* Bella Voce ▲ 7003 [AAD]

Beethoven, L. van:Missa Solemnis, w. G. Janowitz (sop), C. Ludwig (mez), W. Berry (bass), H. von Karajan (cnd), Berlin PO, Vienna Singverein [L] Deutsche Grammophon ("Galleria" series) 2-▲ 423913-2 [ADD]

Beethoven, L. van:Songs, w. Hubert Giesen (pno)—Ich liebe dich; Adelaide; Resignation; Der Kuss Deutsche Grammophon ("Dokumente" series) ▲ 429933-2 [ADD]

Beethoven, L. van:Songs, w. Hubert Giesen (pno)—Adelaide, Op. 46; Mailied, Op. 52/4; Der Wachtelschlag; Resignation; Der Kuss, Op. 128 *(rec Salzburg, Aug 19, 1965)* Orfeo d'or ("Festspiel Dikumente" series) ▲ C 432961 (m) [ADD]

Beethoven, L. van:Songs, w. Hubert Giesen (pno) *(rec Salzburg August 1965)* Acanta ▲ CD 43529

Beethoven, L. van:Songs, w. H. Giesen (pno)—Adelaide, Op. 46; Resignation; Der Wachtelschlag; Mailied, Op. 52, No. 4; Der Küss, Op. 128 [G] *(rec Mar. 24, 1966)* Myto ▲ MCD 93278

Beethoven, L. van:Songs, w. Hubert Giesen (pno)—Adelaide, Op. 46; Resignation, WoO 149; Mailied, Op. 52/4; Der Kuss, Op. 128 *(rec Hannover, Mar 24, 1966)* Bella Voce ▲ 7003 [AAD]

Beethoven, L. van:Sym 9, "Choral Sym", w. W. Lipp (sop), F. Crass (bass), O. Klemperer (cnd), Philharmonia Orch, Vienna Singverein Arkadia ▲ 759

Berg, A.:Wozzeck, w. E. Lear (sop—Marie), F. Wunderlich (ten—Andres), G. Stoltze (ten—The Captain), D. Fischer-Dieskau (bar—Wozzeck), K. Böhm (cnd), German Opera Orch, German Opera Chorus [G] *(rec 1965)* Deutsche Grammophon 3-▲ 435705-2 [ADD]

Cherubini, L.:Les Deux journées, w. H. Hillebrecht (sop), M. Cordes (bar), R. Hoyem (sgr), H. Müller-Kray (cnd), Stockholm RSO, Stockholm Radio Chorus *(rec live, Stockholm 1960)* Melodram ▲ CDM 19507 [ADD]

Fall, L.:Der fidele Bauer (sels), w. Sonja Knittel (sop), Brigette Fassbaender (mez), Heinz Hoppe (ten), Benno Kusche (bass), C. Michalski (cnd), Graunke SO, Rudolf Lamy Singers Emperor Operetta ▲ KO 86353

Fall, L.:Die Rose von Stambul (sels), w. Christine Gorner (sop), Melita Muszely (sop), C. Michalski (cnd), Graunke SO Emperor Operetta ▲ KO 86353

Fritz Wunderlich's Last Concert, w. Hubert Giesen (pno) *(rec Edinburgh, Sept 17, 1966)* Myto ▲ MCD 890.11 (m) [ADD]

Gluck, C.W.:Iphigénie en Tauride, w. S. Jurinac (sop), H. Prey (bar), K. Engen (bass), R. Kubelik (cnd), Bavarian RSO, Bavarian Radio Chorus [1781 J.B. von Alxinger-Gluck German-language version] *(rec live, Munich 1965)* Myto 2-▲ 2 MCD 91544 [ADD]

The Great German Tenor EMI Classics 3-▲ CDZC 62993

Handel, G.F.:Alcina, w. J. Sutherland (sop), N. Procter (cta), N. Monti (ten), T. Hemsley (bar), F. Leitner (cnd), Cappella Coloniensis, Cologne Radio Chorus Melodram 3-▲ CDM 37002

Handel, G.F.:Arias, *(various orchs)*—3 arias each from Alcina, Julius Caesar, Messiah, Serse *(rec live 1959-1965)* Melodram 2-▲ MEL 28026 [AAD]

Handel, G.F.:Arias—2 arias from Serse Melodram 3-▲ MEL 37059 [AAD]

Handel, G.F.:Arias—2 arias each from Alcina *(w. Ferdinand Leitner, Cappella Coloniensis Orch., rec. 1959)* & Serse *(w. Rafael Kubelik, Bavarian RSO, rec. 1962)* Myto 2-▲ 2 MCD 91752 [ADD]

Handel, G.F.:Giulio Cesare in Egitto, w. Lucia Popp (sop), Christa Ludwig (mez), Walter Berry (bass), F. Leitner (cnd), Munich PO, Bavarian Radio Chorus Melodram 3-▲ MEL 37059 [AAD]

Handel, G.F.:Giulio Cesare in Egitto, w. Lucia Popp (sop), Christa Ludwig (mez), Walter Berry (bass), F. Leitner (cnd), Munich PO, Bavarian Radio Chorus [G] *(rec live, Munich 7/1-5/65)* Verona 3-▲ 27035/37 [AAD]

Handel, G.F.:Judas Maccabaeus, w. Agnes Giebel (sop), Julianna Falk (cta), L. Welter (bar), Pöld (sgr), R. Kubelik (cnd), Bavarian RSO, Bavarian Chorus [G] *(rec live 10/25/63)* Melodram 2-▲ MEL 28026 [AAD]

Handel, G.F.:Serse, w. Ingeborg Hallstein (sop), et al., R. Kubelik (cnd), Bavarian RSO, Bavarian Radio Chorus [G] *(rec 10/22-28/62)* Verona 3-▲ 27032/34 (m) [AAD]

Haydn, J.:Die Jahreszeiten, w. Agnes Giebel (sop—Hanne), Fritz Wünderlich (ten—Lukas), Kieth Engen (bass—Simon), H. Müller-Kray (cnd), Stuttgart South Radio Orch, Hesse Radio Chorus *(rec Schwetzingen, May 24, 1959)* Bella Voce 2-▲ 7204 [AAD]

Haydn, J.:Die Schöpfung, w. Gundula Janowitz (sop—Gabriel), Fritz Wünderlich (ten—Uriel), Kim Borg (bass—Raphael), H. von Karajan (cnd), Vienna PO, Vienna Singverein *(rec Salzburg, Aug 29, 1965)* Bella Voce 2-▲ 7204 [AAD]

Haydn, J.:Die Schöpfung, w. Gunalda Janowitz (sop), Dietrich Fischer-Dieskau (bass), H. von Karajan (cnd), Berlin PO, Vienna Singverein *(rec 1966 & 1968)* Deutsche Grammophon ("Galleria" series) 2-▲ 435077-2 [ADD]

Janácek, L.:The Excursions of Mr. Brouček, w. Antonie Fahberg (sop—Piccolo), Wilma Lipp (sop—Málinka), Lilian Benningsen (cta—Fanny Nowak), Paul Kuen (ten—Trambahn-Kondukteur), Karl Ostertag (ten—Vorsitzender des Hausbesitzerverbandes), Fritz Wunderlich (ten—Mazal), Kurt Böhme (b-bar—Sakristan von St. Veit), Kieth Engen (bass—Würfl), J. Keilberth (cnd), Bavarian SO *(rec live, Prinzregententheater, Nov. 19, 1959)* Orfeo 2-▲ 354942 (m)

Kálmán, I.:Gräfin Mariza, w. A. Görner (sop), B. Kusche (bar), Hartung (sgr), Hofmann (sgr), Marszalek (cnd), Cologne Radio Orch, Cologne Radio Chorus [G] Acanta ▲ CD 42479 [DDD]

The Legendary Voice of Fritz Wunderlich Acanta ▲ CD 43567

Lehár, F.:Der Zarewitsch (sels), w. Christine Gorner (sop), Melita Muszely (sop), Willy Hagara (bar), C. Michalski (cnd), Bavarian SO Emperor Operetta ▲ KO 86341

Mahler, G.:Das Lied von der Erde, w. C. Ludwig (mez), O. Klemperer (cnd), Philharmonia Orch [G] EMI Classics ▲ CDC 47231

Mozart, W.A.:Arias, w. I. Cotrubas (sop), E. Gruberova (sop), L. Price (sop), J. Varady (sop), L. Popp (mez), F. Araiza (ten), P. Domingo (ten), P. de Palma (ten), P. Schreier (ten), S. Milnes (bar), A. Titus (bar), M. Talvela (bass)—sels. from Entführung aus dem Serail, Così fan tutte, Don Giovanni, Idomeneo, Die Zauberflöte, Le nozze di Figaro Eurodisc ▲ 69256-2-RG [ADD]

Mozart, W.A.:Don Giovanni, w. L. Price (sop), H. Gueden (sop), G. Sciurri (sop), E. Wächter (bar), W. Berry (bass), H. von Karajan (cnd), Vienna PO, Vienna State Opera Chorus [I] *(rec live, 1963)* Verona 3-▲ 27065/67 (m) [AAD]

Wunderlich, Fritz (ten) (cont.)

Mozart, W.A.:Entführung, w. Reri Grist (sop—Blondchen), Anneliese Rothenberger (sop—Konstanze), Gerhard Unger (ten—Pedrillo), Fritz Wunderlich (ten—Belmonte), Fernando Corena (bass—Osmin), Michael Heltau (nar—Selim), Z. Mehta (cnd), Vienna PO, Vienna State Opera Chorus *(rec July 28, 1965)* Orfeo d'or ("Festspiel Dokumente" series) 2–▲ 392952 (m)

Mozart, W.A.:Entführung (sels), w. I. Kertész (cnd), Vienna PO—Konstanze, dich wiederzusehen Orfeo d'or ("Festspiel Dokumente" series) ▲ 394301

Mozart, W.A.:Requiem, w. L. Price (sop), H. Rössl–Majdan (mez), W. Berry (bass), H. von Karajan (cnd), Vienna PO, Vienna Singverein [L] *(rec live, Salzburg Festival, Aug. 24, 1960)* Melodram ▲ MEL 18003

Mozart, W.A.:Zauberflöte (sels), w. E. Lear (sop), R. Peters (sop), L. Otto (sop), F. Lenz (ten), D. Fischer–Dieskau (bar), F. Crass (bass), K. Böhm (cnd), Berlin PO, Berlin RIAS Chamber Choir—Scenes & Arias Deutsche Grammophon ▲ 429825–2 [ADD] ■ 429825–4

Opera & Operetta Arias Acanta ▲ 43267

Pfitzner, H.:Palestrina, w. S. Jurinac (sop), C. Ludwig (mez), G. Stolze (ten), O. Wiener (bar), G. Frick (bass), W. Berry (bass), R. Heger (cnd), Vienna State Opera Orch, Vienna State Opera Chorus *(rec live, Vienna 12/16/64)* Myto 3–▲ 3 MCD 92259 [ADD]

Rosenmüller, J.:Lamentationes Jeremiae, w. Lisedor Praetorius (hpd), Fred Buck (vc) *(rec Stuttgart, Mar 24, 1957)* Bella Voce ▲ 7003 [AAD]

Rossini, G.:Il barbiere di Siviglia, w. R. Grist (sop), E. Wächter (bar), O. Czerwenka (bass), Kunz (sgr), K. Böhm (cnd), Vienna State Opera Orch, Vienna State Opera Chorus *(rec live, Vienna 4/28/66)* Myto 2–▲ 2 MCD 91752 [ADD]

Schmidt, F.:Das Buch mit sieben Siegeln, w. H. Gueden (sop), I. Malaniuk (cta), A. Dermota (ten), W. Berry (bass), D. Mitropoulos (cnd), Vienna PO, Vienna Singverein *(rec live, Salzburg Festival 1959)* Melodram 2–▲ MEL 27078

Schmidt, F.:Das Buch mit sieben Siegeln, w. Hilde Gueden (sop), Ira Malaniuk (cta), Anton Dermota (ten), Walter Berry (bass), D. Mitropoulos (cnd), Vienna PO, Vienna Singverein Sony Classical ("Festspiel Dokumente:Salzburger Festspiele" series) 2–▲ SM2K 68442

Schubert, Franz:Fierrabras, w. H. Plümacher (cta), R. Wolansky (bar), O. von Rohr (bass), H. Müller–Kray (cnd), Bern State Orch, Berlin RIAS Chamber Choir, South Swiss Radio Chorus—abridged performance *(rec l959)* Myto ▲ MCD 89001 [ADD]

Schubert, Franz:Die Forelle, w. Hubert Giesen (pno) *(rec Hochschule for Music, Munich, Nov 1965)* Deutsche Grammophon ("The Originals" series) ▲ 447452–2 [ADD]

Schubert, Franz:Frühlingsglaube, w. Hubert Giesen (pno) *(rec Hochschule for Music, Munich, Nov 1965)* Deutsche Grammophon ("The Originals" series) ▲ 447452–2 [ADD]

Schubert, Franz:Heidenröslein, w. Hubert Giesen (pno) *(rec Hochschule for Music, Munich, Nov 1965)* Deutsche Grammophon ("The Originals" series) ▲ 447452–2 [ADD]

Schubert, Franz:Die Schöne Müllerin, w. H. Giesen (pno) [G] *(rec 1965 broadcast)* Verona ▲ 2701 [AAD]

Schubert, Franz:Die Schöne Müllerin, w. Hubert Giesen (pno) *(rec Acad. der Wissenschaften, Munich, July 1966)* Deutsche Grammophon ("The Originals" series) ▲ 447452–2 [ADD]

Schubert, Franz:Songs (misc), w. H. Giesen (pno)—6 songs [G]—D.360, 672, 764, 795/7, 891, 905 *(rec live, Salzburg 8/19/65)* Myto 2–▲ 2 MCD 91544 [ADD]

Schubert, Franz:Songs (misc), w. Hubert Giesen (pno)—Der Einsame, D.800; Nachtstück, D.672; An die Laute, D.905; Lied eines Schiffers an die Dioskuren, D.360; An Sylvia, D.891; Der Musensohn, D.764; Im Abendrot, D.799; Ungeduld aus Die schöne Müllerin, D.795 *(rec Salzburg, Aug 19, 1965)* Orfeo d'or ("Festspiel Dikumente" series) ▲ C 432961 (m) [ADD]

Schubert, Franz:Songs (misc), w. H. Giesen (pno)—9 songs Deutsche Grammophon ("Dokumente" series) ▲ 429933–2 [ADD]

Schubert, Franz:Songs (misc), w. H. Giesen (pno)—Der Einsame, Op. 41; Nachtstuck, Op. 36, No. 2; An die Laute, Op. 81, No. 2; Lied eines Schiffers an die Dioskuren, Op. 65, No. 1; An Silvia, Op. 106, No. 4; Der Musensohn, Op. 92, No. 1; Frühlingsglaube, Op. 20, No. 2; An die Musik, Op. 88, No. 4 [G] *(rec Mar. 24, 1966)* Myto ▲ MCD 93278

Schubert, Franz:Songs (misc), w. H. Giesen (pno)—4 songs—D.360, 672, 800, 905 [G] *(rec live, Salzburg, 8/19/65)* Myto 2–▲ 2 MCD 91648 [ADD]

Schubert, Franz:Songs (misc), w. H. Giesen (pno) *(rec Salzburg, 8/65)* Acanta ▲ CD 43529

Schumann, R.:Dichterliebe, w. Hubert Giesen (pno) *(rec Salzburg, Aug 19, 1965)* Orfeo d'or ("Festspiel Dikumente" series) ▲ C 432961 (m) [ADD]

Schumann, R.:Dichterliebe, w. H. Giesen (pno) [G] *(rec Mar. 24, 1966)* Myto ▲ MCD 93278

Schumann, R.:Dichterliebe, w. H. Giesen (pno) [G] *(rec live, Salzburg 8/19/65)* Myto 2–▲ 2 MCD 91544 [ADD]

Schumann, R.:Dichterliebe, w. H. Giesen (pno) [G] *(rec live, 9/17/66)* Myto ▲ 1 MCD 89011 (m) [ADD]

Schumann, R.:Dichterliebe, w. H. Giesen (pno) Deutsche Grammophon ("Dokumente" series) ▲ 429933–2 [ADD]

Schumann, R.:Dichterliebe, w. H. Giesen (pno) *(rec Salzburg, 8/65)* Acanta ▲ CD 43529

Smetana, B.:The Bartered Bride, w. P. Lorengar (sop), G. Frick (bass), R. Kempe (cnd), Bamberg SO, Bamberg RIAS Chorus [G] *(rec ca. 1963)* EMI Classics ("Studio" series) 2–▲ CDMB 64002

Strauss, R.:Daphne, w. H. Gueden (sop), J. King (ten), P. Schöffler (bass), K. Böhm (cnd), Vienna SO, Vienna State Opera Chorus *(rec live 1963)* Deutsche Grammophon 2–▲ 445322–2

Strauss, R.:Der Rosenkavalier, w. Erika Köth (sop—Sophie), Annelie Waas (sop—Marianne), Claire Watson (sop—Marschallin), Hertha Töpper (mez—Octavian), Brigitte Fassbaender (cta—Annina), Gerhard Stolze (ten—Valzacchi), Fritz Wunderlich (ten—Singer), Otto Wiener (bar—Faninal), Kurt Böhme (bass—Baron), J. Keilberth (cnd), Bavarian State Opera Orch, Bavarian State Opera Chorus *(rec Munich Opera Festival, National Theater, May 21, 1965)* Orfeo d'or 3–▲ 425963

Strauss, R.:Die Schweigsame Frau, w. G. von Milinkovic (mez), H. Hotter (b–bar), H. Prey (bar), K. Böhm (cnd), Vienna PO, Vienna State Opera Chorus *(rec live, Salzburg Festival, 8/8/59)* Melodram 2–▲ MEL 27071 (m) [AAD]

Strauss, R.:Die Schweigsame Frau, w. H. Güden (sop), H. Prey (bar), H. Hotter (b–bar), K. Böhm (cnd), Vienna PO *(rec Salzburg Festival, 1959)* Deutsche Grammophon 2–▲ 445335–2 (m) [ADD]

Verdi, G.:Requiem Mass, w. M. Stader (sop), M. Höffgen (cta), G. Frick (bass), H. Müller–Kray (cnd), South German RSO, South German Radio Sym Chorus *(rec live, Stuttgart, 11/2/60)* Myto 2–▲ 2 MCD 91648 [ADD]

Verdi, G.:La traviata (sels), w. T. Stratas (sop), H. Prey (bar), G. Patanè (cnd), Bavarian State Opera Orch, Bavarian State Opera Chorus—substantial selections from Acts 1–3 *(rec live, Munich, 3/28/65)* Myto 2–▲ 2 MCD 91648 [ADD]

Wagner, R.:Der fliegende Holländer, w. M. Schech (sop), S. Wagner (mez), G. Frick (ten), R. Schock (ten), D. Fischer–Dieskau (bar), F. Konwitschny (cnd), Berlin Staatskapelle Berlin Classics ("Eterna" series) 2–▲ BER 2097 [ADD]

Wagner, R.:Der fliegende Holländer (sels), w. Marianne Schech (sop), Dietrich Fischer–Dieskau (bar), Gottlob Frick (bass), F. Konwitschny (cnd), Berlin Staatskapelle Berlin Classics ▲ BER 9080 [ADD]

Wagner, R.:Tannhäuser, w. E. Grümmer (sop), M. Schech (sop), H. Hopf (ten), D. Fischer–Dieskau (bar), G. Frick (bass), F. Konwitschny (cnd), Berlin State Opera Orch, Berlin State Opera Chorus [G] EMI Classics ("Studio" series) 3–▲ CDMC 63214 [ADD]

Wünzer, Rudolf (bass)

Orff, C.:Der Mond—Ein kleines Welttheater, w. Karl Erb (nar), Paul Kuen (ten—Lad 3), Josef Knapp (bar—Lad 2), Benno Kusche (bar—Lad 1), Georg Hann (bass—St. Peter), Georg Wieter (bass—Lad 4), Rudolf Wünzer (bass—The Farmer), Karl Hanft (sgr—Innkeeper), Willy Rösner (sgr—The Major), R. Alberth (cnd), Bavarian RSO, Bavarian Radio Chorus *(rec Studio 1, Bavarian Radio, Jan. 19–20, 1950)* Calig ▲ CAL 50948 (m) [ADD]

Wyatt, Walker (bass)

Bach, J.S.:Cant 21, w. P. Esswood (ct), K. Equiluz (ten), N. Harnoncourt (cnd), Vienna Concentus Musicus, Chorus Viennensis, Vienna Boys' Choir [G] Teldec 2–▲ 2292–42502–2 [AAD]

Wyckoff, Lou Ann (sop)

Puccini, G.:Suor angelica, w. Elisabeth Carron (sop—Angelica), Joan Summers (sop—Genovieffa), Donna Owen (sop—Dolcina), Lou Ann Wyckoff (sop—Alms collector), Hanna Owen (sop—novice), Anthea De Forest (sop—novice), Charlotte Povia (mez—Abbess), Beverly Evans (mez—Monitress), Kay Creed (mez—Mistress), La Vergne Monette (sop/mez—lay sister), Joan August (sop/mez—lay sister), Pearle Goldsmith (sop/mez—other sister), Lila Herbert (sop/mez—other sister), Jodell Kenting (sop/mez—other sister), Ann Pretzat (sop/mez—other sister), Evelyn Sachs (cta—Princess), F. Patanè (cnd), *(orch unknown) (rec New York, Feb 23, 1967)* Legato Classics ▲ LCD 212–1 [ADD]

Wyner, Susan Davenny (mez)

Fine, I.:Childhood Fables for Grownups, w. Y. Wyner (pno) [E] CRI ▲ CD 574 [ADD]

Ravel, M.:L'Enfant et les sortilèges, w. Arleen Augér (sop), Marilyn Richardson (sop), Jane Berbié (mez), Linda Finnie (mez), Jocelyne Taillon (mez), Philip Langridge (ten), Philippe Huttenlocher (bar), Jules Bastin (bass), A. Previn (cnd), London SO, Ambrosian Opera Chorus Classics for Pleasure ("Eminence" series) ▲ CFP 2241

Wyner, Y.:Intermedio, w. Y. Wyner (cnd), *(orch unknown) (rec Mar 21, 1976)* CRI ("American Masters" series) ▲ CD 701 [ADD]

Wyner, Y.:Memorial Music, w. Mary Posses (fl), Jonathan Drexler (fl), Peter Standaart (fl) *(rec Dwight Chapel, Yale University, 1975)* CRI ("American Masters" series) ▲ CD 701 [ADD]

Wynn, K. (sgr)

Berlin, I.:Annie Get Your Gun, w. J. Garland (sgr), H. Keel (sgr), F. Morgan (sgr), *(other artists unknown) (rec 1949 soundtrack)* Sandy Hook ▲ CSH 2053

Wynn, N. (sgr)

Kern, J.:Cover Girl, w. Gene Kelly (sgr), P. Silvers (sgr) *(rec 1944)* Curtain Calls ▲ CC 100/24

Kern, J.:Cover Girl, w. Gene Kelly (sgr), P. Silvers (sgr) *(rec 1944)* Hollywood Soundstage ▲ HSCD 4005

Kern, J.:You Were Never Lovelier, w. F. Astaire (sgr) *(rec 1942)* Curtain Calls ▲ CC 100/24

Kern, J.:You Were Never Lovelier, w. F. Astaire (sgr), L. Romay (sgr) *(rec 1942)* Hollywood Soundstage ▲ HSCD 4005

Wyn–Rogers, Catherine (cta)

Beethoven, L. van:Sym 9, "Choral Sym", w. Gillian Webster (sop), Martyn Hill (ten), Robert Hayward (bar), R. Leppard (cnd), Royal PO, Ambrosian Singers Tring ("Royal Philharmonic Collection" series) ▲ TRP 51 [DDD]

Britten, H.:A Boy Was Born, w. Susan Gritton (sgr), David Goode (org), Stephen Layton (cnd), Holst Singers Hyperion ▲ CDA 66825

Britten, H.:Choral Music, w. Susan Gritton (sgr), David Goode (org), Stephen Layton (cnd), Holst Singers—Christ's Nativity; A Shepherd's Carol; Jubilate in C Hyperion ▲ CDA 66825

Britten, H.:A Hymn to the Virgin, w. Susan Gritton (sgr), David Goode (org), Stephen Layton (cnd), Holst Singers Hyperion ▲ CDA 66825

Britten, H.:Te Deum, w. Susan Gritton (sgr), David Goode (org), Stephen Layton (cnd), Holst Singers Hyperion ▲ CDA 66825

Haydn, J.:Mass 7, "Kleine Orgelmesse", w. Linda Russell (alto), William Kendall (ten), Michael George (bass), D. Hill (cnd), Brandenburg Orch, Winchester Cathedral Choir Hyperion ▲ CDA 66508 [DDD]

Haydn, J.:Mass 14, "Harmoniemesse", w. Linda Russell (alto), William Kendall (ten), Michael George (bass), D. Hill (cnd), Brandenburg Orch, Winchester Cathedral Choir Hyperion ▲ CDA 66508 [DDD]

Mozart, W.A.:Missa, K.317, w. Barbara Bonney (sop), Jamie MacDougall (ten), Stephen Gadd (bass), T. Pinnock (cnd), English CO, English Concert Choir Archive ▲ 445353–2

Mozart, W.A.:Vesperae solennes, w. Barbara Bonney (sop), Jamie MacDougall (ten), Stephen Gadd (bass), T. Pinnock (cnd), English CO, English Concert Choir Archive ▲ 445353–2

Schubert, Franz:Songs (misc), w. Lorna Anderson (sop), Jamie McDougall (ten) Simon Keenlyside (bar), Graham Johnson (pno), London Schubert Chorale—Das Leben ist ein Traum; Das Grab; Trinklied; Punschlied; Vaterlandslied; Selma und Selmar; Morgenlied; An die Sonne; Hermann und Thusnelda; Cora und die Sonne; Lorna; Genugsamkeit; Der Abend; Das Mädchen aus dem Fremde; Am Rosa (I); Am Rosa (II); An Sie; Gebet während der Schlacht; Das Abendroth; Die drei Sänger; Die Sterne; Cronnan; Furcht der Geliebten; Die Erscheinung; Stolie; Das Bild; Lob des Tokayers Hyperion ▲ CDJ 33022

Vaughan Williams, R.:Magnificat, w. M. Best (cnd), City of London Sinfonia, Corydon Singers [E] Hyperion ▲ CDA 66569 [DDD]

Vivaldi, A.:Gloria, RV.589, w. P. Kwella (sop), E. Priday (sop), A. Carwood (ten), S. Darlington (cnd), Hanover Band, Christ Church Cathedral Choir Oxford Nimbus ▲ NI 5278 [DDD]

Vivaldi, A.:Gloria (& Intro), RV.588, w. P. Kwella (sop), E. Priday (sop), A. Carwood (ten), S. Darlington (cnd), Hanover Band, Christ Church Cathedral Choir Oxford Nimbus ▲ NI 5278 [DDD]

Yachmi–Caucig, Rohangiz (cta)

Mozart, W.A.:Così fan tutte, w. J. Borowska (sop—Fiordiligi), P. Coles (sop—Despina), R. Yachmi (mez—Dorabella), J. Dickie (ten—Ferrando), A. Martin (bar—Guglielmo), P. Mikulaš (b–bar—Don Alfonso), J. Wildner (cnd), Capella Istropolitana, Slovak Phil Chorus [I] *(rec Feb.–Mar. 1990)* Naxos 3–▲ 8.660008/10 [DDD]

Mozart, W.A.:Così fan tutte (sels), w. Joanna Borowska (sop—Fiordiligi), Priti Coles (sop—Despina), Rohangiz Yachmi (mez—Dorabella), John Dickie (ten—Ferrando), Andrea Martin (bar—Guglielmo), Peter Mikulaš (bass—Don Alfonso), Milada Synkova (hpd), J. Wildner (cnd), Capella Istropolitana, Slovak Phil Chorus—Ov.; [Act I] La mia Dorabella capace non è; È la fede della femmine; Una bella serenata; Ah guarda, sorella; Vorrei dir, e cor non ho; Sento, o Dio; Bella vita militar!; Soave sia il vento; Smanie implacabili; In uomini, in soldati; Alla bella Despinetta; Come Scoglio; Non siate ritrosi; Un'aura amorosa; [Act II] Una donna a quindici anni; Prenderò quel brunettino; La mano a me date; Ei parte...senti...ah no!; Donne mie la fate a tanti a tanti; Fra gle amplessi; Fortunato l'uom che prende *(rec Slovak Philharmonic Moyzes Hall, Bratislava, Feb.–Apr. 1990)* Naxos ▲ 8.553172 [DDD]

Strauss (II), Joh.:Die Fledermaus (sels), w. Ariane Calix (sop—Ida), Gabriele Fontana (sop—Rosalinde), Brigitte Karwautz (sop—Adele), Rohangiz Yachmi–Caucig (cta—Orlofsky), John Dickie (ten—Eisenstein), Josef Hopferwieser (ten—Alfred), Erich Wessner (ten—Dr. Blind), Andrea Martin (bar—Falke), Alfred Werner (bar—Frank), J. Wildner (cnd), Czech–Slovak RSO Bratislava, Bratislava City Chorus—Ov.; [Act I] Täubchen, das entflattert ist...; Ach, ich darf nicht hin zu dir; Nein, mit solchen Advokaten; Komm mit mir zum Souper; So muss allein ich bleiben; Trinke, Liebchen, trinke schnell; [Act II] Ein Souper heut' uns winkt; Ich lade gern mir Gäste ein; Mein Herr Marquis, ein Mann wie Sie; Dieser Anstand, so manierlich; Klänge der Heimat; Im Feuerstrom der Reben; Marianka komm und tanz me hier; [Act III] Entr'acte; Spiel' ich die Unschuld vom Lande; O Fledermaus, o Fledermaus *(rec Slovak Radio Concert Hall, Bratislava)* Naxos ▲ 8.553171 [DDD]

Yakar, Rachel (sop)

Campra, A.:L'Europe galante, w. M. Kweksilber (sop), R. Jacobs (ct), S. Nimsgern (bar), G. Leonhardt (cnd), La Petite Bande Editio Classica 2–▲ 77059–2–RG [ADD]

Collet, H.:Los Amantes de galioia, w. Claude Lavoix (pno) *(rec Théatre de Poissy, Paris, Nov. 30–Dec. 2, 1994)* Claves ▲ CD 9506 [DDD]

Collet, H.:Canciones populares castellanas (5), w. Claude Lavoix (pno) *(rec Théatre de Poissy, Paris, Nov. 30–Dec. 2, 1994)* Claves ▲ CD 9506 [DDD]

Collet, H.:Chansons populaires de Burgos (7), w. Claude Lavoix (pno) *(rec Théatre de Poissy, Paris, Nov. 30–Dec. 2, 1994)* Claves ▲ CD 9506 [DDD]

Collet, H.:La Pena, w. Claude Lavoix (pno) *(rec Théatre de Poissy, Paris, Nov. 30–Dec. 2, 1994)* Claves ▲ CD 9506 [DDD]

Collet, H.:Poema de un día, w. Claude Lavoix (pno) *(rec Théatre de Poissy, Paris, Nov. 30–Dec. 2, 1994)* Claves ▲ CD 9506 [DDD]

Collet, H.:Songs, w. Claude Lavoix (pno)—Canciones populaires castellanas, Op. 69; Chansons populaires de Burgos, Op. 80; Poema de un dia, Op. 48; La Pena; Los amantes de Galicia; Songs of Castille, Op. 42/1 & 2 Claves ▲ 50–9506

Lully, J.–B.:Le Bourgeois gentilhomme, w. M. Kweksilber (sop), R. Jacobs (ct), S. Nimsgern (bar), G. Leonhardt (cnd), La Petite Bande Editio Classica 2–▲ 77059–2–RG [ADD]

Lully, J.–B.:Phaëton, w. V. Gens (sop), J. Smith (sop), H. Crook (ten), J.–P. Fouchécourt (ten), M. Minkowski (cnd), Musiciens du Louvres Erato 2–▲ 91737

Mendelssohn, F.:St. Paul, w. B. Baileys (mez), M. Schäfer (ten), T. Hampson (bar), M. Corboz (cnd), Lisbon Gulbenkian Foundation Orch, Lisbon Gulbenkian Foundation Chorus Erato 2–▲ 45279–2

1482

▲ = CD ♦ = Enhanced CD Δ = MD ■ = Cassette Tape □ = DCC

Yakar, Rachel (sop) (cont.)
Mozart, W.A.:Requiem, w. Ortrun Wenkel (cta), Kurt Equiluz (ten), Robert Holl (bass), N. Harnoncourt (cnd), Vienna Concentus Musicus, Vienna State Opera Chorus [L] Teldec ▲ 2292-42911-2
Poulenc, F.:Dialogues des Carmélites, w. C. Dubosc (sop), R. Gorr (mez), M. Dupuy (mez), J. Van Dam (b-bar), K. Nagano (cnd), Lyon Opera Orch Virgin Classics ▲ CDCB 59227
Purcell, H.:Dido & Aeneas, w. A. Murray (mez), A. Scharinger (bass), N. Harnoncourt (cnd), Vienna Concentus Musicus [E] Teldec ▲ 2292-42959-2
Purcell, H.:Dido & Aeneas, w. A. Murray (mez), A. Scharinger (bass), N. Harnoncourt (cnd), Vienna Concentus Musicus, Arnold Schoenberg Choir Teldec ("Das alte Werke" series) ▲ 93686
Stravinsky, I.:Cant Sop, w. M. LeCocq (ten), O.G. Blarr (cnd), Ensemble 1971 [E] Koch Schwann ▲ CD 313 050 [ADD]

Yakovenko, Sergei (bar)
Mussorgsky, M.:Songs & Dances, w. I. Scheps (pno) Russian Season ("Russian Season" series) ▲ LDC 288031 [DDD]
Mussorgsky, M.:Songs (misc), w. I. Scheps (pno)—13 songs Russian Season ("Russian Season" series) ▲ LDC 288031 [DDD]
Mussorgsky, M.:Sunless, w. I. Scheps (pno) Russian Season ("Russian Season" series) ▲ LDC 288031 [DDD]
Russian Musical Satire, w. Yakovenko, Sergei (bar), I. Scheps (pno), State Sym Cappella Choir [cnd:V. Poliansky] Russian Season ▲ LDC 288075

Yakovlev, S. (bar)
Prokofiev, S.:Maddalena, w. S. Kulikova (sgr), N. Zagorinskaya (sgr), Y. Melnikova (sgr), S. Donets (sgr), C. Tikhonov (cnd), Moscow Helikon Theater Chamber Ensemble [R] MK ▲ MKA 417056 [DDD]
Stravinsky, I.:Mavra, w. S. Kulikova (sgr), N. Zagorinskaya (sgr), Y. Melnikova (sgr), S. Donets (sgr), C. Tikhonov (cnd), Moscow Helikon Theater Chamber Ensemble MK ▲ MKA 417056 [DDD]

Yamada, C. (voc)
Satoh, T.:Music of, w. Alba Musica Kyo Ensemble [F, J]—Pèlerinage au Rollant (1981); Kobanashi (1985); Komori-uta (1982-91) Channel Classics ▲ CCS 3291 [DDD]

Yamaj, Yoshihisa (ten)
Albinoni, T.:Il Nascimento de l'Aurora, w. June Anderson (sop), Susanne Klare (sop), Margarita Zimmermann (sop), Sandra Browne (alt), C. Scimone (cnd), Venice Solisti Erato 2-▲ ERA SEL 96374 [DDD]

Yamashita, T. (sgr)
Pugnani, G.:Werther, w. M. Cei (sgr), A. Andreani (sgr), A. Flint (sgr), M. Andreae (cnd), Swiss-Italian Radio-TV Orch *(rec Dec. 14, 1989)* Bongiovanni 2-▲ GB 5028/29 [DDD]

Yamins, R. (sgr)
Lebaron, A.:Lamentation/Invocation, w. A. Shearer (sgr), M. Shapiro (vc), N. Kellman (perc), L. Bouchard (tpt), New Music Consort [E] Mode ▲ 30

Yankovic, "Weird Al" (nar)
Carlos, W.:Carnival of Animals:Part II, w. W. Carlos (cnd), LSI PO CBS ▲ MK 44567 [DDD]
Prokofiev, S.:Peter & the Wolf, w. W. Carlos (cnd), LSI PO [all-synthesized orchestra] CBS ▲ MK 44567 [DDD]

Yanukov (bar)
Orff, C.:Carmina burana, w. R. Bareva (sop), H. Kamenov (ten), G. Robev (cnd), Sofia PO, Bulgarian choirs [G, L] Forlane ▲ FOR 16556 [DDD]

Yarnell, B. (sgr)
Berlin, I.:Annie Get Your Gun, w. E. Merman (sgr), *(other artists unknown)* [1966 Lincoln Center cast] RCA ▲ 1124 2 RC [ADD] ■ 1124 4 R

Yaroslavtsev, Valeri (bass)
Glinka, M.:Russian & Ludmilla, w. Nina Fomina (sop—Gorislava), Bela Rudenko (sop—Ludmilla), Tamara Sinyavskaya (mez—Ratmir), Boris Morozov (bass—Farlaf), Evgeny Nesterenko (bass—Russlan), Valeri Yaroslavtsev (bass—Svetozar), Y. Simonov (cnd), Bolshoi Theater Orch, Bolshoi Theater Chorus *(rec Moscow, 1978-1979)* Melodiya ("The Russian Opera" series) 3-▲ 74321-29348-2 [ADD]

Yauger, Margaret (mez)
Verdi, G.:Rigoletto, w. P. Wise (sop—Gilda), B. Evans (sop—Giovanna), M. Yauger (mez—Maddalena), J. Carreras (ten—Duke), L. Quilico (bar—Rigoletto), J. Rudel (cnd), *(orch unknown) (rec Apr. 22, 1973)* Standing Room Only 2-▲ SRO 843 [ADD]

Yaw, Ellen Beach (sgr)
The Recordings (1899-1913) Pearl ▲ PEA 9239 (m) [AAD]

Yeend, Frances (sop)
Mario Lanza & Frances Yeend, w. Mario Lanza (ten), Hollywood Bowl Orch [cnd:Eugene Ormandy] *(rec live at the Hollywood Bowl, 8/27/47)* Melodram ▲ CDM 16512 (m) [AAD]
Unforgettable Recitals:Mario Lanza & Frances Yeend, w. Mario Lanza (ten) *(rec Hollywood Bowl, 1947)* Melodram ▲ CDI 104001 [ADD]

Yevtushenko, Yevgeni (reciter)
Shostakovich, D.:Sym 13, w. S. Leiferkus (bass), K. Masur (cnd), New York PO, New York Choral Artists Men's Voices Teldec ▲ 90848

Yoder, Paul (bar)
Henze, H.-W.:El Cimarrón, w. M. Faust (fl), R. Evers (gtr), Mircea Ardeleanu (perc) Koch Schwann 2-▲ 314 030 [DDD]

Yoko, Nagashima (cta)
Steffani, A.:Enrico Leone, w. R. Popken (alt), M. Frimmer (sop), S. Szameit (sop), C. Guber (cta), D. Diwiak (ten), G. Faulstich (bar), L. Rovatkay (cnd), Cappela Agostino Steffani [period instrs] [I] Calig ▲ CAL 50855 [DDD]

York, Deborah (sop)
Hasse, J.A.:Salve Regina, w. James Bowman (ct), R. King (cnd), King's Consort Hyperion ▲ CDA 66875
Scarlatti, A.:Cants, w. James Bowman (ct), Crispian Steele-Perkins (tpt), R. King (cnd), King's Consort—3 cants Hyperion ▲ CDA 66875
Scarlatti, D.:Salve Regina, w. James Bowman (ct), R. King (cnd), King's Consort Hyperion ▲ CDA 66875
Vivaldi, A.:Sacred Choral Music, w. Catherine Denley (sop), James Bowman (ct), R. King (cnd), King's Consort Hyperion ▲ CDA 66779

York, Michael (nar)
Hovhaness, A.:Rubaiyat, w. Diane Schmidt (acc), G. Schwarz (cnd), Seattle SO *(rec Seattle Opera House, June 6-7, 1994)* Delos ▲ DE 3168 [DDD]

Yost, Riccardo (bar)
Verdi, G.:Rigoletto, w. Renata Scotto (sop—Gilda), Stella Maris Silva (sop—Giovanna), Martha Carrizo (mez—Page), Carmen de la Mata (mez—Countess Ceprano), Noemi Souza (cta—Maddalena), Horacio Mastrango (ten—Borso), Richard Tucker (ten—Duke of Mantua), Cornell MacNeil (bar—Rigoletto), Riccardo Yost (bar—Marullo), Guerrino Boschetti (bass—Usher), Tulio Gagliardo (bass—Count Ceprano), Victor de Narké (bass—Monterone), William Wilderman (bass—Sparafucile), F. Previtali (cnd), Buenos Aires Teatro Colón Orch, Buenos Aires Teatro Colón Chorus *(rec Colon Theater, Buenos Aires, Aug. 22, 1967)* Legato Classics 2-▲ LCD 198-2

Young, Alexander (ten)
Beethoven, L van:Sym 9, "Choral Sym", w. Heather Harper (sop), Helem Watts (cta), Donald McIntyre (bass), L. Stokowski (cnd), London SO, London Sym Chorus *(rec London, Sept 23, 1967)* Music & Arts ▲ MUA CD 943
Handel, G.F.:Judas Maccabaeus, w. Heather Harper (sop), Helen Watts (cta), John Shirley-Quirk (bass), J. Somary (cnd), English CO, Amor Artis Chorale [E] *(rec 1979)* Vanguard Classics 2-▲ OVC 4071/72 [ADD]
Handel, G.F.:Judas Maccabaeus (sels), w. Heather Harper (sop), Helen Watts (cta), John Shirley-Quirk (bar), J. Somary (cnd), English CO, Amor Artis Chorale Vanguard Classics ▲ OVC 4073 [ADD]
Handel, G.F.:Messiah, w. Margaret Price (sop), Yvonne Minton (mez), Justino Diaz (bass), J. Somary (cnd), English CO, Amor Artis Chorale [E] *(rec 1970)* Vanguard Classics ▲ OVC 4020 [ADD]
Handel, G.F.:Messiah, w. Margaret Price (sop), Yvonne Minton (mez), Justino Diaz (bass), J. Somary (cnd), English CO, Amor Artis Chorale [E] *(rec 1970)* Vanguard Classics 2-▲ OVC 4018/19 [ADD]
Handel, G.F.:Theodora, w. H. Harper (sop), M. Lehane (mez), M. Forrester (cta), J. Lawrenson (bar), J. Somary (cnd), English CO, Amor Artis Chorale [E] *(rec 1968)* Vanguard Classics 2-▲ OVC 4074/5 [ADD]

Young, Alexander (ten) (cont.)
Haydn, J.:Die Schöpfung, w. Judith Raskin (sop), John Reardon (bar), L. Bernstein (cnd), New York PO, Camerata Singers [G] *(rec 1966)* Sony Classical ("Bernstein:The Royal Edition" series) 2-▲ SM2K 47560 [ADD]
Mozart, W.A.:Requiem, w. Elsie Morison (sop), Monica Sinclair (cta), Marian Nowakowski (bass), T. Beecham (cnd), Royal PO, BBC Sym Chorus *(rec 1958)* Theorema ▲ TH 121151
Stravinsky, I.:The Rake's Progress, w. J. Raskin (sop), J. Reardon (bar), I. Stravinsky (cnd), Royal PO *(rec 1964)* Sony Classical 2-▲ SM2K 46299
Sullivan, A.:The Gondoliers, w. G. Evans (bar), O. Brannigan (bass), R. Lewis (ten), M. Sargent (cnd), Pro Arte Orch, Glyndebourne Festival Chorus EMI Classics 2-▲ CDMB 64394
Sullivan, A.:Patience, w. J. Shaw (bar), T. Anthony (bass), G. Baker (bar), M. Sargent (cnd), Pro Arte Orch, Glyndebourne Festival Chorus EMI Classics 2-▲ CDMB 64406
Sullivan, A.:The Yeomen of the Guard, w. R. Lewis (ten), J. Cameron (bar), M. Sargent (cnd), Pro Arte Orch, Glyndebourne Festival Chorus EMI Classics 2-▲ CDMB 64415
Wagner, R.:Die Meistersinger von Nürnberg (sels), w. Heather Harper (sop), Helem Watts (cta), Donald McIntyre (bass), L. Stokowski (cnd), London SO, London Sym Chorus—Suite:Prelude Act III, Dance of the Apprentices, Entrance of the Mastersingers *(rec London, Sept 23, 1967)* Music & Arts ▲ MUA CD 943

Young, Jean (sgr)
Floyd, C.:Susannah, w. Phyllis Curtin (sop—Susannah Polk), Richard Cassilly (ten—Sam Polk), Norman Treigle (bass—Olin Blitch), Marietta Muhs Cosenza (sgr—Mrs. McLean), Marilyn Davidson (sgr—Mrs. Gleaton), Kay Long (sgr—Mrs. Hayes), Jean Young (sgr—Mrs. Ott), Alton Brim (sgr—Elder Hayes), Thomas Carter (sgr—Elder Gleaton), Jack Davis (sgr—Elder McLean), Keith Kaldenberg (sgr—Little Bat McLean), Burton Parker (sgr—Elder Ott), K. Andersson (cnd), New Orleans Opera Orch, New Orleans Opera Chorus *(rec Mar 31, 1962)* VAI Audio 2-▲ VAIA 1115-2 [ADD]

Young, R. (sgr)
Partch, H.:Revelation in the Courthouse Park, w. S. Costallos (sgr—Mom & Agave), C. Durham (ten—Sonny & Pentheus), M. Kimbrough (bar—Vendor & Herdsman), E. Earle (b-bar—Hobo & Tiresias), O. Babatunde (sgr—Dion & Dionysus), C. Roos (sgr—Mayor & Cadmus), O. Williams (sgr—Korypheus), R. Young (sgr—Cop & Guard), D. Mitchell (cnd), Partch Instrumentalists, marching band, *(chorus unknown)* [E] *(rec 10/87)* Tomato 2-▲ R2 70390 [DDD]

Young, Thomas (ten)
Clair de Lune & Sister Moon, w. Jay Leonhart (bass), Mike Renzi (pno), Grady Tate (dr) *(rec Nola Recording Studio, NYC, Oct 21 & 23, 1996)* Ocean ▲ OR 104

Young, Thomas J. (ten)
Black Christmas:Spirituals in the African-American Tradition, w. Vanessa Ayers (mez), Robert Mosley (bar), Dinard Smith (pno), Ronald Isaac (cnd) ESS.A.Y ▲ ESS 1011 [DDD]
Davis, A.:X, The Life & Times of Malcolm X, w. Priscilla Baskerville (sop), Hilda Harris (mez), Eugene Perry (bar—Malcolm), Herbert Perry (bass), W. H. Curry (cnd), Orch of St. Luke, Episteme [E] Gramavision 2-▲ R2-79470 [DDD]

Yovanovitch, Nikola (ten)
Salieri, A.:La passione di Gesù Cristo, w. Daniela Citino (sop), Maria Teresa Toso (alt), Mario Scardoni (bass), Giovanna Scardoni (voc), A. Turco (cnd), Verona Cathedral Cappella Musicale *(rec Verona Cathedral, Italy, Mar 30, 1995)* Bongiovanni ▲ GB 2190 [DDD]

Yule, Don (sgr)
Puccini, G.:Tosca, w. Birgit Nilsson (sop—Floria Tosca), Puli Toro (mez—Shepherd), Jose Carreras (ten—Mario Cavaradossi), Joaquin Romaguera (ten—Spoleta), James Billings (bar—Sacristan), Richard Fredricks (bar—Baron Scarpa), Samuel Ramey (bass—Cesare Angelotti), William Ledbetter (sgr—Sciarrone), Richard Park (sgr—Cardinal), Don Yule (sgr—Jailer), J. Rudel (cnd), *(orch & chorus unknown) (rec Nov 13, 1974)* Legato Classics 2-▲ LCD-200-2

Yurisich, Gregory (bar)
Mozart, W.A.:Don Giovanni, w. N. Argenta (sop), A. Halgrimson (sop), L. Dawson (sop), J. M. Ainsley (ten), G. Finley (ten), A. Miles (bar), A. Schmidt (bar), R. Norrington (cnd), London Classical Players, Schütz Choir London EMI Classics ▲ CDCB 54859
Puccini, G.:Tosca, w. Jane Eaglen (sop—Floria Tosca), Charbel Michael (alt—Shepherd Boy), John Daszak (ten—Spoletta), Dennis O'Neill (ten—Mario Cavaradossi), Christopher Booth-Jones (bar—Sciarrone), Ashley Holland (bar—Jailor), Gregory Yurisich (bar—Baron Scarpia), Peter Rose (bass—Cesare Angelotti), Andrew Shore (bass—Sacristan), D. Parry (cnd), Philharmonia Orch, Geoffrey Mitchell Choir, Peter Kay Children's Chorus Chandos ("Opera in English" series) 2-▲ CHAN 3000

Zabelich, Nicolai (cant)
Hymns to the Mother of God at the Moleben, w. [cnd:Archmandrite Matfei], Trinity-St. Sergius Laura Monks' Choir, Moscow Theological Academy Choir, Nicolai Ivanov (cant) *(rec Cathedral of the Dormition, Trinity-St. Sergiy Lavra, June 1987)* Russian Compact Disc ▲ RCD 15002 [AAD]

Zaccaria, Nicola (bass)
Bellini, V.:I Capuleti e i Montecchi, w. M. Rinaldi (sop—Giulietta), G. Aragall (ten—Romeo), L. Pavarotti (ten—Tebaldo), N. Zaccaria (bass—Capellio), C. Abbado (cnd), Residentie Orch The Hague, Bologna Chorus [I] *(rec live, Amsterdam 6/30/66)* Verona 2-▲ 28001/2
Bellini, V.:I Capuleti e i Montecchi, w. M. Rinaldi (sop), G. Aragall (ten), L. Pavarotti (ten), C. Abbado (cnd), Residentie Orch The Hague, Bologna Chorus *(rec live, Amsterdam 6/30/66)* Melodram 2-▲ MEL 27001
Bellini, V.:Norma, w. M. Callas (sop), C. Ludwig (mez), F. Corelli (ten), T. Serafin (cnd), La Scala Orch, La Scala Chorus [I] EMI Classics ("Studio" series) 3-▲ CDMC 63000 [ADD]
Bellini, V.:Norma, w. M. Callas (sop), G. Simionato (mez), M. Del Monaco (ten), A. Votto (cnd), La Scala Orch, La Scala Chorus *(rec 12/7/55)* HRE 2-▲ 1007-2
Bellini, V.:Norma, w. Maria Callas (sop), Gabriella Carturan (mez), Giulietta Simionato (mez), Mario del Monaco (ten), Giuseppe Zampieri (ten), A. Votto (cnd), La Scala Orch, La Scala Chorus Melodram 2-▲ CDM 26036
Bellini, V.:Norma (sels), w. M. Callas (sop), C. Ludwig (mez), F. Corelli (ten), T. Serafin (cnd), La Scala Orch, La Scala Chorus EMI Classics ▲ ZDM 63091
Bellini, V.:La sonnambula, w. M. Callas (sop), F. Cossotto (mez), N. Monti (ten), A. Votto (cnd), La Scala Orch, La Scala Chorus [I] EMI Classics 2-▲ CDCB 47377 (m)
Bellini, V.:La sonnambula, w. M. Callas (sop), F. Cossotto (mez), N. Monti (ten), A. Votto (cnd), La Scala Orch, La Scala Chorus [I] *(rec live 1957)* Arkadia 2-▲ 503 (m) [AAD]
Bellini, V.:La sonnambula, w. M. Callas (sop), F. Cossotto (mez), N. Monti (ten), A. Votto (cnd), La Scala Orch, La Scala Chorus [I] *(rec live 1957)* Verona 2-▲ 2704/05 (m) [AAD]
Bellini, V.:La sonnambula, w. M. Callas (sop), F. Cossotto (mez), N. Monti (ten), A. Votto (cnd), La Scala Orch, La Scala Chorus [I] *(rec live 1957)* Melodram 2-▲ MEL 26003
Bellini, V.:La sonnambula, w. Maria Callas (sop), Fiorenza Cossotto (mez), Nicola Monti (ten), Franco Ricciardi (ten), Dino Mantovani (bar), A. Votto (cnd), La Scala Orch, La Scala Chorus Melodram 2-▲ CDM 26037
Bellini, V.:La sonnambula (sels), w. M. Callas (sop), F. Cossotto (mez), N. Monti (ten), A. Votto (cnd), La Scala Orch, La Scala Chorus, from Act 2—Oh! se una volta sola rivederio; Ah, non creda mirarti [I] *(rec live, 7/4/57)* Myto 2-▲ 2 MCD 89006 (m) [ADD]
Cherubini, L.:Médée, w. M. Callas (sop), T. Berganza (mez), J. Vickers (ten), N. Rescigno (cnd), Dallas SO *(rec live, Dallas Civic Opera, State Fair Music Hall 11/6/58)* Melodram 2-▲ MEL 26016
Cherubini, L.:Médée, w. M. Callas (sop), F. Cossotto (mez), J. Vickers (ten), N. Rescigno (cnd), Royal Opera House Orch, Royal Opera House Chorus Covent Garden [I] *(rec live, Covent Garden, 6/30/59)* Melodram 2-▲ MEL 26005
Debussy, C.:Pelléas et Mélisande, w. A. Martino (soprano), A. Reynolds (mez), G. Bacquier (bar), T. Rovetta (bar), L. Maazel (cnd), *(orch unknown) (rec 1969* Great Opera Performances 3-▲ GOP 711
Donizetti, G.:Belisario, w. L. Gencer (sop), M. Pecile (cta), U. Grilli (ten), G. Taddei (bar), G. Gavazzeni (cnd), Venice Teatro La Fenice Orch, Venice Teatro La Fenice Chorus [I] *(rec live, Venice 5/14/69)* Melodram 2-▲ MEL 27051 [AAD]
Donizetti, G.:Belisario, w. L. Gencer (sop), M. Pecile (cta), U. Grilli (ten), G. Taddei (bar), G. Gavazzeni (cnd), Venice Teatro La Fenice Orch, Venice Teatro La Fenice Chorus [I] *(rec live in Venice, 5/14/69)* Verona 2-▲ 27048/49 (m) [AAD]
Donizetti, G.:La favorita, w. S. Zanolli (sop), G. Simionato (mez), G. Raimondi (ten), M. Zanasi (bar), F. Previtali (cnd), Naples Teatro San Carlo Orch, Naples Teatro San Carlo Chorus [I] *(rec live, Naples 5/12/63)* Golden Age of Opera 2-▲ GAO 105/06 [ADD]

Zaccaria, Nicola (bass) (cont.)

Donizetti, G.:Lucia di Lammermoor, w. M. Callas (sop), G. di Stefano (ten), R. Panerai (bar), H. von Karajan (cnd), RIAS SO, La Scala Chorus [I] *(rec 9/29/55)* Verona 2-▲ 2709/10 (m) [AAD]
Donizetti, G.:Lucia di Lammermoor, w. M. Callas (sop), G. di Stefano (ten), R. Panerai (bar), H. von Karajan (cnd), RIAS SO, La Scala Chorus [I] *(rec 9/29/55)* Melodram 2-▲ MEL 26004
Donizetti, G.:Lucia di Lammermoor, w. M. Callas (sop), G. di Stefano (ten), R. Panerai (bar), H. von Karajan (cnd), RIAS SO, La Scala Chorus [I] *(rec live, 1955)* EMI Classics (Studio) 2-▲ CDMB 63631 [ADD]
Donizetti, G.:Poliuto, w. M. Callas (sop), F. Corelli (ten), E. Bastianini (bar), A. Votto (cnd), La Scala Orch, La Scala Chorus [I] *(rec live, Milan 12/7/60)* Verona 2-▲ 28003/04
Donizetti, G.:Poliuto, w. M. Callas (sop), F. Corelli (ten), E. Bastianini (bar), A. Votto (cnd), La Scala Orch, La Scala Chorus [I] *(rec live, 12/7/60)* Melodram 2-▲ MEL 26006
Donizetti, G.:Poliuto, w. M. Callas (sop), F. Corelli (ten), E. Bastianini (bar), A. Votto (cnd), La Scala Orch, La Scala Chorus [I] *(rec live, 12/7/60)* Arkadia 2-▲ 520 (m) [AAD]
Meyerbeer, G.:Les Huguenots, w. A. Pastori (sop), A. de Cavalieri (mez), G. Lauri-Volpi (ten), G. Taddei (bar), G. Tozzi (bass), T. Serafin (cnd), Milan RAI SO, Milan RAI Chorus *(rec 1956)* Memories 3-▲ MEM 4566 [ADD]
Puccini, G.:Tosca, w. Renata Tebaldi (sop—Floria Tosca), Guiseppe di Stefano (ten—Mario Cavardossi), Rinaldo Pelizzoni (ten—Spoletta), Ettore Bastianini (bar—Baron Scarpia), Carlo Badioli (bass—Sacristan), Guiseppe Moresi (bass—Sciarrone), Franco Piva (bass—Jailer), Nicola Zaccaria (bass—Cesare Angelotti), G. Gavazzeni (cnd) *(rec Great Auditorium, Brussels World Fair, 1958)* Legato Classics 2-▲ LCD 2092 [ADD]
Puccini, G.:Turandot, w. M. Callas (sop), E. Schwarzkopf (sop), E. Fernandi (ten), T. Serafin (cnd), La Scala Orch, La Scala Chorus [I] *(rec 1957)* EMI Classics 2-▲ CDCB 47971 (m) [ADD]
Rossini, G.:Il barbiere di Siviglia, w. M. Callas (sop), L. Alva (ten), T. Gobbi (bar), F. Ollendorf (bass), A. Galliera (cnd), Philharmonia Orch EMI Classics ▲ ZDM 63076
Rossini, G.:L'italiana in Algeri, w. K. Battle (sop), M. Horne (mez), E. Palacio (ten), S. Ramey (bass), C. Scimone (cnd), Venice Solisti, Prague Phil Chorus [I] Erato ("Libretto" series) 2-▲ 2292-45404-2
Rossini, G.:Stabat Mater, w. T. Zylis-Gara (sop), S. Verrett (mez), L. Pavarotti (ten), C. M. Giulini (cnd), Rome RAI Orch, Rome RAI Chorus [L] *(rec live 12/22/67)* Melodram 2-▲ MEL 28012
Rossini, G.:Stabat Mater, w. T. Zylis-Gara (sop), S. Verrett (mez), L. Pavarotti (ten), C.M. Giulini (cnd), Rome Radio Orch, Rome RAI Chorus [L] *(rec live 12/22/67)* Verona 2-▲ 27060/61 (m) [AAD]
Rossini, G.:Stabat Mater, w. Teresa Zylis-Gara (sop), Shirley Verrett (mez), Luciano Pavarotti (ten), C. M. Giulini (cnd), Rome RAI Orch, Rome RAI Chorus *(rec Rome, Dec. 1967)* Emozioni ▲ ARCD 2041
Spontini, G.:La vestale, w. M. Callas (sop), N. Rossi-Lemeni (bass), F. Corelli (ten), E. Sordello (bar), V. Tatozzi (bar), A. Votto (cnd), La Scala Orch, La Scala Chorus Great Opera Performances ▲ GOP 741
Verdi, G.:Aida, w. M. Callas (sop), F. Barbieri (mez), G. Tucker (ten), T. Gobbi (ten), T. Serafin (cnd), La Scala Orch, La Scala Chorus [I] EMI Classics 3-▲ CDCC 49030 [ADD]
Verdi, G.:Aida, w. Antonietta Stella (sop—Aida), Mirella Parutto (sop—Priestess), Giulietta Simionato (mez—Amneris), Giuseppe DiStefano (ten—Radames), Giuseppe Zampiere (ten—Messenger), Giangiacomo Guelfi (bar—Amonasro), Silvio Maionica (bass—King of Egypt), A. Votto (cnd), La Scala Orch, La Scala Chorus *(rec Milan, Dec 7, 1956)* Legato Classics 2-▲ LCD 204-2 [ADD]
Verdi, G.:Requiem Mass, w. Gré Brouwenstijn (sop), Oralia Dominguez (mez), Giuseppe Zampieri (ten), G. Solti (cnd), West German Radio Orch, West German Radio Chorus Globe 2-▲ GLO 5141 [ADD]
Verdi, G.:Requiem Mass, w. Gré Brouwenstijn (sop), Oralia Dominguez (mez), Giuseppe Zampieri (ten), G. Solti (cnd), Cologne RSO, Cologne Radio Chorus *(rec Nov 17, 1958)* Bella Voce 2-▲ 107.201 [AAD]
Vivaldi, A.:Orlando Furioso, w. V. de los Angeles (sop), M. Horne (mez), L. Valentini-Terrani (mez), C. Gonzales (mez), Kosma (sgr), S. Bruscantini (bar), C. Scimone (cnd), Venice Solisti Erato 3-▲ 2292-45147-2 ZB

Zadek, Hilde (sop)

Beethoven, L. van:Leonore (opera), w. A. Dermota (ten), P. Schöffler (b-bar), O. von Rohr (bass), F. Leitner (cnd), Vienna SO, Vienna State Opera Chorus [G] *(rec live, Bregenz 1960)* Melodram 2-▲ CDM 27085 [AAD]
Bruckner, A.:Te Deum, w. Hilde Güden (sop), Erich Majkut (ten), Gottlob Frick (bass), B. Walter (cnd), Vienna PO, Vienna State Opera Chorus *(rec live, 1955)* Enterprise ("Palladio" series) ▲ ENTPD 4209 [ADD]
Strauss (II), Joh.:Der Zigeunerbaron, w. Emmy Loose (sop), Rosette Anday (cta), Julius Patzak (ten), Karl Dönch (bar), Alfred Poell (bar), Steffi Leverenz (sgr), C. Krauss (cnd), Vienna PO, Vienna State Opera Chorus Phonographe 2-▲ PHG 5020 [AAD]
Verdi, G.:Requiem Mass, w. Margarete Klose (cta), Helge Roswaenge (ten), Boris Christoff (bass), H. von Karajan (cnd), Vienna PO, Vienna Singverein Stradivarius 2-▲ STV DTM 12323 [ADD]
Wagner, R.:Das Liebesverbot, w. L. Sorell (mez), A. Dermota (ten), K. Equiluz (ten), L. Welter (bar), Imdahl (sgr), R. Heger (cnd), Austrian RSO, Austrian Radio Chorus *(rec live, Vienna, 1962)* Melodram 2-▲ MEL 27052 [AAD]

Zádori, Mária (sop)

Esterházy, P.:Harmonia caelestis, w. M. Fers (sop), K. Gémes (mez), K. Károlyi (cta), G. Kállay (ten), J. Moldvay (bass), P. Németh (cnd), Capella Savaria, Savaria Vocal Ensemble [period instrs] [L] Hungaroton 2-▲ HCD 31148/49 [DDD]
Graun, K.H.:Der Tod Jesu, w. M. Fers (sop), M. Klietmann (ten), K. Mertens (b-bar), P. Németh (cnd), Capella Savaria Musique d'Abord ▲ HMA 1903061
Handel, G.F.:Brockes-Passion, w. K. Farkas (sop), D. Minter (alt), J. Bándi (ten), M. Klietmann (ten), G. de Mey (ten), I. Gáti (bar), N. McGegan (cnd), Capella Savaria, Hallé State Chorus [period instrs] [G] Hungaroton 3-▲ HCD 12734/36 [DDD]
Lickl, J.G.:Missa solemnis, w. Judith Nemet (mez), Boldizsar Keönch (ten), Tamas Bator (bass), H. Williams (cnd), Pécs SO, Pécs Chamber Choir Koch Schwann ▲ SCH 312962
Lickl, J.G.:Requiem, w. Judith Nemet (mez), Boldizsar Keönch (ten), Tamas Bator (bass), H. Williams (cnd), Pécs SO, Pécs Chamber Choir Koch Schwann ▲ SCH 312962
Telemann, G.P.:Brockes Passion, w. A. Markert (cta), M. Klietmann (ten), G. De Mey (ten), I. Gáti (bar), N. McGegan (cnd), Capella Savaria, Hallé State Chorus [period instrs] Hungaroton 3-▲ HCD 31130/32 [DDD]
Vivaldi, A.:Juditha triumphans devicta Holofernes barbarie, w. J. Németh (mez), K. Gémes (mez), G. Banditelli (cta), A. Markert (cta), N. McGegan (cnd), Capella Savaria, Savaria Vocal Ensemble [L] Hungaroton 2-▲ HCD 31063/64 [DDD]
Vivaldi, A.:Motets, w. P. Németh (cnd), Capella Savaria—Canta in prato, ride in monte, RV.623; O qui coeli terraeque serenitas, RV.631; Nulla in mundo pax sincera, RV.630; In furore iustissimae irae, RV.626; Carae rosae respirate, RV.624; Vos aurae per montes, RV.634 *(rec 1992)* Musique d'Abord ▲ HMA 1903063

Zadvorny, Sergey (bass)

Rossini, G.:Armida, w. R. Fleming (sop), C. Bosi (ten), B. Fowler (ten), J. Francis (ten), D. Kaasch (ten), G. Kunde (ten), I. Zennaro (ten), I. D'Arcangelo (bass), D. Gatti (cnd), Bologna Teatro Comunale Orch, Bologna Teatro Comunale Chorus *(rec Pesaro, Italy, Aug. 6-17, 1993)* Sony Classical 3-▲ S3K 58968 [DDD]

Zaepffel, Alain (ct)

Boësset, A.:Music of, w. Marcel Bozonnet (nar), Véronique Dietschy (sop), Christophe Le Paludier (ten), Jacques Bone (bass), Claire Antonini (lt), Marianne Muller (vl)—Madame de la fayette; Airs de cour; La princesse de cleves (sels) Adès ▲ ADE 204722
Charpentier, M.-A.:Judicum Salomonis, w. J. Benet (ten), Elwes (ten), G. Ragon (ten), J. Cabré (bar), G. Reinhart (bar), P. Colléaux (cnd), Stradivaria Ensemble, Nantes Vocal Ensemble [L] Arion ▲ ARN 68037 [DDD]
Gluck, C.W.:Orfeo ed Euridice (sels), w. D. Cuiller (cnd), Stradivaria Ensemble, Nantes Vocal Ensemble—Ballo; Che Puro Ciel Adda ▲ ADD 581050
Handel, G.F.:Music of, St. John's Smith Square Orch—sels. from Solomon & Xerxes LaserLight ▲ 15502 [ADD]
Handel, G.F.:Samson (sels), w. D. Cuiller (cnd), Stradivaria Ensemble, Paul Colleaux (cnd), Nantes Vocal Ensemble—The Body Comes; Return Oh God of Hosts Adda ▲ ADD 581050
Handel, G.F.:Serse (sels), w. M. Pommer (cnd), New Bach Collegium Musicum Laserlight ▲ 15 502

Zaepffel, Alain (ct) (cont.)

Handel, G.F.:Theodora (sels), w. D. Cuiller (cnd), Stradivaria Ensemble, Paul Colleaux (cnd), Nantes Vocal Ensemble—Sweet Rose & Lily; Unhappy, Happy Crew; Kind Heaven; Go Gen'rous Pious Youth Adda ▲ ADD 581050
Hasse, J.A.:Il trionfo di Clelia (sels), w. D. Cuiller (cnd), Stradivaria Ensemble, Nantes Vocal Ensemble—Resta Cara Adda ▲ ADD 581050
Leçons de ténèbres et raga de la nuit avancée, w. Véronique Dietschy (sop), Sulochana Brahaspati (voc), Ensemble Gradiva K617 ▲ 7017 [DDD]
Piccinni, N.:Tigrane (sels), w. D. Cuiller (cnd), Stradivaria Ensemble, Paul Colleaux (cnd), Nantes Vocal Ensemble—Ah Cleopatra Adda ▲ ADD 581050
Scarlatti, A.:Cants & Duets, w. Véronique Dietschy (sop), Marianne Muller (vl), Macha Yanuchevskaia (vc), Aline Zylberajch (hpd/org), Yasurnori Imamura (thb)—Il Sonno; Clori e Mirtillo; Marcantonio e Cleopatra; Doralbo e Niso Adès ▲ ADE 202172 [DDD]
Traetta, T.:Ifigenia in Tauride (sels), w. D. Cuiller (cnd), Stradivaria Ensemble, Nantes Vocal Ensemble—Scène avec Shoeurs Adda ▲ ADD 581050

Zagonara, Adelio (ten)

Giordano, U.:Andrea Chénier, w. Maria Caniglia (sop—Maddalena), Maria Huder (mez—Bersi), Vittoria Palombini (mez—Madelon), Giulietta Simionato (mez—Contessa), Beniamino Gigli (ten—Andrea), Adelio Zagonara (ten—Incroyable/Abbé), Gino Bechi (bar—Carlo), Leone Paci (bar—Mathieu), Giuseppe Taddei (b-bar—Pietro/Fouquier), Italo Tajo (b-bar—Roucher), Gino Conti (bass—Master/Schmidt), O. de Fabritiis (cnd), La Scala Orch, La Scala Chorus *(rec Nov 1941)* Arkadia ("The 78's" series) 2-▲ 78012 [ADD]
Puccini, G.:La fanciulla del West (sels), w. Magda Olivero (sop—Minnie), Corinna Vozza (mez—Wowkle), Paolo Caroli (ten—Harry), Giacomo Lauri-Volpi (ten—Dick Johnson), Marco Rogani (ten—Pony Express Rider), Salvatore di Tommaso (ten—Trin), Adelio Zagonara (ten—Nick), Virgilio Ascorro (bar—Sid), Alfredo Colella (bar—Jake Wallace), Giuseppe Forgione (bar—Bello), Giancarlo Guelfi (bar—Jack Rance), Arturo la Porta (bar—Sonora), Gino Conti (bass—José Castro), Piere Passarotti (bass—Bill), Enzo Titta (bass—Larkens), Giulio Tomei (bass—Ashby), V. Bellezza (cnd), Rome Opera Orch, Rome Opera Chorus—Minnie, dalla mia casa son partito; Laggiù nel Soledad; Chi c'è per farmi i ricci; Oh! Mister Johnson, siete rimasto; Non so ben neppur io; Io non son che una povera fanciulla; No, Minnie, non piangete; Vorrei mettermi queste; Hallo!; Oh, se sapeste; Credo che abbiate torto; Ma ti giuro ch'io non ti lascio più; Vieni fuori!; Una parola sola!...Or son sei mesi; Che c'è di nuovo Jack?; È là; Siete pronto; Ch'ella mi creda; È Minnie!...È Minnie! *(rec Rome, Mar. 30, 1957)* Golden Age of Opera ▲ GAO 180 [ADD]
Puccini, G.:Madama Butterfly, w. Toti dal Monte (sop—Madama Butterfly), Maria Huder (mez—Kate Pinkerton), Beniamino Gigli (ten—B.F. Pinkerton), Adelio Zagonara (ten—Goro), Mario Basiola (bar—Sharpless), Gino Conti (bass—Principe Yamadori), Ernesto Dominici (bass—Il Bonzo), Vittoria Paolombini (sgr—Suzuki), O. de Fabritiis (cnd), Rome Opera Orch, Giuseppe Conca (cnd), Rome Opera Chorus *(rec Aug 1939)* Arkadia 2-▲ CD 78004 (m) [ADD]
Puccini, G.:Turandot, w. Birgit Nilsson (sop—Turandot), Renata Tebaldi (sop—Liù), Jussi Björling (ten—Calaf), Alessio De Paolis (ten—Emperor Altoum), Piero de Palma (ten—Pang), Mario Sereni (bar—Ping), Adelio Zagonara (bar—Prince of Persia), Giorgio Tozzi (bass—Timur), Tommaso Frascati (bass—Pong), Leonardo Monreale (bass—Mandarin), E. Leinsdorf (cnd), Rome Opera Orch, Rome Opera Chorus *(rec Rome Opera House, July 3-11, 1959)* RCA Living Stereo 2-▲ 09026-62687-2 [ADD]
Verdi, G.:La traviata, w. Maria Caniglia (sop—Violetta), Maria Huder (mez—Flora), Gladys Palmer (cta—Annina), Octave Dua (ten—Giuseppe), Beniamino Gigli (ten—Alfredo), Booth Hitchen (ten—D'Obigny), Adelio Zagonara (bar—Gastone), Aristide Baracchi (bar—Douphol), Mario Basiola (bar—Germont), Norman Walker (bass—Dr. Grenville), V. Gui (cnd), London PO, London Phil Chorus *(rec Royal Opera House, Covent Garden, May 22, 1939)* Minerva 2-▲ MN A28/29 (m) [ADD]

Zagorinskaya, Natalia (sop)

Denisov, E.:Sun of the Incas, w. Moscow Contemporary Music Ensemble *(rec Mosfilm Studio, June 5-7 & 19, 1995)* Triton ▲ 17003 [DDD]
Mosolov, A.:Children's Songs, w. Moscow Contemporary Music Ensemble *(rec Mosfilm Studio, Jan 1995)* Triton ▲ 17004 [DDD]
Mosolov, A.:Newspaper, w. Moscow Contemporary Music Ensemble *(rec Mosfilm Studio, Jan 1995)* Triton ▲ 17004 [DDD]
Prokofiev, S.:Maddalena, w. S. Kulikova (sgr), Y. Melnikova (sgr), S. Donets (sgr), S. Yakovlev (sgr), C. Tikhonov (cnd), Moscow Helikon Theater Chamber Ensemble [R] MK ▲ MKA 417056 [DDD]
Stravinsky, I.:Mavra, w. S. Kulikova (sgr), Y. Melnikova (sgr), S. Donets (sgr), S. Yakovlev (bar), C. Tikhonov (cnd), Moscow Helikon Theater Chamber Ensemble MK ▲ MKA 417056 [DDD]

Zagórzanka, Barbara (sop)

Moniuszko, S.:Halka, w. R. Racewicz (mez), W. Ochman (ten), A. Hiolski (bar), J. Ostapuik (bass), R. Satanowski (cnd), Warsaw Teatr Wielki Orch, Warsaw Teatr Wielki Chorus *(rec live, 10/14/86)* CPO 2-▲ CPO 999032-2 [DDD]
Szymanowski, K.:King Roger, w. A. Malewicz-Madey (cta), H. Grychnik (ten), W. Ochman (ten), A. Hiolski (bar), L. A. Mròz (bass), K. Stryja (cnd), Polish State PO Katowice, Cracow Phil Boys' Chorus, Polish State Phil Chorus *(rec Apr. 7-9, 1990)* Marco Polo ("Opera Classics" series) 2-▲ 8.223339/40 [DDD]
Szymanowski, K.:King Roger, w. B. Zagórzanka (sop—Roger), S. Kowalski (ten—Shepherd), Z. Nikodem (ten—Edrisi), F. Skulski (bar—Roger II), R. Satanowski (cnd), Warsaw Teatr Wielki Orch, Warsaw Teatr Wielki Chorus [Polish] Koch Schwann 2-▲ CD 314 014 [DDD]
Szymanowski, K.:Veni Creator, w. K. Stryja (cnd), Polish State PO, Polish State Phil Chorus Marco Polo ▲ 8.223293 [DDD]

Zahradnicek, Jiří (ten)

Smetana, B.:The 2 Widows, w. N. Sormova (sop), M. Machotková (sop), F. Jílek (cnd), Prague National Theater Orch, Prague National Theater Chorus [Cz] *(rec 1975)* Supraphon 2-▲ SUP 11 2122 [AAD]

Zajick, Dolora (mez)

James Levine's 25th Anniversary Metropolitan Opera Gala, w. J. Levine (cnd), Metropolitan Opera Orch, Ileana Cotrubas (sop), Renée Fleming (sop), Hei-Kyung Hong (sop), Karita Mattila (sop), Birgit Nilsson (sop), Ruth Ann Swenson (sop), Kiri Te Kanawa (sop), Deborah Voigt (sop), Grace Bumbry (mez), Heidi Grant Murphy (mez), Anne Sofie von Otter (mez) *(rec live, Metropolitan Opera House, New York, Apr 27, 1996)* Deutsche Grammophon ▲ 449177-2 [DDD]
Massenet, J.:Hérodiade, w. Renée Fleming (sop—Salome), Dolora Zajick (mez—Hérodiade), Plácido Domingo (ten—Jean), Juan Pons (bar—Erode), Kenneth Cox (bass—Phanuel), V. Gergiev (cnd), San Francisco Opera Orch, San Francisco Opera Chorus Sony Classical 2-▲ S2K 66847
Massenet, J.:Hérodiade (sels), w. Renée Fleming (sop), Kristin Clayton (sgr), Plácido Domingo (ten), Kenneth Cox (bass), Juan Pons (bar), Hector Vásquez (sgr), V. Gergiev (cnd), San Francisco Opera Orch, San Francisco Opera Chorus—highlights *(rec San Francisco Opera, Nov 1994)* Sony Classical ▲ SK 61965
Massenet, J.:Hérodiade (sels), w. Renée Fleming (sop—Salomé), Dolora Zajick (mez—Hérodiade), Plácido Domingo (ten—Jean), Juan Pons (bar—Hérode), Hector Vásquez (bar—Vitellius), Kenneth Cox (bass—Phanuel), V. Gergiev (cnd), San Francisco Opera Orch, San Francisco Opera Chorus Sony Classical ▲ SK 61965
Verdi, G.:Aida, w. A. Millo (sop), P. Domingo (ten), J. Morris (bass), S. Ramey (bass), J. Levine (cnd), Metropolitan Opera Orch, New York Metropolitan Opera Chorus [I] Sony Classical 3-▲ S3K 45973 [DDD] 3-■ S3T 45973 (D)
Verdi, G.:Aida (sels), w. A. Millo (sop), P. Domingo (ten), J. Morris (bar), S. Ramey (bass), T. Cook (bass), J. Levine (cnd), Metropolitan Opera Orch, New York Metropolitan Opera Chorus *(rec New York, May 18-26, 1990)* Sony Classical ("Opera Highlights" series) ▲ SMK 53506 [DDD]
Verdi, G.:Don Carlos (sels), w. J. Bunnell (sop), A. Millo (sop), M. Sylvester (ten), V. Chernov (bar), F. Furlanetto (bass), P. Plishka (bass), J. Levine (cnd), Metropolitan Opera Orch, New York Metropolitan Opera Chorus *(rec New York, Apr. 20-May 14, 1992)* Sony Classical ("Opera Highlights" series) ▲ SMK 53507 [DDD]
Verdi, G.:Il trovatore, w. A. Millo (sop), S. Kelly (cta), P. Domingo (ten), T. Willson (ten), A. Laciura (ten), J. Morris (bass), G. Bater (bass), J. Levine (cnd), Metropolitan Opera Orch, New York Metropolitan Opera Chorus *(rec June 18, 1991)* Sony Classical 2-▲ S2K 48070 [DDD]

1484

▲ = CD ♦ = Enhanced CD Δ = MD ■ = Cassette Tape □ = DCC

Zajíčkova, Kamila (sop)
Bach, J.S.:Cant 209, Musica Aeterna *(rec Moyzes Hall of the Slovak Philharmonic, Bratislava, Jan 20–23, 1993)* Slovart ▲ SR 0003-2-131 [DDD]
Handel, G.F.:Cants, Musica Aeterna—Cant HWV 97, "Crudel tiranno Amor" *(rec Moyzes Hall of the Slovak Philharmonic, Bratislava, Jan 20–23, 1993)* Slovart ▲ SR 0003-2-131 [DDD]
Telemann, G.P.:Cants, Musica Aeterna—Der Weiberorden *(rec Moyzes Hall of the Slovak Philharmonic, Bratislava, Jan 20–23, 1993)* Slovart ▲ SR 0003-2-131 [DDD]

Zakai, Mira (cta)
Berg, A.:Songs, Op. 2, w. Y. Zak (pno) [G] Koch International Classics ▲ KIC 7021-2 [DDD] ■ 3-7021-4 (D)
Handel, G.F.:Cants, w. A. Biron (fl), A. Shavel (hpd)—"Mal palpita il cor" [I] Koch International Classics ▲ KIC 7021-2 [DDD] ■ 3-7021-4 (D)
Mahler, G.:Songs, w. Y. Zak (pno)—6 early songs:Ablösung im Sommer; Erinnerung; Frühlingsmorgen; Phantasie; Schneiden und Meiden; Serenade [G] Koch International Classics ▲ KIC 7021-2 [DDD] ■ 3-7021-4 (D)
Mahler, G.:Sym 2, w. I. Buchanan (sop), G. Solti (cnd), Chicago SO, Chicago Sym Chorus [G] London 2-▲ 410202-2 [DDD]
Ravel, M.:Chansons madécasses, w. A. Biron (fl), M. Haran (vc), Y. Zak (pno) [F] Koch International Classics ▲ KIC 7021-2 [DDD] ■ 3-7021-4 (D)
Schoenberg, A.:Moses und Aaron, w. B. Bonney (sop), P. Langridge (ten), F. Mazura (bar), A. Haugland (bass), G. Solti (cnd), Chicago SO, Chicago Sym Chorus, Glen Ellyn Children's Chorus [G] London 2-▲ 414264-2 [DDD]
Webern, A.:Songs from *Der siebente Ring*, Op. 3, w. Y. Zak (pno) [G] Koch International Classics ▲ KIC 7021-2 [DDD] ■ 3-7021-4 (D)

Zambalis, S. (sop)
Taneyev, S.:Duet for Romeo & Juliet, w. J. Daniecki (ten), P. Tiboris (cnd), Moscow Radio-TV SO Bridge ▲ BCD 9034 [DDD]

Zamballi, Elisa Savani (sop)
Liszt, F.:Via Crucis, w. Simone Alberghini (bar), Allesandra Mazzanti (org), Bonifacio Manduchi (cnd), Fabio de Bologne Polyphonic Chorus [orig version] Studio SM 2-▲ 2515 [DDD]

Zambelli, Corrado (ten)
Verdi, G.:Otello, w. Maria Carbone (sgr), Nicola Fusati (ten), Piero Girardi (ten), Apollo Granforte (bar), Enrico Spada (sgr), C. Sabajno (cnd), La Scala Orch, La Scala Chorus Grammofono 2000 2-▲ GRM 78651
Verdi, G.:Il trovatore, w. G. Cigna (sop—Leonora), G. Wettergren (mez—Azucena), M. Huder (mez—Ines), J. Björling (ten—Manrico), O. Dua (ten—Ruiz), C. Zambelli (ten—Ferrando), M. Basiola (bar—Count di Luna), L. Horsman (bar—Old Gypsy), V. Gui (cnd), Royal Opera Orch, Royal Opera House Chorus Covent Garden *(rec May 12, 1939)* Legato Classics 2-▲ LCD 173-2 [ADD]

Zambon, Amadeo (ten)
Bellini, V.:La straniera, w. M. Caballé (sop), B. M. Casoni (cta), A. Guadagno (cnd), American Opera Society Orch, American Opera Society Chorus *(rec 1969)* Melodram 2-▲ MLO 270111 [DDD]
Bellini, V.:La straniera (sels), w. M. Caballé (sop), A. Guadagno (cnd), *(orch unknown)*— 5 arias [I] *(rec live, Carnegie Hall, 3/22/69)* Verona 2-▲ 27097/98
Cilea, F.:Adriana Lecouvreur, w. L. Gencer (sop—Adriana), A. Lazzarini (mez—Princess), F. Ricciardi (ten—Abbot), A. Zambon (ten—Maurizio), E. Sordello (bar—Michonnet), A. Zerbini (bass—Prince), O. de Fabritiis (cnd), Naples Teatro San Carlo Orch, Naples Teatro San Carlo Chorus *(rec Dec. 17, 1966)* Golden Age of Opera 2-▲ GAO 143/44 [ADD]

Zambon, Giuseppe (ct)
Gesualdo, D.C.:Madrigals, w. Elena Cecchi Fedi (sop), Roberta Invernizzi (sop), Daniela Del Monaco (cta), Roberto Balconi (ct), Gian Paolo Fagotto (ten), Giovanni Dagnino (bass), A. Curtis (cnd), I Fegi Armonici—Book 6 [Se la Mia Morte Brami; Beltà Poi Che T'Assenti; Tu Piangi O Fille Mia; Resta di Darmi Noia; Chiaro Risplender Suole; others] Symphonia ▲ SYM 94133
Pergolesi, G.B.:Stabat mater, w. Lina Maria Akerlund (sop), C. Chiarappa (cnd), Accademia Bizantina Denon ▲ CO 78904 [DDD]
Peri, J.:Euridice, w. Monica Benvenuti (sop—Ninfa I/Venere), Rossana Bertini (sop—Dafne/Ninfa II), Gloria Banditelli (cta—Euridice/Ninfa III/Tragedia/Proserpina), Mario Cecchetti (ten—Aminta/Radamanto), Paolo Da Col (ten—Tirsi), Gianpaolo Fagotto (ten—Orfeo), Giuseppe Zambon (ct—Arcetro), Sergio Foresti (bass—Caronte/Pastore), Furio Zanasi (bass—Plutone), R. de Caro (cnd), Arpeggione Ensemble *(rec Bologna, Italy, Nov 1992)* Arts Music 2-▲ 47276-2 [DDD]

Zamboni, Maria (sop)
Puccini, G.:Manon Lescaut, w. Francesco Merli (ten), Lorenzo Conati (sgr), L. Molajoli (cnd), La Scala Orch, La Scala Chorus *(rec Milan, 1930)* Melodram 2-▲ IMC 202001
Puccini, G.:Manon Lescaut, w. Maria Zamboni (sop—Manon), Anna Masetti-Bassi (mez—Singer), Francesco Merli (ten—Chevalier), Giuseppe Nessi (ten—Edmondo/Dancing Master/ Lamplighter), Lorenzo Conati (bar—Lescaut), Aristide Baracchi (bass—Innkeeper/Sergeant), Attilio Bordonali (bass—Geronte), Natale Villa (bass—Naval Captain), L. Molajoli (cnd), La Scala Orch, Vittore Veneziani (cnd), La Scala Chorus *(rec 1930)* Arkadia ("The 78's" series) 2-▲ 78014 [ADD]
Puccini, G.:Manon Lescaut, w. Francesco Merli (ten), Lorenzo Conati (sgr), L. Molajoli (cnd), La Scala Orch, La Scala Chorus *(rec Milan, 1930)* Phonographie 2-▲ PHC 5006 [ADD]

Zamfir, Mihaï (ten)
Rossini, G.:Stabat Mater, w. O. Liani (sop), J. Jaques (mez), T. Krause (bar), P. Crispini (cnd), Geneva Elans Orch Ensemble, Geneva Elans Vocal Ensemble [L] Gallo ▲ CD 487

Zampieri, Giuseppe (ten)
Beethoven, L. van:Fidelio, w. C. Goltz (sop), S. Jurinac (sop), P. Schöffler (b-bar), O. Edelmann (bass), H. von Karajan (cnd), Vienna PO, Vienna State Opera Chorus [G] *(rec live, Salzburg Festival 7/27/57)* Claque 2-▲ CLQ 2007 (m)
Bellini, V.:Norma, w. Maria Callas (sop), Gabriella Carturan (mez), Giulietta Simionato (mez), Mario del Monaco (ten), Nicola Zaccaria (bass), A. Votto (cnd), La Scala Orch, La Scala Chorus Melodram 2-▲ CDM 26036
Donizetti, G.:Lucia di Lammermoor, w. M. Callas (sop), G. di Stefano (ten), R. Panerai (bar), G. Modesti (bass), H. von Karajan (cnd), La Scala Orch, La Scala Chorus *(rec 1954)* Melodram 2-▲ MLO 26040 [DDD]
Strauss (II), Joh.:Die Fledermaus, w. H. Gueden (sop), E. Köth (sop), R. Resnik (mez), W. Kmentt (ten), E. Wächter (bar), W. Berry (bass), E. Kunz (bar), H. von Karajan (cnd), Vienna PO, Vienna State Opera Chorus, with Gala Sequence [G] London 2-▲ 421046-2 [ADD]
Strauss (II), Joh.:Die Fledermaus, w. H. Gueden (sop), R. Streich (sop), G. Di Stefano (ten), G. Stolze (ten), E. Wächter (bar), W. Berry (bass), E. Kunz (bar), H. von Karajan (cnd), Vienna State Opera Orch, Vienna State Opera Chorus [G] Arkadia 3-▲ 215 (m) [ADD]
Verdi, G.:Aida, w. Antonietta Stella (sop—Aida), Mirella Parutto (sop—Priestess), Giulietta Simionato (mez—Amneris), Giuseppe DiStefano (ten—Radames), Giuseppe Zampiere (ten—Messenger), Giangiacomo Guelfi (bar—Amonasro), Silvio Maionica (bass—King of Egypt), Nicola Zaccaria (bass-Ramfis), A. Votto (cnd), La Scala Orch, La Scala Chorus *(rec Milan, Dec 7, 1956)* Legato Classics 2-▲ LCD 204-2 [ADD]
Verdi, G.:Un ballo in maschera, w. G. Bouwenstijn (sop); E. Ratti (sop), A. Delori (cta), F. Molinari-Pradelli (cnd), Netherlands Opera Orch, Netherlands Opera Chorus *(rec live 1958)* Globe 2-▲ GLO 5109
Verdi, G.:Requiem Mass, w. Gré Brouwenstijn (sop), Oralia Dominguez (mez), Nicola Zaccaria (bass), G. Solti (cnd), West German Radio Orch, West German Radio Chorus Globe 2-▲ GLO 5141 [ADD]
Verdi, G.:Requiem Mass, w. Gré Brouwenstijn (sop), Oralia Dominguez (mez), Nicola Zaccaria (bass), G. Solti (cnd), Cologne RSO, Cologne Radio Chorus *(rec Nov 17, 1958)* Bella Voce 2-▲ 107.201 [AAD]
Verdi, G.:Simon Boccanegra, w. Leyla Gencer (sop), Glade Peterson (ten), Tito Gobbi (bar), Rolando Panerai (bar), Vito Susca (bass), Giorgio Tozzi (bass), G. Gavazzeni (cnd), *(orch unknown)* Great Opera Performances 2-▲ GOP 767
Verdi, G.:La traviata, w. A. Moffo (sop), G. Janowitz (sop), E. Bastianini (bar), B. Klobucar (cnd), Vienna State Opera Orch, Vienna State Opera Chorus [I] *(rec live, Vienna, 1964)* Melodram (Connaisseur) 2-▲ CDM 27510 [ADD]

Zampieri, Mara (sop)
Galuppi, B.:Adamo, w. Susanna Rigacci (sop—Angelo di Misericordia), Mara Zampieri (sop—Eva), Marilyn Schmiege (mez—Angelo di Giustizia), Ernesto Palacio (ten—Adamo), C. Scimone (cnd), Venice Solisti Erato 2-▲ ERA SEL 12984 [ADD]
Puccini, G.:La fanciulla del West, w. P. Domingo (ten), J. Pons (bar), L. Maazel (cnd), La Scala Orch, La Scala Chorus *(rec live 1991)* Sony Classical 2-▲ S2K 47189

Zanasi (sgr)
Puccini, G.:Tosca, w. Raina Kabaivanska (sop), Plácido Domingo (ten), F.M. Pradelli (cnd), La Scala Orch *(rec live, May 17, 1974)* Arkadia ("Historical Performances" series) 2-▲ 496

Zanasi, Alfredo (bass)
Verdi, G.:La traviata, w. M. Callas (sop), C. Valletti (ten), N. Rescigno (cnd), Royal Opera House Orch, Royal Opera House Chorus Covent Garden [I] *(rec live 6/20/58)* Verona 2-▲ 27054/55 (m) [AAD]
Verdi, G.:La traviata, w. M. Callas (sop), C. Valletti (ten), N. Rescigno (cnd), Royal Opera House Orch, Royal Opera House Chorus Covent Garden [I] *(rec live 6/20/58)* Melodram 2-▲ MEL 26007 (m)

Zanasi, Furio (bass)
Handel, G.F.:Giulio Cesare in Egitto, w. Barbara Schlick (sop), Jennifer Larmore (mez), Marianne Rørholm (mez), Bernarda Fink (cta), Derek Lee Ragin (ct), Dominique Visse (ct), Oliver Lallouette (bass), R. Jacobs (cnd), Concerto Cologne [period instrs] Harmonia Mundi France 3-▲ HMC 901385/87
Peri, J.:Euridice, w. Monica Benvenuti (sop—Ninfa I/Venere), Rossana Bertini (sop—Dafne/Ninfa II), Gloria Banditelli (cta—Euridice/Ninfa III/Tragedia/Proserpina), Mario Cecchetti (ten—Aminta/Radamanto), Paolo Da Col (ten—Tirsi), Gianpaolo Fagotto (ten—Orfeo), Giuseppe Zambon (ct—Arcetro), Sergio Foresti (bass—Caronte/Pastore), Furio Zanasi (bass—Plutone), R. de Caro (cnd), Arpeggione Ensemble *(rec Bologna, Italy, Nov 1992)* Arts Music 2-▲ 47276-2 [DDD]

Zanasi, Mario (bar)
Bellini, V.:Beatrice di Tenda, w. L. Gencer (sop), J. Oncina (ten), V. Gui (cnd), Venice Teatro La Fenice Orch, Venice Teatro La Fenice Chorus *(rec 1964)* Memories 2-▲ MEM 4543 [ADD]
Donizetti, G.:La favorita, w. S. Zanolli (sop), G. Simionato (mez), G. Raimondi (ten), N. Zaccaria (bass), F. Previtali (cnd), Naples Teatro San Carlo Orch, Naples Teatro San Carlo Chorus [I] *(rec live, Naples 5/12/63)* Golden Age of Opera 2-▲ GAO 105/06 [ADD]
Verdi, G.:Un ballo in maschera, w. R. Orlandi Malaspina (sop—Ameilia), D. Mazzuccato (sop—Oscar), A. Lazzarini (mez—Ulrica), L. Pavarotti (ten—Riccardo), M. Zanasi (bar—Renato), A. Zerbini (bass—Samuel), G. Casarini (bass—Tom), G. Zecchillo (bass—Sil) Golden Age of Opera 2-▲ GAO 164/65 [ADD]
Verdi, G.:Un ballo in maschera, w. Leyla Gencer (sop), Adriana Lazzarini (mez), Carlo Bergonzi (ten), O. de Fabritiis (cnd), Bologna Teatro Comunale Orch, Bologna Teatro Comunale Chorus *(rec live, Nov 28, 1961)* Arkadia 2-▲ 622
Verdi, G.:La traviata, w. B. Sills (sop), M. Zotti (sop), G. Borelli (mez), A. Kraus (ten), A. Ceccato (cnd), Naples Teatro San Carlo Orch, Naples Teatro San Carlo Chorus *(rec live 1/17/70)* Melodram 2-▲ MEL 27063 (m) [AAD]
Verdi, G.:Il trovatore, w. M. Caballé (sop), G. Tucker (ten), T. Schippers (cnd), Florence Maggio Musicale Orch, Florence Maggio Musicale Chorus [I] *(rec live 1968)* Melodram 2-▲ MEL 27035
Verdi, G.:Il trovatore, w. M. Caballé (sop), G. Tucker (ten), T. Schippers (cnd), Florence Maggio Musicale Orch, Florence Maggio Musicale Chorus *(rec 1968)* Memories ▲ MEM 4521 [ADD]

Zancanaro, Giorgio (bar)
Bizet, G.:Carmen, w. M. Chiara (sop—Micaela), A. Caminada (mez—Mercedes), F. Cossotto (mez—Carmen), F. Andreoli (ten—Il Remendado), P. M. Ferraro (ten—Don José), R. Bruson (bar—Escamillo), G. Zancanaro (bar—Morales), A. Carusi (bass—Il Dancairo), P. Maag (cnd), Venice Teatro La Fenice Orch, Venice Teatro La Fenice Chorus *(rec 1971)* Myto 2-▲ MCD 93487
Giordano, U.:Andrea Chénier, w. E. Martón (sop), J. Carreras (ten), G. Patanè (cnd), Hungarian State Orch, Hungarian State Chorus [I] CBS 2-▲ M2K 42369 [DDD]
Rossini, G.:Guillaume Tell, w. C. Studer (sop), C. Merritt (ten), R. Muti (cnd), La Scala Orch, La Scala Chorus [I] *(rec live, 12/7/88)* Philips 4-▲ 422391-2 [DDD]
Verdi, G.:Attila, w. S. Studer (sop), N. Shicoff (ten), S. Ramey (bass), R. Muti (cnd), La Scala Orch, La Scala Chorus [I] EMI Classics 2-▲ CDCB 49952 [DDD]
Verdi, G.:Giovanna d'Arco, w. Edita Gruberova (sop), Salvatore Fisichella (ten), G.-F. Masini (cnd), Vienna SO *(rec live, 1985)* Serenissima 2-▲ SER 360133
Verdi, G.:La traviata, w. E. Gruberova (sop), N. Shicoff (ten), C. Rizzi (cnd), London SO, Ambrosian Singers Teldec 2-▲ 9031-76348-2 PL
Verdi, G.:La traviata (sels), w. E. Gruberova (sop), N. Shicoff (ten), C. Rizzi (cnd), London SO [I] Teldec ▲ 4509-91975-2
Verdi, G.:Il trovatore, w. R. Kabaivanska (sop), M. Cortez (ten), F. Bonisolli (ten), B. Bartoletti (cnd), Berlin State Opera Orch, Berlin State Opera Chorus [I] Acanta 2-▲ CD 43301 [DDD]

Zanchetta, Renato (sgr)
Giordano, U.:Fedora, w. Mirella Freni (sop—Principessa Fedora), Adelina Scarabelli (sop—Contessa Olga), Silvia Mazzoni (mez—Dimitri), Monica Minarelli (sgr—Savoiardo), Placido Domingo (ten—Conte Loris), Ernesto Gavazzi (ten—Desiré), Aldo Bottion (ten—Barone Rouvel), Alessandro Corbelli (bar—Siriex), Luigi Roni (bass—Cirillo), Silvostro Sammaritano (bass—Baroff), Alfredo Giacomotti (bass—Gretch), Ernesto Panariello (bass—Lorek), Vincenzo Alaimo (sgr—Nicola), Arnold Bosman (sgr—Boleslao), Bruno Capisani (sgr—Sergio), Renato Zanchetta (sgr—Michele), G. Gavazzeni (cnd), La Scala Orch, La Scala Chorus *(rec La Scala, Apr 5, 1993)* Legato 2-▲ LCD 213-2 [ADD]

Zancu, Dan (bass)
Puccini, G.:La Bohème, w. Elvira Cirje-Druica (sop—Musetta), Eugenia Moldoveanu (sop—Mimi), Andrei Borsos (ten—Parpignol), Constantin Gabor (ten—Alcindoro), Ludovic Spiess (ten—Rodolfo), Lucian Marinescu (bar—Schaunard), David Ohanesian (bar—Marcello), Pompei Harasteanu (bass—Benoit), Dan Zancu (bass—Colline), C. Petrovici (cnd), Romanian Opera Orch, Romanian Opera Chorus *(rec 1982)* Vox Box 2-▲ CDX 5156

Zanelli, Renato (ten)
Renato Zanelli *(rec between 1919–1929)* Pearl ▲ PEA 9028 [AAD]
Rich & Rare:The Voice of Margaret Sheridan, w. Margaret Sheridan (sop), Aureliano Pertile (ten), Hubert Greenslade (pno), Carlo Sabajno (cnd), La Scala Orch, Queens Hall Orch *(rec 1926–29)* Time Machine ▲ 0100

Zanetti, Monique (sop)
Campra, A.:Messe de Requiem, w. E. Baudry (sop), J. Benet (ten), J. Elwes (ten), S. Varcoe (bar), P. Herreweghe (cnd), La Chapelle Royale Orch [L] Harmonia Mundi France ▲ HMC 901251
Charpentier, M.-A.:Le Malade imaginaire, w. C. Brua (sop), N. Rime (sop), D. Visse (ct), H. Crook (ten), J.-F. Gardeil (bar), W. Christie (cnd), Les Arts Florissants [F] Harmonia Mundi France ▲ HMC 901336
Charpentier, M.-A.:Médée, w. Isabelle Desrochers (sop—Cleone), Lorraine Hunt (sop—Medee), Noemi Rime (sop—Nerine), Monique Zanetti (sop—Creuse), Mark Padmore (ten—Jason), François Bazola (bar—Arcas), Jean-Marc Salzmann (bar—Oronte), Bernard Deletre (bass-Creon), W. Christie (cnd), Les Arts Florissants Erato 3-▲ 96558-2
Hasse, J.A.:Motets, w. Jennifer Lane (mez), M. Gester (cnd), Parlement de Musique—Gentes barbarae, Tartarae turbae; Alta nubes illustrata; Salva R. in A; Salva R. in G Opus 111 ▲ OPS 30-100
Perti, G.A.:Gesù al sepolcro, w. L. M. Akerlund (sop), C. Cavina (alt), M. Cecchetti (ten), A. W. Schultze (bass), S. Vartolo (cnd), San Petronio Cappella Musicale Orch [I] Tactus ▲ TC 661601

Zanibelli (sgr)
Verdi, G.:Il trovatore, w. Katia Ricciarelli (sop), Richard Tucker (ten), Renato Bruson (bar), A. Erede (cnd), Parma Teatro Regio Orch *(rec Parma, 1971)* Golden Age of Opera 2-▲ GAO 193/194

Zannini, Laura (mez)
Rossini, G.:L'italiana in Algeri, w. T. Berganza (sop), U. Benelli (ten), E. Dara (bar), A. Romero (bar), P. Montarsolo (bass), C. Abbado (cnd), Florence Teatro Comunale Orch, Florence Teatro Comunale Chorus *(rec 1973)* Great Opera Performances ▲ GOP 740

Zanolli, A. (sop)
Verdi, G.:La traviata, w. M. Callas (sop), L. Mandelli (sop), G. Raimondi (ten), E. Bastianini (bar), C. M. Giulini (cnd), La Scala Orch, La Scala Chorus *(rec live 1/19/56)* Myto 2-▲ MCD 89003 (m) [ADD]

Zanolli, Silvana (sop)
Donizetti, G.:La favorita, w. G. Simionato (mez), G. Raimondi (ten), M. Zanasi (bar), N. Zaccaria (bass), F. Previtali (cnd), Naples Teatro San Carlo Orch, Naples Teatro San Carlo Chorus [I] *(rec live, Naples 5/12/63)* Golden Age of Opera 2-▲ GAO 105/06 [ADD]

Zäpffel (sgr)
Handel, G.F.:The Choice of Hercules, w. Arleen Augér (sop), Venceslava Hruba-Freiberger (sop), Eberhard Büchner (ten), M. Pommer (cnd), Leipzig New Bach Collegium Musicum, Leipzig Univ Choir [E] Capriccio ▲ CDC 10019 [DDD]

Zara, Meredith (sop)
Mozart, W.A.:Mitridate, w. E. Gabry (sgr), G. Stanley (sgr), L. Hager (cnd), Salzburg Mozarteum Orch [I] *(rec live in Salzburg, Jan. 31, 1970)* Memories 2-▲ HR 4156/57 (m) [ADD]

Zaradníček, Jiří (ten)
Martinů, B.:The Epic of Gilgamesh, w. M. Machotková (sop), V. Zítek (ten), K. Průša (bass), J. Belohlávek (cnd), Prague SO, Czech Phil Chorus Supraphon ▲ SUP 11 1824 [ADD]

Zaramella (sgr)
Astorga, E. d':Stabat Mater, w. Elisabetta Battaglia (sop), Mapelli (sgr), Narita (sgr), Concentus Musicae Antiqua Nuova Era ("Ancient Music" series) ▲ NUO 7198 [DDD]

Zaramella, Sonia (alt)
Haydn, J.:Stabat Mater, w. R. Lampo (sop), V. Martino (ten), P. Turner (bass), D. Ferrari (cnd), Milan Sinfonietta, Concentus Musicae Antiquae Vocal Group Nuova Era ▲ NUO 7170 [DDD]

Zardo, Carlo (bass)
Catalani, A.:Dejanice, w. C. Basto (sop), M. L. Garbato (sop), O. Garaventa (ten), R. Massis (bar), J. Latham-König (cnd), Lucca Teatro Comunale del Giglio Orch, Lucca Teatro Comunale del Giglio Chorus [I] *(rec 9/6/85)* Bongiovanni 2-▲ GB 2031/32 [DDD]
Smareglia, A.:Nozze istrane, w. Maria Chiara (sop—Marussa), Eleonora Iancovich (cta—Luze), Ruggero Bondino (ten—Lorenzo), Alessandro Cassis (bar—Nicola), Alessandro Maddalena (bar—Biagio), Carlo Zardo (bass—Bara Menico), M. Wolf-Ferrari (cnd), Trieste Teatro Comunale Giuseppe Verdi Orch, Trieste Teatro Comunale G. Verdi Chorus *(rec Trieste, Feb 17, 1973)* Bongiovanni ("Il Mito dell'Opera" series) 2-▲ 1133/34-2 [ADD]

Zaremba, Elena (mez)
Rimsky-Korsakov, N.:Christmas Eve, w. Ekaterina Koudriavtchenko (sop), Vladimir Bogtatchov (ten), Alexei Maslennikov (ten), Viatcheslav Voinarovski (ten), Viatcheslav Verestnikov (bar), Maxime Mikhailov (bass), Stanislav Souleimanov (bass), M. Yurovski (cnd), Moscow Forum Theater Orch, Yurloff Academic Choir Russian Season 4-▲ CMX 388054
Shostakovich, D.:Lady Macbeth of Mtsensk, w. M. Ewing (sop), P. Langridge (ten), H. Zednik (ten), A. Haugland (bass), A. Kotcherga (bass), K. Moll (bass), S. Larin (bass), M.-W. Chung (cnd), Bastille Opera Orch, Bastille Opera Chorus Deutsche Grammophon 2-▲ 437511-2
Wagner, R.:Das Rheingold, w. Gabriele Fontana (sop—Woglinde), Nancy Gustafson (sop—Freia), Ildiko Komlosi (mez—Wellgunde), Hanna Schwarz (mez—Fricka), Elena Zaremba (mez—Erda), Margareta Hintermeier (cta—Flosshilde), Kim Begley (ten—Loge), Peter Schreier (ten—Mime), Thomas Sunnegardh (ten—Froh), Robert Hale (bass-bar—Wotan), Walter Fink (bass—Fafner), Franz-Josef Kapellmann (bass—Alberich), Jan-Hendrik Rootering (bass—Fasolt), Eike Wilm Schulte (bass—Donner), C. von Dohnányi (cnd), Cleveland Orch *(rec Severance Hall, Cleveland, Ohio, Dec 1993)* London 2-▲ 443690-2

Zareska, Eugenia (cta)
Mahler, G.:Sym 2, w. E. Selig (sop), C. Schuricht (cnd), Paris National Orch, Paris National Chorus [G] *(rec live, Paris 2/20/58)* Melodram ("Connaisseur" series) 2-▲ CD 27504 (m) [AAD]
Martin, F.:Pilate, w. Ariette Chedel (cta), Eric Tappy (ten), Derrik Olsen (bar), Jean-Christoph Benoit (bar), E. Ansermet (cnd), Swiss Romande Orch, Lausanne Pro Arte Choir Cascavelle 2-▲ CVL 2006 [ADD]

Zarmeba, Eléna (mez)
Mussorgsky, M.:Boris Godunov, w. V. Valente (sop—Xenia), E. Gorochovskaya (mez—Nurse), L. Nichiteanu (mez—Fyodor), E. Zarmeba (mez—Hostess), M. Lipovšek (cta—Marina), P. Langridge (ten—Prince Shuisky), H. Wildhaber (ten—Misail), A. Fedin (ten—Simpleton), S. Leiferkus (bar—Rangoni), A. Kotcherga (bass—B. Godounov), A. Shagidullin (bass—Shchelkalov), S. Ramey (bass—Pimen), S. Larin (bass—Girgory), G. Nikolsky (bass—Varlaam), C. Abbado (cnd), Berlin PO, Tölz Boys' Choir, Berlin Radio Chorus, Slovak Phil Chorus *(rec Nov. 7-30, 1993)* Sony Classical 3-▲ S3K 58977 [DDD]

Zarrelli, Gioacchino (bar)
Rossini, G.:La pietra del paragone, w. Tiziana Carraro (sop—Fulvia), Elisabetta Gutierrez (mez—Baronessa Aspasia), Sara Mingardo (cta—Clarice), William Matteuzzi (ten—Giocondo), Marco Camastra (bar—Pacuvio), Pietro Spagnoli (bar—Conte Asdrubale), Gioacchino Zarrelli (bar—Fabrizio), Josè Fardilha (bass—Macrobio), B. Aprea (cnd), Graz SO, Sluk Chamber Chorus Bratislava *(rec 1993)* Bongiovanni 2-▲ GB 2179/80 [DDD]

Zawisza, P. (bar)
Weisgall, H.:Six Characters in Search of an Author, w. E. Byrne (sop—Stepdaughter), S. Foster (sop—Prompter), E. Furtal (sop—Coloratura), J. King (mez—Mezzo), N. Maultsby (mez—Mother), P. LoVerne (cta—Madame Pace), D. Pritchett (alt—Wardrobe Mistress), B. Fowler (ten—Tenore Boffo), K. Anderson (ten—Director), A. Schroeder (bar—Accompanist), P. Zawisza (bar—Stage Manager), R. Orth (bar—Father), G. Lehman (bar—Son), M. Wadsworth (b-bar—Basso Cantante), L. Schaenen (cnd), Chicago Lyric Opera Orch, Lyric Opera Center Chorus *(rec Chicago, June 14 & 16, 1990)* New World 2-▲ 80454-2

Zbrueva, Evgenia (cta)
The World of Singing, Vol. 2:Singers of Imperial Russia, w. Nina Koshetz (sop), Nicolai Figner (ten), Feodor Chaliapin (bass), Nina Friede (sgr), Maria Kouznetsova (sgr), Anastasia Vialtzeva (sgr) Enterprise ("Vocal Archives" series) 2-▲ ENT VA 2102

Zbytovská, Eva (sgr)
Bruckner, A.:Mass 3, w. Dagmar Masková (sgr), Vladimír Nacházel (sgr), Jiří Novotný (sgr), Jiří Seiler (sgr), Jiří Uherek (sgr), Jan Votava (trbn), Josef Kšica (org), Josef Pancík (cnd), Prague Chamber Choir Orfeo ▲ 327 951 [DDD]
Bruckner, A.:Motets, w. Dagmar Masková (sgr), Vladimír Nacházel (sgr), Jiří Novotný (sgr), Jiří Seiler (sgr), Jiří Uherek (sgr), Jan Votava (trbn), Josef Kšica (org), Josef Pancík (cnd), Prague Chamber Choir—Locus iste; Afferentur regi; Ave Maria (2); Pange lingua; Pange lingua (phrygisch); Tantum ergo (2); Libera me; Os iusti; Virga jesse; Vexilla regis; Christus factus est; Tota pulchra es Maria; Ecce sacerdos magnus Orfeo ▲ 327 951 [DDD]

Zeani, Virginia (sop)
Classics Go to the Movies, Vol. 5, w. Hannes Käster (org), Salzburg Mozarteum Orch, Bavarian RSO, Ludovic Spiess (ten), Rumanian Opera Orch, Rumanian Radio-TV Studio Orch, Sofia PO, Budapest SO, Philharmonia Orch LaserLight ▲ 15 645
Mascagni, P.:Il piccolo Marat, w. Clara Betner (mez), Umberto Borso (ten), Nicola Rossi-Lemeni (bass), O. de Fabritiis (cnd), Teatro La Gran Guardia Orch, Teatro La Gran Guardia Chorus [I] *(rec live, 10/26/61)* Fonè 2-▲ 88 F 17-37 [ADD]
Massenet, J.:Manon (sels), w. A. Kraus (ten), U. Rapalo (cnd), Naples Teatro San Carlo Orch—2 tenor arias & 2 soprano-tenor duets *(rec live, Naples 2/29/64)* Bongiovanni 2-▲ GB 550/51
Massenet, J.:Werther, w. A. Kraus (ten), D. Trimarchi (bar), M. Basiola (bar), A. Votto (cnd), *(orch unknown) (rec Palermo, 1971)* Great Opera Performances 2-▲ GOP 749
Mercadante, S.:Elisa e Claudio, w. Agostino Lazzari (ten), Domenico Trimarchi (bar), Ugo Trama (bass), Fiorini (sgr), U. Rapalo (cnd), Naples Teatro San Carlo Orch, Naples Teatro San Carlo Chorus *(rec live, Naples, 1/31/71)* Melodram 2-▲ MEL 27099 [ADD]
Il mito dell'opera Bongiovanni ▲ 1112
Puccini, G.:Tosca, w. Virginia Zeani (sop—Floria Tosca), Emilia Oprea (mez—Shepherd), Nicolae Andreescu (ten—Spoletta), Corneliu Fanateanu (ten—Mario Cavaradossi), Nicolae Herlea (bar—Baron Scarpia), Gheorghe Crasnaru (bass—Cesare Angelotti), Constantin Gabor (bass—Sacristan), Pompei Harasteanu (bass—Jailer), Adrian Stefanescu (bass—Sciarrone), C. Trailescu (cnd), Romanian Opera Orch, Romanian Opera Chorus *(rec Sept 1977)* Vox Box 2-▲ CDX 5153
Rossini, G.:Zelmira, w. Anna Maria Rota (cta), Enrico Campi (bass), Guido Mazzini (bass), Paolo Washington (bass), Gastone Limarilli (sgr), Giuseppe Moretti (sgr), Nicola Tagger (sgr), C. Franci (cnd), *(orch unknown)* Great Opera Performances 2-▲ GOP 780

Zeani, Virginia (sop) (cont.)
Verdi, G.:Alzira, w. G. Cecchele (ten), C. MacNeil (bar), C. Cava (bass), F. Capuana (cnd), Rome Opera Orch, Rome Opera Chorus [I] *(rec live, 3/16/67)* Verona 2-▲ 27042/43 (m) [AAD]
Verdi, G.:Alzira, w. G. Cecchele (ten), C. MacNeil (bar), C. Cava (bass), F. Capuana (cnd), Rome Opera Orch, Rome Opera Chorus [I] *(rec live 3/16/67)* Melodram 2-▲ MEL 27013 (m) [AAD]
Verdi, G.:La traviata, w. G. Raimondi (ten), U. Savarese (bar), A. Questa (cnd), Naples Teatro San Carlo Orch, Naples Teatro San Carlo Chorus [I] *(rec live, Naples 8/11/57)* Golden Age of Opera 2-▲ GAO 103/04 [ADD]
Verdi, G.:La traviata, w. Elena Simionescu (sop—Annina), Virginia Zeani (sop—Violetta Valery), Elisabeta Neculce-Cartis (mez—Flora Bervoix), Ion Buzea (ten—Alfredo Germont), Vasile Moldoveanu (ten—Gastone/Viconte de Letorieres/Giuseppe), Teodor Panea (ten—Flora's Servant), Constantin Dumitru (bar—Commissioner/Baron Douphol), Nicolae Herlea (bar—Giorgio Germont), Valentin Loghin (bass—Marchese D'Obigny), Nicolae Rafael (bass—Doctor Grenvil), J. Bobescu (cnd), Romanian Opera Orch, Stelian Olariu (cnd), Romanian Opera Chorus *(rec 1968)* Vox Box 2-▲ CDX 5154
Verdi, G.:La traviata (sels), w. Buzea (sgr), Herlea (sgr), J. Bobescu (cnd), Bucharest State Opera Orch [I] Allegretto ▲ ACD 8084 [ADD] ■ ACS 8084
Virginia Zeani, w. various Italian orchs *(rec live, 1957-1969)* Bongiovanni ▲ GB 1060-2 [ADD]
Virginia Zeani, Soprano Arias, w. Nicola Rossi-Lemeni (bass), Turin Radio Orch [cnd:Fulvio Vernizzi] Melodram 2-▲ CDM 27013 (m) [AAD]

Zec, Nikolaus (bass)
Wagner, R.:Parsifal (sels), w. Fred Destal (bar—Amfortas), Herbert Alsen (bass—Gurnemanz), H. Knappertsbusch (cnd), Vienna State Opera Orch *(rec Nov. 1, 1937)* Koch Schwann 2-▲ SCH 314632 [ADD]
Wagner, R.:Das Rheingold (sels), w. A. Konetzni (sop—Fricka), J. Prohaska (bar—Wotan), N. Zec (b-bar—Fasolt), H. Alsen (bass—Fafner), J. Krips (cnd), Vienna State Opera Orch, Vienna State Opera Chorus *(rec Jan. 18, 1937)* Koch Schwann 2-▲ SCH 314592

Zecchillo, Giuseppe (bass)
Verdi, G.:Un ballo in maschera, w. R. Orlandi Malaspina (sop—Ameilia), D. Mazzuccato (sop—Oscar), A. Lazzarini (mez—Ulrica), L. Pavarotti (ten—Riccardo), M. Zanasi (bar—Renato), A. Zerbini (bass—Samuel), G. Casarini (bass—Tom), G. Zecchillo (bass—Sil) Golden Age of Opera 2-▲ GAO 164/65 [ADD]

Zedelius, Maria (sop)
Telemann, G.P.:St. Matthew Passion, w. A. Browner (alt), H.P. Blochwitz (ten), W. Schmidt (bar), A. Scharinger (bass), W. Seeliger (cnd), Darmstadt CO, Darmstadt Concert Choir Christophorus ▲ 77149 [DDD]

Zednik, Heinz (ten)
Berg, A.:Wozzeck, w. H. Behrens (sop), P. Langridge (ten), F. Grundheber (bar), A. Haugland (bass), C. Abbado (cnd), Vienna PO, Vienna State Opera Chorus, Vienna Boys' Choir [G] *(rec live, 6/88)* Deutsche Grammophon 2-▲ 423587-2 [DDD]
Berg, A.:Wozzeck, w. A. Silja (sop), G. Jahn (mez), H. Laubenthal (ten), E. Waechter (bar), C. von Dohnányi (cnd), Vienna PO London 2-▲ 417348-2 [DDD]
Mozart, W.A.:Entführung, w. E. Gruberova (sop), K. Battle (sop), G. Winbergh (ten), M. Talvela (bass), Will Quadflieg (nar), G. Solti (cnd), Vienna PO [G] London 2-▲ 417402-2 [DDD]
Prokofiev, S.:The Fiery Angel, w. N. Secunde (sop), R. Engert-Ely (mez), S. Lorenz (bar), K. Moll (bass), N. Järvi (cnd), Gothenburg SO, Gothenburg Sym Chorus [R] Deutsche Grammophon 2-▲ 431669-2 [DDD]
Schoenberg, A.:The Cabaret Songs, w. K. Leitner (pno) [G] Preiser ▲ 93401 [DDD]
Shostakovich, D.:Lady Macbeth of Mtsensk, w. M. Ewing (sop), E. Zaremba (mez), P. Langridge (ten), A. Haugland (bass), A. Kotcherga (bass), K. Moll (bass), S. Larin (bass), M.-W. Chung (cnd), Bastille Opera Orch, Bastille Opera Chorus Deutsche Grammophon 2-▲ 437511-2
Strauss, R.:Salome, w. E. Martón (sop), B. Fassbaender (mez/sop), R. Lewis (ten), B. Weikl (bar), Z. Mehta (cnd), Berlin PO *(rec live)* Sony Classical 2-▲ S2K 46717
Strauss, R.:Songs, w. K. Leitner (pno)—Krämerspiegel (12 songs), Op. 66 [G] Preiser ▲ 93401 [DDD]
Wagner, R.:Das Rheingold, w. H. Schwarz (mez), H. Becht (bar), D. McIntyre (b-bar), P. Boulez (cnd), Bayreuth Festival Orch, Bayreuth Festival Chorus [G] Philips 2-▲ 434421-2 [DDD]
Wagner, R.:Das Rheingold, w. M. Lipovšek (mez), J. Rappé (ten), P. Haage (ten), A. Schmidt (bar), T. Adam (b-bar), H. Tschammer (bass), K. Rydl (bass), J. Morris (bass), B. Haitink (cnd), Bavarian RSO [G] EMI Classics 2-▲ CDCB 49853 [DDD]
Wagner, R.:Das Rheingold, w. B. Svendén (sop), C. Ludwig (mez), S. Jerusalem (ten), E. Wlaschiha (bar), J. Morris (bass), J. Levine (cnd), Metropolitan Opera Orch [G] Deutsche Grammophon 3-▲ 427607-2 [DDD]
Wagner, R.:Siegfried, w. G. Jones (sop), H. Becht (bar), D. McIntyre (b-bar), P. Boulez (cnd), Bayreuth Festival Orch, Bayreuth Festival Chorus [G] Philips 3-▲ 434423-2 [DDD]
Werfel, A.M.:Songs, w. K. Leitner (pno)—Die stille Stadt; In meines Vaters Garten; Laue Sommernacht; Bei dir ist es traut; Ich wandle unter Blumen; Der Erkennende; Ekstase [G] Preiser ▲ 93401 [DDD]

Zeller, Richard (bar)
Thomson, V.:Lord Byron, w. J. Ommerlé (sop), D. Fortunato (mez), M. Lord (ten), R. Johnson (bar), J. Bolle (cnd), Monadnock Music Festival Orch [E] *(rec live, Aug. 31 & Sept. 2, 1991)* Koch International Classics 2-▲ KIC 7124-2 [DDD]

Zellweger, Daniel (alt)
Kraft, Walter:Christus, w. Anna Senn-Dähler (sop), Barbara Künzler (sop), Barbara Sutter (sop), Christine Guy (alt), Heidi Uhlmann (alt), Matthias Senn (ten), Mikoto Usami (ten), Wolfgang Pailer (bass), Heinz Suter (bass), Klaus Knall (cnd), Evangelische Singgemeinde Choirs *(rec Ostdorf bei Balingen, Oct. 8-11, 1986)* Cantate 2-▲ 58004 [DDD]

Ze-Luis (sgr)
Chevalier, C.:Music of, w. Teca Calazans (sgr), Regina Machado (sgr), Nigel Scragg (fl/a sax), Rosihna de Valenca (gtr), Jean-Yves Candela (pno), Wilson das Neves (perc), Regina Machado (perc), Silvano Michelino (perc)—Comme d'habitude; Couleur café; Une histoire d'amour; Les feuilles mortes; Les moulins de mon coeur; Syracuse; Je t'aimerai; Ces petits rien; La valse des lilas; L'absent; Que reste-il de nos amours; Un homme et une femme *(rec Studio Bastille)* Iris ▲ 010 [DDD]

Zemenkova, Elena (sop)
Rimsky-Korsakov, N.:Snow Maiden, w. Stefka Evstatieva (sop—Kupava), Elena Zemenkova (sop—Snow Maiden), Alexandrina Milcheva (mez—Spring Fairy), Vessela Zorova (mez—wife), Stefka Mineva (alt—Lehl), Avram Andreev (ten—Tsar), Lyubomir Dyakovski (ten—Cottager, Sprite), Lyubomir Videnov (bar—Misgir), Nicola Ghiuselev (bass—King), S. Angelov (cnd), Bulgarian RSO, Bulgarian National Chorus *(rec Sofia, 1985)* Capriccio 3-▲ 10749-51 [DDD]

Zempléni, Maria (sop)
Gluck, C.W.:Orfeo ed Euridice, w. V. Kincses (sop), J. Hamari (mez), E. Lukács (cnd), Hungarian State Opera Orch, Hungarian State Opera Chorus LaserLight ▲ 14113 [DDD]
Vivaldi, A.:L'Olimpiade (sels), w. T. Takács (mez), Horváth (sgr), Káplán (sgr), L. Miller (bar), I. Gáti (bar), K. Kováts (bass), F. Szekeres (cnd), Hungarian State Orch, Budapest Madrigal Choir [I] White Label ▲ HRC 073 [ADD]

Zenatello, Giovanni (ten)
The Collected Recordings, Vol. 1 *(rec 1903, 1905-11)* Pearl 4-▲ PEA 9073 [AAD]
The Complete Destinn, w. Emmy Destinn (sop), E. Caruso (ten), J. McCormack (ten), K. Jörn (ten), G. Martinelli (ten), et al. Supraphon 12-▲ SUP 112136 [ADD]
Giovanni Zenatello (1876-1949), w. Rosario Bourdon (cnd), Carlo Sabajno (cnd) *(rec 1926-1930 for HMV)* Preiser ("Lebendige Vergangenheit" series) ▲ PRE 89038 (m) [AAD]
The Harold Wayne Collection, Vol. 17:The Fonotipia Recordings, w. (rec. 1908-10) Symposium ▲ SYM 1148
The Harold Wayne Collection, Vol. 19:G. Zenatello—The Fonotipia Recordings, w. *(rec 1906-12)* Symposium ▲ SYM 1168
Leoncavallo, R.:Pagliacci (sels), w. Enrico Caruso (ten), Antonio Paoli (ten), Amedeo Bassi (ten), Hermann Jadlowker (ten), Fernand Ansseau (ten), Hipolito Lazaro (ten), Nino (Filippo) Piccaluga (ten), Mario Chamlee (ten), Giacomo Lauri-Volpi (ten), Miguel Fleta (ten), Giovanni Martinelli (ten), Aureliano Pertile (ten), Georges Thill (ten), Alessandro Valente (ten), Francesco Merli (ten), Lauritz Melchior (ten), Marcel Wittrisch (ten), Joseph Schmidt (ten), Beniamino Gigli (ten), Giuseppe Lugo (ten), Helge Roswaenge (ten), Jussi Bjoerling (ten)—23 versions of the tenor aria "Vesti la giubba" *(rec 1907-1944)* Bongiovanni ▲ GB 1071 [ADD]

▲ = CD ♦ = Enhanced CD Δ = MD ■ = Cassette Tape □ = DCC

Zenatello, Giovanni (ten) (cont.)
Verdi, G.:Arias—Il Trovatore:Ai nostri monti (w. Parsi–Pettinella); Tace la notte; Mal reggendo (w. Bruno); Di quella pira; Ah, quell'infame (w. Bruno & Mazzoleni); La Traviata:De miei bollenti spiriti; Questa donna conoscete?; Parigi o cara (w. Cannetti); Gran' Dio, morir si giovane (w. Cannetti); Un ballo in maschera:La rivedro nell'estasi; Di tu se fedele; Non sai tu (w. Burzio); La riverdro nell'estasi; Di tu se fedele; Non sai tu (w. Mazzoleni); La forza del destino:O tu che in seno; Aida:Gia i sacerdoti (w. Frascani) Symposium ▲ SYM 1138
Verdi, G.:Un ballo in maschera (sels), w. Maria Caniglia (sop), Gina Cigna (sop), Fedora Barbieri (mez), Enrico Carusa (ten), Beniamino Gigli (ten), Carlo Galeffi (bar), Lawrence Tibbett (bar), *(various orchs & cnds) (rec 1911–43)* Grammofono 2000 ▲ GRM 78527 (m)
Verdi, G.:Otello (sels), w. Sabajno, Bellezza (cnd), La Scala Orch, Royal Opera House Orch Covent Garden, Royal Opera House Chorus Covent Garden Phonographe ("Great Voices" series) ▲ PHG 5048
Verdi, G.:Il trovatore (sels), w. J. Biel (ten), F. Tamagno (ten), L.-A. Escalaïs (ten), M. Gilion (ten), E. Caruso (ten), A. Paoli (ten), J. Sembach (ten), L. Slezak (ten), F. Constantino (ten), G. Martinelli (ten), B. De Muro (ten), N. Fusati (ten), N. Piccaluga (ten), G. Lauri-Volpi (ten), A. Pertile (ten), E. Bergamaschi (ten), R. Tauber (ten), J. O'Sullivan (ten), H. Roswaenge (ten), G. Taccani (ten), V. Lois (ten), H. Lazaro (ten), A. Lindi (ten), A. Cortis (ten), F. Merli (ten), F. Völker (ten), J. Kiepura (ten), J. Schmidt (ten), J. Bjoerling (ten), B. Gigli (ten), A. Salvarezza (ten), J. Soler (ten), M. Filippeschi (ten)—34 performances of the Act III tenor aria "Di quella pira!," *(rec from 1903–1956)* Bongiovanni ▲ GB 1051 [AAD]
The World of Singing, Vol 4:The Italian School Part 1:Tenors before World War I, Book 2, w. Edoardo Garbin (ten), Fiorello Giraud (ten), Florencio Costantino (ten), Antonio Paoli (ten), Giuseppe Borgatti (ten), Carlo Albani (ten), Enrico Caruso (ten), Amedeo Bassi (ten), Piero Schivazzi (ten), Elvino Ventura (ten), Giovanni Zenatello (ten) Enterprise ("Vocal Archives" series) 3-▲ ENT VA 2107

Zennaro, Iorio (ten)
Mascagni, P.:Messa di gloria, w. P. Spagnoli (bar), F. Colusso (cnd), Seicentonovecento Ensemble Musicaimmagine ▲ MR 10001 [DDD]
Rossini, G.:Armida, w. R. Fleming (sop), C. Bosi (ten), B. Fowler (ten), J. Francis (ten), D. Kaasch (ten), G. Kunde (ten), I. D'Arcangelo (bass), S. Zadvorny (bass), D. Gatti (cnd), Bologna Teatro Comunale Orch, Bologna Teatro Comunale Chorus *(rec Pesaro, Italy, Aug. 6–17, 1993)* Sony Classical 3-▲ S3K 58968 [DDD]
Rossini, G.:L'inganno felice, w. A. Felle (sop), F. Previati (bar), N. de Carolis (b-bar), D. Serraiocco (b-bar), M. Viotti (cnd), English CO [I] Claves 8-▲ CD 9200 [DDD]
Rossini, G.:L'inganno felice, w. Amelia Felle (sop), Fabio Previati (bar), Natale de Carolis (b-bar), Danilo Serraiocco (bass), M. Viotti (cnd), English CO Claves ▲ 50-9211
Rossini, G.:L'occassione fa il ladro, w. M. Bayo (sop), F. Provvisionato (mez), F. Massa (ten), F. Previati (bar), N. de Carolis (b-bar), M. Viotti (cnd), English CO [I] Claves 8-▲ CD 9200 [DDD]
Rossini, G.:L'occassione fa il ladro, w. Maria Bayo (sop), Francesca Provvisionato (mez), Fulvio Massa (ten), Fabio Previati (bar), Natale de Carolis (b-bar), M. Viotti (cnd), English CO Claves 2-▲ 50-9208/9

Zentai, Anna (sop)
Kacsóh, P.:János Vitéz, w. Mária Gyurkovics (sop), Anna Zentai (sop—Iluska), Tivadar Bilicsi (sgr), Hilda Gobbi (sgr), Sándor Pethes (sgr—Bartoló), Róbert Ilosfalvy (ten—Kukorica), György Melis (bar—Bagó), György Radnai (bar—Strázsamester), László Domahidy (bass—Csősz), E. Lukács (cnd), Hungarian State Opera Orch, Hungarian Radio-TV Chorus *(rec Budapest, 1961)* Classical Diamonds 2-▲ CLD 4011-12 [AAD]

Zerbini, Antonio (bass)
Cilea, F.:Adriana Lecouvreur, w. L. Gencer (sop—Adriana), A. Lazzarini (mez—Princess), F. Ricciardi (ten—Abbot), A. Zambon (ten—Maurizio), E. Sordello (bar—Michonnet), A. Zerbini (bass—Prince), O. de Fabritiis (cnd), Naples Teatro San Carlo Orch, Naples Teatro San Carlo Chorus *(rec Dec. 17, 1966)* Golden Age of Opera 2-▲ GAO 143/44 [ADD]
Cilea, F.:L'Arlesiana, w. L. di Lelio (sop), P. Tassinari (sop), F. Tagliavini (ten), G. Galli (bar), P. Silveri (bar), B. Carmassi (bass), A. Basile (cnd), Turin RAI Orch, Turin RAI Chorus *(rec 1951)* Cetra Classics ▲ CDO 21 [AAD]
Donizetti, G.:Lucia di Lammermoor, w. M. Callas (sop), G. Raimondi (ten), R. Panerai (bar), F. Molinari-Pradelli (cnd), Naples Teatro San Carlo Orch, Naples Teatro San Carlo Chorus [I] *(rec live, 3/22/56)* Myto ▲ 2 MCD 90319 (m) [ADD]
Massenet, J.:Manon (sels), w. Mirella Freni (sop), Luciano Pavarotti (ten), Franco Ricciardi (ten), Wladimiro Ganzarolli (bar), Giuseppe Morresi (bass), Ida Farina (sgr), P. Maag (cnd), La Scala Orch, La Scala Chorus *(rec live, Milan, 1969)* Budget ("The Greatest Voice in Opera" series) ▲ SYP 110
Verdi, G.:Un ballo in maschera, w. R. Orlandi Malaspina (sop—Ameilia), D. Mazzuccato (sop—Oscar), A. Lazzarini (mez—Ulrica), L. Pavarotti (ten—Riccardo), M. Zanasi (bar—Renato), A. Zerbini (bass—Samuel), G. Casarini (bass—Tom), G. Zecchillo (bass—Sil) Golden Age of Opera 2-▲ GAO 164/65 [ADD]
Verdi, G.:Rigoletto, w. L. Pagluighi (sop—Gilda), I. Colasanti (mez—Maddalena), F. Tagliavini (ten—Duca), A. Albertini (bar—Il Cavaliere Marullo), G. Taddei (bar—Rigoletto), G. Neri (bass—Sparafucile), A. Zerbini (bass—Conte di Monterone), A. Questa (cnd), Turin RSO, Turin Radio Chorus *(rec 1953)* Cetra Classics 2-▲ CDO 11 [AAD]

Zerial, Dario (ten)
Smareglia, A.:La falena, w. Leyla Gencer (sop—La Falena), Rita Lantieri (sop—Albina, sua figlia), Ruggero Bondino (ten—Re Stellio), Dario Zerial (ten—Il ladro), Mario D'Anna (bar—Il vecchio Uberto), Aurio Tomicich (bass—Morio), Giuseppe Botta (sgr—Un marinaio), G. Gavazzeni (cnd), Trieste Teatro Comunale Giuseppe Verdi Orch, Trieste Teatro Comunale G. Verdi Chorus *(rec Trieste, Mar 18, 1876)* Bongiovanni 2-▲ GB 1131/32

Zeumer, Gerti (sop)
Mahler, G.:Syms, w. J. Blegen (sop), B. Hendricks (sop), M. Price (sop), H. Wittek (trb), A. Baltsa (mez), C. Ludwig (mez), K. Riegel (ten), H. Prey (bar), A. Schmidt (bar), J. Van Dam (b-bar), L. Bernstein (cnd), New York PO, Royal Concertgebouw Orch, Vienna PO, Westminster Choir, New York Choral Artists, Brooklyn Boys' Choir, Vienna Boys' Choir, Vienna State Opera Chorus, Vienna Singverein Deutsche Grammophon 13-▲ 435162-2 [DDD]
Mahler, G.:Sym 8, w. J. Blegen (sop), M. Price (sop), A. Baltsa (mez), K. Riegel (ten), H. Prey (bar), A. Schmidt (bar), J. Van Dam (b-bar), L. Bernstein (cnd), Vienna PO, Vienna State Opera Chorus, Vienna Boys' Choir *(rec Salzburg Festival, 1975)* Deutsche Grammophon 2-▲ 435102-2 [ADD]
Schubert, Franz:Stabat mater, w. D. Ellenbeck (ten), E. G. Schramm (bass), R. Bader (cnd), Berlin RSO, Berlin Radio Chorus Koch Schwann ▲ CD 313 055 [DDD]

Zhang, Jianyi (ten)
Liszt, F.:A Faust Sym, w. E. Inbal (cnd), Berlin RSO, Berlin Radio Chorus Denon ▲ CO 75634 [DDD]

Zhou, Zheng (bar)
Somary, J.:Songs of Innocence, w. Andrea Matthews (sop), J. Somary (cnd), Bronx Arts Ensemble Premier ▲ PRCD 1042 [DDD]

Zickwolf, Udo (nar)
Platz, R.H.:Dunkles Haus, w. Maria Husmann (sop—Woman), Michael Busch (bar—Man), Udo Zickwolf (nar—Child/Bird/Man), Carin Levine (a fl/b fl), R. Platz (cnd), Marstall Ensemble of the Bavarian State Opera *(rec 1991)* Thorofon ▲ CTH 2170

Zídek, Ivo (ten)
Dvořák, A.:Rusalka, w. Milada Šubrtová (sop), Eduard Haken (bass), Z. Chalabala (cnd), Prague National Theater Orch, Prague National Theater Chorus Supraphon 2-▲ SUP 0013 [AAD]
Fibich, Z.:The Bride of Messina, w. G. Benackova (sop), L. Marova (mez), F. Jílek (cnd), Prague National Theater Orch, Prague National Theater Chorus Supraphon 2-▲ SUP 111492 [ADD]
Ivo Zídek Operatic Recital, w. Prague National Theater Orch Supraphon ▲ SUP 3189
Janácek, L.:Jenůfa, w. Libuse Domininská (sop—Jenufa), Nadeshda Kniplová (sop—Kostelnicka), Vilém Přibyl (ten—Laca), Ivo Zídek (ten—Steva), B. Gregor (cnd), Prague National Theater Orch, Prague National Theater Chorus EMI Classics 2-▲ CDMB 65476
Janácek, L.:The Makropulos Affair, w. Libuse Prylova (sop), Helena Tattermuschová (sop), Rudolf Vanasek (ten), B. Gregor (cnd), Prague National Orch, Prague National Theater Chorus *(rec mid 1960's)* Supraphon 2-▲ SUP 108351 [AAD]
Martinů, B.:Julietta, w. M. Tauberová (sop), J. Krombholc (cnd), Prague National Theater Orch, Prague National Theater Chorus [Cz] *(rec 1964)* Supraphon 3-▲ 10 8176-2 [AAD]
Smetana, B.:The Bartered Bride, w. Drahomira Tikalová (sop), Eduard Haken (bass), Z. Chalabala (cnd), Prague National Theater Orch, Prague National Theater Chorus Supraphon 2-▲ SUP 0040 [AAD]

Ziegler, Delores (mez)
Bach, J.S.:Mass in b, BWV 232, w. A. M. Blasi (sop), J. Rappé (cta), K. Equiluz (ten), R. Holl (bass), N. Harnoncourt (cnd), Vienna Concentus Musicus, Arnold Schoenberg Choir [L] Teldec 2-▲ 2292-42676-2 [DDD]
Bach, J.S.:Mass in b, BWV 232, w. S. McNair (sop), G. Simpson (mez), J. Aler (ten), W. Stone (bar), T. Paul (bass), R. Shaw (cnd), Atlanta SO, Atlanta Chamber Chorus [L] Telarc 2-▲ CD 80233 [DDD]
Bertoni, F.:Orfeo ed Euridice, w. Cecilia Gasdia (sop—Euridice), Delores Ziegler (mez—Orfeo), Bruce Ford (ten—Imeneo), C. Scimone (cnd), Venice Solisti, John McCarthy (cnd), Ambrosian Opera Chorus *(rec Vicenza, Italy, Aug 3–7, 1990)* Arts Music ▲ 47118-2 [DDD]
Donizetti, G.:Anna Bolena, w. Edita Gruberová (sop), Stefano Palatchi (bass), E. Boncompagni (cnd), Hungarian RSO, Hungarian Radio Chorus Nightingale Classics 3-▲ NIG 70565
Donizetti, G.:Roberto Devereux, w. Edita Gruberová (sop), Don Bernardini (sgr), Ettore Kim (sgr), F. Haider (cnd), Strasbourg PO, Rhine Opera Chorus Nightingale Classics 2-▲ NIG 70563
Haydn, J.:Mass 10, "Kriegsmesse", "Paukenmesse", w. Sylvia McNair (sop), Hans-Peter Blochwitz (ten), Andreas Schmidt (bar), J. Levine (cnd), Berlin SO, Berlin RIAS Chamber Choir Deutsche Grammophon ▲ 435853-2
Mozart, W.A.:Clemenza, w. Christine Barbaux (sop—Servilia), Carol Vaness (sop—Viellia), Martha Senn (mez—Annio), Delores Ziegler (mez—Sesto), Gösta Winbergh (ten—Tito), László Polgár (bass—Publio), R. Muti (cnd), Vienna PO, Vienna State Opera Chorus *(rec live, Salzburg Festival, 1988)* EMI Classics 2-▲ CDCB 55489
Mozart, W.A.:Clemenza, w. L. Popp (sop), R. Ziesack (sop), A. Murray (mez), P. Langridge (ten), L. Polgar (bass), T. Grabowski (hpd), C. Hermann (vc), N. Harnoncourt (cnd), Zurich Opera Orch, Zurich Opera House Chorus Teldec 2-▲ 90857-2
Mozart, W.A.:Così fan tutte, w. Carol Vaness (sop), C. Watson (cta), J. Aler (ten), D. Duesing (bar), C. Desderi (bar), B. Haitink (cnd), London PO, Glyndebourne Festival Chorus EMI Classics 3-▲ CDCC 47727
Mozart, W.A.:Così fan tutte (sels), w. C. Margiono (sop), van der Walt (sop), G. Cachemaille (bar), N. Harnoncourt (cnd), Royal Concertgebouw Orch Teldec ▲ 9031-76455-2
Mozart, W.A.:Missa, K.317, w. S. McNair (sop), H.P. Blochwitz (ten), A. Schmidt (bar), J. Levine (cnd), Berlin SO, Berlin RIAS Chamber Choir Deutsche Grammophon ▲ 435853-2
Mozart, W.A.:Missa, K.427, w. Edith Wiens (sop), John Aler (ten), William Stone (bar), R. Shaw (cnd), Atlanta SO, Atlanta Sym Chorus [L] Telarc 2-▲ CD 80150 [DDD]
Mozart, W.A.:Requiem, w. A. Augér (sop), J. Hadley (ten), T. Krause (bar), R. Shaw (cnd), Atlanta SO, Atlanta Sym Chorus [L] Telarc ▲ CD 80128 [DDD]
Verdi, G.:Falstaff, w. Maureen O'Flynn (sop), Daniela Dessi (sop), Bernadette Manca di Nissa (mez), Ramon Vargas (ten), Ernesto Gavazzi (ten), Paolo Barbacini (ten), Juan Pons (bar), Roberto Frontali (bar), Luigi Roni (bass), R. Muti (cnd), La Scala Orch, La Scala Chorus *(rec Milan La Scala Theater, Italy, Mar. 29 & 31)* Sony Classical ▲ S2K 58961 [DDD]
Weber, C.M. von:Oberon, w. D. Voigt (sop), G. Lakes (ten), B. Heppner (ten), J. Conlon (cnd), Cologne PO, Cologne Opera Chorus EMI Classics 2-▲ CDCB 54739

Ziemba, K. (sgr)
Porter, C.:Fifty Million Frenchmen, w. H. McGillin (sgr), K. Criswell (sop), K. McClelland (sgr), S. Powell (sgr), J. Graae (sgr), J. Harder (sgr), S. Waara (sgr), P. Cass (sgr), J. LeClerc (sgr) [1991 studio cast] New World ▲ 80417-2 [DDD]

Ziesak, Ruth (sop)
Bach, J.S.:Christmas Oratorio, w. Monica Groop (alt), Christoph Pregardien (ten), Klaus Mertens (bass), R. Otto (cnd), Concerto Cologne, Frankfurt Vocal Ensemble *(rec Festeburgkirche Frankfurt, Jan 9–16, 1991 & May 12–1)* Capriccio 2-▲ 60025-2 [DDD]
Beethoven, L. van:Egmont (incidental music), w. U. Tukur (sgr), G. Albrecht (cnd), Hamburg State PO [G] Orfeo ▲ 288921 [DDD]
Beethoven, L. van:Fidelio (sels), w. Evelyn Herlitzius (sop—Leonore), Ruth Ziesak (sop—Marzelline), Stig Andersen (ten—Florestan), Herbert Lippert (ten—Jaquino), Albert Dohmen (bar—Don Pizarro), Andreas Kohn (bass—Don Fernando), Hans Tschammer (bass—Rocco), G. Solti (cnd), World Orch for Peace, London Voices—Finale Act II *(rec Victoria Hall, Geneva, July 5, 1995)* London ▲ 448901-2 [DDD]
Haydn, J.:Die Schöpfung, w. Ruth Ziesak (sop—Eve & Gabriel), Herbert Lippert (ten—Uriel), Rene Papé (bass—Raphael), Anton Scharinger (bass—Adam), G. Solti (cnd), Chicago SO, Chicago Sym Chorus London 2-▲ 443445-2 [DDD]
Hindemith, P.:Die Serenaden, w. Lajos Lencses (ob), Gunter Teuffel (va), Ansgar Schneider (vc) CPO ▲ CPO 999332
Humperdinck, E.:Hänsel und Gretel, w. H. Behrens (sop—Gertrud, the Stepmother), R. Ziesak (sop—Gretel), R. Joshua (sop—Sandman), C. Schäfer (sop—Dew Fairy), J. Larmore (mez—Hänsel), H. Schwarz (cta—Nibblewitch), B. Weikl (bar—Peter, the Father), D. Runnicles (cnd), Bavarian RSO, Tölz Boys' Choir *(rec Munich, Feb. 1994)* Teldec 2-▲ 94549-2 [DDD]
Mahler, G.:Sym 2, w. C. Hellekant (mez), H. Blomstedt (cnd), San Francisco SO, San Francisco Sym Chorus London ▲ 443350-2
Mozart:Missa Solemnis & Salieri:Te Deum (The Coronation Mass for Leopold II in Prague, September 1791), w. Vienna Academy, E. von Magnus (moz), H. Wildahaber (ten), G. Hornik (bass), Hugo Distler Chorus, Vienna Hofburg Chapel Choir Novalis ▲ 150087 [DDD]
Mozart, W.A.:Clemenza, w. L. Popp (sop), A. Murray (mez), D. Ziegler (mez), P. Langridge (ten), L. Polgar (bass), T. Grabowski (hpd), C. Hermann (vc), N. Harnoncourt (cnd), Zurich Opera Orch, Zurich Opera House Chorus Teldec 2-▲ 90857-2
Mozart, W.A.:Missa solemnis, K.337, w. E. von Magnus (alt), H. Wildhaber (ten), G. Hornik (bar), H. Hüttler (cant), M. Jankowitsch (cant), P. Jelosits (cant), I. Rainer (org), M. Haselböck (cnd), Vienna Academy, Vienna Hofburg Chapel Choir [L] *(rec Apr. 1992)* Novalis ▲ 150087 [DDD]
Mozart, W.A.:Requiem, w. Nancy Maultsby (mez), Richard Croft (ten), David Arnold (bar), M. Pearlman (cnd), Boston Baroque Orch [completion by Robert Levin; performed on period instruments] *(rec Campion Center, Weston, MA, Nov 2–3, 1994)* Telarc ▲ CD 80410 [DDD]
Mozart, W.A.:Zauberflöte, w. S. Jo (sop), U. Heilmann (ten), A. Kraus (ten), K. Moll (bass), G. Solti (cnd), Vienna PO, Vienna State Opera Chorus London 2-▲ 433210-2 [DDD]
Mozart, W.A.:Zauberflöte (sels), w. S. Jo (sop), U. Heilmann (ten), A. Kraus (ten), K. Moll (bass), G. Solti (cnd), Vienna PO, Vienna State Opera Chorus London ▲ 433667-2 [DDD]
Orff, C.:Catulli Carmina, w. M. Schäfer (ten), *(other artists unknown)*, W. Schäfer (cnd), Frankfurt Kantorei [L] Koch Schwann ▲ 314 021 [DDD]
Weber, C.M. von:Der Freischütz, w. S. Sweet (sop), A. Schmidt (bar), M. Hölle (bass), M. Janowski (cnd), German SO, Berlin Radio Chorus RCA Red Seal 2-▲ 09026-62538-2
Wolf, H.:Goethe-Lieder (sels), w. U. Eisenlohr (pno)—Blumengruss; Gleich und Gliech; Anakreons Grab; Die Spröde; Die Bekehrte; Der Schäfer; Philine; Epiphanias; Nimmer will ich dich verlieren; Phänomen; Hochbeglückt in deiner Liebe *(rec Oct. 8–10, 1992)* Sony Classical ▲ SK 53278 [DDD]
Wolf, H.:Mörike-Lieder (sels), w. U. Eisenlohr (pno)—Elfenlied; Zitronenfalter im April; Auf eine Christblume I; Auf eine Christblume II; Der Gärtner; Er ist's; Denk es, O Seele; Schlafendes Jesuskind; Auf ein altes Bild; Frage und Antwort; Im Frühling; Gesang Weylas; Die Geister am Mummelsee; Nixe Binsefuss *(rec Oct. 8–10, 1992)* Sony Classical ▲ SK 53278 [DDD]
Zemlinsky, A. von:Songs (misc), w. Iris Vermillion (mez), Hans Peter Blochwitz (ten), Andreas Schmidt (bar), Cord Garben (pno)—Die schlanke Wasserlilie; Gute Nacht; Liebe und Frühling; Ich sah mein eigen Angesicht; In der Ferne; Waldgespräch; Der Rosenband; Abendstern; Des Mädchens Klage; Der Morgenstern; Wandl' ich im Wald des Abends; Orientalisches Sonett; Süsse, süsse Sommernacht; Herbsten; Nun schwillt der See so bang; In der Sonnengasse; Herr Bombardil; Es war ein alter König; Über eine Wiege; Mädel, kommst du mit zum Tanz?; Jane Grey; Der verlorene Haufen; Vorspiel; Ansturm; Auf See; Noch spür ich ihren Atem; Hörtest du denn nicht hinein; Die Beiden; Harmonie des Abends; Und einmal gehst du *(rec Stuttgart & Berlin, Germany, Mar. 30–June 8, 1993)* Sony Classical ▲ SK 57960

Zijlstra, Nancy (sop)
Charpentier, M.-A.:Motets for Double Choir, w. B. Schlick (sop), K. Wessel (alt), D. Visse (ct), H. van Berne (ten), C. Prégardien (ten), P. Kooy (bass), K. Martens (bass), T. Koopman (cnd), Amsterdam Baroque Orch—Canticum pro pace; Josué; Mors Saulis et Jonathae; Praelium Michaelis; Quam dilecta; 3 Leçons de Ténèbres Erato (Musifrance) ▲ 2292-45822-2 ZA

Zika, Zdenka (sgr)
Wagner, R.:Lohengrin (sels), w. Franz Völker (ten—Lohengrin), Josef von Manowarda (bass—King Henry), Zdenka Zika (sgr—Titurel), F. Rühlmann (cnd), Vienna State Opera Orch *(rec Vienna, June 3, 1933)* Koch Schwann 2-▲ SCH 314662 [ADD]

Zikmundová, Eva (mez)
Dvořák, A.:St Ludmilla, w. Vera Soukupová (mez), Beno Blachut (ten), Richard Novák (bass), V. Smetáček (cnd), Prague SO, Czech Phil Chorus *(rec 1963)* Supraphon 2-▲ SUP 112141 [AAD]
Janácek, L.:The Cunning Little Vixen, w. Helena Tattermuschova (sop—Cunning Little Vixen), Eva Zikmundová (sop—The Fox), B. Gregor (cnd), Prague National Theater Orch, Prague National Theater Chorus *(rec 1970)* Supraphon 2-▲ SUP 3071

Ziliani, Alessandro (ten)
Verdi, G.:La traviata, w. Olga de Franco (sop—Flora Bervoix/Annina), Anna Rosza (sop—Violetta Valery), Giordano Callegari (ten—Gastone), Alessandro Ziliani (ten—Alfredo Germont), Luigi Borgonovo (bar—Giorgio Germont), Arnoldo Lenzi (bar—Barone Douphol), Antonio Gelli (bass—Marchese d'Obigny/Dottor Grenvil), C. Sabajno (cnd), La Scala Orch, Vittore Veneziani (cnd), La Scala Chorus *(rec Oct–Nov 1930)* Arkadia 2-▲ CD 78001 (m) [ADD]
Verdi, G.:La traviata, w. Olga de Franco (sop—Flora Bervoix/Annina), Anna Rosza (sop—Violetta Valéry), Giordano Callegari (ten—Gastone), Alessandro Ziliani (ten—Alfredo Germont), Luigi Borgonovo (bar—Giorgio Germont), Arnoldo Lenzi (bar—Baron Douphol), Antonio Gelli (bass—Marquis d'Obigny/Dr. Grenvil), C. Sabajno (cnd), La Scala Orch, La Scala Chorus *(rec La Scala Theatre, Milan, Oct.–Nov. 1930)* VAI Audio 2-▲ VAIA 1108-2

Zilio, Elena (mez)
Bellini, V.:Beatrice di Tenda, w. A. Gulin (sop), J. Carreras (ten), R. Bruson (bar), F. Mannino (cnd), Turin RAI Orch, Turin RAI Chorus [I] *(rec live Oct. 9, 1973)* Golden Age of Opera 2-▲ GAO 158/59 [ADD]
Bellini, V.:La straniera, w. R. Scotto (sop), R. Cioni (ten), D. Trimarchi (bar), E. Campi (bass), N. Sanzogno (cnd), Palermo Teatro Massimo Orch, Palermo Teatro Massimo Chorus [I] *(rec live, Palermo, 1968)* Verona 2-▲ 27097/98
Bellini, V.:La straniera, w. R. Scotto (sop), R. Cioni (ten), D. Trimarchi (bar), E. Campi (bass), N. Sanzogno (cnd), Palermo Teatro Massimo Orch, Palermo Teatro Massimo Chorus [I] *(rec live, Palermo, 1968)* Melodram 2-▲ 27039
Cavalli, P.F.:Ormindo, w. V. Manno (ten), G. Gatti (bar), A. Rinaldi (bar), R. Fasano (cnd), Rome Virtuosi Stradivarius 2-▲ DAT 12307
Cilea, F.:L'Arlesiana, w. M. Spacagna (sop), P. Kelen (ten), B. Póka (bar), T. Clementis (bass), C. Rosekrans (cnd), Hungarian State Orch, Hungarian State Chorus Quintana 2-▲ QUI 903067/68
Donizetti, G.:Gianni di Parigi, w. L. Serra (sop), G. Morino (ten), E. Fissore (bar), A. Romero (bar), S. Manga (sgr), C. F. Cillario (cnd), Milan RAI Orch, Milan RAI Chorus [I] *(rec live)* Nuova Era 2-▲ 6752/53 [DDD]
Donizetti, G.:Maria di Rohan, w. R. Scotto (sop—Maria), E. Zilio (mez—Armando di Gondi), U. Grilli (ten—Riccardo), R. Bruson (bar—Enrico), G. Gavazzeni (cnd), Venice Teatro La Fenice Orch, Venice Teatro La Fenice Chorus *(rec live Mar. 26, 1974)* Golden Age of Opera 2-▲ GAO 156/57 [ADD]
Pergolesi, G.B.:Il flaminio, w. D. Dessi (sop—Flaminio), F. Pediconi (sop—Agata), E. Zilio (mez—Giustina), M. Ferrugia (ten—Fernando), G. Sica (ten—Polidoro), V. Baiano (bass—Checa), S. Pagliuca (bass—Bastiano), M. Panni (cnd), Naples Teatro San Carlo Orch *(rec Nov. 12, 1983)* Fonit Cetra 3-▲ CDC 39 [ADD]
Piccinni, N.:La cecchina, ossia la buona figliola, w. Lucia Alberti (sop—Il Cavaliere Armidoro), Emilia Ravaglia (sop—La Marchesa), Margherita Rinaldi (sop—Cecchina), Elena Zilio (mez—Paoluccia), Ugo Benelli (bar—Il Marchese della Conchiglia), Alessandro Corbelli (bar—Mengotto), Enzo Dara (bar—Tagliaferro), Renata Baldisseri (sgr—Sandrina), G. Gelmetti (cnd), Rome Opera Orch, Rome Opera Chorus *(rec Rome, Feb 4, 1981)* Italia 2-▲ CDC 95 [ADD]

Zilková, Jarmila (sop)
Novák, V.:Storm, w. Jarmila Smycková (sop), Frantisek Livora (ten), Z. Košler (cnd), Czech PO, Czech Phil Chorus Supraphon ▲ SUP CD 3088

Zimbalist Jr., E. (nar)
Warren, E.R.:Good Morning, America!, w. S. Kawalla (cnd), Cracow Polish Radio–TV SO, Cracow Polish Radio–TV Chorus [E] Cambria ▲ CD 1042 [DDD]

Zimmer, Darynn (sop)
Beydts, L.:Chansons pour les Oiseaux, w. R. Wilson (cnd), New York Solisti New Albion ▲ NA 078
Delage, M.:Chants de la jungle (3), w. R. Wilson (cnd), New York Solisti New Albion ▲ NA 078
Delage, M.:Haï-kaï, w. R. Wilson (cnd), New York Solisti *(rec American Academy of Arts & Letters, New York City)* New Albion ▲ NA 078
Delage, M.:Poèmes désenchantés, w. R. Wilson (cnd), New York Solisti *(rec American Academy of Arts & Letters, New York City)* New Albion ▲ NA 078
Gounod, C.:Songs, w. Gaït Sirguey (pno), R. Wilson (cnd), New York Solisti—Les Deux pigeons; Le Soir; Le Temps des roses; L'Absent; Viens! Les Gazons sont verts! *(rec American Academy of Arts & Letters, New York City)* New Albion ▲ NA 078
Massenet, J.:Songs, w. Gaït Sirguey (pno), R. Wilson (cnd), New York Solisti—Oh! Si les fleurs avaient des yeux; Crépuscule; Souvenez-vous, vierge Marie!; C'est l'amour New Albion ▲ NA 078

Zimmer, Wolfgang (bar)
Max Lorenz:Recital, 1933–1957, w. Max Lorenz (ten), Maria Reining (sop), Berlin RSO [cnd:Artur Rother], Bayreuth Festival Orch [cnd:Heinz Tietjen, Richard Strauss], German Large RSO [cnd:Rudolf Moralt, Max Schönherr, Anton Paulik], Hessen RSO [cnd:Kurt Schröder], Brenda Lewis (sop), Eberhard Wächter (ten) *(rec 1933–57)* Myto ▲ MCD 934.88

Zimmermann, Erich (ten)
Wagner, R.:Die Meistersinger von Nürnberg (sels), w. V. Ursuleac (sop—Eva), M. Lorenz (ten—Walther), E. Zimmermann (ten—David), A. Jerger (b-bar—Hans Sachs), C. Krauss (cnd), Vienna State Opera Orch, Vienna State Opera Chorus *(rec Feb. 26, 1933)* Koch Schwann 2-▲ SCH 314562 [ADD]
Wagner, R.:Die Meistersinger von Nürnberg (sels), w. Maria Reining (sop—Eva), Max Lorenz (ten—Walther), Erich Zimmermann (ten—David), Karl Kamann (bar—Hans Sachs), W. Furtwängler (cnd), Vienna State Opera Orch *(rec Vienna, Nov. 25, 1937)* Koch Schwann 2-▲ SCH 314702 [ADD]
Wagner, R.:Das Rheingold (sels), w. Erich Zimmermann (ten—Mime), Herrmann Wiedemann (bar—Alberich), Josef von Manowarda (bass—Wotan), C. Krauss (cnd), Vienna State Opera Orch *(rec Feb. 28, 1933)* Koch Schwann 2-▲ SCH 314642 [ADD]
Wagner, R.:Der Ring des Nibelungen (sels), w. Adele Kern (sop), Anny Konetzni (sop), Hilde Konetzni (sop), Elisabeth Schumann (sop), Enid Szantho (cta), Josef Kalenberg (ten), Max Lorenz (ten), Set Svanholm (ten), Hans Hotter (bar), Jaro Prohaska (bar), Emil Schipper (bar), Paul Schöffler (b-bar), Ludwig Hoffmann (bass), H. Knappertsbusch (cnd), Vienna State Opera Orch *(rec Vienna, 1937–1943)* Koch Schwann 2-▲ SCH 314742 [ADD]
Wagner, R.:Siegfried (sels), w. G. Kappel (sop—Brünhilde), R. Schubert (ten—Siegfried), E. Zimmermann (ten—Mime), R. Heger (cnd), Vienna State Opera Orch, Vienna State Opera Chorus *(rec June 13, 1933)* Koch Schwann 2-▲ SCH 314592

Zimmermann, Margarita (mez)
Berlioz, H.:L'Enfance du Christ, w. J. Aler (ten), E. Wilm Schulte (bass), S. Dean (bass), P. Kang (bass), E. Inbal (cnd), Frankfurt RSO, Cologne Radio Chorus [F] Denon 2-▲ CO 76863/4 [DDD]
Vivaldi, A.:Catone in Utica, w. Cecilia Gasdia (sop), Susanna Rigacci (sop), Marilyn Schmiege (sop), Lucretia Lendi (mez), C. Scimone (cnd), Venice Solisti Erato 2-▲ ERA SEL 11232 [DDD]

Zimmermann, Margarita (sop)
Albinoni, T.:Il Nascimento de l'Aurora, w. June Anderson (sop), Susanne Klare (sop), Sandra Browne (alt), Yoshihisa Yamaj (ten), C. Scimone (cnd), Venice Solisti Erato 2-▲ ERA SEL 96374 [DDD]

Zimnenko, Leonid (sgr)
Rubinstein, A.:The Demon, w. Ludmilla Andrew (sop—Nanny), Marina Mescheriakova (sop—Tamara), Alison Browner (mez—Angel), Anatoly Lochak (sgr—Demon), Richard Robson (sgr—Old Servant), Valery Serkin (sgr—Prince Sinodal), Wjacheslav Weinorowski (sgr—Messenger), Leonid Zimnenko (sgr—Prince Gudal), A. Anissimov (cnd), Irish National SO, Gregory Rose (cnd), Wexford Festival Opera Chorus *(rec Wexford, Oct & Nov, 1994)* Marco Polo 2-▲ 8.223781-2 [DDD]

Zimpel, Peter (sgr)
Cavalli, P.F.:Vespero della beata Vergine Maria, w. Barbara Borden (sop), Emily van Evera (sop), Markus Brutscher (ten), Mark Padmore (ten), Rodrigo del Pozo (ten), Gerd Türk (ten), Harry van der Kamp (bass), Bruce Dickey (sackbut), Charles Toet (sackbut), Concerto Palatino, Schola Cantorum Basiliensis Harmonia Mundi France ("Documenta" series) 2-▲ HMC 905219/20

Zinetti, Giuseppina (sop)
Verdi, G.:Il trovatore, w. Bianca Scacciati (sop), Francesco Merli (ten), Enrico Molinari (bar), L. Molajoli (cnd), Milan SO, La Scala Chorus *(rec live, 1930)* Melodram ▲ CDI 202002

Zítek, Vaclav (bar)
Dvořák, A.:The Cunning Peasant, w. Eva Depoltová (sop), Karel Berman (bass), F. Vajnar (cnd), Prague RSO, Prague Radio Chorus Supraphon 2-▲ SUP 0019 [DDD]
Fibich, Z.:Šárka, w. Eva Depoltová (sop), Eva Randová (mez), Vilém Přibyl (ten), J. Stych (cnd), Brno State PO, J. Pancik (cnd), Janáček Opera Chorus *(rec 1978)* Supraphon 2-▲ SUP 0036
Janácek, L.:Amarus, w. Kvetoslava Nemeckova (sop), Leo Marian Vodicka (ten), Jan Hora (org), C. Mackerras (cnd), Czech PO, Lubomír Mátl (cnd), Czech Phil Chorus *(rec 1984)* Supraphon ▲ SUP CD 3045
Janácek, L.:From the House of the Dead, w. D. Jedlička (bass), C. Mackerras (cnd), Vienna PO, Vienna Opera Chorus London 2-▲ 430375-2 [DDD]
Janácek, L.:The Makropulos Affair, w. E. Söderström (sop), V. Krejčík (ten), Z. Švehla (ten), D. Jedlička (bass), C. Mackerras (cnd), Vienna PO, Vienna Opera Chorus London 2-▲ 430372-2 [ADD]
Martinů, B.:The Epic of Gilgamesh, w. M. Machotková (sop), J. Zaradníček (ten), K. Průša (bass), J. Bělohlávek (cnd), Prague SO, Czech Phil Chorus Supraphon ▲ SUP 11 1824 [ADD]
Martinů, B.:Field Mass, w. V. Neumann (cnd), Czech PO, Czech Phil Chorus Panton ▲ PAN 811217
Smetana, B.:Libuše, w. G. Benackova (sop), V. Soupukova (sop), Z. Košler (cnd), Prague National Theater Orch, Prague National Theater Chorus Supraphon 3-▲ SUP 111276 [DDD]

Zivojinovic, Snezana (nar)
Schibler, A.:La Folie de Tristan, w. Audrey Michael (sop—Iseut), Arlette Chédel (mez—Brangien), Pierre-André Blaser (ten—Tristan), Philippe Huttenlocher (bar—Le roi Marc/Le pêcheur/Le portier), André Fauré (nar), William Jacques (nar), J. Auberson (cnd), Lausanne CO, Romande Instrumental Group Rockband, Swiss Romande Radio Choir *(rec live, Festival de Montreux, Sept 15, 1980)* Jecklin ▲ JD 695

Zizich, P. (bass)
Bellini, V.:La straniera, w. L. Alberti (sop—Alaide), S. Mingardo (mez—Isoletta), V. Bello (ten—Arturo), R. Frontale (bar—Il Barone di Valdeburgo), V. Sagona (bass—Il signore di Montalino), P. Zizich (bass—Osburgo), G. Masini (cnd), Trieste Teatro Comunale Giuseppe Verdi Orch, Trieste Teatro Comunale G. Verdi Chorus *(rec Dec. 1990)* Ricordi ▲ RFCD 2015 [DDD]

Zlobin, A. (ten)
Rachmaninoff, S.:All-Night Vigil, w. Y. Necheporenko (ten), R. Sevostyanov (ten), O. Shepel (cnd), Voronezh Chamber Choir Globe ▲ GLO 5077 [DDD]

Zoll, Emmanuelle (sop)
Aperghis, G.:L'origine des espèces, w. Françoise Degeorges (sop), Donatienne Michel-Dansac (sop), Valérie Joly (mez), Frédérique Wolf-Michaux (cta), Elena Andreyev (vc) Musique Française d'Aujourd'hui ▲ MFA 216004

Zollenkopf, Ursula (cta)
Beethoven, L. van:Syms (comp), w. I. Wenglor (sop), Hans Joachim Rotzsch (ten), T. Adam (bass-bar), F. Konwitschny (cnd), Leipzig Gewandhaus Orch, Leipzig Radio Chorus *(rec 1959–1961)* Berlin Classics ("Eterna" series) 6-▲ BER 2005 [ADD]
Beethoven, L. van:Sym 9, "Choral Sym", w. Ingeborg Wenglor (sop), Hans Jochim Rotzsch (ten), Theo Adam (bass), F. Konwitschny (cnd), Leipzig Gewandhaus Orch, Leipzig Radio Chorus Polskie Nagrania Edition ▲ ECD 028

Zoranca, Giorgio (sgr)
Verdi, G.:Don Carlos, w. Katia Ricciarelli (sop), Fiorenza Cossotto (mez), Guido Fabbris (ten), Veriano Luchetti (ten), Piero Cappuccilli (bar), Gianfranco Casarini (bass), Nicolai Ghiaurov (bass), Alessandro Maddalena (bass), Aracelly Haengel (sgr), Marisa Salimbeni (sgr), G. Prêtre (cnd), *(orch unknown)* Great Opera Performances 3-▲ GOP 777

Zorina, Vera (nar)
Milhaud, D.:Choéphores, w. Virginia Babikian (sop), Irene Jordan (sop), McHenry Boatwright (bar), L. Bernstein (cnd), New York PO, New York Schola Cantorum Sony Classical ("Masterworks Heritage" series) ▲ MHK 62352
Walton, W.:Façade, w. E. Ormandy (cnd), Philadelphia Orch Sony Classical ("Essential Classics" series) ▲ SBK 62400 ■ SBT 62400

Zorova, Vessela (mez)
Mahler, G.:Sym 2, w. Tiha Genova (sop), E. Tabakov (cnd), Sofia PO, Bulgarian National Chorus *(rec Bulgarian Concert Hall, Sofia, Jan 1987)* Capriccio 15-▲ 49043 [DDD]
Mussorgsky, M.:Boris Godunov, w. Eirian James (mez), Samuel Ramey (bass), E. de Waart (cnd), Swiss Romande Orch *(rec live, 1993)* Serenissima 2-▲ SER 360109 [DDD]
Rimsky-Korsakov, N.:Snow Maiden, w. Stefka Evstatieva (sop—Kupava), Elena Zemenkova (sop—Snow Maiden), Alexandrina Milcheva (mez—Spring Fairy), Vessela Zorova (mez—wife), Stefka Mineva (alt—Lehl), Avram Andreev (ten—Tsar), Lyubomir Dyakovski (ten—Cottager, Sprite), Lyubomir Videnov (bar—Misgir), Nicola Ghiuselev (bass—King), S. Angelov (cnd), Bulgarian RSO, Bulgarian National Chorus *(rec Sofia, 1985)* Capriccio 3-▲ 10749–51 [DDD]

Zotti, Marisa (sop)
Donizetti, G.:La favorita (sels), w. F. Cossotto (mez), A. Kraus (ten), R. Raimondi (bass), O. de Fabritiis (cnd), NHK SO *(rec Sept. 13, 1971)* Myto 2-▲ MCD 93276
Verdi, G.:La traviata, w. B. Sills (sop), G. Borelli (mez), A. Kraus (ten), M. Zanasi (bar), A. Ceccato (cnd), Naples Teatro San Carlo Orch, Naples Teatro San Carlo Chorus *(rec live 1/17/70)* Melodram 2-▲ MEL 27063 (m) [AAD]

Zuchetto, Gérard (sgr)
Tensons e partimens de Trobairitz, Vol. 3, w. Katia Caré (sgr), Gisela Bellsolà (sgr), Patrice Brient (voc/h-g/rebeck), Guy Robert (medieval lt/oud/hp) Gallo ▲ CD 769 [DDD]
Troubador Songs of the 12th & 13th Centuries, w. Patrice Brient (instr), Jacques Khoudir (perc) Gallo ▲ CD 529
Troubador Songs of the 12th & 13th Centuries, Vol. 2, w. Dominique Regef (rebec/israj/hurdy-gurdy), Jacques Khoudir (perc) Gallo ▲ CD 684 [DDD]

Zukof, William (ct)
Camilo, M.:Batey, w. P. E. Clark (sop), C.B. Rowe (sop), L. Bennett (ten), W. L. Lee (ten), E. Levine (bar), Puntilla (sgr), New Generation Western Wind ▲ WW 2001
Darling, D.:Blessings:A Prayer for the Planet, w. P.E. Clark (sop), C.B. Rowe (sop), L. Bennett (ten), W.L. Lee (ten), E. Levine (bar), D. Darling (acoustic & electric vc/syn/voice) Western Wind ▲ WW 2001
Darling, D.:Blessings (sels), w. P.E. Clark (sop), C.B. Rowe (sop), L. Bennett (ten), W.L. Lee (ten), E. Levine (bar), D. Darling (acoustic & electric vc/syn/voice) Western Wind ▲ WW 2001

Zürcher, Liliane (mez)
Casella, A.:L'Adieu à la vie, w. G. Garbarino (cnd), Villa Marigola Festival Orch [F] Nuova Era 2-▲ 7143/44 [DDD]

Zvetanov, Boiko (sgr)
Verdi, G.:Rigoletto (sels), w. Daniella Lojarro (sop), Elizabeth Carter (sgr), Roberto Servile (bar)—Ov; Questa o quella; Pari siamo! Io la lingua—Figlia! Mio Padre; Giovanna, ho Dei rimorsi; Gualtier Maldé - Caro nome; Ella mi fu rapita!; Scorrendo uniti remota via; Cortigiani, vil razza danata; plus others Laserlight ▲ 14207 [DDD]

Zylis-Gara, Teresa (sop)
Handel, G.F.:Dixit Dominus (sels), w. Janet Baker (mez), Robert Tear (ten), D. Willcocks (cnd), King's College Choir Cambridge—Dixit Dominus [chorus w. solos]; Gloria [chorus] *(rec King's College Chapel, Cambridge, Aug. 1965)* EMI Classics ▲ CDK 65336 [ADD]
Lalo, E.:Songs, w. Christian Ivaldi (pno)—5 Lieder (1879); 6 mélodies [after V. Hugo], Op. 17 (1856); 3 mélodies [after A. de Musset] (?c.1870); 3 mélodies (1887); Si j'étais petit oiseau; La pauvre femme [both from 6 romances populaires]; Chant breton; Aubade; Humoresque; Marine; Ballade à la lune; Le rouge-gorge *(rec Paris, Mar 18 & 19, 1987)* Phoenix ▲ PX 904.1 [DDD]

▲ = CD ♦ = Enhanced CD △ = MD ■ = Cassette Tape □ = DCC

Zylis-Gara, Teresa (sop) (cont.)
Mahler, G.:Das Klagende Lied, w. A. Reynolds (mez), A. Kaposy (ten), W. Morris (cnd), New Philharmonia Orch, Ambrosian Singers   IMP Classics ▲ IMPCD 1053 [DDD]
Mahler, G.:Das Klagende Lied, w. A. Reynolds (mez), A. Kaposy (ten), W. Morris (cnd), New Philharmonia Orch, Ambrosian Singers [G] *(rec 1967)*   Nimbus ▲ NI 5085 [AAD]
Moniuszko, S.:Songs, w. Christian Ivaldi (pno)—La filatrice; Adorazione; Le ragazze di Cracovia; Canto della follia d'Ofelia; Piccola quaglia; Il fiorellino; Conversione; L'usignolo; Lacrima; Il gattino; La rondinella; La piccola Sofia; Il ritorno della primavera; Il messaggero d'amor piumato; La vecchia filatrice; Il violinista girovago; Le quattro stagioni; Sofia; Il pesciolino d'oro; Una fanciulla dal cuore di pietra; Sul fiume; La rosellina; Conosci il paese dove...; Il bocciuolo; Primavera *(rec Studio 107, Radio France, Paris, Dec 12-13, 1984)*   Agorá Music ("Phoenix" series) ▲ 902 [DDD]
Mozart, W.A:Don Giovanni, w. G. Janowitz (sop), M. Freni (sop), A. Kraus (ten), R. Panerai (bar), V. von Halem (bass), N. Ghiaurov (bass), H. von Karajan (cnd), Vienna PO, Vienna State Opera Chorus [I] *(rec live, Salzburg, Aug. 1, 1969)*   Memories 3-▲ HR 4362/64 (m) [ADD]
Mozart, W.A.:Don Giovanni (sels), w. A. Tomowa-Sintow (sop), E. Mathis (sop), S. Milnes (bar), W. Berry (bass), K. Böhm (cnd), Vienna PO, Vienna State Opera Chorus—Scenes & Arias   Deutsche Grammophon ▲ 429823-2 [ADD]
Polish Stars Sing the Carols, w. Wiesław Ochman (ten), Polish Radio-TV SO (cnd:Stefan Stuligrosz), Warsaw CO, Poznan State PO Men's & Boys' Choir   Polskie Nagrania Edition ▲ ECD 025
Rossini, G.:Mosè in Egitto, w. Shirley Verrett (mez), Ottavio Garaventa (ten), Giampaolo Corradi (bass), Nicolai Ghiaurov (bass), Mario Petri (bass), W. Sawallisch (cnd), Rome RAI Orch, Rome RAI Chorus *(rec live, Rome, 1968)*   Italian Opera Rarities 2-▲ IOR 7724 [ADD]
Rossini, G.:Stabat Mater, w. Shirley Verrett (mez), Luciano Pavarotti (ten), Nicola Zaccaria (bass), C. M. Giulini (cnd), Rome RAI Orch, Rome RAI Chorus *(rec Rome, Dec. 1967)*   Emozioni ▲ ARCD 2041
Rossini, G.:Stabat Mater, w. S. Verrett (mez), L. Pavarotti (ten), N. Zaccaria (bass), C. M. Giulini (cnd), Rome RAI Orch, Rome RAI Chorus [L] *(rec live 12/22/67)*   Melodram 2-▲ MEL 28012
Rossini, G.:Stabat Mater, w. S. Verrett (mez), L. Pavarotti (ten), N. Zaccaria (bass), C.M. Giulini (cnd), Rome Radio Orch, Rome RAI Chorus [L] *(rec live 12/22/67)*   Verona 2-▲ 27060/61 (m) [AAD]

Zylstra, Nancy (sop)
Bach, J.S.:Mass in b, BWV 232, w. J. Baird (sop), J. Nelson (sop), J. Lane, Z. Muñoz, S. Rickards, P. Romano, W. Sharp, J. Weaver (bass), J. Thomas (cnd), American Bach Soloists   Koch International Classics 2-▲ KIC 7194-2 [DDD]
Out of the Orient Crystall Skyes, w. Margriet Tindemans (vl), Jillion Stopples Dupree (hpd/org), Michael Sand (baroque vn/vl), Linda Melsted (baroque vn), Olga Hauptmann (baroque va), Ellen Siebert (vl), Russell Paige (vl)   Wildboar ▲ WLBR 8901 [DDD]

Zywietz, Detelf (sgr)
Schultze, N.:Das kalte Herz, w. Grit van Jüten (sop), Elisabeth Steiner (mez), Heinz Kruse (ten), N. Schutze (cnd), Cologne RSO, Händel Collegium   Koch Schwann 2-▲ SCH 318002 [DDD]

MISCELLANEOUS

Amirkhanian, Charles (cmpt processing)
Amirkhanian, C.:Politics As Usual Centaur ▲ CRC 2194
Apple, Jacki (elec)
Apple, J.:Voices in the Dark, w. Anna Holmer (voc), David Moss (voc) ¿What Next? ▲ WN 0014
Arel, Bülent (elecs)
Arel, B.:Stereo Elec Music 2 CRI ▲ CD 611 [ADD]
Armin, A. (elec)
Celona, J.:Sum over Histories, w. B. Degazio (sgr), S. Peet (sgr), R. Sacks (sgr), R. Armin (elecs), J. Brownell (elecs), D. Hutton (elecs), G. Martynec (elecs), D. Mott (elecs), C. Sokol (elecs) Soundprints ▲ SP 9301
Degazio, B.:Digital Rituals, w. J. Brownell (elec), B. Degazio (elec), D. Hutton (elec), G. Martynec (elec), D. Mott (elec), S. Peet (elec), R. Sacks (elec), C. Sokol (elec) Soundprints ▲ SP 9301
Mott, D.:Oh! Mysterious Magnum, w. R. Armin (elec), J. Brownell (elec), B. Degazio (elec), D. Hutton (elec), G. Martynec (elec), D. Mott (elec), S. Peet (elec), R. Sacks (elec), C. Sokol (elec) Soundprints ▲ SP 9301
Tenney, J.:Tableaux Vivants, w. R. Armin (elec), J. Brownell (elec), B. Degazio (elec), D. Hutton (elec), G. Martynec (elec), D. Mott (elec), S. Peet (elec), R. Sacks (elec), C. Sokol (elec) [electronic music] Soundprints ▲ SP 9301
Armin, R. (elec)
Celona, J.:Sum over Histories, w. B. Degazio (sgr), S. Peet (sgr), R. Sacks (sgr), A. Armin (elecs), J. Brownell (elecs), D. Hutton (elecs), G. Martynec (elecs), D. Mott (elecs), C. Sokol (elecs) Soundprints ▲ SP 9301
Mott, D.:Oh! Mysterious Magnum, w. A. Armin (elec), J. Brownell (elec), B. Degazio (elec), D. Hutton (elec), G. Martynec (elec), D. Mott (elec), S. Peet (elec), R. Sacks (elec), C. Sokol (elec) Soundprints ▲ SP 9301
Tenney, J.:Tableaux Vivants, w. A. Armin (elec), J. Brownell (elec), B. Degazio (elec), D. Hutton (elec), G. Martynec (elec), D. Mott (elec), S. Peet (elec), R. Sacks (elec), C. Sokol (elec) [electronic music] Soundprints ▲ SP 9301
Ashley, Robert (cmpt/syn)
Ashley, R.:Tract, w. Thomas Bruckner (bar), Nathaniel Reichman (cmpt/syn), Tom Hamilton (syn) *(rec 10 Beach St, NYC)* New World ▲ 80460-2
Austin, Linda (elec)
Subotnick, M.:Trembling, w. R. Davidovici (vn), A. Wodnicki (pno), J. La Barbara (recorded voc) *(rec Dec. 1992)* Centaur ▲ CRC 2170 [DDD]
Bacalov, Daniel (elecs)
La Camera Astratta [The Abstract Room], w. P. Milesi (elecs) Cuneiform ▲ Rune 18
Bahn, Curtis (tape)
Rulon, C.B.:Self Requiem, w. C. Bryan Rulon (cnd), Musicians' Accord CRI ▲ CD 729 [DDD]
Baker, Jeffrey Reid (elec)
A Composer's Christmas, w. J. R. Baker (elec) *(rec JeRBil, Inc., Huntington, NY, May 30–June 2, 1996)* JRB ▲ JRB 2001 [DDD]
Bandt, Ros (elec)
Bandt, R.:Electronic Music—Stargazer; After Medtation; Pipe Dance; Genesis; Spring Flute; Invading the Landscape; Mee-Ow; Subterra; Mary at the Dairy; Starzones Vox Australis ▲ VAST 004-2
Behrman, David (elec)
Behrman, D.:Figure in a Clearing, w. David Gibson (vc), Kim-1 (cmpt) *(rec State Univ of New York, Albany, June 9, 1977)* Lovely Music ▲ LCD 1041 [ADD]
Behrman, D.:On the Other Ocean, w. Maggi Payne (fl), Arthur Stidfole (bn), Kim-1 (computer) *(rec Mills College, Oakland, CA, Sep 18, 1977)* Lovely Music ▲ LCD 1041 [ADD]
Bimstein, P. K. (elec)
Bimstein, P.K.:Dark Winds Rising, w. Turtle Island String Quartet Starkland ▲ ST 205 [DDD]
Bimstein, P.K.:The Door Starkland ▲ ST 205 [DDD]
Bimstein, P.K.:Garland Hirschi's Cows Starkland ▲ ST 205 [DDD]
Bimstein, P.K.:Vox=Dominum Starkland ▲ ST 205 [DDD]
Braack, Steve (elec)
O'Rourke, J.:Terminal Pharmacy, w. Tony Burr (cl), Jeff Cortazzo (b trbn), John McEntire (dr), Rob Prosser (acc), Isha Suftin (acc), Mike Dockter (vc), Hattie Franck (vc), Robert Keck (vc), Mary LaBreque (vc), Dan Loch (vc), Stan Saderk (vc), Lisa Hemmer (fl), Sue Oberg (fl), Wendi Lev (fl), Jim Vanden (fl), Jim O'Rourke (gtr) Tzadik ▲ TZA 7011 [DDD]
Brand, Robert Gibby (actor)
Moore, D.:Devil & Daniel Webster, w. Joyce Guyer (sop—Mary Stone), Benjamin Bongers (ten—Walter Butler), Michael Philip Davis (ten—Simon Girty), Matthew Foerschler (ten—Miser Stephens), Darren Keith Woods (ten—Mr. Scratch), Michael Lanman (bass—Blackbeard Teach), David Soxman (bass—Clerk), Brian Steele (bass—Daniel Webster), John Stephens (bass—Jabez Stone), Andrew Stuckey (bass—King Philip), Robert Gibby Brand (actor), Cary Miller (actor), Russell Patterson (cnd), Kansas City SO, Kansas City Lyric Opera Chorus *(rec Sept 1995)* Newport Classic ▲ NPD 85585 [DDD]
Bresnick, Martin (elec)
Bresnick, M.:Lady Neil's Dumpe Centaur ▲ CRC 2039 [DDD]
Brown, Chris (elecs)
Brown, C.:Lava, w. William Winant (perc), Toyoji Tomita (trbn), Tom Dill (tpt), Peter Wahrhaftig (tuba)—Crack; Eruption; Fountain; River; Crest; Pahoehoe Tzadik ("The Composers" series) ▲ TZA 7002 [DDD]
Riley, T.:In C, w. Bruce Ackley, Steve Adams, Don R. Baker, George Brooks, Steve Coughlin, Blake Derby, Bill Douglass, Mihr'un'Nisa Douglass, Hank Dutt, David Harrington, Don Howe, Joan Jeanrenaud, Alden Jenks, Warner Jepson, Henry Kaiser, Jaron Lanier, Bill Maginnis, George Marsh, Shabda Owens, Jon Raskin, Gyan Riley, Terry Riley, Gino Robair, John Sackett, Ramón Sender, John Sherba, Toyji Tomita, Danny Tunick, William Winant, Evan Ziporyn *(rec Jan. 14, 1990)* New Albion ▲ NA 071
Brownell, J. (elec)
Celona, J.:Sum over Histories, w. B. Degazio (sgr), S. Peet (sgr), R. Sacks (sgr), A. Armin (elecs), R. Armin (elecs), D. Hutton (elecs), G. Martynec (elecs), D. Mott (elecs), C. Sokol (elecs) Soundprints ▲ SP 9301
Degazio, B.:Digital Rituals, w. A. R. Armin (elec), B. Degazio (elec), D. Hutton (elec), G. Martynec (elec), D. Mott (elec), S. Peet (elec), R. Sacks (elec), C. Sokol (elec) Soundprints ▲ SP 9301
Mott, D.:Oh! Mysterious Magnum, w. A. Armin (elec), R. Armin (elec), B. Degazio (elec), D. Hutton (elec), G. Martynec (elec), D. Mott (elec), S. Peet (elec), R. Sacks (elec), C. Sokol (elec) Soundprints ▲ SP 9301
Tenney, J.:Tableaux Vivants, w. A. Armin (elec), R. Armin (elec), B. Degazio (elec), D. Hutton (elec), G. Martynec (elec), D. Mott (elec), S. Peet (elec), R. Sacks (elec), C. Sokol (elec) [electronic music] Soundprints ▲ SP 9301
Buck, T. (elec)
Dean, R.T.:Electronic Music, w. R. Dean (elec), S. Evans (elec)—Dye pulse; Pinnacles; Even suite time varies; Moving the landscapes; Hardly moving; Reel choice; Alela; Drums are-ticulate [E] *(rec 1991)* Tall Poppies ▲ TP 007 [DDD]
Butlers, Steven (microtonal metals)
Powell, Morgan: Orphans, w. John Fonville (microtonal fls) *(rec Urbana, IL, Oct 5, 1995)* New World ▲ 80499-2
Carlos, Wendy (elec)
Bach, J.S.:Brandenburg Cons
Cassara, Frank (boo/spoils of war/kithara 2)
Partch, H.:Daphne of the Dunes, w. Dominic Donato (b mar/surrogate kithara/boo), Dean Drummond (harmonic canons/kithara 2/spoils of war/kithara), Nina Kellman (kithara 2/harmonic canon/surrogate kithara), Michael Lipsey (cloud-chamber bowls), Ted Mook (vc/gourd tree/cone gongs), James Pugliese (diamond mar), Elizabeth Rodgers (chromelodeon/harmonic canon) *(rec Queens, NY, Mar. 12, 1991)* Mode ▲ MODE 33
Celli, Joseph (elec)
Garcia, O.J.:Improvisation with Metallic Materials O.O. Discs ▲ OO 6 [DDD]
Chadabe, J. (elec)
Chadabe, J.:Modalities Centaur ▲ CRC 2047 [DDD]
Stravinsky, I.:The Rake's Progress, w. J. West (sop—Anne Trulove), S. Love (mez—Mother Goose), W. White (mez—Baba the Turk), J. Garrison (ten—Tome Rakewell), M. Lowrey (ten—Sellem), A. Woodley (bar—Father Truelove), *(orch unknown)* MusicMasters 2-▲ 01612-67131-2 [DDD]
Chafe, C. (elec)
Chafe, C.:Duo Improvisation, w. D. Morrill (elecs) Centaur ▲ CRC 2133 [DDD]
Chiappetta, Quentin (sampler/pno/cpsr)
Gisberg:Music of, w. Christine Bard (perc), Christina Sun (erhu), Jeff O'Malley (nar), Jacqueline Leclair (ob), Reuben Radding (bass instrument), Gisburg (voice/fl/cpsr)—Opening; No Stranger Not At All; Imaginary Movielandscape 1; Portrait; "Jowohl"; Mein Herz hat nicht vergessen [tango]; Ritual; Dying Takes Its Time; Fruits; Mic' N Drums Tzadik ("The Composers" series) ▲ TZA 7007 [DDD]
Choloniewski, Marek (cmpt)
Schaeffer, B.:Con 3 Pno, w. Boguslaw Schaeffer (pno), Bogdan Oledzki (cnd), Polish National RSO Katowice Pro Viva ▲ ISPV 168 [ADD]
Cole, Cinnie (sampler)
Exquisite Corpses from P.S. 122, w. D. Watson (shears/stick vn/gtr/tpt), Judy Dunaway (gtr/balloons), Anthony Coleman (sampler), Raissa St. Pierre (drums), Guy Yarden (vn/pno), Leslie Ross (bn), Linda Austin (gtr), Bruce Kaplan (gtr), Doug Henderson (peckhorn/bass/toy pno), Sue Ann Harkey (gtr), et al. ¿What Next? ▲ WN 0002 [ADD]
Coleman, Anthony (sampler)
Exquisite Corpses from P.S. 122, w. Watson, David (shears/stick vn/gtr/tpt), Judy Dunaway (gtr/balloons), Raissa St. Pierre (drums), Guy Yarden (vn/pno), Leslie Ross (bn), Linda Austin (gtr), Bruce Kaplan (gtr), Doug Henderson (peckhorn/bass/toy pno), Sue Ann Harkey (gtr), Cinnie Cole (sampler), et al. ¿What Next? ▲ WN 0002 [ADD]
Collins, Nicolas (elec)
Sato, M.:Improvs, w. Michihiro Sato (tsugaru shamisen), Bill Frisell (elec gtr), Fred Frith (elec gtr), Tenko (sgr), Mark Miller (elec bass), Christian Marclay (turntables), Steve Colemann (sax), Tom Cora (vc), Joey Baron (perc), Mark Dresser (elec bass), Gerry Hemingway (perc), Toh Ban Djan [Ikue Mori (perc), Luli Shioi (elec bass/sgr)], Semantics [Elliott Sharp (electric gtr/bass), Samm Bennett (perc), Ned Rothenberg (sax)]—23 improvisations with various accompaniment combinations *(rec Baby Monster Studio, NY, Apr. 11–16, 1988)* Hat Hut ▲ hat ART CD 6015 [ADD]
Cope, D. (elecs)
Bach by Design: Experiments in Musical Intelligence Centaur ▲ CRC 2184
Creshevsky, Noah (cmpt)
Creshevsky, N.:Borrowed Time Centaur ▲ CRC 2194
Creshevsky, N.:Coup d'état Centaur ▲ CRC 2194
Creshevsky, N.:Electronic Music—Electric Partita (1990); Electric String Quartet (1988); Memento Mori (1989); Talea (1991); Variations (1987) Centaur ▲ CRC 2126 [DDD]
Curran, Alvin (sampler)
Curran, A.:Animal Behavior, w. Annie Sprinkle (moans/groans) Tzadik ("The Composers" series) ▲ TZA 7001 [DDD]
Dashow, James (cmpt)
Dashow, J.:Reconstructions, w. Lucia Bova (hp) *(rec Studio Wonderland, Rome, June 1993)* Pro Viva ▲ ISPV 177 CD [DDD]
Dashow, James (elec)
Dashow, J.:Mappings, w. Luca Paccagnella (vc) *(rec Studio Lead, Rome, May 1991)* Pro Viva ▲ ISPV 177 CD [DDD]
Dean, Roger (elec)
Dean, R.T.:Electronic Music, w. T. Buck (elec), S. Evans (elec)—Dye pulse; Pinnacles; Even suite time varies; Moving the landscapes; Hardly moving; Reel choice; Alela; Drums are-ticulate [E] *(rec 1991)* Tall Poppies ▲ TP 007 [DDD]
Degazio, B. (elec)
Degazio, B.:Digital Rituals, w. A. R. Armin (elec), J. Brownell (elec), D. Hutton (elec), G. Martynec (elec), D. Mott (elec), S. Peet (elec), R. Sacks (elec), C. Sokol (elec) Soundprints ▲ SP 9301
Mott, D.:Oh! Mysterious Magnum, w. A. Armin (elec), R. Armin (elec), J. Brownell (elec), D. Hutton (elec), G. Martynec (elec), D. Mott (elec), S. Peet (elec), R. Sacks (elec), C. Sokol (elec) Soundprints ▲ SP 9301
Tenney, J.:Tableaux Vivants, w. A. Armin (elec), R. Armin (elec), J. Brownell (elec), D. Hutton (elec), G. Martynec (elec), D. Mott (elec), S. Peet (elec), R. Sacks (elec), C. Sokol (elec) [electronic music] Soundprints ▲ SP 9301
Dockstader, Tod (elec)
Dockstader, T.:Electroacoustic Music—Quatermass (1964); Two Moons of Quatermass (1964); Water Music (1963) Starkland ▲ ST 201 [AAD]
Dockstader, T.:Music of—Traveling Music; Luna Park; 2 Fragments from Apocalypse; Apocalypse; Drone; 4 Telemetry Tapes Starkland ▲ ST 202 [AAD]
Dorsey, Don (elec)
Bachbusters (elecs) Telarc ▲ CD 80123 [DDD] ■ CS 30123 (D)
Beethoven or Bust (elecs) Telarc ▲ CD 80153 [DDD] ■ CS 30153 (D)
Beethoven, L. van: Music of Telarc ▲ CD 80153 [DDD] ■ CS 30153 (D)
Dresher, Paul (elec)
Dresher, P.:Dark Blue Circumstance *(rec 1987)* New Albion ▲ NA 053
Dresher, P.:Other Fire, Starkland ▲ ST 204
Dresher, P.:Underground Starkland ▲ ST 204
Dresher, P.:Water Dreams, w. Sarah Willner (va samples) Lovely Music ▲ LCD 2011 [ADD]
Dunn, David (elec)
Dunn, D.:Chaos & the Emergent Mind—location recordings from ponds in North America & Africa ¿What Next? ▲ WN 0009 ■ WN 0009
Dunn, D.:Tabula Angelorum Bonorum 49 ¿What Next? ▲ WN 0009 ■ WN 0009
Eagle, David (MIDI controller)
Eagle, D.:Solitudes New Concert Discs ▲ NCD 0294 [DDD]
Englert, G. (elec)
Duggan, M.:Sopra la girolmeta Grammont ▲ CTSP 49-2
Evans, D. (elecs)
Brody, M.:Moments musicaux, w. C. Fisk (pno) CRI ▲ CD 594 [DDD]
Evans, S. (elec)
Dean, R.T.:Electronic Music, w. T. Buck (elec), R. Dean (elec)—Dye pulse; Pinnacles; Even suite time varies; Moving the landscapes; Hardly moving; Reel choice; Alela; Drums are-ticulate [E] *(rec 1991)* Tall Poppies ▲ TP 007 [DDD]
Fast, L. (elec)
Weill, K.:Songs, w. H. Schneider (sop), B. Coyle (pno) CBS ▲ MK 45703 [DDD] ■ FMT 45703 (D)
Festi, Valerio (fireworks)
Milesi, P.:Kings' Night for Fireworks—The Procession; Three figurations: the Braid, the Rhombus, the Star; The Waterfall Cuneiform ▲ Rune 7

▲ = CD ♦ = Enhanced CD Δ = MD ■ = Cassette Tape □ = DCC

Fraser, Scott (tape)
Cage, J.:Europera 3, w. Suzan Hanson (sop), Ruby Hinds (mez), Patricia McAfee (mez), Michael Lyon (ten), Richard Powell (ten), Kevin Bell (bass), Brian Pezzone (pno), Vicki Ray (pno), Hannes Geiger (record players), Joseph Giri (record players), William Houston (record players), Dren McDonald (record players), Ronda Rindone (record players), Clarice Ross (record players), Andrew Culver (cnd), Long Beach Opera Orch *(rec Center Theater, Long Beach, CA, Nov. 13, 1993)* Mode 2-▲ MODE 38/39
Cage, J.:Europera 4, w. Anne-Marie Ketchum (sop), Daisetta Kim (sop), Brian Pezzone (pno), Jerry Wheeler (victrola), Andrew Culver (cnd), Long Beach Opera Orch *(rec Center Theater, Long Beach, CA, Nov. 13, 1993)* Mode 2-▲ MODE 38/39

Frohmader, Peter (elecs)
Macrocosm Cuneiform ▲ Rune 23

Fujieda, Mamoru (cmpt)
Fujieda, M.:Music of, w. Makiko Sakurai (shomyo/Buddhist chant), Mineko Grimmer (audible sculptures), Kodo Uesugi (fukimono), Kazuko Takada (hikimono), Toshiyuki Matsukura (uchimono), Satoshi Sakai (uchimono), Koshin Ebihara (jumon)—The Night Chant III; Wind Chant; Cocoon Chant; Duct Chant; Falling Chant; The Night Chant I Tzadik ("The Composers" series) ▲ TZA 7003 [DDD]

Geiger, Hannes (record players)
Cage, J.:Europera 3, w. Suzan Hanson (sop), Ruby Hinds (mez), Patricia McAfee (mez), Michael Lyon (ten), Richard Powell (ten), Kevin Bell (bass), Brian Pezzone (pno), Vicki Ray (pno), Joseph Giri (record players), William Houston (record players), Dren McDonald (record players), Ronda Rindone (record players), Clarice Ross (record players), Scott Fraser (tape), Andrew Culver (cnd), Long Beach Opera Orch *(rec Center Theater, Long Beach, CA, Nov. 13, 1993)* Mode 2-▲ MODE 38/39

Geisler, Kathy (cmpt)
Josquin Desprez:Missa, "Hercules Dux Ferrariae" [realized by K. Geisler] Well-Tempered Productions ▲ WPT 5165 [DDD]
Ockeghem, J.:Missa prolationum [realized by K. Geisler] Well-Tempered Productions ▲ WPT 5165 [DDD]
Vivaldi, A.:Cons Vn, Op. 8/1-4, "The Four Seasons" [realized by K. Geisler] Well-Tempered Productions ▲ WPT 5166 [DDD]

Geisler, Kathy (cmpt/ob)
Albinoni, T.:Cons Obs—in d *(rec Center for Computer Research in Music & Acoustics, Stanford & Mobius Music, San Francisco)* Well-Tempered Productions ▲ WTP 5167 [DDD]
Bach, J.S.:Con Ob d'amore *(rec Center for Computer Research in Music & Acoustics, Stanford & Mobius Music, San Francisco)* Well-Tempered Productions ▲ WTP 5167 [DDD]
Handel, G.F.:Cons (3) Ob—in g *(rec Center for Computer Research in Music & Acoustics, Stanford & Mobius Music, San Francisco)* Well-Tempered Productions ▲ WTP 5167 [DDD]
Marcello, A.:Cons Ob—in d *(rec Center for Computer Research in Music & Acoustics, Stanford & Mobius Music, San Francisco)* Well-Tempered Productions ▲ WTP 5167 [DDD]
Telemann, G.P.:Cons Ob Orch—in d *(rec Center for Computer Research in Music & Acoustics, Stanford & Mobius Music, San Francisco)* Well-Tempered Productions ▲ WTP 5167 [DDD]
Vivaldi, A.:Cons Ob—in F, R.455 *(rec Center for Computer Research in Music & Acoustics, Stanford & Mobius Music, San Francisco)* Well-Tempered Productions ▲ WTP 5167 [DDD]

Geisler, Kathy (elec)
Handel, G.F.:Messiah (sels)—Symphony; And he shall purify; For behold, darkness shall cover the earth; The people that walked in darkness; Pifa; There were shepherds abiding in the field; And lo, the angel of the Lord came upon them; And the angel said unto them; And suddenly there was with the angel; Glory to God in the highest; His yoke is easy, His burthen is light; Surely, He hath borne our griefs & carried our sorrow; And with his stripes we are healed; All we like sheep have gone astray; All they that see Him, laugh Him to scorn; He trusted in God; Thou art gone up on high; How beautiful are the feet of them; Why do the nations so furiously rage together; Let us break their bonds assunder; He that dwelleth in heaven; Thou shalt break them with a rod of iron; I know that my redeemer liveth; O death, where is thy sting?; But thanks be to God Well-Tempered Productions ▲ WTP 5162 [DDD]
Six Concertos for Oboe & Virtual Orchestra Well-Tempered Productions ▲ WTP 5167 [DDD]
21st Century Bach Well-Tempered Productions ▲ WTP 5160 [DDD]

Ghezzo, Dinu (elec)
Ghezzo, D.:Prayers (2), w. Catherine Rowe (sop) *(rec Aaron Copland School of Music, Queens College, NYC)* Capstone ▲ CPS 8616 [ADD]

Giri, Joseph (record players)
Cage, J.:Europera 3, w. Suzan Hanson (sop), Ruby Hinds (mez), Patricia McAfee (mez), Michael Lyon (ten), Richard Powell (ten), Kevin Bell (bass), Brian Pezzone (pno), Vicki Ray (pno), Hannes Geiger (record players), William Houston (record players), Dren McDonald (record players), Ronda Rindone (record players), Clarice Ross (record players), Scott Fraser (tape), Andrew Culver (cnd), Long Beach Opera Orch *(rec Center Theater, Long Beach, CA, Nov. 13, 1993)* Mode 2-▲ MODE 38/39

Gordon, Peter (elec)
Ashley, R.:Perfect Lives [Private Parts], w. R. Ashley (nar), "Blue" G. Tyranny (kbds), J. Kroesen (voc), D. Van Thiegem (voc) Lovely Music 3-▲ LCD 4917.3 [ADD] 2-■ LMC 4913/4947

Grimmer, Mineko (audible sculptures)
Fujieda, M.:Music of, w. Mamoru Fujueda (cmpt), Makiko Sakurai (shomyo/Buddhist chant), Kodo Uesugi (fukimono), Kazuko Takada (hikimono), Toshiyuki Matsukura (uchimono), Satoshi Sakai (uchimono), Koshin Ebihara (jumon)—The Night Chant III; Wind Chant; Cocoon Chant; Duct Chant; Falling Chant; The Night Chant I Tzadik ("The Composers" series) ▲ TZA 7003 [DDD]

Grippe, Ragnar (elec)
Grippe, R.:Situation I *(rec 1976)* BIS ▲ CD 241 [AAD]
Grippe, R.:Ten Temperaments *(rec Nov. 1981)* BIS ▲ CD 241 [AAD]
Grippe, R.:Ur Undrens Tid *(rec 1975)* BIS ▲ CD 241 [AAD]

Hamilton, Tom (cmpt/syn)
Ashley, R.:Superior 7, w. Barbara Held (cmpt), Robert Ashley (syn) *(rec 10 Beach St, NYC)* New World ▲ 80460-2

Hamilton, Tom (syn)
Ashley, R.:Tract, w. Thomas Bruckner (bar), Robert Ashley (cmpt/syn), Nathaniel Reichman (cmpt/syn) *(rec 10 Beach St, NYC)* New World ▲ 80460-2

Hamilton, Tom (syn/elec)
Hamilton, T.:Off-Hour Wait State, w. Thomas Buckner (voc), Roscoe Mitchell (a sax), Ralph Samuelson (shak), Peter Zummo (trbn), Jonathan Haas (perc) O.O. Discs ▲ OO 26 [DDD]

Harvey, Jonathan (elec)
Harvey, J.:Ritual Melodies Bridge ▲ BCD 9031 [DDD]

Hays, Sorrel (elec)
Hays, S.:Structure 123 New World ▲ 805202 [DDD]

Hays, Sorrel (elec/elec sax)
Hays, S.:Take a Back Country Road, w. Brian Charles (ob), Marilyn Ries (elec) New World ▲ 805202 [DDD]

Held, Barbara (cmpt)
Ashley, R.:Superior 7, w. Tom Hamilton (cmpt/syn), Robert Ashley (syn) *(rec 10 Beach St, NYC)* New World ▲ 80460-2

Henry, Pierre (elecs)
Henry, P.:Vars for a Door & a Sigh Musique d'Abord ▲ HMA 1905200
Henry, P.:The Veil of Orpheus Musique d'Abord ▲ HMA 1905200

Holland, John (elec/kbd)
Holland, J.:Etudes 1-24 Titanic ▲ Ti 180 [DDD]

Holmes, R. (elecs)
Holmes, R.:Drumfire Opus One ▲ CD 162
Holmes, R.:Electric Syms Opus One ▲ CD 162

Houston, William (record players)
Cage, J.:Europera 3, w. Suzan Hanson (sop), Ruby Hinds (mez), Patricia McAfee (mez), Michael Lyon (ten), Richard Powell (ten), Kevin Bell (bass), Brian Pezzone (pno), Vicki Ray (pno), Hannes Geiger (record players), Joseph Giri (record players), Dren McDonald (record players), Ronda Rindone (record players), Clarice Ross (record players), Scott Fraser (tape), Andrew Culver (cnd), Long Beach Opera Orch *(rec Center Theater, Long Beach, CA, Nov. 13, 1993)* Mode 2-▲ MODE 38/39

Hughes, Chris (elecs)
Hughes, C.:Shift Philips ▲ 314518-2 [DDD]

Hunt, Jerry (elec)
Hunt, J.:Cantegral Segments CRI ▲ CRI 713 [ADD]
Hunt, J.:Chimanzzi, w. J. Henry (vn/elec) O.O. Discs ▲ OO 9 [DDD]
Hunt, J.:Haramand Plane ¿What Next? ▲ WN 0015
Hunt, J.:Kernel CRI ▲ CRI 713 [ADD]
Hunt, J.:Lattice CRI ▲ CRI 713 [ADD]
Hunt, J.:Talk, w. Rod Stasick (elec) O.O. Discs ▲ OO 9 [DDD]
Hunt, J.:Transform CRI ▲ CRI 713 [ADD]
Hunt, J.:Transform O.O. Discs ▲ OO 9 [DDD]
Hunt, J.:Transphalba CRI ▲ CRI 713 [ADD]

Hutton, D. (elec)
Celona, J.:Sum over Histories, w. B. Degazio (sgr), S. Peet (sgr), R. Sacks (sgr), A. Armin (elecs), R. Armin (elecs), J. Brownell (elecs), G. Martynec (elecs), D. Mott (elecs), C. Sokol (elecs) Soundprints ▲ SP 9301
Degazio, B.:Digital Rituals, w. A. R. Armin (elec), J. Brownell (elec), B. Degazio (elec), G. Martynec (elec), D. Mott (elec), S. Peet (elec), R. Sacks (elec), C. Sokol (elec) Soundprints ▲ SP 9301
Mott, D.:Oh! Mysterious Magnum, w. A. Armin (elec), R. Armin (elec), J. Brownell (elec), B. Degazio (elec), G. Martynec (elec), D. Mott (elec), S. Peet (elec), R. Sacks (elec), C. Sokol (elec) Soundprints ▲ SP 9301
Tenney, J.:Tableaux Vivants, w. A. Armin (elec), R. Armin (elec), J. Brownell (elec), B. Degazio (elec), G. Martynec (elec), D. Mott (elec), S. Peet (elec), R. Sacks (elec), C. Sokol (elec) [electronic music] Soundprints ▲ SP 9301

Jackson, Glenda (actor)
Peaslee, R.:Marat/Sade, w. Peter Brook (cnd), *(orch unknown)*, Royal Shakespeare Company *(this is a reissue of the 1966 New York Original Cast recording)* Premier ▲ PRCD 1022 [ADD]
Peaslee, R.:US, w. Peter Brook (cnd), *(orch unknown)*, Royal Shakespeare Company *(this is a reissue of the 1966 London Original Cast recording)* Premier ▲ PRCD 1022 [ADD]

James, Bob (elec)
Keyboard Pieces on Synthesized Instruments CBS ▲ MK 39540 [DDD]

Karpen, R. (elec)
Karpen, R.:Denouement Centaur ▲ CRC 2144 [DDD]
Karpen, R.:Saxonomy, w. M. Brockman (saxs) Centaur ▲ CRC 2144 [DDD]

Katzer, Georg (elec)
Katzer, G.:Aide Memoire ReR ▲ CMCD [DDD]

Keable, Michel (actor)
Gratton, H.:Imagerie:Christmas Pastoral, w. S. Léonard (actor), J.-L. Millette (actor), M. Laferrière (sop), C. Rioux (mez), B. Levasseur (bar), N. Richard (b-bar), L. Lavigueur (cnd), Louis Lavigueur Instrumental Ensemble, Louis Lavigueur Vocal Ensemble [F] *(rec 5/91)* CBC ("SM 5000" series) ▲ SMCD 5109 [DDD]

Kim-1, (cmpt)
Behrman, D.:Figure in a Clearing, w. David Behrman (elec), David Gibson (vc) *(rec State Univ of New York, Albany, June 9, 1977)* Lovely Music ▲ LCD 1041 [ADD]
Behrman, D.:On the Other Ocean, w. David Behrman (elec), Maggi Payne (fl), Arthur Stidfole (bn) *(rec Mills College, Oakland, CA, Sep 18, 1977)* Lovely Music ▲ LCD 1041 [ADD]

Krček, Jaroslav (elec)
Krček, J.:Sonaty Slavickove ReR ▲ CMCD [DDD]

Kucharz, L. (elec)
Kucharz, L.:Computer Music—Aquarids (1991 No. 5); Ethereal Proportions for A.W. (1976 No. 7) [realization of instrumental work]; Radiant (1987 No. 9); Cosmology for C.B. (1992 No. 9); Lunar Bells (1982 No. 3); Celestial Mechanics (1982 No. 3); Radial Velocity (1983 No. 6); Luminous Precession (1977 No. 11) [realization of instrumental work]; Lyrids (1992 No. 8) International Audiochrome ▲ IA 24
Kucharz, L.:Computer Music—1987 No. 7; 1976 No. 3 [realization of instrumental work]; 1986 No. 4; 1990 No. 4; 1987 No. 11; 1989 No. 2; 1975 No. 5 [realization of instrumental work]; 1988 No. 8; 1988 No. 9 International Audiochrome ▲ IA 23

Lansky, Paul (cmpt)
Lansky, P.:Computer Music—Idle Chatter; Word Color; just_more_idle_chatter; The Lesson; Notjustmoreidlechatter; Memory Pages Bridge ▲ BCD 9050 [DDD]

Lansky, Paul (cmpt/gtr/vn)
Lansky, P.:Music of—Strut; Tender Ladies; Delta; Ash Grove; Hammer; Barbara Allen; Howl; Pine Ridge; Wayfaring Stranger; Pretty Polly; Blue Wine; Motherless Child Bridge ▲ BCD 9060 [DDD]

Lansky, Paul (elec)
Lansky, P.:Fants on a Poem by Thomas Campion CRI ▲ CD 683 [DDD]
Lansky, P.:Still Time CRI ▲ CD 683 [DDD]
Six fantasies on a Poem by Thomas Campion CRI ▲ S 456

Lansky, Paul (elec/sgr)
Lansky, P.:Smalltalk & August, w. H. McKay (sgr) New Albion ▲ NA 030 [DDD]

Lansky, Paul (hands)
Lansky, P.:Music for Computer-Processed Natural Sounds, w. J. Lansky (perc), C. Lansky (perc), H. MacKay (nar), J. Moses (hands)—Table's Clear (percussive kitchen paraphernalia); Night Traffic (traffic sounds); Now and Then (speech-music); Quakerbridge (people in a suburban shopping mall); The Sound of Two Hands Bridge ▲ BCD 9035 [DDD]

Léonard, S. (actor)
Gratton, H.:Imagerie:Christmas Pastoral, w. M. Keable (actor), J.-L. Millette (actor), M. Laferrière (sop), C. Rioux (mez), B. Levasseur (bar), N. Richard (b-bar), L. Lavigueur (cnd), Louis Lavigueur Instrumental Ensemble, Louis Lavigueur Vocal Ensemble [F] *(rec 5/91)* CBC ("SM 5000" series) ▲ SMCD 5109 [DDD]

Lewis, Peter Tod (elec)
Lewis, P.T.:Music of, w. J. Ferrell (vn), J. Avery (pno), S. Schick (perc), Center for New Music Ensemble, Columbia String Quartet—Bricolage (1979); Gestes (1973); Manestar (1970); ...of bells...and time (1967); Signs & Circuits—String Quartet No. 2 (1969) *(rec 1978-82)* CRI ▲ CD 619 [ADD]

Lockwood, Annea (elec)
Lockwood, A.:A Sound Map of the Hudson River—Lockwood traces the course of the Hudson through on-site recordings of its flow at 15 separate locations; an enclosed color fold-out map correlates numbered sites with the recording sections Lovely Music ▲ LCD 2081 [ADD]

Lucier, Alvin (elec)
Lucier, A.:Clocker *(rec North Gallery of the Center for the Arts, Wesleyan Univ., June 11, 1991)* Lovely Music ▲ LCD 1019 [DDD]
Lucier, A.:Music on a Long Thin Wire Lovely Music ▲ LCD 1011 [ADD]

Luening, Otto (elec)
Luening, O.:Electronic Music—Fantasy in Space; Invention in 12 Tones; Low Speed; Moonflight CRI ▲ CD 611 [ADD]
Luening, O.:Incantation, w. Ussachevsky (elec) CRI ▲ CD 611 [ADD]
Luening, O.:Poem in Cycles & Bells, w. Ussachevsky (elec), Royal Danish Radio Orch CRI ■ ACS 6011

Lundsten, R. (elec)
Lundsten, R.:Nordic Nature Sym 4—Cloud Dreams; The Remembering Castle *(rec Saltsjö-Boo, Sweden, Apr. 1994)* GNP/Crescendo ▲ GNPD 2241
Lundsten, R.:Nordic Nature Sym 5—The Endless Tale *(rec Saltsjö-Boo, Sweden, Apr. 1994)* GNP/Crescendo ▲ GNPD 2241
Lundsten, R.:Sym of Joy *(rec. Saltsjö-Boo, Sweden, Apr. 1994)* GNP/Crescendo ▲ GNPD 2241
Lundsten, R.:Sym of Light *(rec Saltsjö-Boo, Sweden, Apr. 1994)* GNP/Crescendo ▲ GNPD 2241
Lundsten, R.:Sym of Love *(rec Saltsjö-Boo, Sweden, Apr. 1994)* GNP/Crescendo ▲ GNPD 2241

McDonald, Dren (record players)
Cage, J.:Europera 3, w. Suzan Hanson (sop), Ruby Hinds (mez), Patricia McAfee (mez), Michael Lyon (ten), Richard Powell (ten), Kevin Bell (bass), Brian Pezzone (pno), Vicki Ray (pno), Hannes Geiger (record players), Joseph Giri (record players), William Houston (record players), Ronda Rindone (record players), Clarice Ross (record players), Scott Fraser (tape), Andrew Culver (cnd), Long Beach Opera Orch *(rec Center Theater, Long Beach, CA, Nov. 13, 1993)* Mode 2–▲ MODE 38/39

Machover, Tod (elec)
Machover, T.:Bug-Mudra, w. D. Starobin (gtr), O. Fader (elec gtr), D. Kennedy (perc) *(rec live, Tokyo)* Bridge ▲ BCD 9022 [DDD]
Machover, T.:Valis, w. A. Azéma (sop), J. Felty (mez), T. Edwards (ten), P. Mason (bar), T. Machover (cnd), *(ensemble unknown)* [E] Bridge ▲ BCD 9007 [DDD] ■ BCS 7007 (D)

McLean, Barton (elec)
McLean, B.:A Little Night Music Centaur ▲ CRC 2047 [DDD]
McLean, B.:Visions of a Summer Night *(rec)* Capstone ▲ CPS 8622
McLean, P.:Dance of Shiva *(rec)* Capstone ▲ CPS 8622

Maderna, Bruno (elec)
Maderna, B.:Dimensioni 2, w. C. Berberian (sop), M. Zuccheri (elec) Stradivarius ▲ STR 33349
Maderna, B.:Elec Music, w. M. Zuccheri (elec)—Notturno (1955); Syntaxis (1957); Continuo (1958); Serenata III (1962); Le rire (1964) Stradivarius ▲ STR 33349
Maderna, B.:Musica su due dimensioni, w. Renato Rivolta (fl), M. Zuccheri (elec) Stradivarius ▲ STR 33349

Mahin, Bruce (digital delay)
Mahin, B.:Time Chants II. Monhegan Island, August 1992, w. Caryl Conger (pno) *(rec Radford University's Preston Hall, May 8–9, 1994)* Capstone ♦ CPS 8624 [DDD]

Marclay, Christian (turntables)
Sato, M.:Improvs, w. Michihiro Sato (tsugaru shamisen), Bill Frisell (elec gtr), Fred Frith (elec gtr), Tenko (sgr), Mark Miller (elec bass), Nicolas Collins (elec), Steve Colemann (sax), Tom Cora (vc), Joey Baron (perc), Mark Dresser (elec bass), Gerry Hemingway (perc), Toh Ban Djan (Ikue Mori (perc), Luli Shioi (elec bass/sgr)], Semantics [Elliott Sharp (electric gtr/bass), Samm Bennett (perc), Ned Rothenberg (sax)]—23 improvisations with various accompaniment combinations *(rec Baby Monster Studio, NY, Apr. 11–16, 1988)* Hat Hut ▲ hat ART CD 6015 [ADD]

Marinis, Paul de (computer-altered voice)
de Marinis, P.:Music as 2nd Language—Leçon par l'aiguille; Fonetica Francese; Odd Evening; An Appeal; The Sand Clock; Cincinnati; The Power of Suggestion; Beneath the Numbered Sky Lovely Music ▲ LCD 3011 [ADD]

Marshall, Ingram (elec)
Marshall, I.:Alcatraz New Albion ▲ NA 040 [DDD]

Marshall, Ingram (elec/gambuh)
Marshall, I.:Gambuh 1, w. Foster Reed (tape delay) New Albion ▲ NA 002 [ADD]
Marshall, I.:Gradual Requiem, w. Foster Reed (tape delay) New Albion ▲ NA 002 [ADD]

Martirano, Salvatore (cmpt/kbd)
Martirano, S.:Elec & Cmpt Music, w. Dorothy Martirano (zeta vn)—SATBehind Demo; Look at the Back of My Head for Awhile; 4 Not 2; Electronic Dance No. 1 Centaur ▲ CRC 2266 [DDD]

Martynec, G. (elec)
Celona, J.:Sum over Histories, w. B. Degazio (sgr), S. Peet (sgr), R. Sacks (sgr), A. Armin (elecs), R. Armin (elecs), J. Brownell (elecs), D. Hutton (elecs), D. Mott (elecs), C. Sokol (elecs) Soundprints ▲ SP 9301
Degazio, B.:Digital Rituals, w. A. R. Armin (elec), J. Brownell (elec), B. Degazio (elec), D. Hutton (elec), D. Mott (elec), S. Peet (elec), R. Sacks (elec), C. Sokol (elec) Soundprints ▲ SP 9301
Mott, D.:Oh! Mysterious Magnum, w. A. Armin (elec), R. Armin (elec), J. Brownell (elec), B. Degazio (elec), D. Hutton (elec), D. Mott (elec), S. Peet (elec), R. Sacks (elec), C. Sokol (elec) Soundprints ▲ SP 9301
Tenney, J.:Tableaux Vivants, w. A. Armin (elec), R. Armin (elec), J. Brownell (elec), B. Degazio (elec), D. Hutton (elec), D. Mott (elec), S. Peet (elec), R. Sacks (elec), C. Sokol (elec) [electronic music] Soundprints ▲ SP 9301

Mattila, Edward (elec)
Mattila, E.:Primordius Capstone ▲ SCI 6

Mavrides, Anastasi (arr/syn)
Country Evening Real Music ▲ 67777-2 [DDD]
Country Morning, w. Manken Palmboom (kbd) Real Music ▲ 65555-2 [DDD]

Melby, John (elec)
Melby, J.:Chor der Waisen Centaur ▲ CRC 2045 [DDD]

Metz, Don (tape)
Cage, J.:Europera 5, w. M. Herr (sop), G. Burgess (ten), Y. Mikhashoff (pno), J. Wiliams (victrola [78 rpm]) *(rec Apr. 12, 1991)* Mode ▲ MOD 36 [DDD]

Milesi, Piero (elecs)
La Camera Astratta [The Abstract Room], w. Daniel Bacalov (elecs) Cuneiform ▲ Rune 18

Miller, Cary (actor)
Moore, D.:Devil & Daniel Webster, w. Joyce Guyer (sop—Mary Stone), Benjamin Bongers (ten—Walter Butler), Michael Philip Davis (ten—Simon Girty), Matthew Foerschler (ten—Miser Stephens), Darren Keith Woods (ten—Mr. Scratch), Michael Lanman (bass—Blackbeard Teach), David Soxman (bass—Clerk), Brian Steele (bass—Daniel Webster), John Stephens (bass—Jabez Stone), Andrew Stuckey (bass—King Philip), Robert Gibby Brand (actor), Cary Miller (actor), Russell Patterson (cnd), Kansas City SO, Kansas City Lyric Opera Chorus *(rec Sept 1995)* Newport Classic ▲ NPD 85585 [DDD]

Millette, Jean-Louis (actor)
Gratton, H.:Imagerie:Christmas Pastoral, w. M. Keable (actor), S. Léonard (actor), M. Laferrière (sop), C. Rioux (mez), B. Levasseur (bar), N. Richard (b-bar), L. Lavigueur (cnd), Louis Lavigueur Instrumental Ensemble, Louis Lavigueur Vocal Ensemble [F] *(rec 5/91)* CBC ("SM 5000" series) ▲ SMCD 5109 [DDD]

Mondshine, C. (sound effects)
Behrman, D.:Music of, w. T. Kosugi (vn), B. Neill (tpt), R. Chatham (tpt), jakino (keyboard improvisation)—Interspecies Small Talk (1984); Leapday Night (1983–86); A Traveller's Dream Journal (1988–90) Lovely Music ▲ LCD 1042 [ADD]

Moore, Steve (elec)
Moore, S.:Quiet Gathering ReR ▲ CMCD [DDD]

Morrill, D. (elec)
Morrill, D.:6 Dark Questions *(rec June 1991 & June 1992)* Centaur ▲ CRC 2143 [DDD]
Morrill, D.:Walden Nocturnes *(rec June 1991 & June 1992)* Centaur ▲ CRC 2143 [DDD]

Morrill, D. (elecs)
Chafe, C.:Duo Improvisation, w. C. Chafe (elecs) Centaur ▲ CRC 2133 [DDD]

Moses, J. (hands)
Lansky, P.:Music for Computer-Processed Natural Sounds, w. J. Lansky (perc), C. Lansky (perc), H. MacKay (nar), P. Lansky (hands)—Table's Clear (percussive kitchen paraphernalia); Night Traffic (traffic sounds); Now and Then (speech–music); Quakerbridge (people in a suburban shopping mall); The Sound of Two Hands Bridge ▲ BCD 9035 [DDD]

Mott, D. (elec)
Celona, J.:Sum over Histories, w. B. Degazio (sgr), S. Peet (sgr), R. Sacks (sgr), A. Armin (elecs), R. Armin (elecs), J. Brownell (elecs), B. Hutton (elecs), G. Martynec (elecs), C. Sokol (elecs) Soundprints ▲ SP 9301
Degazio, B.:Digital Rituals, w. A. R. Armin (elec), J. Brownell (elec), B. Degazio (elec), D. Hutton (elec), G. Martynec (elec), S. Peet (elec), R. Sacks (elec), C. Sokol (elec) Soundprints ▲ SP 9301
Mott, D.:Oh! Mysterious Magnum, w. A. Armin (elec), R. Armin (elec), J. Brownell (elec), B. Degazio (elec), D. Hutton (elec), G. Martynec (elec), S. Peet (elec), R. Sacks (elec), C. Sokol (elec) Soundprints ▲ SP 9301
Tenney, J.:Tableaux Vivants, w. A. Armin (elec), R. Armin (elec), J. Brownell (elec), B. Degazio (elec), D. Hutton (elec), G. Martynec (elec), S. Peet (elec), R. Sacks (elec), C. Sokol (elec) [electronic music] Soundprints ▲ SP 9301

Mowitz, Ira (elec)
Mowitz, I.J.:Computer Music—A la Memoire d'un Ami; Darkening; Shimmering New Albion ▲ NA 047

Nageak, J. (Iñupiat Eskimo performer)
Adams, J.L.:Earth & the Great Weather, w. R. Lorentz (vn/perc), R. Lawrence (va), M. Finckel (vc), R. Black (db/perc), A. Knoles (perc), J. L. Adams (perc), D. Simmonds (Iñupiat Eskimo performer), L. Tritt (Gwich'in Indian performer), A. P. Raboff (Gwich'in Indian performer), D. Hunsaker (Latin voice), John Luthers Adams (cnd) *(rec Fairbanks, Mar. 8–11, 1993)* New World ▲ 80459-2

Nelson, M. (elec tape)
Corwell, N.:New England Reveries *(rec 12/90–1/91)* Crystal ▲ CD 691

Nikolais, Alwin (elec)
Nikolais, A.:Dance Music CRI ▲ CD 651 [DDD]

Panis, Jan (sound projection)
Boogman, W.:La Disciplina Dei sentimenti, w. Charlotte Riedijk (nar), Hans Tutschku (sound projection), Mark Foster (cnd), Asko Ensemble, Asko Choir *(rec Muziekcentrum Vredenburg Utrecht, Netherlands, Dec 17, 1993)* Donemus ▲ CV 57 [DDD]

Peet, S. (elec)
Degazio, B.:Digital Rituals, w. A. R. Armin (elec), J. Brownell (elec), B. Degazio (elec), D. Hutton (elec), G. Martynec (elec), D. Mott (elec), R. Sacks (elec), C. Sokol (elec) Soundprints ▲ SP 9301
Mott, D.:Oh! Mysterious Magnum, w. A. Armin (elec), R. Armin (elec), J. Brownell (elec), B. Degazio (elec), D. Hutton (elec), G. Martynec (elec), D. Mott (elec), R. Sacks (elec), C. Sokol (elec) Soundprints ▲ SP 9301
Tenney, J.:Tableaux Vivants, w. A. Armin (elec), R. Armin (elec), J. Brownell (elec), B. Degazio (elec), D. Hutton (elec), G. Martynec (elec), D. Mott (elec), R. Sacks (elec), C. Sokol (elec) [electronic music] Soundprints ▲ SP 9301

Pimenta, Emanuel (elec)
Pimenta, E.D. de M.:Electro-Acoustic Music—Rings (1989); Rozart (1989); Structures II (1988); Short Waves 1985 (1985) Mode ▲ 21 [ADD]

Pugliese, Michael (9 clay pots/tapes)
Cage, J.:Five Stone Wind, w. T. Kosugi (amplified vn/live elec/bamboo fl), D. Tudor (live elec) Mode ▲ 24

Pugliese, Michael (phonograph cartidges & amplified small objects)
Cage, J.:Cartridge Music, w. T. Kosugi (phonograph cartidges & amplified small objects), D. Tudor (phonograph cartidges & amplified small objects) Mode ▲ 24

Raboff, A. P. (Gwich'in Indian performer)
Adams, J.L.:Earth & the Great Weather, w. R. Lorentz (vn/perc), R. Lawrence (va), M. Finckel (vc), R. Black (db/perc), A. Knoles (perc), J. L. Adams (perc), J. Nageak (Iñupiat Eskimo performer), D. Simmonds (Iñupiat Eskimo performer), L. Tritt (Gwich'in Indian performer), D. Hunsaker (Latin voice), John Luthers Adams (cnd) *(rec Fairbanks, Mar. 8–11, 1993)* New World ▲ 80459-2

Rahn, John (elec)
Rahn, J.:Kali Centaur ▲ CRC 2144 [DDD]
Rahn, J.:Miranda Centaur ▲ CRC 2144 [DDD]

Rechtman, I. (cmpt)
Vivaldi, A.:Cons Vn, Op. 8/1–4, "The Four Seasons", w. P. Saint-Denis (fl) *(rec Oct. 1992)* Omega ▲ OCD 3020 [DDD]

Reed, Foster (tape delay)
Marshall, I.:Gambuh 1, w. I. Marshall (elec/gambuh) New Albion ▲ NA 002 [ADD]
Marshall, I.:Gradual Requiem, w. I. Marshall (elec/gambuh) New Albion ▲ NA 002 [ADD]

Reich, Steve (elec)
Reich, S.:Come Out Elektra/Nonesuch ▲ 79169-2 [DDD] ■ 79169-4 (D)
Reich, S.:It's Gonna Rain Elektra/Nonesuch ▲ 79169-2 [DDD] ■ 79169-4 (D)

Reichman, Nathaniel (cmpt/syn)
Ashley, R.:Tract, w. Thomas Bruckner (bar), Robert Ashley (cmpt/syn), Tom Hamilton (syn) *(rec 10 Beach St, NYC)* New World ▲ 80460-2

Reynolds, K. (elec)
Reynolds, R.:Ping, w. R. Reynolds (elec), *(ensemble unknown)* CRI ■ C 285
Reynolds, R.:Traces, w. R. Reynolds (elec), *(ensemble unknown)* CRI ■ C 285

Reynolds, R. (elec)
Reynolds, R.:Ping, w. K. Reynolds (elec), *(ensemble unknown)* CRI ■ C 285
Reynolds, R.:Traces, w. K. Reynolds (elec), *(ensemble unknown)* CRI ■ C 285

Richard, André (tapes/sound effects)
Nono, L.:Lontananza, w. I. Arditti (vn), Montaigne ▲ MO 782004 [DDD]
Nono, L.:Madrigale per piu "caminantes", w. I. Arditti (vn) Montaigne ▲ MO 782004 [DDD]

Ries, Marilyn (elec)
Hays, S.:Take a Back Country Road, w. Brian Charles (ob), Sorrel Hays (elec sax/elec) New World ▲ 805202 [DDD]

Riley, Terry (elec)
Riley, T.:Descending Moonshine Dervishes Kuckuck ▲ 12047-2
Riley, T.:Descending Moonshine Dervishes Kuckuck ■ 11047-4
Riley, T.:Poppy Nogood's Phantom Band CBS ▲ MK 07315 [ADD]
Riley, T.:Shri Camel CBS ▲ MK 35164 [ADD]

Rindone, Ronda (record players)
Cage, J.:Europera 3, w. Suzan Hanson (sop), Ruby Hinds (mez), Patricia McAfee (mez), Michael Lyon (ten), Richard Powell (ten), Kevin Bell (bass), Brian Pezzone (pno), Vicki Ray (pno), Hannes Geiger (record players), Joseph Giri (record players), William Houston (record players), Dren McDonald (record players), Clarice Ross (record players), Scott Fraser (tape), Andrew Culver (cnd), Long Beach Opera Orch *(rec Center Theater, Long Beach, CA, Nov. 13, 1993)* Mode 2–▲ MODE 38/39

Risdall, Cora (baby)
Oswald, J.:Parade, w. John Oswald (kbd/a sax/elec), Paul Plimley (kbd), Alex Varty (gtr) ReR ▲ CMCD [DDD]

Rockmore, Clara (elecs)
The Art of the Theremin: transcriptions Delos ▲ DCD 1014 [AAD]

Rodger, Eckhard (ring modulator)
Kelemen, M.:Mirabilia, w. Gerhard Erber (pno), Max Pommer (cnd), Leipzig RSO Berlin Classics ▲ BER 1144 [ADD]

Rolnick, Neil B. (elec)
Kabat, J.:Child & the Moon-Tree, w. J. Kabat (voice) Centaur ▲ CRC 2047 [DDD]
Rolnick, N.B.:Elec Music, w. Gamelan Son of Lion members—Balkanization (for MIDI performance system); Macedonian AirDrumming (for MIDI & AirDrums); ReRebong (for gamelan instruments & real-time digital processing); Sanctus (computer generated tape) Bridge ▲ BCD 9030 [DDD]
Rolnick, N.B.:The Persistance of the Clavé Centaur ▲ CRC 2133 [DDD]
Rolnick, N.B.:A Robert Johnson Sampler Centaur ▲ CRC 2047 [DDD]
Rolnick, N.B.:Vocal Chords, w. K. Myers (voc) Centaur ▲ CRC 2047 [DDD]
Rolnick, N.B.:What Is The Use? Centaur ▲ CRC 2039 [DDD]

Rosenboom, David (elec)
Rosenboom, D.:A Precipice in Time, w. A. Braxton (sax), W. Winant (perc), et al. Centaur ▲ CRC 2110 [DDD]
Rosenboom, D.:Systems of Judgement Centaur ▲ CRC 2077 [DDD]

Ross, Clarice (record players)
Cage, J.:Europera 3, w. Suzan Hanson (sop), Ruby Hinds (mez), Patricia McAfee (mez), Michael Lyon (ten), Richard Powell (ten), Kevin Bell (bass), Brian Pezzone (pno), Vicki Ray (pno), Hannes Geiger (record players), Joseph Giri (record players), William Houston (record players), Dren McDonald (record players), Ronda Rindone (record players), Scott Fraser (tape), Andrew Culver (cnd), Long Beach Opera Orch *(rec Center Theater, Long Beach, CA, Nov. 13, 1993)* Mode 2–▲ MODE 38/39

Rúbio, Javier (elec)
Manchado, M.:Ov RNE/Spanish National Radio ▲ M3/12 [ADD]

Sacks, R. (elec)
Degazio, B.:Digital Rituals, w. A. R. Armin (elec), J. Brownell (elec), B. Degazio (elec), D. Hutton (elec), G. Martynec (elec), D. Mott (elec), S. Peet (elec), C. Sokol (elec) Soundprints ▲ SP 9301

1492 ▲ = CD ♦ = Enhanced CD Δ = MD ■ = Cassette Tape ◻ = DCC

Sacks, R. (elec) (cont.)
Mott, D.:Oh! Mysterious Magnum, w. A. Armin (elec), R. Armin (elec), J. Brownell (elec), B. Degazio (elec), D. Hutton (elec), G. Martynec (elec), D. Mott (elec), S. Peet (elec), C. Sokol (elec)
Soundprints ▲ SP 9301
Tenney, J.:Tableaux Vivants, w. A. Armin (elec), R. Armin (elec), J. Brownell (elec), B. Degazio (elec), D. Hutton (elec), G. Martynec (elec), D. Mott (elec), S. Peet (elec), C. Sokol (elec) (electronic music)
Soundprints ▲ SP 9301

Satoh, Somei (elec)
Satoh, S.:Mantra
New Albion ▲ NA 016 [DAD]

Scaletti, Carla (elec)
Scaletti, C.:sunSurgeAutomata
Centaur ▲ CRC 2045 [DDD]

Scholz, C. (elec)
Oliveros, P.:Lion's Tale
Centaur ▲ CRC 2047 [DDD]

Schwartz, Elliott (tape)
Schwartz, E.:Cycles & Gongs, w. L Raver (org), A. Dean (tpt)
CRI ▲ CD 598 [ADD]
Schwartz, E.:Extended Cl, w. J. Bunke (cl)
CRI ▲ CD 598 [ADD]

Scott, D. (elec)
Scott, D.:Interlude & Fant
Centaur ▲ CRC 2170 [DDD]

Shea, David (sampler/pno/turntables)
Shea, D.:Hsi-Yu Chi, w. Sim Cain (perc), Hideki Kato (bass instrument), Wu Man (pipa), Zeena Parkins (hp/pno/acc), Jim Pugliese (perc), Mark Ribot (gtr/banjo), Alex Tobias (celtic dr/misc.), Rebecca Wilson (screaming), John Zorn (a sax)
Tzadik ("The Composers" series) ▲ TZA 7005 [DDD]

Shea, David (turntables)
Zorn, J.:Elegy, w. Mike Patton (sgr), Barbara Chaffe (fl), David Abel (vn), Scummy (gtr), David Slusser (sound effects), William Winant (perc)
Tzadik ▲ TZA 7302 [ADD]

Simmonds, D. (Iñupiat Eskimo performer)
Adams, J.L.:Earth & the Great Weather, w. R. Lorentz (vn/perc), R. Lawrence (va), M. Finckel (vc), R. Black (db/perc), A. Knoles (perc), J. L Adams (perc), J. Nageak (Iñupiat Eskimo performer), L. Tritt (Gwich'in Indian performer), A. P. Raboff (Gwich'in Indian performer), D. Hunsaker (Latin voice), John Luthers Adams (cnd) (rec Fairbanks, Mar. 8–11, 1993)
New World ▲ 80459-2

Slusser, David (sound effects)
Zorn, J.:Elegy, w. Mike Patton (sgr), Barbara Chaffe (fl), David Abel (vn), Scummy (gtr), David Shea (turntables), William Winant (perc)
Tzadik ▲ TZA 7302 [ADD]

Smiley, P. (elec)
Smiley, P.:Kolyosa
CRI ▲ CD 611 [ADD]

Sokol, C. (elec)
Celona, J.:Sum over Histories, w. B. Degazio (sgr), S. Peet (sgr), R. Sacks (sgr), A. Armin (elecs), R. Armin (elecs), J. Brownell (elecs), D. Hutton (elecs), G. Martynec (elecs), D. Mott (elecs)
Soundprints ▲ SP 9301
Degazio, B.:Digital Rituals, w. A. R. Armin (elec), J. Brownell (elec), B. Degazio (elec), D. Hutton (elec), G. Martynec (elec), D. Mott (elec), S. Peet (elec), R. Sacks (elec)
Soundprints ▲ SP 9301
Mott, D.:Oh! Mysterious Magnum, w. A. Armin (elec), R. Armin (elec), J. Brownell (elec), B. Degazio (elec), D. Hutton (elec), G. Martynec (elec), D. Mott (elec), S. Peet (elec), R. Sacks (elec)
Soundprints ▲ SP 9301
Tenney, J.:Tableaux Vivants, w. A. Armin (elec), R. Armin (elec), J. Brownell (elec), B. Degazio (elec), D. Hutton (elec), G. Martynec (elec), D. Mott (elec), S. Peet (elec), R. Sacks (elec)
Soundprints ▲ SP 9301

Spek, Jaap (elec)
Stockhausen, K.:Kontakte, w. J. Avery (pno/perc), S. Schick (perc)
Music & Arts ▲ CD 648 [AAD/ADD]

Sprinkle, Annie (moans/groans)
Curran, A.:Animal Behavior, w. Alvin Curran (sampler)
Tzadik ("The Composers" series) ▲ TZA 7001 [DDD]

Stasick, Rod (elec)
Hunt, J.:Talk, w. Jerry Hunt (elec)
O.O. Discs ▲ OO 9 [DDD]

Steiger, Rand (cmpt)
Subotnick, M.:The Key to Songs, w. Rand Steiger (cnd), California EAR Unit Yamaha Computer Assisted Music System
New Albion ▲ NA 012
Subotnick, M.:Return, w. Rand Steiger (cnd), California EAR Unit Yamaha Computer Assisted Music System
New Albion ▲ NA 012

Swearington, Donald (elec)
Swearingen, D.:Salvation at 1 AM—recordings from late night TV programs
¿What Next? ▲ WN 0014

Tcherepnin, Ivan (elecs)
Tcherepnin, I.:Flores musicales, w. Peggy Pearson (ob), Wilma Smith (vn) (rec Harvard Univ. Electronic Music Studio, Oct. & Dec. 1981)
CRI ▲ CD 684 [ADD]
Tcherepnin, I.:Santur Live
CRI ▲ CD 684 [ADD]
Tcherepnin, I.:Songs Cta, w. Marion Dry (cta), Jean-Pierre Dautricourt (fl) (rec Harvard University Electronic Music Studio, Oct. & Dec. 1981)
CRI ▲ CD 684 [ADD]

Tecayehuatzin, V. S. (elec)
Tecayehuatzin, V.S.:Fluxions
Capstone ▲ CPS 8609 CD

Teitelbaum, Richard (elec)
Teitelbaum, R.:Con Grosso, w. Anthony Braxton (ww), George Lewis (trbn) (rec Klaviere & Computer Festival, Cologne, May 3, 1985)
Hat Hut ▲ hat ART CD 6004 [AAD]
Teitelbaum, R.:Golem I
Centaur ▲ CRC 2039 [DDD]

Thorington, Helen (elec)
Thorington, H.:Partial Perceptions, w. Shelley Hirsch (sgr), Joseph Celli (instrs)
¿What Next? ▲ WN 0013

Tone, Yasunao (elec)
Tone, Y.:Music of—Jiao Liao Fruits, Solar Eclipse in October
Lovely Music ▲ LOV 3041 [DDD]

Tritt, L (Gwich'in Indian performer)
Adams, J.L.:Earth & the Great Weather, w. R. Lorentz (vn/perc), R. Lawrence (va), M. Finckel (vc), R. Black (db/perc), A. Knoles (perc), J. L. Adams (perc), J. Nageak (Iñupiat Eskimo performer), D. Simmonds (Iñupiat Eskimo performer), A. P. Raboff (Gwich'in Indian performer), D. Hunsaker (Latin voice), John Luthers Adams (cnd) (rec Fairbanks, Mar. 8–11, 1993)
New World ▲ 80459-2

Trochu, P. (elec)
Trochu, P.:Eros
Centrediscs ▲ CD 3288

Trythall, Richard (elec)
Trythall, R.:Ommagio a Jerry Lee Lewis
ReR ▲ CMCD [DDD]

Tudor, David (elec)
Cage, J.:Five Stone Wind, w. T. Kosugi (amplified vn/live elec/bamboo fl), M. Pugliese (9 clay pots/tapes)
Mode ▲ 24
Cage, J.:Indeterminacy, w. J. Cage (speaker)
Smithsonian/Folkways 2–▲ SF 40804/5 [AAD]
Tudor, D.:Elec Music—Neural Syntheses Nos. 6, 7, 8 & 9 (rec)
Lovely Music 2–▲ LCD 1602 [DDD]
Tudor, D.:Phonemes
Lovely Music ▲ LCD 1601 [ADD]
Tudor, D.:Pulsers, w. Takehisa Kosugi (elec vn)
Lovely Music ▲ LCD 1601 [ADD]
Tudor, D.:Untitled, w. Takehisa Kosugi (sgr)
Lovely Music ▲ LCD 1601 [ADD]

Tudor, David (phonograph cartridges & amplified small objects)
Cage, J.:Cartridge Music, w. T. Kosugi (phonograph cartridges & amplified small objects), M. Pugliese (phonograph cartridges & amplified small objects)
Mode ▲ 24

Tutschku, Hans (sound projection)
Boogman, W.:La Disciplina Dei sentimenti, w. Charlotte Riedijk (nar), Jan Panis (sound projection), Mark Foster (cnd), Asko Ensemble, Asko Choir (rec Muziekcentrum Vredenburg Utrecht, Netherlands, Dec 17, 1993)
Donemus ▲ CV 57 [DDD]

Ungvary, T. (elec)
Ungvary, T.:Gypsy Children's Giant Dance with Lil Fourier
Wergo ▲ WER 2032-2

Unrau, Lucia (elec)
Terry, P.:Aria & Accidental Music
Cambria ▲ CD 1088

Ussachevsky, Vladimir (elec)
Luening, O.:Incantation, w. Otto Luening (elec)
CRI ▲ CD 611 [ADD]
Luening, O.:Poem in Cycles & Bells, w. Otto Luening (elec), Royal Danish Radio Orch
CRI ■ ACS 6011

Ussachevsky, Vladimir (elec) (cont.)
Ussachevsky, V.:Elec Music—Computer Piece No. 1; Piece for Tape Recorder; Sonic Contours; Two Sketches for a Computer Piece
CRI ▲ CD 611 [ADD]
Ussachevsky, V.:Line of Apogee
New World ▲ NW 80389-2 [AAD]
Ussachevsky, V.:No Exit
New World ▲ NW 80389-2 [AAD]

Vandermaelen, Johan (elec)
Crumb, G.:Black Angels (Images I), w. Filip Suys (vn), Marleen Ydiers (vn), Annemarie Vercauteren (va), Arne Deforce (vc) (rec Steurbaut Sound Recording Ctr)
René Gailly ▲ CD87 118 [DDD]

Vennonen, Kimmo (samples)
Machine For Making Sense:On 2nd Thoughts, w. Machine for Making Sense
O.O. Discs ▲ OO 19 [ADD]

Ward, Peter (elecs)
Oliveros, P.:The Roots of the Moment, w. Pauline Oliveros (acc/elecs) (rec Studio Lussi, Allschwil, Switzerland, Nov. 10, 1987)
Hat Hut ("NOW." series) ▲ hat ART CD 6009 [ADD]

Waschka, R. (elec/comp/vox)
Waschka (II), R.:Help Me Remember (rec Dec. 1992)
Centaur ▲ CRC 2170 [DDD]

Wesley-Smith, Martin (cmpt)
Wesley-Smith, M.:Japanese Pictures (rec Electronic Music Studio, Sydney Conservatorium of Music)
Tall Poppies ▲ TP 072 [DDD]
Wesley-Smith, M.:Riffs (rec Electronic Music Studio, Sydney Conservatorium of Music)
Tall Poppies ▲ TP 072 [DDD]

Wesley-Smith, Martin (elec)
Wesley-Smith, M.:Beta-Globin DNA (rec Electronic Music Studio, Sydney Conservatorium of Music)
Tall Poppies ▲ TP 072 [DDD]
Wesley-Smith, M.:Snark-Hunting 2, w. Olivia Wesley-Smith (sgr) [excerpts from Boojum! (1986)] (rec Electronic Music Studio, Sydney Conservatorium of Music)
Tall Poppies ▲ TP 072 [DDD]
Wesley-Smith, M.:VENCEREMOS, w. Robert Constable (prepared pno), Michael Askill (perc) (rec Electronic Music Studio, Sydney Conservatorium of Music)
Tall Poppies ▲ TP 072 [DDD]
Wesley-Smith, M.:Vietnam Image
Tall Poppies ▲ TP 072 [DDD]
Wesley-Smith, M.:Wattamolla Red (rec Electronic Music Studio, Sydney Conservatorium of Music)
Tall Poppies ▲ TP 072 [DDD]

Wheeler, Jerry (victrola)
Cage, J.:Europera 4, w. Anne-Marie Ketchum (sop), Daisetta Kim (sop), Brian Pezzone (pno), Scott Fraser (tape), Andrew Culver (cnd), Long Beach Opera Orch (rec Center Theater, Long Beach, CA, Nov. 13, 1993)
Mode 2–▲ MODE 38/39

Whitehead, Gregory (elec)
Whitehead, Gregory: Pressures of the Unspeakable
¿What Now? ▲ WN 0014

Wiliams, J. (victrola)
Cage, J.:Europera 5, w. M. Herr (sop), G. Burgess (ten), Y. Mikhashoff (pno), J. Wiliams (victrola [78 rpm]), D. Metz (tape) (rec Apr. 12, 1991)
Mode ▲ MOD 36 [DDD]

Wilson, Rebecca (screaming)
Shea, D.:Hsi-Yu Chi, w. Sim Cain (perc), Hideki Kato (bass instrument), Wu Man (pipa), Zeena Parkins (hp/pno/acc), Jim Pugliese (perc), Mark Ribot (gtr/banjo), David Shea (sampler/pno/turntables), Alex Tobias (celtic dr/misc.), John Zorn (a sax)
Tzadik ("The Composers" series) ▲ TZA 7005 [DDD]

Wimuno-Pearson, B. (elec)
Melby, J.:Con Fl & Sounds, w. T. Lane (fl)
Zuma Records ▲ ZMA 104

Zappa, Frank (elec)
Zappa, F.:Civilization Phaze III, w. Ensemble Modern (rec Apostolic Studio, NYC, Utility Muffin Research Kitchen, Hollywood & Joe's Garage, North Hollywood, 1967 & 1991–92)
Barking Pumpkin 2–▲ UMRK 01

Zuccheri, Marino (elec)
Maderna, B.:Dimensioni 2, w. C. Berberian (sop), B. Maderna (elec)
Stradivarius ▲ STR 33349
Maderna, B.:Elec Music, w. B. Maderna (elec)—Notturno (1955); Syntaxis (1957); Continuo (1958); Serenata III (1962); Le rire (1964)
Stradivarius ▲ STR 33349
Maderna, B.:Musica su due dimensioni, w. Renato Rivolta (fl), B. Maderna (elec)
Stradivarius ▲ STR 333490

LABEL ADDRESSES

Academy: (distr. Albany)
Acanta: (distr. Pilz Compact Disc)
Accent: (distr. Qualiton)
Acoma: Acoma Company P.O. Box 62056 Victoria Park Terrace Toronto OT M4A 2W1 Canada: tel./fax 416-757-5966; e-mail Acoma@compuserve.com (distr. Bayside)
Acoustic Music Resource: 1610 Crestview Ave Seal Beach CA 90740: tel. 310-431-1608
Adagio: (distr. Allegro)
Adams Disques: 1414 Elmwood Evanston IL 60201: tel 847-869-6150
Adda: (distr. Allegro)
Aerial: (distr. Nonsequitur)
Agora: (distr. Qualiton)
Albany Music Distributors, Inc.: P.O. Box 5011 Albany NY 12205: tel. 518-453-2203
Alden Productions: Alden Productions, Inc. P.O. Box 894 Highland Park IL 60035-0894; fax 708-433-4312 (distr. Collegium)
Alienor: (distr. Harmonia Mundi)
Allegretto: (distr. Vox Music Group)
Allegro: 14134 NE Airport Way Portland OR 97230-3443: tel. 503-257-8480/800-288-2007
Almaviva: (distr. Qualiton)
Alphée: (distr. Qualiton)
Alshire: Alshire International Box 7107 Burbank CA 91510: tel. 213-849-4671/800 423-2936
Altarus: (distr. Albany)
Amadeus Press: 133 S.W. 2nd St. Ste 450 Portland OR 97204-3527 tel: 503-227-2878; fax: 503-227-3070
Amati: (distr. Qualiton)
Amatius Classics: Amatius Classics Productions P.O. Box 341 Charlemont MA 01339: tel. 413-339-8539; fax 413-774-3056
Ambient: (distr. Instinct/Caroline)
Ambitus: (distr. Allegro)
AmCam: AmCam Recordings, Inc. P.O. Box 1502 Wheaton MD 20902 (distr. Albany)
American Choral Catalog, Ltd.: P.O. Box 528 205 Water St. South Northfield MN 55057: tel. 507-645-4695; fax 507-645-2474
American Gramophone: American Gramophone Records, Inc. 9130 Mormon Bridge Rd. Omaha NE 68134: tel. 402-457-4341
AMG Classic Recordings: Antara Music Group Classic Recordings P.O. Box 389 Anderson IN 46015-0389: tel. 800-468-7232; fax 317-622-3599; e-mail 76122.2704@compuserve.com
AMG Distribution:: tel. 800-546-1546
Amphion: (distr. Allegro)
Approche: (distr. Qualiton)
APR: (distr. Albany)
Arbiter: P.O. Box 541336 Linden Hill Station New York NY 11354: tel 718-939-6971 (distr Qualiton)
Arc: Arc Recordings (distr. Original Cast)
Arcana: (distr. Koch)
Archetype: Archetype Records 56 Paul St 2nd Floor Newton Center MA 02159: tel 617-796-9989
Archipon: (distr. Albany)
Archive Documents: (distr. JEM)
Arcobaleno: (distr. Empire)
Arizona Friends of Chamber Music: P.O. Box 40802 Tucson AZ 85717: tel. 520-298-5806
Arkadia: formerly Hunt Productions
Arkadia Classical: (distr. Arkadia Records)
Arkadia Records: Arkadia Entertainment Corp. 34 East 23 St. New York NY 10010: tel. 212-674-5550; fax 212-979-0266
Arkadia-Akademia: (distr. Qualiton)
Arlecchino: (distr. JEM Music Corp.)
Ars Production: (distr. Allegro)
ARSIS: ARSIS 138 Ipswich St. Boston MA 02215 tel: 617-236-1935; fax: 617-236-0261 (distr. Allegro)
Artist-Direct: Blue Mounds WI 53517
Artists: (distr. Allegro)
Arts: (distr. Albany)
Arts Music: (distr. Albany)
AS Disc: (distr. Allegro)
AS Disc (Notes): (distr. Allegro)
Ascencion: Ascención Recordings P.O. Box 1406 Elizabeth City NC 27906: tel 919-331-5898; email ascencion.recordings@internetmci.com
Ashlar: Ashlar Records 714 Ninth Avenue Suite 526 New York NY 10019: tel. 212-265-0714; fax 212-399-0577
Astrée: (distr. Harmonia Mundi)
ASV/Gaudeamus: (distr. Koch)
Athene: (distr. Albany)
Attacca: (distr. Koch)
Audio Advancements: P.O. Box 100 Lincoln Park NJ 07035: tel. 201-633-1151
Audio Art: P.O. Box 230704 Encinitas CA 92023-0704: tel. 619-942-3950; e-mail 102115.1475@compuserve.com
Audiofon: Audiofon Records/PM & J Productions, Inc. 1725 Courthouse Tower 44 West Flagler St. Miami FL 33130: tel. 305-373-3101 (distr. Bayside)
Audiophile Classics: (distr. Qualiton)
Audioquest: P.O. Box 6040 San Clemente CA 92674: tel. 714-498-1977; fax 714-498-6223
Aura Classics: (distr. Empire)
Auracle: (distr. Newport Classic/Allegro)
B & V: Bischof & Vitacco Inc 119 East 74th St New York NY 10021: tel 800-243-1941
Bayside Record Distributing Company: 2609 Del Monte St. West Sacramento CA 95691: tel. 916-373-2548/800-525-5709; fax 916-373-2511
The Beecham Collection: (distr. JEM)
Bel Age: (distr. Qualiton)
Bella Voce: (distr. Qualiton)
Bequest: (distr. East Coast Music)
Bianco e Nero: (distr. JEM)
Biddulph: Biddulph Recordings 35 St. George Street Hanover Square London W1R 9FA England (distr. VAI)
Biograph: Biograph Records 35 Medford St. Suite 203 Somerville MA 02143: tel. 617-627-9050; fax 617-627-9051; e-mail CD@biograph.com
Bison Tales: Bison Tales Publishing P.O. Box 334 Waldoboro ME 04572: tel. 207-832-2007
BKM: BKM Associates Box 22 Wilmington MA 01887
BMG: Bertelsman Music Group 8750 Wilshire Blvd Beverly Hills CA 90211: tel. 310-358-4900
BMG: Bertelsman Music Group 1540 Broadway Times Square New York NY 10036: tel. 212-930-4000
BOMR: Book-of-the-Month Club Records, Inc. BOMR Retail Division 1225 S. Market St. Mechanicsburg PA 17055
Boston Ballet Orchestra: Boston Ballet 19 Clarendon St. Boston MA 02116-6100: tel. 617-695-6950, ext 307 or 350; fax: 617-695-6995
Boston Brass: R. Barron 18 Turner Terrace Newtonville MA 02160: tel. 617-965-3957

Boston Records: 80 Island Creek Road Duxbury MA 02332: tel. 617-934-0411; fax 617-934-9017 (distr. Albany)
Boston Skyline: 73 Hemenway Street #508 Boston MA 02115: tel. 617-536-5464; fax 617-266-1575; e-mail BosSkyline@aol.com
Brassissimo: (distr. Albany)
BSO Classics: (distr. Allegro)
Butterfly Music: (distr. Allegro)
Caedmon: HarperAudio 10 East 53rd St. New York NY 10022: tel. 212-207-7000; fax 212-207-7759; e-mail harperaudio@harpercollins.com
Callisto: Callisto Distribution 146 S. Main St. Suite 212 Orange CA 92668: tel. 714-633-5232; fax 714-633-5232
Cambrix: Cambrix Publishing, Inc. 6269 Variel Avenue Suite B Woodland Hills CA 91367: tel. 818-992-8484; fax 818-992-8781
Canadian Music Centre Distribution Service (CMC): 20 St. Joseph St. Toronto Ontario M4Y 1J9 Canada: tel. 416-961-6601; fax 416-961-7198; e-mail cmc@interlog.com
Cane: Cane Records Univ of Miami, P.O. Box 248165 204 Volpe Bldg Coral Gables FL 33124-7322: tel 305-465-2263; fax 305-284-2290
Cantabile: (distr. Lyric Distribution)
Cantate: (distr. Qualiton)
Canyon: 4143 N. 16th St. Phoenix AZ 85016: tel. 602-266-4823
Canyon Classics: (distr. Qualiton)
Canzone: (distr. Kontrapunkt/Allegro)
Cappella: (distr. Discovery Systems)
Carlton: (distr. Allegro)
Carmel: Carmel Records 2331 Carmel Drive Palo Alto CA 94303: tel. 415-856-3650; fax 415-856-0371
Cascavelle: (distr. Allegro)
CBS: CBS Records, Inc. 51 West 52nd St. New York NY 10019: tel. 212-975-4321
CBS Masterworks: (distr. Sony)
Cedille: Cedille Records 700 W. Barry Ave. Suite 3E Chicago IL 60657-4587: tel. 312-404-0758; fax 312-404-0759 (distr. Qualiton)
Celestial Harmonies: P.O. Box 30122 Tucson AZ 85712: tel. 602-326-4400
Cembal d'Amour: (distr. JEM)
Centrediscs: 20 St. Joseph St Toronto Ontario M4Y 1J9: tel. 416-961-6601; fax 416-961-7188 (distr. Albany or Canadian Music Centre)
Cetra Classic: (distr. Qualiton)
Chaconne: Chaconne Records 245 8th Ave, Ste 136 New York NY 10011: tel. 212-924-4353
Chandos Brass: (distr. Koch)
Channel Productions: P.O. Box 454 Twin Falls ID 83303: tel. 208-734-8668; fax 208-734-6550
Chansons Actuelites: (distr. Qualiton)
Chant du Monde: (distr. Harmonia Mundi)
Chanterelle: (distr. JEM)
Chanticleer: Chanticleer Records 650 Fifth St. Suite 311 San Francisco CA 94107: tel. 415-896-5866 (distr. Allegro)
Cherbourne: (distr. Empire)
Chesky: Chesky Records Box 1268 Radio City Station New York NY 10101: tel. 212-586-7799
Christophorus: (distr. Albany)
Chroma: Chroma Disc 2409 Dunbar St. Vancouver B.C. Canada V6R 3N2: tel. 604-739-9272; fax 604-739-8047
Citadel: (distr. Klavier/Albany)
C.L. Barnhouse Co.: P.O. Box 680 205 Cowan Avenue West Oskaloosa IA 52577: tel 515-673-8397; fax 515-673-4718
Claque: (distr. Allegro)
Claremont: (distr. Albany)
Clarinet Classics: (distr. Qualiton)
Clarity: Clarity Recordings P.O. Box 411407 San Francisco CA 94141-1407: tel. 800-205-9668; fax 415-626-4190
Classic Jewel: 6437 Calder Beaumont TX 77706: tel. 409-860-3684
Classic Masters: (distr. Allegro)
Classic Records: Classic Records 1444 N. Highland Ave. Hollywood CA 90028: tel. 213-466-9694; fax 213-466-9825
Classic Studio Berlin: (distr. Allegro)
The Classical Collector: (distr. Qualiton)
Classical Diamonds: (distr. Qualiton)
A Classical Record: (distr. JEM)
Classical Recording Co.: Classical Recording Co. 21 Meades Lane Chesham Bucks HP5 1SP England (distr. Amadeus Press)
ClassiCDigital: 16018 Northfield St Pacific Palisades CA 90272: tel/fax 310-459-2326
Classico: (distr. Qualiton)
Classics for Pleasure: (distr. Allegro)
Claves: (distr. Empire Music)
Col Legno: (distr. Albany)
Collegium: Collegium Records 12606 South 70th Street Omaha NE 68133-2634: tel. 800-367-9059; fax 402-597-1254
Collins Classics: (distr. Allegro)
Collins Quest: (distr. Allegro)
Colorado Children's Chorale: 910 15th Street, Ste 1020 Denver CO 80202: tel. 303-892-5600
Composers Recordings, Inc.: (see CRI)
Concerto: (distr. Qualiton)
Concerto Bayreuth: (distr. Allegro)
Concord Concerto: (distr. Concord Jazz)
Concord Jazz: Concord Jazz, Inc. Box 845 Concord CA 94522: tel. 510-682-6770
Conifer Classics: (distr. BMG)
Connoisseur Society: 2211 Broadway New York NY 10024: tel. 212-873-6769; fax 212-787-9747 (distr. In Sync Labs)
Consensus: Consensus Management 3479 NW Yeon Portland OR 97210: tel. 503-228-5113
Consonance: (distr. Albany)
Continuum: (distr. Allegro)
Coronet: Coronet Recording Co. 4971 North High St. Columbus OH 43214: tel. 614-888-6624
Corvus: 2070 Bingham Ct. Reston VA 20191-1304: tel. 703-860-1937; email abeetem@wizard.net
CPI: CPI Records 70 Lincoln St. Boston MA 02111: tel. 617-542-1880, xt 132; fax 617-423-8837; e-mail mbchico@aol.com
CPO: (distr. Naxos)
CP²: (distr. Albany)
CRD: (distr. Qualiton)
CRI: Composers Recordings, Inc. 73 Spring St. Room 506 New York NY 10012: tel. 212-941-9673 (distr. Koch)
Critics Choice: Critics Choice Records Box 27 Smithtown NY 11787: tel. 516-864-2439; fax 516-864-2397
Crown Classics: (distr. Allegro)

CRS: Contemporary Recording Studios/Contemporary Record 724 Winchester Rd. Broomall PA 19008: tel. 215-544-5920 (distr. VAI Audio)
Crystal: Crystal Records, Inc. 28818 NE Hancock Rd. Camas WA 98607: tel. 360-834-7022; fax 360-834-9680
Crystal Clear: Crystal Clear Sound 4902 Don Drive Dallas TX 75247: tel. 214-630-2957; fax 214-630-5936; e-mail crstlclr@onramp.net
Cultured Kids: Cultured Kids 62 King Rd PO Box 349 Etna NH 03750: tel. 508-468-2930; fax 508-468-2930
Cuneiform: P.O. Box 8427 Silver Spring MD 20907-8427
Cypres: (distr. Qualiton)
D A Music USA: 362 Pinehurst Lane Marietta GA 30068: tel. 404-977-4172/404-325-0832; fax 404-977-4173
Dana Recording Project: Youngstown State University Youngstown OH 44555-3636: tel. 216-742-1837
Denacord: (distr. JEM Music Corp.)
Danica: (distr. Albany)
Dante: (distr. JEM Music Corp.)
Dargason: Dargason Music Box 189 Burbank CA 91503: tel. 818-846-4981; fax 818-846-2294
Daring: (distr. Rounder)
Datum: (distr. Albany)
D'Blue: 1006 E. Cooper Ave. Aspen CO 81611: tel. 970-925-2202/800-696-7664
DCC Compact Classics: 9301 Jordan Ave. Suite 105 Chatsworth CA 91324: tel. 818-993-8822; fax 818-993-0605; e-mail DCCompact@aol.com
Delfon: Delfon Recording Society 305 Third Avenue West Newark NJ 07107: tel. 201-484-6438
Dell'Arte: (distr. Albany)
Delos: Delos International, Inc. 1645 North Vine St. Suite 340 Hollywood CA 90028: tel. 213-962-2626; fax 213-962-2636
Delta: Delta Music Inc. 2500 Broadway Ave. Suite 380 Santa Monica CA 90404-3061: tel. 310-453-9504; fax 310-828-1435
Denon: Denon Records 3343 Peachtree Rd N.E. Suite 333 Atlanta GA 30326: tel. 404-240-2947; fax 404-240-2959
Denon Canada, Inc.: 17 Denison St. Markham Ontario L3R 1B5 Canada
Denon/PCM Digital: (distr. Denon/Allegro)
Deutsche Grammophon: Polygram Classics & Jazz Worldwide Plaza 825 Eighth Avenue New York NY 10019: tel. 212-333-8331; fax 212-333-8402 (distr. Polygram Classics)
Deutsche Harmonia Mundi: (distr. BMG Classics/BMG)
Deutsche Schallplatten: (distr. Empire)
Diamante: Diamante Music Group 1000 Quail Street Suite 110 Newport Beach CA 92660: tel. 800-766-4DMG/714-442-7531; fax 714-442-7543
Digital Fossils: Source Music P.O. Box 1066 Cooper Station New York NY 10276: tel. 212-388-0747 (distr. Albany)
Direct-To-Tape Recording: Direct-To-Tape Recording Co. 14 Station Avenue Haddon Heights NJ 08035-1456: tel. 609-547-6890 (distr. JEM)
Discover International: P.O. Box 874 New York NY 10023: tel. 212-769-2644
Discovery: Discovery Records: Warner Music Discovery Inc. 2034 Broadway Santa Monica CA 90404: tel. 310-828-1033; fax 310-828-1584; e-mail info@discoveryrec.com
Discovery Systems: 7001 Discovery Boulevard Dublin OH 43017: tel. 614-761-2000
Distribution North America: One Camp Street Cambridge MA 02140: tel. 617-354-0700; fax 617-491-1970
Divertimento: (distr. Qualiton)
Divox: (distr. Empire)
d'Note: 40 Platt Ave Sausalito CA 94965: tel. 415-331-2130/800-995-2657; fax 415-331-0853; e-mail mkelly@dNote.com (distr. Allegro)
d'Note Classics: (distr. Allegro)
Dolphin: Dolphin Records (distr. Allegro; City Hall)
Donemus: (distr. Albany)
Donsuemor: Donsuemor 836 Cragmont Ave. Berkeley CA 94708: tel. 510-524-1502
Dorchester Classics: (distr. Allegro)
Dorchester Recordings: (distr. Allegro)
Doremi: P.O. Box 433 Islington Station A Islington OT M9A 4X4 Canada: tel. 416-225-8834; fax 416-225-2723 (distr. Allegro)
Dorian Discovery: (distr. Dorian Recordings/Allegro)
Dorian Recordings: The Dorian Group, Ltd. 8 Brunswick Road Troy NY 12180: tel. 518-274-5475 (distr. Allegro)
Doron: (distr. Qualiton)
Dove Audio: (distr. Allegro)
Doyen: (distr. Empire)
DRG: DRG Records, Inc. 130 West 57th St. New York NY 10019: tel. 212-582-3040; fax 212-459-9437 (distr. Koch)
Drive: (distr. Allegro)
Ducale: (distr. Allegro)
Duo: (distr. Allegro)
Dutton Laboratories: (distr. Allegro)
Dynamic: (distr. Qualiton)
E D Arts: Fine Arts 38660 Mentor Ave. Willoughby OH 44094: tel. 216-951-7500
Earthbeat: (distr. Music For Little People/WEA)
East Coast Music Distributors: 311 Willowbrook Road Staten Island NY 10314-1969: tel. 718-698-7552; fax 718-761-6411
EastWest Records America: (distr. Atlantic/WEA)
ebs: (distr. Qualiton)
ECM: 1540 Broadway New York NY 10036-4098: tel. 212-930-4989; fax 212-930-4278 (distr. BMG)
ECM New Series: (distr. BMG)
ECM/Watt: (distr. BMG)
EcoClassics: P.O. Box 6834 Holliston MA 01746: tel. 508-429-6977
EDA: (distr. Albany)
Edi Pan: (distr. Albany)
Ediciones Albert Moraleda: (distr. Albany)
Editio Classica: (distr. BMG Classics/BMG)
Eigenart: (distr. JEM)
Eklipse: (distr. VAI Audio)
Elan: Box 101 Riverdale MD 20738: tel. 301-864-0499; fax 301-209-8573 (distr. Albany)
Electrecord: (distr. Harmonia Mundi)
Elektra: Elektra Entertainment 75 Rockefeller Plaza New York NY 10019: tel. 212-275-4000 (distr. WEA)
Elektra/Nonesuch: (distr. Elektra Entertainment/WEA)
Elysium: (distr. Qualiton)
EMD: EMD Music Distribution 21700 Oxnard St. #700 Woodland Hills CA 91367: tel. 818-587-4000; fax 818-999-9206
Emergo: (distr. Qualiton)
EMI Classics: (distr. EMD)
Emperor Operetta: (distr. Empire)
Empire Music Group, Inc.: 170 West 74th St. New York NY 10023: tel. 212-580-5959
L'Empreinte Digitale: (distr. Harmonia Mundi)
Endeca: Endeca Corporation 935 North Calvert Street #D Baltimore MD 21202: tel. 410-625-5791
Enja: (distr. Koch)
Enterprise: (distr. Allegro)
Entr'acte: (distr. Fifth Continent Music/Koch)
Entrée: (distr. Christophorus/Qualiton; Allegro)

Epiphany: tel 800-342-0220 (distr. Albany)
EPM: (distr. Allegro; Qualiton)
EPM (Rym Musique): (distr. Allegro)
EPR (Encore Performance Recording): Ron Meyer Recordings 1613 Duke Court Plano TX 75093
Erasmus: (distr. Qualiton)
Erato: (distr. Albany)
E.R.M.: Editions de la Rue Margot, Paris 3712 N. Broadway #264 Chicago IL 60613: tel. 312-935-1676; fax 312-725-5055
Ermitage: (distr. Qualiton)
Eroica: Eroica Classical Recordings P.O. Box 15208 Santa Fe NM 87506: tel. 505-471-8334/800-9-BARTOK
Esoldun: (distr. Qualiton)
ESS.A.Y: ESS.A.Y Recordings 145 Palisade St. 4th Floor Dobbs Ferry NY 10522: tel. 914-693-5595; fax 914-693-7040 (distr. Allegro)
Essex Entertainment, Inc.: 560 Sylvan Avenue Englewood Cliffs NJ 07632: tel. 201-894-8700; fax 201-894-8630
Etcetera: (distr. Qualiton)
Eufoda: (distr. Albany)
Eurodisc: (distr. BMG Classics/BMG)
Everest: (distr. Omega)
Exclusive: (distr. Koch)
Exultate Chamber Singers: Exultate Chamber Singers 383 Huron St. Toronto OT M5S 2G5 Canada
Eye of the Storm: (distr. Allegro)
Facet: (distr. Delos)
Fanfare: (distr. Intersound International)
Fantasy: Fantasy Inc. 10th & Parker Berkeley CA 94710: tel. 510-549-2500
Fat Boy: (distr. Empire)
Feedback, Inc.: Feedback, Inc. Music Distribution 524 Windy Point Drive Glendale Hights IL 60139: tel. 800-326-3472; fax 708-545-9191
Festivo: (distr. Organ Literature Foundation)
Fifth Continent Music: 18 Malvern Rd. Leura NSW 2780 Australia: tel. 61-47-842-814; fax 61-47-842-814 (distr. Koch)
Fine Arts Company: P.O. Box 2064 Station A Berkeley CA 94702-0064
Finlandia: (distr. Albany)
Finnadar: (distr. Atlantic/WEA)
Flat Town Music Co.: P.O. Drawer 10 Ville Platte LA 70586: tel. 318-363-2177
Fleur de Son: P.O. Box 44 Buffalo NY 14207: tel. 716-836-5884; fax 716-842-0220 (distr. Qualiton)
FNAC Music: (distr. Qualiton)
Focus: (distr. Albany)
Folger Consort: (distr. Albany)
Fone: (distr. Allegro; Empire)
Fonit Cetra: (distr. Albany)
Fontalis: (distr. Auvidis/Harmonia Mundi)
Fonti Musicali: (distr. Qualiton)
Forlane: (distr. Albany)
Fortissimo: (distr. Albany)
Fortuna: (distr. Celestial Harmonies)
Four Winds: Four Winds Records 16830 Ventura Blvd., Suite 515, Encino CA 91436: tel. 818-907-8783/800-547-7715; fax 800-423-4741
4-Tay: 4-Tay Records, Inc 73 Ireland Place Ste 108 Amityville NY 11701: tel/fax 516-797-9166 (distr. Albany)
Foyer: (distr. Allegro)
Fredonia: 3947 Fredonia Drive Los Angeles CA 90068
Freshwater: Freshwater Records P.O. Box 27713 Los Angeles CA 90027-0713: tel. 213-660-5444/800-776-8932; fax 213-660-2743; e-mail TSPW91A@Prodigy.com
Freshwater Classical: (distr. Freshwater)
FSM: (distr. Allegro)
FSM-Adagio: (distr. Allegro)
FSM-Fono: (distr. Allegro)
FTC: P.O. Box 27245 Los Angeles CA 90027: tel. 800-444-7931; fax 213-655-7998
FY: (distr. Allegro)
Gajo: Gajo Records P.O. Box 140777 Dallas TX 75214-0777: tel. 214-821-6540
Gallo: (distr. Albany)
Gamut Classics: (distr. Allegro)
Gasparo: Gasparo Records P.O. Box 3090 Peterborough NH 03458-3090: tel. 603-924-4483; fax 603-924-4493 (distr. Allegro)
Gasparo Gallante: (distr. Gasparo/Allegro)
Gega: (distr. Qualiton)
Genesis: Genesis P.O. Box 1619 Santa Monica CA 70406: tel. 310-476-1941; fax 310-476-7290 (distr. Crystal)
GHA: (distr. Qualiton)
GHB: (distr. C.R.C.; City Hall)
GIA: GIA Publications, Inc. 7404 S. Mason Avenue Chicago IL 60638: tel. 708-496-3800/800-442-1358; fax 708-496-3828 (distr. Allegro)
Gimell: (distr. PGD)
Giulia: (distr. Albany)
GLME: (see Great Lakes Music Enterprises)
Globe: Globe Records P.O. Box 5523 Mill Valley CA 94117: tel. 415-381-1702; e-mail emcee@globerecords.com (also distr. Qualiton)
Glossa: (distr. Albany)
GM: GM Recordings 167 Dudley Road Newton Centre MA 02159: tel. 617-332-6328; fax 617-969-1079; email gunmar@aol.com (distr. Allegro)
GNP Crescendo: 8400 Sunset Blvd Suite 4A Los Angeles CA 90069: tel. 213-656-2614; fax 213-656-0693
Golden Age of Opera: (distr. Qualiton)
Golden Apple: 3706 North 17th St. Arlington VA 22207: tel. 703-525-7550 (distr. Albany)
Golden Harp: (distr. JEM)
Golden Melodram: (distr. Albany)
Golden String: Golden String Audiophile Repertory (distr. Albany)
Golden Tone: Golden Tone Records P.O. Box 923265 Sylmar CA 91392-3265: tel. 213-669-5324
Goldies: (distr. Albany)
Gothic: Gothic Records P.O. Box 6406 Anaheim CA 92816: tel. 714-999-1061; fax 714-999-0572; e-mail gothicrec@aol.com (distr. Koch)
Gramavision: (distr. Rykodisc)
Grammofono 2000: (distr. Allegro)
Grammont: (distr. Albany)
Great Lakes Music Enterprises (GLME): P.O. Box 804 Mentor OH 44061: tel/fax 216-257-0413
Great Opera Performances: (distr. Albany)
Grenadilla: Grenadilla Productions 52 Kohring Circle South Harrington Park NJ 07640: tel. 201-768-0971 (distr. Grenadilla/Crystal)
Greystone: Greystone Records P.O. Box 282 Greenvale NY 11548: tel. 516-621-6551; fax 516-365-4271
Griffin: Griffin Music P.O. Box 87587 Carol Stream IL 60188-7587: tel. 708-858-7801; fax 708-858-7806; e-mail GrifMus@aol.com (distr. Feedback, Inc.)
GRP: GRP Records Inc. 555 West 57th St. New York NY 10019: tel. 212-424-1000; fax 212-424-1007 (distr. UNI)
GSP: GSP Recordings 514 Bryant St. San Francisco CA 94107-1217: tel. 415-896-1122/415-896-1144; fax 415-896-1155 (distr. Allegro)

Guild: (distr. Qualiton)
Halcyon: Halcyon Productions P.O. Box 1342 Olney MD 20830-1342 tel/fax: 301-774-0881
Hannibal: (distr. Rykodisc)
Hänssler Classic: (distr. AMG Classic Recordings)
Happy Days: (distr. Empire)
Harmonia Mundi: Harmonia Mundi USA 2037 Granville Avenue Los Angeles CA 90025-6103: tel. 310-478-1311; fax 310-996-1389
Harmonia Mundi France: (distr. Harmonia Mundi)
Harmonia Mundi/Nightingale: (distr. Harmonia Mundi)
Harmonia Mundi Plus: (distr. Harmonia Mundi)
Hat Art: (distr. Hat Hut)
Hat Hut: Hat Hut Records LTD. Box 461 4106 Therwil Switzerland: tel. 41.61.721.66.55; fax 41.61.721.66.55 (distr. North Country)
Haydn Society: Esoteric, Inc. 119 Knollwood Rd. West Hartford CT 06110-1736: tel. 203-561-2839
Helicon: Helicon Music, Ltd. 7 New York Ave. White Plains NY 10606: tel. 914-761-6931; fax 914-682-2946
Helicon Classics: (distr. Helicon)
Herald: (distr. Albany)
Hester Park: Hester Park NW 310 Wawawai Rd. Pullman WA 99163-2959: tel. 509-334-4660/800-543-5429; fax 509-334-3551 (distr. Albany)
Historical Performers: (distr. Allegro)
Honest: Honest Entertainment P.O. Box 23468, Dept H/L Nashville TN 37202: tel. 1-800-493-5540; fax 615-242-4453; email onebna@aol.com (also distr. Acoustic Music Resource)
HoneyRock: HoneyRock RD 4, Box 87 Everett, PA 15537: tel. 814-652-9184
Horizon: (distr. A&M/PGD)
HPC (Historical Piano Collection): (distr. JEM)
HRE: (distr. Lyric Distribution)
Hungaroton: (distr. Qualiton)
Hyperion: (distr. Harmonia Mundi)
Imaginary Road: (distr. PGD)
IMG/Pickwick: (distr. Pickwick/Allegro)
Imogena: (distr. Allegro)
IMP: Innovative Music Productions (distr. Allegro)
IMP Allegro: (distr. Allegro)
IMP Classics: (distr. Allegro)
IMP Collectors Series: (distr. Allegro)
IMP Masters: (distr. Allegro)
In Sync: In Sync Labs Inc. 2211 Broadway Suite 10E New York NY 10024: tel. 212-873-6769
Incontri Memorabili: (distr. Qualiton)
Indiana Univ Press: 601 N. Morton St Bloomington IN 47404-3797: tel 800-842-6796; fax 812-855-7931
Indiana Univ School of Music: (distr Indiana Univ Press or Albany)
Infinity Digital: (distr. Sony)
Innova: The Minnesota Composers Forum 26 East Exchange St. Suite 200 St. Paul MN 55101: tel. 612-228-1407 (distr. Albany)
Insights: (distr. Albany)
Intaglio: (distr. Koch)
Integra Classics: (distr. AMG)
Intercord: (distr. Four Winds)
Intermezzo Media: (distr. Albany)
International Audiochrome, Inc.: P.O. Box 1068 Rye NY 10580: tel. 914-921-0194; e-mail intaudiocr@aol.com
Intersound: Intersound International, Inc. 11810 Wills Rd. P.O. Box 1724 Roswell GA 30077: tel. 770-664-9262; fax 770-664-7316; e-mail intersound@intersoundmusic.com
Intim Musik: (distr. Albany)
Intrada: 1488 Vallejo St. San Francisco CA 94109: tel. 415-776-1333 (distr. Koch)
Iridisc: Iridisc Digital Media 4005 Holland St. Wheat Ridge CO 80033; fax 303-421-2577; e-mail http://www.csn.net/beatty
Iris: (distr. Qualiton)
Iris: Iris Records P.O. Box 422 Port Washington NY 11050: tel. 516-944-7905
Iron Needle: (distr. Qualiton)
ISBA: ISBA Music (distr. Koch)
Island: Island Records, Inc. 400 Lafayette St. 5th Floor New York NY 10003: tel. 212-995-7800; fax 212-477-5918 (distr. PGD)
Italia: (distr. Qualiton)
Italian Opera Rarities: (distr. Allegro)
ITM: (distr. Albany)
Jacek Music: (distr. Poland Import Export)
Jackal: Jackal Records 1756 Plymouth Rd. Ste 260 Ann Arbor MI 48105: tel/fax 313-769-9256
Jadan: Jadan P.O. Box 84 St. John VI 00831: tel. 809-776-6423; fax 809-779-4323
Jade: (distr. Harmonia Mundi)
Janus: (distr. Quicksilver)
Janus: 839 Garfield Ave South Pasadena CA 91030: tel. 818-403-1972; fax 818-799-7331
JB: JB Records 6689 Orchard Lake Rd. Suite 116 West Bloomfield MI 48322: tel. 800-321-PIANO 7426/810-681-2417/; fax 810-681-2437
Jecklin: (distr. Albany)
Jecklin-Disco: (distr. Albany)
Jem: Jem Music Corporation 303 Fifth Ave. New York NY 10016: tel. 212-684-6768; fax 212-684-3341; e-mail musjem@aol.com
John Hammond Music: (distr. Sony)
John Marks: (distr. Allegro)
JRB: JRB Records P.O. Box 441 Huntington NY 11743-0441 tel: 516-424-7964/888-572-2322; fax: 516-424-6519; email: jerbil@jrb-cd.com/http://www.jrb-cd.com (distr. Collegium)
Jupiter: 15 James Farm Lee NH 03824: tel. 603-659-8468
Just A Memory: (distr. Qualiton)
Justice: Justice Records 3100 Alabama Court Houston TX 77027: tel. 713-520-6669; fax 713-525-4444
KEM: KEM Enterprises 200 Winston Dr Cliffside Park NJ 07010
Kem Disc: (distr. Phoenix Records)
Kicco Classic: (distr. Qualiton)
Klavier: Klavier Records 27134 Paseo Espada #202 San Juan Capistrano CA 92675: tel. 714-248-7234; fax 714-248-7527 (distr. Albany)
Koch: Koch International L.P. 2 Tri-Harbor Court Port Washington NY 11050-4617: tel. 516-484-1000; fax 516-484-4746 (distr. consumer mail order service div: MusiMail, PO Box 1110, Port Washington, NY 11050: tel. 800-688-3482)
Koch Historic: (distr. Koch)
Koch International Classics: (distr. Koch)
Koch Präsent: (distr. Koch)
Koch Schwann: (distr. Koch)
Koch Treasure: (distr. Koch)
Kontrapunkt: (distr. Allegro)
Koss Classics: Koss Classics, Ltd.: Koss Corporation 4129 North Port Washington Ave. Milwaukee WI 53212: tel. 414-964-5000 (distr. Albany)
K/S Records: (distr. Carmel)
K617: (distr. Qualiton)
K2B2: (distr. FTC)
Kuckuck: (distr. Celestial Harmonies)
Label "X": (distr. Koch)

Labor: Box 1601 Canal Street Station New York NY 10013-0879: tel. 718-833-4430; fax 718-833-7165
Landmark: (distr. Koch)
Largo: (distr. Qualiton)
Larrikin: (distr. Allegro)
Laserlight: 2275 S. Carmelina Ave. Los Angeles CA 90064: tel. 213-826-6151 (distr. Delta Music Inc.)
Laudis: (distr. Allegro)
Laurel: 2451 Nichols Canyon Los Angeles CA 90046-1798: tel. 213-876-6040 (distr. Albany)
Legato Classics: (distr. Lyric Distribution)
Legend: (distr. Albany)
Léman Classics: (distr. Qualiton or JEM)
Leo: Leo Records (distr. Leo Lab/North Country)
Leo Lab: The Cottage 6 Anerly Hill London SE192AA UK: tel. 011-44-81-778-3853; fax 011-44-81-659-6422 (distr. North Country)
Leonarda: Leonarda Productions, Inc. Box 1736 Cathedral Station New York NY 10025: tel. 212-666-7697 (distr. Albany)
LFO: (distr. Professional Media Service Corp.)
Library of Congress: (distr. Koch)
Ligia Digital: (distr. Qualiton)
Lind: The Lind Institute P.O. Box 14487 San Francisco CA 94114: tel. 415-864-3396
Linn: (distr. Honest; Allegro)
Live Classics: (distr. Qualiton)
London: 825 Eighth Avenue 26th Floor New York NY 10019: tel. 212-333-8327; fax 212-333-8402 (distr. PGD)
Lorelt: (distr. Albany)
Lotos: (distr. Qualiton)
Louisville Orchestra: (distr. Albany)
Lovely Music: Lovely Communications Ltd. 10 Beach St. New York NY 10013: tel. 212-941-8911; fax 212-334-5149 (distr. Albany)
Lydian: (distr. Naxos)
Lyra House: Lyra House LTD 12629 N. Tatum Blvd. Suite 467 Phoenix AZ 85032: tel. 602-261-6036
Lyric Distribution: 18 Madison Avenue Hicksville NY 11801: tel. 516-932-5503
Lyrichord: Lyrichord Discs, Inc. 141 Perry St. New York NY 10014: tel. 212-929-8234 (distr. Koch)
Lyrinx: (distr. Albany)
Lyrita: (distr. Harmonia Mundi)
LYS: (distr. JEM Music Corp.)
Maggie's Music: P.O. Box 4144 Annapolis MD 21403: tel. 410-268-3394; fax 410-267-7061; e-mail connie@maggiesmusic.com
Maguelone: (distr. Qualiton)
Mahler Fest: (distr. Empire Group)
Mandala: (distr. Harmonia Mundi)
Manu: (distr. Allegro)
MAP: (distr. JEM)
Marco Polo: (distr. Naxos)
Marco Polo/Decapo: (distr. Naxos)
Mark: Mark Custom Recording Service, Inc. P.O. Box 406 Clarence NY 14031-0406: tel 716-759-2600; fax 716-759-2329
Marquis: (distr. Allegro)
Mask: (distr. Albany)
Master Digital: (distr. Delta Music Inc.)
Master Musicians Collective: see MMC
Master of Arts: (distr. Qualiton)
Mastersound: (distr. Albany)
May Audio Marketing: 646 Blvd Guimond Longueuil Quebec J4G 1P8 Canada: tel. 514-651-5707/514-651-9740
MCA: MCA Records International 70 Universal City Plaza Universal City CA 91608: tel. 818-777-4500; fax 818-760-1176 (distr. UNI)
MCA Classics: (distr. UNI)
MCA Classics/Melodiya: (distr. Mobile Fidelity)
MCM: Michael Cave Music 1525 Walnut Ave. Venice CA 90291: tel. 213-399-5333
MCP Productions: Manchester Chamber Players P.O. Box 712 Manchester VT 05254: tel. 802-362-7162
MD + G: Musikproduktion Dabringhaus und Grimm (distr. Koch)
Media 7: (distr. Qualiton)
Medici Quartet: (distr. Allegro)
Meet The Composer: (distr. Elektra/Nonesuch/WEA)
Megadisc: (distr. Qualiton)
Melodiya: Melodiya America Distributors Inc 265 Great Neck Rd. Great Neck NY 11021: tel. 516-829-7373 (distr. BMG)
Melodram: (distr. Albany)
Melodram/Koch: Melodram Connoisseur series (distr. Koch)
Memoir Classics: (distr. Qualiton)
Memoire Vive: (distr. Qualiton)
Memoria: (distr. Empire)
Memories: (distr. Koch)
Mercury: (distr. PGD)
Mercury Living Presence: (distr. PGD)
Meridian: (distr. Albany)
Mesa: Mesa/Bluemoon Recordings 209 East Alameda Ave. Suite 101 Burbank CA 91502: tel. 818-841-8585 (distr. Rhino/WEA)
Metro: Metro Records 3674 19th St. San Francisco CA 94110: tel. 415-487-1361 (distr. Better Music)
Metronome: (distr. Qualiton)
Meyer: Meyer Creative Productions 208 North 4th St., P.O. Box 1738, Bismarck ND 58502: tel. 701-223-7316/800-286-9903; fax 701-255-8287
Mezhdunarodnaya Kniga: (distr. Qualiton)
Milan: Milan Entertainment, Inc. 1540 Broadway 29th floor, Suite D New York NY 10036: tel. 212-782-1086; fax 212-782-1078 (distr. BMG)
Minerva: (distr. Qualiton)
Minmax: (distr. Albany)
Mirabilis: (distr. Albany)
Miramax Hollywood: (distr. PGD)
MITRA: (distr. Organ Literature Foundation)
MK: (distr. Allegro)
MKA: (distr. Allegro)
MMC: (distr. Albany)
MMG: 50 S. Buckhout St. Irvington NY 10533: tel. 914-591-5100
Mobile Fidelity: Mobile Fidelity Sound Lab 105 Morris St. Sebastopol CA 95472-3857: tel. 707-829-0134/800-423-5759
Mobius: 3950 Huron Avenue Culver City CA 90232: tel. 310-839-4899
Mode: Mode Records Box 1026 New York NY 10016: tel. 212-979-1027; fax 212-979-1027 (distr. V.S.O.P.)
Monitor: Monitor Recordings, Inc. 10 Fiske Place Suite 517 Mount Vernon NY 10550: tel. 914-667-2020
Montaigne: (distr. Harmonia Mundi)
Montilla: (distr. Qualiton)
Motette: (distr. Koch)
MP Classics: (distr. Empire)
Multisonic: (distr. Allegro)

Music & Arts: P.O. Box 771 Berkeley CA 94701; tel. 510-525-4583; fax 510-524-2111 (distr. Koch)
Music From Iceland: (distr. Albany)
Music Memoria: (distr. Allegro)
Music of the Baroque: 100 N. LaSalle St Ste 1610 Chicago IL 60602; tel 312-551-1415
Music of the World: Music of the World, Ltd. P.O. Box 3620 Chapel Hill NC 27515-3620; tel. 919-932-9600; fax 919-932-9700; e-mail motw1@aol.com (distr. Allegro)
Musica D'Oggi: (distr. Qualiton)
Música Mundial: Música Mundial Productions P.O. Box 6097 Santa Fe NM 87502
Musica Oscura: (distr. Koch)
Musica Svecias: (distr. Allegro)
Musica Viva: (distr. CBC Records/Allegro)
Musicaimagine: (distr. Qualiton)
Musical Arts Society: 2746 Broadway Evanston IL 60201; tel. 312-864-0539
Musicales Actes Sud: (distr. Harmonia Mundi)
Musicaphon: (distr. Qualiton)
MusicMasters: 1710 Highway 35 Oakhurst NJ 07755-2910; tel. 908-531-3375; fax 908-531-1505; e-mail MusMasters@aol.com (distr. BMG)
Musicon: (distr. Poland Import Export)
Musidisc: (distr. Allegro)
Musique D'Abord: (distr. Harmonia Mundi)
Musique Française d'Aujourdhui: (distr. Harmonia Mundi)
Musiques Suisses: (distr. Qualiton)
Myto: (distr. Qualiton)
Nannerl: Nannerl Recordings P.O. Box 7692 Louisville KY 40257-0692; tel. 502-897-5719
Naxos: Naxos of America 1165 Marlcrest Suites E & F Cherry Hill NJ 08003; tel. 609-751-4744/800-75NAXOS; fax 609-751-7721
Neuma: (distr. Albany)
New Albion: 584 Castro St. #515 San Francisco CA 94114; tel. 415-621-5757; fax 415-621-4711 (distr. Harmonia Mundi)
New Classic Colours: (distr. Allegro)
New Concert Discs: (distr. Canadian Music Centre)
New Millennium: New Millennium Records P.O. Box 532 Planetarium Station New York NY 10024-0532; tel 212-769-4076; fax 212-799-4704 (distr Albany)
New World: New World Records 701 Seventh Ave. New York NY 10036; tel. 212-302-0460; fax 212-944-1922
Newport Classic: 11 Willow St. #4 Newport RI 02840; tel. 401-848-2442; fax 401-848-0060 (distr. Allegro)
Nexus: William L. Cahn 8740 Wesley Road Holcomb NY 14469; tel. 716-582-2508 (distr. Canadian Music Centre Distribution Service)
Nickson: P.O. Box 25523 Rochester NY 14635-06523; tel. 716-381-5381
Nigel Classics: Nigel Classics P.O. Box 144153 Coral Gables FL 33114; tel. 305-461-1322/800-583-9909; fax 305-446-1555
Nightingale Classics: (distr. Lyric Distribution)
Nimbus: Nimbus Records P.O. Box 7746 Charlottesville VA 22906-7746; tel. 804-985-8555; fax 804-985-3953
Nine Winds: (distr. FTC)
NKF: (distr. Qualiton)
NM Classics: (distr. Allegro)
NMC: (distr. Allegro)
Nonesuch: (see also Elektra/Nonesuch) (distr. Atlantic/WEA)
Nonsequitur: Nonsequitur Foundation P.O. Box 344 Albuquerque NM 87103; tel. 505-224-9483
Nord-Disc: (distr. Qualiton)
North Country: North Country Distribution Cadence Bdg Redwood NY 13679; tel. 315-287-2852; fax 315-287-2860; email cadence@northnet.org
North/South Recordings: (distr. Albany)
Northeastern (Classical Arts series): Northeastern Records P.O. Box 3589 Saxonville MA 01701-0605; tel. 508-820-4440; fax 508-820-7769 (distr. Koch)
Northwestern Univ School of Music: Northwestern Univ Press Chicago Distribution Center 11030 S. Langley Ave Chicago IL 60628; tel. 800-621-2736
Norway Music: (distr. Qualiton)
Novadisc: Novadisc 276 Carlaw Ave Ste 211 Toronto OT M4M 3L1 Canada
Novalis: (distr. Qualiton)
Nuova Era: (distr. Koch)
Oak Leaf: (distr. Albany)
Ocean: Ocean Records 315 East 62nd St. 6th Floor New York NY 10021; tel. 212-715-0470; fax 212-715-0461; email 74771.3034@compuserve.com
Ocora: (distr. Harmonia Mundi)
Ode/New Zealand: (distr. Allegro)
Odyssey: (distr. Sony)
L'Oiseau-Lyre: (distr. Polygram Classics)
Olympia: (distr. Allegro)
OMD: (distr. Qualiton)
Omega: Omega Record Group, Inc. 27 West 72nd St. New York NY 10023; tel. 212-769-3060; fax 212-769-3195
Ondine: (distr. Koch)
One Way: 1 Prospect Avenue P.O. Box 6429 Albany NY 12206-0429; tel. 518-489-3288
One-Eleven: One-Eleven, Ltd. (distr. Albany)
Ongaku: Ongaku Records 6 Royal Circle Lexington MA 02173; tel. 617-863-6108/800-647-9509; fax 617-863-6105
Onyx: (distr. Organ Historical Society)
O.O. Discs: 261 Grovers Avenue Black Rock CT 06605-3452; tel. 203-367-7917 (distr. Albany)
O.O. Imports: (distr. Albany)
Opal: (distr. Koch)
Open Loop: Open Loop Recordings P.O. Box 206 Medfield MA 02052; tel. 508-359-7004; fax 508-359-7988 (distr. Albany)
Opera Rara: (distr. Lyric Distribution)
Opera tres: (distr. Qualiton)
Opus One: Box 604 Greenville ME 04441 (distr. Albany)
Opus 111: (distr. Harmonia Mundi)
Opus 3: (distr. Albany)
Orata: Carkal Co. 570 Pelham Road New Rochelle NY 10805; tel. 914-633-5783 (distr. Allegro)
Orfeo: (distr. Qualiton)
Orfeo d'or: (distr. Qualiton)
Organ Historical Society: The Organ Historical Society P.O. Box 26811 Richmond VA 23261; tel. 804-353-9226 (distr. Albany)
Organ Literature Foundation: 45 Norfolk Rd. Braintree MA 02184-5915; tel. 617-848-1388
Original Cast: Box 496 Georgetown CT 06829; tel. 203-544-8288; fax 203-544-8288
Originals: (distr. Allegro)
Orion: (distr. Naxos)
Ornamenti: (distr. Qualiton)
Ottavo: (distr. Qualiton)
Our Musical Past: (distr. Koch)
Owl: (distr. Qualiton)
Oxymoron P&D, Inc: 9532 Quakertown Ave. Chatsworth CA 91311-5521; tel. 818-886-2650
Pablo Today: (distr. Fantasy)
Pan Classics: (distr. Qualiton)
Pantheon: (distr. Allegro)
Panton: (distr. Albany)

Paraclete: Paraclete Press Box 1568 Orleans MA 02653; tel. 800-451-5006/508-255-4685 (distr. Koch)
Parade: (distr. Empire)
Partridge: (distr. Albany)
Paula: (distr. Albany)
Pavane: (distr. Qualiton)
Pearl: (distr. Koch)
Pentagon: (distr. Qualiton)
PGD: Polygram Group Distribution Worldwide Plaza 825 Eighth Ave. New York NY 10019; tel. 212-333-8000
PGM: PGM Recordings 1600 Broadway Ste 610 New York NY 10019-7485; tel. 212-586-4200; fax 212-586-5339; e-mail info@pgm.com; http://www.pgm.com (distr. Allegro)
Phaedra: (distr. Albany)
PHD: (distr. Allegro)
Philips: (distr. Polygram Classics)
Philomel: (distr. JEM)
Phoenix: (distr. Albany)
Phono Suecia: (distr. Allegro)
Phonographe: (distr. Koch)
Pianissimo: (distr. Albany)
Pickwick: (distr. Allegro)
Pierre Verany: (distr. Allegro)
Pilz: Pilz America, Inc. P.O. Box 220 54 Conchester Rd. Concordville PA 19331; tel. 610-459-5035; fax 610-459-5958
Piu Mosso: 27 Cliff St, Ste 303 New York NY 10038; tel 212-732-7424; fax 212-732-7309; email 74504.13@compuserve.com
Platz: (distr. Allegro)
Playasound: (distr. Allegro)
Plaza: (distr. Empire)
PMG: (distr. Pilz Compact Disc)
Point: Point Records (distr. Albany)
Point Music: (distr. Polygram Classics)
Poland Import Export: P.O. Box 1352 Belmont CA 94002; tel. 415-341-3541; fax 415-341-7359
Polecat: (distr. Premier/Empire Group)
Polskie Nagrania: (distr. Poland Import Export)
Polskie Nagrania Edition: (distr. Empire)
Polydor: (distr. PGD)
Polygram Classics, Inc.: Worldwide Plaza 825 Eighth Ave. New York NY 10019; tel. 212-333-8000
Polygram Records, Inc.: see PGD
Pope: Kathy Pope 640 E. Valley View Circle N.S.L. UT 84054; tel 801-298-3035
PopeMusic: 82 E. Allendale Rd. Saddle River NJ 07458; tel 201-825-7900; fax 201-825-0493
Posh Boy: P.O. Box 4474 Palm Desert CA 92281; tel. 619-341-8264
Positively Armenian: Armenian General Benevolent Union 585 Saddle River Rd. Saddle Brook NJ 07662
Praga: (distr. Harmonia Mundi)
Preamble: Fifth Continent Music/Koch
Preiser: (distr. Koch)
Prelude: (distr. Albany)
Preludio: (distr. Albany)
Premier: Premier Recordings, Inc. P.O. Box 1214 Gracie Station New York NY 10028-0008 (distr. Empire)
Prezioso: (distr. Qualiton)
Priory: (distr. Allegro)
Private Music: 9014 Melrose Avenue Los Angeles CA 90069 (distr. BMG)
Pro Arte: (distr. Intersound International)
Pro Arte/Fanfare: (distr. Intersound International)
Pro Organo: Pro Organo America P.O. Box 6494 South Bend IN 46660; tel. 800-336-2224 (distr. Zarex)
Pro Piano: Pro Piano Records 85 Jane St. New York NY 10014; tel. 212-206-8794; fax 212-633-1207 (distr. Albany)
Pro Viva: Intersound GmbH Schleibingerstrasse 10 D-8000 Munich 80 Federal Republic of Germany (distr. Albany)
PROdigital: P.O. Box 27831 Los Angeles CA 90027; tel. 213-665-2332 (distr. Albany)
Producciones Fonograficas: (distr. Qualiton)
Professional Media Service Corp.: 19122 S. Vermont Ave Gardenia CA 90248; tel. 800-223-7672
Prophone: (distr. JEM)
Propius: (distr. JEM)
Protone: Protone Records 970 Bel Air Rd. Los Angeles CA 90077; tel. 310-472-5344 (distr. Bayside)
PWK Classics: (distr. Pickwick)
Pyramid: (distr. Albany)
Quadrivium: (distr. Qualiton)
Qualiton: Qualiton Imports, Ltd. 24-02 40th Ave. Long Island City NY 11101; tel. 718-937-8515; fax 718-729-3239
Quantum: Azure International P.O. Box 182 Temple NH 03084-0182; tel. 603-878-0539 (distr. Albany)
Quintana: (distr. Harmonia Mundi)
Quintessence: (distr. Intersound International)
Radio Katowice: (distr. Poland Import Export)
Raptoria Caam: (distr. Albany)
Raptus: (distr. Qualiton)
Raven: (distr. Organ Historical Society)
RBW: P.O. Box 14187 Parkville MO 64152; tel. 816-587-5358; fax 816-421-6095
RCA Gold Seal: (distr. BMG Classics/BMG)
RCA Living Stereo: (distr. BMG)
RCA Papillon Collection: (distr. BMG Classics/BMG)
RCA Red Seal: (distr. BMG Classics/BMG)
RCA Silver Seal: (distr. BMG Classics/BMG)
RCA Victor: RCA Records (distr. BMG)
RCB: RCBB Recordings P.O. Box 6436 Pittsburgh PA 15212
RCM: (distr. Allegro)
RealTime: M&K Sound Corp. 10391 Jefferson Blvd. Culver City CA 90230; tel. 213-204-2854
Records Ltd., Inc.: P.O. Box 20136 Los Angeles CA 90006; tel. 213-737-2611
Redcliffe: Redcliffe Recordings 68 Barrowgate Rd London W4 4QU England (distr. Albany)
Reference: Reference Recordings Box 77225X San Francisco CA 94107; tel. 415-355-1892/800-336-8866
Regis Tro: (distr. Qualiton)
Relief: (distr. Albany)
REM: (distr. Allegro)
Renaissance: 770 E. Green St. #102 Pasadena CA 91101; tel. 818-398-7254
René Gailly: (distr. Qualiton)
Replay: (distr. Qualiton)
RêR: RêR Megacorp 79 Beulah Rd. Thornton Heath Surrey CR7 8JG UK; tel. 0181-771-1063 (distr. Cuneiform)
Resmiranda: 179 West State Street Windsor VT 05089; tel. 802-674-5886; fax 802-674-5886
Rhino: Rhino Records, Inc. 10635 Santa Monica Blvd. Los Angeles CA 90025-4900; tel. 310-474-4778; fax 310-441-6578 (distr. Atlantic/WEA)
Ricercar: (distr. Qualiton)
Ricercar In Ecco: (distr. Qualiton)
Ricordi: (distr. Qualiton)

Rising Star: Rising Star Records & Publishers 52 Executive Park South Suite 5203 Atlanta GA 30329: tel. 404-636-2050; fax 404-636-5051; e-mail info@ristar.com
River City Brass Band: (distr. Empire)
Rivoalto: (distr. Allegro)
RNE/Spanish National Radio: (distr. Albany)
Romophone: (distr. Bayside)
Rondo: (distr. Albany)
Rondo Grammophon: (distr. Albany)
Rossi: (distr. Woodwind Service Inc.)
Round Top: Round Top Records P.O. Drawer 89 Round Top TX 78954: tel. 409-249-3129; fax 409-249-5078
Rounder: Rounder Records One Camp St. Cambridge MA 02140: tel. 617-354-0700
Royal Classics: (distr. Empire)
The Royal Philharmonic Collection: (distr. Allegro)
RPO: (distr. Allegro)
RPO Records Impact: (distr. Allegro)
RS Applausi: (distr. Qualiton)
RS Prestige: (distr. Qualiton)
Russian Compact Disc: (distr. Albany)
Russian Disc: (distr. Albany)
Russian Season: (distr. Chant du Monde/Harmonia Mundi)
Rykodisc: Shetland Park 27 Congress Street Salem MA 01970: tel. 508-744-7678/800-232-7385; fax 508-741-4506; e-mail rykodisc@aol.com/rykodisc@delphi.com
Saga Classics: (distr. Qualiton)
St. Paul Books & Media: 50 St. Paul's Avenue Boston MA 02130: tel. 617-522-8911
St. Louis Symphony: tel. 314-533-2500
Salabert: (distr. Harmonia Mundi)
Sanctus: (distr. Qualiton)
Sanjo Music: P.O. Box 16422 San Francisco CA 94116: tel. 415-333-3999
Sarx: (distr. Allegro)
Saydisc: (distr. Qualiton)
Schoolkids': Schoolkids' Records 523 E. Liberty Ann Arbor MI 48104: tel. 313-994-8031
Screen Trax: (distr. Albany)
Seamus: Society for Electro-Acoustic Music in the US 2550 Beverly Boulevard Los Angeles CA 90057: tel. 213-388-0476
Seda: Seda Productions 45 Common Street Belmont MA 02178-3022: tel. 617-489-1848
Selene: (distr. Poland Import Export)
Serenissima: (distr. Allegro)
Seven Seas: (distr. Koch)
Shanachie: Shanachie Records Corp. 37 East Clinton St. Newton NJ 07860: tel. 201-579-7763 (distr. Koch)
Sheffield Lab: Sheffield Lab, Inc. 408 Bryant Circle Suite C Ojai CA 93023: tel. 800-576-4745/805-640-2900; fax 805-640-2901; e-mail 75242,1421.compuserve.com (distr. Allegro)
Sierra: Sierra Records Books & Home Video P.O. Box 5853 Pasadena CA 91117-0853: tel. 818-355-0181 (also distr. Allegro)
Sierra Classical: (distr. Sierra)
Signum: (distr. Qualiton)
Silva America: (distr. Silva Screen/Koch)
Silva Classics: (distr. Silva Screen/Koch)
Silva Screen: Silva Screen Records America, Inc. 1600 Broadway Suite 910 New York NY 10019: tel. 212-757-1616; fax 212-757-2374 (distr. Koch)
Silva Treasury: (distr. Silva Screen/Koch)
Simax: (distr. Qualiton)
Siperio Dischi: (distr. Albany)
Skarbo: (distr. Albany)
Skowronski Classical: Skowronski Classical Recordings 1726 Sherman Ave #2 Evanston IL 60201: tel 847-491-9155
SKR Classical: (distr. Schoolkids')
Skylark: (distr. Schoolkids')
Slovart: (distr. Empire Music Group)
Smithsonian Collection: Smithsonian Collection of Recordings (distr. Koch)
Smithsonian/Folkways: Office of Folklife Programs 955 l'Enfant Plaza Suite 2600 Washington DC 20560: tel. 202-287-3262 (distr. Koch)
SNE: (distr. Allegro)
Snedeker: 404 N Sampson St Ellensburg WA 98926: tel 509-963-1226; fax 509-963-1239; email snedeker@ewu.edu
Socadisc: (distr. Qualiton)
Soli Deo Gloria: SDG Records 3402 Woolsworth Ave. Omaha NE 68105-1944
Solstice: (distr. Allegro)
Somerset: (distr. Fine Arts Company)
SOMM: (distr. Albany)
Song Lion Productions: (distr. JEM)
Sonora: Sonora Productions P.O. Box 1187 Melrose MA 02176: tel. 617-665-9642 (distr. Bayside or JEM)
Sonpact: (distr. Qualiton)
Sony: Sony Music Entertainment Inc. 550 Madison Ave. New York NY 10022-3211: tel. 212-833-8000
Sony Broadway: (distr. Sony)
Sony Classical: (distr. Sony)
Sony Masterworks: (distr. Sony)
Sound Products Holland: (distr. Allegro)
Sound Solutions: 39 Veronica Avenue Somerset NJ 08875-6150: tel. 908-846-0055; fax 908-846-7769
Soundprints: 192 Spadina Ave Ste 512 Toronto OT M5T 2C2 Canada: tel. 416-504-9353; fax 416-504-9354; email sndprnts@mail.north.net
Soundspells: Soundspells Productions 86 Livingston St. Rhinebeck NY 12572: tel. 914-876-6295 (distr. Albany)
Southern Cross: (distr. Fifth Continent Music/Koch)
Spartacus: (distr. Qualiton or Albany)
Special Music Co.: (distr. Essex Entertainment)
Sphere Marketing and Distribution, Inc.: JFK Airport Cargo Bldg. 80 Room 2A Jamaica NY 11430: tel. 718-656-6220; fax 718-244-1804
Standing Room Only: (distr. Lyric Distribution)
Star Sounds: P.O. Box 3, Little Silver NJ 07739: tel. 908-530-6887; fax 908-842-5041 (distr. DA Music)
Starkland: P.O. Box 2190 Boulder CO 80306: tel. 303-449-6510 (distr. Albany)
Starstruck: Starstruck Records, Inc. P.O. Box 19204 Indianapolis IN 46219: tel. 818-769-8782
Start Classics: (distr. Empire)
Stash: 140 West 22nd Street 12th Floor New York NY 10011: tel. 212-243-4321
Stereophile: Stereophile Magazine P.O. Box 5529 Santa Fe NM 87502 (distr. Albany)
Sterling: (distr. Qualiton)
Stradivari Classics: (distr. Essex Entertainment)
Stradivarius: (distr. Qualiton)
Strings in the Mountains: 33250 Storm Meadows Drive P.O. Box 774627 Steamboat Springs CO 80477: tel. 303-879-5056
Studio Matous: (distr. Allegro)
Studio SM: (distr. Qualiton)
Sugo: (distr. Allegro)

Suite: (distr. Allegro)
Summit: Summit Records & Books P.O. Box 26850 Tempe AZ 85285-6850: tel: 602-470-0694/800-543-5156: fax: 602-470-0696 (distr. Allegro)
Sunrise: (distr. Qualiton)
Suoni e Colori: (distr. JEM)
Supraphon: (distr. Koch)
Supraphon Collection: (distr. Koch)
Supraphonet: (distr. Koch)
Swedish Society: (distr. May Audio Marketing)
Swedish Society Discofil: (distr. Jem)
Symphonia: (distr. Allegro)
Symposium: (distr. Albany)
Syrinx: (distr. Qualiton)
Tacet: (distr. Qualiton or JEM)
Tactus: (distr. Qualiton)
Tahra: (distr. JEM)
Talent: (distr. Qualiton)
Tall Poppies: (distr. Albany)
TCC: Turtle Creek Chorale Sammons Center For The Arts PO Box 190806 Dallas TX 75219-0806: tel. 800-746-4412; fax 214-528-0673
Te Deum: 105 Victoria St. Dundas Ontario L9H 2C1 Canada: tel. 905-628-4533; fax 905-628-9204
Telarc: Telarc Records 23307 Commerce Park Road Cleveland OH 44122: tel. 216-464-2313
Teldec: (distr. Allegro)
Temple: (distr. Rounder)
Ten Thousand Lakes: The Schubert Club 302 Landmark Center St. Paul MN 55102: tel. 612-292-3267
TER Limited: (distr. Records Ltd., Inc.)
Tessitura: Tessitura Music 52 West Pomfret St. Carlisle PA 17013: tel. 717-258-4664
Testament: (distr. Allegro)
Theorema: (distr. Albany)
Thesis: (distr. Qualiton)
Thorofon: (distr. Qualiton)
Time Machine: (distr. VAI Audio)
Timpani: (distr. Qualiton)
Titanic: Box 204 Somerville MA 02144 (distr. Allegro)
Tomato: (distr. Rhino/WEA)
Topazio: (distr. Allegro)
Topnotch: Topnotch Entertainment Corp. Box 1515 Sanibel Island FL 33957-1515: tel. 941-982-1515/818-505-9006; fax 941-472-5033
Town Hall: Box 199 Chatham NY 12037: tel. 800-327-4212 (distr. Albany)
Travelling: (distr. Auvidis/Harmonia Mundi)
Tremula: (distr. Albany)
Trevak: (distr. Allegro)
Tring: (distr. Allegro)
Triton: (distr. Albany)
Troost Press: Troost Press Box 424313 Denton TX 76204: tel. 817-387-8798; e-mail f_flohr@twu.edu (distr. Crystal Clear)
Troubadisc: (distr. Albany)
Truemedia: (distr. Great Lakes Music Enterprises)
Tudor: (distr. Albany)
Tutl: (distr. Albany)
Tuxedo: (distr. Qualiton)
TW Classics: Touchwood Records 1650 Broadway Ste 1210 New York NY 10019: tel. 212-977-7800; fax 212-977-7963
Tzadik: (distr. Koch)
Ummus: (distr. Albany)
UNI Distribution Corp.: 60 Universal City Plaza Universal City CA 91608: tel. 818-777-4400
Unical: Faculty of Fine Arts The University of Calgary 2500 University Drive NW Calgary Alberta T2N 1N4 Canada: tel. 403-220-5497 (distr. Canadian Music Centre Distribution Service)
Unicorn–Kanchana: (distr. Harmonia Mundi)
Unison: Unison Music Distribution 404 BNA Drive Bldg. 200, Suite 600 Nashville TN 37217: tel. 800-251-4000/800-726-1990; fax 615-883-7851
United: (distr. Allegro)
Urtext: (distr. Allegro)
VAI Audio: VAI Audio 158 Linwood Plaza Suite 301 Fort Lee NJ 07024-3790: tel. 201-944-0099/800-477-7146; fax 201-947-8850
Valhalla: Valhalla Records 16 N. Beverwyck Rd P.O. Box 131 Lake Hiawatha NJ 07034-0131: tel. 201-335-0111; fax 201-335-2882; email ValhallRec@aol.com
Valois: (distr. Harmonia Mundi)
Vanguard Classics: (distr. Omega)
Vanguard Classics (Historical Anthology): (distr. Omega)
Vanguard Everyman Classics: (distr. Omega)
Vanguard Twofer: (distr. Welk Music Group)
Vanstory: (distr. Albany)
Varèse Sarabande: Varèse Sarabande Records Inc. Box 801896 Santa Clarita CA 91380: tel. 818-753-4143; fax 818-753-7596 (distr. UNI)
VDE: (distr. Albany)
Vedantic Arts: Vedantic Arts Recordings 30 W 71st St New York NY 10023: tel 212-877-4730/212-787-5384; fax 212-769-4280; email VedWestCom@aol.com
Venture: (distr. Atlantic/WEA)
Verdi Classics: (distr. Empire)
Veritas: (distr. Virgin Classics/EMD)
Vernissage: (distr. East Coast Music)
Verona: (distr. Allegro)
Verve: (distr. PGD)
Vestige: Vestige 4408 West Lakeshore Drive Baton Rouge LA 70808: tel. 504-766-8809
Victoria: (distr. Qualiton)
Vienna Modern Masters (VMM): (distr. Albany)
Vintage Jazz Classics: (distr. Stash)
Virgin: Virgin Records 1790 Broadway 6th Floor New York NY 10019: tel. 212-977-8020 (distr. EMD)
Virgin Classics: (distr. EMD)
Vital Music: VTL The Vital Sound 2591 Pomona Blvd. Pomona CA 91768: tel. 909-613-1323; fax 909-594-9652
Vivace: Sound Products Holland (distr. Allegro)
VM: VM Music P.O. Box 298 Pittsford NY 14534: tel 716-264-1705
Vocalia: (distr. Qualiton)
Voce della Luna: (distr. JEM Music Corp.)
Vox Australis: (distr. Albany)
Vox Box: (distr. Vox Music Group)
Vox Cameo Classics: (distr. Vox Music Group)
Vox Classics: (distr. Vox Music Group)
Vox Legends: (distr. Vox Music Group)
Vox Music Group: Essex Entertainment 560 Sylvan Avenue Englewood Cliffs NJ 07632: tel. 201-894-8700; fax 201-894-8630
VQR Digital: Vogt Quality Recordings Box 302 Needham MA 02192: tel. 617-444-8687
V.S.O.P.: c/o Magnebit 4343 B. Viewridge Ave. San Diego CA 92123: tel. 619-573-0727; fax 619-573-0731
Walking Frog: (distr C.L. Barnhouse Company)

Walsingham Classics: (distr. Allegro)
Walt Disney: Walt Disney Records 500 S. Buena Vista St. Burbank CA 91521: tel. 818-567-5328
Warner Bros.: 3300 Warner Blvd. Burbank CA 91510: tel. 818-846-9090
WEA: Warner/Elektra/Atlantic Corp. 111 N. Hollywood Way Burbank CA 91505: tel. 818-843-6311
WEB: Eaken Piano Trio Dickinson College P.O. Box 1773 Carlisle PA 17013-2896: tel 717-245-1433; fax 717-245-1937; email Baun@Dickinson.edu
Welk Music Group: 1299 Ocean Ave. Suite 800 Santa Monica CA 90401
Well-Tempered Productions: 1678 Shattuck Ave. Suite 156 Berkeley CA 94709: tel. 510-526-5608; fax 510-526-6826 (distr. Allegro)
Weltbild Classics: (distr. Albany)
Wergo: (distr. Harmonia Mundi)
Western Wind: 263 West 86th St. New York NY 10024: tel. 212-873-2848 (distr. Albany)
¿What Next?: (distr. Nonsequitor)
White Label: (distr. Qualiton)
Wild Iris: Wild Iris Records Rt. 19 Box 116AL Santa Fe NM 87505: tel. 505-989-7212
Wildboer: 2430 Bancroft Way Berkeley CA 94704: tel. 888-BWV-1079; fax 510-849-9214 (distr. Albany)
Woodwind Service Inc.: P.O. Box 206 Medfield MA 02052: tel. 800-527-6647; fax 508-359-7988
Work: (distr. Sony)
Work Music: (distr. Harmonia Mundi)
World Wind: World Wind Music (distr. Great Lakes Music Enterprises)
XI Compact Discs: P.O. Box 1754 Canal Street Station New York NY 10013: tel. 212-431-5127; fax 212-431-4486
XLNT: XLNT Music, Inc. 38-62 240th St. Little Neck NY 11363: tel. 718-279-4139 (distr. Albany)
Yellow River: (distr. Harmonia Mundi)
Yellowtail: (distr. Allegro)
Zarex: Zarex Corp. Edison Park Station PO Box 8338 South Bend IN 46660-8338: tel. 219-271-9151/800-336-2224; fax 219-271-9191
Zuma Records: Zuma Records Inc. (distr. Empire)

Notes

Notes

Notes

Notes

Notes